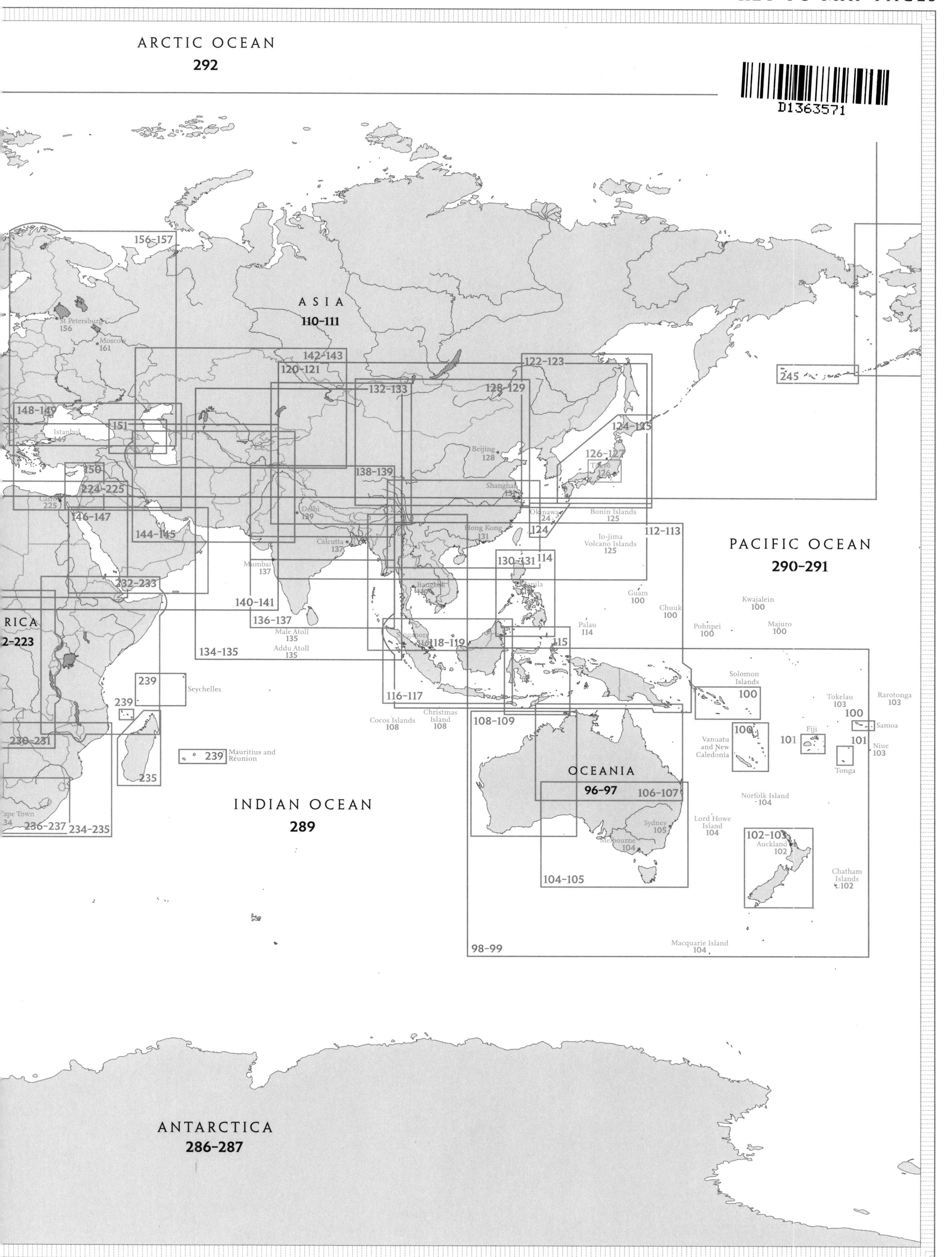
ARCTIC OCEAN
292
ASIA
110-111
St Petersburg 156
Moscow 161
156-157
142-143
120-121
132-133
122-123
128-129
124-125
126-127
Tokyo 126
Beijing 128
Shanghai 131
148-149
Istanbul 149
151
150
224-225
Cairo 225
146-147
144-145
138-139
Delhi 139
Calcutta 137
Mumbai 137
Hong Kong 131
Okinawa 124
Bonin Islands 125
Io-jima Volcano Islands 125
112-113
130-131
114
Bangkok 116
Manila
140-141
136-137
Male Atoll 135
Addu Atoll 135
134-135
232-233
Singapore 116
118-119
115
116-117
Cocos Islands 108
Christmas Island 108
108-109
PACIFIC OCEAN
290-291
Guam 100
Chuuk 100
Kwajalein 100
Majuro 100
Palau 114
Pohnpei 100
Solomon Islands 100
Tokelau 103
100
Rarotonga 103
Samoa
100
Vanuatu and New Caledonia
101
Fiji
101
Niue 103
Tonga
OCEANIA
96-97
106-107
Norfolk Island 104
Lord Howe Island 104
Sydney 105
Melbourne 104
102-103
Auckland 102
Chatham Islands 102
104-105
98-99
Macquarie Island 104
245
RICA
2-223
239
Seychelles
239
235
239
Mauritius and Réunion
230-231
Cape Town 34
236-237
234-235
INDIAN OCEAN
289
ANTARCTICA
286-287

ATLAS OF THE WORLD

THE TIMES CONCISE ATLAS OF THE WORLD

Times Books, 77-85 Fulham Palace Road, London W6 8JB

First Edition 1972
Second Edition 1975
Third Edition 1978
Fourth Edition 1980
Fifth Edition 1986
Sixth Edition 1992
Seventh Edition 1995
Eighth Edition 2000
Ninth Edition 2004
Tenth Edition 2006

Eleventh Edition 2009

Printed in Thailand by Imago

British Library Cataloguing in Publication Data
A catalogue record for this book is available from the British Library

ISBN 978 0 00 731199 6

All mapping in this atlas is generated from Collins Bartholomew digital databases. Collins Bartholomew, the UK's leading independent geographical information supplier, can provide a digital, custom, and premium mapping service to a variety of markets.
For further information:
Tel: +44 (0) 141 306 3752
e-mail: collinsbartholomew@harpercollins.co.uk
or visit our website at www.collinsbartholomew.com

The world's most authoritative and prestigious maps and atlases
www.timesatlas.com

THE TIMES CONCISE
ATLAS OF THE WORLD

TIMES BOOKS
LONDON

Pages	Title	Scale
	HISTORICAL MAPPING	
2–3	THE WORLD ON MERCATOR'S PROJECTION 1858	
4–5	POLITICAL MAP OF THE WORLD 1914	
6–7	WORLD POLITICAL DIVISIONS 1936	
8–9	WORLD POLITICAL CHART 1963	
10–11	STATES OF THE WORLD 1982	
12–13	AFRICA 1898	
14–15	INDIAN EMPIRE 1914	
16–17	EUROPE POLITICAL 1922	
18	WORLD POWERS 1957	
	IMAGES OF EARTH	
20–21	OCEANIA	
22–23	ASIA	
24–25	EUROPE	
26–27	AFRICA	
28–29	NORTH AMERICA	
30–31	SOUTH AMERICA	
32–33	ANTARCTICA	
34–35	TAYLOR VALLEY, ANTARCTICA	
36–37	NEW CALEDONIA	
38–39	GRAND COULEE DAM, USA	
40–41	PALM ISLANDS, UAE	
42–43	PARIS, FRANCE	
	THE WORLD TODAY	
44–45	THE PLANETS	
46–47	EARTHQUAKES AND VOLCANOES	
48–49	THE OCEANS	
50–51	CLIMATE	
52–53	ENVIRONMENT	
54–55	BIODIVERSITY	
56–57	POPULATION	
58–59	URBANIZATION	
60–61	ENERGY	
62–63	COMMUNICATIONS	
64–65	THE EVOLUTION OF MAPPING	
66–67	REVOLUTONS IN CARTOGRAPHY	
	GEOGRAPHICAL INFORMATION	
68–71	PHYSICAL FEATURES	
72–86	STATES AND TERRITORIES OF THE WORLD	
	ATLAS OF THE WORLD	
88–89	INTRODUCTION	
90–91	SYMBOLS AND ABBREVIATIONS	
	WORLD	
92–93	WORLD Physical Features	1:70 000 000
94–95	WORLD Countries	1:70 000 000
	OCEANIA	
96–97	OCEANIA	1:27 000 000
98–99	AUSTRALASIA and SOUTHWEST PACIFIC1:18 000 000	
100–101	PACIFIC OCEAN ISLANDS Samoa and American Samoa Vanuatu and New Caledonia Fiji Tonga French Polynesia Solomon Islands Marshall Islands: Majuro and Kwajalein Guam Micronesia: Pohnpei and Chuuk	

Pages	Title	Scale
102–103	NEW ZEALAND Auckland Niue Cook Islands Rarotonga Tokelau Chatham Islands	1:3 000 000
104–105	AUSTRALIA Southeast Melbourne Sydney Macquarie Island Lord Howe Island Norfolk Island	1:6 000 000
106–107	AUSTRALIA Northeast	1:6 000 000
108–109	AUSTRALIA West Christmas Island Cocos Islands	1:6 000 000
	ASIA	
110–111	ASIA	1:24 000 000
112–113	ASIA Southeast	1:13 000 000
114	PHILIPPINES Manila Palau	1:6 000 000
115	INDONESIA Central	1:6 000 000
116–117	INDONESIA West, MALAYSIA and SINGAPORE	1:6 000 000
118–119	MYANMAR, THAILAND, LAOS, CAMBODIA and VIETNAM Bangkok	1:6 600 000
120–121	ASIA East	1:13 000 000
122–123	ASIA Northeast	1:6 000 000
124–125	JAPAN Ryūkyū Islands Bonin Islands and Volcano Islands	1:3 600 000
126–127	JAPAN Tokyo to Osaka Tōkyō	1:1 200 000
128–129	CHINA North and MONGOLIA Beijing	1:6 000 000
130–131	CHINA South Shanghai Hong Kong	1:6 000 000
132–133	CHINA West	1:6 000 000
134–135	ASIA Central and South Maldives: Addu Atoll and Male Atoll	1:12 000 000
136–137	INDIA South and SRI LANKA Mumbai Calcutta	1:6 000 000
138–139	INDIA North and BANGLADESH Delhi	1:6 000 000
140–141	ASIA Southwest	1:11 000 000
142–143	KAZAKHSTAN, UZBEKISTAN and KYRGYZSTAN	1:6 000 000
144–145	IRAN, TURKMENISTAN, TAJIKISTAN, AFGHANISTAN and PAKISTAN	1:6 000 000
146–147	ARABIAN PENINSULA	1:6 000 000
148–149	TURKEY, IRAQ, SYRIA, JORDAN and TRANS-CAUCASIAN REPUBLICS Istanbul	1:6 000 000
150	MIDDLE EAST	1:3 000 000
151	CAUCASUS	1:3 000 000
152–153	RUSSIAN FEDERATION	1:18 000 000
	EUROPE	
154–155	EUROPE	1:15 000 000
156–157	RUSSIAN FEDERATION West St Petersburg	1:7 200 000
158–159	UKRAINE and MOLDOVA	1:3 000 000
160–161	ESTONIA, LATVIA, LITHUANIA and RUSSIA Moscow Region Moscow	1:3 000 000
162–163	ICELAND, NORWAY, SWEDEN and FINLAND	1:4 000 000
164–165	NORWAY South, SWEDEN South and DENMARK	1:2 250 000

Pages	Title	Scale
166–167	UNITED KINGDOM and IRELAND	1:3 000 000
168	UK Scotland	1:1 500 000
169	IRELAND	1:1 500 000
170–171	UK England North and Scotland South	1:1 200 000
172–173	UK England South and Wales	1:1 200 000
174	UK London	1:125 000
175	FRANCE Paris	1:125 000
176–177	FRANCE	1:3 000 000
178–179	FRANCE Northeast	1:1 200 000
180–181	FRANCE Northwest	1:1 200 000
182–183	FRANCE Southeast	1:1 200 000
184–185	FRANCE Southwest	1:1 200 000
186–187	NETHERLANDS, BELGIUM and LUXEMBOURG	1:1 200 000
188–189	EUROPE North Central	1:3 000 000
190–191	GERMANY Northwest	1:1 200 000
192–193	GERMANY Northeast Berlin	1:1 200 000
194–195	GERMANY South	1:1 500 000
196–197	POLAND	1:1 800 000
198–199	CZECH REPUBLIC, SLOVAKIA and HUNGARY	1:1 800 000
200–201	AUSTRIA	1:1 200 000
202–203	SPAIN and PORTUGAL Canary Islands	1:3 000 000
204–205	SPAIN North and PORTUGAL North Madrid	1:1 500 000
206–207	SPAIN South and PORTUGAL South Gibraltar Madeira	1:1 500 000
208–209	SPAIN East Barcelona	1:1 500 000
210–211	ITALY, SLOVENIA, CROATIA and BOSNIA-HERZEGOVINA	1:3 000 000
212–213	ITALY North and SWITZERLAND	1:1 500 000
214–215	ITALY Central Rome	1:1 500 000
216–217	ITALY South Malta	1:1 500 000
218–219	HUNGARY, ROMANIA and THE BALKANS	1:3 000 000
220–221	GREECE and TURKEY West Athens	1:2 250 000

AFRICA

Pages	Title	Scale
222–223	AFRICA	1:24 000 000
224–225	AFRICA Northeast Cairo	1:7 500 000
226–227	AFRICA Northwest	1:7 500 000
228–229	AFRICA West Cape Verde	1:7 500 000
230–231	AFRICA West Central	1:7 500 000
232–233	AFRICA East Central	1:7 500 000
234–235	AFRICA South Cape Town	1:7 500 000
236–237	REPUBLIC OF SOUTH AFRICA	1:3 300 000
238–239	ATLANTIC and INDIAN OCEAN ISLANDS St Helena and Dependencies: Ascension and Tristan da Cunha Azores: São Miguel, Terceira, São Jorge, Faial and Pico, Canary Islands: Tenerife and La Gomera, Fuerteventura, Lanzarote, La Palma, Gran Canaria, El Hierro Seychelles Mauritius and Réunion Comoros and Mayotte	

Pages	Title	Scale
	NORTH AMERICA	
240–241	NORTH AMERICA	1:27 000 000
242–243	CANADA	1:15 000 000
244–245	USA Alaska and CANDA Yukon	1:6 000 000
246–247	CANADA West	1:6 000 000
248–249	CANADA Central and East	1:6 000 000
250–251	THE GREAT LAKES Chicago	1:3 000 000
252–253	UNITED STATES OF AMERICA	1:12 000 000
254–255	USA East The Bahamas: New Providence Bermuda	1:6 000 000
256–257	USA Northeast	1:3 000 000
258–259	USA Washington to New York New York Washington	1:1 000 000
260–261	USA Central	1:6 000 000
262–263	USA West Los Angeles San Francisco	1:6 000 000
264–265	USA Southwest Hawaiian Islands	1:3 000 000
266–267	MEXICO and CENTRAL AMERICA	1:6 600 000
268–269	MEXICO Central Mexico	1:3 000 000
270–271	CARIBBEAN Puerto Rico St Kitts and Nevis, Antigua and Barbuda, Montserrat, Guadeloupe and Dominica Martinique, St Lucia, St Vincent and the Grenadines Trinidad and Tobago Grenada Aruba Bonaire Curaçao Jamaica	1:6 600 000
	SOUTH AMERICA	
272–273	SOUTH AMERICA	1:27 000 000
274–275	SOUTH AMERICA North Galapagos Islands	1:7 500 000
276–277	SOUTH AMERICA Central Juan Fernandez Islands	1:7 500 000
278-279	SOUTH AMERICA East Rio de Janeiro	1:7 500 000
280–281	BRAZIL Southeast São Paulo	1:3 300 000
282–283	SOUTH AMERICA South Buenos Aires	1:7 500 000
284–285	CHILE Central, ARGENTINA Central and URUGUAY	1:3 300 000
	OCEANS AND POLAR REGIONS	
286–287	ANTARCTICA	1:18 000 000
288	ATLANTIC OCEAN	1:48 000 000
289	INDIAN OCEAN	1:48 000 000
290–291	PACIFIC OCEAN	1:48 000 000
292	THE ARCTIC	1:24 000 000
	INDEX AND ACKNOWLEDGEMENTS	
293-296	GLOSSARY	
297	INTRODUCTION TO THE INDEX	
298–439	INDEX	
440	ACKNOWLEDGEMENTS	

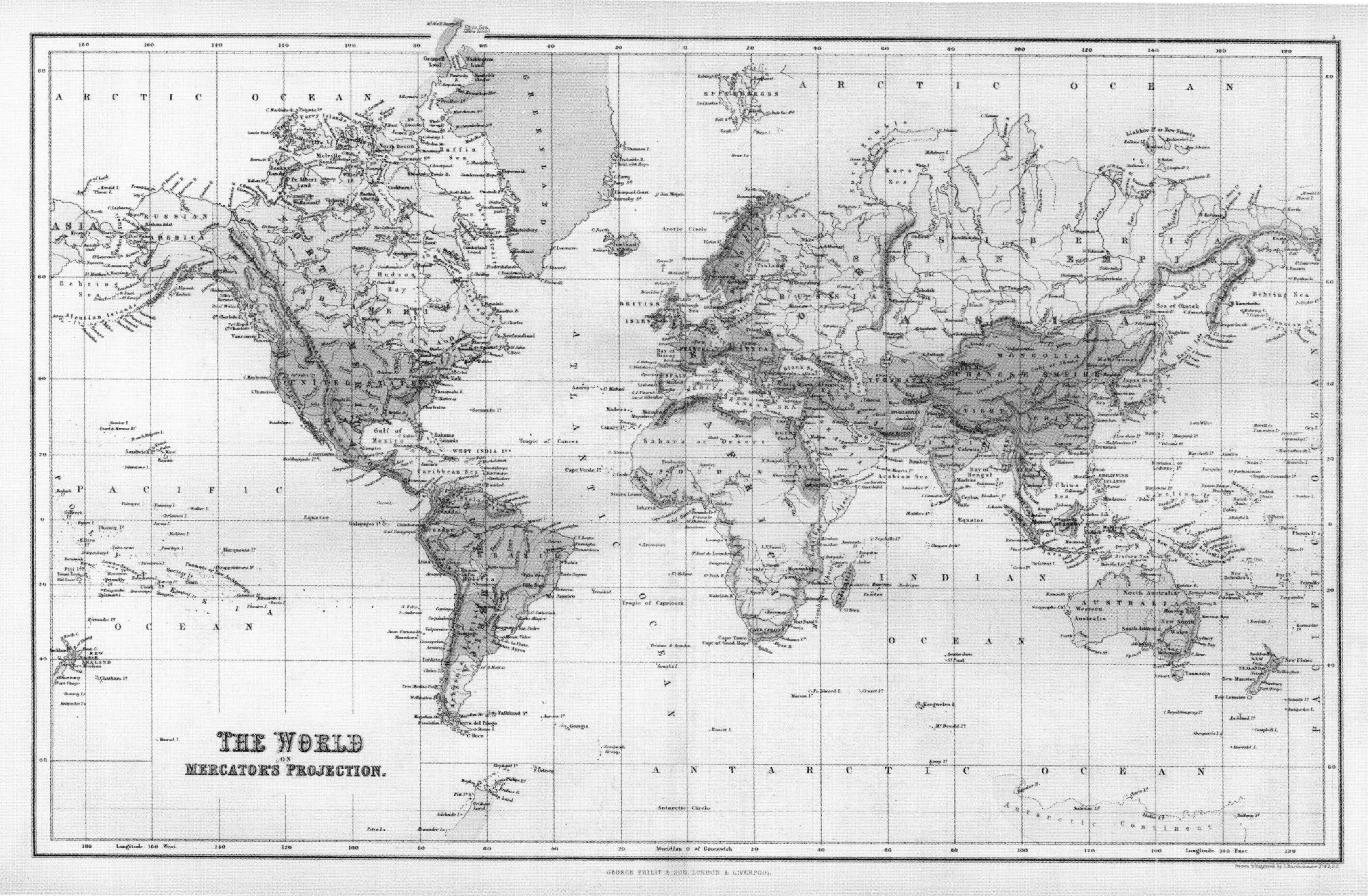

2–3 THE WORLD ON MERCATOR'S PROJECTION 1858

From the *Family Atlas of Physical, General and Classical Geography.* Drawn and engraved by J. Bartholomew Jr F.R.G.S.

The 19th century was known as the 'Age of Empire', when all the major European powers harboured imperial ambitions and used their commercial and military might to extend their influence. In the first half of the century, the process had been gradual. Britain had emerged as the pre-eminent overseas power, extending the boundaries of her established colonial possessions in North America, India and Australia. In the second half of the century, the pace of imperial expansion increased markedly and the world depicted here was on a cusp of a dramatic change.

4–5 POLITICAL DIVISIONS OF THE WORLD 1914

From the *International Reference Atlas of the World.* Cartography by J. G. Bartholomew LL.D., F.R.G.S., Cartographer to the King.

This map shows the imperial divisions of the world at the onset of the First World War in 1914. European colonial empires had grown rapidly over the past century and by now the Great Powers of Europe had engrossed nine-tenths of Africa and much of Asia. Prior to 1914, Europe had been run on balance-of-power politics, where a status quo was maintained between the major powers, often with unofficial agreements and alliances.

6–7 WORLD POLITICAL DIVISIONS 1936

From the *Advanced Atlas, Fifth Edition.* Cartography by John Bartholomew M.C., M.A., F.R.S.E., F.R.G.S. Cartographer to the King.

The political situation of the world three years before the outbreak of the Second World War can be seen from this map. The power of empires had waned significantly after the First World War, and a number of treaties and pacts were signed between countries to safeguard against military attacks. Growing political and social conflict was leading to nationalist uprisings, while both communism and fascism were on the rise in Europe.

8–9 WORLD POLITICAL CHART 1963

From the *Edinburgh World Atlas, Fifth Edition.* Cartography by John Bartholomew C.B.E., M.C., LL.D., F.R.S.E., F.R.G.S.

Almost twenty years on from the end of the Second World War, the 'Age of Empire' was close to its end. International politics had instead become dominated by two superpowers – the United States and the Union of Soviet Socialist Republics (USSR) – who were opposed to each other during the lengthy Cold War. Significant changes affected French and British possessions worldwide at this time. After the war, European powers no longer had the military strength to defend against nationalist movements, nor the economic strength to enforce their rule. Decolonisation in Africa increased.

10–11 STATES OF THE WORLD 1982

From the *Bartholomew World Atlas, Twelfth Edition.* Cartography by John Bartholomew, M.A., F.R.S.E., Director, the Geographical Institute, Edinburgh.

This map represents a transition between one extensive series of changes and another - beforehand, the decolonisation which had gone on, especially in Africa; and afterwards, the collapse of communist regimes in the 1990s. One of the inset maps plots the many changes of sovereignty that had occurred since 1939. Britain sought to maintain association with its former colonies through the Commonwealth. The changes that came after this map was published mostly resulted from political changes in the Soviet Union and its Warsaw Pact allies.

12–13 AFRICA 1898

From the *Citizen's Atlas.* Cartography by J. G. Bartholomew, F.R.G.S.

A comparison between the maps of Africa on p.2–3 [World 1858] and this one dramatically illustrates the speed with which the continent was parcelled up between the competing European powers in the latter half of the 19th century. In 1880, the 'Scramble for Africa' began in earnest with Britain in many ways the chief beneficiary. A primary motivation was to secure communication channels with India, the keystone of her empire. It was for this reason that Egypt was effectively annexed in 1882 to protect the strategically vital Suez Canal.

14–15 INDIAN EMPIRE 1914

From the *International Reference Atlas of the World.* Cartography by J. G. Bartholomew LL.D., F.R.G.S., Cartographer to the King.

Dating from immediately before the outbreak of the First World War, this map illustrates the reach of British imperial power on the Indian subcontinent. Extending far beyond the political borders of modern India, it also included the present-day states of Pakistan, Bangladesh and Myanmar (Burma). Although not officially part of British India, the Crown colony of Ceylon (now Sri Lanka) and the northern kingdoms of Nepal and Bhutan also fell under its influence. The map also shows the mixture of direct rule and local autonomy that was vital to the smooth administration of such a vast and diverse territory.

16–17 EUROPE POLITICAL 1922

From *The Times Survey Atlas of the World.* Prepared at "The Edinburgh Geographical Institute" under the direction of J. G. Bartholomew, LL.D., F.R.S.E., F.R.G.S., Cartographer to the King.

The aftermath of the First World War and the Treaty of Versailles in 1919 redrew the world map and brought an end to the centuries of dynastic power in central and eastern Europe. The new separate states of Austria, Hungary, Czechoslovakia and Yugoslavia emerged after the demise of the Habsburg dynasty. At this time, ethnic nationalism was threatening European colonial empires with ideas of democracy and social reform. The newly independent Baltic states would be occupied by the USSR within twenty years.

18–19 WORLD POWERS 1957

From *The Times Atlas of the World, Mid-Century Edition 1958.* Cartography by John Bartholomew, M.C., LL.D.

The most striking feature of this map is its unusual viewpoint (or projection). Devised in 1948 by John Bartholomew, the Atlantis Projection abandons the common atlas convention of showing the Arctic at the top and the Antarctic at the bottom. Here the projection is tilted to focus on the Atlantic Ocean. In this instance it is particularly effective in conveying the combative nature of relations between the United States and the Soviet Union, the two 'superpowers' which emerged to dominate the new world order following the Second World War.

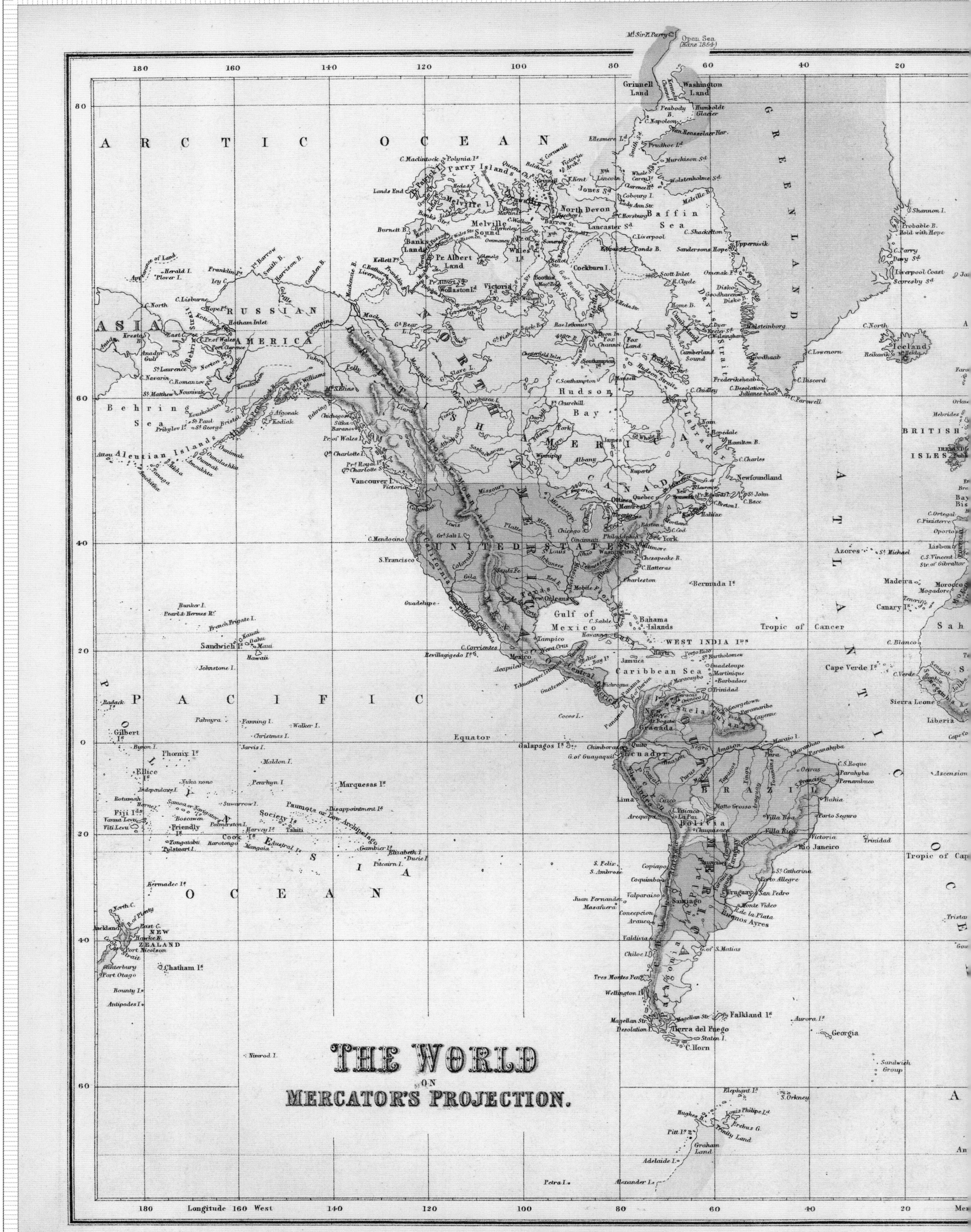
THE WORLD
ON
MERCATOR'S PROJECTION.
ARCTIC OCEAN
PACIFIC
OCEAN
POLYNESIA
NORTH AMERICA
UNITED STATES
CANADA
RUSSIAN AMERICA
ASIA
GREENLAND
ATLANTIC
SOUTH AMERICA
BRAZIL
Behring Sea
Aleutian Islands
Hudson Bay
Baffin Sea
Gulf of Mexico
Caribbean Sea
WEST INDIA I^{DS}
Tropic of Cancer
Equator
Tropic of Capricorn
Sandwich I^{ds}
Iceland
BRITISH ISLES
Azores
Bahama Islands
Galapagos I^s
Falkland I^s
Terra del Fuego
C. Horn
Newfoundland
Vancouver I.
Chatham I^s
NEW ZEALAND
Fiji I^{ds}
Marquesas I^s
Longitude 160 West
GEORGE PHILIP

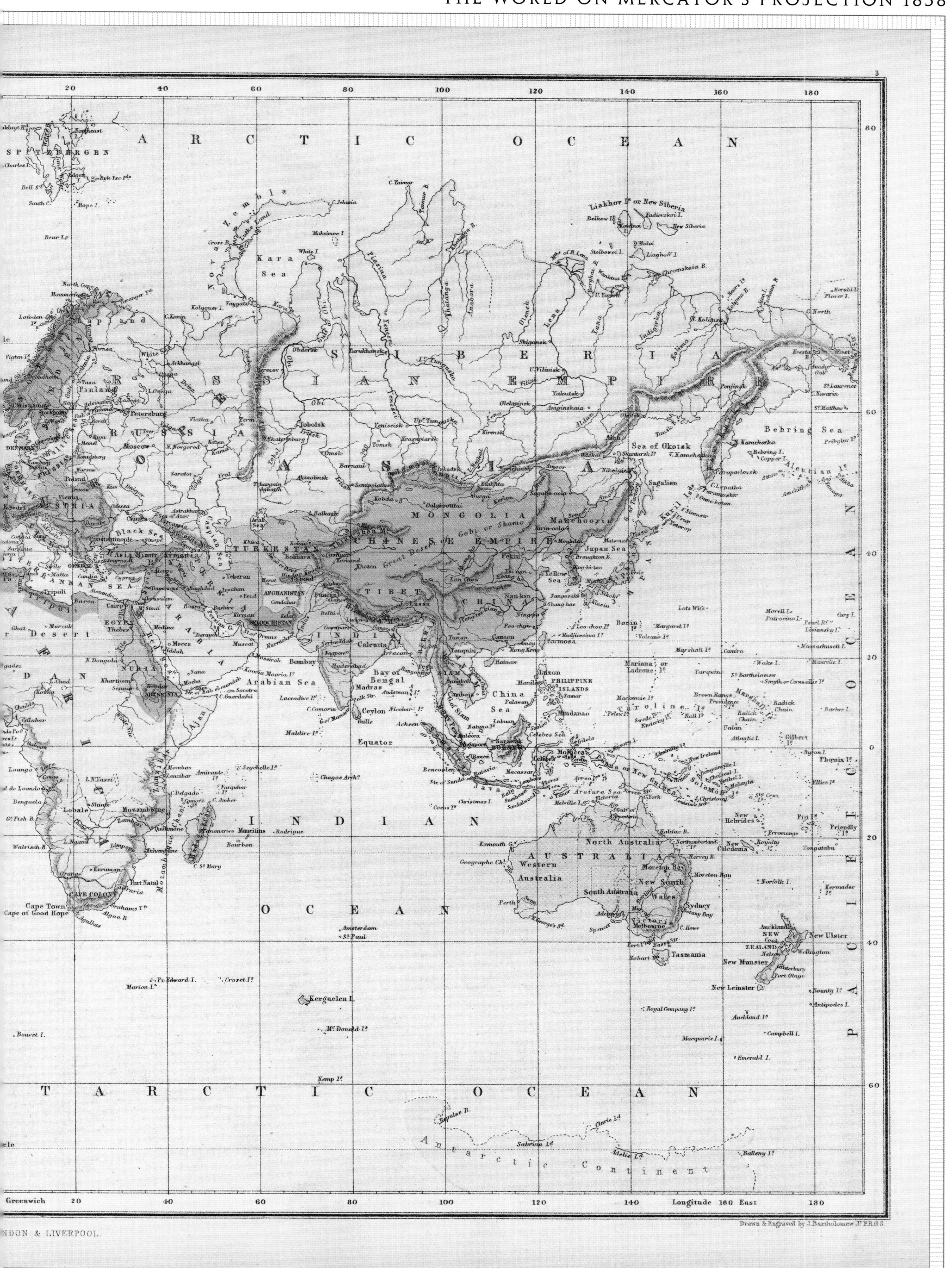

ARCTIC OCEAN
SPITZBERGEN
Nova Zembla
Kara Sea
Liakhov Is or New Siberia
SIBERIA
RUSSIAN EMPIRE
RUSSIA
ASIA
Sea of Okotsk
Behring Sea
Kamchatka
Aleutian Is
MONGOLIA
Gobi or Shamo
CHINESE EMPIRE
Manchooria
Japan Sea
Pekin
Yellow Sea
TURKESTAN
Black Sea
Caspian Sea
Aral Sea
Constantinople
Asia Minor
Teheran
AFGHANISTAN
BELOOCHISTAN
TIBET
CHINA
Nankin
Canton
Formosa
Arabian Sea
Bombay
Madras
Calcutta
Bay of Bengal
Ceylon
ARABIA
Persian G.
Mecca
NUBIA
ABYSSINIA
Mozambique
Cape Town
Cape of Good Hope
CAPE COLONY
Madagascar
Mauritius
Bourbon
Equator
China Sea
PHILIPPINE ISLANDS
Manilla
BORNEO
Celebes
Java
Mindanao
Caroline Is
Marshall
Mariana or Ladrone Is
New Guinea
Solomon Is
New Hebrides
New Caledonia
Fiji Is
INDIAN OCEAN
North Australia
AUSTRALIA
Western Australia
South Australia
New South Wales
Moreton Bay
Sydney
Victoria
Melbourne
Tasmania
Bass Str.
NEW ZEALAND
New Ulster
New Munster
New Leinster
Auckland
Wellington
PACIFIC OCEAN
Kerguelen I.
Amsterdam
St Paul
ANTARCTIC OCEAN
Antarctic Continent
Sabrina Ld
Adelie Ld
Clarie Ld
Balleny Is
Greenwich
Longitude 160 East
20
40
60
80
100
120
140
160
180
Drawn & Engraved by J. Bartholomew Jr F.R.G.S.
NDON & LIVERPOOL

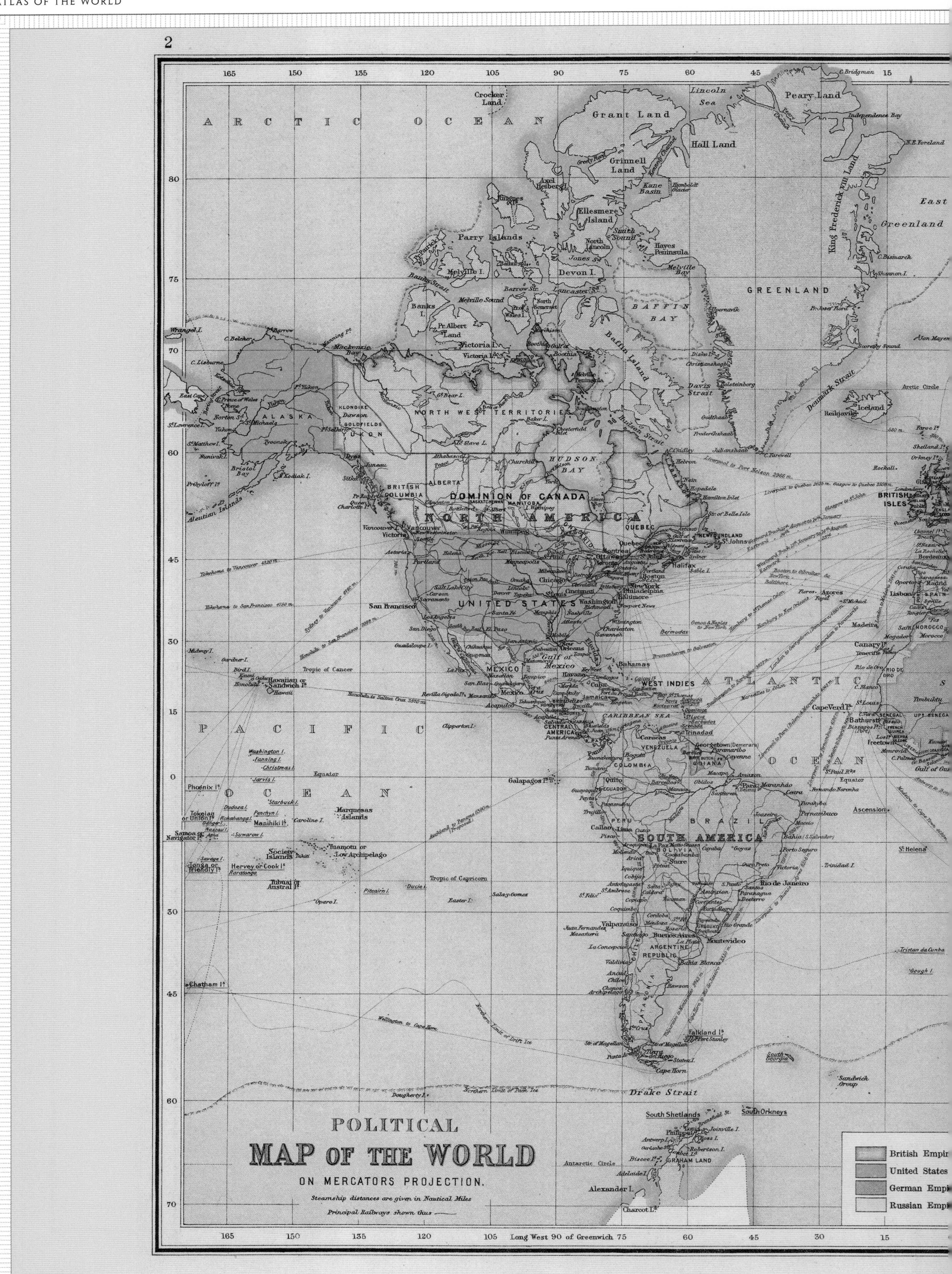
2
POLITICAL
MAP OF THE WORLD
ON MERCATORS PROJECTION.
Steamship distances are given in Nautical Miles
Principal Railways shown thus
Long West 90 of Greenwich
British Empir
United States
German Empi
Russian Empi
ARCTIC OCEAN
PACIFIC OCEAN
ATLANTIC OCEAN
NORTH AMERICA
SOUTH AMERICA
DOMINION OF CANADA
UNITED STATES
GREENLAND
ALASKA
NORTH WEST TERRITORIES
YUKON
HUDSON BAY
BAFFIN BAY
MEXICO
WEST INDIES
BRAZIL
ARGENTINE REPUBLIC
BRITISH ISLES
Drake Strait
Tropic of Cancer
Equator
Tropic of Capricorn
Antarctic Circle
Arctic Circle
GRAHAM LAND
South Shetlands
South Orkneys

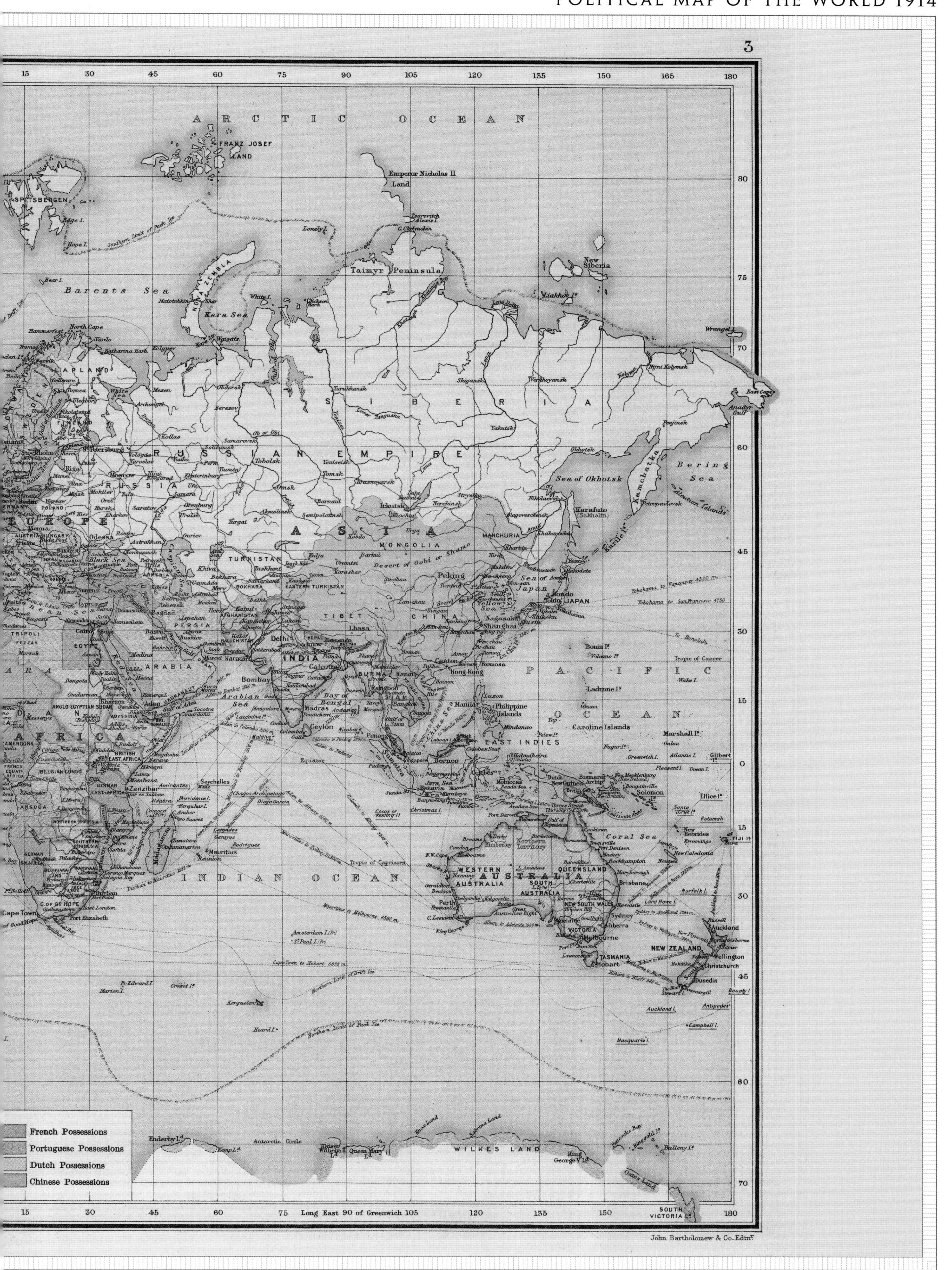
3
ARCTIC OCEAN
FRANZ JOSEF LAND
Emperor Nicholas II Land
SPITSBERGEN
Barents Sea
NOVAYA ZEMLYA
Kara Sea
Taimyr Peninsula
New Siberia
SIBERIA
RUSSIAN EMPIRE
RUSSIA
EUROPE
ASIA
MONGOLIA
TURKISTAN
MANCHURIA
Sea of Okhotsk
Kamchatka
Bering Sea
Sea of Japan
JAPAN
TIBET
CHINA
PERSIA
ARABIA
INDIA
Arabian Sea
Bay of Bengal
SIAM
Philippine Islands
EAST INDIES
PACIFIC OCEAN
Caroline Islands
Marshall Is
AFRICA
BRITISH EAST AFRICA
GERMAN EAST AFRICA
BELGIAN CONGO
ANGOLA
ANGLO-EGYPTIAN SUDAN
ABYSSINIA
EGYPT
TRIPOLI
Madagascar
INDIAN OCEAN
Tropic of Capricorn
Tropic of Cancer
Equator
WESTERN AUSTRALIA
SOUTH AUSTRALIA
QUEENSLAND
NEW SOUTH WALES
VICTORIA
TASMANIA
AUSTRALIA
Coral Sea
NEW ZEALAND
WILKES LAND
SOUTH VICTORIA L.D
Antarctic Circle
French Possessions
Portuguese Possessions
Dutch Possessions
Chinese Possessions
Long East 90 of Greenwich 105
John Bartholomew & Co. Edin

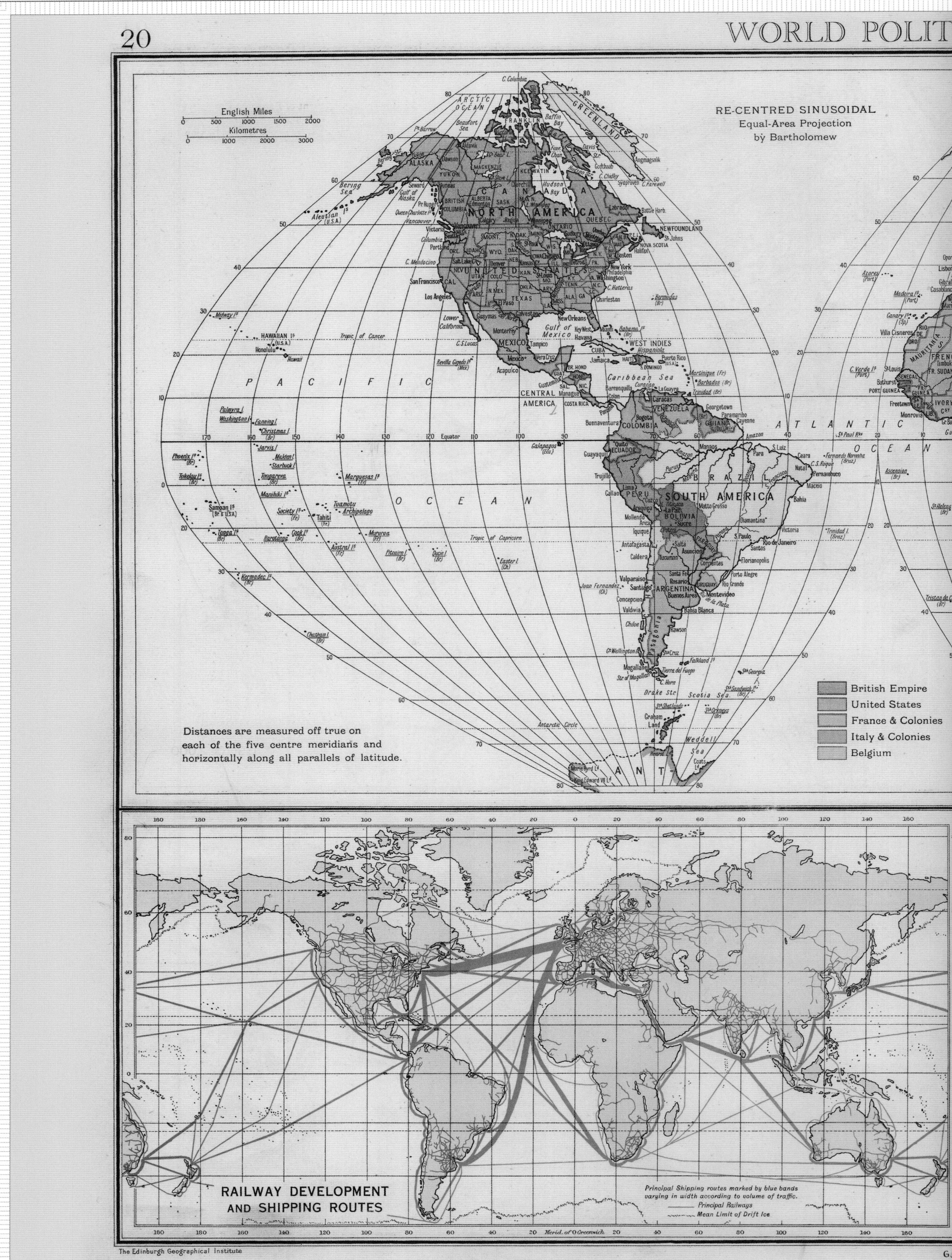
20
WORLD POLIT
RE-CENTRED SINUSOIDAL
Equal-Area Projection
by Bartholomew
English Miles
0 500 1000 1500 2000
Kilometres
0 1000 2000 3000
ARCTIC OCEAN
GREENLAND
NORTH AMERICA
CANADA
UNITED STATES
MEXICO
CENTRAL AMERICA
WEST INDIES
Gulf of Mexico
Caribbean Sea
PACIFIC
OCEAN
ATLANTIC
OCEAN
SOUTH AMERICA
BRAZIL
COLOMBIA
VENEZUELA
ECUADOR
PERU
BOLIVIA
ARGENTINA
Tropic of Cancer
Tropic of Capricorn
Equator
Antarctic Circle
Distances are measured off true on each of the five centre meridians and horizontally along all parallels of latitude.
British Empire
United States
France & Colonies
Italy & Colonies
Belgium
RAILWAY DEVELOPMENT AND SHIPPING ROUTES
Principal Shipping routes marked by blue bands varying in width according to volume of traffic.
Principal Railways
Mean Limit of Drift Ice
Merid. of Greenwich
The Edinburgh Geographical Institute

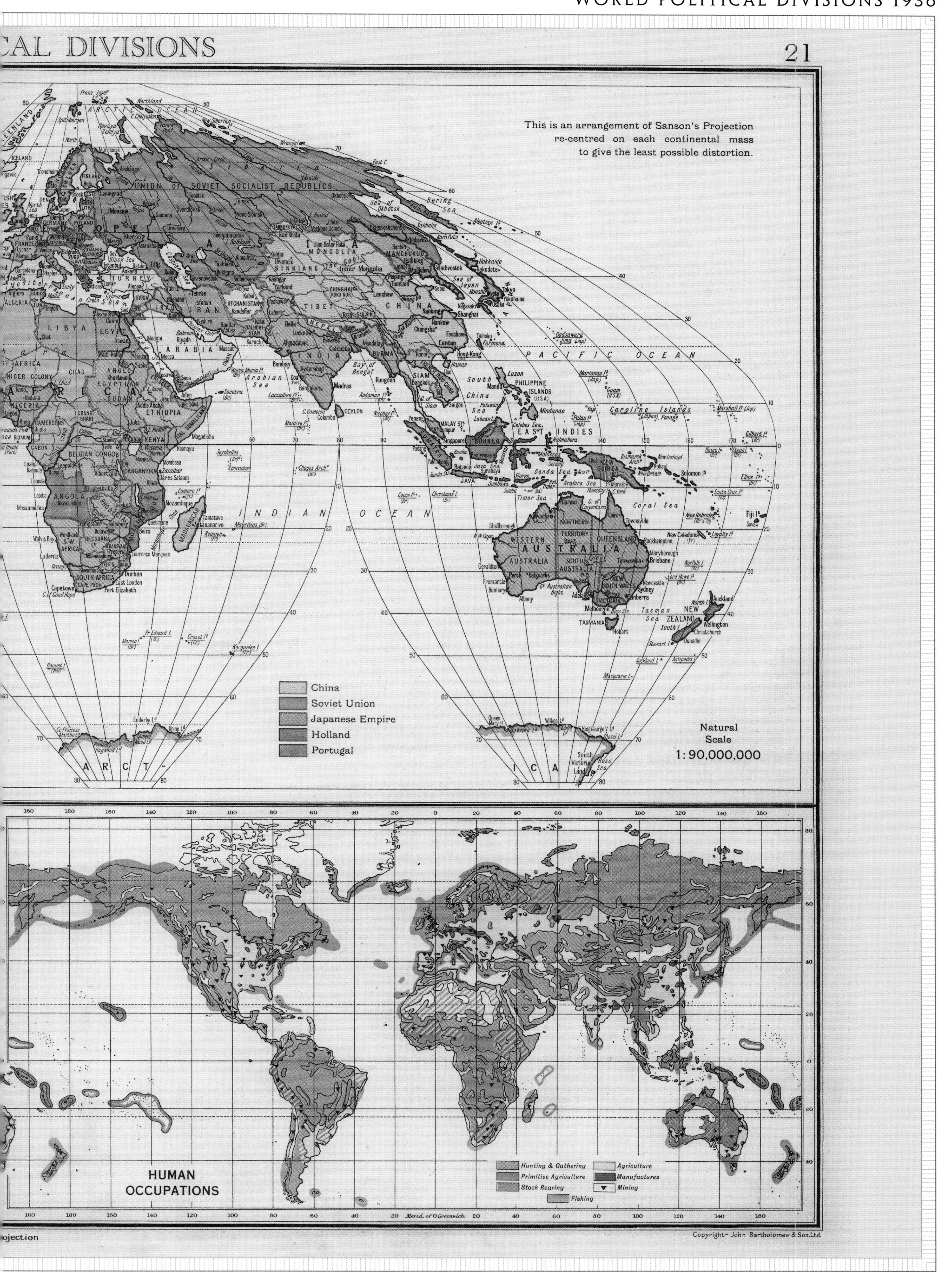
CAL DIVISIONS
21
This is an arrangement of Sanson's Projection re-centred on each continental mass to give the least possible distortion.
ARCTIC OCEAN
UNION OF SOVIET SOCIALIST REPUBLICS
EUROPE
ASIA
Siberia
MONGOLIA
SINKIANG
MANCHUKUO
CHINA
TIBET
INDIA
JAPAN
AFGHANISTAN
IRAN
IRAQ
TURKEY
ARABIA
LIBYA
EGYPT
AFRICA
ANGLO-EGYPTIAN SUDAN
ETHIOPIA
BELGIAN CONGO
ANGOLA
SOUTH AFRICA
MADAGASCAR
PACIFIC OCEAN
INDIAN OCEAN
PHILIPPINE ISLANDS
EAST INDIES
BORNEO
NEW GUINEA
AUSTRALIA
WESTERN AUSTRALIA
NORTHERN TERRITORY
QUEENSLAND
SOUTH AUSTRALIA
NEW SOUTH WALES
VICTORIA
TASMANIA
NEW ZEALAND
Coral Sea
Tasman Sea
Arabian Sea
Bay of Bengal
South China Sea
Caroline Islands
China
Soviet Union
Japanese Empire
Holland
Portugal
Natural Scale
1:90,000,000
HUMAN OCCUPATIONS
Hunting & Gathering
Primitive Agriculture
Stock Rearing
Fishing
Agriculture
Manufactures
Mining
Merid. of Greenwich
ojection
Copyright- John Bartholomew & Son Ltd.

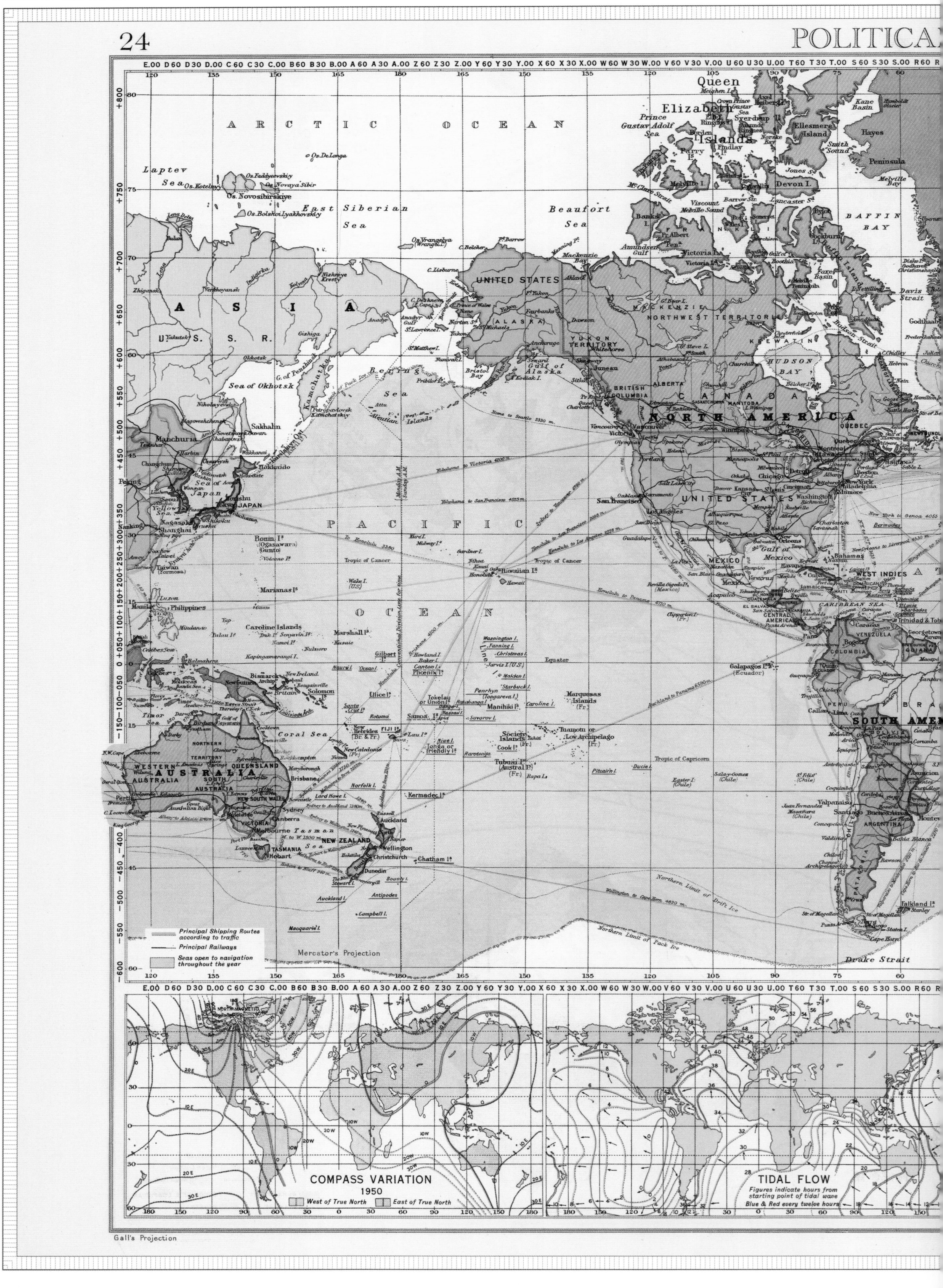

24

POLITICA

Principal Shipping Routes according to traffic

Principal Railways

Seas open to navigation throughout the year

Mercator's Projection

COMPASS VARIATION
1950

West of True North

East of True North

TIDAL FLOW
Figures indicate hours from starting point of tidal wave
Blue & Red every twelve hours

Gall's Projection

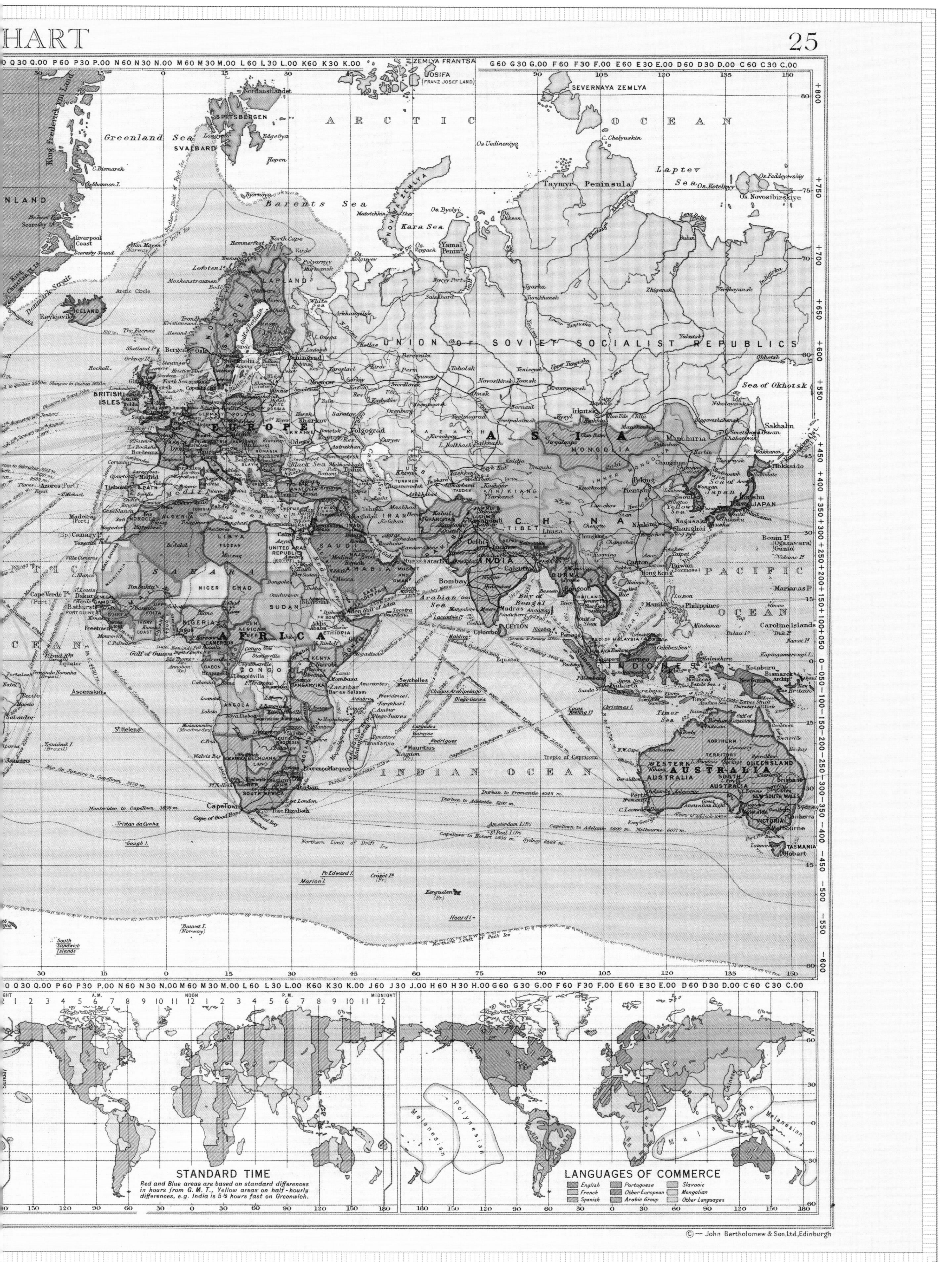
HART
25
ARCTIC OCEAN
UNION OF SOVIET SOCIALIST REPUBLICS
EUROPE
ASIA
AFRICA
CHINA
INDIA
AUSTRALIA
INDIAN OCEAN
PACIFIC OCEAN
STANDARD TIME
Red and Blue areas are based on standard differences in hours from G. M. T., Yellow areas on half-hourly differences, e.g. India is 5½ hours fast on Greenwich.
LANGUAGES OF COMMERCE
English
French
Spanish
Portuguese
Other European
Arabic Group
Slavonic
Mongolian
Other Languages
Melanesian
Polynesian
Malay
©— John Bartholomew & Son,Ltd,Edinburgh

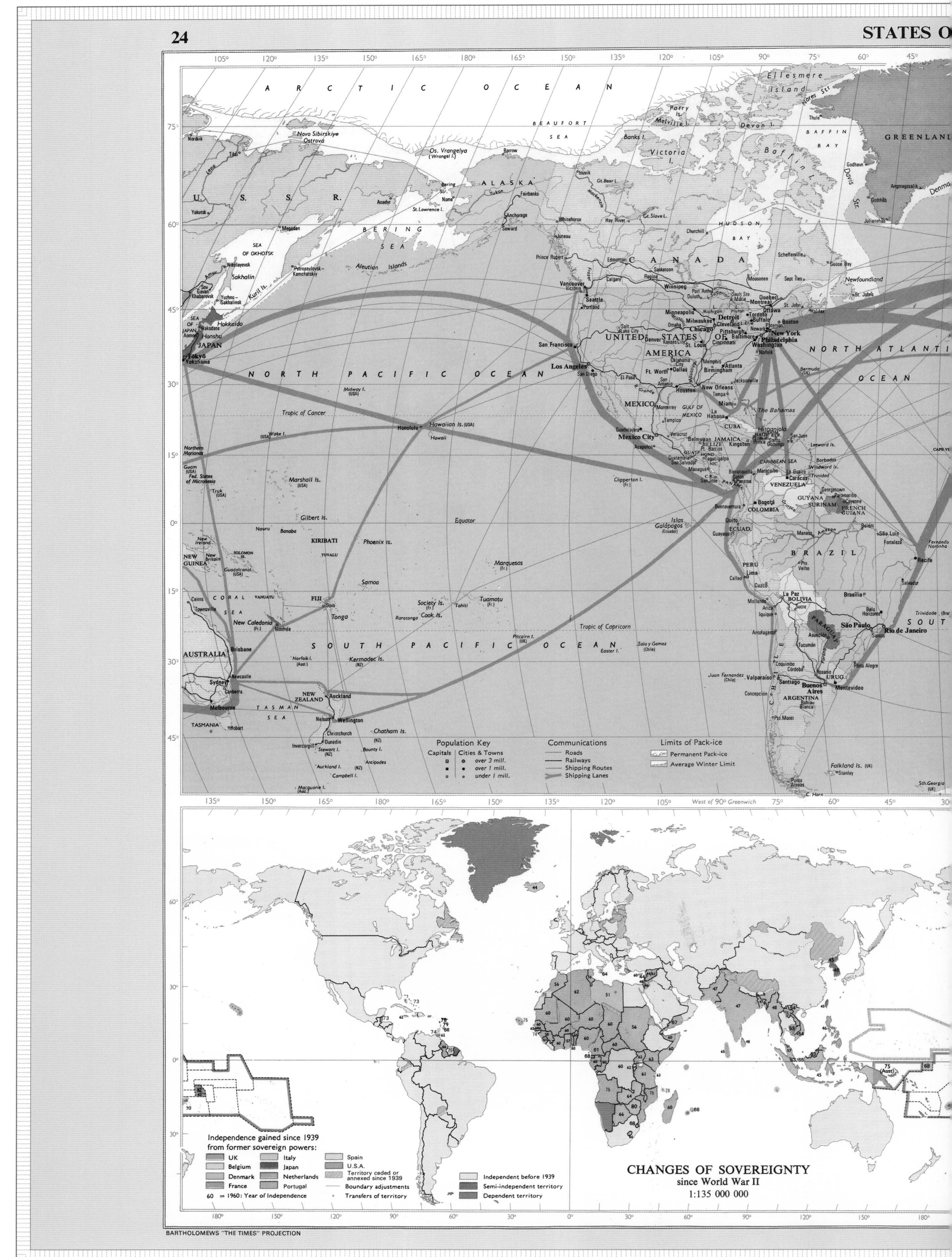
24
ARCTIC OCEAN
NORTH PACIFIC OCEAN
SOUTH PACIFIC OCEAN
NORTH ATLANTIC OCEAN
CANADA
UNITED STATES OF AMERICA
MEXICO
BRAZIL
AUSTRALIA
NEW ZEALAND
JAPAN
Population Key
Capitals
Cities & Towns
over 3 mill.
over 1 mill.
under 1 mill.
Communications
Roads
Railways
Shipping Routes
Shipping Lanes
Limits of Pack-ice
Permanent Pack-ice
Average Winter Limit
West of 90° Greenwich
Independence gained since 1939 from former sovereign powers:
UK
Belgium
Denmark
France
Italy
Japan
Netherlands
Portugal
Spain
U.S.A.
Territory ceded or annexed since 1939
Boundary adjustments
Transfers of territory
60 = 1960: Year of Independence
Independent before 1939
Semi-independent territory
Dependent territory
CHANGES OF SOVEREIGNTY
since World War II
1:135 000 000
BARTHOLOMEWS "THE TIMES" PROJECTION

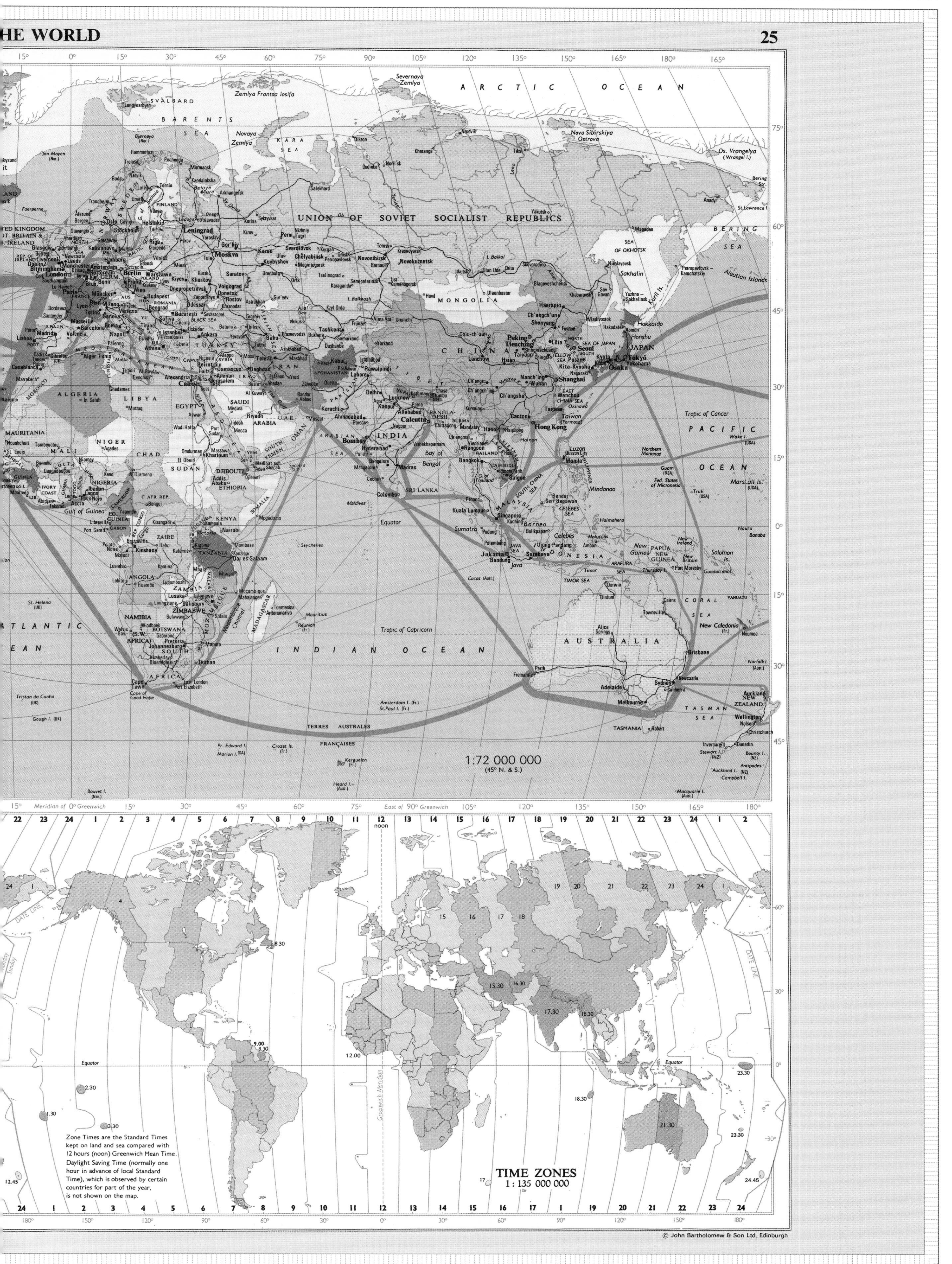
HE WORLD
25
ARCTIC OCEAN
SVALBARD
BARENTS SEA
KARA SEA
Zemlya Frantsa Iosifa
Severnaya Zemlya
Novaya Zemlya
Novo Sibirskiye Ostrova
Os. Vrangelya (Wrangel I.)
UNION OF SOVIET SOCIALIST REPUBLICS
BERING SEA
SEA OF OKHOTSK
Sakhalin
Kuril Is.
Aleutian Islands
MONGOLIA
CHINA
JAPAN
Hokkaido
Honshu
SEA OF JAPAN
TIBET
INDIA
ARABIAN SEA
Bay of Bengal
SRI LANKA
BANGLADESH
BURMA
THAILAND
SOUTH CHINA SEA
PHILIPPINES
Taiwan (Formosa)
Hong Kong
MALAYSIA
INDONESIA
Borneo
Sumatra
Java
Celebes
Moluccas
New Guinea
PAPUA NEW GUINEA
AUSTRALIA
TASMANIA
TASMAN SEA
NEW ZEALAND
CORAL SEA
ARAFURA SEA
TIMOR SEA
PACIFIC OCEAN
Tropic of Cancer
Tropic of Capricorn
Equator
INDIAN OCEAN
ATLANTIC OCEAN
Gulf of Guinea
ALGERIA
LIBYA
EGYPT
NIGER
CHAD
SUDAN
MAURITANIA
MALI
NIGERIA
ETHIOPIA
KENYA
ZAIRE
TANZANIA
ANGOLA
ZAMBIA
ZIMBABWE
MOZAMBIQUE
NAMIBIA (S.W. AFRICA)
BOTSWANA
SOUTH AFRICA
MADAGASCAR
SAUDI ARABIA
IRAN
TURKEY
AFGHANISTAN
PAKISTAN
TERRES AUSTRALES FRANÇAISES
1:72 000 000 (45° N. & S.)
Meridian of 0° Greenwich
East of 90° Greenwich
TIME ZONES
1 : 135 000 000
Zone Times are the Standard Times kept on land and sea compared with 12 hours (noon) Greenwich Mean Time. Daylight Saving Time (normally one hour in advance of local Standard Time), which is observed by certain countries for part of the year, is not shown on the map.
DATE LINE
Greenwich Meridian
© John Bartholomew & Son Ltd, Edinburgh

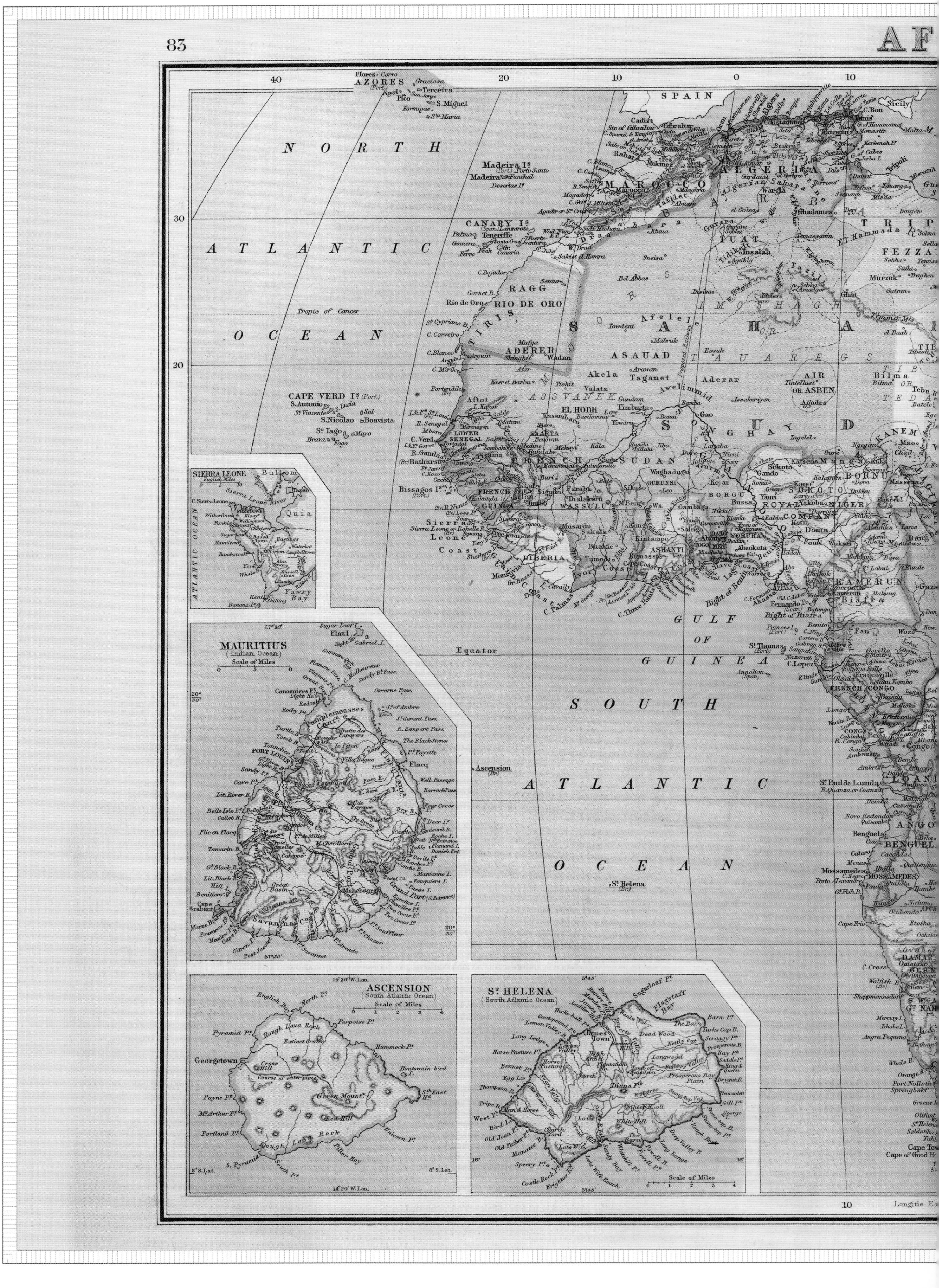

AF

NORTH ATLANTIC OCEAN

Tropic of Cancer

Equator

GULF OF GUINEA

SOUTH ATLANTIC OCEAN

AZORES (Port.)

Madeira Is. (Port.)

CANARY Is. (Span.)

CAPE VERD Is. (Port.)

SPAIN

MAROCCO

ALGERIA

SAHARA

SUDAN

FRENCH SUDAN

LIBERIA

FRENCH CONGO

Ascension (Br.)

St. Helena (Br.)

SIERRA LEONE
English Miles

MAURITIUS
(Indian Ocean)
Scale of Miles

ASCENSION
(South Atlantic Ocean)
Scale of Miles

St. HELENA
(South Atlantic Ocean)
Scale of Miles

Longitde East

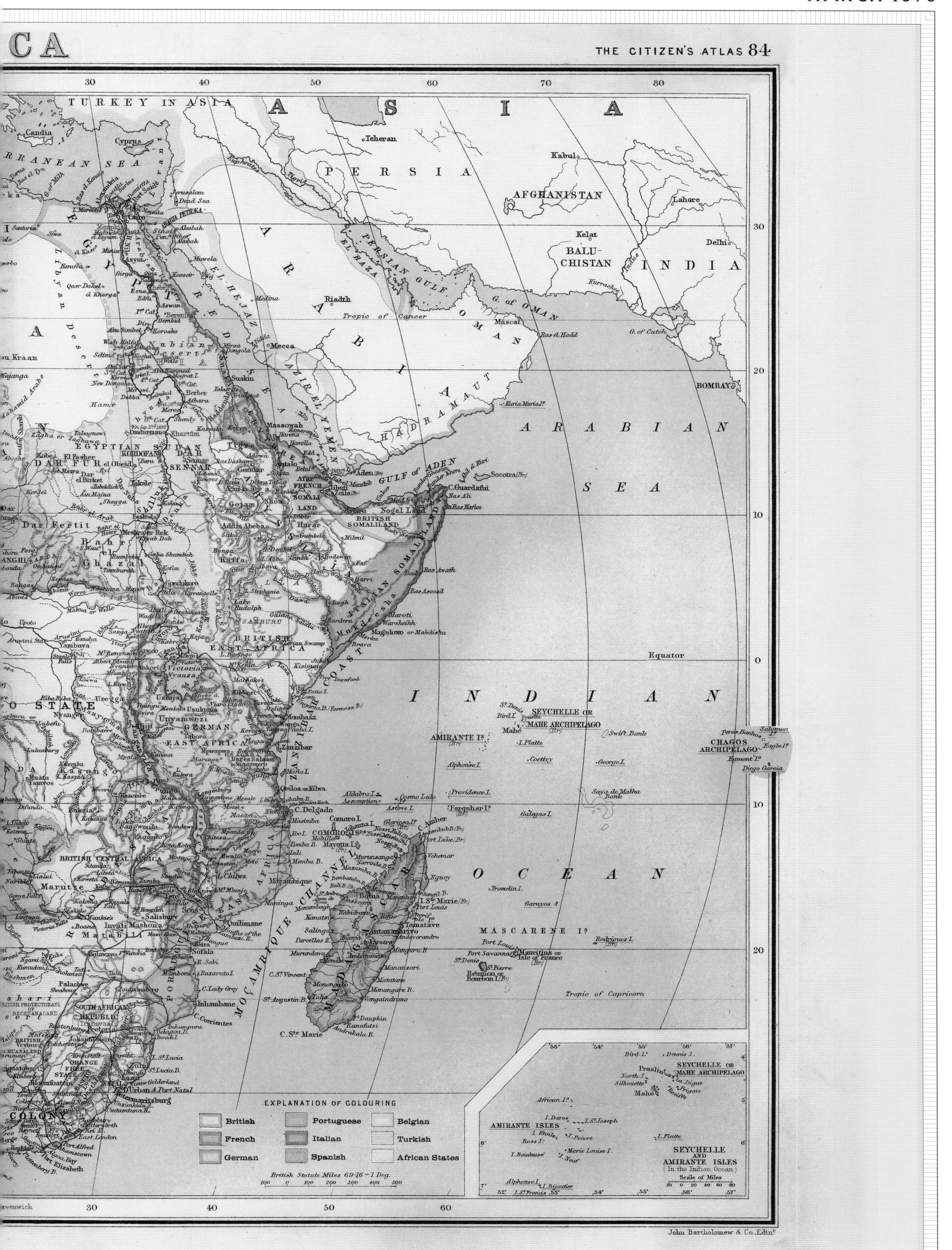
CA
THE CITIZEN'S ATLAS 84
TURKEY IN ASIA
A S I A
PERSIA
AFGHANISTAN
BALU-CHISTAN
INDIA
ARABIA
HADRAMAUT
OMAN
PERSIAN GULF
G. of OMAN
Tropic of Cancer
ARABIAN SEA
GULF of ADEN
BRITISH SOMALILAND
ITALIAN SOMALILAND
BRITISH EAST AFRICA
GERMAN EAST AFRICA
BRITISH CENTRAL AFRICA
MOÇAMBIQUE CHANNEL
MADAGASCAR
INDIAN OCEAN
SEYCHELLE OR MAHE ARCHIPELAGO
AMIRANTE Is
CHAGOS ARCHIPELAGO
MASCARENE Is
Equator
Tropic of Capricorn
EGYPT
DAR FUR
KORDOFAN
SENNAR
SOUTH AFRICAN REPUBLIC
ORANGE FREE STATE
COLONY
Teheran
Kabul
Lahore
Delhi
Kelat
BOMBAY
Riadth
Mecca
Muscat
Cairo
Khartum
Massowah
Aden
Socotra
C. Guardafui
Magadoxo
Mombasa
Zanzibar
Tabora
Moçambique
Salisbury
Sofala
Inhambane
Tamatave
Antananarivo
Port Louis
Mauritius or Isle of France
Réunion or Bourbon I.
Pietermaritzburg
Durban & Port Natal
Port Elizabeth
EXPLANATION OF COLOURING
British
French
German
Portuguese
Italian
Spanish
Belgian
Turkish
African States
British Statute Miles 69·16 = 1 Deg.
SEYCHELLE AND AMIRANTE ISLES (In the Indian Ocean)
Scale of Miles
30
40
50
60
70
80
John Bartholomew & Co. Edinr.

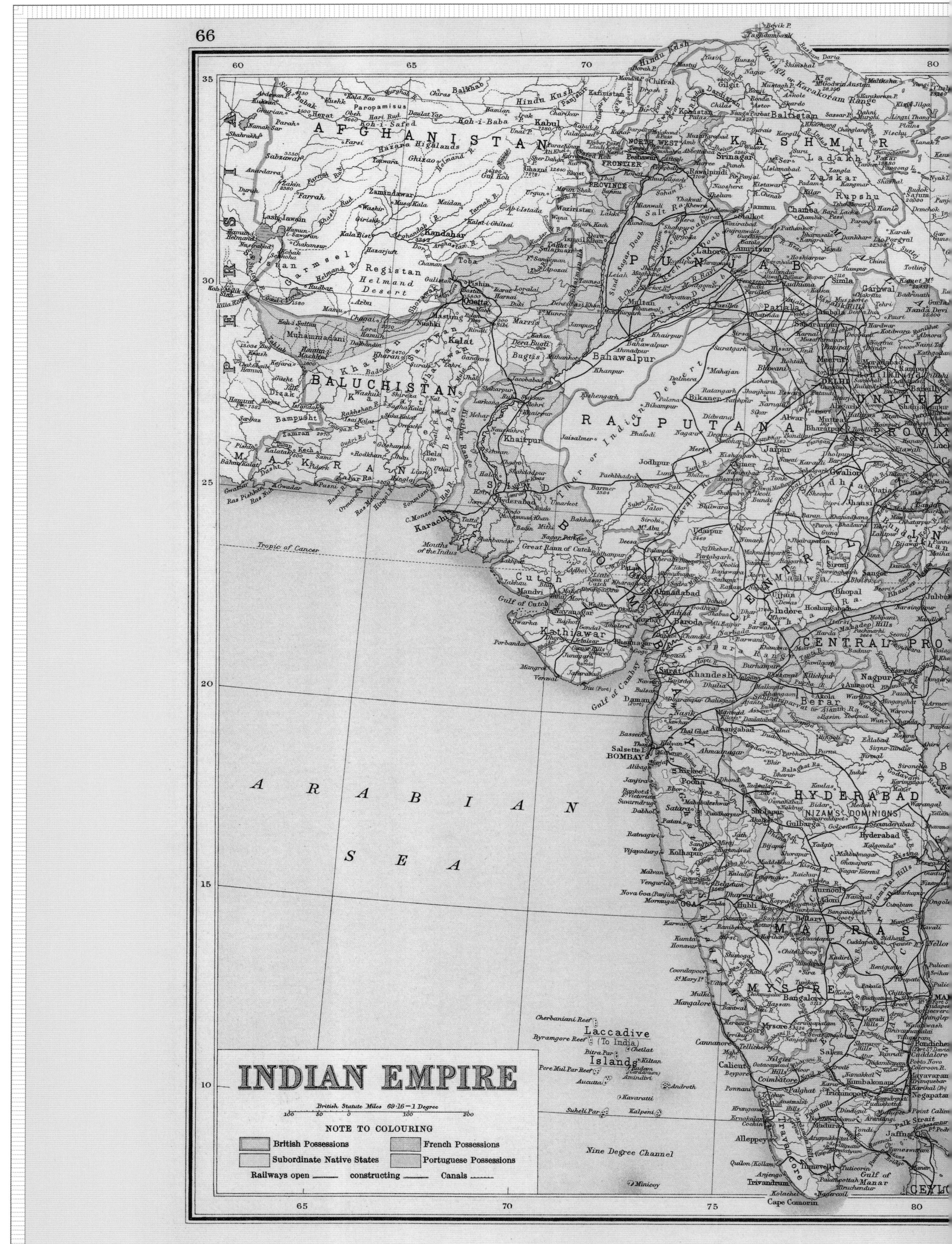
66
INDIAN EMPIRE
British Statute Miles 69·16 = 1 Degree
NOTE TO COLOURING
British Possessions
French Possessions
Subordinate Native States
Portuguese Possessions
Railways open
constructing
Canals
AFGHANISTAN
BALUCHISTAN
MAKRAN
PUNJAB
KASHMIR
RAJPUTANA
CENTRAL
HYDERABAD
NIZAM'S DOMINIONS
MADRAS
MYSORE
ARABIAN SEA
Laccadive
(To India)
Islands
Tropic of Cancer
Gulf of Cutch
Gulf of Cambay
Nine Degree Channel
Kabul
Kandahar
Quetta
Kalat
Karachi
Hyderabad
Lahore
Multan
Bahawalpur
Ahmadabad
Baroda
Surat
BOMBAY
Poona
Goa
Bangalore
Mangalore
Calicut
Cochin
Trivandrum
Cape Comorin
Delhi
Agra
Jaipur
Ajmer
Indore
Bhopal
Nagpur
Jodhpur
Simla
Srinagar
Peshawar
Rawalpindi
NORTH WEST FRONTIER PROVINCE
Thar or Indian Desert
Great Rann of Cutch
Kathiawar
Khandesh
Berar
Mouths of the Indus
60
65
70
75
80
35
30
25
20
15
10

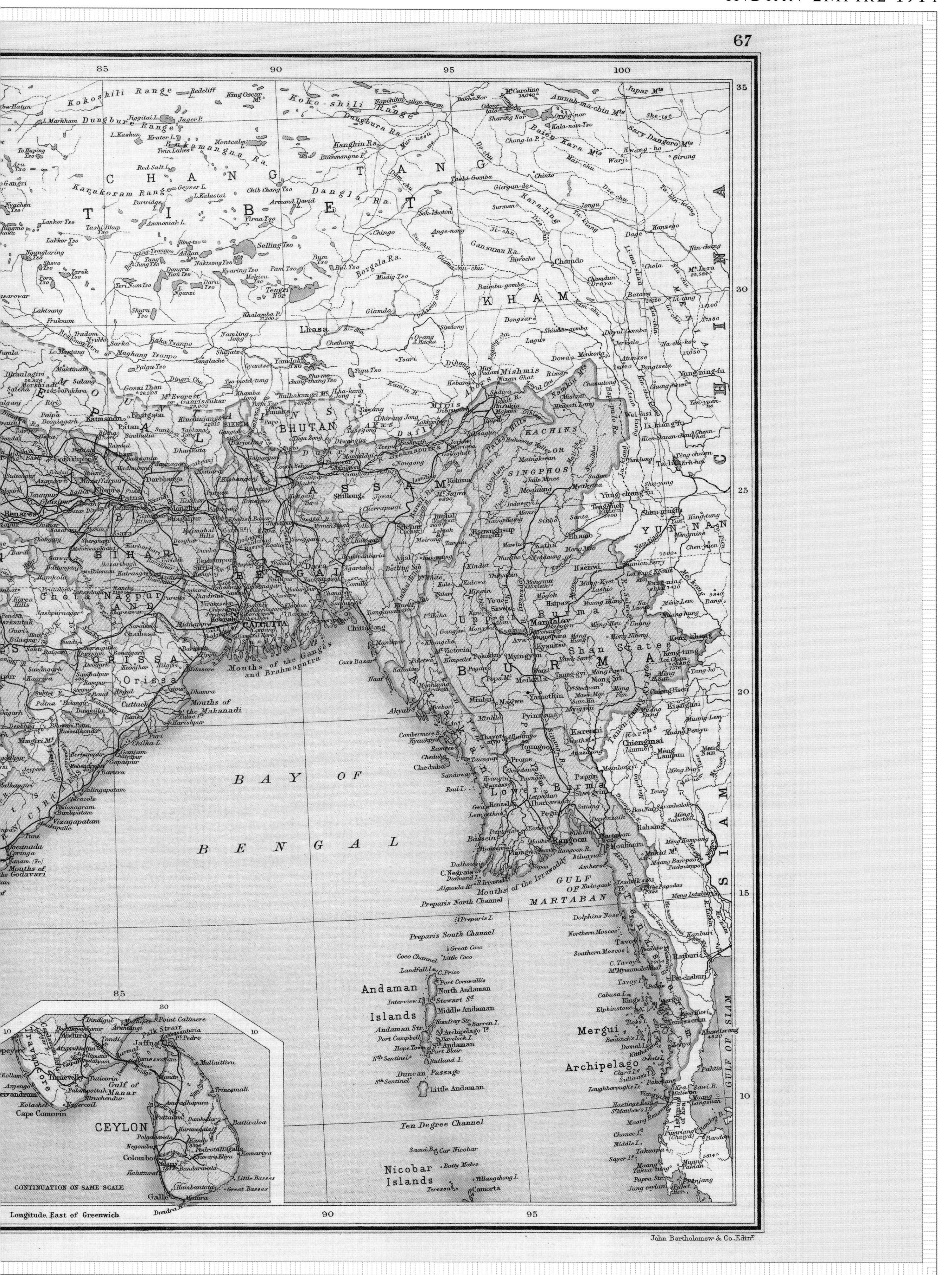
67
Kokoshili Range
Dungbura Ra.
C H A N G - T A N G
T I B E T
K H A M
Lhasa
BHUTAN
SIKKIM
A S S A M
KACHINS
SINGPHOS
YUN-NAN
CHINA
B E N G A L
CALCUTTA
Mouths of the Ganges and Brahmaputra
ORISSA
Mouths of the Mahanadi
Upper Burma
B U R M A
Shan States
Mandalay
Lower Burma
Rangoon
Mouths of the Irrawaddy
GULF OF MARTABAN
Moulmein
SIAM
GULF OF SIAM
B A Y O F B E N G A L
Preparis North Channel
Preparis South Channel
Coco Channel
Andaman Islands
Duncan Passage
Little Andaman
Ten Degree Channel
Car Nicobar
Nicobar Islands
Mergui Archipelago
CEYLON
Palk Strait
Jaffna
Gulf of Manar
Cape Comorin
Colombo
Galle
CONTINUATION ON SAME SCALE
Longitude East of Greenwich
John Bartholomew & Co. Edin[r]

"The Times" ATLAS
EUROP
Scale 1: 10,000,000
English Miles
Kilometres
ARCTIC
ICELAND
Arctic Circle
BRITISH ISLES
SCOTLAND
IRELAND
ENGLAND
NORTH SEA
ATLANTIC OCEAN
ENGLISH CHANNEL
Skager Rack
Cattegat
DENMARK
BALTIC
GERMANY
CZECHO
FRANCE
SWITZERLAND
AUSTRIA
HUNGA
YUGOSL
BAY OF BISCAY
SPAIN
CORSICA
SARDINIA
Balearic Islands
TYRRHENIAN SEA
MEDITERRANEAN
IONIAN SEA
SICILY
MOROCCO
ALGERIA
TUNIS
Gulf of Lions
Gulf of Venice
Faroes
Shetland I.s
Orkney I.s
Bay of Biscay
Longitude East
THE EDINBURGH GEOGRAPHICAL INSTITUTE

POLITICAL
PLATE 10
OCEAN
Kolguev I.
Vaygach I.
Kola Peninsula
White Sea
Archangel
FINLAND
Lake Ladoga
Lake Onega
PETROGRAD
Gulf of Finland
ESTHONIA
Helsinki
Gulf of Riga
Riga
LITHUANIA
Vilnius
Minsk
Smolensk
MOSCOW
Tula
Nizhniy Novgorod
Kazan
RUSSIA
SIBERIA
Tobolsk
Ekaterinburg
Perm
Ufa
Samara
Simbirsk
Penza
Saratov
Voronezh
Kursk
Orel
Kharkov
Kiev
Chernigov
Poltava
UKRAINE
Ekaterinoslav
Kherson
Odessa
Nikolayev
RUMANIA
TRANSYLVANIA
CRIMEA
Sevastopol
SEA OF AZOV
Rostov
Tsaritsyn
Astrakhan
CASPIAN SEA
Caucasus Mountains
Elbruz
Tiflis
Baku
GEORGIA
AZERBAIJAN
ARMENIA
Erivan
Batum
Trebizond
BLACK SEA
BULGARIA
Varna
CONSTANTINOPLE
Sea of Marmara
TURKEY
ANATOLIA
Angora
SMYRNA
Konia
Taurus Mounts
Adana
Aleppo
SYRIA
Syrian Desert
CYPRUS
Rhodes
CRETE OR CANDIA
Archipelago
MESOPOTAMIA
Mosul
Baghdad
PERSIA
Tabriz
Hamadan
Erzerum
Van
Kars
Volga
R. Ural
Orenburg
R. Ob
GULF OF OB
Ural Mountains
Timan Mountains
Uvalli
JOHN BARTHOLOMEW & SON. LTD.

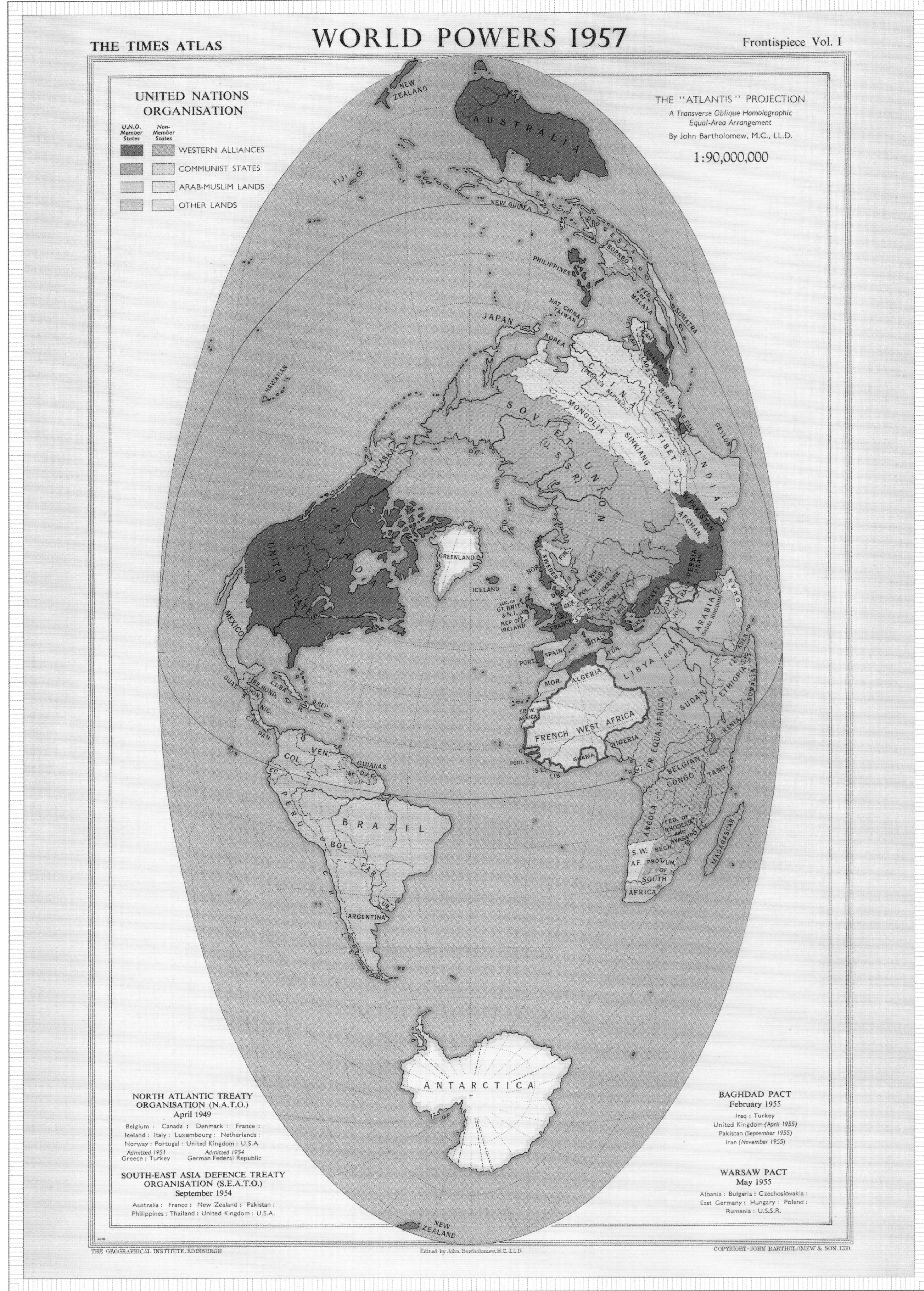
THE TIMES ATLAS
WORLD POWERS 1957
Frontispiece Vol. I
UNITED NATIONS ORGANISATION
U.N.O. Member States
Non-Member States
WESTERN ALLIANCES
COMMUNIST STATES
ARAB-MUSLIM LANDS
OTHER LANDS
THE "ATLANTIS" PROJECTION
A Transverse Oblique Homolographic Equal-Area Arrangement
By John Bartholomew, M.C., LL.D.
1:90,000,000
NEW ZEALAND
AUSTRALIA
FIJI
NEW GUINEA
INDONESIA
BORNEO
PHILIPPINES
FED. OF MALAYA
SUMATRA
NAT. CHINA TAIWAN
JAPAN
KOREA
CHINA (PEOPLE'S REPUBLIC)
MONGOLIA
SINKIANG
TIBET
BURMA
E. PAK.
CEYLON
INDIA
HAWAIIAN IS.
SOVIET UNION (U.S.S.R.)
ALASKA
CANADA
UNITED STATES
GREENLAND
ICELAND
NOR.
SWEDEN
FIN.
POL.
UKRAINE
U.K. OF GT. BRIT. & N.I.
REP. OF IRELAND
FRANCE
GER.
ROM.
BUL.
TURKEY
AFGHAN.
W. PAKISTAN
PERSIA (IRAN)
ARABIA (SAUDI KINGDOM)
OMAN
ADEN
SPAIN
PORT.
ITALY
TUN.
MOR.
ALGERIA
LIBYA
EGYPT
SUDAN
ETHIOPIA
SOMALIA
KENYA
SP. W. AFRICA
FRENCH WEST AFRICA
NIGERIA
GHANA
PORT. G.
S.L.
LIB.
FR. EQUA. AFRICA
BELGIAN CONGO
TANG.
ANGOLA
FED. OF RHODESIA AND NYASALAND
MADAGASCAR
S.W. AF.
BECH. PROT.
UN. OF SOUTH AFRICA
MEXICO
CUBA
BR. HOND.
GUAT.
HON.
NIC.
C.R.
PAN.
D. REP.
H.
VEN.
COL.
GUIANAS
Br. Du. Fr.
EC.
PERU
BRAZIL
BOL.
PAR.
CHILE
UR.
ARGENTINA
ANTARCTICA
NORTH ATLANTIC TREATY ORGANISATION (N.A.T.O.)
April 1949
Belgium : Canada : Denmark : France : Iceland : Italy : Luxembourg : Netherlands : Norway : Portugal : United Kingdom : U.S.A.
Admitted 1951 Greece : Turkey
Admitted 1954 German Federal Republic
SOUTH-EAST ASIA DEFENCE TREATY ORGANISATION (S.E.A.T.O.)
September 1954
Australia : France : New Zealand : Pakistan : Philippines : Thailand : United Kingdom : U.S.A.
BAGHDAD PACT
February 1955
Iraq : Turkey
United Kingdom (April 1955)
Pakistan (September 1955)
Iran (November 1955)
WARSAW PACT
May 1955
Albania : Bulgaria : Czechoslovakia : East Germany : Hungary : Poland : Rumania : U.S.S.R.
THE GEOGRAPHICAL INSTITUTE, EDINBURGH
Edited by John Bartholomew, M.C., LL.D.
COPYRIGHT - JOHN BARTHOLOMEW & SON LTD.

Grand Coulee Dam
NORTH AMERICA
EUROPE
Paris
ASIA
Palm Islands and World Islands
AFRICA
SOUTH AMERICA
New Caledonia
OCEANIA
Taylor Valley
ANTARCTICA

SATELLITE IMAGES

20–21 OCEANIA
22–23 ASIA
24–25 EUROPE
26–27 AFRICA
28–29 NORTH AMERICA
30–31 SOUTH AMERICA
32–33 ANTARCTICA
34–35 TAYLOR VALLEY Antarctica
36–37 NEW CALEDONIA South Pacific Ocean
38–39 GRAND COULEE DAM Washington State USA
40–41 PALM ISLANDS and WORLD ISLANDS Dubai UAE
42–43 PARIS France

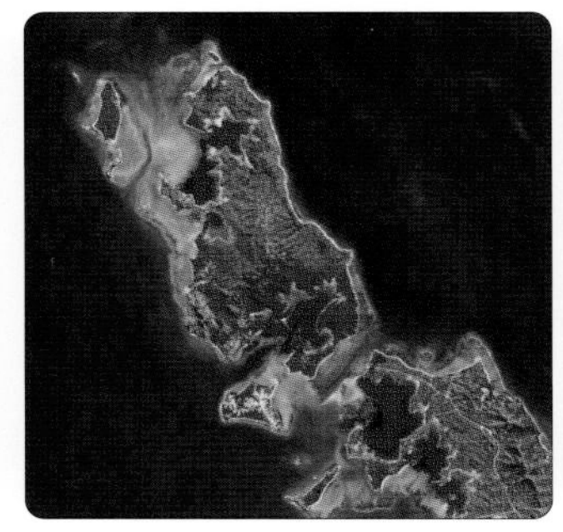

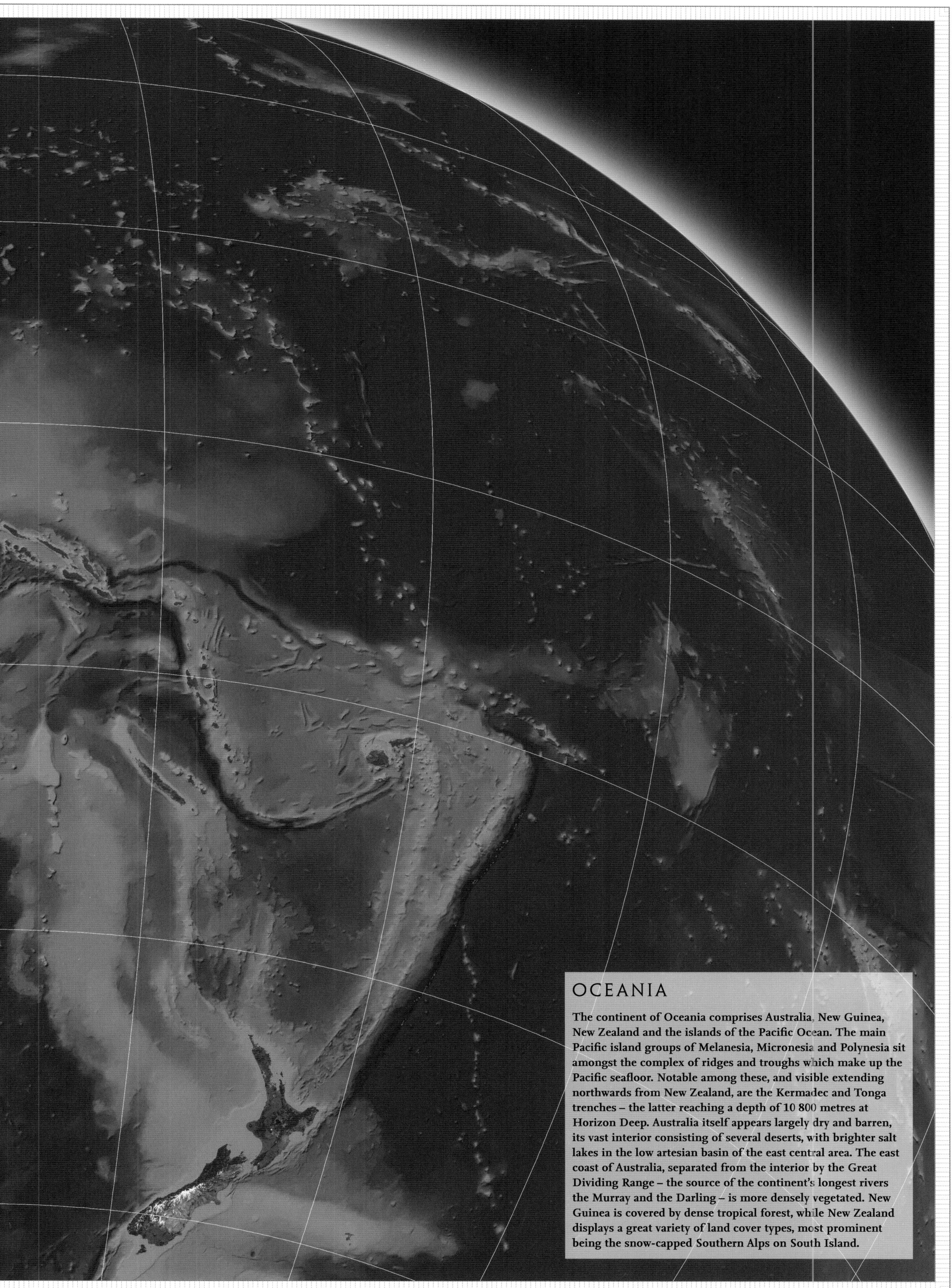

OCEANIA

The continent of Oceania comprises Australia, New Guinea, New Zealand and the islands of the Pacific Ocean. The main Pacific island groups of Melanesia, Micronesia and Polynesia sit amongst the complex of ridges and troughs which make up the Pacific seafloor. Notable among these, and visible extending northwards from New Zealand, are the Kermadec and Tonga trenches – the latter reaching a depth of 10 800 metres at Horizon Deep. Australia itself appears largely dry and barren, its vast interior consisting of several deserts, with brighter salt lakes in the low artesian basin of the east central area. The east coast of Australia, separated from the interior by the Great Dividing Range – the source of the continent's longest rivers the Murray and the Darling – is more densely vegetated. New Guinea is covered by dense tropical forest, while New Zealand displays a great variety of land cover types, most prominent being the snow-capped Southern Alps on South Island.

ASIA

This vast continent – the world's largest – covers an enormous area and contains a great variety of landscapes, evident on this image. It stretches from the Mediterranean Sea in the west to the far east of the Russian Federation and Japan, and from arctic Siberia in the north to the tropical islands of Indonesia. The Caspian Sea – the world's largest lake – is prominent in the west. The snow-capped Caucasus mountains stretching from the Caspian Sea to the Black Sea clearly mark the divide between Asia and Europe. Just east of the Caspian Sea lies the complex shape of the Aral Sea. This was once the world's fourth largest lake, but is now drastically reduced in size because of climate change and the extraction of water for irrigation. In the centre of the image, the long arc of the mountain ranges of the Himalaya, Karakoram, Hindu Kush and Tien Shan circle the featureless Tarim Pendi basin and the lake-riddled Plateau of Tibet.

EUROPE

The generally densely vegetated continent of Europe contains some dramatic geographical features. Its northern and western limits are marked by the complex coastlines of Iceland, Scandinavia and north western Russian Federation, while the British Isles sit on the flat, wide continental shelf. Europe's mountain ranges divide the continent – in the southwest, the Pyrenees separate France from the drier Iberian Peninsula, the wide arc of the Alps separates Italy from the rest of western Europe, the Carpathian Mountains, appearing as a dark curve between the Alps and the Black Sea, mark the edge of the vast European plains, and the Caucasus, stretching between the Black Sea and the Caspian Sea, create a prominent barrier between Europe and Asia. Two of Europe's greatest rivers are also clearly visible on this image – the Volga, Europe's longest river, flowing south from the Ural Mountains into the Caspian Sea and the Dnieper flowing across the plains into the northern Black Sea.

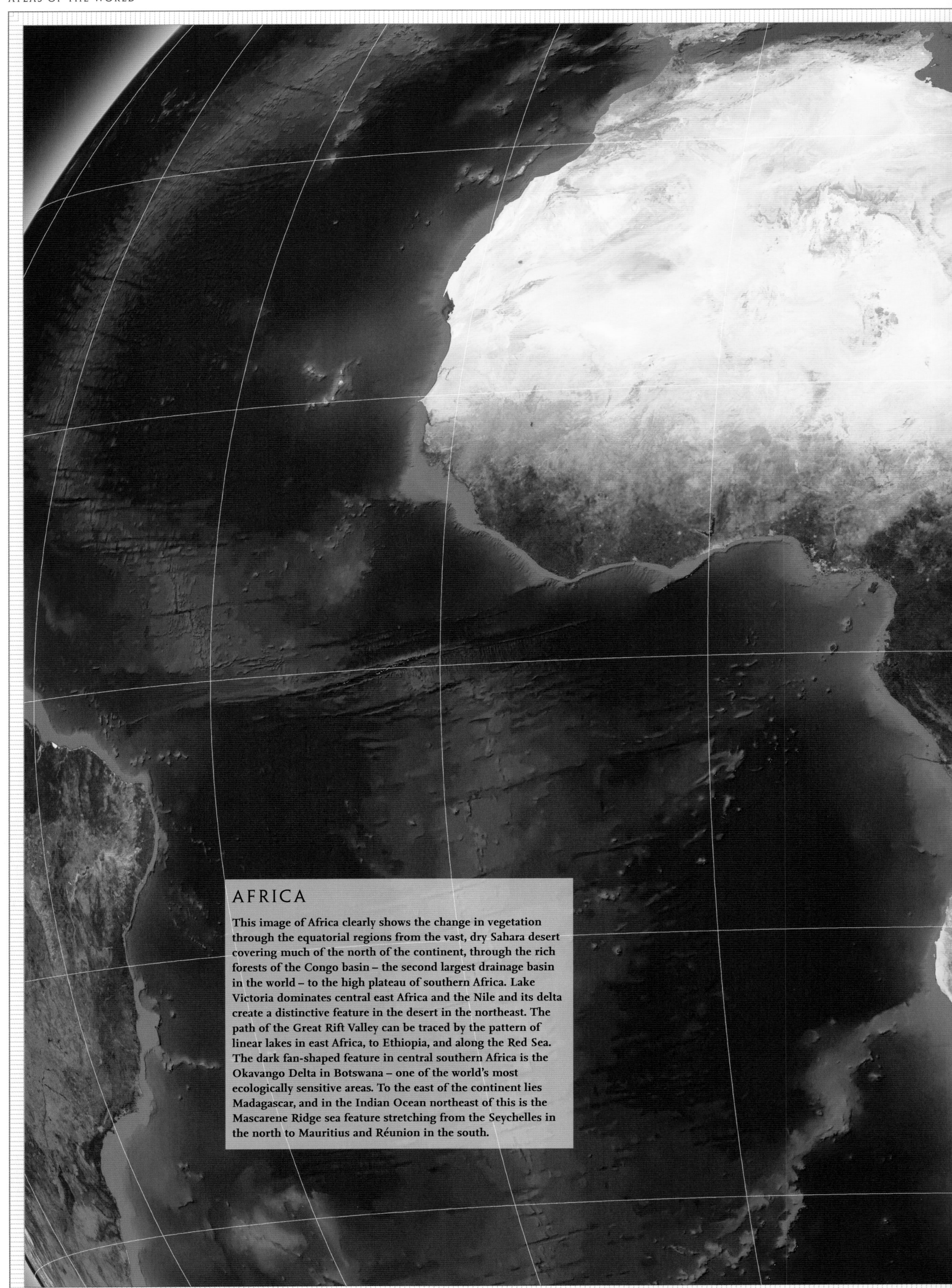

AFRICA

This image of Africa clearly shows the change in vegetation through the equatorial regions from the vast, dry Sahara desert covering much of the north of the continent, through the rich forests of the Congo basin – the second largest drainage basin in the world – to the high plateau of southern Africa. Lake Victoria dominates central east Africa and the Nile and its delta create a distinctive feature in the desert in the northeast. The path of the Great Rift Valley can be traced by the pattern of linear lakes in east Africa, to Ethiopia, and along the Red Sea. The dark fan-shaped feature in central southern Africa is the Okavango Delta in Botswana – one of the world's most ecologically sensitive areas. To the east of the continent lies Madagascar, and in the Indian Ocean northeast of this is the Mascarene Ridge sea feature stretching from the Seychelles in the north to Mauritius and Réunion in the south.

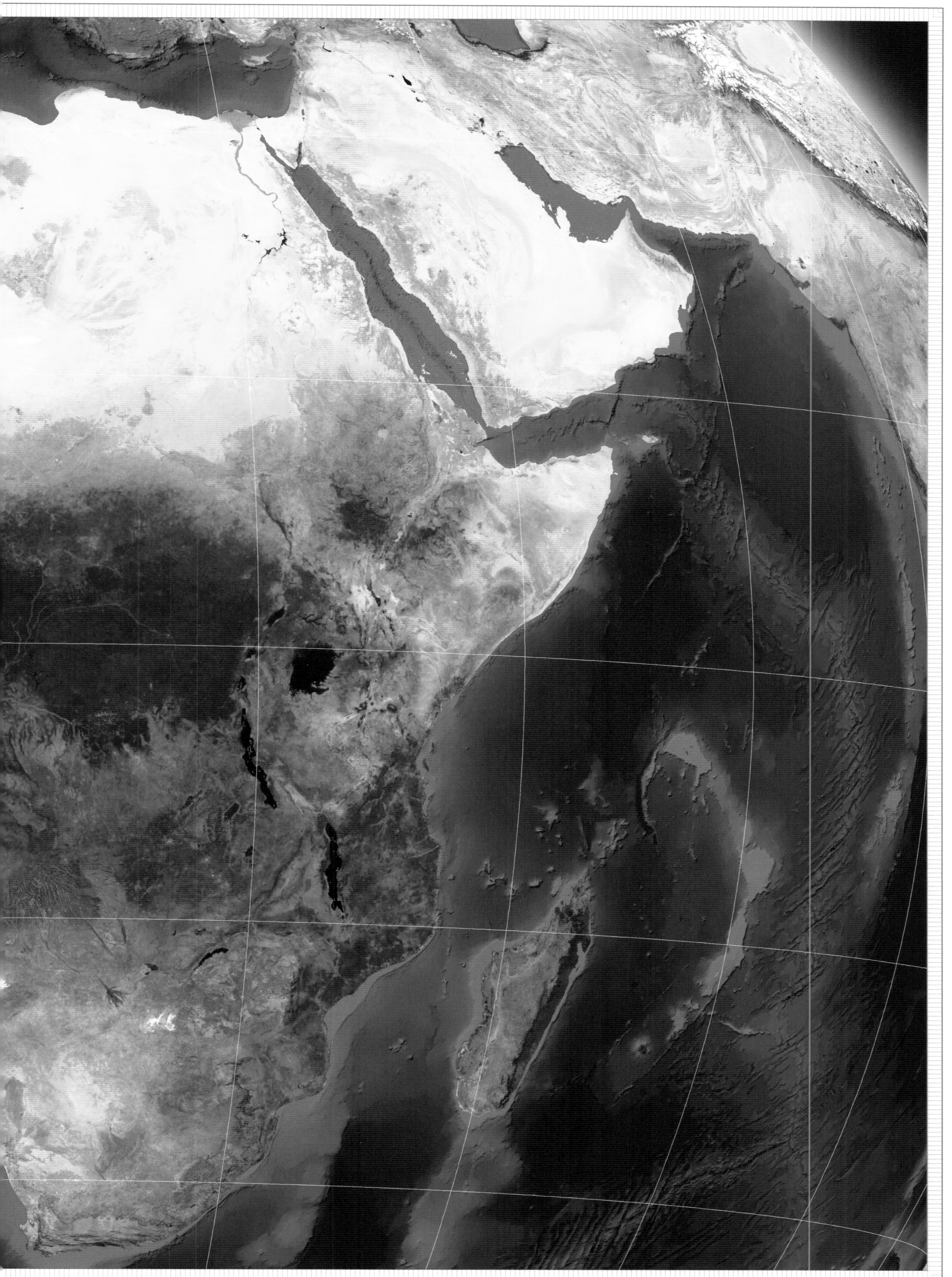

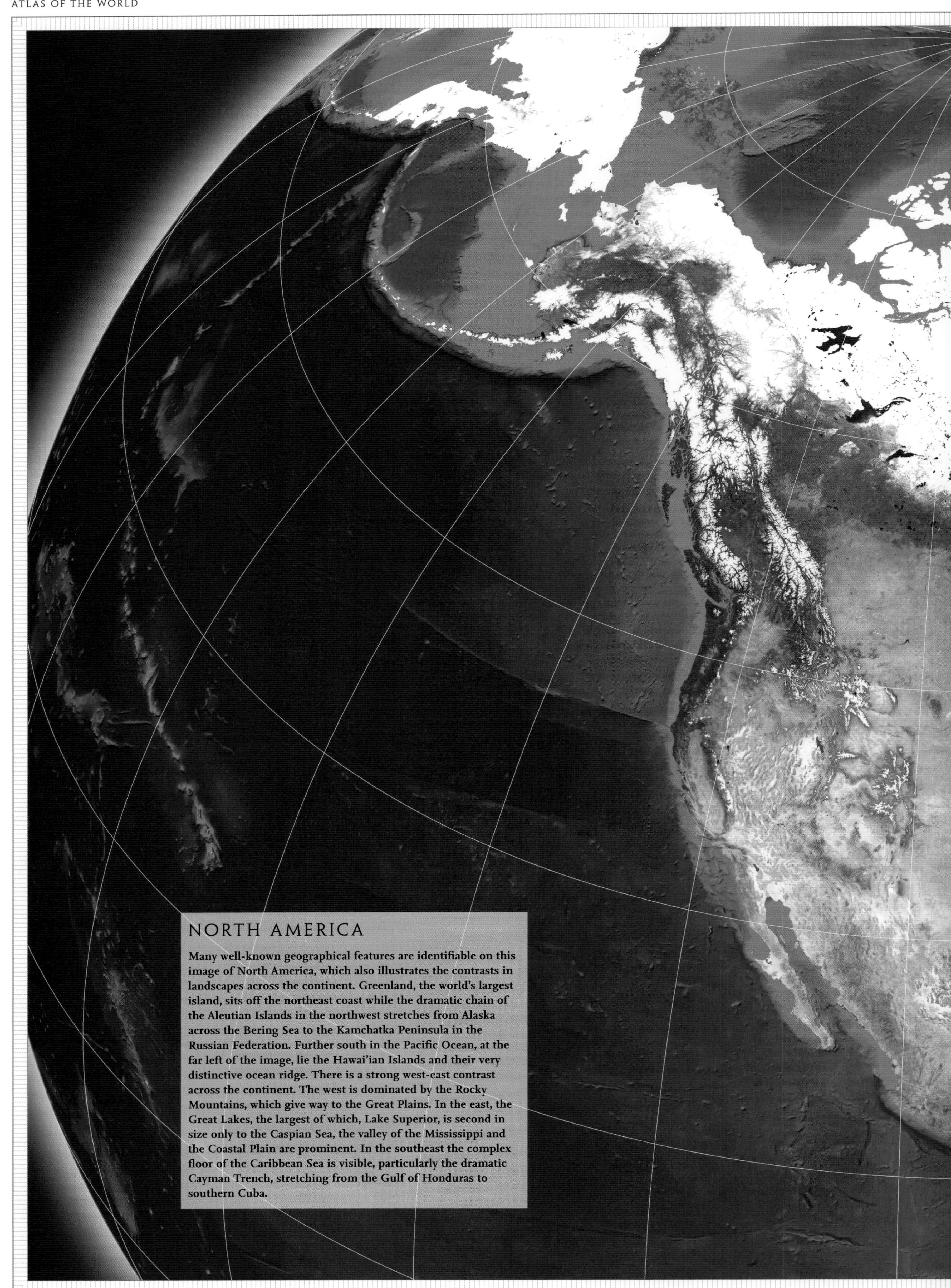

NORTH AMERICA

Many well-known geographical features are identifiable on this image of North America, which also illustrates the contrasts in landscapes across the continent. Greenland, the world's largest island, sits off the northeast coast while the dramatic chain of the Aleutian Islands in the northwest stretches from Alaska across the Bering Sea to the Kamchatka Peninsula in the Russian Federation. Further south in the Pacific Ocean, at the far left of the image, lie the Hawai'ian Islands and their very distinctive ocean ridge. There is a strong west-east contrast across the continent. The west is dominated by the Rocky Mountains, which give way to the Great Plains. In the east, the Great Lakes, the largest of which, Lake Superior, is second in size only to the Caspian Sea, the valley of the Mississippi and the Coastal Plain are prominent. In the southeast the complex floor of the Caribbean Sea is visible, particularly the dramatic Cayman Trench, stretching from the Gulf of Honduras to southern Cuba.

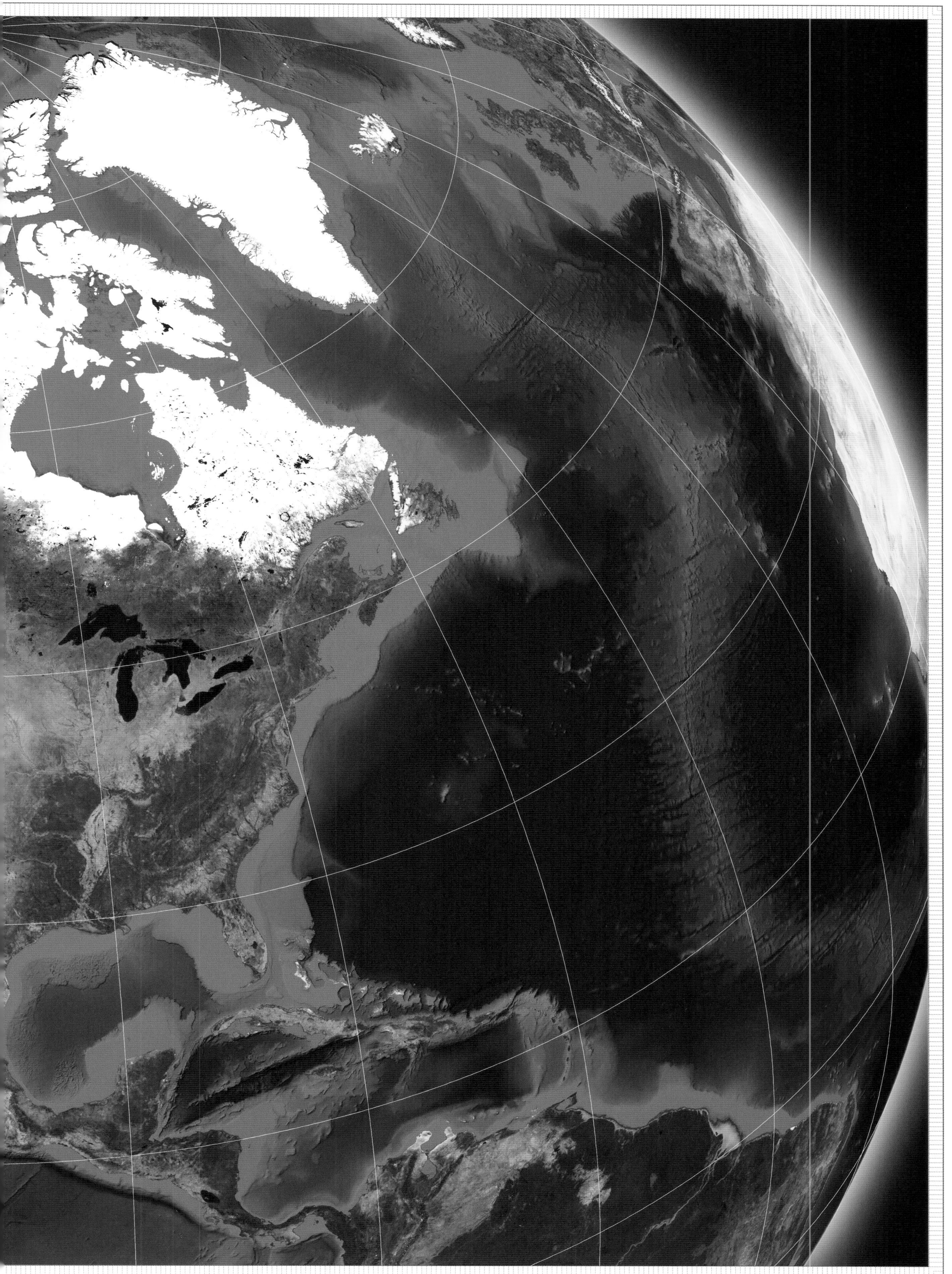

SOUTH AMERICA

The Andes mountains stretch along the whole length of the west coast of South America, widening into the high plains of the Altiplano in Bolivia and Peru in the centre of the continent. Lake Titicaca, the world's highest large navigable lake, lies on the Altiplano, straddling the Bolivia-Peru border. Running parallel to the Andes, just off the west coast, is the Peru-Chile Trench which marks the active boundary between the Nazca and South American tectonic plates. Movement between these plates gives rise to numerous volcanoes in the Andes. The Amazon river runs across almost the whole width of the continent in the north, meeting the Atlantic Ocean in its wide delta on the northeast coast. The vast Amazon basin is one of the most ecologically diverse areas of the Earth. In the south, the wide continental shelf stretches eastward from the tip of the continent to the Falkland Islands and South Georgia on the bottom edge of the image.

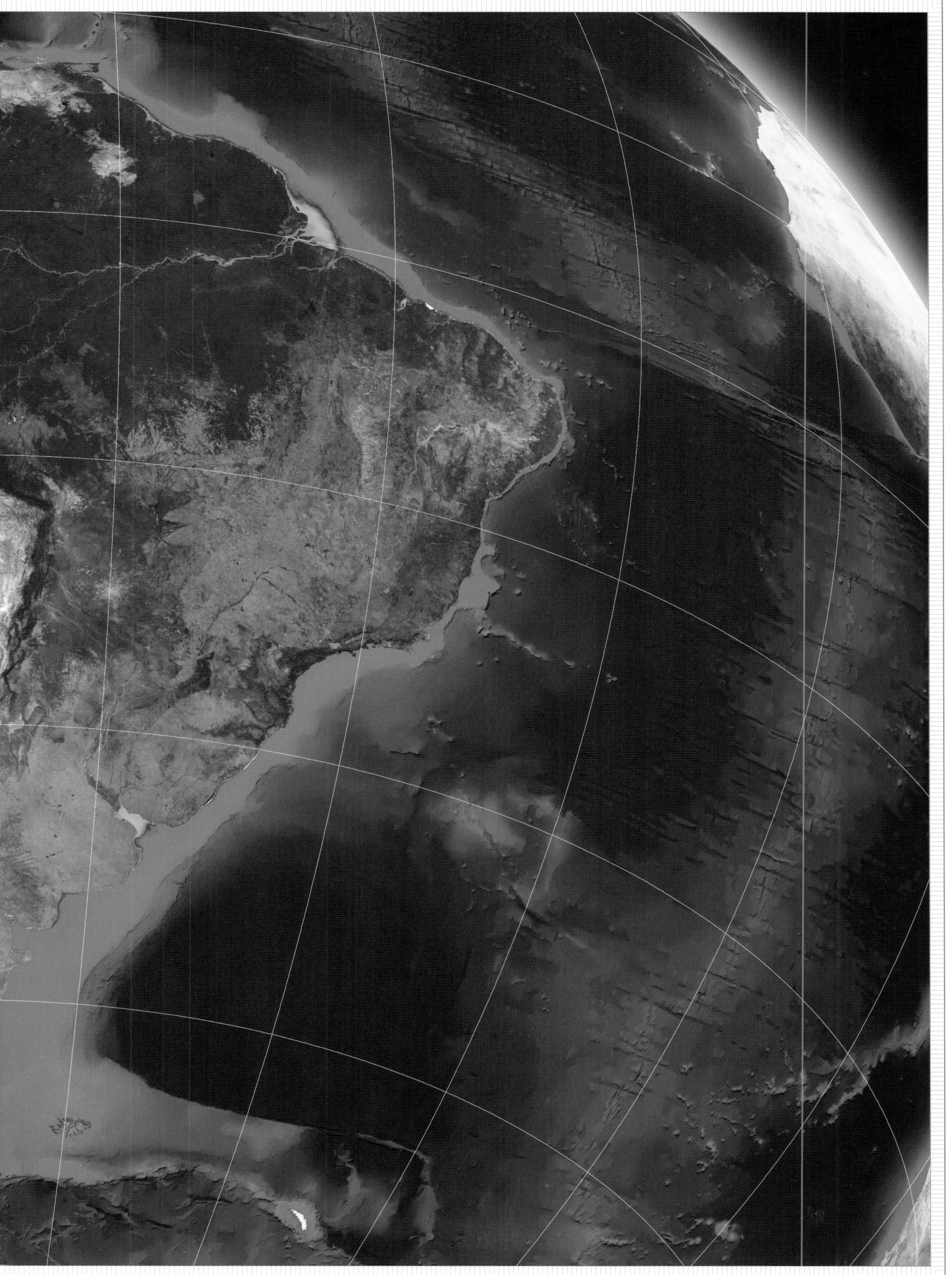

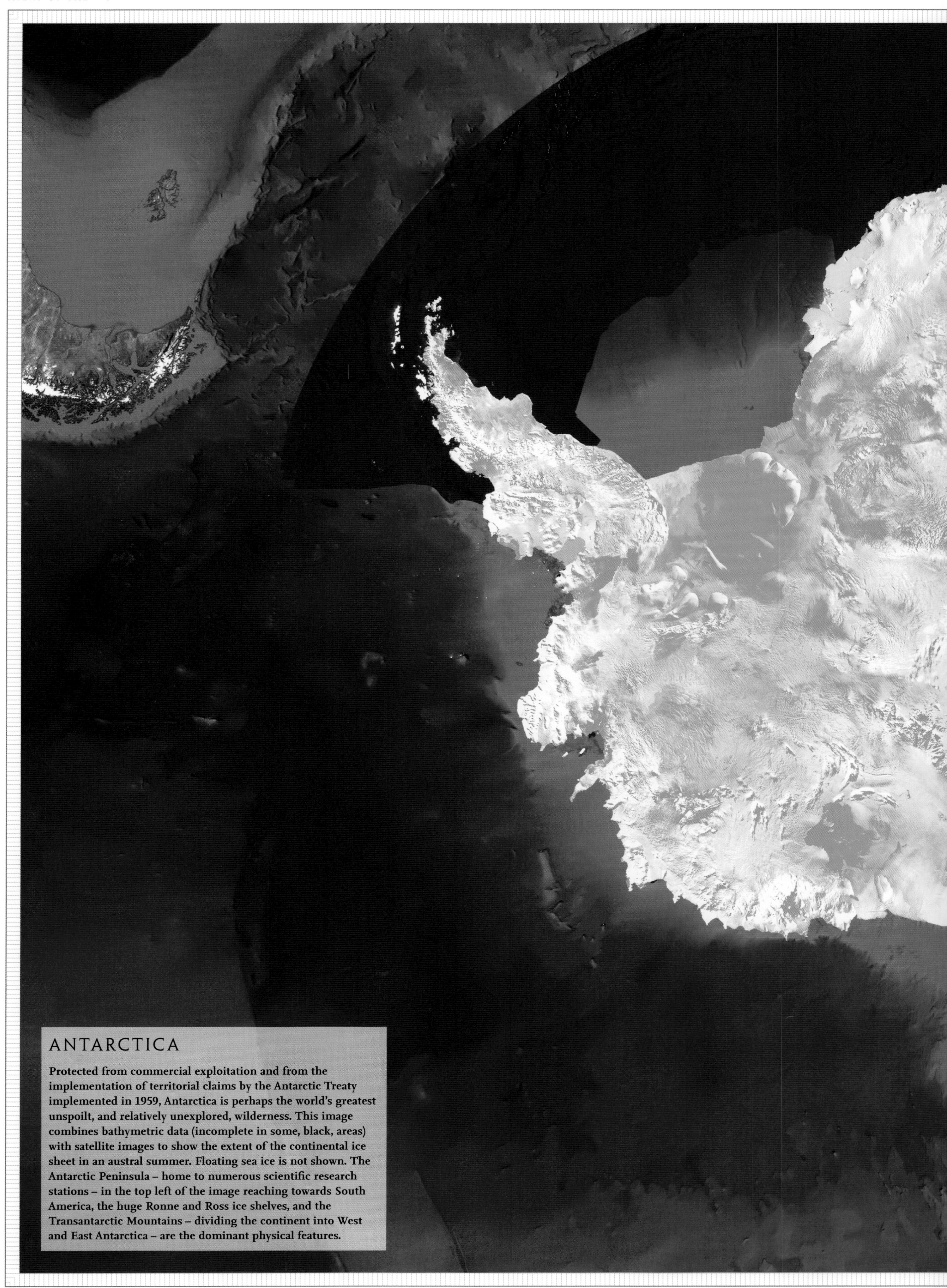

ANTARCTICA

Protected from commercial exploitation and from the implementation of territorial claims by the Antarctic Treaty implemented in 1959, Antarctica is perhaps the world's greatest unspoilt, and relatively unexplored, wilderness. This image combines bathymetric data (incomplete in some, black, areas) with satellite images to show the extent of the continental ice sheet in an austral summer. Floating sea ice is not shown. The Antarctic Peninsula – home to numerous scientific research stations – in the top left of the image reaching towards South America, the huge Ronne and Ross ice shelves, and the Transantarctic Mountains – dividing the continent into West and East Antarctica – are the dominant physical features.

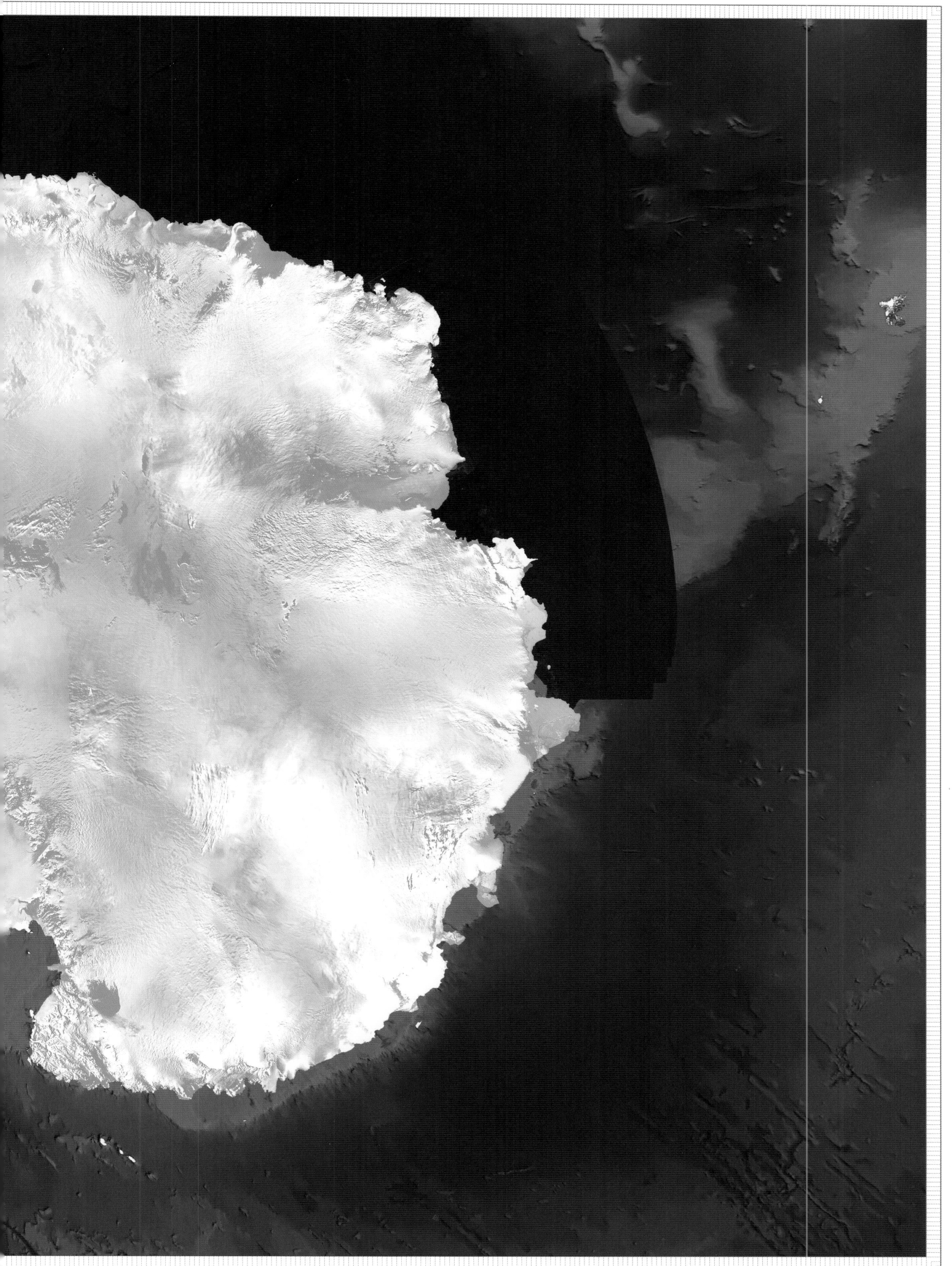

TAYLOR VALLEY
ANTARCTICA

Antarctica may be known for ice and snow, but parts of it are kept snow free by cold dry winds. In this image we can see part of the area known as the Dry Valleys. They lie between the Ross Sea and the East Antarctica Ice Sheet and at the bottom of the image is the Taylor Valley in which we can see several ice-covered lakes. The Taylor Valley lakes include Lake Bonney, which sits below the Taylor Glacier. This glacier-lake junction has an unusual feature as iron oxide seeps out of the Taylor Glacier leading to a red colouring to the ice and the name Blood Falls.

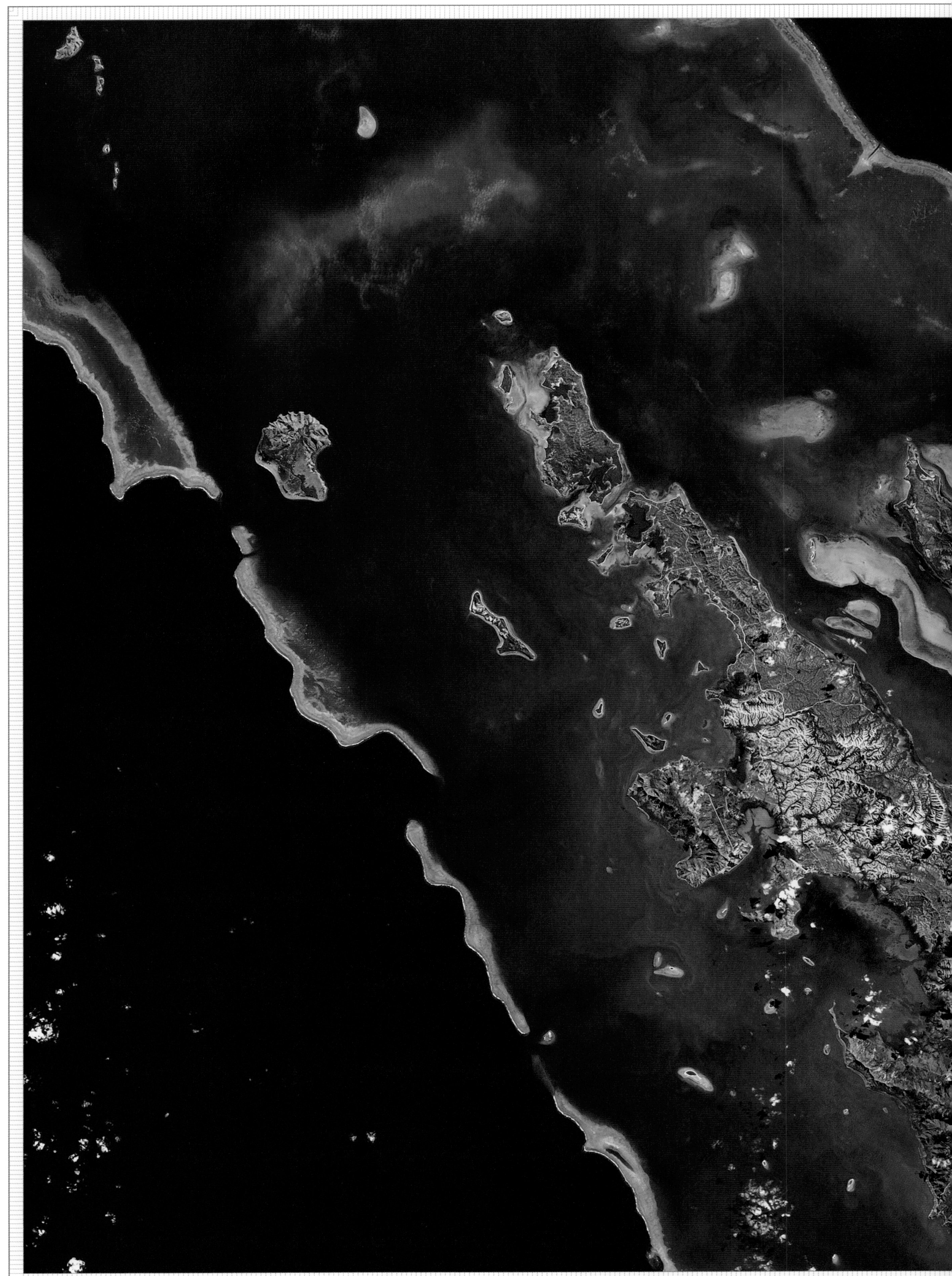

NEW CALEDONIA
SOUTH PACIFIC OCEAN

New Caledonia is a French-governed archipelago around 1 200 km (745 miles) east of Australia. It has the third largest coral reef area in the world, enclosing shallow lagoons with high biodiversity. In 2008 UNESCO announced that six areas of lagoon around New Caledonia were to be inscribed as a new World Heritage Site called Lagoons of New Caledonia: Reef Diversity and Associated Ecosystems. This image shows part of the area covered by one of these, the Zone du Grand Logon Nord, the northern tip of the main island of Grande Terra and various islands and reefs surrounding it. The New Caledonian coral reefs have a large diversity of species and include the world's third largest population of the threatened dugong (a large herbivorous marine mammal).

GRAND COULEE DAM
WASHINGTON STATE USA

The Grand Coulee Dam in Washington State was completed in 1942 after nine years work. This major hydroelectric gravity dam is on the Columbia river and created the Frankiln D. Roosevelt Lake, which can be seen covering the top right part of the image. The Grand Coulee Dam is located at the change in the river course. This happened after the last glacier blocking the Columbia river retreated. The modern channel snakes off to the north and west while the historic channel in the Grand Coulee canyon to the south west can now be seen where Banks Lake has been created. This summer image shows a patchwork of cultivated land to the south, including several distinctive circles where point-pivot irrigation is being used.

PALM ISLANDS AND WORLD ISLANDS 2008

DUBAI UAE

The Palm Islands and The World, an archipelago of over 300 artificial islands, have been created off the coast of Dubai, in the United Arab Emirates. The main image is a mosaic of two scenes from late 2008 showing the progress of the work. The three smaller insets show the development of the first Palm, called Palm Jumeirah in 2002, 2003 and 2004. The Palms were created from sand dredged from the Gulf, and have a protective rock-based crescent shaped breakwater. The building of the Palms and The World islands have changed the coastal ecology and are also affecting the sediment deposition and erosion along what was a well established coastline.

2002

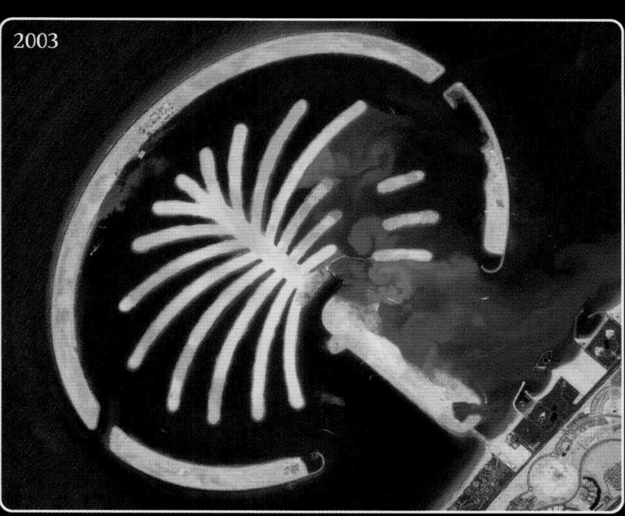
2003

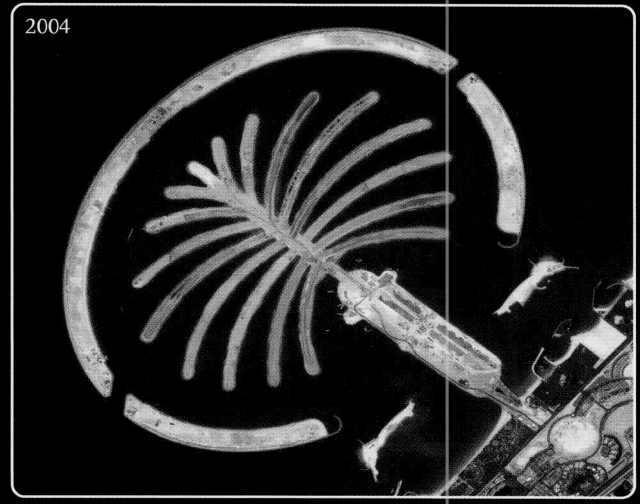
2004

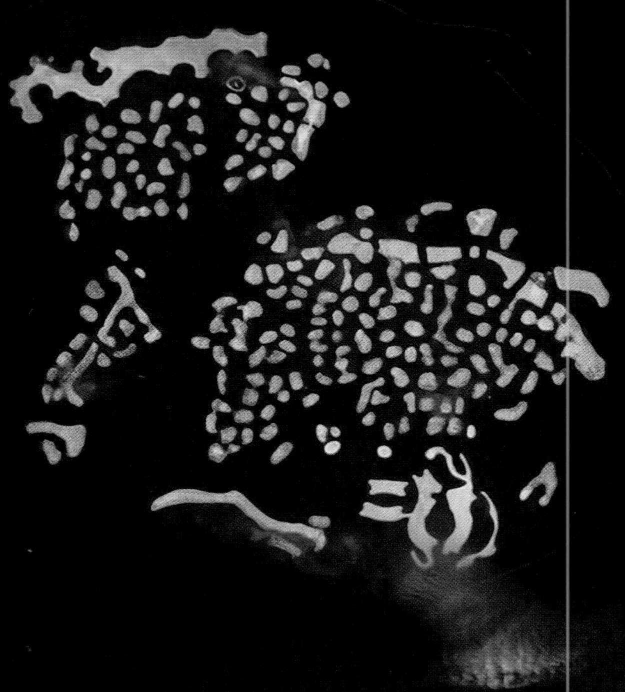

PARIS
FRANCE

Paris is the capital of, and largest city in France. It is located on the river Seine and contains many historic monuments and gardens. This image covers part of central Paris. South of the river, just on the bend is the distinctive shape of the Eiffel Tower facing the Jardin du Trocadero and the curving wings of the Palais de Chaillot just across the river. To the north east of the Palais is the wheel shaped Place Charles de Gaulle with the Arc de Triomphe in the centre. The Avenue des Champs-Elysées runs from the Arc de Triomphe south-east to the Jardin des Tuileries and the Louvre museum with the Pyramid at its entrance.

ORIGINS OF THE SOLAR SYSTEM

The nature and origin of our Solar System has been a subject of much debate. Early ideas of an Earth-centred system took many hundreds of years to be discarded in favour of Copernicus' heliocentric, or sun-centred model. More refined theories followed with Kepler's laws of orbital motion, and Newton's laws of gravity. The question of origin remained unanswered, and was regarded more as a philosophical matter.

The fact that the Sun and the planets rotate in the same direction suggests a common formation mechanism - that of a large collapsing cloud or nebula. It is now believed that this did happen, about 4 600 million years ago. The nebula consisted of predominantly hydrogen and helium, but with a small amount of heavier elements. Over time, the cloud collapsed to form a rotating disk around a dense core. As core collapse continued and pressure in the core increased, material was heated enough to allow the nuclear fusion of hydrogen. Meanwhile as the disk cooled, the heavier elements began to condense and agglomerate. Larger bodies grew rapidly by sweeping up much of the remaining smaller material. As the core began to shine, its radiation pushed back much of the nearby volatile disk material into the outer Solar System, where it condensed and accumulated on the more distant planetary cores. This left the Inner Planets as small rocky bodies, and produced the Gas Giants of the outer system. Bombardment of the planets by a decreasing number of small bodies continued for several hundred million years, causing the craters now seen on many of the planets and moons.

THE SOLAR SYSTEM

ASTEROIDS

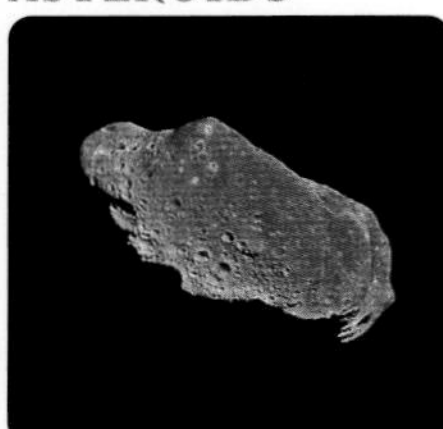

Asteroids are small irregularly shaped rocky objects which orbit the Sun and which are remnants from the formation of the planets. The largest concentration of asteroids exists in a belt, 180 million km in width, which lies between the orbits of Mars and Jupiter. Over 100 000 asteroids are estimated to have diameters greater than 1 km and yet only a dozen or so are known to have diameters greater than 250 km. The entire mass of the asteroid belt is approximately one-thousandth of the Earth's mass. One-third of this mass is accounted for by Ceres, the largest asteroid known with a diameter of 913 km. Another group of asteroids known as the Trojans orbit the Sun in two broad clouds centred 60° ahead of and 60° behind Jupiter.

Hundreds, possibly thousands of asteroids, of varying sizes, cross the Earth's orbit and on 13 April 2029 asteroid number 99942 Apophis will fly within 40 000 km of the Earth.

THE SUN

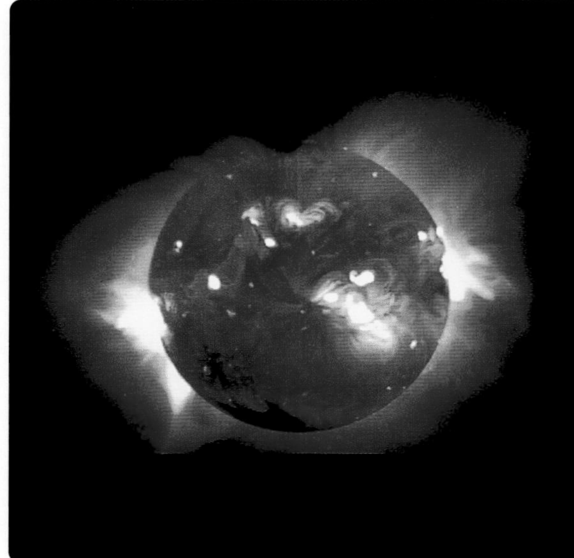

The Sun is a typical star and the closest one to Earth. It accounts for 99.85 per cent of the total mass contained within the Solar System, ensuring that it provides a dominating gravitational hold on its orbiting planets. The tremendous amount of heat and light produced by the Sun is the result of nuclear fusion reactions which occur in its core. In this process, hydrogen is converted into helium to produce a core temperature of roughly 15 million°C. Intense magnetic fields can induce cooling zones seen as dark sun spots on the Sun's surface. The Sun constantly emits a stream of charged particles which form the solar wind and cause auroral activity which can be seen on Earth.

	Sun	Mercury	Venus	Earth	Mars	Jupiter	Saturn	Uranus	Neptune
Mass (Earth=1)	332 830	0.055	0.815	1(6 x 10^{24})	0.107	317.82	95.161	14.371	17.147
Volume (Earth=1)	1 306 000	0.05	0.88	1	0.15	1 316	755	52	44
Density (Water=1)	1.41	5.43	5.24	5.52	3.94	1.33	0.70	1.30	1.76
Equatorial diameter (km)	1 392 000	4 879.4	12 103.6	12 756.3	6 794	142 984	120 536	51 118	49 528
Polar flattening	0	0	0	0.003	0.007	0.065	0.098	0.023	0.017
Surface gravity (Earth=1)	27.5	0.38	0.91	1	0.38	2.53	1.07	0.90	1.14
Number of satellites > 100km	-	0	0	1	0	7	13	8	6
Total number of satellites	-	0	0	1	2	63	47	27	13
Rotation period (Earth days)	25–36	58.65	-243	23hr 56m 4s	1.03	0.41	0.44	-0.72	0.67
Year (Earth days/years)	-	88 days	224.7 days	365.24 days	687 days	11.86 years	29.42 years	83.8 years	163.8 years
Mean orbital distance (million km)	-	57.9	108.2	149.6	227.9	778.4	1 426.7	2 871.0	4 498.3
Orbital eccentricity	-	0.2056	0.0068	0.0167	0.0934	0.0484	0.0542	0.0472	0.0086
Mean orbital velocity (km/s)	-	47.87	35.02	29.79	24.13	13.07	9.67	6.84	5.48
Inclination of equator to orbit (deg.)	7.25	0	177.3	23.45	25.19	3.12	26.73	97.86	29.58
Orbital inclination (w.r.t. ecliptic)	-	7.005	3.395	0.00005	1.851	1.305	2.485	0.770	1.769
Mean surface temperature (°C)	5 700	167	457	15–20	-90– -5	-108	-139	-197	-200
Atmospheric pressure (bars)	-	-	90	1	0.007–0.010	0.3	0.4	-	-
Atmospheric composition (selected gas components)	H_2 92.1% He 7.8% O_2 0.061%	-	CO_2 96% N_2 3%	N_2 77% O_2 21% Ar 1.6%	CO_2 95.3% N_2 2.7%	H_2 90% He 10%	H_2 97% He 3%	H_2 83% He 15% CH_4 2%	H_2 85% He 13% CH_4 2%

RELATIVE SIZES OF PLANETS

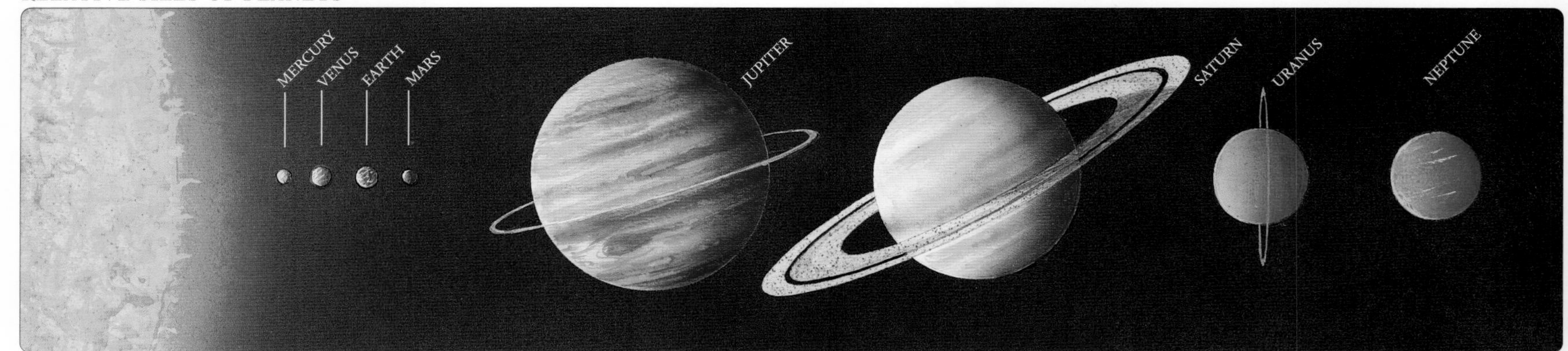

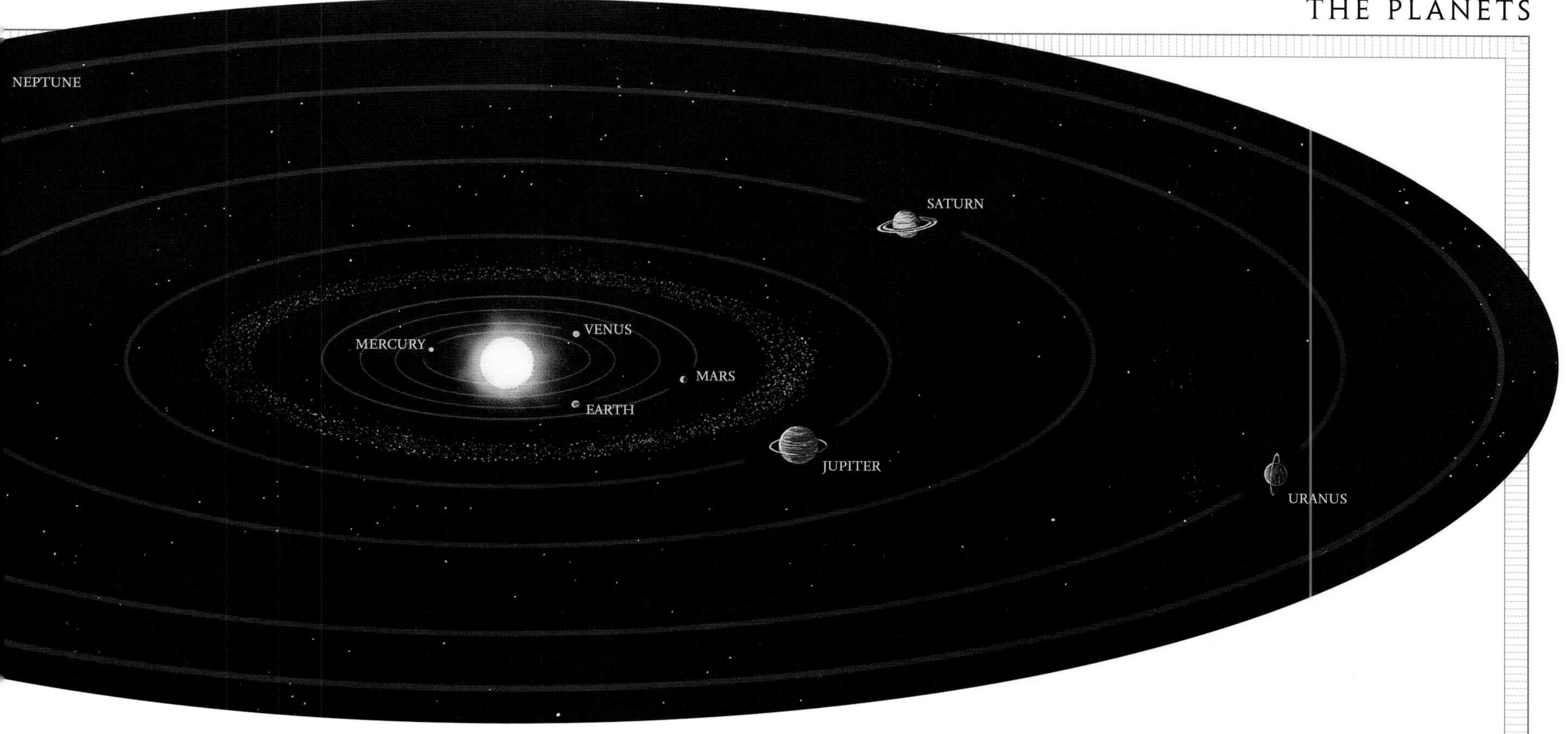

MERCURY

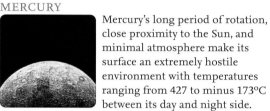

Mercury's long period of rotation, close proximity to the Sun, and minimal atmosphere make its surface an extremely hostile environment with temperatures ranging from 427 to minus 173°C between its day and night side. Mercury is similar to Earth's Moon in size and appearance; its cratered surface was first photographed in detail in the mid-1970s by the Mariner 10 space probe. However the internal structure differs from the Moon. Analysis of its magnetic field suggests that the core consists of molten iron, believed to be 40 per cent of the planet's volume. Mercury has a very eccentric orbit with its distance from the Sun varying from 46 to 70 million km.

VENUS

Venus' thick atmosphere of carbon dioxide and nitrogen creates not only a huge surface pressure of ninety times that on Earth but also a greenhouse effect producing temperatures in excess of 450°C. Traces of sulphur dioxide and water vapour form clouds of dilute sulphuric acid, making the atmosphere extremely corrosive. The thick clouds reflect almost all incident light and hide the surface from view. In 1990 use of radar imaging enabled the Magellan space probe to see through the cloud. Magellan mapped 98 per cent of the planet during three years to find a surface covered in craters, volcanoes, mountains and solidified lava flows. Venus is the brightest object in the sky after the Sun and Moon and is unusual in that its year is less than its rotation period.

EARTH

Earth is the largest and densest of the Inner Planets. Created some 4 500 million years ago, the core, rocky mantle and crust are similar in structure to Venus. The Earth's core is composed almost entirely of iron and oxygen compounds which exist in a molten state at temperatures of approximately 5 000°C. Earth is the only planet with vast quantities of life-sustaining water, with the oceans covering 70.8 per cent of its surface. The action of plate tectonics has created vast mountain ranges and is responsible for volcanic activity. The Moon is Earth's only natural satellite and with a diameter of over one quarter that of the Earth's, makes the Earth-Moon system a near double-planet.

MARS

Named after the Roman god of war because of its blood-red appearance, Mars is the last of the Inner Planets. The red colour comes from the high concentration of iron oxides on its surface. Mars has impressive surface features, including the highest known peak in the Solar System, Olympus Mons, an inactive volcano reaching a height of 23 km above the surrounding plains, and Valles Marineris, a 2 500 km long canyon four times as deep as the Grand Canyon. Mars has polar caps composed of water and carbon dioxide ice which partially evaporate during its summer. NASA's surface rovers Spirit and Opportunity, which landed in 2004, have provided clear evidence that water once flowed on Mars, increasing the likelihood that life once existed there.

JUPITER

Jupiter is by far the most massive of all the planets and is the dominant body in the Solar System after the Sun. It is the innermost of the Gas Giants. The dense surface atmosphere is predominantly hydrogen, with helium, water vapour, and methane. Below this is a layer of liquid hydrogen, then an even deeper layer of metallic hydrogen and possibly a small rocky core. Unlike solid bodies, Jupiter's rotation period is somewhat ill-defined, with equatorial regions rotating faster than the polar caps. This, combined with convection currents in lower layers, cause intense magnetic fields and rapidly varying surface features. Most notable of these is the Great Red Spot, a giant circular storm visible since the first telescopic observations of Jupiter, which shows no signs of abating.

SATURN

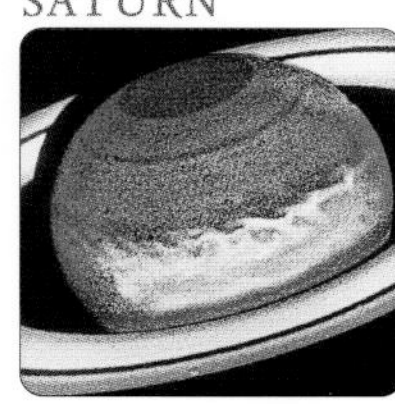

Although only slightly smaller than Jupiter, Saturn is a mere one-third of Jupiter's mass, and the least dense of all the planets – less dense than water. The low mass, combined with a fast rotation rate, leads to the planet's significant polar flattening. Saturn exhibits a striking ring system, more than twice the diameter of the planet. The rings consist of countless small rock and ice clumps which vary in size from a grain of sand to tens of metres in diameter. It is believed that the rings were formed from a stray moon coming too close to, and being ripped apart by Saturn. Distinct bands and gaps in the rings are the result of complex interactions between Saturn and its closer moons. Recent rare opportunities to view Saturn's rings edgeways have led to the discovery of at least two other moons.

URANUS

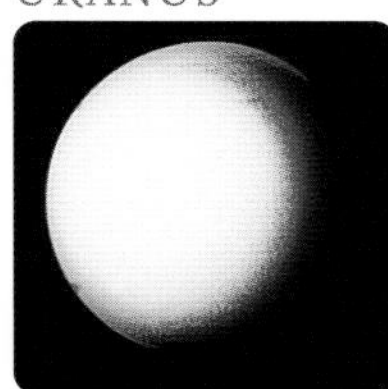

Uranus has many surprising features; the most prominent of these is the tilt of its rotation axis by over 90 degrees caused by a large collision in its early history. Like the other Gas Giants, Uranus is predominantly hydrogen and helium with a small proportion of methane and other gases. However, because Uranus is colder than Jupiter and Saturn, the methane forms ice crystals which give Uranus a featureless blue-green colour. The interior is also different from that expected. Instead of having a gaseous atmosphere above liquid and metallic hydrogen layers, Uranus has a super-dense gaseous atmosphere extending down to its core. Uranus' magnetic field is inclined at 60 degrees to the rotation axis, and is off centre by one-third of the planet's radius, which suggests that it is not generated by the core.

NEPTUNE

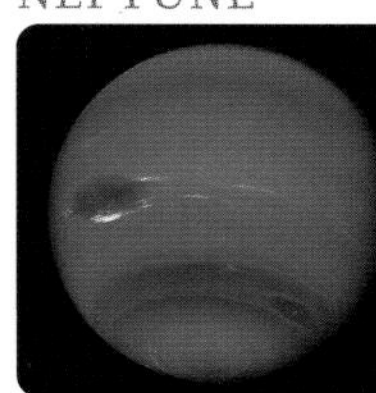

Neptune has always been associated with Uranus because of its similar size, composition and appearance, but, unexpectedly, Neptune's atmosphere is more active than that of Uranus. This was shown by Voyager 2 in 1989 with the observation of the Great Dark Spot, Neptune's equivalent to Jupiter's Great Red Spot. Voyager 2 recorded the fastest winds ever seen in the Solar System, 2 000 km per hour, around the Dark Spot. This feature disappeared in 1994, but has been replaced by a similar storm in the northern polar cap. Like Uranus, Neptune has a magnetic field highly inclined to the planet's axis of rotation and off-centre by more than half of the planet's radius. The cause of this magnetic field is convection currents in conducting fluid layers outside the core.

PLUTO AND THE KUIPER BELT

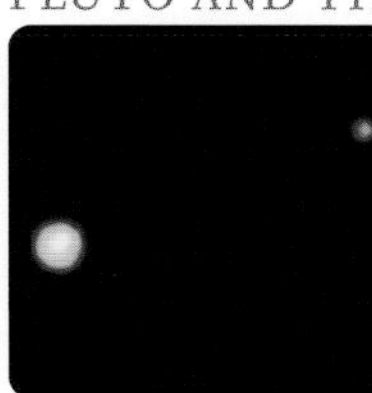

Discovered in 1930, Pluto was long considered to be the 'ninth planet' but since 1992 many hundreds of similar objects have been found in a flattened disk beyond Neptune. Astronomers often call this region of trans-Neptunian bodies the 'Kuiper Belt'. As more and more Kuiper Belt Objects, some about the same size as Pluto and many having moons of their own, were discovered, a debate about Pluto's status erupted. Finally, in 2006 the International Astronomical Union decided to re-classify Pluto, and some of the larger Kuiper Belt Objects such as Eris and Sedna, as a new class of 'dwarf-planets'.

THE EARTH'S STRUCTURE

The interior of the Earth can be divided into three principal regions (*see 1*). The outermost region is known as the crust, which is extremely thin. Under the continents the crust is about 33 km thick on average, under the oceans the crust is even thinner: perhaps a third of its continental thickness. Over the course of geological time the Earth's crust has broken up into large fragments. These lithospheric plates are slowly moving – a process known as continental drift.

The next layer down is the mantle which is about 2 850 km thick. There is a weak zone in the upper mantle, called the asthenosphere, which behaves like a fluid when under stress. The outermost 70 km or so of the mantle, together with the crust, is known as the lithosphere and is much stronger. Below the mantle is the Earth's core, which is mainly made up of iron. The greater part of the core is completely liquid; however, there is a solid inner core. It is the dynamic processes operating in the upper parts of the Earth's interior which give rise to very dramatic and violent expressions of the huge energies involved: earthquakes and volcanoes.

1. THE EARTH'S INTERIOR

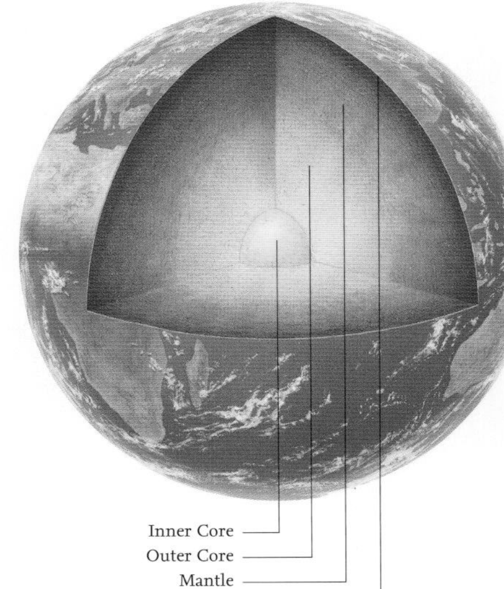

2. DISTRIBUTION OF MAJOR EARTHQUAKES AND VOLCANOES

Winkel Tripel Projection
scale approximately 1:109 000 000

DISTRIBUTION OF EARTHQUAKES AND VOLCANOES

Any map showing the distribution of earthquakes and volcanoes will inevitably look very similar to a map showing the boundaries of the tectonic plates. This is because both phenomena are largely controlled by the processes of plate tectonics. The vast majority of the world's earthquakes occur at plate boundaries as a result of one plate pushing past, or under, another. Even those earthquakes which occur away from plate margins are still mostly due to stresses in the rocks which result indirectly from plate movements.

3. TECTONIC PLATE BOUNDARIES

scale 1:271 000 000

Constructive boundary - mid ocean ridge
Destructive boundary
Conservative boundary
→7.2 Rate of movement (cm per year)

VOLCANOES

A volcano forms where a vent allows molten rock (magma) from the interior of the Earth to reach the surface. The magma originates ultimately in the mantle, but is often stored in a magma reservoir within the crust as it moves upwards. It then erupts either as a stream of liquid rock (called lava when it appears at the surface) or as fine particles of ash or cinder. Either way, the erupted material builds up over time into a mountain, typically conical in shape. The exact shape of the volcano is controlled by the type of material erupted. Volcanoes in oceanic locations (such as Hawaii) tend to erupt very basic (non-acidic) lava which flows relatively easily. Because it can run quite far before cooling, this produces a very flat volcano with gentle slopes, known as a shield volcano. Continental volcanoes produce more ash and acidic lava which flows more slowly, forming steeper-sided cones. Such volcanoes also tend to erupt more explosively, because of the greater amount of steam or gas in the lava, and are generally more dangerous. They can produce what is know as a pyroclastic flow, a fast-moving cloud of super-heated ash and gases, which is what destroyed Pompeii in AD 79. Gas is sometimes a significant by-product of volcanic eruptions. The 1991 eruption of Mt Pinatubo in the Philippines injected vast amounts of sulphur dioxide into the atmosphere.

Volcanic ash is formed when magma, blown into fine drops by escaping gas, solidifies as tiny particles of rock.

Volcanoes can also be classified according to their eruptive history. Active volcanoes are those that are currently erupting. An eruption can go on intermittently for years, and some volcanoes, such as Stromboli in Italy, are almost permanently active. However, most volcanoes erupt much less frequently, and those that have not erupted for tens or hundreds of years, but may be expected to erupt again, are said to be dormant. Lastly, there are extinct volcanoes which were once active but which cannot possibly erupt again today.

Lava erupting into the Pacific Ocean on Big Island, Hawaii

MAJOR VOLCANIC ERUPTIONS 1980–2009

Year	Volcano	Country
1980	Mt St Helens	USA
1982	El Chichónal	Mexico
1982	Gunung Galunggung	Indonesia
1983	Kilauea	Hawaii, USA
1983	Ō-yama	Japan
1985	Nevado del Ruiz	Colombia
1991	Mt Pinatubo	Philippines
1991	Unzen-dake	Japan
1993	Mayon	Philippines
1993	Volcán Galeras	Colombia
1994	Volcán Llaima	Chile
1994	Rabaul	Papua New Guinea
1997	Soufrière Hills	Montserrat
2000	Hekla	Iceland
2001	Mount Etna	Italy
2002	Nyiragongo	Democratic Republic of the Congo

ARTHQUAKES

ı earthquake is produced by a sudden breaking of rock the Earth's crust as the stresses become too great for e strength of the rock to withstand. Naturally, this is ost likely to happen where the rock is weakest. Where e rock breaks, a fracture line, known as a fault, is left, d because there is now a break, future movements are ely to happen along the same weakness. Once the fault s formed, it may produce earthquakes again and again roughout geological history as long as similar forces ntinue to act upon it. These forces derive mostly from e movements of the Earth's tectonic plates.

The force with which the rock breaks releases a large nount of energy in the form of waves which travel rough the Earth. These radiate outwards from where e fault has ruptured. The point on the fault at which e rupture begins is known as the hypocentre. This is usually at a depth of 10 to 30 km for shallow earthquakes. However, earthquakes in subduction zones can be as deep as 600 km below the Earth's surface. The point on the Earth's surface directly above the hypocentre is called the epicentre. The magnitude of an earthquake, commonly measured on the Richter scale, is a logarithmic approximation of the total amount of energy released.

The strength of shaking at any point is known as the intensity, and this decreases with distance from the epicentre. A large earthquake which may be severely damaging at the epicentre, is less strongly felt by people at greater distances. The further the waves spread out, the more the energy is dispersed and absorbed, and the less severe the shaking at the surface is.

ICHTER SCALE

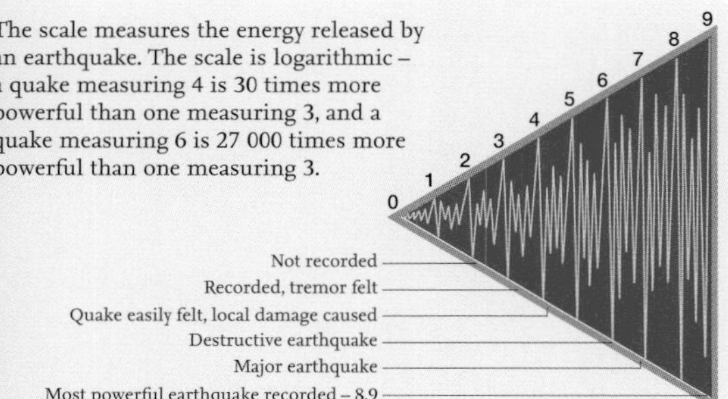

The scale measures the energy released by
ın earthquake. The scale is logarithmic –
ı quake measuring 4 is 30 times more
powerful than one measuring 3, and a
quake measuring 6 is 27 000 times more
powerful than one measuring 3.

Not recorded
Recorded, tremor felt
Quake easily felt, local damage caused
Destructive earthquake
Major earthquake
Most powerful earthquake recorded – 8.9

TSUNAMIS

Earthquakes can sometimes give rise to another phenomenon which can cause even more destruction and loss of life – the tsunami. Tsunami is a Japanese word, meaning 'harbour wave', and is used today in preference to the expression 'tidal wave' (tides are not involved). When an earthquake occurs offshore, it may cause a sudden change in the shape of the ocean floor, as a result of submarine landslides or vertical fault movement. This causes a massive displacement of water, which in turn produces a powerful wave or series of waves, able to travel over huge distances.

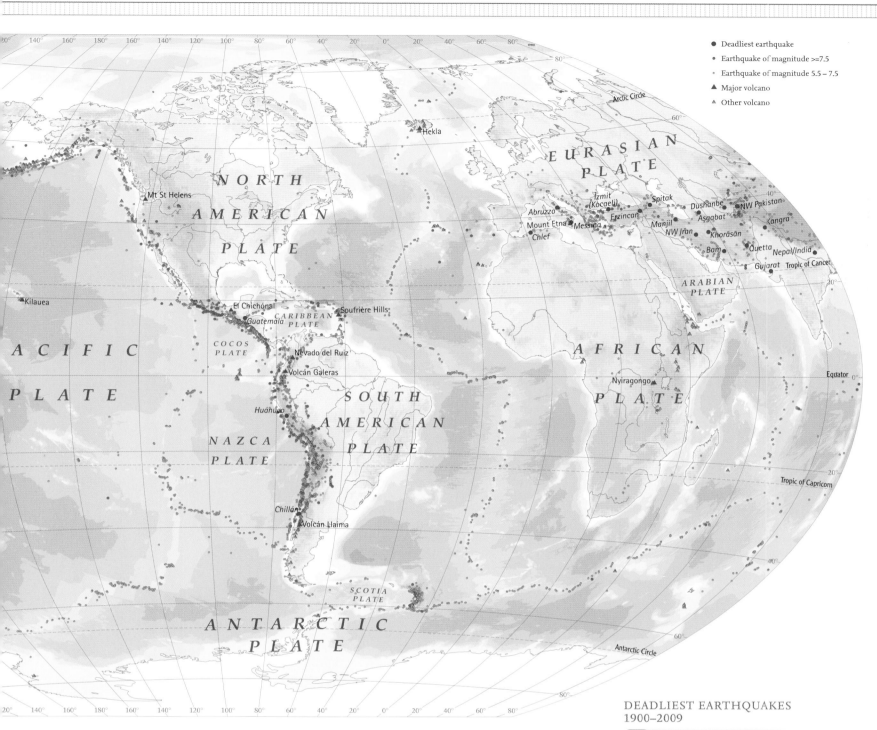

DEADLIEST EARTHQUAKES 1900–2009

Year	Location	Deaths
1905	**Kangra,** India	19 000
1907	west of **Dushanbe,** Tajikistan	12 000
1908	**Messina,** Italy	110 000
1915	**Abruzzo,** Italy	35 000
1917	**Bali,** Indonesia	15 000
1920	**Ningxia Province,** China	200 000
1923	**Tōkyō,** Japan	142 807
1927	**Qinghai Province,** China	200 000
1932	**Gansu Province,** China	70 000
1933	**Sichuan Province,** China	10 000
1934	**Nepal/India**	10 700
1935	**Quetta,** Pakistan	30 000
1939	**Chillán,** Chile	28 000
1939	**Erzincan,** Turkey	32 700
1948	**Aşgabat,** Turkmenistan	19 800
1962	northwest **Iran**	12 225
1970	**Huánuco Province,** Peru	66 794
1974	**Yunnan** and **Sichuan Provinces,** China	20 000
1975	**Liaoning Province,** China	10 000
1976	central **Guatemala**	22 778
1976	**Tangshan,** Hebei Province, China	255 000
1978	**Khorāsān Province,** Iran	20 000
1980	**Chlef,** Algeria	11 000
1988	**Spitak,** Armenia	25 000
1990	**Manjīl,** Iran	50 000
1999	**İzmit (Kocaeli),** Turkey	17 000
2001	**Gujarat,** India	20 000
2003	**Bam,** Iran	26 271
2004	**Sumatera,** Indonesia/Indian Ocean	226 435
2005	northwest **Pakistan**	74 648
2008	**Sichuan Province,** China	87 476

OBSERVING THE OCEANS

The oceans cover nearly three-quarters of the Earth's surface, and exert an extraordinary influence on the physical processes of the Earth and its atmosphere. The oceanic and atmospheric circulations, and the exchange of water between them, have a profound influence on our climate and therefore on human life. Any study of the Earth's climate relies upon a clear understanding of the role of the oceans and of the complex processes within them. The precise nature and effect of the processes varies geographically, but individual instances cannot be considered in isolation from the overall processes involved. Methods of direct and indirect observation of the oceans, by sampling and through the application of satellite remote sensing, for example, have developed enormously over the last fifty years. These techniques have provided the amount and quality of data required to greatly develop our understanding of the oceans and their role in the Earth's climate. For example, we now appreciate that the ocean is changing in response to global warming – currents are changing, the ocean is warming and sea level is rising. These changes are manifest in both the upper ocean circulation driven by the wind and in a global circulation driven by regional differences in the temperature and salinity.

Until the advent of Earth-observation satellites in the late 1970s all ocean observations were made from ships. The first global survey of the oceans, their bathymetry and their physical and biological characteristics, was made by HMS Challenger between 1872 and 1876.

Throughout the 20th century, comprehensive descriptions of the distributions of temperature and salinity were made through numerous regional and global expeditions. Analysis of the temperature and salinity characteristics of a water sample allowed its origins to be determined, and enabled overall patterns of water circulation to be deduced.

Until the 1960s there was no means of directly measuring currents below the ocean surface. Parallel developments produced two solutions to this problem. In the USA, current-recording meters were designed which returned records of current speed and direction, and water temperature. In the UK, devices were produced which could be made to drift with the currents at a predetermined depth and which could be tracked from an attendant ship. Such floats can now be used globally, independent of ships.

Earth observation satellites have become increasingly important in observing the oceans. Radiometers allow sea surface temperatures to be monitored and radar altimeters permit ocean surface currents to be inferred from measurements of sea surface height. Such developments meant that by the early 1990s routine monitoring of ocean surface currents was possible. The combination of satellite altimetry and other observation methods has also allowed a detailed picture of the ocean floor to be established (*see 1*).

1. GLOBAL SEAFLOOR TOPOGRAPHY

The range of colours represents different depths of the ocean – from orange and yellow on the shallow continental shelves to dark blues in the deepest ocean trenches.

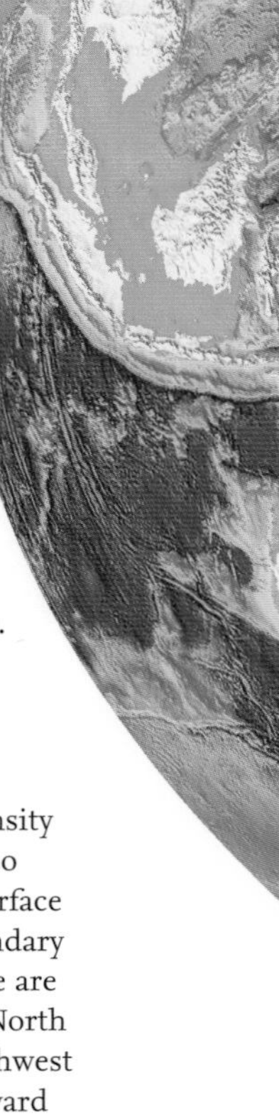

OCEAN CIRCULATION

Most of the Earth's incoming solar radiation is absorbed in the top few tens of metres of the ocean. Thus the upper ocean is warmed, the warming being greatest around the equator. Sea water has a high thermal capacity in comparison with the atmosphere or lithosphere and as a consequence, the ocean is an extremely effective store of thermal energy. Slow ocean currents play a major role in redistributing this heat around the globe and the oceans and their circulation are thus key elements in the climate system.

Global circulation consists of two parts: wind driven currents circulating in ocean-wide horizontal gyres; and a vertical thermohaline circulation where upper, warmer ocean water moves towards the poles and deep, cooler water moves towards the equator. Although conceptually we separate the wind driven and thermohaline circulations, in reality they are intimately connected by the exchange of energy – creating the global circulation known as the global ocean conveyor belt (*see 2*).

Ocean currents are influenced by winds, by density gradients and by the Earth's rotation. They are also constrained by the topography of the seafloor. Surface currents are usually strong, narrow, western-boundary currents flowing towards the poles. Some of these are well known, for example the Gulf Stream in the North Atlantic Ocean, the Kuroshio Current in the northwest Pacific, and the Brazil Current (*see 3*). These poleward flows are returned towards the equator in broad, slow, interior flows which complete a gyre in each hemisphere basin. Sea surface circulation is reflected in variations in sea surface height which can vary greatly across currents (*see 4*). For example, differences in sea surface height of over 1m are evident across the Kuroshio Current. At high latitudes, winter cooling produces high density water which sinks towards the ocean floor and flows towards the equator, being constrained by the sea floor topography. This fills the deep ocean basins with water at temperatures close to 0°C.

2. GLOBAL OCEAN CONVEYOR BELT

Circulation of light, warmer surface water (red) and deep, cooler water (blue).

3. OCEAN SURFACE CURRENTS

Surface wind-driven circulation.

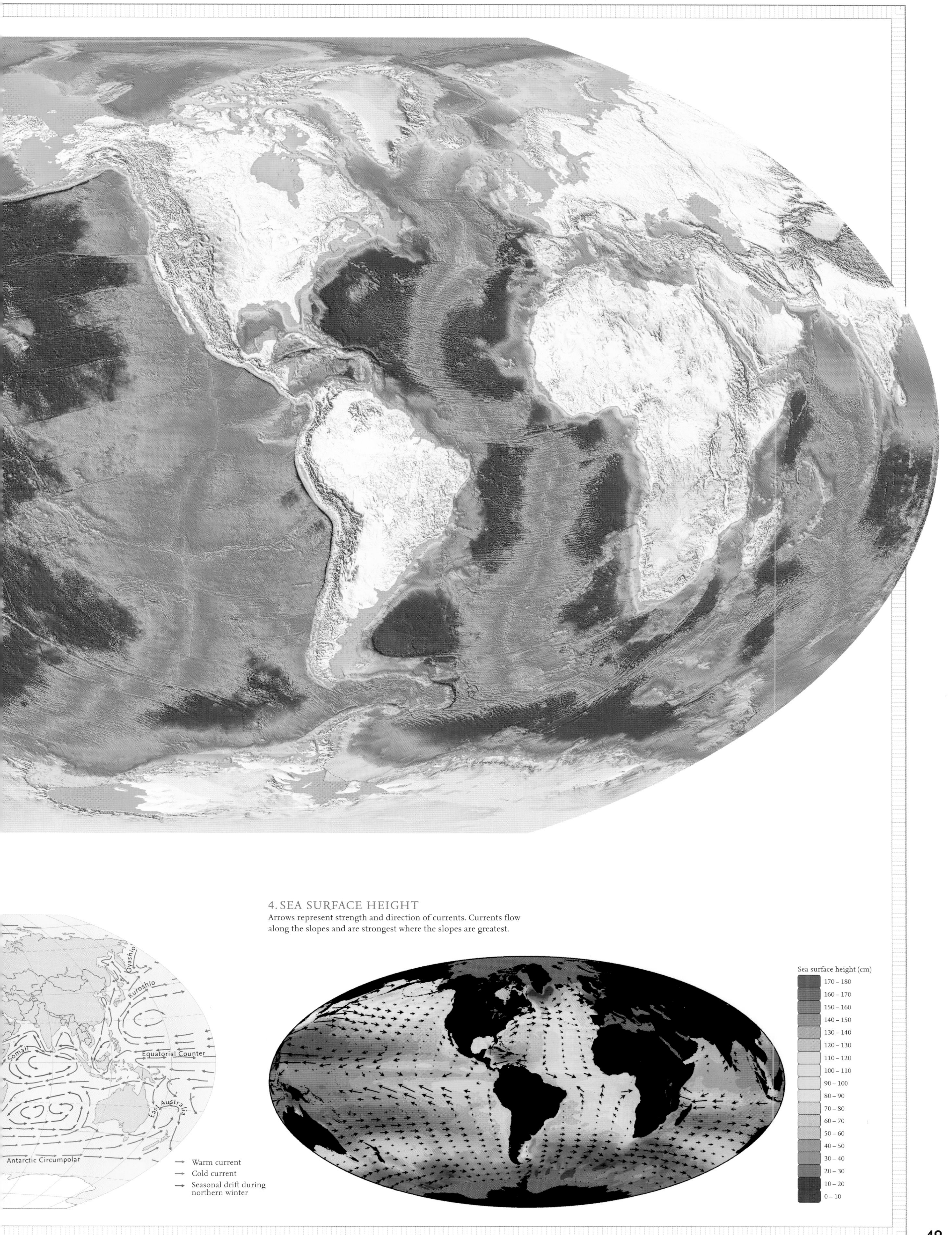

4. SEA SURFACE HEIGHT

Arrows represent strength and direction of currents. Currents flow along the slopes and are strongest where the slopes are greatest.

THE CLIMATE SYSTEM

The Earth's climate system is a highly complex interactive system involving the atmosphere, hydrosphere (oceans, lakes and rivers), biosphere (the Earth's living resources), cryosphere (particularly sea ice and polar ice caps) and lithosphere (the Earth's crust and upper mantle). This results in a great variety of climate types (*see 1*). Man's activities are affecting this system, and the monitoring of climate change, and of human influences upon it, is now a major issue.

Greenhouse gases such as carbon dioxide, methane and chlorofluorocarbons (CFCs) act to trap outgoing long-wave radiation, keeping the Earth's surface and lower atmosphere warmer than it would be otherwise. This is the phenomenon usually referred to as the greenhouse effect. Human activity has increased the atmospheric concentration of some of these gases and has therefore contributed to the effect. As a result of this, the world is about 0.6°C warmer than it was a hundred years ago with the three warmest years globally (in decreasing order) being 1998, 2005 and 2003.

1. MAJOR CLIMATIC REGIONS AND SUB-TYPES 2006

Köppen classification system
Winkel Tripel Projection
scale 1:110 000 000

• Climate graph location
○ Weather extreme location

Polar		Cooler humid		Warmer humid		Dry		Tropical humid	
EF	Ice cap	Dc Dd	Subarctic	Cb Cc	Temperate	BS	Steppe	Aw As	Savanna
ET	Tundra	Db	Continental cool summer	Ca	Humid subtropical	BW	Desert	Af Am	Rain forest
		Da	Continental warm summer	Cs	Mediterranean				

A Rainy climate with no winter: coolest month above 18°C (64.4°F).

B Dry climates; limits are defined by formulae based on rainfall effectiveness:
BS Steppe or semi-arid climate.
BW Desert or arid climate.

*C Rainy climates with mild winters: coolest month above 0°C (32°F), but below 18°C (64.4°F); warmest month above 10°C (50°F).

*D Rainy climates with severe winters: coldest month below 0°C (32°F); warmest month above 10°C (50°F).

E Polar climates with no warm season: warmest month below 10°C (50°F).
ET Tundra climate: warmest month below 10°C (50°F) but above 0°C (32°F).
EF Perpetual frost: all months below 0°C (32°F).

a Warmest month above 22°C (71.6°F).

b Warmest month below 22°C (71.6°F).

c Less than four months over 10°C (50°F).

d As 'c', but with severe cold: coldest month below -38°C (-36.4°F).

f Constantly moist rainfall throughout the year.

*h Warmer dry: all months above 0°C (32°F).

*k Cooler dry: at least one month below 0°C (32°F).

m Monsoon rain: short dry season, but is compensated by heavy rains during rest of the year.

n Frequent fog.

s Dry season in summer.

w Dry season in winter.

*** Modification of Köppen definition**

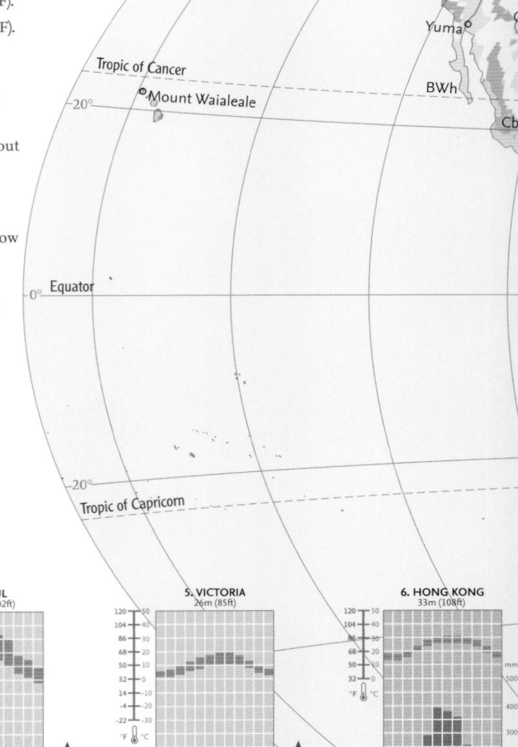

2. CLIMATE GRAPHS

These graphs relate by number, name and colour to the selected stations on the map and present mean temperature and precipitation values for each month. Red bars show average daily maximum and minimum temperatures for each month in degrees centigrade and fahrenheit. Vertical blue columns depict precipitation in millimetres and inches, with the total mean annual precipitation shown under the graph. The altitude of each station above sea level is given in metres and feet.

Precipitation (average monthly total) Temperature (average daily maximum and minimum)

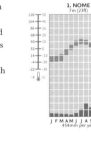

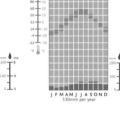

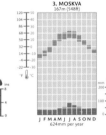

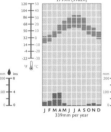

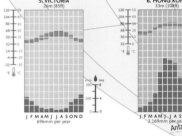

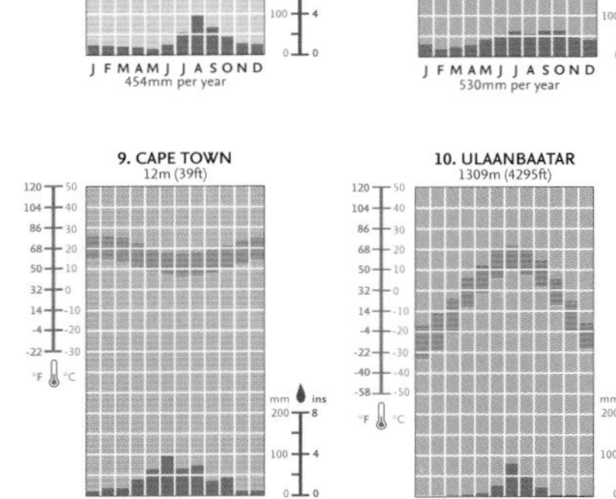

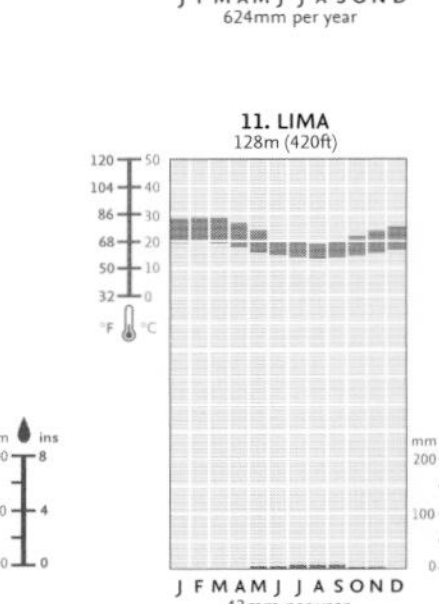

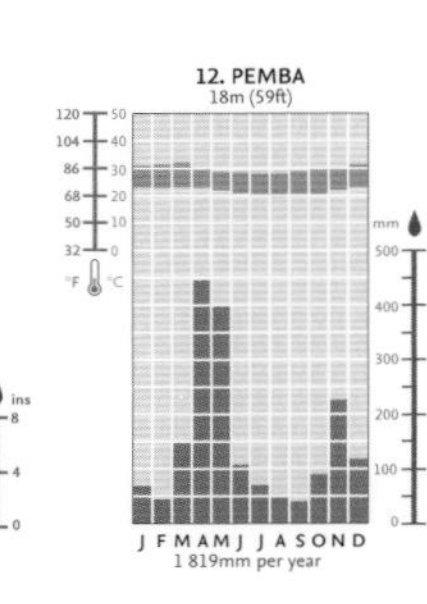

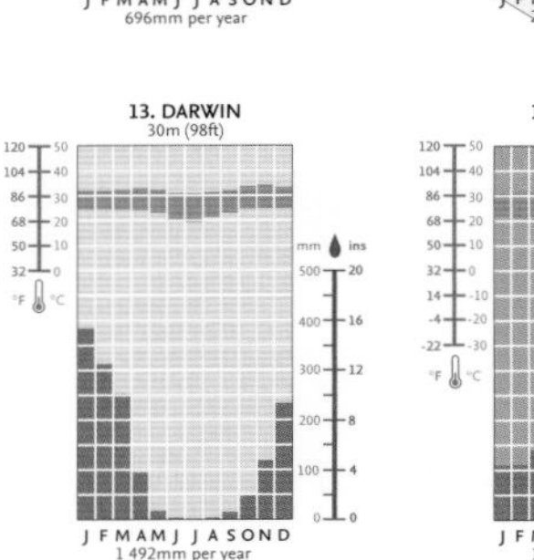

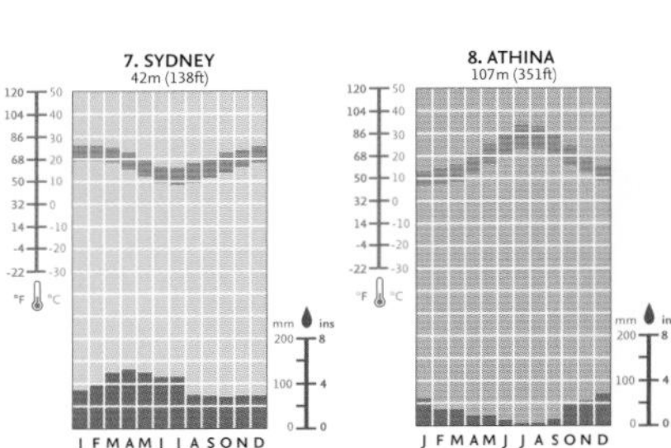

11. LIMA 128m (420ft) 43mm per year
12. PEMBA 18m (59ft) 1 819mm per year
13. DARWIN 30m (98ft) 1 492mm per year
14. KISANGANI 415m (1362ft) 1 704mm per year

CLIMATE CHANGE

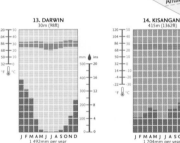

Future climate change depends on how quickly and to what extent the concentration of greenhouse gases and aerosols in the atmosphere increases. If we assume that no action is taken to limit future greenhouse gas emissions, then a warming during the 21st century of 0.2 to 0.3°C per decade is likely. Such a rate of warming would be greater than anything that has occurred over the last 10 000 years.

Projections based on the models assessed by the Intergovernmental Panel on Climate Change (IPCC) suggest likely further global warming of between 1.0 and 6.4°C by the end of the 21st century. Sea level is projected to rise by between 28 cm and 58 cm, threatening a number of coastal cities, low-lying deltas and small islands. Change will not be spread uniformly around the world. Some regions will warm faster than the global average, while others will warm more slowly (*see 3*). Faster warming is expected near the poles, as the melting snow and sea ice exposes the darker underlying land and ocean surfaces which then absorb more of the sun's radiation instead of reflecting it back to space in the way that brighter ice and snow do. Changes in precipitation are also expected to vary from place to place (*see 4*). In the high-latitude regions the year-round average precipitation is projected to increase, while in most sub-tropical land regions it is projected to decrease by as much as 20 per cent. This would increase the risk of drought and, in combination with higher temperatures, threaten agricultural productivity.

3. PROJECTION OF GLOBAL TEMPERATURES 2090–2099

Based on IPCC scenario A1B. Change relative to 1980–1999.

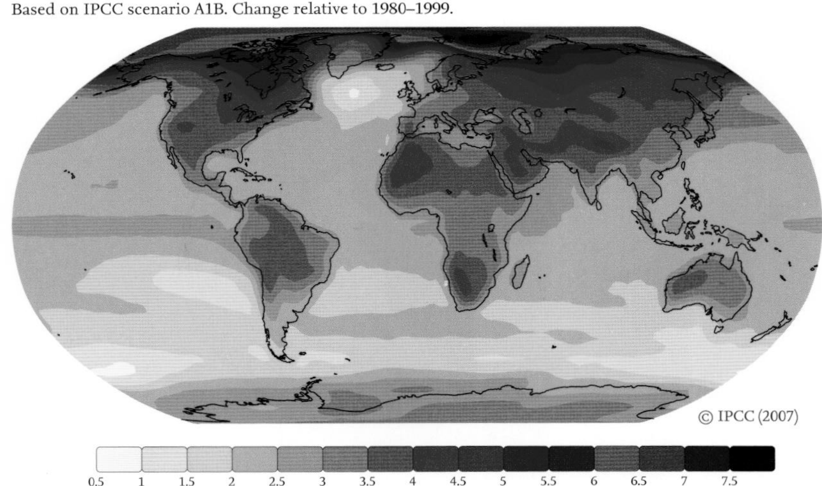

© IPCC (2007)

0.5 1 1.5 2 2.5 3 3.5 4 4.5 5 5.5 6 6.5 7 7.5

Change in average surface temperature (°C)

4. PROJECTION OF GLOBAL PRECIPITATION 2090–2099

Based on IPCC scenario A1B. Change relative to 1980–1999.

White areas represent areas of less than two-thirds agreement between scenarios; dots represent areas of over 90 per cent agreement.

© IPCC (2007)

-20 -10 -5 5 10 20

Change in precipitation (%) June–July–August average

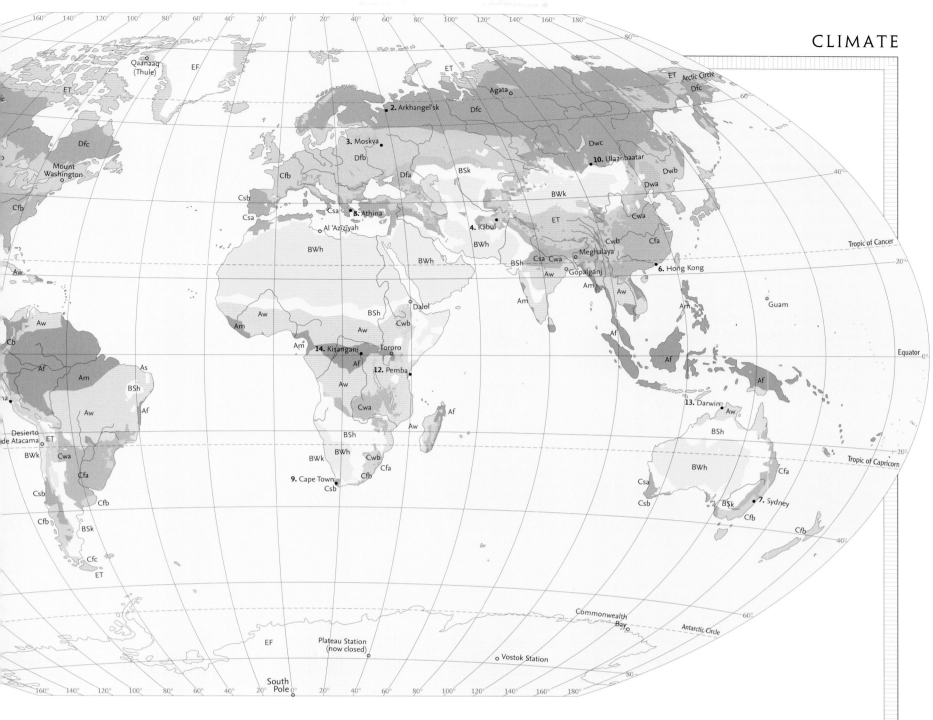

ROPICAL STORMS

opical storms develop, and have different names, in ferent parts of the world: hurricanes in the north lantic and east Pacific; typhoons in the northwest cific; and cyclones in the Indian Ocean region. There also many local names for these events.

Tropical storms are among the most powerful and structive weather systems on Earth. Of the eighty to e hundred which develop annually over the tropical eans, many make landfall and cause considerable mage to property and loss of life as a result of high nds and heavy rain.

The majority of tropical storms originate in the rthwest Pacific, where as typhoons they commonly ect areas from the Philippines through to China and an. They are also found as cyclones in the Bay of ngal, either developing locally or on occasion being remnants of typhoons which have moved westwards ross Thailand. These storms bring heavy rains to stern India or to the Ganges Delta in Bangladesh. In se places the land is so close to sea level that the rise water levels has great potential for heavy loss of life.

The conditions required for the development of pical storms – warm (over 26.5°C) ocean waters to a pth of at least 50 m; pre-existing cyclonic (low essure) systems; thunderstorm activity; and moist ers of air in the mid-troposphere (around 5 km above Earth's surface) – mean that most occur in mid- to e-summer in the areas concerned *(see 6)*.

5. WORLD WEATHER EXTREMES

	Location
Highest shade temperature	57.8°C/136°F Al 'Azīzīyah, Libya (13th September 1922)
Hottest place — Annual mean	34.4°C/93.9°F Dalol, Ethiopia
Driest place — Annual mean	0.1 mm/0.004 inches Atacama Desert, Chile
Most sunshine — Annual mean	90% Yuma, Arizona, USA (over 4 000 hours)
Least sunshine	Nil for 182 days each year, South Pole
Lowest screen temperature	-89.2°C/-128.6°F Vostok Station, Antarctica (21st July 1983)
Coldest place — Annual mean	-56.6°C/-69.9°F Plateau Station, Antarctica
Wettest place — Annual mean	11 873 mm/467.4 inches Meghalaya, India
Most rainy days	Up to 350 per year Mount Waialeale, Hawaii, USA
Windiest place	322 km per hour/200 miles per hour in gales, Commonwealth Bay, Antarctica

	Location
Highest surface wind speed	
High altitude	372 km per hour/231 miles per hour Mount Washington, New Hampshire, USA (12th April 1934)
Low altitude	333 km per hour/207 miles per hour Qaanaaq (Thule), Greenland (8th March 1972)
Tornado	512 km per hour/318 miles per hour Oklahoma City, Oklahoma, USA (3rd May 1999)
Greatest snowfall	31 102 mm/1 224.5 inches Mount Rainier, Washington, USA (19th February 1971 — 18th February 1972)
Heaviest hailstones	1 kg/2.21 lb Gopalganj, Bangladesh (14th April 1986)
Thunder-days average	251 days per year Tororo, Uganda
Highest barometric pressure	1 083.8 mb Agata, Siberia, Rus. Fed. (31st December 1968)
Lowest barometric pressure	870 mb 483 km/300 miles west of Guam, Pacific Ocean (12th October 1979)

6. TRACKS OF TROPICAL STORMS

(wind speeds often over 160 km per hour)
scale 1:247 000 000

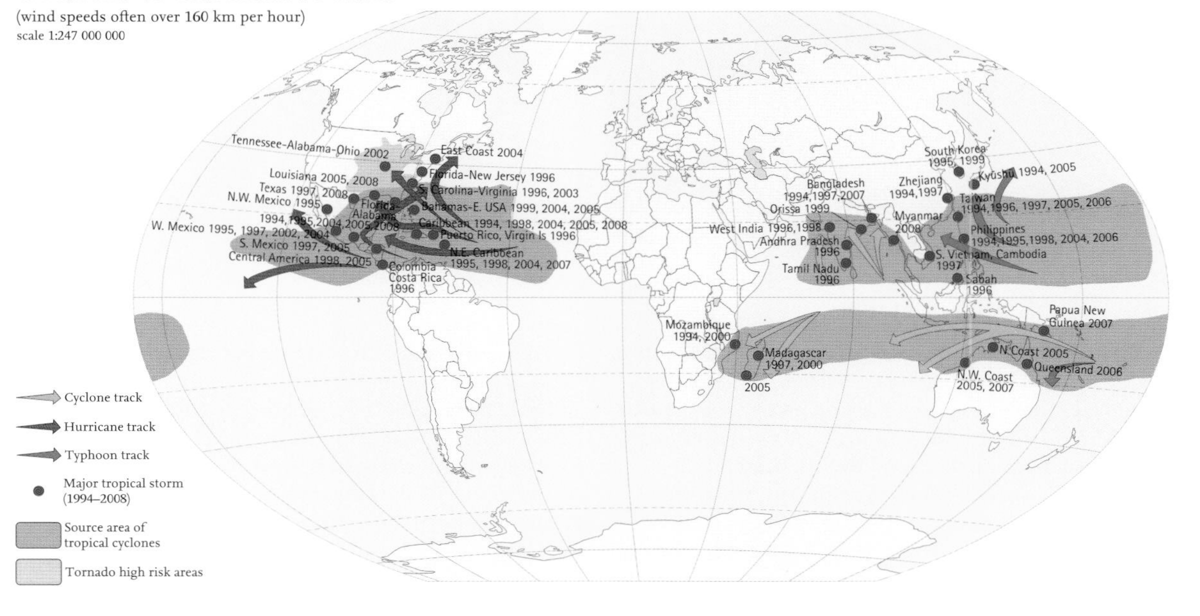

GLOBAL LAND COVER

Throughout history people have altered the natural environment, influencing landscapes, land cover, biodiversity, and the chemical composition of air, land, and water. The rate of change has accelerated dramatically since the industrial revolution, as a result of advances in technology, changing lifestyles and associated patterns of production and consumption, and the rapidly growing global population. As the human population has increased, so too has demand for the Earth's natural resources, leading in many areas to environmental degradation such as habitat loss and pollution, including increasing greenhouse gas emissions. These changes have had significant impacts on people's lives in many parts of the world. Among the most affected are the world's poor, especially those living in rural areas, whose livelihoods depend most directly on the goods and services that are derived from the natural environment. While there is a growing understanding of the factors underpinning a more sustainable future for societies and economies, there is a pressing need to put them into practice more widely.

Arctic Circle
Tropic of Cancer
0° Equator
Tropic of Capricorn
Antarctic Circle

- Irrigated croplands
- Rain fed croplands
- Mosaic croplands/vegetation
- Mosaic vegetation/croplands
- Closed to open broadleaved evergreen or semi-deciduous forest
- Closed broadleaved deciduous forest
- Open broadleaved deciduous forest
- Closed needle leaved evergreen forest
- Open needle leaved deciduous or evergreen forest
- Closed to open mixed broadleaved and needle leaved forest
- Mosaic forest – shrubland/grassland
- Mosaic grassland – forest/shrubland
- Closed to open shrubland
- Closed to open grassland
- Sparse vegetation
- Closed to open broadleaved forest regularly flooded (fresh-brackish water)
- Closed broadleaved forest permanently flooded (saline-brackish water)
- Closed to open vegetation regularly flooded
- Artificial areas
- Bare areas
- Water bodies
- Permanent snow and ice
- No data

PRODUCTIVITY AND CONSUMPTION

One key measure of environmental productivity is plant growth rate, measured as 'net primary productivity' (NPP). This is the net amount of solar energy converted to plant organic matter through the process of photosynthesis. The pattern of this 'greenness' is reflected in the map of world land cover (*see 1*). Areas of highest photosynthetic activity occur in forested areas with progressively lower levels in areas of cropland, grassland and shrubland, and the lowest levels in barren or sparsely vegetated regions. The distribution of NPP is determined not only by the amount of sunlight, but also moisture availability, soil nutrients, carbon dioxide (CO2) concentration, and temperature variability. Rising global temperature and CO2 levels are both resulting in increased NPP and, in conjunction with land use changes, will dramatically affect the future distribution of forest and other vegetation types, as well as agricultural productivity.

One measure of people's demand on the environment is the 'ecological footprint'. Calculations indicate that demand has been exceeding Earth's capacity to provide renewable resources and absorb waste since the late 1980s (*see 2*). Currently, humanity's demand on nature exceeds by a quarter what Earth can renew. The ecological footprint adds up the area of biologically productive land and water used to provide resources and services, including waste absorption. The area needed to absorb excess carbon dioxide emissions is included. This footprint is then compared to the available biocapacity of the planet or a region. Typically, industrialized countries and urban areas have greater per capita footprints than developing nations and rural populations. This results from their greater demand for cropland, grazing land, forest, and fishing grounds to produce food, fibre, and timber, to absorb their waste, and to provide space for their infrastructure.

2. ECOLOGICAL FOOTPRINT

Humanity's ecological footprint by component 1961–2003.

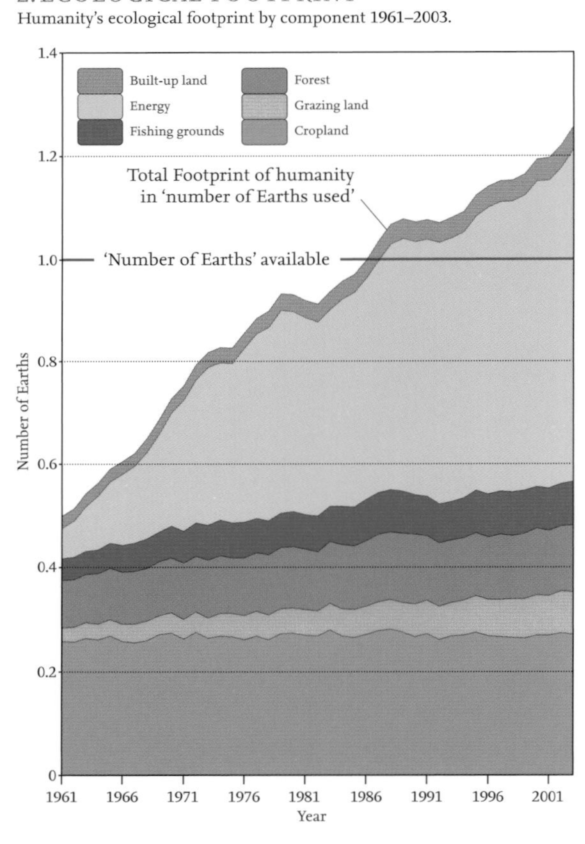

3. GLOBAL FRESH WATER AVAILABILITY

Cubic metres per person per year.

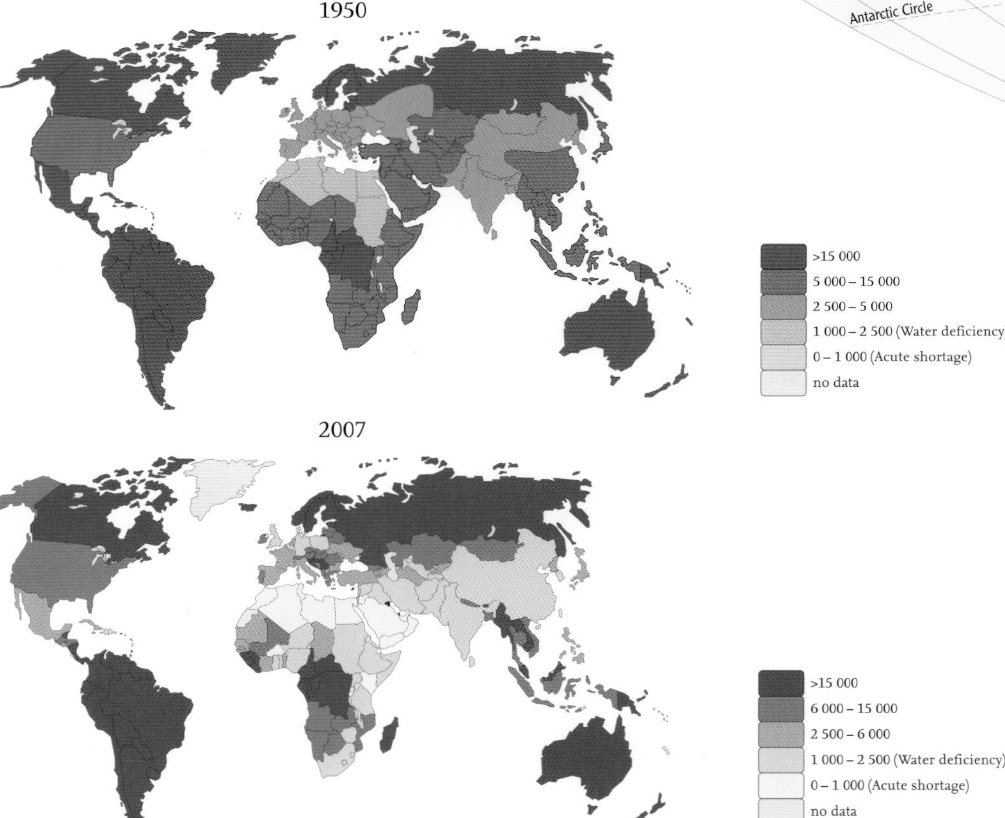

WATER RESOURCES

Forests and mountains in particular, play a critical role in regulating and supplying clean, stable supplies of fresh water. Fresh water is crucial for food production, human health, and economic development. However, fresh water is not equally available around the world, and its availability changes through the year. More than one billion people do not have access to sufficient fresh water to meet their basic needs, and only 15 per cent of the world's population have a surplus of water supply (*see 3*).

The availability of fresh water is particularly threatened by withdrawals from non-renewable groundwater, the overuse of renewable water sources such as rivers and lakes, and the degradation of the forest and mountain ecosystems, which regulate water flow. Overuse of fresh water occurs in all continents, particularly in areas where water is required for irrigated agriculture. Supplies of good quality fresh water are also affected by pollution, especially in cultivated and urban landscapes, and in dryland areas. Increasing demand for fresh water has resulted in damage to natural habitats, changes in the flow regime of rivers, and the disruption of migration routes of aquatic species such as salmon. Very high volume transfers of water between river basins have affected many of the world's largest rivers, including the Nile, Yellow, and North American Colorado.

Arctic Circle
Tropic of Cancer
Equator
Tropic of Capricorn
Antarctic Circle

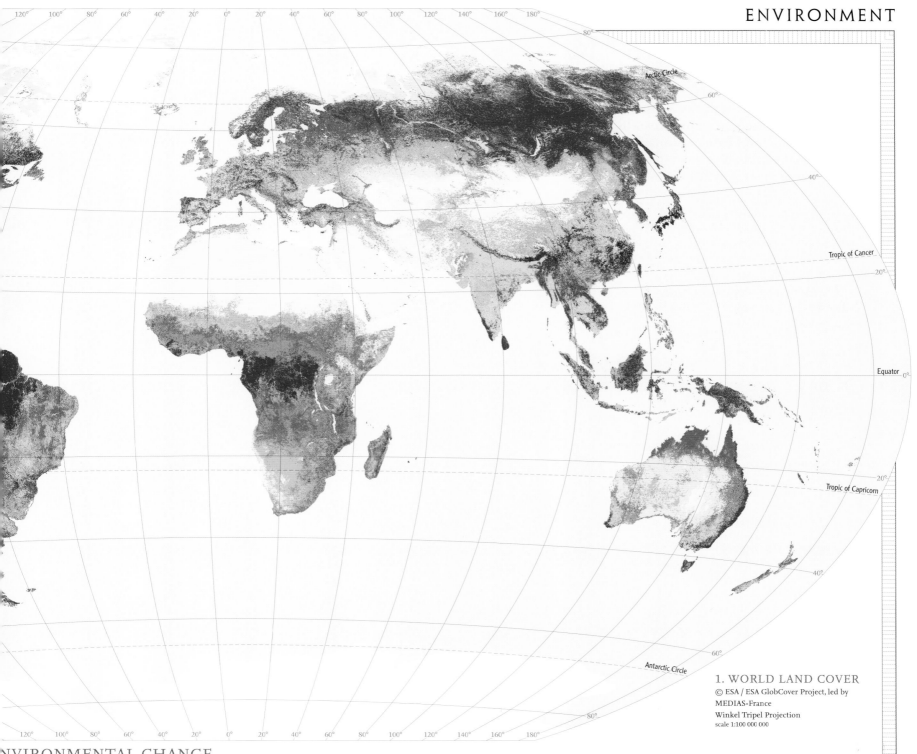

1. WORLD LAND COVER

Winkel Tripel Projection
scale 1:100 000 000

NVIRONMENTAL CHANGE

nd cover has changed more over the past fifty years in at any time in human history (*see 4*). Much of this ange has been due to the conversion of natural osystems to agricultural land to help meet demand for od production, particularly in developing regions. arly a quarter of the Earth's land surface is currently der cultivation, while urbanization is also continuing *pages 58–59*), and over 50 per cent of the world's pulation now live in urban areas.

Wetlands and other freshwater environments have o been dramatically affected by changes in land cover d use, for example, up to 65 per cent of inland tlands in Europe and North America were drained for intensive agriculture by 1985. Fragmentation and the modification of river flow have resulted from the construction of dams and other structures along rivers, affecting almost 60 per cent of the large river systems in the world.

Dryland and mountain environments are particularly vulnerable. Drylands have relatively low productivity and yet are home to the world's poorest people, who depend on the land for their livelihoods and well-being. Mountains are subject to both natural and human-induced threats, including volcanic and seismic events, and the loss of vegetation and soils as a result of agriculture, forestry, and extraction activities.

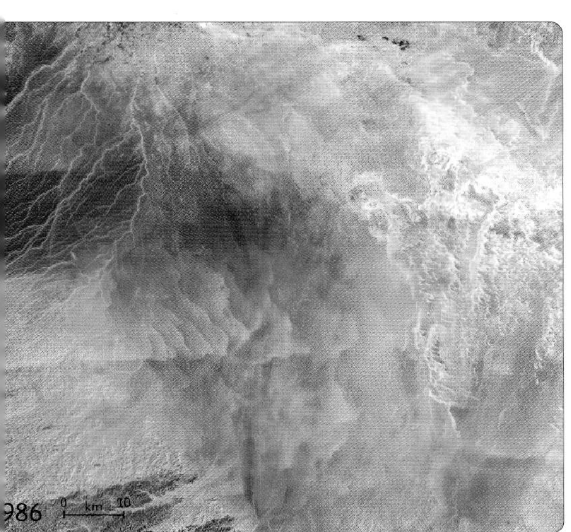

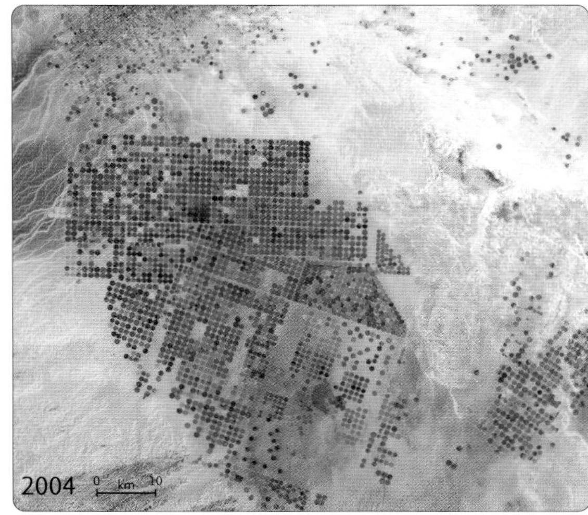

velopment of centre-pivot irrigation system in the desert at Wādī an Sirhān, di Arabia.

4. LAND DEGRADATION

Degradation extent	Cause
6 800 000 sq km	Overgrazing • About 20 per cent of the world's pasture and rangelands have been damaged.
5 800 000 sq km	Deforestation • Degradation of forests by large-scale logging and clearance for farm and urban use.
5 500 000 sq km	Agricultural mismanagement • Water erosion causes soil losses of about 25 000 million tonnes annually. • Soil salinization and waterlogging affect about 40 million hectares of land globally.
1 370 000 sq km	Fuelwood consumption • About 1.7 million m^3 of fuelwood are harvested annually from forests and plantations. Woodfuel is the primary source of energy in many developing countries.
195 000 sq km	Industry and urbanization • Urban growth, road construction, mining and industry are major factors in land degradation in different regions. Valuable agricultural land is often lost.

GLOBAL BIODIVERSITY

Biodiversity, derived from the term 'biological diversity', is the name given to the variety and processes of all life on Earth, including individual living organisms, their genes, and the habitats or ecosystems of which they are part, whether terrestrial, freshwater or marine. The diversity of life is not evenly distributed around the world, and based on the number of species in a location, or 'species richness', a general pattern emerges of considerably more biodiversity in the tropics than at higher latitudes (*see 1*).

To date approximately two million species have been identified and described. However, the total number of species on Earth is likely to be nearer 10–12 million, with most estimates ranging between 5 and 30 million. Much of this uncertainty relates to a lack of knowledge about the most species-rich groups, including invertebrates (*see 2*). By including bacteria, about which very little is known, the total estimate would increase still further.

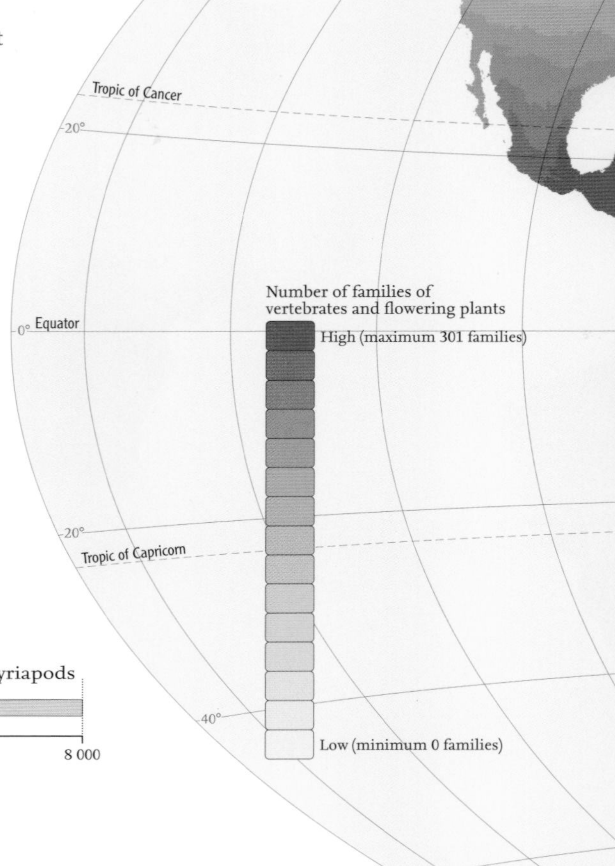

1. GLOBAL BIODIVERSITY
Diversity of terrestrial vertebrates and flowering plants.
scale approximately 1:100 000 000

2. NUMBER OF SPECIES EXISTING AND ESTIMATED

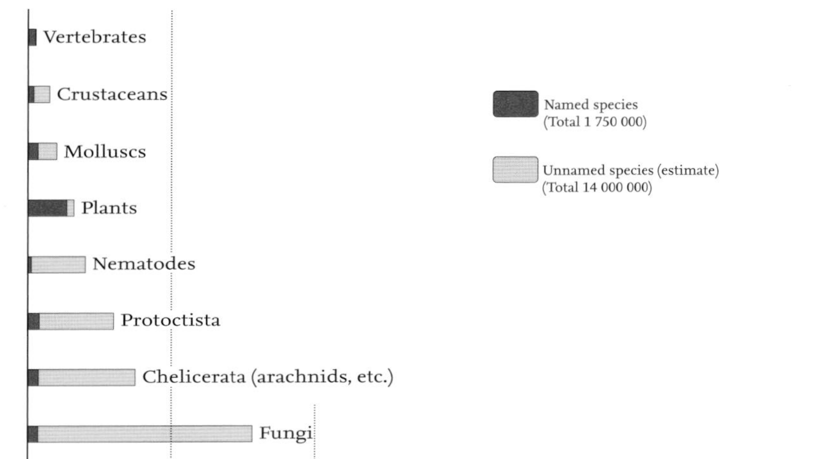

THE VALUE OF BIODIVERSITY

Genetic diversity provides the basis for living organisms to respond to natural selection and adapt to their environment. As such, genes play a role in the capacity of biodiversity to adapt to global change, such as through climate change or the emergence of novel diseases. Genetic diversity also provides many direct benefits to people, for example through its use in improving yield and disease resistance of crops and for developing medicines.

Ecosystems consist of living creatures interacting with one another and with the air, water, and soil around them. People and the millions of species with which they share the planet are all dependent on the health and functioning of the world's ecosystems. They provide the basic necessities of human life such as food, materials for shelter, and clean water. They also offer protection from natural disasters and disease, and contribute in many non-material ways to our well-being. These 'ecosystem services' also support and maintain the essential life processes of the planet, such as primary production and nutrient cycling (*see 3*).

Changes in biodiversity affect the functioning of ecosystems, and can leave them more vulnerable to disturbances, and less able to supply benefits to people through ecosystem services. An increasing number of studies show that managing ecosystems in a more sustainable way, for a wider range of ecosystem services, can yield greater total overall benefit than managing for a specific, even high-value, product such as timber.

3. ECOSYSTEM SERVICES

	Examples
Provisioning services (ecosystem goods)	Food, fibre, fuel, genetic resources, biochemicals.
Regulating services	Pollination, seed dispersal, climate regulation, pest regulation, disease regulation, natural hazard protection, invasion resistance, erosion regulation, water purification.
Supporting services	Primary production, provision of habitat, nutrient cycling, soil formation and retention, production of atmospheric oxygen, water cycling.
Cultural services	Spiritual and religious values, education and inspiration, recreation and aesthetic values.

TRENDS IN BIODIVERSITY

Biodiversity is declining globally, largely as a result of human activities. Over the past few hundred years species extinction rates have increased by as much as 1 000 times the natural rates of extinction. Between 10 and 50 per cent of well-studied groups of species (mammals, birds, amphibians, conifers, and cycads) are currently threatened with extinction, and there has been a consistent decline in populations of species, of about 40 per cent between 1970 and 2003 (*see 4*). Exceptions to this general decline include a few species which have been protected through specific conservation measures, and those which thrive well in human-modified landscapes.

Virtually all of the planet's ecosystems have now been dramatically transformed through human actions. Although human impacts on biodiversity are not a recent phenomenon, changes have been occurring more rapidly in the past fifty years than at any time in human history. Global deforestation, for example, took place at an estimated average rate of over 350 sq km per day between 1990 and 2005. Between 1960 and 2000 reservoir storage capacity quadrupled, so that the amount of water stored behind large dams is now estimated to be three to six times the amount held by rivers. Approximately one-third of mangrove ecosystems have been removed, and up to 40 per cent of known coral reefs have been destroyed or degraded in the last few decades.

The pressures causing changes in, and loss of, biodiversity are diverse and numerous. Five main threats are commonly identified: habitat change, overexploitation, pollution (including that caused by excess nutrients from agriculture and industry), climate change, and the spread of invasive non-native species. Ultimately it is a combination of patterns of consumption and human population distribution which is underlying the threats placed on the planet's living resources (*see 5*).

4. LIVING PLANET INDEX
Trends in population of terrestrial, freshwater and marine species 1970–2003.

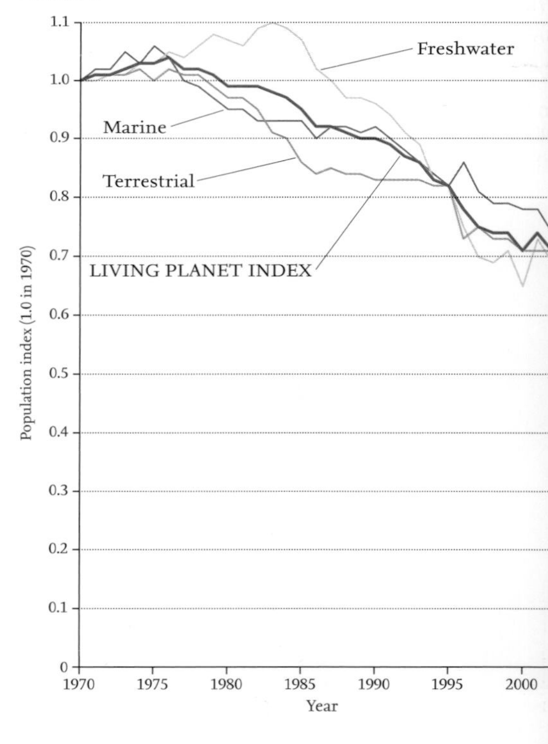

)NSERVATION

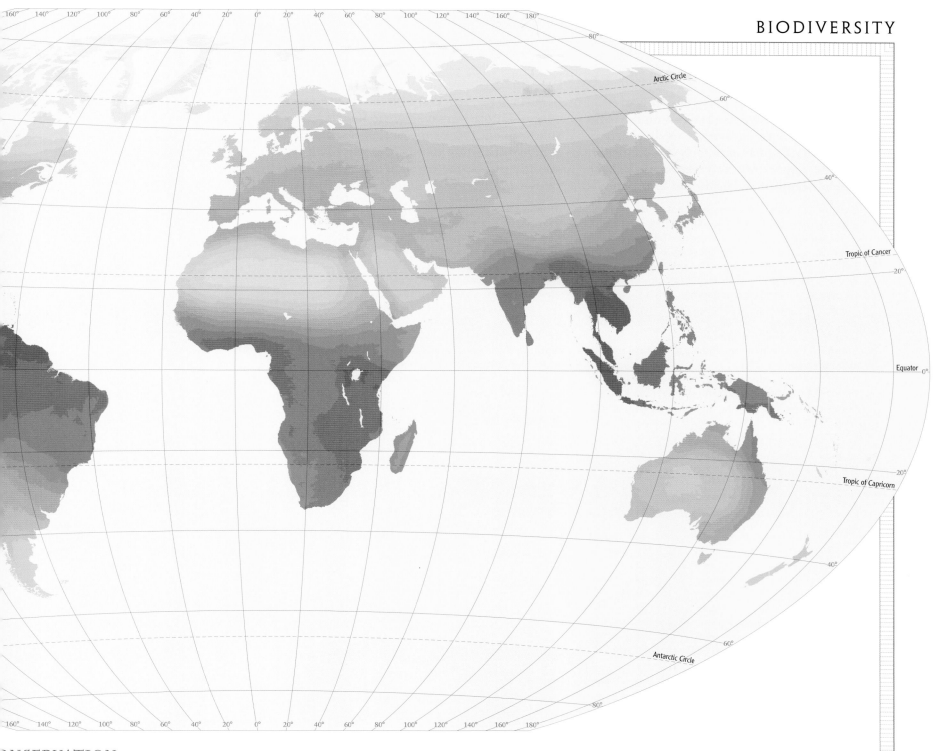

ıcern over the loss of biodiversity led to the creation, .992 of a global treaty, the Convention on Biological ersity (CBD). In 2002, national governments, through CBD and other forums, adopted a target to greatly ıce the rate of loss of biodiversity by 2010.

)ne of the best-known conservation tools is the ıblishment and management of Protected Areas. 1872 the world's first Protected Area at Yellowstone ional Park, USA. Presently over 19 000 000 sq km per cent of the world's land surface) is now included within over 107 000 designated Protected Areas worldwide. However, there is great variation in the degree to which different ecosystem types are protected (*see 6*). Protection of terrestrial ecosystems varies considerably, but all fare better than freshwater or marine ecosystems. Restoration activities are now common in many countries for wetlands, forests, grasslands, and coastal systems. However, restoration is generally far more costly than the conservation and sustainable use of the original ecosystem, and only in rare cases can this be fully restored.

Recently there has been an increasing emphasis on a more holistic approach to biodiversity conservation. This integrates management of land, water and living resources, promoting conservation and sustainable use in an equitable way, recognizing that people are an integral component of ecosystems. Successful implementation will be central to achieving dual goals of conservation and sustainable development.

3IODIVERSITY UNDER THREAT

ıber of threatened species of amphibians, mammals birds compared to human population density.

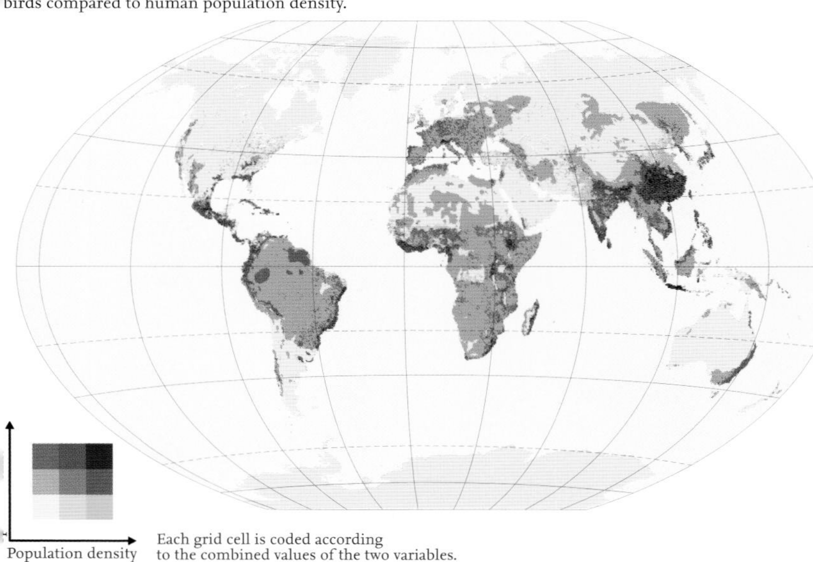

6. PROTECTED AREAS OF THE WORLD

Proportion of large marine ecosystems and terrestrial ecoregions under protection.

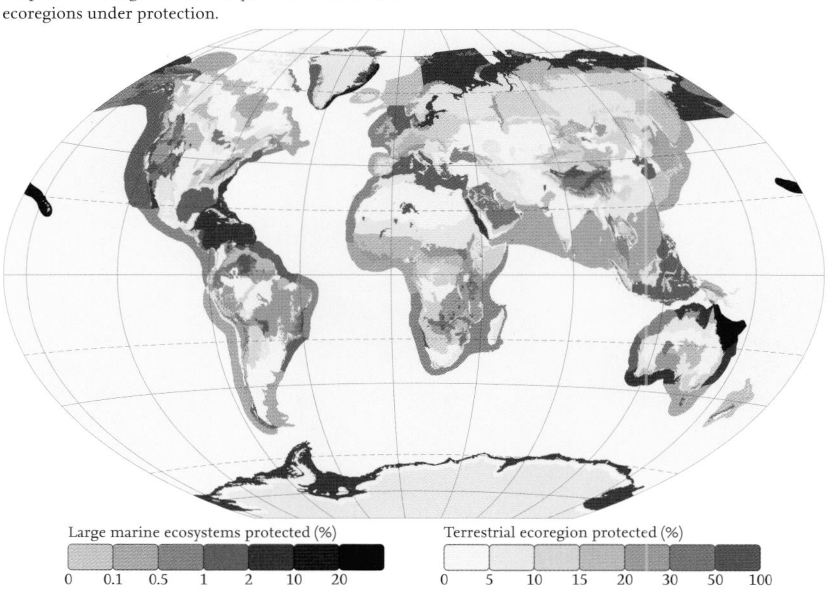

POPULATION DISTRIBUTION AND GROWTH

People are distributed very unevenly over the face of the planet. As shown on the main map (*see 1*), over a quarter of the land area is uninhabited or has extremely low population density. Approximately a quarter of the land area is occupied at densities of 25 or more persons per square km, with the three largest concentrations of east Asia, the Indian subcontinent and Europe accounting for over half the world total. China and India dominate the scene, together accounting for nearly two-fifths of world population (*see 2*).

Over the past half century world population has been growing faster than it has ever done before. Whereas world population did not pass the one billion mark until 1804 and took another 123 years to reach two billion in 1927, it then added the third billion in 33 years, the fourth in 14 years and the fifth in 13 years, with the 6 billion mark being passed only 12 years after this in 1999. It is expected that another three billion people will have been added to the world's population by 2050 (*see 5*). Recent projections looking even further into the future estimate that the total will have risen to around 9 billion by 2300.

Population growth since 1950 has been spread very unevenly between the continents. While overall numbers have been growing extremely rapidly since 1950, a massive 89 per cent increase has taken place in the less developed regions, especially southern and eastern Asia, while Europe's population is now stationary and ageing rapidly. Africa was the second largest contributor and represents by far the highest growth rate of all the continents. The latest trends in population growth at country level (*see 4*) emphasize the continuing contrast between the more and less developed regions. Annual growth rates of 1.1 per cent or more are very common in Latin America, Africa and the southern half of Asia. A number of countries have rates in excess of 2.8 per cent, which if continued would lead to the doubling of their populations in 25 years or less.

1. WORLD POPULATION DISTRIBUTION

Winkel Tripel Projection
scale 1:100 000 000

Density of inhabitants
per sq mile

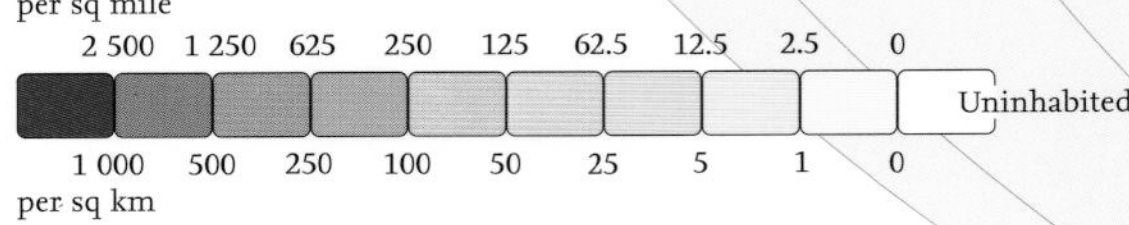

per sq km

2. TOP TEN COUNTRIES BY POPULATION AND POPULATION DENSITY 2009

Total population	Country	Rank	Country*	Inhabitants per sq mile	Inhabitants per sq km
1 330 265 000	China	1	Bangladesh	2 918	1 127
1 198 003 000	India	2	Taiwan	1 650	637
314 659 000	United States of America	3	South Korea	1 261	487
229 965 000	Indonesia	4	Netherlands	1 035	400
193 734 000	Brazil	5	India	1 012	391
180 808 000	Pakistan	6	Haiti	936	362
162 221 000	Bangladesh	7	Belgium	904	349
154 729 000	Nigeria	8	Japan	872	337
140 874 000	Russian Federation	9	Sri Lanka	799	308
127 156 000	Japan	10	Philippines	794	307

*Only countries with a population of over 10 million are considered.

3. KEY POPULATION STATISTICS FOR MAJOR REGIONS

	Population 2009 (millions)	Growth (per cent)	Infant mortality rate	Total fertility rate	Life expectancy (years)	% aged 60 and over 2010	% aged 60 and over 2050
World	6 829	1.2	47	2.6	68	11	22
More developed regions[1]	1 223	0.1	6	1.6	77	22	33
Less developed regions[2]	5 596	1.4	52	2.7	66	9	20
Africa	1 010	2.4	83	4.6	54	5	11
Asia	4 121	1.2	42	2.4	69	10	24
Europe[3]	732	-0.1	7	1.5	75	22	34
Latin America and the Caribbean[4]	582	1.3	22	2.3	73	10	26
North America	348	0.6	6	2.0	79	18	28
Oceania	35	1.0	23	2.4	76	15	24

Except for population and % aged 60 and over figures, the data are annual averages projected for the period 2005–2010.

1. Europe, North America, Australia, New Zealand and Japan.
2. Africa, Asia (excluding Japan), Latin America and the Caribbean, and Oceania (excluding Australia and New Zealand).
3. Includes Russian Federation.
4. South America, Central America (including Mexico) and all Caribbean Islands.

4. POPULATION CHANGE 2005–2010

Average annual rate of population change (per cent) and the top ten contributors to world population growth (net annual addition).

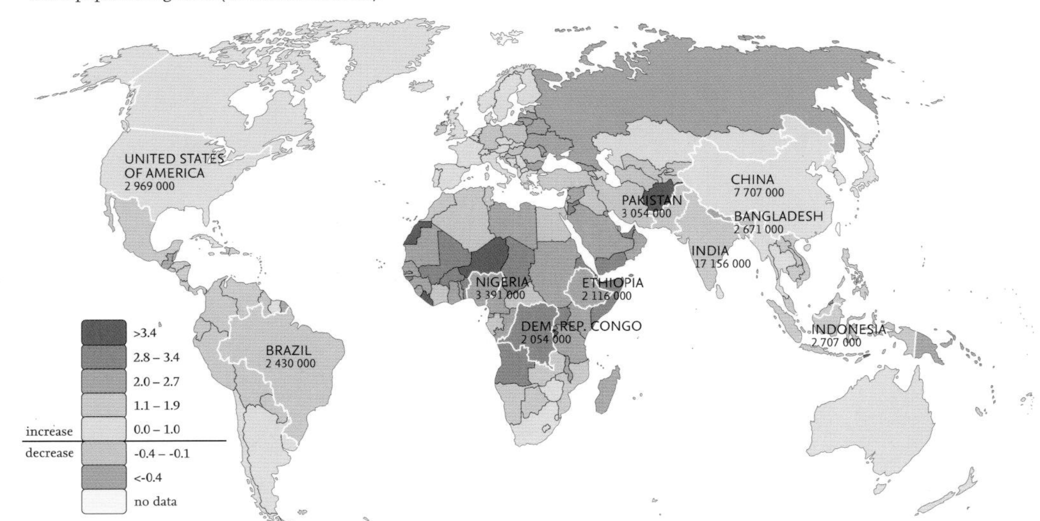

5. WORLD POPULATION GROWTH 1750–2050

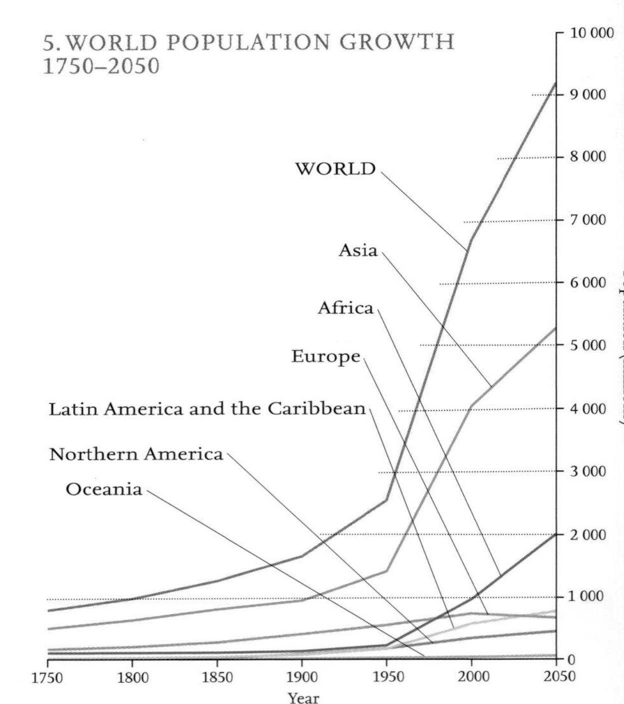

Arctic Circle
Tropic of Cancer
Equator
Tropic of Capricorn
Antarctic Circle

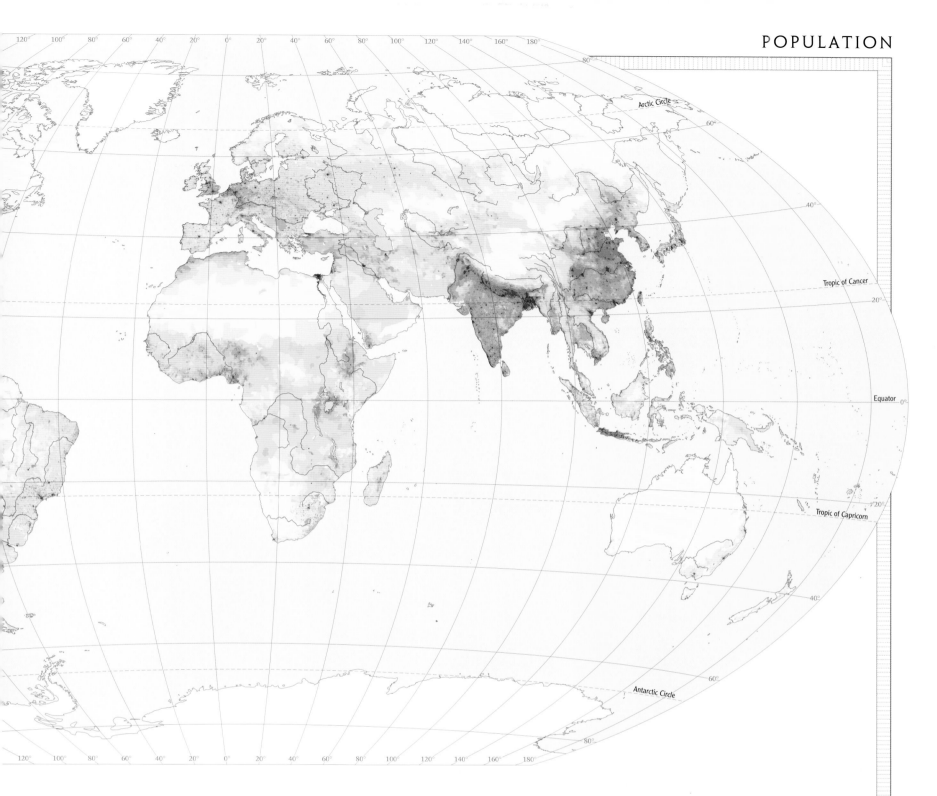

:MOGRAPHIC TRANSITION

ind patterns of population growth lies the nographic transition' process, where countries pass ugh a phase of falling death rates and then a phase alling fertility. Most parts of the world have passed ugh the first phase, with the average life expectancy 6 years in the less developed world now not far ind that of 77 years in the more developed regions 3). Even so, infant mortality – a very good indicator uman development levels – remains a major lenge in the less developed regions (*see 6*). Here, verage of fifty-two out of every one thousand babies die before their first birthday, compared to only six out of every one thousand in the more developed regions. Sub-Saharan Africa started this transitional phase later than most other parts of the world and has so far seen life expectancy rise to only 51.5 years, with progress being hampered by continuing high levels of infant mortality and by rising numbers of AIDS-related deaths.

Reductions in fertility rate (*see 7*) hold the key to the successful completion of the transition and the future stabilization of population growth. Much of the more developed world is well advanced in this process. In particular, Europe's total fertility rate (broadly the average number of babies born to each woman) is now down to 1.5 – well below the 'replacement rate' of 2.1 needed to give a constant population in the long term. Predictions indicate that there will be a major increase in the number of older people throughout the world especially in less developed regions (*see 3*). Europe's proportion of people aged 60 and over will rise from one-fifth to one-third whereas Latin America's will almost treble from 10 to 26 per cent.

6. INFANT MORTALITY RATE 2005–2010

Deaths of infants less than one year old per 1 000 live births.

7. TOTAL FERTILITY RATE 2005–2010

Estimate of the number of children a woman will bear through her child-bearing years.

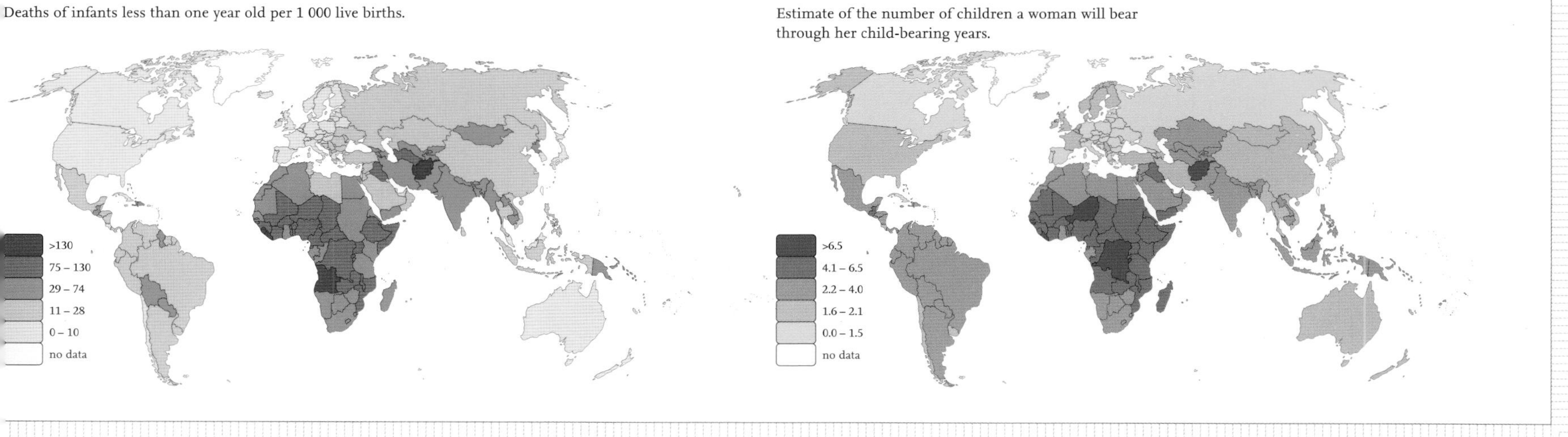

TOWARDS AN URBANIZED WORLD

World population is urbanizing rapidly but the current level of urbanization – the proportion of the population living in urban conditions – varies greatly across the world, as does its rate of increase. In the hundred years up to 1950 the greatest changes in urban population patterns took place in Europe and North America. Relatively few large cities developed elsewhere and most of these were in coastal locations with good trading connections with the imperial and industrial nations.

This legacy is still highly visible on the world map of major cities (*see 1*). The main feature of the past half century has been the massive growth in the numbers of urban dwellers in the less developed regions. This process is still accelerating, posing an even greater logistical challenge during the next few decades than it did in the closing decades of the twentieth century.

The year 2008 was a momentous point in world history, as for the first time urban dwellers outnumbered those living in traditionally rural areas, according to UN data. The annual rise in the percentage of the world's population living in cities has been accelerating steadily since the 1970s and will be running at unprecedentedly high levels until at least 2030. As a result, by then, 59.7 per cent of the world's population will be urbanites compared to 36.0 per cent in 1970 and 50.6 per cent in 2010 (*see 2*). In absolute terms, the global urban population more than doubled between 1970 and 2000 and is expected to rise by a further 2.1 billion by 2030 (*see 3*).

1. THE WORLD'S MAJOR CITIES

Urban agglomerations with over 1 million inhabitants
Winkel Tripel Projection
scale 1:111 000 000

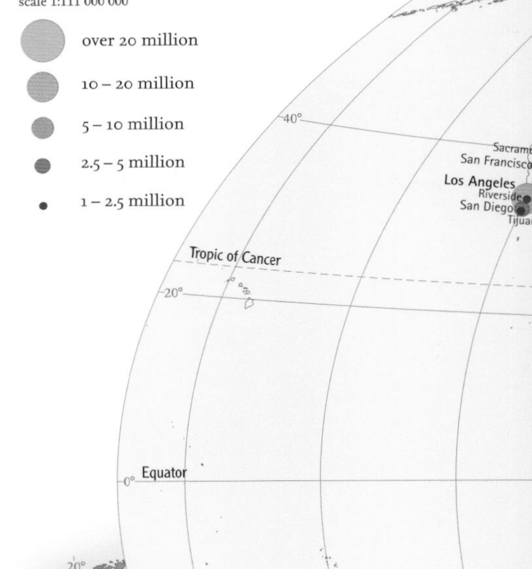

2. LEVEL OF URBANIZATION BY MAJOR REGION

Urban population as a percentage of total population 1970–2030.

	1970	2010	2030
World	36	50.6	59.7
More developed regions[1]	64.6	75	80.6
Less developed regions[2]	25.3	45.3	56
Africa	23.6	39.9	50
Asia	22.7	42.5	54.1
Europe[3]	62.8	72.6	77.8
Latin America and the Caribbean[4]	57	79.4	84.6
Northern America	73.8	82.1	86.7
Oceania	70.8	70.6	72.6

1. Europe, Northern America, Australia, New Zealand and Japan.
2. Africa, Asia (excluding Japan), Latin America and the Caribbean, and Oceania (excluding Australia and New Zealand).
3. Includes Russian Federation.
4. South America, Central America (including Mexico) and all Caribbean Islands.

PATTERNS OF URBANIZATION

There is a broad contrast in the levels of urbanization between the more and less developed regions. In the more developed regions as a whole, three-quarters of the population now live in urban places. Excluding the smallest countries, levels range from 97.4 per cent for Belgium to under 50 per cent for Albania, Bosnia, Moldova and Slovenia. Many countries have seen very little increase in their level of urbanization over several decades, with some reporting renewed population growth in rural areas. Only 45.3 per cent of the population in the less developed regions are urbanites, but this represents a big jump from the 25.3 per cent figure for 1970. Africa and Asia both currently average less than this, but will be seeing the greatest changes in the future, with their urban proportions likely to pass the 50 per cent mark by 2030 and 2025, respectively.

Alongside the rise in the world's urban population has occurred a massive increase in the number and size of cities, especially of the very large cities or 'megacities'. In 1950, New York was the only agglomeration with over 10 million inhabitants, but the number of such cities had grown to six by 1980, to eighteen by 2000 and to nineteen by 2007. This increase has been principally an Asian phenomenon; by 2007 North America's tally had risen to only two, Latin America possessed four, Africa and Europe had one each, but Asia had acquired eleven. According to United Nations figures there are expected to be twenty-four megacities by 2025 (*see 4*). This marked growth in the number of megacities in recent years is due to a combination of in-migration and natural increase, together with the physical outward expansion of their built-up areas and the incorporation of nearby settlements.

3. TOTAL URBAN POPULATION OF MAJOR REGIONS

Total population living in urban areas 1950–2030.

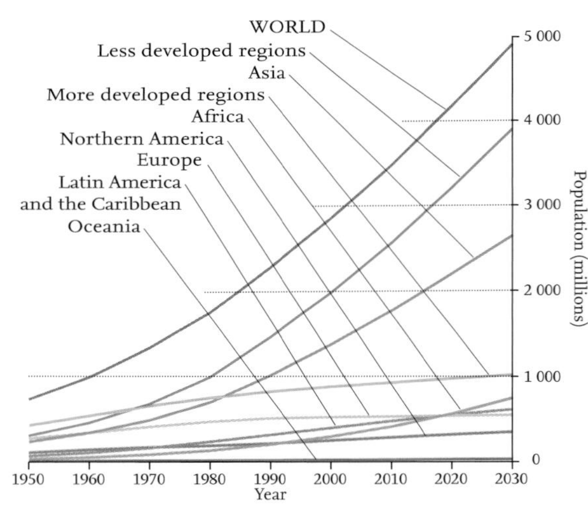

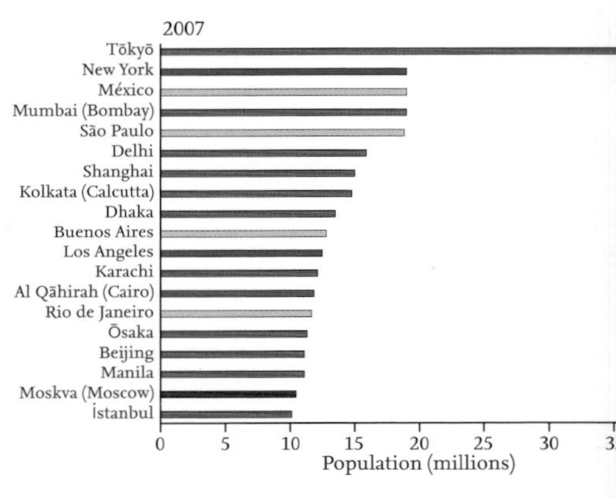

4. CITIES OF OVER 10 MILLION INHABITANTS

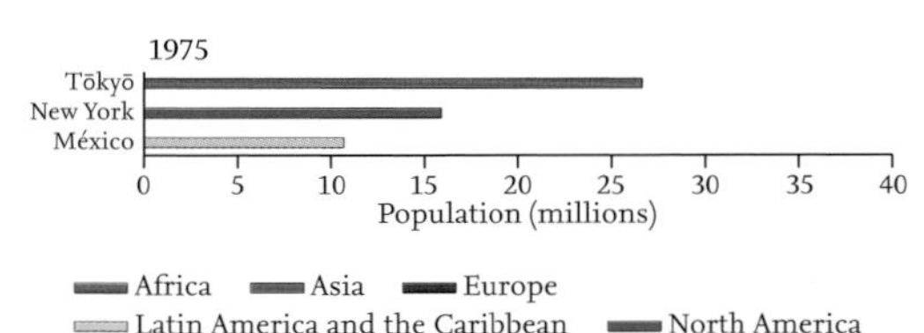

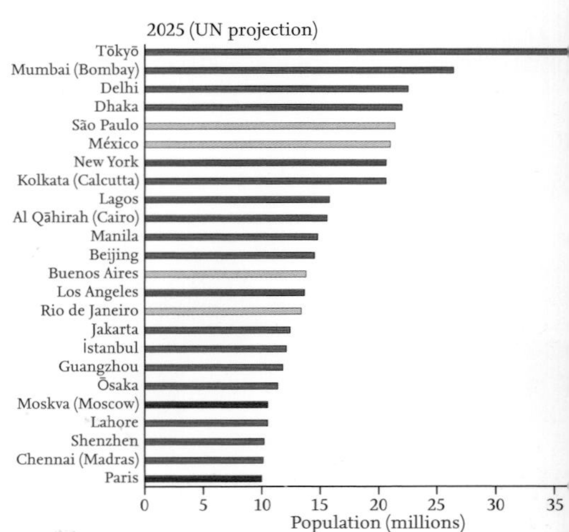

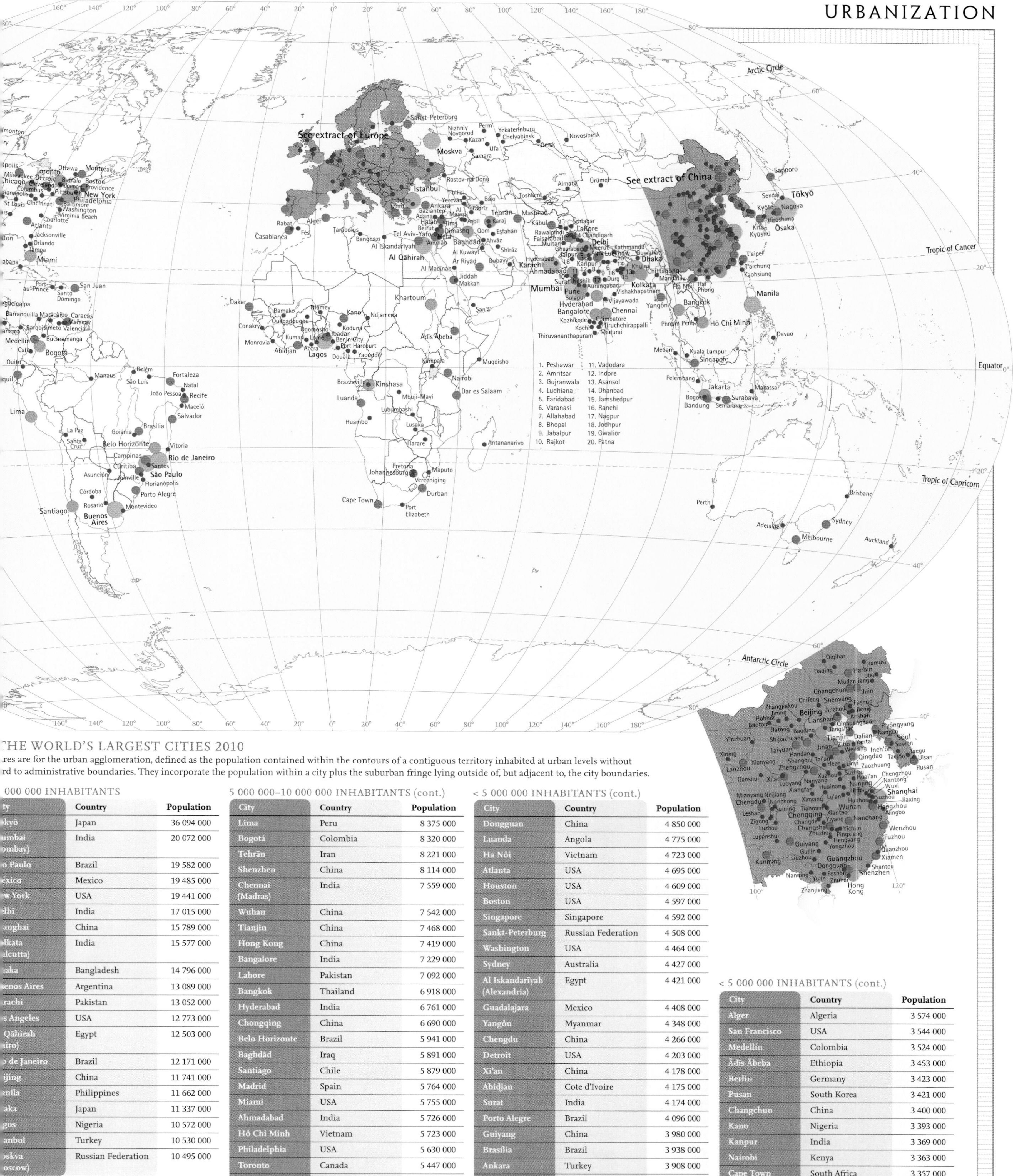

THE WORLD'S LARGEST CITIES 2010

ures are for the urban agglomeration, defined as the population contained within the contours of a contiguous territory inhabited at urban levels without ard to administrative boundaries. They incorporate the population within a city plus the suburban fringe lying outside of, but adjacent to, the city boundaries.

000 000 INHABITANTS

ty	Country	Population
kyō	Japan	36 094 000
umbai (ombay)	India	20 072 000
o Paulo	Brazil	19 582 000
éxico	Mexico	19 485 000
w York	USA	19 441 000
lhi	India	17 015 000
anghai	China	15 789 000
lkata (alcutta)	India	15 577 000
aka	Bangladesh	14 796 000
enos Aires	Argentina	13 089 000
rachi	Pakistan	13 052 000
s Angeles	USA	12 773 000
Qāhirah (iro)	Egypt	12 503 000
o de Janeiro	Brazil	12 171 000
ijing	China	11 741 000
anila	Philippines	11 662 000
aka	Japan	11 337 000
gos	Nigeria	10 572 000
anbul	Turkey	10 530 000
oskva (oscow)	Russian Federation	10 495 000

0 000–10 000 000 INHABITANTS

ty	Country	Population
ris	France	9 958 000
ul (eul)	South Korea	9 762 000
karta	Indonesia	9 703 000
angzhou	China	9 447 000
icago	USA	9 211 000
nshasa	Dem. Rep. Congo	9 052 000
ndon	United Kingdom	8 607 000

5 000 000–10 000 000 INHABITANTS (cont.)

City	Country	Population
Lima	Peru	8 375 000
Bogotá	Colombia	8 320 000
Tehrān	Iran	8 221 000
Shenzhen	China	8 114 000
Chennai (Madras)	India	7 559 000
Wuhan	China	7 542 000
Tianjin	China	7 468 000
Hong Kong	China	7 419 000
Bangalore	India	7 229 000
Lahore	Pakistan	7 092 000
Bangkok	Thailand	6 918 000
Hyderabad	India	6 761 000
Chongqing	China	6 690 000
Belo Horizonte	Brazil	5 941 000
Baghdād	Iraq	5 891 000
Santiago	Chile	5 879 000
Madrid	Spain	5 764 000
Miami	USA	5 755 000
Ahmadabad	India	5 726 000
Hô Chi Minh	Vietnam	5 723 000
Philadelphia	USA	5 630 000
Toronto	Canada	5 447 000
Khartoum	Sudan	5 185 000
Barcelona	Spain	5 057 000
Chittagong	Bangladesh	5 012 000
Pune	India	5 010 000

< 5 000 000 INHABITANTS

City	Country	Population
Dallas	USA	4 955 000
Shenyang	China	4 952 000
Ar Riyāḑ (Riyadh)	Saudi Arabia	4 856 000

< 5 000 000 INHABITANTS (cont.)

City	Country	Population
Dongguan	China	4 850 000
Luanda	Angola	4 775 000
Ha Nôi	Vietnam	4 723 000
Atlanta	USA	4 695 000
Houston	USA	4 609 000
Boston	USA	4 597 000
Singapore	Singapore	4 592 000
Sankt-Peterburg	Russian Federation	4 508 000
Washington	USA	4 464 000
Sydney	Australia	4 427 000
Al Iskandarīyah (Alexandria)	Egypt	4 421 000
Guadalajara	Mexico	4 408 000
Yangôn	Myanmar	4 348 000
Chengdu	China	4 266 000
Detroit	USA	4 203 000
Xi'an	China	4 178 000
Abidjan	Cote d'Ivoire	4 175 000
Surat	India	4 174 000
Porto Alegre	Brazil	4 096 000
Guiyang	China	3 980 000
Brasília	Brazil	3 938 000
Ankara	Turkey	3 908 000
Monterrey	Mexico	3 901 000
Melbourne	Australia	3 851 000
Recife	Brazil	3 831 000
Nanjing	China	3 813 000
Montréal	Canada	3 781 000
Kābul	Afghanistan	3 768 000
Harbin	China	3 753000
Salvador	Brazil	3 695 000
Phoenix	USA	3 687 000
Johannesburg	South Africa	3 618 000
Fortaleza	Brazil	3599000

< 5 000 000 INHABITANTS (cont.)

City	Country	Population
Alger	Algeria	3 574 000
San Francisco	USA	3 544 000
Medellín	Colombia	3 524 000
Ādīs Ābeba	Ethiopia	3 453 000
Berlin	Germany	3 423 000
Pusan	South Korea	3 421 000
Changchun	China	3 400 000
Kano	Nigeria	3 393 000
Kanpur	India	3 369 000
Nairobi	Kenya	3 363 000
Cape Town	South Africa	3 357 000
P'yŏngyang	North Korea	3 346 000
Dalian	China	3 335 000
Roma (Rome)	Italy	3 333 000
Curitiba	Brazil	3 320 000
Dar es Salaam	Tanzania	3 319 000
Hangzhou	China	3 269 000
Nagoya	Japan	3 267 000
Casablanca	Morocco	3 267 000
Athina (Athens)	Greece	3 256 000

ENERGY PRODUCTION AND CONSUMPTION

The world's energy resources are unevenly distributed (*see 1*). Similarly, the geography of energy production and consumption is highly uneven, with three countries, the USA, the Russian Federation and China, dominating both the production and consumption of energy (*see 2 and 3*). Some countries – typically the oil-exporting states, such as Saudi Arabia, Iran and Nigeria – produce much more than they consume, but many of the most advanced industrial economies, such as the USA and Japan, as well as relatively newly industrialized countries, such as South Korea and Taiwan, are net consumers. Peripheral countries, including Burkina, Chad and The Gambia, and some of the richest countries, including Singapore, are energy 'paupers' which produce no energy and are wholly reliant upon imports.

The USA is the largest primary energy consumer and, despite having only 5 per cent of the world's population, it consumes over a quarter of the world's energy. Together with Canada and Mexico, the USA's primary energy consumption increased by 8 per cent between 1992–2007, while the Middle East, South and Central America and Africa experienced higher growth rates from much lower base levels. Highest per capita energy consumption occurs in countries including Australia, Belgium and Canada as well as the USA. Lowest per capita energy consumption occurs in the world's poorest countries, including Benin, Burkina and Burundi. Uneven production and consumption mean that energy sources are the largest single items in international trade. Mexico and South and Central America, the Middle East, West and North Africa, Former Soviet Union and Canada are net oil exporters. The USA, Europe, eastern and South Africa, Australasia, China and Japan are net oil importers and generate wealth elsewhere to be able to pay for their imports.

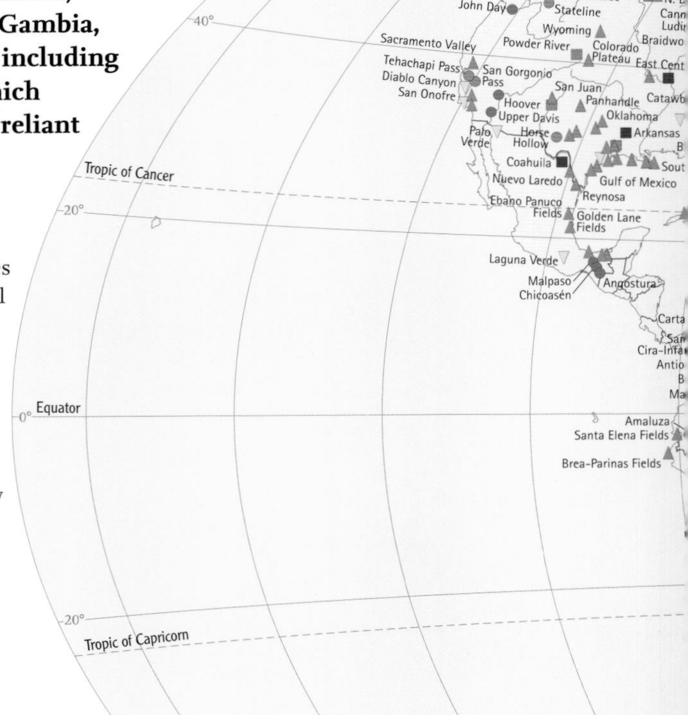

1. DISTRIBUTION OF RESOURCES
Winkel Tripel Projection
scale 1:100 000 000

- Major oil fields
- Major gas fields
- Major coal deposits
- Major lignite deposits
- Major nuclear reactors
- Major hydro plants
- Major wind farms

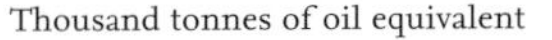

2. ENERGY PRODUCTION 2006
Thousand tonnes of oil equivalent

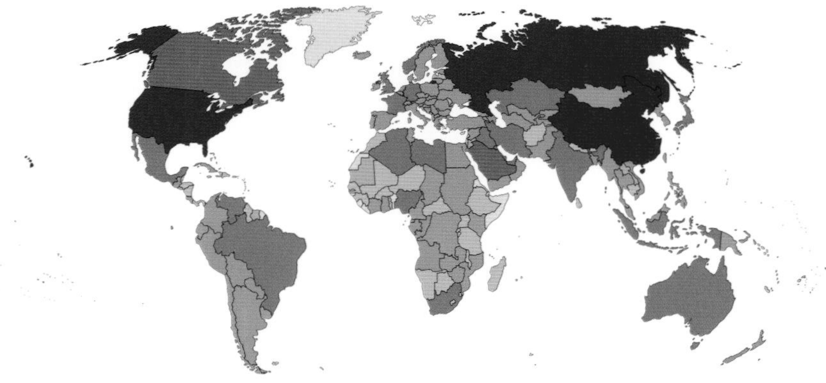

3. ENERGY CONSUMPTION 2006
Thousand tonnes of oil equivalent

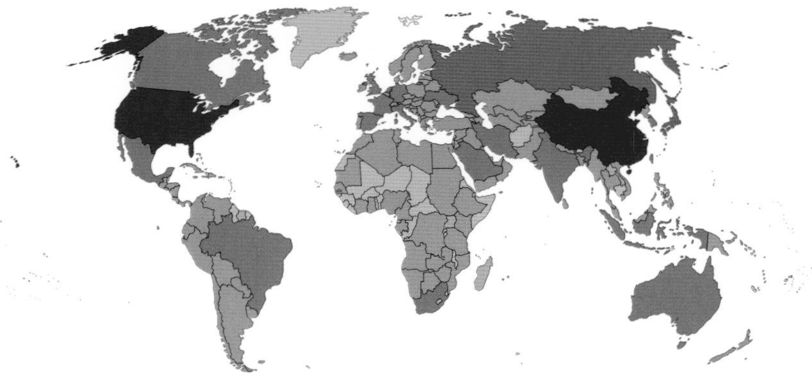

5. PRIMARY ENERGY CONSUMPTION

Million tonnes of oil equivalent
WORLD
Former Soviet Union[2]
South and Central America
Middle East
Africa
Asia Pacific
North America[1]
Europe
Year

1. Canada, USA and Mexico. 2. *See* footnote 2 for table 4.

6. NUCLEAR ENERGY CONSUMPTION

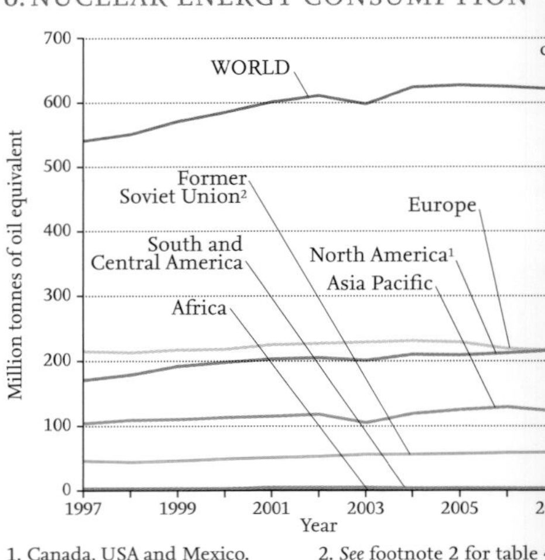

1. Canada, USA and Mexico. 2. *See* footnote 2 for table 4

ENERGY RESERVES AND RATES OF CONSUMPTION

Proven energy reserves are also unevenly distributed (*see 4*). Nearly two-thirds of proven oil reserves are concentrated in the Middle East. Reserves in the USA and Russian Federation have declined and Europe's reserves are expected to dry up early this century. Central America and Africa are expected to cease oil exports around 2025. Major import-dependent regions will be reliant upon the Middle East, underlining issues of security of supply in the context of global geopolitical instability. Proven reserves of natural gas are dominated by the Former Soviet Union and the Middle East while coal reserves are more evenly distributed between the Asia-Pacific region, North America and the Former Soviet Union.

Global energy use has grown historically and further growth is expected due to developing world industrialization. Between 1992 and 2007, global primary energy consumption increased by 24 per cent (*see 5*), led by the Middle East with a 56 per cent increase. Elsewhere, relatively costly energy in Europe depressed consumption to the relatively low level of 6 per cent while the dissolution of the Soviet Union led to the collapse in consumption which is now recovering. If rates of energy consumption were to remain constant then it has been estimated that the proven oil reserves would last forty years, natural gas sixty years and coal three hundred years. However, energy consumption rates are increasing and these estimates need regular revision.

4. PROVEN ENERGY RESERVES 2007

	Oil	%	Natural Gas	%	Coal	%
North America[1]	69.3	5.6	7.98	4.5	250 510	29.6
South and Central America	111.2	9.0	7.73	4.4	16 276	1.9
Europe	14.2	1.1	5.71	3.2	50 063	5.9
Former Soviet Union[2]	129.5	10.5	53.70	30.2	222 183	26.2
Middle East	755.3	61.0	73.20	41.3	1386	0.20
Africa	117.5	9.5	14.58	8.2	49 605	5.8
Asia Pacific	40.8	3.3	14.46	8.2	257 465	30.4
World	**1237.9**	**100**	**177.36**	**100**	**847 488**	**100**

1. Canada, USA and Mexico. 2. Comprises: Russian Federation, Estonia, Latvia, Lithuania, Belarus, Ukraine, Moldova, Georgia, Armenia, Azerbaijan, Kazakhstan, Uzbekistan, Turkmenistan, Tajikistan and Kyrgyzstan.

Oil (thousand million barrels) Natural Gas (trillion cubic metres) Coal (million tonnes)

ONSERVATION AND RENEWABLE RESOURCES

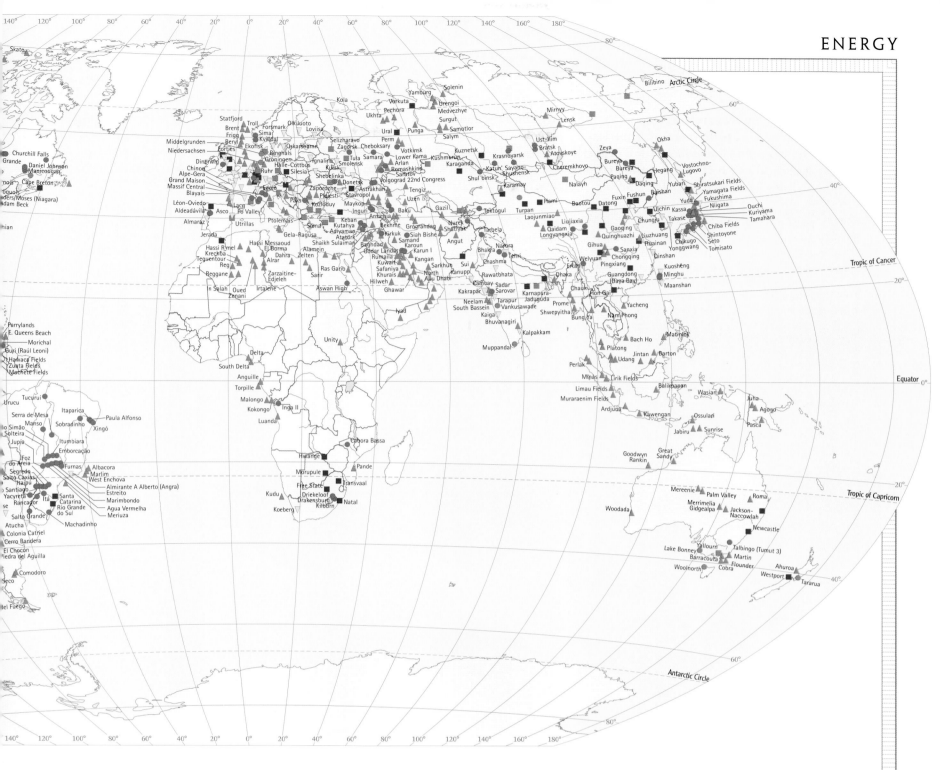

stainability has underpinned the search for ewable energy sources that are less detrimental environmental quality. Energy conservation aims extend the life of non-renewable resources, ucing their environmental damage and increasing rgy efficiency. Renewable energy sources may be other solution, although they currently only represent per cent of world total primary energy supply (*see 7*). blems of cost and technical inefficiency are being dressed through technological advances and supportive government policy and growth is expected due to the longer-term constraints upon primary and non-renewable sources.

Biomass (wood and organic wastes) is prevalent in developing countries. Geothermal power is generated from underground water heated by the Earth's molten core. New Zealand utilizes this obtaining 10 per cent of its electricity from geothermal sources. Energy derived from water – hydroelectric power – is another renewable energy source. World hydroelectricity consumption has risen over 20 per cent between 1992 and 2007 (*see 8*). Solar energy has the benefit of being renewable on a daily basis and being available globally, although it varies by season and latitude. Currently Japan, the USA and Germany account for 80 per cent of installed generation capacity. Wind power requires the right conditions in terms of terrain and weather to be commercially viable. Installed generation capacity has increased more than tenfold in the last decade, concentrated in Germany, the USA, Spain and Denmark.

7. FUEL SHARES IN WORLD TOTAL PRIMARY ENERGY SUPPLY 2007

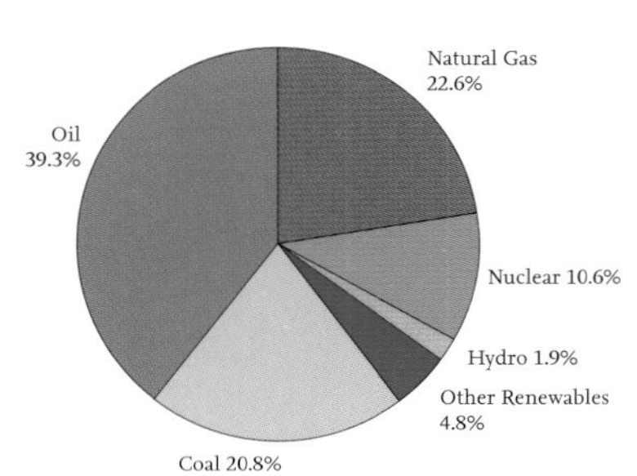

8. HYDROELECTRICITY CONSUMPTION

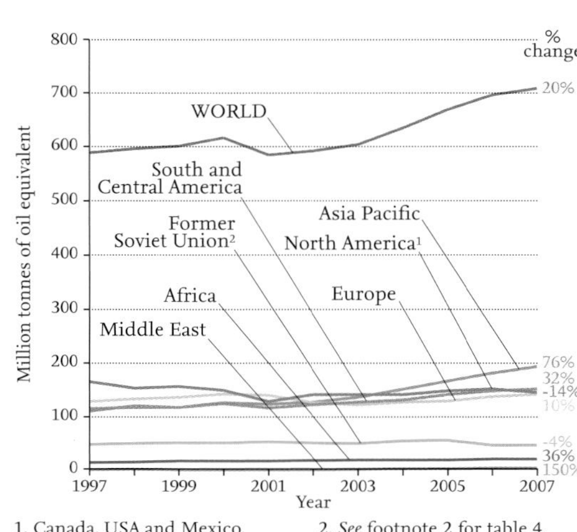

1. Canada, USA and Mexico. 2. *See* footnote 2 for table 4.

9. SOLAR, WIND, TIDE AND WAVE ENERGY FOR ELECTRICITY PRODUCTION

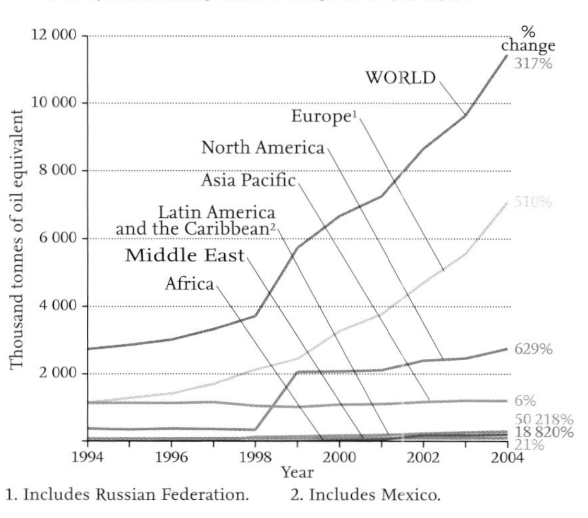

1. Includes Russian Federation. 2. Includes Mexico.

INTERNATIONAL TELECOMMUNICATIONS

Increased availability and ownership of telecommunications equipment over the last thirty years has aided the globalization of the world economy. Over half of the world's fixed telephone lines have been installed since 1987, and the majority of the world's Internet hosts (computers on which World Wide Web sites are stored) have come on-line since 1997 (*see 1*). Network access is uneven, however. Nearly half of existing telephone lines and cellular phones are in North America and Europe. Internet users in Asia, North America and Europe make up over 85 per cent of the world total (*see 2*).

This means that there is strong competition in the traditional telephone market in many parts of the world. In North America and Europe consumers have a wide choice available to them. This is not the case everywhere. For example, in many African countries there is little or no competition and consumers have little choice in the service they subscribe to. This is also affecting the development of broadband internet access (*see 3*). An interesting development that is affecting the number of fixed telephone lines, is the increase in mobile-only households. These are most common in households with occupants under the age of 35, where often new householders moving out of the parental home choose not to have a fixed line.

One measure of the perceived 'death of distance' is the steady rise in international telephone calls, which has increased by 381 per cent between 1991 and 2004. The map (*see 4*) shows accessibility to telephone lines and telephone traffic between countries in different continents for routes using at least 100 million minutes of telecommunications time in 2007. In that year, thes[e] streams totalled 111.5 billion minutes, 43 per cent of global international TDM traffic. The routes data in th[e] map reflects TDM traffic only. Changes are taking pla[ce] in the international telephone market. Many people now access low cost or free international calls through the internet by means of specialist software. Others make use of satellite or cellular phones to make their international calls, or they send a text message or use electronic mail.

1. WORLD COMMUNICATIONS EQUIPMENT 1993–2007

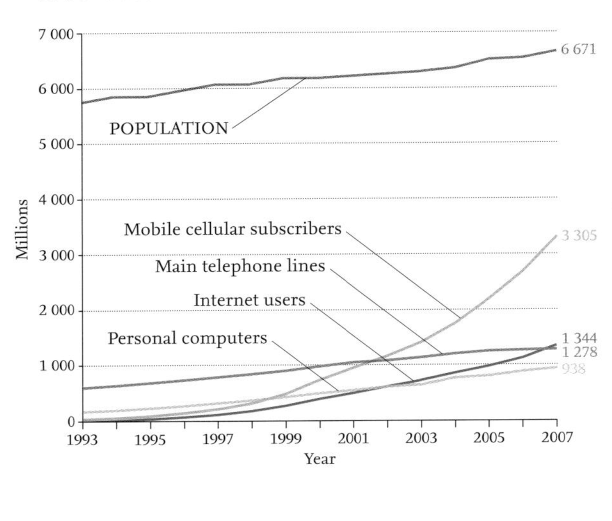

2. INTERNATIONAL TELECOMMUNICATIONS INDICATORS BY REGION 2007

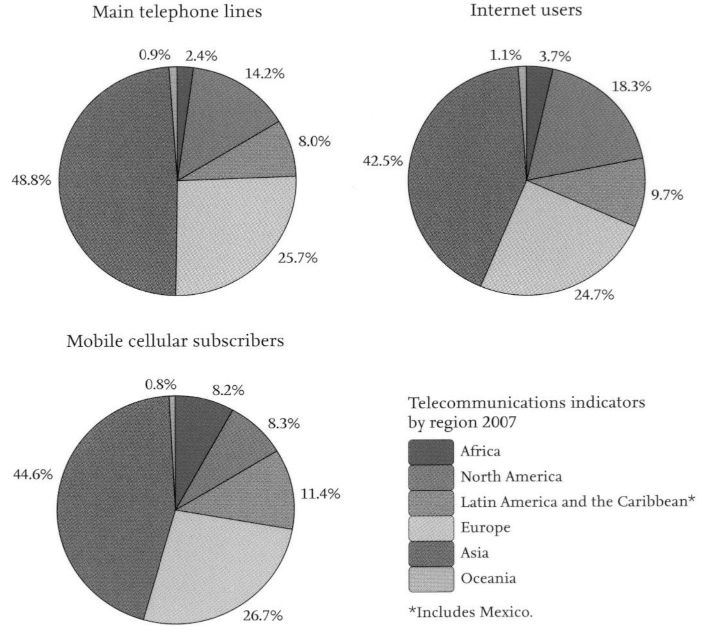

3. TOP BROADBAND ECONOMIES 2007

Countries with the highest broadband penetration ra[te] subscribers per 100 inhabitants

	Top Economies	Rate
1	Denmark	36.3
2	Iceland	34.8
3	Netherlands	33.5
4	Finland	33.3
5	Switzerland	32.1
6	South Korea	30.6
7	Norway	29.0
8	Sweden	25.9
9	United Kingdom	25.6
10	France	25.2
11	Luxembourg	24.2
12	Germany	24.0
13	Canada	22.9
14	Belgium	22.6
15	Japan	22.1
16	Israel	22.1
17	Australia	21.7
18	Estonia	20.8
19	Barbados	20.5
20	Singapore	19.9

4. INTERNATIONAL TELECOMMUNICATIONS TRAFFIC 2007

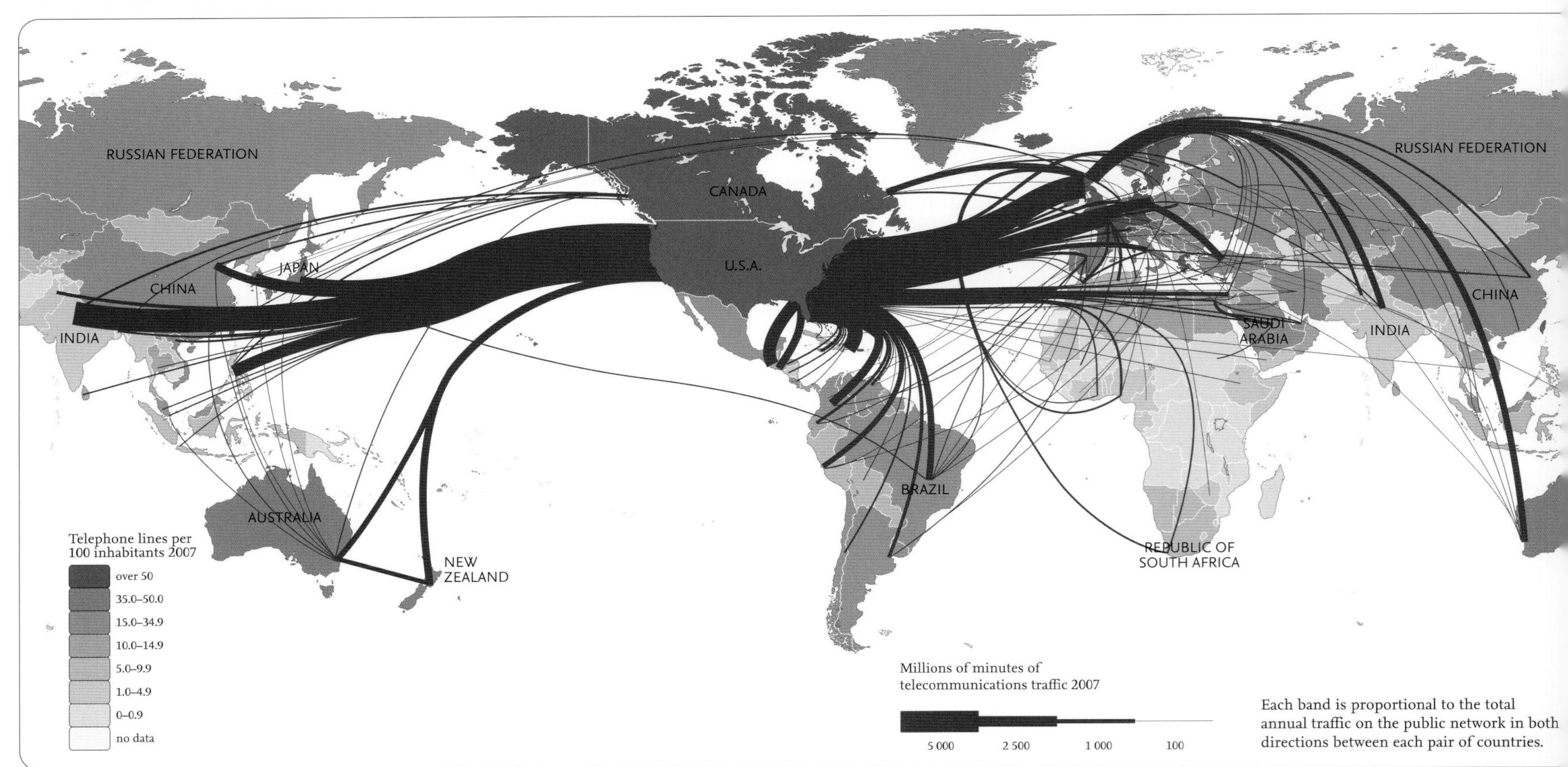

Each band is proportional to the total annual traffic on the public network in both directions between each pair of countries.

ATELLITE AND INTERNET OMMUNICATIONS

ernational telecommunications use either fibre-optic les or satellites as transmission media. Although les carry the vast majority of traffic around the world, nmunications satellites are important for person-to-son communication, including cellular telephones, l for broadcasting. Growing volumes of data traffic, ticularly from the Internet (*see 5*), have boosted nand for international transmission capacity. Most fic is routed over fibre-optic cables. In 1999, the rld's trans-oceanic cables could carry approximately gigabits per second (Gbps), which is equivalent to 5 million simultaneous phone calls. By 2003, ernational cable capacity had grown seventeen-fold l it continues to increase.

Unlike submarine cables, which must connect at fixed nts, satellites can transmit information between th stations located anywhere within a satellite's radio m, or 'footprint'. Geostationary satellites, which orbit 36 000 kilometres above the Earth (*see 6*), may have tprints spanning over 1000 kilometres, thus viding a broad service area for point to multi-point ce, video and data communications. The positions of nmunications satellites are critical to their use, and ect the demand for such communications in each t of the world. Satellites placed in 'geostationary' it sit above the equator and this means that they ve at the same speed as the Earth and remain fixed ve a single point on the Earth's surface.

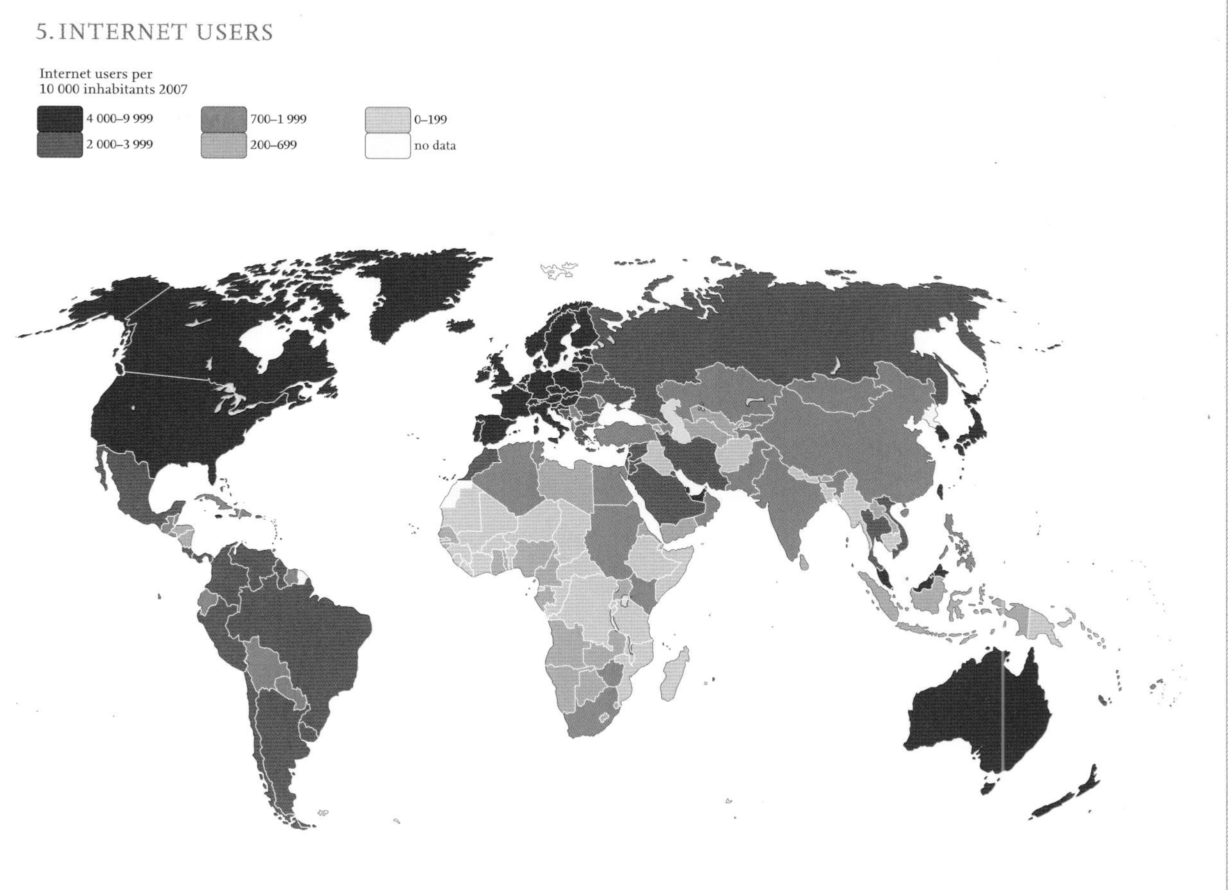

GEOSTATIONARY COMMUNICATIONS SATELLITES AND MOBILE CELLULAR SUBSCRIBERS

stationary munications lites
In service
Inclined orbit
Planned

Mobile cellular subscribers per 100 inhabitants 2007
over 100
80 – 100
60 – 79.9
40 – 59.9
20 – 39.9
0 – 19.9
no data

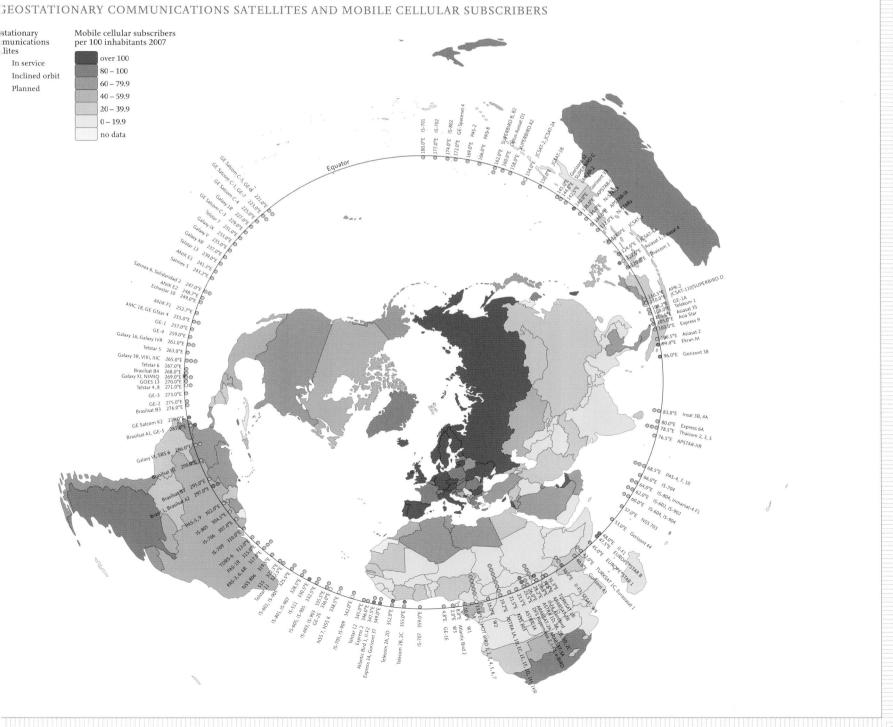

Equator

PREHISTORIC AND CLASSICAL CARTOGRAPHY (500 BC–AD 500)

The evolution of mapping has been inextricably linked to people's knowledge of the world and to related scientific and technological developments. Mapping skills have been influenced by factors such as way of life and the nature of the physical environment, and maps can therefore provide an excellent insight into cultures and civilizations.

Surviving examples of ancient maps are rare. Their limits of coverage tended to be the extent of the producers' accurate geographical knowledge. Beyond the local area, maps appeared to reflect a speculative or cosmological approach *(see 1)*.

The most significant contribution of the Greeks to cartography was theoretical rather than practical. It is primarily the work of Claudius Ptolemy, a Greek mathematician, astronomer and geographer living in the 2nd century AD, which provides us with information about the level of geographical knowledge at this time. Ptolemy's work *Geographia* included theoretical principles of cartography, lists of place names and computed co-ordinates. Later maps, based on this work, show how he believed the world to look at that time *(see 2)*.

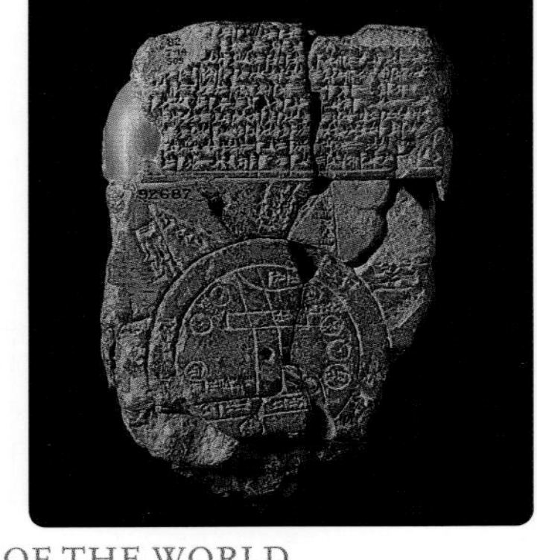

1. MAP OF THE WORLD
Carved on a Babylonian clay tablet, c. 600 BC. Babylon is shown as a rectangle intersected by vertical lines representing the Euphrates river. Small circles show other cities and countries, and the world is encircle by an ocean – the 'Bitter River'.
British Museum, Department of Western Asiatic Antiquities, London,

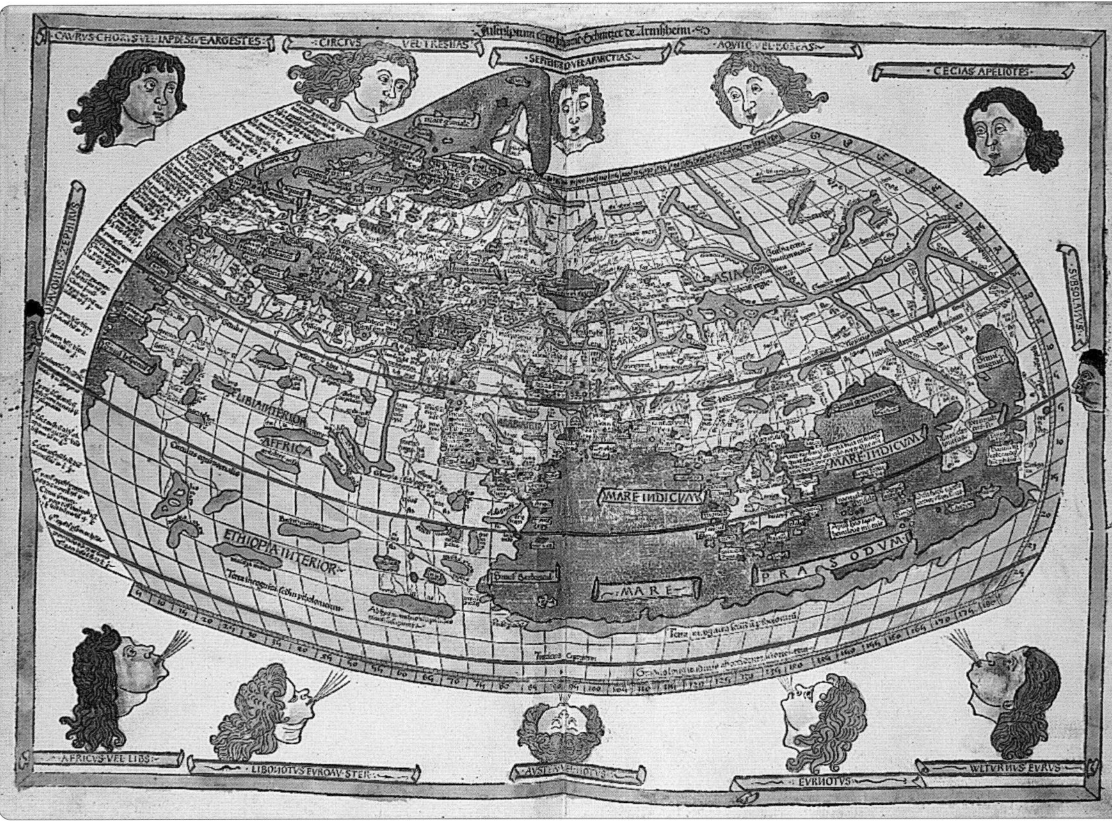

2. PTOLEMAIC WORLD MAP
Based on the work of Claudius Ptolemy, produced by Donis Nicolaus in Ulm, Germany, 1630. The map includes lines of latitude and longitude which give a sense of accuracy. The figures represent different wind directions.
British Library, London, UK.

3. THE MADABA MOSAIC MAP
Detail from the Madaba map (c. AD 550) showing the walled city of Jerusalem and the surrounding area. Approximately a quarter of the original map, which covered 94 square metres of floor, is still intact.

4. THE HEREFORD MAPPA MUNDI
Produced on vellum, and attributed to Richard of Haldingham and Lafford, c. 1290. The map follows the form of a T-O map, centred on Jerusalem, with east to the top. The continents of Asia (top), Africa (lower right) and Europe (lower left) are separated by the Mediterranean Sea and the Nile and Don rivers.
Hereford Cathedral, Hereford, UK.

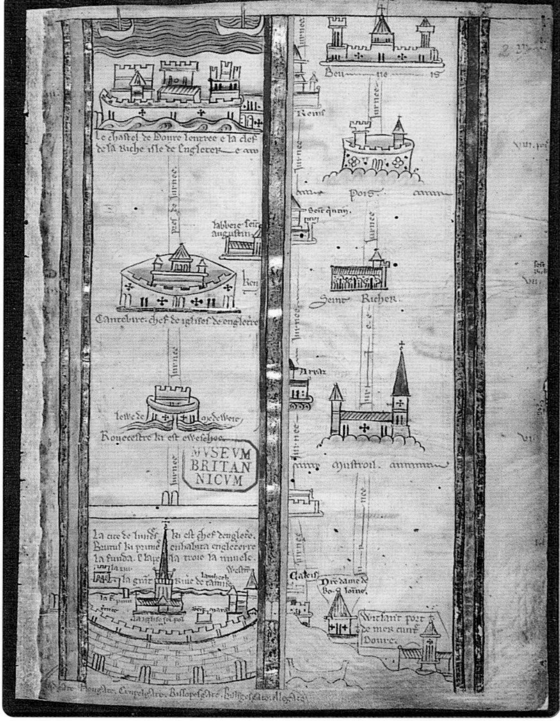

5. ITINERARY MAP OF A ROUTE FROM LONDON TO ITALY
Produced by Matthew Paris, c. 1250. This is a fine, early example of a road map in strip form. This extract includes Rochester, Canterbury and Dover.
British Library, London, UK.

AD 500–1600

Religious beliefs played an important part in the cartography of this period. One particularly significan product was the Madaba map (c. AD 550) – a Christian map in the form of a floor mosaic discovered in a chu in Madaba, Jordan, depicting biblical Palestine *(see 3)*. Also during this period, maps originating in the classi tradition were overlain with later Christian elements. Such maps were usually oval or circular in shape, schematic in content, and centred on Jerusalem. These world maps *(mappæmundi)* conveyed a Christian perspective of the world, and their detail ranged from virtually diagrammatic to the highly complex *(see 4)*.

Maps from the later medieval period include sea charts, town plans and local, district and route maps. C these, portolan charts – sea charts designed primarily navigation – were by far the most significant and provided impressively detailed and accurate informati on coastlines, harbours and related navigational matte Route maps, for the use of pilgrims and merchants travelling overland, also developed over this period, as exemplified by Matthew Paris' map of the route from London to Otranto, Italy produced around AD 1250 *(see*

The 15th and 16th centuries were essentially the age exploration and discovery, a period which witnessed a explosion of global knowledge and a veritable renaissance in cartography. The period saw a great development of world maps, many of which began to include the coastal detail of the earlier portolan charts and to show the latest geographical information resulting from the voyages of discovery. Rome and Ver dominated European map production from 1550 to 15 but later in the period dominance in mapmaking pass to the Low Countries. This 'Golden Age' of Dutch cartography is exemplified by the first printed 'atlas' o map sheets by Abraham Ortelius in 1570 – the *Theatru Orbis Terrarum*. The term 'atlas' was coined by Gerard Mercator the Flemish cartographer – perhaps the mos widely known figure in the history of cartography. His work, in particular his map projection published in 15 makes him the geographical colossus of the period.

›00–1900

rtography in the earlier years of the 17th century was minated by the Low Countries, epitomized by the ·eu publishing house *(see 6)* but, by the late 17th ntury, the world centre for cartographic production l shifted from Amsterdam to Paris. France was one of first countries to recognize the importance of ablishing a national survey and mapping programme. ere, the Cassini family established the national survey France well ahead of other such surveys in western rope *(see 7)*.

The colonial scramble for North America, and the nerican War of Independence (1775–1783), drove the velopment of cartography in North America, and it s an age, too, when the exploration of Australia, smania and New Zealand resulted in their appearance world maps. Such exploration was aided by great velopments in navigation and particularly the ability establish longitude more precisely.

During the 19th century special maps appeared in greater numbers reflecting scientific and social observation and analysis. One significant example of this development of thematic mapping was the *Physikalischer Atlas* of Heinrich Berghaus, published in two volumes in 1845 and 1848 *(see 8)*. Lithographic printing of maps was developed in the early years of the century allowing the production of multiple copies of maps very much more cheaply, stimulating a proliferation of maps for mass consumption and for educational purposes.

As the 19th century progressed, factors such as exploration and emigration were reflected in extended world coverage of maps and charts. Work on national surveys proceeded, one particularly notable national cartographic achievement being the Great Trigonometrical Survey (GTS) of India which facilitated the creation of extensive and detailed topographic maps of the sub-continent.

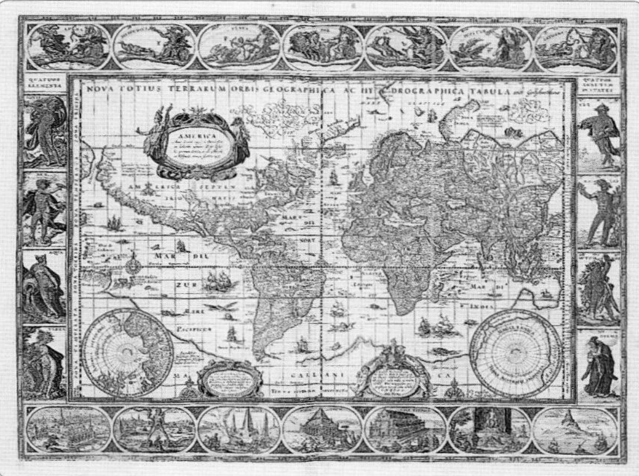

6. WORLD MAP
Produced in Amsterdam by Willem Blaeu, 1630. This is one of the finest examples of early maps on Mercator's projection.
British Library, London, UK.

7. CARTE DE FRANCE
Detail from the first sheet – Sheet No. 1 Paris – by Cassini de Thury, 1736. Original scale 1:86 400.
National Library of Scotland, Edinburgh, UK.

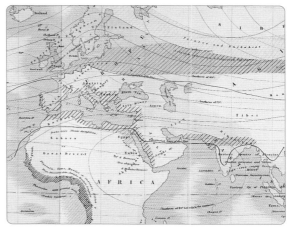

8. THEMATIC ATLAS MAP
Extract from a map of the *Survey of the geographical distribution and cultivation of the most important plants which are used as food for man: with indications of the isotheres and isokhimenes*, 1842. Published in the *Physikalischer Atlas* by Heinrich Berghaus,1845 and 1848. This English language version appeared as Plate 44 in W & A K Johnston's *National Atlas of Historical, Commercial and Political Geography*, 1847.
National Library of Scotland, Edinburgh, UK.

)TH CENTURY

r, politics and technological development were trumental in prompting the expansion of map and art coverage throughout the 20th century. The velopment of aviation and, in turn, space exploration, d photography and imagery possible through them, ve been particularly significant in recent velopments in cartography and have spawned a new e in map making. The development of the computer s led to the production of digital maps and the consequent development of Geographical Information Systems (GIS). New digital cartographic techniques allow users to combine and manipulate geographical data sets, and also support new forms of output and visualization *(see 9)*.

There has been a significant increase in map coverage throughout the world, and yet the fact that comprehensive national topographic mapping has been produced does not mean that it is readily available to the public. Many countries, particularly in Africa and Asia, impose strict restrictions on the release of their mapping. The question of national map coverage and availability is complicated by the activities of external mapping organizations. The former USSR had extensive programmes producing topographic mapping of countries throughout the world *(see 10)*. Easy access to this previously classified military mapping has recently served to extend map availability.

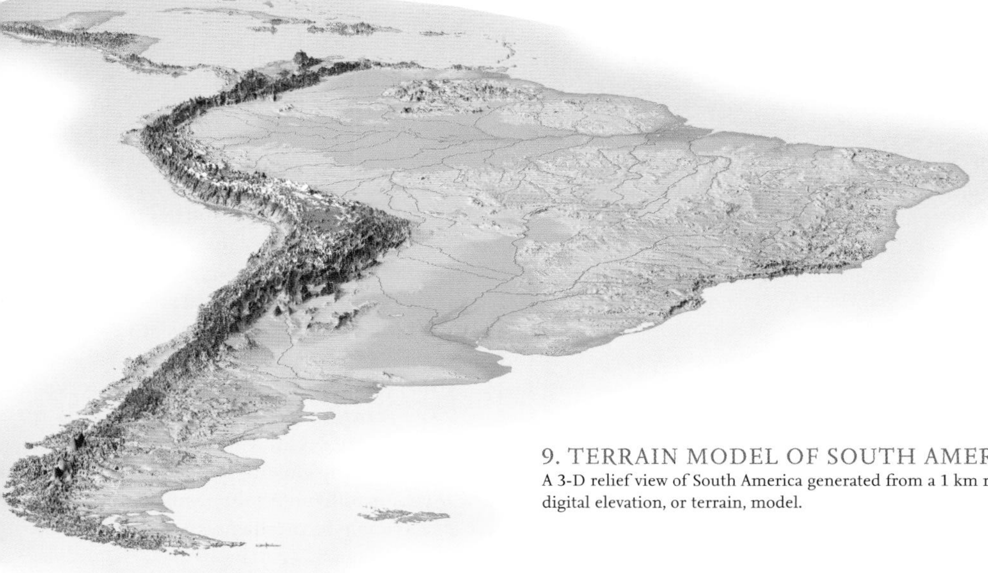

9. TERRAIN MODEL OF SOUTH AMERICA
A 3-D relief view of South America generated from a 1 km resolution digital elevation, or terrain, model.

10. GROZNYY, RUSSIAN FEDERATION
Extract from a Russian military topographic map 1:500 000, 1988.

CHANGES IN MAPPING

Although we retain our internal cognitive mapping abilities, the value of a pencil and paper (or a stick and some sand for our ancestors, or just for convenience – *see 5*) to support the spatial thinking process is self evident, and was the genesis of the great developments in mapping we have seen.

During the past two thousand years most fundamental theory and practical knowledge had been acquired. The great achievement of recent centuries was the introduction of printing which opened up markets and financial incentives to make high quality maps available to all.

However, the introduction of computers in the mid-20th century has had a much greater impact. Not only has it transformed the production and use of maps but it has also changed the relationships between people, maps and spatial data forever.

Printed maps are still being provided by national and commercial agencies to satisfy established markets, but compilation, as in the case of this atlas (*see 1*), is increasingly from digital databases, and their design and production increasingly uses Geographic Information System (GIS) and graphic software. Major reference databases now contain fundamental, often non-generalized information, with greater potential to satisfy the more specific needs of narrower groups within the geospatial information community, generally via the Internet.

1. ATLAS MAP COMPILATION
Maps for publication now make use of digital geographic data and powerful graphics software to ensure high levels of accuracy and the highest standards of reproduction.

2. WORLD MAP PROJECTIONS

Goode's Homolosine Projection

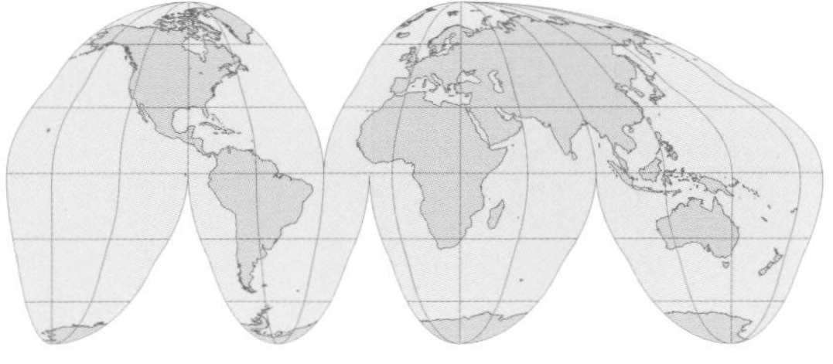

Winkel Tripel Projection

Mercator Projection

Briesemeister Projection

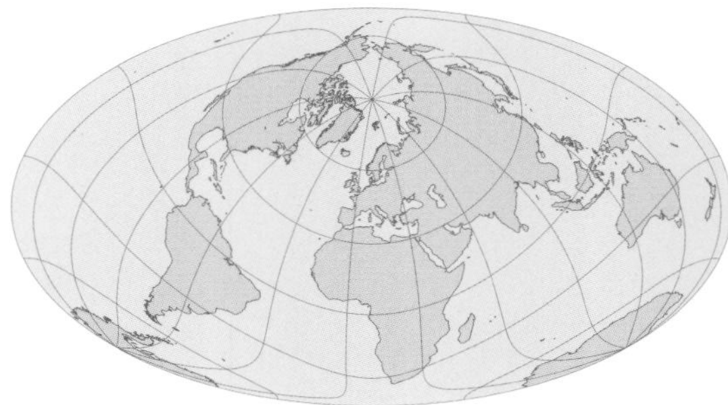

MAP PROJECTIONS

One of the main challenges of cartography is how to depict a sphere on a plane surface. It is impossible to d this while preserving correct shapes and areas and compromises have to be reached. Transformations of the globe onto a flat surface are referred to as projections. The earliest examples (6th – 1st centuries BC) were vaguely 'cylindrical' (i.e. constructed as if the Earth's graticule is projected onto a cylinder of paper wrapped around the globe). These produce a rectangul pattern of lines of latitude and longitude. Ptolemy's written work of the 2nd century AD contained some of the most detailed cartographic instructions and in his Geography he also describes simple conic projections (produced as if projected onto a cone). The other main type of projection is azimuthal, with the graticule 'projected' onto a flat piece of paper in contact with, or cutting through the globe. Perhaps the most famous projection of all time is that of Mercator. Cylindrical i form, the lines of latitude are spaced to allow loxodromes (lines of constant compass bearing) to appear as straight lines to satisfy the convenience of th mariner who navigates by compass. This projection an variations of it are still used today for detailed topographic mapping. Although the projection does preserve shape around each point, areas, especially in high latitudes, are very distorted. Thus when the whole world is depicted, a hectare of forest in northern Cana would appear over 1000% larger than the equivalent ground area in central Africa. For this reason its use in an atlas to depict the world distribution of forest cover for example, could be justly criticized. Today there are numerous map projections to choose from (*see 2*), man of which are appropriate for small-scale world maps.

3. SATELLITE IMAGE OF FLINDERS RIVER, AUSTRALIA
This satellite image taken on 18 February 2009, shows the extreme flooding along the Flinders River System in northern Queensland, Australia. Western Australia, Queensland and New South Wales suffered severe flooding in February 2009 during the annual wet season. Satellite imagery is an invaluable tool for assessing and mapping environmental phenomena.

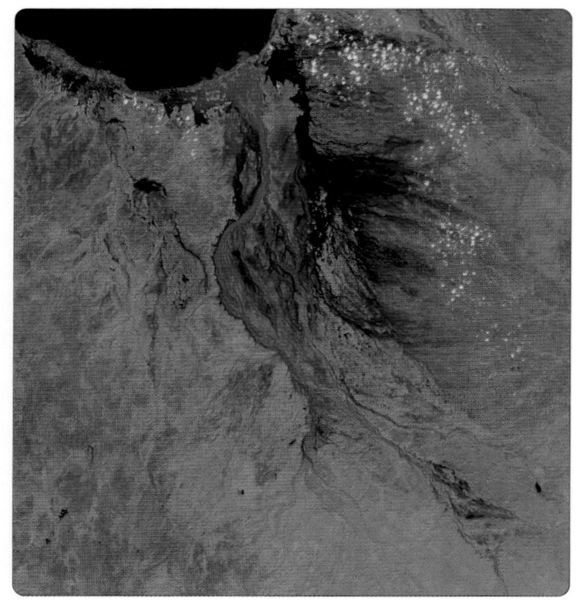

CARTOGRAPHIC DATA

Following the Dark Ages (AD 500–1300) mapping expanded both within Europe and globally with the growth of colonialism and world trade. The development of printing in the 15th century increased the demand from mariners for sea charts, and from the military for topographic maps of the land. Survey accuracy, an essential characteristic of such products, requires the measurement procedure of working from the whole (control frameworks at global and regional scales) to the part (detailed mapping at local level). With horizontal and vertical control in place, mapping progressed, initially with ground surveying techniques but later using aerial photography and photogrammetry (taking measurements from stereographic aerial photographs). New technologies such as satellite Global Positioning Systems (GPS), originally developed in the USA for military use, are now employed for navigation, establishing control and for detailed survey work. While topographic base maps are essential for many purposes, the growing need to map and monitor global issues ha led to the employment of advanced techniques including radar imagery and satellite imaging systems (*see 3*). Recent high-resolution (sub-metre) scanners on the Quick Bird and IKONOS satellites (*see 4*) are even adding fine metric data and permitting these images to act directly as map substitutes for some tasks. With the development of digital systems in recent decades the storage, manipulation, transmission and visualization o all this data are becoming much simpler and more routine. Such data, essential for producing accurate maps, are therefore much in demand by environmental scientists and planners.

Recently these high resolution images have become more accessible to the general public via the internet permitting the user to view high resolution satellite images of many major towns and cities throughout the world.

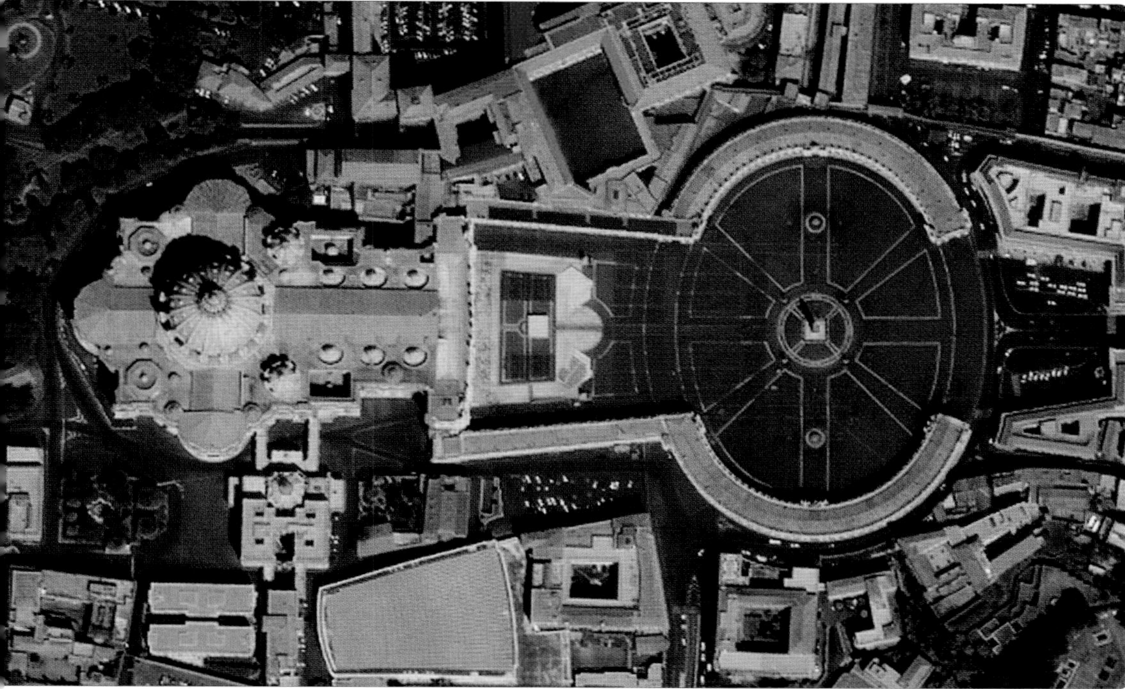

SATELLITE IMAGE OF VATICAN CITY
gh resolution satellite images such as this one of Vatican City can provide huge amounts of data for cartographers and urban planners. They can 've as source material for the compilation of large-scale maps, or may sometimes be used directly as a map base.

5. SAND MAP
Members of the US Pennsylvania National Guard examine a rudimentary map drawn in sand before an exercise. Maps can be 'externalized' in many ways using the most convenient and readily available media.

NTERACTING WITH GEOGRAPHIC INFORMATION

atial knowledge of the environment, structured as gnitive (mental) maps, is essential for human survival d routine activities. Although some people can retain mplex geographies in their minds, most require ternal (for example, printed) maps for them to amine their surroundings and consider spatial oblems or tasks in more detail. Cognitive maps can externalized in several ways, for example verbally, rough hand gestures (such as pointing) or through etch maps, whether on paper or in sand (*see 5*). The st of these provide continuity between our instinctive ilities to make and use maps and what has become e professional discipline of cartography.

In the past, maps were used for both data storage d visualization. Once compiled, designed and inted they were normally sold and archived. owever, because of the time-lapse introduced by ese processes, maps can often be out of date or ay not contain exactly the information required. ndamental changes have followed the introduction computers. Maps and geographic information are now stored in digital databases which can be constantly maintained, with direct updating possible from survey and satellite data. This procedure is increasingly being employed by national and commercial mapping agencies where maps, particularly at large scales, are compiled digitally and printed on demand rather than as part of a publishing programme or printed series. This means that choices are now available for the provision of geographic or cartographic information – through printing or via computer-based mapping systems on CD-ROM or the Internet. The latter may carry some disadvantages (such as the need for the latest hardware, and the restricted view of a monitor screen) but these systems can also offer revolutionary advantages for the viewer. Not only can geographic information be selected and combined at will but the user may also have interactive control over the design and content of the image (*see 6*). Animation may also be provided as well as hyper-links to other parts of the database for images, video-clips or sounds.

Geographic information systems (GIS) – combining software and hardware for the manipulation and analysis of spatial data – develop these ideas much farther and are now used extensively within government, industry and commerce. Digital geographic data and cartographic facilities are now also being employed in what are often referred to as location-based services (LBS), including in-car navigation systems (*see 7*), mobile phones and personal digital assistants. These can incorporate GPS receivers and respond to geographic triggers such as the input of a town name, street name or postcode. The precise position of the user can then be identified and route guidance and local information provided directly. However, new technology need not change completely how we access and use maps. We still travel on foot, by bicycle, motorcar or aircraft as circumstances demand. Thus the future can be interpreted as offering a wider spectrum of cartographic sources and facilities for different uses – from high quality publications produced by cartographic specialists, to personal interactive experiences.

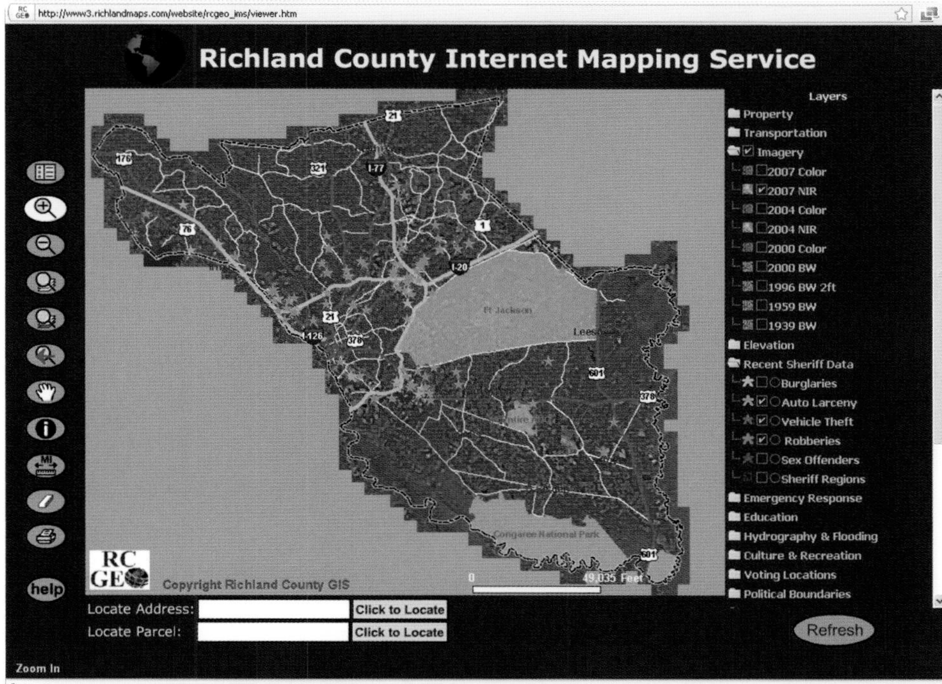

6. INTERACTIVE WEB MAPPING
Richland County Geographic Information Systems (RC GEO), South Carolina, use data from across several departments to develop spatial databases and mapping services for use by local government, the general public and businesses. Integration of the data within a geographic information system (GIS) allows each point on a map to become an index to cultural, environmental, demographic and political information about that location, and allows users to manipulate and output maps for their specific needs.

7. MOBILE MAPPING
The latest in-car systems use Bluetooth technology to facilitate 'hands-free' navigation, and real-time traffic information is also now available. This permits routes to be calculated around traffic bottlenecks, and road incidents affecting traffic are graphically represented on-screen as icons on the navigation map. It is also possible for the user to load customized points of interest (POIs) such as speed cameras to add to a pre-loaded POI database.

AUSTRALASIA Total Land Area 8 844 516 sq km / 3 414 887 sq miles (includes New Guinea and Pacific Island nations)

Puncak Jaya, Indonesia

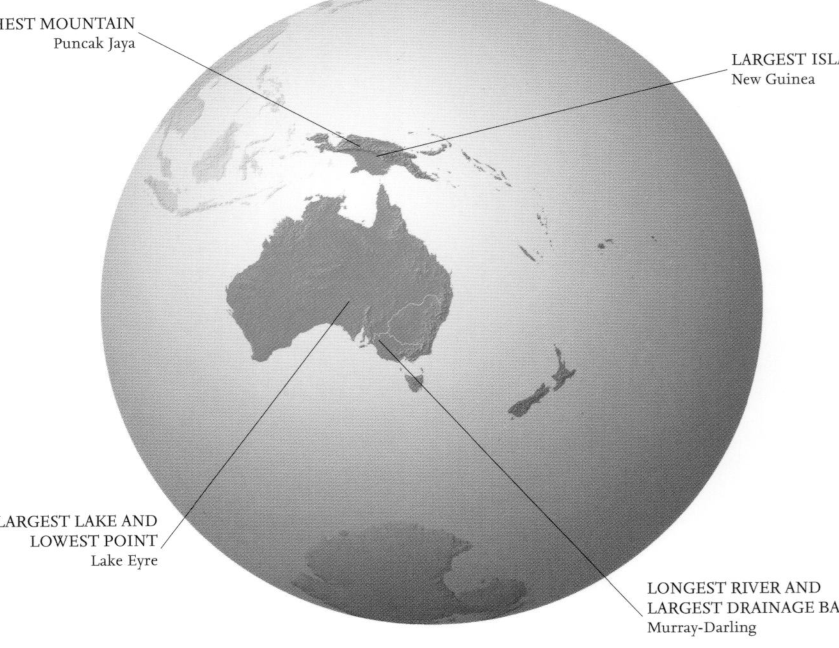

New Guinea

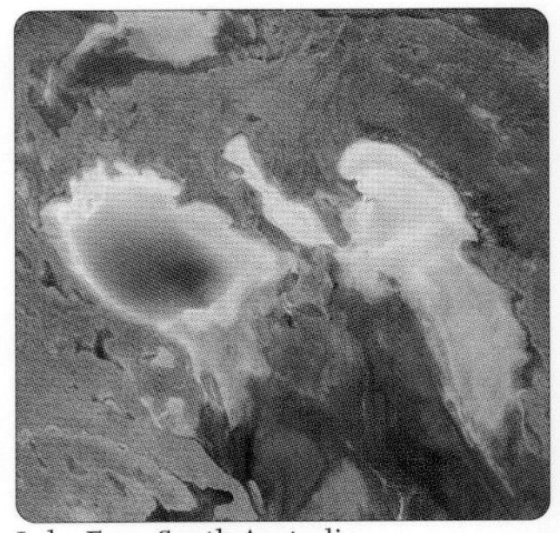
Lake Eyre, South Australia

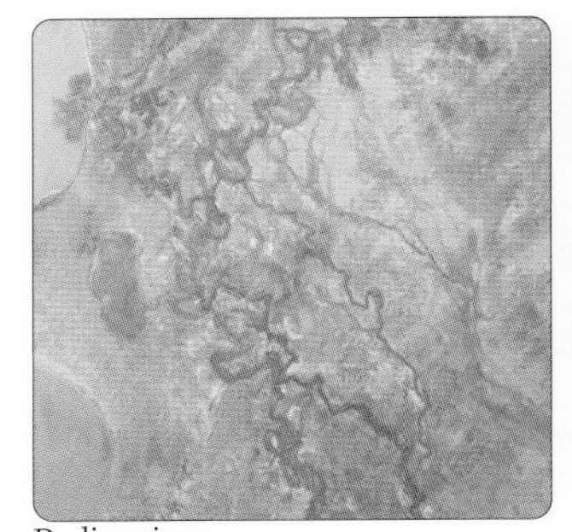
Darling river,
New South Wales, Australia

HIGHEST MOUNTAINS	metres	feet
Puncak Jaya, Indonesia	5 030	16 502
Puncak Trikora, Indonesia	4 730	15 518
Puncak Mandala, Indonesia	4 700	15 420
Puncak Yamin, Indonesia	4 595	15 075
Mt Wilhelm, Papua New Guinea	4 509	14 793
Mt Kubor, Papua New Guinea	4 359	14 301

LARGEST ISLANDS	sq km	sq miles
New Guinea	808 510	312 167
South Island, New Zealand	151 215	58 384
North Island, New Zealand	115 777	44 701
Tasmania	67 800	26 178

LONGEST RIVERS	km	miles
Murray-Darling	3 750	2 330
Darling	2 739	1 702
Murray	2 589	1 609
Murrumbidgee	1 690	1 050
Lachlan	1 480	920
Macquarie	950	590

LARGEST LAKES	sq km	sq miles
Lake Eyre	0–8 900	0–3 436
Lake Torrens	0–5 780	0–2 232

ASIA Total Land Area 45 036 492 sq km / 17 388 686 sq miles

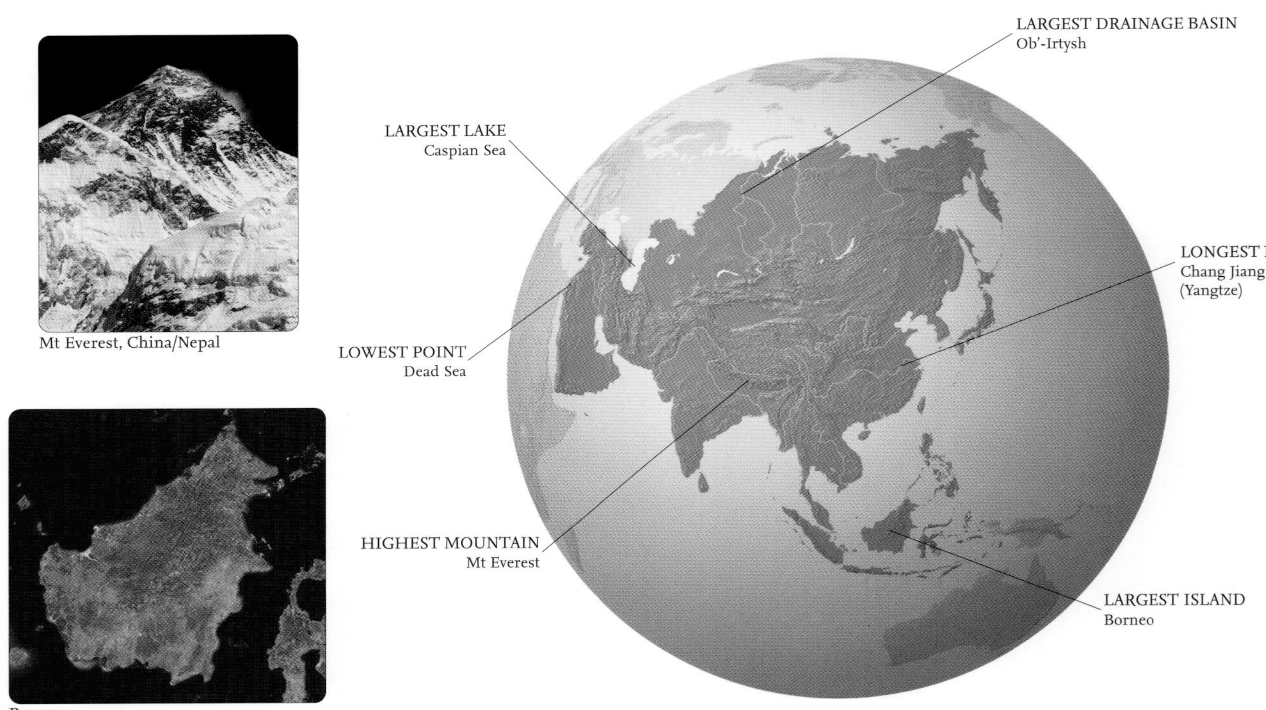

Mt Everest, China/Nepal

Borneo

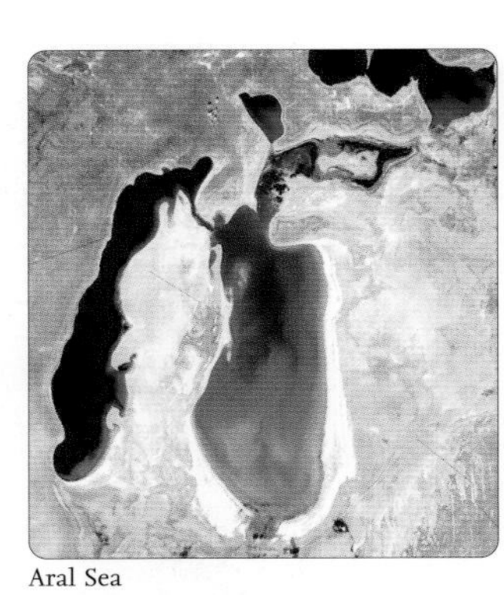
Aral Sea

Chang Jiang (Yangtze), China

HIGHEST MOUNTAINS	metres	feet
Mt Everest (Sagarmatha/ Qomolangma Feng), China/Nepal	8 848	29 028
K2 (Qogir Feng), China/Pakistan	8 611	28 251
Kangchenjunga, India/Nepal	8 586	28 169
Lhotse, China/Nepal	8 516	27 939
Makalu, China/Nepal	8 463	27 765
Cho Oyu, China/Nepal	8 201	26 906

LARGEST ISLANDS	sq km	sq miles
Borneo	745 561	287 861
Sumatera (Sumatra)	473 606	182 859
Honshū	227 414	87 805
Sulawesi (Celebes)	189 216	73 056
Jawa (Java)	132 188	51 038
Luzon	104 690	40 421

LONGEST RIVERS	km	miles
Chang Jiang (Yangtze)	6 380	3 965
Ob'-Irtysh	5 568	3 460
Yenisey-Angara-Selenga	5 550	3 449
Huang He (Yellow River)	5 464	3 395
Irtysh	4 440	2 759
Mekong	4 425	2 750

LARGEST LAKES	sq km	sq miles
Caspian Sea	371 000	143 243
Ozero Baykal (Lake Baikal)	30 500	11 776
Ozero Balkhash (Lake Balkhash)	17 400	6 718
Aral'skoye More (Aral Sea)	17 158	6 625
Ysyk-Köl	6 200	2 394

EUROPE Total Land Area 9 908 599 sq km / 3 825 731 sq miles

El'brus, Russian Federation

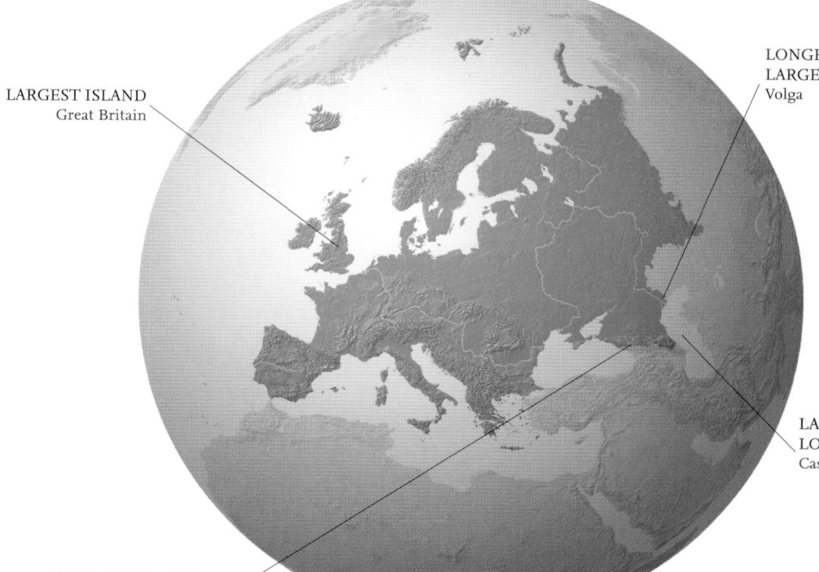

Caspian Sea

Great Britain

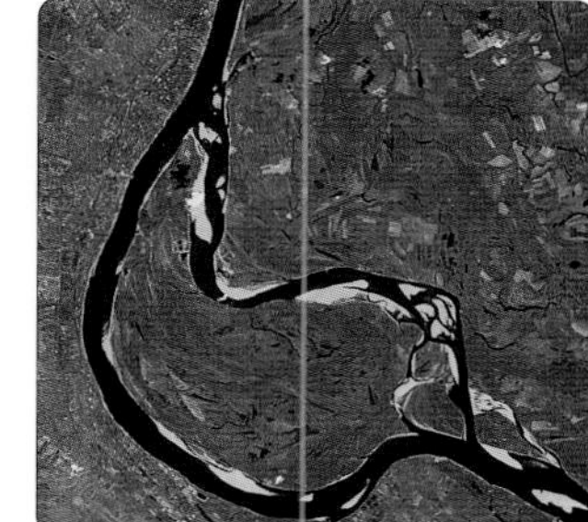
Volga, Russian Federation

HIGHEST MOUNTAINS	metres	feet
El'brus, Russian Federation	5 642	18 510
Gora Dykh-Tau, Russian Federation	5 204	17 073
Shkhara, Georgia/Russian Federation	5 201	17 063
Kazbek, Georgia/Russian Federation	5 047	16 558
Mont Blanc, France/Italy	4 808	15 774
Dufourspitze, Italy/Switzerland	4 634	15 203

LARGEST ISLANDS	sq km	sq miles
Great Britain	218 476	84 354
Iceland	102 820	39 699
Novaya Zemlya	90 650	35 000
Ireland	83 045	32 064
Spitsbergen	37 814	14 600
Sicilia (Sicily)	25 426	9 817

LONGEST RIVERS	km	miles
Volga	3 688	2 292
Danube	2 850	1 771
Dnieper	2 285	1 420
Kama	2 028	1 260
Don	1 931	1 200
Pechora	1 802	1 120

LARGEST LAKES	sq km	sq miles
Caspian Sea	371 000	143 243
Ladozhskoye Ozero (Lake Ladoga)	18 390	7 100
Onezhskoye Ozero (Lake Onega)	9 600	3 707
Vänern	5 585	2 156
Rybinskoye Vodokhranilishche	5 180	2 000

AFRICA Total Land Area 30 343 578 sq km / 11 715 721 sq miles

Kilimanjaro, Tanzania

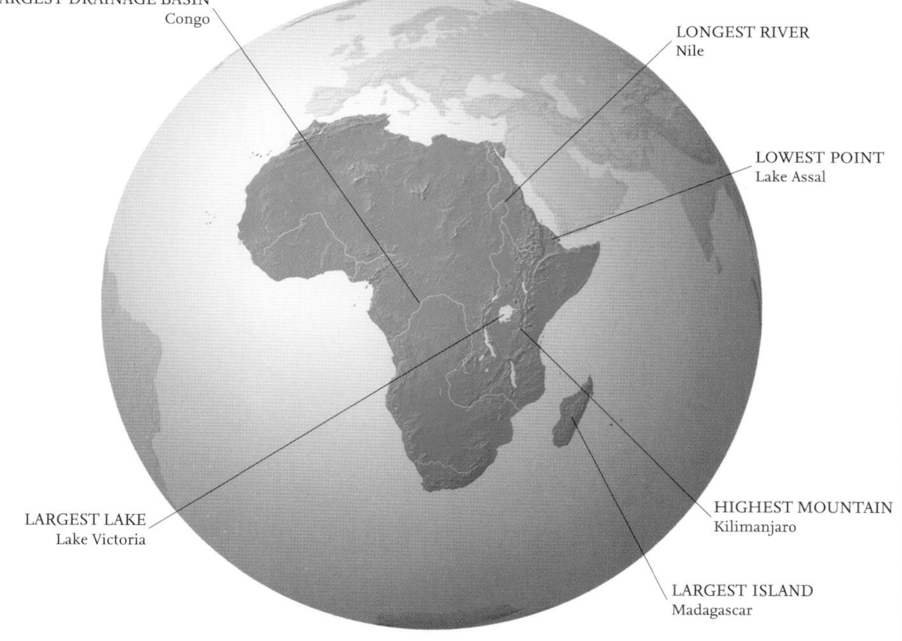

Lake Victoria, Kenya/Tanzania/Uganda

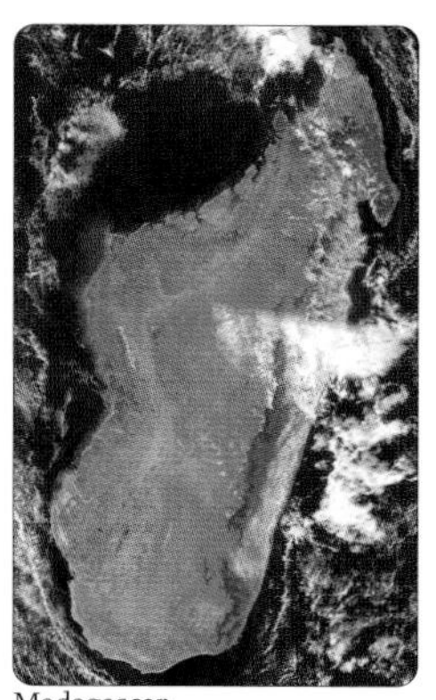
Madagascar

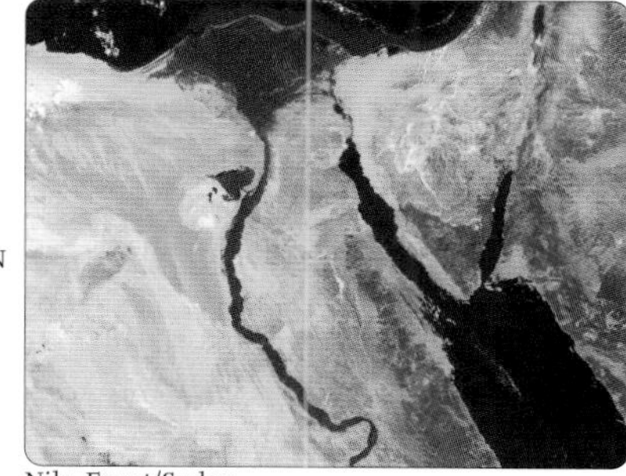
Nile, Egypt/Sudan

HIGHEST MOUNTAINS	metres	feet
Kilimanjaro, Tanzania	5 892	19 330
Kirinyaga (Mt Kenya), Kenya	5 199	17 057
Margherita Peak (Mt Stanley), Democratic Republic of the Congo/Uganda	5 110	16 765
Meru, Tanzania	4 565	14 977
Ras Dejen, Ethiopia	4 533	14 872
Mt Karisimbi, Rwanda	4 510	14 796

LARGEST ISLANDS	sq km	sq miles
Madagascar	587 040	226 656

LONGEST RIVERS	km	miles
Nile	6 695	4 160
Congo	4 667	2 900
Niger	4 184	2 600
Zambezi (Zambeze)	2 736	1 700
Webi Shabeelle	2 490	1 547
Ubangi	2 250	1 398

LARGEST LAKES	sq km	sq miles
Lake Victoria	68 870	26 591
Lake Tanganyika	32 600	12 587
Lake Nyasa (Lake Malawi)	29 500	11 390
Lake Volta	8 482	3 275
Lake Turkana	6 500	2 510
Lake Albert	5 600	2 162

NORTH AMERICA Total Land Area 24 680 331 sq km / 9 529 129 sq miles (including Hawaiian Islands)

Mt McKinley, United States of America

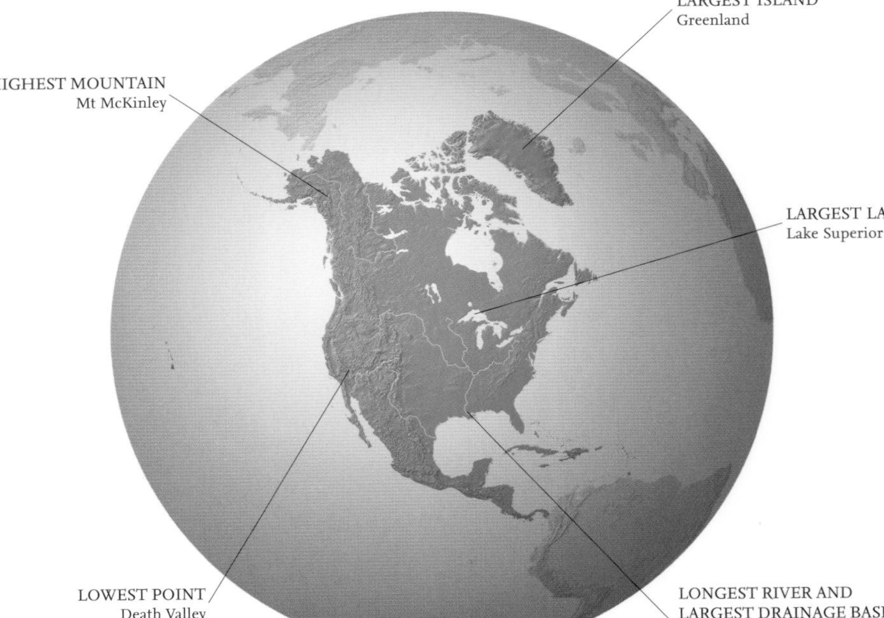

Lake Superior, USA/Canada

Mississippi-Missouri, United States of America

Greenland

HIGHEST MOUNTAINS	metres	feet
Mt McKinley, USA	6 194	20 321
Mt Logan, Canada	5 959	19 550
Pico de Orizaba, Mexico	5 610	18 405
Mt St Elias, USA	5 489	18 008
Volcán Popocatépetl, Mexico	5 452	17 887
Mt Foraker, USA	5 303	17 398

LARGEST ISLANDS	sq km	sq miles
Greenland	2 175 600	839 999
Baffin Island	507 451	195 927
Victoria Island	217 291	83 896
Ellesmere Island	196 236	75 767
Cuba	110 860	42 803
Newfoundland	108 860	42 031
Hispaniola	76 192	29 418

LONGEST RIVERS	km	miles
Mississippi-Missouri	5 969	3 709
Mackenzie-Peace-Finlay	4 241	2 635
Missouri	4 086	2 539
Mississippi	3 765	2 340
Yukon	3 185	1 979
Rio Grande (Río Bravo del Norte)	3 057	1 900

LARGEST LAKES	sq km	sq miles
Lake Superior	82 100	31 699
Lake Huron	59 600	23 012
Lake Michigan	57 800	22 317
Great Bear Lake	31 328	12 096
Great Slave Lake	28 568	11 030
Lake Erie	25 700	9 923
Lake Winnipeg	24 387	9 416
Lake Ontario	18 960	7 320

SOUTH AMERICA Total Land Area 17 815 420 sq km / 6 878 572 sq miles

Cerro Aconcagua, Argentina

LONGEST RIVER AND
LARGEST DRAINAGE BASIN
Amazonas

LARGEST LAKE
Lago Titicaca

LOWEST POINT
Laguna del Carbón

HIGHEST MOUNTAIN
Cerro Aconcagua

LARGEST ISLAND
Isla Grande de Tierra del Fuego

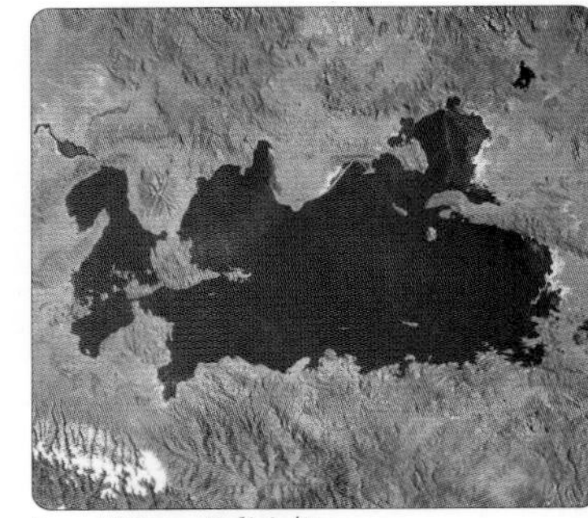

Lago Titicaca, Bolivia/Peru

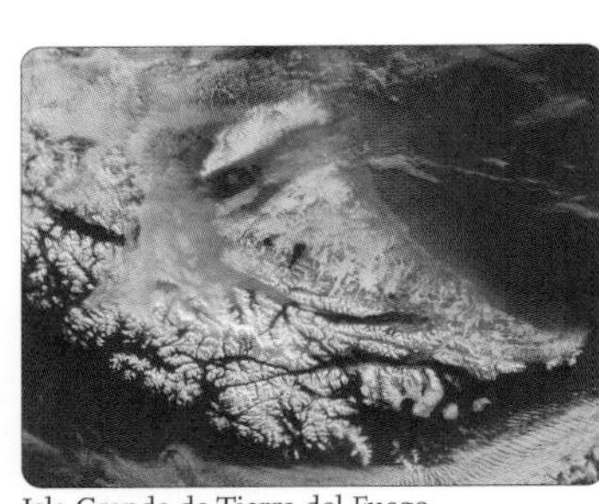

Isla Grande de Tierra del Fuego, Argentina/Chile

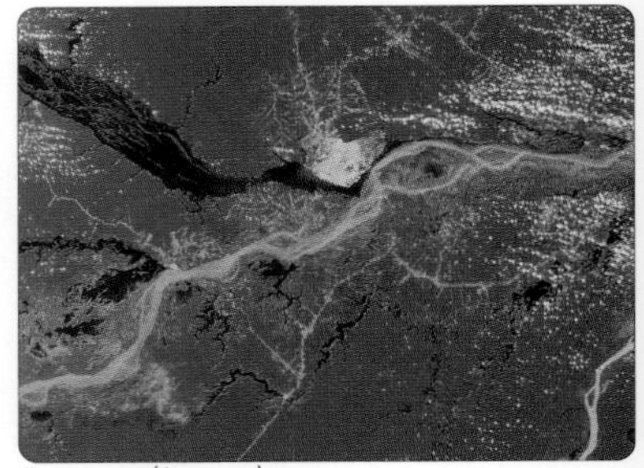

Amazonas (Amazon)

HIGHEST MOUNTAINS	metres	feet
Cerro Aconcagua, Argentina	6 959	22 831
Nevado Ojos del Salado, Argentina/Chile	6 908	22 664
Cerro Bonete, Argentina	6 872	22 546
Cerro Pissis, Argentina	6 858	22 500
Cerro Tupungato, Argentina/Chile	6 800	22 309
Cerro Mercedario, Argentina	6 770	22 211

LARGEST ISLANDS	sq km	sq miles
Isla Grande de Tierra del Fuego	47 000	18 147
Isla de Chiloé	8 394	3 241
East Falkland	6 760	2 610
West Falkland	5 413	2 090

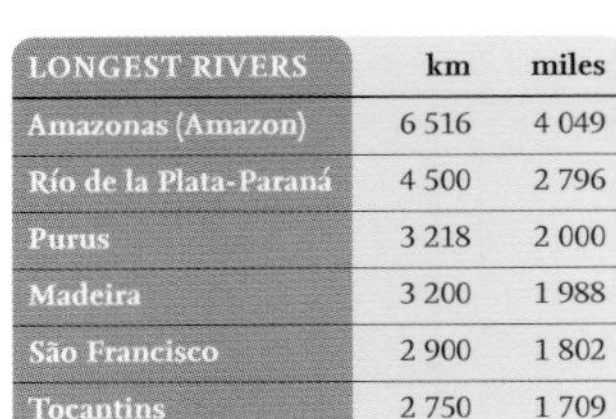

LONGEST RIVERS	km	miles
Amazonas (Amazon)	6 516	4 049
Río de la Plata-Paraná	4 500	2 796
Purus	3 218	2 000
Madeira	3 200	1 988
São Francisco	2 900	1 802
Tocantins	2 750	1 709

LARGEST LAKES	sq km	sq miles
Lake Titicaca	8 340	3 220

OCEANS AND POLES

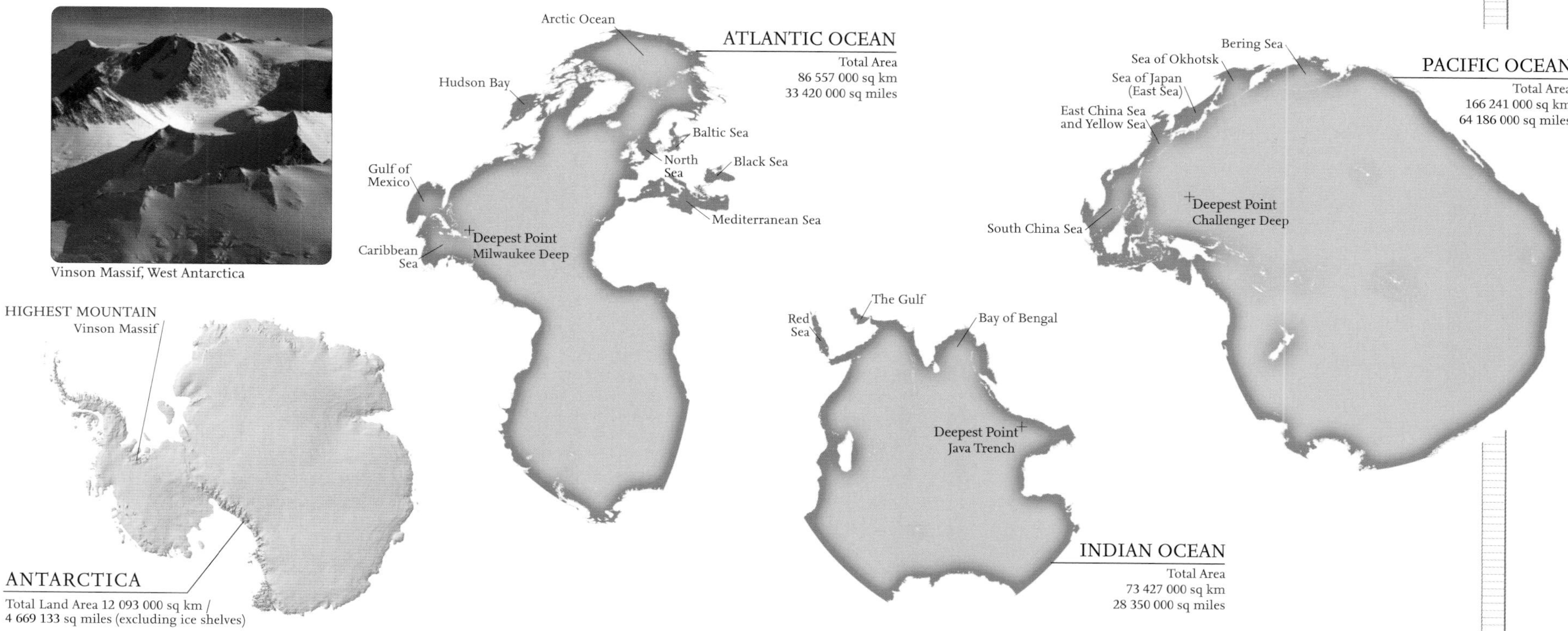

Vinson Massif, West Antarctica

HIGHEST MOUNTAINS	metres	feet
Vinson Massif	4 897	16 066
Mt Tyree	4 852	15 918
Mt Kirkpatrick	4 528	14 855
Mt Markham	4 351	14 275
Mt Jackson	4 190	13 747
Mt Sidley	4 181	13 717

ATLANTIC OCEAN	Area sq km	Area sq miles	Deepest Point metres	Deepest Point feet
Extent	86 557 000	33 420 000	8 605	28 231
Arctic Ocean	9 485 000	3 662 000	5 450	17 880
Caribbean Sea	2 512 000	970 000	7 680	25 196
Mediterranean Sea	2 510 000	969 000	5 121	16 800
Gulf of Mexico	1 544 000	596 000	3 504	11 495
Hudson Bay	1 233 000	476 000	259	849
North Sea	575 000	222 000	661	2 168
Black Sea	508 000	196 000	2 245	7 365
Baltic Sea	382 000	147 000	460	1 509

INDIAN OCEAN	Area sq km	Area sq miles	Deepest Point metres	Deepest Point feet
Extent	73 427 000	28 350 000	7 125	23 376
Bay of Bengal	2 172 000	839 000	4 500	14 763
Red Sea	453 000	175 000	3 040	9 973
The Gulf	238 000	92 000	73	239

PACIFIC OCEAN	Area sq km	Area sq miles	Deepest Point metres	Deepest Point feet
Extent	166 241 000	64 186 000	10 920	35 826
South China Sea	2 590 000	1 000 000	5 514	18 090
Bering Sea	2 261 000	873 000	4 150	13 615
Sea of Okhotsk	1 392 000	537 000	3 363	11 033
Sea of Japan (East Sea)	1 013 000	391 000	3 743	12 280
East China Sea and Yellow Sea	1 202 000	464 000	2 717	8 913

WORLD

HIGHEST MOUNTAINS	metres	feet	Location
Mt Everest	8 848	29 028	China/Nepal
K2	8 611	28 251	China/Jammu and Kashmir
Kangchenjunga	8 586	28 169	India/Nepal
Lhotse	8 516	27 939	China/Nepal
Makalu	8 463	27 765	China/Nepal
Cho Oyu	8 201	26 906	China/Nepal
Dhaulagiri	8 167	26 794	Nepal
Manaslu	8 163	26 781	Nepal
Nanga Parbat	8 126	26 660	Jammu and Kashmir
Annapurna I	8 091	26 545	Nepal
Gasherbrum I	8 068	26 469	China/Jammu and Kashmir
Broad Peak	8 047	26 401	China/Jammu and Kashmir
Gasherbrum II	8 035	26 361	China/Jammu and Kashmir
Xixabangma Feng	8 012	26 286	China
Annapurna II	7 937	26 040	Nepal
Nuptse	7 885	25 869	Nepal
Himalchul	7 864	25 800	Nepal
Masherbrum	7 821	25 659	Jammu and Kashmir
Nanda Devi	7 816	25 643	India
Rakaposhi	7 788	25 551	Jammu and Kashmir

LARGEST ISLANDS	sq km	sq miles	Location
Greenland	2 175 600	839 999	North America
New Guinea	808 510	312 166	Australasia
Borneo	745 561	287 861	Asia
Madagascar	587 040	226 656	Africa
Baffin Island	507 451	195 927	North America
Sumatera (Sumatra)	473 606	182 859	Asia
Honshū	227 414	87 805	Asia
Great Britain	218 476	84 354	Europe
Victoria Island	217 291	83 896	North America
Ellesmere Island	196 236	75 767	North America
Sulawesi (Celebes)	189 216	73 056	Asia
South Island, New Zealand	151 215	58 384	Australasia
Jawa (Java)	132 188	51 038	Asia
North Island, New Zealand	115 777	44 701	Australasia
Cuba	110 860	42 803	North America
Newfoundland	108 860	42 031	North America
Luzon	104 690	40 421	Asia
Iceland	102 820	39 699	Europe
Mindanao	94 630	36 537	Asia
Novaya Zemlya	90 650	35 000	Europe

LARGEST RIVERS	km	miles	Location
Nile	6 695	4 160	Africa
Amazonas (Amazon)	6 516	4 049	South America
Chang Jiang (Yangtze)	6 380	3 965	Asia
Mississippi-Missouri	5 969	3 709	North America
Ob'-Irtysh	5 568	3 460	Asia
Yenisey-Angara-Selenga	5 550	3 449	Asia
Huang He (Yellow River)	5 464	3 395	Asia
Congo	4 667	2 900	Africa
Río de la Plata-Paraná	4 500	2 796	South America
Irtysh	4 440	2 759	Asia
Mekong	4 425	2 750	Asia
Heilong Jiang (Amur)-Argun'	4 416	2 744	Asia
Lena-Kirenga	4 400	2 734	Asia
Mackenzie-Peace-Finlay	4 241	2 635	North America
Niger	4 184	2 600	Africa
Yenisey	4 090	2 542	Asia
Missouri	4 086	2 539	North America
Mississippi	3 765	2 340	North America
Murray-Darling	3 750	2 330	Australasia
Ob'	3 701	2 300	Asia

LARGEST DRAINAGE BASINS	sq km	sq miles	Continent
Amazonas (Amazon)	7 050 000	2 722 000	South America
Congo	3 700 000	1 429 000	Africa
Nile	3 349 000	1 293 000	Africa
Mississippi-Missouri	3 250 000	1 255 000	North America
Río de la Plata-Paraná	3 100 000	1 197 000	South America
Ob'-Irtysh	2 990 000	1 154 000	Asia
Yenisey-Angara-Selenga	2 580 000	996 000	Asia
Lena-Kirenga	2 490 000	961 000	Asia
Chang Jiang (Yangtze)	1 959 000	756 000	Asia
Niger	1 890 000	730 000	Africa
Heilong Jiang (Amur)-Argun'	1 855 000	716 000	Asia
Mackenzie-Peace-Finlay	1 805 000	697 000	North America
Ganga (Ganges)-Brahmaputra	1 621 000	626 000	Asia
St Lawrence-St Louis	1 463 000	565 000	North America
Volga	1 380 000	533 000	Europe
Zambezi (Zambeze)	1 330 000	514 000	Africa
Indus	1 166 000	450 000	Asia
Nelson-Saskatchewan	1 150 000	444 000	North America
Shaṭṭ al'Arab	1 114 000	430 000	Asia
Murray-Darling	1 058 000	409 000	Australasia

LARGEST LAKES	sq km	sq miles	Location
Caspian Sea	371 000	143 243	Asia/Europe
Lake Superior	82 100	31 699	North America
Lake Victoria	68 870	26 591	Africa
Lake Huron	59 600	23 012	North America
Lake Michigan	57 800	22 317	North America
Lake Tanganyika	32 600	12 587	Africa
Great Bear Lake	31 328	12 096	North America
Ozero Baykal (Lake Baikal)	30 500	11 776	Asia
Lake Nyasa (Lake Malawi)	29 500	11 390	Africa
Great Slave Lake	28 568	11 030	North America
Lake Erie	25 700	9 923	North America
Lake Winnipeg	24 387	9 416	North America
Lake Ontario	18 960	7 320	North America
Ladozhskoye Ozero (Lake Ladoga)	18 390	7 100	Europe
Ozero Balkhash	17 400	6 718	Asia
Aral Sea (Aral'skoye More)	17 158	6 625	Asia
Onezhskoye Ozero (Lake Onega)	9 600	3 707	Europe
Lake Volta	8 482	3 275	Africa
Lake Titicaca	8 340	3 220	South America
Lago de Nicaragua	8 150	3 147	North America

EARTH'S DIMENSIONS	
Mass	5.974 x 10^{21} tonnes
Total area	509 450 000 sq km / 196 698 645 sq miles
Land area	149 450 000 sq km / 57 702 645 sq miles
Water area	360 000 000 sq km / 138 996 000 sq miles
Volume	1 083 207 x 10^{6} cubic km / 259 911 x 10^{6} cubic miles
Equatorial diameter	12 756 km / 7 926 miles
Polar diameter	12 714 km / 7 901 miles
Equatorial circumference	40 075 km / 24 903 miles
Meridional circumference	40 008 km / 24 861 miles

STATES AND TERRITORIES

All 195 independent countries and all populated dependent and disputed territories are included in this list of the states and territories of the world; the list is arranged in alphabetical order by the conventional name form. For independent states, the full name is given below the conventional name, if this is different; for territories, the status is given. The capital city name is given in the local form as shown on the reference maps.

Area and population statistics are the latest available and include estimates. The information on languages and religions is based on the latest information on 'de facto' speakers of the language or 'de facto' adherents of the religion. This varies greatly from country to country because some countries include questions in censuses while others do not, in which case best estimates are used. The order of the languages and religions reflects their relative importance within the country; generally, languages or religions are included when more than one per cent of the population are estimated to be speakers or adherents.

Membership of selected international organizations is shown by the abbreviations below; dependent territories do not normally have separate memberships of these organizations.

APEC	Asia-Pacific Economic Cooperation
ASEAN	Association of Southeast Asian Nations
CARICOM	Caribbean Community
CIS	Commonwealth of Independent States
Comm.	The Commonwealth
EU	European Union
NATO	North Atlantic Treaty Organization
OECD	Organisation for Economic Co-operation and Development
OPEC	Organization of Petroleum Exporting Countries
SADC	Southern African Development Community
UN	United Nations

AFGHANISTAN

Islamic State of Afghanistan

Area Sq Km	652 225	**Currency**	Afghani
Area Sq Miles	251 825	**Languages**	Dari, Pushtu, Uzbek, Turkmen
Population	28 150 000	**Religions**	Sunni Muslim, Shi'a Muslim
Capital	Kābul	**Organizations**	UN

A landlocked country in central Asia with central highlands bordered by plains in the north and southwest, and by the mountains of the Hindu Kush in the northeast. The climate is dry continental. Over the last thirty years war has disrupted the economy, which is highly dependent on farming and livestock rearing. Most trade is with the former USSR, Pakistan and Iran.

Map page 144–145

ALBANIA

Republic of Albania

Area Sq Km	28 748	**Currency**	Lek
Area Sq Miles	11 100	**Languages**	Albanian, Greek
Population	3 155 000	**Religions**	Sunni Muslim, Orthodox, Roman Catholic
Capital	Tiranë (Tirana)	**Organizations**	NATO, UN

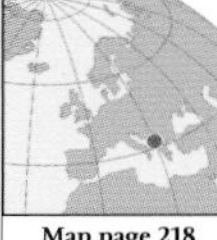

Map page 218

Albania lies in the western Balkan Mountains in southeastern Europe, bordering the Adriatic Sea. It is mountainous, with coastal plains where half the population lives. The economy is based on agriculture and mining. Albania is one of the poorest countries in Europe and relies heavily on foreign aid.

ALGERIA

People's Democratic Republic of Algeria

Area Sq Km	2 381 741	**Currency**	Algerian dinar
Area Sq Miles	919 595	**Languages**	Arabic, French, Berber
Population	34 895 000	**Religions**	Sunni Muslim
Capital	Alger (Algiers)	**Organizations**	OPEC, UN

Map page 226–227

Algeria, the second largest country in Africa, lies on the Mediterranean coast of northwest Africa and extends southwards to the Atlas Mountains and the dry sandstone plateau and desert of the Sahara. The climate ranges from Mediterranean on the coast to semi-arid and arid inland. The most populated areas are the coastal plains and the fertile northern slopes of the Atlas Mountains. Oil, natural gas and related products account for over ninety-five per cent of export earnings. Agriculture employs about a quarter of the workforce, producing mainly food crops. Algeria's main trading partners are Italy, France and the USA.

American Samoa

United States Unincorporated Territory

Area Sq Km	197	**Currency**	United States dollar
Area Sq Miles	76	**Languages**	Samoan, English
Population	67 000	**Religions**	Protestant, Roman Catholic
Capital	Fagatogo		

Lying in the south Pacific Ocean, American Samoa consists of five main islands and two coral atolls. The largest island is Tutuila. Tuna and tuna products are the main exports, and the main trading partner is the USA.

Map page 100

ANDORRA

Principality of Andorra

Area Sq Km	465	**Currency**	Euro
Area Sq Miles	180	**Languages**	Spanish, Catalan, French
Population	86 000	**Religions**	Roman Catholic
Capital	Andorra la Vella	**Organizations**	UN

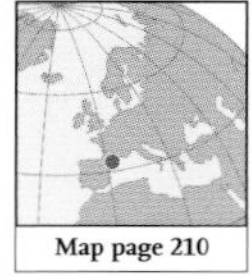

Map page 210

A landlocked state in southwest Europe, Andorra lies in the Pyrenees mountain range between France and Spain. It consists of deep valleys and gorges, surrounded by mountains. Tourism, encouraged by the development of ski resorts, is the mainstay of the economy. Banking is also an important economic activity.

ANGOLA

Republic of Angola

Area Sq Km	1 246 700	**Currency**	Kwanza
Area Sq Miles	481 354	**Languages**	Portuguese, Bantu, local languages
Population	18 498 000	**Religions**	Roman Catholic, Protestant, traditional beliefs
Capital	Luanda	**Organizations**	OPEC, SADC, UN

Angola lies on the Atlantic coast of south central Africa. Its small northern province, Cabinda, is separated from the rest of the country by part of the Democratic Republic of the Congo. Much of Angola is high plateau. In the west is a narrow coastal plain and in the southwest is desert. The climate is equatorial in the north but desert in the south. Over eighty per cent of the population relies on subsistence agriculture. Angola is rich in minerals (particularly diamonds), and oil accounts for approximately ninety per cent of export earnings. The USA, South Korea and Portugal are its main trading partners.

Map page 231

Anguilla

United Kingdom Overseas Territory

Area Sq Km	155	**Currency**	East Caribbean dollar
Area Sq Miles	60	**Languages**	English
Population	15 000	**Religions**	Protestant, Roman Catholic
Capital	The Valley		

Anguilla lies at the northern end of the Leeward Islands in the eastern Caribbean. Tourism and fishing form the basis of the economy.

Map page 271

ANTIGUA AND BARBUDA

Area Sq Km	442	**Currency**	East Caribbean dollar
Area Sq Miles	171	**Languages**	English, creole
Population	88 000	**Religions**	Protestant, Roman Catholic
Capital	St John's	**Organizations**	CARICOM, Comm., UN

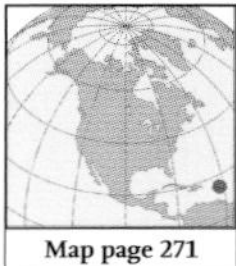

Map page 271

The state comprises the islands of Antigua, Barbuda and the tiny rocky outcrop of Redonda, in the Leeward Islands in the eastern Caribbean. Antigua, the largest and most populous island, is mainly hilly scrubland, with many beaches. The climate is tropical, and the economy relies heavily on tourism. Most trade is with other eastern Caribbean states and the USA.

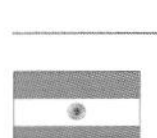

ARGENTINA

Argentine Republic

Area Sq Km	2 766 889	**Currency**	Argentinian peso
Area Sq Miles	1 068 302	**Languages**	Spanish, Italian, Amerindian languages
Population	40 276 000	**Religions**	Roman Catholic, Protestant
Capital	Buenos Aires	**Organizations**	UN

Argentina, the second largest state in South America, extends from Bolivia to Cape Horn and from the Andes mountains to the Atlantic Ocean. It has four geographical regions: subtropical forests and swampland in the northeast; temperate fertile plains or Pampas in the centre; the wooded foothills and valleys of the Andes in the west; and the cold, semi-arid plateaus of Patagonia in the south. The highest mountain in South America, Cerro Aconcagua, is in Argentina. Nearly ninety per cent of the population lives in towns and cities. The country is rich in natural resources including petroleum, natural gas, ores and precious metals. Agricultural products dominate exports, which also include motor vehicles and crude oil. Most trade is with Brazil and the USA.

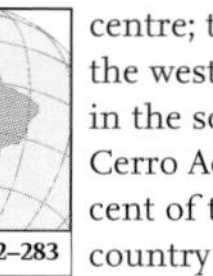

Map page 282–283

ARMENIA

Republic of Armenia

Area Sq Km	29 800	**Currency**	Dram
Area Sq Miles	11 506	**Languages**	Armenian, Azeri
Population	3 083 000	**Religions**	Armenian Orthodox
Capital	Yerevan (Erevan)	**Organizations**	CIS, UN

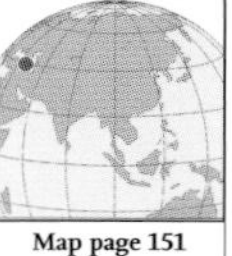

Map page 151

A landlocked state in southwest Asia, Armenia lies in the south of the Lesser Caucasus mountains. It is a mountainous country with a continental climate. One-third of the population lives in the capital, Yerevan (Erevan). Exports include diamonds, scrap metal and machinery. Many Armenians depend on remittances from abroad.

Aruba

Self-governing Netherlands Territory

Area Sq Km	193	**Currency**	Aruban florin
Area Sq Miles	75	**Languages**	Papiamento, Dutch, English
Population	107 000	**Religions**	Roman Catholic, Protestant
Capital	Oranjestad		

The most southwesterly of the islands in the Lesser Antilles in the Caribbean, Aruba lies just off the coast of Venezuela. Tourism, offsh finance and oil refining are the most important sectors of the economy. The USA is the main trading partner.

Map page 271

Ascension

Dependency of St Helena

Area Sq Km (Miles) 88 (34) **Population** 1 100 **Capital** Georgetown

A volcanic island in the south Atlantic Ocean about 1 300 kilometre (800 miles) northwest of St Helena.

Map page 238

AUSTRALIA

Commonwealth of Australia

Area Sq Km	7 692 024	**Currency**	Australian dollar
Area Sq Miles	2 969 907	**Languages**	English, Italian, Greek
Population	21 293 000	**Religions**	Protestant, Roman Catholic, Orthodox
Capital	Canberra	**Organizations**	APEC, Comm., OECD, UN

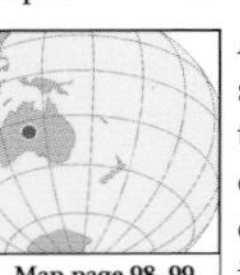

Map page 98–99

Australia, the world's sixth largest country, occupies tl smallest, flattest and driest continent. The western ha the continent is mostly arid plateaus, ridges and vast deserts. The central eastern area comprises the lowlan of river systems draining into Lake Eyre, while to the is the Great Dividing Range, a belt of ridges and plate running from Queensland to Tasmania. Climatically, more than two-thirds of the country is arid or semi-arid. The north is tropical mons the east subtropical, and the southwest and southeast temperate. The majority of Australia's highly urbanized population lives along the eas southeast and southwest coasts. Australia has vast mineral deposits an various sources of energy. It is among the world's leading producers c iron ore, bauxite, nickel, copper and uranium. It is a major producer c coal, and oil and natural gas are also being exploited. Although accounting for only five per cent of the workforce, agriculture continu to be an important sector of the economy, with food and agricultural materials making up most of Australia's export earnings. Fuel, ores an metals, and manufactured goods, account for the remainder of export Japan and the USA are Australia's main trading partners.

Australian Capital Territory (Federal territory)			
Area Sq Km (Miles) 2 358 (910)		**Population** 346 400	**Capital** Canberra
Jervis Bay Territory (Territory)			
Area Sq Km (Miles) 73 (28)		**Population** 611	**Capital**
New South Wales (State)			
Area Sq Km (Miles) 800 642 (309 130)		**Population** 7 017 100	**Capital** Sydney
Northern Territory (Territory)			
Area Sq Km (Miles) 1 349 129 (520 902)		**Population** 221 100	**Capital** Darwin
Queensland (State)			
Area Sq Km (Miles) 1 730 648 (668 207)		**Population** 4 320 100	**Capital** Brisbane
South Australia (State)			
Area Sq Km (Miles) 983 482 (379 725)		**Population** 1 607 700	**Capital** Adelaide
Tasmania (State)			
Area Sq Km (Miles) 68 401 (26 410)		**Population** 498 900	**Capital** Hobart
Victoria (State)			
Area Sq Km (Miles) 227 416 (87 806)		**Population** 5 340 300	**Capital** Melbourne
Western Australia (State)			
Area Sq Km (Miles) 2 529 875 (976 790)		**Population** 2 188 500	**Capital** Perth

AUSTRIA

Republic of Austria

Area Sq Km	83 855	**Currency**	Euro
Area Sq Miles	32 377	**Languages**	German, Croatian, Turkish
Population	8 364 000	**Religions**	Roman Catholic, Protestant
Capital	Wien (Vienna)	**Organizations**	EU, OECD, UN

Map page 200–201

Two-thirds of Austria, a landlocked state in central Europe, lies within the Alps, with lower mountains to the north. The only lowlands are in the east. The Danube river valley in the northeast contains almost a the agricultural land and most of the population. Although the climate varies with altitude, in general summers are warm and winters cold with heavy snowfalls. Manufacturing industry and tourism are the most important sectors c the economy. Exports are dominated by manufactured goods. Germa is Austria's main trading partner.

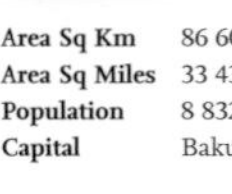

AZERBAIJAN

Republic of Azerbaijan

Area Sq Km	86 600	**Currency**	Azerbaijani manat
Area Sq Miles	33 436	**Languages**	Azeri, Armenian, Russian, Lezgian
Population	8 832 000	**Religions**	Shi'a Muslim, Sunni Muslim, Russian and Armenian Orthodox
Capital	Baku	**Organizations**	CIS, UN

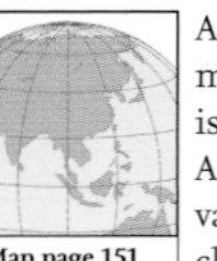

Map page 151

Azerbaijan lies to the southeast of the Caucasus mountains, on the Caspian Sea. Its region of Naxçıvar is separated from the rest of the country by part of Armenia. It has mountains in the northeast and west, valleys in the centre, and a low coastal plain. The climate is continental. It is rich in energy and minera resources. Oil production, onshore and offshore, is the main industry and the basis of heavy industries. Agriculture is important, with cotto and tobacco the main cash crops.

THE BAHAMAS

Commonwealth of the Bahamas

Area Sq Km	13 939	**Currency**	Bahamian dollar
Area Sq Miles	5 382	**Languages**	English, creole
Population	342 000	**Religions**	Protestant, Roman Catholic
Capital	Nassau	**Organizations**	CARICOM, Comm., UN

e Bahamas, an archipelago made up of approximately seven
ndred islands and over two thousand cays, lies to the northeast of

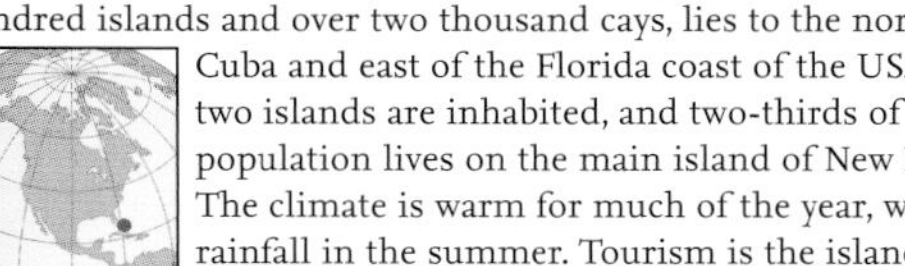
Map page 253

Cuba and east of the Florida coast of the USA. Twenty-two islands are inhabited, and two-thirds of the population lives on the main island of New Providence. The climate is warm for much of the year, with heavy rainfall in the summer. Tourism is the islands' main industry. Offshore banking, insurance and ship
istration are also major foreign exchange earners.

BAHRAIN

Kingdom of Bahrain

Sq Km	691	Currency	Bahraini dinar
Sq Miles	267	Languages	Arabic, English
lation	791 000	Religions	Shi'a Muslim, Sunni Muslim, Christian
tal	Al Manāmah (Manama)	Organizations	UN

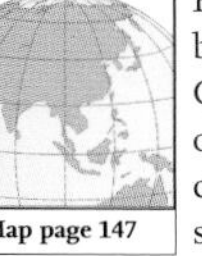
Map page 147

Bahrain consists of more than thirty islands lying in a bay in The Gulf, off the coasts of Saudi Arabia and Qatar. Bahrain Island, the largest island, is connected to other islands and to the mainland of Arabia by causeways. Oil production and processing are the main sectors of the economy.

BANGLADESH

People's Republic of Bangladesh

Sq Km	143 998	Currency	Taka
Sq Miles	55 598	Languages	Bengali, English
lation	162 221 000	Religions	Sunni Muslim, Hindu
tal	Dhaka (Dacca)	Organizations	Comm., UN

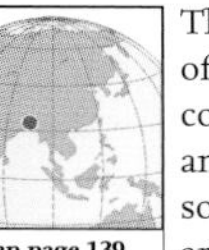
Map page 139

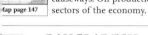

The south Asian state of Bangladesh is in the northeast of the Indian subcontinent, on the Bay of Bengal. It consists almost entirely of the low-lying alluvial plains and deltas of the Ganges and Brahmaputra rivers. The southwest is swampy, with mangrove forests in the delta area. The north, northeast and southeast have low
ested hills. Bangladesh is one of the world's most densely populated
l least developed countries. The economy is based on agriculture,
ugh the garment industry is the main export sector. Floods and
lones during the summer monsoon season often cause devastating
oding and crop destruction. The country relies on large-scale foreign
and remittances from workers abroad.

BARBADOS

Sq Km	430	Currency	Barbados dollar
Sq Miles	166	Languages	English, creole
lation	256 000	Religions	Protestant, Roman Catholic
tal	Bridgetown	Organizations	CARICOM, Comm., UN

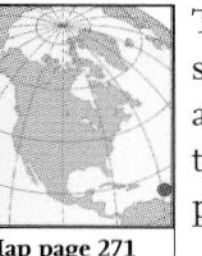
Map page 271

The most easterly of the Caribbean islands, Barbados is small and densely populated. It has a tropical climate and is subject to hurricanes. The economy is based on tourism, financial services, light industries and sugar production.

BELARUS

Republic of Belarus

Sq Km	207 600	Currency	Belarus rouble
Sq Miles	80 155	Languages	Belorussian, Russian
lation	9 634 000	Religions	Belorussian Orthodox, Roman Catholic
tal	Minsk	Organizations	CIS, UN

arus, a landlocked state in eastern Europe, consists of low hills and
ins, with many lakes, rivers and, in the south, extensive marshes.
ests cover approximately one-third of the country. It has a continental climate. Agriculture contributes one-third of national income, with beef cattle and grains as the major products. Manufacturing industries produce a range of items, from construction equipment to textiles. The Russian Federation and Ukraine are the main trading partners.

p page 156–157

BELGIUM

Kingdom of Belgium

Sq Km	30 520	Currency	Euro
Sq Miles	11 784	Languages	Dutch (Flemish), French (Walloon), German
ulation	10 647 000	Religions	Roman Catholic, Protestant
tal	Bruxelles (Brussels)	Organizations	EU, NATO, OECD, UN

gium lies on the North Sea coast of western Europe. Beyond low sand
nes and a narrow belt of reclaimed land, fertile plains extend to the
nbre-Meuse river valley. The land rises to the forested Ardennes plateau in the southeast. Belgium has mild winters and cool summers. It is densely populated and has a highly urbanized population. With few mineral resources, Belgium imports raw materials for processing and manufacture. The agricultural sector is small, but provides for most food needs. A large services sector
lects Belgium's position as the home base for over eight hundred
ernational institutions. The headquarters of the European Union are
the capital, Brussels.

Map page 187

BELIZE

Sq Km	22 965	Currency	Belize dollar
Sq Miles	8 867	Languages	English, Spanish, Mayan, creole
lation	307 000	Religions	Roman Catholic, Protestant
tal	Belmopan	Organizations	CARICOM, Comm., UN

lize lies on the Caribbean coast of central America and includes
merous cays and a large barrier reef offshore. The coastal areas are

Map page 267

flat and swampy. To the southwest are the Maya Mountains. Tropical jungle covers much of the country and the climate is humid tropical, but tempered by sea breezes. A third of the population lives in the capital. The economy is based primarily on agriculture, forestry and fishing, and exports include raw sugar, orange concentrate and bananas.

BENIN

Republic of Benin

Area Sq Km	112 620	Currency	CFA franc
Area Sq Miles	43 483	Languages	French, Fon, Yoruba, Adja, local languages
Population	8 935 000	Religions	Traditional beliefs, Roman Catholic, Sunni Muslim
Capital	Porto-Novo	Organizations	UN

Map page 229

Benin is in west Africa, on the Gulf of Guinea. The climate is tropical in the north, equatorial in the south. The economy is based mainly on agriculture and transit trade. Agricultural products account for two-thirds of export earnings. Oil, produced offshore, is also a major export.

Bermuda

United Kingdom Overseas Territory

Area Sq Km	54	Currency	Bermuda dollar
Area Sq Miles	21	Languages	English
Population	65 000	Religions	Protestant, Roman Catholic
Capital	Hamilton		

In the Atlantic Ocean to the east of the USA, Bermuda comprises a group of small islands with a warm and humid climate. The economy is based on international business and tourism.

Map page 255

BHUTAN

Kingdom of Bhutan

Area Sq Km	46 620	Currency	Ngultrum, Indian rupee
Area Sq Miles	18 000	Languages	Dzongkha, Nepali, Assamese
Population	697 000	Religions	Buddhist, Hindu
Capital	Thimphu	Organizations	UN

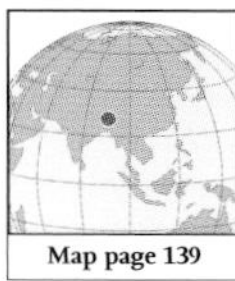
Map page 139

Bhutan lies in the eastern Himalaya mountains, between China and India. It is mountainous in the north, with fertile valleys. The climate ranges between permanently cold in the far north and subtropical in the south. Most of the population is involved in livestock rearing and subsistence farming. Bhutan is the world's largest producer of cardamom. Tourism is an increasingly important foreign currency earner.

BOLIVIA

Republic of Bolivia

Area Sq Km	1 098 581	Currency	Boliviano
Area Sq Miles	424 164	Languages	Spanish, Quechua, Aymara
Population	9 863 000	Religions	Roman Catholic, Protestant, Baha'i
Capital	La Paz/Sucre	Organizations	UN

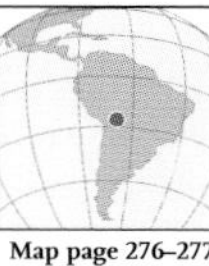
Map page 276–277

Bolivia is a landlocked state in central South America. Most Bolivians live on the high plateau within the Andes mountains. The lowlands range between dense rainforest in the northeast and semi-arid grasslands in the southeast. Bolivia is rich in minerals (zinc, tin and gold), and sales generate approximately half of export income. Natural gas, timber and soya beans are also exported. The USA is the main trading partner.

Bonaire part of Netherlands Antilles

Area Sq Km (Miles) 288 (111) **Population** 12 103 **Capital** Kralendijk

An island in the Caribbean Sea off the north coast of Venezuela, known for its fine beaches; tourism is the mainstay of the economy.

Map page 271

BOSNIA-HERZEGOVINA

Republic of Bosnia and Herzegovina

Area Sq Km	51 130	Currency	Marka
Area Sq Miles	19 741	Languages	Bosnian, Serbian, Croatian
Population	3 767 000	Religions	Sunni Muslim, Orthodox, Roman Catholic, Protestant
Capital	Sarajevo	Organizations	UN

Bosnia-Herzegovina lies in the western Balkan Mountains of southern Europe, on the Adriatic Sea. It is mountainous, with ridges running northwest–southeast. The main lowlands are around the Sava valley in the north. Summers are warm, but winters can be very cold. The economy relies heavily on overseas aid.

Map page 210

BOTSWANA

Republic of Botswana

Area Sq Km	581 370	Currency	Pula
Area Sq Miles	224 468	Languages	English, Setswana, Shona, local languages
Population	1 950 000	Religions	Traditional beliefs, Protestant, Roman Catholic
Capital	Gaborone	Organizations	Comm., SADC, UN

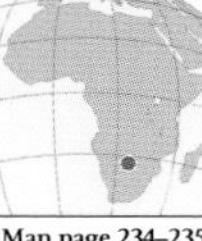
Map page 234–235

Botswana is a landlocked state in southern Africa. Over half of the country lies within the Kalahari Desert, with swamps to the north and salt-pans to the northeast. Most of the population lives near the eastern border. The climate is subtropical, but drought-prone. The economy was founded on cattle rearing, and although beef remains an important export, the economy is now based on mining. Diamonds account for seventy per cent of export earnings. Copper-nickel matte is also exported. Most trade is with members of the South African Customs Union.

BRAZIL

Federative Republic of Brazil

Area Sq Km	8 514 879	Currency	Real
Area Sq Miles	3 287 613	Languages	Portuguese
Population	193 734 000	Religions	Roman Catholic, Protestant
Capital	Brasília	Organizations	UN

Brazil, in eastern South America, covers almost half of the continent, and is the world's fifth largest country. The northwest contains the vast basin of the Amazon, while the centre-west is largely a vast plateau of savanna and rock escarpments. The northeast is mostly semi-arid plateaus, while to the east and south are rugged mountains, fertile valleys and narrow, fertile coastal plains. The Amazon basin is hot, humid and wet; the rest of the country is cooler and drier, with seasonal variations. The northeast is drought-prone. Most Brazilians live in urban areas along the coast and on the central plateau. Brazil has well-developed agricultural, mining and service sectors, and the economy is larger than that of all other South American countries combined. Brazil is the world's biggest producer of coffee, and other agricultural crops include grains and sugar cane. Mineral production includes iron, aluminium and gold. Manufactured goods include food products, transport equipment, machinery and industrial chemicals. The main trading partners are the USA and Argentina. Despite its natural wealth, Brazil has a large external debt and a growing poverty gap.

Map page 278–279

British Indian Ocean Territory

United Kingdom Overseas Territory

Area Sq Km (Miles) 60 (23) **Population** uninhabited

The territory consists of the Chagos Archipelago in the central Indian Ocean. The islands are uninhabited apart from the joint British-US military base on Diego Garcia.

Map page 110

BRUNEI

Brunei Darussalam

Area Sq Km	5 765	Currency	Brunei dollar
Area Sq Miles	2 226	Languages	Malay, English, Chinese
Population	400 000	Religions	Sunni Muslim, Buddhist, Christian
Capital	Bandar Seri Begawan	Organizations	APEC, ASEAN, Comm., UN

The southeast Asian oil-rich state of Brunei lies on the northwest coast of the island of Borneo, on the South China Sea. Its two enclaves are surrounded by the Malaysian state of Sarawak. Tropical rainforest covers over two-thirds of the country. The economy is dominated by the oil and gas industries.

Map page 117

BULGARIA

Republic of Bulgaria

Area Sq Km	110 994	Currency	Lev
Area Sq Miles	42 855	Languages	Bulgarian, Turkish, Romany, Macedonian
Population	7 545 000	Religions	Bulgarian Orthodox, Sunni Muslim
Capital	Sofiya (Sofia)	Organizations	EU, NATO, UN

Map page 219

Bulgaria, in southern Europe, borders the western shore of the Black Sea. The Balkan Mountains separate the Danube plains in the north from the Rhodope Mountains and the lowlands in the south. The economy has a strong agricultural base. Manufacturing industries include machinery, consumer goods, chemicals and metals. Most trade is with the Russian Federation, Italy and Germany.

BURKINA

Democratic Republic of Burkina Faso

Area Sq Km	274 200	Currency	CFA franc
Area Sq Miles	105 869	Languages	French, Moore (Mossi), Fulani, local languages
Population	15 757 000	Religions	Sunni Muslim, traditional beliefs, Roman Catholic
Capital	Ouagadougou	Organizations	UN

Map page 228–229

Burkina, a landlocked country in west Africa, lies within the Sahara desert to the north and semi-arid savanna to the south. Rainfall is erratic, and droughts are common. Livestock rearing and farming are the main activities, and cotton, livestock, groundnuts and some minerals are exported. Burkina relies heavily on foreign aid, and is one of the poorest and least developed countries in the world.

BURUNDI

Republic of Burundi

Area Sq Km	27 835	Currency	Burundian franc
Area Sq Miles	10 747	Languages	Kirundi (Hutu, Tutsi), French
Population	8 303 000	Religions	Roman Catholic, traditional beliefs, Protestant
Capital	Bujumbura	Organizations	UN

The densely populated east African state of Burundi consists of high plateaus rising from the shores of Lake Tanganyika in the southwest. It has a tropical climate and depends on subsistence farming. Coffee is its main export, and its main trading partners are Germany and Belgium. The country has been badly affected by internal conflict since the early 1990s.

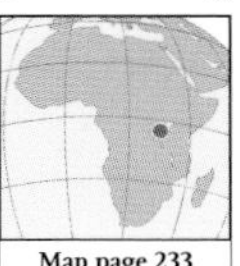
Map page 233

CAMBODIA

Kingdom of Cambodia

Area Sq Km	181 035	**Currency**	Riel
Area Sq Miles	69 884	**Languages**	Khmer, Vietnamese
Population	14 805 000	**Religions**	Buddhist, Roman Catholic, Sunni Muslim
Capital	Phnum Pénh	**Organizations**	ASEAN, UN

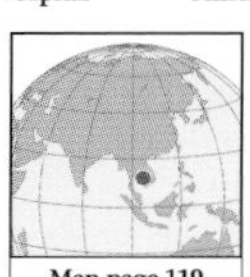

Map page 119

Cambodia lies in southeast Asia on the Gulf of Thailand, and occupies the Mekong river basin, with the Tônlé Sap (Great Lake) at its centre. The climate is tropical monsoon. Forests cover half the country. Most of the population lives on the plains and is engaged in farming (chiefly rice growing), fishing and forestry. The economy is recovering slowly following the devastation of civil war in the 1970s.

CAMEROON

Republic of Cameroon

Area Sq Km	475 442	**Currency**	CFA franc
Area Sq Miles	183 569	**Languages**	French, English, Fang, Bamileke, local languages
Population	19 522 000	**Religions**	Roman Catholic, traditional beliefs, Sunni Muslim, Protestant
Capital	Yaoundé	**Organizations**	Comm., UN

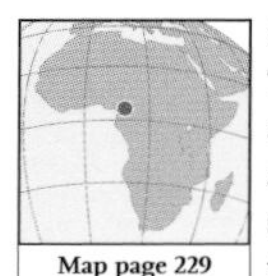

Map page 229

Cameroon is in west Africa, on the Gulf of Guinea. The coastal plains and southern and central plateaus are covered with tropical forest. Despite oil resources and favourable agricultural conditions Cameroon still faces problems of underdevelopment. Oil, timber and cocoa are the main exports. France is the main trading partner.

CANADA

Area Sq Km	9 984 670	**Currency**	Canadian dollar
Area Sq Miles	3 855 103	**Languages**	English, French, local languages
Population	33 573 000	**Religions**	Roman Catholic, Protestant, Orthodox, Jewish
Capital	Ottawa	**Organizations**	APEC, Comm., NATO, OECD, UN

The world's second largest country, Canada covers the northern two-fifths of North America and has coastlines on the Atlantic, Arctic and Pacific Oceans. In the west are the Coast Mountains, the Rocky Mountains and interior plateaus. In the centre lie the fertile Prairies. Further east, covering about half the total land area, is the Canadian Shield, a relatively flat area of infertile lowlands around Hudson Bay, extending to Labrador on the east coast. The Shield is bordered to the south by the fertile Great Lakes-St Lawrence lowlands. In the far north climatic conditions are polar, while the rest has a continental climate. Most Canadians live in the urban areas of the Great Lakes-St Lawrence basin. Canada is rich in mineral and energy resources. Only five per cent of land is arable. Canada is among the world's leading producers of wheat, of wood from its vast coniferous forests, and of fish and seafood from its Atlantic and Pacific fishing grounds. It is a major producer of nickel, uranium, copper, iron ore, zinc and other minerals, as well as oil and natural gas. Its abundant raw materials are the basis for many manufacturing industries. Main exports are machinery, motor vehicles, oil, timber, newsprint and paper, wood pulp and wheat. Since the 1989 free trade agreement with the USA and the 1994 North America Free Trade Agreement, trade with the USA has grown and now accounts for around seventy-five per cent of imports and around eighty-five per cent of exports.

Map page 242–243

Province/Territory	Area Sq Km (Miles)	Population	Capital
Alberta (Province)	661 848 (255 541)	3 610 782	Edmonton
British Columbia (Province)	944 735 (364 764)	4 405 534	Victoria
Manitoba (Province)	647 797 (250 116)	1 210 547	Winnipeg
New Brunswick (Province)	72 908 (28 150)	747 790	Fredericton
Newfoundland and Labrador (Province)	405 212 (156 453)	508 944	St John's
Northwest Territories (Province)	1 346 106 (519 734)	43 151	Yellowknife
Nova Scotia (Province)	55 284 (21 345)	939 125	Halifax
Nunavut (Territory)	2 093 190 (808 185)	31 522	Iqaluit (Frobisher Bay)
Ontario (Province)	1 076 395 (415 598)	12 977 059	Toronto
Prince Edward Island (Province)	5 660 (2 185)	140 750	Charlottetown
Québec (Province)	1 542 056 (595 391)	7 771 854	Québec
Saskatchewan (Province)	651 036 (251 366)	1 020 847	Regina
Yukon Territory (Territory)	482 443 (186 272)	33 372	Whitehorse

CAPE VERDE

Republic of Cape Verde

Area Sq Km	4 033	**Currency**	Cape Verde escudo
Area Sq Miles	1 557	**Languages**	Portuguese, creole
Population	506 000	**Religions**	Roman Catholic, Protestant
Capital	Praia	**Organizations**	UN

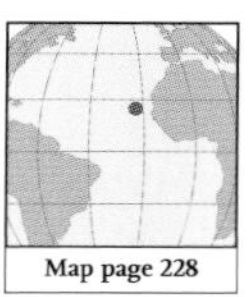

Map page 228

Cape Verde is a group of semi-arid volcanic islands lying off the coast of west Africa. The economy is based on fishing and subsistence farming but relies on emigrant workers' remittances and foreign aid.

Cayman Islands

United Kingdom Overseas Territory

Area Sq Km	259	**Currency**	Cayman Islands dollar
Area Sq Miles	100	**Languages**	English
Population	56 000	**Religions**	Roman Catholic, Protestant
Capital	George Town		

A group of islands in the Caribbean, northwest of Jamaica. There are three main islands: Grand Cayman, Little Cayman and Cayman Brac. The Cayman Islands are one of the world's major offshore financial centres. Tourism is also important to the economy.

Map page 270

CENTRAL AFRICAN REPUBLIC

Area Sq Km	622 436	**Currency**	CFA franc
Area Sq Miles	240 324	**Languages**	French, Sango, Banda, Baya, local languages
Population	4 422 000	**Religions**	Protestant, Roman Catholic, trad. beliefs, Muslim
Capital	Bangui	**Organizations**	UN

Map page 230

A landlocked country in central Africa, the Central African Republic is mainly savanna plateau, drained by the Ubangi and Chari river systems, with mountains to the east and west. The climate is tropical, with high rainfall. Most of the population lives in the south and west, and a majority of the workforce is involved in subsistence farming. Some cotton, coffee, tobacco and timber are exported, but diamonds account for around half of export earnings.

CHAD

Republic of Chad

Area Sq Km	1 284 000	**Currency**	CFA franc
Area Sq Miles	495 755	**Languages**	Arabic, French, Sara, local languages
Population	11 206 000	**Religions**	Sunni Muslim, Roman Catholic, Protestant, traditional beliefs
Capital	Ndjamena	**Organizations**	UN

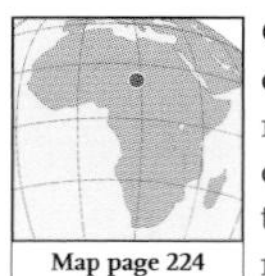

Map page 224

Chad is a landlocked state of north-central Africa. It consists of plateaus, the Tibesti mountains in the north and the Lake Chad basin in the west. Climatic conditions range between desert in the north and tropical forest in the southwest. With few natural resources, Chad relies on subsistence farming, exports of raw cotton, and foreign aid. The main trading partners are France, Portugal and Cameroon.

CHILE

Republic of Chile

Area Sq Km	756 945	**Currency**	Chilean peso
Area Sq Miles	292 258	**Languages**	Spanish, Amerindian languages
Population	16 970 000	**Religions**	Roman Catholic, Protestant
Capital	Santiago	**Organizations**	APEC, UN

Chile lies along the Pacific coast of the southern half of South America. Between the Andes in the east and the lower coastal ranges is a central valley, with a mild climate, where most Chileans live. To the north is the arid Atacama Desert and to the south is cold, wet forested grassland. Chile has considerable mineral resources and is the world's leading exporter of copper. Nitrates, molybdenum, gold and iron ore are also mined. Agriculture (particularly viticulture), forestry and fishing are also important to the economy.

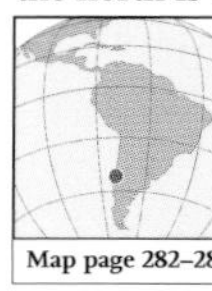

Map page 282–283

CHINA

People's Republic of China

Area Sq Km	9 584 492	**Currency**	Yuan, Hong Kong dollar, Macao pataca
Area Sq Miles	3 700 593	**Languages**	Mandarin, Wu, Cantonese, Hsiang, regional languages
Population	1 330 265 000		
Capital	Beijing (Peking)	**Religions**	Confucian, Taoist, Buddhist, Christian, Muslim
		Organizations	APEC, UN

China, the world's most populous and fourth largest country, occupies a large part of east Asia, borders fourteen states and has coastlines on the Yellow, East China and South China Seas. It has a huge variety of landscapes. The southwest contains the high Plateau of Tibet, flanked by the Himalaya and Kunlun Shan mountains. The north is mountainous with arid basins and extends from the Tien Shan and Altai Mountains and the vast Taklimakan Desert in the west to the plateau and Gobi Desert in the centre-east. Eastern China is predominantly lowland and is divided broadly into the basins of the Yellow River (Huang He) in the north, the Yangtze (Chang Jiang) in the centre and the Pearl River (Xi Jiang) in the southeast. Climatic conditions and vegetation are as diverse as the topography: much of the country experiences temperate conditions, while the southwest has an extreme mountain climate and the southeast enjoys a moist, warm subtropical climate. Nearly seventy per cent of China's huge population lives in rural areas, and agriculture employs around half of the working population. The main crops are rice, wheat, soya beans, peanuts, cotton, tobacco and hemp. China is rich in coal, oil and natural gas and has the world's largest potential in hydroelectric power. It is a major world producer of iron ore, molybdenum, copper, asbestos and gold. Economic reforms from the early 1980's led to an explosion in manufacturing development concentrated on the 'coastal economic open region'. The main exports are machinery, textiles, footwear, toys and sports goods. Japan and the USA are China's main trading partners.

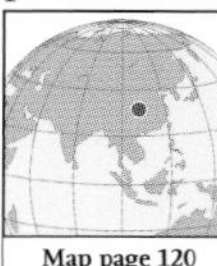

Map page 120

Province/Region	Area Sq Km (Miles)	Population	Capital
Anhui (Province)	139 000 (53 668)	61 180 000	Hefei
Beijing (Municipality)	16 800 (6 487)	16 330 000	Beijing (Peking)
Chongqing (Municipality)	23 000 (8 880)	28 160 000	Chongqing
Fujian (Province)	121 400 (46 873)	35 810 000	Fuzhou
Gansu (Province)	453 700 (175 175)	26 170 000	Lanzhou
Guangdong (Province)	178 000 (68 726)	94 490 000	Guangzhou (Canton)
Guangxi Zhuangzu Zizhiqu (Autonomous Region)	236 000 (91 120)	47 680 000	Nanning
Guizhou (Province)	176 000 (67 954)	37 620 000	Guiyang
Hainan (Province)	34 000 (13 127)	8 450 000	Haikou
Hebei (Province)	187 700 (72 471)	69 430 000	Shijiazhuang
Heilongjiang (Province)	454 600 (175 522)	38 240 000	Harbin
Henan (Province)	167 000 (64 479)	93 600 000	Zhengzhou
Hong Kong (Special Administrative Region)	1 075 (415)	6 926 000	Hong Kong
Hubei (Province)	185 900 (71 776)	56 990 000	Wuhan
Hunan (Province)	210 000 (81 081)	63 550 000	Changsha
Jiangsu (Province)	102 600 (39 614)	76 250 000	Nanjing
Jiangxi (Province)	166 900 (64 440)	43 680 000	Nanchang
Jilin (Province)	187 000 (72 201)	27 300 000	Changchun
Liaoning (Province)	147 400 (56 911)	42 980 000	Shenyang
Macao (Special Administrative Region)	17 (7)	526 000	Macao
Nei Mongol Zizhiqu (Inner Mongolia) (Autonomous Region)	1 183 000 (456 759)	24 050 000	Hohhot
Ningxia Huizu Zizhiqu (Autonomous Region)	66 400 (25 637)	6 100 000	Yinchuan
Qinghai (Province)	721 000 (278 380)	5 520 000	Xining
Shaanxi (Province)	205 600 (79 383)	37 480 000	Xi'an
Shandong (Province)	153 300 (59 189)	93 670 000	Jinan
Shanghai (Municipality)	6 300 (2 432)	18 580 000	Shanghai
Shanxi (Province)	156 300 (60 348)	33 930 000	Taiyuan
Sichaun (Province)	569 000 (219 692)	81 270 000	Chengdu
Tianjin (Municipality)	11 300 (4 363)	11 150 000	Tianjin
Xinjiang Uygur Zizhiqu (Sinkiang) (Autonomous Region)	1 600 000 (617 763)	20 950 000	Ürümqi
Xizang Zizhiqu (Tibet) (Autonomous Region)	1 228 400 (474 288)	2 840 000	Lhasa
Yunnan (Province)	394 000 (152 124)	45 140 000	Kunming
Zhejiang (Province)	101 800 (39 305)	50 600 000	Hangzhou

Taiwan: The People's Republic of China claims Taiwan as its 23rd Province

Christmas Island

Australian External Territory

Area Sq Km	135	**Currency**	Australian dollar
Area Sq Miles	52	**Languages**	English
Population	1 351	**Religions**	Buddhist, Sunni Muslim, Protestant, Roman Catholic
Capital	The Settlement		

The island is situated in the east of the Indian Ocean, to the south of Indonesia. The economy was formerly based on phosphate extraction although reserves are now nearly depleted. Tourism is developing and is a major employer.

Map page 108

Cocos Islands (Keeling Islands)

Australian External Territory

Area Sq Km	14	**Currency**	Australian dollar
Area Sq Miles	5	**Languages**	English
Population	621	**Religions**	Sunni Muslim, Christian
Capital	West Island		

The Cocos Islands consist of numerous islands on two coral atolls in the eastern Indian Ocean between Sri Lanka and Australia. Most of the population lives on West Island or Home Island. Coconuts are the only cash crop, and the main export.

Map page 108

COLOMBIA
Republic of Colombia

q Km	1 141 748	Currency	Colombian peso
q Miles	440 831	Languages	Spanish, Amerindian languages
ation	45 660 000	Religions	Roman Catholic, Protestant
	Bogotá	Organizations	UN

mbia, in northwest South America, has coastlines on the Pacific he Caribbean. Most Colombians live in high valleys and plateaus in the Andes. To the southeast are grasslands and the forests of the zon. The climate is tropical, varying with altitude. Only five per of land is cultivable. Colombia is the world's second largest ucer of coffee and the largest producer of emeralds. Also important are sugar, bananas, cotton and flowers for export; and coal, nickel, gold, silver and platinum. Oil and its products are the main export. The main trade partner is the USA. Internal violence - both politically motivated and drugs-related - continues to hinder development.

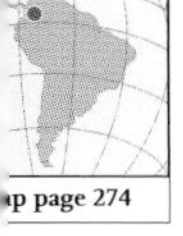
p page 274

COMOROS
Union of the Comoros

q Km	1 862	Currency	Comoros franc
q Miles	719	Languages	Comorian, French, Arabic
ation	676 000	Religions	Sunni Muslim, Roman Catholic
l	Moroni	Organizations	UN

state, in the Indian Ocean off the east African coast, comprises volcanic islands of Ngazidja (Grande Comore), Nzwani (Anjouan) and Mwali (Mohéli), and some coral atolls. These tropical islands are mountainous, with poor soil and few natural resources. Subsistence farming predominates. Vanilla, cloves and ylang-ylang (an essential oil) are exported, and the economy relies heavily on workers' remittances from abroad.

p page 239

CONGO
Republic of the Congo

q Km	342 000	Currency	CFA franc
q Miles	132 047	Languages	French, Kongo, Monokutuba, local languages
ation	3 683 000	Religions	Roman Catholic, Protestant, trad. beliefs, Sunni Muslim
l	Brazzaville	Organizations	UN

Congo, in central Africa, is mostly a forest or savanna-covered plateau drained by the Ubangi-Congo river systems. Sand dunes and lagoons line the short Atlantic coast. The climate is hot and tropical. Most Congolese live in the southern third of the country. Half of the workforce are farmers, growing food and crops including sugar, coffee, cocoa and oil palms. Oil and ber are the mainstays of the economy, and oil generates over fifty cent of export revenues.

page 230–231

CONGO, DEMOCRATIC REPUBLIC OF THE

q Km	2 345 410	Currency	Congolese franc
q Miles	905 568	Languages	French, Lingala, Swahili, Kongo, local languages
ation	66 020 000	Religions	Christian, Sunni Muslim
l	Kinshasa	Organizations	SADC, UN

s central African state, formerly Zaire, consists of the basin of the go river flanked by plateaus, with high mountain ranges to the east and a short Atlantic coastline to the west. The climate is tropical, with rainforest close to the Equator and savanna to the north and south. Fertile land allows a range of food and cash crops to be grown, chiefly coffee. The country has vast mineral resources, with copper, cobalt and diamonds being the most important.

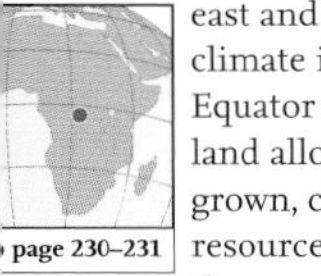
page 230–231

Cook Islands
New Zealand Overseas Territory

Sq Km	293	Currency	New Zealand dollar
Sq Miles	113	Languages	English, Maori
lation	20 000	Religions	Protestant, Roman Catholic
al	Avarua		

se consist of groups of coral atolls and volcanic islands in the hwest Pacific Ocean. The main island is Rarotonga. Distance from ign markets and restricted natural resources hinder development.

ap page 103

COSTA RICA
Republic of Costa Rica

Sq Km	51 100	Currency	Costa Rican colón
Sq Miles	19 730	Languages	Spanish
lation	4 579 000	Religions	Roman Catholic, Protestant
al	San José	Organizations	UN

a Rica, in central America, has coastlines on the Caribbean Sea and Pacific Ocean. From tropical coastal plains, the land rises to mountains and a temperate central plateau, where most of the population lives. The economy depends on agriculture and tourism, with ecotourism becoming increasingly important. Main exports are textiles, coffee and bananas, and almost half of all trade is with the USA.

ap page 266

CÔTE D'IVOIRE (Ivory Coast)
Republic of Côte d'Ivoire

Sq Km	322 463	Currency	CFA franc
Sq Miles	124 504	Languages	French, creole, Akan, local languages
lation	21 075 000	Religions	Sunni Muslim, Roman Catholic, traditional beliefs, Protestant
tal	Yamoussoukro	Organizations	UN

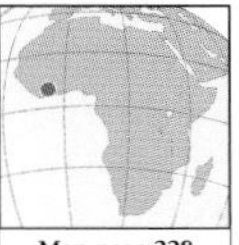
Map page 228

Côte d'Ivoire (Ivory Coast) is in west Africa, on the Gulf of Guinea. In the north are plateaus and savanna; in the south are low undulating plains and rainforest, with sand-bars and lagoons on the coast. Temperatures are warm, and rainfall is heavier in the south. Most of the workforce is engaged in farming. Côte d'Ivoire is a major producer of cocoa and coffee, and agricultural products (also including cotton and timber) are the main exports. Oil and gas have begun to be exploited.

CROATIA
Republic of Croatia

Area Sq Km	56 538	Currency	Kuna
Area Sq Miles	21 829	Languages	Croatian, Serbian
Population	4 416 000	Religions	Roman Catholic, Serbian Orthodox, Sunni Muslim
Capital	Zagreb	Organizations	NATO, UN

The southern European state of Croatia has a long coastline on the Adriatic Sea, with many offshore islands. Coastal areas have a Mediterranean climate; inland is cooler and wetter. Croatia was once strong agriculturally and industrially, but conflict in the early 1990s, and associated loss of tourist revenue, caused economic problems from which recovery has been slow.

Map page 210

CUBA
Republic of Cuba

Area Sq Km	110 860	Currency	Cuban peso
Area Sq Miles	42 803	Languages	Spanish
Population	11 204 000	Religions	Roman Catholic, Protestant
Capital	La Habana (Havana)	Organizations	UN

The country comprises the island of Cuba (the largest island in the Caribbean), and many islets and cays. A fifth of Cubans live in and around Havana. Cuba is slowly recovering from the withdrawal of aid and subsidies from the former USSR. Sugar remains the basis of the economy, although tourism is developing and is, together with remittances from workers abroad, an important source of revenue.

Map page 270

Curaçao part of Netherlands Antilles

Area Sq Km (Miles) 444 (171) Population 140 796 Capital Willemstad

An island in the Caribbean Sea off the north coast of Venezuela, it is the largest and most populous island of the Netherlands Antilles. Oil refining and tourism form the basis of the economy.

Map page 271

CYPRUS
Republic of Cyprus

Area Sq Km	9 251	Currency	Euro
Area Sq Miles	3 572	Languages	Greek, Turkish, English
Population	871 000	Religions	Greek Orthodox, Sunni Muslim
Capital	Lefkosia (Nicosia)	Organizations	Comm., EU, UN

The eastern Mediterranean island of Cyprus has hot dry summers and mild winters. The economy of the Greek south is based mainly on specialist agriculture and tourism, though shipping and offshore banking are also major sources of income. The Turkish north depends on agriculture, tourism and aid from Turkey. Cyprus joined the European Union in May 2004.

Map page 150

CZECH REPUBLIC

Area Sq Km	78 864	Currency	Koruna
Area Sq Miles	30 450	Languages	Czech, Moravian, Slovakian
Population	10 369 000	Religions	Roman Catholic, Protestant
Capital	Praha (Prague)	Organizations	EU, NATO, OECD, UN

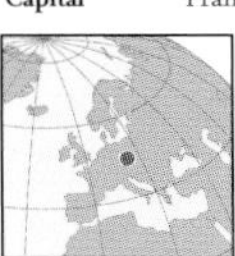
Map page 198–199

The landlocked Czech Republic in central Europe consists of rolling countryside, wooded hills and fertile valleys. The climate is continental. The country has substantial reserves of coal and lignite, timber and some minerals, chiefly iron ore. It is highly industrialized, and major manufactured goods include industrial machinery, consumer goods, cars, iron and steel, chemicals and glass. Germany is the main trading partner. The Czech Republic joined the European Union in May 2004.

DENMARK
Kingdom of Denmark

Area Sq Km	43 075	Currency	Danish krone
Area Sq Miles	16 631	Languages	Danish
Population	5 470 000	Religions	Protestant
Capital	København (Copenhagen)	Organizations	EU, NATO, OECD, UN

In northern Europe, Denmark occupies the Jutland (Jylland) peninsula and nearly five hundred islands in and between the North and Baltic Seas. The country is low-lying, with long, indented coastlines. The climate is cool and temperate, with rainfall throughout the year. A fifth of the population lives in and around the capital, Copenhagen (København), on the largest of the islands, Zealand (Sjælland). The country's main natural resource is its agricultural potential: two-thirds of the total area is fertile farmland or pasture. Agriculture is high-tech, and with forestry and fishing employs only around six per cent of the workforce. Denmark is self-sufficient in oil and natural gas, produced from fields in the North Sea. Manufacturing, largely based on imported raw materials, accounts for over half of all exports, which include machinery, food, furniture, and pharmaceuticals. The main trading partners are Germany and Sweden.

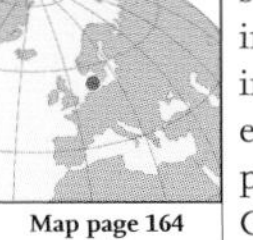
Map page 164

DJIBOUTI
Republic of Djibouti

Area Sq Km	23 200	Currency	Djibouti franc
Area Sq Miles	8 958	Languages	Somali, Afar, French, Arabic
Population	864 000	Religions	Sunni Muslim, Christian
Capital	Djibouti	Organizations	UN

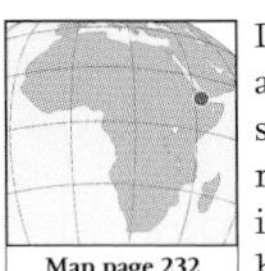
Map page 232

Djibouti lies in northeast Africa, on the Gulf of Aden at the entrance to the Red Sea. Most of the country is semi-arid desert with high temperatures and low rainfall. More than two-thirds of the population live in the capital. There is some camel, sheep and goat herding, but with few natural resources the economy is based on services and trade. Djibouti serves as a free trade zone for northern Africa, and the capital's port is a major transhipment and refuelling destination. It is linked by rail to Addis Ababa in Ethiopia.

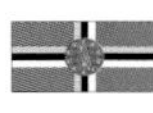

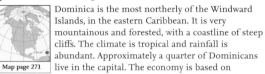

DOMINICA
Commonwealth of Dominica

Area Sq Km	750	Currency	East Caribbean dollar
Area Sq Miles	290	Languages	English, creole
Population	67 000	Religions	Roman Catholic, Protestant
Capital	Roseau	Organizations	CARICOM, Comm., UN

Dominica is the most northerly of the Windward Islands, in the eastern Caribbean. It is very mountainous and forested, with a coastline of steep cliffs. The climate is tropical and rainfall is abundant. Approximately a quarter of Dominicans live in the capital. The economy is based on agriculture, with bananas (the major export), coconuts and citrus fruits the most important crops. Tourism is a developing industry.

Map page 271

DOMINICAN REPUBLIC

Area Sq Km	48 442	Currency	Dominican peso
Area Sq Miles	18 704	Languages	Spanish, creole
Population	10 090 000	Religions	Roman Catholic, Protestant
Capital	Santo Domingo	Organizations	UN

The state occupies the eastern two-thirds of the Caribbean island of Hispaniola (the western third is Haiti). It has a series of mountain ranges, fertile valleys and a large coastal plain in the east. The climate is hot tropical, with heavy rainfall. Sugar, coffee and cocoa are the main cash crops. Nickel (the main export), and gold are mined, and there is some light industry. The USA is the main trading partner. Tourism is the main foreign exchange earner.

Map page 270–271

EAST TIMOR
Democratic Republic of Timor-Leste

Area Sq Km	14 874	Currency	United States dollar
Area Sq Miles	5 743	Languages	Portuguese, Tetun, English
Population	1 134 000	Religions	Roman Catholic
Capital	Dili	Organizations	UN

The island of Timor is part of the Indonesian archipelago, to the north of Western Australia. East Timor occupies the eastern section of the island, and a small coastal enclave (Ocussi) to the west. A referendum in 1999 ended Indonesia's occupation, after which the country was under UN transitional administration until full independence was achieved in 2002. The economy is in a poor state and East Timor is heavily dependent on foreign aid.

Map page 115

ECUADOR
Republic of Ecuador

Area Sq Km	272 045	Currency	United States dollar
Area Sq Miles	105 037	Languages	Spanish, Quechua, and other Amerindian languages
Population	13 625 000		
Capital	Quito	Religions	Roman Catholic
		Organizations	OPEC, UN

Map page 274

Ecuador is in northwest South America, on the Pacific coast. It consists of a broad coastal plain, high mountain ranges in the Andes, and part of the forested upper Amazon basin to the east. The climate is tropical, moderated by altitude. Most people live on the coast or in the mountain valleys. Ecuador is one of South America's main oil producers, and mineral reserves include gold. Most of the workforce depends on agriculture. Petroleum, bananas, shrimps, coffee and cocoa are exported. The USA is the main trading partner.

EGYPT
Arab Republic of Egypt

Area Sq Km	1 000 250	Currency	Egyptian pound
Area Sq Miles	386 199	Languages	Arabic
Population	82 999 000	Religions	Sunni Muslim, Coptic Christian
Capital	Al Qāhirah (Cairo)	Organizations	UN

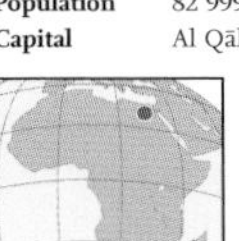
Map page 224–225

Egypt, on the eastern Mediterranean coast of north Africa, is low-lying, with areas below sea level in the Qattara depression. It is a land of desert and semi-desert, except for the Nile valley, where ninety-nine per cent of Egyptians live. The Sinai peninsula in the northeast of the country forms the only land bridge between Africa and Asia. The summers are hot, the winters mild and rainfall is negligible. Less than four per cent of land (chiefly around the Nile floodplain and delta) is cultivated. Farming employs about one-third of the workforce; cotton is the main cash crop. Egypt imports over half its food needs. There are oil and natural gas reserves, although nearly a quarter of electricity comes from hydroelectric power. Main exports are oil and oil products, cotton, textiles and clothing.

EL SALVADOR
Republic of El Salvador

Area Sq Km	21 041	**Currency**	El Salvador colón, United States dollar
Area Sq Miles	8 124	**Languages**	Spanish
Population	6 163 000	**Religions**	Roman Catholic, Protestant
Capital	San Salvador	**Organizations**	UN

Located on the Pacific coast of central America, El Salvador consists of a coastal plain and volcanic mountain ranges which enclose a densely populated plateau area. The coast is hot, with heavy summer rainfall; the highlands are cooler. Coffee (the chief export), sugar and cotton are the main cash crops. The main trading partners are the USA and Guatemala.

Map page 267

EQUATORIAL GUINEA
Republic of Equatorial Guinea

Area Sq Km	28 051	**Currency**	CFA franc
Area Sq Miles	10 831	**Languages**	Spanish, French, Fang
Population	676 000	**Religions**	Roman Catholic, traditional beliefs
Capital	Malabo	**Organizations**	UN

The state consists of Rio Muni, an enclave on the Atlantic coast of central Africa, and the islands of Bioco, Annobón and the Corisco group. Most of the population lives on the coastal plain and upland plateau of Rio Muni. The capital city, Malabo, is on the fertile volcanic island of Bioco. The climate is hot, humid and wet. Oil production started in 1992, and oil is now the main export, along with timber. The economy depends heavily on foreign aid.

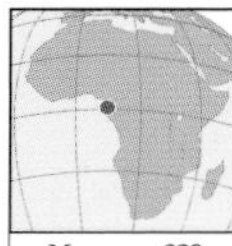
Map page 229

ERITREA
State of Eritrea

Area Sq Km	117 400	**Currency**	Nakfa
Area Sq Miles	45 328	**Languages**	Tigrinya, Tigre
Population	5 073 000	**Religions**	Sunni Muslim, Coptic Christian
Capital	Asmara	**Organizations**	UN

Eritrea, on the Red Sea coast of northeast Africa, consists of a high plateau in the north with a coastal plain which widens to the south. The coast is hot; inland is cooler. Rainfall is unreliable. The agriculture-based economy has suffered from over thirty years of war and occasional poor rains. Eritrea is one of the least developed countries in the world.

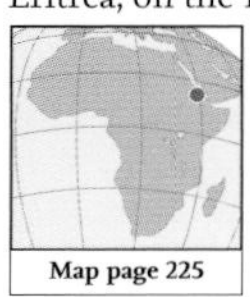
Map page 225

ESTONIA
Republic of Estonia

Area Sq Km	45 200	**Currency**	Kroon
Area Sq Miles	17 452	**Languages**	Estonian, Russian
Population	1 340 000	**Religions**	Protestant, Estonian and Russian Orthodox
Capital	Tallinn	**Organizations**	EU, NATO, UN

Estonia is in northern Europe, on the Gulf of Finland and the Baltic Sea. The land, over one-third of which is forested, is generally low-lying with many lakes. Approximately one-third of Estonians live in the capital, Tallinn. Exported goods include machinery, wood products, textiles and food products. The main trading partners are the Russian Federation, Finland and Sweden. Estonia joined the European Union in May 2004.

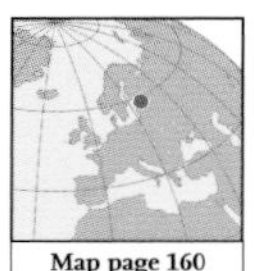
Map page 160

ETHIOPIA
Federal Democratic Republic of Ethiopia

Area Sq Km	1 133 880	**Currency**	Birr
Area Sq Miles	437 794	**Languages**	Oromo, Amharic, Tigrinya, local languages
Population	82 825 000	**Religions**	Ethiopian Orthodox, Sunni Muslim, trad. beliefs
Capital	Ādīs Ābeba (Addis Ababa)	**Organizations**	UN

A landlocked country in northeast Africa, Ethiopia comprises a mountainous region in the west which is traversed by the Great Rift Valley. The east is mostly arid plateau land. The highlands are warm with summer rainfall. Most people live in the central–northern area. In recent years civil war, conflict with Eritrea and poor infrastructure have hampered economic development. Subsistence farming is the main activity, although droughts have led to frequent famines. Coffee is the main export and there is some light industry. Ethiopia is one of the least developed countries in the world.

Map page 232

Falkland Islands
United Kingdom Overseas Territory

Area Sq Km	12 170	**Currency**	Falkland Islands pound
Area Sq Miles	4 699	**Languages**	English
Population	2 955	**Religions**	Protestant, Roman Catholic
Capital	Stanley		

Lying in the southwest Atlantic Ocean, northeast of Cape Horn, two main islands, West Falkland and East Falkland and many smaller islands, form the territory of the Falkland Islands. The economy is based on sheep farming and the sale of fishing licences.

Map page 283

Faroe Islands
Self-governing Danish Territory

Area Sq Km	1 399	**Currency**	Danish krone
Area Sq Miles	540	**Languages**	Faroese, Danish
Population	50 000	**Religions**	Protestant
Capital	Tórshavn (Thorshavn)		

A self-governing territory, the Faroe Islands lie in the north Atlantic Ocean between the UK and Iceland. The islands benefit from the North Atlantic Drift ocean current, which has a moderating effect on the climate. The economy is based on deep-sea fishing.

Map page 166

FIJI
Republic of the Fiji Islands

Area Sq Km	18 330	**Currency**	Fiji dollar
Area Sq Miles	7 077	**Languages**	English, Fijian, Hindi
Population	849 000	**Religions**	Christian, Hindu, Sunni Muslim
Capital	Suva	**Organizations**	Comm., UN

The southwest Pacific republic of Fiji comprises two mountainous and volcanic islands, Vanua Levu and Viti Levu, and over three hundred smaller islands. The climate is tropical and the economy is based on agriculture (chiefly sugar, the main export), fishing, forestry, gold mining and tourism.

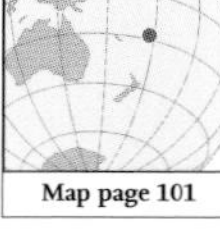
Map page 101

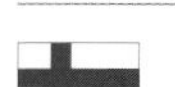

FINLAND
Republic of Finland

Area Sq Km	338 145	**Currency**	Euro
Area Sq Miles	130 559	**Languages**	Finnish, Swedish
Population	5 326 000	**Religions**	Protestant, Greek Orthodox
Capital	Helsinki (Helsingfors)	**Organizations**	EU, OECD, UN

Finland is in northern Europe, and nearly one-third of the country lies north of the Arctic Circle. Forests cover over seventy per cent of the land area, and ten per cent is covered by lakes. Summers are short and warm, and winters are long and severe, particularly in the north. Most of the population lives in the southern third of the country, along the coast or near the lakes. Timber is a major resource and there are important minerals, chiefly chromium. Main industries include metal working, electronics, paper and paper products, and chemicals. The main trading partners are Germany, Sweden and the UK.

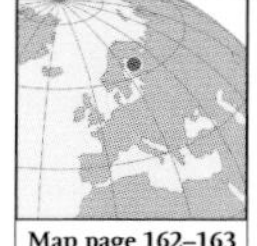
Map page 162–163

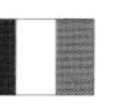

FRANCE
French Republic

Area Sq Km	543 965	**Currency**	Euro
Area Sq Miles	210 026	**Languages**	French, Arabic
Population	62 343 000	**Religions**	Roman Catholic, Protestant, Sunni Muslim
Capital	Paris	**Organizations**	EU, NATO, OECD, UN

France lies in western Europe and has coastlines on the Atlantic Ocean and the Mediterranean Sea. It includes the Mediterranean island of Corsica. Northern and western regions consist mostly of flat or rolling countryside, and include the major lowlands of the Paris basin, the Loire valley and the Aquitaine basin, drained by the Seine, Loire and Garonne river systems respectively. The centre-south is dominated by the hill region of the Massif Central. To the east are the Vosges and Jura mountains and the Alps. In the southwest, the Pyrenees form a natural border with Spain. The climate is temperate with warm summers and cool winters, although the Mediterranean coast has hot, dry summers and mild winters. Over seventy per cent of the population lives in towns, with almost a sixth of the population living in the Paris area. The French economy has a substantial and varied agricultural base. It is a major producer of both fresh and processed food. There are relatively few mineral resources; it has coal reserves, and some oil and natural gas, but it relies heavily on nuclear and hydroelectric power and imported fuels. France is one of the world's major industrial countries. Main industries include food processing, iron, steel and aluminium production, chemicals, cars, electronics and oil refining. The main exports are transport equipment, plastics and chemicals. Tourism is a major source of revenue and employment. Trade is predominantly with other European Union countries.

Map page 176

French Guiana
French Overseas Department

Area Sq Km	90 000	**Currency**	Euro
Area Sq Miles	34 749	**Languages**	French, creole
Population	226 000	**Religions**	Roman Catholic
Capital	Cayenne		

French Guiana, on the north coast of South America, is densely forested. The climate is tropical, with high rainfall. Most people live in the coastal strip, and agriculture is mostly subsistence farming. Forestry and fishing are important, but mineral resources are largely unexploited and industry is limited. French Guiana depends on French aid. The main trading partners are France and the USA.

Map page 275

FRENCH POLYNESIA
French Overseas Country

Area Sq Km	3 265	**Currency**	CFP franc
Area Sq Miles	1 261	**Languages**	French, Tahitian, Polynesian languages
Population	269 000	**Religions**	Protestant, Roman Catholic
Capital	Papeete		

Extending over a vast area of the southeast Pacific Ocean, French Polynesia comprises more than one hundred and thirty islands and coral atolls. The main island groups are the Marquesas Islands, the Tuamotu Archipelago and the Society Islands. The capital, Papeete, is on Tahiti in the Society Islands. The climate is subtropical, and the economy is based on tourism. The main export is cultured pearls.

Map page 101

French Southern and Antarctic Lands
French Overseas Territory

Area Sq Km (Miles) 439 580 (169 723) **Population** uninhabited

This territory includes the Crozet Islands, Kerguelen, Amsterdam Island and St Paul Island. All are uninhabited apart from scientific research staff. In accordance with the Antarctic Treaty, French (and a other) territorial claims in Antarctica have been suspended.

Map page 95

GABON
Gabonese Republic

Area Sq Km	267 667	**Currency**	CFA franc
Area Sq Miles	103 347	**Languages**	French, Fang, local languages
Population	1 475 000	**Religions**	Roman Catholic, Protestant, traditional beliefs
Capital	Libreville	**Organizations**	UN

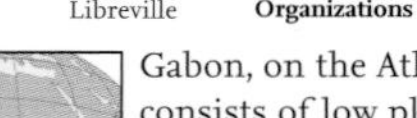

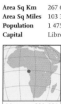

Gabon, on the Atlantic coast of central Africa, consists of low plateaus and a coastal plain lined by lagoons and mangrove swamps. The climate is tropical and rainforests cover over three-quarters of the land area. Over seventy per cent of the population lives in towns. The economy is heavily dependent on oil, which accounts for around seventy-five per cent of exports; manganese, uranium and timber are the other main exports. Agriculture is mainly at subsistence level.

Map page 230–231

THE GAMBIA
Republic of The Gambia

Area Sq Km	11 295	**Currency**	Dalasi
Area Sq Miles	4 361	**Languages**	English, Malinke, Fulani, Wolof
Population	1 705 000	**Religions**	Sunni Muslim, Protestant
Capital	Banjul	**Organizations**	Comm., UN

The Gambia, on the coast of west Africa, occupies a strip of land along the lower Gambia river. Sandy beaches are backed by mangrove swamps, beyond which is savanna. The climate is tropical, with most rainfall in the summer. Over seventy per cent of Gambians are farmers, growing chiefly groundnuts (the main export), cotton, oil palms and food crops. Livestock rearing and fishing are important, while manufacturing is limited. Re-expor mainly from Senegal, and tourism are major sources of income.

Map page 228

Gaza Semi-autonomous region

Area Sq Km	363	**Currency**	Israeli shekel
Area Sq Miles	140	**Languages**	Arabic
Population	1 486 816	**Religions**	Sunni Muslim, Shi'a Muslim
Capital	Gaza		

Gaza is a narrow strip of land on the southeast corner of the Mediterranean Sea, between Egypt and Israel. This Palestinian territ has internal autonomy, but Israel exerts full control over its border with Israel. All Israeli settlers were evacuated in 2005. Hostilities between the two parties continue to restrict its economic developme

Map page 150

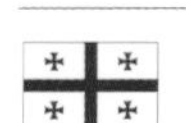

GEORGIA
Republic of Georgia

Area Sq Km	69 700	**Currency**	Lari
Area Sq Miles	26 911	**Languages**	Georgian, Russian, Armenian, Azeri, Ossetian, Ab
Population	4 260 000	**Religions**	Georgian Orthodox, Russian Orthodox, Sunni M
Capital	T'bilisi	**Organizations**	CIS, UN

Georgia is in the northwest Caucasus area of southwest Asia, on the eastern coast of the Black Se Mountain ranges in the north and south flank the Kura and Rioni valleys. The climate is generally mil and along the coast it is subtropical. Agriculture is important, with tea, grapes, and citrus fruits the main crops. Mineral resources include manganese ore and oil, and the main industries are steel, oil refining and machine building. The main trading partners are the Russian Federation and Turkey.

Map page 151

GERMANY
Federal Republic of Germany

Area Sq Km	357 022	**Currency**	Euro
Area Sq Miles	137 849	**Languages**	German, Turkish
Population	82 167 000	**Religions**	Protestant, Roman Catholic
Capital	Berlin	**Organizations**	EU, NATO, OECD, UN

The central European state of Germany borders nine countries an has coastlines on the North and Baltic Seas. Behind the indented coastline, and covering about one-third of the country, is the nort German plain, a region of fertile farmland and sandy heaths drained by the country's major rivers. The central highlands are a belt of forested hills and plateaus which stretch from the Eifel region in the west to the mountains of the Erzgebirge along the border with the Czech Republic. Farther south the land rises to the Swabian Alps (Schwäbische Alb), with the high rugged and forested Black Forest (Schwarzwald) in the southwest. In the far south the Bavarian Alps form the border with Austria. The climate is temperate, with continental condition in eastern areas. The population is highly urbanized, with over eighty-five per cent living in cities and towns. With the exception of coal, lignite, potash and baryte, Germany lacks minerals and other industrial raw materials. It has a small agricultural base, although a few products (chiefly wines and beers) enjoy an international reputation. Germany is the world's third ranking economy after the USA and Japan. Its industries are amongst the world's most technologically advanced. Exports include machinery vehicles and chemicals. The majority of trade is with other countries in the European Union, the USA and Japan.

Map page 188–189

…n-Württemberg (State)		
…q Km (Miles) 35 752 (13 804)	Population 10 751 000	Capital Stuttgart
…rn (State)		
…q Km (Miles) 70 550 (27 240)	Population 12 521 000	Capital München (Munich)
…n (State)		
…q Km (Miles) 892 (344)	Population 3 426 000	Capital Berlin
…denburg (State)		
…q Km (Miles) 29 476 (11 381)	Population 2 528 000	Capital Potsdam
…men (State)		
…q Km (Miles) 404 (156)	Population 661 000	Capital Bremen
…burg (State)		
…q Km (Miles) 755 (292)	Population 1 772 000	Capital Hamburg
…sen (State)		
…q Km (Miles) 21 114 (8 152)	Population 6 072 000	Capital Wiesbaden
…klenburg-Vorpommern (State)		
…q Km (Miles) 23 173 (8 947)	Population 1 670 000	Capital Schwerin
…ersachsen (State)		
…q Km (Miles) 47 616 (18 385)	Population 7 959 000	Capital Hannover
…rhein-Westfalen (State)		
…q Km (Miles) 34 082 (13 159)	Population 17 964 000	Capital Düsseldorf
…inland-Pfalz (State)		
…q Km (Miles) 19 847 (7 663)	Population 4 037 000	Capital Mainz
…land (State)		
…q Km (Miles) 2 568 (992)	Population 1 033 000	Capital Saarbrücken
…sen (State)		
…q Km (Miles) 18 413 (7 109)	Population 4 200 000	Capital Dresden
…sen-Anhalt (State)		
…q Km (Miles) 20 447 (7 895)	Population 2 393 000	Capital Magdeburg
…eswig-Holstein (State)		
…q Km (Miles) 15 761 (6 085)	Population 2 836 000	Capital Kiel
…ringen (State)		
…q Km (Miles) 16 172 (6 244)	Population 2 274 000	Capital Erfurt

GHANA
Republic of Ghana

…q Km	238 537	Currency	Cedi
…q Miles	92 100	Languages	English, Hausa, Akan, local languages
…ation	23 837 000	Religions	Christian, Sunni Muslim, traditional beliefs
…l	Accra	Organizations	Comm., UN

A west African state on the Gulf of Guinea, Ghana is a land of plains and low plateaus covered with savanna and rainforest. In the east is the Volta basin and Lake Volta. The climate is tropical, with the highest rainfall in the south, where most of the population lives. Agriculture employs around sixty per cent of the workforce. Main …rts are gold, timber, cocoa, bauxite and manganese ore.

…page 228–229

Gibraltar
United Kingdom Overseas Territory

…q Km	7	Currency	Gibraltar pound
…q Miles	3	Languages	English, Spanish
…ation	31 000	Religions	Roman Catholic, Protestant, Sunni Muslim
…l	Gibraltar		

…altar lies on the south coast of Spain at the western entrance to …Mediterranean Sea. The economy depends on tourism, offshore …king and shipping services.

…ap page 207

GREECE
Hellenic Republic

…q Km	131 957	Currency	Euro
…q Miles	50 949	Languages	Greek
…ation	11 161 000	Religions	Greek Orthodox, Sunni Muslim
…l	Athina (Athens)	Organizations	EU, NATO, OECD, UN

Greece comprises a mountainous peninsula in the Balkan region of southeastern Europe and many islands in the Ionian, Aegean and Mediterranean Seas. The islands make up over one-fifth of its area. Mountains and hills cover much of the country. The main lowland areas are the plains of Thessaly in the centre and around …ssaloniki in the northeast. Summers are hot and dry while winters …mild and wet, but colder in the north with heavy snowfalls in the …ntains. One-third of Greeks live in the Athens area. Employment in …ulture accounts for approximately twenty per cent of the workforce, …exports include citrus fruits, raisins, wine, olives and olive oil. …minium and nickel are mined and a wide range of manufactures are …uced, including food products and tobacco, textiles, clothing, and …nicals. Tourism is an important industry and there is a large services …r. Most trade is with other European Union countries.

…page 220–221

GREENLAND
Self-governing Danish Territory

…q Km	2 175 600	Currency	Danish krone
…q Miles	840 004	Languages	Greenlandic, Danish
…ation	57 000	Religions	Protestant
…l	Nuuk (Godthåb)		

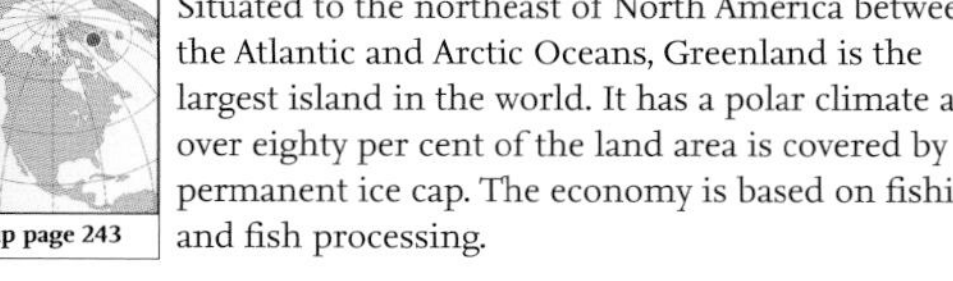

Situated to the northeast of North America between the Atlantic and Arctic Oceans, Greenland is the largest island in the world. It has a polar climate and over eighty per cent of the land area is covered by permanent ice cap. The economy is based on fishing and fish processing.

…ap page 243

GRENADA

Area Sq Km	378	Currency	East Caribbean dollar
Area Sq Miles	146	Languages	English, creole
Population	104 000	Religions	Roman Catholic, Protestant
Capital	St George's	Organizations	CARICOM, Comm., UN

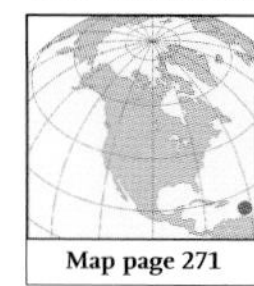

Map page 271

The Caribbean state comprises Grenada, the most southerly of the Windward Islands, and the southern islands of the Grenadines. Grenada has wooded hills, with beaches in the southwest. The climate is warm and wet. Agriculture is the main activity, with bananas, nutmeg and cocoa the main exports. Tourism is the main foreign exchange earner.

Guadeloupe
French Overseas Department

Area Sq Km	1 780	Currency	Euro
Area Sq Miles	687	Languages	French, creole
Population	465 000	Religions	Roman Catholic
Capital	Basse-Terre		

Guadeloupe, in the Leeward Islands in the Caribbean, consists of two main islands (Basse-Terre and Grande-Terre, connected by a bridge), Marie-Galante, and a few outer islands. The climate is tropical, but moderated by trade winds. Bananas, sugar and rum are the main exports and tourism is a major source of income.

Map page 271

Guam
United States Unincorporated Territory

Area Sq Km	541	Currency	United States dollar
Area Sq Miles	209	Languages	Chamorro, English, Tagalog
Population	178 000	Religions	Roman Catholic
Capital	Hagåtña (Agana)		

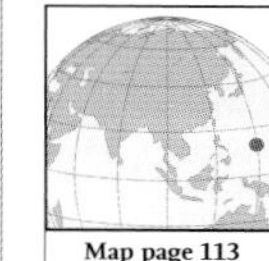

Map page 113

Lying at the south end of the Northern Mariana Islands in the western Pacific Ocean, Guam has a humid tropical climate. The island has a large US military base and the economy relies on that and on tourism, which has grown rapidly.

GUATEMALA
Republic of Guatemala

Area Sq Km	108 890	Currency	Quetzal, United States dollar
Area Sq Miles	42 043	Languages	Spanish, Mayan languages
Population	14 027 000	Religions	Roman Catholic, Protestant
Capital	Guatemala	Organizations	UN

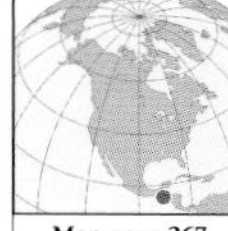

Map page 267

The most populous country in Central America after Mexico, Guatemala has long Pacific and short Caribbean coasts separated by a mountain chain which includes several active volcanoes. The climate is hot tropical in the lowlands and cooler in the highlands, where most of the population lives. Farming is the main activity and coffee, sugar and bananas are the main exports. There is some manufacturing of clothing and textiles. The main trading partner is the USA.

Guernsey
United Kingdom Crown Dependency

Area Sq Km	78	Currency	Pound sterling
Area Sq Miles	30	Languages	English, French
Population	64 801	Religions	Protestant, Roman Catholic
Capital	St Peter Port		

Guernsey is one of the Channel Islands, lying off northern France. The dependency also includes the nearby islands of Alderney, Sark and Herm. Financial services are an important part of the island's economy.

Map page 180

GUINEA
Republic of Guinea

Area Sq Km	245 857	Currency	Guinea franc
Area Sq Miles	94 926	Languages	French, Fulani, Malinke, local languages
Population	10 069 000	Religions	Sunni Muslim, traditional beliefs, Christian
Capital	Conakry	Organizations	UN

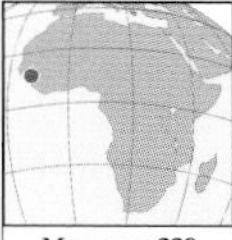

Map page 228

Guinea is in west Africa, on the Atlantic Ocean. There are mangrove swamps along the coast, while inland are lowlands and the Fouta Djallon mountains and plateaus. To the east are savanna plains drained by the upper Niger river system. The southeast is hilly. The climate is tropical, with high coastal rainfall. Agriculture is the main activity, employing nearly eighty per cent of the workforce, with coffee, bananas and pineapples the chief cash crops. There are huge reserves of bauxite, which accounts for more than seventy per cent of exports. Other exports include aluminium oxide, gold, coffee and diamonds.

GUINEA-BISSAU
Republic of Guinea-Bissau

Area Sq Km	36 125	Currency	CFA franc
Area Sq Miles	13 948	Languages	Portuguese, crioulo, local languages
Population	1 611 000	Religions	Traditional beliefs, Sunni Muslim, Christian
Capital	Bissau	Organizations	UN

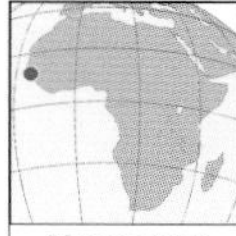

Map page 228

Guinea-Bissau is on the Atlantic coast of west Africa. The mainland coast is swampy and contains many estuaries. Inland are forested plains, and to the east are savanna plateaus. The climate is tropical. The economy is based mainly on subsistence farming. There is little industry, and timber and mineral resources are largely unexploited. Cashews account for seventy per cent of exports. Guinea-Bissau is one of the least developed countries in the world.

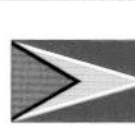

GUYANA
Co-operative Republic of Guyana

Area Sq Km	214 969	Currency	Guyana dollar
Area Sq Miles	83 000	Languages	English, creole, Amerindian languages
Population	762 000	Religions	Protestant, Hindu, Roman Catholic, Sunni Muslim
Capital	Georgetown	Organizations	CARICOM, Comm., UN

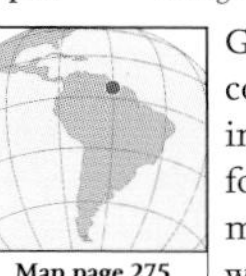

Map page 275

Guyana, on the northeast coast of South America, consists of highlands in the west and savanna uplands in the southwest. Most of the country is densely forested. A lowland coastal belt supports crops and most of the population. The generally hot, humid and wet conditions are modified along the coast by sea breezes. The economy is based on agriculture, bauxite, and forestry. Sugar, bauxite, gold, rice and timber are the main exports.

HAITI
Republic of Haiti

Area Sq Km	27 750	Currency	Gourde
Area Sq Miles	10 714	Languages	French, creole
Population	10 033 000	Religions	Roman Catholic, Protestant, Voodoo
Capital	Port-au-Prince	Organizations	CARICOM, UN

Haiti, occupying the western third of the Caribbean island of Hispaniola, is a mountainous state with small coastal plains and a central valley. The Dominican Republic occupies the rest of the island. The climate is tropical, and is hottest in coastal areas. Haiti has few natural resources, is densely populated and relies on exports of local crafts and coffee, and remittances from workers abroad.

Map page 270

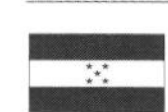

HONDURAS
Republic of Honduras

Area Sq Km	112 088	Currency	Lempira
Area Sq Miles	43 277	Languages	Spanish, Amerindian languages
Population	7 466 000	Religions	Roman Catholic, Protestant
Capital	Tegucigalpa	Organizations	UN

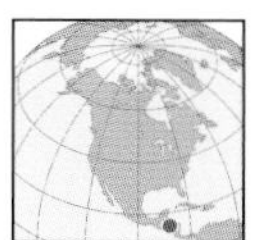

Map page 266

Honduras, in central America, is a mountainous and forested country with lowland areas along its long Caribbean and short Pacific coasts. Coastal areas are hot and humid with heavy summer rainfall; inland is cooler and drier. Most of the population lives in the central valleys. Coffee and bananas are the main exports, along with shellfish and zinc. Industry involves mainly agricultural processing.

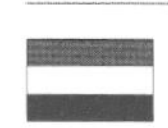

HUNGARY
Republic of Hungary

Area Sq Km	93 030	Currency	Forint
Area Sq Miles	35 919	Languages	Hungarian
Population	9 993 000	Religions	Roman Catholic, Protestant
Capital	Budapest	Organizations	EU, NATO, OECD, UN

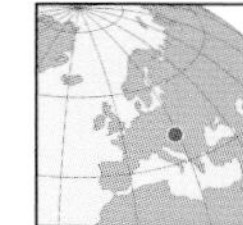

Map page 198–199

The Danube river flows north-south through central Hungary, a landlocked country in eastern Europe. In the east lies a great plain, flanked by highlands in the north. In the west low mountains and Lake Balaton separate a smaller plain and southern uplands. The climate is continental. Sixty per cent of the population lives in urban areas, and one-fifth lives in the capital, Budapest. Some minerals and energy resources are exploited, chiefly bauxite, coal and natural gas. Hungary has an industrial economy based on metals, machinery, transport equipment, chemicals and food products. The main trading partners are Germany and Austria. Hungary joined the European Union in May 2004.

ICELAND
Republic of Iceland

Area Sq Km	102 820	Currency	Icelandic króna
Area Sq Miles	39 699	Languages	Icelandic
Population	323 000	Religions	Protestant
Capital	Reykjavík	Organizations	NATO, OECD, UN

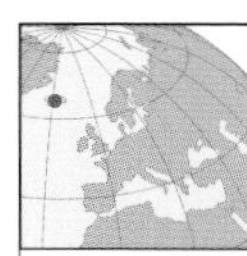

Map page 162

Iceland lies in the north Atlantic Ocean near the Arctic Circle, to the northwest of Scandinavia. The landscape is volcanic, with numerous hot springs, geysers, and approximately two hundred volcanoes. One-tenth of the country is covered by ice caps. Only coastal lowlands are cultivated and settled, and over half the population lives in the Reykjavik area. The climate is mild, moderated by the North Atlantic Drift ocean current and by southwesterly winds. The mainstays of the economy are fishing and fish processing, which account for seventy per cent of exports. Agriculture involves mainly sheep and dairy farming. Hydroelectric and geothermal energy resources are considerable. The main industries produce aluminium, ferro-silicon and fertilizers. Tourism, including ecotourism, is growing in importance.

INDIA
Republic of India

Area Sq Km	3 064 898	Currency	Indian rupee
Area Sq Miles	1 183 364	Languages	Hindi, English, many regional languages
Population	1 198 003 000	Religions	Hindu, Sunni Muslim, Shi'a Muslim, Sikh, Christian
Capital	New Delhi	Organizations	Comm., UN

The south Asian country of India occupies a peninsula that juts out into the Indian Ocean between the Arabian Sea and Bay of Bengal. The heart of the peninsula is the Deccan plateau, bordered on either side by ranges of hills, the Western Ghats and the lower Eastern Ghats, which fall away to narrow coastal plains. To the north is a broad plain, drained by the Indus, Ganges and Brahmaputra rivers and their tributaries. The plain is intensively farmed and is the most populous region. In the west is the Thar Desert. The mountains of the Himalaya form India's northern border, together with parts of the

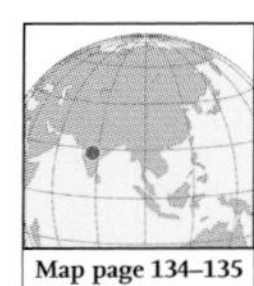
Map page 134–135

Karakoram and Hindu Kush ranges in the northwest. The climate shows marked seasonal variation: a hot season from March to June; a monsoon season from June to October; and a cold season from November to February. Rainfall ranges between very high in the northeast Assam region to negligible in the Thar Desert. Temperatures range from very cold in the Himalaya to tropical heat over much of the south. Over seventy per cent of the huge population – the second largest in the world – is rural, although Delhi, Mumbai (Bombay) and Kolkata (Calcutta) all rank among the ten largest cities in the world. Agriculture, forestry and fishing account for a quarter of national output and two-thirds of employment. Much of the farming is on a subsistence basis and involves mainly rice and wheat. India is a major world producer of tea, sugar, jute, cotton and tobacco. Livestock is reared mainly for dairy products and hides. There are major reserves of coal, reserves of oil and natural gas, and many minerals, including iron, manganese, bauxite, diamonds and gold. The manufacturing sector is large and diverse – mainly chemicals and chemical products, textiles, iron and steel, food products, electrical goods and transport equipment; software and pharmaceuticals are also important. All the main manufactured products are exported, together with diamonds and jewellery. The USA, Germany, Japan and the UK are the main trading partners.

INDONESIA

Republic of Indonesia

Area Sq Km	1 919 445	**Currency**	Rupiah
Area Sq Miles	741 102	**Languages**	Indonesian, local languages
Population	229 965 000	**Religions**	Sunni Muslim, Protestant, Roman Catholic, Hindu, Buddhist
Capital	Jakarta	**Organizations**	APEC, ASEAN, OPEC, UN

Map page 112–113

Indonesia, the largest and most populous country in southeast Asia, consists of over thirteen thousand islands extending between the Pacific and Indian Oceans. Sumatra, Java, Sulawesi, Kalimantan (two-thirds of Borneo) and Papua (formerly Irian Jaya, western New Guinea) make up ninety per cent of the land area. Most of Indonesia is mountainous and covered with rainforest or mangrove swamps, and there are over three hundred volcanoes, many active. Two-thirds of the population lives in the lowland areas of the islands of Java and Madura. The climate is tropical monsoon. Agriculture is the largest sector of the economy and Indonesia is among the world's top producers of rice, palm oil, tea, coffee, rubber and tobacco. Many goods are produced, including textiles, clothing, cement, tin, fertilizers and vehicles. Main exports are oil, natural gas, timber products and clothing. Main trading partners are Japan, the USA and Singapore. Indonesia is a relatively poor country, and ethnic tensions and civil unrest often hinder economic development.

IRAN

Islamic Republic of Iran

Area Sq Km	1 648 000	**Currency**	Iranian rial
Area Sq Miles	636 296	**Languages**	Farsi, Azeri, Kurdish, regional languages
Population	74 196 000	**Religions**	Shi'a Muslim, Sunni Muslim
Capital	Tehrān	**Organizations**	OPEC, UN

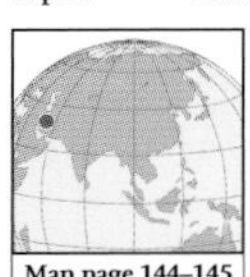
Map page 144–145

Iran is in southwest Asia, and has coasts on The Gulf, the Caspian Sea and the Gulf of Oman. In the east is a high plateau, with large salt pans and a vast sand desert. In the west the Zagros Mountains form a series of ridges, and to the north lie the Elburz Mountains. Most farming and settlement is on the narrow plain along the Caspian Sea and in the foothills of the north and west. The climate is one of extremes, with hot summers and very cold winters. Most of the light rainfall is in the winter months. Agriculture involves approximately one-third of the workforce. Wheat is the main crop, but fruit (especially dates) and pistachio nuts are grown for export. Petroleum (the main export) and natural gas are Iran's leading natural resources. Manufactured goods include carpets, clothing, food products and construction materials.

IRAQ

Republic of Iraq

Area Sq Km	438 317	**Currency**	Iraqi dinar
Area Sq Miles	169 235	**Languages**	Arabic, Kurdish, Turkmen
Population	30 747 000	**Religions**	Shi'a Muslim, Sunni Muslim, Christian
Capital	Baghdād	**Organizations**	OPEC, UN

Iraq, in southwest Asia, has at its heart the lowland valley of the Tigris and Euphrates rivers. In the southeast, where the two rivers join, are the Mesopotamian marshes and the Shaṭṭ al 'Arab waterway. Northern Iraq is hilly, while western Iraq is desert. Summers are hot and dry, while winters are mild with light, unreliable rainfall. One in five of the population lives in the capital, Baghdād. The economy has suffered following the 1991 Gulf War and the invasion of US-led coalition forces in 2005. The latter resulted in the overthrow of the dictator Saddam Hussein, but there is continuing internal instability. Oil is normally the main export.

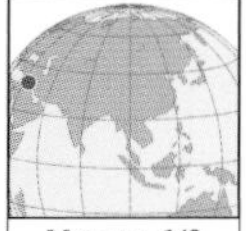
Map page 149

IRELAND

Republic of Ireland

Area Sq Km	70 282	**Currency**	Euro
Area Sq Miles	27 136	**Languages**	English, Irish
Population	4 515 000	**Religions**	Roman Catholic, Protestant
Capital	Dublin (Baile Átha Cliath)	**Organizations**	EU, OECD, UN

The Irish Republic occupies some eighty per cent of the island of Ireland, in northwest Europe. It is a lowland country of wide valleys, lakes and peat bogs, with isolated mountain ranges around the coast. The west coast is rugged and indented with many bays. The climate is mild due to the modifying effect of the North Atlantic Drift ocean current and rainfall is plentiful, although highest in the west. Nearly sixty per cent of the population lives in urban areas, Dublin and Cork being the main cities. Resources include natural gas, peat, lead and zinc. Agriculture, the traditional mainstay, now employs less than ten per cent of the workforce, while industry employs nearly thirty per cent. The main industries are electronics, pharmaceuticals and engineering as well as food processing, brewing and textiles. Service industries are expanding, with tourism a major earner. The UK is the main trading partner.

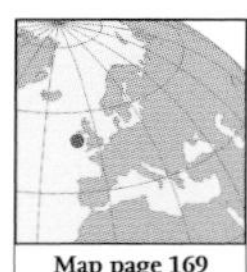
Map page 169

Isle of Man

United Kingdom Crown Dependency

Area Sq Km	572	**Currency**	Pound sterling
Area Sq Miles	221	**Languages**	English
Population	80 000	**Religions**	Protestant, Roman Catholic
Capital	Douglas		

The Isle of Man lies in the Irish Sea between England and Northern Ireland. The island is self-governing, although the UK is responsible for its defence and foreign affairs. It is not part of the European Union, but has a special relationship with the EU which allows for free trade. Eighty per cent of the economy is based on the service sector, particularly financial services.

Map page 170

ISRAEL

State of Israel

Area Sq Km	20 770	**Currency**	Shekel
Area Sq Miles	8 019	**Languages**	Hebrew, Arabic
Population	7 170 000	**Religions**	Jewish, Sunni Muslim, Christian, Druze
Capital	Jerusalem (Yerushalayim) (El Quds) De facto capital. Disputed	**Organizations**	UN

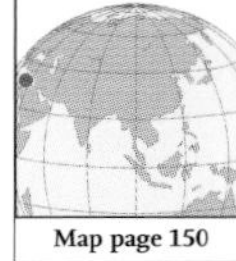
Map page 150

Israel lies on the Mediterranean coast of southwest Asia. Beyond the coastal Plain of Sharon are the hills and valleys of Samaria, with the Galilee highlands to the north. In the east is a rift valley, which extends from Lake Tiberias (Sea of Galilee) to the Gulf of Aqaba and contains the Jordan river and the Dead Sea. In the south is the Negev, a triangular semi-desert plateau. Most of the population lives on the coastal plain or in northern and central areas. Much of Israel has warm summers and mild, wet winters. The south is hot and dry. Agricultural production was boosted by the occupation of the West Bank in 1967. Manufacturing makes the largest contribution to the economy, and tourism is also important. Israel's main exports are machinery and transport equipment, software, diamonds, clothing, fruit and vegetables. The country relies heavily on foreign aid. Security issues relating to the West Bank and Gaza have still to be resolved.

ITALY

Italian Republic

Area Sq Km	301 245	**Currency**	Euro
Area Sq Miles	116 311	**Languages**	Italian
Population	59 870 000	**Religions**	Roman Catholic
Capital	Roma (Rome)	**Organizations**	EU, NATO, OECD, UN

Most of the southern European state of Italy occupies a peninsula that juts out into the Mediterranean Sea. It includes the islands of Sicily and Sardinia and approximately seventy much smaller islands in the surrounding seas. Italy is mountainous, dominated by the Alps, which form its northern border, and the various ranges of the Apennines, which run almost the full length of the peninsula. Many of Italy's mountains are of volcanic origin, and its active volcanoes are Vesuvius, near Naples, Etna and Stromboli. The main lowland area, the Po river valley in the northeast, is the main agricultural and industrial area and is the most populous region. Italy has a Mediterranean climate, although the north experiences colder, wetter winters, with heavy snow in the Alps. Natural resources are limited, and only about twenty per cent of the land is suitable for cultivation. The economy is fairly diversified. Some oil, natural gas and coal are produced, but most fuels and minerals used by industry are imported. Agriculture is important, with cereals, vines, fruit and vegetables the main crops. Italy is the world's largest wine producer. The north is the centre of Italian industry, especially around Turin, Milan and Genoa. Leading manufactures include industrial and office equipment, domestic appliances, cars, textiles, clothing, leather goods, chemicals and metal products. There is a strong service sector, and with over twenty-five million visitors a year, tourism is a major employer and accounts for five per cent of the national income. Finance and banking are also important. Most trade is with other European Union countries.

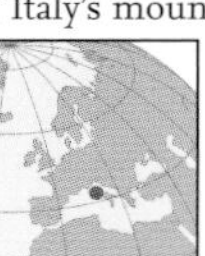
Map page 210–211

JAMAICA

Area Sq Km	10 991	**Currency**	Jamaican dollar
Area Sq Miles	4 244	**Languages**	English, creole
Population	2 719 000	**Religions**	Protestant, Roman Catholic
Capital	Kingston	**Organizations**	CARICOM, Comm., UN

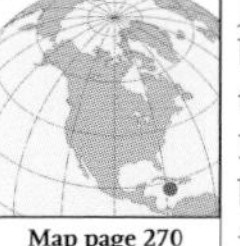
Map page 270

Jamaica, the third largest Caribbean island, has beaches and densely populated coastal plains traversed by hills and plateaus rising to the forested Blue Mountains in the east. The climate is tropical, but cooler and wetter on high ground. The economy is based on tourism, agriculture, mining and light manufacturing. Bauxite, aluminium oxide, sugar and bananas are the main exports. The USA is the main trading partner. Foreign aid is also significant.

Jammu and Kashmir

Disputed territory (India, Pakistan, China)

Area Sq Km (Miles) 222 236 (85 806) **Population** 13 000 000 **Capital** Srinagar

A disputed region in the north of the Indian subcontinent, to the w of the Karakoram and Himalaya mountains. The 'Line of Control' separates the northwestern, Pakistani-controlled area and the southeastern, Indian-controlled area. China occupies the Himalaya section known as the Aksai Chin, which is also claimed by India.

Map page 138

JAPAN

Area Sq Km	377 727	**Currency**	Yen
Area Sq Miles	145 841	**Languages**	Japanese
Population	127 156 000	**Religions**	Shintoist, Buddhist, Christian
Capital	Tōkyō	**Organizations**	APEC, OECD, UN

Japan lies in the Pacific Ocean off the coast of eastern Asia and consists of four main islands – Hokkaidō, Honshū, Shikoku and Kyūshū – and more than three thousand smaller islands in the surrounding Sea of Japan, East China Sea and Pacifi Ocean. The central island of Honshū accounts for s per cent of the total land area and contains eighty p cent of the population. Behind the long and deeply indented coastline, nearly three-quarters of the country is mountainous and heavily forested. Japan has over sixty active volcanoes, and is subject to frequent earthquak and typhoons. The climate is generally temperate maritime, with warm summers and mild winters, except in western Hokkaidō and northwest Honshū, where the winters are very cold with heavy snov Only fourteen per cent of the land area is suitable for cultivation, a its few raw materials (coal, oil, natural gas, lead, zinc and copper) ar insufficient for its industry. Most materials must be imported, including about ninety per cent of energy requirements. Yet Japan the world's second largest industrial economy, with a range of modern heavy and light industries centred mainly around the maj ports of Yokohama, Ōsaka and Tōkyō. It is the world's largest manufacturer of cars, motorcycles and merchant ships, and a majo producer of steel, textiles, chemicals and cement. It is also a leadin producer of many consumer durables, such as washing machines, a electronic equipment, chiefly office equipment and computers. Jap has a strong service sector, banking and finance being particularly important, and Tōkyō has one of the world's major stock exchange Owing to intensive agricultural production, Japan is seventy per ce self-sufficient in food. The main food crops are rice, barley, fruit, wheat and soya beans. Livestock rearing (chiefly cattle, pigs and chickens) and fishing are also important, and Japan has one of the largest fishing fleets in the world. A major trading nation, Japan ha trade links with many countries in southeast Asia and in Europe, although its main trading partner is the USA.

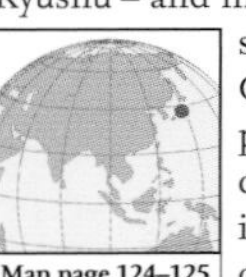
Map page 124–125

Jersey

United Kingdom Crown Dependency

Area Sq Km	116	**Currency**	Pound sterling
Area Sq Miles	45	**Languages**	English, French
Population	90 800	**Religions**	Protestant, Roman Catholic
Capital	St Helier		

One of the Channel Islands lying off the west coast of the Cherbou peninsula in northern France. Financial services are the most important part of the economy.

Map page 170

JORDAN

Hashemite Kingdom of Jordan

Area Sq Km	89 206	**Currency**	Jordanian dinar
Area Sq Miles	34 443	**Languages**	Arabic
Population	6 316 000	**Religions**	Sunni Muslim, Christian
Capital	'Ammān	**Organizations**	UN

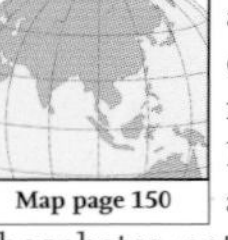
Map page 150

Jordan, in southwest Asia, is landlocked apart from a short coastline on the Gulf of Aqaba. Much of th country is rocky desert plateau. To the west of the mountains, the land falls below sea level to the Dead Sea and the Jordan river. The climate is hot and dry. Most people live in the northwest. Phosphates, potash, pharmaceuticals, fruit and vegetables are the main exports. The tourist industry is important, and the economy relies on workers' remittances from abroad and foreign aid.

KAZAKHSTAN

Republic of Kazakhstan

Area Sq Km	2 717 300	**Currency**	Tenge
Area Sq Miles	1 049 155	**Languages**	Kazakh, Russian, Ukrainian, German, Uzbek, T
Population	15 637 000	**Religions**	Sunni Muslim, Russian Orthodox, Protestant
Capital	Astana (Akmola)	**Organizations**	CIS, UN

Stretching across central Asia, Kazakhstan covers a vast area of step land and semi-desert. The land is flat in the west, with large lowlan around the Caspian Sea, rising to mountains in the southeast. The climate is continental. Agriculture and livestock rearing are import and cotton and tobacco are the main cash crops. Kazakhstan is very rich in minerals, including coal, chromium, gold, molybdenum, lead and zinc, and has substantial reserves of oil and gas. Mining, metallurgy, machin building and food processing are major industries. gas and minerals are the main exports, and the Rus Federation is the dominant trading partner.

Map page 142–143

KENYA
Republic of Kenya

q Km	582 646	Currency	Kenyan shilling
q Miles	224 961	Languages	Swahili, English, local languages
tion	39 802 000	Religions	Christian, traditional beliefs
	Nairobi	Organizations	Comm., UN

page 232–233

Kenya is in east Africa, on the Indian Ocean. Inland beyond the coastal plains the land rises to plateaus interrupted by volcanic mountains. The Great Rift Valley runs north-south to the west of the capital, Nairobi. Most of the population lives in the central area. Conditions are tropical on the coast, semi-desert in the h and savanna in the south. Hydroelectric power from the Upper river provides most of the country's electricity. Agricultural ucts, mainly tea, coffee, fruit and vegetables, are the main exports. t industry is important, and tourism, oil refining and re-exports for locked neighbours are major foreign exchange earners.

KIRIBATI
Republic of Kiribati

q Km	717	Currency	Australian dollar
q Miles	277	Languages	Gilbertese, English
tion	98 000	Religions	Roman Catholic, Protestant
	Bairiki	Organizations	Comm., UN

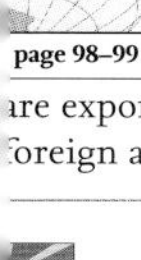
page 98–99

Kiribati, in the Pacific Ocean, straddles the Equator and comprises coral islands in the Gilbert, Phoenix and Line Island groups and the volcanic island of Banaba. Most people live on the Gilbert Islands, and the capital, Bairiki, is on Tarawa island in this group. The climate is hot, and wetter in the north. Copra and are exported. Kiribati relies on remittances from workers abroad foreign aid.

KOSOVO

Republic of Kosovo

q Km	10 908	Currency	Euro
q Miles	4 212	Languages	Albanian, Serbian
ation	2 153 139	Religions	Sunni Muslim, Serbian Orthodox,
l	Prishtinë (Priština)		

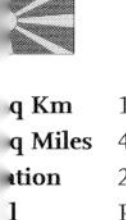

page 218–219

Kosovo, traditionally an autonomous southern province of Serbia, was the focus of ethnic conflict between Serbs and the majority ethnic Albanians in the 1990s until international intervention in 1999, after which it was administered by the UN. Kosovo declared its independence from Serbia in February 2008. The scape is largely hilly or mountainous, especially along the southern western borders.

KUWAIT

State of Kuwait

q Km	17 818	Currency	Kuwaiti dinar
q Miles	6 880	Languages	Arabic
tion	2 985 000	Religions	Sunni Muslim, Shi'a Muslim, Christian, Hindu
	Al Kuwayt (Kuwait)	Organizations	OPEC, UN

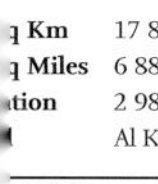
p page 149

Kuwait lies on the northwest shores of The Gulf in southwest Asia. It is mainly low-lying desert, with irrigated areas along the bay, Kuwait Jun, where most people live. Summers are hot and dry, and winters are cool with some rainfall. The oil industry, which accounts for eighty per cent of exports, has largely vered from the damage caused by the Gulf War in 1991. Income is derived from extensive overseas investments. Japan and the USA he main trading partners.

KYRGYZSTAN
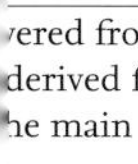

Kyrgyz Republic

q Km	198 500	Currency	Kyrgyz som
q Miles	76 641	Languages	Kyrgyz, Russian, Uzbek
ation	5 482 000	Religions	Sunni Muslim, Russian Orthodox
	Bishkek (Frunze)	Organizations	CIS, UN

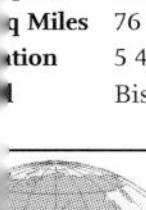
p page 143

A landlocked central Asian state, Kyrgyzstan is rugged and mountainous, lying to the west of the Tien Shan mountain range. Most of the population lives in the valleys of the north and west. Summers are hot and winters cold. Agriculture (chiefly livestock farming) is the main activity. Some oil and gas, coal, gold, antimony and cury are produced. Manufactured goods include machinery, metals metal products, which are the main exports. Most trade is with many, the Russian Federation, Kazakhstan and Uzbekistan.

LAOS

Lao People's Democratic Republic

q Km	236 800	Currency	Kip
q Miles	91 429	Languages	Lao, local languages
ation	6 320 000	Religions	Buddhist, traditional beliefs
l	Viangchan (Vientiane)	Organizations	ASEAN, UN

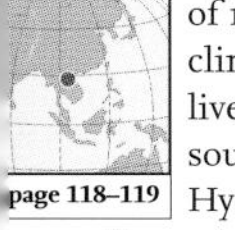
page 118–119

A landlocked country in southeast Asia, Laos is a land of mostly forested mountains and plateaus. The climate is tropical monsoon. Most of the population lives in the Mekong valley and the low plateau in the south, where food crops, chiefly rice, are grown. Hydroelectricity from a plant on the Mekong river, ber, coffee and tin are exported. Laos relies heavily on foreign aid.

LATVIA

Republic of Latvia

q Km	64 589	Currency	Lats
q Miles	24 938	Languages	Latvian, Russian
ation	2 249 000	Religions	Protestant, Roman Catholic, Russian Orthodox
l	Rīga	Organizations	EU, NATO, UN

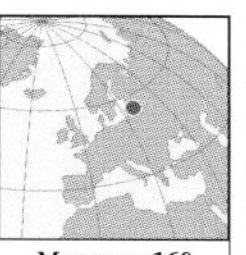
Map page 160

Latvia is in northern Europe, on the Baltic Sea and the Gulf of Riga. The land is flat near the coast but hilly with woods and lakes inland. The country has a modified continental climate. One-third of the people live in the capital, Rīga. Crop and livestock farming are important. There are few natural resources. Industries and main exports include food products, transport equipment, wood and wood products and textiles. The main trading partners are the Russian Federation and Germany. Latvia joined the European Union in May 2004.

LEBANON

Republic of Lebanon

Area Sq Km	10 452	Currency	Lebanese pound
Area Sq Miles	4 036	Languages	Arabic, Armenian, French
Population	4 224 000	Religions	Shi'a Muslim, Sunni Muslim, Christian
Capital	Beirut (Beyrouth)	Organizations	UN

Map page 150

Lebanon lies on the Mediterranean coast of southwest Asia. Beyond the coastal strip, where most of the population lives, are two parallel mountain ranges, separated by the Bekaa Valley (El Beq'a). The economy and infrastructure have been recovering since the 1975-1991 civil war crippled the traditional sectors of financial services and tourism. Italy, France and the UAE are the main trading partners.

LESOTHO

Kingdom of Lesotho

Area Sq Km	30 355	Currency	Loti, South African rand
Area Sq Miles	11 720	Languages	Sesotho, English, Zulu
Population	2 067 000	Religions	Christian, traditional beliefs
Capital	Maseru	Organizations	Comm., SADC, UN

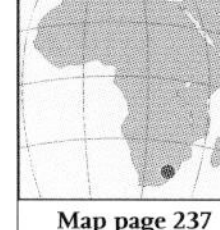
Map page 237

Lesotho is a landlocked state surrounded by the Republic of South Africa. It is a mountainous country lying within the Drakensberg mountain range. Farming and herding are the main activities. The economy depends heavily on South Africa for transport links and employment. A major hydroelectric plant completed in 1998 allows the sale of water to South Africa. Exports include manufactured goods (mainly clothing and road vehicles), food, live animals, wool and mohair.

LIBERIA

Republic of Liberia

Area Sq Km	111 369	Currency	Liberian dollar
Area Sq Miles	43 000	Languages	English, creole, local languages
Population	3 955 000	Religions	Traditional beliefs, Christian, Sunni Muslim
Capital	Monrovia	Organizations	UN

Map page 228

Liberia is on the Atlantic coast of west Africa. Beyond the coastal belt of sandy beaches and mangrove swamps the land rises to a forested plateau and highlands along the Guinea border. A quarter of the population lives along the coast. The climate is hot with heavy rainfall. Liberia is rich in mineral resources and forests. The economy is based on the production and export of basic products. Exports include diamonds, iron ore, rubber and timber. Liberia has a huge international debt and relies heavily on foreign aid.

LIBYA
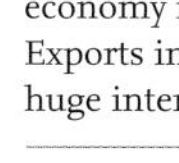
Great Socialist People's Libyan Arab Jamahiriya

Area Sq Km	1 759 540	Currency	Libyan dinar
Area Sq Miles	679 362	Languages	Arabic, Berber
Population	6 420 000	Religions	Sunni Muslim
Capital	Ṭarābulus (Tripoli)	Organizations	OPEC, UN

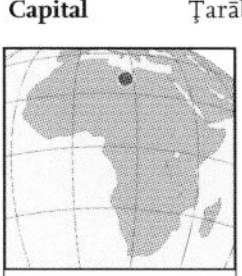
Map page 224

Libya lies on the Mediterranean coast of north Africa. The desert plains and hills of the Sahara dominate the landscape and the climate is hot and dry. Most of the population lives in cities near the coast, where the climate is cooler with moderate rainfall. Farming and herding, chiefly in the northwest, are important but the main industry is oil. Libya is a major producer, and oil accounts for virtually all of its export earnings. Italy and Germany are the main trading partners.

LIECHTENSTEIN

Principality of Liechtenstein

Area Sq Km	160	Currency	Swiss franc
Area Sq Miles	62	Languages	German
Population	36 000	Religions	Roman Catholic, Protestant
Capital	Vaduz	Organizations	UN

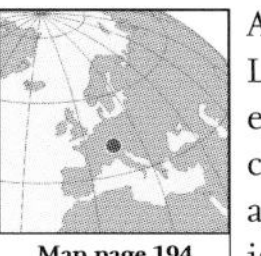
Map page 194

A landlocked state between Switzerland and Austria, Liechtenstein has an industrialized, free-enterprise economy. Low business taxes have attracted companies to establish offices which provide approximately one-third of state revenues. Banking is also important. Major products include precision instruments, ceramics and textiles.

LITHUANIA

Republic of Lithuania

Area Sq Km	65 200	Currency	Litas
Area Sq Miles	25 174	Languages	Lithuanian, Russian, Polish
Population	3 287 000	Religions	Roman Catholic, Protestant, Russian Orthodox
Capital	Vilnius	Organizations	EU, NATO, UN

Map page 160

Lithuania is in northern Europe on the eastern shores of the Baltic Sea. It is mainly lowland with many lakes, rivers and marshes. Agriculture, fishing and forestry are important, but manufacturing dominates the economy. The main exports are machinery, mineral products and chemicals. The Russian Federation and Germany are the main trading partners. Lithuania joined the European Union in May 2004.

LUXEMBOURG
Grand Duchy of Luxembourg

Area Sq Km	2 586	Currency	Euro
Area Sq Miles	998	Languages	Letzeburgish, German, French
Population	486 000	Religions	Roman Catholic
Capital	Luxembourg	Organizations	EU, NATO, OECD, UN

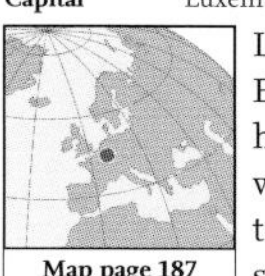
Map page 187

Luxembourg, a small landlocked country in western Europe, borders Belgium, France and Germany. The hills and forests of the Ardennes dominate the north, with rolling pasture to the south, where the main towns, farms and industries are found. The iron and steel industry is still important, but light industries (including textiles, chemicals and food products) are growing. Luxembourg is a major banking centre. Main trading partners are Belgium, Germany and France.

MACEDONIA (F.Y.R.O.M.)

Republic of Macedonia

Area Sq Km	25 713	Currency	Macedonian denar
Area Sq Miles	9 928	Languages	Macedonian, Albanian, Turkish
Population	2 042 000	Religions	Macedonian Orthodox, Sunni Muslim
Capital	Skopje	Organizations	UN

Map page 218–219

The Former Yugoslav Republic of Macedonia is a landlocked state in southern Europe. Lying within the southern Balkan Mountains, it is traversed northwest-southeast by the Vardar valley. The climate is continental. The economy is based on industry, mining and agriculture, but conflicts in the region have reduced trade and caused economic difficulties. Foreign aid and loans are now assisting in modernization and development of the country.

MADAGASCAR

Republic of Madagascar

Area Sq Km	587 041	Currency	Malagasy ariary, Malagasy franc
Area Sq Miles	226 658	Languages	Malagasy, French
Population	19 625 000	Religions	Traditional beliefs, Christian, Sunni Muslim
Capital	Antananarivo	Organizations	SADC, UN

Map page 235

Madagascar lies off the east coast of southern Africa. The world's fourth largest island, it is mainly a high plateau, with a coastal strip to the east and scrubby plain to the west. The climate is tropical, with heavy rainfall in the north and east. Most of the population lives on the plateau. Although the amount of arable land is limited, the economy is based on agriculture. The main industries are agricultural processing, textile manufacturing and oil refining. Foreign aid is important. Exports include coffee, vanilla, cotton cloth, sugar and shrimps. France is the main trading partner.

MALAWI
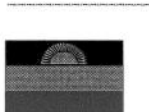
Republic of Malawi

Area Sq Km	118 484	Currency	Malawian kwacha
Area Sq Miles	45 747	Languages	Chichewa, English, local languages
Population	15 263 000	Religions	Christian, traditional beliefs, Sunni Muslim
Capital	Lilongwe	Organizations	Comm., SADC, UN

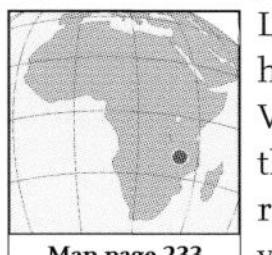
Map page 233

Landlocked Malawi in central Africa is a narrow hilly country at the southern end of the Great Rift Valley. One-fifth is covered by Lake Nyasa. Most of the population lives in rural areas in the southern regions. The climate is mainly subtropical, with varying rainfall. The economy is predominantly agricultural, with tobacco, tea and sugar the main exports. Malawi is one of the world's least developed countries and relies heavily on foreign aid. South Africa is the main trading partner.

MALAYSIA

Federation of Malaysia

Area Sq Km	332 965	Currency	Ringgit
Area Sq Miles	128 559	Languages	Malay, English, Chinese, Tamil, local languages
Population	27 468 000	Religions	Sunni Muslim, Buddhist, Hindu, Christian, traditional beliefs
Capital	Kuala Lumpur/ Putrajaya	Organizations	APEC, ASEAN, Comm., UN

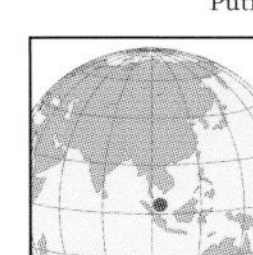
Map page 116–117

Malaysia, in southeast Asia, comprises two regions, separated by the South China Sea. The western region occupies the southern Malay Peninsula, which has a chain of mountains dividing the eastern coastal strip from wider plains to the west. East Malaysia, consisting of the states of Sabah and Sarawak in the north of the island of Borneo, is mainly rainforest-covered hills and mountains with mangrove swamps along the coast. Both regions have a tropical climate with heavy rainfall. About eighty per cent of the population lives in Peninsular Malaysia. The country is rich in natural resources and has reserves of minerals and fuels. It is an important producer of tin, oil, natural gas and tropical hardwoods. Agriculture remains a substantial part of the economy, but industry is the most important sector. The main exports are transport and electronic equipment, oil, chemicals, palm oil, wood and rubber. The main trading partners are Japan, the USA and Singapore.

MALDIVES

Republic of the Maldives

Area Sq Km	298	Currency	Rufiyaa
Area Sq Miles	115	Languages	Divehi (Maldivian)
Population	309 000	Religions	Sunni Muslim
Capital	Male	Organizations	Comm., UN

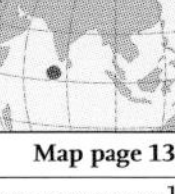
Map page 135

The Maldive archipelago comprises over a thousand coral atolls (around two hundred of which are inhabited), in the Indian Ocean, southwest of India. Over eighty per cent of the land area is less than one metre above sea level. The main atolls are North and South Male and Addu. The climate is hot, humid and monsoonal. There is little cultivation and almost all food is imported. Tourism has expanded rapidly and is the most important sector of the economy.

MALI
Republic of Mali

Area Sq Km	1 240 140	Currency	CFA franc
Area Sq Miles	478 821	Languages	French, Bambara, local languages
Population	13 010 000	Religions	Sunni Muslim, traditional beliefs, Christian
Capital	Bamako	Organizations	UN

Map page 228–229

A landlocked state in west Africa, Mali is generally low-lying. Northern regions lie within the Sahara desert. To the south are marshes and savanna grassland. Rainfall is unreliable. Most of the population lives along the Niger and Falémé rivers. Exports include cotton, livestock and gold. Mali relies heavily on foreign aid.

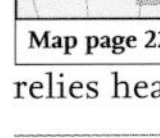

MALTA
Republic of Malta

Area Sq Km	316	Currency	Euro
Area Sq Miles	122	Languages	Maltese, English
Population	409 000	Religions	Roman Catholic
Capital	Valletta	Organizations	Comm., EU, UN

Map page 217

The islands of Malta and Gozo lie in the Mediterranean Sea, off the coast of southern Italy. The islands have hot, dry summers and mild winters. The economy depends on foreign trade, tourism and the manufacture of electronics and textiles. Main trading partners are the USA, France and Italy. Malta joined the European Union in May 2004.

MARSHALL ISLANDS
Republic of the Marshall Islands

Area Sq Km	181	Currency	United States dollar
Area Sq Miles	70	Languages	English, Marshallese
Population	62 000	Religions	Protestant, Roman Catholic
Capital	Delap-Uliga-Djarrit	Organizations	UN

Map page 97

The Marshall Islands consist of over a thousand atolls and islands in the north Pacific Ocean. The main atolls are Majuro (home to half the population), Kwajalein, Jaluit, Enewetak and Bikini. The climate is tropical. About half the workforce is employed in farming or fishing. Tourism is a small source of foreign exchange and the islands depend heavily on aid from the USA.

Martinique
French Overseas Department

Area Sq Km	1 079	Currency	Euro
Area Sq Miles	417	Languages	French, creole
Population	405 000	Religions	Roman Catholic, traditional beliefs
Capital	Fort-de-France		

Martinique, one of the Caribbean Windward Islands, has volcanic peaks in the north, a populous central plain, and hills and beaches in the south. Tourism is a major source of income, and substantial aid comes from France. The main trading partners are France and Guadeloupe.

Map page 271

MAURITANIA
Islamic Arab and African Republic of Mauritania

Area Sq Km	1 030 700	Currency	Ouguiya
Area Sq Miles	397 955	Languages	Arabic, French, local languages
Population	3 291 000	Religions	Sunni Muslim
Capital	Nouakchott	Organizations	UN

Map page 226

Mauritania is on the Atlantic coast of northwest Africa and lies almost entirely within the Sahara desert. Oases and a fertile strip along the Senegal river to the south are the only areas suitable for cultivation. The climate is generally hot and dry. About a quarter of Mauritanians live in the capital, Nouakchott. Most of the workforce depends on livestock rearing and subsistence farming. There are large deposits of iron ore which account for more than half of total exports. Mauritania's coastal waters are among the richest fishing grounds in the world. The main trading partners are France, Japan and Italy.

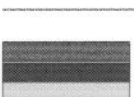

MAURITIUS
Republic of Mauritius

Area Sq Km	2 040	Currency	Mauritius rupee
Area Sq Miles	788	Languages	English, creole, Hindi, Bhojpuri, French
Population	1 288 000	Religions	Hindu, Roman Catholic, Sunni Muslim
Capital	Port Louis	Organizations	Comm., SADC, UN

Map page 239

The state comprises Mauritius, Rodrigues and some twenty small islands in the Indian Ocean, east of Madagascar. The main island of Mauritius is volcanic in origin and has a coral coast, rising to a central plateau. Most of the population lives on the north and west sides of the island. The climate is warm and humid. The economy is based on sugar production, light manufacturing (chiefly clothing) and tourism.

Mayotte
French Departmental Collectivity

Area Sq Km	373	Currency	Euro
Area Sq Miles	144	Languages	French, Mahorian
Population	194 000	Religions	Sunni Muslim, Christian
Capital	Dzaoudzi		

Lying in the Indian Ocean off the east coast of central Africa, Mayotte is geographically part of the Comoro archipelago. The economy is based on agriculture, but Mayotte depends heavily on aid from France.

Map page 239

MEXICO
United Mexican States

Area Sq Km	1 972 545	Currency	Mexican peso
Area Sq Miles	761 604	Languages	Spanish, Amerindian languages
Population	109 610 000	Religions	Roman Catholic, Protestant
Capital	México	Organizations	APEC, OECD, UN

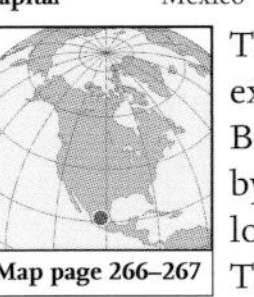
Map page 266–267

The largest country in Central America, Mexico extends south from the USA to Guatemala and Belize. Most of the country is high plateau flanked by the Sierra Madre mountains. The principal lowland is the Yucatán peninsula in the southeast. The climate is hot and humid in the lowlands, warm on the plateau and cool with cold winters in the mountains. The north is arid, while the far south has heavy rainfall. Mexico City is the second largest conurbation in the world and the country's economic centre. Agriculture involves a fifth of the workforce; crops include grains, coffee, cotton and vegetables. Mexico is rich in minerals, including copper, zinc, lead, tin, sulphur, and silver. It is one of the world's largest producers of oil, from vast reserves in the Gulf of Mexico. The oil and petrochemical industries still dominate the economy, but a variety of goods are produced, including iron and steel, motor vehicles, textiles, chemicals and food and tobacco products. Over three-quarters of all trade is with the USA.

MICRONESIA, FEDERATED STATES OF

Area Sq Km	701	Currency	United States dollar
Area Sq Miles	271	Languages	English, Chuukese, Pohnpeian, local languages
Population	111 000	Religions	Roman Catholic, Protestant
Capital	Palikir	Organizations	UN

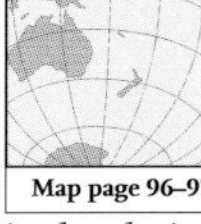
Map page 96–97

Micronesia comprises over six hundred atolls and islands of the Caroline Islands in the north Pacific Ocean. A third of the population lives on Pohnpei. The climate is tropical, with heavy rainfall. Fishing and subsistence farming are the main activities. Fish, garments and bananas are the main exports. Income is also derived from tourism and the licensing of foreign fishing fleets. The islands depend heavily on aid from the USA.

MOLDOVA
Republic of Moldova

Area Sq Km	33 700	Currency	Moldovan leu
Area Sq Miles	13 012	Languages	Romanian, Ukrainian, Gagauz, Russian
Population	3 604 000	Religions	Romanian Orthodox, Russian Orthodox
Capital	Chişinău (Kishinev)	Organizations	CIS, UN

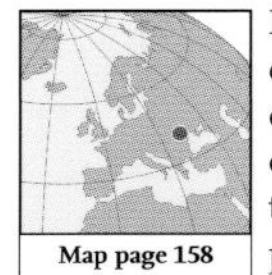
Map page 158

Moldova lies between Romania and Ukraine in eastern Europe. It consists of hilly steppe land, drained by the Prut and Dniester rivers. The economy is mainly agricultural, with sugar beet, tobacco, wine and fruit the chief products. Food processing, machinery and textiles are the main industries. The Russian Federation is the main trading partner.

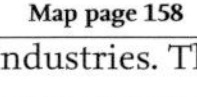

MONACO
Principality of Monaco

Area Sq Km	2	Currency	Euro
Area Sq Miles	1	Languages	French, Monégasque, Italian
Population	33 000	Religions	Roman Catholic
Capital	Monaco-Ville	Organizations	UN

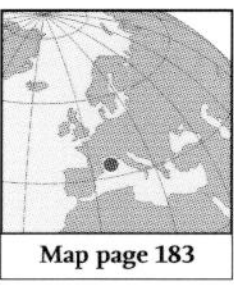
Map page 183

The principality occupies a rocky peninsula and a strip of land on France's Mediterranean coast. Monaco's economy depends on service industries (chiefly tourism, banking and finance) and light industry.

MONGOLIA

Area Sq Km	1 565 000	Currency	Tugrik (Tögrög)
Area Sq Miles	604 250	Languages	Khalka (Mongolian), Kazakh, local languages
Population	2 671 000	Religions	Buddhist, Sunni Muslim
Capital	Ulaanbaatar	Organizations	UN

Mongolia is a landlocked country in eastern Asia between the Russian Federation and China. Much of it is high steppe land, with mountains and lakes in the west and north. In the south is the Gobi Desert. Mongolia has long, cold winters and short, mild summers. A quarter of the population lives in the capital, Ulaanbaatar. Livestock breeding and agricultural processing are important. There are substantial mineral resources. Copper and textiles are the main exports.

Map page 128–129

MONTENEGRO

Area Sq Km	13 812	Currency	Euro
Area Sq Miles	5 333	Languages	Serbian (Montenegrin), Albanian
Population	624 000	Religions	Montenegrin Orthodox, Sunni Muslim
Capital	Podgorica	Organizations	UN

Map page 218

Montenegro, previously a constituent republic of the former Yugoslavia, became an independent nation in June 2006 when it opted to split from the state union of Serbia and Montenegro. Montenegro separates the much larger Serbia from the Adriatic coast. The landscape is rugged and mountainous, and the climate Mediterranean.

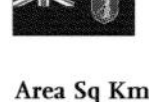

Montserrat
United Kingdom Overseas Territory

Area Sq Km	100	Currency	East Caribbean dollar
Area Sq Miles	39	Languages	English
Population	4 655	Religions	Protestant, Roman Catholic
Capital	Brades	Organizations	CARICOM

An island in the Leeward Islands group in the Lesser Antilles, in th Caribbean. From 1995 to 1997 the volcanoes in the Soufrière Hills erupted for the first time since 1630. Over sixty per cent of the isl was covered in volcanic ash and Plymouth, the capital was, virtuall destroyed. Many people emigrated, and the remaining population moved to the north of the island. Brades has replaced Plymouth as temporary capital. Reconstruction is being funded by aid from the

Map page 271

MOROCCO
Kingdom of Morocco

Area Sq Km	446 550	Currency	Moroccan dirham
Area Sq Miles	172 414	Languages	Arabic, Berber, French
Population	31 993 000	Religions	Sunni Muslim
Capital	Rabat	Organizations	UN

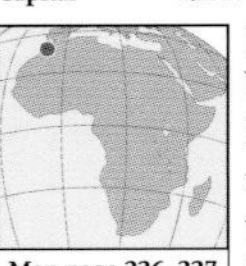
Map page 226–227

Lying in the northwest corner of Africa, Morocco h both Atlantic and Mediterranean coasts. The Atlas Mountains separate the arid south and disputed region of Western Sahara from the fertile regions o the west and north, which have a milder climate. Most Moroccans live on the Atlantic coastal plain. The economy is based on agriculture, phosphate mining and tourism; the most important industries are food processing, textile and chemicals. France is the main trading partner.

MOZAMBIQUE
Republic of Mozambique

Area Sq Km	799 380	Currency	Metical
Area Sq Miles	308 642	Languages	Portuguese, Makua, Tsonga, local languages
Population	22 894 000	Religions	Traditional beliefs, Roman Catholic, Sunni M
Capital	Maputo	Organizations	Comm., SADC, UN

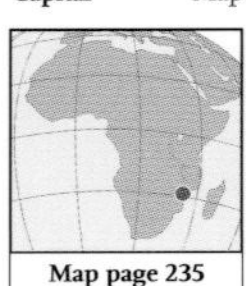
Map page 235

Mozambique lies on the east coast of southern Afric The land is mainly a savanna plateau drained by the Zambezi and Limpopo rivers, with highlands to the north. Most of the population lives on the coast or i the river valleys. In general the climate is tropical wi winter rainfall, but droughts occur. The economy is based on subsistence agriculture. Exports include shrimps, cashews, cotton and sugar, but Mozambique relies heavily on aid, and remair one of the least developed countries in the world.

MYANMAR (Burma)
Union of Myanmar

Area Sq Km	676 577	Currency	Kyat
Area Sq Miles	261 228	Languages	Burmese, Shan, Karen, local languages
Population	50 020 000	Religions	Buddhist, Christian, Sunni Muslim
Capital	Nay Pyi Taw/ Yangôn (Rangoon)	Organizations	ASEAN, UN

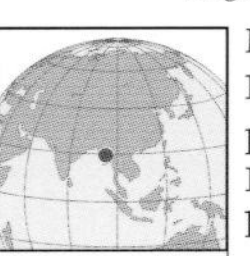
Map page 118–119

Myanmar (Burma) is in southeast Asia, bordering th Bay of Bengal and the Andaman Sea. Most of the population lives in the valley and delta of the Irrawaddy river, which is flanked by mountains and high plateaus. The climate is hot and monsoonal, an rainforest covers much of the land. Most of the workforce is employed in agriculture. Myanmar is rich in minerals, including zinc, lead, copper and silver. Political and social unrest ar lack of foreign investment have affected economic development.

NAMIBIA
Republic of Namibia

Area Sq Km	824 292	Currency	Namibian dollar
Area Sq Miles	318 261	Languages	English, Afrikaans, German, Ovambo, local langu
Population	2 171 000	Religions	Protestant, Roman Catholic
Capital	Windhoek	Organizations	Comm., SADC, UN

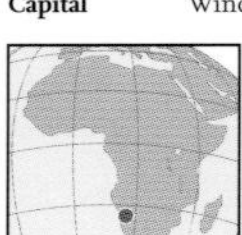
Map page 234

Namibia lies on the southern Atlantic coast of Afric Mountain ranges separate the coastal Namib Deser from the interior plateau, bordered to the south an east by the Kalahari Desert. The country is hot and dry, but some summer rain in the north supports crops and livestock. Employment is in agriculture and fishing, although the economy is based on mineral extraction diamonds, uranium, lead, zinc and silver. The economy is closely linked to the Republic of South Africa.

NAURU
Republic of Nauru

Area Sq Km	21	Currency	Australian dollar
Area Sq Miles	8	Languages	Nauruan, English
Population	10 000	Religions	Protestant, Roman Catholic
Capital	Yaren	Organizations	Comm., UN

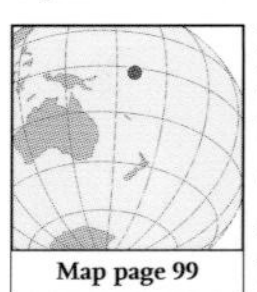
Map page 99

Nauru is a coral island near the Equator in the Pacific Ocean. It has a fertile coastal strip and a barren central plateau. The climate is tropical. The economy is based on phosphate mining, but reserves are near exhaustion and replacement of th income is a serious long-term problem.

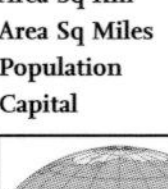

NEPAL
Federal Democratic Republic of Nepal

Area Sq Km	147 181	Currency	Nepalese rupee
Area Sq Miles	56 827	Languages	Nepali, Maithili, Bhojpuri, English, local langua
Population	29 331 000	Religions	Hindu, Buddhist, Sunni Muslim
Capital	Kathmandu	Organizations	UN

Map page 138–139

Nepal lies in the eastern Himalaya mountains betw India and China. High mountains (including Evere dominate the north. Most people live in the tempe central valleys and subtropical southern plains. The economy is based largely on agriculture and forestr There is some manufacturing, chiefly of textiles an carpets, and tourism is important. Nepal relies heavily on foreign a

NETHERLANDS

Kingdom of the Netherlands

q Km	41 526	Currency	Euro
q Miles	16 033	Languages	Dutch, Frisian
ation	16 592 000	Religions	Roman Catholic, Protestant, Sunni Muslim
l	Amsterdam/ 's-Gravenhage (The Hague)	Organizations	EU, NATO, OECD, UN

Netherlands lies on the North Sea coast of western Europe. Apart low hills in the far southeast, the land is flat and low-lying, much below sea level. The coastal region includes the delta of five rivers polders (reclaimed land), protected by sand dunes, dykes and s. The climate is temperate, with cool summers and mild winters. fall is spread evenly throughout the year. The Netherlands is a densely populated and highly urbanized country, with the majority of the population living in the cities of Amsterdam, Rotterdam and The Hague. Horticulture and dairy farming are important activities, although they employ less than four per cent of the workforce. The Netherlands ranks as the world's third agricultural rter, and is a leading producer and exporter of natural gas from ves in the North Sea. The economy is based mainly on national trade and manufacturing industry. The main industries uce food products, chemicals, machinery, electrical and electronic s and transport equipment. Germany is the main trading partner, wed by other European Union countries.

page 186–187

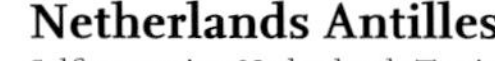

Netherlands Antilles

Self-governing Netherlands Territory

q Km	800	Currency	Netherlands Antilles guilder
q Miles	309	Languages	Dutch, Papiamento, English
ation	198 000	Religions	Roman Catholic, Protestant
l	Willemstad		

territory comprises two island groups: Curaçao and Bonaire off coast of Venezuela, and Saba, Sint Eustatius and Sint Maarten in esser Antilles. Tourism, oil refining and offshore finance are mainstays of the economy. The main trading partners are the Venezuela and Mexico. Plans were in place for the dissolution e territory in December 2008. Under these plans, which have postponed indefinitely, Curaçao and Sint Maarten will become governing Netherlands Territories, and Bonaire, Saba and Sint atius will be governed directly from the Netherlands.

p page 271

New Caledonia

French Overseas Collectivity

q Km	19 058	Currency	CFP franc
q Miles	7 358	Languages	French, local languages
ation	250 000	Religions	Roman Catholic, Protestant, Sunni Muslim
l	Nouméa		

sland group lying in the southwest Pacific, with a sub-tropical ate. New Caledonia has over one-fifth of the world's nickel rves, and the main economic activity is metal mining. Tourism so important. New Caledonia relies on aid from France.

p page 100

NEW ZEALAND

q Km	270 534	Currency	New Zealand dollar
q Miles	104 454	Languages	English, Maori
ation	4 266 000	Religions	Protestant, Roman Catholic
l	Wellington	Organizations	APEC, Comm., OECD, UN

New Zealand comprises two main islands. Both are mountainous. The North Island, with three-quarters of the population, has broad fertile valleys and a central plateau with volcanoes and hot springs. The South Island has the Southern Alps, with the Canterbury Plains the only significant lowland. The climate is perate, although South Island has colder winters. New Zealand is a ing producer of beef, lamb and mutton, and wool and dairy lucts; fruit and fish are also important. Hydroelectric and hermal power provide most energy needs. Other industries uce timber, wood pulp, iron, aluminium, machinery and nicals. Tourism is growing. Main trading partners are Australia, USA and Japan.

page 102–103

NICARAGUA

Republic of Nicaragua

q Km	130 000	Currency	Córdoba
q Miles	50 193	Languages	Spanish, Amerindian languages
ation	5 743 000	Religions	Roman Catholic, Protestant
l	Managua	Organizations	UN

Nicaragua lies at the heart of Central America, with both Pacific and Caribbean coasts. Mountain ranges separate the east, which is largely rainforest, from the more developed western regions, which include Lake Nicaragua and some active volcanoes. The highest land is in the north. The climate is tropical. Nicaragua is of the western hemisphere's poorest countries, and the economy rgely agricultural. Exports include coffee, seafood, cotton and nas. The USA is the main trading partner. Nicaragua has a huge onal debt, and relies heavily on foreign aid.

ap page 266

NIGER

Republic of Niger

q Km	1 267 000	Currency	CFA franc
q Miles	489 191	Languages	French, Hausa, Fulani, local languages
ation	15 290 000	Religions	Sunni Muslim, traditional beliefs
l	Niamey	Organizations	UN

ndlocked state of west Africa, Niger lies mostly within the Sahara rt, but with savanna in the south and in the Niger valley area. The ntains of the Massif de l'Aïr dominate central regions. Much of the country is hot and dry. The south has some summer rainfall, although droughts occur. The economy depends on subsistence farming and herding, and uranium exports, but Niger is one of the world's least developed countries and relies heavily on foreign aid. France is the main trading partner.

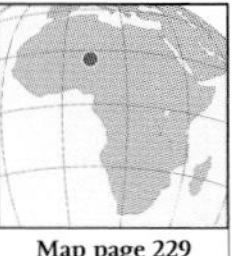

Map page 229

NIGERIA

Federal Republic of Nigeria

Area Sq Km	923 768	Currency	Naira
Area Sq Miles	356 669	Languages	English, Hausa, Yoruba, Ibo, Fulani, local languages
Population	154 729 000	Religions	Sunni Muslim, Christian, traditional beliefs
Capital	Abuja	Organizations	Comm., OPEC, UN

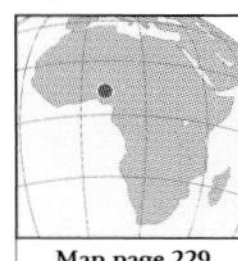

Map page 229

Nigeria is in west Africa, on the Gulf of Guinea, and is the most populous country in Africa. The Niger delta dominates coastal areas, fringed with sandy beaches, mangrove swamps and lagoons. Inland is a belt of rainforest which gives way to woodland or savanna on high plateaus. The far north is the semi-desert edge of the Sahara. The climate is tropical, with heavy summer rainfall in the south but low rainfall in the north. Most of the population lives in the coastal lowlands or in the west. About half the workforce is involved in agriculture, mainly growing subsistence crops. Agricultural production, however, has failed to keep up with demand, and Nigeria is now a net importer of food. Cocoa and rubber are the only significant export crops. The economy is heavily dependent on vast oil resources in the Niger delta and in shallow offshore waters, and oil accounts for over ninety per cent of export earnings. Nigeria also has natural gas reserves and some mineral deposits, but these are largely undeveloped. Industry involves mainly oil refining, chemicals (chiefly fertilizers), agricultural processing, textiles, steel manufacture and vehicle assembly. Political instability in the past has left Nigeria with heavy debts, poverty and unemployment.

Niue

Self-governing New Zealand Overseas Territory

Area Sq Km	258	Currency	New Zealand dollar
Area Sq Miles	100	Languages	English, Niuean
Population	1 625	Religions	Christian
Capital	Alofi		

Niue, one of the largest coral islands in the world, lies in the south Pacific Ocean about 500 kilometres (300 miles) east of Tonga. The economy depends on aid and remittances from New Zealand. The population is declining because of migration to New Zealand.

Map page 103

Norfolk Island

Australian External Territory

Area Sq Km	35	Currency	Australian dollar
Area Sq Miles	14	Languages	English
Population	2 523	Religions	Protestant, Roman Catholic
Capital	Kingston		

In the south Pacific Ocean, Norfolk Island lies between Vanuatu and New Zealand. Tourism has increased steadily and is the mainstay of the economy and provides revenues for agricultural development.

Map page 104

Northern Mariana Islands

United States Commonwealth

Area Sq Km	477	Currency	United States dollar
Area Sq Miles	184	Languages	English, Chamorro, local languages
Population	87 000	Religions	Roman Catholic
Capital	Capitol Hill		

A chain of islands in the northwest Pacific Ocean, extending over 550 kilometres (350 miles) north to south. The main island is Saipan. Tourism is a major industry, employing approximately half the workforce.

Map page 96

NORTH KOREA

Democratic People's Republic of Korea

Area Sq Km	120 538	Currency	North Korean won
Area Sq Miles	46 540	Languages	Korean
Population	23 906 000	Religions	Traditional beliefs, Chondoist, Buddhist
Capital	P'yŏngyang	Organizations	UN

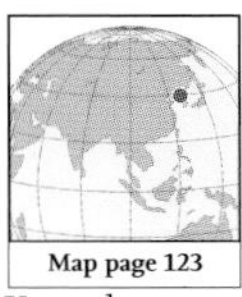

Map page 123

Occupying the northern half of the Korean peninsula in eastern Asia, North Korea is a rugged and mountainous country. The principal lowlands and the main agricultural areas are the plains in the southwest. More than half the population lives in urban areas, mainly on the coastal plains. North Korea has a continental climate, with cold, dry winters and hot, wet summers. Approximately one-third of the workforce is involved in agriculture, mainly growing food crops on cooperative farms. Various minerals, notably iron ore, are mined and are the basis of the country's heavy industries. Exports include minerals (lead, magnesite and zinc) and metal products (chiefly iron and steel). The economy declined after 1991, when ties to the former USSR and eastern bloc collapsed, and there have been serious food shortages.

NORWAY

Kingdom of Norway

Area Sq Km	323 878	Currency	Norwegian krone
Area Sq Miles	125 050	Languages	Norwegian
Population	4 812 000	Religions	Protestant, Roman Catholic
Capital	Oslo	Organizations	NATO, OECD, UN

Norway stretches along the north and west coasts of Scandinavia, from the Arctic Ocean to the North Sea. Its extensive coastline is indented with fjords and fringed with many islands. Inland, the terrain is mountainous, with coniferous forests and lakes in the south. The only major lowland areas are along the southern North Sea and Skagerrak coasts, where most of the population lives. The climate is modified by the effect of the North Atlantic Drift ocean current. Norway has vast petroleum and natural gas resources in the North Sea. It is one of western Europe's leading producers of oil and gas, and exports of oil account for approximately half of total export earnings. Related industries include engineering (oil and gas platforms) and petrochemicals. More traditional industries process local raw materials, particularly fish, timber and minerals. Agriculture is limited, but fishing and fish farming are important. Norway is the world's leading exporter of farmed salmon. Merchant shipping and tourism are major sources of foreign exchange.

Map page 162–163

OMAN

Sultanate of Oman

Area Sq Km	309 500	Currency	Omani riyal
Area Sq Miles	119 499	Languages	Arabic, Baluchi, Indian languages
Population	2 845 000	Religions	Ibadhi Muslim, Sunni Muslim
Capital	Masqaṭ (Muscat)	Organizations	UN

In southwest Asia, Oman occupies the east and southeast coasts of the Arabian Peninsula and an enclave north of the United Arab Emirates. Most of the land is desert, with mountains in the north and south. The climate is hot and mainly dry. Most of the population lives on the coastal strip on the Gulf of Oman. The majority depend on farming and fishing, but the oil and gas industries dominate the economy with around eighty per cent of export revenues coming from oil.

Map page 147

PAKISTAN

Islamic Republic of Pakistan

Area Sq Km	803 940	Currency	Pakistani rupee
Area Sq Miles	310 403	Languages	Urdu, Punjabi, Sindhi, Pushtu, English
Population	180 808 000	Religions	Sunni Muslim, Shi'a Muslim, Christian, Hindu
Capital	Islamabad	Organizations	Comm., UN

Pakistan is in the northwest part of the Indian subcontinent in south Asia, on the Arabian Sea. The east and south are dominated by the great basin of the Indus river system. This is the main agricultural area and contains most of the predominantly rural population. To the north the land rises to the mountains of the Karakoram, Hindu Kush and Himalaya mountains. The west is semi-desert plateaus and mountain ranges. The climate ranges between dry desert, and arctic tundra on the mountain tops. Temperatures are generally warm and rainfall is monsoonal. Agriculture is the main sector of the economy, employing approximately half of the workforce, and is based on extensive irrigation schemes. Pakistan is one of the world's leading producers of cotton and a major exporter of rice. Pakistan produces natural gas and has a variety of mineral deposits including coal and gold, but they are little developed. The main industries are textiles and clothing manufacture and food processing, with fabrics and ready-made clothing the leading exports. Pakistan also produces leather goods, fertilizers, chemicals, paper and precision instruments. The country depends heavily on foreign aid and remittances from workers abroad.

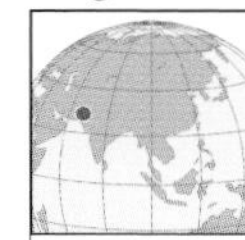

Map page 145

PALAU

Republic of Palau

Area Sq Km	497	Currency	United States dollar
Area Sq Miles	192	Languages	Palauan, English
Population	20 000	Religions	Roman Catholic, Protestant, traditional beliefs
Capital	Melekeok	Organizations	UN

Palau comprises over three hundred islands in the western Caroline Islands, in the west Pacific Ocean. The climate is tropical. The economy is based on farming, fishing and tourism, but Palau is heavily dependent on aid from the USA.

Map page 114

PANAMA

Republic of Panama

Area Sq Km	77 082	Currency	Balboa
Area Sq Miles	29 762	Languages	Spanish, English, Amerindian languages
Population	3 454 000	Religions	Roman Catholic, Protestant, Sunni Muslim
Capital	Panamá	Organizations	UN

Panama is the most southerly state in central America and has Pacific and Caribbean coasts. It is hilly, with mountains in the west and jungle near the Colombian border. The climate is tropical. Most of the population lives on the drier Pacific side. The economy is based mainly on services related to the Panama Canal: shipping, banking and tourism. Exports include bananas, shrimps, coffee, clothing and fish products. The USA is the main trading partner.

Map page 266

PAPUA NEW GUINEA

Independent State of Papua New Guinea

Area Sq Km	462 840	Currency	Kina
Area Sq Miles	178 704	Languages	English, Tok Pisin (creole), local languages
Population	6 732 000	Religions	Protestant, Roman Catholic, traditional beliefs
Capital	Port Moresby	Organizations	APEC, Comm., UN

Papua New Guinea occupies the eastern half of the island of New Guinea and includes many island groups. It has a forested and mountainous interior, bordered by swampy plains, and a tropical monsoon climate. Most of the workforce are farmers. Timber, copra, coffee and cocoa are important, but exports are dominated by minerals, chiefly gold and copper. The country depends on foreign aid. Australia, Japan and Singapore are the main trading partners.

Map page 99

PARAGUAY

Republic of Paraguay

Area Sq Km	406 752	**Currency**	Guaraní
Area Sq Miles	157 048	**Languages**	Spanish, Guaraní
Population	6 349 000	**Religions**	Roman Catholic, Protestant
Capital	Asunción	**Organizations**	UN

Map page 277

Paraguay is a landlocked country in central South America, bordering Bolivia, Brazil and Argentina. The Paraguay river separates a sparsely populated western zone of marsh and flat alluvial plains from a more developed, hilly and forested region to the east and south. The climate is subtropical. Virtually all electricity is produced by hydroelectric plants, and surplus power is exported to Brazil and Argentina. The hydroelectric dam at Itaipú is one of the largest in the world. The mainstay of the economy is agriculture and related industries. Exports include cotton, soya bean and edible oil products, timber and meat. Brazil and Argentina are the main trading partners.

PERU

Republic of Peru

Area Sq Km	1 285 216	**Currency**	Sol
Area Sq Miles	496 225	**Languages**	Spanish, Quechua, Aymara
Population	29 165 000	**Religions**	Roman Catholic, Protestant
Capital	Lima	**Organizations**	APEC, UN

Map page 276

Peru lies on the Pacific coast of South America. Most Peruvians live on the coastal strip and on the plateaus of the high Andes mountains. East of the Andes is the Amazon rainforest. The coast is temperate with low rainfall while the east is hot, humid and wet. Agriculture involves one-third of the workforce and fishing is also important. Agriculture and fishing have both been disrupted by the El Niño climatic effect in recent years. Sugar, cotton, coffee and, illegally, coca are the main cash crops. Copper and copper products, fishmeal, zinc products, coffee, petroleum and its products, and textiles are the main exports. The USA and the European Union are the main trading partners.

PHILIPPINES

Republic of the Philippines

Area Sq Km	300 000	**Currency**	Philippine peso
Area Sq Miles	115 831	**Languages**	English, Filipino, Tagalog, Cebuano, local languages
Population	91 983 000	**Religions**	Roman Catholic, Protestant, Sunni Muslim
Capital	Manila	**Organizations**	APEC, ASEAN, UN

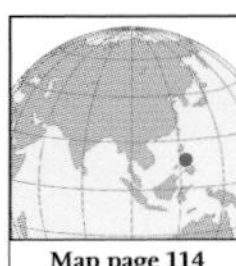

Map page 114

The Philippines, in southeast Asia, consists of over seven thousand islands and atolls lying between the South China Sea and the Pacific Ocean. The islands of Luzon and Mindanao account for two-thirds of the land area. They and nine other fairly large islands are mountainous and forested. There are active volcanoes, and earthquakes and tropical storms are common. Most of the population lives in the plains on the larger islands or on the coastal strips. The climate is hot and humid with heavy monsoonal rainfall. Rice, coconuts, sugar cane, pineapples and bananas are the main agricultural crops, and fishing is also important. Main exports are electronic equipment, machinery and transport equipment, garments and coconut products. Foreign aid and remittances from workers abroad are important to the economy, which faces problems of high population growth rate and high unemployment. The USA and Japan are the main trading partners.

Pitcairn Islands

United Kingdom Overseas Territory

Area Sq Km	45	**Currency**	New Zealand dollar
Area Sq Miles	17	**Languages**	English
Population	66	**Religions**	Protestant
Capital	Adamstown		

An island group in the southeast Pacific Ocean consisting of Pitcairn Island and three uninhabited islands. It was originally settled by mutineers from *HMS Bounty* in 1790.

Map page 97

POLAND

Polish Republic

Area Sq Km	312 683	**Currency**	Złoty
Area Sq Miles	120 728	**Languages**	Polish, German
Population	38 074 000	**Religions**	Roman Catholic, Polish Orthodox
Capital	Warszawa (Warsaw)	**Organizations**	EU, NATO, OECD, UN

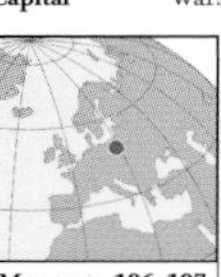

Map page 196–197

Poland lies on the Baltic coast of eastern Europe. The Oder (Odra) and Vistula (Wisła) river deltas dominate the coast. Inland, much of the country is low-lying, with woods and lakes. In the south the land rises to the Sudeten Mountains and the western part of the Carpathian Mountains, which form the borders with the Czech Republic and Slovakia respectively. The climate is continental. Around a quarter of the workforce is involved in agriculture, and exports include livestock products and sugar. The economy is heavily industrialized, with mining and manufacturing accounting for forty per cent of national income. Poland is one of the world's major producers of coal, and also produces copper, zinc, lead, sulphur and natural gas. The main industries are machinery and transport equipment, shipbuilding, and metal and chemical production. Exports include machinery and transport equipment, manufactured goods, food and live animals. Germany is the main trading partner. Poland joined the European Union in May 2004.

PORTUGAL

Portuguese Republic

Area Sq Km	88 940	**Currency**	Euro
Area Sq Miles	34 340	**Languages**	Portuguese
Population	10 707 000	**Religions**	Roman Catholic, Protestant
Capital	Lisboa (Lisbon)	**Organizations**	EU, NATO, OECD, UN

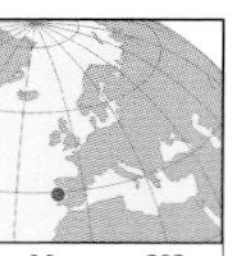

Map page 202

Portugal lies in the west of the Iberian peninsula in southwest Europe. The island groups of the Azores and Madeira are parts of Portugal. The climate in the he south is warmer, with dry, mild winters. Most Portuguese live near the coast, particularly around Lisbon (Lisboa). Agriculture, fishing and forestry involve only a tenth of the workforce: mining and manufacturing are the main economic sectors, producing kaolin, copper, tin, zinc, tungsten and salt. Exports include textiles, clothing and footwear, electrical machinery and transport equipment, cork and wood products, and chemicals. Tourism and banking are important, as are remittances from workers abroad. Most trade is with other EU countries.

PUERTO RICO

United States Commonwealth

Area Sq Km	9 104	**Currency**	United States dollar
Area Sq Miles	3 515	**Languages**	Spanish, English
Population	3 982 000	**Religions**	Roman Catholic, Protestant
Capital	San Juan		

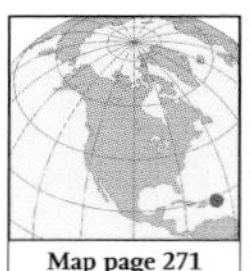

Map page 271

The Caribbean island of Puerto Rico has a forested, hilly interior, coastal plains and a tropical climate. Half of the population lives in the San Juan area. The economy is based on manufacturing (chiefly chemicals, electronics and food), tourism and agriculture. The USA is the main trading partner.

QATAR

State of Qatar

Area Sq Km	11 437	**Currency**	Qatari riyal
Area Sq Miles	4 416	**Languages**	Arabic
Population	1 409 000	**Religions**	Sunni Muslim
Capital	Ad Dawḩah (Doha)	**Organizations**	OPEC, UN

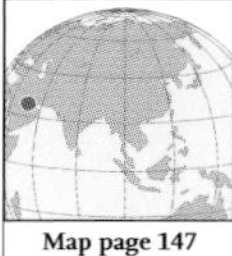

Map page 147

Qatar occupies a peninsula in southwest Asia that extends northwards from east-central Saudi Arabia into The Gulf. The land is flat and barren with sand dunes and salt pans. The climate is hot and mainly dry. Most people live in the area of the capital, Doha. The economy is heavily dependent on oil and natural gas production and the oil-refining industry. Income also comes from overseas investment. Japan is the largest trading partner.

Réunion

French Overseas Department

Area Sq Km	2 551	**Currency**	Euro
Area Sq Miles	985	**Languages**	French, creole
Population	827 000	**Religions**	Roman Catholic
Capital	St-Denis		

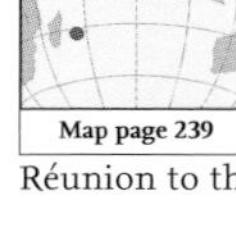

Map page 239

The Indian Ocean island of Réunion is mountainous, with coastal lowlands and a warm climate. The economy depends on tourism, French aid, and exports of sugar. In 2005 France transferred the administration of various small uninhabited islands in the seas around Madagascar from Réunion to the French Southern and Antarctic Lands.

ROMANIA

Area Sq Km	237 500	**Currency**	Romanian leu
Area Sq Miles	91 699	**Languages**	Romanian, Hungarian
Population	21 275 000	**Religions**	Romanian Orthodox, Protestant, Roman Catholic
Capital	București (Bucharest)	**Organizations**	EU, NATO, UN

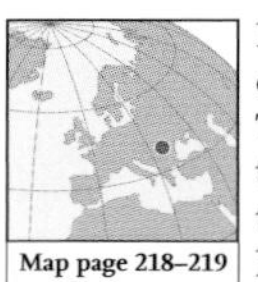

Map page 218–219

Romania lies in eastern Europe, on the northwest coast of the Black Sea. Mountains separate the Transylvanian Basin in the centre of the country from the populous plains of the east and south and from the Danube delta. The climate is continental. Romania has mineral resources (zinc, lead, silver and gold) and oil and natural gas reserves. Economic development has been slow and sporadic, but measures to accelerate change were introduced in 1999. Agriculture employs over one-third of the workforce. The main exports are textiles, mineral products, chemicals, machinery and footwear. The main trading partners are Germany and Italy.

RUSSIAN FEDERATION

Area Sq Km	17 075 400	**Currency**	Russian rouble
Area Sq Miles	6 592 849	**Languages**	Russian, Tatar, Ukrainian, local languages
Population	140 874 000	**Religions**	Russian Orthodox, Sunni Muslim, Protestant
Capital	Moskva (Moscow)	**Organizations**	APEC, CIS, UN

The Russian Federation occupies much of eastern Europe and all of northern Asia, and is the world's largest country. It borders fourteen countries to the west and south and has long coastlines on the Arctic and Pacific Oceans to the north and east. European Russia lies west of the Ural Mountains. To the south the land rises to uplands and the Caucasus mountains on the border with Georgia and Azerbaijan. East of the Urals lies the flat West Siberian Plain and the Central Siberian Plateau. In the south-east is Lake Baikal, the world's deepest lake, and the Sayan ranges on the border with Kazakhstan and Mongolia. Eastern Siberia is rugged and mountainous, with many active volcanoes in the Kamchatka Peninsula. The country's major rivers are the Volga in the west and the Ob', Irtysh, Yenisey, Lena and Amur in Siberia. The climate and vegetation range between arctic tundra in the north and semi-arid steppe towards the Black and Caspian Sea coasts in the south. In general, the climate is continental with extreme temperatures. The majority of the population (the eighth largest in the world), and industry and agriculture are concentrated in European Russia. The economy is dependent on exploitation of raw materials and on heavy industry. Russia has a wealth of mineral resources,

Map page 152–153

although they are often difficult to exploit because of climate and remote locations. It is one of the world's leading producers of petroleum, natural gas and coal as well as iron ore, nickel, copper, bauxite, and many precious and rare metals. Forests cover over forty per cent of the land area and supply an important timber, paper and pulp industry. Approximately eight per cent of the land is suitable for cultivation, but farming is generally inefficient and food, especially grains, must be imported. Fishing is important and Russia has a large fleet operating around the world. The transition to a market economy has been slow and difficult, with considerable underemployment. As well as mining and extractive industries there is a wide range of manufacturing industry, from steel mills to aircraft and space vehicles, shipbuilding, synthetic fabrics, plastics, cotton fabrics, consumer durables, chemicals and fertilizers. Exports include fuels, metals, machinery, chemicals and forest products. The most important trading partners include Germany, the USA and Belarus.

RWANDA

Republic of Rwanda

Area Sq Km	26 338	**Currency**	Rwandan franc
Area Sq Miles	10 169	**Languages**	Kinyarwanda, French, English
Population	9 998 000	**Religions**	Roman Catholic, traditional beliefs, Protestant
Capital	Kigali	**Organizations**	UN

Rwanda, the most densely populated country in Africa, is situated in the mountains and plateaus to the east of the western branch of the Great Rift Valley in east Africa. The climate is warm with a summer dry season. Rwanda depends on subsistence farming, coffee and tea exports, light industry and foreign aid. The country is slowly recovering from serious internal conflict which caused devastation in the early 1990s.

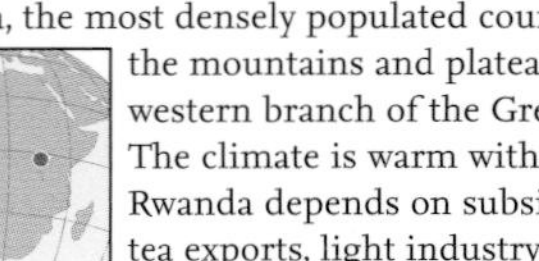

Map page 233

Saba part of Netherlands Antilles

Area Sq Km (Miles) 13 (5)	**Population** 1 524	**Capital** Bottom

An island in the Leeward Islands in the Lesser Antilles, in the Caribbean to the south of St-Martin.

Map page 271

St-Barthélemy French Overseas Collectivity

Area Sq Km	21	**Currency**	Euro
Area Sq Miles	8	**Languages**	French
Population	8 450	**Religions**	Roman Catholic
Capital	Gustavia		

An island in the Leeward Islands in the Lesser Antilles, in the Caribbean south of St-Martin. Tourism is the main economic activity.

Map page 271

St Helena

United Kingdom Overseas Territory

Area Sq Km	121	**Currency**	St Helena pound
Area Sq Miles	47	**Languages**	English
Population	4 255	**Religions**	Protestant, Roman Catholic
Capital	Jamestown		

St Helena and its dependencies Ascension and Tristan da Cunha are isolated island groups lying in the south Atlantic Ocean. St Helena is a rugged island of volcanic origin. The main activity is fishing, but the economy relies on financial aid from the UK. Main trading partners are the UK and South Africa.

Map page 238

ST KITTS AND NEVIS

Federation of St Kitts and Nevis

Area Sq Km	261	**Currency**	East Caribbean dollar
Area Sq Miles	101	**Languages**	English, creole
Population	52 000	**Religions**	Protestant, Roman Catholic
Capital	Basseterre	**Organizations**	CARICOM, Comm., UN

Map page 271

St Kitts and Nevis are in the Leeward Islands, in the Caribbean. Both volcanic islands are mountainous and forested, with sandy beaches and a warm, wet climate. About three-quarters of the population lives on St Kitts. Agriculture is the main activity, with sugar the main product. Tourism and manufacturing (chiefly garment and electronic components) and offshore banking are important activi

ST LUCIA

Area Sq Km	616	**Currency**	East Caribbean dollar
Area Sq Miles	238	**Languages**	English, creole
Population	172 000	**Religions**	Roman Catholic, Protestant
Capital	Castries	**Organizations**	CARICOM, Comm., UN

St Lucia, one of the Windward Islands in the Caribbean Sea, is a volcanic island with forested mountains, hot springs, sandy beaches and a wet tropical climate. Agriculture is the main activity, with bananas accounting for approximately forty per cent of export earnings. Tourism, agricultural processing and light manufacturing are increasingly important.

Map page 271

St-Martin French Overseas Collectivity

Area Sq Km	54	**Currency**	Euro
Area Sq Miles	21	**Languages**	French
Population	35 692	**Religions**	Roman Catholic
Capital	Marigot		

The northern part of one of the Leeward Islands, in the Caribbean. The other part of the island is part of the Netherlands Antilles (Sint Maarten). Tourism is the main source of income.

Map page 271

St Pierre and Miquelon
French Territorial Collectivity

q Km	242	Currency	Euro
q Miles	93	Languages	French
ation	6 125	Religions	Roman Catholic
l	St-Pierre		

oup of islands off the south coast of Newfoundland in eastern ıda. The islands are largely unsuitable for agriculture, and fishing fish processing are the most important activities. The islands rely ily on financial assistance from France.

ıp page 249

ST VINCENT AND THE GRENADINES

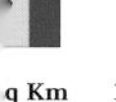

q Km	389	Currency	East Caribbean dollar
q Miles	150	Languages	English, creole
ation	109 000	Religions	Protestant, Roman Catholic
l	Kingstown	Organizations	CARICOM, Comm., UN

incent, whose territory includes islets and cays in the Grenadines, the Windward Islands, in the Caribbean. St Vincent itself is forested and mountainous, with an active volcano, Soufrière. The climate is tropical and wet. The economy is based mainly on agriculture and tourism. Bananas account for approximately one-third of export earnings and arrowroot is also important. Most trade is with the USA and other CARICOM countries.

ıp page 271

SAMOA
Independent State of Samoa

q Km	2 831	Currency	Tala
q Miles	1 093	Languages	Samoan, English
ation	179 000	Religions	Protestant, Roman Catholic
l	Apia	Organizations	Comm., UN

Samoa consists of two larger mountainous and forested islands, Savai'i and Upolu, and seven smaller islands, in the south Pacific Ocean. Over half the population lives on Upolu. The climate is tropical. The economy is based on agriculture, with some fishing and light manufacturing. Traditional exports are ›nut products, fish and beer. Tourism is increasing, but the islands ›nd on workers' remittances and foreign aid.

ıp page 100

SAN MARINO
Republic of San Marino

q Km	61	Currency	Euro
q Miles	24	Languages	Italian
ation	31 000	Religions	Roman Catholic
l	San Marino	Organizations	UN

Landlocked San Marino lies in northeast Italy. A third of the people live in the capital. There is some agriculture and light industry, but most income comes from tourism. Italy is the main trading partner.

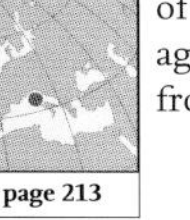

ıp page 213

SÃO TOMÉ AND PRÍNCIPE
Democratic Republic of São Tomé and Príncipe

q Km	964	Currency	Dobra
q Miles	372	Languages	Portuguese, creole
ation	163 000	Religions	Roman Catholic, Protestant
l	São Tomé	Organizations	UN

The two main islands and adjacent islets lie off the coast of west Africa in the Gulf of Guinea. São Tomé is the larger island, with over ninety per cent of the population. Both São Tomé and Príncipe are mountainous and tree-covered, and have a hot and humid climate. The economy is heavily dependent on oa, which accounts for around ninety per cent of export earnings.

ıp page 229

SAUDI ARABIA
Kingdom of Saudi Arabia

q Km	2 200 000	Currency	Saudi Arabian riyal
q Miles	849 425	Languages	Arabic
ation	25 721 000	Religions	Sunni Muslim, Shi'a Muslim
l	Ar Riyāḍ (Riyadh)	Organizations	OPEC, UN

Saudi Arabia occupies most of the Arabian Peninsula in southwest Asia. The terrain is desert or semi-desert plateaus, which rise to mountains running parallel to the Red Sea in the west and slope down to plains in the southeast and along The Gulf in the east. Over eighty per cent of the population lives in urban areas. There around four million foreign workers in Saudi Arabia, employed nly in the oil and service industries. Summers are hot, winters are m and rainfall is low. Saudi Arabia has the world's largest reserves il and significant natural gas reserves, both onshore and in The f. Crude oil and refined products account for over ninety per cent xport earnings. Other industries and irrigated agriculture are ıg encouraged, but most food and raw materials are imported. di Arabia has important banking and commercial interests. Japan the USA are the main trading partners.

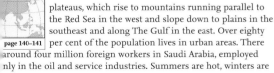

page 140–141

SENEGAL
Republic of Senegal

q Km	196 720	Currency	CFA franc
q Miles	75 954	Languages	French, Wolof, Fulani, local languages
lation	12 534 000	Religions	Sunni Muslim, Roman Catholic, traditional beliefs
tal	Dakar	Organizations	UN

egal lies on the Atlantic coast of west Africa. The north is arid i-desert, while the south is mainly fertile savanna bushland. The ıate is tropical with summer rains, although droughts occur.

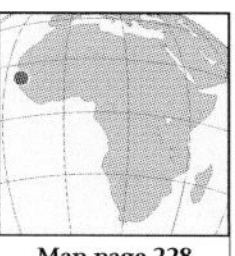

One-fifth of the population lives in and around Dakar, the capital and main port. Fish, groundnuts and phosphates are the main exports. France is the main trading partner.

Map page 228

SERBIA
Republic of Serbia

Area Sq Km	77 453	Currency	Serbian dinar
Area Sq Miles	29 904	Languages	Serbian, Hungarian
Population	9 850 000	Religions	Serbian Orthodox, Roman Catholic, Sunni Muslim
Capital	Beograd (Belgrade)	Organizations	UN

Following ethnic conflict and the break-up of Yugoslavia through the 1990s, the state union of Serbia and Montenegro retained the name Yugoslavia until 2003. The two then became separate independent countries in 2006. The southern Serbian province of Kosovo declared its independence from Serbia in February 2008. The landscape is rugged, mountainous and forested in the south, while the north is low-lying and drained by the Danube river system.

Map page 218–219

SEYCHELLES
Republic of the Seychelles

Area Sq Km	455	Currency	Seychelles rupee
Area Sq Miles	176	Languages	English, French, creole
Population	84 000	Religions	Roman Catholic, Protestant
Capital	Victoria	Organizations	Comm., SADC, UN

The Seychelles comprises an archipelago of over one hundred granitic and coral islands in the western Indian Ocean. Over ninety per cent of the population lives on the main island, Mahé. The climate is hot and humid with heavy rainfall. The economy is based mainly on tourism, fishing and light manufacturing.

Map page 239

SIERRA LEONE
Republic of Sierra Leone

Area Sq Km	71 740	Currency	Leone
Area Sq Miles	27 699	Languages	English, creole, Mende, Temne, local languages
Population	5 696 000	Religions	Sunni Muslim, traditional beliefs
Capital	Freetown	Organizations	Comm., UN

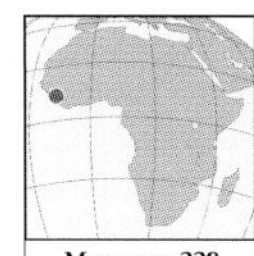

Sierra Leone lies on the Atlantic coast of west Africa. Its coastline is heavily indented and is lined with mangrove swamps. Inland is a forested area rising to savanna plateaus, with mountains to the northeast. The climate is tropical and rainfall is heavy. Most of the workforce is involved in subsistence farming. Cocoa and coffee are the main cash crops. Diamonds and rutile (titanium ore) are the main exports. Sierra Leone is one of the world's poorest countries, and the economy relies on substantial foreign aid.

Map page 228

SINGAPORE
Republic of Singapore

Area Sq Km	639	Currency	Singapore dollar
Area Sq Miles	247	Languages	Chinese, English, Malay, Tamil
Population	4 737 000	Religions	Buddhist, Taoist, Sunni Muslim, Christian, Hindu
Capital	Singapore	Organizations	APEC, ASEAN, Comm., UN

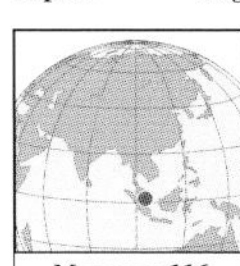

The state comprises the main island of Singapore and over fifty other islands, lying off the southern tip of the Malay Peninsula in southeast Asia. Singapore is generally low-lying and includes land reclaimed from swamps and the sea. It is hot and humid, with heavy rainfall throughout the year. There are fish farms and vegetable gardens in the north and east of the island, but most food is imported. Singapore also lacks mineral and energy resources. Manufacturing industries and services are the main sectors of the economy. Their rapid development has fuelled the nation's impressive economic growth during recent decades. Main industries include electronics, oil refining, chemicals, pharmaceuticals, ship repair, food processing and textiles. Singapore is also a major financial centre. Its port is one of the world's largest and busiest and acts as an entrepôt for neighbouring states. Tourism is also important. Japan, the USA and Malaysia are the main trading partners.

Map page 116

Sint Eustatius part of Netherlands Antilles

Area Sq Km (Miles) 21 (8) **Population** 2 754 **Capital** Oranjestad

An island in the Leeward Islands, in the Caribbean south of St-Martin (Sint Maarten). It has a developing tourism industry.

Map page 271

Sint Maarten part of Netherlands Antilles

Area Sq Km (Miles) 34 (13) **Population** 40 007 **Capital** Philipsburg

The southern part of one of the Leeward Islands, in the Caribbean; the other part of the island is a dependency of France. Tourism and fishing are the most important industries.

Map page 271

SLOVAKIA
Slovak Republic

Area Sq Km	49 035	Currency	Euro
Area Sq Miles	18 933	Languages	Slovak, Hungarian, Czech
Population	5 406 000	Religions	Roman Catholic, Protestant, Orthodox
Capital	Bratislava	Organizations	EU, NATO, OECD, UN

A landlocked country in central Europe, Slovakia is mountainous in the north, but low-lying in the southwest. The climate is continental. There is a range of manufacturing industries, and the main exports are machinery and transport equipment, but in recent years there have been economic difficulties and growth has been slow. Slovakia joined the European Union in May 2004. Most trade is with other EU countries, especially the Czech Republic.

Map page 198–199

SLOVENIA
Republic of Slovenia

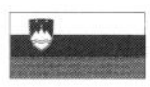

Area Sq Km	20 251	Currency	Euro
Area Sq Miles	7 819	Languages	Slovene, Croatian, Serbian
Population	2 020 000	Religions	Roman Catholic, Protestant
Capital	Ljubljana	Organizations	EU, NATO, UN

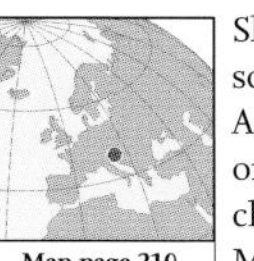

Slovenia lies in the northwest Balkan Mountains of southern Europe and has a short coastline on the Adriatic Sea. It is mountainous and hilly, with lowlands on the coast and in the Sava and Drava river valleys. The climate is generally continental inland and Mediterranean nearer the coast. The main agricultural products are potatoes, grain and sugar beet; the main industries include metal processing, electronics and consumer goods. Trade has been re-orientated towards western markets and the main trading partners are Germany and Italy. Slovenia joined the European Union in May 2004.

Map page 210

SOLOMON ISLANDS

Area Sq Km	28 370	Currency	Solomon Islands dollar
Area Sq Miles	10 954	Languages	English, creole, local languages
Population	523 000	Religions	Protestant, Roman Catholic
Capital	Honiara	Organizations	Comm., UN

The state consists of the Solomon, Santa Cruz and Shortland Islands in the southwest Pacific Ocean. The six main islands are volcanic, mountainous and forested, although Guadalcanal, the most populous, has a large lowland area. The climate is generally hot and humid. Subsistence farming, forestry and fishing predominate. Exports include timber products, fish, copra and palm oil. The islands depend on foreign aid.

Map page 100

SOMALIA
Somali Republic

Area Sq Km	637 657	Currency	Somali shilling
Area Sq Miles	246 201	Languages	Somali, Arabic
Population	9 133 000	Religions	Sunni Muslim
Capital	Muqdisho (Mogadishu)	Organizations	UN

Somalia is in northeast Africa, on the Gulf of Aden and Indian Ocean. It consists of a dry scrubby plateau, rising to highlands in the north. The climate is hot and dry, but coastal areas and the Jubba and Webi Shabeelle river valleys support crops and most of the population. Subsistence farming and livestock rearing are the main activities. Exports include livestock and bananas. Frequent drought and civil war have prevented economic development. Somalia is one of the poorest, most unstable and least developed countries in the world.

Map page 232

SOUTH AFRICA, REPUBLIC OF

Area Sq Km	1 219 090	Currency	Rand
Area Sq Miles	470 689	Languages	Afrikaans, English, nine other official languages
Population	50 110 000	Religions	Protestant, Roman Catholic, Sunni Muslim, Hindu
Capital	Pretoria (Tshwane)/ Cape Town	Organizations	Comm., SADC, UN

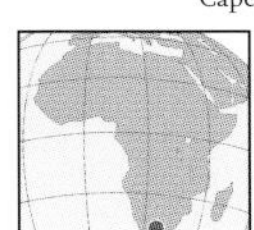

The Republic of South Africa occupies most of the southern part of Africa. It surrounds Lesotho and has a long coastline on the Atlantic and Indian Oceans. Much of the land is a vast plateau, covered with grassland or bush and drained by the Orange and Limpopo river systems. A fertile coastal plain rises to mountain ridges in the south and east, including Table Mountain near Cape Town and the Drakensberg range in the east. Gauteng is the most populous province, with Johannesburg and Pretoria its main cities. South Africa has warm summers and mild winters. Most of the country has the majority of its rainfall in summer, but the coast around Cape Town has winter rains. South Africa has the largest economy in Africa, although wealth is unevenly distributed and unemployment is very high. Agriculture employs approximately one-third of the workforce, and produce includes fruit, wine, wool and maize. The country is the world's leading producer of gold and chromium and an important producer of diamonds. Many other minerals are also mined. The main industries are mineral and food processing, chemicals, electrical equipment, textiles and motor vehicles. Financial services are also important.

Map page 234–235

SOUTH KOREA
Republic of Korea

Area Sq Km	99 274	Currency	South Korean won
Area Sq Miles	38 330	Languages	Korean
Population	48 333 000	Religions	Buddhist, Protestant, Roman Catholic
Capital	Sŏul (Seoul)	Organizations	APEC, OECD, UN

The state consists of the southern half of the Korean Peninsula in eastern Asia and many islands lying off the western and southern coasts in the Yellow Sea. The terrain is mountainous, although less rugged than that of North Korea. Population density is high and the country is highly urbanized; most of the population lives on the western coastal plains and in the river basins of the Han-gang in the northwest and the Naktong-gang in the southeast. The climate is continental, with hot, wet summers and dry, cold winters. Arable land is limited by the mountainous terrain, but because of intensive farming South Korea is nearly self-sufficient in food. Sericulture (silk) is important, as is fishing, which contributes to exports. South Korea has few mineral resources, except for coal and tungsten. It has

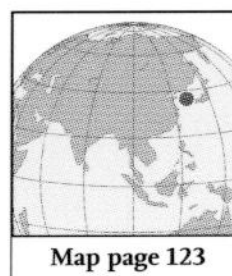
Map page 123

achieved high economic growth based mainly on export manufacturing. The main manufactured goods are cars, electronic and electrical goods, ships, steel, chemicals and toys, as well as textiles, clothing, footwear and food products. The USA and Japan are the main trading partners.

SPAIN

Kingdom of Spain

Area Sq Km	504 782	**Currency**	Euro
Area Sq Miles	194 897	**Languages**	Castilian, Catalan, Galician, Basque
Population	44 904 000	**Religions**	Roman Catholic
Capital	Madrid	**Organizations**	EU, NATO, OECD, UN

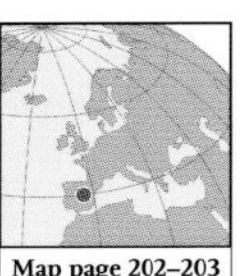
Map page 202–203

Spain occupies the greater part of the Iberian peninsula in southwest Europe, with coastlines on the Atlantic Ocean and Mediterranean Sea. It includes the Balearic Islands in the Mediterranean, the Canary Islands in the Atlantic, and two enclaves in north Africa (Ceuta and Melilla). Much of the mainland is a high plateau drained by the Douro (Duero), Tagus (Tajo) and Guadiana rivers. The plateau is interrupted by a low mountain range and bounded to the east and north also by mountains, including the Pyrenees, which form the border with France and Andorra. The main lowland areas are the Ebro basin in the northeast, the eastern coastal plains and the Guadalquivir basin in the southwest. Over three-quarters of the population lives in urban areas. The plateau experiences hot summers and cold winters. Conditions are cooler and wetter to the north, and warmer and drier to the south. Agriculture involves about ten per cent of the workforce, and fruit, vegetables and wine are exported. Fishing is an important industry, and Spain has a large fishing fleet. Mineral resources include lead, copper, mercury and fluorspar. Some oil is produced, but Spain has to import most energy needs. The economy is based mainly on manufacturing and services. The principal products are machinery, transport equipment, motor vehicles and food products, with a wide variety of other manufactured goods. With approximately fifty million visitors a year, tourism is a major industry. Banking and commerce are also important. Approximately seventy per cent of trade is with other European Union countries.

SRI LANKA

Democratic Socialist Republic of Sri Lanka

Area Sq Km	65 610	**Currency**	Sri Lankan rupee
Area Sq Miles	25 332	**Languages**	Sinhalese, Tamil, English
Population	20 238 000	**Religions**	Buddhist, Hindu, Sunni Muslim, Roman Catholic
Capital	Sri Jayewardenepura Kotte	**Organizations**	Comm., UN

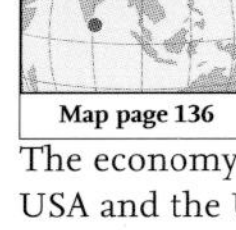
Map page 136

Sri Lanka lies in the Indian Ocean off the southeast coast of India in south Asia. It has rolling coastal plains, with mountains in the centre-south. The climate is hot and monsoonal. Most people live on the west coast. Manufactures (chiefly textiles and clothing), tea, rubber, copra and gems are exported. The economy relies on foreign aid and workers' remittances. The USA and the UK are the main trading partners.

SUDAN

Republic of the Sudan

Area Sq Km	2 505 813	**Currency**	Sudanese pound (Sudani)
Area Sq Miles	967 500	**Languages**	Arabic, Dinka, Nubian, Beja, Nuer, local languages
Population	42 272 000	**Religions**	Sunni Muslim, traditional beliefs, Christian
Capital	Khartoum	**Organizations**	UN

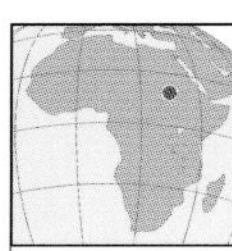
Map page 224–225

Africa's largest country, the Sudan is in the northeast of the continent, on the Red Sea. It lies within the upper Nile basin, much of which is arid plain but with swamps to the south. Mountains lie to the northeast, west and south. The climate is hot and arid with light summer rainfall, and droughts occur. Most people live along the Nile and are farmers and herders. Cotton, gum arabic, livestock and other agricultural products are exported. The government is working with foreign investors to develop oil resources, but civil war in the south continues to restrict the growth of the economy. Main trading partners are Saudi Arabia, China and Libya.

SURINAME

Republic of Suriname

Area Sq Km	163 820	**Currency**	Suriname guilder
Area Sq Miles	63 251	**Languages**	Dutch, Surinamese, English, Hindi
Population	520 000	**Religions**	Hindu, Roman Catholic, Protestant, Sunni Muslim
Capital	Paramaribo	**Organizations**	CARICOM, UN

Map page 275

Suriname, on the Atlantic coast of northern South America, consists of a swampy coastal plain (where most of the population lives), central plateaus, and highlands in the south. The climate is tropical, and rainforest covers much of the land. Bauxite mining is the main industry, and alumina and aluminium are the chief exports, with shrimps, rice, bananas and timber also exported. The main trading partners are the Netherlands, Norway and the USA.

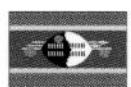

SWAZILAND

Kingdom of Swaziland

Area Sq Km	17 364	**Currency**	Emalangeni, South African rand
Area Sq Miles	6 704	**Languages**	Swazi, English
Population	1 185 000	**Religions**	Christian, traditional beliefs
Capital	Mbabane	**Organizations**	Comm., SADC, UN

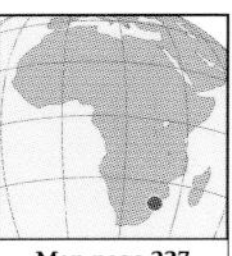
Map page 237

Landlocked Swaziland in southern Africa lies between Mozambique and the Republic of South Africa. Savanna plateaus descend from mountains in the west towards hill country in the east. The climate is subtropical, but temperate in the mountains. Subsistence farming predominates. Asbestos and diamonds are mined. Exports include sugar, fruit and wood pulp. Tourism and workers' remittances are important to the economy. Most trade is with South Africa.

SWEDEN

Kingdom of Sweden

Area Sq Km	449 964	**Currency**	Swedish krona
Area Sq Miles	173 732	**Languages**	Swedish
Population	9 249 000	**Religions**	Protestant, Roman Catholic
Capital	Stockholm	**Organizations**	EU, OECD, UN

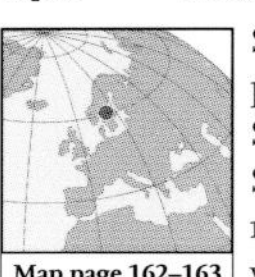
Map page 162–163

Sweden occupies the eastern part of the Scandinavian peninsula in northern Europe and borders the Baltic Sea, the Gulf of Bothnia, and the Kattegat and Skagerrak, connecting with the North Sea. Forested mountains cover the northern half, part of which lies within the Arctic Circle. The southern part of the country is a lowland lake region where most of the population lives. Sweden has warm summers and cold winters, which are more severe in the north. Natural resources include coniferous forests, mineral deposits and water resources. Some dairy products, meat, cereals and vegetables are produced in the south. The forests supply timber for export and for the important pulp, paper and furniture industries. Sweden is an important producer of iron ore and copper. Zinc, lead, silver and gold are also mined. Machinery and transport equipment, chemicals, pulp and wood, and telecommunications equipment are the main exports. The majority of trade is with other European Union countries.

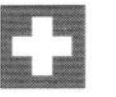

SWITZERLAND

Swiss Confederation

Area Sq Km	41 293	**Currency**	Swiss franc
Area Sq Miles	15 943	**Languages**	German, French, Italian, Romansch
Population	7 568 000	**Religions**	Roman Catholic, Protestant
Capital	Bern (Berne)	**Organizations**	OECD, UN

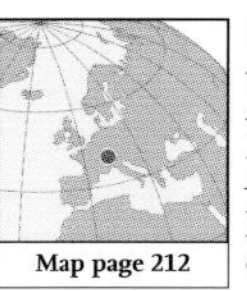
Map page 212

Switzerland is a mountainous landlocked country in west central Europe. The southern regions lie within the Alps, while the northwest is dominated by the Jura mountains. The rest of the land is a high plateau, where most of the population lives. The climate varies greatly, depending on altitude and relief, but in general summers are mild and winters are cold with heavy snowfalls. Switzerland has one of the highest standards of living in the world, yet it has few mineral resources, and most food and industrial raw materials are imported. Manufacturing makes the largest contribution to the economy. Engineering is the most important industry, producing precision instruments and heavy machinery. Other important industries are chemicals and pharmaceuticals. Banking and financial services are very important, and Zürich is one of the world's leading banking cities. Tourism, and international organizations based in Switzerland, are also major foreign currency earners. Germany is the main trading partner.

SYRIA

Syrian Arab Republic

Area Sq Km	185 180	**Currency**	Syrian pound
Area Sq Miles	71 498	**Languages**	Arabic, Kurdish, Armenian
Population	21 906 000	**Religions**	Sunni Muslim, Shi'a Muslim, Christian
Capital	Dimashq (Damascus)	**Organizations**	UN

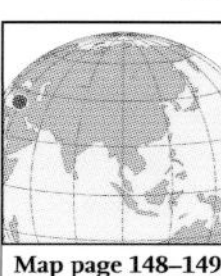
Map page 148–149

Syria is in southwest Asia, has a short coastline on the Mediterranean Sea, and stretches inland to a plateau traversed northwest-southeast by the Euphrates river. Mountains flank the southwest borders with Lebanon and Israel. The climate is Mediterranean in coastal regions, hotter and drier inland. Most Syrians live on the coast or in the river valleys. Cotton, cereals and fruit are important products, but the main exports are petroleum and related products, and textiles.

TAIWAN

Area Sq Km	36 179	**Currency**	Taiwan dollar
Area Sq Miles	13 969	**Languages**	Mandarin, Min, Hakka, local languages
Population	23 046 000	**Religions**	Buddhist, Taoist, Confucian, Christian
Capital	T'aipei	**Organizations**	APEC

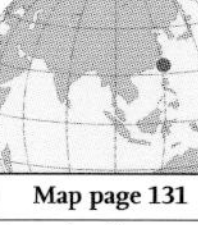
Map page 131

The east Asian state consists of the island of Taiwan, separated from mainland China by the Taiwan Strait, and several much smaller islands. Much of Taiwan is mountainous and forested. Densely populated coastal plains in the west contain the bulk of the population and most economic activity. Taiwan has a tropical monsoon climate, with warm, wet summers and mild winters. Agriculture is highly productive. The country is virtually self-sufficient in food and exports some products. Coal, oil and natural gas are produced and a few minerals are mined, but none of them are of great significance to the economy. Taiwan depends heavily on imports of raw materials and exports of manufactured goods. The main manufactures are electrical and electronic goods, including television sets, personal computers and calculators, textiles, fertilizers, clothing, footwear and toys. The main trading partners are the USA, Japan and Germany. The People's Republic of China claims Taiwan as its 23rd Province.

TAJIKISTAN

Republic of Tajikistan

Area Sq Km	143 100	**Currency**	Somoni
Area Sq Miles	55 251	**Languages**	Tajik, Uzbek, Russian
Population	6 952 000	**Religions**	Sunni Muslim
Capital	Dushanbe	**Organizations**	CIS, UN

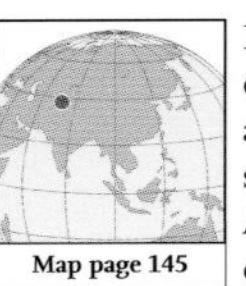
Map page 145

Landlocked Tajikistan in central Asia is a mountaino country, dominated by the mountains of the Alai Ra and the Pamir. In the less mountainous western area summers are warm, although winters are cold. Agriculture is the main sector of the economy, chiefl cotton growing and cattle breeding. Mineral deposits include lead, zinc, and uranium. Processed metals, textiles and cloth are the main manufactured goods; the main exports are aluminium cotton. Uzbekistan, Kazakhstan and the Russian Federation are the main trading partners.

TANZANIA

United Republic of Tanzania

Area Sq Km	945 087	**Currency**	Tanzanian shilling
Area Sq Miles	364 900	**Languages**	Swahili, English, Nyamwezi, local languages
Population	43 739 000	**Religions**	Shi'a Muslim, Sunni Muslim, traditional belie Christian
Capital	Dodoma	**Organizations**	Comm., SADC, UN

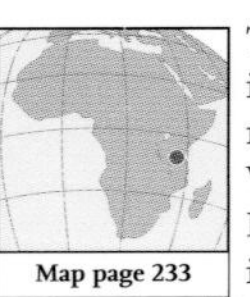
Map page 233

Tanzania lies on the coast of east Africa and includes t island of Zanzibar in the Indian Ocean. Most of the mainland is a savanna plateau lying east of the Great Valley. In the north, near the border with Kenya, is Kilimanjaro, the highest mountain in Africa. The clim is tropical. The economy is predominantly based on agriculture, which employs an estimated ninety per cent of the workfc Agricultural processing and gold and diamond mining are the main industries, although tourism is growing. Coffee, cotton, cashew nuts a tobacco are the main exports, with cloves from Zanzibar. Most export trade is with India and the UK. Tanzania depends heavily on foreign a

THAILAND

Kingdom of Thailand

Area Sq Km	513 115	**Currency**	Baht
Area Sq Miles	198 115	**Languages**	Thai, Lao, Chinese, Malay, Mon-Khmer langua
Population	67 764 000	**Religions**	Buddhist, Sunni Muslim
Capital	Bangkok (Krung Thep)	**Organizations**	APEC, ASEAN, UN

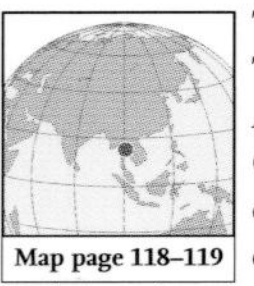
Map page 118–119

The largest country in the Indo-China peninsula, Thailand has coastlines on the Gulf of Thailand and Andaman Sea. Central Thailand is dominated by the Chao Phraya river basin, which contains Bangkok, th capital city and centre of most economic activity. To east is a dry plateau drained by tributaries of the Mekong river, while to the north, west and south, extending down n of the Malay peninsula, are forested hills and mountains. Many sma islands line the coast. The climate is hot, humid and monsoonal. Ab half the workforce is involved in agriculture. Fishing and fish processing are important. Thailand produces natural gas, some oil a lignite, minerals (chiefly tin, tungsten and baryte) and gemstones. Manufacturing is the largest contributor to national income, with electronics, textiles, clothing and footwear, and food processing the main industries. With around seven million visitors a year, tourism the major source of foreign exchange. Thailand is one of the world's leading exporters of rice and rubber, and a major exporter of maize tapioca. Japan and the USA are the main trading partners.

TOGO

Republic of Togo

Area Sq Km	56 785	**Currency**	CFA franc
Area Sq Miles	21 925	**Languages**	French, Ewe, Kabre, local languages
Population	6 619 000	**Religions**	Traditional beliefs, Christian, Sunni Muslim
Capital	Lomé	**Organizations**	UN

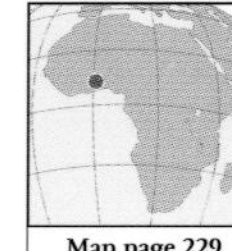
Map page 229

Togo is a long narrow country in west Africa with a sl coastline on the Gulf of Guinea. The interior consists plateaus rising to mountainous areas. The climate is tropical, and is drier inland. Agriculture is the mainst of the economy. Phosphate mining and food processi are the main industries. Cotton, phosphates, coffee ar cocoa are the main exports. Lomé, the capital, is an entrepôt trade cer

Tokelau New Zealand Overseas Territory

Area Sq Km	10	**Currency**	New Zealand dollar
Area Sq Miles	4	**Languages**	English, Tokelauan
Population	1 466	**Religions**	Christian

Tokelau consists of three atolls, Atafu, Nukunonu and Fakaofa, lying the Pacific Ocean north of Samoa. Subsistence agriculture is the ma activity, and the islands rely on aid from New Zealand and remittanc from workers overseas.

Map page 103

TONGA

Kingdom of Tonga

Area Sq Km	748	**Currency**	Pa'anga
Area Sq Miles	289	**Languages**	Tongan, English
Population	104 000	**Religions**	Protestant, Roman Catholic
Capital	Nuku'alofa	**Organizations**	Comm., UN

Tonga comprises some one hundred and seventy islands in the sout Pacific Ocean, northeast of New Zealand. The three main groups are Tongatapu (where sixty per cent of Tongans live), Ha'apai and Vava'u. The climate is warm and wet, and the economy relies heavily on agriculture. Tourism and light industry ar also important to the economy. Exports include squa fish, vanilla beans and root crops. Most trade is with New Zealand, Japan and Australia.

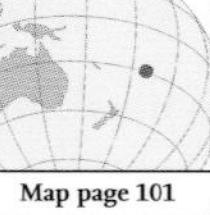
Map page 101

TRINIDAD AND TOBAGO

Republic of Trinidad and Tobago

q Km	5 130	Currency	Trinidad and Tobago dollar
q Miles	1 981	Languages	English, creole, Hindi
tion	1 339 000	Religions	Roman Catholic, Hindu, Protestant, Sunni Muslim
	Port of Spain	Organizations	CARICOM, Comm., UN

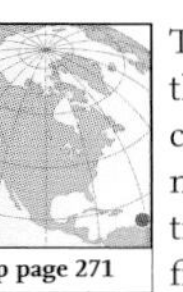

p page 271

Trinidad, the most southerly Caribbean island, lies off the Venezuelan coast. It is hilly in the north, with a central plain. Tobago, to the northeast, is smaller, more mountainous and less developed. The climate is tropical. The main crops are cocoa, sugar cane, coffee, fruit and vegetables. Oil and petrochemical industries inate the economy. Tourism is also important. The USA is the trading partner.

stan da Cunha Dependency of St Helena

q Km (Miles) 98 (38) Population 264 Capital Settlement of Edinburgh

oup of volcanic islands in the south Atlantic Ocean: the other islands in the group are Nightingale Island and Inaccessible d. The group is over 2 000 kilometres (1 250 miles) south of elena. The economy is based on fishing, fish processing and culture. Ecotourism is increasingly important.

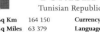

p page 238

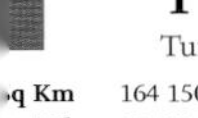

TUNISIA

Tunisian Republic

q Km	164 150	Currency	Tunisian dinar
q Miles	63 379	Languages	Arabic, French
ation	10 272 000	Religions	Sunni Muslim
l	Tunis	Organizations	UN

p page 227

Tunisia is on the Mediterranean coast of north Africa. The north is mountainous with valleys and coastal plains, has a Mediterranean climate and is the most populous area. The south is hot and arid. Oil and phosphates are the main resources, and the main crops are olives and citrus fruit. Tourism is an important stry. Exports include petroleum products, textiles, fruit and phorus. Most trade is with European Union countries.

TURKEY

Republic of Turkey

q Km	779 452	Currency	Lira
q Miles	300 948	Languages	Turkish, Kurdish
ation	74 816 000	Religions	Sunni Muslim, Shi'a Muslim
l	Ankara	Organizations	NATO, OECD, UN

page 148–149

Turkey occupies a large peninsula of southwest Asia and has coastlines on the Black, Mediterranean and Aegean Seas. It includes eastern Thrace, which is in southeastern Europe and separated from the rest of the country by the Bosporus, the Sea of Marmara and the Dardanelles. The Asian mainland consists of the -arid Anatolian plateau, flanked to the north, south and east by ntains. Over forty per cent of Turks live in central Anatolia and e Marmara and Aegean coastal plains. The coast has a iterranean climate, but inland conditions are more extreme with dry summers and cold, snowy winters. Agriculture involves about per cent of the workforce, and products include cotton, grain, cco, fruit, nuts and livestock. Turkey is a leading producer of mium, iron ore, lead, tin, borate, and baryte. Coal is also mined. main manufactured goods are clothing, textiles, food products, and vehicles. Tourism is a major industry, with nine million ors a year. Germany and the USA are the main trading partners. ittances from workers abroad are important to the economy.

TURKMENISTAN

Republic of Turkmenistan

q Km	488 100	Currency	Turkmen manat
q Miles	188 456	Languages	Turkmen, Uzbek, Russian
ation	5 110 000	Religions	Sunni Muslim, Russian Orthodox
l	Aşgabat (Ashkhabad)	Organizations	UN

page 144–145

Turkmenistan, in central Asia, comprises the plains of the Karakum Desert, the foothills of the Kopet Dag mountains in the south, the Amudar'ya valley in the north and the Caspian Sea plains in the west. The climate is dry, with extreme temperatures. The economy is based mainly on irrigated agriculture efly cotton growing), and natural gas and oil. Main exports are ral gas, oil and cotton fibre. Ukraine, Iran, Turkey and the Russian eration are the main trading partners.

Turks and Caicos Islands

United Kingdom Overseas Territory

Sq Km	430	Currency	US dollar
Sq Miles	166	Languages	English
ation	33 000	Religions	Protestant
al	Grand Turk (Cockburn Town)		

state consists of over forty low-lying islands and cays in the hern Caribbean. Only eight islands are inhabited, and two-fifths e people live on Grand Turk and Salt Cay. The climate is tropical, the economy is based on tourism, fishing and offshore banking.

p page 270

TUVALU

Sq Km	25	Currency	Australian dollar
Sq Miles	10	Languages	Tuvaluan, English
lation	10 000	Religions	Protestant
al	Vaiaku	Organizations	Comm., UN

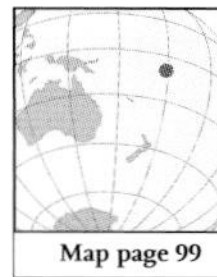

Map page 99

Tuvalu comprises nine low-lying coral atolls in the south Pacific Ocean. One-third of the population lives on Funafuti, and most people depend on subsistence farming and fishing. The islands export copra, stamps and clothing, but rely heavily on foreign aid. Most trade is with Fiji, Australia and New Zealand.

UGANDA

Republic of Uganda

Area Sq Km	241 038	Currency	Ugandan shilling
Area Sq Miles	93 065	Languages	English, Swahili, Luganda, local languages
Population	32 710 000	Religions	Roman Catholic, Protestant, Muslim, trad. beliefs
Capital	Kampala	Organizations	Comm., UN

Map page 232

A landlocked country in east Africa, Uganda consists of a savanna plateau with mountains and lakes. The climate is warm and wet. Most people live in the southern half of the country. Agriculture employs around eighty per cent of the workforce and dominates the economy. Coffee, tea, fish and fish products are the main exports. Uganda relies heavily on aid.

UKRAINE

Area Sq Km	603 700	Currency	Hryvnia
Area Sq Miles	233 090	Languages	Ukrainian, Russian
Population	45 708 000	Religions	Ukrainian Orthodox, Ukrainian Catholic, Roman Catholic
Capital	Kyiv (Kiev)	Organizations	CIS, UN

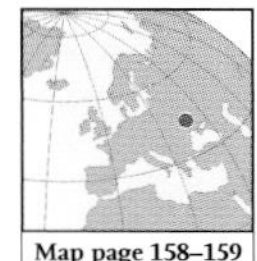

Map page 158–159

The country lies on the Black Sea coast of eastern Europe. Much of the land is steppe, generally flat and treeless, but with rich black soil, and it is drained by the river Dnieper. Along the border with Belarus are forested, marshy plains. The only uplands are the Carpathian Mountains in the west and smaller ranges on the Crimean peninsula. Summers are warm and winters are cold, with milder conditions in the Crimea. About a quarter of the population lives in the mainly industrial areas around Donets'k, Kiev and Dnipropetrovs'k. The Ukraine is rich in natural resources: fertile soil, substantial mineral and natural gas deposits, and forests. Agriculture and livestock rearing are important, but mining and manufacturing are the dominant sectors of the economy. Coal, iron and manganese mining, steel and metal production, machinery, chemicals and food processing are the main industries. The Russian Federation is the main trading partner.

UNITED ARAB EMIRATES

Federation of Emirates

Area Sq Km	77 700	Currency	United Arab Emirates dirham
Area Sq Miles	30 000	Languages	Arabic, English
Population	4 599 000	Religions	Sunni Muslim, Shi'a Muslim
Capital	Abū Ẓabī (Abu Dhabi)	Organizations	OPEC, UN

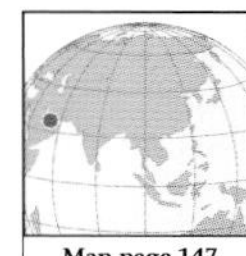

Map page 147

The UAE lies on the Gulf coast of the Arabian Peninsula. Six emirates are on The Gulf, while the seventh, Fujairah, is on the Gulf of Oman. Most of the land is flat desert with sand dunes and salt pans. The only hilly area is in the northeast. Over eighty per cent of the population lives in three of the emirates - Abu Dhabi, Dubai and Sharjah. Summers are hot and winters are mild, with occasional rainfall in coastal areas. Fruit and vegetables are grown in oases and irrigated areas, but the Emirates' wealth is based on hydrocarbons found in Abu Dhabi, Dubai, Sharjah and Ras al Khaimah. The UAE is one of the major oil producers in the Middle East. Dubai is an important entrepôt trade centre. The main trading partner is Japan.

Abū Ẓabī (Abu Dhabi) (Emirate)
Area Sq Km (Miles) 67 340 (26 000) Population 1 559 000 Capital Abū Ẓabī (Abu Dhabi)

'Ajman (Emirate)
Area Sq Km (Miles) 259 (100) Population 237 000 Capital 'Ajman

Dubayy (Dubai) (Emirate)
Area Sq Km (Miles) 3 885 (1 500) Population 1 596 000 Capital Dubayy (Dubai)

Al Fujayrah (Emirate)
Area Sq Km (Miles) 1 165 (450) Population 143 000 Capital Al Fujayrah

Ra's al Khaymah (Emirate)
Area Sq Km (Miles) 1 684 (650) Population 231 000 Capital Ra's al Khaymah

Ash Shāriqah (Sharjah) (Emirate)
Area Sq Km (Miles) 2 590 (1 000) Population 946 000 Capital Ash Shāriqah (Sharjah)

Umm al Qaywayn (Emirate)
Area Sq Km (Miles) 777 (300) Population 53 000 Capital Umm al Qaywayn

UNITED KINGDOM

United Kingdom of Great Britain and Northern Ireland

Area Sq Km	243 609	Currency	Pound sterling
Area Sq Miles	94 058	Languages	English, Welsh, Gaelic
Population	61 565 000	Religions	Protestant, Roman Catholic, Muslim
Capital	London	Organizations	Comm., EU, NATO, OECD, UN

The United Kingdom, in northwest Europe, occupies the island of Great Britain, part of Ireland, and many small adjacent islands. Great Britain comprises England, Scotland and Wales. England covers over half the land area and supports over four-fifths of the population, at its densest in the southeast. The English landscape is flat or rolling with some uplands, notably the Cheviot Hills on the Scottish border, the Pennines in the centre-north, and the hills of the Lake District in the northwest. Scotland consists of southern uplands, central lowlands, the Highlands (which include the UK's highest peak) and many islands. Wales is a land of hills, mountains and river valleys. Northern Ireland contains uplands, plains and the UK's largest lake, Lough Neagh. The climate of the UK is mild, wet and variable. There

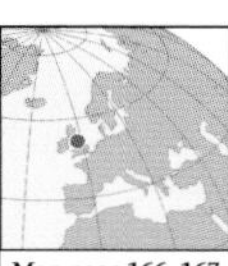

Map page 166–167

are few mineral deposits, but important energy resources. Agricultural activities involve sheep and cattle rearing, dairy farming, and crop and fruit growing in the east and southeast. Productivity is high, but approximately one-third of food is imported. The UK produces petroleum and natural gas from reserves in the North Sea and is self-sufficient in energy in net terms. Major manufactures are food and drinks, motor vehicles and parts, aerospace equipment, machinery, electronic and electrical equipment, and chemicals and chemical products. However, the economy is dominated by service industries, including banking, insurance, finance and business services. London, the capital, is one of the world's major financial centres. Tourism is also a major industry, with approximately twenty-five million visitors a year. International trade is also important, equivalent to one-third of national income. Over half of the UK's trade is with other European Union countries.

England (Constituent country)
Area Sq Km (Miles) 130 433 (50 360) Population 51 092 000 Capital London

Northern Ireland (Province)
Area Sq Km (Miles) 13 576 (5 242) Population 1 759 100 Capital Belfast

Scotland (Constituent country)
Area Sq Km (Miles) 78 822 (30 433) Population 5 144 200 Capital Edinburgh

Wales (Principality)
Area Sq Km (Miles) 20 778 (8 022) Population 2 980 000 Capital Cardiff

UNITED STATES OF AMERICA

Federal Republic

Area Sq Km	9 826 635	Currency	United States dollar
Area Sq Miles	3 794 085	Languages	English, Spanish
Population	314 659 000	Religions	Protestant, Roman Catholic, Sunni Muslim, Jewish
Capital	Washington D.C.	Organizations	APEC, NATO, OECD, UN

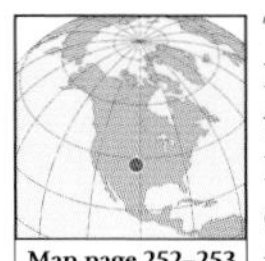

Map page 252–253

The USA comprises forty-eight contiguous states in North America, bounded by Canada and Mexico, plus the states of Alaska, to the northwest of Canada, and Hawaii, in the north Pacific Ocean. The populous eastern states cover the Atlantic coastal plain (which includes the Florida peninsula and the Gulf of Mexico coast) and the Appalachian Mountains. The central states occupy a vast interior plain drained by the Mississippi-Missouri river system. To the west lie the Rocky Mountains, separated from the Pacific coastal ranges by intermontane plateaus. The Pacific coastal zone is also mountainous, and prone to earthquakes. Hawaii is a group of some twenty volcanic islands. Climatic conditions range between arctic in Alaska to desert in the intermontane plateaus. Most of the USA has a temperate climate, although the interior has continental conditions. There are abundant natural resources, including major reserves of minerals and energy resources. The USA has the largest and most technologically advanced economy in the world, based on manufacturing and services. Although agriculture accounts for approximately two per cent of national income, productivity is high and the USA is a net exporter of food, chiefly grains and fruit. Cotton is the major industrial crop. The USA produces iron ore, copper, lead, zinc, and many other minerals. It is a major producer of coal, petroleum and natural gas, although being the world's biggest energy user it imports significant quantities of petroleum and its products. Manufacturing is diverse. The main industries are petroleum, steel, motor vehicles, aerospace, telecommunications, electronics, food processing, chemicals and consumer goods. Tourism is a major foreign currency earner, with approximately forty-five million visitors a year. Other important service industries are banking and finance, Wall Street in New York being one of the world's major stock exchanges. Canada and Mexico are the main trading partners.

Alabama (State)
Area Sq Km (Miles) 135 765 (52 419) Population 4 661 900 Capital Montgomery

Alaska (State)
Area Sq Km (Miles) 1 717 854 (663 267) Population 686 293 Capital Juneau

Arizona (State)
Area Sq Km (Miles) 295 253 (113 998) Population 6 500 180 Capital Phoenix

Arkansas (State)
Area Sq Km (Miles) 137 733 (53 179) Population 2 855 390 Capital Little Rock

California (State)
Area Sq Km (Miles) 423 971 (163 696) Population 36 756 666 Capital Sacramento

Colorado (State)
Area Sq Km (Miles) 269 602 (104 094) Population 4 939 456 Capital Denver

Connecticut (State)
Area Sq Km (Miles) 14 356 (5 543) Population 3 501 252 Capital Hartford

Delaware (State)
Area Sq Km (Miles) 6 446 (2 489) Population 873 092 Capital Dover

District of Columbia (District)
Area Sq Km (Miles) 176 (68) Population 591 833 Capital Washington

Florida (State)
Area Sq Km (Miles) 170 305 (65 755) Population 18 328 340 Capital Tallahassee

Georgia (State)
Area Sq Km (Miles) 153 910 (59 425) Population 9 685 744 Capital Atlanta

Hawaii (State)
Area Sq Km (Miles) 28 311 (10 931) Population 1 288 198 Capital Honolulu

Idaho (State)
Area Sq Km (Miles) 216 445 (83 570) Population 1 523 816 Capital Boise

Illinois (State)
Area Sq Km (Miles) 149 997 (57 914) Population 12 901 563 Capital Springfield

Indiana (State)
Area Sq Km (Miles) 94 322 (36 418) Population 6 376 792 Capital Indianapolis

Iowa (State)
Area Sq Km (Miles) 145 744 (56 272) Population 3 002 555 Capital Des Moines

Kansas (State)
Area Sq Km (Miles) 213 096 (82 277) Population 2 802 134 Capital Topeka

State	Area Sq Km (Miles)	Population	Capital
Kentucky (State)	104 659 (40 409)	4 269 245	Frankfort
Louisiana (State)	134 265 (51 840)	4 410 796	Baton Rouge
Maine (State)	91 647 (35 385)	1 316 456	Augusta
Maryland (State)	32 134 (12 407)	5 633 597	Annapolis
Massachusetts (State)	27 337 (10 555)	6 497 967	Boston
Michigan (State)	250 493 (96 716)	10 003 422	Lansing
Minnesota (State)	225 171 (86 939)	5 220 393	St Paul
Mississippi (State)	125 433 (48 430)	2 938 618	Jackson
Missouri (State)	180 533 (69 704)	5 911 605	Jefferson City
Montana (State)	380 837 (147 042)	967 440	Helena
Nebraska (State)	200 346 (77 354)	1 783 432	Lincoln
Nevada (State)	286 352 (110 561)	2 600 167	Carson City
New Hampshire (State)	24 216 (9 350)	1 315 809	Concord
New Jersey (State)	22 587 (8 721)	8 682 661	Trenton
New Mexico (State)	314 914 (121 589)	1 984 356	Santa Fe
New York (State)	141 299 (54 556)	19 490 297	Albany
North Carolina (State)	139 391 (53 819)	9 222 414	Raleigh
North Dakota (State)	183 112 (70 700)	641 481	Bismarck
Ohio (State)	116 096 (44 825)	11 485 910	Columbus
Oklahoma (State)	181 035 (69 898)	3 642 361	Oklahoma City
Oregon (State)	254 806 (98 381)	3 790 060	Salem
Pennsylvania (State)	119 282 (46 055)	12 448 279	Harrisburg
Rhode Island (State)	4 002 (1 545)	1 050 788	Providence
South Carolina (State)	82 931 (32 020)	4 479 800	Columbia
South Dakota (State)	199 730 (77 116)	804 194	Pierre
Tennessee (State)	109 150 (42 143)	6 214 888	Nashville
Texas (State)	695 622 (268 581)	24 326 974	Austin
Utah (State)	219 887 (84 899)	2 736 424	Salt Lake City
Vermont (State)	24 900 (9 614)	621 270	Montpelier
Virginia (State)	110 784 (42 774)	7 769 089	Richmond
Washington (State)	184 666 (71 300)	6 549 224	Olympia
West Virginia (State)	62 755 (24 230)	1 814 468	Charleston
Wisconsin (State)	169 639 (65 498)	5 627 967	Madison
Wyoming (State)	253 337 (97 814)	532 668	Cheyenne

URUGUAY

Oriental Republic of Uruguay

Area Sq Km	176 215	**Currency**	Uruguayan peso
Area Sq Miles	68 037	**Languages**	Spanish
Population	3 361 000	**Religions**	Roman Catholic, Protestant, Jewish
Capital	Montevideo	**Organizations**	UN

Map page 282

Uruguay, on the Atlantic coast of central South America, is a low-lying land of prairies. The coast and the River Plate estuary in the south are fringed with lagoons and sand dunes. Almost half the population lives in the capital, Montevideo. Uruguay has warm summers and mild winters. The economy is based on cattle and sheep ranching, and the main industries produce food products, textiles, and petroleum products. Meat, wool, hides, textiles and agricultural products are the main exports. Brazil and Argentina are the main trading partners.

UZBEKISTAN

Republic of Uzbekistan

Area Sq Km	447 400	**Currency**	Uzbek som
Area Sq Miles	172 742	**Languages**	Uzbek, Russian, Tajik, Kazakh
Population	27 488 000	**Religions**	Sunni Muslim, Russian Orthodox
Capital	Toshkent	**Organizations**	CIS, UN

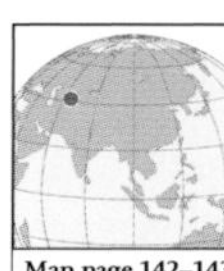

Map page 142–143

A landlocked country of central Asia, Uzbekistan consists mainly of the flat Kyzylkum Desert. High mountains and valleys are found towards the southeast borders with Kyrgyzstan and Tajikistan. Most settlement is in the Fergana basin. The climate is hot and dry. The economy is based mainly on irrigated agriculture, chiefly cotton production. Uzbekistan is rich in minerals, including gold, copper, lead, zinc and uranium, and it has one of the largest gold mines in the world. Industry specializes in fertilizers and machinery for cotton harvesting and textile manufacture. The Russian Federation is the main trading partner.

VANUATU

Republic of Vanuatu

Area Sq Km	12 190	**Currency**	Vatu
Area Sq Miles	4 707	**Languages**	English, Bislama (creole), French
Population	240 000	**Religions**	Protestant, Roman Catholic, traditional beliefs
Capital	Port Vila	**Organizations**	Comm., UN

Map page 100

Vanuatu occupies an archipelago of approximately eighty islands in the southwest Pacific. Many of the islands are mountainous, of volcanic origin and densely forested. The climate is tropical, with heavy rainfall. Half of the population lives on the main islands of Éfaté and Espíritu Santo, and the majority of people are employed in agriculture. Copra, beef, timber, vegetables, and cocoa are the main exports. Tourism is becoming important to the economy. Australia, Japan and Germany are the main trading partners.

VATICAN CITY

Vatican City State or Holy See

Area Sq Km	0.5	**Currency**	Euro
Area Sq Miles	0.2	**Languages**	Italian
Population	557	**Religions**	Roman Catholic
Capital	Vatican City (Città del Vaticano)		

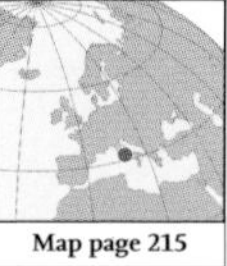

Map page 215

The world's smallest sovereign state, the Vatican City occupies a hill to the west of the river Tiber within the Italian capital, Rome. It is the headquarters of the Roman Catholic church, and income comes from investments, voluntary contributions and tourism.

VENEZUELA

Republic of Venezuela

Area Sq Km	912 050	**Currency**	Bolívar fuerte
Area Sq Miles	352 144	**Languages**	Spanish, Amerindian languages
Population	28 583 000	**Religions**	Roman Catholic, Protestant
Capital	Caracas	**Organizations**	OPEC, UN

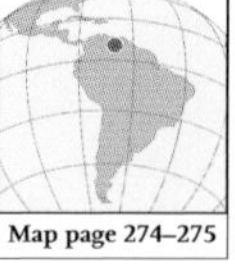

Map page 274–275

Venezuela is in northern South America, on the Caribbean. Lake Maracaibo is a major inlet of the sea. Mountain ranges enclose a central zone of grasslands drained by the Orinoco. To the south are the Guiana Highlands, which contain the Angel Falls, the world's highest waterfall. Almost ninety per cent of the population lives in towns. The climate is tropical. Cattle ranching and dairy farming are important; coffee, maize, rice and sugar cane are produced. Oil accounts for about seventy-five per cent of exports. Aluminium, iron ore, copper and gold are mined, and manufactures include steel, textiles and food products. The USA and Puerto Rico are the main trading partners.

VIETNAM

Socialist Republic of Vietnam

Area Sq Km	329 565	**Currency**	Dong
Area Sq Miles	127 246	**Languages**	Vietnamese, Thai, Khmer, Chinese, local languages
Population	88 069 000	**Religions**	Buddhist, Taoist, Roman Catholic, Cao Dai, Hoa Hao
Capital	Ha Nôi (Hanoi)	**Organizations**	APEC, ASEAN, UN

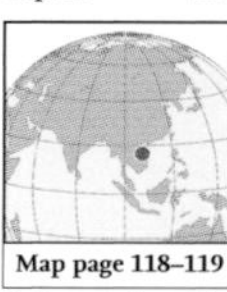

Map page 118–119

Vietnam lies in southeast Asia on the west coast of the South China Sea. The Red River delta lowlands in the north are separated from the huge Mekong delta in the south by long, narrow coastal plains backed by the mountainous and forested terrain of the Annam Highlands. Most of the population lives in the river deltas. The climate is tropical, with summer monsoon rains. Over three-quarters of the workforce is involved in agriculture, forestry and fishing. Coffee, tea and rubber are important cash crops, but Vietnam is the world's second largest rice exporter. Oil, coal and copper are produced, and other main industries are food processing, clothing and footwear, cement and fertilizers. Exports include oil, coffee, rice, clothing, fish and fish products. Japan and Singapore are the main trading partners.

Virgin Islands (U.K.)

United Kingdom Overseas Territory

Area Sq Km	153	**Currency**	United States dollar
Area Sq Miles	59	**Languages**	English
Population	23 000	**Religions**	Protestant, Roman Catholic
Capital	Road Town		

The Caribbean territory comprises four main islands and over thirty islets at the eastern end of the Virgin Islands group. Apart from the flat coral atoll of Anegada, the islands are volcanic in origin and hilly. The climate is subtropical, and tourism is the main industry.

Map page 271

Virgin Islands (U.S.A.)

United States Unincorporated Territory

Area Sq Km	352	**Currency**	United States dollar
Area Sq Miles	136	**Languages**	English, Spanish
Population	110 000	**Religions**	Protestant, Roman Catholic
Capital	Charlotte Amalie		

The territory consists of three main islands and over fifty islets in the Caribbean's western Virgin Islands. The islands are hilly, of volcanic origin, and the climate is subtropical. The economy is based on tourism, with some manufacturing, including a major oil refinery on St Croix.

Map page 271

Wallis and Futuna Islands

French Overseas Collectivity

Area Sq Km	274	**Currency**	CFP franc
Area Sq Miles	106	**Languages**	French, Wallisian, Futunian
Population	15 000	**Religions**	Roman Catholic
Capital	Matā'utu		

The south Pacific territory comprises the volcanic islands of the Wallis archipelago and the Hoorn Islands. The climate is tropical. The islands depend on subsistence farming, the sale of licences to foreign fishing fleets, workers' remittances from abroad and French aid.

Map page 97

West Bank

Disputed Territory

Area Sq Km	5 860	**Currency**	Jordanian dinar, Israeli shekel
Area Sq Miles	2 263	**Languages**	Arabic, Hebrew
Population	2 448 433	**Religions**	Sunni Muslim, Jewish, Shi'a Muslim, Christian

The territory consists of the west bank of the river Jordan and parts of Judea and Samaria. The land was annexed by Israel in 1967, but some areas have been granted autonomy under agreements between Israel and the Palestinian Authority. Conflict between the Israelis and the Palestinians continues to restrict economic development.

Map page 150

Western Sahara

Disputed Territory (Morocco)

Area Sq Km	266 000	**Currency**	Moroccan dirhamr
Area Sq Miles	102 703	**Languages**	Arabic
Population	513 000	**Religions**	Sunni Muslim
Capital	Laâyoune		

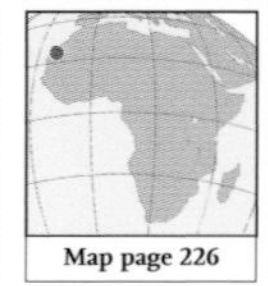

Map page 226

Situated on the northwest coast of Africa, the territory of the Western Sahara is now effectively controlled by Morocco. The land is low, flat desert with higher land in the northeast. There is little cultivation and only about twenty per cent of the land is pasture. Livestock herding, fishing and phosphate mining are the main activities. All trade is controlled by Morocco.

YEMEN

Republic of Yemen

Area Sq Km	527 968	**Currency**	Yemeni riyal
Area Sq Miles	203 850	**Languages**	Arabic
Population	23 580 000	**Religions**	Sunni Muslim, Shi'a Muslim
Capital	Şan'ā'	**Organizations**	UN

Map page 146–147

Yemen occupies the southwestern part of the Arabian Peninsula, on the Red Sea and the Gulf of Aden. Beyond the Red Sea coastal plain the land rises to a mountain range and then descends to desert plateaus. Much of the country is hot and arid, but there is more rainfall in the west, where most of the population lives. Farming and fishing are the main activities, with cotton the main cash crop. The main exports are crude oil, fish, coffee and dried fruit. Despite some oil resources Yemen is one of the poorest countries in the Arab world. Main trading partners are Thailand, China, South Korea and Saudi Arabia.

ZAMBIA

Republic of Zambia

Area Sq Km	752 614	**Currency**	Zambian kwacha
Area Sq Miles	290 586	**Languages**	English, Bemba, Nyanja, Tonga, local languages
Population	12 935 000	**Religions**	Christian, traditional beliefs
Capital	Lusaka	**Organizations**	Comm., SADC, UN

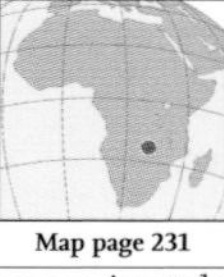

Map page 231

A landlocked state in south central Africa, Zambia consists principally of high savanna plateaus and is bordered by the Zambezi river in the south. Most people live in the Copperbelt area in the centre-north. The climate is tropical, with a rainy season from November to May. Agriculture employs approximately eighty per cent of the workforce, but is mainly at subsistence level. Copper mining is the mainstay of the economy, although reserves are declining. Copper and cobalt are the main exports. Most trade is with South Africa.

ZIMBABWE

Republic of Zimbabwe

Area Sq Km	390 759	**Currency**	Zimbabwean dollar
Area Sq Miles	150 873	**Languages**	English, Shona, Ndebele
Population	12 523 000	**Religions**	Christian, traditional beliefs
Capital	Harare	**Organizations**	SADC, UN

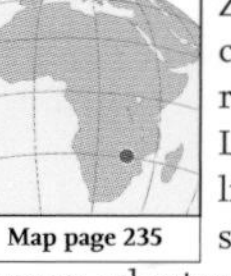

Map page 235

Zimbabwe, a landlocked state in south-central Africa, consists of high plateaus flanked by the Zambezi river valley and Lake Kariba in the north and the Limpopo river in the south. Most of the population lives in the centre of the country. There are significant mineral resources, including gold, nickel, copper, asbestos, platinum and chromium. Agriculture is a major sector of the economy, with crops including tobacco, maize, sugar cane and cotton. Beef cattle are also important. Exports include tobacco, gold, ferroalloys, nickel and cotton. South Africa is the main trading partner. The economy has suffered recently through significant political unrest and instability.

ATLAS OF THE WORLD

ATLAS MAPPING

The Atlas of the World includes a variety of styles and scales of mapping which together provide comprehensive coverage of all parts of the world; the map styles and editorial policies followed are introduced here. The area covered by each map is shown on the front and back endpapers.

Each continent is introduced by a politically coloured map followed by reference maps of sub-continental regions and then more detailed reference mapping of regions and individual countries. Scales for continental maps (*see 1*) range between 1:15 000 000 and 1:27 000 000 and regional maps (*see 2*) are in the range 1:11 000 000 to 1:13 000 000. Mapping for most countries is at scales between 1:3 000 000 and 1:7 500 000 (*see 3*) although selected, more densely populated areas of Europe, North America and Asia are mapped at larger scales, up to 1:1 000 000 (*see 4*). Large-scale city plans of a selection of the world's major cities (*see 8*), are included on the appropriate map pages. A suite of maps covering the world's oceans and poles (*see 9*) at a variety of scales, concludes the main reference map section.

The symbols and place name abbreviations used on the maps are fully explained on pages 90–91 and a glossary of geographical terms is included at the back of the atlas on pages 293–296. The alphanumeric reference system used in the index is based on latitude and longitude, and the number and letter for each graticule square are shown within each map frame, in brown. The numbers of adjoining or overlapping pages are shown by arrows in the page frame and accompanying numbers in the margin.

BOUNDARIES

The status, names and boundaries of nations are shown in this atlas as they were at the time of going to press, as far as can be ascertained. Where an international boundary symbol appears in the sea or ocean it does not necessarily infer a legal maritime boundary, but shows which off-shore islands belong to which country.

Where international boundaries are the subject of dispute it may be that no portrayal of them will meet with the approval of any of the countries involved, but it is not seen as the function of this atlas to try to adjudicate between the rights and wrongs of political issues. The atlas aims to take a neutral viewpoint of all such cases. Although reference mapping at atlas scales is not the ideal medium for indicating territorial claims, every reasonable attempt is made to show where an active territorial dispute exists, and where there is an important difference between 'de facto' (existing in fact, on the ground) and 'de jure' (according to law) boundaries. This is done by the use of a different symbol where international boundaries are disputed, or where the alignment is unconfirmed, to that used for settled international boundaries. Cease-fire lines are also shown by a separate symbol. For clarity, disputed boundaries and areas are annotated where this is considered necessary but it is impossible to represent all the complexities of territorial disputes on maps at atlas scales.

The latest internal administrative division boundaries are shown on the maps for selected countries where the combination of map scale and the number of divisions permits, with recent changes to local government systems being taken into account as far as possible. Towns which are first-order and second-order administrative centres are also symbolized where scale permits.

2. SOUTHEAST ASIA 1:13 000 000
(extract from pages 112–113)

3. EAST CENTRAL AFRICA 1:7 500 000
(extract from pages 232–233)

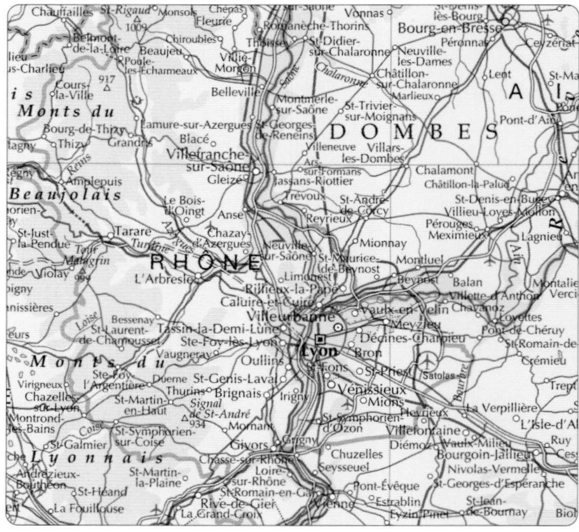

4. SOUTHEAST FRANCE 1:1 200 000
(extract from pages 182–183)

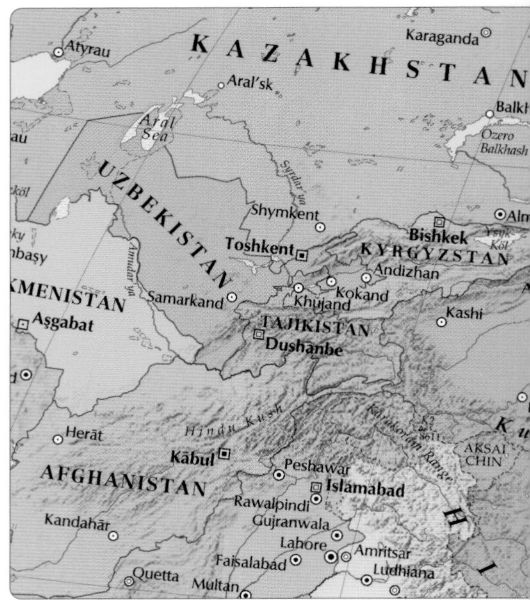

1. CONTINENTAL MAP OF ASIA
(extract from pages 110–111)

PLACE NAMES

NAME FORM POLICY

The spelling of place names on maps has always been matter of great complexity, because of the variety of th world's languages and the systems used to write them down. There is no standard way of spelling names or converting them from one alphabet, or symbol set, to another. Instead, conventional ways of spelling have evolved in each of the world's major languages, and th results often differ significantly from the name as it is spelled in the original language. Familiar examples of English conventional names include Munich (Münch Florence (Firenze) and Moscow (from the transliterate form, Moskva).

In this atlas, local name forms are used where they in the Roman alphabet. These local forms are those which are recognized by the government of the count concerned, usually as represented by its official mapp agency. This is a basic principle laid down by the Unit Kingdom government's Permanent Committee on Geographical Names for British Official Use (PCGN).

For languages in non-Roman alphabets or symbol s names need to be 'Romanized' through a process of transliteration (the conversion of characters or symbo from one alphabet into another) or transcription (conversion of names based on pronunciation). Differ systems often exist for this process, but PCGN and its United States counterpart, the Board on Geographic Names (BGN), usually follow the same Romanization principles, and the general policy for this atlas is to follow their lead. One notable change in this edition i that PCGN and BGN principles are now followed for Arabic names in Egypt ('Al' style – for example Al Qāhirah for Cairo), where previous editions followed PCGN's former policy of using a local Survey of Egypt system ('El' style – El Qâhira).

Local name form mapping is the nearest that the cartographer can achieve to an international standard is in fact impossible, and perhaps unnecessary, to provide English names for the majority of mapped features, and translating names into English is fraugh with linguistic hazards. Consequently, a local name fo map is more internally consistent than a partly-anglicized one.

Although local forms in this atlas are given precedence, prominent English-language conventiona names and historic names are not neglected. The nam of countries, continents, oceans, seas and underwater features in international waters appear in English throughout the atlas, as do those of other internationa features where such an English form exists. Significan superseded names and other alternative spellings are included in brackets on the maps where space permit and variants and former names are cross-referenced i the index.

AP PROJECTIONS

creation of computer-generated maps presents the ortunity to select projections specifically for the area scale of each map. As the only way to show the Earth absolute accuracy is on a globe, all map projections compromises. Some projections seek to maintain ect area relationships (equal area projections), true ances and bearings from a point (equidistant ections) or correct angles and shapes (conformal ections); others attempt to achieve a balance between these properties. The choice of projections used in this atlas has been made on an individual continental and regional basis. Projections used, and their individual parameters, have been defined to minimize distortion and to reduce scale errors (shown as percentage figures in the accompanying diagrams) as much as possible.

For world maps, the Bartholomew version of the Winkel Tripel Projection is used. This projection combines elements of conformality with that of equal area, and shows, over the world as a whole, relatively true shapes and reasonably equal areas. The Mercator Projection (*see 5*) has been selected for the regional maps of southeast Asia along the Equator , while in higher latitudes, particularly in Europe and to some extent in North America, the Conic Equidistant Projection (*see 6*) has been used extensively for regional mapping. The Lambert Azimuthal Equal Area Projection (*see 7*) has been employed in both South America and Australia.

ERCATOR PROJECTION

rectangular or cylindrical projection is constructed on the basis of a der in contact with the globe, in this case around the Equator. Scale is ct along the Equator and distortion increases away from it in both tions.

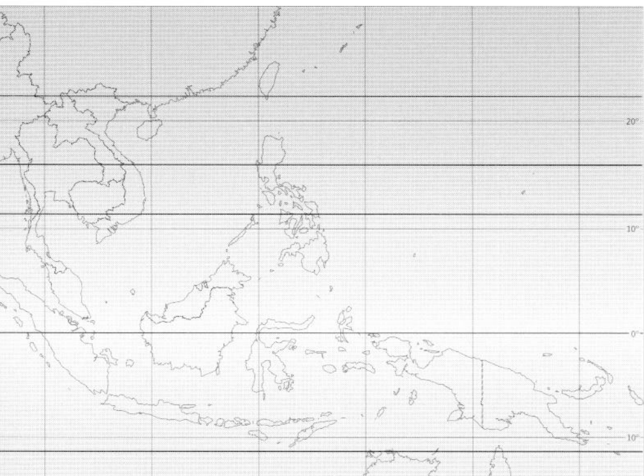

6. CONIC EQUIDISTANT PROJECTION

Constructed on the basis of a cone intersecting the globe along two standard parallels (55°N and 75°N in this illustration), along both of which scale is correct. Lines of equal scale error are parallel to the standard lines, with distortion increasing away from each.

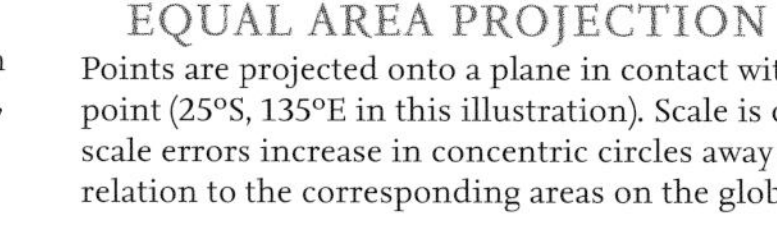

7. LAMBERT AZIMUTHAL EQUAL AREA PROJECTION

Points are projected onto a plane in contact with the globe at the centre point (25°S, 135°E in this illustration). Scale is correct at the centre, and scale errors increase in concentric circles away from it. Areas are true in relation to the corresponding areas on the globe.

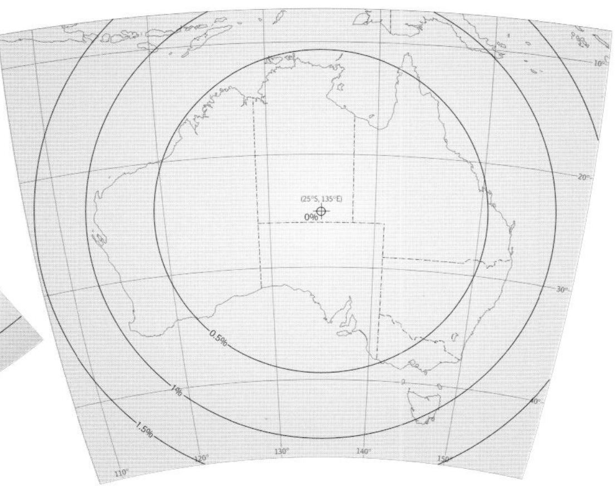

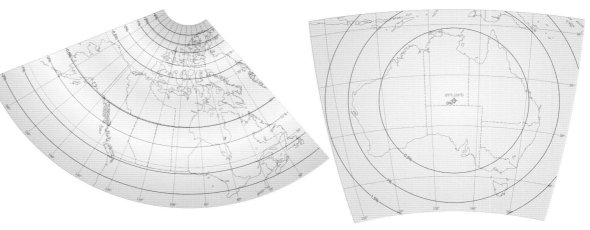

ACE NAMES

ME CHANGES

tinuing changes in official languages, in writing ems and in Romanization methods, have to be taken account by cartographers. In many countries erent languages are in use in different regions or -by-side in the same region, and there is potential widely varying name forms even within a single ntry. A worldwide trend towards national, regional ethnic self-determination is operating at the same e as pressure towards increased international dardization.

lace names are, to an extent, a mirror for the changes continue to transform the political world. Changes erritorial control may have a significant effect on ne forms. Yet even in countries where name forms ld be expected to have long been largely dardized, there are sometimes continuing issues for cartographer to address. In the UK, for example, e is a trend for more Gaelic and Welsh-language nes to be given official recognition. Similarly, there been an increase in the official recognition and use ndigenous name forms in for instance New Zealand ori) and Canada (Inuit and Indian names). Name lling issues are, in fact, likely to emerge in almost any of the world.

eflecting trends across the world, systematic rations affecting various countries are reflected in atlas. The dissolution of the former USSR has given to the greatest changes in recent years, and this atlas tinues the policy established in the previous edition ames being converted from Russian to the main onal language in Belarus, Ukraine, Moldova, nenia, Georgia, Azerbaijan, Kyrgyzstan and Tajikistan. ekistan is the latest to have been converted in this using the new Uzbek Roman alphabet. Russian urally continues to be used as the main form in the sian Federation and also continues to be used as the ne language on maps of Kazakhstan. Here, local-guage name forms (derived from Kazakh Cyrillic) are uded for main place names where space permits on the maps, with additional alternatives in the index. In Turkmenistan, main Turkmen Cyrillic-derived names are similarly covered, but native sources are starting to apply a finalized Roman alphabet, pointing the way to a future in which Cyrillic names will be dropped entirely. Main examples of new Turkmen forms are included as cross-references in the index.

In Spain, account is taken of the official prominence now given to Catalan, Galician and some Basque spellings, which results in name forms such as Eivissa for Ibiza and A Coruña for La Coruña. Reflecting these changes, many names are now represented in dual form on official Spanish mapping. Depending on their specific treatment on local mapping, some of these are shown in this atlas as hyphenated (for example Donostia-San Sebastián, Gijón-Xixón, Elche-Elx) while others include the second forms as alternative names.

Chinese name forms, which were fully converted to the official Pinyin Romanization system some years ago in earlier editions of this atlas, continue to change. Name forms have been brought into line with the latest official sources, continuing to follow the principle whereby numerous towns which are the centres of administrative units such as the county or 'xian' officially take the name of the county itself. The alternative place name in common local use is shown in brackets on the map. The index also includes numerous cross-references for Chinese name forms as they were before the introduction of Pinyin – taking account of the main so-called 'Post Office' spellings such as Tientsin (now Tianjin), and more particularly of the long-familiar Wade-Giles Romanization, which gives, for instance, Pei-ching as against the Pinyin form Beijing.

As well as systematic changes in name forms such as those outlined above, occasionally places are given entirely new names for a variety of reasons. This atlas accounts for any such recent changes. One significant example is the official renaming of Calcutta as Kolkata, following earlier changes by the Indian authorities to Bombay (now Mumbai) and Madras (now Chennai).

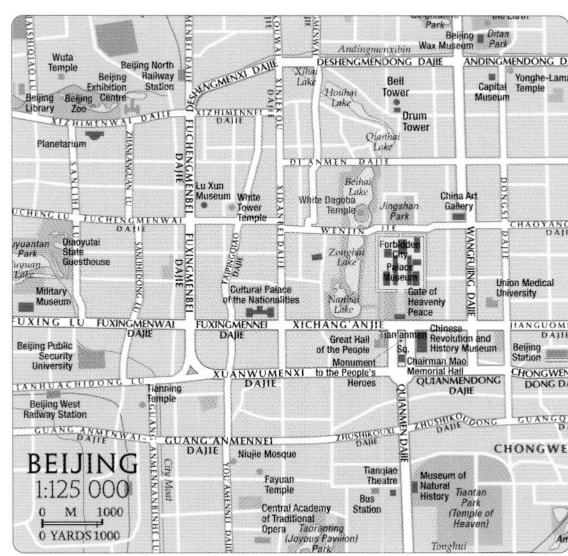

8. BEIJING CITY PLAN
(extract from page 128)

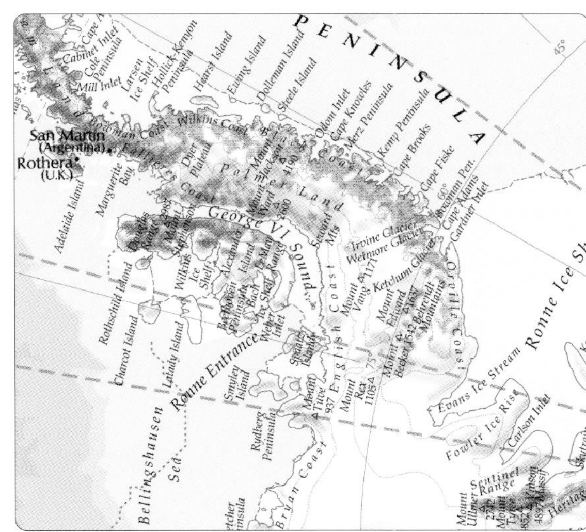

9. ANTARCTICA 1:18 000 000
(extract from pages 286–287)

REFERENCE MAPS

CITIES AND TOWNS

Population	National Capital	Administrative Capital (Shown for selected countries only.) First order	Administrative Capital Second order (Scales larger than 1:9 000 000.)	Other City or Town
over 10 million	TŌKYŌ	Karachi	Los Angeles	New York
5 million to 10 million	SANTIAGO	Tianjin	Chicago	Hong Kong
1 million to 5 million	KĀBUL	Sydney	Tangshan	Kaohsiung
500 000 to 1 million	BANGUI	Trujillo	Mysore	Anyang
100 000 to 500 000	WELLINGTON	Mansa	Naogaon	Apucarana
50 000 to 100 000	PORT OF SPAIN	Potenza	Trier	Arecibo
10 000 to 50 000	MALABO	Chinhoyi	Willimantic	Ceres
1 000 to 10 000	VALLETTA	Ati	Nepalganj	Abla
under 1000 Scales 1: 4 000 000 and larger		Chhukha	Carmel	Lopigna

Built-up area

MISCELLANEOUS FEATURES

National park
Regional park
Reserve or special land area
Site of specific interest
Wall

RELIEF

Contour intervals used in layer-colouring for land height and sea depth

Scales 1:4 000 000 and larger	Scales 1:4 000 000 and larger (Europe only)	Scales smaller than 1:4 000 000	Oceans and Antarctica (Pages 286–292)
6000 / 19686	6000 / 19686	6000 / 19686	6000 / 19686
5000 / 16404	5000 / 16404	5000 / 16404	5000 / 16404
4000 / 13124	4000 / 13124	4000 / 13124	4000 / 13124
3000 / 9843	3000 / 9843	3000 / 9843	3000 / 9843
2000 / 6562	2000 / 6562	2000 / 6562	2000 / 6562
1500 / 4921	1500 / 4921	1000 / 3281	1000 / 3281
1000 / 3281	1000 / 3281	500 / 1640	500 / 1640
500 / 1640	500 / 1640	200 / 656	200 / 656
200 / 656	200 / 656	0 / 0 LAND BELOW SEA LEVEL	0 / 0 LAND BELOW SEA LEVEL
100 / 328	100 / 328	200 / 656	200 / 656
0 / 0 LAND BELOW SEA LEVEL	0 / 0 LAND BELOW SEA LEVEL	2000 / 6562	2000 / 6562
200 / 656	50 / 164	4000 / 13124	3000 / 9843
1000 / 3281	200 / 656	6000 / 19686	4000 / 13124
2000 / 6562	1000 / 3281	M / FT	5000 / 16409
M / FT	2000 / 6562		6000 / 19686
	M / FT		7000 / 22967
			9000 / 29529
			M / FT

1234 Summit
Height in metres.

-123 Spot height
Surface height in metres for depressions and areas below sea level.

5678 Ocean deep
In metres.
Ocean pages only.

STYLES OF LETTERING

Cities and towns are explained separately

Country	FRANCE
Overseas Territory/Dependency	Guadeloupe
Disputed Territory	AKSAI CHIN
Administrative name, first order internal division. Shown for selected countries only.	SCOTLAND
Administrative name, second order internal division. Scales 1:4 000 000 and larger. Shown for selected countries only.	MANCHE
Area name	ARTOIS

Physical features	
Island	*Gran Canaria*
Lake	*LAKE ERIE*
Mountain	*Mt Blanc*
River	*Thames*
Region	*PAMPAS*

BOUNDARIES

International boundary
Disputed international boundary or alignment unconfirmed
Undefined international boundary in the sea. All land within this boundary is part of state or territory named.
Administrative boundary, first order internal division. Scales 1:4 000 000 and larger. Shown for selected countries only.
Administrative boundary, first order internal division. Scales smaller than 1:4 000 000. Shown for selected countries only.
Administrative boundary, second order internal division. Scales 1:4 000 000 and larger. Shown for selected countries only.
Disputed administrative boundary. Scales 1:4 000 000 and larger. Shown for selected countries only.
Ceasefire line or other boundary described on the map

LAND AND SEA FEATURES

Rock desert
Sand desert / Dunes
Oasis
Lava field
1234 Volcano
Height in metres.
Marsh
Ice cap / Glacier
Nunatak
Coral reef
Escarpment
Flood dyke
123 Pass
Height in metres.
Ice shelf

LAKES AND RIVERS

Lake
Impermanent lake
Salt lake or lagoon
Impermanent salt lake
Dry salt lake or salt pan
123 Lake height
Surface height above sea level, in metres.
River
Impermanent river
Wadi or watercourse
Waterfall
Dam
Barrage

TRANSPORT

under construction — Motorway
Scales 1:4 000 000 and larger.
under construction — Main road
under construction — Secondary road
Motorway tunnel
Road tunnel
Track
under construction — Main railway
under construction — Secondary railway
under construction — Railway tunnel
Canal
Minor canal
Main airport
Regional airport

NTINENTAL MAPS

UNDARIES

——	International boundary
-----	Disputed international boundary or alignment unconfirmed
/——	Undefined international boundary in the sea. All land within this boundary is part of state or territory named.
••••••	Ceasefire line
- - - -	Administrative boundary Shown for selected countries only.

CITIES AND TOWNS

Population	National Capital	Other City or Town
over 10 million	México	Mumbai
5 million to 10 million	London	Belo Horizonte
1 million to 5 million	Kābul	Kaohsiung
500 000 to 1 million	Bangui	Anyang
100 000 to 500 000	Wellington	Iquitos
50 000 to 100 000	Port of Spain	Naga
10 000 to 50 000	Malabo	Ushuaia
under 10 000	Valletta	Arviat

TY PLANS

Built-up area | Cemetery | Park

Place of worship | General place of interest | Transport location | Academic / municipal building

BREVIATIONS

C.T.	Australian Capital Territory		
rch.	Archipelago		
	Archipiélago	Spanish	archipelago
B.	Bay		
	Bahia, Baía	Portuguese	bay
	Bahía	Spanish	bay
	Baie	French	bay
Bol.	Bol'shaya, Bol'shoy, Bol'shoye	Russian	big
C.	Cape		
	Cabo	Portuguese, Spanish	cape, headland
	Cap	Catalan, French	cape, headland
ach.	Cachoeira	Portuguese	waterfall, rapids
Can.	Canal	French, Portuguese, Spanish	canal, channel
Cd	Ciudad	Spanish	city, town
han.	Channel		
Co	Cerro	Spanish	hill, mountain, peak
ord.	Cordillera	Spanish	mountain range
Cr.	Creek		
uch.	Cuchilla	Spanish	hills, mountain range
D.	Dağ, Dağı	Turkish	mountain
	Dāgh	Farsi	mountain, mountains
	Dağları	Turkish	mountain range
	Danau	Indonesian, Malay	lake
Div.	Division		
Dr	Doctor		
E.	East, Eastern		
mb.	Embalse	Spanish	reservoir
Est.	Estero	Spanish	estuary, inlet
	Estrecho	Spanish	strait
Fj.	Fjörður	Icelandic	fjord, inlet
Ft	Fort		
G.	Gebel	Arabic	hill, mountain
	Golfo	Italian, Spanish	gulf, bay
	Gora	Russian	mountain
	Gunung	Indonesian, Malay	hill, mountain
Gd	Grand	French	big
Gde	Grande	French, Italian, Portuguese, Spanish	big
Geb.	Gebergte	Afrikaans, Dutch	mountain range
Gen.	General		
Gl.	Glacier		
Gp	Group		
Gt	Great		
Harb.	Harbour		
Hd	Head		

I.	Island, Isle		
	Ilha	Portuguese	island
	Isla	Spanish	island
Î.	Île	French	island
im.	imeni	Russian	'in the name of'
Ind. Res.	Indian Reservation		
Ing.	Ingeniero	Spanish	engineer
Is	Islands, Isles		
	Islas	Spanish	islands
Îs	Îles	French	islands
J.	Jabal, Jebel	Arabic	mountain, mountains
Kep.	Kepulauan	Indonesian, Malay	archipelago, islands
Khr.	Khrebet	Russian	mountain range
L.	Lake		
	Loch	(Scotland)	lake
	Lough	(Ireland)	lake
	Lac	French	lake
	Lago	Portuguese, Spanish	lake
Lag.	Laguna	Spanish	lagoon
M.	Mys	Russian	cape, point
Mt	Mount		
	Mont	French	hill, mountain
Mt.	Mountain		
Mte	Monte	Portuguese, Spanish	hill, mountain
Mts	Mountains		
	Monts	French	hills, mountains
N.	North, Northern		
Nev.	Nevado	Spanish	peak
Nat.	National		
Nat. Park	National Park		
Nat. Res.	Nature Reserve		
Nizh.	Nizhniy, Nizhnyaya	Russian	lower
N.E.	Northeast, Northeastern		
N.H.S.	National Heritage Site		
N.W.	Northwest, Northwestern		
O.	Ostrov	Russian	island
O-va	Ostrova	Russian	islands
Oz.	Ozero	Russian, Ukrainian	lake
P.	Paso	Spanish	pass
	Pulau	Indonesian, Malay	island
Pass.	Passage		
Peg.	Pegunungan	Indonesian, Malay	mountain range
Pen.	Peninsula		
	Península	Spanish	peninsula
Pk	Peak		
	Puncak	Indonesian	mountain, peak
P-ov	Poluostrov	Russian	peninsula

P. P.	Pulau-pulau	Indonesian	islands
Psa	Presa	Spanish	reservoir
Pt	Point		
Pta	Punta	Italian, Spanish	cape, point
Pte	Pointe	French	cape, point
Pto	Porto	Portuguese	harbour, port
	Puerto	Spanish	harbour, port
R.	River		
	Rio	Portuguese	river
	Río	Spanish	river
	Rivière	French	river
	Rūd	Farsi	river
Ra.	Range		
Rec.	Recreation		
Res.	Reservation, Reserve		
Resr	Reservoir		
S.	South, Southern		
	Salar, Salina, Salinas	Spanish	salt pan, salt pans
Sa	Serra	Portuguese	mountain range
	Sierra	Spanish	mountain range
Sd	Sound		
S.E.	Southeast, Southeastern		
Serr.	Serranía	Spanish	mountain range
Sk.	Shuiku	Chinese	reservoir
Sr.	Sredniy, Srednyaya	Russian	middle, central
St	Saint		
	Sankt	German, Russian	saint
	Sint	Dutch	saint
Sta	Santa	Italian, Portuguese, Spanish	saint
Ste	Sainte	French	saint
Sto	Santo	Italian, Portuguese, Spanish	saint
Str.	Strait		
S.W.	Southwest, Southwestern		
Tg	Tanjong, Tanjung	Indonesian, Malay	cape, point
Tk	Teluk, Telukan	Indonesian, Malay	bay, gulf
Tte	Teniente	Spanish	lieutenant
Va	Villa	Spanish	town
Vdkhr.	Vodokhranilishche	Russian	reservoir
Verkh.	Verkhniy, Verkhnyaya	Russian	upper
Vol.	Volcano		
	Volcan	French	volcano
	Volcán	Spanish	volcano
Vozv.	Vozvyshennost'	Russian	hills, upland
W.	West, Western		
	Wadi, Wâdi, Wādī	Arabic	watercourse

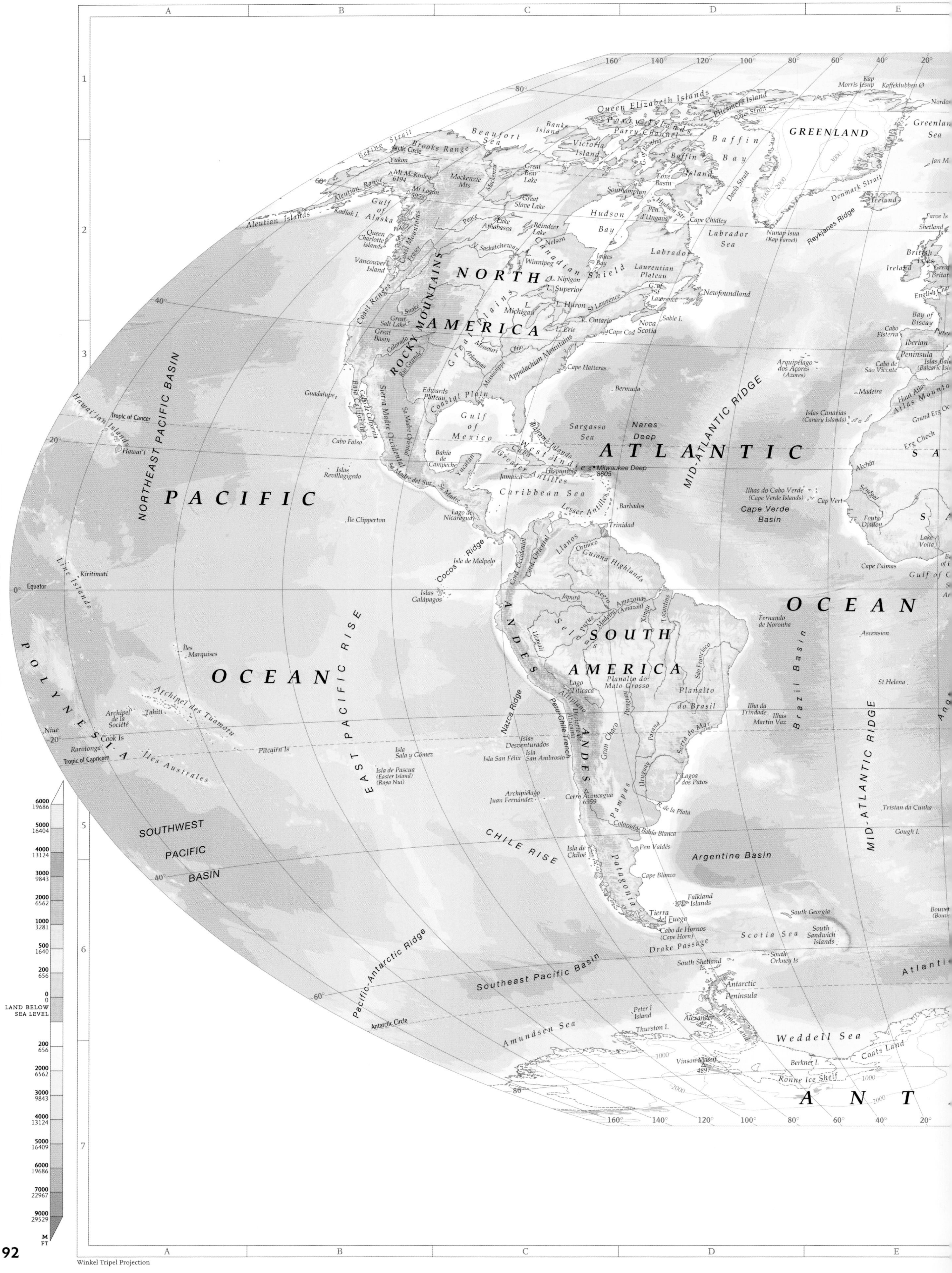

A B C D E

1 2 3 4 5 6 7

160° 140° 120° 100° 80° 60° 40° 20°

80°

Queen Elizabeth Islands
Ellesmere Island
Nares Strait
Kap Morris Jesup
Kaffeklubben Ø
Nordos
Parry Islands
Parry Channel
Banks Island
Beaufort Sea
Victoria Island
Baffin Bay
Baffin Island
GREENLAND
Greenland Sea
Jan M
Bering Strait
Arctic Circle
Brooks Range
Yukon
Mt McKinley 6194
Mt Logan 5959
Mackenzie Mts
Mackenzie
Great Bear Lake
Great Slave Lake
Southampton I.
Foxe Basin
Davis Strait
Denmark Strait
Iceland
60°
Aleutian Range
Aleutian Islands
Kodiak I.
Gulf of Alaska
Hudson Str.
Pen. d'Ungava
Cape Chidley
Hudson Bay
Lake Athabasca
Peace
Reindeer Lake
Nelson
Labrador Sea
Nunap Isua (Kap Farvel)
Reykjanes Ridge
Faroe Is
Shetland
Queen Charlotte Islands
Coast Mountains
Fraser
N. Saskatchewan
Canadian Shield
James Bay
Labrador
Laurentian Plateau
British Isles
Ireland
Great Britain
Vancouver Island
NORTH
Winnipeg
L. Nipigon
L. Superior
G. of St Lawrence
Newfoundland
English Channel
40°
Coast Ranges
Snake
ROCKY MOUNTAINS
Great Plains
L. Michigan
L. Huron
St Lawrence
L. Ontario
Sable I.
Bay of Biscay
Great Salt Lake
Great Basin
AMERICA
L. Erie
Cape Cod
Nova Scotia
Cabo Fisterra
Pyrenees
Iberian Peninsula
Colorado
Missouri
Ohio
Appalachian Mountains
Rio Grande
Arkansas
Mississippi
Cape Hatteras
Arquipélago dos Açores (Azores)
Cabo de São Vicente
Islas Baleares (Balearic Islands)
NORTHEAST PACIFIC BASIN
Guadalupe
Baja California
Golfo de California
Sierra Madre Occidental
Sierra Madre Oriental
Edwards Plateau
Coastal Plain
Bermuda
MID-ATLANTIC RIDGE
Madeira
Haut Atlas
Atlas Mountains
Hawai'ian Islands
Tropic of Cancer
Gulf of Mexico
Sargasso Sea
Nares Deep
Islas Canarias (Canary Islands)
Grand Erg Occidental
20°
Hawai'i
Cabo Falso
Bahía de Campeche
Yucatán
Bahama Islands
West Indies
Cuba
ATLANTIC
Erg Chech
SA
Islas Revillagigedo
Sierra Madre del Sur
Greater Antilles
Jamaica
Hispaniola
Milwaukee Deep 8605
Akchâr
PACIFIC
Sierra Madre
Caribbean Sea
Ilhas do Cabo Verde (Cape Verde Islands)
Cap Vert
Sénégal
Cape Verde Basin
Île Clipperton
Lago de Nicaragua
Lesser Antilles
Barbados
Trinidad
Fouta Djallon
Lake Volta
NORTHEAST PACIFIC BASIN
Cocos Ridge
Isla de Malpelo
Cord. Occidental
Cord. Oriental
Llanos
Orinoco
Guiana Highlands
Kiritimati
Line Islands
Cape Palmas
Gulf of Guinea
0°
Equator
Islas Galápagos
Japurá
Negro
Amazonas (Amazon)
Tocantins
Xingu
Madeira
Purus
Selvas
OCEAN
Fernando de Noronha
Ascension
EAST PACIFIC RISE
Îles Marquises
Ucayali
ANDES
SOUTH AMERICA
São Francisco
Brazil Basin
POLYNESIA
OCEAN
Lago Titicaca
Altiplano
Planalto do Mato Grosso
Planalto do Brasil
St Helena
Archipel des Tuamotu
Archipel de la Société
Tahiti
Nazca Ridge
Peru-Chile Trench
Desierto de Atacama
Paraguay
Paraná
Serra do Mar
Ilha da Trindade
Ilhas Martin Vaz
MID-ATLANTIC RIDGE
Niue
Cook Is
Rarotonga
Tropic of Capricorn
Îles Australes
Pitcairn Is
Islas Desventuradas
Isla San Félix
Isla San Ambrosio
Isla Sala y Gómez
Isla de Pascua (Easter Island) (Rapa Nui)
Gran Chaco
Uruguay
Lagoa dos Patos
Archipiélago Juan Fernández
Cerro Aconcagua 6959
Pampas
R. de la Plata
Tristan da Cunha
SOUTHWEST PACIFIC BASIN
CHILE RISE
Colorado
Bahía Blanca
Gough I.
Isla de Chiloé
Pen Valdés
Argentine Basin
40°
Patagonia
Cape Blanco
Falkland Islands
Tierra del Fuego
Cabo de Hornos (Cape Horn)
South Georgia
Scotia Sea
South Sandwich Islands
Bouvet (Bouv
Pacific-Antarctic Ridge
Drake Passage
South Orkney Is
South Shetland Is
Southeast Pacific Basin
Atlantic
Antarctic Peninsula
60°
Antarctic Circle
Peter I Island
Alexander I.
Palmer Land
Thurston I.
Amundsen Sea
Weddell Sea
Coats Land
Vinson Massif 4897
Berkner I.
Ronne Ice Shelf
ANT
80°

6000 19686
5000 16404
4000 13124
3000 9843
2000 6562
1000 3281
500 1640
200 656
0 0
LAND BELOW SEA LEVEL
200 656
2000 6562
3000 9843
4000 13124
5000 16409
6000 19686
7000 22967
9000 29529
M FT

Winkel Tripel Projection

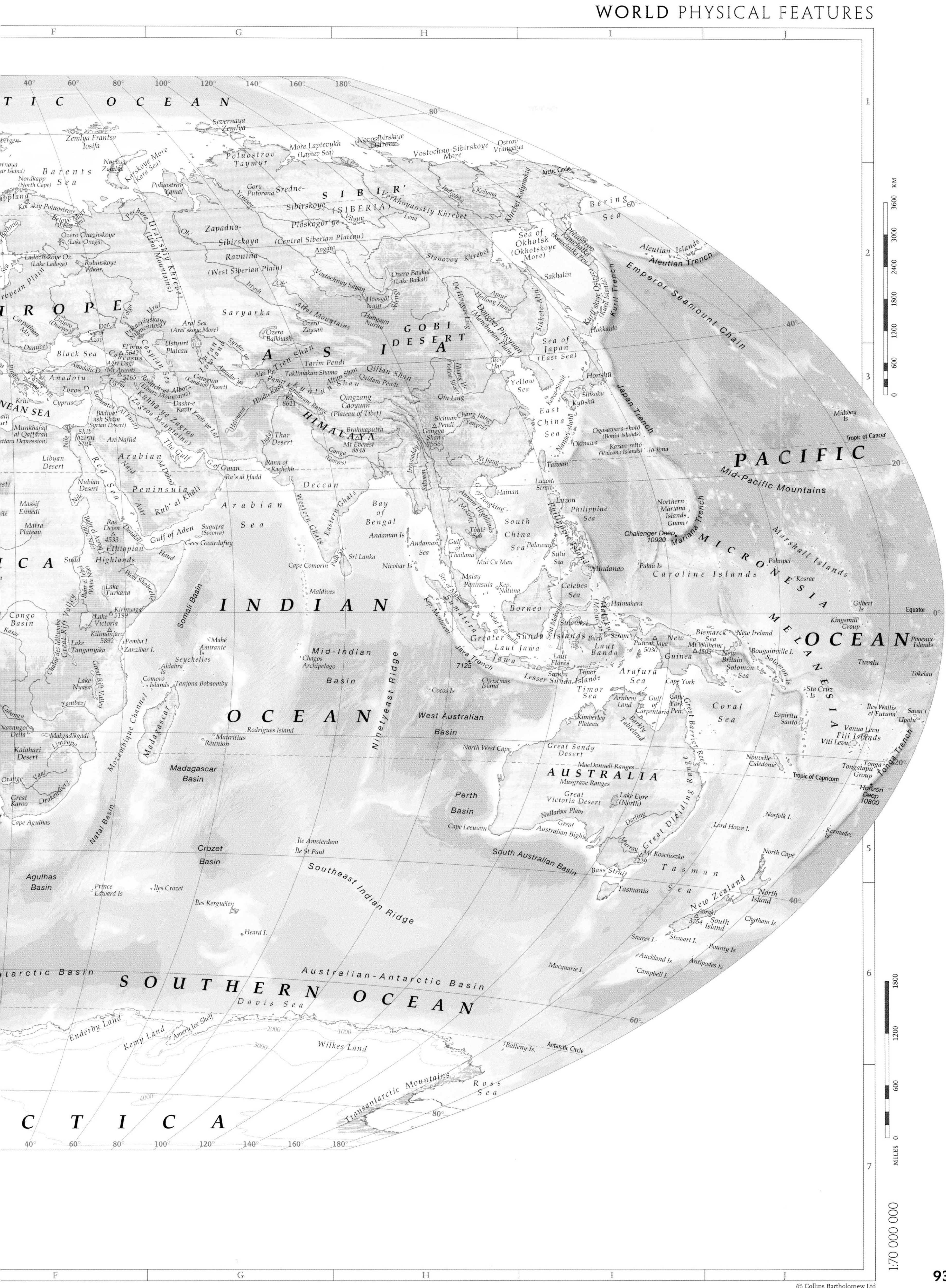
F
G
H
I
J
1
2
3
4
5
6
7
ARCTIC OCEAN
Severnaya Zemlya
Zemlya Frantsa Iosifa
Barents Sea
Karskoye More (Kara Sea)
Novaya Zemlya
Nordkapp (North Cape)
Poluostrov Taymyr
More Laptevykh (Laptev Sea)
Novosibirskiye Ostrova
Vostochno-Sibirskoye More
Ostrov Vrangelya
Arctic Circle
Poluostrov Yamal
Gory Putorana
Sredne-Sibirskoye Ploskogor'ye (Central Siberian Plateau)
SIBIR' (SIBERIA)
Verkhoyanskiy Khrebet
Kolyma
Khrebet Kolymskiy
Bering Sea
Beloye More (White Sea)
Kol'skiy Poluostrov
Ozero Onezhskoye (Lake Onega)
Ladozhskoye Oz. (Lake Ladoga)
Rybinskoye Vdkhr.
Ural'skiy Khrebet (Ural Mountains)
Zapadno-Sibirskaya Ravnina (West Siberian Plain)
Sea of Okhotsk (Okhotskoye More)
Poluostrov Kamchatka (Kamchatka Pen.)
Aleutian Islands
Aleutian Trench
Stanovoy Khrebet
Ozero Baykal (Lake Baikal)
Sakhalin
Kuril Trench
Emperor Seamount Chain
EUROPE
Saryarka
Aral Sea (Aral'skoye More)
Ozero Balkhash
Altai Mountains
GOBI DESERT
ASIA
Black Sea
Caspian Sea
Caucasus
El'brus 5642
Ustyurt Plateau
Turan Lowland
Karakum (Karakum Desert)
Tien Shan
Tarim Pendi
Taklimakan Shamo
Qilian Shan
Qaidam Pendi
Kunlun Shan
Sea of Japan (East Sea)
Hokkaidō
Honshū
Yellow Sea
Anadolu
Toros D.
Cyprus
Kriti
MEDITERRANEAN SEA
Reshteh-ye Alborz (Elburz Mountains)
Kūhhā-ye Zagros (Zagros Mountains)
Dasht-e Kavīr
Bādiyat ash Shām (Syrian Desert)
Qingzang Gaoyuan (Plateau of Tibet)
HIMALAYA
Mt Everest 8848
K2 8611
Karakoram Range
Hindu Kush
Sichuan Pendi
Gongga Shan 7556
Chang Jiang (Yangtze)
East China Sea
Japan Trench
Kyūshū
Shikoku
Nansei-shotō
Ogasawara-shotō (Bonin Islands)
Kazan-rettō (Volcano Islands)
Iō-jima
Midway Is
Tropic of Cancer
Okinawa
Taiwan
Xi Jiang
Munkhafaḑ al Qaţţārah (Qattara Depression)
Libyan Desert
An Nafūd
Arabian Peninsula
Ad Dahnā'
The Gulf
G. of Oman
Ra's al Ḥadd
Rann of Kachchh
Thar Desert
Brahmaputra
Ganga (Ganges)
PACIFIC
Mid-Pacific Mountains
Nubian Desert
Red Sea
Rub' al Khālī
Arabian Sea
Deccan
Bay of Bengal
Hainan
Luzon Strait
Luzon
Philippine Sea
Northern Mariana Islands
Guam
Challenger Deep 10920
Mariana Trench
MICRONESIA
Marshall Islands
Massif Ennedi
Marra Plateau
Ras Dejen 4533
Ethiopian Highlands
Gulf of Aden
Suquţrá (Socotra)
Gees Gwardafuy
Western Ghats
Eastern Ghats
Andaman Is
Andaman Sea
Gulf of Thailand
Tônlé Sab
South China Sea
Palawan
Sulu Sea
Philippine Islands
Mindanao
Palau Is
Caroline Islands
Pohnpei
Kosrae
Sudd
Nile
Lake Turkana
Cape Comorin
Sri Lanka
Nicobar Is
Mui Ca Mau
Malay Peninsula
Kep. Natuna
Celebes Sea
Halmahera
Gilbert Is
Equator
Congo Basin
Lake Victoria
Kirinyaga 5199
Kilimanjaro 5892
Somali Basin
INDIAN
Maldives
Sumatera
Borneo
Sulawesi
Maluku (Moluccas)
Kingsmill Group
Kasai
Lake Tanganyika
Pemba I.
Zanzibar I.
Mahé
Amirante Is
Seychelles
Mid-Indian Basin
Chagos Archipelago
Ninetyeast Ridge
Java Trench 7125
Greater Sunda Islands
Laut Jawa
Laut Flores
Laut Banda
Seram
Buru
Puncak Jaya 5030
New Guinea
Bismarck Sea
Mt Wilhelm 4509
New Ireland
New Britain
Bougainville I.
Solomon Islands
Solomon Sea
MELANESIA
OCEAN
Phoenix Islands
Tuvalu
Tokelau
Great Rift Valley
Lake Nyasa
Aldabra Is
Comoro Islands
Tanjona Bobaomby
Zambezi
Christmas Island
Cocos Is
Lesser Sunda Islands
Sumba
Timor
Timor Sea
Arafura Sea
Cape York
Cape York Pen.
Gulf of Carpentaria
Arnhem Land
Coral Sea
Sta Cruz Is
Espiritu Santo
Îles Wallis et Futuna
Savai'i
'Upolu
Mozambique Channel
Madagascar
Cubango
Okavango Delta
Makgadikgadi
Limpopo
Kalahari Desert
OCEAN
Rodrigues Island
Mauritius
Réunion
West Australian Basin
Kimberley Plateau
Barkly Tableland
Great Barrier Reef
Vanua Levu
Fiji Islands
Viti Levu
North West Cape
Great Sandy Desert
MacDonnell Ranges
AUSTRALIA
Musgrave Ranges
Nouvelle-Calédonie
Tropic of Capricorn
Tonga
Tongatapu Group
Tonga Trench
Horizon Deep 10800
Orange
Vaal
Drakensberg
Great Karoo
Cape Agulhas
Madagascar Basin
Natal Basin
Perth Basin
Great Victoria Desert
Lake Eyre (North)
Nullarbor Plain
Great Australian Bight
Cape Leeuwin
Darling
Great Dividing Range
Norfolk I.
Lord Howe I.
Kermadec Is
Crozet Basin
Île Amsterdam
Île St Paul
South Australian Basin
Murray
Mt Kosciuszko 2229
Bass Strait
Tasmania
Tasman Sea
North Cape
North Island
New Zealand
Aoraki 3754
South Island
Chatham Is
Agulhas Basin
Prince Edward Is
Îles Crozet
Southeast Indian Ridge
Îles Kerguélen
Heard I.
Snares I.
Stewart I.
Bounty Is
Auckland Is
Antipodes Is
Campbell I.
Macquarie I.
Antarctic Basin
Australian-Antarctic Basin
SOUTHERN OCEAN
Davis Sea
Enderby Land
Kemp Land
Amery Ice Shelf
Wilkes Land
Balleny Is.
Antarctic Circle
Transantarctic Mountains
Ross Sea
ANTARCTICA
KM
0
600
1200
1800
2400
3000
3600
MILES
0
600
1200
1800
1:70 000 000

Winkel Tripel Projection

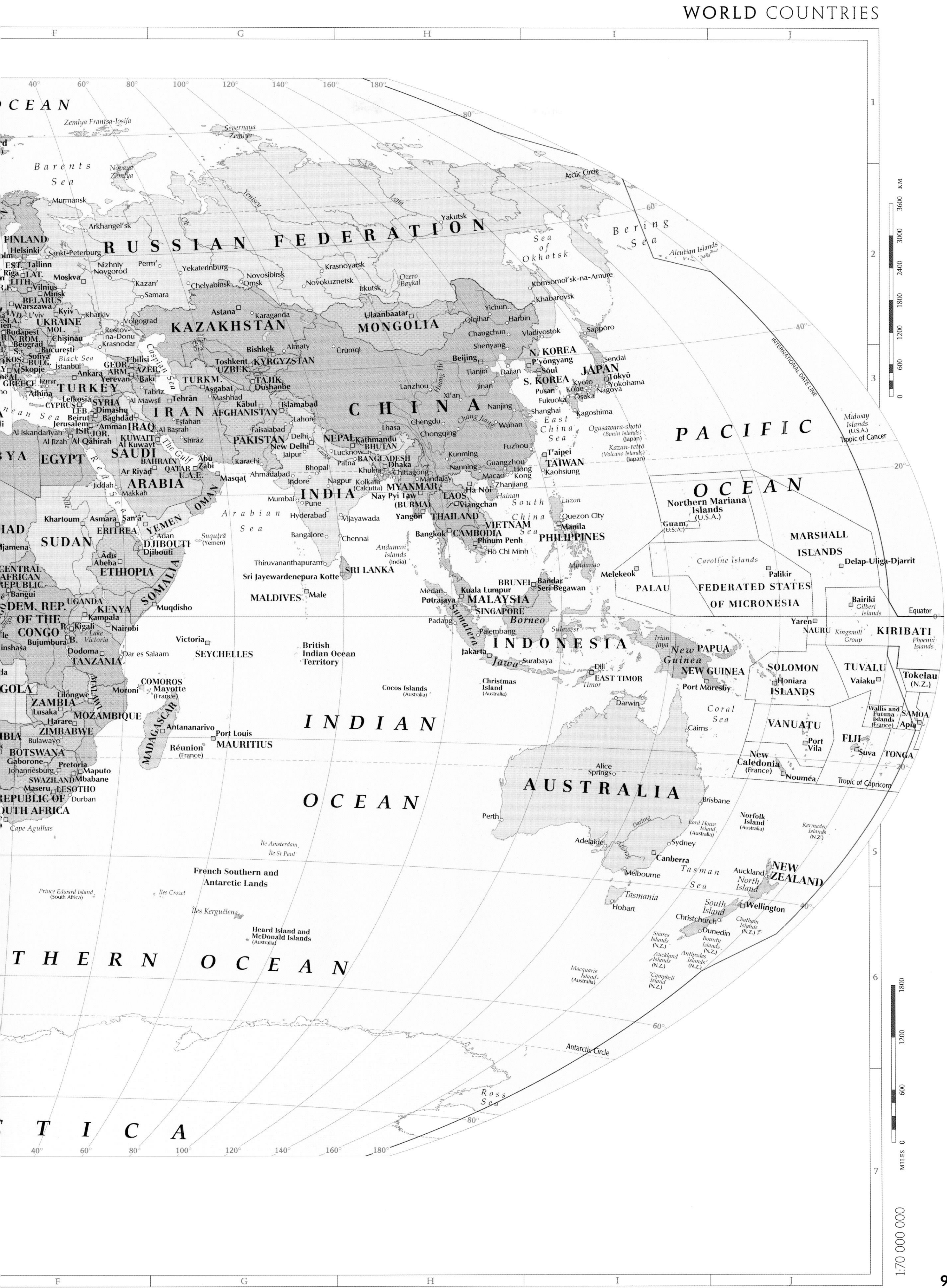
F
G
H
I
J
1
2
3
5
6
7
OCEAN
Zemlya Frantsa-Iosifa
Severnaya Zemlya
Barents Sea
Novaya Zemlya
Murmansk
Arkhangel'sk
FINLAND
Helsinki
Sankt-Peterburg
RUSSIAN FEDERATION
EST. Tallinn
Riga LAT.
LITH.
Moskva
Nizhniy Novgorod
Perm'
Yekaterinburg
Novosibirsk
Krasnoyarsk
Yakutsk
Vilnius
Minsk
BELARUS
Warszawa
Kazan'
Samara
Chelyabinsk
Omsk
Novokuznetsk
Irkutsk
Ozero Baykal
Kyiv
L'viv
Kharkiv
UKRAINE
Volgograd
Astana
Karaganda
KAZAKHSTAN
Ulaanbaatar
MONGOLIA
Budapest
MOL.
Chișinău
Rostov-na-Donu
Krasnodar
Aral Sea
Bucureşti
Beograd
Sofiya
BULG.
Skopje
Istanbul
Black Sea
T'bilisi
GEOR.
AZER.
ARM.
Yerevan
Baki
Caspian Sea
Bishkek
Almaty
Toshkent
KYRGYZSTAN
UZBEK.
TURKM.
Aşgabat
TAJIK.
Dushanbe
Ürümqi
GREECE
Izmir
Ankara
Athina
TURKEY
Lefkosia
CYPRUS
SYRIA
LEB.
Dimashq
Beirut
Jerusalem
ISR.
JOR.
'Ammān
Baghdād
IRAQ
Al Mawsil
Tabriz
Tehrān
Mashhad
IRAN
Kābul
AFGHANISTAN
Islamabad
Lahore
Eşfahan
Al Başrah
Shīrāz
KUWAIT
Al Kuwayt
Al Iskandariyah
Al Jīzah
Al Qāhirah
EGYPT
SAUDI ARABIA
Ar Riyāḑ
BAHRAIN
QATAR
Abū Zabi
U.A.E.
The Gulf
Masqaṭ
OMAN
Jiddah
Makkah
Red Sea
Nile
Faisalabad
PAKISTAN
Karachi
Delhi
New Delhi
Jaipur
Ahmadabad
Indore
Bhopal
Nagpur
Mumbai
Pune
Hyderabad
Vijayawada
Bangalore
Chennai
INDIA
Ganga
Lucknow
Patna
Kolkata (Calcutta)
Khulna
NEPAL
Kathmandu
BHUTAN
BANGLADESH
Dhaka
Chittagong
MYANMAR (BURMA)
Mandalay
Nay Pyi Taw
Yangon
Lhasa
CHINA
Chengdu
Chongqing
Lanzhou
Xi'an
Huang He
Chang Jiang
Wuhan
Nanjing
Shanghai
Beijing
Tianjin
Jinan
Dalian
Shenyang
Changchun
Harbin
Qiqihar
Yichun
Vladivostok
Kunming
Nanning
Guangzhou
Hong Kong
Macao
Zhanjiang
Fuzhou
Hainan
Ha Nôi
LAOS
Viangchan
THAILAND
Bangkok
CAMBODIA
Phnum Penh
VIETNAM
Hô Chi Minh
N. KOREA
P'yŏngyang
Sŏul
S. KOREA
Pusan
JAPAN
Sapporo
Sendai
Tōkyō
Yokohama
Nagoya
Kyōto
Kōbe
Ōsaka
Fukuoka
Kagoshima
Komsomol'sk-na-Amure
Khabarovsk
Sea of Okhotsk
Bering Sea
Aleutian Islands
Arctic Circle
Yenisey
Ob'
Lena
East China Sea
T'aipei
TAIWAN
Kaohsiung
South China Sea
Luzon
Quezon City
Manila
PHILIPPINES
Mindanao
Ogasawara-shotō (Bonin Islands) (Japan)
Kazan-rettō (Volcano Islands) (Japan)
PACIFIC OCEAN
Midway Islands (U.S.A.)
Tropic of Cancer
INTERNATIONAL DATE LINE
Northern Mariana Islands (U.S.A.)
Guam (U.S.A.)
MARSHALL ISLANDS
Delap-Uliga-Djarrit
Caroline Islands
Palikir
FEDERATED STATES OF MICRONESIA
Melekeok
PALAU
Bairiki
Gilbert Islands
Equator
Yaren
NAURU
Kingsmill Group
KIRIBATI
Phoenix Islands
TUVALU
Vaiaku
Tokelau (N.Z.)
SOLOMON ISLANDS
Honiara
Wallis and Futuna Islands (France)
SAMOA
Apia
VANUATU
Port Vila
FIJI
Suva
TONGA
New Caledonia (France)
Nouméa
Tropic of Capricorn
Arabian Sea
Suquṭrā (Yemen)
YEMEN
Şan'ā'
Adan
DJIBOUTI
Djibouti
ERITREA
Asmara
Khartoum
SUDAN
Ādīs Ābeba
ETHIOPIA
SOMALIA
Muqdisho
Andaman Islands (India)
Thiruvananthapuram
Sri Jayewardenepura Kotte
SRI LANKA
MALDIVES
Male
BRUNEI
Bandar Seri Begawan
Medan
Kuala Lumpur
Putrajaya
MALAYSIA
SINGAPORE
Sumatera
Borneo
Padang
Palembang
Sulawesi
Jakarta
INDONESIA
Jawa
Surabaya
Irian Jaya
New Guinea
PAPUA NEW GUINEA
Port Moresby
Dili
EAST TIMOR
Timor
Darwin
Coral Sea
Cairns
UGANDA
KENYA
Kampala
Nairobi
Kigali
Lake Victoria
Bujumbura
Dodoma
TANZANIA
Dar es Salaam
Victoria
SEYCHELLES
British Indian Ocean Territory
DEM. REP. OF THE CONGO
Bangui
CENTRAL AFRICAN REPUBLIC
Ndjamena
COMOROS
Moroni
Mayotte (France)
Lilongwe
MALAWI
ZAMBIA
Lusaka
Harare
ZIMBABWE
MOZAMBIQUE
Bulawayo
BOTSWANA
Gaborone
Pretoria
Johannesburg
Maputo
SWAZILAND
Mbabane
Maseru
LESOTHO
REPUBLIC OF SOUTH AFRICA
Durban
Cape Agulhas
MADAGASCAR
Antananarivo
Port Louis
MAURITIUS
Réunion (France)
Cocos Islands (Australia)
Christmas Island (Australia)
INDIAN OCEAN
AUSTRALIA
Alice Springs
Brisbane
Perth
Adelaide
Darling
Murray
Sydney
Canberra
Melbourne
Tasmania
Hobart
Lord Howe Island (Australia)
Norfolk Island (Australia)
Kermadec Islands (N.Z.)
Tasman Sea
Auckland
North Island
NEW ZEALAND
Wellington
South Island
Christchurch
Dunedin
Chatham Islands (N.Z.)
Bounty Islands (N.Z.)
Antipodes Islands (N.Z.)
Snares Islands (N.Z.)
Auckland Islands (N.Z.)
Campbell Island (N.Z.)
Macquarie Island (Australia)
Île Amsterdam
Île St Paul
French Southern and Antarctic Lands
Prince Edward Islands (South Africa)
Îles Crozet
Îles Kerguelen
Heard Island and McDonald Islands (Australia)
SOUTHERN OCEAN
Antarctic Circle
Ross Sea
ANTARCTICA
KM 0 600 1200 1800 2400 3000 3600
MILES 0 600 1200 1800
1:70 000 000

Orthographic Projection

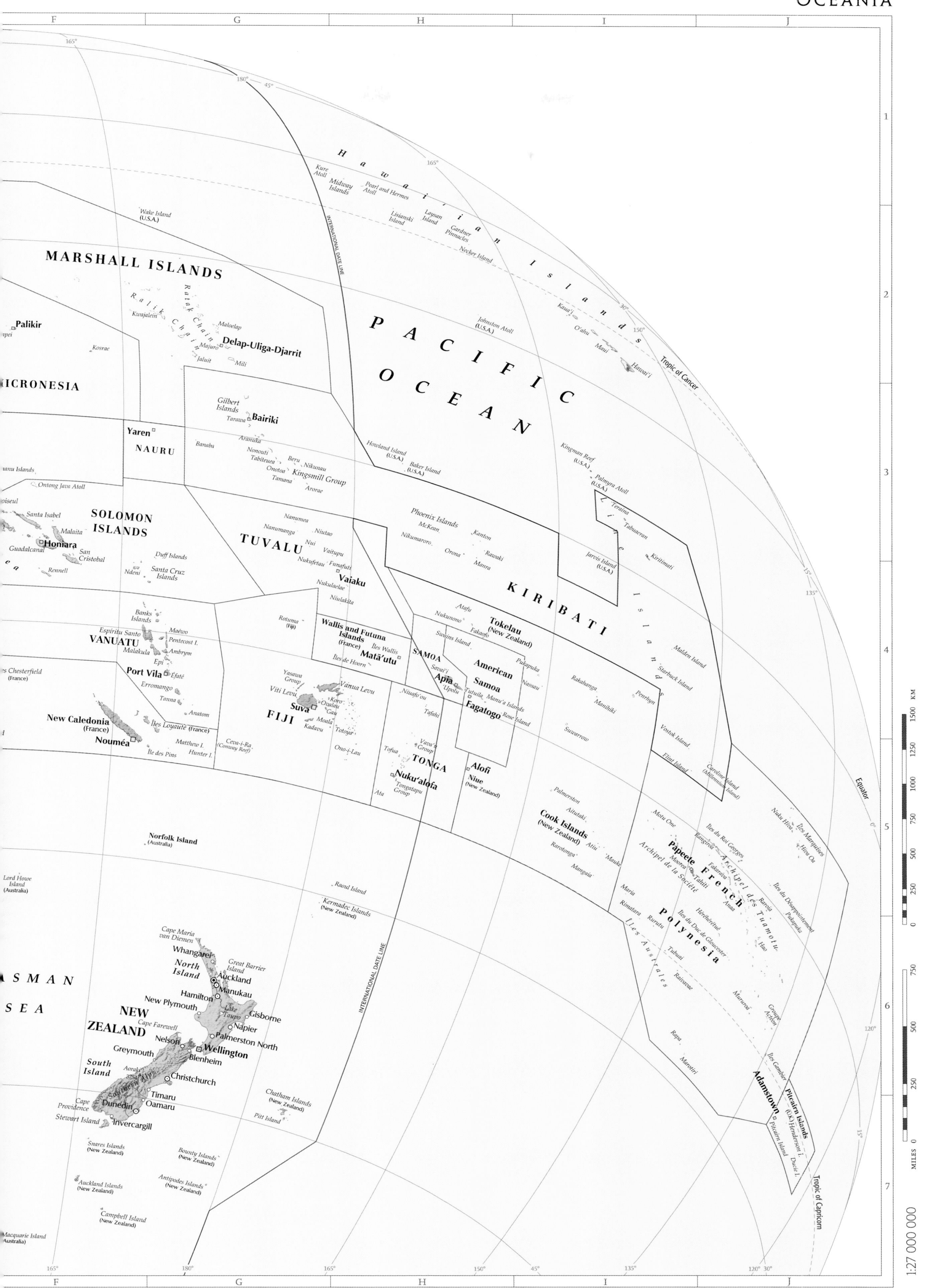
PACIFIC OCEAN
Hawaiian Islands
MARSHALL ISLANDS
Delap-Uliga-Djarrit
Palikir
MICRONESIA
Yaren
NAURU
Bairiki
SOLOMON ISLANDS
Honiara
TUVALU
Vaiaku
KIRIBATI
Tokelau (New Zealand)
Wallis and Futuna Islands (France)
Matā'utu
SAMOA
Apia
American Samoa
Fagatogo
VANUATU
Port Vila
FIJI
Suva
New Caledonia (France)
Nouméa
TONGA
Nuku'alofa
Alofi
Niue (New Zealand)
Cook Islands (New Zealand)
Papeete
French Polynesia
Pitcairn Islands (U.K.)
Adamstown
Norfolk Island (Australia)
Lord Howe Island (Australia)
Kermadec Islands (New Zealand)
NEW ZEALAND
North Island
South Island
Auckland
Hamilton
Wellington
Christchurch
Dunedin
Invercargill
Chatham Islands (New Zealand)
Auckland Islands (New Zealand)
Campbell Island (New Zealand)
Macquarie Island (Australia)
TASMAN SEA
INTERNATIONAL DATE LINE
Tropic of Cancer
Equator
Tropic of Capricorn
1:27 000 000

Lambert Azimuthal Equal Area Projection

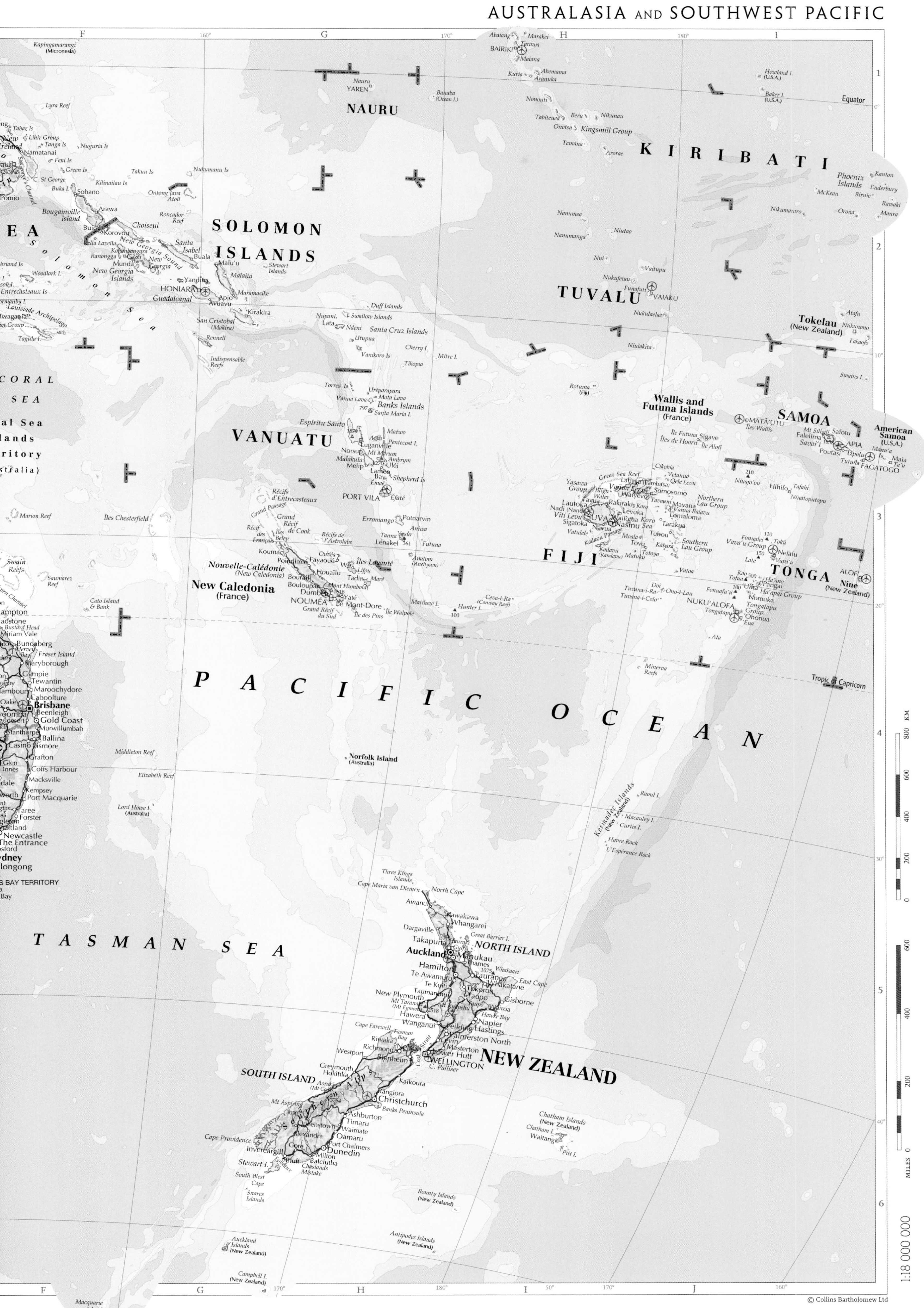
NAURU
KIRIBATI
SOLOMON ISLANDS
TUVALU
Tokelau (New Zealand)
Wallis and Futuna Islands (France)
SAMOA
American Samoa (U.S.A.)
VANUATU
FIJI
TONGA
Niue (New Zealand)
New Caledonia (France)
Nouvelle-Calédonie (New Caledonia)
CORAL SEA
PACIFIC OCEAN
TASMAN SEA
NEW ZEALAND
NORTH ISLAND
SOUTH ISLAND
Norfolk Island (Australia)
Kermadec Islands (New Zealand)
Chatham Islands (New Zealand)
Bounty Islands (New Zealand)
Antipodes Islands (New Zealand)
Auckland Islands (New Zealand)
Campbell I. (New Zealand)
Macquarie Island (Australia)
Lord Howe I. (Australia)
HONIARA
PORT VILA
NOUMÉA
SUVA
APIA
NUKU'ALOFA
WELLINGTON
Auckland
Christchurch
Dunedin
Brisbane
Sydney
Newcastle
Equator
Tropic of Capricorn
1:18 000 000
© Collins Bartholomew Ltd

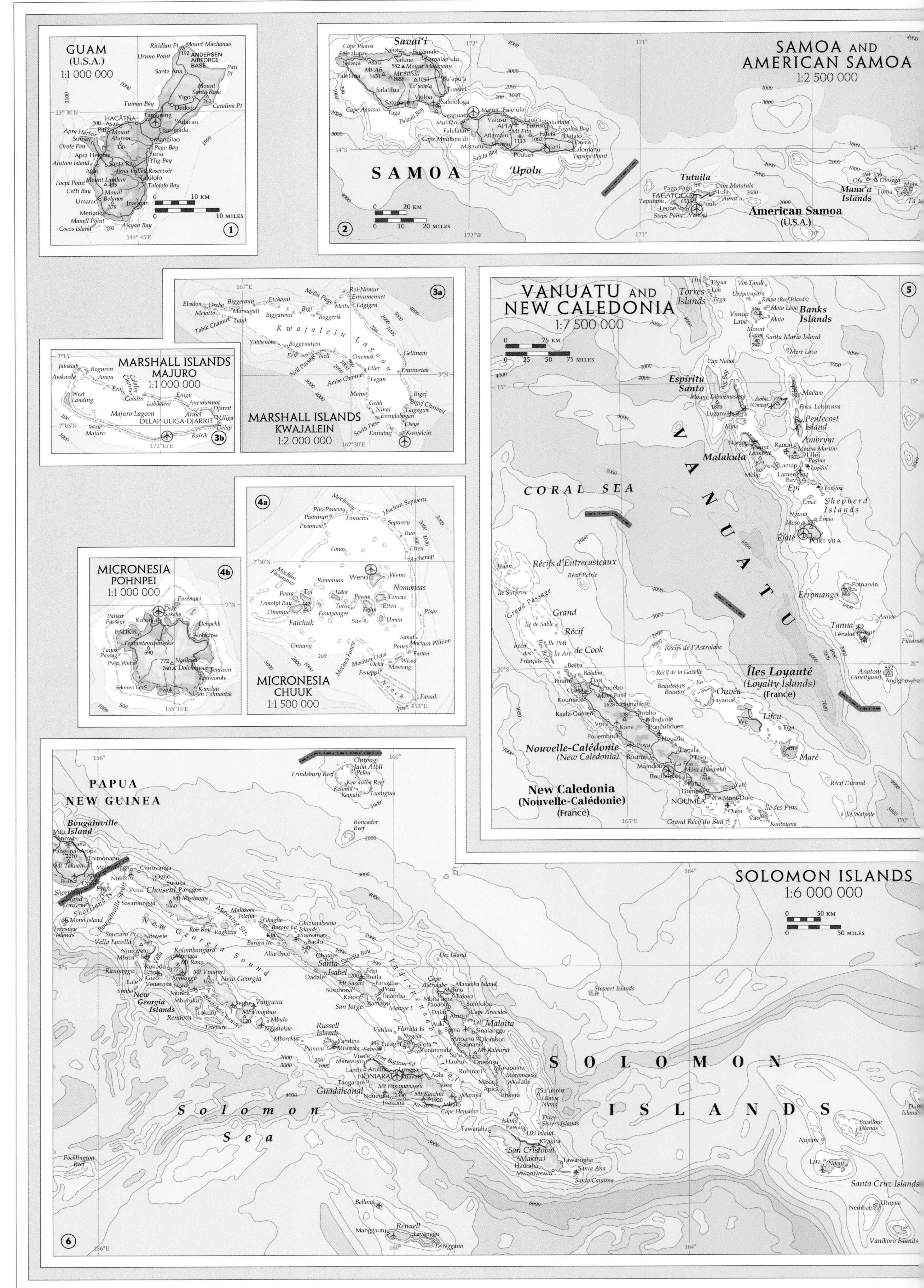
GUAM
(U.S.A.)
1:1 000 000
SAMOA AND AMERICAN SAMOA
1:2 500 000
MARSHALL ISLANDS
MAJURO
1:1 000 000
MARSHALL ISLANDS
KWAJALEIN
1:2 000 000
VANUATU AND NEW CALEDONIA
1:7 500 000
MICRONESIA
POHNPEI
1:1 000 000
MICRONESIA
CHUUK
1:1 500 000
SOLOMON ISLANDS
1:6 000 000

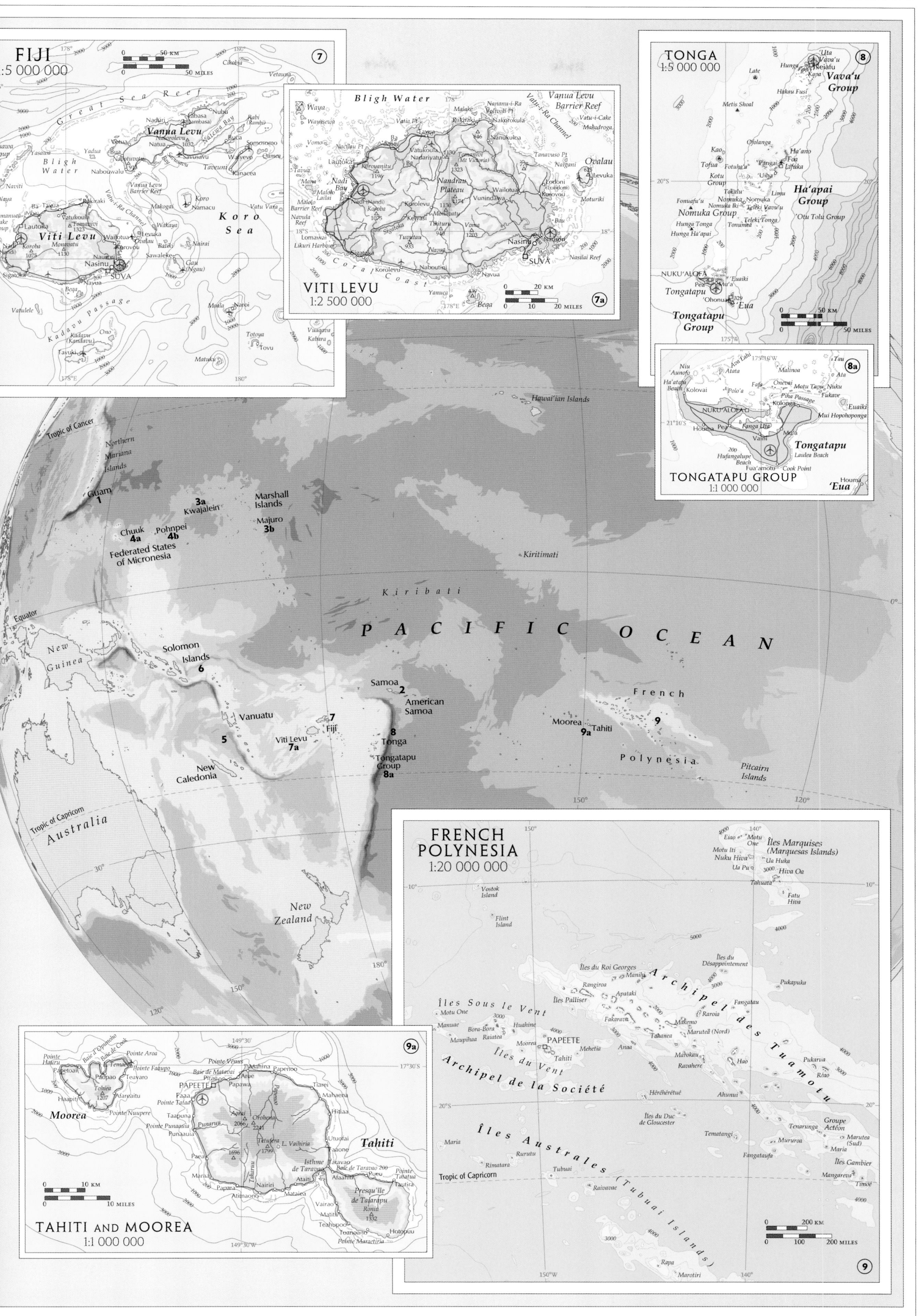
FIJI
1:5 000 000
VITI LEVU
1:2 500 000
TONGA
1:5 000 000
TONGATAPU GROUP
1:1 000 000
FRENCH POLYNESIA
1:20 000 000
TAHITI AND MOOREA
1:1 000 000
PACIFIC OCEAN
Kiribati
Marshall Islands
Federated States of Micronesia
Solomon Islands
Vanuatu
New Caledonia
Fiji
Tonga
Samoa
American Samoa
French Polynesia
Pitcairn Islands
Hawai'ian Islands
Kiritimati
Australia
New Zealand
New Guinea
Tropic of Cancer
Equator
Tropic of Capricorn

NORTH ISLAND
TASMAN SEA
NORTHLAND
AUCKLAND
WAIKATO
BAY OF PLENTY
GISBORNE
HAWKE'S BAY
TARANAKI
MANAWATU-WANGANUI
Bay of Plenty
Hawke Bay
Hauraki Gulf
Coromandel Peninsula
North Cape
C. Reinga
Three Kings Islands
Ninety Mile Beach
Kaipara Harbour
Auckland
Hamilton
Napier
New Plymouth
Wanganui
Taupo
AUCKLAND
1:30 000
Waitemata Harbour
Auckland Domain
CHATHAM ISLANDS
1:3 000 000
Chatham Island (Rekohua)
Pitt Island
Pitt Strait
Conic Equidistant Projection
6000 19686
5000 16404
4000 13124
3000 9843
2000 6562
1500 4921
1000 3281
500 1640
200 656
100 328
0 0
LAND BELOW SEA LEVEL
200 656
1000 3281
2000 6562
M FT

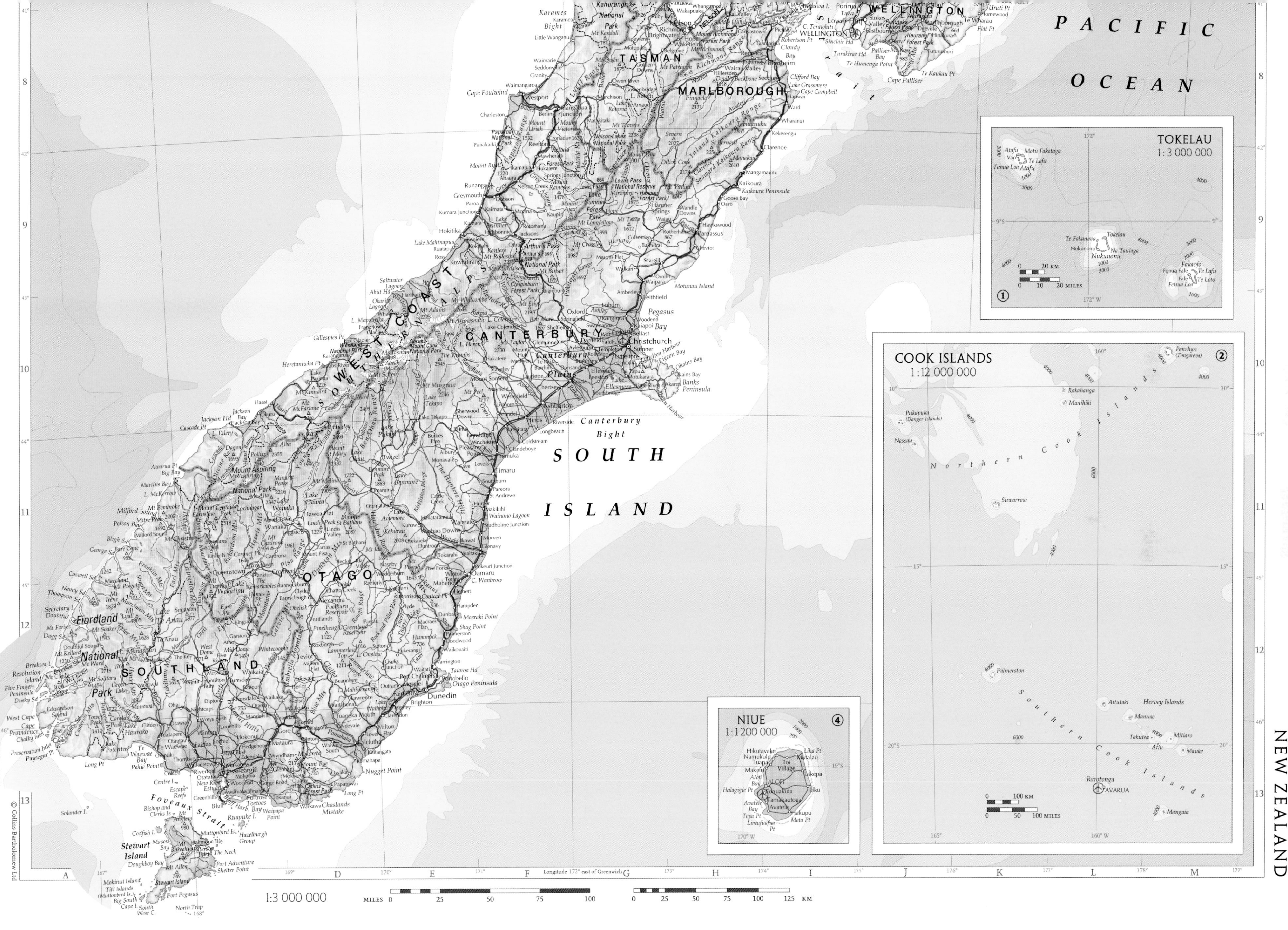

PACIFIC OCEAN
SOUTH ISLAND
Canterbury Bight
WELLINGTON
TASMAN
MARLBOROUGH
CANTERBURY
WEST COAST
SOUTHERN ALPS
OTAGO
SOUTHLAND
Fiordland National Park
Stewart Island
Foveaux Strait
Christchurch
Dunedin
TOKELAU
1:3 000 000
COOK ISLANDS
1:12 000 000
Northern Cook Islands
Southern Cook Islands
NIUE
1:1 200 000
1:3 000 000
Longitude 172° east of Greenwich

106
109
WESTERN AUSTRALIA
SOUTH AUSTRALIA
GREAT VICTORIA DESERT
Great Victoria Desert Nature Reserve
Anangu Pitjantjatjara Aboriginal Lands
Maralinga-Tjarutja Aboriginal Lands
Woomera Prohibited Area
Nullarbor Plain
Nullarbor Regional Reserve
Nullarbor National Park
GREAT AUSTRALIAN BIGHT
Musgrave Ranges
Simpson Desert
Sturt Stony Desert
Lake Eyre (North)
Lake Eyre (South)
Lake Torrens
Lake Gairdner
FLINDERS RANGES
Gawler Ranges
Eyre Peninsula
Spencer Gulf
Gulf St Vincent
Investigator Strait
Kangaroo Island
Adelaide
Port Augusta
Port Pirie
Port Lincoln
Whyalla
Coober Pedy
Woomera
Ceduna
Mount Gambier
NORFOLK ISLAND ①
1:900 000
LORD HOWE ISLAND ②
1:900 000
MACQUARIE ISLAND ③
1:900 000
MELBOURNE
1:30 000
LAND BELOW SEA LEVEL
M
FT
Lambert Azimuthal Equal Area Projection
Longitude 140° east of Greenwich

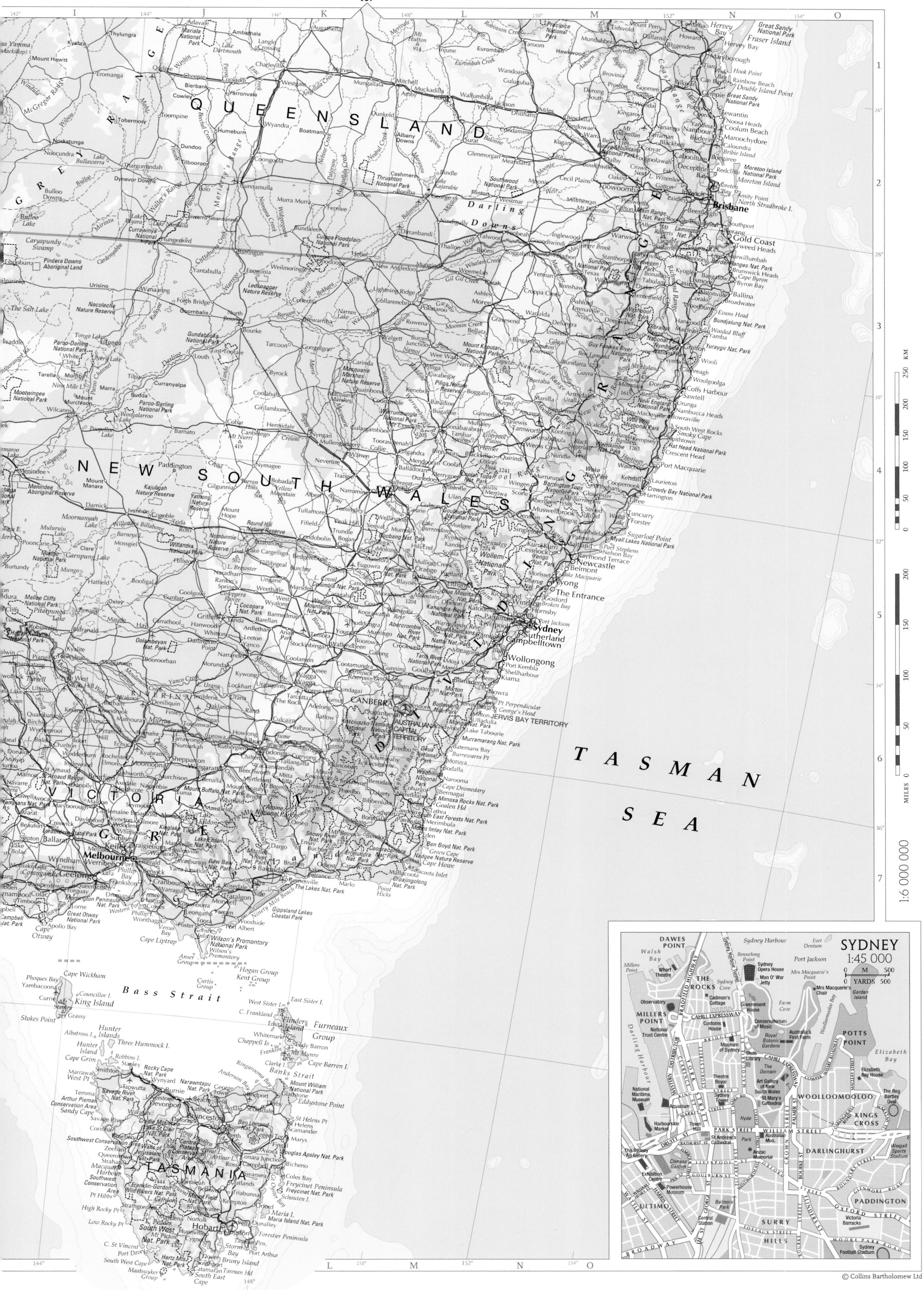
107
QUEENSLAND
NEW SOUTH WALES
VICTORIA
TASMANIA
TASMAN SEA
GREY RANGE
GREAT DIVIDING RANGE
AUSTRALIAN CAPITAL TERRITORY
JERVIS BAY TERRITORY
CANBERRA
Sydney
Melbourne
Brisbane
Hobart
Newcastle
Wollongong
Gold Coast
Geelong
Bass Strait
Banks Strait
King Island
Flinders Island
Furneaux Group
Darling Downs
Fraser Island
Moreton Island
North Stradbroke I.
Port Macquarie
Coffs Harbour
Tamworth
Armidale
Dubbo
Orange
Bathurst
Wagga Wagga
Albury
Bendigo
Ballarat
Launceston
Devonport
Toowoomba
Bundaberg
Maryborough
1:6 000 000
KM
MILES
SYDNEY
1:45 000
DAWES POINT
THE ROCKS
MILLERS POINT
POTTS POINT
WOOLLOOMOOLOO
KINGS CROSS
DARLINGHURST
PADDINGTON
SURRY HILLS
ULTIMO
Sydney Harbour
Port Jackson
Sydney Opera House
Darling Harbour
Hyde Park
The Domain
Royal Botanic Gardens
Farm Cove
Sydney Football Stadium

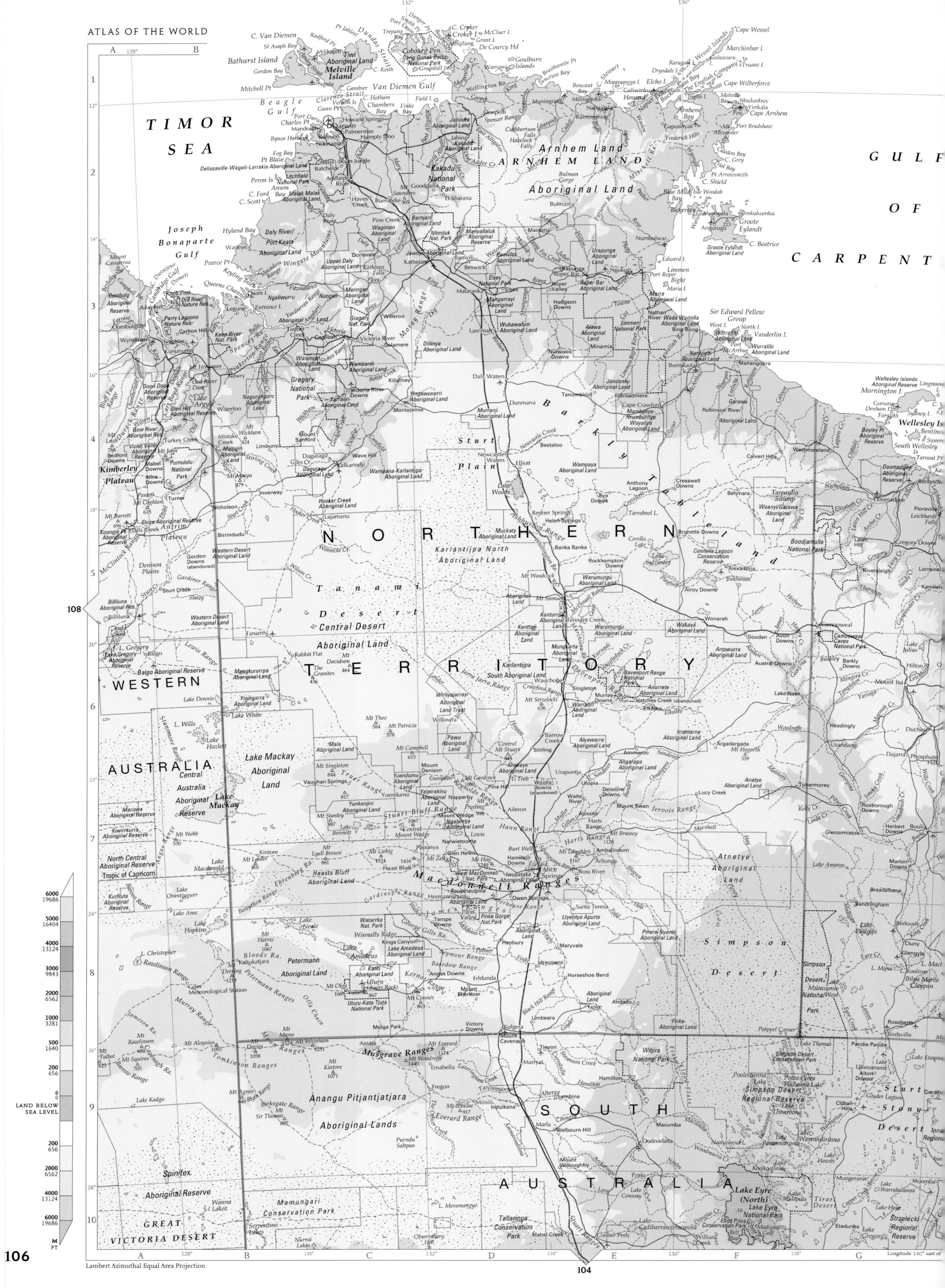

TIMOR SEA
Joseph Bonaparte Gulf
Beagle Gulf
Van Diemen Gulf
GULF OF CARPENT
Melville Island
Bathurst Island
Tiwi Aboriginal Land
Cobourg Pen.
Darwin
Palmerston
Kakadu National Park
Arnhem Land
ARNHEM LAND
Aboriginal Land
Groote Eylandt
Katherine
Mataranka
Roper River
Daly Waters
Kimberley Plateau
Sturt Plain
Barkly Tableland
NORTHERN TERRITORY
Tanami Desert
Central Desert Aboriginal Land
Karlantijpa North Aboriginal Land
Tennant Creek
Lake Mackay Aboriginal Land
Central Australia Aboriginal Reserve
Lake Mackay
WESTERN AUSTRALIA
Macdonnell Ranges
Alice Springs
Haasts Bluff Aboriginal Land
Petermann Aboriginal Land
Uluru
Simpson Desert
Atnetye Aboriginal Land
Mount Isa
Musgrave Ranges
Anangu Pitjantjatjara Aboriginal Lands
SOUTH AUSTRALIA
Lake Eyre (North)
Coober Pedy
Sturt Stony Desert
Spinifex Aboriginal Reserve
Mamungari Conservation Park
GREAT VICTORIA DESERT
Tallaringa Conservation Park
6000
19686
5000
16404
4000
13124
3000
9843
2000
6562
1000
3281
500
1640
200
656
0
0
LAND BELOW SEA LEVEL
200
656
2000
6562
4000
13124
6000
19686
M
FT
Lambert Azimuthal Equal Area Projection

108
104

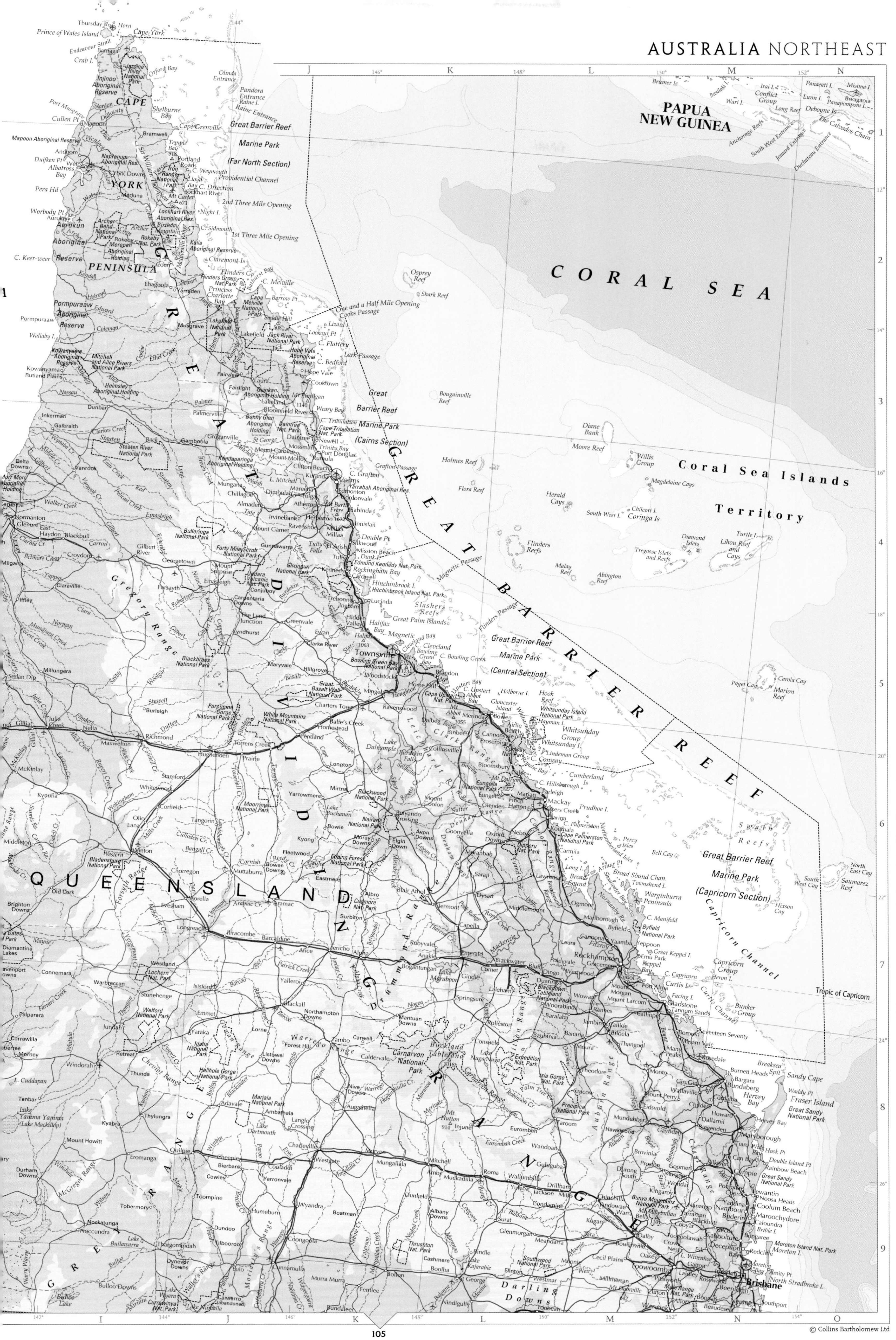

CORAL SEA

PAPUA NEW GUINEA

Coral Sea Islands Territory

GREAT BARRIER REEF

GREAT DIVIDING RANGE

QUEENSLAND

CAPE YORK PENINSULA

Great Barrier Reef Marine Park (Far North Section)

Great Barrier Reef Marine Park (Cairns Section)

Great Barrier Reef Marine Park (Central Section)

Great Barrier Reef Marine Park (Capricorn Section)

Tropic of Capricorn

Townsville

Cairns

Mackay

Rockhampton

Brisbane

Darling Downs

1:6 000 000

© Collins Bartholomew Ltd

105

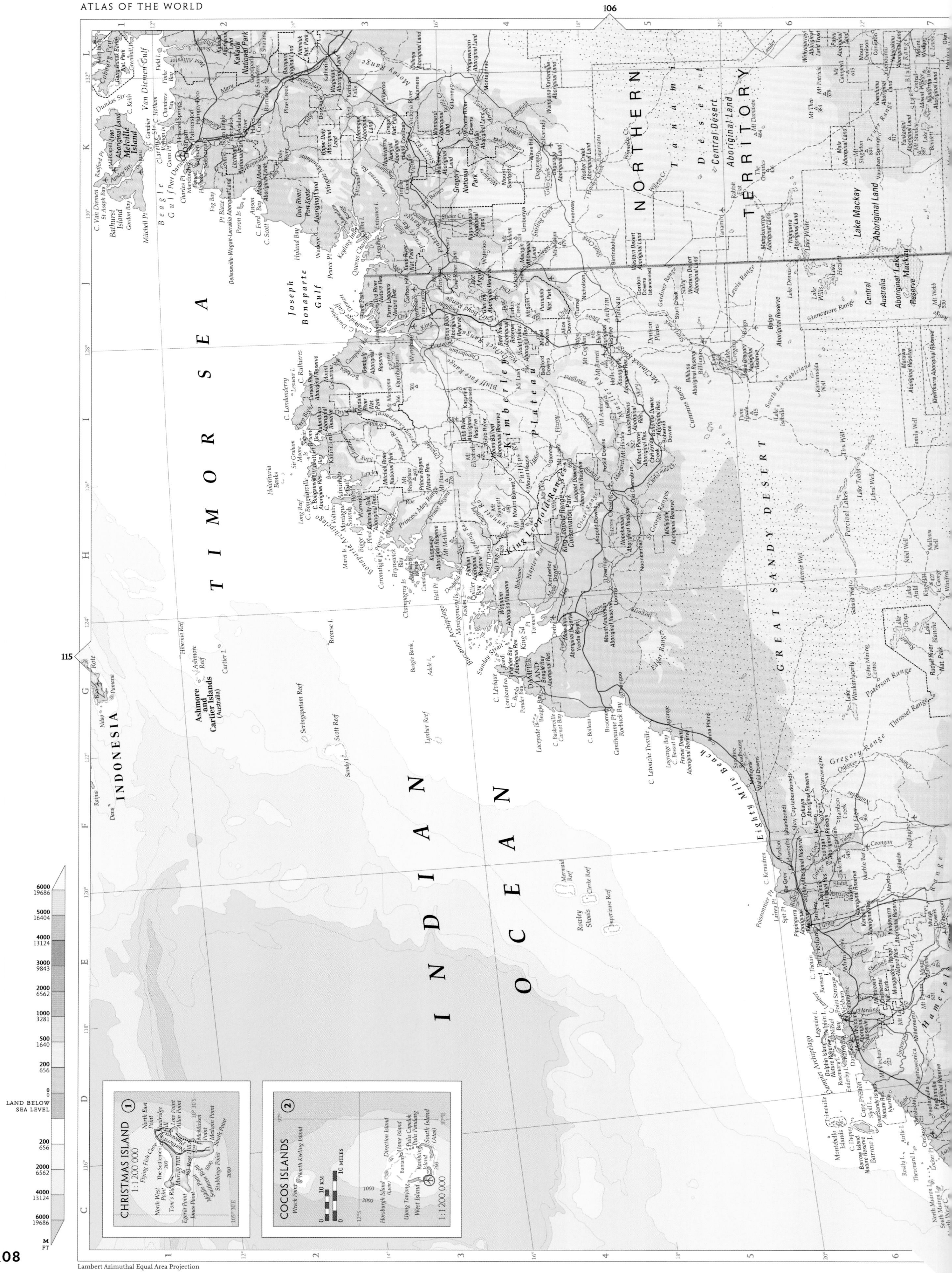

106

115

TIMOR SEA

INDIAN OCEAN

NORTHERN TERRITORY

GREAT SANDY DESERT

INDONESIA

Ashmore and Cartier Islands (Australia)

Joseph Bonaparte Gulf

Kimberley Plateau

CHRISTMAS ISLAND ①
1:1 200 000

COCOS ISLANDS ②
1:1 200 000

M	FT
6000	19686
5000	16404
4000	13124
3000	9843
2000	6562
1000	3281
500	1640
200	656
0	0
LAND BELOW SEA LEVEL	
200	656
2000	6562
4000	13124
6000	19686

Lambert Azimuthal Equal Area Projection

104
WESTERN AUSTRALIA
SOUTH AUSTRALIA
GREAT AUSTRALIAN BIGHT
GREAT VICTORIA DESERT
Nullarbor Plain
Little Sandy Desert
Perth
Kalgoorlie
Geraldton
Carnarvon
Shark Bay
Houtman Abrolhos
Archipelago of the Recherche
Tropic of Capricorn
1:6 000 000
MILES 0 50 100 150 200
0 50 100 150 200 250 KM
Longitude 120° east of Greenwich

Orthographic Projection

OCEAN
Bering Strait
Tiksi
SREDNE-SIBIRSKOYE
PLOSKOGOR'YE
Verkhoyanskiy Khrebet
Khrebet Kolymskiy
Arctic Circle
Ugol'nyye Kopi
Susuman
BERING SEA
Pribilof Islands
FEDERATION
Mirnyy
Yakutsk
Magadan
Aldan
Sea of Okhotsk
Poluostrov Kamchatka
Aleutian Islands
Bodaybo
Ust'- Kut
Stanovoy Khrebet
Petropavlovsk-Kamchatskiy
Bratsk
Tynda
Ozero Baykal
Amur
Komsomol'sk-na-Amure
Sakhalin
Irkutsk
Chita
Ulan-Ude
Blagoveshchensk
Hövsgöl Nuur
Hailar
Da Hinggan Ling
Khabarovsk
Yuzhno-Sakhalinsk
Korsakov
Kuril'skiye Ostrova
Darhan
Ulaanbaatar
Qiqihar
Suihua
Jiamusi
Daqing
Harbin
Wakkanai
MONGOLIA
Matad
GOBI
Changchun
Jilin
Lake Khanka
Hokkaidō
Sapporo
Hakodate
Vladivostok
Dalandzadgad
NEI MONGOL ZIZHIQU (INNER MONGOLIA)
Fushun
Shenyang
Anshan
Benxi
Ch'ŏngjin
NORTH KOREA
Sea of Japan (East Sea)
Akita
Sendai
Jining
Zhangjiakou
Baotou
Hohhot
Beijing
Wuhai
Datong
Huang He (Yellow River)
Tangshan
Tianjin
Bo Hai
Dalian
Korea Bay
P'yŏngyang
Niigata
Yinchuan
Shijiazhuang
Taiyuan
Yantai
Puch'ŏn
Sŏul
Inch'ŏn
Suwŏn
SOUTH KOREA
Taejŏn
Kanazawa
Tōkyō
Yokohama
Honshū
JAPAN
Qinghai Hu
Xining
Handan
Jinan
Zibo
Qingdao
Kwangju
Taegu
Pusan
Kyōto
Kōbe
Nagoya
Ōsaka
Lanzhou
Xinxiang
Jining
Yellow Sea
Lianyungang
Mokp'o
Kita-Kyūshū
Hiroshima
Izu-shotō (Japan)
Weinan
Xi'an
Luoyang
Zhengzhou
Xuzhou
Fukuoka
Shikoku
Pingdingshan
Huainan
Nagasaki
Kumamoto
Kyūshū
CHINA
Hefei
Nanjing
Changzhou
Kagoshima
Suizhou
Wuhu
Wuxi
Shanghai
Chengdu
Nanchong
Wuhan
Jiaxing
Hangzhou
East China Sea
Neijiang
Chongqing
Yueyang
Jingdezhen
Ningbo
Yibin
Changde
Quzhou
Nanchang
Changsha
Wenzhou
Ogasawara-shotō (Japan)
Zhaotong
PACIFIC
Tropic of Cancer
Panzhihua
Guiyang
Hengyang
Okinawa
Fuzhou
Kazan-rettō (Japan)
Nansei-shotō (Japan)
T'aipei
Qujing
Taiwan Strait
Kunming
Liuzhou
Xiamen
TAIWAN
Meizhou
Nanning
Guangzhou
Shenzhen
Shantou
T'aitung
Kaohsiung
Macao
Hong Kong
OCEAN
Ha Nôi
Hai Phong
Zhanjiang
Batan Islands
Pagan
Gulf of Tongking
Luzon Strait
Northern Mariana Islands
Louangphrabang
Haikou
Chiang Mai
Hainan
Aparri
LAOS
Viangchan
Luzon
PHILIPPINES
Saipan
Tinian
Rota
VIETNAM
Huê
Paracel Islands
Quezon City
Guam
Da Nâng
THAILAND
SOUTH CHINA SEA
Manila
Nakhon Ratchasima
Naga
Bangkok
Mindoro
Tônlé Sab
Masbate
Samar
CAMBODIA
Nha Trang
Panay
Yap
Gulf of Thailand
Phnum Penh
Iloilo
Cebu
Surigao
Sihanoukville
Hô Chi Minh
Caroline Islands
Chuuk
Negros
Spratly Islands
Palawan
Dipolog
PALAU
Melekeok
Nakhon Si Thammarat
Sulu Sea
Mindanao
Davao
Mortlock Islands
Zamboanga
Kota Bharu
Kota Kinabalu
Sandakan
Sulu Archipelago
SABAH
Kepulauan Talaud
BRUNEI
Bandar Seri Begawan
Kepulauan Sangir
Ipoh
MALAYSIA
Equator
Kuala Lumpur
Celebes Sea
Molucca Sea
Strait of Malacca
Putrajaya
SARAWAK
Manado
Halmahera
Kuching
Sibu
Singapore
Sri Aman
Ketapang
Sumatera
Borneo
Maluku
Jazirah Doberai
Jayapura
Bismarck Archipelago
Bismarck Sea
Palu
Pontianak
Kepulauan Sula
Kepulauan Lingga
Balikpapan
Macassar Strait
Seram Sea
Seram
Pegunungan Van Rees
New Britain
Ketapang
Sulawesi
Bangka
Buru
NEW GUINEA
Bougainville Island
Palembang
Parepare
Banda Sea
Solomon Sea
Java Sea
Banjarmasin
Buton
Bengkulu
Ujung Pandang
Kepulauan Aru
Bandar Lampung
INDONESIA
Enggano
Selat Sunda
Jakarta
Madura
Kepulauan Tanimbar
Gulf of Papua
Semarang
Bali Sea
Flores Sea
Wetar
Dili
Bandung
Jawa (Java)
Surabaya
Surakarta
Bali
Raba
Flores
EAST TIMOR
Arafura Sea
Torres Strait
OCEANIA
Yogyakarta
Lombok
Sumbawa
Sumba
Sawu Sea
Timor
Kupang
Rote
Melville Island
Cape York Peninsula
CORAL SEA
KM 0 250 500 750 1000 1250
MILES 0 250 500 750
1:24 000 000
F G H I J
1 2 3 4 5 6 7

CHINA
LAOS
VIETNAM
THAILAND
CAMBODIA
MYANMAR (BURMA)
MALAYSIA
BRUNEI
SINGAPORE
INDONESIA
TAIWAN
SOUTH CHINA SEA
Gulf of Tongking
Gulf of Thailand
LAUT JAWA (JAVA SEA)
INDIAN OCEAN
SULU SEA
CELEBES SEA
GREATER SUNDA ISLANDS
Lesser Sunda Islands
SUMATERA
BORNEO
KALIMANTAN
SARAWAK
SABAH
SULAWESI (CELEBES)
JAWA (JAVA)
HAINAN
LUZON
Palawan
Hong Kong
BANGKOK (Krung Thep)
HANOI
Hô Chi Minh (Saigon)
KUALA LUMPUR
JAKARTA
MANILA
T'AIPEI
The People's Republic of China claims Taiwan as its 23rd province
LAND BELOW SEA LEVEL
Mercator Projection

PACIFIC OCEAN
Northern Mariana Islands (U.S.A.)
FEDERATED STATES OF MICRONESIA
PALAU
Caroline Islands
Guam (U.S.A.)
HAGÅTÑA
CAPITOL HILL
Saipan
Tinian
Rota
MELEKEOK
Colonia
Yap
Weno
Chuuk
Okino-Tori-shima (Japan)
Kazan-rettō (Volcano Islands) (Japan)
Tropic of Cancer
Equator
PAPUA NEW GUINEA
NEW GUINEA
PAPUA (IRIAN JAYA)
Bismarck Archipelago
Bismarck Sea
Solomon Sea
Gulf of Papua
ARAFURA SEA
PORT MORESBY
Jayapura
Madang
Lae
Wewak
Rabaul
New Britain
New Ireland
Halmahera
Ternate
Ambon
Seram
EAST TIMOR
AUSTRALIA
Thursday Island
1:13 000 000
KM
MILES
Longitude 130° east of Greenwich
© Collins Bartholomew Ltd

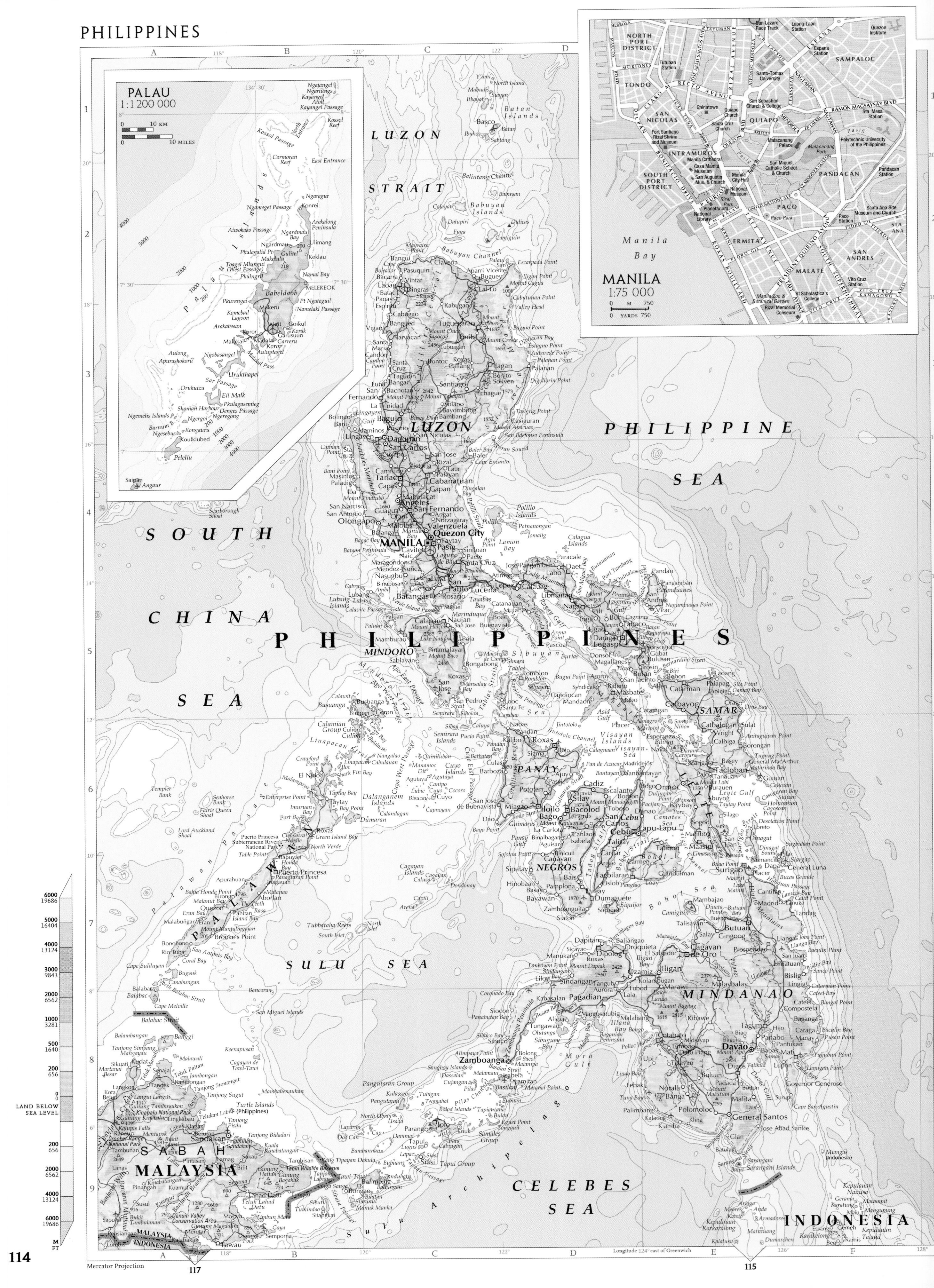
PALAU
1:1 200 000
MANILA
1:75 000
LUZON STRAIT
PHILIPPINE SEA
SOUTH CHINA SEA
PHILIPPINES
LUZON
MINDORO
PANAY
NEGROS
SAMAR
LEYTE
BOHOL
MINDANAO
PALAWAN
SULU SEA
CELEBES SEA
Sulu Archipelago
SABAH
MALAYSIA
INDONESIA
Manila Bay
Babuyan Islands
Batan Islands
Visayan Islands
Quezon City
MANILA
Cebu
Davao
Zamboanga
Mercator Projection
Longitude 124° east of Greenwich
LAND BELOW SEA LEVEL
117
115

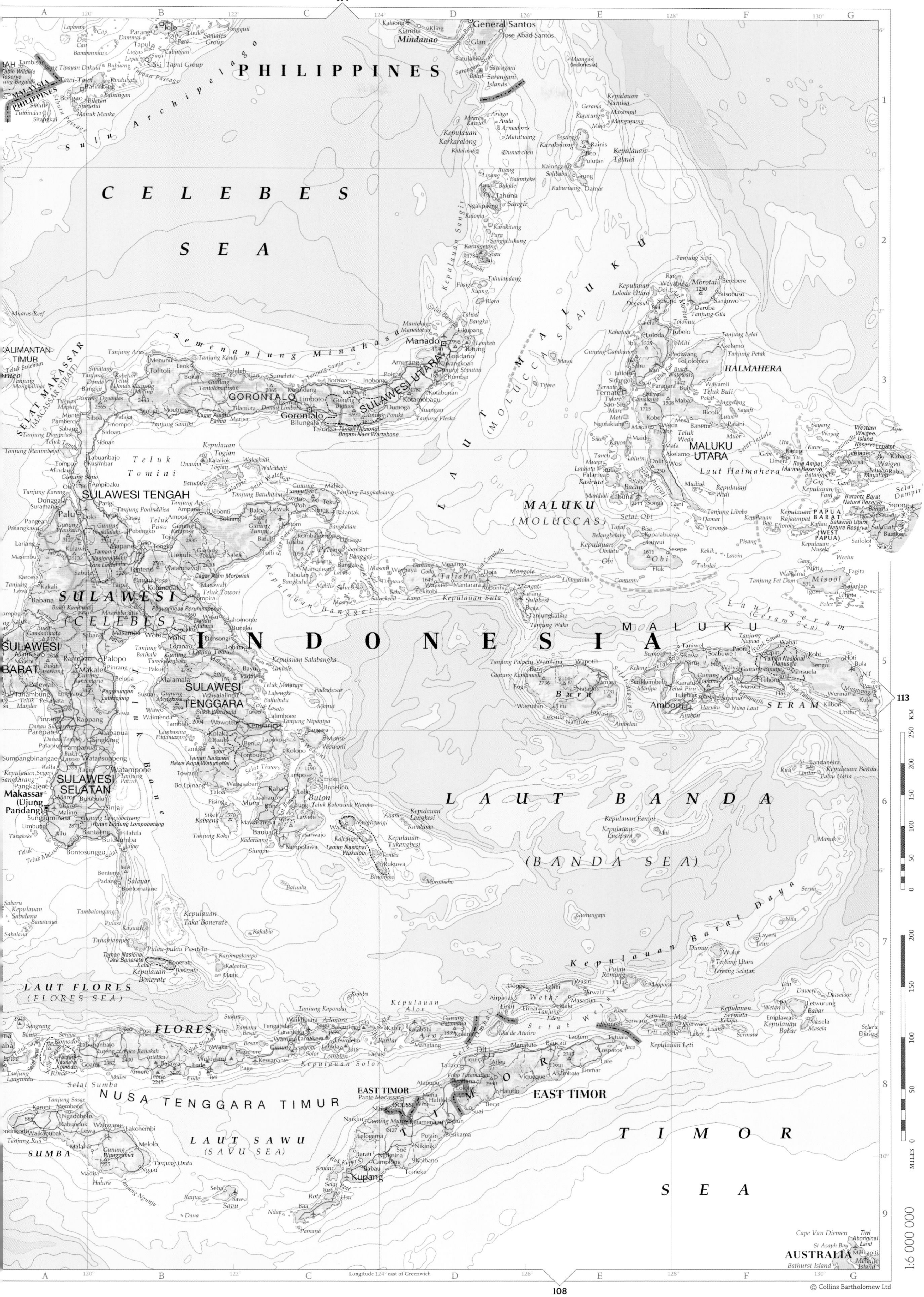

114

PHILIPPINES

CELEBES SEA

Sulu Archipelago

Mindanao

General Santos

LAUT MALUKU (MOLUCCA SEA)

SULAWESI (CELEBES)

INDONESIA

MALUKU (MOLUCCAS)

HALMAHERA

LAUT BANDA (BANDA SEA)

LAUT FLORES (FLORES SEA)

FLORES

NUSA TENGGARA TIMUR

LAUT SAWU (SAVU SEA)

SUMBA

TIMOR

EAST TIMOR

TIMOR SEA

AUSTRALIA

SULAWESI TENGAH

SULAWESI TENGGARA

SULAWESI SELATAN

SULAWESI UTARA

GORONTALO

MALUKU UTARA

SERAM

Ambon

Kupang

Manado

Makassar (Ujung Pandang)

113

1:6 000 000

108

Longitude 124° east of Greenwich

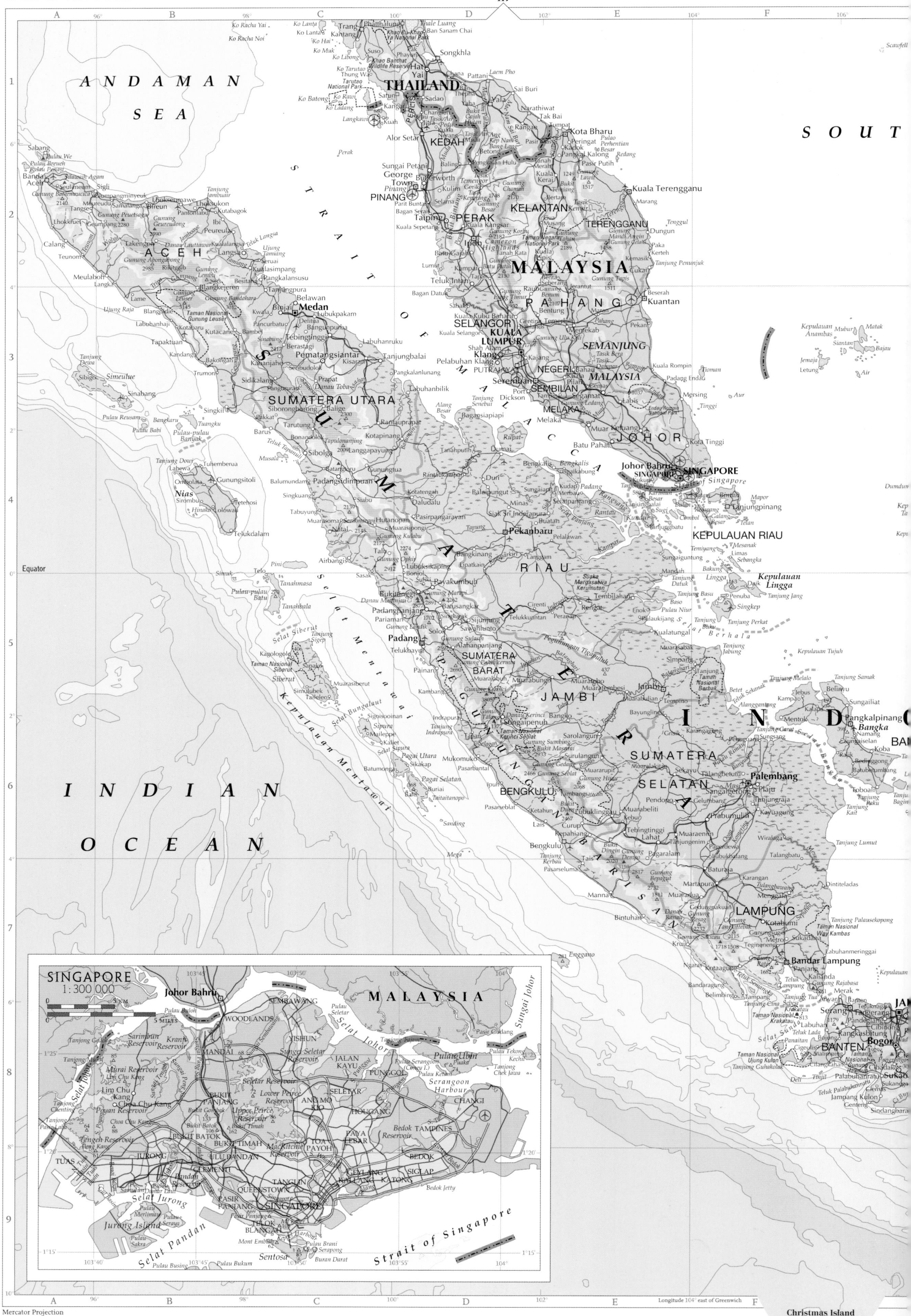

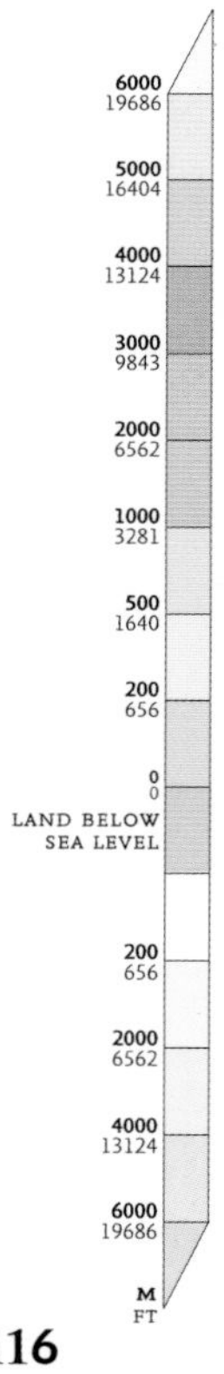

ANDAMAN SEA

STRAIT OF MALACCA

THAILAND

MALAYSIA

SOUT

INDIAN OCEAN

SUMATERA

PEGUNUNGAN BARISAN

KEPULAUAN RIAU

ACEH

SUMATERA UTARA

RIAU

SUMATERA BARAT

JAMBI

BENGKULU

SUMATERA SELATAN

LAMPUNG

BANTEN

KEDAH

PERAK

KELANTAN

TERENGGANU

PAHANG

SELANGOR

KUALA LUMPUR

NEGERI SEMBILAN

MELAKA

JOHOR

SEMENANJUNG MALAYSIA

SINGAPORE

Medan

Padang

Pekanbaru

Palembang

Bandar Lampung

Kuantan

Kota Bharu

Kuala Terengganu

Johor Bahru

Equator

SINGAPORE
1:300 000

MALAYSIA

Johor Bahru

Strait of Singapore

Selat Johor

Selat Jurong

Selat Pandan

Jurong Island

Sentosa

WOODLANDS

JURONG

QUEENSTOWN

CHANGI

BEDOK

TAMPINES

ANG MO KIO

BUKIT TIMAH

TOA PAYOH

Pulau Ubin

Pulau Tekong

M FT

6000 19686

5000 16404

4000 13124

3000 9843

2000 6562

1000 3281

500 1640

200 656

0 0

LAND BELOW SEA LEVEL

200 656

2000 6562

4000 13124

6000 19686

Mercator Projection

Longitude 104° east of Greenwich

Christmas Island (Australia)

SULU SEA
PHILIPPINES
CELEBES SEA
BRUNEI
SABAH
SARAWAK
MALAYSIA
KALIMANTAN TIMUR
KALIMANTAN BARAT
KALIMANTAN TENGAH
KALIMANTAN SELATAN
BORNEO
SULAWESI TENGAH
SULAWESI BARAT
SULAWESI SELATAN
SULAWESI (CELEBES)
SELAT MAKASSAR (MACASSAR STRAIT)
LAUT JAWA (JAVA SEA)
LAUT BALI (BALI SEA)
LAUT FLORES (FLORES SEA)
JAWA TENGAH
JAWA TIMUR
YOGYAKARTA
BALI
NUSA TENGGARA BARAT
SUMBAWA
Madura
Lombok
Equator
Kota Kinabalu
Sandakan
Tawau
Kuching
Pontianak
Banjarmasin
Balikpapan
Samarinda
Tarakan
Palu
Makassar
Surabaya
Semarang
Denpasar
Mataram
1:6 000 000

131

130

133

M	FT
6000	19686
5000	16404
4000	13124
3000	9843
2000	6562
1000	3281
500	1640
200	656
0	0
LAND BELOW SEA LEVEL	
200	656
2000	6562
4000	13124
6000	19686

CHINA

MYANMAR (BURMA)

LAOS

THAILAND

VIETNAM

INDIA

GULF OF TONGKING

BAY OF BENGAL

HAINAN

Mercator Projection

139

137

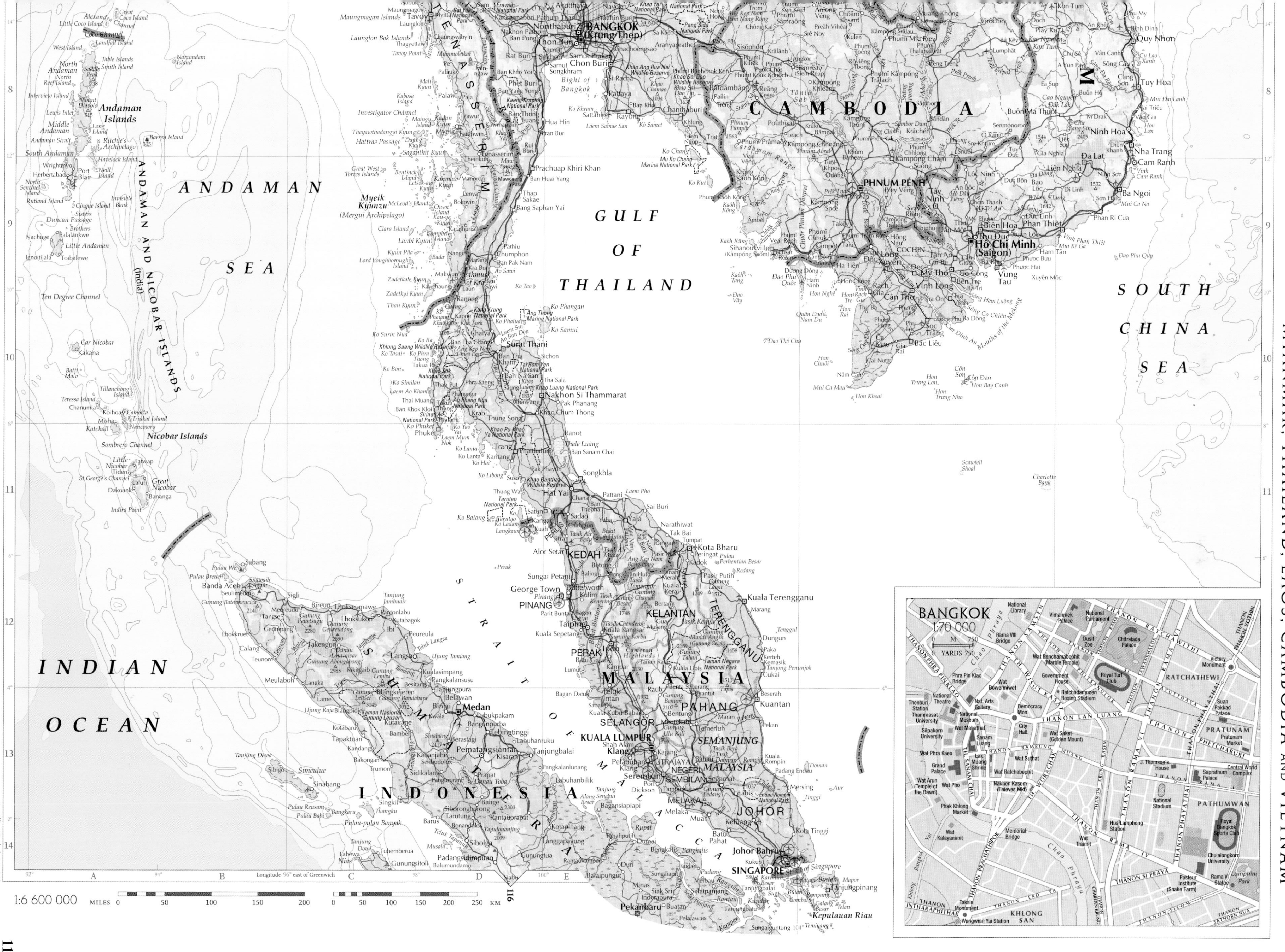

BANGKOK 1:70 000
SOUTH CHINA SEA
GULF OF THAILAND
ANDAMAN SEA
INDIAN OCEAN
STRAIT OF MALACCA
CAMBODIA
MALAYSIA
INDONESIA
SUMATERA
ANDAMAN AND NICOBAR ISLANDS (India)
BANGKOK (Krung Thep)
PHNUM PENH
Hô Chi Minh (Saigon)
KUALA LUMPUR
SINGAPORE
Medan
Nicobar Islands
Andaman Islands
Myeik Kyunzu (Mergui Archipelago)
116
1:6 600 000

152

134

M	FT
6000	19686
5000	16404
4000	13124
3000	9843
2000	6562
1000	3281
500	1640
200	656
0	0
LAND BELOW SEA LEVEL	
200	656
2000	6562
4000	13124
6000	19686

Albers Equal Area Conic Projection

112

153

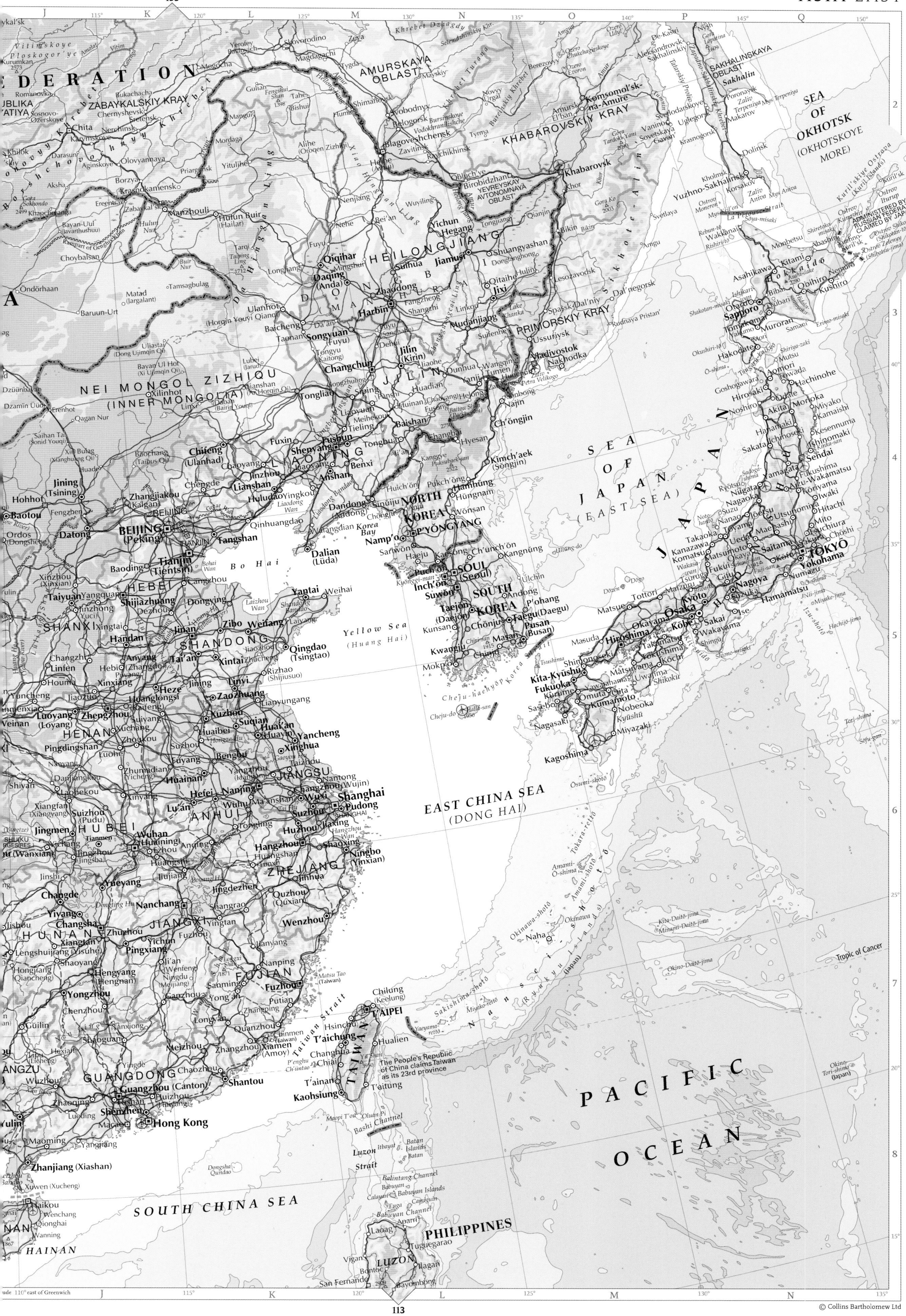
SEA OF OKHOTSK (OKHOTSKOYE MORE)
SEA OF JAPAN (EAST SEA)
JAPAN
Hokkaidō
Honshū
Shikoku
Kyūshū
TŌKYŌ
Yokohama
Nagoya
Ōsaka
Kyōto
Kōbe
Hiroshima
Sapporo
Sendai
Fukuoka
Kita-Kyūshū
Kagoshima
NORTH KOREA
P'YŎNGYANG
SOUTH KOREA
SOUL (Seoul)
Pusan (Busan)
Inch'ŏn
Taegu (Daegu)
Kwangju
Yellow Sea (Huang Hai)
Bo Hai
EAST CHINA SEA (DONG HAI)
SOUTH CHINA SEA
PACIFIC OCEAN
PHILIPPINES
LUZON
Luzon Strait
Bashi Channel
Balintang Channel
Babuyan Channel
TAIWAN
T'AIPEI
Kaohsiung
Taiwan Strait
The People's Republic of China claims Taiwan as its 23rd province
Tropic of Cancer
BEIJING (Peking)
Tianjin (Tientsin)
Shanghai
Hong Kong
Guangzhou (Canton)
Shenzhen
Nanjing
Wuhan
Hangzhou
Qingdao (Tsingtao)
Dalian (Lüda)
Shenyang
Harbin
Changchun
HEILONGJIANG
JILIN
LIAONING
HEBEI
SHANDONG
SHANXI
HENAN
JIANGSU
ANHUI
HUBEI
ZHEJIANG
JIANGXI
HUNAN
FUJIAN
GUANGDONG
HAINAN
NEI MONGOL ZIZHIQU (INNER MONGOLIA)
FEDERATION
ZABAYKALSKIY KRAY
AMURSKAYA OBLAST'
KHABAROVSKIY KRAY
PRIMORSKIY KRAY
SAKHALINSKAYA OBLAST'
YEVREYSKAYA AVTONOMNAYA OBLAST'
Vladivostok
Khabarovsk
Sakhalin
Kuril'skiye Ostrova (Kuril Islands)
ADMINISTERED BY RUSSIAN FEDERATION, CLAIMED BY JAPAN
Nansei-shotō (Ryukyu Islands) (Japan)
Okinawa-shotō
Naha
1:13 000 000
KM
MILES
0 100 200 300 400 500 600
0 100 200 300 400

113

153

6000
19686
5000
16404
4000
13124
3000
9843
2000
6562
1000
3281
500
1640
200
656
0
LAND BELOW
SEA LEVEL
0
200
656
2000
6562
4000
13124
6000
19686
M
FT

Conic Equidistant Projection

129

SEA OF JAPAN
(EAST SEA)
JAPAN
PACIFIC OCEAN
YELLOW SEA
(HUANG HAI)
Korea Bay
Bohai Haixia
NORTH KOREA
SOUTH KOREA
CHINA
SHIKOKU
KYŪSHŪ
P'YŎNGYANG
Seoul
TŌKYŌ
Ōsaka
Nagoya
Kyōto
Hiroshima
Fukuoka
Kita-Kyūshū
Pusan (Busan)
Taegu (Daegu)
Kwangju
Taejŏn (Daejeon)
Inch'ŏn
Nagasaki
Kagoshima
Sendai
Niigata
Kanazawa
Yokohama
Dalian (Lüda)
Yantai
Liancourt Rocks
Claimed and administered by South Korea as Tok-tō; claimed by Japan as Take-shima
Longitude 132° east of Greenwich
1:6 000 000
MILES 0 50 100 150 200
0 50 100 150 200 250 KM

131

RYUKYU ISLANDS
CONTINUATION AT THE SAME SCALE
Okinawa
1:1 000 000
10 KM
10 MILES
EAST CHINA SEA
(DONG HAI)
NANSEI-SHOTŌ
(RYUKYU ISLANDS)
OKINAWA
KAGOSHIMA
Ōsumi-shotō
Amami-shotō
Okinawa-shotō
Sakishima-shotō
Miyako-jima
Naha
HOKKAIDŌ
Sea of Okhotsk
(Okhotskoye More)
Kuril'skiye Ostrova
(Kuril Islands)
ADMINISTERED BY RUSSIAN FEDERATION, CLAIMED BY JAPAN
La Pérouse Strait
Wakkanai
Asahikawa
Sapporo
Otaru
Tomakomai
Muroran
Obihiro
Kushiro
Kitami
Hakodate
AOMORI
Hachinohe
Hirosaki
AKITA
IWATE
Morioka
YAMAGATA
MIYAGI
Sendai
JAPAN
6000
19686
5000
16404
4000
13124
3000
9843
2000
6562
1500
4921
1000
3281
500
1640
200
656
100
328
0
0
LAND BELOW SEA LEVEL
200
656
1000
3281
2000
6562
M
FT
Polyconic Projection

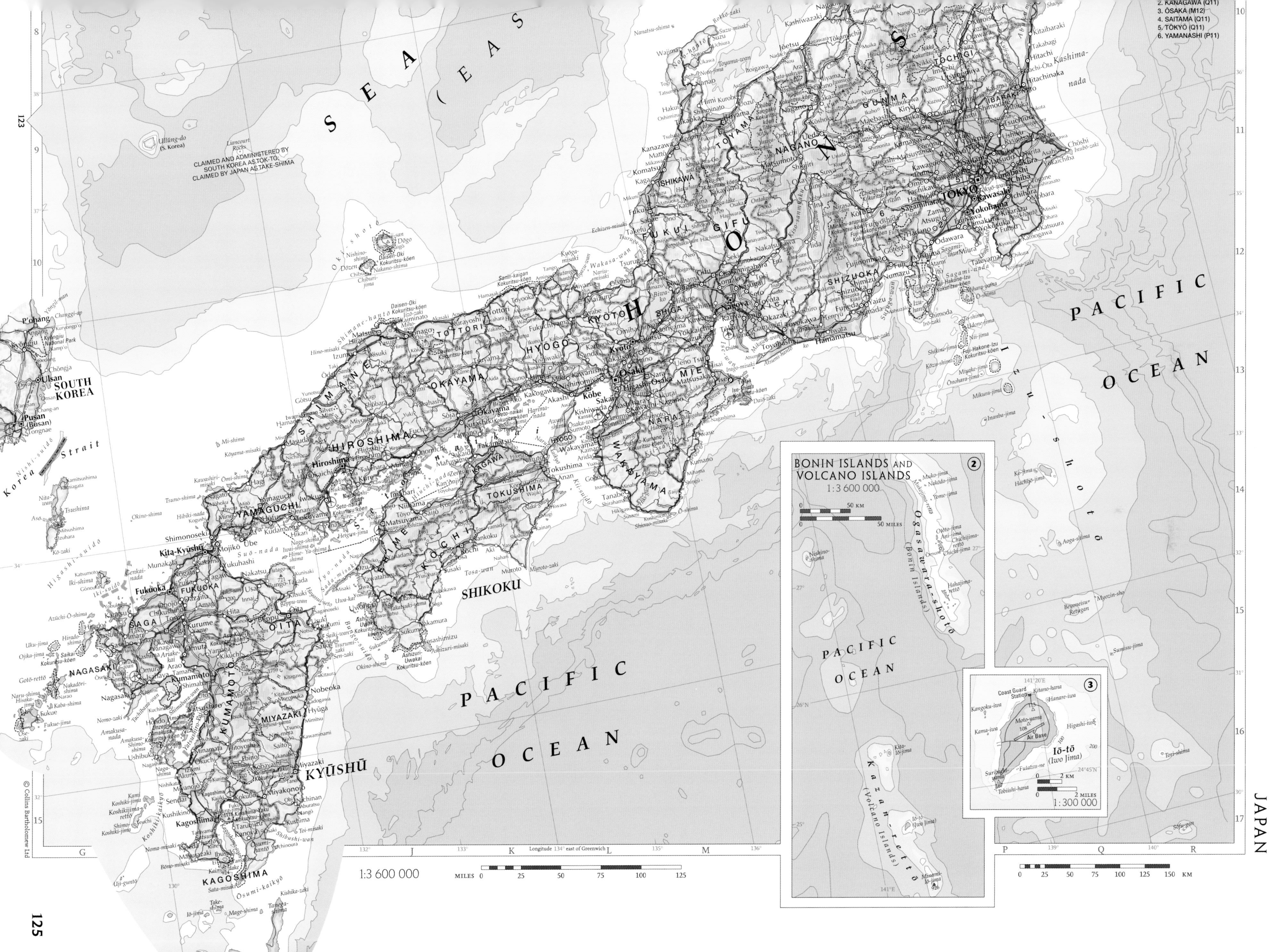
2. KANAGAWA (Q11)
3. ŌSAKA (M12)
4. SAITAMA (Q11)
5. TŌKYŌ (Q11)
6. YAMANASHI (P11)
SEA (EAS
PACIFIC OCEAN
PACIFIC OCEAN
SHIKOKU
KYŪSHŪ
SOUTH KOREA
CLAIMED AND ADMINISTERED BY SOUTH KOREA AS TOK-TO; CLAIMED BY JAPAN AS TAKE-SHIMA
Korea Strait
TŌKYŌ
Yokohama
Kawasaki
Nagoya
Kyoto
Ōsaka
Kobe
Hiroshima
Fukuoka
Kita-Kyūshū
Kagoshima
Nagasaki
BONIN ISLANDS AND VOLCANO ISLANDS
1:3 600 000
Ogasawara-shotō (Bonin Islands)
PACIFIC OCEAN
Kazan-rettō (Volcano Islands)
Iō-tō (Iwo Jima)
1:300 000
1:3 600 000
Longitude 134° east of Greenwich
123

SEA OF JAPAN (EAST SEA)

TOKYO 1:125 000

Conic Equidistant Projection

125

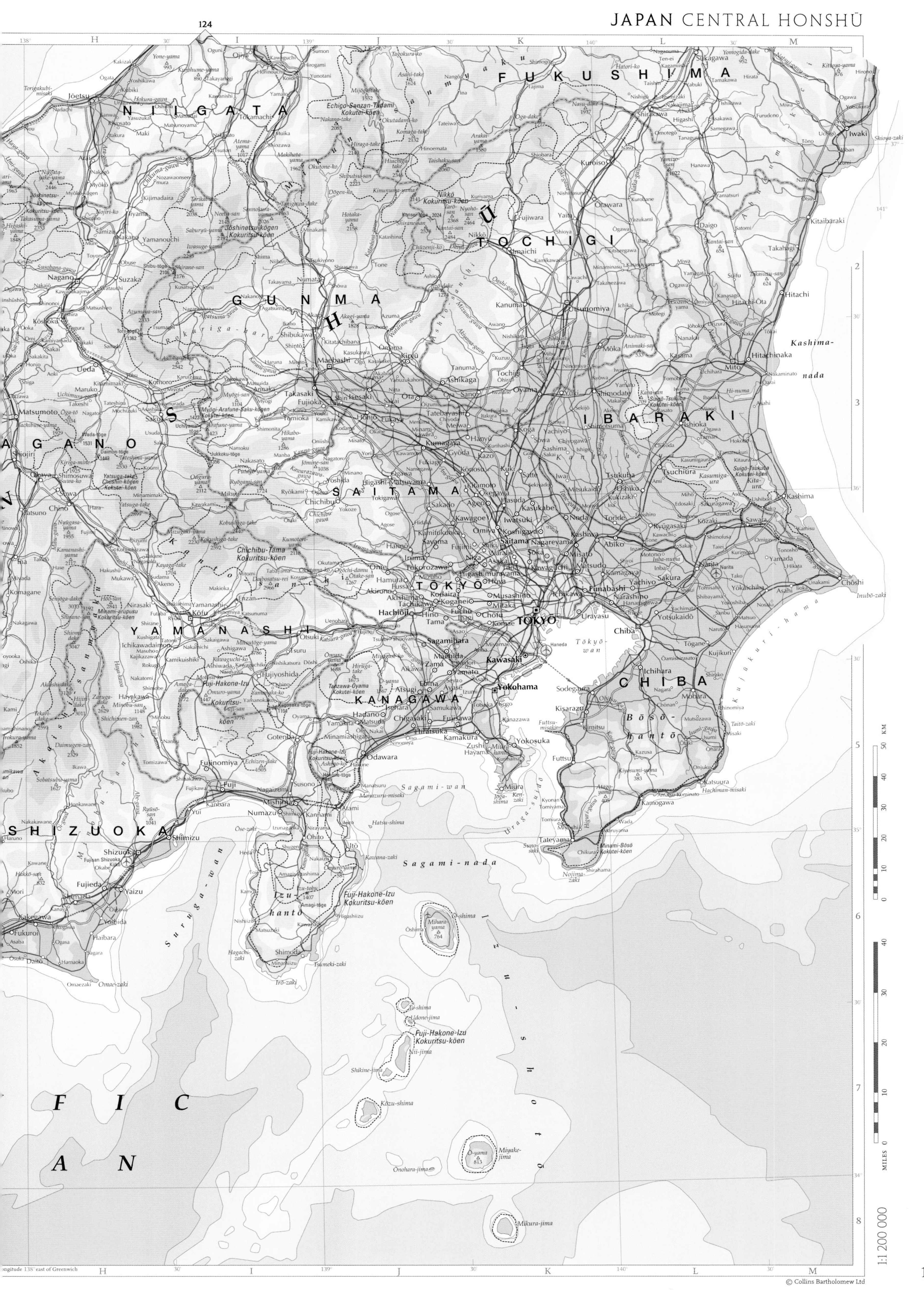
124
FUKUSHIMA
NIIGATA
TOCHIGI
GUNMA
IBARAKI
NAGANO
SAITAMA
TŌKYŌ
YAMANASHI
KANAGAWA
CHIBA
SHIZUOKA
HONSHŪ
Jōetsu
Nagano
Ueda
Matsumoto
Maebashi
Takasaki
Kumagaya
Utsunomiya
Mito
Hitachi
Iwaki
Kashima
Chōshi
Narita
Chiba
Funabashi
Kawaguchi
Saitama
Hachiōji
Kōfu
Kawasaki
Yokohama
Yokosuka
Sagamihara
Odawara
Numazu
Mishima
Fuji
Fujinomiya
Shimizu
Shizuoka
Fujieda
Yaizu
Shimoda
Itō
Atami
Tateyama
Kisarazu
Kashima-nada
Tōkyō-wan
Sagami-wan
Sagami-nada
Suruga-wan
Izu-hantō
Bōsō-hantō
Kujūkuri-hama
Inubō-zaki
Nojima-zaki
Ō-shima
Toshima
Nii-jima
Shikine-jima
Kōzu-shima
Miyake-jima
Mikura-jima
Izu-shotō
Nikkō Kokuritsu-kōen
Chichibu-Tama Kokuritsu-kōen
Fuji-Hakone-Izu Kokuritsu-kōen
Minami-Bōsō Kokutei-kōen
PACIFIC OCEAN
Longitude 138° east of Greenwich
KM 0 10 20 30 40 50
MILES 0 10 20 30 40
1:1 200 000

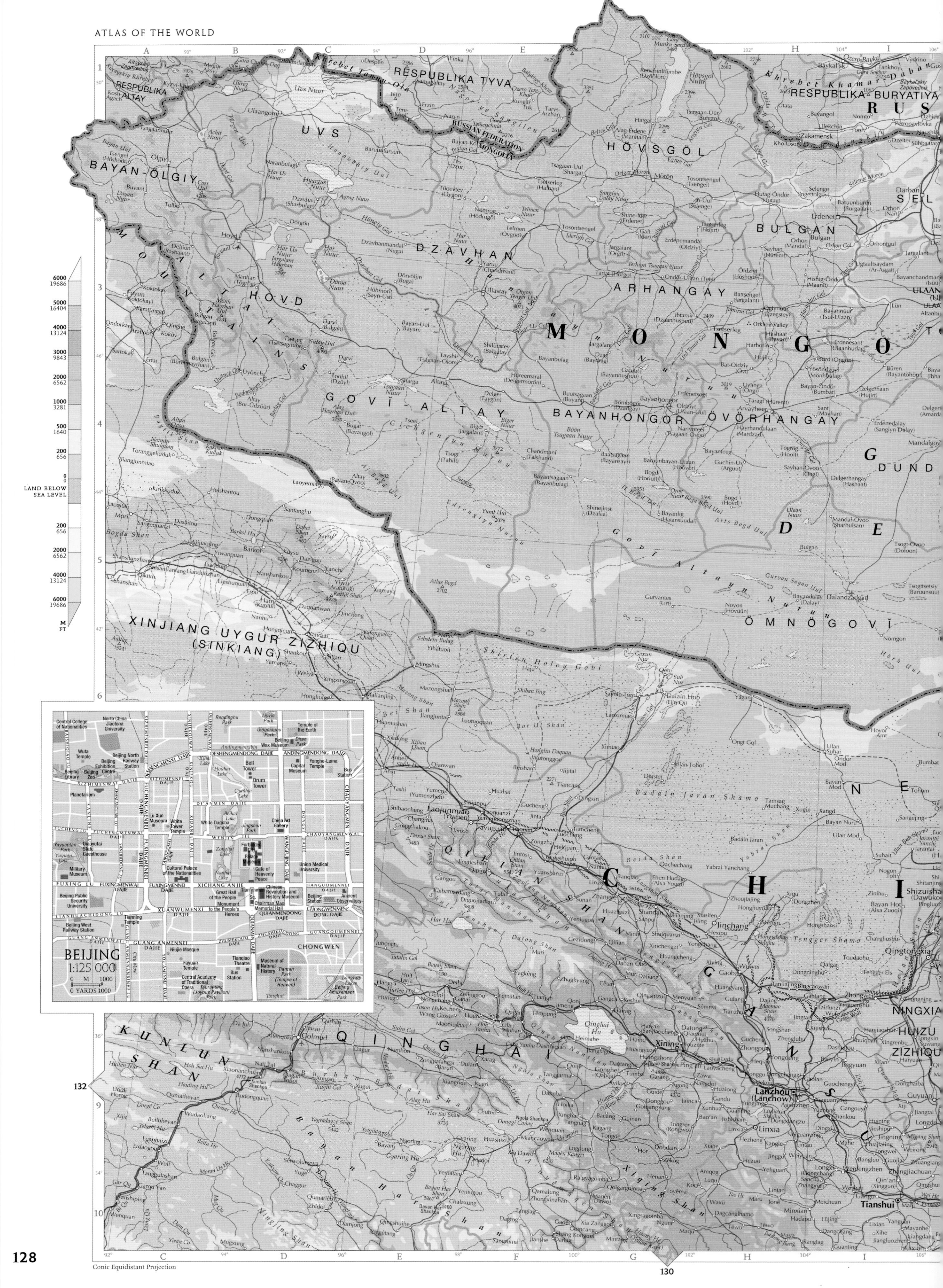

Conic Equidistant Projection

153

122

123

131

1:6 000 000

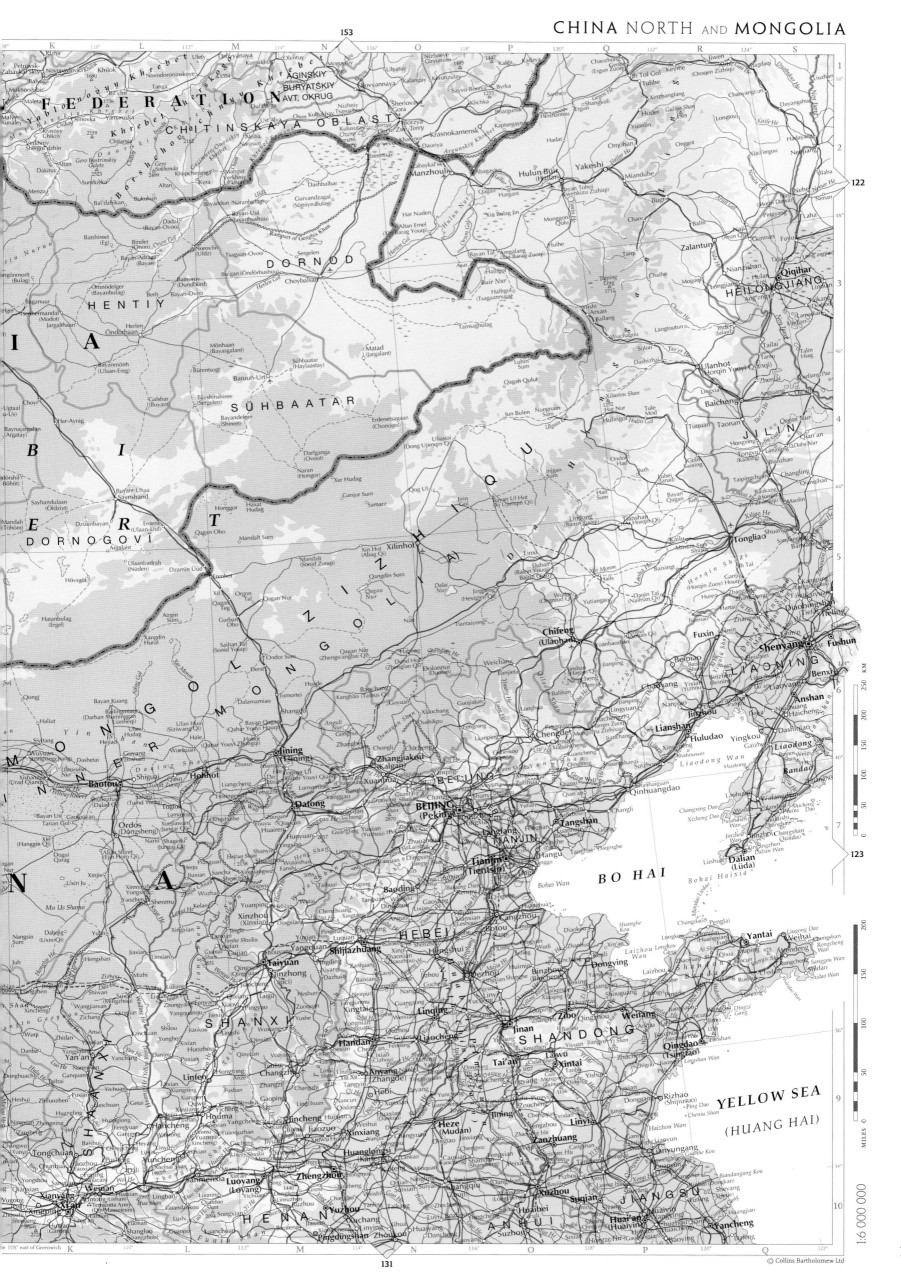

128

133

118

QINGHAI
GANSU
SHAANXI
SICHUAN
XIZANG ZIZHIQU
(TIBET)
CHONGQING
GUIZHOU
YUNNAN
CHINA
GUANGXI ZHUANGZU ZIZHIQU
MYANMAR
(BURMA)
KACHIN
SHAN
THAILAND
LAOS
VIETNAM
TONKIN
HAINAN
GULF OF
TONGKING
INDIA
MYANMAR
Chengdu
Chongqing
Kunming
Guiyang
Nanning
Xi'an
Lanzhou
Tianshui
Mianyang
Nanchong
Leshan
Zigong
Yibin
Neijiang
Suining
Panzhihua
(Dukou)
Dali
(Xiaguan)
Qujing
Zunyi
Liuzhou
Hanzhong
Ankang
Wanzhou
(Wanxian)
Xianyang
Weinan
Baoji
Guangyuan
Xichang
Zhaotong
Lupanshui
(Zhongshan)
Anshun
(Xixiu)
Kaiyuan
Gejiu
Yuxi
Chuxiong
Baoshan
Dongchuan
Xingyi
(Huangcaoba)
Kaili
Duyun
Bose
Qinzhou
Beihai
Yulin
Zhanjiang
(Xiashan)
HA NOI
Hai Phong
Thanh Hoa
Vinh
Nam Dinh
VIANGCHAN
(Vientiane)
Louangphabang
Chiang Mai
Chiang Rai
Lampang
Nong Khai
Myitkyina
Bhamo
Tropic of Cancer
Conic Equidistant Projection
6000
19686
5000
16404
4000
13124
3000
9843
2000
6562
1000
3281
500
1640
200
656
0
0
LAND BELOW
SEA LEVEL
200
656
2000
6562
4000
13124
6000
19686
M
FT

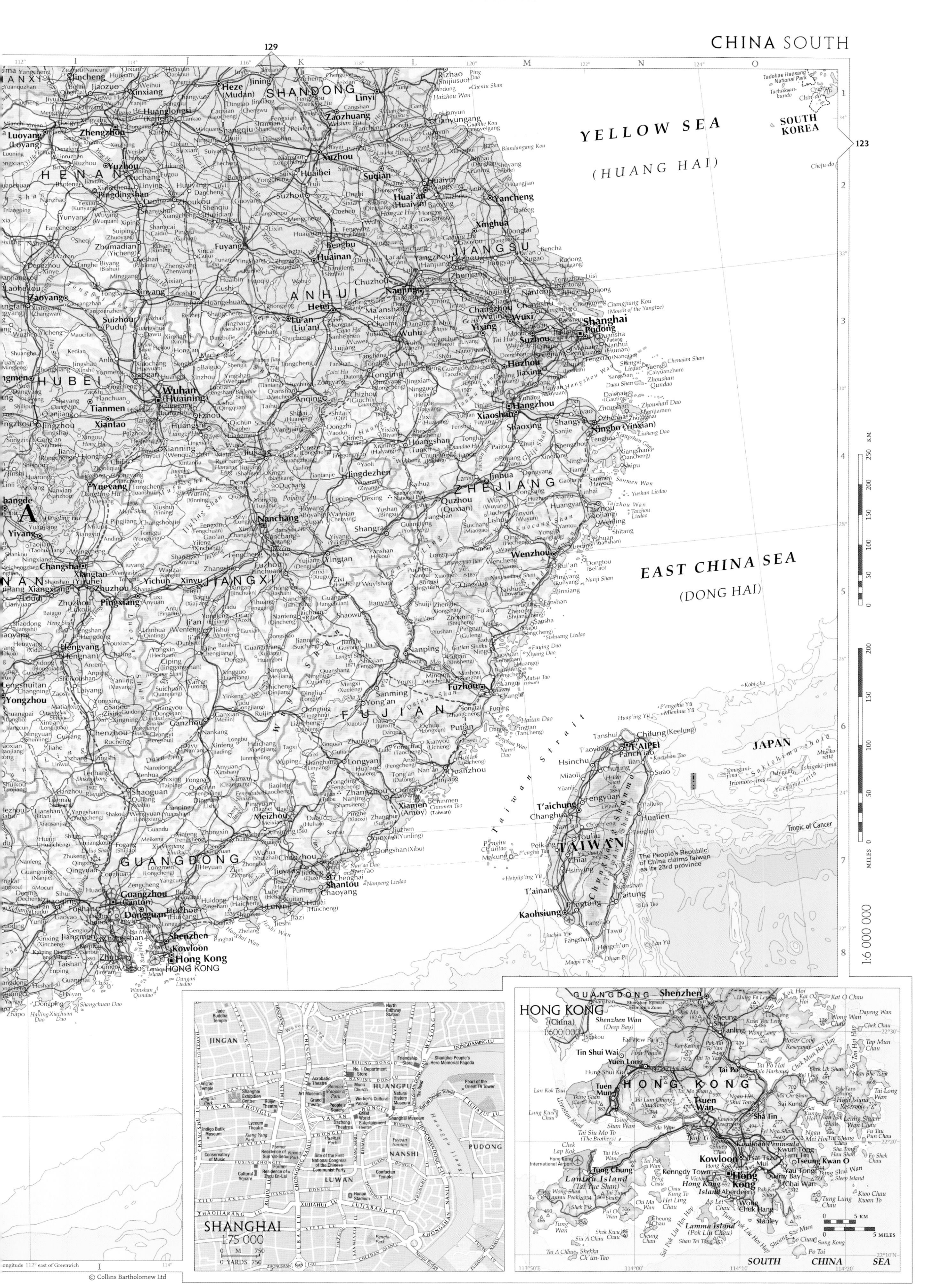
129
123
YELLOW SEA
(HUANG HAI)
EAST CHINA SEA
(DONG HAI)
SOUTH KOREA
JAPAN
SHANDONG
HENAN
JIANGSU
ANHUI
HUBEI
ZHEJIANG
JIANGXI
FUJIAN
GUANGDONG
TAIWAN
HONG KONG
Taiwan Strait
Tropic of Cancer
The People's Republic of China claims Taiwan as its 23rd province
Shanghai
Pudong
Nanjing
Hefei
Hangzhou
Ningbo (Yinxian)
Wuhan (Huaining)
Nanchang
Changsha
Fuzhou
Xiamen (Amoy)
Quanzhou
Shantou
Guangzhou (Canton)
Shenzhen
Kowloon
Hong Kong
Macao
Zhengzhou
Xuzhou
Wenzhou
T'AIPEI
Kaohsiung
T'aichung
T'ainan
1:6 000 000
KM
MILES
0
50
100
150
200
250
HONG KONG (China)
1:600 000
SOUTH CHINA SEA
Lantau Island (Tai Yue Shan)
Lamma Island (Pok Liu Chau)
Hong Kong International Airport
SHANGHAI
1:75 000
HUANGPU
NANSHI
LUWAN
JINGAN
PUDONG
Longitude 112° east of Greenwich

128

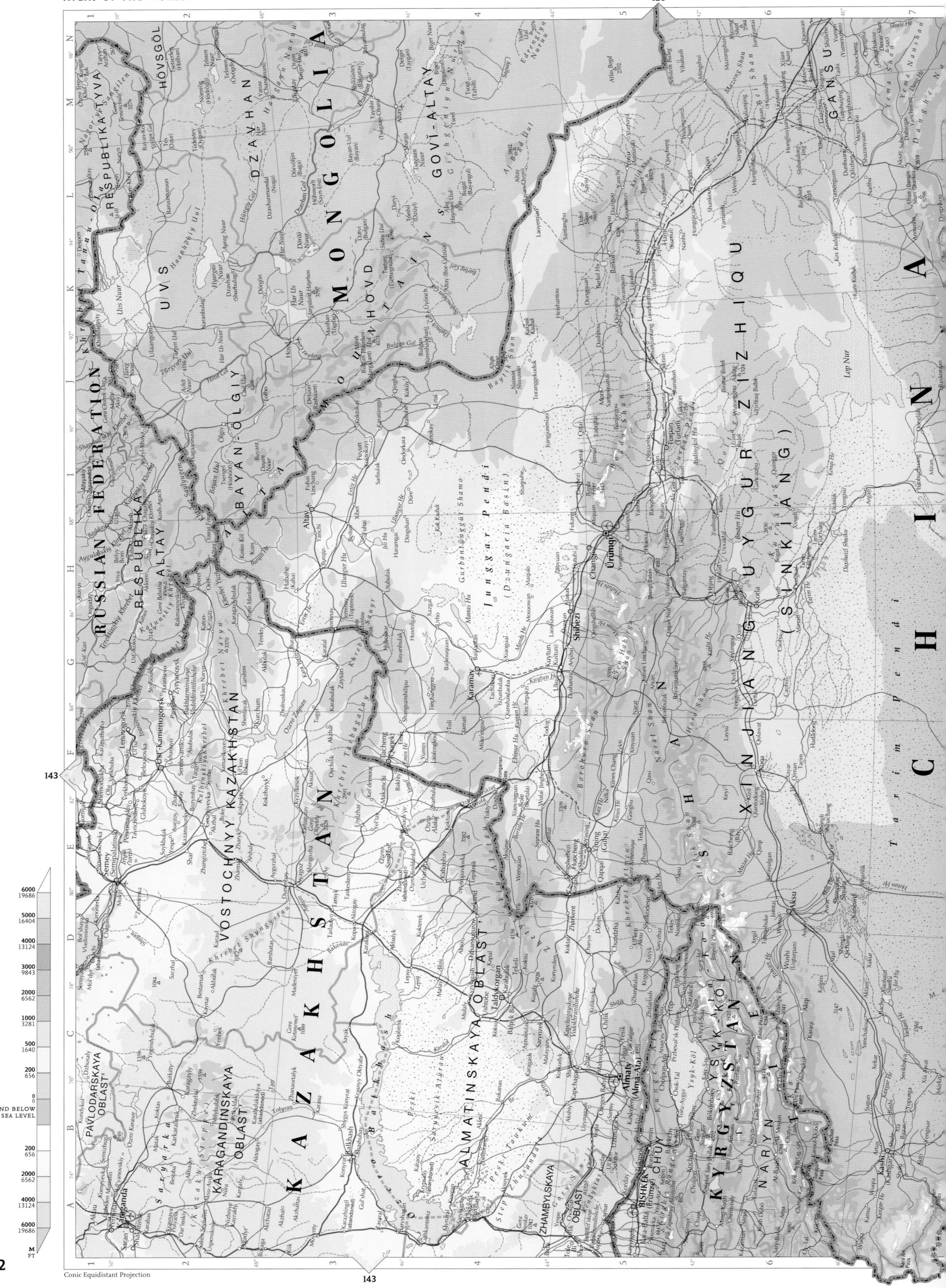

143

RUSSIAN FEDERATION

RESPUBLIKA TYVA

RESPUBLIKA ALTAY

MONGOLIA

KAZAKHSTAN

KYRGYZSTAN

CHINA

XINJIANG UYGUR ZIZHIQU (SINKIANG)

VOSTOCHNYY KAZAKHSTAN

KARAGANDINSKAYA OBLAST'

PAVLODARSKAYA OBLAST'

ALMATINSKAYA OBLAST'

ZHAMBYLSKAYA OBLAST'

M	FT
6000	19686
5000	16404
4000	13124
3000	9843
2000	6562
1000	3281
500	1640
200	656
0	0
LAND BELOW SEA LEVEL	
200	656
2000	6562
4000	13124
6000	19686

Conic Equidistant Projection

143

1:6 000 000

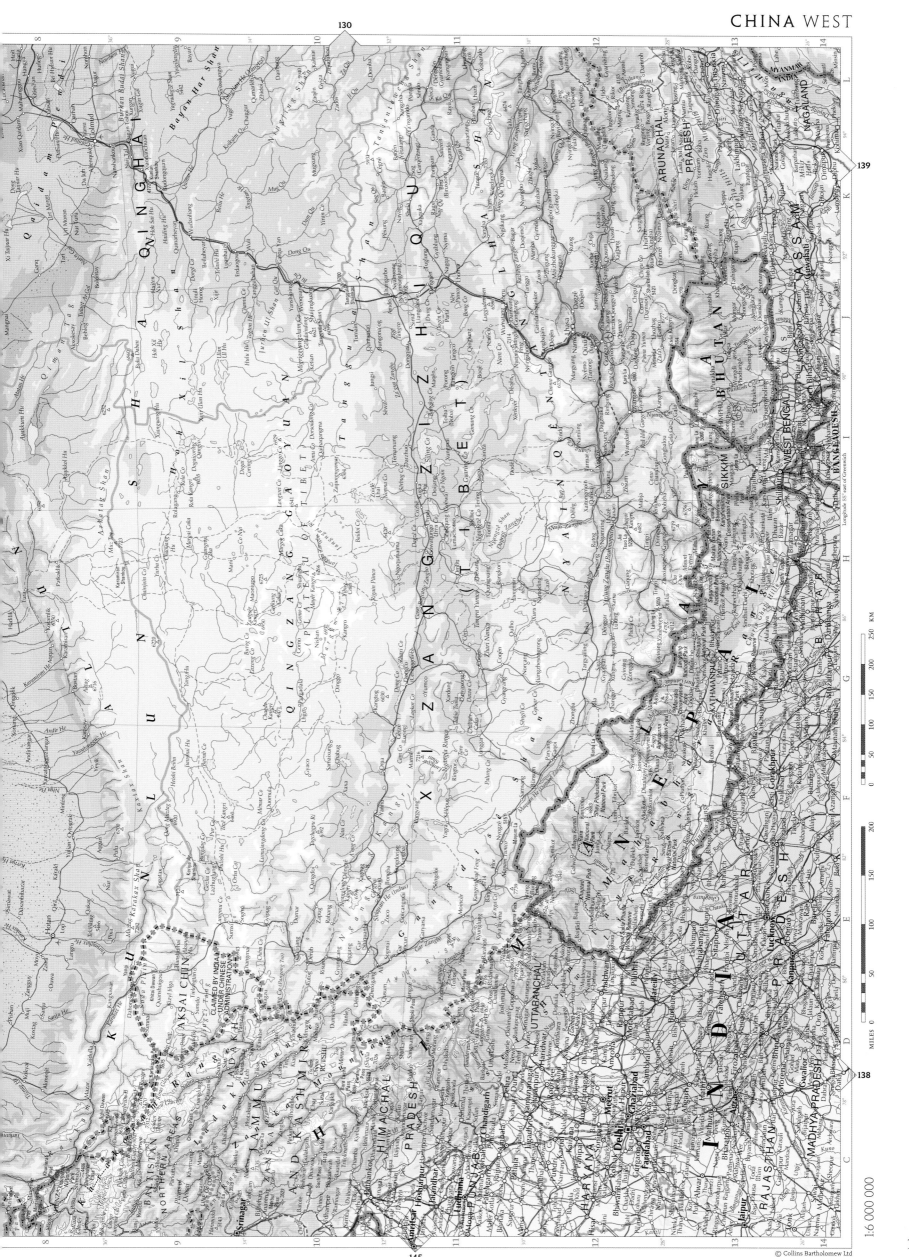

120

152

M	FT
6000	19686
5000	16404
4000	13124
3000	9843
2000	6562
1000	3281
500	1640
200	656
0	0
LAND BELOW SEA LEVEL	
200	656
2000	6562
4000	13124
6000	19686

Albers Equal Area Conic Projection

141

ARABIAN SEA
BAY OF BENGAL
INDIAN OCEAN
ANDAMAN SEA
INDIA
MYANMAR (BURMA)
SRI LANKA
MALDIVES
INDONESIA
ANDAMAN AND NICOBAR ISLANDS (India)
LAKSHADWEEP (India)
Laccadive Islands
MAHARASHTRA
ANDHRA PRADESH
TAMIL NADU
KARNATAKA
ORISSA
CHHATTISGARH
JHARKHAND
MADHYA PRADESH
GUJARAT
WEST BENGAL
Mumbai (Bombay)
Chennai (Madras)
Kolkata (Calcutta)
Bangalore (Bengaluru)
Hyderabad
Ahmadabad
Pune (Poona)
Nagpur
Vishakhapatnam
Colombo
SRI JAYEWARDENEPURA KOTTE
YANGON (Rangoon)
Chittagong
Khulna
Mandalay
Malabar Coast
Coromandel Coast
Palk Strait
Gulf of Mannar
Eight Degree Channel
Nine Degree Channel
Ten Degree Channel
One and a Half Degree Channel
Equator
MALDIVES MALE ATOLL 1:1 200 000
North Male Atoll
South Male Atoll
MALE
MALDIVES ADDU ATOLL 1:1 200 000
Addu Atoll
1:12 000 000

138

Conic Equidistant Projection

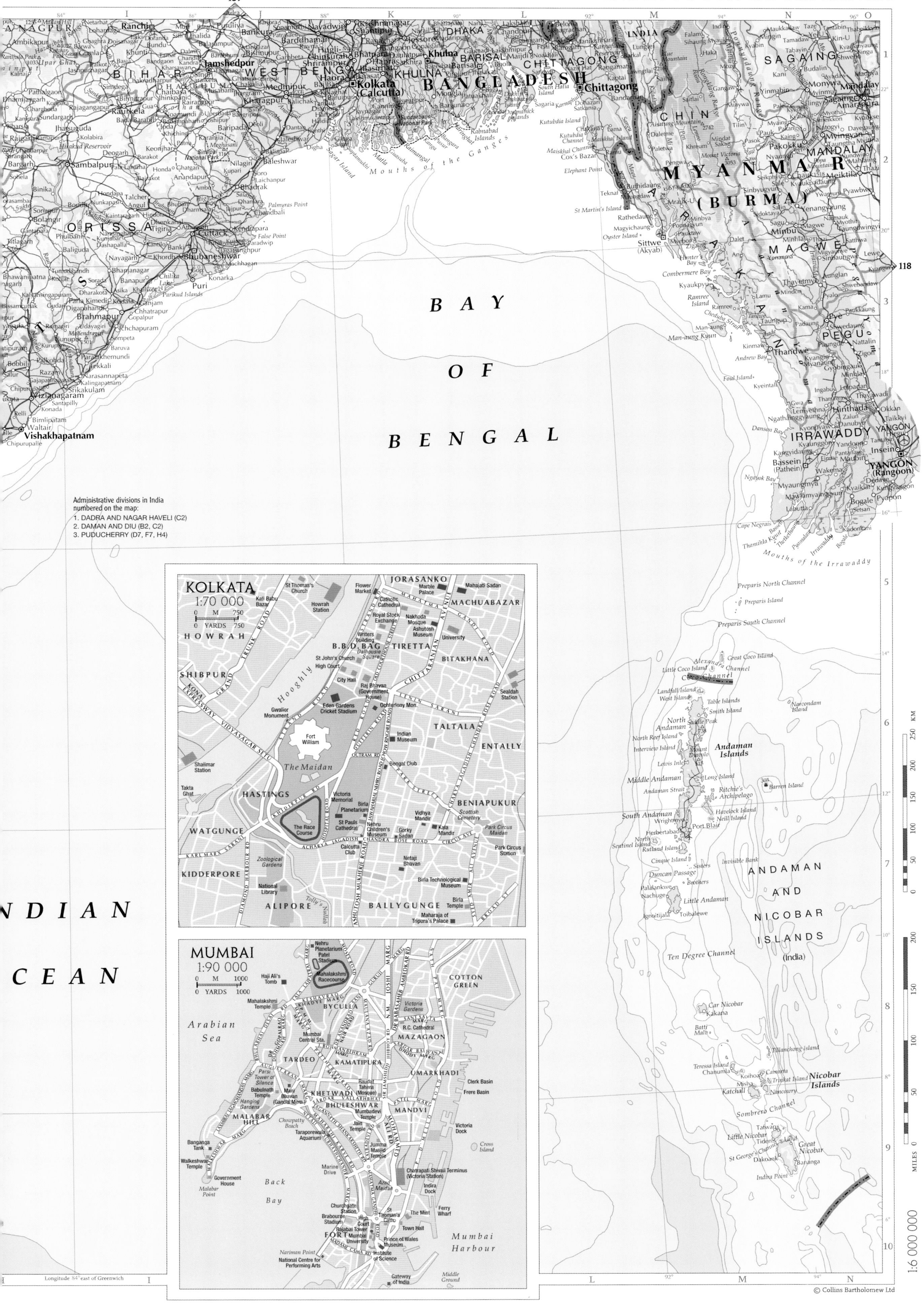
139
118
BAY
OF
BENGAL
INDIAN
OCEAN
BANGLADESH
MYANMAR
(BURMA)
WEST BENGAL
BIHAR
ORISSA
CHITTAGONG
BARISAL
KHULNA
DHAKA
CHIN
SAGAING
MANDALAY
MAGWE
PEGU
IRRAWADDY
YANGON
Kolkata
(Calcutta)
Chittagong
Ranchi
Jamshedpur
Cuttack
Bhubaneshwar
Puri
Brahmapur
Vishakhapatnam
Sittwe
(Akyab)
Mandalay
Yangon
(Rangoon)
Bassein
(Pathein)
Mouths of the Ganges
Mouths of the Irrawaddy
Andaman Islands
Port Blair
Barren Island
Ten Degree Channel
Car Nicobar
Nicobar Islands
ANDAMAN AND NICOBAR ISLANDS
(India)
Great Nicobar
Administrative divisions in India
numbered on the map:
1. DADRA AND NAGAR HAVELI (C2)
2. DAMAN AND DIU (B2, C2)
3. PUDUCHERRY (D7, F7, H4)
KOLKATA
1:70 000
HOWRAH
SHIBPUR
B.B.D. BAG
TIRETTA
BITAKHANA
JORASANKO
MACHUABAZAR
TALTALA
ENTALLY
HASTINGS
WATGUNGE
BENIAPUKUR
KIDDERPORE
ALIPORE
BALLYGUNGE
The Maidan
Fort William
Hooghly
MUMBAI
1:90 000
Arabian Sea
BYCULLA
COTTON GREEN
MAZAGAON
TARDEO
KAMATIPURA
UMARKHADI
KHETWADI
BHULESHWAR
MANDVI
MALABAR HILL
FORT
Back Bay
Mumbai Harbour
KM 0 50 100 150 200 250
MILES 0 50 100 150 200
1:6 000 000
Longitude 84° east of Greenwich

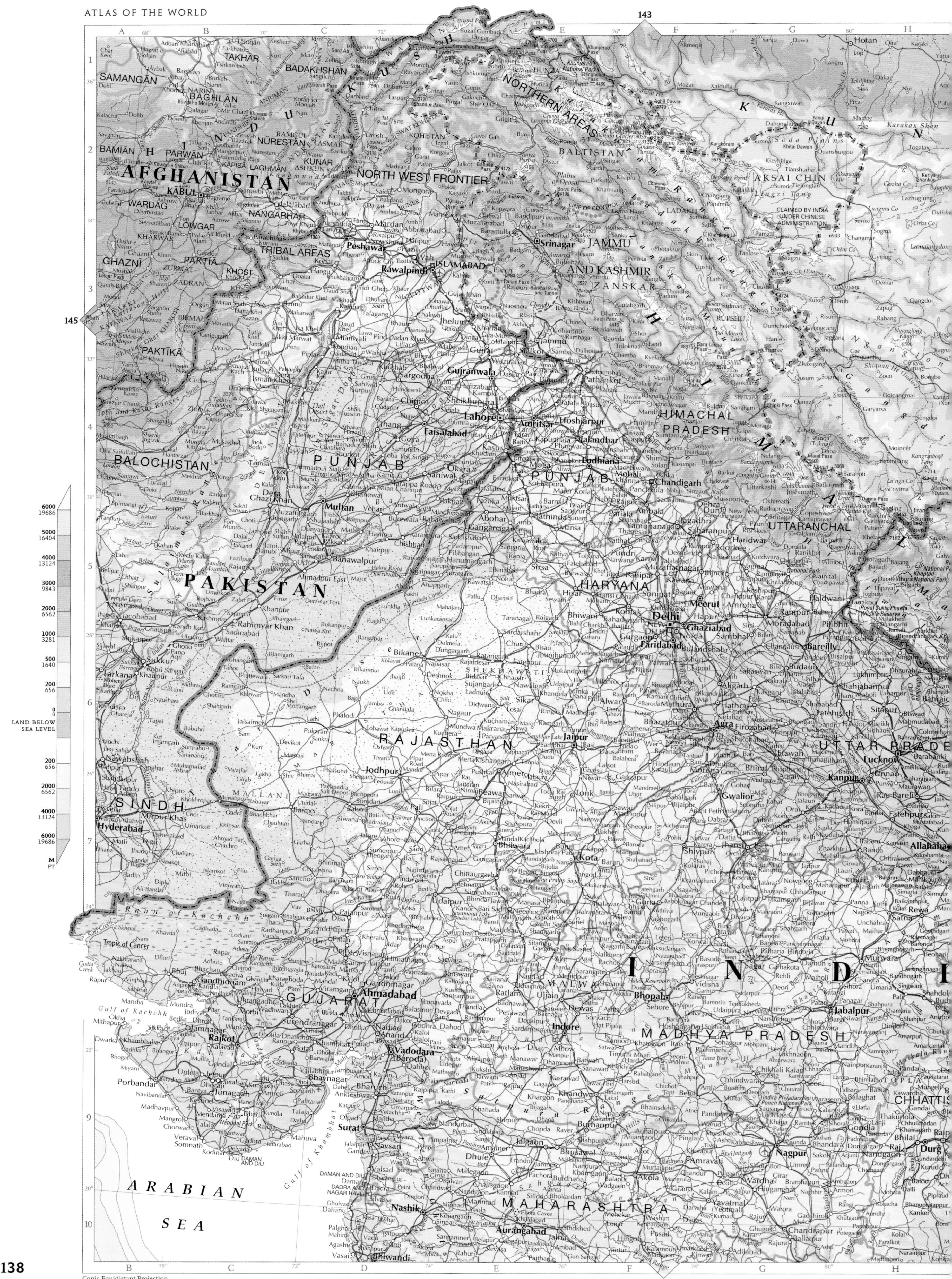

Conic Equidistant Projection

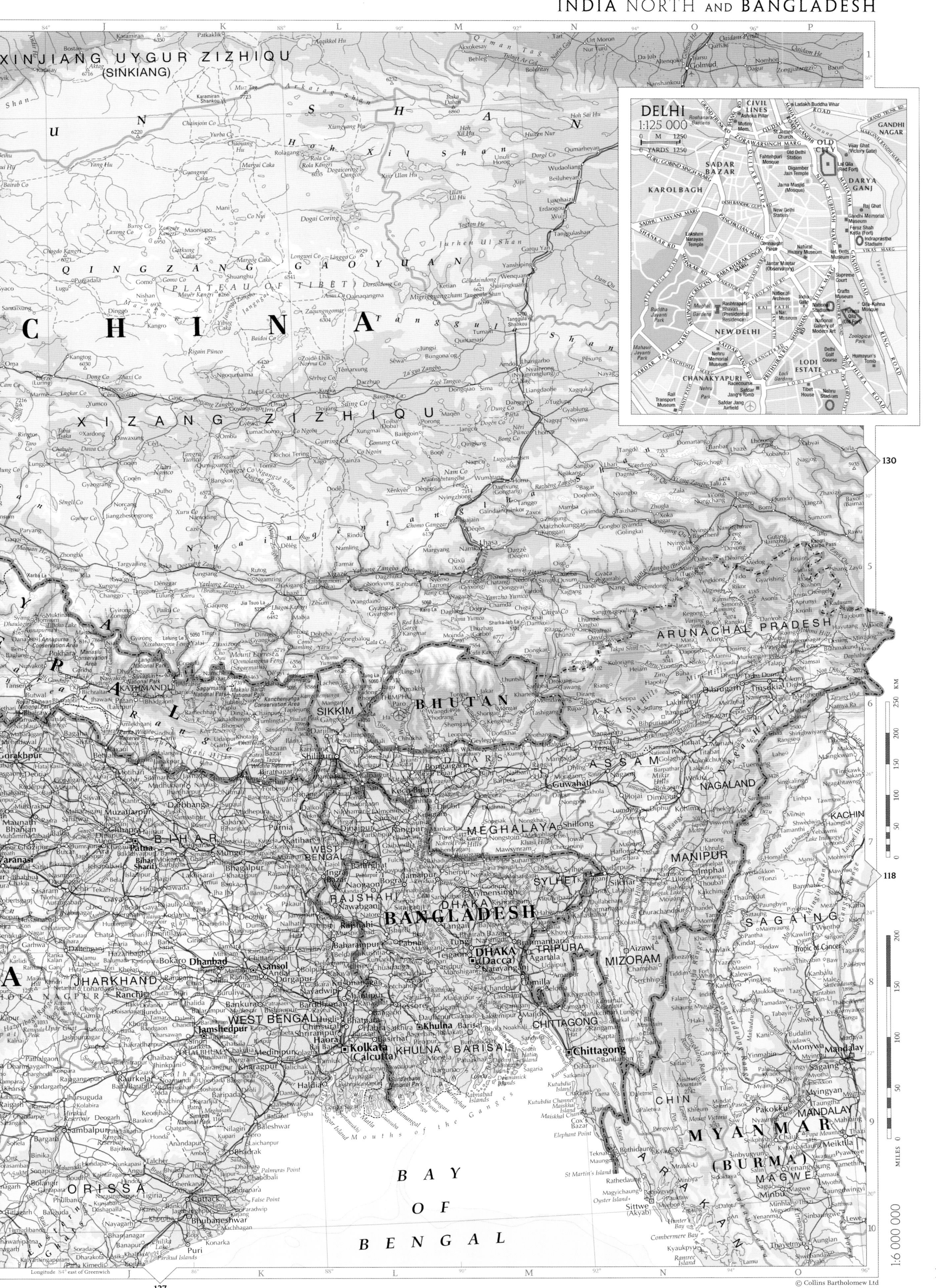
XINJIANG UYGUR ZIZHIQU
(SINKIANG)
QINGZANG GAOYUAN
(PLATEAU OF TIBET)
CHINA
XIZANG ZIZHIQU
DELHI
1:125 000
CIVIL LINES
SADAR BAZAR
KAROLBAGH
OLD CITY
DARYA GANJ
NEW DELHI
CHANAKYAPURI
LODI ESTATE
GANDHI NAGAR
ARUNACHAL PRADESH
BHUTAN
SIKKIM
ASSAM
NAGALAND
MEGHALAYA
MANIPUR
BIHAR
WEST BENGAL
BANGLADESH
RAJSHAHI
DHAKA
SYLHET
TRIPURA
MIZORAM
JHARKHAND
KHULNA
BARISAL
CHITTAGONG
ORISSA
SAGAING
KACHIN
CHIN
MYANMAR
(BURMA)
MAGWE
MANDALAY
ARAKAN
BAY OF BENGAL
Mouths of the Ganges
Kolkata (Calcutta)
DHAKA (Dacca)
Chittagong
Patna
Lhasa
Guwahati
Shillong
Imphal
Mandalay
Sittwe (Akyab)
Bhubaneshwar
130
118
137
1:6 000 000
Longitude 84° east of Greenwich

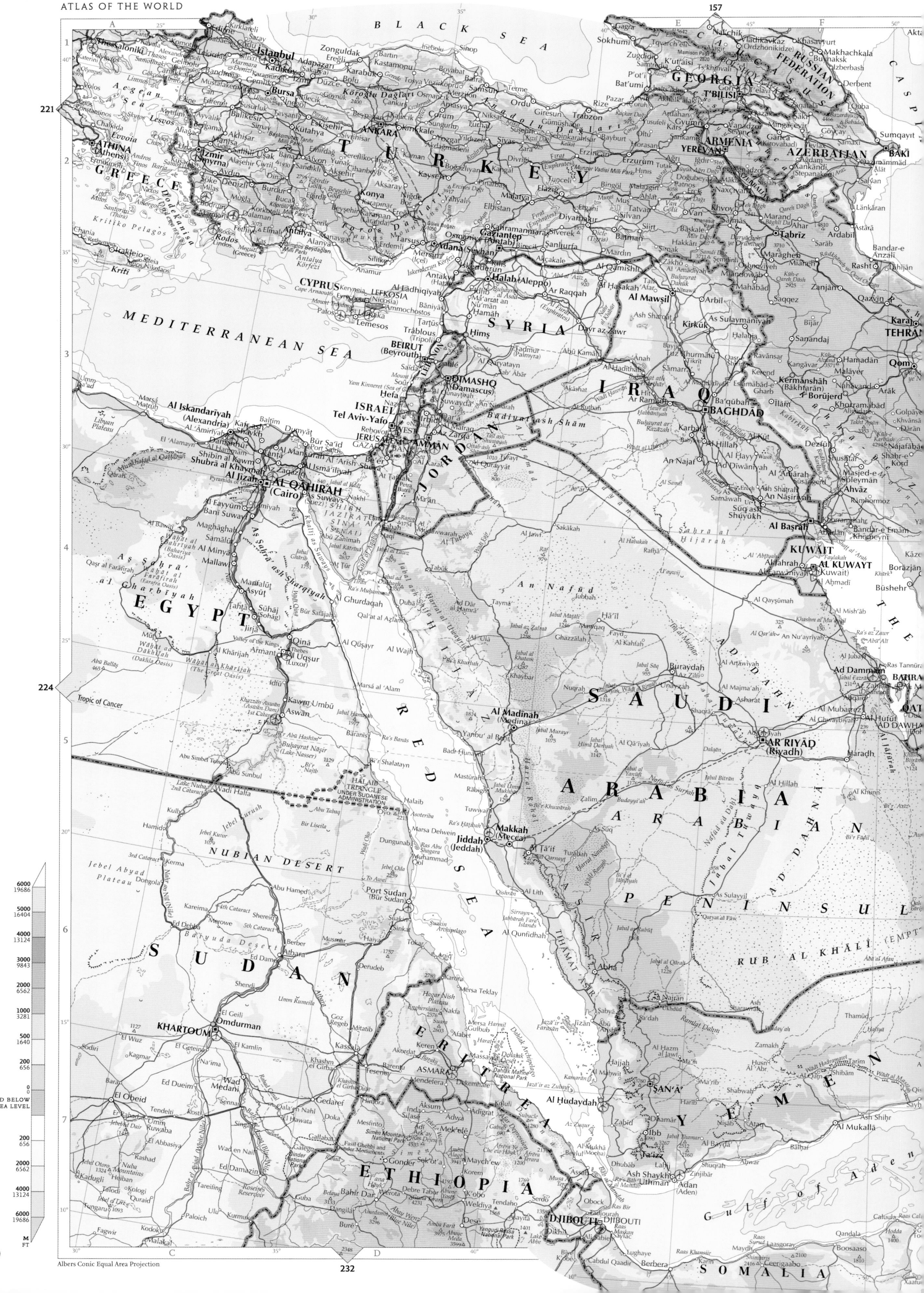

157

221

224

BLACK SEA

MEDITERRANEAN SEA

RED SEA

TURKEY

GREECE

CYPRUS

SYRIA

LEBANON

ISRAEL

JORDAN

IRAQ

KUWAIT

EGYPT

SUDAN

ERITREA

ETHIOPIA

DJIBOUTI

SOMALIA

YEMEN

SAUDI ARABIA

ARABIAN PENINSULA

GEORGIA

ARMENIA

AZERBAIJAN

RUSSIAN FEDERATION

NUBIAN DESERT

RUB' AL KHĀLĪ (EMPTY

Gulf of Aden

Tropic of Cancer

HALAIB TRIANGLE UNDER SUDANESE ADMINISTRATION

M / FT
6000 / 19686
5000 / 16404
4000 / 13124
3000 / 9843
2000 / 6562
1000 / 3281
500 / 1640
200 / 656
0 / 0
LAND BELOW SEA LEVEL
200 / 656
2000 / 6562
4000 / 13124
6000 / 19686

Albers Conic Equal Area Projection

232

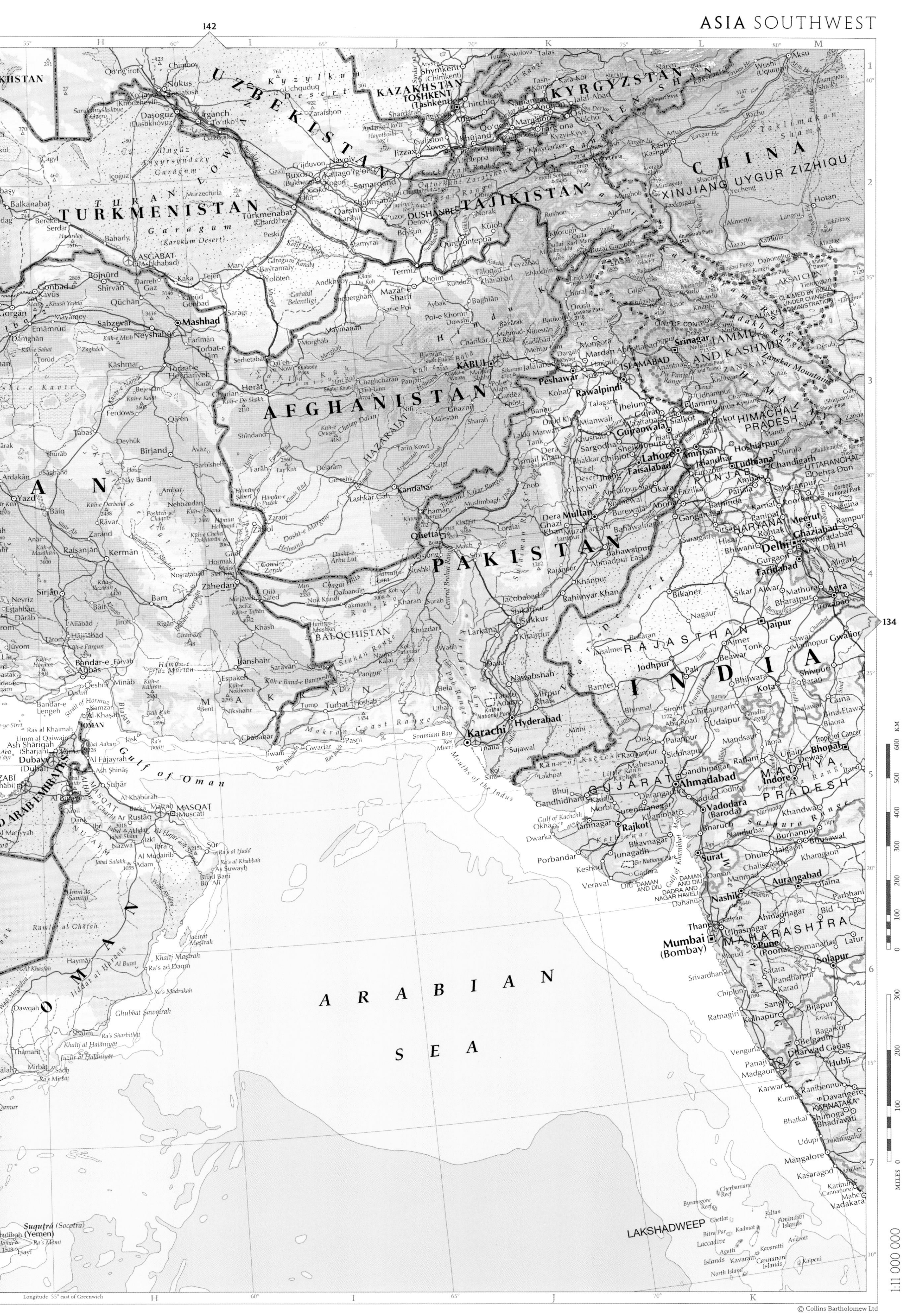
142
134
UZBEKISTAN
KAZAKHSTAN
KYRGYZSTAN
TAJIKISTAN
TURKMENISTAN
AFGHANISTAN
PAKISTAN
INDIA
CHINA
XINJIANG UYGUR ZIZHIQU
OMAN
UNITED ARAB EMIRATES
ARABIAN SEA
Gulf of Oman
Gulf of Kachchh
Gulf of Khambhat
Strait of Hormuz
Mouths of the Indus
TOSHKENT (Tashkent)
DUSHANBE
AŞGABAT (Ashkhabad)
KABUL
ISLAMABAD
NEW DELHI
MASQAT (Muscat)
Mashhad
Herāt
Kandahār
Quetta
Karachi
Hyderabad
Peshawar
Rawalpindi
Lahore
Faisalabad
Multan
Amritsar
Delhi
Agra
Jaipur
Ahmadabad
Vadodara (Baroda)
Surat
Mumbai (Bombay)
Pune
Nashik
Aurangabad
Kermān
Zāhedān
Samarqand
Buxoro
Dubayy (Dubai)
Srinagar
JAMMU AND KASHMIR
HIMACHAL PRADESH
PUNJAB
HARYANA
UTTARANCHAL
RAJASTHAN
GUJARAT
MADHYA PRADESH
MAHARASHTRA
KARNATAKA
LAKSHADWEEP
BALOCHISTAN
HAZARAJAT
AKSAI CHIN
CLAIMED BY INDIA UNDER CHINESE ADMINISTRATION
LINE OF CONTROL
Thar Desert
Tropic of Cancer
Suquṭrá (Socotra) (Yemen)
Longitude 55° east of Greenwich
1:11 000 000
KM
MILES

156

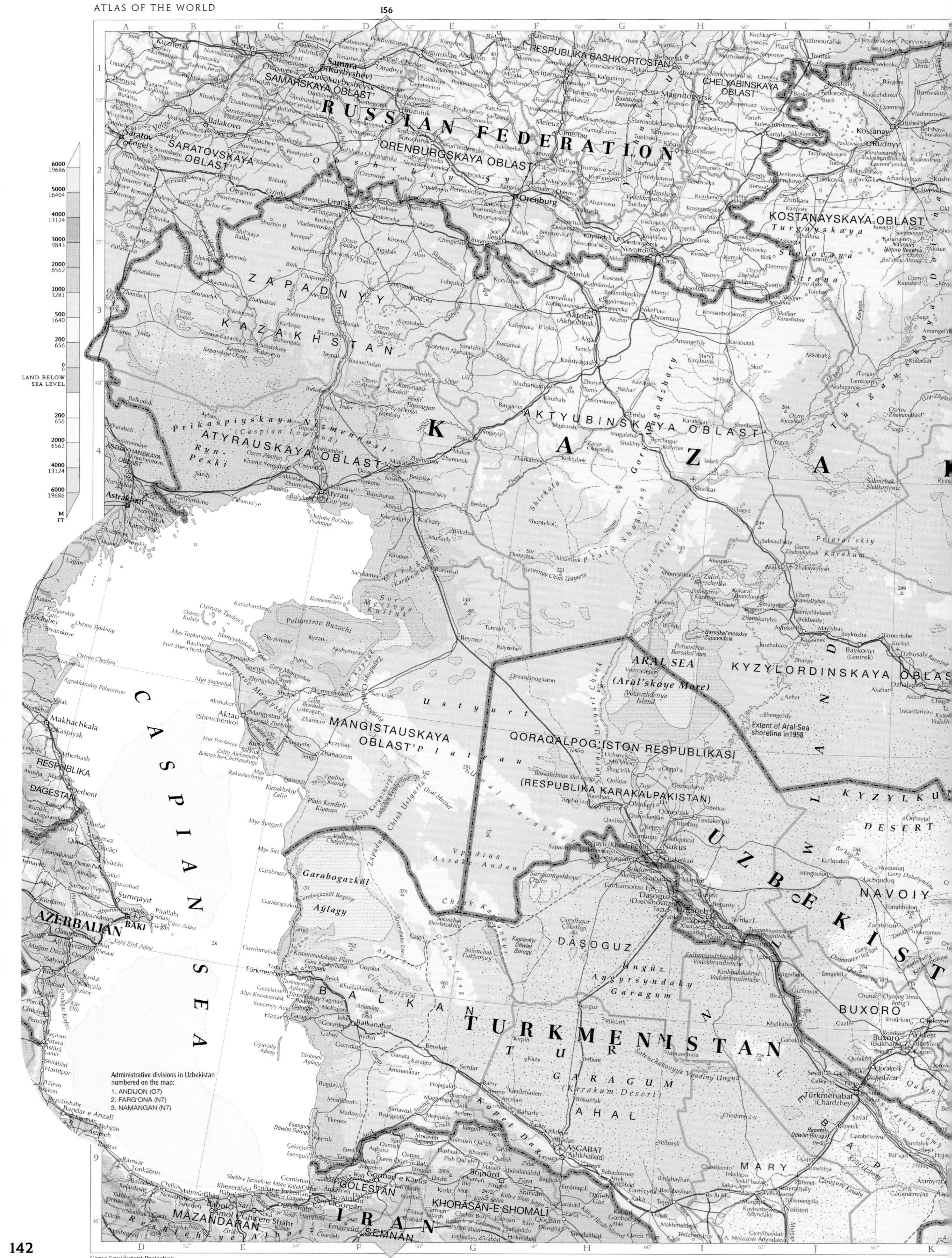

Conic Equidistant Projection

144

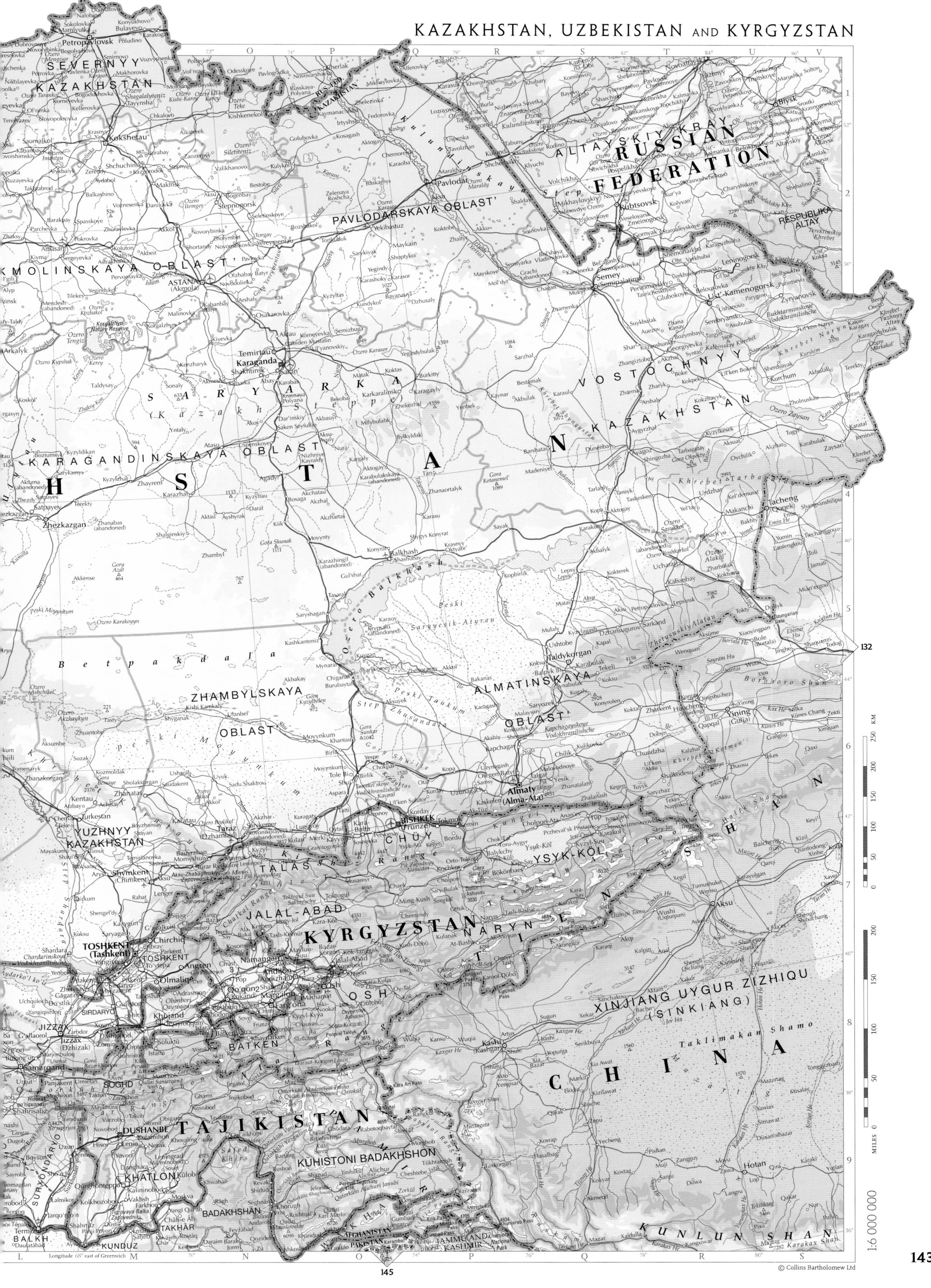
RUSSIAN FEDERATION
ALTAYSKIY KRAY
RESPUBLIKA ALTAY
SEVERNYY KAZAKHSTAN
AKMOLINSKAYA OBLAST'
PAVLODARSKAYA OBLAST'
KARAGANDINSKAYA OBLAST'
VOSTOCHNYY KAZAKHSTAN
ALMATINSKAYA OBLAST'
ZHAMBYLSKAYA OBLAST'
YUZHNYY KAZAKHSTAN
KYRGYZSTAN
CHUY
TALAS
JALAL-ABAD
NARYN
YSYK-KÖL
OSH
BATKEN
TAJIKISTAN
SOGHD
KHATLON
KŬHISTONI BADAKHSHON
TOSHKENT
SIRDARYO
JIZZAX
SURXONDARYO
BADAKHSHAN
TAKHAR
XINJIANG UYGUR ZIZHIQU (SINKIANG)
CHINA
KUNLUN SHAN
Taklimakan Shamo
Betpakdala
Saryarka (Kazakh Steppe)
Ozero Balkhash
Ysyk-Köl
ASTANA (Akmola)
Karaganda
Pavlodar
Semey (Semipalatinsk)
Ust'-Kamenogorsk
Petropavlovsk
Kokshetau
Balkhash
Taldykorgan
Almaty (Alma-Ata)
BISHKEK (Frunze)
Taraz (Dzhambul)
Shymkent (Chimkent)
TOSHKENT (Tashkent)
Namangan
Andijon
Osh
Farg'ona
Khujand
Jizzax (Dzhizak)
Samarqand
DUSHANBE
Kashi (Kashgar)
Aksu
Hotan
Yining (Gulja)
Tacheng (Qoqek)
Zhezkazgan
Biysk
Rubtsovsk
132
145
Longitude 68° east of Greenwich
1:6 000 000
KM
MILES
© Collins Bartholomew Ltd

Conic Equidistant Projection

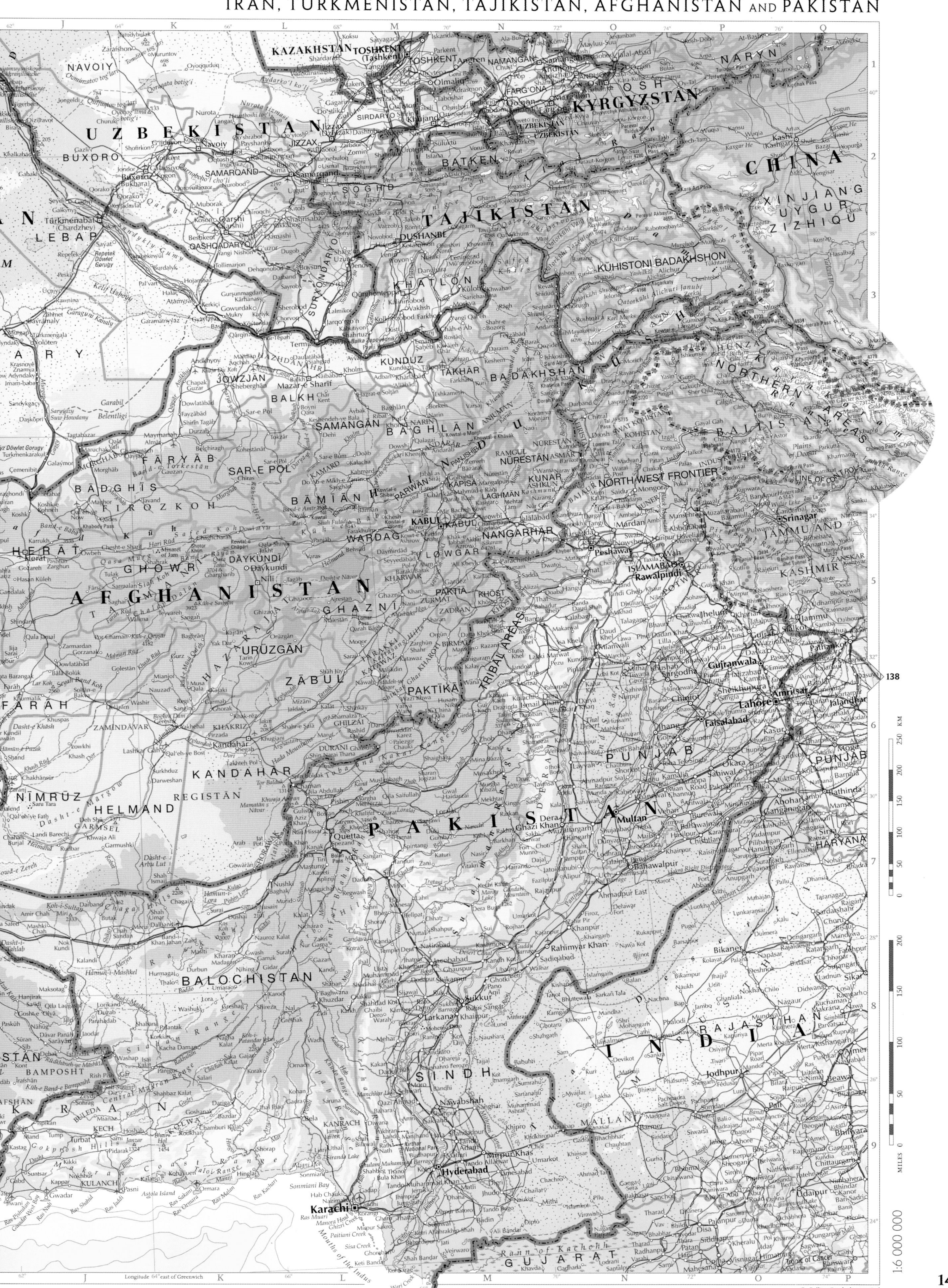
KAZAKHSTAN
UZBEKISTAN
KYRGYZSTAN
TAJIKISTAN
AFGHANISTAN
PAKISTAN
CHINA
INDIA
XINJIANG UYGUR ZIZHIQU
NORTHERN AREAS
BALTISTAN
JAMMU AND KASHMIR
NORTH WEST FRONTIER
TRIBAL AREAS
PUNJAB
SINDH
BALOCHISTAN
RAJASTHAN
GUJARAT
HARYANA
NAVOIY
BUXORO
SAMARQAND
QASHQADARYO
SURXONDARYO
LEBAP
SOGHD
KHATLON
KUHISTONI BADAKHSHON
BATKEN
NARYN
OSH
JOWZJAN
BALKH
KUNDUZ
TAKHAR
BADAKHSHAN
SAMANGAN
BAGHLAN
FARYAB
SAR-E POL
BADGHIS
HERAT
GHOWR
DAYKUNDI
BAMIAN
PARWAN
KAPISA
NURESTAN
KUNAR
LAGHMAN
NANGARHAR
KABUL
WARDAG
LOWGAR
PAKTIA
KHOST
GHAZNI
URUZGAN
ZABUL
PAKTIKA
FARAH
NIMRUZ
HELMAND
KANDAHAR
REGISTAN
Kabul
Dushanbe
Toshkent (Tashkent)
Samarqand
Bukhara
Türkmenabat (Chardzhey)
Mazar-e Sharif
Herat
Kandahar
Quetta
Peshawar
ISLAMABAD
Rawalpindi
Srinagar
Jammu
Gujranwala
Lahore
Amritsar
Faisalabad
Multan
Bahawalpur
Sukkur
Larkana
Hyderabad
Karachi
Nawabshah
Jodhpur
Bikaner
Udaipur
Kashi (Kashgar)
Jalandhar
Rahimyar Khan
Dera Ghazi Khan
Rann of Kachchh
Mouths of the Indus
Longitude 64° east of Greenwich
138
1:6 000 000

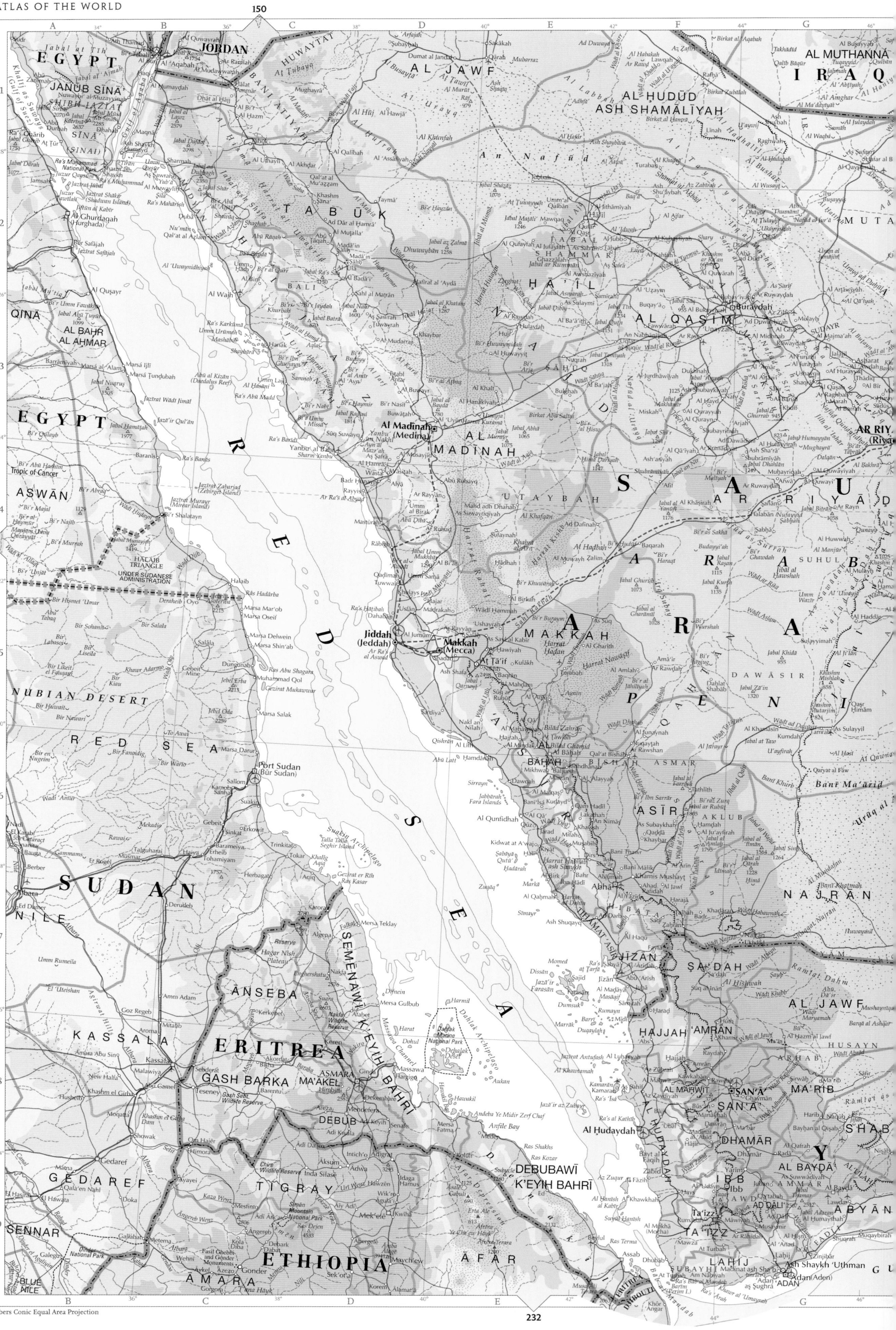

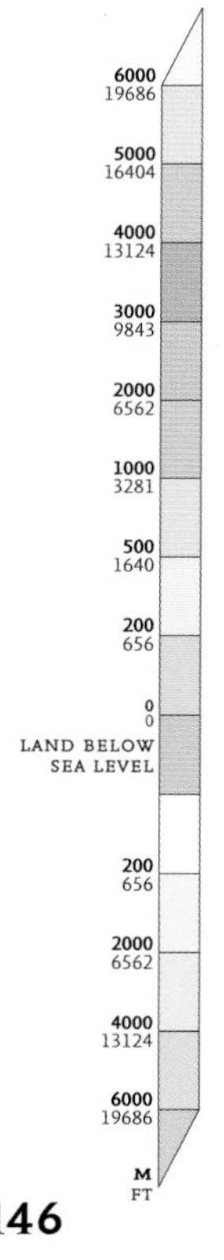

150

225

EGYPT

JORDAN

IRAQ

SAUDI ARABIA

SUDAN

ERITREA

ETHIOPIA

RED SEA

M	FT
6000	19686
5000	16404
4000	13124
3000	9843
2000	6562
1000	3281
500	1640
200	656
0	0
LAND BELOW SEA LEVEL	
200	656
2000	6562
4000	13124
6000	19686

Albers Conic Equal Area Projection

232

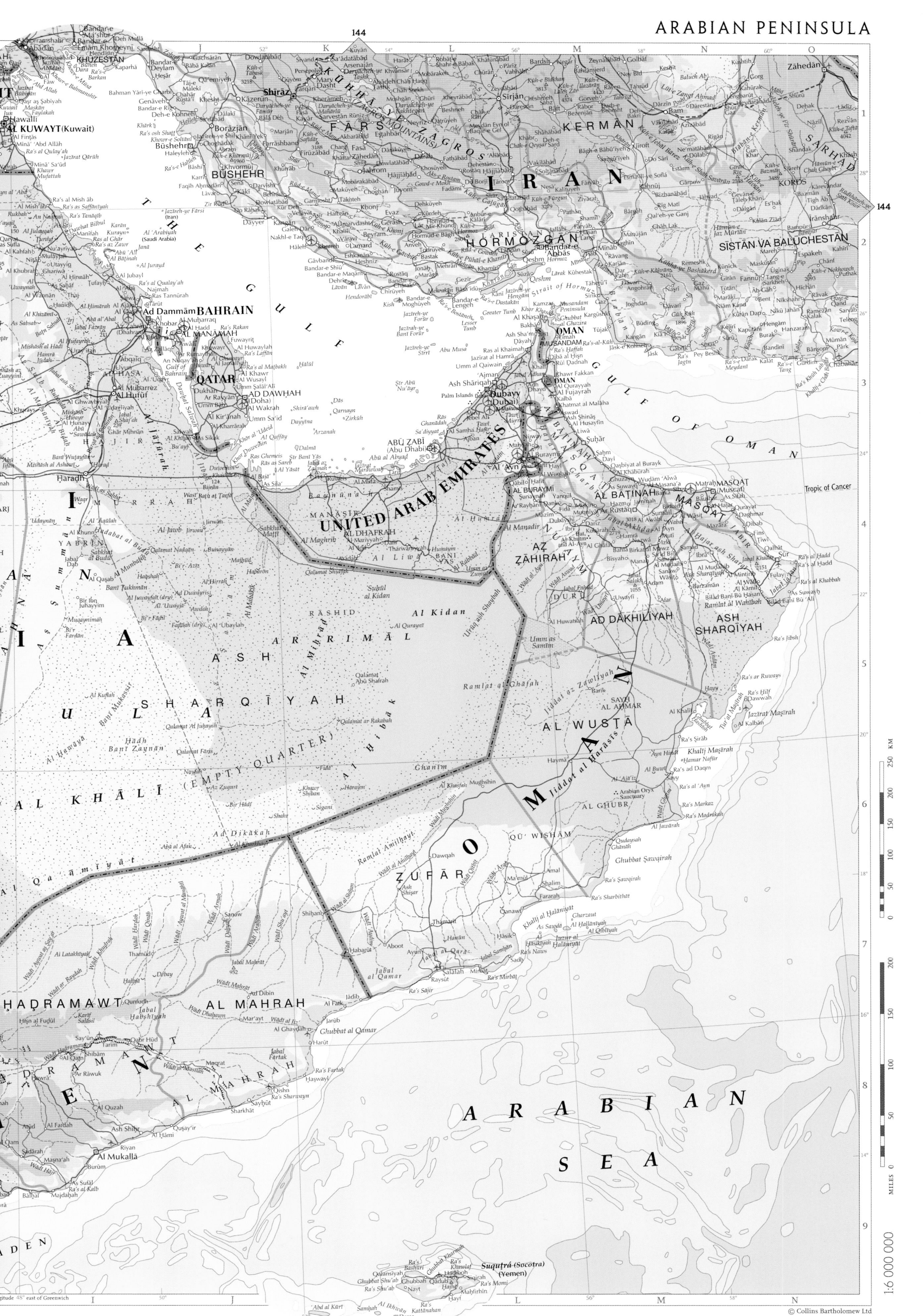
IRAN
FARS
KERMAN
HORMOZGAN
SISTAN VA BALUCHESTAN
BUSHEHR
KHUZESTAN
ZAGROS MOUNTAINS
THE GULF
GULF OF OMAN
BAHRAIN
QATAR
AD DAWHAH (Doha)
AL MANAMAH
AL KUWAYT (Kuwait)
UNITED ARAB EMIRATES
ABU ZABI (Abu Dhabi)
Dubayy (Dubai)
OMAN
MASQAT (Muscat)
RUB' AL KHALI (EMPTY QUARTER)
AL MAHRAH
HADRAMAWT
ARABIAN SEA
Suqutra (Socotra) (Yemen)
Tropic of Cancer
1:6 000 000
© Collins Bartholomew Ltd

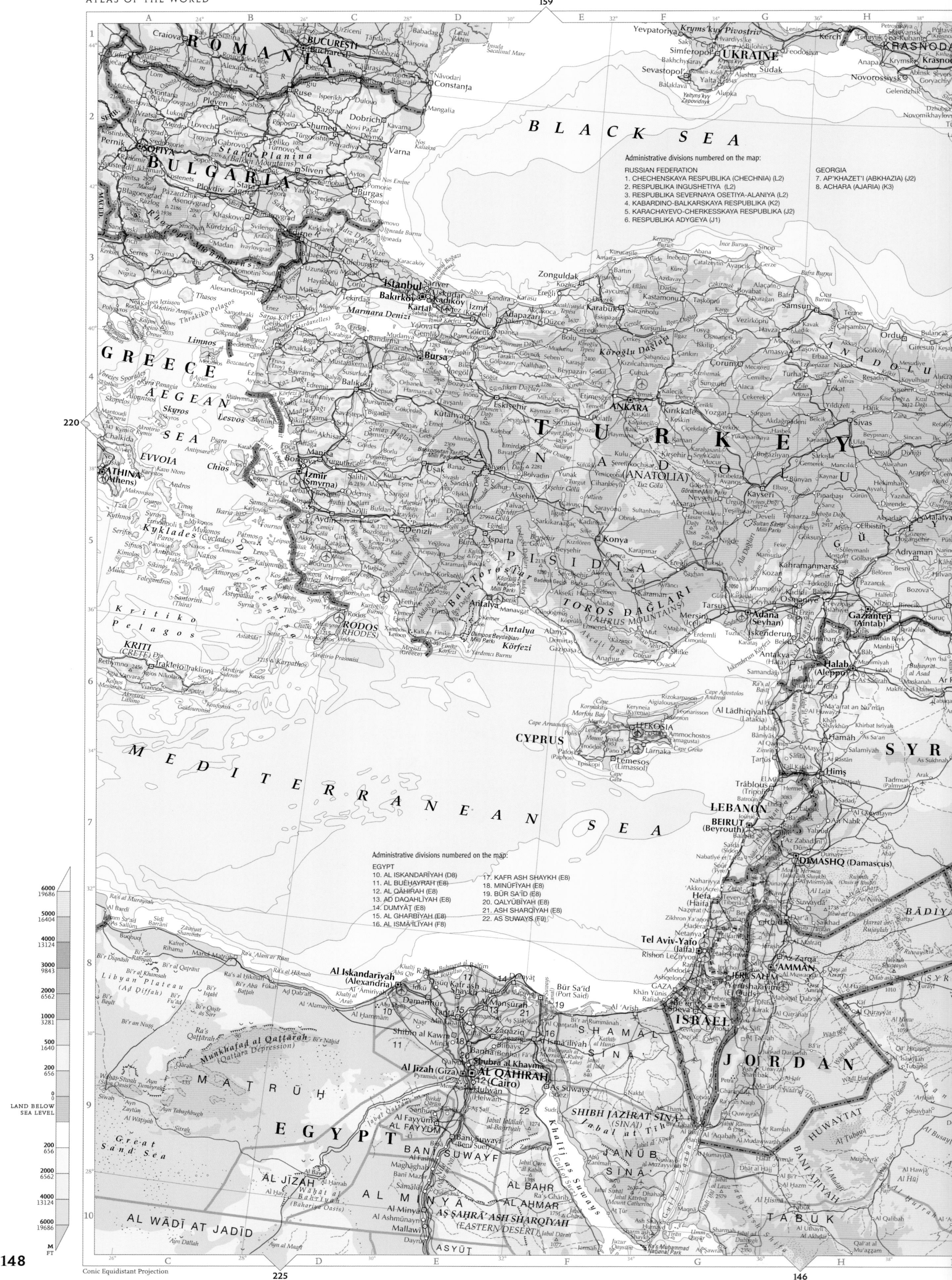
159
220
225
146
BLACK SEA
MEDITERRANEAN SEA
AEGEAN SEA
ROMANIA
BULGARIA
GREECE
TURKEY
ANATOLIA
CYPRUS
LEBANON
ISRAEL
JORDAN
EGYPT
SYR
KRASNODA
UKRAINE
BUCUREȘTI (Bucharest)
SOFIYA
ATHINA (Athens)
İstanbul
ANKARA
İzmir (Smyrna)
Bursa
Konya
Adana (Seyhan)
Halab (Aleppo)
BEIRUT (Beyrouth)
DIMASHQ (Damascus)
Tel Aviv-Yafo (Jaffa)
JERUSALEM Yerushalayim El Quds
AMMAN
Al Iskandarīyah (Alexandria)
AL QĀHIRAH (Cairo)
Al Jīzah (Giza)
LEFKOSIA (Nicosia)
KRITI (CRETE)
RODOS (RHODES)
Kyklades (Cyclades)
Limnos
Lesvos
Chios
Samos
Evvoia
Kritiko Pelagos
Marmara Denizi
Krymsʼkyy Pivostriv
Sevastopolʼ
Constanța
Varna
Burgas
Antalya Körfezi
TOROS DAĞLARI (TAURUS MOUNTAINS)
Munkhafaḍ al Qaṭṭārah (Qattara Depression)
Great Sand Sea
Libyan Plateau (Aḍ Diffah)
SHIBH JAZĪRAT SĪNĀ (SINAI)
AL WĀDĪ AT JADĪD
AṢ ṢAḤRĀʼ ASH SHARQĪYAH (EASTERN DESERT)
BANI SUWAYF
AL MINYĀ
AL BAḤR AL AḤMAR
MATRŪḤ
TABŪK
HUWAYṬAT
BĀDIYA
Administrative divisions numbered on the map:
RUSSIAN FEDERATION
1. CHECHENSKAYA RESPUBLIKA (CHECHNIA) (L2)
2. RESPUBLIKA INGUSHETIYA (L2)
3. RESPUBLIKA SEVERNAYA OSETIYA-ALANIYA (L2)
4. KABARDINO-BALKARSKAYA RESPUBLIKA (K2)
5. KARACHAYEVO-CHERKESSKAYA RESPUBLIKA (J2)
6. RESPUBLIKA ADYGEYA (J1)
GEORGIA
7. APʼKHAZETʼI (ABKHAZIA) (J2)
8. ACHARA (AJARIA) (K3)
Administrative divisions numbered on the map:
EGYPT
10. AL ISKANDARĪYAH (D8)
11. AL BUḤAYRAH (E8)
12. AL QĀHIRAH (E8)
13. AD DAQAHLĪYAH (E8)
14. DUMYĀṬ (E8)
15. AL GHARBĪYAH (E8)
16. AL ISMĀʻĪLĪYAH (F8)
17. KAFR ASH SHAYKH (E8)
18. MINŪFĪYAH (E8)
19. BŪR SAʻĪD (E8)
20. QALYŪBĪYAH (E8)
21. ASH SHARQĪYAH (E8)
22. AS SUWAYS (F9)
6000 19686
5000 16404
4000 13124
3000 9843
2000 6562
1000 3281
500 1640
200 656
0 0
LAND BELOW SEA LEVEL
200 656
2000 6562
4000 13124
6000 19686
M FT
Conic Equidistant Projection

RUSSIAN FEDERATION
STAVROPOL'SKIY KRAY
GEORGIA
T'BILISI
ARMENIA
YEREVAN
AZERBAIJAN
BAKI
RESPUBLIKA DAGESTAN
CASPIAN SEA
KAZAKHSTAN
MANGISTAUSKAYA OBLAST'
UZBEKISTAN
TURKMENISTAN
BALKAN
IRAN
TEHRAN
TEHRĀN
AZARBAYJAN-E SHARQI
AZARBAYJAN-E GHARBI
ARDABIL
GILAN
MAZANDARAN
GOLESTAN
SEMNĀN
QAZVIN
ZANJAN
KORDESTĀN
HAMADAN
KERMĀNSHĀH
LORESTĀN
ĪLĀM
KHŪZESTĀN
FARS
BŪSHEHR
IRAQ
BAGHDAD
NĪNAWĀ
DAHŪK
ARBĪL
AT TA'MĪM
AS SULAYMĀNIYAH
ṢALĀḤ AD DĪN
DIYĀLĀ
AL ANBĀR
WĀSIṬ
BĀBIL
KARBALĀ'
AL QĀDISIYAH
MAYSĀN
DHĪ QĀR
AN NAJAF
AL BAṢRAH
AL MUTHANNĀ
KUWAIT
AL KUWAYT (Kuwait)
SAUDI ARABIA
AL ḤUDŪD ASH SHAMĀLĪYAH
ASH SHARQĪYAH
THE GULF
ISTANBUL
1:60 000
1:6 000 000
142
144
147

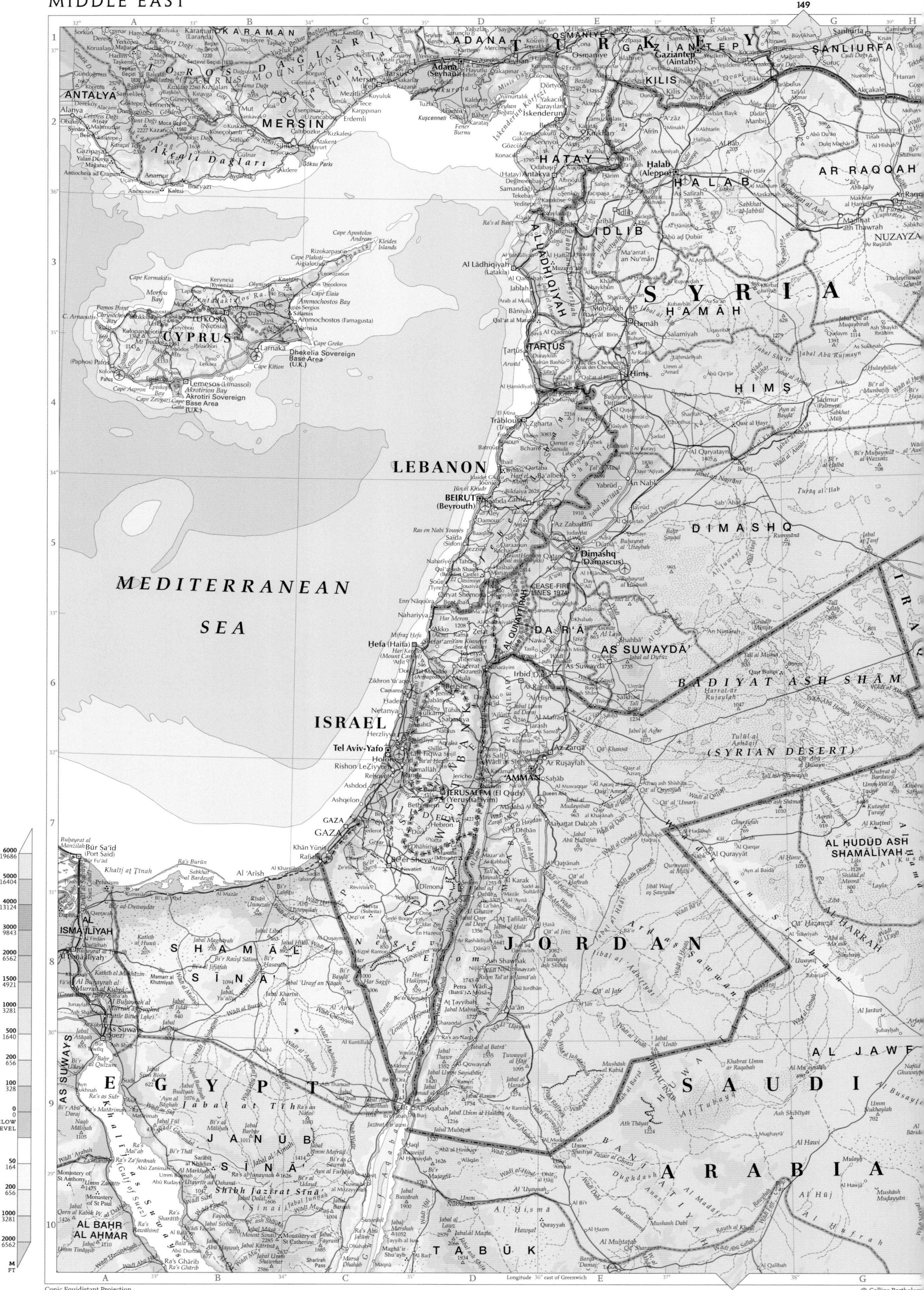

Conic Equidistant Projection

1:3 000 000

Equidistant Projection

© Collins Bartholomew Ltd

Conic Equidistant Projection

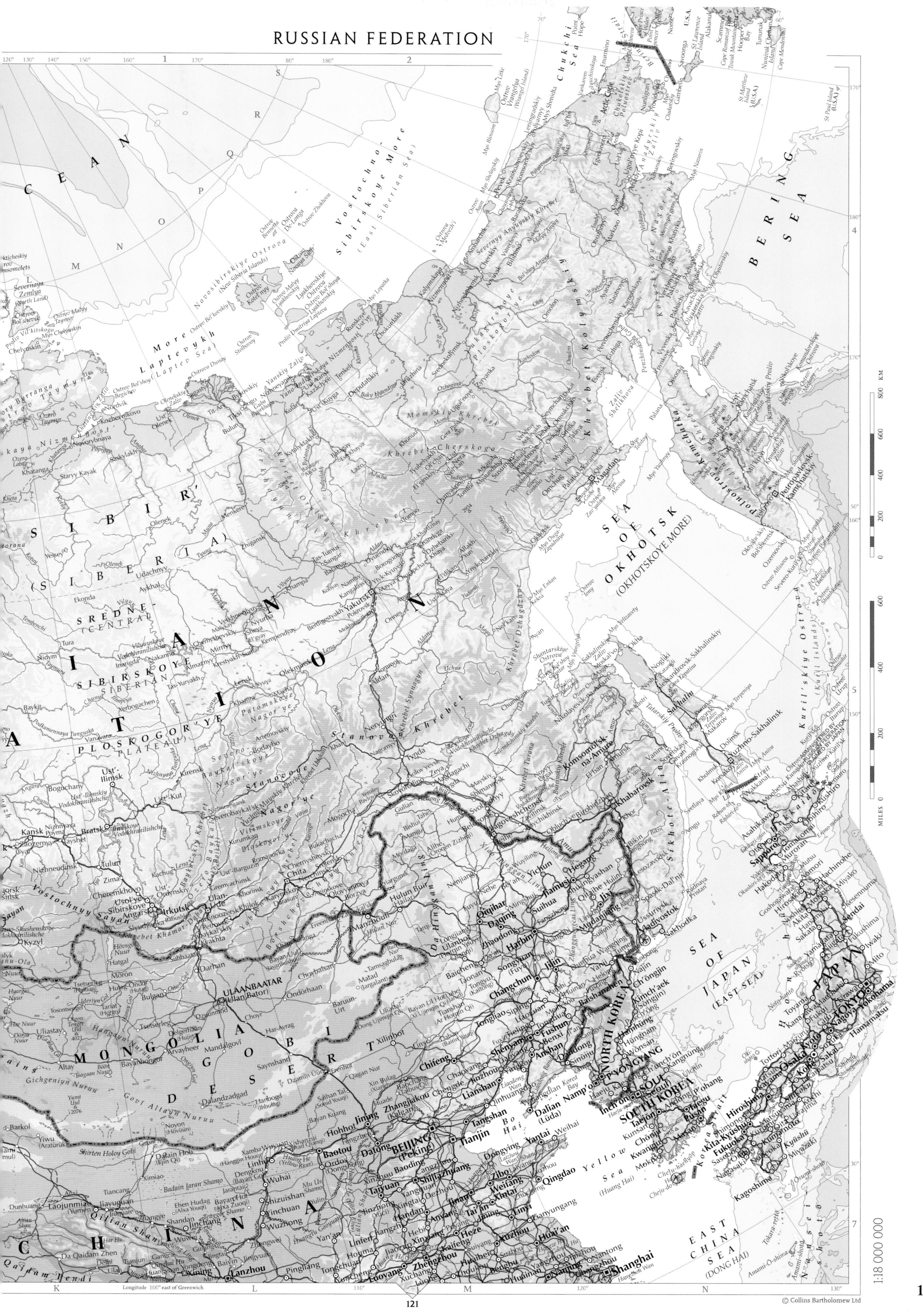
BERING SEA
SEA OF OKHOTSK
(OKHOTSKOYE MORE)
SEA OF JAPAN
(EAST SEA)
EAST CHINA SEA
(DONG HAI)
Yellow Sea
(Huang Hai)
Bo Hai
More Laptevykh
(Laptev Sea)
Vostochno-Sibirskoye More
(East Siberian Sea)
Chukchi Sea
Novosibirskiye Ostrova
(New Siberia Islands)
Severnaya Zemlya
(North Land)
SIBIR'
(SIBERIA)
SREDNE-SIBIRSKOYE PLOSKOGOR'YE
(CENTRAL SIBERIAN PLATEAU)
Khrebet Cherskogo
Khrebet Kolymskiy
Stanovoy Khrebet
Poluostrov Kamchatka
Kuril'skiye Ostrova
(Kuril Islands)
Sakhalin
MONGOLIA
GOBI DESERT
CHINA
NORTH KOREA
SOUTH KOREA
JAPAN
ULAANBAATAR
(Ulan Bator)
BEIJING
(Peking)
P'YONGYANG
SEOUL
TOKYO
Yakutsk
Magadan
Petropavlovsk-Kamchatskiy
Khabarovsk
Vladivostok
Irkutsk
Chita
Bratsk
Harbin
Shenyang
Tianjin
Dalian
Shanghai
Sapporo
Osaka
Busan
Lanzhou
Baotou
1:18 000 000
Longitude 100° east of Greenwich

121

NORTH AMERICA
Baffin Bay
Greenland
Arctic Circle
Greenland Sea
Spitsbergen
Nordaustlandet
Svalbard (Norway)
Longyearbyen
Bjørnøya (Norway)
BARENTS SEA
Nordkapp
Jan Mayen (Norway)
Denmark Strait
ICELAND
Reykjavík
NORWEGIAN SEA
NORWAY
SWEDEN
Trondheim
Faroe Islands (Denmark)
Tórshavn
Shetland Islands
Bergen
Oslo
Vänern
Göteborg
Orkney Islands
Outer Hebrides
Skagerrak
Kattegat
Ålborg
DENMARK
København
Odense
British Isles
SCOTLAND
Glasgow
Edinburgh
NORTH SEA
NORTHERN IRELAND
Belfast
UNITED KINGDOM
Dublin
IRELAND
Leeds
Manchester
Liverpool
Birmingham
WALES
ENGLAND
Cardiff
London
English Channel
Hamburg
Bremen
Hannover
Bielefeld
NETHERLANDS
Amsterdam
's-Gravenhage
Rotterdam
Essen
Düsseldorf
Köln
Aachen
Bonn
Bruxelles
BELGIUM
Lille
LUXEMBOURG
Luxembourg
Frankfurt am Main
Mannheim
ATLANTIC OCEAN
Channel Islands
Paris
Brest
Rennes
Orléans
Loire
Strasbourg
Dijon
Zürich
Bern
Nantes
FRANCE
Genève
Lyon
Milano
Torino
Bay of Biscay
Bordeaux
A Coruña
Toulouse
Marseille
Nice
Bilbao
Pyrenees
Andorra la Vella
ANDORRA
Ebro
Zaragoza
Barcelona
Porto
Salamanca
Madrid
SPAIN
PORTUGAL
Valencia
Islas Baleares
Menorca
Mallorca
Eivissa
Lisboa
Córdoba
Sevilla
Cartagena
Cádiz
Málaga
Gibraltar (U.K.)
Ceuta (Spain)
Melilla (Spain)
Corse
Sardegna
Corvo
Flores
Arquipélago dos Açores
São Jorge
Faial
Pico
Terceira
Azores (Portugal)
São Miguel
Ponta Delgada
Santa Maria
Arquipélago da Madeira
Madeira (Portugal)
Ilha de Porto Santo
Funchal
Orthographic Projection

RUSSIAN FEDERATION
ASIA
UKRAINE
BELARUS
ESTONIA
LATVIA
LITHUANIA
POLAND
SLOVAKIA
HUNGARY
ROMANIA
MOLDOVA
CROATIA
BOSNIA-HERZEGOVINA
SERBIA
MONTENEGRO
KOSOVO
BULGARIA
MACEDONIA
GREECE
TURKEY
ITALY
MALTA
Moskva
Sankt-Peterburg
Helsinki
Tallinn
Riga
Vilnius
Minsk
Kyiv
Warszawa
Chişinău
Bucureşti
Budapest
Bratislava
Beograd
Sofiya
Zagreb
Sarajevo
Podgorica
Prishtinë
Skopje
Tiranë
Athina
Valletta
İstanbul
Black Sea
Caspian Sea
Aral Sea
Sea of Azov
Aegean Sea
Ionian Sea
Adriatic Sea
MEDITERRANEAN SEA
The Gulf
Beloye More
Ural'skiy Khrebet (Ural Mountains)
Carpathian Mountains
Caucasus
Kuhhā-ye Zagros (Zagros Mountains)
Altai Mountains
Hindu Kush
Volga
Don
Ob'
Yenisey
Irtysh
Cyprus
Kriti
Rodos
Sicilia
Dodekanisa
Arkhangel'sk
Syktyvkar
Vorkuta
Petrozavodsk
Vologda
Yaroslavl'
Nizhniy Novgorod
Kazan'
Perm'
Kirov
Izhevsk
Ufa
Samara
Orenburg
Ul'yanovsk
Penza
Saratov
Tula
Smolensk
Voronezh
Volgograd
Astrakhan'
Rostov-na-Donu
Krasnodar
Stavropol'
Groznyy
Novorossiysk
Simferopol'
Odesa
Mykolayiv
Dnipropetrovs'k
Donets'k
Kharkiv
Belgorod
Sumy
Chernihiv
Homyel'
Mahilyow
Vitsyebsk
Hrodna
Brest
Rivne
L'viv
Kirovohrad
Kraków
Katowice
Wrocław
Łódź
Białystok
Košice
Debrecen
Oradea
Szeged
Timişoara
Braşov
Iaşi
Craiova
Pleven
Varna
Burgas
Edirne
Thessaloniki
Larisa
Bari
Napoli
Cosenza
Messina
Palermo
Siracusa
Split
Trieste
Brno
Wien
1:15 000 000
MILES
KM

152

ST PETERSBURG
1:125 000
6000
19686
5000
16404
4000
13124
3000
9843
2000
6562
1000
3281
500
1640
200
656
0
0
LAND BELOW
SEA LEVEL
200
656
2000
6562
4000
13124
6000
19686
M
FT
BARENTS SEA
Pechorskoye More
BELOYE MORE (WHITE SEA)
BALTIC SEA
Gulf of Finland
Gulf of Riga
RUSSIA
FINLAND
SWEDEN
ESTONIA
LATVIA
LITHUANIA
RESPUBLIKA KARELIYA
MURMANSKAYA OBLAST'
ARKHANGEL'SKAYA OBLAST'
VOLOGODSKAYA OBLAST'
LENINGRADSKAYA OBLAST'
PSKOVSKAYA OBLAST'
NOVGORODSKAYA OBLAST'
TVERSKAYA OBLAST'
YAROSLAVSKAYA OBLAST'
IVANOVSKAYA OBLAST'
KOSTROMSKAYA OBLAST'
KIROVSKAYA OBLAST'
RESPUBLIKA MARIY EL
UDMURTSKAYA RESPUBLIKA
RESPUBLIKA KOMI
NENETSKIY AVTONOMNYY OKRUG
PERMSKIY KRAY
KHANTY-MANSIYSKIY AVTONOMNYY OKRUG-YUGRA
SVERDLOVSKAYA OBLAST'
URAL'SKIY KHREBET
URAL MOUNTAINS
Sankt-Peterburg
HELSINKI (Helsingfors)
TALLINN
RIGA
STOCKHOLM
Arkhangel'sk
Severodvinsk
Murmansk
Petrozavodsk
Syktyvkar
Ukhta
Vorkuta
Kotlas
Vologda
Cherepovets
Yaroslavl'
Kostroma
Ivanovo
Izhevsk
Perm'
Nizhniy Novgorod

162

142

144

148

197

160

189

219

BELARUS

POLAND

UKR

MOLDOVA

ROMANIA

SLOVAKIA

HUNGARY

SERBIA

HRODZYENSKAYA VOBLASTS'

MINSKAYA VOBLASTS'

MAHILYOWSKAYA VOBLASTS'

BRESTSKAYA VOBLASTS'

HOMYEL'SKAYA VOBLAS

PRIPET MARSHES

VOLYNS'KA OBLAST'

RIVNENS'KA OBLAST'

ZHYTOMYRS'KA OBLAST'

L'VIVS'KA OBLAST'

TERNOPILS'KA OBLAST'

KHMEL'NYTS'KA OBLAST'

IVANO-FRANKIVS'KA OBLAST'

VINNYTS'KA OBLAST'

ZAKARPATS'KA OBLAST

CHERNIVETS'KA OBLAST

ODES'KA

KYIVS

CARPATHIAN MOUNTAINS

CARPAŢII MERIDIONALI (TRANSYLVANIAN ALPS)

NIZINA MAZOWIECKA

WYŻYNA LUBELSKA

WARSZAWA (Warsaw)

BUCUREŞTI (Bucharest)

CHIŞINĂU (Kishinev)

6000 19686

5000 16404

4000 13124

3000 9843

2000 6562

1500 4921

1000 3281

500 1640

200 656

100 328

0 0

LAND BELOW SEA LEVEL

50 164

200 656

1000 3281

2000 6562

M FT

Conic Equidistant Projection

219

161
RUSSIAN
FEDERATION
BRYANSKAYA OBLAST'
ORLOVSKAYA OBLAST'
LIPETSKAYA OBLAST'
TAMBOVSKAYA OBLAST'
KURSKAYA OBLAST'
VORONEZHSKAYA OBLAST'
BELGORODSKAYA OBLAST'
SUMS'KA OBLAST'
POLTAVS'KA OBLAST'
KHARKIVS'KA OBLAST'
LUHANS'KA OBLAST'
DONETS'KA OBLAST'
DNIPROPETROVS'KA OBLAST'
ZAPORIZ'KA OBLAST'
KHERSONS'KA OBLAST'
ROSTOVSKAYA OBLAST'
KRASNODARSKIY KRAY
RESPUBLIKA KRYM (CRIMEA)
Kharkiv
Dnipropetrovs'k
Zaporizhzhya
Donets'k
Luhans'k
Poltava
Sumy
Kursk
Belgorod
Voronezh
Kryvyy Rih
Mykolayiv
Kherson
Melitopol'
Mariupol'
Berdyans'k
Rostov-na-Donu
Taganrog
Krasnodar
Kerch
Simferopol'
Sevastopol
Yalta
Novorossiysk
Sea of Azov
BLACK SEA
Gulf of Taganrog
Longitude 32° east of Greenwich
1:3 000 000
157
KM
MILES

163

165

189

GULF OF BOTHNIA

GULF OF FINLAND

BALTIC SEA

GULF OF RIGA

Gulf of Gdańsk

SWEDEN

FINLAND

ESTONIA

LATVIA

LITHUANIA

RUSSIAN FEDERATION

KALININGRADSKAYA OBLAST'

POLAND

BELARUS

LÄNSI-SUOMI

ETELÄ-SUOMI

UPPSALA

STOCKHOLM

GOTLAND

PSKOVSKAYA

VITSYEBSKAYA VOBLASTS'

MINSKAYA VOBLASTS'

HRODZYENSKAYA VOBLASTS'

BRESTSKAYA VOBLASTS'

POJEZIERZE MAZURSKIE

NIZINA MAZOWIECKA

M	FT
6000	19686
5000	16404
4000	13124
3000	9843
2000	6562
1500	4921
1000	3281
500	1640
200	656
100	328
0	0
LAND BELOW SEA LEVEL	
50	164
200	656
1000	3281
2000	6562

Conic Equidistant Projection

158

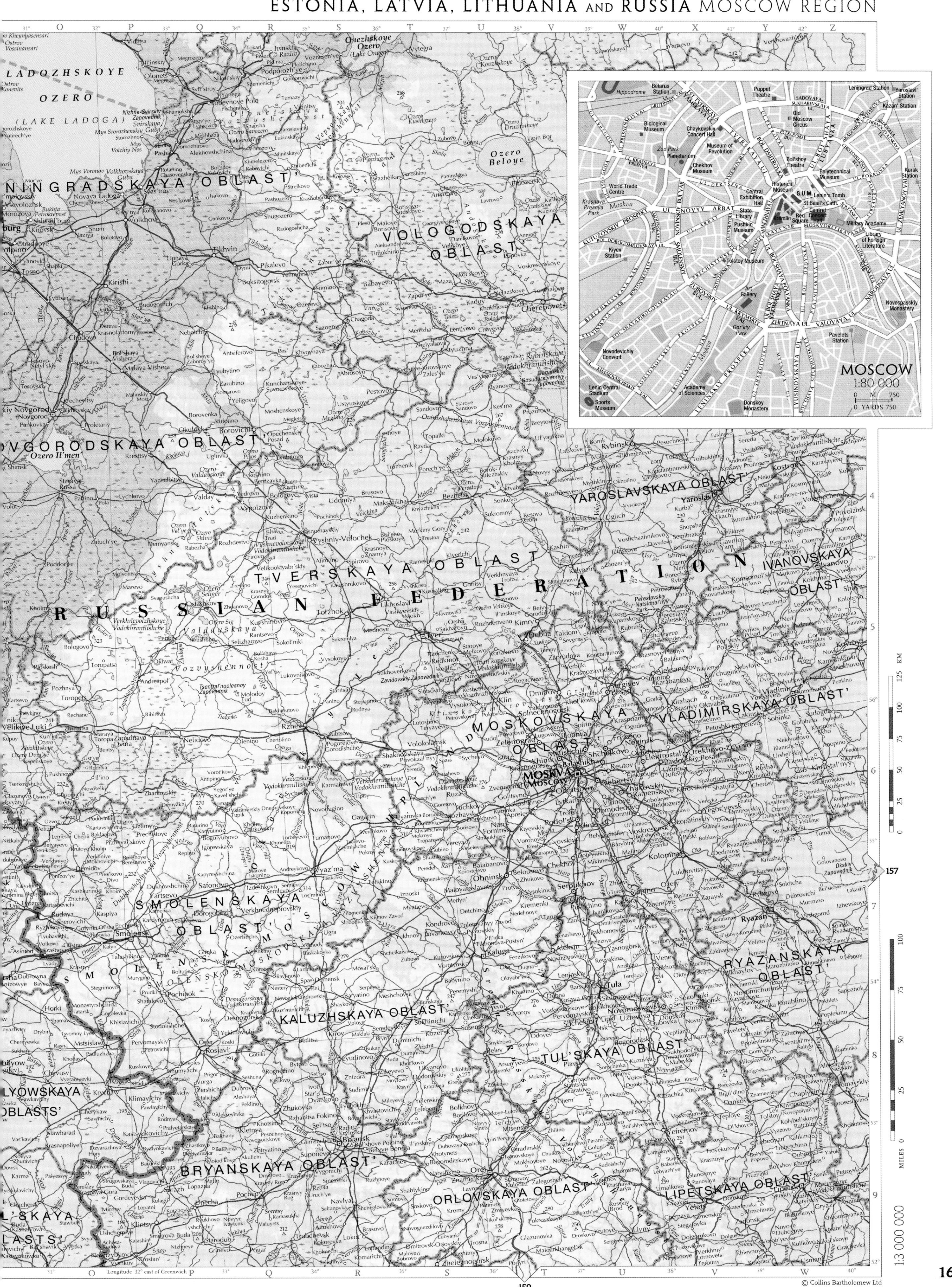
LADOZHSKOYE OZERO
(LAKE LADOGA)
Onezhskoye Ozero
(Lake Onega)
Ozero Beloye
Ozero Il'men'
VOLOGODSKAYA OBLAST'
NOVGORODSKAYA OBLAST'
TVERSKAYA OBLAST
YAROSLAVSKAYA OBLAST'
IVANOVSKAYA OBLAST'
VLADIMIRSKAYA OBLAST'
MOSKOVSKAYA OBLAST'
SMOLENSKAYA OBLAST'
KALUZHSKAYA OBLAST'
TUL'SKAYA OBLAST'
RYAZANSKAYA OBLAST'
BRYANSKAYA OBLAST'
ORLOVSKAYA OBLAST'
LIPETSKAYA OBLAST'
RUSSIAN FEDERATION
MOSKVA (Moscow)
Tver'
Yaroslavl'
Kostroma
Ivanovo
Vladimir
Ryazan'
Tula
Kaluga
Smolensk
Bryansk
Orel
Cherepovets
Rybinsk
Velikiy Novgorod
Rzhev
Vyaz'ma
Kolomna
Serpukhov
Obninsk
MOSCOW
1:80 000
1:3 000 000
Longitude 32° east of Greenwich
157
159

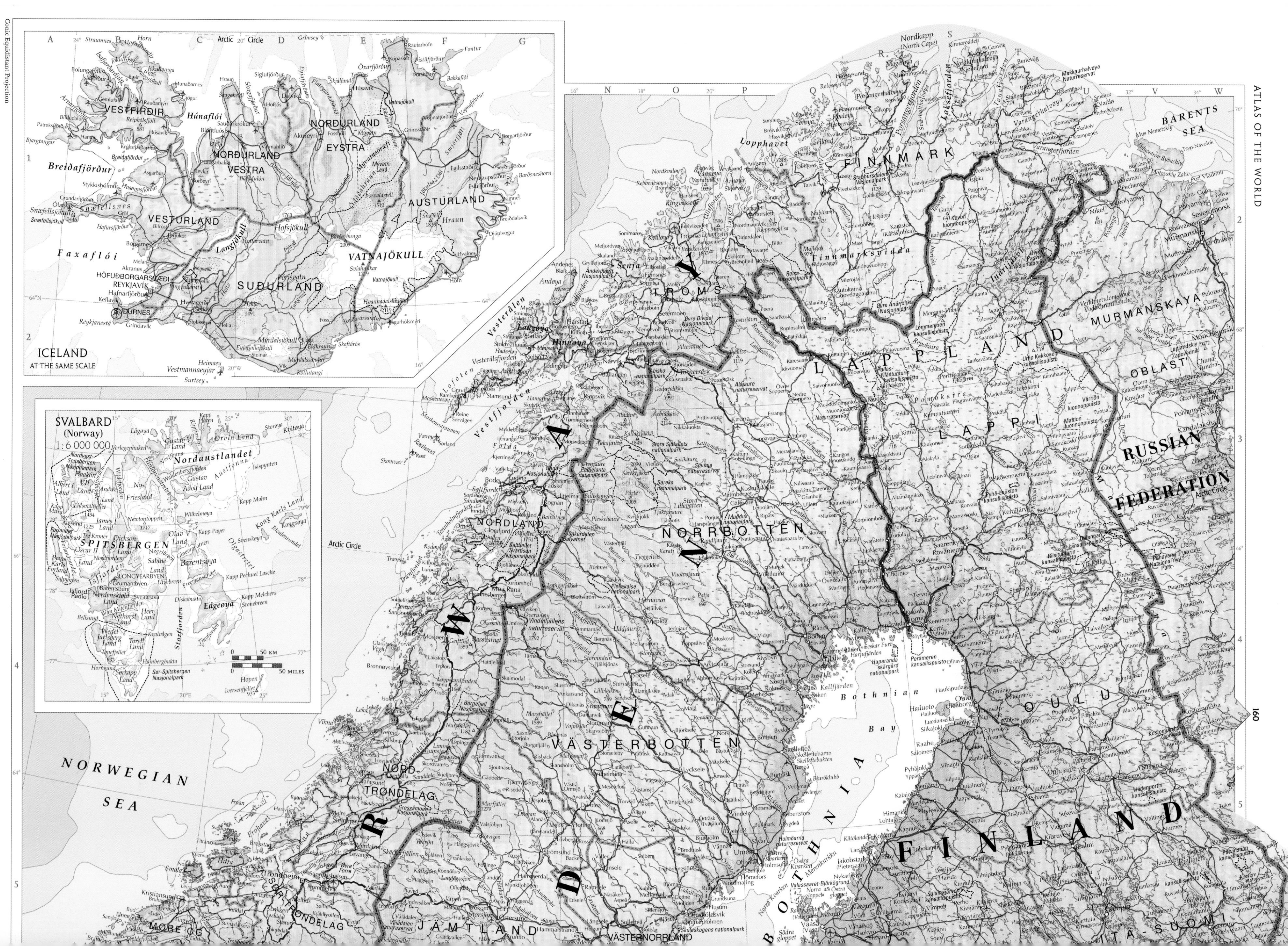
NORWAY
SWEDEN
FINLAND
BARENTS SEA
NORWEGIAN SEA
RUSSIAN FEDERATION
MURMANSKAYA OBLAST'
FINNMARK
TROMS
NORDLAND
NORD-TRØNDELAG
SØR-TRØNDELAG
MØRE OG
NORRBOTTEN
VÄSTERBOTTEN
JÄMTLAND
VÄSTERNORRLAND
OULU
LAPPI
LAPPLAND
Bothnian Bay
GULF OF BOTHNIA
Arctic Circle
Nordkapp (North Cape)
Lofoten
Vestfjorden
Vesterålen
Lopphavet
Finnmarksvidda
ICELAND
AT THE SAME SCALE
VESTFIRÐIR
VESTURLAND
NORÐURLAND VESTRA
NORÐURLAND EYSTRA
AUSTURLAND
SUÐURLAND
VATNAJÖKULL
HÖFUÐBORGARSVÆÐI
REYKJAVÍK
SUÐURNES
Faxaflói
Breiðafjörður
Húnaflói
SVALBARD
(Norway)
1:6 000 000
Nordaustlandet
SPITSBERGEN
Barentsøya
Edgeøya
Storfjorden
50 KM
50 MILES

1:4 000 000

© Collins Bartholomew Ltd

162

Conic Equidistant Projection

190

192

GÄVLEBORG
DALARNA
UPPSALA
Uppland
VÄSTMANLAND
STOCKHOLM
ÖREBRO
SÖDERMANLAND
ÖSTERGOTLAND
JÖNKÖPING
KALMAR
KRONOBERG
BLEKINGE
SWEDEN
Åland
(Ahvenanmaa)
FINLAND
LÄNSI-SUOMI
Ålands Hav
Södra Kvarken
ESTONIA
Hiiumaa
Saaremaa
Gotska Sandön
(Sweden)
GOTLAND
GOTLAND
(Sweden)
ÖLAND
Kalmarsund
BALTIC SEA
Hanöbukten
Bornholm Strait
Bornholm
(Denmark)
Irbe Strait
LATVIA
LITHUANIA
RUSSIAN FEDERATION
Courland Lagoon
Gulf of Gdańsk
POLAND
Gdańsk
Gdynia
Kaliningrad
Klaipėda
Liepāja
Ventspils
Visby
Uppsala
Gävle
Norrköping
Linköping
Västerås
Karlskrona
Kalmar
Växjö
Slupsk
Koszalin
Kołobrzeg
1:2 250 000
MILES
KM
160
197

Conic Equidistant Projection

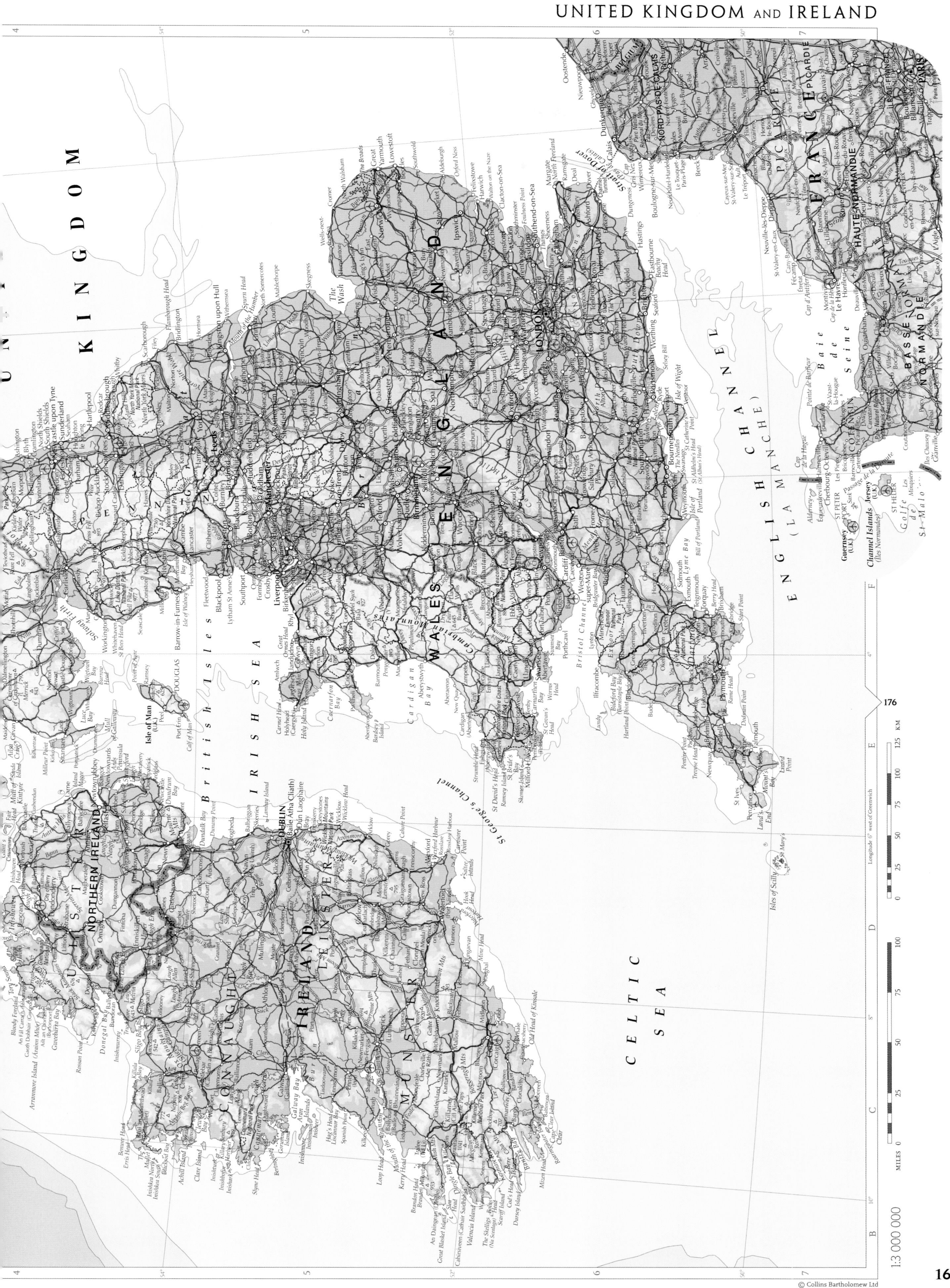

UNITED KINGDOM
ENGLAND
WALES
NORTHERN IRELAND
IRELAND
ULSTER
CONNAUGHT
LEINSTER
MUNSTER
FRANCE
LONDON
DUBLIN
Baile Átha Cliath
IRISH SEA
British Isles
CELTIC SEA
ENGLISH CHANNEL
(LA MANCHE)
St George's Channel
Bristol Channel
Cardigan Bay
Isle of Man (U.K.)
DOUGLAS
Channel Islands (Îles Normandes)
Guernsey (U.K.)
Jersey (U.K.)
Isles of Scilly
Liverpool
Manchester
Leeds
Birmingham
Cardiff
Swansea
Bristol
Plymouth
Southampton
Brighton
Ipswich
Norwich
Great Yarmouth
Lowestoft
The Wash
Kingston upon Hull
Newcastle upon Tyne
Sunderland
Belfast
Londonderry
Cork
Galway
Limerick
Waterford
Wexford
PICARDIE
HAUTE-NORMANDIE
BASSE-NORMANDIE
NORD-PAS-DE-CALAIS
PARIS
Strait of Dover
Baie de Seine
Cambrian Mountains
176
MILES
KM
1:3 000 000

176

ST KILDA
AT THE SAME SCALE
ATLANTIC OCEAN
THE MINCH
ORKNEY
SHETLAND ISLANDS
AT THE SAME SCALE
OUTER HEBRIDES
WESTERN ISLES
(NA H-EILEANAN AN IAR)
Isle of Lewis
North Uist
South Uist
Sea of the Hebrides
Little Minch
SKYE
MULL
JURA
ISLAY
ARRAN
CAITHNESS
SUTHERLAND
HIGHLAND
MORAY
ABERDEENSHIRE
ANGUS
PERTH AND KINROSS
FIFE
STIRLING
ARGYLL AND BUTE
NORTH AYRSHIRE
EAST AYRSHIRE
SOUTH AYRSHIRE
SOUTH LANARKSHIRE
SCOTTISH BORDERS
DUMFRIES AND GALLOWAY
NORTHUMBERLAND
SCOTLAND
GRAMPIAN MOUNTAINS
SOUTHERN UPLANDS
NORTH SEA
NORTH CHANNEL
NORTHERN IRELAND
ENGLAND
Moray Firth
Firth of Forth
Solway Firth
Firth of Clyde
Firth of Lorn
Pentland Firth
Inverness
Aberdeen
Dundee
Perth
Edinburgh
Glasgow
Stirling
Fort William
Local authorities in the UK numbered on the map:
SCOTLAND
1. ABERDEEN (L8)
2. CLACKMANNANSHIRE (I10)
3. DUNDEE (K10)
4. EAST DUNBARTONSHIRE (H11)
5. EAST LOTHIAN (K11)
6. EAST RENFREWSHIRE (H11)
7. EDINBURGH (J11)
8. FALKIRK (I11)
9. GLASGOW (H11)
10. INVERCLYDE (G11)
11. MIDLOTHIAN (J11)
12. NORTH LANARKSHIRE (I11)
13. RENFREWSHIRE (G11)
14. WEST DUNBARTONSHIRE (G11)
15. WEST LOTHIAN (I11)
6000 19686
5000 16404
4000 13124
3000 9843
2000 6562
1500 4921
1000 3281
500 1640
200 656
100 328
0 0
LAND BELOW SEA LEVEL
50 164
200 656
1000 3281
2000 6562
M FT
Conic Equidistant Projection
Longitude 3° west of Greenwich
169
171

ATLANTIC OCEAN

NORTHERN IRELAND

UNITED KINGDOM

SCOTLAND

NORTH CHANNEL

IRELAND

ST GEORGE'S CHANNEL

CELTIC SEA

ULSTER

CONNAUGHT

LEINSTER

MUNSTER

DONEGAL

LONDONDERRY

ANTRIM

TYRONE

FERMANAGH

ARMAGH

DOWN

MONAGHAN

CAVAN

LOUTH

LEITRIM

SLIGO

MAYO

ROSCOMMON

LONGFORD

WESTMEATH

MEATH

GALWAY

OFFALY

KILDARE

DUBLIN

WICKLOW

LAOIS

CARLOW

KILKENNY

WEXFORD

CLARE

TIPPERARY

LIMERICK

KERRY

CORK

WATERFORD

Longitude 8° west of Greenwich

1:1 500 000

168

170

168

169

M	FT
6000	19686
5000	16404
4000	13124
3000	9843
2000	6562
1500	4921
1000	3281
500	1640
200	656
100	328
0	0
LAND BELOW SEA LEVEL	
50	164
200	656
1000	3281
2000	6562

NORTHERN IRELAND

IRELAND

UNITED

IRISH SE

NORTH CHANNEL

Isle of Man (U.K.)

ARGYLL AND BUTE

DONEGAL · LONDONDERRY · ANTRIM · TYRONE · FERMANAGH · ARMAGH · DOWN · MONAGHAN · CAVAN · LEITRIM · LONGFORD · LOUTH · MEATH · WESTMEATH · OFFALY · KILDARE · DUBLIN · WICKLOW · LAOIS · CARLOW · KILKENNY · TIPPERARY · WEXFORD · ULSTER · LEINSTER

NORTH AYRSHIRE · EAST AYRSHIRE · SOUTH AYRSHIRE · DUMFRIES · STIRLING · ISLE OF ANGLESEY

Conic Equidistant Projection

Local authorities in the UK numbered on the map:
SCOTLAND
1. CLACKMANNANSHIRE (J1)
2. EAST DUNBARTONSHIRE (I2)
3. EAST LOTHIAN (L2)
4. EAST RENFREWSHIRE (I2)
5. EDINBURGH (K2)
6. FALKIRK (J2)
7. GLASGOW (I2)
8. INVERCLYDE (H2)
9. MIDLOTHIAN (K2)
10. NORTH LANARKSHIRE (J2)
11. PERTH AND KINROSS (K1)
12. RENFREWSHIRE (H2)
13. WEST DUNBARTONSHIRE (H2)
14. WEST LOTHIAN (J2)
ENGLAND
15. BLACKPOOL (K6)
16. CHESHIRE EAST (M7)
17. CHESHIRE WEST & CHESTER (L7)
18. DARLINGTON (N4)
19. HARTLEPOOL (O4)
20. KINGSTON UPON HULL (Q6)
21. MIDDLESBROUGH (O4)
22. NORTH EAST LINCOLNSHIRE (Q6)
23. STOCKTON-ON-TEES (O4)
24. STOKE-ON-TRENT (M7)
NORTH SEA
UNITED KINGDOM
ENGLAND
SCOTTISH BORDERS
NORTHUMBERLAND
TYNE AND WEAR
DURHAM
CUMBRIA
NORTH YORKSHIRE
EAST RIDING OF YORKSHIRE
LANCASHIRE
WEST YORKSHIRE
SOUTH YORKSHIRE
MERSEYSIDE
GREATER MANCHESTER
NORTH LINCOLNSHIRE
LINCOLNSHIRE
DERBYSHIRE
NOTTINGHAMSHIRE
STAFFORDSHIRE
SHROPSHIRE
LEICESTERSHIRE
RUTLAND
FLINTSHIRE
DENBIGHSHIRE
WREXHAM
POWYS
TELFORD AND WREKIN
Firth of Forth
The Wash
Greenwich Meridian
MILES
KM
1:1 200 000

173

Local authorities in the UK numbered on the map:

ENGLAND	WALES
1. BATH AND N.E. SOMERSET (H5)	27. BLAENAU GWENT (F4)
2. BRACKNELL FOREST (K5)	28. BRIDGEND (E4)
3. BRIGHTON AND HOVE (L6)	29. CAERPHILLY (F4)
4. BRISTOL (G5)	30. CARDIFF (F5)
5. BOURNEMOUTH (I6)	31. MERTHYR TYDFIL (F4)
6. CENTRAL BEDFORDSHIRE (L3)	32. NEWPORT (G4)
7. CHESHIRE EAST (H1)	33. RHONDDA CYNON TAFF (F4)
8. CHESHIRE WEST & CHESTER (G1)	34. TORFAEN (F4)
9. GREATER MANCHESTER (H1)	
10. LUTON (L4)	
11. MILTON KEYNES (K3)	
12. NOTTINGHAM (J2)	
13. PLYMOUTH (D7)	
14. POOLE (I6)	
15. PORTSMOUTH (J6)	
16. READING (J5)	
17. SLOUGH (K4)	
18. SOUTHAMPTON (J6)	
19. SOUTHEND (N4)	
20. STOKE-ON-TRENT (H1)	
21. SWINDON (I4)	
22. THURROCK (M5)	
23. TORBAY (E7)	
24. WEST MIDLANDS (I3)	
25. WINDSOR AND MAIDENHEAD (K5)	
26. WOKINGHAM (K5)	

ISLES OF SCILLY
CONTINUATION AT THE SAME SCALE

M	FT
6000	19686
5000	16404
4000	13124
3000	9843
2000	6562
1500	4921
1000	3281
500	1640
200	656
100	328
0	0
LAND BELOW SEA LEVEL	
50	164
200	656
1000	3281
2000	6562

Conic Equidistant Projection

NORTH SEA
ENGLISH CHANNEL
(LA MANCHE)
Strait of Dover
(Pas de Calais)
The Wash
KINGDOM
ENGLAND
SOUTH YORKSHIRE
DERBYSHIRE
NOTTINGHAMSHIRE
LINCOLNSHIRE
LEICESTERSHIRE
RUTLAND
NORFOLK
SUFFOLK
CAMBRIDGESHIRE
NORTHAMPTONSHIRE
WARWICKSHIRE
BEDFORD
BUCKINGHAMSHIRE
OXFORDSHIRE
HERTFORDSHIRE
ESSEX
GREATER LONDON
LONDON
MEDWAY
KENT
SURREY
WEST BERKSHIRE
HAMPSHIRE
WEST SUSSEX
EAST SUSSEX
ISLE OF WIGHT
FRANCE
NORD-PAS-DE-CALAIS
PICARDIE
HAUTE-NORMANDIE
Sheffield
Lincoln
Nottingham
Derby
Leicester
Peterborough
Northampton
Cambridge
Norwich
Great Yarmouth
Lowestoft
Ipswich
Colchester
Chelmsford
Southend-on-Sea
Luton
Oxford
Reading
Swindon
Salisbury
Winchester
Southampton
Portsmouth
Brighton
Hastings
Eastbourne
Canterbury
Margate
Dover
Folkestone
Calais
Boulogne-sur-Mer
Dungeness
Beachy Head
Selsey Bill
St Catherine's Point
Greenwich 0° meridian
1:1 200 000
KM
MILES
178

1:125 000
YARDS 0 1000 2000 3000 4000 5000 6000 7000
0 1000 2000 3000 4000 5000 6000 M
CENTRAL LONDON
1:30 000
REDBRIDGE
WALTHAM FOREST
HARINGEY
BRENT
CAMDEN
ISLINGTON
HACKNEY
NEWHAM
TOWER HAMLETS
WESTMINSTER
EALING
HAMMERSMITH AND FULHAM
KENSINGTON AND CHELSEA
GREENWICH
SOUTHWARK
LAMBETH
WANDSWORTH
HOUNSLOW
RICHMOND UPON THAMES
LEWISHAM
MERTON
KINGSTON UPON THAMES
BROMLEY
CROYDON
SUTTON
SURREY
Heathrow Airport (London)
Richmond Park
Wimbledon Common
Bushy Park
Hampton Court Park
Thames
NORTH CIRCULAR ROAD
SOUTH CIRCULAR ROAD
© Collins Bartholomew

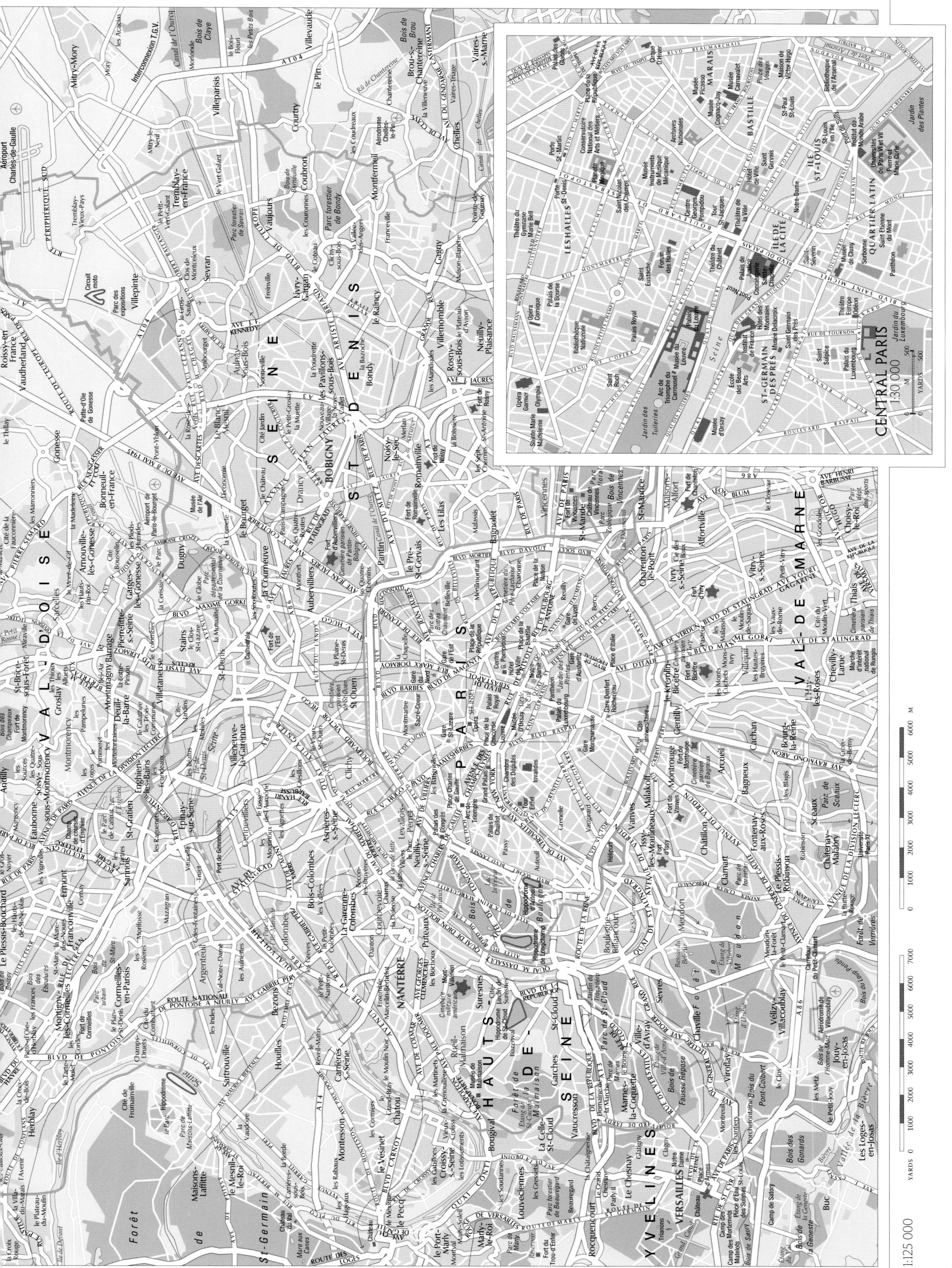
CENTRAL PARIS
1:30 000
VAL-D'OISE
SEINE-ST-DENIS
PARIS
VAL-DE-MARNE
HAUTS-DE-SEINE
YVELINES
1:125 000

ENGLAND
U.K.
ENGLISH CHANNEL
(LA MANCHE)
Strait of Dover
(Pas de Calais)
Channel Islands
(Îles Normandes)
Guernsey
(U.K.)
Jersey
(U.K.)
Baie de Seine
Golfe de St-Malo
Isles of Scilly
Plymouth
Southampton
Portsmouth
Bournemouth
Brighton
Hastings
Calais
Dunkerque
Boulogne-sur-Mer
Amiens
Le Havre
Rouen
Caen
Cherbourg-Octeville
St-Malo
Brest
Quimper
Lorient
Vannes
Rennes
Le Mans
Angers
Nantes
St-Nazaire
Tours
Poitiers
La Rochelle
Angoulême
Limoges
Bordeaux
Toulouse
Montauban
Pau
Bayonne
Biarritz
Orléans
Chartres
PARIS
NORD-
PICARDIE
HAUTE-NORMANDIE
BASSE-NORMANDIE
BRETAGNE
PAYS DE LA LOIRE
CENTRE
POITOU-CHARENTES
LIMOUSIN
AQUITAINE
MIDI-PYRÉNÉES
ÎLE-DE-FRANCE
FRANCE
BAY OF BISCAY
Golfe de Gascogne
Mar Cantábrico
PYRENEES
ANDORRA
SPAIN
ASTURIAS
CANTABRIA
PAÍS VASCO
NAVARRA
LA RIOJA
CASTILLA Y LEÓN
ARAGÓN
CATALUÑA
Gijón-Xixón
Santander
Bilbao
Donostia-San Sebastián
Vitoria-Gasteiz
Pamplona (Iruña)
Logroño
Burgos
Valladolid
Huesca
6000 19686
5000 16404
4000 13124
3000 9843
2000 6562
1500 4921
1000 3281
500 1640
200 656
100 328
0 0
LAND BELOW SEA LEVEL
50 164
200 656
1000 3281
2000 6562
M FT
Conic Equidistant Projection
Greenwich 0° meridian

203

188

BELGIUM

LUXEMBOURG

GERMANY

RHEINLAND-PFALZ

HESSEN

SAARLAND

BADEN-WÜRTTEMBERG

BAYERN

LORRAINE

CHAMPAGNE-ARDENNE

ALSACE

FRANCHE-COMTÉ

BOURGOGNE

SWITZERLAND

LIECHTENSTEIN

AUSTRIA

TRENTINO-ALTO ADIGE

LOMBARDIA

VENETO

VALLE D'AOSTA

PIEMONTE

RHÔNE-ALPES

ITALY

EMILIA-ROMAGNA

LIGURIA

TOSCANA

PROVENCE-ALPES-CÔTE D'AZUR

MONACO

CORSE (CORSICA) (France)

GOLFE DU LION

LIGURIAN SEA

MEDITERRANEAN SEA

Golfo di Genova

1:3 000 000

KM 0 25 50 75 100 125

MILES 0 25 50 75 100

210

173

Administrative Departments in France numbered on the map:

1. HAUTS-DE-SEINE (D6)
2. PARIS (D6)
3. SEINE-ST-DENIS (D6)
4. VAL-DE-MARNE (D6)

181

M	FT
6000	19686
5000	16404
4000	13124
3000	9843
2000	6562
1500	4921
1000	3281
500	1640
200	656
100	328
0	0
LAND BELOW SEA LEVEL	
50	164
200	656
1000	3281
2000	6562

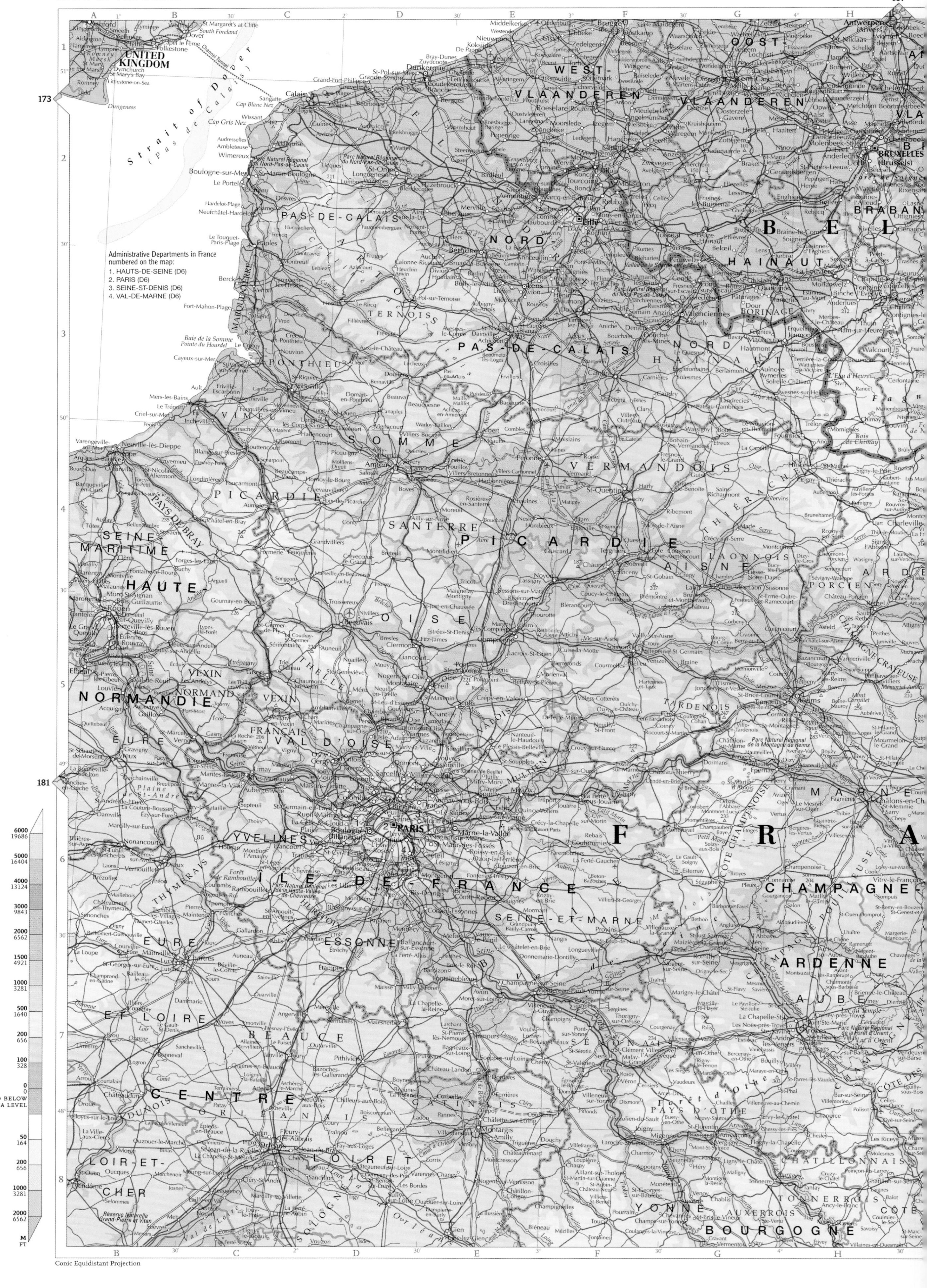

Conic Equidistant Projection

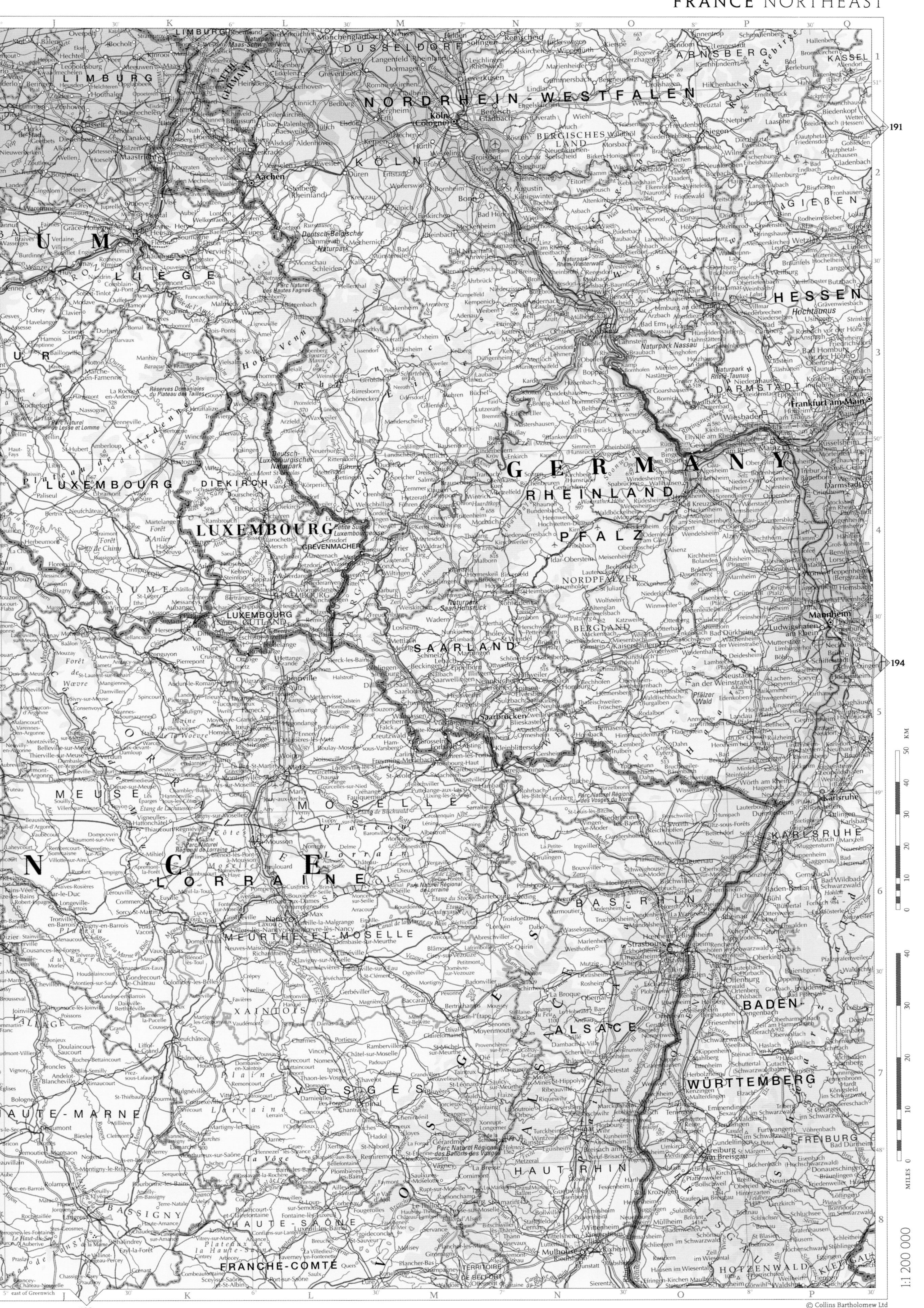
LIMBURG
DÜSSELDORF
NORDRHEIN-WESTFALEN
ARNSBERG
KASSEL
KÖLN
Köln (Cologne)
BERGISCHES LAND
Aachen
LIEGE
GIESSEN
HESSEN
Hochtaunus
DARMSTADT
Frankfurt am Main
Wiesbaden
Mainz
Darmstadt
GERMANY
RHEINLAND
PFALZ
NORDPFÄLZER BERGLAND
Pfälzer Wald
Mannheim
Ludwigshafen am Rhein
LUXEMBOURG
DIEKIRCH
GREVENMACHER
SAARLAND
Saarbrücken
Metz
MOSELLE
MEUSE
LORRAINE
Nancy
MEURTHE-ET-MOSELLE
BAS-RHIN
Strasbourg
Karlsruhe
KARLSRUHE
BADEN-
WÜRTTEMBERG
FREIBURG
Freiburg im Breisgau
ALSACE
HAUT-RHIN
Colmar
Mulhouse
VOSGES
Épinal
XAINTOIS
HAUTE-MARNE
BASSIGNY
HAUTE-SAÔNE
FRANCHE-COMTÉ
TERRITOIRE DE BELFORT
HOTZENWALD
191
194
182
1:1 200 000
MILES
KM
east of Greenwich

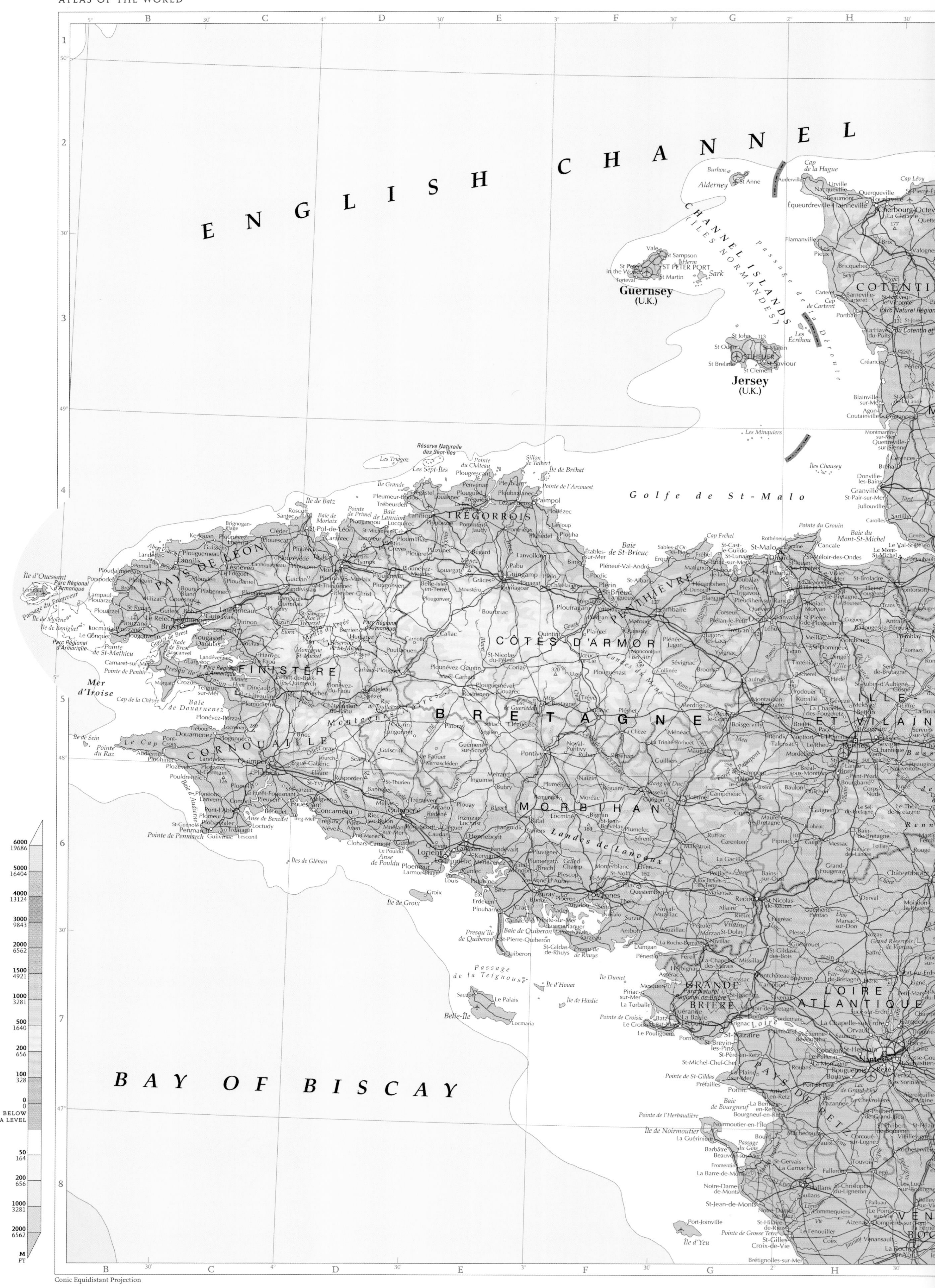

Conic Equidistant Projection

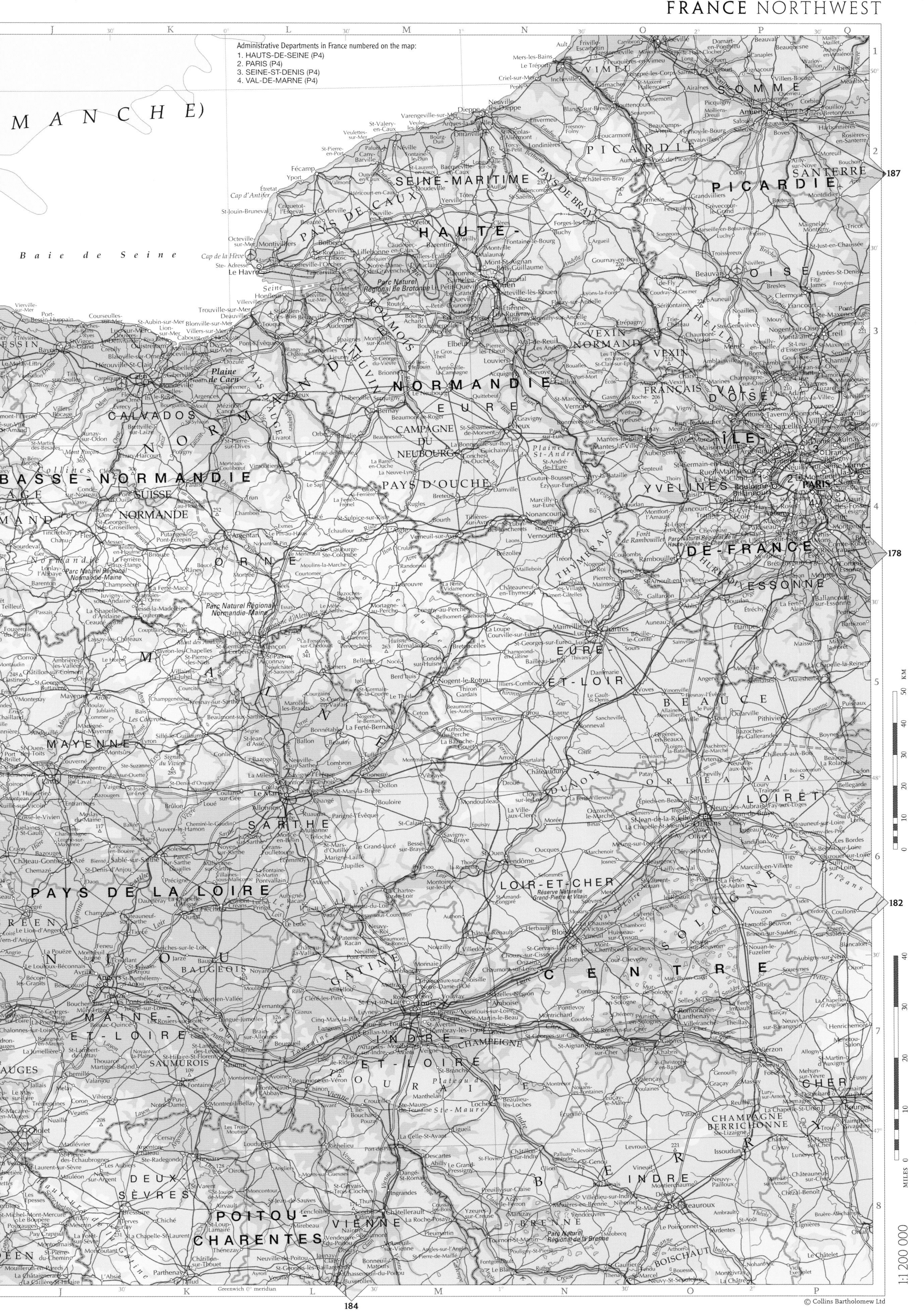
Administrative Departments in France numbered on the map:
1. HAUTS-DE-SEINE (P4)
2. PARIS (P4)
3. SEINE-ST-DENIS (P4)
4. VAL-DE-MARNE (P4)
MANCHE)
Baie de Seine
HAUTE-NORMANDIE
SEINE-MARITIME
PICARDIE
SOMME
OISE
EURE
CALVADOS
BASSE-NORMANDIE
ORNE
MAYENNE
SARTHE
PAYS DE LA LOIRE
MAINE-ET-LOIRE
DEUX-SÈVRES
POITOU-CHARENTES
VIENNE
INDRE-ET-LOIRE
LOIR-ET-CHER
EURE-ET-LOIR
YVELINES
ÎLE-DE-FRANCE
ESSONNE
VAL-D'OISE
LOIRET
CENTRE
CHER
INDRE
BERRY
SOLOGNE
BEAUCE
PARIS
187
178
182
184
Greenwich 0° meridian
1:1 200 000
KM
MILES

194

178

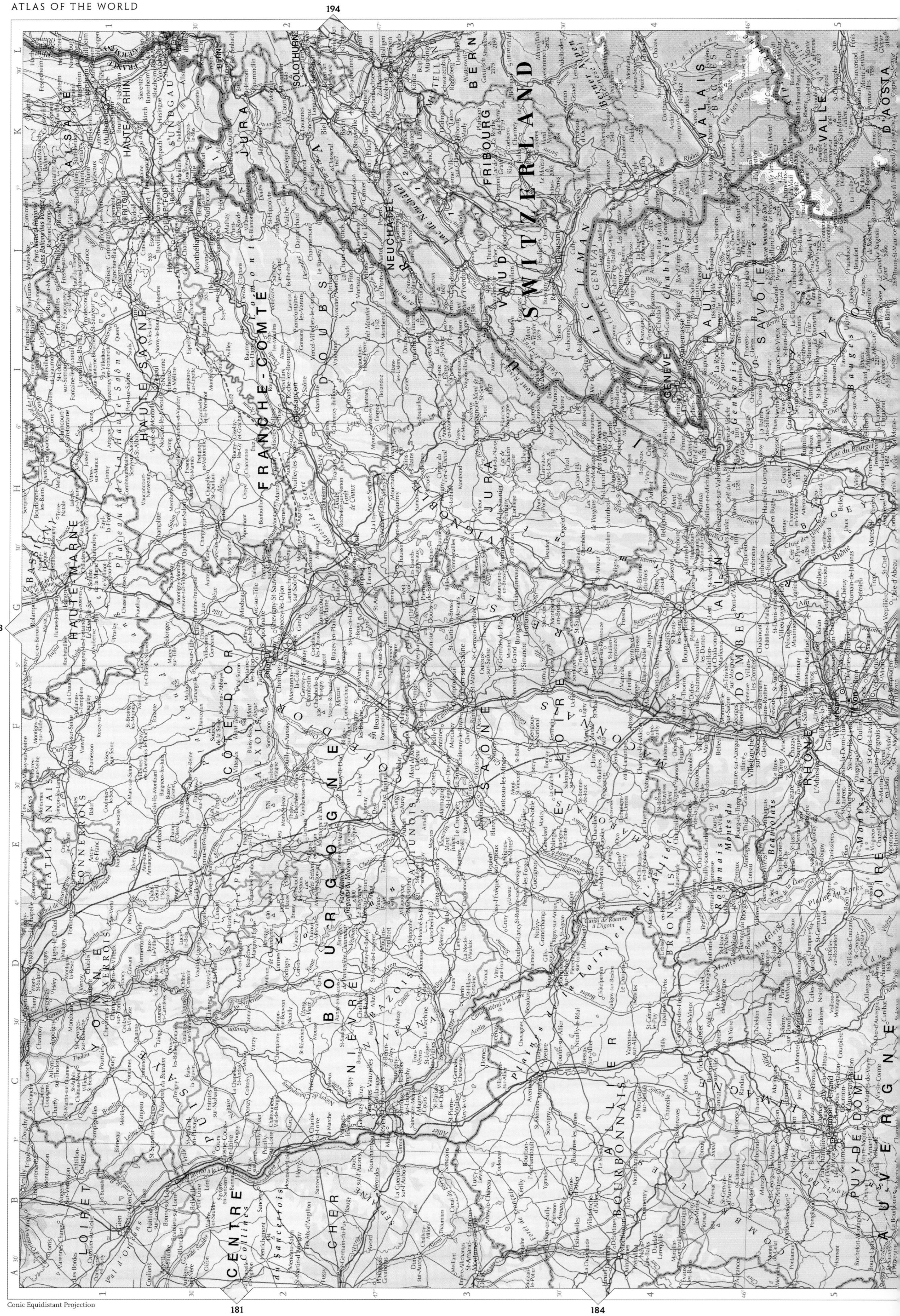

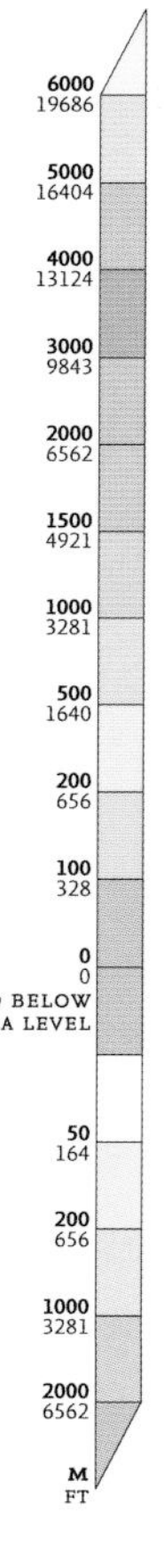

M	FT
6000	19686
5000	16404
4000	13124
3000	9843
2000	6562
1500	4921
1000	3281
500	1640
200	656
100	328
0	0
LAND BELOW SEA LEVEL	
50	164
200	656
1000	3281
2000	6562

Conic Equidistant Projection

181

184

Swiss Cantons numbered on the map:
1. FRIBOURG (J3)
2. VAUD (K3)
ITALY
PIEMONTE
TORINO
CUNEO
MONACO
PROVENCE-ALPES-CÔTE D'AZUR
ALPES-MARITIMES
ALPES-DE-HAUTE-PROVENCE
HAUTES-ALPES
VAR
VAUCLUSE
BOUCHES-DU-RHÔNE
DRÔME
ARDÈCHE
HAUTE-LOIRE
LOZÈRE
GARD
HÉRAULT
AUDE
AVEYRON
CANTAL
LANGUEDOC-ROUSSILLON
MIDI-PYRÉNÉES
MASSIF CENTRAL
CAMARGUE
GOLFE DU LION
Marseille
Toulon
Nice
Montpellier
Avignon
Valence
Grenoble
MILES 0 10 20 30 40
0 10 20 30 40 50 KM
1:1 200 000

185

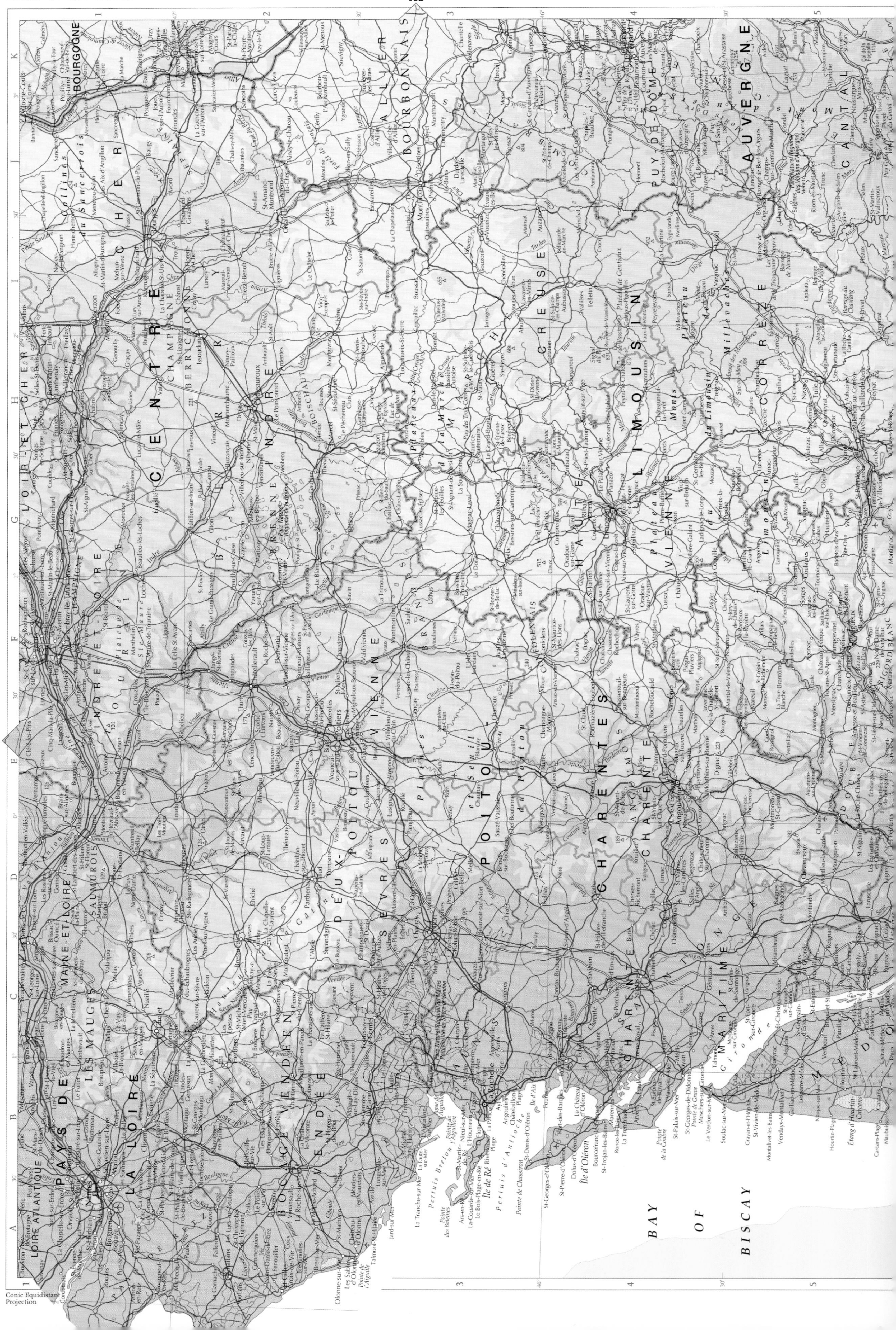

182

181

PAYS DE LA LOIRE
CENTRE
POITOU-CHARENTES
LIMOUSIN
AUVERGNE
BAY OF BISCAY

M	FT
6000	19686
5000	16404
4000	13124
3000	9843
2000	6562
1500	4921
1000	3281
500	1640
200	656
100	328
0	0
LAND BELOW SEA LEVEL	
50	164
200	656
1000	3281
2000	6562

Conic Equidistant Projection

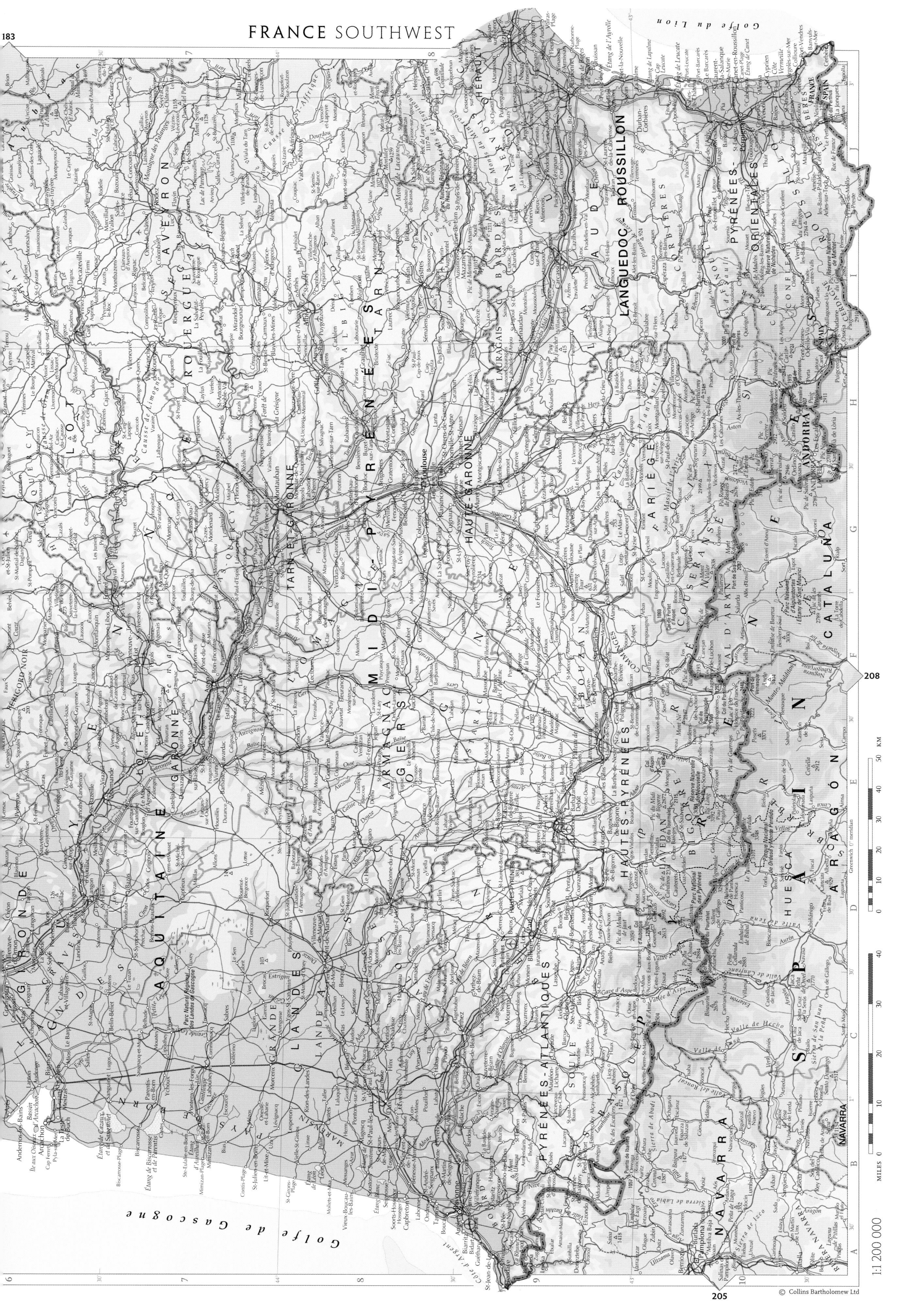
183
208
205
Golfe de Gascogne
Golfe du Lion
AQUITAINE
MIDI-PYRÉNÉES
LANGUEDOC-ROUSSILLON
GIRONDE
LANDES
GERS
TARN-ET-GARONNE
HAUTE-GARONNE
AVEYRON
TARN
AUDE
ARIÈGE
HÉRAULT
LOT
LOT-ET-GARONNE
PYRÉNÉES-ATLANTIQUES
HAUTES-PYRÉNÉES
PYRÉNÉES-ORIENTALES
ANDORRA
NAVARRA
ARAGÓN
CATALUÑA
HUESCA
Toulouse
Montauban
Bayonne
Pamplona
1:1 200 000
KM
MILES

190

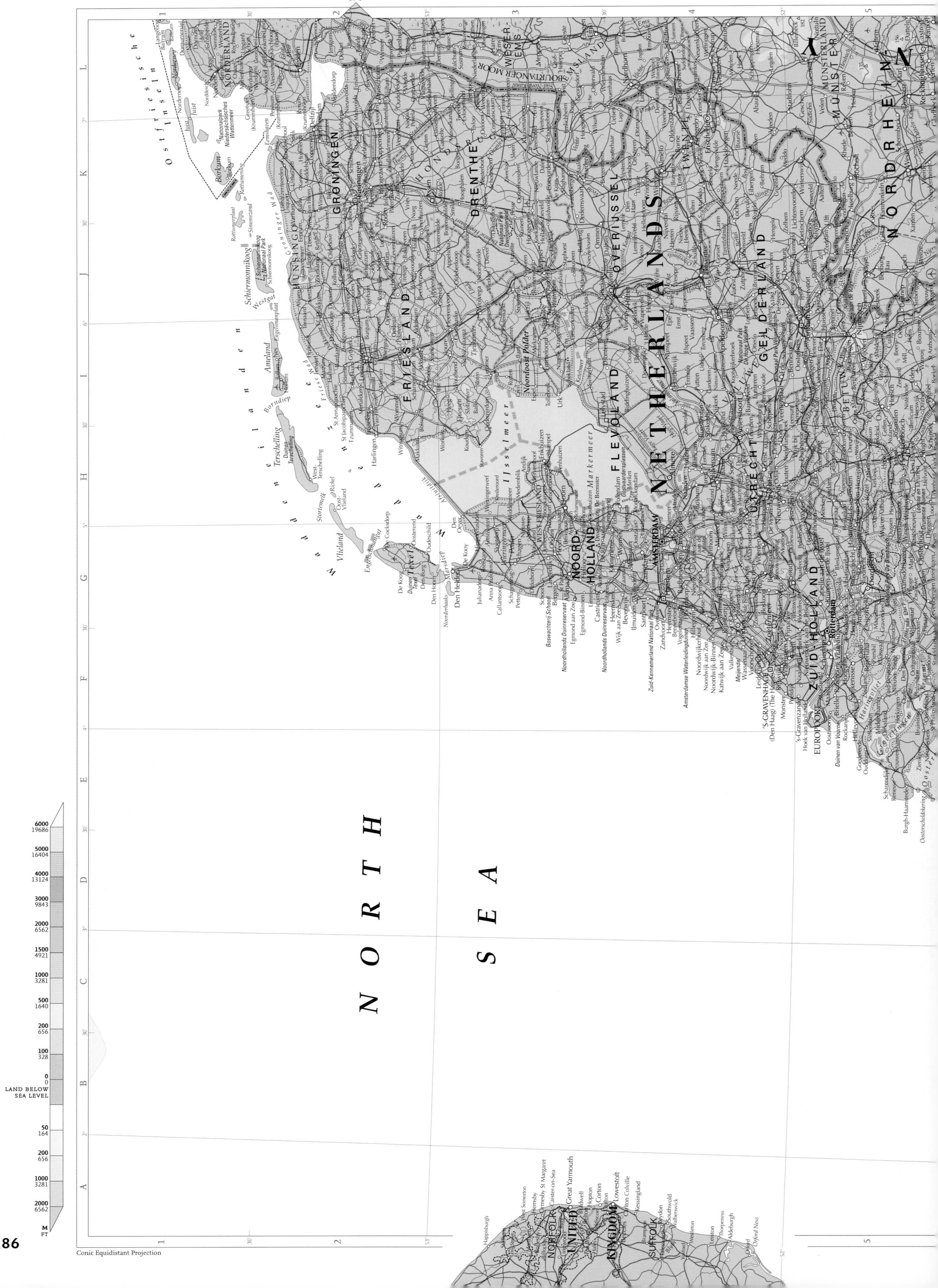

NORTH SEA

NETHERLANDS

GRONINGEN

FRIESLAND

DRENTHE

OVERIJSSEL

FLEVOLAND

GELDERLAND

UTRECHT

NOORD-HOLLAND

ZUID-HOLLAND

NORDRHEIN-

MÜNSTER

WESER-EMS

UNITED KINGDOM

NORFOLK

SUFFOLK

M	FT
6000	19686
5000	16404
4000	13124
3000	9843
2000	6562
1500	4921
1000	3281
500	1640
200	656
100	328
0	0
LAND BELOW SEA LEVEL	
50	164
200	656
1000	3281
2000	6562

Conic Equidistant Projection

191

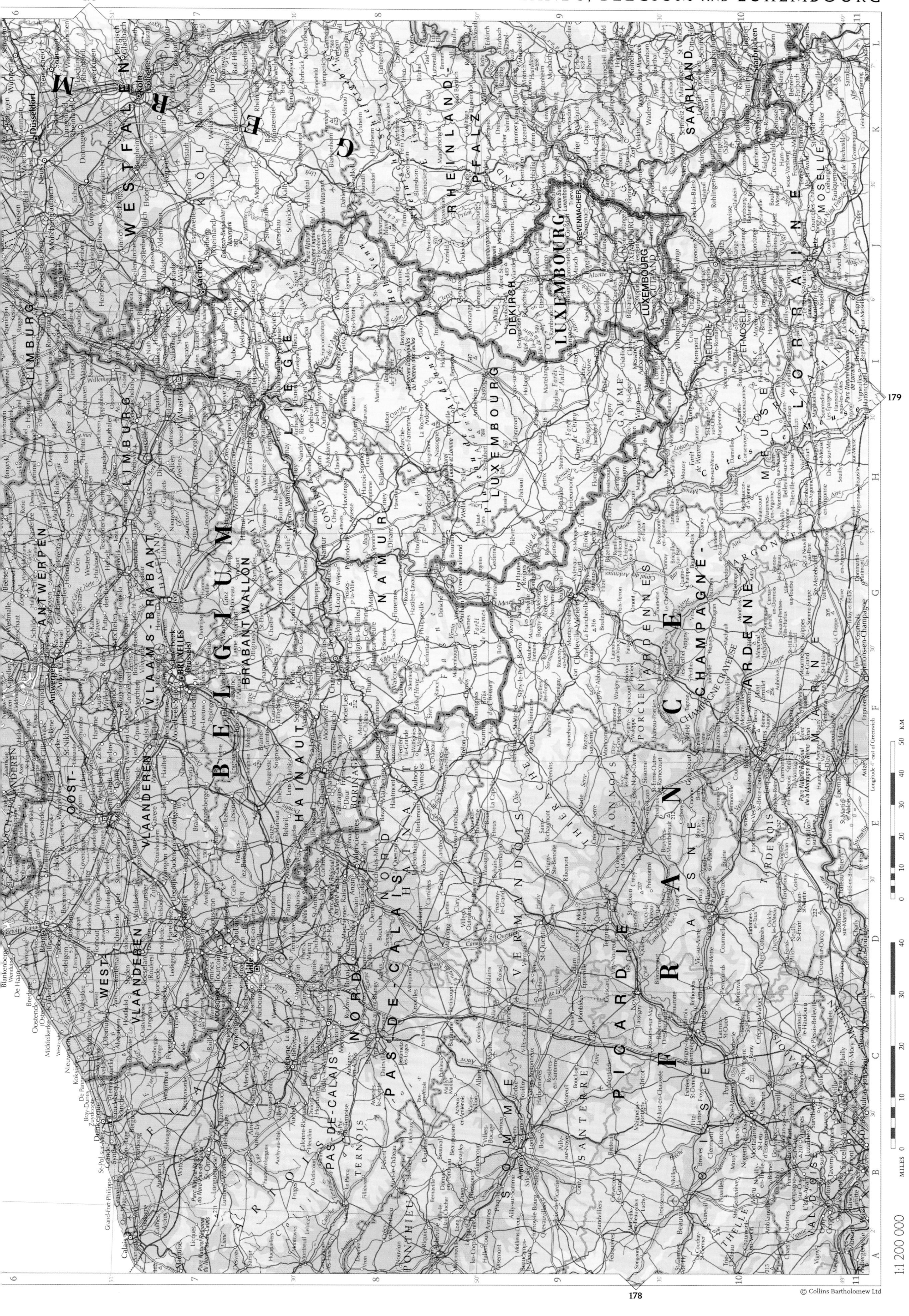

179

1:1 200 000

178

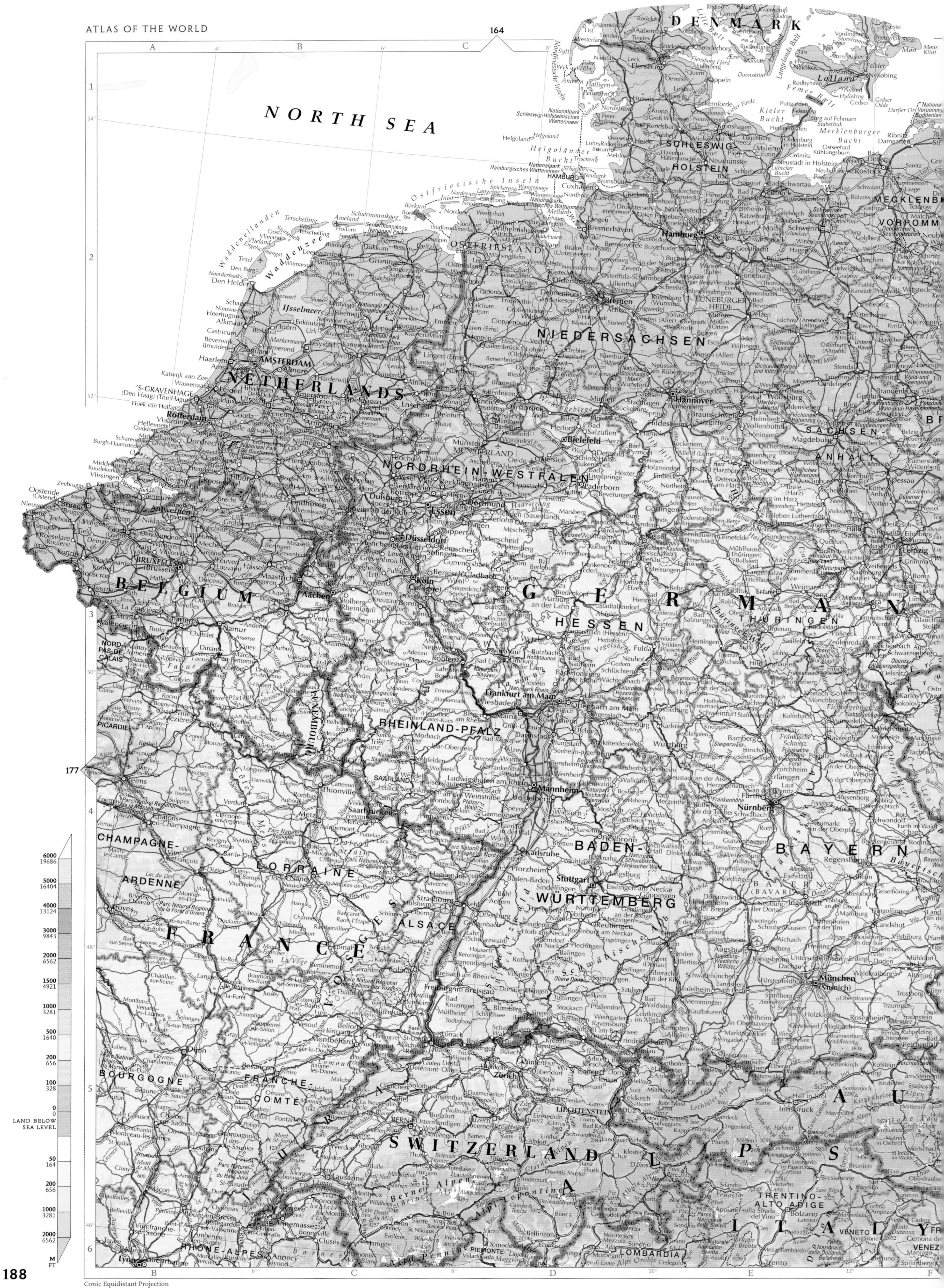

Conic Equidistant Projection

BALTIC SEA
Gulf of Gdańsk
Pomeranian Bay
RUSSIAN FEDERATION
LITHUANIA
POLAND
CZECH REPUBLIC
SLOVAKIA
HUNGARY
ROMANIA
SLOVENIA
CROATIA
SERBIA
UKRAINE
CARPATHIAN MOUNTAINS
POJEZIERZE POMORSKIE
POJEZIERZE MAZURSKIE
NIZINA MAZOWIECKA
WYŻYNA LUBELSKA
WYŻYNA MAŁOPOLSKA
WARSZAWA (Warsaw)
PRAHA (Prague)
WIEN (Vienna)
BRATISLAVA
BUDAPEST
Gdańsk
Poznań
Wrocław
Kraków
Łódź
Katowice
156
158
218
1:3 000 000
KM
MILES
0 25 50 75 100
0 25 50 75
14° east of Greenwich

192

164

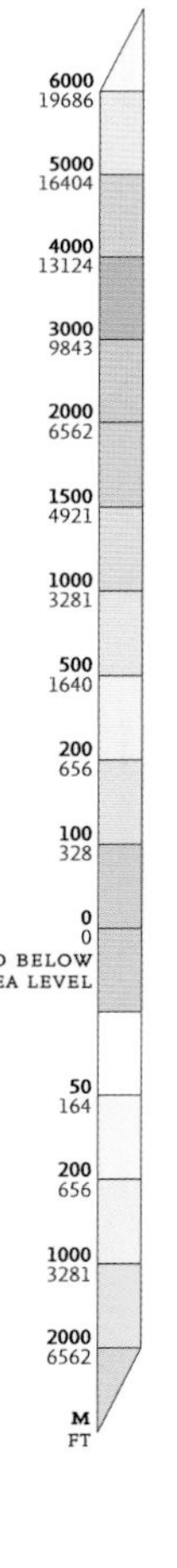

M	FT
6000	19686
5000	16404
4000	13124
3000	9843
2000	6562
1500	4921
1000	3281
500	1640
200	656
100	328
0	0
LAND BELOW SEA LEVEL	
50	164
200	656
1000	3281
2000	6562

Conic Equidistant Projection

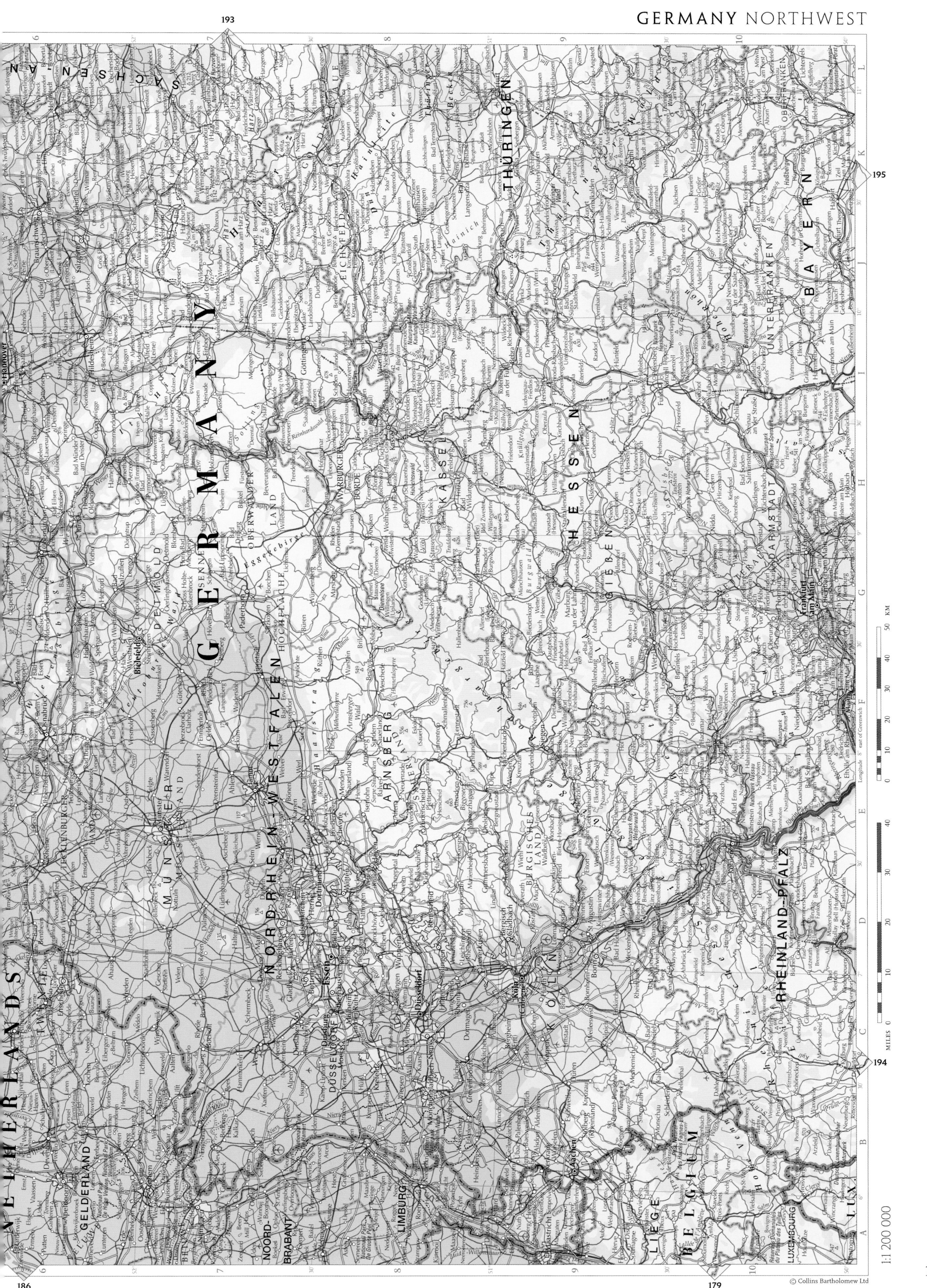
GERMANY
NETHERLANDS
BELGIUM
LUX.
NORDRHEIN-WESTFALEN
HESSEN
THÜRINGEN
RHEINLAND-PFALZ
BAYERN
LIEGE
LIMBURG
LUXEMBOURG
GELDERLAND
NOORD-BRABANT
Köln
Düsseldorf
Essen
Dortmund
Bielefeld
Kassel
Göttingen
Frankfurt am Main
Hannover
Braunschweig
Aachen
1:1 200 000
© Collins Bartholomew Ltd

Conic Equidistant Projection

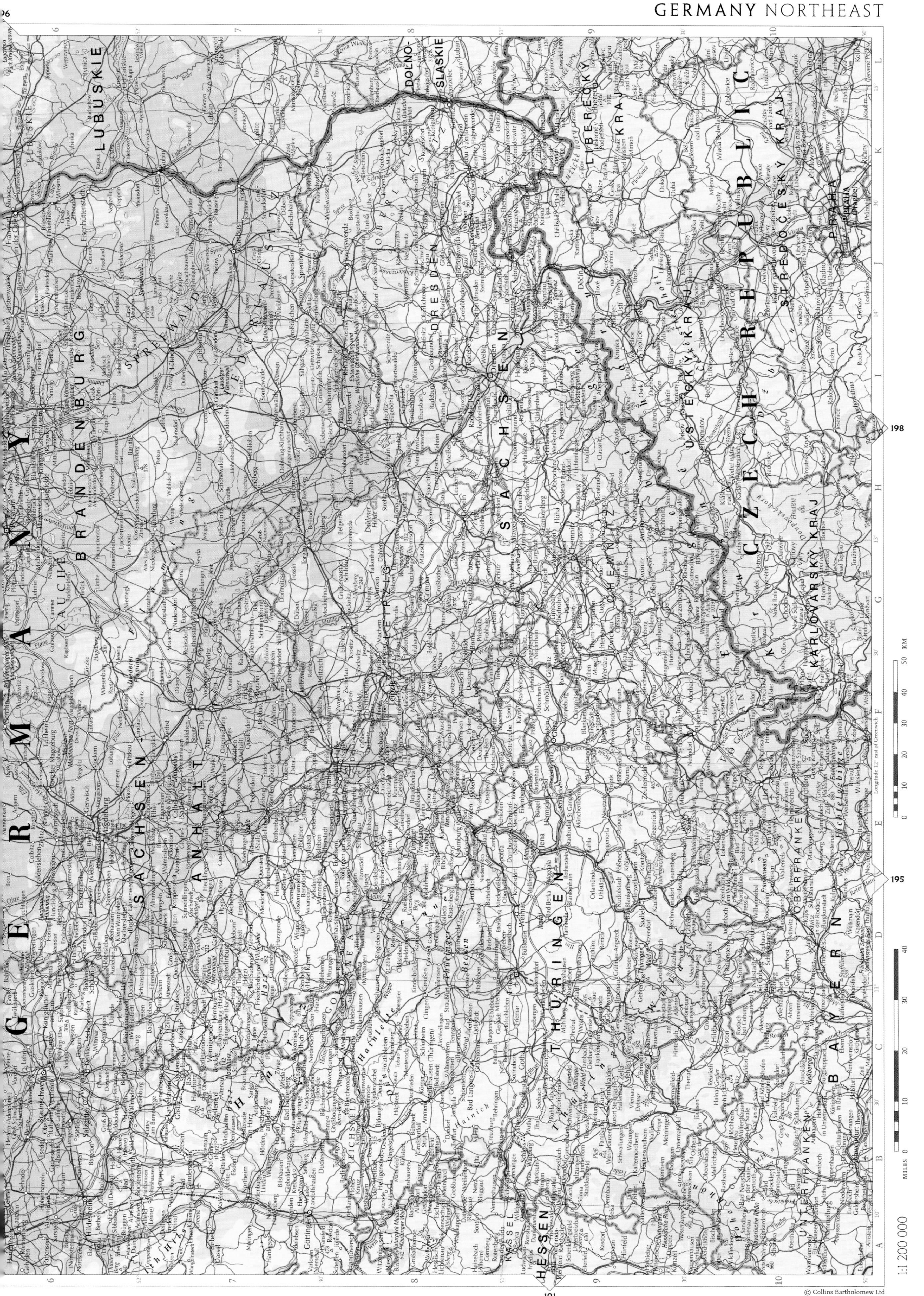
GERMANY
CZECH REPUBLIC
BRANDENBURG
SACHSEN-ANHALT
SACHSEN
THÜRINGEN
BAYERN
HESSEN
LUBUSKIE
DOLNOŚLĄSKIE
OBERFRANKEN
UNTERFRANKEN
LIBERECKÝ KRAJ
ÚSTECKÝ KRAJ
STŘEDOČESKÝ KRAJ
KARLOVARSKÝ KRAJ
PRAHA
Dresden
Leipzig
Chemnitz
Halle
Magdeburg
Erfurt
KASSEL
1:1 200 000
MILES
KM
198
195
191

191

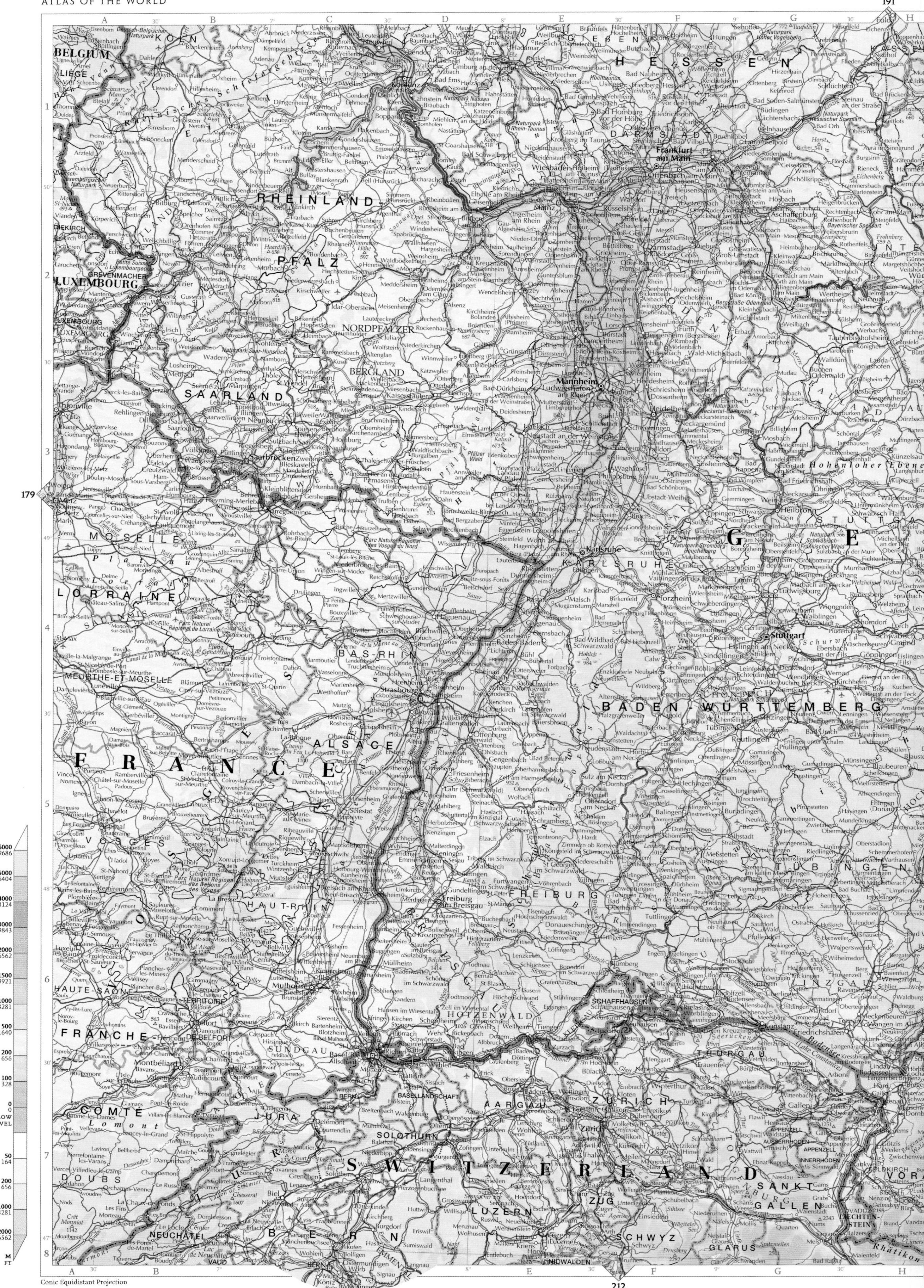

179

Conic Equidistant Projection

212

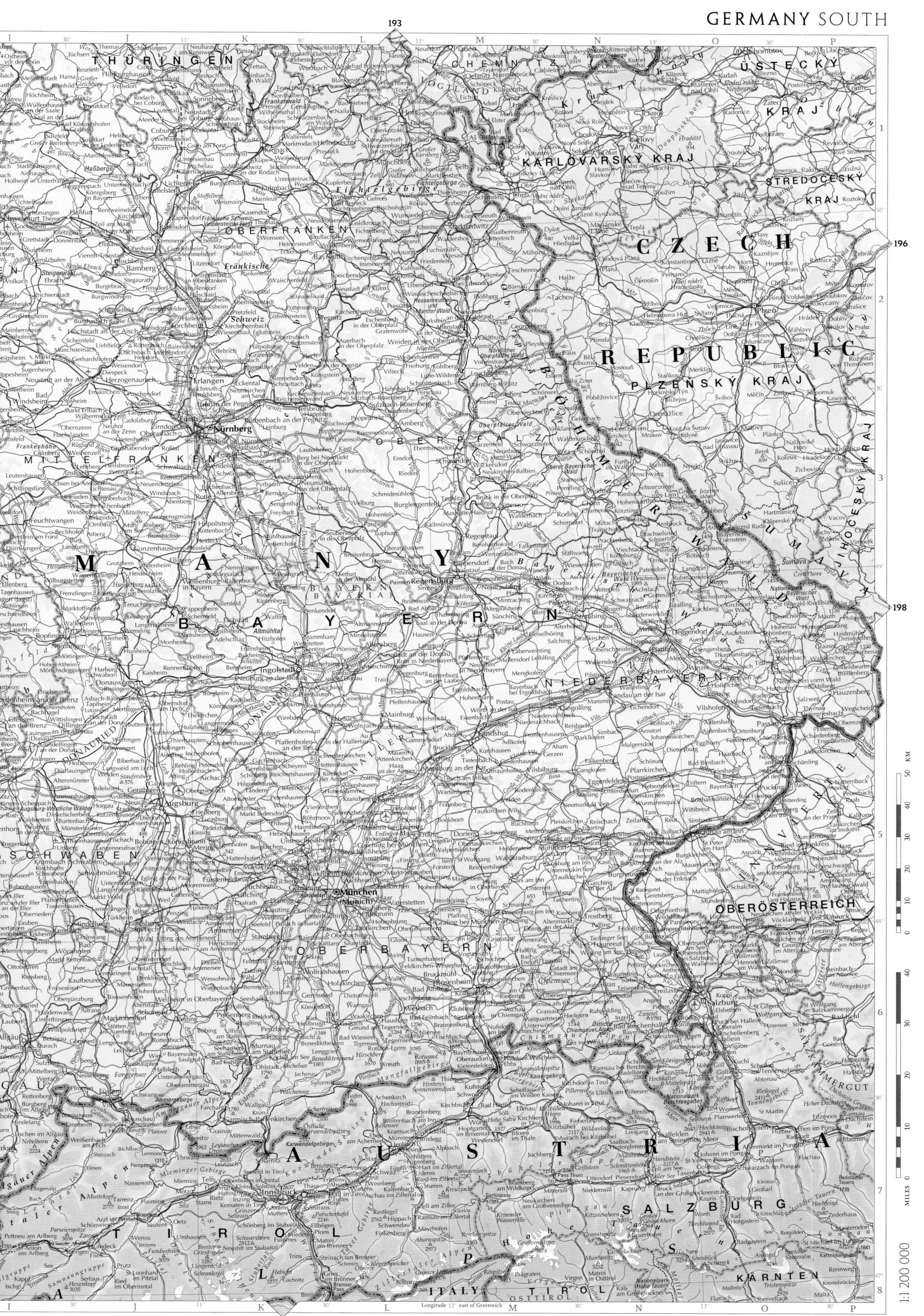
193
196
198
200
THÜRINGEN
OBERFRANKEN
MITTELFRANKEN
OBERPFALZ
BAYERN
BAVARIA
NIEDERBAYERN
OBERBAYERN
SCHWABEN
GERMANY
CZECH REPUBLIC
ÚSTECKÝ KRAJ
KARLOVARSKÝ KRAJ
STŘEDOČESKÝ KRAJ
PLZEŇSKÝ KRAJ
JIHOČESKÝ KRAJ
AUSTRIA
OBERÖSTERREICH
SALZBURG
TIROL
OSTTIROL
KÄRNTEN
ITALY
Nürnberg
München
Munich
Augsburg
Regensburg
Ingolstadt
Innsbruck
Salzburg
Longitude 12° east of Greenwich
1:1 200 000
KM
MILES

BALTIC SEA

Pomeranian Bay

MECKLENBURG-VORPOMMERN

BRANDENBURG

GERMANY

SACHSEN

POMORSKIE

ZACHODNIOPOMORSKIE

KUJAWSKO-POMORSKIE

LUBUSKIE

WIELKOPOLSKIE

POLAND

DOLNOŚLĄSKIE

OPOLSKIE

LIBERECKÝ KRAJ

ÚSTECKÝ KRAJ

KRÁLOVÉHRADECKÝ KRAJ

STŘEDOČESKÝ KRAJ

PARDUBICKÝ KRAJ

OLOMOUCKÝ KRAJ

MORAVSKOSLEZSKÝ KRAJ

PLZEŇSKÝ KRAJ

JIHOČESKÝ KRAJ

VYSOČINA

JIHOMORAVSKÝ KRAJ

ZLÍNSKÝ KRAJ

CZECH REPUBLIC

M	FT
6000	19686
5000	16404
4000	13124
3000	9843
2000	6562
1500	4921
1000	3281
500	1640
200	656
100	328
0	0
LAND BELOW SEA LEVEL	
50	164
200	656
1000	3281
2000	6562

Longitude 18° east of Greenwich

Conic Equidistant Projection

193
195
198

160
RUSSIAN FEDERATION
LITHUANIA
WARMIŃSKO-MAZURSKIE
POJEZIERZE MAZURSKIE
PODLASKIE
HRODZYENSKAYA VOBLASTS'
BELARUS
NIZINA MAZOWIECKA
MAZOWIECKIE
BRESTSKAYA VOBLASTS'
WARSZAWA
(Warsaw)
Białystok
Olsztyn
Elbląg
Kaliningrad
Hrodna
Brest
MAZOWIECKA
ŁÓDZKIE
LUBELSKIE
Lublin
Radom
Kielce
WYŻYNA LUBELSKA
WYŻYNA MAŁOPOLSKA
ŚWIĘTOKRZYSKIE
UKRAINE
Kraków
Tarnów
Rzeszów
MAŁOPOLSKIE
PODKARPACKIE
CARPATHIAN MOUNTAINS
PREŠOVSKÝ KRAJ
POLAND
SLOVAKIA
158
199
1:1 800 000
KM
MILES

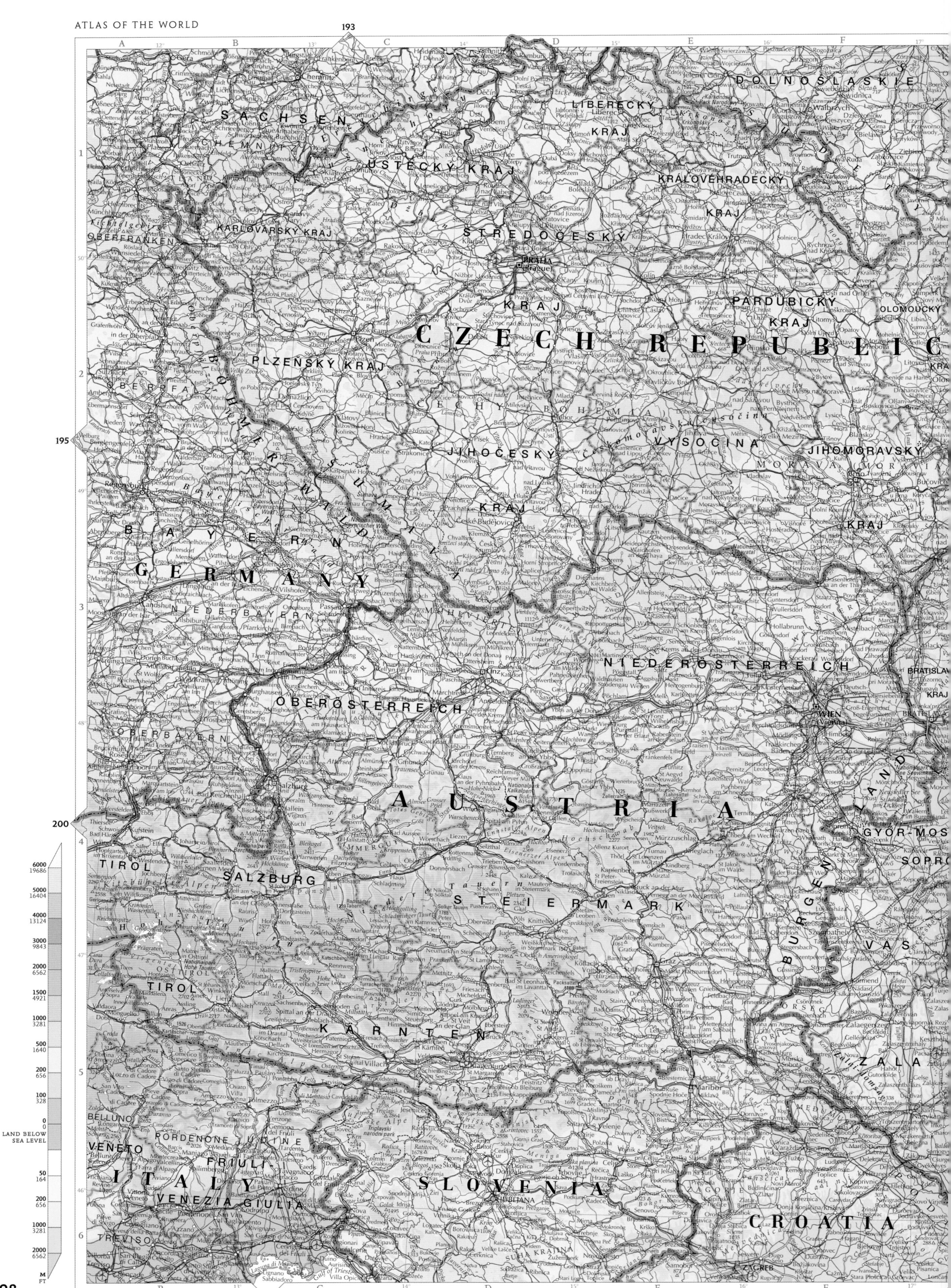

Conic Equidistant Projection

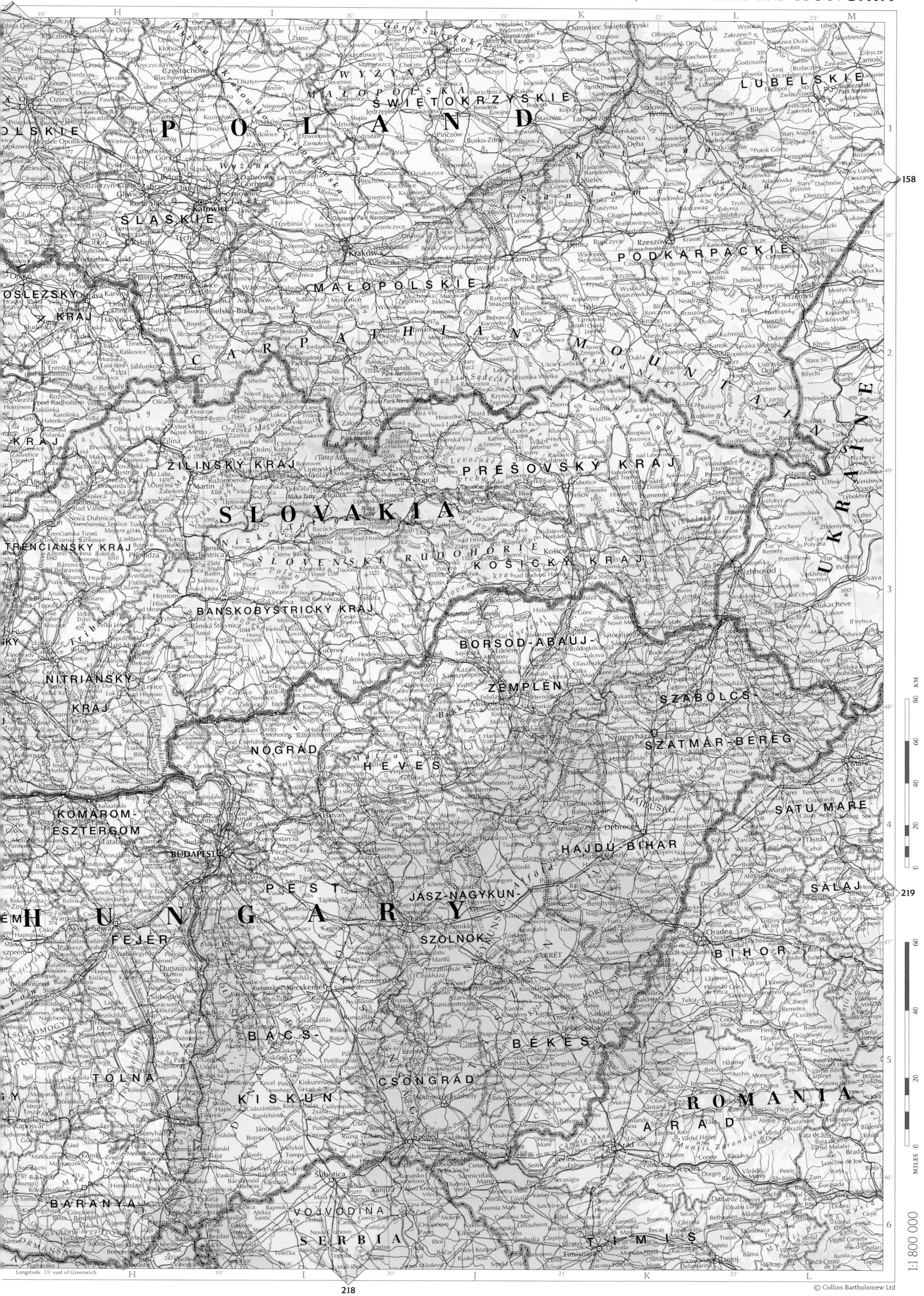

196

POLAND

SLOVAKIA

HUNGARY

UKRAINE

ROMANIA

SERBIA

CARPATHIAN MOUNTAINS

ŚWIĘTOKRZYSKIE

MAŁOPOLSKIE

ŚLĄSKIE

PODKARPACKIE

LUBELSKIE

ŽILINSKÝ KRAJ

PREŠOVSKÝ KRAJ

KOŠICKÝ KRAJ

TRENČIANSKY KRAJ

BANSKOBYSTRICKÝ KRAJ

NITRIANSKY KRAJ

BORSOD-ABAÚJ-ZEMPLÉN

SZABOLCS-SZATMÁR-BEREG

NÓGRÁD

HEVES

KOMÁROM-ESZTERGOM

BUDAPEST

PEST

HAJDÚ-BIHAR

JÁSZ-NAGYKUN-SZOLNOK

FEJÉR

BÁCS-KISKUN

BÉKÉS

CSONGRÁD

TOLNA

BARANYA

VOJVODINA

SATU MARE

SĂLAJ

BIHOR

ARAD

TIMIȘ

158

219

218

MILES 0 20 40 60

0 20 40 60 80 KM

1:1 800 000

Longitude 18° east of Greenwich

195

194

212

GERMANY

BAYERN

MITTELFRANKEN

OBERPFALZ

NIEDERBAYERN

OBERBAYERN

SCHWABEN

BADEN-WÜRTTEMBERG

STUTTGART

TÜBINGEN

ALLGÄU

München
Munich

AUSTRIA

TIROL

VORARLBERG

SALZBURG

OSTTIROL

ALPS

SWITZERLAND

GRAUBÜNDEN

ITALY

BOLZANO

TRENTINO

ALTO ADIGE

TRENTO

LOMBARDIA

SONDRIO

BERGAMO

BRESCIA

VENETO

BELLUNO

VICENZA

TREVISO

FRIULI

PORDENONE

VENEZIA GIULIA

M	FT
6000	19686
5000	16404
4000	13124
3000	9843
2000	6562
1500	4921
1000	3281
500	1640
200	656
100	328
0	0
LAND BELOW SEA LEVEL	
50	164
200	656
1000	3281
2000	6562

A B C D E F G

1 2 3 4 5 6 7 8

Longitude 12° east of Greenwich

Conic Equidistant Projection

196

CZECH REPUBLIC
JIHOČESKÝ KRAJ
VYSOČINA
JIHOMORAVSKÝ KRAJ
NIEDERÖSTERREICH
WIEN
ÖSTERREICH
AUSTRIA
STEIERMARK
BURGENLAND
KÄRNTEN
GYOR-MOSON-SOPRON
VAS
HUNGARY
ZALA
SLOVENIA
CROATIA
SLOVAKIA
Wien (Vienna)
Graz
Linz
Maribor
Ljubljana
Zagreb
Trieste
Gulf of Trieste
MILES
KM
1:1 200 000

199

213

Conic Equidistant Projection

226

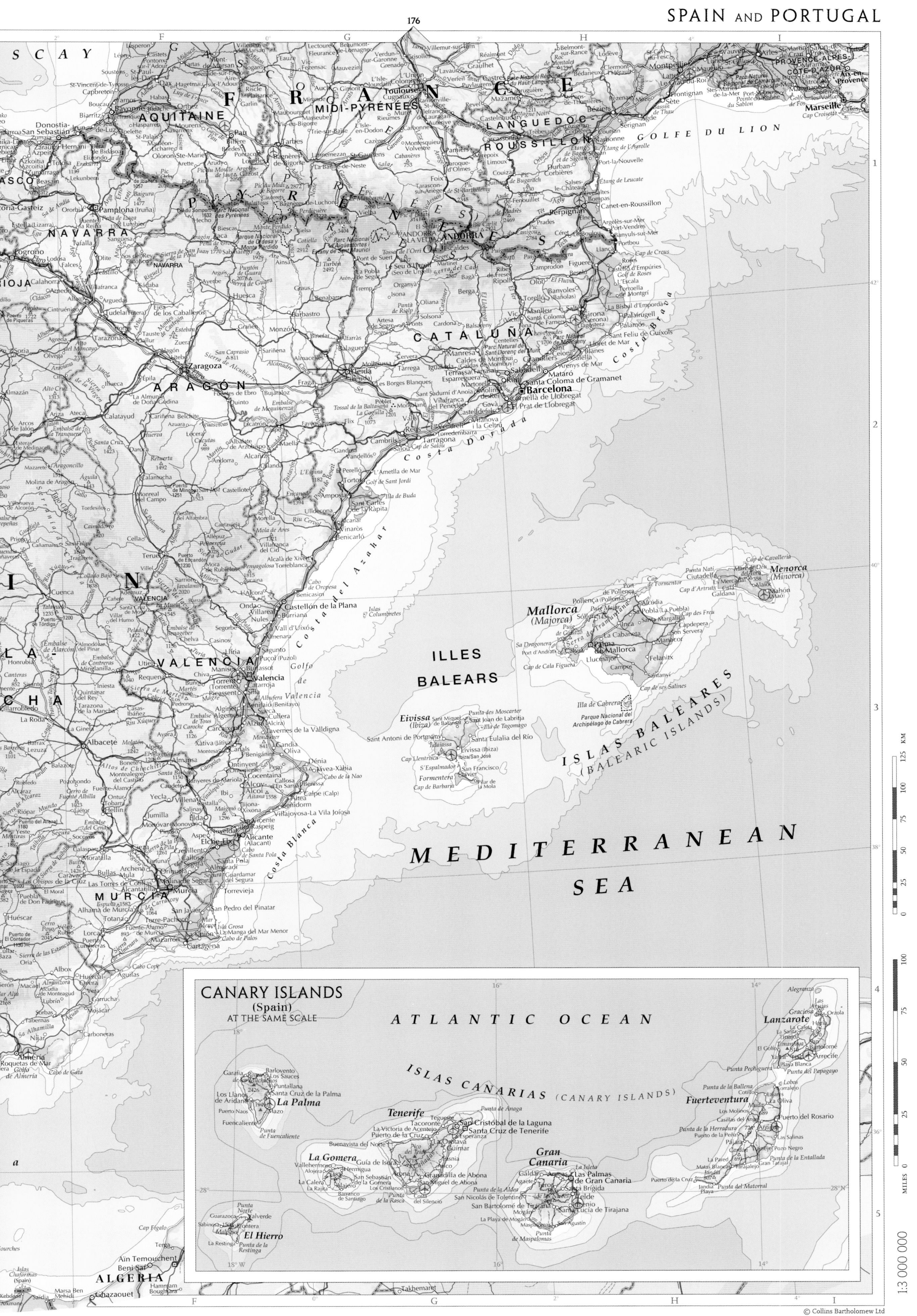
176
FRANCE
AQUITAINE
MIDI-PYRÉNÉES
LANGUEDOC-ROUSSILLON
PROVENCE-ALPES-CÔTE-D'AZUR
GOLFE DU LION
PYRENEES
NAVARRA
ARAGÓN
CATALUÑA
VALENCIA
MURCIA
ANDORRA
Toulouse
Montpellier
Marseille
Perpignan
Pamplona (Iruña)
Zaragoza
Lleida (Lérida)
Barcelona
Tarragona
Castellón de la Plana
Valencia
Alicante (Alacant)
Albacete
Murcia
Cartagena
Almería
Costa Brava
Costa Dorada
Costa del Azahar
Costa Blanca
Golfo de Valencia
ILLES BALEARS
ISLAS BALEARES (BALEARIC ISLANDS)
Mallorca (Majorca)
Palma de Mallorca
Menorca (Minorca)
Eivissa (Ibiza)
Formentera
MEDITERRANEAN SEA
ALGERIA
CANARY ISLANDS (Spain)
AT THE SAME SCALE
ATLANTIC OCEAN
ISLAS CANARIAS (CANARY ISLANDS)
La Palma
Tenerife
La Gomera
El Hierro
Gran Canaria
Fuerteventura
Lanzarote
Santa Cruz de Tenerife
Las Palmas de Gran Canaria
Puerto del Rosario
Arrecife
1:3 000 000

Conic Equidistant Projection

206

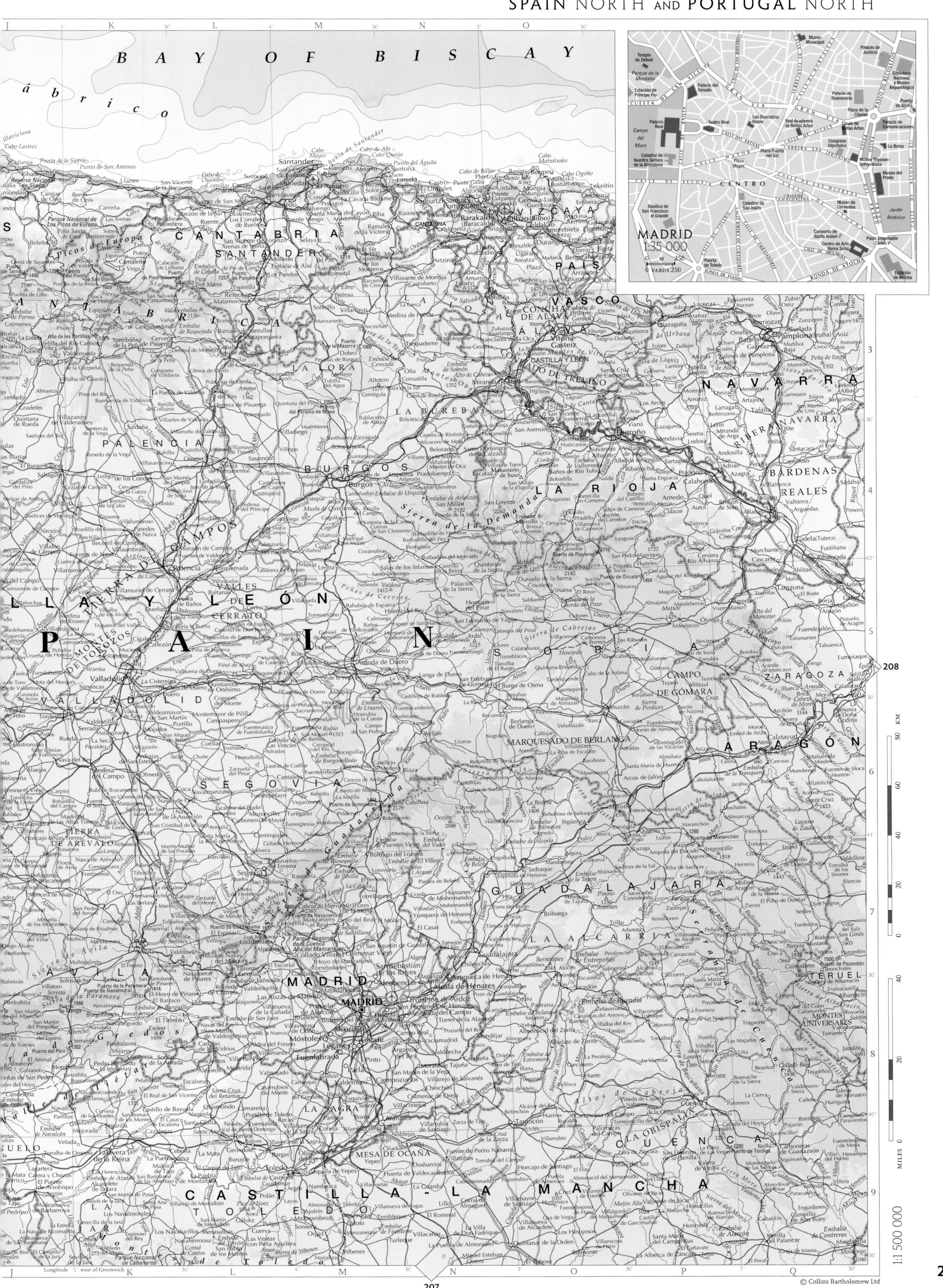

BAY OF BISCAY
Cantábrico
MADRID
1:35 000
CANTABRIA
SANTANDER
PAÍS VASCO
ÁLAVA
NAVARRA
BARDENAS REALES
LA RIOJA
CASTILLA Y LEÓN
SPAIN
PALENCIA
BURGOS
VALLADOLID
SORIA
ZARAGOZA
ARAGON
SEGOVIA
AVILA
MADRID
GUADALAJARA
LA ALCARRIA
CUENCA
TERUEL
TOLEDO
CASTILLA-LA MANCHA
MESA DE OCAÑA
LA SAGRA
1:1 500 000
208
207
Longitude 5° west of Greenwich

204

PORTUGAL

GOLFO DE CÁDIZ

MADEIRA (Portugal)

1:1 250 000

Arquipélago da Madeira

Ilha da Madeira

Ilha de Porto Santo

Ilhas Desertas

FUNCHAL

0 20 KM

0 10 20 MILES

M	FT
6000	19686
5000	16404
4000	13124
3000	9843
2000	6562
1500	4921
1000	3281
500	1640
200	656
100	328
0	0
LAND BELOW SEA LEVEL	
50	164
200	656
1000	3281
2000	6562

Conic Equidistant Projection

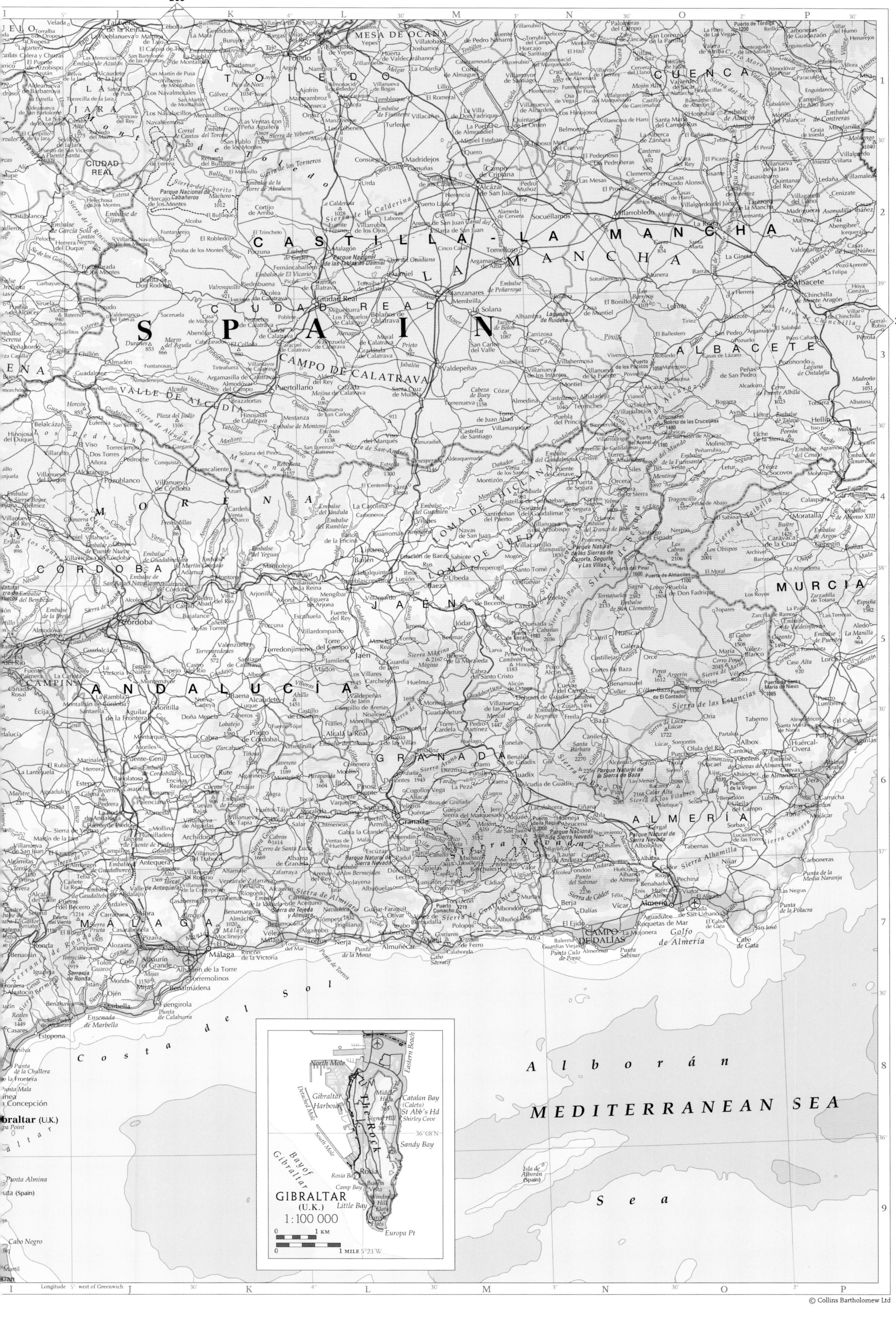

205

209

SPAIN

CASTILLA-LA MANCHA

ANDALUCÍA

MURCIA

TOLEDO

CIUDAD REAL

CUENCA

ALBACETE

JAÉN

CÓRDOBA

GRANADA

MÁLAGA

ALMERÍA

LA MANCHA

CAMPO DE CALATRAVA

Sierra Morena

Sierra Nevada

Costa del Sol

Alborán Sea

MEDITERRANEAN SEA

Golfo de Almería

GIBRALTAR
(U.K.)
1:100 000

North Mole

Eastern Beach

Catalan Bay (Caleta)

St Abb's Hd

Shirley Cove

Sandy Bay

The Rock

Gibraltar Harbour

Detached Mole

South Mole

Bay of Gibraltar

Rosia Bay

Camp Bay

Little Bay

Windmill Hill Flats

Europa Pt

36°08'N

5°21'W

0 1 KM

0 1 MILE

1:1 500 000

MILES 0 20 40

KM 0 20 40 60 80

Longitude 5° west of Greenwich

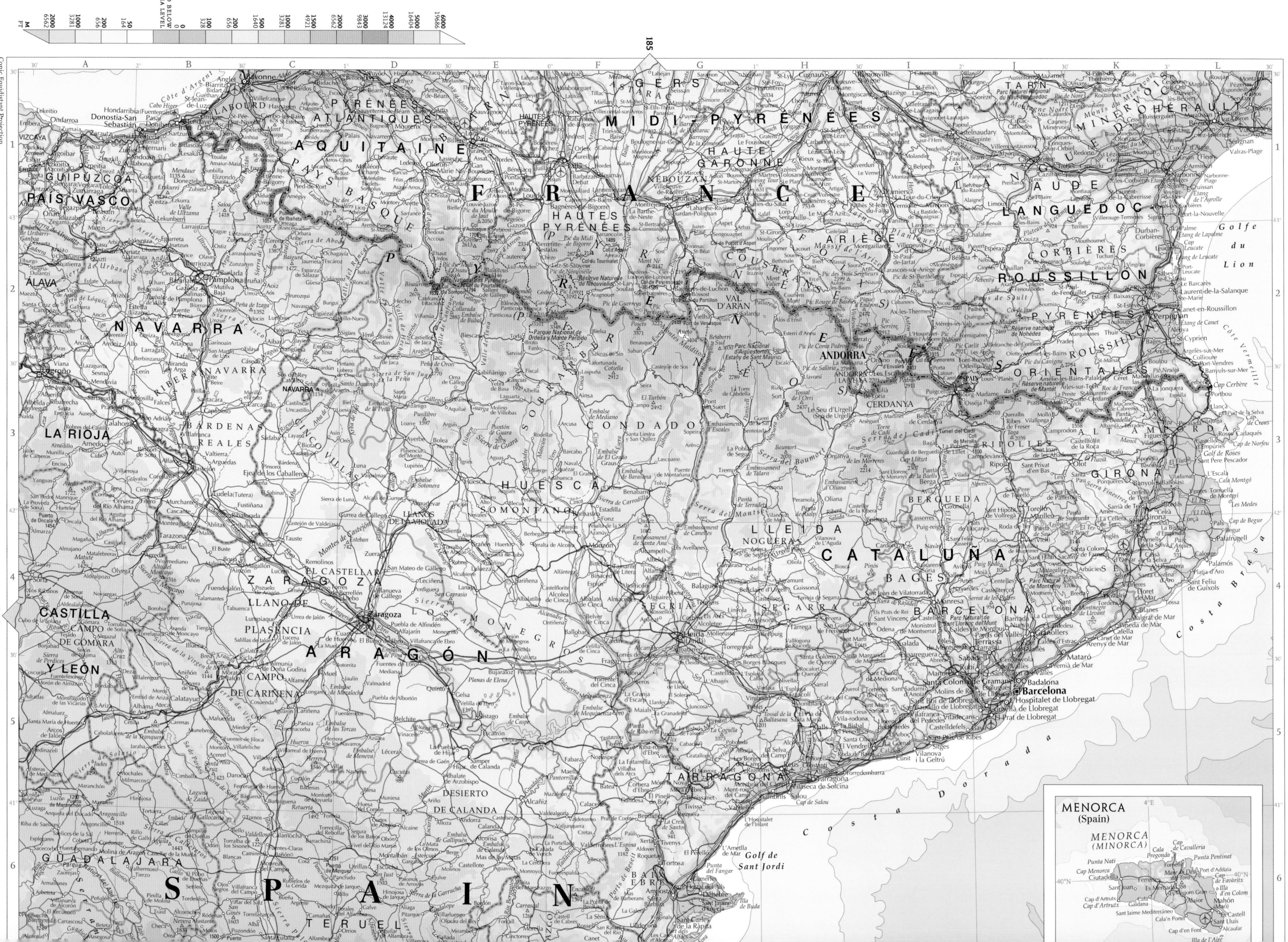

Conic Equidistant Projection

MEDITERRANEAN
SEA
ILLES BALEARS
Islas Baleares (Balearic Islands)
MALLORCA (MAJORCA)
Palma de Mallorca
EIVISSA (IBIZA)
Formentera
Illa de Cabrera
Golfo de Valencia
Costa del Azahar
Costa Blanca
Valencia
Alicante (Alacant)
Castellón de la Plana
Albacete
Murcia
Cartagena
CASTILLA-LA MANCHA
VALENCIA
MURCIA
ANDALUCÍA
BARCELONA
1:60 000
EIXAMPLE
SANT ANTONI
EL RAVAL
BARRI GÒTIC
RIBERA
POBLE SEC
MONTJUÏC
SANTS MONTJUÏC
LA BARCELONETA
EL FORT PIUS
EL PORT
1:1 500 000
MILES
KM
207

188
189
218
177
SLOVAKIA
HUNGARY
AUSTRIA
SLOVENIA
CROATIA
BOSNIA-HERZEGOVINA
REPUBLIKA SRPSKA
FEDERACIJA BOSNA I HERCEGOVINA
MONTENEGRO
GERMANY
BAYERN
BADEN-WÜRTTEMBERG
SWITZERLAND
LIECHTENSTEIN
FRANCE
ALSACE
LORRAINE
FRANCHE-COMTÉ
RHÔNE-ALPES
PROVENCE-ALPES-CÔTE D'AZUR
TRENTINO-ALTO ADIGE
FRIULI-VENEZIA GIULIA
VENETO
LOMBARDIA
PIEMONTE
VALLE D'AOSTA
LIGURIA
EMILIA-ROMAGNA
TOSCANA
UMBRIA
MARCHE
SAN MARINO
MONACO
ADRIATIC
LIGURIAN SEA
Gulf of Venice
Golfo di Genova
BUDAPEST
WIEN (Vienna)
BRATISLAVA
LJUBLJANA
ZAGREB
SARAJEVO
München (Munich)
Milano (Milan)
Venezia (Venice)
Torino (Turin)
Genova (Genoa)
Firenze (Florence)
6000
19686
5000
16404
4000
13124
3000
9843
2000
6562
1500
4921
1000
3281
500
1640
200
656
100
328
0
0
LAND BELOW SEA LEVEL
50
164
200
656
1000
3281
2000
6562
M
FT
Conic Equidistant Projection

TYRRHENIAN SEA
IONIAN SEA
MEDITERRANEAN SEA
SICILIAN CHANNEL
SARDEGNA (SARDINIA) (Italy)
CORSE (CORSICA) (France)
SICILIA (SICILY)
MALTA
VALLETTA
ROMA (Rome)
Napoli (Naples)
Palermo
Messina
Catania
Taranto
Bari
Cagliari
Sassari
TUNIS
TUNISIA
ALGERIA
ANNABA
LAZIO
MOLISE
CAMPANIA
PUGLIA
BASILICATA
CALABRIA
Golfo di Taranto
Golfe de Tunis
Golfe de Hammamet
Isole Pelagie (Italy)
1:3 000 000
MILES 0 25 50
0 25 50 75 KM
Longitude 10° east of Greenwich
227
© Collins Bartholomew Ltd

194
182
183
FRANCHE-COMTÉ
FRANCE
DOUBS
NEUCHÂTEL
JURA
VAUD
FRIBOURG
BERN
SOLOTHURN
BASELLANDSCHAFT
AARGAU
ZÜRICH
THURGAU
SANKT GALLEN
LUZERN
ZUG
SCHWYZ
GLARUS
OBWALDEN
NIDWALDEN
URI
SWITZERLAND
GRAUBÜNDEN
VORARLBERG
LIECHTENSTEIN
LAC LÉMAN
(LAKE GENEVA)
Genève
VALAIS
TICINO
HAUTE-SAVOIE
SAVOIE
RHÔNE-ALPES
VALLE D'AOSTA
CUSIO OSSOLA
VERBANO
VERCELLI
BIELLA
NOVARA
VARESE
COMO
LECCO
BERGAMO
SONDRIO
LOMBARDI
Milano (Milan)
TORINO
Torino (Turin)
PIEMONTE
CANAVESE
PAVIA
LODI
CREMONA
ITA
PIACENZA
ASTI
ALESSANDRIA
CUNEO
GENOVA
Genova
LIGURIA
SAVONA
IMPERIA
LA SPEZIA
MASSA E CARRARA
PARM
EMI
ISÈRE
HAUTES-ALPES
FRANCE
PROVENCE
ALPES-DE-HAUTE-PROVENCE
ALPES-MARITIMES
CÔTE D'AZUR
VAR
MONACO
Nice
Golfo di Genova
LIGURIAN SEA
6000
19686
5000
16404
4000
13124
3000
9843
2000
6562
1500
4921
1000
3281
500
1640
200
656
100
328
0
LAND BELOW SEA LEVEL
50
164
200
656
1000
3281
2000
6562
M
FT
Swiss Cantons numbered on the map:
1. APPENZELL AUSSERRHODEN (G1)
2. APPENZELL INNERRHODEN (G1)
3. FRIBOURG (B2)
4. VAUD (C2)
Italian Provinces numbered on the map:
5. MONZA E BRIANZA (G4)
6. MILANO (G4)
Conic Equidistant Projection

200
198
218
215
AUSTRIA
TIROL
SALZBURG
STEIERMARK
OSTTIROL
KÄRNTEN
BOLZANO
TRENTINO-
ALTO ADIGE
TRENTO
BELLUNO
FRIULI-
VENEZIA GIULIA
UDINE
PORDENONE
TREVISO
VICENZA
VENETO
VERONA
PADOVA
VENEZIA
ROVIGO
FERRARA
ROMAGNA
BOLOGNA
RAVENNA
FORLÌ-
CESENA
RIMINI
SAN MARINO
PESARO
E URBINO
ANCONA
MARCHE
MACERATA
PERUGIA
UMBRIA
AREZZO
FIRENZE
TOSCANA
SIENA
SLOVENIA
CROATIA
GORSKI KOTAR
Gulf of Venice
Gulf of Trieste
ADRIATIC SEA
Longitude 11° east of Greenwich
KM
MILES
1:1 500 000

LIGURIAN SEA

CORSE
(CORSICA)
(France)

HAUTE-CORSE

CORSE-DU-SUD

Strait of Bonifacio

SARDEGNA
(SARDINIA)
(Italy)

SASSARI

OLBIA-TEMPIO

NUORO

ORISTANO

OGLIASTRA

MEDIO CAMPIDANO

CARBONIA-IGLESIAS

CAGLIARI

TOSCANA

PISA

LIVORNO

SIENA

GROSSETO

AREZZO

Arcipelago Toscano

TYRRHENIAN

M	FT
6000	19686
5000	16404
4000	13124
3000	9843
2000	6562
1500	4921
1000	3281
500	1640
200	656
100	328
0	0
LAND BELOW SEA LEVEL	
50	164
200	656
1000	3281
2000	6562

Conic Equidistant Projection

CROATIA
Vis
Hvar
Biševo
Sušac
ADRIATIC
SEA
Palagruža (Croatia)
Isole Pianosa
Isole Tremiti (Italy)
San Domino
Isole San Nicola
MARCHE
MACERATA
FERMO
ASCOLI PICENO
Parco Nazionale dei Monti Sibillini
San Benedetto del Tronto
TERAMO
PESCARA
Pescara
Francavilla al Mare
Ortona
Punta di Ferruccio
ABRUZZO
L'AQUILA
L'Aquila
Parco Nazionale del Gran Sasso e Monti della Laga
Parco Nazionale della Maiella
CHIETI
Chieti
Vasto
Termoli
Punta della Penna
RIETI
LAZIO
ROMA
Tivoli
Anzio
Latina
LATINA
FROSINONE
Parco Nazionale del Circeo
Lago di Sabaudia
San Felice Circeo
Golfo di Terracina
Gaeta
Golfo di Gaeta
Isola Zannone
Isola Palmarola
Isola di Ponza
Isola di Gavi
Isole Ponziane
Isola Ventotene
ITALY
MOLISE
ISERNIA
CAMPOBASSO
FOGGIA
Foggia
Golfo di Manfredonia
Manfredonia
Vieste
Testa del Gargano
Parco Nazionale del Gargano
Promontorio del Gargano
Lago di Lesina
Lago di Varano
PUGLIA
BARLETTA-ANDRIA-TRANI
Barletta
Trani
Andria
BARI
Parco Nazionale dell'Alta Murgia
Margherita di Savoia
BENEVENTO
CASERTA
AVELLINO
CAMPANIA
NAPOLI
Napoli (Naples)
Golfo di Napoli
Vesuvio
Isola d'Ischia
Capri
Isola di Capri
Punta Campanella
Sorrento
Salerno
Golfo di Salerno
SALERNO
Agropoli
Paestum
Parco Nazionale del Cilento e del Vallo di Diano
Golfo di Policastro
BASILICATA
POTENZA
Potenza
MATERA
Matera
Altamura
Parco Nazionale del Pollino
COSENZA
Cosenza
CALABRIA
Paola
Amantea
Tyrrhenian Sea (...EA)
ROME 1:50 000
VATICAN CITY
Basilica di San Pietro
Musei Vaticani
Castel Sant'Angelo
Piazza del Popolo
Villa Borghese
Stazione Roma-Viterbo
TRIONFALE
SALARIO
Trinità dei Monti
Palazzo Barberini
Fontana di Trevi
Palazzo del Quirinale
Pantheon
Piazza Navona
Terme di Diocleziano
Stazione Centrale
Museo Nazionale Romano
Santa Maria Maggiore
Monumento a Vittorio Emanuele II
Foro Romano
Teatro di Marcello
Colosseo
Arco di Costantino
Circo Massimo
Palazzo Corsini
Santa Maria in Trastevere
TRASTEVERE
Villa Abamelek
Villa Doria Pamphili
Terme di Caracalla
Parco di Porta Capena
217
1:1 500 000
KM
MILES

TYRRHENIAN SEA

SICILIA (SICILY)

SICILIAN CHANNEL

TUNISIA

Isola di Ustica

Isole Ponziane

Isola di Pantelleria (Italy)

Isole Egadi

Golfo di Napoli

Golfo di Gela

Napoli (Naples)

Palermo

M	FT
6000	19686
5000	16404
4000	13124
3000	9843
2000	6562
1500	4921
1000	3281
500	1640
200	656
100	328
0	0
LAND BELOW SEA LEVEL	
50	164
200	656
1000	3281
2000	6562

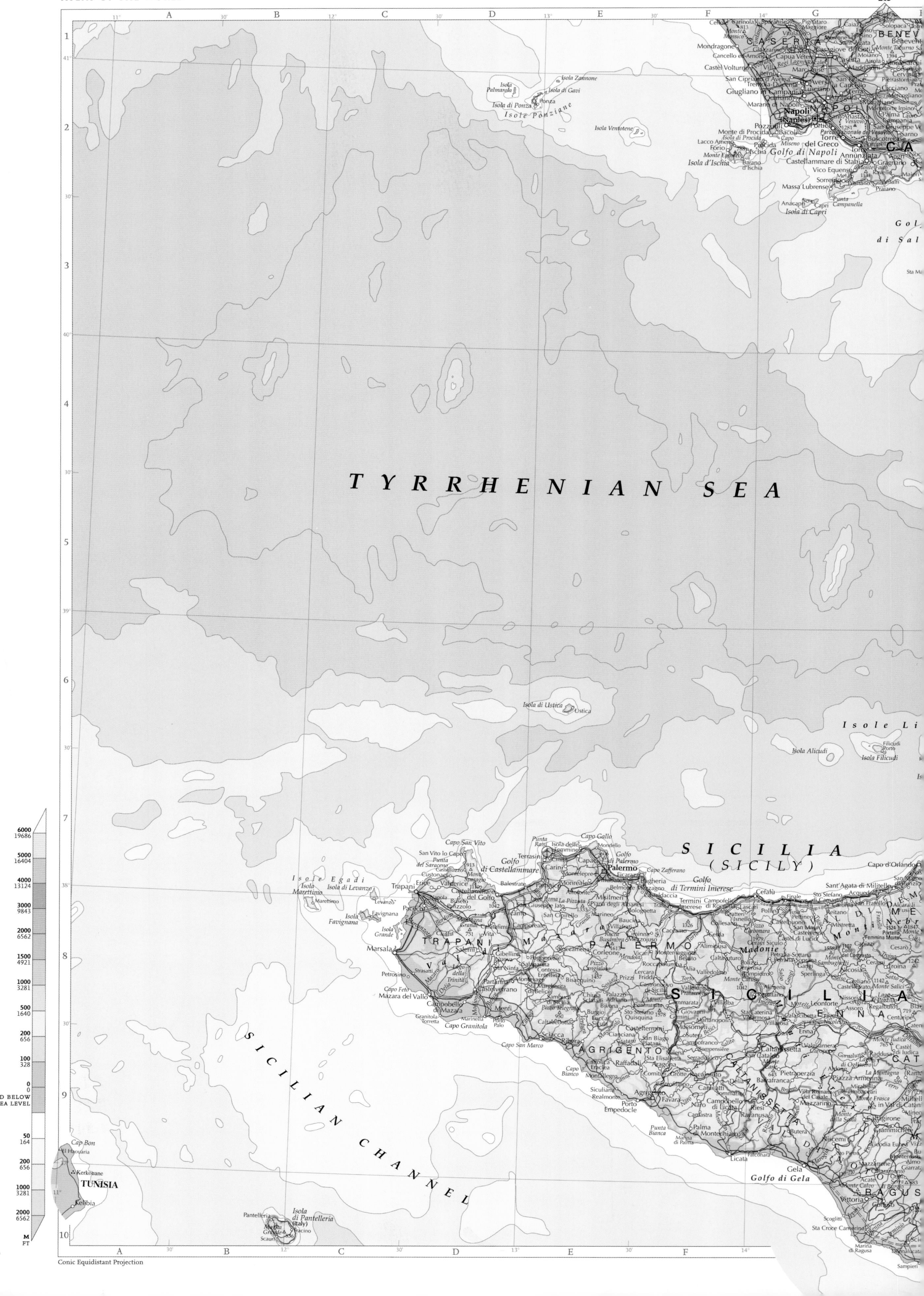

Conic Equidistant Projection

ADRIATIC SEA
Strait of Otranto
GOLFO DI TARANTO
IONIAN SEA
PUGLIA
BASILICATA
CALABRIA
FOGGIA
BARLETTA-ANDRIA-TRANI
BARI
TARANTO
BRINDISI
LECCE
POTENZA
MATERA
COSENZA
CROTONE
CATANZARO
VIBO VALENTIA
REGGIO DI CALABRIA
Golfo di Policastro
Golfo di Corigliano
Golfo di Santa Eufemia
Golfo di Squillace
Golfo di Gioia
Golfo di Catania
Golfo di Noto
MALTA
1:500 000
Gozo (Ghawdex)
Kemmuna (Comino)
Malta
Valletta
1:1 500 000
Longitude 16° east of Greenwich

189

210

CZECH REPUBLIC

GERMANY

BAYERN

AUSTRIA

SLOVAKIA

HUNGARY

SLOVENIA

CROATIA

ITALY

FRIULI-VENEZIA GIULIA

VENETO

EMILIA-ROMAGNA

MARCHE

UMBRIA

ABRUZZO

LAZIO

MOLISE

CAMPANIA

PUGLIA

BASILICATA

BOSNIA-HERZEGOVINA

REPUBLIKA SRPSKA

FEDERACIJA BOSNA I HERCEGOVINA

DAYTON ACCORD LINE 1996

VOJVODINA

SERBIA

MONTENEGRO

KOSOVO

ALBANIA

Gulf of Venice

ADRIATIC SEA

M	FT
6000	19686
5000	16404
4000	13124
3000	9843
2000	6562
1500	4921
1000	3281
500	1640
200	656
100	328
0	0
LAND BELOW SEA LEVEL	
50	164
200	656
1000	3281
2000	6562

Conic Equidistant Projection

211

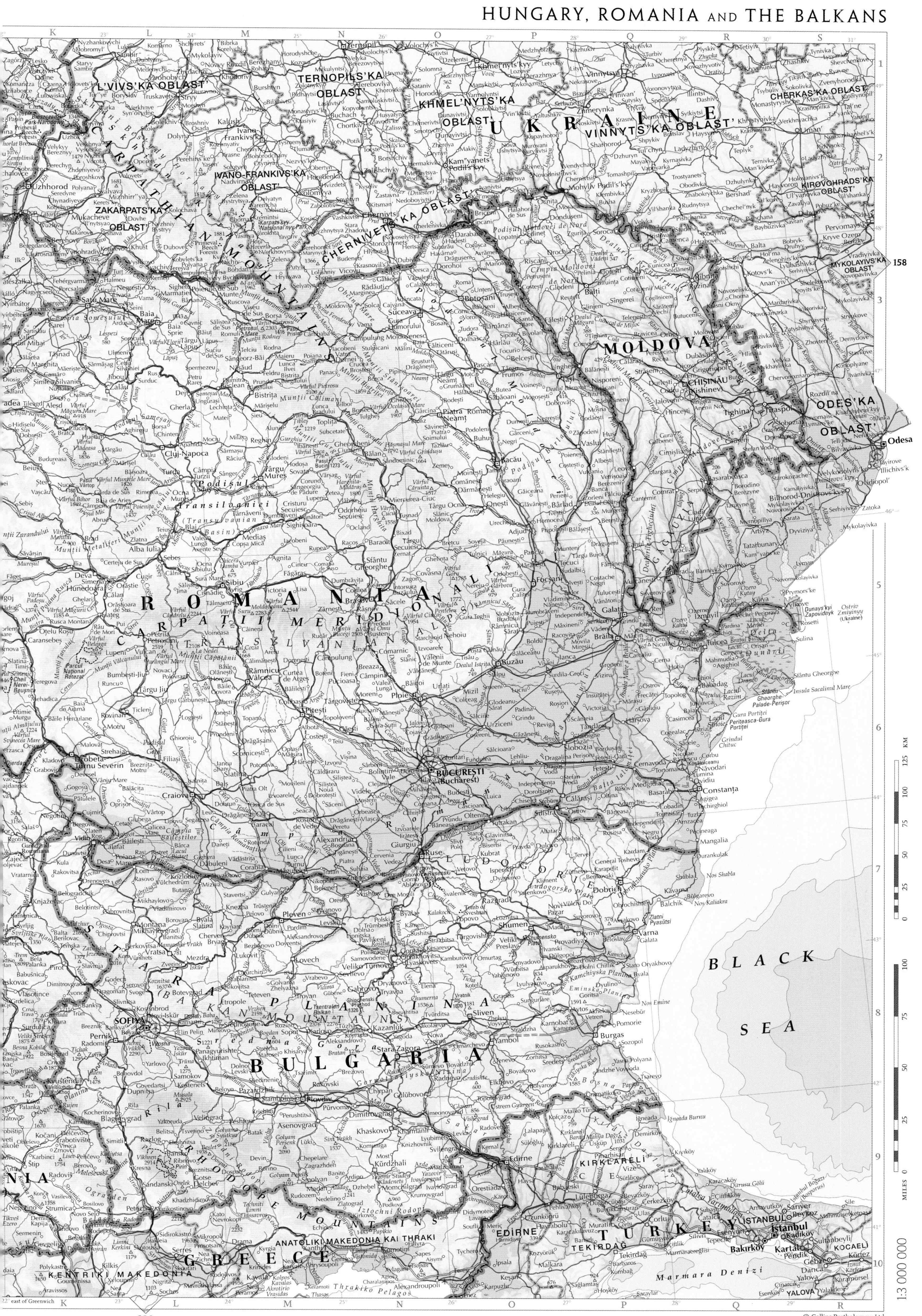
UKRAINE
MOLDOVA
ROMANIA
BULGARIA
GREECE
TURKEY
BLACK SEA
CARPATHIAN MOUNTAINS
CARPAȚII MERIDIONALI
TRANSYLVANIAN ALPS
STARA PLANINA
(BALKAN MOUNTAINS)
RHODOPE MOUNTAINS
L'VIVS'KA OBLAST'
TERNOPIL'S'KA OBLAST'
KHMEL'NYTS'KA OBLAST'
VINNYTS'KA OBLAST'
CHERKAS'KA OBLAST'
IVANO-FRANKIVS'KA OBLAST'
ZAKARPATS'KA OBLAST'
CHERNIVETS'KA OBLAST'
KIROVOHRADS'KA OBLAST'
MYKOLAYIVS'KA OBLAST'
ODES'KA OBLAST'
ANATOLIKI MAKEDONIA KAI THRAKI
KENTRIKI MAKEDONIA
EDIRNE
KIRKLARELI
TEKIRDAĞ
KOCAELI
YALOVA
BUCUREȘTI
(Bucharest)
CHIȘINĂU
SOFIYA
Odesa
Constanța
Varna
Burgas
İstanbul
Marmara Denizi
Thrakiko Pelagos
158
220
MILES 0 25 50 75 100
0 25 50 75 100 125 KM
1:3 000 000
east of Greenwich

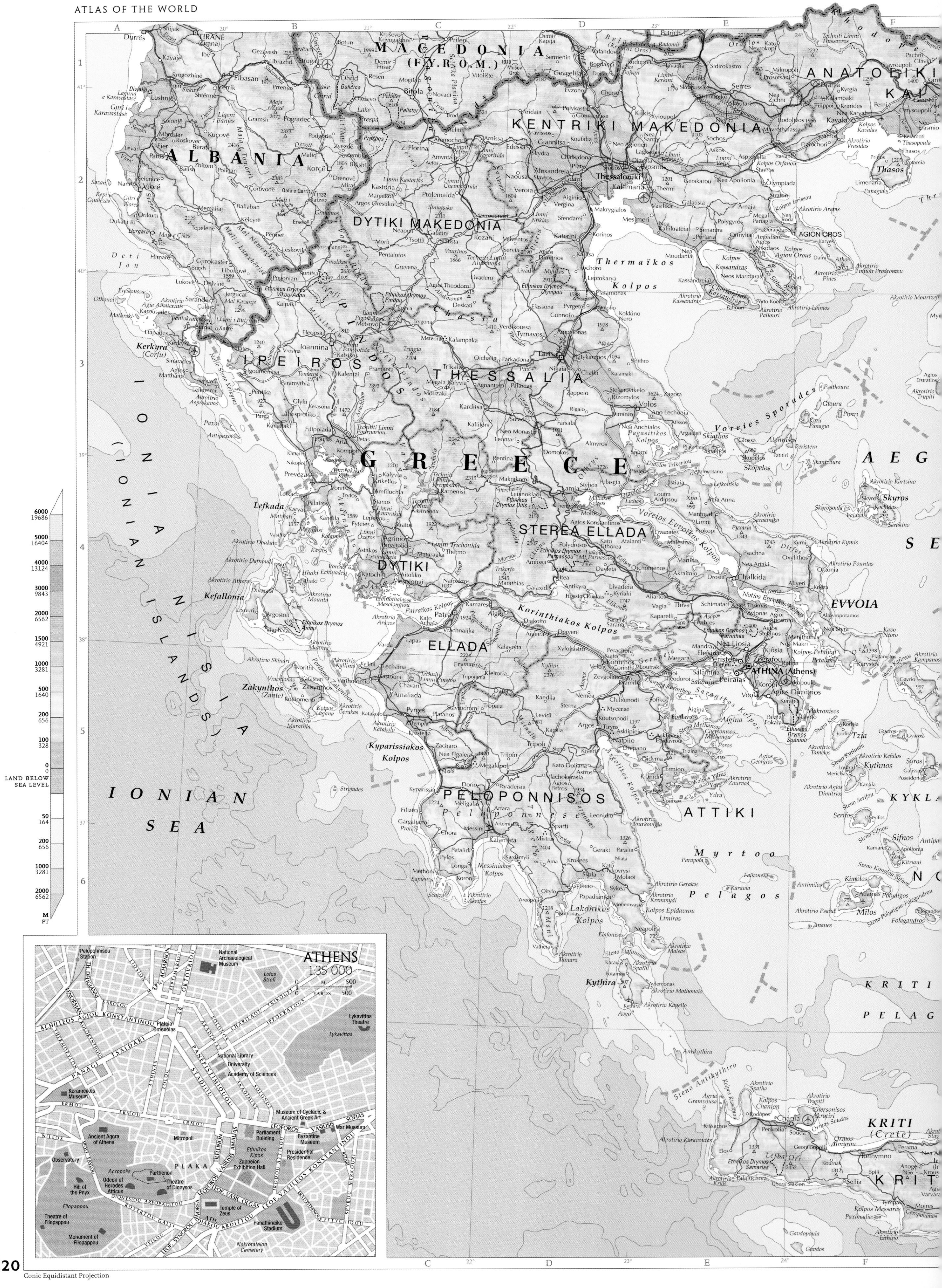

MACEDONIA (F.Y.R.O.M.)

ALBANIA

KENTRIKI MAKEDONIA

ANATOLIKI

DYTIKI MAKEDONIA

IPEIROS

THESSALIA

GREECE

STEREA ELLADA

DYTIKI ELLADA

EVVOIA

PELOPONNISOS

ATTIKI

IONIAN SEA

IONIA NISIA (IONIAN ISLANDS)

Thermaïkos Kolpos

Voreies Sporades

Korinthiakos Kolpos

Saronikos Kolpos

Myrtoo Pelagos

KRITI (Crete)

Kerkyra (Corfu)

Kefallonia

Lefkada

Zakynthos (Zante)

Thasos

Skyros

Kythira

ATHINA (Athens)

Thessaloniki

M	FT
6000	19686
5000	16404
4000	13124
3000	9843
2000	6562
1500	4921
1000	3281
500	1640
200	656
100	328
0	
LAND BELOW SEA LEVEL	
50	164
200	656
1000	3281
2000	6562

ATHENS
1:35 000

National Archaeological Museum

Lofos Strefi

Lykavittos Theatre

Plateia Omonias

National Library

University

Academy of Sciences

Kerameikos Museum

Museum of Cycladic & Ancient Greek Art

Parliament Building

War Museum

Byzantine Museum

Ancient Agora of Athens

Mitropoli

Ethnikos Kipos

Zappeion Exhibition Hall

Presidential Residence

Observatory

Acropolis

Parthenon

PLAKA

Odeon of Herodes Atticus

Theatre of Dionysos

Hill of the Pnyx

Filopappou

Theatre of Filopappou

Temple of Zeus

Panathinaiko Stadium

Monument of Filopappou

Nekrotafeion Cemetery

Conic Equidistant Projection

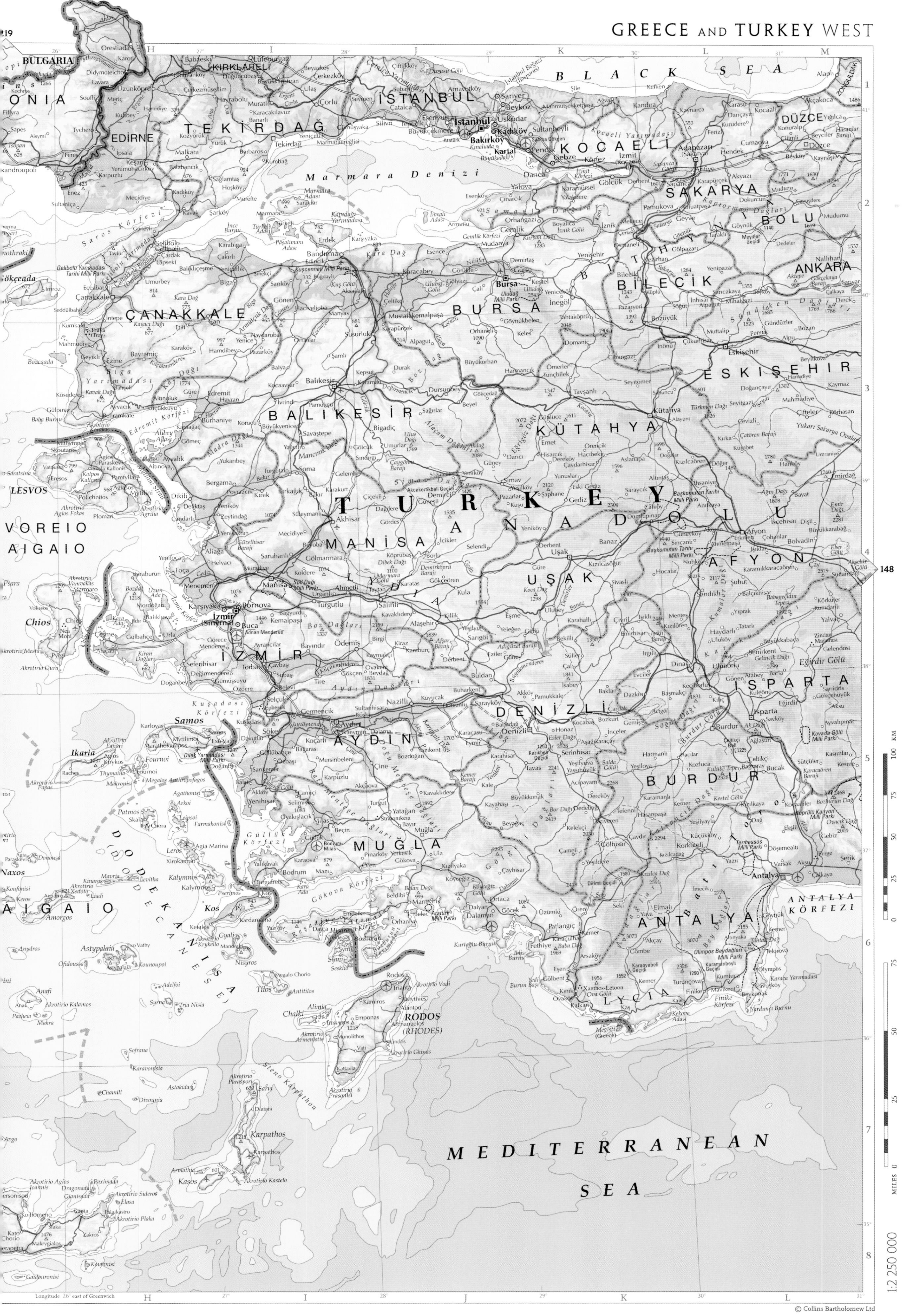
BLACK SEA
BULGARIA
EDİRNE
TEKİRDAĞ
KIRKLARELİ
İSTANBUL
KOCAELİ
SAKARYA
DÜZCE
BOLU
ANKARA
BİLECİK
BURSA
ÇANAKKALE
ESKİŞEHİR
BALIKESİR
KÜTAHYA
MANİSA
TURKEY
ANADOLU
UŞAK
AFYON
İZMİR
DENİZLİ
ISPARTA
AYDIN
BURDUR
MUĞLA
ANTALYA
LYCIA
Marmara Denizi
Samos
Ikaria
Chios
LESVOS
VOREIO AIGAIO
NOTIO AIGAIO
DODEKANISA (DODECANESE)
Kos
RODOS (RHODES)
Karpathos
Kasos
MEDITERRANEAN SEA
ANTALYA KÖRFEZİ
148
1:2 250 000
KM 0 25 50 75 100
MILES 0 25 50 75
Longitude 26° east of Greenwich

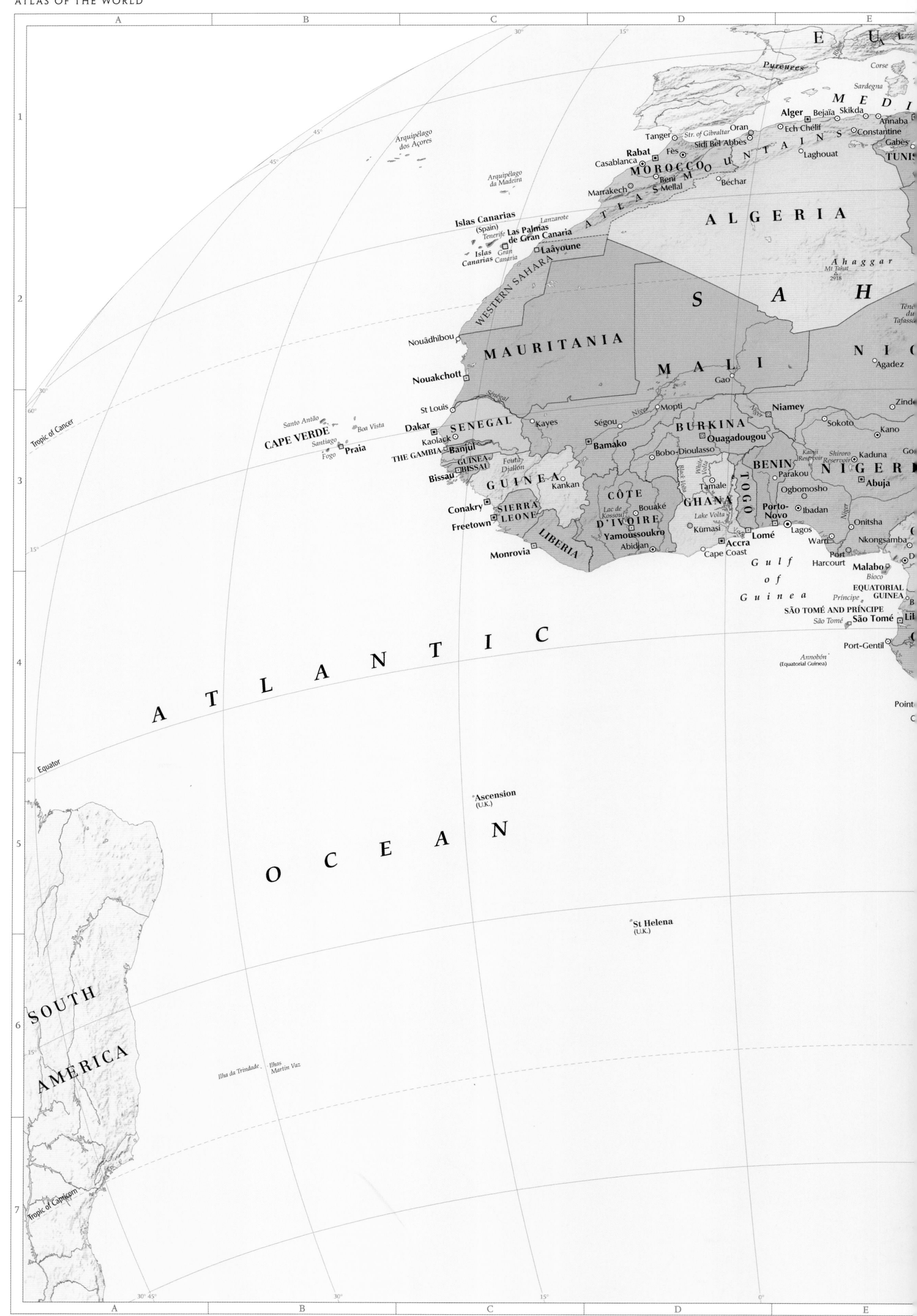

Orthographic Projection

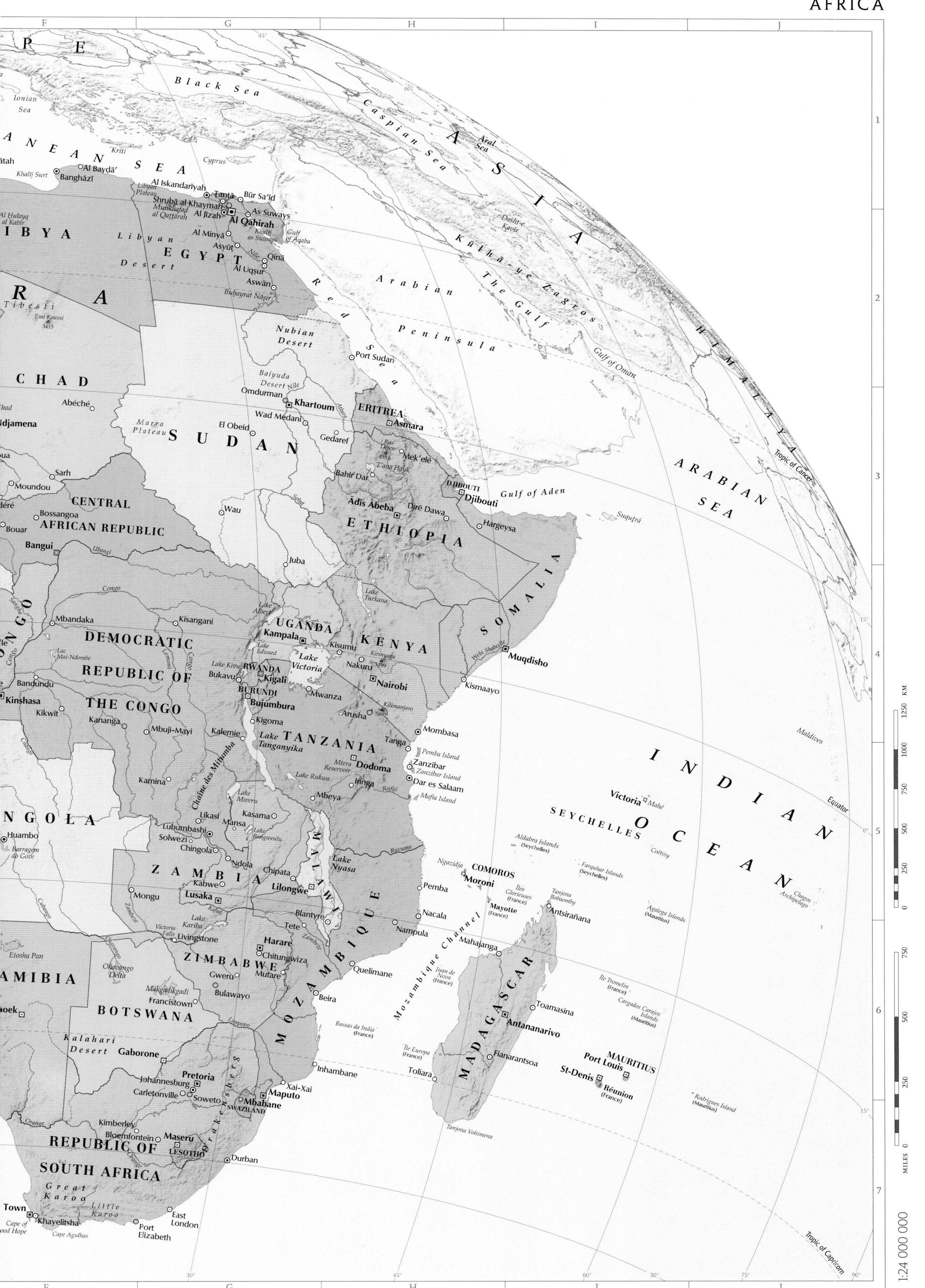
Black Sea
Caspian Sea
Aral Sea
ASIA
MEDITERRANEAN SEA
Cyprus
LIBYA
EGYPT
Al Qāhirah
Al Iskandarīyah
Libyan Desert
Arabian Peninsula
Red Sea
Nubian Desert
Port Sudan
CHAD
SUDAN
Khartoum
Omdurman
ERITREA
Asmara
Kūhhā-ye Zagros
The Gulf
Gulf of Oman
HIMALAYA
Tropic of Cancer
ARABIAN SEA
Gulf of Aden
DJIBOUTI
Djibouti
ETHIOPIA
Ādīs Ābeba
SOMALIA
Muqdisho
CENTRAL AFRICAN REPUBLIC
Bangui
DEMOCRATIC REPUBLIC OF THE CONGO
Kinshasa
UGANDA
Kampala
KENYA
Nairobi
RWANDA
Kigali
BURUNDI
Bujumbura
Lake Victoria
TANZANIA
Dodoma
Lake Tanganyika
Dar es Salaam
Zanzibar
Mombasa
INDIAN OCEAN
SEYCHELLES
Victoria
Equator
Maldives
Chagos Archipelago
ANGOLA
ZAMBIA
Lusaka
MALAWI
Lilongwe
Lake Nyasa
COMOROS
Moroni
Mayotte (France)
MOZAMBIQUE
Maputo
Mozambique Channel
ZIMBABWE
Harare
NAMIBIA
BOTSWANA
Gaborone
Kalahari Desert
MADAGASCAR
Antananarivo
MAURITIUS
Port Louis
St-Denis
Réunion (France)
Rodrigues Island (Mauritius)
Pretoria
Johannesburg
SWAZILAND
Mbabane
LESOTHO
Maseru
REPUBLIC OF SOUTH AFRICA
Durban
Port Elizabeth
Cape Agulhas
Great Karoo
Tropic of Capricorn

1:24 000 000

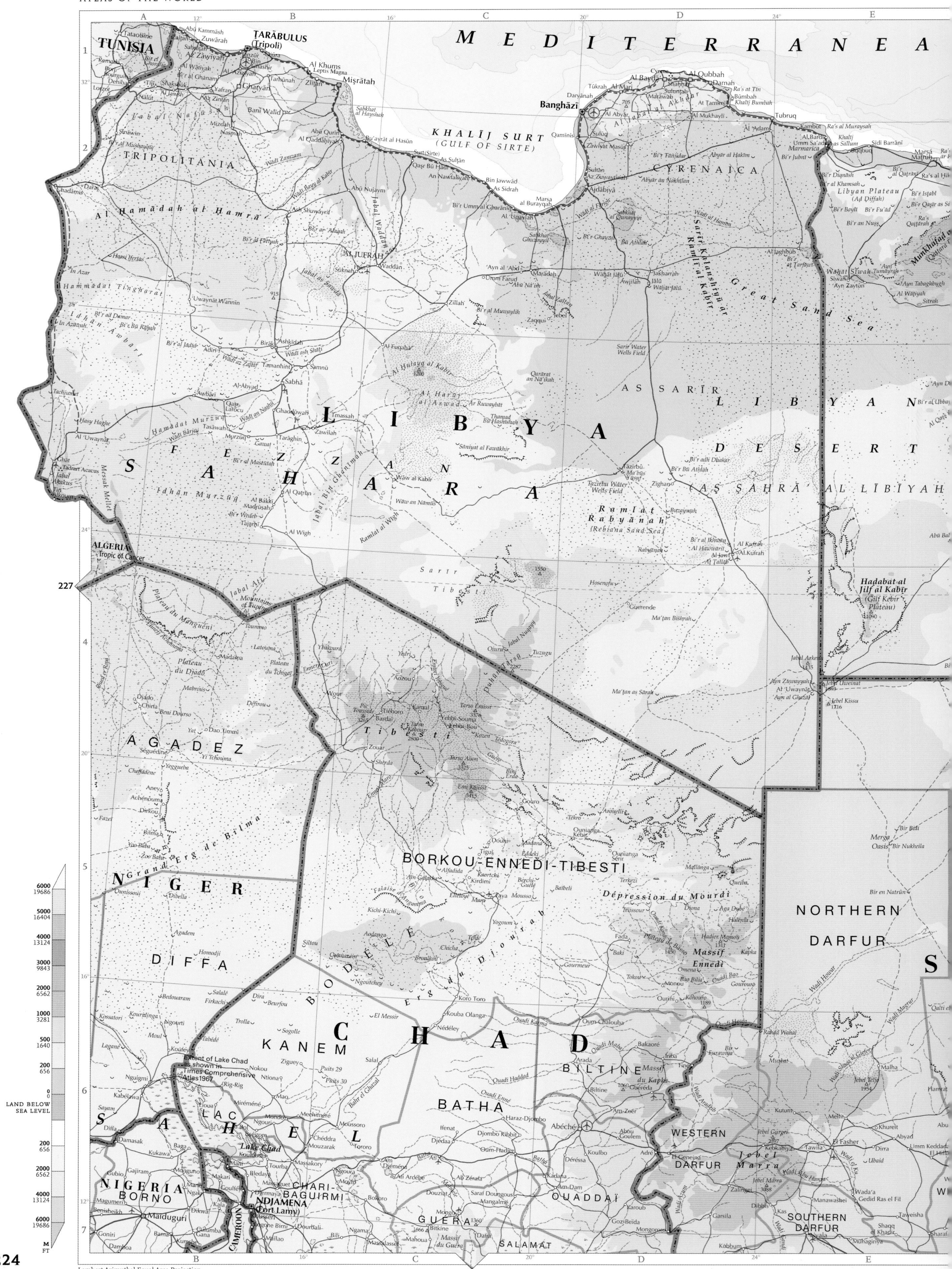

Lambert Azimuthal Equal Area Projection

140

146

232

SEA

LEBANON

SYRIA

DIMASHQ (Damascus)

IRAQ

BĀDIYAT ASH SHĀM (SYRIAN DESERT)

Tel Aviv-Yafo (Jaffa)

WEST BANK

GAZA

ISRAEL

JORDAN

'AMMAN

Jerusalem

AL QĀHIRAH (Cairo)

Al Jīzah (Giza)

EGYPT

Bûr Sa'îd (Port Said)

As Suways (Suez)

Jazīrat Sīnā' (Sinai)

Al Uqşur (Luxor)

Aswān

Buḩayrat Nāşir (Lake Nasser)

RED SEA

AL ḨIJĀZ

SAUDI ARABIA

Al Madīnah (Medina)

Jiddah (Jeddha)

Makkah (Mecca)

Tropic of Cancer

HALAIB TRIANGLE UNDER SUDANESE ADMINISTRATION

NUBIAN DESERT

Port Sudan (Būr Sudan)

SUDAN

NORTHERN

NILE

KHARTOUM

Omdurman

KASSALA

NORTHERN KORDOFAN

EL GEZIRA

GEDAREF

SENNAR

WHITE NILE

BLUE NILE

SOUTHERN KORDOFAN

ERITREA

ASMARA

ANSEBA

GASH BARKA

DEBUB

SEMENAWI K'EYIH BAHRĪ

DEBUBAWI K'EYIH BAHRĪ

ETHIOPIA

TIGRAY

ĀMARA

ĀFAR

DJIBOUTI

YEMEN

ŞAN'Ā'

Al Ḩudaydah

Ta'izz

ASĪR

CAIRO

1:60 000

METRES 500

YARDS 500

Zamalek Island

Gezira

GEZIRA

BULAQ

AL AZBAKIYA

BAB EL-SHA'RIYA

AL-MUSKI

'ĀBDĪN

GARDEN CITY

Roda Island

AD DARB AL AHMAR

AS SAYYIDAH ZAYNAB

GEZIRET

Nile

0 100 200 300 400 KM

0 100 200 MILES

1:7 500 000

Longitude 32° east of Greenwich

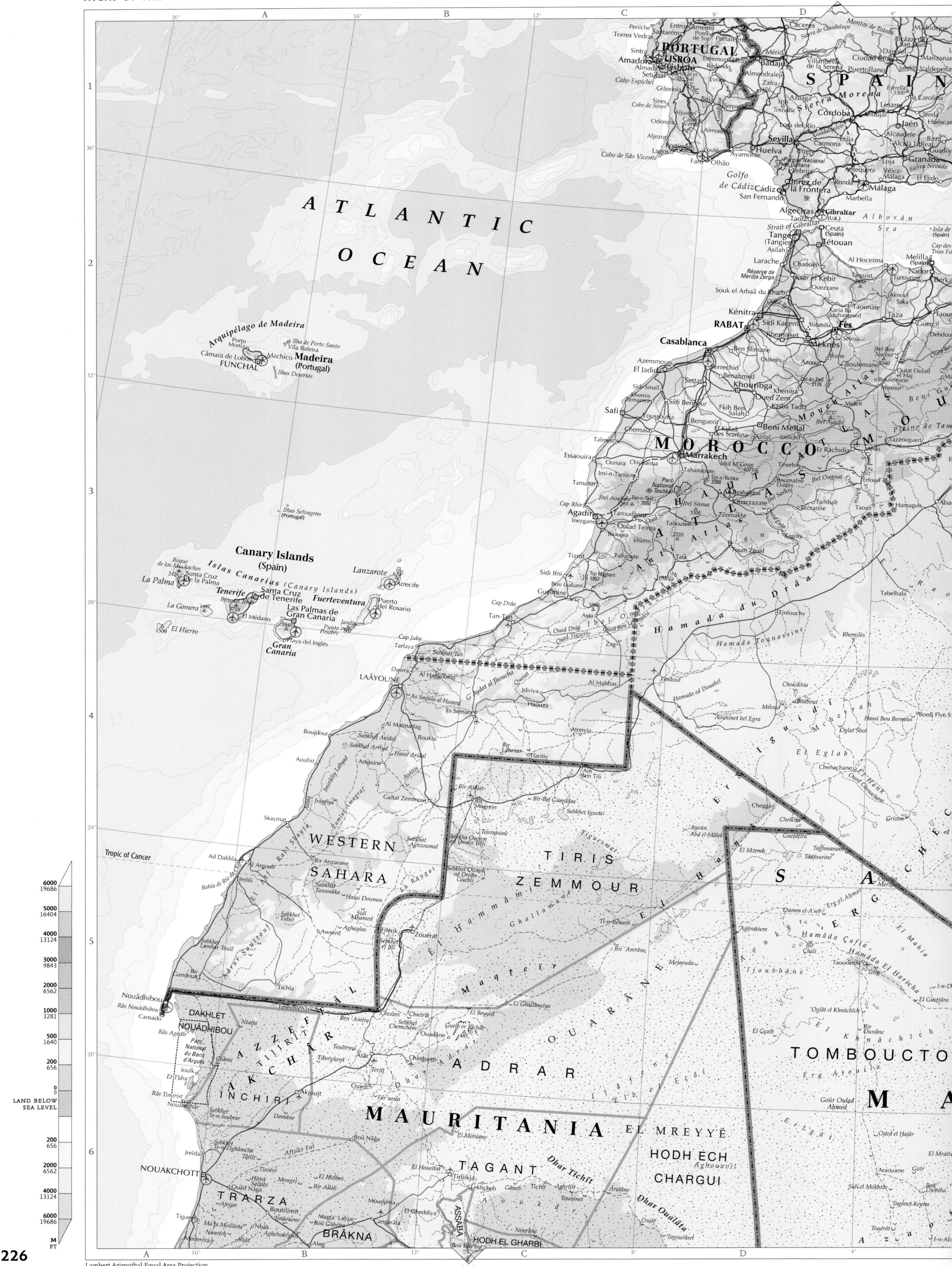

Lambert Azimuthal Equal Area Projection

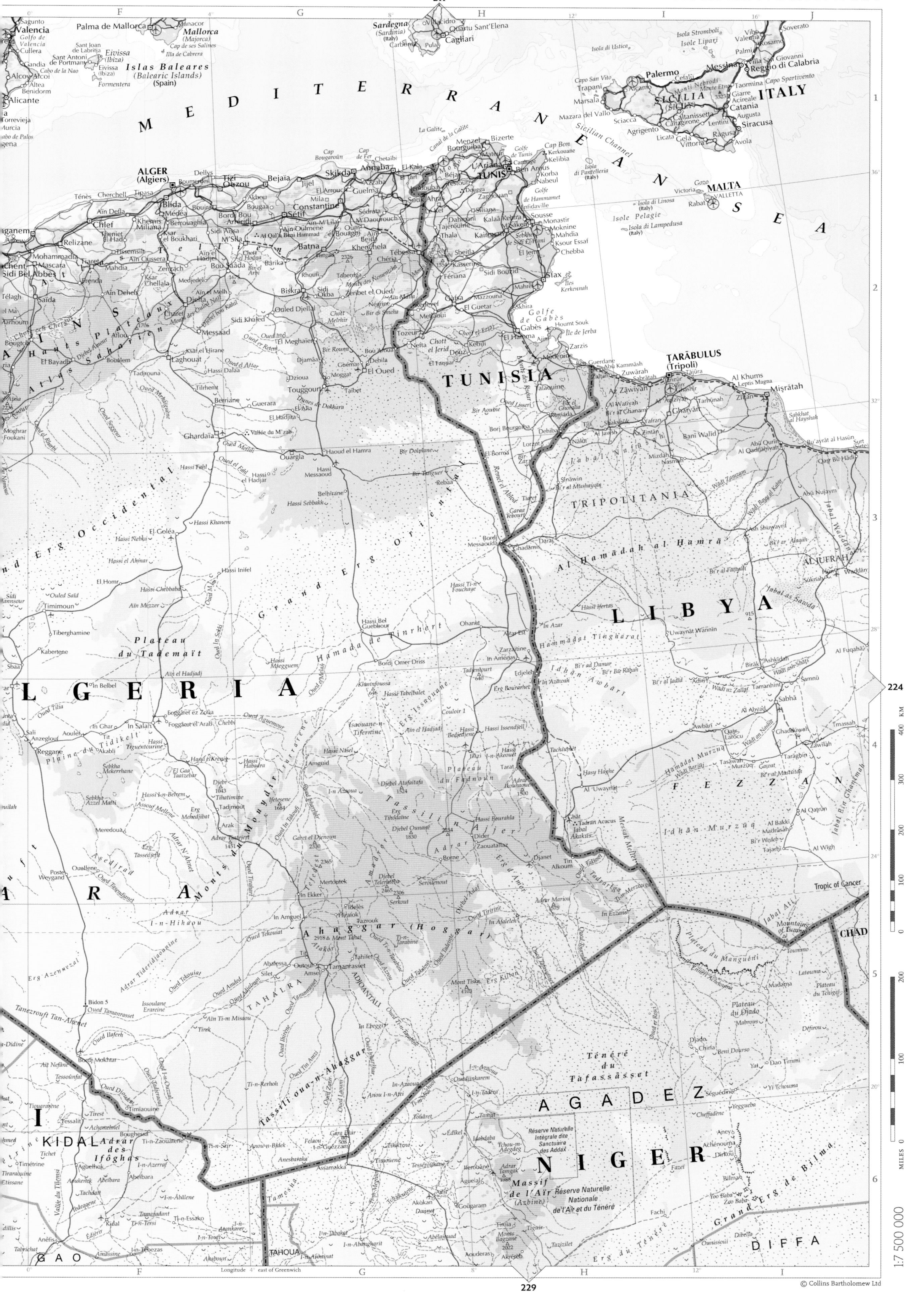

211

MEDITERRANEAN SEA

ALGERIA

TUNISIA

LIBYA

NIGER

CHAD

ITALY

MALTA

Islas Baleares (Balearic Islands) (Spain)

Sardegna (Sardinia) (Italy)

Sicilia (Sicily)

ALGER (Algiers)

TUNIS

ṬARĀBULUS (Tripoli)

VALLETTA

Sicilian Channel

Golfe de Tunis

Golfe de Hammamet

Golfe de Gabès

Grand Erg Occidental

Grand Erg Oriental

Hauts Plateaux

Atlas Saharien

Tell Atlas

Plateau du Tademaït

Tassili n'Ajjer

Ahaggar (Hoggar)

Tassili oua-n-Ahaggar

Adrar des Ifôghas

Massif de l'Aïr (Azbine)

Ténéré du Tafassâsset

Grand Erg de Bilma

Erg du Ténéré

Plateau du Manguéni

Plateau du Djado

TRIPOLITANIA

FEZZAN

Al Ḥamādah al Ḥamrā'

Idhān Awbārī

Idhān Murzūq

Jabal Nafūsah

AGADEZ

DIFFA

KIDAL

GAO

TAHOUA

AL JUFRAH

Réserve Naturelle Intégrale dite Sanctuaire des Addax

Réserve Naturelle Nationale de l'Aïr et du Ténéré

Tropic of Cancer

224

KM 0 100 200 300 400

MILES 0 100 200

1:7 500 000

Longitude 4° east of Greenwich

229

MAURITANIA
SENEGAL
THE GAMBIA
GUINEA-BISSAU
GUINEA
SIERRA LEONE
LIBERIA
CÔTE D'IVOIRE
ATLANTIC OCEAN
NOUAKCHOTT
DAKAR
BANJUL
BISSAU
CONAKRY
FREETOWN
MONROVIA
BAMAKO
YAMOUSSOUKRO
Abidjan
OUAGADOUGOU
CAPE VERDE
AT THE SAME SCALE
Ilhas do Cabo Verde
PRAIA
LAND BELOW SEA LEVEL
Lambert Azimuthal Equal Area Projection
Longitude 4° west of Greenwich

227
224
230
ALGERIA
NIGER
NIGERIA
BENIN
TOGO
CHAD
CAMEROON
CENTRAL AFRICAN REPUBLIC
EQUATORIAL GUINEA
GABON
CONGO
SÃO TOMÉ AND PRÍNCIPE
KIDAL
GAO
TILLABÉRI
TAHOUA
AGADEZ
DOSSO
MARADI
ZINDER
DIFFA
NIAMEY
Niamey
Agadez
Zinder
Maradi
Tahoua
Sokoto
Kano
Kaduna
Zaria
Jos
ABUJA
Lagos
Ibadan
Benin City
Port Harcourt
Calabar
Enugu
Maiduguri
Porto-Novo
Cotonou
LOMÉ
Douala
YAOUNDÉ
MALABO
Bioco
Libreville
LIBREVILLE
São Tomé
Príncipe
Annobón (Equatorial Guinea)
NDJAMENA (Fort Lamy)
Garoua
Maroua
Ngaoundéré
Bight of Benin
Slave Coast
GULF OF GUINEA
Mouths of the Niger
EQUATORIAL GUINEA
Lake Chad
Massif de l'Aïr
Ténéré du Tafassâsset
Grand Erg de Bilma
Adrar des Ifôghas
KANEM
LAC
BORKOU-ENNEDI-TIBESTI
MAYO-KEBBI
CHARI-BAGUIRMI
BORNO
YOBE
JIGAWA
KATSINA
ZAMFARA
KEBBI
KANO
KADUNA
BAUCHI
GOMBE
ADAMAWA
PLATEAU
NIGER
KWARA
OYO
OSUN
OGUN
LAGOS
ONDO
EKITI
KOGI
BENUE
NASSARAWA
TARABA
EDO
DELTA
ANAMBRA
ENUGU
EBONYI
IMO
ABIA
RIVERS
BAYELSA
AKWA IBOM
CROSS RIVER
FEDERAL CAPITAL TERRITORY
EXTRÊME-NORD
NORD
ADAMAOUA
NORD OUEST
OUEST
SUD OUEST
LITTORAL
CENTRE
EST
SUD
RÍO MUNI
WOLEU-NTEM
ESTUAIRE
MOYEN-OGOOUÉ
OGOOUÉ-IVINDO
OGOOUÉ-LOLO
HAUT-OGOOUÉ
NGOUNIÉ
OGOOUÉ MARITIME
SANGHA
CUVETTE
Extent of Lake Chad as shown in Times Comprehensive Atlas 1967
1:7 500 000
KM
MILES

224
232
229
SUDAN
CHAD
CENTRAL AFRICAN REPUBLIC
DEMOCRATIC REPUBLIC
CAMEROON
NIGERIA
GABON
CONGO
EQUATORIAL GUINEA
RWANDA
NORTHERN DARFUR
WESTERN DARFUR
SOUTHERN DARFUR
WESTERN KORDOFAN
SOUTHERN KORDOFAN
NORTHERN BAHR EL GHAZAL
WESTERN BAHR EL GHAZAL
WARAB
WAHDA
EL BUHEYRAT
WESTERN EQUATORIA
OUADDAÏ
SALAMAT
GUÉRA
MOYEN-CHARI
CHARI-BAGUIRMI
MAYO-KEBBI
TANDJILÉ
LOGONE OCCIDENTAL
LOGONE ORIENTAL
VAKAGA
HAUTE-KOTTO
HAUT-MBOMOU
MBOMOU
BAMINGUI-BANGORAN
OUAKA
BASSE-KOTTO
NANA-GRÉBIZI
KÉMO
OUHAM
OUHAM-PENDÉ
OMBELLA-MPOKO
LOBAYE
NANA-MAMBÉRÉ
MAMBÉRÉ-KADÉÏ
SANGHA-MBAÉRÉ
BANGUI
ITURI
HAUT-UELE
BAS-UELE
TSHOPO
NORD-KIVU
NORD-UBANGI
SUD-UBANGI
MONGALA
TSHUAPA
EQUATEUR
LIKOUALA
SANGHA
CUVETTE
CUVETTE OUEST
PLATEAUX
EXTRÊME-NORD
NORD
ADAMAOUA
EST
CENTRE
SUD
LITTORAL
OUEST
NORD-OUEST
SUD-OUEST
BORNO
YOBE
JIGAWA
KANO
BAUCHI
GOMBE
ADAMAWA
TARABA
PLATEAU
NASSARAWA
KADUNA
BENUE
CROSS RIVER
RIO MUNI
WOLEU-NTEM
OGOOUÉ-IVINDO
HAUT-OGOOUÉ
OGOOUÉ-LOLO
MOYEN-OGOOUÉ
NGOUNIÉ
ESTUAIRE
OGOOUÉ-MARITIME
NDJAMENA (Fort Lamy)
YAOUNDÉ
LIBREVILLE
Douala
MALABO
Bioco
Kano
BANGUI
Kisangani
Mbandaka
Equator
Congo Basin
Cameroon Highlands
Lambert Azimuthal Equal Area Projection
6000 19686
5000 16404
4000 13124
3000 9843
2000 6562
1000 3281
500 1640
200 656
0
LAND BELOW SEA LEVEL
200 656
2000 6562
4000 13124
6000 19686
M FT

233
234
ATLANTIC
OCEAN
ANGOLA
CONGO
ZAMBIA
NAMIBIA
BOTSWANA
ZIMBABWE
TANZANIA
LUANDA
KINSHASA
BRAZZAVILLE
LUSAKA
Huambo
Benguela
Lobito
Namibe
Lubumbashi
Pointe-Noire
CABINDA (Angola)
1:7 500 000
MILES
KM

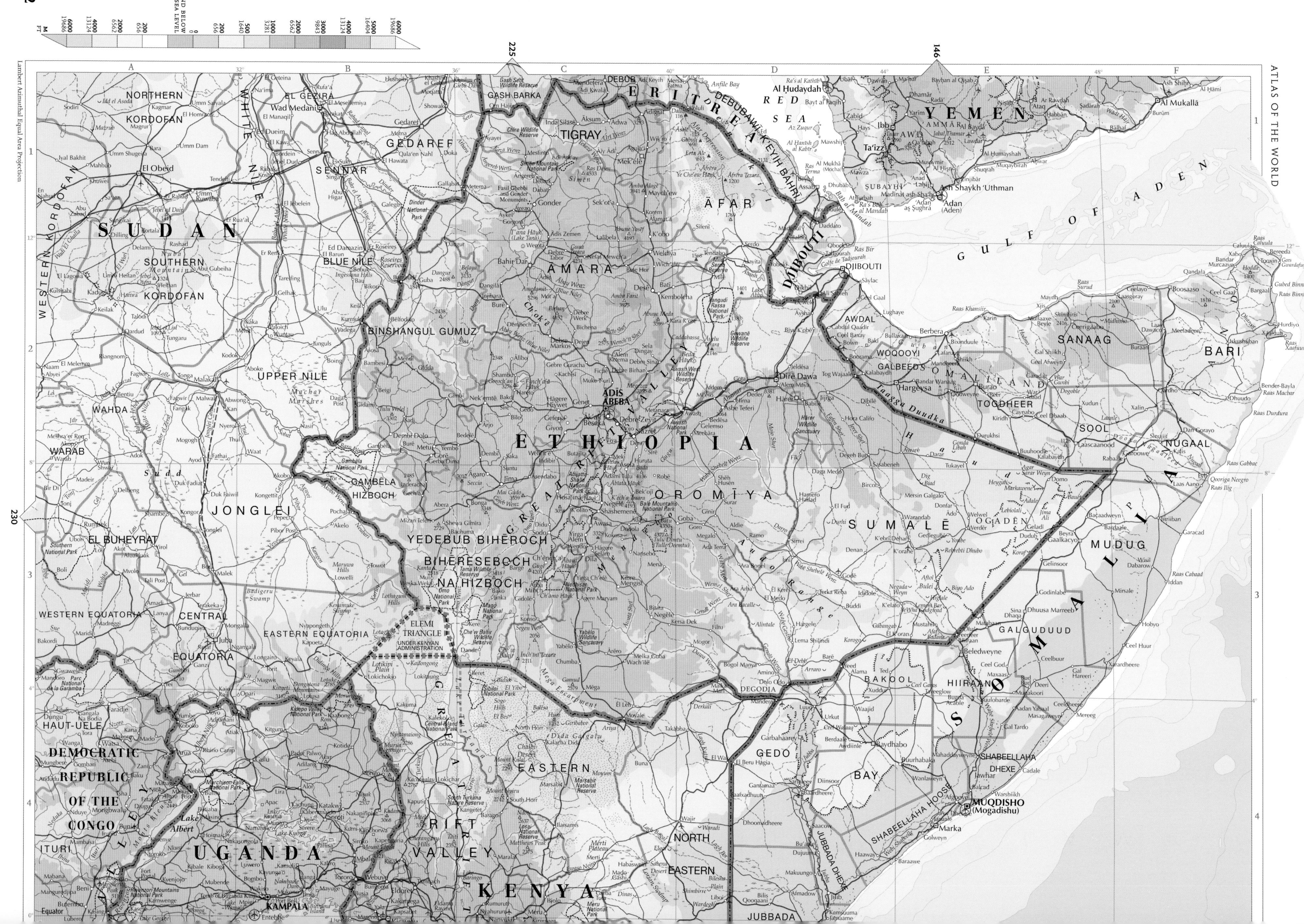
146
225
230
6000
19686
5000
16404
4000
13124
3000
9843
2000
6562
1000
3281
500
1640
200
656
0
LAND BELOW
SEA LEVEL
200
656
2000
6562
4000
13124
6000
19686
M
FT
YEMEN
GULF OF ADEN
RED SEA
DJIBOUTI
ERITREA
ETHIOPIA
SOMALIA
SUDAN
KENYA
UGANDA
DEMOCRATIC REPUBLIC OF THE CONGO
ADIS ABEBA
MUQDISHO (Mogadishu)
KAMPALA
TIGRAY
AMARA
ĀFAR
OROMĪYA
SUMALĒ
GAMBELA HIZBOCH
BINSHANGUL GUMUZ
DEBUBAWĪ KEYIH BAHRĪ
GASH BARKA
GEDAREF
SENNAR
BLUE NILE
UPPER NILE
JONGLEI
WHITE NILE
NORTHERN KORDOFAN
SOUTHERN KORDOFAN
WESTERN KORDOFAN
EL GEZIRA
WAHDA
WARAB
EL BUHEYRAT
CENTRAL EQUATORIA
EASTERN EQUATORIA
WESTERN EQUATORIA
ELEMI TRIANGLE
UNDER KENYAN ADMINISTRATION
HAUT-UÉLÉ
ITURI
NORTH EASTERN
EASTERN
RIFT VALLEY
GEDO
BAY
BAKOOL
HIIRAAN
GALGUDUUD
MUDUG
NUGAAL
BARI
SANAAG
SOOL
TOGDHEER
WOQOOYI GALBEED
AWDAL
SHABEELLAHA HOOSE
SHABEELLAHA DHEXE
JUBBADA DHEXE
Lambert Azimuthal Equal Area Projection

INDIAN OCEAN
Administrative regions numbered on the map:
TANZANIA (C6)
1. PEMBA NORTH
2. PEMBA SOUTH
3. ZANZIBAR NORTH
4. ZANZIBAR SOUTH
5. ZANZIBAR WEST
Aldabra Islands (Seychelles)
Farquhar Islands (Seychelles)
Îles Glorieuses (Seychelles)
COMOROS
MORONI
Mayotte (France)
MOZAMBIQUE CHANNEL
MADAGASCAR
ANTSIRAÑANA
MAHAJANGA
Mahajanga
TANZANIA
Dar es Salaam
Zanzibar Island
Pemba Island
Mafia Island
Mombasa
COAST
ARUSHA
KILIMANJARO
MANYARA
TANGA
MOROGORO
PWANI
LINDI
MTWARA
RUVUMA
IRINGA
MBEYA
SINGIDA
DODOMA
TABORA
SHINYANGA
MWANZA
MARA
KAGERA
KIGOMA
RUKWA
RWANDA
KIGALI
BURUNDI
BUJUMBURA
MALAWI
LILONGWE
CENTRAL
NORTHERN
SOUTHERN
Blantyre
ZAMBIA
NORTHERN
LUAPULA
EASTERN
CENTRAL
LUSAKA
HAUT-KATANGA
DEM. REP. CONGO
MOZAMBIQUE
CABO DELGADO
NIASSA
NAMPULA
Nampula
Nacala
Pemba
ZAMBÉZIA
TETE
ZIMBABWE
MASHONALAND WEST
Lake Tanganyika
Lake Malawi
GREAT RIFT VALLEY
Selous Game Reserve
Parque Nacional das Quirimbas
Longitude 32° east of Greenwich
1:7 500 000
MILES 0 100 200
0 100 200 300 400 KM
231
235

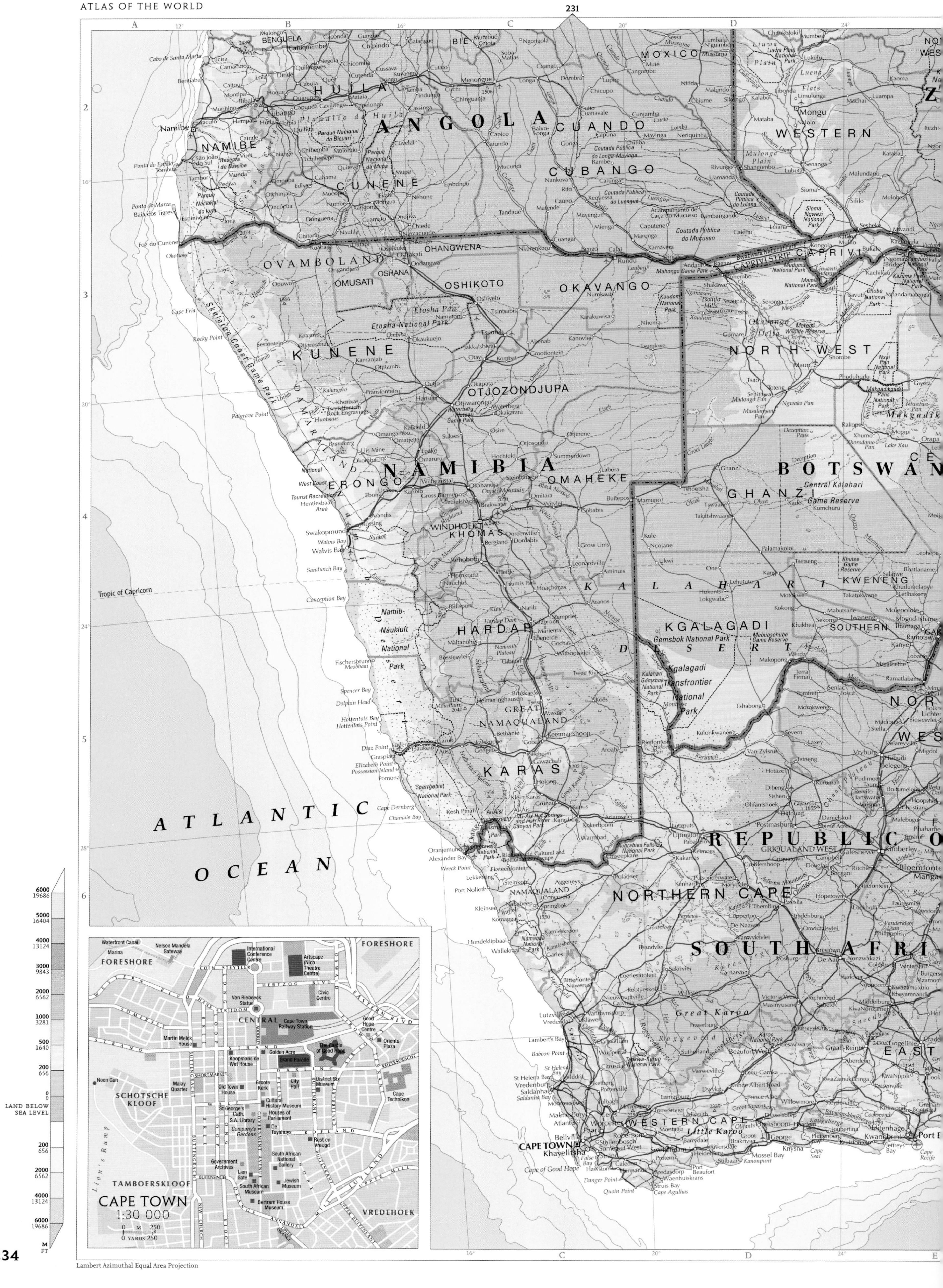

231

ANGOLA

NAMIBIA

BOTSWANA

REPUBLIC OF SOUTH AFRICA

ATLANTIC OCEAN

Tropic of Capricorn

HUÍLA · NAMIBE · CUNENE · CUANDO CUBANGO · MOXICO · OHANGWENA · OVAMBOLAND · OMUSATI · OSHANA · OSHIKOTO · OKAVANGO · KUNENE · OTJOZONDJUPA · ERONGO · OMAHEKE · KHOMAS · HARDAP · KARAS · GHANZI · KGALAGADI · KWENENG · SOUTHERN · NORTH-WEST · WESTERN · NORTHERN CAPE · WESTERN CAPE

KALAHARI DESERT

CAPE TOWN

1:30 000

LAND BELOW SEA LEVEL

M	FT
6000	19686
5000	16404
4000	13124
3000	9843
2000	6562
1000	3281
500	1640
200	656
0	
200	656
2000	6562
4000	13124
6000	19686

Lambert Azimuthal Equal Area Projection

1:7 500 000

MADAGASCAR
AT THE SAME SCALE

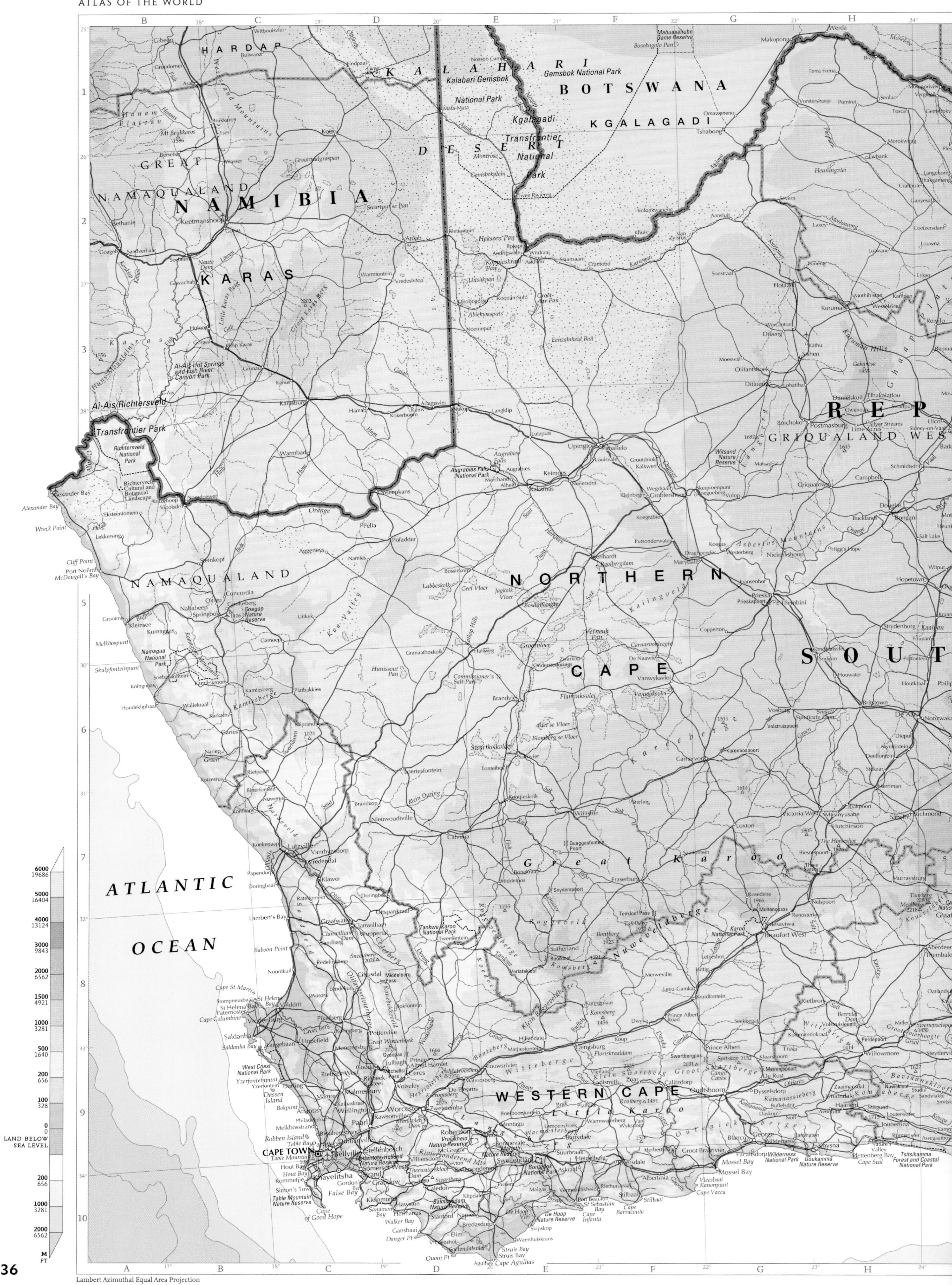
HARDAP
KALAHARI
DESERT
Kalahari Gemsbok National Park
Gemsbok National Park
BOTSWANA
KGALAGADI
Kgalagadi Transfrontier National Park
GREAT NAMAQUALAND
NAMIBIA
KARAS
Ai-Ais Hot Springs and Fish River Canyon Park
Al-Ais/Richtersveld Transfrontier Park
Richtersveld National Park
Richtersveld Cultural and Botanical Landscape
Augrabies Falls National Park
NAMAQUALAND
NORTHERN CAPE
Goegap Nature Reserve
Namaqua National Park
Witsand Nature Reserve
GRIQUALAND WES
REP
SOUT
Great Karoo
Tankwa-Karoo National Park
Karoo National Park
West Coast National Park
WESTERN CAPE
Little Karoo
Wilderness National Park
Goukamma Nature Reserve
Tsitsikamma Forest and Coastal National Park
Table Mountain Nature Reserve
Bontebok National Park
De Hoop Nature Reserve
ATLANTIC OCEAN
CAPE TOWN
Alexander Bay
Wreck Point
Cliff Point
Port Nolloth
McDougall's Bay
Melkbospunt
Skulpfonteinpunt
Lambert's Bay
Baboon Point
Cape St Martin
St Helena Bay
Cape Columbine
Saldanha
Saldanha Bay
Dassen Island
Robben Island
Table Bay
False Bay
Cape of Good Hope
Cape Agulhas
Mossel Bay
Upington
Springbok
Kuruman
Prieska
Beaufort West
Oudtshoorn
George
Knysna
Stellenbosch
Worcester
Paarl
Keetmanshoop
Karasburg
Lambert Azimuthal Equal Area Projection
6000
19686
5000
16404
4000
13124
3000
9843
2000
6562
1500
4921
1000
3281
500
1640
200
656
100
328
0
0
LAND BELOW SEA LEVEL
200
656
1000
3281
2000
6562
M
FT

234

MPUMALANGA
GAUTENG
PRETORIA
Tshwane
Johannesburg
Soweto
Vereeniging
MAPUTO
MOZAMBIQUE
SWAZILAND
HHOHHO
MANZINI
LUBOMBO
SHISELWENI
FREE STATE
Bloemfontein
Mangaung
MASERU
LESOTHO
KWAZULU-NATAL
Pietermaritzburg
Durban
Richards Bay
Port Shepstone
EASTERN CAPE
GRIQUALAND EAST
East London
Port Elizabeth
Uitenhage
Grahamstown
Queenstown
King William's Town
Mdantsane
Algoa Bay
St Francis Bay
Kimberley
Welkom
Newcastle
Ladysmith
iSimangaliso Wetland Park
Maluti Mountains
Drakensberg
INDIAN OCEAN
1:3 300 000
Longitude 26° east of Greenwich
KM
MILES

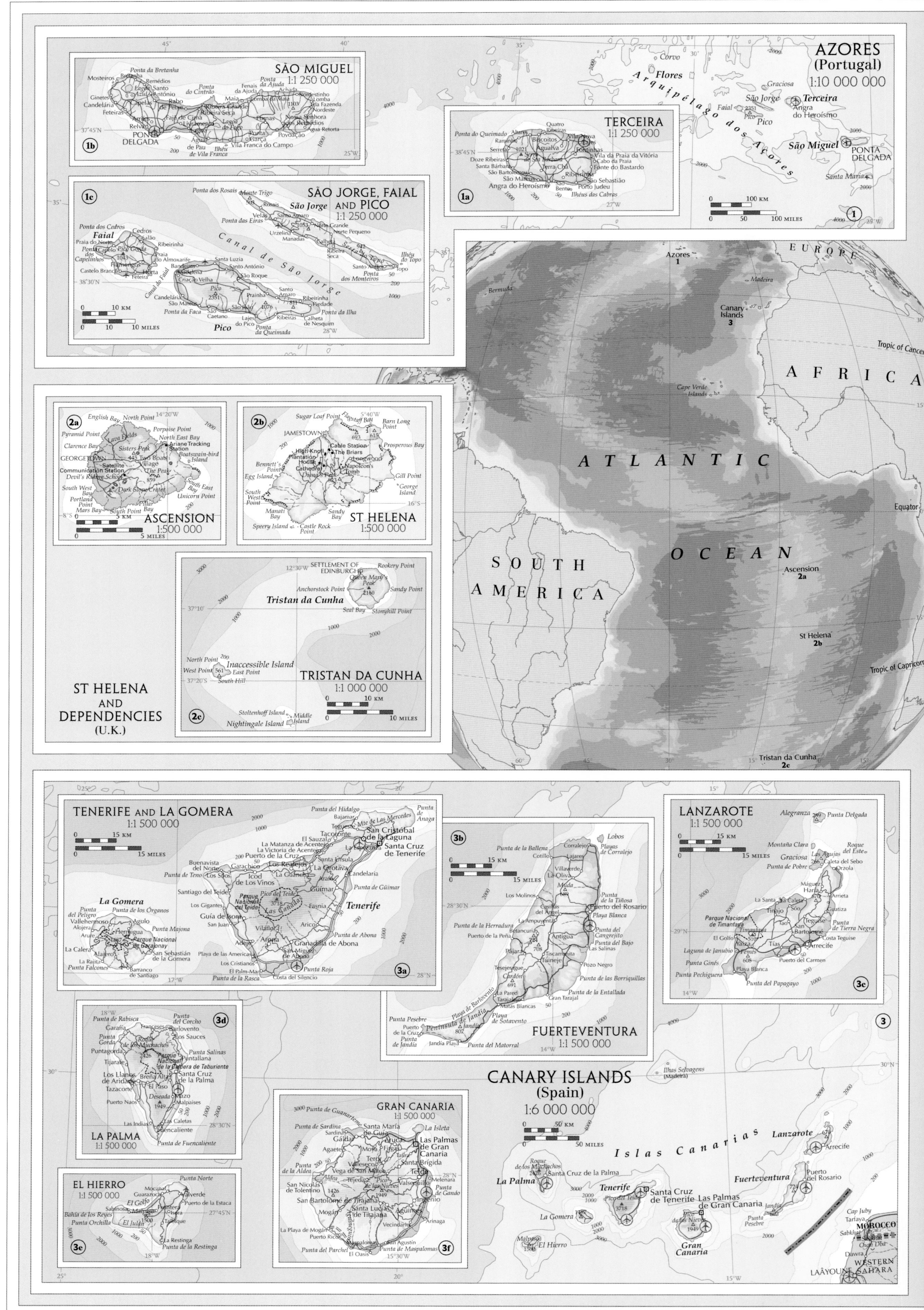

AZORES
(Portugal)
1:10 000 000
Arquipélago dos Açores
Corvo
Flores
Graciosa
São Jorge
Terceira
Angra do Heroísmo
Faial
Pico
São Miguel
PONTA DELGADA
Santa Maria
SÃO MIGUEL
1:1 250 000
TERCEIRA
1:1 250 000
SÃO JORGE, FAIAL AND PICO
1:1 250 000
Canal de São Jorge
EUROPE
Azores
Madeira
Bermuda
Canary Islands
Tropic of Cancer
AFRICA
Cape Verde Islands
ATLANTIC
OCEAN
Equator
SOUTH AMERICA
Ascension
St Helena
Tropic of Capricorn
Tristan da Cunha
ASCENSION
1:500 000
GEORGETOWN
ST HELENA
1:500 000
JAMESTOWN
TRISTAN DA CUNHA
1:1 000 000
SETTLEMENT OF EDINBURGH
Tristan da Cunha
Inaccessible Island
Nightingale Island
ST HELENA AND DEPENDENCIES
(U.K.)
TENERIFE AND LA GOMERA
1:1 500 000
Santa Cruz de Tenerife
Tenerife
La Gomera
FUERTEVENTURA
1:1 500 000
LANZAROTE
1:1 500 000
Arrecife
LA PALMA
1:1 500 000
Santa Cruz de la Palma
EL HIERRO
1:1 500 000
GRAN CANARIA
1:1 500 000
Las Palmas de Gran Canaria
CANARY ISLANDS
(Spain)
1:6 000 000
Islas Canarias
Ilhas Selvagens (Madeira)
La Palma
La Gomera
El Hierro
Gran Canaria
Fuerteventura
Lanzarote
Puerto del Rosario
MOROCCO
WESTERN SAHARA
LAÂYOUNE

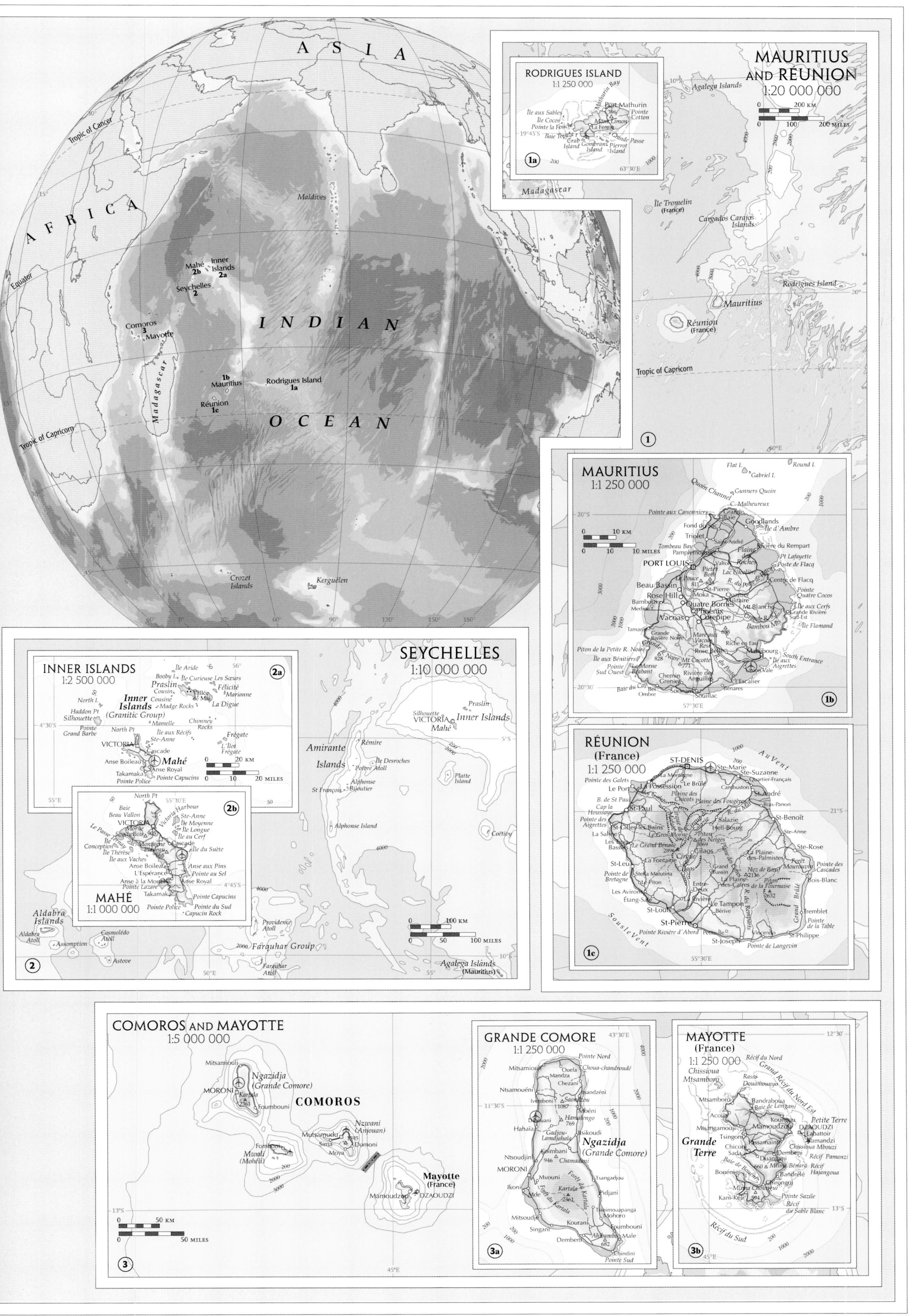
ASIA
AFRICA
INDIAN OCEAN
MAURITIUS AND RÉUNION
1:20 000 000
RODRIGUES ISLAND
1:1 250 000
MAURITIUS
1:1 250 000
RÉUNION
(France)
1:1 250 000
SEYCHELLES
1:10 000 000
INNER ISLANDS
1:2 500 000
MAHÉ
1:1 000 000
COMOROS AND MAYOTTE
1:5 000 000
GRANDE COMORE
1:1 250 000
MAYOTTE
(France)
1:1 250 000
Tropic of Cancer
Tropic of Capricorn
Equator
Maldives
Madagascar
Crozet Islands
Kerguélen
PORT LOUIS
ST-DENIS
VICTORIA
MORONI
DZAOUDZI
MAMOUDZOU

Orthographic Projection

E U R O P E
A F R I C A
A T L A N T I C
O C E A N
Greenland
(Kalaallit Nunaat)
(Denmark)
Greenland Sea
Denmark Strait
Iceland
Baffin Bay
Baffin Island
Davis Strait
Labrador Sea
Hudson Strait
HUDSON BAY
Nuuk
Ilulissat
Ammassalik
Iqaluit
NEWFOUNDLAND AND LABRADOR
QUÉBEC
ONTARIO
Ottawa
Montréal
Québec
Toronto
Boston
New York
Philadelphia
Washington
Bermuda
(U.K.)
GULF OF MEXICO
CARIBBEAN SEA
THE BAHAMAS
Nassau
CUBA
La Habana
JAMAICA
Kingston
HAITI
DOMINICAN REPUBLIC
Santo Domingo
Puerto Rico
(U.S.A.)
BELIZE
Belmopan
GUATEMALA
HONDURAS
Tegucigalpa
NICARAGUA
Managua
EL SALVADOR
San Salvador
COSTA RICA
San José
PANAMA
Panamá
SOUTH AMERICA
Tropic of Cancer
Equator
Arquipélago dos Açores
Arquipélago da Madeira
Islas Canarias
Ilhas do Cabo Verde
1:27 000 000

BERING SEA
RUSSIAN FEDERATION
ARCTIC OCEAN
BEAUFORT SEA
Chukchi Sea
Bering Strait
ALEUTIAN ISLANDS
Pribilof Islands
Fox Islands
Andreanof Islands
U.S.A.
ALASKA
Brooks Range
Philip Smith Mountains
Alaska Range
Kuskokwim Mountains
Ahklun Mts
Bristol Bay
Cook Inlet
Anchorage
Shelikof Strait
Kodiak
GULF OF ALASKA
Yakutat Bay
Alexander Archipelago
Prince of Wales Island
Dixon Entrance
Queen Charlotte Islands
Queen Charlotte Sound
Vancouver Island
PACIFIC OCEAN
YUKON TERRITORY
NORTHWEST TERRITORIES
Mackenzie Mountains
Great Bear Lake
Great Slave Lake
Yellowknife
Banks Island
Amundsen Gulf
BRITISH COLUMBIA
ROCKY MOUNTAINS
Coast Mountains
ALBERTA
Edmonton
Calgary
SASKATCHEWAN
Saskatoon
Regina
Vancouver
Victoria
Seattle
Tacoma
WASHINGTON
Spokane
Portland
Salem
Eugene
OREGON
IDAHO
Boise
Snake River Plain
MONTANA
Great Falls
Billings
WYOMING
NEVADA
Reno
UTAH
Salt Lake City
CALIFORNIA
Sacramento
San Francisco
Oakland
San Jose
Stockton
Modesto
Fresno
Salinas
UNITED STATES OF AMERICA
Lambert Conformal Conic Projection
LAND BELOW SEA LEVEL
M
FT
153
252

Greenland
(Kalaallit Nunaat)
(Denmark)
GREENLAND SEA
ICELAND
Denmark Strait
BAFFIN BAY
Davis Strait
LABRADOR SEA
ATLANTIC OCEAN
HUDSON BAY
James Bay
Hudson Strait
Foxe Basin
Ungava Bay
NUNAVUT
NUNAVIK
QUÉBEC
ONTARIO
NEWFOUNDLAND AND LABRADOR
NEW BRUNSWICK
NOVA SCOTIA
PRINCE EDWARD ISLAND
MANITOBA
CANADIAN SHIELD
QUEEN ELIZABETH ISLANDS
Ellesmere Island
Devon Island
Baffin Island
Southampton Island
Lake Superior
Lake Michigan
Lake Huron
Lake Erie
MINNESOTA
WISCONSIN
MICHIGAN
IOWA
PENNSYLVANIA
NEW YORK
VERMONT
NEW HAMPSHIRE
MAINE
Gulf of St Lawrence
Gulf of Maine
Cabot Strait
OTTAWA
Montréal
Québec
Toronto
Boston
New York
Philadelphia
Chicago
Milwaukee
Detroit
Cleveland
Minneapolis
Halifax
St John's
Thunder Bay
Longitude 70° west of Greenwich
1:15 000 000
KM
MILES

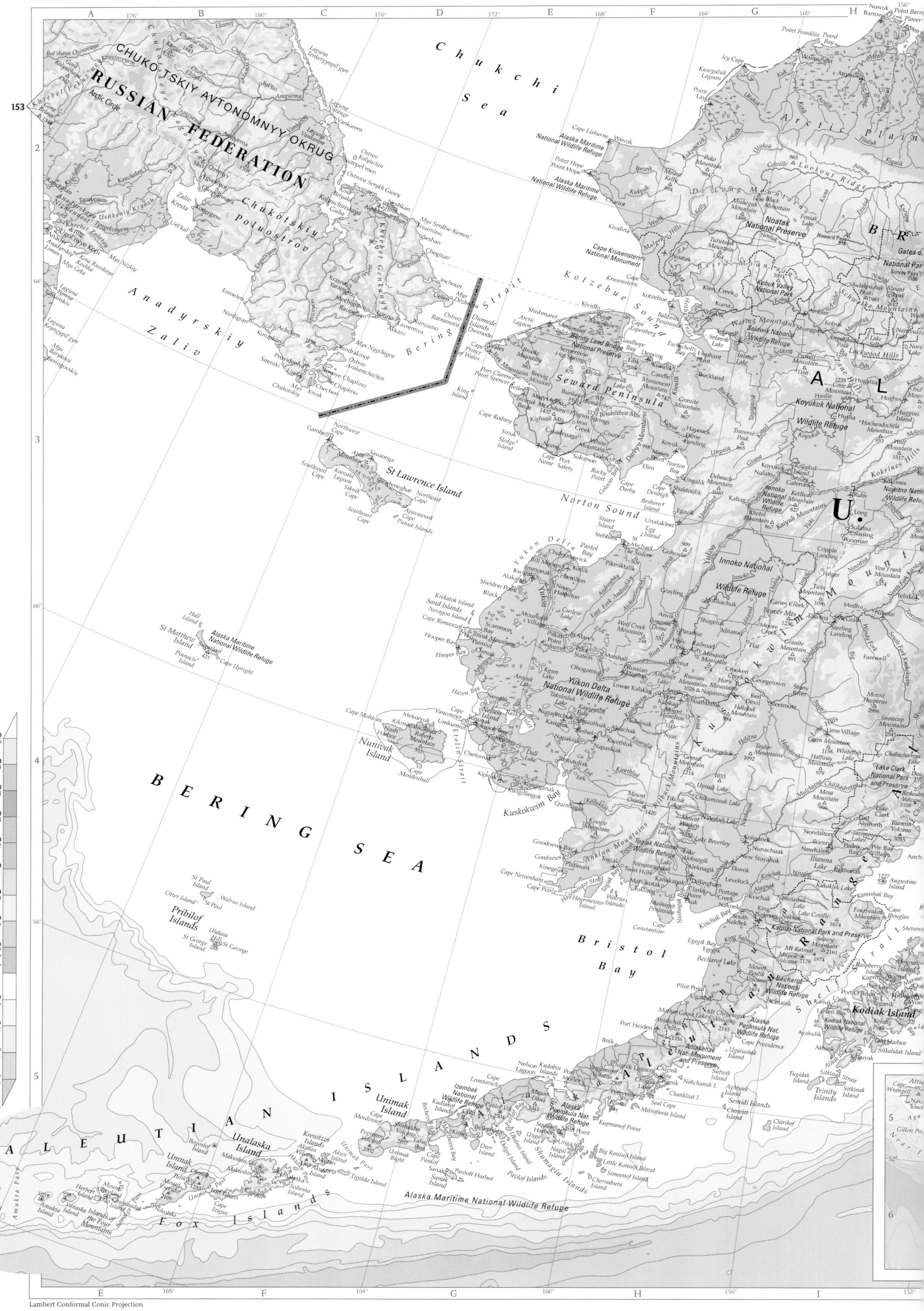

CHUKOTSKIY AVTONOMNYY OKRUG

RUSSIAN FEDERATION

Chukchi Sea

Chukotskiy Poluostrov

Anadyrskiy Zaliv

Bering Strait

Kotzebue Sound

Seward Peninsula

St Lawrence Island

Norton Sound

Nunivak Island

BERING SEA

Pribilof Islands

Bristol Bay

ALEUTIAN ISLANDS

Unimak Island

Unalaska Island

Fox Islands

Alaska Maritime National Wildlife Refuge

Kodiak Island

Lambert Conformal Conic Projection

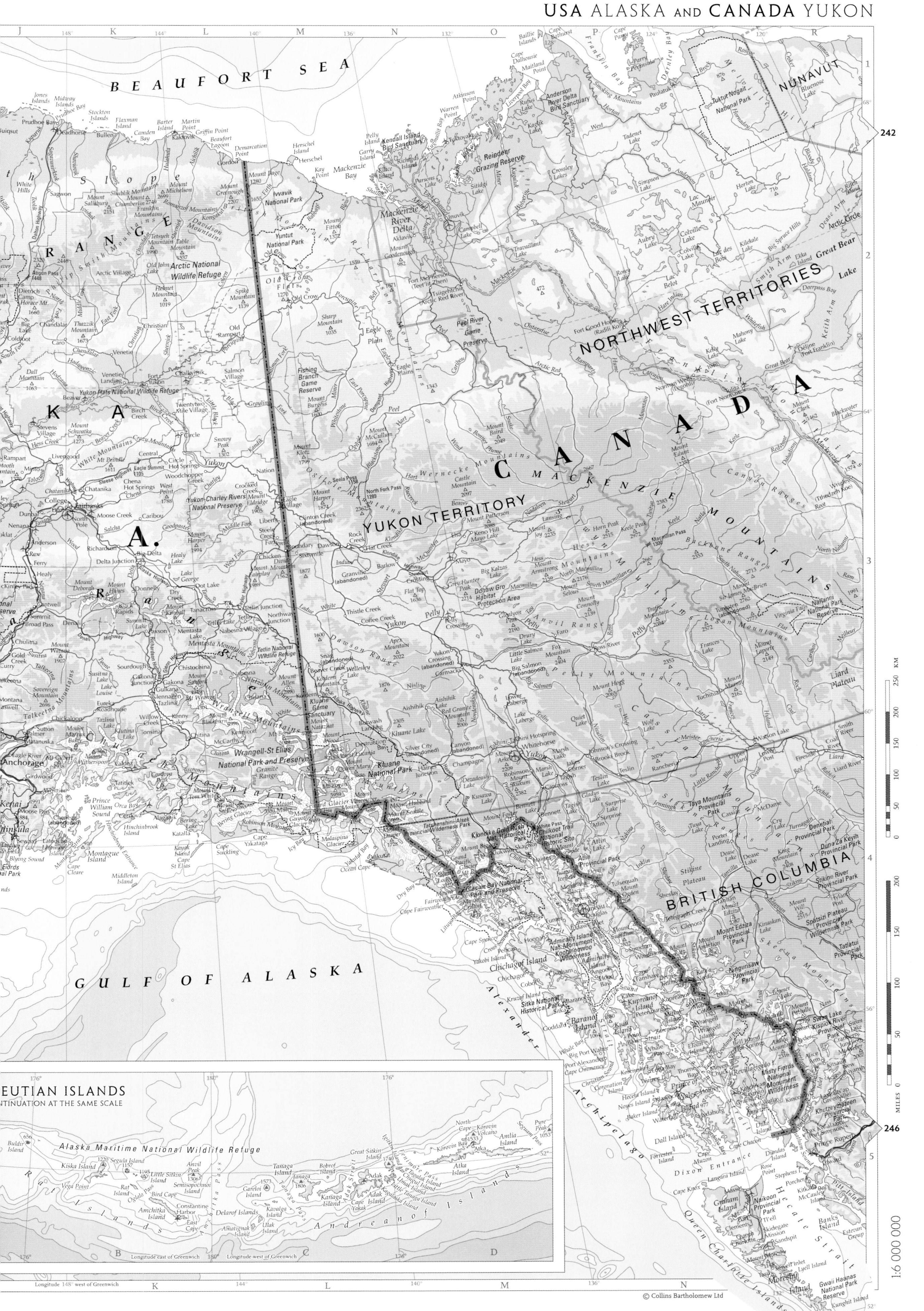
BEAUFORT SEA
GULF OF ALASKA
CANADA
YUKON TERRITORY
NORTHWEST TERRITORIES
BRITISH COLUMBIA
NUNAVUT
ALEUTIAN ISLANDS
CONTINUATION AT THE SAME SCALE
1:6 000 000

245
242
245
262
YUKON TERRITORY
NORTHWEST TERR
MACKENZIE MOUNTAINS
ALASKA
U.S.A.
BRITISH
COLUMBIA
ALBERT
COAST MOUNTAINS
COLUMBIA MOUNTAINS
ROCKY MOUNTAINS
SELKIRK MOUNTAINS
CARIBOO MOUNTAINS
WASHINGTON
IDAHO
MO
CANADA
U.S.A.
PACIFIC
OCEAN
Great Bear Lake
Great Slave Lake
Liard Plateau
Stikine Plateau
Fraser Plateau
Horn Mountains
Cariboo Mountains
Cassiar Mountains
Pelly Mountains
Selwyn Mountains
Alexander Archipelago
Queen Charlotte Islands
Queen Charlotte Sound
Hecate Strait
Dixon Entrance
Vancouver Island
Strait of Georgia
Graham Island
Yakutat Bay
Dry Bay
Whitehorse
Dawson Range
Carmacks
Faro
Ross River
Watson Lake
Teslin
Juneau
Sitka
Ketchikan
Prince Rupert
Terrace
Kitimat
Stewart
Smithers
Fort St James
Prince George
Quesnel
Williams Lake
Fort Nelson
Fort St John
Dawson Creek
Grande Prairie
Peace River
Hay River
Fort Simpson
Fort Providence
Yellowknife
Kamloops
Kelowna
Vernon
Penticton
Revelstoke
Golden
Banff
Calgary
Red Deer
Edson
Hinton
Jasper National Park
Vancouver
North Vancouver
Burnaby
Coquitlam
Surrey
Langley
Abbotsford
Chilliwack
Victoria
Nanaimo
Port Alberni
Campbell River
Courtenay
Port Hardy
Bella Coola
Tofino
Cape Flattery
Cape Scott
Cape St James
Mount Waddington
Kluane National Park
Glacier Bay National Park
Nahanni National Park Reserve
Great Bear Lake
Mackenzie
Liard
Fraser
Peace
Stikine
Skeena
Yukon
Pelly
Conic Equidistant Projection
6000
19686
5000
16404
4000
13124
3000
9843
2000
6562
1000
3281
500
1640
200
656
0
LAND BELOW
SEA LEVEL
200
656
2000
6562
4000
13124
6000
19686
M
FT

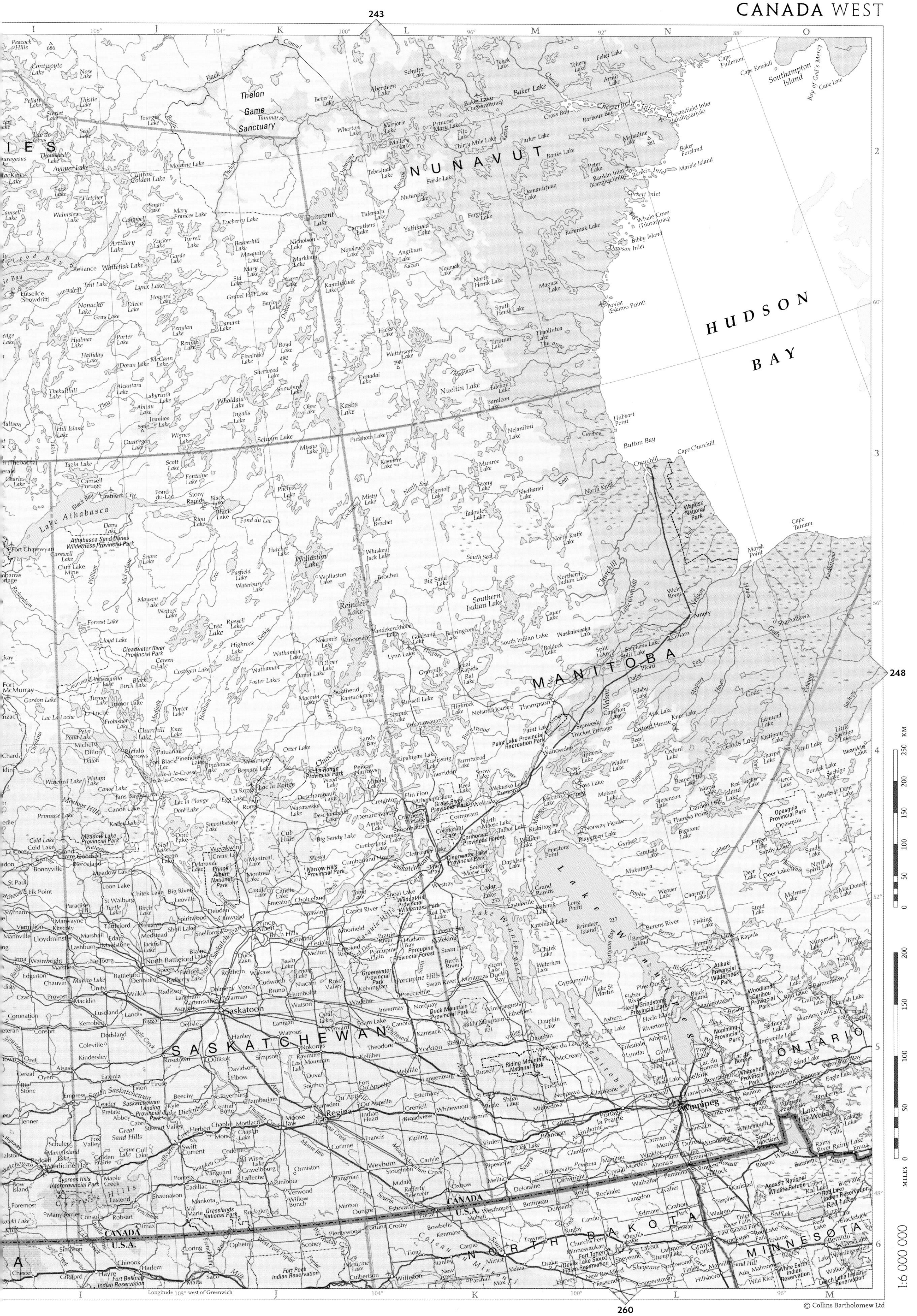
243
248
260
NUNAVUT
MANITOBA
SASKATCHEWAN
ONTARIO
NORTH DAKOTA
MINNESOTA
HUDSON BAY
CANADA
U.S.A.
Thelon Game Sanctuary
Southampton Island
Lake Athabasca
Reindeer Lake
Southern Indian Lake
Lake Winnipeg
Lake Winnipegosis
Lake Manitoba
Lake of the Woods
Prince Albert National Park
Riding Mountain National Park
Wapusk National Park
Grasslands National Park
Churchill
Thompson
Flin Flon
The Pas
Prince Albert
Saskatoon
Regina
Moose Jaw
Swift Current
Medicine Hat
Brandon
Winnipeg
Yorkton
Lloydminster
North Battleford
Baker Lake (Qamanittuaq)
Rankin Inlet (Kangiqcliniq)
Arviat (Eskimo Point)
Chesterfield Inlet (Igluligaarjuk)
Whale Cove (Tikirarjuaq)
Grand Forks
Minot
Longitude 108° west of Greenwich
KM
MILES
1:6 000 000

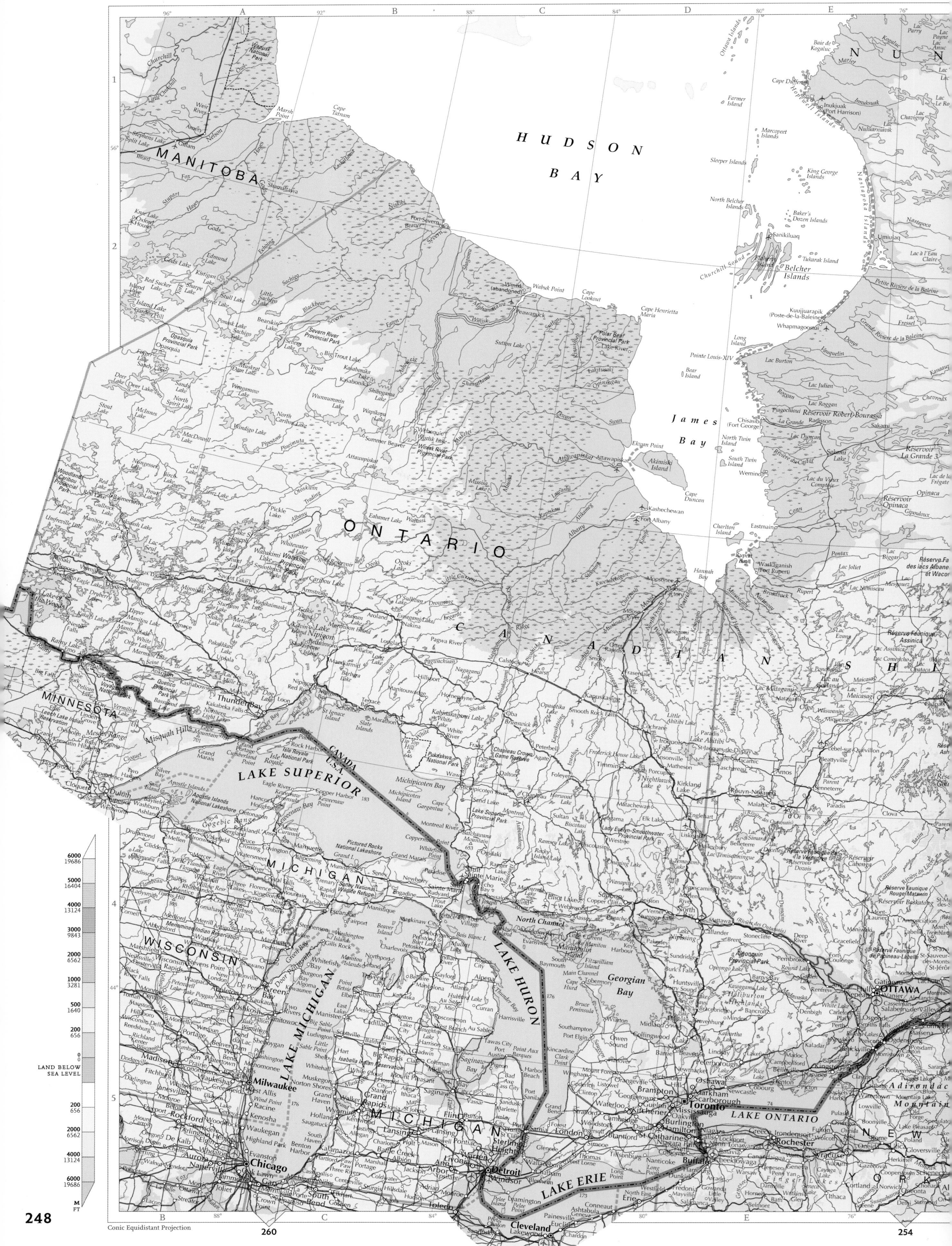

HUDSON BAY

James Bay

MANITOBA

ONTARIO

CANADIAN SHIELD

MINNESOTA

WISCONSIN

MICHIGAN

NEW YORK

LAKE SUPERIOR

LAKE MICHIGAN

LAKE HURON

LAKE ERIE

LAKE ONTARIO

Georgian Bay

M	FT
6000	19686
5000	16404
4000	13124
3000	9843
2000	6562
1000	3281
500	1640
200	656
0	0
LAND BELOW SEA LEVEL	
200	656
2000	6562
4000	13124
6000	19686

Conic Equidistant Projection

260

254

LABRADOR SEA
NEWFOUNDLAND AND LABRADOR
LABRADOR
Newfoundland
GULF OF ST LAWRENCE
Cabot Strait
Détroit d'Honguedo
ATLANTIC OCEAN
Ungava Bay
Gulf of Maine
Bay of Fundy
NEW BRUNSWICK
NOVA SCOTIA
PRINCE EDWARD ISLAND
MAINE
NEW HAMPSHIRE
QUÉBEC
St Pierre and Miquelon (France)
Île d'Anticosti
Îles de la Madeleine
Cape Breton Island
Sable Island
Smallwood Reservoir
Lake Melville
Péninsule de la Gaspésie
Torngat Mountains
Mealy Mountains
Long Range Mountains
Strait of Belle Isle
Halifax
Saint John
Fredericton
Charlottetown
St John's
Québec
Boston
Portland
Bangor
Happy Valley-Goose Bay
Sept-Îles
Chicoutimi
Rimouski
Moncton
Sydney
Corner Brook
Gander
1:6 000 000
MILES
KM

248

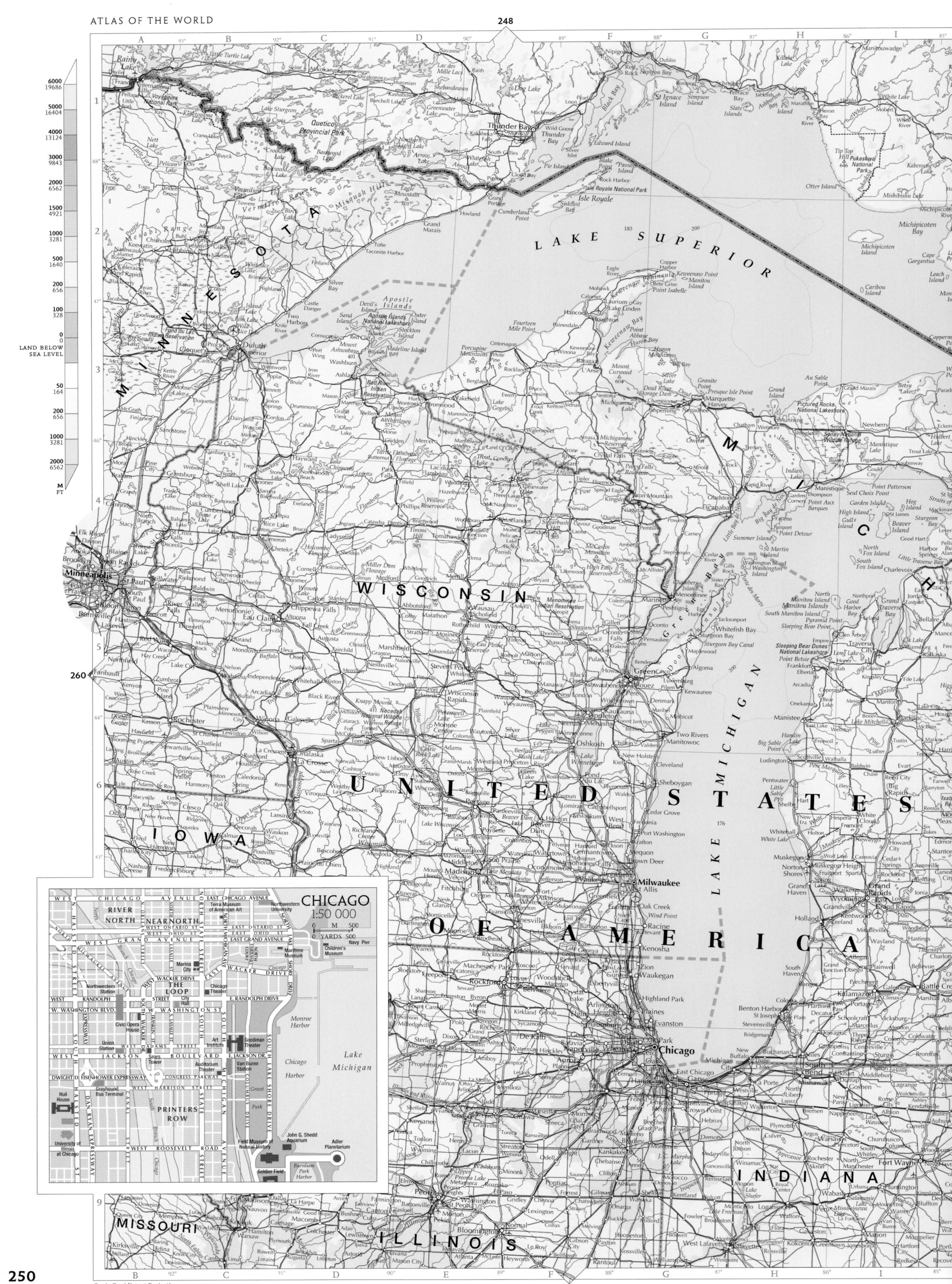

260

254

Conic Equidistant Projection

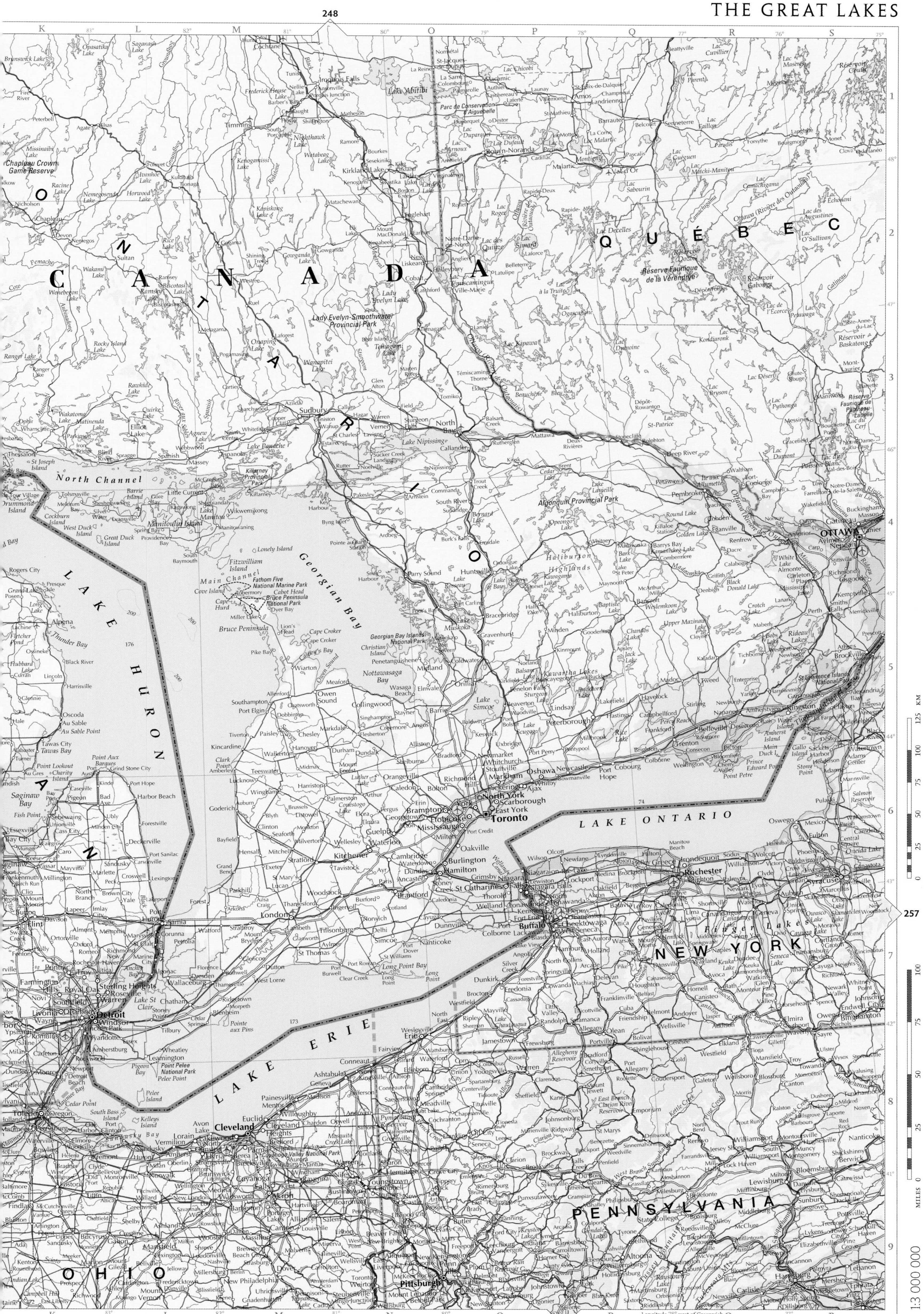
248
CANADA
ONTARIO
QUÉBEC
NEW YORK
PENNSYLVANIA
OHIO
LAKE HURON
LAKE ONTARIO
LAKE ERIE
Georgian Bay
North Channel
Lake Nipissing
Lake Simcoe
Lake St Clair
Algonquin Provincial Park
Lady Evelyn-Smoothwater Provincial Park
Chapleau Crown Game Reserve
Réserve Faunique de la Vérendrye
Georgian Bay Islands National Park
Bruce Peninsula National Park
Fathom Five National Marine Park
Point Pelee National Park
St Lawrence Islands National Park
Cuyahoga Valley National Park
Manitoulin Island
Bruce Peninsula
Finger Lakes
OTTAWA
Toronto
Detroit
Cleveland
Buffalo
Rochester
Pittsburgh
Sudbury
Timmins
Hamilton
Kitchener
London
Kingston
Syracuse
Erie
Toledo
Windsor
257
254
1:3 000 000
KM
MILES
Longitude 78° west of Greenwich

242

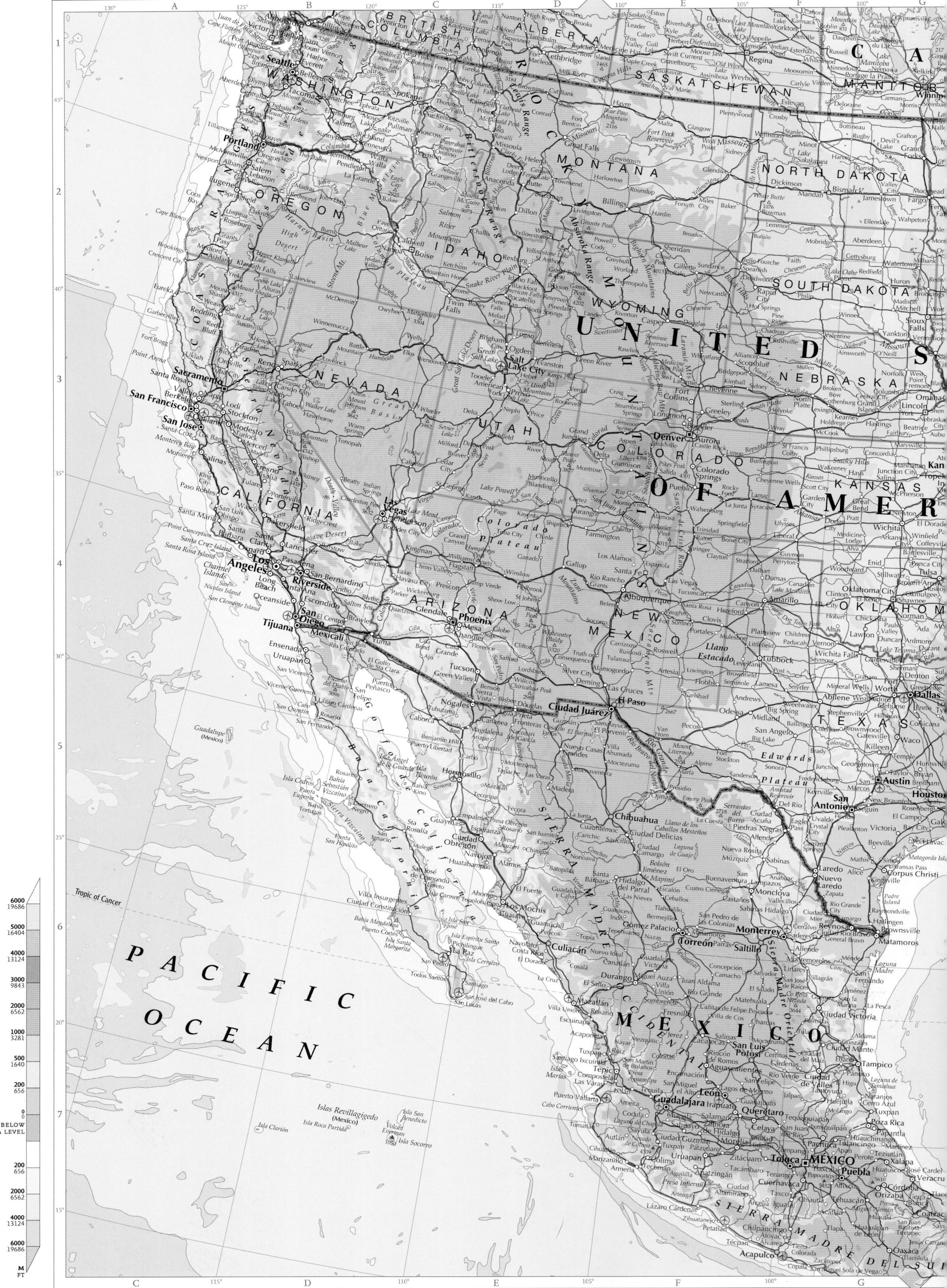

Lambert Conformal Conic Projection

266

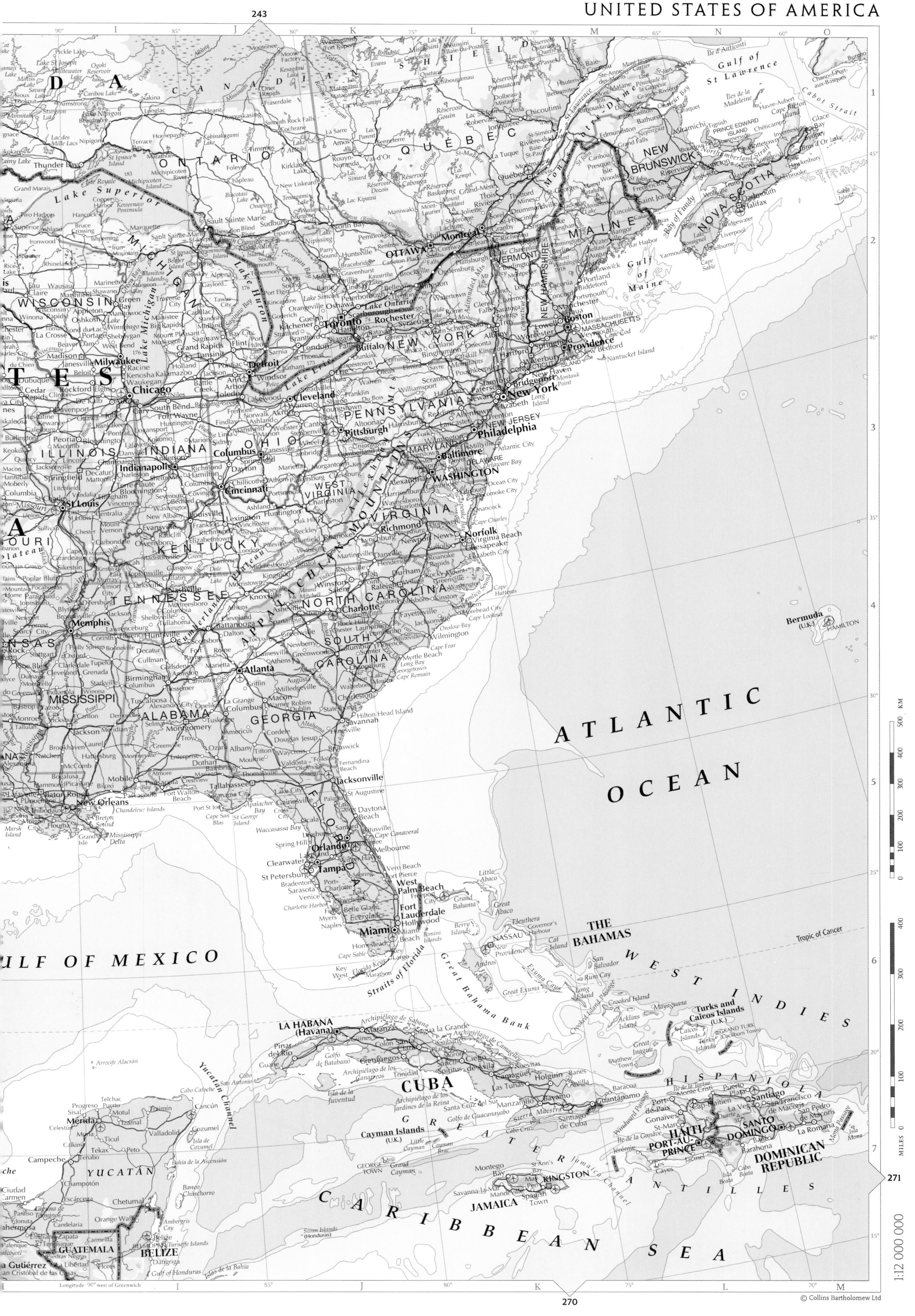
243
271
270
ATLANTIC OCEAN
GULF OF MEXICO
CARIBBEAN SEA
WEST INDIES
GREATER ANTILLES
Gulf of St Lawrence
Gulf of Maine
ONTARIO
QUÉBEC
NEW BRUNSWICK
NOVA SCOTIA
PRINCE EDWARD ISLAND
MAINE
VERMONT
NEW HAMPSHIRE
MASSACHUSETTS
NEW YORK
PENNSYLVANIA
NEW JERSEY
MARYLAND
DELAWARE
WEST VIRGINIA
VIRGINIA
NORTH CAROLINA
SOUTH CAROLINA
GEORGIA
FLORIDA
ALABAMA
MISSISSIPPI
TENNESSEE
KENTUCKY
OHIO
INDIANA
ILLINOIS
MICHIGAN
WISCONSIN
APPALACHIAN MOUNTAINS
Lake Superior
Lake Michigan
Lake Huron
Lake Erie
Lake Ontario
OTTAWA
Montréal
Québec
Toronto
Chicago
Detroit
Cleveland
Pittsburgh
Buffalo
Boston
Providence
New York
Philadelphia
Baltimore
WASHINGTON
Richmond
Norfolk
Charlotte
Atlanta
Jacksonville
Orlando
Tampa
Miami
Memphis
Nashville
St Louis
Indianapolis
Columbus
Cincinnati
Milwaukee
New Orleans
Halifax
Bermuda (U.K.)
HAMILTON
THE BAHAMAS
NASSAU
Tropic of Cancer
LA HABANA (Havana)
CUBA
Cayman Islands (U.K.)
JAMAICA
KINGSTON
HISPANIOLA
HAITI
PORT-AU-PRINCE
DOMINICAN REPUBLIC
SANTO DOMINGO
Turks and Caicos Islands (U.K.)
YUCATÁN
BELIZE
GUATEMALA
Straits of Florida
Yucatan Channel
Longitude 90° west of Greenwich
MILES
KM
1:12 000 000

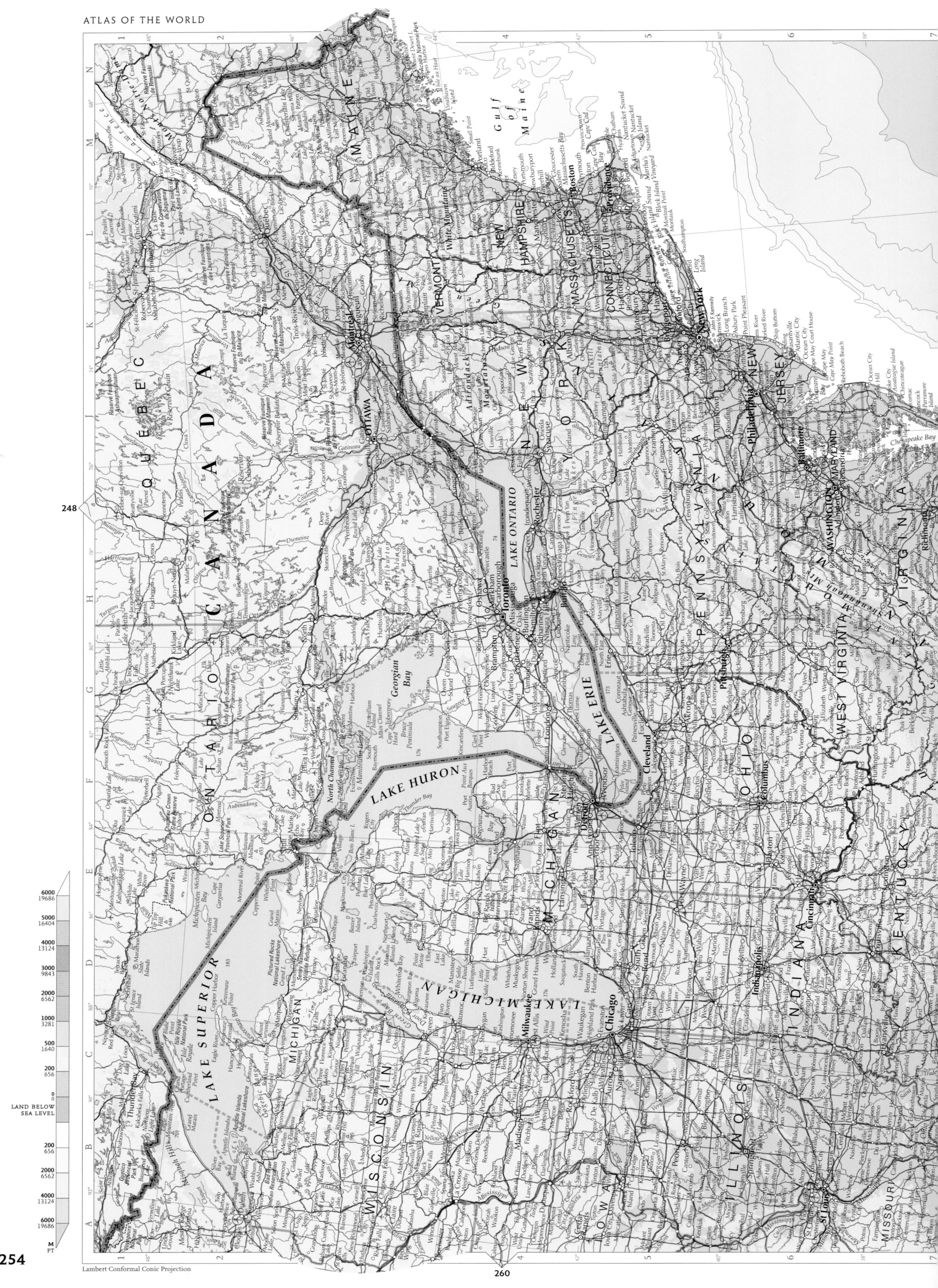

Lambert Conformal Conic Projection

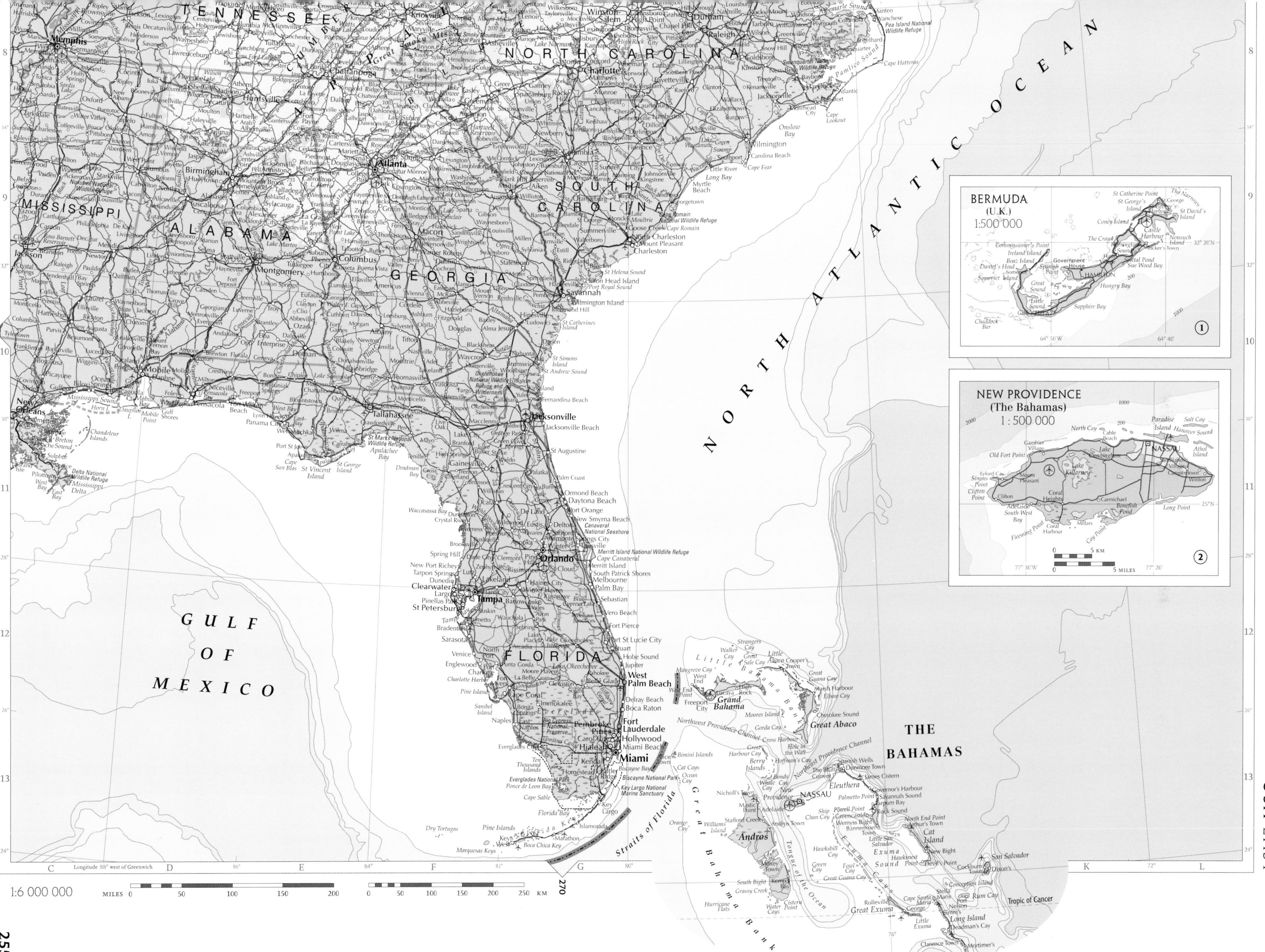
NORTH ATLANTIC OCEAN
GULF OF MEXICO
THE BAHAMAS
BERMUDA
(U.K.)
1:500 000
NEW PROVIDENCE
(The Bahamas)
1 : 500 000
NASSAU
TENNESSEE
NORTH CAROLINA
SOUTH CAROLINA
GEORGIA
ALABAMA
MISSISSIPPI
FLORIDA
Memphis
Atlanta
Charlotte
Raleigh
Birmingham
Montgomery
Columbus
Macon
Savannah
Charleston
Wilmington
Jacksonville
Tallahassee
Mobile
Pensacola
New Orleans
Orlando
Tampa
St Petersburg
Clearwater
West Palm Beach
Fort Lauderdale
Hollywood
Miami
Grand Bahama
Great Abaco
Andros
Eleuthera
Great Exuma
Long Island
Cat Island
San Salvador
Straits of Florida
Great Bahama Bank
Tongue of the Ocean
Tropic of Cancer
Longitude 88° west of Greenwich
1:6 000 000
MILES 0 50 100 150 200
0 50 100 150 200 250 KM

261

270

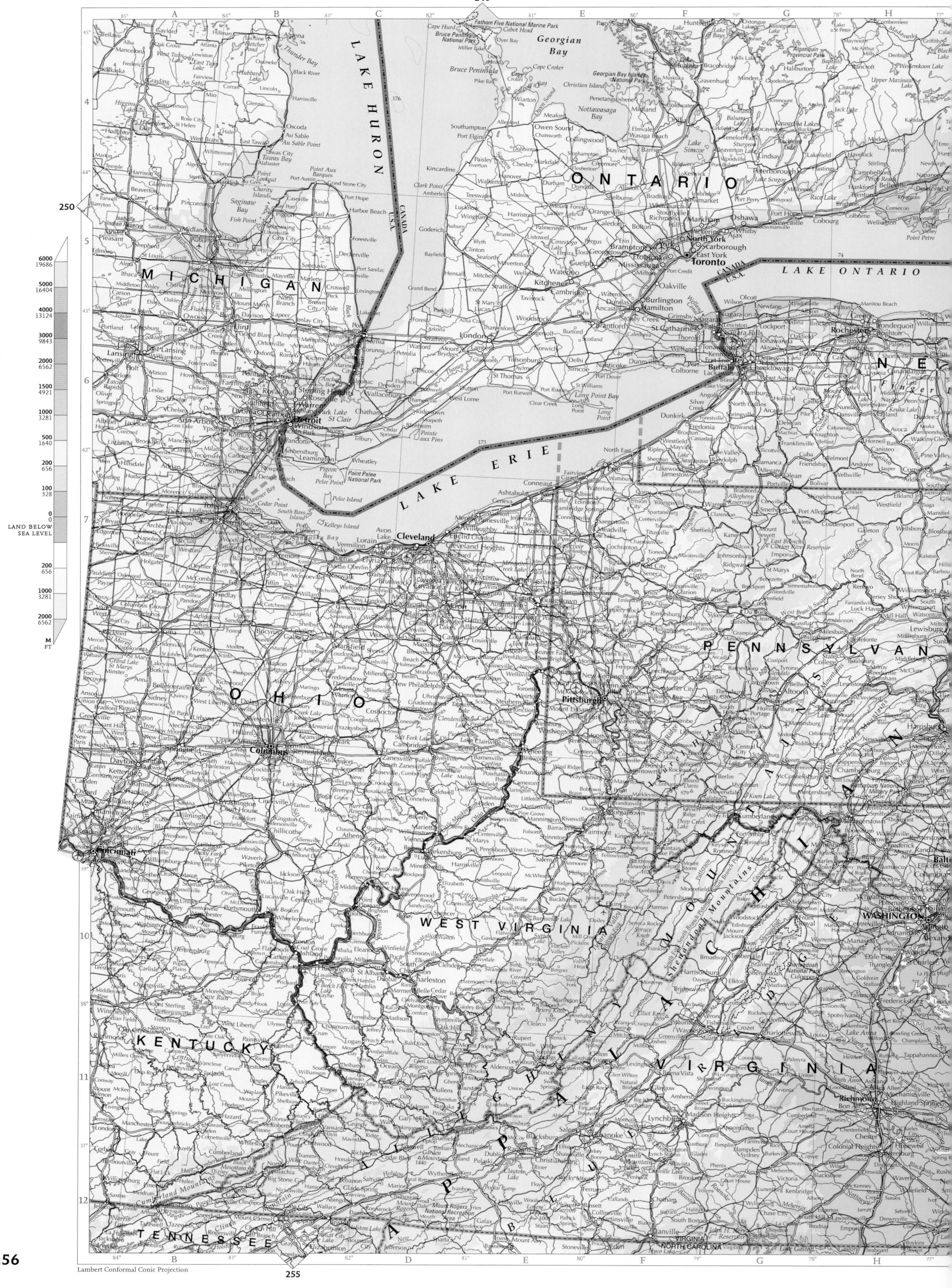

248

250

M	FT
6000	19686
5000	16404
4000	13124
3000	9843
2000	6562
1500	4921
1000	3281
500	1640
200	656
100	328
0	0
LAND BELOW SEA LEVEL	
200	656
1000	3281
2000	6562

MICHIGAN

ONTARIO

LAKE HURON

Georgian Bay

LAKE ONTARIO

LAKE ERIE

OHIO

PENNSYLVANIA

WEST VIRGINIA

KENTUCKY

VIRGINIA

TENNESSEE

NORTH CAROLINA

APPALACHIAN MOUNTAINS

WASHINGTON

Lambert Conformal Conic Projection

255

MAINE
CONTINUATION AT THE SAME SCALE

1:3 000 000

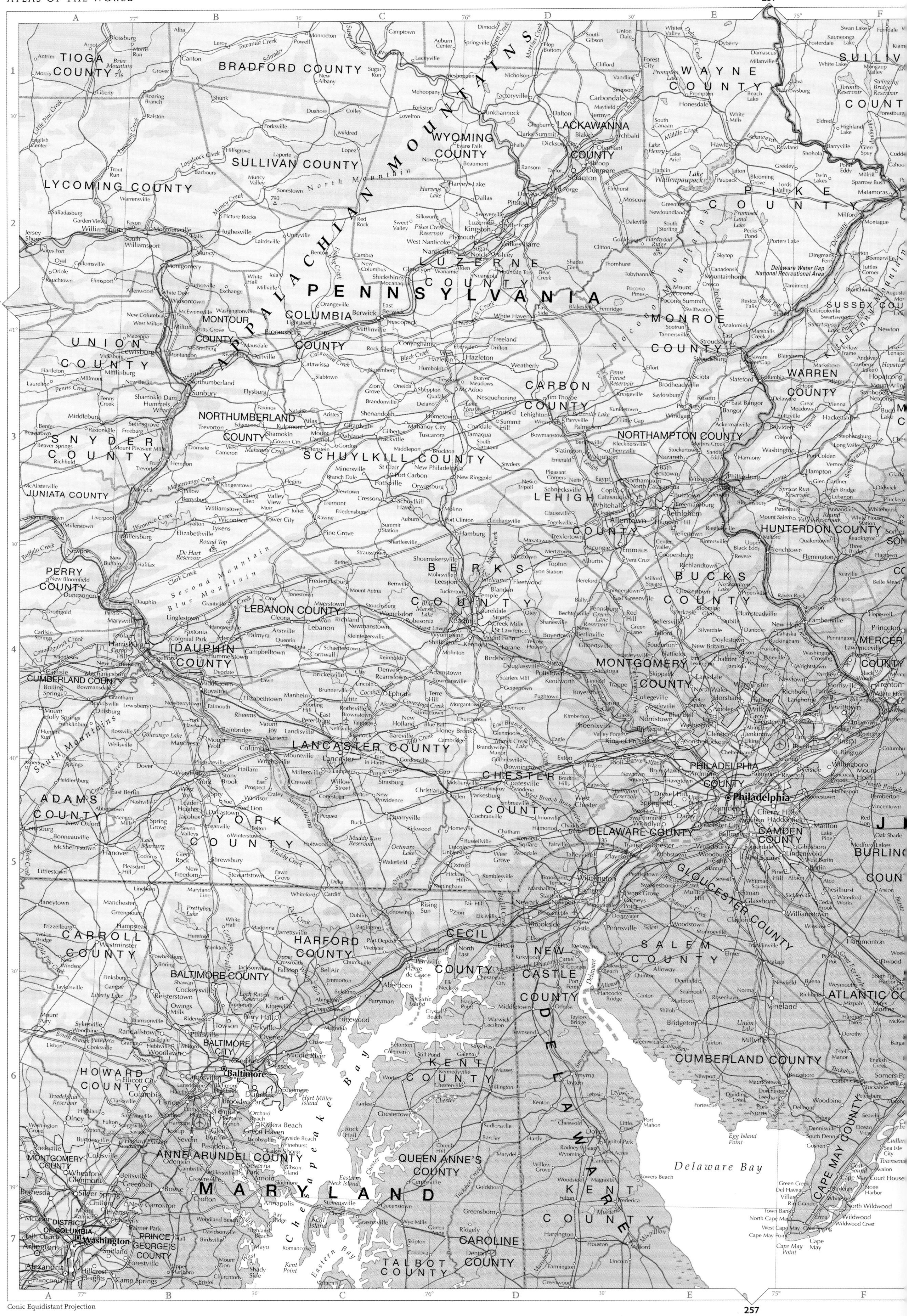

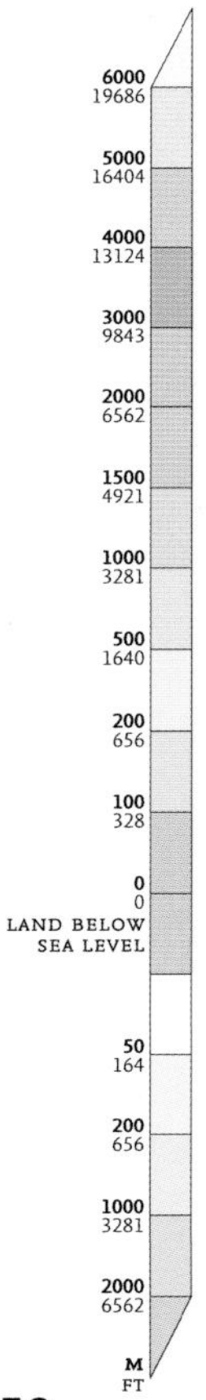

257

PENNSYLVANIA

APPALACHIAN MOUNTAINS

MARYLAND

DELAWARE

TIOGA COUNTY

BRADFORD COUNTY

WAYNE COUNTY

SULLIVAN COUNTY

WYOMING COUNTY

LACKAWANNA COUNTY

LYCOMING COUNTY

PIKE COUNTY

LUZERNE COUNTY

MONTOUR COUNTY

COLUMBIA COUNTY

MONROE COUNTY

UNION COUNTY

SUSSEX COUNTY

WARREN COUNTY

CARBON COUNTY

NORTHUMBERLAND COUNTY

SNYDER COUNTY

SCHUYLKILL COUNTY

NORTHAMPTON COUNTY

JUNIATA COUNTY

LEHIGH COUNTY

HUNTERDON COUNTY

PERRY COUNTY

BERKS COUNTY

BUCKS COUNTY

LEBANON COUNTY

DAUPHIN COUNTY

MERCER COUNTY

CUMBERLAND COUNTY

MONTGOMERY COUNTY

LANCASTER COUNTY

CHESTER COUNTY

PHILADELPHIA COUNTY

ADAMS COUNTY

YORK COUNTY

DELAWARE COUNTY

CAMDEN COUNTY

BURLINGTON COUNTY

GLOUCESTER COUNTY

CARROLL COUNTY

HARFORD COUNTY

CECIL COUNTY

SALEM COUNTY

NEW CASTLE COUNTY

BALTIMORE COUNTY

ATLANTIC COUNTY

HOWARD COUNTY

KENT COUNTY

CUMBERLAND COUNTY

ANNE ARUNDEL COUNTY

QUEEN ANNE'S COUNTY

CAPE MAY COUNTY

MONTGOMERY COUNTY

DISTRICT OF COLUMBIA

PRINCE GEORGE'S COUNTY

CAROLINE COUNTY

TALBOT COUNTY

Philadelphia

Baltimore

Washington

Chesapeake Bay

Delaware Bay

M	FT
6000	19686
5000	16404
4000	13124
3000	9843
2000	6562
1500	4921
1000	3281
500	1640
200	656
100	328
0	0
LAND BELOW SEA LEVEL	
50	164
200	656
1000	3281
2000	6562

Conic Equidistant Projection

257

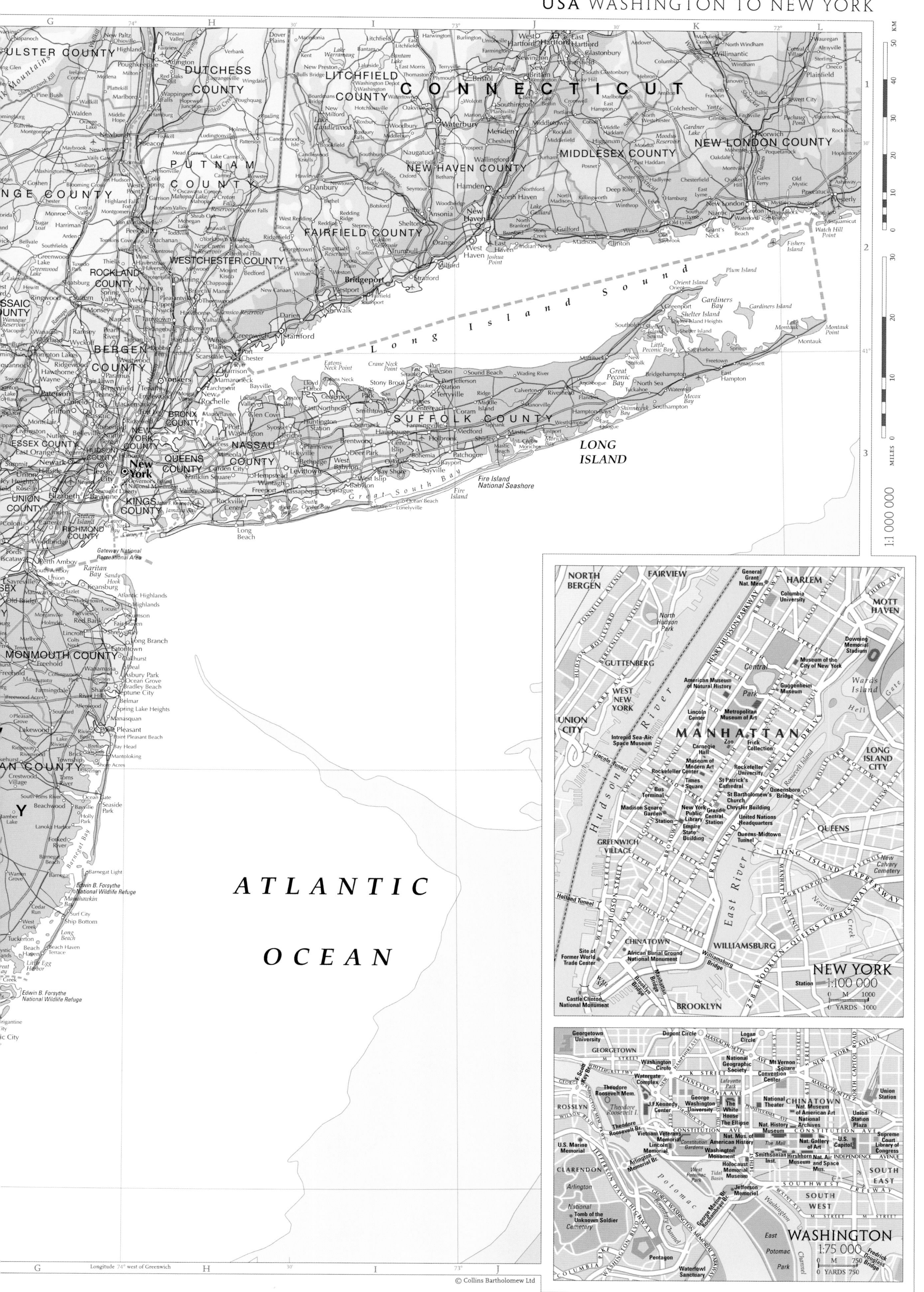
CONNECTICUT
LITCHFIELD COUNTY
NEW HAVEN COUNTY
MIDDLESEX COUNTY
NEW LONDON COUNTY
FAIRFIELD COUNTY
DUTCHESS COUNTY
PUTNAM COUNTY
WESTCHESTER COUNTY
ROCKLAND COUNTY
BERGEN COUNTY
ESSEX COUNTY
HUDSON COUNTY
UNION COUNTY
RICHMOND COUNTY
KINGS COUNTY
QUEENS COUNTY
NASSAU COUNTY
SUFFOLK COUNTY
BRONX COUNTY
NEW YORK COUNTY
MONMOUTH COUNTY
ULSTER COUNTY
Long Island Sound
LONG ISLAND
Great South Bay
Fire Island National Seashore
ATLANTIC
OCEAN
NEW YORK
1:100 000
MANHATTAN
HARLEM
BROOKLYN
WILLIAMSBURG
CHINATOWN
GREENWICH VILLAGE
QUEENS
LONG ISLAND CITY
WASHINGTON
1:75 000
GEORGETOWN
ROSSLYN
CLARENDON
SOUTH WEST
SOUTH EAST
1:1 000 000
© Collins Bartholomew Ltd

254

247

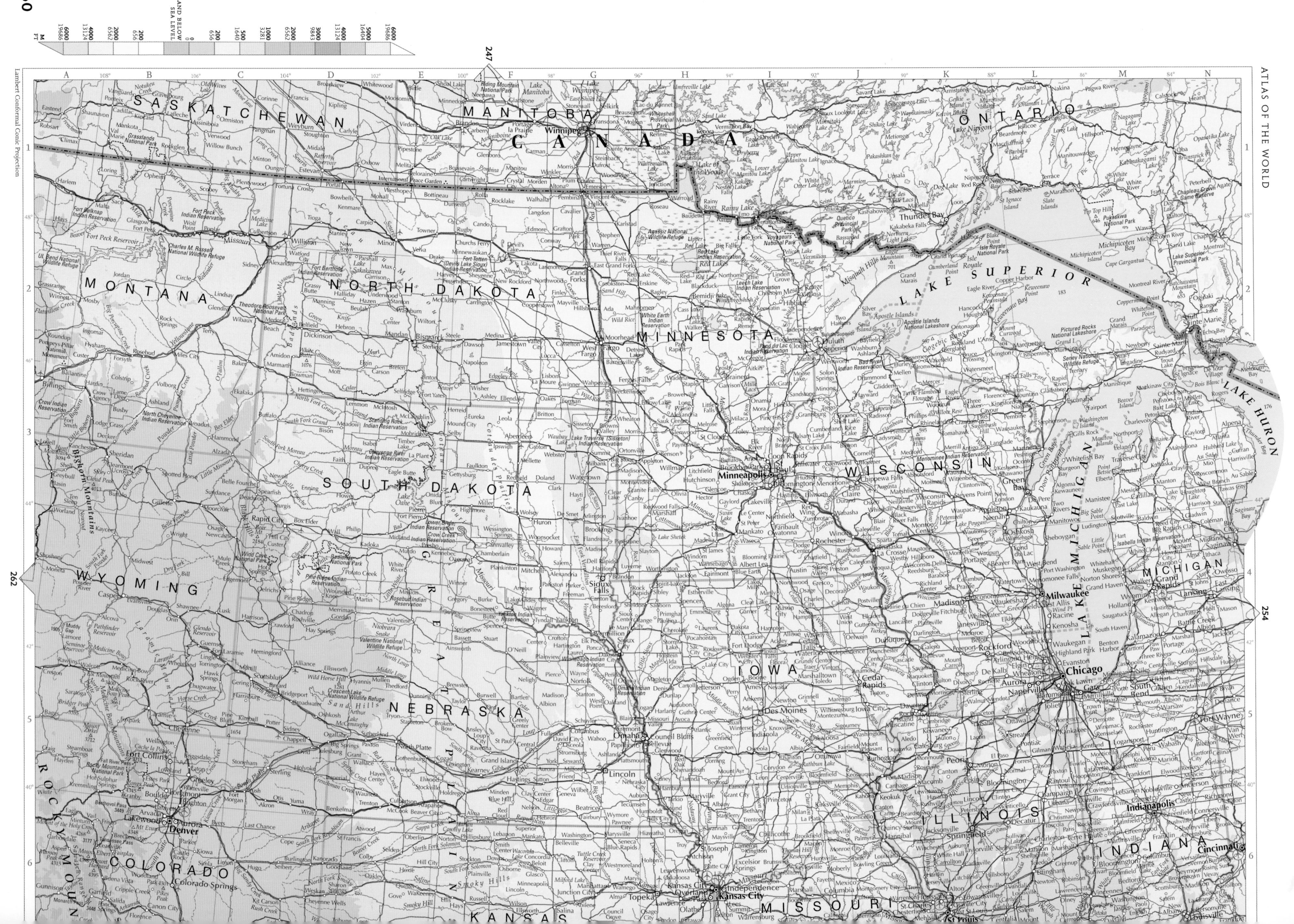

Lambert Conformal Conic Projection

262

255

267

263

1:6 000 000

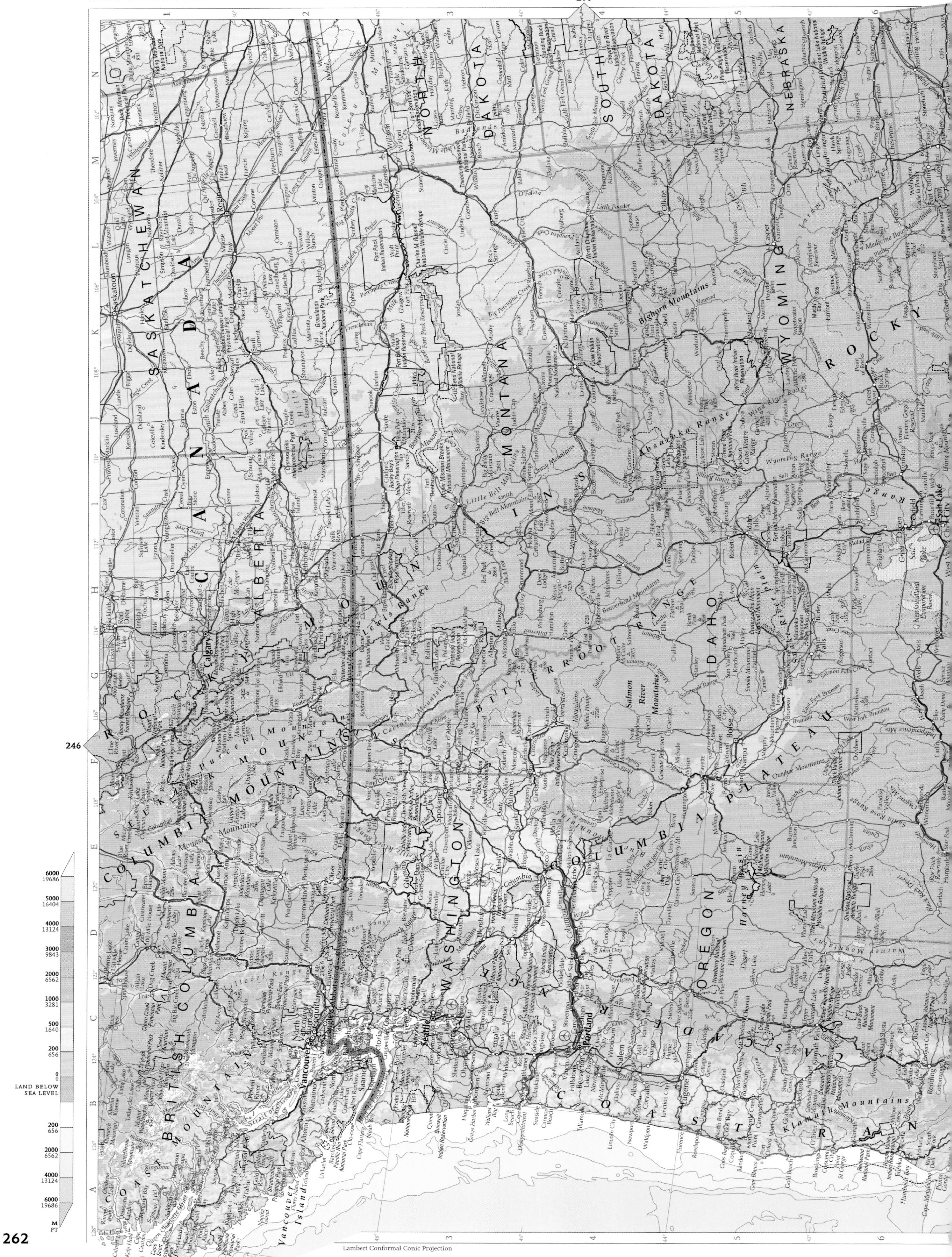
260
246
6000
19686
5000
16404
4000
13124
3000
9843
2000
6562
1000
3281
500
1640
200
656
0
LAND BELOW
SEA LEVEL
200
656
2000
6562
4000
13124
6000
19686
M
FT
SASKATCHEWAN
ALBERTA
BRITISH COLUMBIA
CANADA
NORTH DAKOTA
SOUTH DAKOTA
NEBRASKA
MONTANA
WYOMING
IDAHO
WASHINGTON
OREGON
COLUMBIA PLATEAU
BITTERROOT RANGE
ROCKY MOUNTAINS
CASCADE RANGE
COAST MOUNTAINS
COLUMBIA MOUNTAINS
Bighorn Mountains
Salmon River Mountains
Wind River Range
Absaroka Range
Saskatoon
Regina
Calgary
Lethbridge
Vancouver
Victoria
Seattle
Tacoma
Spokane
Portland
Salem
Eugene
Boise
Great Falls
Billings
Casper
Cheyenne
Salt Lake City
Pocatello
Idaho Falls
Rapid City
Kamloops
Kelowna
Vancouver Island
Lambert Conformal Conic Projection

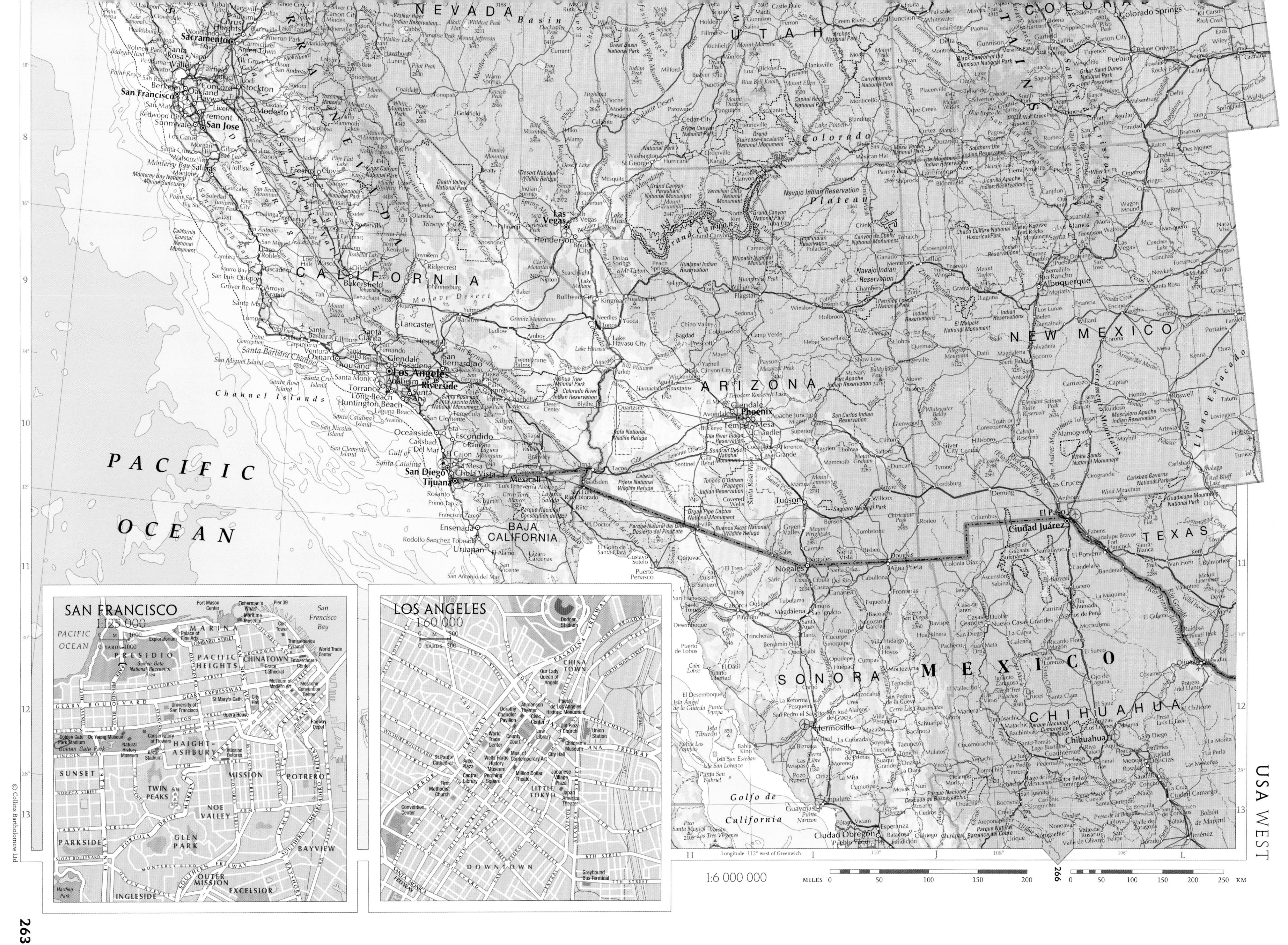

PACIFIC OCEAN
CALIFORNIA
NEVADA
ARIZONA
NEW MEXICO
UTAH
TEXAS
MEXICO
CHIHUAHUA
SONORA
BAJA CALIFORNIA
Golfo de California
Channel Islands
Plateau
Mojave Desert
Sacramento Mountains
Llano Estacado
San Francisco
Los Angeles
San Diego
Tijuana
Phoenix
Tucson
Las Vegas
Albuquerque
El Paso
Ciudad Juárez
Chihuahua
Hermosillo
Sacramento
San Jose
Fresno
Bakersfield
Mexicali
Nogales
Longitude 112° west of Greenwich
1:6 000 000
MILES 0 50 100 150 200
266
0 50 100 150 200 250 KM
SAN FRANCISCO
1:125 000
LOS ANGELES
1:60 000

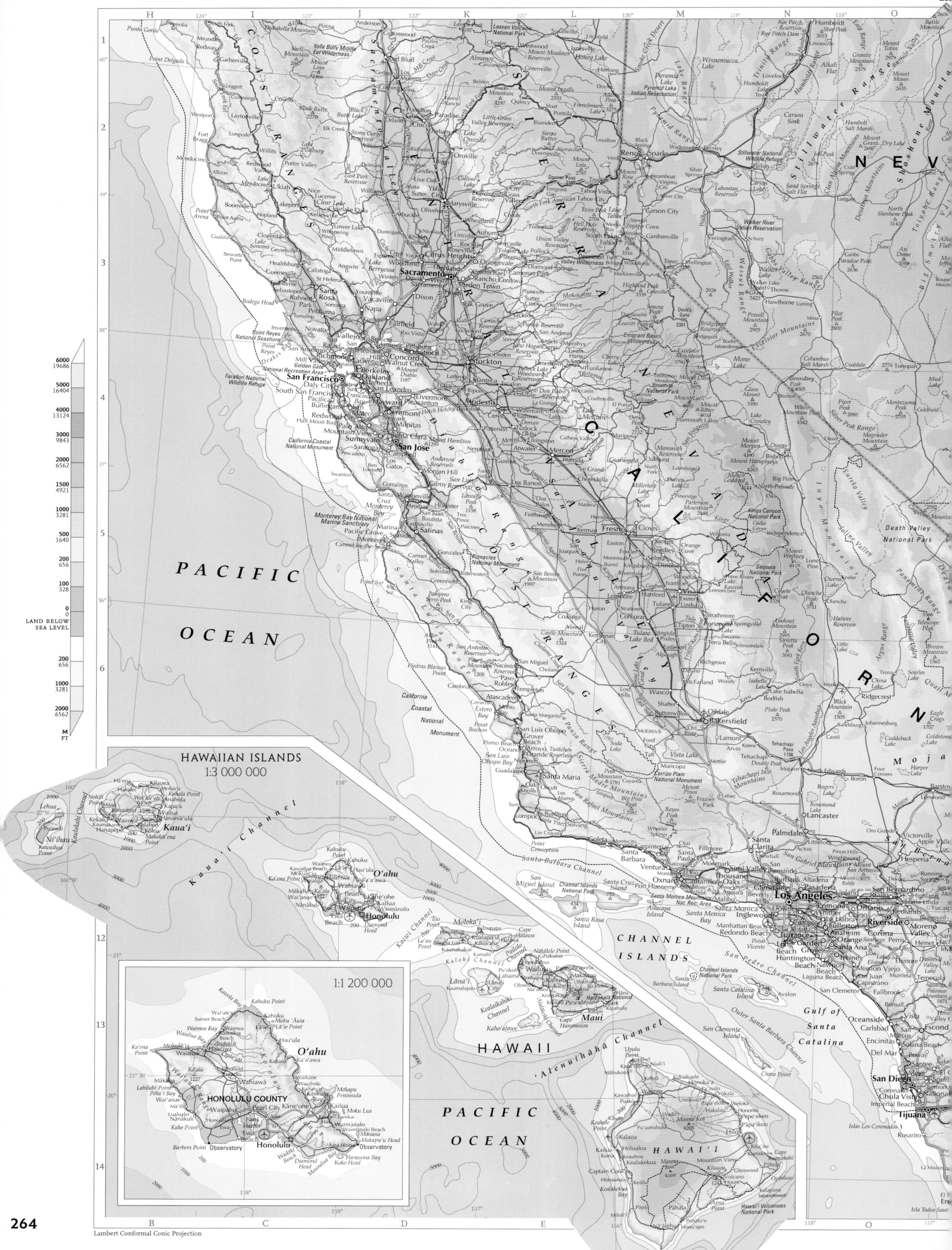

PACIFIC OCEAN

CALIFORNIA

NEVADA

COAST RANGES

SIERRA NEVADA

CENTRAL VALLEY

CHANNEL ISLANDS

Gulf of Santa Catalina

Kaua'i Channel

HAWAIIAN ISLANDS
1:3 000 000

1:1 200 000

HONOLULU COUNTY

O'ahu

HAWAII

PACIFIC OCEAN

HAWAI'I

M	FT
6000	19686
5000	16404
4000	13124
3000	9843
2000	6562
1500	4921
1000	3281
500	1640
200	656
100	328
0	0
LAND BELOW SEA LEVEL	
200	656
1000	3281
2000	6562

Lambert Conformal Conic Projection

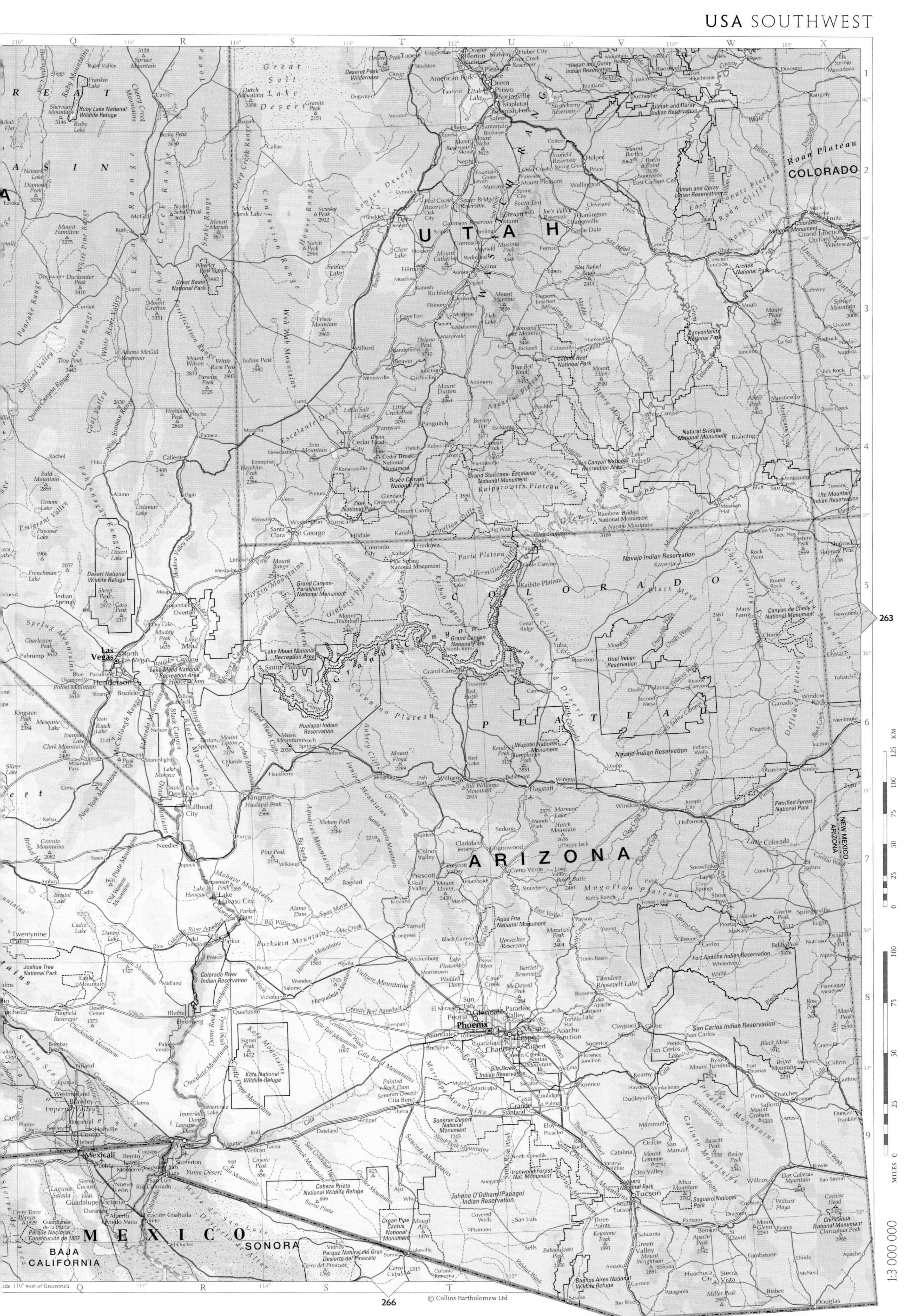
UTAH
ARIZONA
COLORADO
NEW MEXICO
ARIZONA
MEXICO
BAJA CALIFORNIA
SONORA
GREAT BASIN
COLORADO PLATEAU
WASATCH RANGE
Great Salt Lake Desert
Salt Lake City
Provo
Orem
Las Vegas
North Las Vegas
Henderson
Boulder City
Phoenix
Glendale
Mesa
Tempe
Chandler
Tucson
Flagstaff
Kingman
Prescott
Yuma
Mexicali
St George
Cedar City
Moab
Grand Canyon
Lake Mead
Lake Powell
Grand Canyon National Park
Navajo Indian Reservation
Hopi Indian Reservation
Fort Apache Indian Reservation
San Carlos Indian Reservation
Tohono O'Odham (Papago) Indian Reservation
Mogollon Plateau
Kaibab Plateau
Coconino Plateau
Painted Desert
Sonoran Desert National Monument
Salton Sea
Yuma Desert
Roan Plateau
Uintah and Ouray Indian Reservation
263
266
1:3 000 000
MILES
KM

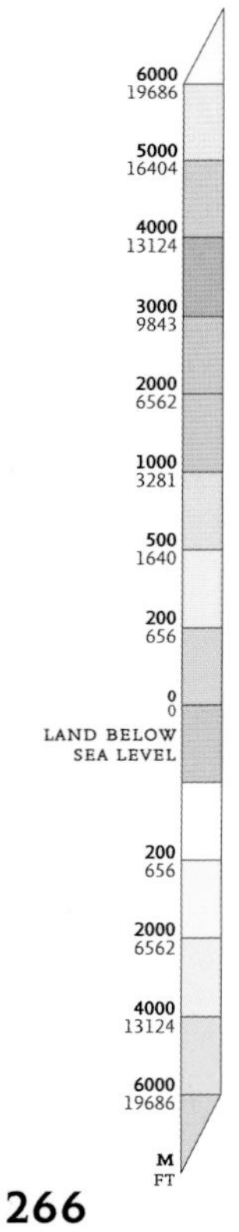

263

274

CENTRAL AMERICA
CONTINUATION AT THE SAME SCALE

M	FT
6000	19686
5000	16404
4000	13124
3000	9843
2000	6562
1000	3281
500	1640
200	656
0	0
LAND BELOW SEA LEVEL	
200	656
2000	6562
4000	13124
6000	19686

Lambert Conformal Conic Projection

GULF OF MEXICO

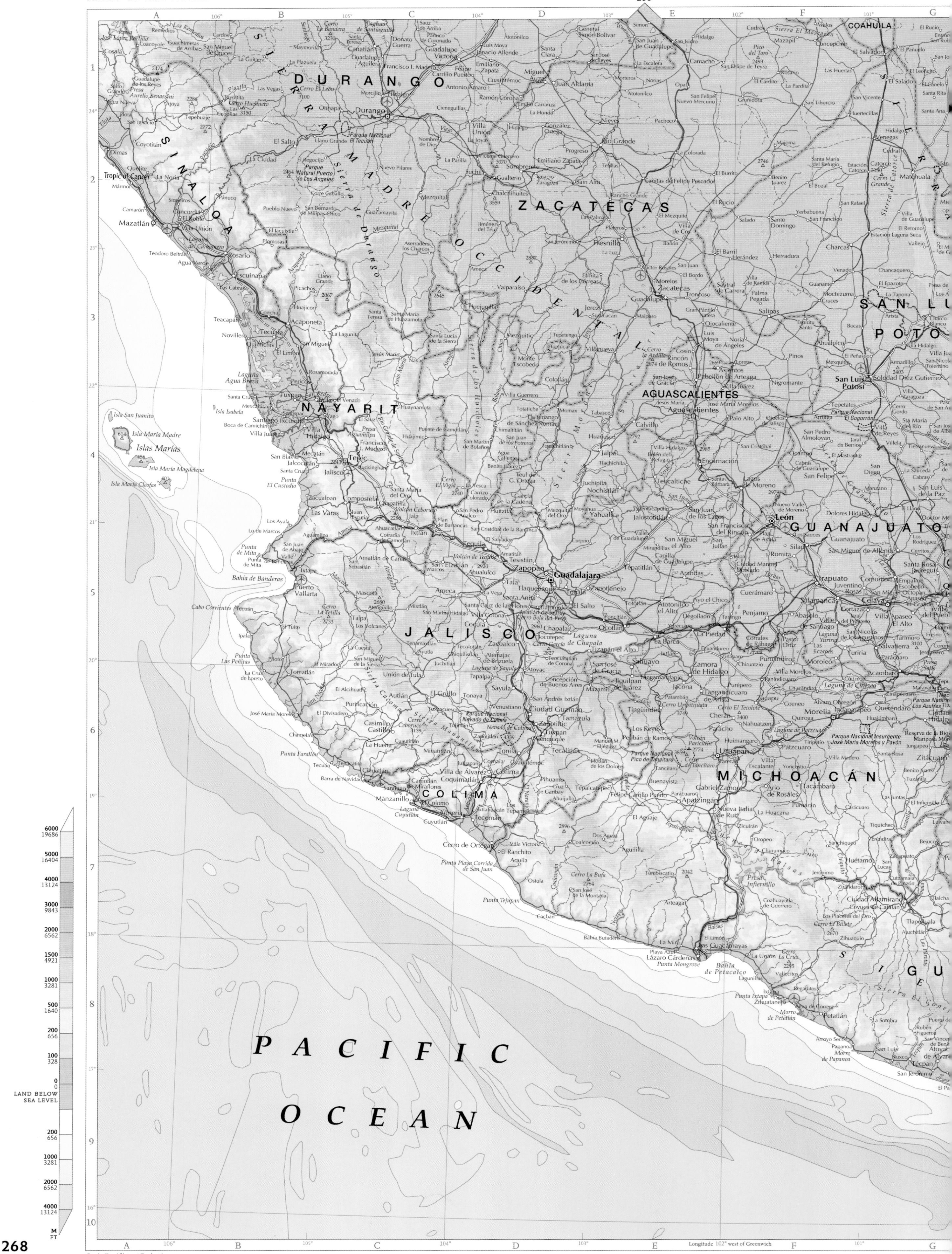

266

DURANGO

SINALOA

SIERRA MADRE OCCIDENTAL

ZACATECAS

NAYARIT

AGUASCALIENTES

JALISCO

GUANAJUATO

COLIMA

MICHOACÁN

PACIFIC OCEAN

6000 19686
5000 16404
4000 13124
3000 9843
2000 6562
1500 4921
1000 3281
500 1640
200 656
100 328
0 0
LAND BELOW SEA LEVEL
200 656
1000 3281
2000 6562
4000 13124
M FT

Longitude 102° west of Greenwich

Conic Equidistant Projection

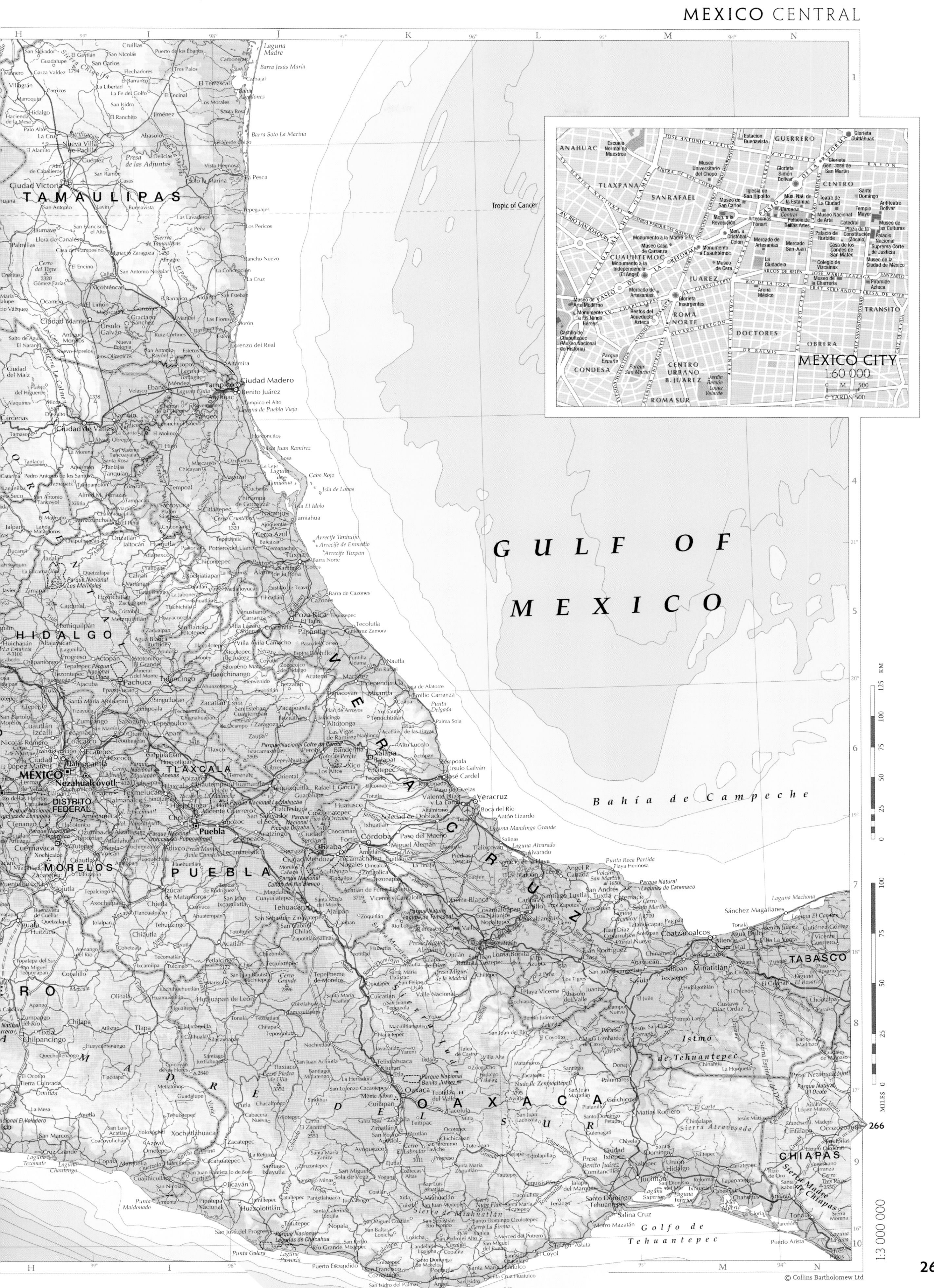
GULF OF MEXICO
Bahía de Campeche
Tropic of Cancer
TAMAULIPAS
HIDALGO
MEXICO
DISTRITO FEDERAL
TLAXCALA
MORELOS
PUEBLA
VERACRUZ
OAXACA
TABASCO
CHIAPAS
SIERRA MADRE ORIENTAL
SIERRA MADRE DEL SUR
Istmo de Tehuantepec
Golfo de Tehuantepec
Sierra Atravesada
Sierra Madre de Chiapas
Ciudad Victoria
Ciudad Madero
Tampico
Ciudad Mante
Ciudad de Valles
Pachuca
México
Nezahualcóyotl
Puebla
Tlaxcala
Cuernavaca
Chilpancingo
Xalapa
Veracruz
Córdoba
Orizaba
Poza Rica
Tuxpan
Papantla
Coatzacoalcos
Minatitlán
Oaxaca
Juchitán
Salina Cruz
Puerto Escondido
Laguna Madre
Cabo Rojo
Laguna Superior
Laguna Inferior
Puerto Arista
MEXICO CITY
1:60 000
ANAHUAC
TLAXPANA
SAN RAFAEL
GUERRERO
CENTRO
CUAUHTEMOC
JUAREZ
ROMA NORTE
DOCTORES
OBRERA
TRANSITO
CONDESA
CENTRO URBANO B.JUAREZ
ROMA SUR
PASEO DE LA REFORMA
Zócalo
Palacio Nacional
Catedral
Alameda Central
Palacio de Bellas Artes
Monumento a la Revolución
Monumento a la Independencia (El Ángel)
Castillo de Chapultepec (Museo Nacional de Historia)
266
1:3 000 000

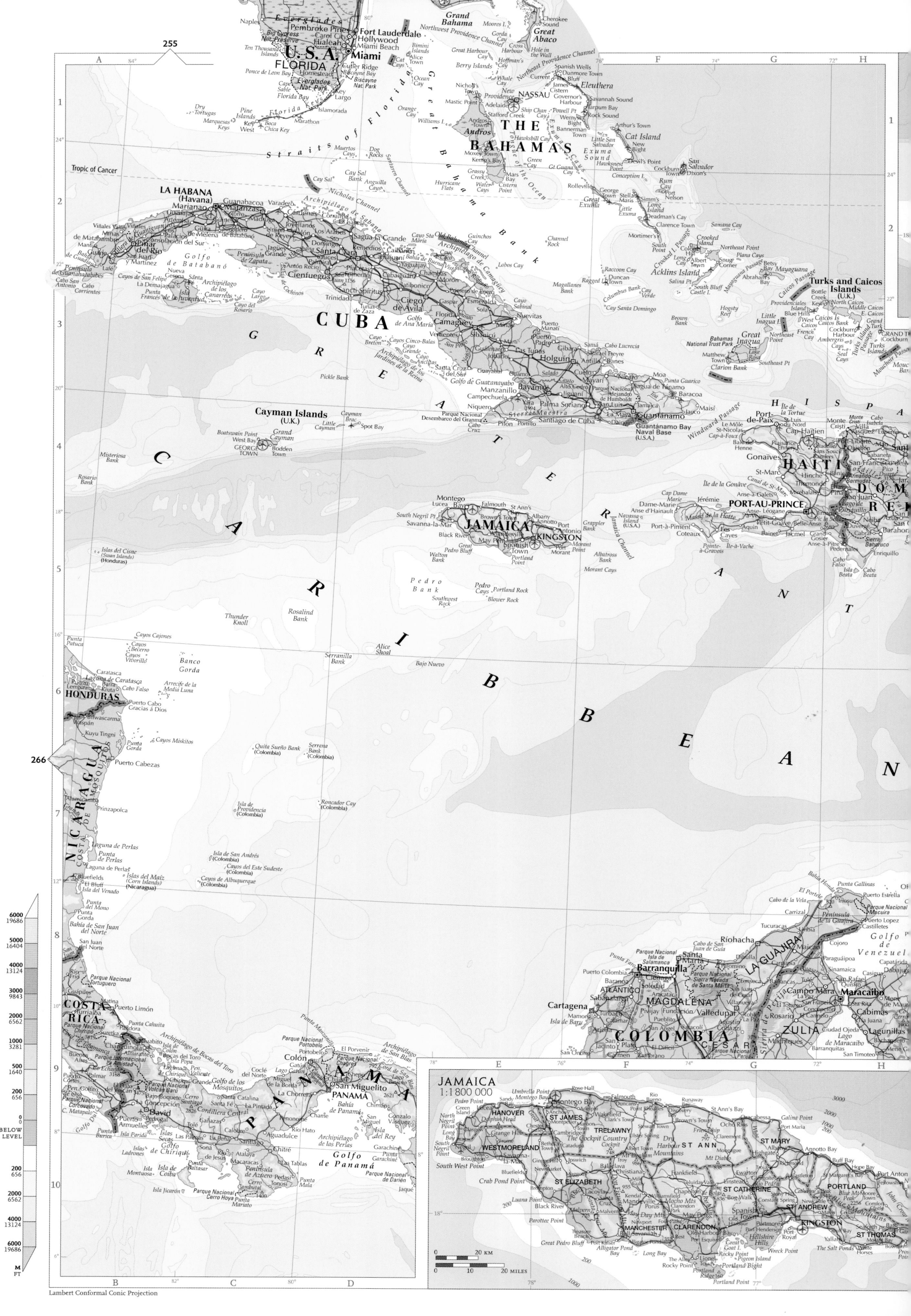

Lambert Conformal Conic Projection

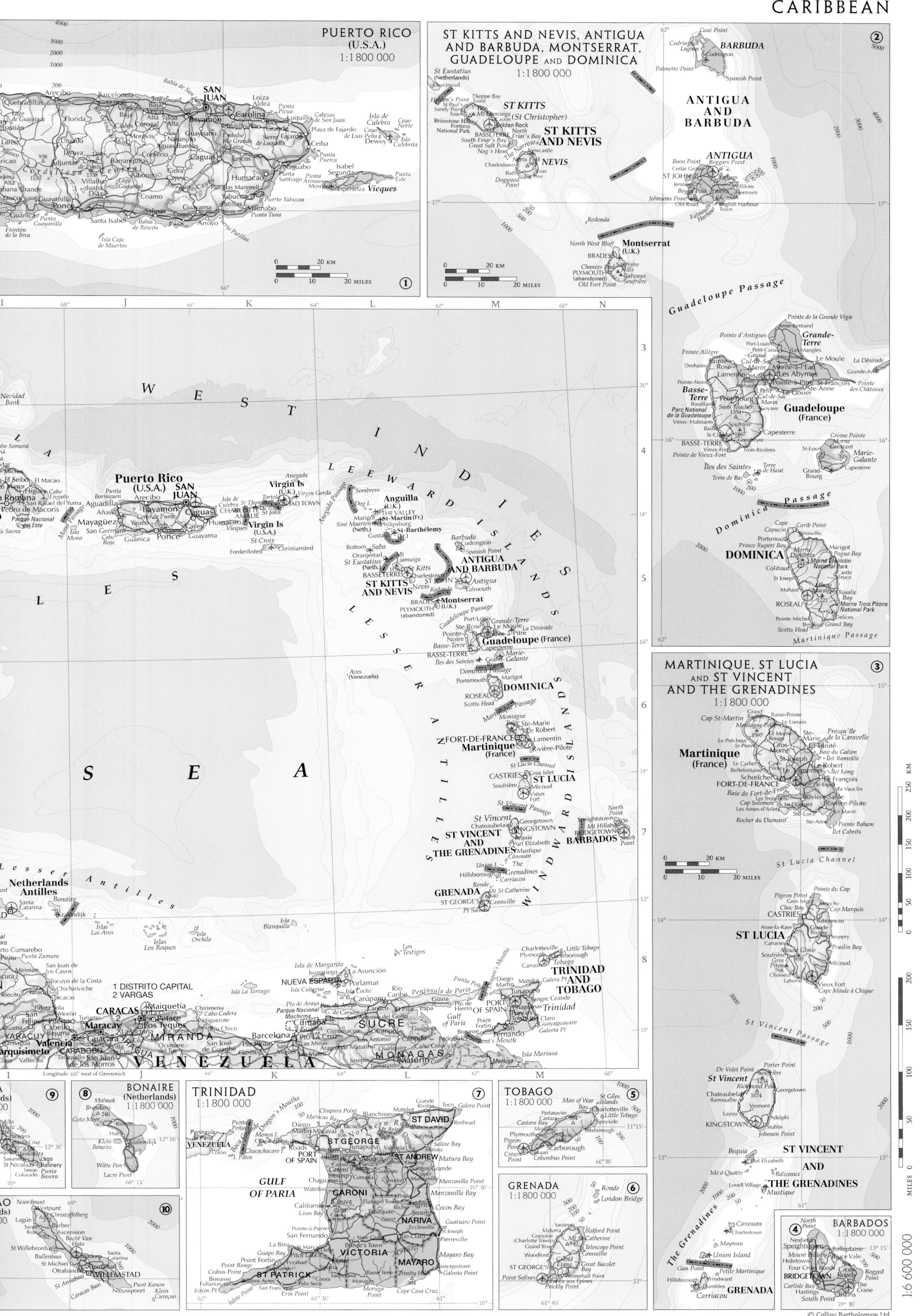
PUERTO RICO
(U.S.A.)
1:1 800 000
ST KITTS AND NEVIS, ANTIGUA AND BARBUDA, MONTSERRAT, GUADELOUPE AND DOMINICA
1:1 800 000
MARTINIQUE, ST LUCIA AND ST VINCENT AND THE GRENADINES
1:1 800 000
BARBADOS
1:1 800 000
TRINIDAD
1:1 800 000
TOBAGO
1:1 800 000
GRENADA
1:1 800 000
BONAIRE
(Netherlands)
1:1 800 000
W E S T I N D I E S
LEEWARD ISLANDS
LESSER ANTILLES
WINDWARD ISLANDS
S E A
VENEZUELA
1 DISTRITO CAPITAL
2 VARGAS
1:6 600 000

Orthographic Projection

F
G
H
I
J
1
2
3
4
5
6
7
Anguilla
Virgin Is
Barbuda
Antigua
St Kitts-Nevis
Montserrat
Guadeloupe
Dominica
Martinique
St Lucia
Barbados
St Vincent and the Grenadines
Grenada
Tobago
Trinidad
Caracas
Cumaná
Ciudad Bolívar
Orinoco
Georgetown
Paramaribo
Cayenne
GUYANA
SURINAME
French Guiana
Guiana Highlands
Boa Vista
Macapá
Mouths of the Amazon
Manaus
Amazonas (Amazon)
Santarém
Belém
São Luís
Carauari
Madeira
Purus
Tapajós
Xingu
Iriri
Tocantins
Represa Tucuruí
Marabá
Parnaíba
Teresina
Fortaleza
Araguaína
Porto Velho
BRAZIL
Natal
João Pessoa
Recife
Maceió
Aracaju
Floresta
Juazeiro
Barragem de Sobradinho
Palmas
São Francisco
Trinidad
Guaporé
Cuiabá
Brasília
Represa Serra da Mesa
Goiânia
Salvador
Ilhéus
BOLIVIA
Santa Cruz
Sucre
Tarija
Campo Grande
Patos de Minas
Uberaba
Teófilo Otôni
PARAGUAY
Pedro Juan Caballero
Araçatuba
Ribeirão Preto
Belo Horizonte
Vitória
San Salvador de Jujuy
San Miguel de Tucumán
Gran Chaco
Asunción
Formosa
Coronel Oviedo
Maringá
Campinas
São Paulo
Santos
Rio de Janeiro
Resistencia
Corrientes
Encarnación
Posadas
Curitiba
Salinas de Ambargasta
Florianópolis
Laguna Mar Chiquita
Santa Maria
Córdoba
Santa Fé
Concórdia
Lagoa dos Patos
Porto Alegre
Paraná
Rosario
Paysandú
Rio Grande
San Luis
Buenos Aires
URUGUAY
Montevideo
La Plata
Río de la Plata
Pampas
Mar del Plata
Bahía Blanca
Negro
Viedma
Golfo San Matías
Trelew
Comodoro Rivadavia
Falkland Islands (U.K.)
Stanley
Isla de los Estados
Shag Rocks
South Georgia (U.K.)
South Shetland Islands
South Orkney Islands
South Sandwich Islands (U.K.)
Traversay Islands
Candlemas Island
Saunders Island
Montagu Island
Southern Thule
Bristol Island
Arquipélago da Madeira
Islas Canarias
Gran Canaria
Santo Antão
Ilhas do Cabo Verde
Boa Vista
Santiago
Tropic of Cancer
Sénégal
Niger
São Pedro e São Paulo (Brazil)
Atol das Rocas
Fernando de Noronha (Brazil)
AFRICA
Gulf of Guinea
Equator
Ascension
ATLANTIC OCEAN
Ilha da Trindade (Brazil)
Ilhas Martin Vaz (Brazil)
St Helena
Tropic of Capricorn
Tristan da Cunha
Orange
Cape of Good Hope
KM
0
250
500
750
1000
1250
1500
MILES
0
250
500
750
1:27 000 000

270

266

Administrative regions numbered on the map:

COLOMBIA
1. SANTAFÉ DE BOGOTÁ (C3)

ECUADOR
2. BOLÍVAR (B5)
3. CHIMBORAZO (B5)
4. TUNGURAHUA (B5)
5. ZAMORA-CHINCHIPE (B5)

VENEZUELA
1. DISTRITO CAPITAL (E2)
2. VARGAS (E2)

CARIBBEAN SEA

PACIFIC OCEAN

COLOMBIA

ECUADOR

PERU

PANAMA

GALAPAGOS ISLANDS
(Ecuador)
AT THE SAME SCALE

M	FT
6000	19686
5000	16404
4000	13124
3000	9843
2000	6562
1000	3281
500	1640
200	656
0	0
LAND BELOW SEA LEVEL	
200	656
2000	6562
4000	13124
6000	19686

Lambert Azimuthal Equal Area Projection

276

271

ATLANTIC OCEAN

GRENADA

TRINIDAD AND TOBAGO

GUYANA

SURINAME

French Guiana

BRAZIL

VENEZUELA

NUEVA ESPARTA

SUCRE

MONAGAS

ANZOÁTEGUI

DELTA AMACURO

BOLÍVAR

GUIANA HIGHLANDS

RORAIMA

AMAZONAS

AMAPÁ

PARÁ

RONDÔNIA

MATO GROSSO

GEORGETOWN

PARAMARIBO

CAYENNE

PORT OF SPAIN

ST GEORGE'S

Mouths of the Amazon

Ilha de Marajó

Pakaraima Mountains

Serra Tumucumaque

Serra do Cachimbo

Serra dos Carajás

1:7 500 000

KM 0 100 200 300

MILES 0 100 150

278

277

Longitude 64° west of Greenwich

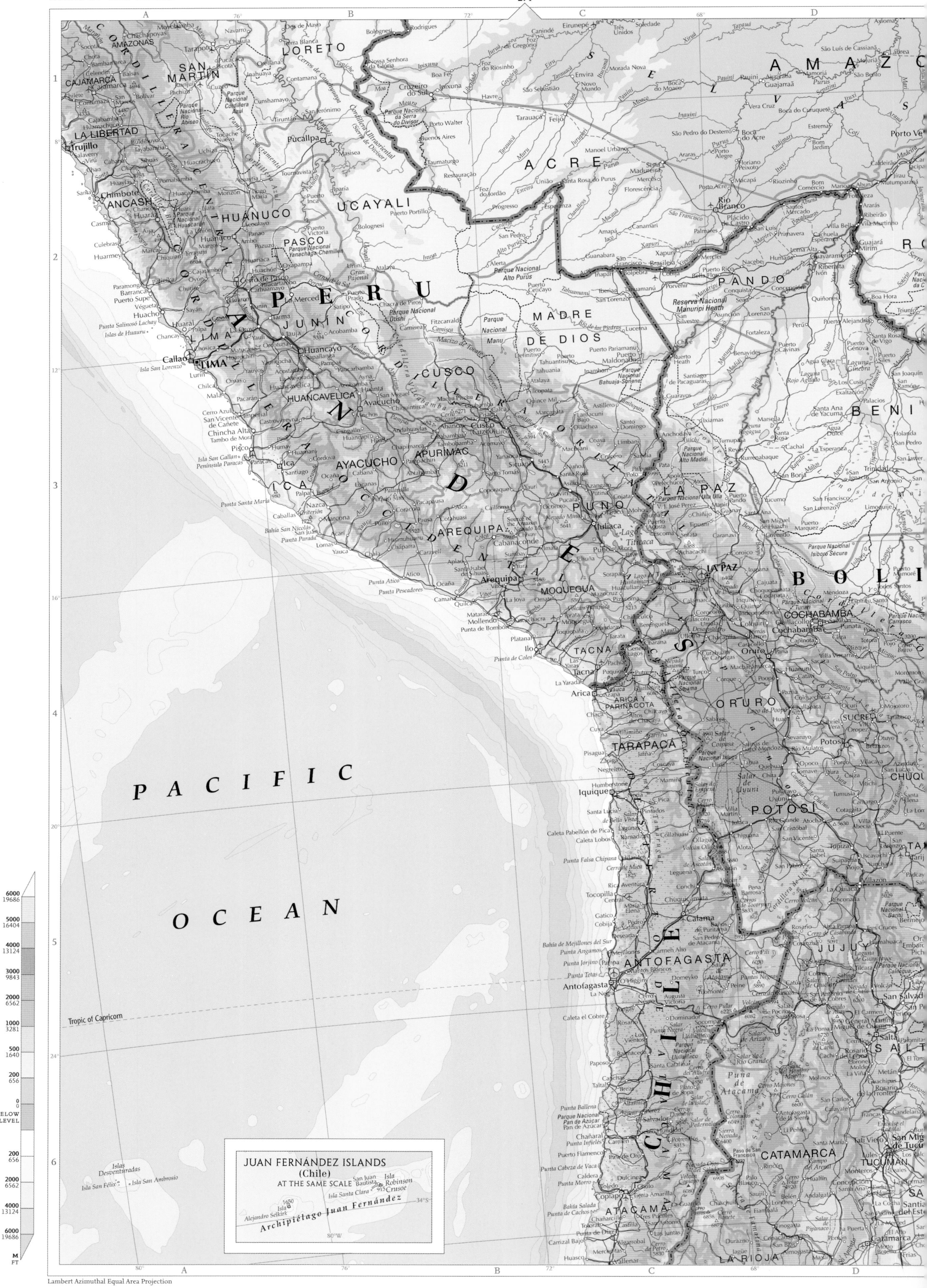

274

PERU

BOLIVIA

CHILE

PACIFIC OCEAN

CORDILLERA CENTRAL

CORDILLERA OCCIDENTAL

CORDILLERA ORIENTAL

ANDES

AMAZONAS

SAN MARTIN

LORETO

LA LIBERTAD

CAJAMARCA

ANCASH

HUÁNUCO

UCAYALI

PASCO

JUNÍN

LIMA

HUANCAVELICA

AYACUCHO

APURÍMAC

CUSCO

MADRE DE DIOS

ICA

AREQUIPA

PUNO

MOQUEGUA

TACNA

ACRE

PANDO

BENI

LA PAZ

COCHABAMBA

ORURO

POTOSÍ

ARICA Y PARINACOTA

TARAPACÁ

ANTOFAGASTA

ATACAMA

CATAMARCA

JUJUY

LA RIOJA

Tropic of Capricorn

JUAN FERNÁNDEZ ISLANDS (Chile)

AT THE SAME SCALE

Archipiélago Juan Fernández

Isla Robinson Crusoe

Isla Alejandro Selkirk

Isla Santa Clara

San Juan Bautista

Islas Desventuradas

Isla San Félix

Isla San Ambrosio

M / FT

6000 / 19686

5000 / 16404

4000 / 13124

3000 / 9843

2000 / 6562

1000 / 3281

500 / 1640

200 / 656

0 / 0

LAND BELOW SEA LEVEL

200 / 656

2000 / 6562

4000 / 13124

6000 / 19686

Lambert Azimuthal Equal Area Projection

275

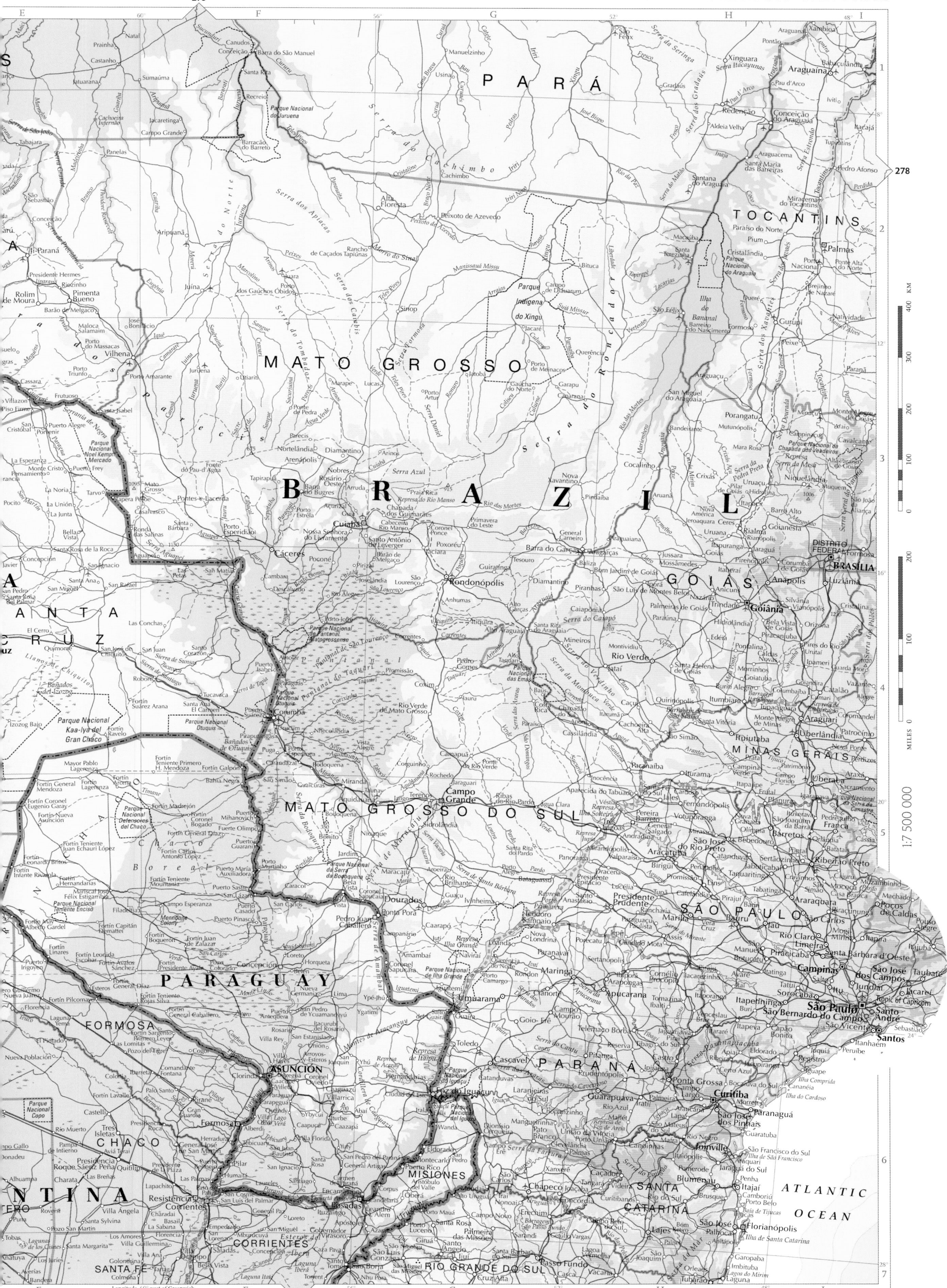
PARÁ
TOCANTINS
MATO GROSSO
BRAZIL
GOIÁS
DISTRITO FEDERAL
BRASÍLIA
MINAS GERAIS
MATO GROSSO DO SUL
SÃO PAULO
PARANÁ
SANTA CATARINA
RIO GRANDE DO SUL
PARAGUAY
ASUNCIÓN
FORMOSA
CHACO
ARGENTINA
MISIONES
CORRIENTES
SANTA FE
SANTA CRUZ
ATLANTIC OCEAN
Goiânia
Campo Grande
Cuiabá
Curitiba
São Paulo
Campinas
Florianópolis
Santos
Tropic of Capricorn
Longitude 60° west of Greenwich
1:7 500 000
MILES
KM

278

282

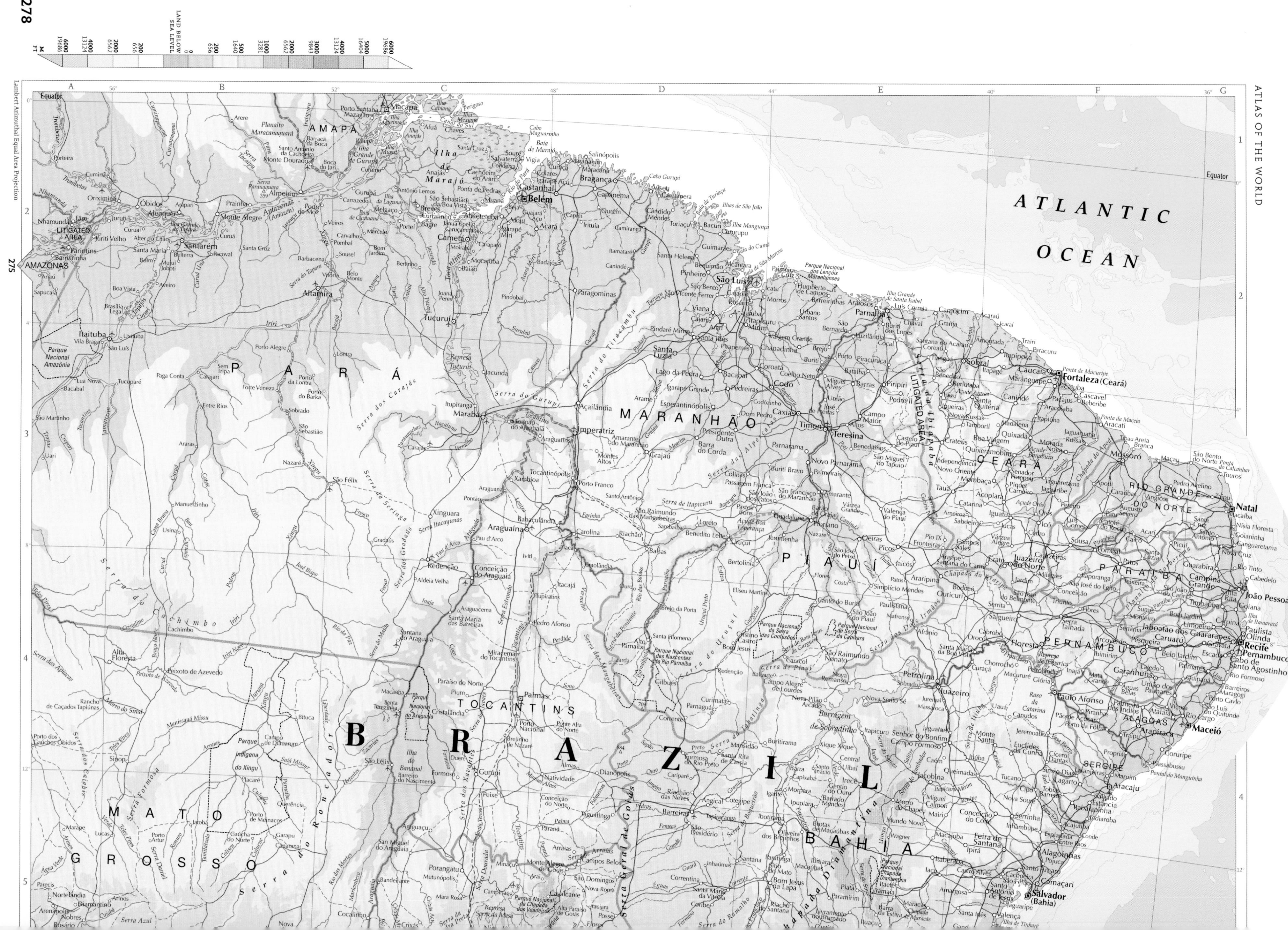
ATLANTIC
OCEAN
B R A Z I L
P A R Á
M A R A N H Ã O
P I A U Í
C E A R Á
RIO GRANDE DO NORTE
P A R A Í B A
P E R N A M B U C O
A L A G O A S
SERGIPE
B A H I A
T O C A N T I N S
M A T O G R O S S O
AMAPÁ
AMAZONAS
LITIGATED AREA
Equator
Natal
João Pessoa
Recife (Pernambuco)
Maceió
Aracaju
Salvador (Bahia)
Fortaleza (Ceará)
Teresina
São Luís
Belém
Macapá
Santarém
Palmas
Ilha de Marajó
Serra da Ibiapaba
Serra Geral de Goiás
Serra do Roncador
Serra do Cachimbo
Parque Nacional Amazônia
6000
19686
5000
16404
4000
13124
3000
9843
2000
6562
1000
3281
500
1640
200
656
0
LAND BELOW SEA LEVEL
200
656
2000
6562
4000
13124
6000
19686
M
FT
Lambert Azimuthal Equal Area Projection
275

ATLANTIC
OCEAN
RIO DE JANEIRO
1:125 000
Tropic of Capricorn
MINAS GERAIS
GOIÁS
SÃO PAULO
PARANÁ
SANTA CATARINA
RIO GRANDE DO SUL
MATO GROSSO DO SUL
ESPÍRITO SANTO
RIO DE JANEIRO
PARAGUAY
ARGENTINA
URUGUAY
MISIONES
CORRIENTES
Belo Horizonte
Rio de Janeiro
São Paulo
Vitória
Curitiba
Florianópolis
Porto Alegre
Goiânia
Campo Grande
Campinas
Santos
Londrina
Maringá
Uberlândia
Ribeirão Preto
Juiz de Fora
Nova Iguaçu
Joinville
Pelotas
Dourados
Lagoa dos Patos
1:7 500 000
282
277

A B C D

1 2 3 4 5 6

DISTRITO FEDERAL
BRASÍLIA

MATO GROSSO

GOIÁS

MATO GROSSO DO SUL

SÃO PAULO

PARANÁ

MI

279

Tropic of Capricorn

M	FT
6000	19686
5000	16404
4000	13124
3000	9843
2000	6562
1500	4921
1000	3281
500	1640
200	656
100	328
0	0
LAND BELOW SEA LEVEL	
200	656
1000	3281
2000	6562

Conic Equidistant Projection

Longitude 48° west of Greenwich

279

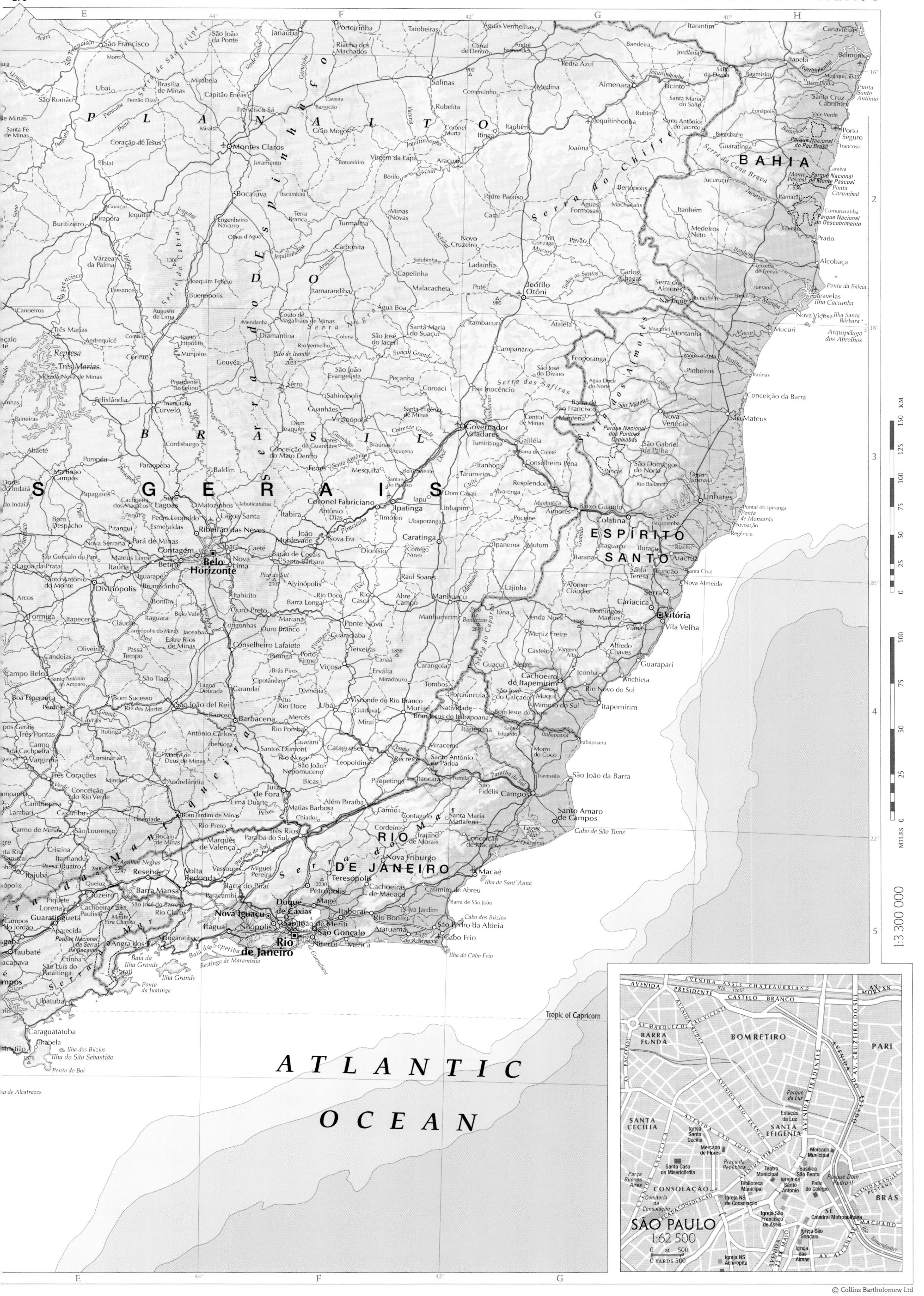
E
F
G
H
44°
42°
40°
16°
18°
20°
22°
2
3
4
5
P L A N A L T O
B R A S I L
S G E R A I S
BAHIA
ESPÍRITO SANTO
RIO DE JANEIRO
ATLANTIC
OCEAN
Serra do Espinhaço
Serra do Chifre
Serra dos Aimorés
Serra da Mantiqueira
Serra do Mar
Tropic of Capricorn
Montes Claros
Belo Horizonte
Governador Valadares
Teófilo Otôni
Vitória
Vila Velha
Rio de Janeiro
Niterói
Nova Iguaçu
Duque de Caxias
Petrópolis
Teresópolis
Nova Friburgo
Campos
Macaé
Cabo Frio
Juiz de Fora
Barbacena
São João del Rei
Ipatinga
Coronel Fabriciano
Colatina
Linhares
Cachoeiro de Itapemirim
Guarapari
São Mateus
Caravelas
Porto Seguro
Alcobaça
Mucuri
Diamantina
Curvelo
Divinópolis
Contagem
Betim
Ouro Preto
Conselheiro Lafaiete
Muriaé
Volta Redonda
Resende
Barra Mansa
Angra dos Reis
Ubatuba
Caraguatatuba
Ilhabela
Taubaté
Guaratinguetá
Cabo de São Tomé
Ilha Grande
Arquipélago dos Abrolhos
Parque Nacional do Pau Brasil
Parque Nacional do Descobrimento
Parque Nacional dos Pontões Capixabas
Parque Nacional da Serra da Bocaina
Represa Três Marias
KM
MILES
0
25
50
75
100
125
150
1:3 300 000
SÃO PAULO
1:62 500
BARRA FUNDA
BOMRETIRO
PARI
SANTA CECILIA
SANTA EFIGÊNIA
CONSOLAÇÃO
BRÁS
SÉ
AVENIDA ASSIS CHATEAUBRIAND
AVENIDA PRESIDENTE CASTELO BRANCO
AVENIDA TIRADENTES
AVENIDA RIO BRANCO
AVENIDA SÃO JOÃO
Parque da Luz
Estação da Luz
Mercado Municipal
Teatro Municipal
Catedral Metropolitana
Praça da República

279

M	FT
6000	19686
5000	16404
4000	13124
3000	9843
2000	6562
1000	3281
500	1640
200	656
0	0
LAND BELOW SEA LEVEL	
200	656
2000	6562
4000	13124
6000	19686

277

276

PACIFIC OCEAN

Lambert Azimuthal Equal Area Projection

BUENOS AIRES
1:125 000
ATLANTIC OCEAN
Falkland Islands
(U.K.)
West Falkland
East Falkland
STANLEY
SOUTH GEORGIA
(U.K.)
AT THE SAME SCALE
1:7 500 000
RÍO NEGRO
CHUBUT
SANTA CRUZ
AISÉN
LOS LAGOS
LOS RÍOS
MAGALLANES Y ANTÁRTICA CHILENA
TIERRA DEL FUEGO
Golfo San Matías
Golfo San Jorge
Comodoro Rivadavia
Rawson
Trelew
Puerto Madryn
Viedma
Puerto Montt
Osorno
Valdivia
Punta Arenas
Río Gallegos
Ushuaia

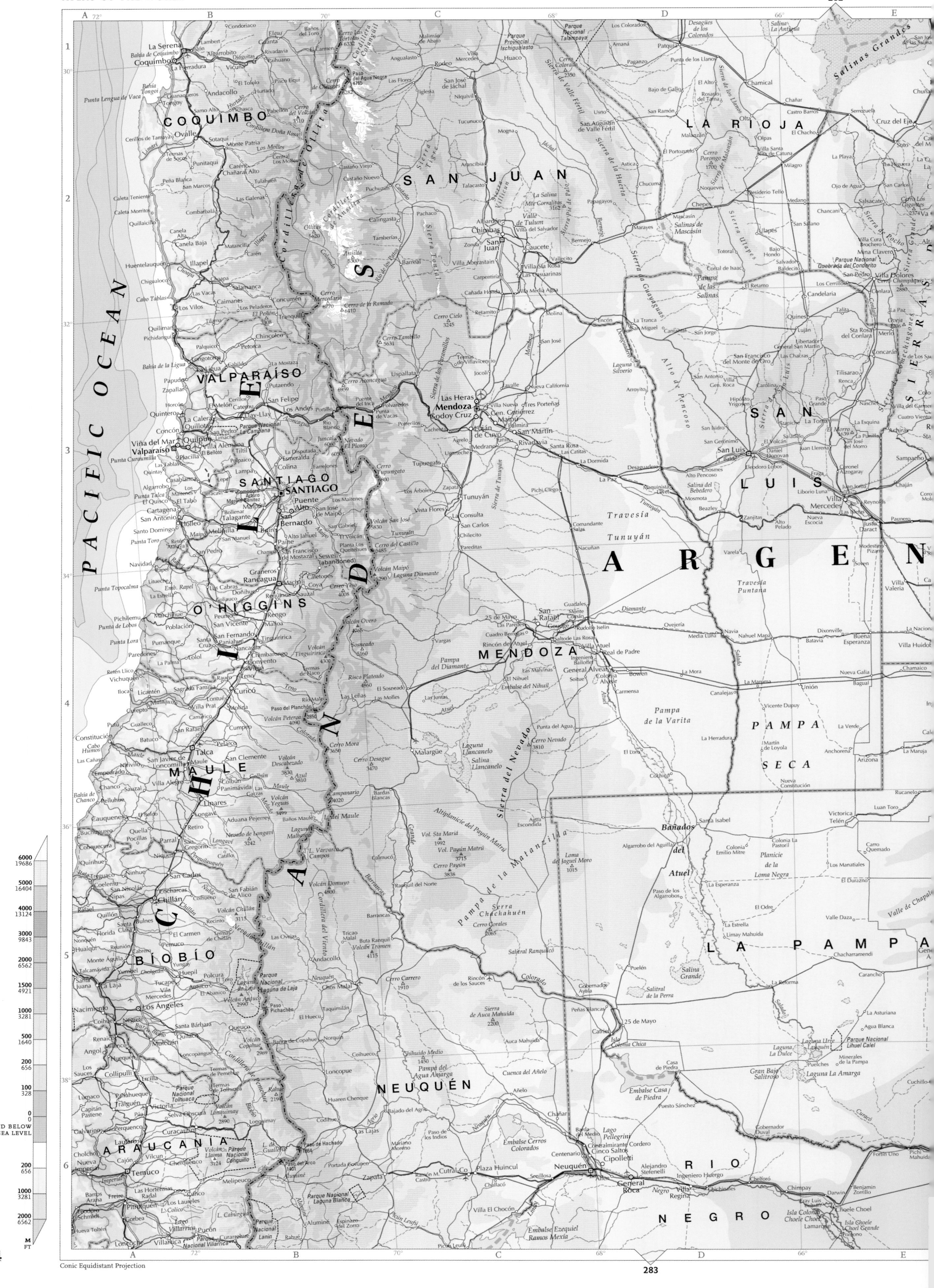

282

PACIFIC OCEAN

CHILE

ARGENTINA

ANDES

COQUIMBO · VALPARAÍSO · SANTIAGO · O'HIGGINS · MAULE · BÍOBÍO · ARAUCANÍA · SAN JUAN · LA RIOJA · MENDOZA · SAN LUIS · NEUQUÉN · LA PAMPA · RIO NEGRO

M	FT
6000	19686
5000	16404
4000	13124
3000	9843
2000	6562
1500	4921
1000	3281
500	1640
200	656
100	328
0	0
LAND BELOW SEA LEVEL	
200	656
1000	3281
2000	6562

Conic Equidistant Projection

283

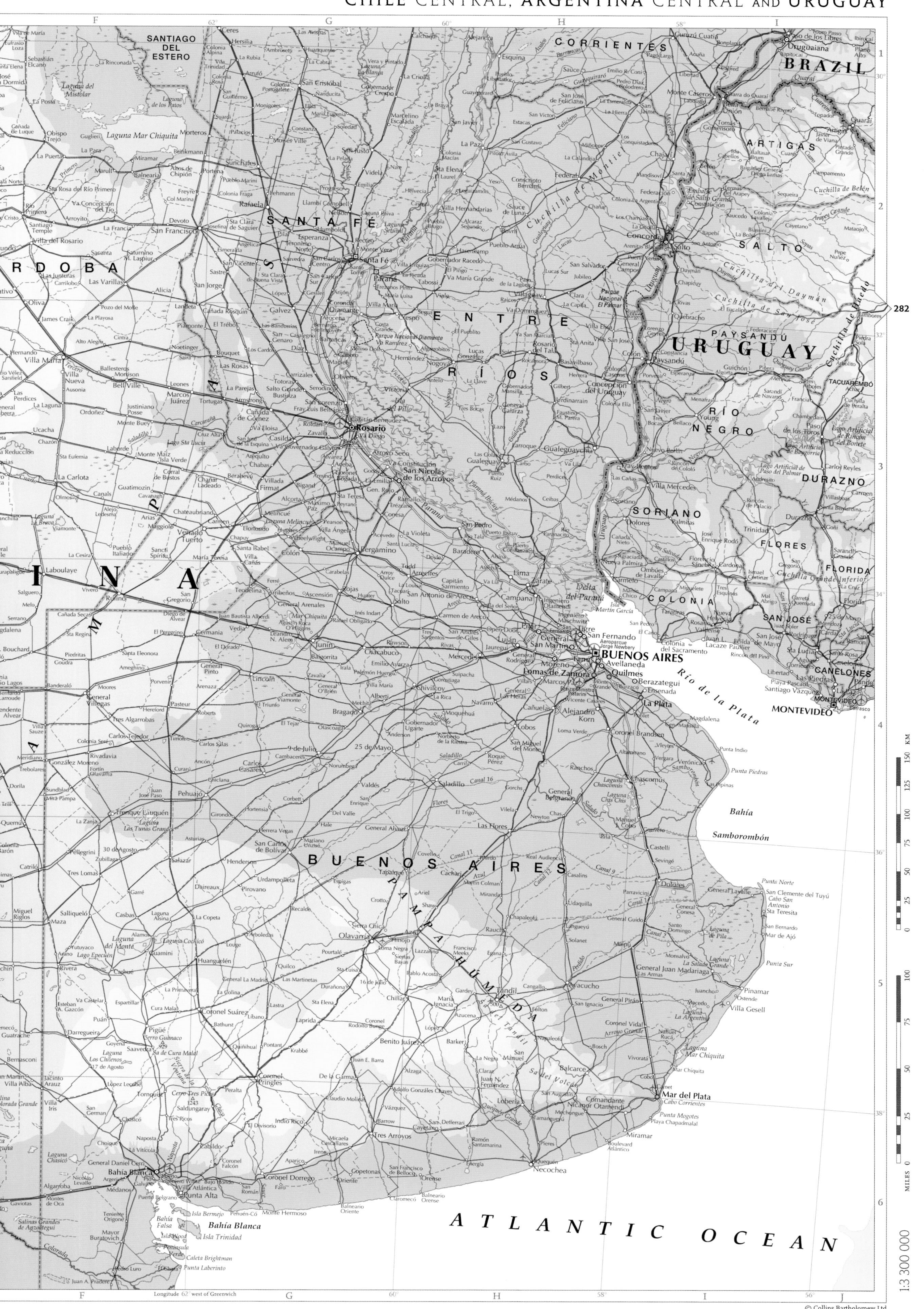
SANTIAGO DEL ESTERO
CORRIENTES
BRAZIL
ARTIGAS
SALTO
SANTA FÉ
ENTRE RÍOS
PAYSANDÚ
URUGUAY
RÍO NEGRO
TACUAREMBÓ
DURAZNO
SORIANO
FLORES
FLORIDA
COLONIA
SAN JOSÉ
CANELONES
MONTEVIDEO
BUENOS AIRES
Río de la Plata
Bahía Samborombón
BUENOS AIRES
PAMPA HÚMEDA
Rosario
Santa Fé
Paraná
Mar del Plata
Bahía Blanca
ATLANTIC OCEAN
282
KM
MILES
1:3 300 000
Longitude 62° west of Greenwich

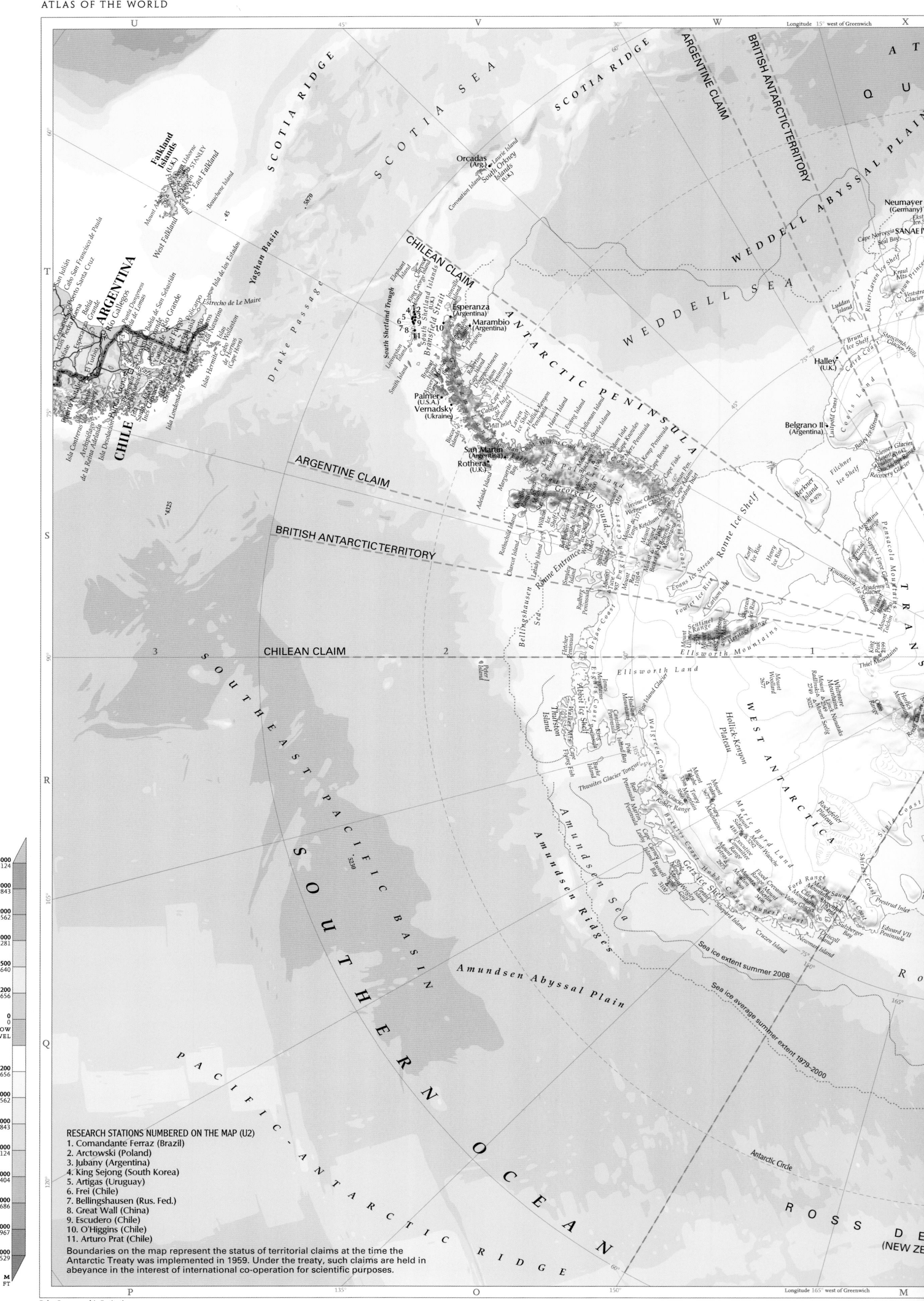

Polar Stereographic Projection

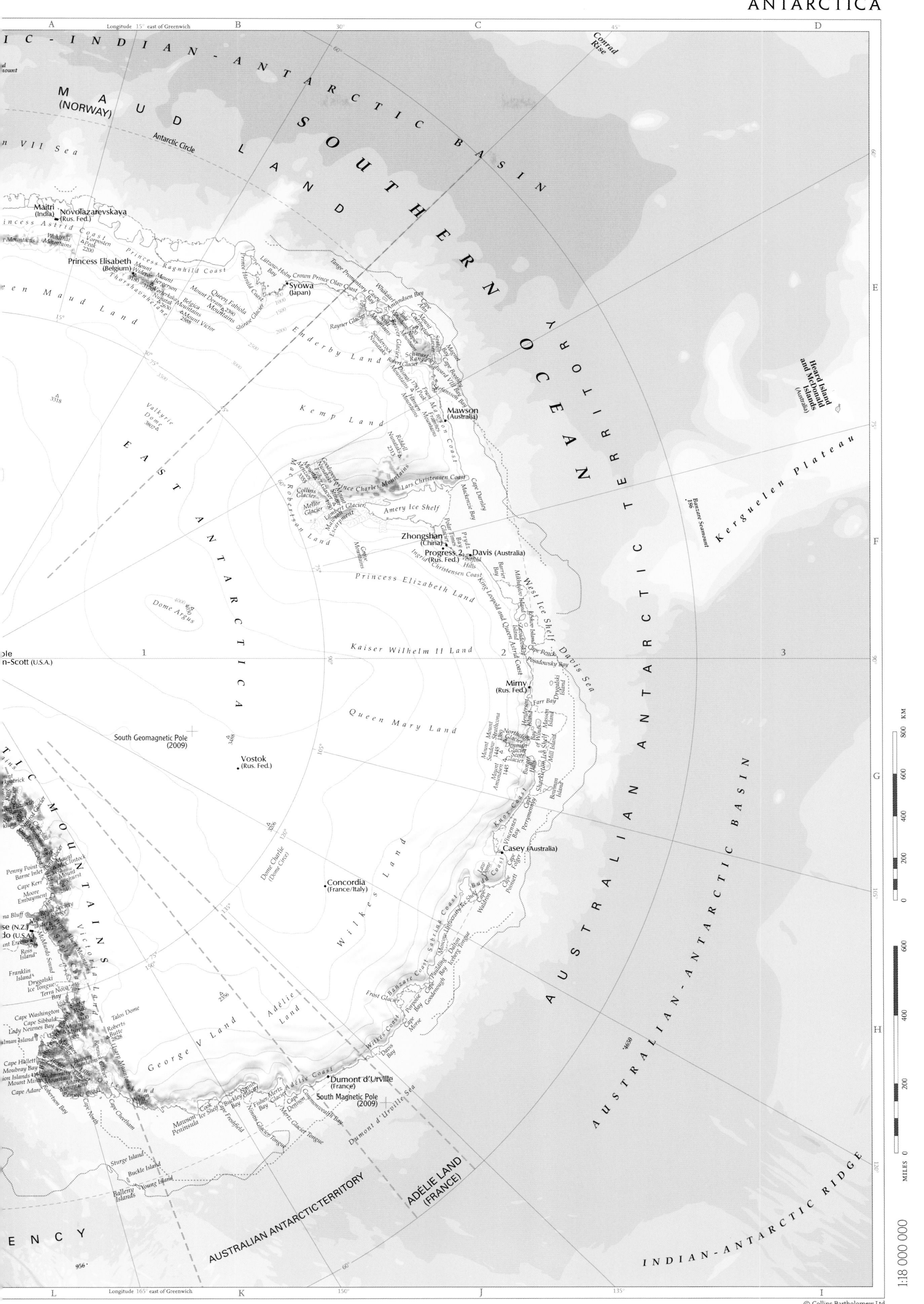
SOUTHERN OCEAN
EAST ANTARCTICA
QUEEN MAUD LAND (NORWAY)
AUSTRALIAN ANTARCTIC TERRITORY
ADÉLIE LAND (FRANCE)
AUSTRALIAN-ANTARCTIC BASIN
INDIAN-ANTARCTIC RIDGE
Kerguelen Plateau
Heard Island and McDonald Islands (Australia)
Enderby Land
Kemp Land
Mac. Robertson Land
Princess Elizabeth Land
Kaiser Wilhelm II Land
Queen Mary Land
Wilkes Land
George V Land
Adélie Land
Amery Ice Shelf
West Ice Shelf
Davis Sea
Dumont d'Urville Sea
Mawson (Australia)
Zhongshan (China)
Progress 2 (Rus. Fed.)
Davis (Australia)
Mirny (Rus. Fed.)
Casey (Australia)
Vostok (Rus. Fed.)
Concordia (France/Italy)
Dumont d'Urville (France)
South Magnetic Pole (2009)
South Geomagnetic Pole (2009)
Syowa (Japan)
Princess Elisabeth (Belgium)
Maitri (India)
Novolazarevskaya (Rus. Fed.)
Antarctic Circle
TRANSANTARCTIC MOUNTAINS
Longitude 15° east of Greenwich
Longitude 165° east of Greenwich
1:18 000 000
KM
MILES

Lambert Azimuthal Equal Area Projection

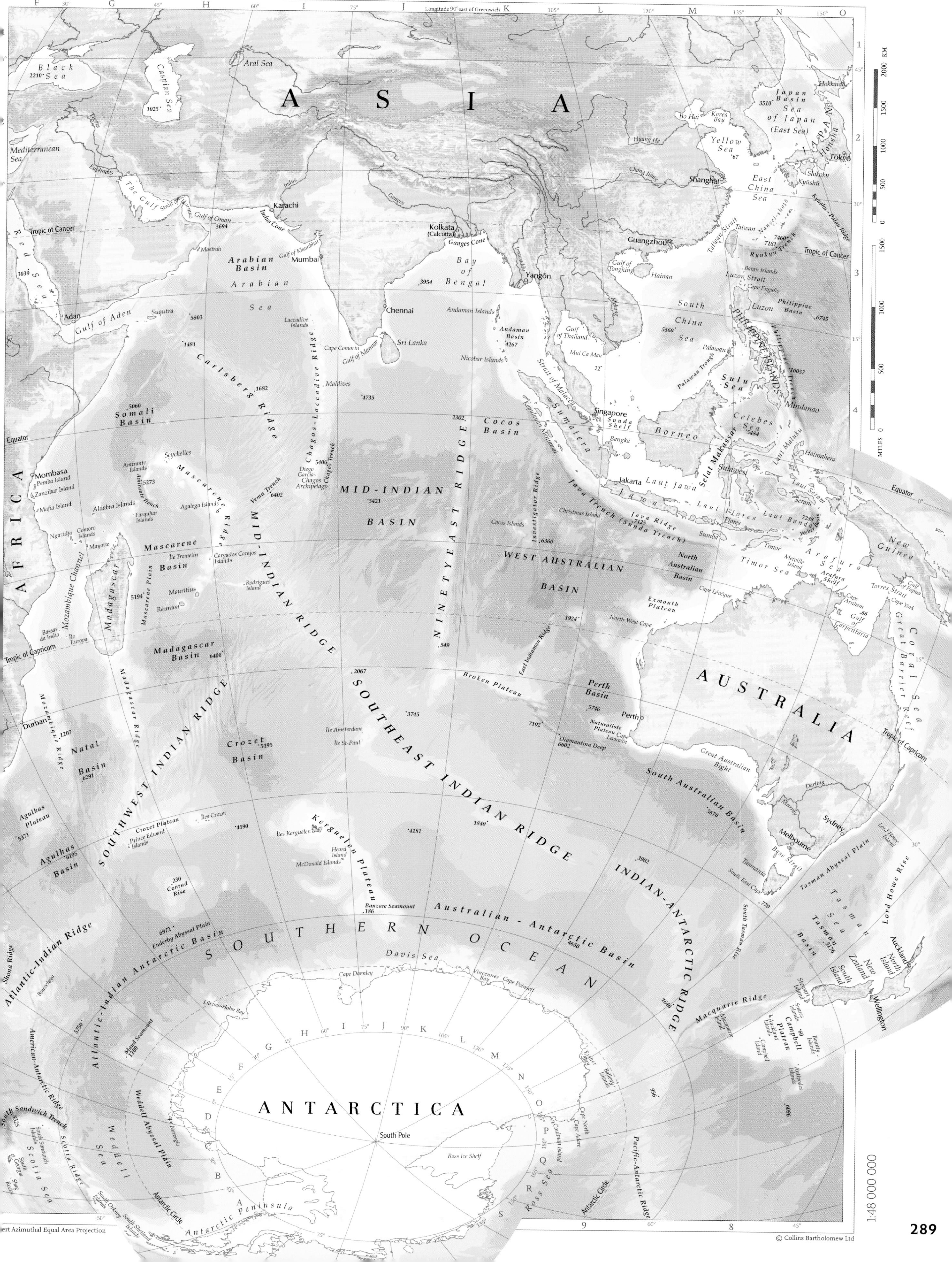
ASIA
AFRICA
AUSTRALIA
ANTARCTICA
SOUTHERN OCEAN
Arabian Sea
Bay of Bengal
South China Sea
MID-INDIAN BASIN
WEST AUSTRALIAN BASIN
NINETYEAST RIDGE
SOUTHEAST INDIAN RIDGE
SOUTHWEST INDIAN RIDGE
MID-INDIAN RIDGE
INDIAN-ANTARCTIC RIDGE
Carlsberg Ridge
Chagos-Laccadive Ridge
Mascarene Basin
Madagascar Basin
Crozet Basin
Kerguelen Plateau
Australian - Antarctic Basin
South Australian Basin
Perth Basin
Somali Basin
Arabian Basin
Tropic of Cancer
Equator
Tropic of Capricorn
Antarctic Circle
South Pole
Lambert Azimuthal Equal Area Projection
1:48 000 000
© Collins Bartholomew Ltd

4000 13124
3000 9843
2000 6562
1000 3281
500 1640
200 656
0 0
LAND BELOW SEA LEVEL
200 656
2000 6562
3000 9843
4000 13124
5000 16404
6000 19686
7000 22967
9000 29529
M FT

Lambert Azimuthal Equal Area Projection

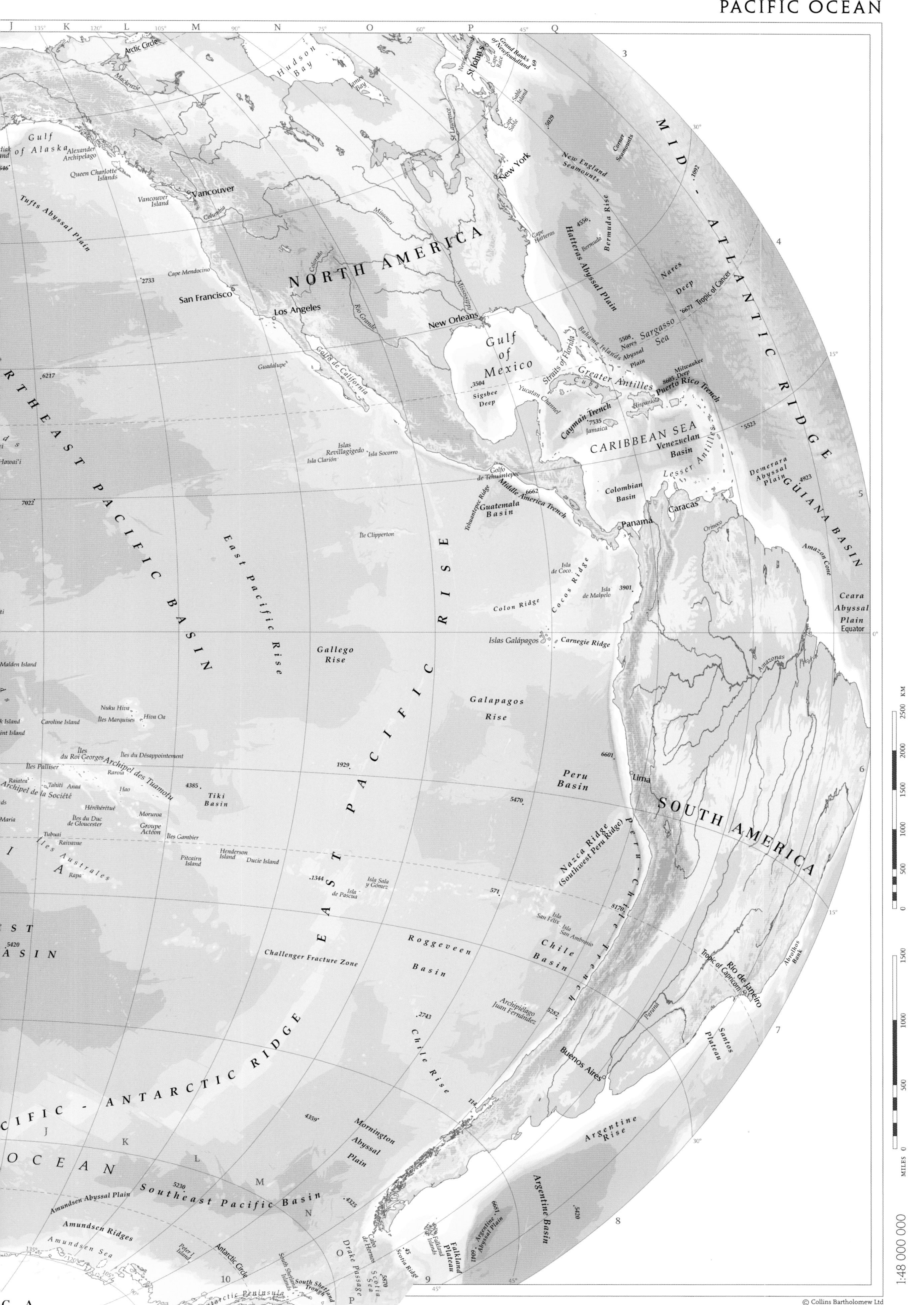
NORTH AMERICA
SOUTH AMERICA
Hudson Bay
James Bay
Gulf of Alaska
Alexander Archipelago
Queen Charlotte Islands
Vancouver Island
Vancouver
Tufts Abyssal Plain
Cape Mendocino
San Francisco
Los Angeles
New Orleans
New York
St John's
Grand Banks of Newfoundland
Newfoundland Basin
New England Seamounts
Corner Seamounts
Bermuda Rise
Hatteras Abyssal Plain
Cape Hatteras
Bermuda
Nares Deep
Tropic of Cancer
Sargasso Sea
MID - ATLANTIC RIDGE
Gulf of Mexico
Sigsbee Deep
Straits of Florida
Bahama Islands
Nares Abyssal Plain
Greater Antilles
Milwaukee Deep
Puerto Rico Trench
Yucatan Channel
Cayman Trench
Jamaica
Hispaniola
CARIBBEAN SEA
Venezuelan Basin
Lesser Antilles
Colombian Basin
Caracas
Panama
Demerara Abyssal Plain
GUIANA BASIN
Amazon Cone
Ceara Abyssal Plain
Equator
Golfo de California
Guadalupe
Islas Revillagigedo
Isla Socorro
Isla Clarión
Golfo de Tehuantepec
Middle America Trench
Tehuantepec Ridge
Guatemala Basin
Île Clipperton
Isla de Coco
Cocos Ridge
Isla de Malpelo
Colon Ridge
Islas Galápagos
Carnegie Ridge
NORTHEAST PACIFIC BASIN
East Pacific Rise
EAST PACIFIC RISE
Gallego Rise
Galapagos Rise
Malden Island
Caroline Island
Nuku Hiva
Îles Marquises
Hiva Oa
Îles du Désappointement
Îles du Roi Georges
Îles Palliser
Archipel des Tuamotu
Raroia
Tahiti
Anaa
Hao
Archipel de la Société
Hérèhérètué
Îles du Duc de Gloucester
Moruroa
Groupe Actéon
Îles Gambier
Tubuai
Raivavae
Îles Australes
Rapa
Pitcairn Island
Henderson Island
Ducie Island
Tiki Basin
Peru Basin
Lima
Nazca Ridge (Southwest Peru Ridge)
Peru-Chile Trench
Isla Sala y Gómez
Isla de Pascua
Isla San Félix
Isla San Ambrosio
Chile Basin
Roggeveen Basin
Challenger Fracture Zone
Archipiélago Juan Fernández
Chile Rise
PACIFIC - ANTARCTIC RIDGE
Tropic of Capricorn
Rio de Janeiro
Abrolhos Bank
Paraná
Santos Plateau
Buenos Aires
Argentine Rise
Mornington Abyssal Plain
Argentine Basin
Argentine Abyssal Plain
Falkland Plateau
Falkland Islands
Cabo de Hornos
Scotia Ridge
Scotia Sea
Drake Passage
South Shetland Trough
South Shetland Islands
Antarctic Peninsula
Antarctic Circle
Peter I Island
Amundsen Sea
Amundsen Ridges
Amundsen Abyssal Plain
Southeast Pacific Basin
OCEAN
1:48 000 000
MILES 0 500 1000 1500
0 500 1000 1500 2000 2500 KM

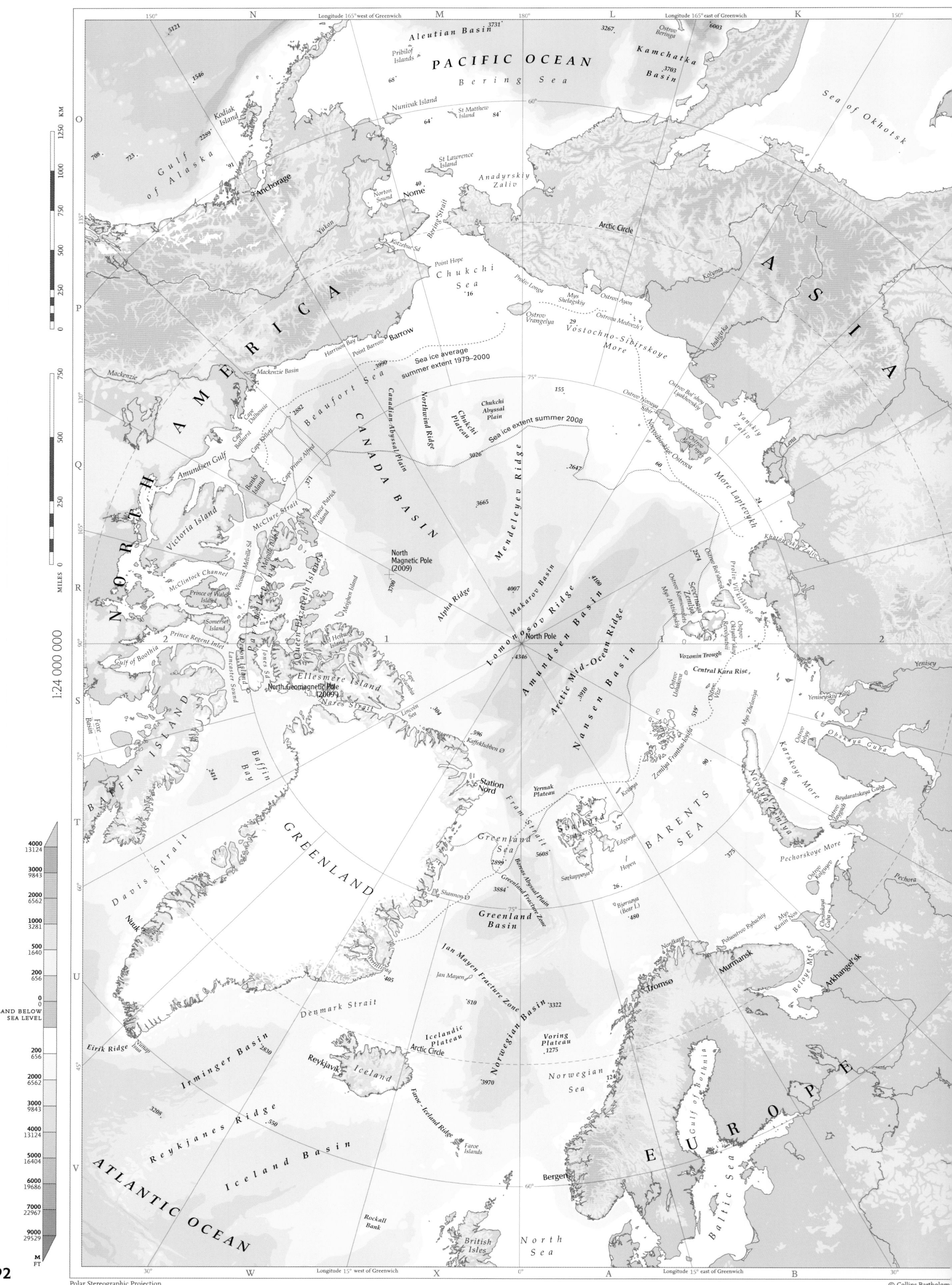

Polar Stereographic Projection

A

Geographical term	Language	Meaning
-á	Icelandic	river
-å	Danish	river
Āb	Farsi	river
Abajo	Spanish	lower
Abbaye	French	abbey
Abhainn	Gaelic	river
Abyār	Arabic	wells
Açude	Portuguese	reservoir
Adası	Azeri, Turkish	island
Adrar	Berber	hills, mountains
Agia, Agios	Greek	saint
Agioi	Greek	saints
Aiguille	French	peak
Ain, ‘Ain, ‘Aîn, Aïn, ’Aïn	Arabic	spring, well
Akra	Greek	cape, point
Ala-	Finnish	lower
Allt	Gaelic	river
Alpi	Italian	mountain range
Alpe	Slovene	mountain range
Alpen	German	mountain range
Alpes	French	mountain range
Alt-	German	old
Alta	Italian, Portuguese, Spanish	upper
Altiplanicie	Spanish	high plain
Alto	Italian, Portuguese, Spanish	upper
Alto	Spanish	summit
-älv, -älven	Swedish	river
Ano	Greek	upper
Anou, Ânou	Berber	well
Anse	French	bay
Ao	Thai	bay
Archipel	French	archipelago
Archipiélago	Spanish	archipelago
Arenas	Spanish	sands
Argelanots’	Armenian	reserve
Arkhipelag	Russian	archipelago
Arquipélago	Portuguese	archipelago
Arrecife	Spanish	reef
Arriba	Spanish	upper
Arroio	Portuguese	watercourse
Arroyo	Spanish	watercourse
Augstiene	Latvian	hill region
Aust-	Norwegian	east, eastern
Austur-	Icelandic	east, eastern
Avtonomnaya, Avtonomnyy	Russian	autonomous
Āw	Kurdish	river
‘Ayn	Arabic	spring, waterhole, well

B

Geographical term	Language	Meaning
Baai, -baai	Afrikaans, Dutch	bay
Bāb	Arabic	strait
Bad	German	spa
Badia	Catalan	bay
Bādiyah	Arabic	desert
Bælt	Danish	strait
Bagh	Gaelic	bay
Bahia	Portuguese	bay
Bahía	Spanish	bay
Bahr, Baḩr, Baḩr	Arabic	bay, lake, canal, river, watercourse
Bahra, Baḩra	Arabic	lagoon, lake
Baía	Portuguese	bay
Baie	French	bay
Baixa, Baixo	Portuguese	lower
Baja	Spanish	lower
Bajja	Maltese	bay
Bajo	Spanish	depression, lower
Bālā	Farsi	upper
Ban	Laotian, Thai	village
Banc	Welsh	hill
Banco	Spanish	shoal
Bandao	Chinese	peninsula
Bandar	Arabic, Farsi, Somali	anchorage, inlet, port, harbour
Bandar	Malay	port, town
Banī	Arabic	desert
Banjaran	Malay	mountain range
Baraj, Barajı	Turkish	dam
Barat	Indonesian, Malay	west, western
Barra	Portuguese, Spanish	sandbank, sandbar, spit
Barrage	French	dam
Barragem	Portuguese	dam, reservoir
Barranco	Spanish	gorge, ravine
Baruun	Mongolian	west, western
Bas, Basse	French	lower
Bassin	French	basin
Bāţin, Baţn	Arabic	depression
-beek	Afrikaans, Dutch	river
Beg, Beag	Gaelic, Irish	small
Bei	Chinese	north, northern
bei	German	at, near
Beinn	Gaelic	mountain
Belogor’ye	Russian	mountain range
Ben	Gaelic	mountain
Bereg	Russian	coastal area
-berg, -berge	German, Norwegian, Swedish, Afrikaans	mountain, mountains
Besar	Indonesian, Malay	big
Bi’ār	Arabic	wells
Bir, Bi’r, Bîr	Arabic	waterhole, well
Birkat	Arabic	waterhole, well
-bjerg	Danish	hill
Boca	Portuguese, Spanish	mouth
Bodden	German	bay
Boğazı	Turkish	strait, pass
Bois	French	forest, wood
Boloto	Russian	marsh
Bol’shaya, Bol’shiye, Bol’shoy, Bol’shoye	Russian	big
-bong	Korean	mountain
Boquerón	Spanish	pass
Bory	Polish	woods
-botn	Norwegian	valley floor
-botten	Swedish	valley floor
Böyük	Azeri	big
Braţul	Romanian	arm, branch
-bre, -breen	Norwegian	glacier
Bredning	Danish	bay
Breg	Croatian, Serbian	hill
-bron	Afrikaans	spring, well
Brücke	German	bridge
Bucht	German	bay
Bugt	Danish	bay
-bugten	Danish	bay
Bukhta	Russian	bay
Bukit	Indonesian, Malay	hill, mountain
-bukt, -bukta	Norwegian	bay
-bukten	Swedish	bay
Bulag	Mongolian	spring
Bulak	Russian, Uighur	spring
Bum	Burmese	mountain
Burnu, Burun	Turkish	cape, point
Büyük	Turkish	big
Bwlch	Welsh	pass

C

Geographical term	Language	Meaning
Cabo	Portuguese, Spanish	cape, point
Cachoeira	Portuguese	waterfall
Caka	Tibetan	salt lake
Cala	Catalan, Italian	bay
Caleta	Spanish	inlet
Câmpia	Romanian	plain
Campo	Italian, Spanish	plain
Cañada, Cañadón	Spanish	ravine, gorge
Canal	French, Portuguese, Spanish	canal, channel
Caño	Spanish	river
Cañon	Spanish	canyon
Caol	Gaelic	hill
Cap	Catalan, French	cape, point
Capo	Italian	cape, point
Carn	Welsh	hill
Castell	Catalan	castle
Causse	French	limestone plateau
Çay, -çay, Çayı, -çayı	Azeri, Turkish	river
Cayo	Spanish	island
Cefn	Welsh	hill, ridge
Cerro	Spanish	hill, mountain, peak
Česká, České, Český	Czech	Czech
Chaco	Spanish	plain
Chāh	Farsi	river
Chaîne	French	mountain range
Cham	Kurdish	river
Chapada	Portuguese	hills, uplands
Château	French	castle, palace
Chau	Chinese	island
Chaung	Burmese	river
Chāy	Kurdish	river
Chhu	Dzongkha (Bhutan)	river
Chiang	Thai	town
Chink	Russian	hill range
Chiyā	Kurdish	mountain, hill range
Chott	Arabic	salt lake
Chuan	Chinese	river
Chuŏr Phnum	Cambodian	mountain range
Ci	Indonesian	river
Ciénaga	Spanish	marshy lake
Cima	Italian	peak
Cime	French	peak
Città	Italian	city
Ciudad	Spanish	town, city
Cnoc	Gaelic	hill
Co	Tibetan	lake
Col	French	pass
Collado	Spanish	mountain
Colle	Italian	pass
Colline	French	hill
Cona	Tibetan	lake
Cordillera	Spanish	mountain range
Corno	Italian	peak
Coronel	Spanish	colonel
Costa	Catalan, Italian, Portuguese, Spanish	coastal area
Côte	French	coast, hill region, slope
Coutada	Portuguese	reserve
Coxilha	Portuguese	mountain pasture
Cratère	French	crater
Creag	Gaelic	mountain
Cruz	Spanish	cross
Cu Lao	Vietnamese	island
Cuchilla	Spanish	mountain range
Cuenca	Spanish	deep valley, river basin
Cueva	Spanish	cave
Cumbre	Spanish	mountain
-cun	Chinese	village

D

Geographical term	Language	Meaning
Da	Chinese	big
Da	Vietnamese	river
Dağ, Dağı	Azeri, Turkish	hill(s), mountain(s)
Dāgh	Farsi	mountain(s)
Dağları	Turkish	mountains
-dake	Japanese	hill, mountain
-dal	Afrikaans, Danish, Swedish	valley
-dal, -dalen	Norwegian	valley
-dalur	Icelandic	valley
-dan	Korean	cape, point
Danau	Indonesian, Malay	lake
Dao	Chinese	island
Đao	Vietnamese	island
Daqq	Farsi	salt flat, salt lake
-dara	Tajik	river
Darreh	Farsi	valley
Dar’ya	Russian	river
Daryācheh	Farsi	lake
Dashan	Chinese	mountain
Dasht	Farsi	desert
Dataran Tinggi	Malay	plateau
Davan	Kazakh	pass
Dawḩat	Arabic	bay
Dayr	Arabic	monastery
Dealul	Romanian	hill, mountain
Dealurile	Romanian	hills
Deh	Farsi	village
Deir	Arabic	monastery
Denizi	Turkish	sea
Deresi	Turkish	river
Desierto	Spanish	desert
Détroit	French	channel
-diep	Dutch	channel
Dingzi	Chinese	hill, small mountain
Djebel	Arabic	mountain
-do	Korean	island
Dolna, Dolni	Bulgarian	lower
Dolna, Dolne, Dolny	Polish	lower
Dolní	Czech	lower
Dong	Chinese	east, eastern
-dong	Korean	village
Donja, Donji	Croatian, Serbian	lower
Dorf	German	village
-dorp	Afrikaans, Dutch	village
Druim	Gaelic	hill, mountain
Dund	Mongolian	middle, central
Düzü	Azeri	plain
-dyngja	Icelandic	hill, mountain
Dzüün	Mongolian	east, eastern

E

Geographical term	Language	Meaning
Eilean	Gaelic	island
-elv, -elva	Norwegian	river
Embalse	Spanish	reservoir
‘Emeq	Hebrew	plain
Ensenada	Spanish	bay
Erg, ’Erg, ‘Erg	Arabic	sand dunes
Eski	Turkish	old
Estany	Catalan	pond
Estero	Spanish	estuary, inlet, lagoon
Estrada	Spanish	bay
Estrecho	Spanish	strait
Étang	French	lagoon, lake
-ey, -eyjar	Icelandic	island, islands
-eyri	Icelandic	sandbar
ežeras	Lithuanian	lake
ezers	Latvian	lake

F

Geographical term	Language	Meaning
Falaise	French	cliff, escarpment
Farihy	Malagasy	lake
Fayéat	Arabic	waterhole
-fell	Icelandic	hill, mountain
Fels	German	rock
Feng	Chinese	mountain
Fiume	Italian	river
-fjäll, -fjällen, -fjället	Swedish	hill(s), mountain(s)
-fjallgarður	Icelandic	mountains
-fjara	Icelandic	beach
-fjell, -fjellet	Norwegian	mountain
-fjöll	Icelandic	hill(s), mountain(s)
Fjord, -fjord, -fjorden	Danish, Norwegian, Swedish	fjord
-fjörður	Icelandic	fjord
Fliegu	Maltese	channel
-fljót	Icelandic	river
-flói	Icelandic	bay
-főcsatorna	Hungarian	canal
Foel	Welsh	hill
Förde	German	inlet
Forêt	French	forest
Forst	German	forest
-foss	Icelandic	waterfall

Geographical term	Language	Meaning
-foss, -fossen	Norwegian	rapids, waterfall
Fuente	Spanish	source, well
Fulayj	Arabic	watercourse

G

Geographical term	Language	Meaning
-gan	Japanese	rock
Gang	Dzongkha (Bhutan)	mountain
Gang	Chinese	bay, river
-gang	Korean	river
Gaoyuan	Chinese	plateau
Gardaneh	Farsi	pass
-gat	Dutch	channel
-gata	Japanese	inlet, lagoon, lake
Gau	German	district
Gave	French	torrent
-gawa	Japanese	river
Gebel	Arabic	mountain
Gebergte	Dutch	mountain range
Gebiet	German	district, region
Gebirge	German	mountains
Geodha	Gaelic	inlet
Gezâ'ir	Arabic	islands
Gezirat	Arabic	island
Ghard	Arabic	sand dunes
Ghubba, Ghubbat	Arabic	bay
Gjiri	Albanian	bay
Gletscher	German	glacier
Gobernador	Spanish	governor
Gobi	Mongolian	desert
Gol	Mongolian	river
Göl	Azeri	lake
Golets	Russian	mountain
Golf	Catalan	gulf
Golfe	French	bay, gulf
Golfo	Italian, Spanish	bay, gulf
Gölü	Azeri, Turkish	lake
Gora	Bulgarian, Croatian, Russian, Serbian	mountain(s)
Gorges	French	gorge
Górka	Polish	hill
Gornja, Gornje, Gornji	Croatian, Serbian	upper
Gorno-	Russian	mountainous
Gory	Russian	mountains
Góry	Polish	mountains
Gou	Chinese	river
Graben	German	trench
-grad	Bulgarian, Croatian, Russian, Serbian	town
Grand, Grande	French	big
-gród	Polish	town
Groot	Afrikaans, Dutch	big
Gross, Grosse, Grossen, Grosser (also Groß-)	German	big
Grotta	Italian	cave
Grotte	French	cave
Grotte	Italian	caves
Groupe	French	group
Grund	German	ground, valley
Gruppo	Italian	group
Gryada	Russian	mountains
Guan	Chinese	pass
Guba	Russian	bay, gulf
Gubed	Somali	bay
-guntō	Japanese	islands
Gunung	Indonesian, Malay	mountain
Guri	Albanian	peak

H

Geographical term	Language	Meaning
Ḥafar	Arabic	wells
Hafen	German	port, harbour
Haff	German	bay
Hai	Chinese	lake, sea
Haixia	Chinese	channel, strait
-háls	Icelandic	ridge
-halvøya	Norwegian	peninsula
Hamada, Hammada	Arabic	plateau
-hamn	Norwegian, Swedish	port, harbour
-hamrar	Icelandic	cliffs
Hāmūn	Farsi	marsh, salt pan
-hantō	Japanese	peninsula
Har	Hebrew	mountain
Hara	Belorussian	hill
Hardt	German	wooded hills
Ḥarrat, Ḥarrāt	Arabic	lava field
Hassi	Arabic	well
-haug, -haugen	Norwegian	hill
-havn	Danish, Faroese, Norwegian	bay, harbour, port
Hawr	Arabic	lake, impermanent lake, marsh
Häyk'	Amharic	lake
He	Chinese	river
-hegység	Hungarian	hills, mountains
-hei	Norwegian	heath, moor
-heide	Dutch	heath, marsh
Heide	German	heath, moor
-heiði	Icelandic	heath
Helodrano	Malagasy	bay
Higashi-	Japanese	east, eastern
-hisar	Turkish	castle
Ḥiṣn	Arabic	fort
Hka	Burmese	river
-hnjúkur	Icelandic	hill
-ho	Korean	lake
-hø	Norwegian	peak
Hoch	German	high
Hoek	Dutch	cape, point
-höfði	Icelandic	hill, mountain
-höfn	Icelandic	cove
Hög	Swedish	height, high
-högda	Norwegian	height
Höhe	German	height
Hohen-	German	high
Hoi, Hoi Hap	Chinese	bay, channel, harbour, inlet
-høj, -høje	Danish	hill, hills
Hon	Vietnamese	island
Hoog	Dutch	high
Hora, Hory	Czech, Ukrainian	mountain(s)
-horn	Icelandic	cape, point, peak
Horn, -horn	German	mountain, peak
Horná, Horné, Horní, Horný	Czech	upper
Ḥorvot	Hebrew	ruins
-hot	Mongolian	town
-hrad	Czech	town
-hraun	Icelandic	lava field
Hu	Chinese	lake

I

Geographical term	Language	Meaning
Idd	Arabic	well
Île	French	island
Ilha, Ilhéu	Portuguese	island
Illa	Catalan	island
im	German	in
imeni	Russian	in the name of
Inish	Irish	island
Insel, Inseln	German	island, islands
Insula	Romanian	island
Irq, 'Irq	Arabic	hill, sand dune, sand dunes
Isla	Spanish	island
Iso-	Finnish	big
Isola, Isole	Italian	island, islands
Islote	Catalan	island
Isthme	French	isthmus
Istmo	Spanish	isthmus
-iwa	Japanese	island

J

Geographical term	Language	Meaning
Jabal	Arabic	mountain
järv	Estonian	lake
-järvi	Finnish	lake
Jasiired	Somali	island
Jaun-	Latvian	new
-jaure	Lappish	lake
Jazīrah, Jazīreh, Jazīrat	Arabic	island
Jbel, Jebel	Arabic	mountain
Jezero, jezero	Croatian, Serbian, Slovene	lake
Jezioro	Polish	lake
Jiang	Chinese	river
Jiao	Chinese	cape, point
Jibāl	Arabic	mountains
-jima	Japanese	island
Jing	Chinese	well
-jõgi	Estonian	river
-joki	Finnish	river
-jokka	Lappish	river
-jökull, jökullen	Icelandic, Norwegian	glacier, ice cap

K

Geographical term	Language	Meaning
Kaap	Afrikaans	cape, point
-kai	Japanese	bay, channel
-kaigan	Japanese	coastal area
-kaikyō	Japanese	channel, strait
Kali	Indonesian, Malay	river
kalnas, kalnis	Lithuanian	hill
kalns	Latvian	hill
Kamen'	Russian	rock
Kamm	German	ridge, crest
Kâmpóng	Cambodian	town, village
-kanaal	Dutch	canal
Kanal	German, Russian	canal
Kanał	Polish	canal
Kanalı	Azeri	canal
Kaôh	Cambodian	island
Kap	Danish	cape, point
Kapp	Norwegian	cape, point
Karang	Indonesian, Malay	reef
Kato	Greek	lower
Kavīr	Farsi	salt desert
-kawa	Japanese	river
Kecil	Indonesian, Malay	small
K'edi	Georgian	hills
Kefar	Hebrew	village
Kepi	Albanian	cape, point
Kepulauan	Indonesian	islands
Keski-	Finnish	middle, central
Khabrah, Khabrat	Arabic	impermanent lake
Khalīg, Khalīj	Arabic	bay, gulf
Khao	Thai	peak
Khashm	Arabic	hill
Khawr	Arabic	bay, channel
Khor, Khōr	Arabic	bay
Khowr	Farsi	bay, inlet
Khrebet	Russian	mountain range
Kis-	Hungarian	small
Kita-	Japanese	north, northern
Klein	Afrikaans	small
Klein, Kleine, Kleiner	German	small
Klint	Danish	cliff
-kloof	Afrikaans	pass
Knock	Irish	hill
-ko	Japanese	lake
Ko	Thai	island
-kōchi, -kōgen	Japanese	plateau
Koh	Farsi	mountain
Kok	Chinese	cape, point
Köl	Kazakh, Kyrgyz	lake
Kolpos	Greek	gulf
Koog	German	polder (reclaimed land)
-kop	Afrikaans	hill, mountain
Kopf	German	hill
Körfezi	Turkish	bay, gulf
körgustik	Estonian	upland
Kosa	Russian, Ukrainian	spit
Kou	Chinese	river mouth
-köy	Turkish	village
Kraj	Croatian, Czech, Polish, Serbian	region
Krajobrazowy	Polish	regional
Kray	Russian	territory
Kryazh	Russian	hills, ridge
Kuala	Malay	river mouth
Küçük	Turkish	small
Kuduk	Uighur	well
Kūh	Farsi	mountain
Kūhhā	Farsi	mountain range
Kul'	Russian	lake
-kŭl	Tajik	lake
-küla	Estonian	village
Kum	Russian	sandy desert
-kundo	Korean	islands
Kuppe	German	hill top
kurk	Estonian	channel, strait
K'vemo	Georgian	upper
-kvísl, kvíslar	Icelandic	river, rivers
-kylä	Finnish	village
Kyun	Burmese	island

L

Geographical term	Language	Meaning
La	Tibetan	pass
Lac	French	lake
Lacul	Romanian	lake
Laem	Thai	cape, point
Lago	Italian, Portuguese, Spanish	lake
Lagoa	Portuguese	lagoon
Laguna	Spanish	lagoon, lake
Lagune	French	lagoon
laht	Estonian	bay
-laid	Estonian	island
Lam	Thai	river
Län	Swedish	county
Land	German	province
Lande	French	heath, sandy moor
Las	Polish	wood, forest
Laut	Indonesian, Malay	sea
Lerr	Armenian	mountain
Lerrnashght'a	Armenian	mountains
Lich	Armenian	lake
Liedao	Chinese	islands
Liel-	Latvian	big
Lille	Danish, Norwegian	small
Liman	Russian	bay, lagoon, lake
Limni	Greek	lagoon, lake
Limnothalassa	Greek	inlet, lagoon
Ling	Chinese	mountain range
Liqeni	Albanian	lake
Llano	Spanish	plain, prairie
Llyn	Welsh	lake
Loch, Lochan	Gaelic	lake, small lake
Lohatanjona	Malagasy	cape, point
Loi	Burmese	mountain
looduskaitseala	Estonian	reserve
Luonnonpuisto	Finnish	nature reserve
-luoto	Finnish	rocky island
Lyman	Ukrainian	bay, lake

M

Geographical term	Language	Meaning
Macizo	Spanish	mountain range
Madh	Albanian	big
Madīnat	Arabic	town
Mae, Mae Nam	Thai	river
mägi	Estonian	hill
Măgura	Romanian	hill, mountain
Maḥaṭṭat	Arabic	station
Maja	Albanian	mountain
Mal	Albanian	mountain(s)
Mala	Croatian, Serbian	small
Malá	Czech, Slovak	small
Mali	Albanian	mountain
Mali	Croatian, Serbian, Ukrainian	small
Malo	Croatian, Serbian	small
Maloye	Russian	small
Maly, Malyya	Belorussian	small
-man	Korean	bay
Mar	Spanish	lagoon, lake
Marais	French	marsh, swamp
Mare	Italian	sea
Mare	Romanian	big
marios	Lithuanian	lake
Marsa	Arabic	anchorage, bay, inlet
Marsch	German	fen, marsh
Masabb	Arabic	estuary
Massif	French	mountains, upland
Ma'ṭan	Arabic	well
Mayor	Spanish	higher, larger
Maz-	Latvian	small
Meall	Gaelic	hill, mountain
Meer	Dutch, German	lake
Mega, Megalo-	Greek	big
Men	Chinese	gate
Menor	Portuguese, Spanish	smaller, lesser
Mersa	Arabic	anchorage, inlet
Mesa, Meseta	Spanish	tableland
Mesto	Croatian, Serbian	town
Město	Czech	town
Mets	Armenian	big
Mezzo	Italian	middle, central
Miao	Chinese	temple
Miasto	Polish	town
Mic, Mica	Romanian	small
Mikra, Mikri	Greek	small

Geographical term	Language	Meaning
Minā'	Arabic	port, harbour
Minami-	Japanese	south, southern
-mine	Japanese	mountain
-misaki	Japanese	cape, point
Mishāsh	Arabic	well
Mittel-, Mitten-	German	middle, central
Moel	Welsh	hill
Monasterio	Spanish	monastery
Moni	Greek	monastery
Mont	French	hill, mountain
Montagna	Italian	mountain
Montagne	French	mountain
Monte	Italian, Portuguese, Spanish	hill, mountain
Monti	Italian	mountains
Moor	German	marsh, moor, swamp
Moos	German	marsh, moss
More	Russian	sea
Mörön	Mongolian	river
Morro	Portuguese	hill
Morro	Spanish	cape, point
-mose	Danish	marsh, moor
Moyen	French	middle, central
Mt'a	Georgian	mountain
Muang	Laotian, Thai	town
Muara	Indonesian, Malay	estuary
Mui	Vietnamese	cape, point
Mun	Chinese	channel
Munţii	Romanian	mountains
Mynydd	Welsh	mountain
-mýri	Icelandic	marsh
Mys	Russian	cape, point

N

Geographical term	Language	Meaning
na	Croatian, Czech, Russian, Serbian, Slovak, Slovene	on
Nacional	Portuguese, Spanish	national
nacionalinis	Lithuanian	national
nad	Czech, Polish, Slovak	above, over
-nada	Japanese	bay, gulf
Nafūd	Arabic	desert, sand dunes
Nagor'ye	Russian	mountains, plateau
Nagy-	Hungarian	big
Nahr	Arabic	river
Nakhon	Thai	town
Nakrdzali	Georgian	reserve
Nam	Burmese, Laotian	river
Nam	Korean, Vietnamese	south, southern
Nan	Chinese	south, southern
Nanshan	Chinese	mountain range
Narodowy	Polish	national
Nationaal	Dutch	national
Naturreservat	Norwegian, Swedish	nature reserve
Natuurreservaat	Dutch	nature reserve
Naviglio	Italian	canal
Nawa-	Urdu	new
Nazionale	Italian	national
Neder-	Dutch	lower
Nehri	Turkish	river
Nei	Chinese	inner
Nek	Afrikaans	pass
-nes	Icelandic	cape, point
Neu-	German	new
Neuf, Neuve	French	new
Nevado, Nevada	Spanish	snow-covered mountain(s)
Nieder-	German	lower
Nieuw, Nieuwe, Nieuwer	Dutch	new
nina	Estonian	cape, point
Nishi-	Japanese	west, western
Nizhneye, Nizhniy, Nizhniye, Nizhnyaya	Russian	lower
Nizina	Belorussian, Bulgarian, Polish	lowland
Nízke	Slovak	low
Nizmennost'	Russian	lowland
Nižní	Czech	lower
Nižný	Slovak	lower
Noguera	Catalan	river
Noord	Dutch	north, northern
Nord	French, German	north, northern
Nord-, Nordre	Danish	north, northern
Norður	Icelandic	north, northern
Norra	Swedish	north, northern
Nørre	Danish	north, northern
Norte	Portuguese, Spanish	north, northern
Nos	Bulgarian, Russian	cape, point, spit
Nosy	Malagasy	island
Nou	Romanian	new
Nouveau, Nouvelle	French	new
Nova	Bulgarian, Croatian, Portuguese, Serbian, Slovene, Ukrainian	new
Nová	Czech	new
Novaya	Russian	new
Nové	Czech, Slovak	new
Novi	Bulgarian, Croatian, Serbian, Ukrainian	new
Novo	Portuguese, Slovene	new
Novo-, Novoye	Russian	new
Novy	Belorussian	new
Nový	Czech	new
Novyy, Novyye	Russian, Ukrainian	new
Novyya	Belorussian	new
Nowa, Nowe, Nowy	Polish	new
Nueva, Nuevo	Spanish	new
-numa	Japanese	lake
-núpur	Icelandic	hill
Nur	Chinese, Mongolian	lake
Nuruu	Mongolian	mountain range
Nuur	Mongolian	lake
Ny-	Danish, Norwegian, Swedish	new

O

Geographical term	Language	Meaning
-ø	Danish	island
-ö	Swedish	island
oaivi, oaivve	Lappish	hill, mountain
Obanbari	Tajik	reservoir
Ober-	German	upper
Oblast'	Russian, Ukrainian	administrative division
-odde	Danish, Norwegian	cape, point
Oeste	Spanish	west, western
Okrug	Russian	administrative district
-ön	Swedish	island
Öndör-	Mongolian	upper
-oog	German	island
Oost, Ooster	Dutch	east, eastern
-öræfi	Icelandic	lava field
Oriental	Spanish	east, eastern
Ormos	Greek	bay
Oros	Greek	mountain
-ós	Icelandic	river mouth
Ost-	German	east, eastern
Øster-	Danish, Norwegian	east, eastern
Östra-	Swedish	east, eastern
Ostriv	Ukrainian	island
Ostrov, Ostrova	Russian	island, islands
Oud, Oude, Ouden, Ouder	Dutch	old
Oued	Arabic	watercourse
Ovası	Turkish	plain
Over-	Danish, Dutch	upper
Över-, Övre-	Norwegian, Swedish	upper
-oy	Faroese	island
Ozero	Russian, Ukrainian	lake

P

Geographical term	Language	Meaning
-pää	Finnish	hill
Pampa	Spanish	plain
Pantà	Catalan	reservoir
Pantanal	Portuguese	marsh
Pao	Chinese	small lake
Parbat	Urdu	mountain
Parc	French	park
Parc Naturel	French	nature reserve
Parco	Italian	park
parkas	Lithuanian	park
Parque	Portuguese, Spanish	park
-pas	Afrikaans	pass
Paso	Spanish	pass
Paß	German	pass
Passage	French	channel
Passe	French	channel
Passo	Italian	pass
Pasul	Romanian	pass
Pegunungan	Indonesian, Malay	mountain range
Pelabuhan	Malay	port, harbour
Pen	Welsh	hill
Peña	Spanish	cliff, rock
Pendi	Chinese	basin
Península	Spanish	peninsula
Péninsule	French	peninsula
Penisola	Italian	peninsula
Pereval	Russian	pass
Pervo-, Pervyy	Russian	first
Peski	Russian	desert
Petit, Petite	French	small
Phou	Laotian	mountain
Phu	Thai	mountain
Phumĭ	Cambodian	town, village
Pic	Catalan, French	peak
Picacho	Spanish	peak
Pico	Spanish	peak
Pik	Russian	peak
Pingyuan	Chinese	plain
Pivostriv	Ukrainian	peninsula
Pizzo	Italian	peak
-plaat	Dutch	flat, sandbank, shoal
Plage	French	beach
Plaine	French	plain
Planalto	Portuguese	plateau
Planina	Bulgarian, Croatian, Serbian	mountain(s)
Platforma	Romanian	plateau
Plato	Bulgarian, Russian	plateau
Playa	Spanish	beach
Plaza	Spanish	market-place, square
Ploskogor'ye	Russian	plateau
Po	Chinese	lake
pod	Czech, Russian, Slovak	under, sub-, near
Podişul	Romanian	plateau
Pointe	French	cape, point
Pojezierze	Polish	area of lakes
Polje	Croatian, Serbian	plain
Poluostrov	Russian	peninsula
Pont	French	bridge
Ponta	Maltese, Portuguese	cape, point
Ponte	Portuguese	bridge
poolsaar	Estonian	peninsula
Porogi	Russian	rapids
Port	Catalan, French, Maltese, Russian	port, harbour
Portella	Italian	pass
Portillo	Spanish	gap, pass
Porto	Italian, Portuguese, Spanish	bay, port, harbour, pass
Pradesh	Hindi	state
Praia	Portuguese	beach, shore
Prêk	Cambodian	lake, river
près	French	near, beside
Presa	Spanish	reservoir
Presqu'île	French	peninsula
Pri-	Russian	near, by
Proliv	Russian	channel, strait
Protoka	Russian	channel, watercourse
Pueblo	Spanish	village
Puente	Spanish	bridge
Puerta	Spanish	narrow pass
Puerto	Spanish	pass, port, harbour
Puig	Catalan	hill, mountain
Puk-	Korean	north, northern
Pulau	Indonesian, Malay	island
Pulau-pulau	Indonesian, Malay	islands
Puncak	Indonesian, Malay	hill, mountain, summit
Punta	Italian, Spanish	cape, point
Punta	Italian	hill, mountain
Puntan	Marshallese	cape, point
Puy	French	peak

Q

Geographical term	Language	Meaning
Qā'	Arabic	depression, salt flat, impermanent lake
Qabr	Arabic	tomb
Qafa	Albanian	pass
Qala	Maltese	bay
Qalamat	Arabic	well
Qalti	Arabic	well
Qâret	Arabic	hill
Qatorkŭhi	Tajik	mountain range
Qi	Chinese	banner (administrative division)
Qiao	Chinese	bridge
Qiryat	Hebrew	town
Qolleh	Farsi	mountain
Qoor, Qooriga	Somali	bay
qoruğu	Azeri	reserve
Qu	Tibetan	river
Quan	Chinese	spring, well
Quebrada	Spanish	ravine, river
Qullai	Tajik	mountain
Qundao	Chinese	islands

R

Geographical term	Language	Meaning
Raas	Somali	cape, point
Rade	French	harbour
rags	Latvian	cape, point
Rambla	Catalan	river
Ramla	Maltese	bay, harbour
Ramlat	Arabic	sandy desert
-rani	Icelandic	spur
Ras	Arabic, Maltese	cape, point
Ra's	Arabic, Farsi	cape, point
Râs, Răs	Arabic	cape, point
Ravnina	Russian	plain
Récif	French	reef
Represa	Portuguese, Spanish	reservoir
Reserva	Portuguese, Spanish	reserve
Réserve de Faune, Réserve Faunique	French	wildlife reserve
Réserve Naturelle	French	nature reserve
Reshteh	Farsi	mountain range
Respublika	Russian	republic
-rettō	Japanese	island chain, island group
rezervatas	Lithuanian	reserve
-ri	Korean	village
Ri	Tibetan	mountain
Ría	Spanish	estuary, inlet, river mouth
Ribeirão, Ribeiro	Portuguese	river
Rio	Portuguese	river
Río	Spanish	river
Riserva	Italian	reserve
-rivier	Afrikaans	river
Riviera	Italian	coastal area
Rivière	French	river
Roca	Spanish	rock
Rocher	French	rock
Rt	Croatian, Serbian	cape, point
Rū, Rūbār	Kurdish	river
Rubh', Rubha	Gaelic	cape, point
Rūd, Rūdkhāneh	Farsi	river
Rujm	Arabic	hill

S

Geographical term	Language	Meaning
-saar	Estonian	island
-saari	Finnish	island
Sabkhat, Sabkhet	Arabic	impermanent lake, salt flat, salt marsh
Sadd, Saddat	Arabic	dam
Sagar, Sagara	Hindi	lake
Şaghīr, Şaghīr	Arabic	small
Şaḩrā'	Arabic	desert
-saki	Japanese	cape, point
Salar, Salina	Spanish	salt pan
Salto	Portuguese, Spanish	waterfall
San	Italian, Maltese, Portuguese, Spanish	saint
San	Laotian	mountain
-san	Japanese, Korean	mountain
-sanchi	Japanese	mountain range
-sandur	Icelandic	sandy area
Sankt	German, Russian	saint
-sanmaek	Korean	mountain range
-sanmyaku	Japanese	mountain range
Sant	Catalan	saint
Sant'	Italian	saint
Santa	Italian, Portuguese, Spanish	saint
Santo	Italian, Portuguese, Spanish	saint
São	Portuguese	saint
Sar	Kurdish	mountain

Geographical term	Language	Meaning
Sarīr	Arabic	desert
Satu	Romanian	village
Say	Kyrgyz	river
Schloß	German	castle, mansion
Scoglio	Italian	reef, rock
Sebkha, Sebkhet	Arabic	salt flat, salt marsh
See, -see	German	lake
-şehir	Turkish	town
Selat	Indonesian, Malay	channel, strait
Selatan	Indonesian, Malay	south, southern
-selkä	Finnish	lake, open water, ridge
Selo	Croatian, Russian, Serbian	village
Selva	Portuguese, Spanish	forest
Semenanjung	Indonesian, Malay	peninsula
Seno	Spanish	bay, sound
Serra	Catalan, Portuguese	hills, mountains
Serranía	Spanish	mountain range
-seter	Norwegian	mountain pasture
-seto	Japanese	channel, strait
Severnaya, Severnoye, Severnyy, Severo-	Russian	north, northern
Sfântu	Romanian	saint
Sgeir	Gaelic	island
Sgor, Sgorach, Sgorr, Sgurr	Gaelic	hill
Shahr	Farsi	town
Sha'īb	Arabic	watercourse
Shamo	Chinese	desert
Shan	Chinese	hill(s), mountain(s)
Shang	Chinese	next to, upper
Shankou	Chinese	pass
Sharm	Arabic	bay
Shaṭṭ	Arabic	estuary, river mouth, watercourse
Shën-	Albanian	saint
Shet'	Amharic	watercourse
Shi	Chinese	city
-shima	Japanese	island
-sho	Japanese	island
-shotō	Japanese	islands
Shui	Chinese	river
Shui Tong	Chinese	reservoir
Shuiku	Chinese	reservoir
Sierra	Spanish	mountain range
Silsiläsi	Azeri	hills
-sjø	Norwegian	lake
-sjö, -sjön	Swedish	lake
-sjór	Icelandic	lake
-sker	Icelandic	island
-skog	Norwegian	wood
Slieau	Manx	hill, mountain
Slieve	Irish	hill, mountain
Sloboda	Russian	large village
Sø	Danish, Norwegian	lake
Söder, Södra	Swedish	south, southern
Solonchak	Russian	salt lake
Sommet	French	peak, summit
Sønder-, Søndre	Danish	south, southern
Sông	Vietnamese	river
Sopka	Russian	hill, mountain, volcano
Sør-	Norwegian	south, southern
Sor	Russian	salt pan
sous	French	under
Sovkhoz	Russian	state farm
Spitze	German	peak
Sredna, Sredno	Bulgarian	middle, central
Sredne-, Sredneye, Sredniy, Srednyaya	Russian	middle, central
Sron	Gaelic	hill
Stac	Gaelic	hill, stack
-stad	Afrikaans, Norwegian, Swedish	town
-stadt	German	town
-staður	Icelandic	town
Stagno	Italian	lagoon, lake
Stara, Stari	Croatian, Serbian, Ukrainian	old
Stará, Staré, Starý	Czech	old
Staraya, Stary, Staryya	Belorussian	old
Staraya, Staroye, Staryy, Staryye	Russian	old
Stare, Staro-, Staryy	Ukrainian	old
Stausee	German	reservoir
Steno	Greek	strait
Step'	Russian	plain, steppe
Stob	Gaelic	hill, mountain
Stœng	Cambodian	river
Stór-, Stóra, Stóri	Icelandic	big
Stor, Stora	Swedish	big
Store	Danish	big
Strand	Danish, German	beach
-strand	Norwegian, Swedish	beach
Straße	German	street
Stretta	Italian	strait
-strönd	Icelandic	beach
Sud	French	south, southern
Süd-, Süder-	German	south, southern
Suður-	Icelandic	south, southern
Suid	Afrikaans	south, southern
-suidō	Japanese	channel, strait
Sul	Portuguese	south, southern
sul, sull'	Italian	on
Sund	Swedish	strait, sound
Sungai	Indonesian, Malay	river
-suo	Finnish	marsh, swamp
Superior	Spanish	upper
Sūq	Arabic	market
Sur	Spanish	south, southern
sur	French	on
Suur	Estonian	big
Sveti	Croatian, Serbian	saint
Syðra, Syðri	Icelandic	south, southern
sýsla	Icelandic	county
Szent-	Hungarian	saint
-sziget	Hungarian	island

T

Geographical term	Language	Meaning
-tag	Uighur	mountain
-take	Japanese	hill, mountain
Tal	German	valley
Tall	Arabic	hill
Tanjona	Malagasy	cape, point
Tanjong, Tanjung	Indonesian, Malay	cape, point
Tao	Chinese	island
Tassili	Berber	plateau
Tau	Russian	mountain(s)
Taung	Burmese	mountain
Tba	Georgian	lake
Techniti Limni	Greek	reservoir
tekojärvi	Finnish	reservoir
Tell	Arabic	hill, mountain
Teluk, Telukan	Indonesian, Malay	bay, gulf
Tengah	Indonesian, Malay	middle, central
Teniente	Spanish	lieutenant
Tepe, Tepesi	Turkish	hill, mountain
Terara	Amharic	mountain
Terre	French	land
Thale	Thai	lake
Thamad	Arabic	well
Tierra	Spanish	land
Timur	Indonesian, Malay	east, eastern
-tind, -tinden	Norwegian	peak
-tindar	Icelandic	peak
-tindur	Faroese, Icelandic	peak
Tir'at	Arabic	canal, river, watercourse
Tizi	Berber	pass
-tjåkkå	Lappish	mountain
-tjärro	Lappish	mountain
-tó	Hungarian	lake
-tō	Japanese	island
-to	Korean	island
-tōge	Japanese	pass
-tong	Korean	village
Tônlé	Cambodian	lake, river
Too	Kyrgyz	mountain range
-topp, -toppen	Norwegian	peak
T'ou	Chinese	cape, point
Tsentral'nyy	Russian	central
Tso	Tibetan	lake
Tsqalsats'avi	Georgian	reservoir
Tsui	Chinese	cape, point
Túnel	Spanish	tunnel
-tunturi	Finnish	treeless mountain

U

Geographical term	Language	Meaning
Über-	German	upper
-udden	Swedish	cape, point
Ugheltekhili	Georgian	pass
Új-	Hungarian	new
Ujung	Indonesian	cape, point
Unter-, unter	German	below, lower
'Uqlat	Arabic	well
-ura	Japanese	inlet
'Urayq, 'Urūq	Arabic	sand dunes
Ust'-, Ust'ye	Russian	river mouth
Utara	Indonesian, Malay	north, northern
Uttar	Hindi	north, northern
Uul	Mongolian	mountain range
Uval	Russian	hills
'Uyūn	Arabic	springs

V

Geographical term	Language	Meaning
v	Czech	in
-vaara, -vaarat	Finnish	hill(s), mountain(s)
Vaart, -vaart	Dutch	canal
-vaðall	Icelandic	inlet
-våg	Norwegian	bay
-vágur	Faroese	bay
Väike-	Estonian	small
väin	Estonian	bay, channel, strait
Val	French, Portuguese, Spanish	valley
Vale	Portuguese, Romanian	valley
Vall	Catalan, Spanish	valley
Valle	Italian, Spanish	valley
Vallée	French	valley
Valli	Italian	valleys
Vallon	French	small valley
Vârful	Romanian	hill, mountain
-város	Hungarian	town
-varre	Norwegian	mountain
Väster, Västra	Swedish	west, western
-vatn	Icelandic	lake
-vatn, -vatnet	Norwegian	lake
-vatten, -vattnet	Swedish	lake
Vaux	French	valleys
Vechi	Romanian	old
veehoidla	Estonian	lake
-veld	Afrikaans	field
Velha, Velho	Portuguese	old
Velika	Croatian, Slovene, Serbian	big
Velikaya, Velikiy, Velikiye	Russian	big
Velike	Slovene	big
Veliki	Croatian, Serbian	big
Velká, Velké, Velký	Czech	big
Veľká, Veľké, Veľký	Slovak	big
-vellir	Icelandic	plain
Velyka	Ukrainian	big
Verkhne-, Verkhneye, Verkhniy, Verkhnyaya	Russian	upper
-vesi	Finnish	lake, water
Viaduc	French	viaduct
-vidda	Norwegian	plateau
Vieja, Viejo	Spanish	old
Vieux	French	old
Vig	Danish	bay
-vík	Icelandic	bay
-vik	Norwegian	bay, inlet
Vila	Portuguese	small town
Ville	French	town
Vinh	Vietnamese	bay
-víz	Hungarian	river
-víztároló	Hungarian	reservoir
-vlei	Afrikaans	lake, salt pan
-vloer	Afrikaans	salt pan
Voblasts'	Belorussian	province
Vodaskhovishcha	Belorussian	reservoir
Vodná nádrž	Slovak	reservoir
Vodní nádrž	Czech	reservoir
Vodokhranilishche	Russian	reservoir
Vodoskhovyshche	Ukrainian	reservoir
-vogur	Icelandic	bay
Volcán	Spanish	volcano
Vostochno-, Vostochnyy	Russian	east, eastern
-vötn	Icelandic	lakes
Vozvyshennost'	Russian	hills, upland
Vozyera	Belorussian	lake
Vpadina	Russian	depression
Vrchovina	Czech	hills, mountain region
Vrŭkh	Bulgarian	hill, mountain
Vulkan	Russian	volcano
Vyalikaya, Vyalikaye, Vyaliki, Vyalikiya	Belorussian	big
Vyerkhnya	Belorussian	upper
Vysokaya, Vysokoye	Russian	upper

W

Geographical term	Language	Meaning
-waard	Dutch	polder (reclaimed land)
Wad	Dutch	sandflat
Wadi, Wâdi, Wādī	Arabic	watercourse
Wai	Chinese	outer
Wald	German	forest
Wan	Chinese	bay
-wan	Japanese	bay
Wand	German	cliff
Wasser	German	water
Wāw	Arabic	well
Webi	Somali	river
Wenz	Amharic	river, watercourse
Wielka, Wielki, Wielkie, Wielko-	Polish	big
-woud	Dutch	wood, forest
Wysoka, Wysoki, Wysokie	Polish	upper
Wyżna	Polish	lowland
Wzvyshsha	Belorussian	upland

X

Geographical term	Language	Meaning
Xé	Vietnamese	river
Xi	Chinese	river, west, western
Xia	Chinese	gorge, lower
Xian	Chinese	county
Xiao	Chinese	small

Y

Geographical term	Language	Meaning
Yam	Hebrew	lake, sea
-yama	Japanese	mountain
Yang	Chinese	channel
Yangi	Russian	new
Yarımadası	Azeri, Turkish	peninsula
Yazovir	Bulgarian	reservoir
Ye	Burmese	island
Yeni	Turkish	new
Yli-	Finnish	upper
Ynys	Welsh	island
Yoma	Burmese	mountain range
You	Chinese	right
Ytra-, Ytri-	Icelandic	outer
Ytre-	Norwegian	outer
Ytter-	Norwegian, Swedish	outer
Yuan	Chinese	spring
Yumco	Tibetan	lake
Yunhe	Chinese	canal
Yuzhno-, Yuzhnyy	Russian	south, southern

Z

Geographical term	Language	Meaning
Za-	Russian	behind, beyond
-zaki	Japanese	cape, point
Zalew	Polish	bay
Zaliv	Russian	bay, gulf, inlet
-zan	Japanese	mountain
Zand	Dutch	sandbank, sandhill
Zangbo	Tibetan	river
Zapadnaya, Zapadno-, Zapadnyy	Russian	west, western
Zapavyednik	Belorussian	reserve
Zapovednik	Russian	reserve
Zapovidnyk	Ukrainian	reserve
Zatoka	Polish, Ukrainian	bay, gulf, lagoon
-zee	Dutch	lake, sea
Zemlya	Russian	land
Zemo	Georgian	upper
Zhen	Chinese	town
Zhong	Chinese	middle, central
Zhou	Chinese	island
Zizhiqu	Chinese	autonomous region
Zuid, Zuider	Dutch	south, southern
Zuo	Chinese	left

The index includes names shown on the maps in the Atlas of the World. Each entry includes the country or geographical area in which the feature is located, a page number and an alphanumeric reference. Additional details within the entries are explained below. Abbreviations used in the index are explained in the table below.

REFERENCING

Names are referenced by page number, the first element of each entry, and by a grid reference. The grid reference correlates to the alphanumeric values which appear within each map frame. These reflect the graticule on the map – the letter relates to longitude divisions, the number to latitude divisions.

Names are generally referenced to the largest scale map page on which they appear. For large geographical features, including countries, the reference is to the largest scale map on which the feature appears in its entirety, or on which the majority of it appears.

Rivers are referenced to their lowest downstream point – either their mouth or their confluence with another river. The river name will generally be positioned as close to this point as possible, but may not necessarily be in the same grid square.

ALTERNATIVE NAMES

Alternative names or name forms appear as cross-references and refer the user to the entry for the map form of the name.

For rivers with multiple names – for example those which flow through several countries – all alternative name forms are included within the main index entries, with details of the countries in which each form applies. Different types of name used are: alternative forms or spellings currently in use (alt.); English conventional name forms normally used in English-language contexts (conv.); and long names – full forms of names which are most commonly used in the abbreviated form.

ADMINISTRATIVE QUALIFIERS

Entries within the following countries include the main administrative division in which they occur: Australia, Canada, China, India, Serbia, UK and USA. Administrative divisions are also included to differentiate duplicate names – entries of exactly the same name and feature type within the one country – where these division names are shown on the maps. In such cases, duplicate names are alphabetized in the order of the administrative division names.

Additional qualifiers are included for names within selected geographical areas, to indicate more clearly their location. In particular, this has been applied to island nations to indicate the island group, or individual island, on which a feature occurs.

DESCRIPTORS

Entries, other than those for towns and cities, include a descriptor indicating the type of geographical feature. Descriptors are not included where the type of feature is implicit in the name itself, unless there is a town or city of exactly the same name.

INSETS

Entries relating to names appearing on insets are indicated by a small box symbol: ▫, followed by an inset number if there is more than one inset on the page, or by a grid reference if the inset has its own alphanumeric values.

NAME FORMS AND ALPHABETICAL ORDER

Name forms are as they appear on the maps, with additional alternative forms included as cross-references. Names appear in full in the index, although they may appear in abbreviated form on the maps.

The Icelandic characters Þ and þ are transliterated and alphabetized as 'Th' and 'th'. The German character ß is alphabetized as 'ss'. Names beginning with Mac or Mc are alphabetized exactly as they appear. The terms Saint, Sainte, etc, are abbreviated to St, Ste, etc, but alphabetized as if in the full form.

Name form policies are explained in the Introduction to the Atlas (pp 88-89).

NUMERICAL ENTRIES

Entries beginning with numerals appear at the beginning of the index, in numerical order. Elsewhere, numerals appear before 'a'.

PERMUTED TERMS

Names beginning with generic, geographical terms are permuted – the descriptive term is placed after, and the index alphabetized by, the main part of the name. For example, Lake Superior is indexed as Superior, Lake; Mount Everest as Everest, Mount. This policy is applied to all languages. Permuting has not been applied to names of towns, cities or administrative divisions beginning with such geographical terms. These remain in their full form, for example, Lake Isabella, California, USA. The definite article, for example La, Le, Les (French); El, Las, Los (Spanish); Al, Ar, As (Arabic), is not permuted in any language.

INDEX ABBREVIATIONS

A.C.T.	Australian Capital Territory
admin. dist.	administrative district
admin. div.	administrative division
admin. reg.	administrative region
Afgh.	Afghanistan
AK	Alaska
AL	Alabama
Alg.	Algeria
alt.	alternative name form
Alta	Alberta
Andhra Prad.	Andhra Pradesh
AR	Arkansas
Arg.	Argentina
Arun. Prad.	Arunachal Pradesh
Austr.	Australia
aut. comm.	autonomous community
aut. div.	autonomous division
aut. prov.	autonomous province
aut. reg.	autonomous region
aut. rep.	autonomous republic
AZ	Arizona
Azer.	Azerbaijan
b.	bay
Bangl.	Bangladesh
B.C.	British Columbia
B.I.O.T.	British Indian Ocean Territory
Bol.	Bolivia
Bos.-Herz.	Bosnia-Herzegovina
Bulg.	Bulgaria
c.	cape
CA	California
Can.	Canada
C.A.R.	Central African Republic
CO	Colorado
Col.	Colombia
conv.	conventional name form
CT	Connecticut
Czech Rep.	Czech Republic
DC	District of Columbia
DE	Delaware
Dem. Rep. Congo	Democratic Republic of the Congo
depr.	depression
dept	department
des.	desert
Dom. Rep.	Dominican Republic
E.	East, Eastern
Equat. Guinea	Equatorial Guinea
esc.	escarpment
est.	estuary
Eth.	Ethiopia
Fin.	Finland
FL	Florida
for.	forest
Fr. Guiana	French Guiana
Fr. Polynesia	French Polynesia
g.	gulf
GA	Georgia
Gd Bahama	Grand Bahama
Ger.	Germany
Guat.	Guatemala
hd	headland
Heilong.	Heilongjiang
HI	Hawaii
Hima. Prad.	Himachal Pradesh
H.K.	Hong Kong
Hond.	Honduras
i.	island
is	islands
IA	Iowa
ID	Idaho
IL	Illinois
imp. l.	impermanent lake
IN	Indiana
Indon.	Indonesia
isth.	isthmus
Kazakh.	Kazakhstan
KS	Kansas
KY	Kentucky
Kyrg.	Kyrgyzstan
l.	lake
LA	Louisiana
lag.	lagoon
Lith.	Lithuania
Lux.	Luxembourg
MA	Massachusetts
Madag.	Madagascar
Madh. Prad.	Madhya Pradesh
Mahar.	Maharashtra
Man.	Manitoba
Maur.	Mauritania
MD	Maryland
ME	Maine
Mex.	Mexico
MI	Michigan
MN	Minnesota
MO	Missouri
Moz.	Mozambique
MS	Mississippi
MT	Montana
mt.	mountain
mts	mountains
mun.	municipality
N.	North
N.B.	New Brunswick
NC	North Carolina
ND	North Dakota
NE	Nebraska
Neth.	Netherlands
Nfld.	Newfoundland
NH	New Hampshire
Nic.	Nicaragua
NJ	New Jersey
NM	New Mexico
N.S.	Nova Scotia
N.S.W.	New South Wales
N.T.	Northern Territory
NV	Nevada
N.W.T.	Northwest Territories
NY	New York
N.Z.	New Zealand
OH	Ohio
OK	Oklahoma
Ont.	Ontario
OR	Oregon
PA	Pennsylvania
Pak.	Pakistan
Para.	Paraguay
P.E.I.	Prince Edward Island
pen.	peninsula
Phil.	Philippines
plat.	plateau
P.N.G.	Papua New Guinea
Pol.	Poland
Port.	Portugal
pref.	prefecture
prov.	province
Qld	Queensland
Que.	Québec
r.	river
r. mouth	river mouth
reg.	region
Rep.	Republic
research stn	research station
resr	reservoir
rf	reef
RI	Rhode Island
Rus. Fed.	Russian Federation
S.	South
S.A.	South Australia
Sask.	Saskatchewan
SC	South Carolina
SD	South Dakota
sea chan.	sea channel
Sing.	Singapore
str.	strait
Switz.	Switzerland
Tajik.	Tajikistan
Tanz.	Tanzania
Tas.	Tasmania
terr.	territory
Thai.	Thailand
TN	Tennessee
Trin. and Tob.	Trinidad and Tobago
tun.	tunnel
Turkm.	Turkmenistan
TX	Texas
U.A.E.	United Arab Emirates
U.K.	United Kingdom
Ukr.	Ukraine
Uru.	Uruguay
U.S.A.	United States of America
UT	Utah
Uttar Prad.	Uttar Pradesh
Uzbek.	Uzbekistan
VA	Virginia
val.	valley
Venez.	Venezuela
Vic.	Victoria
vol.	volcano
vol. crater	volcanic crater
VT	Vermont
W.	West, Western
W.A.	Western Australia
WA	Washington
WI	Wisconsin
WV	West Virginia
WY	Wyoming
Y.T.	Yukon Territory

1

225 G3 1st Cataract rapids Egypt
107 J2 1st Three Mile Opening sea chan. Qld Austr.
225 F4 2nd Cataract rapids Sudan
107 I2 2nd Three Mile Opening sea chan. Qld Austr.
225 F5 3rd Cataract rapids Sudan
225 G5 4th Cataract rapids Sudan
225 G5 5th Cataract rapids Sudan
285 G4 9 de Julio Arg.
285 G5 16 de Julio Arg.
285 F5 17 de Agosto Arg.
284 C4 25 de Mayo Mendoza Arg.
285 G4 25 de Mayo Buenos Aires Arg.
284 D5 25 de Mayo La Pampa Arg.
285 I4 25 de Mayo Uru.
285 F5 30 de Agosto Arg.
237 N4 42nd Hill S. Africa
246 F5 70 Mile House B.C. Can.
246 F5 100 Mile House B.C. Can.
246 F4 150 Mile House B.C. Can.

A

178 D1 Aa r. France
191 B7 Aa r. Ger.
191 E7 Aa r. Ger.
164 F6 Aabenraa Denmark
194 F6 Aach Ger.
194 G6 Aach r. Ger.
191 B9 Aachen Ger.
232 E4 Aadan Yabaal Somalia
212 F1 Aadorf Switz.
165 K6 Aakirkeby Bornholm Denmark
164 F4 Aalborg Denmark
164 G5 Aalborg Bugt b. Denmark
195 I4 Aalen Ger.
164 F5 Aalestrup Denmark
Aalesund Norway see Ålesund
Aaley Lebanon see Aley
186 G4 Aalsmeer Neth.
187 F7 Aalst Belgium
187 H6 Aalst Neth.
186 K5 Aalten Neth.
187 D6 Aalter Belgium
Aanaar Fin. see Inari
162 R5 Äänekoski Fin.
236 G2 Aansluit S. Africa
Aar r. Switz. see Aare
135 □1 Aarah i. N. Male Maldives
212 E1 Aarau Switz.
212 C1 Aarberg Switz.
212 D1 Aarburg Switz.
187 D6 Aardenburg Neth.
212 E1 Aare r. Switz.
162 Q3 Aareavaara Sweden
212 E1 Aargau canton Switz.
Aarhus Denmark see Århus
186 I6 Aarle Neth.
Aarlen Belgium see Arlon
204 D2 A Armada Spain
164 F5 Aars Denmark
187 G7 Aarschot Belgium
187 F6 Aartselaar Belgium
164 G6 Aarup Denmark
194 D7 Aarwangen Switz.
243 M3 Aasiaat Greenland
Aath Belgium see Ath
162 Q3 Aavasaksa Fin.
130 C2 Aba Sichuan China
230 F4 Aba Dem. Rep. Congo
199 H4 Aba Hungary
229 G5 Aba Nigeria
146 G2 Abā ad Dūd Saudi Arabia
147 J6 Abā al Afan oasis Saudi Arabia
150 D9 Abā al Hinshan Saudi Arabia
275 G6 Abacaxis r. Brazil
144 C6 Ābādān Iran
144 H2 Abadan Turkm.
144 C6 Ābādān, Jazīrah i. Iran/Iraq
144 F3 Ābādān Tappeh Iran
144 E6 Ābādeh Iran
144 E7 Ābādeh Ţashk Iran
204 G7 Abadengo reg. Spain
205 L7 Abades Spain
280 D3 Abadia dos Dourados Brazil
280 C2 Abadiânia Brazil
204 F2 Abadín Spain
226 E3 Abadla Alg.
199 J4 Abádszalók Hungary
151 B1 Abadzekhskaya Rus. Fed.
281 E3 Abaeté Brazil
281 E3 Abaeté r. Brazil
278 C2 Abaetetuba Brazil
129 O2 Abagaytuy Rus. Fed.
Abagnar Qi Nei Mongol China see Xilinhot
Abag Qi Nei Mongol China see Xin Hot
277 G6 Abaí Para.
99 H1 Abaiang atoll Kiribati
204 D2 A Baiuca Spain
229 G4 Abaji Nigeria
265 W4 Abajo Peak UT U.S.A.
229 H5 Abakaliki Nigeria
120 F1 Abakan Rus. Fed.
120 E1 Abakanskiy Khrebet mts Rus. Fed.
230 B5 Abala Congo
229 F3 Abala Niger
229 G3 Abalak Niger
227 G5 Abalessa Alg.
160 N7 Abalyanka r. Belarus
148 G3 Abana Turkey
205 P7 Abánades Spain
276 B3 Abancay Peru
230 A5 Abanga r. Gabon
209 C11 Abanilla Spain
213 L5 Abano Terme Italy
276 E4 Abapó Bol.
209 C11 Abarán Spain
Abariringa atoll Phoenix Is Kiribati see Kanton
144 E6 Abarkūh Iran
144 E6 Abarkūh, Kavīr-e des. Iran
204 E3 A Barrela Spain
Abarshahr Iran see Neyshābūr
199 J4 Abasár Hungary
151 D3 Abasha Georgia
124 V2 Abashiri Japan
124 V3 Abashiri-ko l. Japan
124 V2 Abashiri-wan b. Japan
268 F5 Abasolo Guanajuato Mex.
269 I1 Abasolo Tamaulipas Mex.
269 L8 Abasolo del Valle Mex.
151 D4 Abast'umani Georgia
233 C5 Abasula waterhole Kenya
113 K9 Abau P.N.G.
199 K3 Abaújszántó Hungary
160 E4 Abava r. Latvia
143 O3 Abay Karagandinskaya Oblast' Kazakh.
Abay Vostochnyy Kazakhstan Kazakh. see Karaul
Abaya, Lake Eth. see Ābaya Hāyk'
232 C3 Ābaya Hāyk' l. Eth.
Abay Bazar Kazakh. see Abay
232 B2 Ābay Wenz r. Eth. alt. Azraq, Bahr el (Sudan), conv. Blue Nile
120 F1 Abaza Rus. Fed.
230 B3 Abba C.A.R.
214 H2 Abbadia San Salvatore Italy
149 P8 'Abbāsābād Fārs Iran
144 H5 'Abbāsābād Khorāsān Iran
144 G3 'Abbāsābād Iran
144 F5 'Abbāsābād Mehr Jān Iran
214 B7 Abbasanta Sardegna Italy
Abbatis Villa France see Abbeville
250 F3 Abbaye, Point MI U.S.A.
232 D2 Abbe, Lake Djibouti/Eth.
173 N4 Abberton Reservoir England U.K.
178 C3 Abbeville France
255 E10 Abbeville AL U.S.A.
255 F10 Abbeville GA U.S.A.
261 I11 Abbeville LA U.S.A.
255 F8 Abbeville SC U.S.A.
247 I5 Abbey Sask. Can.
169 C8 Abbeydorney Ireland
169 D8 Abbeyfeale Ireland
168 I13 Abbey Head Scotland U.K.
169 H7 Abbeyleix Ireland
171 K4 Abbeytown Cumbria, England U.K.
212 F5 Abbiategrasso Italy
162 O4 Abborrträsk Sweden
107 K6 Abbot, Mount Qld Austr.
107 K5 Abbot Bay Qld Austr.
286 R2 Abbot Ice Shelf Antarctica
173 I2 Abbots Bromley Staffordshire, England U.K.
172 G6 Abbotsbury Dorset, England U.K.
246 F5 Abbotsford B.C. Can.
250 D5 Abbotsford WI U.S.A.
173 L4 Abbots Langley Hertfordshire, England U.K.
258 B5 Abbotstown PA U.S.A.
263 L8 Abbott NM U.S.A.
256 E11 Abbott VA U.S.A.
256 E10 Abbott WV U.S.A.
145 O4 Abbottabad Pak.
160 M7 Abchuha Belarus
186 G4 Abcoude Neth.
199 G4 Abda Hungary
149 J5 'Abd al 'Azīz, Jabal hill Syria
147 K9 'Abd al Kūrī i. Yemen
149 N9 'Abd Allah, Khawr sea chan. Iraq/Kuwait
150 G8 Abd al Ma'asīr well Saudi Arabia
144 B5 Ābdānān Iran
156 J5 Abdi Rus. Fed.
144 G4 'Abdolābād Iran
144 G3 'Abdollāhābād Khorāsān Iran
144 E4 'Abdollāhābād Semnān Iran
142 E1 Abdulino Rus. Fed.
224 D6 Abéché Chad
144 G5 Ab-e Garm, Chashmeh-ye spring Iran
127 H6 Abe-gawa r. Japan
229 F2 Abeïbara Mali
229 F2 Abeïbara well Mali
205 O5 Abejar Spain
209 D8 Abejuela Spain
229 G5 Abejukolo Nigeria
206 B4 Abela Port.
229 G2 Abélajouad well Niger
228 E2 Abelbod well Mali
187 C7 Abele Belgium
204 C4 Abelleiro, Punta pt Spain
Abellinum Italy see Avellino
103 H7 Abel Tasman National Park South I. N.Z.
162 K4 Abelvær Norway
99 H1 Abemama atoll Gilbert Is Kiribati
234 C3 Abenab Namibia
195 J3 Abenberg Ger.
207 P2 Abengibre Spain
228 E5 Abengourou Côte d'Ivoire
207 K3 Abenójar Spain
Åbenrå Denmark see Aabenraa
195 L4 Abens r. Ger.
195 L4 Abensberg Ger.
229 F5 Abeokuta Nigeria
232 B3 Abera Eth.
172 D3 Aberaeron Ceredigion, Wales U.K.
172 F4 Aberaman Rhondda Cynon Taff, Wales U.K.
172 E4 Aberavon Neath Port Talbot, Wales U.K.
180 B4 Aber Benoît inlet France
172 F4 Abercanaid Merthyr Tydfil, Wales U.K.
172 B4 Abercastle Pembrokeshire, Wales U.K.
168 K7 Aberchirder Aberdeenshire, Scotland U.K.
Abercorn Zambia see Mbala
105 L5 Abercrombie r. N.S.W. Austr.
105 L6 Abercrombie River National Park N.S.W. Austr.
172 F4 Abercynon Rhondda Cynon Taff, Wales U.K.
172 F4 Aberdare Rhondda Cynon Taff, Wales U.K.
232 C5 Aberdare National Park Kenya
172 C2 Aberdaron Gwynedd, Wales U.K.
Aberdaugleddau Pembrokeshire, Wales U.K. see Milford Haven
105 M5 Aberdeen N.S.W. Austr.
131 □J7 Aberdeen H.K. China
236 I8 Aberdeen S. Africa
168 L8 Aberdeen Aberdeen, Scotland U.K.
168 L8 Aberdeen admin. div. Scotland U.K.
258 C6 Aberdeen MD U.S.A.
261 K9 Aberdeen MS U.S.A.
256 B10 Aberdeen OH U.S.A.
260 F3 Aberdeen SD U.S.A.
262 C3 Aberdeen WA U.S.A.
Aberdeen Island H.K. China see Ap Lei Chau
247 L1 Aberdeen Lake Nunavut Can.
236 I8 Aberdeen Road S. Africa
168 K8 Aberdeenshire admin. div. Scotland U.K.
168 J10 Aberdour Fife, Scotland U.K.
172 D2 Aberdovey Gwynedd, Wales U.K.
Aberdyfi Gwynedd, Wales U.K. see Aberdovey
168 I9 Aberfeldy Perth and Kinross, Scotland U.K.
172 D1 Aberffraw Isle of Anglesey, Wales U.K.
171 O6 Aberford West Yorkshire, England U.K.
168 H10 Aberfoyle Stirling, Scotland U.K.
172 F4 Abergavenny Monmouthshire, Wales U.K.
232 C1 Ābergelē Eth.
172 E1 Abergele Conwy, Wales U.K.
Abergwaun Pembrokeshire, Wales U.K. see Fishguard
172 E3 Abergwesyn Powys, Wales U.K.
172 E2 Abergynolwyn Gwynedd, Wales U.K.
Aberhonddu Powys, Wales U.K. see Brecon
172 E4 Aberkenfig Bridgend, Wales U.K.
168 K10 Aberlady East Lothian, Scotland U.K.
168 K9 Aberlemno Angus, Scotland U.K.
168 J8 Aberlour Moray, Scotland U.K.
Abermaw Gwynedd, Wales U.K. see Barmouth
261 E9 Abernathy TX U.S.A.
168 J10 Abernethy Perth and Kinross, Scotland U.K.
Aberpennar Wales U.K. see Mountain Ash
172 C3 Aberporth Ceredigion, Wales U.K.
172 C2 Abersoch Gwynedd, Wales U.K.
172 F4 Abersychan Torfaen, Wales U.K.
198 B1 Abertamy Czech Rep.
Abertawe Swansea, Wales U.K. see Swansea
Aberteifi Ceredigion, Wales U.K. see Cardigan
172 F4 Abertillery Blaenau Gwent, Wales U.K.
206 H2 Abertura Spain
168 I10 Aberuthven Perth and Kinross, Scotland U.K.
180 B4 Aber Vrac'h inlet France
172 D3 Aberystwyth Ceredigion, Wales U.K.
Abeshr Chad see Abéché
156 M2 Abez' Rus. Fed.
200 G6 Abfaltersbach Austria
144 H8 Āb Gāh Iran
157 I6 Abganerovo Rus. Fed.
146 F6 Abhā Saudi Arabia
146 E3 Abhā, Jabal hill Saudi Arabia
168 B7 Abhainnsuidhe Western Isles, Scotland U.K.
138 H9 Abhanpur Chhattisgarh India
144 C3 Abhar Iran
144 C4 Abhar Rūd r. Iran
229 G5 Abia state Nigeria
225 G6 Abiad, Bahr el r. Sudan/Uganda alt. Jebel, Bahr el, conv. White Nile
205 P8 Abia de la Obispalía Spain
232 C3 Ābīata Hāyk' l. Eth.
274 B2 Abibe, Serranía de mts Col.
228 D5 Abidjan Côte d'Ivoire
208 E3 Abiego Spain
236 E3 Abiekwasputs salt pan S. Africa
232 C3 Abijatta-Shalla National Park Eth.
127 L4 Abiko Japan
190 G1 Abild Denmark
260 G6 Abilene KS U.S.A.
261 F9 Abilene TX U.S.A.
181 M8 Abilly France
173 J4 Abingdon Oxfordshire, England U.K.
258 C6 Abingdon MD U.S.A.
256 C12 Abingdon VA U.S.A.
Abingdon Island Islas Galápagos Ecuador see Pinta, Isla
168 I12 Abington South Lanarkshire, Scotland U.K.
257 O6 Abington MA U.S.A.
258 E4 Abington PA U.S.A.
107 L5 Abington Reef Coral Sea Is Terr. Austr.
157 G7 Abinsk Rus. Fed.
205 N5 Abión r. Spain
Ab-i-Panja r. Afgh./Tajik. see Panj
162 O2 Abisko nationalpark nat. park Sweden
247 J2 Abitau Lake N.W.T. Can.
248 D3 Abitibi r. Ont. Can.
248 D3 Abitibi, Lake Ont./Que. Can.
Abkhazia aut. rep. Georgia see Ap'khazet'i
144 G4 Ab Khūr Iran
207 N6 Abla Spain
178 C6 Ablis France
205 Q5 Ablitas Spain
225 F3 Abnūb Egypt
Åbo Fin. see Turku
208 C2 Abodi, Sierra de mts Spain
138 E4 Abohar Punjab India
204 D5 Aboim das Choças Port.
228 E5 Aboisso Côte d'Ivoire
232 B2 Aboke Sudan
229 F5 Abomey Benin
238 □3a Abona, Punta de pt Tenerife Canary Is
182 J4 Abondance France
116 B2 Abongabong, Gunung mt. Indon.
229 I6 Abong Mbang Cameroon
199 J4 Abony Hungary
228 E5 Abooso Ghana
147 K7 Aboot Oman
114 B7 Aborlan Palawan Phil.
126 G3 Abō-tōge pass Japan
230 C2 Abou Déia Chad
224 D6 Abou Goulem Chad
230 B5 Aboumi Gabon
230 E2 Abourasséin, Mont mt. C.A.R.
229 G3 Abouraya well Niger
151 F5 Abovyan Armenia
168 K8 Aboyne Aberdeenshire, Scotland U.K.
147 I3 Abqaiq Saudi Arabia
283 B9 Abra, Canal sea chan. Chile
283 E6 Abra, Laguna del l. Arg.
146 H8 Abrād, Wādī watercourse Yemen
204 D6 Abragão Port.
270 G2 Abraham's Bay Mayaguana Bahamas
229 G5 Abraka Nigeria
199 L4 Abram Romania
171 L6 Abram Greater Manchester, England U.K.
156 H2 Abramov, Mys pt Rus. Fed.
159 U2 Abramovka Rus. Fed.
250 F5 Abrams WI U.S.A.
199 L4 Abrămuţ Romania
206 C2 Abrantes Port.
282 D1 Abra Pampa Arg.
151 G6 Äbraqunis Azer.
159 Q9 Abrau-Dyurso Rus. Fed.
204 E7 Abraveses Port.
281 F4 Abre Campo Brazil
204 F6 Abreiro Port.
266 C4 Abreojos, Punta pt Mex.
208 I4 Abrera Spain
179 N6 Abreschviller France
182 C4 Abrest France
225 F4 'Abri Sudan
183 J7 Abriès France
281 H3 Abrolhos, Arquipélago dos is Brazil
288 G7 Abrolhos Bank sea feature S. Atlantic Ocean
161 S3 Abrosovo Rus. Fed.
207 N6 Abrucena Spain
219 L4 Abrud Romania
160 F3 Abruka i. Estonia
Abruzzi admin. reg. Italy see Abruzzo
215 L3 Abruzzo admin. reg. Italy
215 L4 Abruzzo, Parco Nazionale d' nat. park Italy
146 F7 'Abs Yemen
286 W1 Absalom, Mount Antarctica
200 E5 Absam Austria
262 I4 Absaroka Range mts WY U.S.A.
195 J3 Absberg Ger.
201 M3 Absdorf Austria
259 G6 Absecon NJ U.S.A.
259 G6 Absecon Bay NJ U.S.A.
151 K5 Abşeron Yarımadası pen. Azer.
160 K6 Absterna, Vozyera l. Belarus
150 F4 Abtar, Jabal al hills Syria
201 H4 Abtenau Austria
194 H4 Abtsgmünd Ger.
125 I12 Abu Japan
150 F3 Abū aḑ Ḑuhūr Syria
147 K3 Abū al Abyaḑ i. U.A.E.
150 G6 Abū al Ḩusayn, Qā' imp. l. Jordan
147 I2 Abū 'Alī i. Saudi Arabia
146 C3 Abū al Kizān rf Saudi Arabia
150 E8 Abū 'Āmūd, Wādī watercourse Jordan
146 F7 Abū 'Arīsh Saudi Arabia
224 E3 Abū Ballāş hill Egypt
146 G7 Abū Dā'ir des. Yemen
225 G6 Abu Deleiq Sudan
Abu Dhabi U.A.E. see Abū Ẓabī
146 D4 Abū Ḑībā' waterhole Saudi Arabia
150 G2 Abū Du'ān Syria
150 B10 Abū Durbah Egypt
275 F6 Abufari Brazil
230 E2 Abu Gabra Sudan
225 H6 Abu Gamel Sudan
225 G5 Abu Ghirban Sudan
232 A2 Abu Gubeiha Sudan
150 B10 Abū Ḩad, Wādī watercourse Egypt
150 G6 Abū Ḩafnah, Wādī watercourse Jordan
150 E7 Abū Ḩallūfah, Jabal hill Jordan
225 G5 Abu Hamed Sudan
224 E6 Abu Hamra, Wadi watercourse Sudan
225 G5 Abu Haraz Sudan
225 G5 Abu Hashim Sudan
150 B10 Abū Ḩaşwah, Jabal hill Egypt
135 □2 Abuhera i. Addu Atoll Maldives
225 G6 Abu Higar Sudan
229 G4 Abuja Nigeria
150 C10 Abū Jalūm, Ra's pt Egypt
147 H3 Abū Jifān well Saudi Arabia
150 D8 Abū Jurdhān Jordan
149 J6 Abū Kamāl Syria
224 A1 Abū Kammāsh Libya
197 M2 Abukhava Belarus
127 L1 Abukuma-gawa r. Japan
127 M2 Abukuma-kōchi plat. Japan
225 F6 Abu La'ot watercourse Sudan
146 E6 Abū Latt i. Saudi Arabia
146 C3 Abū Madd, Ra's hd Saudi Arabia
230 E2 Abu Matariq Sudan
148 D8 Abu Mena tourist site Egypt
230 D4 Abumombazi Dem. Rep. Congo
147 L3 Abu Musa i. The Gulf
Abū Mūsá, Jazīreh-ye i. The Gulf see Abu Musa
276 D2 Abunã r. Bol./Brazil
276 D2 Abunã Brazil
274 E5 Abunai Brazil
224 C2 Abū Nā'im well Libya
232 C1 Ābune Yosēf mt. Eth.
224 B2 Abū Nujaym Libya
150 F4 Abū Qa'ţūr Syria
148 E8 Abū Qīr, Khalīj b. Egypt
224 B2 Abū Qurīn Libya
146 C2 Abū Rāqah well Saudi Arabia
150 C9 Abū Rawthah, Jabal mt. Egypt
126 E4 Aburazaka-tōge pass Japan
230 F4 Aburo mt. Dem. Rep. Congo
138 D7 Abu Road Rajasthan India
146 D4 Abū Rubayq Saudi Arabia
150 B10 Abū Rudays Egypt
150 G4 Abū Rujmayn, Jabal mts Syria
146 E3 Abū Salīm, Birkat waterhole Saudi Arabia
150 F10 Abū Sallah, Wādī watercourse Saudi Arabia
147 I3 Abū Sawādah well Saudi Arabia
225 H4 Abu Shagara, Ras pt Sudan
224 E6 Abu Shanab Sudan
225 F4 Abu Simbel Temple tourist site Egypt
149 L8 Abū Şukhayr Iraq
225 F4 Abū Sunbul Egypt
124 R4 Abuta Japan
225 G4 Abu Tabaq well Sudan
146 C2 Abū Ţāqah Saudi Arabia
150 B9 Abū Ţarfā', Wādī watercourse Egypt
103 E10 Abut Head South I. N.Z.
225 F3 Abū Tīj Egypt
225 G3 Abū Ţuyūr, Jabal mt. Egypt
225 F6 Abu Uruq well Sudan
150 C8 Abū 'Uwayqilah well Egypt
232 C2 Abuye Meda mt. Eth.
114 E6 Abuyog Leyte Phil.
225 F6 Abu Zabad Sudan
147 L3 Abū Ẓabī U.A.E.
144 C6 Abūzam Iran
225 G2 Abū Zanīmah Egypt
144 D5 Abū Zeydābād Iran
232 B2 Abwong Sudan
165 M3 Åby Sweden
224 E6 Abyad Sudan
150 F4 Abyaḑ, Jabal al mts Syria
146 G9 Abyān governorate Yemen
224 D2 Abyār al Hakīm well Libya
224 D2 Abyār an Nakhīlan well Libya
108 E6 Abydos W.A. Austr.
230 F2 Abyei Sudan
149 O5 Ābyek Iran
162 P4 Åbyn Sweden
Abyssinia country Africa see Ethiopia
142 H1 Abzakovo Rus. Fed.
142 G2 Abzanovo Rus. Fed.
224 C6 Ab Zérafa Chad
274 C4 Acacias Col.
Acacus, Jabal mts Libya see Akakus, Jabal
Academician Vernadskiy research stn Antarctica see Vernadsky
Academy Bay Rus. Fed. see Akademii, Zaliv
286 T1 Academy Glacier Antarctica
Acadia prov. Can. see Nova Scotia
257 □Q4 Acadia National Park ME U.S.A.
280 B5 Açaí Brazil
278 D3 Açailândia Brazil
278 F4 Acajutiba Brazil
267 O11 Acajutla El Salvador
267 M9 Acala Mex.
Acamarachi mt. Chile see Pili, Cerro
268 G5 Acambaro Mex.
269 H6 Acambay Mex.
231 D9 Acampamento de Caça do Mucusso Angola
267 O7 Acancéh Mex.
274 B2 Acandí Col.
204 D4 A Cañiza Spain
268 B3 Acaponeta Mex.
268 B3 Acaponeta r. Mex.
269 H9 Acapulco Mex.
Acapulco de Juárez Mex. see Acapulco
278 C2 Acará Brazil
278 C2 Acará r. Brazil
275 F6 Acará, Lago l. Brazil
275 G4 Acarai Mountains hills Brazil/Guyana
278 C2 Acará Miri r. Brazil
278 E2 Acaraú Brazil
278 E2 Acaraú r. Brazil
277 G6 Acaray, Represa de resr Para.
204 C2 A Carballa Spain
278 F3 Acarí Brazil
281 E1 Acari r. Brazil
276 B3 Acarí Peru
276 B3 Acarí r. Peru
274 D2 Acarigua Venez.
204 D2 A Carreira Spain
219 K3 Acâş Romania
216 G9 Acate Sicilia Italy
269 J5 Acateno Mex.
269 I7 Acatlán Mex.
269 K6 Acatlán Mex.
268 D5 Acatlán de Juárez Mex.
269 K7 Acatlán de Pérez Figueroa Mex.
269 J7 Acatzingo Mex.
282 D2 Acay, Nevado de mt. Arg.
269 M8 Acayucán Mex.
215 O5 Accadia Italy
212 B7 Acceglio Italy
215 Q7 Accettura Italy
Accho Israel see 'Akko
215 L3 Acciano Italy
257 J11 Accomac VA U.S.A.
Accomack VA U.S.A. see Accomac
185 C10 Accous France
228 E5 Accra Ghana
171 M6 Accrington Lancashire, England U.K.
215 K2 Accumoli Italy
285 G3 Aceba Arg.
204 G8 Acebo Spain
206 H2 Acedera Spain
205 P3 Acedo Spain
282 G3 Aceguá Brazil
116 B2 Aceh admin. dist. Indon.
204 G9 Acehuche Spain
204 H8 Aceituna Spain
205 Q6 Acered Spain
215 P6 Acerenza Italy
215 O6 Acerno Italy
215 M6 Acerra Italy
206 G3 Aceuchal Spain
285 G3 Acevedo Arg.
200 G3 Ach Austria
195 K4 Ach r. Ger.
195 K6 Ach r. Ger.
276 C4 Achacachi Bol.
238 □1b Achada São Miguel Azores
206 □ Achadas da Cruz Madeira
168 C6 Achadh Mòr Western Isles, Scotland U.K.
274 D3 Achaguas Venez.
138 F9 Achalpur Mahar. India
136 F4 Achampet Andhra Prad. India
122 J4 Achan Rus. Fed.
204 D4 A Chan Spain
136 G4 Achanta Andhra Prad. India
285 I3 Achar Uru.
151 D4 Achara aut. rep. Georgia
168 E9 Acharacle Highland, Scotland U.K.
151 C4 Acharistsqali r. Georgia
168 J6 Achavanich Highland, Scotland U.K.
153 S3 Achayvayam Rus. Fed.
224 A5 Achegour well Niger
Acheh admin. dist. Indon. see Aceh
187 H6 Achel Belgium
220 C4 Acheloos r. Greece
224 B4 Achelouma, Enneri watercourse Niger
227 F5 Achemelmel well Mali
228 D2 Achemmîm well Maur.
122 E6 Acheng Heilong. China
200 E4 Achenkirch Austria
229 I2 Achénouma Niger
200 E5 Achensee l. Austria
194 E4 Achern Ger.
229 H3 Achétinamou well Niger
178 E3 Acheux-en-Amiénois France
168 G6 Achfary Highland, Scotland U.K.
138 H9 Achhota Chhattisgarh India
126 G5 Achi Japan
178 E3 Achicourt France
151 C3 Ach'igvara Georgia
151 F1 Achikulak Rus. Fed.
169 B5 Achill Head Ireland
169 B5 Achill Island Ireland
169 C5 Achill Sound Ireland
168 F6 Achiltibuie Highland, Scotland U.K.
190 H4 Achim Ger.
Achin admin. dist. Indon. see Aceh
153 K4 Achinsk Rus. Fed.
168 F8 Achintee Highland, Scotland U.K.
284 E3 Achiras Arg.
143 M6 Achisay Kazakh.
151 I3 Achisu Rus. Fed.
156 L4 Achit Rus. Fed.
128 B2 Achit Nuur l. Mongolia
151 G2 Achkhoy-Martan Rus. Fed.
221 G6 Achlada, Akrotirio pt Greece
150 B3 Achna Cyprus
168 F7 Achnasheen Highland, Scotland U.K.
161 O9 Achosa-Rudnya Belarus
168 D9 Achosnich Highland, Scotland U.K.
195 N4 Achslach Ger.
194 H5 Achstetten Ger.
190 H1 Achtrup Ger.
157 G7 Achuyevo Rus. Fed.
217 I8 Aci Castello Sicilia Italy
217 I8 Aci Catena Sicilia Italy
221 K5 Acıgöl l. Turkey
151 H4 Acınohur depr. Azer.
221 K5 Acıpayam Turkey
217 I8 Acireale Sicilia Italy
217 I8 Aci Sant'Antonio Sicilia Italy
261 K9 Ackerman MS U.S.A.
258 E3 Ackermanville PA U.S.A.
260 I4 Ackley IA U.S.A.
270 F2 Acklins Island Bahamas
171 O6 Ackworth Moor Top West Yorkshire, England U.K.
173 P2 Acle Norfolk, England U.K.
276 B3 Acobamba Huancavelica Peru
276 B2 Acobamba Junín Peru
182 C3 Acolin r. France
276 C3 Acomayo Cusco Peru
276 A2 Acomayo Huánuco Peru
171 M4 Acomb Northumberland, England U.K.
284 B3 Aconcagua r. Chile
284 B3 Aconcagua, Cerro mt. Arg.
278 F3 Acopiara Brazil
276 C3 Acora Peru
238 □1 Açores, Arquipélago dos is N. Atlantic Ocean
204 D2 A Coruña Spain
204 D2 A Coruña prov. Spain
276 B3 Acostambo Peru
239 □3b Acoua Mayotte
266 □Q12 Acoyapa Nic.
216 H6 Acquacalda Isole Lipari Italy
213 N8 Acqualagna Italy
217 L4 Acquaniti r. Italy
214 H2 Acquapendente Italy
215 P9 Acquappesa Italy
217 K6 Acquaro Italy
212 F3 Acquarossa Switz.
215 K2 Acquasanta Terme Italy
215 J2 Acquasparta Italy
215 L2 Acquaviva Picena Italy
216 H7 Acquedolci Sicilia Italy
178 B5 Acquigny France
212 E6 Acqui Terme Italy
257 K6 Acra NY U.S.A.
Acragas Sicilia Italy see Agrigento
104 E5 Acraman, Lake salt flat S.A. Austr.
276 D2 Acre r. Brazil
276 C2 Acre state Brazil
Acre Israel see 'Akko
280 B2 Acreúna Brazil
217 K5 Acri Italy
204 F3 A Cruz do Incio Spain
199 H4 Ács Hungary
199 I4 Acsa Hungary
Actaeon Group is Arch. des Tuamotu Fr. Polynesia see Actéon, Groupe
101 □9 Actéon, Groupe is Arch. des Tuamotu Fr. Polynesia
269 I7 Acteopan Mex.
251 N6 Acton Ont. Can.
173 N3 Acton Suffolk, England U.K.
264 N7 Acton CA U.S.A.
269 I5 Actopán Mex.
269 K6 Actopan Mex.
276 D1 Açuã r. Brazil
281 F3 Açuçena Brazil
269 H5 Aculco de Espinosa Mex.
269 J7 Acultzingo Mex.
285 I1 Acuña Arg.
280 C6 Acungui Brazil
Acunum Acusio France see Montélimar
229 H6 Acurenam Equat. Guinea
277 F3 Açurizal Brazil
215 K4 Acuto Italy
229 F5 Ada Ghana
218 I5 Ada Vojvodina Serbia
260 G2 Ada MN U.S.A.
256 B8 Ada OH U.S.A.
261 G8 Ada OK U.S.A.
232 C3 Ādaba Eth.
Adabazar Turkey see Adapazarı
100 □1 Adacao Guam
227 H5 Adaf, Djebel mts Alg.
159 Q8 Adagum r. Rus. Fed.
208 E3 Adahuesca Spain
250 D9 Adair IL U.S.A.
205 K5 Adaja r. Spain
162 O4 Adak Sweden
245 □C6 Adak AK U.S.A.
245 □C6 Adak Island AK U.S.A.
151 B6 Adaklı Bingöl Turkey
150 F1 Adaklı Gaziantep Turkey
245 □C6 Adak Strait AK U.S.A.
232 E3 Adale well Eth.
Adalia Turkey see Antalya
147 M4 Adam Oman
283 F8 Adam, Mount hill Falkland Is
280 B4 Adamantina Brazil
229 I5 Adamaoua prov. Cameroon
229 I5 Adamaoua, Massif de l' mts Cameroon
220 F6 Adamas Milos Greece
229 H4 Adamawa state Nigeria
219 P6 Adamclisi Romania
212 J3 Adamello mt. Italy
212 I3 Adamello-Brenta, Parco Naturale nature res. Italy
105 L7 Adaminaby N.S.W. Austr.
232 C3 Ādamī Tulu Eth.
196 E6 Adamov Czech Rep.
142 H2 Adamovka Rus. Fed.
197 K4 Adamów Lubelskie Pol.
197 L5 Adamów Lubelskie Pol.
197 K5 Adamówka Pol.
158 G4 Adampil' Ukr.
256 C10 Adams KY U.S.A.
257 L6 Adams MA U.S.A.
250 B6 Adams MN U.S.A.
257 I5 Adams NY U.S.A.
250 E6 Adams WI U.S.A.
286 T2 Adams, Cape Antarctica
103 E10 Adams, Mount South I. N.Z.
136 F8 Adam's Bridge sea feature India/Sri Lanka
257 I5 Adams Center NY U.S.A.
258 A5 Adams County county PA U.S.A.
246 G5 Adams Lake B.C. Can.
265 Q3 Adams McGill Reservoir NV U.S.A.
245 O5 Adams Mountain AK U.S.A.
Adam's Peak Sri Lanka see Sri Pada
264 L2 Adams Peak CA U.S.A.
169 I8 Adamstown Ireland
258 C4 Adamstown PA U.S.A.
207 J4 Adamuz Spain
146 G9 'Adan Yemen
146 G9 'Adan governorate Yemen
148 G5 Adana Turkey
150 D1 Adana prov. Turkey
Adana Yemen see 'Adan
146 G9 'Adan aş Şughrá Yemen
219 O3 Adâncata Romania
199 H5 Ádánd Hungary
205 K7 Adanero Spain
117 L5 Adang, Teluk b. Indon.
229 G5 Adani Nigeria
204 F8 Adão Port.
221 L2 Adapazarı Turkey
146 G9 Adaran, Jabal mt. Yemen
169 E7 Adare Ireland
287 L2 Adare, Cape Antarctica
146 B5 Adarmo, Khawr watercourse Sudan
124 R9 Adatara-san vol. Japan
232 D3 Ada Terra Eth.
107 J8 Adavale Qld Austr.
160 H4 Ādaži Latvia
145 M3 Adban Afgh.
139 I9 Adbhar Chhattisgarh India
212 H5 Adda r. Italy
224 F2 Aḑ Ḑab'ah Egypt
Ad Dabbah Sudan see Ed Debba
146 E4 Ad Dafīnah Saudi Arabia
149 L7 Ad Daghghārah Iraq
146 H5 Ad Dahnā' des. Saudi Arabia
147 M5 Ad Dākhilīyah admin. reg. Oman
226 B5 Ad Dakhla Western Sahara
146 G9 Aḑ Ḑāli' Yemen
146 G9 Aḑ Ḑāli' governorate Yemen
Ad Damir Sudan see Ed Damer
147 J2 Ad Dammām Saudi Arabia
136 F5 Addanki Andhra Prad. India
212 H4 Adda Nord, Parco dell' park Italy
148 E8 Ad Daqahlīyah governorate Egypt
146 C2 Ad Dār al Ḩamrā' Saudi Arabia
146 F7 Ad Darb Saudi Arabia
212 H5 Adda Sud, Parco dell' park Italy
136 H4 Addatigala Andhra Prad. India
146 G3 Ad Dawādimī Saudi Arabia
147 J3 Ad Dawḩah Qatar
149 K6 Ad Dawr Iraq
150 F4 Ad Daww plain Syria
229 H2 Addax, Réserve Naturelle Intégrale dite Sanctuaire des nature res. Niger
149 M8 Ad Dayr Iraq
173 J3 Adderbury Oxfordshire, England U.K.
146 H2 Ad Dibdibah plain Saudi Arabia
147 J7 Ad Dibīn Yemen
Aḑ Ḑiffah plat. Egypt/Libya see Libyan Plateau
147 J6 Ad Dikākah des. Saudi Arabia
147 H4 Ad Dilam Saudi Arabia
171 N6 Addingham West Yorkshire, England U.K.
146 H3 Ad Dir'īyah Saudi Arabia
Addis Ababa Eth. see Ādīs Ābeba
256 H6 Addison NY U.S.A.
149 L8 Ad Dīwānīyah Iraq
Ad Dīwānīyah governorate Iraq see Al Qādisīyah
173 L5 Addlestone Surrey, England U.K.
237 J9 Addo S. Africa
237 J9 Addo Elephant National Park S. Africa
135 □2 Addu Atoll Maldives
149 K8 Ad Duwayd well Saudi Arabia
146 G2 Ad Duwayḩirah Saudi Arabia
Ad Duwaym Sudan see Ed Dueim
147 J4 Ad Duwayris well Saudi Arabia
238 □3a Adeje Tenerife Canary Is
255 F10 Adel GA U.S.A.
260 H5 Adel IA U.S.A.
104 G6 Adelaide S.A. Austr.
106 C2 Adelaide r. N.T. Austr.
270 E1 Adelaide New Prov. Bahamas
237 K8 Adelaide S. Africa
286 T2 Adelaide Island Antarctica
106 C2 Adelaide River N.T. Austr.
212 D3 Adelboden Switz.
191 I7 Adelebsen Ger.
108 G3 Adele Island W.A. Austr.
217 L1 Adelfia Italy
221 H6 Adelfoi i. Greece
190 J5 Adelheidsdorf Ger.
285 E3 Adelia María Arg.
Adélie Coast reg. Antarctica see Adélie Land
287 J2 Adélie Land reg. Antarctica
194 H4 Adelmannsfelden Ger.
105 L6 Adelong N.S.W. Austr.
109 F10 Adelong Aboriginal Reserve W.A. Austr.
270 □ Adelphi Jamaica
271 □3 Adelphi St Vincent
195 K4 Adelschlag Ger.
195 J2 Adelsdorf Ger.
194 G3 Adelsheim Ger.
195 J5 Adelsried Ger.
195 K5 Adelzhausen Ger.
209 C7 Ademuz Spain
209 C7 Ademuz, El Rincón de reg. Spain
Aden Yemen see 'Adan
140 F7 Aden, Gulf of Somalia/Yemen
256 E8 Adena OH U.S.A.
191 C10 Adenau Ger.
190 J4 Adendorf Ger.
236 I8 Adendorp S. Africa
191 I7 Adenstedt Ger.
229 G3 Aderbissinat Niger
Aderno Sicilia Italy see Adrano
138 C8 Adesar Gujarat India
232 C2 Ādēt Eth.
Adhámas Milos Greece see Adamas
147 M3 Adhan, Jabal mt. U.A.E.
146 G8 Adhanah, Wādī watercourse Yemen
147 L3 Adh Dhayd U.A.E.
146 G2 Adh Dhāyūf well Saudi Arabia
149 J9 'Adhfā' well Saudi Arabia
145 N5 Adhi Kot Pak.
150 E8 'Ādhirīyāt, Jibāl al mts Jordan
138 C8 Adhoi Gujarat India
113 H7 Adi i. Papua Indon.
228 E5 Adiaké Côte d'Ivoire
232 C1 Ādī Ārk'ay Eth.
206 E4 Adiça, Serra da hills Port.
274 D2 Adícora Venez.
146 D8 Ādī Da'iro Eth.
225 F6 'Adid Umm Inderab well Sudan
213 M5 Adige r. Italy
Adigey Autonomous Oblast aut. rep. Rus. Fed. see Adygeya, Respublika
232 C1 Ādīgrat Eth.
221 K4 Adıgüzel Barajı resr Turkey
225 H6 Adi Keyih Eritrea
225 H6 Adi Kwala Eritrea
136 F3 Adilabad Andhra Prad. India
232 B4 Adilang Uganda
149 K4 Adilcevaz Turkey
262 D6 Adin CA U.S.A.
Adîncata Romania see Adâncata
187 C6 Adinkerke Belgium
224 B3 Adīrī Libya
257 K4 Adirondack Mountains NY U.S.A.
232 C2 Ādīs Ābeba Eth.
232 C1 Ādīs Zemen Eth.
Adi Ugri Eritrea see Mendefera
148 I5 Adıyaman Turkey
Adjaria aut. rep. Georgia see Achara
227 F5 Adjelman, Oued watercourse Alg.
219 P4 Adjud Romania
232 A4 Adjumani Uganda
271 □1 Adjuntas Puerto Rico
269 I2 Adjuntas, Presa de las resr Mex.
249 J2 Adlavik Islands Nfld and Lab. Can.
151 A2 Adler Rus. Fed.
171 L6 Adlington Lancashire, England U.K.
212 F1 Adliswil Switz.
195 M4 Adlkofen Ger.
108 H3 Admiralty Gulf W.A. Austr.
108 H3 Admiralty Gulf Aboriginal Reserve W.A. Austr.
243 J2 Admiralty Inlet Nunavut Can.
243 H3 Admiralty Island Nunavut Can.
245 N4 Admiralty Island AK U.S.A.
245 N4 Admiralty Island National Monument-Kootznoow[...] Wilderness nat. park AK
104 □2 Admiralty Islands Lord [...] Austr.
113 K7 Admiralty Islands P.N.G.
287 L2 Admiralty Mountains A[...]
201 J4 Admont Austria
221 I4 Adnan Menderes airpor[...]
232 E3 Ādo Eth.
229 G5 Ado-Ekiti Nigeria
126 D5 Adogawa Japan
126 D5 Ado-gawa r. Japan
230 F2 Adok Sudan
285 G6 Adolfo Gonzáles Chave[...]
269 N9 Adolfo López Mateos M[...]
162 N3 Adolfsström Sweden
108 J3 Adolphus Island W.A. A[...]
115 C8 Adonara i. Indon.
136 E5 Adoni Andhra Prad. Ind[...]
199 H4 Adony Hungary
193 F10 Adorf Sachsen Ger.
193 G9 Adorf Sachsen Ger.
191 G8 Adorf (Diemelsee) Ger.
206 A2 A-dos-Cunhados Port.
122 M3 Ado-Tymovo Sakhalin R[...]
204 E6 Adoufe Port.
185 A8 Adour r. France
139 K8 Adra W. Bengal India
207 M7 Adra Spain
207 N7 Adra r. Spain
150 E5 'Adrā' Syria
205 P6 Adradas Spain
205 L6 Adrados Spain
Adramyttium Turkey see[...]
Adramyttium, Gulf of T[...] Edremit Körfezi
216 H8 Adrano Sicilia Italy
227 E4 Adrar Alg.
227 G4 Adrar mts Alg.
Adrar hills Mali see Ifôghas, Adrar des
226 C5 Adrar admin. reg. Maur.
228 B2 Adrar, Dhar hills Maur.
Adrar des Iforas hills M[...] Ifôghas, Adrar des
227 G5 Adrar Tedjorart well Alg[...]
150 B2 Adras Dağı mt. Turkey
145 J5 Adraskand r. Afgh.
145 M1 Adrasmon Tajik.
224 D6 Adré Chad
213 M5 Adria Italy
251 J8 Adrian MI U.S.A.
261 D8 Adrian TX U.S.A.
Adrianople Turkey see E[...]
Adrianopolis Turkey see[...]
210 D3 Adriatic Sea Europe
184 F3 Adriers France
169 C9 Adrigole Ireland
Adua Eth. see Ādwa
284 B5 Aduana Pejerrey Chile
186 J2 Aduard Neth.
212 G3 Adula Gruppe mts Switz[...]
Adunara i. Indon. see Ad[...]
136 E8 Adur Kerala India
230 F4 Adusa Dem. Rep. Cong[...]
224 E5 Adusa, Qalti el well Sud[...]
160 J6 Adutiškis Lith.
Aduwa Eth. see Ādwa
108 G6 Adverse Well W.A. Austr.
232 C1 Ādwa Eth.
171 O6 Adwick le Street South [...] England U.K.
228 E5 Adwufia Ghana
153 O3 Adycha r. Rus. Fed.
151 C1 Adyge-Khabl' Rus. Fed.
Adygeya aut. rep. Rus. Fe[...] Adygeya, Respublika
151 B1 Adygeya, Respublika au[...] Rus. Fed.
157 G7 Adygeysk Rus. Fed.
Adygeyskaya Avtonomn[...] Oblast' aut. rep. Rus. Fed[...] Adygeya, Respublika
157 I7 Adyk Rus. Fed.
159 L5 Adzhamka Ukr.
Adzharia aut. rep. Georg[...] Achara
228 E5 Adzopé Côte d'Ivoire
156 M2 Adz'va r. Rus. Fed.
156 L2 Adz'vavom Rus. Fed.
221 F4 Aegean Sea Greece/Tur[...]
Aegeri, Lake of Switz. se[...] Ägerisee
Aegina i. Greece see Aig[...]
160 H2 Aegna i. Estonia
160 I2 Aegviidu Estonia
Aegyptus country Africa [...]
Aela Jordan see Al 'Aqab[...]
Aelana Jordan see Al 'Aq[...]
Aelia Capitolina Israel/[...] see Jerusalem
Aelönlaplap atoll Marsh[...] Ailinglaplap
Aenus Turkey see Enez
164 G7 Ærø i. Denmark
159 N8 Aeroflots'kyy Ukr.
172 D3 Aeron r. Wales U.K.
190 J1 Ærøskøbing Denmark
191 H6 Aerzen Ger.
204 C3 A Escusa Spain
Aesernia Italy see Isernia
204 C4 A Esfarrapada Spain
204 D3 A Estrada Spain
220 C2 Aetos Greece
163 Q6 Äetsä Fin.
101 □9a Afaahiti Tahiti Fr. Polyne[...]
225 H5 Afabet Eritrea
232 E3 Afaf Badane well Eth.
Afal watercourse Saudi A[...] 'Ifāl, Wādī
149 L5 Āfān Iran
159 R3 Afanas'yevka Rus. Fed.
156 K4 Afanas'yevo Rus. Fed.
Afándou Rodos Greece s[...] Afantou
221 J6 Afantou Rodos Greece
232 D1 Āfar admin. reg. Eth.
147 M4 Afar Oman
225 I6 Afar Depression Eritrea[...]
101 □9a Afareaitu Moorea Fr. Pol[...]
232 D2 Āfdem Eth.
204 E2 A Feira do Monte Spain
180 G6 Aff r. France
228 E5 Afféri Côte d'Ivoire
215 K4 Affile Italy
195 J5 Affing Ger.
212 E1 Affoltern am Albis Switz[...]
Affreville Alg. see Khemi[...]
168 F8 Affric, Loch l. Scotland U[...]
Afghānestān country Asia[...] Afghanistan
145 K5 Afghanistan country Asia
232 E4 Afgooye Somalia
100 □2 Afi, Mount Samoa
100 □2 Afiamalu Samoa
146 F4 'Afif Saudi Arabia
204 C5 Afife Port.
229 G5 Afikpo Nigeria
161 R4 Afim'ino Rus. Fed.
159 R9 Afipskiy Rus. Fed.
150 D6 Afiq Syria
220 E3 Afissos Greece
Afiun Karahissar Turkey[...] Afyon
144 D4 Afjeh Iran
162 K5 Åfjord Norway
187 D6 Afleidingskanaal van de[...] canal Belgium
201 L4 Aflenz Kurort Austria
227 F2 Aflou Alg.
232 D4 Afmadow Somalia
244 I4 Afognak AK U.S.A.
244 I4 Afognak Island AK U.S.A.
228 B2 Afojjar well Maur.
204 F2 A Fonsagrada Spain
281 G4 Afonso Cláudio Brazil
204 E4 A Forxa Galicia Spain
204 E4 A Forxa Galicia Spain
213 M8 Afra r. Italy
215 M6 Afragola Italy
278 E4 Afrânio Brazil
232 D1 Āfrēra Terara vol. Eth.
232 D1 Āfrēra YeChe'ew Hāyk' l.[...]

Africa continent
Africa Nova country Africa see Tunisia
E2 'Afrīn Syria
E2 'Afrīn, Nahr r. Syria/Turkey
I6 Afritz Austria
J4 Afşar Barajı resr Turkey
H4 Afşin Turkey
H3 Afsluitdijk barrage Neth.
E4 Aftar Iran
E3 Aftol well Eth.
J6 Afton NY U.S.A.
I5 Afton WY U.S.A.
H12 Afton Bridgend East Ayrshire, Scotland U.K.
B2 Aftoût Faï depr. Maur.
Afuá Brazil
D6 'Afula Israel
L4 Afyon Turkey
L4 Afyon prov. Turkey
Afyonkarahisar Turkey see Afyon
F9 Aga Ger.
N1 Aga Rus. Fed.
N1 Aga r. Rus. Fed.
Aga-Buryat Autonomous Okrug admin. div. Rus. Fed. see Aginskiy Buryatskiy Avtonomnyy Okrug
Agadem well Niger
Agadès Niger see Agadez
Agadez Niger
Agadez dept Niger
Agadir Morocco
Agâdîr, Râs pt Maur.
Aga Dubé well Chad
Agadyr' Kazakh.
Agaete Gran Canaria Canary Is
Agaie Nigeria
Agalega Islands Mauritius
Agallas Spain
Agalta nat. park Hond.
Agalta, Sierra de mts Hond.
Agana Guam see Hagåtña
A Gándara Galicia Spain
A Gándara de Altea Galicia Spain
Aganzhen Gansu China
Agapovka Rus. Fed.
Agar Madh. Prad. India
Agara Georgia
Agârak well Niger
Agâraktem well Mali
Āgaro Eth.
Agar Sarar Weyn well Eth.
Agartala Tripura India
Ágasegyháza Hungary
Agashi Mahar. India
Agassiz National Wildlife Refuge nature res. MN U.S.A.
Agat Guam
Agate Ont. Can.
Agathe France see Agde
Agathonisi i. Greece
Agatsuma Japan
Agatsuma-gawa r. Japan
Agatti i. India
Agattu Island AK U.S.A.
Agattu Strait AK U.S.A.
Agawa r. Ont. Can.
Agayani Georgia see Aghaiani
Agbor Bojiboji Nigeria
Agboville Côte d'Ivoire
Ağcabädi Azer.
Ağcaşar Turkey
Ağdam Azer.
Ağdam Azer.
Ağdärä Dağlıq Qarabağ Azer.
Ağdärä Azer.
Ağdaş Azer.
Agdash Azer. see Ağdaş
Agde France
Agdzhabedi Azer. see Ağcabädi
Agedabia Libya see Ajdābiyā
Agematsu Japan
Agen France
Agenais reg. France
Agenebode Nigeria
Agenois reg. France see Agenais
Ageo Japan
Àger Spain
Agerbæk Denmark
Āgere Maryam Eth.
Ägerisee l. Switz.
Ageyevo Rus. Fed.
Ágfalva Hungary
Aggeneys S. Africa
Agger r. Ger.
Aggershus county Norway see Akershus
Aggius Sardegna Italy
Ağgöl salt flat Azer.
Ağgöl Qoruğu nature res. Azer.
Aggsbach Markt Austria
Aggteleki nat. park Hungary
Aghaboe Ireland
Aghadoon Ireland
Aghagallon Northern Ireland U.K.
Aghaiani Georgia
Āghā Jārī Iran
Aghalee Northern Ireland U.K.
Aghamore Ireland
Aghanloo Northern Ireland U.K.
Aghavannagh Ireland
Aghaylas well Western Sahara
Aghchoûrguit well Maur.
Aghern Ireland
Aghezzaf well Mali
Aghil Dawan pass China
Aghione Corse France
Aghireşu Romania
Aghiyuk Island AK U.S.A.
Aghla Mountain hill Ireland
Aghnacliff Ireland
Aghnjadzor Armenia
Aghouavil des. Maur.
Aghrîjît well Maur.
Aghstev r. Armenia
Aghzoumal, Sabkhat salt pan Western Sahara
Agia Greece
Agia Aikaterinis, Akrotirio pt Kerkyra Greece
Agia Anna Greece
Agiabampo Mex.
Agia Eirinis, Akrotirio pt Limnos Greece
Agia Marina Greece
Agia Paraskevi Greece
Agiasos Lesvos Greece
Agia Varvara Kriti Greece
Agigea Romania
Agighiol Romania
Agiguan i. N. Mariana Is see Aguijan
Ağın Turkey
Agincourt France see Azincourt
Ağın Dağı mt. Turkey
Aginskoye Rus. Fed.
Aginum France see Agen
Agioi Apostoloi Greece
Agioi Theodoroi Dytiki Makedonia Greece
Agioi Theodoroi Peloponnisos Greece
Agion Oros admin. div. Greece
Agios Charalampos Greece
Agios Dimitrios Attiki Greece
Agios Dimitrios Kentriki Makedonia Greece
Agios Dimitrios, Akrotirio pt Kythnos Greece
Agios Efstratios Greece
Agios Efstratios i. Greece
Agios Fokas, Akrotirio pt Lesvos Greece
Agios Georgios Greece
Agios Georgios i. Greece
Agios Ioannis, Akrotirio pt Kriti Greece
Agios Kirykos Ikaria Greece
Agios Konstantinos Greece
Agios Matthaios Kerkyra Greece
Agios Nikolaos Kentriki Makedonia Greece
Agios Nikolaos Kriti Greece
221 H3 Agios Paraskevi Lesvos Greece
220 D5 Agios Petros Greece
150 B3 Agios Sergios Cyprus
220 E4 Agios Stefanos Greece
150 C3 Agios Theodoros Cyprus
220 E4 Agios Thomas Greece
220 E2 Agiou Orous, Kolpos b. Greece
216 H8 Agira Sicilia Italy
225 G5 Agirwat Hills Sudan
237 J2 Agisanang S. Africa
170 D3 Agivey Northern Ireland U.K.
194 F3 Aglasterhausen Ger.
221 L5 Ağlasun Turkey
213 K8 Agliana Italy
214 C5 Aglientu Sardegna Italy
185 K10 Agly r. France
212 H5 Agnadello Italy
220 C3 Agnantero Greece
181 I3 Agneaux France
183 J7 Agnel, Col pass France
215 L5 Agnena r. Italy
104 B2 Agnes, Mount hill S.A. Austr.
109 F10 Agnew W.A. Austr.
251 M3 Agnew Lake Ont. Can.
169 K3 Agnew's Hill Northern Ireland U.K.
228 E5 Agnibilékrou Côte d'Ivoire
219 M5 Agnita Romania
122 K3 Agniye-Afanas'yevsk Rus. Fed.
213 K4 Agno r. Italy
212 F3 Agno Switz.
215 M4 Agnone Italy
126 E7 Ago Japan
229 F4 Ago-Are Nigeria
212 F5 Agogna r. Italy
228 E5 Agogo Ghana
Agoitz Spain see Aoiz
204 D3 Agolada Spain
228 E5 Agona Ghana
184 F5 Agonac France
228 E5 Agona Junction Ghana
180 H3 Agon-Coutainville France
128 G8 Agong Qinghai China
213 M3 Agordo Italy
139 I7 Agori Uttar Prad. India
127 J4 Agose Japan
209 D11 Agost Spain
185 D9 Agos-Vidalos France
199 K4 Ágotapuszta nature res. Hungary
228 E2 Agounni Jefal well Mali
264 N7 Agoura CA U.S.A.
229 F2 Agous-n-Ehsel well Mali
185 H8 Agout r. France
126 E7 Ago-wan b. Japan
151 A1 Agoy Rus. Fed.
138 G6 Agra Uttar Prad. India
285 H3 Agraciada Uru.
220 C4 Agrafiotis r. Greece
151 I2 Agrakhanskiy Poluostrov pen. Rus. Fed.
Agram Croatia see Zagreb
207 P4 Agramón Spain
208 H4 Agramunt Spain
212 G4 Agrate Brianza Italy
205 Q5 Agreda Spain
284 C3 Agrelo Arg.
209 E10 Agrés Spain
215 R7 Agri r. Italy
149 K4 Ağrı Turkey
151 E6 Ağrı prov. Turkey
220 E7 Agria Gramvousa i. Greece
214 C2 Agriates, Désert des hills Corse France
151 F6 Ağrı Dağı mt. Turkey
Agrigan i. N. Mariana Is see Agrihan
216 F9 Agrigento Sicilia Italy
216 E8 Agrigento prov. Sicilia Italy
Agrigentum Sicilia Italy see Agrigento
113 K3 Agrihan i. N. Mariana Is
219 L3 Agrii r. Romania
221 H3 Agrilia, Akrotirio pt Lesvos Greece
220 C4 Agrinio Greece
284 C6 Agrio r. Arg.
206 G5 Agrio, Embalse de resr Spain
220 E3 Agriovotano Greece
204 F5 Agrochão Port.
215 N7 Agropoli Italy
156 K4 Agryz Rus. Fed.
162 L3 Ågskaret Norway
151 G4 Ağstafa Azer.
151 J5 Ağsu Azer.
114 C4 Agta Point Phil.
237 J8 Agter Sneeuberg S. Africa
237 J6 Agtertang S. Africa
209 D12 Agua, Cabo de c. Spain
206 H4 Agua, Sierra del hills Spain
284 C6 Agua Amarga, Pampa del plain Arg.
284 E5 Agua Blanca Arg.
269 I5 Agua Blanca Iturbide Mex.
281 F2 Água Boa Brazil
268 B3 Agua Brava, Laguna lag. Mex.
268 D4 Agua Caliente Mex.
276 D3 Agua Clara Bol.
280 A4 Água Clara Brazil
274 C3 Aguaclara Col.
267 N8 Aguada Mex.
271 □1 Aguada Puerto Rico
271 I8 Aguada Grande Venez.
274 C3 Aguadas Col.
268 F8 Agua de Correra Mex.
238 □1b Água de Pau São Miguel Azores
271 □1 Aguadilla Puerto Rico
283 D6 Aguado Cecilio Arg.
281 G3 Agua Doce do Norte Brazil
280 C5 Aguados, Serra dos mts Brazil
276 D3 Agua Dulce Bol.
269 M7 Agua Dulce Mex.
266 □S13 Aguadulce Panama
207 J6 Aguadulce Andalucía Spain
207 N7 Aguadulce Andalucía Spain
284 C5 Agua Escondida Arg.
265 T8 Agua Fria r. AZ U.S.A.
265 T7 Agua Fria National Monument nat. park AZ U.S.A.
280 D5 Aguaí Brazil
238 □1a Agualva Terceira Azores
268 B5 Aguamilpa Mex.
268 C4 Aguamilpa, Presa l. Mex.
268 D1 Aguanaval r. Mex.
206 E5 Água Negra hill Port.
284 C2 Agua Negra, Paso del pass Arg./Chile
264 P8 Aguanga CA U.S.A.
249 I3 Aguanish r. Que. Can.
266 □P11 Aguanqueterique Hond.
266 F5 Agua Nueva Mex.
277 F4 Aguapeí Brazil
280 B4 Aguapeí r. Brazil
277 F3 Aguapeí r. Brazil
277 F4 Aguapeí, Serra hills Brazil
266 E2 Agua Prieta Mex.
276 E5 Aguaragüe, Cordillera de mts Bol.
282 E1 Aguaray Arg.
204 C5 A Guarda Spain
238 □1b Agua Retorta São Miguel Azores
274 E2 Aguaro-Guariquito, Parque Nacional nat. park Venez.
208 C5 Aguarón Spain
266 F5 Aguaruto Mex.
208 E3 Aguas Spain
207 P6 Aguas r. Spain
278 F4 Águas Belas Brazil
204 D9 Águas Belas Port.
271 □1 Aguas Buenas Puerto Rico
268 E4 Aguascalientes Mex.
268 E4 Aguascalientes state Mex.
285 I4 Aguas Corrientes Uru.
281 G2 Águas Formosas Brazil
204 F5 Águas Frias Port.
281 G1 Águas Vermelhas Brazil
208 E5 Aguasvivas r. Spain
277 F3 Água Verde r. Brazil
268 B3 Agua Verde Mex.
280 B3 Água Vermelha, Represa resr Brazil
208 E6 Aguaviva Spain
276 B2 Aguaytia Peru
204 F4 A Gudiña Spain
207 J3 Agudo Spain
280 C5 Agudos Brazil
204 D7 Águeda Port.
204 G6 Águeda r. Port./Spain
204 H7 Agueda, Embalse de resr Spain
229 H2 Âguelal Niger
229 F2 Aguelhok Mali
227 F4 Aguemour, Oued watercourse Alg.
205 N2 Agüera r. Spain
183 C8 Aguessac France
229 H2 Aguessis well Niger
213 O8 Agugliano Italy
126 E6 Agui Japan
206 D4 Aguiar Port.
204 E7 Aguiar da Beira Port.
229 G3 Aguié Niger
204 D8 Aguieira, Barragem da resr Port.
113 K4 Aguijan i. N. Mariana Is
205 Q7 Águila mt. Spain
265 S8 Aguila AZ U.S.A.
205 N2 Águila, Punta del pt Spain
205 L6 Aguilafuente Spain
263 L8 Aguilar CO U.S.A.
208 D6 Aguilar de Alfambra Spain
205 L3 Aguilar de Campóo Spain
205 L3 Aguilar de Campóo, Embalse de resr Spain
207 J5 Aguilar de la Frontera Spain
205 Q5 Aguilar del Río Alhama Spain
207 P6 Águilas Spain
268 E7 Aguililla Mex.
204 D8 Aguim Port.
238 □3f Agüimes Gran Canaria Canary Is
238 □3f Aguineguin r. Gran Canaria Canary Is
114 D6 Aguisan Negros Phil.
205 N6 Aguisejo r. Spain
232 C1 Āgula'i Eth.
206 □ Agulha, Ponta da pt Madeira
236 E10 Agulhas S. Africa
236 E10 Agulhas, Cape S. Africa
288 K9 Agulhas Basin sea feature Southern Ocean
281 E5 Agulhas Negras mt. Brazil
289 F7 Agulhas Plateau sea feature Southern Ocean
288 J8 Agulhas Ridge sea feature S. Atlantic Ocean
208 K3 Agullana Spain
209 D10 Agullent Spain
238 □3a Agulo La Gomera Canary Is
124 □E20 Aguni-jima i. Nansei-shotō Japan
Aguntum Italy see San Candido
114 E7 Agusan r. Mindanao Phil.
270 G8 Agustín Codazzi Col.
285 G4 Agustín Roca O'Higgins Arg.
114 C6 Agutaya Phil.
114 C6 Agutaya i. Phil.
221 K1 Ağva Turkey
151 H3 Agvali Rus. Fed.
229 G4 Agwarra Nigeria
232 B3 Agwei r. Sudan
151 I4 Ağyazı Azer.
Agyrium Sicilia Italy see Agira
124 □1 Aha Okinawa Japan
146 F6 Ahad Rafidah Saudi Arabia
227 G5 Ahaggar plat. Alg.
227 G5 Ahaggar, Tassili oua-n- plat. Alg.
106 D7 Ahakeye Aboriginal Land res. N.T. Austr.
169 C9 Ahakista Ireland
144 H2 Ahal admin. div. Turkm.
195 M4 Aham Ger.
144 I5 Āhangarān Iran
144 B2 Ahar Iran
103 F9 Ahaura South I. N.Z.
103 F9 Ahaura r. South I. N.Z.
191 D6 Ahaus Ger.
190 H4 Ahausen Ger.
169 H8 Ahenny Ireland
169 E9 Aherla Ireland
169 G8 Aherlow r. Ireland
239 □3a Ahibambo hill Njazidja Comoros
204 H8 Ahigal Spain
204 H6 Ahigal de Villarino Spain
207 K5 Ahillo mt. Spain
206 H4 Ahillones Spain
102 K5 Ahimanawa Range mts North I. N.Z.
158 E1 Ahinski Kanal canal Belarus
102 H2 Ahipara North I. N.Z.
102 H2 Ahipara Bay North I. N.Z.
136 G3 Ahiri Mahar. India
102 I5 Ahititi North I. N.Z.
160 K3 Ahja r. Estonia
244 G4 Ahklun Mountains AK U.S.A.
149 K4 Ahlat Turkey
192 J3 Ahlbeck Ger.
192 J3 Ahlbeck, Seebad Ger.
190 I5 Ahlden (Aller) Ger.
191 E7 Ahlen Ger.
190 H4 Ahlerstedt Ger.
190 F5 Ahlhorn Ger.
193 D7 Ahlsdorf Ger.
138 D8 Ahmadabad Gujarat India
149 P8 Aḥmadābād Iran
144 H4 Aḥmadābād Khorāsān Iran
144 I4 Aḥmadābād Khorāsān Iran
150 D9 Aḥmad al Bāqir, Jabal mt. Jordan
151 I6 Ähmädbäyli Azer.
136 D3 Ahmadnagar Mahar. India
136 E3 Ahmadpur Mahar. India
145 N7 Ahmadpur East Pak.
145 N6 Ahmadpur Sial Pak.
145 N9 Ahmad Tar Pak.
232 D2 Ahmar mts Eth.
Ahmedabad Gujarat India see Ahmadabad
Ahmednagar Mahar. India see Ahmadnagar
221 I4 Ahmetli Turkey
221 L4 Ahmetpaşa Turkey
190 J5 Ahnsbeck Ger.
229 G5 Ahoada Nigeria
169 J3 Ahoghill Northern Ireland U.K.
266 E5 Ahome Mex.
138 D7 Ahore Rajasthan India
191 K10 Ahorn Ger.
200 E5 Ahornspitze mt. Austria
255 I7 Ahoskie NC U.S.A.
191 D9 Ahr r. Ger.
144 D7 Ahram Iran
Ahrâmât el Jîzah tourist site Egypt see Pyramids of Giza
159 N8 Ahrarne Ukr.
139 I7 Ahraura Uttar Prad. India
144 E6 Āhravān Iran
217 □ Ahrax, Il-Ponta ta' l- pt Malta
191 C10 Ahrbrück Ger.
190 K2 Ahrensbök Ger.
190 J3 Ahrensburg Ger.
192 I5 Ahrensfelde Ger.
192 G2 Ahrenshagen Ger.
192 F2 Ahrenshoop, Ostseebad Ger.
191 E7 Ahse r. Ger.
156 D3 Ähtäri Fin.
160 K2 Ahtme Estonia
144 C6 Āhū Iran
268 C4 Ahuacatlán Mex.
267 O11 Ahuachapán El Salvador
268 D5 Ahualulco Jalisco Mex.
268 F3 Ahualulco San Luis Potosí Mex.
269 I7 Ahuatempan Mex.
269 I5 Ahuazotepec Mex.
268 D6 Ahuijullo Mex.
184 I3 Ahun France
160 K3 Ahunapalu Estonia
101 □9 Ahunui atoll Arch. des Tuamotu Fr. Polynesia
103 E11 Ahuriri r. South I. N.Z.
102 I3 Ahuroa North I. N.Z.
165 K6 Åhus Sweden
144 C6 Ahvāz Iran
Ahvenanmaa is Åland Fin. see Åland
138 D9 Ahwa Gujarat India
146 H9 Aḥwar Yemen
Ahwāz Iran see Ahvāz
229 F3 Ahzar, Vallée de l' watercourse Niger
115 F6 Ai i. Maluku Indon.
234 C5 Ai-Ais Namibia
234 C5 Ai-Ais Hot Springs and Fish River Canyon Park nature res. Namibia
234 C5 Ai-Ais/Richtersveld Transfrontier Park Namibia/S. Africa
275 F6 Aiapuá, Lago l. Brazil
274 D4 Aiari r. Brazil
129 L5 Aibag Gol r. China
205 R3 Aibar Spain
124 T3 Aibetsu Japan
201 L6 Aibl Austria
271 □1 Aibonito Puerto Rico
195 K5 Aichach Ger.
194 E5 Aichhalden Ger.
126 F6 Aichi pref. Japan
126 F5 Aichi-kōgen Kokutei-kōen park Japan
245 L1 Aichilik r. AK U.S.A.
195 I6 Aichstetten Ger.
138 F7 Aichwara Madh. Prad. India
256 C10 Aid OH U.S.A.
125 L12 Aida Japan
195 O4 Aidenbach Ger.
191 J10 Aidhausen Ger.
216 G9 Aidone Sicilia Italy
264 □D12 'Aiea HI U.S.A.
215 Q9 Aiello Calabro Italy
215 P8 Aieta Italy
184 D3 Aiffres France
220 D4 Aigeira Greece
201 J4 Aigen im Ennstal Austria
201 I2 Aigen im Mühlkreis Austria
221 G6 Aigiali Greece
150 C3 Aigialousa Cyprus
220 E5 Aigina Greece
220 E5 Aigina i. Greece
220 D2 Aiginio Greece
220 D4 Aigio Greece
212 B3 Aigle Switz.
184 I5 Aigle, Barrage de l' dam France
183 J7 Aigle de Chambeyron mt. France
183 I8 Aiglun France
185 E8 Aignan France
178 I8 Aignay-le-Duc France
183 D8 Aigoual, Mont mt. France
184 E4 Aigre France
184 C3 Aigrefeuille-d'Aunis France
180 I7 Aigrefeuille-sur-Maine France
239 □1b Aigrettes, Île aux i. Mauritius
239 □1c Aigrettes, Pointe des pt Réunion
204 D4 A Igrexa Spain
282 G4 Aiguá Uru.
182 F2 Aigue, Mont hill France
182 I5 Aiguebelle France
251 P1 Aiguebelle, Parc de Conservation d' nature res. Que. Can.
182 J5 Aigueblanche France
182 C4 Aigueperse France
183 F8 Aigues r. France
209 E10 Aigües Spain
183 E9 Aigues-Mortes France
183 D10 Aigues-Mortes, Golfe d' b. France
208 G2 Aigüestortes i Estany de Sant Maurici, Parc Nacional d' nat. park Spain
183 B10 Aigues-Vives Languedoc-Roussillon France
183 E9 Aigues-Vives Languedoc-Roussillon France
185 H10 Aigues-Vives Midi-Pyrénées France
183 H7 Aiguille, Mont mt. France
184 A3 Aiguille, Pointe de l' pt France
182 K5 Aiguille d'Argentière mt. France/Switz.
182 K5 Aiguille de la Grande Sassière mt. France
183 J6 Aiguille de Péclet mt. France
183 J6 Aiguille de Scolette mt. France/Italy
182 J5 Aiguille du Midi mt. France
183 J7 Aiguilles France
183 I6 Aiguilles d'Arves mts France
182 J5 Aiguilles des Glaciers mts France
102 J3 Aiguilles Island North I. N.Z.
182 J5 Aiguille Verte mt. France
185 E7 Aiguillon France
184 B3 Aiguillon, Anse de l' b. France
184 B3 Aiguillon, Pointe de l' pt France
184 H3 Aigurande France
123 D8 Ai He r. China
Aihua Yunnan China see Yunxian
Aihui Heilong. China see Heihe
276 A2 Aija Peru
Aijal Mizoram India see Aizawl
127 J4 Aikawa Kanagawa Japan
124 P8 Aikawa Niigata Japan
255 G9 Aiken SC U.S.A.
130 C6 Ailao Shan mts Yunnan China
106 D7 Aileron N.T. Austr.
115 D8 Aileu East Timor
266 □T13 Ailigandi Panama
130 G6 Ailing Guangxi China
Ailinglabelab atoll Marshall Is see Ailinglaplap
290 G6 Ailinglaplap atoll Marshall Is
178 F8 Aillant-sur-Tholon France
185 D7 Aillas France
183 J10 Aille r. France
179 L8 Aillevillers-et-Lyaumont France
178 C3 Ailly-le-Haut-Clocher France
178 D4 Ailly-sur-Noye France
178 D4 Ailly-sur-Somme France
251 M6 Ailsa Craig Ont. Can.
168 F12 Ailsa Craig i. Scotland U.K.
169 F3 Ailt an Chorráin Ireland
183 E9 Aimargues France
182 J5 Aime France
Aimeo i. Fr. Polynesia see Moorea
115 B8 Aimere Flores Indon.
282 D3 Aimogasta Arg.
281 G3 Aimorés Brazil
281 G2 Aimorés, Serra dos hills Brazil
182 G4 Ain dept France
182 G5 Ain r. France
264 □D12 'Āina Haina HI U.S.A.
182 B3 Ainay-le-Château France
160 H4 Ainaži Latvia
227 G2 Aïn Beïda Alg.
226 E2 Aïn Beni Mathar Morocco
226 C4 'Aïn Ben Tili Maur.
228 C2 Aïn Biré well Maur.
227 F1 Aïn Defla Alg.
227 F2 Aïn Deheb Alg.
195 J4 Aindling Ger.
211 B7 Aïn Draham Tunisia
227 F3 Aïn el Hadjadj well Alg.
227 G4 Aïn el Hadjadj well Alg.
227 F2 Aïn el Hadjel Alg.
227 G2 Aïn el Melh Alg.
200 G6 Ainet Austria
224 C5 Aïn Galakka spring Chad
185 B9 Ainhoa France
227 G2 Aïn Mdila well Alg.
227 F3 Aïn Mezzer well Alg.
227 G1 Aïn-M'Lila Alg.
Aïn Mokra Alg. see Berrahal
220 B4 Ainou, Ethnikos Drymos nat. park Kefallonia Greece
227 G2 Aïn Oulmene Alg.
227 F2 Aïn Oussera Alg.
195 N6 Ainring Ger.
208 F3 Ainsa Spain
Ain Salah Alg. see In Salah
171 K6 Ainsdale Merseyside, England U.K.
227 E2 Aïn Sefra Alg.
249 I4 Ainslie, Lake N.S. Can.
260 F4 Ainsworth NE U.S.A.
Aintab Turkey see Gaziantep
227 E2 Aïn Temouchent Alg.
227 F5 Aïn Ti-m Misaou well Alg.
171 L7 Aintree Merseyside, England U.K.
205 R5 Ainzón Spain
125 L12 Aioi Japan
274 C4 Aipe Col.
276 D4 Aiquile Bol.
116 G3 Air i. Indon.
229 H2 Aïr, Massif de l' mts Niger
114 □ Airai Palau
178 C4 Airaines France
275 F5 Airão Brazil
212 C6 Airasca Italy
116 C4 Airbangis Sumatera Indon.
168 C7 Aird Asaig Western Isles, Scotland U.K.
168 E8 Aird of Sleat Highland, Scotland U.K.
246 H5 Airdrie Alta Can.
168 I11 Airdrie North Lanarkshire, Scotland U.K.
179 I5 Aire r. France
178 E2 Aire, Canal d' France
208 □ Aire, Illa de l' i. Spain
171 N6 Airedale val. England U.K.
185 D8 Aire-sur-l'Adour France
178 D2 Aire-sur-la-Lys France
229 H2 Aïr et du Ténéré, Réserve Naturelle Nationale de l' nature res. Niger
243 K3 Air Force Island Nunavut Can.
129 L5 Airgin Sum Nei Mongol China
117 I6 Airhitam r. Indon.
117 I6 Airhitam, Teluk b. Indon.
168 C6 Airidh a'Bhruaich Western Isles, Scotland U.K.
107 L6 Airlie Beach Qld Austr.
108 C6 Airlie Island W.A. Austr.
116 D1 Air Muda, Tasik l. Malaysia
215 N5 Airola Italy
212 F2 Airolo Switz.
115 D7 Airpanas Maluku Indon.
116 D1 Air Pedu, Tasik l. Malaysia
247 J4 Air Ronge Sask. Can.
168 I10 Airth Falkirk, Scotland U.K.
171 M5 Airton North Yorkshire, England U.K.
184 D2 Airvault France
118 A4 Aisatung Mountain Myanmar
195 K2 Aisch r. Ger.
283 B7 Aisén admin. reg. Chile
178 I8 Aisey-sur-Seine France
275 G4 Aishalton Guyana
129 Q8 Ai Shan hill Shandong China
245 M3 Aishihik Y.T. Can.
245 M3 Aishihik Lake Y.T. Can.
Aisími Greece see Aisymi
195 I4 Aislingen Ger.
178 G4 Aisne dept France
179 E5 Aisne r. France
227 E2 Aïssa, Djebel mt. Alg.
182 I2 Aïssey France
221 G1 Aisymi Greece
182 E1 Aisy-sur-Armançon France
162 R3 Aitamännikkö Fin.
209 E10 Aitana mt. Spain
113 J7 Aitape P.N.G.
226 D3 Aït Benhaddou tourist site Morocco
195 N4 Aiterach r. Ger.
195 N4 Aiterhofen Ger.
168 K4 Aith Orkney, Scotland U.K.
260 I2 Aitkin MN U.S.A.
227 F5 Aït Nefâne well Mali
126 D5 Aitō Japan
220 C4 Aitoliko Greece
208 F5 Aitona Spain
142 F1 Aitova Rus. Fed.
195 I6 Aitrach Ger.
195 J6 Aitrang Ger.
103 □2 Aitutaki i. Cook Is
219 L4 Aiud Romania
160 I5 Aiviekste r. Latvia
114 □ Aiwokako Passage Palau
Aix France see Aix-en-Provence
182 E5 Aix r. France
184 B3 Aix, Île d' i. France
178 G7 Aix-en-Othe France
183 G9 Aix-en-Provence France
184 G4 Aixe-sur-Vienne France
Aix-la-Chapelle Ger. see Aachen
182 H5 Aix-les-Bains France
232 C1 Āīy Ādī Eth.
Aiyiáli Greece see Aigiali
Aíyina i. Greece see Aigina
Aiyínion Greece see Aiginio
Aíyion Greece see Aigio
Aíyira Greece see Aigeira
139 N8 Aizawl Mizoram India
180 H8 Aizenay France
160 I5 Aizkraukle Latvia
205 Q3 Aizpún Spain
160 E5 Aizpute Latvia
125 Q9 Aizu-Wakamatsu Japan
146 E2 Ajā, Jibāl mts Saudi Arabia
144 A3 'Ajab Shīr Iran
214 B4 Ajaccio Corse France
Ajaccio airport Corse France see Campo dell'Oro
214 B4 Ajaccio, Golfe d' b. Corse France
269 H5 Ajacuba Mex.
138 H7 Ajaigarh Madh. Prad. India
274 C4 Ajajú r. Col.
199 L3 Ajak Hungary
269 J7 Ajalpán Mex.
151 D3 Ajamet'is Nakrdzali nature res. Georgia
138 E9 Ajanta Mahar. India
Ajanta Range hills India see Sahyadriparvat Range
229 G5 Ajaokuta Nigeria
Ajaria aut. rep. Georgia see Achara
229 G4 Ajasse Nigeria
184 G5 Ajat France
251 O6 Ajax Ont. Can.
103 G9 Ajax, Mount South I. N.Z.
Ajayameru Rajasthan India see Ajmer
100 □1 Ajayan Bay Guam
147 L3 Ajban U.A.E.
128 D4 Aj Bogd Uul mts Mongolia
224 D2 Ajdābiyā Libya
210 D3 Ajdovščina Slovenia
a-Jiddét des. Oman see Ḥarāsīs, Jiddat al
124 R6 Ajigasawa Japan
227 H2 Ajim Tunisia
139 L7 Ajimganj W. Bengal India
127 J5 Ajiro Japan
227 G4 Ajjer, Tassili n' plat. Alg.
199 G4 Ajka Hungary
150 D6 'Ajlūn Jordan
146 B1 'Ajmah, Jabal al mts Egypt
150 B9 'Ajmah, Jabal al plat. Egypt
147 L3 'Ajman U.A.E.
138 E6 Ajmer Rajasthan India
Ajmer-Merwara Rajasthan India see Ajmer
138 E4 Ajnala Punjab India
205 M2 Ajo Spain
265 T9 Ajo AZ U.S.A.
205 M1 Ajo, Cabo de c. Spain
265 T9 Ajo, Mount AZ U.S.A.
205 M9 Ajofrín Spain
212 B1 Ajoie reg. Switz.
100 □3b Ajokwola i. Majuro Marshall Is
269 J4 Ajoquentla Mex.
268 A1 Ajoya Mex.
136 D4 Ajra Mahar. India
145 L5 Ajrestan Afgh.
268 G7 Ajuchitlán Mex.
238 □1b Ajuda, Ponta da pt São Miguel Azores
276 D1 Ajuricaba Brazil
114 D6 Ajuy Panay Phil.
144 F3 Ajyyap Turkm.
126 F6 Akabane Japan
124 T3 Akabira Japan
227 F4 Akabli Alg.
127 J3 Akabori Japan
229 F2 Akaboun well Mali
122 K1 Akademii, Zaliv b. Rus. Fed.
Akademii Nauk, Khrebet mt. Tajik. see Akademiyai Fanho, Qatorkŭhi
145 N2 Akademiyai Fanho, Qatorkŭhi mt. Tajik.
125 P9 Akadomari Japan
124 Q8 Aka-gawa r. Japan
233 A5 Akagera, Parc National de l' nat. park Rwanda
127 J2 Akagi Gunma Japan
125 J12 Akagi Shimane Japan
127 J2 Akagi-yama vol. Japan
127 H5 Akaishi-dake mt. Japan
127 G6 Akaishi-sanmyaku mts Japan
232 C2 Āk'ak'ī Beseka Eth.
224 A3 Akakus, Jabal mts Libya
136 E4 Akalkot Mahar. India
Akama, Akra c. Cyprus see Arnaoutis, Cape
Akamagaseki Japan see Shimonoseki
229 H5 Akamkpa Nigeria
124 V3 Akan Japan
230 A4 Akanda, Parc National d' nat. park Estuaire Gabon
124 U3 Akan-ko l. Japan
124 V3 Akan Kokuritsu-kōen nat. park Japan
229 G3 Akarkar well Niger
220 B4 Akarnanika mts Greece
103 G10 Akaroa South I. N.Z.
103 G10 Akaroa Harbour South I. N.Z.
139 N6 Akas reg. India
125 K11 Akasaki Japan
225 F4 Akasha Sudan
140 D3 'Akāshāt Iraq
149 I7 Akāshat Iraq
126 A6 Akashi Japan
126 A6 Akashi-kaikyō str. Japan
127 G3 Akashina Japan
237 M1 Akasia S. Africa
162 Q3 Äkäsjoki r. Fin.
162 Q3 Äkäsjokisuu Fin.
199 I5 Akasztó Hungary
103 J8 Akatarawa North I. N.Z.
151 C5 Akbaba Turkey
143 O5 Akbakay Kazakh.
143 R4 Akbalyk Kazakh.
145 M4 Akbar Afgh.
144 E7 Akbarābād Iran
138 H6 Akbarpur Uttar Prad. India
139 I6 Akbarpur Uttar Prad. India
142 I4 Akbasty Kazakh.
143 P3 Akbauyr Kazakh.
Akbaytal Kŭhistoni Badakhshon Tajik. see Rabotoqbaytal
145 O2 Akbaytal, Pereval pass Tajik.
143 N2 Akbeit Kazakh.
150 E2 Akbez Turkey
227 G1 Akbou Alg.
143 R3 Akbulak Kazakh.
143 U3 Akbulak Kazakh.
142 D3 Akbulak Kazakh.
142 F2 Akbulak Rus. Fed.
151 A4 Akçaabat Turkey
148 H4 Akçadağ Turkey
151 E6 Akça Dağ mt. Turkey
148 I5 Akçakale Turkey
221 J3 Akcakertikbeli Geçidi pass Turkey
221 M1 Akçakoca Turkey
150 F2 Akçakoyunlu Turkey
148 F5 Akçali Dağ mt. Turkey
150 A2 Akçalı Dağları mts Turkey
221 I5 Akçaova Turkey
221 K6 Akçay Antalya Turkey
151 E5 Akçay Kars Turkey
221 J5 Akçay r. Turkey
228 B2 Akchâr reg. Maur.
143 O4 Akchatau Kazakh.
Akchi Kazakh. see Akshiy
151 C6 Akdağ mt. Turkey
221 J3 Akdağ mt. Turkey
221 J5 Akdağ mts Turkey
221 L5 Ak Dağı mt. Turkey
221 K6 Akdağlar mts Turkey
148 G4 Akdağmadeni Turkey
151 E5 Akdam Turkey
144 H1 Akdepe Turkm.
150 B2 Akdere Turkey
Akdoğan Cyprus see Lysi
151 C6 Akdoğan Dağı mts Turkey
126 F5 Akechi Japan
115 E4 Akelamo Halmahera Indon.
115 F3 Akelamo Halmahera Indon.
171 M2 Akeld Northumberland, England U.K.
146 D8 Akele Guzai prov. Eritrea
232 B3 Akelo Sudan
193 F7 Aken Ger.
127 L3 Akeno Ibaraki Japan
127 H4 Akeno Yamanashi Japan
165 O2 Åkersberga Sweden
164 H1 Akershus county Norway
186 G3 Akersloot Neth.
165 N2 Åkers styckebruk Sweden
163 K6 Åkerstrømmen Norway
142 I4 Akespe Kazakh.
230 D4 Aketi Dem. Rep. Congo
144 F1 Akgyr Erezi hills Turkm.
Akkyr, Gory hills Turkm. see Akgyr Erezi
144 E5 Ā Khakh Iran
151 F3 Akhalgori Georgia
Akhali-Afoni Georgia see Akhali Ap'oni
151 B2 Akhali Ap'oni Georgia
151 E4 Akhalk'alak'i Georgia
Akhal Oblast admin. div. Turkm. see Ahal
151 D4 Akhalts'ikhe Georgia
224 D2 Akhḍar, Al Jabal al mts Libya
147 M4 Akhḍar, Jabal mts Oman
150 E10 Akhḍar, Wādī al watercourse Saudi Arabia
Akhelóös r. Greece see Acheloos
219 P8 Akheloy Bulg.
244 I4 Akhiok AK U.S.A.
221 I4 Akhisar Turkey
151 F4 Akhk'erp'i Georgia
151 G3 Akhmeta Georgia
151 C1 Akhmetovskaya Rus. Fed.
225 F3 Akhmīm Egypt
138 E3 Akhnoor Jammu and Kashmir India
151 E3 Akhsau Rus. Fed.
Akhsu Azer. see Ağsu
Akhta Armenia see Hrazdan
149 P10 Akhtar Iran
150 F2 Akhtarīn Syria
157 I6 Akhtubinsk Rus. Fed.
151 I4 Akhty Rus. Fed.
Akhtyrka Ukr. see Okhtyrka
159 R9 Akhtyrskiy Rus. Fed.
142 H1 Akhunovo Rus. Fed.
151 I4 Akhvay, Gora mt. Azer./Rus. Fed.
125 K13 Aki Japan
244 G3 Akiachak AK U.S.A.
230 B5 Akiéni Gabon
248 D2 Akimiski Island Nunavut Can.
Akıncılar İzmir Turkey see Selçuk
148 I3 Akıncılar Sivas Turkey
135 □1 Akinfushi i. N. Male Maldives
127 J4 Akiruno Japan
127 J4 Akishima Japan
122 H2 Akishma r. Rus. Fed.
124 R7 Akita Japan
124 R7 Akita pref. Japan
102 K7 Akitio North I. N.Z.
127 K3 Akiyama-gawa r. Japan
228 B2 Akjoujt Maur.
226 C3 Akka Morocco
142 J3 Akkabak Kazakh.
162 N3 Akkajaure l. Sweden
244 E2 Akkani Rus. Fed.
142 I2 Akkarga Kazakh.
151 C4 Akkaya Turkey
132 H1 Akkem Rus. Fed.
143 M4 Akkense Kazakh.
Akkerman Ukr. see Bilhorod-Dnistrovs'kyy
142 H2 Akkermanovka Rus. Fed.
124 V3 Akkeshi Japan
124 W3 Akkeshi-ko l. Japan
124 V4 Akkeshi-wan b. Japan
142 D4 Akkistau Kazakh.
150 D6 'Akko Israel
143 N1 Akkol' Akmolinskaya Oblast' Kazakh.
143 P5 Akkol' Almatinskaya Oblast' Kazakh.
157 J7 Akkol' Atyrauskaya Oblast' Kazakh.
143 N6 Akkol' Zhambylskaya Oblast' Kazakh.
143 N6 Akkol', Ozero salt l. Kazakh.
221 I5 Akköy Aydın Turkey
221 K5 Akköy Denizli Turkey
186 I2 Akkrum Neth.
143 Q2 Akku Kazakh.
Akkul' Kazakh. see Akkol'
142 K5 Akkum Kazakh.
148 H3 Akkuş Turkey
229 F4 Aklampa Benin
245 N1 Aklavik N.W.T. Can.
138 F7 Aklera Rajasthan India
Akli well Mali see I-n-Akli
146 G6 Aklub reg. Saudi Arabia
Ak-Mechet Kazakh. see Kyzylorda
160 F6 Akmena r. Lith.
160 F5 Akmenė Lith.
160 E5 Akmeņrags pt Latvia
133 C8 Akmeqit Xinjiang China
143 N3 Akmeshit Kazakh.
Akmola Kazakh. see Astana
Akmola Oblast admin. div. Kazakh. see Akmolinskaya Oblast'
Akmolinsk Kazakh. see Astana
143 N2 Akmolinskaya Oblast' admin. div. Kazakh.
143 Q7 Ak-Moyun Kyrg.
160 I5 Aknīste Latvia
226 E2 Aknoul Morocco
125 L12 Akō Japan
232 B3 Akobo Sudan
232 B3 Akobo Wenz r. Eth./Sudan
138 F8 Akodia Madh. Prad. India
229 G2 Akokan Niger
136 D3 Akola Mahar. India
138 F9 Akola Mahar. India
229 H6 Akom II Cameroon
132 C6 Akongkür Xinjiang China
229 I6 Akonolinga Cameroon
230 F2 Akop Sudan
225 H6 Akordat Eritrea
221 L4 Akören Afyon Turkey
148 F5 Akören Konya Turkey
138 F9 Akot Mahar. India
230 F3 Akot Sudan
228 E5 Akoupé Côte d'Ivoire
143 O3 Akoy Kazakh.
243 L3 Akpatok Island Nunavut Can.
132 D6 Akqi Xinjiang China
220 E4 Akraifnio Greece
162 □B1 Akranes Iceland
164 B2 Åkrehamn Norway
229 H2 Akrérèb Niger
220 C6 Akritas, Akrotirio pt Greece
260 D5 Akron CO U.S.A.
250 H8 Akron IN U.S.A.
256 G5 Akron NY U.S.A.
256 D7 Akron OH U.S.A.
258 C4 Akron PA U.S.A.
220 F7 Akrotiri, Chersonisos pen. Kriti Greece
Akrotiri Bay Cyprus see Akrotirion Bay
150 B4 Akrotirion Bay Cyprus
Akrotiriou, Kolpos b. Cyprus see Akrotirion Bay
150 A4 Akrotiri Sovereign Base Area military base Cyprus
133 D9 Aksai Chin terr. Asia
221 J2 Aksakal Turkey
219 P7 Aksakovo Bulg.
157 K5 Aksakovo Rus. Fed.
148 G4 Aksaray Turkey
152 H3 Aksarka Rus. Fed.
151 C2 Aksaut r. Rus. Fed.
132 L7 Aksay Gansu China
142 E2 Aksay Kazakh.
143 P7 Ak-Say r. Kyrg.
157 G7 Aksay Rostovskaya Oblast' Rus. Fed.
157 I7 Aksay Volgogradskaya Oblast' Rus. Fed.
159 S6 Aksay r. Rus. Fed.
133 D9 Aksayqin Hu l. Aksai Chin
148 E4 Akşehir Turkey
221 M4 Akşehir Gölü l. Turkey
148 E5 Akseki Turkey
142 F1 Aksenovo Rus. Fed.
144 F7 Aks-e Rostam r. Iran
129 M1 Aksha Rus. Fed.
142 F3 Akshatau Kazakh.
142 J3 Akshiganak Kazakh.
143 Q6 Akshiy Kazakh.
142 D6 Akshukur Kazakh.
142 E5 Akshymyrau Kazakh.
132 E5 Aksu Xinjiang China
132 E6 Aksu Xinjiang China
143 N1 Aksu Akmolinskaya Oblast' Kazakh.
143 R5 Aksu Almatinskaya Oblast' Kazakh.
143 Q1 Aksu Pavlodarskaya Oblast' Kazakh.
143 M6 Aksu Kazakh.
142 E2 Aksu Zapadnyy Kazakhstan Kazakh.
143 R4 Aksu r. Kazakh.
Aksu r. Tajik. see Oqsu
221 L6 Aksu Antalya Turkey
151 B5 Aksu Erzurum Turkey
221 M5 Aksu Isparta Turkey
221 L6 Aksu r. Turkey
142 K2 Aksuat Kostanayskaya Oblast' Kazakh.
143 T4 Aksuat Vostochnyy Kazakhstan Kazakh.
Aksuat, Ozero salt l. Kazakh. see Bol'shoy Aksuat, Ozero
143 O3 Aksu-Ayuly Kazakh.
157 J5 Aksubayevo Rus. Fed.
132 E6 Aksu He r. China
232 C1 Āksum Eth.
143 L5 Aksumbe Kazakh.
132 E4 Aksüme Xinjiang China
143 P5 Aksuyek Kazakh.
143 N6 Aksu-Zhabaglinskiy Zapovednik nature res. Kazakh.
133 G8 Aktag mt. Xinjiang China
132 D7 Aktam Xinjiang China
156 K5 Aktanysh Rus. Fed.
143 L3 Aktas Kazakh.
150 E2 Aktaş Hatay Turkey
151 B4 Aktaş Rize Turkey
149 L4 Aktas Dağı mt. Turkey
149 K3 Aktaş Gölü l. Georgia
132 H1 Aktash Rus. Fed.
151 I2 Aktash r. Rus. Fed.
Aktash Uzbek. see Oqtosh
143 N4 Aktau Karagandinskaya Oblast' Kazakh.
143 O2 Aktau Karagandinskaya Oblast' Kazakh.
142 D6 Aktau Mangistauskaya Oblast' Kazakh.
150 E2 Aktepe Turkey
221 M2 Aktepe hill Turkey
132 C7 Akto Xinjiang China
142 G2 Aktobe Aktyubinskaya Oblast' Kazakh.
143 P3 Aktogay Karagandinskaya Oblast' Kazakh.
143 P1 Aktogay Pavlodarskaya Oblast' Kazakh.
143 R4 Aktogay Vostochnyy Kazakhstan Kazakh.
150 F1 Aktoprak Turkey
161 N6 Aktsyabrskaya Belarus
160 L9 Aktsyabrski Homyel'skaya Voblasts' Belarus
160 M7 Aktsyabrski Vitsyebskaya Voblasts' Belarus
143 L3 Aktuma (abandoned) Kazakh.
142 G4 Aktumsyk Kazakh.
142 H5 Aktumsyk, Mys pt Uzbek.
143 P6 Ak-Tüz Kyrg.
Aktyubinsk Aktyubinskaya Oblast' Kazakh. see Aktobe
142 H3 Aktyubinskaya Oblast' admin. div. Kazakh.
Aktyubinsk Oblast admin. div. Kazakh. see Aktyubinskaya Oblast'
Aktyuz Kyrg. see Ak-Tüz
162 S2 Akujärvi Fin.
230 D4 Akula Dem. Rep. Congo
161 Q8 Akulichi Rus. Fed.
243 K3 Akulivik Que. Can.
228 E5 Akumadan Ghana
125 H14 Akune Japan
244 F5 Akun Island AK U.S.A.
232 B4 Akur mt. Uganda
151 G4 Akura Georgia
229 G5 Akure Nigeria
136 G9 Akuressa Sri Lanka
162 □D1 Akureyri Iceland
124 □G17 Akuseki-jima i. Nansei-shotō Japan

151 I3 **Akusha** Rus. Fed.
244 F5 **Akutan** *AK* U.S.A.
244 F5 **Akutan Island** *AK* U.S.A.
244 F5 **Akutan Pass** *sea channel AK* U.S.A.
244 F5 **Akutan Volcano** *AK* U.S.A.
229 G5 **Akwa Ibom** *state* Nigeria
229 H4 **Akwanga** Nigeria
229 H5 **Akwaya** Cameroon
133 J8 **Akxokesay** *Qinghai* China
Akyab Myanmar *see* **Sittwe**
151 E5 **Akyaka** Turkey
142 H2 **Ak"yar** Rus. Fed.
150 D2 **Akyatan Gölü** *salt l.* Turkey
221 L2 **Akyazı** Turkey
143 O4 **Akzhal** *Karagandinskaya Oblast'* Kazakh.
143 S3 **Akzhal** *Vostochnyy Kazakhstan* Kazakh.
142 G2 **Akzhar** Kazakh.
142 K5 **Akzhar** *Kyzylordinskaya Oblast'* Kazakh.
143 T4 **Akzhar** *Vostochnyy Kazakhstan* Kazakh.
143 N6 **Akzhar** *Zhambylskaya Oblast'* Kazakh.
143 O4 **Akzhartas** Kazakh.
143 L5 **Akzhaykyn, Ozero** *salt l.* Kazakh.
148 I5 **Akziyaret** Turkey
164 E1 **Ål** Norway
160 M9 **Ala** *r.* Belarus
213 K4 **Ala** Italy
150 E3 **'Alā, Jabal al** *hills* Syria
214 C6 **Alà, Monti di** *mts Sardegna* Italy
147 I2 **Al 'Abā** Saudi Arabia
255 D10 **Alabama** *r. AL* U.S.A.
255 D9 **Alabama** *state* U.S.A.
255 D9 **Alabaster** *AL* U.S.A.
251 K5 **Alabaster** *MI* U.S.A.
103 C11 **Alabaster, Lake** *South I.* N.Z.
149 L9 **Al 'Abṭīyah** *well* Iraq
143 N7 **Ala-Buka** Kyrg.
224 B3 **Al Abyaḍ** Libya
224 D1 **Al Abyār** Libya
217 L6 **Alaca** *r.* Italy
148 G3 **Alaca** Turkey
151 C4 **Alaca Dağı** *mt.* Turkey
148 H4 **Alacahan** Turkey
148 G3 **Alaçam** Turkey
221 J3 **Alaçam Dağları** *mts* Turkey
150 A2 **Alacami** Turkey
Alacant Spain *see* **Alicante**
221 H4 **Alaçatı** Turkey
267 O6 **Alacrán, Arrecife** *rf* Mex.
219 N9 **Aladag** *mt.* Bulg.
148 F5 **Aladağ** Turkey
151 D5 **Aladağ** *mt.* Turkey
149 K4 **Ala Dag** *mt.* Turkey
149 K4 **Ala Dağlar** *mts* Turkey
148 G5 **Ala Dağları** *mts* Turkey
224 D2 **Al 'Adam** Libya
214 C6 **Alà dei Sardi** *Sardegna* Italy
212 C5 **Ala di Stura** Italy
205 J6 **Alaejos** Spain
132 E6 **Ala'er** *Xinjiang* China
146 H5 **Al Aflāj** *reg.* Saudi Arabia
275 F4 **Alagadiço** Brazil
245 K3 **Alaganik** *AK* U.S.A.
136 F7 **Alagapuram** *Tamil Nadu* India
128 F1 **Alag-Erdene** *Hövsgöl* Mongolia
Alagez *mt.* Armenia *see* **Aragats Lerr**
128 D4 **Alag Hayrhan Uul** *mt.* Mongolia
128 E9 **Alag Hu** *l. Qinghai* China
151 F2 **Alagir** Rus. Fed.
244 H4 **Alagnak** *r. AK* U.S.A.
212 D4 **Alagna Valsesia** Italy
183 C6 **Alagnon** *r.* France
204 C3 **A Lagoa** Spain
278 F4 **Alagoas** *state* Brazil
278 F5 **Alagoinhas** Brazil
208 C4 **Alagón** Spain
204 G9 **Alagón** *r.* Spain
132 I5 **Ala Gou** *r.* China
151 D4 **Alagöz Dağı** *mt.* Turkey
114 E8 **Alah** *r. Mindanao* Phil.
116 D5 **Alahanpanjang** *Sumatera* Indon.
162 Q5 **Alahärmä** Fin.
149 N9 **Al Aḥmadī** Kuwait
Alaid, Ostrov *i. Kuril'skiye O-va* Rus. Fed. *see* **Atlasova, Ostrov**
185 I9 **Alaigne** France
208 □ **Alaior** Spain
145 N2 **Alai Range** *mts* Asia
144 E4 **Ālaivān** Iran
150 D3 **Ālājah** Syria
147 M6 **Al 'Ajā'iz** *well* Oman
147 I2 **Al Ajām** Saudi Arabia
206 F5 **Alájar** Spain
162 Q5 **Alajärvi** Fin.
162 P2 **Alajaure naturreservat** *nature res.* Sweden
238 □[3a] **Alajero** *La Gomera* Canary Is
146 F2 **Al Ajfar** Saudi Arabia
160 K2 **Alajõgi** *r.* Estonia
150 C8 **Al 'Ajrūd** *well* Egypt
266 □Q12 **Alajuela** Costa Rica
144 B2 **Alajujeh** Iran
235 □J4 **Alak Ambohimaha** Madag.
244 F3 **Alakanuk** *AK* U.S.A.
151 B2 **Alakhadzi** Georgia
146 C1 **Al Akhḍar** Saudi Arabia
151 I4 **Alakhundag, Gora** *mt.* Rus. Fed.
138 G4 **Alaknanda** *r.* India
143 S4 **Alakol', Ozero** *salt l.* Kazakh.
244 I1 **Alaktak** *AK* U.S.A.
Ala Kul *salt l.* Kazakh. *see* **Alakol', Ozero**
162 U3 **Alakurtti** Rus. Fed.
162 R3 **Alakylä** Fin.
264 □E13 **'Alalākeiki Channel** *HI* U.S.A.
225 F2 **Al 'Alamayn** Egypt
275 F5 **Alalaú** *r.* Brazil
146 E6 **Al 'Alayyah** Saudi Arabia
Alalia *Corse* France *see* **Aléria**
232 D3 **Alama** Somalia
149 K5 **Al 'Amādīyah** Iraq
113 K3 **Alamagan** *i.* N. Mariana Is
Alamaguan *i.* N. Mariana Is *see* **Alamagan**
146 G3 **Al 'Amār** Saudi Arabia
149 M8 **Al 'Amārah** Iraq
224 E2 **'Alam ar Rūm, Ra's** *pt* Egypt
144 E8 **'Alāmarvdasht** Iran
144 E7 **'Alāmarvdasht** *watercourse* Iran
232 C1 **Ālamat'ā** Eth.
144 A2 **Alamdar** Iran
207 J6 **Alameda** Spain
264 J4 **Alameda** *CA* U.S.A.
207 M2 **Alameda de Cervera** Spain
205 M8 **Alameda de la Sagra** Spain
149 L9 **Al Amghar** *waterhole* Iraq
266 □Q11 **Alamicamba** Nic.
207 J3 **Alamillo** Spain
114 B3 **Alaminos** *Luzon* Phil.
148 D8 **Al 'Āmirīyah** Egypt
263 L12 **Alamito Creek** *r. TX* U.S.A.
266 H4 **Alamítos, Sierra de los** *mt.* Mex.
146 F5 **Al Amlah** Saudi Arabia
269 J5 **Álamo** Mex.
206 E4 **Álamo** *r.* Port.
206 H8 **Alamo** *r.* Spain
255 F9 **Alamo** *GA* U.S.A.
265 Q4 **Alamo** *NV* U.S.A.
261 K8 **Alamo** *TN* U.S.A.
265 S7 **Alamo Dam** *AZ* U.S.A.
263 L10 **Alamogordo** *NM* U.S.A.
261 F11 **Alamo Heights** *TX* U.S.A.
274 A6 **Alamor** Ecuador
285 F5 **Alamos** Arg.
266 D3 **Alamos** *Sonora* Mex.
266 E4 **Alamos** *Sonora* Mex.
267 I4 **Alamos** *r.* Mex.
266 E4 **Alamos, Sierra** *mts* Mex.
263 L8 **Alamosa** *CO* U.S.A.
263 K10 **Alamosa** *watercourse NM* U.S.A.
263 L9 **Alamosa Creek** *r. NM* U.S.A.
266 F2 **Alamos de Peña** Mex.
136 F5 **Alampur** *Andhra Prad.* India
213 R5 **Alan** Croatia
146 G9 **Al 'Anad** Yemen
162 S3 **Ala-Nampa** Fin.
162 M4 **Alanäs** Sweden
149 J6 **Al Anbār** *governorate* Iraq
163 O6 **Åland** *is* Åland Fin.
192 E4 **Aland** *r.* Ger.
136 E4 **Aland** *Karnataka* India
144 A2 **Aland** *r.* Iran
151 C4 **Alan Dağı** *mt.* Turkey
150 F3 **Al Andarīn** Syria
165 L3 **Åländern** *l.* Sweden
Åland Islands *Åland* Fin. *see* **Åland**
133 L11 **Alando** *Xizang* China
206 E3 **Alandroal** Port.
163 O7 **Ålands Hav** *sea chan.* Fin./Sweden
136 G6 **Alandur** *Tamil Nadu* India
117 L2 **Alang** *Kalimantan* Indon.
144 F3 **Alang, Kūh-e** *mt.* Iran
117 L6 **Alangalang, Tanjung** *pt* Indon.
116 D3 **Alang Besar** *i.* Indon.
206 G3 **Alange** Spain
206 G3 **Alange, Embalse de** *resr* Spain
116 F5 **Alanggantang** *i.* Indon.
Alania *aut. reg.* Georgia *see* **Samkhret' Oset'i**
206 H4 **Alanís** Spain
250 J4 **Alanson** *MI* U.S.A.
229 I4 **Alantika Mountains** Cameroon/Nigeria
148 F5 **Alanya** Turkey
144 F6 **'Alā' od Dīn** Iran
199 H5 **Alap** Hungary
255 F10 **Alapaha** *r. GA* U.S.A.
136 F7 **Alapakam** *Tamil Nadu* India
221 M1 **Alaplı** Turkey
136 E8 **Alappuzha** *Kerala* India
138 G6 **Alapur** *Uttar Prad.* India
Alapuzha *Kerala* India *see* **Alappuzha**
150 D9 **Al 'Aqabah** Jordan
150 D9 **'Alāqān** Saudi Arabia
146 E5 **Al 'Aqīq** Saudi Arabia
269 H3 **Alaquines** Mex.
147 I4 **Al 'Āqūlah** *well* Saudi Arabia
147 J2 **Al 'Arabiyah** *i. Ash Sharqīyah* Saudi Arabia
Al 'Arabīyah as Sa'ūdīyah *country* Asia *see* **Saudi Arabia**
205 J7 **Alaraz** Spain
205 P9 **Alarcón** Spain
205 P9 **Alarcón, Embalse de** *resr* Spain
205 L3 **Alar del Rey** Spain
226 B5 **Al Argoub** Western Sahara
146 F7 **Al 'Āriḍah** Saudi Arabia
146 F6 **Al Arīn** Saudi Arabia
225 G2 **Al 'Arīsh** Egypt
209 K8 **Alaró** Spain
146 G3 **Al Arṭāwī** Saudi Arabia
146 G2 **Al Arṭāwīyah** Saudi Arabia
117 L9 **Alas** *Sumbawa* Indon.
117 L9 **Alas, Selat** *sea chan.* Indon.
221 J4 **Alaşehir** Turkey
151 G5 **Äläsgärli** Azer.
Alashiya *country* Asia *see* **Cyprus**
225 F3 **Al Ashmūnayn** Egypt
149 K8 **Al 'Āshūrīyah** *well* Iraq
245 L3 **Alaska** *state* U.S.A.
235 F3 **Alaska** Zimbabwe
245 K4 **Alaska, Gulf of** *AK* U.S.A.
245 L3 **Alaska Highway** Can./U.S.A.
245 □B5 **Alaska Maritime National Wildlife Refuge** *nature res.* *AL* U.S.A.
244 G5 **Alaska Peninsula** *AK* U.S.A.
244 H4 **Alaska Peninsula National Wildlife Refuge** *nature res.* *AK* U.S.A.
245 J3 **Alaska Range** *mts AK* U.S.A.
117 K9 **Alas Purwo, Taman Nasional** *nat. park* Indon.
146 D1 **Al 'Assāfīyah** Saudi Arabia
212 E7 **Alassio** Italy
163 Q6 **Alastaro** Fin.
151 K6 **Älät** Azer.
Alat Uzbek. *see* **Olot**
214 B4 **Alata** *Corse* France
Alataw Shankou *pass* China/Kazakh. *see* **Dzungarian Gate**
244 I2 **Alatna** *AK* U.S.A.
244 I2 **Alatna** *r. AK* U.S.A.
209 C9 **Alatoz** Spain
215 K4 **Alatri** Italy
151 J5 **Älät Tiräsi** *plat.* Azer.
199 J4 **Alattyán** Hungary
146 F1 **Al Atwā'** *well* Saudi Arabia
157 I5 **Alatyr'** Rus. Fed.
157 I5 **Alatyr'** *r.* Rus. Fed.
160 I4 **Alauksts** *l.* Latvia
274 B5 **Alausí** Ecuador
205 O3 **Álava** *prov.* Spain
151 F4 **Alaverdi** Armenia
162 R4 **Alavieska** Fin.
144 D5 **'Alavījeh** Iran
162 T4 **Ala-Vuokki** Fin.
162 Q5 **Alavus** Fin.
172 D1 **Alaw, Llyn** *resr Wales* U.K.
106 E3 **Alawa Aboriginal Land** *res.* *N.T.* Austr.
147 M4 **Al Awābī** Oman
118 C2 **Alawbum** Myanmar
146 G3 **Al 'Awdah** Saudi Arabia
104 H6 **Alawoona** *S.A.* Austr.
146 E2 **Al Awshazīyah** Saudi Arabia
Alaykel' Kyrg. *see* **Kök-Art**
Alaykuu *Osh* Kyrg. *see* **Kök-Art**
Alay Kyrka Toosu *mts* Asia *see* **Alai Range**
147 M4 **Al 'Ayn** Oman
146 D3 **Al 'Ayn** Saudi Arabia
147 L3 **Al 'Ayn** U.A.E.
150 D8 **Al 'Aynā** Jordan
Alayskiy Khrebet *mts* Asia *see* **Alai Range**
221 L3 **Alayunt** Turkey
151 H4 **Alazani** *r.* Azer./Georgia
153 Q2 **Alazeya** *r.* Rus. Fed.
149 L7 **Al 'Azīzīyah** Iraq
224 B1 **Al 'Azīzīyah** Libya
150 E7 **Al Azraq al Janūbī** Jordan
194 E6 **Alb** *r.* Ger.
212 E6 **Alba** Italy
208 C6 **Alba** Spain
250 J5 **Alba** *MI* U.S.A.
258 B1 **Alba** *PA* U.S.A.
103 C11 **Alba, Mount** *South I.* N.Z.
205 K3 **Alba, Sierra de** *mts* Spain
215 L2 **Alba Adriatica** Italy
146 E2 **Al Ba'ā'ith** Saudi Arabia
150 F2 **Al Bāb** Syria
207 P2 **Albacete** Spain
207 P3 **Albacete** *prov.* Spain
150 D10 **Al Bad'** Saudi Arabia
146 D2 **Al Badā'i'** Saudi Arabia
205 I7 **Alba de Tormes** Spain
146 H5 **Al Badī'** Saudi Arabia
149 L8 **Al Bādiyah al Janūbīyah** *des.* Iraq
164 G4 **Ålbæk** Denmark
164 G4 **Ålbæk Bugt** *b.* Denmark
214 B8 **Albagiara** *Sardegna* Italy
146 E5 **Al Bāḥah** Egypt
146 E5 **Al Bāḥah** Saudi Arabia
146 E5 **Al Bāḥah** *prov.* Saudi Arabia
150 D3 **Al Bahlūlīyah** Syria
150 A10 **Al Baḥr al Aḥmar** *governorate* Egypt
Al Baḥrayn *country* Asia *see* **Bahrain**
209 E10 **Albaida** Spain
219 L4 **Alba Iulia** Romania
147 J3 **Al Bajā'** *well* U.A.E.
146 F3 **Al Ba'jah** Saudi Arabia
136 G3 **Albaka** *Andhra Prad.* India
146 H3 **Al Bakhrā** *well* Saudi Arabia
224 B3 **Al Bakkī** Libya
207 N3 **Albaladejo** Spain
206 G2 **Albalá del Caudillo** Spain
150 B10 **Al Balā'im** Egypt
150 B10 **Al Balā'im** *b.* Egypt
183 F7 **Alba-la-Romaine** France
208 E5 **Albalate de Arzobispo** Spain
208 F4 **Albalate de Cinca** Spain
205 P8 **Albalate de las Nogueras** Spain
205 O8 **Albalate de Zorita** Spain
208 E4 **Albalatillo** Spain
225 F3 **Al Balyanā** Egypt
185 I8 **Alban** France
207 O6 **Albánchez** Spain
249 F3 **Albanel, Lac** *l. Que.* Can.
215 O7 **Albanella** Italy
249 F3 **Albanel-Mistassini et Waconichi, Réserve Faunique des lacs** *nature res. Que.* Can.
218 H9 **Albania** *country* Europe
275 G5 **Albano** Brazil
215 J4 **Albano, Lago** *l.* Italy
215 Q6 **Albano di Lucania** Italy
215 J4 **Albano Laziale** Italy
109 D13 **Albany** *W.A.* Austr.
248 D2 **Albany** *r. Ont.* Can.
270 □ **Albany** Jamaica
255 E10 **Albany** *GA* U.S.A.
260 H5 **Albany** *MO* U.S.A.
257 L6 **Albany** *NY* U.S.A.
256 C9 **Albany** *OH* U.S.A.
262 C4 **Albany** *OR* U.S.A.
261 F9 **Albany** *TX* U.S.A.
208 K3 **Albanyà** Spain
107 L9 **Albany Downs** *Qld* Austr.
282 G4 **Albardão do João Maria** *coastal area* Brazil
224 E2 **Al Bardī** Libya
284 C2 **Albardón** Arg.
212 H3 **Albaredo per San Marco** Italy
204 D4 **Albarellos, Encoro de** *resr* Spain
183 C7 **Albaret-le-Comtal** France
212 H7 **Albareto** Italy
183 C7 **Albaret-Ste-Marie** France
150 H9 **Al Bāridah** *hills* Saudi Arabia
182 G5 **Albarine** *r.* France
227 H4 **Al Barkāt** *well* Libya
183 E9 **Albaron** France
205 R8 **Albarracín** Spain
205 Q8 **Albarracín, Sierra de** *mts* Spain
206 F2 **Albarragena** *r.* Spain
146 G3 **Al Barrah** Saudi Arabia
146 G3 **Al Barūd** Saudi Arabia
159 R7 **Albasi** *r.* Rus. Fed.
149 M8 **Al Baṣrah** Iraq
149 M8 **Al Baṣrah** *governorate* Iraq
172 D6 **Albaston** *Cornwall, England* U.K.
207 P3 **Albatana** Spain
208 G4 **Albatàrrec** Spain
209 D11 **Albatera** Spain
149 L8 **Al Baṭḥa'** *marsh* Iraq
147 M4 **Al Bāṭinah** *admin. reg.* Oman
147 M3 **Al Bāṭinah** *reg.* Oman
147 I2 **Al Bāṭinah** *i.* Saudi Arabia
270 F5 **Albatross Bank** *sea feature* Jamaica
107 H2 **Albatross Bay** *Qld* Austr.
105 J9 **Albatross Island** *Tas.* Austr.
102 I5 **Albatross Point** *North I.* N.Z.
225 F2 **Al Bawīṭī** Egypt
224 D1 **Al Bayḍā'** Libya
146 G9 **Al Bayḍā'** Yemen
146 G8 **Al Bayḍā'** *governorate* Yemen
114 D5 **Albay Gulf** *Luzon* Phil.
194 E6 **Albbruck** Ger.
179 N6 **Albe** *r.* France
214 G2 **Albegna** *r.* Italy
208 F4 **Albelda** Spain
205 P4 **Albelda de Iregua** Spain
208 E3 **Albella** Spain
255 G8 **Albemarle** *NC* U.S.A.
Albemarle Island *Islas Galápagos* Ecuador *see* **Isabela, Isla**
255 I8 **Albemarle Sound** *sea chan.* *NC* U.S.A.
205 P7 **Albendea** Spain
207 K5 **Albendín** Spain
212 E7 **Albenga** Italy
182 H5 **Albens** France
209 D7 **Albentosa** Spain
209 C12 **Alberca de las Torres** *Murcia* Spain
205 K9 **Alberche** *r.* Spain
277 F6 **Alberdi** Para.
104 E2 **Alberga** *watercourse S.A.* Austr.
204 D7 **Albergaria-a-Velha** Port.
204 C9 **Albergaria dos Doze** Port.
212 B5 **Albergian, Monte** *mt.* Italy
209 E9 **Alberic** Spain
205 P4 **Alberite** Spain
201 J3 **Alberndorf in der Riedmark** Austria
206 D5 **Albernoa** Port.
208 E3 **Albero Alto** Spain
217 M2 **Alberobello** Italy
213 M5 **Alberoni** Italy
200 A5 **Alberschwende** Austria
190 H2 **Albersdorf** Ger.
105 K5 **Albert** *N.S.W.* Austr.
106 G4 **Albert** *r. Qld* Austr.
178 E4 **Albert** France
104 G6 **Albert, Lake** *S.A.* Austr.
232 A4 **Albert, Lake** Dem. Rep. Congo/Uganda
Albert, Parc National *nat. park* Dem. Rep. Congo *see* **Virunga, Parc National des**
246 H4 **Alberta** *prov.* Can.
256 H12 **Alberta** *VA* U.S.A.
214 B3 **Albertacce** *Corse* France
212 G6 **Alberta Ligure** Italy
237 O5 **Albert Falls Nature Reserve** S. Africa
285 G4 **Alberti** Arg.
162 □ **Albert I Land** *reg.* Svalbard
236 F10 **Albertinia** S. Africa
199 I4 **Albertirsa** Hungary
187 H7 **Albert Kanaal** *canal* Belgium
260 I4 **Albert Lea** *MN* U.S.A.
232 B4 **Albert Nile** *r.* Sudan/Uganda
283 C9 **Alberto de Agostini, Parque Nacional** *nat. park* Chile
249 H4 **Alberton** *P.E.I.* Can.
237 M2 **Alberton** S. Africa
262 G3 **Alberton** *MT* U.S.A.
265 Q9 **Alberto Oviedo Mota** Mex.
237 J3 **Albertshoek** S. Africa
195 I2 **Albertshofen** Ger.
270 F2 **Albert Town** Bahamas
270 □ **Albert Town** Jamaica
103 D11 **Albert Town** *South I.* N.Z.
Albertville Dem. Rep. Congo *see* **Kalemie**
182 I5 **Albertville** France
255 D8 **Albertville** *AL* U.S.A.
208 E4 **Alberuela de Tubo** Spain
208 G4 **Albesa** Spain
219 P3 **Albeşti** *Botoşani* Romania
219 P4 **Albeşti** *Vaslui* Romania
179 M6 **Albestroff** France
185 I8 **Albi** France
260 I5 **Albia** *IA* U.S.A.
146 D4 **Al Bi'ār** Saudi Arabia
185 G7 **Albias** France
147 I3 **Al Bīḍah** *des.* Saudi Arabia
217 K4 **Albidona** Italy
185 H8 **Albigeois** *reg.* France
213 L5 **Albignasego** Italy
275 H3 **Albina** Suriname
146 C2 **Al Binī** Saudi Arabia
212 H4 **Albino** Italy
264 I2 **Albion** *CA* U.S.A.
254 E5 **Albion** *IN* U.S.A.
250 J7 **Albion** *MI* U.S.A.
260 F5 **Albion** *NE* U.S.A.
258 F5 **Albion** *NJ* U.S.A.
256 G5 **Albion** *NY* U.S.A.
256 E7 **Albion** *PA* U.S.A.
146 G3 **Al Bīr** Saudi Arabia
146 C1 **Al Bi'r** Saudi Arabia
205 J4 **Albires** Spain
146 E6 **Al Birk** Saudi Arabia
146 E4 **Al Birkah** Saudi Arabia
194 E2 **Albisheim (Pfrimm)** Ger.
212 F7 **Albisola Marina** Italy
212 F7 **Albisola Superiore** Italy
146 H5 **Al Biyāḍh** *reg.* Saudi Arabia
186 G5 **Alblasserdam** Neth.
214 C7 **Albo, Monte** *mts Sardegna* Italy
209 F7 **Albocàsser** Spain
207 N6 **Alboloduy** Spain
183 F6 **Albon** France
207 M7 **Albondón** Spain
207 M9 **Alborán, Isla de** *i.* Spain
202 D4 **Alboran Sea** Europe
209 C9 **Alborea** Spain
Ålborg Denmark *see* **Aalborg**
144 C3 **Alborz, Reshteh-ye** *mts* Iran
219 M6 **Albota** Romania
207 O6 **Albox** Spain
199 H2 **Albrechtice** Czech Rep.
172 H2 **Albrighton** *Shropshire, England* U.K.
107 K7 **Albro** *Qld* Austr.
194 G5 **Albstadt** Ger.
195 H4 **Albuch** *hills* Ger.
147 J2 **Al Budayyi'** Bahrain
190 K1 **Albuen** *pen.* Denmark
206 C6 **Albufeira** Port.
148 E8 **Al Buḥayrah** *governorate* Egypt
209 C12 **Albujón** Spain
146 F2 **Al Bukayrīyah** Saudi Arabia
212 G2 **Albula** *r.* Switz.
212 H3 **Albula Alpen** *mts* Switz.
207 M7 **Albuñol** Spain
207 L7 **Albuñuelas** Spain
263 K9 **Albuquerque** *NM* U.S.A.
270 C7 **Albuquerque, Cayos de** *is* Caribbean Sea
150 E4 **Al Burayj** Syria
147 L3 **Al Buraymī** Oman
147 L4 **Al Buraymī** *admin reg.* U.S.A.
257 L4 **Alburg** *VT* U.S.A.
150 C9 **Al Burj** Jordan
215 O6 **Alburno, Monte** *mt.* Italy
206 F2 **Alburquerque** Spain
258 D3 **Alburtis** *PA* U.S.A.
105 K7 **Albury** *N.S.W.* Austr.
103 E11 **Albury** *South I.* N.Z.
149 J6 **Al Buṣayrah** Syria
148 I9 **Al Busayṭā'** *plain* Saudi Arabia
149 M8 **Al Buṣayyah** Iraq
146 G1 **Al Bushūk** *well* Saudi Arabia
146 G2 **Al Buṭayn** *plain* Saudi Arabia
146 D3 **Al Buwayr** Saudi Arabia
147 M6 **Al Buwī** *well* Oman
182 I5 **Alby-sur-Chéran** France
276 B3 **Alca** Peru
206 A3 **Alcabideche** Port.
206 B4 **Alcácer do Sal** Port.
206 C4 **Alcáçovas** Port.
206 C4 **Alcáçovas** *r.* Port.
207 P3 **Alcadozo** Spain
208 D6 **Alcaine** Spain
204 F9 **Alcains** Port.
206 H6 **Alcalá de Guadaira** Spain
208 D3 **Alcalá de Gurrea** Spain
205 N8 **Alcalá de Henares** Spain
209 D7 **Alcalá de la Selva** Spain
209 C9 **Alcalá del Júcar** Spain
206 H8 **Alcalá de los Gazules** Spain
206 H5 **Alcalá del Río** Spain
207 I7 **Alcalá del Valle** Spain
209 F7 **Alcalà de Xivert** Spain
207 L6 **Alcalá la Real** Spain
282 C3 **Alcalde, Punta** *pt* Chile
216 D8 **Alcamo** *Sicilia* Italy
208 F4 **Alcampell** Spain
208 F4 **Alcanadre** *r.* Spain
208 F6 **Alcanar** Spain
206 B2 **Alcanede** Port.
206 B2 **Alcanena** Port.
206 B2 **Alcanhões** Port.
204 H5 **Alcañices** Spain
208 E5 **Alcañiz** Spain
278 D2 **Alcântara** Brazil
204 G9 **Alcántara** Spain
204 G9 **Alcántara, Embalse de** *resr* Spain
204 H9 **Alcántara II, Embalse de** *resr* Spain
247 I2 **Alcantara Lake** *N.W.T.* Can.
209 C12 **Alcantarilla** Spain
205 P7 **Alcantud** Spain
207 J4 **Alcaracejos** Spain
216 H7 **Alcara li Fusi** *Sicilia* Italy
207 O3 **Alcaraz** Spain
207 N3 **Alcaraz, Sierra de** *mts* Spain
285 H2 **Alcaraz Segundo** Arg.
206 D6 **Alcaria do Cume** *hill* Port.
206 D5 **Alcaria Ruiva** Port.
202 C4 **Alcaria Ruiva** *hill* Port.
206 E4 **Alcarrache** *r.* Port./Spain
208 G4 **Alcarràs** Spain
209 E9 **Alcàsser** Spain
281 E6 **Alcatrazes, Ilha de** *i.* Brazil
207 K7 **Alcaucín** Spain
207 K5 **Alcaudete** Spain
205 K9 **Alcaudete de la Jara** Spain
208 □ **Alcaufar** Spain
185 C9 **Alçay-Alçabéhéty-Sunharette** France
206 F3 **Alcazaba** *r.* Spain
205 O8 **Alcázar del Rey** Spain
207 M2 **Alcázar de San Juan** Spain
205 K6 **Alcazarén** Spain
Alcazarquivir Morocco *see* **Ksar el Kebir**
173 I3 **Alcester** *Warwickshire, England* U.K.
159 R5 **Alchevs'k** Ukr.
284 E3 **Alcira** Arg.
Alcira *Valencia* Spain *see* **Alzira**
207 K2 **Alcoba** Spain
281 H2 **Alcobaça** Brazil
204 C9 **Alcobaça** Port.
205 M7 **Alcobendas** Spain
206 B2 **Alcobertas** Port.
Alcocebre Spain *see* **Alcossebre**
205 O8 **Alcocer** Spain
205 N4 **Alcocero de Mola** Spain
206 B3 **Alcochete** Port.
206 B2 **Alcoentre** Port.
204 D7 **Alcofra** Port.
207 J5 **Alcolea** *Andalucía* Spain
207 N7 **Alcolea** *Andalucía* Spain
207 K3 **Alcolea de Calatrava** Spain
208 F4 **Alcolea de Cinca** Spain
205 P6 **Alcolea del Pinar** Spain
206 H5 **Alcolea del Río** Spain
208 G4 **Alcoletge** Spain
206 H2 **Alcollarín** Spain
206 E3 **Alconchel** Spain
206 G4 **Alconera** Spain
207 N6 **Alcóntar** Spain
106 E7 **Alcoota** *N.T.* Austr.
205 M8 **Alcorcón** Spain
208 E6 **Alcorisa** Spain
205 O6 **Alcorlo, Embalse de** *resr* Spain
206 F2 **Alcorneo** *r.* Port./Spain
205 Q7 **Alcoroches** Spain
285 G3 **Alcorta** Arg.
209 F7 **Alcossebre** Spain
206 E6 **Alcoutim** Port.
262 K5 **Alcova** *WY* U.S.A.
208 H5 **Alcover** Spain
209 E10 **Alcoy-Alcoi** Spain
199 H4 **Alcsútdoboz** Hungary
208 E4 **Alcubierre** Spain
208 D4 **Alcubierre, Sierra de** *mts* Spain
205 N5 **Alcubilla de Avellaneda** Spain
207 M3 **Alcubillas** Spain
209 D8 **Alcublas** Spain
209 L8 **Alcúdia** Spain
207 J3 **Alcudia** *r.* Spain
209 L8 **Alcúdia, Badia d'** *b.* Spain
207 J3 **Alcudia, Sierra de** *mts* Spain
207 J3 **Alcudia, Valle de** *reg.* Spain
Alcudia de Carlet Spain *see* **L'Alcudia**
207 M6 **Alcudia de Guadix** Spain
203 E4 **Alcudia de Monteagud** Spain
206 G2 **Alcuéscar** Spain
239 □[2] **Aldabra Atoll** *Aldabra Is* Seychelles
239 □[2] **Aldabra Islands** Seychelles
266 G3 **Aldama** *Chihuahua* Mex.
269 I3 **Aldama** *Tamaulipas* Mex.
153 N4 **Aldan** Rus. Fed.
153 N3 **Aldan** *r.* Rus. Fed.
173 I5 **Aldbourne** *Wiltshire, England* U.K.
171 Q6 **Aldbrough** *East Riding of Yorkshire, England* U.K.
173 O3 **Alde** *r. England* U.K.
238 □[3f] **Aldea** *r. Gran Canaria* Canary Is
238 □[3f] **Aldea, Punta de la** *pt Gran Canaria* Canary Is
206 H1 **Aldeacentenera** Spain
204 G6 **Aldeadávila, Embalse de** *resr* Port./Spain
204 G6 **Aldeadávila de la Ribera** Spain
206 G2 **Aldea del Cano** Spain
205 L8 **Aldea del Fresno** Spain
204 G7 **Aldea del Obispo** Spain
207 L3 **Aldea del Rey** Spain
204 I9 **Aldea de Trujillo** Spain
205 P5 **Aldealafuente** Spain
205 P5 **Aldealpozo** Spain
205 K5 **Aldeamayor de San Martín** Spain
205 J9 **Aldeanueva de Barbarroya** Spain
204 I6 **Aldeanueva de Figueroa** Spain
204 I8 **Aldeanueva del Camino** Spain
205 J9 **Aldeanueva de San Bartolomé** Spain
207 M4 **Aldeaquemada** Spain
204 I6 **Aldearrodrigo** Spain
205 K6 **Aldeaseca** Spain
204 I7 **Aldeatejada** Spain
205 L7 **Aldeavieja** Spain
186 I2 **Aldeboarn** Neth.
173 P3 **Aldeburgh** *Suffolk, England* U.K.
204 H7 **Aldehuela de la Bóveda** Spain
204 H7 **Aldehuela de Yeltes** Spain
206 D2 **Aldeia da Mata** Port.
204 G8 **Aldeia da Ponte** Port.
204 F8 **Aldeia do Bispo** Port.
206 C5 **Aldeia dos Elvas** Port.
206 C5 **Aldeia dos Palheiros** Port.
278 C4 **Aldeia Velha** Brazil
204 G8 **Aldeia Velha** *Guarda* Port.
206 C2 **Aldeia Velha** *Portalegre* Port.
231 B7 **Aldeia Viçosa** Angola
258 C2 **Alden** *PA* U.S.A.
173 L4 **Aldenham** *Hertfordshire, England* U.K.
191 B9 **Aldenhoven** Ger.
213 K4 **Aldeno** Italy
173 I5 **Alderbury** *Wiltshire, England* U.K.
257 J5 **Alder Creek** *NY* U.S.A.
169 J3 **Aldergrove** *Northern Ireland* U.K.
173 I6 **Alderholt** *Dorset, England* U.K.
171 M7 **Alderley Edge** *Cheshire, England* U.K.
180 G2 **Alderney** *i.* Channel Is
264 K6 **Alder Peak** *CA* U.S.A.
195 O4 **Aldersbach** Ger.
173 K5 **Aldershot** *Hampshire, England* U.K.
256 E11 **Alderson** *WV* U.S.A.
147 K4 **Al Dhafrah** *reg.* U.A.E.
232 D3 **Aldie** Eth.
218 J9 **Aldinci** Macedonia
194 F5 **Aldingen** Ger.
171 K5 **Aldingham** *Cumbria, England* U.K.
173 N5 **Aldington** *Kent, England* U.K.
237 P5 **Aldinville** S. Africa
208 G6 **Aldover** Spain
173 I2 **Aldridge** *West Midlands, England* U.K.
185 B9 **Aldudes** France
164 I5 **Åled** Sweden
207 P5 **Aledo** Spain
260 J5 **Aledo** *IL* U.S.A.
228 B2 **Aleg** Maur.
238 □[3c] **Alegranza** *i.* Canary Is
281 G4 **Alegre** *Espírito Santo* Brazil
280 D3 **Alegre** *Minas Gerais* Brazil
279 B9 **Alegrete** Brazil
206 E2 **Alegrete** Port.
205 P3 **Alegría-Dulantzi** Spain
263 J9 **Alegros Mountain** *NM* U.S.A.
285 H1 **Alejandra** Arg.
285 H4 **Alejandro Korn** Arg.
285 F3 **Alejandro Roca** Arg.
276 □ **Alejandro Selkirk, Isla** *i.* S. Pacific Ocean
284 D6 **Alejandro Stefenelli** Arg.
285 F3 **Alejo Ledesma** Arg.
161 Q1 **Alekhovshchina** Rus. Fed.
244 H4 **Aleknagik** *AK* U.S.A.
244 H4 **Aleknagik, Lake** *AK* U.S.A.
122 K1 **Aleksandra, Mys** *hd* Rus. Fed.
142 D6 **Aleksandra Bekovicha-Cherkasskogo, Zaliv** *b.* Kazakh.
Aleksandriya Ukr. *see* **Oleksandriya**
151 I2 **Aleksandriyskaya** Rus. Fed.
151 H2 **Aleksandro-Nevskaya** Rus. Fed.
161 X8 **Aleksandro-Nevskiy** Rus. Fed.
Aleksandropol Armenia *see* **Gyumri**
161 V5 **Aleksandrov** Rus. Fed.
218 J7 **Aleksandrovac** *Aleksandrovac* Serbia
Aleksandrov Dar Ukr. *see* **Rakhmanivka**
142 C2 **Aleksandrov Gay** Rus. Fed.
157 K5 **Aleksandrovka** *Orenburgskaya Oblast'* Rus. Fed.
142 G1 **Aleksandrovka** *Respublika Bashkortostan* Rus. Fed.
159 S7 **Aleksandrovka** *Rostovskaya Oblast'* Rus. Fed.
219 M7 **Aleksandrovo** *Lovech* Bulg.
219 N8 **Aleksandrovo** *Stara Zagora* Bulg.
156 L4 **Aleksandrovsk** Rus. Fed.
Aleksandrovsk Ukr. *see* **Zaporizhzhya**
161 T2 **Aleksandrovskaya** Rus. Fed.
Aleksandrovskiy Rus. Fed. *see* **Aleksandrovsk**
151 D1 **Aleksandrovskoye** *Stavropol'skiy Kray* Rus. Fed.
149 L1 **Aleksandrovskoye** *Stavropol'skiy Kray* Rus. Fed.
152 I3 **Aleksandrovskoye** *Tomskaya Oblast'* Rus. Fed.
122 M3 **Aleksandrovsk-Sakhalinskiy** *Sakhalin* Rus. Fed.
197 I3 **Aleksandrów** Pol.
196 G3 **Aleksandrów Kujawski** Pol.
197 H4 **Aleksandrów Łódzki** Pol.
152 F1 **Aleksandry, Zemlya** *i. Zemlya Frantsa-Iosifa* Rus. Fed.
199 I6 **Aleksa Šantić** *Vojvodina* Serbia
151 J4 **Alekseyevka** Azer.
Alekseyevka *Akmolinskaya Oblast'* Kazakh. *see* **Akkol'**
Alekseyevka *Vostochnyy Kazakhstan* Kazakh. *see* **Terekty**
122 E2 **Alekseyevka** *Amurskaya Oblast'* Rus. Fed.
157 G6 **Alekseyevka** *Belgorodskaya Oblast'* Rus. Fed.
157 G6 **Alekseyevka** *Belgorodskaya Oblast'* Rus. Fed.
161 P8 **Alekseyevka** *Bryanskaya Oblast'* Rus. Fed.
159 T4 **Alekseyevo-Lozovskoye** Rus. Fed.
157 H6 **Alekseyevskaya** Rus. Fed.
161 U7 **Aleksin** Rus. Fed.
219 J7 **Aleksinac** *Aleksinac* Serbia
161 W6 **Aleksino-Shatur** Rus. Fed.
165 M5 **Ålem** Sweden
229 I7 **Alembé** Congo
230 A5 **Alèmbé** Gabon
232 C2 **'Alem Ketema** Eth.
232 D2 **'Alem Maya** Eth.
281 F4 **Além Paraíba** Brazil
162 K5 **Ålen** Norway
181 L5 **Alençon** France
181 L5 **Alençon, Campagne d'** *plain* France
182 D3 **Alène** *r.* France
275 H5 **Alenquer** Brazil
206 B2 **Alenquer** Port.
206 B2 **Alenquer** *r.* Port.
206 C4 **Alentejo** *reg.* Port.
264 □E14 **'Alenuihāhā Channel** *HI* U.S.A.
185 J10 **Alénya** France
Alep Syria *see* **Ḥalab**
228 E5 **Alépé** Côte d'Ivoire
Aleppo Syria *see* **Ḥalab**
136 F4 **Aler** *r.* India
195 J4 **Alerheim** Ger.
214 D3 **Aléria** *Corse* France
208 E3 **Alerre** Spain
243 L1 **Alert** *Nunavut* Can.
276 C2 **Alerta** Peru
246 E5 **Alert Bay** *B.C.* Can.
183 E8 **Alès** France
214 B8 **Ales** *Sardegna* Italy
219 K3 **Aleşd** Romania
Aleshki Ukr. *see* **Tsyurupyns'k**
161 Q8 **Aleshnya** Rus. Fed.
Alesia France *see* **Alise-Ste-Reine**
Aleşkirt Turkey *see* **Eleşkirt**
205 O4 **Alesón** Spain
212 F6 **Alessandria** Italy
212 F6 **Alessandria** *prov.* Italy
217 K4 **Alessandria del Carretto** Italy
217 O4 **Alessano** Italy
Alessio Albania *see* **Lezhë**
162 I5 **Ålesund** Norway
185 I9 **Alet-les-Bains** France
Aletrium Italy *see* **Alatri**
212 D3 **Aletschhorn** *mt.* Switz.
290 G2 **Aleutian Basin** *sea feature* Bering Sea
244 D5 **Aleutian Islands** *AK* U.S.A.
244 H4 **Aleutian Range** *mts AK* U.S.A.
290 H2 **Aleutian Trench** *sea feature* N. Pacific Ocean
153 Q4 **Alevina, Mys** *c.* Rus. Fed.
Alevişik Turkey *see* **Samandağı**
260 D2 **Alexander** *ND* U.S.A.
286 T2 **Alexander, Cape** Antarctica
106 F2 **Alexander, Mount** *hill N.T.* Austr.
109 C7 **Alexander, Mount** *hill W.A.* Austr.
245 M4 **Alexander Archipelago** *is* *AK* U.S.A.
236 A4 **Alexander Bay** *b.* Namibia/S. Africa
236 A4 **Alexander Bay** S. Africa
255 E9 **Alexander City** *AL* U.S.A.
286 T2 **Alexander Island** Antarctica
144 E3 **Alexander's Wall** *tourist site* Iran
144 F3 **Alexander's Wall** *tourist site* Iran
105 J7 **Alexandra** *Vic.* Austr.
106 G5 **Alexandra** *r. Qld* Austr.
103 D12 **Alexandra** *South I.* N.Z.
283 □ **Alexandra, Cape** S. Georgia
137 M5 **Alexandra Channel** *Andaman & Nicobar Is* India
246 G2 **Alexandra Falls** *N.W.T.* Can.
Alexandra Land *i. Zemlya Frantsa-Iosifa* Rus. Fed. *see* **Aleksandry, Zemlya**
220 D2 **Alexandreia** Greece
Alexandretta Turkey *see* **İskenderun**
Alexandria Afgh. *see* **Ghaznī**
106 F5 **Alexandria** *N.T.* Austr.
246 F4 **Alexandria** *B.C.* Can.
248 F4 **Alexandria** *Ont.* Can.
219 N7 **Alexandria** Romania
237 K9 **Alexandria** S. Africa
Alexandria Turkm. *see* **Mary**
168 G11 **Alexandria** *West Dunbartonshire, Scotland* U.K.
256 A10 **Alexandria** *KY* U.S.A.
261 I10 **Alexandria** *LA* U.S.A.
260 H3 **Alexandria** *MN* U.S.A.
260 G4 **Alexandria** *SD* U.S.A.
258 A7 **Alexandria** *VA* U.S.A.
Alexandria Arachoton Afgh. *see* **Kandahār**
Alexandria Areion Afgh. *see* **Herāt**
257 J4 **Alexandria Bay** *NY* U.S.A.
Alexandria Prophthasia Afgh. *see* **Farāh**
104 G6 **Alexandrina, Lake** *S.A.* Austr.
221 G2 **Alexandroupoli** Greece
280 C2 **Alexânia** Brazil
249 J2 **Alexis** *r. Nfld and Lab.* Can.
246 F4 **Alexis Creek** *B.C.* Can.
150 D5 **Aley** Lebanon
143 T1 **Aley** *r.* Rus. Fed.
144 G3 **Aleyak** Iran
143 T1 **Aleysk** Rus. Fed.
217 O3 **Alezio** Italy
191 D10 **Alf** Ger.
207 L6 **Alfacar** Spain
208 G6 **Alfacs, Port dels** *b.* Spain
224 C5 **Alfadida** *well* Chad
209 E9 **Alfafar** Spain
204 G8 **Alfaiates** Port.
208 D4 **Alfajarín** Spain
269 H5 **Alfajayucan** Mex.
208 C6 **Alfambra** Spain
208 C7 **Alfambra** *r.* Spain
206 B6 **Alfambras** Port.
208 C5 **Alfamén** Spain
204 G6 **Alfândega da Fé** Port.
208 F4 **Alfántega** Spain
147 I8 **Al Fardah** Yemen
204 C8 **Alfarelos** Port.
207 K6 **Alfarnate** Spain
205 Q4 **Alfaro** Spain
208 G4 **Alfarràs** Spain
147 I3 **Al Farūq** *reg.* Saudi Arabia
144 B7 **Al Farwānīyah** Kuwait
149 M9 **Al Farwānīyah** Kuwait
Al Fas Morocco *see* **Fès**
225 F2 **Al Fashn** Egypt
219 P7 **Alfatar** Bulg.
149 K6 **Al Fatḥah** Iraq
147 K7 **Al Fatk** Yemen
149 N9 **Al Fāw** Iraq
225 F2 **Al Fayyūm** Egypt
148 E9 **Al Fayyūm** *governorate* Egypt
146 F8 **Al Fāzih** Yemen
194 H4 **Alfdorf** Ger.
215 M4 **Alfedena** Italy
220 C5 **Alfeios** *r.* Greece
204 B9 **Alfeizerão** Port.
191 I7 **Alfeld (Leine)** Ger.
204 C6 **Alfena** Port.
281 E4 **Alfenas** Brazil
206 C6 **Alferce** Port.
143 Q1 **Alferovka** Rus. Fed.
206 C2 **Alferrarede** Port.
191 E5 **Alfhausen** Ger.
149 N9 **Al Finṭās** Kuwait
Alfíos *r.* Greece *see* **Alfeios**
150 A8 **Al Firdān** Egypt
199 J5 **Alföld** *plain* Hungary
213 M7 **Alfonsine** Italy
207 P4 **Alfonso XIII, Embalse de** *resr* Spain
168 K8 **Alford** *Aberdeenshire, Scotland* U.K.
171 R7 **Alford** *Lincolnshire, England* U.K.
208 G5 **Alforja** Spain
257 K3 **Alfred** *Ont.* Can.
257 □O5 **Alfred** *ME* U.S.A.
109 H8 **Alfred and Marie Range** *hills* *W.A.* Austr.
269 I4 **Alfred M. Terrazas** Mex.
281 G4 **Alfredo Chaves** Brazil
102 J7 **Alfredton** *North I.* N.Z.
171 O7 **Alfreton** *Derbyshire, England* U.K.
163 N6 **Alfta** Sweden
147 M3 **Al Fujayrah** U.A.E.
206 C4 **Alfundão** Port.
224 C3 **Al Fuqahā'** Libya
140 F3 **Al Furāt** *r.* Iraq/Syria *alt.* **Fırat (Turkey),** *conv.* **Euphrates**
146 G3 **Al Furūthi** Saudi Arabia
142 G3 **Alga** Kazakh.
142 E2 **Algabas** Kazakh.
209 K8 **Algaida** Spain
214 B2 **Algajola** *Corse* France
207 I6 **Algámitas** Spain
206 H7 **Algar** Spain
164 B3 **Ålgård** Norway
207 K6 **Algarinejo** Spain
285 F6 **Algarroba** Arg.
282 C3 **Algarrobal** Chile
284 B1 **Algarrobito** Chile
285 G3 **Algarrobitos** Arg.
284 B3 **Algarrobo** Chile
207 K7 **Algarrobo** Spain
209 C12 **Algarrobo** *hill* Spain
284 D5 **Algarrobo del Aguilla** Arg.
206 C6 **Algarve** *reg.* Port.
157 H5 **Algasovo** Rus. Fed.
207 I7 **Algatocín** Spain
122 I1 **Algazeya** Rus. Fed.
207 I8 **Algeciras** Spain
Algeciras, Bahía de *b.* Gibraltar/Spain *see* **Gibraltar, Bay of**
209 E9 **Algemesí** Spain
225 H5 **Algena** Eritrea
227 F1 **Alger** Alg.
251 J5 **Alger** *MI* U.S.A.
227 F3 **Algeria** *country* Africa
191 I6 **Algermissen** Ger.
208 G4 **Algerri** Spain
205 N7 **Algete** Spain
151 G4 **Alget'i** *r.* Georgia
151 F4 **Alget'is Nakrdzali** *natu…* Georgia
209 C12 **Algezares** Spain
Algha Kazakh. *see* **Alga**
147 M4 **Al Ghāfāt** Oman
149 L8 **Al Ghammās** Iraq
148 E8 **Al Gharbīyah** *governora…*
Al Ghardaqah Egypt *see* **Al Ghurdaqah**
146 E5 **Al Gharīth** Saudi Arabia
146 G2 **Al Ghāṭ** Saudi Arabia
150 D7 **Al Ghawr** *plain* Jordan/…
150 D8 **Al Ghawr** *plain* Jordan/…
147 K7 **Al Ghayḍah** Yemen
146 H4 **Al Ghayl** Saudi Arabia
214 A6 **Alghero** *Sardegna* Italy
147 M6 **Al Ghubr** *reg.* Oman
225 G3 **Al Ghurdaqah** *Al Baḥr…* Egypt
147 J3 **Al Ghuwayr** *well* Qatar
147 I3 **Al Ghwaybiyah** Saudi A…
206 C6 **Algibre** *r.* Port.
Algiers Alg. *see* **Alger**
209 E9 **Alginet** Spain
237 J9 **Algoa Bay** S. Africa
274 D5 **Algodón** *r.* Peru
207 I7 **Algodonales** Spain
269 J1 **Algodones, Bahía** *b.* M…
205 M9 **Algodor** *r.* Spain
250 G5 **Algoma** *WI* U.S.A.
260 H4 **Algona** *IA* U.S.A.
251 L7 **Algonac** *MI* U.S.A.
248 E4 **Algonquin Park** *Ont.* C…
251 P4 **Algonquin Provincial P…** *Ont.* Can.
205 O7 **Algora** Spain
205 O2 **Algorta** Spain
285 I3 **Algorta** Uru.
204 G6 **Algoso** Port.
206 C6 **Algoz** Port.
179 L5 **Algrange** France
162 N4 **Älgsjö** Sweden
208 G4 **Alguaire** Spain
209 C11 **Alguazas** Spain
Algueirao Moz. *see* **Ha…**
206 A3 **Algueirão-Mem Martin…**
209 D11 **Algueña** Spain
149 K9 **Al Habakah** *well* Saudi …
149 K7 **Al Ḥabbānīyah** Iraq
207 N7 **Alhabia** Spain
146 G1 **Al Ḥadaqah** *well* Saudi …
204 C8 **Alhadas** Port.
146 F4 **Al Ḥadbah** *reg.* Saudi A…
147 J2 **Al Ḥadd** Bahrain
146 G5 **Al Haddār** Saudi Arabia
149 K9 **Al Hadhālīl** *plat.* Saudi …
150 E3 **Al Ḥadīdīyah** Syria
149 K6 **Al Ḥadīthah** Iraq
150 F7 **Al Ḥadīthah** Saudi Arab…
149 K6 **Al Ḥaḍr** Iraq
146 E1 **Al Ḥafár** *well* Saudi Ara…
150 E3 **Al Ḥaffah** Syria
226 B4 **Al Haggounia** Western …
146 H3 **Al Ḥā'ir** Saudi Arabia
147 N4 **Al Hajar** Oman
147 M3 **Al Ḥajar al Gharbī** *mts*
147 N4 **Al Ḥajar ash Sharqī** *mt…*
147 H7 **Al Ḥajr** Yemen
147 M7 **Al Ḥallānīyah** *i.* Oman
207 L6 **Alhama** *r.* Spain
205 Q4 **Alhama** *r.* Spain
150 G7 **Al Ḥamād** *plain* Asia
207 N7 **Alhama de Almería** Spa…
205 Q6 **Alhama de Aragón** Spa…
207 L6 **Alhama de Granada** Sp…
209 C12 **Alhama de Murcia** Spa…
146 H4 **Al Ḥamar** Saudi Arabia
207 M3 **Alhambra** Spain
147 I8 **Al Ḥāmi** Yemen
150 D4 **Al Ḥamīdīyah** Syria
207 O7 **Alhamilla, Sierra** *hills* S…
225 F2 **Al Ḥammām** Egypt
149 K8 **Al Hammām** *well* Iraq
146 D4 **Al Ḥamrā'** Saudi Arabi…
150 E4 **Al Ḥamrāt** Syria
146 E3 **Al Ḥanākīyah** Saudi Ar…
206 A3 **Alhandra** Port.
146 F9 **Al Ḥanīsh al Kabīr** *i.* Ye…
149 L9 **Al Haniyah** *esc.* Iraq
150 F3 **Al Ḥānūtah** Syria
146 F7 **Al Haqū** Saudi Arabia
146 H4 **Al Hariq** Saudi Arabia
225 F2 **Al Ḥarrah** Egypt
150 G8 **Al Ḥarrah** *reg.* Saudi Ar…
224 C3 **Al Harūj al Aswad** *hills*
150 D8 **Al Ḥasā** Jordan
147 I3 **Al Hasa** *reg.* Saudi Arab…
149 J5 **Al Ḥasakah** Syria
146 C3 **Al Ḥasāni** *i.* Saudi Arab…
146 L7 **Al Hāshimīyah** Iraq
146 G5 **Al Ḥasī** *well* Saudi Arab…
147 L7 **Al Ḥāsikīyah** *i.* Oman
146 G2 **Al Ḥatīfah** *plain* Saudi …
207 J7 **Alhaurín de la Torre** Sp…
207 J7 **Alhaurín el Grande** Spa…
147 I5 **Al Ḥawāyā** *des.* Saudi A…
150 G9 **Al Hawi** *salt pan* Saudi …
146 E5 **Al Ḥawīyah** Saudi Arab…
146 D1 **Al Ḥawjā'** Saudi Arabia
147 H9 **Al Ḥawrā** Yemen
147 H4 **Al Ḥawṭah** *reg.* Saudi A…
224 D3 **Al Hawwārīī** *oasis* Libya
146 F3 **Al Ḥayd** Saudi Arabia
149 M7 **Al Ḥayy** Iraq
148 D9 **Al Ḥayz** Egypt
148 H8 **Al Hazīm** Jordan
146 C1 **Al Ḥazm** Saudi Arabia
146 G7 **Al Ḥazm al Jawf** Yemen
236 E4 **Alheit** S. Africa
207 L6 **Alhendín** Spain
147 K6 **Al Ḥibāk** *des.* Saudi Ara…
150 E5 **Al Hījānah** Syria
149 L7 **Al Ḥillah** Iraq
Al Ḥillah *governorate* Ir… **Bābil**
146 H4 **Al Ḥillah** Saudi Arabia
146 H4 **Al Ḥilwah** Saudi Arabia
147 I2 **Al Ḥimārah** *well* Saudi
149 L7 **Al Hindīyah** Iraq
147 I2 **Al Ḥinnāh** Saudi Arabia
148 I8 **Al Ḥinw** *mt.* Saudi Arab…
147 J4 **Al Hirrah** *well* Saudi Ar…
150 H2 **Al Hīshah** Syria
146 G7 **Al Ḥishwah** *hills* Yemen
146 B1 **Al Ḥismā** *plain* Saudi A…
150 D6 **Al Ḥiṣn** Jordan
146 G9 **Al Ḥiṣn** Yemen
226 E2 **Al Hoceima** Morocco
202 D5 **Al Hoceima** *prov.* Moro…
204 E7 **Alhões** Port.
205 O7 **Alhóndiga** Spain
282 E2 **Alhuampa** Arg.
146 F8 **Al Ḥudaydah** Yemen
146 F8 **Al Ḥudaydah** *governora…*
146 F1 **Al Ḥudūd ash Shamālī** Saudi Arabia
147 I2 **Al Ḥufayrah** *well* Saudi
146 G3 **Al Ḥufayyirah** Saudi Ar…
146 D1 **Al Ḥufrah** *reg.* Saudi A…
147 I3 **Al Hufūf** Saudi Arabia
146 D1 **Al Hūj** *hills* Saudi Arabi…
224 C3 **Al Ḥulayq al Kabīr** *hills*
148 G9 **Al Ḥumayḍah** Saudi Ar…
146 G9 **Al Ḥumayshah** Yemen
147 L4 **Al Ḥumrah** *reg.* U.A.E.
147 I3 **Al Ḥunayy** Saudi Arabi…
146 G3 **Al Hurayyiq** Saudi Arab…
147 M3 **Al Husayfīn** Oman
147 M5 **Al Huwatsah** Oman
147 J3 **Al Huwaylah** Qatar
147 H8 **Al Ḥuwaymi** Yemen
146 E3 **Al Ḥuwayyiṭ** Saudi Arab…
150 E3 **Al Ḥuwayz** *Ḥamāh* Syri…
150 E3 **Al Ḥuwayz** *Ḥamāh* Syri…
146 G4 **Al Huwwah** Saudi Arab…
133 D10 **Ali** *Xizang* China
217 I7 **Alì** *Sicilia* Italy
216 F8 **Alia** *Sicilia* Italy
207 I2 **Alía** Spain
145 M3 **'Alīābād** Afgh.
151 H4 **Äliabad** Azer.
144 F3 **'Alīābād** *Golestān* Iran

'Alīābād *Hormozgan* Iran
'Alīābād *Khorāsān* Iran
'Alīābād *Kordestān* Iran
'Alīābād *Kordestān* Iran
'Alīābād *Qom* Iran
'Alīābād, Kūh-e *mt.* Iran
Aliaga Spain
Aliağa Turkey
Aliaguilla Spain
Aliakmona, Techniti Limni *l.* Greece
Aliakmonas *r.* Greece
'Alī al Gharbī Iraq
Aliambata East Timor
Aliano Italy
Aliartos Greece
Alibag *Mahar.* India
Ali Bandar Pak.
Älibäyli Azer.
Äli Bayramlı Azer.
Alibey Adası *i.* Turkey
Ālībo Eth.
Alibunar *Vojvodina* Serbia
Älicançay *r.* Azer.
Alicante Spain
Alicante *prov.* Spain
Alicante, Bahía de *b.* Spain
Alice *Qld* Austr.
Alice *r. Qld* Austr.
Alice *watercourse Qld* Austr.
Alice S. Africa
Alice *TX* U.S.A.
Alice, Punta *pt* Italy
Alice Arm B.C. Can.
Alicedale S. Africa
Alice Downs *W.A.* Austr.
Alice Shoal *sea feature* Caribbean Sea
Alice Springs *N.T.* Austr.
Alice Town Bahamas
Aliceville *AL* U.S.A.
Aliçeyrek Turkey
Alichur Tajik.
Alichur *r.* Tajik.
Alichuri Janubí, Qatorkŭhi *mts* Tajik.
Alicia Arg.
Alicia *Mindanao* Phil.
Alick Creek *r. Qld* Austr.
Alicudi, Isola *i. Isole Lipari* Italy
Alicún de Ortega Spain
Al 'Idd U.A.E.
Al 'Idwah *well* Saudi Arabia
Aliero Nigeria
Alife Italy
Alifuatpaşa Turkey
Aligarh *Rajasthan* India
Aligarh *Uttar Prad.* India
Alīgūdarz Iran
Alihe *Nei Mongol* China
Alija del Infantado Spain
Alija de los Melones Spain *see* **Alija del Infantado**
Alijó Port.
'Alījūq, Kūh-e *mt.* Iran
Alikamerli Turkey
Alikazgan *r.* Rus. Fed.
'Alī Kheyl Afgh.
Al Ikhwān *is* Yemen
Alikovo Rus. Fed.
Alima *r.* Congo
Al Imārāt al 'Arabīyah at Muttaḥidah *country* Asia *see* **United Arab Emirates**
Alimena *Sicilia* Italy
Alimia *i.* Greece
A Limia *reg.* Spain
Aliminusa *Sicilia* Italy
Alimpaya Point *Mindanao* Phil.
Alindao C.A.R.
Alindau *Sulawesi* Indon.
Alinghar *r.* Afgh.
Alingsås Sweden
Alintale *well* Eth.
Aliova *r.* Turkey
Alipur *Mahar.* India
Alipur Pak.
Alipur Duar *W. Bengal* India
Aliquippa *PA* U.S.A.
Alirajpur *Madh. Prad.* India
Ali Sabieh Djibouti
Al 'Īsāwīyah Saudi Arabia
Aliseda Spain
Alise-Ste-Reine France
'Alī Shāh Iran
Al Iskandarīyah Egypt
Al Iskandarīyah *governorate* Egypt
Al Iskandarīyah Iraq
Aliskerovo Rus. Fed.
Al Ismā'īlīyah Egypt
Al Ismā'īlīyah *governorate* Egypt
Alisofu Turkey
Aliste *r.* Spain
Alitåive *mt.* Sweden
Alitak Bay *AK* U.S.A.
Alì Terme *Sicilia* Italy
Al Ittihab Yemen *see* **Madīnat ash Sha'b**
Aliveri Greece
Aliwal *Punjab* India
Aliwal North S. Africa
Alix *Alta* Can.
Aliyaha *r.* Ukr.
Alizai Pak.
Alizay France
Al Jafr Jordan
Al Jāfūrah *des.* Saudi Arabia
Al Jaghbūb Libya
Al Jahrah Kuwait
Al Jamalīyah Qatar
Aljaraque Spain
Al Jarāwī *well* Saudi Arabia
Al Jarf *mts* Saudi Arabia
Al Jauf Saudi Arabia *see* **Dumat al Jandal**
Al Jawārah *well* Oman
Al Jawb *reg.* Saudi Arabia
Al Jawf Libya
Al Jawf *'Asīr* Saudi Arabia
Al Jawf Saudi Arabia
Al Jawf *prov.* Saudi Arabia
Al Jawf *governorate* Yemen
Al Jawlān *hills* Syria *see* **Golan**
Al Jawsh Libya
Al Jaza'ir Alg. *see* **Alger**
Alj Beyk Iran
Aljezur Port.
Al Jībān *reg.* Saudi Arabia
Aljibe *mt.* Spain
Al Ji'lān *hills* Saudi Arabia
Al Jilh *esc.* Saudi Arabia
Al Jithāmīyah Saudi Arabia
Al Jīzah Egypt
Al Jīzah *governorate* Egypt
Al Jīzah Jordan
Al Ju'ayfirah Saudi Arabia
Aljubarrota Port.
Al Jubayl Saudi Arabia
Al Jubayl *hills* Saudi Arabia
Al Jubaylah Saudi Arabia
Al Jubb Saudi Arabia
Aljucén Spain
Aljucén *r.* Spain
Al Jufayfah Saudi Arabia
Al Jufrah *oasis* Libya
Al Julaydah *well* Saudi Arabia
Al Julayqah *well* Saudi Arabia
Al Jumah Saudi Arabia
Al Jumūm Saudi Arabia
Al Junaynah Saudi Arabia
Al Jurayd *i.* Saudi Arabia
Al Jurayfah Saudi Arabia
Al Jurayr *well* Saudi Arabia
Al Jurdhāwīyah Saudi Arabia
Aljustrel Port.
Al Juwayf *depr.* Syria
Al Juwayfah *well* Saudi Arabia
Al Kahfah *Al Qaşīm* Saudi Arabia
Al Kahfah *Ash Sharqīyah* Saudi Arabia
Al Kalbān Oman
Alkali Lake B.C. Can.
Alkaliya *r.* Ukr.

229 H3 **Alkamari** Niger
147 N4 **Al Kāmil** Oman
150 D7 **Al Karak** Jordan
150 D7 **Al Karāmah** Jordan
143 N1 **Alkaterek** Kazakh.
149 L7 **Al Kāẓimīyah** Iraq
187 H7 **Alken** Belgium
147 M4 **Al Khābūrah** Oman
146 F1 **Al Khaḍrā'** *well* Saudi Arabia
147 H2 **Al Khafaq** *well* Saudi Arabia
146 E4 **Al Khafqān** *salt pan* Saudi Arabia
146 E3 **Al Khalf** Saudi Arabia
147 N5 **Al Khalīf** Oman
Al Khalīl West Bank *see* **Hebron**
149 L7 **Al Khāliş** Iraq
146 G5 **Al Khamāsīn** Saudi Arabia
146 H4 **Al Kharfah** Saudi Arabia
225 F3 **Al Khārijah** Egypt
147 H4 **Al Kharj** *reg.* Saudi Arabia
147 J6 **Al Kharkhayr** *oasis* Saudi Arabia
147 J3 **Al Kharrārah** Qatar
150 B7 **Al Kharrūbah** Egypt
147 M2 **Al Khaşab** Oman
147 L6 **Al Khasfah** *well* Oman
146 F4 **Al Khāşirah** Saudi Arabia
147 L3 **Al Khatam** *reg.* U.A.E.
150 G7 **Al Khaṭīmī** *vol.* Saudi Arabia
146 F9 **Al Khawkhah** Yemen
147 J3 **Al Khawr** Qatar
146 F8 **Al Khawtamah** *i.* Yemen
149 L8 **Al Khiḍr** Iraq
147 J3 **Al Khīşah** *well* Saudi Arabia
147 I2 **Al Khizāmī** *well* Saudi Arabia
147 J2 **Al Khobar** Saudi Arabia
147 I2 **Al Khubrah** Saudi Arabia
146 G3 **Al Khuff** *reg.* Saudi Arabia
224 B1 **Al Khums** Libya
146 D1 **Al Khunfah** *sand area* Saudi Arabia
147 I4 **Al Khunn** Saudi Arabia
150 D5 **Al Khushnīyah** Syria
147 J2 **Al Khuwayr** Qatar
147 L4 **Al Kidan** *well* Saudi Arabia
149 L7 **Al Kifl** Iraq
147 J3 **Al Kir'ānah** Qatar
150 E5 **Al Kiswah** Syria
186 G3 **Alkmaar** Neth.
201 J3 **Alkoven** Austria
150 A8 **Al Kūbrī** Egypt
149 L7 **Al Kūfah** Iraq
147 I5 **Al Kuflah** *well* Saudi Arabia
224 D3 **Al Kufrah** Libya
224 D3 **Al Kufrah** *oasis* Libya
146 F2 **Al Kuhayfīyah** Saudi Arabia
149 M7 **Al Kumayt** Iraq
150 C9 **Al Kuntillah** Egypt
146 D3 **Al Kurá** *lava field* Saudi Arabia
150 G7 **Al Kusūr** *hills* Saudi Arabia
149 L7 **Al Kūt** Iraq
Al Kuwayt *country* Asia *see* **Kuwait**
149 M9 **Al Kuwayt** Kuwait
150 D8 **Al La'bān** Jordan
149 J9 **Al Labbah** *plain* Saudi Arabia
229 F5 **Allada** Benin
150 D3 **Al Lādhiqīyah** Syria
150 D3 **Al Lādhiqīyah** *governorate* Syria
136 F5 **Allagadda** *Andhra Prad.* India
257 □P1 **Allagash** *r. ME* U.S.A.
257 □P2 **Allagash Lake** *ME* U.S.A.
138 H7 **Allahabad** *Uttar Prad.* India
151 D5 **Allahüekber Dağları** *mts* Turkey
151 D5 **Allahüekber Tepe** *mt.* Turkey
214 B8 **Allai** *Sardegna* Italy
178 E4 **Allaines** France
178 C7 **Allaines-Mervilliers** France
180 G6 **Allaire** France
150 E6 **Al Lajā** *lava field* Syria
244 I2 **Allakaket** *AK* U.S.A.
153 O3 **Allakh-Yun'** Rus. Fed.
258 F3 **Allamuchy** *NJ* U.S.A.
183 F7 **Allan** France
183 B6 **Allanche** France
237 L4 **Allandale** S. Africa
108 □[1] **Allan Point** Christmas I.
237 K3 **Allanridge** S. Africa
170 J2 **Allanton** *North Lanarkshire, Scotland* U.K.
136 G3 **Allapalli** *Mahar.* India
225 G4 **'Allāqī, Wādī al** *watercourse* Egypt
151 J6 **Allar** Azer.
249 H4 **Allardville** N.B. Can.
100 □[6] **Allardyce** *Sta Isabel* Solomon Is
204 E4 **Allariz** Spain
179 N7 **Allarmont** France
184 G5 **Allassac** France
147 I7 **Al Latakhīyah** *well* Yemen
183 G10 **Allauch** France
235 F4 **Alldays** S. Africa
212 C1 **Alle** Switz.
250 I7 **Allegan** *MI* U.S.A.
256 G6 **Allegany** *NY* U.S.A.
213 M3 **Alleghe** Italy
256 F8 **Allegheny** *r. PA* U.S.A.
256 C12 **Allegheny Mountains** U.S.A.
256 G7 **Allegheny Reservoir** *PA* U.S.A.
183 D6 **Allègre** France
271 □[2] **Allègre, Pointe** *pt* Guadeloupe
183 G9 **Alleins** France
237 L4 **Allemanskraaldam** *resr* S. Africa
183 I6 **Allemond** France
284 D6 **Allen** Arg.
114 E5 **Allen** *Samar* Phil.
170 D7 **Allen** Ireland
256 A7 **Allen** *MI* U.S.A.
169 F4 **Allen, Lough** *l.* Ireland
103 B14 **Allen, Mount** *hill Stewart I.* N.Z.
245 L3 **Allen, Mount** *AK* U.S.A.
255 G9 **Allendale** *SC* U.S.A.
171 M4 **Allendale Town** *Northumberland, England* U.K.
267 I3 **Allende** *Coahuila* Mex.
267 I5 **Allende** *Nuevo León* Mex.
269 M7 **Allende** *Veracruz* Mex.
191 G8 **Allendorf (Eder)** Ger.
191 G9 **Allendorf (Lumda)** Ger.
251 M5 **Allenford** *Ont.* Can.
171 M4 **Allenheads** *Northumberland, England* U.K.
194 G6 **Allensbach** Ger.
Allenstein Pol. *see* **Olsztyn**
256 C9 **Allensville** *OH* U.S.A.
256 H8 **Allensville** *PA* U.S.A.
258 F4 **Allentown** *NJ* U.S.A.
258 D3 **Allentown** *PA* U.S.A.
201 L2 **Allentsteig** Austria
169 I6 **Allenwood** Ireland
259 G4 **Allenwood** *NJ* U.S.A.
258 B2 **Allenwood** *PA* U.S.A.
Alleppey India *see* **Alappuzha**
208 D7 **Allepuz** Spain
190 H5 **Aller** *r.* Ger.
182 F3 **Allerey-sur-Saône** France
214 H2 **Allerona** Italy
195 K3 **Allersberg** Ger.
195 L5 **Allershausen** Ger.
183 I6 **Allevard** France
183 F7 **Allex** France
195 I6 **Allgäu** *reg.* Ger.
200 B5 **Allgäuer Alpen** *mts* Austria
173 N5 **Allhallows** *Medway, England* U.K.
275 H3 **Allianc** Suriname
260 D4 **Alliance** *NE* U.S.A.
256 D8 **Alliance** *OH* U.S.A.
178 H6 **Allibaudières** France
Al Lībīyah *country* Africa *see* **Libya**
182 C4 **Allier** *dept* France
182 C3 **Allier** *r.* France
149 K8 **Al Līfīyah** *well* Iraq
107 H4 **Alligator Point** *Qld* Austr.
270 □ **Alligator Pond** Jamaica
270 □ **Alligator Pond Bay** Jamaica
182 E2 **Alligny-en-Morvan** France
147 H2 **Al Lihābah** *well* Saudi Arabia
169 B9 **Allihies** Ireland
136 E3 **Allikher** *Karnataka* India
182 I4 **Allinges** France
165 K6 **Allinge-Sandvig** *Bornholm* Denmark
146 H2 **Al Lişāfah** *well* Saudi Arabia
150 D7 **Al Lisān** *pen.* Jordan
260 I4 **Allison** *IA* U.S.A.
217 O4 **Alliste** Italy
251 O5 **Alliston** *Ont.* Can.
146 E5 **Al Līth** Saudi Arabia

147 K4 **Al Liwā'** *oasis* U.A.E.
194 H5 **Allmendingen** Ger.
205 P3 **Allo** Spain
168 I10 **Alloa** *Clackmannanshire, Scotland* U.K.
181 P7 **Allogny** France
171 K4 **Allonby** *Cumbria, England* U.K.
184 E1 **Allonnes** *Pays de la Loire* France
181 L6 **Allonnes** *Pays de la Loire* France
185 D7 **Allons** France
105 N3 **Allora** *Qld* Austr.
183 J8 **Allos** France
183 J8 **Allos, Col d'** *pass* France
184 F3 **Alloue** France
250 F5 **Allouez** *WI* U.S.A.
169 E8 **Allow** *r.* Ireland
168 G12 **Alloway** *South Ayrshire, Scotland* U.K.
258 E5 **Alloway** *NJ* U.S.A.
258 D6 **Alloway Creek** *r. NJ* U.S.A.
205 Q3 **Alloz, Embalse de** *resr* Spain
208 D6 **Alloza** Spain
212 D1 **Allschwil** Switz.
193 D8 **Allstedt** Ger.
115 A6 **Allu** *Sulawesi* Indon.
146 F8 **Al Luḥayyah** Yemen
251 Q4 **Allumettes, Île aux** *i. Que.* Can.
214 H3 **Allumiere** Italy
136 G5 **Allur** *Andhra Prad.* India
136 G5 **Alluru Kottapatnam** *Andhra Prad.* India
149 K8 **Al Lussuf** *well* Iraq
182 D2 **Alluy** France
249 G3 **Alma** *Que.* Can.
255 F10 **Alma** *GA* U.S.A.
260 G6 **Alma** *KS* U.S.A.
250 J6 **Alma** *MI* U.S.A.
260 F5 **Alma** *NE* U.S.A.
149 K8 **Al Ma'ānīyah** Iraq
Alma-Ata Kazakh. *see* **Almaty**
Alma-Ata Oblast *admin. div.* Kazakh. *see* **Almatinskaya Oblast'**
208 F4 **Almacelles** Spain
207 K7 **Almáchar** Spain
207 O5 **Almaciles, Puerto de** *pass* Spain
206 A3 **Almada** Port.
146 C1 **Al Madāfi'** *plat.* Saudi Arabia
149 L9 **Al Ma'danīyāt** *well* Iraq
146 F7 **Al Maḍāyā** Saudi Arabia
107 J4 **Almaden** *Qld* Austr.
207 J3 **Almadén** Spain
206 G5 **Almadén de la Plata** Spain
207 J3 **Almadenejos** Spain
207 P4 **Almadenes, Embalse de** *resr* Spain
144 B6 **Al Madīnah** Iraq
146 D3 **Al Madīnah** Saudi Arabia
146 E3 **Al Madīnah** *prov.* Saudi Arabia
150 E6 **Al Mafraq** Jordan
285 E3 **Almafuerte** Arg.
147 K4 **Al Maghrib** *reg.* U.A.E.
269 I2 **Almagre** Mex.
114 E6 **Almagro** *i.* Phil.
207 L3 **Almagro** Spain
209 B13 **Almagro, Sierra de** *hills* Spain
147 J4 **Al Mahākik** *reg.* Saudi Arabia
225 F3 **Al Maḥārīq** Egypt
146 E5 **Al Maḥāwiyah** Saudi Arabia
226 C4 **Al Mahbas** Western Sahara
146 E5 **Al Mahḍam** Saudi Arabia
150 F2 **Al Mahdum** Syria
146 D2 **Al Maḥiā** *depr.* Saudi Arabia
149 L7 **Al Maḥmūdīyah** Iraq
147 J7 **Al Mahrah** *governorate* Yemen
147 J8 **Al Mahrah** *reg.* Yemen
146 F8 **Al Maḥwīt** Yemen
146 F8 **Al Maḥwīt** *governorate* Yemen
147 J4 **Al Majann** *ridge* Saudi Arabia
205 P5 **Almajano** Spain
146 G3 **Al Majma'ah** Saudi Arabia
219 K6 **Almăjului, Munții** *mts* Romania
225 F3 **Al Maks al Baḥrī** Egypt
151 H4 **Almalı** Azer.
147 I3 **Al Malsūnīyah** *reg.* Saudi Arabia
205 P6 **Almaluez** Spain
Almalyk Uzbek. *see* **Olmaliq**
147 L4 **Al Manadir** *reg.* Oman
147 J2 **Al Manāmah** Bahrain
146 G4 **Al Manjūr** *well* Saudi Arabia
264 K1 **Almanor, Lake** *CA* U.S.A.
209 C10 **Almansa** Spain
209 C10 **Almansa, Embalse de** *resr* Spain
206 C6 **Almansil** Port.
206 B3 **Almansor** *r.* Port.
225 F2 **Al Manşūrah** Egypt
149 L6 **Al Manşūrīyah** Iraq
205 J3 **Almanza** Spain
205 J8 **Almanzor** *mt.* Spain
207 P6 **Almanzora** *r.* Spain
146 E6 **Al Ma'qaş** Saudi Arabia
149 M8 **Al Ma'qil** Iraq
145 K4 **Almār** Afgh.
205 J7 **Almar** *r.* Spain
204 I9 **Almaraz** Spain
207 I6 **Almargen** Spain
147 K4 **Al Mariyyah** U.A.E.
224 D1 **Al Marj** Libya
150 B9 **Al Markhah** *spring* Egypt
205 P5 **Almarza** Spain
278 D4 **Almas** Brazil
199 L5 **Almaş** Romania
219 L3 **Almaş** *r.* Romania
280 C1 **Almas, Rio das** *r.* Brazil
147 M4 **Al Masana'a** Oman
199 H4 **Almásfüzitő** Hungary
199 G6 **Almás-patak** *r.* Hungary
Almassora *Valencia* Spain *see* **Almazora**
148 F8 **Al Maṭarīyah** Egypt
143 Q5 **Almatinskaya Oblast'** *admin. div.* Kazakh.
226 B4 **Al Matmarfag** Western Sahara
143 Q6 **Almaty** Kazakh.
Almaty Oblast *admin. div.* Kazakh. *see* **Almatinskaya Oblast'**
Almaty Oblysy *admin. div.* Kazakh. *see* **Almatinskaya Oblast'**
149 K5 **Al Mawşil** Iraq
149 J6 **Al Mayādīn** Syria
205 O6 **Almazán** Spain
150 B7 **Al Mazār** Egypt
153 M3 **Almaznyy** Rus. Fed.
209 E8 **Almazora** Spain
150 D7 **Al Mazra'ah** Jordan
205 P5 **Almazul** Spain
195 P4 **Alm Berg** *mt.* Ger.
191 G7 **Alme** *r.* Ger.
209 C11 **Almeces** *mt.* Spain
207 N3 **Almedina** Spain
207 K6 **Almedinilla** Spain
204 G7 **Almeida** Port.
204 H6 **Almeida de Sayago** Spain
275 H5 **Almeirim** Brazil
206 B2 **Almeirim** Port.
186 K4 **Almelo** Neth.
208 G4 **Almenar** Spain
281 G2 **Almenara** Brazil
209 E8 **Almenara** Spain
209 B12 **Almenara** *hill* Spain
209 B12 **Almenara, Sierra de** *hills* Spain
207 O3 **Almenaras** *mt.* Spain
205 P5 **Almenar de Soria** Spain
204 F6 **Almendra** Port.
204 H6 **Almendra** Spain
204 H6 **Almendra, Embalse de** *resr* Spain
206 F3 **Almendral** Spain
206 G3 **Almendralejo** Spain
207 P6 **Almendricos** Spain
186 H4 **Almere** Neth.
207 O7 **Almería** Spain
207 O6 **Almería** *prov.* Spain
207 O7 **Almería, Golfo de** *b.* Spain
207 N7 **Almerimar** Spain
Almetievsk Rus. Fed. *see* **Al'met'yevsk**
157 K5 **Al'met'yevsk** Rus. Fed.
165 K5 **Älmhult** Sweden
146 G3 **Al Midhnab** Saudi Arabia
147 K5 **Al Miḥrāḍ** *reg.* Saudi Arabia
207 L7 **Almijara, Sierra de** *mts* Spain
207 I9 **Almina, Punta** *pt Ceuta* Spain
146 E5 **Al Mindak** Saudi Arabia
147 N4 **Al Mintirib** Oman
225 F2 **Al Minyā** Egypt

148 E9 **Al Minyā** *governorate* Egypt
283 C9 **Almirantazgo, Seno del** *sea chan.* Chile
266 □R13 **Almirante** Panama
280 C6 **Almirante Tamandaré** Brazil
147 K3 **Al Mirfa** U.A.E.
Almirós Greece *see* **Almyros**
147 I1 **Al Mish'āb** Saudi Arabia
150 E5 **Al Mismīyah** Syria
186 G5 **Almkerk** Neth.
206 C5 **Almodôvar** Port.
205 M8 **Almodóvar** *hill* Spain
206 H8 **Almodóvar** *r.* Spain
207 K3 **Almodóvar del Campo** Spain
205 Q9 **Almodóvar del Pinar** Spain
207 I5 **Almodóvar del Río** Spain
204 E7 **Almofala** Port.
207 J7 **Almogía** Spain
206 B5 **Almograve** Port.
205 O8 **Almoguera** Spain
206 G2 **Almoharín** Spain
268 G7 **Almoloya** Mex.
205 R6 **Almonacid de la Sierra** Spain
205 O9 **Almonacid del Marquesado** Spain
205 O8 **Almonacid del Zorita** Spain
205 M9 **Almonacid de Toledo** Spain
206 F5 **Almonaster la Real** Spain
168 J10 **Almond** *r. Scotland* U.K.
168 I10 **Almondbank** *Perth and Kinross, Scotland* U.K.
172 G4 **Almondsbury** *South Gloucestershire, England* U.K.
251 K7 **Almont** *MI* U.S.A.
251 R4 **Almonte** *Ont.* Can.
206 F6 **Almonte** Spain
204 H9 **Almonte** *r.* Spain
138 G5 **Almora** *Uttaranchal* India
209 D11 **Almoradí** Spain
207 I3 **Almorchón** Spain
205 L8 **Almorox** Spain
199 K4 **Álmosd** Hungary
204 D9 **Almoster** Port.
206 B2 **Almoster** *r.* Port.
229 G3 **Al Mota** *well* Niger
229 F2 **Almoustarat** Mali
201 I4 **Almsee** *l.* Austria
191 I6 **Almstedt** Ger.
150 G9 **Al Mu'ayzīlah** *hill* Saudi Arabia
147 I3 **Al Mubarrez** Saudi Arabia
147 N4 **Al Muḍaibī** Oman
147 N4 **Al Muḍairib** Oman
146 D3 **Al Mudarraj** Saudi Arabia
150 E9 **Al Mudawwarah** Jordan
208 D3 **Almudévar** Spain
147 J2 **Al Muḥarraq** Bahrain
150 E10 **Al Muḥtaṭab** *depr.* Saudi Arabia
147 I8 **Al Mukallā** Yemen
146 F9 **Al Mukhā** Yemen
224 D1 **Al Mukhaylī** Libya
146 G4 **Al Mulayḥ** Saudi Arabia
147 I4 **Al Munbaṭiḥ** *des.* Saudi Arabia
146 G6 **Al Mundafan** *pass* Saudi Arabia
207 L7 **Almuñécar** Spain
208 E4 **Almuniente** Spain
201 I4 **Almünster** Austria
149 L7 **Al Muqdādīyah** Iraq
207 M3 **Almuradiel** Spain
Al Mūrītānīyah *country* Africa *see* **Mauritania**
206 D2 **Almuro** *r.* Port.
149 I9 **Al Murūt** *well* Saudi Arabia
148 H3 **Almus** Turkey
146 H1 **Al Musannāh** *ridge* Saudi Arabia
146 D3 **Al Musayjīd** Saudi Arabia
209 E9 **Almussafes** Spain
146 C2 **Al Muṭalla'** Saudi Arabia
149 L8 **Al Muthanná** *governorate* Iraq
150 E7 **Al Muwaqqar** Jordan
146 E4 **Al Muwayh** Saudi Arabia
146 B2 **Al Muwayliḥ** Saudi Arabia
220 F4 **Almyropotamos** Greece
220 D3 **Almyros** Greece
220 F7 **Almyrou, Ormos** *b. Kriti* Greece
259 L1 **Almyville** *CT* U.S.A.
168 H7 **Alness** *Highland, Scotland* U.K.
Alness *r. Scotland* U.K. *see* **Averon**
171 N3 **Alnmouth** *Northumberland, England* U.K.
171 N3 **Alnwick** *Northumberland, England* U.K.
209 C7 **Alobras** Spain
205 O7 **Alocén** Spain
103 □[4] **Alofi** Niue
99 I3 **Alofi, Île** *i.* Wallis and Futuna Is
103 □[4] **Alofi Bay** Niue
100 □[4b] **Alohkapw** *Pohnpei* Micronesia
232 B4 **Aloi** Uganda
160 H4 **Aloja** Latvia
238 □[3a] **Alojera** *La Gomera* Canary Is
160 M5 **Alol'** Rus. Fed.
160 L5 **Alolya** *r.* Rus. Fed.
139 O5 **Along** *Arun. Prad.* India
122 B3 **Alongshan** *Nei Mongol* China
220 E3 **Alonnisos** *i.* Greece
280 B6 **Alonso** *r.* Brazil
115 D8 **Alor** *i.* Indon.
115 D8 **Alor, Kepulauan** *is* Indon.
115 C8 **Alor, Selat** *sea chan.* Indon.
207 J7 **Álora** Spain
116 D1 **Alor Setar** Malaysia
Alor Star Malaysia *see* **Alor Setar**
208 H2 **Alós d'Ensil** Spain
206 E5 **Alosno** Spain
Alost Belgium *see* **Aalst**
138 E8 **Alot** *Madh. Prad.* India
276 D5 **Alota** Bol.
113 L9 **Alotau** P.N.G.
181 J8 **Alouettes, Mont des** *hill* France
205 N7 **Alovera** Spain
182 F2 **Aloxe-Corton** France
109 J9 **Aloysius, Mount** *W.A.* Austr.
207 J7 **Alozaina** Spain
156 E2 **Alozero** Rus. Fed.
208 I3 **Alp** Spain
285 F5 **Alpachiri** Arg.
284 E3 **Alpa Corral** Arg.
221 J3 **Alpagut** *Bursa* Turkey
221 L2 **Alpagut** *Eskişehir* Turkey
206 D2 **Alpalhão** Port.
205 O6 **Alpanseque** Spain
264 M6 **Alpaugh** *CA* U.S.A.
200 E5 **Alpbach** Austria
205 L7 **Alpedrete** Spain
204 F8 **Alpedrinha** Port.
204 C9 **Alpedriz** Port.
191 C7 **Alpen** Ger.
251 K4 **Alpena** *MI* U.S.A.
191 E9 **Alpenrod** Ger.
208 J3 **Alpens** Spain
209 C10 **Alpera** Spain
278 D3 **Alpercatas, Serra das** *hills* Brazil
183 I8 **Alpes-de-Haute-Provence** *dept* France
183 K9 **Alpes-Maritimes** *dept* France
Alpes Maritimes *mts* France/Italy *see* **Maritime Alps**
200 D6 **Alpetta, Punta dell'** *mt.* Italy
212 E3 **Alpe Veglia e dell'Alpe Devero, Parco Naturale dell'** *nature res.* Italy
107 K7 **Alpha** *Qld* Austr.
237 P3 **Alpha** S. Africa
107 K7 **Alpha Creek** *r. Qld* Austr.
292 P1 **Alpha Ridge** *sea feature* Arctic Ocean
186 G6 **Alphen** Neth.
186 G4 **Alphen aan den Rijn** Neth.
239 □[2] **Alphonse** *i.* Seychelles
239 □[2] **Alphonse Island** Seychelles
212 I7 **Alpi Apuane, Parco Naturale delle** *nature res.* Italy
206 B2 **Alpiarça** Port.
208 G4 **Alpicat** Spain
Alpi Dolomitiche *mts* Italy *see* **Dolomiti**
183 F9 **Alpilles** *hills* France
183 F9 **Alpilles, Canal des** France
Alpi Marittime *mts* France/Italy *see* **Maritime Alps**
265 W8 **Alpine** *AZ* U.S.A.
264 P9 **Alpine** *CA* U.S.A.
251 R7 **Alpine** *NY* U.S.A.
261 D10 **Alpine** *TX* U.S.A.

262 I5 **Alpine** *WY* U.S.A.
105 K7 **Alpine National Park** *Vic.* Austr.
280 D4 **Alpinópolis** Brazil
194 E5 **Alpirsbach** Ger.
212 E2 **Alpnach** Switz.
201 O5 **Alpokalja** *mts* Hungary
213 K5 **Alpone** *r.* Italy
206 D6 **Alportel** *r.* Port.
212 B5 **Alps** *mts* Europe
221 L3 **Alpu** Turkey
209 D8 **Alpuente** Spain
150 B10 **Al Qā'** *val.* Egypt
146 E5 **Al Qā'** *Makkah* Saudi Arabia
146 E6 **Al Qā'** *Makkah* Saudi Arabia
147 H7 **Al Qa'āmīyāt** *reg.* Saudi Arabia
224 B2 **Al Qaddāḥīyah** Libya
149 L8 **Al Qādisīyah** *governorate* Iraq
150 E3 **Al Qadmūs** Syria
147 K3 **Al Qaffāy** *i.* U.A.E.
146 G8 **Al Qafrah** Yemen
225 F2 **Al Qāhirah** Egypt
148 E9 **Al Qāhirah** *governorate* Egypt
146 E6 **Al Qaḥmah** Saudi Arabia
146 F3 **Al Qā'īyah** Saudi Arabia
146 G2 **Al Qā'īyah** *well* Saudi Arabia
227 G2 **Al Qal'a Beni Hammad** *tourist site* Alg.
146 C1 **Al Qalībah** Saudi Arabia
149 J5 **Al Qāmishlī** Syria
225 G2 **Al Qanṭarah** Egypt
146 H2 **Al Qar'ah** *well* Saudi Arabia
150 E6 **Al Qar'ah** *lava field* Syria
150 E3 **Al Qardāḥah** Syria
225 I5 **Al Qarḥah** Saudi Arabia
147 H8 **Al Qarn** Yemen
150 F7 **Al Qarqar** Saudi Arabia
150 F4 **Al Qaryatayn** Syria
146 G3 **Al Qaşab** *Ar Riyāḍ* Saudi Arabia
147 I4 **Al Qaşab** *Ash Sharqīyah* Saudi Arabia
146 F3 **Al Qaşīm** *prov.* Saudi Arabia
225 F3 **Al Qaşr** Egypt
146 E2 **Al Qaşr** Saudi Arabia
224 E3 **Al Qaşş Abū Sa'īd** *plat.* Egypt
147 J2 **Al Qaṭīf** Saudi Arabia
147 I8 **Al Qaṭn** Yemen
150 E7 **Al Qaṭrānah** Jordan
224 B3 **Al Qaṭrūn** Libya
146 G5 **Al Qawnas** *reg.* Saudi Arabia
146 H1 **Al Qayşūmah** Saudi Arabia
149 K9 **Al Qāyşūmah** *well* Saudi Arabia
147 M7 **Al Qiblīyah** *i.* Oman
224 D1 **Al Qubbah** *Darnah* Libya
206 D4 **Alqueva** Port.
206 E4 **Alqueva, Barragem de** *resr* Port.
208 F3 **Alquézar** Spain
146 E2 **Al Qufayfah** Saudi Arabia
207 M6 **Alquife** Spain
Al Qumur *country* Africa *see* **Comoros**
150 D5 **Al Qunayṭirah** Syria
150 D5 **Al Qunayṭirah** *governorate* Syria
146 E6 **Al Qunfidhah** Saudi Arabia
146 F3 **Al Qurayn** Saudi Arabia
147 K5 **Al Qurayni** *oasis* Saudi Arabia
146 F3 **Al Qurayyah** Saudi Arabia
147 M3 **Al Qurayyah** U.A.E.
148 H8 **Al Qurayyāt** Saudi Arabia
149 M8 **Al Qurnah** Iraq
150 C8 **Al Quşaymah** Egypt
225 G3 **Al Quşayr** Egypt
149 L8 **Al Qusayr** Iraq
150 E4 **Al Quşayr** Syria
150 E5 **Al Quṭayfah** Syria
146 F2 **Al Quwārah** Saudi Arabia
146 G4 **Al Quwayi'** Saudi Arabia
146 G3 **Al Quwayīyah** Saudi Arabia
150 D9 **Al Quwayrah** Jordan
147 I8 **Al Quzah** Yemen
147 L4 **Al Rabbād** *reg.* U.A.E.
183 B8 **Alrance** France
227 H3 **Alrar Est** Alg.
173 O4 **Alresford** *Essex, England* U.K.
173 I2 **Alrewas** *Staffordshire, England* U.K.
106 F5 **Alroy Downs** *N.T.* Austr.
164 F6 **Als** *i.* Denmark
205 M2 **Alsa, Embalse de** *resr* Spain
179 N7 **Alsace** *admin. reg.* France
179 N7 **Alsace** *reg.* France
179 N8 **Alsace, Plaine d'** *val.* France
171 M7 **Alsager** *Cheshire, England* U.K.
144 F9 **Al Samha** U.A.E.
149 K8 **Al Samīt** *well* Iraq
247 I5 **Alsask** *Sask.* Can.
Alsasua Spain *see* **Altsasu**
Alsatia *reg.* France *see* **Alsace**
194 F2 **Alsbach** Ger.
191 B9 **Alsdorf** Ger.
245 M4 **Alsek** *r. AK* U.S.A.
194 D3 **Alsenborn** Ger.
212 H6 **Alseno** Italy
194 D2 **Alsenz** Ger.
191 H9 **Alsfeld** Ger.
190 I1 **Als Fjord** *inlet* Denmark
168 E8 **Alsh, Loch** *sea chan. Scotland* U.K.
194 E2 **Alsheim** Ger.
285 H3 **Alsína** Arg.
122 J1 **Al'skiy Khrebet** *mt.* Rus. Fed.
193 E7 **Alsleben (Saale)** Ger.
199 I4 **Alsónémedi** Hungary
199 G4 **Alsóörs** Hungary
199 J3 **Alsóvadász** Hungary
199 J3 **Alsózsolca** Hungary
165 M5 **Alsterån** *r.* Sweden
165 L5 **Alstermo** Sweden
179 M5 **Alsting** France
171 M4 **Alston** *Cumbria, England* U.K.
105 N3 **Alstonville** *N.S.W.* Austr.
160 E5 **Alsunga** Latvia
160 J4 **Alsviķi** Latvia
162 Q2 **Alta** Norway
165 O2 **Älta** Sweden
103 C11 **Alta, Mount** *South I.* N.Z.
212 H1 **Altach** Austria
213 K2 **Altacroce, Monte** *mt.* Italy
264 N7 **Altadena** *CA* U.S.A.
162 Q2 **Altaelva** *r.* Norway
162 Q1 **Altafjorden** *sea chan.* Norway
277 F2 **Alta Floresta** Brazil
208 H5 **Altafulla** Spain
284 E2 **Alta Gracia** Arg.
266 □Q12 **Alta Gracia** Nic.
132 H2 **Altai Mountains** Asia
285 E4 **Alta Italia** Arg.
255 G10 **Altamaha** *r. GA* U.S.A.
274 E4 **Altamira** *Amazonas* Brazil
275 H5 **Altamira** *Pará* Brazil
282 C2 **Altamira** Chile
274 C4 **Altamira** Col.
266 □Q12 **Altamira** Costa Rica
269 J3 **Altamíra** Mex.
205 L2 **Altamira, Cuevas de** *tourist site* Spain
207 I1 **Altamira, Sierra de** *mts* Spain
285 H4 **Altamirano** Arg.
267 M9 **Altamirano** *Chiapas* Mex.
269 K6 **Altamirano** *Veracruz* Mex.
255 G11 **Altamonte Springs City** *FL* U.S.A.
208 K3 **Alt Ampordà** *reg.* Spain
215 R6 **Altamura** Italy
217 K1 **Alta Murgia, Parco Nazionale dell'** *nat. park* Italy
129 K2 **Altan** *Chitinskaya Oblast'* Rus. Fed.
129 L2 **Altan** *Chitinskaya Oblast'* Rus. Fed.
128 J3 **Altanbulag** Mongolia
129 O2 **Altan Emel** *Nei Mongol* China
214 A9 **Altano, Capo** *c. Sardegna* Italy
128 B4 **Altan Ovoo** *mt.* China/Mongolia
129 K7 **Altan Shiret** *Nei Mongol* China
Altan Xiret *Nei Mongol* China *see* **Altan Shiret**
278 D5 **Alta Paraiso de Goiás** Brazil
275 E2 **Altapirire** Venez.
266 D2 **Altar** Mex.
263 I11 **Altar** *r.* Mex.
266 B1 **Altar, Desierto de** *des.* Mex.
212 E7 **Altare** Italy
238 □[1a] **Altares** *Terceira* Azores
266 F5 **Altata** Mex.
201 I4 **Altaussee** Austria
201 I4 **Altausseer See** *l.* Austria

212 D7 **Alta Valle Pesio, Parco Naturale dell'** *nature res.* Italy
212 D4 **Alta Val Sesia, Parco Naturale** *nature res.* Italy
216 H2 **Altavilla Irpina** Italy
215 O6 **Altavilla Silentina** Italy
256 F11 **Altavista** *VA* U.S.A.
132 I3 **Altay** *Xinjiang* China
128 D4 **Altay** *Govĭ-Altay* Mongolia
128 E3 **Altay** Mongolia
128 C4 **Altay** Mongolia
128 A1 **Altay, Respublika** *aut. rep.* Rus. Fed.
Altay Kray *admin. div.* Rus. Fed. *see* **Altayskiy Kray**
143 U2 **Altayskiy** Rus. Fed.
Altayskiy Khrebet *mts* Asia *see* **Altai Mountains**
143 T2 **Altayskiy Kray** *admin. div.* Rus. Fed.
128 A1 **Altayskiy Zapovednik** *nature res.* Rus. Fed.
193 J7 **Altdöbern** Ger.
195 M4 **Altdorf** Ger.
212 F2 **Altdorf** Switz.
195 K3 **Altdorf bei Nürnberg** Ger.
190 I2 **Alt Duvenstedt** Ger.
206 C6 **Alte** Port.
209 E10 **Altea** Spain
192 D4 **Alte Elde** *r.* Ger.
192 H2 **Altefähr** Ger.
195 M4 **Alteglofsheim** Ger.
162 Q1 **Alteidet** Norway
191 E8 **Altena** Ger.
191 C9 **Altenahr** Ger.
191 J7 **Altenau** Ger.
191 G7 **Altenbeken** Ger.
193 I9 **Altenberg** Ger.
191 D6 **Altenberge** Ger.
190 G3 **Altenbruch-Westerende** Ger.
194 G2 **Altenbuch** Ger.
193 F9 **Altenburg** Ger.
191 E10 **Altendiez** Ger.
191 K9 **Altenfeld** Ger.
201 I3 **Altenfelden** Austria
194 C2 **Altenglan** Ger.
191 K8 **Altengottern** Ger.
192 E2 **Altenhagen** Ger.
194 D5 **Altenheim** Ger.
192 I5 **Altenhof** Ger.
190 J2 **Altenholz** Ger.
192 H1 **Altenkirchen** Ger.
191 E9 **Altenkirchen (Westerwald)** Ger.
190 K2 **Altenkrempe** Ger.
195 N5 **Altenmarkt an der Alz** Ger.
201 M3 **Altenmarkt an der Triesting** Austria
201 K4 **Altenmarkt bei Sankt Gallen** Austria
201 H5 **Altenmarkt im Pongau** Austria
190 K4 **Altenmedingen** Ger.
195 J5 **Altenmünster** Ger.
128 D8 **Altenqoke** *Qinghai* China
195 I5 **Altenstadt** *Bayern* Ger.
195 J6 **Altenstadt** *Bayern* Ger.
191 G10 **Altenstadt** *Hessen* Ger.
195 M2 **Altenstadt an der Waldnaab** Ger.
194 F4 **Altensteig** Ger.
192 H3 **Altentreptow** Ger.
193 E7 **Altenweddingen** Ger.
192 J5 **Alte Oder** *r.* Ger.
275 H5 **Alter do Chão** Brazil
206 D2 **Alter do Chão** Port.
206 D2 **Alter Pedroso** *hill* Port.
193 H6 **Altes Lager** Ger.
162 O2 **Altevatnet** *l.* Norway
195 M5 **Altfraunhofen** Ger.
195 K5 **Althegnenberg** Ger.
200 H3 **Altheim** Austria
194 G5 **Altheim** Ger.
195 I4 **Altheim (Alb)** Ger.
194 F4 **Althengstett** Ger.
201 J6 **Althofen** Austria
151 J5 **Altıağaç** Azer.
183 D8 **Altier** France
183 D8 **Altier** *r.* France
151 A6 **Altınbasak** Turkey
151 A5 **Altındere** *park* Turkey
157 F8 **Altınkaya Barajı** *resr* Turkey
149 L6 **Altin Köprü** Iraq
221 H3 **Altınoluk** Turkey
280 D4 **Altinópolis** Brazil
221 H3 **Altınova** *Balıkesir* Turkey
150 F1 **Altınova** *Şanlıurfa* Turkey
150 E2 **Altınözü** Turkey
221 L3 **Altıntaş** Turkey
221 L6 **Altınyaka** Turkey
276 C4 **Altiplano** *plain* Bol.
151 E6 **Altıyol** Turkey
182 K1 **Altkirch** France
193 F9 **Altkirchen** Ger.
192 D4 **Alt Krenzlin** Ger.
192 I5 **Altlandsberg** Ger.
195 L4 **Altmannstein** Ger.
192 D5 **Altmark** *reg.* Ger.
193 G9 **Altmittweida** Ger.
195 L4 **Altmühl** *r.* Ger.
195 K4 **Altmühltal** *park* Ger.
168 G9 **Altnafeadh** *Highland, Scotland* U.K.
168 H6 **Altnaharra** *Highland, Scotland* U.K.
250 I7 **Alto** *MI* U.S.A.
213 L5 **Alto, Monte** *hill* Italy
285 F3 **Alto Alegre** Arg.
280 A2 **Alto Araguaia** Brazil
270 F3 **Alto Cedro** Cuba
231 C7 **Alto Chicapa** Angola
205 P5 **Alto Cruz** *mt.* Spain
267 N10 **Alto Cuchumatanes** *mts* Guat.
269 H2 **Alto de Caballeros** Mex.
205 N3 **Alto de Cabezas** *mt.* Spain
204 F4 **Alto de Covelo** *pass* Spain
205 K3 **Alto de las Portillas** *pass* Spain
205 Q5 **Alto del Moncayo** *mt.* Spain
204 I3 **Alto del Rabizo** *pass* Spain
284 D3 **Alto de Pencoso** *hills* Arg.
207 M6 **Alto de San Juan** *mt.* Spain
204 F4 **Alto do Canizo** *pass* Spain
204 D8 **Alto do Trevim** *mt.* Port.
204 F5 **Alto Douro Wine Region** *reg.* Port.
216 E7 **Altofonte** *Sicilia* Italy
279 B6 **Alto Garças** Brazil
284 B3 **Alto Jahuel** Chile
235 H2 **Alto Ligonha** Moz.
269 K6 **Alto Lucero** Mex.
276 C3 **Alto Madidi, Parque Nacional** *nat. park* Bol.
205 O8 **Altomira, Sierra de** *mts* Spain
235 H2 **Alto Molócuè** Moz.
215 Q8 **Altomonte** Italy
195 K5 **Altomünster** Ger.
173 K5 **Alton** *Hampshire, England* U.K.
173 I2 **Alton** *Staffordshire, England* U.K.
260 J6 **Alton** *IL* U.S.A.
261 J7 **Alton** *MO* U.S.A.
257 □N5 **Alton** *NH* U.S.A.
246 F3 **Altona** B.C. Can.
247 L5 **Altona** *Man.* Can.
104 G2 **Alton Downs** *S.A.* Austr.
283 B7 **Alto Nevado** *mt.* Chile
256 G8 **Altoona** *PA* U.S.A.
250 C5 **Altoona** *WI* U.S.A.
275 I5 **Alto Pacajá** *r.* Brazil
278 D4 **Alto Parnaíba** Brazil
213 J8 **Altopascio** Italy
284 D3 **Alto Pelado** Arg.
284 D3 **Alto Pencoso** Arg.
280 A6 **Alto Piquiri** Brazil
276 C2 **Alto Purús** *r.* Peru
276 C2 **Alto Purús, Parque Nacional** *nat. park* Peru
204 E5 **Alto Rabagão, Barragem do** *resr* Port.
281 F4 **Alto Rio Doce** Brazil
283 C7 **Alto Río Senguerr** Arg.
280 A3 **Alto Rio Verde** Brazil
208 F4 **Altorricón** Spain
278 E3 **Altos** Brazil
205 O8 **Altos de Cabrejas** *mts* Spain
276 C4 **Altos de Chacaya** Chile
207 P3 **Altos de Chinchilla** *mts* Spain
285 F2 **Altos de Chipión** Arg.

280 A3 **Alto Sucuriú** Brazil
205 P7 **Alto Tajo, Parque Natural del** *nature res.* Spain
280 A2 **Alto Taquarí** Brazil
205 M3 **Altotero** *mt.* Spain
269 J6 **Altotonga** Mex.
195 N5 **Altötting** Ger.
279 B8 **Alto Uruguai** Brazil
271 □[9] **Alto Vista** *hill* Aruba
192 J5 **Altranft** Ger.
194 B2 **Altrich** Ger.
171 M7 **Altrincham** *Greater Manchester, England* U.K.
192 G5 **Alt Ruppin** Ger.
205 P3 **Altsasu** Spain
192 F3 **Alt Schwerin** Ger.
194 H6 **Altshausen** Ger.
212 H1 **Altstätten** Switz.
151 E2 **Altud** Rus. Fed.
161 R9 **Altukhovo** Rus. Fed.
151 B6 **Altunkent** Turkey
132 K7 **Altun Shan** *mt. Qinghai* China
133 H8 **Altun Shan** *mts* China
209 E8 **Altura** Spain
262 D6 **Alturas** *CA* U.S.A.
261 F8 **Altus** *OK* U.S.A.
195 I6 **Altusried** Ger.
191 J6 **Alt Wallmoden** Ger.
159 M2 **Altynivka** Ukr.
Altyn-Topkan Tajik. *see* **Oltintopkan**
160 H2 **Alu** Estonia
235 H2 **Alua** Moz.
230 F3 **Aluakluak** Sudan
147 J4 **Al 'Ubaylah** Saudi Arabia
148 I3 **Alucra** Turkey
147 I3 **Al 'Uḍaylīyah** Saudi Arabia
146 F9 **Al 'Udayn** Yemen
160 K4 **Alūksne** Latvia
160 K4 **Alūksnes** *l.* Latvia
146 C2 **Al 'Ulā** Saudi Arabia
146 G8 **Al'ulah** *reg.* Yemen
144 C5 **Alūm** Iran
256 E9 **Alum Bridge** *WV* U.S.A.
256 C8 **Alum Creek Lake** *OH* U.S.A.
284 B6 **Aluminé** Arg.
284 B6 **Aluminé** *r.* Arg.
284 B6 **Aluminé, Lago** *l.* Arg.
165 O1 **Alunda** Sweden
219 M4 **Aluniş** Romania
159 N9 **Alupka** Ukr.
224 C2 **Al 'Uqaylah** Libya
Al 'Uqaylah Saudi Arabia *see* **An Nabk**
147 J3 **Al 'Uqayr** Saudi Arabia
225 G3 **Al Uqşur** Egypt
136 E5 **Alur** *Andhra Prad.* India
148 I9 **Al 'Urayq** *des.* Saudi Arabia
Al 'Urdun *country* Asia *see* **Jordan**
Alur Setar Malaysia *see* **Alor Setar**
159 N9 **Alushta** Ukr.
205 Q7 **Alustante** Spain
144 A4 **'Ālūt** Iran
146 C1 **Al Uthaylī** Saudi Arabia
100 □[1] **Alutom, Mount** *hill* Guam
100 □[1] **Alutom Island** Guam
Aluva *Kerala* India *see* **Alwaye**
146 G4 **Al 'Uwayjā'** *well* Saudi Arabia
147 J4 **Al 'Uwayjā'** *well* Saudi Arabia
147 I2 **Al 'Uwaynah** *well* Saudi Arabia
224 E4 **Al 'Uwaynāt** *Al Kufrah* Libya
224 A3 **Al 'Uwaynāt** *Awbārī* Libya
146 C2 **Al 'Uwaynidhiyah** *i.* Saudi Arabia
149 K8 **Al 'Uwayqīlah** Saudi Arabia
146 H3 **Al 'Uyaynah** Saudi Arabia
150 E10 **Al 'Uyaynah** *well* Saudi Arabia
146 D3 **Al 'Uyūn** *Al Madīnah* Saudi Arabia
146 F2 **Al 'Uyūn** *Al Qaşīm* Saudi Arabia
146 F2 **Al 'Uẓaym** Saudi Arabia
149 M8 **Al 'Uzayr** Iraq
204 D8 **Alva** *r.* Port.
168 I10 **Alva** *Clackmannanshire, Scotland* U.K.
261 F7 **Alva** *OK* U.S.A.
204 D9 **Alvaiázere** Port.
206 C5 **Alvalade** Port.
151 I5 **Älvänd** Azer.
144 C4 **Alvand, Kūh-e** *mt.* Iran
212 H2 **Alvaneu** Switz.
204 E6 **Alvão, Parque Natural do** *nature res.* Port.
204 E6 **Alvão, Serra de** *mts* Spain
151 C6 **Alvar** Turkey
269 L7 **Alvarado** Mex.
261 G9 **Alvarado** *TX* U.S.A.
269 L7 **Alvarado, Laguna** *lag.* Mex.
275 E5 **Alvarães** Brazil
204 C5 **Alvarães** Port.
281 G3 **Alvarenga** Brazil
204 D7 **Alvarenga** Port.
204 D8 **Álvares** Port.
280 B5 **Álvares Machado** Brazil
285 G3 **Alvarez** Arg.
204 E9 **Álvaro** Port.
268 F6 **Álvaro Obregón** Mex.
269 I4 **Álvaro Obregón** Mex.
163 M6 **Älvdalen** Sweden
163 J1 **Älvdalen** *val.* Sweden
173 I3 **Alvechurch** *Worcestershire, England* U.K.
204 D2 **Alvedro** *airport* Spain
206 C2 **Alvega** Port.
172 H3 **Alveley** *Shropshire, England* U.K.
204 D9 **Alvelos, Serra de** *mts* Port.
206 A3 **Alverca** Port.
204 F7 **Alverca da Beira** Port.
187 C6 **Alveringem** Belgium
168 J7 **Alves** *Moray, Scotland* U.K.
190 I3 **Alveslohe** Ger.
165 K5 **Alvesta** Sweden
172 G4 **Alveston** *South Gloucestershire, England* U.K.
215 I2 **Alviano** Italy
168 I8 **Alvie** *Highland, Scotland* U.K.
185 H6 **Alvignac** France
164 C1 **Ålvik** Norway
163 N5 **Alvik** Sweden
261 H11 **Alvin** *TX* U.S.A.
250 F4 **Alvin** *WI* U.S.A.
281 F4 **Alvinópolis** Brazil
204 E7 **Alvite** Port.
215 L4 **Alvito** Italy
206 D4 **Alvito** Port.
206 D4 **Alvito, Barragem do** *resr* Port.
165 N1 **Älvkarleby** Sweden
215 P6 **Alvo** *r.* Italy
204 E8 **Alvoco da Serra** Port.
206 B6 **Alvor** Port.
162 P4 **Älvsbyn** Sweden
148 C10 **Al Wādī at Jadīd** *governorate* Egypt
147 N4 **Al Wāfī** Oman
149 M9 **Al Wafrah** Kuwait
146 C2 **Al Wajh** Saudi Arabia
147 J3 **Al Wakrah** Qatar
147 I2 **Al Wannān** Saudi Arabia
146 G1 **Al Waqbá** *well* Saudi Arabia
138 F6 **Alwar** *Rajasthan* India
147 H2 **Al Warī'ah** Saudi Arabia
147 N4 **Al Wāsiṭ** Oman
224 E2 **Al Wāṭiyah** *well* Egypt
224 A1 **Al Watīyah** Libya
136 E7 **Alwaye** *Kerala* India
172 E1 **Alwen Reservoir** *Wales* U.K.
197 H5 **Alwernia** Pol.
149 J7 **Al Widyān** *plat.* Iraq/Saudi Arabia
224 B3 **Al Wīgh** Libya
147 M4 **Al Wuqbah** Oman
147 J3 **Al Wusayl** Qatar
146 G1 **Al Wusayṭ** *well* Saudi Arabia
147 M5 **Al Wusṭá** *admin. reg.* Oman
Alxa Youqi *Nei Mongol* China *see* **Ehen Hudag**
Alxa Zuoqi *Nei Mongol* China *see* **Bayan Hot**
146 D4 **'Alyā** Saudi Arabia
147 H3 **Al Yamāmah** Saudi Arabia
106 F2 **Alyangula** *N.T.* Austr.
147 J3 **Al Yāsāt** *i.* U.A.E.
106 E6 **Alyawarra Aboriginal Land** *res.* N.T. Austr.
146 F6 **Āl Yazīd** Saudi Arabia
143 L2 **Alyp** Kazakh.

168 J9 Alyth Perth and Kinross, Scotland U.K.
160 H7 Alytus Lith.
195 N5 Alz r. Ger.
262 L4 Alzada MT U.S.A.
285 H5 Alzaga Arg.
212 H4 Alzano Lombardo Italy
191 H10 Alzenau in Unterfranken Ger.
187 J9 Alzette r. Lux.
194 E2 Alzey Ger.
209 E9 Alzira Spain
183 C9 Alzon France
185 I9 Alzonne France
237 L8 Amabele S. Africa
274 D5 Amacayacu, Parque Nacional nat. park Col.
269 H8 Amacuzac r. Mex.
163 M6 Åmådalen Sweden
106 C8 Amadeus, Lake salt flat N.T. Austr.
230 F3 Amadi Sudan
243 K3 Amadjuak Lake Nunavut Can.
265 U10 Amado AZ U.S.A.
206 A3 Amadora Port.
227 G4 Amadror plain Alg.
274 C3 Amaga Col.
127 I5 Amaga-dake mt. Japan
259 K3 Amagansett NY U.S.A.
126 B6 Amagasaki Japan
164 I6 Amager i. Denmark
125 H13 Amagi Japan
127 I6 Amagi-san vol. Japan
127 I6 Amagi-tōge pass Japan
127 I6 Amagiyugashima Japan
178 I4 Amagne France
126 D5 Amagoi-dake mt. Japan
115 F5 Amahai Seram Indon.
146 F5 Amā'ir Saudi Arabia
208 C1 Amaiur-Maia Spain
269 I4 Amajac r. Mex.
127 G2 Amakazari-yama mt. Japan
125 H14 Amakusa-Kami-shima i. Japan
125 G14 Amakusa-nada b. Japan
125 H14 Amakusa-Shimo-shima i. Japan
147 L6 Amal Oman
164 I2 Åmål Sweden
229 F3 Amalaoulaou well Mali
136 H4 Amalapuram Andhra Prad. India
121 K1 Amalat r. Rus. Fed.
215 N6 Amalfi Italy
237 J3 Amalia S. Africa
220 C5 Amaliada Greece
138 E9 Amalner Mahar. India
197 L1 Amalvas l. Lith.
113 I7 Amamapare Papua Indon.
277 G5 Amambaí Brazil
277 G5 Amambaí, Serra de hills Brazil/Para.
124 □G18 Amami-Ō-shima i. Nansei-shotō Japan
124 □F20 Amami-shotō is Japan
230 E5 Amamula Dem. Rep. Congo
163 M6 Amån r. Sweden
284 D2 Amaná Arg.
275 E5 Amanã, Lago l. Brazil
274 E5 Amana, Reserva de Desenvolvimento Sustentável nature res. Brazil
179 L8 Amance France
179 K8 Amance r. France
178 H7 Amance, Lac l. France
182 I2 Amancey France
256 C9 Amanda OH U.S.A.
215 K2 Amandola Italy
142 H3 Amangel'dy Aktyubinskaya Oblast' Kazakh.
142 K2 Amangel'dy Kostanayskaya Oblast' Kazakh.
142 K1 Amankaragay Kazakh.
Amankeldi Aktyubinskaya Oblast' Kazakh. see Amangel'dy
Amankeldi Kostanayskaya Oblast' Kazakh. see Amangel'dy
165 M2 Åmänningen l. Sweden
142 I4 Amanotkel' Kazakh.
Amanqaraghay Kazakh. see Amankaragay
215 Q9 Amantea Italy
235 E3 Amanzamnyama watercourse Zimbabwe
237 O6 Amanzimtoti S. Africa
276 C2 Amapá Acre Brazil
275 I4 Amapá Amapá Brazil
275 I4 Amapá state Brazil
269 K7 Amapa r. Mex.
266 □P11 Amapala Hond.
275 I4 Amapari r. Brazil
232 C2 Āmara admin. reg. Eth.
225 G6 Amara Abu Sin Sudan
219 L6 Amaradia r. Romania
'Amārah Iraq see Al 'Amārah
279 B9 Amaral Ferrador Brazil
278 E3 Amarante Brazil
204 D6 Amarante Port.
278 D3 Amarante do Maranhão Brazil
118 C4 Amarapura Myanmar
136 F7 Amaravati r. India
225 F4 Amara West Sudan
Amardalay Mongolia see Delgertsogt
204 D5 Amarela, Serra mts Port.
206 E4 Amareleja Port.
204 D5 Amares Port.
278 F5 Amargosa Brazil
263 F8 Amargosa watercourse CA U.S.A.
265 P5 Amargosa Desert NV U.S.A.
264 P5 Amargosa Range mts CA U.S.A.
265 P5 Amargosa Valley NV U.S.A.
207 M2 Amarguillo r. Spain
Amargura Island Tonga see Fonualei
261 E8 Amarillo TX U.S.A.
282 C4 Amarillo, Cerro mt. Arg.
138 H8 Amarkantak Chhattisgarh India
215 M3 Amaro, Monte mt. Italy
217 K6 Amaroni Italy
106 G7 Amaroo, Lake salt flat Qld Austr.
138 H8 Amarpur Madh. Prad. India
139 M8 Amarpur Tripura India
138 G8 Amarwara Madh. Prad. India
250 F3 Amasa MI U.S.A.
126 E1 Ama-saki pt Japan
215 K5 Amaseno Italy
215 K5 Amaseno r. Italy
151 E5 Amasia Armenia
Amasia Turkey see Amasya
226 B4 Amasine Western Sahara
148 F3 Amasra Turkey
229 F2 Amâssine well Mali
148 G3 Amasya Turkey
104 C2 Amata S.A. Austr.
275 G5 Amatari Brazil
274 D5 Amataurá Brazil
267 M9 Amatenango Mex.
268 G7 Amatepec Mex.
245 □C6 Amatignak Island AK U.S.A.
237 P5 Amatikulu S. Africa
266 □O10 Amatique, Bahía de b. Guat.
268 D5 Amatitán Mex.
269 K7 Amatlán Mex.
268 C5 Amatlán de Cañas Mex.
217 K6 Amato r. Italy
237 K8 Amatola Range mts S. Africa
215 K2 Amatrice Italy
127 L5 Amatsu-Kominato Japan
259 H2 Amawalk NY U.S.A.
187 H7 Amay Belgium
205 L3 Amaya mt. Spain
122 B2 Amazar Rus. Fed.
122 B2 Amazar r. Rus. Fed.
275 I4 Amazon r. S. America alt. Amazonas
275 I4 Amazon, Mouths of the Brazil
276 C3 Amazon, Source of the Peru
275 E6 Amazonas state Brazil
274 D5 Amazonas dept Col.
274 B6 Amazonas dept Peru
275 I4 Amazonas r. S. America conv. Amazon
275 E4 Amazonas state Venez.
288 F5 Amazon Cone sea feature S. Atlantic Ocean
275 G6 Amazónia, Parque Nacional nat. park Brazil
145 O4 Amb Pak.
232 C1 Āmba Ālagē mt. Eth.
136 D3 Ambad Mahar. India
232 C2 Amba Farit mt. Eth.
235 □I4 Ambahikily Madag.
136 E3 Ambajogai Mahar. India
138 F4 Ambala Haryana India
235 □J3 Ambalajanakomby Madag.
235 □J2 Ambalakida Madag.
235 □K2 Ambalakirajy Madag.
136 G9 Ambalangoda Sri Lanka
235 □J4 Ambalatany Madag.
235 □J4 Ambalavao Madag.
106 E7 Ambalindum N.T. Austr.
229 H6 Ambam Cameroon
235 □K2 Ambanja Madag.
144 H6 Ambar Iran
153 R3 Ambarchik Rus. Fed.
184 D6 Ambarès-et-Lagrave France
282 D3 Ambargasta, Salinas de salt pan Arg.
156 F2 Ambarnyy Rus. Fed.
205 J3 Ambasaguas Spain
136 E8 Ambasamudram Tamil Nadu India
139 M8 Ambassa Tripura India
107 J8 Ambathala Qld Austr.
274 B5 Ambato Ecuador
282 D3 Ambato, Sierra mts Arg.
235 □J3 Ambato Boeny Madag.
235 □J4 Ambato Finandrahana Madag.
235 □J4 Ambatolahy Madag.
235 □J3 Ambatolampy Madag.
235 □J3 Ambatomainty Madag.
235 □J3 Ambatomanoina Madag.
235 □K3 Ambatondrazaka Madag.
235 □K2 Ambatosia Madag.
235 □K3 Ambatosoratra Madag.
184 G4 Ambazac France
184 G4 Ambazac, Monts d' hills France
Ambejogai Mahar. India see Ambajogai
145 O4 Ambela Pak.
115 E5 Ambelau i. Maluku Indon.
Ambelón Greece see Ampelonas
Amber Rajasthan India see Amer
195 L3 Amberg Ger.
250 G4 Amberg WI U.S.A.
171 O7 Ambergate Derbyshire, England U.K.
267 P8 Ambergris Cay i. Belize
270 H3 Ambergris Cays is Turks and Caicos Is
182 G5 Ambérieu-en-Bugey France
251 M5 Amberley Ont. Can.
103 G10 Amberley South I. N.Z.
187 I8 Amberloup Belgium
182 D5 Ambert France
184 C5 Ambès France
138 H9 Ambgaon Mahar. India
185 I8 Ambialet France
Ambianum France see Amiens
228 C3 Ambidédi Mali
182 D4 Ambierle France
138 D9 Ambika r. India
139 I8 Ambikapur Chhattisgarh India
114 C5 Ambil i. Phil.
235 □J4 Ambila Madag.
181 L7 Ambillou France
235 □K2 Ambilobe Madag.
245 O4 Ambition, Mount B.C. Can.
178 D5 Amblainville France
171 N3 Amble Northumberland, England U.K.
172 H3 Amblecote West Midlands, England U.K.
244 H2 Ambler AK U.S.A.
258 E4 Ambler PA U.S.A.
244 H2 Ambler r. AK U.S.A.
171 L5 Ambleside Cumbria, England U.K.
178 C2 Ambleteuse France
187 I8 Amblève r. Belgium
187 I8 Amblève, Vallée de l' val. Belgium
139 K9 Ambo Orissa India
276 A2 Ambo Peru
235 □J5 Amboasary Madag.
235 □K3 Amboasary Gara Madag.
235 □K3 Amboavory Madag.
100 □3a Ambo Channel Kwajalein Marshall Is
235 □K3 Ambodifotatra Madag.
235 □K4 Ambodiharina Madag.
235 □K3 Ambodilazana Madag.
235 □J3 Ambohidratrimo Madag.
235 □K3 Ambohijanahary Madag.
235 □J4 Ambohimahasoa Madag.
235 □I4 Ambohimahavelona Madag.
235 □J3 Ambohipaky Madag.
235 □K2 Ambohitra mt. Madag.
235 □K2 Ambohitralanana Madag.
Amboina Maluku Indon. see Ambon
184 F1 Amboise France
231 B7 Amboiva Angola
180 F6 Ambon France
115 F5 Ambon Maluku Indon.
115 E5 Ambon i. Maluku Indon.
235 □J5 Ambondro Madag.
178 H5 Ambonnay France
276 D4 Amboró, Parque Nacional nat. park Bol.
233 C5 Amboseli National Park Kenya
235 □J4 Ambositra Madag.
235 □J5 Ambovombe Madag.
Ambow i. Fiji see Bau
265 Q7 Amboy CA U.S.A.
250 E8 Amboy IL U.S.A.
181 O8 Ambrault France
Ambre, Cap d' c. Madag. see Bobaomby, Tanjona
239 □1b Ambre, Île d' i. Mauritius
181 J5 Ambrières-les-Vallées France
Ambrim i. Vanuatu see Ambrym
231 B6 Ambriz Angola
231 B6 Ambriz, Coutada do nature res. Angola
Ambrizete Angola see N'zeto
151 E3 Ambrolauri Georgia
182 G4 Ambronay France
173 J4 Ambrosden Oxfordshire, England U.K.
285 G2 Ambrosetti Arg.
274 D5 Ambrosio Brazil
100 □5 Ambrym i. Vanuatu
117 J9 Ambulu Jawa Indon.
117 J8 Ambunten Jawa Indon.
136 F6 Ambur Tamil Nadu India
107 L9 Amby Qld Austr.
245 □B6 Amchitka Island AK U.S.A.
245 □C5 Amchitka Pass sea channel AK U.S.A.
164 E2 Åmdals Verk Norway
224 D6 Am-Dam Chad
227 F5 Amded, Oued watercourse Alg.
152 H3 Amderma Rus. Fed.
229 E2 Amdillis well Mali
224 C6 Am Djéména Chad
133 J10 Amdo Xizang China
268 G5 Amealco Mex.
268 C5 Ameca Jalisco Mex.
268 D3 Ameca Zacatecas Mex.
268 B5 Ameca r. Mex.
269 I6 Amecameca Mex.
232 C2 Amedamit mt. Eth.
285 F4 Ameghino Arg.
212 H7 Ameglia Italy
201 I2 Ameisberg hill Austria
206 D6 Ameixial Port.
187 J8 Amel Belgium
186 I2 Ameland i. Neth.
215 I2 Amelia Italy
256 H11 Amelia Court House VA U.S.A.
185 J11 Amélie-les-Bains-Palalda France
190 J4 Amelinghausen Ger.
138 H6 Amellu Uttar Prad. India
204 D9 Amêndoa Port.
206 D5 Amendoeira Port.
217 L4 Amendolara Italy
217 J8 Amendolea r. Italy
257 L7 Amenia NY U.S.A.
225 F5 Amentego Sudan
133 B13 Amer Rajasthan India
208 K3 Amer Spain
227 H4 Amer, Erg d' des. Alg.
209 L8 Amer, Punta pt Spain
195 M6 Amerang Ger.
204 E4 A Merca Spain
264 K3 American, North Fork r. CA U.S.A.
280 D5 Americana Brazil
288 H9 American-Antarctic Ridge sea feature S. Atlantic Ocean
262 H5 American Falls ID U.S.A.
262 H5 American Falls Reservoir ID U.S.A.
265 U1 American Fork UT U.S.A.
100 □2 American Samoa terr. S. Pacific Ocean
255 E9 Americus GA U.S.A.
201 K5 Ameringkogel mt. Austria
186 H5 Amerongen Neth.
186 H4 Amersfoort Neth.
237 N3 Amersfoort S. Africa
173 K4 Amersham Buckinghamshire, England U.K.
247 M3 Amery Man. Can.
287 E2 Amery Ice Shelf Antarctica
260 I4 Ames IA U.S.A.
173 I5 Amesbury Wiltshire, England U.K.
257 O6 Amesbury MA U.S.A.
138 D7 Amet Rajasthan India
138 H6 Amethi Uttar Prad. India
208 A1 Amezketa Spain
204 F4 A Mezquita Spain
220 C4 Amfilochia Greece
220 D4 Amfissa Greece
181 M3 Amfreville-la-Campagne France
153 O3 Amga Rus. Fed.
129 P2 Amgalang Nei Mongol China
122 J6 Amgu Rus. Fed.
153 T3 Amguema Rus. Fed.
227 G4 Amguid Alg.
121 O1 Amgun' r. Rus. Fed.
249 H4 Amherst N.S. Can.
257 M6 Amherst MA U.S.A.
256 C7 Amherst OH U.S.A.
256 F11 Amherst VA U.S.A.
108 I5 Amherst, Mount hill W.A. Austr.
251 K7 Amherstburg Ont. Can.
256 D11 Amherstdale WV U.S.A.
251 R5 Amherst Island Ont. Can.
251 R5 Amherstview Ont. Can.
127 L3 Ami Japan
206 B2 Amiais de Baixo Port.
214 H2 Amiata, Monte mt. Italy
Amida Turkey see Diyarbakır
260 D2 Amidon ND U.S.A.
206 D4 Amieira Port.
204 E9 Amieira do Tejo Port.
178 D4 Amiens France
149 J7 'Amīj, Wādī watercourse Iraq
148 H5 Amik Ovası marsh Turkey
147 K6 Amilḥayt, Ramlat des. Oman
147 K6 Amilḥayt, Wādī al r. Oman
178 E8 Amilly France
144 E6 Amīnābād Iran
Amíndhaion Greece see Amyntaio
Amindivi atoll India see Amini
136 C7 Amindivi Islands Lakshadweep India
136 C7 Amini atoll India
232 D3 Amino Eth.
126 B4 Amino Japan
234 C4 Aminuis Namibia
150 D4 Amioun Lebanon
138 G5 Amipshahr Uttar Prad. India
145 L4 Amīr, Band-e lakes Afgh.
144 D5 Amīrābād Eşfahān Iran
144 B5 Amīrābād Īlām Iran
Amirabad Iran see Fūlād Maīalleh
239 □2 Amirante Islands Seychelles
289 H5 Amirante Trench sea feature Indian Ocean
145 J7 Amir Chah Pak.
247 K4 Amisk Lake Sask. Can.
Amistad, Represa de resr Mex./U.S.A. see Amistad Reservoir
267 I3 Amistad Reservoir Mex./U.S.A.
Amisus Turkey see Samsun
261 J10 Amite LA U.S.A.
261 J10 Amite Creek r. MS U.S.A.
107 N9 Amity Point Qld Austr.
138 E8 Amjhera Madh. Prad. India
138 G9 Amla Madh. Prad. India
146 F6 Amlaḥ, Jabal al hill Saudi Arabia
229 F5 Amlamé Togo
144 D3 Amlash Iran
139 J6 Amlekhganj Nepal
164 E3 Åmli Norway
245 □D5 Amlia Island AK U.S.A.
172 D1 Amlwch Isle of Anglesey, Wales U.K.
225 H5 'Amm Adam Sudan
150 D7 'Ammān Jordan
144 F2 Ammanazar Turkm.
172 E4 Ammanford Carmarthenshire, Wales U.K.
156 E2 Ämmänsaari Fin.
146 G8 'Ammār reg. Yemen
150 E6 'Ammār, Tall hill Syria
162 N4 Ammarnäs Sweden
106 E6 Ammaroo N.T. Austr.
104 D2 Ammaroodinna watercourse S.A. Austr.
243 O3 Ammassalik Greenland
195 K6 Ammer r. Ger.
162 N5 Ammerån r. Sweden
194 F4 Ammerbuch Ger.
200 C5 Ammergauer Alpen mts Austria/Ger.
195 J6 Ammergebirge nature res. Ger.
190 E4 Ammerland reg. Ger.
191 J8 Ammern Ger.
190 J3 Ammersbek Ger.
179 N7 Ammerschwihr France
195 K6 Ammersee l. Ger.
220 C2 Ammochori Greece
150 B3 Ammochostos Cyprus
150 C3 Ammochostos Bay Cyprus
146 F9 Am Nābiyah Yemen
Amne Machin Range mts China see A'nyêmaqên Shan
179 L5 Amnéville France
Amnok-kang r. China/N. Korea see Yalu Jiang
138 D9 Amod Gujarat India
204 E4 Amoeiro Spain
130 D7 Amo Jiang r. Yunnan China
144 E3 Āmol Iran
277 F4 Amolar Brazil
159 N2 Amon' Rus. Fed.
204 C5 Amonde Port.
191 G9 Amöneburg Ger.
278 F2 Amontada Brazil
205 L9 Amor mt. Spain
194 G2 Amorbach Ger.
205 O2 Amorebieta País Vasco Spain
282 F3 Amores r. Arg.
221 G6 Amorgos i. Greece
280 B2 Amorinópolis Brazil
261 K8 Amory MS U.S.A.
248 E3 Amos Que. Can.
164 H6 Åmose r. Denmark
164 F2 Åmot Buskerud Norway
164 D2 Åmot Telemark Norway
163 N6 Åmot Sweden
Amota i. Vanuatu see Mota
274 A6 Amotape, Cerros de mts Peru
164 I2 Åmotfors Sweden
185 C8 Amou France
220 E2 Amouliani i. Greece
227 F2 Amour, Djebel mts Alg.
228 D2 Amourj Maur.
Amoy Fujian China see Xiamen
269 I6 Amozoc Mex.
117 K5 Ampah Kalimantan Indon.
115 B4 Ampana Sulawesi Indon.
235 □K2 Ampanefena Madag.
137 H3 Ampani Orissa India
235 □J5 Ampanihy Madag.
235 □K3 Ampanotoamaizina Madag.
235 □J2 Amparafaka, Tanjona pt Madag.
235 □K3 Amparafaravola Madag.
136 G9 Amparai Sri Lanka
280 D5 Amparo Brazil
235 □K3 Ampasimanolotra Madag.
235 □K3 Ampasimbe Madag.
200 D5 Ampass Austria
220 D3 Ampelonas Greece
117 L9 Ampenan Lombok Indon.
195 L5 Amper r. Ger.
229 H4 Amper Nigeria
288 I3 Ampere Seamount sea feature N. Atlantic Ocean
213 N3 Ampezzo Italy
195 M5 Ampfing Ger.
195 P5 Ampflwang im Hausruckwald Austria
112 D3 Amphitrite Group is Paracel Is
115 B4 Ampibaku Sulawesi Indon.
235 □K2 Ampisikinana Madag.
Ampitsikinana Madag. see Ampisikinana
182 E5 Amplepuis France
115 B4 Ampoa Sulawesi Indon.
173 I5 Amport Hampshire, England U.K.
208 G6 Amposta Spain
173 L3 Ampthill Bedfordshire, England U.K.
205 K5 Ampudia Spain
205 N2 Ampuero Spain
183 I9 Ampus France
128 H9 Amqog Gansu China
249 H3 Amqui Que. Can.
146 F3 'Amrah, Jabal hill Saudi Arabia
146 F8 'Amrān Yemen
146 F7 'Amrān governorate Yemen
Amraoti Mahar. India see Amravati
138 F9 Amravati Mahar. India
138 C9 Amreli Gujarat India
145 M8 Amri Pak.
139 N7 Amring Assam India
212 G1 Amriswil Switz.
138 E4 Amritsar Punjab India
138 G5 Amroha Uttar Prad. India
190 F1 Amrum i. Ger.
227 G5 Amsel Alg.
162 O4 Åmsele Sweden
186 G3 Amstelmeer l. Neth.
186 G4 Amstelveen Neth.
186 G4 Amsterdam Neth.
237 O2 Amsterdam S. Africa
257 K6 Amsterdam NY U.S.A.
256 E8 Amsterdam OH U.S.A.
289 J7 Amsterdam, Île i. Indian Ocean
186 H5 Amsterdam-Rijnkanaal canal Neth.
186 F4 Amsterdamse Waterleidingduinen nature res. Neth.
201 K3 Amstetten Austria
194 H4 Amstetten Ger.
259 K1 Amston CT U.S.A.
230 D2 Am Timan Chad
151 C2 Amtqeli Georgia
194 H6 Amtzell Ger.
274 C4 Amú r. Col.
133 I10 Amu Co l. Xizang China
142 H5 Amudar'ya r. Asia
Amudaryo r. Asia see Amudar'ya
244 E5 Amukta Island AK U.S.A.
244 D5 Amukta Pass sea channel AK U.S.A.
243 I2 Amund Ringnes Island Nunavut Can.
287 G2 Amundsen, Mount Antarctica
291 K10 Amundsen Abyssal Plain sea feature Southern Ocean
292 B1 Amundsen Basin sea feature Arctic Ocean
287 D2 Amundsen Bay Antarctica
286 O1 Amundsen Coast Antarctica
286 N1 Amundsen Glacier Antarctica
242 F2 Amundsen Gulf N.W.T. Can.
291 K10 Amundsen Ridges sea feature Southern Ocean
287 A1 Amundsen-Scott research stn Antarctica
286 Q2 Amundsen Sea Antarctica
117 K6 Amuntai Kalimantan Indon.
Amur China see Jingtao
122 I4 Amur r. Rus. Fed. alt. Heilong Jiang (China)
225 G5 'Amur, Wadi watercourse Sudan
115 D3 Amurang Sulawesi Indon.
Amur Oblast admin. div. Rus. Fed. see Amurskaya Oblast'
205 O2 Amurrio Spain
122 J3 Amursk Rus. Fed.
122 F2 Amurskaya Oblast' admin. div. Rus. Fed.
159 N8 Amurs'ke Ukr.
142 H1 Amurskiy Rus. Fed.
122 L2 Amurskiy Liman str. Rus. Fed.
122 G5 Amurzet Rus. Fed.
217 K7 Amusa r. Italy
205 L4 Amusco Spain
122 C1 Amutkachi Rus. Fed.
220 C4 Amvrakia, Limni l. Greece
220 B4 Amvrakikos Kolpos b. Greece
159 R6 Amvrosiyivka Ukr.
Amyderya r. Asia see Amudar'ya
220 C2 Amyntaio Greece
250 J1 Amyot Ont. Can.
219 Q7 Amzacea Romania
229 F2 Amzérakad well Mali
224 D6 Am-Zoer Chad
118 B5 An Myanmar
221 I1 Ana r. Turkey
101 □9 Anaa atoll Arch. des Tuamotu Fr. Polynesia
144 G4 Anābad Iran
115 B5 Anabanua Sulawesi Indon.
153 M2 Anabar r. Rus. Fed.
105 H6 Ana Branch r. N.S.W. Austr.
150 D6 Anabtā West Bank
264 M7 Anacapa Island CA U.S.A.
215 M6 Anacapri Italy
275 E2 Anaco Venez.
262 H3 Anaconda MT U.S.A.
262 C2 Anacortes WA U.S.A.
114 C3 Anacuao, Mount Phil.
261 F8 Anadarko OK U.S.A.
204 D8 Anadia Port.
221 J4 Anadolu reg. Turkey
148 H3 Anadolu Dağları mts Turkey
153 S3 Anadyr' Rus. Fed.
153 S3 Anadyr' r. Rus. Fed.
Anadyr, Gulf of Rus. Fed. see Anadyrskiy Zaliv
244 B2 Anadyrskiy Liman b. Rus. Fed.
153 T3 Anadyrskiy Zaliv b. Rus. Fed.
221 G6 Anafi Greece
221 G6 Anafi i. Greece
238 □3a Anaga, Punta de pt Tenerife Canary Is
169 F2 Anagaire Ireland
278 E5 Anagé Brazil
215 K4 Anagni Italy
Anagnia Italy see Anagni
149 J6 'Ānah Iraq
264 O8 Anaheim CA U.S.A.
246 E4 Anahim Lake B.C. Can.
264 □B11 Anahola HI U.S.A.
267 I4 Anáhuac Nuevo León Mex.
269 J3 Anáhuac Veracruz Mex.
261 H11 Anahuac TX U.S.A.
264 □C12 'Anahulu r. HI U.S.A.
136 E7 Anaimalai Hills India
136 E7 Anai Mudi Kerala India
169 C6 An Aird Mhóir Ireland
Anaiteum i. Vanuatu see Anatom
275 I5 Anajás Brazil
275 I5 Anajás, Ilha i. Brazil
278 D2 Anajatuba Brazil
235 □I4 Anakao Madag.
137 H4 Anakapalle Andhra Prad. India
107 K7 Anakie Qld Austr.
245 J1 Anaktuvuk r. AK U.S.A.
245 J1 Anaktuvuk Pass AK U.S.A.
235 □J2 Analalava Madag.
235 □K3 Analamaitso mts Madag.
280 D5 Analândia Brazil
235 □I4 Analavelona mts Madag.
258 E2 Analomink PA U.S.A.
275 F5 Anamã Brazil
270 D3 Ana María, Golfo de b. Cuba
116 F3 Anambas, Kepulauan is Indon.
229 G5 Anambra state Nigeria
126 E1 Anamizu Japan
Anamooka i. Tonga see Nomuka
260 J4 Anamosa IA U.S.A.
275 G4 Anamu r. Brazil
148 F5 Anamur Turkey
127 G5 Anan Nagano Japan
126 A8 Anan Tokushima Japan
205 O3 Añana-Gesaltza Spain
138 D8 Anand Gujarat India
139 K9 Anandapur Orissa India
138 F4 Anandpur Punjab India
139 K8 Anandpur r. W. Bengal India
220 F6 Ananes i. Greece
143 Q6 Anan'ev Kyrg.
104 C2 Anangu Pitjantjatjara Aboriginal Lands res. S.A. Austr.
115 D6 Anano i. Indon.
136 E5 Anantapur Andhra Prad. India
138 E3 Anantnag Jammu and Kashmir India
138 G6 Anant Peth Madh. Prad. India
Ananyev Ukr. see Anan'yiv
Anan'yevo Kyrg. see Anan'ev
158 I6 Anan'yiv Ukr.
157 G7 Anapa Rus. Fed.
217 I9 Anapo r. Sicilia Italy
220 G8 Anapodiaris r. Kriti Greece
280 C2 Anápolis Brazil
275 I5 Anapú r. Brazil
Anár Fin. see Inari
144 F6 Anār Iran
144 E5 Anārak Iran
144 D4 Anarbar r. Iran
199 L3 Anarcs Hungary
145 I5 Anardara Afgh.
287 L2 Anare Mountains Antarctica
104 □3 Anare Station S. Pacific Ocean
169 B8 Anascaul Ireland
271 □1 Añasco Puerto Rico
271 □1 Añasco, Río Grande de r. Puerto Rico
162 P4 Ånäset Sweden
159 R6 Anastasiyevka Rus. Fed.
159 Q8 Anastasiyevskaya Rus. Fed.
113 K3 Anatahan i. N. Mariana Is
Anatajan i. N. Mariana Is see Anatahan
Anatolia reg. Turkey see Anadolu
220 G1 Anatoliki Makedonia kai Thraki admin. reg. Greece
100 □5 Anatom i. Vanuatu
282 E3 Añatuya Arg.
106 F7 Anatye Aboriginal Land res. N.T. Austr.
275 F4 Anauá r. Brazil
280 A5 Anaurilândia Brazil
275 F5 Anavilhanas, Arquipélago das is Brazil
205 J7 Anaya de Alba Spain
Anaypazari Turkey see Gülnar
150 E10 Anaz mts Saudi Arabia
169 B9 An Baile Breac Kerry Ireland
144 C2 'Anbarān Iran
128 E6 Anbei Gansu China
Anbu Guangdong China see Chao'an
144 C3 Anbūh Iran
169 F2 An Bun Beag Ireland
144 F8 Anbūr-e Kālārī Iran
123 E9 Anbyon N. Korea
204 C8 Ançã Port.
204 F3 Ancares, Serra dos mts Spain
169 E6 An Carn Mór Ireland
276 A2 Ancash dept Peru
251 O6 Ancaster Ont. Can.
173 K2 Ancaster Lincolnshire, England U.K.
282 D3 Ancasti, Sierra mts Arg.
183 D7 Ance r. France
183 I7 Ancelle France
180 I7 Ancenis France
179 J6 Ancerville France
283 D6 Anchán Arg.
130 E3 Anchang Sichuan China
169 E3 An Charraig Donegal Ireland
229 H4 Anchau Nigeria
169 C6 An Cheathru Rua Ireland
281 G4 Anchieta Brazil
276 C3 Anchodaya Bol.
245 J3 Anchorage AK U.S.A.
Anchorage Island atoll Cook Is see Suwarrow
107 M1 Anchorage Reefs P.N.G.
251 L7 Anchor Bay MI U.S.A.
284 E4 Anchorena Arg.
244 J4 Anchor Point AK U.S.A.
238 □2c Anchorstock Point Tristan da Cunha S. Atlantic Ocean
270 □ Anchovy Jamaica
136 E8 Anchuthengu Kerala India
Anci Hebei China see Langfang
197 L1 Ančia l. Lith.
160 F6 Ančia r. Lith.
205 P3 Ancín Spain
270 D3 Anclitas, Cayo i. Cuba
169 G3 An Clochán Donegal Ireland
169 B8 An Clochán Kerry Ireland
169 F3 An Clochán Liath Ireland
An Cóbh Ireland see Cobh
169 G3 An Coimín Ireland
285 G4 Ancón Arg.
276 A2 Ancón Peru
213 P8 Ancona Italy
213 N9 Ancona prov. Italy
178 D4 Ancre r. France
168 K11 Ancrum Scottish Borders, Scotland U.K.
233 C8 Ancuabe Moz.
235 G3 Ancuaze Moz.
283 B6 Ancud Chile
283 B6 Ancud, Golfo de g. Chile
178 H8 Ancy-le-Franc France
Ancyra Turkey see Ankara
122 D5 Anda Heilong. China
Anda Heilong. China see Daqing
115 D1 Anda i. Indon.
163 I6 Anda Norway
284 B5 Andacollo Arg.
284 B2 Andacollo Chile
106 E8 Andado N.T. Austr.
276 B3 Andahuaylas Peru
169 B8 An Daingean Ireland
235 □K3 Andaingo Gara Madag.
139 K8 Andal W. Bengal India
Andalaly Rus. Fed. see Nozhay-Yurt
282 D2 Andalgalá Arg.
213 K3 Andalo Italy
162 I5 Åndalsnes Norway
207 K5 Andalucía aut. comm. Spain
Andalusia S. Africa see Jan Kempdorp
Andalusia aut. comm. Spain see Andalucía
255 D10 Andalusia AL U.S.A.
147 N5 Andām, Wādī r. Oman
119 A9 Andaman and Nicobar Islands union terr. India
289 K4 Andaman Basin sea feature Indian Ocean
137 M6 Andaman Islands Andaman & Nicobar Is India
119 B9 Andaman Sea Indian Ocean
137 M6 Andaman Strait Andaman & Nicobar Is India
104 F4 Andamooka S.A. Austr.
183 F6 Andance France
235 □K2 Andapa Madag.
234 D3 Andara Namibia
145 M4 Andarāb Afgh.
207 N7 Andarax r. Spain
145 N3 Andarob Tajik.
201 P4 Andau Austria
204 I5 Andavías Spain
130 F7 Ande Guangxi China
146 E8 Andeba Ye Midir Zerf Chaf pt Eritrea
195 K6 Andechs Ger.
212 G2 Andeer Switz.
156 K2 Andeg Rus. Fed.
Andegavum France see Angers
212 F1 Andelfingen Switz.
178 B5 Andelle r. France
179 J7 Andelot-Blancheville France
182 H3 Andelot-en-Montagne France
200 A5 Andelsbuch Austria
186 I5 Andelst Neth.
162 N2 Andenes Norway
187 H8 Andenne Belgium
229 F3 Andéramboukane Mali
162 N2 Ånderdalen Nasjonalpark nat. park Norway
187 F7 Anderlecht Belgium
187 F8 Anderlues Belgium
212 F2 Andermatt Switz.
191 D10 Andernach Ger.
185 B6 Andernos-les-Bains France
Anderob Tajik. see Andarob
165 N1 Andersbo Sweden
100 □1 Andersen Airforce Base Guam
285 G4 Anderson Arg.
245 O1 Anderson r. N.W.T. Can.
245 J2 Anderson AK U.S.A.
264 J1 Anderson CA U.S.A.
254 E5 Anderson IN U.S.A.
261 H7 Anderson MO U.S.A.
255 F8 Anderson SC U.S.A.
105 K9 Anderson Bay Tas. Austr.
264 K4 Anderson Reservoir CA U.S.A.
256 B9 Andersonville OH U.S.A.
191 E5 Andervenne Ger.
274 C3 Andes Col.
276 B3 Andes mts S. America
206 E5 Andévalo, Sierra de hills Spain
162 N2 Andfjorden sea chan. Norway
Andhíparos i. Greece see Antiparos
136 C3 Andhra Lake India
136 F4 Andhra Pradesh state India
151 H3 Andi Rus. Fed.
205 Q3 Andía, Sierra de mts Spain
186 H3 Andijk Neth.
143 O7 Andijon Andijon Uzbek.
143 O7 Andijon admin. div. Uzbek.
Andijon Wiloyati admin. div. Uzbek. see Andijon
Andikíra Greece see Antikyra
Andikithira i. Greece see Antikythira
235 □K3 Andilamena Madag.
235 □K3 Andilanatoby Madag.
179 K8 Andilly-en-Bassigny France
144 C5 Andīmeshk Iran
Andímilos i. Greece see Antimilos
131 I4 Anding Hunan China
Andípaxoi i. Greece see Antipaxoi
Andípsara i. Greece see Antipsara
280 B5 Andirá Brazil
133 F8 Andir He r. China
148 H5 Andırın Turkey
133 F8 Andirlangar Xinjiang China
151 H3 Andiyskoye Koysu r. Rus. Fed.
136 E7 Andiyur Tamil Nadu India
Andizhan Andijon Uzbek. see Andijon
Andizhan Oblast admin. div. Uzbek. see Andijon
145 K3 Andkhui r. Afgh.
145 K3 Andkhvoy Afgh.
179 N7 Andlau France
179 O6 Andlau r. France
208 A1 Andoain Spain
235 □K2 Andoany Madag.
274 B5 Andoas Peru
274 B5 Andoas Nuevo Ecuador
199 G5 Andocs Hungary
161 U2 Andoga r. Rus. Fed.
161 U2 Andogskaya Gryada hills Rus. Fed.
235 □J5 Andohahela, Parc National d' nature res. Madag.
235 □K2 Andohajango Madag.
230 A4 Andok Foula Gabon
136 F4 Andol Andhra Prad. India
136 E4 Andola Karnataka India
179 N7 Andolsheim France
Andong Liaoning China see Dandong
129 P9 Andong Shandong China
123 F10 Andong S. Korea
107 H2 Andoom Qld Austr.
201 I3 Andorf Austria
199 J4 Andornaktálya Hungary
212 E4 Andorno Micca Italy
208 I2 Andorra country Europe
208 E6 Andorra Spain
208 I2 Andorra, Valls d' val. Andorra
208 I2 Andorra la Vella Andorra
Andorra la Vieja Andorra see Andorra la Vella
205 Q4 Andosilla Spain
181 J5 Andouillé France
199 H4 Andovce Slovakia
173 J5 Andover Hampshire, England U.K.
259 K1 Andover CT U.S.A.
257 N6 Andover MA U.S.A.
257 N5 Andover NH U.S.A.
258 F3 Andover NJ U.S.A.
256 H6 Andover NY U.S.A.
256 E7 Andover OH U.S.A.
162 M2 Andøya i. Norway
161 U2 Andozero, Ozero l. Rus. Fed.
183 E6 Andrable r. France
280 D5 Andradas Brazil
265 R9 Andrade CA U.S.A.
280 B4 Andradina Brazil
Andraitx Spain see Andratx
235 □J3 Andramasina Madag.
235 □J3 Andramy Madag.
217 O4 Andrano Italy
235 □J3 Andranomavo Madag.
235 □K3 Andranomena Madag.
235 □I4 Andranopasy Madag.
235 □K2 Andranovondronina Madag.
235 □J4 Andranovory Madag.
209 J8 Andratx Spain
244 G3 Andreafsky r. AK U.S.A.
244 G3 Andreafsky, East Fork r. AK U.S.A.
245 □C6 Andreanof Islands AK U.S.A.
161 P5 Andreapol' Rus. Fed.
170 I5 Andreas Isle of Man
162 □ Andrée Land reg. Svalbard
230 D2 André Félix, Parc National d' nat. park C.A.R.
281 G1 André Fernandes Brazil
281 E4 Andrelândia Brazil
281 E3 Andrequicé Brazil
285 I3 Andresito Uru.
197 H4 Andrespol Pol.
185 E9 Andrest France
247 H4 Andrew Alta Can.
118 B5 Andrew Bay Myanmar
255 H9 Andrews SC U.S.A.
261 D9 Andrews TX U.S.A.
142 D1 Andreyevka Rus. Fed.
Andreyevskoye Rus. Fed. see Dneprovskoye
159 M1 Andreykovichi Rus. Fed.
161 R6 Andreykovo Rus. Fed.
182 E5 Andrézieux-Bouthéon France
215 Q5 Andria Italy
235 □J3 Andriamena Madag.
235 □J3 Andriba Madag.
199 L4 Andrid Romania
236 I9 Andrieskraal S. Africa
236 E2 Andriesvale S. Africa
218 H8 Andrijevica Andrijevica Montenegro
235 □J4 Andringitra mts Madag.
159 P7 Andrivka Ukr.
158 G3 Andriyevychi Ukr.
159 P6 Andriyivka Dnipropetrovs'ka Oblast' Ukr.
159 Q6 Andriyivka Donets'ka Oblast' Ukr.
159 P4 Andriyivka Kharkivs'ka Oblast' Ukr.
159 M9 Andriyivka Respublika Krym Ukr.
159 M3 Andriyivka Sums'ka Oblast' Ukr.
159 P6 Andriyivka Zaporiz'ka Oblast' Ukr.
235 □J5 Androka Madag.
235 □K2 Androna reg. Madag.
161 W4 Androniki Rus. Fed.
Andropov Rus. Fed. see Rybinsk
270 D1 Andros i. Bahamas
220 F5 Andros Andros Greece
220 F5 Andros i. Greece
257 P5 Androscoggin r. ME/NH U.S.A.
142 C1 Androsovka Rus. Fed.
270 E1 Andros Town Andros Ba
136 C7 Androtti i. India
Andrushevka Ukr. see Andrushivka
158 I3 Andrushivka Ukr.
158 I4 Andrushky Ukr.
197 H6 Andrychów Pol.
197 K3 Andrzejewo Pol.
162 O2 Andselv Norway
162 P1 Andsnes Norway
230 F4 Andudu Dem. Rep. Cor
144 G6 Andūhjerd Iran
207 K4 Andújar Spain
231 C7 Andulo Angola
169 C5 An Dumhach Bheag Ir
183 D8 Anduze France
151 E1 Andzhiyevskiy Rus. Fed
109 J7 Anec, Lake salt flat W.A.
283 C6 Anecón Grande mt. Arg
Āneen-Kio N. Pacific O Wake Island
229 F2 Anéfis Mali
228 E2 Anéfis well Mali
271 K4 Anegada i. Virgin Is (U.
283 E6 Anegada, Bahía b. Arg.
271 L4 Anegada Passage Virgi
265 T9 Anegam AZ U.S.A.
229 F5 Aného Togo
Aneityum i. Vanuatu se
'Aneiza, Jabal hill Iraq s 'Unayzah, Jabal
100 □3b Aneju i. Majuro Marsha
136 E6 Anekal Karnataka India
100 □5 Anelghowhat Vanuatu
284 C6 Añelo Arg.
150 A2 Anemourion tourist site
100 □3b Anemwanot i. Majuro M
158 I7 Anenii Noi Moldova
227 G6 Anesbaraka well Alg.
178 B6 Anet France
Anetchom, Île i. Vanua Anatom
208 G2 Aneto mt. Spain
Ānewetak atoll Marsha Enewetak
229 I2 Aney Niger
Aneytioum, Île i. Vanua Anatom
169 F2 An Fál Carrach Ireland
169 B4 An Fál Mór Ireland
225 I6 Anfile Bay Eritrea
200 B8 Anfo Italy
131 J5 Anfu Jiangxi China
136 E7 Angadippuram Kerala
235 □J2 Angadoka, Lohatanjon Madag.
105 I8 Angahook Lorne State nature res. Vic. Austr.
106 C3 Angalarri r. N.T. Austr.
224 C5 Angamma, Falaise d' e
283 B8 Angamos, Isla i. Chile
276 C5 Angamos, Punta pt Ch
268 G6 Angangueo Mex.
129 R3 Ang'angxi Heilong. Chi
120 H1 Angara r. Rus. Fed.
229 F4 Angaradébou Benin
106 E7 Angarapa Aboriginal L N.T. Austr.
120 H1 Angarsk Rus. Fed.
106 D8 Angas Downs N.T. Aus
108 J7 Angas Range hills W.A.
104 G6 Angaston S.A. Austr.
114 C4 Angat Luzon Phil.
Angatau atoll Arch. des Fr. Polynesia see Fanga
280 C5 Angatuba Brazil
114 □ Angaur i. Palau
163 M5 Ånge Sweden
169 B4 An Geata Mór Ireland
204 C7 Angeja Port.
275 F3 Angel, Salto waterfall V
266 C3 Ángel de la Guarda, Is
114 C4 Angeles Luzon Phil.
Angel Falls Venez. see Angel, Salto
164 I5 Ängelholm Sweden
162 R2 Angeli Fin.
285 G2 Angelica Arg.
261 H10 Angelina r. TX U.S.A.
107 K9 Angellala Creek r. Qld
190 I1 Angeln reg. Ger.
109 D7 Angelo r. W.A. Austr.
269 L7 Angel R. Cabada Mex.
264 L3 Angels Camp CA U.S.A
165 J5 Angelstad Sweden
182 E1 Angely France
195 N6 Anger Ger.
232 C1 Āngereb Eth.
232 C1 Āngereb Wenz r. Eth.
162 N5 Ångermanälven r. Swe
192 J4 Angermünde Ger.
193 E6 Angern Ger.
201 O3 Angern an der March
181 J7 Angers France
178 D7 Angerville France
183 K9 Anges, Baie des b. Fran
117 L5 Anggana Kalimantan I
213 M8 Anghiari Italy
278 D4 Angical Brazil
278 F3 Angicos Brazil
247 L2 Angikuni Lake Nunavu
264 M6 Angiola CA U.S.A.
220 E2 Angistis r. Greece
119 F8 Angkor tourist site Cam
184 C5 Anglade France
184 I5 Anglards-de-Salers Fr
172 B4 Angle Pembrokeshire, W
103 B13 Anglem, Mount hill Stewart I. N.Z.
246 G5 Anglemont B.C. Can.
185 J8 Anglès France
208 K4 Anglès Spain
172 D1 Anglesey i. Wales U.K.
208 H4 Anglesona Spain
181 M8 Angles-sur-l'Anglin Fr
185 A9 Anglet France
261 H11 Angleton TX U.S.A.
251 O2 Angliers Que. Can.
181 L8 Angliers France
184 F2 Anglin r. France
Anglo-Egyptian Sudan Africa see Sudan
214 B6 Anglona reg. Sardegna
178 G6 Anglure France
Angmagssalik Greenla Ammassalik
116 □ Ang Mo Kio Sing.
230 E3 Ango Dem. Rep. Cong
235 H3 Angoche Moz.
144 G8 Angohrān Iran
169 G8 An Goirtín Waterford Ir
184 G5 Angoisse France
284 A5 Angol Chile
231 C7 Angola country Africa
254 E5 Angola IN U.S.A.
256 F6 Angola NY U.S.A.
288 I7 Angola Basin sea featu S. Atlantic Ocean
235 G2 Angonia, Planalto de
245 N4 Angoon AK U.S.A.
Angora Turkey see Ank
268 G3 Angostura San Luis Po
266 E5 Angostura Sinaloa Me
184 E4 Angoulême France
184 B3 Angoulins France
184 D4 Angoumois reg. France
238 □1a Angra do Heroísmo T Azores
281 E5 Angra dos Reis Brazil
143 N7 Angren Uzbek.
215 N6 Angri Italy
136 C4 Angria's Bank sea featu
181 J6 Angrie France
165 M2 Ängsö naturreservat n Sweden
119 E7 Ang Thong Thai.
119 D10 Ang Thong Marine Na Park Thai.
230 E4 Angu Dem. Rep. Cong
284 C2 Angualasto Arg.
129 R4 Anguang Jilin China
208 E3 Angüés Spain
205 O4 Anguiano Spain
285 F5 Anguil Arg.

Anguilla terr. West Indies
Anguilla Cays is Bahamas
Anguillara Sabazia Italy
Anguillara Veneta Italy
Anguille, Cape Nfld and Lab. Can.
Anguita Spain
Angul Orissa India
Anguli Nur l. China
Anguo Hebei China
Angurugu N.T. Austr.
Angus Ont. Can.
Angus admin. div. Scotland U.K.
Angustura Brazil
Angutikada Peak AK U.S.A.
Angwin CA U.S.A.
Anhanguera Brazil
Anhée Belgium
Anholt i. Denmark
Anhua Hunan China
Anhui prov. China
Anhumas Brazil
Anhwei prov. China see **Anhui**
Ani Japan
Ani tourist site Turkey
Ania r. Italy
Aniak AK U.S.A.
Aniak r. AK U.S.A.
Aniakchak Crater AK U.S.A.
Aniakchak National Monument and Preserve nat. park AK U.S.A.
Aniane Franc
Aniche France
Anicuns Brazil
Ánidhros i. Greece see **Anydros**
Anié Togo
Anie, Pic d' mt. France
Aniene r. Italy
Anif Austria
Ani-jima i. Ogasawara-shotō Japan
Anikhovka Rus. Fed.
Anikovo Rus. Fed.
Animaki-san hill Japan
Animas r. CO U.S.A.
Anin Myanmar
Anina Romania
Anini Arun. Prad. India
Aniñón Spain
Anishino Rus. Fed.
Añisoc Equat. Guinea
Anitaguipan Point Samar Phil.
Anitápolis Brazil
Anıtkaya Turkey
Anıtlı Turkey
Aniva Sakhalin Rus. Fed.
Aniva, Mys c. Sakhalin Rus. Fed.
Aniva, Zaliv b. Sakhalin Rus. Fed.
Anivorano Madag.
Anivorano Avaratra Madag.
Aniwa WI U.S.A.
Aniwa i. Vanuatu
Anizy-le-Château France
Anjad Madh. Prad. India
Anjadip i. India
Anjafy mt. Madag.
Anjalankoski Fin.
Anjangaon Mahar. India
Anjar Gujarat India
Anjengo India see **Anchuthengu**
Anji Zhejiang China
Anji Mahar. India
Anjiang Hunan China see **Qianyang**
Anjihai Xinjiang China
Anjir Avand Iran
Anjō Japan
Anjoman Iran
Anjou reg. France
Anjou, Val d' val. France
Anjouan i. Comoros see **Nzwani**
Anjozorobe Madag.
Anjŭ N. Korea
Anjum Neth.
Anjuman reg. Afgh.
Anka Nigeria
Ankaboa, Tanjona pt Madag.
Ankang Shaanxi China
Ankara Turkey
Ankara prov. Turkey
Ankaran Slovenia
Ankaratra mts Madag.
Ankarsrum Sweden
Ankarsund Sweden
Ankasa National Park Western Ghana
Ankatafa Madag.
Ankavandra Madag.
Ankazoabo Madag.
Ankazobe Madag.
Ankazomiriotra Madag.
Ankeny IA U.S.A.
Ankerika Madag.
Ankershagen Ger.
An Khê Vietnam
Ankiliabo Madag.
Anklam Ger.
Ankleshwar Gujarat India
Anklesvar Gujarat India see **Ankleshwar**
Ankofa mt. Madag.
Ankogel mt. Austria
Ankola Karnataka India
Ankouzhen Gansu China
An'kovo Rus. Fed.
Ankpa Nigeria
Ankum Ger.
Anlaby East Riding of Yorkshire, England U.K.
Anlauter r. Ger.
Anlezy France
Anlier, Forêt d' for. Belgium
Anling Henan China see **Yanling**
An Lôc Vietnam
Anloga Ghana
Anlong Guizhou China
Ânlong Vêng Cambodia
Anlu Hubei China
An Machaire Ireland
An Mám Ireland
Anmoore WV U.S.A.
An Muileann gCearr Ireland see **Mullingar**
Anmyŏn-do i. S. Korea
Ann, Cape Antarctica
Ann, Cape MA U.S.A.
Anna Rus. Fed.
Anna Spain
Anna OH U.S.A.
Anna, Lake VA U.S.A.
Anna, Pulo i. Palau
Annaba Alg.
Annaba prov. Alg.
Annaberg Austria
Annaberg-Buchholtz Ger.
An Nabhānīyah Saudi Arabia
An Nabk Saudi Arabia
An Nabk Syria
Annaburg Ger.
Annacotty Ireland
An Nafūd des. Saudi Arabia
Annagry Ireland see **Anagaire**
Annahütte Ger.
Annai Guyana
An Najaf Iraq
An Najaf governorate Iraq
Annaka Japan
Annalee r. Ireland
Annalong Northern Ireland U.K.
Annam reg. Vietnam
Annam Highlands mts Laos/Vietnam
Annamoe Ireland
Annan Dumfries and Galloway, Scotland U.K.
Annan r. Scotland U.K.
'Annān, Wādī al watercourse Syria
Annanba Gansu China
Annandale val. Scotland U.K.
Annandale NJ U.S.A.
Annandale VA U.S.A.
Anna Paulowna Neth.
Anna Plains W.A. Austr.
Annapolis MD U.S.A.
249 H4 **Annapolis Royal** N.S. Can.
139 J5 **Annapurna Conservation Area** nature res. Nepal
139 I5 **Annapurna I** mt. Nepal
147 I2 **An Naqīrah** well Saudi Arabia
251 K7 **Ann Arbor** MI U.S.A.
275 G3 **Anna Regina** Guyana
193 D7 **Annarode** Ger.
An Nás Ireland see **Naas**
149 M8 **An Nāşirīyah** Iraq
237 J4 **Annaspan** imp. l. S. Africa
224 C2 **An Nawfalīyah** Libya
169 I4 **Annayalla** Ireland
168 G12 **Annbank** South Ayrshire, Scotland U.K.
215 Q9 **Annea** r. Italy
109 E9 **Annean, Lake** salt flat W.A. Austr.
258 B7 **Anne Arundel County** county MD U.S.A.
Anne Arundel Town MD U.S.A. see **Annapolis**
182 I5 **Annecy** France
182 I5 **Annecy, Lac d'** l. France
182 I5 **Annecy-le-Vieux** France
Annel Fin. see **Angeli**
249 I2 **Anne Marie Lake** Nfld and Lab. Can.
182 I4 **Annemasse** France
186 K2 **Annen** Neth.
184 F5 **Annesse-et-Beaulieu** France
172 □ **Annet** i. England U.K.
245 O5 **Annette Island** AK U.S.A.
183 F6 **Anneyron** France
171 N4 **Annfield Plain** Durham, England U.K.
170 H2 **Annick** r. Scotland U.K.
107 I3 **Annie** r. Qld Austr.
160 J2 **Annikvere** Estonia
150 F6 **An Nimārah** Syria
146 F6 **An Nimāş** Saudi Arabia
130 D6 **Anning** Yunnan China
130 C5 **Anning He** r. Sichuan China
161 X9 **Annino** Lipetskaya Oblast' Rus. Fed.
161 U2 **Annino** Vologodskaya Oblast' Rus. Fed.
255 E9 **Anniston** AL U.S.A.
229 G7 **Annobón** i. Equat. Guinea
178 E2 **Annœullin** France
183 F6 **Annonay** France
212 G4 **Annone, Lago di** l. Italy
183 J9 **Annot** France
270 □ **Annotto Bay** Jamaica
170 F5 **Annsborough** Northern Ireland U.K.
147 I2 **An Nu'ayrīyah** Saudi Arabia
149 L7 **An Nu'mānīyah** Iraq
147 J3 **An Nuqay'ah** Qatar
256 B11 **Annville** KY U.S.A.
258 B4 **Annville** PA U.S.A.
194 D3 **Annweiler am Trifels** Ger.
126 D6 **Anō** Japan
100 □6 **Anoano** Malaita Solomon Is
208 A1 **Anoeta** Spain
220 F7 **Anogeia** Kriti Greece
250 A4 **Anoka** MN U.S.A.
220 E3 **Ano Lechonia** Greece
205 Q5 **Añón** Spain
Anonima atoll Micronesia see **Namonuito**
161 X6 **Anopino** Rus. Fed.
178 H4 **Anor** France
207 J4 **Añora** Spain
275 F5 **Anori** Brazil
233 F8 **Anorontany, Tanjona** hd Madag.
235 □K3 **Anosibe An'Ala** Madag.
227 G5 **Anou I-n-Atei** well Alg.
179 M7 **Anould** France
229 F2 **Ânou Mellene** well Mali
227 G6 **Anou-n-Bidek** well Alg.
205 M9 **Añover de Tajo** Spain
Anóyia Kriti Greece see **Anogeia**
131 I5 **Anping** Hunan China
130 H8 **Anpu** Guangdong China
130 G8 **Anpu Gang** b. China
131 K3 **Anqing** Anhui China
129 P8 **Anqiu** Shandong China
205 P7 **Anquela del Ducado** Spain
200 G6 **Anras** Austria
An Ráth Ireland see **Charleville**
131 I5 **Anren** Hunan China
169 G8 **An Rinn** Ireland
191 F7 **Anröchte** Ger.
An Rubha pen. Scotland U.K. see **Eye Peninsula**
187 I7 **Ans** Belgium
164 F5 **Ans** Denmark
184 F4 **Ansac-sur-Vienne** France
129 K8 **Ansai** Shaanxi China
195 J3 **Ansbach** Ger.
182 F5 **Anse** France
270 G4 **Anse-à-Galets** Haiti
239 □2b **Anse à la Mouche** Mahé Seychelles
270 H4 **Anse-à-Pitre** Haiti
270 G4 **Anse-à-Veau** Haiti
225 H5 **Ānseba** prov. Eritrea
146 C7 **Anseba Shet** watercourse Eritrea
271 □2 **Anse-Bertrand** Guadeloupe
239 □2b **Anse Boileau** Mahé Seychelles
270 F4 **Anse d'Hainault** Haiti
214 G3 **Ansedonia** Italy
271 □3 **Anse-la-Raye** St Lucia
187 G8 **Anseremme** Belgium
105 K8 **Anser Group** is Tas. Austr.
274 C3 **Anserma** Col.
239 □2b **Anse Royal** Mahé Seychelles
201 J3 **Ansfelden** Austria
168 I9 **An Sgarsoch** mt. Scotland U.K.
129 R6 **Anshan** Liaoning China
130 E5 **Anshun** Guizhou China
130 D4 **Anshunchang** Sichuan China
204 D9 **Ansião** Port.
213 M3 **Ansiei** r. Italy
284 C2 **Ansilta** mt. Arg.
284 C2 **Ansilta, Cordillera de** mts Arg.
282 G3 **Ansina** Uru.
162 N5 **Ansjö** Sweden
260 F5 **Ansley** NE U.S.A.
208 D2 **Ansó** Spain
208 D2 **Ansó, Valle de** val. Spain
261 F9 **Anson** TX U.S.A.
106 C2 **Anson Bay** N.T. Austr.
104 □1 **Anson Bay** Norfolk I.
229 F3 **Ansongo** Mali
229 F3 **Ansongo-Ménaka, Réserve Partielle de Faune d'** nature res. Mali
259 I2 **Ansonia** CT U.S.A.
256 A8 **Ansonia** OH U.S.A.
248 D3 **Ansonville** Ont. Can.
169 D6 **An Spidéal** Ireland
193 H9 **Ansprung** Ger.
256 D10 **Ansted** WV U.S.A.
168 K10 **Anstruther** Fife, Scotland U.K.
Ansu Hebei China see **Xushui**
173 P2 **Ant** r. England U.K.
138 F7 **Anta** Rajasthan India
276 B3 **Anta** Peru
276 B3 **Antabamba** Peru
148 H5 **Antakya** Turkey
235 □K2 **Antalaha** Madag.
221 L6 **Antalya** Turkey
221 L5 **Antalya** prov. Turkey
221 L6 **Antalya Körfezi** g. Turkey
235 □K3 **Antanambao Manampotsy** Madag.
235 □K3 **Antanambe** Madag.
235 □J3 **Antananarivo** Madag.
235 □J3 **Antananarivo** prov. Madag.
235 □J3 **Antanifotsy** Madag.
235 □J5 **Antanimora Atsimo** Madag.
An tAonach Ireland see **Nenagh**
286 **Antarctica**
286 T2 **Antarctic Peninsula** Antarctica
235 □J5 **Antaritarika** Madag.
204 F7 **Antas** Port.
207 P6 **Antas** Spain
207 P6 **Antas** r. Spain
204 E3 **Antas de Ulla** Spain
169 C6 **An Teach Dóite** Ireland
168 F7 **An Teallach** mt. Scotland U.K.
169 G2 **An Tearmann** Ireland
285 G3 **Antelo** Arg.
265 P2 **Antelope Range** mts NV U.S.A.
164 I3 **Anten** l. Sweden
184 D4 **Antenne** r. France
207 J6 **Antequera** Spain
200 F6 **Anterselva di Sopra** Italy
258 A2 **Antes Fort** PA U.S.A.
183 J10 **Anthéor** France
200 H4 **Anthering** Austria
182 D2 **Anthien** France
261 F7 **Anthony** KS U.S.A.
263 K10 **Anthony** NM U.S.A.
104 D3 **Anthony, Lake** salt flat S.A. Austr.
106 E4 **Anthony Lagoon** N.T. Austr.
226 C3 **Anti Atlas** mts Morocco
183 K9 **Antibes** France
183 K9 **Antibes, Cap d'** c. France
249 I3 **Anticosti, Île d'** i. Que. Can.
Anticosti Island Que. Can. see **Anticosti, Île d'**
181 L2 **Antifer, Cap d'** c. France
250 E4 **Antigo** WI U.S.A.
249 I4 **Antigonish** N.S. Can.
271 □2 **Antigua** i. Antigua and Barbuda
238 □3b **Antigua** Fuerteventura Canary Is
Antigua Guat. see **Antigua Guatemala**
Antigua country West Indies see **Antigua and Barbuda**
271 □2 **Antigua and Barbuda** country West Indies
267 N10 **Antigua Guatemala** Guat.
271 □2 **Antigues, Pointe d'** pt Guadeloupe
269 H3 **Antiguo-Morelos** Mex.
220 D4 **Antikyra** Greece
220 E7 **Antikythira** i. Greece
220 E7 **Antikythiro, Steno** sea chan. Greece
Anti Lebanon mts Lebanon/Syria see **Sharqī, Jabal ash**
282 D2 **Antilla** Arg.
270 F3 **Antilla** Cuba
217 I8 **Antillo** Sicilia Italy
220 F6 **Antimilos** i. Greece
265 U3 **Antimony** UT U.S.A.
An tInbhear Mór Ireland see **Arklow**
264 K3 **Antioch** CA U.S.A.
250 F7 **Antioch** IL U.S.A.
150 A2 **Antiocheia ad Cragum** tourist site Turkey
Antiochia Turkey see **Antakya**
274 C3 **Antioquia** Col.
274 C3 **Antioquia** dept Col.
220 G5 **Antiparos** i. Greece
220 B3 **Antipaxoi** i. Greece
161 Q6 **Antipino** Rus. Fed.
99 H6 **Antipodes Islands** N.Z.
221 G4 **Antipsara** i. Greece
214 C3 **Antisanti** Corse France
221 I6 **Antitilos** i. Greece
Antium Italy see **Anzio**
261 H8 **Antlers** OK U.S.A.
An t-Òb Western Isles, Scotland U.K. see **Leverburgh**
276 C5 **Antofagasta** Chile
276 C5 **Antofagasta** admin. reg. Chile
282 D2 **Antofagasta de la Sierra** Arg.
187 D7 **Antoing** Belgium
199 H3 **Antol** Slovakia
212 G6 **Antola, Monte** mt. Italy
235 □J2 **Antonhibe** Madag.
280 C6 **Antonina** Brazil
168 I11 **Antonine Wall** tourist site Scotland U.K.
158 F4 **Antoniny** Ukr.
217 L5 **Antonio** r. Italy
268 C1 **Antonio Amaro** Mex.
281 F4 **Antônio Carlos** Brazil
283 D7 **Antonio de Biedma** Arg.
281 F3 **Antônio Dias** Brazil
António Enes Moz. see **Angoche**
275 I5 **Antônio Lemos** Brazil
158 I4 **Antoniv** Ukr.
159 L3 **Antonivka** Chernihivs'ka Oblast' Ukr.
159 L7 **Antonivka** Khersons'ka Oblast' Ukr.
199 L3 **Antonivka** Zakarpats'ka Oblast' Ukr.
159 O6 **Antonivka** Zaporiz'ka Oblast' Ukr.
269 L6 **Antón Lizardo** Mex.
184 F5 **Antonne-et-Trigonant** France
270 C2 **Antón Recio** Cuba
178 D6 **Antony** France
158 D1 **Antopal'** Belarus
183 E7 **Antraigues-sur-Volane** France
180 I5 **Antrain** France
159 S5 **Antratsyt** Ukr.
169 D5 **An Trian** Ireland
169 J3 **Antrim** Northern Ireland U.K.
169 J3 **Antrim** county Northern Ireland U.K.
258 A1 **Antrim** PA U.S.A.
169 J2 **Antrim Hills** Northern Ireland U.K.
108 J5 **Antrim Plateau** W.A. Austr.
215 K3 **Antrodoco** Italy
156 H4 **Antropovo** Rus. Fed.
235 □K2 **Antsahabe** Madag.
235 □K2 **Antsahanoro** Madag.
235 □K2 **Antsakabary** Madag.
235 □J3 **Antsalova** Madag.
235 □K2 **Antsambalahy** Madag.
Antseranana Madag. see **Antsirañana**
161 Q3 **Antsiferovo** Rus. Fed.
235 □J3 **Antsirabe** Madag.
235 □K2 **Antsirabe Avaratra** Madag.
235 □K2 **Antsirañana** Madag.
235 □K2 **Antsirañana** prov. Madag.
160 J4 **Antsla** Estonia
235 □J2 **Antsohihy** Madag.
235 □K2 **Antsohimbondrona** Madag.
235 □J3 **Antsondrodava** Madag.
162 Q3 **Anttis** Sweden
163 S6 **Anttola** Fin.
Antu Jilin China see **Songjiang**
An Tuc Vietnam see **An Khê**
284 B5 **Antuco** Chile
284 B5 **Antuco, Volcán** vol. Chile
146 F8 **Antufash, Jazīrat** i. Yemen
Antufush Island Yemen see **Antufash, Jazīrat**
182 E3 **Antully** France
Antunnacum Ger. see **Andernach**
Antwerp Belgium see **Antwerpen**
257 J4 **Antwerp** NY U.S.A.
187 F6 **Antwerpen** Belgium
187 G6 **Antwerpen** prov. Belgium
208 A1 **Antzuola** Spain
An Uaimh Ireland see **Navan**
248 F1 **Anuc, Lac** l. Que. Can.
122 H7 **Anuchino** Rus. Fed.
283 C6 **Anueque, Sierra** mts Arg.
123 E11 **Anŭi** S. Korea
138 D5 **Anupgarh** Rajasthan India
138 H8 **Anuppur** Madh. Prad. India
136 G8 **Anuradhapura** Sri Lanka
106 E6 **Anurrete Aboriginal Land** res. N.T. Austr.
144 F8 **Anveh** Iran
Anvers Belgium see **Antwerpen**
286 T2 **Anvers Island** Antarctica
244 G3 **Anvik** AK U.S.A.
244 G3 **Anvik** r. AK U.S.A.
245 □B5 **Anvil Peak** vol. AK U.S.A.
245 N3 **Anvil Range** mts Y.T. Can.
178 D3 **Anvin** France
131 L6 **Anxi** Fujian China
128 D6 **Anxi** Gansu China
Anxian Sichuan China see **Anchang**
130 E3 **Anxian** Sichuan China
131 I4 **Anxiang** Hunan China
129 N7 **Anxin** Hebei China
104 E5 **Anxious Bay** S.A. Austr.
Anxur Italy see **Terracina**
228 D5 **Anyama** Côte d'Ivoire
Anyang Guangxi China see **Du'an**
129 N8 **Anyang** Henan China
123 E10 **Anyang** S. Korea
116 F8 **Anyar** Jawa Indon.
221 G6 **Anydros** i. Greece
128 F9 **A'nyêmaqên Shan** mts China
131 J4 **Anyi** Jiangxi China
160 I6 **Anykščiai** Lith.
237 O3 **Anysspruit** S. Africa
131 I5 **Anyuan** Jiangxi China
131 J6 **Anyuan** Jiangxi China
156 L3 **An'yudin** Rus. Fed.
130 E3 **Anyue** Sichuan China
122 J4 **Anyuy** r. Rus. Fed.
153 R3 **Anyuysk** Rus. Fed.
212 E3 **Anza** r. Italy
247 I3 **Anzac** Alta Can.
246 F4 **Anzac** B.C. Can.
208 D3 **Anzánigo** Spain
215 O5 **Anzano di Puglia** Italy
183 C6 **Anzat-le-Luguet** France
129 M8 **Anze** Shanxi China
187 D7 **Anzegem** Belgium
227 F4 **Anzeglouf** Alg.
195 L2 **Anzelberg** hill Ger.
182 K4 **Anzère** Switz.
152 J4 **Anzhero-Sudzhensk** Rus. Fed.
230 D5 **Anzi** Dem. Rep. Congo
215 P6 **Anzi** Italy
178 F3 **Anzin** France
198 A3 **Anzing** Ger.
215 J5 **Anzio** Italy
285 F6 **Anzoátegui** Arg.
275 E2 **Anzoátegui** state Venez.
285 F6 **Anzoátegui, Salinas Grandes de** salt pan Arg.
207 J6 **Anzur** r. Spain
127 K4 **Aoba** Japan
100 □5 **Aoba** i. Vanuatu
126 B4 **Aoba-yama** hill Japan
224 C5 **Aodanga** well Chad
126 B5 **Aogaki** Japan
125 Q14 **Aoga-shima** i. Japan
Aohan Qi Nei Mongol China see **Xinhui**
205 R3 **Aoiz** Spain
119 D10 **Ao Kham, Laem** pt Thai.
127 H3 **Aoki** Japan
100 □6 **Aola** Guadalcanal Solomon Is
Aomen Macau China see **Macao**
124 R6 **Aomori** Japan
124 S6 **Aomori** pref. Japan
168 F8 **Aonach Buidhe** hill Scotland U.K.
133 E10 **A'ong Co** l. Xizang China
220 B2 **Aoos** r. Greece
119 D10 **Ao Phang Nga National Park** Thai.
168 D11 **Aoradh** Argyll and Bute, Scotland U.K.
101 □9a **Aorai** mt. Tahiti Fr. Polynesia
103 E10 **Aoraki** South I. N.Z.
103 E10 **Aoraki** mt. South I. N.Z.
103 E10 **Aoraki/Mount Cook National Park** South I. N.Z.
119 G8 **Aôral, Phnum** mt. Cambodia
Aorangi mt. South I. N.Z. see **Aoraki**
103 J8 **Aorangi Mountains** North I. N.Z.
103 G7 **Aorere** r. South I. N.Z.
205 R3 **Aós** Spain
126 A8 **Ao-shima** i. Japan
212 C4 **Aosta** Italy
182 H5 **Aoste** France
102 I5 **Aotea Harbour** North I. N.Z.
Aotearoa country Oceania see **New Zealand**
229 H2 **Aouderas** Niger
226 B4 **Aoufist** Western Sahara
226 D4 **Aouhinet bel Egra** well Alg.
230 C2 **Aouk, Bahr** r. C.A.R./Chad
230 D2 **Aoukalé** r. C.A.R./Chad
230 D2 **Aouk-Aoakole, Réserve de Faune de l'** nature res. C.A.R.
226 D5 **Aoukâr** reg. Mali/Maur.
229 F2 **Aoukenek** well Mali
227 F4 **Aoulef** Alg.
226 C3 **Aoulime, Jbel** mt. Morocco
228 C3 **Aourou** Mali
183 G7 **Aouste-sur-Sye** France
Aoxi Jiangxi China see **Le'an**
125 L11 **Aoya** Japan
126 D6 **Aoyama** Japan
Aoyang Jiangxi China see **Shanggao**
224 C4 **Aozou** Chad
277 F5 **Apa** r. Brazil
219 L3 **Apa** Romania
232 B4 **Apac** Uganda
201 M6 **Apače** Slovenia
265 W10 **Apache** AZ U.S.A.
261 F8 **Apache** OK U.S.A.
265 U8 **Apache, Lake** AZ U.S.A.
265 U8 **Apache Junction** AZ U.S.A.
265 V10 **Apache Peak** AZ U.S.A.
276 D5 **Apagado, Volcán** vol. Bol.
199 K4 **Apagy** Hungary
219 L4 **Apahida** Romania
280 C5 **Apaiaí** r. Brazil
Apaiang atoll Kiribati see **Abaiang**
199 I4 **Apaj** Hungary
255 E11 **Apalachee Bay** FL U.S.A.
255 E11 **Apalachicola** FL U.S.A.
255 E11 **Apalachicola** r. FL U.S.A.
255 E11 **Apalachicola Bay** FL U.S.A.
228 E5 **Apam** Ghana
Apamama atoll Gilbert Is Kiribati see **Abemama**
Apamea Turkey see **Dinar**
269 I6 **Apan** Mex.
179 L8 **Apance** r. France
269 H8 **Apango** Mex.
274 D5 **Apaporis** r. Col.
117 L6 **Apar, Teluk** b. Indon.
151 F5 **Aparan** Armenia
281 E5 **Aparecida** Brazil
280 C2 **Aparecida de Goiânia** Brazil
280 B3 **Aparecida do Rio Doce** Brazil
280 B4 **Aparecida do Tabuado** Brazil
199 H5 **Aparhant** Hungary
285 G6 **Aparico** Arg.
Aparima South I. N.Z. see **Riverton**
103 C13 **Aparima** r. South I. N.Z.
114 C2 **Aparri** Luzon Phil.
275 F3 **Aparurén** Venez.
283 D6 **Apas, Sierra** hills Arg.
160 H5 **Apaščia** r. Lith.
268 G5 **Apaseo El Grande** Mex.
101 □9 **Apataki** atoll Arch. des Tuamotu Fr. Polynesia
199 K5 **Apateu** Romania
199 J5 **Apátfalva** Hungary
218 G5 **Apatin** Vojvodina Serbia
156 F2 **Apatity** Rus. Fed.
275 H3 **Apatou** Fr. Guiana
201 O7 **Apatovac** Croatia
268 E6 **Apatzingán** Mex.
244 E3 **Apavawook Cape** AK U.S.A.
269 H7 **Apaxtla** Mex.
160 J4 **Ape** Latvia
213 M8 **Apecchio** Italy
277 E2 **Apediá** r. Brazil
204 D4 **A Pedreira** Spain
186 I4 **Apeldoorn** Neth.
191 H6 **Apelern** Ger.
190 E4 **Apen** Ger.
192 D5 **Apenburg** Ger.
190 I4 **Apensen** Ger.
276 D3 **Apere** r. Bol.
204 E4 **A Peroxa** Spain
245 M3 **Apex Mountain** Y.T. Can.
244 F3 **Aphrewn** r. AK U.S.A.
230 E4 **Api** Dem. Rep. Congo
138 H4 **Api** mt. Nepal
Api i. Vanuatu see **Epi**
115 B4 **Api, Tanjung** pt Indon.
274 C3 **Apia** Col.
Apia atoll Kiribati see **Abaiang**
100 □2 **Apia** Samoa
277 F2 **Apiacas, Serra dos** hills Brazil
280 C6 **Apiaí** Brazil
275 F4 **Apiaú, Serra do** mts Brazil
215 N5 **Apice** Italy
204 C3 **A Picota** Spain
100 □6 **Apio** Malaita Solomon Is
269 H7 **Apipilulco** Mex.
213 O9 **Apiro** Italy
261 D6 **Apishapa** r. CO U.S.A.
102 J6 **Apiti** North I. N.Z.
269 I6 **Apizaco** Mex.
266 H5 **Apizolaya** Mex.
151 C2 **Ap'khazet'i** aut. rep. Georgia
276 B4 **Aplao** Peru
131 □J7 **Ap Lei Chau** i. H.K. China
114 E8 **Apo, Mount** vol. Mindanao Phil.
204 F3 **A Pobla de Brollón** Spain
204 F3 **A Pobra de San Xiao** Spain
204 F4 **A Pobra de Trives** Spain
204 C3 **A Pobra do Caramiñal** Spain
159 Q2 **Apochka** r. Rus. Fed.
278 F3 **Apodi** Brazil
278 F3 **Apodi, Chapada do** hills Brazil
114 C5 **Apo East Passage** Phil.
275 G3 **Apoera** Suriname
193 E8 **Apolda** Ger.
Apollinopolis Magna Egypt see **Idfū**
105 I8 **Apollo Bay** Vic. Austr.
Apollonia Bulg. see **Sozopol**
220 F6 **Apollonia** Sifnos Greece
276 C3 **Apolo** Bol.
204 F2 **A Pontenova** Spain
204 C2 **A Pontepedra** Spain
255 G11 **Apopka** FL U.S.A.
279 B6 **Aporé** Goiás Brazil
280 B3 **Aporé** Mato Grosso do Sul Brazil
280 B3 **Aporé** r. Brazil
275 I4 **Aporema** Brazil
199 H5 **Apostag** Hungary
250 D3 **Apostle Islands** WI U.S.A.
250 D2 **Apostle Islands National Lakeshore** nature res. WI U.S.A.
243 N3 **Apostolens Tommelfinger** mt. Greenland
282 G2 **Apóstoles** Arg.
150 C3 **Apostolos Andreas, Cape** Cyprus
159 M6 **Apostolove** Ukr.
275 G3 **Apoteri** Guyana
Apoucaroua atoll Arch. des Tuamotu Fr. Polynesia see **Pukarua**
114 C5 **Apo West Passage** Phil.
256 C12 **Appalachia** VA U.S.A.
256 B12 **Appalachian Mountains** U.S.A.
Appalla i. Fiji see **Kabara**
186 J3 **Appelscha** Neth.
Appenines mts Italy
Appennino mts Italy see **Appenines**
215 K3 **Appennino Abruzzese** mts Italy
215 M4 **Appennino Campano** mts Italy
215 P6 **Appennino Lucano** mts Italy
215 O5 **Appennino Napoletano** mts Italy
213 I8 **Appennino Tosco-Emiliano** mts Italy
213 M9 **Appennino Umbro-Marchigiano** mts Italy
194 D4 **Appenweier** Ger.
212 G1 **Appenzell** Switz.
212 G1 **Appenzell Ausserrhoden** canton Switz.
212 G1 **Appenzell Innerrhoden** canton Switz.
213 K3 **Appiano sulla Strada del Vino** Italy
214 B3 **Appietto** Corse France
213 O9 **Appignano** Italy
186 K2 **Appingedam** Neth.
171 M4 **Appleby-in-Westmorland** Cumbria, England U.K.
168 E8 **Applecross** Highland, Scotland U.K.
172 D5 **Appledore** Devon, England U.K.
173 N5 **Appledore** Kent, England U.K.
260 G3 **Appleton** MN U.S.A.
250 F5 **Appleton** WI U.S.A.
171 L7 **Appleton Thorn** Warrington, England U.K.
264 O7 **Apple Valley** CA U.S.A.
178 G8 **Appoigny** France
256 G11 **Appomattox** VA U.S.A.
183 G6 **Apprieu** France
100 □1 **Apra Harbor** inlet Guam
100 □1 **Apra Heights** Guam
161 U6 **Aprelevka** Rus. Fed.
182 H2 **Apremont** France
179 K6 **Apremont-la-Forêt** France
212 I3 **Aprica** Italy
215 O4 **Apricena** Italy
217 K5 **Aprigliano** Italy
215 J4 **Aprilia** Italy
204 G3 **A Proba** Spain
139 O5 **Aprunyi** Arun. Prad. India
151 A1 **Apsheronsk** Rus. Fed.
Apsheronskaya Rus. Fed. see **Apsheronsk**
Apsheronskiy Poluostrov pen. Azer. see **Abşeron Yarımadası**
104 H7 **Apsley** Vic. Austr.
251 P5 **Apsley** Ont. Can.
106 C1 **Apsley Strait** N.T. Austr.
183 G9 **Apt** France
212 I7 **Apuane, Alpi** mts Italy
264 □F14 **'Āpua Point** HI U.S.A.
280 B5 **Apucarana** Brazil
280 B5 **Apucarana, Serra da** hills Brazil
269 I5 **Apulco** Mex.
204 C6 **Apúlia** Port.
Apulum Romania see **Alba Iulia**
114 B7 **Apurahuan** Palawan Phil.
114 □ **Apurashokoru** i. Palau
274 E3 **Apure** r. Venez.
274 D3 **Apure** state Venez.
276 B3 **Apurímac** dept Peru
276 B3 **Apurimac** r. Peru
274 D3 **Apurito** Venez.
Aq"a Georgia see **Sokhumi**
'Aqaba Jordan see **Al 'Aqabah**
146 B1 **Aqaba, Gulf of** Asia
149 K8 **'Aqabah, Birkat al** well Iraq
150 B8 **'Aqabah, Wādī al** watercourse Egypt
Aqadyr Kazakh. see **Agadyr'**
132 D6 **Aqal** Xinjiang China
Aqbalyq Kazakh. see **Akbalyk**
Aqbaūyr Kazakh. see **Akbauyr**
Aqbeyit Kazakh. see **Akbeit**
145 L3 **Āqchah** Afgh.
149 L4 **Aq Chai** r. Iran
144 E5 **'Aqdā** Iran
144 B3 **Aqdoghmish** r. Iran
149 N5 **Āq Gadūk, Gardaneh-ye** pass Iran
225 H5 **Aqiq** Sudan
146 D6 **Aqiq, Khalîg** b. Sudan
146 E3 **Aqiq, Wādī al** watercourse Saudi Arabia
128 B6 **Aqitag** mt. Xinjiang China
Aqköl Akmolinskaya Oblast' Kazakh. see **Akkol'**
Aqköl Atyrauskaya Oblast' Kazakh. see **Akkol'**
146 C3 **Aqla** well Saudi Arabia
Aqmola Kazakh. see **Astana**
Aqmola Oblysy admin. div. Kazakh. see **Akmolinskaya Oblast'**
144 F3 **Āq Qal'eh** Iran
133 E8 **Aqqan** Xinjiang China
133 G8 **Aqqan** Xinjiang China
133 I8 **Aqqikkol Hu** salt l. China
Aqqystaū Kazakh. see **Akkistau**
150 D6 **'Aqraba** West Bank
149 K5 **'Aqrah** Iraq
150 G7 **'Aqran** hill Saudi Arabia
Aqsay Kazakh. see **Aksay**
Aqsayqin Hit terr. Asia see **Aksai Chin**
Aqshataū Kazakh. see **Akchatau**
Aqshī Kazakh. see **Akshiy**
142 H6 **Aqsho'laq** Uzbek.
Aqshuqyr Kazakh. see **Akshukur**
Aqsū Akmolinskaya Oblast' Kazakh. see **Aksu**
Aqsū Almatinskaya Oblast' Kazakh. see **Aksu**
Aqsū Pavlodarskaya Oblast' Kazakh. see **Aksu**
Aqsūat Kazakh. see **Aksuat**
Aqsū-Ayuly Kazakh. see **Aksu-Ayuly**
Aqtas Kazakh. see **Aktas**
Aqtaū Kazakh. see **Aktau**
Aqtöbe Kazakh. see **Aktobe**
Aqtöbe Oblysy admin. div. Kazakh. see **Aktyubinskaya Oblast'**
Aqtoghay Karagandinskaya Oblast' Kazakh. see **Aktogay**
Aqtoghay Pavlodarskaya Oblast' Kazakh. see **Aktogay**
Aquae Grani Ger. see **Aachen**
Aquae Gratianae France see **Aix-les-Bains**
Aquae Mortuae France see **Aigues-Mortes**
Aquae Sextiae France see **Aix-en-Provence**
Aquae Statiellae Italy see **Acqui Terme**
265 S7 **Aquarius Mountains** AZ U.S.A.
265 U4 **Aquarius Plateau** UT U.S.A.
217 L2 **Aquaviva delle Fonti** Italy
259 J3 **Aquebogue** NY U.S.A.
277 F5 **Aquidabánmi** r. Para.
277 G5 **Aquidauana** Brazil
277 F4 **Aquidauana** r. Brazil
268 D7 **Aquila** Mex.
201 H8 **Aquilêia** Italy
266 F3 **Aquiles** Mex.
215 O6 **Aquilonia** Italy
208 E3 **Aquilué** Spain
270 G4 **Aquin** Haiti
Aquincum Hungary see **Budapest**
215 L5 **Aquino** Italy
Aquinum Italy see **Aquino**
Aquiry r. Brazil see **Acre**
Aquisgranum Ger. see **Aachen**
269 H4 **Aquismón** Mex.
185 D7 **Aquitaine** admin. reg. France
Aqzhal Kazakh. see **Akzhal**
Aqzhar Kazakh. see **Akzhar**
Aqzhayqyn Köli salt l. Kazakh. see **Akzhaykyn, Ozero**
139 J7 **Ara** Bihar India
208 F3 **Ara** r. Spain
232 D3 **Āra Ārba** Eth.
145 K6 **Arab** Afgh.
255 D8 **Arab** AL U.S.A.
230 F2 **Arab, Bahr el** watercourse Sudan
225 F2 **'Arab, Khalīj al** b. Egypt
144 G5 **'Arabābād** Iran
232 D3 **Ara Bacalle** well Eth.
150 A9 **'Arabah, Wādī** watercourse Egypt
147 J7 **'Arabah, Wādī** r. Yemen
150 D9 **'Arabah, Wādī al** watercourse Israel/Jordan
150 D3 **'Arab al Mulk** Syria
159 N8 **Arabats'ka Strilka, Kosa** spit Ukr.
Arabatskaya Strelka spit Ukr. see **Arabats'ka Strilka, Kosa**
159 O8 **Arabats'ka Zatoka** b. Ukr.
275 E3 **Arabelo** Venez.
209 C10 **Arabí** mt. Spain
289 I4 **Arabian Basin** sea feature Indian Ocean
Arabian Gulf Asia see **The Gulf**
147 M6 **Arabian Oryx Sanctuary** tourist site Saudi Arabia
147 J5 **Arabian Peninsula** Asia
141 J6 **Arabian Sea** Indian Ocean
151 J4 **Arablinskoye** Rus. Fed.
232 D3 **Ara Bonel** Eth.
275 F3 **Arabopó** Venez.
151 J5 **Äräb Qubalı** Azer.
185 G10 **Arac** r. France
148 F3 **Araç** Turkey
275 F5 **Araça** r. Brazil
278 F4 **Aracaju** Brazil
277 G6 **Aracanguy, Montes de** hills Para.
282 D2 **Aracar, Volcán** vol. Arg.
270 F8 **Aracataca** Col.
278 F3 **Aracati** Brazil
278 E5 **Aracatu** Brazil
280 B4 **Araçatuba** Brazil
206 F5 **Aracena** Spain
206 G5 **Aracena, Embalse de** resr Spain
283 C9 **Aracena, Isla** i. Chile
206 E5 **Aracena, Sierra de** hills Spain
220 C3 **Arachthos** r. Greece
100 □6 **Aracides, Cape** Malaita Solomon Is
278 F3 **Aracoiaba** Brazil
281 G3 **Aracruz** Brazil
281 F2 **Araçuaí** Brazil
281 F2 **Araçuaí** r. Brazil
150 D7 **'Arad** Israel
218 J4 **Arad** Romania
199 K5 **Arad** county Romania
224 D6 **Arada** Chad
204 D7 **Arada, Serra de** mts Port.
147 K4 **'Arādah** U.A.E.
144 E4 **Arādān** Iran
206 B6 **Arade** r. Port.
206 C6 **Arade, Barragem do** resr Port.
224 D6 **Aradeib, Wadi** watercourse Sudan
217 O3 **Aradeo** Italy
199 J5 **Aradului, Câmpia** plain Romania
238 □3a **Arafo** Tenerife Canary Is
127 I3 **Arafune-yama** mt. Japan
98 D2 **Arafura Sea** Austr./Indon.
290 D6 **Arafura Shelf** sea feature Austr./Indon.
280 A1 **Aragarças** Brazil
151 F5 **Aragats Lerr** mt. Armenia
127 H1 **Ara-gawa** r. Japan
127 K4 **Ara-gawa** r. Japan
185 E10 **Aragnouet** France
205 Q6 **Aragón** aut. comm. Spain
205 Q4 **Aragón** r. Spain
208 C4 **Aragón, Canal Imperial de** Spain
216 F9 **Aragona** Sicilia Italy
205 P7 **Aragoncillo** Spain
205 P7 **Aragoncillo** mt. Spain
274 E2 **Aragua** state Venez.
278 C4 **Araguacema** Brazil
278 C5 **Araguaçu** Brazil
275 E2 **Aragua de Barcelona** Venez.
275 F2 **Aragua de Maturín** Venez.
280 C **Araguaia** r. Brazil
278 C4 **Araguaia, Parque Nacional do** nat. park Brazil
280 B1 **Araguaiana** Brazil
278 C3 **Araguaína** Brazil
280 A2 **Araguainha** Brazil
277 H1 **Araguana** Brazil
275 F2 **Araguao, Boca** r. mouth Venez.
275 F2 **Araguapiche, Punta** pt Venez.
280 C3 **Araguari** Brazil
280 C3 **Araguari** r. Brazil
275 I4 **Araguari** r. Brazil
278 C3 **Araguatins** Brazil
151 F4 **Aragvi** r. Georgia
146 F9 **'Ārah, Ra's** pt Yemen
147 L7 **'Ārah, Wādī** r. Oman
278 D5 **Arai** Brazil
127 H2 **Arai** Niigata Japan
126 G6 **Arai** Shizuoka Japan
205 P3 **Araia** Spain
Árainn Mhór i. Ireland see **Arranmore Island**
278 E2 **Araiosos** Brazil
227 F4 **Arak** Alg.
144 C4 **Arāk** Iran
150 G4 **Arak** Syria
127 K1 **Arakai-yama** mt. Japan
275 F3 **Arakaka** Guyana
118 A4 **Arakan** state Myanmar
118 B4 **Arakan Yoma** mts Myanmar
124 □1 **Arakawa** Okinawa Japan
Arakhthos r. Greece see **Arachthos**
126 F3 **Araki-gawa** r. Japan
102 M5 **Arakihi** hill North I. N.Z.
136 F6 **Arakkonam** Tamil Nadu India
151 B5 **Araklı** Turkey
151 F6 **Arak's** r. Armenia alt. **Aras Nehri (Turkey)**, alt. **Araz (Azerbaijan/Iran)**, conv. **Aras**, hist. **Araxes**
151 I4 **Arakul** Rus. Fed.
133 J7 **Aral** Qinghai China
Aral Kazakh. see **Aral'sk**
Aral Tajik. see **Vose**
208 A1 **Aralar, Sierra de** mts Spain
151 F6 **Aralık** Turkey
142 I5 **Aral Sea** salt l. Kazakh./Uzbek.
142 I4 **Aral'sk** Kazakh.
Aral'skoye More salt l. Kazakh./Uzbek. see **Aral Sea**
142 C3 **Aralsor, Ozero** l. Kazakh.
142 E3 **Aralsor, Ozero** salt l. Kazakh.
Aral Tengizi salt l. Kazakh./Uzbek. see **Aral Sea**
128 B3 **Araltobe** Xinjiang China
107 J7 **Aramac** Qld Austr.
107 J7 **Aramac Creek** watercourse Qld Austr.
146 H3 **Aramah** plat. Saudi Arabia
204 C3 **A Ramallosa** Spain
269 H1 **Aramberri** Mex.
278 D3 **Arame** Brazil
113 J8 **Aramia** r. P.N.G.
185 C9 **Aramits** France
183 F9 **Aramon** France
151 H5 **Aran** Azer.
136 F3 **Aran** r. India
208 G2 **Aran, Val d'** reg. Spain
207 M6 **Arana, Sierra** mts Spain
151 J6 **Ārānchī** Iran
284 C2 **Arancibia** Arg.
205 R5 **Aranda** r. Spain
205 M5 **Aranda de Duero** Spain
205 Q5 **Aranda de Moncayo** Spain
149 M6 **Arandān** Iran
268 E5 **Arandas** Mex.
218 I6 **Aranđelovac** Aranđelovac Serbia
234 B4 **Arandis** Namibia
138 I9 **Arang** Chhattisgarh India
204 F8 **Aranhas** Port.
136 F6 **Arani** Tamil Nadu India
169 C6 **Aran Islands** Ireland
205 M8 **Aranjuez** Spain
285 F5 **Arano** Arg.
234 C5 **Aranos** Namibia
261 G12 **Aransas Pass** TX U.S.A.
136 F7 **Arantangi** Tamil Nadu India
280 B3 **Arantes** r. Brazil
204 I9 **Arañuelo, Campo** reg. Spain
99 H1 **Aranuka** atoll Gilbert Is Kiribati
119 F8 **Aranyaprathet** Thai.
199 L3 **Aranyosapáti** Hungary
205 N8 **Aranzueque** Spain
125 H14 **Arao** Japan
228 E2 **Araouane** Mali
261 F8 **Arapaho** OK U.S.A.
260 F5 **Arapahoe** NE U.S.A.
275 H5 **Arapari** Brazil
103 I8 **Arapawa Island** South I. N.Z.
285 I2 **Arapey Grande** r. Uru.
148 I4 **Arapgir** Turkey
274 B5 **Arapicos** Ecuador
204 I7 **Arapiles** Spain
278 F4 **Arapiraca** Brazil
220 F2 **Arapis, Akrotirio** pt Greece
280 B5 **Arapongas** Brazil
280 C6 **Arapoti** Brazil
Arapsun Turkey see **Gülşehir**
280 A4 **Arapuá** Brazil
102 J5 **Arapuni** North I. N.Z.
279 C8 **Araquari** Brazil
149 J8 **'Ar'ar** Saudi Arabia
149 K8 **'Ar'ar, Wādī** watercourse Iraq/Saudi Arabia
275 F5 **Arara** r. Brazil
274 C5 **Araracuara** Col.
274 C5 **Araracuara, Cerros de** hills Col.
139 J6 **Araraj** Bihar India
279 C9 **Araranguá** Brazil
280 C6 **Ararapira** Brazil
280 C4 **Araraquara** Brazil
276 C2 **Araras** Amazonas Brazil
275 H6 **Araras** Pará Brazil
280 D5 **Araras** São Paulo Brazil
276 D2 **Ararás** Brazil
278 E3 **Araras, Açude** resr Brazil
280 A3 **Araras, Serra das** hills Brazil
280 A6 **Araras, Serra das** mts Brazil
151 F6 **Ararat** Armenia
105 I7 **Ararat** Vic. Austr.
Ararat, Mount Turkey see **Ağrı Dağı**
278 D2 **Arari** Brazil
139 K6 **Araria** Bihar India
278 E3 **Araripe** Brazil
278 E3 **Araripe, Chapada do** hills Brazil
278 E3 **Araripina** Brazil
281 F5 **Araruama** Brazil
281 F5 **Araruama, Lago de** lag. Brazil
149 L4 **Aras** r. Asia alt. **Arak's (Armenia)**, alt. **Aras Nehri (Turkey)**, alt. **Araz (Azerbaijan/Iran)**, hist. **Araxes**
205 P3 **Aras** Spain
149 K4 **Aras** Turkey
124 □1 **Ara-saki** c. Okinawa Japan
144 F4 **Arāsavān** Iran
209 C8 **Aras de los Olmos** Spain
Ar-Asgat Mongolia see **Ugtaaltsaydam**
151 G6 **Aras Govşaghyuyn** resr Azer./Iran
151 D6 **Aras Güneyi Dağları** mts Turkey
126 E4 **Arashima-dake** mt. Japan
271 □9 **Arasji** Aruba
151 C6 **Aras Nehri** r. Turkey alt. **Arak's (Armenia)**, alt. **Araz (Azerbaijan/Iran)**, conv. **Aras**, hist. **Araxes**
284 E4 **Arata** Arg.
279 F5 **Arataca** Brazil
228 C2 **Araţâne** well Maur.
275 I5 **Arataú** r. Brazil
Aratürük Xinjiang China see **Yiwu**
116 D1 **Arau** Malaysia
276 D2 **Arauã** r. Brazil
275 F6 **Arauá** r. Brazil
274 D3 **Arauca** Col.
274 D3 **Arauca** dept Col.
274 E3 **Arauca** r. Venez.
284 A6 **Araucanía** admin. reg. Chile
279 C8 **Araucária** Brazil
282 B5 **Arauco** Chile
282 B5 **Arauco, Golfo de** b. Chile
183 E6 **Araules** France
274 D3 **Arauquita** Col.
274 D2 **Araure** Venez.
265 V9 **Aravaipa Creek** watercourse AZ U.S.A.
138 D7 **Aravalli Range** mts India
160 I2 **Aravete** Estonia
205 P5 **Araviana** r. Spain
182 I5 **Aravis** mts France
182 I5 **Aravis, Col des** pass France
220 D2 **Aravissos** Greece
100 □6 **Arawa** P.N.G.
233 D5 **Arawale National Reserve** nature res. Kenya
Arawata r. South I. N.Z. see **Arawhata**
102 L5 **Arawhana** mt. North I. N.Z.
103 C11 **Arawhata** r. South I. N.Z.
280 D3 **Araxá** Brazil
220 C4 **Araxos, Akrotirio** pt Greece
Araya Spain see **Araia**
275 E2 **Araya, Península de** pen. Venez.
271 K8 **Araya, Punta de** pt Venez.
148 E4 **Arayıt Dağı** mt. Turkey
151 J6 **Araz** r. Azer. alt. **Arak's (Armenia)**, alt. **Aras Nehri (Turkey)**, conv. **Aras**, hist. **Araxes**
204 C8 **Arazede** Port.
208 C4 **Arba** r. Spain
208 C3 **Arba de Biel** r. Spain
208 C3 **Arba de Luesia** r. Spain
Arbailu Iraq see **Arbīl**

232 C3 Ārba Minch Eth.
185 F10 Arbas France
149 L6 Arbat Iraq
214 D8 Arbatax Sardegna Italy
156 J4 Arbazh Rus. Fed.
208 G4 Arbeca Spain
179 K8 Arbecey France
212 G3 Arbedo Switz.
Arbela Iraq see Arbīl
182 H4 Arbent France
185 D10 Arbéost France
195 J3 Arberg Ger.
Arberth Pembrokeshire, Wales U.K. see Narberth
201 K2 Arbesbach Austria
205 P7 Arbeteta Spain
213 K9 Arbia r. Italy
149 L5 Arbīl Iraq
149 K6 Arbīl governorate Iraq
205 P3 Arbizu Spain
165 L2 Arboga Sweden
182 H3 Arbois France
207 O6 Arboleas Spain
285 G5 Arboledas Arg.
274 B2 Arboletes Col.
285 I3 Arbolito Uru.
212 G1 Arbon Switz.
214 B8 Arborea Sardegna Italy
214 B8 Arborea reg. Sardegna Italy
247 K4 Arborfield Sask. Can.
247 L5 Arborg Man. Can.
212 E5 Arborio Italy
163 N6 Arbrå Sweden
168 K9 Arbroath Angus, Scotland U.K.
208 K4 Arbúcies Spain
264 J2 Arbuckle CA U.S.A.
145 J7 Arbu Lut, Dasht-e des. Afgh.
185 C9 Arbus France
214 B8 Arbus Sardegna Italy
159 K6 Arbuzynka Ukr.
183 G9 Arc r. France
183 I5 Arc r. France
185 B6 Arcachon France
185 B6 Arcachon, Bassin d' inlet France
256 G6 Arcade NY U.S.A.
255 G12 Arcadia FL U.S.A.
261 I9 Arcadia LA U.S.A.
250 H5 Arcadia MI U.S.A.
256 G8 Arcadia PA U.S.A.
250 C5 Arcadia WI U.S.A.
182 I5 Arcalod, Pointe d' mt. France
256 A9 Arcanum OH U.S.A.
267 N7 Arcas, Cayos is Mex.
262 B6 Arcata CA U.S.A.
264 O3 Arc Dome mt. NV U.S.A.
215 L4 Arce Italy
268 G7 Arcelia Mex.
186 J6 Arcen Neth.
179 J8 Arc-en-Barrois France
184 C4 Arces France
178 G7 Arces-Dilo France
182 H2 Arc-et-Senans France
213 N8 Arcevia Italy
Archangel Rus. Fed. see Arkhangel'sk
Archangel Oblast admin. div. Rus. Fed. see Arkhangel'skaya Oblast'
221 J6 Archangelos Rodos Greece
219 K7 Archar r. Bulg.
258 D2 Archbald PA U.S.A.
256 A7 Archbold OH U.S.A.
209 C11 Archena Spain
107 H2 Archer r. Qld Austr.
107 I2 Archer Bend National Park Qld Austr.
261 F9 Archer City TX U.S.A.
179 M7 Arches France
265 W3 Arches National Park UT U.S.A.
228 E2 Arch Henda well Mali
184 D4 Archiac France
207 K6 Archidona Spain
106 G5 Archie Creek r. Qld Austr.
249 I3 Archipel-de-Mingan, Réserve du Parc National de l' nat. park Que. Can.
209 K9 Archipiélago de Cabrera, Parque Nacional del nat. park Illes Balears Spain
199 L5 Archiş Romania
207 P4 Archivel Spain
214 B8 Arci, Monte hill Italy
214 H2 Arcidosso Italy
214 C5 Arcipelago de la Maddalena, Parco Nazionale dell' nat. park Sardegna Italy
214 E2 Arcipelago Toscano, Parco Nazionale dell' nat. park Italy
178 H6 Arcis-sur-Aube France
144 C2 Ärçivan Azer.
104 E3 Arckaringa watercourse S.A. Austr.
182 H2 Arc-lès-Gray France
144 G2 Arçman Turkm.
213 J4 Arco Italy
262 H5 Arco ID U.S.A.
284 B6 Arco, Paso del pass Chile
206 □ Arco da Calheta Madeira
204 E6 Arco de Baúlhe Port.
212 H7 Arcola Italy
256 H10 Arcola VA U.S.A.
182 I3 Arçon France
182 D4 Arconce r. France
181 L5 Arçonnay France
281 E4 Arcos Brazil
206 D3 Arcos Port.
205 M4 Arcos Spain
205 P6 Arcos de Jalón Spain
206 H7 Arcos de la Frontera Spain
209 C8 Arcos de las Salinas Spain
204 D5 Arcos de Valdevez Port.
136 F6 Arcot Tamil Nadu India
180 E4 Arcouest, Pointe de l' pt France
278 F4 Arcoverde Brazil
204 C5 Arcozelo Braga Port.
204 E7 Arcozelo Guarda Port.
204 C6 Arcozelo Porto Port.
204 C5 Arcozelo Viana do Castelo Port.
182 G2 Arc-sur-Tille France
243 J2 Arctic Bay Nunavut Can.
Arctic Institute Islands Rus. Fed. see Arkticheskogo Instituta, Ostrova
244 F2 Arctic Lagoon AK U.S.A.
292 B1 Arctic Mid-Ocean Ridge sea feature Arctic Ocean
245 K1 Arctic National Wildlife Refuge nature res. AK U.S.A.
292 Arctic Ocean
245 N2 Arctic Red r. N.W.T. Can.
Arctic Red River N.W.T. Can. see Tsiigehtchic
245 K1 Arctic Village AK U.S.A.
286 N8 Arctowski research stn Antarctica
214 B8 Arcuentu, Monte hill Italy
208 F3 Arcusa Spain
182 D1 Arcy-sur-Cure France
219 N9 Arda r. Bulg. alt. Ardas (Greece)
212 I5 Arda r. Italy
144 C2 Ardabīl Iran
144 B2 Ardabīl prov. Iran
201 K3 Ardagger Markt Austria
169 D8 Ardagh Ireland
149 K3 Ardahan Turkey
151 D4 Ardahan prov. Turkey
144 H3 Ardāk Iran
144 E6 Ardakān Fārs Iran
144 E5 Ardakān Yazd Iran
144 D6 Ardal Iran
163 I6 Årdal Norway
205 N5 Ardal mt. Spain
207 J7 Ardales Spain
164 D3 Ardalsknapen hill Norway
163 I6 Årdalstangen Norway
169 J7 Ardanairy Ireland
185 B10 Ardanaz Spain
151 D4 Ardanuç Turkey
214 B6 Ardara Sardegna Italy
169 F3 Ardara Ireland
219 O9 Ardas r. Greece alt. Arda (Bulgaria)
150 F8 Ard aş Şawwān plain Jordan
157 H5 Ardatov Nizhegorodskaya Oblast' Rus. Fed.
157 I5 Ardatov Respublika Mordoviya Rus. Fed.
170 D8 Ardattin Ireland
251 N4 Ardbeg Ont. Can.
168 F11 Ard Bheinn hill Scotland U.K.
170 E6 Ardcath Ireland
168 D10 Ardchiavaig Argyll and Bute, Scotland U.K.
169 F7 Ardconry Ireland
215 J4 Ardea Italy
183 E7 Ardèche dept France
183 F8 Ardèche r. France
183 E8 Ardèche, Gorges de l' France
169 I5 Ardee Ireland
168 G10 Arden Argyll and Bute, Scotland U.K.
259 G2 Arden NY U.S.A.
104 F5 Arden, Mount hill S.A. Austr.
187 G9 Ardenne, Plateau de l' Belgium
Ardennes plat. Belgium see Ardenne, Plateau de l'
178 I4 Ardennes dept France
178 H5 Ardennes r. France
179 I4 Ardennes, Canal des France
184 H2 Ardentes France
168 G10 Ardentinny Argyll and Bute, Scotland U.K.
264 K3 Arden Town CA U.S.A.
169 G6 Arderin hill Ireland
168 H7 Ardersier Highland, Scotland U.K.
183 C6 Ardes France
151 C4 Ardeşen Turkey
144 E5 Ardestān Iran
212 I2 Ardez Switz.
169 C8 Ardfert Ireland
169 G8 Ardfinnan Ireland
168 H7 Ardgay Highland, Scotland U.K.
169 F8 Ardglass Ireland
169 K4 Ardglass Northern Ireland U.K.
151 B6 Ardıcın Dağı mt. Turkey
206 E4 Ardila r. Port.
219 N9 Ardino Bulg.
168 B8 Ardivachar Point Scotland U.K.
102 L5 Ardkeen North I. N.Z.
169 K4 Ardkeen Northern Ireland U.K.
168 F11 Ardlamont Point Scotland U.K.
173 N4 Ardleigh Essex, England U.K.
105 K6 Ardlethan N.S.W. Austr.
168 G10 Ardlui Argyll and Bute, Scotland U.K.
168 E10 Ardlussa Argyll and Bute, Scotland U.K.
168 F7 Ardmair Highland, Scotland U.K.
168 E11 Ardminish Argyll and Bute, Scotland U.K.
168 E9 Ardmolich Highland, Scotland U.K.
Ardmore Ireland see An Aird Mhóir
261 G8 Ardmore OK U.S.A.
258 E4 Ardmore PA U.S.A.
169 G9 Ardmore Bay Ireland
168 D9 Ardmore Point Scotland U.K.
169 E7 Ardnacrusha Ireland
168 D9 Ardnamurchan pen. Scotland U.K.
168 D9 Ardnamurchan, Point of Scotland U.K.
169 E6 Ardnasodan Ireland
159 L1 Ardon' Rus. Fed.
151 F2 Ardon Rus. Fed.
151 F2 Ardon r. Rus. Fed.
212 C3 Ardon Switz.
187 D7 Ardooie Belgium
217 K7 Ardore Italy
169 E8 Ardpatrick Ireland
168 E11 Ardpatrick Point Scotland U.K.
169 E6 Ardrahan Ireland
178 C2 Ardres France
168 F10 Ardrishaig Argyll and Bute, Scotland U.K.
104 F6 Ardrossan S.A. Austr.
168 G11 Ardrossan North Ayrshire, Scotland U.K.
170 D7 Ardscull Ireland
259 H2 Ardsley NY U.S.A.
169 L4 Ards Peninsula Northern Ireland U.K.
169 H3 Ardstraw Northern Ireland U.K.
219 L3 Ardusat Romania
168 E8 Ardvasar Highland, Scotland U.K.
168 A8 Ardvule, Rubha pt Scotland U.K.
162 L5 Åre Sweden
280 D4 Areado Brazil
205 O2 Areatza Spain
230 F4 Arebi Dem. Rep. Congo
182 J5 Arèches France
271 □[1] Arecibo Puerto Rico
285 H3 Areco r. Arg.
219 M5 Arefu Romania
282 F2 Areguá Para.
278 F3 Areia Branca Brazil
204 D9 Areias Port.
114 □ Arekalong Peninsula Palau
158 C2 Arekhava Belarus
161 N7 Arekhawsk Belarus
Arel Belgium see Arlon
Arelas France see Arles
Arelate France see Arles
164 H2 Aremark Norway
191 C10 Aremberg hill Ger.
208 G3 Arén Spain
114 C7 Arena rf Phil.
264 I3 Arena, Point CA U.S.A.
266 E6 Arena, Punta pt Mex.
266 E5 Arena de la Ventana, Punta pt Mex.
282 D2 Arenal, Campo del plain Arg.
207 O4 Arenal, Puerto del pass Spain
266 □Q12 Arenal, Volcán vol. Costa Rica
114 D5 Arena Point Luzon Phil.
277 F3 Arenápolis Brazil
271 □[1] Arenas, Punta pt Puerto Rico
283 C9 Arenas, Punta de pt Arg.
205 L2 Arenas de Iguña Spain
207 L7 Arenas del Rey Spain
207 M2 Arenas de San Juan Spain
205 J8 Arenas de San Pedro Spain
285 G4 Arenaza Arg.
164 E3 Arendal Norway
187 H6 Arendonk Belgium
192 D5 Arendsee l. Ger.
192 D5 Arendsee (Altmark) Ger.
185 C7 Arengosse France
172 E2 Arenig Fawr hill Wales U.K.
205 O6 Arenillas Spain
285 I2 Arenitas Blancas Uru.
209 D7 Arenos, Embalse de resr Spain
207 K4 Arenosillo r. Spain
207 K4 Arenoso r. Spain
191 I8 Arenshausen Ger.
217 K5 Arente r. Italy
208 K4 Arenys de Mar Spain
212 F7 Arenzano Italy
220 D6 Areopoli Greece
204 C5 Areosa Port.
266 F4 Areponapuchi Mex.
276 C4 Arequipa Peru
276 B3 Arequipa dept Peru
285 G3 Arequito Arg.
212 H4 Arera, Pizzo mt. Italy
275 H5 Arere Brazil
232 C3 Ārēro Eth.
185 B6 Arès France
204 D2 Ares Spain
160 L9 Aresa r. Belarus
195 K4 Aresing Ger.
205 N2 Arespalditza Spain
144 F5 Arestān Iran
185 C9 Arette France
185 C10 Arette-Pierre-St-Martin France
205 J7 Arevalillo Spain
205 K6 Arevalillo r. Spain
205 K6 Arévalo Spain
205 K6 Arévalo, Tierra de reg. Spain
206 D2 Arez Port.
146 D8 Areza Eritrea
Arezzaf well Mali see Aghezzaf
213 L9 Arezzo Italy
213 L8 Arezzo prov. Italy
148 I8 'Arfajah well Saudi Arabia
220 D5 Arfara Greece
185 I9 Arfons France
205 Q4 Arga r. Spain
106 F6 Argadargada N.T. Austr.
129 L4 Argalant Mongolia
220 E3 Argalasti Greece
206 H3 Argallanes, Sierra de los hills Spain
207 I4 Argallón Spain
207 M2 Argamasilla de Alba Spain
207 K3 Argamasilla de Calatrava Spain
207 O3 Argamasón Spain
132 I6 Argan Xinjiang China
205 N8 Arganda del Rey Spain
204 D8 Arganil Port.
204 G3 Arganza Spain
114 D7 Argao Cebu Phil.
138 F9 Argaon Mahar. India
Argatay Mongolia see Bayanjargalan
215 L4 Argatone, Monte mt. Italy
212 G4 Argegno Italy
Argel Alg. see Alger
185 D9 Argelès-Gazost France
185 K10 Argelès-sur-Mer France
183 B10 Argeliers France
209 E7 Argelita Spain
194 H6 Argen r. Ger.
194 H6 Argenbühl Ger.
181 K3 Argences France
183 J10 Argens r. France
213 L6 Argenta Italy
181 K4 Argentan France
214 G3 Argentario, Monte hill Italy
184 H5 Argentat France
208 C6 Argente Spain
212 B7 Argentera Italy
212 C7 Argentera, Cima dell' mt. Italy
212 C7 Argentera, Parco Naturale dell' nature res. Italy
178 D6 Argenteuil France
194 D2 Argenthal Ger.
214 A6 Argentiera Sardegna Italy
182 J5 Argentière France
212 D8 Argentina r. Italy
282 D4 Argentina country S. America
286 V1 Argentina Range mts Antarctica
182 I6 Argentine France
288 F9 Argentine Abyssal Plain sea feature S. Atlantic Ocean
288 G8 Argentine Basin sea feature S. Atlantic Ocean
Argentine Republic country S. America see Argentina
288 F8 Argentine Rise sea feature S. Atlantic Ocean
283 B8 Argentino, Lago l. Arg.
184 D1 Argenton r. France
181 K8 Argenton-Château France
Argentoratum France see Strasbourg
181 J5 Argentre France
181 I5 Argentré-du-Plessis France
181 P6 Argent-sur-Sauldre France
285 F6 Argerich Arg.
207 O5 Argerín mt. Spain
219 O6 Argeş r. Romania
205 L9 Argés Spain
219 M6 Argeşel r. Romania
145 K6 Arghandab r. Afgh.
145 K6 Arghastan r. Afgh.
170 B6 Arghavas Ireland
225 F5 Argo Sudan
220 D5 Argolikos Kolpos b. Greece
182 I5 Argonay France
179 I5 Argonne reg. France
250 F4 Argonne WI U.S.A.
220 D5 Argos Greece
207 P4 Argos r. Spain
250 H8 Argos IN U.S.A.
207 P4 Argos, Embalse de resr Spain
220 C2 Argos Orestiko Greece
220 B4 Argostoli Kefallonia Greece
180 I5 Argouges France
Argovie canton Switz. see Aargau
151 E2 Argudan Rus. Fed.
205 Q4 Arguedas Spain
178 C4 Argueil France
207 O4 Arguellite Spain
180 G4 Arguenon r. France
208 E3 Arguís Spain
205 Q9 Arguisuelas Spain
204 I6 Argujillo Spain
122 B2 Argun' r. China/Rus. Fed.
151 H2 Argun r. Georgia/Rus. Fed.
151 G2 Argun Rus. Fed.
229 G3 Argungu Nigeria
122 A3 Argunsk Rus. Fed.
129 O2 Argunskiy Khrebet mts Rus. Fed.
287 F1 Argus, Dome ice feature Antarctica
264 O6 Argus Range mts CA U.S.A.
Arguut Mongolia see Guchin-Us
249 H5 Argyle N.S. Can.
250 C9 Argyle IA U.S.A.
250 E7 Argyle WI U.S.A.
108 J4 Argyle, Lake W.A. Austr.
168 F10 Argyll reg. Scotland U.K.
168 F11 Argyll and Bute admin. div. Scotland U.K.
Argyrokastron Albania see Gjirokastër
146 G8 Arḥab reg. Yemen
128 G3 Arhangay prov. Mongolia
151 C4 Arhavi Turkey
Ar Horqin Qi Nei Mongol China see Tianshan
164 G5 Århus Denmark
164 G5 Århus Bugt b. Denmark
164 G5 Århus-Tirstrup airport Denmark
244 G3 Arhymot Lake AK U.S.A.
102 I5 Aria North I. N.Z.
217 H7 Aria, Monte hill Isole Lipari Italy
122 I6 Ariadnoye Rus. Fed.
115 D1 Ariaga i. Indon.
105 K6 Ariah Park N.S.W. Austr.
125 H13 Ariake-kai b. Japan
234 C6 Ariamsvlei Namibia
238 □[2a] Ariane Tracking Station research stn Ascension S. Atlantic Ocean
213 M6 Ariano, Isola d' i. Italy
215 O5 Ariano Irpino Italy
213 M6 Ariano nel Polesine Italy
285 F3 Arias Arg.
135 D11 Ari Atoll Maldives
275 G5 Ariaú Brazil
208 C2 Aribe Spain
275 F2 Aribí r. Venez.
228 E3 Aribinda Burkina
276 C4 Arica Chile
274 D5 Arica Col.
274 C5 Arica Peru
274 D2 Aricagua Venez.
276 C4 Arica y Parinacota admin. reg. Chile
215 J4 Ariccia Italy
238 □[3a] Arico Tenerife Canary Is
109 G12 Arid, Cape W.A. Austr.
126 B7 Arida Japan
126 B7 Arida-gawa r. Japan
151 E6 Arı Dağı mt. Turkey
220 D2 Aridaia Greece
226 B4 Aridal, Sabkhat salt pan Western Sahara
239 □[2a] Aride, Île i. Inner Islands Seychelles
Arid Island North I. N.Z. see Rakitu Island
185 G10 Ariège dept France
185 G8 Ariège r. France
285 H5 Ariel Arg.
219 L4 Arieş r. Romania
199 L5 Arieşeni Romania
219 L4 Arieşul Mic r. Romania
221 L2 Arifiye Turkey
145 O6 Arifwala Pak.
128 G1 Arigiyn Gol r. Mongolia
150 E3 Arīḥā Syria
Arīḥā West Bank see Jericho
205 M3 Arija Spain
285 G2 Arijón Arg.
260 E5 Arikaree r. CO U.S.A.
218 I7 Arilje Arilje Serbia
275 F6 Arimã Brazil
271 □[7] Arima Trin. and Tob.
126 F3 Arimine-ko resr Japan
Ariminum Italy see Rimini
275 G3 Arimu Mine Guyana
146 F6 'Arīn, Wādī al watercourse Saudi Arabia
238 □[3f] Arinaga Gran Canaria Canary Is
168 C9 Arinagour Argyll and Bute, Scotland U.K.
208 D5 Ariño Spain
277 G3 Arinos Mato Grosso Brazil
281 D1 Arinos Minas Gerais Brazil
277 F2 Arinos r. Brazil
182 H4 Arinthod France
268 F6 Ario de Rosáles Mex.
160 G6 Ariogala Lith.
271 □[7] Aripo, Mount hill Trin. and Tob.
274 D3 Ariporo r. Col.
277 F2 Aripuanã Brazil
275 F6 Aripuanã r. Brazil
277 E2 Ariquemes Brazil
279 B6 Ariranhá r. Brazil
168 E9 Arisaig Highland, Scotland U.K.
168 E9 Arisaig, Sound of sea chan. Scotland U.K.
275 G3 Arisaru Falls Guyana
150 B7 'Arīsh, Wādī al watercourse Egypt
274 D2 Arismendi Venez.
268 G3 Arista Mex.
246 D4 Aristazabal Island B.C. Can.
258 C3 Aristes PA U.S.A.
283 D7 Aristizábal, Cabo c. Arg.
282 G2 Aristóbulo del Valle Arg.
214 C8 Aritzo Sardegna Italy
235 □J3 Arivonimamo Madag.
Arixang Xinjiang China see Wenquan
232 C4 Ariya waterhole Kenya
136 F7 Ariyalur Tamil Nadu India
204 E7 Ariz Port.
205 P6 Ariza Spain
282 D2 Arizaro, Salar de salt flat Arg.
185 G9 Arize r. France
185 G10 Arize, Massif de l' mts France
205 O2 Arizgoiti Spain
205 Q3 Arizola Spain
284 E4 Arizona Arg.
265 U7 Arizona state U.S.A.
266 D2 Arizpe Mex.
146 G3 'Arjah Saudi Arabia
164 I2 Årjäng Sweden
117 K8 Arjasa Jawa Indon.
162 N3 Arjeplog Sweden
232 C2 Ārjo Eth.
274 C2 Arjona Col.
207 K5 Arjona Spain
207 K5 Arjonilla Spain
139 I9 Arjuni Chhattisgarh India
138 H9 Arjuni Mahar. India
157 H6 Arkadak Rus. Fed.
261 I8 Arkadelphia AR U.S.A.
159 Q4 Arkadivka Ukr.
153 P3 Arkagala Rus. Fed.
168 F9 Arkaig, Loch l. Scotland U.K.
136 E6 Arkalgud Karnataka India
220 G7 Arkalochori Kriti Greece
143 L2 Arkalyk Kazakh.
261 J9 Arkansas r. AR U.S.A.
261 I8 Arkansas state U.S.A.
261 J9 Arkansas City AR U.S.A.
261 G7 Arkansas City KS U.S.A.
219 K8 Arkata r. Bulg.
133 I8 Arkatag Shan mts China
245 N3 Arkell, Mount Y.T. Can.
224 E4 Arkenu, Jabal mt. Libya
156 H2 Arkhangel'sk Rus. Fed.
156 H3 Arkhangel'skaya Oblast' admin. div. Rus. Fed.
157 L5 Arkhangel'skoye Respublika Bashkortostan Rus. Fed.
151 F1 Arkhangel'skoye Stavropol'skiy Kray Rus. Fed.
161 U8 Arkhangel'skoye Tul'skaya Oblast' Rus. Fed.
159 T2 Arkhangel'skoye Voronezhskaya Oblast' Rus. Fed.
159 M7 Arkhanhel's'ka Sloboda Ukr.
159 M6 Arkhanhel's'ke Ukr.
122 F4 Arkhara Rus. Fed.
122 F4 Arkhara r. Rus. Fed.
151 H4 Arkhilos Kalo Georgia
159 R9 Arkhipo-Osipovka Rus. Fed.
161 Y5 Arkhipovka Ivanovskaya Oblast' Rus. Fed.
122 H7 Arkhipovka Primorskiy Kray Rus. Fed.
161 O7 Arkhipovka Smolenskaya Oblast' Rus. Fed.
151 F2 Arkhonskaya Rus. Fed.
151 C2 Arkhyz Rus. Fed.
Árki i. Greece see Arkoi
151 J6 Ärkivan Azer.
168 G6 Arkle hill Scotland U.K.
169 J7 Arklow Ireland
221 H5 Arkoi i. Greece
251 M6 Arkona Ont. Can.
192 H1 Arkona, Kap c. Ger.
Arkonam Tamil Nadu India see Arakkonam
165 M3 Arkösund Sweden
153 K1 Arkticheskiy, Mys c. Rus. Fed.
152 J2 Arkticheskogo Instituta, Ostrova is Rus. Fed.
156 J4 Arkul' Rus. Fed.
165 M2 Ärla Sweden
183 D6 Arlanc France
144 F2 Arlandag mt. Turkm.
205 L4 Arlanza r. Spain
205 N4 Arlanzón Spain
205 L4 Arlanzón r. Spain
205 N4 Arlanzón, Embalse de resr Spain
205 O8 Arlas r. Spain
200 B5 Arlbergpass pass Austria
190 D3 Arle (Großheide) Ger.
183 D7 Arlempdes France
214 H3 Arlena di Castro Italy
183 F9 Arles France
173 L3 Arlesey Bedfordshire, England U.K.
169 H7 Arless Ireland
185 J11 Arles-sur-Tech France
182 E2 Arleuf France
178 F3 Arleux France
229 F4 Arli Burkina
229 F4 Arli, Parc National de l' nat. park Burkina
229 F4 Arli, Réserve Partielle de l' nature res. Burkina
250 E8 Arlington IL U.S.A.
259 H1 Arlington NY U.S.A.
256 B8 Arlington OH U.S.A.
262 D4 Arlington OR U.S.A.
260 G3 Arlington SD U.S.A.
258 A7 Arlington VA U.S.A.
250 E6 Arlington WI U.S.A.
250 F7 Arlington Heights IL U.S.A.
229 G2 Arlit Niger
187 I9 Arlon Belgium
106 E7 Arltunga N.T. Austr.
212 F4 Arluno Italy
182 I5 Arly r. France
160 M6 Arlyeya Belarus
247 J5 Arm r. Sask. Can.
206 C6 Armação de Pêra Port.
256 C6 Armada MI U.S.A.
109 C12 Armadale W.A. Austr.
168 I11 Armadale West Lothian, Scotland U.K.
268 G3 Armadillo Mex.
115 D1 Armadores i. Indon.
Armageddon tourist site Israel see Tel Megiddo
169 I4 Armagh Northern Ireland U.K.
169 I4 Armagh county Northern Ireland U.K.
185 E8 Armagnac reg. France
147 J7 Armah, Wādī r. Yemen
205 P7 Armallones Spain
204 E6 Armamar Port.
178 G8 Armance r. France
178 G8 Armançon r. France
270 H4 Armando Bermudez nat. park Dom. Rep.
225 G3 Armant Egypt
162 Q3 Armasjärvi Sweden
221 H7 Armathia i. Greece
151 F5 Armavir Armenia
157 H7 Armavir Rus. Fed.
185 B9 Armendarits France
151 F5 Armenia country Asia
274 C3 Armenia Col.
151 F6 Armenian Monastic Buildings tourist site Iran
221 I6 Armenistis, Akrotirio pt Rodos Greece
161 X4 Armenki Rus. Fed.
212 E4 Armeno Italy
Armenopolis Romania see Gherla
269 I9 Armenta Mex.
205 J7 Armenteros Spain
178 E2 Armentières France
215 Q7 Armento Italy
268 D7 Armeria Mex.
268 D7 Armería r. Mex.
211 E7 Armi, Capo dell' c. Italy
105 M4 Armidale N.S.W. Austr.
207 L6 Armilla Spain
285 G3 Arminda Arg.
262 I3 Armington MT U.S.A.
183 C10 Armissan France
171 N8 Armitage Staffordshire, England U.K.
247 N1 Armit Lake Nunavut Can.
264 M5 Armona CA U.S.A.
138 H9 Armori Mahar. India
180 D5 Armorique, Parc Régional d' park France
260 F4 Armour SD U.S.A.
169 J2 Armoy Northern Ireland U.K.
194 E2 Armsheim Ger.
285 G3 Armstrong Arg.
106 C4 Armstrong r. N.T. Austr.
246 G5 Armstrong B.C. Can.
248 B3 Armstrong Ont. Can.
245 N3 Armstrong, Mount Y.T. Can.
Armstrong Island Cook Is see Rarotonga
256 E9 Armstrong Mills OH U.S.A.
122 J5 Armu r. Rus. Fed.
205 L6 Armuña Spain
214 C8 Armungia Sardegna Italy
204 I3 Armunia Spain
136 F3 Armur Andhra Prad. India
221 I3 Armutçuk Dağı mts Turkey
221 J2 Armutlu Turkey
Armutova Turkey see Gömeç
159 M7 Armyans'k Ukr.
Armyanskaya S.S.R. country Asia see Armenia
164 E7 Arnå r. Denmark
220 D6 Arna Greece
184 G5 Arnac-Pompadour France
212 D4 Arnad Italy
166 D1 Árnafjall hill Faroe Is
181 L6 Arnage France
220 E2 Arnaia Greece
150 A3 Arnaoutis, Cape Cyprus
162 □A1 Arnarfjörður inlet Iceland
249 G1 Arnaud r. Que. Can.
Arnauti, Cape Cyprus see Arnaoutis, Cape
221 J1 Arnavutköy Turkey
145 N4 Arnawai Pak.
182 E2 Arnay-le-Duc France
195 N3 Arnbruck Ger.
171 M5 Arncliffe North Yorkshire, England U.K.
172 H6 Arne Dorset, England U.K.
192 F5 Arneburg Ger.
205 P4 Arnedillo Spain
205 P4 Arnedo Spain
204 D3 Arnego r. Spain
185 B9 Arnéguy France
278 E3 Arneiroz Brazil
162 P4 Arnemark Sweden
186 E6 Arnemuiden Neth.
164 H1 Årnes Norway
208 F6 Arnes Spain
261 F7 Arnett OK U.S.A.
201 L6 Arnfels Austria
186 I5 Arnhem Neth.
106 F2 Arnhem, Cape N.T. Austr.
106 F2 Arnhem Bay N.T. Austr.
106 D2 Arnhem Land reg. N.T. Austr.
106 E2 Arnhem Land Aboriginal Land res. N.T. Austr.
100 □[3b] Arniel i. Majuro Marshall Is
160 I6 Arnionys 1 Lith.
168 E8 Arnisdale Highland, Scotland U.K.
220 C2 Arnissa Greece
213 I8 Arno r. Italy
104 F5 Arno Bay S.A. Austr.
204 D4 Arnoia r. Spain
168 C6 Arnol Western Isles, Scotland U.K.
171 O7 Arnold Nottinghamshire, England U.K.
258 B6 Arnold MD U.S.A.
250 G3 Arnold MI U.S.A.
260 J6 Arnold MO U.S.A.
249 K4 Arnold's Cove Nfld and Lab. Can.
201 I6 Arnoldstein Austria
184 I1 Arnon r. France
Arnon r. Jordan see Mawjib, Wādī al
199 J3 Arnót Hungary
258 A1 Arnot PA U.S.A.
251 O1 Arnoux, Lac l. Que. Can.
162 P1 Arnøya i. Norway
Arnoya r. Spain see Arnoia
248 E4 Arnprior Ont. Can.
170 I1 Arnprior Stirling, Scotland U.K.
191 F8 Arnsberg Ger.
191 F8 Arnsberg admin. reg. Ger.
191 F8 Arnsberger Wald hills Ger.
195 N3 Arnschwang Ger.
193 I8 Arnsdorf bei Dresden Ger.
191 K9 Arnstadt Ger.
251 O4 Arnstein Ont. Can.
193 A11 Arnstein Ger.
195 N4 Arnstorf Ger.
251 O1 Arntfield Que. Can.
205 M2 Arnuero Spain
275 E3 Aro r. Venez.
271 I8 Aroa Venez.
101 □[9a] Aroa, Pointe pt Moorea Fr. Polynesia
234 C5 Aroab Namibia
285 G3 Arocena Arg.
206 F5 Aroche Spain
206 E4 Aroche, Sierra de hills Spain
279 B7 Aroeira Brazil
204 D7 Arões Aveiro Port.
204 D6 Arões Braga Port.
199 J4 Ároktő Hungary
248 C3 Aroland Ont. Can.
212 C3 Arolla Switz.
191 H8 Arolsen Ger.
225 H6 Aroma Sudan
264 K5 Aromas CA U.S.A.
181 J5 Aron France
182 C3 Aron r. Bourgogne France
181 J5 Aron r. Pays de la Loire France
138 F7 Aron Madh. Prad. India
238 □[3a] Arona Tenerife Canary Is
212 F4 Arona Italy
257 □R2 Aroostook N.B. Can.
257 □R2 Aroostook r. ME U.S.A.
100 □[6] Aropa P.N.G.
244 G3 Aropuk Lake AK U.S.A.
99 H2 Arorae i. Gilbert Is Kiribati
103 □[3] Arorangi Rarotonga Cook Is
Arore i. Gilbert Is Kiribati see Arorae
114 D5 Aroroy Masbate Phil.
266 E3 Aros r. Mex.
204 D5 Arosa Port.
212 H2 Arosa Switz.
Arosa, Ría de est. Spain see Arousa, Ría de
Arossi i. Solomon Is see San Cristobal
204 D7 Arouca Port.
271 □[7] Arouca Trin. and Tob.
224 D5 Arouelli well Chad
204 C3 Arousa, Illa de i. Spain
204 B4 Arousa, Ría de est. Spain
151 F6 Arp'a r. Armenia
151 E5 Arpa r. Armenia/Turkey
143 P7 Arpa Kyrg.
149 K3 Arpaçay Turkey
150 C2 Arpaçsakarlar Turkey
178 D6 Arpajon France
185 I6 Arpajon-sur-Cère France
215 L4 Arpino Italy
Arpinum Italy see Arpino
Arqalyq Kazakh. see Arkalyk
215 K2 Arquata del Tronto Italy
212 F6 Arquata Scrivia Italy
185 I10 Arques Languedoc-Roussillon France
178 D2 Arques Nord-Pas-de-Calais France
208 K4 Arques, Puig d' hill Spain
178 B4 Arques-la-Bataille France
207 M4 Arquillos Spain
235 G4 Arquipélago de Bazaruto, Parque Nacional de nat. park Moz.
238 □[1] Arquipélago dos Açores aut. reg. N. Atlantic Ocean
145 K9 Arra r. Pak.
150 D7 Ar Rabbah Jordan
206 B3 Arrábida, Parque Natural da nature res. Port.
107 H9 Arrabury Qld Austr.
195 N3 Arrach Ger.
179 M6 Arracourt France
225 G3 Ar Radīsīyah Baḥrī Egypt
180 F6 Arradon France
146 G3 Ar Raghbah Saudi Arabia
228 E5 Arrah Côte d'Ivoire
Arrah Bihar India see Ara
149 K7 Ar Raḥḥālīyah Iraq
146 G9 Ar Rāhidah Yemen
278 D5 Arraias Brazil
278 B4 Arraias r. Brazil
278 D5 Arraias, Serra de hills Brazil
206 D3 Arraiolos Port.
149 K7 Ar Ramādī Iraq
150 D9 Ar Ramlah Jordan
169 F7 Arra Mountains hills Ireland
150 E6 Ar Ramthā Jordan
168 F11 Arran i. Scotland U.K.
179 K5 Arrancy-sur-Crusne France
206 A3 Arranhó Port.
169 E3 Arranmore Island Ireland
150 H3 Ar Raqqah Syria
150 G2 Ar Raqqah governorate Syria
232 D3 Arraro well Eth.
178 E3 Arras France
146 D4 Ar Ra's al Abyaḍ pt Saudi Arabia
205 P2 Arrasate Spain
185 D10 Arras-en-Lavedan France
150 D8 Ar Rashādīyah Jordan
146 F3 Ar Rass Saudi Arabia
150 E4 Ar Rastān Syria
185 F7 Arrats r. France
185 B9 Arraute-Charritte France
149 K9 Ar Rawḍ well Saudi Arabia
146 E2 Ar Rawḍah Ḥā'il Saudi Arabia
146 F5 Ar Rawḍah Makkah Saudi Arabia
147 H8 Ar Rawḍah Yemen
146 F5 Ar Rawshan Saudi Arabia
147 I8 Ar Rāwuk Yemen
147 L4 Ar Rayḥānī Oman
146 G4 Ar Rayn Saudi Arabia
147 J3 Ar Rayyān Qatar
146 D4 Ar Rayyān Al Madīnah Saudi Arabia
146 D5 Ar Rayyān Makkah Saudi Arabia
185 E10 Arreau France
274 D4 Arrecifal Col.
238 □[3c] Arrecife Lanzarote Canary Is
285 G4 Arrecifes Arg.
205 M2 Arredondo Spain
180 C5 Arrée, Monts d' hills France
185 D9 Arrens, Gave d' r. France
178 I7 Arrentières France
164 I6 Arresø l. Denmark
Arretium Italy see Arezzo
201 I6 Arriach Austria
269 N9 Arriagá Mex.
268 F4 Arriaga Mex.
207 I7 Arriate Spain
285 G4 Arribeños Arg.
238 □[3c] Arrieta Lanzarote Canary Is
149 M8 Ar Rifā'ī Iraq
204 D7 Arrifana Aveiro Port.
204 D8 Arrifana Coimbra Port.
204 F7 Arrifana Guarda Port.
238 □[1b] Arrifes São Miguel Azores
178 I6 Arrigny France
205 O2 Arrigorriaga Spain
149 L8 Ar Rihāb salt flat Iraq
147 K5 Ar Rimāl des. Saudi Arabia
256 G11 Arrington VA U.S.A.
109 C10 Arrino W.A. Austr.
205 J2 Arriondas Spain
146 H3 Ar Riyāḍ Saudi Arabia
146 G3 Ar Riyāḍ prov. Saudi Arabia
226 B4 Arriyd, Sabkhat salt pan Western Sahara
207 J2 Arroba de los Montes Spain
204 H8 Arrobuey mt. Spain
168 G10 Arrochar Argyll and Bute, Scotland U.K.
282 G4 Arroio Grande Brazil
181 J3 Arromanches-les-Bains France
206 E2 Arronches Port.
215 J2 Arrone Italy
214 H3 Arrone r. Lazio Italy
215 I4 Arrone r. Lazio Italy
205 P3 Arroniz Spain
185 D8 Arros r. France
212 E7 Arroscia r. Italy
178 B7 Arrou France
182 D4 Arroux r. France
250 E1 Arrow r. Ont. Can.
172 G3 Arrow r. England U.K.
169 F4 Arrow, Lough l. Ireland
262 J3 Arrow Creek r. MT U.S.A.
250 D1 Arrow Lake Ont. Can.
103 E10 Arrowsmith, Mount South I. N.Z.
106 F2 Arrowsmith, Point N.T. Austr.
103 C11 Arrowtown South I. N.Z.
205 L3 Arroyal Spain
285 G4 Arroy Dulce Arg.
285 F2 Arroyito Córdoba Arg.
284 D3 Arroyito Mendoza Arg.
271 □[1] Arroyo Puerto Rico
206 F1 Arroyo de la Luz Spain
206 G3 Arroyo de San Serván Spain
264 L6 Arroyo Grande CA U.S.A.
206 G4 Arroyomolinos de León Spain
285 G3 Arroyo Seco Arg.
268 F8 Arroyo Seco Guerrero Mex.
269 H4 Arroyo Seco Querétaro Mex.
277 F6 Arroyos-y-Esteros Para.
146 D4 Ar Rubaḍ Saudi Arabia
146 G2 Ar Rubay'iyah Saudi Arabia
277 F3 Arruda Brazil
206 A3 Arruda dos Vinhos Port.
285 G2 Arrufó Arg.
146 F3 Ar Rumādīyat Saudi Arabia
147 J3 Ar Rumaythah Bahrain
149 L8 Ar Rumaythah Iraq
150 D6 Ar Rummān Jordan
146 H1 Ar Ruq'ī well Saudi Arabia
150 G3 Ar Ruṣāfah Syria
150 E6 Ar Ruṣayfah Jordan
147 M4 Ar Rustāq Oman
149 J7 Ar Ruṭbah Iraq
224 C3 Ar Ruwaybāt well Libya
146 G2 Ar Ruwayḍah Ar Riyāḍ Saudi Arabia
146 G4 Ar Ruwayḍah Ar Riyāḍ Saudi Arabia
150 F3 Ar Ruwayḍah Syria
106 F6 Arruwurra Aboriginal Land res. N.T. Austr.
179 L5 Arry France
144 B3 Ars Iran
221 K6 Arsaköy Turkey
144 F1 Ärsarybaba Erezi hills Turkm.
208 I3 Arsèguel Spain
144 E7 Arsenajān Iran
246 H1 Arseno Lake N.W.T. Can.
184 A3 Ars-en-Ré France
122 M5 Arsent'evka Rus. Fed.
122 H6 Arsen'yev Rus. Fed.
161 T8 Arsen'yevo Rus. Fed.
143 O2 Arshaly Akmolinskaya Oblast' Kazakh.
143 S3 Arshaly Vostochnyy Kazakhstan Kazakh.
160 M7 Arshanskaye Wzvyshsha hills Belarus
213 L4 Arsiè Italy
213 K4 Arsiero Italy
136 E6 Arsikere Karnataka Ind…
151 A5 Arsin Turkey
156 J4 Arsk Rus. Fed.
Arslanbob Kyrg. see Ars…
215 K3 Arsoli Italy
182 F5 Ars-sur-Formans Franc…
179 L5 Ars-sur-Moselle France
145 O1 Arstanban Kyrg.
100 □[5] Art, Île i. New Caledoni…
220 B3 Arta Greece
209 L8 Artà Spain
205 Q3 Artajona Spain
151 G3 Art'ana Georgia
209 E8 Artana Spain
212 C4 Artanavaz r. Italy
181 M7 Artannes-sur-Indre Fra…
151 F6 Artashat Armenia
267 I5 Arteaga Coahuila Mex.
268 E7 Arteaga Michoacán Mex…
122 H7 Artem Rus. Fed.
182 H5 Artemare France
270 B2 Artemisa Cuba
220 D5 Artemisia Greece
159 R6 Artemivka Donets'ka Ob…
159 Q4 Artemivka Kharkivs'ka … Ukr.
159 O4 Artemivka Poltavs'ka Ob…
159 R5 Artemivs'k Donets'ka O…
159 R5 Artemivs'k Luhans'ka O…
Artemovsk Ukr. see Arte…
153 M4 Artemovskiy Irkutskaya Rus. Fed.
122 H7 Artemovskiy Primorskiy Rus. Fed.
213 L3 Artèn Italy
215 J4 Artena Italy
178 C7 Artenay France
193 D8 Artern (Unstrut) Ger.
208 I4 Artés Spain
208 H4 Artesa de Segre Spain
265 W9 Artesia AZ U.S.A.
263 L10 Artesia NM U.S.A.
212 F1 Arth Switz.
185 I8 Arthès France
185 D9 Arthez-d'Asson France
185 C9 Arthez-de-Béarn Franc…
181 O8 Arthon France
180 H7 Arthon-en-Retz France
109 C8 Arthur r. W.A. Austr.
251 N6 Arthur Ont. Can.
260 E5 Arthur NE U.S.A.
256 B12 Arthur TN U.S.A.
104 F4 Arthur, Lake salt flat S.A…
237 J8 Arthur, Lake S. Africa
256 E8 Arthur, Lake PA U.S.A.
105 K9 Arthur Lake Tas. Austr.
105 J9 Arthur Pieman Conserv… Area nature res. Tas. Aus…
107 M7 Arthur Point Qld Austr.
103 F9 Arthur's Pass South I. N…
103 F9 Arthur's Pass National … South I. N.Z.
270 F1 Arthur's Town Cat I. Ba…
170 D3 Articlave Northern Irelar…
208 D2 Artieda Spain
208 G2 Arties Spain
170 C4 Artigarvan Northern Irel…
286 U2 Artigas research stn Anta…
285 I2 Artigas Uru.
285 I2 Artigas dept Uru.
185 G9 Artigat France
151 E5 Art'ik Armenia
247 I2 Artillery Lake N.W.T. Ca…
234 E5 Artisia Botswana
185 C9 Artix France
160 J1 Artjärvi Fin.
190 J4 Artlenburg Ger.
212 I4 Artogne Italy
178 C2 Artois reg. France
178 C2 Artois, Collines d' hills …
149 K4 Artos Dağı mt. Turkey
148 H3 Artova Turkey
208 □ Artrutx, Cap d' c. Spain
Artsakh aut. reg. Azer. s… Dağlıq Qarabağ
128 G4 Arts Bogd Uul mts Mor…
Artsiz Ukr. see Artsyz
158 I8 Artsyz Ukr.
183 I9 Artuby r. France
Artur de Paiva Angola se…
286 U2 Arturo Prat research stn …
132 C7 Artux Xinjiang China
149 J3 Artvin Turkey
151 C4 Artvin prov. Turkey
144 H3 Artyk Turkm.
205 N2 Artziniega Spain
230 F4 Aru Dem. Rep. Congo
113 H8 Aru, Kepulauan is Indon…
204 F4 A Rúa Spain
232 A4 Arua Uganda
274 E6 Aruajá Brazil
278 C5 Aruanã Brazil
271 □[9] Aruba terr. West Indies
238 □[3f] Arucas Gran Canaria Ca…
151 F5 Aruch Armenia
185 D9 Arudy France
101 □[9a] Arue Tahiti Fr. Polynesia
280 D5 Arujá Brazil
100 □[6] Aruliho Guadalcanal So…
275 F6 Arumã Brazil
124 □[1] Arume Okinawa Japan
124 □[1] Arume-wan b. Okinawa …
139 K6 Arun r. Nepal
139 N6 Arunachal Pradesh stat…
103 F10 Arundel South I. N.Z.
173 K6 Arundel West Sussex, En…
129 S3 Arun Gol r. China
Arun Qi Nei Mongol Ch… Naji
136 F8 Aruppukkottai Tamil Na…
238 □[3a] Arure La Gomera Canary…
115 B3 Arus, Tanjung pt Indon.
233 C5 Arusha Tanz.
233 C5 Arusha admin. reg. Tanz.
233 C5 Arusha National Park T…
117 I6 Arut r. Indon.
275 E5 Aruti Brazil
230 D4 Aruwimi r. Dem. Rep. C…
260 C6 Arvada CO U.S.A.
169 G5 Arvagh Ireland
183 I6 Arvan r. France
128 H3 Arvayheer Mongolia
182 I4 Arve r. France
184 B4 Arvert France
185 D6 Arveyres France
138 G9 Arvi Mahar. India
247 M2 Arviat Nunavut Can.
254 L1 Arvida Que. Can.
162 O4 Arvidsjaur Sweden
183 B8 Arvieu France
183 J7 Arvieux France
164 I2 Arvika Sweden
162 P1 Årviksand Norway
264 N6 Arvin CA U.S.A.
217 K5 Arvo, Lago l. Italy
256 G11 Arvonia VA U.S.A.
146 G4 Arwā' Saudi Arabia
150 D4 Arwād i. Syria
115 E7 Arwala Maluku Indon.
129 P3 Arxan Nei Mongol China
132 G5 Arxan Xinjiang China
Aryanah Tunisia see L'A…
156 K4 Aryazh Rus. Fed.
143 M1 Arykbalyk Kazakh.
Aryqbayq Kazakh. see Ar…
143 M6 Arys Kazakh.
143 M6 Arys' r. Kazakh.
143 L5 Arys, Ozero salt l. Kazak…
214 C5 Arzachena Sardegna Ital…
185 D8 Arzacq-Arraziguet Franc…
157 H5 Arzamas Rus. Fed.
214 D8 Arzana Sardegna Italy
147 K3 Arzanah i. U.A.E.
180 E6 Arzano France
191 E10 Arzbach Ger.
193 F10 Arzberg Bayern Ger.
193 H7 Arzberg Sachsen Ger.
185 I9 Arzens France
227 E2 Arzew Alg.
191 B10 Arzfeld Ger.
157 I7 Arzgir Rus. Fed.
213 K4 Arzignano Italy
Arzila Morocco see Asila

C5 Arzl im Pitztal Austria
D6 Arzon r. France
D8 Arzúa Spain
I6 As Belgium
B1 Aš Czech Rep.
C5 Asa waterhole Kenya
I4 Åsa Sweden
G4 Asaa Denmark
B1 Asab Namibia
G6 Asaba Japan
G5 Asaba Nigeria
G2 Asad, Buḩayrat al resr Syria
N4 Asadābād Afgh.
C4 Asadābād Hamadān Iran
H4 Asadābād Khorāsān Iran
E6 Asadābād Yazd Iran
H5 Aşağı Ağcakänd Azer.
G4 Aşağı Āskipara Azer.
G5 Aşağı Ayıblı Azer.
E5 Aşağı Dağ mt. Turkey
E5 Aşağıdalören Turkey
K5 Aşağıkaraçay Turkey
C5 Aşağıkatıklı Turkey
Aşağı Köynük Azer.
E6 Aşağıküpkıran Turkey
H5 Aşağı Oratağ Azer.
F7 Aşağısağmallı Turkey
E6 Aşağısöylemez Turkey
D5 Asagny, Parc National d' nat. park Côte d'Ivoire
A5 Asago Japan
C3 Asahan r. Indon.
F5 Asahi Aichi Japan
M4 Asahi Chiba Japan
D4 Asahi Fukui Japan
F3 Asahi Gifu Japan
M3 Asahi Ibaraki Japan
K5 Asahi Kanagawa Japan
E5 Asahi Mie Japan
G3 Asahi Nagano Japan
G2 Asahi Toyama Japan
D8 Asahi-dake mt. Japan
Asahi-dake vol. Japan
K12 Asahi-gawa r. Japan
Asahikawa Japan
L1 Asahi-take mt. Japan
Asaka Japan
Asaka Uzbek.
Asakawa Japan
Asake-gawa r. Japan
'Asal Egypt
Āsalē l. Eth.
Asālem Iran
'Asalū, Chāh-e well Iran
Asamaga-take hill Japan
Asama-yama vol. Japan
Asamankese Ghana
Asan Guam
Asankranguaa Ghana
Asan-man b. S. Korea
Asansol W. Bengal India
Asanwenso Ghana
Asao Japan
Asar Nei Mongol China
Asashina Japan
Asarp-Arros France
Asau Samoa
Asava i. Fiji see Yasawa
Āsayita Eth.
Asbach Ger.
Asbach-Bäumenheim Ger.
Asbestos Que. Can.
Asbestos Hill Que. Can. see Purtuniq
Asbestos Mountains S. Africa
Āsbe Teferi Eth.
Åsbro Sweden
Asbury Park NJ U.S.A.
Ascain France
Ascalon Israel see Ashqelon
Ascea Italy
Ascensión Arg.
Ascensión Bol.
Ascensión Chihuahua Mex.
Ascensión Nuevo León Mex.
Ascension atoll Micronesia see Pohnpei
Ascension Curaçao Neth. Antilles
Ascension i. S. Atlantic Ocean
Ascensión, Bahía de la b. Mex.
Ascha Ger.
Ascha r. Ger.
Aschach an der Donau Austria
Aschaffenburg Ger.
Aschau im Zillertal Austria
Aschau im Chiemgau Ger.
Aschbach Markt Austria
Ascheberg Ger.
Ascheberg (Holstein) Ger.
Aschenstein hill Ger.
Aschères-le-Marché France
Aschersleben Ger.
Aschheim Ger.
Asciano Italy
Ascione, Colle d' pass Italy
Asco Corse France
Ascochinga Arg.
Ascoli Piceno Italy
Ascoli Piceno prov. Italy
Ascoli Satriano Italy
Ascona Switz.
Ascot Windsor and Maidenhead, England U.K.
Ascotán Chile
Ascotán, Salar de salt flat Chile
Ascou France
As Covas Spain
Asculum Italy see Ascoli Piceno
Asculum Picenum Italy see Ascoli Piceno
Ascutney VT U.S.A.
Asdhu i. N. Male Maldives
Asdu i. N. Male Maldives see Asdhu
Åse Norway
Āseb Eritrea see Assab
Åseda Sweden
Asedjrad plat. Alg.
Asekeyevo Rus. Fed.
Āsela Eth.
Åsele Sweden
Åsen Sweden
Asendabo Eth.
Asendorf Niedersachsen Ger.
Asendorf Niedersachsen Ger.
Asenovgrad Bulg.
Åseral Norway
Aseri Estonia
A Serra de Outes Spain
Aserradero los Charcos Mex.
Aşfar, Jabal al mt. Jordan
Aşfar, Tall al hill Syria
Asfeld France
Asfordby Leicestershire, England U.K.
Aşgabat Turkm.
Ásgarður Iceland
Ash Kent, England U.K.
Ash Surrey, England U.K.
Asha Rus. Fed.
Ashahi-dake mt. Japan
Ashanti admin. reg. Ghana
Ashap Rus. Fed.
Asharat Saudi Arabia
Ash'arīyah Saudi Arabia
Ashaway RI U.S.A.
Ashbourne Ireland
Ashbourne Derbyshire, England U.K.
Ashburn GA U.S.A.
Ashburton watercourse W.A. Austr.
Ashburton South I. N.Z.
Ashburton r. South I. N.Z.
Ashburton Devon, England U.K.
Ashburton Bay Ont. Can.
Ashburton Range hills N.T. Austr.
Ashbury Oxfordshire, England U.K.
Ashby de la Zouch Leicestershire, England U.K.
Ashchikol', Ozero salt l. Kazakh.
Ashchurch Gloucestershire, England U.K.
Ashchysay Kazakh. see Achisay
Ashcott Somerset, England U.K.
246 F5 Ashcroft B.C. Can.
150 C7 Ashdod Israel
261 H9 Ashdown AR U.S.A.
173 M5 Ashdown Forest reg. England U.K.
255 H8 Asheboro NC U.S.A.
261 G8 Asher OK U.S.A.
247 L5 Ashern Man. Can.
255 F8 Asheville NC U.S.A.
160 M4 Ashevo Rus. Fed.
248 C2 Asheweig r. Ont. Can.
105 M3 Ashford N.S.W. Austr.
169 J6 Ashford Ireland
173 I6 Ashford Hampshire, England U.K.
173 N5 Ashford Kent, England U.K.
173 L5 Ashford Surrey, England U.K.
265 T6 Ash Fork AZ U.S.A.
102 J7 Ashhurst North I. N.Z.
124 T3 Ashibetsu Japan
127 I4 Ashigawa Japan
127 J3 Ashikaga Japan
125 H14 Ashikita Japan
173 N2 Ashill Norfolk, England U.K.
171 N3 Ashington Northumberland, England U.K.
127 J5 Ashino-ko l. Japan
127 J2 Ashio Japan
127 J3 Ashio-sanchi mts Japan
250 F6 Ashippun WI U.S.A.
124 S6 Ashiro Japan
127 I4 Ashiwada Japan
126 B6 Ashiya Japan
125 K14 Ashizuri-misaki pt Japan
125 J14 Ashizuri-Uwakai Kokuritsu-kōen nat. park Japan
144 F6 Ashkazar Iran
Ashkelon Israel see Ashqelon
Ashkhabad Turkm. see Aşgabat
Ashkhabadskaya Oblast' admin. div. Turkm. see Ahal
224 B3 Ashkidah Libya
168 K12 Ashkirk Scottish Borders, Scotland U.K.
250 G9 Ashkum IL U.S.A.
145 N4 Ashkun reg. Afgh.
255 E9 Ashland AL U.S.A.
261 F7 Ashland KS U.S.A.
256 C10 Ashland KY U.S.A.
257 □Q2 Ashland ME U.S.A.
261 K8 Ashland MS U.S.A.
262 K4 Ashland MT U.S.A.
260 G5 Ashland NE U.S.A.
257 N5 Ashland NH U.S.A.
256 C8 Ashland OH U.S.A.
262 C5 Ashland OR U.S.A.
258 C3 Ashland PA U.S.A.
256 H11 Ashland VA U.S.A.
250 D3 Ashland WI U.S.A.
255 D7 Ashland City TN U.S.A.
105 L3 Ashley N.S.W. Austr.
103 G10 Ashley r. South I. N.Z.
173 M3 Ashley Cambridgeshire, England U.K.
250 I8 Ashley IN U.S.A.
250 J6 Ashley MI U.S.A.
260 F2 Ashley ND U.S.A.
256 C8 Ashley OH U.S.A.
258 D2 Ashley PA U.S.A.
108 G2 Ashmore and Cartier Islands terr. Austr.
108 G2 Ashmore Reef Ashmore & Cartier Is Austr.
160 I7 Ashmyanskaye Wzvyshsha hills Belarus
160 I7 Ashmyany Hrodzyenskaya Voblasts' Belarus
160 J7 Ashmyany Hrodzyenskaya Voblasts' Belarus
138 F7 Ashoknagar Madh. Prad. India
124 U3 Ashoro Japan
151 E4 Ashots'k' Armenia
146 G7 Ashqar, Barqā al reg. Yemen
150 C7 Ashqelon Israel
146 F6 Ash Sha'ār Saudi Arabia
149 K8 Ash Shabakah Iraq
225 F4 Ash Shabb well Egypt
149 J5 Ash Shaddādah Syria
146 E5 Ash Shafa Saudi Arabia
150 A8 Ash Shallūfah Egypt
Ash Sham Syria see Dimashq
147 M2 Ash Sha'm U.A.E.
149 L8 Ash Shanāfīyah Iraq
149 J9 Ash Shaqīq well Saudi Arabia
146 G3 Ash Sha'rā' Saudi Arabia
150 D8 Ash Sharāh mts Jordan
146 H7 Ash Sharawrah Saudi Arabia
147 L3 Ash Shāriqah U.A.E.
149 K6 Ash Sharqāţ Iraq
148 E8 Ash Sharqīyah governorate Egypt
147 N5 Ash Sharqīyah admin. reg. Oman
147 N4 Ash Sharqīyah reg. Oman
147 J5 Ash Sharqīyah prov. Saudi Arabia
149 M8 Ash Shaţrah Iraq
150 E2 Ash Shaţţ Egypt
150 D8 Ash Shawbak Jordan
146 E1 Ash Shaybānī well Saudi Arabia
151 B1 Ash Shaykh Ḩumayd Saudi Arabia
150 G3 Ash Shaykh Ibrāhīm Syria
146 G9 Ash Shaykh 'Uthman Yemen
150 F9 Ash Shiblīyāt hill Saudi Arabia
147 I8 Ash Shiḩr Yemen
147 M3 Ash Shināş Oman
147 K6 Ash Shişar well Oman
146 F2 Ash Shu'aybah Saudi Arabia
146 G1 Ash Shu'bah Saudi Arabia
146 F3 Ash Shubaykīyah Saudi Arabia
147 H2 Ash Shumlūl Saudi Arabia
146 F7 Ash Shuqayq Saudi Arabia
Ash Shurayf Saudi Arabia see Khaybar
224 B2 Ash Shuwayrif Libya
138 F8 Ashta Madh. Prad. India
136 D4 Ashta Mahar. India
256 E7 Ashtabula OH U.S.A.
151 F5 Ashtarak Armenia
136 D3 Ashti Mahar. India
136 F3 Ashti Mahar. India
138 G9 Ashti Mahar. India
236 E9 Ashton S. Africa
271 □3 Ashton St Vincent
171 L7 Ashton Cheshire, England U.K.
262 I4 Ashton ID U.S.A.
250 E8 Ashton IL U.S.A.
258 A6 Ashton MD U.S.A.
171 M7 Ashton-under-Lyne Greater Manchester, England U.K.
151 I4 Ashty Rus. Fed.
249 H2 Ashuanipi r. Nfld and Lab. Can.
249 H2 Ashuanipi Lake Nfld and Lab. Can.
254 K1 Ashuapmushuan r. Que. Can.
248 F3 Ashuapmushuan, Réserve Faunique nature res. Que. Can.
Ashur Iraq see Ash Sharqāţ
173 I6 Ashurst Hampshire, England U.K.
173 M5 Ashurst Kent, England U.K.
255 D9 Ashville AL U.S.A.
257 □Q4 Ashville ME U.S.A.
256 G8 Ashville PA U.S.A.
250 D3 Ashwabay, Mount hill WI U.S.A.
250 F5 Ashwaubenon WI U.S.A.
172 G5 Ashwick Somerset, England U.K.
150 E4 'Āşī r. Lebanon alt. 'Āşī, Nahr al (Syria), alt. Asi (Turkey), hist. Orontes
150 E3 Asi r. Turkey alt. 'Āşī (Lebanon), alt. 'Āşī, Nahr al (Syria), hist. Orontes
150 E2 'Āşī, Nahr al r. Syria alt. 'Āşī (Lebanon), alt. Asi (Turkey), hist. Orontes
110 Asia Continent
213 L4 Asiago Italy
114 D5 Asid Gulf Masbate Phil.
268 E3 Asientos Mex.
136 F3 Asifabad Andhra Prad. India
137 I3 Asika Orissa India
163 R6 Asikkala Fin.
226 D2 Asilah Morocco
273 C3 Asillo Peru
220 G7 Asimi Kriti Greece
208 C3 Asín Spain
214 B6 Asinara, Golfo dell' b. Sardegna Italy
214 A5 Asinara, Isola i. Sardegna Italy
138 E7 Asind Rajasthan India
152 J4 Asino Rus. Fed.
161 N7 Asintorf Belarus
160 L8 Asipovichy Belarus
144 E8 Asīr Iran
146 E5 'Asīr prov. Saudi Arabia
146 E5 'Asīr reg. Saudi Arabia
Asisium Italy see Assisi
160 E1 Askainen Fin.
138 E2 Askale Pak.
149 J4 Aşkale Turkey
159 M7 Askaniya Nova Ukr.
159 M7 Askaniya Nova, Zapovidnyk nature res. Ukr.
158 H1 Askarovo Rus. Fed.
169 E7 Askeaton Ireland
237 L7 Askeaton S. Africa
163 G2 Asker Norway
151 A7 Asker Dağı mt. Turkey
171 O6 Askern South Yorkshire, England U.K.
165 K3 Askersund Sweden
236 E2 Askham S. Africa
169 F4 Askill Ireland
164 H2 Askim Norway
149 K5 Askī Mawşil Iraq
154 L4 Askino Rus. Fed.
229 I4 Askira Nigeria
168 D9 Askival hill Scotland U.K.
120 F1 Askiz Rus. Fed.
165 E5 Asklipieio Greece
190 L1 Askø i. Denmark
163 R6 Askola Fin.
165 M2 Åsköping Sweden
220 E2 Askos Greece
138 H5 Askot Uttaranchal India
164 B1 Askøy i. Norway
236 E10 Askraal S. Africa
163 H6 Askvoll Norway
151 H6 Askyaran Azer.
146 G5 Aslam, Wādī watercourse Saudi Arabia
221 K3 Aslanapa Turkey
144 B2 Aşlāndūz Iran
160 M8 Asliwka r. Belarus
Aslóközpont Hungary see Mórahalom
145 N4 Asmar Afgh.
145 N4 Asmar reg. Afgh.
146 F6 Asmar reg. Saudi Arabia
225 H6 Asmara Eritrea
146 E2 Asmarah, Jabal mts Saudi Arabia
204 D2 As Mariñas reg. Spain
Āsmera Eritrea see Asmara
165 K5 Åsnen l. Sweden
204 D2 As Neves Galicia Spain
204 D4 As Neves Galicia Spain
204 F3 As Nogais Spain
215 L1 Aso r. Italy
127 L4 Asō Japan
275 G4 Asoenangka Brazil
125 I14 Aso-Kuju Kokuritsu-kōen nat. park Japan
212 I5 Asola Italy
213 L4 Asolo Italy
207 P2 Asomadilla hill Spain
139 O5 Asonli Arun. Prad. India
220 D5 Asopos r. Greece
220 E4 Asopos r. Greece
232 B2 Āsosa Eth.
125 I14 Aso-san vol. Japan
225 H4 Asoteriba, Jebel mt. Sudan
262 F3 Asotin WA U.S.A.
199 I5 Ásotthalom Hungary
125 G12 Asō-wan b. Japan
156 L4 Aspa Rus. Fed.
201 H3 Aspach Austria
201 N4 Aspang-Markt Austria
144 C3 Aspar Iran
143 O6 Aspara Kazakh.
201 N2 Asparn an der Zaya Austria
219 P8 Asparukhovo Bulg.
162 M5 Aspås Sweden
171 K4 Aspatria Cumbria, England U.K.
209 D11 Aspe Spain
185 C9 Aspe, Gave d' r. France
185 C10 Aspe, Vallée d' val. France
162 N5 Aspeå Sweden
263 K7 Aspen CO U.S.A.
186 H5 Asperen Neth.
164 H2 Asperen l. Norway
194 G4 Asperg Ger.
261 E9 Aspermont TX U.S.A.
258 A5 Aspers PA U.S.A.
185 F9 Aspet France
185 E10 Aspin, Col d' pass France
151 E4 Aspindza Georgia
183 C9 Aspiran France
103 C11 Aspiring, Mount South I. N.Z.
204 E2 As Pontes de García Rodríguez Spain
183 H7 Aspremont France
183 H7 Aspres-sur-Buëch France
185 I6 Asprières France
Aspro, Cape Cyprus see Aspron, Cape
220 B3 Asprokavos, Akrotirio pt Kerkyra Greece
217 J7 Aspromonte, Parco Nazionale dell' nat. park Italy
150 A4 Aspron, Cape Cyprus
Aspropotamos r. Greece see Acheloos
220 E2 Asprovalta Greece
138 E8 Aspur Rajasthan India
247 J4 Asquith Sask. Can.
204 F2 As Rodrigas Spain
213 K4 Assa r. Italy
226 C3 Assa Morocco
151 G2 Assa r. Rus. Fed.
150 F3 As Sa'an Syria
225 I6 Assab Eritrea
228 C2 Assaba admin. reg. Maur.
146 E2 As Sab'ān Saudi Arabia
150 H3 As Sabkhah Syria
147 I2 As Sabsab well Saudi Arabia
124 R5 Assabu Japan
150 E5 Aş Şafā lava field Syria
Aş Şafāqis Tunisia see Sfax
225 F2 Aş Şaff Egypt
150 D7 Aş Şāfī Jordan
150 F2 Aş Şafīrah Syria
146 D3 Aş Şafrā Al Madīnah Saudi Arabia
146 F2 Aş Şafrā Ḩā'il Saudi Arabia
147 I2 Aş Şaḩāf Saudi Arabia
146 F8 Aş Şahīf Yemen
Aş Şaḩrā' des. Egypt/Libya see Libyan Desert
225 F3 Aş Şaḩrā' al Gharbīyah des. Egypt
225 G3 Aş Şaḩrā' ash Sharqīyah des. Egypt
229 H4 Assaikio Nigeria
Assake Uzbek. see Asaka
142 G6 Assake-Audan, Vpadina depr. Uzbek.
225 I7 'Assal, Lac l. Djibouti
147 H3 As Salamīyah Saudi Arabia
148 F8 Aş Şāliḩīyah Egypt
149 J6 Aş Şāliḩīyah Syria
148 B8 As Sallūm Egypt
149 L8 As Salmān Iraq
150 D6 As Salţ Jordan
139 M6 Assam state India
229 G2 Assamakka Niger
149 L8 As Samāwah Iraq
150 E6 As Samrā' Jordan
194 H3 Assamstadt Ger.
147 J5 Aş Şanām reg. Saudi Arabia
150 E5 Aş Şanamayn Syria
226 B4 Assaq watercourse Western Sahara
226 B4 As Saquia al Hamra watercourse Western Sahara
146 G2 As Sarīf well Saudi Arabia
224 D3 As Sarīr reg. Libya
185 D9 Assat France
257 J10 Assateague Island MD U.S.A.
257 J11 Assateague Island National Seashore nature res. VA U.S.A.
146 G4 As Sawādah reg. Saudi Arabia
147 L7 As Sawdā i. Oman
171 O2 Aş Şawrah Al Madīnah Saudi Arabia
146 B2 Aş Şawrah Tabūk Saudi Arabia
146 H4 As Sayḩ Saudi Arabia
146 E5 As Sayl al Kabīr Saudi Arabia
187 F7 Asse Belgium
183 H9 Asse r. France
236 I9 Assegaaibos S. Africa
214 C9 Assemini Sardegna Italy
186 K2 Assen Neth.
186 G4 Assendelft Neth.
187 E6 Assenede Belgium
164 F6 Assens Denmark
180 G7 Assérac France
215 L3 Assergi Italy
187 H8 Assesse Belgium
224 C2 As Sidrah Libya
185 H6 Assier France
147 N4 As Sīfah Oman
249 H2 Assigny, Lac l. Nfld and Lab. Can.
147 J3 As Sikak Saudi Arabia
147 J4 As Sila' U.A.E.
247 J5 Assiniboia Sask. Can.
247 L5 Assiniboine r. Man./Sask. Can.
246 H5 Assiniboine, Mount Alta/B.C. Can.
248 F3 Assinica, Réserve Faunique nature res. Que. Can.
280 B5 Assis Brazil
280 A6 Assis Chateaubriand Brazil
215 J1 Assisi Italy
191 F9 Aßlar Ger.
200 G6 Assling Austria
195 M6 Aßling Ger.
212 G4 Asso Italy
228 □ Assomada Santiago Cape Verde
239 □2 Assomption i. Aldabra Is Seychelles
185 D9 Asson France
216 G8 Assoro Sicilia Italy
227 F4 Assouf Mellene watercourse Alg.
149 M9 Aş Şubayḩīyah Kuwait
146 F6 As Subaykhah Saudi Arabia
147 I8 As Sufāl Yemen
146 G1 Aş Şufayrī well Saudi Arabia
150 G4 As Sukhnah Syria
149 L6 As Sulaymānīyah Iraq
149 L6 As Sulaymānīyah governorate Iraq
146 E2 As Sulaymī Saudi Arabia
146 G5 As Sulayyil Saudi Arabia
147 I3 Aş Şulb reg. Saudi Arabia
224 C2 As Sulţān Libya
206 E2 Assumar Port.
146 H2 Aş Şummān plat. Saudi Arabia
147 I5 Aş Şummān plat. Saudi Arabia
146 E5 As Sūq Saudi Arabia
As Sūrīyah country Asia see Syria
149 J6 Aş Şuwar Syria
150 E6 As Suwaydā' Syria
150 E6 As Suwaydā' governorate Syria
147 N4 As Suwayḩ Oman
147 M4 As Suwayq Oman
149 L7 Aş Şuwayrah Iraq
146 E4 As Suwayriqīyah Saudi Arabia
225 G2 As Suways Egypt
150 A9 As Suways governorate Egypt
146 G8 As Suwwādīyah Yemen
168 F6 Assynt, Loch l. Scotland U.K.
163 K6 Asta r. Norway
213 L3 Asta, Cima d' mt. Italy
Astacus Turkey see İzmit
185 F7 Astaffort France
221 H7 Astakida i. Greece
220 C4 Astakos Greece
Astalu Island Pak. see Astola Island
143 N2 Astana Kazakh.
144 C3 Āstaneh Iran
144 C2 Āstārā Iran
185 E8 Astarac reg. France
185 F9 Astarac, Barrage de l' dam France
164 J1 Åsteby Sweden
201 J3 Asten Austria
187 I6 Asten Neth.
Asterabad Iran see Gorgān
212 E6 Asti Italy
212 E6 Asti prov. Italy
284 D2 Astica Arg.
213 L4 Astico r. Italy
199 L4 Aştileu Romania
276 C3 Astillero Peru
Astin Tag mts China see Altun Shan
Astipálaia i. Greece see Astypalaia
145 J9 Astola Island Pak.
185 H10 Aston r. France
237 I10 Aston Bay S. Africa
173 K4 Aston Clinton Buckinghamshire, England U.K.
138 E2 Astor Pak.
145 P4 Astor r. Pak.
280 B5 Astorga Brazil
204 H4 Astorga Spain
250 D9 Astoria IL U.S.A.
262 C3 Astoria OR U.S.A.
164 I5 Åstorp Sweden
239 □2 Astove i. Aldabra Is Seychelles
283 D7 Astra Arg.
Astrabad Iran see Gorgān
Astrakhan' Kazakh. see Astrakhanka
142 C4 Astrakhan' Rus. Fed.
Astrakhan' Bazar Azer. see Cälilabad
143 M2 Astrakhanka Kazakh.
159 O7 Astrakhanka Ukr.
Astrakhan Oblast admin. div. Rus. Fed. see Astrakhanskaya Oblast'
142 B4 Astrakhanskaya Oblast' admin. div. Rus. Fed.
160 I7 Astravyets Belarus
151 J5 Astraxanka Azer.
Astrida Rwanda see Butare
100 □6 Astrolabe, Cape Malaita Solomon Is
100 □5 Astrolabe, Récifs de l' rf New Caledonia
220 D5 Astros Greece
160 M6 Astrowna Belarus
160 H8 Astryna Belarus
161 O8 Astsyor r. Belarus
205 L4 Astudillo Spain
215 J5 Astura r. Italy
285 F5 Asturias Arg.
204 H1 Asturias airport Spain
204 H2 Asturias aut. comm. Spain
Asturica Augusta Spain see Astorga
173 I3 Astwood Bank Worcestershire, England U.K.
221 H6 Astypalaia Greece
221 H6 Astypalaia i. Greece
143 T3 Asubulak Kazakh.
Asūbulaq Kazakh. see Asubulak
100 □2 Asuisui, Cape Samoa
126 C7 Asuka Japan
126 F5 Asuke Japan
276 D2 Asunción Bol.
263 H11 Asunción r. Mex.
113 K3 Asuncion i. N. Mariana Is
277 F6 Asunción Para.
267 O10 Asunción Mita Guat.
165 O4 Asunden i. Sweden
164 J4 Åsunden l. Sweden
165 L4 Åsunden l. Sweden
214 B8 Asuni Sardegna Italy
126 D3 Asuwa-gawa r. Japan
160 L5 Asvyeya Belarus
160 L5 Asvyeyskaye, Vozyera l. Belarus
232 A4 Aswa r. Uganda
147 M3 Aswad Oman
146 D5 Aswad, Ar Ra's al pt Saudi Arabia
147 L5 Aswad, Wādī watercourse Oman
225 G3 Aswān Egypt
146 A3 Aswān governorate Egypt
225 G3 Aswān, Khazzān dam Egypt
Aswan Dam Egypt see Aswān, Khazzān
225 F3 Asyūţ Egypt
148 E10 Asyūţ governorate Egypt
199 J3 Aszaló Hungary
101 □8a Ata i. Tonga
274 E3 Atabapo r. Col./Venez.
143 M6 Atabay Kazakh.
221 L5 Atabey Turkey
282 C2 Atacama admin. reg. Chile
282 C2 Atacama, Desierto de des. Chile
282 D2 Atacama, Puna de plat. Arg.
276 C5 Atacama, Salar de salt flat Chile
274 B4 Atacames Ecuador
274 C4 Ataco Col.
227 G4 Atafaitafa, Djebel mt. Alg.
103 □1 Atafu atoll Tokelau
103 □1 Atafu i. Tokelau
126 C5 Atago-san hill Japan
127 K5 Atago-yama hill Japan
101 □9a Ataiti Tahiti Fr. Polynesia
143 M7 Atakent Kazakh.
150 C2 Atakent Turkey
151 J5 Atakişili Azer.
227 G5 Atakor mts Alg.
229 F4 Atakora, Chaîne de l' mts Benin
229 F5 Atakpamé Togo
278 G4 Atalaia Brazil
206 B4 Atalaia hill Port.
206 B6 Atalaia, Ponta da pt Port.
274 D6 Atalaia do Norte Brazil
Atalándi Greece see Atalanti
220 E4 Atalanti Greece
266 □S13 Atalaya Panama
276 C3 Atalaya Madre de Dios Peru
276 B2 Atalaya Ucayali Peru
207 P6 Atalaya Arabe hill Spain
281 G3 Ataléia Brazil
98 C2 Atambua Timor Indon.
127 J5 Atami Japan
282 E3 Atamisqui Arg.
243 M3 Atammik Greenland
145 K3 Atamyrat Turkm.
Ataniya Turkey see Adana
136 E4 Atanur Karnataka India
199 J4 Átány Hungary
205 M4 Atapuerca tourist site Spain
115 D8 Atapupu Timor Indon.
146 H8 'Ataq Yemen
150 A9 'Atāqah, Jabal hill Egypt
205 K6 Ataquines Spain
226 B5 Atâr Maur.
118 C6 Ataran r. Myanmar
269 H4 Atarjea Mex.
Atas i. Cocos Is see South Island
264 L6 Atascadero CA U.S.A.
261 F11 Atascosa watercourse TX U.S.A.
144 E4 Ātashān Iran
143 N3 Atasu Kazakh.
101 □8a Atata i. Tonga
133 I7 Atatan He r. China
148 D3 Atatürk airport Turkey
221 J6 Atatürk Milli Parkı nat. park Turkey
115 D8 Ataúro, Ilha de i. East Timor
Atáviros mt. Rodos Greece see Attavyros
144 H1 Ataýap Turkm.
150 B2 Atayurt Turkey
225 G5 Atbara Sudan
225 G5 Atbara r. Sudan
143 M2 Atbasar Kazakh.
143 P7 At-Bashy Kyrg.
261 J11 Atchafalaya Bay LA U.S.A.
260 H6 Atchison KS U.S.A.
244 G3 Atchueelinguk r. AK U.S.A.
258 F5 Atco NJ U.S.A.
205 Q6 Atea Spain
228 E5 Atebubu Ghana
205 Q6 Ateca Spain
204 E6 Atei Port.
204 F4 A Teixeira Spain
215 M4 Ateleta Italy
215 P6 Atella Italy
215 P6 Atella r. Italy
268 D5 Atemajac de Brizuela Mex.
127 I1 Atema-yama mt. Japan
276 C3 Aten Bol.
215 P7 Atena Lucana Italy
269 H7 Atenango del Río Mex.
268 C4 Atengo r. Mex.
268 C5 Atenguillo Mex.
268 C5 Atenguillo r. Mex.
268 D6 Atenquique Mex.
Ateransk Kazakh. see Atyrau
215 L3 Aterno r. Italy
145 I5 Āteshkhāneh, Kūh-e hill Afgh.
215 M3 Atessa Italy
146 G7 'Aţfayn, Wādī watercourse Yemen
258 D5 Atglen PA U.S.A.
187 E7 Ath Belgium
246 H4 Athabasca Alta Can.
246 I3 Athabasca r. Alta Can.
247 I3 Athabasca, Lake Alta/Sask. Can.
247 I3 Athabasca Sand Dunes Wilderness Provincial Park nature res. Sask. Can.
139 J9 Athagarh Orissa India
256 C10 Athalia OH U.S.A.
247 K4 Athapapuskow Lake Man. Can.
145 O6 Atharan Hazari Pak.
169 I5 Athboy Ireland
169 D8 Athea Ireland
Athenae Greece see Athina
169 E6 Athenry Ireland
251 S5 Athens Ont. Can.
Athens Greece see Athina
255 D8 Athens AL U.S.A.
255 F9 Athens GA U.S.A.
257 L6 Athens NY U.S.A.
256 C9 Athens OH U.S.A.
256 I7 Athens PA U.S.A.
255 E8 Athens TN U.S.A.
261 H9 Athens TX U.S.A.
191 K7 Athenstedt Ger.
220 B4 Atheras, Akrotirio pt Kefallonia Greece
172 D6 Atherington Devon, England U.K.
173 I2 Atherstone Warwickshire, England U.K.
107 J4 Atherton Qld Austr.
171 M6 Atherton Greater Manchester, England U.K.
233 C5 Athi r. Kenya
178 E4 Athies France
178 G4 Athies-sous-Laon France
220 E5 Athina Greece
Athínai Greece see Athina
233 C5 Athi River Kenya
181 K4 Athis-de-l'Orne France
178 D6 Athis-Mons France
169 E8 Athlacca Ireland
169 F5 Athleague Ireland
169 G6 Athlone Ireland
150 G6 Athnā', Wādī al watercourse Jordan
136 D4 Athni Karnataka India
103 C12 Athol South I. N.Z.
257 M6 Athol MA U.S.A.
255 □2 Athol Island New Prov. Bahamas
168 H9 Atholl, Forest of reg. Scotland U.K.
220 F2 Athos mt. Greece
Athos, Mount admin. div. Greece see Agion Oros
225 G2 Ath Thamad Egypt
150 E9 Ath Thāyat mt. Saudi Arabia
146 G2 Ath Thumāmī well Saudi Arabia
169 I7 Athy Ireland
224 C6 Ati Chad
224 B4 Ati, Jabal mts Libya
144 H4 Aţīābād Iran
232 B4 Atiak Uganda
102 K5 Atiamuri North I. N.Z.
224 C6 Ati Ardébé Chad
280 D5 Atibaia Brazil
276 B4 Atico Peru
276 B4 Atico, Punta pt Peru
230 E3 Atiedo Sudan
205 O6 Atienza Spain
245 J1 Atigun Pass AK U.S.A.
268 F7 Atijo Mex.
247 L5 Atikaki Provincial Wilderness Park Man. Can.
246 H4 Atikameg Alta Can.
248 D2 Atikameg r. Ont. Can.
247 M4 Atik Lake Man. Can.
248 B3 Atikokan Ont. Can.
249 H2 Atikonak Lake Nfld and Lab. Can.
101 □9a Atimaono Tahiti Fr. Polynesia
114 C4 Atimonan Luzon Phil.
215 L4 Atina Italy
267 O10 Atiquizaya El Salvador
136 F7 Atirampattinam Tamil Nadu India
267 N10 Atitlán Guat.
267 N10 Atitlán, Parque Nacional nat. park Guat.
103 □2 Atiu i. Cook Is
Atjeh admin. dist. Indon. see Aceh
146 H2 'Atk, Wādī al watercourse Saudi Arabia
153 Q3 Atka Rus. Fed.
245 □D5 Atka AK U.S.A.
245 □D5 Atka Island AK U.S.A.
199 I4 Atkár Hungary
157 I6 Atkarsk Rus. Fed.
261 I8 Atkins AR U.S.A.
245 O1 Atkinson Point pt N.W.T. Can.
115 G4 Atkri Papua Indon.
269 H6 Atlacomulco Mex.
237 L1 Atlanta S. Africa
255 E9 Atlanta GA U.S.A.
250 E9 Atlanta IL U.S.A.
251 J4 Atlanta MI U.S.A.
261 H9 Atlanta TX U.S.A.
148 F4 Atlantı Turkey
260 H5 Atlantic IA U.S.A.
257 □Q4 Atlantic ME U.S.A.
255 I8 Atlantic NC U.S.A.
257 K9 Atlantic City NJ U.S.A.
258 F6 Atlantic County county NJ U.S.A.
259 G4 Atlantic Highlands NJ U.S.A.
286 X2 Atlantic-Indian-Antarctic Basin sea feature S. Atlantic Ocean
289 D8 Atlantic-Indian Ridge sea feature Southern Ocean
274 C2 Atlántico dept Col.
288 Atlantic Ocean
262 J5 Atlantic Peak WY U.S.A.
236 C9 Atlantis S. Africa
269 I4 Atlapexco Mex.
258 C3 Atlas PA U.S.A.
128 E5 Atlas Bogd mt. Mongolia
Atlas Méditerranéen mts Alg. see Atlas Tellien
226 D3 Atlas Mountains Africa
153 Q4 Atlasova, Ostrov i. Kuril'skiye O-va Rus. Fed.
227 F2 Atlas Saharien mts Alg.
227 F2 Atlas Tellien mts Alg.
269 I7 Atlatlahucan Mex.
245 N4 Atlin B.C. Can.
245 N4 Atlin Lake B.C./Y.T. Can.
246 C3 Atlin Provincial Park B.C. Can.
150 C6 'Atlit Israel
269 I7 Atlixco Mex.
269 I8 Atlixtac Mex.
136 F5 Atmakur Andhra Prad. India
244 G3 Atmautluak AK U.S.A.
255 D10 Atmore AL U.S.A.
163 K6 Atna Norway
138 F9 Atner Madh. Prad. India
106 F7 Atnetye Aboriginal Land res. N.T. Austr.
125 I12 Atō Japan
276 D5 Atocha Bol.
261 G8 Atoka OK U.S.A.
231 B7 Atome Angola
226 C4 Atonyia Western Sahara
100 □6 Atori Malaita Solomon Is
269 I5 Atotonico El Grande Mex.
268 D1 Atotonilco Durango Mex.
268 E1 Atotonilco Zacatecas Mex.
268 E5 Atotonilco el Alto Mex.
118 H6 Atouat mt. Laos
206 A2 Atouguia da Baleia Port.
226 D5 Atouila, Erg des. Mali
268 D5 Atoyac Mex.
269 I7 Atoyac r. Mex.
269 J9 Atoyac r. Mex.
269 K6 Atoyac r. Mex.
268 G8 Atoyac de Álvarez Mex.
136 D4 Atpadi Mahar. India
Atqan Xinjiang China see Aqqan
244 H1 Atqasuk AK U.S.A.
139 L7 Atrai r. India
Atrak r. Iran/Turkm. see Atrek
164 I5 Ätran r. Sweden
138 G6 Atranh Uttar Prad. India
274 B2 Atrato r. Col.
269 M9 Atravesada, Sierra mts Mex.
144 G3 Atrek r. Iran/Turkm. alt. Atrak (Iran/Turkm.), alt. Etrek (Iran/Turkm.)
215 L2 Atri Italy
Atria Italy see Adria
215 N6 Atripalda Italy
Atropatene country Asia see Azerbaijan
151 D3 Ats'ana Georgia
220 G3 Atsiki Limnos Greece
258 F5 Atsion NJ U.S.A.
127 J5 Atsugi Japan
229 H5 Atsuku Nigeria
126 F6 Atsumi Aichi Japan
124 Q8 Atsumi Yamagata Japan
126 F6 Atsumi-hantō pen. Japan
124 S3 Atsuta Japan
147 L3 Aţ Ţaff reg. U.A.E.
150 D8 Aţ Ţafīlah Jordan
146 E5 Aţ Ţā'if Saudi Arabia
199 H5 Attala Hungary
Attalea Turkey see Antalya
Attalia Turkey see Antalya
255 D8 Attalla AL U.S.A.
224 D3 Aţ Ţallāb oasis Libya
149 K6 At Ta'mīm governorate Iraq
224 D1 At Tamīmī Libya
170 C8 Attanagh Ireland
119 H7 Attapu Laos
227 G2 Attar, Oued el watercourse Alg.
217 □ Attard Malta
169 C4 Attavalley Ireland
221 I6 Attavyros mt. Rodos Greece
248 D2 Attawapiskat Ont. Can.
248 D2 Attawapiskat r. Ont. Can.
248 C2 Attawapiskat Lake Ont. Can.
225 H2 Aţ Ţawīl mts Saudi Arabia
146 E5 Aţ Ţāwlah Saudi Arabia
146 F1 At Taysīyah plat. Saudi Arabia
150 D8 Aţ Ţayyibah Jordan
102 H7 Attempt Hill South I. N.Z.
191 E8 Attendorn Ger.
195 L4 Attenkirchen Ger.
237 M1 Atteridgeville S. Africa
201 I4 Attersee Austria
201 I4 Attersee l. Austria
187 I9 Attert Belgium
187 J9 Attert r. Lux.
254 D5 Attica IN U.S.A.
256 G6 Attica NY U.S.A.
256 C7 Attica OH U.S.A.
169 J4 Attical Northern Ireland U.K.
178 F5 Attichy France
215 I2 Attigliano Italy
182 G4 Attignat France
178 I5 Attigny France
249 H2 Attikamagen Lake Nfld and Lab. Can.
220 E5 Attiki admin. reg. Greece
150 A7 Aţ Ţīnah Egypt
136 E8 Attingal Kerala India
257 N7 Attleboro MA U.S.A.
173 O2 Attleborough Norfolk, England U.K.
173 O2 Attlebridge Norfolk, England U.K.
201 I3 Attnang Austria
145 O5 Attock City Pak.
Attopeu Laos see Attapu
243 M3 Attu Greenland
244 □A5 Attu AK U.S.A.
148 H9 Aţ Ţubayq reg. Saudi Arabia
244 □A5 Attu Island AK U.S.A.
146 G2 Aţ Ţulayḩī well Saudi Arabia
105 M4 Attunga N.S.W. Austr.
At Tūnisīyah country Africa see Tunisia
225 G2 Aţ Ţūr Egypt
136 E7 Attur Tamil Nadu India
136 F7 Attur Tamil Nadu India
146 F9 At Turbah Ta'izz Yemen
146 G9 At Turbah Ta'izz Yemen
146 E2 Aţ Ţuwayyah well Saudi Arabia
169 E6 Attymon Ireland
285 H3 Atucha Arg.
147 I8 Atūd Yemen
284 D5 Atuel r. Arg.
284 D5 Atuel, Bañados del marsh Arg.
244 E3 Atuk Mountain hill AK U.S.A.
184 F5 Atur France
165 L3 Åtvidaberg Sweden
139 L6 Atwari Bangl.
264 L4 Atwater CA U.S.A.
260 E6 Atwood KS U.S.A.
157 I5 Atyashevo Rus. Fed.
142 D4 Atyrau Kazakh.
Atyrau Oblast admin. div. Kazakh. see Atyrauskaya Oblast'
Atyraū Oblysy admin. div. Kazakh. see Atyrauskaya Oblast'
142 D4 Atyrauskaya Oblast' admin. div. Kazakh.
157 H5 Atyur'yevo Rus. Fed.
159 L2 Atyusha Ukr.
214 C8 Atzara Sardegna Italy
201 M3 Atzenbrugg Austria
193 E7 Atzendorf Ger.
209 E10 Atzeneta d'Albaida Spain
209 E7 Atzeneta del Maestrat Spain
200 A5 Au Austria
212 H1 Au Switz.
274 E5 Auati-Paraná r. Brazil
195 I2 Aub Ger.
191 H10 Aubach r. Ger.
183 H10 Aubagne France
183 E9 Aubais France
187 I9 Aubange Belgium
114 D3 Aubarede Point Luzon Phil.
184 H5 Aubazines France
181 M4 Aube France
178 H7 Aube dept France
178 G6 Aube r. France
235 H3 Aúbe Moz.
187 I7 Aubel Belgium
183 E7 Aubenas France
178 H4 Aubenton France
178 C6 Aubergenville France
178 H5 Aubérive France
179 J8 Auberive France
184 E5 Aubeterre-sur-Dronne France
178 F6 Aubetin r. France
178 B5 Aubevoye France
185 F8 Aubiet France
183 G8 Aubignan France
181 L6 Aubigné-Racan France
183 H8 Aubignosc France
178 E3 Aubigny-en-Artois France
181 P7 Aubigny-sur-Nère France
185 I6 Aubin France
248 D4 Aubinadong r. Ont. Can.
185 D10 Aubisque, Col d' pass France
212 A2 Aubonne Switz.
183 E9 Aubord France
179 K5 Auboué France
183 B7 Aubrac mts France
179 J5 Aubreville France
265 T6 Aubrey Cliffs mts AZ U.S.A.
245 P2 Aubry Lake N.W.T. Can.
107 M8 Auburn r. Qld Austr.
251 M6 Auburn Ont. Can.
255 E9 Auburn AL U.S.A.
264 K3 Auburn CA U.S.A.
260 K6 Auburn IL U.S.A.
254 E5 Auburn IN U.S.A.
257 N6 Auburn MA U.S.A.
257 □O4 Auburn ME U.S.A.
251 J6 Auburn MI U.S.A.
260 H5 Auburn NE U.S.A.
256 I6 Auburn NY U.S.A.
258 C3 Auburn PA U.S.A.
262 C3 Auburn WA U.S.A.
258 C1 Auburn Center PA U.S.A.
250 D5 Auburndale WI U.S.A.
107 M8 Auburn Range hills Qld Austr.
184 I4 Aubusson France
178 F3 Auby France
284 C5 Auca Mahuida Arg.
284 C5 Auca Mahuida, Sierra de mt. Arg.
185 G8 Aucamville France
160 F5 Auce Latvia
185 F8 Auch France
168 J9 Auchallater Aberdeenshire, Scotland U.K.
170 G2 Auchbraad Argyll and Bute, Scotland U.K.
118 C2 Auche Myanmar
178 D2 Auchel France
168 L9 Auchenblae Aberdeenshire, Scotland U.K.
168 F11 Auchenbreck Argyll and Bute, Scotland U.K.
168 I13 Auchencairn Dumfries and Galloway, Scotland U.K.
168 L11 Auchencrow Scottish Borders, Scotland U.K.
229 G5 Auchi Nigeria
168 H12 Auchinleck East Ayrshire, Scotland U.K.
168 K9 Auchmull Angus, Scotland U.K.
168 L8 Auchnagatt Aberdeenshire, Scotland U.K.
168 J8 Aucholzie Aberdeenshire, Scotland U.K.
168 K9 Auchronie Angus, Scotland U.K.
168 I10 Auchterarder Perth and Kinross, Scotland U.K.
168 J10 Auchtermuchty Fife, Scotland U.K.
178 D2 Auchy-au-Bois France
102 I3 Auckland North I. N.Z.
102 I3 Auckland admin. reg. North I. N.Z.
99 G6 Auckland Islands N.Z.
185 D10 Aucun France
183 A10 Aude dept France
183 C10 Aude r. France
248 C3 Auden Ont. Can.
Audenarde Belgium see Oudenaarde
185 B6 Audenge France
180 H2 Auderville France
257 □O3 Audet Que. Can.
182 H2 Audeux France
180 B5 Audierne France
180 C6 Audierne, Baie d' b. France
182 J2 Audincourt France
172 G2 Audlem Cheshire, England U.K.
171 M7 Audley Staffordshire, England U.K.
232 D3 Audo mts Eth.
185 C8 Audon France
178 C2 Audresselles France
160 H3 Audru Estonia
178 D2 Audruicq France
260 H5 Audubon IA U.S.A.
258 E5 Audubon NJ U.S.A.
179 K5 Audun-le-Roman France
193 G9 Aue Ger.
190 E4 Aue r. Niedersachsen Ger.
191 J5 Aue r. Niedersachsen Ger.
195 O4 Auerbach Bayern Ger.
193 F9 Auerbach Sachsen Ger.
193 G9 Auerbach Sachsen Ger.
195 L2 Auerbach in der Oberpfalz Ger.
193 G10 Auersberg mt. Ger.
201 O3 Auersthal Austria
193 G9 Auerswalde Ger.
143 S3 Auezov Kazakh.
178 B4 Auffay France
195 M4 Aufhausen Ger.
107 K8 Augathella Qld Austr.
169 H4 Augher Northern Ireland U.K.
169 I4 Aughnacloy Northern Ireland U.K.
169 F6 Aughrim Galway Ireland
169 J7 Aughrim Wicklow Ireland
171 L6 Aughton Lancashire, England U.K.
171 O7 Aughton South Yorkshire, England U.K.
184 F4 Augignac France
Augila Libya see Awjilah
236 E4 Augrabies S. Africa
236 E4 Augrabies Falls S. Africa
236 E4 Augrabies Falls National Park S. Africa
251 K5 Au Gres MI U.S.A.
195 J5 Augsburg Ger.
200 C3 Augsburg airport Ger.
195 J5 Augsburg-Westliche Wälder park Ger.
160 I4 Augšlīgatne Latvia
160 J5 Augšzemes augstiene hills Latvia
109 C13 Augusta W.A. Austr.

217 I9 **Augusta** *Sicilia* Italy
261 J8 **Augusta** *AR* U.S.A.
255 F9 **Augusta** *GA* U.S.A.
250 D9 **Augusta** *IL* U.S.A.
261 G7 **Augusta** *KS* U.S.A.
256 A10 **Augusta** *KY* U.S.A.
257 □P4 **Augusta** *ME* U.S.A.
262 H3 **Augusta** *MT* U.S.A.
258 F2 **Augusta** *NJ* U.S.A.
250 C5 **Augusta** *WI* U.S.A.
256 G9 **Augusta** *WV* U.S.A.
217 I9 **Augusta, Golfo di** *b. Sicilia* Italy
Augusta Auscorum France *see* **Auch**
Augusta Taurinorum Italy *see* **Torino**
Augusta Treverorum Ger. *see* **Trier**
276 C6 **Augusta Victoria** Chile
Augusta Vindelicorum Ger. *see* **Augsburg**
190 I1 **Augustenborg** Denmark
244 I4 **Augustine Island** *AK* U.S.A.
251 S2 **Augustines, Lac des** *l. Que.* Can.
Augusto Cardosa Moz. *see* **Metangula**
281 E3 **Augusto de Lima** Brazil
Augustodunum France *see* **Autun**
278 F3 **Augusto Severo** Brazil
197 K2 **Augustów** Pol.
197 L3 **Augustowo** Pol.
197 L2 **Augustowska, Puszcza** *for.* Pol.
197 L2 **Augustowski, Kanał** *canal* Pol.
109 D8 **Augustus, Mount** W.A. Austr.
193 H9 **Augustusburg** Ger.
108 H3 **Augustus Island** W.A. Austr.
191 H6 **Auhagen** Ger.
195 L4 **Au in der Hallertau** Ger.
179 I7 **Aujon** *r.* France
Aujuittuq *Nunavut* Can. *see* **Grise Fiord**
146 E8 **Aukan** Eritrea
245 N4 **Auke Bay** *AK* U.S.A.
100 □6 **Auki** *Malaita* Solomon Is
190 I2 **Aukrug** Ger.
160 J6 **Aukštaitijos nacionalinis parkas** *nat. park* Lith.
160 G6 **Aukštelkai** Lith.
160 G6 **Aukštelkė** Lith.
160 I7 **Aukštojo kalnas** *hill* Lith.
162 O4 **Auktsjaur** Sweden
242 G2 **Aulavik National Park** *N.W.T.* Can.
108 G7 **Auld, Lake** *salt flat* W.A. Austr.
168 I7 **Auldearn** *Highland, Scotland* U.K.
191 K8 **Auleben** Ger.
212 H7 **Aulella** *r.* Italy
194 H6 **Aulendorf** Ger.
215 O6 **Auletta** Italy
Auliye Ata Kazakh. *see* **Taraz**
142 K1 **Auliyekol'** Kazakh.
212 H7 **Aulla** Italy
214 C4 **Aullène** *Corse* France
182 C5 **Aulnat** France
182 C5 **Aulnat** *airport* France
184 D3 **Aulnay** France
178 E6 **Aulnay-sous-Bois** France
180 C5 **Aulne** *r.* France
247 M5 **Aulneau Peninsula** *Ont.* Can.
179 L6 **Aulnois-sur-Seille** France
178 G3 **Aulnoye-Aymeries** France
Aulon Albania *see* **Vlorë**
185 F9 **Aulon** France
114 □ **Aulong** *i.* Palau
192 E5 **Aulosen** Ger.
178 B3 **Ault** France
168 E7 **Aultbea** *Highland, Scotland* U.K.
168 G7 **Aultguish Inn** *Highland, Scotland* U.K.
164 E5 **Aulum** Denmark
114 □ **Auluptagel** *i.* Palau
185 G10 **Aulus-les-Bains** France
193 E9 **Auma** Ger.
178 C4 **Aumale** France
182 B3 **Aumance** *r.* France
179 K5 **Aumetz** France
182 H3 **Aumont** France
183 C7 **Aumont-Aubrac** France
190 J3 **Aumühle** Ger.
229 G4 **Auna** Nigeria
182 D2 **Aunay-en-Bazois** France
181 J3 **Aunay-sur-Odon** France
138 H9 **Aundhi** *Chhattisgarh* India
178 C7 **Auneau** France
178 D5 **Auneuil** France
118 C4 **Aungban** Myanmar
118 B5 **Aunglan** Myanmar
164 G5 **Auning** Denmark
184 B3 **Aunis** *reg.* France
205 O7 **Auñón** Spain
100 □2 **'Aunu'u** *i.* American Samoa
234 D5 **Auob** *watercourse* Namibia/S. Africa
213 O3 **Aupa** *r.* Italy
249 G1 **Aupaluk** *Que.* Can.
115 D4 **Auponhia** *Maluku* Indon.
183 I9 **Aups** France
116 F3 **Aur** *i.* Malaysia
163 Q6 **Aura** Fin.
195 I3 **Aurach** Ger.
200 F5 **Aurach bei Kitzbühel** Austria
136 E3 **Aurad** *Karnataka* India
185 G8 **Auradé** France
191 I10 **Aura im Sinngrund** Ger.
138 G6 **Auraiya** *Uttar Prad.* India
160 F1 **Aurajoki** *r.* Fin.
139 J7 **Aurangabad** *Bihar* India
136 D3 **Aurangabad** *Mahar.* India
180 F6 **Auray** France
181 I3 **Aure** *r.* France
162 J5 **Aure** Norway
185 E10 **Aure, Vallée d'** *val.* France
183 E6 **Aurec-sur-Loire** France
185 E9 **Aureilhan** France
185 B7 **Aureilhan, Étang d'** *l.* France
183 F9 **Aureille** France
183 G8 **Aurel** *Provence-Alpes-Côte d'Azur* France
183 G7 **Aurel** *Rhône-Alpes* France
268 A1 **Aurelio Benassini, Presa** *resr* Mex.
185 D8 **Aurensan** France
190 D4 **Aurich** Ger.
280 B4 **Auriflama** Brazil
185 F9 **Aurignac** France
Aurigny *i.* Channel Is *see* **Alderney**
280 B2 **Aurilândia** Brazil
184 I6 **Aurillac** France
208 E2 **Aurín** *r.* Spain
213 L2 **Aurino** *r.* Italy
183 H10 **Auriol** France
107 M1 **Auriora Island** P.N.G.
213 P4 **Aurisina** Italy
208 C2 **Auritz** Spain
117 I5 **Aurkuning** *Kalimantan* Indon.
102 I6 **Auroa** *North I.* N.Z.
201 H3 **Aurolzmünster** Austria
183 J8 **Auron** France
182 A2 **Auron** *r.* France
213 M2 **Auronzo di Cadore** Italy
114 D8 **Aurora** *Mindanao* Phil.
236 C8 **Aurora** S. Africa
262 L7 **Aurora** *CO* U.S.A.
250 F8 **Aurora** *IL* U.S.A.
257 □Q4 **Aurora** *ME* U.S.A.
250 B2 **Aurora** *MN* U.S.A.
261 I7 **Aurora** *MO* U.S.A.
260 G5 **Aurora** *NE* U.S.A.
256 D7 **Aurora** *OH* U.S.A.
265 U3 **Aurora** *UT* U.S.A.
Aurora Island Vanuatu *see* **Maéwo**
104 □3 **Aurora Point** S. Pacific Ocean
185 D6 **Auros** France
183 D7 **Auroux** France
136 F7 **Auroville** *Tamil Nadu* India
107 H2 **Aurukun** *Qld* Austr.
107 H2 **Aurukun Aboriginal Reserve** *Qld* Austr.
215 K5 **Aurunci, Monti** *mts* Italy
234 C5 **Aus** Namibia
136 E3 **Ausa** *Mahar.* India
213 O4 **Ausa** *r.* Italy
251 K5 **Au Sable** *MI* U.S.A.
251 K5 **Au Sable** *r. MI* U.S.A.
257 L4 **Ausable** *r. NY* U.S.A.
257 L4 **Au Sable Forks** *NY* U.S.A.
250 H3 **Au Sable Point** *MI* U.S.A.
251 K5 **Au Sable Point** *MI* U.S.A.
213 O4 **Ausa-Corno** Italy
Auschwitz Pol. *see* **Oświęcim**
Ausculum Italy *see* **Ascoli Satriano**
Ausculum Apulum Italy *see* **Ascoli Satriano**
205 P4 **Ausejo** Spain
215 L5 **Ausente** *r.* Italy
199 L4 **Auşeu** Romania
168 K4 **Auskerry** *i. Scotland* U.K.
193 D6 **Ausleben** Ger.
215 K5 **Ausoni, Monti** *mts* Italy
285 F3 **Ausonia** Arg.
215 L5 **Ausonia** Italy
185 G9 **Ausseing Tour** *hill* France
200 F6 **Außervillgraten** Austria
185 I8 **Aussillon** France
183 J6 **Aussois** France
185 G8 **Aussonne** France
185 C9 **Aussurucq** France
162 K4 **Austafjord** Norway
164 E3 **Aust-Agder** *county* Norway
162 □D1 **Austari-Jökulsá** *r.* Iceland
162 T1 **Austertana** Norway
163 H6 **Austfjorden** *inlet* Norway
162 □ **Austfonna** *ice cap* Svalbard
250 B6 **Austin** *MN* U.S.A.
264 O2 **Austin** *NV* U.S.A.
261 G10 **Austin** *TX* U.S.A.
109 E9 **Austin, Lake** *salt flat* W.A. Austr.
256 E7 **Austintown** *OH* U.S.A.
214 C7 **Austis** *Sardegna* Italy
106 F6 **Austral Downs** *N.T.* Austr.
101 □9 **Australes, Îles** *is* Fr. Polynesia
98 C4 **Australia** *country* Oceania
289 K8 **Australian-Antarctic Basin** *sea feature* Southern Ocean
287 J2 **Australian Antarctic Territory** Antarctica
105 L6 **Australian Capital Territory** *admin. div.* Austr.
109 C12 **Australind** W.A. Austr.
201 H5 **Austria** *country* Europe
160 F5 **Austrumkursas augstiene** *hills* Latvia
162 □F1 **Austurland** *constituency* Iceland
162 M2 **Austvågøy** *i.* Norway
275 G5 **Autazes** Brazil
185 G9 **Auterive** France
Autesiodorum France *see* **Auxerre**
182 H1 **Autet** France
178 C3 **Authie** *r.* France
251 P1 **Authier** *Que.* Can.
181 K7 **Authion** *r.* France
181 M6 **Authon** *Centre* France
183 I8 **Authon** *Provence-Alpes-Côte d'Azur* France
181 M5 **Authon-du-Perche** France
268 C6 **Autlán** Mex.
205 P4 **Autol** Spain
183 H6 **Autrans** France
179 K7 **Autreville** France
182 G2 **Autrey-lès-Gray** France
179 I5 **Autry** France
162 S3 **Autti** Fin.
182 E3 **Autun** France
182 E3 **Autunois** *reg.* France
178 I5 **Auve** France
187 G8 **Auvelais** Belgium
239 □1c **Au Vent** *reg.* Réunion
182 C5 **Auvergne** *admin. reg.* France
183 A7 **Auvergne** *reg.* France
182 B5 **Auvergne, Monts d'** *mts* France
181 K6 **Auvers-le-Hamon** France
178 D5 **Auvers-sur-Oise** France
184 F5 **Auvézère** *r.* France
185 E7 **Auvignon** *r.* France
185 F7 **Auvillar** France
178 H4 **Auvillers-les-Forges** France
178 G8 **Auxerre** France
178 G8 **Auxerrois** *reg.* France
178 D3 **Auxi-le-Château** France
182 F2 **Auxois** *reg.* France
182 G2 **Auxonne** France
182 E3 **Auxy** France
275 F3 **Auyan Tepuí** *plat.* Venez.
243 L3 **Auyuittuq National Park** *Nunavut* Can.
182 A4 **Auzances** France
185 G10 **Auzat** France
183 C6 **Auzat-sur-Allier** France
184 I5 **Auze** *r.* France
185 I7 **Auzits** France
183 C6 **Auzon** France
185 E7 **Auzoue** *r.* France
118 B4 **Ava** Myanmar
261 I7 **Ava** *MO* U.S.A.
257 J5 **Ava** *NY* U.S.A.
103 □3 **Avaavaroa Passage** *Rarotonga* Cook Is
280 C5 **Avaí** Brazil
184 F3 **Availles-Limouzine** France
101 □8a **Ava Lahi** *sea chan.* Tonga
244 H1 **Avalik** *r. AK* U.S.A.
182 D1 **Avallon** France
181 K5 **Avaloirs, Mont des** *hill* France
264 N8 **Avalon** *CA* U.S.A.
258 F6 **Avalon** *NJ* U.S.A.
249 K4 **Avalon Peninsula** *Nfld and Lab.* Can.
249 K4 **Avalon Wilderness** *nature res. Nfld and Lab.* Can.
285 H2 **Avalos** *r.* Arg.
268 F1 **Ávalos** Mex.
151 F2 **Avalov** Rus. Fed.
144 B2 **Avān** Iran
136 E7 **Avanashi** *Tamil Nadu* India
204 C7 **Avanca** Port.
185 E7 **Avance** *r.* France
183 I7 **Avançon** France
275 G3 **Avanganna** *mt.* Guyana
136 G4 **Avanigadda** *Andhra Prad.* India
148 G4 **Avanos** Turkey
178 H7 **Avant-lès-Ramerupt** France
Avarau *atoll* Cook Is *see* **Palmerston**
280 C5 **Avaré** Brazil
Avaricum France *see* **Bourges**
149 M4 **Āvārsin** Iran
151 H3 **Avarskoye Koysu** *r.* Rus. Fed.
103 □3 **Avarua** *Rarotonga* Cook Is
103 □3 **Avarua Harbour** *Rarotonga* Cook Is
103 □4 **Avatele** Niue
103 □4 **Avatele Bay** Niue
103 □3 **Avatiu** *Rarotonga* Cook Is
103 □3 **Avatiu Harbour** *Rarotonga* Cook Is
162 N4 **Avaträsk** Sweden
162 O4 **Avaviken** Sweden
256 B11 **Avawam** *KY* U.S.A.
144 I5 **Āvāz** Iran
Avdeyevka Ukr. *see* **Avdiyivka**
220 F2 **Avdira** Greece
159 Q5 **Avdiyivka** Ukr.
204 C6 **Ave** *r.* Port.
173 I5 **Avebury** *Wiltshire, England* U.K.
204 G4 **A Veiga** Spain
206 B2 **Aveiras de Cima** Port.
275 H5 **Aveiro** Brazil
204 C7 **Aveiro** Port.
204 C7 **Aveiro** *admin. dist.* Port.
204 C7 **Aveiro, Ria de** *est.* Port.
144 C4 **Āvej** Iran
204 D9 **Avelar** Port.
204 D5 **Aveleda** *Braga* Port.
204 G5 **Aveleda** *Bragança* Port.
173 M5 **Aveley** *Thurrock, England* U.K.
187 D7 **Avelgem** Belgium
285 E2 **Avellanada** Arg.
285 H4 **Avellaneda** *Buenos Aires* Arg.
282 F3 **Avellaneda** *Santa Fé* Arg.
215 N6 **Avellino** Italy
215 O6 **Avellino** *prov.* Italy
180 D6 **Aven** *r.* France
264 L5 **Avenal** *CA* U.S.A.
178 H5 **Avenay-Val-d'Or** France
212 C2 **Avenches** Switz.
183 C9 **Avène** France
186 G3 **Avenhorn** Neth.
204 D1 **Avenida do Marqués de Figueroa** Spain
Avenio France *see* **Avignon**
Aventicum Switz. *see* **Avenches**
282 E3 **Averías** Arg.
182 C3 **Avermes** France
165 L3 **Avern** *l.* Sweden
190 J1 **Avernakø** *i.* Denmark
168 H7 **Averon** *r. Scotland* U.K.
162 I5 **Averøya** *i.* Norway
212 H3 **Avers** Switz.
215 M6 **Aversa** Italy
271 L6 **Aves** *i.* West Indies
Aves *is* West Indies *see* **Las Aves, Islas**
178 E3 **Avesnes-le-Comte** France
178 G3 **Avesnes-sur-Helpe** France
165 M1 **Avesta** Sweden
212 G6 **Aveto** *r.* Italy
217 N3 **Avetrano** Italy
183 B8 **Aveyron** *dept* France
185 G7 **Aveyron** *r.* France
215 K3 **Avezzano** Italy
150 B1 **Avgan Geçidi** *pass* Turkey
220 E6 **Avgo** *i. Kythira* Greece
221 G7 **Avgo** *i. Kythira* Greece
208 I3 **Avià** Spain
204 D4 **Avia** *r.* Spain
213 N3 **Aviano** Italy
282 E2 **Aviá Terai** Arg.
168 F10 **Avich, Loch** *l. Scotland* U.K.
168 I8 **Aviemore** *Highland, Scotland* U.K.
103 E11 **Aviemore, Lake** *South I.* N.Z.
212 C5 **Avigliana** Italy
215 P6 **Avigliano** Italy
215 I2 **Avigliano Umbro** Italy
183 F9 **Avignon** France
185 H9 **Avignonet-Lauragais** France
205 K7 **Ávila** Spain
205 K7 **Ávila** *prov.* Spain
205 J7 **Ávila, Sierra de** *mts* Spain
204 E1 **A Vila da Igrexa** Spain
204 I1 **Avilés** Spain
204 I1 **Avilés, Ría de** *inlet* Spain
182 I2 **Avilley** France
159 R6 **Avilo-Uspenka** Rus. Fed.
204 D1 **Aviño** Spain
204 C6 **Avintes** Port.
160 J3 **Avinurme** Estonia
208 I4 **Avinyó** Spain
213 J4 **Avio** Italy
178 E3 **Avion** France
204 D4 **Avión** *mt.* Spain
179 J4 **Avioth** France
206 D2 **Avis** Port.
213 K3 **Avisio** *r.* Italy
178 H6 **Avize** France
150 B2 **Avlama Dağı** *mt.* Turkey
220 E6 **Avlemonas** *Kythira* Greece
Avlona Albania *see* **Vlorë**
220 E4 **Avlonas** Greece
156 I3 **Avnyugskiy** Rus. Fed.
105 K9 **Avoca** *Tas.* Austr.
105 I7 **Avoca** *Vic.* Austr.
105 I6 **Avoca** *r. Vic.* Austr.
169 J7 **Avoca** Ireland
237 P1 **Avoca** S. Africa
260 H5 **Avoca** *IA* U.S.A.
256 H6 **Avoca** *NY* U.S.A.
168 H7 **Avoch** *Highland, Scotland* U.K.
181 L7 **Avoine** France
217 I10 **Avola** *Sicilia* Italy
214 G3 **Avoltore, Punta** *pt* Italy
109 D11 **Avon** *r.* W.A. Austr.
178 E7 **Avon** France
172 E7 **Avon** *r. Devon, England* U.K.
172 G5 **Avon** *r. England* U.K.
173 H3 **Avon** *r. England* U.K.
173 I6 **Avon** *r. England* U.K.
250 D9 **Avon** *IL* U.S.A.
256 H6 **Avon** *NY* U.S.A.
258 C4 **Avon** *PA* U.S.A.
169 J7 **Avonbeg** *r.* Ireland
171 J2 **Avonbridge** *Falkirk, Scotland* U.K.
265 T8 **Avondale** *AZ* U.S.A.
258 D5 **Avondale** *PA* U.S.A.
259 L2 **Avondale** *RI* U.S.A.
106 F6 **Avon Downs** *N.T.* Austr.
107 K6 **Avon Downs** *Qld* Austr.
256 C7 **Avon Lake** *OH* U.S.A.
169 J7 **Avonmore** *r.* Ireland
172 G4 **Avonmouth** *Bristol, England* U.K.
255 G12 **Avon Park** *FL* U.S.A.
236 H9 **Avontuur** S. Africa
182 B2 **Avord** France
182 J4 **Avoriaz** France
160 H5 **Avoti** Latvia
182 I2 **Avoudrey** France
219 O2 **Avrămeni** Romania
219 J4 **Avram Iancu** Romania
180 I4 **Avranches** France
178 D4 **Avre** *r.* France
181 N4 **Avre** *r.* France
179 M6 **Avricourt** France
219 M5 **Avrig** Romania
179 K5 **Avril** France
184 B3 **Avrillé** *Pays de la Loire* France
181 J6 **Avrillé** *Pays de la Loire* France
151 C5 **Avsek Dağı** *mt.* Turkey
100 □6 **Avuavu** *Guadalcanal* Solomon Is
Avveel Fin. *see* **Ivalo**
Avvil Fin. *see* **Ivalo**
124 □1 **Awa** *Okinawa* Japan
150 D5 **A'waj** *r.* Syria
126 B6 **Awaji** Japan
126 A7 **Awaji-shima** *i.* Japan
102 K5 **Awakeri** *North I.* N.Z.
102 I5 **Awakino** *North I.* N.Z.
147 J2 **'Awālī** Bahrain
117 L9 **Awang** *Lombok* Indon.
127 K3 **Awano** Japan
187 H7 **Awans** Belgium
102 H2 **Awanui** *North I.* N.Z.
126 D3 **Awara** Japan
117 J8 **Awarawar, Tanjung** *pt* Indon.
232 E2 **Āwarē** Eth.
150 H4 **'Awāriḍ, Wādī al** *watercourse* Syria
146 H6 **Awārik, 'Urūq al** *des.* Saudi Arabia
103 C13 **Awarua** *South I.* N.Z.
103 C11 **Awarua Point** *South I.* N.Z.
232 C3 **Āwasa** Eth.
232 D2 **Āwash** Eth.
232 D2 **Āwash** *r.* Eth.
124 Q8 **Awa-shima** *i.* Japan
232 C2 **Āwash National Park** Eth.
232 C2 **Āwash West Wildlife Reserve** *nature res.* Eth.
132 E6 **Awat** *Xinjiang* China
232 C3 **Āwatā Shet'** *r.* Eth.
103 I8 **Awatere** *r. South I.* N.Z.
224 B3 **Awbārī** Libya
224 A3 **Awbārī, Idhān** *des.* Libya
169 F8 **Awbeg** *r.* Ireland
146 G9 **Awd** *reg.* Yemen
147 J4 **'Awdah** *well* Saudi Arabia
149 M8 **'Awdah, Hawr al** *imp. l.* Iraq
232 D2 **Awdal** *admin. div.* Somalia
232 E4 **Aw Dheegle** Somalia
232 D4 **Awdiinle** Somalia
168 F10 **Awe, Loch** *l. Scotland* U.K.
230 E2 **Aweil** Sudan
229 G5 **Awgu** Nigeria
224 D2 **Awjilah** Libya
229 G5 **Awka** Nigeria
226 B4 **Awlitis** *watercourse* Western Sahara
115 B5 **Awo** *r.* Indon.
172 H4 **Awre** *Gloucestershire, England* U.K.
246 H2 **Awry Lake** *N.W.T.* Can.
226 B5 **Awserd** Western Sahara
115 D2 **Awu** *vol.* Indon.
244 I1 **Awuna** *r. AK* U.S.A.
122 C3 **Awuni** *Nei Mongol* China
200 D5 **Axams** Austria
185 I10 **Axat** France
172 F6 **Axe** *r. Devon/Dorset, England* U.K.
172 G5 **Axe** *r. North Somerset/Somerset, England* U.K.
105 J7 **Axedale** *Vic.* Austr.
187 E6 **Axel** Neth.
286 N1 **Axel Heiberg Glacier** Antarctica
243 I2 **Axel Heiberg Island** *Nunavut* Can.
219 M4 **Axente Sever** Romania
228 E5 **Axim** Ghana
275 G6 **Axinim** Brazil
275 E6 **Axioma** Brazil
220 D2 **Axios** *r.* Greece *alt.* **Vardar** (Macedonia)
185 H10 **Ax-les-Thermes** France
163 N6 **Axmars naturreservat** *nature res.* Sweden
172 G6 **Axminster** *Devon, England* U.K.
269 I7 **Axochiapan** Mex.
190 G4 **Axstedt** Ger.
Axum Eth. *see* **Āksum**
269 I7 **Axutla** Mex.
178 H5 **Ay** France
143 S4 **Ay** Kazakh.
126 B5 **Ayabe** Japan
226 D2 **Ayachi, Jbel** *mt.* Morocco
285 H5 **Ayacucho** Arg.
276 B3 **Ayacucho** Peru
276 B3 **Ayacucho** *dept* Peru
118 B3 **Ayadaw** Myanmar
143 S4 **Ayagoz** Kazakh.
143 R4 **Ayagoz** *watercourse* Kazakh.
Ayaguz Kazakh. *see* **Ayagoz**
Ayakkuduk Uzbek. *see* **Oyoqquduq**
133 I8 **Ayakkum Hu** *salt l.* China
Ayaköz Kazakh. *see* **Ayagoz**
244 I4 **Ayakulik** *AK* U.S.A.
126 D6 **Ayama** Japan
228 E5 **Ayamé** Côte d'Ivoire
229 H6 **Ayamiken** Equat. Guinea
206 E6 **Ayamonte** Spain
153 O4 **Ayan** Rus. Fed.
148 G3 **Ayancık** Turkey
123 D9 **Ayang** N. Korea
229 G5 **Ayangba** Nigeria
153 R3 **Ayanka** Rus. Fed.
274 C3 **Ayapel, Serranía de** *mts* Col.
148 F3 **Ayaş** Turkey
127 J5 **Ayase** Japan
269 K7 **Ayautla** Mex.
276 C3 **Ayaviri** Peru
232 C1 **Ayayei** Eth.
145 M3 **Āybak** Afgh.
142 C4 **Aybas** Kazakh.
171 N4 **Aycliffe** *Durham, England* U.K.
143 M1 **Aydabol** Kazakh.
159 R3 **Aydar** Rus. Fed.
159 S5 **Aydar** *r.* Ukr.
143 L7 **Aydarko'l ko'li** *l.* Uzbek.
142 K5 **Aydarly** Kazakh.
182 B5 **Aydat** France
144 G2 **Aydere** Turkm.
147 K7 **'Aydim, Wādī** *r.* Oman
221 I5 **Aydın** Turkey
221 J5 **Aydın** *prov.* Turkey
150 B2 **Aydıncık** Turkey
221 I4 **Aydın Dağları** *mts* Turkey
132 I5 **Aydingkol Hu** *marsh* China
151 B6 **Aydınlar** *Bingöl* Turkey
151 D7 **Aydınlar** *Bitlis* Turkey
151 B5 **Aydıntepe** Turkey
144 F2 **Aýdyň** Turkm.
205 P4 **Ayedo** *mt.* Spain
232 D2 **Āyelu Terara** *vol.* Eth.
230 A5 **Ayem** Gabon
184 G5 **Ayen** France
257 N6 **Ayer** *MA* U.S.A.
208 D3 **Ayerbe** Spain
116 □ **Ayer Chawan, Pulau** *i.* Sing.
116 □ **Ayer Merbau, Pulau** *i.* Sing.
Ayers Rock *hill N.T.* Austr. *see* **Uluru**
Ayeyarwady *r.* Myanmar *see* **Irrawaddy**
132 H1 **Aygulakskiy Khrebet** *mts* Rus. Fed.
143 S3 **Aygyrzhal** Kazakh.
Ayiá Greece *see* **Agia**
Ayiásos *Lesvos* Greece *see* **Agiasos**
133 D10 **Ayila Ri'gyü** *mts Xizang* China
195 L6 **Aying** Ger.
Áyion Óros *admin. div.* Greece *see* **Agion Oros**
Áyios Dhimítrios Greece *see* **Agios Dimitrios**
Áyios Dhimítris, Ákra *pt Kythnos* Greece *see* **Agios Dimitrios, Akrotirio**
Áyios Evstrátios *i.* Greece *see* **Agios Efstratios**
Áyios Nikólaos *Kriti* Greece *see* **Agios Nikolaos**
Áyios Yeóryios *i.* Greece *see* **Agios Georgios**
142 I2 **Ayke, Ozero** *l.* Kazakh.
232 C1 **Āykel** Eth.
153 M3 **Aykhal** Rus. Fed.
156 J3 **Aykino** Rus. Fed.
132 E6 **Aykol** *Xinjiang* China
103 G10 **Aylesbury** *South I.* N.Z.
173 K4 **Aylesbury** *Buckinghamshire, England* U.K.
173 M5 **Aylesford** *Kent, England* U.K.
173 O5 **Aylesham** *Kent, England* U.K.
256 H11 **Aylett** *VA* U.S.A.
205 N6 **Ayllón** Spain
205 N6 **Ayllón, Sierra de** *mts* Spain
251 N7 **Aylmer** *Ont.* Can.
251 S4 **Aylmer** *Que.* Can.
247 I1 **Aylmer Lake** *N.W.T.* Can.
173 O2 **Aylsham** *Norfolk, England* U.K.
212 C4 **Aymavilles** Italy
147 M6 **'Ayn, Ra's al** *c.* Oman
147 L4 **'Ayn, Wādī al** *watercourse* Oman
276 B3 **Ayna** Peru
207 O3 **Ayna** Spain
143 Q5 **Aynabulak** Kazakh.
185 H6 **Aynac** France
224 C2 **'Ayn al 'Abd** Libya
147 I1 **'Ayn al 'Abd** *well* Saudi Arabia
150 B9 **'Ayn al Bāghah** *well* Egypt
150 F7 **'Ayn al Baidā'** Saudi Arabia
150 F4 **'Ayn al Bayḍā'** *well* Syria
150 C9 **'Ayn al Furṭājah** *well* Egypt
224 E4 **'Ayn al Ghazāl** *spring* Libya
225 F3 **'Ayn al Maqfī** *spring* Egypt
146 D3 **'Ayn al Mazr'ah** *well* Saudi Arabia
225 F3 **'Ayn 'Āmūr** *spring* Egypt
147 H9 **'Ayn Bā Ma'bad** Yemen
224 E3 **'Ayn Dāllah** *spring* Egypt
147 M6 **'Ayn Hindī** *oasis* Oman
145 M2 **Ayní** Tajik.
146 E5 **'Aynīn** *well* Saudi Arabia
148 I5 **'Ayn 'Īsá** Syria
150 A9 **'Ayn Sukhnah** Egypt
224 E2 **'Ayn Tabaghbugh** *spring* Egypt
224 E2 **'Ayn Tumayrah** *spring* Egypt
224 E2 **'Ayn Zaytūn** Egypt
224 E4 **'Ayn Zuwayyah** *spring* Libya
232 A2 **Ayod** Sudan
268 E5 **Ayo el Chico** Mex.
153 R3 **Ayon, Ostrov** *i.* Rus. Fed.
204 H4 **Ayoo de Vidriales** Spain
269 K9 **Ayoquezco** Mex.
209 C9 **Ayora** Spain
229 F3 **Ayorou** Niger
229 I6 **Ayos** Cameroon
226 D4 **'Ayoûn 'Abd el Mâlek** *well* Maur.
228 C2 **'Ayoûn el 'Atroûs** Maur.
107 K5 **Ayr** *Qld* Austr.
251 N6 **Ayr** *Ont.* Can.
168 G12 **Ayr** *South Ayrshire, Scotland* U.K.
168 G12 **Ayr** *r. Scotland* U.K.
172 F1 **Ayr, Point of** *Wales* U.K.
128 C2 **Ayrag Nuur** *salt l.* Mongolia
150 F1 **Ayran** Turkey
148 F5 **Ayrancı** Turkey
221 I4 **Ayrancılar** Turkey
170 I5 **Ayre, Point of** Isle of Man
151 H4 **Äyriçay** *r.* Azer.
183 C10 **Ayrolle, Étang de l'** *lag.* France
181 L8 **Ayron** France
151 F4 **Ayrum** Armenia
Aysarinskoye Kazakh. *see* **Zaozernyy**
Aysary Kazakh. *see* **Zaozernyy**
171 N5 **Aysgarth** *North Yorkshire, England* U.K.
232 D2 **Āysha** Eth.
143 N4 **Ayshyrak** Kazakh.
195 J5 **Aystetten** Ger.
142 J5 **Ayteke Bi** Kazakh.
219 P8 **Aytos** Bulg.
219 P8 **Aytoska Reka** *r.* Bulg.
184 B3 **Aytré** France
115 G3 **Ayu** *i. Papua* Indon.
115 G3 **Ayu, Kepulauan** *atoll Papua* Indon.
205 O3 **Ayuda** *r.* Spain
159 N9 **Ayudah, Mys** *pt* Ukr.
206 F2 **Ayuela** *r.* Spain
147 K7 **Ayun** Oman
119 I8 **A Yun, Ia** *r.* Vietnam
119 I8 **A Yun Pa** Vietnam
Ayuthia Thai. *see* **Ayutthaya**
159 T6 **Ayutinskiy** Rus. Fed.
269 H9 **Ayutla** *Guerrero* Mex.
268 C5 **Ayutla** *Jalisco* Mex.
269 L8 **Ayutla** *Oaxaca* Mex.
119 E7 **Ayutthaya** Thai.
274 B5 **Ayuy** Ecuador
221 H3 **Ayvacık** Turkey
Ayvadzh Tajik. *see* **Ayvaj**
145 M3 **Ayvaj** Tajik.
151 C5 **Ayvalı** *Erzurum* Turkey
148 H4 **Ayvalı** *Malatya* Turkey
221 H3 **Ayvalık** Turkey
221 M5 **Ayvalıpınar** Turkey
187 I8 **Aywaille** Belgium
147 J7 **'Aywat al Manāhīl, Wādī** *r.* Yemen
147 I7 **'Aywat aş Şay'ar, Wādī** *r.* Yemen
159 M9 **Ayya, Mys** *pt* Ukr.
229 G2 **Aza** *well* Niger
266 □P10 **Azacualpa** Hond.
151 J6 **Āzādlū** Iran
144 F3 **Āzād Shahr** Iran
205 Q4 **Azagra** Spain
126 D5 **Azai** Japan
208 E5 **Azaila** Spain
Azak Rus. Fed. *see* **Azov**
124 □1 **Azama** *Okinawa* Japan
206 B2 **Azambuja** Port.
206 D4 **Azambuja** *r.* Port.
139 I6 **Azamgarh** *Uttar Prad.* India
276 C3 **Azangaro** Peru
218 I6 **Azanja** *Smederevska Palanka* Serbia
179 J5 **Azannes-et-Soumazannes** France
208 F4 **Azanúy** Spain
228 E2 **Azaouâd** *reg.* Mali
229 F2 **Azaouagh, Vallée de** *watercourse* Mali/Niger
276 C4 **Azapa** Chile
229 G2 **Azar** *watercourse* Niger
282 G3 **Azara** Arg.
Azaran Iran *see* **Hashtrud**
Azärbayjan *country* Asia *see* **Azerbaijan**
144 A2 **Āzarbāyjān-e Gharbī** *prov.* Iran
144 B3 **Āzarbāyjān-e Sharqī** *prov.* Iran
229 H4 **Azare** Nigeria
206 D3 **Azaruja** Port.
160 M9 **Azarychy** Belarus
143 M4 **Azat, Gory** *hill* Kazakh.
151 G5 **Azatamut** Armenia
161 U2 **Azatskoye, Ozero** *l.* Rus. Fed.
151 E4 **Azavret'i** Georgia
181 N8 **Azay-le-Ferron** France
181 L7 **Azay-le-Rideau** France
150 F2 **A'zāz** Syria
Azbine *mts* Niger *see* **Aïr, Massif de l'**
Azcoitia Spain *see* **Azkoitia**
148 F3 **Azdavay** Turkey
181 J6 **Azé** France
229 H2 **Azélik** *well* Niger
226 C2 **Azemmour** Morocco
227 E5 **Azennezal, Erg** *des.* Alg.
184 G3 **Azerables** France
151 J5 **Azerbaijan** *country* Asia
Azerbaydzhanskaya S.S.R. *country* Asia *see* **Azerbaijan**
182 F5 **Azergues** *r.* France
206 E4 **Azevel** *r.* Port.
232 C1 **Āzezo** Eth.
144 B2 **Āzghān** Iran
142 I5 **Azhar** Kazakh.
151 F5 **Azhdahak Lerr** *mt.* Armenia
226 D2 **Azilal** Morocco
251 M3 **Azilda** *Ont.* Can.
183 B10 **Azille** France
178 D3 **Azincourt** France
230 A5 **Azingo** Gabon
206 B2 **Azinhaga** Port.
206 E6 **Azinhal** Port.
204 G6 **Azinhoso** Port.
257 □O3 **Aziscohos Lake** *ME* U.S.A.
144 H7 **'Azīzābād** Iran
Azizbekov Armenia *see* **Vayk'**
Aziziye Turkey *see* **Pınarbaşı**
208 A1 **Azkoitia** Spain
146 B2 **Aẓlam, Wādī** *watercourse* Saudi Arabia
157 K5 **Aznakayevo** Rus. Fed.
206 G6 **Aznalcázar** Spain
206 G5 **Aznalcóllar** Spain
206 H7 **Aznar, Sierra de** *mts* Spain
274 B5 **Azogues** Ecuador
206 A4 **Azóia** Port.
156 I2 **Azopol'ye** Rus. Fed.
Azores *is* N. Atlantic Ocean *see* **Açores, Arquipélago dos**
Azores *aut. reg.* Port. *see* **Arquipélago dos Açores**
288 H3 **Azores-Biscay Rise** *sea feature* N. Atlantic Ocean
151 C5 **Azot Geçidi** *pass* Turkey
Azotus Israel *see* **Ashdod**
230 D2 **Azoum, Bahr** *watercourse* Chad
157 G7 **Azov** Rus. Fed.
159 P7 **Azov, Sea of** Rus. Fed./Ukr.
159 N7 **Azovo-Sivas'kyy Zapovidnyk** *nature res.* Ukr.
Azovs'ke More *sea* Rus. Fed./Ukr. *see* **Azov, Sea of**
159 T6 **Azovskiy Kanal** *canal* Rus. Fed.
Azovskoye More *sea* Rus. Fed./Ukr. *see* **Azov, Sea of**
159 N8 **Azovs'kyy Kanal** *canal* Ukr.
269 I9 **Azoyú** Mex.
208 A1 **Azpeitia** Spain
230 C2 **Azrak, Bahr** *watercourse* Chad
225 G6 **Azraq, Bahr el** *r.* Sudan *alt.* **Ābay Wenz (Ethiopia),** *conv.* **Blue Nile**
150 E7 **Azraq ash Shīshān** Jordan
226 D2 **Azrou** Morocco
227 G5 **Azrou, Oued** *watercourse* Alg.
145 M4 **Azrow** Afgh.
263 J8 **Aztec** *NM* U.S.A.
270 H4 **Azua** Dom. Rep.
206 H4 **Azuaga** Spain
208 D5 **Azuara** Spain
274 B5 **Azuay** *prov.* Ecuador
282 C2 **Azúcar** *r.* Chile
285 H5 **Azucena** Arg.
126 D5 **Azuchi** Japan
125 G13 **Azuchi-Ō-shima** *i.* Japan
207 K4 **Azuel** Spain
205 P3 **Azuelo** Spain
207 L2 **Azuer** *r.* Spain
266 □S14 **Azuero, Península de** *pen.* Panama
282 C2 **Azufre, Cerro del** *mt.* Chile
285 H5 **Azul** Arg.
285 H5 **Azul** *r.* Arg.
284 B4 **Azul** *vol.* Chile
267 O9 **Azul** *r.* Mex.
274 □ **Azul, Cerro** *vol. Islas Galápagos* Ecuador
276 B2 **Azul, Cordillera** *mts* Peru
238 □1b **Azul, Lagoa** *l. São Miguel* Azores
277 G3 **Azul, Serra** *hills* Brazil
266 □P10 **Azul Meambar, Parque Nacional** *nat. park* Hond.
224 D6 **Azum, Wadi** *watercourse* Sudan
127 J2 **Azuma** *Gunma* Japan
127 J3 **Azuma** *Gunma* Japan
127 L4 **Azuma** *Ibaraki* Japan
124 R9 **Azuma-san** *vol.* Japan
127 H2 **Azumaya-san** *mt.* Japan
127 G3 **Azumi** Japan
205 N7 **Azuqueca de Henares** Spain
185 B8 **Azur** France
204 C6 **Azurara** Port.
276 D5 **Azurduy** Bol.
126 G3 **Azusa-ko** *resr* Japan
205 J9 **Azután** Spain
205 K9 **Azután, Embalse de** *resr* Spain
197 N2 **Azyarnitsa** Belarus
182 C3 **Azy-le-Vif** France
160 H8 **Azyory** Belarus
'Azza Gaza *see* **Gaza**
227 G1 **Azzaba** Alg.
150 E5 **Az Zabadānī** Syria
146 F2 **Az Zabīrah** *well* Saudi Arabia
225 I5 **Aẓ Ẓafīr** Saudi Arabia
149 K8 **Aẓ Ẓafīrī** *reg.* Iraq
147 M4 **Aẓ Ẓāhirah** *admin. reg.* Oman
147 J2 **Aẓ Ẓahrān** Saudi Arabia
147 J3 **Az Zallāq** Bahrain
213 N4 **Azzano Decimo** Italy
225 F2 **Az Zaqāzīq** Egypt
150 E2 **Az Zarbah** Syria
150 E6 **Az Zarqā'** Jordan
224 B1 **Az Zāwīyah** Libya
146 F8 **Az Zaydīyah** Yemen
226 B5 **Azzeffâl** *hills* Maur./W. Sahara
227 F4 **Azzel Matti, Sebkha** *salt pan* Alg.
146 G2 **Az Zilfī** Saudi Arabia
224 B2 **Az Zintān** Libya
212 I4 **Azzone** Italy
149 M8 **Az Zubayr** Iraq
146 F8 **Az Zuhrah** Yemen
146 F8 **Az Zuqur** *i.* Yemen
147 J6 **Az Zuqurt** *oasis* Saudi Arabia
224 D2 **Az Zuwaytīnah** Libya

B

101 □7a **Ba** *Viti Levu* Fiji
101 □7a **Ba** *r. Viti Levu* Fiji
119 I8 **Ba, Sông** *r.* Vietnam
115 C9 **Baa** Indon.
100 □5 **Baâba** *i.* New Caledonia
150 D5 **Baabda** Lebanon
117 L4 **Baai** *r.* Indon.
150 E4 **Ba'albek** Lebanon
193 E7 **Baalberge** Ger.
186 K3 **Baalder** Neth.
150 D7 **Ba'al Ḥazor** *mt.* West Bank
179 J5 **Baâlon** France
150 D5 **Baaqline** Lebanon
194 F6 **Baar** *reg.* Ger.
212 F1 **Baar** Switz.
232 D4 **Baardheere** Somalia
195 K4 **Baar-Ebenhausen** Ger.
187 G6 **Baarle-Hertog** Belgium
187 G6 **Baarle-Nassau** Neth.
186 H4 **Baarn** Neth.
128 F4 **Baatsagaan** Mongolia
138 G6 **Bab** *Uttar Prad.* India
219 L8 **Baba** *mt.* Bulg.
201 K1 **Baba** *hill* Czech Rep.
145 J4 **Bābā, Band-e** *mts* Afgh.
144 H5 **Bābā, Chāh-e** *well* Iran
145 M4 **Bābā, Kūh-e** *mts* Afgh.
228 B2 **Bababé** Maur.
221 H3 **Baba Burnu** *pt* Turkey
278 D3 **Babaçulândia** Brazil
151 J4 **Babadağ** *mt.* Azer.
219 Q6 **Babadag** Romania
221 J5 **Babadağ** Turkey
221 K6 **Baba Dağ** *mt.* Turkey
219 Q6 **Babadagului, Podişul** *plat.* Romania
144 H3 **Babadurmaz** Turkm.
221 I1 **Babaeski** Turkey
221 L4 **Babageçidin Tepesi** *mt.* Turkey
274 B5 **Babahoyo** Ecuador
138 H5 **Babai** *r.* Nepal
149 M4 **Bābājān** Iran
151 G6 **Babăk** Azer.
114 E8 **Babak** Phil.
144 D6 **Bābā Kalān** Iran
Bābā Khalāt Iran *see* **Bābā Khaled**
144 E5 **Bābā Khaled** Iran
151 A5 **Babakonağı** Turkey
229 H3 **Babakourimigana** *well* Niger
225 I6 **Bāb al Mandab** *str.* Africa/Asia
146 F9 **Bāb al Mandab, Ra's** *c.* Yemen
115 A5 **Babana** *Sulawesi Barat* Indon.
229 F4 **Babana** Nigeria
237 P4 **Babanango** S. Africa
237 M4 **Babangiboni** *mt.* S. Africa
229 H5 **Babanki** Cameroon
230 E2 **Babanusa** Sudan
Babao *Qinghai* China *see* **Qilian**
130 E7 **Babao** *Yunnan* China
115 F7 **Babar** *i. Maluku* Indon.
115 F7 **Babar, Kepulauan** *is Maluku* Indon.
117 J8 **Babat** *Jawa* Indon.
233 B6 **Babati** Tanz.
115 C9 **Babau** *Timor* Indon.
161 S2 **Babayevo** Rus. Fed.
159 N4 **Babaykivka** Ukr.
151 H2 **Babayurt** Rus. Fed.
172 F6 **Babbacombe Bay** *England* U.K.
245 M1 **Babbage** *r. Y.T.* Can.
109 B8 **Babbage Island** W.A. Austr.
186 J5 **Babberich** Neth.
114 □ **Babeldaob** *i.* Palau
237 M1 **Babelegi** S. Africa
Babelthuap *i.* Palau *see* **Babeldaob**
195 I5 **Babenhausen** *Bayern* Ger.
194 F2 **Babenhausen** *Hessen* Ger.
219 M6 **Băbeni** Romania
230 E4 **Babenza** Dem. Rep. Congo
138 H7 **Baberu** *Uttar Prad.* India
116 B3 **Babi, Pulau** *i.* Indon.
204 H3 **Babia** *reg.* Spain
197 H6 **Babia Góra** *mt.* Pol.
197 I1 **Babiak** *Warmińsko-Mazurskie* Pol.
196 G3 **Babiak** *Wielkopolskie* Pol.
130 C7 **Babian Jiang** *r. Yunnan* China
198 G2 **Babice** Czech Rep.
197 H5 **Babice** Pol.
149 L7 **Bābil** *governorate* Iraq
205 J7 **Babilafuente** Spain
232 D2 **Babīlē** Eth.
196 D3 **Babimost** Pol.
161 N7 **Babinavichy** Belarus
107 J4 **Babinda** *Qld* Austr.
242 F4 **Babine** *r. B.C.* Can.
246 E4 **Babine** *r. B.C.* Can.
246 E4 **Babine Lake** *B.C.* Can.
246 E4 **Babine Range** *mts B.C.* Can.
231 C5 **Babinga** Dem. Rep. Congo
197 H6 **Babiogórski Park Narodowy** *nat. park* Pol.
160 G5 **Babītes ezers** *l.* Latvia
213 R4 **Babno Polje** Slovenia
113 H7 **Babo** *Papua* Indon.
198 G5 **Babócsa** Hungary
144 E3 **Bābol** Iran
199 G4 **Bábolna** Hungary
144 E3 **Bābol Sar** Iran
229 I5 **Babongo** Cameroon
271 □3 **Babonneau** St Lucia
236 C8 **Baboon Point** S. Africa
265 U10 **Baboquivari Peak** *AZ* U.S.A.
196 F5 **Baborów** Pol.
197 I3 **Baboszewo** Pol.
230 B3 **Baboua** C.A.R.
160 M8 **Babruysk** Belarus
122 H4 **Babstovo** Rus. Fed.
160 G6 **Babtai** Lith.
Babu *Guangxi* China *see* **Hezhou**
138 B6 **Babuhri** *Rajasthan* India
219 J9 **Babuna Planina** *mts* Macedonia
145 P4 **Babusar Pass** Pak.
120 I1 **Babushkin** Rus. Fed.
156 H4 **Babushkina, imeni** Rus. Fed.
219 K7 **Babušnica** *Babušnica* Serbia
114 B7 **Babuyan** *Palawan* Phil.
114 C2 **Babuyan** *i.* Phil.
114 C2 **Babuyan Channel** Phil.
114 C2 **Babuyan Islands** Phil.
171 P7 **Babworth** *Nottinghamshire, England* U.K.
149 L7 **Babylon** *tourist site* Iraq
259 I3 **Babylon** *NY* U.S.A.
161 S7 **Babynino** Rus. Fed.
218 H5 **Bač** *Vojvodina* Serbia
232 E3 **Bacaadweyn** Somalia
274 D5 **Bacaba** *r.* Brazil
266 E4 **Bacabáchi** Mex.
278 D3 **Bacabal** *Maranhão* Bra
275 G6 **Bacabal** *Pará* Brazil
275 I5 **Bacajá** *r.* Brazil
148 E3 **Bacakliyayla Tepesi** *mt.*
267 O8 **Bacalar** Mex.
267 P8 **Bacalar Chico, Boca** *se* Mex.
115 E4 **Bacan** *i. Maluku* Indon
185 F10 **Bacanère, Pic de** *mt.* F
128 G9 **Bacang** *Qinghai* China
266 E3 **Bacanora** Mex.
207 O6 **Bacares** Spain
114 C2 **Bacarra** *Luzon* Phil.
219 O4 **Bacău** Romania
179 M7 **Baccarat** France
249 H5 **Baccaro Point** *N.S.* Car
213 M5 **Bacchiglione** *r.* Italy
212 E3 **Baceno** Italy
118 H4 **Băc Giang** Vietnam
200 B5 **Bach** Austria
122 H4 **Bacha** *Heilong.* China
195 M3 **Bach an der Donau** Ge
274 D2 **Bachaquero** Venez.
191 E10 **Bacharach** Ger.
160 M6 **Bacheykava** Belarus
195 I4 **Bachhagel** Ger.
286 T2 **Bach Ice Shelf** Antarcti
263 K12 **Bachiniva** Mex.
118 H4 **Bach Long Vi, Đao** *i.* V
197 K6 **Bachórz** Pol.
196 G3 **Bachorze, Kanał** *canal*
132 D7 **Bachu** *Xinjiang* China
232 B3 **Bachuma** Eth.
197 K3 **Baciki Bliższe** Pol.
107 I4 **Back** *r. Qld* Austr.
247 M1 **Back** *r. N.W.T./Nunavut*
218 H4 **Bačka** *reg.* Hungary/Se
168 K4 **Backaland** *Orkney, Scot*
218 H5 **Bačka Palanka** *Vojvodir*
218 H5 **Bačka Topola** *Vojvodina*
256 F9 **Backbone Mountain** *M*
245 O3 **Backbone Ranges** *mts N.W.T.* Can.
162 N5 **Backe** Sweden
164 I3 **Bäckefors** Sweden
165 K2 **Bäckhammar** Sweden
199 H6 **Bački Breg** *Vojvodina* S
199 H6 **Bački Monoštor** *Vojvod*
218 H5 **Bački Petrovac** *Vojvodir*
247 I2 **Back Lake** *N.W.T.* Can.
194 G4 **Backnang** Ger.
218 I5 **Bačko Gradište** *Vojvodi*
197 J5 **Baćkowice** Pol.
104 F6 **Backstairs Passage** *S.A*
168 J9 **Backwater Reservoir** *Scotland* U.K.
172 G5 **Backwell** *North Somers England* U.K.
119 G10 **Bac Liêu** Vietnam
118 H4 **Bac Ninh** Vietnam
114 C3 **Bacnotan** *Luzon* Phil.
114 C5 **Baco, Mount** *Mindoro*
266 D2 **Bacoachi** Mex.
263 I12 **Bacoachi** *watercourse* M
266 E4 **Bacobampo** Mex.
215 M6 **Bacoli** Italy
114 D6 **Bacolod** *Negros* Phil.
Bacou, Pic de *mt.* Fran **Guerreys, Pic de**
248 F1 **Bacqueville, Lac** *l. Que.*
178 A4 **Bacqueville-en-Caux** F
199 I5 **Bácsalmás** Hungary
199 I5 **Bácsbokod** Hungary
199 I5 **Bácsborsód** Hungary
199 I5 **Bács-Kiskun** *county* Hu
Bactra Afgh. *see* **Balkh**
266 F5 **Bacubirito** Mex.
199 I3 **Bacúch** Slovakia
114 F8 **Baculin Bay** *Mindanao*
114 F7 **Baculin Point** *Mindana*
171 M6 **Bacup** *Lancashire, Engle*
278 D2 **Bacuri** Brazil
196 D3 **Baczyna** Pol.
260 E3 **Bad** *r. SD* U.S.A.
Bada *Guangxi* China *see*
232 C3 **Bada** *mt.* Eth.
119 D9 **Bada** *i.* Myanmar
139 J8 **Bada Barabil** *Orissa* In
144 I3 **Badabaýhan** *Akhal'skay* Turkm.
195 M4 **Bad Abbach** Ger.
198 G5 **Badacsonyi** *park* Hunga
195 M6 **Bad Aibling** Ger.
128 H7 **Badain Jaran** *Nei Mong*
128 G6 **Badain Jaran Shamo** *de Mongol* China
275 F5 **Badajós** *Amazonas* Braz
278 D2 **Badajós** *Pará* Brazil
275 F5 **Badajós, Lago** *l.* Brazil
206 F3 **Badajoz** Spain
206 G3 **Badajoz** *prov.* Spain
145 N3 **Badakhshān** *prov.* Afgh
Badakhshan *aut. rep.* Ta **Kŭhistoni Badakhshon**
Badakhshoni Kŭhí *aut. see* **Kŭhistoni Badakhsh**
208 J5 **Badalona** Spain
212 D8 **Badalucco** Italy
205 N2 **Bádames** Spain
136 D5 **Badami** *Karnataka* Indi
139 K8 **Badampaharh** *Orissa* In
149 J8 **Badanah** Saudi Arabia
168 H6 **Badanloch, Loch** *l. Scot*
Badaojiang *Jilin* China **Baishan**
205 O4 **Badarán** Spain
138 G4 **Badarinath** *Uttaranchal*
Badarinath *mts Uttaran see* **Chaukhamba**
139 N7 **Badarpur** *Assam* India
117 K2 **Badas** Brunei
116 G4 **Badas, Kepulauan** *is* In
138 H7 **Badausa** *Uttar Prad.* Ind
201 I4 **Bad Aussee** Austria
251 L6 **Bad Axe** *MI* U.S.A.
190 G3 **Bad Bederkesa** Ger.
191 D6 **Bad Bentheim** Ger.
190 E5 **Badbergen** Ger.
194 D3 **Bad Bergzabern** Ger.
193 D9 **Bad Berka** Ger.
191 F8 **Bad Berleburg** Ger.
193 E10 **Bad Berneck im Fichtelgebirge** Ger.
191 D10 **Bad Bertrich** Ger.
190 K4 **Bad Bevensen** Ger.
193 E8 **Bad Bibra** Ger.
195 O5 **Bad Birnbach** Ger.
193 D9 **Bad Blankenburg** Ger.
201 I6 **Bad Bleiberg** Austria
191 J10 **Bad Bocklet** Ger.
193 F10 **Bad Brambach** Ger.
190 I3 **Bad Bramstedt** Ger.
191 D10 **Bad Breisig** Ger.
191 I10 **Bad Brückenau** Ger.
194 H5 **Bad Buchau** Ger.
191 F10 **Bad Camberg** Ger.
168 F7 **Badcaul** *Highland, Scotl*
249 I4 **Baddeck** *N.S.* Can.
191 J6 **Baddeckenstedt** Ger.
162 Q2 **Badderen** Norway
145 K7 **Baddo** *r.* Pak.
192 E2 **Bad Doberan** Ger.
191 H7 **Bad Driburg** Ger.
193 G7 **Bad Düben** Ger.
194 E3 **Bad Dürkheim** Ger.
193 F8 **Bad Dürrenberg** Ger.
194 F5 **Bad Dürrheim** Ger.
193 D7 **Badeborn** Ger.
184 G5 **Badefols-d'Ans** France
229 G3 **Badéguichéri** Niger
191 H6 **Bad Eilsen** Ger.
193 F10 **Bad Elster** Ger.
Bademli Turkey *see* **Alad**
148 E5 **Bademli Geçidi** *pass* Tu
191 E10 **Bad Ems** Ger.
201 N3 **Baden** Austria
180 F6 **Baden** France
212 E1 **Baden** Switz.
208 C5 **Bádenas** Spain
194 E4 **Baden-Baden** Ger.

Bad Endbach Ger.
Bad Endorf Ger.
Badenhausen Ger.
Badenoch reg. Scotland U.K.
Badenscoth Aberdeenshire, Scotland U.K.
Badenweiler Ger.
Baden-Württemberg land Ger.
Badér Niger
Baderna Croatia
Badersleben Ger.
Badesi Sardegna Italy
Bad Essen Ger.
Bad Feilnbach Ger.
Bad Freienwalde Ger.
Bad Friedrichshall Ger.
Bad Füssing Ger.
Badgam Jammu and Kashmir India
Bad Gams Austria
Bad Gandersheim Ger.
Badgastein Austria
Badger Nfld and Lab. Can.
Bādghīs prov. Afgh.
Bad Gleichenberg Austria
Bad Goisern Austria
Bad Gottleuba, Kurort Ger.
Bad Großpertholz Austria
Bad Grund (Harz) Ger.
Bad Hall Austria
Bad Häring Austria
Bad Harzburg Ger.
Bad Heilbrunn Ger.
Bad Herrenalb Ger.
Bad Hersfeld Ger.
Badhoevedorp Neth.
Bad Hofgastein Austria
Bad Homburg vor der Höhe Ger.
Bad Honnef Ger.
Badi r. Guinea
Badia Italy
Badia Calavena Italy
Badia Gran Spain
Badia Polesine Italy
Badia Tedalda Italy
Bad Iburg Ger.
Badiel r. Spain
Badigeru Swamp Sudan
Badillo Col.
Badin Pak.
Badín Slovakia
Badinko, Réserve du nature res. Mali
Badiraguato Mex.
Bad Ischl Austria
Bādiyat ash Shām des. Asia
Badje-Sohppar Sweden see Övre Soppero
Bad Karlshafen Ger.
Bad Kissingen Ger.
Bad Kleinen Ger.
Bad Kleinkirchheim Austria
Bad Klosterlausnitz Ger.
Bad Kohlgrub Ger.
Bad König Ger.
Bad Königsdorff Pol. see Jastrzębie-Zdrój
Bad Königshofen im Grabfeld Ger.
Bad Kösen Ger.
Bad Kreuzen Austria
Bad Kreuznach Ger.
Bad Krozingen Ger.
Bad Laasphe Ger.
Bad Laer Ger.
Badlands reg. ND U.S.A.
Badlands reg. SD U.S.A.
Badlands National Park SD U.S.A.
Bad Langensalza Ger.
Bad Lauchstädt Ger.
Bad Lausick Ger.
Bad Lauterberg im Harz Ger.
Bad Leonfelden Austria
Bad Liebenwerda Ger.
Bad Liebenzell Ger.
Bad Lippspringe Ger.
Badlipster Highland, Scotland U.K.
Bad Mergentheim Ger.
Bad Mitterndorf Austria
Bad Münder am Deister Ger.
Bad Münster am Stein-Ebernburg Ger.
Bad Münstereifel Ger.
Bad Muskau Ger.
Bad Nauheim Ger.
Badnawar Madh. Prad. India
Bad Nenndorf Ger.
Badnera Mahar. India
Bad Neuenahr-Ahrweiler Ger.
Bad Neustadt an der Saale Ger.
Bad Oeynhausen Ger.
Badolato Italy
Badolatosa Spain
Bad Oldesloe Ger.
Badong Hubei China
Ba Đông Vietnam
Badonviller France
Bad Orb Ger.
Badou Shandong China
Badou Togo
Badovinci Bogatić Serbia
Bad Peterstal Ger.
Bad Pirawarth Austria
Badplaas S. Africa
Bad Pyrmont Ger.
Badr Saudi Arabia
Bad Radkersburg Austria
Bad Ragaz Switz.
Badrah Iraq
Bad Rappenau Ger.
Bad Reichenhall Ger.
Badr Ḥunayn Saudi Arabia
Badrinath Peaks Uttaranchal India see Chaukhamba
Bad River Indian Reservation res. WI U.S.A.
Bad Rothenfelde Ger.
Bad Saarow-Pieskow Ger.
Bad Sachsa Ger.
Bad Säckingen Ger.
Bad Salzdetfurth Ger.
Bad Salzschlirf Ger.
Bad Salzuflen Ger.
Bad Salzungen Ger.
Bad Sankt Leonhard im Lavanttal Austria
Bad Sassendorf Ger.
Bad Schallerbach Austria
Bad Schandau Ger.
Bad Schmiedeberg Ger.
Bad Schönborn Ger.
Bad Schussenried Ger.
Bad Schwalbach Ger.
Bad Schwartau Ger.
Bad Segeberg Ger.
Badsey Worcestershire, England U.K.
Bad Sobernheim Ger.
Bad Soden-Salmünster Ger.
Bad Sooden-Allendorf Ger.
Bad Steben Ger.
Bad Suderode Ger.
Bad Sulza Ger.
Bad Sülze Ger.
Bad Tennstedt Ger.
Bad Tölz Ger.
Badu Fujian China
Bad Überkingen Ger.
Badu Island Qld Austr.
Badules Spain
Badulla Sri Lanka
Bad Urach Ger.
Badvel Andhra Prad. India
Bad Vilbel Ger.
Bad Vöslau Austria
Bad Waldsee Ger.
Bad Waltersdorf Austria
Bad Wiessee Ger.
Bad Wildbad im Schwarzwald Ger.
Bad Wildungen Ger.
Bad Wilsnack Ger.
194 G3 Bad Wimpfen Ger.
201 I3 Bad Wimsbach-Neydharting Austria
195 I2 Bad Windsheim Ger.
195 J6 Bad Wörishofen Ger.
194 H6 Bad Wurzach Ger.
201 K3 Bad Zell Austria
122 I3 Badzhal Rus. Fed.
122 H4 Badzhal'skiy Khrebet mts Rus. Fed.
191 H8 Bad Zwesten Ger.
190 F4 Bad Zwischenahn Ger.
Bae Cinmel Conwy, Wales U.K. see Kinmel Bay
Bae Colwyn Conwy, Wales U.K. see Colwyn Bay
162 □B1 Bæir Iceland
192 E4 Baek Ger.
164 F6 Bække Denmark
164 E5 Bækmarksbro Denmark
187 I7 Baelen Belgium
208 I3 Baells, Pantà de la resr Spain
207 K5 Baena Spain
Bae Penrhyn Conwy, Wales U.K. see Penrhyn Bay
191 B9 Baesweiler Ger.
274 B5 Baeza Ecuador
207 M5 Baeza Spain
229 H5 Bafang Cameroon
228 B3 Bafatá Guinea-Bissau
145 O4 Baffa Pak.
243 L2 Baffin Bay sea Can./Greenland
243 L3 Baffin Island Nunavut Can.
229 H5 Bafia Cameroon
229 F4 Bafilo Togo
228 C3 Bafing r. Guinea/Mali
228 C3 Bafing, Réserve du nature res. Mali
228 C3 Bafing Makana Mali
186 K2 Baflo Neth.
228 C3 Bafoulabé Mali
229 H5 Bafoussam Cameroon
144 F6 Bāfq Iran
148 G3 Bafra Turkey
148 G3 Bafra Burnu pt Turkey
144 G7 Bāft Iran
230 E4 Bafwaboli Dem. Rep. Congo
230 E4 Bafwamboma Dem. Rep. Congo
230 E4 Bafwasende Dem. Rep. Congo
199 I4 Bag Hungary
229 I3 Baga Nigeria
208 I3 Bagà Spain
128 G4 Baga Bogd Uul mts Mongolia
114 C4 Bagac Bay Luzon Phil.
139 J6 Bagaha Bihar India
117 M2 Bagahak, Gunung hill Malaysia
217 J7 Bagaladi Italy
136 D4 Bagalkot Karnataka India
144 E5 Bagam Iran
199 K4 Bagamér Hungary
233 C6 Bagamoyo Tanz.
143 Q1 Bagan Rus. Fed.
229 G5 Bagana Nigeria
Bagan Datoh Malaysia see Bagan Datuk
116 D3 Bagan Datuk Malaysia
114 F8 Baganga Mindanao Phil.
234 D3 Bagani Namibia
114 D8 Baganian Peninsula Mindanao Phil.
116 D2 Bagan Serai Malaysia
116 D3 Bagansiapiapi Sumatera Indon.
129 K3 Baganuur Mongolia
212 I6 Baganza r. Italy
133 K11 Bagar Xizang China
221 I5 Bağarası Turkey
183 E8 Bagard France
229 G3 Bagaré well Niger
229 G3 Bagaroua Niger
231 C5 Bagata Dem. Rep. Congo
274 C6 Bagazán Peru
225 F6 Bagbag Sudan
265 S7 Bagdad AZ U.S.A.
Bagdadi Georgia see Baghdat'i
282 G3 Bagé Brazil
182 F4 Bâgé-le-Châtel France
169 I7 Bagenalstown Ireland
190 K1 Bagenkop Denmark
136 E6 Bagepalli Karnataka India
139 L8 Bagerhat Bangl.
185 J10 Bages France
208 I4 Bages reg. Spain
183 B10 Bages et de Sigean, Étang de lag. France
138 G5 Bageshwar Uttaranchal India
165 L2 Baggå Sweden
262 K6 Baggs WY U.S.A.
172 D5 Baggy Point England U.K.
138 E8 Bagh Madh. Prad. India
145 O5 Bagh Pak.
144 F6 Bāgh, Chāh-e well Iran
Bagh a'Chaisteil Western Isles, Scotland U.K. see Castlebay
145 K7 Baghak Pak.
168 B8 Baghasdail, Loch inlet Scotland U.K.
144 I3 Bagh Baghū Iran
149 L7 Baghdād Iraq
149 L7 Baghdād governorate Iraq
151 D3 Baghdat'i Georgia
144 G7 Bāgh-e Bābū'īyeh Iran
144 C6 Bāgh-e Malek Iran
Bagherhat Bangl. see Bagerhat
216 F7 Bagheria Sicilia Italy
144 G6 Bāghīn Iran
145 M3 Baghlān Afgh.
145 M4 Baghlān prov. Afgh.
144 B2 Bāghlī Da hill Iran
151 E5 Baghramyan Armenia
145 K5 Baghrān Afgh.
145 L8 Baghwana Pak.
172 F1 Bagillt Flintshire, Wales U.K.
116 G6 Baginda, Tanjung pt Indon.
151 A6 Bağırpaşa Dağı mts Turkey
Bağırsak Deresi r. Syria/Turkey see Sājūr, Nahr
151 C7 Bağlar Turkey
260 H2 Bagley MN U.S.A.
245 J4 Bagley Icefield AK U.S.A.
139 I5 Baglung Nepal
163 J6 Bagn Norway
213 L7 Bagnacavallo Italy
185 I6 Bagnac-sur-Célé France
217 J7 Bagnara Calabra Italy
212 G6 Bagnaria Italy
213 O4 Bagnaria Arsa Italy
212 E7 Bagnasco Italy
178 E7 Bagneaux-sur-Loing France
185 E9 Bagnères-de-Bigorre France
185 F10 Bagnères-de-Luchon France
212 C3 Bagnes reg. Switz.
212 C3 Bagnes, Val des val. Switz.
212 H3 Bagni di Masino Italy
213 J3 Bagni di Rabbi Italy
213 L8 Bagno di Romagna Italy
181 K4 Bagnoles-de-l'Orne France
215 M4 Bagnoli del Trigno Italy
213 L5 Bagnoli di Sopra Italy
215 O6 Bagnoli Irpino Italy
213 J6 Bagnolo in Piano Italy
212 I5 Bagnolo Mella Italy
183 K7 Bagnolo Piemonte Italy
213 J5 Bagnolo San Vito Italy
183 J9 Bagnols-en-Forêt France
183 D7 Bagnols-les-Bains France
183 F8 Bagnols-sur-Cèze France
212 I7 Bagnone Italy
214 I2 Bagnoregio Italy
139 K7 Bagnuiti r. Nepal
Bago Myanmar see Pegu
Bago admin. div. Myanmar see Pegu
114 D6 Bago Negros Phil.
198 F5 Bagod Hungary
228 D3 Bagoé r. Côte d'Ivoire/Mali
212 I4 Bagolino Italy
Bagong Guizhou China see Sansui
160 D7 Bagrationovsk Rus. Fed.
Bagrax Xinjiang China see Bohu
Bagrax Hu l. China see Bosten Hu
275 I5 Bagre Brazil
221 L5 Bağsaray Turkey
173 K5 Bagshot Surrey, England U.K.
274 B6 Bagua Peru
284 E4 Bagual Arg.
229 G4 Bagudo Nigeria
208 C5 Báguena Spain
114 C3 Baguio Luzon Phil.
114 E8 Baguio Mindanao Phil.
114 D3 Baguio Point Luzon Phil.
Bagur Spain see Begur
Bagur, Cabo c. Spain see Begur, Cap de
198 G4 Bágyogszovát Hungary
221 I4 Bağyurdu Turkey
229 H2 Bagzane, Monts mts Niger
205 M5 Bahabón de Esgueva Spain
159 R4 Bahachka Ukr.
133 F13 Bahadurganj Nepal
138 F5 Bahadurgarh Haryana India
145 N5 Bahadur Khel Pak.
145 I9 Bāhā Kālāt Iran
271 □3 Baham, Pointe pt Martinique
Bahāmabād Iran see Rafsanjān
Bahamas country West Indies see The Bahamas
145 L8 Bahara Pak.
139 L7 Baharampur W. Bengal India
145 M9 Bahardipur Pak.
Bahariya Oasis Egypt see Bahrīyah, Wāḥāt al
144 G2 Baharly Turkm.
159 N8 Bahate Ukr.
159 P6 Bahatyr Ukr.
117 L3 Bahau r. Indon.
116 E3 Bahau Malaysia
117 K6 Bahaur Kalimantan Indon.
145 O7 Bahawalnagar Pak.
145 N7 Bahawalpur Pak.
150 D2 Bahçe Adana Turkey
148 H5 Bahçe Osmaniye Turkey
151 B6 Bahçeköy Turkey
221 H3 Bahçeli Çanakkale Turkey
151 C5 Bahçeli Erzurum Turkey
130 F3 Ba He r. China
Bäherden Turkm. see Baharly
138 G5 Baheri Uttar Prad. India
233 B6 Bahi Tanz.
Bahia Brazil see Salvador
281 G1 Bahia state Brazil
266 □P9 Bahía, Islas de la is Hond.
285 F6 Bahía Blanca Arg.
268 E7 Bahía Bufadero Mex.
283 D7 Bahía Bustamante Arg.
274 A5 Bahía de Caráquez Ecuador
114 B7 Bahia Honda Point Palawan Phil.
266 D3 Bahía Kino Mex.
283 D8 Bahía Laura Arg.
277 F5 Bahía Negra Para.
283 E6 Bahía San Blas Arg.
266 B4 Bahía Tortugas Mex.
205 K4 Bahíllo Spain
232 C2 Bahir Dar Eth.
138 E5 Bahl Haryana India
147 M4 Bahlā Oman
219 P3 Bahlui r. Romania
144 C7 Bahmanshīr, Khowr-e r. Iran
144 D7 Bahman Yārī-ye Gharbī Iran
115 B5 Bahomonte Sulawesi Indon.
198 G3 Báhoň Slovakia
146 E6 Bahr Saudi Arabia
138 H6 Bahraich Uttar Prad. India
147 J2 Bahrain country Asia
147 J3 Bahrain, Gulf of Asia
144 C3 Bahrāmābād Iran
144 C3 Bahrām Beyg Iran
138 H6 Bahramghat Uttar Prad. India
144 G7 Bahrāmjerd Iran
151 I6 Bährämtäpä Azer.
193 D6 Bahrdorf Ger.
190 G5 Bahrenborstel Ger.
225 F3 Bahrīyah, Wāḥāt al oasis Egypt
138 F6 Bahror Rajasthan India
276 C3 Bahuaja-Sonene, Parque Nacional nat. park Peru
115 C5 Bahubulu i. Indon.
161 N7 Bahushewsk Belarus
219 O3 Baia Suceava Romania
219 Q6 Baia Tulcea Romania
219 K6 Baia de Aramă Romania
219 L4 Baia de Arieș Romania
199 L5 Baia de Criș Romania
215 Q4 Baia della Zagare Italy
231 A9 Baía dos Tigres Angola
231 B8 Baía Farta Angola
219 L3 Baia Mare Romania
275 I5 Baião Brazil
204 D6 Baião Port.
205 O3 Baias r. Spain
219 L3 Baia Sprie Romania
216 D8 Baiata r. Sicilia Italy
144 F5 Baiazeh Iran
139 K5 Baiba Xizang China
224 D5 Baïbeli well Chad
230 B3 Baïbokoum Chad
Baicheng Henan China see Xiping
129 R4 Baicheng Jilin China
132 E6 Baicheng Xinjiang China
219 N5 Băicoi Romania
Baidoa Somalia see Baydhabo
133 H10 Baidoi Co l. Xizang China
131 K6 Baidu Guangdong China
132 L6 Baidunzi Gansu China
128 I8 Baidunzi Gansu China
Baie-aux-Feuilles Que. Can. see Tasiujaq
249 G3 Baie-Comeau Que. Can.
270 G4 Baie de Henne Haiti
Baie-du-Poste Que. Can. see Mistissini
249 I3 Baie-Johan-Beetz Que. Can.
271 □2 Baie-Mahault b. Guadeloupe
194 H6 Baienfurt Ger.
195 K5 Baierbrunn Ger.
194 E4 Baiersbronn Ger.
195 K2 Baiersdorf Ger.
249 G4 Baie-St-Paul Que. Can.
249 H3 Baie-Trinité Que. Can.
249 J3 Baie Verte Nfld and Lab. Can.
184 D5 Baignes-Ste-Radegonde France
182 F1 Baigneux-les-Juifs France
285 G4 Baigorrita Arg.
129 O7 Baigou He r. China
Baiguan Zhejiang China see Shangyu
131 J3 Baiguo Hubei China
131 I5 Baiguo Hunan China
205 R3 Baigura mt. Spain
130 B5 Baihanchang Yunnan China
138 H8 Baihar Madh. Prad. India
122 F7 Baihe Jilin China
130 H2 Baihe Shaanxi China
131 I2 Bai He r. China
129 O6 Bai He r. China
Baiji Iraq see Bayjī
132 G4 Baijiantan Xinjiang China
138 F3 Baijnath Hima. Prad. India
138 G5 Baijnath Uttaranchal India
Baikal, Lake Rus. Fed. see Baykal, Ozero
122 C2 Baikalu Shan mt. Heilong. China
138 H7 Baikanthpur Madh. Prad. India
132 G4 Baikouquan Xinjiang China
139 I8 Baikunthpur Chhattisgarh India
129 Q3 Bailang Nei Mongol China
171 N6 Baildon West Yorkshire, England U.K.
Baile Ailein Scotland U.K. see Balallan
Baile an Bhuinneánaigh Ireland see Ballybunion
Baile an Chinnéidigh Ireland see Newtown Mount Kennedy
169 D6 Baile an Dúlaigh Ireland
169 B9 Baile an Sceilg Ireland
Baile Átha Cliath Ireland see Dublin
Baile Átha Luain Ireland see Athlone
169 E6 Baile Chláir Ireland
219 M5 Băile Govora Romania
219 K6 Băile Herculane Romania
168 B7 Baile Mhartainn Western Isles, Scotland U.K.
169 D9 Baile Mhic Íre Ireland
207 L4 Bailén Spain
169 F3 Baile na Finne Ireland
219 M5 Băile Olănești Romania
169 I5 Baile Órthaí Ireland
219 L6 Băilești Romania
219 L6 Băileștilor, Câmpia plain Romania
237 K7 Bailey S. Africa
109 G10 Bailey Range hills W.A. Austr.
256 C12 Baileyton TN U.S.A.
131 J3 Bailianhe Shuiku resr China
130 H6 Bailicun Guangxi China
169 I5 Bailieborough Ireland
129 L6 Bailingmiao Nei Mongol China
275 I4 Bailique Brazil
178 B7 Bailleau-le-Pin France
178 E2 Bailleul France
247 J1 Baillie r. Nunavut Can.
245 O1 Baillie Islands N.W.T. Can.
271 □2 Baillif Guadeloupe
187 H8 Baillonville Belgium
208 D2 Bailo Spain
Bailong Gansu China see Hadapu
130 E2 Bailong Jiang r. Gansu/Qinghai China
231 B8 Bailundo Angola
130 C2 Baima Qinghai China
Baima Xizang China see Baxoi
131 K3 Baima Jian mt. Anhui China
130 G9 Baimajing Hainan China
171 Q7 Bain r. England U.K.
Bainang Xizang China see Norkyung
171 M5 Bainbridge North Yorkshire, England U.K.
255 E10 Bainbridge GA U.S.A.
257 J6 Bainbridge NY U.S.A.
256 B9 Bainbridge OH U.S.A.
258 B4 Bainbridge PA U.S.A.
180 H6 Bain-de-Bretagne France
194 H6 Baindt Ger.
136 D6 Bainduru Karnataka India
270 G4 Bainet Haiti
133 J11 Baingoin Xizang China
Baini Guizhou China see Yuqing
183 D6 Bains France
179 L7 Bains-les-Bains France
180 G6 Bains-sur-Oust France
171 P6 Bainton East Riding of Yorkshire, England U.K.
204 C2 Baio Spain
204 C4 Baiona Spain
130 C2 Baiqên Qinghai China
122 E5 Baiquan Heilong. China
150 E8 Bā'ir Jordan
150 F7 Bā'ir, Wādī watercourse Jordan/Saudi Arabia
133 F9 Bairab Co l. China
139 J6 Bairagnia Bihar India
261 F9 Baird TX U.S.A.
245 N2 Baird, Mount Y.T. Can.
244 F3 Baird Inlet AK U.S.A.
244 H2 Baird Mountains AK U.S.A.
99 H1 Bairiki Kiribati
129 P5 Bairin Qiao Nei Mongol China
Bairin Youqi Nei Mongol China see Daban
Bairin Zuoqi Nei Mongol China see Lindong
143 M6 Bairkum Kazakh.
105 K7 Bairnsdale Vic. Austr.
206 D3 Bairro dos Canaviais Port.
180 I5 Bais Bretagne France
181 K5 Bais Pays de la Loire France
114 D7 Bais Negros Phil.
185 E7 Baïse r. France
130 F4 Baisha Chongqing China
130 G9 Baisha Hainan China
131 J5 Baisha Jiangxi China
130 G3 Baisha Sichuan China
Baishan Guangxi China see Mashan
122 E7 Baishan Jilin China
123 E8 Baishan Jilin China
132 K6 Bai Shan mt. Gansu China
129 Q6 Baishi Shuiku resr Liaoning China
129 K9 Baishui Shaanxi China
130 E2 Baishui Jiang r. Sichuan China
213 J7 Baiso Italy
219 L4 Băișoara Romania
160 G6 Baisogala Lith.
229 H5 Baissa Nigeria
199 L5 Băița Romania
138 H5 Baitadi Nepal
130 A2 Baitang Qinghai China
118 G5 Bai Thương Vietnam
123 F8 Baitou Shan mt. China/N. Korea
219 M3 Băiuț Romania
183 F7 Baix France
206 A3 Baixa da Banheira Port.
185 J10 Baixas France
208 F6 Baix Ebre reg. Spain
Baixi Sichuan China see Yibin
129 N8 Baixiang Hebei China
129 Q5 Baixingt Nei Mongol China
238 □1c Baixo, Ilhéu de i. Azores
206 □ Baixo, Ilhéu de i. Madeira
281 G3 Baixo Guandu Brazil
231 C8 Baixo-Longa Angola
129 O7 Baiyang Dian resr China
132 I5 Baiyanghe Xinjiang China
Baiyashi Hunan China see Dong'an
128 I8 Baiyin Gansu China
130 B3 Baiyü Sichuan China
225 G5 Baiyuda Desert Sudan
130 C2 Baiyügoinba Qinghai China
129 J8 Baiyu Shan mts China
199 H5 Baja Hungary
266 B3 Baja, Punta pt Mex.
266 B2 Baja California pen. Mex.
266 B3 Baja California state Mex.
266 C5 Baja California Sur state Mex.
284 B6 Bajado del Agrio Arg.
144 C3 Bājalān Iran
238 □3a Bajamar Tenerife Canary Is
267 I4 Bajan Mex.
138 H5 Bajang Nepal
116 G3 Bajau i. Indon.
145 N4 Bajaur reg. Pak.
115 B8 Bajawa Flores Indon.
139 L8 Baj Baj W. Bengal India
199 H4 Bajč Slovakia
217 □ Bajda Ridge Malta
144 H3 Bājgīrān Iran
146 F8 Bājil Yemen
218 H7 Bajina Bašta Bajina Bašta Serbia
139 M7 Bajitpur Bangl.
218 H5 Bajmok Vojvodina Serbia
199 H4 Bajna Hungary
138 E8 Bajna Madh. Prad. India
238 □3b Bajo, Punta del pt Fuerteventura Canary Is
274 B3 Bajo Baudó Col.
266 □R13 Bajo Boquete Panama
283 C7 Bajo Caracoles Arg.
284 D2 Bajo de Gallo Arg.
229 H4 Bajoga Nigeria
283 C7 Bajo Grande Arg.
206 H6 Bajo Guadalquivir, Canal del Spain
285 G6 Bajo Hondo Buenos Aires Arg.
284 E2 Bajo Hondo La Rioja Arg.
235 H3 Bajone Moz.
270 D6 Bajo Nuevo sea feature Col.
107 M7 Bajool Qld Austr.
199 H4 Bajót Hungary
205 J6 Bajoz r. Spain
139 J9 Bajrakot Orissa India
218 I8 Bajram Curri Albania
199 I6 Bajša Vojvodina Serbia
198 F5 Bak Hungary
199 G4 Baka Slovakia
117 J5 Baka, Bukit mt. Indon.
230 C3 Bakaba Chad
230 D3 Bakala C.A.R.
197 K1 Bakałarzewo Pol.
156 K5 Bakaly Rus. Fed.
143 Q5 Bakanas Kazakh.
143 R4 Bakanas watercourse Kazakh.
224 D6 Bakaoré Chad
213 R5 Bakar Croatia
228 A3 Bakau Gambia
117 L6 Bakaucengal Kalimantan Indon.
117 L3 Bakayan, Gunung mt. Indon.
159 L3 Bakayivka Ukr.
186 I6 Bakel Neth.
228 B3 Bakel Senegal
265 P6 Baker CA U.S.A.
262 H4 Baker ID U.S.A.
261 J10 Baker LA U.S.A.
262 L3 Baker MT U.S.A.
265 R2 Baker NV U.S.A.
262 F4 Baker OR U.S.A.
256 G9 Baker WV U.S.A.
262 D2 Baker, Mount vol. WA U.S.A.
265 U7 Baker Butte mt. AZ U.S.A.
247 N2 Baker Foreland hd Nunavut Can.
99 I1 Baker Island N. Pacific Ocean
245 N5 Baker Island AK U.S.A.
109 I9 Baker Lake salt flat W.A. Austr.
247 M1 Baker Lake Nunavut Can.
247 M1 Baker Lake l. Nunavut Can.
257 □P2 Baker Lake l. ME U.S.A.
107 L6 Bakers Creek Qld Austr.
248 E1 Baker's Dozen Islands Nunavut Can.
264 N6 Bakersfield CA U.S.A.
255 F7 Bakersville NC U.S.A.
237 K1 Bakerville S. Africa
119 H8 Bâ Kêv Cambodia
171 N7 Bakewell Derbyshire, England U.K.
147 M2 Bakhā Oman
161 Q8 Bakhany Rus. Fed.
Bakharden Turkm. see Baharly
144 I4 Bākharz, Kūhhā-ye mts Iran
138 C7 Bakhasar Rajasthan India
Bakhchisaray Ukr. see Bakhchysaray
159 M9 Bakhchysaray Ukr.
122 F3 Bakhirevo Rus. Fed.
159 L2 Bakhmach Ukr.
Bakhmut Ukr. see Artemivs'k
159 R5 Bakhmut r. Ukr.
161 R5 Bakhmutovo Rus. Fed.
152 J3 Bakhta Rus. Fed.
Bākhtarān Iran see Kermānshāh
Bākhtarān prov. Iran see Kermānshāh
144 E7 Bakhtegan, Daryācheh-ye l. Iran
144 C5 Bakhtiari Country reg. Iran
139 J7 Bakhtiyarpur Bihar India
143 T4 Bakhty Kazakh.
275 G3 Bakhuis Gebergte mts Suriname
151 K5 Bakı Azer.
224 D5 Baki well Chad
232 D2 Baki Somalia
229 H3 Bakin Birji Niger
221 I3 Bakır Turkey
221 I4 Bakır r. Turkey
221 J2 Bakırköy Turkey
151 K5 Bakıxanov Azer.
162 □F1 Bakkaflói b. Iceland
186 J2 Bakkeveen Neth.
221 K5 Baklan Turkey
161 O6 Baklanovo Rus. Fed.
138 E3 Bakloh Hima. Prad. India
228 D4 Bako Côte d'Ivoire
232 C2 Bako Oromīya Eth.
232 C3 Bako YeDebub Bihēroch Bihēreseboch na Hizboch Eth.
117 I4 Bako National Park Malaysia
116 B3 Bakongan Sumatera Indon.
199 K4 Bakonszeg Hungary
199 G4 Bakony hills Hungary
199 G4 Bakonybél Hungary
199 G4 Bakonynána Hungary
199 H4 Bakonysárkány Hungary
199 G4 Bakonyszentkirály Hungary
199 G4 Bakonyszombathely Hungary
232 D4 Bakool admin. reg. Somalia
230 F3 Bakordi Sudan
229 G4 Bakori Nigeria
230 D5 Bakota Dem. Rep. Congo
230 D3 Bakouma C.A.R.
230 B5 Bakoumba Gabon
201 N6 Bakovci Slovenia
193 K10 Bakov nad Jizerou Czech Rep.
228 C3 Bakoy r. Mali
145 M8 Bakrani Pak.
199 H6 Baksa Hungary
151 E2 Baksan Rus. Fed.
151 F2 Baksan r. Rus. Fed.
151 E2 Baksanenok Rus. Fed.
151 E2 Baksanges Rus. Fed.
199 L4 Baktalórántháza Hungary
Baku Azer. see Bakı
230 F4 Baku Dem. Rep. Congo
190 F5 Bakum Ger.
116 F4 Bakung i. Indon.
160 H9 Bakuny Belarus
151 E4 Bakuriani Georgia
151 E4 Bakurianis Andeziti Georgia
286 P2 Bakutis Coast Antarctica
Baky Azer. see Bakı
153 P3 Baky Uyandino r. Rus. Fed.
148 F4 Balâ Turkey
172 E2 Bala Gwynedd, Wales U.K.
276 C3 Bala, Cerros de mts Bol.
114 A7 Balabac Phil.
114 A8 Balabac i. Phil.
117 L1 Balabac Strait Malaysia/Phil.
144 E5 Balābād, Gardaneh-ye pass Iran
117 L6 Balabalangan, Kepulauan atolls Indon.
221 H2 Balabancık Turkey
161 T6 Balabanovo Rus. Fed.
100 □5 Balabio i. New Caledonia
145 J5 Bālā Bolūk Afgh.
159 O6 Balabyne Ukr.
219 P5 Bălăceanu Romania
219 L6 Bălăcița Romania
270 □ Balaclava Jamaica
149 L6 Balad Iraq
144 D7 Bālā Deh Iran
144 D3 Baladeh Māzandarān Iran
144 D3 Baladeh Māzandarān Iran
122 H2 Baladek Rus. Fed.
138 H9 Balaghat Madh. Prad. India
136 D3 Balaghat Range hills India
214 B2 Balagne reg. Corse France
208 G4 Balaguer Spain
138 F6 Balahera Rajasthan India
144 H6 Bālā Ḥowz Iran
117 I5 Balaiberkuak Kalimantan Indon.
117 I4 Balaikarangan Kalimantan Indon.
116 D4 Balaipungut Sumatera Indon.
117 I6 Balairiam Kalimantan Indon.
185 D10 Balaïtous mt. France
233 B8 Balaka Malawi
151 H4 Balakän Azer.
230 C3 Balakété C.A.R.
156 H4 Balakhna Rus. Fed.
161 V5 Balakirevo Rus. Fed.
104 G6 Balaklava S.A. Austr.
159 M9 Balaklava Ukr.
Balakleya Ukr. see Balakliya
159 P4 Balakliya Ukr.
142 B1 Balakovo Rus. Fed.
172 E2 Bala Lake Wales U.K.
168 C6 Balallan Western Isles, Scotland U.K.
235 H2 Balama Moz.
117 L1 Balambangan i. Malaysia
179 I4 Balan Champagne-Ardenne France
182 G5 Balan Rhône-Alpes France
138 C6 Balan Rajasthan India
219 N4 Bălan Romania
267 N9 Balancán Mex.
Balanda Rus. Fed. see Kalininsk
221 J6 Balan Dağı hill Turkey
159 K5 Balandyne Ukr.
158 H6 Bălănești Moldova
114 C4 Balanga Luzon Phil.
230 C4 Balangala Dem. Rep. Congo
136 G9 Balangoda Sri Lanka
115 C4 Balantak Sulawesi Indon.
138 F9 Balapur Mahar. India
139 K8 Balarampur W. Bengal India
183 D10 Balaruc-les-Bains France
115 B5 Balase r. Indon.
219 P4 Bălășești Romania
142 C2 Balashi Rus. Fed.
161 U6 Balashikha Rus. Fed.
157 H6 Balashov Rus. Fed.
138 D8 Balasinor Gujarat India
199 I3 Balassagyarmat Hungary
199 J5 Balástya Hungary
221 I5 Balat Turkey
198 G5 Baláta-tó l. Hungary
199 G5 Balaton l. Hungary
Balaton, Lake Hungary see Balaton
199 H4 Balatonalmádi Hungary
199 G5 Balatonboglár Hungary
199 G5 Balaton-felvidék hills Hungary
199 G5 Balatonföldvár Hungary
199 G5 Balatonfüred Hungary
199 H4 Balatonfűzfő Hungary
199 H4 Balatonkenese Hungary
198 G5 Balatonkeresztúr Hungary
199 G5 Balatonlelle Hungary
199 H5 Balatonszabadi Hungary
199 G5 Balatonszemes Hungary
198 G5 Balatonszentgyörgy Hungary
199 H5 Balatonvilágos Hungary
115 C8 Balauring Indon.
207 O3 Balazote Spain
160 G7 Balbieriškis Lith.
182 E5 Balbigny France
275 G5 Balbina Brazil
275 G5 Balbina, Represa de resr Brazil
168 H7 Balblair Highland, Scotland U.K.
169 J5 Balbriggan Ireland
199 L4 Balc Romania
232 E4 Balcad Somalia
104 G4 Balcanoona S.A. Austr.
285 H5 Balcarce Arg.
168 I13 Balcary Point Scotland U.K.
269 J4 Balcázar Mex.
219 Q7 Balchik Bulg.
221 L4 Balçıkhisar Turkey
150 A2 Balcılar Turkey
103 D13 Balclutha South I. N.Z.
173 L5 Balcombe West Sussex, England U.K.
284 D3 Balde Arg.
284 E2 Baldecito Arg.
212 E1 Baldegger See l. Switz.
171 M4 Balderhead Reservoir England U.K.
171 P7 Balderton Nottinghamshire, England U.K.
109 D13 Bald Head W.A. Austr.
281 F3 Baldim Brazil
261 J8 Bald Knob AR U.S.A.
256 D11 Bald Knob WV U.S.A.
265 Q4 Bald Mountain NV U.S.A.
173 L4 Baldock Hertfordshire, England U.K.
247 L3 Baldock Lake Man. Can.
201 H6 Baldramsdorf Austria
173 N6 Baldslow East Sussex, England U.K.
214 C5 Baldu r. Italy
251 O5 Baldwin Ont. Can.
255 F10 Baldwin FL U.S.A.
250 I6 Baldwin MI U.S.A.
250 B5 Baldwin WI U.S.A.
244 G2 Baldwin Peninsula AK U.S.A.
257 I5 Baldwinsville NY U.S.A.
257 M6 Baldwinville MA U.S.A.
246 G5 Baldy Mount B.C. Can.
247 K5 Baldy Mountain hill Man. Can.
265 W8 Baldy Peak AZ U.S.A.
129 L2 Bal'dzhikan Rus. Fed.
213 P5 Bale Croatia
116 D6 Bale Indon.
Bâle Switz. see Basel
228 C3 Baléa Mali
209 H9 Baleares, Islas is Spain
Baleares Insulae is Spain see Baleares, Islas
Balearic Islands is Spain see Baleares, Islas
117 J3 Baleh r. Malaysia
281 H2 Baleia, Ponta da pt Brazil
248 E2 Baleine, Grande Rivière de la r. Que. Can.
248 E2 Baleine, Petite Rivière de la r. Que. Can.
249 H1 Baleine, Rivière à la r. Que. Can.
184 A3 Baleines, Pointe des pt France
206 D4 Baleizão Port.
168 C10 Balemartine Argyll and Bute, Scotland U.K.
232 C3 Bale Mountains National Park Eth.
187 H6 Balen Belgium
219 N6 Băleni Romania
114 D5 Baleno Masbate Phil.
114 C4 Baler Luzon Phil.
114 C4 Baler Bay Luzon Phil.
207 N7 Balerma Spain
232 C4 Balesa well Kenya
168 B7 Baleshare i. Scotland U.K.
139 K9 Baleshwar Orissa India
163 I6 Balestrand Norway
216 E7 Balestrate Sicilia Italy
214 C6 Balestrieri, Punta mt. Italy
229 F3 Baléyara Niger
156 K4 Balezino Rus. Fed.
266 □P10 Balfate Hond.
107 J6 Balfe's Creek Qld Austr.
246 G5 Balfour B.C. Can.
103 C12 Balfour South I. N.Z.
237 K8 Balfour Eastern Cape S. Africa
237 M2 Balfour Mpumalanga S. Africa
168 K4 Balfour Orkney, Scotland U.K.
108 F7 Balfour Downs W.A. Austr.
168 H10 Balfron Stirling, Scotland U.K.
Balgatay Mongolia see Shilüüstey
190 H5 Balge Ger.
108 I6 Balgo W.A. Austr.
108 J6 Balgo Aboriginal Reserve W.A. Austr.
168 D7 Balgown Highland, Scotland U.K.
233 C5 Balguda well Kenya
132 H5 Balguntay Xinjiang China
147 I8 Bālḥaf Yemen
232 D1 Balho Djibouti
138 D7 Bali Rajasthan India
138 D7 Bali Rajasthan India
117 K9 Bali i. Indon.
117 K9 Bali prov. Indon.
229 H5 Bali Nigeria
146 C2 Bali reg. Saudi Arabia
117 K8 Bali, Laut sea Indon.
117 K9 Bali, Selat sea chan. Indon.
114 D7 Baliangao Mindanao Phil.
139 K9 Baliapal Orissa India
117 K9 Bali Barat, Taman Nasional nat. park Bali Indon.
271 □3 Baliceaux i. St Vincent
139 K8 Balichak W. Bengal India
116 C3 Balige Sumatera Indon.
197 K6 Baligród Pol.
139 I9 Baliguda Orissa India
129 P6 Balihan Nei Mongol China
221 I3 Balıkesir Turkey
221 J3 Balıkesir prov. Turkey
149 K4 Balık Gölü l. Turkey
150 H3 Balīkh r. Syria/Turkey
221 I2 Balıklıçeşme Turkey
221 H4 Balıklıova Turkey
117 L5 Balikpapan Kalimantan Indon.
117 L5 Balikpapan, Teluk b. Indon.
219 M5 Bălilești Romania
114 B9 Balimbing Phil.
136 H3 Balimila Reservoir India
113 J8 Balimo P.N.G.
129 R2 Balin Nei Mongol China
116 D2 Baling Malaysia
165 N2 Bälinge Sweden
194 F5 Balingen Ger.
117 J3 Balingian Sarawak Malaysia
117 J3 Balingian r. Malaysia
199 H4 Balinka Hungary
Balinqiao Nei Mongol China see Bairin Qiao
199 K6 Balinț Romania
114 C2 Balintang Channel Phil.
168 I7 Balintore Highland, Scotland U.K.
Balira r. Andorra/Spain see Valira
Bali Sea Indon. see Bali, Laut
230 D3 Balitondo C.A.R.
114 C9 Baliungan i. Phil.
280 A2 Baliza Brazil
190 H3 Balje Ger.
146 E6 Baljurshī Saudi Arabia
186 I3 Balk Neth.
144 F1 Balkan admin. div. Turkm.
144 F2 Balkanabat Turkm.
Balkan Mountains Bulg./Yugo. see Stara Planina
Balkan Oblast admin. div. Turkm. see Balkan
199 K4 Balkány Hungary
143 M1 Balkashino Kazakh.
186 J3 Balkbrug Neth.
145 L3 Balkh Afgh.
145 L3 Balkh prov. Afgh.
145 L3 Balkhab r. Afgh.
143 P4 Balkhash Kazakh.
Balkhash, Lake Kazakh. see Balkhash, Ozero
143 O5 Balkhash, Ozero l. Kazakh.
136 F3 Balkonda Andhra Prad. India
142 B4 Balkuduk Kazakh.
139 M7 Balla Bangl.
Balla Balla Zimbabwe see Mbalabala
220 B2 Ballaban Albania
170 H5 Ballabeg Isle of Man
212 G4 Ballabio Italy
168 F9 Ballachulish Highland, Scotland U.K.
109 G12 Balladonia W.A. Austr.
105 L4 Balladoran N.S.W. Austr.
169 J5 Ballagan Point Ireland
169 E5 Ballaghaderreen Ireland
178 D6 Ballancourt-sur-Essonne France
162 N2 Ballangen Norway
181 M7 Ballan-Miré France
262 J4 Ballantine MT U.S.A.
168 G12 Ballantrae South Ayrshire, Scotland U.K.
214 C8 Ballao Sardegna Italy
105 I7 Ballarat Vic. Austr.
109 F10 Ballard, Lake salt flat W.A. Austr.
136 F3 Ballarpur Mahar. India
170 H5 Ballasalla Isle of Man
168 J8 Ballater Aberdeenshire, Scotland U.K.
170 H5 Ballaugh Isle of Man
104 □1 Ball Bay Norfolk I.
228 C3 Ballé Mali
181 K6 Ballée France
282 C2 Ballena, Punta pt Chile
238 □3b Ballena, Punta de la pt Fuerteventura Canary Is
168 I12 Ballencleuch Law hill Scotland U.K.
283 C9 Ballenero, Canal sea chan. Chile
287 K2 Balleny Islands Antarctica
181 J3 Balleroy France
164 I6 Ballerup Denmark
285 F3 Ballesteros Arg.
139 J7 Ballia Uttar Prad. India
170 C8 Ballickmoyler Ireland
105 N3 Ballina N.S.W. Austr.
169 D4 Ballina Ireland
169 B6 Ballinaboy Ireland
169 H6 Ballinagar Ireland
169 H5 Ballinagh Ireland
169 H7 Ballinakill Ireland
169 H5 Ballinalack Ireland
169 G5 Ballinalee Ireland
169 G4 Ballinamallard Northern Ireland U.K.
169 F5 Ballinameen Ireland
169 G4 Ballinamore Ireland
169 G8 Ballinamult Ireland
169 E9 Ballinascarthy Ireland
169 F6 Ballinasloe Ireland
169 C8 Ballinclogher Ireland
169 E6 Ballinderreen Ireland
169 F6 Ballinderry Ireland
169 I3 Ballinderry r. Northern Ireland U.K.
169 E5 Ballindine Ireland
Ballindooly Ireland see Baile an Dúlaigh
169 E9 Ballineen Ireland
169 E8 Ballingarry Limerick Ireland
169 G7 Ballingarry Tipperary Ireland
Ballingeary Ireland see Béal Átha an Ghaorthaidh
261 F10 Ballinger TX U.S.A.
168 J10 Ballingry Fife, Scotland U.K.
169 D9 Ballingurteen Ireland
169 E9 Ballinhassig Ireland
169 E5 Ballinlough Ireland
168 I9 Ballinluig Perth and Kinross, Scotland U.K.
169 D5 Ballinrobe Ireland
169 E7 Ballinruan Ireland
Ballinskelligs Ireland see Baile an Sceilg
169 E9 Ballinspittle Ireland
169 J2 Ballintoy Northern Ireland U.K.
168 J9 Ballintuim Perth and Kinross, Scotland U.K.
169 G7 Ballinure Ireland
169 I6 Ballitore Ireland
169 I5 Ballivor Ireland
195 I4 Ballmertshofen Ger.
208 F4 Ballobar Spain
168 G11 Balloch West Dunbartonshire, Scotland U.K.
181 L5 Ballon France
170 D8 Ballon Ireland
179 M8 Ballon d'Alsace mt. France
179 M8 Ballons des Vosges, Parc Naturel Régional des nature res. France
199 I5 Ballószög Hungary
181 I6 Ballots France
220 A2 Ballsh Albania
104 □2 Ball's Pyramid i. Lord Howe I. Austr.
191 K8 Ballstädt Ger.
257 L5 Ballston Spa NY U.S.A.
186 I2 Ballum Neth.
169 F3 Ballure Ireland
258 D4 Bally PA U.S.A.
169 E8 Ballyagran Ireland
169 I4 Ballybay Ireland
169 G3 Ballybofey Ireland
169 J5 Ballyboghil Ireland
169 I2 Ballybogy Northern Ireland U.K.
Ballybrack Ireland see An Baile Breac
169 J6 Ballybrack Dublin Ireland
169 G7 Ballybrophy Ireland
169 C7 Ballybunion Ireland
169 G7 Ballycahill Ireland
169 H7 Ballycallan Ireland
169 J7 Ballycanew Ireland
169 I7 Ballycarney Ireland
169 K3 Ballycarry Northern Ireland U.K.
169 D4 Ballycastle Ireland
169 J2 Ballycastle Northern Ireland U.K.
169 K3 Ballyclare Northern Ireland U.K.
169 B6 Ballyconneely Ireland
169 B6 Ballyconneely Bay Ireland
169 G4 Ballyconnell Cavan Ireland
169 E4 Ballyconnell Sligo Ireland
169 G9 Ballycotton Bay Ireland
169 C4 Ballycroy Ireland
169 G6 Ballycumber Ireland
169 F6 Ballydangan Ireland
169 F6 Ballydavid Ireland
169 B8 Ballydavid Head Ireland
169 D9 Ballydehob Ireland
169 D8 Ballydesmond Ireland
169 F8 Ballyduff Ireland
169 D5 Ballyfarnagh Ireland
169 F4 Ballyfarnon Ireland
169 F9 Ballyfeard Ireland
170 C7 Ballyfin Ireland
169 F6 Ballyforan Ireland
169 H6 Ballyfore Ireland
169 K3 Ballygalley Northern Ireland U.K.
169 F5 Ballygar Ireland
169 J7 Ballygarrett Ireland
169 H4 Ballygawley Northern Ireland U.K.
169 D5 Ballyglass Mayo Ireland
169 E5 Ballyglass Mayo Ireland
169 H2 Ballygorman Ireland
169 K3 Ballygowan Northern Ireland U.K.
168 D11 Ballygrant Argyll and Bute, Scotland U.K.
169 I8 Ballyhack Ireland
169 E8 Ballyhaght Ireland
169 D7 Ballyhahill Ireland
170 C5 Ballyhaise Ireland

169 L4 **Ballyhalbert** *Northern Ireland* U.K.
169 E5 **Ballyhaunis** Ireland
169 C8 **Ballyheigue** Ireland
169 C8 **Ballyheigue Bay** Ireland
169 F8 **Ballyhooly** Ireland
169 K4 **Ballyhornan** *Northern Ireland* U.K.
169 E8 **Ballyhoura Mountains** *hills* Ireland
169 H5 **Ballyjamesduff** Ireland
169 G6 **Ballykeeran** Ireland
169 H2 **Ballykelly** *Northern Ireland* U.K.
169 H6 **Ballykilleen** Ireland
169 F8 **Ballylanders** Ireland
169 F5 **Ballyleague** Ireland
170 D5 **Ballyleny** *Northern Ireland* U.K.
169 H2 **Ballyliffin** Ireland
169 D7 **Ballylongford** Ireland
169 H7 **Ballylynan** Ireland
169 G8 **Ballymacarberry** Ireland
169 C8 **Ballymacelligott** Ireland
169 H7 **Ballymack** Ireland
170 C5 **Ballymackilroy** *Northern Ireland* U.K.
169 G8 **Ballymacmague** Ireland
169 G9 **Ballymacoda** Ireland
169 H3 **Ballymagorry** *Northern Ireland* U.K.
169 G5 **Ballymahon** Ireland
Ballymakeery Ireland *see* **Baile Mhic Íre**
169 K4 **Ballymartin** *Northern Ireland* U.K.
169 J3 **Ballymena** *Northern Ireland* U.K.
169 F5 **Ballymoe** Ireland
169 I2 **Ballymoney** *Northern Ireland* U.K.
169 G2 **Ballymore** *Donegal* Ireland
169 G6 **Ballymore** *Westmeath* Ireland
169 E4 **Ballymote** Ireland
169 I7 **Ballymurphy** Ireland
169 F5 **Ballymurry** Ireland
169 I8 **Ballynabola** Ireland
169 D9 **Ballynacarriga** Ireland
170 B6 **Ballynacarrigy** Ireland
169 H5 **Ballynafid** Ireland
169 C6 **Ballynahinch** Ireland
169 K4 **Ballynahinch** *Northern Ireland* U.K.
169 G6 **Ballynahowen** Ireland
169 B5 **Ballynakill Bay** Ireland
169 E8 **Ballynamona** Ireland
169 C8 **Ballynaskreena** Ireland
169 E7 **Ballyneety** Ireland
170 E7 **Ballynockan** Ireland
169 F8 **Ballynoe** Ireland
169 K3 **Ballynure** *Northern Ireland* U.K.
169 F8 **Ballyporeen** Ireland
169 L4 **Ballyquintin Point** *Northern Ireland* U.K.
169 H7 **Ballyragget** Ireland
169 H7 **Ballyroan** Ireland
169 I3 **Ballyronan** *Northern Ireland* U.K.
169 C9 **Ballyroon** Ireland
169 F3 **Ballyshannon** Ireland
169 E7 **Ballysteen** Ireland
169 I8 **Ballyteige Bay** Ireland
169 D6 **Ballyvaughan** Ireland
169 F6 **Ballyvoneen** Ireland
169 J2 **Ballyvoy** *Northern Ireland* U.K.
169 G8 **Ballyvoyle** Ireland
169 L3 **Ballywalter** *Northern Ireland* U.K.
170 E5 **Ballyward** *Northern Ireland* U.K.
169 I8 **Ballywilliam** Ireland
168 E8 **Balmacara** *Highland, Scotland* U.K.
283 C7 **Balmaceda** *Aisén* Chile
276 C6 **Balmaceda** *Antofagasta* Chile
168 G10 **Balmaha** *Stirling, Scotland* U.K.
Balmartin *Western Isles, Scotland* U.K. *see* **Baile Mhartainn**
205 N2 **Balmaseda** Spain
199 K4 **Balmazújváros** Hungary
212 C5 **Balme** Italy
168 L8 **Balmedie** *Aberdeenshire, Scotland* U.K.
Balmer *Rajasthan* India *see* **Barmer**
247 M5 **Balmertown** *Ont.* Can.
212 D3 **Balmhorn** *mt.* Switz.
104 H7 **Balmoral** *Vic.* Austr.
103 G9 **Balmoral** *South I.* N.Z.
261 D10 **Balmorhea** *TX* U.S.A.
212 E4 **Balmuccia** Italy
168 F8 **Balnacra** *Highland, Scotland* U.K.
168 D10 **Balnahard** *Argyll and Bute, Scotland* U.K.
168 H7 **Balnapaling** *Highland, Scotland* U.K.
285 F2 **Balnearia** Arg.
208 E2 **Balneario de Panticosa Huesca** Spain
285 H6 **Balneario Orense** Arg.
285 G6 **Balneario Oriente** Arg.
115 C4 **Baloa** *Sulawesi* Indon.
212 E5 **Balocco** Italy
145 L7 **Balochistan** *prov.* Pak.
141 I4 **Balochistan** *reg.* Pak.
138 H9 **Balod** *Chhattisgarh* India
139 I8 **Baloda** *Chhattisgarh* India
138 I9 **Baloda Bazar** *Chhattisgarh* India
198 F4 **Balogunyom** Hungary
117 G6 **Balok, Teluk** *b.* Indon.
231 B8 **Balombo** Angola
105 L3 **Balonne** *r. Qld* Austr.
115 D2 **Balontohe** *i.* Indon.
178 H8 **Balot** France
199 I5 **Balotaszállás** Hungary
138 D7 **Balotra** *Rajasthan* India
151 D6 **Balotu** Turkey
158 D1 **Baloty** Belarus
192 E4 **Balow** Ger.
143 R5 **Balpyk Bi** Kazakh.
Balqash Kazakh. *see* **Balkhash**
Balqash Köli *l.* Kazakh. *see* **Balkhash, Ozero**
168 H10 **Balquhidder** *Stirling, Scotland* U.K.
138 I6 **Balrampur** *Uttar Prad.* India
105 I6 **Balranald** *N.S.W.* Austr.
169 J5 **Balrath** Ireland
169 J5 **Balrothery** Ireland
219 M6 **Balș** Romania
209 C9 **Balsa de Ves** Spain
251 O3 **Balsam Creek** *Ont.* Can.
251 P5 **Balsam Lake** *l. Ont.* Can.
250 B4 **Balsam Lake** *WI* U.S.A.
209 C12 **Balsapintada** Spain
274 B6 **Balsapuerto** Peru
208 I4 **Balsareny** Spain
278 D3 **Balsas** Brazil
269 H7 **Balsas** Mex.
268 E8 **Balsas** *r.* Mex.
274 B6 **Balsas** Peru
278 D3 **Balsas, Rio das** *r.* Brazil
161 N9 **Bal'shavik** Belarus
209 D12 **Balsicas** Spain
215 L4 **Balsorano** Italy
165 N2 **Bålsta** Sweden
212 D1 **Balsthal** Switz.
168 □O1 **Balta** *i. Scotland* U.K.
158 I6 **Balta** Ukr.
219 K7 **Balta Berilovac** *Knjaževac* Serbia
205 L5 **Baltanás** Spain
204 E5 **Baltar** Spain
208 H5 **Baltasana, Tossal de la** *mt.* Spain
285 I2 **Baltasar Brum** Uru.
156 J4 **Baltasi** Rus. Fed.
168 □O1 **Baltasound** *Shetland, Scotland* U.K.
142 B1 **Baltay** Rus. Fed.
158 G6 **Bălți** Moldova
259 K1 **Baltic** *CT* U.S.A.
165 M6 **Baltic Sea** *g.* Europe
225 F2 **Balṭīm** Egypt
169 D10 **Baltimore** Ireland
235 F4 **Baltimore** S. Africa
258 B6 **Baltimore** *MD* U.S.A.
256 C9 **Baltimore** *OH* U.S.A.
258 B6 **Baltimore City** *county MD* U.S.A.
258 B6 **Baltimore County** *county MD* U.S.A.
258 B6 **Baltimore Highlands** *MD* U.S.A.
160 K5 **Baltinava** Latvia
169 I7 **Baltinglass** Ireland
138 E2 **Baltistan** *reg.* Pak.
160 C7 **Baltiysk** Rus. Fed.
197 H1 **Baltiyskaya Kosa** *spit* Rus. Fed.
160 I7 **Baltoji Vokė** Lith.
138 F2 **Baltoro Glacier** Pak.
197 J4 **Bałtów** Pol.
190 D3 **Baltrum** Ger.
190 D3 **Baltrum** *i.* Ger.
268 A3 **Baluarie** *r.* Mex.
278 E4 **Baluarte** Brazil
261 G12 **Baluarte, Arroyo** *watercourse TX* U.S.A.
144 H7 **Baluch Ab** *well* Iran
Baluchistan *reg.* Pak. *see* **Balochistan**
117 J3 **Balui** *r.* Malaysia
139 J8 **Balumath** *Jharkhand* India
104 F5 **Balumbah** *S.A.* Austr.
116 C4 **Balumundam** *Sumatera* Indon.
160 J5 **Balupe** *r.* Latvia
117 J5 **Baluran, Gunung** *mt.* Indon.
117 K8 **Baluran, Taman Nasional** *nat. park* Indon.
139 L7 **Balurghat** *W. Bengal* India
219 O3 **Bălușeni** Romania
114 E9 **Balut** *i.* Phil.
215 P6 **Balvano** Italy
162 M3 **Balvatnet** *l.* Norway
191 E8 **Balve** Ger.
160 K4 **Balvi** Latvia
221 I3 **Balya** Turkey
129 K1 **Balyaga** Rus. Fed.
143 Q6 **Balykchy** Kyrg.
142 D4 **Balykshi** Kazakh.
128 E1 **Balyktyg-Khem** *r.* Rus. Fed.
Balyqshy Kazakh. *see* **Balykshi**
217 □ **Balzan** Malta
274 B5 **Balzar** Ecuador
194 H7 **Balzers** Liechtenstein
144 H7 **Bam** Iran
144 G3 **Bām** Iran
130 F6 **Bama** *Guangxi* China
229 I4 **Bama** Nigeria
107 I1 **Bamaga** *Qld* Austr.
248 B3 **Bamaji Lake** *Ont.* Can.
228 D3 **Bamako** Mali
230 C3 **Bamba** *r.* C.A.R.
231 C6 **Bamba** Dem. Rep. Congo
228 E2 **Bamba** Mali
230 B5 **Bambama** Congo
274 B6 **Bambamarca** Peru
114 C3 **Bambang** *Luzon* Phil.
231 D9 **Bambangando** Angola
114 C9 **Bambannan** *i.* Phil.
230 D3 **Bambari** C.A.R.
231 C9 **Bambe** Angola
116 B3 **Bambel** *Sumatera* Indon.
171 L6 **Bamber Bridge** *Lancashire, England* U.K.
195 J2 **Bamberg** Ger.
255 G9 **Bamberg** *SC* U.S.A.
259 G5 **Bamber Lake** *NJ* U.S.A.
232 B2 **Bambesi** Eth.
228 A3 **Bambey** Senegal
230 E4 **Bambili** Dem. Rep. Congo
230 C4 **Bambio** C.A.R.
237 K7 **Bamboesberg** *mts* S. Africa
228 E4 **Bamboi** Ghana
108 F6 **Bamboo Creek** *W.A.* Austr.
228 E2 **Bambou** *well* Mali
228 C3 **Bambouk** *reg.* Mali
239 □[1b] **Bambou Mountains** *hills* Mauritius
239 □[1b] **Bambous** Mauritius
230 E3 **Bambouti** C.A.R.
232 B2 **Bambudi** Eth.
281 E4 **Bambuí** Brazil
117 K5 **Bambulung** *Kalimantan* Indon.
171 N2 **Bamburgh** *Northumberland, England* U.K.
130 A3 **Bamda** *Xizang* China
144 C6 **Bāmdezh** Iran
229 H5 **Bamenda** Cameroon
229 H5 **Bamendjing, Lac de** *l.* Cameroon
246 E5 **Bamfield** *B.C.* Can.
145 L4 **Bāmīān** Afgh.
145 L4 **Bāmīān** *prov.* Afgh.
129 S5 **Bamiancheng** *Liaoning* China
Bamiantong *Heilong.* China *see* **Muling**
230 D3 **Bamingui** C.A.R.
230 C2 **Bamingui** *r.* C.A.R.
230 D2 **Bamingui-Bangoran** *pref.* C.A.R.
230 C2 **Bamingui-Bangoran, Parc National du** *nat. park* C.A.R.
145 M4 **Bamiyan** *r.* Afgh.
115 G4 **Bamkeri** *Papua* Indon.
194 F3 **Bammental** Ger.
229 H3 **Bammo** *well* Niger
119 G8 **Bâmnak** Cambodia
118 E7 **Bamnet Narong** Thai.
266 E5 **Bamoa** Mex.
138 G6 **Bamor** *Madh. Prad.* India
138 G8 **Bamori** *Madh. Prad.* India
145 J8 **Bamposht** *reg.* Iran
172 F6 **Bampton** *Devon, England* U.K.
173 I4 **Bampton** *Oxfordshire, England* U.K.
144 I8 **Bampūr** Iran
144 H8 **Bampūr** *watercourse* Iran
144 I5 **Bamrūd** Iran
Bami Turkm. *see* **Bamy**
144 G2 **Bamy** Turkm.
106 D3 **Bamyili** *N.T.* Austr.
228 E3 **Ban** Burkina
199 G4 **Bana** Hungary
146 G9 **Bana, Wādī** *watercourse* Yemen
99 G2 **Banaba** *i.* Kiribati
278 F3 **Banabuiu, Açude** *resr* Brazil
114 C4 **Banahao, Mount** *vol. Luzon* Phil.
230 E4 **Banalia** Dem. Rep. Congo
228 D3 **Banamba** Mali
266 D3 **Banámichi** Mex.
130 F4 **Banan** *Chongqing* China
107 M8 **Banana** *Qld* Austr.
228 B4 **Banana Islands** Sierra Leone
278 C4 **Bananal, Ilha do** *i.* Brazil
137 M9 **Bananga** *Andaman & Nicobar Is* India
228 C4 **Banankoro** Guinea
137 I3 **Banapur** *Orissa* India
214 B6 **Banari** *Sardegna* Italy
221 I1 **Banarlı** Turkey
138 F7 **Banas** *r.* India
225 G4 **Banās, Ra's** *pt* Egypt
183 C8 **Banassac** France
218 J5 **Banatski Karlovac** *Vojvodina* Serbia
199 J5 **Banatsko Aranđelovo** *Vojvodina* Serbia
199 J6 **Banatsko Veliko Selo** *Vojvodina* Serbia
115 A7 **Banawaya** *i.* Indon.
221 K4 **Banaz** Turkey
221 K4 **Banaz** *r.* Turkey
118 F5 **Ban Ban** Laos
146 H3 **Banbān, 'Irq** *des.* Saudi Arabia
133 L11 **Banbar** *Xizang* China
130 C9 **Ban Bo** Laos
169 J4 **Banbridge** *Northern Ireland* U.K.
118 E7 **Ban Bua Chum** Thai.
118 F7 **Ban Bua Yai** Thai.
118 H7 **Ban Bungxai** Laos
173 J3 **Banbury** *Oxfordshire, England* U.K.
185 B9 **Banca** France
219 P4 **Banca** Romania
118 F4 **Ban Cang** Vietnam
226 A5 **Banc d'Arguin, Parc National du** *nat. park* Maur.
118 F6 **Ban Chiang** *tourist site* Thai.
168 L8 **Banchory** *Aberdeenshire, S cotland* U.K.
114 B8 **Bancoran** *i.* Phil.
248 E4 **Bancroft** *Ont.* Can.
Bancroft Zambia *see* **Chililabombwe**
229 I4 **Banda** Cameroon
231 A5 **Banda** Congo
230 E3 **Banda** Dem. Rep. Congo
138 G7 **Banda** *Madh. Prad.* India
138 H7 **Banda** *Uttar Prad.* India
115 F6 **Banda, Kepulauan** *is Maluku* Indon.
115 G6 **Banda, Laut** *sea* Indon.
116 A2 **Banda Aceh** *Sumatera* Indon.
105 N4 **Banda Banda, Mount** *N.S.W.* Austr.
145 N5 **Banda Daud Shah** Pak.
116 B3 **Bandahara, Gunung** *mt.* Indon.
124 Q9 **Bandai-Asahi Kokuritsu-kōen** *nat. park* Japan
164 E2 **Bandak** *l.* Norway
228 D5 **Bandama** *r.* Côte d'Ivoire
228 D4 **Bandama Blanc** *r.* Côte d'Ivoire
144 I6 **Bandān** Iran
115 F6 **Bandaneira** *Maluku* Indon.
144 I6 **Bandān Kūh** *mts* Iran
Bandar *Andhra Prad.* India *see* **Machilipatnam**
235 G3 **Bandar** Moz.
Bandar Abbas Iran *see* **Bandar-e 'Abbās**
116 F7 **Bandaragung** *Sumatera* Indon.
136 G9 **Bandarawela** Sri Lanka
139 N8 **Bandarban** Bangl.
144 G8 **Bandar-e 'Abbās** Iran
144 C3 **Bandar-e Anzalī** Iran
144 F8 **Bandar-e Chārak** Iran
144 D6 **Bandar-e Deylam** Iran
144 C6 **Bandar-e Emām Khomeynī** Iran
144 F8 **Bandar-e Lengeh** Iran
144 E8 **Bandar-e Maqām** Iran
144 C6 **Bandar-e Ma'shur** Iran
144 F8 **Bandar-e Moghūyeh** Iran
Bandar-e Pahlavī Iran *see* **Bandar-e Anzalī**
144 D7 **Bandar-e Rīg** Iran
Bandar-e Shāh Iran *see* **Bandar-e Torkeman**
Bandar-e Shāhpūr Iran *see* **Bandar-e Emām Khomeynī**
144 E8 **Bandar-e Shīū'** Iran
144 E3 **Bandar-e Torkeman** Iran
116 F7 **Bandar Lampung** *Sumatera* Indon.
232 F2 **Bandar Murcaayo** Somalia
138 G4 **Bandarpunch** *mt. Uttaranchal* India
117 K2 **Bandar Seri Begawan** Brunei
232 E2 **Bandar Wanaag** Somalia
Banda Sea Indon. *see* **Banda, Laut**
204 E4 **Bande** Spain
145 L3 **Band-e Amīr, Daryā-ye** *r.* Afgh.
145 J8 **Band-e Bamposht, Kūh-e** *mts* Iran
281 G1 **Bandeira** Brazil
278 C5 **Bandeirante** Brazil
280 B5 **Bandeirantes** Brazil
238 □[1c] **Bandeiras** *Pico* Azores
281 G4 **Bandeiras, Pico de** *mt.* Brazil
192 D4 **Bandenitz** Ger.
218 H7 **Bander** *pass* Montenegro/Serbia
282 E3 **Bandera** Arg.
261 F11 **Bandera** *TX* U.S.A.
285 F4 **Banderaló** Arg.
266 G2 **Banderas** Mex.
268 B5 **Banderas, Bahía de** *b.* Mex.
269 K6 **Banderilla** Mex.
144 F4 **Band-e Sar Qom** Iran
139 J8 **Bandgaon** *Jharkhand* India
145 M8 **Bandhi** Pak.
138 H8 **Bandhogarh** *Madh. Prad.* India
190 L1 **Bandholm** Denmark
138 D7 **Bandi** *r. Rajasthan* India
138 E6 **Bandi** *r. Rajasthan* India
136 G3 **Bandia** *r.* India
228 E3 **Bandiagara** Mali
228 E3 **Bandiagara, Falaise de** *esc.* Mali
145 K7 **Band-i-Khan Jahan** Pak.
138 F6 **Bandikui** *Rajasthan* India
144 H9 **Bandīnī** Iran
138 E2 **Bandipur** *Jammu and Kashmir* India
139 J6 **Bandipur** Nepal
136 E7 **Bandipur National Park** India
221 I2 **Bandırma** Turkey
Bandjarmasin *Kalimantan* Indon. *see* **Banjarmasin**
183 H10 **Bandol** France
169 E9 **Bandon** Ireland
169 E9 **Bandon** *r.* Ireland
Ban Don Thai. *see* **Surat Thani**
262 B5 **Bandon** *OR* U.S.A.
119 D10 **Ban Don, Ao** *b.* Thai.
135 □[1] **Bandos** *i. N. Male* Maldives
151 K6 **Bändovan Burnu** *pt* Azer.
144 C6 **Band Qīr** Iran
136 C3 **Bandra** *Mahar.* India
239 □[3b] **Bandraboua** Mayotte
239 □[3b] **Bandrélé** Mayotte
235 G3 **Bandua** Moz.
235 G3 **Bandula** Moz.
117 G8 **Bandung** *Jawa* Indon.
109 G10 **Bandya** *W.A.* Austr.
219 P6 **Băneasa** *Constanța* Romania
219 O6 **Băneasa** *Giurgiu* Romania
144 A4 **Bāneh** Iran
115 F3 **Banemo** *Halmahera* Indon.
138 E7 **Banera** *Rajasthan* India
270 F3 **Banes** Cuba
228 C4 **Banfèlè** Guinea
246 H5 **Banff** *Alta* Can.
168 K7 **Banff** *Aberdeenshire, Scotland* U.K.
246 G5 **Banff National Park** *Alta* Can.
228 D4 **Banfora** Burkina
230 B3 **Bang** C.A.R.
117 J4 **Bang, Gunung** *mt.* Indon.
231 B7 **Banga** Angola
231 D6 **Banga** Dem. Rep. Congo
114 E8 **Banga** *Mindanao* Phil.
114 E8 **Banga** *r. Mindanao* Phil.
230 E3 **Bangadi** Dem. Rep. Congo
114 F8 **Bangai Point** *Mindanao* Phil.
107 J7 **Bangall Creek** *watercourse Qld* Austr.
136 E6 **Bangalore** *Karnataka* India
105 N3 **Bangalow** *N.S.W.* Austr.
230 D3 **Bangana** C.A.R.
136 F5 **Banganapalle** *Andhra Prad.* India
138 G6 **Banganga** *r.* India
229 H5 **Bangangté** Cameroon
139 L8 **Bangaon** *W. Bengal* India
117 K2 **Bangar** Brunei
114 C3 **Bangar** *Luzon* Phil.
139 L9 **Bangara** *r.* Bangl.
136 F6 **Bangarapet** *Karnataka* India
230 D3 **Bangassou** C.A.R.
230 C3 **Bangba** C.A.R.
133 E9 **Bangdag Co** *salt l.* China
118 G6 **Bangfai, Xé** *r.* Laos
115 C4 **Banggai** *Sulawesi* Indon.
115 C4 **Banggai** *i.* Indon.
115 C4 **Banggai, Kepulauan** *is* Indon.
112 F7 **Banggai, Kepulauan** *is* Indon.
117 L1 **Banggi** *i.* Malaysia
224 D1 **Banghāzī** Libya
118 G6 **Banghiang, Xé** *r.* Laos
117 J8 **Bangil** *Jawa* Indon.
116 G6 **Bangka** *i.* Indon.
115 D3 **Bangka** *i.* Indon.
116 F6 **Bangka, Selat** *sea chan.* Indon.
115 D2 **Bangka, Selat** *sea chan.* Indon.
116 G6 **Bangka-Belitung** *prov.* Indon.
117 J6 **Bangkal** *Kalimantan* Indon.
115 A6 **Bangkala, Teluk** *b.* Indon.
117 J8 **Bangkalan** *Jawa* Indon.
115 C4 **Bangkalan** *i.* Indon.
116 B3 **Bangkaru** *i.* Indon.
116 D4 **Bangkinang** *Sumatera* Indon.
115 B3 **Bangkir** *Sulawesi* Indon.
116 E6 **Bangko** *Sumatera* Indon.
133 I11 **Bangkog Co** *salt l.* China
119 E8 **Bangkok** Thai.
119 E8 **Bangkok, Bight of** *b.* Thai.
133 H11 **Bangkor** *Xizang* China
117 K6 **Bangkuang** *Kalimantan* Indon.
115 C4 **Bangkulu** *i.* Indon.
117 M9 **Bangkulua** *Sumbawa* Indon.
Bangla *state* India *see* **West Bengal**
139 L8 **Bangladesh** *country* Asia
119 E11 **Bang Lang, Ang Kep Nam** Thai.
128 I9 **Bangluo** *Gansu* China
130 B7 **Bangma Shan** *mts Yunnan* China
118 E6 **Bang Mun Nak** Thai.
162 M4 **Bångnäs** Sweden
119 I9 **Ba Ngoi** Vietnam
228 D5 **Bangolo** Côte d'Ivoire
138 G3 **Bangong Co** *salt l.* China/India
172 D1 **Bangor** *Gwynedd, Wales* U.K.
169 K3 **Bangor** *Northern Ireland* U.K.
257 □Q4 **Bangor** *ME* U.S.A.
250 H7 **Bangor** *MI* U.S.A.
258 E3 **Bangor** *PA* U.S.A.
230 D2 **Bangoran** C.A.R.
139 K8 **Bangriposi** *Orissa* India
265 S5 **Bangs, Mount** *AZ* U.S.A.
117 L5 **Bangsalsepulun** *Kalimantan* Indon.
119 D9 **Bang Saphan Yai** Thai.
162 K4 **Bangsund** Norway
230 C5 **Bangu** *Équateur* Dem. Rep. Congo
231 D7 **Bangu** *Katanga* Dem. Rep. Congo
114 C3 **Bangued** *Luzon* Phil.
230 C3 **Bangui** C.A.R.
114 C2 **Bangui** *Luzon* Phil.
230 C4 **Bangui-Motaba** Congo
233 B8 **Bangula** Malawi
116 C3 **Bangunpurba** *Sumatera* Indon.
230 E4 **Banguru** Dem. Rep. Congo
231 F7 **Bangweulu, Lake** Zambia
225 F2 **Banhā** *Qalyūbīyah* Egypt
173 O3 **Banham** *Norfolk, England* U.K.
235 G4 **Banhine, Parque Nacional de** *nat. park* Moz.
118 F5 **Ban Hin Heup** Laos
Ban Houei Sai Laos *see* **Huayxay**
118 E5 **Ban Huai Khon** Thai.
119 D9 **Ban Huai Yang** Thai.
229 E3 **Bani** Burkina
230 D3 **Bani** C.A.R.
270 H4 **Baní** Dom. Rep.
228 D3 **Bani** *r.* Mali
114 B3 **Bani** *Luzon* Phil.
226 C3 **Bani, Jbel** *ridge* Morocco
230 C3 **Bania** C.A.R.
148 H9 **Bani Atiyah** *reg.* Saudi Arabia
229 F3 **Bani-Bangou** Niger
270 H4 **Bánica** Dom. Rep.
196 C2 **Banie** Pol.
197 K1 **Banie Mazurskie** Pol.
228 D3 **Banifing** *r.* Mali
228 D3 **Banifing** *r.* Mali
144 F8 **Banī Forūr, Jazīreh-ye** *i.* Iran
138 E3 **Banihal Pass and Tunnel** *Jammu and Kashmir* India
146 E6 **Banī 'Īsá** Saudi Arabia
229 F4 **Banikoara** Benin
146 F6 **Banī Mālik** Saudi Arabia
225 F2 **Banī Mazār** Egypt
114 B4 **Bani Point** *Luzon* Phil.
199 L4 **Bănișor** Romania
256 G12 **Banister** *r. VA* U.S.A.
225 F2 **Banī Suwayf** *Banī Suwayf* Egypt
148 D9 **Banī Suwayf** *governorate* Egypt
219 N9 **Banite** Bulg.
146 F6 **Banī Thawr** Saudi Arabia
219 L7 **Banitsa** Bulg.
224 B2 **Banī Walīd** Libya
147 I3 **Banī Wuṭayfān** *well* Saudi Arabia
150 D5 **Bāniyās** *Al Qunayṭirah* Syria
150 D3 **Bāniyās** *Ṭarṭūs* Syria
147 L4 **Bani Yas** *reg.* U.A.E.
218 H7 **Banja** *Priboj* Serbia
210 F3 **Banja Luka** Bos.-Herz.
138 F4 **Banjar** *Hima. Prad.* India
117 K6 **Banjarbaru** *Kalimantan* Indon.
117 K6 **Banjarmasin** *Kalimantan* Indon.
218 I10 **Banjës, Liqeni i** *resr* Albania
132 I5 **Banjiegou** *Xinjiang* China
129 O6 **Banjieta** *Hebei* China
201 I7 **Banjšice** *plat.* Slovenia
228 A3 **Banjul** Gambia
151 K6 **Bankä** Azer.
139 K7 **Banka** *Bihar* India
106 E5 **Banka Banka** *N.T.* Austr.
119 G7 **Ban Kadian** Laos
136 D5 **Bankapur** *Karnataka* India
228 E3 **Bankass** Mali
165 K4 **Bankeryd** Sweden
168 I9 **Bankfoot** *Perth and Kinross, Scotland* U.K.
119 E8 **Ban Khai** Thai.
119 D8 **Ban Khao Yoi** Thai.
119 D10 **Ban Khok Kloi** Thai.
139 J9 **Banki** *Orissa* India
229 F3 **Bankilaré** Niger
229 H5 **Bankim** Cameroon
237 O2 **Bankkop** S. Africa
228 C4 **Banko, Massif de** *mt.* Guinea
117 L7 **Bankobankoang** *i.* Indon.
136 C4 **Bankol** *Mahar.* India
228 C4 **Bankon** Guinea
245 O5 **Banks Island** *B.C.* Can.
242 F2 **Banks Island** *N.W.T.* Can.
100 □[5] **Banks Islands** Vanuatu
247 M2 **Banks Lake** *Nunavut* Can.
262 E3 **Banks Lake** *WA* U.S.A.
103 H10 **Banks Peninsula** *South I.* N.Z.
105 L9 **Banks Strait** *Tas.* Austr.
139 K8 **Bankura** *W. Bengal* India
219 K8 **Bankya** *Pernik* Bulg.
219 L8 **Bankya** *Sofiya-Grad* Bulg.
119 F7 **Ban Lamduan** Thai.
130 G6 **Banlan** *Guangxi* China
118 D7 **Ban Le Kathe** Thai.
218 J5 **Banloc** Romania
118 C5 **Ban Mae La Luang** Thai.
118 D5 **Ban Mae Mo** Thai.
118 D5 **Ban Mae Suya** Thai.
118 B2 **Banmauk** Myanmar
130 C9 **Ban Mouang** Laos
169 I7 **Bann** *r.* Ireland
169 I2 **Bann** *r. Northern Ireland* U.K.
118 G6 **Ban Nakham** Laos
180 D6 **Bannalec** France
118 G5 **Ban Napè** Laos
119 D10 **Ban Na San** Thai.
182 B2 **Bannay** France
270 E1 **Bannerman Town** *Eleuthera* Bahamas
256 E12 **Bannertown** *NC* U.S.A.
192 D2 **Bannesdorf auf Fehmarn** Ger.
264 P8 **Banning** *CA* U.S.A.
Banningville Dem. Rep. Congo *see* **Bandundu**
158 H8 **Bannivka** Ukr.
103 D12 **Bannockburn** *South I.* N.Z.
168 I10 **Bannockburn** *Stirling, Scotland* U.K.
118 C6 **Ban Noi** Myanmar
118 E4 **Ban Nong Kha** Laos
118 H7 **Ban Nongmek** Laos
169 I8 **Bannow** Ireland
145 N5 **Bannu** Pak.
141 K3 **Bannu** *admin. div.* Pak.
204 G7 **Bañobárez** Spain
Bañolas Spain *see* **Banyoles**
183 H8 **Banon** France
268 E2 **Bañón** Mex.
208 C6 **Bañón** Spain
274 B5 **Baños de Agua Santa** Ecuador
284 B5 **Baños de Copahue** Arg.
207 L4 **Baños de la Encina** Spain
284 B1 **Baños del Toro** Chile
204 E4 **Baños de Molgas** Spain
204 I8 **Baños de Montemayor** Spain
276 C5 **Baños de Puritama** Chile
205 O4 **Baños de Río Tobía** Spain
205 M5 **Baños de Valdearados** Spain
284 B5 **Baños Maule** Chile
199 G3 **Bánov** Czech Rep.
199 H3 **Bánov** Slovakia
199 H3 **Bánovce nad Bebravou** Slovakia
210 G3 **Banovići** Bos.-Herz.
Banow Afgh. *see* **Andarāb**
118 E5 **Ban Pak-Leng** Laos
119 D9 **Ban Pak Nam** Thai.
118 G6 **Ban Phaeng** Thai.
118 F6 **Ban Phai** Thai.
118 F5 **Ban Phôn-Hông** Laos
118 D7 **Banphot Phisai** Thai.
118 D6 **Ban Phran Katai** Thai.
119 D8 **Ban Pong** Thai.
128 G7 **Banqiao** *Gansu* China
130 B6 **Banqiao** *Yunnan* China
130 E5 **Banqiao** *Yunnan* China
119 E11 **Ban Sanam Chai** Thai.
228 B3 **Bansang** Gambia
119 D9 **Ban Sawi** Thai.
139 I6 **Bansgaon** *Uttar Prad.* India
169 F8 **Bansha** Ireland
139 K7 **Bansi** *Bihar* India
138 E7 **Bansi** *Rajasthan* India
138 G7 **Bansi** *Uttar Prad.* India
139 I6 **Bansi** *Uttar Prad.* India
139 L7 **Bansihari** *W. Bengal* India
192 J3 **Bansin, Seebad** Ger.
199 I3 **Banská Bystrica** Slovakia
199 H3 **Banská Štiavnica** Slovakia
219 L9 **Bansko** Bulg.
199 I3 **Banskobystrický kraj** *admin. reg.* Slovakia
139 K7 **Bansloi** *r.* India
144 I9 **Bānsont** Iran
173 L5 **Banstead** *Surrey, England* U.K.
118 D6 **Ban Sut Ta** Thai.
136 E3 **Banswada** *Andhra Prad.* India
138 E8 **Banswara** *Rajasthan* India
186 I3 **Bant** Neth.
115 A8 **Banta** *i.* Indon.
115 A6 **Bantaeng** *Sulawesi* Indon.
108 □[2] **Bantam** Cocos Is
Bantam *Jawa* Indon. *see* **Banten**
259 I1 **Bantam** *CT* U.S.A.
259 I1 **Bantam Lake** *CT* U.S.A.
118 F5 **Ban Taviang** Laos
114 D6 **Bantayan** *i.* Phil.
229 F4 **Bantè** Benin
169 E8 **Banteer** Ireland
116 G8 **Banten** *Jawa* Indon.
116 G8 **Banten** *prov.* Indon.
119 D10 **Ban Tha Chang** Thai.
119 D10 **Ban Tha Kham** Thai.
172 E7 **Bantham** *Devon, England* U.K.
118 C6 **Ban Tha Song Yang** Thai.
Banthat *mts* Cambodia *see* **Cardamom Range**
118 E7 **Ban Tha Tako** Thai.
118 D4 **Ban Tha Ton** Thai.
118 F7 **Ban Tha Tum** Thai.
119 E11 **Ban Thepha** Thai.
179 J5 **Bantheville** France
119 D8 **Ban Thung Luang** Thai.
118 H6 **Ban Tôp** Laos
169 D9 **Bantry** Ireland
169 C9 **Bantry Bay** Ireland
117 I8 **Bantul** Indon.
138 C9 **Bantva** *Gujarat* India
136 D6 **Bantval** *Karnataka* India
118 D6 **Ban Wang Chao** Thai.
118 G6 **Ban Wang Ta Mua** Thai.
172 G5 **Banwell** *North Somerset, England* U.K.
118 F5 **Ban Woen** Laos
118 H7 **Ban Xepian** Laos
116 B3 **Banyak, Pulau-pulau** *is* Indon.
209 K8 **Banyalbufar** Spain
119 D8 **Ban Yang Yong** Thai.
159 M2 **Banychi** Ukr.
209 D10 **Banyeres de Mariola** Spain
229 H5 **Banyo** Cameroon
208 K3 **Banyoles** Spain
116 F6 **Banyuasin** *r.* Indon.
185 K11 **Banyuls-sur-Mer** France
117 H8 **Banyumas** *Jawa* Indon.
117 K9 **Banyuwangi** *Jawa* Indon.
287 I2 **Banzare Coast** Antarctica
289 J8 **Banzare Seamount** *sea feature* Indian Ocean
Banzart Tunisia *see* **Bizerte**
215 Q6 **Banzi** Italy
192 E3 **Banzkow** Ger.
Banzyville Dem. Rep. Congo *see* **Mobayi-Mbongo**
Bao, Embalse del *resr* Spain *see* **Vao, Embalse de**
224 D5 **Bao, Ouadi** *watercourse* Chad
Bao'an *Guangdong* China *see* **Shenzhen**
128 H9 **Bao'an** *Qinghai* China
Bao'an *Shaanxi* China *see* **Zhidan**
224 D5 **Bao Bilia** *well* Chad
129 N6 **Baochang** *Nei Mongol* China
Baocheng *Hainan* China *see* **Baoting**
130 F2 **Baocheng** *Shaanxi* China
129 O7 **Baodi** *Tianjin* China
129 N7 **Baoding** *Hebei* China
131 I2 **Baofeng** *Henan* China
Baohe *Yunnan* China *see* **Weixi**
129 J9 **Baoji** *Shaanxi* China
129 J9 **Baoji** *Shaanxi* China
131 H3 **Baokang** *Hubei* China
129 R4 **Baokang** *Nei Mongol* China
118 G3 **Bao Lac** Vietnam
122 F6 **Baolin** *Heilong.* China
100 □[6] **Baolo** *Sta Isabel* Solomon Is
119 H9 **Bao Lôc** Vietnam
122 H5 **Baoqing** *Heilong.* China
230 B3 **Baoro** C.A.R.
131 M3 **Baoshan** *Shanghai* China
130 B6 **Baoshan** *Yunnan* China
130 G9 **Baoting** *Hainan* China
129 L6 **Baotou** *Nei Mongol* China
228 C3 **Baoulé** *r.* Mali
228 D3 **Baoulé** *r.* Mali
130 D3 **Baoxing** *Sichuan* China
130 D7 **Baoxiu** *Yunnan* China
131 L2 **Baoying** *Jiangsu* China
Baoyou *Hainan* China *see* **Ledong**
138 D6 **Bap** *Rajasthan* India
136 G5 **Bapatla** *Andhra Prad.* India
178 E3 **Bapaume** France
251 P4 **Baptiste Lake** *Ont.* Can.
Bapu *Sichuan* China *see* **Meigu**
146 F2 **Baq'ā'** *oasis* Saudi Arabia
150 A7 **Baqar, Maṣrif Baḥr al** *canal* Egypt
146 F4 **Baqarah** Saudi Arabia
133 K10 **Baqên** *Xizang* China
133 L11 **Baqên** *Xizang* China
131 J5 **Baqiu** *Jiangxi* China
146 E5 **Baqrān** Saudi Arabia
Baqty Kazakh. *see* **Bakhty**
149 L7 **Ba'qūbah** Iraq
179 I4 **Bar** *r.* France
218 H8 **Bar** *Bar* Montenegro
129 J1 **Bar** Rus. Fed.
158 G4 **Bar** Ukr.
138 H7 **Bara** *Uttar Prad.* India
115 E5 **Bara** *Buru* Indon.
229 H4 **Bara** Nigeria
199 K6 **Bara** Romania
225 F6 **Bara** Sudan
230 E2 **Bara** *well* Sudan
232 E4 **Baraawe** Somalia
117 K6 **Barabai** *Kalimantan* Indon.
138 H6 **Barabanki** *Uttar Prad.* India
161 V7 **Barabanovo** Rus. Fed.
199 L3 **Barabás** Hungary
122 G6 **Barabash-Levada** Rus. Fed.
Barabhas *Western Isles, Scotland* U.K. *see* **Barvas**
139 K8 **Barabhum** *W. Bengal* India
152 I4 **Barabinsk** Rus. Fed.
250 E6 **Baraboo** *WI* U.S.A.
250 E6 **Baraboo** *r. WI* U.S.A.
228 E3 **Baraboulé** Burkina
158 J7 **Baraboy** *r.* Ukr.
Baracaldo *País Vasco* Spain *see* **Barakaldo**
270 F3 **Baracoa** Cuba
199 H5 **Baracs** Hungary
199 H4 **Baracska** Hungary
150 E5 **Baradá, Nahr** *r.* Syria
150 F3 **Baradah** Syria
285 H3 **Baradero** Arg.
105 L4 **Baradine** *N.S.W.* Austr.
105 L4 **Baradine** *r. N.S.W.* Austr.
250 F3 **Baraga** *MI* U.S.A.
219 P6 **Bărăganului, Câmpia** *plain* Romania
215 P6 **Baragiano** Italy
232 C4 **Baragoi** Kenya
274 D2 **Baragua** Venez.
274 D2 **Baragua, Sierra de** *mts* Venez.
270 H4 **Barahona** Dom. Rep.
205 O6 **Barahona** Spain
138 G4 **Barahoti** *Uttaranchal* India
139 N7 **Barail Range** *mts* India
228 E2 **Bara Issa** *r.* Mali
205 O8 **Barajas de Melo** Spain
218 I6 **Barajevo** *Ripanj* Serbia
145 N3 **Barak** Afgh.
139 N7 **Barak** *r.* India
225 H5 **Baraka** *watercourse* Eritrea/Sudan
205 O2 **Barakaldo** Spain
232 B1 **Barakat** Sudan
145 M5 **Barakī Barak** Afgh.
237 I8 **Barakke** S. Africa
139 J9 **Barakot** *Orissa* India
161 W7 **Barakovo** Rus. Fed.
143 L1 **Barakpay** Kazakh.
107 L8 **Baralaba** *Qld* Austr.
138 F3 **Bara Lacha Pass** *Hima. Prad.* India
151 E4 **Baralet'i** Georgia
204 F3 **Baralla** Spain
247 L3 **Baralzon Lake** *Man.* Can.
139 K8 **Baram** *W. Bengal* India
117 J2 **Baram** *r.* Malaysia
117 J2 **Baram, Tanjung** *pt* Malaysia
275 G3 **Baramanni** Guyana
136 D3 **Baramati** *Mahar.* India
107 M8 **Barambah** *r. Qld* Austr.
225 H5 **Barameiya** Sudan
138 E2 **Baramulla** *Jammu and Kashmir* India
161 N7 **Baran'** Belarus
138 F7 **Baran** *Rajasthan* India
151 I6 **Barān** Iran
145 M9 **Baran** *r.* Pak.
144 I5 **Bārān, Kūh-e** *mts* Iran
145 O6 **Barana** Pak.
205 Q3 **Barañain** Spain
160 J8 **Baranavichy** Belarus
205 O2 **Baranbio** Spain
199 K4 **Báránd** Hungary
215 N4 **Baranello** Italy
153 R3 **Baranikha** Rus. Fed.
225 G4 **Baranīs** Egypt
158 G3 **Baranivka** Ukr.
138 H7 **Barannda** *Madh. Prad.* India
270 F8 **Baranoa** Col.
215 L6 **Barano d'Ischia** Italy
245 N4 **Baranof** *AK* U.S.A.
245 N4 **Baranof Island** *AK* U.S.A.
Baranovichi Belarus *see* **Baranavichy**
142 B1 **Baranovka** Rus. Fed.
197 K4 **Baranów** *Lubelskie* Pol.
196 G4 **Baranów** *Wielkopolskie* Pol.
Baranowicze Belarus *see* **Baranavichy**
197 J2 **Baranowo** Pol.
197 J5 **Baranów Sandomierska** Pol.
160 K6 **Barany** Belarus
199 H5 **Baranya** *county* Hungary
199 H6 **Baranyai-dombság** *hills* Hungary
281 F3 **Barão de Cocais** Brazil
278 E3 **Barão de Grajaú** Brazil
277 G4 **Barão de Melgaço** Brazil
277 E2 **Barão de Melgaco** Brazil
206 B6 **Barão de São Miguel** Port.
219 N4 **Baraolt** Romania
228 D3 **Baraouéli** Mali
Baraqbay Kazakh. *see* **Barakpay**
187 I8 **Baraque de Fraiture** *hill* Belgium
185 I7 **Baraqueville** France
277 F1 **Bararati** *r.* Brazil
158 H3 **Barashi** Ukr.
208 F3 **Barasona, Embalse de** *resr* Spain
115 D7 **Barat Daya, Kepulauan** *is Maluku* Indon.
115 C8 **Barati** *Timor* Indon.
159 L7 **Barativka** Ukr.
104 G5 **Baratta (abandoned)** *S.A.* Austr.
275 F4 **Barauaná, Serra** *mts* Brazil
138 F5 **Baraut** *Uttar Prad.* India
160 L6 **Baravukha** Belarus
274 C4 **Baraya** Col.
281 F4 **Barbacena** *Minas Gerais* Brazil
275 H5 **Barbacena** *Pará* Brazil
206 E3 **Barbacena** Port.
274 E2 **Barbacoas** Venez.
204 E4 **Barbadás** Spain
Barba de Puerco Spain *see* **Puerto Seguro**
205 N4 **Barbadillo de Herreros** Spain
205 N4 **Barbadillo del Mercado** Spain
205 N4 **Barbadillo del Pez** Spain
271 □[4] **Barbados** *country* West Indies
214 C7 **Barbagia** *mts Sardegna* Italy
213 Q5 **Barban** Croatia
150 B9 **Barbar, Jabal** *mt.* Egypt
248 C3 **Barbara Lake** *Ont.* Can.
213 L5 **Barbarano Vicentino** Italy
269 J3 **Barbarena** *r.* Mex.
209 H10 **Barbaria, Cap de** *c.* Spain
213 P5 **Barbariga, Rt** *pt* Croatia
221 I2 **Barbaros** Turkey
185 E7 **Barbaste** France
208 F3 **Barbastro** Spain
213 R6 **Barbat** Croatia
206 H8 **Barbate** *r.* Spain
206 H8 **Barbate, Embalse de** *resr* Spain
206 H8 **Barbate de Franco** Spain
180 G8 **Barbâtre** France
185 F9 **Barbazan** France
185 E9 **Barbazan-Debat** France
243 K1 **Barbeau Peak** *mt.* Can.
266 F4 **Barbechitos** Mex.
160 H5 **Bārbele** Latvia
183 F9 **Barbentane** France
271 □[10] **Barber** *Curaçao* Neth. Antilles
213 K7 **Barberino di Mugello** Italy
251 N1 **Barber's Bay** *Ont.* Can.
237 J2 **Barberspan Nature Reserve** S. Africa
264 □C12 **Barbers Point** *HI* U.S.A.
237 P1 **Barberton** S. Africa
256 D7 **Barberton** *OH* U.S.A.
184 D5 **Barbezieux-St-Hilaire** France
139 J7 **Barbigha** *Bihar* India
178 E7 **Barbizon** France
171 L5 **Barbon** *Cumbria, England* U.K.
178 G6 **Barbonne-Fayel** France
274 C3 **Barbosa** Col.
185 D8 **Barbotan-les-Thermes** France
247 M2 **Barbour Bay** *Nunavut* Can.
258 B2 **Barbours** *PA* U.S.A.
256 B12 **Barbourville** *KY* U.S.A.
114 D6 **Barboza** *Panay* Phil.
271 □[2] **Barbuda** *i.* Antigua and Barbuda
173 J3 **Barby** *Northamptonshire, England* U.K.
193 E7 **Barby (Elbe)** Ger.
219 L7 **Bârca** Romania
205 O6 **Barca** Spain
208 F3 **Barcabo** Spain
204 G6 **Barca de Alva** Port.
271 □[9] **Barcadera** Aruba
107 J7 **Barcaldine** *Qld* Austr.
206 F3 **Barcarrota** Spain
219 J3 **Barcău** *r.* Romania
Barce Libya *see* **Al Marj**
204 C5 **Barcelinhos** Port.
217 I7 **Barcellona Pozzo di Gotto** *Sicilia* Italy
208 J5 **Barcelona** Spain
208 I4 **Barcelona** *prov.* Spain
275 E2 **Barcelona** Venez.
271 □[1] **Barceloneta** Puerto Rico
185 D8 **Barcelonne-du-Gers** France
183 J8 **Barcelonnette** France
275 F5 **Barcelos** Brazil
204 C5 **Barcelos** Port.
204 G3 **Bárcena, Embalse de** *resr* Spain
204 G2 **Bárcena del Monasterio** Spain
205 L2 **Bárcena de Pie de Concha** Spain
205 M2 **Barcenillas de Cerezos** Spain
191 J9 **Barchfeld** Ger.
197 J1 **Barciany** Pol.
183 H8 **Barcillonnette** France
196 F3 **Barcin** Pol.
196 E1 **Barcino** Pol.
Barcino Spain *see* **Barcelona**
213 N3 **Barcis** Italy
258 D6 **Barclay** *MD* U.S.A.
Barclay de Tolly *atoll Arch. des Tuamotu* Fr. Polynesia *see* **Raroia**
228 C5 **Barclayville** Liberia
205 O6 **Barcones** Spain
107 I8 **Barcoo** *watercourse Qld* Austr.
Barcoo Creek *watercourse Qld/S.A.* Austr. *see* **Cooper Creek**
Barcoo National Park *Qld* Austr. *see* **Welford National Park**
204 E6 **Barcos** Port.
198 G6 **Barcs** Hungary
199 G5 **Barcsi Ősborókás** *park*
185 C9 **Barcus** France
197 I2 **Barczewo** Pol.
182 E2 **Bard, Montagne de** *hill*
151 I5 **Bärdä** Azer.
156 K4 **Barda** Rus. Fed.
232 E3 **Bardaale** Somalia
284 C6 **Barda del Medio** Arg.
224 C4 **Bardaï** Chad
162 □E1 **Bárðarbunga** *mt.* Icelan
284 C4 **Bardas Blancas** Arg.
144 G4 **Bardāskan** Iran
150 G7 **Bardawil, Khabrat al** *salt* Saudi Arabia
150 B7 **Bardawīl, Sabkhat al** *lag.*
139 K8 **Barddhaman** *W. Bengal*
199 K2 **Bardejov** Slovakia
208 C3 **Bárdena** Spain
205 Q4 **Bárdenas Reales** *reg.* Sp
193 G6 **Bardenitz** Ger.
Bardera Somalia *see* **Baa**
108 G4 **Bardi** *W.A.* Austr.
138 I7 **Bardi** *Madh. Prad.* India
212 H6 **Bardi** Italy
212 E7 **Bardineto** Italy
171 Q7 **Bardney** *Lincolnshire, England* U.K.
196 E5 **Bardo** Pol.
213 J4 **Bardolino** Italy
212 B5 **Bardonecchia** Italy
185 B9 **Bardos** France
190 J4 **Bardowick** Ger.
171 K5 **Bardsea** *Cumbria, Englan*
172 C2 **Bardsey Island** *Wales* U.
172 C2 **Bardsey Sound** *sea chan. Wales* U.K.
144 D5 **Bard Shāh** Iran
144 G7 **Bardsīr** Iran
162 □G1 **Barðsneshorn** *pt* Iceland
254 E7 **Bardstown** *KY* U.S.A.
199 G5 **Bárdudvarnok** Hungary
Barduli Italy *see* **Barletta**
261 K7 **Bardwell** *KY* U.S.A.
229 H5 **Baré** Cameroon
232 D3 **Barē** Eth.
103 B11 **Bare Cone** *hill South I.* N
185 E10 **Barèges** France
138 G5 **Bareilly** *Uttar Prad.* India
102 L6 **Bare Island** *North I.* N.Z.
138 G8 **Bareli** *Madh. Prad.* India
105 K6 **Barellan** *N.S.W.* Austr.
190 G5 **Barenburg** Ger.
190 K4 **Barendorf** Ger.
139 M7 **Barengapara** *Meghalaya*
193 K7 **Bärenklau** Ger.
193 H10 **Bärenstein** *Sachsen* Ger.
193 I9 **Bärenstein** *Sachsen* Ger.
178 A4 **Barentin** France
181 J4 **Barenton** France
162 □ **Barentsburg** Svalbard
Barents Island Svalbard *see* **Barentsøya**
162 □ **Barentsøya** *i.* Svalbard
292 C1 **Barents Sea** Arctic Ocea
225 H6 **Barentu** Eritrea
117 K3 **Bareo** *Sarawak* Malaysia
258 C4 **Bareville** *PA* U.S.A.
180 I2 **Barfleur** France
180 I2 **Barfleur, Pointe de** *pt* Fr
133 E11 **Barga** *Xizang* China
212 I7 **Barga** Italy
232 F2 **Bargaal** Somalia
212 G7 **Bargagli** Italy
144 G8 **Bārgāh** Iran
258 F6 **Bargaintown** *NJ* U.S.A.
107 N8 **Bargara** *Qld* Austr.
139 I9 **Bargarh** *Orissa* India
205 L9 **Bargas** Spain
232 C3 **Bargē** Eth.
212 C6 **Barge** Italy
183 J9 **Bargemon** France
212 F1 **Bargen** Switz.
190 H2 **Bargenstedt** Ger.
212 I4 **Barghe** Italy
138 G8 **Bargi** *Madh. Prad.* India
Bargiri Turkey *see* **Murac**
192 I3 **Bargischow** Ger.
197 K2 **Bargłów Kościelny** Pol.
172 F4 **Bargoed** *Caerphilly, Wales*
168 G12 **Bargrennan** *Dumfries an Galloway, Scotland* U.K.
190 H4 **Bargstedt** Ger.
190 J3 **Bargteheide** Ger.
185 F7 **Barguelonne** *r.* France
139 M8 **Barguna** Bangl.
136 E7 **Bargur** *Tamil Nadu* India
151 H6 **Bärgüşad** *r.* Azer.
230 E3 **Barh** C.A.R.
139 J7 **Barh** *Bihar* India
139 I6 **Barhaj** *Uttar Prad.* India
139 I6 **Barhalganj** *Uttar Prad.* I
105 J6 **Barham** *N.S.W.* Austr.
173 O5 **Barham** *Kent, England* U.
257 □Q4 **Bar Harbor** *ME* U.S.A.
139 K7 **Barharwa** *Jharkhand* Ind
173 M3 **Bar Hill** *Cambridgeshire, England* U.K.
230 C4 **Bari** Dem. Rep. Congo
138 F6 **Bari** *Rajasthan* India
217 L1 **Bari** Italy
215 R6 **Bari** *prov.* Italy
232 F2 **Bari** *admin. reg.* Somalia
119 H9 **Ba Ria** Vietnam
233 B5 **Bariadi** Tanz.
146 C3 **Barīdī, Ra's** *hd* Saudi Ara
145 O6 **Bari Doab** *lowland* Pak.
147 M5 **Barik** Oman
227 G2 **Barika** Alg.
145 N4 **Barikot** Afgh.
138 I5 **Barikot** Nepal
215 P6 **Barile** Italy
146 F9 **Barīm** *i.* Yemen
275 G2 **Barima** *r.* Guyana
209 C11 **Barinas** Spain
274 D2 **Barinas** Venez.
274 D2 **Barinas** *state* Venez.
250 B9 **Baring** *MO* U.S.A.
230 D4 **Baringa** Dem. Rep. Cong
232 C4 **Baringo, Lake** Kenya
139 K9 **Baripada** *Orissa* India
280 C5 **Bariri** Brazil
225 F3 **Bārīs** Egypt
138 E7 **Bari Sadri** *Rajasthan* Ind
151 F3 **Barisakho** Georgia
139 M8 **Barisal** Bangl.
139 M8 **Barisal** *admin. div.* Bangl.
116 D5 **Barisan, Pegunungan** *m*
214 D8 **Bari Sardo** *Sardegna* Italy
215 L3 **Barisciano** Italy
117 K6 **Barito** *r.* Indon.
282 D1 **Baritú, Parque Nacional** Arg.
Barium Italy *see* **Bari**
183 E8 **Barjac** France
183 I9 **Barjaude, Montagne de** France
183 I9 **Barjols** France
139 K8 **Barjora** *W. Bengal* India
224 B3 **Barjūj, Wādī** *watercourse*
146 C7 **Barka** *prov.* Eritrea
147 M4 **Barkā** Oman
139 N8 **Barkal** Bangl.
130 D3 **Barkam** *Sichuan* China
144 C6 **Barkan, Ra's-e** *pt* Iran
160 J5 **Barkava** Latvia
190 I1 **Barkelsby** Ger.
285 H5 **Barker** Arg.
109 F11 **Barker, Lake** *salt flat* W.A.
246 F4 **Barkerville** *B.C.* Can.
228 B2 **Barkéwol el Abiod** Maur.
145 M7 **Barkhan** Pak.
138 F8 **Barkhera** *Madh. Prad.* Inc
139 J7 **Barki Saria** *Jharkhand* Inc
251 Q4 **Bark Lake** *Ont.* Can.
254 D7 **Barkley, Lake** *KY* U.S.A.
246 E5 **Barkley Sound** *inlet* B.C.
106 G6 **Barkly Downs** *Qld* Austr.
237 L6 **Barkly East** S. Africa
237 L7 **Barkly Pass** S. Africa
106 E5 **Barkly Tableland** *reg.* N.T
236 I4 **Barkly West** S. Africa
128 C5 **Barkol** *Xinjiang* China
128 C5 **Barkol Hu** *salt l. Xinjiang*

Barkot *Uttaranchal* India
Barkowo Pol.
Barkway *Hertfordshire, England* U.K.
Barla Turkey
Bârlad Romania
Bârladului, Podişul *plat.* Romania
Barlag Gol *watercourse* Mongolia
Barlaston *Staffordshire, England* U.K.
Barlborough *Derbyshire, England* U.K.
Barle *r. England* U.K.
Barleben Ger.
Bar-le-Duc France
Barlee, Lake *salt flat W.A.* Austr.
Barlee Range *hills W.A.* Austr.
Barlee Range Nature Reserve W.A. Austr.
Barles France
Barletta Italy
Barletta - Andria - Trani *admin. div.* Italy
Barley *Hertfordshire, England* U.K.
Barlin France
Barlinecko-Gorzowski Park Krajobrazowy Pol.
Barlinek Pol.
Barlo Point Sierra Leone
Barlovento *La Palma* Canary Is
Barlow *Y.T.* Can.
Barlow Lake *N.W.T.* Can.
Barmashove Ukr.
Barmedman *N.S.W.* Austr.
Barmen-Elberfeld Ger. *see* **Wuppertal**
Barmer *Rajasthan* India
Barmera *S.A.* Austr.
Barm Fīrūz, Kūh-e *mt.* Iran
Barmouth *Gwynedd, Wales* U.K.
Barmouth Bay *Wales* U.K.
Barmstedt Ger.
Barna Ireland *see* **Bearna**
Bârna Romania
Barnagar *Madh. Prad.* India
Barnala *Punjab* India
Barnard, Mount Can./U.S.A.
Barnard Castle *Durham, England* U.K.
Barnato *N.S.W.* Austr.
Barnatra Ireland *see* **Barr na Trá**
Bärnau Ger.
Barnaul Rus. Fed.
Barnbach Austria
Barnegat *NJ* U.S.A.
Barnegat Bay *NJ* U.S.A.
Barnegat Beach *NJ* U.S.A.
Barnegat Light *NJ* U.S.A.
Barne Inlet Antarctica
Barnes *N.S.W.* Austr.
Barnesboro *PA* U.S.A.
Barnes Icecap *Nunavut* Can.
Barnesville *GA* U.S.A.
Barnesville *MN* U.S.A.
Barnesville *OH* U.S.A.
Barnet *Greater London, England* U.K.
Barnet *VT* U.S.A.
Barneveld Neth.
Barneville-Carteret France
Barnewitz Ger.
Barneycarroll Ireland
Barneys Lake *imp. l. N.S.W.* Austr.
Barney Top *mt. UT* U.S.A.
Barnhart *TX* U.S.A.
Barnim *reg.* Ger.
Barningham *Suffolk, England* U.K.
Barnjarn Aboriginal Land *res.* N.T. Austr.
Barn Long Point St Helena
Barnmeen *Northern Ireland* U.K.
Barnoldswick *Lancashire, England* U.K.
Bârnova, Dealul *hill* Romania
Barnowko Pol.
Barnsdall *OK* U.S.A.
Barnsley *South Yorkshire, England* U.K.
Barnstable *MA* U.S.A.
Barnstädt Ger.
Barnstaple *Devon, England* U.K.
Barnstaple Bay *England* U.K.
Barnstorf Ger.
Barnton *Cheshire, England* U.K.
Barntrup Ger.
Barnum Bay Palau
Barnwell *SC* U.S.A.
Baro Nigeria
Baroda *Gujarat* India *see* **Vadodara**
Baroda *Madh. Prad.* India
Baroda S. Africa
Baroe S. Africa
Bärofen *mt.* Austria
Baronda *Madh. Prad.* India
Barone, Monte *mt.* Italy
Barong *Sichuan* China
Baronia *reg. Sardegna* Italy
Baron'ki Belarus
Baronnies *reg.* France
Barons Range *hills W.A.* Austr.
Baronville France
Barora Fa *i.* Solomon Is
Barora Ite *i.* Solomon Is
Baroua C.A.R.
Baro Wenz *r.* Eth.
Barowghīl, Kowtal-e *pass* Afgh.
Barowka Belarus
Barpathar *Assam* India
Barpeta *Assam* India
Bar Pla Soi Thai. *see* **Chon Buri**
Barqā Damaj *well* Saudi Arabia
Barqah, Jabal *mt.* Egypt
Barqueros Spain
Barques, Point Aux *MI* U.S.A.
Barques, Point Aux *MI* U.S.A.
Barquinha Port.
Barquisimeto Venez.
Barr France
Barr *South Ayrshire, Scotland* U.K.
Barra Brazil
Barra *i. Scotland* U.K.
Barra, Sound of *sea chan. Scotland* U.K.
Barraba *N.S.W.* Austr.
Barra Bonita Brazil
Barra Bonita, Represa *resr* Brazil
Barraca da Boca Brazil
Barracão do Barreto Brazil
Barracas Spain
Barrachina Spain
Barrackville *WV* U.S.A.
Barracouta, Cape S. Africa
Barra da Estiva Brazil
Barra de Cazones Mex.
Barra de Navidad Mex.
Barra de Santos *inlet* Brazil
Barra de São Francisco Brazil
Barra de São João Brazil
Barra do Bugres Brazil
Barra do Corda Brazil
Barra do Cuanza Angola
Barra do Cuieté Brazil
Barra do Garças Brazil
Barrado Mendes Brazil
Barra do Piraí Brazil
Barra do Quaraí Brazil
Barra do São Manuel Brazil
Barra do Turvo Brazil
Barra do Una Brazil
Barra Falsa, Ponta da *pt* Moz.
Barrafranca *Sicilia* Italy
Barraigh *i. Scotland* U.K. *see* **Barra**
Barra Kruta Hond.
Barral Spain
Barrali *Sardegna* Italy
Barra Longa Brazil
Barra Mansa Brazil
Barrāmīyah Egypt
Barran France
Barranca Peru
Barranca Venez.
Barrancabermeja Col.
Barranca del Cobre, Parque Natural *nature res.* Mex.

284 C5 **Barrancas** *Neuquén* Arg.
285 G3 **Barrancas** *Santa Fé* Arg.
284 C5 **Barrancas** *r.* Arg.
285 H2 **Barrancas** *r.* Arg.
270 G8 **Barrancas** Col.
274 D2 **Barrancas** *Barinas* Venez.
275 F2 **Barrancas** *Monagas* Venez.
274 C2 **Barranco de Loba** Col.
238 □[3a] **Barranco de Santiago** *La Gomera* Canary Is
206 D6 **Barranco do Velho** Port.
206 F4 **Barrancos** Port.
207 P4 **Barranda** Spain
269 J5 **Barra Norte** Mex.
274 C2 **Barranquilla** *Atlántico* Col.
274 C4 **Barranquilla** *Guaviare* Col.
274 B6 **Barranquita** Peru
271 □[1] **Barranquitas** Puerto Rico
274 C2 **Barranquitas** Venez.
168 C10 **Barrapoll** *Argyll and Bute, Scotland* U.K.
278 E3 **Barras** Brazil
251 Q1 **Barraute** *Que.* Can.
207 O2 **Barrax** Spain
257 M6 **Barre** *MA* U.S.A.
257 M4 **Barre** *VT* U.S.A.
215 L4 **Barrea, Lago di** *l.* Italy
284 C2 **Barreal** Arg.
183 D8 **Barre-des-Cévennes** France
183 I7 **Barre des Écrins** *mt.* France
278 D5 **Barreiras** Brazil
275 G5 **Barreirinha** Brazil
278 E2 **Barreirinhas** Brazil
279 B5 **Barreiro** *r.* Brazil
206 A3 **Barreiro** Port.
278 C4 **Barreiro do Nascimento** Brazil
278 G4 **Barreiros** Brazil
183 I9 **Barrême** France
137 M6 **Barren Island** *Andaman & Nicobar Is* India
Barren Island Kiribati *see* **Starbuck Island**
244 I4 **Barren Islands** *AK* U.S.A.
280 C4 **Barretos** Brazil
264 P9 **Barrett** *CA* U.S.A.
108 I5 **Barrett, Mount** *hill W.A.* Austr.
246 H4 **Barrhead** *Alta* Can.
168 H11 **Barrhead** *East Renfrewshire, Scotland* U.K.
103 F10 **Barrhill** *South I.* N.Z.
168 G12 **Barrhill** *South Ayrshire, Scotland* U.K.
146 F7 **Barrī** *i.* Saudi Arabia
208 J4 **Barriada Nueva** Spain
248 E4 **Barrie** *Ont.* Can.
204 C3 **Barrié de la Maza, Encoro de** *resr* Spain
251 L4 **Barrie Island** *Ont.* Can.
102 J3 **Barrier, Cape** *North I.* N.Z.
287 F2 **Barrier Bay** Antarctica
246 F5 **Barrière** *B.C.* Can.
104 H4 **Barrier Range** *hills N.S.W.* Austr.
267 O9 **Barrier Reef** Belize
100 □[1] **Barrigada** Guam
249 H5 **Barrington** *N.S.* Can.
236 G9 **Barrington** S. Africa
105 M5 **Barrington, Mount** *N.S.W.* Austr.
Barrington Island *Islas Galápagos* Ecuador *see* **Santa Fé, Isla**
247 K3 **Barrington Lake** *Man.* Can.
105 M5 **Barrington Tops National Park** *N.S.W.* Austr.
105 J3 **Barringun** *N.S.W.* Austr.
209 D12 **Barrio del Peral** Spain
209 E8 **Barrio Mar** Spain
204 I3 **Barrios de Luna, Embalse de** *resr* Spain
169 C4 **Barr na Trá** Ireland
204 E6 **Barrô** Port.
278 C5 **Barro Alto** Brazil
204 E8 **Barroca** Port.
281 F2 **Barrocão** Brazil
204 D4 **Barroças e Taias** Port.
179 J6 **Barrois, Plateau du** France
281 H2 **Barrolândia** Brazil
250 C4 **Barron** *WI* U.S.A.
250 C4 **Barronett** *WI* U.S.A.
206 G3 **Barros, Tierra de** *reg.* Spain
284 A6 **Barros Arana** Chile
204 C5 **Barroselas** Port.
281 F4 **Barroso** Brazil
267 I4 **Barroterán** Mex.
271 □[3] **Barrouallie** St Vincent
285 G6 **Barrow** Arg.
169 I8 **Barrow** *r.* Ireland
244 H1 **Barrow** *AK* U.S.A.
244 H1 **Barrow, Point** *pt AK* U.S.A.
173 K2 **Barrowby** *Lincolnshire, England* U.K.
106 D6 **Barrow Creek** *N.T.* Austr.
171 M6 **Barrowford** *Lancashire, England* U.K.
171 K5 **Barrow-in-Furness** *Cumbria, England* U.K.
108 C6 **Barrow Island** *W.A.* Austr.
108 C6 **Barrow Island Nature Reserve** *W.A.* Austr.
107 J3 **Barrow Point** *Qld* Austr.
109 I9 **Barrow Range** *hills W.A.* Austr.
243 I2 **Barrow Strait** *Nunavut* Can.
171 Q6 **Barrow upon Humber** *North Lincolnshire, England* U.K.
109 F9 **Barr Smith Range** *hills W.A.* Austr.
204 G6 **Barruecopardo** Spain
205 L3 **Barruelo de Santullan** Spain
172 F5 **Barry** *Vale of Glamorgan, Wales* U.K.
236 E9 **Barrydale** S. Africa
105 K7 **Barry Mountains** *Vic.* Austr.
248 E4 **Barrys Bay** *Ont.* Can.
256 A5 **Barryton** *MI* U.S.A.
102 J5 **Barryville** *North I.* N.Z.
258 F2 **Barryville** *NY* U.S.A.
199 L5 **Bârsa** Romania
185 D6 **Barsac** France
142 H5 **Barsakel'mes, Poluostrov** *pen.* Kazakh.
142 I5 **Barsakel'messkiy Zapovednik** *nature res.* Kazakh.
228 E3 **Barsalogo** Burkina
138 D5 **Barsalpur** *Rajasthan* India
219 M3 **Bârsana** Romania
190 J3 **Barsbüttel** Ger.
143 R3 **Barshatas** Kazakh.
Barshi *Mahar.* India *see* **Barsi**
136 D3 **Barsi** *Mahar.* India
191 H6 **Barsinghausen** Ger.
164 F6 **Barsø** *i.* Denmark
139 K7 **Barsoi** *Bihar* India
190 E4 **Barßel** Ger.
264 O7 **Barstow** *CA* U.S.A.
160 E5 **Barstyčiai** Lith.
161 U7 **Barsuki** Rus. Fed.
136 G3 **Barsur** *Chhattisgarh* India
178 I7 **Bar-sur-Aube** France
178 H7 **Bar-sur-Seine** France
160 E5 **Bārta** Latvia
160 E5 **Bārta** *r.* Latvia
145 N2 **Bartang** Tajik.
145 N3 **Bartang** *r.* Tajik.
182 K1 **Bartenheim** France
194 H3 **Bartenstein** Ger.
245 L1 **Barter Island** *AK* U.S.A.
192 G2 **Barth** Ger.
192 G2 **Barthe** *r.* Ger.
194 H4 **Bartholomä** Ger.
261 I9 **Bartholomew, Bayou** *r. LA* U.S.A.
Bartholomew Island Vanuatu *see* **Malo**
275 G3 **Bartica** Guyana
148 F3 **Bartın** Turkey
107 J4 **Bartle Frere, Mount** *Qld* Austr.
256 C10 **Bartles** *OH* U.S.A.
265 V2 **Bartles, Mount** *UT* U.S.A.
261 G7 **Bartlesville** *OK* U.S.A.
260 F5 **Bartlett** *NE* U.S.A.
257 N4 **Bartlett** *NH* U.S.A.
246 G2 **Bartlett Lake** *N.W.T.* Can.
265 U8 **Bartlett Reservoir** *AZ* U.S.A.
102 L5 **Bartletts** *North I.* N.Z.
197 I2 **Bartniki** Pol.
197 L1 **Bartninkai** Lith.
171 L6 **Barton** *Lancashire, England* U.K.
257 M4 **Barton** *VT* U.S.A.

173 L4 **Barton-le-Clay** *Bedfordshire, England* U.K.
173 I2 **Barton-under-Needwood** *Staffordshire, England* U.K.
171 Q6 **Barton-upon-Humber** *North Lincolnshire, England* U.K.
250 E9 **Bartonville** *IL* U.S.A.
165 Q7 **Bartoszyce** Pol.
255 G12 **Bartow** *FL* U.S.A.
162 N3 **Barturte** *mt.* Sweden
160 E5 **Bartuva** *r.* Lith.
274 C2 **Baru, Isla de** *i.* Col.
197 H3 **Baruchowo** Pol.
139 L8 **Baruipur** *W. Bengal* India
206 E2 **Barulho** Port.
214 C8 **Barumini** *Sardegna* Italy
116 D3 **Barumun** *r.* Indon.
128 E8 **Barun** *Qinghai* China
117 J9 **Barung** *i.* Indon.
Barunga *N.T.* Austr. *see* **Bamyili**
129 N1 **Barun-Torey, Ozero** *l.* Rus. Fed.
116 C3 **Barus** *Sumatera* Indon.
193 I6 **Baruth** *Brandenburg* Ger.
193 K8 **Baruth** *Sachsen* Ger.
128 G4 **Baruunbayan-Ulaan** Mongolia
128 I2 **Baruunbüren** Mongolia
Baruunharaa Mongolia *see* **Bayangol**
Baruunsuu Mongolia *see* **Tsogttsetsiy**
128 D2 **Baruunturuun** Mongolia
129 M3 **Baruun-Urt** Mongolia
137 I3 **Baruva** *Andhra Prad.* India
168 C6 **Barvas** *Western Isles, Scotland* U.K.
187 H8 **Barvaux** Belgium
190 G5 **Barver** Ger.
159 Q5 **Barvinkove** Ukr.
139 J8 **Barwa** *Jharkhand* India
138 F8 **Barwah** *Madh. Prad.* India
138 C8 **Barwala** *Gujarat* India
138 E5 **Barwala** *Haryana* India
138 E8 **Barwani** *Madh. Prad.* India
138 G7 **Barwa Sagar** *Uttar Prad.* India
190 K5 **Barwedel** Ger.
Barwéli Mali *see* **Baraouéli**
196 E2 **Barwice** Pol.
105 K4 **Barwon** *r. N.S.W.* Austr.
161 R7 **Baryatino** Rus. Fed.
161 U6 **Barybino** Rus. Fed.
196 E4 **Barycz** *r.* Pol.
Barygaza *Gujarat* India *see* **Bharuch**
160 L7 **Barysaw** Belarus
157 I5 **Barysh** Rus. Fed.
159 K3 **Baryshivka** Ukr.
147 N4 **Barzamān** Oman
204 I2 **Bárzana** Spain
199 L5 **Bârzava** Romania
145 K3 **Basaga** Turkm.
144 F8 **Bāsa'īdū** Iran
282 F2 **Basail** Arg.
119 G9 **Basăk, Tônlé** *r.* Cambodia
107 J5 **Basalt** *r. Qld* Austr.
Basalt Island *H.K.* China *see* **Fo Shek Chau**
231 E6 **Basanga** Dem. Rep. Congo
230 C4 **Basankusu** Dem. Rep. Congo
139 K6 **Basantpur** *Bihar* India
136 E3 **Basar** *Mahar.* India
158 H7 **Basarabeasca** Moldova
219 Q6 **Basarabi** Romania
Basargechar Armenia *see* **Vardenis**
136 E4 **Basavakalyan** *Karnataka* India
136 E4 **Basavana Bagevadi** *Karnataka* India
285 H3 **Basavilbaso** Arg.
114 D7 **Basay** *Negros* Phil.
151 C5 **Başçakmak** Turkey
219 O5 **Bâsca Mică** *r.* Romania
208 K3 **Bàscara** Spain
179 K4 **Bascharage** Lux.
172 G2 **Baschurch** *Shropshire, England* U.K.
215 L2 **Basciano** Italy
114 C1 **Basco** Phil.
104 E5 **Bascombe Well Conservation Park** *nature res. S.A.* Austr.
205 M3 **Basconcillos del Tozo** Spain
185 D8 **Bascons** France
185 E8 **Bascous** France
282 C3 **Bascuñán, Cabo** *c.* Chile
205 P8 **Bascuñana, Sierra de** *mts* Spain
190 H4 **Basdahl** Ger.
192 H5 **Basdorf** Ger.
151 A5 **Başdurak** Turkey
187 E7 **Basècles** Belgium
106 D8 **Basedow Range** *hills N.T.* Austr.
212 D1 **Basel** Switz.
213 K3 **Baselga di Pinè** Italy
215 N5 **Baselice** Italy
212 D1 **Basellandschaft** *canton* Switz.
182 L1 **Basel-Mulhouse** *airport* France
183 E6 **Bas-en-Basset** France
215 Q6 **Basentello** *r.* Italy
215 R7 **Basento** *r.* Italy
185 F10 **Baserca, Embalse de** *resr* Spain
219 P3 **Başeu** *r.* Romania
114 E6 **Basey** *Samar* Phil.
144 H8 **Bashākerd, Kūhhā-ye** *mts* Iran
Bashan *Jiangxi* China *see* **Chongren**
Bashanta Rus. Fed. *see* **Gorodovikovsk**
246 H4 **Bashaw** *Alta* Can.
143 U2 **Bashchelakskiy Khrebet** *mts* Rus. Fed.
237 M8 **Bashee** *r.* S. Africa
237 M7 **Bashee Bridge** S. Africa
145 N4 **Bashgul** *r.* Afgh.
144 D7 **Bāshī** Iran
112 F2 **Bashi Channel** Taiwan
231 E6 **Bashimuke** Dem. Rep. Congo
132 H1 **Bashkaus** *r.* Rus. Fed.
Bashkiria *aut. rep.* Rus. Fed. *see* **Bashkortostan, Respublika**
Bashkirskaya A.S.S.R. *aut. rep.* Rus. Fed. *see* **Bashkortostan, Respublika**
142 G1 **Bashkirskiy Zapovednik** *nature res.* Rus. Fed.
151 F4 **Bashk'oi** Georgia
142 G1 **Bashkortostan, Respublika** *aut. rep.* Rus. Fed.
157 H5 **Bashmakovo** Rus. Fed.
Bāsh Qal'eh Iran *see* **Pīsh Qal'eh**
144 D6 **Bāsht** Iran
159 L6 **Bashtanka** Ukr.
147 K9 **Bashūrī, Ra's** *pt Suquṭrā* Yemen
138 F6 **Basi** *Rajasthan* India
139 J8 **Basia** *Jharkhand* India
205 O2 **Basigo** Spain
107 M1 **Basilaki Island** P.N.G.
114 C8 **Basilan** *i.* Phil.
114 D8 **Basilan Strait** Phil.
173 M4 **Basildon** *Essex, England* U.K.
261 I10 **Basile** *LA* U.S.A.
229 H6 **Basile, Pico** *vol.* Equat. Guinea
213 O3 **Basiliano** Italy
215 P6 **Basilicata** *admin. reg.* Italy
217 I6 **Basiluzzo, Isola** *i. Isole Lipari* Italy
262 J4 **Basin** *WY* U.S.A.
165 M1 **Bäsingen** *l.* Sweden
173 J5 **Basingstoke** *Hampshire, England* U.K.
247 J4 **Basin Lake** *Sask.* Can.
149 L6 **Bāsīra** *r.* Iraq
144 H6 **Başīrān** Iran
139 L8 **Basirhat** *W. Bengal* India
150 D3 **Basīṭ, Ra's al** *pt* Syria
159 O2 **Basivka** Ukr.
210 E3 **Baška** Croatia
199 H2 **Baška** Czech Rep.
257 □R3 **Baskahegan Lake** *ME* U.S.A.
161 R7 **Baskakovka** Rus. Fed.
149 L4 **Başkale** Turkey
143 P1 **Baskamys** Kazakh.
248 F4 **Baskatong, Réservoir** *resr Que.* Can.
108 G4 **Baskerville, Cape** *W.A.* Austr.
221 L4 **Başkomutan Tarıhı Milli Parkı** *nat. park* Turkey
221 L4 **Başkomutan Tarıhı Milli Parkı** *nat. park* Turkey

151 B5 **Başköy** *Erzurum* Turkey
150 A2 **Başköy** *Karaman* Turkey
157 I6 **Baskunchak, Ozero** *l.* Rus. Fed.
151 I4 **Baş Layski** Azer.
Basle Switz. *see* **Basel**
151 H6 **Başlıbel** Azer.
171 N7 **Baslow** *Derbyshire, England* U.K.
221 L5 **Başmakçı** Turkey
136 E3 **Basmat** *Mahar.* India
151 J6 **Baş Muğan Kanalı** *canal* Azer.
116 E5 **Baso** *i.* Indon.
138 F8 **Basoda** *Madh. Prad.* India
212 E3 **Basodino** *mt.* Italy/Switz.
230 D4 **Basoko** Dem. Rep. Congo
145 K9 **Basol** *r.* Pak.
231 D6 **Basongo** Dem. Rep. Congo
Basora, Punt *pt* Aruba *see* **Basora, Punta**
271 □[9] **Basora, Punta** *pt* Aruba
233 B6 **Basotu** Tanz.
151 I5 **Baş Qärvänd** Azer.
Basque Country *aut. comm.* Spain *see* **País Vasco**
185 F7 **Bas-Quercy** *reg.* France
Basra Iraq *see* **Al Başrah**
179 O6 **Bas-Rhin** *dept* France
Bass, Îlots de *is Îs Australes* Fr. Polynesia *see* **Marotiri**
214 C5 **Bassacutena** *Sardegna* Italy
214 C5 **Bassacutena** *r.* Italy
220 C5 **Bassae** *tourist site* Greece
247 H5 **Bassano** *Alta* Can.
213 L4 **Bassano del Grappa** Italy
214 I3 **Bassano Romano** Italy
229 F4 **Bassar** Togo
289 G6 **Bassas da India** *rf* Indian Ocean
136 C6 **Bassas de Pedro Padua Bank** *sea feature* India
228 D4 **Bassawa** Côte d'Ivoire
212 C1 **Bassecourt** Switz.
180 I7 **Basse-Goulaine** France
118 B6 **Bassein** Myanmar
118 B6 **Bassein** *r.* Myanmar
230 D3 **Basse-Kotto** *pref.* C.A.R.
181 K4 **Basse-Normandie** *admin. reg.* France
171 K4 **Bassenthwaite Lake** *England* U.K.
271 □[3] **Basse-Pointe** Martinique
Basses-Alpes *dept* France *see* **Alpes-de-Haute-Provence**
228 B3 **Basse Santa Su** Gambia
Basses-Pyrénées *dept* France *see* **Pyrénées-Atlantiques**
271 □[2] **Basse-Terre** Guadeloupe
271 □[2] **Basse-Terre** *i.* Guadeloupe
271 □[2] **Basseterre** St Kitts and Nevis
271 □[7] **Basse Terre** Trin. and Tob.
260 F4 **Bassett** *NE* U.S.A.
256 F12 **Bassett** *VA* U.S.A.
265 V9 **Bassett Peak** *AZ* U.S.A.
257 □Q4 **Bass Harbor** *ME* U.S.A.
215 K4 **Bassiano** Italy
185 G10 **Bassiès, Pic Rouge de** *mt.* France
179 J8 **Bassigny** *reg.* France
228 D3 **Bassikounou** Maur.
229 F4 **Bassila** Benin
173 L3 **Bassingbourn** *Cambridgeshire, England* U.K.
171 P7 **Bassingham** *Lincolnshire, England* U.K.
224 D5 **Basso, Plateau de** Chad
185 E8 **Bassoues** France
168 K10 **Bass Rock** *i. Scotland* U.K.
105 K8 **Bass Strait** *Tas./Vic.* Austr.
190 G5 **Bassum** Ger.
248 B3 **Basswood Lake** *Ont.* Can.
250 C1 **Basswood Lake** *MN* U.S.A.
182 H5 **Bassy** France
164 I5 **Båstad** Sweden
144 F8 **Bastak** Iran
149 Q5 **Basṭām** Iran
144 B3 **Bāstānābād** Iran
215 J2 **Bastardo** Italy
214 C3 **Bastelica** *Corse* France
214 B4 **Bastelicaccia** *Corse* France
185 C8 **Bastennes** France
191 J10 **Bastheim** Ger.
139 I6 **Basti** *Uttar Prad.* India
214 C2 **Bastia** *Corse* France
Bastia *airport Corse* France *see* **Poretta**
215 J1 **Bastia** Italy
256 D11 **Bastian** *VA* U.S.A.
187 I8 **Bastogne** Belgium
192 E2 **Bastorf** Ger.
280 B4 **Bastos** Brazil
261 J9 **Bastrop** *LA* U.S.A.
261 G10 **Bastrop** *TX* U.S.A.
162 P4 **Bastuträsk** Sweden
158 F1 **Bastyn'** Belarus
116 E5 **Basu, Tanjung** *pt* Indon.
230 E4 **Bas-Uele** *prov.* Dem. Rep. Congo
Basuo *Hainan* China *see* **Dongfang**
Basutoland *country* Africa *see* **Lesotho**
161 O8 **Basya** *r.* Belarus
150 A2 **Başyayla** Turkey
210 F4 **Bat** *mt.* Croatia
147 M4 **Bat, Al Khutm and Al Ayn** *tourist site* Oman
229 H6 **Bata** Equat. Guinea
199 H5 **Báta** Hungary
199 L5 **Bata** Romania
114 C4 **Bataan Peninsula** *Luzon* Phil.
270 B2 **Batabanó, Golfo de** *b.* Cuba
114 C2 **Batac** *Luzon* Phil.
266 E4 **Batacosa** Mex.
153 O3 **Batagay** Rus. Fed.
153 O3 **Batagay-Alyta** Rus. Fed.
280 A4 **Bataguassu** Brazil
280 A5 **Bataiporã** Brazil
219 M9 **Batak** Bulg.
117 K7 **Batakan** *Kalimantan* Indon.
138 E4 **Batala** *Punjab* India
278 E3 **Batalha** Brazil
204 C9 **Batalha** Port.
116 F4 **Batam** *i.* Indon.
230 E4 **Batama** Dem. Rep. Congo
153 N3 **Batamay** Rus. Fed.
142 H2 **Batamshinskiy** Kazakh.
Batamshy Kazakh. *see* **Batamshinskiy**
131 M1 **Batan** *Jiangsu* China
114 D1 **Batan** *i.* Phil.
114 E5 **Batan** *i.* Phil.
130 B3 **Batang** *Sichuan* China
117 H8 **Batang** *Jawa* Indon.
230 A5 **Batanga** Gabon
230 C3 **Batangafo** C.A.R.
117 J4 **Batang Ai National Park** Malaysia
114 C5 **Batangas** *Luzon* Phil.
116 F5 **Batanghari** *r.* Indon.
115 G4 **Batangpele** *i. Papua* Indon.
117 I4 **Batangtarang** *Kalimantan* Indon.
116 C4 **Batangtoru** *Sumatera* Indon.
114 D1 **Batan Islands** Phil.
115 G4 **Batanta** *i. Papua* Indon.
199 K5 **Batăr** Romania
199 H5 **Bátaszék** Hungary
280 D4 **Batatais** Brazil
284 E4 **Batavia** Arg.
Batavia *Jawa* Indon. *see* **Jakarta**
275 H3 **Batavia** Suriname
250 F8 **Batavia** *IL* U.S.A.
256 G6 **Batavia** *NY* U.S.A.
256 A9 **Batavia** *OH* U.S.A.
161 P8 **Batayeva** Rus. Fed.
157 G7 **Bataysk** Rus. Fed.
114 C6 **Batbatan** *i.* Phil.
251 J2 **Batchawana** *Ont.* Can.
251 J3 **Batchawana** *r. Ont.* Can.
250 J3 **Batchawana Bay** *Ont.* Can.
248 C4 **Batchawana Mountain** *hill Ont.* Can.
106 C2 **Batchelor** *N.T.* Austr.
119 F8 **Bătdâmbâng** Cambodia
208 F5 **Batea** Spain
116 A2 **Bateemeucica, Gunung** *mt.* Indon.
231 B5 **Batéké, Plateaux** Congo
105 M6 **Batemans Bay** *N.S.W.* Austr.
162 S1 **Båteng** Norway

207 J3 **Baterno** Spain
104 □[1] **Bates, Mount** *hill* Norfolk I.
255 G9 **Batesburg** *SC* U.S.A.
109 F9 **Bates Range** *hills W.A.* Austr.
261 J8 **Batesville** *AR* U.S.A.
261 K8 **Batesville** *MS* U.S.A.
161 N3 **Batetskiy** Rus. Fed.
249 H4 **Bath** *N.B.* Can.
251 R5 **Bath** *Ont.* Can.
270 □ **Bath** Jamaica
271 □[2] **Bath** St Kitts and Nevis
172 H5 **Bath** *Bath and North East Somerset, England* U.K.
250 D9 **Bath** *IL* U.S.A.
257 □P5 **Bath** *ME* U.S.A.
256 H6 **Bath** *NY* U.S.A.
258 E3 **Bath** *PA* U.S.A.
224 C6 **Batha** *pref.* Chad
224 C6 **Batha** *watercourse* Chad
172 H5 **Bath and North East Somerset** *admin. div. England* U.K.
172 H5 **Batheaston** *Bath and North East Somerset, England* U.K.
172 H5 **Bathford** *Bath and North East Somerset, England* U.K.
168 I11 **Bathgate** *West Lothian, Scotland* U.K.
138 E4 **Bathinda** *Punjab* India
186 J4 **Bathmen** Neth.
285 G5 **Bathurst** Arg.
105 L5 **Bathurst** *N.S.W.* Austr.
249 H4 **Bathurst** *N.B.* Can.
Bathurst Gambia *see* **Banjul**
237 K9 **Bathurst** S. Africa
245 P1 **Bathurst, Cape** *N.W.T.* Can.
107 J3 **Bathurst Bay** *Qld* Austr.
242 H3 **Bathurst Inlet** *inlet Nunavut* Can.
242 H3 **Bathurst Inlet (abandoned)** *Nunavut* Can.
106 C1 **Bathurst Island** *N.T.* Austr.
243 I2 **Bathurst Island** *Nunavut* Can.
145 I4 **Bathyz Döwlet Gorugy** *nature res.* Turkm.
232 D2 **Batī** Eth.
229 F4 **Batia** Benin
228 E4 **Batié** Burkina
115 B5 **Batikala, Tanjung** *pt* Indon.
101 □[7] **Batiki** *i.* Fiji
179 K5 **Batilly** France
221 I5 **Batı Menteşe Dağları** *mts* Turkey
146 H1 **Bāṭin, Wādī al** *watercourse* Asia
199 H6 **Batina** Croatia
278 E4 **Batista, Serra da** *hills* Brazil
221 L6 **Batı Toroslar** *mts* Turkey
199 J2 **Batizovce** Slovakia
143 N7 **Batken** Kyrg.
143 N8 **Batken** *admin. div.* Kyrg.
151 H3 **Batlaich** Rus. Fed.
144 E5 **Bāṭlāq-e Gavkhūnī** *marsh* Iran
171 N6 **Batley** *West Yorkshire, England* U.K.
105 L6 **Batlow** *N.S.W.* Austr.
149 J5 **Batman** Turkey
227 G2 **Batna** Alg.
129 L3 **Batnorov** Mongolia
127 L2 **Batō** Japan
218 J6 **Batočina** *Batočina* Serbia
116 □ **Batok, Bukit** Sing.
116 □ **Batok, Bukit** *hill* Sing.
231 E9 **Batoka** Zambia
128 H3 **Bat-Öldziy** Mongolia
119 D11 **Batong, Ko** *i.* Thai.
261 J10 **Baton Rouge** *LA* U.S.A.
199 I4 **Bátonyterenye** Hungary
266 F4 **Batopilas** Mex.
199 H4 **Bátorove Kosihy** Slovakia
197 K5 **Batorz** Pol.
138 E3 **Batote** *Jammu and Kashmir* India
230 B4 **Batouala** Gabon
229 I5 **Batouri** Cameroon
199 H3 **Bátovce** Slovakia
Batrā' *tourist site* Jordan *see* **Petra**
146 C3 **Batrā, Jabal** *mt.* Saudi Arabia
150 D9 **Batrā', Jabal al** *mt.* Jordan
199 L5 **Bătrâna, Vârful** *mt.* Romania
119 H9 **Ba Tri** Vietnam
150 D4 **Batroûn** Lebanon
162 T1 **Båtsfjord** Norway
129 L2 **Batshireet** Mongolia
258 F5 **Batsto** *r. NJ* U.S.A.
128 J2 **Batsümber** *Töv* Mongolia
Battambang Cambodia *see* **Bătdâmbâng**
191 G8 **Battenberg (Eder)** Ger.
212 D1 **Bätterkinden** Switz.
138 E4 **Batti** *Punjab* India
136 G9 **Batticaloa** Sri Lanka
137 M8 **Batti Malv** *i. Andaman & Nicobar Is* India
215 N6 **Battipaglia** Italy
247 I4 **Battle** *r. Alta/Sask.* Can.
173 M6 **Battle** *East Sussex, England* U.K.
106 C3 **Battle Creek** *r. N.T.* Austr.
247 I5 **Battle Creek** *r.* Can./U.S.A.
250 I7 **Battle Creek** *MI* U.S.A.
235 F3 **Battlefields** Zimbabwe
247 I4 **Battleford** *Sask.* Can.
264 P1 **Battle Mountain** *NV* U.S.A.
264 O1 **Battle Mountain** *mt. NV* U.S.A.
199 K5 **Battonya** Hungary
128 G3 **Battsengel** *Arhangay* Mongolia
138 E1 **Battura Glacier** Pak.
232 C3 **Batu** *mt.* Eth.
117 J3 **Batu, Bukit** *mt.* Malaysia
116 C5 **Batu, Pulau-pulau** *is* Indon.
117 M3 **Batu, Tanjung** *pt* Indon.
115 C7 **Batuata** *i.* Indon.
117 K4 **Batuayau, Bukit** *mt.* Indon.
116 G6 **Batubetumbang** Indon.
117 K3 **Batu Bora, Bukit** *mt.* Malaysia
284 B4 **Batuco** Chile
115 B4 **Batudaka** *i.* Indon.
116 D2 **Batu Gajah** Malaysia
115 C4 **Batuhitam, Tanjung** *pt* Indon.
115 C4 **Batui** *Sulawesi* Indon.
114 E9 **Batulaki** *Mindanao* Phil.
117 L6 **Batulicin** *Kalimantan* Indon.
117 K4 **Batulilangmebang, Gunung** *mt.* Indon.
Batum Georgia *see* **Bat'umi**
151 C4 **Bat'umi** Georgia
116 D6 **Batumonga** Indon.
116 E4 **Batu Pahat** Malaysia
116 D2 **Batu Putih, Gunung** *mt.* Malaysia
116 F7 **Baturaja** *Sumatera* Indon.
117 I9 **Baturetno** *Jawa* Indon.
161 P6 **Baturino** Rus. Fed.
159 L2 **Baturyn** Ukr.
116 D5 **Batusangkar** *Sumatera* Indon.
199 H5 **Bátya** Hungary
197 M5 **Batyatychi** Ukr.
157 I5 **Batyrevo** Rus. Fed.
Batys Qazaqstan Oblysy *admin. div.* Kazakh. *see* **Zapadnyy Kazakhstan**
180 C4 **Batz, Île de** *i.* France
180 G7 **Batz-sur-Mer** France
275 H6 **Bau** *r.* Brazil
101 □[7a] **Bau** *i.* Fiji
117 I4 **Bau** *Sarawak* Malaysia
232 B2 **Bau** Sudan
115 C6 **Baubau** *Sulawesi* Indon.
115 E8 **Baucau** East Timor
229 H4 **Bauchi** Nigeria
229 H4 **Bauchi** *state* Nigeria
216 F8 **Baucina** *Sicilia* Italy
180 E6 **Baud** France
260 H1 **Baudette** *MN* U.S.A.
274 B3 **Baudo, Serranía de** *mts* Col.
Baudouinville Dem. Rep. Congo *see* **Moba**
183 I9 **Bauduen** France
212 F2 **Bauen** Switz.
104 □[3] **Bauer Bay** S. Pacific Ocean
232 E3 **Bauet** *well* Eth.
181 K6 **Baugé** France
181 K6 **Baugeois** *reg.* France
182 I5 **Bauges** *mts* France
173 J5 **Baughurst** *Hampshire, England* U.K.
182 B2 **Baugy** France
107 L8 **Bauhinia** *Qld* Austr.
Baukau East Timor *see* **Baucau**
115 B6 **Baula** *Sulawesi* Indon.

194 G3 **Bauland** *reg.* Ger.
249 K3 **Bauld, Cape** *Nfld and Lab.* Can.
180 H6 **Baulon** France
243 J2 **Baumann Fiord** *inlet Nunavut* Can.
182 I2 **Baume-les-Dames** France
194 C2 **Baumholder** Ger.
191 K11 **Baunach** Ger.
191 K11 **Baunach** *r.* Ger.
100 □[6] **Baunani** *Malaita* Solomon Is
138 E3 **Baundal** *Hima. Prad.* India
214 D7 **Baunei** *Sardegna* Italy
169 C8 **Baurtregaum** *hill* Ireland
280 C5 **Bauru** Brazil
280 A3 **Baús** Brazil
191 C10 **Bausendorf** Ger.
147 N4 **Baushar** Oman
160 H5 **Bauska** Latvia
142 D5 **Bautino** Kazakh.
193 J8 **Bautzen** Ger.
143 N6 **Bauyrzhan Momyshuly** Kazakh.
144 E6 **Bavānāt** Iran
182 J2 **Bavans** France
Bavaria *reg.* Ger. *see* **Bayern**
178 G3 **Bavay** France
136 C4 **Bavda** *Mahar.* India
186 G5 **Bavel** Neth.
214 C4 **Bavella, Col de** *pass* France
165 M2 **Båven** *l.* Sweden
212 F4 **Baveno** Italy
236 H9 **Baviaanskloofberge** *mts* S. Africa
182 J1 **Bavilliers** France
266 E2 **Bavispe** Mex.
266 E3 **Bavispe** *r.* Mex.
138 D8 **Bavla** *Gujarat* India
161 W5 **Bavleny** Rus. Fed.
157 K5 **Bavly** Rus. Fed.
198 D2 **Bavorov** Czech Rep.
230 C3 **Bavula** Dem. Rep. Congo
118 B3 **Baw** Myanmar
138 F5 **Bawal** *Haryana* India
117 I6 **Bawal** *i.* Indon.
117 J5 **Bawan** *Kalimantan* Indon.
117 H5 **Bawang, Tanjung** *pt* Indon.
105 K7 **Baw Baw National Park** *Vic.* Austr.
173 O2 **Bawdeswell** *Norfolk, England* U.K.
173 O3 **Bawdsey** *Suffolk, England* U.K.
118 C3 **Bawdwin** Myanmar
117 J7 **Bawean** *i.* Indon.
190 D5 **Bawinkel** Ger.
228 E4 **Bawku** Ghana
118 C5 **Bawlake** Myanmar
170 B5 **Bawnboy** Ireland
130 C4 **Bawolung** *Sichuan* China
171 O7 **Bawtry** *South Yorkshire, England* U.K.
130 D2 **Baxi** *Sichuan* China
Baxian *Chongqing* China *see* **Banan**
Baxian *Hebei* China *see* **Bazhou**
132 J7 **Baxkorgan** *Xinjiang* China
255 F10 **Baxley** *GA* U.S.A.
130 A3 **Baxoi** *Xizang* China
257 □Q2 **Baxter State Park** *ME* U.S.A.
Bay *Xinjiang* China *see* **Baicheng**
232 D4 **Bay** *admin. reg.* Somalia
114 C4 **Bay, Laguna de** *lag. Luzon* Phil.
228 E3 **Bay, Réserve de** *nature res.* Mali
228 E5 **Baya** *r.* Côte d'Ivoire
211 B8 **Bayad** Alg.
270 E3 **Bayamo** Cuba
271 □[1] **Bayamón** Puerto Rico
151 H5 **Bayan** Azer.
122 E5 **Bayan** *Heilong.* China
128 E9 **Bayan** *Qinghai* China
Bayan *Qinghai* China *see* **Hualong**
117 L9 **Bayan** *Lombok* Indon.
129 J3 **Bayan** *Töv* Mongolia
Bayan Mongolia *see* **Bayan-Uul**
Bayan Mongolia *see* **Hashaat**
Bayan Mongolia *see* **Bayan-Adraga**
145 K4 **Bāyan, Band-e** *mts* Afgh.
138 F6 **Bayana** *Rajasthan* India
129 L2 **Bayan-Adraga** *Hentiy* Mongolia
143 P2 **Bayanauyl** Kazakh.
128 F3 **Bayanbulag** *Bayanhongor* Mongolia
Bayanbulag Mongolia *see* **Bayantsagaan**
Bayanbulag Mongolia *see* **Ömnödelger**
132 G3 **Bayanbulak** *Xinjiang* China
132 G5 **Bayanbulak** *Xinjiang* China
128 J2 **Bayanchandmanī** Mongolia
128 H5 **Bayandalay** Mongolia
129 M4 **Bayandelger** Mongolia
129 K3 **Bayandelger** Mongolia
129 M2 **Bayandun** *Dornod* Mongolia
117 H4 **Bayang, Pegunungan** *mts* Indon.
230 C4 **Bayanga** C.A.R.
230 B3 **Bayanga-Didi** C.A.R.
Bayan Gol *Nei Mongol* China *see* **Dengkou**
128 J2 **Bayangol** Mongolia
Bayangol Mongolia *see* **Bugat**
128 H1 **Bayangol** Rus. Fed.
130 A1 **Bayan Har Shan** *mt. Qinghai* China
128 D9 **Bayan Har Shan** *mts* China
128 E9 **Bayan Har Shankou** *pass Qinghai* China
128 G3 **Bayanhongor** Mongolia
128 F4 **Bayanhongor** *prov.* Mongolia
128 I7 **Bayan Hot** *Nei Mongol* China
Bayanhushuu Mongolia *see* **Galuut**
129 J4 **Bayanjargalan** Mongolia
128 E2 **Bayan-Kol** Rus. Fed.
129 K6 **Bayan Kuang** *Nei Mongol* China
128 G4 **Bayanlig** Mongolia
128 I6 **Bayan Mod** *Nei Mongol* China
129 K3 **Bayanmönh** Mongolia
128 I6 **Bayan Nuru** *Nei Mongol* China
128 I3 **Bayannuur** Mongolia
266 □T13 **Bayano, Lago** *l.* Panama
128 A2 **Bayan-Ölgiy** *prov.* Mongolia
128 I3 **Bayan-Öndör** Mongolia
128 I3 **Bayan-Önjüül** Mongolia
129 M3 **Bayan-Ovoo** *Hentiy* Mongolia
128 J5 **Bayan-Ovoo** *Ömnögovī* Mongolia
Bayan-Ovoo Mongolia *see* **Altay**
Bayan-Ovoo Mongolia *see* **Dadal**
129 M6 **Bayan Qagan** *Nei Mongol* China
129 Q4 **Bayan Qagan** *Nei Mongol* China
Bayansayr Mongolia *see* **Baatsagaan**
128 E8 **Bayan Shan** *mt.* China
132 G5 **Bayansumküre** *Xinjiang* China
129 O2 **Bayan Tal** *Nei Mongol* China
128 G4 **Bayanteeg** Mongolia
129 P2 **Bayan Tohoi** *Nei Mongol* China
Bayantöhöm Mongolia *see* **Büren**
128 F4 **Bayantsagaan** *Bayanhongor* Mongolia
129 J3 **Bayantsagaan** Mongolia
129 O4 **Bayan Ul Hot** *Nei Mongol* China
129 K6 **Bayan Us** *Nei Mongol* China
129 M2 **Bayan-Uul** Mongolia
128 D3 **Bayan-Uul** *Govī-Altay* Mongolia
128 A2 **Bayan Uul** *mts* Mongolia
207 N6 **Bayárcal** Spain
260 D5 **Bayard** *NE* U.S.A.
256 F9 **Bayard** *WV* U.S.A.
183 I7 **Bayard, Col** *pass* France
179 J6 **Bayard-sur-Marne** France
Bayasgalant Mongolia *see* **Mönhaan**
221 L4 **Bayat** *Afyon* Turkey
Bayat *Antalya* Turkey *see* **Akçay**
114 D7 **Bayawan** *Negros* Phil.
144 F6 **Bayāẕ** Iran
114 E6 **Baybay** *Leyte* Phil.
255 I8 **Bayboro** *NC* U.S.A.
256 C7 **Bay Bridge** *OH* U.S.A.
249 K4 **Bay Bulls** *Nfld and Lab.* Can.
149 J3 **Bayburt** Turkey
151 B5 **Bayburt** *prov.* Turkey
158 I5 **Baybuzivka** Ukr.
119 H10 **Bay Canh, Hon** *i.* Vietnam
142 E4 **Baychunas** Kazakh.
251 K6 **Bay City** *MI* U.S.A.

261 G11 **Bay City** *TX* U.S.A.
171 K5 **Baycliff** *Cumbria, England* U.K.
146 D3 **Baydā, Jabal al** *hill* Saudi Arabia
152 H3 **Baydaratskaya Guba** Rus. Fed.
232 D4 **Baydhabo** Somalia
Baydrag Mongolia *see* **Dzag**
128 F4 **Baydrag Gol** *r.* Mongolia
249 K3 **Bay du Nord Wilderness** *nature res. Nfld and Lab.* Can.
Baydzhansay Kazakh. *see* **Bayzhansay**
230 D3 **Baye** Dem. Rep. Congo
178 G6 **Baye** France
144 D3 **Bāyeh** Iran
179 I7 **Bayel** France
229 G5 **Bayelsa** *state* Nigeria
195 O5 **Bayerbach** Ger.
195 M4 **Bayerbach bei Ergoldsbach** Ger.
195 O3 **Bayerisch Eisenstein** Ger.
191 I10 **Bayerische Rhön** *park* Ger.
194 G2 **Bayerischer Spessart** *park* Ger.
195 M3 **Bayerischer Wald** *mts* Ger.
195 N3 **Bayerischer Wald** *nat. park* Ger.
195 O4 **Bayerischer Wald, Nationalpark** *nat. park* Ger.
195 N6 **Bayerisch Gmain** Ger.
193 C10 **Bayern** *reg.* Ger.
200 D2 **Bayern** *reg.* Ger.
195 K6 **Bayersoien** Ger.
181 J3 **Bayeux** France
161 O7 **Bayeva** Belarus
143 S1 **Bayevo** Rus. Fed.
251 M6 **Bayfield** *Ont.* Can.
250 D3 **Bayfield** *WI* U.S.A.
142 F3 **Bayganin** Kazakh.
143 L5 **Baygekum** Kazakh.
142 J1 **Baygora** Kazakh.
159 S1 **Baygora** *r.* Rus. Fed.
285 I3 **Baygorria, Lago Artificial de** *resr* Uru.
146 G8 **Bayḩan al Qişab** Yemen
259 G4 **Bay Head** *NJ* U.S.A.
129 O9 **Bayiji** *Jiangsu* China
151 I5 **Bāyimli** Azer.
221 I4 **Bayındır** Turkey
221 J5 **Bayır** Turkey
Bay Islands *is* Hond. *see* **Bahía, Islas de la**
Bayizhen China *see* **Nyingchi**
149 K6 **Bayjī** Iraq
Baykadam Kazakh. *see* **Saudakent**
128 I1 **Baykal, Ozero** *l.* Rus. Fed.
122 F2 **Baykal-Amur Magistral** Rus. Fed.
Baykal Range *mts* Rus. Fed. *see* **Baykal'skiy Khrebet**
128 I1 **Baykal'sk** Rus. Fed.
120 I1 **Baykal'skiy Khrebet** *mts* Rus. Fed.
128 I1 **Baykal'skiy Zapovednik** *nature res.* Rus. Fed.
149 J4 **Baykan** Turkey
156 L5 **Baykibashevo** Rus. Fed.
153 K3 **Baykit** Rus. Fed.
Baykonur Kazakh. *see* **Baykonyr**
142 L4 **Baykonur** *Karagandinskaya Oblast'* Kazakh.
142 J5 **Baykonyr** *Gorod Baykonyr* Kazakh.
142 J5 **Baykozha** Kazakh.
106 G4 **Bayley Point Aboriginal Reserve** *Qld* Austr.
142 H1 **Baymak** Rus. Fed.
255 D10 **Bay Minette** *AL* U.S.A.
147 K4 **Baynūna'h** *reg.* U.A.E.
Bayo Spain *see* **Baio**
102 I2 **Bay of Islands Maritime and Historic Park** *nature res. North I.* N.Z.
102 K4 **Bay of Plenty** *admin. reg. North I.* N.Z.
114 C3 **Bayombong** *Luzon* Phil.
179 L7 **Bayon** France
Bayona *Galicia* Spain *see* **Baiona**
185 B9 **Bayonne** France
259 G3 **Bayonne** *NJ* U.S.A.
114 C6 **Bayo Point** *Panay* Phil.
274 A6 **Bayóvar** Peru
114 B6 **Bay Point** Phil.
251 K6 **Bay Port** *MI* U.S.A.
259 I3 **Bayport** *NY* U.S.A.
Bayqadam Kazakh. *see* **Saudakent**
Bayqongyr Kazakh. *see* **Baykonyr**
159 N4 **Bayrak** Ukr.
151 E5 **Bayraktutan** Turkey
145 J3 **Bayramaly** Turkm.
221 H3 **Bayramiç** Turkey
195 L2 **Bayreuth** Ger.
258 C7 **Bay Ridge** *MD* U.S.A.
195 M6 **Bayrischzell** Ger.
Bayrūt Lebanon *see* **Beirut**
248 E4 **Bays, Lake of** *Ont.* Can.
261 K10 **Bay St Louis** *MS* U.S.A.
146 F7 **Baysh** *watercourse* Saudi Arabia
Bayshonas Kazakh. *see* **Baychunas**
259 I3 **Bay Shore** *NY* U.S.A.
258 C6 **Bayside Beach** *MD* U.S.A.
261 K10 **Bay Springs** *MS* U.S.A.
172 G2 **Bayston Hill** *Shropshire, England* U.K.
Baysun Uzbek. *see* **Boysun**
143 L8 **Baysuntau, Gory** *mts* Uzbek.
146 F8 **Bayt al Faqīh** Yemen
128 B4 **Baytik Shan** *mts* China
Bayt Lahm West Bank *see* **Bethlehem**
261 H11 **Baytown** *TX* U.S.A.
115 C5 **Bayu** *Sulawesi* Indon.
205 O5 **Bayubas de Abajo** Spain
116 E5 **Bayunglincir** *Sumatera* Indon.
102 K6 **Bay View** *North I.* N.Z.
259 G5 **Bayville** *NJ* U.S.A.
259 H3 **Bayville** *NY* U.S.A.
224 B2 **Bayy al Kabīr, Wādī** *watercourse* Libya
Bayyrqum Kazakh. *see* **Bairkum**
143 M6 **Bayzhansay** Kazakh.
207 N5 **Baza** Spain
207 N5 **Baza** *r.* Spain
207 N6 **Baza, Sierra de** *mts* Spain
198 F5 **Bázakerettye** Hungary
158 F4 **Bazaliya** Ukr.
178 H5 **Bazancourt** France
143 T3 **Bazar** *watercourse* Kazakh.
158 I2 **Bazar** Ukr.
145 M4 **Bāzārak** Afgh.
142 D3 **Bazarchulan** Kazakh.
151 I4 **Bazardyuzyu, Gora** *mt.* Azer./Rus. Fed.
144 C3 **Bāzār-e Māsāl** Iran
149 L4 **Bāzārgān** Iran
143 M8 **Bazarkhanym, Gora** *mt.* Uzbek.
143 O7 **Bazar-Korgon** Kyrg.
Bazar Kurgan Kyrg. *see* **Bazar-Korgon**
142 B1 **Bazarnyy Karabulak** Rus. Fed.
157 I5 **Bazarnyy Syzgan** Rus. Fed.
Bazarshulan Kazakh. *see* **Bazarchulan**
142 D3 **Bazartobe** Kazakh.
235 G4 **Bazaruto, Ilha do** *i.* Moz.
185 D7 **Bazas** France
159 N6 **Bazavluk** *r.* Ukr.
145 K8 **Bazdar** Pak.
179 I4 **Bazeilles** France
185 E9 **Bazet** France
151 G1 **Bazhigan** Rus. Fed.
130 F3 **Bazhong** *Sichuan* China
129 O7 **Bazhou** *Hebei* China
Bazhou *Sichuan* China *see* **Bazhong**
185 H9 **Baziège** France
185 E9 **Bazillac** France
248 F4 **Bazin** *r. Que.* Can.
228 C4 **Baziwehn** Liberia
144 I8 **Bazmān** Iran
144 I7 **Bazmān, Kūh-e** *mt.* Iran
182 D2 **Bazoches** France
181 K4 **Bazoches-au-Houlme** France
178 D7 **Bazoches-les-Gallerandes** France
181 L4 **Bazoches-sur-Hoëne** France
144 D6 **Bāzoft, Āb-e** *r.* Iran
182 D2 **Bazois** *reg.* France
181 J5 **Bazougers** France
181 J6 **Bazouges** France
180 H5 **Bazouges-la-Pérouse** France

208 C1 **Baztán, Valle del** val. France/Spain
150 E4 **Bcharré** Lebanon
Bé, Nossi i. Madag. see **Bé, Nosy**
235 □K2 **Bé, Nosy** i. Madag.
119 H9 **Be, Sông** r. Vietnam
260 D2 **Beach** ND U.S.A.
251 R4 **Beachburg** Ont. Can.
256 D8 **Beach City** OH U.S.A.
259 G3 **Beach Glen** NJ U.S.A.
259 G5 **Beach Haven** NJ U.S.A.
259 G5 **Beach Haven Terrace** NJ U.S.A.
258 E1 **Beach Lake** PA U.S.A.
104 H7 **Beachport** S.A. Austr.
259 G5 **Beachwood** NJ U.S.A.
173 M6 **Beachy Head** England U.K.
109 D11 **Beacon** W.A. Austr.
257 L7 **Beacon** NY U.S.A.
237 L8 **Beacon Bay** S. Africa
259 I2 **Beacon Falls** CT U.S.A.
105 K9 **Beaconsfield** Tas. Austr.
173 K4 **Beaconsfield** Buckinghamshire, England U.K.
171 N2 **Beadnell** Northumberland, England U.K.
171 N2 **Beadnell Bay** England U.K.
170 B3 **Beagh, Lough** l. Ireland
283 C9 **Beagle, Canal** sea chan. Arg.
108 G3 **Beagle Bank** rf W.A. Austr.
108 G4 **Beagle Bay** W.A. Austr.
108 G4 **Beagle Bay Aboriginal Reserve** W.A. Austr.
106 B2 **Beagle Gulf** N.T. Austr.
109 C10 **Beagle Island** W.A. Austr.
235 □K2 **Bealanana** Madag.
Béal an Átha Ireland see **Ballina**
169 F3 **Béal an Átha Móir** Ireland
169 C4 **Béal an Mhuirthead** Ireland
169 D9 **Béal Átha an Ghaorthaidh** Ireland
Béal Átha na Sluaighe Ireland see **Ballinasloe**
169 C4 **Béal Deirg** Ireland
169 E9 **Bealnablath** Ireland
261 E9 **Beals Creek** r. TX U.S.A.
172 G6 **Beaminster** Dorset, England U.K.
235 □J5 **Beampingaratra** mts Madag.
205 Q8 **Beamud** Spain
235 □K2 **Beandrarezona** Madag.
262 H6 **Bear** r. ID U.S.A.
169 C9 **Beara** reg. Ireland
Bearalváhki Norway see **Berlevåg**
258 D2 **Bear Creek** PA U.S.A.
261 E7 **Bear Creek** r. KS U.S.A.
248 C3 **Beardmore** Ont. Can.
287 L1 **Beardmore Glacier** Antarctica
260 J5 **Beardstown** IL U.S.A.
Bear Island i. Arctic Ocean see **Bjørnøya**
251 N3 **Bear Island** Ont. Can.
248 D2 **Bear Island** i. Nunavut Can.
204 D4 **Beariz** Spain
247 L4 **Bear Lake** l. Man. Can.
250 H5 **Bear Lake** MI U.S.A.
262 I5 **Bear Lake** l. ID U.S.A.
138 G7 **Bearma** r. Madh. Prad. India
260 D4 **Bear Mountain** SD U.S.A.
185 C9 **Béarn** reg. France
169 D6 **Bearna** Ireland
Bearnaraigh i. Scotland U.K. see **Berneray**
Bearnaraigh i. Western Isles, Scotland U.K. see **Berneray**
262 J2 **Bear Paw Mountain** MT U.S.A.
262 J2 **Bearpaw Mountains** MT U.S.A.
286 Q2 **Bear Peninsula** Antarctica
168 H11 **Bearsden** East Dunbartonshire, Scotland U.K.
247 N4 **Bearskin Lake** Ont. Can.
173 N5 **Bearsted** Kent, England U.K.
138 E4 **Beas** r. India
206 F6 **Beas** Spain
208 A1 **Beasain** Spain
207 M6 **Beas de Granada** Spain
207 N4 **Beas de Segura** Spain
270 H5 **Beata, Cabo** c. Dom. Rep.
270 H5 **Beata, Isla** i. Dom. Rep.
260 G5 **Beatrice** NE U.S.A.
235 F3 **Beatrice** Zimbabwe
106 F3 **Beatrice, Cape** N.T. Austr.
168 J12 **Beattock** Dumfries and Galloway, Scotland U.K.
246 F3 **Beatton** r. B.C. Can.
264 P5 **Beatty** NV U.S.A.
248 E3 **Beattyville** Que. Can.
256 B11 **Beattyville** KY U.S.A.
239 □1b **Beau Bassin** Mauritius
183 F9 **Beaucaire** France
178 C4 **Beaucamps-le-Vieux** France
178 C7 **Beauce** reg. France
183 F7 **Beauchastel** France
251 P3 **Beauchêne, Lac** l. Que. Can.
283 F9 **Beauchene Island** Falkland Is
182 J2 **Beaucourt** France
181 J7 **Beaucouzé** France
185 E9 **Beaudéan** France
107 N9 **Beaudesert** Qld Austr.
Beauduc, Golfe de b. France see **Stes Maries, Golfe des**
181 L5 **Beaufay** France
105 I7 **Beaufort** Vic. Austr.
182 G3 **Beaufort** Franche-Comté France
182 J5 **Beaufort** Rhône-Alpes France
117 K2 **Beaufort** Sabah Malaysia
169 C8 **Beaufort** Ireland
255 I8 **Beaufort** NC U.S.A.
255 G9 **Beaufort** SC U.S.A.
Beaufort Castle tourist site Lebanon see **Shaqīf, Qal'at ash**
184 D1 **Beaufort-en-Vallée** France
182 J5 **Beaufortin** mts France
Beaufort Island H.K. China see **Lo Chau**
245 L1 **Beaufort Lagoon** AK U.S.A.
242 F2 **Beaufort Sea** Can./U.S.A.
236 G8 **Beaufort West** S. Africa
178 C8 **Beaugency** France
257 L3 **Beauharnois** Que. Can.
183 I8 **Beaujeu** Provence-Alpes-Côte d'Azur France
182 F4 **Beaujeu** Rhône-Alpes France
182 E4 **Beaujolais, Monts du** hills France
183 E9 **Beaulieu** France
181 N7 **Beaulieu-lès-Loches** France
184 H6 **Beaulieu-sur-Dordogne** France
182 B1 **Beaulieu-sur-Loire** France
182 D3 **Beaulon** France
168 H8 **Beauly** Highland, Scotland U.K.
168 H8 **Beauly** r. Scotland U.K.
168 H8 **Beauly Firth** est. Scotland U.K.
185 E8 **Beaumarchés** France
172 D1 **Beaumaris** Isle of Anglesey, Wales U.K.
167 E5 **Beaumaris Castle** tourist site Wales U.K.
183 G8 **Beaumes-de-Venise** France
181 M3 **Beaumesnil** France
178 E3 **Beaumetz-lès-Loges** France
187 F8 **Beaumont** Belgium
185 F6 **Beaumont** Aquitaine France
182 C5 **Beaumont** Auvergne France
180 H2 **Beaumont** Basse-Normandie France
181 L8 **Beaumont** Poitou-Charentes France
103 D12 **Beaumont** South I. N.Z.
264 P8 **Beaumont** CA U.S.A.
261 K10 **Beaumont** MS U.S.A.
258 D2 **Beaumont** PA U.S.A.
261 H10 **Beaumont** TX U.S.A.
185 F8 **Beaumont-de-Lomagne** France
183 H9 **Beaumont-de-Pertuis** France
179 J4 **Beaumont-en-Argonne** France
181 L7 **Beaumont-en-Véron** France
181 M6 **Beaumont-la-Ronce** France
181 M3 **Beaumont-le-Roger** France
181 M5 **Beaumont-les-Autels** France
183 F7 **Beaumont-lès-Valence** France
178 D5 **Beaumont-sur-Oise** France
181 L5 **Beaumont-sur-Sarthe** France
182 F2 **Beaune** France
178 D7 **Beaune-La Rolande** France
181 J7 **Beaupréau** France
178 D3 **Beauquesne** France
187 G8 **Beauraing** Belgium
182 K5 **Beauregard, Lago di** l. Italy
183 G6 **Beaurepaire** France
182 G3 **Beaurepaire-en-Bresse** France
183 H7 **Beaurières** France
247 L5 **Beauséjour** Man. Can.
179 J6 **Beausite** France
183 K9 **Beausoleil** France
100 □5 **Beautemps Beaupré** atoll Îles Loyauté New Caledonia
178 F4 **Beautor** France
178 D5 **Beauvais** France
247 J4 **Beauval** Sask. Can.
178 D3 **Beauval** France
239 □2b **Beau Vallon, Baie** b. Mahé Seychelles
183 J8 **Beauvezer** France
185 F7 **Beauville** France
180 G8 **Beauvoir-sur-Mer** France
184 D3 **Beauvoir-sur-Niort** France
183 E9 **Beauvoisin** France
183 E6 **Beauzac** France
185 G8 **Beauzelle** France
247 J4 **Beaver** r. Alta/Sask. Can.
248 C2 **Beaver** r. Ont. Can.
245 N3 **Beaver** r. Y.T. Can.
246 E3 **Beaver** r. Y.T. Can.
245 K2 **Beaver** AK U.S.A.
261 E7 **Beaver** OK U.S.A.
265 T3 **Beaver** UT U.S.A.
261 E7 **Beaver** r. OK U.S.A.
265 T2 **Beaver** r. UT U.S.A.
260 F5 **Beaver City** NE U.S.A.
245 L3 **Beaver Creek** Y.T. Can.
245 K2 **Beaver Creek** r. AK U.S.A.
261 I7 **Beaver Creek** r. MO U.S.A.
262 K2 **Beaver Creek** r. MT U.S.A.
260 E2 **Beaver Creek** r. ND U.S.A.
260 F5 **Beaver Creek** r. NE U.S.A.
254 D7 **Beaver Dam** KY U.S.A.
250 F6 **Beaver Dam** WI U.S.A.
250 F6 **Beaver Dam Lake** WI U.S.A.
256 E8 **Beaver Falls** PA U.S.A.
287 D2 **Beaver Glacier** Antarctica
262 H4 **Beaverhead** r. MT U.S.A.
262 H4 **Beaverhead Mountains** MT U.S.A.
247 H4 **Beaverhill Lake** Alta Can.
247 M4 **Beaver Hill Lake** Man. Can.
247 J2 **Beaverhill Lake** N.W.T. Can.
250 I4 **Beaver Island** MI U.S.A.
261 I7 **Beaver Lake** resr AR U.S.A.
246 G4 **Beaverlodge** Alta Can.
258 D3 **Beaver Meadows** PA U.S.A.
244 H3 **Beaver Mountains** AK U.S.A.
256 F8 **Beaver Run Reservoir** PA U.S.A.
258 A3 **Beaver Springs** PA U.S.A.
248 E4 **Beaverton** Ont. Can.
250 J6 **Beaverton** MI U.S.A.
262 C4 **Beaverton** OR U.S.A.
258 A3 **Beavertown** PA U.S.A.
138 E6 **Beawar** Rajasthan India
284 D3 **Beazley** Arg.
199 J5 **Beba Veche** Romania
284 D3 **Bebedero, Salina del** salt pan Arg.
230 C2 **Bébédjia** Chad
280 C4 **Bebedouro** Brazil
278 F3 **Beberibe** Brazil
193 D6 **Bebertal** Ger.
171 K7 **Bebington** Merseyside, England U.K.
230 C2 **Béboto** Chad
191 I9 **Bebra** Ger.
130 A3 **Bêca** Qinghai China
209 K8 **Beca, Punta** pt Spain
182 J5 **Becca du Lac** mt. France
173 P3 **Beccles** Suffolk, England U.K.
213 K4 **Becco di Filadonna** mt. Italy
204 I8 **Becedas** Spain
208 F6 **Beceite** Spain
218 I5 **Bečej** Vojvodina Serbia
204 F3 **Becerreá** Spain
207 J6 **Becerrero** hill Spain
205 K4 **Becerril de Campos** Spain
266 □R10 **Becerro, Cayos** is Hond.
226 E3 **Béchar** Alg.
244 H4 **Becharof Lake** AK U.S.A.
244 H4 **Becharof National Wildlife Refuge** nature res. AK U.S.A.
194 D2 **Becherbach** Ger.
180 H5 **Bécherel** France
244 G5 **Bechevin Bay** AK U.S.A.
156 G4 **Bechevinka** Rus. Fed.
195 J3 **Bechhofen** Bayern Ger.
194 C3 **Bechhofen** Rheinland-Pfalz Ger.
193 J10 **Bechlín** Czech Rep.
258 D4 **Bechtelsville** PA U.S.A.
194 E2 **Bechtheim** Ger.
Bechuanaland country Africa see **Botswana**
198 D2 **Bechyně** Czech Rep.
199 K6 **Becicherecu Mic** Romania
205 J4 **Becilla de Valderaduey** Spain
221 I5 **Beçin** Turkey
190 I4 **Beckdorf** Ger.
191 H6 **Beckedorf** Ger.
190 G5 **Beckeln** Ger.
286 T1 **Becker, Mount** Antarctica
194 B3 **Beckingen** Ger.
171 P7 **Beckingham** Nottinghamshire, England U.K.
256 D11 **Beckley** WV U.S.A.
199 G3 **Beckov** Slovakia
103 D11 **Becks** South I. N.Z.
191 F7 **Beckum** Ger.
265 R2 **Becky Peak** NV U.S.A.
219 M3 **Beclean** Romania
115 D8 **Beco** East Timor
181 J7 **Bécon-les-Granits** France
193 I10 **Bečov** Czech Rep.
198 B1 **Bečov nad Teplou** Czech Rep.
198 F5 **Becsehely** Hungary
198 F5 **Becsvölgye** Hungary
199 G2 **Bečva** r. Czech Rep.
232 D2 **Beda Hāyk'** l. Eth.
171 N5 **Bedale** North Yorkshire, England U.K.
230 C2 **Bédan** Chad
183 C9 **Bédarieux** France
183 F8 **Bédarrides** France
191 C9 **Bedburg** Ger.
191 B7 **Bedburg-Hau** Ger.
172 F4 **Beddau** Rhondda Cynon Taff, Wales U.K.
172 D1 **Beddgelert** Gwynedd, Wales U.K.
173 M6 **Beddingham** East Sussex, England U.K.
257 □Q4 **Beddington** ME U.S.A.
Bedeau Alg. see **Râs el Ma**
180 H5 **Bédée** France
201 M7 **Bedekovčina** Croatia
Bedel', Pereval pass China/Kyrg. see **Bedel Pass**
232 C2 **Bedelē** Eth.
132 D6 **Bedel Pass** China/Kyrg.
232 D2 **Bedēsa** Eth.
156 L5 **Bedeyeva Polyana** Rus. Fed.
249 I4 **Bedford** N.S. Can.
257 M3 **Bedford** Que. Can.
237 K8 **Bedford** Eastern Cape S. Africa
237 O4 **Bedford** KwaZulu-Natal S. Africa
173 L3 **Bedford** Bedfordshire, England U.K.
173 K3 **Bedford** admin. div. England U.K.
260 H5 **Bedford** IA U.S.A.
254 D6 **Bedford** IN U.S.A.
254 E6 **Bedford** KY U.S.A.
259 H2 **Bedford** NY U.S.A.
256 G8 **Bedford** PA U.S.A.
256 F11 **Bedford** VA U.S.A.
107 J3 **Bedford, Cape** Qld Austr.
108 I4 **Bedford Downs** W.A. Austr.
256 D7 **Bedford Heights** OH U.S.A.
259 H2 **Bedford Hills** NY U.S.A.
173 L3 **Bedford Level (Middle Level)** lowland England U.K.
173 L2 **Bedford Level (North Level)** lowland England U.K.
173 M3 **Bedford Level (South Level)** lowland England U.K.
271 □6 **Bedford Point** Grenada
105 K5 **Bedgerebong** N.S.W. Austr.
138 C8 **Bedi** Gujarat India
151 F4 **Bediani** Georgia
116 G6 **Bedinggong** Indon.
197 H4 **Będków** Pol.
138 D7 **Bedla** Rajasthan India
171 N3 **Bedlington** Northumberland, England U.K.
197 H3 **Bedlno** Pol.
207 M5 **Bedmar** Spain
201 M7 **Bednja** Croatia
210 F2 **Bednja** r. Croatia
183 G8 **Bédoin** France
116 □ **Bedok** Sing.
116 □ **Bedok, Sungai** r. Sing.
116 □ **Bedok Jetty** Sing.
116 □ **Bedok Reservoir** Sing.
213 K3 **Bedollo** Italy
212 H6 **Bedonia** Italy
229 I3 **Bedouaram** well Niger
106 G8 **Bedourie** Qld Austr.
185 C9 **Bedous** France
265 X3 **Bedrock** CO U.S.A.
185 H6 **Béduer** France
186 K2 **Bedum** Neth.
172 F4 **Bedwas** Caerphilly, Wales U.K.
173 J3 **Bedworth** Warwickshire, England U.K.
197 H5 **Będzin** Pol.
196 D1 **Będzino** Pol.
168 B8 **Bee, Loch** l. Scotland U.K.
107 J9 **Beechal Creek** watercourse Qld Austr.
250 G8 **Beecher** IL U.S.A.
257 N3 **Beecher Falls** VT U.S.A.
256 C10 **Beech Fork Lake** WV U.S.A.
105 K7 **Beechworth** Vic. Austr.
247 J5 **Beechy** Sask. Can.
190 J5 **Beedenbostel** Ger.
171 Q6 **Beeford** East Riding of Yorkshire, England U.K.
186 I5 **Beek** Gelderland Neth.
186 I5 **Beek** Noord-Brabant Neth.
186 I4 **Beekbergen** Neth.
109 C10 **Beekeepers Nature Reserve** W.A. Austr.
193 G6 **Beelitz** Ger.
258 F2 **Beemerville** NJ U.S.A.
193 D6 **Beendorf** Ger.
107 N9 **Beenleigh** Qld Austr.
192 H4 **Beenz** Ger.
232 E2 **Beer** Somalia
172 F6 **Beer** Devon, England U.K.
194 F2 **Beerfelden** Ger.
109 D10 **Beeringgnurding, Mount** hill W.A. Austr.
150 D8 **Be'ér Menuḥa** Israel
187 D6 **Beernem** Belgium
150 C9 **Be'ér Ora** Israel
186 I5 **Beers** Neth.
187 G6 **Beerse** Belgium
187 F7 **Beersel** Belgium
Beersheba Israel see **Be'ér Sheva'**
150 C7 **Be'ér Sheva'** Israel
150 C7 **Be'ér Sheva'** watercourse Israel
187 C6 **Beerst** Belgium
186 L2 **Beerta** Neth.
236 H9 **Beervlei Dam** S. Africa
193 E7 **Beesenstedt** Ger.
193 J6 **Beeskow** Ger.
237 L1 **Beestekraal** S. Africa
191 E6 **Beesten** Ger.
173 J2 **Beeston** Nottinghamshire, England U.K.
106 D4 **Beetaloo** N.T. Austr.
286 T2 **Beethoven Peninsula** Antarctica
173 N2 **Beetley** Norfolk, England U.K.
186 J2 **Beetsterzwaag** Neth.
192 D5 **Beetzendorf** Ger.
193 G6 **Beetzsee** l. Ger.
261 G11 **Beeville** TX U.S.A.
230 D4 **Befale** Dem. Rep. Congo
235 □I4 **Befandriana Atsimo** Madag.
235 □K2 **Befandriana Avaratra** Madag.
235 □J4 **Befasy** Madag.
230 D4 **Befori** Dem. Rep. Congo
235 □J4 **Befotaka** Fianarantsoa Madag.
235 □K2 **Befotaka** Mahajanga Madag.
169 J3 **Beg, Lough** l. Northern Ireland U.K.
105 L7 **Bega** N.S.W. Austr.
115 D5 **Bega** Maluku Indon.
219 J5 **Bega** r. Romania
185 C8 **Bégaar** France
184 C5 **Bégadan** France
139 M8 **Begamganj** Bangl.
180 E4 **Bégard** France
145 M7 **Begari** r. Pak.
199 K5 **Begécsivíztároló** resr Hungary
271 □2 **Beggars Point** Antigua and Barbuda
Begicheva, Ostrov i. Rus. Fed. see **Bol'shoy Begichev, Ostrov**
207 L5 **Begíjar** Spain
187 G6 **Begijnendijk** Belgium
185 C6 **Bègles** France
180 D6 **Beg-Meil** France
164 G1 **Begna** r. Norway
204 E2 **Begonte** Spain
228 E5 **Begoro** Ghana
Begovat Uzbek. see **Bekobod**
138 E7 **Begun** Rajasthan India
208 L4 **Begur** Spain
208 L4 **Begur, Cap de** c. Spain
139 K7 **Begusarai** Bihar India
144 H5 **Behābād** Iran
144 F6 **Behābād** Iran
275 I3 **Béhague, Pointe** pt Fr. Guiana
235 □J5 **Behara** Madag.
144 D6 **Behbehān** Iran
246 G2 **Behchokô** N.W.T. Can.
133 J8 **Behleg** Qinghai China
190 K3 **Behlendorf** Ger.
246 D4 **Behm Canal** sea chan. AK U.S.A.
221 H3 **Behramkale** Turkey
286 T2 **Behrendt Mountains** Antarctica
179 M5 **Behren-lès-Forbach** France
192 G2 **Behren-Lübchin** Ger.
191 K8 **Behringen** Ger.
144 E7 **Behrūsī** Iran
144 E3 **Behshahr** Iran
145 L4 **Behsūd** Afgh.
237 I8 **Behulpsaam** S. Africa
122 E4 **Bei'an** Heilong. China
Bei'ao Zhejiang China see **Dongtou**
130 F2 **Beiba** Shaanxi China
130 F4 **Beibei** Chongqing China
130 E3 **Beichuan** Sichuan China
Beida Libya see **Al Bayḍā'**
128 F7 **Beida He** r. Gansu China
128 G7 **Beida Shan** mts Nei Mongol China
193 G9 **Beierfeld** Ger.
Beigang Taiwan see **Peikang**
171 O7 **Beighton** South Yorkshire, England U.K.
232 B2 **Beigi** Eth.
212 F7 **Beigua, Monte** mt. Italy
130 G8 **Beihai** Guangxi China
133 L8 **Bei Hulsan Hu** salt l. Qinghai China
131 I7 **Bei Jiang** r. China
129 O7 **Beijing** Beijing China
129 O6 **Beijing** mun. China
186 K3 **Beilen** Neth.
130 H7 **Beiliu** Guangxi China
195 K3 **Beilngries** Ger.
193 H7 **Beilrode** Ger.
194 G3 **Beilstein** Ger.
133 K9 **Beilu He** r. Qinghai China
128 C9 **Beiluheyan** Qinghai China
194 H5 **Beimerstetten** Ger.
230 B2 **Béinamar** Chad
212 D5 **Beinasco** Italy
178 H5 **Beine-Nauroy** France
212 D7 **Beinette** Italy
Beining China see **Beizhen**
170 F2 **Beinn an Tuirc** hill Scotland U.K.
168 E8 **Beinn Bhan** hill Scotland U.K.
168 D11 **Beinn Bheigeir** hill Scotland U.K.
170 F1 **Beinn Bhreac** hill Argyll and Bute, Scotland U.K.
168 F10 **Beinn Bhreac** hill Argyll and Bute, Scotland U.K.
168 F11 **Beinn Bhreac** hill Argyll and Bute, Scotland U.K.
168 D8 **Beinn Bhreac** hill Highland, Scotland U.K.
168 G10 **Beinn Bhuidhe** hill Scotland U.K.
168 F10 **Beinn Chapull** hill Scotland U.K.
168 G7 **Beinn Dearg** mt. Highland, Scotland U.K.
168 I9 **Beinn Dearg** mt. Perth and Kinross, Scotland U.K.
168 G9 **Beinn Dorain** mt. Scotland U.K.
166 E3 **Beinn Heasgarnich** mt. Scotland U.K.
168 G10 **Beinn Ime** mt. Scotland U.K.
168 G6 **Beinn Leoid** hill Scotland U.K.
168 C6 **Beinn Mholach** hill Scotland U.K.
168 F10 **Beinn Mhòr** hill Scotland U.K.
168 B8 **Beinn Mhòr** hill Western Isles, Scotland U.K.
168 C7 **Beinn Mhòr** hill Western Isles, Scotland U.K.
Beinn na Faoghla i. Scotland U.K. see **Benbecula**
168 G9 **Beinn na Lap** hill Scotland U.K.
168 E8 **Beinn na Seamraig** hill Scotland U.K.
168 E9 **Beinn Resipol** hill Scotland U.K.
168 E8 **Beinn Sgritheall** hill Scotland U.K.
168 F9 **Beinn Sgulaird** hill Scotland U.K.
168 H7 **Beinn Tharsuinn** hill Scotland U.K.
168 H9 **Beinn Udlamain** mt. Scotland U.K.
212 E1 **Beinwil** Switz.
130 F6 **Beipan Jiang** r. Guizhou China
129 Q6 **Beipiao** Liaoning China
235 G3 **Beira** Moz.
Beira prov. Moz. see **Sofala**
206 E2 **Beirã** Port.
204 E7 **Beira Alta** reg. Port.
204 F9 **Beira Baixa** reg. Port.
204 D8 **Beira Litoral** reg. Port.
205 Q4 **Beire** Spain
131 J2 **Beiru He** r. China
150 D5 **Beirut** Lebanon
246 H5 **Beiseker** Alta Can.
128 F6 **Beishan** Nei Mongol China
128 D6 **Bei Shan** mts China
235 F4 **Beitbridge** Zimbabwe
168 G11 **Beith** North Ayrshire, Scotland U.K.
150 D7 **Beit Jālā** West Bank
162 K5 **Beitstadfjorden** sea chan. Norway
132 H3 **Beitun** Xinjiang China
219 K4 **Beiuș** Romania
122 D4 **Beixing** Heilong. China
Bei Yunhe canal China see **Jinghang Yunhe**
129 Q6 **Beizhen** Liaoning China
278 C2 **Beja** Brazil
206 D4 **Beja** Port.
206 C5 **Beja** admin. dist. Port.
227 H1 **Béja** Tunisia
211 B7 **Béja** admin. div. Tunisia
227 G1 **Bejaïa** Alg.
204 I8 **Béjar** Spain
144 H4 **Bejestān** Iran
145 M7 **Beji** r. Pak.
209 D8 **Bejís** Spain
268 G7 **Bejucos** Mex.
271 I8 **Bejuma** Venez.
229 I6 **Bek** r. Cameroon
229 I5 **Béka** Adamaoua Cameroon
229 I5 **Béka** Est Cameroon
229 I4 **Béka** Nord Cameroon
Bekabad Uzbek. see **Bekobod**
136 D6 **Bekal** Kerala India
235 □J3 **Bekapaika** Madag.
116 G8 **Bekasi** Jawa Indon.
142 J5 **Bekbauly** Kazakh.
142 E4 **Bekbike** Kazakh.
231 E7 **Beke** Dem. Rep. Congo
199 K5 **Békés** Hungary
199 K5 **Békés** county Hungary
199 K5 **Békéscsaba** Hungary
199 J5 **Békéssámson** Hungary
199 J5 **Békésszentandrás** Hungary
156 G3 **Beketovskaya** Rus. Fed.
159 L7 **Bekhtery** Ukr.
221 K4 **Bekilli** Turkey
235 □J5 **Bekily** Madag.
235 □J3 **Bekipay** Madag.
235 □J5 **Bekitro** Madag.
124 W3 **Bekkai** Japan
141 J1 **Bekobod** Uzbek.
235 □J3 **Bekodoka** Madag.
232 C3 **BeK'ojī** Eth.
235 □J3 **Bekopaka** Madag.
235 □I4 **Bekoropoka-Antongo** Madag.
157 H5 **Bekovo** Rus. Fed.
228 E5 **Bekwai** Ghana
228 E5 **Bekyem** Ghana
139 J7 **Bela** Bihar India
138 H7 **Bela** Uttar Prad. India
145 L8 **Bela** Pak.
199 H2 **Belá** Slovakia
145 M7 **Belab** r. Pak.
235 F5 **Bela-Bela** S. Africa
229 I5 **Bélabo** Cameroon
184 G2 **Bélâbre** France
218 J6 **Bela Crkva** Vojvodina Serbia
199 H3 **Beladice** Slovakia
199 H2 **Belá-Dulice** Slovakia
117 J3 **Belaga** Sarawak Malaysia
143 S2 **Bel'agash** Kazakh.
180 F5 **Bel Air** hill France
258 C5 **Bel Air** MD U.S.A.
230 D5 **Belaka** Dem. Rep. Congo
207 I3 **Belalcázar** Spain
198 B2 **Bělá nad Radbuzou** Czech Rep.
115 D3 **Belang** Sulawesi Indon.
115 E4 **Belangbelang** i. Maluku Indon.
219 K7 **Bela Palanka** Bela Palanka Serbia
199 J3 **Bélapátfalva** Hungary
198 D1 **Bělá pod Bezdězem** Czech Rep.
198 G1 **Bělá pod Pradědem** Czech Rep.
136 D3 **Belapur** Mahar. India
157 E5 **Belarus** country Europe
205 Q3 **Belascoáin** Spain
Belasica mts Bulg./Macedonia see **Belasitsa**
219 K9 **Belasitsa** mts Bulg./Macedonia
Belau country N. Pacific Ocean see **Palau**
231 B6 **Bela Vista** Bengo Angola
Bela Vista Huambo Angola see **Katchiungo**
274 E4 **Bela Vista** Amazonas Brazil
277 F5 **Bela Vista** Mato Grosso do Sul Brazil
235 G5 **Bela Vista** Moz.
280 C2 **Bela Vista de Goiás** Brazil
116 C3 **Belawan** Sumatera Indon.
232 C2 **Belaya** mt. Eth.
159 O2 **Belaya** Rus. Fed.
153 S3 **Belaya** r. Rus. Fed.
159 S8 **Belaya** r. Rus. Fed.
159 M1 **Belaya Berezka** Rus. Fed.
157 H7 **Belaya Glina** Rus. Fed.
157 H6 **Belaya Kalitva** Rus. Fed.
156 J4 **Belaya Kholunitsa** Rus. Fed.
117 L5 **Belayan** r. Indon.
117 K4 **Belayan, Gunung** mt. Indon.
161 W5 **Belaya Rechka** Rus. Fed.
Belaya Tserkva Ukr. see **Bila Tserkva**
204 D7 **Belazaima do Chão** Port.
229 G3 **Belbédji** Niger
212 F6 **Belbo** r. Italy
185 H10 **Belcaire** France
258 C6 **Belcamp** MD U.S.A.
169 D5 **Belcarra** Ireland
185 I7 **Belcastel** France
219 P3 **Belcești** Romania
197 H4 **Bełchatów** Pol.
194 D6 **Belchen** mt. Ger.
256 C11 **Belcher** KY U.S.A.
248 E1 **Belcher Islands** Nunavut Can.
145 K4 **Belchiragh** Afgh.
208 D5 **Belchite** Spain
198 C2 **Bělčice** Czech Rep.
148 H4 **Belcik** Turkey
218 I9 **Belčišta** Debarca Macedonia
169 E6 **Belclare** Ireland
251 Q1 **Belcourt** Que. Can.
139 L8 **Beldanga** W. Bengal India
197 J2 **Bełdany, Jezioro** l. Pol.
264 K1 **Belden** CA U.S.A.
Belderg Ireland see **Béal Deirg**
221 J6 **Beldibi** Turkey
250 I6 **Belding** MI U.S.A.
Beleapani rf India see **Cherbaniani Reef**
142 F1 **Belebey** Rus. Fed.
198 G4 **Beled** Hungary
232 E3 **Beledweyne** Somalia
228 C5 **Belefuanai** Liberia
213 Q6 **Belej** Croatia
144 E2 **Belek** Turkm.
228 D3 **Béléko** Mali
229 I5 **Bélèl** Cameroon
229 I4 **Belel** Nigeria
278 C2 **Belém** Brazil
230 B2 **Bélèm** Chad
282 D2 **Belén** Arg.
277 F5 **Belén** Para.
150 A2 **Belen** Antalya Turkey
148 H5 **Belen** Hatay Turkey
285 I2 **Belén** Uru.
263 K9 **Belen** NM U.S.A.
285 I2 **Belén, Cuchilla de** hills Uru.
205 N7 **Beleña, Embalse de** resr Spain
268 E4 **Belén del Refugio** Mex.
219 N7 **Belene** Bulg.
159 P3 **Belenikhino** Rus. Fed.
205 J2 **Beleño** Spain
100 □5 **Belep, Îles** is New Caledonia
204 E3 **Belesar, Encoro de** resr Spain
185 H10 **Bélesta** France
161 T8 **Belev** Rus. Fed.
221 I4 **Belevi** Turkey
198 F5 **Belezna** Hungary
103 G10 **Belfast** South I. N.Z.
237 O1 **Belfast** S. Africa
169 K3 **Belfast** Northern Ireland U.K.
257 □P4 **Belfast** ME U.S.A.
256 G6 **Belfast** NY U.S.A.
170 E4 **Belfast International** airport Northern Ireland U.K.
169 K3 **Belfast Lough** inlet Northern Ireland U.K.
187 J6 **Belfeld** Neth.
260 D2 **Belfield** ND U.S.A.
232 B2 **Bēlfodiyo** Eth.
171 N2 **Belford** Northumberland, England U.K.
182 J1 **Belfort** France
179 M8 **Belfort, Territoire de** dept France
185 H7 **Belfort-du-Quercy** France
215 K1 **Belforte del Chienti** Italy
136 D5 **Belgaum** Karnataka India
183 I10 **Belgentier** France
193 H8 **Belgern** Ger.
193 G8 **Belgershain** Ger.
Belgian Congo country Africa see **Congo, Democratic Republic of the**
Belgicafjella mts Antarctica see **Belgica Mountains**
287 C2 **Belgica Mountains** Antarctica
België country Europe see **Belgium**
212 G5 **Belgioioso** Italy
Belgique country Europe see **Belgium**
187 F7 **Belgium** country Europe
214 C2 **Belgodère** Corse France
157 G6 **Belgorod** Rus. Fed.
Belgorod-Dnestrovskyy Ukr. see **Bilhorod-Dnistrovs'kyy**
Belgorod Oblast admin. div. Rus. Fed. see **Belgorodskaya Oblast'**
157 G6 **Belgorodskaya Oblast'** admin. div. Rus. Fed.
Belgrade Beograd Serbia see **Beograd**
257 □P4 **Belgrade** ME U.S.A.
262 I4 **Belgrade** MT U.S.A.
286 V1 **Belgrano II** research stn Antarctica
103 G8 **Belgrove** South I. N.Z.
185 C7 **Belhade** France
227 G3 **Belhirane** Alg.
178 B6 **Belhomert-Guéhouville** France
213 Q5 **Beli** Croatia
228 B4 **Béli** Guinea-Bissau
208 H4 **Belianes** Spain
201 O7 **Belica** Croatia
216 D8 **Belice** r. Sicilia Italy
206 E6 **Beliche** r. Port.
216 F8 **Belici** r. Sicilia Italy
218 I8 **Beli Drim** r. Albania/Serbia
151 J4 **Belidzhi** Rus. Fed.
Beliliou i. Palau see **Peleliu**
219 O7 **Beli Lom** r. Bulg.
210 G3 **Beli Manastir** Croatia
116 F7 **Belimbing** Sumatera Indon.
119 I14 **Belimbing, Tanjung** pt Indon.
185 C7 **Belin-Béliet** France
205 N8 **Belinchón** Spain
230 B4 **Bélinga** Gabon
256 F9 **Belington** WV U.S.A.
Belingwe Zimbabwe see **Mberengwa**
157 H5 **Belinskiy** Rus. Fed.
219 J5 **Belinț** Romania
116 F5 **Belinyu** Indon.
219 K6 **Beli Timok** r. Serbia
197 N2 **Belitsa** Belarus
219 L9 **Belitsa** Bulg.
159 O2 **Belitsa** Rus. Fed.
117 H6 **Belitung** i. Indon.
199 L5 **Beliu** Romania
231 B6 **Belize** Angola
267 O9 **Belize** Belize
267 O9 **Belize** country Central America
275 H3 **Bélizon** Fr. Guiana
Beljak Austria see **Villach**
219 J6 **Beljanica** mt. Serbia
244 G5 **Belkofski** AK U.S.A.
153 O2 **Bel'kovskiy, Ostrov** i. Novosibirskiye O-va Rus. Fed.
107 M9 **Bell** Qld Austr.
105 L5 **Bell** r. N.S.W. Austr.
248 E3 **Bell** r. Que. Can.
245 M2 **Bell** r. Y.T. Can.
191 D10 **Bell** Ger.
237 L9 **Bell** S. Africa
191 D10 **Bell (Hunsrück)** Ger.
104 D5 **Bell, Point** S.A. Austr.
215 P6 **Bella** Italy
246 D4 **Bella Bella** B.C. Can.
184 G3 **Bellac** France
182 I5 **Bellacha, Mont** mt. France
285 I3 **Bellaco** Uru.
246 E4 **Bella Coola** B.C. Can.
246 E4 **Bella Coola** r. B.C. Can.
169 C4 **Bellacorick** Ireland
276 D2 **Bella Flor** Bol.
169 E5 **Bellaghy** Ireland
169 I3 **Bellaghy** Northern Ireland U.K.
212 G4 **Bellagio** Italy
250 I5 **Bellaire** MI U.S.A.
261 H11 **Bellaire** TX U.S.A.
169 F5 **Bellanagare** Ireland
169 G4 **Bellanaleck** Northern Ireland U.K.
Bellanamore Ireland see **Béal an Átha Móir**
169 F6 **Bellaneeny** Ireland
212 G3 **Bellano** Italy
215 L2 **Bellante** Italy
213 M7 **Bellaria** Italy
136 E5 **Bellary** Karnataka India
105 L3 **Bellata** N.S.W. Austr.
285 I2 **Bella Unión** Uru.
170 B5 **Bellavally Gap** pass Ireland
169 D5 **Bellavary** Ireland
282 F3 **Bella Vista** Corrientes Arg.
283 C8 **Bella Vista** Santa Cruz Arg.
277 E3 **Bella Vista** Bol.
277 F5 **Bella Vista** Para.
274 B6 **Bellavista** Cajamarca Peru
274 C5 **Bellavista** Loreto Peru
214 D8 **Bellavista, Capo** c. Sardegna Italy
276 C5 **Bella Vista, Salar de** salt flat Chile
102 I6 **Bell Block** North I. N.Z.
107 M6 **Bell Cay** rf Qld Austr.
208 G4 **Bellclaire d'Urgell** Spain
256 D10 **Belle** WV U.S.A.
270 G4 **Belle-Anse** Haiti
193 E7 **Belleben** Ger.
183 H6 **Belledonne** mts France
183 H6 **Belledonne, Grand Pic de** mt. France
169 F4 **Belleek** Northern Ireland U.K.
169 J4 **Belleek** Northern Ireland U.K.
179 L7 **Bellefontaine** France
271 □3 **Bellefontaine** Martinique
256 B8 **Bellefontaine** OH U.S.A.
256 H8 **Bellefonte** PA U.S.A.
260 D3 **Belle Fourche** SD U.S.A.
260 D3 **Belle Fourche** r. SD U.S.A.
178 D8 **Bellegarde** Centre France
183 F9 **Bellegarde** Languedoc-Roussillon France
184 I4 **Bellegarde-en-Marche** France
182 H4 **Bellegarde-sur-Valserine** France
255 G12 **Belle Glade** FL U.S.A.
180 E7 **Belle-Île** i. France
249 K3 **Belle Isle** i. Nfld and Lab. Can.
249 J3 **Belle Isle, Strait of** Nfld and Lab. Can.
180 E4 **Belle-Isle-en-Terre** France
181 M5 **Bellême** France
258 F4 **Belle Mead** NJ U.S.A.
265 U6 **Bellemont** AZ U.S.A.
182 C4 **Bellenaves** France
195 I5 **Bellenberg** Ger.
178 B4 **Bellencombre** France
271 □4 **Belleplaine** Barbados
182 C4 **Bellerive-sur-Allier** France
179 M6 **Belles-Forêts** France
248 E4 **Belleterre** Que. Can.
178 F5 **Belleu** France
182 J4 **Bellevaux** France
182 G3 **Bellevesvre** France
248 E4 **Belleville** Ont. Can.
182 F4 **Belleville** France
260 G6 **Belleville** KS U.S.A.
259 G3 **Belleville** NJ U.S.A.
182 B1 **Belleville-sur-Loire** France
179 J5 **Belleville-sur-Meuse** France
180 I8 **Belleville-sur-Vie** France
254 B4 **Bellevue** IA U.S.A.
250 I7 **Bellevue** MI U.S.A.
260 H5 **Bellevue** NE U.S.A.
256 C7 **Bellevue** OH U.S.A.
262 C3 **Bellevue** WA U.S.A.
183 D6 **Bellevue-la-Montagne** France
182 H5 **Belley** France
228 C5 **Belle Yella** Liberia
250 F9 **Bellflower** IL U.S.A.
194 E3 **Bellheim** Ger.
182 J2 **Bellherbe** France
182 H4 **Bellignat** France
Bellin Que. Can. see **Kangirsuk**
105 N4 **Bellingen** N.S.W. Austr.
171 M3 **Bellingham** Northumberland, England U.K.
262 C2 **Bellingham** WA U.S.A.
286 U2 **Bellingshausen** research stn Antarctica
Bellingshausen Island atoll Arch. de la Société Fr. Polynesia see **Motu One**
286 S2 **Bellingshausen Sea** Antarctica
186 L2 **Bellingwolde** Neth.
212 F4 **Bellinzago Novarese** Italy
212 G3 **Bellinzona** Switz.
249 K3 **Bell Island** Nfld and Lab. Can.
245 O5 **Bell Island Hot Springs** AK U.S.A.
215 N6 **Bellizzi** Italy
258 E5 **Bellmawr** NJ U.S.A.
274 C3 **Bello** Col.
205 R7 **Bello** Spain
185 C8 **Bellocq** France
100 □6 **Bellona** i. Solomon Is
181 K4 **Bellou-en-Houlme** France
257 M5 **Bellows Falls** VT U.S.A.
145 M7 **Bellpat** Pak.
208 H4 **Bellpuig** Spain
168 L10 **Bell Rock** i. Scotland U.K.
168 H11 **Bellshill** North Lanarkshire, Scotland U.K.
162 □ **Bellsund** inlet Svalbard
213 M3 **Belluno** Italy
213 M3 **Belluno** prov. Italy
259 G2 **Bellvale** NY U.S.A.
208 I3 **Bellver de Cerdanya** Spain
285 F3 **Bell Ville** Arg.
236 C9 **Bellville** S. Africa
256 C8 **Bellville** OH U.S.A.
261 G11 **Bellville** TX U.S.A.
256 G8 **Bellwood** PA U.S.A.
246 H5 **Belly** r. Alta Can.
191 F6 **Belm** Ger.
259 G4 **Belmar** NJ U.S.A.
199 K5 **Bélmegyer** Hungary
207 I4 **Bélmez** Spain
207 M5 **Bélmez de la Moraleda** Spain
105 M5 **Belmont** N.S.W. Austr.
185 E8 **Belmont** France
236 I5 **Belmont** S. Africa
168 □O1 **Belmont** Shetland, Scotland U.K.
257 N5 **Belmont** NH U.S.A.
256 G6 **Belmont** NY U.S.A.
182 E4 **Belmont-de-la-Loire** France
281 H1 **Belmonte** Brazil
204 F8 **Belmonte** Port.
204 H2 **Belmonte** Asturias Spain
205 O9 **Belmonte** Castilla-La Mancha Spain
215 Q9 **Belmonte Calabro** Italy
215 M4 **Belmonte del Sannio** Italy
215 J3 **Belmonte in Sabina** Italy
216 E7 **Belmonte Mezzagno** Sicilia Italy
183 B9 **Belmont-sur-Rance** France
267 O9 **Belmopan** Belize
107 H5 **Belmore Creek** r. Qld Austr.
Belmullet Ireland see **Béal an Mhuirthead**
235 □J4 **Belo** Madag.
279 E5 **Belo Campo** Brazil
187 E7 **Belœil** Belgium
143 T1 **Beloglazovo** Rus. Fed.
122 F3 **Belogorsk** Rus. Fed.
Belogorsk Ukr. see **Bilohirs'k**
159 T3 **Belogor'ye** Rus. Fed.
219 K7 **Belogradchik** Bulg.
235 □J5 **Beloha** Madag.
274 E5 **Belo Horizonte** Amazonas Brazil
281 F3 **Belo Horizonte** Minas Gerais Brazil
260 F6 **Beloit** KS U.S.A.
250 E7 **Beloit** WI U.S.A.
278 F4 **Belo Jardim** Brazil
Belokamensk Ukr. see **Inkerman**
230 B3 **Béloko** C.A.R.
143 U2 **Belokurikha** Rus. Fed.
239 □1b **Bel Ombre** Mauritius
275 I5 **Belo Monte** Pará Brazil
Belo Monte Piauí Brazil see **Batalha**
156 F2 **Belomorsk** Rus. Fed.
139 M8 **Belonia** Tripura India
161 W7 **Beloomut** Rus. Fed.
281 F3 **Belo Oriente** Brazil
Beloozersk Belarus see **Byelaazyorsk**
161 V6 **Beloozerskiy** Rus. Fed.
115 B5 **Belopa** Sulawesi Indon.
Belopol'ye Ukr. see **Bilopillya**
205 N4 **Belorado** Spain
157 G7 **Belorechensk** Rus. Fed.
Belorechenskaya Rus. Fed. see **Belorechensk**
148 H5 **Belören** Adıyaman Turkey
148 F5 **Belören** Konya Turkey
142 H1 **Beloretsk** Rus. Fed.
Belorussia country Europe see **Belarus**
Belorusskaya S.S.R. country Europe see **Belarus**
219 P7 **Beloslav** Bulg.
Belostok Pol. see **Białystok**
245 P2 **Belot, Lac** l. N.W.T. Can.
151 F3 **Belot'i** Georgia
199 G2 **Bělotín** Czech Rep.
219 K7 **Belotintsi** Bulg.
235 □J3 **Belo Tsiribihina** Madag.
246 B2 **Beloud Post** Y.T. Can.
143 T2 **Belousovka** Kazakh.
161 T6 **Belousovo** Rus. Fed.
281 E4 **Belo Vale** Brazil
160 G9 **Belovezhskaya Pushcha, Natsyyanal'ny Park** Bela
219 M8 **Belovo** Bulg.
122 F3 **Beloyarovo** Rus. Fed.
156 G2 **Beloye** Rus. Fed.
161 U1 **Beloye, Ozero** l. Rus. Fed
162 V3 **Beloye More** Rus. Fed.
156 G2 **Beloye More** sea Rus. Fe
156 K4 **Beloyevo** Rus. Fed.
142 F1 **Belozerka** Rus. Fed.
161 U1 **Belozersk** Rus. Fed.
Belozerskoye Ukr. see **Bi**
212 C2 **Belp** Switz.
194 D8 **Belp** airport Switz.
216 H8 **Belpasso** Sicilia Italy
185 H9 **Belpech** France
171 O7 **Belper** Derbyshire, Englar
256 D9 **Belpre** OH U.S.A.
171 N3 **Belsay** Northumberland, England U.K.
197 I4 **Belsk Duży** Pol.
161 X7 **Bel'skoye** Rus. Fed.
104 G4 **Beltana** S.A. Austr.
104 F3 **Belt Bay** salt flat S.A. Aus
265 P4 **Belted Range** mts NV U.
275 H5 **Belterra** Brazil
128 F1 **Beltes Gol** r. Mongolia
191 D10 **Beltheim** Ger.
201 N6 **Beltinci** Slovenia
199 L4 **Beltiug** Romania
173 P2 **Belton** Norfolk, England
260 H6 **Belton** MO U.S.A.
261 G10 **Belton** TX U.S.A.
142 I6 **Beltov** Uzbek.
169 D5 **Beltra** Mayo Ireland
169 E4 **Beltra** Sligo Ireland
169 D5 **Beltra Lough** l. Ireland
186 K4 **Beltrum** Neth.
Bel'ts' Moldova see **Bălți**
258 B6 **Beltsville** MD U.S.A.
Bel'tsy Moldova see **Bălți**
169 H4 **Belturbet** Ireland
258 D3 **Beltzville Lake** PA U.S.A.
214 B8 **Belu** r. Sardegna Italy
244 J3 **Beluga Lake** AK U.S.A.
134 G2 **Belukha, Gora** mt. Kazakh./Rus. Fed.
136 D6 **Belur** Karnataka India
117 L2 **Beluran** Sabah Malaysia
199 H2 **Beluša** Slovakia
156 I2 **Belush'ye** Rus. Fed.
256 D10 **Belva** WV U.S.A.
214 B4 **Belvédère-Campomoro** France
215 P8 **Belvedere Marittimo** Ital
206 D1 **Belver** Port.
208 F4 **Belver de Cinca** Spain
185 G6 **Belvès** France
185 I9 **Belvèze-du-Razès** France
183 E8 **Belvézet** France
250 F7 **Belvidere** IL U.S.A.
258 E3 **Belvidere** NJ U.S.A.
169 D4 **Belville** Ireland
205 K9 **Belvís de la Jara** Spain
200 B7 **Belviso, Lago** l. Italy
107 K6 **Belyando** r. Qld Austr.
107 K6 **Belyando Crossing** Qld A
142 G2 **Belyayevka** Rus. Fed.
Belyayevka Ukr. see **Bilya**
161 O6 **Belyayevo** Rus. Fed.
106 C2 **Belyuen** N.T. Austr.
161 P6 **Belyy** Rus. Fed.
152 I2 **Belyy, Ostrov** i. Rus. Fed.
132 H1 **Belyy Bom** Rus. Fed.
161 R8 **Belyye Berega** Rus. Fed.
161 U6 **Belyye Stolby** Rus. Fed.
161 U5 **Belyy Gorodok** Rus. Fed.
159 R3 **Belyy Kolodez'** Rus. Fed.
152 J4 **Belyy Yar** Rus. Fed.
180 E6 **Belz** France
158 D3 **Belz** Ukr.
197 L5 **Bełżec** Pol.
193 G6 **Belzig** Ger.
261 J9 **Belzoni** MS U.S.A.
197 K4 **Bełżyce** Pol.
235 □K2 **Bemanevika** Madag.
235 □J3 **Bemaraha, Plateau du M**
231 B6 **Bembe** Angola
229 F4 **Bembèrèkè** Benin
207 I5 **Bembézar** r. Spain
207 I5 **Bembézar, Embalse del** Spain
204 H3 **Bembibre** Castilla y León
204 C2 **Bembibre** Galicia Spain
231 C7 **Bembo** Angola
173 J6 **Bembridge** Isle of Wight, England U.K.
260 H2 **Bemidji** MN U.S.A.
261 K8 **Bemis** TN U.S.A.
186 I5 **Bemmel** Neth.
204 H6 **Bemposta** Bragança Port.
206 C2 **Bemposta** Santarém Port.
171 Q5 **Bempton** East Riding of Y England U.K.
228 D3 **Béna** Burkina
208 F3 **Benabarre** Spain
231 D6 **Bena Dibele** Dem. Rep. C
209 C8 **Benagéber, Embalse de** Spain
117 K5 **Benagin** Kalimantan Indo
209 D8 **Benaguasil** Spain
207 O7 **Benahadux** Spain
207 I7 **Benahavís** Spain
226 D2 **Benahmed** Morocco
168 J7 **Ben Aigan** hill Scotland U
207 I4 **Benajarafe** r. Spain
168 H9 **Ben Alder** mt. Scotland U
105 J7 **Benalla** Vic. Austr.
207 J7 **Benalmádena** Spain
207 M6 **Benalúa de Guadix** Spain
207 L6 **Benalúa de las Villas** Spa
206 H8 **Benalup de Sidonia** Spai
207 K7 **Benamargosa** Spain
207 N5 **Benamaurel** Spain
207 J6 **Benamejí** Spain
226 B5 **Ben 'Amîra** well Maur.
207 K7 **Benamocarra** Spain
207 I7 **Benaocaz** Spain
207 I7 **Benaoján** Spain
Benares Uttar Prad. India **Varanasi**
239 □1b **Benares** Mauritius
227 H1 **Ben Arous** Tunisia
211 B7 **Ben Arous** admin. div. Tur
209 E7 **Benasal** Spain
209 E10 **Benasau** Spain
208 G2 **Benasque** Spain
184 E2 **Benassay** France
183 I10 **Bénat, Cap** c. France
198 D1 **Benátky nad Jizerou** Czec
231 D6 **Bena-Tshadi** Dem. Rep. C
206 B3 **Benavente** Port.
204 I4 **Benavente** Spain
276 D3 **Benavides** Bol.
204 I4 **Benavides de Orbigo** Spa
206 D2 **Benavila** Port.
168 J8 **Ben Avon** mt. Scotland U.
169 J2 **Benbane Head** Northern Ireland U.K.
169 C5 **Benbaun** hill Ireland
168 B8 **Benbecula** i. Scotland U.K
105 M7 **Ben Boyd National Park** N.S.W. Austr.
169 F4 **Benbulben** hill Ireland
169 I4 **Benburb** Northern Ireland
169 C5 **Benbury** hill Ireland
206 E3 **Bencatel** Port.
131 M2 **Bencha** Jiangsu China
Bencheng Hebei China se **Luannan**
168 I10 **Ben Chonzie** hill Scotland
169 C5 **Bencorr** hill Ireland
168 F10 **Ben Cruachan** mt. Scotlar
109 D11 **Bencubbin** W.A. Austr.
262 D4 **Bend** OR U.S.A.
237 L7 **Bendearg** mt. S. Africa
231 C5 **Bendela** Dem. Rep. Cong
244 F2 **Bendeleben, Mount** AK U
244 F2 **Bendeleben Mountains** A
105 M4 **Bendemeer** N.S.W. Austr.
Bender Moldova see **Tigh**
232 F2 **Bender-Bayla** Somalia

Benderville WI U.S.A.
Bendery Moldova see Tighina
Bendestorf Ger.
Bendieuta watercourse S.A. Austr.
Bendigo Vic. Austr.
Bendoc Vic. Austr.
Bendorf Ger.
Bendzin Pol. see Będzin
Bēne Latvia
Bene Moz.
Beneden-Leeuwen Neth.
Benedict, Mount hill Nfld and Lab. Can.
Benedicta ME U.S.A.
Benediktbeuren Ger.
Benediktenwand mt. Ger.
Benedita Port.
Beneditinos Brazil
Benedito Leite Brazil
Benegiles Spain
Beneixama Spain
Bénéjacq France
Benejúzar Spain
Bénéna Mali
Benenden Kent, England U.K.
Benenitra Madag.
Benešov Czech Rep.
Benešov nad Černou Czech Rep.
Benešov nad Ploučnicí Czech Rep.
Bénesse-Maremne France
Benestare Italy
Bénestroff France
Benet France
Benetutti Sardegna Italy
Bene Vagienna Italy
Bénévent-l'Abbaye France
Benevento Italy
Benevento prov. Italy
Beneventum Italy see Benevento
Benezette PA U.S.A.
Benfeld France
Benfer PA U.S.A.
Benfica do Ribatejo Port.
Beng, Nam r. Laos
Benga i. Fiji see Beqa
Benga Malawi
Bengal, Bay of sea Indian Ocean
Bengaluru Karnataka India see Bangalore
Bengamisa Dem. Rep. Congo
Bengbis Cameroon
Bengbu Anhui China
Ben Geary hill Scotland U.K.
Benghajsa, Il-Ponta ta' pt Malta
Benghazi Libya see Banghāzī
Beng He r. China
Benghisa Point Malta see Benghajsa, Il-Ponta ta'
Bengkalis Sumatera Indon.
Bengkalis i. Indon.
Bengkayang Kalimantan Indon.
Bengkulu Sumatera Indon.
Bengkulu prov. Indon.
Bengkung Kalimantan Indon.
Bengo Cuando Cubango Angola
Bengo Uíge Angola
Bengo prov. Angola
Bengoi Seram Indon.
Bengorm hill Ireland
Bengtsfors Sweden
Benguela Angola
Benguela prov. Angola
Ben Guerdane Tunisia
Benguerir Morocco
Benguérua, Ilha i. Moz.
Benha Qalyūbīyah Egypt see Banhā
Ben Hee hill Scotland U.K.
Ben Hiant hill Scotland U.K.
Ben Hope hill Scotland U.K.
Ben Horn hill Scotland U.K.
Beni dept Bol.
Beni r. Bol.
Beni Dem. Rep. Congo
Beni Nepal
Beni Abbès Alg.
Benia de Onís Spain
Beniah Lake N.W.T. Can.
Beniarrés Spain
Beniarrés, Embalse de resr Spain
Beni Boufrah Morocco
Benicarló Spain
Benicasim Spain
Benicia CA U.S.A.
Benidorm Spain
Benidorm, Isolte de i. Spain
Beni Dourso well Niger
Beniel Spain
Benifaió Spain
Benifallet Spain
Benifallim Spain
Benifayo Valencia Spain see Benifaió
Benigánim Spain
Beniguet, Île de i. France
Beni Guil reg. Morocco
Benilloba Spain
Beni Mellal Morocco
Benin country Africa
Benin r. Nigeria
Benin, Bight of g. Africa
Benin City Nigeria
Beni Ounif Alg.
Beni Saf Alg.
Benisheikh Nigeria
Benissa Spain
Benissanet Spain
Beni Suef Banī Suwayf Egypt see Banī Suwayf
Benitachell Spain
Benithora r. India
Bénitiers, Île aux i. Mauritius
Benito r. Equat. Guinea see Mbini
Benito, Islas is Mex.
Benito Juárez Arg.
Benito Juárez Baja California Mex.
Benito Juarez Michoacán Mex.
Benito Juarez San Luis Potosí Mex.
Benito Juárez Tabasco Mex.
Benito Juárez Veracruz Mex.
Benito Juárez Veracruz Mex.
Benito Juárez Zacatecas Mex.
Benito Juárez, Parque Nacional nat. park Mex.
Benito Juárez, Presa resr Mex.
Benito Soliven Luzon Phil.
Benizalón Spain
Benízar Spain
Benjamim Constant Brazil
Benjamin TX U.S.A.
Benjamin, Isla i. Chile
Benjamín Hill Mex.
Benjamin Zorrillo Arg.
Benjina Maluku Indon.
Benkei-misaki pt Japan
Benkelman NE U.S.A.
Benken Switz.
Ben Klibreck hill Scotland U.K.
Benkovac Croatia
Benkovski Bulg.
Ben Lawers mt. Scotland U.K.
Ben Ledi hill Scotland U.K.
Benllech Isle of Anglesey, Wales U.K.
Benlloch Spain
Ben Lomond mt. N.S.W. Austr.
Ben Lomond hill Scotland U.K.
Ben Lomond CA U.S.A.
Ben Lomond National Park Tas. Austr.
Ben Loyal hill Scotland U.K.
Ben Lui mt. Scotland U.K.
Ben Macdhui mt. Lesotho
Ben Macdui mt. Scotland U.K.
Ben Mahidi Alg.
Benmara N.T. Austr.
Ben More mt. South I. N.Z.
Ben More hill Scotland U.K.
Ben More mt. Scotland U.K.
Benmore, Lake South I. N.Z.
Ben More Assynt hill Scotland U.K.
103 E11 Benmore Peak South I. N.Z.
168 F12 Bennan Head Scotland U.K.
193 D7 Benndorf Ger.
186 G4 Bennebroek Neth.
191 K7 Benneckenstein (Harz) Ger.
186 I4 Bennekom Neth.
245 N4 Bennett B.C. Can.
250 C3 Bennett WI U.S.A.
106 C7 Bennett, Lake salt flat N.T. Austr.
153 P2 Bennetta, Ostrov i. Novosibirskiye O-va Rus. Fed.
Bennett Island Novosibirskiye O-va Rus. Fed. see Bennetta, Ostrov
245 N4 Bennett Lake B.C. Can.
169 H7 Bennettsbridge Ireland
238 □2b Bennett's Point St Helena
255 H8 Bennettsville SC U.S.A.
168 F9 Ben Nevis mt. Scotland U.K.
102 J5 Benneydale North I. N.Z.
257 N5 Bennington NH U.S.A.
257 L6 Bennington VT U.S.A.
193 E8 Bennstedt Ger.
193 D8 Bennungen Ger.
180 C6 Bénodet France
180 C6 Benodet, Anse de b. France
103 D11 Ben Ohau Range mts South I. N.Z.
116 □ Benoi Basin dock Sing.
237 M2 Benoni S. Africa
229 I4 Bénoué r. Cameroon
229 I4 Bénoué, Parc National de la nat. park Cameroon
230 C2 Bénoye Chad
204 F8 Benquerença Port.
185 C8 Benquet France
168 J8 Ben Rinnes hill Scotland U.K.
206 B6 Bensafrim Port.
193 F6 Bensdorf Ger.
191 K9 Benshausen Ger.
194 F2 Bensheim Ger.
226 D2 Ben Slimane Morocco
173 J4 Benson Oxfordshire, England U.K.
265 V10 Benson AZ U.S.A.
260 H3 Benson MN U.S.A.
228 C5 Bensonville Liberia
256 D9 Bens Run WV U.S.A.
168 F9 Ben Starav mt. Scotland U.K.
144 H8 Bent Iran
116 D2 Benta Seberang Malaysia
186 K4 Bentelo Neth.
115 B7 Benteng Sulawesi Indon.
118 G5 Ben Thuy Vietnam
228 B4 Benti Guinea
231 B8 Bentiaba Angola
202 E5 Ben Tieb Morocco
106 G4 Bentinck Island Qld Austr.
119 D9 Bentinck Island Myanmar
168 J9 Ben Tirran hill Scotland U.K.
230 F2 Bentiu Sudan
150 D5 Bent Jbaïl Lebanon
246 H4 Bentley Alta Can.
171 O6 Bentley South Yorkshire, England U.K.
256 E8 Bentleyville PA U.S.A.
277 F4 Bento Gomes r. Brazil
257 □R3 Benton N.B. Can.
261 I8 Benton AR U.S.A.
264 N4 Benton CA U.S.A.
260 K6 Benton IL U.S.A.
261 K7 Benton KY U.S.A.
261 I9 Benton LA U.S.A.
261 K7 Benton MO U.S.A.
258 C2 Benton PA U.S.A.
255 E8 Benton TN U.S.A.
Bentong Malaysia see Bentung
250 H7 Benton Harbor MI U.S.A.
261 H7 Bentonville AR U.S.A.
256 B10 Bentonville OH U.S.A.
119 H9 Bên Tre Vietnam
161 O5 Bentsy Rus. Fed.
116 D3 Bentung Malaysia
192 F2 Bentwisch Ger.
192 H3 Bentzin Ger.
115 C6 Benua Sulawesi Indon.
116 G4 Benua i. Indon.
117 J4 Benuamartinus Kalimantan Indon.
229 G5 Benue r. Nigeria
229 H5 Benue state Nigeria
116 E3 Benum, Gunung mt. Malaysia
199 I3 Beňuš Slovakia
168 G10 Ben Vorlich hill Argyll and Bute, Scotland U.K.
168 H10 Ben Vorlich hill Perth and Kinross/Stirling, Scotland U.K.
231 E7 Benwa Zambia
169 C4 Benwee Head Ireland
256 E8 Benwood WV U.S.A.
168 G7 Ben Wyvis mt. Scotland U.K.
129 R6 Benxi Liaoning China
226 E3 Ben Zireg Alg.
207 I9 Benzu Morocco
115 E1 Beo Sulawesi Indon.
218 I6 Beograd Beograd Serbia
138 H7 Beohari Madh. Prad. India
228 D5 Béoumi Côte d'Ivoire
116 E7 Bepagut, Gunung mt. Indon.
125 I13 Beppu Japan
125 I13 Beppu-wan b. Japan
101 □7a Beqa i. Fiji
271 □3 Bequia i. St Vincent
278 D2 Bequimão Brazil
139 L7 Bera Bangl.
116 E3 Bera, Tasik l. Malaysia
285 G3 Berabevú Arg.
138 E7 Berach r. India
208 B1 Bera de Bidasoa Spain
169 H3 Beragh Northern Ireland U.K.
235 □J5 Beraketa Madag.
235 □K2 Beramanja Madag.
218 H8 Berane Berane Montenegro
205 M2 Beranga Spain
117 L6 Berangas Kalimantan Indon.
205 O2 Berango Spain
205 O3 Berantevilla Spain
249 G1 Bérard, Lac l. Que. Can.
138 F8 Berasia Madh. Prad. India
116 C3 Berastagi Sumatera Indon.
220 A2 Berat Albania
185 G9 Bérat France
117 L5 Beratus, Gunung mt. Indon.
195 L3 Beratzhausen Ger.
117 L3 Berau r. Indon.
113 H7 Berau, Teluk b. Papua Indon.
235 □J3 Beravina Madag.
285 H4 Berazategui Arg.
116 F5 Berbak, Taman Nasional nat. park Indon.
208 E4 Berbegal Spain
225 G5 Berber Sudan
232 E2 Berbera Somalia
230 B3 Berbérati C.A.R.
237 P3 Berbice S. Africa
205 Q3 Berbinzana Spain
205 N2 Bercedo Spain
199 I4 Bercel Hungary
178 G7 Bercenay-en-Othe France
205 J5 Bercero Spain
212 H6 Berceto Italy
187 E7 Berchem Belgium
212 B2 Bercher Switz.
214 C6 Berchidda Sardegna Italy
224 C5 Berchi-Guélé well Chad
195 K3 Berching Ger.
142 H3 Berchogur Kazakh.
195 O6 Berchtesgaden Ger.
195 N6 Berchtesgaden, Nationalpark nat. park Ger.
195 N6 Berchtesgadener Alpen mts Ger.
207 M7 Bérchules Spain
204 I4 Bercianos del Páramo Spain
178 C3 Berck France
199 L4 Bercu Romania
151 G5 Berd Armenia
159 P7 Berda r. Ukr.
232 D4 Berdaale Somalia
181 M5 Berd'huis France
Berdichev Ukr. see Berdychiv
153 N3 Berdigestyakh Rus. Fed.
152 J4 Berdsk Rus. Fed.
204 G2 Berducedo Spain
208 D2 Berdún Spain
159 P7 Berdyans'k Ukr.
159 P7 Berdyans'ka Kosa spit Ukr.
Berdyanskaya Kosa spit Ukr. see Berdyans'ka Kosa
159 P7 Berdyans'ka Zatoka b. Ukr.
158 H4 Berdychiv Ukr.
230 C2 Béré Chad
256 A11 Berea KY U.S.A.
256 D7 Berea OH U.S.A.
172 D7 Bere Alston Devon, England U.K.
115 F2 Berebere Maluku Indon.
Béréby Côte d'Ivoire see Grand-Bérébi
232 F2 Bereeda Somalia
172 D7 Bere Ferrers Devon, England U.K.
161 U1 Bereg Rus. Fed.
199 L3 Beregdaróc Hungary
Beregovo Ukr. see Berehove
122 E1 Beregovoy Rus. Fed.
212 G5 Bereguardo Italy
158 E5 Berehomet Ukr.
159 O8 Berehove Respublika Krym Ukr.
158 B5 Berehove Zakarpats'ka Oblast' Ukr.
113 K8 Bereina P.N.G.
169 C9 Bere Island i. Ireland
201 O8 Berek Croatia
159 P4 Bereka Ukr.
159 P4 Bereka r. Ukr.
199 K4 Berekböszörmény Hungary
144 F2 Bereket Turkm.
235 □J4 Bereketa Madag.
199 J4 Berekfürdő Hungary
233 B6 Bereku Tanz.
271 □2 Berekua Dominica
228 E5 Berekum Ghana
143 V3 Berel' Kazakh.
199 H6 Beremend Hungary
161 W5 Berendeyevo Rus. Fed.
276 C4 Berenguela Bol.
Berenice Libya see Banghāzī
247 L4 Berens r. Man. Can.
247 L4 Berens Island Man. Can.
247 L4 Berens River Man. Can.
235 □J4 Berenty Madag.
172 H6 Bere Regis Dorset, England U.K.
249 H4 Beresford N.B. Can.
260 G4 Beresford SD U.S.A.
158 E3 Berestechko Ukr.
219 P4 Bereşti Romania
159 M3 Berestivka Ukr.
159 O4 Berestova r. Ukr.
159 P5 Berestove Kharkivs'ka Oblast' Ukr.
159 P6 Berestove Zaporiz'ka Oblast' Ukr.
159 O4 Berestoven'ka Ukr.
159 L2 Berestovets' Ukr.
158 E3 Berestyane Ukr.
199 K4 Berettyó r. Hungary
199 K4 Berettyóújfalu Hungary
235 □J3 Berevo Madag.
235 □J3 Berevo-Ranobe Madag.
Bereza Belarus see Byaroza
159 K3 Berezan' Ukr.
159 K7 Berezanka Ukr.
159 S8 Berezanskaya Rus. Fed.
159 K7 Berezans'kiy Lyman l. Ukr.
161 Q4 Berezayka Rus. Fed.
158 G3 Berezdiv Ukr.
219 Q4 Berezeni Romania
158 D4 Berezhany Ukr.
Berezino Minskaya Voblasts' Belarus see Byerazino
Berezino Vitsyebskaya Voblasts' Belarus see Byerazino
159 L3 Berezivka Chernihivs'ka Oblast' Ukr.
159 L6 Berezivka Kirovohrads'ka Oblast' Ukr.
158 J6 Berezivka Odes'ka Oblast' Ukr.
158 G4 Berezivka Zhytomyrs'ka Oblast' Ukr.
158 H3 Berezivka Zhytomyrs'ka Oblast' Ukr.
159 K2 Berezna Ukr.
158 F2 Berezne Ukr.
159 L6 Bereznehuvate Ukr.
156 H3 Bereznik Rus. Fed.
156 L4 Berezniki Rus. Fed.
158 G3 Bereznyky Ukr.
Berezov Rus. Fed. see Berezovo
156 L3 Berezovaya r. Rus. Fed.
158 G2 Berezove Ukr.
156 I3 Berezovik Rus. Fed.
Berezovka Belarus see Byarozawka
122 E3 Berezovka Amurskaya Oblast' Rus. Fed.
161 V8 Berezovka Lipetskaya Oblast' Rus. Fed.
142 H1 Berezovka Orenburgskaya Oblast' Rus. Fed.
156 L4 Berezovka Permskaya Oblast' Rus. Fed.
Berezovka Ukr. see Berezivka
152 H3 Berezovo Rus. Fed.
122 I3 Berezovyy Rus. Fed.
158 I7 Berezyne Ukr.
194 H6 Berg Baden-Württemberg Ger.
193 E10 Berg Bayern Ger.
195 K6 Berg Bayern Ger.
191 C9 Berg Rheinland-Pfalz Ger.
187 J9 Berg Lux.
194 E4 Berg (Pfalz) Ger.
193 D8 Berga Sachsen-Anhalt Ger.
193 F9 Berga Thüringen Ger.
208 I3 Berga Spain
221 I3 Bergama Turkey
212 H4 Bergamo Italy
212 H4 Bergamo prov. Italy
208 E6 Bergantes, Riu r. Spain
204 C2 Bergantiños reg. Spain
205 P2 Bergara Spain
194 H6 Bergatreute Ger.
195 K3 Berg bei Neumarkt in der Oberpfalz Ger.
201 I2 Berg bei Rohrbach Austria
163 N6 Bergby Sweden
192 E4 Berge Brandenburg Ger.
190 E5 Berge Niedersachsen Ger.
208 E6 Berge Spain
212 E7 Bergeggi Italy
195 N6 Bergen Bayern Ger.
192 H2 Bergen Mecklenburg-Vorpommern Ger.
190 I5 Bergen Niedersachsen Ger.
186 G3 Bergen Neth.
164 B1 Bergen Norway
237 O3 Bergen S. Africa
256 H5 Bergen NY U.S.A.
190 K5 Bergen (Dumme) Ger.
259 G3 Bergen County county NJ U.S.A.
259 H3 Bergenfield NJ U.S.A.
186 F6 Bergen op Zoom Neth.
186 K3 Bergentheim Neth.
185 E6 Bergerac France
178 H6 Bergères-lès-Vertus France
287 B2 Bergerson, Mount Antarctica
182 F4 Bergesserin France
187 H6 Bergeyk Neth.
192 H5 Bergfelde Ger.
193 I9 Berggießhübel, Kurort Ger.
102 H1 Berghan Point North I. N.Z.
186 I5 Bergharen Neth.
194 D5 Berghaupten Ger.
200 H4 Bergheim Austria
195 K4 Bergheim Ger.
191 H8 Bergheim (Edertal) Ger.
191 C9 Bergheim (Erft) Ger.
186 I5 Berghem Neth.
193 H6 Bergholz-Rehbrücke Ger.
194 H5 Berghülen Ger.
200 H6 Berg im Drautal Austria
191 D9 Bergisches Land reg. Ger.
191 D9 Bergisch Gladbach Ger.
191 E7 Bergkamen Ger.
195 K5 Bergkirchen Ger.
234 C4 Bergland Namibia
250 E3 Bergland MI U.S.A.
162 N4 Bergnäs Sweden
162 O3 Bergnäsviken Sweden
191 E8 Bergneustadt Ger.
Bergomum Italy see Bergamo
256 E10 Bergoo WV U.S.A.
191 J10 Bergrheinfeld Ger.
165 O2 Bergshamra Sweden
163 N6 Bergsjö Sweden
194 G2 Bergstraße-Odenwald park Ger.
162 P4 Bergsviken Sweden
195 I2 Bergtheim Ger.
208 I3 Bergueda reg. Spain
205 N3 Berguenda Spain
178 D2 Bergues France
212 H2 Bergün Switz.
237 N4 Bergville S. Africa
193 G7 Bergwitz Ger.
129 L3 Berh Mongolia
116 E5 Berhala, Selat sea chan. Indon.
Berhampur W. Bengal India see Baharampur
219 P4 Berheci r. Romania
199 H4 Berhida Hungary
116 G6 Berikat, Tanjung pt Indon.
151 J3 Berikey Rus. Fed.
281 F2 Berilo Brazil
153 R4 Beringa, Ostrov i. Rus. Fed.
109 D8 Beringarra W.A. Austr.
187 I6 Beringe Neth.
206 D4 Beringel Port.
187 H6 Beringen Belgium
245 L3 Bering Glacier AK U.S.A.
245 K3 Bering Lake AK U.S.A.
244 F2 Bering Land Bridge National Preserve nature res. AK U.S.A.
153 S3 Beringovskiy Rus. Fed.
242 A4 Bering Sea N. Pacific Ocean
242 B3 Bering Strait Rus. Fed./U.S.A.
173 J4 Berinsfield Oxfordshire, England U.K.
145 I9 Berīs, Ra's pt Iran
Berislav Ukr. see Beryslav
239 □1c Bérive Réunion
158 J6 Berizky Ukr.
207 N7 Berja Spain
191 J9 Berka Ger.
162 K5 Berkåk Norway
226 E2 Berkane Morocco
186 F5 Berkel Neth.
186 J4 Berkel r. Neth.
108 I3 Berkeley r. W.A. Austr.
172 H4 Berkeley Gloucestershire, England U.K.
264 J4 Berkeley CA U.S.A.
259 G3 Berkeley Heights NJ U.S.A.
256 G9 Berkeley Springs WV U.S.A.
190 K3 Berkenthin Ger.
173 K4 Berkhamsted Hertfordshire, England U.K.
195 I5 Berkheim Ger.
186 H3 Berkhout Neth.
286 U1 Berkner Island Antarctica
219 L7 Berkovitsa Bulg.
258 D4 Berks County county PA U.S.A.
173 J5 Berkshire Downs hills England U.K.
257 L6 Berkshire Hills MA U.S.A.
173 I3 Berkswell West Midlands, England U.K.
186 J3 Berkum Neth.
187 G6 Berlaar Belgium
178 G3 Berlaimont France
246 G4 Berland r. Alta Can.
206 H4 Berlanga Spain
205 O6 Berlanga de Duero Spain
187 F6 Berlare Belgium
206 A2 Berlenga i. Port.
162 T1 Berlevåg Norway
186 H5 Berlicum Neth.
186 I2 Berlikum Neth.
192 H5 Berlin Ger.
193 H5 Berlin land Ger.
259 J1 Berlin CT U.S.A.
257 J10 Berlin MD U.S.A.
257 □N4 Berlin NH U.S.A.
258 F5 Berlin NJ U.S.A.
256 D8 Berlin OH U.S.A.
256 G9 Berlin PA U.S.A.
250 F6 Berlin WI U.S.A.
286 O1 Berlin, Mount Antarctica
191 J8 Berlingerode Ger.
243 J2 Berlinguet Inlet Nunavut Can.
103 F8 Berlins South I. N.Z.
258 D3 Berlinsville PA U.S.A.
218 J6 Berlişte Romania
193 D8 Berlstedt Ger.
105 M7 Bermagui N.S.W. Austr.
194 G6 Bermatingen Ger.
144 G2 Berme Turkm.
283 E6 Bermeja, Punta pt Arg.
207 I8 Bermeja, Sierra mts Spain
207 L7 Bermejales, Embalse de los resr Spain
266 H5 Bermejíllo Mex.
284 D2 Bermejo Arg.
284 D3 Bermejo r. Arg.
282 F2 Bermejo r. Arg./Bol.
276 D5 Bermejo Bol.
285 G6 Bermejo, Isla i. Arg.
249 G2 Bermen, Lac l. Que. Can.
205 O2 Bermeo Spain
204 H6 Bermillo de Sayago Spain
255 □1 Bermuda terr. N. Atlantic Ocean
288 E4 Bermuda Rise sea feature N. Atlantic Ocean
212 C2 Bern Switz.
212 D2 Bern canton Switz.
285 I2 Bernabé Rivera Uru.
185 E9 Bernac-Dessus France
217 L3 Bernalda Italy
263 K9 Bernalillo NM U.S.A.
280 C5 Bernardino de Campos Brazil
251 O4 Bernard Lake Ont. Can.
285 G3 Bernardo de Irigoyen Arg.
285 F4 Bernardo Larroude Arg.
283 B8 Bernardo O'Higgins, Parque Nacional nat. park Chile
205 L6 Bernardos Spain
258 F3 Bernardsville NJ U.S.A.
198 D2 Bernartice Czech Rep.
285 F5 Bernasconi Arg.
194 E6 Bernau Baden-Württemberg Ger.
192 I5 Bernau Brandenburg Ger.
195 M6 Bernau am Chiemsee Ger.
183 J6 Bernaude, Roche mt. France/Italy
178 D3 Bernaville France
181 M3 Bernay France
195 J6 Bernbeuren Ger.
193 E7 Bernburg (Saale) Ger.
201 N4 Berndorf Austria
190 F4 Berne Ger.
Berne Switz. see Bern
250 J9 Berne IN U.S.A.
199 H3 Bernecebaráti Hungary
205 P3 Bernedo Spain
212 C3 Berner Alpen mts Switz.
168 B7 Berneray i. Western Isles, Scotland U.K.
168 A9 Berneray i. Western Isles, Scotland U.K.
Bernese Alps mts Switz. see Berner Alpen
204 I4 Bernesga r. Spain
182 J4 Bernex France
195 K3 Berngau Ger.
201 O2 Bernhardsthal Austria
195 M3 Bernhardswald Ger.
243 J2 Bernier Bay Nunavut Can.
109 B8 Bernier Island W.A. Austr.
183 H6 Bernin France
212 I3 Bernina Pass Switz.
205 O7 Berninches mt. Spain
168 D8 Bernisdale Highland, Scotland U.K.
187 E8 Bernissart Belgium
192 E3 Bernitt Ger.
194 C2 Bernkastel-Kues Ger.
185 D7 Bernos-Beaulac France
195 K6 Bernried Bayern Ger.
195 N4 Bernried Bayern Ger.
193 J8 Bernsdorf Ger.
195 I4 Bernstadt Baden-Württemberg Ger.
193 K8 Bernstadt Sachsen Ger.
256 A11 Bernstadt KY U.S.A.
201 N5 Bernstein Austria
258 C4 Bernville PA U.S.A.
Beroea Greece see Veroia
Beroea Syria see Ḥalab
212 E1 Beromünster Switz.
235 □J4 Beroroha Madag.
198 D2 Beroun Czech Rep.
198 D2 Berounka r. Czech Rep.
Berovina Madag. see Beravina
219 K9 Berovo Macedonia
213 L6 Berra Italy
211 A7 Berrahal Alg.
183 B10 Berre r. France
183 G10 Berre, Étang de lag. France
226 D2 Berrechid Morocco
183 G10 Berre-l'Étang France
104 H6 Berri S.A. Austr.
227 F2 Berriane Alg.
183 E8 Berrias-et-Casteljau France
105 L7 Berridale N.S.W. Austr.
168 I6 Berriedale Highland, Scotland U.K.
168 I6 Berriedale Water r. Scotland U.K.
180 D5 Berrien France
105 J6 Berrigan N.S.W. Austr.
205 Q3 Berriozar Spain
206 F5 Berrocal Spain
284 E3 Berrotarán Arg.
227 F1 Berrouaghia Alg.
172 F5 Berrow Somerset, England U.K.
178 H5 Berru France
105 M6 Berry N.S.W. Austr.
184 H2 Berry reg. France
182 B3 Berry, Canal du France
178 G5 Berry-au-Bac France
247 I5 Berry Creek r. Alta Can.
264 J3 Berryessa, Lake CA U.S.A.
172 F7 Berry Head England U.K.
270 E1 Berry Islands Bahamas
258 B3 Berrysburg PA U.S.A.
261 I7 Berryville AR U.S.A.
256 H9 Berryville VA U.S.A.
236 B2 Berseba Namibia
190 E5 Bersenbrück Ger.
158 I5 Bershad' Ukr.
184 C5 Berson France
213 J4 Bersone Italy
193 I7 Berste r. Ger.
142 I1 Bersuat Rus. Fed.
151 C4 Berta r. Turkey
116 E2 Bertam Malaysia
204 C3 Bertamirans Spain
249 G3 Berté, Lac l. Que. Can.
193 J8 Berthelsdorf Ger.
183 B8 Bertholène France
178 E3 Bertincourt France
275 I5 Bertinho Brazil
213 M7 Bertinoro Italy
187 I8 Bertogne Belgium
278 E3 Bertolínia Brazil
281 G2 Bertópolis Brazil
229 I5 Bertoua Cameroon
169 C6 Bertraghboy Bay Ireland
187 J9 Bertrange Lux.
179 M7 Bertrichamps France
187 H9 Bertrix Belgium
213 M6 Bertuzzi, Valle lag. Italy
99 H2 Beru atoll Gilbert Is Kiribati
190 D3 Berumbur Ger.
142 I7 Beruniy Uzbek.
275 F5 Beruri Brazil
136 F9 Beruwala Sri Lanka
219 K3 Berveni Romania
168 L9 Bervie Water r. Scotland U.K.
181 L3 Berville-sur-Mer France
105 J8 Berwick Vic. Austr.
257 O5 Berwick ME U.S.A.
251 R8 Berwick PA U.S.A.
171 M2 Berwick-upon-Tweed Northumberland, England U.K.
172 F2 Berwyn hills Wales U.K.
258 E4 Berwyn PA U.S.A.
159 M7 Beryslav Ukr.
Berytus Lebanon see Beirut
219 J6 Berzasca Romania
160 J5 Bērzaune Latvia
160 G6 Beržė r. Lith.
198 G5 Berzence Hungary
197 L1 Berźniki Pol.
207 I2 Berzocana Spain
160 K5 Bērzpils Latvia
183 C7 Bès r. France
117 L3 Besah Kalimantan Indon.
235 □J3 Besalampy Madag.
208 K3 Besalú Spain
182 I2 Besançon France
205 K3 Besande Spain
115 C8 Besar i. Indon.
117 K6 Besar, Gunung mt. Indon.
116 D2 Besar, Gunung mt. Malaysia
205 L2 Besaya r. Spain
142 F4 Besbay Kazakh.
244 G2 Besboro Island AK U.S.A.
182 D3 Besbre r. France
208 K4 Bescanó Spain
161 O9 Besed' r. Rus. Fed.
159 P2 Besedino Rus. Fed.
191 F10 Beselich-Obertiefenbach Ger.
199 H3 Bešeňov Slovakia
199 J4 Besenyőtelek Hungary
199 J4 Besenyszög Hungary
116 E3 Beserah Malaysia
143 N7 Beshariq Uzbek.
Besharyk Uzbek. see Beshariq
142 K8 Beshkent Uzbek.
138 F8 Beshnagar Madh. Prad. India
144 F7 Beshneh Iran
151 F4 Besht'asheni Georgia
Besh-Ter, Gora mt. Kyrg./Uzbek. see Besh-Ter Toosu
143 N6 Besh-Ter Toosu mt. Kyrg./Uzbek.
Beshtor Toghi mt. Kyrg./Uzbek. see Besh-Ter Toosu
208 G2 Besiberri Sud mt. Spain
115 D8 Besikama Timor Indon.
142 K8 Beşir Turkm.
149 J5 Beşiri Turkey
116 C2 Besitang Sumatera Indon.
197 J6 Beskid Niski hills Pol.
197 I6 Beskid Sądecki mts Pol.
Beskra Alg. see Biskra
199 H2 Beskydy park Czech Rep.
151 F2 Beslan Rus. Fed.
219 L9 Beslet mt. Bulg.
219 K8 Besna Kobila mt. Serbia
247 J4 Besnard Lake Sask. Can.
148 H5 Besni Turkey
143 P3 Besoba Kazakh.
150 C7 Besor watercourse Israel
212 F4 Besozzo Italy
Beşparmak Dağları mts Cyprus see Pentadaktylos Range
161 U7 Besputa r. Rus. Fed.
171 O6 Bessacarr South Yorkshire, England U.K.
Bessa Monteiro Angola see Kindeje
230 B3 Bessan C.A.R.
183 C10 Bessan France
230 B3 Béssao Chad
Bessarabka Moldova see Basarabeasca
182 C4 Bessay-sur-Allier France
143 M6 Bessaz, Gora mt. Kazakh.
169 J4 Bessbrook Northern Ireland U.K.
183 I6 Besse France
182 B5 Besse-et-St-Anastaise France
183 E8 Bessèges France
255 D9 Bessemer AL U.S.A.
250 D3 Bessemer MI U.S.A.
256 E8 Bessemer PA U.S.A.
182 F5 Bessenay France
194 G2 Bessenbach Ger.
181 M6 Bessé-sur-Braye France
183 I10 Besse-sur-Issole France
142 E5 Besshoky, Gora hill Kazakh.
185 H8 Bessières France
181 J3 Bessin reg. France
184 G3 Bessines-sur-Gartempe France
151 C1 Besskorbnaya Rus. Fed.
159 P3 Bessonovka Belgorodskaya Oblast' Rus. Fed.
157 I5 Bessonovka Penzenskaya Oblast' Rus. Fed.
184 I4 Bessou, Mont de hill France
186 H5 Best Neth.
142 F3 Bestamak Aktyubinskaya Oblast' Kazakh.
143 R3 Bestamak Vostochnyy Kazakhstan Kazakh.
193 I6 Bestensee Ger.
237 N4 Besters S. Africa
143 O1 Bestobe Kazakh.
165 L3 Bestorp Sweden
156 H3 Bestuzhevo Rus. Fed.
191 F8 Bestwig Ger.
106 D3 Beswick N.T. Austr.
106 D3 Beswick Aboriginal Land res. N.T. Austr.
235 □J3 Betafo Madag.
235 □J3 Betanantanana Madag.
238 □3b Betancuria Fuerteventura Canary Is
276 D4 Betanzos Bol.
204 D2 Betanzos Spain
204 D2 Betanzos, Ría de est. Spain
229 I5 Bétaré Oya Cameroon
274 B3 Beté Col.
250 G2 Bete Grise MI U.S.A.
232 C2 Bete Hor Eth.
208 B1 Betelu Spain
209 E8 Bétera Spain
229 F4 Bétérou Benin
116 F5 Betet i. Indon.
205 P7 Beteta Spain
150 C7 Bet Guvrin Israel
226 D2 Beth, Oued r. Morocco
237 N2 Bethal S. Africa
234 C5 Bethanie Namibia
259 J2 Bethany CT U.S.A.
260 H5 Bethany MO U.S.A.
261 G8 Bethany OK U.S.A.
139 I6 Bethari Nepal
199 K6 Bethausen Romania
244 G3 Bethel AK U.S.A.
259 I2 Bethel CT U.S.A.
257 □O4 Bethel ME U.S.A.
256 A10 Bethel OH U.S.A.
258 C4 Bethel PA U.S.A.
191 I6 Betheln Ger.
256 E8 Bethel Park PA U.S.A.
237 J9 Bethelsdorp S. Africa
270 □ Bethel Town Jamaica
178 H5 Bétheny France
173 N5 Bethersden Kent, England U.K.
172 D1 Bethesda Gwynedd, Wales U.K.
258 A7 Bethesda MD U.S.A.
256 D8 Bethesda OH U.S.A.
237 I7 Bethesdaweg S. Africa
178 E5 Béthisy-St-Pierre France
102 K4 Bethlehem North I. N.Z.
237 M4 Bethlehem S. Africa
258 E3 Bethlehem PA U.S.A.
150 D7 Bethlehem West Bank
185 G10 Bethmale France
178 G6 Bethon France
259 I3 Bethpage NY U.S.A.
237 J6 Bethulie S. Africa
178 E2 Béthune France
178 B4 Béthune r. France
145 M7 Beti Pak.
274 D2 Betijoque Venez.
281 E3 Betim Brazil
235 □J4 Betioky Madag.
117 J9 Betiri, Gunung mt. Indon.
Bet Lehem West Bank see Bethlehem
161 Q7 Betlitsa Rus. Fed.
138 E8 Betma Madh. Prad. India
178 F6 Beton-Bazoches France
117 I4 Betong Sarawak Malaysia
119 E12 Betong Thai.
106 H8 Betoota Qld Austr.
232 C2 Beto Shet' r. Eth.
230 C4 Bétou Congo
143 N5 Betpakdala plain Kazakh.
235 □J3 Betrandraka Madag.
235 □J4 Betroka Madag.
179 O6 Betschdorf France
150 D6 Bet She'an Israel
249 G3 Betsiamites Que. Can.
249 G3 Betsiamites r. Que. Can.
235 □J2 Betsiboka r. Madag.
250 H5 Betsie, Point MI U.S.A.
126 E3 Betsu-zan mt. Japan
270 G2 Betsy Bay Mayaguana Bahamas
250 I3 Betsy Lake MI U.S.A.
179 L5 Bettelainville France
200 E5 Bettelwurf mt. Austria
187 J9 Bettembourg Lux.
187 J9 Bettendorf Lux.
258 C6 Betterton MD U.S.A.
139 J6 Bettiah Bihar India
237 N2 Bettiesdam S. Africa
194 A2 Bettingen Ger.
245 J2 Bettles AK U.S.A.
165 M3 Bettna Sweden
212 H6 Bettola Italy
180 H5 Betton France
215 J1 Bettona Italy
168 H5 Bettyhill Highland, Scotland U.K.
169 J5 Bettystown Ireland
138 F9 Betul Madh. Prad. India
115 D8 Betun Timor Indon.
117 J4 Betung Kerihun, Taman Nasional Indon.
186 I5 Betuwe reg. Neth.
138 G7 Betwa r. India
172 E1 Betws-y-coed Conwy, Wales U.K.
209 E8 Betxi Spain
160 G6 Betygala Lith.
196 E2 Betyń, Jezioro l. Pol.
178 E5 Betz France
191 E9 Betzdorf Ger.
187 J9 Betzdorf Lux.
195 K2 Betzenstein Ger.
195 I6 Betzigau Ger.
231 B6 Béu Angola
183 J8 Beuil France
105 I6 Beulah Vic. Austr.
172 E3 Beulah Powys, Wales U.K.
250 H5 Beulah MI U.S.A.
260 E2 Beulah ND U.S.A.
173 M5 Beult r. England U.K.
186 I5 Beuningen Neth.
191 J8 Beuren Ger.
224 B6 Beurfou well Chad
194 F5 Beuron Ger.
179 I7 Beurville France
Beuthen Pol. see Bytom
182 E3 Beuvray, Mont hill France
182 D2 Beuvron r. France
181 N7 Beuvron r. France
178 E2 Beuvry France
181 L3 Beuzeville France
215 J2 Bevagna Italy
212 B2 Bevaix Switz.
191 E6 Bever r. Ger.
183 L9 Bévéra r. France
109 D12 Beverley W.A. Austr.
171 Q6 Beverley East Riding of Yorkshire, England U.K.
244 H4 Beverley, Lake AK U.S.A.
257 O6 Beverly MA U.S.A.
258 F4 Beverly NJ U.S.A.
256 D9 Beverly OH U.S.A.
264 N7 Beverly Hills CA U.S.A.
247 K1 Beverly Lake Nunavut Can.
191 H7 Bevern Ger.
190 G4 Beverstedt Ger.
191 H7 Beverungen Ger.
186 G4 Beverwijk Neth.
178 C7 Béville-le-Comte France
172 H3 Bewdley Worcestershire, England U.K.
173 M5 Bewl Water resr England U.K.
212 C3 Bex Switz.
194 C3 Bexbach Ger.
173 M6 Bexhill East Sussex, England U.K.
221 J5 Beyağaç Turkey
149 M6 Beyānlū Iran
221 I1 Beyazköy Turkey
Beyce Turkey see Orhaneli
185 D6 Beychac-et-Caillau France
221 M2 Beyciler Turkey
221 J4 Beydağ Turkey
221 L6 Bey Dağları mts Turkey
151 B7 Beydoğan Turkey
221 J3 Beyel Turkey
193 E6 Beyendorf Ger.
221 L6 Beykonak Turkey
221 M2 Beyköy Bolu Turkey
221 L2 Beyköy Eskişehir Turkey
221 K1 Beykoz Turkey
228 C4 Beyla Guinea
Beylagan Azer. see Beyläqan
151 I6 Beyläqan Azer.
221 M3 Beylikova Turkey
225 I6 Beylul Eritrea
185 G6 Beynac-et-Cazenac France
184 H5 Beynat France
187 I7 Beyne-Heusay Belgium
142 F5 Beyneu Kazakh.
182 G5 Beynost France
221 I4 Beyoba Turkey
125 Q15 Beyoneisu-retsugan i. Japan
125 Q15 Beyoneisu Retugan i. Japan
148 E3 Beypazarı Turkey
148 H4 Beypınarı Turkey
136 D7 Beypore Kerala India
232 E3 Beyra Somalia
144 E8 Beyram Iran
Beyrouth Lebanon see Beirut
148 E5 Beyşehir Turkey
148 E5 Beyşehir Gölü l. Turkey
159 S8 Beysug Rus. Fed.
159 R7 Beysug r. Rus. Fed.
159 R7 Beysugskiy Liman lag. Rus. Fed.
159 R8 Beysuzhek r. Rus. Fed.
122 D2 Beytonovo Rus. Fed.
149 K5 Beytüşşebap Turkey
183 G7 Bez r. France
144 G4 Bezameh Iran
209 C7 Bezas Spain
200 A5 Bezau Austria
156 J4 Bezbozhnik Rus. Fed.
218 G5 Bezdan Vojvodina Serbia
182 G2 Bèze France
151 E2 Bezengi Rus. Fed.
144 G7 Bezenjān Iran
198 G4 Bezenye Hungary
160 M5 Bezhanitskaya Vozvyshennost' hills Rus. Fed.
160 M5 Bezhanitsy Rus. Fed.
219 M7 Bezhanovo Bulg.
161 T4 Bezhetsk Rus. Fed.
161 T4 Bezhetskiy Verkh reg. Rus. Fed.
151 H3 Bezhta Rus. Fed.
183 C10 Béziers France
197 I1 Bezledy Pol.
Bezmein Turkm. see Abadan
183 F9 Bezouce France
199 L3 Bežovce Slovakia
Bezwada Andhra Prad. India see Vijayawada
138 C7 Bhabhar Gujarat India
139 I7 Bhabhua Bihar India
138 E8 Bhabra Madh. Prad. India
138 C8 Bhachau Gujarat India
138 C7 Bhachbhar Rajasthan India
138 B9 Bhadar r. India
138 E3 Bhadarwah Jammu and Kashmir India
145 P6 Bhadaur Punjab India
138 F7 Bhadaura Madh. Prad. India
Bhadgaon Nepal see Bhaktapur
139 I7 Bhadohi Uttar Prad. India
138 E5 Bhadra Rajasthan India
136 G4 Bhadrachalam Andhra Prad. India
Bhadrachalam Road Station Andhra Prad. India see Kottagudem
138 D7 Bhadrajan Rajasthan India
139 K9 Bhadrak Orissa India
136 D6 Bhadra Reservoir India
136 D6 Bhadravati Karnataka India
145 L7 Bhag Pak.
133 C10 Bhaga r. India
139 K7 Bhagalpur Bihar India
139 L8 Bhagirathi r. India
136 E3 Bhainsa Andhra Prad. India
138 F9 Bhainsdehi Madh. Prad. India
139 M7 Bhairab Bazar Bangl.
139 I6 Bhairawa Nepal
Bhairawaha Nepal see Bhairawa
141 I4 Bhairi Hol mt. Pak.
145 N6 Bhakkar Pak.
139 J6 Bhaktapur Nepal
Bhaleshear i. Scotland U.K. see Baleshare
136 E3 Bhalki Karnataka India
145 O5 Bhalwal Pak.
138 F9 Bhamgarh Madh. Prad. India
118 C2 Bhamo Myanmar
136 G3 Bhamragarh Mahar. India
138 G9 Bhandara Mahar. India
138 G7 Bhander Madh. Prad. India
138 H6 Bhangaha Uttar Prad. India
138 B8 Bhangor Gujarat India
137 I3 Bhanjanagar Orissa India
138 E7 Bhanpura Madh. Prad. India
138 G8 Bhanrer Range hills Madh. Prad. India
138 H9 Bhanupratappur Chhattisgarh India
Bharat country Asia see India
138 F6 Bharatpur Rajasthan India
139 J6 Bharatpur Nepal
139 N6 Bhareli r. India
145 J9 Bhari r. Pak.
138 G6 Bharthana Uttar Prad. India
138 D9 Bharuch Gujarat India
138 H9 Bhatapara Chhattisgarh India
Bhatarsaigh i. Scotland U.K. see Vatersay
136 C3 Bhatghar Lake India
139 L8 Bhatiapara Ghat Bangl.
Bhatinda Punjab India see Bathinda
136 D6 Bhatkal Karnataka India
Bhatnair Rajasthan India see Hanumangarh
139 L8 Bhatpara W. Bengal India
145 O5 Bhaun Pak.
136 E7 Bhavani Tamil Nadu India
136 E7 Bhavani r. India
136 E7 Bhavani Sagar l. India
138 D9 Bhavnagar Gujarat India
145 O6 Bhawana Pak.
137 H3 Bhawanipatna Orissa India
Bhearnaraigh, Eilean i. Western Isles, Scotland U.K. see Berneray
Bheemavaram Andhra Prad. India see Bhimavaram
237 O3 Bhekuzulu S. Africa
138 H7 Bhelki Madh. Prad. India
145 O5 Bhera Pak.
138 H5 Bheri r. Nepal
136 D3 Bhigvan Mahar. India
138 H9 Bhilai Chhattisgarh India
138 D7 Bhildi Gujarat India
138 E7 Bhilwara Rajasthan India
136 E4 Bhima r. India
138 C6 Bhimar Rajasthan India
136 G4 Bhimavaram Andhra Prad. India
145 P5 Bhimber Pak.
138 H8 Bhimlath Madh. Prad. India
139 K6 Bhimnagar Bihar India
139 J6 Bhimphedi Nepal
138 G6 Bhind Madh. Prad. India
138 E7 Bhindar Rajasthan India
138 H6 Bhinga Uttar Prad. India
136 D3 Bhingar Mahar. India
138 D7 Bhinmal Rajasthan India
237 L8 Bhisho S. Africa
136 C3 Bhiwandi Mahar. India
138 F5 Bhiwani Haryana India
138 G6 Bhogaipur Uttar Prad. India
138 B9 Bhogat Gujarat India
138 F8 Bhojpur Madh. Prad. India
139 K6 Bhojpur Nepal
138 E9 Bhokardan Mahar. India
139 M8 Bhola Bangl.
138 G6 Bhongaon Uttar Prad. India
136 F4 Bhongir Andhra Prad. India
237 N6 Bhongweni S. Africa
138 F8 Bhopal Madh. Prad. India
136 G3 Bhopalpatnam Chhattisgarh India
136 C3 Bhor Mahar. India
Bhrigukaccha Gujarat India see Bharuch
139 J9 Bhuban Orissa India
139 J9 Bhubaneshwar Orissa India
Bhubaneswar Orissa India see Bhubaneshwar
139 N7 Bhuban Hills India
138 B8 Bhuj Gujarat India
237 P2 Bhunya Swaziland

138 E9 **Bhusawal** Mahar. India
139 M6 **Bhutan** country Asia
138 C6 **Bhuttewala** Rajasthan India
136 F7 **Bhuvanagiri** Tamil Nadu India
274 E5 **Biá** r. Brazil
231 E7 **Bia, Monts** mts Dem. Rep. Congo
118 F5 **Bia, Phou** mt. Laos
144 G8 **Bīabān** mts Iran
232 E3 **Biad** well Eth.
196 F4 **Biadki** Pol.
133 B9 **Biafo Glacier** Pak.
Biafra, Bight of g. Africa see **Benin, Bight of**
113 I7 **Biak** Papua Indon.
115 C4 **Biak** Sulawesi Indon.
113 I7 **Biak** i. Papua Indon.
196 F5 **Biała** Pol.
197 I5 **Biała** r. Pol.
196 F5 **Biała** r. Pol.
196 G4 **Biała-Parcela Pierwsza** Pol.
197 K2 **Biała Piska** Pol.
197 L3 **Biała Podlaska** Pol.
197 I4 **Biała Rawska** Pol.
196 F2 **Białe Błota** Pol.
197 K4 **Białka** r. Pol.
197 I4 **Białobrzegi** Mazowieckie Pol.
197 K5 **Białobrzegi** Podkarpackie Pol.
196 D2 **Białogard** Pol.
196 F2 **Białośliwie** Pol.
197 L3 **Białowieski Park Narodowy** nat. park Pol.
197 L3 **Białowieża** Pol.
196 E2 **Biały Bór** Pol.
197 I6 **Biały Dunajec** Pol.
197 L2 **Białystok** Pol.
216 F9 **Bianca, Punta** pt Sicilia Italy
216 H8 **Biancavilla** Sicilia Italy
217 K7 **Bianco** Italy
213 L5 **Bianco, Canale** canal Italy
216 E9 **Bianco, Capo** c. Sicilia Italy
212 D4 **Bianco, Corno** mt. Italy
Bianco, Monte mt. France/Italy see **Blanc, Mont**
129 Q9 **Biandangang Kou** r. mouth China
212 E5 **Biandrate** Italy
230 D3 **Bianga** C.A.R.
228 D5 **Biankouma** Côte d'Ivoire
228 E5 **Bianouan** Côte d'Ivoire
182 I3 **Bians-les-Usiers** France
212 E5 **Bianzè** Italy
129 R4 **Bianzhao** Jilin China
Bianzhuang Shandong China see **Cangshan**
114 E8 **Biao** Mindanao Phil.
138 F8 **Biaora** Madh. Prad. India
209 D10 **Biar** Spain
144 F3 **Biārjomand** Iran
115 D2 **Biaro** i. Indon.
185 A9 **Biarritz** France
Biarritz airport France see **Parme**
185 B8 **Biarrotte** France
184 H6 **Biars-sur-Cère** France
146 G3 **Bi'ār Tabrāk** well Saudi Arabia
185 B7 **Bias** Aquitaine France
185 F7 **Bias** Aquitaine France
212 F3 **Biasca** Switz.
285 I2 **Biassini** Uru.
199 H4 **Biatorbágy** Hungary
225 F2 **Bibā** Egypt
124 S3 **Bibai** Japan
231 B8 **Bibala** Angola
230 A4 **Bibas** Gabon
105 L7 **Bibbenluke** N.S.W. Austr.
213 L8 **Bibbiena** Italy
213 J9 **Bibbona** Italy
247 M2 **Bibby Island** Nunavut Can.
229 I4 **Bibémi** Cameroon
194 E5 **Biberach** Ger.
194 H5 **Biberach an der Riß** Ger.
195 J4 **Biberbach** Ger.
195 J3 **Bibert** r. Ger.
228 E5 **Bibiani** Ghana
136 G9 **Bibile** Sri Lanka
213 O4 **Bibione** Italy
161 P5 **Bibirevo** Rus. Fed.
139 M7 **Bibiyana** r. Bangl.
194 E2 **Biblis** Ger.
Biblos Lebanon see **Jbail**
158 D4 **Bibrka** Ukr.
173 I4 **Bibury** Gloucestershire, England U.K.
160 J5 **Bicānu ezers** l. Latvia
281 F4 **Bicas** Brazil
199 M4 **Bicaz** Maramureș Romania
219 O4 **Bicaz** Neamț Romania
215 O5 **Biccari** Italy
148 E4 **Biçer** Turkey
173 J4 **Bicester** Oxfordshire, England U.K.
138 D7 **Bichabhera** Rajasthan India
271 □7 **Biche** Trin. and Tob.
232 C2 **Bichena** Eth.
Bicheng Chongqing China see **Bishan**
105 L9 **Bicheno** Tas. Austr.
122 I5 **Bichevaya** Rus. Fed.
229 H3 **Bichi** Nigeria
122 K2 **Bichi** r. Rus. Fed.
195 K6 **Bichl** Ger.
200 C5 **Bichlbach** Austria
136 C5 **Bicholim** Goa India
139 J6 **Bichraltar** Nepal
129 J1 **Bichura** Rus. Fed.
151 B2 **Bichvint'a** Georgia
151 B2 **Bichvint'is Konts'khi** pt Georgia
194 F2 **Bickenbach** Ger.
173 I3 **Bickenhill** West Midlands, England U.K.
106 F2 **Bickerton Island** N.T. Austr.
172 D7 **Bickleigh** Devon, England U.K.
172 E6 **Bickleigh** Devon, England U.K.
173 N4 **Bicknacre** Essex, England U.K.
265 U3 **Bicknell** UT U.S.A.
151 J5 **Bico** Azer.
115 F3 **Bicoli** Halmahera Indon.
209 D9 **Bicorp** Spain
206 C5 **Bicos** Port.
199 H4 **Bicske** Hungary
172 G2 **Bicton** Shropshire, England U.K.
231 B8 **Bicuari, Parque Nacional do** nat. park Angola
136 D3 **Bid** Mahar. India
229 G4 **Bida** Nigeria
185 B9 **Bidache** France
117 M2 **Bidadari, Tanjung** pt Malaysia
136 E4 **Bidar** Karnataka India
185 A9 **Bidart** France
138 E6 **Bidasar** Rajasthan India
147 N4 **Bidbid** Oman
257 □O5 **Biddeford** ME U.S.A.
173 N5 **Biddenden** Kent, England U.K.
186 I4 **Biddinghuizen** Neth.
171 M7 **Biddulph** Staffordshire, England U.K.
168 F9 **Bidean nam Bian** mt. Scotland U.K.
172 D5 **Bideford** Devon, England U.K.
Bideford Bay England U.K. see **Barnstaple Bay**
213 M7 **Bidente** r. Italy
173 I3 **Bidford-on-Avon** Warwickshire, England U.K.
162 Q2 **Bidjovagge** Norway
144 G7 **Bīdkhan, Kūh-e** mt. Iran
144 H4 **Bīdokht** Iran
227 F5 **Bidon 5** tourist site Alg.
185 C9 **Bidos** France
185 B8 **Bidouze** r. France
199 K3 **Bidovce** Slovakia
122 G5 **Bidzhan** Rus. Fed.
122 H5 **Bidzhar** r. Rus. Fed.
Bié Angola see **Kuito**
231 C8 **Bié** prov. Angola
231 B8 **Bié, Planalto do** plat. Angola
191 H10 **Bieber** Ger.
194 E2 **Biebesheim am Rhein** Ger.
197 K2 **Biebrza** r. Pol.
197 K2 **Biebrzański Park Narodowy** nat. park Pol.
197 J6 **Biecz** Pol.
191 G9 **Biedenkopf** Ger.
193 E6 **Biederitz** Ger.
208 D3 **Biel** Spain
212 C1 **Biel** Switz.
199 I1 **Bielańsko-Tyniecki Park Krajobrazowy** Pol.
197 K3 **Bielany-Żyłaki** Pol.
196 E5 **Bielawa** Pol.
191 G6 **Bielefeld** Ger.
199 H2 **Biele Karpaty** park Slovakia
200 B6 **Bielerhöhe** pass Austria
212 C1 **Bieler See** l. Switz.
196 C2 **Bielice** Pol.
197 I5 **Bieliny Kapitulne** Pol.
Bielitz Pol. see **Bielsko-Biała**
212 E4 **Biella** Italy
212 E4 **Biella** prov. Italy
185 D9 **Bielle** France
208 F2 **Bielsa** Spain
197 H3 **Bielsk** Pol.
197 H6 **Bielsko-Biała** Pol.
197 L3 **Bielsk Podlaski** Pol.
191 I8 **Bielstein** hill Ger.
190 J4 **Bienenbüttel** Ger.
119 H9 **Biên Hoa** Vietnam
196 D4 **Bieniów** Pol.
182 H4 **Bienne** r. France
Bienne Switz. see **Biel**
212 I4 **Bienno** Italy
207 N3 **Bienservida** Spain
206 G4 **Bienvenida** Spain
206 G4 **Bienvenida** hill Spain
205 P7 **Bienvenida** mt. Spain
269 J5 **Bienvenido** Mex.
275 H4 **Bienvenue** Fr. Guiana
249 F2 **Bienville, Lac** l. Que. Can.
199 H1 **Bierawa** Pol.
196 G5 **Bierawka** r. Pol.
107 J9 **Bierbank** Qld Austr.
196 G5 **Bierdzany** Pol.
193 E7 **Biere** Ger.
212 A2 **Bière** Switz.
208 E3 **Bierge** Spain
181 J6 **Bierné** France
185 G10 **Biert** France
197 H5 **Bieruń** Pol.
196 F4 **Bierutów** Pol.
196 G3 **Bierzwienna-Długa** Pol.
196 D2 **Bierzwnik** Pol.
208 E2 **Biescas** Spain
192 E5 **Biese** r. Ger.
192 I5 **Biesenthal** Ger.
196 E1 **Biesiekierz** Pol.
237 J2 **Biesiesvlei** S. Africa
179 J7 **Biesles** France
196 E1 **Biesowice** Pol.
236 H7 **Biesrespoort** S. Africa
195 J6 **Biessenhofen** Ger.
197 K6 **Bieszczady** mts Pol.
197 K6 **Bieszczadzki Park Narodowy** nat. park Pol.
194 E4 **Bietigheim** Ger.
194 G4 **Bietigheim-Bissingen** Ger.
192 I4 **Bietikow** Ger.
212 D3 **Bietschhorn** mt. Switz.
187 H9 **Bièvre** Belgium
197 H3 **Bieżuń** Pol.
215 O4 **Biferno** r. Italy
230 A5 **Bifoun** Gabon
162 □C1 **Bifröst** Iceland
124 T2 **Bifuka** Japan
244 I3 **Big** r. AK U.S.A.
264 I2 **Big** r. CA U.S.A.
221 I2 **Biga** Turkey
221 I2 **Biga** r. Turkey
221 J3 **Bigadiç** Turkey
285 G3 **Bigand** Arg.
185 C6 **Biganos** France
209 D11 **Bigastro** Spain
221 H3 **Biga Yarımadası** pen. Turkey
262 I3 **Big Baldy Mountain** MT U.S.A.
246 F5 **Big Bar Creek** B.C. Can.
103 C11 **Big Bay** b. South I. N.Z.
250 G3 **Big Bay** MI U.S.A.
100 □5 **Big Bay** b. Vanuatu
250 G4 **Big Bay de Noc** MI U.S.A.
264 P7 **Big Bear Lake** CA U.S.A.
262 I3 **Big Belt Mountains** MT U.S.A.
237 P2 **Big Bend** Swaziland
261 D11 **Big Bend National Park** TX U.S.A.
261 J9 **Big Black** r. MS U.S.A.
260 G6 **Big Blue** r. NE U.S.A.
172 E7 **Bigbury Bay** England U.K.
172 E7 **Bigbury-on-Sea** Devon, England U.K.
102 □ **Big Bush** Chatham Is S. Pacific Ocean
261 E11 **Big Canyon** watercourse TX U.S.A.
270 C1 **Big Cypress National Preserve** nature res. FL U.S.A.
255 G13 **Big Cypress National Preserve** nature res. FL U.S.A.
245 K2 **Big Delta** AK U.S.A.
104 H6 **Big Desert Wilderness Park** nature res. Vic. Austr.
250 E5 **Big Eau Pleine Reservoir** WI U.S.A.
100 □3a **Bigej** i. Kwajalein Marshall Is
100 □3a **Bigej Channel** Kwajalein Marshall Is
258 D5 **Big Elk Creek** r. MD U.S.A.
128 E4 **Biger** Govĭ-Altay Mongolia
128 E4 **Biger Nuur** salt l. Mongolia
260 I1 **Big Falls** MN U.S.A.
250 A1 **Big Fork** r. MN U.S.A.
247 J4 **Biggar** Sask. Can.
168 I11 **Biggar** South Lanarkshire, Scotland U.K.
248 F3 **Biggar, Lac** l. Que. Can.
100 □3a **Biggarenn** i. Kwajalein Marshall Is
237 N4 **Biggarsberg** S. Africa
108 H3 **Bigge Island** W.A. Austr.
107 N8 **Biggenden** Qld Austr.
245 M4 **Bigger, Mount** B.C. Can.
100 □3a **Biggerann** i. Kwajalein Marshall Is
191 E8 **Biggesee** l. Ger.
173 M5 **Biggin Hill** Greater London, England U.K.
173 L3 **Biggleswade** Bedfordshire, England U.K.
264 K2 **Biggs** CA U.S.A.
262 D4 **Biggs** OR U.S.A.
262 H4 **Big Hole** r. MT U.S.A.
262 K3 **Bighorn** r. MT/WY U.S.A.
262 K4 **Bighorn Mountains** WY U.S.A.
230 D4 **Bigi** Dem. Rep. Congo
100 □3a **Bigi** i. Kwajalein Marshall Is
161 W8 **Bigil'dino** Rus. Fed.
151 I5 **Bığır** Azer.
243 K3 **Big Island** i. Nunavut Can.
246 G2 **Big Island** i. N.W.T. Can.
256 F11 **Big Island** VA U.S.A.
245 N3 **Big Kalzas Lake** Y.T. Can.
244 H5 **Big Koniuji Island** AK U.S.A.
245 J3 **Big Lake** AK U.S.A.
261 E10 **Big Lake** TX U.S.A.
257 □R3 **Big Lake** l. ME U.S.A.
262 H5 **Big Lost** r. ID U.S.A.
Big Moggy Island Stewart I. N.Z. see **Mokinui Island**
262 L2 **Big Muddy Creek** r. MT U.S.A.
180 F6 **Bignan** France
212 F3 **Bignasco** Switz.
228 A3 **Bignona** Senegal
231 E6 **Bigobo** Dem. Rep. Congo
185 D10 **Bigorre** reg. France
256 F11 **Big Otter** r. VA U.S.A.
264 N4 **Big Pine** CA U.S.A.
264 M7 **Big Pine Peak** CA U.S.A.
262 K3 **Big Porcupine Creek** r. MT U.S.A.
245 N4 **Big Port Walter** AK U.S.A.
250 I6 **Big Rapids** MI U.S.A.
250 E5 **Big Rib** r. WI U.S.A.
247 J4 **Big River** Sask. Can.
250 H5 **Big Sable Point** MI U.S.A.
245 N3 **Big Salmon** r. Y.T. Can.
245 N3 **Big Salmon (abandoned)** Y.T. Can.
247 L3 **Big Sand Lake** Man. Can.
262 I2 **Big Sandy** MT U.S.A.
262 J6 **Big Sandy** r. WY U.S.A.
265 S7 **Big Sandy** watercourse AZ U.S.A.
260 D6 **Big Sandy Creek** r. CO U.S.A.
247 J4 **Big Sandy Lake** Sask. Can.
250 A3 **Big Sandy Lake** MN U.S.A.
260 G4 **Big Sioux** r. SD U.S.A.
264 O3 **Big Smokey Valley** NV U.S.A.
103 B14 **Big South Cape Island** Stewart I. N.Z.
261 E9 **Big Spring** TX U.S.A.
260 D5 **Big Springs** NE U.S.A.
247 I5 **Big Stone** Alta Can.
260 G3 **Big Stone City** SD U.S.A.
256 C12 **Big Stone Gap** VA U.S.A.
247 M4 **Bigstone Lake** Man. Can.
261 J9 **Big Sunflower** r. MS U.S.A.
264 K5 **Big Sur** CA U.S.A.
261 H10 **Big Thicket National Preserve** nature res. TX U.S.A.
262 J4 **Big Timber** MT U.S.A.
248 B2 **Big Trout Lake** Ont. Can.
248 B2 **Big Trout Lake** l. Ont. Can.
208 C2 **Bigüézal** Spain
214 C2 **Biguglia** Corse France
214 C2 **Biguglia, Étang de** lag. Corse France
246 H4 **Big Valley** Alta Can.
265 U4 **Big Water** UT U.S.A.
251 O4 **Bigwin** Ont. Can.
210 E3 **Bihać** Bos.-Herz.
139 J7 **Bihar** state India
199 K4 **Biharia** Romania
139 K7 **Bihariganj** Bihar India
199 K4 **Biharkeresztes** Hungary
199 K4 **Biharnagybajom** Hungary
139 J7 **Bihar Sharif** Bihar India
199 K5 **Biharugra** Hungary
199 K5 **Biharugraihalastavak** lakes Hungary
199 L5 **Bihor** county Romania
219 K4 **Bihor, Vârful** mt. Romania
124 V3 **Bihoro** Japan
199 L5 **Bihorului, Munții** mts Romania
139 N6 **Bihpuriagaon** Assam India
142 F4 **Biikzhal** Kazakh.
138 E9 **Bijagarh** Madh. Prad. India
228 A4 **Bijagós, Arquipélago dos** is Guinea-Bissau
138 E7 **Bijainagar** Rajasthan India
138 F6 **Bijaipur** Madh. Prad. India
136 D4 **Bijapur** Karnataka India
144 B4 **Bījār** Iran
136 G3 **Bijarpur** Chhattisgarh India
138 G7 **Bijawar** Madh. Prad. India
138 E3 **Bijbehara** Jammu and Kashmir India
210 G3 **Bijeljina** Bos.-Herz.
210 E3 **Bijelolasica** mt. Croatia
218 H7 **Bijelo Polje** Bijelo Polje Montenegro
138 H8 **Bijeraghogarh** Madh. Prad. India
Bijiang Yunnan China see **Zhiziluo**
130 E5 **Bijie** Guizhou China
136 G3 **Bijji** Chhattisgarh India
139 M6 **Bijni** Assam India
138 G5 **Bijnor** Uttar Prad. India
145 N7 **Bijnot** Pak.
138 E7 **Bijolia** Rajasthan India
239 □2 **Bijoutier** i. Seychelles
147 J3 **Bijrān** well Saudi Arabia
147 J3 **Bijrān, Khashm** hill Saudi Arabia
138 D6 **Bikampur** Rajasthan India
138 D5 **Bikaner** Rajasthan India
150 D5 **Bikfaiya** Lebanon
122 I5 **Bikin** Rus. Fed.
122 I5 **Bikin** r. Rus. Fed.
235 F4 **Bikita** Zimbabwe
232 B2 **Bikori** Sudan
230 C5 **Bikoro** Dem. Rep. Congo
130 E2 **Bikou** Gansu China
130 E2 **Bikou Shuiku** resr Gansu China
199 I6 **Bikovo** Vojvodina Serbia
139 J7 **Bikramganj** Bihar India
159 R4 **Bila** r. Ukr.
159 S4 **Bila** r. Ukr.
114 E7 **Bilaa Point** Mindanao Phil.
151 K5 **Biläcarı** Azer.
147 N5 **Bilād Banī Bū 'Alī** Oman
147 N4 **Bilād Banī Bū Ḥasan** Oman
146 E5 **Bilād Ghāmid** reg. Saudi Arabia
146 E5 **Bilād Zahrān** reg. Saudi Arabia
159 M6 **Bila Krynytsya** Ukr.
151 B7 **Bilaloğlu** Turkey
229 E3 **Bilanga** Burkina
117 M4 **Bilangbilangan** i. Indon.
138 D6 **Bilara** Rajasthan India
138 G5 **Bilari** Uttar Prad. India
138 I8 **Bilaspur** Chhattisgarh India
138 F4 **Bilaspur** Hima. Prad. India
151 J6 **Biläsuvar** Azer.
151 J6 **Biläsuvar** Azer.
114 C9 **Bilatan** i. Phil.
158 J4 **Bila Tserkva** Ukr.
119 D7 **Bilauktaung Range** mts Myanmar/Thai.
205 O2 **Bilbao** Spain
225 F2 **Bilbays** Egypt
Bilbo Spain see **Bilbao**
219 N3 **Bilbor** Romania
168 J6 **Bilbster** Highland, Scotland U.K.
129 L1 **Bil'chir** Rus. Fed.
162 □B1 **Bíldudalur** Iceland
197 M6 **Bile** Ukr.
210 G4 **Bileća** Bos.-Herz.
221 K2 **Bilecik** Turkey
221 L2 **Bilecik** prov. Turkey
210 G4 **Bilećko Jezero** resr Bos.-Herz./Yugo.
218 I5 **Biled** Romania
151 J6 **Bīleh Savār** Iran
199 G2 **Bílé Karpaty** park Czech Rep.
159 Q5 **Bilen'ke** Donets'ka Oblast' Ukr.
159 O6 **Bilen'ke** Zaporiz'ka Oblast' Ukr.
232 D4 **Bilesha Plain** Kenya
197 K5 **Biłgoraj** Pol.
233 A5 **Bilharamulo** Tanz.
138 H6 **Bilhaur** Uttar Prad. India
158 J7 **Bilhorod-Dnistrovs'kyy** Ukr.
230 C2 **Bili** Chad
230 E3 **Bili** Dem. Rep. Congo
230 D3 **Bili** r. Dem. Rep. Congo
153 R3 **Bilibino** Rus. Fed.
233 D8 **Bilibiza** Moz.
151 B6 **Bilice** Turkey
Bīlīköl l. Kazakh. see **Biylikol', Ozero**
118 C6 **Bilin** Myanmar
198 C1 **Bílina** Czech Rep.
215 Q6 **Bilioso** r. Italy
114 E6 **Biliran** i. Phil.
220 B2 **Bilisht** Albania
232 D4 **Bilis Qooqaani** Somalia
117 M2 **Bilit** Sabah Malaysia
129 R7 **Biliu He** r. China
199 M3 **Bilky** Ukr.
262 L5 **Bill** WY U.S.A.
109 C9 **Billabalong** W.A. Austr.
Billabong Creek r. N.S.W. Austr. see **Moulamein Creek**
109 C9 **Billabong Roadhouse** W.A. Austr.
205 O2 **Billao, Cabo de** c. Spain
164 H4 **Billdal** Sweden
190 J3 **Bille** r. Ger.
191 D7 **Billerbeck** Ger.
185 D9 **Billère** France
173 M4 **Billericay** Essex, England U.K.
182 H4 **Billiat** France
104 H6 **Billiat Conservation Park** nature res. S.A. Austr.
194 G3 **Billigheim** Ger.
108 I5 **Billiluna** W.A. Austr.
108 I5 **Billiluna Aboriginal Reserve** W.A. Austr.
289 E1 **Billingford** Norfolk, England U.K.
171 O4 **Billingham** Stockton-on-Tees, England U.K.
171 Q7 **Billinghay** Lincolnshire, England U.K.
262 J4 **Billings** MT U.S.A.
173 L5 **Billingshurst** West Sussex, England U.K.
Billiton i. Indon. see **Belitung**
244 G3 **Bill Moores** AK U.S.A.
173 P2 **Billockby** Norfolk, England U.K.
172 G6 **Bill of Portland** hd England U.K.
182 C5 **Billom** France
164 F6 **Billund** Denmark
163 J9 **Billund** airport Denmark
265 R7 **Bill Williams** r. AZ U.S.A.
265 T6 **Bill Williams Mountain** AZ U.S.A.
182 C4 **Billy** France
229 I2 **Bilma** Niger
229 I2 **Bilma, Grand Erg de** des. Niger
232 C2 **Bīlo** Eth.
107 M8 **Biloela** Qld Austr.
198 F5 **Bilo Gora** hills Croatia
159 N8 **Bilohirs'k** Ukr.
158 F3 **Bilohir"ya** Ukr.
158 F4 **Bilohorodka** Khmel'nyts'ka Oblast' Ukr.
158 J3 **Bilohorodka** Kyivs'ka Oblast' Ukr.
275 G4 **Biloku** Guyana
159 R4 **Bilokurakyne** Ukr.
136 E3 **Biloli** Mahar. India
159 S4 **Biloluts'k** Ukr.
159 N2 **Bilopillya** Ukr.
159 Q7 **Bilosarays'ka Kosa** spit Ukr.
158 F3 **Bilotyn** Ukr.
159 L3 **Bilousivka** Ukr.
199 H2 **Bílovec** Czech Rep.
199 G2 **Bílovice** Czech Rep.
159 S4 **Bilovods'k** Ukr.
261 K10 **Biloxi** MS U.S.A.
159 L7 **Bilozerka** Ukr.
159 Q5 **Bilozers'ke** Ukr.
106 G8 **Bilpa Morea Claypan** salt flat Qld Austr.
191 J7 **Bilshausen** Ger.
158 D4 **Bil'shivtsi** Ukr.
138 G5 **Bilsi** Uttar Prad. India
159 N3 **Bil's'k** Ukr.
158 E2 **Bil's'ka Volya** Ukr.
168 J11 **Bilston** Midlothian, Scotland U.K.
186 H4 **Bilthoven** Neth.
224 D6 **Biltine** Chad
224 D6 **Biltine** pref. Chad
162 P2 **Bilto** Norway
171 Q6 **Bilton** East Riding of Yorkshire, England U.K.
118 C6 **Bilugyun Island** Myanmar
159 O4 **Bilukhivka** Ukr.
115 C3 **Bilungala** Sulawesi Indon.
266 □R10 **Bilwascarma** Nic.
158 J7 **Bilyayivka** Ukr.
197 K6 **Bilychi** Ukr.
159 N4 **Bilyky** Ukr.
158 I4 **Bilylivka** Ukr.
158 I6 **Bilyne** Ukr.
159 Q5 **Bilyts'ke** Ukr.
158 D5 **Bilyy Cheremosh** r. Ukr.
159 Q3 **Bilyy Kolodyaz'** Ukr.
187 I7 **Bilzen** Belgium
230 E4 **Bima** r. Dem. Rep. Congo
117 M9 **Bima** Sumbawa Indon.
117 M9 **Bima, Teluk** b. Sumbawa Indon.
231 B7 **Bimbe** Angola
229 F4 **Bimbila** Ghana
230 C3 **Bimbo** C.A.R.
270 D1 **Bimini Islands** Bahamas
137 H4 **Bimlipatam** Andhra Prad. India
151 H6 **Binä** Dağlıq Qarabağ Azer.
151 L5 **Binä** Azer.
195 N5 **Bina** r. Ger.
199 H4 **Bíňa** Slovakia
149 N5 **Bināb** Iran
208 F4 **Binaced** Spain
138 G7 **Bina-Etawa** Madh. Prad. India
115 F5 **Binaija, Gunung** mt. Seram Indon.
114 D6 **Binalbagan** Negros Phil.
144 H3 **Bīnālūd, Reshteh Kūh-e** mts Iran
231 B6 **Binanga** Dem. Rep. Congo
144 H4 **Binar** pass Iran
197 J6 **Binarowa** Pol.
178 B8 **Binas** France
212 G5 **Binasco** Italy
117 I3 **Binatang** Sarawak Malaysia
107 K6 **Binbee** Qld Austr.
148 H4 **Binboğa Daği** mt. Turkey
171 Q7 **Binbrook** Lincolnshire, England U.K.
187 F8 **Binche** Belgium
129 P8 **Bincheng** Shandong China
Bincheng Shandong China see **Binzhou**
130 C6 **Binchuan** Yunnan China
230 B2 **Binder** Chad
129 L2 **Binder** Mongolia
138 H6 **Bindki** Uttar Prad. India
195 L2 **Bindlach** Ger.
107 L9 **Bindle** Qld Austr.
Bindloe Island Islas Galápagos Ecuador see **Marchena, Isla**
231 C6 **Bindu** Dem. Rep. Congo
235 F3 **Bindura** Zimbabwe
208 F4 **Binefar** Spain
170 D3 **Binevenagh** hill Northern Ireland U.K.
235 E3 **Binga** Zimbabwe
235 G3 **Binga, Monte** mt. Moz.
105 M3 **Bingara** N.S.W. Austr.
136 C7 **Bingaram** i. India
106 F3 **Bing Bong** N.T. Austr.
128 H8 **Bingcaowan** Gansu China
194 G5 **Bingen** Ger.
194 D2 **Bingen am Rhein** Ger.
186 J5 **Bingerden** Neth.
228 E5 **Bingerville** Côte d'Ivoire
173 K2 **Bingham** Nottinghamshire, England U.K.
257 □P3 **Bingham** ME U.S.A.
Binghamstown Ireland see **An Geata Mór**
257 J6 **Binghamton** NY U.S.A.
224 B3 **Bin Ghanīmah, Jabal** hills Libya
224 B1 **Bin Ghashir** Libya
171 N6 **Bingley** West Yorkshire, England U.K.
Bingmei Guizhou China see **Congjiang**
149 J4 **Bingöl** Turkey
151 B6 **Bingöl** prov. Turkey
149 J4 **Bingol Dağı** mt. Turkey
151 C6 **Bingöl Dağları** mts Turkey
Bingxi Jiangxi China see **Yushan**
130 B4 **Bingzhongluo** Yunnan China
119 I8 **Binh Đinh** Vietnam
118 H4 **Binh Gia** Vietnam
180 F4 **Binic** France
114 D7 **Binicuil** Negros Phil.
224 C4 **Bini Erda** well Chad
208 D2 **Biniés** Spain
139 I9 **Binika** Orissa India
209 K8 **Binissalem** Spain
116 C3 **Binjai** Sumatera Indon.
224 C2 **Bin Jawwād** Libya
232 F2 **Binna, Raas** pt Somalia
105 L4 **Binnaway** N.S.W. Austr.
168 G9 **Binnein Mòr** mt. Scotland U.K.
190 H5 **Binnen** Ger.
115 D7 **Binongko** i. Indon.
151 D6 **Binpınar** Turkey
139 K8 **Binpur** W. Bengal India
103 F10 **Binser, Mount** South I. N.Z.
232 B2 **Bīnshangul Gumuz** admin. reg. Eth.
195 J4 **Binswangen** Ger.
116 F4 **Bintan** i. Indon.
116 D2 **Bintang, Bukit** mts Malaysia
114 C5 **Bintuan** Phil.
116 E7 **Bintuhan** Sumatera Indon.
117 J3 **Bintulu** Sarawak Malaysia
114 C5 **Binubusan** Luzon Phil.
122 E6 **Binxian** Heilong. China
129 K9 **Binxian** Shaanxi China
Binxian Shandong China see **Bincheng**
130 G7 **Binyang** Guangxi China
229 G4 **Bin-Yauri** Nigeria
192 I2 **Binz, Ostseebad** Ger.
194 D6 **Binzen** Ger.
Binzhou Guangxi China see **Binyang**
Binzhou Heilong. China see **Binxian**
129 P8 **Binzhou** Shandong China
284 A5 **Bíobío** admin. reg. Chile
284 A5 **Bíobío** r. Chile
229 H6 **Bioco** i. Equat. Guinea
210 E4 **Biograd na Moru** Croatia
218 H8 **Biogradska Gora** nat. park Montenegro
Bioko i. Equat. Guinea see **Bioco**
210 F4 **Biokovo** park Croatia
182 G6 **Biol** France
212 C4 **Bionaz** Italy
208 H4 **Biosca** Spain
183 K9 **Biot** France
208 C3 **Biota** Spain
226 C3 **Biougra** Morocco
190 E5 **Bippen** Ger.
133 K10 **Bi Qu** r. Qinghai China
281 E3 **Biquinhas** Brazil
Bir Mahar. India see **Bid**
232 D2 **Bir, Ras** pt Djibouti
122 H4 **Bira** Rus. Fed.
122 H4 **Bira** r. Rus. Fed.
146 C2 **Bi'r Abā al 'Ajjāj** well Saudi Arabia
225 G4 **Bi'r Abraq** well Egypt
148 C8 **Bi'r Abū Baṭṭah** well Egypt
150 A9 **Bi'r Abū Daraj** well Egypt
225 F5 **Bir Abu Garad** well Sudan
225 G4 **Bi'r Abū Hashīm** well Egypt
225 F4 **Bi'r Abū Ḥuṣayn** well Egypt
150 G2 **Bi'r Abū Jady** oasis Syria
224 E3 **Bi'r Abū Minqār** well Egypt
224 A3 **Bi'r ad Damar** well Libya
150 A8 **Bi'r ad Duwaydār** well Egypt
224 D3 **Bi'r adh Dhakar** well Libya
226 C4 **Bîr Aïdiat** well Maur.
224 B3 **Birāk** Libya
122 G4 **Birakan** Rus. Fed.
150 B7 **Bi'r al 'Abd** Egypt
146 D3 **Bi'r al Amīr** well Saudi Arabia
146 D3 **Bi'r al Aṭbaq** well Saudi Arabia
146 D4 **Bi'r al 'Awādī** well Saudi Arabia
224 B2 **Bi'r al Fātīyah** well Libya
224 B1 **Bi'r al Ghanam** Libya
150 G4 **Bi'r al Ḥalbā** well Syria
225 G4 **Bi'r al Ḥaymūr** well Egypt
146 E3 **Bi'r al Ḥisw** well Saudi Arabia
224 D3 **Bi'r al Ikhwān** well Libya
224 B3 **Bi'r al Jadīd** well Libya
146 F5 **Bi'r al Jāhilīyah** well Saudi Arabia
150 B8 **Bi'r al Jifjāfah** well Egypt
224 E2 **Bi'r al Khamsah** well Egypt
228 B2 **Bir Allah** well Maur.
150 B9 **Bi'r al Māliḥah** well Egypt
225 H3 **Bi'r al Mashī** well Saudi Arabia
224 B3 **Bi'r al Mastūtah** well Libya
149 J7 **Bi'r al Mulūsi** Iraq
150 G4 **Bi'r al Munbaṭiḥ** well Syria
224 A2 **Bi'r al Mushayqīq** well Libya
224 C2 **Bi'r al Muwaylih** well Libya
224 E2 **Bi'r al Qaṭrānī** well Egypt
146 C2 **Bi'r al Qurr** well Saudi Arabia
224 E3 **Bi'r al Ubbayiḍ** well Egypt
150 C10 **Bi'r al 'Udayd** well Egypt
226 C5 **Bir 'Amrâne** well Maur.
156 G3 **Birandozero** Rus. Fed.
224 E2 **Bi'r an Nuṣṣ** well Egypt
226 B5 **Bir Anzarane** Western Sahara
230 D2 **Birao** C.A.R.
227 H2 **Bir Aouine** well Tunisia
224 B2 **Bi'r ar 'Alaqah** well Libya
146 E3 **Bi'r 'Arja** well Saudi Arabia
148 B8 **Bi'r ar Rābiyah** well Egypt
225 G2 **Bi'r ar Rummānah** Egypt
146 F4 **Bi'r as Sakhā** well Saudi Arabia
150 C9 **Bi'r as Sawrah** well Egypt
145 J1 **Birata** Turkm.
132 J6 **Biratar Bulak** spring China
139 K6 **Biratnagar** Nepal
124 T4 **Biratori** Japan
224 E2 **Bi'r aṭ Ṭarfāwī** well Libya
147 J4 **Bi'r 'Azīz** well Saudi Arabia
146 F6 **Bi'raz Zurq** well Saudi Arabia
150 F4 **Bi'r Başīrī** well Syria
150 C8 **Bi'r Bayḍā'** well Egypt
146 C2 **Bi'r Baydā** well Saudi Arabia
224 E2 **Bi'r Baylī** well Egypt
226 C4 **Bîr Bel Guerdâne** well Maur.
226 E4 **Bir Ben Takoul** well Alg.
224 E5 **Bir Bidi** well Sudan
224 D3 **Bi'r Bū Athlah** well Libya
146 D3 **Bi'r Budayy** well Saudi Arabia
224 A3 **Bi'r Bū Rāḥah** well Libya
146 E5 **Bi'r Buraym** well Saudi Arabia
148 I5 **Bi'r Buṭaymān** Syria
246 H3 **Birch** r. Alta Can.
226 D5 **Bir Chali** well Mali
245 K2 **Birch Creek** AK U.S.A.
245 K2 **Birch Creek** r. AK U.S.A.
244 I2 **Birches** AK U.S.A.
247 J4 **Birch Hills** Sask. Can.
173 O5 **Birchington** Kent, England U.K.
105 I6 **Birchip** Vic. Austr.
199 L6 **Birchiș** Romania
246 G5 **Birch Island** B.C. Can.
246 G2 **Birch Lake** N.W.T. Can.
247 M5 **Birch Lake** Ont. Can.
247 I4 **Birch Lake** Sask. Can.
250 C2 **Birch Lake** MN U.S.A.
246 H3 **Birch Mountains** Alta Can.
247 K4 **Birch River** Man. Can.
256 E10 **Birch River** WV U.S.A.
251 K6 **Birch Run** MI U.S.A.
250 C4 **Birchwood** WI U.S.A.
232 D3 **Bircot** Eth.
197 K6 **Bircza** Pol.
245 □B6 **Bird Cape** AK U.S.A.
169 F7 **Birdhill** Ireland
230 F3 **Bir Di** Sudan
225 F4 **Bi'r Dibs** well Egypt
258 C4 **Bird in Hand** PA U.S.A.
224 E2 **Bi'r Diqnāsh** well Egypt
Bird Island N. Mariana Is see **Farallon de Medinilla**
227 H3 **Bir Dolmane** well Alg.
258 D4 **Birdsboro** PA U.S.A.
265 U2 **Birdseye** UT U.S.A.
106 G8 **Birdsville** Qld Austr.
258 B7 **Birdsville** MD U.S.A.
106 D3 **Birdum** r. N.T. Austr.
148 H5 **Birecik** Turkey
226 E4 **Bir ed Deheb** well Alg.
227 G2 **Bir el Arbi** well Alg.
227 H2 **Bir el Ghoralia** well Tunisia
227 E4 **Bir El Hadjaj** well Alg.
Birendranagar Nepal see **Surkhet**
233 A5 **Birenga** Rwanda
224 E5 **Bir en Natrûn** well Sudan
225 G5 **Bir en Nugeim** well Sudan
227 G2 **Bir es Smeha** well Alg.
116 B2 **Bireun** Sumatera Indon.
147 I4 **Bi'r Fāḍil** well Saudi Arabia
146 C1 **Bi'r Fajr** well Saudi Arabia
225 G5 **Bir Fanoidig** well Sudan
147 I4 **Bi'r Fardān** well Saudi Arabia
224 E2 **Bi'r Fu'ād** well Egypt
224 D6 **Bir Furawiya** well Sudan
145 I8 **Bīrg, Kūh-e** mts Iran
226 A5 **Bir Gandouz** Western Sahara
146 G4 **Bi'r Ghawdah** well Saudi Arabia
224 D2 **Bi'r Ghayzal** well Libya
221 J4 **Birgi** Turkey
217 □ **Birgu** Malta
147 J6 **Bir Hādī** oasis Saudi Arabia
150 H4 **Bi'r Ḥajal** well Syria
232 C2 **Birhan** mt. Eth.
146 F4 **Bi'r Haraqī** well Saudi Arabia
150 B8 **Bi'r Ḥasanah** well Egypt
225 G4 **Bir Hatab** well Sudan
146 D3 **Bi'r Ḥaymir** well Saudi Arabia
146 D2 **Bi'r Ḥayzān** well Saudi Arabia
225 G4 **Bir Hismet 'Umar** well Sudan
146 F4 **Bi'r Ḥudūf** well Saudi Arabia
225 G4 **Bir Huwait** well Sudan
146 E3 **Bi'r Ḥuwaymidah** well Saudi Arabia
114 E5 **Biri** i. Phil.
146 C3 **Bi'r Ibn Ghunayn** well Saudi Arabia
Bi'r Ibn Hirmās Saudi Arabia see **Al Bi'r**
147 I4 **Bir Ibn Juhayyim** Saudi Arabia
146 F6 **Bi'r Ibn Sarrār** well Saudi Arabia
146 G6 **Bi'r Īdīmah** well Saudi Arabia
280 B4 **Birigüi** Brazil
150 E3 **Bīrīn** Syria
151 G4 **Birinci Şıxlı** Azer.
230 D3 **Birini** C.A.R.
224 E2 **Bi'r Isṭabl** well Egypt
144 H5 **Bīrjand** Iran
146 C2 **Bi'r Jaydah** well Saudi Arabia
146 G8 **Bi'r Jifah** well Yemen
224 E2 **Bi'r Jubnī** well Libya
146 F5 **Bi'r Jugjug** well Saudi Arabia
147 M4 **Birkat al Mawz** Oman
164 E3 **Birkeland** Norway
194 F2 **Birkenau** Ger.
194 F4 **Birkenfeld** Baden-Württemberg Ger.
194 H2 **Birkenfeld** Bayern Ger.
194 C2 **Birkenfeld** Rheinland-Pfalz Ger.
171 K7 **Birkenhead** Merseyside, England U.K.
191 E9 **Birken-Honigsessen** Ger.
192 H5 **Birkenwerder Berlin** Ger.
190 L1 **Birket** Denmark
201 M5 **Birkfeld** Austria
190 J1 **Birkholm** i. Denmark
146 C2 **Bi'r Khurbah** well Saudi Arabia
146 E4 **Bi'r Khuwārah** well Saudi Arabia
225 G4 **Bir Kiau** well Sudan
149 L5 **Bīrkim** Iraq
217 □ **Birkirkara** Malta
104 C2 **Birksgate Range** hills S.A. Austr.
191 J8 **Birkungen** Ger.
225 F4 **Bi'r Kusaybah** well Egypt
159 N3 **Birky** Ukr.
225 G4 **Bir Labasoi** well Sudan
Bîrlad Romania see **Bârlad**
150 B7 **Bi'r Lahfān** well Egypt
226 C4 **Bir Lahmar** Western Sahara
143 O5 **Birlik** Zhambylskaya Oblast' Kazakh.
143 O6 **Birlik** Zhambylskaya Oblast' Kazakh.
225 G4 **Bir Likeit el Fauqani** well Sudan
225 G4 **Bir Liseila** well Sudan
225 G4 **Bi'r Majal** well Egypt
145 M5 **Birmal** reg. Afgh.
146 F4 **Bi'r Malīyah** well Saudi Arabia
173 I3 **Birmingham** West Midlands, England U.K.
255 D9 **Birmingham** AL U.S.A.
224 E4 **Bi'r Misāḥa** well Egypt
139 J8 **Birmitrapur** Orissa India
226 C4 **Bîr Mogreïn** Maur.
150 G4 **Bi'r Muḥaymid al Wazwaz** well Syria
150 D9 **Bi'r Mujayfil** well Saudi Arabia
225 G4 **Bi'r Murrah** well Egypt
146 C3 **Bi'r Nabt** well Saudi Arabia
225 F2 **Bi'r Nāḥid** oasis Egypt
225 G4 **Bi'r Najīb** well Egypt
146 D3 **Bi'r Nasīf** Saudi Arabia
225 G4 **Bir Nawari** well Sudan
200 G6 **Birnbaum** Austria
200 G5 **Birnhorn** mt. Austria
229 F4 **Birni** Benin
100 □5 **Birnie** i. Kiribati
229 F3 **Birnin-Gaouré** Niger
229 G4 **Birnin-Gwari** Nigeria
229 G3 **Birnin-Kebbi** Nigeria
229 G3 **Birnin Konni** Niger
229 H4 **Birnin Kudu** Nigeria
229 H3 **Birniwa** Nigeria
224 E5 **Bir Nukheila** well Sudan
122 H4 **Birobidzhan** Rus. Fed.
122 H4 **Birofel'd** Rus. Fed.
185 F6 **Biron** France
114 B7 **Birong** Palawan Phil.
230 B5 **Birougou, Parc National de** nat. park Gabon
226 E4 **Bir Ould Brini** well Alg.
226 E5 **Bir Ounâne** well Mali
139 K6 **Birpur** Bihar India
224 E2 **Bi'r Qaṣīr as Sirr** well Egypt
225 G3 **Bi'r Qulayb** well Egypt
169 G6 **Birr** Ireland
150 B8 **Bi'r Rawḍ Sālim** well Egypt
191 C10 **Birresborn** Ger.
105 K3 **Birrie** r. N.S.W. Austr.
106 B5 **Birrindudu** N.T. Austr.
227 G2 **Bir Roumi** well Alg.
149 K7 **Bi'r Sābil** Iraq
225 F4 **Bi'r Şafşaf** well Egypt
225 F4 **Bi'r Şaḥrā'** well Egypt
225 G4 **Bir Salala** well Sudan
Bîrsana Romania see **Bârsana**
168 J4 **Birsay** Orkney, Scotland U.K.
212 D1 **Birse** r. Switz.
225 G4 **Bi'r Shalatayn** Egypt
150 H2 **Bi'r Shamandūr** well Syria
Birshoghyr Kazakh. see **Berchogur**
156 K5 **Birsk** Rus. Fed.
225 G4 **Bir Sohanit** well Sudan
173 J2 **Birstall** Leicestershire, England U.K.
191 H10 **Birstein** Ger.
160 H7 **Birštonas** Lith.
150 C9 **Bi'r Ṭābah** Egypt
146 H4 **Bir Ṭalḥah** well Saudi Arabia
227 H3 **Bir Tanguer** well Alg.
224 D2 **Bi'r Tānjidar** well Libya
225 F4 **Bi'r Ṭarfāwī** well Egypt
162 P2 **Birtavarre** Norway
150 B9 **Bi'r Thāl** well Egypt
107 I2 **Birthday Mountain** hill Qld Austr.
247 K5 **Birtle** Man. Can.
171 N4 **Birtley** Tyne and Wear, England U.K.
133 K11 **Biru** Xizang China
150 A9 **Bi'r Udayb** well Egypt
158 H6 **Biruința** Moldova
Biruintsa Moldova see **Ştefan Vodă**
224 C2 **Bi'r Umm al Gharānīq** Libya
146 A3 **Bi'r Umm Fawākhīr** well Egypt
146 C3 **Bi'r Umm Missā** well Saudi Arabia
Biruni Uzbek. see **Beruniy**
225 G4 **Bi'r 'Unjāt** well Egypt
136 D6 **Birur** Karnataka India
146 H4 **Bi'r Usaylīlah** well Saudi Arabia
225 G5 **Bir Wario** well Sudan
224 B3 **Bi'r Wedeb** well Libya
146 F5 **Bi'r Wurshah** well Saudi Arabia
159 R3 **Biryuch** Rus. Fed.
151 I2 **Biryuchek** Rus. Fed.
160 H5 **Biržai** Lith.
227 H3 **Bir Zar** well Tunisia
217 □ **Birżebbuġa** Malta
201 M6 **Biš** Slovenia
115 E4 **Bisa** i. Maluku Indon.
215 O5 **Bisaccia** Italy
216 E8 **Bisacquino** Sicilia Italy
126 E5 **Bisai** Japan
138 G5 **Bisalpur** Uttar Prad. India
138 E5 **Bisau** Rajasthan India
208 D2 **Bisaurín** mt. Spain
265 W10 **Bisbee** AZ U.S.A.
Biscari Sicilia Italy see **Acate**
185 B7 **Biscarrosse** France
185 B7 **Biscarrosse et de Parentis, Étang de** l. France
185 B7 **Biscarrosse-Plage** France
176 B4 **Biscay, Bay of** sea France/Spain
288 I3 **Biscay Abyssal Plain** sea feature N. Atlantic Ocean
255 G13 **Biscayne Bay** FL U.S.A.
255 G13 **Biscayne National Park** FL U.S.A.
215 R5 **Bisceglie** Italy
195 J2 **Bischberg** Ger.
194 G2 **Bischbrunn** Ger.
179 O6 **Bischheim** France
191 F9 **Bischoffen** Ger.
191 J8 **Bischofferode** Ger.
195 L1 **Bischofsgrün** Ger.
194 E2 **Bischofsheim** Ger.
191 J10 **Bischofsheim an der Rhön** Ger.
200 H5 **Bischofshofen** Austria
195 O4 **Bischofsmais** Ger.
193 J8 **Bischofswerda** Ger.
195 N6 **Bischofswiesen** Ger.
212 G1 **Bischofszell** Switz.
179 M6 **Bischwald, Étang de** l. France
179 O6 **Bischwiller** France
286 T2 **Biscoe Islands** Antarctica
238 □1a **Biscoitos** Terceira Azores
248 D4 **Biscotasi Lake** Ont. Can.
248 D4 **Biscotasing** Ont. Can.
124 □1 **Bise** Okinawa Japan
230 E3 **Bisellia** Sudan
215 L2 **Bisenti** Italy
214 H2 **Bisentina, Isola** i. Italy
156 L4 **Biser** Rus. Fed.
156 K4 **Biserovo** Rus. Fed.
156 L4 **Bisert'** r. Rus. Fed.
219 O7 **Bisertsi** Bulg.
210 E4 **Biševo** i. Croatia
124 □1 **Bise-zaki** pt Okinawa Jap
130 D7 **Bisezhai** Yunnan China
225 H6 **Bisha** Eritrea
146 F6 **Bīshah** reg. Saudi Arabia
146 G5 **Bīshah, Wādī** watercours Saudi Arabia
130 F4 **Bishan** Chongqing China
Bishbek Kyrg. see **Bishke**
149 N7 **Bīsheh** Iran
139 P5 **Bishemnagar** Arun. Prac
143 P6 **Bishkek** Kyrg.
139 K8 **Bishnupur** W. Bengal Inc
264 N4 **Bishop** CA U.S.A.
103 B13 **Bishop and Clerks Islan** Stewart I. N.Z.
171 N4 **Bishop Auckland** Durha England U.K.
168 H11 **Bishopbriggs** East Dunbartonshire, Scotland
246 G1 **Bishop Lake** N.W.T. Can
172 G3 **Bishop's Castle** Shropshi England U.K.
172 H4 **Bishop's Cleeve** Glouces England U.K.
172 F5 **Bishop's Hull** Somerset, England U.K.
173 J3 **Bishop's Itchington** War England U.K.
172 F5 **Bishop's Lydeard** Somer England U.K.
173 M4 **Bishop's Stortford** Hertf England U.K.
172 D5 **Bishop's Tawton** Devon, England U.K.
172 E6 **Bishopsteignton** Devon, England U.K.
173 J6 **Bishop's Waltham** Ham England U.K.
168 H11 **Bishopton** Renfrewshire, Scotland U.K.
255 G8 **Bishopville** SC U.S.A.
148 I6 **Bishrī, Jabal** hills Syria
122 C2 **Bishui** Heilong. China
Bishui Henan China see
237 N6 **Bisi** S. Africa
215 Q8 **Bisignano** Italy
274 D3 **Bisinaca** Col.
194 F5 **Bisingen** Ger.
227 G2 **Biskra** Alg.
197 K4 **Biskupice** Lubelskie Pol.
196 G4 **Biskupice** Opolskie Pol.
199 I3 **Biskupice** Slovakia
197 H2 **Biskupiec** Warmińsko-M Pol.
197 I2 **Biskupiec** Warmińsko-M Pol.
172 H4 **Bisley** Gloucestershire, England U.K.
114 F7 **Bislig** Mindanao Phil.
114 F7 **Bislig Bay** Mindanao Ph
260 E2 **Bismarck** ND U.S.A.
113 K7 **Bismarck Archipelago** is
98 E2 **Bismarck Range** mts P.N
113 K7 **Bismarck Sea** P.N.G.
192 E5 **Bismark (Altmark)** Ger.
149 J5 **Bismil** Turkey
163 J6 **Bismo** Norway
260 D3 **Bison** SD U.S.A.
144 B4 **Bīsotūn** Iran
162 N5 **Bispgården** Sweden
190 J4 **Bispingen** Ger.
137 H3 **Bissamcuttak** Orissa Ind
228 B4 **Bissau** Guinea-Bissau
229 H5 **Bissaula** Nigeria
187 J9 **Bissen** Lux.
191 F6 **Bissendorf** Ger.
190 I5 **Bissendorf (Wedemark)**
247 M5 **Bissett** Man. Can.
228 C4 **Bissikrima** Guinea
200 C7 **Bissina, Lago di** l. Italy
195 J4 **Bissingen** Ger.
228 B3 **Bissorã** Guinea-Bissau
212 E6 **Bistagno** Italy
246 G3 **Bistcho Lake** Alta Can.
218 I9 **Bistra** mt. Macedonia
218 I8 **Bistra** mt. Macedonia/Se
219 K5 **Bistra** r. Romania
219 L7 **Bistreț** Romania
219 L7 **Bistreț, Lacul** l. Romania
201 M7 **Bistrica** Šmarje pri Jelšah
201 J7 **Bistrica** Tržič Slovenia
219 M3 **Bistrița** Romania
219 M3 **Bistrița** r. Romania
219 O4 **Bistrița** r. Romania
219 M3 **Bistrița Bârgăului** Roma
219 N3 **Bistriței, Munții** mts Ror
219 L9 **Bistritsa** r. Bulg.
114 C6 **Bisucay** i. Phil.
138 H6 **Biswan** Uttar Prad. India
147 M4 **Bīsyah** Oman
165 Q7 **Bisztynek** Pol.
135 □1 **Bitadhoo** i. S. Male Mald
Bitadoo i. S. Male Maldiv **Bitadhoo**
230 A4 **Bitam** Gabon
232 C3 **Bitata** Eth.
194 B2 **Bitburg** Ger.
179 N5 **Bitche** France
217 L1 **Bitetto** Italy
138 H6 **Bithur** Uttar Prad. India
221 K2 **Bithynia** reg. Turkey
142 D2 **Bitik** Kazakh.
230 E3 **Bitilifondi** C.A.R.
230 C2 **Bitkine** Chad
149 K4 **Bitlis** Turkey
218 J9 **Bitola** Macedonia
Bitolj Macedonia see **Bit**
217 L1 **Bitonto** Italy
146 G4 **Bitrān, Jabal** hill Saudi A
136 C7 **Bitra Par** rf India
179 N8 **Bitschwiller-lès-Thann** F
265 W2 **Bitter Creek** r. UT U.S.A.
262 J6 **Bitter Creek** r. WY U.S.A.
193 F7 **Bitterfeld** Ger.
236 C7 **Bitterfontein** S. Africa
262 G3 **Bitterroot** r. MT U.S.A.
262 G3 **Bitterroot Range** mts ID
264 L5 **Bitterwater** CA U.S.A.
214 C7 **Bitti** Sardegna Italy
193 E6 **Bittkau** Ger.
172 H5 **Bitton** South Gloucestersh England U.K.
229 E4 **Bittou** Burkina
278 B4 **Bituca** Brazil
115 D3 **Bitung** Sulawesi Indon.
237 M7 **Bityi** S. Africa
157 G6 **Bityug** r. Rus. Fed.
194 G5 **Bitz** Ger.
229 I4 **Biu** Nigeria
231 D7 **Biula** Angola
205 Q3 **Biurrun** Spain
237 P3 **Bivane** r. S. Africa
212 H3 **Bivio** Switz.
219 P3 **Bivolari** Romania
216 E8 **Bivona** Sicilia Italy
250 B2 **Biwabik** MN U.S.A.
126 C5 **Biwa-ko** l. Japan
126 D5 **Biwa-ko Kokutei-kōen** pc
Biwmares Wales U.K. see **Beaumaris**
219 N4 **Bixad** Romania
232 E2 **Bixinduule** Somalia
168 □N2 **Bixter** Shetland, Scotland
143 U1 **Biya** r. Rus. Fed.
Biyang Anhui China see Y
131 I2 **Biyang** Henan China
232 D2 **Bīye K'obē** Eth.
143 N6 **Biylikol', Ozero** l. Kazakh
232 E3 **Biyo Ado** well Eth.
143 U1 **Biysk** Rus. Fed.
237 N6 **Bizana** S. Africa
183 B10 **Bizanet** France
185 D9 **Bizanos** France
200 A5 **Bizau** Austria
183 B10 **Bize-Minervois** France
125 L12 **Bizen** Japan
Bizerta Tunisia see **Bizert**
227 H1 **Bizerte** Tunisia
211 B7 **Bizerte** admin. div. Tunisi
144 H8 **Bīzhanābād** Iran
162 □A1 **Bjargtangar** hd Iceland

Bjarkøy Norway
Bjärnum Sweden
Bjärsjölagård Sweden
Bjästa Sweden
Bjelasica mts Montenegro
Bjelašnica mts Bos.-Herz.
Bjelovar Croatia
Bjerkvik Norway
Bjerreby Denmark
Bjerringbro Denmark
Bjøllånes Norway
Bjoneroa Norway
Björbo Sweden
Bjordal Norway
Bjørgan Norway
Bjørkelangen Norway
Björkfjället mts Sweden
Björkliden Sweden
Björklinge Sweden
Bjørknes Akershus Norway
Bjørknes Finnmark Norway
Björkö Sweden
Björkö i. Sweden
Björksele Sweden
Bjorli Norway
Björna Sweden
Bjørnafjorden b. Norway
Bjørnanuten mt. Norway
Björneborg Fin. see Pori
Bjornesfjorden l. Norway
Bjørnevatn Norway
Bjørnfjell Norway
Bjørnøya i. Arctic Ocean
Bjørnstad Norway
Bjurberget Sweden
Bjurholm Sweden
Bjuröklubb pt Sweden
Bjursås Sweden
Bla Mali
Bla Bheinn hill Scotland U.K.
Blacé France
Blace Blace Serbia
Blachownia Pol.
Black r. Man. Can.
Black r. Ont. Can.
Black r. Ont. Can.
Black r. Can./U.S.A.
Black r. Jamaica
Black Mauritius see Grande Rivière Noire
Black AK U.S.A.
Black r. AR U.S.A.
Black r. AR U.S.A.
Black r. AZ U.S.A.
Black r. MI U.S.A.
Black r. SC U.S.A.
Black r. WI U.S.A.
Blackadder Water r. Scotland U.K.
Blackall Qld Austr.
Black Bay Ont. Can.
Black Bay Sask. Can.
Blackbear r. Ont. Can.
Blackberry MN U.S.A.
Black Birch Lake Sask. Can.
Blackbourne, Point Norfolk I.
Black Bourton Oxfordshire, England U.K.
Blackbraes National Park nat. park Australia
Blackbull Qld Austr.
Black Bull Ireland
Blackburn Aberdeenshire, Scotland U.K.
Blackburn Blackburn with Darwen, England U.K.
Blackburn West Lothian, Scotland U.K.
Blackburn, Mount AK U.S.A.
Blackburn with Darwen admin. div. England U.K.
Blackbutt Qld Austr.
Black Butte mt. CA U.S.A.
Black Butte Lake CA U.S.A.
Black Canyon gorge AZ U.S.A.
Black Canyon City AZ U.S.A.
Black Canyon of the Gunnison National Park CO U.S.A.
Black Coast Antarctica
Black Combe hill England U.K.
Blackcraig Hill Scotland U.K.
Black Creek WI U.S.A.
Black Creek r. PA U.S.A.
Black Creek watercourse AZ U.S.A.
Black Dome mt. B.C. Can.
Black Donald Lake Ont. Can.
Black Down Hills England U.K.
Blackdown Tableland National Park Qld Austr.
Blackduck MN U.S.A.
Blacken b. Sweden
Blackfalds Alta Can.
Blackfeet Indian Reservation res. MT U.S.A.
Blackfield Hampshire, England U.K.
Blackfoot ID U.S.A.
Black Foot r. MT U.S.A.
Blackfoot Reservoir ID U.S.A.
Blackford Perth and Kinross, Scotland U.K.
Black Forest mts Ger. see Schwarzwald
Black Head Ireland
Black Head England U.K.
Black Head Northern Ireland U.K.
Black Hill England U.K.
Black Hill Range hills N.T. Austr.
Black Hills SD U.S.A.
Black Hills SD U.S.A.
Blackhope Scar hill Scotland U.K.
Black Island Man. Can.
Black Isle pen. Scotland U.K.
Black Lake Sask. Can.
Black Lake l. Sask. Can.
Black Lake l. MI U.S.A.
Blacklion Ireland
Blacklunans Perth and Kinross, Scotland U.K.
Blackman's Barbados
Black Mesa mt. AZ U.S.A.
Black Mesa ridge AZ U.S.A.
Blackmoor Gate Devon, England U.K.
Blackmore Essex, England U.K.
Black Mountain hills Wales U.K.
Black Mountain AK U.S.A.
Black Mountain CA U.S.A.
Black Mountain KY U.S.A.
Black Mountains hills Wales U.K.
Black Mountains AZ U.S.A.
Black Nossob watercourse Namibia
Black Notley Essex, England U.K.
Black Pagoda Orissa India see Konarka
Black Point H.K. China see Lan Kok Tsui
Blackpool Blackpool, England U.K.
Black Range State Park nature res. Vic. Austr.
Black Rapids AK U.S.A.
Black River Jamaica
Black River MI U.S.A.
Black River NY U.S.A.
Black River r. Vietnam see Đa, Sông
Black River Falls WI U.S.A.
Black Rock hill Jordan see 'Unāb, Jabal al
Blackrock Ireland
Black Rock Desert NV U.S.A.
Blacksburg VA U.S.A.
Black Sea Asia/Europe
Blacks Fork r. WY U.S.A.
Blacks Harbour N.B. Can.
Blackshear GA U.S.A.
Blacksod Bay Ireland
Black Springs NV U.S.A.
Blackstairs Mountains hills Ireland
Blackstone r. N.W.T. Can.
Blackstone r. Y.T. Can.
Blackstone VA U.S.A.
Black Sturgeon r. Ont. Can.

105 M4 Black Sugarloaf mt. N.S.W. Austr.
249 K2 Black Tickle Nfld and Lab. Can.
169 G3 Blacktown Northern Ireland U.K.
237 P4 Black Umfolozi r. S. Africa
105 M4 Blackville N.S.W. Austr.
228 E4 Black Volta r. Africa alt. Mouhoun, alt. Volta Noire
107 L7 Blackwater Qld Austr.
107 J8 Blackwater watercourse Qld Austr.
246 E2 Blackwater r. N.W.T. Can.
169 I3 Blackwater r. N. Ireland/Ireland
169 J8 Blackwater Ireland
169 I5 Blackwater r. Ireland
169 G8 Blackwater r. Ireland
173 N4 Blackwater r. England U.K.
168 H6 Black Water r. Highland, Scotland U.K.
168 H7 Black Water r. Highland, Scotland U.K.
256 I12 Blackwater r. VA U.S.A.
261 E9 Blackwater watercourse NM/TX U.S.A.
168 F12 Blackwaterfoot North Ayrshire, Scotland U.K.
245 Q3 Blackwater Lake N.W.T. Can.
168 G9 Blackwater Reservoir Scotland U.K.
170 D5 Blackwatertown Northern Ireland U.K.
109 C13 Blackwood r. W.A. Austr.
172 F4 Blackwood Caerphilly, Wales U.K.
107 K6 Blackwood National Park Qld Austr.
187 H6 Bladel Neth.
107 I7 Bladensburg National Park Qld Austr.
172 E2 Blaenau Ffestiniog Gwynedd, Wales U.K.
172 F4 Blaenau Gwent admin. div. Wales U.K.
172 F4 Blaenavon Torfaen, Wales U.K.
172 E4 Blaengarw Bridgend, Wales U.K.
172 E4 Blaengwrach Neath Port Talbot, Wales U.K.
162 L4 Blåfjellshatten mt. Norway
172 G5 Blagdon North Somerset, England U.K.
185 G8 Blagnac France
179 J4 Blagny France
157 H7 Blagodarnyy Rus. Fed.
159 N2 Blagodatnoye Rus. Fed.
219 L8 Blagoevgrad Bulg.
143 L1 Blagoveshchenka Kazakh.
143 R1 Blagoveshchenka Rus. Fed.
122 E3 Blagoveshchensk Amurskaya Oblast' Rus. Fed.
156 L5 Blagoveshchensk Respublika Bashkortostan Rus. Fed.
Blagoveshchenskoye Severnyy Kazakhstan Kazakh. see Blagoveshchenka
201 K7 Blagovica Slovenia
159 N7 Blahodatne Khersons'ka Oblast' Ukr.
159 K6 Blahodatne Mykolayivs'ka Oblast' Ukr.
159 N6 Blahovishchenka Zaporiz'ka Oblast' Ukr.
159 P6 Blahovishchenka Zaporiz'ka Oblast' Ukr.
195 N3 Blaibach Ger.
168 F9 Blaich Highland, Scotland U.K.
195 I6 Blaichach Ger.
246 H5 Blaikiston, Mount B.C. Can.
180 H7 Blain France
256 H8 Blain PA U.S.A.
250 A4 Blaine MN U.S.A.
262 C2 Blaine WA U.S.A.
247 J4 Blaine Lake Sask. Can.
179 L6 Blainville-sur-l'Eau France
180 H3 Blainville-sur-Mer France
181 K3 Blainville-sur-Orne France
260 G5 Blair NE U.S.A.
250 C5 Blair WI U.S.A.
107 K7 Blair Athol Qld Austr.
168 I9 Blair Atholl Perth and Kinross, Scotland U.K.
237 K1 Blairbeth S. Africa
168 J9 Blairgowrie Perth and Kinross, Scotland U.K.
256 F12 Blairs VA U.S.A.
264 L2 Blairsden CA U.S.A.
258 F3 Blairstown NJ U.S.A.
255 F8 Blairsville GA U.S.A.
256 F8 Blairsville PA U.S.A.
179 I6 Blaise r. France
179 I7 Blaiserives France
182 F2 Blaisy-Bas France
219 L4 Blaj Romania
185 F9 Blajan France
199 L5 Blăjeni Romania
142 I2 Blak Rus. Fed.
Blakang Mati, Pulau i. Sing. see Sentosa
255 E10 Blakely GA U.S.A.
258 D2 Blakely PA U.S.A.
172 H4 Blakeney Gloucestershire, England U.K.
173 O2 Blakeney Norfolk, England U.K.
173 N2 Blakeney Point England U.K.
250 F1 Blake Point MI U.S.A.
258 D2 Blakeslee PA U.S.A.
228 C5 Blama Sierra Leone
117 K9 Blambangan, Semenanjung pen. Indon.
179 M6 Blâmont France
185 I8 Blan France
209 K9 Blanc, Cap c. Spain
185 B8 Blanc, Étang l. France
182 J5 Blanc, Mont mt. France/Italy
209 C11 Blanca Spain
285 G6 Blanca, Bahía b. Arg.
276 A2 Blanca, Cordillera mts Peru
207 J7 Blanca, Sierra mts Spain
263 L10 Blanca, Sierra mt. NM U.S.A.
181 Q6 Blancafort France
263 L8 Blanca Peak CO U.S.A.
205 R7 Blancas Spain
170 E7 Blanchardstown Ireland
183 I8 Blanche r. France
104 E5 Blanche, Cape S.A. Austr.
104 G3 Blanche, Lake salt flat S.A. Austr.
108 G7 Blanche, Lake salt flat W.A. Austr.
183 I8 Blanche, Montagne de la ridge France
100 □6 Blanche Channel New Georgia Is Solomon Is
256 B9 Blanchester OH U.S.A.
104 G6 Blanchetown S.A. Austr.
271 □7 Blanchisseuse Trin. and Tob.
178 C2 Blanc Nez, Cap c. France
282 C3 Blanco r. Arg.
276 D3 Blanco r. Bol.
274 C6 Blanco r. Peru
236 G9 Blanco S. Africa
207 I5 Blanco r. Spain
266 □Q13 Blanco, Cabo c. Costa Rica
Blanco, Cabo c. Spain see Blanc, Cap
262 B5 Blanco, Cape OR U.S.A.
249 J3 Blanc-Sablon Que. Can.
105 K5 Bland r. N.S.W. Austr.
256 D11 Bland VA U.S.A.
162 □C1 Blanda r. Iceland
172 H6 Blandford Camp Dorset, England U.K.
172 H6 Blandford Forum Dorset, England U.K.
265 W4 Blanding UT U.S.A.
250 D9 Blandinsville IL U.S.A.
258 D4 Blandon PA U.S.A.
208 K4 Blanes Spain
250 I3 Blaney Park MI U.S.A.
116 □ Blangah, Telok b. Sing.
116 B3 Blangkejeren Sumatera Indon.
116 B3 Blangpidie Sumatera Indon.
181 L3 Blangy-le-Château France
178 C4 Blangy-sur-Bresle France
198 D2 Blanice r. Czech Rep.
198 D2 Blanice r. Czech Rep.
198 D2 Blaník park Czech Rep.
165 M4 Blankaholm Sweden
192 E3 Blankenberg Ger.

187 D6 Blankenberge Belgium
191 K7 Blankenburg (Harz) Ger.
193 H6 Blankenfelde Ger.
193 F9 Blankenhain Sachsen Ger.
193 D9 Blankenhain Thüringen Ger.
191 C10 Blankenheim Nordrhein-Westfalen Ger.
193 D7 Blankenheim Sachsen-Anhalt Ger.
191 D10 Blankenrath Ger.
192 H4 Blankensee Ger.
193 E10 Blankenstein Ger.
185 C6 Blanquefort France
275 E2 Blanquilla, Isla i. Venez.
206 H8 Blanquilla, Sierra mts Spain
207 N4 Blanquillo mt. Spain
198 F2 Blansko Czech Rep.
233 B8 Blantyre Malawi
184 E5 Blanzac-Porcheresse France
182 C5 Blanzat France
184 E3 Blanzay France
182 E3 Blanzy France
186 H4 Blaricum Neth.
169 E9 Blarney Ireland
256 G6 Blasdell NY U.S.A.
185 D6 Blasimon France
164 C2 Blåsjø l. Norway
163 I6 Blaskavlen mt. Norway
169 A8 Blasket Sound sea chan. Ireland
162 L5 Blåstöten mt. Sweden
196 G4 Błaszki Pol.
198 C2 Blatná Czech Rep.
198 G3 Blatné Slovakia
187 E7 Blaton Belgium
162 N4 Blattniksele Sweden
115 C3 Blau Sulawesi Indon.
194 H5 Blaubeuren Ger.
194 H3 Blaufelden Ger.
190 G2 Blauort i. Ger.
194 H5 Blaustein Ger.
164 E6 Blåvands Huk pt Denmark
Blaven hill Scotland U.K. see Bla Bheinn
180 E6 Blavet r. France
156 B2 Blåviksjön Sweden
183 D6 Blavozy France
171 N4 Blaydon Tyne and Wear, England U.K.
184 C5 Blaye France
185 I7 Blaye-les-Mines France
183 I8 Blayeul mt. France
105 L5 Blayney N.S.W. Austr.
106 C2 Blaze, Point N.T. Austr.
197 L6 Blazhiv Ukr.
158 G2 Blazhove Ukr.
197 J4 Błaziny Górne Pol.
201 O1 Blažovice Czech Rep.
197 K6 Błażowa Pol.
207 I4 Blázquez Spain
173 O5 Blean Kent, England U.K.
190 K4 Bleckede Ger.
208 E3 Blecua Spain
201 J7 Bled Slovenia
224 B6 Bledaya Chad
197 I4 Błędów Pol.
196 G2 Błędowo Pol.
196 D3 Bledzew Pol.
117 J8 Blega Jawa Indon.
201 J7 Blegoš mt. Slovenia
187 D7 Bléharies Belgium
191 B10 Bleialf Ger.
201 K6 Bleiburg Austria
191 K8 Bleicherode Ger.
191 F10 Bleidenstadt Ger.
162 M2 Bleik Norway
200 H4 Bleikogel mt. Austria
193 E9 Bleilochtalsperre resr Ger.
186 G4 Bleiswijk Neth.
190 K2 Blekendorf Ger.
165 K5 Blekinge county Sweden
171 K4 Blencathra hill England U.K.
178 D2 Blendecques France
190 H5 Blender Ger.
178 E8 Bléneau France
248 D5 Blenheim Ont. Can.
103 H8 Blenheim South I. N.Z.
173 J4 Blenheim Palace tourist site England U.K.
179 L6 Blénod-lès-Pont-à-Mousson France
179 K6 Blénod-lès-Toul France
183 H8 Bléone r. France
214 I3 Blera Italy
178 F4 Blérancourt France
184 F1 Bléré France
187 J6 Blerick Neth.
208 D5 Blesa Spain
186 G5 Bleskensgraaf Neth.
183 C6 Blesle France
236 I3 Blesmanspos S. Africa
169 I6 Blessington Ireland
169 I6 Blessington Lakes Ireland
182 B3 Blet France
173 K3 Bletchley Milton Keynes, England U.K.
164 F2 Bletoppen mt. Norway
182 G3 Bletterans France
251 P3 Bleu, Lac l. Que. Can.
230 F4 Bleus, Monts mts Dem. Rep. Congo
173 J4 Blewbury Oxfordshire, England U.K.
190 G3 Blexen (Nordenham) Ger.
199 J3 Blh r. Slovakia
227 F1 Blida Alg.
190 I4 Bliedersdorf Ger.
194 C3 Blies r. Ger.
194 C3 Blieskastel Ger.
103 B11 Bligh Sound inlet South I. N.Z.
101 □7a Bligh Water b. Fiji
178 I7 Bligny France
182 F2 Bligny-sur-Ouche France
186 L2 Blijham Neth.
204 I2 Blimea Spain
201 K3 Blindenmarkt Austria
192 I4 Blindow Ger.
248 D4 Blind River Ont. Can.
237 K8 Blinkwater S. Africa
104 G4 Blinman S.A. Austr.
212 E3 Blinnenhorn mt. Italy/Switz.
262 G5 Bliss ID U.S.A.
251 K8 Blissfield MI U.S.A.
256 D8 Blissfield OH U.S.A.
173 K3 Blisworth Northamptonshire, England U.K.
117 J9 Blitar Jawa Indon.
196 G4 Blizanów Pol.
195 N3 Blížejov Czech Rep.
198 E3 Blížkovice Czech Rep.
197 J6 Blizne Pol.
Bliznetsy Ukr. see Blyznyuky
Bliznyuki Ukr. see Blyznyuky
197 I4 Bliżyn Pol.
218 I8 Bllacë Suharekë Kosovo
257 N7 Block Island RI U.S.A.
257 N7 Block Island i. RI U.S.A.
257 N7 Block Island Sound sea chan. RI U.S.A.
173 I3 Blockley Gloucestershire, England U.K.
237 O3 Bloedrivier S. Africa
237 K5 Bloemfontein S. Africa
237 J3 Bloemhof S. Africa
237 J3 Bloemhof Dam S. Africa
237 J3 Bloemhof Dam Nature Reserve S. Africa
181 N6 Blois France
186 I3 Blokzijl Neth.
191 H7 Blomberg Ger.
236 E6 Blomberg se Vloer salt pan S. Africa
164 A1 Blomøy i. Norway
162 □D1 Blöndulón l. Iceland
162 □C1 Blönduós Iceland
117 L9 Blongas Lombok Indon.
197 H3 Błonie Łódzkie Pol.
197 I3 Błonie Mazowieckie Pol.
193 G7 Blönsdorf Ger.
181 L3 Blonville-sur-Mer France
106 B8 Bloods Range mts N.T. Austr.
257 I10 Bloodsworth Island MD U.S.A.
247 L5 Bloodvein r. Man. Can.
245 Q2 Bloody r. N.W.T. Can.
169 F2 Bloody Foreland pt Ireland
250 C4 Bloomer WI U.S.A.

251 Q6 Bloomfield Ont. Can.
260 I5 Bloomfield IA U.S.A.
254 D6 Bloomfield IN U.S.A.
261 K7 Bloomfield MO U.S.A.
263 K8 Bloomfield NM U.S.A.
107 J3 Bloomfield River Qld Austr.
259 G1 Bloomingburg NY U.S.A.
259 G2 Bloomingdale NJ U.S.A.
258 E4 Blooming Glen PA U.S.A.
259 G2 Blooming Grove NY U.S.A.
258 E2 Blooming Grove PA U.S.A.
250 A6 Blooming Prairie MN U.S.A.
250 F9 Bloomington IL U.S.A.
254 D6 Bloomington IN U.S.A.
250 A5 Bloomington MN U.S.A.
251 R8 Bloomsburg PA U.S.A.
107 L6 Bloomsbury Qld Austr.
258 E3 Bloomsbury NJ U.S.A.
117 I8 Blora Jawa Indon.
251 Q8 Blossburg PA U.S.A.
243 P3 Blosseville Kyst coastal area Greenland
153 S2 Blossom, Mys pt Rus. Fed.
182 K1 Blotzheim France
235 F4 Blouberg Nature Reserve S. Africa
236 C9 Bloubergstrand S. Africa
237 K4 Bloudrif S. Africa
255 E10 Blountstown FL U.S.A.
256 C12 Blountville TN U.S.A.
185 E9 Blousson-Sérian France
198 C2 Blovice Czech Rep.
245 M1 Blow r. Y.T. Can.
192 E3 Blowatz Ger.
270 E5 Blower Rock i. Jamaica
173 J3 Bloxham Oxfordshire, England U.K.
171 N6 Blubberhouses North Yorkshire, England U.K.
200 A5 Bludenz Austria
200 A5 Bludesch Austria
245 O4 Blue r. B.C. Can.
261 H9 Blue r. OK U.S.A.
265 W8 Blue watercourse AZ U.S.A.
170 B7 Blue Ball Ireland
258 C4 Blue Ball PA U.S.A.
258 E4 Blue Bell PA U.S.A.
265 U3 Blue Bell Knoll mt. UT U.S.A.
246 F3 Blueberry r. B.C. Can.
237 J9 Blue Cliff S. Africa
Blue Creek r. Mex. see Azul
255 G12 Blue Cypress Lake FL U.S.A.
265 Q5 Blue Diamond NV U.S.A.
260 H4 Blue Earth MN U.S.A.
260 H3 Blue Earth r. MN U.S.A.
256 D11 Bluefield VA U.S.A.
256 D11 Bluefield WV U.S.A.
270 □ Bluefields Jamaica
266 □R11 Bluefields Nic.
169 D8 Blueford Ireland
237 L6 Bluegums S. Africa
257 □Q4 Blue Hill ME U.S.A.
260 F5 Blue Hill NE U.S.A.
270 G3 Blue Hills Turks and Caicos Is
256 G8 Blue Knob hill PA U.S.A.
231 E8 Blue Lagoon National Park Zambia
258 C4 Blue Marsh Lake PA U.S.A.
249 J3 Blue Mountain hill Nfld and Lab. Can.
139 N8 Blue Mountain Mizoram India
258 B4 Blue Mountain ridge PA U.S.A.
257 K5 Blue Mountain Lake NY U.S.A.
237 L5 Blue Mountain Pass Lesotho
270 □ Blue Mountain Peak Jamaica
105 L5 Blue Mountains N.S.W. Austr.
270 □ Blue Mountains Jamaica
103 D13 Blue Mountains South I. N.Z.
262 E4 Blue Mountains OR U.S.A.
105 M5 Blue Mountains National Park N.S.W. Austr.
106 F2 Blue Mud Bay N.T. Austr.
225 G6 Blue Nile r. Eth./Sudan alt. Ābay Wenz (Ethiopia), alt. Azraq, Bahr el (Sudan)
232 B2 Blue Nile state Sudan
245 R1 Bluenose Lake Nunavut Can.
260 G6 Blue Rapids KS U.S.A.
255 E8 Blue Ridge GA U.S.A.
256 F11 Blue Ridge VA U.S.A.
256 E12 Blue Ridge mts VA U.S.A.
246 G4 Blue River B.C. Can.
169 F3 Blue Stack Mountains hills Ireland
256 E11 Bluestone Lake WV U.S.A.
107 L7 Bluff Qld Austr.
103 C13 Bluff South I. N.Z.
265 W4 Bluff UT U.S.A.
256 C12 Bluff City TN U.S.A.
265 U1 Bluffdale UT U.S.A.
108 I4 Bluff Face Range hills W.A. Austr.
103 C13 Bluff Harbour South I. N.Z.
Bluff Island H.K. China see Sha Tong Hau Shan
109 E13 Bluff Knoll mt. W.A. Austr.
109 C9 Bluff Point W.A. Austr.
254 E5 Bluffton IN U.S.A.
256 B8 Bluffton OH U.S.A.
201 N5 Blumau in Steiermark Austria
194 F6 Blumberg Baden-Württemberg Ger.
192 I5 Blumberg Brandenburg Ger.
279 C8 Blumenau Brazil
192 I3 Blumenhagen Ger.
192 H4 Blumenholz Ger.
192 F4 Blumenthal Ger.
212 D3 Blümlisalp mt. Switz.
260 E3 Blunt SD U.S.A.
246 F5 Blustry Mountain B.C. Can.
262 D5 Bly OR U.S.A.
245 J4 Blying Sound sea channel AK U.S.A.
159 K2 Blystova Ukr.
106 E2 Blyth r. N.T. Austr.
251 M6 Blyth Ont. Can.
171 N3 Blyth Northumberland, England U.K.
171 O7 Blyth Nottinghamshire, England U.K.
173 P3 Blyth r. England U.K.
168 J11 Blyth Bridge Scottish Borders, Scotland U.K.
265 R8 Blythe CA U.S.A.
237 P5 Blythedale Beach S. Africa
261 K8 Blytheville AR U.S.A.
109 J9 Blyth Range hills W.A. Austr.
171 P7 Blyton Lincolnshire, England U.K.
159 P5 Blyznyuky Ukr.
164 F2 Bø Norway
228 C5 Bo Sierra Leone
114 C5 Boac Phil.
266 □Q11 Boaco Nic.
204 H7 Boada Spain
208 K3 Boadella, Pantà de resr Spain
205 M8 Boadilla del Monte Spain
205 K4 Boadilla de Rioseco Spain
277 E1 Boa Esperança Amazonas Brazil
281 E4 Boa Esperança Minas Gerais Brazil
275 F4 Boa Esperança Roraima Brazil
278 E3 Boa Esperança, Açude resr Brazil
280 C4 Boa Esperança do Sul Brazil
276 B1 Boa Fé Brazil
276 D2 Boa Hora Brazil
129 M9 Bo'ai Henan China
130 F7 Bo'ai Yunnan China
170 B4 Boa Island Northern Ireland U.K.
204 G2 Boal Spain
204 D5 Boalhosa Port.
230 C3 Boali C.A.R.
256 H8 Boalsburg PA U.S.A.
237 Q2 Boane Moz.
115 E5 Boano i. Maluku Indon.
115 E5 Boano, Selat sea chan. Maluku Indon.
278 E5 Boa Nova Brazil
213 L5 Boara Pisani Italy
256 E7 Boardman OH U.S.A.
259 I1 Boardmans Bridge CT U.S.A.
168 H7 Boath Highland, Scotland U.K.
234 E4 Boatlaname Botswana
107 K9 Boatman Qld Austr.
168 I8 Boat of Garten Highland, Scotland U.K.

238 □2a Boatswain-bird Island Ascension S. Atlantic Ocean
270 C4 Boatswain Point Cayman Is
206 □ Boaventura Madeira
278 F3 Boa Viagem Brazil
274 C6 Boa Vista Amazonas Brazil
275 E5 Boa Vista Amazonas Brazil
275 H5 Boa Vista Pará Brazil
275 F4 Boa Vista Roraima Brazil
228 □ Boa Vista i. Cape Verde
204 C9 Boa Vista Port.
255 □1 Boaz Island Bermuda
105 K5 Bobadah N.S.W. Austr.
207 J6 Bobadilla Andalucía Spain
205 O4 Bobadilla La Rioja Spain
205 J6 Bobadilla del Campo Spain
130 H7 Bobai Guangxi China
235 □K1 Bobaomby, Tanjona c. Madag.
235 □K2 Bobasakoa Madag.
193 F7 Bobbau Ger.
137 H3 Bobbili Andhra Prad. India
212 G6 Bobbio Italy
212 C6 Bobbio Pellice Italy
251 P5 Bobcayegon Ont. Can.
194 E2 Bobenheim-Roxheim Ger.
158 F2 Bober r. Ukr.
158 B4 Boberka Ukr.
204 G2 Bobia mt. Spain
204 G2 Bobia, Sierra de la mts Spain
196 E2 Bobięcińskie Wielkie, Jezioro l. Pol.
178 D6 Bobigny France
195 K6 Böbing Ger.
195 J5 Bobingen Ger.
192 D3 Bobitz Ger.
161 W6 Bobkovo Rus. Fed.
194 G4 Böblingen Ger.
197 M4 Bobly Ukr.
228 D4 Bobo-Dioulasso Burkina
196 E2 Bobolice Pol.
114 E5 Bobon Samar Phil.
235 F4 Bobonong Botswana
204 D4 Boborás Spain
199 L4 Bobota Romania
Bobotov Kuk mt. Montenegro see Durmitor
219 L8 Bobovdol Bulg.
199 L3 Bobove Ukr.
197 I6 Bobowa Pol.
196 G2 Bobowo Pol.
143 N7 Boboyob, Gora mt. Uzbek.
160 M7 Bobr Belarus
160 L7 Bobr r. Belarus
196 D3 Bóbr r. Pol.
195 O3 Böbrach Ger.
Bobriki Rus. Fed. see Novomoskovsk
Bobrinets Ukr. see Bobrynets'
245 □C6 Bobrof Island AK U.S.A.
157 H6 Bobrov Rus. Fed.
199 I2 Bobrov Slovakia
199 I2 Bobrovec Slovakia
Bobrovitsa Ukr. see Bobrovytsya
159 Q2 Bobrovo-Dvorskoye Rus. Fed.
159 K3 Bobrovytsya Ukr.
193 L7 Bobrowice Pol.
196 D3 Bobrówko Pol.
196 G3 Bobrowniki Kujawsko-Pomorskie Pol.
197 L2 Bobrowniki Podlaskie Pol.
197 H2 Bobrowo Pol.
Bobruysk Belarus see Babruysk
160 J9 Bobryk r. Belarus
158 J6 Bobryk-Druhyy Ukr.
159 L5 Bobrynets' Ukr.
159 P2 Bobryshevo Rus. Fed.
251 R5 Bobs Lake Ont. Can.
130 D2 Bobso Sichuan China
256 F9 Bobtown PA U.S.A.
232 B2 Bobuk Sudan
274 D2 Bobures Venez.
235 □J4 Boby mt. Madag.
201 M7 Boč hill Slovenia
204 H7 Bocacara Spain
255 G13 Boca Chica Key i. FL U.S.A.
268 B4 Boca de Camichin Mex.
205 K3 Boca de Huérgano Spain
283 D6 Boca de la Travesía Arg.
275 E2 Boca del Pao Venez.
269 K6 Boca del Río Mex.
275 F2 Boca de Macareo Venez.
275 F2 Boca de Uracoa Venez.
276 D2 Boca do Acre Brazil
275 F6 Boca do Capanã Brazil
276 D2 Boca do Curuquetê Brazil
275 I5 Boca do Jari Brazil
276 C1 Boca do Moaco Brazil
181 I4 Bocage Normand reg. France
181 I8 Bocage Vendéen reg. France
271 □7 Boca Grande r. mouth Trin. and Tob./Venez.
281 E5 Bocaina de Minas Brazil
209 D10 Bocairent Spain
281 F2 Bocaiúva Brazil
280 C6 Bocaiúva do Sul Brazil
275 E4 Boca Mavaca Venez.
228 D5 Bocanda Côte d'Ivoire
199 J6 Bočar Vojvodina Serbia
230 B3 Bocaranga C.A.R.
255 G12 Boca Raton FL U.S.A.
268 F3 Bocas Mex.
266 □R13 Bocas del Toro Panama
266 □R13 Bocas del Toro, Archipiélago de is Panama
217 L5 Bocchigliero Italy
205 M6 Boceguillas Spain
198 F5 Bocfölde Hungary
275 F3 Bochinche Venez.
197 I6 Bochnia Pol.
187 I6 Bocholt Belgium
191 C7 Bocholt Ger.
198 C1 Bochov Czech Rep.
191 D8 Bochum Ger.
Bochum S. Africa see Senwabarwana
192 G2 Bock i. Ger.
191 J6 Bockenem Ger.
195 L5 Bockhorn Bayern Ger.
190 F4 Bockhorn Niedersachsen Ger.
190 E4 Bockhorst Ger.
197 L3 Boćki Pol.
214 C3 Bocognano Corse France
231 B8 Bocoio Angola
199 J4 Boconád Hungary
266 F4 Bocoyna Mex.
187 G8 Bocq r. Belgium
199 J3 Bőcs Hungary
199 I5 Bócsa Hungary
219 J5 Bocşa Caraş-Severin Romania
199 L4 Bocşa Sălaj Romania
199 K5 Bocsig Romania
196 C3 Boczów Pol.
230 C3 Boda C.A.R.
163 M6 Boda Sweden
165 N4 Böda Öland Sweden
197 L5 Bodaczów Pol.
165 K4 Bodafors Sweden
165 L5 Boda glasbruk Sweden
199 H4 Bodajk Hungary
105 M7 Bodalla N.S.W. Austr.
109 E11 Bodallin W.A. Austr.
153 M4 Bodaybo Rus. Fed.
168 M8 Boddam Aberdeenshire, Scotland U.K.
168 □N3 Boddam Shetland, Scotland U.K.
270 C4 Bodden Town Cayman Is
192 D3 Boddin Ger.
109 D12 Boddington W.A. Austr.
193 E7 Bode r. Ger.
264 I3 Bodega Head CA U.S.A.
186 G4 Bodegraven Neth.
194 F5 Bodelshausen Ger.
172 F1 Bodelwyddan Denbighshire, Wales U.K.
162 P4 Boden Sweden
191 I7 Bodenfelde Ger.
172 G3 Bodenham Herefordshire, England U.K.
194 E2 Bodenheim Ger.
195 M5 Bodenkirchen Ger.
195 O3 Bodenmais Ger.
194 G6 Bodensee l. Ger./Switz.
190 K5 Bodenteich Ger.
191 I7 Bodenwerder Ger.

201 K4 Bodenwies mt. Austria
195 M3 Bodenwöhr Ger.
169 G5 Boderg, Lough l. Ireland
229 G4 Bode-Sadu Nigeria
219 O3 Bodeşti Romania
264 N6 Bodfish CA U.S.A.
136 E3 Bodhan Andhra Prad. India
139 J7 Bodh Gaya Bihar India
173 J3 Bodicote Oxfordshire, England U.K.
264 M3 Bodie (abandoned) CA U.S.A.
136 E7 Bodinayakkanur Tamil Nadu India
206 F4 Bodión r. Spain
194 G6 Bodman Ger.
172 C7 Bodmin Cornwall, England U.K.
172 C6 Bodmin Moor moorland England U.K.
194 H6 Bodnegg Ger.
162 M3 Bodø Norway
278 F3 Bodocó Brazil
194 H6 Bodolz Ger.
206 F4 Bodonal de la Sierra Spain
128 C4 Bodonchiyn Gol watercourse Mongolia
277 F4 Bodoquena Mato Grosso do Sul Brazil
277 F5 Bodoquena Mato Grosso do Sul Brazil
277 F5 Bodoquena, Serra da hills Brazil
230 C3 Bodoukpa C.A.R.
199 K3 Bodrog r. Hungary
199 K3 Bodroghalom Hungary
221 I5 Bodrum Turkey
148 C5 Bodrum-Milas airport Turkey
162 M5 Bodsjö Sweden
162 P3 Bodträskfors Sweden
135 □1 Boduhali i. N. Male Maldives
199 J3 Bódva r. Hungary
199 J3 Bodva r. Slovakia
199 J3 Bódvaszilas Hungary
197 I3 Bodzanów Pol.
197 I5 Bodzentyn Pol.
185 F7 Boé France
228 B4 Boé Guinea-Bissau
187 F6 Boechout Belgium
205 K5 Boecillo Spain
205 L4 Boedo r. Spain
182 I4 Boëge France
236 G4 Boegoeberg S. Africa
186 I5 Boekel Neth.
187 E6 Boekhoute Belgium
182 E5 Boën France
230 D5 Boende Dem. Rep. Congo
115 B6 Bo Epinang Sulawesi Indon.
236 E9 Boerboonfontein S. Africa
261 F11 Boerne TX U.S.A.
237 K9 Boesmans r. S. Africa
237 K7 Boesmans hoekpas pass S. Africa
261 J10 Boeuf r. LA U.S.A.
204 H3 Boeza Spain
204 G3 Boeza r. Spain
280 C5 Bofete Brazil
228 B4 Boffa Guinea
183 F7 Boffres France
191 H7 Boffzen Ger.
169 G5 Bofin, Lough l. Ireland
164 F2 Bøfjell hill Norway
162 T1 Boftsa Norway
139 O5 Boga Arun. Prad. India
199 J4 Bogács Hungary
204 G7 Bogajo Spain
232 D4 Bogal, Lagh watercourse Kenya/Somalia
118 B6 Bogale Myanmar
118 B7 Bogale r. Myanmar
261 K10 Bogalusa LA U.S.A.
105 K3 Bogan r. N.S.W. Austr.
229 E3 Bogandé Burkina
105 K5 Bogan Gate N.S.W. Austr.
230 C3 Bogangolo C.A.R.
115 C3 Bogani Nani Wartabone, Taman Nasional nat. park Indon.
107 K7 Bogantungan Qld Austr.
207 O3 Bogarra Spain
218 H6 Bogatić Bogatić Serbia
156 J4 Bogatye Saby Rus. Fed.
196 C5 Bogatynia Pol.
151 I2 Bogatyrevka Rus. Fed.
148 G4 Boğazlıyan Turkey
230 C4 Bogbonga Dem. Rep. Congo
133 H11 Bogcang Zangbo r. Xizang China
128 G4 Bogd Mongolia
128 H4 Bogd Övörhangay Mongolia
199 K6 Bogda Romania
132 I5 Bogda Feng mt. Xinjiang China
219 M8 Bogdan mt. Bulg.
219 N7 Bogdana Romania
219 K9 Bogdanci Macedonia
199 L4 Bogdand Romania
196 D3 Bogdaniec Pol.
Bogdanovka Georgia see Ninotsminda
142 E1 Bogdanovka Rus. Fed.
128 A5 Bogda Shan mts China
122 A3 Bogdat' Rus. Fed.
195 N4 Bogen Ger.
142 I4 Bogen Kazakh.
162 N2 Bogen Norway
143 O1 Bogenbay Kazakh.
164 G6 Bogense Denmark
105 M3 Boggabilla Qld Austr.
105 M4 Boggabri N.S.W. Austr.
100 □3a Boggenatjen i. Kwajalein Marshall Is
169 D8 Boggeragh Mountains hills Ireland
100 □3a Boggerik i. Kwajalein Marshall Is
109 D7 Boggola hill W.A. Austr.
271 □2 Boggy Peak hill Antigua and Barbuda
Boghari Alg. see Ksar el Boukhari
145 K6 Boghra Dam Afgh.
113 J7 Bogia P.N.G.
107 K6 Bogie r. Qld Austr.
168 K8 Bogie r. Scotland U.K.
212 G7 Bogliasco Italy
164 H6 Bognæs nature res. Denmark
212 E3 Bognanco Italy
168 K7 Bogniebrae Aberdeenshire, Scotland U.K.
173 K6 Bognor Regis West Sussex, England U.K.
178 I4 Bogny-sur-Meuse France
229 I4 Bogo Cameroon
192 F1 Bogø Denmark
192 F1 Bogo i. Denmark
114 E6 Bogo Cebu Phil.
Bogodukhov Ukr. see Bohodukhiv
143 M1 Bogodukhovka Kazakh.
169 H6 Bog of Allen reg. Ireland
122 I5 Bogoladza, Khrebet mts Rus. Fed.
232 D3 Bogol Manya Eth.
143 M1 Bogolyubovo Kazakh.
161 P6 Bogolyubovo Smolenskaya Oblast' Rus. Fed.
161 X5 Bogolyubovo Vladimirskaya Oblast' Rus. Fed.
105 K7 Bogong, Mount Vic. Austr.
116 G8 Bogor Jawa Indon.
197 J5 Bogoria Pol.
161 V8 Bogoroditsk Rus. Fed.
161 S8 Bogoroditskoye Rus. Fed.
156 H4 Bogorodsk Rus. Fed.
122 L2 Bogorodskoye Khabarovskiy Kray Rus. Fed.
156 J4 Bogorodskoye Kirovskaya Oblast' Rus. Fed.
244 E5 Bogoslof Island AK U.S.A.
274 C3 Bogotá Col.
199 K3 Bogota hill Slovakia
152 J4 Bogotol Rus. Fed.
156 I4 Bogovarovo Rus. Fed.
218 J9 Bogovinje Bogovinje Macedonia
Bogoyavlenskoye Rus. Fed. see Pervomayskiy
139 L7 Bogra Bangl.
153 K4 Boguchany Rus. Fed.
157 H6 Boguchar Rus. Fed.
159 T4 Boguchar r. Rus. Fed.
197 J6 Boguchwała Pol.
228 B2 Bogué Maur.
261 K10 Bogue Chitto r. MS U.S.A.
Boguslav Ukr. see Bohuslav

196 E5 Boguszów-Gorce Pol.
270 □ Bog Walk Jamaica
199 H5 Bogyiszló Hungary
117 K4 Boh r. Indon.
129 P7 Bo Hai g. China
129 Q7 Bohai Haixia sea chan. China
178 F4 Bohain-en-Vermandois France
129 O7 Bohai Wan b. China
180 C5 Bohars France
158 D5 Bohdan Ukr.
159 O7 Bohdanivka Ukr.
201 M3 Böheimkirchen Austria
Bohemia reg. Czech Rep. see Čechy
259 I3 Bohemia NY U.S.A.
108 I5 Bohemia Downs W.A. Austr.
108 I5 Bohemia Downs Aboriginal Reserve W.A. Austr.
Bohemian Forest mts Ger. see Böhmer Wald
169 F7 Boher Ireland
170 B7 Boheraphuca Ireland
229 F5 Bohicon Benin
201 I7 Bohinjska Bistrica Slovenia
201 I7 Bohinjsko jezero l. Slovenia
160 J6 Bohinskaye, Vozyera l. Belarus
194 E3 Böhl Ger.
193 F8 Böhlen Ger.
193 F8 Böhlitz-Ehrenberg Ger.
237 M4 Bohlokong S. Africa
190 H5 Böhme Ger.
190 H5 Böhme r. Ger.
Böhmen reg. Czech Rep. see Čechy
195 M2 Böhmer Wald mts Ger.
191 F6 Bohmte Ger.
192 F5 Böhne Ger.
159 O3 Bohodukhiv Ukr.
159 L4 Bohodukhivka Ukr.
114 E7 Bohol i. Phil.
169 D5 Bohola Ireland
114 E7 Bohol Sea Phil.
114 D7 Bohol Strait Phil.
198 G5 Böhönye Hungary
201 L7 Bohor mt. Slovenia
158 D5 Bohorodchany Ukr.
Böhöt Mongolia see Öndörshil
205 J8 Bohoyo Spain
138 E1 Bohrt Pak.
132 H6 Bohu Xinjiang China
199 H2 Bohumín Czech Rep.
198 G2 Bohuňovice Czech Rep.
164 H3 Bohuslän reg. Sweden
158 J4 Bohuslav Ukr.
198 C2 Bohutín Czech Rep.
185 C10 Boí France
214 C9 Boi, Capo c. Sardegna Italy
281 E5 Boi, Ponta do pt Brazil
275 F5 Boiaçu Brazil
199 L4 Boianu Mare Romania
236 H4 Boichoko S. Africa
113 J8 Boigu Island Qld Austr.
237 K2 Boikhutso S. Africa
235 H3 Boila Moz.
108 G4 Boileau, Cape W.A. Austr.
258 A4 Boiling Springs PA U.S.A.
275 H5 Boim Brazil
232 B2 Boing Sudan
228 E5 Boin National Park nat. park Western Ghana
118 A3 Boinu r. Myanmar
278 F5 Boipeba, Ilha i. Brazil
204 C3 Boiro de Arriba Spain
280 B3 Bois r. Brazil
245 P2 Bois, Lac des l. N.W.T. Can.
239 □1c Bois-Blanc Réunion
251 J4 Bois Blanc Island MI U.S.A.
181 O8 Boischaut reg. France
178 D7 Boiscommun France
182 I3 Bois-d'Amont France
260 G3 Bois de Sioux r. MN U.S.A.
262 F5 Boise ID U.S.A.
262 F5 Boise r. ID U.S.A.
261 D7 Boise City OK U.S.A.
180 G5 Boisgervilly France
178 B5 Bois-Guillaume France
178 E7 Bois-le-Roi France
183 E9 Boisseron France
185 I6 Boisset France
183 E8 Boisset-et-Gaujac France
247 K5 Boissevain Man. Can.
185 I8 Boissezon France
213 M3 Boite r. Italy
237 J3 Boitumelong S. Africa
280 D5 Boituva Brazil
192 I4 Boitzenburg Ger.
184 E2 Boivre r. France
190 K4 Boize r. Ger.
190 K4 Boizenburg Ger.
196 D4 Bojadła Pol.
215 M5 Bojano Italy
197 J5 Bojanów Pol.
196 E4 Bojanowo Pol.
114 C2 Bojeador, Cape Luzon Phil.
199 H3 Bojná Slovakia
199 H3 Bojnice Slovakia
219 J7 Bojnik Bojnik Serbia
144 G3 Bojnūrd Iran
117 I8 Bojonegoro Jawa Indon.
116 G8 Bojong Jawa Indon.
229 H5 Boju-Ega Nigeria
282 H3 Bojuru Brazil
230 C3 Bokada Dem. Rep. Congo
139 N6 Bokajan Assam India
230 C5 Bokanda Congo
142 J6 Bo'kantov tog'lari hills Uzbek.
139 J8 Bokaro Jharkhand India
115 B3 Bokat Sulawesi Indon.
230 C5 Bokatola Dem. Rep. Congo
228 B4 Boké Guinea
143 S3 Boke Kazakh.
190 G4 Bokel Ger.
230 D5 Bokela Dem. Rep. Congo
230 D4 Bokenda Dem. Rep. Congo
236 D8 Bokfontein S. Africa
105 K3 Bokhara r. N.S.W. Austr.
Bo Kheo Cambodia see Bâ Kêv
229 H5 Bokito Cameroon
190 I1 Böklund Ger.
164 B2 Boknafjorden sea chan. Norway
231 B6 Boko Congo
231 C6 Boko Dem. Rep. Congo
199 H4 Bokod Hungary
230 C4 Bokode Dem. Rep. Congo
230 E3 Bokoko Dem. Rep. Congo
230 A5 Bokolo Gabon
Bokombayevskoye Kyrg. see Bökönbaev
143 Q6 Bökönbaev Kyrg.
Bokonbayevo Kyrg. see Bökönbaev
237 M5 Bokong Lesotho
199 K4 Bököny Hungary
224 C6 Bokoro Chad
230 C5 Bokoro Dem. Rep. Congo
231 B6 Boko-Songho Congo
230 D5 Bokote Dem. Rep. Congo
Bokovo-Antratsit Ukr. see Antratsyt
157 H6 Bokovskaya Rus. Fed.
236 C9 Bokpunt pt S. Africa
119 D9 Bokpyin Myanmar
237 M2 Boksburg S. Africa
161 Q2 Boksitogorsk Rus. Fed.
236 E2 Bokspits S. Africa
122 J3 Boktor Rus. Fed.
230 D5 Bokungu Dem. Rep. Congo
144 H2 Bokurdak Turkm.
230 D5 Bokwankusu Dem. Rep. Congo
224 B6 Bol Chad
230 C2 Bola, Bahr watercourse Chad
115 C4 Bolaang Sulawesi Indon.
268 D5 Bola del Viejo, Cerro mt. Mex.
231 E5 Bolaiti Dem. Rep. Congo
228 B4 Bolama Guinea-Bissau
145 L7 Bolan r. Pak.
230 E3 Bolanda, Jebel mt. Sudan
194 E2 Bolanden Ger.
182 I2 Bolandoz France
139 I9 Bolangir Orissa India
212 H7 Bolano Italy
268 C4 Bolaños r. Mex.
100 □1 Bolanos, Mount Guam
207 L3 Bolaños de Calatrava Spain

145 L7 **Bolan Pass** Pak.
205 O8 **Bolarque, Embalse de** *resr* Spain
118 H7 **Bolavén, Phouphiang** *plat.* Laos
181 L2 **Bolbec** France
229 F3 **Bolbol** Niger
199 H5 **Bölcske** Hungary
144 D6 **Boldājī** Iran
192 I3 **Boldekow** Ger.
190 H1 **Bolderslev** Denmark
199 K3 **Boldogkőváralja** Hungary
171 O4 **Boldon** *Tyne and Wear, England* U.K.
173 I6 **Boldre** *Hampshire, England* U.K.
219 P5 **Boldu** Romania
144 H1 **Boldumsaz** Turkm.
199 K6 **Boldur** Romania
199 J3 **Boldva** Hungary
132 F4 **Bole** *Xinjiang* China
228 E4 **Bole** Ghana
208 D3 **Bolea** Spain
158 C4 **Bolekhiv** Ukr.
230 C5 **Boleko** Dem. Rep. Congo
122 I3 **Bolen** Rus. Fed.
230 C4 **Bolena** Dem. Rep. Congo
199 G3 **Boleráz** Slovakia
197 I5 **Bolesław** Pol.
196 D4 **Bolesławiec** *Dolnośląskie* Pol.
196 G4 **Bolesławiec** *Łódzkie* Pol.
196 C3 **Boleszkowice** Pol.
157 J5 **Bolgar** Rus. Fed.
228 E4 **Bolgatanga** Ghana
160 L5 **Bolgatovo** Rus. Fed.
Bolgrad Ukr. *see* **Bolhrad**
158 H8 **Bolhrad** Ukr.
122 G6 **Boli** *Heilong.* China
230 F3 **Boli** Sudan
230 C5 **Bolia** Dem. Rep. Congo
162 P4 **Boliden** Sweden
Bolifuri *i. S. Male* Maldives *see* **Bolifushi**
135 □[1] **Bolifushi** *i. S. Male* Maldives
197 I3 **Bolimów** Pol.
189 J2 **Bolimowski Park Krajobrazowy** Pol.
114 B3 **Bolinao** *Luzon* Phil.
219 N6 **Bolintin-Vale** Romania
274 B3 **Bolívar** *Antioquia* Col.
274 B4 **Bolívar** *Cauca* Col.
274 C2 **Bolívar** *dept* Col.
276 A1 **Bolívar** Peru
261 I7 **Bolivar** *MO* U.S.A.
256 G6 **Bolivar** *NY* U.S.A.
261 K8 **Bolivar** *TN* U.S.A.
275 F3 **Bolívar** *state* Venez.
276 D4 **Bolivia** *country* S. America
219 J7 **Boljevac** *Boljevac* Serbia
150 B1 **Bolkar Dağları** *mts* Turkey
161 T8 **Bolkhov** Rus. Fed.
251 K1 **Bolkow** *Ont.* Can.
192 E2 **Bölkow** Ger.
196 E5 **Bolków** Pol.
194 H4 **Boll** Ger.
164 I4 **Bollebygd** Sweden
284 B3 **Bollenar** Chile
183 F8 **Bollène** France
212 D5 **Bollengo** Italy
212 C2 **Bolligen** Switz.
190 H1 **Bollingstedt** Ger.
171 M7 **Bollington** *Cheshire, England* U.K.
163 N6 **Bollnäs** Sweden
105 K3 **Bollon** *Qld* Austr.
164 I2 **Bollsbyn** Sweden
194 D6 **Bollschweil** Ger.
162 N5 **Bollstabruk** Sweden
188 E3 **Bollstedt** Ger.
206 F6 **Bollullos Par del Condado** Spain
179 N8 **Bollwiller** France
165 J5 **Bolmen** *l.* Sweden
173 L3 **Bolnhurst** *Bedfordshire, England* U.K.
151 F4 **Bolnisi** Georgia
114 D6 **Bolo** *Panay* Phil.
230 C5 **Bolobo** Dem. Rep. Congo
114 C8 **Bolod Islands** Phil.
122 I3 **Bolodzhak** Rus. Fed.
213 K7 **Bologna** Italy
213 K7 **Bologna** *prov.* Italy
179 J7 **Bologne** France
274 C6 **Bolognesi** *Loreto* Peru
276 B2 **Bolognesi** *Ucayali* Peru
216 E8 **Bolognetta** *Sicilia* Italy
215 K2 **Bolognola** Italy
161 O5 **Bologovo** Rus. Fed.
161 R4 **Bologoye** Rus. Fed.
237 J5 **Bolokanang** S. Africa
161 U7 **Bolokhovo** Rus. Fed.
230 C4 **Bolomba** Dem. Rep. Congo
230 D4 **Bolombo** *r.* Dem. Rep. Congo
Bolon' Rus. Fed. *see* **Achan**
267 O7 **Bolonchén de Rejón** Mex.
230 C5 **Bolondo** Dem. Rep. Congo
229 H6 **Bolondo** Equat. Guinea
114 D8 **Bolong** *Mindanao* Phil.
231 B7 **Bolongongo** Angola
214 B7 **Bolotana** *Sardegna* Italy
161 P2 **Bolotovo** Rus. Fed.
237 L7 **Bolotwa** S. Africa
230 B4 **Bolozo** Congo
276 C2 **Bolpebra** Bol.
139 K8 **Bolpur** *W. Bengal* India
151 J6 **Bolqarçay** *r.* Azer.
282 C3 **Bolsa, Cerro** *mt.* Arg.
214 H2 **Bolsena** Italy
214 H2 **Bolsena, Lago di** *l.* Italy
160 E7 **Bol'shakovo** Rus. Fed.
151 H1 **Bol'shaya Areshevka** Rus. Fed.
156 J4 **Bol'shaya Atnya** Rus. Fed.
159 R1 **Bol'shaya Bereyka** Rus. Fed.
159 R1 **Bol'shaya Boyevka** Rus. Fed.
142 D1 **Bol'shaya Chernigovka** Rus. Fed.
142 K1 **Bol'shaya Churakovka** Kazakh.
142 D1 **Bol'shaya Glushitsa** Rus. Fed.
156 F2 **Bol'shaya Imandra, Ozero** *l.* Rus. Fed.
159 Q3 **Bol'shaya Khalan'** Rus. Fed.
156 I4 **Bol'shaya Kokshaga** *r.* Rus. Fed.
161 Q5 **Bol'shaya Kosha** Rus. Fed.
159 U1 **Bol'shaya Lipovitsa** Rus. Fed.
157 H7 **Bol'shaya Martinovka** Rus. Fed.
Bol'shaya Novoselka Ukr. *see* **Velyka Novosilka**
156 M1 **Bol'shaya Oyu** *r.* Rus. Fed.
156 J2 **Bol'shaya Pyssa** Rus. Fed.
156 M2 **Bol'shaya Rogovaya** *r.* Rus. Fed.
156 L2 **Bol'shaya Synya** *r.* Rus. Fed.
Bol'shaya Tsarevshchina Rus. Fed. *see* **Volzhskiy**
156 K4 **Bol'shaya Usa** Rus. Fed.
161 P3 **Bol'shaya Vishera** Rus. Fed.
143 R2 **Bol'shaya Vladimirovka** Kazakh.
159 R3 **Bol'she Bykovo** Rus. Fed.
159 S6 **Bol'shekrepinskaya** Rus. Fed.
161 S4 **Bol'she-Ploskoye** Rus. Fed.
153 Q4 **Bol'sheretsk** Rus. Fed.
159 Q3 **Bol'shetroitskoye** Rus. Fed.
153 L2 **Bol'shevik, Ostrov** *i. Severnaya Zemlya* Rus. Fed.
156 K2 **Bol'shezemel'skaya Tundra** *lowland* Rus. Fed.
142 H4 **Bol'shiye Barsuki, Peski** *des.* Kazakh.
156 I3 **Bol'shiye Chirki** Rus. Fed.
156 G2 **Bol'shiye Kozly** Rus. Fed.
161 U8 **Bol'shiye Medvedki** Rus. Fed.
142 D4 **Bol'shiye Peshnyye, Ostrova** *is* Kazakh.
159 S6 **Bol'shiye Saly** Rus. Fed.
142 K2 **Bol'shoy Aksuat, Ozero** *salt l.* Kazakh.
153 R3 **Bol'shoy Anyuy** *r.* Rus. Fed.
153 M2 **Bol'shoy Begichev, Ostrov** *i.* Rus. Fed.
160 L1 **Bol'shoy Berezovyy, Ostrov** *i.* Rus. Fed.
161 V6 **Bol'shoye Alekseyevskoye** Rus. Fed.
161 P6 **Bol'shoye Beresnevo** Rus. Fed.
159 Q3 **Bol'shoye Gorodishche** Rus. Fed.
157 I5 **Bol'shoye Ignatovo** Rus. Fed.
161 W7 **Bol'shoye Korovino** Rus. Fed.
161 V5 **Bol'shoye Mikhaylovskoye** Rus. Fed.
156 I5 **Bol'shoye Murashkino** Rus. Fed.
162 V2 **Bol'shoye Ozerko** Rus. Fed.
161 R8 **Bol'shoye Polpino** Rus. Fed.
161 W9 **Bol'shoye Popovo** Rus. Fed.
156 G4 **Bol'shoye Selo** Rus. Fed.
159 O2 **Bol'shoye Soldatskoye** Rus. Fed.
143 R1 **Bol'shoye Topol'noye, Ozero** *salt l.* Rus. Fed.
161 Q3 **Bol'shoye Zaborov'ye** Rus. Fed.
161 V7 **Bol'shoye Zhokovo** Rus. Fed.
142 F2 **Bol'shoy Ik** *r.* Rus. Fed.
142 B2 **Bol'shoy Irgiz** *r.* Rus. Fed.
122 H7 **Bol'shoy Kamen'** Rus. Fed.
Bol'shoy Kavkaz *mts* Asia/Europe *see* **Caucasus**
161 W9 **Bol'shoy Khomutets** Rus. Fed.
161 Q1 **Bol'shoy Kokovichi** Rus. Fed.
151 F1 **Bol'shoy Levoberezhnyy, Kanal** *canal* Rus. Fed.
153 P2 **Bol'shoy Lyakhovskiy, Ostrov** *i. Novosibirskiye O-va* Rus. Fed.
156 L2 **Bol'shoy Patok** *r.* Rus. Fed.
153 K3 **Bol'shoy Porog** Rus. Fed.
153 O4 **Bol'shoy Shantar, Ostrov** *i.* Rus. Fed.
Bol'shoy Tokmak Kyrg. *see* **Tokmok**
Bol'shoy Tokmak Ukr. *see* **Tokmak**
161 O4 **Bol'shoy Tuder** *r.* Rus. Fed.
160 K2 **Bol'shoy Tyuters, Ostrov** *i.* Estonia
142 C3 **Bol'shoy Uzen'** *r.* Kazakh./Rus. Fed.
151 C1 **Bol'shoy Zelenchuk** *r.* Rus. Fed.
266 G4 **Bolsón de Mapimí** *des.* Mex.
171 O7 **Bolsover** *Derbyshire, England* U.K.
186 I2 **Bolsward** Neth.
196 G1 **Bolszewo** Pol.
208 F3 **Boltaña** Spain
171 O5 **Boltby** *North Yorkshire, England* U.K.
192 D3 **Boltenhagen, Ostseebad** Ger.
172 E7 **Bolt Head** *England* U.K.
212 C2 **Boltigen** Switz.
251 O6 **Bolton** *Ont.* Can.
114 E8 **Bolton** *Mindanao* Phil.
171 M6 **Bolton** *Greater Manchester, England* U.K.
171 L5 **Bolton-le-Sands** *Lancashire, England* U.K.
161 P7 **Boltutino** Rus. Fed.
159 N5 **Boltyshka** Ukr.
148 E3 **Bolu** Turkey
221 M2 **Bolu** *prov.* Turkey
162 □B1 **Bolungarvík** Iceland
133 K8 **Boluntay** *Qinghai* China
131 J7 **Boluo** *Guangdong* China
169 B9 **Bolus Head** Ireland
161 R8 **Bolva** *r.* Rus. Fed.
221 M4 **Bolvadin** Turkey
172 C6 **Bolventor** *Cornwall, England* U.K.
199 H6 **Bóly** Hungary
219 O8 **Bolyarovo** Bulg.
213 K3 **Bolzano** Italy
213 K2 **Bolzano** *prov.* Italy
231 B6 **Boma** Dem. Rep. Congo
105 M6 **Bomaderry** *N.S.W.* Austr.
229 G5 **Bomadi** Nigeria
130 B4 **Bomai** *Sichuan* China
187 I8 **Bomal** Belgium
230 C4 **Bomassa** Congo
215 M3 **Bomba** Italy
105 L7 **Bombala** *N.S.W.* Austr.
206 A2 **Bombarral** Port.
Bombay *Mahar.* India *see* **Mumbai**
102 I4 **Bombay** *North I.* N.Z.
265 Q8 **Bombay Beach** *CA* U.S.A.
113 H7 **Bomberai, Semenanjung** *pen. Papua* Indon.
231 B5 **Bombo** *r.* Dem. Rep. Congo
232 B4 **Bombo** Uganda
128 F3 **Bömbögör** Mongolia
229 G6 **Bom Bom, Ilha** *i.* São Tomé and Príncipe
230 C4 **Bomboma** Dem. Rep. Congo
276 D2 **Bom Comércio** Brazil
281 E3 **Bom Despacho** Brazil
139 N6 **Bomdila** *Arun. Prad.* India
172 G2 **Bomere Heath** *Shropshire, England* U.K.
133 L12 **Bomi** *Xizang* China
230 E4 **Bomili** Dem. Rep. Congo
276 D2 **Bom Jardim** *Amazonas* Brazil
275 I5 **Bom Jardim** *Pará* Brazil
278 G3 **Bom Jardim** *Pernambuco* Brazil
280 A2 **Bom Jardim de Goiás** Brazil
281 E4 **Bom Jardim de Minas** Brazil
231 B7 **Bom Jesus** Angola
278 D4 **Bom Jesus** *Piauí* Brazil
279 C9 **Bom Jesus** *Rio Grande do Sul* Brazil
278 E4 **Bom Jesus da Gurgueia, Serra do** *hills* Brazil
278 E5 **Bom Jesus da Lapa** Brazil
280 C3 **Bom Jesus de Goiás** Brazil
281 G4 **Bom Jesus do Itabapoana** Brazil
281 G4 **Bom Jesus do Norte** Brazil
164 B2 **Bomlafjorden** *sea chan.* Norway
190 I5 **Bomlitz** Ger.
164 B2 **Bømlo** *i.* Norway
230 E4 **Bomokandi** *r.* Dem. Rep. Congo
230 C4 **Bomongo** Dem. Rep. Congo
185 J10 **Bompas** France
216 F9 **Bompensiere** *Sicilia* Italy
216 G8 **Bompietro** *Sicilia* Italy
279 C8 **Bom Retiro** Brazil
281 E4 **Bom Sucesso** *Minas Gerais* Brazil
280 B5 **Bom Sucesso** *Paraná* Brazil
230 D3 **Bomu, Réserve de Faune de la** *nature res.* Dem. Rep. Congo
227 H1 **Bon, Cap** *c.* Tunisia
119 C10 **Bon, Ko** *i.* Thai.
Bona Alg. *see* **Annaba**
182 C2 **Bona** France
245 L3 **Bona, Mount** *AK* U.S.A.
144 B3 **Bonāb** Iran
185 F10 **Bonac-Irazein** France
212 G2 **Bonaduz** Switz.
256 H11 **Bon Air** *VA* U.S.A.
271 □[8] **Bonaire** *i.* Neth. Antilles
105 N3 **Bonalbo** *N.S.W.* Austr.
217 K7 **Bonamico** *r.* Italy
116 C4 **Bonandolok** *Sumatera* Indon.
266 □Q11 **Bonanza** Nic.
206 G7 **Bonanza** Spain
270 H4 **Bonao** Dom. Rep.
108 H3 **Bonaparte Archipelago** *is* W.A. Austr.
246 F5 **Bonaparte Lake** *B.C.* Can.
205 J3 **Boñar** Spain
168 H7 **Bonar Bridge** *Highland, Scotland* U.K.
214 B7 **Bonarcado** *Sardegna* Italy
244 G3 **Bonasila Dome** *hill AK* U.S.A.
271 □[7] **Bonasse** Trin. and Tob.
212 H7 **Bonassola** Italy
249 K3 **Bonavista** *Nfld and Lab.* Can.
249 K3 **Bonavista Bay** *Nfld and Lab.* Can.
182 H2 **Bonboillon** France
104 E4 **Bon Bon** *S.A.* Austr.
181 J5 **Bonchamp-lès-Laval** France
168 K12 **Bonchester Bridge** *Scottish Borders, Scotland* U.K.
212 C1 **Boncourt** Switz.
159 S4 **Bondarevo** Rus. Fed.
157 H5 **Bondari** Rus. Fed.
213 K6 **Bondeno** Italy
230 D5 **Bondo** *Équateur* Dem. Rep. Congo
230 D4 **Bondo** *Orientale* Dem. Rep. Congo
114 D5 **Bondoc Peninsula** *Luzon* Phil.
115 A8 **Bondokodi** *Sumba* Indon.
194 F4 **Bondorf** Ger.
228 E4 **Bondoukou** Côte d'Ivoire
228 E4 **Bondoukui** Burkina
117 J8 **Bondowoso** *Jawa* Indon.
255 I13 **Bonds Cay** *i.* Bahamas
250 F5 **Bonduel** *WI* U.S.A.
178 F2 **Bondues** France
156 K3 **Bondyug** Rus. Fed.
Bondyuzhskiy Rus. Fed. *see* **Mendeleyevsk**
Bône Alg. *see* **Annaba**
115 C6 **Bone** *Sulawesi* Indon.
115 B6 **Bone, Teluk** *b.* Indon.
190 J2 **Bönebüttel** Ger.
229 G6 **Bone de Jókei, Ilha** *i.* São Tomé and Príncipe
255 □[2] **Bonefish Pond** *New Prov.* Bahamas
215 N4 **Bonefro** Italy
236 E7 **Bonekraal** S. Africa
250 B4 **Bone Lake** *WI* U.S.A.
115 C6 **Bonelipu** *Sulawesi* Indon.
191 E7 **Bönen** Ger.
185 F7 **Bon-Encontre** France
115 B7 **Bonerate** *Sulawesi* Indon.
115 B7 **Bonerate** *i.* Indon.
115 B7 **Bonerate, Kepulauan** *is* Indon.
168 I10 **Bo'ness** *Falkirk, Scotland* U.K.
260 F4 **Bonesteel** *SD* U.S.A.
209 C10 **Bonete** Spain
282 C2 **Bonete, Cerro** *mt.* Arg.
281 E4 **Bonfim** Brazil
280 A2 **Bonfim** *r.* Brazil
281 E2 **Bonfinópolis de Minas** Brazil
232 C3 **Bonga** Eth.
114 C5 **Bongabong** *Mindoro* Phil.
139 M6 **Bongaigaon** *Assam* India
230 D4 **Bongandanga** Dem. Rep. Congo
236 H5 **Bongani** S. Africa
114 B9 **Bongao** Phil.
107 N9 **Bongaree** *Qld* Austr.
133 E10 **Bongba** *Xizang* China
133 J11 **Bong Co** *l.* China
115 B4 **Bongka** *r.* Indon.
228 C5 **Bong Mountains** *hills* Liberia
231 D6 **Bongo** Dem. Rep. Congo
114 E8 **Bongo** *i.* Phil.
230 D2 **Bongo, Massif des** *mts* C.A.R.
231 B7 **Bongo, Serra do** *mts* Angola
235 □J3 **Bongolava** *mts* Madag.
230 B2 **Bongor** Chad
228 D5 **Bongouanou** Côte d'Ivoire
230 B5 **Bongoville** Gabon
119 I7 **Bông Sơn** Vietnam
261 G9 **Bonham** *TX* U.S.A.
162 O5 **Bönhamn** Sweden
228 E3 **Boni** Mali
205 Q9 **Boniches** Spain
228 D4 **Boniéredougou** Côte d'Ivoire
196 G3 **Boniewo** Pol.
214 C5 **Bonifacio** *Corse* France
Bonifacio, Bocche di *str.* France/Italy *see* **Bonifacio, Strait of**
Bonifacio, Bouches de *str.* France/Italy *see* **Bonifacio, Strait of**
214 B5 **Bonifacio, Strait of** France/Italy
215 P8 **Bonifati** Italy
255 E10 **Bonifay** *FL* U.S.A.
212 D2 **Bönigen** Switz.
196 E1 **Bonin** Pol.
233 D5 **Boni National Reserve** *nature res.* Kenya
Bonin Islands N. Pacific Ocean *see* **Ogasawara-shotō**
255 G12 **Bonita Springs** *FL* U.S.A.
277 F5 **Bonito** Brazil
280 B2 **Bonito** *r.* Brazil
168 K12 **Bonjedward** *Scottish Borders, Scotland* U.K.
116 D4 **Bonjol** *Sumatera* Indon.
229 F3 **Bonkoukou** Niger
191 D9 **Bonn** Ger.
Bonna Ger. *see* **Bonn**
185 H9 **Bonnac** France
214 B6 **Bonnanaro** *Sardegna* Italy
184 H3 **Bonnat** France
182 F3 **Bonnay** France
194 E6 **Bonndorf im Schwarzwald** Ger.
183 H7 **Bonne** *r.* France
258 A5 **Bonneauville** *PA* U.S.A.
185 E9 **Bonnefont** France
262 F2 **Bonners Ferry** *ID* U.S.A.
164 G5 **Bønnerup Strand** Denmark
247 M5 **Bonnet, Lac du** *resr Man.* Can.
181 L5 **Bonnétable** France
245 N2 **Bonnet Plume** *r. Y.T.* Can.
181 M8 **Bonneuil-Matours** France
178 B7 **Bonneval** *Centre* France
182 J5 **Bonneval** *Rhône-Alpes* France
183 K6 **Bonneval-sur-Arc** France
182 I3 **Bonnevaux** France
182 I4 **Bonneville** France
104 H7 **Bonney, Lake** *S.A.* Austr.
178 C5 **Bonnières-sur-Seine** France
109 E11 **Bonnie Rock** *W.A.* Austr.
183 G9 **Bonnieux** France
236 E9 **Bonnievale** S. Africa
194 G3 **Bönnigheim** Ger.
190 I3 **Bönningstedt** Ger.
185 C8 **Bonnut** France
229 G5 **Bonny** Nigeria
168 I10 **Bonnybridge** *Falkirk, Scotland* U.K.
107 J4 **Bonny Glen Aboriginal Holding** *res. Qld* Austr.
237 N6 **Bonny Ridge** S. Africa
168 J11 **Bonnyrigg** *Midlothian, Scotland* U.K.
257 □S3 **Bonny River** *N.B.* Can.
182 B1 **Bonny-sur-Loire** France
247 I4 **Bonnyville** *Alta* Can.
180 F6 **Bono** France
214 C7 **Bono** *Sardegna* Italy
114 A7 **Bonobono** *Palawan* Phil.
125 H15 **Bōno-misaki** *pt* Japan
Bononia Italy *see* **Bologna**
214 B7 **Bonorva** *Sardegna* Italy
228 E5 **Bonoua** Côte d'Ivoire
285 I1 **Bonpland** Arg.
103 C11 **Bonpland, Mount** *South I.* N.Z.
264 O8 **Bonsall** *CA* U.S.A.
182 I4 **Bons-en-Chablais** France
105 M3 **Bonshaw** *N.S.W.* Austr.
182 E5 **Bonson** France
117 L4 **Bontang** *Kalimantan* Indon.
236 F8 **Bontberg** *mt.* S. Africa
236 D9 **Bonteberg** *mts* S. Africa
236 E10 **Bontebok National Park** S. Africa
228 B5 **Bonthe** Sierra Leone
114 C3 **Bontoc** *Luzon* Phil.
115 B7 **Bontomatane** *Sulawesi* Indon.
115 A6 **Bontosunggu** *Sulawesi* Indon.
237 N6 **Bontrand** S. Africa
237 J9 **Bontrug** S. Africa
199 G4 **Bőny** Hungary
199 H5 **Bonyhád** Hungary
106 B7 **Bonython Range** *hills N.T.* Austr.
165 O2 **Boo** Sweden
115 F4 **Boo, Kepulauan** *is Papua* Indon.
239 □[2a] **Booby Island** *Inner Islands* Seychelles
192 J4 **Boock** Ger.
109 G8 **Boodie Boodie Range** *hills* W.A. Austr.
104 D4 **Bookabie** *S.A.* Austr.
265 W2 **Book Cliffs** *ridge UT* U.S.A.
230 D5 **Booke** Dem. Rep. Congo
261 E7 **Booker** *TX* U.S.A.
228 C4 **Boola** Guinea
105 L3 **Boolba** *Qld* Austr.
104 G5 **Booleroo Centre** *S.A.* Austr.
169 H8 **Booley Hills** Ireland
105 J5 **Booligal** *N.S.W.* Austr.
109 C8 **Boologooro** *W.A.* Austr.
105 L3 **Boomi** *N.S.W.* Austr.
250 I5 **Boon** *MI* U.S.A.
107 N9 **Boonah** *Qld* Austr.
263 L7 **Boone** *CO* U.S.A.
260 I4 **Boone** *IA* U.S.A.
255 G7 **Boone** *NC* U.S.A.
256 C12 **Boone Lake** *TN* U.S.A.
256 F11 **Boones Mill** *VA* U.S.A.
261 I8 **Booneville** *AR* U.S.A.
256 B11 **Booneville** *KY* U.S.A.
261 K8 **Booneville** *MS* U.S.A.
271 □[2] **Boon Point** Antigua and Barbuda
237 L1 **Boons** S. Africa
256 H9 **Boonsboro** *MD* U.S.A.
259 G3 **Boonton** *NJ* U.S.A.
128 F4 **Böön Tsagaan Nuur** *salt l.* Mongolia
264 I3 **Boonville** *CA* U.S.A.
254 D6 **Boonville** *IN* U.S.A.
260 I6 **Boonville** *MO* U.S.A.
257 J5 **Boonville** *NY* U.S.A.
276 D3 **Boopi** *r.* Bol.
109 F11 **Boorabin National Park** *W.A.* Austr.
232 D2 **Boorama** Somalia
105 J6 **Booroorban** *N.S.W.* Austr.
105 L6 **Boorowa** *N.S.W.* Austr.
105 I7 **Boort** *Vic.* Austr.
187 G7 **Boortmeerbeek** Belgium
178 B5 **Boos** France
195 I5 **Boos** Ger.
232 F2 **Boosaaso** Somalia
190 J2 **Boostedt** Ger.
257 □P5 **Boothbay Harbor** *ME* U.S.A.
287 D2 **Boothby, Cape** Antarctica
243 J3 **Boothia, Gulf of** *Nunavut* Can.
243 I2 **Boothia Peninsula** *Nunavut* Can.
171 K5 **Bootle** *Cumbria, England* U.K.
171 L7 **Bootle** *Merseyside, England* U.K.
230 A5 **Booué** Gabon
195 I4 **Bopfingen** Ger.
228 C5 **Bopolu** Liberia
191 E10 **Boppard** Ger.
133 J11 **Boqê** *Xizang* China
282 G3 **Boqueirão** Brazil
278 D5 **Boqueirão, Serra do** *hills* Brazil
271 □[1] **Boquerón** Puerto Rico
266 G4 **Boquilla, Presa de la** *resr* Mex.
266 H3 **Boquillas del Carmen** Mex.
266 H5 **Boquillas del Refugio** Mex.
198 B2 **Bor** Czech Rep.
156 I4 **Bor** Rus. Fed.
219 K6 **Bor** *Bor* Serbia
232 A3 **Bor** Sudan
148 G5 **Bor** Turkey
232 D4 **Bor, Lagh** *watercourse* Kenya/Somalia
101 □[9] **Bora-Bora** *is Arch. de la Société* Fr. Polynesia
151 J7 **Boradigah** Azer.
233 C5 **Boragi** *waterhole* Kenya
235 □K3 **Boraha, Nosy** *i.* Madag.
262 H4 **Borah Peak** *ID* U.S.A.
138 H9 **Borai** *Chhattisgarh* India
237 L1 **Borakalalo Nature Reserve** S. Africa
Boran Kazakh. *see* **Buran**
142 F4 **Borankul** Kazakh.
178 D5 **Boran-sur-Oise** France
118 E7 **Boraphet, Bung** *l.* Thai.
Boraraigh *i. Western Isles, Scotland* U.K. *see* **Boreray**
164 I4 **Borås** Sweden
139 I9 **Borasambar** *Orissa* India
144 D7 **Borāzjān** Iran
275 G6 **Borba** Brazil
206 E3 **Borba** Port.
212 F6 **Borbera** *r.* Italy
204 G8 **Borbollón, Embalse del** *resr* Spain
114 E6 **Borbon** *Cebu* Phil.
212 E6 **Borbore** *r.* Italy
280 C4 **Borborema** Brazil
278 F3 **Borborema, Planalto da** *plat.* Brazil
219 N3 **Borca** Romania
219 P6 **Borcea, Brațul** *watercourse* Romania
Borchalo Georgia *see* **Marneuli**
191 G7 **Borchen** Ger.
287 K2 **Borchgrevink Coast** Antarctica
149 J3 **Borçka** Turkey
186 K4 **Borculo** Neth.
108 G4 **Borda, Cape** *W.A.* Austr.
280 D5 **Borda da Mata** Brazil
221 K5 **Bor Dağı** *mt.* Turkey
205 P6 **Bordalba** Spain
199 I5 **Bordány** Hungary
185 C6 **Bordeaux** France
138 G8 **Bordehi** *Madh. Prad.* India
225 G6 **Bordein** Sudan
206 B6 **Bordeira** Port.
190 G1 **Bordelum** Ger.
109 E13 **Borden** *W.A.* Austr.
249 I4 **Borden-Carleton** *P.E.I.* Can.
243 G2 **Borden Island** *N.W.T.* Can.
243 J2 **Borden Peninsula** *Nunavut* Can.
258 F4 **Bordentown** *NJ* U.S.A.
185 E10 **Bordères-Louron** France
185 E9 **Bordères-sur-l'Échez** France
105 N3 **Border Ranges National Park** *N.S.W.* Austr.
Borders *admin. div. Scotland* U.K. *see* **Scottish Borders**
104 H7 **Bordertown** *S.A.* Austr.
185 D9 **Bordes** *Aquitaine* France
185 E9 **Bordes** *Midi-Pyrénées* France
190 J2 **Bordesholm** Ger.
162 □C1 **Borðeyri** Iceland
212 D8 **Bordighera** Italy
208 K3 **Bordils** Spain
216 D8 **Bordino** *r. Sicilia* Italy
227 G1 **Bordj Bou Arréridj** Alg.
226 E4 **Bordj Flye Ste-Marie** Alg.
227 H3 **Bordj Messaouda** Alg.
227 F5 **Bordj Mokhtar** Alg.
Bordj Omar Driss Alg. *see* **Bordj Omer Driss**
227 G3 **Bordj Omer Driss** Alg.
208 E6 **Bordón** Spain
166 D1 **Borðoy** *i.* Faroe Is
143 P6 **Bordu** Kyrg.
Bordunskiy Kyrg. *see* **Bordu**
219 P6 **Bordușani** Romania
212 H6 **Bore** Italy
228 E3 **Boré** Mali
286 X2 **Boreas Nunatak** Antarctica
173 N4 **Boreham** *Essex, England* U.K.
173 L4 **Borehamwood** *Hertfordshire, England* U.K.
195 O3 **Borek** *hill* Czech Rep.
197 I5 **Borek** Pol.
196 F5 **Borek Strzeliński** Pol.
196 F4 **Borek Wielkopolski** Pol.
249 G1 **Borel** *r. Que.* Can.
168 J12 **Boreland** *Dumfries and Galloway, Scotland* U.K.
158 E3 **Boremel'** Ukr.
165 L3 **Boren** *l.* Sweden
165 L3 **Borensberg** Sweden
168 C8 **Boreraig** *Highland, Scotland* U.K.
168 B7 **Boreray** *i. Western Isles, Scotland* U.K.
168 □[1] **Boreray** *i. Western Isles, Scotland* U.K.
201 O2 **Bořetice** Czech Rep.
194 A2 **Borg** Ger.
Borgå Fin. *see* **Porvoo**
162 M4 **Borgafjäll** Sweden
162 □G1 **Borgarfjörður** Iceland
162 □C1 **Borgarnes** Iceland
162 L4 **Børgefjell Nasjonalpark** *nat. park* Norway
191 H7 **Borgentreich** Ger.
190 E5 **Börger** Ger.
186 K3 **Borger** Neth.
261 E8 **Borger** *TX* U.S.A.
209 L8 **Borges** *r.* Spain
212 F6 **Borghetto di Borbera** Italy
165 M5 **Borgholm** *Öland* Sweden
191 F6 **Borgholzhausen** Ger.
217 L6 **Borgia** Italy
168 H5 **Borgie** *r. Scotland* U.K.
187 H7 **Borgloon** Belgium
214 C2 **Borgo** *Corse* France
213 J8 **Borgo a Mozzano** Italy
212 E5 **Borgo d'Ale** Italy
213 J5 **Borgoforte** Italy
212 D4 **Borgofranco d'Ivrea** Italy
217 O3 **Borgo Grappa** Italy
212 F5 **Borgo-lavezzaro** Italy
212 E4 **Borgomanero** Italy
212 D8 **Borgomaro** Italy
212 C5 **Borgone Susa** Italy
212 G5 **Borgonovo Val Tidone** Italy
213 K6 **Borgo Panigale** *airport* Italy
215 K3 **Borgorose** Italy
212 C7 **Borgo San Dalmazzo** Italy
213 K8 **Borgo San Lorenzo** Italy
212 F5 **Borgo San Martino** Italy
212 E4 **Borgosesia** Italy
213 L7 **Borgo Tossignano** Italy
212 H7 **Borgo Val di Taro** Italy
213 K3 **Borgo Valsugana** Italy
215 K3 **Borgo Velino** Italy
212 E5 **Borgo Vercelli** Italy
192 H5 **Borgsdorf** Ger.
164 E1 **Borgsjåbrotet** *mt.* Norway
190 I2 **Borgstedt** Ger.
168 H13 **Borgue** *Dumfries and Galloway, Scotland* U.K.
138 E8 **Bori** *Madh. Prad.* India
138 G9 **Bori** *Mahar.* India
138 E9 **Bori** *r.* India
229 G5 **Bori** Nigeria
118 F5 **Borikhan** Laos
Börili Kazakh. *see* **Burli**
142 E2 **Borili** Kazakh.
161 S8 **Borilovo** Rus. Fed.
187 E8 **Borinage** *reg.* Belgium
258 B5 **Boring** *MD* U.S.A.
219 M9 **Borino** Bulg.
271 □[1] **Borinquen, Punta** *pt* Puerto Rico
161 W9 **Borinskoye** Rus. Fed.
Borislav Ukr. *see* **Boryslav**
157 H6 **Borisoglebsk** Rus. Fed.
161 W4 **Borisoglebskiy** Rus. Fed.
Borisov Belarus *see* **Barysaw**
157 G6 **Borisovka** Rus. Fed.
161 T6 **Borisovo** Rus. Fed.
161 T2 **Borisovo-Sudskoye** Rus. Fed.
Borispol' Ukr. *see* **Boryspil'**
230 E3 **Bo River Post** Sudan
235 □J2 **Boriziny** Madag.
210 F3 **Borja** *mts* Bos.-Herz.
274 B6 **Borja** Peru
205 Q5 **Borja** Spain
205 P5 **Borjabad** Spain
144 G4 **Borjak** Iran
201 H7 **Borjana** Slovenia
Borjas Blancas Spain *see* **Les Borges Blanques**
227 H2 **Borj Bourguiba** Tunisia
151 E4 **Borjomi** Georgia
151 E4 **Borjomis Nakrdzali** *nature res.* Georgia
160 L6 **Borkavichy** Belarus
145 M3 **Borkeh** Afgh.
191 C7 **Borken** Ger.
191 H8 **Borken (Hessen)** Ger.
162 N2 **Borkenes** Norway
193 G6 **Borkheide** Ger.
197 M3 **Borki** Belarus
197 K4 **Borki** Pol.
159 R1 **Borki** Rus. Fed.
224 C5 **Borkou** *reg.* Chad
224 C5 **Borkou-Ennedi-Tibesti** *pref.* Chad
156 J2 **Borkovskaya** Rus. Fed.
197 I4 **Borkowice** Pol.
190 C3 **Borkum** Ger.
190 C3 **Borkum** *i.* Ger.
165 L1 **Borlänge** Sweden
163 I6 **Borlaug** Norway
221 J4 **Borlu** Turkey
183 I10 **Bormes, Rade de** *inlet* France
183 I10 **Bormes-les-Mimosas** France
212 F6 **Bormida** *r.* Italy
212 I3 **Bormio** Italy
193 D6 **Born** Ger.
193 G8 **Borna** *Sachsen* Ger.
193 H8 **Borna** *Sachsen* Ger.
192 G2 **Born am Darß** Ger.
191 J8 **Born-Berge** *hill* Ger.
186 I2 **Borndiep** *sea chan.* Neth.
227 G4 **Borne** Alg.
182 I4 **Borne** *r.* France
186 K4 **Borne** Neth.
178 D5 **Bornel** France
187 F6 **Bornem** Belgium
112 D6 **Borneo** *i.* Asia
186 K4 **Bornerbroek** Neth.
182 J5 **Bornes** *mts* France
204 G6 **Bornes** Port.
204 F6 **Bornes, Serra de** *mts* Port.
204 E5 **Bornes de Aguiar** Port.
196 E2 **Borne Sulinowo** Pol.
191 C9 **Bornheim** Ger.
191 E10 **Bornhofen** Ger.
165 L7 **Bornholm** *i. Bornholm* Denmark
165 K6 **Bornholm Strait** *str.* Denmark/Sweden
190 J2 **Bornhöved** Ger.
191 E10 **Bornich** Ger.
229 I4 **Borno** *state* Nigeria
206 H7 **Bornos** Spain
206 H7 **Bornos, Embalse de** *resr* Spain
205 O7 **Bornova** *r.* Spain
221 I4 **Bornova** Turkey
190 J4 **Börnsen** Ger.
193 D8 **Bornstedt** Ger.
205 Q5 **Borobia** Spain
117 H8 **Borobudur** *tourist site* Indon.
199 L5 **Borod** Romania
159 N5 **Borodayivka** Ukr.
152 J3 **Borodino** *Krasnoyarskiy Kray* Rus. Fed.
161 S6 **Borodino** *Moskovskaya Oblast'* Rus. Fed.
161 S6 **Borodino** *Moskovskaya Oblast'* Rus. Fed.
158 I7 **Borodino** Ukr.
160 M1 **Borodinskoye** Rus. Fed.
158 I3 **Borodyanka** Ukr.
153 O3 **Borogontsy** Rus. Fed.
132 F4 **Borohoro Shan** *mts* China
198 F1 **Borohrádek** Czech Rep.
161 V3 **Borok** Rus. Fed.
115 C3 **Boroko** *Sulawesi* Indon.
161 T4 **Borok-Sulezhskiy** Rus. Fed.
230 D2 **Boromata** C.A.R.
159 N3 **Boromlya** Ukr.
159 O3 **Boromlya** *r.* Ukr.
228 E4 **Boromo** Burkina
228 D4 **Boron** Côte d'Ivoire
228 D3 **Boron** Mali
264 O7 **Boron** *CA* U.S.A.
136 H3 **Borondi** *Orissa* India
114 E6 **Borongan** *Samar* Phil.
196 G5 **Boronów** Pol.
214 B7 **Borore** *Sardegna* Italy
107 M8 **Bororen** *Qld* Austr.
196 G5 **Boroszów** Pol.
199 I5 **Borota** Hungary
228 D4 **Borotou** Côte d'Ivoire
171 O5 **Boroughbridge** *North Yorkshire, England* U.K.
173 M5 **Borough Green** *Kent, England* U.K.
159 Q4 **Borova** *Kharkivs'ka Oblast'* Ukr.
158 J3 **Borova** *Kyivs'ka Oblast'* Ukr.
159 R5 **Borova** *r.* Ukr.
219 L7 **Borovan** Bulg.
198 D3 **Borovany** Czech Rep.
158 E2 **Borove** *Rivnens'ka Oblast'* Ukr.
158 G2 **Borove** *Rivnens'ka Oblast'* Ukr.
161 Q3 **Borovenka** Rus. Fed.
161 Q3 **Borovichi** Rus. Fed.
143 U1 **Borovlyanka** Rus. Fed.
201 J8 **Borovnica** Slovenia
210 G3 **Borovo Selo** Croatia
156 J4 **Borovoy** *Kirovskaya Oblast'* Rus. Fed.
156 F2 **Borovoy** *Respublika Kareliya* Rus. Fed.
156 K3 **Borovoy** *Respublika Komi* Rus. Fed.
161 T6 **Borovsk** Rus. Fed.
142 K1 **Borovskoy** Kazakh.
197 J5 **Borów** Pol.
197 J5 **Borowa** Pol.
197 J4 **Borowie** Pol.
205 M8 **Borox** Spain
281 E3 **Borrachudo** *r.* Brazil
280 B5 **Borrazópolis** Brazil
165 K6 **Borrby** Sweden
192 F1 **Borre** Denmark
265 P8 **Borrego Springs** *CA* U.S.A.
192 G3 **Borrentin** Ger.
184 G6 **Borrèze** France
209 E7 **Borriol** Spain
238 □[3b] **Borriquillas, Punta de las** *pt Fuerteventura* Canary Is
169 I7 **Borris** Ireland
169 G7 **Borris-in-Ossory** Ireland
169 F7 **Borrisokane** Ireland
106 F4 **Borroloola** *N.T.* Austr.
171 K4 **Borrowdale** *Cumbria, England* U.K.
199 K4 **Borș** Romania
162 K5 **Børsa** Norway
219 L4 **Borșa** *Cluj* Romania
219 M3 **Borșa** *Maramureș* Romania
199 K3 **Borša** Slovakia
138 D8 **Borsad** *Gujarat* India
142 G6 **Borsakelmas sho'rxogi** *salt marsh* Uzbek.
187 G6 **Borsbeek** Belgium
193 G8 **Borsdorf** Ger.
219 N4 **Borsec** Romania
162 R1 **Børselv** Norway
220 A2 **Borsh** Albania
159 T2 **Borshchevskiye Peski** Rus. Fed.
158 I6 **Borshchi** Ukr.
158 F5 **Borshchiv** Ukr.
158 E4 **Borshchivka** Ukr.
129 K2 **Borshchovochnyy Khrebet** *mts* Rus. Fed.
197 M6 **Borshchovychi** Ukr.
149 L7 **Borsippa** *tourist site* Iraq
142 D1 **Borskoye** Rus. Fed.
Borský Jur Slovakia *see* **Borský Svätý Jur**
201 P2 **Borský Svätý Jur** Slovakia
199 K3 **Borsod-Abaúj-Zemplén** *county* Hungary
199 J3 **Borsodbóta** Hungary
199 J3 **Borsodnádasd** Hungary
199 J3 **Borsodszentgyörgy** Hungary
187 E6 **Borssele** Neth.
191 K6 **Börßum** Ger.
190 G5 **Borstel** Ger.
193 H9 **Borstendorf** Ger.
Bortala *Xinjiang* China *see* **Bole**
132 F4 **Bortala He** *r.* China
172 D3 **Borth** *Ceredigion, Wales* U.K.
214 B7 **Bortigali** *Sardegna* Italy
214 C6 **Bortigiadas** *Sardegna* Italy
184 I5 **Bort-les-Orgues** France
184 J5 **Bort-les-Orgues, Barrage de** *dam* France
Bor-Üdzüür Mongolia *see* **Altay**
144 D6 **Borūjen** Iran
144 C5 **Borūjerd** Iran
128 F6 **Bor Ul Shan** *mts* China
144 H4 **Borūn** Iran
219 N8 **Borushtitsa** Bulg.
214 B6 **Borutta** *Sardegna* Italy
168 D8 **Borve** *Highland, Scotland* U.K.
158 B4 **Borynya** Ukr.
158 C4 **Boryslav** Ukr.
158 J3 **Boryspil'** Ukr.
197 K4 **Borzechów** Pol.
196 F4 **Borzęciczki** Pol.
159 L2 **Borzenka** *r.* Ukr.
158 B5 **Borzhava** *r.* Ukr.
Borzhomi Georgia *see* **Borjomi**
159 L2 **Borzna** Ukr.
212 G7 **Borzonasca** Italy
199 H4 **Börzsöny** *hills* Hungary
199 H4 **Börzsönyi** *park* Hungary
129 O1 **Borzya** Rus. Fed.
129 N1 **Borzya** *r.* Rus. Fed.
196 F1 **Borzytuchom** Pol.
214 B7 **Bosa** *Sardegna* Italy
199 G3 **Bošáca** Slovakia
143 O4 **Bosaga** Kazakh.
Bosagha Kazakh. *see* **Bosaga**
Bosaginskiy Kazakh. *see* **Bosaga**
214 A7 **Bosa Marina** *Sardegna* Italy
219 O3 **Bosanci** Romania
210 F3 **Bosanska Dubica** Bos.-Herz.
210 F3 **Bosanska Gradiška** Bos.-Herz.
210 F3 **Bosanska Kostajnica** Bos.-Herz.
210 F3 **Bosanska Krupa** Bos.-Herz.
210 G3 **Bosanski Brod** Bos.-Herz.
210 F3 **Bosanski Novi** Bos.-Herz.
210 F3 **Bosanski Petrovac** Bos.-Herz.
210 G3 **Bosanski Šamac** Bos.-Herz.
210 F3 **Bosansko Grahovo** Bos.-Herz.
199 H3 **Bošany** Slovakia
198 G4 **Bősárkány** Hungary
190 J2 **Bosau** Ger.
237 K4 **Bosberg** *mt.* S. Africa
172 H3 **Bosbury** *Herefordshire, England* U.K.
172 C6 **Boscastle** *Cornwall, England* U.K.
257 N5 **Boscawen** *NH* U.S.A.
Boscawen Island Tonga *see* **Niuatoputopu**
285 H5 **Bosch** Arg.
215 I1 **Bosco** Italy
250 D6 **Boscobel** *WI* U.S.A.
213 K4 **Bosco Chiesanuova** Italy
212 E5 **Bosco della Partecipiano e Lucedio, Parco Naturale** *nature res.* Italy
212 F6 **Bosco Marengo** Italy
215 M6 **Boscotrecase** Italy
190 J2 **Bösdorf** Ger.
236 E5 **Bosduiflaagte** *salt pan* S. Africa
130 F7 **Bose** *Guangxi* China
190 E4 **Bösel** Ger.
268 G6 **Bosencheve, Parque Nacional** *nat. park* Mex.
173 K6 **Bosham** *West Sussex, England* U.K.
Boshchakul' Kazakh. *see* **Bozshakol'**
122 M4 **Boshnyakovo** *Sakhalin* Rus. Fed.
237 L1 **Boshoek** S. Africa
237 J4 **Boshof** S. Africa
144 G5 **Boshrūyeh** Iran
219 K8 **Bosilegrad** *Bosilegrad* Serbia
Bosiljgrad *Bosilegrad* Serbia *see* **Bosilegrad**
219 K9 **Bosilovo** *Bosilovo* Macedonia
194 F5 **Bösingen** Ger.
142 I1 **Boskol'** Kazakh.
186 G4 **Boskoop** Neth.
198 F2 **Boskovice** Czech Rep.
275 H3 **Boslanti** Suriname
210 G3 **Bosna** *r.* Bos.-Herz.
219 P8 **Bosna** *hills* Bulg.
Bosna i Hercegovina *country* Europe *see* **Bosnia-Herzegovina**
Bosna Saray Bos.-Herz. *see* **Sarajevo**
Bosnia and Herzegovina, Federation of *aut. div.* Bos.-Herz. *see* **Federacija Bosna i Hercegovina**
210 F3 **Bosnia-Herzegovina** *country* Europe
230 D4 **Boso** Dem. Rep. Congo
236 G1 **Bosobogolo Pan** *salt pan* Botswana
230 C3 **Bosobolo** Dem. Rep. Congo
127 L5 **Bōsō-hantō** *pen.* Japan
230 D3 **Bososama** Dem. Rep. Congo
Bosost Spain *see* **Bòssost**
201 O1 **Bošovice** Czech Rep.
237 K2 **Bospoort** S. Africa
Bosporus *str.* Turkey *see* **İstanbul Boğazı**
Bossaga Turkm. *see* **Basaga**
230 C3 **Bossangoa** C.A.R.
163 M6 **Bössbod** Sweden
230 C3 **Bossembélé** C.A.R.
Bossemptélé C.A.R. *see* **Bossentélé**
230 C3 **Bossentélé** C.A.R.
184 E6 **Bosset** France
236 E5 **Bossiekom** S. Africa
261 I9 **Bossier City** *LA* U.S.A.
234 C5 **Bossiesvlei** Namibia
228 D4 **Bossora** Burkina
208 G2 **Bòssost** Spain
237 L1 **Bosspruit** S. Africa
108 F5 **Bossut, Cape** *W.A.* Austr.
133 G8 **Bostan** *Xinjiang* China
144 B6 **Bostān** Iran
145 L6 **Bostan** Pak.
142 C3 **Bostandyk** Kazakh.
144 F8 **Bostāneh, Ra's-e** *pt* Iran
132 H6 **Bosten Hu** *l.* China
169 E6 **Boston** Ireland
173 L2 **Boston** *Lincolnshire, England* U.K.
257 N6 **Boston** *MA* U.S.A.
104 E6 **Boston Bay** *S.A.* Austr.
251 O1 **Boston Creek** *Ont.* Can.
261 H8 **Boston Mountains** *AR*
171 O6 **Boston Spa** *West Yorksh England* U.K.
210 G3 **Bosut** *r.* Croatia
186 G3 **Boswachterij Schoorl** *r* Neth.
250 G9 **Boswell** *IN* U.S.A.
256 F8 **Boswell** *PA* U.S.A.
138 C8 **Botad** *Gujarat* India
159 M8 **Botanichne** Ukr.
228 C5 **Botata** Liberia
162 N5 **Boteå** Sweden
237 Q2 **Boteler Point** S. Africa
219 N5 **Boteni** Romania
173 O3 **Botesdale** *Suffolk, Engl*
234 E4 **Boteti** *r.* Botswana
157 D8 **Botev** *mt.* Bulg.
219 L8 **Botevgrad** Bulg.
237 K3 **Bothaville** S. Africa
190 I4 **Bothel** Ger.
171 K4 **Bothel** *Cumbria, Englar*
262 C3 **Bothell** *WA* U.S.A.
172 G6 **Bothenhampton** *Dorse England* U.K.
163 O6 **Bothnia, Gulf of** Fin./S
162 Q4 **Bothnian Bay** *g.* Fin./S
105 K10 **Bothwell** *Tas.* Austr.
251 M7 **Bothwell** *Ont.* Can.
204 E5 **Boticas** Port.
210 G4 **Botin** *mt.* Bos.-Herz.
201 M8 **Botinec Stupnički** Cro
159 O7 **Botiyeve** Ukr.
199 L4 **Botiz** Romania
256 A8 **Botkins** *OH* U.S.A.
157 I6 **Botkul', Ozero** *l.* Kazakh./Rus. Fed.
151 H3 **Botlikh** Rus. Fed.
229 H6 **Bot Makak** Cameroon
158 I7 **Botna** *r.* Moldova
208 C4 **Botorrita** Spain
219 O3 **Botoșani** Romania
129 O7 **Botou** *Hebei* China
217 L6 **Botricello** Italy
228 D5 **Botro** Côte d'Ivoire
237 J1 **Botsalano Game Reser** *nature res.* S. Africa
259 I2 **Botsford** *CT* U.S.A.
237 K5 **Botshabelo** S. Africa
162 P4 **Botsmark** Sweden
164 D2 **Botsvatn** *l.* Norway
234 D5 **Botswana** *country* Afric
217 K5 **Botte Donato, Monte** *r*
191 G8 **Bottendorf (Burgwald)**
190 K5 **Bottendorf (Obernhol**
173 K2 **Bottesford** *Leicestershir England* U.K.
171 P6 **Bottesford** *North Linco England* U.K.
214 C7 **Bottidda** *Sardegna* Italy
260 E1 **Bottineau** *ND* U.S.A.
270 G3 **Bottle Creek** Turks and
271 L5 **Bottom** *Saba* Neth. Ant
191 C7 **Bottrop** Ger.
280 C5 **Botucatu** Brazil
281 F2 **Botumirim** Brazil
218 I9 **Botun** Macedonia
Botushany Moldova *see*
249 K3 **Botwood** *Nfld and Lab.*
194 D5 **Bötzingen** Ger.
228 D5 **Bouaflé** Côte d'Ivoire
178 B5 **Bouafles** France
202 D5 **Bou Ahmed** Morocco
228 D5 **Bouaké** Côte d'Ivoire
227 F2 **Boualem** Alg.
228 D4 **Bouandougou** Côte d'I
230 C5 **Bouanga** Congo
230 B3 **Bouar** C.A.R.
211 B7 **Bou Arada** Tunisia
226 E2 **Bouârfa** Morocco
227 G2 **Bou Aroua** Alg.
180 H7 **Bouaye** France
229 I4 **Bouba Ndjida, Parc Na** *nat. park* Cameroon
198 C2 **Boubin** *mt.* Czech Rep.
228 C2 **Boû Bleï'îne** *well* Maur.
226 D4 **Boubout** *well* Alg.
230 C3 **Bouca** C.A.R.
185 B8 **Boucau** France
106 E2 **Boucaut Bay** *N.T.* Austr
183 G10 **Bouc-Bel-Air** France
181 K4 **Boucé** France
178 F3 **Bouchain** France
211 A7 **Bouchegouf** Alg.
181 J7 **Bouchemaine** France
Boucher, Île *i. Îles Loya* New Caledonia *see* **Tiga**
257 L3 **Boucherville** *Que.* Can.
183 G9 **Bouches-du-Rhône** *dep*
251 S3 **Bouchette** *Que.* Can.
178 E4 **Bouchoir** France
228 C3 **Boucle du Baoulé, Parc de la** *nat. park* Mali
249 H4 **Bouctouche** *N.B.* Can.
230 A5 **Bouda** Gabon
187 D6 **Boudewijn Kanaal** *cana*
139 J9 **Boudh** *Orissa* India
202 E5 **Boudinar** Morocco
228 E2 **Boû Djébéha** *well* Mali
230 C3 **Boudoua** C.A.R.
212 B2 **Boudry** Switz.
178 G3 **Boué** France
239 □[3b] **Bouéni** Mayotte
239 □[3b] **Bouéni, Baie de** *b.* May
231 B6 **Bouenza** *admin. reg.* Co
231 B6 **Bouenza** *r.* Congo
181 K6 **Bouessay** France
181 O8 **Bouesse** France
230 C3 **Boufore** C.A.R.
227 G1 **Bougaa** Alg.
108 I2 **Bougainville, Cape** *W.A.*
115 G4 **Bougainville, Selat** *sea Papua* Indon.
113 L8 **Bougainville Island** P.N
107 K3 **Bougainville Reef** *Coral Terr.* Austr.
100 □[6] **Bougainville Strait** Solo
227 G1 **Bougaroûn, Cap** *c.* Alg.
228 B2 **Boû Ghbeïra** *spring* Mau
229 F2 **Boughessa** Mali
Bougie Alg. *see* **Bejaïa**
185 E7 **Bouglon** France
230 B2 **Bougoumen** Chad
228 D4 **Bougouni** Mali
227 F2 **Bougtob** Alg.
180 H7 **Bouguenais** France
228 D2 **Boû Guendoûz** *well* Ma
185 G8 **Bouillac** France
271 □[2] **Bouillante** Guadeloupe
183 E9 **Bouillargues** France
187 H9 **Bouillon** Belgium
178 G7 **Bouilly** France
180 G8 **Bouin** France
227 F1 **Bouira** Alg.
226 C3 **Bou Izakarn** Morocco
182 I3 **Boujailles** France
183 C10 **Boujan-sur-Libron** Frar
226 B4 **Boujdour** Western Saha
227 F2 **Bou Kahil, Djebel** *mts* A
229 F4 **Boukoumbé** Benin
226 B4 **Boukra** Western Sahara
230 C2 **Boukta** Chad
230 C2 **Boula Bouda** Chad
228 C3 **Boulal** Mali
179 L5 **Boulay-Moselle** France
184 F5 **Boulazac** France
183 F9 **Boulbon** France
109 F11 **Boulder** *W.A.* Austr.
262 L6 **Boulder** *CO* U.S.A.
262 H3 **Boulder** *MT* U.S.A.
265 U4 **Boulder** *UT* U.S.A.
265 R5 **Boulder Canyon** *gorge*
265 R6 **Boulder City** *NV* U.S.A.
226 C3 **Bou Legmaden, Oued** *watercourse* Alg./Morocc
226 D2 **Boulemane** *Fez-Boulma* Morocco
226 D2 **Boulemane** *Fez-Boulma* Morocco
265 P9 **Boulevard** *CA* U.S.A.
285 H6 **Boulevard Atlántico** Arg
229 F3 **Boulgou** Burkina
Boulhaut Morocco *see* **Ben Slimane**
106 G7 **Boulia** *Qld* Austr.

Bouligny France
Bouloc France
Boulogne France see Boulogne-sur-Mer
Boulogne r. France
Boulogne-Billancourt France
Boulogne-sur-Gesse France
Boulogne-sur-Mer France
Bouloire France
Boulou r. C.A.R.
Boulouba C.A.R.
Bouloupari New Caledonia
Boulouris France
Boulsa Burkina
Boulsworth Hill England U.K.
Boult-aux-Bois France
Boultoum Niger
Boulzicourt France
Boumalne Dadès Morocco
Boumango Gabon
Boumba r. Cameroon
Boumbé I r. C.A.R.
Boumerdes Alg.
Boumort mt. Spain
Boumort, Serra del mts Spain
Bouna Côte d'Ivoire
Bou Naceur, Jbel mt. Morocco
Boû Nâga Maur.
Boundary AK U.S.A.
Boundary Mountains ME U.S.A.
Boundary Peak NV U.S.A.
Bound Brook NJ U.S.A.
Boundiali Côte d'Ivoire
Boundji Congo
Boundjiguire Mali
Boungou C.A.R.
Boungou r. C.A.R.
Bouniagues France
Bounkiling Senegal
Boun Nua Laos
Bountiful UT U.S.A.
Bountiful Island Qld Austr.
Bounty Islands N.Z.
Bounty Trough sea feature S. Pacific Ocean
Bouquet Arg.
Bourail New Caledonia
Bourarhet, Erg des. Alg.
Bourbince r. France
Bourbon reg. France see Bourbonnais
Bourbon terr. Indian Ocean see Réunion
Bourbon-Lancy France
Bourbon-l'Archambault France
Bourbonnais reg. France
Bourbonne-les-Bains France
Bourbourg France
Bourbre r. France
Bourbriac France
Bourcefranc-le-Chapus France
Bourdeaux France
Bourdeilles France
Bourdon, Réservoir du resr France
Bourdonnay France
Bourem Mali
Bouressa Mali see Boughessa
Bouresse France
Bourg France
Bourg-Achard France
Bourganeuf France
Bourg-Argental France
Bourgbarré France
Bourg-Blanc France
Bourg-de-Péage France
Bourg-de-Thizy France
Bourg-de-Visa France
Bourg-Dun France
Bourg-en-Bresse France
Bourges France
Bourget Ont. Can.
Bourget, Lac du l. France
Bourg-et-Comin France
Bourg-Lastic France
Bourg-lès-Valence France
Bourg-Madame France
Bourgmont Que. Can.
Bourgneuf, Baie de b. France
Bourgneuf-en-Mauges France
Bourgneuf-en-Retz France
Bourgogne France
Bourgogne admin. reg. France
Bourgogne, Canal de France
Bourgoin-Jallieu France
Bourg-St-Andéol France
Bourg-St-Bernard France
Bourg-St-Maurice France
Bourgtheroulde-Infreville France
Bourguébus France
Bourgueil France
Bourke N.S.W. Austr.
Bourkes Ont. Can.
Bourmont France
Bourne r. France
Bourne Lincolnshire, England U.K.
Bournemouth Bournemouth, England U.K.
Bournemouth admin. div. England U.K.
Bournezeau France
Bournoncle-St-Pierre France
Bouro Port.
Bourogne France
Bou Rouhat, Oued watercourse Morocco
Bouroum-Bouroum Burkina
Bourrah Cameroon
Bourran France
Bourriot-Bergonce France
Bourscheid Lux.
Bourtange Neth.
Bourtanger Moor reg. Ger.
Bourth France
Bourton Dorset, England U.K.
Bourton-on-the-Water Gloucestershire, England U.K.
Bourtoutou Chad
Bourzanga Burkina
Bou Saâda Alg.
Bou Salem Tunisia
Bouse AZ U.S.A.
Bouse Wash watercourse AZ U.S.A.
Boussac France
Boussé Burkina
Boussens France
Boussières France
Bousso Chad
Boussois France
Boussu Belgium
Boutersem Belgium
Boû Tezâya well Maur.
Boutilimit Maur.
Boutonne r. France
Boutougou Fara Senegal
Bouttencourt France
Bouveret Switz.
Bouvet Island terr. S. Atlantic Ocean see Bouvetøya
Bouvetøya terr. S. Atlantic Ocean
Bouvières France
Bouvron France
Bouxières-aux-Dames France
Bouxwiller France
Bouy France
Bou Yala Alg.
Bouza Niger
Bouzanne r. France
Bouzonville France
Bouzy France
Bova Italy
Bovalino Italy
Bova Marina Italy
Bovec Slovenia
Bóveda Galicia Spain
Boveda País Vasco Spain
Bovegno Italy
Bovenden Ger.
Boven Kapuas Mountains Indon./Malaysia see Kapuas Hulu, Pegunungan
Bovenkarspel Neth.
Bovensmilde Neth.
178 D4 Boves France
212 D7 Boves Italy
172 E6 Bovey r. England U.K.
250 A2 Bovey MN U.S.A.
172 E6 Bovey Tracey Devon, England U.K.
170 D4 Boviel Northern Ireland U.K.
187 I8 Bovigny Belgium
215 K4 Boville Ernica Italy
172 H6 Bovington Camp Dorset, England U.K.
215 O5 Bovino Italy
213 K5 Bovolone Italy
285 H2 Bovril Arg.
190 I1 Bovrup Denmark
159 L5 Bovtyshka Ukr.
108 J4 Bow r. W.A. Austr.
262 I2 Bow r. Alta Can.
247 I5 Bow r. Alta Can.
Bowa Sichuan China see Muli
260 D1 Bowbells ND U.S.A.
171 N4 Bowburn Durham, England U.K.
270 □ Bowden Jamaica
256 F10 Bowden WV U.S.A.
Bowditch atoll Tokelau see Fakaofo
284 D4 Bowen Arg.
107 L6 Bowen Qld Austr.
107 K6 Bowen r. Qld Austr.
250 C9 Bowen IL U.S.A.
105 L7 Bowen, Mount Vic. Austr.
107 J7 Bowen Downs Qld Austr.
246 F5 Bowen Island B.C. Can.
105 K7 Bowen Mountains Vic. Austr.
106 D1 Bowen Strait N.T. Austr.
107 M9 Bowenville Qld Austr.
258 E6 Bowers Beach DE U.S.A.
287 K2 Bowers Mountains Antarctica
290 G2 Bowers Ridge sea feature Bering Sea
171 M4 Bowes Durham, England U.K.
107 J6 Bowie Qld Austr.
265 W9 Bowie AZ U.S.A.
258 B7 Bowie MD U.S.A.
261 G9 Bowie TX U.S.A.
247 I5 Bow Island Alta Can.
171 L6 Bowland, Forest of reg. England U.K.
254 D7 Bowling Green KY U.S.A.
260 J6 Bowling Green MO U.S.A.
256 B7 Bowling Green OH U.S.A.
256 H10 Bowling Green VA U.S.A.
107 K5 Bowling Green, Cape Qld Austr.
107 K5 Bowling Green Bay Qld Austr.
107 K5 Bowling Green Bay National Park Qld Austr.
260 D2 Bowman ND U.S.A.
246 F5 Bowman, Mount B.C. Can.
286 T2 Bowman Coast Antarctica
287 G2 Bowman Island Antarctica
286 T2 Bowman Peninsula Antarctica
258 B4 Bowmansdale PA U.S.A.
258 D3 Bowmanstown PA U.S.A.
258 C4 Bowmansville PA U.S.A.
251 P6 Bowmanville Ont. Can.
171 M2 Bowmont Water r. England/Scotland U.K.
168 D11 Bowmore Argyll and Bute, Scotland U.K.
232 D2 Bown Somalia
171 K4 Bowness-on-Solway Cumbria, England U.K.
171 L5 Bowness-on-Windermere Cumbria, England U.K.
Bowo Sichuan China see Bomai
Bowo Xizang China see Bomi
105 N4 Bowraville N.S.W. Austr.
108 I4 Bow River Aboriginal Reserve W.A. Austr.
246 F4 Bowron r. B.C. Can.
246 F4 Bowron Lake Provincial Park B.C. Can.
245 O4 Bowser Lake B.C. Can.
172 H5 Box Wiltshire, England U.K.
194 H3 Boxberg Baden-Württemberg Ger.
193 K8 Boxberg Sachsen Ger.
193 I8 Boxdorf Ger.
260 D3 Box Elder SD U.S.A.
260 D3 Box Elder r. SD U.S.A.
165 L3 Boxholm Sweden
129 P8 Boxing Shandong China
186 I5 Boxmeer Neth.
186 H5 Boxtel Neth.
148 G3 Boyabat Turkey
274 C3 Boyacá dept Col.
219 O8 Boyadzhik Bulg.
221 K2 Boyalıca Turkey
Boyalık Turkey see Çiçekdağı
219 L8 Boyana tourist site Bulg.
Boyang China see Poyang
161 R8 Boyanovichi Rus. Fed.
219 O8 Boyanovo Bulg.
109 C12 Boyanup W.A. Austr.
158 J3 Boyarka Ukr.
105 N3 Boyd r. N.S.W. Austr.
109 H8 Boyd Lagoon salt flat W.A. Austr.
247 K2 Boyd Lake N.W.T. Can.
256 G12 Boydton VA U.S.A.
260 H5 Boyer r. IA U.S.A.
230 C5 Boyera Dem. Rep. Congo
258 D4 Boyertown PA U.S.A.
256 H12 Boykins VA U.S.A.
159 Q8 Boykiyevskiy Liman l. Rus. Fed.
246 H4 Boyle Alta Can.
169 F5 Boyle Ireland
107 M7 Boyne r. Qld Austr.
107 M8 Boyne r. Qld Austr.
169 J5 Boyne r. Ireland
250 I4 Boyne City MI U.S.A.
178 D7 Boynes France
145 L3 Boyni Qara Afgh.
230 D3 Boyo C.A.R.
230 E4 Boyoma, Chutes waterfall Dem. Rep. Congo
143 L8 Boysun Uzbek.
277 E5 Boyuibe Bol.
151 I5 Böyük Dähnä Azer.
144 A1 Böyük Hinaldağ mt. Azer.
151 H6 Böyük İşıqlı Dağ mt. Armenia
109 D12 Boyup Brook W.A. Austr.
221 L3 Bozan Turkey
151 B5 Bozan Dağı mt. Turkey
Bozashy Tübegi pen. Kazakh. see Buzachi, Poluostrov
221 J6 Bozburun Turkey
221 M5 Bozburun Dağ mt. Turkey
221 J6 Bozburun Yarımadası pen. Turkey
221 H3 Bozcaada i. Turkey
150 E2 Bozdağ mt. Turkey
221 H4 Bozdağ mt. Turkey
221 J3 Boz Dağ mts Turkey
Bozdag, Khrebet hills Azer. see Bozdağ Silsiläsi
221 I4 Boz Dağları mts Turkey
151 H5 Bozdağ Silsiläsi hills Azer.
151 E6 Bozdağ Tepe mt. Turkey
221 J5 Bozdoğan Turkey
173 K3 Bozeat Northamptonshire, England U.K.
183 J6 Bozel France
262 I4 Bozeman MT U.S.A.
Bozen Italy see Bolzano
197 H3 Bożewo Pol.
131 J2 Bozhou Anhui China
198 F3 Božíce Czech Rep.
201 N8 Božjakovina Croatia
148 F5 Bozkır Turkey
Bozköl Kazakh. see Boskol'
221 K5 Bozkurt Turkey
144 H5 Boznābād Iran
Bozoglan mts Turkey see Bolkar Dağları
183 B8 Bozouls France
230 C3 Bozoum C.A.R.
148 I5 Bozova Turkey
219 K6 Bozovici Romania
144 B3 Bozqūsh, Kūh-e mts Iran
143 P2 Bozshakol' Kazakh.
143 L3 Boztumsyk Kazakh.
221 L3 Bozüyük Turkey
150 A2 Bozyazı Turkey
143 T3 Bozymbay Kazakh.
212 I5 Bozzolo Italy
212 D6 Bra Italy
170 H5 Braaid Isle of Man
168 I9 Braan r. Scotland U.K.
165 L4 Braås Sweden
286 T2 Brabant Island Antarctica
187 G7 Brabant Wallon prov. Belgium
210 F4 Brač i. Croatia
168 D8 Bracadale Highland, Scotland U.K.
168 C8 Bracadale, Loch b. Scotland U.K.
Bracara Port. see Braga
214 I3 Bracciano Italy
214 I3 Bracciano, Lago di l. Italy
248 E4 Bracebridge Ont. Can.
171 P7 Bracebridge Heath Lincolnshire, England U.K.
184 C5 Brach France
191 E9 Brachbach Ger.
181 O6 Bracieux France
170 C7 Brackagh Ireland
162 M5 Bräcke Sweden
190 J4 Brackel Ger.
194 G3 Brackenheim Ger.
261 E11 Brackettville TX U.S.A.
210 F4 Brački Kanal sea chan. Croatia
173 J3 Brackley Northamptonshire, England U.K.
169 H6 Bracknagh Ireland
173 K5 Bracknell Bracknell Forest, England U.K.
173 K5 Bracknell Forest admin. div. England U.K.
277 G2 Braço Norte r. Brazil
219 K4 Brad Romania
215 R7 Bradano r. Italy
255 F12 Bradenton FL U.S.A.
271 □[2] Brades Montserrat
251 O5 Bradford Ont. Can.
171 N6 Bradford West Yorkshire, England U.K.
256 A8 Bradford OH U.S.A.
256 G7 Bradford PA U.S.A.
257 M5 Bradford VT U.S.A.
258 C1 Bradford County county PA U.S.A.
258 D4 Bradford Hills PA U.S.A.
172 H5 Bradford-on-Avon Wiltshire, England U.K.
173 J6 Brading Isle of Wight, England U.K.
250 G8 Bradley IL U.S.A.
259 G4 Bradley Beach NJ U.S.A.
256 B7 Bradner OH U.S.A.
172 F6 Bradninch Devon, England U.K.
172 G6 Bradpole Dorset, England U.K.
171 M6 Bradshaw Greater Manchester, England U.K.
256 D11 Bradshaw WV U.S.A.
108 H3 Bradshaw, Mount hill W.A. Austr.
171 N7 Bradwell Derbyshire, England U.K.
173 P2 Bradwell Norfolk, England U.K.
173 N4 Bradwell Waterside Essex, England U.K.
261 F10 Brady TX U.S.A.
261 F10 Brady Creek r. TX U.S.A.
245 M4 Brady Glacier AK U.S.A.
246 B3 Brady Glacier AK U.S.A.
197 L4 Bradzyatsin Belarus
168 □N2 Brae Shetland, Scotland U.K.
168 H7 Braeantra Highland, Scotland U.K.
168 K9 Braehead of Lunan Angus, Scotland U.K.
104 G5 Braemar S.A. Austr.
168 J8 Braemar Aberdeenshire, Scotland U.K.
216 G9 Braemi r. Sicilia Italy
204 D5 Braga Port.
204 D5 Braga admin. dist. Port.
285 G4 Bragado Arg.
278 D2 Bragança Brazil
204 G5 Bragança Port.
204 G5 Bragança admin. dist. Port.
280 D5 Bragança Paulista Brazil
250 A4 Braham MN U.S.A.
158 J2 Brahin Belarus
158 J2 Brahinka r. Belarus
190 K4 Brahlstorf Ger.
139 P6 Brahmakund Arun. Prad. India
139 M8 Brahmanbaria Bangl.
139 K9 Brahmani r. India
137 I3 Brahmapur Orissa India
139 M8 Brahmaputra r. Asia alt. Dihang (India), alt. Jamuna (Bangladesh), alt. Yarlung Zangbo (China)
138 F3 Brahmaur Hima. Prad. India
105 L6 Braidwood N.S.W. Austr.
250 F8 Braidwood IL U.S.A.
200 F6 Braies, Lago di l. Italy
219 P5 Brăila Romania
219 P6 Brăilei, Insula Mare a i. Romania
173 I2 Brailsford Derbyshire, England U.K.
178 G5 Braine France
187 F7 Braine-l'Alleud Belgium
187 F7 Braine-le-Comte Belgium
260 H2 Brainerd MN U.S.A.
181 L7 Brain-sur-Allonnes France
173 N4 Braintree Essex, England U.K.
171 K4 Braithwaite Cumbria, England U.K.
106 D1 Braithwaite Point N.T. Austr.
187 H7 Braives Belgium
235 F4 Brak r. Limpopo S. Africa
236 E9 Brak r. Western Cape S. Africa
236 C4 Brak watercourse S. Africa
190 F4 Brake (Unterweser) Ger.
187 E7 Brakel Belgium
191 H7 Brakel Ger.
186 H5 Brakel Neth.
228 B2 Brâkna admin. reg. Maur.
165 L5 Bräkneån r. Sweden
237 M2 Brakpan S. Africa
236 H7 Brakpoort S. Africa
237 K2 Brakspruit S. Africa
234 C4 Brakwater Namibia
164 I3 Brålanda Sweden
196 F4 Bralin Pol.
212 G6 Brallo di Pregola Italy
246 F5 Bralorne B.C. Can.
185 I9 Bram France
183 J6 Bramans France
200 F5 Bramberg am Wildkogel Austria
104 E5 Bramfield S.A. Austr.
173 O3 Bramford Suffolk, England U.K.
138 G9 Bramhapuri Mahar. India
171 O7 Bramley South Yorkshire, England U.K.
164 E6 Bramming Denmark
156 B3 Brämön i. Sweden
248 E5 Brampton Ont. Can.
173 L3 Brampton Cambridgeshire, England U.K.
171 L4 Brampton Cumbria, England U.K.
173 P3 Brampton Suffolk, England U.K.
191 D6 Bramsche Niedersachsen Ger.
191 F6 Bramsche Niedersachsen Ger.
165 N1 Bramsöfjärden l. Sweden
190 G4 Bramstedt Ger.
107 I2 Bramwell Qld Austr.
204 I2 Braña Caballo mt. Spain
193 I9 Braňany Czech Rep.
199 H3 Branč Slovakia
217 K8 Brancaleone Italy
173 N2 Brancaster Norfolk, England U.K.
249 K4 Branch Nfld and Lab. Can.
258 C3 Branch Dale PA U.S.A.
258 F2 Branchville NJ U.S.A.
231 D8 Branco Angola
275 F5 Branco r. Roraima Brazil
277 E2 Branco r. Brazil
228 □ Branco i. Cape Verde
200 A5 Brand Austria
195 L2 Brand Ger.
271 □[8] Brandaris hill Bonaire Neth. Antilles
234 B4 Brandberg mt. Namibia
163 N5 Brändbo Sweden
164 G1 Brandbu Norway
164 F6 Brande Denmark
190 I3 Brande-Hörnerkirchen Ger.
200 E5 Brandenberg Austria
193 G6 Brandenburg Ger.
193 H5 Brandenburg land Ger.
254 D7 Brandenburg KY U.S.A.
193 F6 Brandenburger Wald- und Seengebiet park Ger.
193 H9 Brand-Erbisdorf Ger.
184 F3 Brandes reg. France
171 Q6 Brandesburton East Riding of Yorkshire, England U.K.
237 K4 Brandfort S. Africa
193 H7 Brandis Brandenburg Ger.
193 G8 Brandis Sachsen Ger.
236 D7 Brandkop S. Africa
201 L2 Brand-Nagelberg Austria
163 P6 Brändö Åland Fin.
214 C2 Brando Corse France
107 K5 Brandon Qld Austr.
247 L5 Brandon Man. Can.
Brandon Ireland see Cé Bhréanainn
171 N4 Brandon Durham, England U.K.
173 N3 Brandon Suffolk, England U.K.
261 K9 Brandon MS U.S.A.
260 G4 Brandon SD U.S.A.
257 L5 Brandon VT U.S.A.
169 B8 Brandon Bay Ireland
169 B8 Brandon Head Ireland
169 I7 Brandon Hill Ireland
169 B8 Brandon Mountain hill Ireland
258 C3 Brandonville PA U.S.A.
256 F9 Brandonville WV U.S.A.
192 H2 Brandshagen Ger.
258 A4 Brandtsville PA U.S.A.
236 E6 Brandvlei S. Africa
236 D9 Brandvlei Dam resr S. Africa
162 O2 Brandvoll Norway
198 D1 Brandýs nad Labem-Stará Boleslav Czech Rep.
258 D5 Brandywine Creek, East Branch r. PA U.S.A.
258 D5 Brandywine Creek, West Branch r. DE U.S.A.
258 D4 Brandywine Manor PA U.S.A.
259 J2 Branford CT U.S.A.
255 F11 Branford FL U.S.A.
182 G3 Branges France
116 □ Brani, Pulau i. Sing.
201 I8 Branica r. Slovenia
165 P7 Braniewo Pol.
201 I8 Branik Slovenia
199 L6 Brănişca Romania
178 F8 Branlin r. France
162 P4 Brännberg Sweden
185 D6 Branne France
195 M6 Brannenburg Ger.
205 L3 Brañosera Spain
286 T2 Bransfield Strait Antarctica
173 I6 Bransgore Hampshire, England U.K.
197 K3 Brańsk Pol.
261 D7 Branson CO U.S.A.
171 Q7 Branston Lincolnshire, England U.K.
197 J3 Brańszczyk Pol.
117 J8 Brantas r. Indon.
248 D5 Brantford Ont. Can.
173 O4 Brantham Suffolk, England U.K.
199 G1 Brantice Czech Rep.
255 D10 Brantley AL U.S.A.
184 F5 Brantôme France
159 O3 Brantsivka Ukr.
250 D4 Brantwood WI U.S.A.
159 K3 Branytsya Ukr.
212 H3 Branzi Italy
205 M6 Braojos Spain
212 I4 Braone Italy
275 G5 Brás Brazil
183 H10 Bras France
249 I4 Bras d'Or Lake N.S. Can.
204 D8 Brasfemes Port.
274 D6 Brasil Brazil
Brasil country S. America see Brazil
281 G2 Brasil, Planalto do plat. Brazil
280 A4 Brasilândia Mato Grosso do Sul Brazil
280 C1 Brasilândia Minas Gerais Brazil
281 D2 Brasilândia Minas Gerais Brazil
276 C2 Brasileia Brazil
280 D1 Brasília Brazil
281 E2 Brasília de Minas Brazil
275 H5 Brasília Legal Brazil
160 H4 Brasla r. Latvia
Braslav Belarus see Braslaw
160 K6 Braslaw Belarus
219 N5 Braşov Romania
161 R9 Brasovo Rus. Fed.
239 □[1c] Bras-Panon Réunion
281 F4 Brás Pires Brazil
229 G5 Brass Nigeria
185 I8 Brassac France
183 C6 Brassac-les-Mines France
187 F6 Brasschaat Belgium
117 L2 Brassey, Banjaran mts Malaysia
106 E7 Brassey, Mount N.T. Austr.
109 G8 Brassey Range hills W.A. Austr.
257 □P3 Brassua Lake ME U.S.A.
182 D2 Brassy France
164 H3 Brastad Sweden
195 P2 Břasy Czech Rep.
219 N8 Bratan mt. Bulg.
219 K4 Bratca Romania
198 G3 Bratislava Slovakia
198 G3 Bratislavský kraj admin. reg. Slovakia
197 J5 Bratkowice Pol.
153 L4 Bratsk Rus. Fed.
159 K6 Brats'ke Mykolayivs'ka Oblast' Ukr.
159 M8 Brats'ke Respublika Krym Ukr.
Bratskoye Rus. Fed. see Nogamirzin-Yurt
153 L4 Bratskoye Vodokhranilishche resr Rus. Fed.
158 H5 Bratslav Ukr.
257 M6 Brattleboro VT U.S.A.
164 I1 Brattmon Sweden
172 H5 Bratton Wiltshire, England U.K.
162 I5 Brattvåg Norway
210 G3 Bratunac Bos.-Herz.
191 E10 Braubach Ger.
184 C5 Braud-et-St-Louis France
266 □R12 Braulio Carrillo, Parque Nacional nat. park Costa Rica
281 F3 Braúnas Brazil
200 H3 Braunau am Inn Austria
194 B2 Brauneberg Ger.
191 F9 Braunfels Ger.
191 K7 Braunlage Ger.
194 E6 Bräunlingen Ger.
194 H3 Braunsbach Ger.
193 E8 Braunsbedra Ger.
191 K6 Braunschweig Ger.
173 J3 Braunston Northamptonshire, England U.K.
173 J2 Braunstone Leicestershire, England U.K.
172 D5 Braunton Devon, England U.K.
237 L7 Braunville S. Africa
228 □ Brava i. Cape Verde
207 O5 Bravatas r. Spain
256 E9 Brave PA U.S.A.
158 H6 Bravicea Moldova
165 M3 Bråviken inlet Sweden
165 N3 Bråvikens naturreservat nature res. Sweden
276 D4 Bravo, Cerro mt. Bol.
267 K5 Bravo del Norte, Río r. Mex./U.S.A. alt. Rio Grande
206 B6 Bravura, Barragem da resr Port.
265 Q9 Brawley CA U.S.A.
169 J6 Bray Ireland
236 H1 Bray S. Africa
173 K4 Bray Windsor and Maidenhead, England U.K.
172 E6 Bray r. England U.K.
178 E1 Bray-Dunes France
181 M6 Braye r. France
169 B9 Bray Head Ireland
158 H4 Brayiliv Ukr.
243 K3 Bray Island Nunavut Can.
178 F7 Bray-sur-Seine France
171 O6 Brayton North Yorkshire, England U.K.
207 K3 Brazatortas Spain
246 H4 Brazeau r. Alta Can.
246 G4 Brazeau, Mount Alta Can.
237 N7 Brazen Head S. Africa
182 G2 Brazey-en-Plaine France
199 L5 Brazii Romania
278 C4 Brazil country S. America
254 D6 Brazil IN U.S.A.
288 H7 Brazil Basin sea feature S. Atlantic Ocean
261 H11 Brazos r. TX U.S.A.
231 B6 Brazzaville Congo
210 G3 Brčko Bos.-Herz.
196 G2 Brda r. Pol.
196 G3 Brdów Pol.
198 C2 Brdy hills Czech Rep.
Bré Ireland see Bray
205 Q5 Brea Spain
106 G7 Breadalbane Qld Austr.
168 H10 Breadalbane reg. Scotland U.K.
109 H8 Breaden, Lake salt flat W.A. Austr.
205 N8 Brea de Tajo Spain
237 K9 Breakfast Vlei S. Africa
103 A12 Breaksea Island South I. N.Z.
103 A12 Breaksea Sound inlet South I. N.Z.
107 N8 Breaksea Spit Qld Austr.
180 H5 Bréal-sous-Montfort France
172 G4 Bream Gloucestershire, England U.K.
102 I2 Bream Bay North I. N.Z.
102 I2 Bream Head North I. N.Z.
171 M2 Breamish r. England U.K.
102 I3 Bream Tail c. North I. N.Z.
168 B6 Breanais Western Isles, Scotland U.K.
282 C2 Breas Chile
168 C6 Breascleit Western Isles, Scotland U.K.
173 J2 Breaston Derbyshire, England U.K.
181 L2 Bréauté France
219 N5 Breaza Romania
117 H8 Brebes Jawa Indon.
117 H8 Brebes, Tanjung pt Indon.
183 K9 Brec d'Utelle mt. France
180 I4 Brécey France
180 F6 Brech France
178 D5 Brêche r. France
172 D4 Brechfa Carmarthenshire, Wales U.K.
168 K9 Brechin Angus, Scotland U.K.
187 G6 Brecht Belgium
263 K7 Breckenridge CO U.S.A.
260 G2 Breckenridge MN U.S.A.
261 F9 Breckenridge TX U.S.A.
191 D8 Breckerfeld Ger.
173 N3 Breckland lowland England U.K.
283 B9 Brecknock, Península pen. Chile
256 D7 Brecksville OH U.S.A.
198 F3 Břeclav Czech Rep.
172 F4 Brecon Powys, Wales U.K.
172 F4 Brecon Beacons reg. Wales U.K.
172 F4 Brecon Beacons National Park Wales U.K.
186 G5 Breda Neth.
208 K4 Breda Spain
165 J4 Bredaryd Sweden
236 E10 Bredasdorp S. Africa
105 L6 Bredbo N.S.W. Austr.
190 E5 Breddenberg Ger.
192 F5 Breddin Ger.
190 H4 Breddorf Ger.
164 E6 Brede r. Denmark
173 N6 Brede r. England U.K.
187 C6 Bredene Belgium
192 H4 Bredereiche Ger.
172 H3 Bredon Worcestershire, England U.K.
190 G1 Bredstedt Ger.
162 O5 Bredträsk Sweden
162 M3 Bredviken Sweden
142 I1 Bredy Rus. Fed.
187 I6 Bree Belgium
236 E10 Breede r. S. Africa
192 E4 Breese Ger.
186 G3 Breezand Neth.
256 G9 Breezewood PA U.S.A.
194 F6 Breg r. Ger.
219 J9 Bregalnica r. Macedonia
201 M8 Bregana Croatia
213 L4 Breganze Italy
200 A4 Bregenz Austria
200 A5 Bregenzer Wald mts Austria
190 J1 Bregninge Denmark
219 K6 Bregovo Bulg.
213 J4 Breguzzo Italy
180 H4 Bréhal France
180 F5 Bréhan France
180 F4 Bréhat, Île de i. France
191 J8 Brehme Ger.
193 F7 Brehna Ger.
162 □A1 Breiðafjörður b. Iceland
162 B1 Breiðafjörður nature res. Iceland
162 □F1 Breiðdalsvík Iceland
179 N5 Breidenbach France
191 F9 Breidenbach Ger.
260 E2 Breien ND U.S.A.
190 I2 Breiholz Ger.
212 G2 Breil Switz.
183 L9 Breil-sur-Roya France
237 K6 Breipaal S. Africa
194 D5 Breisach am Rhein Ger.
194 D6 Breisgau reg. Ger.
212 D1 Breitenbach Switz.
191 I9 Breitenbach am Herzberg Ger.
200 E5 Breitenbach am Inn Austria
195 P4 Breitenberg Ger.
195 I5 Breitenbrunn Bayern Ger.
195 L3 Breitenbrunn Bayern Ger.
190 I3 Breitenburg Ger.
190 K3 Breitenfelde Ger.
193 E7 Breitenhagen Ger.
200 C5 Breitenwang Austria
191 J8 Breitenworbis Ger.
200 D5 Breiter Grieskogel mt. Austria
192 H4 Breiter Luzinsee l. Ger.
194 E6 Breitnau Ger.
191 F9 Breitscheid Hessen Ger.
191 D9 Breitscheid Rheinland-Pfalz Ger.
191 J9 Breitungen Ger.
162 Q1 Breivikbotn Norway
162 O2 Breivikeidet Norway
206 B6 Brejeira, Serra da mts Port.
278 C4 Brejinho de Nazaré Brazil
278 E2 Brejo Brazil
278 E4 Brejo r. Brazil
278 D4 Brejo da Porta Brazil
190 G1 Breklum Ger.
162 J5 Brekstad Norway
180 B5 Brélès France
212 H4 Brembo r. Italy
190 G4 Bremen Ger.
190 G4 Bremen land Ger.
255 E9 Bremen GA U.S.A.
250 H8 Bremen IN U.S.A.
256 C9 Bremen OH U.S.A.
109 E13 Bremer Bay W.A. Austr.
109 E13 Bremer Bay b. W.A. Austr.
190 G3 Bremerhaven Ger.
109 F12 Bremer Range hills W.A. Austr.
Bremersdorp Swaziland see Manzini
262 C3 Bremerton WA U.S.A.
190 H4 Bremervörde Ger.
212 E1 Bremgarten Switz.
191 D10 Bremm Ger.
245 K3 Bremner r. AK U.S.A.
164 B2 Bremnes Norway
184 A2 Brem-sur-Mer France
197 J5 Breń r. Pol.
207 J5 Breña, Embalse de la resr Spain
238 □[3d] Breña Alta La Palma Canary Is
172 F5 Brendon Hills England U.K.
206 H5 Brenes Spain
261 G10 Brenham TX U.S.A.
206 E4 Brenhas r. Port.
172 E1 Brenig, Llyn resr Wales U.K.
162 L4 Brenna Norway
196 G6 Brenna Pol.
182 G3 Brenne r. France
181 M7 Brenne r. France
181 N8 Brenne reg. France
184 G2 Brenne, Parc Naturel Régional de la nature res. France
213 L2 Brennero Italy
Brennero, Passo di pass Austria/Italy see Brenner Pass
Brennerpaß pass Austria/Italy see Brenner Pass
200 E6 Brenner Pass pass Austria/Italy
162 P2 Brennes Norway
162 P2 Brennfjell Norway
212 I4 Breno Italy
182 H4 Brénod France
185 H8 Brens France
194 F2 Brensbach Ger.
248 E4 Brent Ont. Can.
213 M5 Brenta r. Italy
213 J3 Brenta, Gruppo di mts Italy
172 G5 Brent Knoll Somerset, England U.K.
173 M4 Brentwood Essex, England U.K.
259 I3 Brentwood NY U.S.A.
195 I4 Brenz r. Ger.
213 J4 Brenzone Italy
218 J8 Bresalc Gjilan Kosovo
212 I4 Brescia Italy
212 I4 Brescia prov. Italy
187 E6 Breskens Neth.
Breslau Pol. see Wrocław
178 B3 Bresle r. France
178 D5 Bresles France
249 G2 Brésolles, Lac l. Que. Can.
212 G5 Bressana Bottarone Italy
213 L2 Bressanone Italy
168 □N2 Bressay i. Scotland U.K.
182 G4 Bresse reg. France
185 G8 Bressols France
184 D2 Bressuire France
158 C1 Brest Belarus
180 C5 Brest France
180 C5 Brest, Rade de inlet France
201 L8 Brestanica Slovenia
201 M6 Bresternica Slovenia
Brest-Litovsk Belarus see Brest
Brest Oblast admin. div. Belarus see Brestskaya Voblasts'
219 J7 Brestovac Leskovac Serbia
199 K6 Brestovăţ Romania
Brestskaya Oblast' admin. div. Belarus see Brestskaya Voblasts'
160 I9 Brestskaya Voblasts' admin. div. Belarus
180 F5 Bretagne admin. reg. France
239 □[1c] Bretagne, Pointe de pt Réunion
185 E8 Bretagne-d'Armagnac France
274 C6 Bretana Peru
164 G2 Bretangen b. Norway
238 □[1b] Bretanha São Miguel Azores
238 □[1b] Bretanha, Ponta da pt São Miguel Azores
219 O4 Breţcu Romania
180 H5 Breteil France
185 H6 Bretenoux France
181 M4 Breteuil Haute-Normandie France
178 D4 Breteuil Picardie France
180 H8 Brétignolles-sur-Mer France
178 D6 Brétigny-sur-Orge France
193 J8 Bretnig Ger.
204 I5 Bretocino Spain
246 H4 Breton Alta Can.
270 D3 Breton, Cayo i. Cuba
180 G8 Breton, Marais marsh France
181 M5 Bretoncelles France
261 K11 Breton Sound b. LA U.S.A.
259 G4 Breton Woods NJ U.S.A.
194 F3 Bretten Ger.
172 G1 Bretton Flintshire, Wales U.K.
181 K3 Brettville-sur-Laize France
194 D2 Bretzenheim Ger.
194 G3 Bretzfeld Ger.
276 B2 Breu r. Brazil/Peru
194 G2 Breuberg-Neustadt Ger.
179 L8 Breuches France
179 L8 Breuchin r. France
116 A2 Breueh, Pulau i. Indon.
186 I5 Breugel Neth.
212 D4 Breuil-Cervinia Italy
184 C4 Breuil-Magné France
178 B6 Breuilpont France
186 H4 Breukelen Neth.
191 H8 Breuna Ger.
179 K7 Breuvannes-en-Bassigny France
255 F8 Brevard NC U.S.A.
275 I5 Breves Brazil
244 F2 Brevig Mission AK U.S.A.
164 F2 Brevik Norway
164 I2 Breviken Sweden
182 J4 Brévon r. France
191 H7 Brevörde Ger.
105 K3 Brewarrina N.S.W. Austr.
257 □Q4 Brewer ME U.S.A.
228 C5 Brewerville Liberia
172 H2 Brewood Staffordshire, England U.K.
260 F5 Brewster NE U.S.A.
259 H2 Brewster NY U.S.A.
256 D8 Brewster OH U.S.A.
262 E2 Brewster WA U.S.A.
Brewster, Kap c. Greenland see Kangikajik
105 J5 Brewster, Lake imp. l. N.S.W. Austr.
255 D10 Brewton AL U.S.A.
237 N2 Breyten S. Africa
161 U3 Breytovo Rus. Fed.
199 I2 Breza Slovakia
201 L7 Breze Slovenia
Brezhnev Rus. Fed. see Naberezhnyye Chelny
198 F3 Březí Czech Rep.
210 E3 Brežice Slovenia
201 N7 Breznica Croatia
199 K2 Breznica Slovakia
198 C2 Březnice Czech Rep.
219 K8 Breznik Bulg.
219 L6 Brezniţa-Motru Romania
219 L9 Breznitsa Bulg.
193 H10 Březno Czech Rep.
199 I3 Brezno Slovakia
178 B6 Brézolles France
199 G2 Březová Czech Rep.
199 G3 Brezová pod Bradlom Slovakia
199 L3 Brezovec Slovakia
201 J7 Brezovica Slovenia
219 N8 Brezovo Bulg.
210 F3 Brezovo Polje plain Croatia
230 D3 Bria C.A.R.
122 I2 Briakan Rus. Fed.
184 G4 Briance r. France
183 J7 Briançon France
265 T4 Brian Head mt. UT U.S.A.
172 E3 Brianne, Llyn resr Wales U.K.
259 H2 Briarcliff Manor NY U.S.A.
182 B1 Briare France
178 E8 Briare, Canal de France
185 H8 Briatexte France
217 K6 Briatico Italy
107 N9 Bribie Island Qld Austr.
183 K7 Bric Bouchet mt. France/Italy
158 G5 Briceni Moldova
183 J7 Bric Froid mt. France/Italy
Brichany Moldova see Briceni
212 C6 Bricherasio Italy
169 E5 Brickens Ireland
258 C4 Brickerville PA U.S.A.
258 F6 Bricksboro NJ U.S.A.
259 G4 Brick Township NJ U.S.A.
179 I7 Bricon France
180 H3 Bricquebec France
169 G8 Bride r. Ireland
183 J6 Brides-les-Bains France
173 O5 Bridge Kent, England U.K.
169 H2 Bridge End Ireland
259 K3 Bridgehampton NY U.S.A.
169 I7 Bridgeland Ireland
250 H8 Bridgeman MI U.S.A.
168 K9 Bridgend Angus, Scotland U.K.
168 D11 Bridgend Argyll and Bute, Scotland U.K.
172 E4 Bridgend Bridgend, Wales U.K.
168 J8 Bridgend Moray, Scotland U.K.
172 E4 Bridgend admin. div. Wales U.K.
168 I10 Bridge of Allan Stirling, Scotland U.K.
168 H9 Bridge of Balgie Perth and Kinross, Scotland U.K.
168 J9 Bridge of Cally Perth and Kinross, Scotland U.K.
168 J9 Bridge of Craigisla Angus, Scotland U.K.
168 L8 Bridge of Don Aberdeen, Scotland U.K.
168 K9 Bridge of Dun Angus, Scotland U.K.
168 K9 Bridge of Dye Aberdeenshire, Scotland U.K.
168 J10 Bridge of Earn Perth and Kinross, Scotland U.K.
168 I5 Bridge of Forss Highland, Scotland U.K.
168 G9 Bridge of Orchy Argyll and Bute, Scotland U.K.
168 □M2 Bridge of Walls Shetland, Scotland U.K.
168 G11 Bridge of Weir Renfrewshire, Scotland U.K.
255 E8 Bridgeport AL U.S.A.
264 M3 Bridgeport CA U.S.A.
257 L7 Bridgeport CT U.S.A.
251 K6 Bridgeport MI U.S.A.
260 D5 Bridgeport NE U.S.A.
258 E4 Bridgeport PA U.S.A.
261 G9 Bridgeport TX U.S.A.
264 M3 Bridgeport Reservoir CA U.S.A.
262 J4 Bridger MT U.S.A.
262 K6 Bridger Peak WY U.S.A.
258 E6 Bridgeton NJ U.S.A.
109 D12 Bridgetown W.A. Austr.
271 □[4] Bridgetown Barbados
249 H4 Bridgetown N.S. Can.
169 I8 Bridgetown Ireland
257 J10 Bridgeville DE U.S.A.
105 K10 Bridgewater Tas. Austr.
249 H4 Bridgewater N.S. Can.
257 O7 Bridgewater MA U.S.A.
257 □R2 Bridgewater ME U.S.A.
257 J6 Bridgewater NY U.S.A.
256 G10 Bridgewater VA U.S.A.
104 H8 Bridgewater, Cape Vic. Austr.
172 H2 Bridgnorth Shropshire, England U.K.
257 □O4 Bridgton ME U.S.A.
172 F5 Bridgwater Somerset, England U.K.
172 F5 Bridgwater Bay England U.K.
198 G2 Břidličná Czech Rep.
171 Q5 Bridlington East Riding of Yorkshire, England U.K.
171 Q5 Bridlington Bay England U.K.
105 K9 Bridport Tas. Austr.
172 G6 Bridport Dorset, England U.K.
184 E4 Brie France
178 E7 Brie reg. France
180 D5 Briec France
178 E6 Brie-Comte-Robert France
191 D10 Briedel Ger.
Brieg Pol. see Brzeg
186 F5 Brielle Neth.
178 I7 Brienne-le-Château France
182 E4 Briennon France
178 G7 Brienon-sur-Armançon France
212 E2 Brienz Switz.
215 P7 Brienza Italy
212 E2 Brienzer Rothorn mt. Switz.
212 D2 Brienzer See l. Switz.
180 G7 Brière, Parc Naturel Régional de nature res. France
258 A1 Brier Mountain hill PA U.S.A.
256 E10 Briery Knob mt. WV U.S.A.
193 J6 Briescht Ger.
192 G5 Brieselang Ger.
193 J6 Briesen Ger.
193 I8 Brieske Ger.
193 K6 Brieskow-Finkenheerd Ger.
193 K7 Briesnig Ger.
190 J4 Brietlingen Ger.
179 I5 Brieuilles-sur-Bar France
205 O4 Brieva de Cameros Spain
179 K5 Briey France
212 D3 Brig Switz.
194 F6 Brigach r. Ger.
285 I2 Brigadier General Diego Lamas Uru.
259 G6 Brigantine NJ U.S.A.
171 Q6 Brigg North Lincolnshire, England U.K.
262 L6 Briggsdale CO U.S.A.
250 E6 Briggsville WI U.S.A.
171 K4 Brigham Cumbria, England U.K.
262 H6 Brigham City UT U.S.A.
171 N6 Brighouse West Yorkshire, England U.K.
173 J6 Brighstone Isle of Wight, England U.K.
105 K7 Bright Vic. Austr.
173 O4 Brightlingsea Essex, England U.K.
285 F6 Brightman, Caleta inlet Arg.
251 Q5 Brighton Ont. Can.
103 E12 Brighton South I. N.Z.
173 L6 Brighton Brighton and Hove, England U.K.
262 L7 Brighton CO U.S.A.
251 K7 Brighton MI U.S.A.
256 H5 Brighton NY U.S.A.
256 C10 Brighton WV U.S.A.
173 L6 Brighton and Hove admin. div. England U.K.
107 H7 Brighton Downs Qld Austr.
103 H8 Brightwater South I. N.Z.
182 F5 Brignais France
185 F8 Brignemont France
180 C4 Brignogan-Plage France
183 I10 Brignoles France
168 H10 Brig o'Turk Stirling, Scotland U.K.
173 K3 Brigstock Northamptonshire, England U.K.
205 O7 Brihuega Spain
213 P6 Brijuni nat. park Croatia
228 A3 Brikama Gambia
250 F5 Brillion WI U.S.A.
179 J6 Brillon-en-Barrois France
191 G8 Brilon Ger.
171 O7 Brimington Derbyshire, England U.K.
250 J3 Brimley MI U.S.A.
162 □G1 Brimnes Iceland
250 C2 Brimson MN U.S.A.
271 □[2] Brimstone Hill Fortress National Park St Kitts and Nevis
206 D4 Brinches Port.
204 H6 Brincones Spain
217 N2 Brindisi Italy
217 N2 Brindisi prov. Italy
215 P6 Brindisi Montagna Italy
104 D4 Bring, Lake salt flat S.A. Austr.
210 E3 Brinje Croatia
261 J8 Brinkley AR U.S.A.
285 F2 Brinkmann Arg.
190 E4 Brinkum Niedersachsen Ger.
190 G4 Brinkum Niedersachsen Ger.
104 G5 Brinkworth S.A. Austr.
182 C2 Brinon-sur-Beuvron France
181 P6 Brinon-sur-Sauldre France
171 O7 Brinsley Nottinghamshire, England U.K.
179 L6 Brin-sur-Seille France
171 O7 Brinsworth South Yorkshire, England U.K.
183 C7 Brion France
249 I4 Brion, Île i. Que. Can.
205 O3 Briones Spain
182 E4 Brionnais reg. France
181 M3 Brionne France
183 C6 Brioude France
184 D3 Brioux-sur-Boutonne France
181 K4 Briouze France
249 G2 Brisay Que. Can.
107 N9 Brisbane Qld Austr.
213 L7 Brisighella Italy
181 K7 Brissac-Quincé France
257 □R2 Bristol N.B. Can.
172 G5 Bristol Bristol, England U.K.
172 G5 Bristol admin. div. England U.K.
257 M7 Bristol CT U.S.A.
255 E10 Bristol FL U.S.A.
258 B7 Bristol MD U.S.A.
257 N5 Bristol NH U.S.A.
258 F4 Bristol PA U.S.A.
257 N7 Bristol RI U.S.A.
256 C12 Bristol TN U.S.A.
257 L4 Bristol VT U.S.A.
244 G4 Bristol Bay AK U.S.A.
172 D5 Bristol Channel est. England U.K.
273 G7 Bristol Island S. Sandwich Is
265 Q7 Bristol Lake CA U.S.A.
265 P7 Bristol Mountains CA U.S.A.

173 O2 Briston *Norfolk, England* U.K.
261 G8 Bristow *OK* U.S.A.
172 G6 Brit *r. England* U.K.
Britannia Island *Îles Loyauté* New Caledonia *see* Maré
204 D5 Britelo Port.
286 S2 British Antarctic Territory Antarctica
246 F5 British Columbia *prov.* Can.
243 J1 British Empire Range *mts Nunavut* Can.
British Guiana *country* S. America *see* Guyana
110 C7 British Indian Ocean Territory *terr.* Indian Ocean
162 Q4 British Isles N. Atlantic Ocean
245 L1 British Mountains Can./U.S.A.
British Solomon Islands *country* S. Pacific Ocean *see* Solomon Islands
201 J7 Britof Slovenia
Brito Godins Angola *see* Kiwaba N'zogi
237 L1 Brits S. Africa
236 H6 Britstown S. Africa
169 J6 Brittas Ireland
169 J7 Brittas Bay Ireland
168 D8 Brittle, Loch *b. Scotland* U.K.
260 G3 Britton *SD* U.S.A.
192 I5 Britz Ger.
184 H5 Brive-la-Gaillarde France
183 D6 Brives-Charensac France
205 N3 Briviesca Spain
180 H2 Brix France
200 F5 Brixen im Thale Austria
172 E7 Brixham *Torbay, England* U.K.
Brixia Italy *see* Brescia
200 E5 Brixlegg Austria
173 K3 Brixworth *Northamptonshire, England* U.K.
213 P4 Brkini *reg.* Slovenia
Brlik *Zhambylskaya Oblast'* Kazakh. *see* Birlik
193 K9 Brniště Czech Rep.
198 F2 Brno Czech Rep.
165 N2 Bro Sweden
Broach *Gujarat* India *see* Bharuch
255 G8 Broad *r. SC* U.S.A.
257 K5 Broadalbin *NY* U.S.A.
109 F11 Broad Arrow *W.A.* Austr.
248 E3 Broadback *r. Que.* Can.
172 F6 Broadclyst *Devon, England* U.K.
105 J7 Broadford *Vic.* Austr.
169 E7 Broadford *Clare* Ireland
169 E8 Broadford *Limerick* Ireland
168 E8 Broadford *Highland, Scotland* U.K.
169 C4 Broad Haven *b.* Ireland
172 B4 Broad Haven *Pembrokeshire, Wales* U.K.
172 H3 Broadheath *Worcestershire, England* U.K.
168 J12 Broad Law *hill Scotland* U.K.
172 H6 Broadmayne *Dorset, England* U.K.
106 E4 Broadmere *N.T.* Austr.
173 N6 Broad Oak *East Sussex, England* U.K.
245 J3 Broad Pass *AK* U.S.A.
145 Q4 Broad Peak China/Pak.
107 L7 Broad Sound *sea chan. Qld* Austr.
107 M7 Broad Sound Channel *Qld* Austr.
107 L7 Broadsound Range *hills Qld* Austr.
173 O5 Broadstairs *Kent, England* U.K.
262 L4 Broadus *MT* U.S.A.
247 K5 Broadview *Sask.* Can.
105 N3 Broadwater *N.S.W.* Austr.
260 D5 Broadwater *NE* U.S.A.
169 J8 Broadway Ireland
173 I3 Broadway *Worcestershire, England* U.K.
256 G10 Broadway *VA* U.S.A.
172 H6 Broadwey *Dorset, England* U.K.
172 G6 Broadwindsor *Dorset, England* U.K.
102 H2 Broadwood *North I.* N.Z.
190 I1 Broager Denmark
165 K5 Broby Sweden
212 C2 Broc Switz.
185 C7 Brocas France
160 F5 Brocēni Latvia
168 D8 Brochel *Highland, Scotland* U.K.
247 K3 Brochet *Man.* Can.
247 K3 Brochet, Lac *l. Man.* Can.
249 G3 Brochet, Lac au *l. Que.* Can.
245 Q1 Brock *r. N.W.T.* Can.
171 L6 Brock *r. England* U.K.
190 I4 Brockel Ger.
190 J5 Bröckel Ger.
191 K7 Brocken *mt.* Ger.
173 I6 Brockenhurst *Hampshire, England* U.K.
243 G2 Brock Island *N.W.T.* Can.
108 D7 Brockman, Mount *W.A.* Austr.
256 H5 Brockport *NY* U.S.A.
256 G7 Brockport *PA* U.S.A.
257 N6 Brockton *MA* U.S.A.
258 C3 Brockton *PA* U.S.A.
191 F6 Brockum Ger.
248 F4 Brockville *Ont.* Can.
257 □R3 Brockway *N.B.* Can.
256 G7 Brockway *PA* U.S.A.
172 H4 Brockworth *Gloucestershire, England* U.K.
256 F6 Brocton *NY* U.S.A.
196 E2 Broczyno Pol.
198 G2 Brodek u Přerova Czech Rep.
Broderick Falls Kenya *see* Webuye
192 F2 Broderstorf Ger.
158 H4 Brodets'ke Ukr.
243 J2 Brodeur Peninsula *Nunavut* Can.
250 E7 Brodhead *WI* U.S.A.
258 E3 Brodhead *r. PA* U.S.A.
258 E3 Brodheadsville *PA* U.S.A.
168 F11 Brodick *North Ayrshire, Scotland* U.K.
256 G12 Brodnax *VA* U.S.A.
197 H2 Brodnica *Kujawsko-Pomorskie* Pol.
196 E3 Brodnica *Wielkopolskie* Pol.
189 I2 Brodnicki Park Krajobrazowy Pol.
198 G3 Brodské Slovakia
196 C4 Brody *Lubuskie* Pol.
196 D3 Brody *Lubuskie* Pol.
158 E3 Brody Ukr.
237 J2 Broedersput S. Africa
186 J6 Broekhuizenvorst Neth.
237 J6 Broekpoort *r.* S. Africa
181 M3 Broglie France
191 D10 Brohl Ger.
192 I3 Brohm Ger.
182 G2 Broin France
196 D3 Brójce Pol.
196 D2 Brojce Pol.
197 J3 Brok Pol.
197 J3 Brok *r.* Pol.
190 H3 Brokdorf Ger.
164 E2 Brokefjell *mt.* Norway
109 D13 Broke Inlet *W.A.* Austr.
261 H7 Broken Arrow *OK* U.S.A.
105 M5 Broken Bay *N.S.W.* Austr.
260 F5 Broken Bow *NE* U.S.A.
261 H8 Broken Bow *OK* U.S.A.
261 H8 Broken Bow Reservoir *OK* U.S.A.
256 H10 Brokenburg *VA* U.S.A.
247 L5 Brokenhead *r. Man.* Can.
104 H4 Broken Hill *N.S.W.* Austr.
Broken Hill Zambia *see* Kabwe
289 K7 Broken Plateau *sea feature* Indian Ocean
275 H3 Brokopondo Suriname
Brokopondo Stuwmeer *resr* Suriname *see* Professor van Blommestein Meer
190 I3 Brokstedt Ger.
216 H7 Brolo *Sicilia* Italy
195 J3 Brombachsee *l.* Ger.
Bromberg Pol. *see* Bydgoszcz
190 K5 Brome Ger.
172 G3 Bromfield *Shropshire, England* U.K.
173 K3 Bromham *Bedfordshire, England* U.K.
172 H5 Bromham *Wiltshire, England* U.K.
173 L5 Bromley *Greater London, England* U.K.
164 F1 Bromma Norway
183 B7 Brommat France
165 J3 Brommö *i.* Sweden
162 O1 Bromnes Norway
117 J8 Bromo Tengger Semeru, Taman Nasional *nat. park* Indon.
270 □ Brompton Jamaica
171 O5 Brompton *North Yorkshire, England* U.K.
171 N5 Brompton on Swale *North Yorkshire, England* U.K.
165 M5 Brömsebro Sweden
172 H3 Bromsgrove *Worcestershire, England* U.K.
191 G8 Bromskirchen Ger.
172 G3 Bromyard *Herefordshire, England* U.K.
182 F5 Bron France
172 E2 Bronaber *Gwynedd, Wales* U.K.
205 Q7 Bronchales Spain
164 F4 Brønderslev Denmark
228 E5 Brong-Ahafo *admin. reg.* Ghana
212 G5 Broni Italy
193 K7 Bronice Pol.
237 M1 Bronkhorstspruit S. Africa
161 V6 Bronnitsy Rus. Fed.
162 L4 Brønnøysund Norway
255 F11 Bronson *FL* U.S.A.
250 I8 Bronson *MI* U.S.A.
216 H8 Bronte *Sicilia* Italy
259 H3 Bronx County *county NY* U.S.A.
158 G3 Bronyts'ka Huta Ukr.
212 H4 Bronzone, Monte *mt.* Italy
173 O2 Brooke *Norfolk, England* U.K.
256 H10 Brooke *VA* U.S.A.
169 H4 Brookeborough *Northern Ireland* U.K.
114 A7 Brooke's Point *Palawan* Phil.
259 I1 Brookfield *CT* U.S.A.
260 I6 Brookfield *MO* U.S.A.
250 F6 Brookfield *WI* U.S.A.
261 J10 Brookhaven *MS* U.S.A.
262 B5 Brookings *OR* U.S.A.
260 G3 Brookings *SD* U.S.A.
258 D5 Brookland Terrace *DE* U.S.A.
257 N6 Brookline *MA* U.S.A.
250 D9 Brooklyn *IL* U.S.A.
251 J7 Brooklyn *MI* U.S.A.
258 B6 Brooklyn Park *MD* U.S.A.
250 A4 Brooklyn Park *MN* U.S.A.
256 G11 Brookneal *VA* U.S.A.
250 A4 Brook Park *MN* U.S.A.
247 I5 Brooks *Alta* Can.
257 □P4 Brooks *ME* U.S.A.
256 E11 Brooks *WV* U.S.A.
286 T2 Brooks, Cape Antarctica
245 N3 Brooks Brook *Y.T.* Can.
258 D5 Brookside *DE* U.S.A.
244 F2 Brooks Mountain *hill AK* U.S.A.
246 E5 Brooks Peninsula Provincial Park *B.C.* Can.
245 K1 Brooks Range *mts AK* U.S.A.
250 H9 Brookston *IN* U.S.A.
250 B3 Brookston *MN* U.S.A.
255 F11 Brooksville *FL* U.S.A.
256 A10 Brooksville *KY* U.S.A.
109 D12 Brookton *W.A.* Austr.
257 □R3 Brookton *ME* U.S.A.
254 E6 Brookville *IN* U.S.A.
256 F7 Brookville *PA* U.S.A.
168 F7 Broom, Loch *inlet Scotland* U.K.
108 G4 Broome *W.A.* Austr.
109 D12 Broomehill *W.A.* Austr.
169 I4 Broomfield Ireland
173 M4 Broomfield *Essex, England* U.K.
180 G5 Broons France
183 B8 Broquiès France
168 I6 Brora *Highland, Scotland* U.K.
168 I6 Brora *r. Scotland* U.K.
168 I6 Brora, Loch *l. Scotland* U.K.
165 K6 Brösarp Sweden
172 H2 Broseley *Shropshire, England* U.K.
158 D5 Broshniv Osada Ukr.
169 D8 Brosna Ireland
169 G6 Brosna *r.* Ireland
184 D5 Brossac France
162 N2 Brøstadbotn Norway
219 N3 Broşteni Romania
256 F12 Brosville *VA* U.S.A.
280 C5 Brotas Brazil
206 C3 Brotas Port.
278 E5 Brotas de Macaúbas Brazil
137 M7 Brothers *is Andaman & Nicobar Is* India
262 D5 Brothers *OR* U.S.A.
104 □3 Brothers Point S. Pacific Ocean
208 E2 Broto Spain
181 M3 Brotonne, Parc Naturel Régional de *nature res.* France
191 J9 Brotterode, Kurort Ger.
179 J7 Brottes France
171 P4 Brotton *Redcar and Cleveland, England* U.K.
178 B7 Brou France
171 M4 Brough *Cumbria, England* U.K.
171 P6 Brough *East Riding of Yorkshire, England* U.K.
168 J5 Brough *Highland, Scotland* U.K.
170 B7 Broughal Ireland
168 J4 Brough Head *Scotland* U.K.
168 K5 Brough Ness *pt Scotland* U.K.
169 J3 Broughshane *Northern Ireland* U.K.
172 G1 Broughton *Flintshire, Wales* U.K.
173 K3 Broughton *Northamptonshire, England* U.K.
171 P6 Broughton *North Lincolnshire, England* U.K.
168 J11 Broughton *Scottish Borders, Scotland* U.K.
173 J2 Broughton Astley *Leicestershire, England* U.K.
171 K5 Broughton in Furness *Cumbria, England* U.K.
Broughton Island *Nunavut* Can. *see* Qikiqtarjuaq
168 K4 Broughtown *Orkney, Scotland* U.K.
224 C5 Broulkou *well* Chad
198 F1 Broumov Czech Rep.
179 I7 Brousseval France
179 M7 Brouvelieures France
186 E5 Brouwershaven Neth.
158 J3 Brovary Ukr.
107 M9 Brovinia *Qld* Austr.
164 F4 Brovst Denmark
260 H2 Browerville *MN* U.S.A.
109 E11 Brown, Lake *salt flat W.A.* Austr.
104 G5 Brown, Mount *hill S.A.* Austr.
104 D5 Brown, Point *S.A.* Austr.
270 F3 Brown Bank *sea feature* Bahamas
251 L6 Brown City *MI* U.S.A.
107 I4 Brown Creek *r. Qld* Austr.
250 G6 Brown Deer *WI* U.S.A.
171 M7 Brown Edge *Staffordshire, England* U.K.
109 H8 Browne Range *hills W.A.* Austr.
261 D9 Brownfield *TX* U.S.A.
173 I2 Brownhills *West Midlands, England* U.K.
262 H2 Browning *MT* U.S.A.
264 O6 Brown Mountain *CA* U.S.A.
250 B6 Brownsdale *MN* U.S.A.
258 F5 Browns Mills *NJ* U.S.A.
270 □ Brown's Town Jamaica
254 D6 Brownstown *IN* U.S.A.
258 C4 Brownstown *PA* U.S.A.
260 G3 Browns Valley *MN* U.S.A.
254 D7 Brownsville *KY* U.S.A.
256 F8 Brownsville *PA* U.S.A.
261 K8 Brownsville *TN* U.S.A.
261 G13 Brownsville *TX* U.S.A.
275 H3 Brownsweg Suriname
257 □P3 Brownville *ME* U.S.A.
257 □P3 Brownville Junction *ME* U.S.A.
261 F10 Brownwood *TX* U.S.A.
267 J2 Brownwood, Lake *TX* U.S.A.
108 G3 Browse Island *W.A.* Austr.
168 J11 Broxburn *West Lothian, Scotland* U.K.
212 C2 Broye *r.* Switz.
178 G6 Broyes France
193 J10 Brozany Czech Rep.
204 G9 Brozas Spain
160 M9 Brozha Belarus
212 I4 Brozzo Italy
198 E2 Brtnice Czech Rep.
168 I9 Bruar Water *r. Scotland* U.K.
178 E3 Bruay-la-Bussière France
Bruce Barbados *see* Bruce Vale
261 K9 Bruce *MS* U.S.A.
250 C4 Bruce *WI* U.S.A.
108 E7 Bruce, Mount *W.A.* Austr.
250 E3 Bruce Crossing *MI* U.S.A.
251 M5 Bruce Peninsula *Ont.* Can.
251 M4 Bruce Peninsula National Park *Ont.* Can.
109 E11 Bruce Rock *W.A.* Austr.
271 □4 Bruce Vale Barbados
179 O6 Bruche *r.* France
190 H5 Bruchhausen-Vilsen Ger.
191 G10 Bruchköbel Ger.
194 C3 Bruchmühlbach Ger.
194 F3 Bruchsal Ger.
194 D3 Bruchweiler-Bärenbach Ger.
193 G6 Brück Ger.
200 G5 Bruck an der Großglocknerstraße Austria
201 O3 Bruck an der Leitha Austria
201 L5 Bruck an der Mur Austria
195 L4 Bruckberg Ger.
194 C2 Brücken Ger.
194 C3 Brücken (Pfalz) Ger.
195 M3 Bruck in der Oberpfalz Ger.
201 K6 Brückl Austria
195 L6 Bruckmühl Ger.
217 I9 Brucoli *Sicilia* Italy
197 H3 Brudzeń Duży Pol.
189 I2 Brudzeński Park Krajobrazowy Pol.
196 G3 Brudzew Pol.
172 G5 Brue *r. England* U.K.
183 H9 Brue-Auriac France
192 E3 Brüel Ger.
181 P8 Bruère-Allichamps France
187 E7 Brugelette Belgium
Bruges Belgium *see* Brugge
212 E1 Brugg Switz.
187 D6 Brugge Belgium
191 I6 Brüggen *Niedersachsen* Ger.
191 B8 Brüggen *Nordrhein-Westfalen* Ger.
212 H7 Brugnato Italy
213 N4 Brugnera Italy
185 G8 Bruguières France
162 I5 Bruhagen Norway
194 F3 Brühl *Baden-Württemberg* Ger.
191 C9 Brühl *Nordrhein-Westfalen* Ger.
256 B10 Bruin *KY* U.S.A.
256 F7 Bruin *PA* U.S.A.
186 F5 Bruinisse Neth.
265 V2 Bruin Point *mt. UT* U.S.A.
139 P5 Bruint *Arun. Prad.* India
234 C5 Brukkaros Namibia
236 B1 Brukkaros, Mount Namibia
246 G4 Brûlé *Alta* Can.
250 C3 Brule *WI* U.S.A.
249 I2 Brûlé, Lac *l. Que.* Can.
181 K6 Brûlon France
187 G9 Brûly Belgium
281 E4 Brumadinho Brazil
278 E5 Brumado Brazil
179 O6 Brumath France
107 M1 Brumer Islands P.N.G.
186 J4 Brummen Neth.
199 H2 Brumov-Bylnice Czech Rep.
199 G1 Brumovice Czech Rep.
163 K6 Brumunddal Norway
214 F2 Bruna *r.* Italy
169 J5 Brú Na Bóinne *tourist site* Ireland
192 D5 Brunau Ger.
173 O2 Brundall *Norfolk, England* U.K.
173 O3 Brundish *Suffolk, England* U.K.
Brundisium Italy *see* Brindisi
262 G5 Bruneau *ID* U.S.A.
262 G5 Bruneau *r. ID* U.S.A.
262 G5 Bruneau, East Fork *r. ID/NV* U.S.A.
262 G5 Bruneau, West Fork *r. ID/NV* U.S.A.
178 H4 Brunehamel France
117 K2 Brunei *country* Asia
Brunei Brunei *see* Bandar Seri Begawan
117 K2 Brunei Bay Malaysia
205 M8 Brunete Spain
106 E5 Brunette Downs *N.T.* Austr.
249 K4 Brunette Island *Nfld and Lab.* Can.
162 M5 Brunflo Sweden
213 L2 Brunico Italy
185 H7 Bruniquel France
201 L6 Brunn Austria
Brünn Czech Rep. *see* Brno
192 H3 Brunn Ger.
165 N2 Brunna Sweden
201 N3 Brunn am Gebirge Austria
212 F1 Brunnen Switz.
103 F9 Brunner, Lake *South I.* N.Z.
258 C4 Brunnerville *PA* U.S.A.
247 J4 Bruno *Sask.* Can.
250 B3 Bruno *MN* U.S.A.
190 H3 Brunsbüttel Ger.
187 I7 Brunssum Neth.
179 N8 Brunstatt France
Brunswick Ger. *see* Braunschweig
255 G10 Brunswick *GA* U.S.A.
256 H9 Brunswick *MD* U.S.A.
257 □P5 Brunswick *ME* U.S.A.
260 I6 Brunswick *MO* U.S.A.
256 D7 Brunswick *OH* U.S.A.
283 C9 Brunswick, Península de *pen.* Chile
108 H3 Brunswick Bay *W.A.* Austr.
105 N3 Brunswick Heads *N.S.W.* Austr.
109 C12 Brunswick Junction *W.A.* Austr.
248 D3 Brunswick Lake *Ont.* Can.
198 G2 Bruntál Czech Rep.
286 W2 Brunt Ice Shelf Antarctica
237 O5 Bruntville S. Africa
105 K10 Bruny Island *Tas.* Austr.
218 J7 Brus *Brus* Serbia
Brusa Turkey *see* Bursa
200 D7 Brusago Italy
164 B3 Brusand Norway
156 H3 Brusenets Rus. Fed.
192 D3 Brüsewitz Ger.
260 D5 Brush *CO* U.S.A.
257 K4 Brushton *NY* U.S.A.
212 I3 Brusio Switz.
199 I3 Brusno Slovakia
161 S4 Brusovo Rus. Fed.
279 C8 Brusque Brazil
183 B9 Brusque France
Brussel Belgium *see* Bruxelles
Brussels Belgium *see* Bruxelles
251 M6 Brussels *Ont.* Can.
192 J4 Brüssow Ger.
199 L4 Brusturi Romania
219 O3 Brusturi-Drăgănești Romania
196 F2 Brusy Pol.
158 I3 Brusyliv Ukr.
105 K7 Bruthen *Vic.* Austr.
172 H5 Bruton *Somerset, England* U.K.
191 D10 Bruttig-Fankel Ger.
187 F7 Bruxelles Belgium
179 M7 Bruyères France
178 G4 Bruyères-et-Montbérault France
180 H5 Bruz France
274 D2 Bruzual Venez.
217 K7 Bruzzano, Capo *c.* Italy
218 J9 Brvenica *Brvenica* Macedonia
199 H2 Brvnište Slovakia
197 I3 Brwinów Pol.
260 M5 Bryan *OH* U.S.A.
261 G10 Bryan *TX* U.S.A.
104 G5 Bryan, Mount *hill S.A.* Austr.
286 S2 Bryan Coast Antarctica
159 R5 Bryanka Ukr.
161 R8 Bryansk Rus. Fed.
151 I1 Bryanskaya Kosa, Mys *pt* Rus. Fed.
161 Q8 Bryanskaya Oblast' *admin. div.* Rus. Fed.
Bryansk Oblast *admin. div.* Rus. Fed. *see* Bryanskaya Oblast'
151 H1 Bryanskoye Rus. Fed.
261 I8 Bryant *AR* U.S.A.
250 E4 Bryant *WI* U.S.A.
261 I7 Bryant Creek *r. MO* U.S.A.
257 □O4 Bryant Pond *ME* U.S.A.
265 T4 Bryce Canyon National Park *UT* U.S.A.
265 W8 Bryce Mountain *AZ* U.S.A.
172 □ Bryher *i. England* U.K.
159 M7 Brylivka Ukr.
172 F1 Brymbo *Wrexham, Wales* U.K.
161 S8 Bryn' Rus. Fed.
172 E4 Brynamman *Carmarthenshire, Wales* U.K.
Brynbuga *Wales* U.K. *see* Usk
164 B3 Bryne Norway
172 F1 Brynford *Flintshire, Wales* U.K.
197 H5 Brynica *r.* Pol.
157 G7 Bryn'kovskaya Rus. Fed.
172 F4 Brynmawr *Blaenau Gwent, Wales* U.K.
258 E4 Bryn Mawr *PA* U.S.A.
251 Q3 Bryson, Lac *l. Que.* Can.
255 F8 Bryson City *NC* U.S.A.
157 G7 Bryukhovetskaya Rus. Fed.
158 C4 Bryukhovychi Ukr.
218 I5 Brzava *r.* Romania
196 F5 Brzeg Pol.
196 E4 Brzeg Dolny Pol.
196 G3 Brześć Kujawski Pol.
Brześć nad Bugiem Belarus *see* Brest
197 I6 Brzesko Pol.
197 H6 Brzeszcze Pol.
196 G3 Brzezie *Kujawsko-Pomorskie* Pol.
196 E2 Brzezie *Pomorskie* Pol.
197 H4 Brzeziny *Łódzkie* Pol.
197 J6 Brzeziny *Podkarpackie* Pol.
196 G4 Brzeziny *Wielkopolskie* Pol.
197 H6 Brzeźnica *Małopolskie* Pol.
197 J5 Brzeźnica *Podkarpackie* Pol.
196 G4 Brzeźnio Pol.
197 L4 Brzeźno *Lubelskie* Pol.
196 G3 Brzeźno *Wielkopolskie* Pol.
196 D2 Brzeźno *Zachodniopomorskie* Pol.
197 J6 Brzostek Pol.
199 J3 Brzotín Slovakia
197 J4 Brzóza Pol.
197 K6 Brzozów Pol.
197 K2 Brzozówka *r.* Pol.
197 H2 Brzuze Pol.
197 K5 Brzyska Wola Pol.
178 C6 Bû France
146 G7 Bū *well* Yemen
231 B6 Bua Angola
101 □7 Bua *Vanua Levu* Fiji
164 I4 Bua Sweden
232 D4 Bu'aale Somalia
114 E6 Buad *i.* Phil.
181 J4 Buais France
100 □6 Buala *Sta Isabel* Solomon Is
Buandougou Côte d'Ivoire *see* Bouandougou
115 D2 Buang *i.* Indon.
204 C8 Buarcos Port.
116 D4 Buatan *Sumatera* Indon.
224 D2 Bū Athlah *well* Libya
147 J3 Bu'ayj *well* Saudi Arabia
224 B2 Bu'ayrāt al Hasūn Libya
228 B4 Buba Guinea-Bissau
208 E2 Búbal, Embalse de *resr* Spain
233 A5 Bubanza Burundi
195 K2 Bubenreuth Ger.
235 F4 Bubi *r.* Zimbabwe
149 N9 Būbiyān, Jazīrat *i.* Kuwait
180 E6 Bubry France
114 C8 Bubuan *i.* Phil.
114 C9 Bubuan *i.* Phil.
171 P6 Bubwith *East Riding of Yorkshire, England* U.K.
101 □7 Buca *Vanua Levu* Fiji
221 I4 Buca Turkey
221 L5 Bucak Turkey
199 G3 Bučany Slovakia
151 I4 Bucaq Azer.
274 C3 Bucaramanga Col.
269 H4 Bucareli Mex.
114 E7 Bucas Grande *i.* Phil.
108 G4 Buccaneer Archipelago *is W.A.* Austr.
216 H9 Buccheri *Sicilia* Italy
215 M3 Bucchianico Italy
213 K7 Bucciana, Monte *mt.* Italy
212 G5 Buccinasco Italy
215 O6 Buccino Italy
219 O3 Bucecea Romania
219 N5 Bucegi, Munții *mts* Romania
206 A3 Bucelas Port.
182 H2 Bucey-lès-Gy France
195 I5 Buch Ger.
158 E4 Buchach Ukr.
195 M5 Buch am Erlbach Ger.
105 L7 Buchan *Vic.* Austr.
106 F5 Buchanan *watercourse N.T.* Austr.
228 C5 Buchanan Liberia
255 E9 Buchanan *GA* U.S.A.
250 H8 Buchanan *MI* U.S.A.
259 H2 Buchanan *NY* U.S.A.
256 F11 Buchanan *VA* U.S.A.
107 J6 Buchanan, Lake *salt flat Qld* Austr.
109 G8 Buchanan, Lake *salt flat W.A.* Austr.
261 F10 Buchanan, Lake *TX* U.S.A.
243 K2 Buchan Gulf *Nunavut* Can.
249 J3 Buchans *Nfld and Lab.* Can.
Bucharest Romania *see* București
195 M5 Buchbach Ger.
200 A5 Buchboden Austria
191 D10 Büchel Ger.
190 K4 Büchen Ger.
194 G2 Buchen (Odenwald) Ger.
194 E6 Buchenbach Ger.
195 K3 Büchenbach Ger.
195 I6 Buchenberg Ger.
194 C2 Büchenbeuren Ger.
192 F4 Buchholz Ger.
190 I5 Buchholz (Aller) Ger.
191 D9 Buchholz (Westerwald) Ger.
201 J3 Buchkirchen Austria
195 P4 Büchlberg Ger.
195 J5 Buchloe Ger.
198 G2 Buchlovice Czech Rep.
168 H10 Buchlyvie *Stirling, Scotland* U.K.
190 I4 Bucholz in der Nordheide Ger.
264 L6 Buchon, Point *CA* U.S.A.
212 G1 Buchs Switz.
284 A5 Buchupureo Chile
178 B4 Buchy France
219 N4 Bucin, Pasul *pass* Romania
213 L9 Bucine Italy
258 C5 Buck *PA* U.S.A.
261 E10 Buckburn Draw *watercourse TX* U.S.A.
173 L3 Buckden *Cambridgeshire, England* U.K.
171 M5 Buckden *North Yorkshire, England* U.K.
191 H6 Bückeburg Ger.
190 H5 Bücken Ger.
265 T8 Buckeye *AZ* U.S.A.
172 E7 Buckfastleigh *Devon, England* U.K.
256 E10 Buckhannon *WV* U.S.A.
256 F9 Buckhannon *r. WV* U.S.A.
168 J10 Buckhaven *Fife, Scotland* U.K.
251 P5 Buckhorn *Ont.* Can.
251 P5 Buckhorn Lake *Ont.* Can.
168 K7 Buckie *Moray, Scotland* U.K.
251 S4 Buckingham *Que.* Can.
268 C4 Buckingham Mex.
173 K3 Buckingham *Buckinghamshire, England* U.K.
258 E4 Buckingham *PA* U.S.A.
256 G11 Buckingham *VA* U.S.A.
106 E2 Buckingham Bay *N.T.* Austr.
173 K4 Buckinghamshire *admin. div. England* U.K.
244 G2 Buckland *AK* U.S.A.
244 G2 Buckland *r. AK* U.S.A.
236 H5 Bucklands S. Africa
107 L8 Buckland Tableland *reg. Qld* Austr.
104 F5 Buckleboo *S.A.* Austr.
173 J5 Bucklebury *West Berkshire, England* U.K.
287 K2 Buckle Island Antarctica
104 □3 Buckles Bay S. Pacific Ocean
106 F6 Buckley *watercourse Qld* Austr.
172 F1 Buckley *Flintshire, Wales* U.K.
250 F9 Buckley *IL* U.S.A.
287 J2 Buckley Bay Antarctica
201 M4 Bucklige Welt *reg.* Austria
261 F7 Bucklin *KS* U.S.A.
Buckner Bay *Okinawa* Japan *see* Nakagusuku-wan
192 J5 Buckow Märkische Schweiz Ger.
168 L8 Bucksburn *Aberdeen, Scotland* U.K.
258 E4 Bucks County *county PA* U.S.A.
265 S7 Buckskin Mountains *AZ* U.S.A.
264 K2 Bucks Mountain *CA* U.S.A.
257 □Q4 Bucksport *ME* U.S.A.
192 F5 Bückwitz Ger.
198 G2 Bučovice Czech Rep.
231 B6 Buco-Zau Angola
199 K4 Bucsa Hungary
219 N6 Bucșani Romania
219 O6 București Romania
178 G4 Bucy-lès-Pierrepont France
256 C8 Bucyrus *OH* U.S.A.
197 H4 Buczek Pol.
162 I5 Bud Norway
161 R8 Buda Rus. Fed.
208 G6 Buda, Illa de *i.* Spain
193 L6 Budachów Pol.
199 H4 Budai *park* Hungary
161 N9 Buda-Kashalyova Belarus
199 H4 Budakeszi Hungary
118 B3 Budalin Myanmar
199 H4 Budaörs Hungary
199 I4 Budapest Hungary
138 G5 Budaun *Uttar Prad.* India
105 M6 Budawang National Park *N.S.W.* Austr.
146 F4 Budayyi'ah *well* Saudi Arabia
232 E3 Bud Bud Somalia
109 C10 Budd, Mount *hill W.A.* Austr.
105 J4 Budda *N.S.W.* Austr.
287 H2 Budd Coast Antarctica
193 D6 Büddenstedt Ger.
232 D3 Buddi Eth.
258 F3 Budd Lake *NJ* U.S.A.
168 K10 Buddon Ness *pt Scotland* U.K.
214 C6 Buddusò *Sardegna* Italy
172 C6 Bude *Cornwall, England* U.K.
261 J10 Bude *MS* U.S.A.
172 C6 Bude Bay *England* U.K.
187 I6 Budel Neth.
214 C5 Budelli, Isola *i. Sardegna* Italy
190 I2 Büdelsdorf Ger.
158 E5 Budenets' Ukr.
191 F10 Budenheim Ger.
151 F1 Budennovsk Rus. Fed.
Budennoye Rus. Fed. *see* Krasnogvardeyskoye
206 B6 Budens Port.
107 N9 Buderim *Qld* Austr.
219 O6 Budești Romania
145 M9 Budhapur Pak.
145 P7 Budhlada *Punjab* India
205 O7 Budia Spain
199 I3 Budiná Slovakia
144 G8 Būdīng Iran
191 H10 Büdingen Ger.
201 N7 Budinšćina Croatia
199 G2 Budišov nad Budišovkou Czech Rep.
150 B9 Budīyah, Jabal *hills* Egypt
150 B9 Budīyah, Jabal *mt.* Egypt
230 C4 Budjala Dem. Rep. Congo
196 F5 Budkowiczanka *r.* Pol.
172 F6 Budleigh Salterton *Devon, England* U.K.
161 P2 Budogoshch' Rus. Fed.
213 N3 Budoia Italy
128 C9 Budongquan *Qinghai* China
214 D6 Budoni *Sardegna* Italy
213 L6 Budrio Italy
197 J1 Budry Pol.
Bűdszentmihály Hungary *see* Tiszavasvári
147 I4 Budū, Ḩadabat al *plain* Saudi Arabia
147 I4 Budū', Sabkhat al *salt pan* Saudi Arabia
219 K4 Budureasa Romania
199 L4 Buduslău Romania
218 G8 Budva *Budva* Montenegro
197 K1 Būdviečiai Lith.
Budweis Czech Rep. *see* České Budějovice
193 J10 Budyně nad Ohří Czech Rep.
160 M6 Budzilava Belarus
197 H4 Budziszewice Pol.
197 H6 Budzów Pol.
196 E3 Budzyń Pol.
229 H5 Buea Cameroon
183 H8 Buëch *r.* France
264 L7 Buellton *CA* U.S.A.
208 C6 Bueña Spain
258 F5 Buena *NJ* U.S.A.
205 P9 Buenache de Alarcón Spain
205 P8 Buenache de la Sierra Spain
284 E4 Buena Esperanza Arg.
274 B4 Buenaventura Col.
266 F3 Buenaventura Mex.
205 K8 Buenaventura Spain
276 E4 Buena Vista Bol.
207 □ Buena Vista Gibraltar
268 E6 Buenavista *Michoacán* Mex.
269 I2 Buenavista *Tamaulipas* Mex.
Buena Vista *i.* N. Mariana Is *see* Tinian
114 E7 Buenavista *Mindanao* Phil.
114 C5 Buenavista Phil.
263 K7 Buena Vista *CO* U.S.A.
255 E9 Buena Vista *GA* U.S.A.
256 F11 Buena Vista *VA* U.S.A.
270 D2 Buena Vista, Bahía de *b.* Cuba
269 H7 Buenavista de Cuéllar Mex.
238 □3a Buenavista del Norte *Tenerife* Canary Is
205 K3 Buenavista de Valdavia Spain
205 O8 Buendía Spain
205 O8 Buendia, Embalse de *resr* Spain
231 B6 Buenga *r.* Angola
231 B6 Buengas Angola
280 B1 Buenolândia Brazil
281 E2 Buenópolis Brazil
285 H4 Buenos Aires Arg.
285 G5 Buenos Aires *prov.* Arg.
276 B2 Buenos Aires Brazil
274 D5 Buenos Aires *Amazonas* Col.
274 C4 Buenos Aires *Guaviare* Col.
266 □R13 Buenos Aires Costa Rica
283 B7 Buenos Aires, Lago *l.* Arg./Chile
265 U10 Buenos Aires National Wildlife Refuge *nature res. AZ* U.S.A.
271 □7 Buenos Ayres Trin. and Tob.
283 C7 Buen Pasto Arg.
283 C8 Buen Tiempo, Cabo *c.* Arg.
279 F5 Buerarema Brazil
274 B4 Buesaco Col.
182 J4 Buet, Mont *mt.* France
204 C4 Bueu Spain
207 M3 Buey, Cabeza de *mt.* Spain
209 C11 Buey, Sierra del *mts* Spain
266 G4 Búfalo Mex.
246 H2 Buffalo *r. Alta/N.W.T.* Can.
260 I3 Buffalo *MN* U.S.A.
261 I7 Buffalo *MO* U.S.A.
256 G6 Buffalo *NY* U.S.A.
256 D9 Buffalo *OH* U.S.A.
261 F7 Buffalo *OK* U.S.A.
260 D3 Buffalo *SD* U.S.A.
261 G10 Buffalo *TX* U.S.A.
250 C5 Buffalo *WI* U.S.A.
262 K4 Buffalo *WY* U.S.A.
261 I7 Buffalo *r. AR* U.S.A.
255 D8 Buffalo *r. TN* U.S.A.
250 C5 Buffalo *r. WI* U.S.A.
258 A4 Buffalo Creek *r. PA* U.S.A.
246 G3 Buffalo Head Hills *Y.T.* Can.
246 G3 Buffalo Head Prairie *Alta* Can.
262 G4 Buffalo Hump *mt. ID* U.S.A.
246 H2 Buffalo Lake *N.W.T.* Can.
247 I4 Buffalo Narrows *Sask.* Can.
235 F4 Buffalo Range Zimbabwe
264 O1 Buffalo Valley *NV* U.S.A.
270 □ Buff Bay Jamaica
237 O4 Buffels *r. KwaZulu-Natal* S. Africa
236 E9 Buffels *r. Western Cape* S. Africa
236 B5 Buffels *watercourse* S. Africa
236 G9 Buffelsdrif S. Africa
235 E4 Buffels Drift S. Africa
182 F4 Buffières France
191 K8 Bufleben Ger.
255 E8 Buford *GA* U.S.A.
219 N6 Buftea Romania
192 H1 Bug *pen.* Ger.
197 L4 Bug *r.* Pol.
274 B4 Buga Col.
Buga Mongolia *see* Dörvöljin
229 G4 Buga Nigeria
Buga Buga *i.* Vanuatu *see* Toga
199 I5 Bugac Hungary
232 B5 Bugala Island Uganda
105 L4 Bugaldie *N.S.W.* Austr.
129 J2 Bugant Mongolia
185 I10 Bugarach, Pic de *mt.* France
128 D4 Bugat Mongolia
Bugaz Ukr. *see* Zatoka
173 J3 Bugbrooke *Northamptonshire, England* U.K.
232 E3 Bugda Acable Somalia
221 I2 Buğdaylı Turkey
144 F2 Bugdaýly Turkm.
184 H4 Bugeat France
117 I8 Bugel, Tanjung *pt* Indon.
182 H5 Bugey *reg.* France
187 F6 Buggenhout Belgium
214 A9 Buggerru *Sardegna* Italy
194 D6 Buggingen Ger.
217 □ Buġibba Malta
206 □ Bugio *i.* Madeira
151 C7 Buğlan Geçidi *pass* Turkey
215 L3 Bugnara Italy
185 C9 Bugnein France
210 F3 Bugojno Bos.-Herz.
162 T2 Bugøyfjord Norway
156 J1 Bugrino Rus. Fed.
114 A7 Bugsuk *i.* Phil.
129 Q2 Bugt *Nei Mongol* China
114 C2 Buguey *Luzon* Phil.
114 D5 Bugui Point *Masbate* Phil.
157 K5 Bugul'ma Rus. Fed.
Bügür *Xinjiang* China *see* Luntai
142 E1 Buguruslan Rus. Fed.
199 I4 Bugyi Hungary
139 N6 Buha *Arun. Prad.* India
221 J5 Buharkent Turkey
235 F3 Buhera Zimbabwe
128 F8 Buh He *r.* China
114 D5 Buhi *Luzon* Phil.
194 E4 Bühl Ger.
262 G5 Buhl *ID* U.S.A.
250 B2 Buhl *MN* U.S.A.
194 E4 Bühlertal Ger.
194 H3 Bühlertann Ger.
194 H3 Bühlerzell Ger.
191 K7 Bühne Ger.
233 A6 Buhoro Tanz.
233 B7 Buhoro Flats *plain* Tanz.
158 F3 Buhryn Ukr.
149 K5 Bühtan *r.* Turkey
233 B6 Buhu *r.* Tanz.
219 O4 Buhuşi Romania
213 O3 Buia Italy
246 F3 Buick *B.C.* Can.
168 E10 Buie, Loch *b. Scotland* U.K.
172 F3 Builth Wells *Powys, Wales* U.K.
284 B3 Buin Chile
144 D4 Bū'īn Iran
100 □6 Buin P.N.G.
228 E4 Bui National Park Ghana
157 J5 Buinsk Rus. Fed.
144 B4 Bu'in Soflā Iran
144 D4 Bu'in Zahrā Iran
129 O3 Buir Nur *l.* Mongolia
183 G8 Buis-les-Baronnies France
186 J2 Buitenpost Neth.
234 C4 Buitepos Namibia
205 M7 Buitrago del Lozoya Spain
207 P4 Buitre *mt.* Spain
160 I7 Buivydžiai Lith.
207 K5 Bujalance Spain
219 J8 Bujanovac *Bujanovac* Serbia
208 E5 Bujaraloz Spain
213 P5 Buje Croatia
219 N7 Bujoru Romania
233 A5 Bujumbura Burundi
201 O5 Bük Hungary
196 E3 Buk Pol.
121 K1 Bukachacha Rus. Fed.
197 M6 Bukachivtsi Ukr.
133 J8 Buka Daban *mt. Qinghai/Xinjiang* China
113 L8 Buka Island P.N.G.
234 E3 Bukalo Namibia
231 E7 Bukama Dem. Rep. Congo
144 B3 Būkān Iran
161 R8 Bukan' Rus. Fed.
144 E6 Būkand Iran
143 S1 Bukanskoye Rus. Fed.
230 F5 Bukavu Dem. Rep. Congo
231 C6 Bukedi Dem. Rep. Congo
233 B6 Bukene Tanz.
231 E7 Bukeya Dem. Rep. Congo
Bukhara *Buxoro* Uzbek. *see* Buxoro
Bukhara Oblast *admin. div.* Uzbek. *see* Buxoro
160 M6 Bukhava Belarus
Bukhoro Uzbek. *see* Buxoro
Bukhoro Wiloyati *admin. div.* Uzbek. *see* Buxoro
122 B1 Bukhta Rus. Fed.
143 U3 Bukhtarminskoye Vodokhranilishche *resr* Kazakh.
115 D2 Bukide *i.* Indon.
233 B5 Bukima Tanz.
117 J5 Bukit Baka-Bukit Raya, Taman Nasional *nat. park* Indon.
117 J6 Bukitlidi *Kalimantan* Indon.
116 □ Bukit Timah Sing.
116 D5 Bukittinggi *Sumatera* Indon.
199 J3 Bükk *mts* Hungary
199 J4 Bükkábrány Hungary
199 J4 Bükkalja *hills* Hungary
136 E5 Bukkapatnam *Andhra Prad.* India
199 J3 Bükki *nat. park* Hungary
199 G5 Bükkösd Hungary
199 J4 Bükkzsérc Hungary
193 F7 Buko Ger.
233 A5 Bukoba Tanz.
160 H6 Bukonys Lith.
199 H2 Bukovec Czech Rep.
201 J8 Bukovje Slovenia
199 L2 Bukovské vrchy *hills* Slovakia
197 K5 Bukowa *r.* Pol.
196 F3 Bukowe Pol.
196 F4 Bukowice Pol.
196 G2 Bukowiec *Kujawsko-Pomorskie* Pol.
196 D3 Bukowiec *Lubuskie* Pol.
193 L6 Bukowiec *hill* Pol.
196 F1 Bukowina Pol.
197 I6 Bukowina Tatrzańska Pol.
196 G4 Bukownica Pol.
197 H5 Bukowno Pol.
196 F2 Bukowo Pol.
165 M7 Bukowo, Jezioro *lag.* Pol.
197 K6 Bukowsko Pol.
Bükreş Romania *see* București
116 F5 Buku, Tanjung *pt* Indon.
129 L2 Bukukun Rus. Fed.
116 □ Bukum, Pulau *i.* Sing.
158 J4 Buky Ukr.
144 E6 Būl, Kūh-e *mt.* Iran
228 B3 Bula Guinea-Bissau
115 G5 Bula *Seram* Indon.
231 B7 Bula Atumba Angola
212 F1 Bülach Switz.
Bulag Mongolia *see* Möngönmorīt
Bulagtay Mongolia *see* Hüder
105 N5 Bulahdelah *N.S.W.* Austr.
114 C6 Bulalacao *i.* Phil.
116 E4 Bulan *i.* Indon.
114 D5 Bulan *Luzon* Phil.
114 C8 Bulan *i.* Phil.
148 I3 Bulancak Turkey
138 F5 Bulandshahr *Uttar Pra*
149 K4 Bulanık Turkey
142 F1 Bulanovo Rus. Fed.
225 F3 Būlāq Egypt
122 L3 Bulava Rus. Fed.
115 C3 Bulawa, Gunung *mt.* In
235 F4 Bulawayo Zimbabwe
143 N1 Bulayevo Kazakh.
148 H5 Bulbul Syria
230 E2 Bulbul, Wadi *watercour*
233 C5 Bulbula *waterhole* Keny
221 J4 Buldan Turkey
138 F9 Buldhana *Mahar.* India
276 A2 Buldibuyo Peru
245 □A5 Buldir Island *AK* U.S.A.
138 F4 Buldur *Hima. Prad.* Inc
142 E2 Buldurta Kazakh.
Buldyrty Kazakh. *see* Bu
145 J8 Buleda *reg.* Pak.
232 E3 Bulei *well* Eth.
237 P1 Bulembu Swaziland
228 E4 Bulenga Ghana
173 I5 Bulford *Wiltshire, Engla*
128 B3 Bulgan *Bayan-Ölgiy* Mc
128 H2 Bulgan *Bulgan* Mongol
129 M2 Bulgan Mongolia
128 B3 Bulgan Mongolia
128 H4 Bulgan *Ömnögovĭ* Mon
Bulgan Mongolia *see* D
Bulgan Mongolia *see* Tsagaan-Üür
128 H2 Bulgan *prov.* Mongolia
128 B3 Bulgan Gol *r.* Mongolia
Bulgar Rus. Fed. *see* Bo
219 Q7 Bŭlgarevo Bulg.
219 N8 Bulgaria *country* Europe
Bŭlgariya *country* Europ Bulgaria
146 E3 Bulghah Saudi Arabia
215 O7 Bulgheria, Monte *mt.* I
179 K7 Bulgnéville France
151 D5 Bulgurlu Turkey
159 M9 Bulhanak *r.* Ukr.
115 F3 Buli *Halmahera* Indon.
115 F3 Buli, Teluk *b. Halmaher*
114 A7 Buliluyan, Cape *Palawa*
232 A4 Bulisa Uganda
190 G3 Bülkau Ger.
173 J3 Bulkington *Warwickshir England* U.K.
245 O5 Bulkley Ranges *mts B.C*
197 I3 Bulkowo Pol.
Bulla, Ostrov *is* Azer. *se* Xärä Zirä Adası
207 K3 Bullaque *r.* Spain
207 P4 Bullas Spain
107 I9 Bullawarra, Lake *salt fla Qld* Austr.
232 E2 Bullaxaar Somalia
191 D10 Bullay Ger.
270 □ Bull Bay Jamaica
212 C2 Bulle Switz.
105 H4 Bullea, Lake *salt flat N.*
245 K1 Bullen *AK* U.S.A.
271 □10 Bullenbaai *b. Curaçao* Neth. Antilles
103 F8 Buller *r. South I.* N.Z.
107 I4 Bulleringa National Pa *Qld* Austr.
109 E11 Bullfinch *W.A.* Austr.
265 R6 Bullhead City *AZ* U.S.A.
105 M6 Bulli *N.S.W.* Austr.
187 J8 Büllingen Belgium
265 P7 Bullion Mountains *CA*
162 P4 Bullmark Sweden
106 B3 Bullo *r. N.T.* Austr.
205 P7 Bullones *r.* Spain
105 I3 Bulloo *watercourse Qld*
105 I3 Bulloo Downs *Qld* Aust
105 I3 Bulloo Lake *salt flat Qld*
169 J2 Bull Point *Northern Irel*
102 J7 Bulls *North I.* N.Z.
270 □ Bull Savannah Jamaica
259 I1 Bulls Bridge *CT* U.S.A.
261 I7 Bull Shoals Lake *AR* U.
234 C5 Büllsport Namibia
259 G1 Bullville *NY* U.S.A.
178 E3 Bully-les-Mines France
106 E2 Bulman *N.T.* Austr.
106 E2 Bulman Gorge *N.T.* Aus
246 F2 Bulmer Lake *N.W.T.* Ca
173 N3 Bulmer Tye *Essex, Engla*
284 A5 Bulnes Chile
116 □ Buloh, Pulau *i.* Sing.
105 I7 Buloke, Lake *dry lake Vi*
113 K8 Bulolo P.N.G.
218 I9 Bulqizë Albania
214 C7 Bultei *Sardegna* Italy
237 K4 Bultfontein S. Africa
117 L3 Bulu, Gunung *mt.* Indo
114 E8 Buluan *Mindanao* Phil.
115 B6 Bulubulu *Sulawesi* Indo
232 C3 Buluk *well* Kenya
115 B6 Bulukumba *Sulawesi* In
230 D5 Bulukutu Dem. Rep. Co
153 N2 Bulun Rus. Fed.
145 P2 Bulungkol *Xinjiang* Chi
231 C6 Bulungu *Bandundu* Dem. Rep. Congo
231 D6 Bulungu *Kasaï-Occident* Dem. Rep. Congo
151 E2 Bulungu Rus. Fed.
143 L8 Bulung'ur Uzbek.
114 E5 Bulusan *Luzon* Phil.
236 C1 Bulwana Namibia
237 N5 Bulwer S. Africa
199 L5 Bulz Romania
214 B6 Bulzi *Sardegna* Italy
100 □6 Buma *Malaita* Solomon
231 C6 Bumba *Bandundu* Dem. Rep. Congo
230 D4 Bumba *Équateur* Dem. Rep. Congo
224 D1 Būmbah Libya
224 D1 Būmbah, Khalīj *b.* Libya
128 I6 Bumbat *Nei Mongol* Chi
Bumbat Mongolia *see* Bayan-Öndör
219 L5 Bumbești-Jiu Romania
228 C4 Bumbuna Sierra Leone
118 C1 Bumhkang Myanmar
118 C1 Bumpha Bum *mt.* Myar
231 C5 Buna Dem. Rep. Congo
232 C4 Buna Kenya
Bunacurry Ireland *see* Bun an Churraigh
169 C5 Bun an Churraigh Irelar
147 J4 Bunayyān *well* Saudi Ara
233 A5 Bunazi Tanz.
Bunbeg Ireland *see* An Bun Beag
109 C12 Bunbury *W.A.* Austr.
171 L7 Bunbury *Cheshire, Engla*
169 I7 Bunclody Ireland
169 H2 Buncrana Ireland
233 B5 Bunda Tanz.
107 N8 Bundaberg *Qld* Austr.
105 K3 Bundaleer *Qld* Austr.
105 M4 Bundarra *N.S.W.* Austr.
190 D4 Bunde Ger.
191 G6 Bünde Ger.
194 C2 Bundenbach Ger.
190 D4 Bunderhee Ger.
106 E6 Bundey *watercourse N.T.*
138 E7 Bundi *Rajasthan* India
232 A4 Bundibugyo Uganda
105 N3 Bundjalung National Pa *N.S.W.* Austr.
169 F4 Bundoran Ireland
139 J8 Bundu *Jharkhand* India
232 A3 Bunduqiya Sudan
218 H9 Bunë *r.* Albania/Montene
144 C6 Būneh *i.* Iran
147 I1 Būneh Dara *b.* Iran
145 O4 Buner *reg.* Pak.
229 H3 Bunga *r.* Nigeria
126 C5 Bunga-dake *mt.* Japan
116 C6 Bungalaut, Selat *sea cha*
173 O3 Bungay *Suffolk, England*
105 L6 Bungendore *N.S.W.* Aust
287 G2 Bunger Hills Antarctica
115 C6 Bungi *Sulawesi* Indon.
107 L9 Bungil Creek *r. Qld* Aust

Bungku Sulawesi Indon.
Bungle Bungle National Park W.A. Austr. see **Purnululu National Park**
Bungo Angola
Bungoma Kenya
Bungona'og Xizang China
Bungo-suidō sea chan. Japan
Bungo-Takada Japan
Bunguran, Kepulauan is Indon. see **Natuna, Kepulauan**
Bunguran, Pulau i. Indon. see **Natuna Besar**
Buni, Ci r. Indon.
Bunia Dem. Rep. Congo
Buniel Spain
Bunila Romania
Buningonia well W.A. Austr.
Buni-Yadi Nigeria
Bunji Pak.
Bunker MO U.S.A.
Bunker Group atolls Qld Austr.
Bunker Hill AK U.S.A.
Bunkeya Dem. Rep. Congo
Bunkie LA U.S.A.
Bunkris Sweden
Bunmahon Ireland
Bun na hAbhna Ireland
Bunnahowen Ireland see **Bun na hAbhna**
Bunnanaddan Ireland
Bunnell FL U.S.A.
Bunnik Neth.
Bunnyconnellan Ireland
Bunnythorpe North I. N.Z.
Buñol Spain
Bunschoten-Spakenburg Neth.
Bünsum Xizang China
Bunsuru watercourse Nigeria
Buntești Romania
Buntine W.A. Austr.
Buntingford Hertfordshire, England U.K.
Buntok Kalimantan Indon.
Buntokecil Kalimantan Indon.
Buñuel Spain
Bununu Nigeria
Bunya Mountains National Park Qld Austr.
Bünyan Turkey
Bunyola Spain
Bunyu i. Indon.
Bunza Nigeria
Buoač Bos.-Herz.
Buoddobohki Fin. see **Patoniva**
Buonabitacolo Italy
Buonalbergo Italy
Buonconvento Italy
Buôn Hô Vietnam
Buôn Ma Thuôt Vietnam
Buonvicino Italy
Buorkhaya, Guba b. Rus. Fed.
Bup r. China
Buqay'ā Saudi Arabia
Buqayq Saudi Arabia see **Abqaiq**
Buqbuq Egypt
Buqtyrma Bögeni resr Kazakh. see **Bukhtarminskoye Vodokhranilishche**
Bura Kenya
Buraan Somalia
Burabay Kazakh.
Burak Iran
Burakin W.A. Austr.
Buram Sudan
Buran Kazakh.
Buran Darat rf Sing.
Burang Xizang China
Buranhaém Brazil
Buranhaém r. Brazil
Burannoye Rus. Fed.
Burano r. Italy
Burāq Syria
Burauen Leyte Phil.
Burawai Pak.
Buray r. India
Buraydah Saudi Arabia
Burayevo Rus. Fed.
Burbach Ger.
Burbage Wiltshire, England U.K.
Burbáguena Spain
Burbank CA U.S.A.
Burcei Sardegna Italy
Burchak Ukr.
Burchell Lake Ont. Can.
Burcher N.S.W. Austr.
Burco Somalia
Bürd Mongolia
Burdaard Neth.
Burdalyk Turkm.
Burdekin r. Qld Austr.
Burdekin Falls Qld Austr.
Burdet, Mont mt. France
Burdigala France see **Bordeaux**
Burdinne Belgium
Burdur Turkey
Burdur prov. Turkey
Burdur Gölü l. Turkey
Burdwan W. Bengal India see **Barddhaman**
Burē Āmara Eth.
Burē Oromīya Eth.
Bure r. England U.K.
Bure, Pic de mt. France
Bureå Sweden
Bureinskiy Khrebet mts Rus. Fed.
Bureinskiy Zapovednik nature res. Rus. Fed.
Bureiqa well Sudan
Burejo r. Spain
Burela, Cabo c. Spain
Büren Ger.
Büren Mongolia
Buren Neth.
Büren an der Aare Switz.
Bürenhayrhan Mongolia see **Bulgan**
Bürentsogt Mongolia
Bureo r. Chile
Bures Suffolk, England U.K.
Burewala Pak.
Bureya r. Rus. Fed.
Bureya-Pristan' Rus. Fed. see **Novobureyskiy**
Bureya Range mts Rus. Fed. see **Bureinskiy Khrebet**
Burford Ont. Can.
Burford Oxfordshire, England U.K.
Būr Fu'ād Egypt
Burg France
Burg Ger.
Burg (Dithmarschen) Ger.
Burgaltay Mongolia see **Baruunbüren**
Burganes de Valverde Spain
Burgas Bulg.
Burgau Austria
Burgau Ger.
Burgau Port.
Burg auf Fehmarn Ger.
Burgaw NC U.S.A.
Burg bei Magdeburg Ger.
Burgberg im Allgäu Ger.
Burgbernheim Ger.
Burgbrohl Ger.
Burgdorf Niedersachsen Ger.
Burgdorf Niedersachsen Ger.
Burgdorf Switz.
Burgebrach Ger.
Bürgel Ger.
Burgenland land Austria
Burgeo Nfld and Lab. Can.
Burgersdorp S. Africa
Burgersfort S. Africa
Burgerville S. Africa
Burges, Mount hill W.A. Austr.
Burgess VA U.S.A.
Burgess, Mount Y.T. Can.
Burgess Hill West Sussex, England U.K.
Burget Tuyur waterhole Sudan
Burghaslach Ger.
Burghaun Ger.
Burghausen Ger.
171 K4 **Burgh by Sands** Cumbria, England U.K.
173 J5 **Burghclere** Hampshire, England U.K.
168 J7 **Burghead** Moray, Scotland U.K.
168 I7 **Burghead Bay** Scotland U.K.
195 K4 **Burgheim** Ger.
173 J5 **Burghfield Common** West Berkshire, England U.K.
186 E5 **Burgh-Haamstede** Neth.
172 G3 **Burghill** Herefordshire, England U.K.
171 R7 **Burgh le Marsh** Lincolnshire, England U.K.
216 E8 **Burgio** Sicilia Italy
216 H9 **Burgio, Serra di** hill Sicilia Italy
200 H3 **Burgkirchen** Austria
195 N5 **Burgkirchen an der Alz** Ger.
193 D10 **Burgkunstadt** Ger.
212 G1 **Bürglen** Thurgau Switz.
212 F2 **Bürglen** Uri Switz.
195 M3 **Burglengenfeld** Ger.
195 J3 **Burgoberbach** Ger.
205 K8 **Burgohondo** Spain
205 M6 **Burgomillodo, Embalse de** resr Spain
214 B7 **Burgos** Sardegna Italy
267 J5 **Burgos** Mex.
205 M4 **Burgos** Spain
205 M4 **Burgos** prov. Spain
191 K10 **Burgpreppach** Ger.
194 H5 **Burgrieden** Ger.
195 K3 **Burgsalach** Ger.
191 I10 **Burgsinn** Ger.
194 G2 **Bürgstadt** Ger.
193 G9 **Burgstädt** Ger.
192 H4 **Burg Stargand** Ger.
165 O4 **Burgsvik** Gotland Sweden
195 K3 **Burgthann** Ger.
191 K8 **Burgtonna** Ger.
208 C2 **Burgui** Spain
205 K8 **Burguillo, Embalse de** resr Spain
206 H5 **Burguillos** Spain
206 F4 **Burguillos del Cerro** Spain
186 J2 **Burgum** Neth.
191 G9 **Burgwald** for. Ger.
195 J2 **Burgwindheim** Ger.
139 K9 **Burhabalanga** r. India
128 D9 **Burhan Budai Shan** mts China
221 H3 **Burhaniye** Turkey
138 F9 **Burhanpur** Madh. Prad. India
139 M8 **Burhanuddin** Bangl.
138 H8 **Burhar-Dhanpuri** Madh. Prad. India
190 F3 **Burhave (Butjadingen)** Ger.
139 K7 **Burhi Gandak** r. India
180 G2 **Burhou** i. Channel Is
280 C5 **Buri** Brazil
116 D6 **Buriai** Indon.
114 D5 **Burias** i. Phil.
212 C6 **Buriasco** Italy
Buriat-Mongol Republic aut. rep. Rus. Fed. see **Buryatiya, Respublika**
142 H2 **Buribay** Rus. Fed.
266 □R13 **Burica, Punta** pt Costa Rica
184 D4 **Burie** France
139 I6 **Buri Gandak** r. Nepal
249 K4 **Burin** Nfld and Lab. Can.
249 K4 **Burin Peninsula** Nfld and Lab. Can.
118 F7 **Buriram** Thai.
280 B4 **Buritama** Brazil
278 E2 **Buriti** Brazil
277 F3 **Buriti** r. Brazil
280 C3 **Buriti Alegre** Brazil
278 E3 **Buriti Bravo** Brazil
278 E2 **Buriti dos Lopes** Brazil
278 E4 **Buritirama** Brazil
279 D5 **Buritis** Brazil
281 E2 **Buritizeiro** Brazil
209 E8 **Burjassot** Spain
132 I5 **Burjay** Xinjiang China
145 L6 **Burj Aziz Khan** Pak.
199 L6 **Burjuc** Romania
195 I3 **Burk** Ger.
143 Q7 **Burkan-Suu** r. Kyrg.
191 I10 **Burkardroth** Ger.
261 F8 **Burkburnett** TX U.S.A.
106 G7 **Burke** watercourse Qld Austr.
260 F4 **Burke** SD U.S.A.
246 E5 **Burke Channel** B.C. Can.
286 Q2 **Burke Island** Antarctica
103 E11 **Burkes Pass** South I. N.Z.
254 E7 **Burkesville** KY U.S.A.
106 G4 **Burketown** Qld Austr.
256 G11 **Burkeville** VA U.S.A.
153 P3 **Burkhala** Rus. Fed.
228 E4 **Burkina** country Africa
Burkina Faso country Africa see **Burkina**
143 Q3 **Burkitty** Kazakh.
248 E4 **Burk's Falls** Ont. Can.
143 R1 **Burla** Rus. Fed.
143 R1 **Burla** r. Rus. Fed.
205 Q3 **Burlada** Spain
194 G5 **Burladingen** Ger.
185 I8 **Burlats** France
107 I6 **Burleigh** Qld Austr.
258 F6 **Burleigh** NJ U.S.A.
173 I6 **Burley** Hampshire, England U.K.
262 H5 **Burley** ID U.S.A.
172 G3 **Burley Gate** Herefordshire, England U.K.
171 N6 **Burley in Wharfedale** West Yorkshire, England U.K.
142 I1 **Burli** Kazakh.
264 J4 **Burlingame** CA U.S.A.
248 E5 **Burlington** Ont. Can.
260 D6 **Burlington** CO U.S.A.
259 J1 **Burlington** CT U.S.A.
254 B5 **Burlington** IA U.S.A.
250 H9 **Burlington** IN U.S.A.
260 H6 **Burlington** KS U.S.A.
260 M6 **Burlington** KY U.S.A.
255 H7 **Burlington** NC U.S.A.
258 F4 **Burlington** NJ U.S.A.
257 L4 **Burlington** VT U.S.A.
262 C2 **Burlington** WA U.S.A.
250 F7 **Burlington** WI U.S.A.
258 F5 **Burlington County** county NJ U.S.A.
142 G1 **Burly** Rus. Fed.
Burma country Asia see **Myanmar**
156 J4 **Burmakino** Kirovskaya Oblast' Rus. Fed.
161 X4 **Burmakino** Yaroslavskaya Oblast' Rus. Fed.
156 M3 **Burmantovo** Rus. Fed.
161 X8 **Burminka** Rus. Fed.
200 G4 **Bürmoos** Austria
246 F5 **Burnaby** B.C. Can.
170 C8 **Burnchurch** Ireland
168 K4 **Burness** Orkney, Scotland U.K.
261 F10 **Burnet** TX U.S.A.
107 N8 **Burnett** r. Qld Austr.
107 N8 **Burnett Heads** Qld Austr.
262 D6 **Burney** CA U.S.A.
283 B9 **Burney, Monte** vol. Chile
169 I3 **Burnfoot** Northern Ireland U.K.
169 E8 **Burnfort** Ireland
103 G10 **Burnham** South I. N.Z.
173 K4 **Burnham** Buckinghamshire, England U.K.
257 □P4 **Burnham** ME U.S.A.
256 H8 **Burnham** PA U.S.A.
173 N2 **Burnham Market** Norfolk, England U.K.
173 N4 **Burnham-on-Crouch** Essex, England U.K.
172 G5 **Burnham-on-Sea** Somerset, England U.K.
170 H2 **Burnhouse** North Ayrshire, Scotland U.K.
105 J9 **Burnie** Tas. Austr.
256 B11 **Burning Springs** KY U.S.A.
171 Q5 **Burniston** North Yorkshire, England U.K.
171 M6 **Burnley** Lancashire, England U.K.
168 L11 **Burnmouth** Scottish Borders, Scotland U.K.
171 N4 **Burnopfield** Durham, England U.K.
Burnoye Kazakh. see **Bauyrzhan Momyshuly**
262 E5 **Burns** OR U.S.A.
242 H3 **Burnside** r. Nunavut Can.
109 G8 **Burnside, Lake** salt flat W.A. Austr.
262 F5 **Burns Junction** OR U.S.A.
246 E4 **Burns Lake** B.C. Can.
250 A5 **Burnsville** MN U.S.A.
256 E10 **Burnsville** WV U.S.A.
256 E10 **Burnsville Lake** WV U.S.A.
262 F4 **Burnt** r. OR U.S.A.
168 J10 **Burntisland** Fife, Scotland U.K.
Burnt Lake Que. Can. see **Brûlé, Lac**
104 □[1] **Burnt Pine** Norfolk I.
247 L4 **Burntwood** r. Man. Can.
173 I2 **Burntwood Green** Staffordshire, England U.K.
247 K4 **Burntwood Lake** Man. Can.
133 G9 **Burog Co** l. Xizang China
249 G1 **Buron** r. Que. Can.
151 F3 **Buron** Rus. Fed.
205 J2 **Burón** Spain
212 E5 **Buronzo** Italy
185 D9 **Buros** France
192 H3 **Burow** Ger.
132 H3 **Burqin** Xinjiang China
132 H3 **Burqin He** r. China
150 G6 **Burqu'** Jordan
104 G5 **Burra** S.A. Austr.
168 □N2 **Burra** i. Scotland U.K.
168 □N1 **Burravoe** Shetland, Scotland U.K.
168 K5 **Burray** i. Scotland U.K.
218 I9 **Burrel** Albania
264 M5 **Burrel** CA U.S.A.
168 J9 **Burrelton** Perth and Kinross, Scotland U.K.
169 D6 **Burren** Ireland
169 D5 **Burren** Ireland
169 D6 **Burren** reg. Ireland
170 E5 **Burren** Northern Ireland U.K.
105 L5 **Burrendong, Lake** resr N.S.W. Austr.
105 L4 **Burren Junction** N.S.W. Austr.
105 M6 **Burrewarra Point** N.S.W. Austr.
209 E8 **Burriana** Spain
105 L6 **Burrinjuck Reservoir** N.S.W. Austr.
267 H3 **Burro, Serranías del** mts Mex.
250 C6 **Burr Oak** IA U.S.A.
256 C9 **Burr Oak Reservoir** OH U.S.A.
265 S7 **Burro Creek** watercourse AZ U.S.A.
170 I4 **Burrow Head** Scotland U.K.
106 C2 **Burrundie** N.T. Austr.
282 D2 **Burruyacú** Arg.
172 D4 **Burry Inlet** Wales U.K.
172 D4 **Burry Port** Carmarthenshire, Wales U.K.
200 A5 **Bürs** Austria
221 K2 **Bursa** Turkey
221 J2 **Bursa** prov. Turkey
225 G3 **Būr Safājah** Egypt
225 G2 **Būr Sa'īd** Egypt
148 F8 **Būr Sa'īd** governorate Egypt
171 L6 **Burscough** Lancashire, England U.K.
171 L6 **Burscough Bridge** Lancashire, England U.K.
191 I7 **Bursfelde** Ger.
158 D4 **Burshtyn** Ukr.
122 G3 **Bursinskoye Vodokhranilishche** resr Rus. Fed.
194 E2 **Bürstadt** Ger.
173 L5 **Burstow** Surrey, England U.K.
Būr Sudan Sudan see **Port Sudan**
104 H5 **Burta** N.S.W. Austr.
150 A9 **Būr Tawfiq** Egypt
195 I5 **Burtenbach** Ger.
250 J4 **Burt Lake** MI U.S.A.
160 I4 **Burtnieku ezers** l. Latvia
173 I6 **Burton** Dorset, England U.K.
251 K7 **Burton** MI U.S.A.
248 E2 **Burton, Lac** l. Que. Can.
172 G6 **Burton Bradstock** Dorset, England U.K.
171 L5 **Burton-in-Kendal** Cumbria, England U.K.
173 K3 **Burton Latimer** Northamptonshire, England U.K.
171 O5 **Burton Leonard** North Yorkshire, England U.K.
Burtonport Ireland see **Ailt an Chorráin**
258 B6 **Burtonsville** MD U.S.A.
171 P6 **Burton upon Stather** North Lincolnshire, England U.K.
173 I2 **Burton upon Trent** Staffordshire, England U.K.
162 P4 **Burträsk** Sweden
257 □S2 **Burtts Corner** N.B. Can.
105 I5 **Burtundy** N.S.W. Austr.
106 D7 **Burt Well** N.T. Austr.
115 E5 **Buru** i. Maluku Indon.
143 O5 **Burubaytal** Kazakh.
205 L9 **Burujón** Spain
150 B8 **Burūk, Wādī al** watercourse Egypt
159 N8 **Burul'cha** r. Ukr.
148 E8 **Burullus, Buḩayrat al** lag. Egypt
Burullus, Lake lag. Egypt see **Burullus, Buḩayrat al**
Burultokay Xinjiang China see **Fuhai**
147 I8 **Burūm** Yemen
150 B7 **Burūn, Ra's** pt Egypt
233 A5 **Burundi** country Africa
Burunniy Rus. Fed. see **Tsagan Aman**
233 A5 **Bururi** Burundi
229 G5 **Burutu** Nigeria
172 G3 **Burwarton** Shropshire, England U.K.
173 M6 **Burwash** East Sussex, England U.K.
245 M3 **Burwash Landing** Y.T. Can.
173 M3 **Burwell** Cambridgeshire, England U.K.
260 F5 **Burwell** NE U.S.A.
168 K5 **Burwick** Orkney, Scotland U.K.
171 M6 **Bury** Greater Manchester, England U.K.
Buryatia aut. rep. Rus. Fed. see **Buryatiya, Respublika**
128 H1 **Buryatiya, Respublika** aut. rep. Rus. Fed.
Buryatskaya Mongolskaya A.S.S.R. aut. rep. Rus. Fed. see **Buryatiya, Respublika**
Būrylbaytal Kazakh. see **Burubaytal**
159 M2 **Buryn'** Ukr.
173 N3 **Bury St Edmunds** Suffolk, England U.K.
285 H4 **Burzaco** Arg.
196 G4 **Burzenin** Pol.
183 E7 **Burzet** France
138 E2 **Burzil Pass** Pak.
214 B7 **Busachi** Sardegna Italy
212 F6 **Busalla** Italy
Busan Pusan-si S. Korea see **Pusan**
146 F8 **Būs'ān** Yemen
212 I7 **Busana** Italy
114 D8 **Busan Bay** Mindanao Phil.
230 D5 **Busanga** Dem. Rep. Congo
262 K4 **Busby** MT U.S.A.
212 C6 **Busca** Italy
201 N2 **Buschberg** hill Austria
192 G5 **Buschow** Ger.
190 I2 **Busdorf** Ger.
Buseire Syria see **Al Buşayrah**
216 D7 **Buseto Palizzolo** Sicilia Italy
170 D3 **Bush** r. Northern Ireland U.K.
158 H5 **Busha** Ukr.
158 F3 **Bushcha** Ukr.
144 D7 **Būshehr** Iran
144 D7 **Būshehr** prov. Iran
232 A5 **Bushenyi** Uganda
173 L4 **Bushey** Hertfordshire, England U.K.
Bushire Iran see **Būshehr**
258 E2 **Bushkill** PA U.S.A.
258 F2 **Bush Kill** r. PA U.S.A.
169 I2 **Bushmills** Northern Ireland U.K.
255 F11 **Bushnell** FL U.S.A.
250 D9 **Bushnell** IL U.S.A.
218 I9 **Bushtricë** Albania
232 B4 **Busia** Kenya
178 F3 **Busigny** France
199 I3 **Bušince** Slovakia
116 □ **Busing, Pulau** i. Sing.
230 D4 **Businga** Dem. Rep. Congo
230 C5 **Busira** r. Dem. Rep. Congo
164 J1 **Busjön** l. Sweden
158 D4 **Bus'k** Ukr.
164 E1 **Buskerud** county Norway
197 I5 **Busko-Zdrój** Pol.
Buskul' Kazakh. see **Boskol'**
196 E2 **Buślary** Pol.
115 F2 **Busobuso** Maluku Indon.
150 E6 **Buşrá ash Shām** Syria
179 M8 **Bussang** France
122 E3 **Busse** Rus. Fed.
109 C12 **Busselton** W.A. Austr.
215 P7 **Bussento** r. Italy
230 F3 **Busseri** watercourse Sudan
212 I5 **Busseto** Italy
184 F4 **Bussière-Badil** France
184 H3 **Bussière-Dunoise** France
184 G4 **Bussière-Galant** France
184 F3 **Bussière-Poitevine** France
212 B2 **Bussigny** Switz.
215 L3 **Bussi sul Tirino** Italy
193 D9 **Büßleben** Ger.
213 J5 **Bussolengo** Italy
212 C5 **Bussoleno** Italy
186 H4 **Bussum** Neth.
178 G7 **Bussy-en-Othe** France
182 F1 **Bussy-le-Grand** France
267 I4 **Bustamante** Nuevo León Mex.
269 H2 **Bustamante** Tamaulipas Mex.
Bustandyk Kazakh. see **Bostandyk**
99 F4 **Bustard Head** Qld Austr.
219 N5 **Buşteni** Romania
266 F3 **Bustillos, Lago** l. Mex.
285 G3 **Bustinza** Arg.
204 H1 **Busto, Cabo** c. Spain
212 F4 **Busto Arsizio** Italy
205 O2 **Busturi-Axpe** Spain
114 B5 **Busuanga** Phil.
114 B5 **Busuanga** i. Phil.
230 D4 **Busu-Djanoa** Dem. Rep. Congo
190 G2 **Büsum** Ger.
230 C4 **Busu Modanda** Dem. Rep. Congo
213 O3 **But** r. Italy
230 E4 **Buta** Dem. Rep. Congo
232 C2 **Butajīra** Eth.
145 J7 **Butak** Pak.
219 L7 **Butan** Bulg.
284 C5 **Buta Ranquil** Arg.
233 A5 **Butare** Rwanda
290 G6 **Butaritari** atoll Kiribati
114 D4 **Butauanan** pt Luzon Phil.
168 F11 **Bute** i. Scotland U.K.
168 F11 **Bute, Sound of** sea chan. Scotland U.K.
219 O3 **Butea** Romania
246 D4 **Butedale** B.C. Can.
246 E5 **Bute Inlet** B.C. Can.
230 F4 **Butembo** Dem. Rep. Congo
199 L5 **Buteni** Romania
216 G9 **Butera** Sicilia Italy
187 J8 **Bütgenbach** Belgium
237 M4 **Butha-Buthe** Lesotho
Butha Qi Nei Mongol China see **Zalantun**
118 A4 **Buthidaung** Myanmar
182 K5 **Buthier di Valpelline** r. Italy
279 C9 **Butiá** Brazil
232 A4 **Butiaba** Uganda
190 F3 **Butjadingen** reg. Ger.
261 K9 **Butler** AL U.S.A.
255 E9 **Butler** GA U.S.A.
250 J8 **Butler** IN U.S.A.
256 A10 **Butler** KY U.S.A.
260 H6 **Butler** MO U.S.A.
259 G2 **Butler** NJ U.S.A.
256 F8 **Butler** PA U.S.A.
169 H4 **Butlers Bridge** Ireland
115 C6 **Buton** i. Indon.
115 C6 **Buton, Selat** sea chan. Indon.
158 I6 **Butor** Moldova
159 P3 **Butovo** Rus. Fed.
192 F4 **Bütow** Ger.
206 G4 **Butrera** mt. Spain
197 M1 **Butrimonys** Alytus Lith.
160 I7 **Butrimonys** Vilnius Lith.
220 B3 **Butrint** tourist site Albania
220 B3 **Butrintit, Liqeni i** l. Albania
197 I2 **Butryny** Pol.
212 G1 **Bütschwil** Switz.
197 M4 **Butsyn** Ukr.
261 K9 **Buttahatchee** r. MS U.S.A.
136 G9 **Buttala** Sri Lanka
262 H3 **Butte** MT U.S.A.
260 F4 **Butte** NE U.S.A.
194 F2 **Büttelborn** Ger.
193 D8 **Buttelstedt** Ger.
195 K2 **Buttenheim** Ger.
195 J4 **Buttenwiesen** Ger.
171 K4 **Buttermere** Cumbria, England U.K.
250 D3 **Butternut** WI U.S.A.
171 Q5 **Butterwick** North Yorkshire, England U.K.
116 D2 **Butterworth** Malaysia
237 M8 **Butterworth** S. Africa
264 L2 **Buttes, Sierra** mt. CA U.S.A.
169 E8 **Buttevant** Ireland
194 H2 **Bütthard** Ger.
168 D5 **Butt of Lewis** hd Scotland U.K.
247 M3 **Button Bay** Man. Can.
243 L3 **Button Islands** Nunavut Can.
264 M6 **Buttonwillow** CA U.S.A.
193 D8 **Buttstädt** Ger.
191 J8 **Büttstedt** Ger.
109 F12 **Butty Head** W.A. Austr.
258 E3 **Buttzville** NJ U.S.A.
114 E7 **Butuan** Mindanao Phil.
114 E7 **Butuan Bay** Mindanao Phil.
158 I6 **Butuceni** Moldova
130 D5 **Butuo** Sichuan China
157 H6 **Buturlinovka** Rus. Fed.
139 I6 **Butwal** Nepal
Butysh Rus. Fed. see **Kama**
191 G10 **Butzbach** Ger.
192 E3 **Bützow** Ger.
258 E3 **Butztown** PA U.S.A.
232 E2 **Buuhoodle** Somalia
232 E4 **Buulobarde** Somalia
Buurakan r. Kyrg. see **Burkan-Suu**
233 D5 **Buur Gaabo** Somalia
232 E4 **Buurhabaka** Somalia
186 K4 **Buurse** Neth.
128 F3 **Buutsagaan** Bayanhongor Mongolia
162 M2 **Buvåg** Norway
232 B4 **Buvuma Island** Uganda
150 C10 **Buwārah, Jabal** mt. Saudi Arabia
146 D3 **Buwāţah** Saudi Arabia
139 J7 **Buxar** Bihar India
181 L8 **Buxerolles** France
195 K4 **Buxheim** Ger.
182 B4 **Buxières-les-Mines** France
142 K8 **Buxoro** Buxoro Uzbek.
142 J7 **Buxoro** admin. div. Uzbek.
173 M6 **Buxted** East Sussex, England U.K.
190 I4 **Buxtehude** Ger.
171 N7 **Buxton** Derbyshire, England U.K.
182 F3 **Buxy** France
156 H4 **Buy** Rus. Fed.
156 K4 **Buy** r. Rus. Fed.
128 A2 **Buyant** Bayan-Ölgiy Mongolia
Buyant Mongolia see **Buutsagaan**
Buyant Mongolia see **Galshar**
128 B2 **Buyant Gol** r. Mongolia
128 E3 **Buyant Gol** r. Mongolia
129 J4 **Buyant-Ovoo** Mongolia
129 L4 **Buyant-Uhaa** Mongolia
250 B1 **Buyck** MN U.S.A.
151 I3 **Buynaksk** Rus. Fed.
158 H2 **Buynavichy** Belarus
228 D5 **Buyo** Côte d'Ivoire
228 D5 **Buyo, Lac de** l. Côte d'Ivoire
130 C8 **Buyuan Jiang** r. Yunnan China
221 K2 **Büyükada** i. Turkey
149 L4 **Büyük Ağrı Dağı** mt. Turkey
151 E5 **Büyükçatak** Turkey
221 J1 **Büyükçekmece** Turkey
151 B6 **Büyükgeçit** Turkey
150 G1 **Büyükhan** Turkey
221 L4 **Büyükkabaca** Turkey
221 M4 **Büyükkarabağ** Turkey
221 I1 **Büyükkarıştıran** Turkey
221 K5 **Büyükkonak** Turkey
221 I5 **Büyükmenderes** r. Turkey
221 J3 **Büyükorhan** Turkey
150 F2 **Büyükşahinbey** Turkey
221 I3 **Büyükyenice** Turkey
129 R6 **Buyun Shan** mt. Liaoning China
142 D5 **Buzachi, Poluostrov** pen. Kazakh.
145 P3 **Buzai Gumbad** Afgh.
184 G2 **Buzançais** France
179 I5 **Buzancy** France
219 O5 **Buzău** Romania
219 O5 **Buzău** r. Romania
219 P5 **Buzău** r. Romania
224 D3 **Buzaymah** oasis Libya
157 K5 **Buzdyak** Rus. Fed.
213 P5 **Buzet** Croatia
185 E7 **Buzet-sur-Baïse** France
185 H8 **Buzet-sur-Tarn** France
161 X6 **Buzha** r. Rus. Fed.
235 G3 **Búzi** Moz.
235 G3 **Búzi** r. Moz.
219 J5 **Buziaş** Romania
199 K3 **Buzica** Slovakia
281 G5 **Búzios, Cabo dos** c. Brazil
281 E5 **Búzios, Ilha dos** i. Brazil
Büzmeyin Turkm. see **Abadan**
151 L5 **Buzovna** Azer.
142 E1 **Buzuluk** Rus. Fed.
157 H6 **Buzuluk** r. Rus. Fed.
185 D9 **Buzy** France
143 L2 **Buzylyk** Kazakh.
257 O7 **Buzzards Bay** MA U.S.A.
234 D3 **Bwabwata National Park** nature res. Namibia
113 L9 **Bwagaoia** P.N.G.
233 A5 **Bwanga** Tanz.
Bwcle Flintshire, Wales U.K. see **Buckley**
230 F5 **Bwindi National Park** Uganda
136 D5 **Byadgi** Karnataka India
160 L7 **Byahoml'** Belarus
Byakar Bhutan see **Jakar**
219 N7 **Byala** Ruse Bulg.
219 P8 **Byala** Varna Bulg.
221 H1 **Byala Reka** r. Bulg.
219 L7 **Byala Slatina** Bulg.
160 M8 **Byalynichy** Belarus
161 P8 **Byalynkavichy** Belarus
Byam Martin atoll Arch. des Tuamotu Fr. Polynesia see **Ahunui**
243 H2 **Byam Martin Island** Nunavut Can.
160 I8 **Byarezina** r. Belarus
160 N9 **Byarezina** r. Belarus
160 L7 **Byarezinski Biyasfyerny Zapavyednik** nature res. Belarus
160 H9 **Byaroza** Belarus
160 I8 **Byarozawka** Belarus
197 M3 **Byarozna** Belarus
150 D4 **Byblos** tourist site Lebanon
197 K4 **Bychawa** Pol.
196 G5 **Bycina** Pol.
196 G4 **Byczyna** Pol.
196 F2 **Bydgoski, Kanał** canal Pol.
196 G2 **Bydgoszcz** Pol.
160 I9 **Byelaazyorsk** Belarus
158 F2 **Byelavusha** Belarus
197 L3 **Byelavyezhski** Belarus
197 M2 **Byelaye, Vozyera** l. Belarus
159 P8 **Byelins'ke** Ukr.
161 N9 **Byelitsk** Belarus
160 K6 **Byel'ki** Belarus
Byelorussia country Europe see **Belarus**
197 N1 **Byenyakoni** Belarus
Byerastavitsa Belarus see **Pahranichny**
160 L8 **Byerazino** Minskaya Voblasts' Belarus
160 L7 **Byerazino** Vitsyebskaya Voblasts' Belarus
160 K9 **Byeraznyaki** Belarus
262 L7 **Byers** CO U.S.A.
160 H8 **Byershty** Belarus
160 M6 **Byeshankovichy** Belarus
256 D9 **Byesville** OH U.S.A.
161 O9 **Byesyedz'** r. Belarus
107 M7 **Byfield** Qld Austr.
173 J3 **Byfield** Northamptonshire, England U.K.
107 M7 **Byfield National Park** Qld Austr.
173 L5 **Byfleet** Surrey, England U.K.
162 P4 **Bygdeå** Sweden
162 P4 **Bygdsiljum** Sweden
164 D3 **Bygland** Norway
164 D3 **Byglandsfjord** Norway
164 D3 **Byglandsfjorden** l. Norway
193 J7 **Byhleguhre** Ger.
159 P5 **Byk** r. Ukr.
161 N8 **Bykhaw** Belarus
Bykhov Belarus see **Bykhaw**
158 G3 **Bykivka** Ukr.
164 D2 **Bykle** Norway
159 P3 **Bykovka** Rus. Fed.
159 Q2 **Bykovo** Kurskaya Oblast' Rus. Fed.
157 I6 **Bykovo** Volgogradskaya Oblast' Rus. Fed.
153 N2 **Bykovskiy** Rus. Fed.
265 V8 **Bylas** AZ U.S.A.
172 E1 **Bylchau** Conwy, Wales U.K.
190 H1 **Bylderup-Bov** Denmark
143 P3 **Bylkyldak** Kazakh.
243 K2 **Bylot Island** Nunavut Can.
151 D2 **Bylym** Rus. Fed.
251 N4 **Byng Inlet** Ont. Can.
107 H4 **Bynoe** r. Qld Austr.
106 C2 **Bynoe Harbour** N.T. Austr.
136 B7 **Byramgore Reef** India
287 K1 **Byrd Glacier** Antarctica
129 P1 **Byrka** Rus. Fed.
164 C3 **Byrkjedal** Norway
163 I6 **Byrkjelo** Norway
159 L3 **Byrlivka** Ukr.
105 K4 **Byrock** N.S.W. Austr.
250 E7 **Byron** IL U.S.A.
257 □O4 **Byron** ME U.S.A.
256 B6 **Byron** MI U.S.A.
105 N3 **Byron, Cape** N.S.W. Austr.
105 N3 **Byron Bay** N.S.W. Austr.
Byron Island Gilbert Is Kiribati see **Nikunau**
153 K2 **Byrranga, Gory** mts Rus. Fed.
159 M1 **Byryne** Ukr.
158 I3 **Byshiv** Ukr.
198 D1 **Byšice** Czech Rep.
162 P4 **Byske** Sweden
162 P4 **Byskeälven** r. Sweden
122 G2 **Byssa** Rus. Fed.
122 G2 **Byssa** r. Rus. Fed.
197 H6 **Bystra** Pol.
199 I2 **Bystrá** mt. Slovakia
198 F2 **Bystré** Czech Rep.
199 K2 **Bystré** Slovakia
160 L4 **Bystretsovo** Rus. Fed.
199 H3 **Bystričany** Slovakia
199 H2 **Bystřice** Moravskoslezský kraj Czech Rep.
198 D2 **Bystřice** Středočeský kraj Czech Rep.
198 E1 **Bystřice** r. Czech Rep.
198 F2 **Bystřice nad Pernštejnem** Czech Rep.
199 G2 **Bystřice pod Hostýnem** Czech Rep.
129 L2 **Bystrinskiy Golets, Gora** mt. Rus. Fed.
Bystrovka Kyrg. see **Kemin**
158 D5 **Bystrytsya** Ukr.
158 C4 **Bystrytsya** r. Ukr.
143 U1 **Bystryy Istok** Rus. Fed.
156 K5 **Bystryy Tanyp** r. Rus. Fed.
196 F5 **Bystrzyca** Pol.
196 E4 **Bystrzyca** r. Pol.
197 K4 **Bystrzyca** r. Pol.
196 E5 **Bystrzyca Kłodzka** Pol.
198 F1 **Bystrzyckie, Góry** mts Czech Rep./Pol.
153 O3 **Bytantay** r. Rus. Fed.
199 H2 **Bytča** Slovakia
196 D3 **Bytnica** Pol.
196 G5 **Bytom** Pol.
196 D4 **Bytom Odrzański** Pol.
161 R8 **Bytosh'** Rus. Fed.
165 N7 **Bytów** Pol.
233 A5 **Byumba** Rwanda
144 F2 **Byurgyutli** Turkm.
158 J2 **Byval'ki** Belarus
165 N4 **Byxelkrok** Öland Sweden
Byzantium Turkey see **İstanbul**
198 G3 **Bzenec** Czech Rep.
151 B2 **Bzip'i** r. Georgia
151 B2 **Bzip'is K'edi** hills Georgia
197 I3 **Bzura** r. Pol.
151 A2 **Bzych** Rus. Fed.

C

118 G5 **Ca, Sông** r. Vietnam
277 F6 **Caacupé** Para.
277 F6 **Caaguazú** Para.
277 G6 **Caaguazú, Cordillera de** hills Para.
231 B8 **Caála** Angola
275 F5 **Caapiranga** Brazil
277 F6 **Caapucú** Para.
279 B7 **Caarapó** Brazil
281 E2 **Caatinga** Brazil
277 F6 **Caazapá** Para.
232 F3 **Cabaad, Raas** pt Somalia
277 F3 **Cabaçal** r. Brazil
269 J9 **Cabacera Nueva** Mex.
208 G5 **Cabacés** Spain
270 D2 **Cabaiguán** Cuba
185 D10 **Cabaliros, Pic de** mt. France
276 B3 **Caballas** Peru
207 M6 **Caballo** mt. Spain
274 D5 **Caballococha** Peru
263 K10 **Caballo Reservoir** NM U.S.A.
266 G3 **Caballos Mesteños, Llano de los** plain Mex.
276 A2 **Cabana** Ancash Peru
276 B3 **Cabana** Ayacucho Peru
185 E9 **Cabanac** France
185 C6 **Cabanac-et-Villagrains** France
276 C3 **Cabanaconde** Peru
204 D5 **Cabana Maior** Port.
204 I2 **Cabañaquinta** Spain
206 D6 **Cabanas** Port.
207 N5 **Cabañas** mt. Spain
204 I9 **Cabañas del Castillo** Spain
204 E8 **Cabanas de Viriato** Port.
204 G3 **Cabañas Raras** Spain
114 C4 **Cabanatuan** Luzon Phil.
172 E3 **Caban Coch Reservoir** Wales U.K.
185 G9 **Cabanères** hill France
207 J2 **Cabañeros, Parque Nacional de** nat. park Castilla-La Mancha Spain
209 F7 **Cabanes** Spain
183 F9 **Cabannes** France
249 G4 **Cabano** Que. Can.
210 E3 **Čabar** Croatia
185 I9 **Cabardès** reg. France
183 I10 **Cabasse** France
232 D2 **Cabdul Qaadir** Somalia
204 E4 **Cabe** r. Spain
206 D5 **Cabeça Gorda** Port.
206 C3 **Cabeção** Port.
277 G3 **Cabeceira Rio Manso** Brazil
280 D1 **Cabeceiras** Brazil
204 E5 **Cabeceiras de Basto** Port.
206 D2 **Cabeço de Vide** Port.
204 E9 **Cabeço Rainha** mt. Port.
278 G3 **Cabedelo** Brazil
185 J10 **Cabestany** France
199 L5 **Căbeşti** Romania
269 M9 **Cabestrada** Mex.
204 H6 **Cabeza de Framontanos** Spain
283 C6 **Cabeza del Buey** Arg.
207 I3 **Cabeza del Buey** Spain
204 G6 **Cabeza del Caballo** Spain
282 C2 **Cabeza de Vaca, Punta** pt Chile
206 G4 **Cabeza la Vaca** Spain
205 N9 **Cabezamesada** Spain
265 S9 **Cabeza Prieta National Wildlife Refuge** nature res. AZ U.S.A.
207 K3 **Cabezarados** Spain
277 E4 **Cabezas** Bol.
205 J7 **Cabezas del Villar** Spain
271 □[1] **Cabezas de San Juan** pt Puerto Rico
206 E5 **Cabezas Rubias** Spain
205 Q6 **Cabezo de Morés** mt. Spain
209 C11 **Cabezo de Torres** Spain
206 E5 **Cabezo Gordo** hill Spain
205 K5 **Cabezón** Spain
205 O4 **Cabezón de Cameros** Spain
205 L2 **Cabezón de la Sal** Spain
205 K2 **Cabezón de Liébana** Spain
204 I8 **Cabezuela del Valle** Spain
Cabicorp, Punta pt Spain see **Capicorp, Punta de**
285 G6 **Cabildo** Arg.
284 B3 **Cabildo** Chile
274 D2 **Cabimas** Venez.
231 B6 **Cabinda** Angola
231 B6 **Cabinda** prov. Angola
286 T2 **Cabinet Inlet** Antarctica
262 G2 **Cabinet Mountains** MT U.S.A.
114 C9 **Cabingan** i. Phil.
199 K2 **Čabiny** Slovakia
Cabistra Turkey see **Ereğli**
250 C3 **Cable** WI U.S.A.
255 □[2] **Cable Beach** New Prov. Bahamas
283 D7 **Cabo Blanco** Arg.
238 □[1a] **Cabo da Praia** Terceira Azores
235 H2 **Cabo Delgado** prov. Moz.
278 G4 **Cabo de Santo Agostinho** Brazil
281 F5 **Cabo Frio** Brazil
281 G5 **Cabo Frio, Ilha do** i. Brazil
205 P6 **Cabolafuente** Spain
205 M6 **Cabollera, Peña** mt. Spain
248 E4 **Cabonga, Réservoir** resr Que. Can.
261 I7 **Cabool** MO U.S.A.
107 N9 **Caboolture** Qld Austr.
275 I4 **Cabo Orange, Parque Nacional de** nat. park Brazil
274 C5 **Cabo Pantoja** Peru
Cabora Bassa, Lake resr Moz. see **Cahora Bassa, Lago de**
283 D7 **Cabo Raso** Arg.
266 C2 **Caborca** Mex.
271 □[1] **Cabo Rojo** Puerto Rico
251 M4 **Cabot Head** Ont. Can.
249 I4 **Cabot Strait** Nfld and Lab./N.S. Can.
181 K3 **Cabourg** France
Cabo Verde country N. Atlantic Ocean see **Cape Verde**
228 □ **Cabo Verde, Ilhas do** is N. Atlantic Ocean
Cabo Yubi Morocco see **Tarfaya**
114 C5 **Cabra** i. Phil.
207 K6 **Cabra** Spain
207 J5 **Cabra** r. Spain
204 C5 **Cabração** Port.
208 H5 **Cabra del Camp** Spain
207 M5 **Cabra del Santo Cristo** Spain
209 D7 **Cabra de Mora** Spain
270 H4 **Cabral** Dom. Rep.
281 E2 **Cabral, Serra do** mts Brazil
214 B8 **Cabras** Sardegna Italy
268 G4 **Cabras** Mex.
207 K6 **Cabras** mt. Spain
229 G6 **Cabras, Ilha das** i. São Tomé and Príncipe
238 □[1a] **Cabras, Ilhéus das** is Azores
206 H7 **Cabras, Sierra de las** mts Spain
209 C11 **Cabras, Sierra de las** mts Spain
214 A8 **Cabras, Stagno di** l. Sardegna Italy
268 F4 **Cabras de Guadalupe** Mex.
151 I6 **Cäbrayıl** Azer.
183 H7 **Cabre, Col de** pass France
285 I1 **Cabred** Arg.
204 D5 **Cabreira, Serra da** mts Port.
205 O5 **Cabrejas, Sierra de** mts Spain
205 O5 **Cabrejas del Pinar** Spain
206 C3 **Cabrela** Port.
206 B3 **Cabrela** r. Port.
270 I4 **Cabrera** Dom. Rep.
207 K4 **Cabrera** r. Spain
209 K9 **Cabrera, Freu de** sea chan. Spain
209 K9 **Cabrera, Illa de** i. Spain
207 O6 **Cabrera, Sierra** mts Spain
204 G4 **Cabrera, Sierra de la** mts Spain
185 H6 **Cabrerets** France
284 A5 **Cabrero** Chile
247 I5 **Cabri** Sask. Can.
205 R10 **Cabriel** r. Spain
183 H9 **Cabrières-d'Aigues** France
204 E8 **Cabril** Port.
204 H3 **Cabrillanes** Spain
204 H7 **Cabrillas** Spain
205 P7 **Cabrillas** r. Spain
208 E6 **Cabrillas, Puerto de** pass Spain
271 □[3] **Cabrits, Îlet** i. Martinique
278 F4 **Cabrobó** Brazil
274 E3 **Cabruta** Venez.
114 C3 **Cabugao** Luzon Phil.
114 C6 **Cabulauan** i. Phil.
210 F4 **Čabulja** mt. Bos.-Herz.
266 E2 **Cabullona** Mex.
199 G6 **Cabuna** Croatia
284 B6 **Caburgua, Lago** l. Chile
114 D2 **Cabutunan Point** Luzon Phil.
204 G3 **Cacabelos** Spain
279 C8 **Caçador** Brazil
Cacagoin Sichuan China see **Qagca**
269 I9 **Cacahuatepec** Mex.
218 I7 **Čačak** Cacak Serbia
268 G8 **Cacalutla** Mex.
275 H3 **Cacao** Fr. Guiana
281 E5 **Caçapava** Brazil
279 B9 **Caçapava do Sul** Brazil
256 G9 **Cacapon** r. WV U.S.A.
204 H5 **Caçarelhos** Port.
274 C3 **Cácares** Col.
268 D7 **Cacbán** Mex.
216 F8 **Caccamo** Sicilia Italy
214 A6 **Caccia, Capo** c. Sardegna Italy
215 Q5 **Caccia, Monte** hill Italy
217 L5 **Caccuri** Italy
144 I3 **Çäçe** Turkm.
206 A3 **Cacém** Port.
279 B9 **Cacequi** Brazil
277 F4 **Cáceres** Brazil
206 G2 **Cáceres** Spain
204 H9 **Cáceres** prov. Spain
206 G2 **Cáceres, Embalse de** resr Spain
276 D3 **Cachal** Bol.
285 H5 **Cachari** Arg.
261 K7 **Cache** r. IL U.S.A.
228 A3 **Cacheau** r. Guinea-Bissau
246 F5 **Cache Creek** B.C. Can.
264 K3 **Cache Creek** r. CA U.S.A.
262 L6 **Cache la Poudre** r. CO U.S.A.
262 H5 **Cache Peak** ID U.S.A.
228 A3 **Cacheu** Guinea-Bissau
284 C3 **Cacheuta** Arg.
282 D2 **Cachi** Arg.
282 D2 **Cachi, Nevados de** mts Arg.
278 B4 **Cachimbo** Brazil
278 B4 **Cachimbo, Serra do** hills Brazil
231 D7 **Cachimo** Angola
282 C2 **Cachina** r. Chile
231 C8 **Cachingues** Angola
274 C3 **Cáchira** Col.
278 F5 **Cachoeira** Bahia Brazil
280 B3 **Cachoeira** Mato Grosso do Sul Brazil
280 B3 **Cachoeira Alta** Brazil
280 B2 **Cachoeira de Goiás** Brazil
278 C2 **Cachoeira do Arari** Brazil
281 E3 **Cachoeira dos Macacos** Brazil
279 B9 **Cachoeira do Sul** Brazil
281 E5 **Cachoeira Paulista** Brazil
281 F5 **Cachoeiras de Macacu** Brazil
281 G4 **Cachoeiro de Itapemirim** Brazil
206 D6 **Cachopo** Port.
282 C2 **Cachos, Punta de** pt Chile
199 G3 **Čachtice** Slovakia
276 D2 **Cachuela Esperanza** Bol.
204 C7 **Cacia** Port.
207 L6 **Cacín** Spain
207 K6 **Cacín** r. Spain
228 B4 **Cacine** Guinea-Bissau
275 I4 **Caciporé, Cabo** c. Brazil
231 C7 **Cacolo** Angola
268 B5 **Cacoma, Sierra** mts Mex.
231 B8 **Caconda** Angola
231 B6 **Cacongo** Angola
261 D7 **Cactus** TX U.S.A.
264 O4 **Cactus Range** mts NV U.S.A.
280 B3 **Caçu** Brazil
231 B7 **Cacuaco** Angola
231 B8 **Cacula** Angola
231 C7 **Caculama** Angola
278 E5 **Caculé** Brazil
281 H2 **Cacumba, Ilha** i. Brazil
231 B7 **Cacuso** Angola
206 A2 **Cadafais** Port.
172 E2 **Cadair Idris** hills Wales U.K.
232 E4 **Cadale** Somalia
185 H8 **Cadalen** France
205 L8 **Cadalso de los Vidrios** Spain
170 B7 **Cadamstown** Ireland
208 L3 **Cadaqués** Spain
206 A2 **Cadaval** Port.
199 G6 **Čađavica** Croatia
199 H2 **Čadca** Slovakia
232 D2 **Caddabassa** l. Eth.
173 L4 **Caddington** Bedfordshire, England U.K.
261 I9 **Caddo Lake** TX U.S.A.
213 J6 **Cadelbosco di Sopra** Italy
106 E2 **Cadell** r. N.T. Austr.
107 H7 **Cadell Creek** watercourse Qld Austr.
212 F3 **Cadenazzo** Switz.
190 H3 **Cadenberge** Ger.
183 G9 **Cadenet** France
212 H6 **Cadeo** Italy
267 I5 **Cadereyta** Nuevo León Mex.
269 H5 **Cadereyta** Querétaro Mex.
Cader Idris hills Wales U.K. see **Cadair Idris**
183 F8 **Caderousse** France
Cadí mt. Spain see **Torre de Cadí**
208 I3 **Cadí, Serra del** mts Spain
208 I3 **Cadí, Túnel del** tun. Spain
207 M7 **Cádiar** Spain
104 E3 **Cadibarrawirracanna, Lake** salt flat S.A. Austr.
114 D4 **Cadig Mountains** Luzon Phil.
251 P1 **Cadillac** Que. Can.
247 J5 **Cadillac** Sask. Can.
185 D6 **Cadillac** France
250 I5 **Cadillac** MI U.S.A.
151 D4 **Çadır Dağı** mt. Turkey
151 B6 **Çadırkaya** Turkey
114 D6 **Cadiz** Negros Phil.
206 G7 **Cádiz** Spain
206 H8 **Cádiz** prov. Spain
265 Q7 **Cadiz** CA U.S.A.
254 D7 **Cadiz** KY U.S.A.
256 E8 **Cadiz** OH U.S.A.
206 G7 **Cádiz, Bahía de** b. Spain
206 E7 **Cádiz, Golfo de** g. Spain
265 Q7 **Cadiz Lake** CA U.S.A.
195 J3 **Cadolzburg** Ger.
246 G4 **Cadomin** Alta Can.
213 L5 **Cadoneghe** Italy
213 M3 **Cadore** reg. Italy
250 C5 **Cadott** WI U.S.A.
246 G3 **Cadotte** r. Alta Can.
246 G3 **Cadotte Lake** Alta Can.
185 G8 **Cadours** France
109 D11 **Cadoux** W.A. Austr.
278 E4 **Caém** Brazil
181 K3 **Caen** France
181 K3 **Caen, Plaine de** plain France
172 F5 **Caerau** Cardiff, Wales U.K.
Caerdydd Cardiff, Wales U.K. see **Cardiff**
Caere Italy see **Cerveteri**
Caerffili Caerphilly, Wales U.K. see **Caerphilly**
Caerfyrddin Carmarthenshire, Wales U.K. see **Carmarthen**

172 F1 **Caergwrle** *Flintshire, Wales* U.K.
Caergybi *Isle of Anglesey, Wales* U.K. *see* **Holyhead**
172 E1 **Caerhun** *Conwy, Wales* U.K.
172 G4 **Caerleon** *Newport, Wales* U.K.
172 D1 **Caernarfon** *Gwynedd, Wales* U.K.
172 C1 **Caernarfon Bay** *Wales* U.K.
Caernarvon *Gwynedd, Wales* U.K. *see* **Caernarfon**
172 F4 **Caerphilly** *Caerphilly, Wales* U.K.
172 F4 **Caerphilly** *admin. div. Wales* U.K.
172 F2 **Caersws** *Powys, Wales* U.K.
172 G4 **Caerwent** *Monmouthshire, Wales* U.K.
Caesaraugusta Spain *see* **Zaragoza**
Caesarea Alg. *see* **Cherchell**
150 C6 **Caesarea** *tourist site* Israel
Caesarea Cappadociae Turkey *see* **Kayseri**
Caesarea Philippi Syria *see* **Bāniyās**
Caesarodunum France *see* **Tours**
Caesaromagus *Essex, England* U.K. *see* **Chelmsford**
281 F3 **Caeté** Brazil
276 C2 **Caeté** *r.* Brazil
278 E5 **Caetité** Brazil
212 D5 **Cafasse** Italy
282 D2 **Cafayate** Arg.
280 C4 **Cafelândia** Brazil
Caffa Ukr. *see* **Feodosiya**
226 D5 **Çafia, Hamâda** *des.* Mali
273 D3 **Cafifi** Col.
239 □[1c] **Cafres, Plaine des** *hills* Réunion
275 G4 **Cafuini** *r.* Brazil
206 □ **Cágado, Ponta do** *pt* Madeira
114 C7 **Cagayan** *i.* Phil.
114 C2 **Cagayan** *r. Luzon* Phil.
114 E7 **Cagayan de Oro** *Mindanao* Phil.
114 B8 **Cagayan de Tawi-Tawi** *i.* Phil.
114 C7 **Cagayan Islands** Phil.
215 P6 **Caggiano** Italy
213 N8 **Cagli** Italy
214 C9 **Cagliari** *Sardegna* Italy
214 C9 **Cagliari** *prov. Sardegna* Italy
214 C9 **Cagliari, Golfo di** *b. Sardegna* Italy
214 B9 **Cagliari, Stagno di** *l. Sardegna* Italy
214 B4 **Cagna, Montagne de** *mts Corse* France
185 I8 **Cagnac-les-Mines** France
215 P4 **Cagnano Varano** Italy
183 K9 **Cagnes-sur-Mer** France
114 E6 **Cagosoan Point** Phil.
114 D2 **Cagua, Mount** *vol.* Phil.
274 C5 **Caguán** *r.* Col.
271 □[2] **Caguas** Puerto Rico
144 F1 **Çagyl** Turkm.
144 H1 **Çagyllyşor Çöketligi** *depr.* Turkm.
255 D9 **Cahaba** *r. AL* U.S.A.
231 B9 **Cahama** Angola
169 C9 **Caha Mountains** *hills* Ireland
169 F7 **Caher** Ireland
169 B9 **Cahermore** Ireland
Cahersiveen Ireland *see* **Cahirsiveen**
169 G8 **Cahir** Ireland
169 B9 **Cahirsiveen** Ireland
258 F2 **Cahoonzie** *NY* U.S.A.
231 F2 **Cahora Bassa, Lago de** *resr* Moz.
169 J7 **Cahore Point** Ireland
185 G7 **Cahors** France
276 C4 **Cahuapanas** Peru
274 D5 **Cahuinari, Parque Nacional** *nat. park* Colombia
266 □R13 **Cahuita, Punta** *pt* Costa Rica
158 H8 **Cahul** Moldova
185 H8 **Cahuzac-sur-Vère** France
235 G3 **Caia** Moz.
206 E3 **Caia** Port.
206 E3 **Caia** *r.* Port.
206 E2 **Caia, Barragem do** *resr* Port.
277 F3 **Caiabis, Serra dos** *hills* Brazil
231 D7 **Caianda** Angola
280 B1 **Caiapó** *r.* Brazil
280 A2 **Caiapó, Serra do** *mts* Brazil
280 B2 **Caiapônia** Brazil
231 B8 **Caiaza** Angola
215 M5 **Caiazzo** Italy
271 D2 **Caibarién** Cuba
118 H4 **Cai Bâu, Đao** *i.* Vietnam
119 H9 **Cai Be** Vietnam
275 E3 **Caicara** Venez.
278 F3 **Caicó** Brazil
270 H3 **Caicos Bank** *sea feature* Turks and Caicos Is
270 H3 **Caicos Islands** Turks and Caicos Is
270 G3 **Caicos Passage** Bahamas/Turks and Caicos Is
131 J3 **Caidian** *Hubei* China
Caidu *Henan* China *see* **Shangcai**
231 D7 **Caifuche** Angola
109 H12 **Caiguna** *W.A.* Austr.
130 H3 **Caihua** *Hubei* China
131 K4 **Cailing** *Jiangxi* China
276 C3 **Cailloma** Peru
268 C3 **Caimanero, Laguna del** *lag.* Mex.
284 B2 **Caimanes** Chile
114 B4 **Caiman Point** *Luzon* Phil.
231 B8 **Caimbambo** Angola
205 Q7 **Caimodorro** *mt.* Spain
158 H6 **Căinar** *r.* Moldova
231 B8 **Cainde** Angola
219 M5 **Căineni** Romania
265 U3 **Caineville** *UT* U.S.A.
130 D2 **Cainnyigoin** *Sichuan* China
119 G10 **Cai Nước** Vietnam
204 C2 **Caión** Spain
282 C2 **Caipe** Arg.
183 F8 **Cairanne** France
286 W1 **Caird Coast** Antarctica
Cairinis *Scotland* U.K. *see* **Carinish**
168 F10 **Cairnbaan** *Argyll and Bute, Scotland* U.K.
168 G10 **Cairndow** *Argyll and Bute, Scotland* U.K.
168 I10 **Cairneyhill** *Fife, Scotland* U.K.
168 I8 **Cairn Gorm** *mt. Scotland* U.K.
168 I8 **Cairngorm Mountains** *Scotland* U.K.
168 I8 **Cairngorms National Park** *Scotland* U.K.
244 I3 **Cairn Mountain** *AK* U.S.A.
168 F13 **Cairnryan** *Dumfries and Galloway, Scotland* U.K.
107 J4 **Cairns** *Qld* Austr.
168 H12 **Cairnsmore of Carsphairn** *hill Scotland* U.K.
168 H13 **Cairnsmore of Fleet** *hill Scotland* U.K.
168 I8 **Cairn Toul** *mt. Scotland* U.K.
Cairo Egypt *see* **Al Qāhirah**
255 E10 **Cairo** *GA* U.S.A.
261 K7 **Cairo** *IL* U.S.A.
215 L4 **Cairo, Monte** *mt.* Italy
212 E7 **Cairo Montenotte** Italy
Caisleán an Bharraigh Ireland *see* **Castlebar**
183 E9 **Caissargues** France
168 F11 **Caisteal Abhail** *hill Scotland* U.K.
173 P2 **Caister-on-Sea** *Norfolk, England* U.K.
171 Q7 **Caistor** *Lincolnshire, England* U.K.
168 J6 **Caithness** *reg. Scotland* U.K.
231 B8 **Caitou** Angola
231 C8 **Caiundo** Angola
105 J3 **Caiwarro (abandoned)** *Qld* Austr.
131 K6 **Caixi** *Fujian* China
Caiyuanzhen *Zhejiang* China *see* **Shengsi**
276 D5 **Caiza** Bol.
131 H3 **Caizi Hu** *l.* China
276 A1 **Cajabamba** Peru
271 □[2] **Caja de Muertos, Isla** *i.* Puerto Rico
276 A1 **Cajamarca** Peru
274 B6 **Cajamarca** *dept* Peru
278 D2 **Cajapió** Brazil
185 H7 **Cajarc** France
278 D2 **Cajari** Brazil
276 A2 **Cajatambo** Peru
280 C6 **Cajati** Brazil
278 F3 **Cajàzeiras** Brazil
218 H7 **Čajetina** *Čajetina* Serbia
114 D5 **Cajidiocan** Phil.
199 H3 **Čajkov** Slovakia
210 G4 **Čajniče** Bos.-Herz.
284 A6 **Cajón** Chile
266 □R9 **Cajones, Cayos** *is* Hond.
269 L8 **Cajonos** *r.* Mex.
276 D4 **Cajuata** Bol.
280 D4 **Cajuru** Brazil
219 N3 **Cajvana** Romania
128 F8 **Caka** *Qinghai* China
199 H3 **Čakajovce** Slovakia
Caka'lho *Xizang* China *see* **Yanjing**
128 F8 **Caka Yanhu** *l. Qinghai* China
151 A2 **Çakırkaş** Turkey
221 I2 **Çakırlı** Turkey
151 E5 **Çakmak** Turkey
151 D6 **Çakmak Dağı** *mts* Turkey
210 F2 **Čakovec** Croatia
221 K4 **Çal** *Denizli* Turkey
Çal *Hakkâri* Turkey *see* **Çukurca**
237 L7 **Cala** S. Africa
206 G5 **Cala** Spain
206 G5 **Cala** *r.* Spain
206 G5 **Cala, Embalse de** *resr* Spain
229 H5 **Calabar** Nigeria
209 □13 **Calabardina** Spain
251 R4 **Calabogie** *Ont.* Can.
274 E2 **Calabozo** Venez.
215 Q9 **Calabria** *admin. reg.* Italy
217 L5 **Calabria, Parco Nazionale della** *nat. park* Italy
207 J7 **Calaburra, Punta de** *pt* Spain
208 F5 **Calaceite** Spain
276 C4 **Calacoto** Bol.
214 C3 **Calacuccia** *Corse* France
214 A5 **Cala d'Oliva** *Sardegna* Italy
209 L9 **Cala d'Or** Spain
208 I4 **Calaf** Spain
219 K7 **Calafat** Romania
283 B8 **Calafate** Arg.
208 I5 **Calafell** Spain
214 C9 **Cala Figuera** Spain
209 K9 **Cala Figuera, Cap de** *c.* Spain
219 O3 **Calafindeşti** Romania
208 □ **Cala Galdana** Spain
212 I9 **Calaggio** *r.* Italy
114 B5 **Calagnaan** *i.* Phil.
214 D7 **Cala Gonone** *Sardegna* Italy
266 D4 **Calagua** Mex.
114 D4 **Calagua Islands** Phil.
Calagurris Spain *see* **Calahorra**
207 M7 **Calahonda** Spain
205 Q4 **Calahorra** Spain
231 C9 **Calai** Angola
178 C2 **Calais** France
257 □R3 **Calais** *ME* U.S.A.
267 O8 **Calakmus** *tourist site* Mex.
282 D3 **Calalasteo, Sierra de** *mts* Arg.
100 □[3b] **Calalin** *i. Majuro* Marshall Is
100 □[3b] **Calalin Channel** *Majuro* Marshall Is
213 M3 **Calalzo di Cadore** Italy
277 E2 **Calama** Brazil
276 C5 **Calama** Chile
212 E6 **Calamandrana** Italy
274 C2 **Calamar** *Bolívar* Col.
274 C4 **Calamar** *Guaviare* Col.
276 C4 **Calamarca** Bol.
114 B6 **Calamian Group** *is* Phil.
209 L8 **Cala Millor** Spain
208 C6 **Calamocha** Spain
206 G3 **Calamonte** Spain
209 L9 **Cala Murada** Spain
219 L5 **Călan** Romania
Calanais *Scotland* U.K. *see* **Callanish**
275 E5 **Calanaque** Brazil
206 F5 **Calañas** Spain
212 G3 **Calancasca** *r.* Switz.
208 E6 **Calanda** Spain
208 E5 **Calanda, Desierto de** *reg.* Spain
208 E6 **Calanda, Embalse de** *resr* Spain
114 C6 **Calandagan** *i.* Phil.
231 C7 **Calandula** Angola
116 A2 **Calang** *Sumatera* Indon.
214 C6 **Calangianus** *Sardegna* Italy
217 J7 **Calanna** Italy
208 □ **Cala'n Porter** Spain
114 C5 **Calapan** *Mindoro* Phil.
237 L7 **Calapas** *pass* S. Africa
207 N6 **Calar Alta** *mt.* Spain
158 H6 **Călăraşi** Moldova
219 P6 **Călăraşi** Romania
209 L8 **Cala Ratjada** Spain
207 N4 **Calar del Mundo** *mts* Spain
216 G8 **Calascibetta** *Sicilia* Italy
214 A9 **Calasetta** *Sardegna* Italy
208 D6 **Calasparra** Spain
216 D8 **Calatafimi** *Sicilia* Italy
205 O5 **Calatañazor** Spain
209 H10 **Cala Tarida** Spain
205 Q6 **Calatayud** Spain
205 R5 **Calatorao** Spain
207 K3 **Calatrava, Campo de** *reg.* Spain
193 I7 **Calau** Ger.
114 D5 **Calauag** *Luzon* Phil.
193 I7 **Calau-Altdöbern-Reddern** *park* Ger.
216 H7 **Calavà, Capo** *c. Sicilia* Italy
209 H10 **Cala Vadella** Spain
207 I4 **Calaveruela** *hill* Spain
114 C5 **Calavite Passage** Phil.
114 B5 **Calawit** *i.* Phil.
114 C2 **Calayan** *i.* Phil.
114 E5 **Calbayog** *Samar* Phil.
193 E7 **Calbe (Saale)** Ger.
191 K6 **Calberlah** Ger.
114 E6 **Calbiga** *Samar* Phil.
276 C3 **Calca** Peru
278 C3 **Calcanhar, Ponta do** *pt* Brazil
267 M3 **Calcasieu** *r. LA* U.S.A.
261 I11 **Calcasieu Lake** *LA* U.S.A.
214 C3 **Calcatoggio** *Corse* France
274 A5 **Calceta** Ecuador
285 G1 **Calchaquí** Arg.
212 J8 **Calci** Italy
215 Q6 **Calciano** Italy
212 I5 **Calcinato** Italy
212 H4 **Calcio** Italy
275 I4 **Calçoene** Brazil
Calcutta *W. Bengal* India *see* **Kolkata**
219 M6 **Căldăraru** Romania
270 D7 **Caldaro, Lago di** *l.* Italy
215 K1 **Caldarola** Italy
213 K3 **Caldaro sulla Strada del Vino** Italy
274 C3 **Caldas** *dept* Col.
206 A2 **Caldas da Rainha** Port.
Caldas de Mombuy *Cataluña* Spain *see* **Caldes de Montbui**
206 B6 **Caldas de Monchique** Port.
204 C3 **Caldas de Reis** Spain
204 D6 **Caldas de Vizela** Port.
206 D3 **Caldas Novas** Brazil
171 K4 **Caldbeck** *Cumbria, England* U.K.
208 D3 **Caldearenas** Spain
173 K2 **Caldecott** *Rutland, England* U.K.
276 D2 **Caldeirão** Brazil
206 C6 **Caldeirão, Serra de** *mts* Port.
204 D5 **Caldelas** Port.
206 B5 **Caldelas Taipas** Port.
191 H8 **Calden** Ger.
246 I1 **Calder** *r. N.W.T.* Can.
168 I5 **Calder, Loch** *l. Scotland* U.K.
282 C2 **Caldera** Chile
238 □[3d] **Caldera de Taburiente, Parque Nacional de la** *nat. park La Palma* Canary Is
168 I11 **Caldercruix** *North Lanarkshire, Scotland* U.K.
205 Q7 **Calderereros, Sierra de** *mts* Spain
207 L2 **Calderina, Sierra de la** *mts* Spain
267 O8 **Calderitas** Mex.
172 G4 **Caldicot** *Monmouthshire, Wales* U.K.
151 E6 **Çaldıran** *Van* Turkey
149 K4 **Çaldıran** *Van* Turkey
213 L4 **Caldogno** Italy
213 K3 **Caldonazzo** Italy
213 K3 **Caldonazzo, Lago di** *l.* Italy
171 N4 **Caldwell** *North Yorkshire, England* U.K.
262 F5 **Caldwell** *ID* U.S.A.
261 G7 **Caldwell** *KS* U.S.A.
256 D9 **Caldwell** *OH* U.S.A.
261 G10 **Caldwell** *TX* U.S.A.
251 O6 **Caledon** *Ont.* Can.
237 K6 **Caledon** *r.* Lesotho/S. Africa
236 D10 **Caledon** S. Africa
170 D5 **Caledon** *Northern Ireland* U.K.
106 F2 **Caledon Bay** *N.T.* Austr.
249 H4 **Caledonia** *N.S.* Can.
251 O6 **Caledonia** *Ont.* Can.
Caledonia *admin. div.* U.K. *see* **Scotland**
250 I7 **Caledonia** *MI* U.S.A.
256 C6 **Caledonia** *MN* U.S.A.
256 H6 **Caledonia** *NY* U.S.A.
237 K5 **Caledon Nature Reserve** S. Africa
208 K4 **Calella** Spain
107 L6 **Calen** *Qld* Austr.
204 C6 **Calendário** Port.
214 B2 **Calenzana** *Corse* France
212 H8 **Calenzano** Italy
255 D9 **Calera** *AL* U.S.A.
206 G4 **Calera de León** Spain
205 J9 **Calera y Chozas** Spain
205 N5 **Caleruega** Spain
Caleta *b.* Gibraltar *see* **Catalan Bay**
238 □[3e] **Caleta del Sebo** *Canary Is*
276 C6 **Caleta el Cobre** Chile
283 C9 **Caleta Josefina** Chile
276 C5 **Caleta Lobos** Chile
285 F6 **Caleta Morritos** Chile
276 C5 **Caleta Pabellón de Pica** Chile
284 B2 **Caleta Teniente** Chile
284 B4 **Caletones** Chile
284 E4 **Caleufú** Arg.
265 Q9 **Calexico** *CA* U.S.A.
170 H5 **Calf of Man** *i.* Isle of Man
168 K4 **Calfsound** *Orkney, Scotland* U.K.
246 H5 **Calgary** *Alta* Can.
168 D9 **Calgary** *Argyll and Bute, Scotland* U.K.
238 □[1c] **Calheta** *São Jorge* Azores
206 □ **Calheta** Madeira
206 □ **Calheta, Ponta da** *pt* Madeira
238 □[1c] **Calheta de Nesquim** *Pico* Azores
255 E8 **Calhoun** *GA* U.S.A.
254 D7 **Calhoun** *KY* U.S.A.
274 B4 **Cali** Col.
221 J2 **Çalı** Turkey
114 E6 **Calicoan** *i.* Phil.
Calicut *Kerala* India *see* **Kozhikode**
265 R4 **Caliente** *NV* U.S.A.
271 □[7] **California** Trin. and Tob.
260 I6 **California** *MO* U.S.A.
264 L4 **California** *state* U.S.A.
266 C2 **California, Golfo de** *g.* Mex.
264 K4 **California Aqueduct** *canal CA* U.S.A.
264 N8 **California Coastal National Monument** *nat. park CA* U.S.A.
208 F7 **Calig** Spain
185 E7 **Calignac** France
269 I8 **Calihualá** Mex.
151 J6 **Cälilabad** Azer.
282 D1 **Calilegua** Arg.
282 D1 **Calilegua, Parque Nacional** *nat. park* Arg.
219 M5 **Călimăneşti** Romania
219 M3 **Călimani, Munţii** *mts* Romania
217 O3 **Calimera** Italy
284 C2 **Calingasta** Arg.
Calininsc Moldova *see* **Cupcina**
269 J7 **Calipan** Mex.
265 Q8 **Calipatria** *CA* U.S.A.
264 J3 **Calistoga** *CA* U.S.A.
215 O6 **Calitri** Italy
236 F9 **Calitzdorp** S. Africa
212 E7 **Calizzano** Italy
221 L6 **Çalkaya** *Antalya* Turkey
221 M2 **Çalkaya** *Eskişehir* Turkey
267 N7 **Calkiní** Mex.
221 L4 **Çalköy** Turkey
104 H3 **Callabonna, Lake** *salt flat S.A.* Austr.
180 E5 **Callac** France
256 E11 **Callaghan** *VA* U.S.A.
264 P2 **Callaghan, Mount** *NV* U.S.A.
255 G10 **Callahan** *FL* U.S.A.
169 H7 **Callan** Ireland
170 D5 **Callan** *r. Northern Ireland* U.K.
248 E4 **Callander** *Ont.* Can.
168 H10 **Callander** *Stirling, Scotland* U.K.
256 F12 **Callands** *VA* U.S.A.
114 C3 **Callang** *Luzon* Phil.
168 C6 **Callanish** *Western Isles, Scotland* U.K.
186 G3 **Callantsoog** Neth.
276 A3 **Callao** Peru
265 S2 **Callao** *UT* U.S.A.
183 J9 **Callas** France
108 F6 **Callawa Aboriginal Reserve** *W.A.* Austr.
185 D7 **Callen** France
185 D7 **Calles** Mex.
269 I2 **Callezuela** Spain
208 E2 **Callian** France
183 J9 **Calliano** Italy
212 E5 **Callicoon** *NY* U.S.A.
257 J7 **Callide** *Qld* Austr.
107 M8 **Calling Lake** *Alta* Can.
246 H4 **Calling Lake** *l. Alta* Can.
246 H4 **Callington** *Cornwall, England* U.K.
172 D6 **Calliope** *Qld* Austr.
107 M8 **Callipolis** Turkey *see* **Gelibolu**
Callosa d'En Sarrià Spain
209 E10 **Callosa de Segura** Spain
209 D11 **Callum** *Ont.* Can.
251 N3 **Callyharra Springs** *W.A.* Austr.
109 C8 **Calmar** *Alta* Can.
246 H4 **Calmar** *IA* U.S.A.
250 C6 **Călmăţui** *r.* Romania
219 N6 **Calmont** *Midi-Pyrénées* France
185 H9 **Calmont** *Midi-Pyrénées* France
185 H7 **Calmucó** Arg.
275 J2 **Calnali** Mex.
284 C5 **Calne** *Wiltshire, England* U.K.
269 I5 **Călnic** Romania
172 H5 **Călniştea** *r.* Romania
219 L5 **Calobre** Panama
219 N6 **Calolziocorte** Italy
266 □S13 **Calomarde** Spain
212 G4 **Calonda** Angola
205 Q8 **Calonge** Spain
231 D7 **Calonges** France
208 L4 **Calonne-Ricouart** France
185 F7 **Caloosahatchee** *r. FL* U.S.A.
178 D3 **Calore** Italy
255 G12 **Calore** *r.* Italy
215 N5 **Calore** *r.* Italy
215 M5 **Calotmul** Mex.
215 O6 **Caloundra** *Qld* Austr.
267 O7 **Čalovec** Slovakia *see* **Veľký Meder**
107 N9 **Čalovo** Slovakia *see* **Veľký Meder**
199 G4 **Calp** Spain *see* **Calpe**
209 F10 **Calpe** Spain
250 G7 **Calpoy's Bay** *Ont.* Can.
257 E10 **Calpulalpan** Mex.
269 H5 **Calpulálpan** Mex.
269 I6 **Calstock** *Ont.* Can.
248 C3 **Caltabellotta** *Sicilia* Italy
216 E8 **Caltagirone** *Sicilia* Italy
216 H9 **Caltagirone** *r. Sicilia* Italy
216 G9 **Caltanissetta** *Sicilia* Italy
216 F8 **Caltanissetta** *prov. Sicilia* Italy
216 F8 **Caltavuturo** *Sicilia* Italy
216 F8 **Çaltıbozkır** Turkey
150 B2 **Caltignaga** Italy
212 F4 **Caltojar** Spain
205 O6 **Caltraghlea** Ireland
169 F6 **Caluanga** Angola
231 C7 **Calucinga** Angola
231 C7 **Caluire-et-Cuire** France
182 F5
231 B7 **Calulo** Angola
250 F2 **Calumet** *MI* U.S.A.
250 F2 **Calumet** *MN* U.S.A.
231 D8 **Calunda** Angola
231 C9 **Calunga** Angola
231 B8 **Caluquembe** Angola
114 C7 **Calusa** *i.* Phil.
212 D5 **Caluso** Italy
232 F2 **Caluula** Somalia
232 F2 **Caluula, Raas** *pt* Somalia
114 C6 **Caluya** *i.* Phil.
206 B2 **Calvados** *dept* France
204 C8 **Calvão** Port.
204 I7 **Calvarrasa de Abajo** Spain
204 I7 **Calvarrasa de Arriba** Spain
215 P7 **Calvello** Italy
171 N7 **Calver** *Derbyshire, England* U.K.
169 I6 **Calverstown** Ireland
106 F4 **Calvert** *r. N.T.* Austr.
106 F4 **Calvert Hills** *N.T.* Austr.
246 D5 **Calvert Island** *B.C.* Can.
259 J3 **Calverton** *NY* U.S.A.
109 G7 **Calvert Range** *hills W.A.* Austr.
214 B2 **Calvi** *Corse* France
214 F1 **Calvi, Monte** *hill* Italy
209 K8 **Calvià** Spain
215 J3 **Calvi dell'Umbria** Italy
185 H7 **Calvignac** France
268 E4 **Calvillo** Mex.
168 I9 **Calvine** *Perth and Kinross, Scotland* U.K.
185 I6 **Calvinet** France
236 D7 **Calvinia** S. Africa
215 M5 **Calvi Risorta** Italy
185 I8 **Calvisson** France
204 I8 **Calvitero** *mt.* Spain
216 G10 **Calvo, Monte** *hill* Italy
215 P4 **Calvo, Monte** *mt.* Italy
193 D6 **Calvörde** Ger.
204 E5 **Calvos** Spain
194 F4 **Calw** Ger.
207 L3 **Calzada de Calatrava** Spain
204 I4 **Calzada de Valdunciel** Spain
204 G8 **Calzadilla** Spain
173 M3 **Cam** *r. England* U.K.
231 B7 **Camabatela** Angola
275 F6 **Camaçari** Brazil
206 □ **Camacha** Madeira
206 □ **Camacha** Madeira
264 L3 **Camache Reservoir** *CA* U.S.A.
248 E4 **Camachigama** *r. Que.* Can.
251 R2 **Camachigama, Lac** *l. Que.* Can.
268 E1 **Camacho** Mex.
231 B8 **Camacuio** Angola
231 C8 **Camacupa** Angola
274 E2 **Camaguán** Venez.
270 E3 **Camagüey** Cuba
270 D2 **Camagüey, Archipiélago de** *is* Cuba
212 I8 **Camaiore** Italy
275 G6 **Camaiú** *r.* Brazil
270 D2 **Camajuaní** Cuba
Çamalan Turkey *see* **Gülek**
213 L8 **Camaldoli** Italy
205 K2 **Camaleño** Spain
278 F5 **Camamu** Brazil
276 B4 **Camaná** Peru
276 B4 **Camaná** *r.* Peru
208 C6 **Camañas** Spain
231 D7 **Camanongue** Angola
279 B6 **Camaquã** Brazil
279 C9 **Camaquã** *r.* Brazil
279 C9 **Camaquã** *r.* Brazil
219 K3 **Camăr** Romania
275 F5 **Camará** Brazil
206 □ **Câmara de Lobos** Madeira
274 D4 **Camarão** Brazil
277 F3 **Camararé** *r.* Brazil
208 G4 **Camarasa** Spain
243 J10 **Camarat, Cap** *c.* France
275 L8 **Camarena** Mex.
205 L8 **Camarena** Spain
209 C7 **Camarena** *r.* Spain
205 L8 **Camarena de la Sierra** Spain
183 B9 **Camarès** France
183 F8 **Camaret-sur-Aigues** France
180 B5 **Camaret-sur-Mer** France
276 D5 **Camargo** Bol.
267 J4 **Camargo** Mex.
267 J4 **Camargo, Parque Natural** *nature res.* Mex.
183 F9 **Camargue** *reg.* France
183 F10 **Camargue, Parc Naturel Régional de** *nature res.* France
284 B4 **Camarico** Chile
207 P4 **Camarillas, Embalse de** *resr* Spain
264 M7 **Camarillo** *CA* U.S.A.
206 H8 **Camarinal, Punta** *pt* Spain
204 B2 **Camariñas** Spain
204 B2 **Camariñas, Ría de** *inlet* Spain
268 A2 **Camarón** Mex.
266 □Q10 **Camarón, Cabo** *c.* Hond.
283 D7 **Camarones** Arg.
269 H1 **Camarones** Mex.
283 D7 **Camarones, Bahía** *b.* Arg.
169 I8 **Camaross** Ireland
204 H4 **Camarzana de Tera** Spain
206 G6 **Camas** Spain
262 C4 **Camas** *WA* U.S.A.
262 H4 **Camas** *r. ID* U.S.A.
262 H5 **Camas Creek** *r. ID* U.S.A.
168 F9 **Camasnacroise** *Highland, Scotland* U.K.
216 F9 **Camastra** *Sicilia* Italy
119 G10 **Ca Mau** Vietnam
119 G10 **Ca Mau, Mui** *c.* Vietnam
231 C7 **Camaxilo** Angola
285 G4 **Cambaceres** Arg.
204 C3 **Cambados** Spain
204 C3 **Cambará** Brazil
280 B5 **Cambará** Brazil
277 F4 **Cambay** *Gujarat* India *see* **Khambhat**
280 B5 **Cambay, Gulf of** India *see* **Khambhat, Gulf of**
280 B5 **Cambé** Brazil
173 K5 **Camberley** *Surrey, England* U.K.
185 D6 **Cambes** France
119 G8 **Cambodia** *country* Asia
185 B9 **Cambo-les-Bains** France
178 D5 **Cambon** France
231 B8 **Cambonda, Serra** *mts* Angola
279 C8 **Camboriú** Brazil
172 C7 **Camborne** *Cornwall, England* U.K.
258 C2 **Cambra** *PA* U.S.A.
104 G6 **Cambrai** *S.A.* Austr.
178 F3 **Cambrai** France
204 D2 **Cambre** Spain
181 L3 **Cambremer** France
204 E6 **Cambres** Port.
236 I9 **Cambria** S. Africa
Cambria *admin. div.* U.K. *see* **Wales**
264 K6 **Cambria** *CA* U.S.A.
172 E2 **Cambrian Mountains** *hills Wales* U.K.
248 D5 **Cambridge** *Ont.* Can.
270 □ **Cambridge** Jamaica
102 J4 **Cambridge** *North I.* N.Z.
173 M3 **Cambridge** *Cambridgeshire, England* U.K.
260 J5 **Cambridge** *IL* U.S.A.
257 N6 **Cambridge** *MA* U.S.A.
257 I10 **Cambridge** *MD* U.S.A.
250 A4 **Cambridge** *MN* U.S.A.
257 L5 **Cambridge** *NY* U.S.A.
256 D8 **Cambridge** *OH* U.S.A.
258 D4 **Cambridge** *PA* U.S.A.
250 E6 **Cambridge** *VT* U.S.A.
257 D5 **Cambridge** *WI* U.S.A.
243 H3 **Cambridge Bay** *Nunavut* Can.
108 J3 **Cambridge Gulf** *W.A.* Austr.
173 M3 **Cambridgeshire** *admin. div. England* U.K.
256 E7 **Cambridge Springs** *PA* U.S.A.
249 G1 **Cambrien, Lac** *l. Que.* Can.
208 H5 **Cambrils** Spain
178 E2 **Cambrin** France
178 C3 **Cambron** France
207 M5 **Cambrón, Peña** *mt.* Spain
192 E3 **Cambs** Ger.
280 D5 **Cambuí** Brazil
231 D6 **Cambulo** Angola
231 C7 **Cambundi-Catembo** Angola
281 E4 **Cambuquira** Brazil
193 E8 **Camburg** Ger.
239 □[1c] **Cambuston** Réunion
274 A3 **Cambutal, Cerro** *mt.* Panama
133 F10 **Cam Co** *l. Xizang* China
236 I8 **Camdeboo National Park** *nat. park* S. Africa
105 M6 **Camden** *N.S.W.* Austr.
255 D9 **Camden** *AL* U.S.A.
261 I9 **Camden** *AR* U.S.A.
258 D6 **Camden** *DE* U.S.A.
257 □P4 **Camden** *ME* U.S.A.
255 I7 **Camden** *NC* U.S.A.
258 E5 **Camden** *NJ* U.S.A.
257 J5 **Camden** *NY* U.S.A.
256 A9 **Camden** *OH* U.S.A.
255 G8 **Camden** *SC* U.S.A.
261 K7 **Camden** *TN* U.S.A.
245 K1 **Camden Bay** *AK* U.S.A.
258 E5 **Camden County** *county NJ* U.S.A.
108 H3 **Camden Sound** *sea chan. W.A.* Austr.
260 I6 **Camdenton** *MO* U.S.A.
231 D7 **Cameia** Angola
231 D7 **Cameia, Parque Nacional da** *nat. park* Angola
172 C6 **Camelford** *Cornwall, England* U.K.
221 K5 **Çameli** Turkey
158 H5 **Camenca** Moldova
213 P8 **Camerano** Italy
215 K1 **Camerino** Italy
Camerinum Italy *see* **Camerino**
208 G6 **Camerles** Spain
265 U6 **Cameron** *AZ* U.S.A.
261 I11 **Cameron** *LA* U.S.A.
260 H6 **Cameron** *MO* U.S.A.
261 G10 **Cameron** *TX* U.S.A.
250 C4 **Cameron** *WI* U.S.A.
256 E9 **Cameron** *WV* U.S.A.
116 D2 **Cameron Highlands** *mts* Malaysia
246 G3 **Cameron Hills** *Y.T.* Can.
243 H2 **Cameron Island** *Nunavut* Can.
103 A13 **Cameron Mountains** *South I.* N.Z.
264 L3 **Cameron Park** *CA* U.S.A.
229 I5 **Cameroon** *country* Africa
229 H5 **Cameroon Highlands** *slope* Cameroon/Nigeria
215 O7 **Camerota** Italy
Caméroun *country* Africa *see* **Cameroon**
229 H5 **Cameroun, Mont** *vol.* Cameroon
171 K4 **Camerton** *Cumbria, England* U.K.
285 I5 **Camet** Arg.
275 I5 **Cametá** *Amazonas* Brazil
275 I5 **Cametá** *Pará* Brazil
106 C4 **Camfield** *r. N.T.* Austr.
151 D4 **Çam Geçidi** *pass* Turkey
221 I5 **Çamiçi** Turkey
215 L3 **Camicia, Monte** *mt.* Italy
221 I5 **Çamiçi Gölü** *l.* Turkey
114 C2 **Camiguin** *i.* Phil.
114 E7 **Camiguin** *i.* Phil.
150 D2 **Camili** Turkey
114 C4 **Camiling** *Luzon* Phil.
255 E10 **Camilla** *GA* U.S.A.
190 K4 **Camin** Ger.
276 C5 **Camiña** Chile
274 C4 **Caminha** Port.
204 H8 **Caminomorisco** Spain
206 F6 **Caminreal** Spain
278 D2 **Camiranga** Brazil
276 E5 **Camiri** Bol.
276 B2 **Camisea** Peru
276 B2 **Camisea** *r.* Peru
231 D7 **Camissombo** Angola
151 C5 **Çamlıca** Turkey
150 H1 **Çamlidere** Turkey
151 C4 **Çamlıhemşin** Turkey
151 D5 **Çamlıkale** Turkey
151 C5 **Çamlıkaya** Turkey
151 B5 **Çamlıkoz** Turkey
109 E12 **Camm, Lake** *salt flat W.A.* Austr.
216 F8 **Cammarata** *Sicilia* Italy
216 F8 **Cammarata, Monte** *mt. Sicilia* Italy
193 G6 **Cammer** Ger.
192 F3 **Cammin** Ger.
Cammin Pol. *see* **Kamień Pomorski**
278 E2 **Camocim** Brazil
169 J7 **Camolin** Ireland
178 D4 **Camon** France
212 I4 **Camonica, Val** *val.* Italy
106 G5 **Camooweal** *Qld* Austr.
106 G6 **Camooweal Caves National Park** *Qld* Austr.
275 H4 **Camopi** Brazil
207 J7 **Camorro Alto** *mt.* Spain
180 F6 **Camors** France
137 M8 **Camorta** *i. Andaman & Nicobar Is* India
158 E6 **Camotes Sea** *g.* Phil.
268 D5 **Camotlán de Miraflores** Mex.
169 H3 **Camowen** *r. Northern Ireland* U.K.
169 C8 **Camp** Ireland
213 K7 **Campagna** Italy
216 C8 **Campagnac** France
183 C8 **Campagnatico** Italy
214 G2 **Campagne** *Aquitaine* France
185 G8 **Campagne** *Aquitaine* France
185 G6 **Campagne-lès-Hesdin** France
178 C3 **Campamento** Hond.
266 □P10 **Campamento** Uru.
285 I2 **Campana** Arg.
285 H4 **Campana** Italy
217 L5 **Campana** Mex.
266 H4 **Campana** Uru.
285 I4 **Campana, Isla** *i.* Chile
283 B8 **Campanario** *mt.* Arg./Chile
284 B4 **Campanário** *Mato Grosso do Sul* Brazil
277 G5 **Campanário** *Minas Gerais* Brazil
281 G3 **Campanário** Madeira
206 □ **Campanario** Spain
206 H3 **Campanella, Punta** *pt* Italy
215 M6 **Campanha** Brazil
281 E4 **Campania** *admin. reg.* Italy
215 N5 **Campania Island** *B.C.* Can.
246 D4 **Campano** Spain
206 G3 **Campanquiz, Cerro** *hills* Peru
274 B6 **Camparredondo, Embalse de** *resr* Spain
205 K3 **Campaspe** *r. Qld* Austr.
107 K6 **Campaspero** Spain
205 L6 **Camp Bay** Gibraltar
207 □ **Campbell** S. Africa
236 H4 **Campbell** *CA* U.S.A.
264 K4 **Campbell** *OH* U.S.A.
256 E7 **Campbell, Cape** *South I.* N.Z.
103 I8 **Campbell, Mount** *hill N.T.* Austr.
106 C6 **Campbellford** *Ont.* Can.
248 E4 **Campbell Hill** *OH* U.S.A.
256 B8 **Campbell Island** Myanmar
119 D9 **Campbell Island** N.Z.
99 G6 **Campbell Lake** *N.W.T.* Can.
245 N1 **Campbell Lake** *N.W.T.* Can.
247 J2 **Campbell Plateau** *sea feature* S. Pacific Ocean
290 G9 **Campbell Range** *hills W.A.* Austr.
108 I3 **Campbell River** *B.C.* Can.
246 E5 **Campbell's Bay** *Que.* Can.
251 R5 **Campbellsport** *WI* U.S.A.
250 F6 **Campbellstown** *OH* U.S.A.
256 A9 **Campbellsville** *KY* U.S.A.
254 E7 **Campbellton** *N.B.* Can.
249 H4 **Campbelltown** *N.S.W.* Austr.
105 M6 **Campbell Town** *Tas.* Austr.
105 K9 **Campbelltown** *PA* U.S.A.
258 B4 **Campbeltown** *Argyll and Bute, Scotland* U.K.
168 E12 **Campbon** France
180 H7 **Camp Creek** *WV* U.S.A.
256 D11 **Campeador** Spain
208 J3 **Campeã** Port.
204 E6 **Campeche** Mex.
267 N8 **Campeche** *state* Mex.
267 N8 **Campeche, Bahía de** *g.* Mex.
269 N6 **Campechuela** Cuba
270 E3 **Campello sul Clitunne** Italy
215 J2 **Campelo** Port.
204 D9 **Campelos** Port.
206 A2 **Campénéac** France
180 G6
219 L4 **Câmpeni** Romania
105 I8 **Camperdown** *Vic.* Austr.
255 □[2] **Camperdown** *New Prov.* Bahamas
237 O5 **Camperdown** S. Africa
212 E4 **Campertogno** Italy
280 D4 **Campestre** Brazil
183 G9 **Campestre-et-Luc** France
250 C4 **Camp Hill** *PA* U.S.A.
254 C4 **Campia** *WI* U.S.A.
219 L4 **Câmpia Turzii** Romania
213 K8 **Campi Bisenzio** Italy
214 B8 **Campidano** *reg. Sardegna* Italy
214 F1 **Campiglia Marittima** Italy
212 D4 **Campiglia Soana** Italy
169 I8 **Campile** Ireland
206 C5 **Campilhas** *r.* Port.
206 B5 **Campilhas, Barragem de** *resr* Port.
205 Q9 **Campillo de Alto Buey** Spain
207 L5 **Campillo de Arenas** Spain
206 G5 **Campillo de Dueñas** Spain
206 H3 **Campillo de Llerena** Spain
207 J6 **Campillos** Spain
205 Q9 **Campillos-Paravientos** Spain
219 N5 **Câmpina** Romania
281 G3 **Campina** *reg.* Spain
207 I5 **Campinaçu** Brazil
278 C5 **Campina da Lagoa** Brazil
280 A6 **Campina Grande** Brazil
278 G3 **Campina Grande do Sul** Brazil
280 C6 **Campinas** Brazil
280 D5 **Campina Verde** Brazil
280 C3 **Campinho** Port.
206 E4 **Campisábalos** Spain
205 N6 **Campi Salentina** Italy
217 O3 **Campitello** *Corse* France
214 C2 **Campli** Italy
215 L2 **Camplong** *Timor* Indon.
115 C9 **Campo** Cameroon
229 H6 **Campo** *r.* Cameroon *see* **Ntem**
235 H3 **Campo** Moz.
204 D6 **Campo** Port.
208 F3 **Campo** Spain
229 H6 **Campo, Réserve de** *nature res.* Cameroon
274 C4 **Campoalegre** Col.
278 E4 **Campo Alegre de Lourdes** Brazil
215 N4 **Campobasso** Italy
215 N4 **Campobasso** *prov.* Italy
216 F9 **Campobello di Licata** *Sicilia* Italy
216 D8 **Campobello di Mazara** *Sicilia* Italy
257 □S4 **Campobello Island** *N.B.* Can.
281 E4 **Campo Belo** Brazil
279 C8 **Campo Belo do Sul** Brazil
213 L4 **Campodarsego** Italy
209 D12 **Campo de Cartagena, Canal del** Spain
205 J2 **Campo de Caso** Spain
207 M2 **Campo de Criptana** Spain
278 B4 **Campo de Diauarum** Brazil
212 F4 **Campo dei Fiori, Parco Regionale** *nature res.* Italy
214 B4 **Campo dell'Oro** *airport Corse* France
206 H4 **Campo de San Pedro** Spain
205 M6 **Campodimele** Italy
215 L5 **Campo di Trens** Italy
213 K3 **Campodolcino** Italy
212 G3 **Campo Erê** Brazil
279 B8 **Campo Esperanza** Para.
277 F5 **Campofelice di Roccella** *Sicilia* Italy
216 F8 **Campoformido** Italy
280 C3 **Campo Florido** Brazil
213 O3 **Campo Formoso** Brazil
278 E4 **Campofranco** *Sicilia* Italy
216 F8 **Campofrío** Spain
206 F5 **Campo Gallo** Arg.
282 E2 **Campo Grande** *Amazonas* Brazil
277 F2 **Campo Grande** *Mato Grosso do Sul* Brazil
279 B7 **Campolândia** Brazil
280 B2 **Campo Largo** Brazil
280 C6 **Campolato, Capo** *c. Sicilia* Italy
217 I9 **Campoli Appennino** Italy
215 L4 **Campo Ligure** Italy
212 F6 **Campolongo Maggiore** Italy
213 M5 **Campo Lugar** Spain
206 H2 **Campo Maior** Brazil
278 E3 **Campo Maior** Port.
206 E2 **Campo Mara** Venez.
270 H8 **Campomarino** *Molise* Italy
215 O4 **Campomarino** *Puglia* Italy
217 N3 **Campomoro, Punta di** *pt Corse* France
214 B4 **Campomorone** Italy
212 F6 **Campo Mourão** Brazil
280 A5 **Camponaraya** Spain
204 G3 **Campo Novo** Brazil
279 B8 **Campo Nuevo** Mex.
269 L8 **Campora San Giovanni** Italy
215 Q9 **Campo Real** Spain
205 N8 **Camporeale** *Sicilia* Italy
216 E8 **Campo Redondo** Port.
206 B5 **Camporgiano** Italy
212 I7 **Camporosso** Italy
212 D8 **Camporrobles** Spain
209 C8 **Campos** Brazil
281 G4 **Campos** Port.
204 E5 **Campos** Spain
209 L9 **Campos, Canal de** Spain
204 I5 **Campos, Tierra de** *reg.* Spain
205 J5 **Campos Altos** Brazil
280 D3 **Camposanto** Italy
213 K6 **Campos Belos** Brazil
278 C5 **Campos del Río** Spain
209 C11 **Campos do Jordão** Brazil
281 E5 **Campos Gerais** Brazil
281 E4 **Campos Novos Paulista** Brazil
280 C5 **Campos Sales** Brazil
278 E3 **Campotéjar** Spain
207 L6 **Campo Tencia** *mt.* Switz.
212 F3 **Campotosto** Italy
215 K2 **Campotosto, Lago di** *l.* Italy
215 K2 **Campo Troco** Col.
274 D3 **Campo Tures** Italy
213 L2 **Camp Point** *IL* U.S.A.
260 J5 **Camprodon** Spain
208 J3 **Campsie Fells** *hills Scotland* U.K.
170 I1 **Camps-la-Source** France
183 I10 **Camp Springs** *MD* U.S.A.
258 B7 **Campton** *KY* U.S.A.
256 B11 **Camptown** *Scottish Borders, Scotland* U.K.
168 K12 **Camptown** *PA* U.S.A.
258 C1 **Câmpulung** Romania
219 N5 **Câmpulung la Tisa** Romania
219 L3 **Câmpulung Moldovenesc** Romania
219 N3 **Campuya** Peru
274 C5 **Campuya** *r.* Peru
274 C5 **Camp Verde** *AZ* U.S.A.
265 U7 **Cam Ranh, Vinh** *b.* Vietnam
119 I9 **Cam Ranh Bay** Vietnam *see* **Cam Ranh, Vinh**
Camrose *Alta* Can.
246 H4 **Camrose** *Pembrokeshire, Wales* U.K.
172 B4 **Camsell Lake** *N.W.T.* Can.
247 I2 **Camsell Portage** *Sask.* Can.
247 I3 **Camsell Range** *mts N.W.T.* Can.
246 F2 **Camugnano** Italy
213 K7 **Camulodunum** *Essex, England* U.K. *see* **Colchester**
207 M2 **Camuñas** Spain
151 D6 **Çamurlu Dağ** *mt.* Turkey
150 E2 **Çamuzkışlası** Turkey
221 L5 **Çamyazı** Turkey
150 C2 **Çan** Turkey
221 I2 **Čaňa** Slovakia
199 K3 **Ca Na, Mui** *hd* Vietnam
119 I9 **Canaã** Brazil
281 F4 **Canaan** *r. N.S.* Can.
249 H5 **Canaan** Trin. and Tob.
271 □[5] **Canaan** *CT* U.S.A.
257 L6 **Canaan Peak** *UT* U.S.A.
265 U4 **Canabrava** Brazil
281 F2 **Cana Brava** *r.* Brazil
278 B3 **Cana Brava, Serra da** *hills* Brazil
281 H2 **Canabungan** *i.* Phil.
114 A7 **Canacona** *Goa* India
136 D5 **Canada** *country* N. America
242 J5
209 D10 **Canada** Spain
292 O1 **Canada Basin** *sea feat* Arctic Ocean
208 D6 **Cañada de Benatandu**
285 G3 **Cañada de Gómez** Ar
207 P2 **Cañada del Carrascal**
205 Q9 **Cañada del Hoyo** Spa
285 F2 **Cañada de Luque** Ar
257 □O3 **Canada Falls Lake** *MI*
284 C2 **Cañada Honda** Arg.
285 H3 **Cañada Nieto** Uru.
207 I5 **Cañada Rosal** Spain
285 G3 **Cañada Rosquín** Arg.
285 F4 **Cañada Seca** Arg.
258 E2 **Canadensis** *PA* U.S.A.
261 E8 **Canadian** *TX* U.S.A.
261 H8 **Canadian** *r.* U.S.A.
243 J4 **Canadian Shield** *reg. Ont./Que.* Can.
283 C8 **Cañadón de las Vacas**
283 C7 **Cañadón Grande, Sie**
275 F3 **Canaima, Parque Nac** *nat. park* Venez.
257 K6 **Canajoharie** *NY* U.S.A.
150 H1 **Çanakçı** Turkey
221 H2 **Çanakkale** Turkey
221 H2 **Çanakkale** *prov.* Turke
221 H2 **Çanakkale Boğazı** *str.*
285 I5 **Canal 1** Arg.
285 I5 **Canal 2** Arg.
285 I5 **Canal 9** Arg.
285 H5 **Canal 11** Arg.
285 H5 **Canal 12** Arg.
285 G4 **Canal 16** Arg.
100 □[5] **Canala** New Caledoni
214 C3 **Canale-di-Verde** *Corse*
284 D4 **Canalejas** Arg.
205 P8 **Canalejas del Arroyo**
205 L5 **Canalejas de Peñafiel**
246 H5 **Canal Flats** *B.C.* Can.
206 H4 **Canalizo** *hill* Spain
285 F3 **Canals** Arg.
185 G8 **Canals** France
209 D10 **Canals** Spain
213 L3 **Canàl San Bovo** Italy
256 C9 **Canal Winchester** *OH*
207 K4 **Cañamares** Spain
207 M3 **Cañamares** *r.* Spain
205 O7 **Cañamares** *r.* Spain
276 C2 **Canamari** Brazil
207 I2 **Cañamero** Spain
256 H6 **Canandaigua** *NY* U.S.A
256 H6 **Canandaigua Lake** *NY*
266 D2 **Cananea** Mex.
280 D6 **Cananéia** Brazil
276 D4 **Canapiare, Cerro** *hill* C
178 D3 **Canaples** France
280 C3 **Canápolis** Brazil
274 B5 **Cañar** Ecuador
274 B5 **Cañar** *prov.* Ecuador
278 B5 **Canarana** Brazil
214 C2 **Canari** *Corse* France
238 □[3] **Canarias, Islas** *is* N. Atlantic Ocean
Canarias, Islas *terr.* N. Atlantic Ocean *see* **Canary Islands**
271 □[3] **Canaries** St Lucia
213 L6 **Canaro** Italy
270 B3 **Canarreos, Archipiélag** *is* Cuba
Canary Islands *is* N. Atlantic Ocean *see* **Canarias, Islas**
238 □[3] **Canary Islands** *terr.* N. Atlantic Ocean
267 N8 **Canasayab** Mex.
204 E7 **Canas de Senhorim** Po
256 H6 **Canaseraga** *NY* U.S.A.
257 J5 **Canastota** *NY* U.S.A.
280 D3 **Canastra, Serra da** *mts*
268 C1 **Canatlán** Mex.
204 H9 **Cañaveral** Spain
255 G11 **Canaveral, Cape** *FL* U.
206 F4 **Cañaveral de León** Sp
255 G11 **Canaveral National Se** *nature res. FL* U.S.A.
205 P8 **Cañaveras** Spain
205 O8 **Cañaveruelas** Spain
212 C5 **Canavese** *reg.* Italy
281 H1 **Canavieiras** Brazil
266 □S13 **Cañazas** Panama
213 J3 **Canazei** Italy
105 K6 **Canbelego** *N.S.W.* Aust
105 L6 **Canberra** *A.C.T.* Austr.
262 D6 **Canby** *CA* U.S.A.
260 G3 **Canby** *MN* U.S.A.
180 H4 **Cancale** France
212 I2 **Cancano, Lago di** *l.* Ita
207 P4 **Cancarix** Spain
183 F6 **Cance** *r.* France
215 P4 **Cancellara** Italy
215 M5 **Cancello ed Arnone** It
206 F3 **Canchales, Embalse de** *resr* Spain
282 C2 **Canchas** Chile
178 C2 **Canche** *r.* France
228 A3 **Canchungo** Guinea-Bis
274 C6 **Canchyuaya, Cerros de**
208 E3 **Cancias** *mt.* Spain
185 F6 **Cancon** France
267 P7 **Cancún** Mex.
185 C10 **Candanchú** Spain
Çandar Turkey *see* **Kast**
276 C4 **Candarave** Peru
221 H4 **Çandarlı** Turkey
204 I1 **Candás** Spain
208 B4 **Candasnos** Spain
181 I6 **Candé** France
219 O8 **Candeias** Brazil
281 E4 **Candeias** Brazil
276 E2 **Candeias** *r.* Brazil
215 P5 **Candela** Italy
267 I4 **Candela** Mex.
261 E12 **Candela** *r.* Mex.
282 G2 **Candelaria** *Misiones* Ar
282 D2 **Candelaria** *Salta* Arg.
284 E3 **Candelaria** *San Luis* Ar
238 □[3e] **Candelaria** *Pico* Azores
238 □[3b] **Candelária** *São Miguel*
238 □[3a] **Candelaria** *Tenerife* Can
266 □O10 **Candelaria** Hond.
266 O10 **Candelaria** *Campeche* M
266 F2 **Candelaria** *Chihuahua* M
275 E3 **Candelaria** Venez.
269 K10 **Candelaria Loxicha** Me
204 I8 **Candelario** Spain
204 I8 **Candelario, Sierra de** *m*
215 P4 **Candelaro** *r.* Italy
205 J8 **Candeleda** Spain
105 L7 **Candelo** *N.S.W.* Austr.
212 E4 **Candelo** Italy
204 C5 **Candemil** Port.
Candia *Kriti* Greece *see* **Irakleio**
212 F5 **Candia Lomellina** Italy
278 B6 **Cândido de Abreu** Braz
278 D2 **Cândido Mendes** Brazi
280 B5 **Cândido Mota** Brazil
204 D1 **Candieira, Punta** *pt* Sp
213 N8 **Candigliano** *r.* Italy
204 D3 **Candín** Spain
148 F3 **Çandır** Turkey
244 G2 **Candle** *AK* U.S.A.
247 J4 **Candle Lake** *Sask.* Can.
247 J4 **Candle Lake** *l. Sask.* Ca
273 G7 **Candlemas Island** *S.* Sa
259 I1 **Candlewood, Lake** *CT* U
259 I1 **Candlewood Isle** *CT* U.S
259 I2 **Candlewood Knolls** *CT*
260 F1 **Cando** *ND* U.S.A.
114 C3 **Candon** *Luzon* Phil.
114 C3 **Candon Point** *Luzon* Ph
206 G7 **Candor, Punta** *pt* Spain
237 P3 **Candover** S. Africa
219 L5 **Cândrelu, Vârful** *mt.* Ro
108 C6 **Cane** *r. W.A.* Austr.
219 G9 **Cane, Monte** *hill* Italy
Canea *Kriti* Greece *see* **C**
206 A3 **Canecas** Port.
204 D6 **Canedo** Port.
208 G2 **Canejan** Spain
185 C6 **Canéjean** France
184 B2 **Canela Alta** Chile
284 B2 **Canela Baja** Chile

Canelles, Embassament de resr Spain
Canelli Italy
Canelones Uru.
Canelones dept Uru.
Canelos Ecuador
Canepina Italy
Cane River Conservation Park res. Australia
Canero Spain
Canet Languedoc-Roussillon France
Canet Languedoc-Roussillon France
Canet, Étang de lag. France
Canet de Mar Spain
Cañete Chile
Cañete Spain
Cañete de las Torres Spain
Cañete la Real Spain
Canet-en-Roussillon France
Canet lo Roig Spain
Canet-Plage France
Caney KS U.S.A.
Caney r. KS U.S.A.
Canfranc, Valle de val. Spain
Canfranc-Estación Spain
Cangalha Brazil
Cangallo Arg.
Cangallo Peru
Cangamba Angola
Cängan Azer.
Cangandala Angola
Cangandala, Parque Nacional de nat. park Angola
Çangarâfa Maur.
Cangas Spain
Cangas del Narcea Spain
Cangas de Onís Spain
Cangialoso, Pizzo mt. Italy
Cân Giuôc Vietnam
Canglun Malaysia see Changlun
Cangoa Angola
Cango Caves S. Africa
Cangola Angola
Cangombe Angola
Cangrejito, Punta del pt Fuerteventura Canary Is
Cangshan Shandong China
Canguaretama Brazil
Canguçu Brazil
Canguçu, Serra do hills Brazil
Canguenjo, Serra mts Angola
Cangumbe Angola
Cangxi Sichuan China
Cangyuan Yunnan China
Cangzhou Hebei China
Canha Port.
Canha r. Port.
Canhas Madeira
Canhestros Port.
Caniac-du-Causse France
Caniapiscau Que. Can.
Caniapiscau r. Que. Can.
Caniapiscau, Réservoir de l. Que. Can.
Caniçada, Barragem da resr Port.
Caniçado Moz. see Guija
Caniçal Madeira
Canicattì Sicilia Italy
Canicattini Bagni Sicilia Italy
Caniço Madeira
Canicosa de la Sierra Spain
Canigao Channel Phil.
Canigou, Pic du mt. France
Caniles Spain
Canillas de Aceituno Spain
Canillo Andorra
Canim Lake B.C. Can.
Canim Lake l. B.C. Can.
Canindé Amazonas Brazil
Canindé Ceará Brazil
Canindé Pará Brazil
Canino Italy
Canipo i. Phil.
Canisp hill Scotland U.K.
Canisteo NY U.S.A.
Canisteo r. NY U.S.A.
Canisteo Peninsula Antarctica
Canister Falls Guyana
Canisy France
Cañitas de Felipe Pescador Mex.
Cañizal Spain
Cañizares Spain
Cañizo Spain
Canjáyar Spain
Canjilon NM U.S.A.
Çankırı Turkey
Cankova Slovenia
Cankuzo Burundi
Canlaon Negros Phil.
Canna W.A. Austr.
Canna r. Italy
Canna i. Scotland U.K.
Canna, Sound of sea chan. Scotland U.K.
Cannanore India see Kannur
Cannanore Islands Lakshadweep India
Cannara Italy
Canne r. France
Canne r. Sicilia Italy
Cannero Riviera Italy
Cannes France
Canneto Isole Lipari Italy
Canneto Toscana Italy
Canneto sull'Oglio Italy
Cannich Highland, Scotland U.K.
Canning r. AK U.S.A.
Canning Hill W.A. Austr.
Canningstown Ireland
Cannington Somerset, England U.K.
Cannobio Italy
Cannock Staffordshire, England U.K.
Cannock Chase reg. England U.K.
Cannon r. MN U.S.A.
Cannonball r. ND U.S.A.
Cannon Beach OR U.S.A.
Cannondale CT U.S.A.
Cannoniers Point Mauritius
Cannon Rocks S. Africa
Cannonsburg KY U.S.A.
Cannonvale Qld Austr.
Cann River Vic. Austr.
Cano Port.
Canoa Ecuador
Canoas Brazil
Caño Colorado Col.
Caño Colorado Venez.
Canoeiros Brazil
Canoe Lake Sask. Can.
Canoe Lake l. Sask. Can.
Canohès France
Canoinhas Brazil
Canolo Italy
Canonbie Dumfries and Galloway, Scotland U.K.
Canon City CO U.S.A.
Cañón del Río Blanco, Parque Nacional nat. park Mex.
Cañón del Sumidero, Parque Nacional nat. park Mex.
Cañon Largo watercourse NM U.S.A.
Canoochia r. GA U.S.A.
Canoona Qld Austr.
Canopus S.A. Austr.
Canora Sask. Can.
Caño Riecito Venez.
Canosa di Puglia Italy
Canouan i. St Vincent
Canowindra N.S.W. Austr.
Can Pastilla Spain
Can Picafort Spain
Canredondo Spain
Cansado Western Sahara
Cansano Italy
Canso N.S. Can.
Canso, Cape N.S. Can.
Canso, Strait of N.S. Can.
Canta Peru

205 L2 Cantabria aut. comm. Spain
Cantabrian Mountains Spain see Cantábrica, Cordillera
Cantabrian Sea Spain see Cantábrico, Mar
204 L2 Cantábrica, Cordillera mts Spain
204 G1 Cantábrico, Mar sea Spain
213 K7 Cantagallo Italy
275 G6 Cantagalo Brazil
183 B6 Cantal dept France
205 J6 Cantalapiedra Spain
205 M6 Cantalejo Spain
215 J3 Cantalice Italy
205 N6 Cantalojas Spain
205 J6 Cantalpino Spain
204 C8 Cantanhede Port.
284 D3 Cantantal Arg.
208 E6 Cantavieja Spain
199 I6 Čantavir Vojvodina Serbia
178 B5 Canteleu France
185 B7 Canteloupe r. France
219 Q4 Cantemir Cantemir Moldova
158 H7 Cantemir admin. dist. Moldova
184 C5 Cantenac France
209 C12 Canteras Spain
207 O2 Canteras hill Spain
249 H4 Canterbury N.B. Can.
103 G10 Canterbury admin. reg. South I. N.Z.
173 O5 Canterbury Kent, England U.K.
103 F11 Canterbury Bight b. South I. N.Z.
103 F10 Canterbury Plains South I. N.Z.
215 K4 Canterno, Lago di l. Italy
119 G9 Cân Thơ Vietnam
213 N9 Cantiano Italy
264 O6 Cantil CA U.S.A.
114 E7 Cantilan Mindanao Phil.
206 H5 Cantillana Spain
205 L6 Cantimpalos Spain
278 E4 Canto do Buriti Brazil
212 C5 Cantoira Italy
Canton Guangdong China see Guangzhou
172 F5 Canton Cardiff, Wales U.K.
255 E8 Canton GA U.S.A.
250 D9 Canton IL U.S.A.
260 J5 Canton MO U.S.A.
261 K9 Canton MS U.S.A.
258 E6 Canton NJ U.S.A.
257 J4 Canton NY U.S.A.
256 D8 Canton OH U.S.A.
251 R8 Canton PA U.S.A.
260 G4 Canton SD U.S.A.
261 H9 Canton TX U.S.A.
250 C4 Canton WI U.S.A.
Canton Island atoll Phoenix Is Kiribati see Kanton
207 O6 Cantoria Spain
207 J2 Cantos Negros hill Spain
280 A6 Cantu r. Brazil
212 G4 Cantù Italy
280 B6 Cantu, Serra do hills Brazil
Cantuaria Kent, England U.K. see Canterbury
245 J3 Cantwell AK U.S.A.
277 F1 Canudos Amazonas Brazil
278 F4 Canudos Bahia Brazil
285 H4 Cañuelas Arg.
275 F6 Canumã Amazonas Brazil
275 G6 Canumã Amazonas Brazil
104 H7 Canunda National Park S.A. Austr.
Canusium Italy see Canosa di Puglia
275 E6 Canutama Brazil
261 C12 Canutillo Mex.
103 H8 Canvastown South I. N.Z.
173 N4 Canvey Island Essex, England U.K.
247 J4 Canwood Sask. Can.
235 G3 Canxixe Moz.
181 M2 Cany-Barville France
209 D9 Cànyoles r. Spain
261 E8 Canyon TX U.S.A.
245 M3 Canyon (abandoned) Y.T. Can.
262 E4 Canyon City OR U.S.A.
264 K2 Canyon Creek r. CA U.S.A.
264 K1 Canyondam CA U.S.A.
265 W5 Canyon de Chelly National Monument nat. park AZ U.S.A.
262 I3 Canyon Ferry Lake MT U.S.A.
265 U8 Canyon Lake AZ U.S.A.
265 W3 Canyonlands National Park UT U.S.A.
245 P3 Canyon Ranges mts N.W.T. Can.
262 C5 Canyonville OR U.S.A.
231 D6 Canzar Angola
118 H3 Cao Băng Vietnam
Caocheng Shandong China see Caoxian
128 G8 Cao Daban Qinghai China
Caohai Guizhou China see Weining
Caohe Hubei China see Qichun
123 D8 Cao He r. China
132 G6 Caohu Xinjiang China
132 G6 Caohu Xinjiang China
Caojiahe Hubei China see Qichun
130 B6 Caojian Yunnan China
168 C9 Caolas Argyll and Bute, Scotland U.K.
Caolas Scalpaigh Western Isles, Scotland U.K. see Kyles Scalpay
168 E11 Caolisport, Loch inlet Scotland U.K.
231 C7 Caombo Angola
213 L3 Caorame r. Italy
213 N4 Caorle Italy
129 N9 Caoxian Shandong China
Caozhou Shandong China see Heze
114 C9 Cap i. Phil.
239 □1b Cap, Baie du b. Mauritius
271 □3 Cap, Pointe du pt St Lucia
251 L6 Capac MI U.S.A.
215 O7 Capaccio Italy
215 P5 Capacciotti, Lago di l. Italy
216 E7 Capaci Sicilia Italy
270 G4 Cap-à-Foux c. Haiti
231 D7 Capaia Angola
Çapakçur Turkey see Bingöl
214 G3 Capalbio Italy
199 L5 Căpâlna Romania
115 D4 Capalulu, Selat sea chan. Indon.
274 D5 Capana Brazil
274 E3 Capanaparo r. Venez.
278 D2 Capanema Brazil
214 E2 Capanne, Monte mt. Italy
212 F6 Capanne di Marcarolo, Parco Naturale delle nature res. Italy
213 J8 Capannoli Italy
213 J8 Capannori Italy
280 C6 Capão Bonito Brazil
281 G4 Caparaó, Serra do mts Brazil
206 A3 Caparica Port.
274 D3 Caparo r. Venez.
204 D7 Caparrosa Port.
205 Q4 Caparroso Spain
114 C4 Capas Luzon Phil.
219 L5 Căpățânii, Munții mts Romania
274 D2 Capatárida Venez.
249 I4 Cap-aux-Meules Que. Can.
209 E9 Cap-Blanc Spain
185 B8 Capbreton France
249 H3 Cap-Chat Que. Can.
185 I10 Capcir reg. France
183 D10 Cap d'Agde France
208 □ Cap d'Artrutx Spain
249 F4 Cap-de-la-Madeleine Que. Can.
185 I6 Capdenac France
185 I6 Capdenac-Gare France
208 □ Cap d'en Font Spain
209 L8 Capdepera Spain
107 K6 Cape r. Qld Austr.
109 G12 Cape Arid National Park W.A. Austr.
Cape Bald N.B. Can. see Cap-Pelé
105 L9 Cape Barren Island Tas. Austr.
288 J8 Cape Basin sea feature S. Atlantic Ocean
104 F6 Cape Borda S.A. Austr.
108 I3 Cape Bougainville Aboriginal Reserve W.A. Austr.
249 I4 Cape Breton Highlands National Park N.S. Can.

249 I4 Cape Breton Island N.S. Can.
249 K2 Cape Charles Nfld and Lab. Can.
257 I11 Cape Charles VA U.S.A.
228 E5 Cape Coast Ghana
Cape Coast Castle Ghana see Cape Coast
257 O7 Cape Cod Bay MA U.S.A.
257 O7 Cape Cod Canal MA U.S.A.
257 P7 Cape Cod National Seashore nature res. MA U.S.A.
255 F12 Cape Coral FL U.S.A.
106 E4 Cape Crawford N.T. Austr.
251 M5 Cape Croker Ont. Can.
243 K3 Cape Dorset Nunavut Can.
257 □O5 Cape Elizabeth ME U.S.A.
245 N4 Cape Fanshaw AK U.S.A.
255 I8 Cape Fear r. NC U.S.A.
104 F6 Cape Gantheaume Conservation Park nature res. S.A. Austr.
249 I4 Cape George N.S. Can.
261 K7 Cape Girardeau MO U.S.A.
Cape Juby Morocco see Tarfaya
244 G2 Cape Krusenstern National Monument nat. park AK U.S.A.
109 C12 Capel W.A. Austr.
173 M5 Capel Kent, England U.K.
173 L5 Capel Surrey, England U.K.
280 A3 Capela Brazil
238 □1b Capelas São Miguel Azores
172 E1 Capel Curig Conwy, Wales U.K.
109 G12 Cape Le Grand National Park W.A. Austr.
281 F2 Capelinha Brazil
238 □1c Capelinhos, Ponta dos pt Faial Azores
206 E3 Capelins Port.
107 L7 Capella Qld Austr.
186 G5 Capelle aan de IJssel Neth.
173 O5 Capel le Ferne Kent, England U.K.
187 J9 Capellen Lux.
238 □1c Capelo Faial Azores
108 □2 Capelok, Pulu i. Cocos Is
231 B8 Capelongo Huíla Angola
Capelongo Huíla Angola see Kuvango
214 F3 Capel Rosso, Punta del Italy
173 O3 Capel St Mary Suffolk, England U.K.
258 F7 Cape May NJ U.S.A.
258 F6 Cape May County county NJ U.S.A.
258 F6 Cape May Court House NJ U.S.A.
258 F7 Cape May Point NJ U.S.A.
258 F7 Cape May Point pt NJ U.S.A.
107 J3 Cape Melville National Park Qld Austr.
231 C7 Capenda-Camulemba Angola
185 J9 Capendu France
107 L6 Cape Palmerston National Park Qld Austr.
108 B7 Cape Range hills W.A. Austr.
108 B7 Cape Range National Park W.A. Austr.
255 H9 Cape Romain National Wildlife Refuge nature res. SC U.S.A.
249 H5 Cape Sable Island N.S. Can.
249 J3 Cape St George Nfld and Lab. Can.
246 D5 Cape Scott Provincial Park B.C. Can.
183 C10 Capestang France
271 □2 Capesterre Guadeloupe
215 L3 Capestrano Italy
236 C9 Cape Town S. Africa
107 J3 Cape Tribulation National Park Qld Austr.
107 K5 Cape Upstart National Park Qld Austr.
228 □ Cape Verde country N. Atlantic Ocean
288 G5 Cape Verde Basin sea feature N. Atlantic Ocean
288 G4 Cape Verde Plateau sea feature N. Atlantic Ocean
257 I4 Cape Vincent NY U.S.A.
249 H4 Cape Wolfe P.E.I. Can.
245 L3 Cape Yakataga AK U.S.A.
107 I2 Cape York Peninsula Qld Austr.
185 B6 Cap Ferret France
270 G4 Cap-Haïtien Haiti
274 E4 Capibara Venez.
231 C8 Capico Angola
209 F7 Capicorp, Punta de pt Spain
207 M7 Capileira Spain
207 I3 Capilla Spain
268 E5 Capilla de Guadalupe Mex.
284 E2 Capilla del Monte Arg.
285 H4 Capilla del Señor Arg.
278 D2 Capim Brazil
278 C2 Capim r. Brazil
204 F8 Capinha Port.
280 C3 Capinópolis Brazil
276 D4 Capinota Bol.
215 K4 Capistrello Italy
263 L10 Capitan NM U.S.A.
285 G3 Capitán Bermudez Arg.
284 A6 Capitán Pastene Chile
285 H4 Capitán Sarmiento Arg.
281 F2 Capitão Enéas Brazil
275 F6 Capitari Brazil
258 D6 Capitol Park DE U.S.A.
265 U3 Capitol Reef National Park UT U.S.A.
280 B5 Capivara, Represa resr Brazil
280 D5 Capivari Brazil
278 F5 Capivari r. Bahia Brazil
280 D5 Capivari r. São Paulo Brazil
278 E4 Capixaba Brazil
216 G8 Capizzi Sicilia Italy
199 L4 Căpleni Romania
210 F4 Čapljina Bos.-Herz.
208 I3 Cap Llitzet mt. Spain
114 C6 Capnoyan i. Phil.
235 G2 Capoche r. Moz./Zambia
214 H2 Capodimonte Italy
212 I3 Capo di Ponte Italy
215 M6 Capodochino airport Italy
216 H7 Capo d'Orlando Sicilia Italy
275 G6 Capoeira Brazil
275 G6 Capoeiras, Cachoeira das waterfall Brazil
214 E2 Capoliveri Italy
213 L8 Capolona Italy
217 I10 Capo Passero, Isola i. Sicilia Italy
215 O6 Caposele Italy
214 B9 Capoterra Sardegna Italy
185 H10 Capoulet France
215 K3 Cappadocia Italy
169 E7 Cappagh Ireland
169 F7 Cappagh White Ireland
169 F7 Cappamore Ireland
169 E9 Cappeen Ireland
190 G3 Cappel Ger.
249 H4 Cap-Pelé N.B. Can.
215 M3 Cappelle sul Tavo Italy
190 F5 Cappeln (Oldenburg) Ger.
168 J12 Capplegill Dumfries and Galloway, Scotland U.K.
169 G8 Cappoquin Ireland
214 D9 Cappuccini, Punta dei pt Sardegna Italy
215 M4 Capracotta Italy
214 D1 Capraia, Isola di i. Italy
215 P3 Capraia, Isole is Italy
214 D1 Capraia Isola Italy
214 I3 Capranica Italy
214 A5 Caprara, Punta pt Sardegna Italy
214 I3 Caprarola Italy
214 C5 Caprera, Isola i. Sardegna Italy
215 M6 Capri Italy
215 M6 Capri, Isola di i. Italy
215 M5 Capriati a Volturno Italy
107 M7 Capricorn, Cape Qld Austr.
107 M7 Capricorn Channel Qld Austr.
107 N7 Capricorn Group atolls Qld Austr.
212 G4 Caprino Bergamasco Italy
213 J4 Caprino Veronese Italy
234 D3 Caprivi admin. reg. Namibia
Capsa Tunisia see Gafsa
264 □F14 Captain Cook HI U.S.A.
185 D7 Captieux France
256 E9 Captina r. OH U.S.A.
215 M5 Capua Italy
280 D6 Capuava Brazil

271 □2 Capucin, Cape Dominica
239 □2b Capucin Rock i. Mahé Seychelles
239 □2b Capucins, Pointe pt Mahé Seychelles
269 H6 Capulhuac Mex.
268 G4 Capulín Mex.
231 C8 Capuna Angola
231 B8 Capunda Cavilongo Angola
231 D9 Caputene Angola
193 G6 Caputh Ger.
168 J9 Caputh Perth and Kinross, Scotland U.K.
185 E9 Capvern-les-Bains France
274 C4 Caquetá dept Col.
274 D5 Caquetá r. Col.
274 C3 Cáqueza Col.
205 N8 Carabaña Spain
114 C5 Carabao i. Phil.
276 C3 Carabaya, Cordillera de mts Peru
285 G4 Carabelas Arg.
275 F5 Carabinani r. Brazil
274 E2 Carabobo state Venez.
219 M6 Caracal Romania
275 F4 Caracarai Brazil
274 E2 Caracas Venez.
271 □10 Caracas Baai b. Curaçao Neth. Antilles
277 F5 Caracol Mato Grosso do Sul Brazil
278 E4 Caracol Piauí Brazil
276 D2 Caracol Rondônia Brazil
270 G8 Caracolí Col.
276 D4 Caracollo Bol.
268 F6 Carácuaro Mex.
207 K3 Caracuel de Calatrava Spain
114 F8 Caraga Mindanao Phil.
105 K5 Caragabal N.S.W. Austr.
169 C8 Caragh, Lough l. Ireland
212 C7 Caraglio Italy
281 E5 Caraguatatuba Brazil
283 B5 Carahue Chile
281 G2 Caraí Brazil
169 K1 Cara Island Scotland U.K.
281 H2 Caraiva Brazil
275 H6 Carajari Brazil
275 I6 Carajás, Serra dos hills Brazil
Carales Sardegna Italy see Cagliari
Caralis Sardegna Italy see Cagliari
Caralps Spain see Queralbs
185 H8 Caraman France
215 M3 Caramanico Terme Italy
207 P5 Caramel r. Spain
114 D5 Caramoan Peninsula Luzon Phil.
204 D7 Caramulo Port.
204 D7 Caramulo mt. Port.
204 D8 Caramulo, Serra do mts Port.
277 F3 Caraná r. Brazil
276 D3 Caranavi Bol.
284 E5 Carancho Arg.
199 L5 Cărand Romania
281 F4 Carandaí Brazil
277 E5 Carandaiti Bol.
277 F4 Carandazal Brazil
204 H2 Caranga Spain
281 F4 Carangola Brazil
204 C9 Caranguejeira Port.
219 K5 Caransebeș Romania
180 D4 Carantec France
185 F10 Carants, Tuc de les mt. Spain
275 I5 Carapajó Brazil
274 C5 Cara Paraná r. Col.
277 F6 Carapeguá Para.
215 P5 Carapelle Italy
215 P5 Carapelle r. Italy
215 P5 Carapellotto r. Italy
104 F5 Carappee Hill S.A. Austr.
249 H4 Caraquet N.B. Can.
274 C3 Carare r. Col.
212 G7 Carasco Italy
219 J5 Carașova Romania
199 L4 Carastelec Romania
116 F6 Carat, Tanjung pt Indon.
266 □R10 Caratasca Hond.
266 □R10 Caratasca, Laguna de lag. Hond.
281 F3 Caratinga Brazil
274 D5 Caratué r. Col.
257 □P3 Caratunk ME U.S.A.
274 E6 Carauari Brazil
278 F3 Caraúbas Brazil
Carauná mt. Brazil see Grande, Serra
207 P4 Caravaca de la Cruz Spain
212 H5 Caravaggio Italy
281 H2 Caravelas Brazil
276 B3 Caravelí Peru
271 □3 Caravelle, Presqu'île de la pen. Martinique
269 J1 Carbajal Mex.
204 I5 Carbajales de Alba Spain
204 D4 Carballeda de Avia Spain
204 C2 Carballo Galicia Spain
204 E4 Carballo Galicia Spain
204 H6 Carbellino Spain
247 L5 Carberry Man. Can.
285 H3 Carbo Arg.
266 D3 Carbó Mex.
216 D8 Carboi r. Sicilia Italy
283 C8 Carbón, Laguna del l. Arg.
214 D9 Carbonara, Capo c. Sardegna Italy
214 C9 Carbonara, Golfo di b. Sardegna Italy
216 G8 Carbonara, Pizzo mt. Italy
185 D6 Carbon-Blanc France
258 D3 Carbon County county PA U.S.A.
263 K7 Carbondale CO U.S.A.
261 K7 Carbondale IL U.S.A.
258 D1 Carbondale PA U.S.A.
249 K4 Carbonear Nfld and Lab. Can.
205 O5 Carbonera de Frentes Spain
269 J1 Carboneras Mex.
207 P7 Carboneras Spain
205 Q9 Carboneras de Guadazaón Spain
205 L6 Carbonero El Mayor Spain
207 L4 Carboneros Spain
214 B9 Carbonia Sardegna Italy
214 B9 Carbonia-Iglesias prov. Sardegna Italy
213 M2 Carbonìn Italy
281 F2 Carbonita Brazil
185 G9 Carbonne France
168 D8 Carbost Highland, Scotland U.K.
168 D8 Carbost Highland, Scotland U.K.
169 I6 Carbury Ireland
204 H8 Carcaboso Spain
207 K6 Carcabuey Spain
209 E9 Carcaixent Spain
246 G3 Carcajou Alta Can.
245 O2 Carcajou r. N.W.T. Can.
219 Q5 Carcaliu Romania
184 B5 Carcans France
184 B5 Carcans-Plage France
204 G5 Carção Port.
114 D6 Carcar Cebu Phil.
285 G3 Carcaraña r. Arg.
212 E7 Carcare Italy
185 I9 Carcassonne France
205 R4 Carcastillo Spain
209 C9 Carcelén Spain
183 I10 Carcès France
209 C11 Carche, Sierra del mts Spain
207 L5 Carchelejo Spain
274 B4 Carchi prov. Ecuador
212 E4 Carcoforo Italy
171 O6 Carcroft South Yorkshire, England U.K.
245 N3 Carcross Y.T. Can.
185 H6 Cardaillac France
221 H2 Çardak Çanakkale Turkey
221 K5 Çardak Denizli Turkey
285 I4 Cardal Uru.
Cardamomes, Chaîne des mts Cambodia see Cardamom Range
136 E7 Cardamom Hills India
118 F8 Cardamom Range mts Cambodia
208 J4 Cardedeu Spain
214 D8 Cardedu Sardegna Italy
207 K4 Cardeña Spain
205 M4 Cardeñadijo Spain
270 C2 Cárdenas Cuba
269 H3 Cárdenas San Luis Potosí Mex.
267 M8 Cárdenas Tabasco Mex.
205 Q9 Cardenete Spain
205 K7 Cardeñosa Spain

105 I3 Cardenyabba watercourse N.S.W. Austr.
217 J7 Cardeto Italy
Çardi Turkey see Harmancık
283 C8 Cardiel, Lago l. Arg.
172 F5 Cardiff Cardiff, Wales U.K.
172 F4 Cardiff admin. div. Wales U.K.
258 C5 Cardiff MD U.S.A.
172 F5 Cardiff International airport Wales U.K.
172 C3 Cardigan Ceredigion, Wales U.K.
172 C2 Cardigan Bay Wales U.K.
204 D9 Cardigos Port.
257 J4 Cardinal Ont. Can.
217 K6 Cardinale Italy
246 G3 Cardinal Lake Alta Can.
256 C8 Cardington OH U.S.A.
215 L4 Cardito Italy
238 □3b Cardón hill Fuerteventura Canary Is
266 C4 Cardón, Cerro hill Mex.
208 I4 Cardona Spain
285 I3 Cardona Uru.
269 H5 Cardonal Mex.
208 I4 Cardoner r. Spain
268 B1 Cardos Mex.
280 C4 Cardoso Brazil
280 D6 Cardoso, Ilha do i. Brazil
103 D11 Cardrona South I. N.Z.
103 C11 Cardrona, Mount South I. N.Z.
168 G11 Cardross Argyll and Bute, Scotland U.K.
246 H5 Cardston Alta Can.
107 K5 Cardwell Qld Austr.
281 E5 Careaçu Brazil
247 I3 Careen Lake Sask. Can.
213 K4 Carega, Cima mt. Italy
219 K3 Carei Romania
199 L4 Careilor, Câmpia plain Romania
275 G5 Careiro Brazil
275 F5 Careiro do Castanho Brazil
284 B2 Carén Coquimbo Chile
284 B2 Carén Coquimbo Chile
205 Q6 Carenas Spain
180 I3 Carentan France
180 G6 Carentoir France
205 K2 Cares r. Spain
201 O7 Carevdar Croatia
256 B8 Carey OH U.S.A.
109 G10 Carey, Lake salt flat W.A. Austr.
109 C8 Carey Downs W.A. Austr.
247 K2 Carey Lake N.W.T. Can.
239 □1 Cargados Carajos Islands Mauritius
168 I12 Cargenbridge Dumfries and Galloway, Scotland U.K.
214 B3 Cargèse Corse France
180 D5 Carhaix-Plouguer France
276 A2 Carhuamayo Peru
285 F5 Carhué Arg.
204 F8 Caria Port.
278 F4 Cariacá r. Brazil
281 G4 Cariacica Brazil
271 L8 Cariaco Venez.
271 K8 Cariaco, Golfo de b. Venez.
274 B6 Cariamanga Ecuador
231 B7 Cariango Angola
217 L5 Cariati Italy
270 B4 Caribbean Sea N. Atlantic Ocean
246 F4 Cariboo Mountains B.C. Can.
246 F4 Cariboo Mountains Provincial Park B.C. Can.
247 M3 Caribou r. Man. Can.
245 P3 Caribou r. N.W.T. Can.
245 N2 Caribou r. Y.T. Can.
245 K2 Caribou AK U.S.A.
257 □Q2 Caribou ME U.S.A.
250 I2 Caribou Island Ont. Can.
246 H2 Caribou Islands N.W.T. Can.
248 B3 Caribou Lake Ont. Can.
246 H3 Caribou Mountains Alta Can.
271 □2 Carib Point Dominica
266 F4 Carichic Mex.
114 E6 Carigara Leyte Phil.
114 E6 Carigara Bay Leyte Phil.
179 J4 Carignan France
212 D6 Carignano Italy
105 K4 Carinda N.S.W. Austr.
208 C5 Cariñena Spain
208 C5 Cariñena, Campo de reg. Spain
278 E5 Carinhanha Brazil
278 E5 Carinhanha r. Brazil
216 E7 Carini Sicilia Italy
168 B7 Carinish Western Isles, Scotland U.K.
204 E1 Cariño Spain
215 L5 Carinola Italy
Carinthia land Austria see Kärnten
231 D8 Caripande Angola
278 D4 Cariparé Brazil
275 F2 Caripe Venez.
275 F2 Caripito Venez.
278 E3 Cariris Novos, Serra dos hills Brazil
275 F2 Caris r. Venez.
212 E5 Carisio Italy
213 J3 Carisolo Italy
277 E2 Caritianas Brazil
199 L6 Cârjiți Romania
169 G3 Cark Mountain hill Ireland
185 G9 Carla-Bayle France
Carlabhagh Scotland U.K. see Carloway
Carlabhagh Western Isles, Scotland U.K. see Carloway
169 I3 Carland Northern Ireland U.K.
169 I5 Carlanstown Ireland
215 N4 Carlantino Italy
183 B7 Carlat France
217 I9 Carlentini Sicilia Italy
209 D9 Carlet Spain
251 K7 Carleton MI U.S.A.
249 H4 Carleton, Mount hill N.B. Can.
248 E4 Carleton Place Ont. Can.
237 L2 Carletonville S. Africa
219 N3 Cârlibaba Romania
262 F6 Carlin NV U.S.A.
108 E6 Carlindie Aboriginal Reserve W.A. Austr.
179 M5 Carling France
169 J4 Carlingford Ireland
169 J4 Carlingford Lough inlet Ireland/U.K.
260 K6 Carlinville IL U.S.A.
171 L4 Carlisle Cumbria, England U.K.
256 A10 Carlisle KY U.S.A.
257 K6 Carlisle NY U.S.A.
251 Q9 Carlisle PA U.S.A.
271 □4 Carlisle Bay Barbados
237 K9 Carlisle Bridge S. Africa
109 I10 Carlisle Lakes salt flat W.A. Austr.
258 A4 Carlisle Springs PA U.S.A.
185 H10 Carlit, Pic mt. France
214 A9 Carloforte Sardegna Italy
217 K5 Carlopoli Italy
280 C5 Carlópolis Brazil
168 J11 Carlops Scottish Borders, Scotland U.K.
269 L7 Carlos A. Carrillo Mex.
269 N8 Carlos A. Madrazo Mex.
285 G4 Carlos Casares Arg.
281 G2 Carlos Chagas Brazil
285 I3 Carlos Reyles Uru.
285 G4 Carlos Salas Arg.
285 F4 Carlos Tejedor Arg.
190 K3 Carlow Ger.
169 I7 Carlow Ireland
169 I7 Carlow county Ireland
168 C6 Carloway Western Isles, Scotland U.K.
Carlsbad Czech Rep. see Karlovy Vary
264 O8 Carlsbad CA U.S.A.
263 L10 Carlsbad NM U.S.A.
261 E10 Carlsbad TX U.S.A.
263 L10 Carlsbad Caverns National Park NM U.S.A.
194 E3 Carlsberg Ger.
289 H4 Carlsberg Ridge sea feature Indian Ocean
193 G10 Carlsfeld Ger.
286 S1 Carlson Inlet Antarctica
237 I7 Carlton S. Africa

173 J2 Carlton Nottinghamshire, England U.K.
250 B3 Carlton MN U.S.A.
173 P3 Carlton Colville Suffolk, England U.K.
108 J3 Carlton Hill W.A. Austr.
237 I7 Carlton Hills S. Africa
171 O7 Carlton in Lindrick Nottinghamshire, England U.K.
168 I11 Carluke South Lanarkshire, Scotland U.K.
185 G6 Carlux France
247 K5 Carlyle Sask. Can.
260 K6 Carlyle IL U.S.A.
260 K6 Carlyle Lake IL U.S.A.
245 M3 Carmacks Y.T. Can.
212 D6 Carmagnola Italy
247 L5 Carman Man. Can.
Carmana Iran see Kermān
172 D4 Carmarthen Carmarthenshire, Wales U.K.
172 C4 Carmarthen Bay Wales U.K.
172 D4 Carmarthenshire admin. div. Wales U.K.
185 I7 Carmaux France
254 D6 Carmel IN U.S.A.
257 □P4 Carmel ME U.S.A.
257 L7 Carmel NY U.S.A.
Carmel, Mount hill Israel see Karmel, Har
264 K5 Carmel-by-the-Sea CA U.S.A.
172 C1 Carmel Head Wales U.K.
267 N9 Carmelita Guat.
285 H3 Carmelo Uru.
264 K5 Carmel Valley CA U.S.A.
285 G3 Carmen Arg.
282 C2 Carmen Chile
274 C2 Carmen Col.
267 I5 Carmen Mex.
266 F2 Carmen r. Mex.
114 E7 Carmen Bohol Phil.
285 I3 Carmen Uru.
265 U10 Carmen AZ U.S.A.
266 D5 Carmen, Isla i. Mex.
267 N8 Carmen, Isla del i. Mex.
205 L9 Carmena Spain
276 C5 Carmen Alto Chile
285 H4 Carmen de Areco Arg.
277 F6 Carmen del Paraná Para.
283 E6 Carmen de Patagones Arg.
204 I3 Cármenes Spain
284 D4 Carmensa Arg.
260 K6 Carmi IL U.S.A.
217 O3 Carmiano Italy
255 □2 Carmichael New Prov. Bahamas
264 K3 Carmichael CA U.S.A.
107 L6 Carmila Qld Austr.
281 F4 Carmo Brazil
281 E4 Carmo da Cachoeira Brazil
281 E5 Carmo de Minas Brazil
280 D3 Carmo do Paranaíba Brazil
109 E12 Carmody, Lake salt flat W.A. Austr.
Carmona Angola see Uíge
266 □Q13 Carmona Hond.
206 H6 Carmona Spain
206 G2 Carmonita Spain
281 E4 Carmópolis do Minas Brazil
168 K9 Carmyllie Angus, Scotland U.K.
180 E6 Carnac France
168 G8 Carn a' Chuilinn hill Scotland U.K.
169 I4 Carnagh Northern Ireland U.K.
109 C10 Carnamah W.A. Austr.
109 B8 Carnarvon W.A. Austr.
236 G6 Carnarvon S. Africa
236 F6 Carnarvonleegte salt pan S. Africa
107 K8 Carnarvon National Park Qld Austr.
109 F8 Carnarvon Range hills W.A. Austr.
107 L8 Carnarvon Range mts Qld Austr.
168 K10 Carnbee Fife, Scotland U.K.
168 G7 Carn Chuinneag hill Scotland U.K.
168 G8 Carn Dearg hill Highland, Scotland U.K.
168 H8 Carn Dearg hill Highland, Scotland U.K.
169 H2 Carndonagh Ireland
169 J2 Carnduff Northern Ireland U.K.
168 J8 Carn Ealasaid hill Scotland U.K.
172 E1 Carnedd Llywelyn mt. Wales U.K.
172 E2 Carnedd y Filiast hill Wales U.K.
109 G8 Carnegie W.A. Austr.
109 G9 Carnegie, Lake salt flat W.A. Austr.
291 N6 Carnegie Ridge sea feature S. Pacific Ocean
168 F8 Carn Eige mt. Scotland U.K.
168 I8 Carne na Loine hill Scotland U.K.
282 B5 Carnero, Bahía del b. Chile
207 I8 Carnero, Punta del pt Spain
104 E4 Carnes S.A. Austr.
255 F8 Carnesville GA U.S.A.
169 J7 Carnew Ireland
250 G4 Carney MI U.S.A.
286 P2 Carney Island Antarctica
258 E5 Carneys Point NJ U.S.A.
168 K8 Carnferg hill Scotland U.K.
171 L5 Carnforth Lancashire, England U.K.
168 I8 Carn Glas-choire hill Scotland U.K.
200 G6 Carnic Alps mts Austria
137 M8 Car Nicobar i. Andaman & Nicobar Is India
178 F3 Carnières France
160 H4 Carnikava Latvia
169 K3 Carnlough Northern Ireland U.K.
169 K2 Carnlough Bay Northern Ireland U.K.
168 J8 Carn Mòr hill Scotland U.K.
Carnmore Ireland see An Carn Mór
172 E2 Carno Powys, Wales U.K.
168 H8 Carn Odhar hill Scotland U.K.
180 D5 Carnoët France
183 D9 Carnon-Plage France
230 B3 Carnot C.A.R.
98 D5 Carnot, Cape S.A. Austr.
204 B3 Carnota Spain
108 G4 Carnot Bay W.A. Austr.
183 I10 Carnoules France
168 K9 Carnoustie Angus, Scotland U.K.
183 H10 Carnoux-en-Provence France
169 J8 Carnsore Point Ireland
170 D5 Carnteel Northern Ireland U.K.
245 O1 Carnwath r. N.W.T. Can.
168 I11 Carnwath South Lanarkshire, Scotland U.K.
245 J2 Caro AK U.S.A.
251 K6 Caro MI U.S.A.
275 F4 Caroaebe r. Brazil
Caroch mt. Spain see El Caroche
107 N5 Carola Cay rf Coral Sea Is Terr. Austr.
255 G13 Carol City FL U.S.A.
215 Q9 Carolei Italy
284 D3 Carolina Arg.
278 D3 Carolina Brazil
271 □1 Carolina Puerto Rico
237 O2 Carolina S. Africa
255 I8 Carolina Beach NC U.S.A.
246 H4 Caroline Alta Can.
258 D7 Caroline County county MD U.S.A.
104 □3 Caroline Cove b. S. Pacific Ocean
291 I6 Caroline Island atoll Kiribati
290 E5 Caroline Islands N. Pacific Ocean
103 B12 Caroline Peak South I. N.Z.
180 H4 Carolles France
236 B5 Carolusberg S. Africa
183 G8 Caromb France
212 H3 Carona Italy
274 B4 Carondelet Ecuador
271 □7 Caroni Trinidad Trin. and Tob.
271 □7 Caroni county Trin. and Tob.
275 F2 Caroní r. Venez.
216 G7 Caronia Sicilia Italy
271 □7 Caroni Swamp Trin. and Tob.
274 D2 Carora Venez.
219 R5 C. A. Rosetti Romania
217 M3 Carosino Italy
217 N2 Carovigno Italy

215 M4 Carovilli Italy
251 R4 Carp Ont. Can.
212 H6 Carpaneto Piacentino Italy
199 I2 Carpathian Mountains Europe
Carpații mts Europe see Carpathian Mountains
219 K5 Carpații Meridionali mts Romania
213 M8 Carpegna Italy
212 I5 Carpenedolo Italy
106 G3 Carpentaria, Gulf of N.T./Qld Austr.
107 J5 Carpentaria Downs Qld Austr.
284 C2 Carpentiría Arg.
183 G8 Carpentras France
213 J6 Carpi Italy
217 O3 Carpignano Salentino Italy
212 E4 Carpignano Sesia Italy
278 G3 Carpina Brazil
213 M9 Carpina r. Italy
199 L5 Cărpinet Romania
212 I7 Carpineti Italy
215 K4 Carpineto Romano Italy
218 I5 Cărpiniș Romania
215 P4 Carpino Italy
215 M4 Carpinone Italy
264 M7 Carpinteria CA U.S.A.
205 J6 Carpio Spain
260 E1 Carpio ND U.S.A.
181 K3 Carpiquet France
246 F4 Carp Lake Provincial Park B.C. Can.
180 I7 Carquefou France
183 I10 Carqueiranne France
206 F2 Carquesa hill Spain
169 D5 Carra, Lough l. Ireland
257 □O3 Carrabassett ME U.S.A.
255 E11 Carrabelle FL U.S.A.
169 E5 Carracastle Ireland
204 G3 Carracedelo Spain
168 F11 Carradale East Argyll and Bute, Scotland U.K.
Carraig na Siuire Ireland see Carrick-on-Suir
Carraig Thuathail Ireland see Carrigtohill
274 C2 Carraipía Col.
204 D2 Carral Spain
169 D9 Carran hill Ireland
205 M8 Carranque Spain
169 C9 Carrantuohill mt. Ireland
206 B6 Carrapateira Port.
204 F7 Carrapichana Port.
212 I7 Carrara Italy
Carraroe Ireland see An Cheathru Rua
208 E6 Carrascal mt. Spain
204 I7 Carrascal del Obispo Spain
205 M6 Carrascal del Río Spain
276 D4 Carrasco, Parque Nacional nat. park Bol.
205 P7 Carrascosa Spain
205 O8 Carrascosa del Campo Spain
209 C12 Carrascoy, Sierra de mts Spain
105 J6 Carrathool N.S.W. Austr.
207 J7 Carratraca Spain
204 F6 Carrazeda de Ansiães Port.
275 I5 Carrazedo Brazil
204 F5 Carrazedo de Montenegro Port.
108 J4 Carr Boyd Range hills W.A. Austr.
168 I8 Carrbridge Highland, Scotland U.K.
204 C5 Carreço Port.
206 B2 Carregado Port.
204 E8 Carregal do Sal Port.
204 D9 Carregueiros Port.
204 B3 Carreiro, Punta pt Spain
206 D5 Carreiros r. Port.
205 K2 Carreña Spain
284 C5 Carrero, Cerro mt. Arg.
185 C9 Carresse-Cassaber France
285 I4 Carreta Quemada Uru.
Carrhae Turkey see Harran
271 □3 Carriacou i. Grenada
205 M2 Carriazo Spain
Carrick Ireland see An Charraig
169 I8 Carrick Wexford Ireland
168 G12 Carrick reg. Scotland U.K.
169 H8 Carrickbeg Ireland
169 G5 Carrickboy Ireland
169 K3 Carrickfergus Northern Ireland U.K.
169 I5 Carrickmacross Ireland
169 H3 Carrickmore Northern Ireland U.K.
169 F5 Carrick-on-Shannon Ireland
169 H8 Carrick-on-Suir Ireland
204 C9 Carriço Port.
104 G5 Carrieton S.A. Austr.
169 E9 Carrigadrohid Reservoir Ireland
169 F9 Carrigaline Ireland
169 G5 Carrigallen Ireland
169 D9 Carriganima Ireland
169 H3 Carrigans Ireland
169 D8 Carrigkerry Ireland
169 F9 Carrigtohill Ireland
285 H4 Carril Arg.
266 H4 Carrillo Mex.
285 F2 Carrilobo Arg.
260 F2 Carrington ND U.S.A.
204 D2 Carrio Spain
205 K4 Carrion r. Spain
207 L2 Carrión de Calatrava Spain
206 G6 Carrión de los Céspedes Spain
205 K4 Carrión de los Condes Spain
274 C2 Carrizal Col.
266 F2 Carrizal Mex.
282 C3 Carrizal Bajo Chile
285 G3 Carrizales Arg.
265 V7 Carrizo AZ U.S.A.
268 D4 Carrizo Colorado Mex.
261 D7 Carrizo Creek r. TX U.S.A.
265 V8 Carrizo Creek watercourse AZ U.S.A.
265 Q8 Carrizo Creek watercourse CA U.S.A.
204 I3 Carrizo de la Ribera Spain
264 M7 Carrizo Plain National Monument nat. park CA U.S.A.
269 H1 Carrizos Mex.
207 N3 Carrizosa Spain
261 F11 Carrizo Springs TX U.S.A.
265 W7 Carrizo Wash watercourse AZ/NM U.S.A.
263 L10 Carrizozo NM U.S.A.
207 O2 Carro hill Spain
208 F3 Carrodilla, Sierra de mts Spain
260 H4 Carroll IA U.S.A.
258 A5 Carroll County county MD U.S.A.
261 K9 Carrollton AL U.S.A.
255 E9 Carrollton GA U.S.A.
260 J6 Carrollton IL U.S.A.
254 E6 Carrollton KY U.S.A.
260 I6 Carrollton MO U.S.A.
261 K9 Carrollton MS U.S.A.
256 D8 Carrollton OH U.S.A.
256 G8 Carrolltown PA U.S.A.
107 H4 Carron r. Qld Austr.
168 H7 Carron r. Highland, Scotland U.K.
168 E8 Carron, Loch inlet Scotland U.K.
168 I12 Carronbridge Dumfries and Galloway, Scotland U.K.
284 E5 Carro Quemado Arg.
183 K9 Carros France
247 K4 Carrot r. Sask. Can.
247 K4 Carrot River Sask. Can.
181 K4 Carrouges France
169 G2 Carrowkeel Ireland
169 H2 Carrowkeel Ireland
169 E6 Carrowmore Ireland
169 C4 Carrowmore Lake Ireland
169 E4 Carrowneden Ireland
256 I12 Carrsville VA U.S.A.
212 D7 Carrù Italy
247 K2 Carruthers Lake Nunavut Can.
261 K7 Carruthersville MO U.S.A.
169 K3 Carryduff Northern Ireland U.K.
257 K4 Carry Falls Reservoir NY U.S.A.
183 G10 Carry-le-Rouet France
184 C5 Cars France
185 G6 Carsac-Aillac France
168 E10 Carsaig Argyll and Bute, Scotland U.K.
148 H3 Çarşamba Turkey

151 A4 Çarşıbaşı Turkey
171 N7 Carsington Water resr England U.K.
215 K3 Carsoli Italy
108 I3 Carson r. W.A. Austr.
260 E2 Carson ND U.S.A.
264 M2 Carson r. NV U.S.A.
250 J6 Carson City MI U.S.A.
264 M2 Carson City NV U.S.A.
108 I3 Carson Escarpment W.A. Austr.
264 N2 Carson Lake NV U.S.A.
108 I3 Carson River Aboriginal Reserve W.A. Austr.
264 N2 Carson Sink l. NV U.S.A.
251 L6 Carsonville MI U.S.A.
182 K1 Carspach France
168 H12 Carsphairn Dumfries and Galloway, Scotland U.K.
168 I11 Carstairs South Lanarkshire, Scotland U.K.
Carstensz-top mt. Papua Indon. see Jaya, Puncak
247 I3 Carswell Lake Sask. Can.
284 B3 Cartagena Chile
274 C2 Cartagena Col.
209 D12 Cartagena Spain
274 C3 Cartago Col.
266 □R13 Cartago Costa Rica
207 J7 Cártama Spain
206 B2 Cartaxo Port.
206 E6 Cartaya Spain
183 J10 Cartaya, Cap c. France
184 C5 Cartelègue France
107 I2 Carter, Mount hill Qld Austr.
180 H3 Carteret France
259 G3 Carteret NJ U.S.A.
180 H3 Carteret, Cap de c. France
Carteret Group is P.N.G. see Kilinailau Islands
Carteret Island Solomon Is see Malaita
107 H7 Carters Range hills Qld Austr.
255 E8 Cartersville GA U.S.A.
103 J8 Carterton North I. N.Z.
173 I4 Carterton Oxfordshire, England U.K.
205 L2 Cartes Spain
227 H1 Carthage tourist site Tunisia
250 C9 Carthage IL U.S.A.
261 H7 Carthage MO U.S.A.
255 C9 Carthage MS U.S.A.
255 H8 Carthage NC U.S.A.
257 J5 Carthage NY U.S.A.
255 E7 Carthage TN U.S.A.
261 H9 Carthage TX U.S.A.
Carthago tourist site Tunisia see Carthage
Carthago Nova Spain see Cartagena
251 M3 Cartier Ont. Can.
108 G2 Cartier Island Ashmore & Cartier Is Austr.
171 L5 Cartmel Cumbria, England U.K.
213 N8 Cartoceto Italy
247 L5 Cartwright Man. Can.
249 J2 Cartwright Nfld and Lab. Can.
275 F2 Caruachi Venez.
278 G4 Caruarú Brazil
278 C2 Caruçambaba Brazil
204 G4 Carucedo Spain
215 N4 Carunchio Italy
219 O4 Cărunta, Vârful mt. Romania
275 F2 Carúpano Venez.
278 D2 Carutapera Brazil
204 D9 Carvalhal Santarém Port.
206 B4 Carvalhal Setúbal Port.
275 I5 Carvalho Brazil
204 F6 Carvalho de Egas Port.
256 B11 Carver KY U.S.A.
204 G6 Carviçais Port.
178 E3 Carvin France
206 A2 Carvoeira Port.
275 F5 Carvoeiro Brazil
206 C6 Carvoeiro Port.
206 A2 Carvoeiro, Cabo c. Port.
107 K8 Carwell Qld Austr.
151 J4 Çarxı Azer.
255 H8 Cary NC U.S.A.
105 I3 Caryapundy Swamp Qld Austr.
256 A12 Caryville TN U.S.A.
250 C5 Caryville WI U.S.A.
207 P5 Casa Alta hill Spain
207 K7 Casabermeja Spain
282 D1 Casabindo, Cerro de mt. Arg.
284 B3 Casablanca Chile
226 D2 Casablanca Morocco
280 D4 Casa Branca Brazil
206 C3 Casa Branca Évora Port.
206 D3 Casa Branca Portalegre Port.
215 N4 Casacalenda Italy
271 □[7] Casa Cruz, Cape Trin. and Tob.
266 E2 Casa de Janos Mex.
269 I2 Casa del Campesino Mex.
207 K3 Casa de Michos Spain
244 F2 Casadepaga AK U.S.A.
284 D6 Casa de Piedra Arg.
284 D6 Casa de Piedra, Embalse resr Arg.
215 M5 Casagiove Italy
214 B3 Casaglione Corse France
265 U9 Casa Grande AZ U.S.A.
217 O3 Casa l'Abate Italy
215 M3 Casalanguida Italy
205 O3 Casalarreina Spain
215 N3 Casalbordino Italy
215 O5 Casalbore Italy
215 P7 Casalbuono Italy
212 H5 Casalbuttano ed Uniti Italy
212 F6 Casàl Cermelli Italy
213 K7 Casalecchio di Reno Italy
285 G3 Casalegno Arg.
212 E5 Casale Monferrato Italy
215 P7 Casaletto Spartano Italy
213 L7 Casalfiumanese Italy
213 J6 Casalgrande Italy
212 D6 Casalgrasso Italy
206 B2 Casalinho Port.
285 H5 Casalins Arg.
212 I6 Casalmaggiore Italy
215 O4 Casalnuovo Monterotaro Italy
212 H5 Casalpusterlengo Italy
277 E3 Casalvasco Brazil
215 O4 Casalvecchio di Puglia Italy
215 O7 Casàl Velino Italy
228 A3 Casamance r. Senegal
217 L2 Casamassima Italy
214 C2 Casamozza Corse France
274 D3 Casanare dept Col.
274 D3 Casanare r. Col.
207 J7 Casarabonela Spain
217 O3 Casarano Italy
204 H9 Casar de Cáceres Spain
204 H8 Casar de Palomero Spain
205 N5 Casarejos Spain
266 □P12 Casares Nic.
207 I8 Casares Spain
204 H2 Casares Spain
204 H8 Casares de las Hurdes Spain
207 J6 Casariche Spain
205 L8 Casarrubios del Monte Spain
213 N4 Casarsa della Delizia Italy
212 G7 Casarza Ligure Italy
269 I2 Casas Mex.
209 C7 Casas Altas Spain
207 O2 Casas de Benitez Spain
207 I2 Casas de Don Pedro Spain
207 O2 Casas de Fernando Alonso Spain
207 O2 Casas de Haro Spain
209 C9 Casas de Juan Gil Spain
207 P2 Casas de Juan Núñez Spain
207 O3 Casas de Lázaro Spain
204 I8 Casas del Monte Spain
207 O2 Casas de los Pinos Spain
209 C11 Casas del Puerto Spain
204 H9 Casas de Millán Spain
209 C9 Casas de Ves Spain
266 F2 Casas Grandes Mex.
266 F2 Casas Grandes r. Mex.
207 Q2 Casas-Ibáñez Spain
207 O2 Casasimarro Spain
206 E3 Casas Novas de Mares Port.
205 J5 Casasola de Arión Spain
204 I9 Casatejada Spain
212 G4 Casatenovo Italy
205 K8 Casavieja Spain
285 F5 Casbas Arg.
279 B9 Casca Brazil
266 E3 Cascada de Bassaseachic, Parque Nacional nat. park Mex.
109 F12 Cascade W.A. Austr.
103 C11 Cascade r. South I. N.Z.
239 □[2b] Cascade Mahé Seychelles
260 J4 Cascade IA U.S.A.
262 F4 Cascade ID U.S.A.
262 I3 Cascade MT U.S.A.
104 □[1] Cascade Bay Norfolk I.
103 C11 Cascade Point South I. N.Z.
252 B2 Cascade Range mts Can./U.S.A.
262 F4 Cascade Reservoir ID U.S.A.
239 □[1c] Cascades, Pointe des pt Réunion
262 D5 Cascade Siskiyou National Monument nat. park OR U.S.A.
206 A3 Cascais Port.
266 □Q12 Cascal, Paso del pass Nic.
205 Q4 Cascante Spain
209 C7 Cascante del Río Spain
249 H3 Cascapédia r. Que. Can.
278 F3 Cascavel Ceará Brazil
280 A6 Cascavel Paraná Brazil
215 K2 Cascia Italy
213 J8 Casciana Terme Italy
212 J8 Cascina Italy
219 O6 Căscioarele Romania
250 G5 Casco WI U.S.A.
257 □P5 Casco Bay ME U.S.A.
206 B3 Casebres Port.
205 R3 Cáseda Spain
214 D9 Case della Marina Sardegna Italy
212 F5 Casei Gerola Italy
192 J4 Casekow Ger.
212 F6 Casella Italy
215 P7 Caselle in Pittari Italy
212 D5 Caselle Torinese Italy
213 N3 Cà Selva, Lago di l. Italy
217 L2 Case Perrone Italy
271 □[3] Case-Pilote Martinique
215 M5 Caserta Italy
215 M5 Caserta prov. Italy
206 C5 Casével Port.
251 K6 Caseville MI U.S.A.
287 H2 Casey research stn Antarctica
287 D2 Casey Bay Antarctica
Cas-gwent Wales U.K. see Chepstow
169 G2 Cashel Donegal Ireland
169 E5 Cashel Galway Ireland
169 C6 Cashel Galway Ireland
169 H7 Cashel Laois Ireland
169 G7 Cashel Tipperary Ireland
169 E6 Cashla Ireland
169 B5 Cashleen Ireland
107 L9 Cashmere Qld Austr.
250 D6 Cashton WI U.S.A.
274 D2 Casigua Falcón Venez.
274 C2 Casigua Zulia Venez.
114 D3 Casiguran Luzon Phil.
114 C3 Casiguran Sound sea chan. Luzon Phil.
285 G3 Casilda Arg.
205 K8 Casillas Spain
204 G8 Casillas de Flores Spain
238 □[3b] Casillas del Ángel Fuerteventura Canary Is
219 Q6 Casimcea Romania
219 Q6 Casimcea r. Romania
268 C6 Casimiro Castillo Mex.
281 F5 Casimiro de Abreu Brazil
212 I6 Casina Italy
105 N3 Casino N.S.W. Austr.
209 D8 Casinos Spain
263 I11 Casita Mex.
219 J9 Čaška Čaška Macedonia
169 C6 Casla Ireland
198 E2 Čáslav Czech Rep.
276 A2 Casma Peru
Casnewydd Newport, Wales U.K. see Newport
250 I6 Casnovia MI U.S.A.
114 E6 Casogoran Bay Phil.
204 G4 Casoio r. Spain
212 I7 Casola in Lunigiana Italy
213 L7 Casola Valsenio Italy
213 K9 Casole d'Elsa Italy
215 M3 Casoli Italy
215 M6 Casoria Italy
208 E5 Caspe Spain
208 E5 Caspe, Embalse de resr Spain
262 K5 Casper WY U.S.A.
250 F3 Caspian MI U.S.A.
Caspian Lowland Kazakh./Rus. Fed. see Prikaspiyskaya Nizmennost'
142 C5 Caspian Sea l. Asia/Europe
256 F10 Cass WV U.S.A.
251 K6 Cass r. MI U.S.A.
235 G2 Cassacatiza Moz.
256 F6 Cassadaga NY U.S.A.
208 K4 Cassà de la Selva Spain
185 F9 Cassagnabère-Tournas France
185 J7 Cassagnes-Bégonhès France
231 D7 Cassai Angola
231 D8 Cassamba Angola
185 I6 Cassaniouze France
215 Q8 Cassano allo Ionio Italy
217 L2 Cassano delle Murge Italy
212 F4 Cassano Magnano Italy
212 F6 Cassano Spinola Italy
231 C7 Cassanzade Angola
277 E3 Cassara Brazil
216 H9 Cassaro Sicilia Italy
251 K6 Cass City MI U.S.A.
178 D2 Cassel France
248 F4 Casselman Ont. Can.
260 G2 Casselton ND U.S.A.
185 F7 Casseneuil France
208 I3 Casserres Spain
280 D4 Cássia Brazil
245 O4 Cassiar B.C. Can.
245 O4 Cassiar Mountains B.C. Can.
217 I10 Cassibile Sicilia Italy
217 I10 Cassibile r. Sicilia Italy
280 B3 Cassilândia Brazil
105 L5 Cassilis N.S.W. Austr.
212 F6 Cassine Italy
231 C8 Cassinga Angola
282 G4 Cassino Brazil
215 L5 Cassino Italy
183 H10 Cassis France
260 H2 Cass Lake MN U.S.A.
168 G7 Cassley r. Scotland U.K.
213 L4 Cassola Italy
231 B7 Cassongue Angola
250 H8 Cassopolis MI U.S.A.
183 B7 Cassuéjouls France
261 I7 Cassville MO U.S.A.
198 G3 Častá Slovakia
212 F4 Castagliona Olona Italy
214 B4 Castagna, Punta di a pt Corse France
213 K5 Castagnaro Italy
214 F1 Castagneto Carducci Italy
214 C3 Castagniccia reg. Corse France
212 E6 Castagnole delle Lanze Italy
212 E6 Castagnole Monferrato Italy
209 D10 Castalla Spain
205 J9 Castañar de Ibor Spain
205 O3 Castañares de Rioja Spain
185 H8 Castanet-Tolosan France
275 F6 Castanhal Amazonas Brazil
278 D2 Castanhal Pará Brazil
204 F7 Castanheira Port.
206 □ Castanheira, Ponta da pt Madeira
204 D8 Castanheira de Pêra Port.
275 E5 Castanheiro Brazil
277 E1 Castanho Brazil
284 C2 Castaño r. Arg.
206 F4 Castaño, Sierra del hills Spain
284 C2 Castaño Nuevo Arg.
212 F4 Castano Primo Italy
267 I4 Castaños Mex.
284 C2 Castaño Viejo Arg.
271 □[5] Castara Trin. and Tob.
271 □[5] Castara Bay Trin. and Tob.
212 H3 Castasegna Switz.
212 G5 Casteggio Italy
205 Q4 Castejón Spain
208 C4 Castejón, Montes de mts Spain
208 F4 Castejón del Puente Spain
208 E4 Castejón de Monegros Spain
208 F2 Castejón de Sos Spain
208 D4 Castejón de Valdejasa Spain
215 O5 Castèl Baronia Italy
213 O9 Castelbellino Italy
213 L7 Castèl Bolognese Italy
216 G8 Castelbuono Sicilia Italy
215 O7 Castelcivita Italy
216 F7 Casteldaccia Sicilia Italy
213 J5 Castèl d'Ario Italy
212 C6 Casteldelfino Italy
215 L3 Castèl del Monte Italy
217 K1 Castèl del Monte tourist site Italy
214 H2 Castèl del Piano Italy
213 L7 Castèl del Rio Italy
216 H9 Castèl di Iudica Sicilia Italy
215 L2 Castèl di Lama Italy
216 G8 Castèl di Lucio Sicilia Italy
215 M4 Castèl di Sangro Italy
204 F8 Casteleiro Port.
213 P9 Castelfidardo Italy
213 J8 Castelfiorentino Italy
208 E4 Castelflorite Spain
213 L8 Castèl Focognano Italy
215 L5 Castelforte Italy
215 O6 Castelfranci Italy
213 L8 Castelfranco di Sopra Italy
213 J8 Castelfranco di Sotto Italy
213 K6 Castelfranco Emilia Italy
215 O5 Castelfranco in Miscano Italy
213 L4 Castelfranco Veneto Italy
215 M3 Castèl Frentano Italy
214 H2 Castèl Giorgio Italy
212 I5 Castèl Goffredo Italy
215 O6 Castelgrande Italy
185 E7 Casteljaloux France
195 I2 Castell Ger.
212 E6 Castell'Alfero Italy
215 L2 Castellalto Italy
216 D7 Castellammare, Golfo di b. Sicilia Italy
216 D7 Castellammare del Golfo Sicilia Italy
215 M6 Castellammare di Stabia Italy
212 D5 Castellamonte Italy
217 M2 Castellana Grotte Italy
183 J9 Castellane France
217 L2 Castellaneta Italy
217 L3 Castellaneta Marina Italy
207 N3 Castellanos mt. Spain
205 L4 Castellanos de Castro Spain
207 I8 Castellar de la Frontera Spain
205 Q7 Castellar de la Muela Spain
208 H3 Castellar de la Ribera Spain
207 M3 Castellar de Santiago Spain
207 M4 Castellar de Santisteban Spain
212 H6 Castell'Arquato Italy
214 H2 Castell'Azzara Italy
212 F6 Castellazzo Bormida Italy
208 G5 Castelldans Spain
208 F6 Castell de Cabres Spain
209 E10 Castell de Castells Spain
208 I5 Castelldefels Spain
207 M7 Castell de Ferro Spain
212 H5 Castelleone Italy
212 F4 Castelletto sopra Ticino Italy
208 K3 Castellfollit de la Roca Spain
208 E6 Castellfort Spain
285 I5 Castelli Buenos Aires Arg.
282 E2 Castelli Chaco Arg.
213 K9 Castellina in Chianti Italy
213 J9 Castellina Marittima Italy
215 L4 Castelliri Italy
Castell-nedd Neath Port Talbot, Wales U.K. see Neath
Castell Newydd Emlyn Ceredigion, Wales U.K. see Newcastle Emlyn
209 E8 Castellnovo Spain
183 K7 Castello, Lago di l. Italy
209 E8 Castelló, Plana de plain Spain
213 K6 Castello d'Argile Italy
Castello de Ampurias Spain see Castelló d'Empúries
208 L3 Castelló d'Empúries Spain
209 E10 Castelló de Rugat Spain
212 E6 Castello di Annone Italy
209 E8 Castellón de la Plana Spain
209 E7 Castellón de la Plana prov. Spain
208 E6 Castellote Spain
213 L3 Castello Tesino Italy
208 G4 Castellserá Spain
208 J4 Castellterçol Spain
213 J5 Castellucchio Italy
215 O5 Castelluccio dei Sauri Italy
215 P7 Castelluccio Inferiore Italy
215 O5 Castellucio Valmaggiore Italy
216 H7 Castell'Umberto Sicilia Italy
216 D7 Castelluzzo Sicilia Italy
215 J4 Castèl Madama Italy
213 K6 Càstel Maggiore Italy
212 C7 Castelmagno Italy
213 K5 Castelmassa Italy
185 E7 Castelmoron-sur-Lot France
216 G1 Castèl Morrone Italy
185 G9 Castelnau France
185 F8 Castelnau-Barbarens France
185 H9 Castelnaudary France
185 E8 Castelnau-d'Auzan France
185 F6 Castelnaud-de-Gratecambe France
185 J8 Castelnau-de-Brassac France
184 C5 Castelnau-de-Médoc France
185 H8 Castelnau-de-Montmiral France
185 G8 Castelnau-d'Estréfonds France
183 D9 Castelnau-le-Lez France
185 F9 Castelnau-Magnoac France
185 G7 Castelnau-Montratier France
185 D8 Castelnau-Rivière-Basse France
213 J6 Castelnovo di Sotto Italy
212 I7 Castelnovo ne'Monti Italy
213 L9 Castelnuovo Berardenga Italy
215 O4 Castelnuovo della Daunia Italy
212 I7 Castelnuovo di Garfagnana Italy
214 F1 Castelnuovo di Val di Cecina Italy
212 D5 Castelnuovo Don Bosco Italy
212 F6 Castelnuovo Scrivia Italy
281 G4 Castelo Brazil
204 G7 Castelo Bom Port.
238 □[1c] Castelo Branco Faial Azores
204 G6 Castelo Branco Bragança Port.
204 F9 Castelo Branco Castelo Branco Port.
204 F8 Castelo Branco admin. dist. Port.
204 D9 Castelo de Bode, Barragem do resr Port.
204 D6 Castelo de Paiva Port.
206 E2 Castelo de Vide Port.
204 C5 Castelo do Neiva Port.
278 E3 Castelo do Piauí Brazil
204 D6 Castelões Port.
204 F6 Castelo Melhor Port.
204 G7 Castelo Mendo Port.
204 G7 Castelo Rodrigo Port.
213 O9 Castelplanio Italy
213 O9 Castelraimondo Italy
215 J2 Castèl Ritaldi Italy
213 L2 Castelrotto Italy
185 F7 Castelsagrat France
212 G5 Castèl San Giovanni Italy
213 L8 Castèl San Niccolò Italy
213 L7 Castèl San Pietro Terme Italy
215 K3 Castèl Sant'Angelo Italy
215 K2 Castelsantangelo sul Nera Italy
215 P7 Castelsaraceno Italy
214 B6 Castelsardo Sardegna Italy
185 G7 Castelsarrasin France
208 E6 Castelseras Spain
216 F8 Casteltermini Sicilia Italy
212 H5 Castelverde Italy
215 N5 Castelvetere in Val Fortore Italy
216 D8 Castelvetrano Sicilia Italy
212 H5 Castelvetro Placentino Italy
214 I2 Castèl Viscardo Italy
215 L5 Castèl Volturno Italy
213 K6 Castenaso Italy
185 E8 Castéra-Verduzan France
104 H7 Casterton Vic. Austr.
185 C9 Castetnau-Camblong France
185 B8 Castets France
214 D9 Castiadas Sardegna Italy
209 C7 Castielfabib Spain
208 D2 Castiello de Jaca Spain
214 C2 Castifao Corse France
212 I9 Castiglioncello Italy
213 K7 Castiglione dei Pepoli Italy
214 I1 Castiglione del Lago Italy
214 F2 Castiglione della Pescaia Italy
212 I5 Castiglione delle Stiviere Italy
214 H1 Castiglione d'Orcia Italy
214 I2 Castiglione in Teverina Italy
215 M4 Castiglione Messer Marino Italy
213 L9 Castiglion Fiorentino Italy
215 L2 Castignano Italy
249 G1 Castignon, Lac l. Que. Can.
207 I2 Castilblanco Spain
206 H5 Castilblanco de los Arroyos Spain
256 G6 Castile NY U.S.A.
280 B4 Castilho Brazil
205 R4 Castiliscar Spain
282 C2 Castilla Chile
274 A6 Castilla Peru
205 L4 Castilla, Canal de Spain
205 N10 Castilla-La Mancha aut. comm. Spain
205 L5 Castilla y León aut. comm. Spain
206 G6 Castilleja de la Cuesta Spain
207 N5 Castillejar Spain
205 J6 Castillejo hill Spain
275 F3 Castillejo Venez.
204 G7 Castillejo de Martin Viejo Spain
205 M6 Castillejo de Mesleón Spain
205 N5 Castillejo de Robledo Spain
274 D2 Castilletes Col.
283 B8 Castillo, Canal del sea chan. Chile
284 C3 Castillo, Cerro del mt. Arg.
283 C7 Castillo, Pampa del hills Arg.
205 K8 Castillo de Bayuela Spain
205 P9 Castillo de Garcimuñoz Spain
207 L5 Castillo de Locubín Spain
269 J5 Castillo de Teavo Mex.
183 J9 Castillon, Barrage de dam France
185 G10 Castillon-en-Couserans France
185 D6 Castillon-la-Bataille France
185 F6 Castillonnès France
208 C2 Castillo-Nuevo Spain
282 G4 Castillos Rocha Uru.
285 I3 Castillos Soriano Uru.
282 G4 Castillos, Lago de l. Uru.
205 P5 Castilruiz Spain
212 I4 Castione della Presolana Italy
200 H8 Castiòns di Strada Italy
169 D5 Castlebar Ireland
168 B9 Castlebay Western Isles, Scotland U.K.
169 J5 Castlebellingham Ireland
169 F6 Castleblakeney Ireland
169 I4 Castleblayney Ireland
173 I2 Castle Bromwich West Midlands, England U.K.
271 □[2] Castle Bruce Dominica
171 L4 Castle Carrock Cumbria, England U.K.
172 G5 Castle Cary Somerset, England U.K.
169 H7 Castlecomer Ireland
169 E7 Castleconnell Ireland
169 D4 Castleconor Ireland
265 U2 Castle Dale UT U.S.A.
250 C2 Castle Danger MN U.S.A.
169 I3 Castledawson Northern Ireland U.K.
169 G3 Castlederg Northern Ireland U.K.
169 I7 Castledermot Ireland
265 R8 Castle Dome Mountains AZ U.S.A.
173 J2 Castle Donington Leicestershire, England U.K.
168 I13 Castle Douglas Dumfries and Galloway, Scotland U.K.
169 G3 Castlefinn Ireland
171 O6 Castleford West Yorkshire, England U.K.
169 E9 Castlefreke Ireland
169 F4 Castlegal Ireland
246 G5 Castlegar B.C. Can.
169 B8 Castlegregory Ireland
255 □[1] Castle Harbour b. Bermuda
169 D4 Castlehill Ireland
270 F2 Castle Island Bahamas
169 D8 Castleisland Ireland
170 C7 Castlejordan Ireland
168 G13 Castle Kennedy Dumfries and Galloway, Scotland U.K.
169 J8 Castlellis Ireland
169 F8 Castlelyons Ireland
105 J7 Castlemaine Vic. Austr.
169 C8 Castlemaine Ireland
172 B4 Castlemartin Pembrokeshire, Wales U.K.
169 F9 Castlemartyr Ireland
246 H5 Castle Mountain Alta Can.
245 N2 Castle Mountain Y.T. Can.
264 L6 Castle Mountain CA U.S.A.
Castle Peak hill H.K. China see Tsing Shan
Castle Peak Bay H.K. China see Tsing Shan Wan
103 K7 Castlepoint North I. N.Z.
169 H5 Castlepollard Ireland
169 F5 Castlerea Ireland
105 K4 Castlereagh r. N.S.W. Austr.
169 K3 Castlereagh Northern Ireland U.K.
169 I2 Castlerock Northern Ireland U.K.
263 L7 Castle Rock CO U.S.A.
262 C3 Castle Rock WA U.S.A.
250 D6 Castle Rock Lake WI U.S.A.
238 □[2b] Castle Rock Point St Helena
169 I2 Castleroe Northern Ireland U.K.
171 N4 Castleside Durham, England U.K.
270 □ Castleton Jamaica
171 P5 Castleton North Yorkshire, England U.K.
257 L6 Castleton-On-Hudson NY U.S.A.
170 H5 Castletown Isle of Man
169 D6 Castletown Clare Ireland
169 E9 Castletown Cork Ireland
169 H7 Castletown Laois Ireland
169 I5 Castletown Meath Ireland
168 J5 Castletown Highland, Scotland U.K.
169 F8 Castletownroche Ireland
169 D5 Castleville Ireland
169 K4 Castlewellan Northern Ireland U.K.
247 I4 Castor Alta Can.
248 E2 Castor, Rivière du r. Que. Can.
261 I10 Castor Creek r. LA U.S.A.
Castra Regina Ger. see Regensburg
205 L9 Castrejón, Embalse de resr Spain
205 K3 Castrejón de la Peña Spain
204 F5 Castrelo do Val Spain
185 I8 Castres France
186 G3 Castricum Neth.
183 D9 Castries France
271 □[3] Castries St Lucia
217 O4 Castrignano del Capo Italy
207 N5 Castril Spain
207 N5 Castril r. Spain
205 L5 Castrillo de Don Juan Spain
205 L5 Castrillo de Duero Spain
205 N5 Castrillo de la Reina Spain
205 M5 Castrillo de la Vega Spain
205 L4 Castrillo de Villavega Spain
205 L5 Castrillo Tejeriego Spain
280 C6 Castro Brazil
283 B6 Castro Chile
217 O3 Castro Italy
204 B2 Castro r. Spain
204 H5 Castro, Embalse de resr Spain
278 F5 Castro Alves Brazil
284 E2 Castro Barros Arg.
205 N2 Castrobarto Spain
204 I4 Castrocalbón Spain
213 L7 Castrocaro Terme Italy
204 H4 Castrocontrigo Spain
204 E7 Castro Daire Port.
215 L4 Castro dei Volsci Italy
207 K5 Castro del Río Spain
204 F1 Castro de Ouro Spain
204 F2 Castro de Rei Spain
216 F9 Castrofilippo Sicilia Italy
204 I5 Castrogonzalo Spain
205 L4 Castrojeriz Spain
204 D4 Castro Laboreiro Port.
206 E6 Castro Marim Port.
205 K4 Castromocho Spain
205 J5 Castromonte Spain
204 I5 Castronuevo Spain
205 J6 Castronuño Spain
216 F8 Castronuovo di Sicilia Sicilia Italy
215 N4 Castropignano Italy
204 H3 Castropodame Spain
204 F1 Castropol Spain
191 D7 Castrop-Rauxel Ger.
217 I7 Castroreale Sicilia Italy
205 N2 Castro-Urdiales Spain
204 C4 Castrove hill Spain
206 C5 Castro Verde Port.
204 F2 Castroverde Spain
205 J5 Castroverde de Campos Spain
215 Q8 Castrovillari Italy
264 K5 Castroville CA U.S.A.
276 B3 Castrovirreyna Peru
206 H3 Castuera Spain
128 B2 Cast Uul mt. Mongolia
108 I3 Casuarina, Mount hill W.A. Austr.
245 J3 Caswell AK U.S.A.
103 B11 Caswell Sound inlet South I. N.Z.
149 J4 Çat Turkey
231 C8 Catabola Angola
266 □Q10 Catacamas Hond.
274 A6 Catacaos Peru
274 B6 Catacocha Ecuador
209 D9 Catadau Spain
270 □ Catadupa Jamaica
281 F4 Cataguases Brazil
261 I10 Catahoula Lake LA U.S.A.
114 D5 Cataiñgan Masbate Phil.
150 B2 Çatak İçel Turkey
149 K5 Çatak Van Turkey
151 C7 Çataklı Turkey
207 □ Catalan Bay Gibraltar
280 D3 Catalão Brazil
221 J1 Çatalca Turkey
221 J1 Çatalca Yarımadası pen. Turkey
265 V9 Catalina AZ U.S.A.
100 □[1] Catalina Point Guam
Catalonia aut. comm. Spain see Cataluña
208 I4 Cataluña aut. comm. Spain
Catalunya aut. comm. Spain see Cataluña
148 G3 Çatalzeytin Turkey
105 K10 Catamaran Tas. Austr.
282 D3 Catamarca Arg.
282 D2 Catamarca prov. Arg.
Catambia Moz. see Catandica
Catana Sicilia Italy see Catania
114 D5 Catanauan Luzon Phil.
235 G3 Catandica Moz.
114 E5 Catanduanes i. Phil.
280 C4 Catanduva Brazil
280 A6 Catanduvas Brazil
217 I9 Catania Sicilia Italy
216 H9 Catania prov. Sicilia Italy
217 I9 Catania, Golfo di g. Sicilia Italy
216 H9 Catania, Piana di plain Sicilia Italy
283 C5 Catán Lil Arg.
217 L6 Catanzaro Italy
217 L6 Catanzaro prov. Italy
217 L6 Catanzaro Marina Italy
277 E2 Cataqueamã Brazil
250 D5 Cataract WI U.S.A.
265 T5 Cataract Creek watercourse AZ U.S.A.
278 F3 Catarina Brazil
261 F11 Catarina TX U.S.A.
267 I5 Catarino Rodríguez Mex.
114 E5 Catarman Samar Phil.
114 F8 Catarman Point Mindanao Phil.
209 E9 Catarroja Spain
258 E3 Catasauqua PA U.S.A.
104 E6 Catastrophe, Cape S.A. Austr.
231 B8 Catata Nova Angola
274 C2 Catatumbo Bari nat. park Col.
276 D4 Catavi Bol.
250 D4 Catawba WI U.S.A.
255 G8 Catawba r. SC U.S.A.
251 R9 Catawissa PA U.S.A.
258 C3 Catawissa Creek r. PA U.S.A.
118 H4 Cat Ba, Đao i. Vietnam
114 E6 Catbalogan Samar Phil.
270 D1 Cat Cays is Bahamas
114 F8 Cateel Mindanao Phil.
114 F8 Cateel Bay Mindanao Phil.
231 D9 Catehu Angola
269 L7 Catemaco Mex.
269 L7 Catemaco, Laguna l. Mex.
237 Q2 Catembe Moz.
284 B3 Catemu Chile
214 C7 Catena del Goceano mts Sardegna Italy
214 B7 Catena del Marghine mts Sardegna Italy
216 H8 Catenanuova Sicilia Italy
231 B8 Catengue Angola
173 L5 Caterham Surrey, England U.K.
214 B2 Cateri Corse France
231 B7 Catete Angola
275 H6 Catete r. Brazil
169 B9 Cathair Dónall Ireland
Cathair Saidhbhín Ireland see Cahirsiveen
105 L7 Cathcart N.S.W. Austr.
237 L8 Cathcart S. Africa
265 P8 Cathedral City CA U.S.A.
237 N4 Cathedral Peak Lesotho
246 F5 Cathedral Provincial Park B.C. Can.
Catherdaniel Ireland see Cathair Dónall
255 D9 Catherine AL U.S.A.
Catherine, Mount Egypt see Kātrīnā, Jabal
265 T3 Catherine, Mount UT U.S.A.
270 □ Catherine's Peak hill Jamaica
264 L4 Catheys Valley CA U.S.A.
262 C3 Cathlamet WA U.S.A.
208 F7 Catí Spain
215 L3 Catignano Italy
284 B5 Catillo Chile
228 B4 Catió Guinea-Bissau
275 F3 Catisimiña Venez.
270 F1 Cat Island Bahamas
204 E7 Cativelos Port.
151 C6 Çatkale Turkey
248 B3 Cat Lake Ont. Can.
256 C10 Catlettsburg KY U.S.A.
103 D13 Catlins Forest Park nature res. South I. N.Z.
267 P7 Catoche, Cabo c. Mex.
204 C3 Catoira Spain
99 F4 Cato Island and Bank rf Coral Sea Is Terr. Austr.
278 F3 Catolé do Rocha Brazil
231 C7 Catolo Angola
171 L5 Caton Lancashire, England U.K.
217 J7 Catona r. Italy
258 B6 Catonsville MD U.S.A.
268 G2 Catorce Mex.
268 G2 Catorce, Sierra de mts Mex.
221 L3 Çatören Barajı resr Turkey
231 C8 Catota Angola
204 H3 Catoute mt. Spain
209 D11 Catral Spain
213 N9 Catria, Monte mt. Italy
284 D5 Catriel Arg.
285 F5 Catriló Arg.
275 F4 Catrimani Brazil
275 F4 Catrimani r. Brazil
168 H11 Catrine East Ayrshire, Scotland U.K.
172 H3 Catshill Worcestershire, England U.K.
257 L6 Catskill NY U.S.A.
257 K6 Catskill Mountains NY U.S.A.
179 L5 Cattenom France
191 K9 Catterfeld Ger.
171 N5 Catterick North Yorkshire, England U.K.
171 N5 Catterick Garrison North Yorkshire, England U.K.
168 L9 Catterline Aberdeenshire, Scotland U.K.
103 E11 Cattle Creek South I. N.Z.
213 N8 Cattolica Italy
216 E9 Cattolica Eraclea Sicilia Italy
282 D1 Catúa Arg.
235 G5 Catuane Moz.
235 G2 Catur Moz.
185 G6 Catus France
216 F8 Catuso, Monte mt. Italy
199 L4 Căuaş Romania
278 C2 Cauaxi r. Brazil
114 D7 Cauayan Negros Phil.
249 I1 Caubvick, Mount Nfld and Lab. Can.
274 B4 Cauca dept Col.
274 C2 Cauca r. Col.
278 F2 Caucaia Brazil
274 C3 Caucasia Col.
151 B2 Caucasus mts Asia/Europe
284 C2 Caucete Arg.
282 D1 Cauchari, Salar de salt flat Arg.
247 L4 Cauchon Lake Man. Can.
257 □P2 Caucomgomoc Lake ME U.S.A.
180 E6 Caudan France
184 F6 Caudau r. France
181 M2 Caudebec-en-Caux France
185 F7 Caudecoste France
209 D10 Caudete Spain
209 C8 Caudete de las Fuentes Spain
209 D8 Caudiel Spain
185 I10 Caudiès-de-Fenouillèdes France
178 F3 Caudry France
118 G5 Câu Giat Vietnam
114 F7 Cauit Point Mindanao Phil.
185 G9 Caujac France
180 G5 Caulnes France
217 K7 Caulonia Italy
185 G7 Caumont Midi-Pyrénées France
185 G9 Caumont Midi-Pyrénées France
181 J3 Caumont-l'Éventé France
183 F9 Caumont-sur-Durance France
270 D2 Caunao r. Cuba
185 J9 Caunes-Minervois France
231 C7 Caungula Angola
231 C9 Cauno Angola
284 A4 Cauquenes Chile
275 E3 Caura r. Venez.
275 F5 Caurés r. Brazil
214 B4 Cauro Corse France
249 H3 Causapscal Que. Can.
158 I7 Căuşeni Moldova
169 C8 Causeway Ireland
169 I2 Causeway Head Northern Ireland U.K.
185 H7 Caussade France
276 D3 Cautário r. Brazil
185 D10 Cauterets France
246 E5 Caution, Cape B.C. Can.
270 E3 Cauto r. Cuba
151 J5 Cavad Azer.
215 N6 Cava de'Tirreni Italy
204 C5 Cávado r. Port.
212 E5 Cavaglià Italy
183 G9 Cavaillon France
183 J10 Cavalaire-sur-Mer France
278 D5 Cavalcante Goiás Brazil
276 E2 Cavalcante Rondônia Brazil
206 B5 Cavaleiro Port.
213 K3 Cavalese Italy
260 G1 Cavalier ND U.S.A.
208 □ Cavalleria, Cap de c. Spain
212 D6 Cavallermaggiore Italy
102 H1 Cavalli Islands North I. N.Z.
213 N5 Cavallino Italy
214 C5 Cavallo, Île i. Corse France
215 N3 Cavalluccio, Punta pt Italy
228 D5 Cavally r. Côte d'Ivoire
212 G5 Cava Manara Italy
169 H5 Cavan Ireland
169 H5 Cavan county Ireland
285 F3 Cavanagh Arg.
212 G3 Cavargna Italy
213 M5 Cavarzere Italy
213 O3 Cavazzo Carnico Italy
221 K3 Çavdarhisar Turkey
221 K5 Çavdır Turkey
103 E11 Cave South I. N.Z.
261 J7 Cave City AR U.S.A.
254 E7 Cave City KY U.S.A.
265 U8 Cave Creek AZ U.S.A.
213 P3 Cave del Predil Italy
213 J3 Cavedine, Lago di l. Italy
281 F2 Caveira Brazil
183 E9 Caveirac France
109 J9 Cavenagh Range hills W.A. Austr.
105 I7 Cavendish Vic. Austr.
279 B9 Cavera, Serra do hills Brazil
280 A6 Cavernoso, Serra do mts Brazil
172 H2 Caverswall Staffordshire, England U.K.
256 B10 Cave Run Lake KY U.S.A.
204 E5 Cavês Port.
213 K6 Cavezzo Italy
275 I4 Caviana, Ilha i. Brazil
184 D5 Cavignac France
114 C7 Cavili rf Phil.
114 C4 Cavite Luzon Phil.
213 Q5 Čavle Croatia
219 L3 Cavnic Romania
215 J4 Cavo, Monte hill Italy
214 D9 Cavoli, Isola dei i. Sardegna Italy
217 L3 Cavone r. Italy
231 C8 Cavongo Angola
212 C6 Cavour Italy
250 F4 Cavour WI U.S.A.
212 E5 Cavour, Canale canal Italy
213 J6 Cavriago Italy
213 K8 Cavriglia Italy
148 E4 Çavuşçu Turkey
221 M2 Çavuşdere Turkey
221 L6 Çavuşköy Turkey
168 I7 Cawdor Highland, Scotland U.K.
105 H5 Cawndilla Lake imp. l. N.S.W. Austr.
Cawnpore Uttar Prad. India see Kanpur
171 O6 Cawood North Yorkshire, England U.K.
256 B12 Cawood KY U.S.A.
173 O2 Cawston Norfolk, England U.K.
281 E4 Caxambu Brazil
204 C9 Caxarias Port.
274 D6 Caxias Amazonas Brazil
278 E3 Caxias Maranhão Brazil
279 C9 Caxias do Sul Brazil
231 B7 Caxito Angola
275 I5 Caxiuana, Baía de l. Brazil
221 M4 Çay Turkey
274 B5 Cayambe-Coca, Reserva Ecológica nat. park Ecuador
151 D5 Çayarası Turkey
285 G2 Cayastá Arg.
221 I4 Çaybaşı İzmir Turkey
Çaybaşı Rize Turkey see Çayeli
255 G9 Cayce SC U.S.A.
148 F3 Çaycuma Turkey
149 J3 Çayeli Turkey
275 H3 Cayenne Fr. Guiana
285 I2 Cayetano Uru.
178 C3 Cayeux-sur-Mer France
271 □[1] Cayey Puerto Rico
271 □[1] Cayey, Sierra de hills Puerto Rico
221 J3 Çaygören Barajı resr Turkey
148 G5 Çayhan Turkey
221 J6 Çayhisar Turkey
148 E3 Çayırhan Turkey
151 B6 Çayırlı Turkey
151 B5 Çaykara Turkey
151 H6 Çaylaqqala Azer.
185 H7 Caylus France
270 D4 Cayman Brac i. Cayman Is
270 C4 Cayman Islands terr. West Indies
288 D4 Cayman Trench sea feature Caribbean Sea
232 E2 Caynabo Somalia
172 G3 Caynham Shropshire, England U.K.
183 J8 Cayolle, Col de la pass France
271 □[2] Cayon St Kitts and Nevis
255 □[2] Cay Point New Prov. Bahamas
151 G5 Çay Räsullu Azer.
183 D7 Cayres France
270 C2 Cay Sal i. Bahamas
270 C2 Cay Sal Bank sea feature Bahamas
270 F3 Cay Santa Domingo i. Bahamas
171 P7 Caythorpe Lincolnshire, England U.K.
171 Q5 Cayton North Yorkshire, England U.K.
264 L6 Cayucos CA U.S.A.
251 O7 Cayuga Ont. Can.
256 I6 Cayuga Heights NY U
256 I6 Cayuga Lake NY U.S.A
270 F2 Cay Verde i. Bahamas
231 D7 Cazage Angola
Cazaje Angola see Caz
205 K8 Cazalegas Spain
206 H5 Cazalla de la Sierra Sp
185 G6 Cazals Midi-Pyrénées F
185 H7 Cazals Midi-Pyrénées F
219 P6 Căzăneşti Romania
282 F3 Caza Pava Arg.
185 D8 Cazaubon France
185 B7 Cazaux et de Sanguin de l. France
133 H11 Cazê Xizang China
257 J6 Cazenovia NY U.S.A.
185 G9 Cazères France
185 G7 Cazes-Mondenard Fr
185 I9 Cazilhac France
210 F3 Cažma Croatia
231 D7 Cazombo Angola
269 J5 Cazones Mex.
269 J5 Cazones r. Mex.
207 N5 Cazorla Spain
207 M5 Cazorla, Sierra de mts
185 G6 Cazoulès France
213 N3 Cà Zul, Lago di l. Italy
235 G2 Cazula Moz.
205 K4 Cea Castilla y León Spa
204 E4 Cea Galicia Spain
205 I4 Cea r. Spain
Ceadâr-Lunga Moldo Ciadîr-Lunga
Ceanannus Mór Irela
168 B7 Ceann a' Bhàigh Weste Scotland U.K.
Ceará Brazil see Fortal
278 F3 Ceará state Brazil
288 G6 Ceara Abyssal Plain se S. Atlantic Ocean
168 C6 Cearsiadar Western Isl Scotland U.K.
219 Q5 Ceatalchioi Romania
Ceatharlach Ireland se
181 J5 Ceaucé France
183 D6 Céaux-d'Allègre Franc
266 G4 Ceballos Mex.
204 G1 Cebes, Cabo c. Spain
169 B8 Cé Bhréanainn Irelan
150 A2 Cebireis Dağı mt. Tur
204 E9 Cebolais de Cima Por
205 K9 Cebolla Spain
282 D3 Cebollar Arg.
205 O4 Cebollera, Sierra mts
268 C6 Ceboruco, Cerro mt. M
268 C4 Ceboruco, Volcán vol.
199 I3 Čebovce Slovakia
205 L8 Cebreros Spain
114 D6 Cebu Cebu Phil.
114 D6 Cebu i. Phil.
215 K4 Ceccano Italy
199 H5 Cece Hungary
200 E7 Cece, Cima di mt. Ital
204 D2 Cecebre, Encoro de re
199 K3 Čečejovce Slovakia
198 E2 Čechtice Czech Rep.
198 D1 Čechy reg. Czech Rep.
199 H3 Čechynce Slovakia
250 F5 Cecil WI U.S.A.
258 D5 Cecil County county M
107 M9 Cecil Plains Qld Austr.
109 F8 Cecil Rhodes, Mount W.A. Austr.
258 D6 Cecilton MD U.S.A.
213 J9 Cecina Italy
213 I9 Cecina r. Italy
217 K5 Cecita, Lago di l. Italy
204 G9 Ceclavín Spain
204 F6 Cedães Port.
250 J6 Cedar r. MI U.S.A.
260 E2 Cedar r. ND U.S.A.
260 G5 Cedar r. NE U.S.A.
256 D11 Cedar Bluff VA U.S.A.
265 T4 Cedar Breaks Nationa Monument nat. park U
258 F5 Cedar Brook NJ U.S.A
265 S4 Cedar City UT U.S.A.
261 G9 Cedar Creek Reservoi TX U.S.A.
263 K7 Cedaredge CO U.S.A.
260 I4 Cedar Falls IA U.S.A.
271 □[2] Cedar Grove Antigua and Barbuda
264 N5 Cedar Grove CA U.S.A
250 G6 Cedar Grove WI U.S.A.
256 D10 Cedar Grove WV U.S.A
257 J11 Cedar Island VA U.S.A
247 K4 Cedar Lake Man. Can.
251 P3 Cedar Lake Ont. Can.
256 B7 Cedar Point OH U.S.A
254 B5 Cedar Rapids IA U.S.A
265 U5 Cedar Ridge AZ U.S.A.
250 G4 Cedar River MI U.S.A.
259 G5 Cedar Run NJ U.S.A.
251 L7 Cedar Springs Ont. Ca
250 I6 Cedar Springs MI U.S.
255 E8 Cedartown GA U.S.A.
270 □ Cedar Valley Jamaica
237 N6 Cedarville S. Africa
250 E7 Cedarville IL U.S.A.
251 J4 Cedarville MI U.S.A.
256 B9 Cedarville OH U.S.A.
212 I3 Cedegolo Italy
204 D1 Cedeira Spain
204 C2 Cedeira hill Spain
204 D1 Cedeira, Ría de inlet Sp
205 L9 Cedena r. Spain
266 □P11 Cedeño Hond.
236 C8 Cederberg mts S. Afric
204 F9 Cedillo Spain
204 F9 Cedillo, Embalse de re Port./Spain
205 M8 Cedillo del Condado S
267 P7 Cedral Quintana Roo M
268 G2 Cedral San Luis Potosí
208 D7 Cedrillas Spain
214 D7 Cedrino r. Sardegna Ita
278 F3 Cedro Brazil
238 □[1c] Cedros Faial Azores
266 □P10 Cedros Hond.
266 E4 Cedros Sonora Mex.
268 F1 Cedros Zacatecas Mex.
266 B3 Cedros, Isla i. Mex.
238 □[1c] Cedros, Ponta dos pt F
271 □[7] Cedros Point Trin. anc
196 G1 Cedry Wielkie Pol.
104 D5 Ceduna S.A. Austr.
196 C3 Cedynia Pol.
192 J5 Cedyński Park Krajobr
204 B3 Cee Spain
232 E2 Ceel Afweyn Somalia
232 F2 Ceelayo Somalia
232 D2 Ceel Baxay Somalia
232 E3 Ceelbuur Somalia
232 E2 Ceel Dhaab Somalia
232 E4 Ceeldheere Somalia
232 D2 Ceel Gaal Awdal Soma
232 F2 Ceel Gaal Bari Somalia
232 E3 Ceel Garas well Somal
232 E3 Ceel God Somalia
232 F3 Ceel Huur Somalia
232 D4 Ceel Walaaq well Soma
232 E2 Ceerigaabo Somalia
199 K5 Cefa Romania
216 G7 Cefalù Sicilia Italy
Cefn Bychan Caerphilly U.K. see Newbridge
172 F2 Cefn-mawr Wrexham, V
205 K5 Cega r. Spain
213 N4 Ceggia Italy
199 I4 Cegléd Hungary
199 I4 Ceglédbercel Hungary
217 N2 Ceglie Messapica Italy
197 J3 Cegłów Pol.
133 K10 Cêgnê Xizang China
218 I9 Čegrane Macedonia
199 L4 Cehal Romania
207 P4 Cehegín Spain
130 E6 Ceheng Guizhou China
218 G7 Čehotina r. Montenegr
219 L3 Cehu Silvaniei Roman
271 □[1] Ceiba Puerto Rico
285 H3 Ceibas Arg.
199 L5 Ceica Romania

C9 Ceilhes-et-Rocozels France
Ceinewydd Ceredigion, Wales U.K. see New Quay
J4 Ceinos de Campos Spain
L6 Ceintrey France
D8 Ceira Port.
D8 Ceira r. Port.
F3 Čejč Czech Rep.
K3 Čejkov Slovakia
O2 Čejkovice Czech Rep.
G2 Cekcyn Pol.
G3 Çekerek Turkey
E3 Çekiçler Turkm.
G4 Ceków-Kolonia Pol.
C7 Celadas Spain
Celah, Gunung mt. Malaysia see Mandi Angin, Gunung
D1 Čelákovice Czech Rep.
L3 Celano Italy
E4 Celanova Spain
D10 Celaque, Parque Nacional nat. park Hond.
G5 Celaya Mex.
6 Celbridge Ireland
H7 Célé r. France
Celebes i. Indon. see Sulawesi
B2 Celebes Sea Indon./Phil.
E7 Çelebibağı Turkey
D5 Celeiros Port.
H8 Celemin, Embalse de resr Spain
B6 Celendín Peru
J4 Celenza Valfortore Italy
J7 Celestún Mex.
5 Celico Italy
D6 Çelikli Turkey
M5 Celina OH U.S.A.
E7 Celina TN U.S.A.
E2 Celje Slovenia
E7 Cella Spain
G4 Celldömölk Hungary
5 Celle Ger.
H3 Cellere Italy
D7 Celles Belgium
H10 Celles France
3 Celles-sur-Belle France
5 Celles-sur-Durolle France
J7 Celles-sur-Ource France
6 Cellettes France
3 Cellina r. Italy
2 Cellino Attanasio Italy
3 Cellino San Marco Italy
5 Cellole Italy
4 Celone r. Italy
7 Celorico da Beira Port.
6 Celorico de Basto Port.
Celovec Austria see Klagenfurt
3 Celrà Spain
6 Celtic Sea Ireland/U.K.
2 Celtic Shelf sea feature N. Atlantic Ocean
5 Çeltikçi Burdur Turkey
Çeltikçi Bursa Turkey
5 Çeltikçi Beli pass Turkey
2 Celyn, Llyn l. Wales U.K.
6 Cem r. Turkey
4 Cemaru, Gunung mt. Indon.
3 Cembra Italy
Çemenibit Turkm.
3 Cemilbey Turkey
Çemişgezek Turkey
2 Cemmaes Powys, Wales U.K.
9 Cempi, Teluk b. Sumbawa Indon.
7 Čemšeniška planina mt. Slovenia
6 Cénac-et-St-Julien France
Cenad Romania
4 Cenajo, Embalse del resr Spain
Cencenighe Agordino Italy
Cenderawasih, Teluk b. Papua Indon.
Çendir r. Turkm.
Cendras France
Cendrieux France
Cenei Romania
Ceneselli Italy
Cengio Italy
4 Cenicero Spain
Ceniclentos Spain
Cenis, Col du Mont pass France
Cenizate Spain
Cennetpınar Turkey
Ceno r. Italy
Cenon France
Cenouras, Ilhéu das i. Madeira
Cenrana Sulawesi Barat Indon.
Čenta Vojvodina Serbia
Centallo Italy
Centane S. Africa see Kentani
Centar Župa Centar Župa Macedonia
1 Centaur Peak South I. N.Z.
Centellas Spain see Centelles
Centelles Spain
Centenario Arg.
Centenário do Sul Brazil
Centenary Zimbabwe
Centennial Wash watercourse AZ U.S.A.
Center ND U.S.A.
Center NE U.S.A.
0 Center TX U.S.A.
Centerburg OH U.S.A.
Centereach NY U.S.A.
Center Hill Lake resr TN U.S.A.
Center Moriches NY U.S.A.
5 Center Ossipee NH U.S.A.
Center Point AL U.S.A.
Centerport NY U.S.A.
Center Square PA U.S.A.
Center Valley PA U.S.A.
Centerville IA U.S.A.
Centerville MO U.S.A.
0 Centerville OH U.S.A.
Centerville PA U.S.A.
Centerville PA U.S.A.
Centerville TN U.S.A.
0 Centerville TX U.S.A.
Centerville WV U.S.A.
Cento Italy
Centola Italy
Centraal Suriname Natuurreservaat nature res. Suriname
Centrafricaine, République country Africa see Central African Republic
Central admin. dist. Botswana
Central Brazil
Central Chile
Central admin. reg. Ghana
Central prov. Kenya
Central admin. reg. Malawi
Central AK U.S.A.
Central NM U.S.A.
Central prov. Zambia
Central, Cordillera mts Bol.
Central, Cordillera mts Col.
Central, Cordillera mts Dom. Rep.
3 Central, Cordillera mts Panama
Central, Cordillera mts Peru
Central, Cordillera mts Luzon Phil.
Central, Cordillera mts Puerto Rico
Central African Empire country Africa see Central African Republic
Central African Republic country Africa
Central Australia Aboriginal Reserve W.A. Austr.
Central Bedfordshire admin. div. England U.K.
Central Brahui Range mts Pak.
Central Butte Sask. Can.
Central City IA U.S.A.
Central City NE U.S.A.
Central City PA U.S.A.
Central de Minas Brazil
Central Desert Aboriginal Land res. N.T. Austr.
Central Equatoria state Sudan
Central Falls RI U.S.A.
Centralia IL U.S.A.

262 C3 Centralia WA U.S.A.
232 C4 Central Island National Park Kenya
259 I3 Central Islip NY U.S.A.
234 D4 Central Kalahari Game Reserve nature res. Botswana
284 B2 Central Los Molles Chile
145 K8 Central Makran Range mts Pak.
106 D6 Central Mount Stuart hill N.T. Austr.
106 C7 Central Mount Wedge N.T. Austr.
290 G5 Central Pacific Basin sea feature Pacific Ocean
105 K9 Central Plateau Conservation Area nature res. Tas. Austr.
Central Provinces state India see Madhya Pradesh
237 M5 Central Range mts Lesotho
113 J7 Central Range mts P.N.G.
Central Russian Upland hills Rus. Fed. see Sredne-Russkaya Vozvyshennost'
Central Siberian Plateau Rus. Fed. see Sredne-Sibirskoye Ploskogor'ye
257 I5 Central Square NY U.S.A.
259 G2 Central Valley NY U.S.A.
264 J2 Central Valley val. U.S.A.
259 L1 Central Village CT U.S.A.
229 H5 Centre prov. Cameroon
184 H1 Centre admin. reg. France
255 E8 Centre AL U.S.A.
182 E3 Centre, Canal du France
239 □1b Centre de Flacq Mauritius
103 B13 Centre Island South I. N.Z.
255 D9 Centreville AL U.S.A.
258 C6 Centreville MD U.S.A.
250 I8 Centreville MI U.S.A.
256 H10 Centreville VA U.S.A.
214 C2 Centuri Corse France
237 M1 Centurion S. Africa
216 H8 Centuripe Sicilia Italy
255 D10 Century FL U.S.A.
131 H7 Cenxi Guangxi China
Ceos i. Greece see Tzia
Ceos Scotland U.K. see Keose
185 G6 Céou r. France
215 M3 Cepagatti Italy
Cephaloedium Sicilia Italy see Cefalù
Cephalonia i. Greece see Kefallonia
210 G3 Čepin Croatia
160 H8 Čepkelių nature res. Lith.
204 E7 Cepões Port.
201 I7 Čepovan Slovenia
178 E7 Cepoy France
216 H1 Ceppaloni Italy
215 L4 Ceprano Italy
117 I8 Cepu Jawa Indon.
218 H6 Cer hills Serbia
Ceram i. Maluku Indon. see Seram
216 H8 Cerami Sicilia Italy
216 G8 Cerami r. Sicilia Italy
Ceram Sea Indon. see Seram, Laut
212 F5 Cerano Italy
197 K3 Ceranów Pol.
181 L6 Cérans-Foulletourte France
217 J7 Cerasi Italy
215 O7 Ceraso Italy
214 D6 Ceraso, Capo c. Sardegna Italy
199 L6 Cerbăl Romania
265 R6 Cerbat Mountains AZ U.S.A.
185 K11 Cerbère France
208 L3 Cerbère, Cap c. France/Spain
214 C4 Cerbicale, Îles is Corse France
Cerbol r. Spain see Cervol, Riu
214 F2 Cerboli, Isola i. Italy
206 B2 Cercal Lisboa Port.
206 B5 Cercal Setúbal Port.
206 B5 Cercal hill Port.
206 B5 Cercal, Serra do mts Port.
198 D2 Čerčany Czech Rep.
205 L7 Cercedilla Spain
215 N5 Cercemaggiore Italy
215 L3 Cerchio Italy
198 B2 Čerchov mt. Czech Rep.
182 D3 Cercy-la-Tour France
216 F8 Cerda Sicilia Italy
185 I11 Cerdagne reg. France
Cerdaña reg. France see Cerdagne
208 I3 Cerdanya reg. Spain
208 J5 Cerdanyola del Vallès Spain
204 D3 Cerdedo Spain
204 E8 Cerdeira Port.
181 P6 Cerdon France
185 H6 Cère r. France
213 K5 Cerea Italy
247 I5 Cereal Alta Can.
285 F5 Cereales Arg.
205 N3 Cereceda, Embalse de resr Spain
199 I3 Cered Hungary
172 E3 Ceredigion admin. div. Wales U.K.
213 L5 Ceregnano Italy
196 F3 Cerekwica Pol.
180 I4 Cérences France
217 L5 Cerenzia Italy
285 G1 Ceres Arg.
278 C5 Ceres Brazil
212 C5 Ceres Italy
236 D9 Ceres S. Africa
264 L4 Ceres CA U.S.A.
183 K6 Ceresole, Lago di l. Italy
212 C5 Ceresole Reale Italy
213 L5 Ceresone r. Italy
183 H9 Céreste France
185 J11 Céret France
274 C2 Cereté Col.
205 M6 Cerezo de Abajo Spain
205 M6 Cerezo de Arriba Spain
205 N3 Cerezo de Riotirón Spain
239 □2b Cerf, Île au i. Inner Islands Seychelles
251 S3 Cerf, Lac du l. Que. Can.
187 F8 Cerfontaine Belgium
239 □1b Cerfs, Îles aux is Mauritius
199 K2 Čergov mts Slovakia
178 D5 Cergy France
193 L10 Cerhenice Czech Rep.
133 G11 Cêri Xizang China
212 E7 Ceriale Italy
212 D8 Ceriana Italy
215 P5 Cerignola Italy
Cerigo i. Greece see Kythira
148 F4 Çerikli Turkey
284 B3 Cerillos Chile
284 B2 Cerillos de Tamaya Chile
182 B3 Cérilly France
Cêringgolêb Xizang China see Dongco
178 F7 Cerisiers France
181 J3 Cerisy-la-Forêt France
180 I3 Cerisy-la-Salle France
181 J8 Cerizay France
213 R4 Cerk mt. Slovenia
148 F3 Çerkeş Turkey
221 K2 Çerkeşli Turkey
221 J1 Çerkezköy Turkey
221 I1 Çerkezmüsellim Turkey
201 M8 Cerklje Brežice Slovenia
201 J7 Cerklje Kranj Slovenia
210 E3 Cerknica Slovenia
201 J8 Cerkniško jezero l. Slovenia
201 I7 Cerkno Slovenia
196 D1 Cerkwica Pol.
151 D5 Çerme Turkey
219 J4 Cermei Romania
215 L2 Cermignano Italy
148 I4 Çermik Turkey
219 Q5 Cerna Romania
219 K5 Cerna r. Romania
219 K6 Cerna r. Romania
219 M6 Cerna r. Romania
204 D9 Cernache do Bonjardim Port.
204 H5 Cernadilla, Embalse de resr Spain
198 F2 Černá Hora Czech Rep.
198 C3 Černá hora mt. Czech Rep.
219 O5 Cernat Romania
Cernăuți Ukr. see Chernivtsi
219 Q6 Cernavodă Romania
179 N8 Cernay France
178 I5 Cernay-en-Dormois France

198 C1 Černčice Czech Rep.
205 M3 Cernégula Spain
201 N6 Černelavci Slovenia
212 B1 Cernier Switz.
199 H3 Černík Slovakia
199 L2 Černiny hill Slovakia
212 G4 Cernobbio Italy
198 D2 Černošice Czech Rep.
198 B2 Černošín Czech Rep.
198 D2 Černovice Czech Rep.
185 H7 Cérou r. France
213 Q5 Cerovica Croatia
213 Q5 Cerovlje Croatia
199 I3 Cerovo Slovakia
280 C5 Cerqueira César Brazil
204 G7 Cerralbo Spain
267 J4 Cerralvo Mex.
266 E5 Cerralvo, Isla i. Mex.
205 K5 Cerrato, Valles de reg. Spain
212 I7 Cerreto, Passo del pass Italy
213 N9 Cerreto d'Esi Italy
215 J2 Cerreto di Spoleto Italy
215 N5 Cerreto Sannita Italy
172 E1 Cerrigydrudion Conwy, Wales U.K.
218 H9 Cërrik Albania
282 D2 Cerrillos Arg.
268 G5 Cerritos Guanajuato Mex.
268 G3 Cerritos San Luis Potosí Mex.
215 M4 Cerro al Volturno Italy
280 C6 Cerro Azul Brazil
269 J4 Cerro Azul Mex.
276 A3 Cerro Azul Peru
206 H5 Cerro del Hierro Spain
268 D7 Cerro de Ortega Mex.
276 A2 Cerro de Pasco Peru
268 G4 Cerro Gordo Mex.
266 □S14 Cerro Hoya, Parque Nacional nat. park Panama
283 C9 Cerro Manantiales Chile
207 M7 Cerrón mt. Spain
274 D2 Cerrón, Cerro mt. Venez.
276 C5 Cerro Negro Chile
266 F4 Cerro Prieto Mex.
284 C6 Cerros Colorados, Embalse resr Arg.
274 A5 Cerros de Amotape, Parque Nacional nat. park Peru
181 K7 Cersay France
215 Q7 Cersosimo Italy
213 K8 Certaldo Italy
219 K5 Certeju de Sus Romania
199 K2 Čertižne Slovakia
212 G5 Certosa di Pavia Italy
212 D7 Certosa di Pesio Italy
Ceru Colorado Aruba see Seroe Colorado
204 E6 Cerva Port.
204 C5 Cervães Port.
205 J9 Cervales mt. Spain
109 C11 Cervantes W.A. Austr.
283 B8 Cervantes, Cerro mt. Arg.
215 L5 Cervaro Italy
215 P4 Cervaro r. Italy
215 O7 Cervati, Monte mt. Italy
205 K4 Cervatos de la Cueza Spain
198 F1 Červená Voda Czech Rep.
193 L10 Červené Pečky Czech Rep.
219 N7 Cervenia Romania
198 G2 Červenka Czech Rep.
208 H4 Cervera Spain
208 F6 Cervera, Rambla de r. Spain
205 Q6 Cervera de la Cañada Spain
205 P9 Cervera del Llano Spain
205 K8 Cervera de los Montes Spain
205 Q4 Cervera del Río Alhama Spain
205 L3 Cervera de Pisuerga Spain
214 I4 Cerveteri Italy
213 M7 Cervia Italy
215 O6 Cervialto, Monte mt. Italy
213 O4 Cervignano del Friuli Italy
213 K2 Cervina, Punta mt. Italy
215 N5 Cervinara Italy
198 E2 Červiná Řečice Czech Rep.
214 C3 Cervione Corse France
212 E8 Cervo Italy
212 E5 Cervo r. Italy
204 F1 Cervo Spain
208 G7 Cervol, Riu r. Spain
182 D2 Cervon France
215 Q9 Cerzeto Italy
213 O8 Cesano r. Italy
274 C2 Cesar dept Col.
274 C2 Cesar r. Col.
216 H8 Cesarò Sicilia Italy
200 F8 Cesen, Monte mt. Italy
213 M7 Cesena Italy
213 M7 Cesenatico Italy
212 D7 Cesio Italy
160 I4 Cēsis Latvia
198 D1 Česká Kamenice Czech Rep.
198 D1 Česká Lípa Czech Rep.
Česká Republika country Europe see Czech Republic
198 F1 Česká Skalice Czech Rep.
199 I3 České Brezovo Slovakia
198 D3 České Budějovice Czech Rep.
198 C1 České středohoří hills Czech Rep.
201 K2 České Velenice Austria
198 D2 Českomoravská vysočina hills Czech Rep.
198 D1 Český Brod Czech Rep.
193 K9 Český Dub Czech Rep.
198 D3 Český Krumlov Czech Rep.
198 B2 Český les mts Czech Rep./Ger.
193 L9 Český ráj park Czech Rep.
201 L1 Český Rudolec Czech Rep.
199 H2 Český Těšín Czech Rep.
210 F3 Česma r. Croatia
221 H4 Çeşme Turkey
204 I7 Cespedosa Spain
213 N4 Cessalto Italy
183 B10 Cesse r. France
183 C10 Cessenon-sur-Orb France
182 G5 Cessieu France
105 M5 Cessnock N.S.W. Austr.
180 H5 Cesson-Sévigné France
185 C6 Cestas France
228 C5 Cestos r. Liberia
204 D2 Cesuras Spain
160 J5 Cesvaine Latvia
114 D3 Cetaceo, Mount Phil.
128 G8 Cêtar Qinghai China
199 L4 Cetariu Romania
219 L6 Cetate Romania
Cetatea Albă Ukr. see Bilhorod-Dnistrovs'kyy
210 F4 Cetina r. Croatia
205 Q6 Cetina Spain
218 G8 Cetinje Cetinje Montenegro
212 I3 Ceto Italy
181 M5 Ceton France
214 H2 Cetona Italy
215 P8 Cetraro Italy
185 C10 Cette-Eygun France
100 □1 Cetti Bay Guam
183 H7 Céüse France
183 H7 Céüse, Montagne de mt. France
202 D5 Ceuta N. Africa
209 C11 Ceutí Spain
212 E7 Ceva Italy
99 H4 Ceva-i-Ra rf Fiji
213 J3 Cevedale, Monte mt. Italy
183 C9 Cévennes mts France
183 D8 Cévennes, Parc National des nat. park France
Čevetjävri Fin. see Sevettijärvi
205 L5 Cevico de la Torre Spain
205 L5 Cevico Navero Spain
182 I5 Cevins France
212 F3 Cevio Switz.
151 C5 Cevizli Erzurum Turkey
221 L3 Cevizli Eskişehir Turkey
150 F2 Cevizli Gaziantep Turkey
Cevizlik Turkey see Maçka
196 F1 Cewice Pol.
197 K5 Cewków Pol.
148 G5 Ceyhan Turkey
150 D2 Ceyhan r. Turkey
150 D2 Ceyhan Boğazı r. mouth Turkey
149 J5 Ceylanpınar Turkey
151 K5 Çeyldağ Azer.
Ceylon country Asia see Sri Lanka
151 K5 Ceyranbatan Azer.
183 H10 Ceyreste France

182 G4 Ceyzériat France
184 D5 Cézac France
183 F8 Cèze r. France
204 E5 Chã Port.
186 G6 Chaam Neth.
144 I9 Chābahār Iran
184 F4 Chabanais France
285 G3 Chabas Arg.
183 H8 Chabestan France
183 G7 Chabeuil France
197 H4 Chabielice Pol.
182 J4 Chablais mts France
267 N9 Chablé Mex.
178 G8 Chablis France
184 F4 Chabrac France
183 H8 Chabre ridge France
182 D5 Chabreloche France
181 O7 Chabris France
Chabrol i. Îles Loyauté New Caledonia see Lifou
133 L13 Chabua Assam India
133 F10 Chabug Xizang China
133 G11 Chabyêr Caka salt l. China
276 C4 Chaca Chile
285 G4 Chacabuco Arg.
271 □7 Chacachacare Island Trin. and Tob.
269 L7 Chacaltianguis Mex.
269 J8 Chacaltongo Mex.
276 C4 Chacarilla Bol.
274 B6 Chachapoyas Peru
284 E5 Chacharramendi Arg.
138 F7 Chachaura-Binaganj Madh. Prad. India
Chäche Turkm. see Çäçe
161 N9 Chachersk Belarus
160 M8 Chachevichy Belarus
119 E8 Chachoengsao Thai.
145 N9 Chachro Pak.
204 G6 Chacim Port.
282 E2 Chaco prov. Arg.
277 F5 Chaco Boreal reg. Para.
263 K8 Chaco Culture National Historical Park nat. park NM U.S.A.
245 N5 Chacon, Cape AK U.S.A.
275 G6 Chacorão, Cachoeira da waterfall Brazil
276 B2 Chacra de Piros Peru
224 C6 Chad country Africa
224 B6 Chad, Lake Africa
128 H3 Chadaasan Mongolia
120 F1 Chadan Rus. Fed.
255 □1 Chaddock Bar rf Bermuda
258 D5 Chadds Ford PA U.S.A.
235 G2 Chadiza Zambia
183 D6 Chadrac France
260 D4 Chadron NE U.S.A.
Chadyr-Lunga Moldova see Ciadîr-Lunga
118 D5 Chae Hom Thai.
143 P7 Chaek Kyrg.
123 D9 Chaeryŏng N. Korea
118 D5 Chae Son National Park Thai.
203 E5 Chafarinas, Islas is N. Africa
229 G4 Chafe Nigeria
261 K7 Chaffee MO U.S.A.
283 B7 Chaffers, Isla i. Chile
250 B3 Chaffey WI U.S.A.
274 C4 Chafurray Col.
145 K7 Chagai Pak.
145 J7 Chagai Hills Afgh./Pak.
136 F5 Chagalamarri Andhra Prad. India
142 K5 Chagan Kyzylordinskaya Oblast' Kazakh.
143 R2 Chagan Vostochnyy Kazakhstan Kazakh.
132 I1 Chaganuzun Rus. Fed.
133 G9 Chagdo Kangri mt. China
172 E6 Chagford Devon, England U.K.
133 L9 Chaggur Qinghai China
145 K4 Chaghcharān Afgh.
143 M1 Chaglinka r. Kazakh.
182 F3 Chagny France
161 S2 Chagoda Rus. Fed.
161 S2 Chagoda r. Rus. Fed.
161 T3 Chagodoshcha r. Rus. Fed.
289 I5 Chagos Archipelago is B.I.O.T.
289 I5 Chagos-Laccadive Ridge sea feature Indian Ocean
289 I5 Chagos Trench sea feature Indian Ocean
122 F2 Chagoyan Rus. Fed.
142 C1 Chagra r. Rus. Fed.
Chagrayskoye Plato plat. Kazakh. see Shagyray, Plato
266 □T13 Chagres, Parque Nacional nat. park Panama
271 □7 Chaguanas Trin. and Tob.
271 □7 Chaguaramas Trin. and Tob.
274 E2 Chaguaramas Venez.
144 E1 Chagyllyshor, Vpadina depr. Turkm.
158 I8 Chaha r. Ukr.
145 J6 Chahah Burjal Afgh.
144 H5 Chāhak Iran
144 H5 Chāh Ākhvor Iran
144 E6 Chah 'Ali Iran
144 G4 Chāh 'Ali Akbar Iran
145 N4 Chaharbagh Afgh.
144 D5 Chahār Maḩāll va Bakhtīārī prov. Iran
144 D7 Chahār Rūstā'ī Iran
144 B3 Chahār Ţāq Iran
144 F4 Chah Baba well Iran
144 E5 Chāh Badam Iran
144 I9 Chāh Bahār, Khalīj-e b. Iran
144 I3 Chahchaheh Turkm.
145 M3 Chāh-e Āb Afgh.
144 E6 Chāh-e Dow Chāhī Iran
144 G5 Chāh-e Khoshāb Iran
144 F5 Chāh-e Nūklok Iran
144 F7 Chāh-e Rāh Iran
145 I5 Chah-e Rig Afgh.
144 F5 Chāh-e Shūr Iran
144 I7 Chah Gheybī, Hāmūn-e salt pan Iran
144 F7 Chāh Ḩaqq Iran
144 E6 Chāh Kūh Iran
144 G8 Chāh Lak Iran
145 J7 Chah Sandan Pak.
144 E4 Chah Shirin Iran
144 E7 Chāh Sorkh Iran
269 M9 Chahuites Mex.
139 J8 Chaibasa Jharkhand India
249 H2 Chaigneau, Lac l. Que. Can.
Chaigoubu Hebei China see Huai'an
122 B5 Chaihe Nei Mongol China
122 C7 Chai He r. China
145 M9 Chailar Pak.
173 L6 Chailey East Sussex, England U.K.
184 G3 Chaillac France
181 J5 Chailland France
184 B3 Chaillé-les-Marais France
178 G7 Chailley France
230 A5 Chaillu, Massif du mts Gabon
118 E7 Chainat Thai.
133 H9 Chainjoin Co l. Xizang China
178 H6 Chaintrix-Bierges France
118 D5 Chai Prakan Thai.
119 E8 Chai Si r. Thai.
283 B6 Chaitén Chile
131 □J7 Chai Wan H.K. China
132 H5 Chaiwopu Xinjiang China
119 D10 Chaiya Thai.
118 E7 Chaiyaphum Thai.
284 E3 Chaján Arg.
285 I2 Chajarí Arg.
244 I3 Chakachamna Lake AK U.S.A.
139 K7 Chakai Bihar India
145 O4 Chakai Pak.
145 P5 Chak Amru Pak.
145 M7 Chakar r. Pak.
235 F3 Chakari Zimbabwe
139 N9 Chakaria Bangl.
145 O4 Chakdarra Pak.
233 C6 Chake Chake Tanz.
145 J6 Chakhānsūr Afgh.
139 I7 Chakia Uttar Prad. India
145 O6 Chak Jhumra Pak.
145 L8 Chakku Pak.
249 G1 Chakonipau, Lac l. Que. Can.
139 J8 Chakradharpur Jharkhand India

139 K8 Chakulia Jharkhand India
151 C4 Ch'ak'vi Georgia
145 O5 Chakwal Pak.
276 B3 Chala Peru
233 A6 Chala Tanz.
233 A7 Chalabesa Zambia
185 I10 Chalabre France
Chaladidi Georgia see Sabazho
182 H3 Chalain, Lac de l. France
184 E5 Chalais France
212 D3 Chalais Switz.
182 G4 Chalamont France
145 K5 Chalap Dalan mts Afgh.
182 F4 Chalaronne r. France
266 □O10 Chalatenango El Salvador
235 H3 Chaláua Moz.
128 E9 Chalaxung Qinghai China
232 C4 Chalbi Desert Kenya
Chalcedon Turkey see Kadıköy
268 D2 Chalchihuites Mex.
269 I6 Chalco Mex.
122 A2 Chaldonka Rus. Fed.
173 J6 Chale Isle of Wight, England U.K.
184 F4 Chaleix France
183 F7 Chalencon France
133 K7 Chalengkou Qinghai China
178 E7 Châlette-sur-Loing France
249 H3 Chaleur Bay inlet N.B./Que. Can.
Chaleurs, Baie de inlet N.B./Que. Can. see Chaleur Bay
258 E4 Chalfont PA U.S.A.
173 K4 Chalfont St Peter Buckinghamshire, England U.K.
172 H4 Chalford Gloucestershire, England U.K.
173 J4 Chalgrove Oxfordshire, England U.K.
283 C8 Chalía r. Arg.
197 H3 Chalin Pol.
179 J8 Chalindrey France
131 I5 Chaling Hunan China
233 C6 Chalinze Tanz.
138 E9 Chalisgaon Mahar. India
136 E7 Chalissery Kerala India
182 B3 Chalivoy-Milon France
Chalkar, Ozero salt l. Kazakh. see Shalkar, Ozero
221 I6 Chalki Notio Aigaio Greece
220 D3 Chalki Thessalia Greece
221 I6 Chalki i. Greece
220 E4 Chalkida Greece
220 D2 Chalkidona Greece
103 A13 Chalky Inlet South I. N.Z.
245 L2 Chalkyitsik AK U.S.A.
284 C6 Challacó Arg.
136 E5 Challakere Karnataka India
180 H8 Challans France
276 D4 Challapata Bol.
290 E5 Challenger Deep sea feature N. Pacific Ocean
291 L8 Challenger Fracture Zone sea feature S. Pacific Ocean
178 I5 Challerange France
182 H5 Challes-les-Eaux France
262 G4 Challis ID U.S.A.
261 K11 Chalmette LA U.S.A.
156 G2 Chal'mny-Varre Rus. Fed.
182 D3 Chalmoux France
182 E3 Chaloire r. France
184 C1 Chalonnes-sur-Loire France
178 H6 Châlons-en-Champagne France
Châlons-sur-Marne France see Châlons-en-Champagne
182 F3 Chalon-sur-Saône France
185 C8 Chalosse reg. France
151 E3 Chalovani Georgia
138 E1 Chalt Pak.
151 J5 Chaltan Pass Azer.
159 S6 Chaltyr' Rus. Fed.
122 D7 Chaluhe Jilin China
237 L9 Chalumna S. Africa
184 F4 Châlus France
144 D3 Chālūs Iran
144 D3 Chālūs, Rūd-e r. Iran
195 N3 Cham Ger.
212 E1 Cham Switz.
118 I7 Cham, Cu Lao i. Vietnam
144 D5 Cham, Kūh-e hill Iran
263 K8 Chama NM U.S.A.
263 K8 Chama r. NM U.S.A.
233 B7 Chama Zambia
239 □3a Chamadani hill Njazidja Comoros
116 D2 Chamah, Gunung mt. Malaysia
284 E4 Chamaico Arg.
234 B5 Chamais Bay Namibia
182 C5 Chamalières France
183 G7 Chamaloc France
233 B6 Chamamba Tanz.
145 L6 Chaman Pak.
144 G3 Chaman Bīd Iran
119 E8 Chamao, Khao mt. Thai.
195 N3 Chamb r. Ger.
138 F3 Chamba Hima. Prad. India
235 H2 Chamba Moz.
233 C7 Chamba Tanz.
138 G6 Chambal r. India
151 G5 Chambarak Armenia
183 G6 Chambaran, Plateau de France
270 D2 Chambas Cuba
249 G2 Chambeaux, Lac l. Que. Can.
184 H4 Chamberet France
182 H4 Chambéria France
108 I4 Chamberlain r. W.A. Austr.
247 J5 Chamberlain Sask. Can.
285 I3 Chamberlain Uru.
260 F4 Chamberlain SD U.S.A.
257 □P2 Chamberlain Lake ME U.S.A.
245 K1 Chamberlin, Mount AK U.S.A.
265 W6 Chambers AZ U.S.A.
106 C2 Chambers Bay N.T. Austr.
256 H9 Chambersburg PA U.S.A.
250 G4 Chambers Island WI U.S.A.
182 H5 Chambéry France
233 A7 Chambeshi Zambia
227 H2 Chambi, Jebel mt. Tunisia
274 C6 Chambira r. Peru
179 K5 Chambley-Bussières France
178 D5 Chambly France
181 L4 Chambois France
182 F2 Chambolle-Musigny France
184 H3 Chambon, Lac de l. France
182 B5 Chambon-sur-Lac France
184 I3 Chambon-sur-Voueize France
249 F3 Chambord Que. Can.
181 O6 Chambord France
184 H5 Chamboulive France
181 M7 Chambray-lès-Tours France
113 J7 Chambri Lake P.N.G.
178 G4 Chambry France
145 K8 Chamburi Kalat Pak.
149 L6 Chamchamāl Iraq
139 M5 Chamda Xizang China
Chamdo Xizang China see Qamdo
266 □T13 Chame Panama
183 H6 Chamechaude mt. France
144 C5 Cham-e Ḩannā Iran
268 B6 Chamela Mex.
195 N3 Chamerau Ger.
178 I8 Chamesson France
235 G3 Chametengo Moz.
184 H5 Chameyrat France
226 B5 Châmi well Maur.
284 D2 Chamical Arg.
221 H7 Chamili i. Greece
151 B1 Chamlykskaya Rus. Fed.
232 C3 Ch'amo Hāyk' l. Eth.
212 D4 Chamois Italy
Chamoli Uttaranchal India see Gopeshwar
182 J5 Chamonix-Mont-Blanc France
Chamouchouane r. Que. Can. see Ashuapmushuan
183 H8 Chamouse, Montagne de mt. France
182 I5 Chamoux-sur-Gelon France
284 B3 Champa Chile
139 I8 Champa Chhattisgarh India
184 I5 Champagnac France
184 F5 Champagnac-de-Belair France
183 D6 Champagnac-le-Vieux France
245 M3 Champagne Y.T. Can.
181 L5 Champagné France

178 H6 Champagne-Ardenne admin. reg. France
181 O7 Champagne Berrichonne reg. France
237 N5 Champagne Castle mt. S. Africa
178 H5 Champagne Crayeuse reg. France
182 H5 Champagne-en-Valromey France
178 H7 Champagne Humide reg. France
184 E4 Champagne-Mouton France
178 G7 Champagne Pouilleuse reg. France
178 D5 Champagne-sur-Oise France
178 E7 Champagne-sur-Seine France
179 M8 Champagney France
182 H3 Champagnole France
108 H3 Champagny Islands W.A. Austr.
254 C5 Champaign IL U.S.A.
171 J2 Champany Falkirk, Scotland U.K.
284 E2 Champaqui, Cerro mt. Arg.
276 A2 Champara mt. Peru
119 G7 Champasak Laos
178 G6 Champaubert France
138 H5 Champawat Uttaranchal India
184 F5 Champcevinel France
184 D3 Champdeniers-St-Denis France
182 E1 Champ-d'Oiseau France
249 H2 Champdoré, Lac l. Que. Can.
179 N7 Champ du Feu mt. France
181 M7 Champeigne reg. France
182 C5 Champeix France
212 B3 Champéry Switz.
212 C3 Champex Switz.
182 F3 Champforgeuil France
181 K5 Champgenéteux France
139 N8 Champhai Mizoram India
183 G6 Champier France
181 J6 Champigné France
178 F8 Champignelles France
179 L6 Champigneulles France
178 I7 Champignol-lez-Mondeville France
178 F7 Champigny France
246 H5 Champion Alta Can.
250 G3 Champion MI U.S.A.
257 L4 Champlain NY U.S.A.
256 I10 Champlain VA U.S.A.
248 F4 Champlain, Lake Can./U.S.A.
257 L5 Champlain Canal NY U.S.A.
182 C2 Champlemy France
182 H1 Champlitte France
251 Q1 Champneuf Que. Can.
184 E4 Champniers France
183 I7 Champoléon France
182 D5 Champoly France
267 N8 Champotón Mex.
178 B7 Champrond-en-Gâtine France
181 J4 Champsecret France
183 B6 Champs-sur-Tarentaine-Marchal France
178 G8 Champs-sur-Yonne France
183 H6 Champ-sur-Drac France
183 I8 Champtercier France
180 I7 Champtoceaux France
182 G2 Champvans France
136 E7 Chamrajnagar Karnataka India
183 H6 Chamrousse France
144 D6 Cham Siyāh Iran
133 J9 Chamu Co l. Qinghai China
206 C2 Chamusca Port.
Chamyndy Naryn Kyrg. see Chemyndy
157 I5 Chamzinka Rus. Fed.
119 E11 Chana Thai.
183 C8 Chanac France
Chanak Turkey see Çanakkale
267 M9 Chanal Mex.
285 H2 Chañar Entre Ríos Arg.
284 E2 Chañar La Rioja Arg.
284 C6 Chañar Neuquén Arg.
282 C2 Chañaral Chile
282 C3 Chañaral, Isla i. Chile
284 B2 Chañaral Alto Chile
282 C2 Chañarcillo Chile
285 F3 Chañar Ladeado Arg.
275 F3 Chanaro, Cerro mt. Venez.
183 F6 Chanas France
206 D2 Chança Port.
Chança r. Port./Spain see Chanza
284 E2 Chancani Arg.
268 G3 Chancaquero Mex.
276 A2 Chancay Peru
182 F1 Chanceaux France
181 M7 Chanceaux-sur-Choisille France
184 F5 Chancelade France
204 C9 Chancelaria Port.
271 □2 Chances Peak vol. Montserrat
267 O8 Chanchén Mex.
284 A4 Chanco Chile
284 A4 Chanco, Bahía de b. Chile
276 A2 Chancos Peru
Chanda Mahar. India see Chandrapur
245 J2 Chandalar AK U.S.A.
245 K2 Chandalar r. AK U.S.A.
245 K2 Chandalar, East Fork r. AK U.S.A.
245 J2 Chandalar, Middle Fork r. AK U.S.A.
245 J2 Chandalar, North Fork r. AK U.S.A.
233 C6 Chandama Tanz.
138 H5 Chandan Chauki Uttar Prad. India
139 I9 Chandarpur Chhattisgarh India
138 G5 Chandausi Uttar Prad. India
139 K9 Chandbali Orissa India
139 O7 Chandel Manipur India
261 K11 Chandeleur Islands LA U.S.A.
138 G7 Chanderi Madh. Prad. India
138 H8 Chandia Madh. Prad. India
138 F4 Chandigarh Chandigarh India
138 F4 Chandigarh union terr. India
139 K8 Chandil Jharkhand India
249 H3 Chandler Que. Can.
265 U8 Chandler AZ U.S.A.
261 G8 Chandler OK U.S.A.
245 J1 Chandler r. AK U.S.A.
244 I1 Chandler Lake AK U.S.A.
276 C2 Chandless r. Brazil
128 E4 Chandmanĭ Mongolia
Chandmanĭ Mongolia see Yaruu
251 Q5 Chandos Lake Ont. Can.
139 M8 Chandpur Bangl.
138 G5 Chandpur Uttar Prad. India
136 F6 Chandragiri Andhra Prad. India
136 F3 Chandrapur Mahar. India
204 F4 Chandrexa de Queixa, Encoro de resr Spain
138 G9 Chandur Mahar. India
138 E9 Chandvad Mahar. India
205 L6 Chañe Spain
144 I8 Chānf Iran
119 F8 Chang, Ko i. Thai.
237 Q2 Changalane Moz.
Chang'an Guangxi China see Rong'an
129 K9 Chang'an Shaanxi China
125 G11 Chang-an S. Korea
235 G5 Changane r. Moz.
235 G3 Changara Moz.
123 F8 Changbai Jilin China
123 E8 Changbai Shan mts China/N. Korea
Chang Cheng research stn Antarctica see Great Wall
130 G9 Changcheng Hainan China
130 G9 Changcheng Hainan China
Changchow Fujian China see Zhangzhou
Changchow Jiangsu China see Changzhou
122 D7 Changchun Jilin China
129 Q8 Changdao Shandong China
131 H4 Changde Hunan China
181 J5 Changé Pays de la Loire France
181 L6 Changé Pays de la Loire France
131 K2 Changfeng Anhui China
129 M9 Changge Henan China
123 F10 Changgi-ap pt S. Korea
133 G12 Changgo Xizang China
131 I3 Chang Hu l. China
131 M6 Changhua Taiwan
130 G9 Changhua Jiang r. China
123 E11 Changhŭng S. Korea
116 □ Changi Sing.
116 □ Changi Airport airport Sing.

132 H5 Changji Xinjiang China
130 G9 Changjiang Hainan China
121 L5 Chang Jiang r. China alt. Jinsha Jiang, alt. Tongtian He, conv. Yangtze, long Yangtze Kiang
131 M3 Changjiang Kou r. mouth China
123 E8 Changjin N. Korea
123 E8 Changjin-gang r. N. Korea
Changkiang Guangdong China see Zhanjiang
133 L13 Changlang Arun. Prad. India
131 L6 Changle Fujian China
Changleng Jiangxi China see Xinjian
129 P7 Changli Hebei China
129 R4 Changling Jilin China
128 I7 Changliushui Nei Mongol China
116 D1 Changlun Malaysia
138 F2 Changlung Jammu and Kashmir India
128 E7 Changma Gansu China
133 E9 Changmar Xizang China
131 I5 Changning Hunan China
Changning Jiangxi China see Xunwu
130 E4 Changning Sichuan China
130 B6 Changning Yunnan China
123 D9 Changnyŏn N. Korea
Ch'ang-pai Shan mts China/N. Korea see Changbai Shan
129 O6 Changping Beijing China
Changpu Hunan China see Suining
123 D9 Changsan-got pt N. Korea
131 I4 Changsha Hunan China
131 L4 Changshan Zhejiang China
129 R7 Changshan Qundao is China
130 E5 Changshi Guizhou China
130 F4 Changshou Chongqing China
131 I4 Changshoujie Hunan China
131 M3 Changshu Jiangsu China
123 E11 Changsŏng S. Korea
131 K6 Changtai Fujian China
Changteh Hunan China see Changde
131 K6 Changting Fujian China
122 F6 Changting Heilong. China
122 D7 Changtu Liaoning China
266 □R13 Changuinola Panama
133 K7 Changweiliang Qinghai China
123 F11 Ch'angwŏn S. Korea
129 J9 Changwu Shaanxi China
131 L3 Changxing Zhejiang China
129 Q7 Changxing Dao i. China
182 E4 Changy France
131 H3 Changyang Hubei China
129 P8 Changyi Shandong China
123 D9 Changyŏn N. Korea
Changyuan Chongqing China see Rongchang
129 N9 Changyuan Henan China
129 M8 Changzhi Shanxi China
129 M9 Changzhi Shanxi China
131 L3 Changzhou Jiangsu China
282 D2 Chañi, Nevado de mt. Arg.
220 F7 Chania Kriti Greece
184 C4 Chaniers France
220 E7 Chanion, Kolpos b. Kriti Greece
244 H4 Chankliut Island AK U.S.A.
128 I9 Chankou Gansu China
118 I6 Chân Mây Đông, Mui pt Vietnam
136 D5 Channagiri Karnataka India
136 E6 Channapatna Karnataka India
180 F3 Channel Islands English Chan.
264 M8 Channel Islands CA U.S.A.
264 M7 Channel Islands National Park CA U.S.A.
249 J4 Channel-Port-aux-Basques Nfld and Lab. Can.
270 E2 Channel Rock i. Bahamas
167 H6 Channel Tunnel France/U.K.
250 F3 Channing MI U.S.A.
261 D8 Channing TX U.S.A.
138 D7 Chanod Rajasthan India
204 E3 Chantada Spain
153 S3 Chantal'skiy mt. Rus. Fed.
182 C4 Chantelle France
180 H5 Chantepie France
119 F8 Chanthaburi Thai.
178 D5 Chantilly France
184 B2 Chantonnay France
179 L7 Chantraine France
182 I2 Chantrans France
181 J4 Chanu France
137 M8 Chanumla Andaman & Nicobar Is India
261 H7 Chanute KS U.S.A.
145 O5 Chanuwala Pak.
152 I4 Chany, Ozero salt l. Rus. Fed.
206 D5 Chanza r. Port./Spain
276 A2 Chao Peru
206 □ Chão, Ilhéu i. Madeira
131 K7 Chao'an Guangdong China
129 O7 Chaobai Xinhe r. China
131 K3 Chaohu Anhui China
131 K3 Chao Hu l. China
119 E8 Chao Phraya r. Thai.
129 Q2 Chaor Nei Mongol China
129 R3 Chaor He r. China
226 D2 Chaouèn Morocco
202 D5 Chaouèn prov. Morocco
178 H7 Chaource France
131 K7 Chaoyang Guangdong China
Chaoyang Heilong. China see Jiayin
Chaoyang Jilin China see Huinan
129 Q6 Chaoyang Liaoning China
129 S2 Chaoyangcun Nei Mongol China
133 H9 Chaoyang Hu l. Xizang China
129 Q1 Chaozhong Nei Mongol China
131 K7 Chaozhou Guangdong China
278 E5 Chapada Diamantina, Parque Nacional nat. park Brazil
277 G3 Chapada dos Guimarães Brazil
278 D5 Chapada dos Veadeiros, Parque Nacional da nat. park Brazil
280 A3 Chapadão do Céu Brazil
279 B6 Chapadão do Sul Brazil
278 E2 Chapadinha Brazil
248 F3 Chapais Que. Can.
145 K3 Chapak Guzar Afgh.
268 D5 Chapala Mex.
268 D5 Chapala, Laguna de l. Mex.
284 E5 Chapalcó, Valle de val. Arg.
285 H5 Chapaleofú Arg.
268 C4 Chapalilla Mex.
269 H5 Chapantongo Mex.
276 D3 Chapare r. Bol.
183 H6 Chapareillan France
145 K4 Chāpārī, Kowtal-e pass Afgh.
276 B3 Chaparra Peru
274 C4 Chaparral Col.
159 O4 Chapayeve Ukr.
159 L4 Chapayevka Ukr.
142 D2 Chapayevo Kazakh.
142 C1 Chapayevsk Rus. Fed.
182 B5 Chapdes-Beaufort France
279 B8 Chapecó Brazil
279 B8 Chapecó r. Brazil
171 N7 Chapel-en-le-Frith Derbyshire, England U.K.
171 M4 Chapelfell Top hill England U.K.
255 H8 Chapel Hill NC U.S.A.
187 F8 Chapelle-lez-Herlaimont Belgium
171 R7 Chapel St Leonards Lincolnshire, England U.K.
270 □ Chapelton Jamaica
169 J3 Chapeltown Northern Ireland U.K.
171 O7 Chapeltown South Yorkshire, England U.K.
285 I2 Chapicuy Uru.
276 B3 Chapimarca Peru
205 L8 Chapinería Spain
122 M5 Chaplanovo Rus. Fed.
248 D4 Chapleau Ont. Can.
248 D3 Chapleau Crown Game Reserve nature res. Ont. Can.
247 J5 Chaplin Sask. Can.
Chaplinka Ukr. see Chaplynka
247 J5 Chaplin Lake Sask. Can.

153 T3 Chaplino Rus. Fed.
159 M2 Chapliyivka Ukr.
161 W8 Chaplygin Rus. Fed.
159 P5 Chaplyne Ukr.
159 M7 Chaplynka Ukr.
159 M7 Chaplyns'kyy Kanal canal Ukr.
159 Q2 Chaplyzhnoye Rus. Fed.
246 G5 Chapman, Mount B.C. Can.
256 F7 Chapmanville PA U.S.A.
256 C11 Chapmanville WV U.S.A.
259 H2 Chappaqua NY U.S.A.
260 D5 Chappell NE U.S.A.
105 K9 Chappell Islands Tas. Austr.
Chapra Bihar India see Chhapra
269 I4 Chapulhuacán Mex.
285 G3 Chapuy Arg.
138 F3 Char Jammu and Kashmir India
282 F2 Charadai Arg.
277 E4 Charagua Bol.
276 C4 Charana Bol.
274 C5 Charapita Col.
282 E2 Charata Arg.
266 E4 Charay Mex.
182 E3 Charbonnat France
183 K6 Charbonnel, Pointe de mt. France
268 F2 Charcas Mex.
182 H2 Charcenne France
182 H4 Charchilla France
268 G3 Charco Blanco Mex.
286 S2 Charcot Island Antarctica
247 I4 Chard Alta Can.
172 G6 Chard Somerset, England U.K.
Chardara Kazakh. see Shardara
143 M7 Chardarinskoye Vodokhranilishche resr Kazakh./Uzbek.
144 B5 Chardāvol Iran
144 F3 Chardeh Iran
256 D7 Chardon OH U.S.A.
172 G6 Chardstock Devon, England U.K.
Chardzhev Lebapskaya Oblast' Turkm. see Türkmenabat
Chardzhou Turkm. see Türkmenabat
Chardzhouskaya Oblast' admin. div. Turkm. see Lebap
227 F2 Charef Alg.
226 E2 Charef, Oued watercourse Morocco
184 E4 Charente dept France
184 C4 Charente r. France
184 C4 Charente-Maritime dept France
182 B3 Charenton-du-Cher France
181 M3 Charentonne r. France
151 F5 Ch'arents'avan Armenia
172 H4 Charfield South Gloucestershire, England U.K.
144 E7 Charg Iran
182 H2 Chargey-lès-Gray France
230 B1 Chari r. Cameroon/Chad
144 G6 Chārī Iran
230 C2 Chari-Baguirmi pref. Chad
145 M4 Chārīkār Afgh.
139 K6 Charikot Nepal
173 N5 Charing Kent, England U.K.
244 F1 Chariot AK U.S.A.
260 I5 Chariton IA U.S.A.
260 I6 Chariton r. IA U.S.A.
251 K5 Charity Island MI U.S.A.
159 M6 Charivne Ukr.
Chärjew Turkm. see Türkmenabat
149 O8 Charkas Iran
156 K2 Charkayuvom Rus. Fed.
145 L3 Chār Kent Afgh.
138 G7 Charkhari Uttar Prad. India
138 F5 Charkhi Dadri Haryana India
Charkhlik Xinjiang China see Ruoqiang
173 J4 Charlbury Oxfordshire, England U.K.
237 N2 Charl Cilliers S. Africa
169 I4 Charlemont Northern Ireland U.K.
187 F8 Charleroi Belgium
257 J11 Charles, Cape VA U.S.A.
249 G4 Charlesbourg Que. Can.
250 B6 Charles City IA U.S.A.
256 H11 Charles City VA U.S.A.
Charles Island Islas Galápagos Ecuador see Santa María, Isla
247 I3 Charles Lake Alta Can.
262 K3 Charles M. Russell National Wildlife Refuge nature res. MT U.S.A.
106 C2 Charles Point N.T. Austr.
103 F8 Charleston South I. N.Z.
261 H8 Charleston AR U.S.A.
250 C9 Charleston IA U.S.A.
260 K6 Charleston IL U.S.A.
261 K7 Charleston MO U.S.A.
261 J8 Charleston MS U.S.A.
255 H9 Charleston SC U.S.A.
256 D10 Charleston WV U.S.A.
265 Q5 Charleston Peak NV U.S.A.
169 E5 Charlestown Ireland
237 N3 Charlestown S. Africa
271 □[2] Charlestown St Kitts and Nevis
271 □[3] Charlestown St Vincent
258 D5 Charlestown MD U.S.A.
257 M5 Charlestown NH U.S.A.
257 N7 Charlestown RI U.S.A.
256 H9 Charles Town WV U.S.A.
Charlestown of Aberlour Moray, Scotland U.K. see Aberlour
107 K9 Charleville Qld Austr.
169 E8 Charleville Ireland
178 I4 Charleville-Mézières France
250 I4 Charlevoix MI U.S.A.
245 L2 Charley r. AK U.S.A.
246 F3 Charlie Lake B.C. Can.
182 E4 Charlieu France
250 J7 Charlotte MI U.S.A.
255 G8 Charlotte NC U.S.A.
271 K4 Charlotte Amalie Virgin Is (U.S.A.)
117 G1 Charlotte Bank sea feature S. China Sea
256 G11 Charlotte Court House VA U.S.A.
255 F12 Charlotte Harbor b. FL U.S.A.
246 E4 Charlotte Lake B.C. Can.
164 I2 Charlottenberg Sweden
256 G10 Charlottesville VA U.S.A.
249 I4 Charlottetown P.E.I. Can.
Charlotte Town Grenada see Gouyave
271 □[5] Charlotteville Trin. and Tob.
105 I7 Charlton Vic. Austr.
173 J5 Charlton Hampshire, England U.K.
172 H4 Charlton Wiltshire, England U.K.
248 E2 Charlton Island Nunavut Can.
172 H4 Charlton Kings Gloucestershire, England U.K.
173 L5 Charlwood Surrey, England U.K.
178 F6 Charly France
184 E4 Charmé France
179 L7 Charmes France
183 F7 Charmes-sur-Rhône France
212 C2 Charmey Switz.
172 H6 Charminster Dorset, England U.K.
179 L7 Charmois-l'Orgueilleux France
178 H7 Charmont-sous-Barbuise France
172 G6 Charmouth Dorset, England U.K.
178 F8 Charmoy France
182 F4 Charnay-lès-Mâcon France
206 A3 Charneca Port.
161 N7 Charnitsa r. Belarus
108 H4 Charnley r. W.A. Austr.
178 F8 Charny France
197 M4 Charnyany Belarus
179 J5 Charny-sur-Meuse France
182 E4 Charolais reg. France
182 E4 Charolles France
160 K6 Charomkhava Belarus
181 P8 Chârost France
156 G3 Charozero Rus. Fed.
182 J2 Charquemont France
212 C3 Charrat Switz.
178 I8 Charrey-sur-Seine France
182 D3 Charrin France
247 M4 Charron Lake Man. Can.
184 E3 Charroux France
178 C5 Chars France
145 N4 Charsadda Pak.
Charsk Kazakh. see Shar
160 L6 Charstsvyatskaye, Vozyera l. Belarus
197 H5 Charsznica Pol.
256 B10 Charters KY U.S.A.
107 K6 Charters Towers Qld Austr.
173 O5 Chartham Kent, England U.K.
178 B7 Chartres France
183 H6 Chartreuse, Massif de la mts France
212 C4 Charvensod Italy
182 I4 Charvonnex France
143 R6 Charyn Kazakh.
143 T1 Charysh r. Rus. Fed.
143 T2 Charyshskoye Rus. Fed.
196 F2 Charzykowskie, Jezioro l. Pol.
196 F2 Charzykowy Pol.
196 D1 Charzyno Pol.
285 H4 Chas Arg.
139 K8 Chas Jharkhand India
204 D7 Chās mt. Port.
282 C2 Chaschuil Arg.
285 H4 Chascomús Arg.
285 H4 Chascomús, Laguna l. Arg.
246 G5 Chase B.C. Can.
258 C6 Chase MD U.S.A.
250 I6 Chase MI U.S.A.
256 G12 Chase City VA U.S.A.
145 I3 Chashkent Turkm.
144 F4 Chashmeh Baluch Iran
144 G4 Chashmeh Nūrī Iran
144 E4 Chashmeh Tuleh Iran
144 E4 Chashmeh-ye Palasi Iran
160 M7 Chashniki Belarus
149 P6 Chāsht Khowrān Iran
220 C3 Chasia reg. Greece
285 F6 Chasicó Arg.
283 D6 Chasico Arg.
285 F6 Chasicó, Laguna l. Arg.
159 Q5 Chasiv Yar Ukr.
260 I3 Chaska MN U.S.A.
103 D13 Chaslands Mistake c. South I. N.Z.
123 E8 Chasŏng N. Korea
122 A2 Chasovaya Rus. Fed.
156 H2 Chasovenskaya Arkhangel'skaya Oblast' Rus. Fed.
161 Q1 Chasovenskaya Leningradskaya Oblast' Rus. Fed.
181 L8 Chasseneuil-du-Poitou France
184 E4 Chasseneuil-sur-Bonnieure France
184 F4 Chassenon France
183 D7 Chasseradès France
212 C1 Chasseral mt. Switz.
182 F5 Chasse-sur-Rhône France
183 E8 Chassezac r. France
179 J8 Chassigny-Aisey France
181 K5 Chassillé France
184 B3 Chassiron, Pointe de pt France
144 F5 Chastab, Kūh-e mts Iran
184 I5 Chastang, Barrage du dam France
187 G7 Chastre Belgium
156 K4 Chastyye Rus. Fed.
274 B6 Chasuta Peru
144 F3 Chāt Iran
182 H5 Chat, Mont du mt. France
185 I6 Châtaigneraie reg. France
245 K2 Chatanika AK U.S.A.
245 J2 Chatanika r. AK U.S.A.
250 E9 Chatauqua Lake IL U.S.A.
180 E4 Château, Pointe du pt France
183 H8 Château-Arnoux France
271 □[3] Chateaubelair St Vincent
184 D4 Châteaubernard France
180 I5 Châteaubourg France
285 G3 Chateaubriand Arg.
180 I6 Châteaubriant France
182 D2 Château-Chinon France
212 C3 Château-d'Oex Switz.
184 A2 Château-d'Olonne France
181 L6 Château-du-Loir France
178 B7 Châteaudun France
182 C5 Châteaugay France
257 K4 Chateaugay NY U.S.A.
180 H5 Châteaugiron France
181 J6 Château-Gontier France
257 L3 Châteauguay Que. Can.
249 G1 Châteauguay r. Que. Can.
249 G1 Châteauguay, Lac l. Que. Can.
178 E7 Château-Landon France
181 L6 Château-la-Vallière France
184 F5 Château-l'Évêque France
180 C5 Châteaulin France
183 F9 Châteauneuf-de-Gadagne France
183 F6 Châteauneuf-de-Galaure France
183 D7 Châteauneuf-de-Randon France
180 H4 Châteauneuf-d'Ille-et-Vilaine France
180 D5 Châteauneuf-du-Faou France
183 F8 Châteauneuf-du-Pape France
183 F8 Châteauneuf-du-Rhône France
178 B6 Châteauneuf-en-Thymerais France
184 H4 Châteauneuf-la-Forêt France
182 B4 Châteauneuf-les-Bains France
183 G10 Châteauneuf-les-Martigues France
184 D4 Châteauneuf-sur-Charente France
181 P8 Châteauneuf-sur-Cher France
178 D8 Châteauneuf-sur-Loire France
181 K6 Châteauneuf-sur-Sarthe France
182 C2 Châteauneuf-Val-de-Bargis France
249 J2 Chateau Pond l. Nfld and Lab. Can.
184 G3 Châteauponsac France
178 H4 Château-Porcien France
183 I8 Châteauredon France
178 E8 Châteaurenard Centre France
183 F9 Châteaurenard Provence-Alpes-Côte d'Azur France
182 G3 Châteaurenaud France
181 M6 Château-Renault France
184 H2 Châteauroux Centre France
183 J7 Châteauroux Provence-Alpes-Côte d'Azur France
179 M6 Château-Salins France
178 F5 Château-Thierry France
179 I7 Châteauvillain France
271 □[2] Châteaux, Pointe des pt Guadeloupe
246 G3 Chateh Alta Can.
182 J4 Châtel France
184 B3 Châtelaillon-Plage France
180 F4 Châtelaudren France
182 D1 Châtel-Censoir France
182 D5 Châteldon France
187 G8 Châtelet Belgium
182 E1 Châtel-Gérard France
182 C5 Châtelguyon France
184 F2 Châtellerault France
182 D4 Châtel-Montagne France
182 D4 Châtelperron France
212 B2 Châtel-St-Denis Switz.
179 L7 Châtel-sur-Moselle France
184 I3 Châtelus-Malvaleix France
179 N7 Châtenois Alsace France
179 K7 Châtenois Lorraine France
182 J1 Châtenois-les-Forges France
182 F3 Châtenoy-le-Royal France
250 B6 Chatfield MN U.S.A.
256 C8 Chatfield OH U.S.A.
248 D5 Chatham Ont. Can.
173 N5 Chatham Medway, England U.K.
245 N4 Chatham AK U.S.A.
257 P7 Chatham MA U.S.A.
250 H3 Chatham MI U.S.A.
259 G3 Chatham NJ U.S.A.
257 L6 Chatham NY U.S.A.
258 D5 Chatham PA U.S.A.
256 F12 Chatham VA U.S.A.
283 B8 Chatham, Isla i. Chile
Chatham Island Islas Galápagos Ecuador see San Cristóbal, Isla
Chatham Island Samoa see Savai'i
102 □ Chatham Island Chatham Is S. Pacific Ocean
102 □ Chatham Islands S. Pacific Ocean
290 H8 Chatham Rise sea feature S. Pacific Ocean
245 O5 Chatham Sound sea channel B.C. Can.
245 N4 Chatham Strait AK U.S.A.
187 I9 Châtillon Belgium
212 D4 Châtillon Italy
178 E8 Châtillon-Coligny France
182 D2 Châtillon-en-Bazois France
183 G7 Châtillon-en-Diois France
182 H4 Châtillon-en-Michaille France
182 G5 Châtillon-la-Palud France
178 I8 Châtillonnais reg. France
182 F4 Châtillon-sur-Chalaronne France
181 J5 Châtillon-sur-Colmont France
184 G2 Châtillon-sur-Indre France
182 B1 Châtillon-sur-Loire France
178 G5 Châtillon-sur-Marne France
178 I8 Châtillon-sur-Seine France
181 K8 Châtillon-sur-Thouet France
143 N7 Chatkal r. Kyrg.
143 N7 Chatkal Range mts Kyrg.
261 K10 Chatom AL U.S.A.
139 J7 Chatra Jharkhand India
139 K6 Chatra Nepal
138 E6 Chatsu Rajasthan India
106 H6 Chatsworth Qld Austr.
251 N5 Chatsworth Ont. Can.
255 E8 Chatsworth GA U.S.A.
250 F9 Chatsworth IL U.S.A.
258 F5 Chatsworth NJ U.S.A.
235 F3 Chatsworth Zimbabwe
Chattagam Bangl. see Chittagong
255 E10 Chattahoochee FL U.S.A.
255 E10 Chattahoochee r. GA U.S.A.
255 E8 Chattanooga TN U.S.A.
183 G6 Chatte France
173 M3 Chatteris Cambridgeshire, England U.K.
Chattisgarh state India see Chhattisgarh
103 D12 Chatto Creek South I. N.Z.
171 N2 Chatton Northumberland, England U.K.
118 E7 Chatturat Thai.
183 G7 Chatuzange-le-Goubet France
258 D5 Chatwood PA U.S.A.
Chatyrkël', Ozero l. Kyrg. see Chatyr-Köl
143 P7 Chatyr-Köl l. Kyrg.
143 Q7 Chatyr-Tash Kyrg.
145 N6 Chaubara Pak.
207 L6 Chauchina Spain
159 O8 Chauda, Mys pt Ukr.
179 K8 Chaudenay France
183 C7 Chaudes-Aigues France
183 D7 Chaudeyrac France
187 I7 Chaudfontaine Belgium
119 G9 Châu Đốc Vietnam
181 J7 Chaudron-en-Mauges France
182 E4 Chauffailles France
183 I7 Chauffayer France
138 C7 Chauhtan Rajasthan India
118 B4 Chauk Myanmar
138 H6 Chauka r. India
138 G4 Chaukhamba mts Uttaranchal India
131 □J7 Chau Kung To i. H.K. China
136 C3 Chaul Mahar. India
178 E4 Chaulnes France
182 D2 Chaumeçon, Barrage de dam France
182 G3 Chaumergy France
179 J7 Chaumont France
178 C5 Chaumont-en-Vexin France
178 H4 Chaumont-Porcien France
179 J6 Chaumont-sur-Aire France
181 N7 Chaumont-sur-Loire France
184 E3 Chaunay France
256 C9 Chauncey OH U.S.A.
119 D8 Chaungwabyin Myanmar
153 R3 Chaunskaya Guba b. Rus. Fed.
178 F4 Chauny France
118 I7 Châu Ô Vietnam
Chau Phu Vietnam see Châu Đốc
138 G8 Chaurai Madh. Prad. India
184 D3 Chauray France
180 H4 Chausey, Îles is France
182 G3 Chaussin France
126 G5 Chausu-yama mt. Japan
Chausy Belarus see Chavusy
256 F6 Chautauqua, Lake NY U.S.A.
269 H9 Chautengo, Laguna l. Mex.
145 L6 Chauter Pak.
143 O7 Chauvay Kyrg.
184 F2 Chauvigny France
247 I4 Chauvin Alta Can.
182 H2 Chaux, Forêt de for. France
180 I8 Chavagnes-en-Paillers France
136 G8 Chavakachcheri Sri Lanka
136 D7 Chavakkad Kerala India
278 E2 Chaval Brazil
183 F6 Chavanay France
156 G2 Chavan'ga Rus. Fed.
178 I6 Chavanges France
183 D6 Chavaniac-Lafayette France
182 G5 Chavanoz France
144 B5 Chavār Iran
220 C5 Chavari Greece
179 L7 Chavelot France
275 I5 Chaves Brazil
204 F5 Chaves Port.
274 B6 Chaves Valdivia Peru
248 F1 Chavigny, Lac l. Que. Can.
274 C3 Chaviva Col.
231 D8 Chavuma Zambia
161 N8 Chavusy Belarus
145 L7 Chawal r. Pak.
119 D10 Chawang Thai.
118 G4 Chay, Sông r. Vietnam
Chayan Kazakh. see Shayan
276 D4 Chayanta r. Bol.
122 J2 Chayatyn, Khrebet ridge Rus. Fed.
Chayek Kyrg. see Chaek
161 U3 Chayevo Rus. Fed.
Ch'ayk'end Armenia see Dprabak
156 K4 Chaykovskiy Rus. Fed.
Chăyul Xizang China see Qayü
182 F5 Chazay-d'Azergues France
184 E4 Chazelles France
182 E5 Chazelles-sur-Lyon France
156 K3 Chazhegovo Rus. Fed.
285 F3 Chazón Arg.
269 J7 Chazumba Mex.
257 L4 Chazy NY U.S.A.
171 M7 Cheadle Greater Manchester, England U.K.
173 I2 Cheadle Staffordshire, England U.K.
256 F9 Cheat r. WV U.S.A.
198 B1 Cheb Czech Rep.
250 G8 Chebanse IL U.S.A.
227 H2 Chebba Tunisia
227 F4 Chebbi salt l. Alg.
156 I4 Cheboksarskoye Vodokhranilishche resr Rus. Fed.
156 I4 Cheboksary Rus. Fed.
250 J4 Cheboygan MI U.S.A.
205 Q7 Checa Spain
158 I5 Chechel'nyk Ukr.
151 I2 Chechen', Ostrov i. Rus. Fed.
131 M7 Ch'ech'eng Taiwan
151 G2 Chechenskaya Respublika aut. rep. Rus. Fed.
237 M5 Cheche Pass Lesotho
Chechnia aut. rep. Rus. Fed. see Chechenskaya Respublika
Chechnya aut. rep. Rus. Fed. see Chechenskaya Respublika
123 F10 Chech'ŏn S. Korea
158 D5 Chechva r. Ukr.
197 I5 Chęciny Pol.
261 H8 Checotah OK U.S.A.
178 D8 Chécy France
129 Q8 Chedao Shandong China
173 N3 Chedburgh Suffolk, England U.K.
172 G5 Cheddar Somerset, England U.K.
171 M7 Cheddleton Staffordshire, England U.K.
224 C6 Chéddra Chad
118 A5 Cheduba Strait Myanmar
179 I6 Chée r. France
169 I8 Cheekpoint Ireland
256 G6 Cheektowaga NY U.S.A.
248 D3 Cheepash r. Ont. Can.
107 J9 Cheepie Qld Austr.
287 K2 Cheetham, Cape Antarctica
184 D3 Chef-Boutonne France
229 I2 Cheffadène well Niger
Chefoo Shandong China see Yantai
244 F3 Chefornak AK U.S.A.
122 H3 Chegdomyn Rus. Fed.
Chegem 1 Rus. Fed. see Chegem Pervyy
151 E2 Chegem r. Rus. Fed.
151 E2 Chegem Pervyy Rus. Fed.
226 D4 Chegga Maur.
228 C2 Cheggué watercourse Maur.
228 D2 Chegguet Ti-n-Kerkâz des. Maur.
235 F3 Chegutu Zimbabwe
262 C3 Chehalis WA U.S.A.
262 C3 Chehalis r. WA U.S.A.
144 G3 Chehar Burj Iran
144 G5 Chehardeh Iran
149 M7 Cheheriz tourist site Iraq
144 B4 Chehel Chashmeh, Kūh-e hill Iran
144 I6 Chehel Dokhtarān, Kūh-e mt. Iran
144 G6 Chehel Pāyeh Iran
226 D4 Cheikria well Alg.
219 J5 Cheil Nerei-Beușnița nat. park Romania
220 C2 Cheimaditida, Limni l. Greece
183 J9 Cheiron, Cime du mt. France
123 E12 Cheju S. Korea
123 E12 Cheju-do i. S. Korea
123 E12 Cheju-haehyŏp sea chan. S. Korea
161 T7 Chekalin Rus. Fed.
156 K5 Chekan Rus. Fed.
131 □J7 Chek Chau i. H.K. China
Chek Chue H.K. China see Stanley
161 U6 Chekhov Moskovskaya Oblast' Rus. Fed.
122 L5 Chekhov Sakhalin Rus. Fed.
Chekiang prov. China see Zhejiang
Chekichler Turkm. see Çekiçler
116 □ Chek Jawa, Tanjong pt Sing.
131 □I7 Chek Lap Kok reg. H.K. China
131 □J7 Chek Mun Hoi Hap sea chan. H.K. China
156 H4 Chekshino Rus. Fed.
122 H3 Chekunda Rus. Fed.
231 B9 Chela, Serra da mts Angola
185 F9 Chélan France
262 D3 Chelan WA U.S.A.
262 D2 Chelan, Lake WA U.S.A.
245 J3 Chelatna Lake AK U.S.A.
159 R7 Chelbas r. Rus. Fed.
159 S8 Chelbasskaya Rus. Fed.
206 A3 Cheleiros Port.
206 A3 Cheleiros r. Port.
206 E3 Cheles Spain
284 D6 Chelforó Arg.
235 G4 Cheline Moz.
142 D2 Chelkar Zapadnyy Kazakhstan Kazakh.
209 D9 Chella Spain
197 L4 Chełm Pol.
197 H5 Chełmek Pol.
173 N4 Chelmer r. England U.K.
197 I6 Chełmiec Pol.
196 G2 Chełmno Kujawsko-Pomorskie Pol.
196 G3 Chełmno Wielkopolskie Pol.
220 D5 Chelmos mt. Greece
173 M4 Chelmsford Essex, England U.K.
257 N6 Chelmsford MA U.S.A.
Chelmsford Dam S. Africa see Ntshingwayo Dam
237 N3 Chelmsford Public Resort Nature Reserve S. Africa
158 C2 Chełmski Park Krajobrazowy Pol.
198 F1 Chełmy, Park Krajobrazowy Pol.
196 G2 Chełmża Pol.
251 J7 Chelsea MI U.S.A.
257 M5 Chelsea VT U.S.A.
102 J7 Cheltenham North I. N.Z.
172 H4 Cheltenham Gloucestershire, England U.K.
258 E4 Cheltenham PA U.S.A.
209 D8 Chelva Spain
152 H4 Chelyabinsk Rus. Fed.
142 I1 Chelyabinskaya Oblast' admin. div. Rus. Fed.
Chelyabinsk Oblast admin. div. Rus. Fed. see Chelyabinskaya Oblast'
159 P8 Chelyadinove Ukr.
256 D10 Chelyan WV U.S.A.
153 L2 Chelyuskin Rus. Fed.
153 L2 Chelyuskin, Mys c. Rus. Fed.
226 C2 Chemaïa Morocco
267 P7 Chemax Mex.
181 J6 Chemazé France
235 G3 Chemba Moz.
231 F7 Chembe Zambia
226 B5 Chemchâm, Sebkhet salt flat Maur.
133 D9 Chêm Co l. China
158 F4 Chemerivtsi Ukr.
181 N7 Chémery France
197 M6 Chemeryntsi Ukr.
179 I4 Chémery-sur-Bar France
184 C1 Chemillé France
182 G3 Chemin France
239 □[1b] Chemin Grenier Mauritius
179 I6 Cheminon France
181 K6 Chemiré-le-Gaudin France
Chemmis Egypt see Akhmīm
193 G9 Chemnitz Ger.
193 G9 Chemnitz admin. reg. Ger.
257 □P2 Chemquasabamticook Lake ME U.S.A.
Chemulpo S. Korea see Inch'ŏn
262 D5 Chemult OR U.S.A.
251 R8 Chemung r. NY U.S.A.
143 P7 Chemyndy Naryn Kyrg.
245 K2 Chena r. AK U.S.A.
138 C5 Chenab r. India/Pak.
226 D4 Chenachane Alg.
226 E4 Chenachane, Oued watercourse Alg.
245 K2 Chena Hot Springs AK U.S.A.
257 J6 Chenango r. NY U.S.A.
257 J6 Chenango Bridge NY U.S.A.
144 H3 Chenārān Iran
182 F4 Chénas France
232 C3 Ch'ench'a Eth.
116 D2 Chenderoh, Tasik resr Malaysia
Chendir r. Turkm. see Çendir
182 H2 Chenecey-Buillon France
245 J3 Chenega (abandoned) AK U.S.A.
184 I3 Chénérailles France
261 G7 Cheney Reservoir KS U.S.A.
136 G6 Chengalpattu Tamil Nadu India
136 F6 Chengam Tamil Nadu India
129 N8 Cheng'an Hebei China
130 F6 Chengbihe Shuiku resr China
130 H5 Chengbu Hunan China
129 K9 Chengcheng Shaanxi China
Chengchow Henan China see Zhengzhou
129 O6 Chengde Hebei China
129 P6 Chengde Hebei China
130 E3 Chengdu Sichuan China
Chengel'dy Almatinskaya Oblast' Kazakh. see Shengel'dy
Chengel'dy Kyzylordinskaya Oblast' Kazakh. see Shengel'dy
139 P5 Chengele Arun. Prad. India
130 D6 Chenggong Yunnan China
131 K7 Chenghai Guangdong China
130 C5 Cheng Hai l. China
Chengjiang Jiangxi China see Taihe
130 D6 Chengjiang Yunnan China
130 G3 Chengkou Chongqing China
130 H9 Chengmai Hainan China
129 O9 Chengqian Shandong China
Chengqiao Shanghai China see Chongming
129 R8 Chengshan Shandong China
Chengshou Sichuan China see Yingshan
Chengtu Sichuan China see Chengdu
129 N9 Chengwu Shandong China
130 E2 Chengxian Gansu China
Chengxian Guizhou China see Fuquan
Chengxiang Chongqing China see Wuxi
Chengxiang Jiangxi China see Quannan
Chengyang Shandong China see Juxian
Chengzhong Guangxi China see Ningming
130 A6 Chengzi Yunnan China
179 M7 Cheniménil France
129 P9 Cheniu Shan i. China
136 G9 Chenkaladi Sri Lanka
136 G6 Chennai Tamil Nadu India
250 F9 Chenoa IL U.S.A.
181 N7 Chenonceaux France
182 G2 Chenôve France
131 N3 Chenqian Shan i. China
122 E4 Chenqing Heilong. China
Chenqingqiao Heilong. China see Chenqing
Chenstokhov Pol. see Częstochowa
129 J2 Chentejn Nuruu mts Mongolia
116 □ Chenting, Tanjong pt Sing.
130 H5 Chenxi Hunan China
178 G8 Cheny France
Chenyang Hunan China see Chenxi
Chenying Jiangxi China see Wannian
131 I6 Chenzhou Hunan China
129 N7 Chenzhuang Hebei China
Cheom Ksan Cambodia see Chŏâm Khsant
219 M9 Chepelare Bulg.
274 B6 Chepén Peru
284 D2 Chepes Arg.
159 P4 Chepil' Ukr.
161 O6 Chepli Rus. Fed.
266 □T13 Chepo Panama
172 G4 Chepstow Monmouthshire, Wales U.K.
156 J4 Cheptsa r. Rus. Fed.
178 H6 Chepy France
144 B5 Cheqād Kabūd Iran
250 D3 Chequamegon Bay WI U.S.A.
181 P7 Cher dept France
184 E1 Cher r. France
Chera state India see Kerala
209 D8 Chera Spain
184 D4 Chérac France
217 M3 Cheradi, Isole is Italy
182 H5 Chéran r. France
268 F6 Cherán Mex.
232 B4 Cherangany Hills Kenya
212 D6 Cherasco Italy
145 N5 Cherat Pak.
185 C9 Chéraute France
255 H8 Cheraw SC U.S.A.
136 B6 Cherbaniani Reef India
180 H2 Cherbourg-Octeville France
227 F1 Cherchell Alg.
Cherchen Xinjiang China see Qiemo
157 J5 Cherdakly Rus. Fed.
156 L3 Cherdyn' Rus. Fed.
180 H6 Chère r. France
Chereapani rf India see Byramgore Reef
199 L4 Cherechiu Romania
151 F2 Cherek r. Rus. Fed.
160 L4 Cherekha r. Rus. Fed.
157 G6 Cheremisinovo Rus. Fed.
120 H1 Cheremkhovo Rus. Fed.
143 T1 Cheremnoye Rus. Fed.
122 I6 Cheremshany Rus. Fed.
156 J4 Cheremukhovka Rus. Fed.
214 B6 Cheremule Sardegna Italy
152 J4 Cherepanovo Rus. Fed.
Cherepkovo Moldova see Ciripcău
161 U2 Cherepovets Rus. Fed.
156 I3 Cherevkovo Rus. Fed.
227 E2 Chergui, Chott ech imp. l. Alg.
227 G2 Chéria Alg.
136 F4 Cherial Andhra Prad. India
212 H4 Cherio r. Italy
173 J5 Cheriton Hampshire, England U.K.
257 J11 Cheriton VA U.S.A.
136 C7 Cheriyam atoll India
158 K4 Cherkas'ka Oblast' admin. div. Ukr.
159 O5 Cherkas'ke Dnipropetrovs'ka Oblast' Ukr.
159 Q5 Cherkas'ke Donets'ka Oblast' Ukr.
Cherkas'ke Luhans'ka Oblast' Ukr. see Zymohir"ya
Cherkasskaya Oblast' admin. div. Ukr. see Cherkas'ka Oblast'
Cherkasskoye Ukr. see Zymohir"ya
Cherkassy Ukr. see Cherkasy
159 L4 Cherkasy Ukr.
Cherkasy Oblast admin. div. Ukr. see Cherkas'ka Oblast'
151 D1 Cherkessk Rus. Fed.
161 W5 Cherkutino Rus. Fed.
136 G3 Cherla Andhra Prad. India
143 P1 Cherlak Rus. Fed.
158 F5 Cherlenivka Ukr.
151 F2 Chermen Rus. Fed.
231 D8 Chermenze Angola
156 L4 Chermoz Rus. Fed.
161 T8 Chern' Rus. Fed.
161 T8 Chern' r. Rus. Fed.
244 H5 Chernabura Island AK U.S.A.
143 M6 Chernak Kazakh.
161 V9 Chernava Lipetskaya Oblast' Rus. Fed.
161 W8 Chernava Ryazanskaya Oblast' Rus. Fed.
156 L1 Chernaya Rus. Fed.
156 L1 Chernaya r. Rus. Fed.
160 K3 Chernaya r. Rus. Fed.
159 T3 Chernaya Kalitva r. Rus. Fed.
156 J4 Chernaya Kholunitsa Rus. Fed.
159 M2 Chernecha Sloboda Ukr.
Chernenko Moldova see Șoldănești
159 O4 Cherneshchyna Ukr.
161 V7 Chernevo Moskovskaya Oblast' Rus. Fed.
160 L3 Chernevo Pskovskaya Oblast' Rus. Fed.
Chernigov Ukr. see Chernihiv
122 H6 Chernigovka Rus. Fed.
Chernigov Oblast admin. div. Ukr. see Chernihivs'ka Oblast'
151 A1 Chernigovskaya Rus. Fed.
Chernigovskaya Oblast' admin. div. Ukr. see Chernihivs'ka Oblast'
151 A1 Chernigovskoye Rus. Fed.
159 K2 Chernihiv Ukr.
Chernihiv Oblast admin. div. Ukr. see Chernihivs'ka Oblast'
159 L2 Chernihivs'ka Oblast' admin. div. Ukr.
219 N7 Cherni Lom r. Bulg.
159 P6 Cherninivka Ukr.
197 M6 Cherniv Ukr.
158 F5 Chernivets'ka Oblast' admin. div. Ukr.
Chernivetskaya Oblast' admin. div. Ukr. see Chernivets'ka Oblast'
219 L8 Cherni Vrŭkh mt. Bulg.
158 E5 Chernivtsi Chernivets'ka Oblast' Ukr.
158 H5 Chernivtsi Vinnyts'ka Oblast' Ukr.
Chernivtsi Oblast admin. div. Ukr. see Chernivets'ka Oblast'
158 D5 Cherniyiv Ukr.
Chernobyl' Ukr. see Chornobyl'
120 F1 Chernogorsk Rus. Fed.
151 E1 Chernolesskoye Rus. Fed.
152 J3 Chernoostrovskoye Rus. Fed.
156 K3 Chernorechenskiy Rus. Fed.
151 G2 Chernorech'ye Rus. Fed.
143 Q1 Chernoretsk Kazakh.
161 P1 Chernoushevo Rus. Fed.
156 I4 Chernovskoye Rus. Fed.
Chernovtsy Ukr. see Chernivtsi
Chernovtsy Oblast admin. div. Ukr. see Chernivets'ka Oblast'
Chernoye More sea Asia/Europe see Black Sea
156 L4 Chernushka Rus. Fed.
158 H3 Chernyakhiv Ukr.
160 E7 Chernyakhovsk Rus. Fed.
157 G6 Chernyanka Rus. Fed.
122 D2 Chernyayeve Rus. Fed.
151 I2 Chernyayevskiy Rus. Fed.
161 N7 Chernyewka Belarus
142 H5 Chernysheva, Zaliv b. Kazakh.
121 K1 Chernyshevsk Rus. Fed.
153 M3 Chernyshevskiy Rus. Fed.
157 H6 Chernyshkovskiy Rus. Fed.
159 M8 Chernyshove Ukr.
157 I7 Chernyye Zemli reg. Rus. Fed.
Chernyy Irtysh r. China/Kazakh. see Ertix He
142 F2 Chernyy Otrog Rus. Fed.
156 F3 Chernyy Porog Rus. Fed.
Chernyy Rynok Rus. Fed. see Kochubey
157 I6 Chernyy Yar Rus. Fed.
260 H4 Cherokee IA U.S.A.
261 F7 Cherokee OK U.S.A.
255 F7 Cherokee Lake TN U.S.A.
261 H7 Cherokees, Lake o' the OK U.S.A.
270 E1 Cherokee Sound Gt Abaco Bahamas
178 F7 Chéroy France
161 N5 Cherpessa Rus. Fed.
284 A6 Cherquenco Chile
139 M7 Cherrapunji Meghalaya India
171 Q6 Cherry Burton East Riding of Yorkshire, England U.K.
260 E3 Cherry Creek r. SD U.S.A.
265 R1 Cherry Creek Mountains NV U.S.A.
257 □R4 Cherryfield ME U.S.A.
258 E5 Cherry Hill NJ U.S.A.
99 G3 Cherry Island Solomon Is
264 M3 Cherry Lake CA U.S.A.
251 Q6 Cherry Valley Ont. Can.
258 D3 Cherryville PA U.S.A.
171 Q7 Cherry Willingham Lincolnshire, England U.K.
160 L4 Cherskaya Rus. Fed.
153 R3 Cherskiy Rus. Fed.
Cherskiy Range mts Rus. Fed. see Cherskogo, Khrebet
129 L1 Cherskogo, Khrebet mts Rus. Fed.
153 P3 Cherskogo, Khrebet mts Rus. Fed.
220 D1 Cherso Greece
212 C6 Chersogno, Monte mt. Italy
208 F6 Chert Spain
Cherta Spain see Xerta
136 E8 Cherthala Kerala India
Chertkov Ukr. see Chortkiv
157 H6 Chertkovo Rus. Fed.
161 Q5 Chertolino Rus. Fed.
103 F10 Chertsey South I. N.Z.
173 K5 Chertsey Surrey, England U.K.
161 X6 Cherusti Rus. Fed.
184 G5 Cherveix-Cubas France
219 M7 Cherven Bryag Bulg.
184 D4 Cherves-Richemont France
151 G2 Chervlennaya Rus. Fed.
151 G1 Chervlennyye Buruny Rus. Fed.
159 M5 Chervona Kam"yanka Ukr.
159 N2 Chervone Sums'ka Oblast' Ukr.
158 H4 Chervone Zhytomyrs'ka Oblast' Ukr.
159 Q6 Chervone Pole Ukr.
159 K3 Chervoni Partyzany Ukr.
Chervonoarmeyskoye Ukr. see Vil'nyans'k
Chervonoarmiys'k Donets'ka Oblast' Ukr. see Krasnoarmiys'k
Chervonoarmiys'k Rivnens'ka Oblast' Ukr. see Radyvyliv
158 H3 Chervonoarmiys'k Zhytomyrs'ka Oblast' Ukr.
159 N7 Chervonoarmiys'ke Ukr.
Chervonograd Ukr. see Chervonohrad
158 D3 Chervonohrad Ukr.
159 N6 Chervonohryhorivka Ukr.
159 Q4 Chervonooskil's'ke Vodoskhovyshche resr Ukr.
Chervonopartizansk Ukr. see Chervonopartyzans'k
159 S5 Chervonopartyzans'k Ukr.
159 M3 Chervonozavods'ke Ukr.
158 J6 Chervonoznam"yanka Ukr.
159 P4 Chervonyy Donets' Ukr.
159 M7 Chervonyy Mayak Ukr.
160 L8 Chervyen' Belarus
173 J4 Cherwell r. England U.K.
161 O8 Cherykaw Belarus
251 J6 Chesaning MI U.S.A.
257 I12 Chesapeake VA U.S.A.
258 D5 Chesapeake and Delaware Canal DE U.S.A.
258 C7 Chesapeake Bay MD/VA U.S.A.
256 I10 Chesapeake Beach MD U.S.A.
258 D5 Chesapeake City MD U.S.A.
173 K4 Chesham Buckinghamshire, England U.K.
172 H1 Cheshire admin. div. England U.K.
259 J2 Cheshire CT U.S.A.
257 L6 Cheshire MA U.S.A.
171 M7 Cheshire East admin. div. England U.K.
171 L7 Cheshire Plain England U.K.
171 L7 Cheshire West & Chester admin. div. England U.K.
144 G7 Cheshmeh Sabz Iran
145 I2 Cheshme Vtoroy Turkm.
151 G3 Chesho Georgia
156 I2 Cheshskaya Guba b. Rus. Fed.
145 P3 Cheshtebe Tajik.
145 J4 Chesht-e Sharīf Afgh.
173 L4 Cheshunt Hertfordshire, England U.K.
172 G6 Chesil Beach England U.K.
258 F5 Chesilhurst NJ U.S.A.
251 M5 Chesley Ont. Can.
178 H8 Chesley France
142 I1 Chesma Rus. Fed.
Chesnokovka Rus. Fed. see Novoaltaysk
178 G7 Chessy-les-Prés France
209 D9 Cheste Spain
249 H4 Chester N.S. Can.
171 L7 Chester Cheshire, England U.K.
264 K1 Chester CA U.S.A.
259 K2 Chester CT U.S.A.
260 K7 Chester IL U.S.A.
258 C7 Chester MD U.S.A.
262 I2 Chester MT U.S.A.
258 F3 Chester NJ U.S.A.
259 G2 Chester NY U.S.A.
256 D9 Chester OH U.S.A.
258 E5 Chester PA U.S.A.
255 G8 Chester SC U.S.A.
256 H11 Chester VA U.S.A.
258 C7 Chester r. MD U.S.A.
270 □ Chester Castle Jamaica
258 D4 Chester County county PA U.S.A.
171 O7 Chesterfield Derbyshire, England U.K.
259 K2 Chesterfield CT U.S.A.
260 J6 Chesterfield MO U.S.A.
255 G8 Chesterfield SC U.S.A.
256 H11 Chesterfield VA U.S.A.
99 F3 Chesterfield, Îles is New Caledonia
247 N2 Chesterfield Inlet Nunavut Can.
247 M2 Chesterfield Inlet inlet Nunavut Can.
171 N4 Chester-le-Street Durham, England U.K.
168 K12 Chesters Scottish Borders, Scotland U.K.
258 C6 Chestertown MD U.S.A.
257 L5 Chestertown NY U.S.A.
257 J3 Chesterville Ont. Can.
258 D6 Chesterville MD U.S.A.
256 F8 Chestnut Ridge PA U.S.A.
257 □P2 Chesuncook Lake ME U.S.A.
258 D6 Cheswold DE U.S.A.
227 G1 Chetaïbi Alg.
250 C4 Chetek WI U.S.A.
249 I4 Chéticamp N.S. Can.
136 C7 Chetlat i. India
261 H7 Chetopa KS U.S.A.
267 O8 Chetumal Mex.
103 I7 Chetwode Islands South I. N.Z.
246 F4 Chetwynd B.C. Can.
122 G3 Cheugda Rus. Fed.
131 □J7 Cheung Chau H.K. China
131 □J7 Cheung Chau i H.K. China
244 F3 Chevak AK U.S.A.
183 I8 Cheval Blanc, Sommet du France
184 D5 Chevanceaux France
178 G8 Chevannes France
265 V7 Chevelon Creek r. AZ U.S.A.
199 K6 Chevereșu Mare Romania
258 B7 Cheverly MD U.S.A.
182 G2 Chevigny-St-Sauveur Fran
179 J6 Chevillon France
178 C7 Chevilly France
103 H9 Cheviot South I. N.Z.
256 A9 Cheviot OH U.S.A.
171 L3 Cheviot Hills England U.K.
107 I8 Cheviot Range hills Qld Aus
180 B5 Chèvre, Cap de la c. France
248 F2 Chevreulx r. Que. Can.
178 D6 Chevreuse France
232 C3 Che'w Bahir salt l. Eth.
232 C3 Che'w Bahir Wildlife Rese nature res. Eth.
262 F2 Chewelah WA U.S.A.
172 G5 Chew Magna Bath and No Somerset, England U.K.
172 G5 Chew Valley Lake resr England U.K.
261 F8 Cheyenne OK U.S.A.
262 L6 Cheyenne WY U.S.A.
260 E3 Cheyenne r. SD U.S.A.
260 E3 Cheyenne River Indian Reservation res. SD U.S.A.
260 D6 Cheyenne Wells CO U.S.A.
183 B6 Cheylade France
109 E13 Cheyne Bay W.A. Austr.
136 G6 Cheyur Tamil Nadu India
136 F6 Cheyyar r. India
246 E4 Chezacut B.C. Can.
181 P8 Chezal-Benoît France
239 □[3a] Chezani Njazidja Comoro
185 D10 Chèze France
138 F7 Chhabra Rajasthan India
138 E6 Chhapar Rajasthan India
139 J7 Chhapra Bihar India
138 F6 Chhata Uttar Prad. India
139 M7 Chhatak Bangl.
139 J7 Chhatarpur Jharkhand Ind
138 G7 Chhatarpur Madh. Prad. I
145 M7 Chhatr Pak.
137 I3 Chhatrapur Orissa India
138 H9 Chhattisgarh state India
119 F9 Chhay Arêng, Stœ̆ng r. Ca
138 G6 Chhibramau Uttar Prad. I
138 G8 Chhindwara Madh. Prad. I
138 F7 Chhipa Barod Rajasthan I
138 G4 Chhitkul Hima. Prad. Indi
119 G8 Chhlong, Prêk r. Cambod
138 G8 Chhota Chhindwara Mad India
138 E8 Chhota Udepur Gujarat In
138 H9 Chhuikhadan Chhattisgar
Chhuk Cambodia see Phumĭ Chhuk
139 L6 Chhukha Bhutan
119 F7 Chi, Lam r. Thai.
118 G7 Chi, Mae Nam r. Thai.
281 F4 Chiador Brazil
131 M7 Chiai Taiwan
123 F10 Ch'iak-san National Park S. Korea
233 D5 Chiamboni Kenya
213 K4 Chiampo Italy
213 K5 Chiampo r. Italy
214 H1 Chianciano Terme Italy
118 D5 Chiang Dao Thai.
231 B8 Chiange Angola
118 E5 Chiang Kham Thai.
118 E6 Chiang Khan Thai.
118 D5 Chiang Mai Thai.
118 D5 Chiang Rai Thai.
118 E4 Chiang Saen Thai.
214 I2 Chiani r. Italy
213 J8 Chianni Italy
267 M9 Chiapa Mex.
269 N9 Chiapas state Mex.
267 M9 Chiapilla Mex.
216 H9 Chiaramonte Gulfi Sicilia
214 B6 Chiaramonti Sardegna Ita
213 O8 Chiaravalle Italy
217 K6 Chiaravalle Centrale Italy
212 H4 Chiari Italy
215 Q7 Chiaromonte Italy
213 O3 Chiarso r. Italy
213 M9 Chiascio r. Italy
212 G4 Chiasso Italy
151 E3 Chiat'ura Georgia
269 I6 Chiautempan Mex.
269 I7 Chiautla Mex.
269 I6 Chiautzingo Mex.
212 G7 Chiavari Italy
212 G3 Chiavenna Italy
212 H5 Chiavenna r. Italy
127 L4 Chiba Japan
127 L5 Chiba pref. Japan
235 G4 Chibabava Moz.
124 □[1] Chibana Okinawa Japan
231 B8 Chibemba Angola
131 I4 Chibi Hubei China
Chibi Zimbabwe see Chiv
231 B8 Chibia Angola
132 H1 Chibit Rus. Fed.
Chibizovka Rus. Fed. see Zherdevka
235 G4 Chiboma Moz.
248 F3 Chibougamau Que. Can.
248 F3 Chibougamau r. Que. Ca
248 F3 Chibougamau, Lac l. Qu
125 K10 Chibu Japan
125 K11 Chiburi-jima i. Japan
235 G5 Chibuto Moz.
231 F8 Chibwe Zambia
284 E2 Chica, Sierra mts Arg.
Chicacole Andhra Prad. I Srikakulam
250 G8 Chicago IL U.S.A.
250 G8 Chicago Heights IL U.S.
250 G8 Chicago O'Hare airport
231 C8 Chicala Bié Angola
231 C7 Chicala Moxico Angola
235 G3 Chicamba Moz.
231 D6 Chicapa r. Angola
269 I4 Chicayan Mex.
269 I3 Chicayán r. Mex.
249 H3 Chic-Chocs, Monts mts
249 H3 Chic-Chocs, Réserve Fa des nature res. Que. Can.
219 M5 Chicera Hamba hill Ron
224 C5 Chicha well Chad
245 M4 Chichagof AK U.S.A.
245 N4 Chichagof Island AK U.
145 K8 Chichak r. Pak.
226 C3 Chichaoua Morocco
276 D5 Chichas, Cordillera de
181 K8 Chiché France
129 N6 Chicheng Hebei China
Chicheng Sichuan China Pengxi
267 O7 Chichén Itzá tourist site
173 K6 Chichester West Sussex, England U.K.
108 E7 Chichester Range mts W
138 H9 Chichgarh Mahar. India
127 J4 Chichibu Japan
127 J3 Chichibu-gawa r. Japan
127 I4 Chichibu-Tama Kokurit nat. park Japan
269 K9 Chichicapan Mex.
269 H8 Chichihualco Mex.
125 □[2] Chichi-jima i. Ogasawar Japan
125 □[2] Chichijima-rettō is Ogas shotō Japan

Chichinales Arg.
Chichiriviche Venez.
Chicholi Madh. Prad. India
Chickahominy r. VA U.S.A.
Chickaloon AK U.S.A.
Chickamauga Lake TN U.S.A.
Chickasawhay r. MS U.S.A.
Chickasha OK U.S.A.
Chicken AK U.S.A.
Chickerell Dorset, England U.K.
Chiclana Arg.
Chiclana de la Frontera Spain
Chiclayo Peru
Chico r. Arg.
Chico r. Arg.
Chico r. Arg.
Chico r. Arg.
Chico r. Mex.
Chico CA U.S.A.
Chicoa Moz.
Chicobea i. Fiji see Cikobia
Chicobi, Lac l. Que. Can.
Chicomba Angola
Chicomo Moz.
Chicomucelo Mex.
Chiconamel Mex.
Chiconi Mayotte
Chiconono Moz.
Chicontepec Mex.
Chicopee MA U.S.A.
Chico Sapocoy, Mount Luzon Phil.
Chicots, Plaine des hills Réunion
Chicoutimi Que. Can.
Chicoutimi r. Que. Can.
Chicualacuala Moz.
Chicuma Angola
Chicupo Angola
Chidambaram Tamil Nadu India
Chiddingfold Surrey, England U.K.
Chidenguele Moz.
Chidley, Cape Nfld and Lab./Nunavut Can.
Chido Xizang China see Sêndo
Chido S. Korea
Chiede Angola
Chiefland FL U.S.A.
Chief's Island Botswana
Chiemgauer Alpen mts Ger.
Chieming Ger.
Chiemsee l. Ger.
Chienes Italy
Chiengi Zambia
Chiengmai Thai. see Chiang Mai
Chienti r. Italy
Chieo Lan, Ang Kep Nam Thai.
Chieri Italy
Chiers r. France
Chiesa in Valmalenco Italy
Chieșd Romania
Chiese r. Italy
Chieti Italy
Chieti prov. Italy
Chieuti Italy
Chieveley West Berkshire, England U.K.
Chièvres Belgium
Chifeng Nei Mongol China
Chifre, Serra do mts Brazil
Chifunde Moz.
Chiganak Kazakh.
Chigasaki Japan
Chigil, Ostrov i. Azer. see Çigil Adası
Chiginagak Volcano, Mount AK U.S.A.
Chigla r. Rus. Fed.
Chigmit Mountains AK U.S.A.
Chignahuapán Mex.
Chignecto Bay N.B./N.S. Can.
Chignecto Game Sanctuary nature res. N.S. Can.
Chignik AK U.S.A.
Chignik Bay AK U.S.A.
Chignik Lagoon AK U.S.A.
Chignik Lake AK U.S.A.
Chignik Lake AK U.S.A.
Chignin France
Chigorodó Col.
Chigu Xizang China
Chigualoco Chile
Chiguana Bol.
Chigubo Moz.
Chigu Co l. China
Chigwell Essex, England U.K.
Chihuahua Mex.
Chihuahua state Mex.
Chihuido Medio mt. Arg.
Chiili Kazakh.
Chijinpu Gansu China
Chikaani Georgia
Chikalda Mahar. India
Chikan Guangdong China
Chikaskia r. KS U.S.A.
Chikballapur Karnataka India
Chikhachevo Rus. Fed.
Chikhali Kalan Parasia Madh. Prad. India
Chikhli Mahar. India
Chikishlyar Turkm. see Çekiçler
Chikmagalur Karnataka India
Chikodi Karnataka India
Chikodi Road Karnataka India
Chikola Rus. Fed.
Chikonkomene Zambia
Chikoy Rus. Fed.
Chikoy r. Rus. Fed.
Chikugo Japan
Chikuma-gawa r. Japan
Chikuminuk Lake AK U.S.A.
Chikura Japan
Chikushino Japan
Chikwa Zambia
Chikwawa Malawi
Chikyū-misaki pt Japan
Chila Angola
Chila Mex.
Chila, Laguna l. Mex.
Chilanga Zambia
Chilanko r. B.C. Can.
Chilanko Forks B.C. Can.
Chilapa Guerrero Mex.
Chilapa Oaxaca Mex.
Chilas Pak.
Chilaw Sri Lanka
Chilca Peru
Chilcaya Chile
Chilches Spain
Chilcompton Somerset, England U.K.
Chilcotin r. B.C. Can.
Chilcott Island Coral Sea Is Terr. Austr.
Childers Qld Austr.
Childress TX U.S.A.
Childrey Oxfordshire, England U.K.
Chile country S. America
Chile Basin sea feature S. Pacific Ocean
Chile Chico Chile
Chilecito La Rioja Arg.
Chilecito Mendoza Arg.
Chilengue, Serra do mts Angola
Chile Rise sea feature S. Pacific Ocean
Chilete Peru
Chilgir Rus. Fed.
Chilham Kent, England U.K.
Chilhowie VA U.S.A.
Chilia-Nouă Ukr. see Kiliya
Chilia Veche Romania
Chiliba Angola
Chilibre Panama
Chilik Kazakh.
Chilikadrotna r. AK U.S.A.
Chilika Lake India
Chililabombwe Zambia
Chilimanzi Zimbabwe see Chirumanzu
Chiliomodi Greece
Chilkat r. Can./U.S.A.
Chilko r. B.C. Can.
Chilko Lake B.C. Can.

245 N4 Chilkoot Trail National Historic Site nat. park B.C. Can.
107 J4 Chillagoe Qld Austr.
284 A5 Chillán Chile
284 A5 Chillán r. Chile
284 B5 Chillán, Nevado mts Chile
284 B5 Chillán, Volcán vol. Chile
285 H5 Chillar Arg.
178 D7 Chilleurs-aux-Bois France
250 E9 Chillicothe IL U.S.A.
260 I6 Chillicothe MO U.S.A.
256 C9 Chillicothe OH U.S.A.
276 C4 Chilliculco Peru
138 E1 Chillinji Pak.
246 F5 Chilliwack B.C. Can.
207 J3 Chillón Spain
207 M4 Chilluévar Spain
258 B7 Chillum MD U.S.A.
139 L7 Chilmari Bangl.
138 D6 Chilo Rajasthan India
283 B6 Chiloé, Isla de i. Chile
Chiloé, Isla Grande de i. Chile see Chiloé, Isla de
205 N7 Chiloeches Spain
231 D8 Chilombo Angola
233 A8 Chilonga Zambia
262 D5 Chiloquin OR U.S.A.
269 H8 Chilpancingo Mex.
138 H8 Chilpi Chhattisgarh India
256 B6 Chilson MI U.S.A.
269 K8 Chiltepec Mex.
105 K7 Chiltern Vic. Austr.
173 K4 Chiltern Hills England U.K.
250 F5 Chilton WI U.S.A.
231 D7 Chiluage Angola
231 F7 Chilubi Zambia
233 B7 Chilumba Malawi
131 M6 Chilung Taiwan
233 B8 Chilwa, Lake Malawi
233 B7 Chimala Tanz.
269 M9 Chimalapa Mex.
267 N10 Chimaltenango Guat.
268 D4 Chimaltitán Mex.
266 □T13 Chimán Panama
235 G3 Chimanimani Zimbabwe
131 □J7 Chi Ma Wan H.K. China
187 F8 Chimay Belgium
187 F8 Chimay, Bois de for. Belgium
233 A7 Chimba Zambia
284 B4 Chimbarongo Chile
284 C2 Chimbas Arg.
Chimbay Uzbek. see Chimboy
274 B5 Chimborazo mt. Ecuador
276 A2 Chimbote Peru
142 H6 Chimboy Uzbek.
207 L6 Chimeneas Spain
274 C2 Chimichaguá Col.
Chimishliya Moldova see Cimișlia
Chimkent Kazakh. see Shymkent
Chimkentskaya Oblast' admin. div. Kazakh. see Yuzhnyy Kazakhstan
239 □2a Chimney Rocks is Inner Islands Seychelles
235 G3 Chimoio Moz.
207 J4 Chimorra hill Spain
207 J4 Chimorra, Sierra mts Spain
284 D6 Chimpay Arg.
145 M2 Chimtargha, Qullai mt. Tajik.
Chimtorga, Gora mt. Tajik. see Chimtargha, Qullai
143 N7 Chimyon Uzbek.
118 A4 Chin state Myanmar
120 E4 China country Asia
267 J5 China Mex.
China, Republic of country Asia see Taiwan
China Bakir r. Myanmar see To
266 G5 Chinacates Mex.
267 N9 Chinajá Guat.
264 O6 China Lake CA U.S.A.
257 □P4 China Lake ME U.S.A.
269 M7 Chinameca Mex.
269 J4 Chinampa de Gorostiza Mex.
212 C6 Chinanale Italy
266 □P11 Chinandega Nic.
269 M8 Chinantla Mex.
264 N9 China Point CA U.S.A.
263 L12 Chinati Peak TX U.S.A.
Chinaz Uzbek. see Chinoz
274 B4 Chinca Ecuador
276 A3 Chincha Alta Peru
246 G3 Chinchaga r. Alta Can.
107 M9 Chinchilla Qld Austr.
207 P3 Chinchilla de Monte Aragón Spain
136 E4 Chincholi Karnataka India
205 N8 Chinchón Spain
267 P8 Chinchorro, Banco sea feature Mex.
284 B3 Chincolco Chile
257 J11 Chincoteague VA U.S.A.
257 J11 Chincoteague Bay MD/VA U.S.A.
235 H3 Chinde Moz.
239 □3a Chindini Njazidja Comoros
123 E11 Chindo S. Korea
123 E11 Chin-do i. S. Korea
182 H5 Chindrieux France
130 A2 Chindu Qinghai China
118 B4 Chindwin r. Myanmar
124 □1 Chinen Okinawa Japan
138 E3 Chineni Jammu and Kashmir India
Chinese Turkestan aut. reg. China see Xinjiang Uygur Zizhiqu
235 H2 Chinga Moz.
274 C3 Chingaza, Parque Nacional nat. park Col.
173 L4 Chingford Greater London, England U.K.
Chinghai prov. China see Qinghai
123 D9 Chinghwa N. Korea
142 F2 Chingirlau Kazakh.
Chingleput Tamil Nadu India see Chengalpattu
231 E8 Chingola Zambia
231 C8 Chinguanja Angola
231 C8 Chinguar Angola
226 B5 Chinguețți Maur.
230 C2 Chinguil Chad
123 F11 Chinhae S. Korea
235 G2 Chinhanda Moz.
235 F3 Chinhoyi Zimbabwe
Chini Hima. Prad. India see Kalpa
244 I4 Chiniak AK U.S.A.
244 I4 Chiniak, Cape AK U.S.A.
276 C3 Chiñijo Bol.
Chining Shandong China see Jining
145 O6 Chiniot Pak.
266 E4 Chinipas Mex.
119 G8 Chinit, Stœng r. Cambodia
123 F11 Chinju S. Korea
230 D3 Chinko r. C.A.R.
265 W5 Chinle AZ U.S.A.
265 W5 Chinle Valley AZ U.S.A.
265 W5 Chinle Wash watercourse AZ U.S.A.
131 L6 Chinmen Taiwan
131 L6 Chinmen Tao i. Taiwan
136 G5 Chinna Ganjam Andhra Prad. India
136 E8 Chinnamanur Tamil Nadu India
Chinnamp'o N. Korea see Namp'o
136 F7 Chinna Salem Tamil Nadu India
173 K4 Chinnor Oxfordshire, England U.K.
136 F3 Chinnur Andhra Prad. India
127 H4 Chino Japan
264 O7 Chino CA U.S.A.
265 T7 Chino Creek watercourse AZ U.S.A.
109 E12 Chinocup, Lake salt flat W.A. Austr.
109 E12 Chinocup Nature Reserve W.A. Austr.
184 E1 Chinon France
262 J2 Chinook MT U.S.A.
290 H3 Chinook Trough sea feature N. Pacific Ocean
265 T7 Chino Valley AZ U.S.A.
143 M7 Chinoz Uzbek.
233 B7 Chinsali Zambia
136 G3 Chintalnar Chhattisgarh India
136 F6 Chintamani Karnataka India

219 L4 Chinteni Romania
233 B7 Chintheche Malawi
269 I3 Chintón de las Flores Mex.
274 C2 Chinú Col.
187 H9 Chiny Belgium
187 H9 Chiny, Forêt de for. Belgium
231 D8 Chinyama Litapi Zambia
156 K3 Chin'yavoryk Rus. Fed.
235 G3 Chioco Moz.
213 M5 Chioggia Italy
212 B5 Chiomonte Italy
233 B6 Chiona Tanz.
221 H4 Chios Chios Greece
221 G4 Chios i. Greece
221 H4 Chios Strait Greece
267 N10 Chipam Guat.
235 G3 Chipanga Moz.
233 B8 Chipata Zambia
133 C9 Chip Chap r. China/India
283 C6 Chipchihua, Sierra de mts Arg.
235 G2 Chipera Moz.
231 C8 Chipeta Angola
119 H9 Chiphu Cambodia
231 F7 Chipili Zambia
231 B8 Chipindo Angola
129 O8 Chiping Shandong China
Chipinga Zimbabwe see Chipinge
235 G4 Chipinge Zimbabwe
206 G7 Chipiona Spain
255 E10 Chipley FL U.S.A.
136 C4 Chiplun Mahar. India
249 H4 Chipman N.B. Can.
233 C6 Chipogolo Tanz.
231 C8 Chipoia Angola
172 H5 Chippenham Wiltshire, England U.K.
235 G3 Chipperone, Monte mt. Moz.
260 H3 Chippewa r. MN U.S.A.
250 B5 Chippewa r. WI U.S.A.
250 C4 Chippewa, Lake WI U.S.A.
250 C5 Chippewa Falls WI U.S.A.
173 I3 Chipping Campden Gloucestershire, England U.K.
173 I4 Chipping Norton Oxfordshire, England U.K.
173 M4 Chipping Ongar Essex, England U.K.
172 H4 Chipping Sodbury South Gloucestershire, England U.K.
212 D3 Chippis Switz.
208 E5 Chiprana Spain
219 K7 Chiprovtsi Bulg.
231 F8 Chipundu Central Zambia
231 F8 Chipundu Luapula Zambia
Chipuriro Zimbabwe see Guruve
137 H3 Chipurupalle Andhra Prad. India
137 H4 Chipurupalle Andhra Prad. India
257 □R3 Chiputneticook Lakes Can./U.S.A.
276 A2 Chiquian Peru
267 O9 Chiquibul National Park Belize
267 P7 Chiquilá Mex.
268 D5 Chiquilistlán Mex.
267 O10 Chiquimula Guat.
274 C3 Chiquinquira Col.
276 B3 Chiquintirca Peru
285 G4 Chiquita, Mar l. Arg.
269 H1 Chiquita, Sierra mts Mex.
268 F7 Chiquito r. Mex.
277 E4 Chiquitos, Llanos de plain Bol.
157 H6 Chir r. Rus. Fed.
183 C7 Chirac France
136 G5 Chirada Andhra Prad. India
233 B8 Chiradzulu Malawi
151 I4 Chirag Rus. Fed.
151 J4 Chirakhchay r. Rus. Fed.
136 D7 Chirakkal Kerala India
136 G5 Chirala Andhra Prad. India
235 G3 Chiramba Moz.
274 B3 Chirambirá, Punta pt Col.
145 K4 Chiras Afgh.
133 B12 Chirawa Rajasthan India
172 F2 Chirbury Shropshire, England U.K.
143 M7 Chirchiq Uzbek.
143 M7 Chirchiq r. Uzbek.
235 F4 Chiredzi Zimbabwe
232 C1 Chire Wildlife Reserve nature res. Eth.
224 B4 Chirfa Niger
274 E2 Chirgua r. Venez.
274 C4 Chiribiquete nat. park Col.
265 W9 Chiricahua National Monument nat. park AZ U.S.A.
265 W10 Chiricahua Peak AZ U.S.A.
274 C2 Chiriguaná Col.
244 I5 Chirikof Island AK U.S.A.
271 J8 Chirimena Venez.
274 B6 Chirinos Peru
266 □R13 Chiriquí, Golfo de b. Panama
266 □R13 Chiriquí, Laguna de b. Panama
270 C9 Chiriquí, Punta pt Panama
266 □R13 Chiriquí Grande Panama
123 E11 Chiri-san mt. S. Korea
123 E11 Chiri-san National Park S. Korea
207 O5 Chirivel Spain
151 G2 Chiri-Yurt Rus. Fed.
172 F2 Chirk Wrexham, Wales U.K.
168 L11 Chirnside Scottish Borders, Scotland U.K.
239 □3b Chirongui Mayotte
145 L2 Chiroqchi Uzbek.
182 F4 Chiroubles France
100 □6 Chirovanga Choiseul Solomon Is
219 N8 Chirpan Bulg.
266 □R13 Chirripó, Parque Nacional nat. park Costa Rica
235 F3 Chirumanzu Zimbabwe
235 F3 Chirundu Zimbabwe
268 F5 Chiruntzio Mex.
144 E8 Chīrūyeh Iran
126 F5 Chiryū Japan
231 F8 Chisamba Zambia
245 L3 Chisana AK U.S.A.
245 L3 Chisana r. AK U.S.A.
245 J3 Chisana Glacier AK U.S.A.
231 E8 Chisasa Zambia
248 E2 Chisasibi Que. Can.
285 I4 Chis Chis, Laguna l. Arg.
267 N10 Chisec Guat.
231 E9 Chisekesi Zambia
173 I4 Chiseldon Swindon, England U.K.
219 O6 Chiselet Romania
233 B7 Chisenga Malawi
Chishima-retto is Rus. Fed. see Kuril'skiye Ostrova
157 K5 Chishmy Rus. Fed.
246 H4 Chisholm Alta Can.
257 □O4 Chisholm ME U.S.A.
250 B2 Chisholm MN U.S.A.
145 O7 Chishtian Pak.
130 E4 Chishui Guizhou China
130 E5 Chishui Sichuan China
130 E4 Chishui He r. China
Chisimaio Somalia see Kismaayo
158 H6 Chișinău Moldova
199 L5 Chisindia Romania
219 J4 Chișineu-Criș Romania
199 L4 Chișlaz Romania
212 D6 Chisola r. Italy
212 C6 Chisone r. Italy
239 □3b Chissioua Mbouzi i. Mayotte
239 □3b Chissioua Mtsamboro i. Mayotte
245 K3 Chistochina AK U.S.A.
156 J5 Chistopol' Rus. Fed.
143 L1 Chistopol'ye Kazakh.
Chistyakovo Ukr. see Torez
197 K1 Chistye-Prudy Rus. Fed.
276 D5 Chita Bol.
274 C3 Chita Col.
126 E6 Chita Japan
121 J1 Chita Rus. Fed.
233 B7 Chita Tanz.
144 D6 Chitab Iran
231 B9 Chitado Angola
126 E6 Chita-hantō pen. Japan
Chitaldrug Karnataka India see Chitradurga
138 C7 Chitalwana Rajasthan India
233 A8 Chitambo Zambia
245 J2 Chitanana r. AK U.S.A.
129 L1 Chitanga Rus. Fed.
Chita Oblast admin. div. Rus. Fed. see Chitinskaya Oblast'
231 D6 Chitato Angola

126 E6 Chita-wan b. Japan
156 J3 Chitayevo Rus. Fed.
247 J4 Chitek Lake Sask. Can.
247 L4 Chitek Lake l. Man. Can.
231 C8 Chitembo Angola
213 L8 Chitignano Italy
245 K3 Chitina AK U.S.A.
245 K3 Chitina r. AK U.S.A.
122 A3 Chitinskaya Oblast' admin. div. Rus. Fed.
233 B7 Chitipa Malawi
Chitkul Hima. Prad. India see Chhitkul
235 G4 Chitobe Moz.
231 D8 Chitokoloki Zambia
231 E9 Chitongo Zambia
Chitor Rajasthan India see Chittaurgarh
124 S4 Chitose Japan
136 E5 Chitradurga Karnataka India
138 H7 Chitrakoot Uttar Prad. India
145 N4 Chitral Pak.
145 N4 Chitral r. Pak.
136 F5 Chitravati r. India
266 □S14 Chitré Panama
138 C8 Chitrod Gujarat India
139 M8 Chittagong Bangl.
139 M8 Chittagong admin. div. Bangl.
139 K8 Chittaranjan W. Bengal India
138 E7 Chittaurgarh Rajasthan India
136 F6 Chittoor Andhra Prad. India
Chittorgarh Rajasthan India see Chittaurgarh
136 E7 Chittur Kerala India
233 B8 Chitungulu Zambia
235 F3 Chitungwiza Zimbabwe
233 C7 Chiulezi r. Moz.
Chiu Lung H.K. China see Kowloon
231 D8 Chiume Angola
235 H2 Chiúre Novo Moz.
212 H3 Chiuro Italy
213 L2 Chiusa Italy
212 D7 Chiusa di Pesio Italy
213 O3 Chiusaforte Italy
216 E8 Chiusa Sclafani Sicilia Italy
212 D8 Chiusavecchia Italy
214 G1 Chiusdino Italy
212 D5 Chiusella r. Italy
214 H1 Chiusi Italy
214 H1 Chiusi, Lago di l. Italy
213 L8 Chiusi della Verna Italy
235 G2 Chiúta Moz.
209 D9 Chiva Spain
212 D5 Chivasso Italy
266 D4 Chívato, Punta pt Mex.
276 C3 Chivay Peru
276 C3 Chive Bol.
231 C8 Chiveio Angola
269 M9 Chivela Mex.
235 F3 Chivhu Zimbabwe
235 F4 Chivi Zimbabwe
285 G4 Chivilcoy Arg.
131 I8 Chixi Guangdong China
Chiyirchik, Pereval pass Kyrg. see Chyyyrchyk Ashuusu
127 J3 Chiyoda Gunma Japan
127 L3 Chiyoda Ibaraki Japan
127 K3 Chiyogawa Japan
235 E3 Chizarira Hills Zimbabwe
235 E3 Chizarira National Park Zimbabwe
184 D3 Chizé France
156 I2 Chizha Rus. Fed.
131 K3 Chizhou Anhui China
125 L11 Chizu Japan
Chkalov Rus. Fed. see Orenburg
159 N6 Chkalove Ukr.
143 N1 Chkalovo Kazakh.
Chkalovo Rus. Fed. see Kurchaloy
156 H4 Chkalovsk Rus. Fed.
Chkalovskaya Oblast' admin. div. Rus. Fed. see Orenburgskaya Oblast'
159 P4 Chkalovs'ke Ukr.
122 H6 Chkalovskoye Rus. Fed.
151 D3 Ch'khari Georgia
199 G2 Chlebičov Czech Rep.
199 I2 Chlebnice Slovakia
196 C3 Chlebowo Pol.
227 F1 Chlef Alg.
197 I4 Chlewiska Pol.
199 K3 Chlmec r. Slovakia
197 K6 Chłopice Pol.
265 R6 Chloride AZ U.S.A.
196 E3 Chludowo Pol.
195 O2 Chlumčany Czech Rep.
198 C1 Chlumec Czech Rep.
198 E1 Chlumec nad Cidlinou Czech Rep.
198 D3 Chlum u Třeboně Czech Rep.
122 L2 Chlya, Ozero l. Rus. Fed.
199 H2 Chmeľová hill Slovakia
197 I5 Chmielnik Pol.
196 E2 Chmielno Pol.
197 K4 Chmiel Pierwszy Pol.
116 □ Choa Chu Kang Sing.
116 □ Choa Chu Kang hill Sing.
119 G7 Choâm Khsant Cambodia
284 B2 Choapa Chile
284 B2 Choapa r. Chile
234 E3 Chobe admin. dist. Botswana
234 E3 Chobe National Park Botswana
196 E4 Chobienia Pol.
196 D3 Chobienice Pol.
118 G4 Chô Bo Vietnam
269 J6 Chocamán Mex.
271 □3 Choc Bay St Lucia
198 F1 Choceň Czech Rep.
197 H3 Choceń Pol.
123 E10 Choch'iwŏn S. Korea
199 G3 Chocholná-Velčice Slovakia
118 G4 Chơ Chu Vietnam
196 D4 Chocianów Pol.
196 D2 Chociwel Pol.
274 B3 Chocó dept Col.
265 Q8 Chocolate Mountains AZ/CA U.S.A.
274 C3 Chocontá Col.
255 D10 Choctawhatchee r. FL U.S.A.
196 F4 Chocz Pol.
196 F1 Choczewo Pol.
136 G4 Chodavaram Andhra Prad. India
197 H3 Chodecz Pol.
197 K4 Chodel Pol.
197 J4 Chodelka r. Pol.
123 D9 Cho-do i. N. Korea
198 B1 Chodov Czech Rep.
198 B2 Chodová Planá Czech Rep.
197 K3 Chodów Mazowieckie Pol.
197 H3 Chodów Wielkopolskie Pol.
132 I1 Chodro Rus. Fed.
196 E3 Chodzież Pol.
284 E6 Choele Choel Arg.
284 E6 Choele Choel Grande, Isla i. Arg.
235 F2 Chofombo Moz.
127 K4 Chōfu Japan
144 D7 Choghādak Iran
144 E7 Choghān Iran
144 C6 Choghā Zanbīl tourist site Iran
138 E2 Chogo Lungma Glacier Pak.
Chogori Feng mt. China/Pak. see K2
157 I7 Chograyskoye Vodokhranilishche resr Rus. Fed.
247 J4 Choiceland Sask. Can.
285 F6 Choique Arg.
100 □6 Choiseul i. Solomon Is
271 □3 Choiseul St Lucia
283 F8 Choiseul Sound sea chan. Falkland Is
182 I5 Choisy France
266 E4 Choix Mex.
196 C3 Chojna Pol.
196 F2 Chojnice Pol.
196 D4 Chojnów Pol.
158 A1 Chojnowski Park Krajobrazowy Pol.
124 R7 Chōkai-san vol. Japan
232 C2 Ch'ok'ē mts Eth.
151 D3 Ch'okhatauri Georgia
143 P6 Chokpar Kazakh.
143 Q6 Chok-Tal Kyrg.

Chokue Moz. see Chókwé
153 P2 Chokurdakh Rus. Fed.
235 G5 Chókwé Moz.
130 B3 Cho La pass Sichuan China
264 L6 Cholame CA U.S.A.
264 L6 Cholame Creek r. CA U.S.A.
130 B2 Chola Shan mts Sichuan China
284 A6 Cholchol Chile
184 C1 Cholet France
284 A5 Cholguán Chile
266 □P10 Choloma Hond.
143 P6 Cholpon Kyrg.
143 Q6 Cholpon-Ata Kyrg.
173 J4 Cholsey Oxfordshire, England U.K.
269 I6 Cholula Mex.
266 □P11 Choluteca Hond.
231 E9 Choma Zambia
123 F10 Chŏmch'ŏn S. Korea
183 D6 Chomelix France
183 F7 Chomérac France
133 I12 Chomo Ganggar mt. Xizang China
118 G4 Chơ Moi Vietnam
139 L6 Chomo Lhari mt. Bhutan
118 D5 Chom Thong Thai.
138 E6 Chomun Rajasthan India
198 C1 Chomutov Czech Rep.
198 C1 Chomutovka r. Czech Rep.
153 L3 Chona r. Rus. Fed.
127 L5 Chōnan Japan
123 E10 Ch'ŏnan S. Korea
119 E8 Chon Buri Thai.
283 B6 Chonchi Chile
274 A5 Chone Ecuador
Chong'an Fujian China see Wuyishan
123 D9 Ch'ŏngch'ŏn-gang r. N. Korea
123 F11 Ch'ongdo S. Korea
Chonggye Xizang China see Qonggyai
125 G11 Chŏngja S. Korea
123 F8 Ch'ŏngjin N. Korea
123 D9 Chŏngju N. Korea
123 E10 Ch'ŏngju S. Korea
119 F8 Chông Kal Cambodia
129 N6 Chongli Hebei China
Chonglong Sichuan China see Zizhong
131 M3 Chongming Shanghai China
131 M3 Chongming Dao i. China
233 B8 Chongoni Rock Art tourist site Malawi
231 B8 Chongoroi Angola
123 E9 Chŏngp'yŏng N. Korea
130 F4 Chongqing Chongqing China
Chongqing Sichuan China see Chongzhou
130 F3 Chongqing mun. China
131 J5 Chongren Jiangxi China
123 E11 Chŏngŭp S. Korea
231 F8 Chongwe Zambia
131 J4 Chongyang Hubei China
131 L5 Chongyang Xi r. China
131 J6 Chongyi Jiangxi China
130 D3 Chongzhou Sichuan China
130 F7 Chongzuo Guangxi China
159 N7 Chonhar, Pivostriv pen. Ukr.
123 E11 Chŏnju S. Korea
Chonogol Mongolia see Erdenetsagaan
283 B7 Chonos, Archipiélago de los is Chile
269 N8 Chontalpa Mex.
119 H9 Chơn Thanh Vietnam
139 K5 Cho Oyu mt. China/Nepal
179 I3 Chooz France
158 B5 Chop Ukr.
139 I7 Chopan Uttar Prad. India
138 E9 Chopda Mahar. India
279 B8 Chopimzinho Brazil
158 H3 Chopovychi Ukr.
257 I10 Choptank r. MD U.S.A.
276 D4 Choquecamata Bol.
145 M9 Chor Pak.
220 G6 Chora Greece
220 G6 Chora Greece
220 C5 Chora Greece
221 H5 Chora tourist site Greece
220 F7 Chora Sfakion Kriti Greece
183 I7 Chorges France
207 K2 Chorito, Sierra del mts Spain
171 L6 Chorley Lancashire, England U.K.
173 K4 Chorleywood Hertfordshire, England U.K.
158 I6 Chorna Ukr.
159 M9 Chorna r. Ukr.
158 D5 Chorna Tysa Ukr.
158 E1 Chornaye, Vozyera l. Belarus
197 M5 Chorniyiv Ukr.
159 L4 Chornobay Ukr.
158 J2 Chornobyl' Ukr.
199 L3 Chornoholova Ukr.
159 J7 Chornomors'ke Odes'ka Oblast' Ukr.
157 F7 Chornomors'ke Respublika Krym Ukr.
159 K7 Chornomors'kyy Zapovidnyk nature res. Ukr.
158 I4 Chornorudka Ukr.
159 L3 Chornukhy Ukr.
159 J5 Chornyy Tashlyk r. Ukr.
151 C4 Chorokhi r. Georgia/Turkey
282 C3 Choros, Islas de los is Chile
197 K2 Choroszcz Pol.
107 I7 Chorregon Qld Austr.
278 F4 Chorrochó Brazil
158 E4 Chortkiv Ukr.
145 L3 Chorvoq Uzbek.
143 M7 Chorvoq suv ombori resr Kazakh./Uzbek.
138 C9 Chorwad Gujarat India
123 E9 Ch'ŏrwŏn S. Korea
197 I2 Chorzele Pol.
196 G5 Chorzów Pol.
123 D8 Ch'osan N. Korea
Chōsen-kaikyō sea chan. Japan/S. Korea see Nishi-suidō
127 M4 Chōshi Japan
283 B5 Choshuenco, Volcán vol. Chile
276 A2 Chosica Peru
284 B5 Chos Malal Arg.
284 D3 Chosmes Arg.
196 D2 Choszczno Pol.
274 B6 Chota Peru
139 I8 Chota Nagpur reg. Chhattisgarh India
199 K2 Chotča Slovakia
262 H3 Choteau MT U.S.A.
198 E2 Chotěboř Czech Rep.
195 O2 Chotěšov Czech Rep.
145 N7 Choti Pak.
138 C8 Chotila Gujarat India
199 H4 Chotín Slovakia
239 □3a Choua-chandroudé i. Comoros
226 D4 Chouikhia well Alg.
178 H5 Chouilly France
226 B5 Choûm Maur.
206 C2 Chouto Port.
181 N6 Chouzy-sur-Cisse France
264 L4 Chowchilla CA U.S.A.
244 H5 Chowiet Island AK U.S.A.
104 H5 Chowilla Regional Reserve nature res. S.A. Austr.
246 G4 Chown, Mount Alta Can.
282 D3 Choya Arg.
143 V2 Choya Rus. Fed.
129 N3 Choybalsan Mongolia
182 H2 Choye France
129 K3 Choyr Mongolia
204 I3 Chozas de Abajo Spain
Chozas de la Sierra Spain see Soto del Real
233 B7 Chozi Zambia
198 E2 Chrast Czech Rep.
198 C2 Chrást Czech Rep.
198 D1 Chrastava Czech Rep.
226 B5 Chreïrîk well Maur.
193 J9 Chřibská Czech Rep.
198 G2 Chřiby hills Czech Rep.
260 L6 Chrisman IL U.S.A.
237 O2 Chrissiesmeer S. Africa
103 G10 Christchurch South I. N.Z.
173 I6 Christchurch Dorset, England U.K.

245 K2 Christian AK U.S.A.
245 K2 Christian r. AK U.S.A.
243 L2 Christian, Cape Nunavut Can.
270 □ Christiana Jamaica
237 J3 Christiana S. Africa
258 D5 Christiana PA U.S.A.
Christiania Norway see Oslo
251 N5 Christian Island Ont. Can.
256 E11 Christiansburg VA U.S.A.
164 F6 Christiansfeld Denmark
Christianshåb Greenland see Qasigiannguit
165 L6 Christiansø i. Denmark
245 N5 Christian Sound sea channel AK U.S.A.
271 K5 Christiansted Virgin Is (U.S.A.)
250 D5 Christie WI U.S.A.
247 I2 Christie Bay N.W.T. Can.
247 I3 Christina r. Alta Can.
103 C11 Christina, Mount South I. N.Z.
171 L7 Christleton Cheshire, England U.K.
108 H5 Christmas Creek W.A. Austr.
108 H5 Christmas Creek r. W.A. Austr.
108 □1 Christmas Island terr. Indian Ocean
Christmas Island atoll Kiribati see Kiritimati
171 N2 Christon Bank Northumberland, England U.K.
109 I8 Christopher, Lake salt flat W.A. Austr.
198 E2 Chrudim Czech Rep.
197 H3 Chruślin Pol.
150 A3 Chrysochou Bay Cyprus
Chrysochous, Kolpos b. Cyprus see Chrysochou Bay
220 F2 Chrysoupoli Greece
170 I2 Chryston North Lanarkshire, Scotland U.K.
197 H5 Chrzanów Pol.
196 F4 Chrząstowa Wielka Pol.
196 G5 Chrząstowice Pol.
196 E3 Chrzypsko Wielkie Pol.
Chu Kazakh. see Shu
139 L8 Chuadanga Bangl.
Chuanhui Henan China see Zhoukou
131 M3 Chuansha Shanghai China
244 H3 Chuathbaluk AK U.S.A.
130 B4 Chubalung Sichuan China
159 P6 Chubarivka Ukr.
Chubarovka Ukr. see Polohy
161 T6 Chubarovo Rus. Fed.
Chubartau Kazakh. see Barshatas
262 H5 Chubbuck ID U.S.A.
126 E6 Chūbu airport Aichi Japan
159 R7 Chuburka r. Rus. Fed.
126 G3 Chūbu-Sangaku Kokuritsu-kōen nat. park Japan
283 C6 Chubut prov. Arg.
283 D6 Chubut r. Arg.
128 F9 Chubxi Qinghai China
268 F6 Chucándiro Mex.
199 H2 Chuchelná Czech Rep.
157 H5 Chuchkovo Rus. Fed.
265 Q8 Chuckwalla Mountains CA U.S.A.
285 E3 Chucul Arg.
284 D2 Chucuma Arg.
266 □U13 Chucunaque r. Panama
172 E6 Chudleigh Devon, England U.K.
158 H3 Chudniv Ukr.
196 G5 Chudoba Pol.
161 O2 Chudovo Rus. Fed.
Chudskoye, Ozero l. Estonia/Rus. Fed. see Peipus, Lake
160 J9 Chudzin Belarus
245 K3 Chugach Mountains AK U.S.A.
244 E5 Chuginadak Island AK U.S.A.
125 J12 Chūgoku-sanchi mts Japan
Chugqênsumdo Qinghai China see Jigzhi
Chuguchak Xinjiang China see Tacheng
245 □D6 Chugul Island AK U.S.A.
Chuguyev Ukr. see Chuhuyiv
122 H6 Chuguyevka Rus. Fed.
262 L6 Chugwater WY U.S.A.
Chuhai Guangdong China see Zhuhai
159 P4 Chuhuyiv Ukr.
Chuimatan Gansu China see Jishishan
Chujiang Hunan China see Shimen
130 B4 Chuka Xizang China
Chukai Malaysia see Cukai
122 J2 Chukchagirskoye, Ozero l. Rus. Fed.
Chukchi Peninsula Rus. Fed. see Chukotskiy Poluostrov
292 M1 Chukchi Plateau sea feature Arctic Ocean
244 E1 Chukchi Sea Rus. Fed./U.S.A.
156 H4 Chukhloma Rus. Fed.
153 T3 Chukotskiy, Mys c. Rus. Fed.
153 T3 Chukotskiy Poluostrov pen. Rus. Fed.
159 L7 Chulakivka Ukr.
Chulakkurgan Kazakh. see Sholakkorgan
Chulaktau Kazakh. see Karatau
118 E6 Chulaphon, Ang Kep Nam Thai.
156 I2 Chulasa Rus. Fed.
264 O9 Chula Vista CA U.S.A.
209 D8 Chulilla Spain
245 J3 Chulitna AK U.S.A.
161 T8 Chulkovo Rus. Fed.
207 I8 Chullera, Punta de la pt Spain
172 E6 Chulmleigh Devon, England U.K.
276 C6 Chulo Chile
244 F3 Chuloonawick AK U.S.A.
274 A6 Chulucanas Peru
145 Q4 Chulung Pass Pak.
128 G2 Chuluut Gol r. Mongolia
152 J4 Chulym Rus. Fed.
132 H1 Chulyshman r. Rus. Fed.
156 M2 Chum Rus. Fed.
276 C3 Chuma Bol.
159 N6 Chumaky Ukr.
138 G3 Chumar Jammu and Kashmir India
232 C3 Chumba Eth.
282 D3 Chumbicha Arg.
130 A2 Chumda Qinghai China
132 G2 Chumek Kazakh.
219 N8 Chumerna mt. Bulg.
122 I1 Chumikan Rus. Fed.
151 G4 Ch'umlaqi Georgia
118 F6 Chum Phae Thai.
119 D9 Chumphon Thai.
118 E7 Chum Saeng Thai.
284 E2 Chuña Arg.
153 K4 Chuna r. Rus. Fed.
285 E1 Chuña Huasi Arg.
131 L4 Chun'an Zhejiang China
162 V3 Chuna-Tundra plain Rus. Fed.
123 E10 Ch'unch'ŏn S. Korea
143 R6 Chundzha Kazakh.
231 E8 Chunga Zambia
Chung-hua Jen-min Kung-ho-kuo country Asia see China
Chung-hua Min-kuo country Asia see Taiwan
123 E10 Ch'ungju S. Korea
Chungking Chongqing China see Chongqing
Ch'ungmu S. Korea see T'ongyŏng
123 D9 Chŭngsan N. Korea
233 C7 Chungu Tanz.
131 M7 Chungyang Shanmo mts Taiwan
122 G7 Chunhua Jilin China
130 G1 Chunhua Shaanxi China
267 O8 Chunhuhux Mex.
145 P6 Chunian Pak.
Chunxi Jiangsu China see Gaochun
153 K3 Chunya r. Rus. Fed.
233 B7 Chunya Tanz.
119 G10 Chuôi, Hon i. Vietnam
Chuosijia Sichuan China see Guanyinqiao
156 F2 Chupa Rus. Fed.

159 N3 Chupakhivka Ukr.
271 □7 Chupara Point Trin. and Tob.
144 B3 Chūplū Iran
158 J4 Chupyra Ukr.
276 C5 Chuquicamata Chile
276 D5 Chuquisaca dept Bol.
Chuqung Qinghai China see Chindu
212 H2 Chur Switz.
139 N7 Churachandpur Manipur India
156 K4 Churaki Rus. Fed.
144 F7 Chūrān Iran
153 O3 Churapcha Rus. Fed.
156 K5 Churayevo Rus. Fed.
173 M3 Church End Essex, England U.K.
170 B4 Church Hill Ireland
258 D6 Church Hill MD U.S.A.
256 C12 Church Hill TN U.S.A.
247 M3 Churchill Man. Can.
247 M3 Churchill r. Man. Can.
249 I2 Churchill r. Nfld and Lab. Can.
247 M3 Churchill, Cape Man. Can.
249 I2 Churchill Falls Nfld and Lab. Can.
247 I4 Churchill Lake Sask. Can.
287 K1 Churchill Mountains Antarctica
246 E3 Churchill Peak B.C. Can.
248 E1 Churchill Sound sea chan. Nunavut Can.
171 M7 Church Lawton Cheshire, England U.K.
260 F1 Churchs Ferry ND U.S.A.
172 G2 Church Stretton Shropshire, England U.K.
258 B7 Churchton MD U.S.A.
169 E8 Churchtown Cork Ireland
169 F9 Churchtown Cork Ireland
258 D4 Churchtown PA U.S.A.
258 C5 Churchville MD U.S.A.
256 F10 Churchville VA U.S.A.
128 B1 Churek-Dag, Gora mt. Rus. Fed.
139 J6 Churia Ghati Hills Nepal
161 N6 Churilovo Rus. Fed.
276 A2 Churin Peru
151 H3 Churkey Rus. Fed.
151 H3 Churkeyskoye Vodokhranilishche resr Rus. Fed.
246 F5 Churn Creek Provincial Park B.C. Can.
156 I4 Churov Rus. Fed.
159 L1 Churovichi Rus. Fed.
138 E5 Churu Rajasthan India
Churubay Nura Kazakh. see Abay
250 I8 Churubusco IN U.S.A.
274 D2 Churuguara Venez.
124 U4 Chūrui Japan
145 K1 Churuk Uzbek.
268 F7 Churumuco Mex.
212 H2 Churwalden Switz.
159 N7 Churyuk, Ostriv i. Ukr.
119 I8 Chu Sê Vietnam
138 G3 Chushul Jammu and Kashmir India
265 W5 Chuska Mountains NM U.S.A.
156 L4 Chusovaya r. Rus. Fed.
156 L4 Chusovoy Rus. Fed.
156 L3 Chusovskoye Rus. Fed.
Chust Ukr. see Khust
143 N7 Chust Uzbek.
249 G3 Chute-des-Passes Que. Can.
251 R3 Chute-Rouge Que. Can.
139 N6 Chutia Assam India
159 O4 Chutove Ukr.
131 M6 Chutung Taiwan
100 □4a Chuuk is Micronesia
156 L3 Chuval Rus. Fed.
Chuvashia aut. rep. Rus. Fed. see Chuvashskaya Respublika
Chuvashskaya A.S.S.R. aut. rep. Rus. Fed. see Chuvashskaya Respublika
157 I5 Chuvashskaya Respublika aut. rep. Rus. Fed.
151 I4 Chuvek Rus. Fed.
123 F10 Chuwang-san National Park S. Korea
130 C6 Chuxiong Yunnan China
143 P6 Chüy admin. div. Kyrg.
282 G4 Chuy Uru.
Chuyskaya Oblast' admin. div. Kyrg. see Chüy
182 F5 Chuzelles France
127 J2 Chūzenji-ko l. Japan
131 L2 Chuzhou Anhui China
131 L2 Chuzhou Jiangsu China
126 D5 Chūzu Japan
198 D3 Chvalšiny Czech Rep.
149 L6 Chwārtā Iraq
196 G1 Chwaszczyno Pol.
Chwitffordd Flintshire, Wales U.K. see Whitford
196 G6 Chybie Pol.
158 K6 Chychykliya r. Ukr.
160 M8 Chyhirynskaye Vodaskhovishcha resr Belarus
159 L4 Chyhyryn Ukr.
Chymyshliya Moldova see Cimișlia
158 B5 Chynadiyeve Ukr.
193 J10 Chyňava Czech Rep.
197 J4 Chynów Pol.
160 L9 Chyrvonaya Slabada Belarus
160 K9 Chyrvonaya Slabada Belarus
158 G1 Chyrvonaye, Vozyera l. Belarus
197 M2 Chyrvonaye Syalo Belarus
159 N9 Chysten'ke Ukr.
159 P8 Chystopillya Ukr.
Chystyakove Ukr. see Torez
233 C5 Chyulu Range mts Kenya
143 O7 Chyyyrchyk Ashuusu pass Kyrg.
197 M6 Chyzhykiv Ukr.
218 J5 Ciacova Romania
Ciadâr-Lunga Moldova see Ciadîr-Lunga
158 H7 Ciadîr-Lunga Moldova
185 F9 Ciadoux France
215 P8 Ciagola, Monte mt. Italy
271 □1 Ciales Puerto Rico
214 C4 Ciamannacce Corse France
117 H8 Ciamis Jawa Indon.
215 J4 Ciampino Italy
215 J4 Ciampino airport Italy
216 E8 Cianciana Sicilia Italy
116 G8 Cianjur Jawa Indon.
280 A5 Cianorte Brazil
183 K9 Cians r. France
196 G5 Ciasna Pol.
196 F3 Ciążeń Pol.
116 G8 Cibadak Jawa Indon.
199 J5 Cibakháza Hungary
117 H8 Cibatu Jawa Indon.
265 V7 Cibecue AZ U.S.A.
116 G8 Cibinong Jawa Indon.
233 A5 Cibitoke Burundi
261 G11 Cibolo Creek r. TX U.S.A.
206 C3 Ciborro Port.
266 D2 Cibuta Mex.
266 D2 Cibuta, Sierra mt. Mex.
212 G7 Cicagna Italy
210 D3 Ćićarija mts Croatia
215 N6 Cicciano Italy
148 G4 Çiçekdağı Turkey
150 D2 Çiçekli İçel Turkey
221 J3 Çiçekli Manisa Turkey
215 O7 Cicerale Italy
250 G8 Cicero IL U.S.A.
278 F4 Cícero Dantas Brazil
218 J7 Ćićevac Ćićevac Serbia
196 E4 Cicha Woda r. Pol.
197 L3 Cicibór Duży Pol.
199 G4 Čičov Slovakia
205 Q4 Cidacos r. Spain
116 G8 Cidaun Jawa Indon.
148 F3 Cide Turkey
198 E1 Cidlina r. Czech Rep.
205 O5 Cidones Spain
271 □1 Cidra Puerto Rico
197 I3 Ciechanów Pol.
197 K3 Ciechanowiec Pol.
196 G3 Ciechocinek Pol.
270 D3 Ciego de Ávila Cuba
197 I4 Cielądz Pol.
284 C3 Cielo, Cerro mt. Arg.
116 G8 Ciemas Jawa Indon.
205 M8 Ciempozuelos Spain

274 C2 **Ciénaga** Col.
274 D2 **Ciénagas del Catatumbo** *nat. park* Venez.
267 I5 **Ciénega** Mex.
268 C1 **Cieneguillas** Mex.
270 C2 **Cienfuegos** Cuba
196 F3 **Cienin Zaborny** Pol.
197 J4 **Ciepielów** Pol.
196 E5 **Ciepłowody** Pol.
185 F10 **Cier-de-Luchon** France
199 G3 **Čierna Voda** Slovakia
199 K3 **Čierna voda** *r.* Slovakia
199 H3 **Čierne Kľačany** Slovakia
199 I3 **Čierny Balog** Slovakia
185 F10 **Cierp-Gaud** France
196 F2 **Cierznie** Pol.
204 C4 **Cíes, Illas** *is* Spain
197 L5 **Cieszanów** Pol.
196 F4 **Cieszków** Pol.
196 G6 **Cieszyn** *Śląskie* Pol.
196 F4 **Cieszyn** *Wielkopolskie* Pol.
185 E9 **Cieutat** France
184 G4 **Cieux** France
209 C11 **Cieza** Spain
197 I6 **Ciężkowice** Pol.
150 F2 **Çiflikköy** Turkey
221 M3 **Çifteler** Turkey
Çiftlik Turkey *see* **Kelkit**
151 C6 **Çiftlikköy** *Erzurum* Turkey
221 J1 **Çiftlikköy** *İstanbul* Turkey
205 O7 **Cifuentes** Spain
205 K5 **Cigales** Spain
199 K3 **Cigánd** Hungary
151 C6 **Çiğdemli** Turkey
116 F8 **Cigeulis** *Jawa* Indon.
151 K6 **Çigil Adası** *i.* Azer.
212 E5 **Cigliano** Italy
205 M10 **Cigüela** *r.* Spain
148 F4 **Cihanbeyli** Turkey
221 K3 **Cihangazi** Turkey
268 C6 **Cihuatlán** Mex.
207 J2 **Cíjara, Embalse de** *resr* Spain
199 J6 **Čik** *r.* Serbia
Cikai *Yunnan* China *see* **Gongshan**
117 H8 **Cikalong** *Jawa* Indon.
220 A2 **Çikës, Maja e** *mt.* Albania
101 □7 **Cikobia** *i.* Fiji
210 F4 **Čikola** *r.* Croatia
117 H8 **Cilacap** *Jawa* Indon.
116 G8 **Cilangkahan** *Jawa* Indon.
239 □1c **Cilaos** Réunion
239 □1c **Cilaos, Cirque de** *vol. crater* Réunion
149 K3 **Çıldır** Turkey
149 K3 **Çıldır Gölü** *l.* Turkey
150 F2 **Çıldıroba** Turkey
117 H8 **Ciledug** *Jawa* Indon.
215 O7 **Cilento e del Vallo di Diano, Parco Nazionale del** *nat. park* Italy
151 A5 **Çilhorozdağı Geçidi** *pass* Turkey
131 H4 **Cili** *Hunan* China
150 B2 **Cilicia** *reg.* Turkey
Cilician Gates *pass* Turkey *see* **Gülek Boğazı**
219 M7 **Cilieni** Romania
221 M2 **Çilimli** Turkey
Cill Airne Ireland *see* **Killarney**
205 Q7 **Cillas** Spain
Cill Chainnigh Ireland *see* **Kilkenny**
169 E3 **Cill Charthaigh** Ireland
168 B8 **Cille Bhrighde** *Western Isles, Scotland* U.K.
169 C6 **Cill Éinne** Ireland
204 G8 **Cilleros** Spain
151 F6 **Çilli Geçidi** *pass* Turkey
Cill Mhantáin Ireland *see* **Wicklow**
169 C6 **Cill Rónáin** Ireland
144 F1 **Çilmämmetgum** *des.* Turkm.
149 L5 **Cilo Dağı** *mt.* Turkey
151 L5 **Çilov** Azer.
151 L5 **Çilov Adası** *i.* Azer.
172 E4 **Cilybebyll** *Neath Port Talbot, Wales* U.K.
172 E3 **Cilycwm** *Carmarthenshire, Wales* U.K.
265 Q6 **Cima** *CA* U.S.A.
206 □ **Cima, Ilhéu de** *i.* Madeira
116 G8 **Cimahi** *Jawa* Indon.
204 I3 **Cimanes del Tejar** Spain
261 E7 **Cimarron** *KS* U.S.A.
263 L8 **Cimarron** *NM* U.S.A.
261 G7 **Cimarron** *r. OK* U.S.A.
263 L8 **Cimarron Creek** *r. CO* U.S.A.
205 Q6 **Cimballa** Spain
216 F8 **Ciminna** *Sicilia* Italy
214 I3 **Cimino, Monte** *mt.* Italy
158 H7 **Cimişlia** Moldova
213 M3 **Cimolais** Italy
213 J7 **Cimone, Monte** *mt.* Italy
Cîmpeni Romania *see* **Câmpeni**
Cîmpia Turzii Romania *see* **Câmpia Turzii**
Cîmpina Romania *see* **Câmpina**
Cîmpulung Romania *see* **Câmpulung**
Cîmpulung la Tisa Romania *see* **Câmpulung la Tisa**
Cîmpulung Moldovenesc Romania *see* **Câmpulung Moldovenesc**
116 F7 **Cina, Tanjung** *c.* Indon.
149 J5 **Çınar** Turkey
221 K2 **Çınarcık** Turkey
274 E3 **Cinaruco** *r.* Venez.
274 E3 **Cinaruco-Capanaparo, Parque Nacional** *nat. park* Venez.
208 F3 **Cinca** *r.* Spain
208 F5 **Cinca** *r.* Spain
210 F4 **Cincar** *mt.* Bos.-Herz.
260 M6 **Cincinnati** *OH* U.S.A.
257 J6 **Cincinnatus** *NY* U.S.A.
270 D3 **Cinco-Balas, Cayos** *is* Cuba
207 M2 **Cinco Casas** Spain
Cinco de Outubro Angola *see* **Xá-Muteba**
284 C6 **Cinco Saltos** Arg.
208 C3 **Cinco Villas** *reg.* Spain
208 E6 **Cinctorres** Spain
219 M5 **Cincu** Romania
172 H4 **Cinderford** *Gloucestershire, England* U.K.
221 J5 **Çine** Turkey
221 I5 **Çine** *r.* Turkey
204 I3 **Ciñera** Spain
187 H8 **Ciney** Belgium
204 D6 **Cinfães** Port.
213 O9 **Cingoli** Italy
214 G2 **Cinigiano** Italy
212 G4 **Cinisello Balsamo** Italy
216 E7 **Cinisi** *Sicilia* Italy
169 C6 **Cinn Mhara** Ireland
199 I3 **Cinobaňa** Slovakia
181 L7 **Cinq-Mars-la-Pile** France
217 K7 **Cinquefrondi** Italy
137 M7 **Cinque Island** *Andaman & Nicobar Is* India
212 H7 **Cinque Terre** *reg.* Italy
269 N9 **Cintalapa** Mex.
185 H9 **Cintegabelle** France
214 B3 **Cinto, Monte** *mt.* France
285 F3 **Cintra** Arg.
238 □1b **Cintrão, Ponta do** *pt São Miguel* Azores
179 K8 **Cintrey** France
205 Q4 **Cintruénigo** Spain
237 M8 **Cintsa** S. Africa
280 B5 **Cinzas** *r.* Brazil
219 O6 **Ciolpani** Romania
199 L6 **Ciordan, Dealul** *hill* Romania
210 F4 **Čiovo** *i.* Croatia
117 H8 **Cipatuja** *Jawa* Indon.
131 J5 **Ciping** *Jiangxi* China
278 F4 **Cipó** Brazil
281 E3 **Cipo** *r.* Brazil
284 D6 **Cipolletti** Arg.
281 F4 **Cipotânea** Brazil
151 H5 **Çıraqdärä** Azer.
209 E7 **Cirat** Spain
116 G8 **Cirata, Waduk** *resr Jawa* Indon.
204 I3 **Cirbanal** *mt.* Spain
215 N5 **Circello** Italy
215 K5 **Circeo, Monte** *hill* Italy
215 J5 **Circeo, Parco Nazionale del** *nat. park* Italy
245 K2 **Circle** *AK* U.S.A.
262 L3 **Circle** *MT* U.S.A.
245 K2 **Circle Hot Springs** *AK* U.S.A.
256 C9 **Circleville** *OH* U.S.A.
265 T3 **Circleville** *UT* U.S.A.
117 H8 **Cirebon** *Jawa* Indon.
173 I4 **Cirencester** *Gloucestershire, England* U.K.
Cirene *tourist site* Libya *see* **Cyrene**
116 D5 **Cirenti** *Sumatera* Indon.
179 I7 **Cirey-sur-Blaise** France
179 M6 **Cirey-sur-Vezouze** France
205 Q5 **Ciria** Spain
212 D5 **Ciriè** Italy
215 Q7 **Cirigliano** Italy
158 H5 **Ciripcău** Moldova
160 J5 **Ciriss** *l.* Latvia
217 □ **Cirkewwa, Il-Ponta tac-** *pt* Malta
217 M5 **Cirò** Italy
199 K3 **Cirocha** *r.* Slovakia
217 M5 **Cirò Marina** Italy
185 D6 **Ciron** *r.* France
249 I1 **Cirque Mountain** *Nfld and Lab.* Can.
Cirta Alg. *see* **Constantine**
205 M9 **Ciruelos** Spain
182 E3 **Ciry-le-Noble** France
212 H7 **Cisa, Passo della** *pass* Italy
212 E7 **Cisano sul Neva** Italy
265 W3 **Cisco** *UT* U.S.A.
200 E7 **Cismòn** *r.* Italy
197 K6 **Cisna** Pol.
219 M5 **Cisnădie** Romania
270 B5 **Cisne, Islas del** *is* Caribbean Sea
205 K4 **Cisneros** Spain
282 E3 **Cisnes, Lagunas de los** *lakes* Arg.
213 M4 **Cisòn di Valmarino** Italy
199 J1 **Cisowsko-Orłowiński Park Krajobrazowy** Pol.
181 L8 **Cissé** France
215 J4 **Cisterna di Latina** Italy
217 M2 **Cisternino** Italy
270 E2 **Cistern Point** *Andros* Bahamas
205 J3 **Cistierna** Spain
270 G4 **Citadelle/Sans Souci/Ramiers** *tourist site* Haiti
213 M9 **Citerna** Italy
269 J4 **Citlaltepec** Mex.
Citlaltépetl *vol.* Mex. *see* **Orizaba, Pico de**
210 F4 **Čitluk** Bos.-Herz.
185 J9 **Citou** France
261 K10 **Citronelle** *AL* U.S.A.
236 D8 **Citrusdal** S. Africa
264 K3 **Citrus Heights** *CA* U.S.A.
213 L4 **Cittadella** Italy
215 P8 **Cittadella del Capo** *c.* Italy
214 I2 **Città della Pieve** Italy
213 M9 **Città di Castello** Italy
212 D5 **Città di Torino** *airport* Italy
215 J3 **Cittaducale** Italy
217 K7 **Cittanova** Italy
215 K2 **Cittareale** Italy
215 M2 **Città Sant'Angelo** Italy
212 F4 **Cittiglio** Italy
169 H2 **City of Derry** *airport Northern Ireland* U.K.
219 N5 **Ciucaș, Vârful** *mt.* Romania
219 K4 **Ciucea** Romania
267 I3 **Ciudad Acuña** Mex.
268 G7 **Ciudad Altamirano** Mex.
275 F2 **Ciudad Bolívar** Venez.
266 G4 **Ciudad Camargo** Mex.
266 D5 **Ciudad Constitución** *Baja California Sur* Mex.
267 N10 **Ciudad Cuauhtémoc** Mex.
267 N8 **Ciudad del Carmen** Mex.
277 G6 **Ciudad del Este** Para.
266 G3 **Ciudad Delicias** Mex.
269 H3 **Ciudad del Maíz** Mex.
269 H4 **Ciudad de Valles** Mex.
275 F2 **Ciudad Guayana** Venez.
268 D6 **Ciudad Guzmán** Mex.
268 G6 **Ciudad Hidalgo** Mex.
269 L9 **Ciudad Ixtepec** Mex.
266 F2 **Ciudad Juárez** Mex.
266 H5 **Ciudad Lerdo** Mex.
269 H6 **Ciudad López Mateos** Mex.
269 J3 **Ciudad Madero** Mex.
269 I3 **Ciudad Mante** Mex.
268 F5 **Ciudad Manuel Doblado** Mex.
269 J7 **Ciudad Mendoza** Mex.
267 J4 **Ciudad Mier** Mex.
266 E4 **Ciudad Obregón** Mex.
270 H8 **Ciudad Ojeda** Venez.
275 F3 **Ciudad Piar** Venez.
207 L3 **Ciudad Real** Spain
207 M3 **Ciudad Real** *prov.* Spain
267 J5 **Ciudad Río Bravo** Mex.
204 G7 **Ciudad Rodrigo** Spain
269 J7 **Ciudad Serdán** Mex.
267 M10 **Ciudad Tecún Uman** Guat.
Ciudad Trujillo Dom. Rep. *see* **Santo Domingo**
269 H2 **Ciudad Victoria** Mex.
219 J5 **Ciudanovița** Romania
199 L4 **Ciuhoi** Romania
158 G6 **Ciuhur** *r.* Moldova
158 H6 **Ciulucal de Mijloc** *r.* Moldova
219 N4 **Ciumani** Romania
199 K5 **Ciumeghiu** Romania
208 □ **Ciutadella** Spain
148 H3 **Cıva Burnu** *pt* Turkey
184 F3 **Civaux** France
213 M3 **Civetta, Monte** *mt.* Italy
213 O3 **Cividale del Friuli** Italy
215 Q8 **Civita** Italy
215 I3 **Civita Castellana** Italy
215 K4 **Civita d'Antino** Italy
213 P9 **Civitanova Marche** Italy
215 L3 **Civitaquana** Italy
214 H3 **Civitavecchia** Italy
214 H2 **Civitella, Monte** *mt.* Italy
215 L3 **Civitella Casanova** Italy
214 I2 **Civitella d'Agliano** Italy
213 L7 **Civitella di Romagna** Italy
213 L9 **Civitella in Val di Chiana** Italy
215 K4 **Civitella Roveto** Italy
181 P8 **Civray** *Centre* France
184 E3 **Civray** *Poitou-Charentes* France
221 K4 **Çivril** Turkey
214 C9 **Cixerri** *r. Sardegna* Italy
131 M3 **Cixi** *Zhejiang* China
129 N8 **Cixian** *Hebei* China
129 O9 **Ciyao** *Shandong* China
199 L4 **Cizer** Romania
Cizhou *Hebei* China *see* **Cixian**
193 J10 **Čížkovice** Czech Rep.
149 K5 **Cizre** Turkey
198 C2 **Čkyně** Czech Rep.
168 C9 **Clabhach** *Argyll and Bute, Scotland* U.K.
168 E11 **Clachan** *Argyll and Bute, Scotland* U.K.
168 D8 **Clachan** *Highland, Scotland* U.K.
Clachan Strachur *Scotland* U.K. *see* **Strachur**
262 C4 **Clackamas** *r. OR* U.S.A.
168 I10 **Clackmannanshire** *admin. div. Scotland* U.K.
173 O4 **Clacton-on-Sea** *Essex, England* U.K.
168 F10 **Cladich** *Argyll and Bute, Scotland* U.K.
170 B4 **Clady** *Northern Ireland* U.K.
169 I3 **Clady** *Northern Ireland* U.K.
172 E3 **Claerwen Reservoir** *Wales* U.K.
168 E9 **Claggan** *Highland, Scotland* U.K.
168 C7 **Claidh, Loch** *inlet Scotland* U.K.
184 F2 **Clain** *r.* France
185 E7 **Clairac** France
247 H3 **Claire, Lake** *Alta* Can.
262 C6 **Clair Engle Lake** *resr CA* U.S.A.
246 G4 **Clairmont** *Alta* Can.
178 E5 **Clairoix** France
185 I7 **Clairvaux-d'Aveyron** France
182 H3 **Clairvaux-les-Lacs** France
184 F2 **Claise** *r.* France
183 H6 **Claix** France
182 D2 **Clamecy** France
244 J3 **Clam Gulch** *AK* U.S.A.
250 D3 **Clam Lake** *WI* U.S.A.
170 C4 **Clanabogan** *Northern Ireland* U.K.
264 O2 **Clan Alpine Mountains** *NV* U.S.A.
103 F11 **Clandeboye** *South I.* N.Z.
169 I6 **Clane** Ireland
173 I4 **Clanfield** *Oxfordshire, England* U.K.
183 K8 **Clans** France
255 D9 **Clanton** *AL* U.S.A.
237 L7 **Clanville** S. Africa
236 C8 **Clanwilliam** S. Africa
236 C8 **Clanwilliam Dam** S. Africa
168 F11 **Claonaig** *Argyll and Bute, Scotland* U.K.
173 L3 **Clapham** *Bedfordshire, England* U.K.
171 M5 **Clapham** *North Yorkshire, England* U.K.
168 H6 **Clar, Loch nan** *l. Scotland* U.K.
285 H2 **Clara** Arg.
107 H5 **Clara** *r. Qld* Austr.
169 G6 **Clara** Ireland
283 D6 **Clara, Punta** *pt* Arg.
119 C9 **Clara Island** Myanmar
107 H5 **Claraville** *Qld* Austr.
285 H5 **Claraz** Arg.
171 P7 **Clarborough** *Nottinghamshire, England* U.K.
105 I5 **Clare** *N.S.W.* Austr.
104 G5 **Clare** *S.A.* Austr.
169 E7 **Clare** *county* Ireland
169 D6 **Clare** *r.* Ireland
173 N3 **Clare** *Suffolk, England* U.K.
250 J6 **Clare** *MI* U.S.A.
169 E7 **Clarecastle** Ireland
169 G6 **Clareen** Ireland
Claregalway Ireland *see* **Baile Chláir**
169 B5 **Clare Island** Ireland
270 □ **Claremont** Jamaica
257 M5 **Claremont** *NH* U.S.A.
107 I2 **Claremont Isles** *Qld* Austr.
261 H7 **Claremore** *OK* U.S.A.
169 E5 **Claremorris** Ireland
105 N3 **Clarence** *r. N.S.W.* Austr.
103 H9 **Clarence** *South I.* N.Z.
103 H9 **Clarence** *r. South I.* N.Z.
283 C9 **Clarence, Isla** *i.* Chile
238 □2a **Clarence Bay** *Ascension* S. Atlantic Ocean
286 U2 **Clarence Island** Antarctica
106 C1 **Clarence Strait** *N.T.* Austr.
245 N4 **Clarence Strait** *AK* U.S.A.
270 F2 **Clarence Town** *Long I.* Bahamas
270 □ **Clarendon** *parish* Jamaica
103 E13 **Clarendon** *South I.* N.Z.
261 J8 **Clarendon** *AR* U.S.A.
256 F7 **Clarendon** *PA* U.S.A.
261 E8 **Clarendon** *TX* U.S.A.
270 □ **Clarendon Park** Jamaica
237 M4 **Clarens** S. Africa
249 K3 **Clarenville** *Nfld and Lab.* Can.
246 H5 **Claresholm** *Alta* Can.
183 D9 **Claret** *Languedoc-Roussillon* France
183 H8 **Claret** *Provence-Alpes-Côte d'Azur* France
209 E9 **Clariano** *r.* Spain
107 H4 **Clarina Creek** *r. Qld* Austr.
260 H5 **Clarinda** *IA* U.S.A.
271 K9 **Clarines** Venez.
256 E9 **Clarington** *OH* U.S.A.
260 I4 **Clarion** *IA* U.S.A.
256 F7 **Clarion** *PA* U.S.A.
256 F7 **Clarion** *r. PA* U.S.A.
252 D7 **Clarión, Isla** *i.* Mex.
270 G3 **Clarion Bank** *sea feature* Bahamas
102 J3 **Claris** *North I.* N.Z.
260 G3 **Clark** *SD* U.S.A.
244 I3 **Clark, Lake** *AK* U.S.A.
245 Q2 **Clark, Mount** *N.W.T.* Can.
258 B4 **Clark Creek** *r. PA* U.S.A.
265 T7 **Clarkdale** *AZ* U.S.A.
107 J5 **Clarke** *r. Qld* Austr.
237 M7 **Clarkebury** S. Africa
105 L9 **Clarke Island** *Tas.* Austr.
107 K6 **Clarke Range** *mts Qld* Austr.
107 J5 **Clarke River** *Qld* Austr.
107 H4 **Clarkes Creek** *r. Qld* Austr.
249 K3 **Clarke's Head** *Nfld and Lab.* Can.
255 F8 **Clarkesville** *GA* U.S.A.
262 F2 **Clark Fork** *r. ID* U.S.A.
255 F9 **Clark Hill Reservoir** *GA/SC* U.S.A.
265 Q6 **Clark Mountain** *CA* U.S.A.
286 O1 **Clark Mountains** Antarctica
248 D4 **Clark Point** *Ont.* Can.
259 G4 **Clarksburg** *NJ* U.S.A.
256 E9 **Clarksburg** *WV* U.S.A.
261 J8 **Clarksdale** *MS* U.S.A.
242 G5 **Clarks Fork** *r. MT* U.S.A.
262 J4 **Clark's Fork Yellowstone** *r. MT* U.S.A.
103 E12 **Clarks Junction** *South I.* N.Z.
236 I10 **Clarkson** S. Africa
244 H4 **Clarks Point** *AK* U.S.A.
258 D1 **Clarks Summit** *PA* U.S.A.
262 F3 **Clarkston** *WA* U.S.A.
270 □ **Clark's Town** Jamaica
261 I8 **Clarksville** *AR* U.S.A.
258 B6 **Clarksville** *MD* U.S.A.
255 D7 **Clarksville** *TN* U.S.A.
261 H9 **Clarksville** *TX* U.S.A.
256 G12 **Clarksville** *VA* U.S.A.
280 B1 **Claro** *r.* Brazil
280 B3 **Claro** *r.* Brazil
212 G3 **Claro** Switz.
285 G6 **Claromecó** Arg.
178 F3 **Clary** France
168 H7 **Clashmore** *Highland, Scotland* U.K.
168 F6 **Clashnessie** *Highland, Scotland* U.K.
262 C3 **Clatskanie** *OR* U.S.A.
168 H12 **Clatteringshaws Loch** *l. Scotland* U.K.
261 E8 **Claude** *TX* U.S.A.
281 E4 **Cláudio** Brazil
285 G6 **Claudio Molina** Arg.
169 H3 **Claudy** *Northern Ireland* U.K.
193 H9 **Clausnitz** Ger.
258 D3 **Claussville** *PA* U.S.A.
191 J7 **Clausthal-Zellerfeld** Ger.
213 N3 **Claut** Italy
213 N3 **Clauzetto** Italy
114 C2 **Claveria** *Luzon* Phil.
173 M4 **Clavering** *Essex, England* U.K.
243 P2 **Clavering Ø** *i.* Greenland
172 H2 **Claverley** *Shropshire, England* U.K.
187 H8 **Clavier** Belgium
255 G9 **Claxton** *GA* U.S.A.
258 C4 **Clay** *PA* U.S.A.
256 D10 **Clay** *WV* U.S.A.
257 L4 **Clayburg** *NY* U.S.A.
260 G6 **Clay Center** *KS* U.S.A.
260 F5 **Clay Center** *NE* U.S.A.
256 B11 **Clay City** *KY* U.S.A.
171 O7 **Clay Cross** *Derbyshire, England* U.K.
173 O3 **Claydon** *Suffolk, England* U.K.
178 E6 **Claye-Souilly** France
170 I5 **Clay Head** Isle of Man
265 S4 **Clayhole Wash** *watercourse AZ* U.S.A.
258 E5 **Claymont** *DE* U.S.A.
171 P7 **Claypole** *Lincolnshire, England* U.K.
265 V8 **Claypool** *AZ* U.S.A.
265 V7 **Clay Springs** *AZ* U.S.A.
173 L6 **Clayton** *West Sussex, England* U.K.
255 E10 **Clayton** *AL* U.S.A.
258 D6 **Clayton** *DE* U.S.A.
255 F8 **Clayton** *GA* U.S.A.
258 E5 **Clayton** *NJ* U.S.A.
261 D7 **Clayton** *NM* U.S.A.
257 I4 **Clayton** *NY* U.S.A.
261 H8 **Clayton** *OK* U.S.A.
257 □P2 **Clayton Lake** *ME* U.S.A.
171 M6 **Clayton-le-Moors** *Lancashire, England* U.K.
256 E11 **Claytor Lake** *VA* U.S.A.
285 H3 **Clé** *r.* Arg.
168 D9 **Cleadale** *Highland, Scotland* U.K.
171 O4 **Cleadon** *Tyne and Wear, England* U.K.
169 C9 **Cleady** Ireland
169 C10 **Clear, Cape** Ireland
256 E10 **Clearco** *WV* U.S.A.
251 N7 **Clear Creek** *Ont.* Can.
265 U2 **Clear Creek** *UT* U.S.A.
265 V7 **Clear Creek** *r. AZ* U.S.A.
262 K4 **Clear Creek** *r. WY* U.S.A.
245 K4 **Cleare, Cape** *AK* U.S.A.
256 G7 **Clearfield** *PA* U.S.A.
262 H6 **Clearfield** *UT* U.S.A.
261 F9 **Clear Fork Brazos** *r. TX* U.S.A.
246 G3 **Clear Hills** *Y.T.* Can.
169 D10 **Clear Island** Ireland
260 I4 **Clear Lake** *IA* U.S.A.
260 G3 **Clear Lake** *SD* U.S.A.
250 B4 **Clear Lake** *WI* U.S.A.
264 J2 **Clear Lake** *l. CA* U.S.A.
265 T2 **Clear Lake** *l. UT* U.S.A.
264 J2 **Clearlake Oaks** *CA* U.S.A.
262 D6 **Clear Lake Reservoir** *CA* U.S.A.
262 K4 **Clearmont** *WY* U.S.A.
256 H9 **Clear Spring** *MD* U.S.A.
246 G5 **Clearwater** *B.C.* Can.
246 H4 **Clearwater** *r. Alta* Can.
247 I3 **Clearwater** *r. Alta/Sask.* Can.
255 F12 **Clearwater** *FL* U.S.A.
262 F3 **Clearwater** *r. ID* U.S.A.
260 G2 **Clearwater** *r. MN* U.S.A.
Clear Water Bay *H.K.* China *see* **Tsing Shui Wan**
247 K4 **Clearwater Lake** *l. Man.* Can.
250 E4 **Clearwater Lake** *WI* U.S.A.
247 K4 **Clearwater Lake Provincial Park** *Man.* Can.
262 G4 **Clearwater Mountains** *ID* U.S.A.
247 I3 **Clearwater River Provincial Park** *Sask.* Can.
171 J4 **Cleator Moor** *Cumbria, England* U.K.
261 G9 **Cleburne** *TX* U.S.A.
181 K4 **Clécy** France
180 C4 **Cléder** France
172 G3 **Cleehill** *Shropshire, England* U.K.
262 D3 **Cle Elum** *WA* U.S.A.
171 Q6 **Cleethorpes** *North East Lincolnshire, England* U.K.
179 K7 **Clefmont** France
180 E6 **Cléguer** France
180 E5 **Cléguérec** France
172 G3 **Clehonger** *Herefordshire, England* U.K.
219 N6 **Clejani** Romania
183 H7 **Clelles** France
187 I9 **Clémency** Lux.
275 H4 **Clément** Fr. Guiana
116 □ **Clementi** Sing.
280 B4 **Clementina** Brazil
255 F8 **Clemson** *SC* U.S.A.
256 D10 **Clendenin** *WV* U.S.A.
256 D8 **Clendening Lake** *OH* U.S.A.
190 K5 **Clenze** Ger.
172 H3 **Cleobury Mortimer** *Shropshire, England* U.K.
178 B5 **Cléon** France
258 C4 **Cleona** *PA* U.S.A.
183 F7 **Cléon-d'Andran** France
114 B6 **Cleopatra Needle** *mt. Palawan* Phil.
181 L7 **Cléré-les-Pins** France
178 B4 **Clères** France
178 H7 **Clérey** France
Clerf Lux. *see* **Clervaux**
251 P1 **Cléricy** *Que.* Can.
183 F6 **Clérieux** France
103 A12 **Clerke, Mount** *South I.* N.Z.
108 E4 **Clerke Reef** *W.A.* Austr.
182 F4 **Clermain** France
107 K7 **Clermont** *Qld* Austr.
185 G9 **Clermont** *Midi-Pyrénées* France
178 D5 **Clermont** *Picardie* France
237 O5 **Clermont** S. Africa
255 G11 **Clermont** *FL* U.S.A.
181 K6 **Clermont-Créans** France
184 F6 **Clermont-de-Beauregard** France
Clermont de Tonnère *atoll Arch. des Tuamotu* Fr. Polynesia *see* **Reao**
179 J5 **Clermont-en-Argonne** France
182 C5 **Clermont-Ferrand** France
183 C9 **Clermont-l'Hérault** France
182 J2 **Clerval** France
187 J8 **Clervaux** Lux.
187 J9 **Clervé** *r.* Lux.
178 E7 **Cléry** *r.* France
178 C8 **Cléry-St-André** France
213 K3 **Cles** Italy
104 F5 **Cleve** *S.A.* Austr.
172 G5 **Clevedon** *North Somerset, England* U.K.
255 F8 **Cleveland** *GA* U.S.A.
261 J9 **Cleveland** *MS* U.S.A.
256 D7 **Cleveland** *OH* U.S.A.
255 E8 **Cleveland** *TN* U.S.A.
261 H10 **Cleveland** *TX* U.S.A.
265 V2 **Cleveland** *UT* U.S.A.
256 C12 **Cleveland** *VA* U.S.A.
250 G6 **Cleveland** *WI* U.S.A.
107 K5 **Cleveland, Cape** *Qld* Austr.
262 H2 **Cleveland, Mount** *MT* U.S.A.
244 E5 **Cleveland, Mount** *vol. AK* U.S.A.
107 K5 **Cleveland Bay** *Qld* Austr.
256 D7 **Cleveland Heights** *OH* U.S.A.
171 O5 **Cleveland Hills** *England* U.K.
279 B8 **Clevelândia** Brazil
245 N5 **Cleveland Peninsula** *AK* U.S.A.
171 K6 **Cleveleys** *Lancashire, England* U.K.
Cleves Ger. *see* **Kleve**
169 C5 **Clew Bay** Ireland
237 N1 **Clewer** S. Africa
255 G12 **Clewiston** *FL* U.S.A.
103 B13 **Clifden** *South I.* N.Z.
169 B6 **Clifden** Ireland
106 G4 **Cliffdale** *r. Qld* Austr.
173 M5 **Cliffe** *Medway, England* U.K.
173 M5 **Cliffe Woods** *Medway, England* U.K.
169 F4 **Cliffoney** Ireland
237 L7 **Clifford** S. Africa
258 D1 **Clifford** *PA* U.S.A.
103 I8 **Clifford Bay** *South I.* N.Z.
236 A5 **Cliff Point** S. Africa
256 E10 **Clifftop** *WV* U.S.A.
107 M9 **Clifton** *Qld* Austr.
255 □2 **Clifton** *New Prov.* Bahamas
173 L3 **Clifton** *Bedfordshire, England* U.K.
265 W8 **Clifton** *AZ* U.S.A.
250 G9 **Clifton** *IL* U.S.A.
260 G6 **Clifton** *KS* U.S.A.
259 G3 **Clifton** *NJ* U.S.A.
258 D2 **Clifton** *PA* U.S.A.
107 J4 **Clifton Beach** *Qld* Austr.
256 F11 **Clifton Forge** *VA* U.S.A.
104 G2 **Clifton Hills** *S.A.* Austr.
257 L6 **Clifton Park** *NY* U.S.A.
255 □2 **Clifton Point** *New Prov.* Bahamas
247 I5 **Climax** *Sask.* Can.
250 I7 **Climax** *MI* U.S.A.
256 B12 **Clinch** *r. TN* U.S.A.
256 C11 **Clinchco** *VA* U.S.A.
256 C12 **Clinch Mountain** *mts TN/VA* U.S.A.
256 C12 **Clinchport** *VA* U.S.A.
246 G4 **Cline River** *Alta* Can.
187 F6 **Clinge** Neth.
191 K8 **Clingen** Ger.
246 F5 **Clinton** *B.C.* Can.
248 D5 **Clinton** *Ont.* Can.
103 D13 **Clinton** *South I.* N.Z.
261 I8 **Clinton** *AR* U.S.A.
259 J2 **Clinton** *CT* U.S.A.
254 B5 **Clinton** *IA* U.S.A.
260 K5 **Clinton** *IL* U.S.A.
261 K7 **Clinton** *KY* U.S.A.
261 J10 **Clinton** *LA* U.S.A.
257 □P4 **Clinton** *ME* U.S.A.
251 K7 **Clinton** *MI* U.S.A.
260 I6 **Clinton** *MO* U.S.A.
261 J9 **Clinton** *MS* U.S.A.
255 H8 **Clinton** *NC* U.S.A.
257 J5 **Clinton** *NY* U.S.A.
256 D8 **Clinton** *OH* U.S.A.
261 F8 **Clinton** *OK* U.S.A.
255 E7 **Clinton** *TN* U.S.A.
247 J1 **Clinton-Colden Lake** *N.W.T.* Can.
245 L2 **Clinton Creek (abandoned)** *Y.T.* Can.
250 F5 **Clintonville** *WI* U.S.A.
256 E11 **Clintonville** *WV* U.S.A.
256 C11 **Clintwood** *VA* U.S.A.
255 E10 **Clio** *AL* U.S.A.
251 K6 **Clio** *MI* U.S.A.
181 N8 **Clion** France
240 E7 **Clipperton, Île** *terr.* N. Pacific Ocean
168 C7 **Clisham** *hill Scotland* U.K.
180 I7 **Clisson** France
171 M6 **Clitheroe** *Lancashire, England* U.K.
102 K6 **Clive** *North I.* N.Z.
246 G2 **Clive Lake** *N.W.T.* Can.
276 D4 **Cliza** Bol.
109 B7 **Cloates, Point** *W.A.* Austr.
237 L4 **Clocolan** S. Africa
169 H7 **Clogh** *Kilkenny* Ireland
169 J7 **Clogh** *Wexford* Ireland
169 J3 **Clogh** *Northern Ireland* U.K.
Cloghan Ireland *see* **An Clochán**
169 G6 **Cloghan** *Offaly* Ireland
170 C6 **Cloghan** *Westmeath* Ireland
Cloghane Ireland *see* **An Clochán**
169 E3 **Cloghboy** Ireland
169 G8 **Clogheen** Ireland
169 D5 **Clogher** Ireland
169 H4 **Clogher** *Northern Ireland* U.K.
169 J5 **Clogherhead** Ireland
169 J5 **Clogher Head** Ireland
169 L4 **Cloghy** *Northern Ireland* U.K.
169 I7 **Clohamon** Ireland
180 D6 **Clohars-Carnoët** France
107 H6 **Clonagh** *Qld* Austr.
169 E9 **Clonakilty** Ireland
169 E9 **Clonakilty Bay** Ireland
169 H6 **Clonard** Ireland
170 B7 **Clonaslee** Ireland
106 H6 **Cloncurry** *Qld* Austr.
107 H5 **Cloncurry** *r. Qld* Austr.
169 J6 **Clondalkin** Ireland
169 D9 **Clondrohid** Ireland
169 H8 **Clonea** Ireland
169 J6 **Clonee** Ireland
169 G8 **Cloneen** Ireland
169 I7 **Clonegal** Ireland
169 H4 **Clones** Ireland
169 H2 **Clonmany** Ireland
169 G8 **Clonmel** Ireland
169 H5 **Clonmellon** Ireland
169 I7 **Clonmore** *Carlow* Ireland
169 G7 **Clonmore** *Tipperary* Ireland
169 G6 **Clonony** Ireland
169 G7 **Clonoulty** Ireland
169 I8 **Clonroche** Ireland
169 J6 **Clontarf** Ireland
169 I4 **Clontibret** Ireland
169 H6 **Clonygowan** Ireland
169 E4 **Cloonacool** Ireland
169 D8 **Cloonbannin** Ireland
Cloonboo Ireland *see* **Cluain Bú**
169 G5 **Cloone** Ireland
170 B6 **Clooneagh** Ireland
169 E5 **Cloonfad** *Roscommon* Ireland
169 F6 **Cloonfad** *Roscommon* Ireland
169 D5 **Cloonkeen** Ireland
169 E5 **Cloontia** Ireland
246 E5 **Clo-oose** *B.C.* Can.
190 F5 **Cloppenburg** Ger.
250 B3 **Cloquet** *MN* U.S.A.
250 B2 **Cloquet** *r. MN* U.S.A.
282 F2 **Clorinda** Arg.
168 I12 **Closeburn** *Dumfries and Galloway, Scotland* U.K.
250 E1 **Cloud Bay** *Ont.* Can.
242 H5 **Cloud Peak** *WY* U.S.A.
262 K4 **Cloud Peak** *WY* U.S.A.
103 I8 **Cloudy Bay** *South I.* N.Z.
184 E3 **Clouère** *r.* France
169 K4 **Clough** *Northern Ireland* U.K.
169 J2 **Cloughmills** *Northern Ireland* U.K.
171 Q5 **Cloughton** *North Yorkshire, England* U.K.
168 □N2 **Clousta** *Shetland, Scotland* U.K.
248 F3 **Clova** *Que.* Can.
168 J9 **Clova** *Angus, Scotland* U.K.
172 D5 **Clovelly** *Devon, England* U.K.
168 K11 **Clovenfords** *Scottish Borders, Scotland* U.K.
265 T1 **Clover** *UT* U.S.A.
264 I3 **Cloverdale** *CA* U.S.A.
264 M5 **Clovis** *CA* U.S.A.
261 D8 **Clovis** *NM* U.S.A.
168 F9 **Clovullin** *Highland, Scotland* U.K.
171 O7 **Clowne** *Derbyshire, England* U.K.
178 B8 **Cloyes-sur-le-Loir** France
251 Q5 **Cloyne** *Ont.* Can.
169 F9 **Cloyne** Ireland
169 D6 **Cluain Bú** Ireland
Cluain Meala Ireland *see* **Clonmel**
168 F8 **Cluanie, Loch** *l. Scotland* U.K.
247 I3 **Cluff Lake Mine** *Sask.* Can.
184 H2 **Cluis** France
219 L4 **Cluj-Napoca** Romania
183 I8 **Clumanc** France
172 F3 **Clun** *Shropshire, England* U.K.
172 G3 **Clun** *r. England* U.K.
172 C4 **Clunderwen** *Carmarthenshire, Wales* U.K.
168 G9 **Clunes** *Highland, Scotland* U.K.
106 G8 **Cluny** *Qld* Austr.
182 F4 **Cluny** France
182 G5 **Cluse des Hôpitaux** *gorge* France
182 J4 **Cluses** France
Clusium Italy *see* **Chiusi**
212 H4 **Clusone** Italy
256 G12 **Cluster Springs** *VA* U.S.A.
103 D13 **Clutha** *r. South I.* N.Z.
246 G1 **Clut Lake** *N.W.T.* Can.
109 I8 **Clutterbuck Hills** *W.A.* Austr.
172 G5 **Clutton** *Bath and North East Somerset, England* U.K.
172 F1 **Clwydian Range** *hills Wales* U.K.
172 E4 **Clydach** *Swansea, Wales* U.K.
172 F4 **Clydach Vale** *Rhondda Cynon Taff, Wales* U.K.
246 H4 **Clyde** *Alta* Can.
103 D12 **Clyde** *South I.* N.Z.
168 H11 **Clyde** *r. Scotland* U.K.
256 I5 **Clyde** *NY* U.S.A.
256 C7 **Clyde** *OH* U.S.A.
168 G12 **Clyde, Firth of** *est. Scotland* U.K.
168 H11 **Clydebank** *West Dunbartonshire, Scotland* U.K.
243 L2 **Clyde River** *Nunavut* Can.
168 I11 **Clydesdale** *val. Scotland* U.K.
103 D13 **Clydevale** *South I.* N.Z.
250 F6 **Clyman** *WI* U.S.A.
256 F8 **Clymer** *PA* U.S.A.
172 F3 **Clyro** *Powys, Wales* U.K.
197 J5 **Ćmielów** Pol.
168 I8 **Cnoc Fraing** *hill Scotland* U.K.
168 E12 **Cnoc Moy** *hill Scotland* U.K.
Cnossus *tourist site* Greece *see* **Knosos**
204 F6 **Côa** *r.* Port.
269 H6 **Coacalco** Mex.
265 P8 **Coachella** *CA* U.S.A.
265 P8 **Coachella Canal** *CA* U.S.A.
169 E9 **Coachford** Ireland
268 A1 **Coacoyole** Mex.
269 I9 **Coacoyulichán** Mex.
169 I3 **Coagh** *Northern Ireland* U.K.
268 F7 **Coahuayutla de Guerrero** Mex.
266 H4 **Coahuila** *state* Mex.
245 P4 **Coal** *r. Y.T.* Can.
168 I11 **Coalburn** *South Lanarkshire, Scotland* U.K.
250 F8 **Coal City** *IL* U.S.A.
268 D7 **Coalcomán** Mex.
268 D7 **Coalcomán** *r.* Mex.
247 H5 **Coaldale** *Alta* Can.
264 O3 **Coaldale** *NV* U.S.A.
258 D3 **Coaldale** *PA* U.S.A.
261 G8 **Coalgate** *OK* U.S.A.
256 C10 **Coal Grove** *OH* U.S.A.
246 E5 **Coal Harbour** *B.C.* Can.
264 L5 **Coalinga** *CA* U.S.A.
103 A13 **Coal Island** *South I.* N.Z.
169 I3 **Coalisland** *Northern Ireland* U.K.
256 G8 **Coalport** *PA* U.S.A.
245 P4 **Coal River** *B.C.* Can.
265 Q4 **Coal Valley** *NV* U.S.A.
237 N2 **Coalville** S. Africa
173 J2 **Coalville** *Leicestershire, England* U.K.
262 I6 **Coalville** *UT* U.S.A.
271 □1 **Coamo** Puerto Rico
204 G1 **Coaña** Spain
275 F6 **Coari** Brazil
275 F6 **Coari** *r.* Brazil
275 F6 **Coari, Lago** *l.* Brazil
185 D9 **Coarraze** France
264 M4 **Coarsegold** *CA* U.S.A.
276 C3 **Coasa** Peru
233 D5 **Coast** *prov.* Kenya
Coast *admin. reg.* Tanz. *see* **Pwani**
219 O2 **Coasta Ibăneștilor** *ridge* Romania
261 H10 **Coastal Plain** U.S.A.
246 E4 **Coast Mountains** *B.C.* Can.
107 M8 **Coast Range** *hills Qld* Austr.
264 I1 **Coast Ranges** *mts CA* U.S.A.
168 H11 **Coatbridge** *North Lanarkshire, Scotland* U.K.
269 K9 **Coatecas Altas** Mex.
269 K6 **Coatepec** Mex.
269 H7 **Coatepec Harinas** Mex.
267 N10 **Coatepeque** Guat.
258 D5 **Coatesville** *PA* U.S.A.
249 G4 **Coaticook** *Que.* Can.
269 K9 **Coatlán** Mex.
243 J3 **Coats Island** *Nunavut* Can.
286 V1 **Coats Land** *reg.* Antarctica
269 M7 **Coatzacoalcos** Mex.
269 M7 **Coatzacoalcos** *r.* Mex.
269 J5 **Coatzintla** Mex.
219 Q6 **Cobadin** Romania
251 O2 **Cobalt** *Ont.* Can.
259 J1 **Cobalt** *CT* U.S.A.
267 N10 **Cobán** Guat.
151 G4 **Çobandağ** *hill* Azer./Georgia
221 L4 **Çobanlar** Turkey
151 B6 **Çobantaş Geçidi** *pass* Turkey
105 J4 **Cobar** *N.S.W.* Austr.
105 L7 **Cobargo** *N.S.W.* Austr.
109 I8 **Cobb, Lake** *salt flat W.A.* Austr.
105 I8 **Cobden** *Vic.* Austr.
251 R4 **Cobden** *Ont.* Can.
205 M8 **Cobeja** Spain
205 P7 **Cobeta** Spain
169 F9 **Cobh** Ireland
247 M4 **Cobham** *r. Man./Ont.* Can.
173 L5 **Cobham** *Surrey, England* U.K.
276 C2 **Cobija** Bol.
276 C5 **Cobija** Chile
Coblenz Ger. *see* **Koblenz**
257 K6 **Cobleskill** *NY* U.S.A.
285 I5 **Cobo** Arg.
245 N4 **Cobol** *AK* U.S.A.
269 J5 **Cobos** Mex.
248 E5 **Cobourg** *Ont.* Can.
106 D1 **Cobourg Peninsula** *N.T.* Austr.
284 A5 **Cobquecura** Chile
109 D8 **Cobra** *W.A.* Austr.
105 J6 **Cobram** *Vic.* Austr.
276 D5 **Cobres** Arg.
206 D5 **Cobres** *r.* Port.
233 B8 **Cóbuè** Moz.
191 K10 **Coburg** Ger.
243 K2 **Coburg Island** *Nunavut* Can.
274 B5 **Coca** *Orellana* Ecuador
205 K6 **Coca** Spain
212 I3 **Coca, Pizzo di** *mt.* Italy
276 C4 **Cocachacra** Peru
278 E2 **Cocal** Brazil
258 C4 **Cocalico Creek** *r. PA* U.S.A.
278 C5 **Cocalinho** Brazil
Cocanada *Andhra Prad.* India *see* **Kakinada**
276 D4 **Cocapata** Bol.
215 P7 **Coccovello, Monte** *mt.* Italy
209 E10 **Cocentaina** Spain
276 D4 **Cochabamba** Bol.
276 D4 **Cochabamba** *dept* Bol.
283 B6 **Cochamó** Chile
284 A5 **Cocharcas** Chile
275 F2 **Coche, Isla** *i.* Venez.
191 D10 **Cochem** Ger.
284 D4 **Cochicó** Arg.
285 F5 **Cochicó, Laguna** *l.* Arg.
119 H10 **Co Chiên, Sông** *r. mouth* Vietnam
Cochin *Kerala* India *see* **Kochi**
Cochin India *see* **Kochi**
119 G9 **Cochin** *reg.* Vietnam
270 C2 **Cochinos, Bahía de** *b.* Cuba
265 W9 **Cochise** *AZ* U.S.A.
265 W9 **Cochise Head** *mt. AZ* U.S.A.
255 F9 **Cochran** *GA* U.S.A.
246 H5 **Cochrane** *Alta* Can.
248 D3 **Cochrane** *Ont.* Can.
247 K3 **Cochrane** *r. Sask.* Can.
283 B7 **Cochrane** Chile
283 B7 **Cochrane, Lago** *l.* Arg./Chile
256 E7 **Cochranton** *PA* U.S.A.
258 D5 **Cochranville** *PA* U.S.A.
193 D7 **Cochstedt** Ger.
219 R3 **Cocieri** Moldova
199 L5 **Cociuba Mare** Romania
104 E6 **Cockaleechie** *S.A.* Austr.
168 J8 **Cock Bridge** *Aberdeenshire, Scotland* U.K.
104 H5 **Cockburn** *S.A.* Austr.
270 H3 **Cockburn Harbour** Turks and Caicos Is
248 D4 **Cockburn Island** *Ont.* Can.
168 L11 **Cockburnspath** *Scottish Borders, Scotland* U.K.
270 F1 **Cockburn Town** *San Salvador* Bahamas
Cockburn Town Turks and Caicos Is *see* **Grand Turk**
171 N2 **Cockenheugh** *hill England* U.K.
168 K11 **Cockenzie and Port Seton** *East Lothian, Scotland* U.K.
171 J4 **Cocker** *r. England* U.K.
171 L6 **Cockerham** *Lancashire, England* U.K.
171 K4 **Cockermouth** *Cumbria, England* U.K.
172 E4 **Cockett** *Swansea, Wales* U.K.
258 B6 **Cockeysville** *MD* U.S.A.
109 I12 **Cocklebiddy** *W.A.* Austr.
270 □ **Cockpit** *hill* Jamaica
237 I9 **Cockscomb** *mt.* S. Africa
266 □S13 **Coclé del Norte** Panama
278 C4 **Coco** *r.* Brazil
266 □R10 **Coco** *r.* Hond./Nic.
270 D2 **Coco, Cayo** *i.* Cuba
291 N5 **Coco, Isla de** *i.* N. Pacific Ocean
Cocoa Island *Rodrigues I.* Mauritius *see* **Cocos, Île**
230 A4 **Cocobeach** Gabon
137 M6 **Coco Channel** India
266 F3 **Cocomórachic** Mex.
265 S6 **Coconino Plateau** *AZ* U.S.A.
105 K6 **Cocopara National Park** *N.S.W.* Austr.
105 K5 **Cocoparra Range** *hills N.S.W.* Austr.
274 C3 **Cocorná** Col.
114 C6 **Cocoro** *i.* Phil.
278 D5 **Cocos** Brazil
239 □1a **Cocos, Île** *i. Rodrigues I.* Mauritius
289 K4 **Cocos Basin** *sea feature* Indian Ocean
271 □7 **Cocos Bay** Trin. and Tob.
100 □1 **Cocos Island** Guam
108 □2 **Cocos Islands** *terr.* Indian Ocean
291 N5 **Cocos Ridge** *sea feature* N. Pacific Ocean
239 □1b **Cocotte, Mont** *hill* Mauritius
268 D5 **Cocula** Mex.
185 E7 **Cocumont** France
257 O7 **Cod, Cape** *MA* U.S.A.
214 D6 **Coda Cavallo, Capo** *c. Sardegna* Italy
219 P4 **Codăești** Romania
275 F5 **Codajás** Brazil
171 O5 **Cod Beck** *r. England* U.K.
173 O3 **Coddenham** *Suffolk, Engl*
171 P7 **Coddington** *Nottinghams* *England* U.K.
275 E2 **Codera, Cabo** *c.* Venez.
247 J5 **Coderre** *Sask.* Can.
213 M5 **Codevigo** Italy
103 B13 **Codfish Island** *Stewart I.*
214 D8 **Codi, Monte** *hill* Italy
173 L4 **Codicote** *Hertfordshire, England* U.K.
213 M6 **Codigoro** Italy
284 B6 **Codihue** Arg.
249 I1 **Cod Island** *Nfld and Lab.*
219 N5 **Codlea** Romania
171 O7 **Codnor** *Derbyshire, Engla*
278 E3 **Codó** Brazil
212 H5 **Codogno** Italy
258 B5 **Codorus** *PA* U.S.A.
205 R6 **Codos** Spain
278 D3 **Codózinho** Brazil
271 □2 **Codrington** Antigua and
287 D2 **Codrington, Mount** Anta
271 □2 **Codrington Lagoon** Antigua and Barbuda
213 N4 **Codroipo** Italy
214 B6 **Codrongianos** *Sardegna* I
158 H7 **Codru** Moldova
199 L5 **Codru-Moma, Munții** *m* Romania
172 H2 **Codsall** *Staffordshire, England* U.K.
169 B9 **Cod's Head** Ireland
262 J4 **Cody** *WY* U.S.A.
256 C12 **Coeburn** *VA* U.S.A.
237 J9 **Coega** S. Africa
284 A5 **Coelemu** Chile
278 E3 **Coelho Neto** Brazil
107 I2 **Coen** *Qld* Austr.
107 I2 **Coen** *r. Qld* Austr.
268 F6 **Coeneo** Mex.
237 J9 **Coerney** S. Africa
275 G4 **Coeroeni** *r.* Suriname
191 D7 **Coesfeld** Ger.
239 □2 **Coëtivy** *i.* Seychelles
237 I8 **Coetzeesberg** *mts* S. Afric
236 I2 **Coetzersdam** S. Africa
262 F3 **Coeur d'Alene** *ID* U.S.A.
262 F3 **Coeur d'Alene** *r. ID* U.S.A
262 F3 **Coeur d'Alene Indian Reservation** *res. ID* U.S.A.
262 F3 **Coeur d'Alene Lake** *ID* U
186 K3 **Coevorden** Neth.
180 H8 **Coëx** France
237 N7 **Coffee Bay** S. Africa
245 M3 **Coffee Creek** *Y.T.* Can.
261 K9 **Coffeeville** *MS* U.S.A.
261 H7 **Coffeyville** *KS* U.S.A.
104 E6 **Coffin Bay** *S.A.* Austr.
104 E6 **Coffin Bay** *b. S.A.* Austr.
104 E6 **Coffin Bay National Park** *S.A.* Austr.
104 E6 **Coffin Bay Peninsula** *S.A*
105 N4 **Coffs Harbour** *N.S.W.* Au
237 L8 **Cofimvaba** S. Africa
266 □O10 **Cofradía** Hond.
268 C5 **Cofradia de Camotlán** M
269 J6 **Cofre de Perote** *mt.* Mex.
269 J6 **Cofre de Perote, Parque Nacional** *nat. park* Mex.
209 C9 **Cofrentes** Spain
Cogălniceanu *airport* Ror. *see* **Kogălniceanu**
Cogâlniceni Moldova *see* **Cogîlniceni**
219 Q6 **Cogealac** Romania
205 L5 **Cogeces del Monte** Spair
173 N4 **Coggeshall** *Essex, Englan*
214 B3 **Coggia** *Corse* France
212 E4 **Coggiola** Italy
214 B6 **Coghinas** *r.* Italy
214 C6 **Coghinas, Lago del** *l. Sar* Italy
237 M7 **Coghlan** S. Africa
108 I5 **Coghlan, Mount** *hill W.A.*
208 G3 **Cogigar** *r.* Spain
158 H6 **Cogîlniceni** Moldova
184 D4 **Cognac** France
184 G4 **Cognac-la-Forêt** France
212 C4 **Cogne** Italy
182 H5 **Cognin** France
229 H6 **Cogo** Equat. Guinea
282 F2 **Cogoi** Arg.
212 F7 **Cogoleto** Italy
183 J10 **Cogolin** France
205 M4 **Cogollos** Spain
205 L4 **Cogollos** *r.* Spain
207 L6 **Cogollos Vega** Spain
205 N7 **Cogolludo** Spain
130 C4 **Cogsum** *Sichuan* China
204 F7 **Cogula** Port.
235 G5 **Coguno** Moz.
258 E6 **Cohansey** *r. NJ* U.S.A.
269 I7 **Cohetzala** Mex.
205 L2 **Cohilla, Embalse de** *resr*
162 R2 **Čohkarášša** *mt.* Norway
Čohkkiras Sweden *see* **Jul**
256 H6 **Cohocton** *r. NY* U.S.A.
257 L6 **Cohoes** *NY* U.S.A.
105 J6 **Cohuna** *Vic.* Austr.
266 □S14 **Coiba, Isla de** *i.* Panama
269 I8 **Coicoyán de las Flores** M
286 T3 **Coig** *r.* Arg.
168 F6 **Coigeach, Rubha** *pt Scotl*
283 B7 **Coihaique** Chile
283 C7 **Coihaique Alto** Chile
284 A5 **Coihüe** Chile
284 B5 **Coihueco** Arg.
284 B5 **Coihueco** Chile
136 E7 **Coimbatore** *Tamil Nadu*
204 D8 **Coimbra** Port.
204 D8 **Coimbra** *admin. dist.* Port.
207 J7 **Coín** Spain
178 F5 **Coincy** France
276 C4 **Coipasa, Salar de** *salt flat*
Coire Switz. *see* **Chur**
183 F7 **Coiron, Plateau du** Franc
182 E5 **Coise** *r.* France
269 J8 **Coixtlahuaca** Mex.
204 E8 **Coja** Port.
219 N6 **Cojasca** Romania
276 C3 **Cojata** Peru
274 D2 **Cojedes** *state* Venez.
274 A4 **Cojimíes** Ecuador
274 D2 **Cojoro** Venez.
283 C7 **Cojudo Blanco, Cerro** *mt.*
199 J6 **Čoka** *Vojvodina* Serbia
262 I5 **Cokeville** *WY* U.S.A.
105 I8 **Colac** *Vic.* Austr.
103 B13 **Colac** *South I.* N.Z.
Colair Lake India *see* **Kolleru Lake**
284 C1 **Colangüil, Cordillera de**
150 H2 **Colap** *watercourse* Turkey
278 C2 **Colares** Brazil
281 G3 **Colatina** Brazil
269 I5 **Colatlán** Mex.
185 F7 **Colayrac-St-Cirq** France
191 G9 **Cölbe** Ger.
Colbert Alg. *see* **Aïn Ouln**
170 D7 **Colbinstown** Ireland
193 E6 **Colbitz** Ger.
213 N8 **Colbordola** Italy
251 Q6 **Colborne** *Ont.* Can.
284 B4 **Colbún** Chile
284 B4 **Colbún, Lago** *l.* Chile
260 E6 **Colby** *KS* U.S.A.
250 D5 **Colby** *WI* U.S.A.
276 B3 **Colca** *r.* Peru
219 O6 **Colceag** Romania
237 J9 **Colchester** S. Africa
173 N4 **Colchester** *Essex, Englan*
259 K1 **Colchester** *CT* U.S.A.
250 D9 **Colchester** *IL* U.S.A.
244 G5 **Cold Bay** *AK* U.S.A.
173 J6 **Colden Common** *Hamp* *England* U.K.
245 J2 **Coldfoot** *AK* U.S.A.
168 L11 **Coldingham** *Scottish Bor* *Scotland* U.K.
193 G8 **Colditz** Ger.
193 G8 **Colditzer Forst** *park* Ger.
247 I4 **Cold Lake** *Alta* Can.
247 I4 **Cold Lake** *l. Alta/Sask.* C
258 F7 **Cold Spring** *NJ* U.S.A.

Cold Spring NY U.S.A.
Coldspring TX U.S.A.
Cold Springs NV U.S.A.
Coldstream B.C. Can.
Coldstream South I. N.Z.
Coldstream Scottish Borders, Scotland U.K.
Coldwater Ont. Can.
Coldwater KS U.S.A.
Coldwater MI U.S.A.
Coldwater r. MS U.S.A.
Coldwater Creek r. OK U.S.A.
Coldwell Ont. Can.
Colebrook NH U.S.A.
Coleen r. AK U.S.A.
Coleford S. Africa
Coleford Gloucestershire, England U.K.
Coleford Somerset, England U.K.
Coleman r. Qld Austr.
Coleman MD U.S.A.
Coleman MI U.S.A.
Coleman TX U.S.A.
Coleman WI U.S.A.
Çölemerik Turkey see Hakkâri
Colenso S. Africa
Colentina r. Romania
Cole Peninsula Antarctica
Coleraine Vic. Austr.
Coleraine Northern Ireland U.K.
Coleraine MN U.S.A.
Coleridge, Lake South I. N.Z.
Colerne Wiltshire, England U.K.
Coles, Punta de pt Peru
Coles Bay Tas. Austr.
Colesberg S. Africa
Coleshill Warwickshire, England U.K.
Colesville MD U.S.A.
Colesville NJ U.S.A.
Coleville Sask. Can.
Coleville CA U.S.A.
Colfax CA U.S.A.
Colfax IL U.S.A.
Colfax LA U.S.A.
Colfax WA U.S.A.
Colfax WI U.S.A.
Colgong Bihar India
Colgrave Sound str. Scotland U.K.
Colhué Huapí, Lago l. Arg.
Coliauco Chile
Colibaşi Romania
Colico Italy
Colico, Lago l. Chile
Coligny France
Coligny S. Africa
Colihaut Dominica
Colijnsplaat Neth.
Colima Mex.
Colima state Mex.
Colima, Nevado de vol. Mex.
Colina Brazil
Colina Chile
Colinas Brazil
Colindres Spain
Colintraive Argyll and Bute, Scotland U.K.
Colipa Mex.
Coliseu r. Brazil
Coll i. Scotland U.K.
Collado Bajo mt. Spain
Collado Hermoso Spain
Collado Villalba Spain
Collagna Italy
Collahuasi Chile
Collalto mt. Austria/Italy
Collanzo Spain
Collarada, Peña mt. Spain
Collarenebri N.S.W. Austr.
Collarmele Italy
Collazzone Italy
Collecchio Italy
Colledara Italy
Colle di Val d'Elsa Italy
Colleen Bawn Zimbabwe
Colleferro Italy
College AK U.S.A.
College Park GA U.S.A.
College Station TX U.S.A.
Collegeville PA U.S.A.
Collegno Italy
Colle Isarco Italy
Collelongo Italy
Collepardo Italy
Collepasso Italy
Collerina N.S.W. Austr.
Collesalvetti Italy
Colle Sannita Italy
Collesano Sicilia Italy
Colletorto Italy
Colley PA U.S.A.
Colliano Italy
Colli a Volturno Italy
Collie N.S.W. Austr.
Collie W.A. Austr.
Collier Bay W.A. Austr.
Collier Range hills W.A. Austr.
Collier Range National Park W.A. Austr.
Collierville TN U.S.A.
Collieston Aberdeenshire, Scotland U.K.
Colliford Reservoir England U.K.
Collin Dumfries and Galloway, Scotland U.K.
Collinas Sardegna Italy
Collinée France
Collingham Nottinghamshire, England U.K.
Collinghorst (Rhauderfehn) Ger.
Collingwood Ont. Can.
Collingwood South I. N.Z.
Collingwood Park NJ U.S.A.
Collins MS U.S.A.
Collins Glacier Antarctica
Collins Lake CA U.S.A.
Collinson Peninsula Nunavut Can.
Collinsville Qld Austr.
Collinsville AL U.S.A.
Collinsville OK U.S.A.
Collinsville VA U.S.A.
Collio Italy
Collioure France
Collipulli Chile
Collmberg hill Ger.
Collobrières France
Collombey Switz.
Collomsville PA U.S.A.
Collon Ireland
Collonges France
Collonges-la-Rouge France
Collooney Ireland
Colmar France
Col Marina Arg.
Colmars France
Colmberg Ger.
Colmeal Port.
Colmena Arg.
Colmenar Spain
Colmenar de Montemayor Spain
Colmenar de Oreja Spain
Colmenar Viejo Spain
Colméry France
Colmonell South Ayrshire, Scotland U.K.
Coln r. England U.K.
Colnabaichin Aberdeenshire, Scotland U.K.
Colnbrook Windsor and Maidenhead, England U.K.
Colne Lancashire, England U.K.
Colne r. England U.K.
Colney Heath Hertfordshire, England U.K.
Colnrade Ger.
Colo r. N.S.W. Austr.
Colobraro Italy
Cologna Veneta Italy
Cologne France
Cologne Ger. see Köln
Cologne NJ U.S.A.
Colom, Illa d'en i. Spain
Coloma MI U.S.A.
250 E5 Coloma WI U.S.A.
Colomb-Béchar Alg. see Béchar
181 K3 Colombelles France
178 D6 Colombes France
179 K6 Colombey-les-Belles France
179 I7 Colombey-les-Deux-Églises France
280 C4 Colômbia Brazil
274 C4 Colombia Col.
267 J4 Colombia Mex.
274 C4 Colombia country S. America
288 D5 Colombian Basin sea feature S. Atlantic Ocean
212 B2 Colombier Switz.
182 I5 Colombier, Mont mt. France
185 I7 Colombiès France
280 C6 Colombo Brazil
136 F9 Colombo Sri Lanka
251 O1 Colombourg Que. Can.
205 K2 Colombres Spain
207 L6 Colomera Spain
207 L6 Colomera r. Spain
207 L6 Colomera, Embalse de resr Spain
208 K3 Colomers Spain
185 G8 Colomiers France
285 G3 Colón Buenos Aires Arg.
285 H3 Colón Entre Ríos Arg.
270 C2 Colón Cuba
268 G5 Colón Mex.
266 □T13 Colón Panama
250 I8 Colon MI U.S.A.
271 □7 Colón Venez.
Colón, Archipiélago de is Pacific Ocean see Galápagos, Islas
266 □R13 Colón, Isla de i. Panama
104 D4 Colona S.A. Austr.
138 H6 Colonelganj Uttar Prad. India
270 F2 Colonel Hill Bahamas
266 A2 Colonet, Cabo c. Mex.
282 E2 Colonia Arg.
113 I5 Colonia Yap Micronesia
285 I4 Colonia dept Uru.
259 G3 Colonia NJ U.S.A.
Colonia Agrippina Ger. see Köln
285 F2 Colonia Alpina Arg.
284 D4 Colonia Alvear Arg.
285 F5 Colonia Barón Arg.
284 E3 Colonia Biagorria Arg.
285 H3 Colonia Caseros Arg.
284 D5 Colonia Chica, Isla i. Arg.
284 E6 Colonia Choele Choel, Isla i. Arg.
285 I4 Colonia del Sacramento Uru.
209 L9 Colònia de Sant Jordi Spain
209 L8 Colònia de Sant Pere Spain
266 E2 Colonia Díaz Mex.
282 E3 Colonia Dora Arg.
285 H3 Colonia Elía Arg.
284 D5 Colonia Emilio Mitre Arg.
285 G2 Colonia Fraga Arg.
285 F4 Colonia Hilario Lagos Arg.
Colonia Julia Fenestris Italy see Fano
285 H2 Colonia La Argentina Arg.
284 D5 Colonia La Pastoril Arg.
283 C7 Colonia Las Heras Arg.
285 I2 Colonia Lavalleja Uru.
256 H11 Colonial Heights VA U.S.A.
258 B4 Colonial Park PA U.S.A.
285 H2 Colonia Macías Arg.
285 G2 Colonia Portugalete Arg.
265 T10 Colonia Reforma Mex.
285 G2 Colonia Rosa Arg.
285 F4 Colonia Seré Arg.
282 F4 Colonia Suiza Uru.
217 M5 Colonna, Capo c. Italy
214 A9 Colonne, Punta delle pt Sardegna Italy
215 L2 Colonnella Italy
291 M5 Colon Ridge sea feature Pacific Ocean
168 D10 Colonsay i. Scotland U.K.
285 F6 Colorada Grande, Salina salt l. Arg.
284 C2 Colorado r. Arg.
284 F6 Colorado r. Arg.
282 D3 Colorado r. Arg.
280 B5 Colorado Brazil
284 B4 Colorado r. Chile
269 J9 Colorado r. Mex.
266 B2 Colorado r. Mex./U.S.A.
261 G11 Colorado r. TX U.S.A.
265 X2 Colorado state U.S.A.
284 D2 Colorado, Cerro mt. Arg.
283 E5 Colorado, Delta del Río Arg.
265 S5 Colorado City AZ U.S.A.
261 E9 Colorado City TX U.S.A.
265 P8 Colorado Desert CA U.S.A.
265 X2 Colorado National Monument nat. park CO U.S.A.
265 W4 Colorado Plateau CO U.S.A.
265 R7 Colorado River Aqueduct canal CA U.S.A.
265 R8 Colorado River Indian Reservation res. AZ/CA U.S.A.
282 C2 Colorados, Cerro mt. Arg.
263 L7 Colorado Springs CO U.S.A.
212 I6 Colorno Italy
206 C5 Colos Port.
Colossae Turkey see Honaz
214 D9 Colostrai, Stagno di lag. Sardegna Italy
183 H9 Colostre r. France
269 K10 Colotepec Mex.
269 J10 Colotepec r. Mex.
268 D3 Colotlán Mex.
192 H3 Cölpin Ger.
276 D4 Colquechaca Bol.
168 J11 Colquhar Scottish Borders, Scotland U.K.
276 D4 Colquiri Bol.
255 E10 Colquitt GA U.S.A.
151 K4 Çölquşçu Azer.
179 N7 Colroy-la-Grande France
256 C11 Colson KY U.S.A.
173 K2 Colsterworth Lincolnshire, England U.K.
262 K4 Colstrip MT U.S.A.
173 O2 Coltishall Norfolk, England U.K.
264 O7 Colton CA U.S.A.
257 K4 Colton NY U.S.A.
265 U2 Colton UT U.S.A.
259 G4 Colts Neck NJ U.S.A.
209 C12 Columbares hill Spain
259 K1 Columbia CT U.S.A.
254 E7 Columbia KY U.S.A.
261 I9 Columbia LA U.S.A.
258 B6 Columbia MD U.S.A.
260 I6 Columbia MO U.S.A.
261 K10 Columbia MS U.S.A.
255 I8 Columbia NC U.S.A.
258 E3 Columbia NJ U.S.A.
258 B4 Columbia PA U.S.A.
255 G9 Columbia SC U.S.A.
255 D8 Columbia TN U.S.A.
262 C3 Columbia r. WA U.S.A.
243 K1 Columbia, Cape Nunavut Can.
258 A7 Columbia, District of admin. dist. U.S.A.
246 G4 Columbia, Mount Alta/B.C. Can.
266 B3 Columbia, Sierra mts Mex.
254 E5 Columbia City IN U.S.A.
258 C2 Columbia County county PA U.S.A.
257 □R4 Columbia Falls ME U.S.A.
262 G2 Columbia Falls MT U.S.A.
246 F4 Columbia Mountains B.C. Can.
255 D9 Columbiana AL U.S.A.
256 E8 Columbiana OH U.S.A.
262 E3 Columbia Plateau U.S.A.
236 B8 Columbine, Cape S. Africa
209 G8 Columbretes, Islas is Spain
255 E9 Columbus GA U.S.A.
254 E6 Columbus IN U.S.A.
261 H7 Columbus KS U.S.A.
261 K9 Columbus MS U.S.A.
262 J4 Columbus MT U.S.A.
255 F8 Columbus NC U.S.A.
260 G5 Columbus NE U.S.A.
258 F4 Columbus NJ U.S.A.
263 K11 Columbus NM U.S.A.
256 B9 Columbus OH U.S.A.
256 F7 Columbus PA U.S.A.
261 G11 Columbus TX U.S.A.
250 E6 Columbus WI U.S.A.
270 F3 Columbus Bank sea feature Bahamas
256 A8 Columbus Grove OH U.S.A.
271 □5 Columbus Point Trin. and Tob.
264 N3 Columbus Salt Marsh NV U.S.A.
281 F3 Coluna Brazil
205 J2 Colunga Spain
264 J2 Colusa CA U.S.A.
102 J3 Colville North I. N.Z.
262 F2 Colville WA U.S.A.
245 J1 Colville r. AK U.S.A.
102 J3 Colville, Cape North I. N.Z.
109 I10 Colville, Lake salt flat W.A. Austr.
102 J3 Colville Channel North I. N.Z.
262 E2 Colville Indian Reservation res. WA U.S.A.
245 P2 Colville Lake N.W.T. Can.
245 P2 Colville Lake N.W.T. Can.
173 I2 Colwich Staffordshire, England U.K.
172 E1 Colwyn Bay Conwy, Wales U.K.
184 G5 Coly France
172 F6 Colyton Devon, England U.K.
213 M6 Comacchio Italy
213 M6 Comacchio, Valli di val. Italy
207 M7 Comacho, Puerto pass Spain
133 J12 Comai Xizang China
268 D6 Comala Mex.
267 M8 Comalcalco Mex.
269 I4 Comales r. Mex.
283 C6 Comallo Arg.
219 O6 Comana Romania
219 N5 Comana de Sus Romania
261 F10 Comanche TX U.S.A.
286 U2 Comandante Ferraz research stn Antarctica
282 F2 Comandante Fontana Arg.
283 C8 Comandante Luis Piedra Buena Arg.
285 I6 Comandante Nicanor Otamendi Arg.
284 C3 Comandante Salas Arg.
203 H1 Comanegra, Puig de mt. Spain
219 O4 Comăneşti Romania
208 H2 Coma Pedrosa, Pic de mt. Andorra
219 N5 Comarnic Romania
266 □P10 Comayagua Hond.
255 G9 Combahee r. SC U.S.A.
284 B2 Combarbalá Chile
179 K8 Combeaufontaine France
182 I5 Combe de Savoie val. France
172 D5 Combe Martin Devon, England U.K.
169 K3 Comber Northern Ireland U.K.
251 Q4 Combermere Ont. Can.
118 A5 Combermere Bay Myanmar
173 M3 Comberton Cambridgeshire, England U.K.
172 G6 Combe St Nicholas Somerset, England U.K.
187 I8 Comblain-au-Pont Belgium
182 F2 Comblanchien France
178 E3 Combles France
182 J5 Combloux France
116 E4 Combol i. Indon.
212 I3 Combolo, Monte mt. Italy/Switz.
180 H5 Combourg France
182 A4 Combrailles reg. France
180 C6 Combrit France
182 C5 Combronde France
284 E3 Comechingones, Sierra de mts Arg.
213 N2 Comegliàns Italy
213 N2 Comèlico Superiore Italy
248 F3 Comencho, Lac l. Que. Can.
206 D2 Comenda Port.
280 C3 Comendador Gomes Brazil
281 G2 Comercinho Brazil
271 □1 Comerio Puerto Rico
213 M8 Comero, Monte mt. Italy
107 L7 Comet Qld Austr.
107 L7 Comet r. Qld Austr.
261 F10 Comfort TX U.S.A.
256 D10 Comfort WV U.S.A.
270 □ Comfort Castle Jamaica
139 M8 Comilla Bangl.
205 L2 Comillas Spain
187 C7 Comines Belgium
Comino i. Malta see Kemmuna
214 D6 Comino, Capo c. Sardegna Italy
Cominotto i. Malta see Kemmunett
216 H10 Comiso Sicilia Italy
269 L9 Comitancillo Mex.
267 M9 Comitán de Domínguez Mex.
216 F9 Comitini Sicilia Italy
199 J6 Comloşu Mare Romania
259 I3 Commack NY U.S.A.
251 O4 Commanda Ont. Can.
Commeen Ireland see An Coimín
182 G3 Commenailles France
185 C7 Commensacq France
182 B4 Commentry France
180 H8 Commequiers France
181 J5 Commer France
179 K6 Commercy France
185 F10 Comminges reg. France
255 □1 Commissioner's Point Bermuda
236 D6 Commissioner's Salt Pan S. Africa
243 J3 Committee Bay Nunavut Can.
237 O3 Commondale S. Africa
287 J2 Commonwealth Bay Antarctica
Commonwealth Territory admin. div. Austr. see Jervis Bay Territory
212 G4 Como Italy
212 G4 Como prov. Italy
212 G4 Como, Lago di l. Italy
Como, Lake Italy see Como, Lago di
269 L7 Comoapan Mex.
133 I12 Como Chamling l. China
284 B3 Comodoro Arturo Merino Benitez airport Chile
283 D7 Comodoro Rivadavia Arg.
Comoé r. Côte d'Ivoire see Komoé
228 E4 Comoé, Parc National de la nat. park Côte d'Ivoire
268 G5 Comonfort Mex.
Comores country Africa see Comoros
136 E8 Comorin, Cape India
239 □3 Comoros country Africa
246 E5 Comox B.C. Can.
207 L7 Cómpeta Spain
212 H6 Compiano Italy
178 E5 Compiègne France
185 I7 Compolibat France
206 B4 Comporta Port.
268 C4 Compostela Mex.
114 F8 Compostela Mindanao Phil.
184 G4 Compreignac France
280 D6 Comprida, Ilha i. Brazil
183 J9 Comps-sur-Artuby France
264 N8 Compton CA U.S.A.
250 E8 Compton IL U.S.A.
205 K3 Compuerto, Embalse de resr Spain
158 H7 Comrat Moldova
168 I10 Comrie Perth and Kinross, Scotland U.K.
261 E11 Comstock TX U.S.A.
215 K2 Comunanza Italy
216 G9 Comunelli r. Sicilia Italy
118 G5 Con, Sông r. Vietnam
119 I8 Cơn, Sông r. Vietnam
133 J13 Cona Xizang China
213 M5 Cona Italy
150 E1 Çona Turkey
228 B4 Conakry Guinea
274 B5 Conambo Ecuador
274 B5 Conambo r. Ecuador
283 D6 Cona Niyeo Arg.
105 K9 Conara Junction Tas. Austr.
282 C3 Conay Chile
214 C4 Conca Corse France
213 N8 Conca r. Italy
284 E3 Concarán Arg.
180 D6 Concarneau France
214 D6 Concas Sardegna Italy
275 F5 Conceição Amazonas Brazil
277 F1 Conceição Mato Grosso Brazil
278 F3 Conceição Paraíba Brazil
277 E2 Conceição Rondônia Brazil
275 F4 Conceição Roraima Brazil
280 E2 Conceição r. Brazil
206 D6 Conceição Port.
281 H3 Conceição da Barra Brazil
280 C3 Conceição das Alagoas Brazil
281 G5 Conceição de Macabu Brazil
278 C4 Conceição do Araguaia Brazil
278 F4 Conceição do Coité Brazil
281 F3 Conceição do Mato Dentro Brazil
275 G4 Conceição do Maú Brazil
278 D5 Conceição do Norte Brazil
281 E4 Conceição do Rio Verde Brazil
282 F3 Concepción Corrientes Arg.
282 D2 Concepción Tucumán Arg.
276 D2 Concepción Beni Bol.
277 E4 Concepción Santa Cruz Bol.
282 B5 Concepción Chile
268 F1 Concepción Mex.
266 C2 Concepción r. Mex.
277 F5 Concepción Para.
274 D2 Concepción Venez.
283 B8 Concepción, Canal sea chan. Chile
266 D4 Concepción, Punta pt Mex.
268 D6 Concepción de Buenos Aires Mex.
285 H3 Concepción del Uruguay Arg.
239 □2b Conception, Île i. Inner Islands Seychelles
264 L7 Conception, Point CA U.S.A.
234 B4 Conception Bay Namibia
270 F2 Conception Island Bahamas
212 I4 Concesio Italy
235 F3 Concession Zimbabwe
268 B3 Concha Mex.
205 N2 Concha Spain
205 O3 Concha de Álava reg. Spain
280 C5 Conchas Brazil
263 L9 Conchas NM U.S.A.
204 E5 Conchas, Encoro de resr Spain
263 L9 Conchas Lake NM U.S.A.
178 A6 Conches-en-Ouche France
276 C5 Conchi Chile
266 G4 Concho Mex.
265 W7 Concho AZ U.S.A.
261 F10 Concho r. TX U.S.A.
267 K5 Conchos r. Nuevo León/Tamaulipas Mex.
266 G3 Conchos r. Mex.
284 B3 Concón Chile
264 J4 Concord CA U.S.A.
250 J7 Concord MI U.S.A.
255 G8 Concord NC U.S.A.
257 N5 Concord NH U.S.A.
256 H8 Concord PA U.S.A.
256 G11 Concord VA U.S.A.
257 N4 Concord VT U.S.A.
286 I2 Concordia research stn Antarctica
285 I2 Concordia Arg.
274 E6 Concórdia Amazonas Brazil
279 B8 Concórdia Santa Catarina Brazil
274 C3 Concordia Antioquia Col.
274 C4 Concordia Meta Col.
268 A2 Concordiá Mex.
274 C6 Concordia Peru
236 B5 Concordia S. Africa
260 G6 Concordia KS U.S.A.
213 N4 Concordia Sagittaria Italy
145 O3 Concord Peak Afgh.
185 G6 Concorès France
185 H7 Concots France
284 B2 Concumén Chile
118 G5 Con Cuông Vietnam
231 B7 Conda Angola
208 F3 Condado reg. Spain
206 G6 Condado de Niebla reg. Spain
205 O3 Condado de Treviño reg. Spain
107 M9 Condamine Qld Austr.
107 L9 Condamine r. Qld Austr.
119 H10 Côn Đao Vietnam
183 B6 Condat France
184 G4 Condat-sur-Vienne France
278 F4 Conde Brazil
178 G5 Condé-en-Brie France
266 □P11 Condega Nic.
278 C2 Condeixa Brazil
204 D8 Condeixa-a-Nova Port.
181 M5 Condé-sur-Huisne France
178 G3 Condé-sur-l'Escaut France
181 J4 Condé-sur-Noireau France
181 I3 Condé-sur-Vire France
279 E5 Condeúba Brazil
213 J4 Condino Italy
105 K5 Condobolin N.S.W. Austr.
235 G3 Condoe Moz.
217 J7 Condofuri Italy
185 E8 Condom France
262 D4 Condon OR U.S.A.
274 B6 Condor, Cordillera del mts Ecuador/Peru
284 B1 Condoriaco Chile
212 C5 Condove Italy
172 G2 Condover Shropshire, England U.K.
187 G8 Condroz reg. Belgium
255 D10 Conecuh r. AL U.S.A.
213 M4 Conegliano Italy
266 H4 Conejos Mex.
263 K8 Conejos CO U.S.A.
263 L8 Conejos r. CO/NM U.S.A.
251 O9 Conemaugh r. PA U.S.A.
244 H2 Cone Mountain AK U.S.A.
213 P8 Conero, Monte hill Italy
285 G3 Conesa Arg.
258 C5 Conestoga PA U.S.A.
258 C4 Conestoga Creek r. PA U.S.A.
251 N6 Conestogo Lake Ont. Can.
256 H6 Conesus Lake NY U.S.A.
256 D8 Conesville OH U.S.A.
258 B4 Conewago Creek r. PA U.S.A.
258 B4 Conewago Lake PA U.S.A.
179 L8 Coney r. France
255 □1 Coney Island Bermuda
169 E4 Coney Island Ireland
Coney Island Sing. see Serangoon, Pulau
259 H3 Coney Island NY U.S.A.
179 K5 Conflans-en-Jarnisy France
179 L8 Conflans-sur-Lanterne France
185 I10 Conflent reg. France
215 Q9 Conflenti Italy
113 L9 Conflict Group is P.N.G.
256 F9 Confluence PA U.S.A.
Confoederatio Helvetica country Europe see Switzerland
184 F3 Confolens France
184 F4 Confolentais reg. France
265 S3 Confusion Range mts UT U.S.A.
277 F6 Confuso r. Para.
169 D5 Cong Ireland
130 B3 Conga Xizang China
255 G9 Congaree National Park nat. park SC U.S.A.
172 D6 Congdon's Shop Cornwall, England U.K.
133 H12 Congdü Xizang China
131 I7 Conghua Guangdong China
130 G6 Congjiang Guizhou China
171 M7 Congleton Cheshire, England U.K.
230 B5 Congo country Africa
231 B6 Congo r. Congo/Dem. Rep. Congo
Congo (Brazzaville) country Africa see Congo
Congo (Kinshasa) country Africa see Congo, Democratic Republic of the
230 D5 Congo, Democratic Republic of the country Africa
Congo, Republic of country Africa see Congo
230 D5 Congo Basin Dem. Rep. Congo
231 B6 Congo-Central prov. Dem. Rep. Congo
288 J6 Congo Cone sea feature S. Atlantic Ocean
Congo Free State country Africa see Congo, Democratic Republic of the
281 F4 Congonhas Brazil
280 B5 Congonhinhas Brazil
204 H3 Congosto Spain
205 K3 Congosto de Valdavia Spain
172 G5 Congresbury North Somerset, England U.K.
265 T7 Congress AZ U.S.A.
181 I6 Congrier France
284 B6 Conguillo, Parque Nacional nat. park Chile
284 E5 Conhelo Arg.
267 O8 Conhuas Mex.
103 E12 Conical Peak hill South I. N.Z.
283 C6 Cónico, Cerro mt. Arg.
178 B7 Conie r. France
206 G8 Conil de la Frontera Spain
209 H10 Conillera, Illa sa i. Spain
209 K9 Conills, Illa des i. Spain
105 L6 Conimbla National Park nat. park N.S.W. Austr.
171 Q7 Coningsby Lincolnshire, England U.K.
171 O7 Conisbrough South Yorkshire, England U.K.
106 D7 Coniston N.T. Austr.
248 D4 Coniston Ont. Can.
171 K5 Coniston Cumbria, England U.K.
171 K5 Coniston Water l. England U.K.
107 J5 Conjuboy Qld Austr.
207 M7 Conjuros hill Spain
267 O7 Conkal Mex.
247 I4 Conklin Alta Can.
231 A5 Conkouati, Réserve de Faune nature res. Congo
284 E3 Conlara Arg.
284 E3 Conlara r. Arg.
181 K5 Conlie France
182 H3 Conliège France
169 K3 Conlig Northern Ireland U.K.
248 E2 Conn r. Que. Can.
169 D4 Conn, Lough l. Ireland
Connacht reg. Ireland see Connaught
172 F1 Connah's Quay Flintshire, Wales U.K.
178 G6 Connantre France
251 N1 Connaught Ont. Can.
169 D5 Connaught reg. Ireland
183 F8 Connaux France
256 E7 Conneaut OH U.S.A.
256 E7 Conneaut Lake PA U.S.A.
256 E7 Conneautville PA U.S.A.
259 K2 Connecticut r. CT U.S.A.
257 M7 Connecticut state U.S.A.
168 F10 Connel Argyll and Bute, Scotland U.K.
106 F5 Connells Lagoon Conservation Reserve nature res. N.T. Austr.
256 F8 Connellsville PA U.S.A.
107 I8 Connemara Qld Austr.
167 C5 Connemara reg. Ireland
169 D6 Connemara reg. Ireland
169 C5 Connemara National Park Ireland
106 C8 Conner, Mount hill N.T. Austr.
181 L5 Connerré France
254 E6 Connersville IN U.S.A.
169 D7 Connolly Ireland
245 N3 Connolly, Mount Y.T. Can.
168 D13 Connor Northern Ireland U.K.
107 L6 Connors Range hills Qld Austr.
105 J5 Conoble N.S.W. Austr.
258 B4 Conodoguinet Creek r. PA U.S.A.
274 C5 Cononaco Ecuador
274 C5 Cononaco r. Ecuador
168 H7 Conon Bridge Highland, Scotland U.K.
199 K5 Conop Romania
199 I6 Čonoplja Vojvodina Serbia
250 E3 Conover WI U.S.A.
192 H4 Conow Ger.
258 C5 Conowingo MD U.S.A.
185 I6 Conques France
185 I9 Conques-sur-Orbiel France
276 D2 Conquista Bol.
280 D3 Conquista Brazil
207 J4 Conquista Spain
262 I2 Conrad MT U.S.A.
288 L9 Conrad Rise sea feature Southern Ocean
261 H10 Conroe TX U.S.A.
261 H10 Conroe, Lake TX U.S.A.
213 L6 Consandolo Italy
285 H2 Conscripto Bernardi Arg.
187 J9 Consdorf Lux.
251 Q5 Consecon Ont. Can.
267 O8 Consejo Belize
281 F4 Conselheiro Lafaiete Brazil
281 G3 Conselheiro Pena Brazil
213 L6 Conselice Italy
209 K8 Consell Spain
179 J5 Consenvoye France
171 N4 Consett Durham, England U.K.
258 E4 Conshohocken PA U.S.A.
270 B2 Consolación del Sur Cuba
119 H10 Côn Sơn, Đao i. Vietnam
247 I4 Consort Alta Can.
Constance Ger. see Konstanz
Constance, Lake Ger./Switz. see Bodensee
206 C2 Constância Port.
285 H3 Constancia Uru.
275 F6 Constância dos Baetas Brazil
219 Q6 Constanţa Romania
Constanţa airport Romania see Kogălniceanu
208 H5 Constantí Spain
Constantia tourist site Cyprus see Salamis
Constantia Ger. see Konstanz
204 H5 Constantim Bragança Port.
204 E6 Constantim Vila Real Port.
206 H5 Constantina Spain
227 G1 Constantine Alg.
172 B7 Constantine Cornwall, England U.K.
250 I8 Constantine MI U.S.A.
244 H4 Constantine, Cape AK U.S.A.
245 □B6 Constantine Harbor AK U.S.A.
Constantinople Turkey see İstanbul
270 □ Constant Spring Jamaica
285 G2 Constanza Arg.
205 K7 Constanzana Spain
284 A4 Constitución Chile
285 I2 Constitución Uru.
266 B1 Constitución de 1857, Parque Nacional nat. park Mex.
207 L2 Consuegra Spain
107 L8 Consuelo Qld Austr.
277 E3 Consuelo Brazil
247 I5 Consul Sask. Can.
247 K1 Consul r. Nunavut Can.
262 G6 Contact NV U.S.A.
281 F4 Contagalo Brazil
281 E3 Contagem Brazil
276 B1 Contamana Peru
213 M5 Contarina Italy
278 F5 Contas r. Brazil
214 A7 Conte, Porto b. Sardegna Italy
237 I4 Content S. Africa
216 E8 Contessa Entellina Sicilia Italy
212 C3 Conthey Switz.
215 J3 Contigliano Italy
168 G7 Contin Highland, Scotland U.K.
256 A7 Continental OH U.S.A.
185 B7 Contis-Plage France
257 N5 Contoocook r. NH U.S.A.
267 P7 Contoy, Isla i. Mex.
284 C6 Contralmirante Cordero Arg.
216 G8 Contrasto, Colle del pass Italy
274 C3 Contratación Col.
207 M7 Contraviesa, Sierra de mts Spain
205 Q9 Contreras, Embalse de resr Spain
283 B8 Contreras, Isla i. Chile
184 G1 Contres France
179 K7 Contrexéville France
281 E3 Contria Brazil
215 O6 Controne Italy
282 B5 Contulmo Chile
276 A1 Contumazá Peru
215 O6 Contursi Terme Italy
247 I1 Contwoyto Lake N.W.T./Nunavut Can.
178 D4 Conty France
274 C2 Convención Col.
261 J10 Convent LA U.S.A.
284 B4 Convento Viejo Chile
217 M2 Conversano Italy
256 A8 Convoy OH U.S.A.
237 J7 Conway S. Africa
Conway Conwy, Wales U.K. see Conwy
261 I8 Conway AR U.S.A.
256 A11 Conway KY U.S.A.
260 G1 Conway ND U.S.A.
257 □N5 Conway NH U.S.A.
255 H9 Conway SC U.S.A.
107 L6 Conway, Cape Qld Austr.
104 E3 Conway, Lake salt flat S.A. Austr.
107 L6 Conway National Park Qld Austr.
Conway Reef Fiji see Ceva-i-Ra
261 G7 Conway Springs KS U.S.A.
172 E1 Conwy Conwy, Wales U.K.
172 E1 Conwy admin. div. Wales U.K.
172 E1 Conwy r. Wales U.K.
172 D1 Conwy Bay Wales U.K.
258 C3 Conyngham PA U.S.A.
215 O6 Conza, Lago di l. Italy
104 E3 Coober Pedy S.A. Austr.
Cooch Behar W. Bengal India see Koch Bihar
107 L9 Coogoon r. Qld Austr.
104 C4 Cook S.A. Austr.
250 B2 Cook MN U.S.A.
283 C9 Cook, Bahía de b. Chile
101 □9a Cook, Baie de b. Moorea Fr. Polynesia
246 E5 Cook, Cape B.C. Can.
100 □5 Cook, Grand Récif de rf New Caledonia
245 M3 Cook, Mount Can./U.S.A.
Cook, Mount South I. N.Z. see Aoraki
Cook Atoll Kiribati see Tarawa
263 K10 Cookes Peak NM U.S.A.
255 E7 Cookeville TN U.S.A.
173 K4 Cookham Windsor and Maidenhead, England U.K.
237 J8 Cookhouse S. Africa
287 K2 Cook Ice Shelf Antarctica
244 I3 Cook Inlet sea channel AK U.S.A.
103 □2 Cook Islands S. Pacific Ocean
172 H3 Cookley Worcestershire, England U.K.
101 □8a Cook Point Tongatapu Tonga
Cook's Bay Moorea Fr. Polynesia see Cook, Baie de
257 K6 Cooksburg NY U.S.A.
168 J8 Cook's Cairn hill Scotland U.K.
249 K3 Cook's Harbour Nfld and Lab. Can.
107 J3 Cooks Passage Qld Austr.
169 I3 Cookstown Northern Ireland U.K.
103 I7 Cook Strait South I. N.Z.
258 A6 Cooksville MD U.S.A.
107 J3 Cooktown Qld Austr.
169 F4 Coola Ireland
105 K4 Coolabah N.S.W. Austr.
107 J9 Cooladdi Qld Austr.
105 L4 Coolah N.S.W. Austr.
105 M4 Coolah Tops National Park N.S.W. Austr.
105 K6 Coolamon N.S.W. Austr.
169 E4 Coolaney Ireland
178 H6 Coole France
178 H6 Coole r. France
170 C6 Coole Ireland
109 F11 Coolgardie W.A. Austr.
169 H7 Coolgrange Ireland
169 J7 Coolgreany Ireland
106 C3 Coolibah N.T. Austr.
265 U9 Coolidge AZ U.S.A.
109 C10 Coolimba W.A. Austr.
169 J6 Coolock Ireland
169 H8 Coolroebeg Ireland
107 N9 Coolum Beach Qld Austr.
105 L7 Cooma N.S.W. Austr.
169 B9 Coomacarrea hill Ireland
104 H5 Coombah N.S.W. Austr.
172 C6 Coombe Cornwall, England U.K.
173 I5 Coombe Bissett Wiltshire, England U.K.
169 C9 Coomnadiha hill Ireland
105 L4 Coonabarabran N.S.W. Austr.
104 G6 Coonalpyn S.A. Austr.
105 L4 Coonamble N.S.W. Austr.
109 G11 Coonana W.A. Austr.
109 G11 Coonana Aboriginal Reserve W.A. Austr.
104 H7 Coonawarra S.A. Austr.
104 E4 Coondambo S.A. Austr.
Coondapoor Karnataka India see Kundapura
108 E6 Coongan r. W.A. Austr.
108 E6 Coongan Aboriginal Reserve W.A. Austr.
107 J9 Coongoola Qld Austr.
104 E2 Coongra watercourse S.A. Austr.
250 A4 Coon Rapids MN U.S.A.
106 D2 Cooper r. N.T. Austr.
261 H9 Cooper TX U.S.A.
104 F3 Cooper Creek watercourse Qld/S.A. Austr.
256 C8 Cooperdale OH U.S.A.
105 N4 Coopernook N.S.W. Austr.
258 E3 Coopersburg PA U.S.A.
257 □P4 Coopers Mills ME U.S.A.
255 I12 Cooper's Town Bahamas
260 F2 Cooperstown ND U.S.A.
257 K6 Cooperstown NY U.S.A.
105 L7 Coopracambra National Park Vic. Austr.
271 □7 Coora Trin. and Tob.
104 D4 Coorabie S.A. Austr.
109 D8 Coor-de-Wandy hill W.A. Austr.
104 G7 Coorong National Park S.A. Austr.
109 D10 Coorow W.A. Austr.
107 N9 Cooroy Qld Austr.
255 D9 Coosa r. AL U.S.A.
262 B5 Coos Bay OR U.S.A.
262 B5 Coos Bay b. OR U.S.A.
105 L6 Cootamundra N.S.W. Austr.
169 H4 Cootehill Ireland
136 G6 Cooum r. India
107 M9 Cooyar Qld Austr.
282 D3 Copacabana Arg.
199 L5 Copăcel Romania
284 B5 Copahue, Volcán vol. Chile
267 M9 Copainalá Mex.
269 I9 Copala Mex.
269 H7 Copalillo Mex.
269 K10 Copalita Mex.
269 K10 Copalita r. Mex.
274 C5 Copal Urcu Peru
266 □O10 Copán tourist site Hond.
217 L6 Copanello Italy
260 D6 Cope CO U.S.A.
209 C13 Cope, Cabo c. Spain
169 L3 Copeland Island Northern Ireland U.K.
250 I5 Copemish MI U.S.A.
Copenhagen Denmark see København
277 E4 Copere Bol.
217 O3 Copertino Italy
285 G6 Copetonas Arg.
105 M3 Copeton Reservoir N.S.W. Austr.
118 G6 Cô Pi, Phou mt. Laos/Vietnam
259 I3 Copiague NY U.S.A.
282 C2 Copiapó Chile
282 C2 Copiapo, Volcán vol. Chile
168 K5 Copinsay i. Scotland U.K.
258 E3 Coplay PA U.S.A.
104 G4 Copley S.A. Austr.
171 N4 Copley Durham, England U.K.
171 O6 Copmanthorpe York, England U.K.
277 E6 Copo, Parque Nacional nat. park Arg.
208 I4 Copons Spain
276 C3 Coporaque Peru
212 G5 Coppa r. Italy
213 L6 Copparo Italy
275 G3 Coppename r. Suriname
191 I6 Coppenbrügge Ger.
191 I7 Coppengrave Ger.
245 K3 Copper r. AK U.S.A.
231 E8 Copperbelt prov. Zambia
248 D4 Copper Cliff Ont. Can.
107 I4 Copperfield r. Qld Austr.
250 G2 Copper Harbor MI U.S.A.
Coppermine Nunavut Can. see Kugluktuk
242 G3 Coppermine r. Nunavut Can.
248 C4 Coppermine Point Ont. Can.
235 F3 Copper Queen Zimbabwe
236 G5 Copperton S. Africa
265 T1 Copperton UT U.S.A.
246 H2 Copp Lake N.W.T. Can.
172 E6 Copplestone Devon, England U.K.
219 M4 Copşa Mică Romania
173 L5 Copthorne Surrey, England U.K.
173 I6 Copythorne Hampshire, England U.K.
133 G11 Coqên Xizang China
133 G11 Coqên Xizang China
271 □1 Coqui Puerto Rico
Coquilhatville Dem. Rep. Congo see Mbandaka
Coquille i. Micronesia see Pikelot
262 B5 Coquille OR U.S.A.
268 D6 Coquimatlán Mex.
284 B1 Coquimbo Chile
284 B2 Coquimbo admin. reg. Chile
284 B1 Coquimbo, Bahía de b. Chile
246 F5 Coquitlam B.C. Can.
219 M7 Corabia Romania
281 E2 Coração de Jesus Brazil
217 L6 Corace r. Italy
Coracesium Turkey see Alanya
276 B3 Coracora Peru
205 J3 Corada, Peña mt. Spain
136 C6 Cora Dive sea feature India
105 N3 Coraki N.S.W. Austr.
109 B7 Coral Bay W.A. Austr.
114 A7 Coral Bay b. Palawan Phil.
101 □7a Coral Coast Fiji
284 C5 Corales, Cerro mt. Arg.
255 □2 Coral Harbour New Prov. Bahamas
243 J3 Coral Harbour Nunavut Can.
255 □2 Coral Heights New Prov. Bahamas
100 □5 Coral Sea S. Pacific Ocean
290 F6 Coral Sea Basin S. Pacific Ocean
99 F3 Coral Sea Islands Territory terr. Austr.
169 H6 Coralstown Ireland
259 I3 Coram NY U.S.A.
105 I8 Corangamite, Lake Vic. Austr.
282 D1 Coranzuli Arg.
256 E8 Coraopolis PA U.S.A.
151 K5 Corat Azer.
215 Q5 Corato Italy
180 D5 Coray France
208 D7 Corbalán Spain
169 D4 Corbally Ireland
214 I2 Corbara, Lago di l. Italy
178 D6 Corbeil-Essonnes France
178 E7 Corbeilles France
280 A6 Corbélia Brazil
182 H5 Corbelin France
179 L8 Corbenay France
178 G5 Corbeny France
208 F5 Corbera d'Ebre Spain
285 G4 Corbett Arg.
247 M2 Corbett Inlet Nunavut Can.
138 G5 Corbett National Park India
178 E4 Corbie France
185 I10 Corbières reg. France
212 C2 Corbières Switz.
182 D2 Corbigny France
256 A12 Corbin KY U.S.A.
258 F6 Corbin City NJ U.S.A.
208 G4 Corbins Spain
213 M5 Corbola Italy
207 H5 Corbones r. Spain
171 M4 Corbridge Northumberland, England U.K.
219 Q6 Corbu Romania
173 K3 Corby Northamptonshire, England U.K.
208 L4 Corçà Spain
Corcaigh Ireland see Cork
182 G2 Corcelles-lès-Cîteaux France
215 I3 Corchiano Italy
238 □3d Corcho, Punta del pt La Palma Canary Is
215 I1 Corciano Italy
179 M7 Corcieux France
207 M2 Córcoles r. Spain
264 M5 Corcoran CA U.S.A.
180 H8 Corcoué-sur-Logne France
283 C6 Corcovado Arg.
283 B6 Corcovado, Golfo de sea chan. Chile
266 □R13 Corcovado, Parque Nacional nat. park Costa Rica
204 B3 Corcubión Spain
204 B3 Corcubión, Ría de b. Spain
Corcyra i. Greece see Kerkyra
169 D8 Cordal Ireland
107 N8 Cordalba Qld Austr.
281 F5 Cordeiro Brazil
255 F10 Cordele GA U.S.A.
264 J3 Cordelia CA U.S.A.
261 F8 Cordell OK U.S.A.
180 H7 Cordemais France
213 N4 Cordenòns Italy
185 H7 Cordes France
213 M3 Cordevole r. Italy
213 M4 Cordignano Italy
276 B1 Cordillera Azul, Parque Nacional nat. park Peru
274 C4 Cordillera de los Picachos, Parque Nacional nat. park Col.
114 D6 Cordilleras Range mts Panay Phil.
104 H2 Cordillo Downs S.A. Austr.
204 C8 Cordinhã Port.
281 E3 Cordisburgo Brazil
285 E2 Córdoba Córdoba Arg.
283 C6 Córdoba Río Negro Arg.
285 F3 Córdoba prov. Arg.
274 C2 Córdoba dept Col.
266 H4 Córdoba Durango Mex.
269 K7 Córdoba Veracruz Mex.
207 J5 Córdoba Spain
207 J4 Córdoba prov. Spain
207 J5 Córdoba, Sierra de hills Spain
284 E3 Córdoba, Sierras de mts Arg.
207 J6 Cordobilla, Embalse de resr Spain
206 G2 Cordobilla de Lácara Spain
276 B3 Cordova Peru
Cordova Spain see Córdoba
245 K3 Cordova AK U.S.A.
258 D7 Cordova MD U.S.A.
245 N5 Cordova Bay AK U.S.A.
245 K3 Cordova Peak AK U.S.A.
205 O4 Cordovín Spain
Corduba Spain see Córdoba
205 Q7 Corduente Spain
278 E2 Coreaú Brazil
213 J7 Coreglia Antelminelli Italy
107 H5 Corella r. Qld Austr.
205 Q4 Corella Spain
106 E5 Corella Lake salt flat N.T. Austr.
204 I5 Coreses Spain
172 H6 Corfe Castle Dorset, England U.K.
172 H6 Corfe Mullen Dorset, England U.K.
107 I6 Corfield Qld Austr.
215 L3 Corfinio Italy
Corfu i. Ionioi Nisoi Greece see Kerkyra
256 G6 Corfu NY U.S.A.
204 E6 Corgo r. Port.
279 B6 Corguinho Brazil
215 J4 Cori Italy
204 G9 Coria Spain
206 G6 Coria del Río Spain
213 N8 Coriano Italy
278 D5 Coribe Brazil
105 M5 Coricudgy mt. N.S.W. Austr.
217 L4 Corigliano, Golfo di b. Italy
217 L4 Corigliano Calabro Italy
213 O8 Corinaldo Italy
107 M4 Coringa Islands Coral Sea Is Terr. Austr.
Corinium Gloucestershire, England U.K. see Cirencester
105 J9 Corinna Tas. Austr.

247 J5 **Corinne** Sask. Can.
Corinth Peloponnisos Greece see **Korinthos**
261 K8 **Corinth** MS U.S.A.
257 L5 **Corinth** NY U.S.A.
Corinth, Gulf of sea chan. Greece see **Korinthiakos Kolpos**
Corinthus Greece see **Korinthos**
281 E3 **Corinto** Brazil
266 □P11 **Corinto** Nic.
207 I7 **Coripe** Spain
229 H6 **Corisco** i. Equat. Guinea
277 F4 **Corixa Grande** r. Bol./Brazil
277 F4 **Corixinha** r. Brazil
169 F9 **Cork** Ireland
169 E8 **Cork** county Ireland
180 E5 **Corlay** France
170 B6 **Corlea** Ireland
169 D4 **Corlee** Ireland
216 E8 **Corleone** Sicilia Italy
215 Q7 **Corleto Perticara** Italy
221 I1 **Çorlu** Turkey
221 I1 **Çorlu** r. Turkey
182 F3 **Cormatin** France
204 B2 **Corme e Laxe, Ría de** b. Spain
181 L3 **Cormeilles** France
181 K3 **Cormelles-le-Royal** France
204 C2 **Corme Porto** Spain
184 C4 **Corme-Royal** France
178 G5 **Cormicy** France
213 O4 **Cormons** Italy
275 H4 **Cormontibo** Fr. Guiana
178 H5 **Cormontreuil** France
213 O4 **Cormor** r. Italy
114 □ **Cormoran Reef** Palau
247 K4 **Cormorant** Man. Can.
247 K4 **Cormorant Lake** Man. Can.
247 K4 **Cormorant Provincial Forest** nature res. Man. Can.
215 O5 **Cornacchia, Monte** mt. Italy
169 G6 **Cornafulla** Ireland
205 P4 **Cornago** Spain
Cornamona Ireland see **Corr na Móna**
212 G4 **Cornaredo** Italy
183 F7 **Cornas** France
190 F5 **Cornau** Ger.
191 I8 **Cornberg** Ger.
181 K7 **Corné** France
213 K3 **Cornedo all'Isarco** Italy
185 J10 **Corneilla-del-Vercol** France
237 M3 **Cornelia** S. Africa
280 B5 **Cornélio Procópio** Brazil
282 H3 **Cornélios** Brazil
275 G3 **Corneliskondre** Suriname
250 C4 **Cornell** WI U.S.A.
208 J5 **Cornellà de Llobregat** Spain
208 K3 **Cornellà de Terri** Spain
204 H2 **Cornellana** Spain
249 J3 **Corner Brook** Nfld and Lab. Can.
105 K8 **Corner Inlet** b. Vic. Austr.
207 P5 **Corneros** r. Spain
288 F3 **Corner Seamounts** sea feature N. Atlantic Ocean
158 H6 **Cornești** Moldova
Corneto Italy see **Tarquinia**
213 K4 **Cornetto** mt. Italy
256 B11 **Cornettsville** KY U.S.A.
199 L6 **Cornetu, Vârful** hill Romania
168 K7 **Cornhill** Aberdeenshire, Scotland U.K.
171 M2 **Cornhill-on-Tweed** Northumberland, England U.K.
171 M6 **Cornholme** West Yorkshire, England U.K.
219 O3 **Corni** Romania
214 F2 **Cornia** r. Italy
212 I7 **Corniglio** Italy
178 H5 **Cornillet, Mont** hill France
179 M8 **Cornimont** France
261 J7 **Corning** AR U.S.A.
264 J2 **Corning** CA U.S.A.
260 H5 **Corning** IA U.S.A.
256 H6 **Corning** NY U.S.A.
256 C9 **Corning** OH U.S.A.
107 J7 **Cornish** watercourse Qld Austr.
283 B7 **Cornish, Estrada** b. Chile
Corn Islands is Nic. see **Maíz, Islas del**
215 J2 **Corno** r. Italy
212 I3 **Corno di Campo** mt. Italy/Switz.
215 L3 **Corno Grande** mt. Italy
180 C5 **Cornouaille** reg. France
250 C3 **Cornucopia** WI U.S.A.
213 M4 **Cornuda** Italy
205 N3 **Cornudilla** Spain
183 C9 **Cornus** France
248 F4 **Cornwall** Ont. Can.
249 I4 **Cornwall** P.E.I. Can.
270 □ **Cornwall** reg. Jamaica
172 C6 **Cornwall** admin. div. England U.K.
259 G2 **Cornwall** NY U.S.A.
258 C4 **Cornwall** PA U.S.A.
172 □ **Cornwall, Cape** England U.K.
172 B7 **Cornwall and West Devon Mining Landscape** tourist site UK
243 I2 **Cornwallis Island** Nunavut Can.
243 I2 **Cornwall Island** Nunavut Can.
259 G2 **Cornwall on Hudson** NY U.S.A.
104 F6 **Corny Point** S.A. Austr.
274 D2 **Coro** Venez.
204 F5 **Coroa, Serra da** mts Port.
281 F3 **Coroaci** Brazil
278 D3 **Coroatá** Brazil
276 C4 **Corocoro** Bol.
275 F2 **Corocoro, Isla** i. Venez.
169 D7 **Corofin** Ireland
102 J3 **Coroglen** North I. N.Z.
276 D4 **Coroico** Bol.
280 D3 **Coromandel** Brazil
102 J3 **Coromandel** North I. N.Z.
136 G7 **Coromandel Coast** India
102 J4 **Coromandel Forest Park** nature res. North I. N.Z.
102 J3 **Coromandel Peninsula** North I. N.Z.
102 J3 **Coromandel Range** hills North I. N.Z.
181 J7 **Coron** France
114 C5 **Coron** Phil.
206 C4 **Corona** r. Port.
205 R3 **Corona** mt. Spain
264 O8 **Corona** CA U.S.A.
263 L9 **Corona** NM U.S.A.
229 H6 **Corona, Punta** pt Equat. Guinea
204 C6 **Coronado** Port.
264 O9 **Coronado** CA U.S.A.
266 □R13 **Coronado, Bahía de** b. Costa Rica
114 D8 **Coronado Bay** Mindanao Phil.
283 B6 **Coronados, Golfo de los** b. Chile
247 I4 **Coronation** Alta Can.
242 G3 **Coronation Gulf** Nunavut Can.
286 U2 **Coronation Island** S. Orkney Is Atlantic Ocean
245 N5 **Coronation Island** AK U.S.A.
108 H3 **Coronation Islands** W.A. Austr.
114 C6 **Coron Bay** Phil.
285 G2 **Coronda** Arg.
284 E3 **Coronel Alzogaray** Arg.
285 G3 **Coronel Bogada** Arg.
285 H4 **Coronel Brandsen** Arg.
285 G6 **Coronel Dorrego** Arg.
281 F3 **Coronel Fabriciano** Brazil
285 G6 **Coronel Falcón** Arg.
283 D6 **Coronel Francisco Sosa** Arg.
285 E6 **Coronel Juliá y Echarrán** Arg.
284 E3 **Coronel Moldes** Córdoba Arg.
282 D2 **Coronel Moldes** Salta Arg.
281 F2 **Coronel Murta** Brazil
277 F6 **Coronel Oviedo** Para.
277 G3 **Coronel Ponce** Brazil
274 B5 **Coronel Portillo** Peru
285 G5 **Coronel Pringles** Arg.
285 G5 **Coronel Rodolfo Bunge** Arg.
277 G5 **Coronel Sapucaia** Mato Grosso do Sul Brazil
277 G5 **Coronel Sapucaia** Mato Grosso do Sul Brazil
285 G5 **Coronel Suárez** Arg.
285 I5 **Coronel Vidal** Arg.
268 G5 **Coroneo** Mex.
103 C11 **Coronet Peak** South I. N.Z.
220 B2 **Çorovodë** Albania
105 K6 **Corowa** N.S.W. Austr.
267 O8 **Corozal** Belize
269 I4 **Corozal** Mex.
271 □1 **Corozal** Puerto Rico
275 F2 **Corozal** Venez.
274 E2 **Corozo Pando** Venez.
283 C8 **Corpen Aike** Arg.
183 H7 **Corps** France
180 H6 **Corps-Nuds** France
282 G2 **Corpus** Arg.
261 G12 **Corpus Christi** TX U.S.A.
261 G11 **Corpus Christi, Lake** TX U.S.A.
276 D4 **Corque** Bol.
283 B5 **Corral** Chile
204 I7 **Corral** mt. Spain
205 N9 **Corral de Almaguer** Spain
285 F3 **Corral de Bustos** Arg.
207 K3 **Corral de Calatrava** Spain
205 L9 **Corral de Cantos** mt. Spain
284 D2 **Corral de Isaac** Arg.
238 □3b **Corralejo** Fuerteventura Canary Is
261 C13 **Corrales** Mex.
204 I6 **Corrales** Spain
268 F5 **Corrales de Rábago** Mex.
270 C2 **Corralilla** Cuba
264 K5 **Corralitos** CA U.S.A.
284 D2 **Corralitos, Monte** mt. Arg.
269 L7 **Corral Nuevo** Mex.
207 Q3 **Corral-Rubio** Spain
109 C8 **Corrandibby Range** hills W.A. Austr.
235 H2 **Corrane** Moz.
214 C7 **Corrasi, Punta** mt. Sardegna Italy
169 C5 **Corraun Peninsula** Ireland
179 L8 **Corre** France
268 C2 **Corre Caballo** Mex.
168 K8 **Correen Hills** Scotland U.K.
213 J6 **Correggio** Italy
280 B2 **Córrego do Ouro** Brazil
281 F3 **Córrego Novo** Brazil
278 D4 **Corrente** Brazil
280 B3 **Corrente** r. Brazil
278 E5 **Corrente** r. Brazil
281 F3 **Corrente Grande** r. Brazil
279 B6 **Correntes** Brazil
277 G4 **Correntes** r. Brazil
211 E7 **Correnti, Isola delle** i. Sicilia Italy
278 D5 **Correntina** Brazil
Correntina r. Brazil see **Éguas**
184 H5 **Corrèze** France
184 H5 **Corrèze** dept France
184 G5 **Corrèze** r. France
169 D6 **Corrib, Lough** l. Ireland
213 P9 **Corridonia** Italy
168 F11 **Corrie** North Ayrshire, Scotland U.K.
282 F2 **Corrientes** Arg.
285 H1 **Corrientes** prov. Arg.
282 F3 **Corrientes** r. Arg.
274 C5 **Corrientes** r. Peru
285 I6 **Corrientes, Cabo** c. Arg.
274 B3 **Corrientes, Cabo** c. Col.
270 A3 **Corrientes, Cabo** c. Cuba
268 B5 **Corrientes, Cabo** c. Mex.
261 H10 **Corrigan** TX U.S.A.
109 D12 **Corrigin** W.A. Austr.
173 M4 **Corringham** Thurrock, England U.K.
172 E2 **Corris** Gwynedd, Wales U.K.
275 G3 **Corriverton** Guyana
169 D5 **Corr na Móna** Ireland
178 G6 **Corrobert** France
204 B3 **Corrubedo, Cabo** c. Spain
256 F7 **Corry** PA U.S.A.
105 K7 **Corryong** Vic. Austr.
212 D7 **Corsaglia** r. Italy
217 O4 **Corsano** Italy
214 C3 **Corse** admin. reg. France
214 A3 **Corse** i. France
214 C1 **Corse, Cap** c. Corse France
214 B2 **Corse, Parc Naturel Régional de la** nature res. Corse France
214 B4 **Corse-du-Sud** dept Corse France
168 H12 **Corserine** hill Scotland U.K.
180 G5 **Corseul** France
172 H5 **Corsham** Wiltshire, England U.K.
Corsica i. France see **Corse**
261 G9 **Corsicana** TX U.S.A.
212 G5 **Corsico** Italy
230 A4 **Corsico, Baie de** b. Gabon
168 I12 **Corsock** Dumfries and Galloway, Scotland U.K.
258 F6 **Corson's Inlet** NJ U.S.A.
Cort Adelaer, Kap c. Greenland see **Kangeq**
217 K6 **Cortale** Italy
268 G5 **Cortazar** Mex.
214 C3 **Corte** Corse France
206 F3 **Corte de Peleas** Spain
204 D4 **Cortegada** Spain
206 F5 **Cortegana** Spain
212 E6 **Cortemilia** Italy
212 I3 **Corteno Golgi** Italy
212 G5 **Corteolona** Italy
205 R5 **Cortes** Spain
Cortes, Sea of g. Mex. see **California, Golfo de**
208 D6 **Cortes de Aragón** Spain
207 N5 **Cortes de Baza** Spain
207 I7 **Cortes de la Frontera** Spain
209 D9 **Cortes de Pallás** Spain
263 J8 **Cortez** CO U.S.A.
265 P1 **Cortez Mountains** NV U.S.A.
206 C3 **Cortiçadas do Lavre** Port.
208 G5 **Cortiella** r. Spain
207 K2 **Cortijo de Arriba** Spain
269 I9 **Cortijos** r. Mex.
207 N4 **Cortijos Nuevos** Spain
213 M2 **Cortina d'Ampezzo** Italy
257 I6 **Cortland** NY U.S.A.
256 E7 **Cortland** OH U.S.A.
200 E8 **Corto, Lago del** l. Italy
173 P2 **Corton** Suffolk, England U.K.
213 L9 **Cortona** Italy
228 B4 **Corubal** r. Guinea-Bissau
206 B3 **Coruche** Port.
Çoruh Turkey see **Artvin**
151 C4 **Çoruh** r. Turkey
149 J3 **Çoruh** r. Turkey
204 G3 **Corullón** Spain
148 G3 **Çorum** Turkey
277 F4 **Corumbá** Brazil
280 C3 **Corumbá** r. Brazil
280 C1 **Corumbá de Goiás** Brazil
280 C3 **Corumbaíba** Brazil
280 B5 **Corumbataí** r. Brazil
281 H2 **Corumbaú, Ponta** pt Brazil
204 D2 **Coruña, Ría da** b. Spain
219 N4 **Corund** Romania
199 L4 **Corund** r. Romania
256 C6 **Corunna** Ont. Can.
Corunna Spain see **A Coruña**
251 J7 **Corunna** MI U.S.A.
278 F4 **Coruripe** Brazil
262 C4 **Corvallis** OR U.S.A.
213 L2 **Corvara in Badia** Italy
172 G3 **Corve Dale** val. England U.K.
209 C12 **Corvera** Spain
248 F2 **Corvette, Lac de la** l. Que. Can.
215 J4 **Corvia, Colle** hill Italy
238 □1 **Corvo** i. Azores
172 F2 **Corwen** Denbighshire, Wales U.K.
260 I5 **Corydon** IA U.S.A.
254 D6 **Corydon** IN U.S.A.
173 N4 **Coryton** Thurrock, England U.K.
256 G7 **Coryville** PA U.S.A.
Cos i. Greece see **Kos**
208 C6 **Cosa** Spain
268 A1 **Cosalá** Mex.
269 L7 **Cosamaloapan** Mex.
151 A5 **Coşandere** Turkey
173 J2 **Cosby** Leicestershire, England U.K.
276 C4 **Coscaya** Chile
215 J2 **Coscerno, Monte** mt. Italy
217 L4 **Coscile** r. Italy
269 J6 **Coscomatepec** Mex.
205 P6 **Coscurita** Spain
Cosentia Italy see **Cosenza**
215 Q9 **Cosenza** Italy
215 Q9 **Cosenza** prov. Italy
219 O6 **Coşereni** Romania
217 L4 **Coserie** r. Italy
168 I9 **Coshieville** Perth and Kinross, Scotland U.K.
256 D8 **Coshocton** OH U.S.A.
268 E3 **Cosío** Mex.
212 D7 **Cosio di Arroscia** Italy
205 M8 **Coslada** Spain
239 □2 **Cosmoledo Atoll** Aldabra Is Seychelles
109 G10 **Cosmo Newbery Aboriginal Reserve** W.A. Austr.
280 D5 **Cosmópolis** Brazil
182 B2 **Cosne-Cours-sur-Loire** France
182 B4 **Cosne-d'Allier** France
269 M8 **Cosoleacaque** Mex.
217 J7 **Cosoleto** Italy
284 E2 **Cosquín** Arg.
212 E4 **Cossato** Italy
193 I8 **Cossebaude** Ger.
181 J6 **Cossé-le-Vivien** France
214 B7 **Cossoine** Sardegna Italy
178 B8 **Cosson** r. France
212 B2 **Cossonay** Switz.
278 E3 **Costa** Brazil
206 A4 **Costa Bela** coastal area Port.
209 E11 **Costa Blanca** coastal area Spain
208 L5 **Costa Brava** coastal area Spain
213 N9 **Costacciaro** Italy
219 P5 **Costache Negri** Romania
206 A3 **Costa da Caparica** Port.
206 B4 **Costa da Galé** coastal area Port.
208 G6 **Costa de Fora** coastal area Spain
206 E6 **Costa de la Luz** coastal area Spain
209 E8 **Costa del Azahar** coastal area Spain
238 □3a **Costa del Silencio** Tenerife Canary Is
207 I8 **Costa del Sol** coastal area Spain
266 □R11 **Costa de Mosquitos** coastal area Nic.
206 A3 **Costa do Estoril** coastal area Port.
208 J5 **Costa Dorada** coastal area Spain
206 A3 **Costa do Sol** coastal area Port.
285 G3 **Costa Grande** Arg.
276 D3 **Costa Marques** Brazil
214 D9 **Costa Rei** coastal area Sardegna Italy
280 A3 **Costa Rica** Brazil
270 A8 **Costa Rica** country Central America
266 F5 **Costa Rica** Mex.
214 D5 **Costa Smeralda** coastal area Sardegna Italy
238 □3c **Costa Teguise** Lanzarote Canary Is
214 A9 **Costa Verde** coastal area Sardegna Italy
204 G1 **Costa Verde** coastal area Spain
212 I4 **Costa Volpino** Italy
199 K6 **Coșteiu** Romania
Costelloe Ireland see **Casla**
Costermansville Dem. Rep. Congo see **Bukavu**
173 O2 **Costessey** Norfolk, England U.K.
158 G6 **Costești** Moldova
219 M6 **Costești** Argeș Romania
219 P4 **Costești** Vaslui Romania
257 □Q3 **Costigan** ME U.S.A.
247 J3 **Costigan Lake** Sask. Can.
212 E6 **Costigliole d'Asti** Italy
212 C6 **Costigliole Saluzzo** Italy
208 C5 **Cosuenda** Spain
219 L6 **Coșuștea** r. Romania
193 I8 **Coswig** Sachsen Ger.
193 F7 **Coswig** Sachsen-Anhalt Ger.
276 B3 **Cotabambas** Peru
114 E8 **Cotabato** Mindanao Phil.
276 D4 **Cotacajes** r. Bol.
276 D5 **Cotagaita** Bol.
276 B3 **Cotahuasi** Peru
281 G3 **Cotaxé** r. Brazil
269 K7 **Cotaxtla** Mex.
245 O4 **Cote, Mount** AK U.S.A.
260 F3 **Coteau des Prairies** slope SD U.S.A.
260 D1 **Coteau du Missouri** slope ND U.S.A.
260 E3 **Coteau du Missouri** slope SD U.S.A.
257 K3 **Coteau-Station** Que. Can.
270 F4 **Coteaux** Haiti
178 G6 **Côte Champenoise** reg. France
185 A9 **Côte d'Argent** coastal area France
183 K9 **Côte d'Azur** airport France
183 K9 **Côte d'Azur** coastal area France
178 H7 **Côte des Bars** reg. France
228 D5 **Côte d'Ivoire** country Africa
178 I8 **Côte-d'Or** dept France
182 F3 **Côte d'Or** reg. France
Côte Française de Somalis country Africa see **Djibouti**
278 D4 **Cotegipe** Brazil
180 I3 **Cotentin** pen. France
180 F5 **Côtes-d'Armor** dept France
179 I4 **Côtes de Meuse** ridge France
179 K6 **Côtes de Moselle** hills France
Côtes-du-Nord dept France see **Côtes-d'Armor**
185 K10 **Côte Vermeille** coastal area France
172 D4 **Cothi** r. Wales U.K.
276 D2 **Coti** r. Brazil
Cotiaeum Turkey see **Kütahya**
214 B4 **Coti-Chiavari** Corse France
208 F2 **Cotiella** mt. Spain
183 I9 **Cotignac** France
213 L7 **Cotignola** Italy
268 E6 **Cotija** Mex.
238 □3b **Cotillo** Fuerteventura Canary Is
275 F4 **Cotingo** r. Brazil
158 H6 **Cotiujeni** Moldova
158 H6 **Cotiujenii Mici** Moldova
219 M6 **Cotmeana** r. Romania
118 H4 **Cô Tô, Quân Đao** is Vietnam
Coton, Pointe pt Rodrigues I. Mauritius see **Cotton, Pointe**
206 G5 **Coto Nacional de la Pata del Caballo** nature res. Spain
229 F5 **Cotonou** Benin
274 B5 **Cotopaxi** prov. Ecuador
274 B5 **Cotopaxi, Volcán** vol. Ecuador
270 B2 **Cotorro** Cuba
Cotovsc Moldova see **Hîncești**
217 L5 **Cotronei** Italy
172 H4 **Cotswold Hills** England U.K.
262 C5 **Cottage Grove** OR U.S.A.
215 J3 **Cottanello** Italy
193 J7 **Cottbus** Ger.
136 G6 **Cotteliar** r. India
173 M3 **Cottenham** Cambridgeshire, England U.K.
173 K2 **Cottesmore** Rutland, England U.K.
183 J8 **Cottian Alps** mts France/Italy
275 H4 **Cottica** Suriname
Cottiennes, Alpes mts France/Italy see **Cottian Alps**
171 Q6 **Cottingham** East Riding of Yorkshire, England U.K.
173 K2 **Cottingham** Northamptonshire, England U.K.
250 B2 **Cotton** MN U.S.A.
239 □1a **Cotton, Pointe** pt Rodrigues I. Mauritius
106 G7 **Cottonbush Creek** watercourse Qld Austr.
265 T7 **Cottonwood** AZ U.S.A.
264 J1 **Cottonwood** CA U.S.A.
262 F3 **Cottonwood** ID U.S.A.
260 G6 **Cottonwood** r. KS U.S.A.
260 H3 **Cottonwood** r. MN U.S.A.
261 D10 **Cottonwood Creek** watercourse TX U.S.A.
260 G6 **Cottonwood Falls** KS U.S.A.
265 V7 **Cottonwood Wash** watercourse AZ U.S.A.
270 H4 **Cotuí** Dom. Rep.
261 F11 **Cotulla** TX U.S.A.
219 O2 **Coțușca** Romania
183 D6 **Coubon** France
184 B4 **Coubre, Pointe de la** pt France
182 F3 **Couches** France
108 I3 **Couchman Range** hills W.A. Austr.
206 C3 **Couço** Port.
183 D7 **Coucouron** France
178 F4 **Coucy-le-Château-Auffrique** France
181 N7 **Couddes** France
178 D1 **Coudekerque-Branche** France
256 G7 **Coudersport** PA U.S.A.
249 G4 **Coudres, Île aux** i. Que. Can.
104 F7 **Couedic, Cape du** S.A. Austr.
180 H7 **Couëron** France
180 H4 **Couesnon** r. France
185 G10 **Couflens** France
185 H8 **Coufouleux** France
184 E3 **Couhé** France
185 I10 **Couiza** France
181 L5 **Coulaines** France
178 G8 **Coulanges-la-Vineuse** France
182 C2 **Coulanges-lès-Nevers** France
182 D1 **Coulanges-sur-Yonne** France
181 L5 **Coulans-sur-Gée** France
184 F5 **Coulaures** France
262 E3 **Coulee City** WA U.S.A.
262 E3 **Coulee Dam** WA U.S.A.
182 B3 **Couleuvre** France
181 P6 **Coullons** France
287 L2 **Coulman Island** Antarctica
178 H8 **Coulmier-le-Sec** France
178 C8 **Coulmiers** France
178 C2 **Coulogne** France
178 G5 **Coulognes-Cohan** France
227 H4 **Couloir 1** well Alg.
184 E3 **Coulombiers** France
178 C6 **Coulombs** France
178 F6 **Coulommiers** France
183 F9 **Coulon** r. France
248 E4 **Coulonge** r. Que. Can.
184 C3 **Coulonges-sur-l'Autize** France
184 F5 **Coulounieix-Chamiers** France
168 G10 **Coulport** Argyll and Bute, Scotland U.K.
264 L4 **Coulterville** CA U.S.A.
244 G2 **Council** AK U.S.A.
262 F4 **Council** ID U.S.A.
260 H5 **Council Bluffs** IA U.S.A.
260 G6 **Council Grove** KS U.S.A.
105 J8 **Councillor Island** Tas. Austr.
173 J2 **Countesthorpe** Leicestershire, England U.K.
168 J9 **Coupar Angus** Perth and Kinross, Scotland U.K.
262 C2 **Coupeville** WA U.S.A.
183 B9 **Coupiac** France
181 K5 **Couptrain** France
204 C5 **Coura** Port.
247 I1 **Courageous Lake** N.W.T. Can.
275 G3 **Courantyne** r. Guyana
187 F8 **Courcelles** Belgium
257 □O3 **Courcelles** Que. Can.
179 L5 **Courcelles-Chaussy** France
179 L5 **Courcelles-sur-Nied** France
182 J1 **Courchaton** France
183 J6 **Courchevel** France
181 N6 **Cour-Cheverny** France
181 K5 **Courcité** France
184 C3 **Courçon** France
178 H5 **Courcy** France
204 F4 **Courel, Serra do** mts Spain
181 L5 **Courgains** France
178 G7 **Courgenay** France
212 C1 **Courgenay** Switz.
160 E6 **Courland Lagoon** b. Lith./Rus. Fed.
182 G3 **Courlaoux** France
181 J8 **Courlay** France
178 F7 **Courlon-sur-Yonne** France
212 B4 **Courmayeur** Italy
178 F5 **Courmelles** France
182 C5 **Cournon-d'Auvergne** France
183 D9 **Cournonterral** France
183 G10 **Couronne, Cap** c. France
182 D5 **Courpière** France
212 C1 **Courrendlin** Switz.
185 E8 **Courrensan** France
178 E3 **Courrières** France
182 B2 **Cours** France
184 F5 **Coursac** France
183 C10 **Coursan** France
183 K9 **Coursegoules** France
181 K3 **Courseulles-sur-Mer** France
182 E4 **Cours-la-Ville** France
182 C1 **Courson-les-Carrières** France
212 C1 **Court** Switz.
178 B7 **Courtalain** France
212 C1 **Courtelary** Switz.
182 K1 **Courtelevant** France
246 E5 **Courtenay** B.C. Can.
178 F7 **Courtenay** France
183 F8 **Courthézon** France
178 I6 **Courtisols** France
256 H12 **Courtland** VA U.S.A.
169 E9 **Courtmacsherry** Ireland
169 E9 **Courtmacsherry Bay** Ireland
181 L4 **Courtomer** France
169 J7 **Courtown** Ireland
Courtrai Belgium see **Kortrijk**
187 G7 **Court-St-Etienne** Belgium
178 B7 **Courville-sur-Eure** France
182 G3 **Cousance** France
179 J6 **Cousances-les-Forges** France
185 F10 **Couserans** reg. France
261 I9 **Coushatta** LA U.S.A.
182 D1 **Cousin** r. France
239 □2a **Cousin** i. Inner Islands Seychelles
239 □2a **Cousine** i. Inner Islands Seychelles
204 C4 **Couso, Punta de** pt Spain
184 G4 **Coussac-Bonneval** France
181 M8 **Coussay-les-Bois** France
178 H8 **Coussegrey** France
179 K7 **Coussey** France
183 G9 **Coustellet** France
185 J11 **Coustouges** France
180 I3 **Coutances** France
181 K4 **Couterne** France
Coutinho Moz. see **Ulongue**
281 F3 **Couto de Magalhães de Minas** Brazil
184 D5 **Coutras** France
247 I5 **Coutts** Alta Can.
184 E4 **Couture** r. France
271 □7 **Couva** Trin. and Tob.
212 B2 **Couvet** Switz.
187 G8 **Couvin** Belgium
178 G4 **Couvron-et-Aumencourt** France
185 F6 **Couze** r. France
185 F6 **Couze-et-St-Front** France
184 G4 **Couzeix** France
204 I8 **Covacha del Losar** mt. Spain
204 E3 **Cova da Serpe, Sierra da** mts Spain
205 O5 **Covaleda** Spain
205 N4 **Covarrubias** Spain
199 K5 **Covăsinț** Romania
219 O5 **Covasna** Romania
168 E7 **Cove** Highland, Scotland U.K.
168 L8 **Cove Bay** Aberdeen, Scotland U.K.
265 T3 **Cove Fort** UT U.S.A.
251 M4 **Cove Island** Ont. Can.
285 H5 **Covello** Arg.
264 I2 **Covelo** CA U.S.A.
256 G9 **Cove Mountains** hills PA U.S.A.
274 C2 **Coveñas** Col.
276 D3 **Covendo** Bol.
173 I3 **Coventry** West Midlands, England U.K.
171 N5 **Cover** r. England U.K.
172 B7 **Coverack** Cornwall, England U.K.
265 T9 **Covered Wells** AZ U.S.A.
209 F7 **Coves de Sant Miquel, Riu de les** r. Spain
256 G11 **Covesville** VA U.S.A.
204 F8 **Covilhã** Port.
244 I4 **Coville, Lake** AK U.S.A.
255 F9 **Covington** GA U.S.A.
254 D5 **Covington** IN U.S.A.
256 A9 **Covington** KY U.S.A.
261 J10 **Covington** LA U.S.A.
250 F3 **Covington** MI U.S.A.
256 A8 **Covington** OH U.S.A.
261 K8 **Covington** TN U.S.A.
256 E11 **Covington** VA U.S.A.
251 K2 **Cow** r. Ont. Can.
105 K5 **Cowal, Lake** dry lake N.S.W. Austr.
256 B10 **Cowan** KY U.S.A.
109 F11 **Cowan, Lake** salt flat W.A. Austr.
249 F4 **Cowansville** Que. Can.
173 L2 **Cowbit** Lincolnshire, England U.K.
172 F5 **Cowbridge** Vale of Glamorgan, Wales U.K.
109 D11 **Cowcowing Lakes** salt flat W.A. Austr.
168 J10 **Cowdenbeath** Fife, Scotland U.K.
104 F5 **Cowell** S.A. Austr.
256 E10 **Cowen** WV U.S.A.
105 J8 **Cowes** Vic. Austr.
173 J6 **Cowes** Isle of Wight, England U.K.
173 L6 **Cowfold** West Sussex, England U.K.
171 M4 **Cow Green Reservoir** England U.K.
168 I10 **Cowie** Stirling, Scotland U.K.
107 J9 **Cowley** Qld Austr.
171 M6 **Cowling** North Yorkshire, England U.K.
262 C3 **Cowlitz** r. WA U.S.A.
256 F11 **Cowpasture** r. VA U.S.A.
105 L5 **Cowra** N.S.W. Austr.
171 M4 **Cowshill** Durham, England U.K.
106 E3 **Cox** r. N.T. Austr.
185 G8 **Cox** France
Coxen Hole Hond. see **Roatán**
173 M5 **Coxheath** Kent, England U.K.
171 N4 **Coxhoe** Durham, England U.K.
282 G3 **Coxilha de Santana** hills Brazil/Uru.
279 B9 **Coxilha Grande** hills Brazil
279 B6 **Coxim** Brazil
279 B6 **Coxim** r. Brazil
257 L6 **Coxsackie** NY U.S.A.
139 M9 **Cox's Bazar** Bangl.
171 O5 **Coxwold** North Yorkshire, England U.K.
284 B4 **Coya** Chile
228 B4 **Coyah** Guinea
283 C8 **Coy Aike** Arg.
261 C11 **Coyame** Mex.
261 D10 **Coyanosa Creek** watercourse TX U.S.A.
172 E4 **Coychurch** Bridgend, Wales U.K.
168 H12 **Coylton** South Ayrshire, Scotland U.K.
168 I8 **Coylumbridge** Highland, Scotland U.K.
263 H11 **Coyote** r. Mex.
266 D5 **Coyote, Punta** pt Mex.
264 P6 **Coyote Lake** CA U.S.A.
265 R9 **Coyote Peak** hill AZ U.S.A.
264 N5 **Coyote Peak** CA U.S.A.
268 G5 **Coyotillos** Mex.
268 A2 **Coyotitán** Mex.
268 G9 **Coyuca, Laguna** l. Mex.
268 G8 **Coyuca de Benitez** Mex.
268 G7 **Coyuca de Catalán** Mex.
269 J5 **Coyutla** Mex.
260 F5 **Cozad** NE U.S.A.
207 M3 **Cózar** Spain
184 C4 **Cozes** France
133 H11 **Cozhê** Xizang China
219 M5 **Cozia, Vârful** mt. Romania
Cozie, Alpi mts France/Italy see **Cottian Alps**
267 P7 **Cozumel** Mex.
267 P7 **Cozumel, Isla de** i. Mex.
214 C4 **Cozzano** Corse France
215 Q8 **Cozzo del Pellegrino** mt. Italy
170 E8 **Craanford** Ireland
107 I1 **Crab Island** Qld Austr.
239 □1a **Crab Island** Rodrigues I. Mauritius
270 □ **Crab Pond Point** Jamaica
150 E4 **Crac des Chevaliers** tourist site Syria
180 E6 **Crach** France
215 Q7 **Craco** Italy
Cracovia Pol. see **Kraków**
107 M8 **Cracow** Qld Austr.
Cracow Pol. see **Kraków**
105 K9 **Cradle Mountain Lake St Clair National Park** Tas. Austr.
172 H3 **Cradley** Herefordshire, England U.K.
104 G4 **Cradock** S.A. Austr.
237 J8 **Cradock** S. Africa
102 J3 **Cradock Channel** North I. N.Z.
212 J4 **Craffaro** r. Italy
236 I2 **Crafthole** S. Africa
168 K9 **Craichie** Angus, Scotland U.K.
199 L4 **Craidorolț** Romania
168 F8 **Craig** Highland, Scotland U.K.
245 N5 **Craig** AK U.S.A.
262 K6 **Craig** CO U.S.A.
169 K3 **Craigavad** Northern Ireland U.K.
169 J4 **Craigavon** Northern Ireland U.K.
168 H12 **Craigdarroch** East Ayrshire, Scotland U.K.
168 F11 **Craigendive** Argyll and Bute, Scotland U.K.
105 J7 **Craigieburn** Vic. Austr.
103 F10 **Craigieburn** South I. N.Z.
103 F10 **Craigieburn Forest Park** nature res. South I. N.Z.
168 E10 **Craignure** Argyll and Bute, Scotland U.K.
169 J3 **Craigs** Northern Ireland U.K.
256 F10 **Craigsville** VA U.S.A.
256 E10 **Craigsville** WV U.S.A.
168 K10 **Crail** Fife, Scotland U.K.
195 I3 **Crailsheim** Ger.
219 L6 **Craiova** Romania
199 K5 **Craiva** Romania
258 B5 **Craley** PA U.S.A.
178 G6 **Cramant** France
171 N3 **Cramlington** Northumberland, England U.K.
236 F3 **Cramond** S. Africa
185 H9 **Crampagna** France
170 C3 **Crana** r. Ireland
171 M7 **Cranage** Cheshire, England U.K.
169 H3 **Cranagh** Northern Ireland U.K.
245 O5 **Cranberry Junction** B.C. Can.
258 F3 **Cranberry Lake** NJ U.S.A.
257 K4 **Cranberry Lake** l. NY U.S.A.
247 K4 **Cranberry Portage** Man. Can.
172 H6 **Cranborne Chase** for. England U.K.
105 J8 **Cranbourne** Vic. Austr.
109 D13 **Cranbrook** W.A. Austr.
246 H5 **Cranbrook** B.C. Can.
173 N5 **Cranbrook** Kent, England U.K.
259 F4 **Cranbury** NJ U.S.A.
250 F4 **Crandon** WI U.S.A.
262 E5 **Crane** OR U.S.A.
261 D10 **Crane** TX U.S.A.
247 I5 **Crane Lake** l. Sask. Can.
250 B1 **Crane Lake** MN U.S.A.
259 I3 **Crane Neck Point** NY U.S.A.
173 K3 **Cranfield** Bedfordshire, England U.K.
169 J4 **Cranfield Point** Northern Ireland U.K.
170 B3 **Cranford** Ireland
182 I5 **Cran-Gevrier** France
173 L5 **Cranleigh** Surrey, England U.K.
185 I6 **Cransac** France
168 L11 **Cranshaws** Scottish Borders, Scotland U.K.
212 C3 **Crans-sur-Sierre** Switz.
168 G6 **Cranstackie** hill Scotland U.K.
256 B10 **Cranston** KY U.S.A.
257 N7 **Cranston** RI U.S.A.
171 Q7 **Cranwell** Lincolnshire, England U.K.
Cranz Rus. Fed. see **Zelenogradsk**
278 D3 **Craolândia** Brazil
181 J6 **Craon** France
178 G5 **Craonne** France
219 Q5 **Crapina, Lacul** l. Romania
183 D6 **Craponne-sur-Arzon** France
286 M1 **Crary Ice Rise** Antarctica
286 P1 **Crary Mountains** Antarctica
168 G6 **Crask Inn** Highland, Scotland U.K.
219 K3 **Crasna** Romania
219 K3 **Crasna** r. Romania
158 I7 **Crasnoe** Moldova
262 C5 **Crater Lake National Park** OR U.S.A.
262 H5 **Craters of the Moon National Monument** nat. park ID U.S.A.
278 E3 **Crateús** Brazil
168 J8 **Crathie** Aberdeenshire, Scotland U.K.
215 Q8 **Crati** r. Italy
278 F3 **Crato** Brazil
206 D2 **Crato** Port.
183 F9 **Crau** reg. France
169 E6 **Craughwell** Ireland
212 E4 **Cravagliana** Italy
182 J1 **Cravanche** France
178 G8 **Cravant** France
277 F3 **Cravari** r. Brazil
172 G3 **Craven Arms** Shropshire, England U.K.
280 D4 **Cravinhos** Brazil
274 D3 **Cravo Norte** Col.
260 D4 **Crawford** NE U.S.A.
262 F2 **Crawford Bay** B.C. Can.
168 I12 **Crawfordjohn** South Lanarkshire, Scotland U.K.
114 B6 **Crawford Point** Palawan Phil.
106 D6 **Crawford Range** hills N.T. Austr.
103 F9 **Crawford Range** mts South I. N.Z.
254 D5 **Crawfordsville** IN U.S.A.
255 E10 **Crawfordville** FL U.S.A.
255 F9 **Crawfordville** GA U.S.A.
191 K9 **Crawinkel** Ger.
173 L5 **Crawley** West Sussex, England U.K.
245 K2 **Crazy Mountains** AK U.S.A.
262 I3 **Crazy Mountains** MT U.S.A.
Creag Ghoraidh Scotland U.K. see **Creagorry**
168 G9 **Creag Meagaidh** mt. Scotland U.K.
168 B8 **Creagorry** Western Isles, Scotland U.K.
180 H3 **Créances** France
182 F2 **Créancey** France
247 J4 **Crean Lake** Sask. Can.
204 D4 **Crecente** Spain
182 F4 **Crêches-sur-Saône** France
178 C3 **Crécy-en-Ponthieu** France
178 E6 **Crécy-la-Chapelle** France
178 G4 **Crécy-sur-Serre** France
172 G3 **Credenhill** Herefordshire, England U.K.
172 E6 **Crediton** Devon, England U.K.
247 J3 **Cree** r. Sask. Can.
172 F5 **Creech St Michael** Somerset, England U.K.
263 K8 **Creede** CO U.S.A.
169 D7 **Creegh** Ireland
266 F4 **Creel** Mex.
247 J3 **Cree Lake** Sask. Can.
251 N5 **Creemore** Ont. Can.
169 G2 **Creeslough** Ireland
168 H13 **Creetown** Dumfries and Galloway, Scotland U.K.
169 D4 **Creevagh** Ireland
169 H3 **Creggan** Northern Ireland U.K.
169 I4 **Creggan** Northern Ireland U.K.
169 C5 **Cregganbaun** Ireland
169 F5 **Creggs** Ireland
195 I3 **Creglingen** Ger.
170 H5 **Cregneash** Isle of Man
179 M5 **Créhange** France
247 K4 **Creighton** Sask. Can.
237 N6 **Creighton** S. Africa
178 D5 **Creil** France
186 I3 **Creil** Neth.
183 C8 **Creissels** France
212 H5 **Crema** Italy
182 D5 **Cremeaux** France
205 J3 **Crémenes** Spain
182 G5 **Crémieu** France
191 K6 **Cremlingen** Ger.
246 H5 **Cremona** Alta Can.
212 I5 **Cremona** Italy
212 I5 **Cremona** prov. Italy
178 H7 **Creney-près-Troyes** France
201 N6 **Črenšovci** Slovenia
185 D6 **Créon** France
179 K6 **Crépey** France
275 G6 **Crepori** r. Brazil
178 G4 **Crépy** France
178 E5 **Crépy-en-Valois** France
168 F9 **Creran, Loch** inlet Scotland U.K.
210 E3 **Cres** Croatia
210 E3 **Cres** i. Croatia
262 D5 **Crescent** OR U.S.A.
262 B6 **Crescent City** CA U.S.A.
255 G11 **Crescent City** FL U.S.A.
112 D3 **Crescent Group** is Paracel Is
105 N4 **Crescent Head** N.S.W. Austr.
212 E5 **Crescentino** Italy
265 W3 **Crescent Junction** UT U.S.A.
260 D5 **Crescent Lake National Wildlife Refuge** nature res. NE U.S.A.
265 Q6 **Crescent Peak** NV U.S.A.
264 P1 **Crescent Valley** NV U.S.A.
250 B6 **Cresco** IA U.S.A.
258 E2 **Cresco** PA U.S.A.
212 G5 **Crespi d'Adda** tourist site Italy
213 L6 **Crespino** Italy
285 G3 **Crespo** Arg.
205 K7 **Crespos** Spain
184 H5 **Cressensac** France
194 C7 **Cressier** Switz.
258 C3 **Cressona** PA U.S.A.
106 E5 **Cresswell** watercourse N.T. Austr.
106 E4 **Cresswell Downs** N.T. Austr.
105 I8 **Cressy** Vic. Austr.
183 G7 **Crest** France
114 D3 **Cresta, Mount** Phil.
Crest Hill H.K. China see **Tai Shek Mo**
256 C8 **Crestline** OH U.S.A.
246 G5 **Creston** B.C. Can.
260 H5 **Creston** IA U.S.A.
262 K6 **Creston** WY U.S.A.
255 D10 **Crestview** FL U.S.A.
182 J5 **Crest-Voland** France
259 G5 **Crestwood Village** NJ U.S.A.
171 O7 **Creswell** Derbyshire, England U.K.
258 C5 **Creswell** PA U.S.A.
105 I7 **Creswick** Vic. Austr.
Creta i. Kriti Greece see **Kriti**
213 N2 **Creta Forata, Monte** mt. Italy
208 F6 **Cretas** Spain
182 H4 **Crêt de la Neige** mt. France
182 G5 **Crêt de Pont** mt. France
182 H4 **Crêt des Eculaz** mt. France
182 H4 **Crêt du Nu** mt. France
Crete i. Kriti Greece see **Kriti**
260 G5 **Crete** NE U.S.A.
178 D6 **Créteil** France
182 I2 **Crêt Monniot** mt. France
181 J3 **Creully** France
208 L3 **Creus, Cap de** c. Spain
184 I3 **Creuse** dept France
184 F1 **Creuse** r. France
195 L2 **Creußen** Ger.
195 L2 **Creußen** r. Ger.
179 M5 **Creutzwald** France
191 J8 **Creuzburg** Ger.
182 C4 **Creuzier-le-Vieux** France
213 K6 **Crevalcore** Italy
184 H3 **Crevant** France
286 O1 **Crevasse Valley Glacier** Antarctica
179 L6 **Crévéchamps** France
178 D4 **Crèvecœur-le-Grand** France
209 D11 **Crevillent** Spain
209 D11 **Crevillent, Serra de** mts Spain
171 M7 **Crewe** Cheshire, England U.K.
256 G11 **Crewe** VA U.S.A.
172 G6 **Crewkerne** Somerset, England U.K.
185 F6 **Creysse** France
238 □1c **Criação Velha** Pico Azores
168 G10 **Crianlarich** Stirling, Scotland U.K.
172 D2 **Criccieth** Gwynedd, Wales U.K.
279 C9 **Criciúma** Brazil
172 F4 **Crickhowell** Powys, Wales U.K.
173 I4 **Cricklade** Wiltshire, England U.K.
158 H6 **Cricova** Moldova
219 O6 **Cricovu Sărat** r. Romania
256 A8 **Cridersville** OH U.S.A.
168 I10 **Crieff** Perth and Kinross, Scotland U.K.
178 B3 **Criel-sur-Mer** France
168 I13 **Criffel** hill Scotland U.K.
171 N6 **Crigglestone** West Yorkshire, England U.K.
210 E3 **Crikvenica** Croatia
245 M4 **Crillon, Mount** AK U.S.A.
170 D5 **Crilly** Northern Ireland U.K.
Crimea aut. rep. Ukr. see **Krym, Respublika**
Crimea pen. Ukr. see **Kryms'kyy Pivostriv**
Crimean Republic aut. rep. Ukr. see **Krym, Respublika**
193 F9 **Crimmitschau** Ger.
168 M7 **Crimond** Aberdeenshire, Scotland U.K.
168 E10 **Crinan** Argyll and Bute, Scotland U.K.
173 O2 **Cringleford** Norfolk, Eng
193 I7 **Crinitz** Ger.
263 L7 **Cripple Creek** CO U.S.A.
244 H3 **Cripple Landing** AK U.S
173 N6 **Cripp's Corner** East Sus England U.K.
181 L2 **Criquetot-l'Esneval** Fra
219 R5 **Crișan** Romania
257 J11 **Crisfield** MD U.S.A.
217 M2 **Crispiano** Italy
212 C6 **Crissolo** Italy
280 D2 **Cristais, Serra dos** mts
230 A4 **Cristal, Monts de** mts Equat. Guinea/Gabon
278 C4 **Cristalândia** Brazil
280 D2 **Cristalina** Brazil
Cristalino r. Brazil see **Mariembero**
277 G2 **Cristalino** r. Brazil
213 M2 **Cristallo** mt. Italy
280 C2 **Cristianópolis** Brazil
281 E5 **Cristina** Brazil
278 D4 **Cristino Castro** Brazil
199 L5 **Criștioru de Jos** Roman
204 I8 **Cristóbal** Spain
212 F7 **Cristoforo Colombo** air
219 N4 **Cristuru Secuiesc** Roma
219 J4 **Crișul Alb** r. Romania
219 J4 **Crișul Negru** r. Romani
219 J3 **Crișul Repede** r. Roman
219 J4 **Crișurilor, Câmpia** plain Romania
276 B3 **Criterión** mt. Peru
158 I6 **Criuleni** Moldova
192 E3 **Crivitz** Ger.
250 F4 **Crivitz** WI U.S.A.
278 C5 **Crixás** Brazil
278 C5 **Crixás Açu** r. Brazil
278 C5 **Crixás Mirim** r. Brazil
219 J9 **Crna** r. Macedonia
201 K7 **Črna** Slovenia
199 J6 **Crna Bara** Vojvodina Se
218 H8 **Crna Glava** mt. Monten
Crna Gora country Euro **Montenegro**
218 J8 **Crna Gora** mts Macedo
213 Q6 **Crna Pta, Rt** pt Croatia
219 K8 **Crna Trava** Crna Trava S
218 I9 **Crni Drim** r. Macedonia
213 R5 **Crni Lug** Croatia
219 K7 **Crni Timok** r. Serbia
210 E2 **Črni vrh** mt. Slovenia
210 E3 **Črnomelj** Slovenia
219 K8 **Crnook** mt. Serbia
169 F3 **Croagh** Ireland
169 F3 **Croaghleheen** hill Irelar
169 C5 **Croagh Patrick** hill Irela
105 L7 **Croajingolong National** Vic. Austr.
210 E3 **Croatia** country Europe
217 L6 **Crocchio** r. Italy
217 K7 **Crocco, Monte** mt. Italy
213 K3 **Croce, Monte** mt. Italy
215 P6 **Croce dello Scrivano, P** Italy
215 I2 **Croce di Serra, Monte**
191 K10 **Crock** Ger.
117 K2 **Crocker, Banjaran** mts
117 L2 **Crocker Range Nationa** Malaysia
168 I12 **Crocketford** Dumfries ar Galloway, Scotland U.K.
261 H10 **Crockett** TX U.S.A.
169 G3 **Crockmore** Ireland
184 I4 **Crocq** France
213 M2 **Croda dei Toni** mt. Italy
213 M2 **Croda Rossa** mt. Italy
212 E3 **Crodo** Italy
172 E4 **Croeserw** Neath Port Ta Wales U.K.
172 B4 **Croesgoch** Pembrokeshi Wales U.K.
171 O6 **Crofton** West Yorkshire, England U.K.
258 B6 **Crofton** MD U.S.A.
260 G4 **Crofton** NE U.S.A.
172 D4 **Crofty** Swansea, Wales U
169 F5 **Croghan** Ireland
257 J5 **Croghan** NY U.S.A.
171 L4 **Croglin** Cumbria, Englar
215 K2 **Crognaleto** Italy
169 F3 **Crohy Head** Ireland
168 G7 **Croick** Highland, Scotlar
183 G10 **Croisette, Cap** c. France
180 F7 **Croisic, Pointe de** pt Fra
178 E3 **Croisilles** France
103 H8 **Croisilles Harbour** Sout
212 A5 **Croix de Fer, Col de la** France
183 H7 **Croix-Haute, Col de la** France
212 C5 **Croix-Rousse** mt. Italy
245 R1 **Croker** r. Nunavut Can.
106 D1 **Croker, Cape** N.T. Austr
251 N5 **Croker, Cape** Ont. Can.
106 D1 **Croker Island** N.T. Austr
169 C8 **Cromane** Ireland
168 H7 **Cromarty** Highland, Sco
168 H7 **Cromarty Firth** est. Scot
168 I8 **Cromdale, Hills of** Scot
173 O2 **Cromer** Norfolk, Englan
172 H4 **Cromhall** South Glouces England U.K.
103 D12 **Cromwell** South I. N.Z.
259 J1 **Cromwell** CT U.S.A.
250 B3 **Cromwell** MN U.S.A.
103 F9 **Cronadun** South I. N.Z.
182 D3 **Cronat** France
183 C6 **Cronce** r. France
173 K5 **Crondall** Hampshire, En
171 N4 **Crook** Durham, England
262 D4 **Crooked** r. OR U.S.A.
244 H3 **Crooked Creek** AK U.S.
245 L2 **Crooked Creek** AK U.S.
Crooked Harbour b. H. see **Kat O Hoi**
270 F2 **Crooked Island** Bahama
Crooked Island H.K. Ch **Kat O Chau**
270 F2 **Crooked Island Passage** Bahamas
250 C1 **Crooked Lake** Can./U.S.
247 K4 **Crooked River** Sask. Car
169 C10 **Crookhaven** Ireland
260 G2 **Crookston** MN U.S.A.
169 E9 **Crookstown** Ireland
256 C9 **Crooksville** OH U.S.A.
105 L6 **Crookwell** N.S.W. Austr.
169 E7 **Croom** Ireland
217 L4 **Cropalati** Italy
217 L6 **Cropani** Italy
105 M3 **Croppa Creek** N.S.W. Au
107 I3 **Crosbie** r. Qld Austr.
168 D6 **Crosbost** Western Isles, Scotland U.K.
171 K7 **Crosby** Merseyside, Engl
171 P6 **Crosby** North Lincolnshi England U.K.
260 I2 **Crosby** MN U.S.A.
260 D1 **Crosby** ND U.S.A.
171 L4 **Crosby Ravensworth** Cu England U.K.
261 E9 **Crosbyton** TX U.S.A.
217 L4 **Crosia** Italy
229 H5 **Cross** r. Nigeria
180 G7 **Crossac** France
168 F11 **Crossaig** Argyll and Bute Scotland U.K.
170 C6 **Crossakeel** Ireland
168 C9 **Crossapol Bay** Scotland
247 M2 **Cross Bay** Nunavut Can
171 K4 **Crosscanonby** Cumbria, England U.K.
255 F11 **Cross City** FL U.S.A.
257 □S2 **Cross Creek** N.B. Can.
169 H5 **Crossdoney** Ireland
261 I9 **Crossett** AR U.S.A.
171 M4 **Cross Fell** hill England U
246 H5 **Crossfield** Alta Can.

I11 **Crossford** South Lanarkshire, Scotland U.K.
K4 **Crossgar** Northern Ireland U.K.
I2 **Crossgare** Northern Ireland U.K.
F3 **Crossgates** Powys, Wales U.K.
H11 **Crosshands** East Ayrshire, Scotland U.K.
E1 **Cross Harbour** b. Gt Abaco Bahamas
F9 **Crosshaven** Ireland
G12 **Crosshill** South Ayrshire, Scotland U.K.
H2 **Crosshouse** East Ayrshire, Scotland U.K.
D3 **Cross Inn** Ceredigion, Wales U.K.
C7 **Crosskeys** Ireland
5 **Cross Keys** Ireland
4 **Cross Lake** Man. Can.
4 **Cross Lake** l. Man. Can.
5 **Cross Lake** l. NY U.S.A.
G9 **Crossley, Mount** South I. N.Z.
D1 **Crossley Lakes** N.W.T. Can.
4 **Crossmaglen** Northern Ireland U.K.
R7 **Crossman Peak** AZ U.S.A.
13 **Crossmichael** Dumfries and Galloway, Scotland U.K.
D4 **Crossmolina** Ireland
H5 **Cross River** state Nigeria
M4 **Cross Sound** sea channel AK U.S.A.
E8 **Crossville** TN U.S.A.
F3 **Crossway** Powys, Wales U.K.
6 **Crostolo** r. Italy
6 **Croston** Lancashire, England U.K.
6 **Croswell** MI U.S.A.
R5 **Crotch Lake** Ont. Can.
Croton Italy see **Crotone**
M5 **Crotone** Italy
5 **Crotone** prov. Italy
H2 **Croton Falls** NY U.S.A.
H2 **Croton Falls Reservoir** NY U.S.A.
H2 **Crotonville** NY U.S.A.
7 **Crots** France
10 **Crottendorf** Ger.
5 **Crotto** Arg.
4 **Crouch** r. England U.K.
4 **Croughton** Northamptonshire, England U.K.
2 **Croutelle** France
5 **Crouy** France
5 **Crouy-sur-Ourcq** France
7 **Crouzilles** France
3 **Crove** Ireland
3 **Crow** r. B.C. Can.
4 **Crow Agency** MT U.S.A.
4 **Crowal** watercourse N.S.W. Austr.
5 **Crowborough** East Sussex, England U.K.
6 **Crow Creek** r. CO U.S.A.
3 **Crow Creek Indian Reservation** res. SD U.S.A.
4 **Crowdy Bay National Park** N.S.W. Austr.
3 **Crowell** TX U.S.A.
4 **Crow Hill** Herefordshire, England U.K.
4 **Crow Indian Reservation** res. MT U.S.A.
Crowl watercourse N.S.W. Austr.
2 **Crowland** Lincolnshire, England U.K.
6 **Crowle** North Lincolnshire, England U.K.
0 **Crowley** LA U.S.A.
4 **Crowley, Lake** CA U.S.A.
3 **Crowlin Islands** Scotland U.K.
Crown Point pt Trin. and Tob.
5 **Crown Point** IN U.S.A.
Crownpoint NM U.S.A.
Crown Point NY U.S.A.
2 **Crown Prince Olav Coast** Antarctica
1 **Crown Princess Martha Coast** Antarctica
Crownsville MD U.S.A.
9 **Crows Nest** Qld Austr.
5 **Crowsnest Pass** Alta Can.
5 **Crowsnest Pass** pass Alta/B.C. Can.
Crowthorne Bracknell Forest, England U.K.
2 **Crow Wing** r. MN U.S.A.
7 **Croy** Highland, Scotland U.K.
Croyde Devon, England U.K.
Croydon Qld Austr.
Croydon Greater London, England U.K.
Croydon PA U.S.A.
Crozant France
0 **Crozet** VA U.S.A.
Crozet, Îles is Indian Ocean
Crozet Basin sea feature Indian Ocean
Crozet Plateau sea feature Indian Ocean
Crozier Channel N.W.T. Can.
Crozon France
Crozon, Presqu'île de pen. France
Cruas France
Crucea Romania
Crucero Peru
Cruces Cuba
Cruces Mex.
Cruces, Punta pt Col.
Crucetillas, Puerto de las pass Spain
Crucoli Italy
Cruden Bay Aberdeenshire, Scotland U.K.
Cruillas Mex.
Crùlabhig Western Isles, Scotland U.K.
Crulai France
Crum WV U.S.A.
Crumlin Caerphilly, Wales U.K.
Crumlin Northern Ireland U.K.
Crummock Water l. England U.K.
Cruseilles France
Crusheen Ireland
Crusnes France
Crusnes r. France
Crustepec, Cerro mt. Mex.
Cruz mt. Spain
Cruz Venez.
Cruz, Cabo c. Cuba
Cruz Alta Arg.
Cruz Alta Brazil
Cruz de Garibay Mex.
Cruz del Eje Arg.
Cruzeiro Brazil
Cruzeiro do Oeste Brazil
Cruzeiro do Sul Acre Brazil
Cruzeiro do Sul Paraná Brazil
Cruzen Island Antarctica
Cruz Grande Mex.
Cruzy France
Cruzy-le-Châtel France
Crvenka Vojvodina Serbia
Cry Lake B.C. Can.
Crymych Pembrokeshire, Wales U.K.
Crysdale, Mount B.C. Can.
Crystal NM U.S.A.
Crystal Beach MD U.S.A.
Crystal Brook S.A. Austr.
Crystal City Man. Can.
Crystal City MO U.S.A.
Crystal City TX U.S.A.
Crystal Falls MI U.S.A.
Crystal Lake IL U.S.A.
Crystal River FL U.S.A.
Crystal Springs MS U.S.A.
Csabacsűd Hungary
Csabrendek Hungary
Csaj-tó l. Hungary
Csákánydoroszló Hungary
Csákvár Hungary
Csanádapáca Hungary
Csanádi-hát hills Hungary
Csanádpalota Hungary
Csanytelek Hungary
Császár Hungary
Császártöltés Hungary
199 H5 **Csátalja** Hungary
199 I5 **Csávoly** Hungary
199 I4 **Csécse** Hungary
199 I4 **Csemő** Hungary
199 I5 **Csengele** Hungary
199 L4 **Csenger** Hungary
199 J5 **Csépa** Hungary
198 F4 **Csepreg** Hungary
199 J3 **Cserehát** mts Hungary
199 I4 **Cserhát** hills Hungary
199 I4 **Cserhátsurány** Hungary
199 J5 **Cserkeszőlő** Hungary
199 J3 **Csernely** Hungary
198 G5 **Cserszegtomaj** Hungary
201 O6 **Cserta** r. Hungary
198 F5 **Csesztreg** Hungary
199 G4 **Csetény** Hungary
Csév Hungary see **Piliscsév**
199 I5 **Csikéria** Hungary
199 H4 **Csókakő** Hungary
199 K4 **Csökmő** Hungary
199 G5 **Csököly** Hungary
198 G5 **Csokonyavisonta** Hungary
199 J3 **Csokvaomány** Hungary
199 H4 **Csolnok** Hungary
199 I5 **Csólyospálos** Hungary
199 I4 **Csömör** Hungary
199 J5 **Csongrád** Hungary
199 J5 **Csongrád** county Hungary
199 G5 **Csopak** Hungary
199 H4 **Csór** Hungary
198 G4 **Csorna** Hungary
198 F5 **Csörnyeföld** Hungary
198 F5 **Csörötnek** Hungary
199 J5 **Csorvás** Hungary
199 H4 **Csősz** Hungary
199 G4 **Csót** Hungary
199 H4 **Csóványos** hill Hungary
198 G5 **Csurgó** Hungary
149 L7 **Ctesiphon** tourist site Iraq
204 G3 **Cua** r. Spain
271 J8 **Cúa** Venez.
204 I8 **Cuacos de Yuste** Spain
283 C7 **Cuadrada, Sierra** hills Arg.
284 C4 **Cuadro Berregas** Arg.
204 I3 **Cuadros** Spain
269 I9 **Cuajinicuilapa** Mex.
231 C7 **Cuale** Angola
204 E5 **Cualedro** Spain
231 B9 **Cuamato** Angola
235 H2 **Cuamba** Moz.
231 D9 **Cuando** r. Angola/Zambia
231 C8 **Cuando Cubango** prov. Angola
231 C9 **Cuangar** Angola
231 C8 **Cuango** Cuando Cubango Angola
231 C7 **Cuango** Lunda Norte Angola
231 C6 **Cuango** Uíge Angola
231 C6 **Cuango** r. Angola alt. **Kwango (Dem. Rep. Congo)**
231 B7 **Cuanza** r. Angola
231 B7 **Cuanza Norte** prov. Angola
231 B7 **Cuanza Sul** prov. Angola
285 I2 **Cuareim** r. Uru.
285 I2 **Cuaró** Uru.
285 I2 **Cuaro** r. Uru.
208 D4 **Cuarte de Huerva** Spain
285 F3 **Cuarto** r. Arg.
231 C9 **Cuatir** r. Angola
Cuatretonda Spain see **Quatretonda**
266 H4 **Cuatro Ciénegas** Mex.
276 E4 **Cuatro Ojos** Bol.
284 E3 **Cuatro Vientos** Arg.
266 F3 **Cuauhtémoc** Chihuahua Mex.
268 D6 **Cuauhtémoc** Colima Mex.
268 D1 **Cuauhtémoc** Durango Mex.
268 C6 **Cuautitlán** Mex.
269 I7 **Cuautla** Mex.
269 H6 **Cuautlán Izcalli** Mex.
269 I7 **Cuayuca** Mex.
206 D4 **Cuba** Port.
250 D9 **Cuba** IL U.S.A.
263 K8 **Cuba** NM U.S.A.
256 G6 **Cuba** NY U.S.A.
256 B9 **Cuba** OH U.S.A.
270 C3 **Cuba** country West Indies
265 T10 **Cubabi, Cerro** mt. Mex.
275 E2 **Cubagua, Isla** i. Venez.
231 B8 **Cubal** Angola
231 B7 **Cubal** r. Angola
204 D4 **Cubalhão** Port.
231 D9 **Cubango** r. Angola/Namibia
274 C3 **Cubara** Col.
280 D5 **Cubatão** Brazil
208 G4 **Cubells** Spain
247 J4 **Cub Hills** Sask. Can.
204 H2 **Cubia** r. Spain
207 L6 **Cubillas** r. Spain
205 M4 **Cubillo** r. Spain
184 F5 **Cubjac** France
209 C7 **Cubla** Spain
205 N3 **Cubo de Bureba** Spain
205 P5 **Cubo de la Solana** Spain
158 H6 **Cubolta** r. Moldova
148 F3 **Çubuk** Turkey
267 N10 **Cubulco** Guat.
184 D6 **Cubzac-les-Ponts** France
208 C5 **Cucalón** Spain
283 B6 **Cucao** Chile
265 Q9 **Cucapa, Sierra** mts Mex.
213 N9 **Cucco, Monte** mt. Italy
214 C7 **Cuccuru su Pirastru** hill Sardegna Italy
218 J8 **Čučer-Sandevo** Čučer Sandevo Macedonia
269 J4 **Cucharas** Mex.
231 C8 **Cuchi** Angola
285 I3 **Cuchilla de Peralta** Uru.
282 G4 **Cuchilla Grande** hills Uru.
285 I3 **Cuchilla Grande Inferior** hills Uru.
284 E6 **Cuchillo-Có** Arg.
173 L5 **Cuckfield** West Sussex, England U.K.
173 M6 **Cuckmere** r. England U.K.
219 N4 **Cucu, Vârful** mt. Romania
274 E4 **Cucuí** Brazil
231 C7 **Cucumbi** Angola
183 G9 **Cucuron** France
266 D2 **Cucurpe** Mex.
274 B3 **Cucurrupí** Col.
274 C3 **Cúcuta** Col.
208 D5 **Cucutas** hill Spain
219 P5 **Cudalbi** Romania
271 □9 **Cudarebe** pt Aruba
136 F7 **Cuddalore** Tamil Nadu India
136 F5 **Cuddapah** Andhra Prad. India
107 H8 **Cuddapan, Lake** salt flat Qld Austr.
264 O6 **Cuddeback Lake** CA U.S.A.
258 F2 **Cuddebackville** NY U.S.A.
216 D8 **Cuddia** r. Sicilia Italy
171 L7 **Cuddington** Cheshire, England U.K.
150 H2 **Cudi** watercourse Turkey
150 G2 **Cudi Dağı** hill Turkey
204 H1 **Cudillero** Spain
107 K7 **Cudmore National Park** nat. park Australia
185 D7 **Cudos** France
247 J4 **Cudworth** Sask. Can.
171 O6 **Cudworth** South Yorkshire, England U.K.
109 D9 **Cue** W.A. Austr.
231 C8 **Cuebe** r. Angola
231 D8 **Cueio** r. Angola
271 □1 **Cuelebrita, Isla** i. Puerto Rico
205 L6 **Cuéllar** Spain
231 C8 **Cuemba** Angola
274 B5 **Cuenca** Ecuador
114 C5 **Cuenca** Luzon Phil.
205 P8 **Cuenca** Spain
205 P9 **Cuenca** prov. Spain
205 P7 **Cuenca, Serranía de** mts Spain
205 M7 **Cuenca Alta del Manzanares, Parque Regional de la** park Spain
268 E7 **Cuenca de Balsas** basin Mex.
205 J4 **Cuenca de Campos** Spain
284 C6 **Cuenca del Añelo** reg. Arg.
266 H5 **Cuencamé** Mex.
268 F5 **Cuerámaro** Mex.
205 O5 **Cuerda del Pozo, Embalse de la** resr Spain
205 M7 **Cuerda Larga** ridge Spain
269 H7 **Cuernavaca** Mex.
261 G11 **Cuero** TX U.S.A.
183 I10 **Cuers** France
205 L9 **Cuerva** Spain
205 P7 **Cuervo** r. Spain
265 R9 **Cuervos** Mex.
270 F3 **Cueto** Cuba
269 J5 **Cuetzalán** Mex.
207 K6 **Cuevas Altas** hill Spain
207 K6 **Cuevas Bajas** Spain
207 P6 **Cuevas de Almanzora** Spain
207 P6 **Cuevas de Almanzora, Embalse** resr Spain
207 I7 **Cuevas del Becerro** Spain
207 N5 **Cuevas del Campo** Spain
205 M4 **Cuevas de San Clemente** Spain
208 C7 **Cuevas Labradas** Spain
276 E5 **Cuevo** Bol.
205 K4 **Cueza** r. Spain
173 L4 **Cuffley** Hertfordshire, England U.K.
180 I7 **Cugand** France
183 H10 **Cuges-les-Pins** France
219 L5 **Cugir** Romania
219 L5 **Cugir** r. Romania
214 B7 **Cuglieri** Sardegna Italy
185 G8 **Cugnaux** France
231 C6 **Cugo** r. Angola
180 H5 **Cuguen** France
277 F3 **Cuiabá** Brazil
277 F4 **Cuiabá** r. Brazil
269 K8 **Cuicatlan** Mex.
269 M8 **Cuichapa** Mex.
Cuihua Yunnan China see **Daguan**
Cuijiang Fujian China see **Ninghua**
186 I5 **Cuijk** Neth.
267 N10 **Cuilapa** Guat.
269 K9 **Cuilapan** Mex.
169 G4 **Cuilcagh** hill Ireland/U.K.
168 D8 **Cuillin Hills** Scotland U.K.
168 D8 **Cuillin Sound** sea chan. Scotland U.K.
231 C7 **Cuilo** Angola
231 B6 **Cuilo-Futa** Angola
231 B6 **Cuilo Pombo** Angola
122 F5 **Cuiluan** Heilong. China
231 B6 **Cuimba** Angola
182 G4 **Cuiseaux** France
178 F5 **Cuise-la-Motte** France
182 F3 **Cuisery** France
281 G3 **Cuité** r. Brazil
269 K7 **Cuitláhuac** Mex.
231 D9 **Cuito** r. Angola
231 C8 **Cuito Cuanavale** Angola
268 F6 **Cuitzeo** Mex.
268 F6 **Cuitzeo, Laguna de** l. Mex.
275 F5 **Cuiuni** r. Brazil
260 J6 **Cuivre** r. MO U.S.A.
269 K9 **Cuixtla** Mex.
114 C8 **Cujangan** i. Phil.
219 K6 **Cujmir** Romania
116 E2 **Cukai** Malaysia
220 B3 **Çukë** Albania
151 E6 **Çukurbağ** Turkey
149 K5 **Çukurca** Turkey
151 A5 **Çukurçayır** Turkey
221 L3 **Çukurhisar** Turkey
151 A6 **Çukurköy** Turkey
150 D2 **Çukurova** plat. Turkey
158 H6 **Cula** r. Moldova
129 O8 **Culai Shan** mt. Shandong China
184 I2 **Culan** France
168 J8 **Culardoch** hill Scotland U.K.
114 D6 **Culasi** Panay Phil.
262 L2 **Culbertson** MT U.S.A.
260 E5 **Culbertson** NE U.S.A.
168 H7 **Culbokie** Highland, Scotland U.K.
105 K6 **Culcairn** N.S.W. Austr.
199 M4 **Culciu** Romania
169 H2 **Culdaff** Ireland
168 K8 **Culdrain** Aberdeenshire, Scotland U.K.
271 □1 **Culebra, Isla de** i. Puerto Rico
204 H5 **Culebra, Sierra de la** mts Spain
276 A2 **Culebras** Peru
271 □1 **Culebrinas** r. Puerto Rico
186 H5 **Culemborg** Neth.
151 G7 **Culfa** Azer.
105 K3 **Culgoa Floodplain National Park** nat. park Australia
266 F5 **Culiacán** Mex.
114 B6 **Culion** Phil.
114 B6 **Culion** i. Phil.
170 B5 **Culkey** Northern Ireland U.K.
209 E7 **Culla** Spain
170 C8 **Cullahill** Ireland
207 N5 **Cullar** r. Spain
207 N5 **Cúllar-Baza** Spain
169 I4 **Cullaville** Northern Ireland U.K.
169 D4 **Culleens** Ireland
168 K7 **Cullen** Moray, Scotland U.K.
261 I9 **Cullen** LA U.S.A.
107 H1 **Cullen Point** Qld Austr.
209 E9 **Cullera** Spain
168 H7 **Cullicudden** Highland, Scotland U.K.
169 D5 **Cullin** Ireland
169 D5 **Cullin, Lough** l. Ireland
237 M1 **Cullinan** S. Africa
168 E10 **Cullipool** Argyll and Bute, Scotland U.K.
168 □N1 **Cullivoe** Shetland, Scotland U.K.
255 D8 **Cullman** AL U.S.A.
107 J7 **Culloden Creek** watercourse Qld Austr.
172 F6 **Cullompton** Devon, England U.K.
212 B3 **Cully** Switz.
169 J3 **Cullybackey** Northern Ireland U.K.
169 I4 **Cullyhanna** Northern Ireland U.K.
168 F6 **Cul Mòr** hill Scotland U.K.
169 H2 **Culmore** Northern Ireland U.K.
172 F6 **Culmstock** Devon, England U.K.
168 F7 **Culnacraig** Highland, Scotland U.K.
168 D7 **Culnaknock** Highland, Scotland U.K.
207 N7 **Culo de Perro, Punta** pt Spain
182 H5 **Culoz** France
256 H10 **Culpeper** VA U.S.A.
274 □ **Culpepper, Isla** i. Islas Galápagos Ecuador
168 H7 **Culrain** Highland, Scotland U.K.
168 □M2 **Culswick** Shetland, Scotland U.K.
168 I11 **Culter Fell** hill Scotland U.K.
168 L8 **Cults** Aberdeen, Scotland U.K.
278 B4 **Culuene** r. Brazil
250 H8 **Culver** IN U.S.A.
109 H12 **Culver, Point** W.A. Austr.
103 G9 **Culverden** South I. N.Z.
168 G12 **Culzean Bay** Scotland U.K.
278 D2 **Cumã, Baía do** inlet Brazil
151 E6 **Cumaçay** Turkey
275 E2 **Cumaná** Venez.
271 L8 **Cumanacoa** Venez.
221 L2 **Cumaova** Turkey
280 C3 **Cumari** Brazil
151 H4 **Cumay** Azer.
274 B4 **Cumbal, Nevado de** vol. Col.
256 C12 **Cumberland** KY U.S.A.
256 G9 **Cumberland** MD U.S.A.
256 D9 **Cumberland** OH U.S.A.
256 G11 **Cumberland** VA U.S.A.
250 B4 **Cumberland** WI U.S.A.
256 B12 **Cumberland** r. KY U.S.A.
Cumberland, Cape Vanuatu see **Nahoï, Cap**
254 E7 **Cumberland, Lake** KY U.S.A.
283 □ **Cumberland Bay** S. Georgia
258 E6 **Cumberland County** county NJ U.S.A.
258 A4 **Cumberland County** county PA U.S.A.
247 K4 **Cumberland House** Sask. Can.
107 L6 **Cumberland Islands** Qld Austr.
247 K4 **Cumberland Lake** Sask. Can.
256 B12 **Cumberland Mountains** KY/TN U.S.A.
243 L3 **Cumberland Peninsula** Nunavut Can.
255 E8 **Cumberland Plateau** KY/TN U.S.A.
250 E2 **Cumberland Point** MI U.S.A.
243 L3 **Cumberland Sound** sea chan. Nunavut Can.
168 I11 **Cumbernauld** North Lanarkshire, Scotland U.K.
205 K9 **Cumbre Alta** mt. Spain
283 C7 **Cumbre Negro** mt. Arg.
266 F3 **Cumbres de Majalca, Parque Nacional** nat. park Mex.
267 I5 **Cumbres de Monterey, Parque Nacional** nat. park Mex.
206 F4 **Cumbres de San Bartolomé** Spain
206 F4 **Cumbres Mayores** Spain
171 K4 **Cumbria** admin. div. England U.K.
136 F5 **Cumbum** Andhra Prad. India
206 C6 **Cumeada** Port.
212 C6 **Cumiana** Italy
204 E6 **Cumieira** Port.
275 G5 **Cuminá** Brazil
275 H5 **Cuminapanema** r. Brazil
168 L7 **Cuminestown** Aberdeenshire, Scotland U.K.
192 E4 **Cumlosen** Ger.
255 E8 **Cumming** GA U.S.A.
264 I2 **Cummings** CA U.S.A.
104 E6 **Cummins** S.A. Austr.
108 I5 **Cummins Range** hills W.A. Austr.
105 L5 **Cumnock** N.S.W. Austr.
168 H12 **Cumnock** East Ayrshire, Scotland U.K.
173 J4 **Cumnor** Oxfordshire, England U.K.
266 E2 **Cumpas** Mex.
284 B4 **Cumpeo** Chile
148 F5 **Çumra** Turkey
266 E3 **Cumuripa** Mex.
281 H2 **Cumuruxatiba** Brazil
271 □7 **Cumuto** Trin. and Tob.
275 I4 **Cunani** Brazil
274 C4 **Cuñaré** Col.
181 K7 **Cunault** France
284 A6 **Cunco** Chile
109 G11 **Cundeelee Aboriginal Reserve** W.A. Austr.
109 D11 **Cunderdin** W.A. Austr.
274 C3 **Cundinamarca** dept Col.
237 N4 **Cundycleugh** S. Africa
185 E6 **Cunegès** France
267 N10 **Cunén** Guat.
231 B9 **Cunene** prov. Angola
231 A9 **Cunene** r. Angola/Namibia alt. **Kunene**
212 D7 **Cuneo** Italy
212 D7 **Cuneo** prov. Italy
193 K8 **Cunewalde** Ger.
178 I7 **Cunfin** France
104 E5 **Cungena** S.A. Austr.
119 I8 **Cung Sơn** Vietnam
148 I4 **Çüngüş** Turkey
281 E5 **Cunha** Brazil
204 F7 **Cunha** Port.
231 C8 **Cunhinga** Angola
158 H6 **Cunicea** Moldova
208 I5 **Cunit** Spain
231 D8 **Cunjamba** Angola
182 D5 **Cunlhat** France
105 J3 **Cunnamulla** Qld Austr.
255 □2 **Cunningham, Lake** New Prov. Bahamas
168 □N2 **Cunningsburgh** Shetland, Scotland U.K.
276 B1 **Cunshamayo** Peru
204 C3 **Cuntis** Spain
219 J6 **Cununa** mt. Romania
271 □7 **Cunupia** Trin. and Tob.
212 D5 **Cuorgnè** Italy
168 J10 **Cupar** Fife, Scotland U.K.
275 H5 **Cupari** r. Brazil
199 L4 **Cupari, Dealul** hill Romania
158 G5 **Cupcina** Moldova
215 N3 **Cupello** Italy
274 B3 **Cupica** Col.
215 L1 **Cupra Marittima** Italy
213 O9 **Cupramontana** Italy
218 J7 **Ćuprija** Ćuprija Serbia
266 D5 **Cupula, Pico** mt. Mex.
185 H8 **Cuq-Toulza** France
268 D5 **Cuquio** Mex.
275 F6 **Curaça** Brazil
278 F4 **Curaçá** Brazil
274 D6 **Curaçá** r. Brazil
271 □10 **Curaçao** i. Neth. Antilles
284 B6 **Curacautín** Chile
284 B3 **Curacavi** Chile
284 E6 **Curacó** r. Arg.
231 B8 **Curaculo** Angola
276 C4 **Curahuara de Carangas** Bol.
285 F5 **Cura Malal** Arg.
285 F5 **Cura Malal, Sierra de** hills Arg.
282 B5 **Curanilahue** Chile
276 C2 **Curanja** r. Peru
285 F4 **Curapaligüe** Arg.
274 C5 **Curaray** r. Ecuador
284 B6 **Curarrehue** Chile
285 F4 **Curarú** Arg.
275 F3 **Curatabaca** Venez.
199 L5 **Curățele** Romania
284 B3 **Curaumilla, Punta** pt Chile
282 F3 **Curaya** r. Arg.
104 F4 **Curdlawidny Lagoon** salt flat S.A. Austr.
274 D5 **Curé** r. Col.
182 D1 **Cure** r. France
212 E4 **Cureggio** Italy
239 □1b **Curepipe** Mauritius
284 A4 **Curepto** Chile
182 E3 **Curgy** France
Curia Switz. see **Chur**
275 F2 **Curiapo** Venez.
284 B4 **Curicó** Chile
274 E5 **Curicuriari, Serra** hill Brazil
274 E5 **Curieuriari** r. Brazil
239 □2a **Curieuse, Île** i. Inner Islands Seychelles
278 D4 **Curimata** Brazil
217 K6 **Curinga** Italy
274 C4 **Curiplaya** Col.
280 C6 **Curitiba** Brazil
279 C8 **Curitibanos** Brazil
280 B6 **Curiúva** Brazil
105 M4 **Curlewis** N.S.W. Austr.
244 G3 **Curlew Lake** AK U.S.A.
104 G4 **Curnamona** S.A. Austr.
231 A8 **Curoca** r. Angola
212 F5 **Curone** r. Italy
213 J2 **Curon Venosta** Italy
204 F5 **Curopos** Port.
105 M4 **Currabubula** N.S.W. Austr.
169 J8 **Curracloe** Ireland
169 I6 **Curragh Camp** Ireland
169 F5 **Curraghroe** Ireland
169 E5 **Curragh West** Ireland
169 F8 **Curraglass** Ireland
206 □ **Curral das Freiras** Madeira
281 G1 **Curral de Dentro** Brazil
275 I5 **Curralinho** Brazil
104 E2 **Curralulla** watercourse S.A. Austr.
228 □ **Curral Velho** Cape Verde
251 K5 **Curran** MI U.S.A.
169 B9 **Currane, Lough** l. Ireland
265 Q3 **Currant** NV U.S.A.
105 J4 **Curranyalpa** N.S.W. Austr.
204 C3 **Currás** Spain
107 H8 **Currawilla** Qld Austr.
105 J3 **Currawinya National Park** Qld Austr.
270 E1 **Current** Eleuthera Bahamas
261 J7 **Current** r. MO U.S.A.
105 I8 **Currie** Tas. Austr.
265 R1 **Currie** NV U.S.A.
255 I7 **Currituck** NC U.S.A.
169 E5 **Curry** Ireland
245 J3 **Curry** AK U.S.A.
172 G5 **Curry Rivel** Somerset, England U.K.
217 O3 **Cursi** Italy
199 L6 **Curtea** Romania
219 M5 **Curtea de Argeș** Romania
218 J4 **Curtici** Romania
109 G11 **Curtin** W.A. Austr.
107 N8 **Curtis Channel** Qld Austr.
105 K8 **Curtis Group** is Tas. Austr.
107 M7 **Curtis Island** Qld Austr.
99 I5 **Curtis Island** N.Z.
199 L4 **Curtuișeni** Romania
275 H5 **Curuá** Brazil
275 H6 **Curuá** r. Brazil
275 I4 **Curuá, Ilha** i. Brazil
278 B3 **Curuaés** r. Brazil
275 H5 **Curuaí** Brazil
275 H5 **Curuapanema** r. Brazil
275 H5 **Curuá Una** r. Brazil
278 D2 **Curuçá** Brazil
275 I5 **Curumu** Brazil
116 E6 **Curup** Sumatera Indon.
275 F5 **Curupira** Brazil
275 E4 **Curupira, Serra** mts Brazil/Venez.
277 E3 **Cururú** Bol.
277 F1 **Cururu** r. Brazil
278 D2 **Cururupu** Brazil
275 F3 **Curutú, Cerro** mt. Venez.
285 H1 **Curuzú Cuatiá** Arg.
281 E3 **Curvelo** Brazil
250 F3 **Curwood, Mount** hill MI U.S.A.
214 C2 **Curza, Punta di** pt Corse France
215 N5 **Cusano Mutri** Italy
276 C3 **Cusco** Peru
276 B3 **Cusco** dept Peru
169 J2 **Cushendall** Northern Ireland U.K.
169 J2 **Cushendun** Northern Ireland U.K.
170 C7 **Cushina** Ireland
261 G7 **Cushing** OK U.S.A.
212 I7 **Cusna, Monte** mt. Italy
184 F4 **Cussac** France
184 C5 **Cussac-Fort-Médoc** France
183 D7 **Cussac-sur-Loire** France
234 B2 **Cussava** Angola
182 C4 **Cusset** France
255 E9 **Cusseta** GA U.S.A.
182 E2 **Cussy-les-Forges** France
262 K3 **Custer** MT U.S.A.
260 D4 **Custer** SD U.S.A.
179 L6 **Custines** France
216 D7 **Custonaci** Sicilia Italy
231 C8 **Cutato** Angola
262 H2 **Cut Bank** MT U.S.A.
262 H2 **Cut Bank Creek** r. MT U.S.A.
234 B2 **Cutenda** Angola
255 E10 **Cuthbert** GA U.S.A.
106 D2 **Cuthbertson Falls** N.T. Austr.
213 J7 **Cutigliano** Italy
264 M5 **Cutler** CA U.S.A.
257 □R4 **Cutler** ME U.S.A.
255 G13 **Cutler Ridge** FL U.S.A.
216 H8 **Cutò** r. Sicilia Italy
261 J11 **Cut Off** LA U.S.A.
169 E6 **Cutra, Lough** l. Ireland
284 C6 **Cutral-Co** Arg.
217 L5 **Cutro** Italy
217 O3 **Cutrofiano** Italy
105 J3 **Cuttaburra Creek** r. Qld Austr.
139 J9 **Cuttack** Orissa India
214 B4 **Cuttoli-Corticchiato** Corse France
268 G7 **Cutzamala** r. Mex.
268 G7 **Cutzamala de Pinzón** Mex.
231 B8 **Cuvelai** Angola
230 B5 **Cuvette** admin. reg. Congo
230 B5 **Cuvette-Ouest** admin. reg. Congo
109 B8 **Cuvier, Cape** W.A. Austr.
102 J3 **Cuvier Island** North I. N.Z.
251 R1 **Cuvillier, Lac** l. Que. Can.
185 I9 **Cuxac-Cabardès** France
183 B10 **Cuxac-d'Aude** France
151 J6 **Çuxanlı** Azer.
190 G3 **Cuxhaven** Ger.
151 J5 **Çuxuryurd** Azer.
276 C4 **Cuya** Chile
256 D7 **Cuyahoga Falls** OH U.S.A.
256 D7 **Cuyahoga Valley National Park** OH U.S.A.
264 M7 **Cuyama** CA U.S.A.
264 L7 **Cuyama** r. CA U.S.A.
114 C4 **Cuyapo** Luzon Phil.
114 C6 **Cuyo** Phil.
114 C6 **Cuyo** i. Phil.
114 C6 **Cuyo East Passage** Phil.
114 C6 **Cuyo Islands** Phil.
114 C6 **Cuyo West Passage** Phil.
275 G3 **Cuyuni** r. Guyana
Cuyutingni Nic. see **Kuyu Tingni**
268 C7 **Cuyutlán** Mex.
268 C7 **Cuyutlán, Laguna** lag. Mex.
184 H6 **Cuzance** France
Cuzco Cusco Peru see **Cusco**
276 A1 **Cuzco** San Martín Peru
207 J4 **Cuzna** r. Spain
185 F6 **Cuzorn** France
193 K9 **Cvikov** Czech Rep.
172 F4 **Cwm** Blaenau Gwent, Wales U.K.
172 E4 **Cwmafan** Neath Port Talbot, Wales U.K.
172 F3 **Cwmbach** Powys, Wales U.K.
172 F4 **Cwmbrân** Torfaen, Wales U.K.
172 E4 **Cwmllynfell** Neath Port Talbot, Wales U.K.
233 A5 **Cyangugu** Rwanda
196 C3 **Cybinka** Pol.
196 D2 **Cybowo** Pol.
192 K5 **Cychry** Pol.
Cyclades is Greece see **Kyklades**
197 L4 **Cyców** Pol.
Cydonia Kriti Greece see **Chania**
Cydweli Carmarthenshire, Wales U.K. see **Kidwelly**
Cydweli Wales U.K. see **Kidwelly**
105 K10 **Cygnet** Tas. Austr.
256 B7 **Cygnet** OH U.S.A.
Cymru admin. div. U.K. see **Wales**
172 E3 **Cynghordy** Carmarthenshire, Wales U.K.
172 D4 **Cynin** r. Wales U.K.
256 A10 **Cynthiana** KY U.S.A.
172 D4 **Cynwyl Elfed** Carmarthenshire, Wales U.K.
247 I5 **Cypress Hills** Sask. Can.
247 I5 **Cypress Hills Interprovincial Park** B.C. Can.
150 B3 **Cyprus** country Asia
224 D3 **Cyrenaica** reg. Libya
224 D1 **Cyrene** tourist site Libya
178 F2 **Cysoing** France
Cythera i. Greece see **Kythira**
172 D4 **Cywyn** r. Wales U.K.
196 E3 **Czacz** Pol.
196 G4 **Czajków** Pol.
196 E2 **Czaplinek** Pol.
247 I4 **Czar** Alta Can.
197 J5 **Czarna** Podkarpackie Pol.
197 K5 **Czarna** Podkarpackie Pol.
197 H4 **Czarna** r. Pol.
197 H5 **Czarna** r. Pol.
197 J5 **Czarna** r. Pol.
197 L2 **Czarna Białostocka** Pol.
196 F1 **Czarna Dąbrówka** Pol.
197 K6 **Czarna Górna** Pol.
197 L2 **Czarna Hańcza** r. Pol.
197 I5 **Czarna Nida** r. Pol.
196 G3 **Czarna Struga** r. Pol.
196 G2 **Czarna Woda** Pol.
197 H5 **Czarnca** Pol.
196 E2 **Czarne** Pol.
197 J2 **Czarnia** Pol.
196 E3 **Czarnków** Pol.
192 K5 **Czarnów** Pol.
196 G4 **Czarnożyły** Pol.
197 H6 **Czarny Dunajec** Pol.
199 I2 **Czarny Dunajec** r. Pol.
196 G4 **Czastary** Pol.
197 I6 **Czchów** Pol.
197 H6 **Czechowice-Dziedzice** Pol.
198 E2 **Czech Republic** country Europe
196 E2 **Czechy** Pol.
197 J4 **Czekarzewice** Pol.
197 K4 **Czemierniki** Pol.
196 E3 **Czempiń** Pol.
197 L3 **Czeremcha** Pol.
196 F4 **Czermin** Pol.
196 D4 **Czerna Mała** r. Pol.
196 D4 **Czerna Wielka** r. Pol.
196 F4 **Czernica** Pol.
196 E2 **Czernica** r. Pol.
197 I2 **Czernice Borowe** Pol.
196 F3 **Czerniejewo** Pol.
197 I4 **Czerniewice** Pol.
196 G3 **Czernikowo** Pol.
196 E4 **Czernina** Pol.
Czernowitz Ukr. see **Chernivtsi**
196 F2 **Czersk** Pol.
196 D3 **Czerwieńsk** Pol.
197 J3 **Czerwin** Pol.
197 I3 **Czerwińsk nad Wisłą** Pol.
196 G5 **Czerwionka-Leszczyny** Pol.
196 E3 **Czerwonak** Pol.
193 L8 **Czerwona Woda** Pol.
197 J3 **Czerwonka Włościańska** Pol.
197 H4 **Czestków** Pol.
197 H5 **Częstochowa** Pol.
196 F4 **Czeszów** Pol.
196 E2 **Człopa** Pol.
196 F2 **Człuchów** Pol.
196 F3 **Czmoń** Pol.
193 K8 **Czorneboh** hill Ger.
197 I6 **Czorsztyn, Jezioro** resr Pol.
197 I3 **Czosnów** Pol.
197 J6 **Czudec** Pol.
197 L3 **Czyże** Pol.
197 K3 **Czyżew-Osada** Pol.

D

118 F4 **Đa, Sông** r. Vietnam conv. **Black River**
191 E9 **Daaden** Ger.
129 S4 **Da'an** Jilin China
114 D6 **Daanbantayan** Phil.
186 K4 **Daarle** Neth.
133 D11 **Daba** Xizang China
150 D7 **Ḍabāb, Jabal aḍ** mt. Jordan
233 B7 **Dabaga** Tanz.
274 D2 **Dabajuro** Venez.
228 D4 **Dabakala** Côte d'Ivoire
129 P5 **Daban** Nei Mongol China
128 G8 **Daban Shan** mts China
130 D4 **Dabao** Sichuan China
199 I4 **Dabas** Hungary
130 G2 **Daba Shan** mts China
232 C1 **Dabat** Eth.
Dabba Sichuan China see **Daocheng**
274 B3 **Dabeiba** Col.
118 C6 **Dabein** Myanmar
192 E3 **Dabel** Ger.
138 D8 **Dabhoi** Gujarat India
136 C4 **Dabhol** Mahar. India
150 E7 **Ḍab'ī, Wādī aḍ** watercourse Jordan
196 D3 **Dąbie** Lubuskie Pol.
196 G3 **Dąbie** Wielkopolskie Pol.
196 C2 **Dąbie, Jezioro** l. Pol.
128 D7 **Dabiegai** Gansu China
131 J3 **Dabie Shan** mts China
165 M7 **Dąbki** Pol.
150 E9 **Dabl, Wādī** watercourse Saudi Arabia
179 N6 **Dabo** France
138 G7 **Daboh** Madh. Prad. India
228 C4 **Dabola** Guinea
228 D5 **Dabou** Côte d'Ivoire
228 E4 **Daboya** Ghana
129 K7 **Dabqig** Nei Mongol China
138 G7 **Dabra** Madh. Prad. India
160 J9 **Dabraslawka** Belarus
197 M3 **Dabravolya** Belarus
196 C3 **Dąbroszyn** Lubuskie Pol.
196 G3 **Dąbroszyn** Wielkopolskie Pol.
196 F3 **Dąbrowa** Kujawsko-Pomorskie Pol.
196 F5 **Dąbrowa** Opolskie Pol.
196 F5 **Dąbrowa** Opolskie Pol.
197 L2 **Dąbrowa Białostocka** Pol.
196 G3 **Dąbrowa Biskupia** Pol.
196 G2 **Dąbrowa Chełmińska** Pol.
197 H5 **Dąbrowa Górnicza** Pol.
197 I5 **Dąbrowa Tarnowska** Pol.
197 H3 **Dąbrowice** Pol.
196 D3 **Dąbrówka Wielkopolska** Pol.
197 I2 **Dąbrówno** Pol.
128 D8 **Dabsan** Qinghai China
133 L8 **Dabsan Hu** salt l. Qinghai China
131 K6 **Dabu** Guangdong China
Dabu Guangxi China see **Liucheng**
197 M3 **Dabuchyn** Belarus
219 M7 **Dăbuleni** Romania
Dacca Bangl. see **Dhaka**
195 K5 **Dachau** Ger.
195 K5 **Dachauer Moos** marsh Ger.
128 G7 **Dachechang** Nei Mongol China
129 P6 **Dachengzi** Liaoning China
136 F4 **Dachepalle** Andhra Prad. India
197 L5 **Dachnów** Pol.
191 J8 **Dachrieden** Ger.
195 J2 **Dachsbach** Ger.
201 I4 **Dachstein Gruppe** mts Austria
Dachuan Sichuan China see **Dazhou**
198 E2 **Dačice** Czech Rep.
251 R4 **Dacre** Ont. Can.
171 L4 **Dacre** Cumbria, England U.K.
199 H4 **Dad** Hungary
197 I2 **Dadaj, Jezioro** l. Pol.
129 L2 **Dadal** Hentiy Mongolia
100 □6 **Dadale** Sta Isabel Solomon Is
275 G4 **Dadanawa** Guyana
151 C6 **Dadaş** Turkey
150 F2 **Dādāt** Syria
148 F3 **Daday** Turkey
232 D1 **Daddato** Djibouti
255 F11 **Dade City** FL U.S.A.
255 E9 **Dadeville** AL U.S.A.
145 L7 **Dadhar** Pak.
144 I8 **Dādkān** Iran
Dadong Liaoning China see **Donggang**
185 H8 **Dadou** r. France
138 D9 **Dadra** Dadra India
Dadra Mahar. India see **Achalpur**
138 D9 **Dadra and Nagar Haveli** union terr. India
145 L8 **Dadu** Pak.
130 D4 **Dadu He** r. Sichuan China
Daedalus Reef Saudi Arabia see **Abū al Kizān**
Daegu S. Korea see **Taegu**
Daejŏn S. Korea see **Taejŏn**
114 D4 **Daet** Luzon Phil.
130 E5 **Dafang** Guizhou China
131 M2 **Dafeng** Jiangsu China
147 K4 **Dafīr** U.A.E.
139 N6 **Dafla Hills** India
136 D4 **Daflapur** Mahar. India
220 D5 **Dafni** Dytiki Ellas Greece
220 F2 **Dafni** Kentriki Makedonia Greece
220 B4 **Dafnoudi, Akrotirio** pt Kefallonia Greece
247 M4 **Dafoe** r. Man. Can.
230 C2 **Dafra** Chad
250 J3 **Dafter** MI U.S.A.
199 H4 **Dág** Hungary
138 E8 **Dag** Rajasthan India
221 L5 **Dağ** Turkey
232 D3 **Daga Medo** Eth.
228 B2 **Dagana** Senegal
205 N7 **Daganzo de Arriba** Spain
232 B2 **Daga Post** Sudan
225 G5 **Dagash** Sudan
115 E2 **Dagasuli** i. Maluku Indon.
128 H9 **Dagcanglhamo** Gansu China
151 G5 **Dağ Cäyir** Azer.
151 D5 **Dağcı** Turkey
160 K5 **Dagda** Latvia
221 J4 **Dağdere** Turkey
Dage Hebei China see **Fengning**
190 G1 **Dagebüll** Ger.
Dagenraad atoll Arch. des Tuamotu Fr. Polynesia see **Manihi**
151 I3 **Dagestan, Respublika** aut. rep. Rus. Fed.
Dagestanskaya A.S.S.R. aut. rep. Rus. Fed. see **Dagestan, Respublika**
151 J3 **Dagestanskiye Ogni** Rus. Fed.
151 I1 **Dagestanskiy Zapovednik** nature res. Rus. Fed.
Dagezhen Hebei China see **Fengning**
237 J8 **Daggaboersnek** S. Africa
103 A12 **Dagg Sound** inlet South I. N.Z.
Daghestan aut. rep. Rus. Fed. see **Dagestan, Respublika**
147 N4 **Daghmar** Oman
185 G6 **Daglan** France
151 H6 **Dağlıq Qarabağ** aut. reg. Azer.
133 J12 **Daglung** Xizang China
133 K11 **Dagma** Xizang China
130 A3 **Dagmala Shan** mts Xizang China
188 C5 **Dagmersellen** Luzern Switz.
212 D1 **Dagmersellen** Luzern Switz.
Dagö i. Estonia see **Hiiumaa**
151 A2 **Dagomys** Rus. Fed.
Dagon Myanmar see **Yangôn**
103 C11 **Dagon** mt. South I. N.Z.
228 E4 **Dagonkadi** Ghana
151 B5 **Dağönü** Turkey
150 B2 **Dağpazarı** Turkey
151 E5 **Dağpınar** Turkey
133 H11 **Dagrag Zangbo** r. Xizang China
130 B2 **Dagtog** Qinghai China
129 O7 **Dagu** Tianjin China
130 D5 **Daguan** Yunnan China
230 C2 **Daguéla** Chad
129 Q8 **Dagu He** r. China
122 F6 **Daguokui Shan** hill Heilong. China
114 C3 **Dagupan** Luzon Phil.
128 D8 **Dagur** Qinghai China
106 C4 **Daguragu** N.T. Austr.
106 C4 **Daguragu Aboriginal Land** res. N.T. Austr.
118 C5 **Dagwin** Myanmar
Dagxoi Sichuan China see **Yidun**
Dagxoi Sichuan China see **Sowa**
133 J12 **Dagzê** Xizang China
133 H11 **Dagzê Co** salt l. China
133 I12 **Dagzhuka** Xizang China
146 D5 **Dahabān** Saudi Arabia
245 P3 **Dahadinni** r. N.W.T. Can.
Dahalach, Isole is Eritrea see **Dahlak Archipelago**
Dahana des. Saudi Arabia see **Ad Dahnā'**
136 C3 **Dahanu** Mahar. India
Dahe Guangxi China see **Ziyuan**
128 F9 **Daheba** Qinghai China
122 F5 **Daheiding Shan** mt. China
129 L6 **Dahei He** r. China
128 C5 **Dahei Shan** mt. Xinjiang China
122 D7 **Dahei Shan** mts China
138 D9 **Dahej** Gujarat India
Daheyan Xinjiang China see **Turpan Zhan**
146 E7 **Dahīn, Ḩarrat ad** lava field Saudi Arabia
129 O5 **Da Hinggan Ling** mts China
136 D4 **Dahivadi** Mahar. India
146 G5 **Daḩl, Nafūd ad** des. Saudi Arabia
225 I6 **Dahlak Archipelago** is Eritrea
225 I5 **Dahlak Marine National Park** Eritrea
147 H2 **Daḩl al Furayy** well Saudi Arabia
146 F5 **Daḩlat Shabāb** Saudi Arabia
191 C10 **Dahlem** Ger.
193 H8 **Dahlen** Ger.
190 K4 **Dahlenburg** Ger.
193 H8 **Dahlener Heide** reg. Ger.
193 E6 **Dahlenwarsleben** Ger.
147 H2 **Daḩl Iftākh** well Saudi Arabia
255 F8 **Dahlonega** GA U.S.A.
193 I5 **Dahlwitz-Hoppegarten** Ger.
146 G7 **Dahm, Ramlat** des. Saudi Arabia/Yemen
227 H2 **Dahmani** Tunisia
193 H7 **Dahme** Brandenburg Ger.
192 D2 **Dahme** Schleswig-Holstein Ger.
193 I6 **Dahme** r. Ger.
192 D2 **Dahmeshöved** hd Ger.
194 D3 **Dahn** Ger.
138 E8 **Dahod** Gujarat India
Dahomey country Africa see **Benin**
133 D9 **Dahongliutan** Aksai Chin
Dahra Senegal see **Dara**
190 K5 **Dähre** Ger.
130 G7 **Dahua** Guangxi China
149 K5 **Dahūk** Iraq
149 K5 **Dahūk** governorate Iraq
149 K5 **Dahūk, Buḩayrat** l. Iraq
147 J7 **Ḍaḩyah, Wādī** r. Yemen
115 F7 **Dai** i. Maluku Indon.
127 I4 **Daibosatsu-rei** mt. Japan
129 O7 **Daicheng** Hebei China
Daido r. N. Korea see **Taedong-gang**
127 L2 **Daigo** Japan
129 M6 **Dai Hai** l. China
100 □6 **Dai Island** Solomon Is
116 F5 **Daik** Indon.
162 N4 **Daikanvik** Sweden
118 C6 **Daik-U** Myanmar
119 I8 **Đai Lanh, Mui** pt Vietnam
Dail Bho Thuath Scotland U.K. see **North Dell**
138 H5 **Dailekh** Nepal
256 F10 **Dailey** WV U.S.A.
168 G12 **Dailly** South Ayrshire, Scotland U.K.
125 K10 **Daimanji-san** hill Japan
207 L2 **Daimiel** Spain
126 F2 **Daimon** Japan
127 H3 **Daimon-tōge** pass Japan
127 H5 **Daimugen-zan** mt. Japan
197 M1 **Dainava** Lith.
169 H6 **Daingean** Ireland
261 H9 **Daingerfield** TX U.S.A.
126 E3 **Dainichiga-take** vol. Japan
126 E3 **Dainichi-gawa** r. Japan
126 D3 **Dainichi-zan** mt. Japan
130 A2 **Dainkog** Sichuan China
107 J4 **Daintree** Qld Austr.
107 J4 **Daintree National Park** Qld Austr.
178 E3 **Dainville** France
179 K7 **Dainville-Bertheléville** France
126 E7 **Daiō** Japan
126 E7 **Daiō-zaki** pt Japan
270 F4 **Daiquiri** Cuba
225 F6 **Dair, Jebel ed** mt. Sudan
285 G5 **Daireaux** Arg.
Dairen Liaoning China see **Dalian**
168 K10 **Dairsie** Fife, Scotland U.K.
259 F1 **Dairyland** NY U.S.A.
250 B3 **Dairyland** WI U.S.A.
125 K11 **Dai-sen** vol. Japan
125 K11 **Daisen-Oki Kokuritsu-kōen** nat. park Japan
124 T3 **Daisetsu-zan Kokuritsu-kōen** nat. park Japan
131 N3 **Daishan** Zhejiang China
126 C6 **Daitō** Ōsaka Japan
127 H6 **Daitō** Shizuoka Japan
127 K2 **Daiya-gawa** r. Japan
Daiyue Shanxi China see **Shanyin**
131 L6 **Daiyun Shan** mts China
270 H4 **Dajabón** Dom. Rep.
145 N7 **Dajal** Pak.
126 E5 **Dajan** Japan
106 G6 **Dajarra** Qld Austr.
Dajie Yunnan China see **Jiangchuan**
130 C3 **Dajin Chuan** r. Sichuan China
128 H8 **Dajing** Gansu China
128 D8 **Da Juh** Qinghai China
228 A3 **Dakar** Senegal
225 F5 **Dakar el Arak** well Sudan
150 A10 **Dakhal, Wādī ad** watercourse Egypt
225 F3 **Dākhilah, Wāḩāt ad** oasis Egypt
139 M8 **Dakhin Shahbazpur Island** Bangl.
Dakhla Western Sahara see **Ad Dakhla**
Dakhla Oasis Egypt see **Dākhilah, Wāḩāt ad**
226 A5 **Dakhlet Nouâdhibou** admin. reg. Maur.
151 B1 **Dakhovskaya** Rus. Fed.
229 G4 **Dakingari** Nigeria
129 K2 **Dakituy** Rus. Fed.
119 I8 **Đắk Lăk, Cao Nguyên** plat. Vietnam
137 M9 **Dakoank** Andaman & Nicobar Is India
160 L9 **Dakol'ka** r. Belarus
138 D8 **Dakor** Gujarat India
229 G3 **Dakoro** Niger
260 H4 **Dakota City** IA U.S.A.

260 G4 **Dakota City** *NE* U.S.A.
Đakovica *Gjakovë* Kosovo *see* **Gjakovë**
210 G3 **Đakovo** Croatia
122 E2 **Daktuy** Rus. Fed.
231 D7 **Dala** Angola
199 J5 **Đala** *Vojvodina* Serbia
100 □6 **Dala** *Malaita* Solomon Is
200 B5 **Dalaas** Austria
228 B4 **Dalaba** Guinea
228 B3 **Dalaba** Senegal
168 B8 **Dalabrog** *Western Isles, Scotland* U.K.
Dalad Qi *Nei Mongol* China *see* **Shulinzhao**
Dalai *Jilin* China *see* **Da'an**
128 G6 **Dalain Hob** *Nei Mongol* China
129 O5 **Dalai Nur** *l.* China
144 B4 **Dālā Khānī, Kūh-e** *mt.* Iran
144 D7 **Dālakī** Iran
144 D7 **Dalaki, Rūd-e** *r.* Iran
150 B10 **Dalal, Jabal** *mt.* Egypt
165 N1 **Dalälven** *r.* Sweden
221 J5 **Dalama** Turkey
129 M6 **Dalamamiao** *Nei Mongol* China
221 J6 **Dalaman** Turkey
221 J6 **Dalaman** *r.* Turkey
144 F3 **Daland** Iran
128 I5 **Dalandzadgad** Mongolia
114 C6 **Dalanganem Islands** Phil.
Dalap-Uliga-Darrit *Majuro* Marshall Is *see* **Delap-Uliga-Djarrit**
165 K1 **Dalarna** *county* Sweden
163 L6 **Dalarna** *reg.* Sweden
117 I3 **Dalat** *Sarawak* Malaysia
119 I9 **Đa Lat** Vietnam
Dalatando Angola *see* **N'dalatando**
138 E8 **Dalauda** *Madh. Prad.* India
Dalay Mongolia *see* **Bayandalay**
145 K7 **Dalbandin** Pak.
168 I13 **Dalbeattie** *Dumfries and Galloway, Scotland* U.K.
107 K6 **Dalbeg** *Qld* Austr.
192 D3 **Dalberg-Wendelstorf** Ger.
250 A4 **Dalbo** *MN* U.S.A.
164 I3 **Dalbosjön** *l.* Sweden
107 M9 **Dalby** *Qld* Austr.
170 H5 **Dalby** Isle of Man
164 J6 **Dalby** Sweden
283 B6 **Dalcahue** Chile
164 B1 **Dale** *Hordaland* Norway
163 H6 **Dale** *Sogn og Fjordane* Norway
172 B4 **Dale** *Pembrokeshire, Wales* U.K.
256 H10 **Dale City** *VA* U.S.A.
253 I3 **Dale Hollow Lake** *TN* U.S.A.
191 B10 **Daleiden** Ger.
159 M8 **Daleke** Ukr.
186 K3 **Dalen** Neth.
201 N1 **Dalešice, Vodní nádrž** *resr* Czech Rep.
237 M2 **Daleside** S. Africa
197 I5 **Daleszyce** Pol.
118 A5 **Dalet** Myanmar
118 A4 **Daletme** Myanmar
255 E10 **Daleville** *AL* U.S.A.
258 D2 **Daleville** *PA* U.S.A.
163 M6 **Dalfors** Sweden
186 J3 **Dalfsen** Neth.
144 H8 **Dalgān** Iran
109 D9 **Dalgaranger, Mount** *hill* W.A. Austr.
105 L7 **Dalgety** *N.S.W.* Austr.
109 C8 **Dalgety** *r.* W.A. Austr.
168 J10 **Dalgety Bay** *Fife, Scotland* U.K.
173 N3 **Dalham** *Suffolk, England* U.K.
261 D7 **Dalhart** *TX* U.S.A.
249 H3 **Dalhousie** *N.B.* Can.
138 F3 **Dalhousie** *Hima. Prad.* India
245 O1 **Dalhousie, Cape** *N.W.T.* Can.
129 L9 **Dali** *Shaanxi* China
130 C6 **Dali** *Yunnan* China
150 B3 **Dali** Cyprus
129 Q7 **Dalian** *Liaoning* China
Daliang *Guangdong* China *see* **Shunde**
128 G8 **Daliang** *Qinghai* China
130 D4 **Daliang Shan** *mts Sichuan* China
129 Q7 **Dalian Wan** *b.* China
207 N7 **Dalías** Spain
207 N7 **Dalías, Campo de** *reg.* Spain
Daliburgh *Western Isles, Scotland* U.K. *see* **Dalabrog**
151 H6 **Dälidağ** *mt.* Azer.
129 L8 **Dali He** *r.* China
197 H4 **Dalików** Pol.
151 H5 **Dälilär** Azer.
151 H5 **Dälimämmädli** Azer.
129 R5 **Dalin** *Nei Mongol* China
Dalinghe *Liaoning* China *see* **Linghai**
129 Q6 **Daling He** *r.* China
123 E8 **Dalizi** *Jilin* China
210 G3 **Dalj** Croatia
168 J11 **Dalkeith** *Midlothian, Scotland* U.K.
139 K7 **Dalkola** *W. Bengal* India
244 I3 **Dall, Mount** *AK* U.S.A.
107 N8 **Dallarnil** *Qld* Austr.
168 J7 **Dallas** *Moray, Scotland* U.K.
262 C4 **Dallas** *OR* U.S.A.
258 D2 **Dallas** *PA* U.S.A.
261 G9 **Dallas** *TX* U.S.A.
250 C9 **Dallas City** *IL* U.S.A.
258 B5 **Dallastown** *PA* U.S.A.
Dalles City *OR* U.S.A. *see* **The Dalles**
192 H5 **Dallgow** Ger.
138 H9 **Dalli** *Chhattisgarh* India
245 N5 **Dall Island** *AK* U.S.A.
244 G3 **Dall Lake** *AK* U.S.A.
245 J2 **Dall Mountain** *AK* U.S.A.
232 D1 **Dallol** *vol.* Eth.
229 F3 **Dallol Bosso** *watercourse* Mali/Niger
147 K3 **Dalmā** *i.* U.A.E.
210 E3 **Dalmacija** *reg.* Croatia
285 F3 **Dalmacio Vélez Sarsfield** Arg.
168 G10 **Dalmally** *Argyll and Bute, Scotland* U.K.
199 H5 **Dalmand** Hungary
249 G2 **Dalmas, Lac** *l. Que.* Can.
Dalmatia *reg.* Croatia *see* **Dalmacija**
258 B3 **Dalmatia** *PA* U.S.A.
138 H6 **Dalmau** *Uttar Prad.* India
168 H12 **Dalmellington** *East Ayrshire, Scotland* U.K.
247 J4 **Dalmeny** *Sask.* Can.
139 K8 **Dalmi** *Jharkhand* India
212 H4 **Dalmine** Italy
168 H7 **Dalnavie** *Highland, Scotland* U.K.
122 I6 **Dal'negorsk** Rus. Fed.
122 H6 **Dal'nerechensk** Rus. Fed.
156 I5 **Dal'neye Konstantinovo** Rus. Fed.
156 G1 **Dal'niye Zelentsy** Rus. Fed.
Dalny *Liaoning* China *see* **Dalian**
228 D5 **Daloa** Côte d'Ivoire
107 M1 **Daloloia Group** *is* P.N.G.
130 F5 **Dalou Shan** *mts* China
193 G10 **Dalovice** Czech Rep.
146 G3 **Dalqān** *well* Saudi Arabia
168 G11 **Dalry** *North Ayrshire, Scotland* U.K.
168 G12 **Dalrymple** *East Ayrshire, Scotland* U.K.
107 K6 **Dalrymple, Lake** *Qld* Austr.
107 L6 **Dalrymple, Mount** *Qld* Austr.
160 F1 **Dalsbruk** Fin.
164 I3 **Dals Långed** Sweden
179 L5 **Dalstein** France
171 L4 **Dalston** *Cumbria, England* U.K.
139 J7 **Daltenganj** *Jharkhand* India
248 C3 **Dalton** *Ont.* Can.
237 O5 **Dalton** S. Africa
255 E8 **Dalton** *GA* U.S.A.
257 L6 **Dalton** *MA* U.S.A.
256 D8 **Dalton** *OH* U.S.A.
258 D1 **Dalton** *PA* U.S.A.
Daltonganj *Jharkhand* India *see* **Daltenganj**
287 I2 **Dalton Iceberg Tongue** Antarctica
171 K5 **Dalton-in-Furness** *Cumbria, England* U.K.
251 J1 **Dalton Mills** *Ont.* Can.
169 E8 **Dalua** *r.* Ireland
116 D4 **Daludalu** *Sumatera* Indon.
123 C9 **Dalu Dao** *i.* China
183 J8 **Daluis** France
130 C8 **Daluo** *Yunnan* China
131 I7 **Daluo Shan** *mt. Guangdong* China
114 C2 **Dalupiri** *i.* Phil.
162 □D1 **Dalvík** Iceland
109 D11 **Dalwallinu** *W.A.* Austr.
168 H9 **Dalwhinnie** *Highland, Scotland* U.K.
106 C2 **Daly** *r. N.T.* Austr.
221 J6 **Dalyan** Turkey
264 J4 **Daly City** *CA* U.S.A.
160 J6 **Dalyokiya** Belarus
106 C2 **Daly River** *N.T.* Austr.
106 C3 **Daly River/Port Keats Aboriginal Land** *res. N.T.* Austr.
169 F6 **Dalystown** Ireland
106 D4 **Daly Waters** *N.T.* Austr.
158 C2 **Damachava** Belarus
229 H3 **Damagaram Takaya** Niger
151 D4 **Damal** Turkey
231 F8 **Damalisques de Leshwe** *nature res.* Dem. Rep. Congo
138 D9 **Daman** *Daman* India
138 C9 **Daman and Diu** *union terr.* India
160 I9 **Damanava** Belarus
228 B2 **Damâne** *well* Maur.
144 D5 **Dāmaneh** Iran
225 F2 **Damanhûr** Egypt
247 J2 **Damant Lake** *N.W.T.* Can.
Damão *Daman* India *see* **Daman**
144 C4 **Damaq** Iran
129 N6 **Damaqun Shan** *mts* China
115 E2 **Damar** *Sulawesi* Indon.
115 F4 **Damar** *i. Maluku* Indon.
115 F7 **Damar** *i. Maluku* Indon.
151 C4 **Damar** Turkey
230 C3 **Damara** C.A.R.
234 C4 **Damaraland** *reg.* Namibia
257 □P4 **Damariscotta Lake** *ME* U.S.A.
116 □ **Damar Laut, Pulau** *i.* Sing.
Damas Syria *see* **Dimashq**
229 I3 **Damasak** Nigeria
179 L7 **Damas-aux-Bois** France
Damascus Syria *see* **Dimashq**
256 H9 **Damascus** *MD* U.S.A.
258 E1 **Damascus** *PA* U.S.A.
256 D12 **Damascus** *VA* U.S.A.
196 F3 **Damasławek** Pol.
229 H4 **Damaturu** Nigeria
144 E4 **Damāvand** Iran
144 E4 **Damāvand, Qolleh-ye** *mt.* Iran
185 E7 **Damazan** France
231 B6 **Damba** Angola
179 N7 **Dambach-la-Ville** France
229 F4 **Dambai** Ghana
229 H3 **Dambatta** Nigeria
192 E4 **Dambeck** Ger.
229 I4 **Damboa** Nigeria
201 O1 **Dambořice** Czech Rep.
219 N6 **Dâmbovița** *r.* Romania
136 G9 **Dambulla** Sri Lanka
139 N7 **Damchara** *Assam* India
142 K2 **Damdy** Kazakh.
179 L6 **Damelevières** France
270 F4 **Dame-Marie** Haiti
270 F4 **Dame Marie, Cap** *c.* Haiti
173 I6 **Damerham** *Hampshire, England* U.K.
170 C8 **Damerstown** Ireland
178 G5 **Damery** France
180 F6 **Damgan** France
144 F3 **Dāmghān** Iran
168 E7 **Damh, Loch** *l. Scotland* U.K.
169 I2 **Damhead** *Northern Ireland* U.K.
185 H8 **Damiatte** France
Damietta Egypt *see* **Dumyāṭ**
181 L5 **Damigny** France
129 N8 **Daming** *Hebei* China
130 G7 **Daming Shan** *mt. Guangxi* China
151 J5 **Dämirçi** Azer.
150 D6 **Dāmiyā** Jordan
130 A2 **Damjong** *Qinghai* China
114 C9 **Dammai** *i.* Phil.
Dammam Saudi Arabia *see* **Ad Dammām**
178 C7 **Dammarie** France
212 E2 **Dammastock** *mt.* Switz.
187 D6 **Damme** Belgium
190 F5 **Damme** Ger.
196 F1 **Damnica** Pol.
196 F1 **Damno** Pol.
138 G8 **Damoh** *Madh. Prad.* India
228 E4 **Damongo** Ghana
150 D5 **Damour** Lebanon
190 I1 **Damp** Ger.
116 E3 **Dampar, Tasik** *l.* Malaysia
182 G2 **Damparis** France
115 A3 **Dampelas, Tanjung** *pt* Indon.
108 D6 **Dampier** *W.A.* Austr.
108 D6 **Dampier Archipelago** *is* W.A. Austr.
Dampier Island P.N.G. *see* **Karkar Island**
108 G4 **Dampier Land** *reg. W.A.* Austr.
182 H2 **Dampierre** France
178 E8 **Dampierre-en-Burly** France
182 I1 **Dampierre-sur-Linotte** France
182 H1 **Dampierre-sur-Salon** France
113 K8 **Dampier Strait** P.N.G.
115 G4 **Dampir, Selat** *sea chan. Papua* Indon.
117 J9 **Dampit** *Jawa* Indon.
182 J2 **Damprichard** France
Damqoq Zangbo *r. Xizang* China *see* **Maquan He**
133 K10 **Dam Qu** *r. Qinghai* China
119 G9 **Dâmrei, Chuŏr Phnum** *mts* Cambodia
139 O5 **Damroh** *Arun. Prad.* India
193 G6 **Damsdorf** Ger.
192 D3 **Damshagen** Ger.
192 F1 **Damsholte** Denmark
200 A5 **Damüls** Austria
212 B1 **Damvant** Switz.
178 B6 **Damville** France
179 J5 **Damvillers** France
186 J2 **Damwoude** Neth.
Damxoi *Xizang* China *see* **Comai**
133 J11 **Damxung** *Xizang* China
255 H7 **Dan** *r. NC* U.S.A.
228 D5 **Dan, Monts des** *mts* Côte d'Ivoire
115 B9 **Dana** *i.* Indon.
150 D8 **Ḍānā** Jordan
139 I5 **Dana** Nepal
244 G5 **Dana, Mount** *AK* U.S.A.
264 M4 **Dana, Mount** *CA* U.S.A.
151 H4 **Danaçı** Azer.
207 M4 **Dañador** *r.* Spain
Danakil *reg.* Eritrea/Eth. *see* **Denakil**
228 C5 **Danané** Côte d'Ivoire
118 I6 **Đa Năng** Vietnam
118 I6 **Đa Năng, Vung** *b.* Vietnam
114 E6 **Danao** *Cebu* Phil.
144 F2 **Danata** Turkm.
117 J4 **Danau Sentarum, Taman Nasional** *nature res. Kalimantan* Indon.
129 K8 **Danba** *Shaanxi* China
130 C3 **Danba** *Sichuan* China
258 E4 **Danboro** *PA* U.S.A.
173 N4 **Danbury** *Essex, England* U.K.
257 L7 **Danbury** *CT* U.S.A.
255 G7 **Danbury** *NC* U.S.A.
257 N5 **Danbury** *NH* U.S.A.
250 B3 **Danbury** *WI* U.S.A.
171 P5 **Danby** *North Yorkshire, England* U.K.
257 M5 **Danby** *VT* U.S.A.
265 Q7 **Danby Lake** *CA* U.S.A.
131 J2 **Dancheng** *Henan* China
Dancheng *Zhejiang* China *see* **Xiangshan**
109 C11 **Dandaragan** *W.A.* Austr.
231 B7 **Dande** *r.* Angola
232 C3 **Dande** Eth.
138 H5 **Dandeldhura** Nepal
136 D5 **Dandeli** *Karnataka* India
171 K2 **Danderhall** *Midlothian, Scotland* U.K.
231 C7 **Dando** Angola
123 D8 **Dandong** *Liaoning* China
126 F5 **Dando-san** *mt.* Japan
255 F7 **Dandridge** *TN* U.S.A.
160 E6 **Danė** *r.* Lith.
171 L7 **Dane** *r. England* U.K.
243 P2 **Daneborg** Greenland
173 M5 **Danehill** *East Sussex, England* U.K.
169 G5 **Danesfort** Ireland
219 M7 **Daneți** Romania
Dänew Turkm. *see* **Galkynyş**
130 H2 **Danfeng** *Shaanxi* China
Danfeng *Yunnan* China *see* **Shizong**
257 □R3 **Danforth** *ME* U.S.A.
119 H9 **Dâng, Đa** *r.* Vietnam
131 J7 **Dangan Liedao** *i. Guangdong* China
Dangara Tajik. *see* **Danghara**
122 G6 **Dangbi** Rus. Fed.
128 I9 **Dangchang** *Gansu* China
Dangchengwan *Gansu* China *see* **Subei**
231 B6 **Dange** Angola
229 G3 **Dange** Nigeria
231 B7 **Dange-ia-Menha** Angola
Danger Islands *atoll* Cook Is *see* **Pukapuka**
106 C1 **Danger Point** *N.T.* Austr.
236 D10 **Danger Point** S. Africa
184 F2 **Dangé-St-Romain** France
104 H5 **Danggali Conservation Park** *nature res. S.A.* Austr.
145 M2 **Danghara** Tajik.
128 D6 **Dang He** *r. Gansu* China
128 D7 **Danghe Nanshan** *mts* China
232 C2 **Dangila** Eth.
132 L7 **Dangjin Shankou** *pass Gansu/Qinghai* China
Dangla Shan *mts Xizang* China *see* **Tanggula Shan**
232 F2 **Dan Gorayo** Somalia
139 O6 **Dangori** *Assam* India
133 J11 **Dangqên** *Xizang* China
267 O9 **Dangriga** Belize
129 O9 **Dangshan** *Anhui* China
131 L3 **Dangtu** *Anhui* China
229 G4 **Dan-Gulbi** Nigeria
232 B2 **Dangur** Eth.
232 B2 **Dangur** *mt.* Eth.
232 B2 **Dangur** *mts* Eth.
131 H3 **Dangyang** *Hubei* China
196 G5 **Daniec** Pol.
262 I5 **Daniel** *WY* U.S.A.
278 B5 **Daniel, Serra** *hills* Brazil
284 D3 **Daniel Donovan** Arg.
249 J3 **Daniel's Harbour** *Nfld and Lab.* Can.
255 □1 **Daniel's Head** Bermuda
236 H4 **Daniëlskuil** S. Africa
257 N7 **Danielson** *CT* U.S.A.
237 M3 **Danielsrus** S. Africa
255 F8 **Danielsville** *GA* U.S.A.
161 U2 **Danilkovo** Rus. Fed.
156 H4 **Danilov** Rus. Fed.
218 H8 **Danilovgrad** *Danilovgrad* Montenegro
143 N1 **Danilovka** Kazakh.
157 I6 **Danilovka** Rus. Fed.
156 G4 **Danilovskaya Vozvyshennost'** *hills* Rus. Fed.
129 L8 **Daning** *Shanxi* China
151 K5 **Dänizkänarı** Azer.
Danjiang *Guizhou* China *see* **Leishan**
131 H2 **Danjiangkou** *Hubei* China
131 H2 **Danjiangkou Shuiku** *resr* China
123 F12 **Danjo-guntō** *is* Japan
182 J1 **Danjoutin** France
147 M4 **Ḍank** Oman
146 E9 **Dankalia** *prov.* Eritrea
193 D7 **Dankerode** Ger.
138 G3 **Dankhar** *Hima. Prad.* India
191 J9 **Dankmarshausen** Ger.
161 W8 **Dankov** Rus. Fed.
143 Q7 **Dan'kova, Pik** *mt.* Kyrg.
266 □P10 **Danlí** Hond.
130 D3 **Danling** *Sichuan* China
243 P1 **Danmark Fjord** *inlet* Greenland
191 K6 **Danndorf** Ger.
Dannebrog Ø *i.* Greenland *see* **Qillak**
190 L1 **Dannemare** Denmark
182 K1 **Dannemarie** France
257 L4 **Dannemora** *NY* U.S.A.
192 D4 **Dannenberg (Elbe)** Ger.
192 H4 **Dannenwalde** Ger.
229 G2 **Dannet** *well* Niger
102 K7 **Dannevirke** *North I.* N.Z.
190 I2 **Dannewerk** Ger.
237 O4 **Dannhauser** S. Africa
228 E4 **Dano** Burkina
283 D8 **Dañoso, Cabo** *c.* Arg.
118 E6 **Dan Sai** Thai.
Danshui Taiwan *see* **Tanshui**
118 B6 **Danson Bay** Myanmar
256 H6 **Dansville** *NY* U.S.A.
138 D7 **Danta** *Gujarat* India
139 K9 **Dantan** *W. Bengal* India
256 C12 **Dante** *VA* U.S.A.
136 G3 **Dantewara** *Chhattisgarh* India
219 R5 **Danube** *r.* Europe
alt. **Donau (Austria/Germany),**
alt. **Duna (Hungary),**
alt. **Dunaj (Slovakia),**
alt. **Dunărea (Romania),**
alt. **Dunav (Serbia)**
Danube Delta Romania *see* **Dunării, Delta**
118 B6 **Danubyu** Myanmar
117 K4 **Danumparai** *Kalimantan* Indon.
117 L2 **Danum Valley Conservation Area** *nature res.* Malaysia
261 I8 **Danville** *AR* U.S.A.
254 D5 **Danville** *IL* U.S.A.
254 D6 **Danville** *IN* U.S.A.
254 E7 **Danville** *KY* U.S.A.
256 C8 **Danville** *OH* U.S.A.
251 R9 **Danville** *PA* U.S.A.
256 F12 **Danville** *VA* U.S.A.
257 M4 **Danville** *VT* U.S.A.
Danxian *Hainan* China *see* **Danzhou**
131 L3 **Danyang** *Jiangsu* China
130 F5 **Danzhai** *Guizhou* China
130 G6 **Danzhou** *Guangxi* China
130 G9 **Danzhou** *Hainan* China
Danzhou *Shaanxi* China *see* **Yichuan**
Danzig Pol. *see* **Gdańsk**
Danzig, Gulf of Pol./Rus. Fed. *see* **Gdańsk, Gulf of**
114 C6 **Dao** *Panay* Phil.
204 D8 **Dão** *r.* Port.
130 C4 **Daocheng** *Sichuan* China
Daojiang *Hunan* China *see* **Daoxian**
Daokou *Henan* China *see* **Huaxian**
181 J6 **Daon** France
128 G8 **Daotanghe** *Qinghai* China
Dao Tay Sa *is* S. China Sea *see* **Paracel Islands**
229 I1 **Dao Timmi** Niger
Daoud Alg. *see* **Aïn Beïda**
228 D3 **Daoudi** *well* Maur.
228 E5 **Daoukro** Côte d'Ivoire
180 C5 **Daoulas** France
131 H6 **Daoxian** *Hunan* China
130 F4 **Daozhen** *Guizhou* China
114 F7 **Dapa** Phil.
229 F4 **Dapaong** Togo
229 H3 **Dapchi** Nigeria
131 □J7 **Dapeng Wan** *b. H.K.* China
139 P6 **Daphabum** *mt. Arun. Prad.* India
150 A8 **Daphnae** *tourist site* Egypt
255 D10 **Daphne** *AL* U.S.A.
220 D4 **Daphni** *tourist site* Greece
114 D7 **Dapiak, Mount** *Mindanao* Phil.
Dapingdi *Sichuan* China *see* **Jiankang**
Dapingdi *Yunnan* China *see* **Yanbian**
114 D7 **Dapitan** *Mindanao* Phil.
139 N4 **Daporijo** *Arun. Prad.* India
Dapu *Guangxi* China *see* **Liucheng**
133 L8 **Da Qaidam Zhen** *Qinghai* China
130 D5 **Daqiao** *Yunnan* China
122 D5 **Daqing** *Heilong.* China
129 P7 **Daqinghe** *Hebei* China
129 L6 **Daqing Shan** *mts* China
129 Q5 **Daqin Tal** *Nei Mongol* China
131 L6 **Daqiu** *Fujian* China
144 G5 **Dāq Mashī** Iran
144 F4 **Daqq-e Dombūn** Iran
132 L6 **Daquan** *Gansu* China
128 C5 **Daquanwan** *Xinjiang* China
149 L6 **Dāqūq** Iraq
131 N3 **Daqu Shan** *i.* China
144 C6 **Dara** *i.* Iran
228 B3 **Dara** Senegal
150 E6 **Dar'ā** Syria
150 E6 **Dar'ā** *governorate* Syria
275 E5 **Daraá** *r.* Brazil
144 F7 **Dārāb** Iran
145 N6 **Daraban** Pak.
219 O2 **Darabani** Romania
230 E3 **Daradou** C.A.R.
114 D5 **Daraga** *Luzon* Phil.
225 G3 **Dārah, Jabal** *mt.* Egypt
160 L8 **Darahanava** Belarus
145 N3 **Daraim** Afgh.
235 □K2 **Daraina** Madag.
224 A2 **Daraj** Libya
144 H9 **Darak** Iran
144 F7 **Dārākūyeh** Iran
114 E6 **Daram** *i.* Phil.
144 D5 **Dārān** Iran
199 G6 **Darány** Hungary
232 E2 **Darar** Eth.
121 J1 **Darasun** Rus. Fed.
143 O4 **Darat** Kazakh.
143 O8 **Daraut-Korgon** Kyrg.
Daraut-Kurgan Kyrg. *see* **Daraut-Korgon**
225 G3 **Darāw** Egypt
229 H4 **Darazo** Nigeria
144 G6 **Darband** Iran
145 J7 **Darband** *Balochistan* Pak.
145 N3 **Darband** *North West Frontier* Pak.
143 L8 **Darband** Uzbek.
144 G6 **Darband, Kūh-e** *mt.* Iran
144 I3 **Darband-e Hajjī Boland** Turkm.
160 E5 **Darbėnai** Lith.
202 D5 **Dar Ben Karricha el Behri** Morocco
139 J6 **Darbhanga** *Bihar* India
262 G3 **Darby** *MT* U.S.A.
258 E5 **Darby** *PA* U.S.A.
244 G2 **Darby, Cape** *AK* U.S.A.
244 G2 **Darby Mountains** *AK* U.S.A.
169 B8 **Darby's Bridge** Ireland
130 B2 **Darcang** *Sichuan* China
211 C7 **Dar Chabanne** Tunisia
202 D5 **Dar Chaoui** Morocco
246 F5 **D'Arcy** *B.C.* Can.
210 G3 **Darda** Croatia
261 I8 **Dardanelle** *AR* U.S.A.
264 M3 **Dardanelle** *CA* U.S.A.
261 I8 **Dardanelle, Lake** *AR* U.S.A.
Dardanelles *str.* Turkey *see* **Çanakkale Boğazı**
191 K7 **Dardesheim** Ger.
Dardo *Sichuan* China *see* **Kangding**
213 J3 **Darè** Italy
Dar el Beida Morocco *see* **Casablanca**
148 H4 **Darende** Turkey
233 C6 **Dar es Salaam** Tanz.
144 F7 **Dārestān** *Kermān* Iran
144 H7 **Dārestān** *Kermān* Iran
105 I6 **Dareton** *N.S.W.* Austr.
144 G5 **Dāreyn, Kūh-e** *mt.* Iran
103 G10 **Darfield** *South I.* N.Z.
212 I4 **Darfo Boario Terme** Italy
145 N4 **Dargai** Pak.
102 H2 **Dargaville** *North I.* N.Z.
197 J1 **Dargin, Jezioro** *l.* Pol.
105 K7 **Dargo** *Vic.* Austr.
229 F3 **Dargol** Niger
192 G3 **Dargun** Ger.
128 I2 **Darhan** Mongolia
Darhan Muminggan Lianheqi *Nei Mongol* China *see* **Bailingmiao**
221 K2 **Darıca** Turkey
221 L1 **Darıçayırı** Turkey
221 J3 **Darıcı** Turkey
259 I2 **Darien** *CT* U.S.A.
255 G10 **Darien** *GA* U.S.A.
274 B2 **Darién, Golfo del** *g.* Col.
266 □U14 **Darién, Parque Nacional de** *nat. park* Panama
266 □T13 **Darién, Serranía del** *mts* Panama
145 K8 **Dariga** Pak.
129 M4 **Darīganga** Mongolia
151 A7 **Darıkent** Turkey
143 O3 **Dar'inskiy** Kazakh.
142 D2 **Dar'inskoye** Kazakh.
266 □P11 **Darío** Nic.
221 K5 **Darıveren** Turkey
Darīya Kazakh. *see* **Dar'inskiy**
147 M4 **Darīz** Oman
Darjeeling *W. Bengal* India *see* **Darjiling**
139 L6 **Darjiling** *W. Bengal* India
109 D12 **Darkan** *W.A.* Austr.
104 F5 **Darke Peak** *S.A.* Austr.
144 C6 **Darkhazīneh** Iran
144 C6 **Dārkhovīn** Iran
169 I4 **Darkley** *Northern Ireland* U.K.
238 □2a **Dark Slope Crater** *Ascension* S. Atlantic Ocean
130 B2 **Darlag** *Qinghai* China
105 H6 **Darling** *r. N.S.W.* Austr.
236 C9 **Darling** S. Africa
107 L9 **Darling Downs** *hills Qld* Austr.
191 K7 **Darlingerode** Ger.
243 K2 **Darling Peninsula** *Nunavut* Can.
109 C13 **Darling Range** *hills W.A.* Austr.
171 N4 **Darlington** *Darlington, England* U.K.
171 N4 **Darlington** *admin. div. England* U.K.
258 C5 **Darlington** *MD* U.S.A.
255 H8 **Darlington** *SC* U.S.A.
250 D7 **Darlington** *WI* U.S.A.
237 J9 **Darlington Dam** *resr* S. Africa
105 K6 **Darlington Point** *N.S.W.* Austr.
109 F9 **Darlot, Lake** *salt flat W.A.* Austr.
165 M7 **Darłówko** Pol.
165 M7 **Darłowo** Pol.
219 O4 **Dărmănești** Romania
133 E11 **Darma Pass** China/India
136 F3 **Darmaraopet** *Andhra Prad.* India
144 H5 **Darmīān** Iran
194 F2 **Darmstadt** Ger.
191 G11 **Darmstadt** *admin. reg.* Ger.
138 E9 **Darna** *r.* India
224 D1 **Darnah** Libya
237 P5 **Darnall** S. Africa
178 B5 **Darnétal** France
179 L7 **Darney** France
105 I5 **Darnick** *N.S.W.* Austr.
179 L7 **Darnieulles** France
208 K3 **Darnius** Spain
287 E2 **Darnley, Cape** Antarctica
245 P1 **Darnley Bay** *N.W.T.* Can.
205 R6 **Daroca** Spain
131 L6 **Darong** *Fujian* China
156 H4 **Darovka** Rus. Fed.
156 I4 **Darovskoy** Rus. Fed.
144 G8 **Dar Pahn** Iran
204 C5 **Darque** Port.
107 I7 **Darr** *watercourse Qld* Austr.
168 L7 **Darra** *Aberdeenshire, Scotland* U.K.
169 D7 **Darragh** Ireland
285 F5 **Darregueira** Arg.
144 G5 **Darreh Bīd** Iran
144 H3 **Darreh Gaz** Iran
Darreh Gozaru *r.* Iran *see* **Gīzeh Rūd**
144 F6 **Darreh-ye Bāhābād** Iran
144 B5 **Darreh-ye Shahr** Iran
232 D3 **Darro** *watercourse* Eth.
207 M6 **Darro** Spain
147 K9 **Darsa** *i.* Yemen
136 F5 **Darsi** *Andhra Prad.* India
192 F2 **Darß** *pen.* Ger.
192 G2 **Darßer Ort** *c.* Ger.
172 E7 **Dart** *r. England* U.K.
150 E2 **Dār Ta'izzah** Syria
Dartang *Xizang* China *see* **Baqên**
173 M5 **Dartford** *Kent, England* U.K.
172 E7 **Dartington** *Devon, England* U.K.
172 E6 **Dartmeet** *Devon, England* U.K.
104 H7 **Dartmoor** *Vic.* Austr.
172 D6 **Dartmoor** *hills England* U.K.
172 E6 **Dartmoor National Park** *England* U.K.
249 I4 **Dartmouth** *N.S.* Can.
172 E7 **Dartmouth** *Devon, England* U.K.
107 J9 **Dartmouth, Lake** *salt flat Qld* Austr.
105 K7 **Dartmouth Reservoir** *Vic.* Austr.
171 N6 **Darton** *South Yorkshire, England* U.K.
113 J8 **Daru** P.N.G.
228 C5 **Daru** Sierra Leone
225 G5 **Daru** *waterhole* Sudan
115 F2 **Daruba** *Maluku* Indon.
126 A5 **Daruga-mine** *mt.* Japan
210 F3 **Daruvar** Croatia
168 H11 **Darvel** *East Ayrshire, Scotland* U.K.
128 D3 **Darvi** *Govĭ-Altay* Mongolia
128 C3 **Darvi** *Hovd* Mongolia
161 U3 **Darvinskiy Gosudarstvennyy Zapovednik** *nature res.* Rus. Fed.
144 D7 **Darvīshī** Iran
145 N2 **Darvoz, Qatorkŭhi** *mts* Tajik.
145 L6 **Darwazgai** Afgh.
171 M6 **Darwen** *Blackburn with Darwen, England* U.K.
235 F3 **Darwendale** Zimbabwe
145 K6 **Darweshan** Afgh.
138 F9 **Darwha** *Mahar.* India
284 E6 **Darwin** Arg.
106 C2 **Darwin** *N.T.* Austr.
283 F8 **Darwin** Falkland Is
283 B7 **Darwin, Canal** *sea chan.* Chile
283 C9 **Darwin, Monte** *mt.* Chile
274 □ **Darwin, Volcán** *vol. Islas Galápagos* Ecuador
Darwin Island *Islas Galápagos* Ecuador *see* **Culpepper, Isla**
145 N6 **Darya Khan** Pak.
142 K5 **Dar'yalyktakyr, Ravnina** *plain* Kazakh.
224 D1 **Daryānah** Libya
Dar"yoi Amu *r.* Asia *see* **Amudar'ya**
Dar"yoi Sir *r.* Asia *see* **Syrdar'ya**
133 I10 **Darzhuo** *Xizang* China
144 H7 **Dārzīn** Iran
147 K3 **Dās** *i.* U.A.E.
138 C8 **Dasada** *Gujarat* India
129 N7 **Dasha He** *r.* China
139 J9 **Dashapalla** *Orissa* India
197 M6 **Dashava** Ukr.
129 N2 **Dashbalbar** Mongolia
129 K6 **Dashetai** *Nei Mongol* China
Dashhowuz Turkm. *see* **Daşoguz**
129 R6 **Dashiqiao** *Liaoning* China
128 B5 **Dashitou** *Xinjiang* China
158 I4 **Dashiv** Ukr.
129 Q3 **Dashizhai** *Nei Mongol* China
161 N8 **Dashkawka** Belarus
Dashkesan Azer. *see* **Daşkäsän**
Dashkhovuz *Dashoguzskaya Oblast'* Turkm. *see* **Daşoguz**
Dashkhovuz Oblast *admin. div.* Turkm. *see* **Daşoguz**
Dashköpri Turkm. *see* **Daşköpri**
144 G3 **Dasht** Iran
145 I9 **Dasht** *r.* Pak.
144 G3 **Dashtak** Iran
Dashtak Qal'ehsi Iran *see* **Dashtak**
144 E7 **Dasht-e Palang** *r.* Iran
145 I9 **Dashtiari** Iran
143 M7 **Dashtobod** Uzbek.
128 J8 **Dashuikeng** *Ningxia* China
128 F8 **Dashuiqiao** *Qinghai* China
128 I8 **Dashuitou** *Gansu* China
198 E1 **Dašice** Czech Rep.
195 K5 **Dasing** Ger.
145 P5 **Daska** Pak.
151 H5 **Daşkäsän** Azer.
236 G9 **Daskop** S. Africa
145 J3 **Daşköpri** Turkm.
192 G2 **Daskow** Ger.
144 H1 **Daşoguz** *Dashoguzskaya Oblast'* Turkm.
144 H1 **Daşoguz** *admin. div.* Turkm.
130 E5 **Dasongshu** *Yunnan* China
145 O3 **Daspar** *mt.* Pak.
229 F5 **Dassa** Benin
114 C8 **Dassalan** *i.* Phil.
191 I7 **Dassel** Ger.
190 J4 **Dassendorf** Ger.
236 C9 **Dassen Island** S. Africa
190 K3 **Dassow** Ger.
144 F8 **Dastakān, Ra's-e** *pt* Iran
151 H6 **Dastakert** Armenia
144 H5 **Dastgerd** Iran
144 G4 **Dastgerdān** Iran
122 G7 **Da Suifen He** *r.* China
138 E4 **Dasuya** *Punjab* India
237 M2 **Dasville** S. Africa
197 H3 **Daszyna** Pol.
117 K4 **Datadian** *Kalimantan* Indon.
221 I6 **Datça** Turkey
124 R4 **Date** Japan
265 S7 **Date Creek** *watercourse AZ* U.S.A.
265 S9 **Dateland** *AZ* U.S.A.
138 D9 **Datha** *Gujarat* India
138 G7 **Datia** *Madh. Prad.* India
131 K6 **Datian** *Fujian* China
131 H7 **Datian Ding** *mt. Guangdong* China
263 K9 **Datil** *NM* U.S.A.
131 K3 **Datong** *Anhui* China
Datong *Fujian* China *see* **Tong'an**
122 D6 **Datong** *Heilong.* China
128 G8 **Datong** *Qinghai* China
129 M6 **Datong** *Shanxi* China
128 H8 **Datong He** *r.* China
128 F8 **Datong Shan** *mts* China
122 L4 **Datta** Rus. Fed.
145 M5 **Datta Khel** Pak.
136 F2 **Dattapur** *Mahar.* India
191 D7 **Datteln** Ger.
191 J8 **Datterode (Ringgau)** Ger.
117 H4 **Datu** *i.* Indon.
117 H3 **Datu, Tanjung** *c.* Indon./Malaysia
116 E5 **Datuk, Tanjung** *pt* Indon.
114 E8 **Datu Piang** *Mindanao* Phil.
139 M8 **Daudkandi** Bangl.
145 N5 **Daud Khel** Pak.
139 J7 **Daudnagar** *Bihar* India
160 I5 **Daudzeva** Latvia
160 H7 **Daugai** Lith.
160 I6 **Daugailiai** Lith.
160 H4 **Daugava** *r.* Latvia
alt. **Zakhodnyaya Dzvina,**
alt. **Zapadnaya Dvina,**
conv. **Western Dvina**
160 J6 **Daugavpils** Latvia
160 G5 **Daugyvenė** *r.* Lith.
145 L3 **Daulatābād** Afgh.
Daulatabad Iran *see* **Malāyer**
139 L8 **Daulatpur** Bangl.
274 B5 **Daule** Ecuador
185 G9 **Daumazan-sur-Arize** France
181 K6 **Daumeray** France
191 C10 **Daun** Ger.
136 D3 **Daund** *Mahar.* India
119 D8 **Daung Kyun** *i.* Myanmar
118 B3 **Daungyu** *r.* Myanmar
247 K5 **Dauphin** *Man.* Can.
183 H9 **Dauphin** France
258 B4 **Dauphin** *PA* U.S.A.
258 B4 **Dauphin County** *county PA* U.S.A.
183 G6 **Dauphiné** *reg.* France
183 G7 **Dauphiné, Alpes du** *mts* France
261 K10 **Dauphin Island** *AL* U.S.A.
247 L5 **Dauphin Lake** *Man.* Can.
229 H3 **Daura** Nigeria
109 C8 **Daurie Creek** *r. W.A.* Austr.
129 O2 **Dauriya** Rus. Fed.
129 L2 **Daurskiy Khrebet** *mts* Rus. Fed.
138 F6 **Dausa** *Rajasthan* India
119 H9 **Dâu Tiêng, Hô** *resr* Vietnam
191 G9 **Dautphetal-Friedensdorf** Ger.
191 G9 **Dautphetal-Holzhausen** Ger.
168 I8 **Dava** *Moray, Scotland* U.K.
151 J4 **Däväçi** Azer.
136 D5 **Davangere** *Karnataka* India
114 E8 **Davao** *Mindanao* Phil.
114 E8 **Davao Gulf** *Mindanao* Phil.
144 G6 **Dāvarān** Iran
144 G8 **Dāvarī** *Hormozgan* Iran
144 H8 **Dāvarī** *Hormozgan* Iran
145 J8 **Dāvar Panāh** Iran
237 N2 **Davel** S. Africa
254 B5 **Davenport** *IA* U.S.A.
257 K6 **Davenport** *NY* U.S.A.
262 E3 **Davenport** *WA* U.S.A.
107 H8 **Davenport Downs** *Qld* Austr.
106 E6 **Davenport Range** *hills N.T.* Austr.
106 E6 **Davenport Range National Park** *nat. park* Australia
173 J3 **Daventry** *Northamptonshire, England* U.K.
237 M2 **Daveyton** S. Africa
183 F6 **Davézieux** France
266 □R13 **David** Panama
260 G5 **David City** *NE* U.S.A.
247 J5 **Davidson** *Sask.* Can.
106 C6 **Davidson, Mount** *hill N.T.* Austr.
247 L4 **Davidson Lake** *Man.* Can.
245 L1 **Davidson Mountains** *AK* U.S.A.
258 B7 **Davidsonville** *MD* U.S.A.
104 B2 **Davies, Mount** *S.A.* Austr.
247 K3 **Davin Lake** *Sask.* Can.
280 D3 **Davinópolis** Brazil
168 H8 **Daviot** *Highland, Scotland* U.K.
287 F2 **Davis** *research stn* Antarctica
108 F6 **Davis** *r. W.A.* Austr.
Davis *i.* Myanmar *see* **Than Kyun**
264 K3 **Davis** *CA* U.S.A.
256 F9 **Davis** *WV* U.S.A.
256 F9 **Davis, Mount** *hill PA* U.S.A.
287 I2 **Davis Bay** Antarctica
265 R6 **Davis Dam** *AZ* U.S.A.
265 R6 **Davis Dam** *dam AZ* U.S.A.
249 I2 **Davis Inlet (abandoned)** *Nfld and Lab.* Can.
251 K6 **Davison** *MI* U.S.A.
287 G2 **Davis Sea** Antarctica
243 M3 **Davis Strait** Can./Greenland
220 D4 **Davleia** Greece
157 K5 **Davlekanovo** Rus. Fed.
199 H5 **Dávod** Hungary
217 K6 **Davoli** Italy
212 H2 **Davos** Switz.
151 J6 **Dāvūd Qeshlāqī** Iran
221 I5 **Davutlar** Turkey
256 D11 **Davy** *WV* U.S.A.
151 G2 **Davydenko** Rus. Fed.
158 G1 **Davyd-Haradok** Belarus
197 M6 **Davydiv** Ukr.
159 M6 **Davydiv Brid** Ukr.
159 O7 **Davydivka** Ukr.
Davydkovo Rus. Fed. *see* **Tolbukhino**
159 S2 **Davydovka** Rus. Fed.
161 V4 **Davydovo** Rus. Fed.
247 I3 **Davy Lake** *Sask.* Can.
129 R6 **Dawa** *Liaoning* China
133 G11 **Dawa Co** *l. Xizang* China
Dawahaidy *atoll Arch. des Tuamotu* Fr. Polynesia *see* **Ravahere**
146 G5 **Dawāsir** *reg.* Saudi Arabia
146 G5 **Dawāsir, Wādī ad** *watercourse* Saudi Arabia
232 D3 **Dawa Wenz** *r.* Eth.
133 G11 **Dawaxung** *Xizang* China
130 D3 **Dawê** *Sichuan* China
Dawei Myanmar *see* **Tavoy**
Dawei *r. mouth* Myanmar *see* **Tavoy**
115 G7 **Daweloor** *i. Maluku* Indon.
129 O9 **Dawen He** *r.* China
115 G7 **Dawera** *i. Maluku* Indon.
147 I2 **Dawhat Bilbul** *b.* Saudi Arabia
160 K7 **Dawhinava** Belarus
172 F6 **Dawlish** *Devon, England* U.K.
158 I2 **Dawlyady** Belarus
118 C6 **Dawna Taungdan** *mts* Myanmar/Thai.
Dawo *Qinghai* China *see* **Maqên**
147 L6 **Dawqah** Oman
146 E6 **Dawqah** Saudi Arabia
226 B4 **Dawra** Western Sahara
146 G8 **Ḍawrān** Yemen
169 E3 **Dawros Head** Ireland
107 L7 **Dawson** *r. Qld* Austr.
245 M2 **Dawson** *Y.T.* Can.
255 E10 **Dawson** *GA* U.S.A.
260 F2 **Dawson** *ND* U.S.A.
283 C9 **Dawson, Isla** *i.* Chile
246 G5 **Dawson, Mount** *B.C.* Can.
247 K4 **Dawson Bay** *Man.* Can.
246 F4 **Dawson Creek** *B.C.* Can.
247 M2 **Dawson Inlet** *Nunavut* Can.
245 L3 **Dawson Range** *mts Y.T.* Can.
246 E5 **Dawsons Landing** *B.C.* Can.
255 E8 **Dawsonville** *GA* U.S.A.
131 J3 **Dawu** *Hubei* China
130 C3 **Dawu** *Sichuan* China
Dawu Taiwan *see* **Tawu**
Dawukou *Ningxia* China *see* **Shizuishan**
131 J3 **Dawu Shan** *hill Hubei* China
133 J8 **Dawusi** *Qinghai* China
147 N5 **Dawwah** Oman
185 B8 **Dax** France
Daxian *Sichuan* China *see* **Dazhou**
130 F3 **Daxian** *Sichuan* China
130 D4 **Daxiang Ling** *mts Sichuan* China
132 H6 **Daxihaizi Shuiku** *resr* China
130 F7 **Daxin** *Guangdong* China
Daxing *Yunnan* China *see* **Ninglang**
Daxing *Yunnan* China *see* **Lüchun**
Daxue *Zhejiang* China *see* **Wencheng**
128 E6 **Daxue Shan** *mt.* China
130 C3 **Da Xueshan** *mts Sichuan* China
151 G3 **Day** Rus. Fed.
147 M3 **Ḍayah** U.A.E.
Dayan *Yunnan* China *see* **Lijiang**
133 K13 **Dayang** *r.* India
129 R7 **Dayang He** *r.* China
122 D3 **Dayangqi** *Nei Mongol* China
129 S2 **Dayangshu** *Nei Mongol* China
128 A2 **Dayan Nuur** *l.* Mongolia
130 C6 **Dayao** *Yunnan* China
130 H7 **Dayao Shan** *mts* China
228 E2 **Ḍâyat en Nahârât** *well* Mali
131 J3 **Daye** *Hubei* China
137 O2 **Dayegaung** Myanmar
130 D3 **Dayi** *Sichuan* China
130 E3 **Daying** *Sichuan* China
130 A6 **Daying Jiang** *r.* China
Dayishan *Jiangsu* China *see* **Guanyun**
151 G3 **Daykhokh, Gora** *mt.* Rus. Fed.
147 M3 **Dayl** Oman
105 J7 **Daylesford** *Vic.* Austr.
285 I2 **Daymán** Uru.
285 H2 **Daymán** *r.* Uru.
285 I2 **Daymán, Cuchilla del** *hills* Uru.
145 M4 **Dāymirdād** Afgh.
Dayong *Hunan* China *see* **Zhangjiajie**
150 D6 **Dayr Abū Sa'īd** Jordan
150 E5 **Dayr 'Alī** Syria
150 E4 **Dayr 'Aṭīyah** Syria
149 J6 **Dayr az Zawr** Syria
150 F2 **Dayr Ḥāfir** Syria
150 E3 **Dayr Shumayyil at Taḥtānī** Syria
225 F3 **Dayrūṭ** Egypt
247 H4 **Daysland** *Alta* Can.
250 A4 **Dayton** *MN* U.S.A.
256 A9 **Dayton** *OH* U.S.A.
255 E8 **Dayton** *TN* U.S.A.
261 H11 **Dayton** *TX* U.S.A.
256 G10 **Dayton** *VA* U.S.A.
262 F3 **Dayton** *WA* U.S.A.
255 G11 **Daytona Beach** *FL* U.S.
131 J6 **Dayu** *Jiangxi* China
117 K6 **Dayu** *Kalimantan* Indo
131 I6 **Dayu Ling** *mts* China
262 E4 **Dayville** *OR* U.S.A.
144 D8 **Dayyer** Iran
147 K3 **Dayyīna** *i.* U.A.E.
125 H13 **Dazaifu** Japan
144 A3 **Dazgir** Iran
129 M8 **Dazhai** *Shanxi* China
Dazhe *Guangdong* Chi **Pingyuan**
130 H9 **Dazhipo** *Hainan* China
Dazhongji *Jiangsu* Chi **Dafeng**
130 F3 **Dazhou** *Sichuan* China
130 H9 **Dazhou Dao** *i.* China
130 F3 **Dazhu** *Sichuan* China
128 C5 **Dazigou** *Xinjiang* Chin
221 K5 **Dazkırı** Turkey
130 E4 **Dazu** *Chongqing* China
130 E4 **Dazu Rock Carvings** *tc Chongqing* China
245 N3 **Ddhaw Gro Habitat Pr Area** *nature res. Y.T.* Car
236 I6 **De Aar** S. Africa
169 E7 **Dead** *r.* Ireland
257 □O3 **Dead** *r. ME* U.S.A.
250 G3 **Dead** *r. MI* U.S.A.
245 J1 **Deadhorse** *AK* U.S.A.
255 F11 **Deadman Bay** *FL* U.S.A
270 F2 **Deadman's Cay** *Long I.*
265 R7 **Dead Mountains** *NV* U
250 G3 **Dead River Storage Da** *MI* U.S.A.
150 D7 **Dead Sea** *salt l.* Asia
260 D3 **Deadwood** *SD* U.S.A.
106 D2 **Deaf Adder Creek** *r. N.*
109 J11 **Deakin** *W.A.* Austr.
173 O5 **Deal** *Kent, England* U.K
259 G4 **Deal** *NJ* U.S.A.
237 J4 **Dealesville** S. Africa
246 E4 **Dean** *r. B.C.* Can.
131 J4 **De'an** *Jiangxi* China
172 G4 **Dean, Forest of** *Englan*
246 E4 **Dean Channel** *B.C.* Ca
284 E2 **Deán Funes** Arg.
Deanuvuotna *inlet* Nor **Tanafjorden**
168 J9 **Dean Water** *r. Scotland*
251 K7 **Dearborn** *MI* U.S.A.
171 K4 **Dearham** *Cumbria, Eng*
171 O7 **Dearne** *r. England* U.K.
262 F3 **Deary** *ID* U.S.A.
245 O4 **Dease** *r. B.C.* Can.
245 Q2 **Dease Arm** *b. N.W.T.* C
245 O4 **Dease Lake** *B.C.* Can.
245 O4 **Dease Lake** *B.C.* Can.
242 H3 **Dease Strait** *Nunavut*
264 P5 **Death Valley** *CA* U.S.A.
264 O5 **Death Valley** *depr. CA* U
265 P5 **Death Valley Junction**
264 O5 **Death Valley National** *CA* U.S.A.
181 L3 **Deauville** France
262 J4 **Deaver** *WY* U.S.A.
151 I4 **Deavgay, Gora** *mt.* Rus.
139 L8 **Debagram** *W. Bengal* Ir
117 I4 **Debak** *Sarawak* Malays
159 R5 **Debal'tseve** Ukr.
Debal'tsovo Ukr. *see* **D**
130 F7 **Debao** *Guangxi* China
218 I9 **Debar** Macedonia
232 C1 **Debark** Eth.
244 H2 **Debauch Mountain** *AK*
147 J7 **Debay** *well* Yemen
247 J4 **Debden** *Sask.* Can.
226 E2 **Debdou** Morocco
271 □7 **Debe** Trin. and Tob.
237 N4 **De Beers Pass** S. Africa
173 O3 **Deben** *r. England* U.K.
173 O3 **Debenham** *Suffolk, Eng*
249 I4 **Debert** *N.S.* Can.
156 K4 **Debesy** Rus. Fed.
151 G4 **Debet** *r.* Armenia
197 J5 **Dębica** Pol.
186 G5 **De Biesbosch, Nationa** *nat. park* Neth.
227 G2 **Debila** Alg.
186 H4 **De Bilt** Neth.
153 Q3 **Debin** Rus. Fed.
197 J4 **Dęblin** Pol.
196 F1 **Dębnica Kaszubska** Po
197 I6 **Dębno** *Małopolskie* Pol.
196 C3 **Dębno** *Zachodniopomo*
228 D3 **Débo, Lac** *l.* Mali
245 K3 **Deborah, Mount** *AK* U.
109 E11 **Deborah East, Lake** *sal W.A.* Austr.
109 E11 **Deborah West, Lake** *sa W.A.* Austr.
197 I4 **Dęborzeczka** Pol.
197 L4 **Dębowa Kłoda** Pol.
197 H2 **Dębowa Łąka** Pol.
107 N1 **Deboyne Islands** P.N.G
232 C2 **Debre Birhan** Eth.
199 K4 **Debrecen** Hungary
232 C2 **Debre Markos** Eth.
232 C2 **Debre Sīna** Eth.
218 J9 **Debrešte** Macedonia
232 C2 **Debre Tabor** Eth.
232 C2 **Debre Werk'** Eth.
232 C2 **Debre Zeyit** Eth.
196 F2 **Debrzno** Pol.
196 D2 **Dębsko** Pol.
225 H6 **Debub** *prov.* Eritrea
225 I6 **Debubawī K'eyih Bahri** Eritrea
218 I8 **Deçan** *Deçan* Kosovo
Dečani *Deçan* Kosovo *s*
255 D8 **Decatur** *AL* U.S.A.
255 E9 **Decatur** *GA* U.S.A.
254 C6 **Decatur** *IL* U.S.A.
254 E5 **Decatur** *IN* U.S.A.
250 I7 **Decatur** *MI* U.S.A.
261 K9 **Decatur** *MS* U.S.A.
255 E8 **Decatur** *TN* U.S.A.
261 G9 **Decatur** *TX* U.S.A.
261 K8 **Decaturville** *TN* U.S.A.
185 I6 **Decazeville** France
136 E3 **Deccan** *plat.* India
248 E4 **Decelles, Lac** *resr Que.*
234 E4 **Deception** *watercourse*
107 N9 **Deception Bay** *Qld* Aus
Deception Island Vanu **Moso**
234 D4 **Deception Pans** *salt pa* Botswana
130 D5 **Dechang** *Sichuan* China
Decheng *Guangdong* Ch **Deqing**
199 G3 **Dechtice** Slovakia
214 B9 **Decimomannu** *Sardegr*
214 B9 **Decimoputzu** *Sardegna*
198 D1 **Děčín** Czech Rep.
182 F5 **Décines-Charpieu** Frar
182 C3 **Decize** France
262 K4 **Decker** *MT* U.S.A.
251 L6 **Deckerville** *MI* U.S.A.
186 G2 **De Cocksdorp** Neth.
217 K5 **Decollatura** Italy
250 C6 **Decorah** *IA* U.S.A.
106 D1 **De Courcy Head** *N.T.* A
199 H5 **Decs** Hungary
Dedang *Yunnan* China *s*
Dedap *i.* Indon. *see* **Pen**
118 B6 **Dedaye** Myanmar
173 J4 **Deddington** *Oxfordshire England* U.K.
221 K5 **Dedebağı** Turkey
100 □1 **Dededo** Guam
148 E5 **Dedegöl Dağları** *mts* Tu
191 K6 **Dedeleben** Ger.
221 L2 **Dedeler** Turkey
151 E6 **Dedeli** Turkey
192 I4 **Dedelow** Ger.
190 K5 **Dedelstorf** Ger.
186 J3 **Dedemsvaart** Neth.
232 D2 **Deder** Eth.

Dédestapolcsány Hungary
Dedham Essex, England U.K.
Dedidu Guam see Dededo
Dedinovo Rus. Fed.
Dedo de Deus mt. Brazil
De Doorns S. Africa
Dedop'listsqaro Georgia
Dédougou Burkina
Dedovichi Rus. Fed.
Dedurovka Rus. Fed.
Dedza Malawi
Dedza Mountain Malawi
Dee r. Ireland
Dee est. Wales U.K.
Dee r. England/Wales U.K.
Dee r. Scotland U.K.
Deeg Rajasthan India
Deel r. Ireland
Deel r. Ireland
Deel r. Ireland
Deele r. Ireland
Deelfontein S. Africa
Deensen Ger.
Deep Bay H.K. China see Shenzhen Wan
Deep Bight inlet W.A. Austr.
Deep Creek Lake MD U.S.A.
Deep Creek Range mts UT U.S.A.
Deeping St Nicholas Lincolnshire, England U.K.
Deep River Ont. Can.
Deep River CT U.S.A.
Deepwater N.S.W. Austr.
Deepwater NJ U.S.A.
Deer Creek r. CA U.S.A.
Deer Creek r. MD U.S.A.
Deer Creek Reservoir UT U.S.A.
Deerfield NJ U.S.A.
Deerfield OH U.S.A.
Deeri Somalia
Deering AK U.S.A.
Deering, Mount W.A. Austr.
Deer Island N.B. Can.
Deer Island AK U.S.A.
Deer Island ME U.S.A.
Deer Isle ME U.S.A.
Deer Lake Nfld and Lab. Can.
Deer Lake Ont. Can.
Deer Lake l. Ont. Can.
Deerlijk Belgium
Deer Lodge MT U.S.A.
Deer Park NY U.S.A.
Deer Park WA U.S.A.
Deerpass Bay N.W.T. Can.
Deesa Gujarat India see Disa
Deeth NV U.S.A.
Deetz Ger.
Defanovka Rus. Fed.
Defeng Guizhou China see Liping
Defensores del Chaco, Parque Nacional nat. park Para.
Defereggengebirge mts Austria
Defereggental val. Austria
Defferrari Arg.
Defiance OH U.S.A.
Defiance Plateau AZ U.S.A.
Défilé de Tosaye gorge Mali
Défirou well Niger
De Funiak Springs FL U.S.A.
Dégagnac France
Degana Rajasthan India
Degaña Spain
Degano r. Italy
Deganwy Conwy, Wales U.K.
Dêgê Sichuan China
Degebe r. Port.
Degeberga Sweden
Degeh Bur Eth.
Dégelis Que. Can.
Degema Nigeria
Degerfors Sweden
Deggendorf Ger.
Deggingen Ger.
Degh r. Pak.
Değirmenbaşı Turkey
Değirmencik r. Turkey
Değirmendere Turkey
Değirmenlidere Turkey
Değirmenlik Cyprus see Kythrea
Dego Italy
Degodia reg. Eth.
Degollado Mex.
De Grey W.A. Austr.
De Grey r. W.A. Austr.
De Groote Peel, Nationaal Park nat. park Neth.
Degtevo Rus. Fed.
Degtyarevka Rus. Fed.
De Haan Belgium
Dehaj Iran
Dehak Sīstān va Balūchestān Iran
Dehak Sīstān va Balūchestān Iran
Dehalak Desēt i. Eritrea
Deh'Ali Iran
De Hamert, Nationaal Park nat. park Neth.
De Hart Reservoir PA U.S.A.
Deh Bakrī Iran
Deh Barez Iran see Fāryāb
Deh-Dasht Iran
Dehdez Iran
Deh-e Kohneh Iran
Dehesa de Campoamor Spain
Dehesa de Montejo Spain
Deh-e Sard Iran
Dehesas de Guadix Spain
Dehestān Iran
Deh-e Zamān Iran
Dehgāh Iran
Deh Golān Iran
Dehi Afgh.
Dehiba Tunisia
Deh Khvājeh Iran
Dehkhvār-eqan Iran
Dehkūyeh Iran
Dehlorān Iran
Deh Mollā Iran
De Hoge Veluwe, Nationaal Park nat. park Neth.
De Hoop Nature Reserve S. Africa
De Hoop Vlei l. S. Africa
Dehpehk i. Pohnpei Micronesia
Dehqonobod Uzbek.
Dehra Dun Uttaranchal India
Dehri Bihar India
Dehrīz Iran
Deh Salm Iran
Deh Sheykh Iran
Deh Shū Afgh.
Deh Sūkhteh Iran
Dehua Fujian China
Dehui Jilin China
Deidesheim Ger.
Deifontes Spain
Deilão Port.
Deim Zubeir Sudan
Deining Ger.
Deiningen Ger.
Deinze Belgium
Deir-ez-Zor Syria see Dayr az Zawr
Deißlingen Ger.
Deiva Marina Italy
Dej Romania
Dejë, Mal mt. Albania
Dejen Eth.
Dejguny, Jezioro l. Pol.
Deji Xizang China see Rinbung
Dejiang Guizhou China
Deka Drum Zimbabwe
De Kalb IL U.S.A.
De Kalb MS U.S.A.
De Kalb TX U.S.A.
De Kalb Junction NY U.S.A.
Dekani Slovenia
De-Kastri Rus. Fed.
Dekemhare Eritrea
Dekese Dem. Rep. Congo
Deke Sokehs i. Pohnpei Micronesia
Dekhkanabad Uzbek. see Dehqonobod
Dekina Nigeria
187 F6 De Klinge Belgium
230 C3 Dékoa C.A.R.
186 G2 De Koog Neth.
186 G3 De Kooy Neth.
186 K3 De Krim Neth.
172 C6 Delabole Cornwall, England U.K.
285 G5 De la Garma Arg.
115 D8 Delaki Indon.
265 R4 Delamar Lake NV U.S.A.
106 C3 Delamere N.T. Austr.
171 L7 Delamere Cheshire, England U.K.
230 F2 Delami Sudan
258 F4 Delanco NJ U.S.A.
255 G11 De Land FL U.S.A.
264 M6 Delano CA U.S.A.
258 C3 Delano PA U.S.A.
265 T3 Delano Peak UT U.S.A.
100 □3b Delap i. Majuro Marshall Is
108 G9 De La Poer Range Nature Reserve res. Australia
100 □3b Delap-Uliga-Djarrit Majuro Marshall Is
145 J5 Delārām Afgh.
237 J2 Delareyville S. Africa
245 □C6 Delarof Islands AK U.S.A.
247 J4 Delaronde Lake Sask. Can.
250 E9 Delavan IL U.S.A.
250 F7 Delavan WI U.S.A.
258 E3 Delaware NJ U.S.A.
256 B8 Delaware OH U.S.A.
260 H6 Delaware r. KS U.S.A.
258 E5 Delaware r. NJ/PA U.S.A.
257 J10 Delaware state U.S.A.
257 J7 Delaware, East Branch r. NY U.S.A.
257 J7 Delaware, West Branch r. NY U.S.A.
257 J9 Delaware Bay DE/NJ U.S.A.
258 D5 Delaware City DE U.S.A.
258 E5 Delaware County county PA U.S.A.
258 E3 Delaware Water Gap PA U.S.A.
258 F2 Delaware Water Gap National Recreational Area park NJ/PA U.S.A.
249 G1 Delay r. Que. Can.
256 C11 Delbarton WV U.S.A.
230 F3 Delbeng Sudan
246 H5 Del Bonita Alta Can.
191 G7 Delbrück Ger.
246 H4 Delburne Alta Can.
284 E4 Del Campillo Arg.
219 K9 Delčevo Macedonia
186 K4 Delden Neth.
133 H12 Dêlêg Xizang China
105 L7 Delegate N.S.W. Austr.
204 I9 Deleitosa Spain
201 O7 Đelekovec Croatia
230 D2 Délembé C.A.R.
212 C1 Delémont Switz.
163 P6 Delet b. Fin.
264 J2 Delevan CA U.S.A.
256 G6 Delevan NY U.S.A.
280 D4 Delfinópolis Brazil
186 F4 Delft Neth.
136 F8 Delft Island Sri Lanka
186 K2 Delfzijl Neth.
264 H1 Delgada, Point CA U.S.A.
269 K6 Delgada, Punta pt Mex.
233 D7 Delgado, Cabo c. Moz.
128 E3 Delger Mongolia
128 I3 Delgerhaan Töv Mongolia
128 I4 Delgerhangay Mongolia
Delgermörön Mongolia see Hüreemaral
128 G2 Delger Mörön r. Mongolia
128 J3 Delgertsogt Mongolia
225 F4 Delgo Sudan
258 F6 Del Haven NJ U.S.A.
251 N7 Delhi Ont. Can.
128 E8 Delhi Qinghai China
138 F5 Delhi Delhi India
133 C12 Delhi admin. div. India
264 L4 Delhi CA U.S.A.
263 L8 Delhi CO U.S.A.
261 J9 Delhi LA U.S.A.
257 K6 Delhi NY U.S.A.
128 E8 Delhi Nongchang Qinghai China
116 F8 Deli i. Indon.
149 K4 Deli r. Turkey
216 F9 Delia Sicilia Italy
216 D8 Delia r. Sicilia Italy
217 J7 Delianuova Italy
148 G4 Delice Turkey
148 G3 Delice r. Turkey
271 □2 Delices Dominica
275 H3 Délices Fr. Guiana
215 O5 Deliceto Italy
269 I2 Delicias Mex.
144 D4 Delījān Iran
221 H4 Deliktaş Turkey
245 Q2 Délįne N.W.T. Can.
Delingha Qinghai China see Delhi
Delingha Nongchang Qinghai China see Delhi Nongchang
190 J3 Delingsdorf Ger.
247 J5 Delisle Sask. Can.
106 C2 Delissaville-Wagait-Larrakia Aboriginal Land res. N.T. Austr.
116 C3 Delitua Sumatera Indon.
193 F7 Delitzsch Ger.
200 H6 Dellach Austria
200 H6 Dellach im Drautal Austria
182 K1 Delle France
191 I7 Delligsen Ger.
212 I5 Dello Italy
260 G4 Dell Rapids SD U.S.A.
227 F1 Dellys Alg.
264 O9 Del Mar CA U.S.A.
257 J10 Delmar DE U.S.A.
237 M2 Delmas S. Africa
179 L6 Delme France
190 G4 Delmenhorst Ger.
258 F6 Delmont NJ U.S.A.
256 F8 Delmont PA U.S.A.
106 E7 Delmore Downs N.T. Austr.
210 E3 Delnice Croatia
263 K8 Del Norte CO U.S.A.
153 Q2 De-Longa, Ostrova is Novosibirskiye O-va Rus. Fed.
De Long Islands Novosibirskiye O-va Rus. Fed. see De-Longa, Ostrova
244 G1 De Long Mountains AK U.S.A.
De Long Strait Rus. Fed. see Longa, Proliv
105 K9 Deloraine Tas. Austr.
247 K5 Deloraine Man. Can.
171 M6 Delph Greater Manchester, England U.K.
220 D4 Delphi tourist site Greece
254 D5 Delphi IN U.S.A.
256 A8 Delphos OH U.S.A.
236 I4 Delportshoop S. Africa
255 G12 Delray Beach FL U.S.A.
266 D2 Del Río Mex.
261 E11 Del Rio TX U.S.A.
163 N6 Delsbo Sweden
229 G5 Delta state Nigeria
263 J7 Delta CO U.S.A.
256 A7 Delta OH U.S.A.
258 C5 Delta PA U.S.A.
265 T2 Delta UT U.S.A.
245 K2 Delta r. AK U.S.A.
275 F2 Delta Amacuro state Venez.
107 H4 Delta Downs Qld Austr.
228 A3 Delta du Saloum, Parc National du nat. park Senegal
245 K2 Delta Junction AK U.S.A.
261 K11 Delta National Wildlife Refuge nature res. LA U.S.A.
257 J5 Delta Reservoir NY U.S.A.
208 G6 Deltebre Spain
255 G11 Deltona FL U.S.A.
105 M3 Delungra N.S.W. Austr.
186 L4 De Lutte Neth.
128 B3 Delüün Bayan-Ölgiy Mongolia
138 C9 Delvada Gujarat India
285 G4 Del Valle Arg.
190 H2 Delve Ger.
169 H5 Delvin Ireland
220 B3 Delvinë Albania
158 D5 Delyatyn Ukr.
142 F1 Dema r. Rus. Fed.
117 I8 Demak Jawa Indon.
205 N4 Demanda, Sierra de la mts Spain
179 J6 Demange-aux-Eaux France
245 L1 Demarcation Point pt AK U.S.A.
Demavend mt. Iran see Damāvand, Qolleh-ye
231 D6 Demba Dem. Rep. Congo
231 B7 Demba Chio Angola
160 H6 Dembava Lith.
232 C2 Dembech'a Eth.
239 □3a Dembeni Njazidja Comoros
239 □3b Dembeni Mayotte
232 C2 Dembī Eth.
230 E3 Dembia C.A.R.
232 B2 Dembī Dolo Eth.
199 K3 Demecser Hungary
186 H4 De Meern Neth.
192 E3 Demen Ger.
187 F6 Demer r. Belgium
Demerara Guyana see Georgetown
288 F5 Demerara Abyssal Plain sea feature S. Atlantic Ocean
159 N9 Demerdzhi mt. Ukr.
161 O6 Demidov Rus. Fed.
161 X6 Demidovo Rus. Fed.
182 F3 Demigny France
263 K10 Deming NM U.S.A.
275 F5 Demini r. Brazil
275 F4 Demini, Serras do mts Brazil
221 J3 Demirci Manisa Turkey
151 A5 Demirci Trabzon Turkey
218 J9 Demir Hisar Macedonia
219 K9 Demir Kapija Macedonia
151 E5 Demirkent Turkey
221 J4 Demirköprü Barajı resr Turkey
219 P9 Demirköy Turkey
221 K4 Demirler r. Turkey
151 A5 Demirözü Turkey
148 F5 Demirtaş Antalya Turkey
221 K2 Demirtaş Bursa Turkey
237 I9 Demistkraal S. Africa
192 H3 Demmin Ger.
275 F6 Democracia Brazil
216 G8 Demone, Val di reg. Sicilia Italy
212 C7 Demonte Italy
255 D9 Demopolis AL U.S.A.
254 D5 Demotte IN U.S.A.
116 E7 Dempo, Gunung vol. Indon.
109 G12 Dempster, Point W.A. Austr.
245 M2 Dempster Highway Can.
138 G3 Dêmqog China
185 E8 Dému France
159 P5 Demuryne Ukr.
161 P6 Demyakhi Rus. Fed.
Dem'yanovka Kazakh. see Uzynkol'
156 I3 Dem'yanovo Rus. Fed.
161 P4 Demyansk Rus. Fed.
158 J3 Demydiv Ukr.
158 E3 Demydivka Ukr.
158 J6 Demydove Ukr.
159 R3 Demyno-Oleksandrivka Ukr.
236 F6 De Naawte S. Africa
178 F3 Denain France
264 L4 Denair CA U.S.A.
225 I6 Denakil reg. Eritrea/Eth.
245 K3 Denali AK U.S.A.
Denali AK U.S.A. see McKinley, Mount
245 K3 Denali Highway AK U.S.A.
245 J3 Denali National Park and Preserve AK U.S.A.
232 D3 Denan Eth.
247 K4 Denare Beach Sask. Can.
185 I8 Dénat France
248 E4 Denbigh Ont. Can.
172 F1 Denbigh Denbighshire, Wales U.K.
244 G2 Denbigh, Cape AK U.S.A.
172 F1 Denbighshire admin. div. Wales U.K.
186 F5 Den Bommel Neth.
Den Bosch Neth. see 's-Hertogenbosch
186 G2 Den Burg Neth.
171 N6 Denby Dale West Yorkshire, England U.K.
118 E6 Den Chai Thai.
117 G6 Dendang Indon.
228 D2 Dendâra Maur.
187 F7 Denderleeuw Belgium
187 F6 Dendermonde Belgium
186 H4 Den Dolder Neth.
187 F6 Dendre r. Belgium
186 H5 Den Dungen Neth.
186 L4 Denekamp Neth.
218 J8 Đeneral Janković Kaçanik Kosovo
246 E3 Denetiah Provincial Park nat. park B.C. Can.
156 L3 Denezhkin Kamen', Gora mt. Rus. Fed.
229 H3 Dengas Niger
114 □ Denges Passage Palau
129 M9 Dengfeng Henan China
133 G12 Dênggar Xizang China
229 H4 Dengi Nigeria
Dengjiabu Jiangxi China see Yujiang
Dêngka Gansu China see Têwo
Dêngkagoin Gansu China see Têwo
129 J6 Dengkou Nei Mongol China
133 L11 Dêngqên Xizang China
131 J7 Dengta Guangdong China
185 D9 Denguin France
230 D3 Denguiro C.A.R.
Dengxian Henan China see Dengzhou
133 E10 Dêngzê Xizang China
131 I2 Dengzhou Henan China
Dengzhou Shandong China see Penglai
Den Haag Neth. see 's-Gravenhage
109 B8 Denham W.A. Austr.
108 J3 Denham r. W.A. Austr.
186 K4 Den Ham Neth.
173 L4 Denham Buckinghamshire, England U.K.
270 □ Denham, Mount hill Jamaica
106 G4 Denham Island Qld Austr.
107 L7 Denham Range mts Qld Austr.
109 B8 Denham Sound sea chan. W.A. Austr.
186 G3 Den Helder Neth.
247 I4 Denholm Sask. Can.
168 K12 Denholm Scottish Borders, Scotland U.K.
171 N6 Denholme West Yorkshire, England U.K.
186 G2 Den Hoorn Neth.
209 F10 Dénia Spain
104 D5 Denial Bay S.A. Austr.
104 D5 Denial Bay b. S.A. Austr.
105 J6 Deniliquin N.S.W. Austr.
139 P6 Dening Arun. Prad. India
Deninoo Kue N.W.T. Can. see Fort Resolution
262 E6 Denio NV U.S.A.
159 K1 Deniskovichi Rus. Fed.
260 H4 Denison IA U.S.A.
261 G9 Denison TX U.S.A.
287 J2 Denison, Cape Antarctica
108 J5 Denison Plains W.A. Austr.
142 I1 Denisovka Kazakh.
136 G9 Deniyaya Sri Lanka
221 K5 Denizli Turkey
221 K5 Denizli prov. Turkey
183 J8 Denjuan, Sommet de mt. France
194 G4 Denkendorf Baden-Württemberg Ger.
195 K4 Denkendorf Bayern Ger.
194 F5 Denkingen Baden-Württemberg Ger.
194 G6 Denkingen Baden-Württemberg Ger.
195 J6 Denklingen Ger.
191 K6 Denkte Ger.
105 M5 Denman N.S.W. Austr.
287 G2 Denman Glacier Antarctica
109 D13 Denmark W.A. Austr.
164 G5 Denmark country Europe
250 G5 Denmark WI U.S.A.
Denmark Fjord inlet Greenland see Danmark Fjord
243 P3 Denmark Strait Greenland/Iceland
173 J6 Denmead Hampshire, England U.K.
271 □3 Dennery St Lucia
193 H7 Dennewitz Ger.
237 N1 Dennilton S. Africa
173 O3 Dennington Suffolk, England U.K.
108 J6 Dennis, Lake salt flat W.A. Austr.
256 D8 Dennison OH U.S.A.
258 F6 Dennisville NJ U.S.A.
168 I10 Denny Falkirk, Scotland U.K.
186 H3 Den Oever Neth.
143 L8 Denov Uzbek.
Denow Uzbek. see Denov
117 K9 Denpasar Bali Indon.
115 B5 Densongi Sulawesi Indon.
192 H4 Densow Ger.
212 D3 Dent Blanche mt. Switz.
183 E8 Dent de Rez hill France
187 D7 Dentergem Belgium
195 I3 Dentlein am Forst Ger.
171 M7 Denton Greater Manchester, England U.K.
258 D7 Denton MD U.S.A.
261 G9 Denton TX U.S.A.
183 J6 Dent Parrachée mt. France
109 C13 D'Entrecasteaux, Point W.A. Austr.
100 □5 D'Entrecasteaux, Récifs rf New Caledonia
113 L8 D'Entrecasteaux Islands P.N.G.
109 C13 D'Entrecasteaux National Park W.A. Austr.
212 B3 Dents du Midi mt. Switz.
173 M2 Denver Norfolk, England U.K.
262 L7 Denver CO U.S.A.
258 C4 Denver PA U.S.A.
248 E2 Denys r. Que. Can.
158 I2 Denysovychi Ukr.
194 D5 Denzlingen Ger.
139 J7 Deo Bihar India
138 F5 Deoband Uttar Prad. India
137 H3 Deobhog Chhattisgarh India
258 B4 Deodate PA U.S.A.
139 I7 Deogaon Uttar Prad. India
138 G9 Deogarh Madh. Prad. India
139 J9 Deogarh Orissa India
138 D7 Deogarh Rajasthan India
138 G7 Deogarh Uttar Prad. India
138 I8 Deogarh mt. Madh. Prad. India
139 K7 Deoghar Jharkhand India
138 G9 Deoli Mahar. India
139 K8 Deoli Orissa India
138 E7 Deolia Rajasthan India
184 H2 Déols France
138 G8 Deori Madh. Prad. India
139 I6 Deoria Uttar Prad. India
138 E2 Deosai, Plains of Pak.
138 I8 Deosil Chhattisgarh India
139 M6 Deothang Bhutan
122 E2 Dep r. Rus. Fed.
138 E8 Depalpur Madh. Prad. India
187 C6 De Panne Belgium
249 H2 De Pas, Rivière r. Que. Can.
250 F5 De Pere WI U.S.A.
256 G6 Depew NY U.S.A.
257 J6 Deposit NY U.S.A.
251 R2 Dépôt-Forbes Que. Can.
251 Q3 Dépôt-Rowanton Que. Can.
133 D9 Depsang Point hill Aksai Chin
250 E8 Depue IL U.S.A.
153 O3 Deputatskiy Rus. Fed.
133 J11 Dêqên Xizang China
133 J12 Dêqên Xizang China
Dêqên Xizang China see Dagzê
130 B4 Dêqên Yunnan China
131 H7 Deqing Guangdong China
131 M3 Deqing Zhejiang China
131 L3 Deqing Zhejiang China
261 H8 De Queen AR U.S.A.
261 I10 De Quincy LA U.S.A.
178 I6 Der, Lac du l. France
232 C2 Dera Eth.
138 F4 Dera Hima. Prad. India
145 M7 Dera Bugti Pak.
145 N6 Dera Ghazi Khan Pak.
225 G4 Deraheib reg. Sudan
145 N6 Dera Ismail Khan Pak.
145 N6 Derajat reg. Pak.
287 C2 Deram, Mount Antarctica
145 N7 Derawar Fort Pak.
158 F3 Derazhne Ukr.
158 G4 Derazhnya Ukr.
193 E6 Derben Ger.
151 J3 Derbent Rus. Fed.
221 L2 Derbent Kocaeli Turkey
221 J4 Derbent Manisa Turkey
221 K4 Derbent Uşak Turkey
Derbent Uzbek. see Darband
Derbesiye Turkey see Şenyurt
122 B3 Derbur Nei Mongol China
105 K9 Derby Tas. Austr.
108 G4 Derby W.A. Austr.
237 L1 Derby S. Africa
173 J2 Derby Derby, England U.K.
173 J2 Derby admin. div. England U.K.
259 I2 Derby CT U.S.A.
261 G7 Derby KS U.S.A.
257 M3 Derby Line VT U.S.A.
171 N7 Derbyshire admin. div. England U.K.
151 C5 Derebaşı Turkey
199 K4 Derecske Hungary
173 N2 Dereham Norfolk, England U.K.
150 A1 Dereiçi Turkey
199 J5 Derekegyház Hungary
150 A2 Dereköy Antalya Turkey
221 K5 Dereköy Denizli Turkey
221 K3 Dereköy Kütahya Turkey
191 K7 Derenburg Ger.
191 H7 Derental Ger.
224 D6 Déréssa Chad
161 P2 Dereva Rus. Fed.
159 O5 Derezuvate Ukr.
169 H3 Derg r. Ireland/U.K.
169 G3 Derg, Lough l. Ireland
169 F7 Derg, Lough l. Ireland
142 C2 Dergachi Rus. Fed.
Dergachi Ukr. see Derhachi
104 H7 Dergholm State Park nature res. Vic. Austr.
159 P3 Derhachi Ukr.
138 G7 Deri Uttar Prad. India
261 I10 De Ridder LA U.S.A.
186 G3 De Rijp Neth.
149 J5 Derik Turkey
151 B6 Derinçay Turkey
151 B6 Derindere Turkey
148 G4 Derinkuyu Turkey
159 M5 Deriyivka Ukr.
232 D4 Derkali well Kenya
159 S5 Derkul r. Rus. Fed./Ukr.
191 J9 Dermbach Ger.
Derna Libya see Darnah
199 L4 Derna Romania
234 B5 Dernberg, Cape Namibia
151 B5 Dernekpazarı Turkey
158 E3 Derno Ukr.
130 B4 Dêrong Sichuan China
180 G3 Déroute, Passage de la str. Channel Is/France
142 C9 Derow Iran
169 H5 Derravaragh, Lough l. Ireland
235 H3 Derre Moz.
169 D4 Derreen Ireland
169 C9 Derreendaragh Ireland
169 D9 Derreeny Bridge Ireland
169 F4 Derry Ireland
169 I7 Derry r. Ireland
Derry Northern Ireland U.K. see Londonderry
257 N6 Derry NH U.S.A.
Derrybeg Ireland see Doirí Beaga
169 E6 Derrybrien Ireland
169 D6 Derryerglinna Ireland
169 G4 Derrygonnelly Northern Ireland U.K.
169 F7 Derrygoolin Ireland
169 C6 Derrylea Ireland
170 B5 Derrylin Northern Ireland U.K.
169 G4 Derrynacreeve Ireland
169 D9 Derrynasaggart Mountains hills Ireland
170 C5 Derrynawilt Northern Ireland U.K.
Derryrush Ireland see Doire Iorrais
170 E5 Derrytrasna Northern Ireland U.K.
169 F3 Derryveagh Mountains hills Ireland
219 O3 Dersca Romania
173 N2 Dersingham Norfolk, England U.K.
129 M5 Derst Nei Mongol China
128 G6 Derstei Nei Mongol China
190 D5 Dersum Ger.
133 D10 Dêrub Xizang China
225 H5 Derudeb Sudan
236 G9 De Rust S. Africa
215 I2 Deruta Italy
168 D9 Dervaig Argyll and Bute, Scotland U.K.
180 H6 Derval France
220 D4 Derveni Greece
210 F3 Derventa Bos.-Herz.
212 G3 Dervio Italy
105 K10 Derwent r. Tas. Austr.
173 J2 Derwent r. Derbyshire, England U.K.
171 P6 Derwent r. England U.K.
171 N7 Derwent Reservoir Derbyshire, England U.K.
171 N4 Derwent Reservoir Durham/Northumberland, England U.K.
171 K4 Derwent Water l. England U.K.
159 O1 Deryugino Rus. Fed.
161 R5 Derzha r. Rus. Fed.
142 E1 Derzhavino Rus. Fed.
143 L2 Derzhavinsk Kazakh.
Derzhavinskiy Kazakh. see Derzhavinsk
219 L7 Desa Romania
284 D3 Desaguadero Arg.
284 D4 Desaguadero r. Arg.
276 C4 Desaguadero r. Bol.
284 C4 Desague, Cerro mt. Arg.
284 D1 Desagües de los Colorados marsh Arg.
183 F7 Désaignes France
212 E5 Desana Italy
101 □9 Désappointement, Îles du is Arch. des Tuamotu Fr. Polynesia
261 J8 Des Arc AR U.S.A.
264 O2 Desatoya Mountains NV U.S.A.
251 K3 Desbarats Ont. Can.
173 K3 Desborough Northamptonshire, England U.K.
284 B4 Descabezado, Volcán vol. Chile
277 F4 Descalvado Mato Grosso Brazil
280 D4 Descalvado São Paulo Brazil
204 H8 Descargamaría Spain
184 F2 Descartes France
247 K4 Deschambault Lake Sask. Can.
247 K4 Deschambault Lake l. Sask. Can.
262 D4 Deschutes r. OR U.S.A.
281 H2 Descombrimento, Parque Nacional do nat. park Brazil
232 C2 Desē Eth.
238 □3d Deseada vol. La Palma Canary Is
276 C5 Deseada Chile
283 D7 Deseado Arg.
283 D7 Deseado r. Arg.
199 G5 Deseda-tározó l. Hungary
270 B2 Desembarco del Granma National Park tourist site Cuba
266 C2 Desemboque Mex.
283 D8 Desengaño, Punta pt Arg.
213 J5 Desenzano del Garda Italy
265 T2 Deseret UT U.S.A.
265 T1 Deseret Peak UT U.S.A.
265 T1 Deseret Peak Wilderness nature res. UT U.S.A.
251 Q5 Deseronto Ont. Can.
251 R3 Désert, Lac l. Que. Can.
206 □ Deserta Grande i. Madeira
206 □ Desertas, Ilhas is Madeira
145 M7 Desert Canal Pak.
265 Q8 Desert Center CA U.S.A.
265 P8 Desert Hot Springs CA U.S.A.
182 B4 Désertines France
263 G8 Desert Lake NV U.S.A.
170 D4 Desertmartin Northern Ireland U.K.
265 Q5 Desert National Wildlife Refuge nature res. NV U.S.A.
265 U5 Desert View AZ U.S.A.
207 M4 Desesperada mt. Spain
183 C6 Desges France
271 □2 Deshaies i. Guadeloupe
256 B7 Deshler OH U.S.A.
138 D6 Deshnok Rajasthan India
284 D2 Desiderio Tello Arg.
209 F7 Desierto hill Spain
266 B3 Desierto Central de Baja California, Parque Natural del nature res. Mex.
212 G4 Desio Italy
220 C3 Deskati Greece
201 I7 Deskle Slovenia
260 G3 De Smet SD U.S.A.
260 I5 Des Moines IA U.S.A.
261 D7 Des Moines NM U.S.A.
252 H2 Des Moines r. IA U.S.A.
158 H4 Desna r. Rus. Fed./Ukr.
159 J3 Desna r. Rus. Fed./Ukr.
158 J3 Desna Ukr.
219 L7 Desnățui r. Romania
161 Q7 Desnogorsk Rus. Fed.
161 Q7 Desnogorskoye Vodokhranilishche resr Rus. Fed.
283 C7 Desnudo, Cerro mt. Arg.
283 B9 Desolación, Isla i. Chile
114 E6 Desolation Point Phil.
264 L3 Desolation Valley Wilderness nature res. CA U.S.A.
250 C6 DeSoto WI U.S.A.
237 J9 Despatch S. Africa
128 C1 Despen Rus. Fed.
284 E2 Despeñaderos Arg.
250 G7 Des Plaines IL U.S.A.
218 J6 Despotovac Despotovac Serbia
239 □2 Desroches, Île i. Seychelles
193 F7 Dessau Ger.
187 H6 Dessel Belgium
182 J2 Dessoubre r. France
Dessye Eth. see Desē
186 J4 De Steeg Neth.
187 E6 Destelbergen Belgium
251 P1 Destor Que. Can.
104 F6 D'Estrees Bay S.A. Austr.
204 H4 Destriana Spain
245 M3 Destruction Bay Y.T. Can.
214 C7 Desulo Sardegna Italy
276 A6 Desventuradas, Islas is S. Pacific Ocean
178 C2 Desvres France
196 D3 Deszczno Pol.
199 J5 Deszk Hungary
218 J5 Deta Romania
246 H2 Detah N.W.T. Can.
161 T7 Detchino Rus. Fed.
235 E3 Dete Zimbabwe
190 E4 Detern Ger.
220 A2 Deti Jon b. Albania/Greece
218 I7 Đetinja r. Serbia
199 J4 Detk Hungary
199 G6 Detkovac Croatia
191 G7 Detmold Ger.
191 G7 Detmold admin. reg. Ger.
250 H4 Detour, Point MI U.S.A.
251 K4 De Tour Village MI U.S.A.
265 R5 Detrital Wash watercourse AZ U.S.A.
251 K7 Detroit MI U.S.A.
251 K8 Detroit Beach MI U.S.A.
260 H2 Detroit Lakes MN U.S.A.
Dett Zimbabwe see Dete
195 I2 Dettelbach Ger.
194 G4 Dettingen an der Erms Ger.
195 I5 Dettingen an der Iller Ger.
192 G2 Dettmannsdorf Ger.
191 K6 Dettum Ger.
179 N6 Dettwiller France
119 G7 Det Udom Thai.
199 I3 Detva Slovakia
105 L6 Deua National Park N.S.W. Austr.
193 F8 Deuben Ger.
178 E2 Deûle r. France
191 J8 Deuna Ger.
187 I6 Deurne Neth.
187 J8 Deutsch-Belgischer Naturpark nature res. Belgium
190 J4 Deutsch Evern Ger.
201 L5 Deutschfeistritz Austria
201 M6 Deutsch Goritz Austria
201 J6 Deutsch-Griffen Austria
192 G5 Deutschhof Ger.
201 N5 Deutsch Kaltenbrunn Austria
201 O4 Deutschkreutz Austria
Deutschland country Europe see Germany
201 L6 Deutschlandsberg Austria
191 B11 Deutsch-Luxemburgischer Naturpark nature res. Ger.
193 H9 Deutschneudorf Ger.
201 O3 Deutsch-Wagram Austria
193 F8 Deutzen Ger.
251 P3 Deux-Rivières Ont. Can.
181 K8 Deux-Sèvres dept France
219 K5 Deva Romania
205 K2 Deva r. Spain
Deva Cheshire, England U.K. see Chester
136 E4 Devadurga Karnataka India
136 F8 Devakottai Tamil Nadu India
261 J8 De Valls Bluff AR U.S.A.
Devana Aberdeen, Scotland U.K. see Aberdeen
136 E6 Devanhalli Karnataka India
136 F4 Devarkonda Andhra Prad. India
199 J4 Dévaványa Hungary
199 J4 Dévaványai park Hungary
Deve Bair pass Macedonia see Velbŭzhdki Prokhod
198 G4 Devecser Hungary
148 G4 Develi Turkey
186 J4 Deventer Neth.
212 E3 Devero r. Italy
168 K7 Deveron r. Scotland U.K.
183 D6 Devès, Chaîne du mts France
219 K6 Devesel Romania
151 E6 Devetaş Turkey
198 E2 Devét skal hill Czech Rep.
138 D8 Devgadh Baria Gujarat India
136 C4 Devgarh Mahar. India
Devghar Jharkhand India see Deoghar
138 C6 Devikot Rajasthan India
178 I4 Deville France
244 F2 Devil Mountain hill AK U.S.A.
103 G7 Devil River Peak South I. N.Z.
261 E11 Devils r. TX U.S.A.
103 H8 Devil's Backbone mt. South I. N.Z.
169 G7 Devil's Bit Mountain hill Ireland
172 E3 Devil's Bridge Ceredigion, Wales U.K.
264 M3 Devil's Gate pass CA U.S.A.
250 D2 Devil's Island WI U.S.A.
260 F1 Devil's Lake ND U.S.A.
261 E11 Devil's Lake l. TX U.S.A.
245 N4 Devil's Paw mt. AK U.S.A.
264 M4 Devil's Peak CA U.S.A.
270 F1 Devil's Point Cat I. Bahamas
238 □2a Devil's Riding School vol. crater Ascension S. Atlantic Ocean
245 N4 Devil's Thumb mt. Can./U.S.A.
219 M9 Devin Bulg.
261 F11 Devine TX U.S.A.
159 R2 Devitsa r. Rus. Fed.
173 I5 Devizes Wiltshire, England U.K.
138 E7 Devli Rajasthan India
250 A1 Devlin Ont. Can.
219 P7 Devnya Bulg.
271 □3 De Volet Point St Vincent
218 H10 Devoll r. Albania
183 H7 Dévoluy mts France
251 K2 Devon Ont. Can.
237 M2 Devon S. Africa
172 E6 Devon admin. div. England U.K.
171 P7 Devon r. England U.K.
168 I10 Devon r. Scotland U.K.
243 I2 Devon Island Nunavut Can.
105 K9 Devonport Tas. Austr.
264 O7 Devore CA U.S.A.
285 F2 Devoto Arg.
148 E3 Devrek Turkey
157 F8 Devrekâni Turkey
148 G3 Devrez r. Turkey
136 C4 Devrukh Mahar. India
116 A3 Dewa, Tanjung pt Indon.
117 M7 Dewakang Besar i. Indon.
139 L7 Dewanganj Bangl.
138 F8 Dewas Madh. Prad. India
186 J3 De Weerribben, Nationaal Park nat. park Neth.
232 D2 Dewelē Eth.
237 K5 Dewetsdorp S. Africa
271 □1 Dewey Puerto Rico
186 J3 De Wijk Neth.
261 J8 De Witt AR U.S.A.
260 J5 De Witt IA U.S.A.
257 I5 DeWitt NY U.S.A.
171 N6 Dewsbury West Yorkshire, England U.K.
131 K4 Dexing Jiangxi China
133 L12 Dêxing Xizang China
257 □P3 Dexter ME U.S.A.
251 K7 Dexter MI U.S.A.
250 B6 Dexter MN U.S.A.
261 K7 Dexter MO U.S.A.
263 L10 Dexter NM U.S.A.
257 I4 Dexter NY U.S.A.
250 D5 Dexterville WI U.S.A.
130 E3 Deyang Sichuan China
104 C3 Dey-Dey Lake salt flat S.A. Austr.
144 G5 Deyhūk Iran
159 N3 Deykalivka Ukr.
144 C3 Deylaman Iran
144 H5 Deym Iran
165 R7 Deyma r. Rus. Fed.
Deynau Turkm. see Galkynyş
113 I8 Deyong, Tanjung pt Papua Indon.
144 C6 Dez r. Iran
144 C5 Dez, Sadd-e resr Iran
205 P6 Deza Spain
204 D3 Deza r. Spain
245 M3 Dezadeash Lake Y.T. Can.
144 C5 Dezfūl Iran
153 U3 Dezhneva, Mys c. Rus. Fed.
129 O8 Dezhou Shandong China
Dezhou Sichuan China see Dechang
Dezh Shāhpūr Iran see Marīvān
199 L5 Dezna Romania
212 I4 Dezzo r. Italy
151 D3 Dghnorisa Georgia
151 D4 Dghvani Georgia
139 I6 Dhabarau Uttar Prad. India
139 J6 Dhading Nepal
225 G2 Dhahab Egypt
150 C10 Dhahab, Marsá b. Egypt
146 F5 Dhahab, Wādī watercourse Saudi Arabia
150 D6 Dhahab, Wādī adh r. Syria
147 J7 Dhaḩawn, Wādī r. Yemen
150 C7 Dhāhiriya West Bank
146 G3 Dhahlān, Jabal hill Saudi Arabia
Dhahran Saudi Arabia see Aẓ Ẓahrān
139 M8 Dhaka Bangl.
139 M8 Dhaka admin. div. Bangl.
139 K8 Dhalbhum reg. Jharkhand India
139 M8 Dhaleswari r. Bangl.
139 N7 Dhaleswari r. India
136 D4 Dhalgaon Mahar. India
Dhali Cyprus see Dali
146 G8 Dhamār Yemen
146 G8 Dhamār governorate Yemen
139 K9 Dhamara Orissa India
138 E8 Dhamnod Madh. Prad. India
138 G7 Dhamoni Madh. Prad. India
138 G5 Dhampur Uttar Prad. India
138 H9 Dhamtari Chhattisgarh India
145 M9 Dhana Pak.
145 N6 Dhana Sar Pak.
139 K8 Dhanbad Jharkhand India
138 D8 Dhandhuka Gujarat India
138 D7 Dhanera Gujarat India
138 H5 Dhangarhi Nepal
138 H5 Dhang Range mts Nepal
139 K6 Dhankuta Nepal
138 E5 Dhansia Rajasthan India
136 F8 Dhanushkodi Tamil Nadu India
138 F3 Dhaola Dhar mts India
138 E9 Dhaoli Madh. Prad. India
138 E8 Dhar Madh. Prad. India
137 I3 Dharakota Orissa India
138 D9 Dharampur Gujarat India
139 K6 Dharan Bazar Nepal
136 E7 Dharapuram Tamil Nadu India
145 M8 Dhareja Pak.
138 C9 Dhari Gujarat India
139 N7 Dharmanagar Tripura India
136 F6 Dharmapuri Tamil Nadu India
136 E5 Dharmavaram Andhra Prad. India
139 I8 Dharmjaygarh Chhattisgarh India
138 E4 Dharmkot Punjab India
139 K9 Dharmsala Orissa India
232 F2 Dharoor watercourse Somalia
105 M5 Dharug National Park N.S.W. Austr.
136 E3 Dharur Mahar. India
136 D5 Dharwad Karnataka India
Dharwar Karnataka India see Dharwad
138 F3 Dharwas Hima. Prad. India
138 C9 Dhasa Gujarat India
138 G7 Dhasan r. Madh. Prad. India
148 H9 Dhāt al Ḩājj Saudi Arabia
139 I5 Dhaulagiri mt. Nepal
138 G7 Dhaura Uttar Prad. India
138 H6 Dhaurahra Uttar Prad. India
Dhávlia Greece see Davleia
Dhawlagiri mt. Nepal see Dhaulagiri
Dhebar Lake India see Jaisamand Lake
150 B3 Dhekelia Sovereign Base Area military base Cyprus
139 N6 Dhekiajuli Assam India
139 O6 Dhemaji Assam India
139 J9 Dhenkanal Orissa India
Dheskáti Greece see Deskati
Dhiafánion Karpathos Greece see Diafani
Dhiakoptón Greece see Diakofto
150 D7 Dhībān Jordan
Dhídhima Greece see Didyma
Dhidhimótikhon Greece see Didymoteicho
135 □1 Dhiffushi i. N. Male Maldives
135 □1 Dhigufinolhu i. S. Male Maldives
139 N6 Dhing Assam India
Dhíorix Korínthou b. Greece see Korinthou, Dioryga
149 M8 Dhī Qār governorate Iraq
150 E7 Dhirwah, Wādī adh watercourse Jordan
Dhodhekánisos is Greece see Dodekanisa
Dhofar admin. reg. Oman see Ẓufār
Dhokós i. Greece see Dokos
138 C9 Dhola Gujarat India
138 D8 Dholera Gujarat India
138 D8 Dholka Gujarat India
138 F6 Dholpur Rajasthan India
Dhomokós Greece see Domokos
136 E5 Dhone Andhra Prad. India
232 D4 Dhoomadheere Somalia
170 I5 Dhoon Isle of Man
138 C9 Dhoraji Gujarat India
138 B8 Dhori Gujarat India
Dhragonádha i. Greece see Dragonada
Dhragónisos i. Greece see Tragonisi
138 C8 Dhrangadhra Gujarat India
138 C8 Dhrol Gujarat India
194 B2 Dhron Ger.
Dhrosiá Greece see Drosia
146 F9 Dhubāb Yemen
139 L7 Dhubri Assam India
Dhuburi Assam India see Dhubri
145 O5 Dhudial Pak.
138 E9 Dhule Mahar. India
Dhulia Mahar. India see Dhule
139 K7 Dhulian W. Bengal India
145 O5 Dhulian Pak.
138 G8 Dhuma Madh. Prad. India
139 J6 Dhunche Nepal
232 F2 Dhuudo Somalia
232 E3 Dhuusa Marreeb Somalia
146 D2 Dhuwaybān basin Saudi Arabia
Dhytikí Ellás admin. reg. Greece see Dytiki Ellada
Dhytikí Makedhonía admin. reg. Greece see Dytiki Makedonia
220 G7 Dia i. Greece
183 K8 Diable, Cime du mt. France
270 □ Diablo, Mount hill Jamaica
264 K4 Diablo, Mount CA U.S.A.
266 B2 Diablo, Picacho del mt. Mex.
264 K4 Diablo Range mts CA U.S.A.
233 C7 Diaca Moz.
280 D5 Diadema São Paulo Brazil
221 I7 Diafani Karpathos Greece
228 D3 Diafarabé Mali
284 B2 Diaguitas Chile
228 D3 Diaka r. Mali
220 D4 Diakofto Greece
228 C3 Diakon Mali
199 G3 Diakovce Slovakia
228 C3 Dialafara Mali
228 B3 Dialakoto Senegal
228 E3 Diallassagou Mali
271 □3 Diamant, Rocher du i. Martinique
285 G3 Diamante Arg.
284 D4 Diamante r. Arg.
215 P8 Diamante Italy
284 C4 Diamante, Laguna l. Arg.
284 C4 Diamante, Pampa del plain Arg.
285 G3 Diamante, Parque Nacional nat. park Arg.
107 G9 Diamantina watercourse Qld Austr.
275 F6 Diamantina Amazonas Brazil
281 F3 Diamantina Minas Gerais Brazil
278 E5 Diamantina, Chapada plat. Brazil
289 K7 Diamantina Deep sea feature Indian Ocean
107 H7 Diamantina Gates National Park Qld Austr.
107 H7 Diamantina Lakes Qld Austr.
280 A2 Diamantino Mato Grosso Brazil
277 F3 Diamantino Mato Grosso Brazil
280 A2 Diamantino r. Brazil
139 L8 Diamond Harbour W. Bengal India
264 □D12 Diamond Head HI U.S.A.
264 □D12 Diamond Head HI U.S.A.
107 M4 Diamond Islets Coral Sea Is Terr. Austr.
265 Q2 Diamond Peak NV U.S.A.
264 L3 Diamond Springs CA U.S.A.
264 O8 Diamond Valley Lake resr CA U.S.A.
262 I6 Diamondville WY U.S.A.
228 C3 Diamou Mali
228 B3 Diamounguél Senegal
238 □2b Diana's Peak hill St Helena
131 H8 Dianbai Guangdong China
Dianbu Anhui China see Feidong
130 C6 Diancang Shan mt. Yunnan China
130 D6 Dian Chi l. China
228 C3 Diandioumé Mali
214 D3 Diane, Étang de lag. Corse France
107 L3 Diane Bank sea feature Coral Sea Is Terr. Austr.
228 C3 Diangounté Kamara Mali
228 C5 Diani r. Guinea
130 F3 Dianjiang Chongqing China
212 E6 Diano d'Alba Italy
212 E8 Diano Marina Italy
278 D4 Dianópolis Brazil
228 D4 Dianra Côte d'Ivoire
Dianyang Yunnan China see Shidian

129 R5 Diaobingshan Liaoning China
129 P8 Diaokou Shandong China
122 G6 Diaoling Heilong. China
229 F3 Diapaga Burkina
150 A4 Diarizos r. Cyprus
228 C4 Diatifèrè Guinea
220 D2 Diavata Greece
137 M6 Diavolo, Mount hill Andaman & Nicobar Is India
285 G3 Díaz Arg.
234 B5 Diaz Point Namibia
147 M3 Dibā al Ḥiṣn U.A.E.
147 N4 Ḍibab Oman
Dibang r. India see Dingba Qu
231 D6 Dibaya Dem. Rep. Congo
231 C6 Dibaya-Lubwe Dem. Rep. Congo
224 E6 Dibbis Sudan
173 J6 Dibden Hampshire, England U.K.
221 J4 Dibek Dağı mt. Turkey
229 I2 Dibella well Niger
236 G3 Dibeng S. Africa
232 D2 Dībīlē Eth.
146 E2 Ḍibīy, Jabal hills Saudi Arabia
239 □3a Dibouani Njazidja Comoros
158 I2 Dibrova Kyivs'ka Oblast' Ukr.
158 G2 Dibrova Zhytomyrs'ka Oblast' Ukr.
139 O6 Dibrugarh Assam India
Dibse Syria see Dibsī
150 G3 Dibsī Syria
274 C2 Dibulla Col.
190 F5 Dickel Ger.
261 E9 Dickens TX U.S.A.
257 □P1 Dickey ME U.S.A.
260 D2 Dickinson ND U.S.A.
255 D7 Dickson TN U.S.A.
258 D2 Dickson City PA U.S.A.
162 □ Dickson Land reg. Svalbard
149 K5 Dicle r. Turkey alt. Dijlah, Nahr (Iraq/Syria), conv. Tigris
213 L8 Dicomano Italy
232 C4 Dida Galgalu reg. Kenya
146 G2 Dīdah well Saudi Arabia
186 J5 Didam Neth.
173 J4 Didcot Oxfordshire, England U.K.
191 J6 Didderse Ger.
227 H4 Dider Alg.
151 G3 Didi Borbalo, Mt'a Georgia
114 D2 Didicas i. Phil.
228 C3 Didiéni Mali
151 D3 Didi Inch'khuri Georgia
151 D3 Didi Jikhaishi Georgia
151 F4 Didi Lilo Georgia
232 B3 Didinga Hills Sudan
158 I3 Didivshchyna Ukr.
233 D5 Dido waterhole Kenya
246 H5 Didsbury Alta Can.
232 C3 Didu Eth.
138 E6 Didwana Rajasthan India
235 □K3 Didy Madag.
220 E5 Didyma Greece
221 H1 Didymoteicho Greece
160 J6 Didžiasalis Lith.
160 H7 Didžiulis l. Lith.
183 G7 Die France
191 D10 Dieblich Ger.
228 E4 Diébougou Burkina
194 F2 Dieburg Ger.
199 L5 Dieci Romania
Dieciséis de Julio Arg. see 16 de Julio
Diecisiete de Agosto Arg. see 17 de Agosto
Diedenhofen France see Thionville
195 J5 Diedorf Bayern Ger.
191 J8 Diedorf Thüringen Ger.
247 I5 Diefenbaker, Lake Sask. Can.
184 I5 Diège r. France
205 J7 Diego Álvaro Spain
283 B8 Diego de Almagro, Isla i. Chile
285 F4 Diego de Alvear Arg.
289 I5 Diego Garcia atoll B.I.O.T.
271 □7 Diego Martin Trin. and Tob.
283 C9 Diego Ramirez, Islas is Chile
Diégo Suarez Madag. see Antsirañana
228 C3 Diégrâga well Maur.
228 C5 Diéké Guinea
192 F3 Diekhof Ger.
191 I6 Diekholzen Ger.
187 J9 Diekirch Lux.
187 I9 Diekirch admin. dist. Lux.
212 E1 Dielsdorf Switz.
228 C3 Diéma Mali
228 A3 Diembéreng Senegal
191 H7 Diemel r. Ger.
191 G8 Diemelsee park Ger.
191 G8 Diemel-Stausee resr Ger.
186 G4 Diemen Neth.
182 G5 Diémoz France
Điên Biên Vietnam see Điên Biên Phu
118 F4 Điên Biên Phu Vietnam
118 G5 Diên Châu Vietnam
194 E2 Dienheim Ger.
119 I8 Diên Khanh Vietnam
183 B6 Dienne France
160 H5 Dienvidsusēja r. Latvia
178 I7 Dienville France
191 G6 Diepenau Ger.
187 H7 Diepenbeek Belgium
186 K4 Diepenheim Neth.
186 J4 Diepenveen Neth.
190 F5 Diepholz Ger.
178 B4 Dieppe France
271 □2 Dieppe Bay Town St Kitts and Nevis
236 H6 Dieput S. Africa
191 E9 Dierdorf Ger.
186 J4 Dieren Neth.
192 F2 Dierhagen, Ostseebad Ger.
261 H8 Dierks AR U.S.A.
190 K5 Diesdorf Ger.
193 F8 Dieskau Ger.
195 J2 Diespeck Ger.
186 H6 Diessen Neth.
195 K6 Dießen am Ammersee Ger.
212 F1 Diessenhofen Switz.
187 H7 Diest Belgium
201 J3 Dietachdorf Austria
195 I5 Dietenheim Ger.
195 J3 Dietenhofen Ger.
195 N4 Dietersburg Ger.
195 L3 Dietfurt an der Altmühl Ger.
212 E1 Dietikon Switz.
194 F5 Dietingen Ger.
201 K2 Dietmanns Niederösterreich Austria
201 L2 Dietmanns Niederösterreich Austria
195 I6 Dietmannsried Ger.
195 L6 Dietramszell Ger.
245 J2 Dietrich Camp AK U.S.A.
191 G10 Dietzenbach Ger.
191 F9 Dietzhölztal-Ewersbach Ger.
179 J5 Dieue-sur-Meuse France
183 G7 Dieulefit France
179 L6 Dieulouard France
179 M6 Dieuze France
160 I7 Dieveniškės Lith.
186 J3 Diever Neth.
201 K6 Diex Austria
191 F10 Diez Ger.
207 M6 Diezma Spain
229 I3 Diffa Niger
229 I2 Diffa dept Niger
187 I9 Differdange Lux.
146 D7 Difnein i. Eritrea
232 E3 Dig well Eth.
229 F3 Diga Diga well Niger
137 I3 Digapahandi Orissa India
230 E3 Digba Dem. Rep. Congo
139 O6 Digboi Assam India
249 H4 Digby N.S. Can.
163 M6 Digerbergen hill Sweden
164 J1 Digerberget hill Sweden
138 E6 Diggi Rajasthan India
139 K9 Digha W. Bengal India
151 F4 Dighomi Georgia
260 E6 Dighton KS U.S.A.
136 E3 Diglur Mahar. India
184 E4 Dignac France
213 N3 Dignano Italy
183 I8 Digne-les-Bains France
178 B6 Digny France
182 D4 Digoin France
114 D3 Digollorin Point Luzon Phil.
213 N2 Digòn r. Italy
151 E5 Digor Turkey
151 F2 Digora Rus. Fed.
114 E8 Digos Mindanao Phil.
138 F9 Digras Mahar. India
145 M9 Digri Pak.
113 I8 Digul r. Papua Indon.
128 F7 Diguojiadan Qinghai China
228 E5 Digya National Park Ghana
133 L13 Dihang r. India alt. Jamuna (Bangladesh), alt. Yarlung Zangbo (China), conv. Brahmaputra
249 H1 Dihourse, Lac l. Que. Can.
197 M5 Dihtiv Ukr.
159 L3 Dihtyari Ukr.
146 C4 Diib, Wadi watercourse Sudan
229 I4 Diibao Cameroon
232 D4 Diinsoor Somalia
142 J5 Diirmentobe Kazakh.
149 M8 Dijlah, Nahr r. Iraq/Syria alt. Dicle (Turkey), conv. Tigris
187 G7 Dijle r. Belgium
182 G2 Dijon France
Dijon airport France see Longvic
230 C2 Dik Chad
162 N4 Dikanäs Sweden
151 I6 Dīkdāsh Iran
138 E7 Diken Madh. Prad. India
232 D2 Dikhil Djibouti
139 O6 Dikho r. India
221 H3 Dikili Turkey
187 C7 Dikkebus Belgium
151 G3 Diklosmta mt. Rus. Fed.
151 D5 Dikmeköyü Turkey
228 D4 Dikodougou Côte d'Ivoire
187 C6 Diksmuide Belgium
152 J2 Dikson Rus. Fed.
229 I3 Dikwa Nigeria
232 C3 Dīla Eth.
207 L6 Dilar Spain
207 L6 Dilar r. Spain
144 H6 Dilaram Iran
187 F7 Dilbeek Belgium
151 B5 Dilek Dağı mt. Turkey
221 I5 Dilek Yarımadası Milli Parkı nat. park Turkey
230 E4 Dili Dem. Rep. Congo
115 D8 Dili East Timor
229 I3 Dilia watercourse Niger
151 F5 Dilijan Armenia
151 F5 Dilijan Argelanots' nature res. Armenia
119 I9 Di Linh Vietnam
103 H9 Dilion Cone mt. South I. N.Z.
151 E4 Dilit'i Georgia
Dilizhan Armenia see Dilijan
191 F9 Dillenburg Ger.
261 F11 Dilley TX U.S.A.
228 D3 Dilli Mali
164 G2 Dilling Norway
225 F6 Dilling Sudan
194 B3 Dillingen (Saar) Ger.
195 I4 Dillingen an der Donau Ger.
244 H4 Dillingham AK U.S.A.
106 D3 Dillinya Aboriginal Land res. N.T. Austr.
247 I4 Dillon Sask. Can.
247 I4 Dillon r. Alta/Sask. Can.
262 H4 Dillon MT U.S.A.
255 H8 Dillon SC U.S.A.
251 Q9 Dillsburg PA U.S.A.
256 G11 Dillwyn VA U.S.A.
231 D7 Dilolo Dem. Rep. Congo
221 G5 Dilos i. Greece
187 I6 Dilsen Belgium
149 L7 Diltāwa Iraq
229 I5 Dimako Cameroon
139 N7 Dimapur Nagaland India
213 J3 Dimaro Italy
268 A2 Dimas Mex.
150 E5 Dimashq Syria
150 F5 Dimashq governorate Syria
231 D6 Dimbelenge Dem. Rep. Congo
228 D5 Dimbokro Côte d'Ivoire
105 I7 Dimboola Vic. Austr.
107 J4 Dimbulah Qld Austr.
244 G2 Dime Landing AK U.S.A.
220 D3 Diminio Greece
Dimitrov Ukr. see Dymytrov
219 N8 Dimitrovgrad Bulg.
157 J5 Dimitrovgrad Rus. Fed.
219 K7 Dimitrovgrad Dimitrovgrad Serbia
Dimitrovo Bulg. see Pernik
261 D8 Dimmitt TX U.S.A.
258 D1 Dimock PA U.S.A.
150 D7 Dīmona Israel
114 E6 Dinagat i. Phil.
114 E7 Dinagat Sound sea chan. Phil.
139 L7 Dinajpur Bangl.
217 K6 Dinami Italy
180 G5 Dinan France
138 E3 Dinanagar Punjab India
228 E3 Dinangourou Mali
187 G8 Dinant Belgium
139 J7 Dinapur Bihar India
221 L4 Dinar Turkey
144 D6 Dīnār, Kūh-e mt. Iran
210 F3 Dinara mt. Bos.-Herz.
210 F3 Dinara Planina mts Bos.-Herz./Croatia
180 G4 Dinard France
Dinaric Alps mts Bos.-Herz./Croatia see Dinara Planina
232 C4 Dinas well Kenya
172 C3 Dinas Head Wales U.K.
172 F5 Dinas Powys Vale of Glamorgan, Wales U.K.
Dinbych Denbighshire, Wales U.K. see Denbigh
Dinbych-y-Pysgod Pembrokeshire, Wales U.K. see Tenby
231 B8 Dinde Angola
225 G6 Dinder r. Sudan
146 B9 Dinder el Agaliyin r. Sudan
225 G6 Dinder National Park Sudan
136 F4 Dindi r. India
136 E7 Dindigul Tamil Nadu India
229 H4 Dindima Nigeria
235 G4 Dindiza Moz.
138 H8 Dindori Madh. Prad. India
138 D9 Dindori Mahar. India
180 C5 Dinéault France
221 M3 Dinek Eskişehir Turkey
148 F5 Dinek Konya Turkey
231 C6 Dinga Dem. Rep. Congo
145 O5 Dinga Pak.
114 C4 Dingalan Bay Luzon Phil.
130 H9 Ding'an Hainan China
139 O6 Dingba Qu r. India
129 J8 Dingbian Shaanxi China
131 J3 Dingbujie Anhui China
Dingcheng Anhui China see Dingyuan
Dingcheng Hainan China see Ding'an
231 B6 Dinge Angola
180 H5 Dingé France
191 J8 Dingelstädt Ger.
133 G10 Dinggo Xizang China
116 E6 Dingin, Bukit mt. Indon.
139 K6 Dingla Nepal
Dingle Ireland see An Daingean
169 B8 Dingle pen. Ireland
169 B8 Dingle Bay Ireland
217 □ Dingli Malta
258 F2 Dingmans Ferry PA U.S.A.
131 J6 Dingnan Jiangxi China
107 L7 Dingo Qld Austr.
195 N4 Dingolfing Ger.
Dingping Sichuan China see Linshui
130 B4 Ding Qu r. Sichuan China
114 C2 Dingras Luzon Phil.
132 H3 Dingshan Xinjiang China
129 N9 Dingtao Shandong China
228 C4 Dinguiraye Guinea
249 I4 Dingwall N.S. Can.
168 H7 Dingwall Highland, Scotland U.K.
128 I9 Dingxi Gansu China
Dingxian Hebei China see Dingzhou
129 M7 Dingxiang Shanxi China
128 F6 Dingxin Gansu China
129 N7 Dingxing Hebei China
131 K2 Dingyuan Anhui China
129 N7 Dingzhou Hebei China
129 Q8 Dingzi Gang b. China
132 K7 Dingzikou Qinghai China
119 H10 Đinh An, Cửa r. mouth Vietnam
139 L6 Dinhata W. Bengal India
118 H4 Dinh Lâp Vietnam
113 J8 Dini, Mount P.N.G.
169 H7 Dinin r. Ireland
186 K3 Dinkel r. Neth.
195 I3 Dinkelsbühl Ger.
195 J5 Dinkelscherben Ger.
190 F5 Dinklage Ger.
265 U6 Dinnebito Wash watercourse AZ U.S.A.
168 K8 Dinnet Aberdeenshire, Scotland U.K.
133 H12 Dinngyê Xizang China
171 O7 Dinnington South Yorkshire, England U.K.
215 P8 Dino, Isola di i. Italy
234 E4 Dinokwe Botswana
265 W1 Dinosaur CO U.S.A.
262 J6 Dinosaur National Monument nat. park CO U.S.A.
159 S8 Dinskaya Rus. Fed.
191 C7 Dinslaken Ger.
186 F5 Dinteloord Neth.
186 H5 Dinther Neth.
116 F7 Dintiteladas Sumatera Indon.
264 M5 Dinuba CA U.S.A.
256 H11 Dinwiddie VA U.S.A.
186 J5 Dinxperlo Neth.
228 D3 Dioïla Mali
183 G7 Diois, Massif du mts France
244 E2 Diomede AK U.S.A.
228 C4 Dion r. Guinea
224 D5 Diona well Chad
281 F3 Dionísio Brazil
279 B8 Dionísio Cerqueira Brazil
183 E9 Dions France
280 B2 Diorama Brazil
Dioscurias Georgia see Sokhumi
199 H4 Diósd Hungary
219 K3 Diosig Romania
199 I4 Diósjenő Hungary
Diospolis Magna tourist site Egypt see Thebes
182 D3 Diou France
228 A3 Diouloulou Senegal
228 C3 Dioumara Mali
229 F3 Dioundiou Niger
228 D3 Dioura Mali
228 A3 Diourbel Senegal
145 O6 Dipalpur Pak.
138 H5 Dipayal Nepal
139 N7 Diphu Assam India
215 Q9 Dipignano Italy
Dipkarpaz Cyprus see Rizokarpason
145 M9 Diplo Pak.
114 D7 Dipolog Mindanao Phil.
187 J9 Dippach Lux.
107 L6 Dipperu National Park Qld Austr.
191 I9 Dipperz Ger.
193 I9 Dippoldiswalde Ger.
103 C12 Dipton South I. N.Z.
Dipu Zhejiang China see Anji
229 I5 Dir Cameroon
145 N4 Dir Pak.
145 O4 Dir reg. Pak.
224 B6 Dira well Chad
147 L3 Dīrah U.A.E.
139 N6 Dirang Arun. Prad. India
228 E2 Diré Mali
107 I2 Direction, Cape Qld Austr.
136 C3 Direction Bank sea feature India
108 □2 Direction Island Cocos Is
232 D2 Dirē Dawa Eth.
220 E4 Dirfys mts Greece
160 G2 Dirhami Estonia
266 □P12 Diriamba Nic.
231 D9 Dirico Angola
216 G9 Dirillo r. Sicilia Italy
221 K6 Dirimii Geçidi pass Turkey
180 C5 Dirinon France
109 B8 Dirk Hartog Island W.A. Austr.
229 I2 Dirkou Niger
186 G3 Dirkshorn Neth.
186 F5 Dirksland Neth.
195 J5 Dirlewang Ger.
194 E2 Dirmstein Ger.
224 E6 Dirra Sudan
105 L3 Dirranbandi Qld Austr.
171 M2 Dirrington Great Law hill Scotland U.K.
146 F6 Ḍirs Saudi Arabia
Dirschau Pol. see Tczew
144 C6 Dīrsīyeh Iran
265 V4 Dirty Devil r. UT U.S.A.
138 D7 Disa Gujarat India
139 O6 Disang r. India
286 T2 Disappointment, Cape Antarctica
283 □ Disappointment, Cape S. Georgia
262 B3 Disappointment, Cape WA U.S.A.
109 G7 Disappointment, Lake salt flat W.A. Austr.
Disappointment Islands Arch. des Tuamotu Fr. Polynesia see Désappointement, Îles du
249 I2 Disappointment Lake Nfld and Lab. Can.
195 I4 Dischingen Ger.
104 H8 Discovery Bay b. Vic. Austr.
Discovery Bay b. H.K. China see Tai Pak Wan
270 □ Discovery Bay Jamaica
104 H8 Discovery Bay Coastal Park nature res. Vic. Austr.
288 J8 Discovery Seamounts sea feature S. Atlantic Ocean
212 F2 Disentis Muster Switz.
212 H3 Disgrazia, Monte mt. Italy
144 D6 Dīshmūk Iran
225 G3 Dishnā Egypt
244 H3 Dishna r. AK U.S.A.
Disko i. Greenland see Qeqertarsuaq
Disko Bugt b. Greenland see Qeqertarsuup Tunua
162 □ Diskobukta b. Svalbard
221 M4 Dişli Turkey
106 H5 Dismal Creek r. Qld Austr.
287 D2 Dismal Mountains Antarctica
257 I12 Dismal Swamp VA U.S.A.
178 E6 Disneyland Resort Paris tourist site France
217 O3 Diso Italy
187 I7 Dison Belgium
134 H6 Dispur Assam India
256 H11 Disputanta VA U.S.A.
249 G4 Disraëli Que. Can.
173 O3 Diss Norfolk, England U.K.
146 E7 Dissān i. Saudi Arabia
181 L8 Dissay France
181 L6 Dissay-sous-Courcillon France
191 F6 Dissen am Teutoburger Wald Ger.
228 E4 Dissin Burkina
171 J4 Distington Cumbria, England U.K.
274 E2 Distrito Capital admin. dist. Venez.
280 D1 Distrito Federal admin. dist. Brazil
269 H6 Distrito Federal admin. dist. Mex.
148 E8 Disūq Egypt
114 C6 Dit i. Phil.
193 D7 Ditfurt Ger.
236 G4 Ditloung S. Africa
216 I9 Dittaino r. Sicilia Italy
191 J10 Dittelbrunn Ger.
195 J3 Dittenheim Ger.
173 M5 Ditton Kent, England U.K.
194 G4 Ditzingen Ger.
138 C9 Diu Daman India
114 E7 Diuata Mountains Mindanao Phil.
114 E7 Diuata Point Mindanao Phil.
201 I8 Divača Slovenia
144 B4 Dīvān Darreh Iran
220 B4 Divarata Kefallonia Greece
Divehi country Indian Ocean see Maldives
230 B5 Divénié Congo
212 E3 Diveria r. Italy
181 K3 Dives r. France
181 K3 Dives-sur-Mer France
157 H5 Diveyevo Rus. Fed.
136 G5 Divi, Point India
Divichi Azer. see Däväçi
262 H4 Divide MT U.S.A.
245 L3 Divide Mountain AK U.S.A.
258 E6 Dividing Creek NJ U.S.A.
217 I7 Divieto Sicilia Italy
114 D3 Divilacan Bay Luzon Phil.
199 I3 Divín Slovakia
199 H2 Divina Slovakia
281 F4 Divinésia Brazil
281 E4 Divinópolis Brazil
178 E3 Divion France
280 B2 Divisões, Serra das mts Brazil
Divisor, Sierra de mts Peru see Ultraoriental, Cordillera
220 A2 Divjaka nat. park Albania
157 H7 Divnoye Rus. Fed.
159 O7 Divnyns'ke Ukr.
228 D5 Divo Côte d'Ivoire
161 O6 Divo Rus. Fed.
182 I4 Divonne-les-Bains France
206 C3 Divor r. Port.
206 D3 Divor, Barragem do resr Port.
221 H7 Divounia i. Greece
148 I4 Divriği Turkey
231 D7 Divuma Dem. Rep. Congo
156 L4 Div'ya Rus. Fed.
145 L8 Diwana Pak.
Diwaniyah Iraq see Ad Dīwānīyah
212 C3 Dix, Lac des l. Switz.
228 E5 Dixcove Ghana
257 □O4 Dixfield ME U.S.A.
178 F7 Dixmont France
257 □P4 Dixmont ME U.S.A.
264 K3 Dixon CA U.S.A.
250 E8 Dixon IL U.S.A.
262 G3 Dixon MT U.S.A.
245 N5 Dixon Entrance sea channel Can./U.S.A.
270 F1 Dixon's San Salvador Bahamas
284 E4 Dixonville Arg.
246 G3 Dixonville Alta Can.
257 N3 Dixville Que. Can.
149 K4 Diyadin Turkey
149 L6 Diyālá governorate Iraq
149 L7 Diyālá, Nahr r. Iraq
149 J5 Diyarbakır Turkey
138 C7 Diyodar Gujarat India
145 J8 Diz Pak.
Dizak Iran see Dāvar Panāh
229 H6 Dizangué Cameroon
144 F4 Diz Chah Iran
Dize Turkey see Yüksekova
130 H4 Dizhuang Hunan China
256 B12 Dizney KY U.S.A.
178 G5 Dizy France
178 H4 Dizy-le-Gros France
229 I6 Dja r. Cameroon
229 I6 Dja, Réserve du nature res. Cameroon
224 B4 Djado Niger
224 B4 Djado, Plateau du Niger
Djakarta Jawa Indon. see Jakarta
227 G2 Djamâa Alg.
231 D7 Djamba Katanga Dem. Rep. Congo
231 D7 Djamba Katanga Dem. Rep. Congo
230 B5 Djambala Congo
230 C5 Djampie Dem. Rep. Congo
229 I5 Djampiel Cameroon
227 H4 Djanet Alg.
100 □3b Djarrit i. Majuro Marshall Is
Djarrit-Uliga-Dalap Majuro Marshall Is see Delap-Uliga-Djarrit
113 L7 Djaul Island P.N.G.
227 F4 Djebr mt. Alg.
230 C2 Djébrène Chad
224 C6 Djédaa Chad
227 E4 Djedid well Alg.
227 F2 Djelfa Alg.
230 E3 Djéma C.A.R.
230 C2 Djèmber Chad
Djeneral Jankovič Kaçanik Kosovo see Đeneral Janković
228 D3 Djenné Mali
219 K6 Djerdap nat. park Serbia
224 B6 Djermaya Chad
231 D5 Djia Dem. Rep. Congo
228 E3 Djibo Burkina
228 D4 Djiborosso Côte d'Ivoire
232 D2 Djibouti country Africa
232 D2 Djibouti Djibouti
Djidjelli Alg. see Jijel
228 C3 Djiguéni Maur.
228 D5 Djiroutou Côte d'Ivoire
229 I5 Djohong Cameroon
230 C2 Djoli-Kera, Forêt Classée de nature res. Chad
230 D4 Djolu Dem. Rep. Congo
224 C6 Djombo Kibbit Chad
230 B4 Djoua r. Congo/Gabon
230 D3 Djoubissi C.A.R.
169 J6 Djouce Mountain hill Ireland
227 F5 Djoudem, Oued watercourse Alg.
229 F4 Djougou Benin
229 I6 Djoum Cameroon
230 C4 Djoumbélé Congo
230 B3 Djoumboli Cameroon
224 C6 Djourab, Erg du des. Chad
230 F4 Djugu Dem. Rep. Congo
231 C6 Djuma Dem. Rep. Congo
162 □F1 Djúpivogur Iceland
165 L1 Djurås Sweden
164 J3 Djurö nationalpark nat. park Sweden
165 M3 Djursö i. Sweden
138 E4 Dlairi Punjab India
199 K3 Dlhé Klčovo Slovakia
199 H2 Dlhé Pole Slovakia
198 G2 Dlouhá Loučka Czech Rep.
196 I5 Dłubnia r. Pol.
199 I1 Dłubniański Park Krajobrazowy Pol.
196 F4 Długołęka Dolnośląskie Pol.
197 K2 Długołęka Podlaskie Pol.
197 J3 Długosiodło Pol.
193 L6 Długoszyn Pol.
197 H4 Dłutów Pol.
153 P2 Dmitriya Lapteva, Proliv sea chan. Rus. Fed.
142 D1 Dmitriyevka Samarskaya Oblast' Rus. Fed.
157 H5 Dmitriyevka Tambovskaya Oblast' Rus. Fed.
157 F5 Dmitriyev-L'govskiy Rus. Fed.
Dmitriyevsk Ukr. see Makiyivka
161 U7 Dmitriyevskoye Rus. Fed.
161 U5 Dmitrov Rus. Fed.
161 Q8 Dmitrovo Rus. Fed.
161 W6 Dmitrovskiy Pogost Rus. Fed.
161 S9 Dmitrovsk-Orlovskiy Rus. Fed.
159 S1 Dmitryashevka Rus. Fed.
159 L3 Dmytrivka Chernihivs'ka Oblast' Ukr.
159 N6 Dmytrivka Dnipropetrovs'ka Oblast' Ukr.
159 P5 Dmytrivka Dnipropetrovs'ka Oblast' Ukr.
159 M7 Dmytrivka Khersons'ka Oblast' Ukr.
159 L5 Dmytrivka Kirovohrads'ka Oblast' Ukr.
159 K7 Dmytrivka Mykolayivs'ka Oblast' Ukr.
159 O8 Dmytrivka Respublika Krym Ukr.
159 P7 Dmytrivka Zaporiz'ka Oblast' Ukr.
Dmytriyevs'k Ukr. see Makiyivka
161 N7 Dnepr r. Rus. Fed. alt. Dnipro (Ukraine), alt. Dnyapro (Belarus), conv. Dnieper
Dneprodzerzhinsk Ukr. see Dniprodzerzhyns'k
Dnepropetrovsk Ukr. see Dnipropetrovs'k
Dnepropetrovskaya Oblast' admin. div. Ukr. see Dnipropetrovs'ka Oblast'
Dnepropetrovsk Oblast admin. div. Ukr. see Dnipropetrovs'ka Oblast'
Dneprorudnoye Ukr. see Dniprorudne
161 Q6 Dneprovskoye Rus. Fed.
158 I7 Dnestrovsc Moldova
157 F7 Dnieper r. Europe alt. Dnepr (Rus. Fed.), alt. Dnipro (Ukraine), alt. Dnyapro (Belarus)
158 J7 Dniester r. Ukr./Moldova alt. Dnister (Ukraine), alt. Nistru (Moldova)
159 L7 Dnipro r. Ukr. alt. Dnepr (Rus. Fed.), alt. Dnyapro (Belarus), conv. Dnieper
159 N4 Dnipro-Donbas, Kanal canal Ukr.
159 N5 Dniprodzerzhyns'k Ukr.
159 M5 Dniprodzerzhyns'ke Vodoskhovyshche resr Ukr.
159 M6 Dnipro-Kryvyy Rih, Kanal canal Ukr.
159 O5 Dnipropetrovs'k Ukr.
159 O5 Dnipropetrovs'ka Oblast' admin. div. Ukr.
Dnipropetrovsk Oblast admin. div. Ukr. see Dnipropetrovs'ka Oblast'
159 N6 Dniprorudne Ukr.
159 N8 Dniprovka Respublika Krym Ukr.
159 N6 Dniprovka Zaporiz'ka Oblast' Ukr.
159 O5 Dniprovs'ke Vodoskhovyshche resr Ukr.
159 K7 Dniprovs'kyy Lyman b. Ukr.
159 M7 Dnipryany Ukr.
158 J7 Dnister r. Ukr. alt. Nistru (Moldova), conv. Dniester
158 J7 Dnistrovs'kyy Lyman l. Ukr.
160 M4 Dno Rus. Fed.
161 O7 Dnyapro r. Belarus alt. Dnepr (Rus. Fed.), alt. Dnipro (Ukraine), conv. Dnieper
158 D1 Dnyaprowska-Buhski Kanal canal Belarus
235 G3 Doa Moz.
145 L4 Doāb Afgh.
145 N5 Doaba Pak.
145 L4 Do Āb-e Mīkh-e Zarrīn Afgh.
169 J3 Doagh Northern Ireland U.K.
170 C3 Doagh Isle pen. Ireland
249 H4 Doaktown N.B. Can.
117 L7 Doangdoangan Besar i. Indon.
117 L7 Doangdoangan Kecil i. Indon.
118 G4 Doan Hung Vietnam
235 □K2 Doany Madag.
185 C8 Doazit France
230 C2 Doba Chad
199 L4 Doba Romania
160 N9 Dobasna r. Belarus
192 F3 Dobbertin Ger.
192 F3 Dobbertiner Seenlandschaft park Ger.
213 M2 Dobbiaco Italy
251 M5 Dobbinton Ont. Can.
259 H2 Dobbs Ferry NY U.S.A.
197 I6 Dobczyce Pol.
128 G9 Dobdain Qinghai China
160 G5 Dobele Latvia
193 H8 Döbeln Ger.
113 H7 Doberai, Jazirah pen. Papua Indon.
Doberai Peninsula Papua Indon. see Doberai, Jazirah
193 I7 Doberlug-Kirchhain Ger.
193 K7 Döbern Ger.
201 L2 Dobersberg Austria
193 J8 Doberschau Ger.
190 J2 Dobersdorf Ger.
196 D3 Dobiegniew Pol.
197 J4 Dobieszyn Pol.
201 L6 Dobl Austria
285 E5 Doblas Arg.
113 H8 Dobo Maluku Indon.
210 G3 Doboj Bos.-Herz.
144 F7 Do Borjī Iran
201 M8 Dobova Slovenia
199 K5 Doboz Hungary
197 I6 Dobra Małopolskie Pol.
196 G4 Dobra Wielkopolskie Pol.
196 C2 Dobra Zachodniopomorskie Pol.
196 D2 Dobra Zachodniopomorskie Pol.
199 L6 Dobra Romania
193 E10 Döbraberg hill Ger.
199 I3 Dobrá Niva Slovakia
198 C2 Dobřany Czech Rep.
201 L2 Dobra Stausee resr Austria
201 K2 Dobrá Voda Czech Rep.
196 G3 Dobre Kujawsko-Pomorskie Pol.
197 J3 Dobre Mazowieckie Pol.
159 L6 Dobre Ukr.
165 Q8 Dobre Miasto Pol.
219 K4 Dobrești Romania
219 P7 Dobrich Bulg.
157 H5 Dobrinka Rus. Fed.
198 D2 Dobříš Czech Rep.
193 F6 Dobritz Ger.
195 P2 Dobřív Czech Rep.
201 L7 Dobrna Slovenia
201 K8 Dobrnič Slovenia
205 M3 Dobro Spain
196 G5 Dobrodzień Pol.
199 H5 Döbrököz Hungary
196 E5 Dobromierz Pol.
158 B4 Dobromyl' Ukr.
197 H4 Dobroń Pol.
199 L3 Dobron' Ukr.
198 E2 Dobronín Czech Rep.
159 Q5 Dobropillya Ukr.
Dobropol'ye Ukr. see Dobropillya
197 L5 Dobrosyn Ukr.
196 F4 Dobroszyce Pol.
219 M6 Dobrotești Romania
197 M5 Dobrotvir Ukr.
219 P4 Dobrovăț Romania
193 K10 Dobrovice Czech Rep.
159 P5 Dobrovillya Ukr.
201 N6 Dobrovnik Slovenia
160 F7 Dobrovol'sk Rus. Fed.
197 I5 Dobrowoda Pol.
161 W9 Dobroye Rus. Fed.
160 K3 Dobruchi Rus. Fed.
219 P7 Dobrudzhansko Plato plat. Bulg.
219 M6 Dobrun Romania
159 K1 Dobrush Belarus
159 M8 Dobrushyne Ukr.
198 F1 Dobruška Czech Rep.
156 L4 Dobryanka Rus. Fed.
159 K1 Dobryanka Ukr.
161 U6 Dobrynikha Rus. Fed.
197 I3 Dobrzankowo Pol.
196 D2 Dobrzany Pol.
196 F5 Dobrzeń Wielki Pol.
196 F4 Dobrzyca Pol.
196 E2 Dobrzyca r. Pol.
197 H3 Dobrzyków Pol.
197 H3 Dobrzyń nad Wisłą Pol.
199 J3 Dobšiná Slovakia
197 J1 Dobskie, Jezioro l. Pol.
103 F9 Dobson South I. N.Z.
103 D11 Dobson r. South I. N.Z.
255 G7 Dobson NC U.S.A.
172 C7 Dobwalls Cornwall, England U.K.
143 S6 Dobyn Kazakh.
133 I12 Dobzha Xizang China
199 J5 Dóc Hungary
118 H6 Đôc, Mui pt Vietnam
114 B9 Doc Can rf Phil.
280 B3 Doce r. Brazil
281 H3 Doce r. Brazil
168 H10 Dochart r. Scotland U.K.
168 H8 Dochgarroch Highland, Scotland U.K.
145 M6 Do China Qala Afgh.
173 N2 Docking Norfolk, England U.K.
191 C10 Dockweiler Ger.
Doc Penfro Pembrokeshire, Wales U.K. see Pembroke Dock
268 G2 Doctor Arroyo Mex.
266 F3 Doctor Belisario Domínguez Mex.
261 F13 Doctor Coss Mex.
109 H10 Doctor Hicks Range hills W.A. Austr.
268 G4 Doctor Mora Mex.
Doctor Petru Groza Romania see Ștei
233 C6 Doda Tanz.
145 M7 Dodapur Pak.
136 E6 Dod Ballapur Karnataka India
173 M4 Doddinghurst Essex, England U.K.
171 M2 Doddington Northumberland, England U.K.
133 I11 Dodê Xizang China
Dodecanese is Greece see Dodekanisa
221 I7 Dodekanisa is Greece
186 I5 Dodewaard Neth.
250 B5 Dodge Center MN U.S.A.
261 E7 Dodge City KS U.S.A.
250 D7 Dodgeville WI U.S.A.
213 K4 Dodici, Cima mt. Italy
172 C7 Dodman Point England U.K.
232 C3 Dodola Eth.
233 B6 Dodoma Tanz.
233 B6 Dodoma admin. reg. Tanz.
233 D5 Dodori National Reserve nature res. Kenya
247 I5 Dodsland Sask. Can.
256 B9 Dodsonville OH U.S.A.
186 J4 Doesburg Neth.
186 J5 Doetinchem Neth.
115 D4 Dofa Maluku Indon.
219 N5 Doftana r. Romania
248 B3 Dog r. Ont. Can.
133 I9 Dogai Coring salt l. China
133 I9 Dogaicoring Qangco salt l. China
221 L3 Doğalar Turkey
221 I5 Doğanbey Aydın Turkey
221 H4 Doğanbey İzmir Turkey
221 L3 Doğançayır Turkey
148 H4 Doğanşehir Turkey
151 D6 Doğansu Turkey
246 F5 Dog Creek B.C. Can.
171 Q7 Dogdyke Lincolnshire, England U.K.
133 J11 Dogên Co l. China
127 J2 Dōgen-ko l. Japan
221 L3 Döğer Turkey
194 E6 Dogern Ger.
144 I4 Doghārūn Iran
271 L4 Dog Island Anguilla
249 I1 Dog Island Nfld and Lab. Can.
247 L5 Dog Lake Man. Can.
248 B3 Dog Lake Ont. Can.
248 C3 Dog Lake Ont. Can.
212 D6 Dogliani Italy
219 J5 Dognecea Romania
125 K10 Dōgo i. Japan
228 D4 Dogo Mali
232 E2 Dogoble well Somalia
229 G3 Dogondoutchi Niger
230 C2 Dogoumbo Chad
125 K11 Dōgo-yama mt. Japan
270 D1 Dog Rocks is Bahamas
149 L4 Doğubeyazıt Turkey
151 B5 Doğu Karadeniz Dağları mts Turkey
221 J5 Doğu Menteşe Dağları mts Turkey
271 □2 Dogwood Point St Kitts and Nevis
133 H12 Dogxung Zangbo r. Xizang China
Doha Qatar see Ad Dawḥah
Dohad Gujarat India see Dahod
139 N8 Dohazari Bangl.
193 E10 Döhlau Ger.
193 I9 Dohna Ger.
237 L8 Dohne S. Africa
190 E5 Dohren Ger.
133 F13 Dohrighat Uttar Prad. India
146 D8 Dohul i. Eritrea
99 I4 Doi i. Fiji
115 E2 Doi i. Maluku Indon.
118 D5 Doi Inthanon National Park Thai.
133 I11 Doijang Xizang China
118 D5 Doi Khuntan National Park Thai.
118 D5 Doi Luang National Park Thai.
Doïranis, Limni l. Greece/Macedonia see Dojran, Lake
204 G2 Doiras, Embalse de resr Spain
Doire Northern Ireland U.K. see Londonderry
169 C6 Doire Iorrais Ireland
169 F2 Doirí Beaga Ireland
118 D5 Doi Saket Thai.
139 J8 Doisanagar Jharkhand India
187 G8 Doische Belgium
280 C5 Dois Córregos Brazil
278 E4 Dois Irmãos, Serra dos hills Brazil
206 A2 Dois Portos Port.
118 D5 Doi Suthep-Pui National Park Thai.
198 G3 Dojč Slovakia
219 K9 Dojran Macedonia
219 K9 Dojran, Lake Greece/Macedonia
Dojransko Ezero l. Greece/Macedonia see Dojran, Lake
225 G6 Doka Sudan
144 F5 Dokali Iran
149 L6 Dokan, Sadd dam Iraq
227 G2 Dokhara, Dunes de des. Alg.
163 K6 Dokka Norway
162 P3 Dokkas Sweden
186 I2 Dokkum Neth.
186 I2 Dokkumer Ee r. Neth.
228 C4 Doko Guinea
130 C3 Dokog He r. Sichuan China
220 E5 Dokos i. Greece
145 M8 Dokri Pak.
Dokshukino Rus. Fed. see Nartkala
160 K7 Dokshytsy Belarus
198 D1 Doksy Liberecký kraj Czech Rep.
193 J10 Doksy Středočeský kraj Czech Rep.
124 X2 Dokuchayeva, Mys c. Kuril'skiye O-va Rus. Fed.
159 Q6 Dokuchayevs'k Ukr.
151 C5 Dokumacılar Turkey
221 L2 Dokurcun Turkey
260 F3 Doland SD U.S.A.
172 F2 Dolanog Powys, Wales U.K.
265 R6 Dolan Springs AZ U.S.A.
283 D6 Dolavón Arg.
249 F3 Dolbeau-Mistassini Que. Can.
172 D2 Dolbenmaen Gwynedd, Wales U.K.
212 D8 Dolceacqua Italy
180 H4 Dol-de-Bretagne France
182 G2 Dole France
213 R4 Dolenja Vas Slovenia
201 L8 Dolenjske Toplice Slovenia
182 K5 Dolent, Mont mt. France/Italy
172 F3 Dolfor Powys, Wales U.K.
172 E1 Dolgarrog Conwy, Wales U.K.
159 Q7 Dolgaya, Kosa spit Rus. Fed.
172 E2 Dolgellau Gwynedd, Wales U.K.
192 H4 Dolgen Ger.
257 K5 Dolgeville NY U.S.A.
156 K1 Dolgiy, Ostrov i. Rus. Fed.
156 L1 Dolgiy, Ostrov i. Rus. Fed.
159 O2 Dolgiye Budy Rus. Fed.
244 G5 Dolgoi Island AK U.S.A.
197 I1 Dolgorukovo Kaliningradskaya Oblast' Rus. Fed.
161 V9 Dolgorukovo Lipetskaya Oblast' Rus. Fed.
161 W8 Dolgoye Lipetskaya Oblast' Rus. Fed.
157 G5 Dolgoye Orlovskaya Oblast' Rus. Fed.
161 V9 Dolgusha Rus. Fed.
219 O3 Dolhasca Romania
197 M5 Dołhobyczów Pol.
214 C9 Dolianova Sardegna Italy
196 D2 Dolice Pol.
Dolina Ukr. see Dolyna
165 N7 Dolina Słupi, Park Krajobraz Pol.
199 I1 Dolinki Krakowskie, Park Krajobrazowy Pol.
151 E1 Dolinovka Rus. Fed.
122 M5 Dolinsk Sakhalin Rus. Fed.
189 G3 Doliny Bobru, Park Krajobra Pol.
192 J4 Doliny Dolnej Odry, Park Krajobrazowy Pol.
Dolisie Loubomo Congo see Loubomo
115 E4 Dolit Halmahera Indon.
219 J7 Doljevac Doljevac Serbia
169 F7 Dolla Ireland
168 I10 Dollar Clackmannanshire, Scotland U.K.
190 D4 Dollart Ger.
193 E6 Dolle Ger.
286 T2 Dolleman Island Antarctica
179 N8 Doller r. France
190 I3 Dollern Ger.
193 F8 Döllnitz Ger.
195 K4 Dollnstein Ger.
181 M5 Dollon France
191 K8 Döllstädt Ger.
191 J9 Dolmar hill Ger.
143 M1 Dolmatovo Kazakh.
219 N7 Dolna Lipnitska Bulg.
199 I3 Dolná Strehová Slovakia
218 J9 Dolneni Dolneni Macedonia
199 H3 Dolné Vestenice Slovakia
199 H2 Dolní Benešov Czech Rep.
193 J10 Dolní Beřkovice Czech Rep
201 P2 Dolní Bojanovice Czech Re
198 E1 Dolní Bousov Czech Rep.
201 K1 Dolní Bukovsko Czech Rep.
219 P8 Dolni Chiflik Bulg.
219 M7 Dolni Dŭbnik Bulg.
201 O2 Dolní Dunajovice Czech R
198 D3 Dolní Dvořiště Czech Rep.
198 F2 Dolní Kounice Czech Rep.
199 G3 Dolní Němčí Czech Rep.
198 D1 Dolní Podluží Czech Rep.
193 J9 Dolní Poustevna Czech Re
198 F2 Dolní Újezd Czech Rep.
198 B1 Dolní Žandov Czech Rep.
219 L8 Dolno Kamartsi Bulg.
219 M8 Dolno Levski Bulg.
196 E4 Dolnośląskie prov. Pol.
199 I2 Dolný Kubín Slovakia
Dolný Peter Slovakia see Svätý Peter
199 H3 Dolný Pial Slovakia
199 G4 Dolný Štál Slovakia
115 A4 Dolo Sulawesi Indon.
213 M5 Dolo Italy
212 J7 Dolo r. Italy
100 □4b Dolohmwar hill Pohnpei Micronesia
113 I8 Dolok, Pulau i. Papua Indo
182 H5 Dolomieu France
Dolomites mts Italy see Do
213 L4 Dolomiti mts Italy
213 L3 Dolomiti Bellunesi, Parco Nazionale delle nat. park It
213 M2 Dolomiti di Sesto, Parco Naturale nature res. Italy
Dolon, Pereval pass Kyrg. s Dolon Ashuusu
143 P7 Dolon Ashuusu pass Kyrg.
129 O5 Dolonnur Nei Mongol Chi
232 D3 Dolo Odo Eth.
Doloon Mongolia see Tsog
285 I5 Dolores Arg.
267 O9 Dolores Guat.
266 D5 Dolores Mex.
209 D11 Dolores Spain
285 H3 Dolores Uru.
265 W3 Dolores r. CO U.S.A.
268 G4 Dolores Hidalgo Mex.
218 I6 Dolovo Vojvodina Serbia
283 F8 Dolphin, Cape Falkland Is
242 G3 Dolphin and Union Strait Nunavut Can.
270 □ Dolphin Head hill Jamaica
234 B5 Dolphin Head Namibia
108 D6 Dolphin Island W.A. Austr.
108 D6 Dolphin Island Nature Re W.A. Austr.
171 K2 Dolphinton South Lanarks Scotland U.K.
200 G6 Dölsach Austria
196 F4 Dolsk Pol.
197 M4 Dol's'k Ukr.
197 K3 Dołubowo Pol.
118 G5 Đô Lương Vietnam
184 B4 Dolus-d'Oléron France
158 C5 Dolyna Ukr.
159 L5 Dolyns'ka Ukr.
159 Q7 Dolzhanskaya Rus. Fed.
159 O2 Dolzhenkovo Rus. Fed.
160 M3 Dolzhitsy Rus. Fed.
113 I7 Dom, Gunung mt. Papua
199 J3 Domaháza Hungary
138 G5 Domaila Uttaranchal Indi
221 K3 Domaniç Turkey
197 K3 Domanice Pol.
215 Q9 Domanico Italy
197 H3 Domaniewice Łódzkie Pol.
197 I4 Domaniewice Mazowieck
199 H2 Domaniža Slovakia
139 L6 Domar Bangl.
133 E10 Domar Xizang China
197 J6 Domaradz Pol.
133 L11 Domartang Xizang China
178 D3 Domart-en-Ponthieu Fra
201 O7 Domašinec Croatia
199 J5 Domaszek Hungary
196 E5 Domaszków Pol.
196 F4 Domaszowice Pol.
212 G2 Domat Ems Switz.
178 F7 Domats France
198 B2 Domažlice Czech Rep.
133 L10 Domba Qinghai China
144 B5 Dom Bākh Iran
142 H2 Dombarovskiy Rus. Fed.
163 J5 Dombås Norway
179 J5 Dombasle-en-Argonne F
179 K7 Dombasle-en-Xaintois Fr
179 L6 Dombasle-sur-Meurthe
151 C2 Dombay Rus. Fed.
235 G3 Dombe Moz.
231 B8 Dombe Grande Angola
199 K5 Dombegyház Hungary
182 F4 Dombes reg. France
231 D6 Dombi Dem. Rep. Congo
199 H5 Dombóvár Hungary
231 C8 Dombra Angola
199 K3 Dombrád Hungary
Dombrau Pol. see Dąbrowa Górnicza
212 B1 Dombresson Switz.
Dombrovitsa Ukr. see Dubrovytsya
Dombrowa Pol. see Dąbrowa Górnicza
186 E5 Domburg Neth.
281 F3 Dom Cavati Brazil
Domda Qinghai China se Qingshuihe
182 B5 Dôme, Monts mts France
287 H2 Dome Charlie ice feature Antarctica
Dome Circe ice feature An see Dome Charlie
246 F4 Dome Creek B.C. Can.
200 F7 Domegge di Cadore Italy
160 G7 Domeikava Lith.
Domel Island Myanmar Letsok-aw Kyun
183 H6 Domène France
182 B4 Domérat France
265 R8 Dome Rock Mountains A
193 D6 Domersleben Ger.
214 A9 Domestica, Cala b. Sarde
108 J3 Domett, Cape W.A. Austr.
103 G8 Domett, Mount South I.

K6 Domèvre-en-Haye France
M6 Domèvre-sur-Vezouze France
C5 Domeyko Antofagasta Chile
C3 Domeyko Atacama Chile
C9 Domezain-Berraute France
B9 Dom Feliciano Brazil
J4 Domfront France
K6 Domgermain France
C6 Dominador Chile
G4 Domingos Martins Brazil
E8 Dominguiso Port.
□2 Dominica country West Indies
□R13 Dominical Costa Rica
Dominicana, República country West Indies see Dominican Republic
H4 Dominican Republic country West Indies
□2 Dominica Passage Dominica/Guadeloupe
K3 Dominion, Cape Nunavut Can.
Dominique i. Fr. Polynesia see Hiva Oa
D6 Domiongo Dem. Rep. Congo
D4 Dömitz Ger.
F3 Dom Joaquim Brazil
M6 Domkhar Bhutan
I7 Dommartin-le-Franc France
I6 Dommartin-Varimont France
G6 Domme France
H5 Dommel r. Neth.
D10 Dommershausen Ger.
G7 Dommitzsch Ger.
M5 Domneşti Argeş Romania
N6 Domneşti Bucureşti Romania
E5 Dömnitz r. Ger.
I1 Domnovo Rus. Fed.
E3 Domo Eth.
U6 Domodedovo Rus. Fed.
E3 Domodossola Italy
D3 Domokos Greece
□3 Domoni Nzwani Comoros
D5 Domont France
H4 Dömös Hungary
Q1 Domozhirovo Rus. Fed.
L7 Dompaire France
J6 Dompcevrin France
B9 Dom Pedrito Brazil
D3 Dom Pedro Brazil
E4 Dompierre-les-Ormes France
D3 Dompierre-sur-Besbre France
B3 Dompierre-sur-Mer France
I8 Dompierre-sur-Yon France
M9 Dompu Sumbawa Indon.
K7 Domrémy-la-Pucelle France
I4 Dömsöd Hungary
E4 Domsühl Ger.
B10 Domus de Maria Sardegna Italy
B9 Domusnovas Sardegna Italy
B5 Domuyo, Volcán vol. Arg.
O7 Domuzla r. Ukr.
M3 Domville, Mount hill Qld Austr.
E2 Domžale Slovenia
L5 Don r. Qld Austr.
H6 Don r. France
E4 Don r. India
E4 Don Mex.
L8 Don r. Rus. Fed.
L8 Don r. Scotland U.K.
G7 Don, Xé r. Laos
6 Donabate Ireland
M5 Donada Italy
E2 Donadeu Arg.
H4 Donagh Northern Ireland U.K.
K3 Donaghadee Northern Ireland U.K.
4 Donaghcloney Northern Ireland U.K.
G7 Donaghmore Laois Ireland
6 Donaghmore Meath Ireland
3 Donaghmore Northern Ireland U.K.
8 Donaji Mex.
7 Donald Vic. Austr.
10 Donaldsonville LA U.S.A.
2 Donalnes, Cerro mt. Chile
10 Donalsonville GA U.S.A.
3 Don Álvaro Spain
2 Doña María Cristina, Canal de Spain
5 Doña Mencía Spain
7 Doñana, Parque Nacional de nat. park Spain
6 Donard Ireland
2 Doña Rosa, Cordillera mts Chile
1 Donato Guerra Mex.
2 Donau r. Austria/Ger.
alt. Duna (Hungary),
alt. Dunaj (Slovakia),
alt. Dunărea (Romania),
alt. Dunav (Serbia),
conv. Danube
3 Donau-Auen, Nationalpark nat. park Austria
6 Donaueschingen Ger.
4 Donaumoos reg. Ger.
4 Donauried reg. Ger.
13 Donaustauf Ger.
Donauwörth Ger.
13 Don Benito Spain
5 Donbī Iran
6 Doncaster South Yorkshire, England U.K.
Donchery France
7 Dondo Angola
3 Dondo Moz.
3 Dondo, Tanjung pt Indon.
3 Dondo, Teluk b. Indon.
7 Dondonay i. Phil.
10 Dondra Head Sri Lanka
5 Donduşeni Moldova
Dondyushany Moldova see Donduşeni
3 Donegal Ireland
Donegal county Ireland
3 Donegal Bay Ireland
3 Donemana Northern Ireland U.K.
Dönenbay Kazakh. see Dunenbay
Donetsk Rus. Fed.
6 Donets'k Ukr.
5 Donets'ka Oblast' admin. div. Ukr.
Donetskaya Oblast' admin. div. Ukr. see Donets'ka Oblast'
Donetskaya Seymitsa r. Rus. Fed.
Donetsko-Amrovsiyevka Ukr. see Amvrosiyivka
Donetsk Oblast admin. div. Ukr. see Donets'ka Oblast'
Donets'kyy Ukr.
Donets'kyy Kryazh hills Rus. Fed./Ukr.
Doneztebe Spain
Donfar Eth.
Don Figuerero Mountains hills Jamaica
Dønfoss Norway
4 Donga r. Cameroon/Nigeria
5 Donga Nigeria
5 Dong'an Hunan China
0 Dongara W.A. Austr.
9 Dongargaon Chhattisgarh India
9 Dongargarh Chhattisgarh India
Dongbatu Gansu China
2 Dongbei reg. Heilong. China
Dongbei Pingyuan plain China
Dongbo Xizang China see Mêdog
Dongcheng Guangdong China see Yangdong
Dongchuan Yunnan China see Yao'an
Dongchuan Yunnan China
0 Dongco Xizang China
0 Dong Co l. Xizang China
Dongcun Shandong China see Haiyang
Dongcun Shanxi China see Lanxian
Đông Đăng Vietnam
Dong'e Shandong China
Dongen Neth.
Donges France
Dongfang Hainan China
Dongfanghong Heilong. China

122 D7 Dongfeng Jilin China
115 A4 Donggala Sulawesi Indon.
123 D9 Donggang Liaoning China
129 P9 Donggang Shandong China
128 F9 Donggi Conag l. Qinghai China
Donggou Liaoning China see Donggang
128 G9 Donggou Qinghai China
131 J5 Donggu Jiangxi China
131 I7 Dongguan Guangdong China
118 H6 Đông Ha Vietnam
129 P9 Donghai Jiangsu China
Dong Hai sea N. Pacific Ocean see East China Sea
128 I8 Donghaiba Ningxia China
130 H8 Donghai Dao i. China
130 F3 Dong He r. China
118 H6 Đông Hơi Vietnam
129 K8 Donghuachi Gansu China
Donghuang Guizhou China see Xishui
131 I7 Dong Jiang r. China
112 D1 Dongjiang Shuiku resr Hunan China
122 F6 Dongjingcheng Heilong. China
115 A5 Dongkait, Tanjung pt Indon.
133 J12 Dongkar Xizang China
130 H5 Dongkou Hunan China
129 Q8 Donglai Shandong China
130 F6 Donglan Guangxi China
128 G7 Dongle Gansu China
129 R5 Dongliao He r. China
132 I7 Donglük Xinjiang China
Dongmen Guangxi China see Luocheng
129 N9 Dongming Shandong China
122 G6 Dongning Heilong. China
231 B8 Dongo Angola
231 C6 Dongo Dem. Rep. Congo
212 G3 Dongo Italy
233 B6 Dongobesh Tanz.
225 F5 Dongola Sudan
232 B3 Dongotona Mountains Sudan
230 C4 Dongou Congo
Dong Phaya Yen Range mts Thai. see Phang Hoei, San Khao
118 E7 Dong Phraya Yen esc. Thai.
131 I8 Dongping Guangdong China
Dongping Hunan China see Anhua
129 O8 Dongping Hu l. China
Dongpo Sichuan China see Meishan
133 J11 Dongqiao Xizang China
128 I8 Dongqinghu Nei Mongol China
133 K10 Dong Qu r. Qinghai China
128 C5 Dongquan Xinjiang China
131 K7 Dongshan Fujian China
130 H8 Dongshan Guangdong China
131 M3 Dongshan Jiangsu China
Dongshan Jiangxi China see Shangyou
Dongshan China see Jiangning
131 J5 Dongshao Jiangxi China
112 E2 Dongsha Qundao is China
Dongsheng Nei Mongol China see Ordos
Dongshuan Yunnan China see Tangdan
131 M2 Dongtai Jiangsu China
131 M2 Dongtai He r. China
133 L8 Dong Taijnar Hu l. Qinghai China
131 I4 Dongting Hu l. China
131 M5 Dongtou Zhejiang China
118 H4 Đông Triêu Vietnam
231 B9 Donguena Angola
230 A4 Donguila Gabon
Dong Ujimqin Qi Nei Mongol China see Uliastai
130 E7 Đông Văn Vietnam
Dongxiang Sichuan China see Xuanhan
128 H9 Dongxiangzu Gansu China
130 F8 Dongxing Guangxi China
122 E5 Dongxing Heilong. China
122 H5 Dongxing Heilong. China
131 M4 Dongyang Zhejiang China
129 P8 Dongying Shandong China
131 J7 Dongyuan Guangdong China
128 H7 Dongzhen Gansu China
131 K3 Dongzhi Anhui China
284 B4 Doñihue Chile
173 L2 Donington Lincolnshire, England U.K.
261 J7 Doniphan MO U.S.A.
201 O7 Donja Dubrava Croatia
201 N7 Donja Konjšćina Croatia
201 M8 Donja Stubica Croatia
201 N7 Donja Višnjica Croatia
201 N8 Donja Zelina Croatia
245 L3 Donjek r. Y.T. Can.
179 J7 Donjeux France
210 G3 Donji Miholjac Croatia
219 K6 Donji Milanovac Majdanpek Serbia
210 F3 Donji Vakuf Bos.-Herz.
210 E3 Donji Zemunik Croatia
186 J2 Donkerbroek Neth.
237 J6 Donkerpoort S. Africa
139 M9 Donmanick Islands Bangl.
162 L3 Dønna i. Norway
249 G4 Donnacona Que. Can.
216 H10 Donnalucata Sicilia Italy
212 D4 Donnas Italy
246 G4 Donnelly Alta Can.
245 K3 Donnelly AK U.S.A.
102 H2 Donnellys Crossing North I. N.Z.
178 F7 Donnemarie-Dontilly France
264 L2 Donner Pass CA U.S.A.
201 J5 Donnersbach Austria
194 D2 Donnersberg hill Ger.
195 I2 Donnersdorf Ger.
172 H2 Donnington Telford and Wrekin, England U.K.
109 C12 Donnybrook W.A. Austr.
169 F7 Donohill Ireland
179 N6 Donon mt. France
214 C9 Donori Sardegna Italy
208 B1 Donostia-San Sebastián Spain
169 E9 Donoughmore Ireland
221 G5 Donousa i. Greece
250 G9 Donovan IL U.S.A.
159 Q6 Dons'ke Ukr.
159 T6 Donskoy Rostovskaya Oblast' Rus. Fed.
161 V8 Donskoy Tul'skaya Oblast' Rus. Fed.
161 V9 Donskoye Lipetskaya Oblast' Rus. Fed.
157 H7 Donskoye Stavropol'skiy Kray Rus. Fed.
159 S3 Donskoye Belogor'ye hills Rus. Fed.
114 D5 Donsol Luzon Phil.
118 C6 Donthami r. Myanmar
159 L8 Donuzlav, Ozero l. Ukr.
180 H4 Donville-les-Bains France
142 G4 Donyztau, Sor dry lake Kazakh.
185 F7 Donzac France
194 H4 Donzdorf Ger.
213 M6 Donzella, Isola della i. Italy
184 H5 Donzenac France
183 F8 Donzère France
182 C2 Donzy France
169 B5 Dooagh Ireland
169 E4 Doocastle Ireland
Dooega Ireland see Dumha Éige
Dooghbeg Ireland see An Dumhach Bheag
169 B4 Doogort Ireland
Doohooma Ireland see Dumha Thuama
170 C4 Dooish Northern Ireland U.K.
108 E6 Dooleena hill W.A. Austr.
169 D6 Doolin Ireland
106 G4 Doomadgee Qld Austr.
106 G4 Doomadgee Aboriginal Reserve Qld Austr.
169 F7 Doon Ireland
168 G12 Doon r. Scotland U.K.
168 H12 Doon, Loch l. Scotland U.K.
169 C7 Doonaha Ireland
169 C7 Doonbeg Ireland

169 C7 Doonbeg r. Ireland
169 C7 Doonbeg Bay Ireland
108 J4 Doon Doon Aboriginal Reserve W.A. Austr.
245 J2 Doonerak, Mount AK U.S.A.
169 B6 Doonloughan Ireland
169 B8 Doonmanagh Ireland
169 F3 Doorin Point Ireland
186 H4 Doorn Neth.
186 I4 Doornspijk Neth.
250 G5 Door Peninsula WI U.S.A.
232 F2 Dooxo Nugaaleed val. Somalia
196 E3 Dopiewo Pol.
133 K11 Doqêmo Xizang China
133 J12 Doqoi Xizang China
130 A1 Do Qu r. Qinghai China
145 I6 Dor watercourse Afgh.
144 D5 Dor Iran
150 C6 Dor Israel
161 S6 Dor Rus. Fed.
261 D9 Dora NM U.S.A.
108 G7 Dora, Lake salt flat W.A. Austr.
212 E5 Dora Baltea r. Italy
182 J5 Dora di Ferret r. Italy
182 K5 Dora di Veny r. Italy
266 G4 Dorado Mex.
144 D8 Do Rāhak Iran
145 N3 Dorah Pass Pak.
139 J8 Doranda Jharkhand India
247 I2 Doran Lake N.W.T. Can.
212 D5 Dora Riparia r. Italy
277 E5 D'Orbigny Bol.
Dorbiljin Xinjiang China see Emin
Dorbod Heilong. China see Taikang
Dorbod Qi Nei Mongol China see Ulan Hua
172 H6 Dorchester Dorset, England U.K.
258 F6 Dorchester NJ U.S.A.
234 C4 Dordabis Namibia
178 E7 Dordives France
184 F5 Dordogne dept France
182 B5 Dordogne r. France
173 I2 Dordon Warwickshire, England U.K.
186 G5 Dordrecht Neth.
237 L7 Dordrecht S. Africa
182 C4 Dore r. France
182 B6 Dore, Monts mts France
234 C4 Doreenville Namibia
247 J4 Doré Lake Sask. Can.
247 J4 Doré Lake l. Sask. Can.
183 D6 Dore-l'Église France
200 A5 Doren Austria
191 H6 Dörentrup Ger.
168 H8 Dores Highland, Scotland U.K.
281 F3 Dores de Guanhães Brazil
281 E3 Dores do Indaiá Brazil
228 E3 Dorey Mali
195 M5 Dorfen Ger.
200 H5 Dorfgastein Austria
190 I5 Dorfmark Ger.
192 D3 Dorf Mecklenburg Ger.
214 D7 Dorgali Sardegna Italy
128 C9 Dorgê Co l. Qinghai China
128 C2 Dörgön Mongolia
199 K5 Dorgoş Romania
145 K6 Dori r. Afgh.
229 E3 Dori Burkina
285 F4 Dorila Arg.
236 C7 Doring r. S. Africa
236 D8 Doring r. S. Africa
236 C7 Doringbaai S. Africa
236 D7 Doringbos S. Africa
220 C5 Dorio Greece
106 C3 Dorisvale N.T. Austr.
173 L5 Dorking Surrey, England U.K.
179 N6 Dorlisheim France
228 E5 Dormaa-Ahenkro Ghana
191 C8 Dormagen Ger.
199 J4 Dormánd Hungary
178 G5 Dormans France
212 F4 Dormelletto Italy
194 F5 Dormettingen Ger.
122 I5 Dormidontovka Rus. Fed.
136 G4 Dornakal Andhra Prad. India
201 M7 Dornava Slovenia
191 H8 Dörnberg (Habichtswald) Ger.
200 A5 Dornbirn Austria
193 E8 Dornburg (Saale) Ger.
191 F9 Dornburg-Frickhofen Ger.
190 H3 Dornbusch Ger.
192 H1 Dornbusch pen. Ger.
191 J9 Dorndorf Ger.
193 E8 Dorndorf-Steudnitz Ger.
204 E5 Dornelas Port.
182 C3 Dornes France
191 I8 Dörnhagen (Fuldabrück) Ger.
194 F5 Dornhan Ger.
168 E8 Dornie Highland, Scotland U.K.
193 F6 Dörnitz Ger.
212 F5 Dorno Italy
168 H7 Dornoch Highland, Scotland U.K.
168 H7 Dornoch Firth est. Scotland U.K.
129 N2 Dornod prov. Mongolia
129 K4 Dornogovĭ prov. Mongolia
258 B3 Dornsife PA U.S.A.
194 H5 Dornstadt Ger.
194 E5 Dornstetten Ger.
190 D3 Dornum Ger.
190 D3 Dornumersiel Ger.
228 E2 Doro Mali
219 O6 Dorobanţu Romania
161 U8 Dorobino Rus. Fed.
199 H4 Dorog Hungary
199 I4 Dorogháza Hungary
161 Q7 Dorogobuzh Rus. Fed.
156 I2 Dorogorskoye Rus. Fed.
144 I5 Doroh Iran
219 O3 Dorohoi Romania
197 L4 Dorohusk Pol.
161 T6 Dorokhovo Rus. Fed.
144 H5 Dorokhsh Iran
199 L4 Dorolţ Romania
128 C3 Döröö Nuur salt l. Mongolia
159 K6 Doroshivka Ukr.
Dorostol Bulg. see Silistra
158 E3 Dorosyni Ukr.
162 N4 Dorotea Sweden
258 F6 Dorothy NJ U.S.A.
235 F3 Dorowa Zimbabwe
Dorpat Estonia see Tartu
190 D5 Dörpen Ger.
109 B8 Dorre Island W.A. Austr.
105 N4 Dorrigo N.S.W. Austr.
262 D6 Dorris CA U.S.A.
251 P4 Dorset Ont. Can.
172 H6 Dorset admin. div. England U.K.
256 E7 Dorset OH U.S.A.
172 F6 Dorset and East Devon Coast tourist site U.K.
133 I10 Dorsoidong Co l. Xizang China
191 K6 Dorstadt Ger.
191 C7 Dorsten Ger.
182 H4 Dortan France
191 D7 Dortmund Ger.
191 E7 Dortmund-Ems-Kanal canal Ger.
256 C11 Dorton KY U.S.A.
148 H5 Dörtyol Turkey
196 G4 Doruchów Pol.
144 C5 Dorūd Iran
151 D6 Dorukdibi Turkey
190 G3 Dorum Ger.
230 E3 Doruma Dem. Rep. Congo
144 G4 Dorūneh Iran
144 G4 Dorūneh, Kūh-e mts Iran
190 H5 Dörverden Ger.
128 D3 Dörvöljin Mongolia
Dorylaeum Turkey see Eskişehir
194 H3 Dörzbach Ger.
268 E7 Dos Aguas Mex.
209 D9 Dos Aguas Spain
144 G7 Do Sārī Iran
283 D7 Dos Bahías, Cabo c. Arg.
205 N9 Dosbarrios Spain
265 W9 Dos Cabezas Mountain AZ U.S.A.
274 C6 Dos de Mayo Peru
221 L5 Döşemealtı Turkey
145 I4 Do Shākh, Kūh-e mt. Afgh.
206 H6 Dos Hermanas Spain
127 J4 Dōshi Japan
139 O6 Dosing Arun. Prad. India
267 O9 Dos Lagunos Guat.

118 H4 Đo Sơn Vietnam
264 L5 Dos Palos CA U.S.A.
219 M9 Dospat Bulg.
219 M9 Dospat r. Bulg.
207 N6 Dos Picos mt. Spain
283 D6 Dos Pozos Arg.
192 F5 Dosse r. Ger.
194 F3 Dossenheim Ger.
230 C2 Dosséo, Bahr r. Chad
229 F3 Dosso Niger
229 F3 Dosso dept Niger
229 F3 Dosso, Réserve Partielle de nature res. Niger
212 E3 Dossola, Val val. Italy
142 E4 Dossor Kazakh.
143 M7 Do'stlik Uzbek.
207 J4 Dos Torres Spain
143 T5 Dostyk Kazakh.
Dostyq Kazakh. see Dostyk
255 E10 Dothan AL U.S.A.
245 K3 Dot Lake AK U.S.A.
190 F5 Dötlingen Ger.
194 F5 Dotternhausen Ger.
212 E1 Döttingen Switz.
178 F3 Douai France
226 D4 Douakel, Hamada ed plat. Alg.
228 C4 Douako Guinea
229 H5 Douala Cameroon
229 H6 Douala-Edéa, Réserve nature res. Cameroon
180 C5 Douarnenez France
180 C5 Douarnenez, Baie de b. France
184 E5 Double reg. France
Double Island H.K. China see Wong Wan Chau
107 N8 Double Island Point Qld Austr.
261 E9 Double Mountain Fork r. TX U.S.A.
244 I3 Double Peak AK U.S.A.
264 N6 Double Peak CA U.S.A.
107 K4 Double Point Qld Austr.
255 D8 Double Springs AL U.S.A.
198 E2 Doubrava r. Czech Rep.
182 I3 Doubs France
182 I2 Doubs dept France
182 G3 Doubs r. France/Switz.
108 H3 Doubtful Bay W.A. Austr.
109 E13 Doubtful Island Bay W.A. Austr.
103 B12 Doubtful Sound South I. N.Z.
103 A12 Doubtful Sound inlet South I. N.Z.
102 H1 Doubtless Bay North I. N.Z.
Doucan Shaanxi China see Fuping
178 F8 Douchy France
178 F3 Douchy-les-Mines France
182 H3 Doucier France
181 M2 Doudeville France
184 D1 Doué-la-Fontaine France
228 E3 Douentza Mali
228 E3 Douentza, Réserve de nature res. Mali
170 G2 Dougarie North Ayrshire, Scotland U.K.
227 H1 Dougga tourist site Tunisia
103 B14 Doughboy Bay Stewart I. N.Z.
169 F4 Dough Mountain hill Ireland
167 E4 Douglas Isle of Man
102 I6 Douglas North I. N.Z.
169 F9 Douglas Ireland
236 H5 Douglas S. Africa
168 I11 Douglas South Lanarkshire, Scotland U.K.
245 N4 Douglas AK U.S.A.
265 W10 Douglas AZ U.S.A.
255 F10 Douglas GA U.S.A.
262 L5 Douglas WY U.S.A.
244 I4 Douglas, Cape AK U.S.A.
105 L9 Douglas Apsley National Park Tas. Austr.
170 C4 Douglas Bridge Northern Ireland U.K.
246 D4 Douglas Channel B.C. Can.
104 F3 Douglas Creek watercourse S.A. Austr.
265 X1 Douglas Creek r. CO U.S.A.
286 T2 Douglas Range mts Antarctica
Douglas Reef i. Japan see Okino-Tori-shima
258 D4 Douglassville PA U.S.A.
168 K9 Douglastown Angus, Scotland U.K.
255 E9 Douglasville GA U.S.A.
229 H3 Dougoulé well Niger
224 C5 Douhi Chad
Douhudi Hubei China see Gong'an
220 B4 Doukato, Akrotirio pt Lefkada Greece
179 J7 Doulaincourt-Saucourt France
Douliu Taiwan see Touliu
178 D3 Doullens France
169 B9 Doulus Head Ireland
230 D2 Doum C.A.R.
229 F4 Doumè Benin
229 I5 Doumé Cameroon
229 I5 Doumé r. Cameroon
131 I7 Doumen Guangdong China
228 E3 Douna Mali
168 J4 Dounby Orkney, Scotland U.K.
168 H10 Doune Stirling, Scotland U.K.
168 G10 Doune Hill Scotland U.K.
229 F4 Dounkassa Benin
168 I5 Dounreay Highland, Scotland U.K.
198 C1 Doupovské hory mts Czech Rep.
187 E8 Dour Belgium
280 C3 Dourada, Cachoeira waterfall Brazil
280 B2 Dourada, Serra hills Brazil
278 C5 Dourada, Serra mts Brazil
279 B7 Dourados Brazil
279 B7 Dourados r. Brazil
280 A5 Dourados, Serra dos hills Brazil
230 B2 Dourbali Chad
183 C8 Dourbie r. France
183 C8 Dourbies France
178 D6 Dourdan France
183 A7 Dourdou r. France
183 B9 Dourdou r. France
230 D2 Dourdoura Chad
185 I9 Dourgne France
178 C3 Douriez France
204 C6 Douro r. Port.
alt. Duero (Spain)
204 D6 Douro reg. Port.
204 G6 Douro Internacional, Parque Natural do nature res. Port.
Doushi Hubei China see Gong'an
131 J6 Doushui Shuiku resr China
182 I5 Doussard France
280 A5 Doutor Camargo Brazil
182 I4 Douvaine France
180 I3 Douve r. France
181 K3 Douvres-la-Délivrande France
183 F6 Doux r. France
227 H2 Douz Tunisia
185 D8 Douze r. France
224 C6 Douziat Chad
184 E5 Douzillac France
179 J4 Douzy France
213 L7 Dovadola Italy
158 H3 Dovbysh Ukr.
173 I2 Dove r. Derbyshire/Staffordshire, England U.K.
171 P5 Dove r. North Yorkshire, England U.K.
173 O3 Dove r. Suffolk, England U.K.
249 J2 Dove Brook Nfld and Lab. Can.
243 P2 Dove Bugt b. Greenland
265 X4 Dove Creek CO U.S.A.
105 K10 Dover Tas. Austr.
173 O5 Dover Kent, England U.K.
258 D6 Dover DE U.S.A.
257 □O5 Dover NH U.S.A.
258 F3 Dover NJ U.S.A.
256 D8 Dover OH U.S.A.
258 B5 Dover PA U.S.A.
255 D7 Dover TN U.S.A.
109 H12 Dover, Point W.A. Austr.
167 H6 Dover, Strait of France/U.K.
257 □P3 Dover-Foxcroft ME U.S.A.
173 I2 Doveridge Derbyshire, England U.K.
259 H1 Dover Plains NY U.S.A.

172 E2 Dovey r. Wales U.K.
144 C6 Doveyrich r. Iran/Iraq
158 C5 Dovhe Ukr.
158 E3 Dovhoshyyi Ukr.
197 L1 Dovinė r. Lith.
164 G7 Dovnsklint cliff Denmark
163 J5 Dovrefjell mts Norway
163 J5 Dovrefjell Nasjonalpark nat. park Norway
159 O3 Dovzhyk Ukr.
Dow, Lake Botswana see Xau, Lake
233 B8 Dowa Malawi
250 H8 Dowagiac MI U.S.A.
168 I9 Dowally Perth and Kinross, Scotland U.K.
144 F6 Dow Chāhī Iran
144 H3 Dowghā'ī Iran
116 B4 Dowi, Tanjung pt Indon.
144 F3 Dow Kūh mt. Iran
145 J5 Dowlatābād Afgh.
145 K3 Dowlatābād Afgh.
144 E7 Dowlatābād Būshehr Iran
144 D7 Dowlatābād Fārs Iran
144 F7 Dowlatābād Fārs Iran
144 G3 Dowlatābād Khorāsān Iran
144 H4 Dowlatābād Khorāsān Iran
145 I3 Dowlatābād Khorāsān Iran
145 K4 Dowl at Yār Afgh.
169 K4 Down county Northern Ireland U.K.
264 N8 Downey CA U.S.A.
173 M2 Downham Market Norfolk, England U.K.
264 L2 Downieville CA U.S.A.
250 B9 Downing MO U.S.A.
258 D4 Downingtown PA U.S.A.
169 K4 Downpatrick Northern Ireland U.K.
169 D4 Downpatrick Head Ireland
260 F6 Downs KS U.S.A.
257 K6 Downsville NY U.S.A.
250 C5 Downsville WI U.S.A.
173 I6 Downton Wiltshire, England U.K.
246 E4 Downton, Mount B.C. Can.
169 F4 Dowra Ireland
144 B4 Dow Sar Iran
173 L2 Dowsby Lincolnshire, England U.K.
145 M4 Dowshī Afgh.
161 N8 Dowsk Belarus
161 N6 Dowzha Belarus
133 L12 Doxong Xizang China
182 B4 Doyet France
285 H3 Doyle Arg.
264 L1 Doyle CA U.S.A.
249 J4 Doyles Nfld and Lab. Can.
258 E4 Doylestown PA U.S.A.
219 M7 Doyrentsi Bulg.
144 G8 Dozdān r. Iran
125 J10 Dōzen is Japan
238 □1a Doze Ribeiras Terceira Azores
248 E4 Dozois, Réservoir resr Que. Can.
181 K3 Dozulé France
151 G5 Dprabak Armenia
226 C3 Drâa, Cap c. Morocco
226 C3 Drâa, Hamada du plat. Alg.
226 C3 Drâa, Oued watercourse Morocco
159 L4 Drabiv Ukr.
159 K4 Drabivka Ukr.
183 H6 Drac r. France
280 B4 Dracena Brazil
193 J7 Drachhausen Ger.
160 L8 Drachkava Belarus
195 O3 Drachselsried Ger.
186 J2 Drachten Neth.
196 G2 Dragacz Pol.
219 P6 Dragalina Romania
199 L5 Drăgan r. Romania
162 M4 Dragan l. Sweden
199 L5 Drăgăneşti Romania
219 M6 Drăgăneşti-Olt Romania
219 N6 Drăgăneşti-Vlaşca Romania
219 M6 Drăgăşani Romania
190 J4 Drage Ger.
199 L5 Drăgeşti Romania
236 G5 Draghoender S. Africa
219 K8 Dragoman Bulg.
221 H7 Dragonada i. Greece
Dragonera, Isla i. Spain see Sa Dragonera
282 E1 Dragones Arg.
215 M5 Dragoni Italy
109 E12 Dragon Rocks Nature Reserve W.A. Austr.
271 □7 Dragon's Mouths str. Trin. and Tob./Venez.
265 V9 Dragoon AZ U.S.A.
164 I6 Dragør Denmark
219 P6 Dragoş Vodă Romania
163 Q6 Dragsfjärd Fin.
183 I9 Draguignan France
219 O2 Drăguşeni Botoşani Romania
219 P5 Drăguşeni Galaţi Romania
198 G2 Drahanovice Czech Rep.
158 E1 Drahichyn Belarus
193 I7 Drahnsdorf Ger.
105 N3 Drake N.S.W. Austr.
260 E2 Drake ND U.S.A.
190 H5 Drakenburg Ger.
237 M5 Drakensberg mts Lesotho/S. Africa
235 F5 Drakensberg mts S. Africa
237 N5 Drakensberg Garden S. Africa
237 M6 Draken's Rock mt. S. Africa
288 E9 Drake Passage S. Atlantic Ocean
264 I4 Drakes Bay CA U.S.A.
151 G5 Drakhtik Armenia
158 I8 Drakulya r. Ukr.
220 F1 Drama Greece
164 G2 Drammen Norway
178 D6 Drancy France
119 H8 Drang, Prêk r. Cambodia
162 □B1 Drangajökull ice cap Iceland
169 G7 Drangan Ireland
164 F2 Drangedal Norway
138 M6 Drangme Chhu r. Bhutan
190 G3 Drangstedt Ger.
219 R6 Dranov, Lacul l. Romania
182 J4 Dranse r. France
192 G4 Dranse Ger.
191 I8 Dransfeld Ger.
192 H1 Dranske Ger.
265 U1 Draper UT U.S.A.
245 M4 Draper, Mount AK U.S.A.
169 I3 Draperstown Northern Ireland U.K.
Drapsaca Afgh. see Kunduz
138 E2 Dras Jammu and Kashmir India
145 O3 Drasan Pak.
201 O2 Drasenhofen Austria
201 N4 Draßmarkt Austria
201 K6 Drau r. Austria
alt. Drava (Croatia),
alt. Dráva (Hungary)
210 G3 Drava r. Croatia
alt. Drau (Austria),
alt. Dráva (Hungary)
210 G3 Dráva r. Hungary
alt. Drau (Austria),
alt. Drava (Croatia)
199 G6 Drávafok Hungary
210 E2 Dravinja r. Slovenia
210 E2 Dravograd Slovenia
196 D3 Drawa r. Pol.
196 D2 Drawieński Park Narodowy nat. park Pol.
196 D2 Drawno Pol.
189 H2 Drawski Park Krajobrazowy Pol.
196 E3 Drawsko Pol.
196 E2 Drawsko, Jezioro l. Pol.
196 D2 Drawsko Pomorskie Pol.
173 O2 Drayton Norfolk, England U.K.
173 J4 Drayton Oxfordshire, England U.K.
246 H4 Drayton Valley Alta Can.
197 J2 Drążdżewo Pol.
201 M6 Dražen Vrh Slovenia
201 J7 Dražgoše Slovenia
145 N6 Drazinda Pak.
211 A7 Dréa Alg.
211 A7 Dréan Alg.
190 F5 Drebber Ger.
193 J7 Drebkau Ger.
182 E3 Drée r. France
169 C8 Dreenagh Ireland

192 F5 Dreetz Ger.
172 D4 Drefach Carmarthenshire, Wales U.K.
199 I3 Drégelypalánk Hungary
168 G11 Dreghorn North Ayrshire, Scotland U.K.
191 G10 Dreieich Ger.
200 F5 Dreiherrnspitze mt. Austria
193 D6 Dreileben Ger.
194 B2 Dreis Ger.
194 D5 Dreisam r. Ger.
195 P4 Dreisesselberg mt. Ger.
191 I10 Dreistelzberge hill Ger.
190 J1 Drejø i. Denmark
197 K4 Drelów Pol.
190 H1 Drelsdorf Ger.
171 L1 Drem East Lothian, Scotland U.K.
213 P3 Drenchia Italy
210 G3 Drenovci Croatia
220 B2 Drenovë Albania
219 K7 Drenovets Bulg.
192 I4 Drense Ger.
191 E7 Drensteinfurt Ger.
186 K3 Drenthe prov. Neth.
186 J3 Drentse Hoofdvaart canal Neth.
190 G5 Drentwede Ger.
220 D5 Drepano Greece
251 L7 Dresden Ont. Can.
193 I8 Dresden Ger.
193 J8 Dresden admin. reg. Ger.
261 K7 Dresden TN U.S.A.
156 K1 Dresvyanka Rus. Fed.
160 M6 Dretun' Belarus
196 E1 Dretyń Pol.
186 H5 Dreumel Neth.
178 B6 Dreux France
199 G2 Dřevnice r. Czech Rep.
163 L6 Drevsjø Norway
193 F6 Drewitz Ger.
192 F3 Drewitzer See l. Ger.
196 G1 Drewnica Pol.
256 H12 Drewryville VA U.S.A.
258 E5 Drexel Hill PA U.S.A.
196 D3 Drezdenko Pol.
160 K5 Driceni Latvia
160 K6 Dridža l. Latvia
186 H4 Driebergen Neth.
205 N8 Driebes Spain
191 F9 Driedorf Ger.
199 K3 Drienov Slovakia
186 J2 Driesum Neth.
171 Q5 Driffield East Riding of Yorkshire, England U.K.
173 I4 Driffield Gloucestershire, England U.K.
258 D3 Drifton PA U.S.A.
256 G7 Driftwood PA U.S.A.
262 I5 Driggs ID U.S.A.
107 M9 Drillham Qld Austr.
159 K2 Drimaylivka Ukr.
169 G6 Drimmo Ireland
168 E9 Drimnin Highland, Scotland U.K.
169 D9 Drimoleague Ireland
218 H8 Drin r. Albania
210 G3 Drina r. Bos.-Herz./Yugo.
219 K6 Drincea r. Romania
218 I8 Drini i Zi r. Albania
218 H9 Drinit, Gjiri i b. Albania
220 B2 Drino r. Albania
256 B11 Drip Rock KY U.S.A.
169 E9 Dripsey Ireland
286 O1 Driscoll Island Antarctica
Drissa Belarus see Vyerkhnyadzvinsk
201 J1 Dříteň Czech Rep.
162 J5 Driva Norway
198 F3 Drnholec Czech Rep.
210 F4 Drniš Croatia
201 O7 Drnje Croatia
213 J4 Dro Italy
164 G2 Drøbak Norway
219 K6 Drobeta-Turnu Severin Romania
183 E8 Drobie r. France
197 H3 Drobin Pol.
159 Q4 Drobysheve Ukr.
199 L5 Drocea, Vârful hill Romania
158 G5 Drochia Moldova
190 H3 Drochtersen Ger.
186 J2 Drogeham Neth.
169 J5 Drogheda Ireland
Drogichin Belarus see Drahichyn
Drogobych Ukr. see Drohobych
197 K3 Drohiczyn Pol.
158 C4 Drohobych Ukr.
Droichead Átha Ireland see Drogheda
Droichead Nua Ireland see Newbridge
172 H3 Droitwich Spa Worcestershire, England U.K.
Drokiya Moldova see Drochia
139 M6 Drokung Arun. Prad. India
191 E8 Drolshagen Ger.
169 F4 Dromahair Ireland
105 J8 Dromana Vic. Austr.
169 J4 Dromara Northern Ireland U.K.
183 G7 Drôme dept France
183 F7 Drôme r. France
181 J3 Drôme r. France
105 M7 Dromedary, Cape N.S.W. Austr.
258 A4 Dromgold PA U.S.A.
169 J5 Dromiskin Ireland
190 K5 Drömling reg. Ger.
169 G5 Dromod Ireland
169 H3 Dromore Northern Ireland U.K.
169 J4 Dromore Northern Ireland U.K.
169 E4 Dromore West Ireland
212 C7 Dronero Italy
171 O7 Dronfield Derbyshire, England U.K.
168 H12 Drongan East Ayrshire, Scotland U.K.
187 E6 Drongen Belgium
184 D5 Dronne r. France
243 N3 Dronning Ingrid Land reg. Greenland
243 P2 Dronning Louise Land reg. Greenland
Dronning Maud Land reg. Antarctica see Queen Maud Land
186 I3 Dronten Neth.
186 G3 Droogmakerij De Beemster tourist site Neth.
185 D6 Dropt r. France
201 M2 Drosendorf Austria
145 N4 Drosh Pak.
220 E4 Drosia Greece
201 O2 Drösing Austria
161 U9 Droskovo Rus. Fed.
178 B7 Droué France
129 M1 Drovyanaya Rus. Fed.
248 C3 Drowning r. Ont. Can.
193 F8 Droyßig Ger.
158 G2 Drozdyn' Ukr.
145 N6 Drug Pak.
218 I9 Drugovo Drugovo Macedonia
172 F2 Druid Denbighshire, Wales U.K.
271 □9 Druif Aruba
170 F2 Druimdrishaig Argyll and Bute, Scotland U.K.
160 J6 Drūkšių ežeras l. Belarus/Lith.
Druk-Yul country Asia see Bhutan
179 N6 Drulingen France
169 E7 Drumandoora Ireland
169 H5 Drumanespick Ireland
169 K4 Drumaness Northern Ireland U.K.
168 F6 Drumbeg Highland, Scotland U.K.
169 J4 Drumbilla Ireland
169 G4 Drumcard Northern Ireland U.K.
170 I2 Drumclog South Lanarkshire, Scotland U.K.
169 J6 Drumcondra Ireland
169 I5 Drumcondra Ireland
169 H5 Drumcree Ireland
169 G4 Drumduff Northern Ireland U.K.
182 H5 Drumettaz-Clarafond France
169 H2 Drumfree Ireland
169 F5 Drumharlow, Lough l. Ireland
247 H5 Drumheller Alta Can.
169 F4 Drumkeeran Ireland
170 B5 Drumlea Ireland
169 G5 Drumlish Ireland
168 L9 Drumlithie Aberdeenshire, Scotland U.K.

169 I8 Drummin Ireland
Drummond atoll Gilbert Is Kiribati see Tabiteuea
262 H3 Drummond MT U.S.A.
250 C3 Drummond WI U.S.A.
256 I12 Drummond, Lake VA U.S.A.
Drummond Island Phoenix Is Kiribati see McKean
251 K4 Drummond Island MI U.S.A.
107 K8 Drummond Range hills Qld Austr.
249 F4 Drummondville Que. Can.
168 G13 Drummore Dumfries and Galloway, Scotland U.K.
169 G3 Drumnacross Ireland
168 H8 Drumnadrochit Highland, Scotland U.K.
170 C4 Drumnakilly Northern Ireland U.K.
169 H3 Drumquin Northern Ireland U.K.
170 B7 Drumraney Ireland
169 F4 Drumshanbo Ireland
170 B6 Drumsna Ireland
186 H5 Drunen Neth.
170 C5 Drung Ireland
245 N3 Drury Lake Y.T. Can.
212 F1 Drusberg mt. Switz.
179 O6 Drusenheim France
Druskieniki Lith. see Druskininkai
160 H8 Druskininkai Lith.
160 I4 Drusti Latvia
186 I5 Druten Neth.
160 N8 Druts' r. Belarus
160 K6 Druya Belarus
182 C1 Druyes-les-Belles-Fontaines France
197 H4 Drużbice Pol.
Druzhba Kazakh. see Dostyk
197 J1 Druzhba Rus. Fed.
159 L3 Druzhba Chernihivs'ka Oblast' Ukr.
159 M1 Druzhba Sums'ka Oblast' Ukr.
159 N7 Druzhbivka Ukr.
153 P3 Druzhina Rus. Fed.
161 U1 Druzhinnoye, Ozero l. Rus. Fed.
159 Q5 Druzhkivka Ukr.
Druzhkovka Donets'ka Oblast' Ukr. see Druzhkivka
Druzhkovka Kharkivs'ka Oblast' Ukr. see Lozova
161 N2 Druzhnaya Gorka Rus. Fed.
158 E1 Druzhylavichy Belarus
197 H1 Druzno, Jezioro l. Pol.
199 K3 Družstevná pri Hornáde Slovakia
197 J4 Drwalew Pol.
197 G2 Drwęca r. Pol.
197 H2 Drwęckie, Jezioro l. Pol.
197 I5 Drwinia Pol.
106 D3 Dry r. N.T. Austr.
219 N8 Dryanovo Bulg.
159 S1 Dryazgi Rus. Fed.
160 L3 Dryazhno Rus. Fed.
245 M4 Dry Bay AK U.S.A.
247 M5 Dryberry Lake Ont. Can.
161 O7 Drybin Belarus
172 G4 Drybrook Gloucestershire, England U.K.
261 E7 Dry Cimarron r. KS U.S.A.
245 K3 Dry Creek AK U.S.A.
248 A3 Dryden Ont. Can.
257 I6 Dryden NY U.S.A.
256 C12 Dryden VA U.S.A.
262 L5 Dry Fork r. WY U.S.A.
283 □ Drygalski Fjord inlet S. Georgia
287 L1 Drygalski Ice Tongue Antarctica
287 G2 Drygalski Island Antarctica
197 K2 Drygały Pol.
172 E3 Drygarn Fawr hill Wales U.K.
270 □ Dry Harbour Mountains hills Jamaica
237 I3 Dry Harts r. S. Africa
265 R5 Dry Lake NV U.S.A.
264 O2 Dry Lake l. NV U.S.A.
168 H10 Drymen Stirling, Scotland U.K.
160 K6 Drysa r. Belarus
108 I3 Drysdale r. W.A. Austr.
106 E1 Drysdale Island N.T. Austr.
108 I3 Drysdale River National Park W.A. Austr.
Drysyvaty Vozyera l. Belarus/Lith. see Drūkšių ežeras
255 F13 Dry Tortugas is FL U.S.A.
196 G3 Drzewce Pol.
196 E2 Drzewiany Pol.
197 I4 Drzewica Pol.
196 E2 Drzonowo Zachodniopomorskie Pol.
192 L2 Drzonowo Zachodniopomorskie Pol.
196 G2 Drzycim Pol.
229 H5 Dschang Cameroon
230 D4 Dua r. Dem. Rep. Congo
144 C4 Dūāb r. Iran
271 I8 Duaca Venez.
214 B7 Dualchi Sardegna Italy
130 G7 Du'an Guangxi China
Duancun Shanxi China see Wuxiang
239 □3b Duangani Mayotte
107 L7 Duaringa Qld Austr.
139 M6 Duars reg. Assam India
270 H4 Duarte, Pico mt. Dom. Rep.
280 C5 Duartina Brazil
204 H6 Duas Igrejas Port.
228 E5 Duayaw-Nkwanta Ghana
198 D1 Dubá Czech Rep.
146 B2 Ḑubā Saudi Arabia
Dubai U.A.E. see Dubayy
264 I1 Dubakella Mountain CA U.S.A.
158 I6 Dubăsari Moldova
158 I6 Dubău Moldova
247 L2 Dubawnt r. Nunavut Can.
247 K2 Dubawnt Lake N.W.T./Nunavut Can.
147 M4 Dubayshī Oman
147 L3 Dubayy U.A.E.
146 B2 Dubbagh, Jabal ad mt. Saudi Arabia
105 L5 Dubbo N.S.W. Austr.
228 D5 Dube r. Liberia
158 D2 Dubechne Ukr.
197 L4 Dubeczno Pol.
193 I7 Duben Ger.
193 F7 Düben Ger.
212 F1 Dübendorf Switz.
193 G7 Dübener Heide park Ger.
193 F7 Dübener Heide reg. Ger.
197 K1 Dubeninki Pol.
157 I5 Dubenki Rus. Fed.
142 G2 Dubenskiy Rus. Fed.
Dubesar' Moldova see Dubăsari
168 C10 Dubh Artach i. Scotland U.K.
193 I9 Dubí Czech Rep.
160 H7 Dubičiai Lith.
197 K6 Dubiecko Pol.
197 L4 Dubienka Pol.
218 H8 Dubinës, Maja e mt. Albania
160 I6 Dubingiai Lith.
212 G3 Dubino Italy
158 F5 Dubivka Ukr.
159 K4 Dubiyivka Ukr.
151 H2 Dubki Rus. Fed.
159 N9 Dubky Ukr.
266 F2 Dublán Mex.
250 G1 Dublin Ont. Can.
169 J6 Dublin Ireland
169 J6 Dublin county Ireland
255 F9 Dublin GA U.S.A.
258 C5 Dublin MD U.S.A.
258 E4 Dublin PA U.S.A.
256 E11 Dublin VA U.S.A.
169 J6 Dublin Bay Ireland
198 D2 Dublovice Czech Rep.
158 C4 Dublyany L'vivs'ka Oblast' Ukr.
158 D4 Dublyany L'vivs'ka Oblast' Ukr.
197 M2 Dubna Belarus
160 J5 Dubna r. Latvia
161 U5 Dubna Moskovskaya Oblast' Rus. Fed.
161 T7 Dubna Tul'skaya Oblast' Rus. Fed.
198 G3 Dubňany Czech Rep.
198 D3 Dubné Czech Rep.
199 H3 Dubnica nad Váhom Slovakia

158 E3 Dubno Ukr.
262 H4 Dubois ID U.S.A.
256 G7 Du Bois PA U.S.A.
262 J5 Dubois WY U.S.A.
Dubossary Moldova see Dubăsari
161 T8 Dubovaya Roshcha Rus. Fed.
158 C5 Dubove Ukr.
199 J2 Dubovica Slovakia
159 O5 Dubovi Hryady Ukr.
161 V8 Dubovka Tul'skaya Oblast' Rus. Fed.
157 I6 Dubovka Volgogradskaya Oblast' Rus. Fed.
Dubovo Moldova see Dubău
161 X6 Dubovoye, Ozero l. Rus. Fed.
157 H7 Dubovskoye Rus. Fed.
159 M2 Dubov"yazivka Ukr.
151 J5 Dübrar Dağı mt. Azer.
201 O8 Dubrava Croatia
199 I2 Dúbrava Slovakia
201 M8 Dubravica Croatia
199 I3 Dúbravy Slovakia
228 B4 Dubréka Guinea
Dubris Kent, England U.K. see Dover
158 G3 Dubrivka Ukr.
161 W7 Dubrovichi Rus. Fed.
161 Q8 Dubrovka Bryanskaya Oblast' Rus. Fed.
160 L5 Dubrovka Pskovskaya Oblast' Rus. Fed.
160 M4 Dubrovka Pskovskaya Oblast' Rus. Fed.
210 G4 Dubrovnik Croatia
143 M1 Dubrovnoye Kazakh.
197 L6 Dubrovytsya L'vivs'ka Oblast' Ukr.
158 F2 Dubrovytsya Rivnens'ka Oblast' Ukr.
161 N7 Dubrowna Belarus
254 B4 Dubuque IA U.S.A.
158 J5 Dubynove Ukr.
160 G6 Dubysa r. Lith.
180 G6 Duc, Étang au l. France
119 H9 Đức Bôn Vietnam
101 □9 Duc de Gloucester, Îles du is Arch. des Tuamotu Fr. Polynesia
180 I4 Ducey France
131 K4 Duchang Jiangxi China
107 N1 Duchateau Entrance sea chan. P.N.G.
Ducheng Guangdong China see Yunan
192 I3 Ducherow Ger.
265 V1 Duchesne UT U.S.A.
265 W1 Duchesne r. UT U.S.A.
106 G6 Duchess Qld Austr.
247 I5 Duchess Alta Can.
193 I9 Duchov Czech Rep.
107 I2 Ducie r. Qld Austr.
291 K7 Ducie Island atoll Pitcairn Is
255 D7 Duck r. TN U.S.A.
247 K4 Duck Bay Man. Can.
108 D7 Duck Creek r. W.A. Austr.
173 M4 Duck End Essex, England U.K.
247 J4 Duck Lake Sask. Can.
246 K5 Duck Mountain Provincial Park Man. Can.
262 F6 Duck Valley Indian Reservation res. ID/NV U.S.A.
265 Q3 Duckwater NV U.S.A.
265 Q3 Duckwater Peak NV U.S.A.
181 M3 Duclair France
119 H9 Đức Linh Vietnam
271 □3 Ducos Martinique
119 I7 Đức Phô Vietnam
118 G5 Duc Tho Vietnam
274 C4 Duda r. Col.
199 G4 Dudar Hungary
159 M6 Dudchany Ukr.
171 M2 Duddo Northumberland, England U.K.
171 K5 Duddon r. England U.K.
187 J10 Dudelange Lux.
191 C11 Dudeldorf Ger.
191 J7 Duderstadt Ger.
218 I4 Dudestii Vechi Romania
139 I7 Dudhi Uttar Prad. India
139 M7 Dudhnai Assam India
138 H5 Dudhwa Uttar Prad. India
199 H3 Dudince Slovakia
212 C2 Düdingen Switz.
152 J3 Dudinka Rus. Fed.
172 H2 Dudley West Midlands, England U.K.
265 V9 Dudleyville AZ U.S.A.
136 E3 Dudna r. India
161 S8 Dudorovskiy Rus. Fed.
138 E6 Dudu Rajasthan India
232 E3 Dudub Eth.
237 M2 Duduza S. Africa
210 F2 Dudváh r. Slovakia
168 L8 Dudwick, Hill of Scotland U.K.
122 M3 Due Sakhalin Rus. Fed.
228 D5 Duékoué Côte d'Ivoire
116 E6 Duen, Bukit vol. Indon.
205 K5 Dueñas Spain
165 L7 Dueodde pt Bornholm Denmark
278 C4 Dueré Brazil
204 I4 Duerna r. Spain
182 F5 Duerne France
204 G6 Duero r. Spain
alt. Douro (Portugal)
213 L4 Dueville Italy
251 P1 Dufault, Lac l. Que. Can.
187 G6 Duffel Belgium
248 E1 Dufferin, Cape Que. Can.
262 E6 Duffer Peak NV U.S.A.
173 J2 Duffield Derbyshire, England U.K.
256 C12 Duffield VA U.S.A.
100 □6 Duff Islands Santa Cruz Is Solomon Is
249 G1 Duffreboy, Lac l. Que. Can.
168 J8 Dufftown Moray, Scotland U.K.
212 D4 Dufourspitze mt. Italy/Switz.
247 L5 Dufrost Man. Can.
106 H5 Dugald r. Qld Austr.
210 E3 Duga Resa Croatia
153 P4 Duga-Zapadnaya, Mys c. Rus. Fed.
122 F2 Dugda Rus. Fed.
150 E9 Dughdash mts Saudi Arabia
Dughoba Uzbek. see Dugob
210 E3 Dugi Otok i. Croatia
210 F4 Dugi Rat Croatia
161 T7 Dugna Rus. Fed.
179 J5 Dugny-sur-Meuse France
143 L8 Dugob Uzbek.
210 F4 Dugopolje Croatia
210 F3 Dugo Selo Croatia
129 K7 Dugui Qarag Nei Mongol China
221 I1 Düğüncübaşı Turkey
265 T1 Dugway UT U.S.A.
130 H2 Du He r. China
185 D8 Duhort-Bachen France
224 C4 Duhūn Tārsū mts Chad/Libya
275 E4 Duida-Marahuaca, Parque Nacional nat. park Venez.
107 H2 Duifken Point Qld Austr.
186 H2 Duinen Terschelling nature res. Neth.
186 G2 Duinen Texel nature res. Neth.
186 F5 Duinen van Voorne nature res. Neth.
191 I6 Duingen Ger.
213 P4 Duino Italy
191 C8 Duisburg Ger.
274 C3 Duitama Col.
186 J5 Duiven Neth.
235 F4 Duiwelskloof S. Africa
130 D3 Dujiangyan Sichuan China
232 D4 Dujuuma Somalia
219 K8 Dukat mt. Macedonia
153 Q3 Dukat Rus. Fed.
237 K6 Dukathole S. Africa
220 A2 Dukat i Ri Albania
245 O5 Duke Island AK U.S.A.
Duke of Clarence atoll Tokelau see Nukunonu
Duke of Gloucester Islands Arch. des Tuamotu Fr. Polynesia see Duc de Gloucester, Îles du
Duke of York atoll Tokelau see Atafu
232 A3 Duk Fadiat Sudan
232 A3 Duk Faiwil Sudan
147 J3 Dukhān Qatar
146 F3 Dukhnah Saudi Arabia
142 C1 Dukhovnitskoye Rus. Fed.
161 P6 Dukhovshchina Rus. Fed.
161 O6 Dukhovshchinskaya Vozvyshennost' hills Rus. Fed.
145 M6 Duki Pak.
122 I3 Duki Rus. Fed.
122 I3 Duki r. Rus. Fed.
229 H4 Dukku Nigeria
197 J6 Dukla Pol.
189 J4 Dukla Pass pass Pol./Slovakia
Dukou Sichuan China see Panzhihua
160 J6 Dūkštas Lith.
234 E4 Dukwe Botswana
128 J2 Dulaanhaan Mongolia
144 H7 Dūlab Iran
261 J11 Dulac LA U.S.A.
128 F8 Dulan Qinghai China
Dulawan Mindanao Phil. see Datu Piang
244 H2 Dulbi r. AK U.S.A.
285 F2 Dulce r. Arg.
205 O7 Dulce r. Spain
263 K8 Dulce NM U.S.A.
266 □R13 Dulce, Golfo b. Costa Rica
266 □Q10 Dulce Nombre de Culmí Hond.
282 C2 Dulcinea Chile
129 M1 Dul'durga Rus. Fed.
169 J5 Duleek Ireland
153 O3 Dulgalakh r. Rus. Fed.
219 P7 Dŭlgopol Bulg.
107 I1 Dulhunty r. Qld Austr.
160 K6 Dulina Belarus
133 E9 Dulishi Hu salt l. China
117 J3 Dulit, Pegunungan mts Malaysia
130 G6 Duliu Jiang r. China
114 E6 Duljugan Point Leyte Phil.
139 N7 Dullabchara Assam India
173 M3 Dullingham Cambridgeshire, England U.K.
237 O1 Dullstroom S. Africa
191 D7 Dülmen Ger.
138 D5 Dulmera Rajasthan India
168 I8 Dulnain r. Scotland U.K.
168 I8 Dulnain Bridge Highland, Scotland U.K.
160 L4 Dulovka Rus. Fed.
219 P7 Dulovo Bulg.
150 G2 Dulq Maghār Syria
250 B3 Duluth MN U.S.A.
260 I2 Duluth/Superior airport MN U.S.A.
172 E5 Dulverton Somerset, England U.K.
161 X4 Dulyapino Rus. Fed.
150 E5 Dūmā Syria
114 D7 Dumaguete Negros Phil.
116 D4 Dumai Sumatera Indon.
151 A5 Dumanlı Turkey
151 E5 Dumanlı Dağı mt. Turkey
151 B6 Dumanlı Tepe mt. Turkey
114 D8 Dumanquilas Bay Mindanao Phil.
114 C6 Dumaran i. Phil.
115 D1 Dumarchen i. Indon.
105 M3 Dumaresq r. N.S.W. Austr.
261 J9 Dumas AR U.S.A.
261 E8 Dumas TX U.S.A.
148 I9 Dumat al Jandal Al Jawf Saudi Arabia
150 E5 Ḍumayr Syria
150 E5 Ḍumayr, Jabal mts Syria
Dumbakh Iran see Dom Bākh
168 G11 Dumbarton West Dunbartonshire, Scotland U.K.
237 O3 Dumbe S. Africa
100 □5 Dumbéa New Caledonia
199 I3 Ďumbier mt. Slovakia
109 D12 Dumbleyung W.A. Austr.
109 D12 Dumbleyung, Lake salt flat W.A. Austr.
229 H5 Dumbo Cameroon
199 L6 Dumbrava Romania
219 M4 Dumbrăveni Sibiu Romania
219 P5 Dumbrăveni Vrancea Romania
219 N5 Dumbrăvița Brașov Romania
199 K6 Dumbrăvița Timiș Romania
204 B2 Dumbría Spain
138 G3 Dumchele Jammu and Kashmir India
116 G4 Dumdum i. Indon.
139 O6 Dum Duma Assam India
219 P4 Dumești Romania
180 F7 Dumet, Île i. France
271 □3 Dumfries Grenada
168 I12 Dumfries Dumfries and Galloway, Scotland U.K.
168 I12 Dumfries and Galloway admin. div. Scotland U.K.
169 B5 Dumha Éige Ireland
169 C4 Dumha Thuama Ireland
161 S8 Duminichi Kaluzhskaya Oblast' Rus. Fed.
161 S8 Duminichi Kaluzhskaya Oblast' Rus. Fed.
219 M3 Dumitra Romania
139 K7 Dumka Jharkhand India
151 C5 Dumlu Turkey
151 C5 Dumlu Dağı mt. Turkey
150 A2 Dumlugöze Turkey
221 K4 Dumlupınar Turkey
136 G4 Dummagudem Andhra Prad. India
190 F5 Dümmer l. Ger.
191 F5 Dümmer, Naturpark nature res. Ger.
192 F3 Dummerstorf Ger.
218 J8 Dumnicë e Poshtme Podujevë Kosovo
115 D3 Dumoga Sulawesi Indon.
248 E4 Dumoine r. Que. Can.
251 Q3 Dumoine, Lac l. Que. Can.
251 R3 Dumont, Lac l. Que. Can.
287 J2 Dumont d'Urville research stn Antarctica
287 I2 Dumont d'Urville Sea Antarctica
191 C10 Dümpelfeld Ger.
147 I3 Ḍumrān, Barqā' aḍ esc. Saudi Arabia
139 J7 Dumraon Bihar India
146 F7 Dumsuk i. Saudi Arabia
225 F2 Dumyāṭ Egypt
148 E8 Dumyāṭ governorate Egypt
185 H9 Dun France
191 J8 Dün ridge Ger.
210 G3 Duna r. Hungary
alt. Donau (Austria/Germany),
alt. Dunaj (Slovakia),
alt. Dunărea (Romania),
alt. Dunav (Serbia),
conv. Danube
199 H4 Dunaalmás Hungary
Dünaburg Latvia see Daugavpils
199 H5 Dunaegyháza Hungary
199 H5 Dunafalva Hungary
169 G2 Dunaff Head Ireland
199 H5 Dunaföldvár Hungary
199 I4 Dunaharaszti Hungary
210 F2 Dunaj r. Slovakia
alt. Donau (Austria/Germany),
alt. Duna (Hungary),
alt. Dunărea (Romania),
alt. Dunav (Serbia),
conv. Danube
197 I5 Dunajec r. Pol.
198 G3 Dunajská Lužná Slovakia
199 G4 Dunajská Streda Slovakia
199 I4 Dunakeszi Hungary
198 G4 Dunakiliti Hungary
105 K10 Dunalley Tas. Austr.
Dunanbay Kazakh. see Dunenbay
169 J5 Dunany Point Ireland
199 I5 Dunapataj Hungary
219 Q5 Dunărea r. Romania
alt. Donau (Austria/Germany),
alt. Duna (Hungary),
alt. Dunaj (Slovakia),
alt. Dunav (Serbia),
conv. Danube
219 R5 Dunării, Delta Romania
199 G4 Dunaszeg Hungary
199 H5 Dunaszekcső Hungary
199 H5 Dunaszentgyörgy Hungary
198 G4 Dunasziget Hungary
199 I5 Dunatetétlen Hungary
199 I5 Duna-Tisza Köze reg. Hungary
199 H5 Dunaújváros Hungary
219 P6 Dunav r. Serbia
alt. Donau (Austria/Germany),
alt. Duna (Hungary),
alt. Dunaj (Slovakia),
alt. Dunărea (Romania),
conv. Danube
199 I4 Dunavarsány Hungary
199 H5 Dunavecse Hungary
219 K7 Dunavtsi Bulg.
153 N2 Dunay, Ostrova is Rus. Fed.
158 F4 Dunayivtsi Khmel'nyts'ka Oblast' Ukr.
158 F5 Dunayivtsi Khmel'nyts'ka Oblast' Ukr.
158 I8 Dunays'kyi Zapovidnyk nature res. Ukr.
103 E12 Dunback South I. N.Z.
107 I4 Dunbar Qld Austr.
168 K10 Dunbar East Lothian, Scotland U.K.
245 J2 Dunbar AK U.S.A.
256 F9 Dunbar PA U.S.A.
250 F4 Dunbar WI U.S.A.
256 D10 Dunbar WV U.S.A.
168 J6 Dunbeath Highland, Scotland U.K.
168 I10 Dunblane Stirling, Scotland U.K.
169 J6 Dunboyne Ireland
246 F5 Duncan B.C. Can.
265 W9 Duncan AZ U.S.A.
261 G8 Duncan OK U.S.A.
248 D2 Duncan, Cape Nunavut Can.
248 E2 Duncan, Lac l. Que. Can.
246 G5 Duncan Lake B.C. Can.
246 H2 Duncan Lake N.W.T. Can.
169 I8 Duncannon Ireland
251 Q9 Duncannon PA U.S.A.
169 D8 Duncannon Bridge Ireland
137 M7 Duncan Passage Andaman & Nicobar Is India
270 □ Duncans Jamaica
168 J5 Duncansby Head Scotland U.K.
270 F2 Duncan Town Bahamas
169 B8 Dún Chaoin Ireland
173 J3 Dunchurch Warwickshire, England U.K.
169 I8 Duncormick Ireland
160 F4 Dundaga Latvia
168 E10 Dun da Ghaoithe hill Scotland U.K.
251 N5 Dundalk Ont. Can.
169 J4 Dundalk Ireland
258 B6 Dundalk MD U.S.A.
169 J5 Dundalk Bay Ireland
248 E5 Dundas Ont. Can.
Dundas Greenland see Uummannaq
109 F12 Dundas, Lake salt flat W.A. Austr.
245 O5 Dundas Island B.C. Can.
109 G12 Dundas Nature Reserve W.A. Austr.
242 G2 Dundas Peninsula N.W.T. Can.
106 C1 Dundas Strait N.T. Austr.
Dundbürd Mongolia see Batnorov
Dún Dealgan Ireland see Dundalk
237 O4 Dundee S. Africa
168 K10 Dundee Dundee, Scotland U.K.
168 K10 Dundee admin. div. Scotland U.K.
251 K8 Dundee MI U.S.A.
256 I6 Dundee NY U.S.A.
128 I4 Dundgovĭ prov. Mongolia
129 O5 Dund Hot Nei Mongol China
169 K3 Dundonald Northern Ireland U.K.
168 G11 Dundonald South Ayrshire, Scotland U.K.
107 J9 Dundoo Qld Austr.
168 G8 Dundreggan Highland, Scotland U.K.
168 I13 Dundrennan Dumfries and Galloway, Scotland U.K.
169 J6 Dundrum Dublin Ireland
169 F7 Dundrum Tipperary Ireland
169 K4 Dundrum Northern Ireland U.K.
169 K4 Dundrum Bay Northern Ireland U.K.
138 I6 Dundwa Range mts India/Nepal
248 F1 Dune, Lac l. Que. Can.
168 I11 Duneaton Water r. Scotland U.K.
168 L8 Dunecht Aberdeenshire, Scotland U.K.
103 E12 Dunedin South I. N.Z.
255 F11 Dunedin FL U.S.A.
105 L5 Dunedoo N.S.W. Austr.
143 S3 Dunenbay Kazakh.
185 F7 Dunes France
246 E3 Dune Za Keyih Provincial Park nat. park B.C. Can.
170 B3 Dunfanaghy Ireland
168 J10 Dunfermline Fife, Scotland U.K.
169 I3 Dungannon Northern Ireland U.K.
Dún Garbhán Ireland see Dungarvan
138 E5 Dungargarh Rajasthan India
138 D8 Dungarpur Rajasthan India
169 H7 Dungarvan Kilkenny Ireland
169 G8 Dungarvan Waterford Ireland
195 N4 Dungau reg. Ger.
133 J11 Dung Co l. Xizang China
173 N6 Dungeness hd England U.K.
283 C9 Dungeness, Punta pt Arg.
191 D10 Düngenheim Ger.
169 I3 Dungiven Northern Ireland U.K.
Dungloe Ireland see An Clochán Liath
105 M5 Dungog N.S.W. Austr.
169 F9 Dungourney Ireland
118 I7 Dung Quất, Vung b. Vietnam
230 F4 Dungu Dem. Rep. Congo
116 E2 Dungun Malaysia
225 H4 Dungunab Sudan
171 Q7 Dunholme Lincolnshire, England U.K.
Dunhou Jiangxi China see Ji'an
122 F7 Dunhua Jilin China
132 L6 Dunhuang Gansu China
183 E6 Dunières France
196 E1 Duninowo Pol.
107 L9 Dunkeld Qld Austr.
105 I7 Dunkeld Vic. Austr.
168 I9 Dunkeld Perth and Kinross, Scotland U.K.
169 E6 Dunkellin r. Ireland
201 L3 Dunkelsteiner Wald for. Austria
178 D1 Dunkerque France
169 G7 Dunkerrin Ireland
172 E5 Dunkery Hill England U.K.
169 F3 Dunkineely Ireland
Dunkirk France see Dunkerque
173 N5 Dunkirk Kent, England U.K.
256 F6 Dunkirk NY U.S.A.
256 B8 Dunkirk OH U.S.A.
107 K4 Dunk Island Qld Austr.
228 E5 Dunkwa Ghana
169 J6 Dún Laoghaire Ireland
260 H5 Dunlap IA U.S.A.
250 I8 Dunlap IN U.S.A.
255 E8 Dunlap TN U.S.A.
169 I6 Dunlavin Ireland
169 J5 Dunleer Ireland
184 H3 Dun-le-Palestel France
182 E2 Dun-les-Places France
Dunlewy Ireland see Dún Lúiche
168 G11 Dunlop East Ayrshire, Scotland U.K.
169 J2 Dunloy Northern Ireland U.K.
167 D4 Dunluce tourist site Northern Ireland U.K.
170 A3 Dún Lúiche Ireland
169 C9 Dunmanus Ireland
169 C10 Dunmanus Bay Ireland
169 D9 Dunmanway Ireland
106 D4 Dunmarra N.T. Austr.
169 G8 Dunmoon Ireland
169 E5 Dunmore Ireland
258 D2 Dunmore PA U.S.A.
256 F10 Dunmore WV U.S.A.
169 I8 Dunmore East Ireland
270 E1 Dunmore Town Eleuthera Bahamas
169 K3 Dunmurry Northern Ireland U.K.
255 H8 Dunn NC U.S.A.
255 F11 Dunnellon FL U.S.A.
168 J5 Dunnet Highland, Scotland U.K.
168 J5 Dunnet Bay Scotland U.K.
168 J5 Dunnet Head Scotland U.K.
264 K3 Dunnigan CA U.S.A.
168 I10 Dunning Perth and Kinross, Scotland U.K.
260 E5 Dunning NE U.S.A.
194 F5 Dunningen Ger.
171 P6 Dunnington York, England U.K.
109 E12 Dunn Rock Nature Reserve W.A. Austr.
109 E8 Dunns Range hills W.A. Austr.
251 O7 Dunnville Ont. Can.
178 B8 Dunois reg. France
105 I7 Dunolly Vic. Austr.
168 G11 Dunoon Argyll and Bute, Scotland U.K.
Dunquin Ireland see Dún Chaoin
168 J11 Dun Rig hill Scotland U.K.
168 L11 Duns Scottish Borders, Scotland U.K.
103 G10 Dunsandel South I. N.Z.
109 C12 Dunsborough W.A. Austr.
168 I12 Dunscore Dumfries and Galloway, Scotland U.K.
260 E1 Dunseith ND U.S.A.
190 G5 Dünsen Ger.
169 I5 Dunshaughlin Ireland
262 C6 Dunsmuir CA U.S.A.
173 K4 Dunstable Bedfordshire, England U.K.
103 D12 Dunstan Mountains South I. N.Z.
172 F5 Dunster Somerset, England U.K.
182 B3 Dun-sur-Auron France
179 J5 Dun-sur-Meuse France
168 H8 Duntelchaig, Loch l. Scotland U.K.
103 E11 Duntroon South I. N.Z.
190 E3 Dunum Ger.
170 H3 Dunure South Ayrshire, Scotland U.K.
172 D4 Dunvant Swansea, Wales U.K.
168 C8 Dunvegan Highland, Scotland U.K.
168 C7 Dunvegan, Loch b. Scotland U.K.
168 C7 Dunvegan Head Scotland U.K.
247 J2 Dunvegan Lake N.W.T. Can.
173 P3 Dunwich Suffolk, England U.K.
145 N7 Dunyapur Pak.
129 S2 Duobukur He r. China
Duolun Nei Mongol China see Dolonnur
133 F9 Duomula Xizang China
119 G9 Dương Đông Vietnam
136 F5 Dupadu Andhra Prad. India
131 H6 Dupang Ling mts China
251 O1 Duparquet Que. Can.
251 O1 Duparquet, Lac l. Que. Can.
Duperré Alg. see Aïn Defla
201 K7 Duplica Slovenia
219 L8 Dupnitsa Bulg.
260 E3 Dupree SD U.S.A.
108 C6 Dupuy, Cape W.A. Austr.
146 F7 Duqaylah i. Saudi Arabia
Duque de Bragança Angola see Calandula
281 F5 Duque de Caxias Brazil
283 B8 Duque de York, Isla i. Chile
250 B3 Duquette MN U.S.A.
254 C6 Du Quoin IL U.S.A.
232 C2 Dura r. Eth.
150 D7 Dūrā West Bank
213 M2 Dura, Cima mt. Italy
195 I6 Durach Ger.
98 C3 Durack r. W.A. Austr.
108 I4 Durack Range hills W.A. Austr.
Dura Europos Syria see Aş Şālihīyah
148 G3 Durağan Turkey
138 F8 Duraha Madh. Prad. India
221 J3 Durak Turkey
205 O3 Durana Spain
185 E7 Durance France
183 F9 Durance r. France
251 K7 Durand MI U.S.A.
250 C5 Durand WI U.S.A.
100 □5 Durand, Récif rf New Caledonia
207 J3 Duranes hill Spain
265 Q9 Durango Baja California Mex.
268 C1 Durango Durango Mex.
268 C1 Durango state Mex.
205 O2 Durango Spain
263 K8 Durango CO U.S.A.
268 B2 Durango, Sierra de mts Mex.
145 L6 Durani reg. Afgh.
219 Q7 Durankulak Bulg.
213 M3 Duranno, Monte mt. Italy
285 G5 Durañona Arg.
261 K9 Durant MS U.S.A.
261 G8 Durant OK U.S.A.
185 E6 Duras France
205 L5 Duratón r. Spain
185 G6 Duravel France
150 E4 Duraykīsh Syria
282 C3 Durazno Arg.
285 I3 Durazno Uru.
285 I3 Durazno dept Uru.
Durazzo Albania see Durrës
194 E4 Durbach Ger.
185 G9 Durban France
237 P5 Durban S. Africa
183 B11 Durban-Corbières France
236 C9 Durbanville S. Africa
194 F5 Dürbheim Ger.
256 F10 Durbin WV U.S.A.
179 L7 Durbion r. France
145 K7 Durbun Pak.
187 H8 Durbuy Belgium
207 L7 Dúrcal Spain
207 M7 Dúrcal r. Spain
199 H2 Ďurčiná Slovakia
182 B4 Durdat-Larequille France
181 M2 Durdent r. France
210 F2 Đurđevac Croatia
232 F2 Durdura, Raas pt Somalia
132 I3 Düre Xinjiang China
191 B9 Düren Ger.
144 G5 Düren Iran
183 D9 Durfort France
138 H9 Durg Chhattisgarh India
139 M7 Durgapur Bangl.
139 K8 Durgapur W. Bengal India
251 N5 Durham Ont. Can.
171 N4 Durham Durham, England U.K.
171 M4 Durham admin. div. England U.K.
264 K2 Durham CA U.S.A.
259 J2 Durham CT U.S.A.
255 H8 Durham NC U.S.A.
257 □O5 Durham NH U.S.A.
102 □ Durham, Point Chatham Is S. Pacific Ocean
257 □S2 Durham Bridge N.B. Can.
107 H9 Durham Downs Qld Austr.
171 O4 Durham Tees Valley airport England U.K.
232 D3 Durhi well Eth.
116 D4 Duri Sumatera Indon.
117 H5 Duriansebatang Kalimantan Indon.
168 I12 Durisdeer Dumfries and Galloway, Scotland U.K.
Durlas Ireland see Thurles
158 H6 Durlești Moldova
201 M7 Durmanec Croatia
178 G1 Durme r. Belgium
194 H5 Dürmentingen Ger.
194 E4 Durmersheim Ger.
218 H7 Durmitor mt. Montenegro
218 G7 Durmitor nat. park Montenegro
168 G5 Durness Highland, Scotland U.K.
168 G5 Durness, Kyle of inlet Scotland U.K.
201 O3 Dürnkrut Austria
Durocortorum France see Reims
107 M9 Durong South Qld Austr.
Durostorum Bulg. see Silistra
Durovernum Kent, England U.K. see Canterbury
218 H9 Durrës Albania
106 H8 Durrie Qld Austr.
195 I5 Dürrlauingen Ger.
193 J8 Dürröhrsdorf-Dittersbach Ger.
169 H7 Durrow Ireland
195 I3 Dürrwangen Ger.
169 B9 Dursey Head Ireland
169 B9 Dursey Island Ireland
172 H4 Dursley Gloucestershire, England U.K.
221 J3 Dursunbey Turkey
181 K6 Durtal France
Duru Guizhou China see Wuchuan
230 F4 Duru r. Dem. Rep. Congo
147 M4 Duru reg. Oman
150 F2 Duruca Turkey
205 O5 Duruelo de la Sierra Spain
232 E2 Durukhsi Somalia
221 J1 Durusu Gölü l. Turkey
150 E6 Durūz, Jabal ad mt. Syria
113 I7 D'Urville, Tanjung pt Papua Indon.
102 H7 D'Urville Island South I. N.Z.
258 D2 Duryea PA U.S.A.
168 □N2 Dury Voe inlet Scotland U.K.
145 K4 Durzab Afgh.
144 H3 Duşak Turkm.
160 I6 Dusetos Lith.
145 K7 Dushai Pak.
130 F6 Dushan Guizhou China
145 M2 Dushanbe Tajik.
132 G4 Dushanzi Xinjiang China
159 L1 Dushatino Rus. Fed.
151 F3 Dushet'i Georgia
129 N6 Dushikou Hebei China
251 R8 Dushore PA U.S.A.
160 G7 Dusia l. Lith.
103 A12 Dusky Sound inlet South I. N.Z.
197 M1 Dusmenys Lith.
199 H5 Dusnok Hungary
196 G2 Dusocin Pol.
122 I3 Dusse-Alin', Khrebet mts Rus. Fed.
108 J3 Dussejour, Cape W.A. Austr.
191 C8 Düsseldorf Ger.
191 B7 Düsseldorf admin. reg. Ger.
186 G5 Dussen Neth.
194 G5 Dußlingen Ger.
193 G7 Düßnitz Ger.
145 M3 Dŭstí Tajik.
262 F3 Dusty WA U.S.A.
196 E3 Duszniki Pol.
196 E5 Duszniki-Zdrój Pol.
Dutch East Indies country Asia see Indonesia
258 H1 Dutchess County county NY U.S.A.
Dutch Guiana country S. America see Suriname
242 B4 Dutch Harbor AK U.S.A.
265 S1 Dutch Mountain UT U.S.A.
Dutch New Guinea prov. Indon. see Papua Barat
Dutch West Indies terr. West Indies see Netherlands Antilles
201 I8 Dutovlje Slovenia
229 H4 Dutsan-Wai Nigeria
229 H4 Dutse Nigeria
229 G3 Dutsin-Ma Nigeria
107 I6 Dutton r. Qld Austr.
251 M7 Dutton Ont. Can.
262 I3 Dutton MT U.S.A.
104 F4 Dutton, Lake salt flat S.A. Austr.
265 T3 Dutton, Mount UT U.S.A.
247 J5 Duval Sask. Can.
156 L5 Duvan Rus. Fed.
159 R4 Duvanka r. Ukr.
156 I4 Duvannoye Rus. Fed.
Duvannyy Azer. see Qobustan
Duvannyy, Ostrov i. Azer. see Zänbil Adası
162 L5 Duved Sweden
270 H4 Duvergé Dom. Rep.
249 G1 Duvert, Lac l. Que. Can.
Duvno Bos.-Herz. see Tomislavgrad
133 D8 Duwa Xinjiang China
144 D9 Duweihin well Saudi Arabia
147 J3 Duweihin, Khor b. Saudi Arabia/U.A.E.
149 L5 Duwin Iraq
133 E8 Düxanbibazar Xinjiang China
151 G5 Düyärli Azer.
118 C6 Duyinzeik Myanmar
130 F5 Duyun Guizhou China
145 J8 Duzab Pak.
221 M2 Düzce Turkey
221 M1 Düzce prov. Turkey
151 G4 Düz Cırdaxan Azer.
Duzdab Iran see Zāhedān
151 A5 Düzköy Turkey
158 F1 Dvarets Belarus
219 N7 Dve Mogili Bulg.
160 J5 Dviete Latvia
Dvinsk Latvia see Daugavpils
156 G2 Dvinskaya Guba g. Rus. Fed.
161 O5 Dvin'ye, Ozero l. Rus. Fed.
158 F3 Dvirets' Ukr.
197 M5 Dvirtsi Ukr.
210 F3 Dvor Croatia
199 G2 Dvorce Czech Rep.
159 Q4 Dvorichna Ukr.
161 V5 Dvoriki Rus. Fed.
199 H4 Dvory nad Žitavou Slovakia
161 W6 Dvoyni Rus. Fed.
198 E1 Dvůr Králové Czech Rep.
233 B8 Dwangwa Malawi
138 B8 Dwarka Gujarat India
234 E5 Dwarsberg S. Africa
145 N5 Dwatoi Pak.
217 □ Dwejra, Il-Ponta tad- pt Gozo Malta
109 D12 Dwellingup W.A. Austr.
237 M8 Dwesa Nature Reserve S. Africa
237 O6 Dweshula S. Africa
250 F8 Dwight IL U.S.A.
197 J5 Dwikozy Pol.
186 J3 Dwingelderveld, Nationaal Park nat. park Neth.
186 J3 Dwingeloo Neth.
262 G3 Dworshak Reservoir ID U.S.A.
236 F9 Dwyka S. Africa
236 F9 Dwyka r. S. Africa
159 T4 D'yachenkovo Rus. Fed.
156 H4 D'yakonovo Kostromskaya Oblast' Rus. Fed.
159 O2 D'yakonovo Kurskaya Oblast' Rus. Fed.
159 S6 Dyakove Ukr.
170 D5 Dyan Northern Ireland U.K.
219 O7 Dyankovo Bulg.
161 R8 Dyat'kovo Rus. Fed.
258 E1 Dyberry PA U.S.A.
258 E1 Dyberry Creek r. PA U.S.A.
168 L8 Dyce Aberdeen, Scotland U.K.
196 D4 Dychów Pol.
197 K6 Dydnia Pol.
122 G4 Dydy Rus. Fed.
243 L3 Dyer, Cape Nunavut Can.
251 M4 Dyer Bay Ont. Can.
286 T2 Dyer Plateau Antarctica
261 K7 Dyersburg TN U.S.A.
103 J8 Dyeville North I. N.Z.
Dyffryn Isle of Anglesey, Wales U.K. see Valley
Dyfrdwy r. England/Wales U.K. see Dee
196 D1 Dygowo Pol.
189 H4 Dyje r. Austria/Czech Rep.
159 N4 Dykan'ka Ukr.
168 I7 Dyke Moray, Scotland U.K.
168 J9 Dykehead Angus, Scotland U.K.
151 E2 Dykh-Tau, Gora mt. Rus. Fed.
187 G7 Dyle r. Belgium
198 B2 Dyleň hill Czech Rep.
197 J2 Dylewo Pol.
197 H2 Dylewska Góra hill Pol.
151 H2 Dylym Rus. Fed.
173 N5 Dymchurch Kent, England U.K.
158 J3 Dymer Ukr.
161 Q2 Dymi Rus. Fed.
172 H4 Dymock Gloucestershire, England U.K.
160 M1 Dymovka r. Rus. Fed.
159 Q5 Dymytrov Ukr.
159 L5 Dymytrove Kirovohrads'ka Oblast' Ukr.
159 L5 Dymytrove Kirovohrads'ka Oblast' Ukr.
164 E1 Dyna mt. Norway
105 J3 Dynevor Downs Qld Austr.
197 K6 Dynów Pol.
182 E4 Dyo France
237 M7 Dyoki S. Africa
162 N2 Dyrøyhamn Norway
Dyrrhachium Albania see Durrës
107 L7 Dysart Qld Austr.
172 F1 Dyserth Denbighshire, Wales U.K.
195 P2 Dýšina Czech Rep.
160 J6 Dysna r. Lith.
160 J6 Dysnų ežeras l. Lith.
236 G9 Dysselsdorp S. Africa
220 B4 Dytiki Ellada admin. reg. Greece
220 C2 Dytiki Makedonia admin. reg. Greece
153 O3 Dyuendyu Rus. Fed.
219 P8 Dyulino Bulg.
151 H4 Dyul'tydag, Gora mt. Rus. Fed.
156 K5 Dyurtyuli Rus. Fed.
158 I8 Dyviziya Ukr.
197 I2 Dywity Pol.
Dzaanhushuu Mongolia see Ihtamir
Dzadgay Mongolia see Bömbögör
128 F3 Dzag Mongolia
128 F3 Dzag Gol r. Mongolia
Dzalaa Mongolia see Shinejinst
129 L5 Dzamïn Üüd Mongolia
230 C4 Dzanga-Ndoki, Parc National de nat. park C.A.R.
230 C4 Dzanga-Sangha, Réserve Spéciale de Forêt Dense de nature res. C.A.R.
239 □3b Dzaoudzi Mayotte
Dzaudzhikau Rus. Fed. see Vladikavkaz
128 C2 Dzavhan Mongolia
128 D2 Dzavhan prov. Mongolia
128 C2 Dzavhan Gol r. Mongolia
128 D2 Dzavhanmandal Mongolia
198 C1 Džbán mts Czech Rep.
Dzegstey Mongolia see Ögiynuur
158 F4 Dzelentsi Ukr.
128 I1 Dzelter Mongolia
160 J4 Dzeņi Latvia
Dzerzhinsk Homyel'skaya Voblasts' Belarus see Dzyarzhynsk
Dzerzhinsk Minskaya Voblasts' Belarus see Dzyarzhynsk
156 H4 Dzerzhinsk Rus. Fed.
159 Q5 Dzerzhyns'k Donets'ka Oblast' Ukr.
158 G3 Dzerzhyns'k Zhytomyrs'ka Oblast' Ukr.
122 F2 Dzhagdy, Khrebet mts Rus. Fed.
122 I4 Dzhaki-Unakhta Yakbyyana, Khrebet mts Rus. Fed.
Dzhaksy Kazakh. see Zhaksy
142 K5 Dzhalagash Kazakh.
Dzhalalabad Azer. see Cälilabad
Dzhalal-Abad Kyrg. see Jalal-Abad
Dzhalal-Abadskaya Oblast' admin. div. Kyrg. see Jalal-Abad
156 K5 Dzhalil' Rus. Fed.
122 C2 Dzhalinda Rus. Fed.
Dzhaltyr Kazakh. see Zhaltyr
Dzhambeyty Kazakh. see Zhympity
Dzhambul Kazakh. see Taraz
Dzhambulskaya Oblast' admin. div. Kazakh. see Zhambylskaya Oblast'
Dzhandari Georgia see Jandari
142 D3 Dzhangala Kazakh.
Dzhangi-Dzhol Kyrg. see Jangy-Jol
Dzhankel'dy Uzbek. see Jongeldi
159 N8 Dzhankoy Ukr.
143 R5 Dzhansugurov Kazakh.
Dzhany-Bazar Kyrg. see Jangy-Bazar
Dzhany-Dzhol Kyrg. see Jangy-Jol
Dzhaparidze Georgia see Jap'aridze
Dzharkent Kazakh. see Zharkent
159 L7 Dzharylhach, Ostriv i. Ukr.
159 L7 Dzharylhats'ka Zatoka b. Ukr.
122 K3 Dzhaur r. Rus. Fed.
153 O3 Dzhebariki-Khaya Rus. Fed.
219 N9 Dzhebel Bulg.
Dzhebel Turkm. see Jebel
152 G1 Dzheksona, Ostrov i. Zemlya Frantsa-Iosifa Rus. Fed.
Dzhelondi Tajik. see Jelondí
Dzhergalan Kyrg. see Jyrgalang
Dzhermuk Armenia see Jermuk
Dzheti-Oguz Kyrg. see Jeti-Ögüz
Dzhetygara Kazakh. see Zhitikara
142 K6 Dzhetymtau, Gory hills Uzbek.
Dzhetyoguz Kyrg. see Jeti-Ögüz
Dzhetysay Kazakh. see Zhetysay
Dzhezdy Kazakh. see Zhezdy
Dzhezkazgan Kazakh. see Zhezkazgan
128 J1 Dzhida Rus. Fed.
128 J1 Dzhida r. Rus. Fed.
128 H1 Dzhidinskiy, Khrebet mts Mongolia/Rus. Fed.
Dzhilandy Kŭhistoni Badakhshon Tajik. see Jelondí
Dzhingil'dy Uzbek. see Jongeldi
Dzhirgatal' Tajik. see Jirgatol
Dzhizak Jizzax Uzbek. see Jizzax
Dzhizak Oblast admin. div. Uzbek. see Jizzax
Dzhokhar Ghala Rus. Fed. see Groznyy
Dzhordzhiashvili Georgia see Jorjiashvili
157 G7 Dzhubga Rus. Fed.
153 O4 Dzhugdzhur, Khrebet mts Rus. Fed.
Dzhul'fa Azer. see Culfa
158 I5 Dzhulynka Ukr.
Dzhuma Uzbek. see Juma
143 S5 Dzhungarskiye Vorota val. Kazakh.
143 T5 Dzhungarskiye Vorota val. Kazakh.
151 H3 Dzhurmut r. Rus. Fed.
Dzhurun Kazakh. see Zhuryn
158 H5 Dzhuryn Ukr.
142 K5 Dzhusaly Kazakh.
143 Q2 Dzhusaly Pavlodarskaya Oblast' Kazakh.
197 K3 Dziadkowice Pol.
196 F4 Dziadowa Kłoda Pol.
197 H2 Działdówka r. Pol.
197 I2 Działdowo Pol.
197 I5 Działoszyce Pol.
196 G4 Działoszyn Pol.
197 H2 Działyń Pol.
267 O8 Dzibalchén Mex.
196 F1 Dziemiany Pol.
196 G5 Dziergowice Pol.
197 I3 Dzierząźnia Pol.
196 E3 Dzierżążno Wielkie Pol.
197 H2 Dzierzgoń Pol.
197 I2 Dzierzgowo Pol.
196 E5 Dzierżoniów Pol.
197 J1 Dzietrzychowo Pol.
196 F3 Dziewierzewo Pol.
267 O7 Dzilam de Bravo Mex.
227 G2 Dzioua Alg.
160 L6 Dzisna Belarus
267 O7 Dzitás Mex.
160 I8 Dzitva r. Belarus
158 D2 Dzivin Belarus
196 C2 Dziwna r. Pol.
196 C1 Dziwnów Pol.
197 L3 Dzmitravichy Belarus
229 F5 Dzodze Ghana
Dzogsool Mongolia see Bayantsagaan
Dzöölön Mongolia see Renchinlhümbe
151 F5 Dzoraget r. Armenia
160 H7 Dzūkija nat. park Lith.
Dzungarian Basin China see Junggar Pendi
143 T5 Dzungarian Gate pass China/Kazakh.
Dzur Mongolia see Tes
129 L4 Dzüünbayan Mongolia
128 J2 Dzüünharaa Mongolia
128 J3 Dzuunmod Mongolia
Dzüyl Mongolia see Tonhil
197 I2 Dźwierzuty Pol.
192 L2 Dźwirzyno Pol.
197 K5 Dzwola Pol.
197 H5 Dzwonowice Pol.
160 J9 Dzyaniskavichy Belarus
161 O8 Dzyarazhnya Belarus
161 P8 Dzyarazhnya r. Belarus
160 H8 Dzyarechyn Belarus
158 G2 Dzyarzhynsk Homyel'skaya Voblasts' Belarus
160 K8 Dzyarzhynsk Minskaya Voblc Belarus
160 I8 Dzyatlava Belarus
158 F1 Dzyatlavichy Belarus
160 K6 Dzyerkawshchyna Belarus
158 I2 Dzyornavichy Belarus

E

248 C3 Eabamet Lake Ont. Can.
260 D6 Eads CO U.S.A.
265 W7 Eagar AZ U.S.A.
249 J2 Eagle r. Nfld and Lab. Can.
245 M2 Eagle r. Y.T. Can.
242 D3 Eagle AK U.S.A.
263 K7 Eagle CO U.S.A.
258 D4 Eagle PA U.S.A.
260 E3 Eagle Butte SD U.S.A.
262 F4 Eagle Cap mt. OR U.S.A.
264 O6 Eagle Crags mt. CA U.S.A.
247 J4 Eagle Creek r. Sask. Can.
247 M5 Eagle Lake l. Ont. Can.
257 □Q1 Eagle Lake ME U.S.A.
262 D6 Eagle Lake l. CA U.S.A.
257 □P2 Eagle Lake l. ME U.S.A.
257 □Q1 Eagle Lake l. ME U.S.A.
265 Q8 Eagle Mountain CA U.S.A.
250 D2 Eagle Mountain hill MN U.S
261 G9 Eagle Mountain Lake TX U.
261 E11 Eagle Pass TX U.S.A.
283 F9 Eagle Passage Falkland Is
263 L11 Eagle Peak TX U.S.A.
245 M2 Eagle Plain Y.T. Can.
245 M2 Eagle Plains Y.T. Can.
104 □3 Eagle Point S. Pacific Ocea
245 J3 Eagle River AK U.S.A.
250 F2 Eagle River MI U.S.A.
250 E4 Eagle River WI U.S.A.
256 F11 Eagle Rock VA U.S.A.
171 O4 Eaglescliffe Stockton-on-Tee England U.K.
168 J12 Eaglesfield Dumfries and Galloway, Scotland U.K.
246 G4 Eaglesham Alta Can.
168 H11 Eaglesham East Renfrewshi Scotland U.K.
245 K2 Eagle Summit pass AK U.S.
265 S8 Eagle Tail Mountains AZ U
245 L2 Eagle Village AK U.S.A.
258 E4 Eagleville PA U.S.A.
173 L4 Ealing Greater London, England U.K.
Eap i. Micronesia see Yap
109 F8 Earaheedy W.A. Austr.
168 H9 Earba, Lochan na h- l. Scotland U.K.
171 M6 Earby Lancashire, England U
172 F3 Eardisley Herefordshire, England U.K.
247 M5 Ear Falls Ont. Can.
173 M3 Earith Cambridgeshire, England U.K.
264 M6 Earlimart CA U.S.A.
103 B12 Earl Mountains South I. N.
173 K3 Earls Barton Northamptons England U.K.
173 N4 Earls Colne Essex, England
173 J2 Earl Shilton Leicestershire, England U.K.
168 H10 Earl's Seat hill Scotland U.K
168 K11 Earlston Scottish Borders, Scotland U.K.
173 O3 Earl Stonham Suffolk, England U.K.
251 O2 Earlton Ont. Can.
168 J10 Earn r. Scotland U.K.
103 D12 Earnscleugh South I. N.Z.
103 C11 Earnslaw, Mount South I. N
265 R7 Earp CA U.S.A.
168 B9 Earsairidh Western Isles, Scotland U.K.
261 D8 Earth TX U.S.A.
173 K6 Easebourne West Sussex, England U.K.
171 O4 Easington Durham, Englan
171 R6 Easington East Riding of Yo England U.K.
171 O5 Easingwold North Yorkshire England U.K.
169 E4 Easky Ireland
255 F8 Easley SC U.S.A.
109 G10 East, Mount hill W.A. Austr
106 D2 East Alligator r. N.T. Austr.
287 H1 East Antarctica reg. Antarc
257 J7 East Ararat PA U.S.A.
256 G6 East Aurora NY U.S.A.
168 H12 East Ayrshire admin. div. Scotland U.K.
106 B3 East Baines r. N.T. Austr.
258 E3 East Bangor PA U.S.A.
261 K11 East Bay LA U.S.A.
259 H3 East Bay NY U.S.A.
255 E10 East Bay inlet FL U.S.A.
East Bengal country Asia se Bangladesh
173 O4 East Bergholt Suffolk, England U.K.
259 J1 East Berlin CT U.S.A.
258 B5 East Berlin PA U.S.A.
258 C2 East Berwick PA U.S.A.
103 I8 Eastbourne North I. N.Z.
173 M6 Eastbourne East Sussex, England U.K.
256 F8 East Brady PA U.S.A.
257 J7 East Branch NY U.S.A.
256 G7 East Branch Clarion Rive Reservoir PA U.S.A.
173 K2 East Bridgford Nottinghar England U.K.
171 Q6 Eastburn East Riding of Yo England U.K.
270 H3 East Caicos i. Turks and C
102 M4 East Cape North I. N.Z.
East Cape Rus. Fed. see Dezhneva, Mys
245 □B6 East Cape AK U.S.A.
265 V2 East Carbon City UT U.S.A
290 E5 East Caroline Basin sea fe N. Pacific Ocean
245 N1 East Channel watercourse N.W.T. Can.
250 G8 East Chicago IN U.S.A.
121 M5 East China Sea N. Pacific
102 I3 East Coast Bays North I. N
172 G6 East Coker Somerset, Engl
247 H5 East Coulee Alta Can.
173 M6 East Dean East Sussex, England U.K.
East Dereham England U. Dereham
168 H11 East Dunbartonshire adm Scotland U.K.
247 I5 Eastend Sask. Can.
255 □2 East End Point New Prov. Bahamas
114 □ East Entrance sea chan. Pa
109 B10 Easter Group is W.A. Aust
Easter Island S. Pacific O Pascua, Isla de
228 E5 Eastern admin. reg. Ghana
232 C5 Eastern prov. Kenya
228 C4 Eastern prov. Sierra Leon
233 A8 Eastern prov. Zambia

Eastern Bay MD U.S.A.
Eastern Beach Gibraltar
Eastern Cape prov. S. Africa
Eastern Creek r. Qld Austr.
Eastern Desert Egypt see Aş Şaḩrā' ash Sharqīyah
Eastern Equatoria state Sudan
Eastern Ghats mts India
Eastern Lesser Sunda Islands prov. Indon. see Nusa Tenggara Timur
Eastern Nara canal Pak.
Eastern Neck Island MD U.S.A.
Eastern Samoa terr. S. Pacific Ocean see American Samoa
Eastern Sayan Mountains Rus. Fed. see Vostochnyy Sayan
Eastern Taurus plat. Turkey see Güneydoğu Toroslar
Eastern Transvaal prov. S. Africa see Mpumalanga
Easter Ross reg. Scotland U.K.
Easter Skeld Scotland U.K. see Skeld
Easterville Man. Can.
East Falkland i. Falkland Is
East Falmouth MA U.S.A.
East Fen reg. England U.K.
Eastfield North Yorkshire, England U.K.
East Flanders prov. Belgium see Oost-Vlaanderen
East Frisian Islands Ger. see Ostfriesische Inseln
Eastgate Durham, England U.K.
Eastgate NV U.S.A.
East Grand Forks MN U.S.A.
East Grand Rapids MI U.S.A.
East Greenville PA U.S.A.
East Grinstead West Sussex, England U.K.
East Haddam CT U.S.A.
East Hampton CT U.S.A.
Easthampton MA U.S.A.
East Hampton NY U.S.A.
East Hanney Oxfordshire, England U.K.
East Harling Norfolk, England U.K.
East Hartford CT U.S.A.
East Haven CT U.S.A.
East Haydon Qld Austr.
East Holden ME U.S.A.
East Horsley Surrey, England U.K.
East Huntspill Somerset, England U.K.
East Indiaman Ridge sea feature Indian Ocean
East Island North I. N.Z.
East Jamaica VT U.S.A.
East Jordan MI U.S.A.
East Kazakhstan Oblast admin. div. Kazakh. see Vostochnyy Kazakhstan
East Keal Lincolnshire, England U.K.
East Kilbride South Lanarkshire, Scotland U.K.
East Lake MI U.S.A.
East Lamma Channel H.K. China see Tung Pok Liu Hoi Hap
Eastland TX U.S.A.
East Lansing MI U.S.A.
Eastleigh Hampshire, England U.K.
East Liberty OH U.S.A.
East Linton East Lothian, Scotland U.K.
East Litchfield CT U.S.A.
East Liverpool OH U.S.A.
East Loch Roag inlet Scotland U.K.
East Loch Tarbert inlet Scotland U.K.
East London S. Africa
East Longmeadow MA U.S.A.
East Looe Cornwall, England U.K.
East Lothian admin. div. Scotland U.K.
East Lyme CT U.S.A.
Eastmain Que. Can.
Eastmain r. Que. Can.
East Malling Kent, England U.K.
Eastman Que. Can.
Eastman GA U.S.A.
East Mariana Basin sea feature Pacific Ocean
East Markham Nottinghamshire, England U.K.
Eastmere Qld Austr.
East Middlebury VT U.S.A.
East Midlands airport England U.K.
East Millinocket ME U.S.A.
East Morris CT U.S.A.
East Naples FL U.S.A.
East Northport NY U.S.A.
Eastoft North Lincolnshire, England U.K.
Easton Dorset, England U.K.
Easton CA U.S.A.
Easton CT U.S.A.
Easton MD U.S.A.
Easton PA U.S.A.
Easton-in-Gordano North Somerset, England U.K.
Easton Reservoir CT U.S.A.
East Orange NJ U.S.A.
East Pacific Ridge S. Pacific Ocean
East Pacific Rise sea feature N. Pacific Ocean
East Pakistan country Asia see Bangladesh
East Palestine OH U.S.A.
East Park Reservoir CA U.S.A.
East Peoria IL U.S.A.
East Petersburg PA U.S.A.
East Point Lord Howe I. Austr.
East Point P.E.I. Can.
East Point Tristan da Cunha S. Atlantic Ocean
East Porcupine r. Y.T. Can.
Eastport ME U.S.A.
Eastport MI U.S.A.
Eastport NY U.S.A.
East Preston West Sussex, England U.K.
East Prospect PA U.S.A.
East Quogue NY U.S.A.
East Range mts NV U.S.A.
East Renfrewshire admin. div. Scotland U.K.
East Retford Nottinghamshire, England U.K. see Retford
East Ridge TN U.S.A.
East Riding of Yorkshire admin. div. England U.K.
Eastriggs Dumfries and Galloway, Scotland U.K.
Eastry Kent, England U.K.
East St Louis IL U.S.A.
East Sea N. Pacific Ocean see Japan, Sea of
East Setauket NY U.S.A.
East Shoal Lake Man. Can.
East Siberian Sea Rus. Fed. see Vostochno-Sibirskoye More
East Side PA U.S.A.
East Side Canal r. CA U.S.A.
East Sister Island Tas. Austr.
East Stroudsburg PA U.S.A.
East Sussex admin. div. England U.K.
East Tavaputs Plateau UT U.S.A.
East Tawas MI U.S.A.
East Timor country Asia
East Tons r. India
East Toorale N.S.W. Austr.
East Troy WI U.S.A.
East Twin Lake MI U.S.A.
East Verde r. AZ U.S.A.
Eastview Ont. Can. see Vanier
257 J11 Eastville VA U.S.A.
264 M3 East Walker r. NV U.S.A.
173 K6 East Wittering West Sussex, England U.K.
171 O7 Eastwood Nottinghamshire, England U.K.
173 J5 East Woodhay Hampshire, England U.K.
251 O6 East York Ont. Can.
119 H8 Ea Sup Vietnam
104 D2 Eateringinna Creek watercourse S.A. Austr.
168 C9 Eatharna, Loch inlet Scotland U.K.
109 C12 Eaton W.A. Austr.
262 L6 Eaton CO U.S.A.
254 E6 Eaton OH U.S.A.
173 K4 Eaton Bray Bedfordshire, England U.K.
247 I5 Eatonia Sask. Can.
250 J7 Eaton Rapids MI U.S.A.
259 I3 Eatons Neck NY U.S.A.
259 I3 Eatons Neck Point NY U.S.A.
173 L3 Eaton Socon Cambridgeshire, England U.K.
255 F9 Eatonton GA U.S.A.
259 G4 Eatontown NJ U.S.A.
257 □P1 Eatonville Que. Can.
262 C3 Eatonville WA U.S.A.
250 C5 Eau Claire WI U.S.A.
250 C5 Eau Claire r. WI U.S.A.
248 F1 Eau Claire, Lac à l' l. Que. Can.
178 B4 Eaulne r. France
185 G9 Eaunes France
113 J5 Eauripik atoll Micronesia
290 E5 Eauripik Rise-New Guinea Rise sea feature N. Pacific Ocean
Eaurypyg atoll Micronesia see Eauripik
185 D10 Eaux-Bonnes France
185 E8 Eauze France
100 □3a Ebadon i. Kwajalein Marshall Is
107 I3 Ebagoola Qld Austr.
229 G4 Eban Nigeria
269 I3 Ebano Mex.
200 F4 Ebbs Austria
172 F4 Ebbw Vale Blaenau Gwent, Wales U.K.
229 H6 Ebebiyin Equat. Guinea
191 K8 Ebeleben Ger.
164 G5 Ebeltoft Denmark
200 E5 Eben am Achensee Austria
237 M8 Ebende S. Africa
234 C5 Ebenerde Namibia
201 I6 Ebene Reichenau Austria
201 N4 Ebenfurth Austria
201 H5 Eben im Pongau Austria
256 G8 Ebensburg PA U.S.A.
201 I4 Ebensee Austria
191 K10 Ebensfeld Ger.
201 J6 Ebenthal Austria
194 H6 Ebenweiler Ger.
201 N5 Eberau Austria
194 F3 Eberbach Ger.
221 M4 Eber Gölü l. Turkey
191 J7 Ebergötzen Ger.
194 H5 Eberhardzell Ger.
195 L3 Ebermannsdorf Ger.
195 K2 Ebermannstadt Ger.
191 K10 Ebern Ger.
201 K6 Eberndorf Austria
193 I8 Ebersbach Sachsen Ger.
193 K8 Ebersbach Sachsen Ger.
194 H4 Ebersbach an der Fils Ger.
195 L5 Ebersberg Ger.
201 I3 Eberschwang Austria
201 M5 Ebersdorf Austria
190 H3 Ebersdorf Niedersachsen Ger.
193 E10 Ebersdorf Thüringen Ger.
179 O7 Ebersmunster France
201 K6 Eberstein Austria
192 I5 Eberswalde-Finow Ger.
258 D3 Ebervale PA U.S.A.
199 K4 Ebes Hungary
124 S3 Ebetsu Japan
100 □3a Ebeye Kwajalein Marshall Is
194 F4 Ebhausen Ger.
130 D4 Ebian Sichuan China
212 E1 Ebikon Switz.
127 J5 Ebina Japan
125 H14 Ebino Japan
Ebi Nor salt l. China see Ebinur Hu
132 F4 Ebinur Hu salt l. China
150 E3 Ebla tourist site Syria
212 G1 Ebnat-Kappel Switz.
231 B7 Ebo Angola
230 D4 Ebola r. Dem. Rep. Congo
215 O6 Eboli Italy
229 H6 Ebolowa Cameroon
234 B4 Ebony Namibia
229 H5 Ebonyi state Nigeria
195 I2 Ebrach Ger.
144 A3 Ebrāhim Ḩeşār Iran
Ebre r. Spain see Ebro
201 N4 Ebreichsdorf Austria
182 C4 Ébreuil France
205 O5 Ebrillos r. Spain
194 D6 Ebringen Ger.
205 N3 Ebro r. Spain
205 M2 Ebro, Embalse del resr Spain
209 C7 Ebrón r. Spain
191 G9 Ebsdorfergrund-Dreihausen Ger.
191 G9 Ebsdorfergrund-Rauischholzhausen Ger.
190 J4 Ebstorf Ger.
Eburacum York, England U.K. see York
Eburodunum France see Embrun
Ebusus i. Spain see Eivissa
269 H6 Ecatepec Mex.
187 F7 Écaussinnes-d'Enghien Belgium
Ecbatana Iran see Hamadān
168 J12 Ecclefechan Dumfries and Galloway, Scotland U.K.
171 M7 Eccles Greater Manchester, England U.K.
168 L11 Eccles Scottish Borders, Scotland U.K.
256 D11 Eccles WV U.S.A.
171 O7 Ecclesfield South Yorkshire, England U.K.
172 H2 Eccleshall Staffordshire, England U.K.
171 L6 Eccleston Lancashire, England U.K.
271 □7 Ecclesville Trin. and Tob.
221 H2 Eceabat Turkey
114 C3 Echague Luzon Phil.
212 B2 Echallens Switz.
270 B9 Echandi, Cerro mt. Costa Rica
Echaot'l Koe N.W.T. Can. see Fort Liard
205 Q3 Echarri Spain
Echarri-Aranaz Spain see Etxarri-Aranatz
181 L4 Échauffour France
151 G3 Echeda Rus. Fed.
Echeng Hubei China see Ezhou
182 I1 Échenoz-la-Méline France
266 C3 Echeverria, Pico mt. Mex.
126 D5 Echigawa Japan
127 J1 Echigo-Sanzan-Tadami Kokutei-kōen park Japan
184 C4 Échillais France
195 L5 Eching Bayern Ger.
195 M4 Eching Bayern Ger.
220 F1 Echinos Greece
184 D3 Échiré France
183 H6 Échirolles France
126 D4 Echizen Japan
127 I5 Echizen-dake mt. Japan
126 D3 Echizen-Kaga-kaigan Kokutei-kōen park Japan
126 C4 Echizen-misaki pt Japan
Echmiadzin Armenia see Ejmiatsin
262 E4 Echo OR U.S.A.
105 K10 Echo, Lake Tas. Austr.
242 G3 Echo Bay N.W.T. Can.
248 C4 Echo Bay Ont. Can.
265 U5 Echo Cliffs esc. AZ U.S.A.
247 M4 Echoing r. Man./Ont. Can.
251 S2 Échouani, Lac l. Que. Can.
184 E5 Échourgnac France
201 L2 Echsenbach Austria
187 I6 Echt Neth.
168 L8 Echt Aberdeenshire, Scotland U.K.
191 J7 Echte Ger.
187 J9 Echternach Lux.
105 J7 Echuca Vic. Austr.
191 G10 Echzell Ger.
207 I5 Écija Spain
285 I4 Ecilda Paullier Uru.
170 H1 Eck, Loch l. Scotland U.K.
218 I5 Ečka Vojvodina Serbia
193 E8 Eckartsberga Ger.
179 O6 Eckbolsheim France
195 K2 Eckental Ger.
250 I3 Eckerman MI U.S.A.
190 I2 Eckernförde Ger.
190 J1 Eckernförder Bucht b. Ger.
163 O6 Eckerö Åland Fin.
160 C1 Eckerö i. Fin.
195 L2 Eckersdorf Ger.
168 L11 Eckford Scottish Borders, Scotland U.K.
171 O7 Eckington Derbyshire, England U.K.
172 H3 Eckington Worcestershire, England U.K.
256 D11 Eckman WV U.S.A.
246 H4 Eckville Alta Can.
190 F3 Eckwarden (Butjadingen) Ger.
179 I6 Éclaron-Braucourt-Ste-Livière France
243 J2 Eclipse Sound sea chan. Nunavut Can.
181 L6 Écommoy France
281 G3 Ecoporanga Brazil
251 R2 Écorce, Lac de l' l. Que. Can.
178 C5 Écos France
181 K4 Écouché France
181 J6 Écouflant France
178 B5 Écouis France
183 I7 Écrins, Massif des mts France
183 I7 Écrins, Parc National des nat. park France
179 K6 Écrouves France
199 G4 Écs Hungary
199 I4 Ecséd Hungary
199 I4 Ecseg Hungary
199 J4 Ecsegfalva Hungary
199 I4 Ecser Hungary
274 B5 Ecuador country S. America
268 E5 Ecuandureo Mex.
184 G1 Écueillé France
182 F3 Écuisses France
178 H6 Écury-sur-Coole France
225 I6 Ed Eritrea
164 H3 Ed Sweden
247 I4 Edam Sask. Can.
186 H3 Edam Neth.
168 K4 Eday i. Scotland U.K.
230 E2 Ed Da'ein Sudan
232 B2 Ed Damazin Sudan
225 G5 Ed Damer Sudan
225 F5 Ed Debba Sudan
224 C5 Eddeki well Chad
190 H3 Eddelak Ger.
193 E7 Edderitz Ger.
168 H7 Edderton Highland, Scotland U.K.
249 J3 Eddies Cove Nfld and Lab. Can.
168 F6 Eddrachillis Bay Scotland U.K.
225 G6 Ed Dueim Sudan
105 L9 Eddystone Point Tas. Austr.
261 K7 Eddyville KY U.S.A.
186 I4 Ede Neth.
229 G5 Ede Nigeria
229 H6 Edéa Cameroon
187 F6 Edegem Belgium
247 L2 Edehon Lake Nunavut Can.
280 C2 Edéia Brazil
199 J3 Edelény Hungary
201 L5 Edelschrott Austria
191 J6 Edemissen Ger.
105 L7 Eden N.S.W. Austr.
170 F4 Eden Northern Ireland U.K.
171 K4 Eden r. England U.K.
256 F12 Eden NC U.S.A.
261 F10 Eden TX U.S.A.
262 J5 Eden WY U.S.A.
115 E7 Eden, Tanjung pt Maluku Indon.
173 M5 Edenbridge Kent, England U.K.
237 J5 Edenburg S. Africa
103 C13 Edendale South I. N.Z.
237 O5 Edendale S. Africa
169 H6 Edenderry Ireland
171 M6 Edenfield Lancashire, England U.K.
104 H7 Edenhope Vic. Austr.
194 E3 Edenkoben Ger.
250 A5 Eden Prairie MN U.S.A.
255 I7 Edenton NC U.S.A.
237 M2 Edenvale S. Africa
237 L3 Edenville S. Africa
191 H8 Eder r. Ger.
191 H8 Edermünde Ger.
169 G3 Ederny Northern Ireland U.K.
191 G8 Eder-Stausee resr Ger.
220 D2 Edessa Greece
Edessa Turkey see Şanlıurfa
162 L5 Edevik Sweden
190 E4 Edewecht Ger.
190 E4 Edewechterdamm Ger.
Edfu Egypt see Idfū
260 G5 Edgar NE U.S.A.
108 F6 Edgar, Mount hill W.A. Austr.
108 G5 Edgar Ranges hills W.A. Austr.
257 O7 Edgartown MA U.S.A.
102 K4 Edgecumbe North I. N.Z.
102 K5 Edgecumbe, Mount hill North I. N.Z.
Edgecumbe Island Santa Cruz Is Solomon Is see Utupua
255 G9 Edgefield SC U.S.A.
Edge Island Svalbard see Edgeøya
260 F2 Edgeley ND U.S.A.
258 C6 Edgemere MD U.S.A.
260 D4 Edgemont SD U.S.A.
162 □ Edgeøya i. Svalbard
247 I4 Edgerton Alta Can.
256 A7 Edgerton OH U.S.A.
256 H12 Edgerton VA U.S.A.
250 E7 Edgerton WI U.S.A.
246 G5 Edgewood B.C. Can.
258 C6 Edgewood MD U.S.A.
258 B3 Edgewood PA U.S.A.
169 G5 Edgeworthstown Ireland
100 □3a Edgigen i. Kwajalein Marshall Is
172 H2 Edgmond Telford and Wrekin, England U.K.
Édhessa Greece see Edessa
103 D12 Edievale South I. N.Z.
191 D10 Ediger-Eller Ger.
229 G2 Édîkel well Niger
151 E4 Edik'ilisa Georgia
260 I5 Edina MO U.S.A.
256 E7 Edinboro PA U.S.A.
261 F12 Edinburg TX U.S.A.
256 G10 Edinburg VA U.S.A.
168 J11 Edinburgh Edinburgh, Scotland U.K.
168 J11 Edinburgh admin. div. Scotland U.K.
221 I2 Edincik Turkey
158 G5 Edineţ Moldova
233 B8 Edingeni Malawi
194 F3 Edingen-Neckarhausen Ger.
148 C3 Edirne Turkey
221 H1 Edirne prov. Turkey
151 F3 Edisa Georgia
258 E4 Edison PA U.S.A.
151 F1 Edissiya Rus. Fed.
255 G9 Edisto r. SC U.S.A.
262 I3 Edith, Mount MT U.S.A.
104 F6 Edithburgh S.A. Austr.
246 G4 Edith Cavell, Mount Alta Can.
Edith Ronne Land ice feature Antarctica see Ronne Ice Shelf
109 F8 Edith Withnell, Lake salt flat W.A. Austr.
231 B9 Ediva Angola
227 H4 Edjeleh Libya
229 F2 Édjérir watercourse Mali
109 G10 Edjudina W.A. Austr.
195 M5 Edling Ger.
171 N3 Edlingham Northumberland, England U.K.
201 N4 Edlitz Austria
261 G8 Edmond OK U.S.A.
262 C3 Edmonds WA U.S.A.
169 E5 Edmondstown Ireland
107 J4 Edmonton Qld Austr.
246 H4 Edmonton Alta Can.
254 E7 Edmonton KY U.S.A.
250 I6 Edmore MI U.S.A.
260 F1 Edmore ND U.S.A.
171 N4 Edmundbyers Durham, England U.K.
107 J4 Edmund Kennedy National Park nat. park Qld Austr.
247 M4 Edmund Lake Man. Can.
249 G4 Edmundston N.B. Can.
261 G11 Edna TX U.S.A.
245 N5 Edna Bay AK U.S.A.
Edo Japan see Tōkyō
229 G5 Edo state Nigeria
127 K4 Edo-gawa r. Japan
212 I3 Edolo Italy
150 D8 Edom reg. Israel/Jordan
127 L4 Edosaki Japan
221 I3 Edremit Turkey
221 H3 Edremit Körfezi b. Turkey
128 E4 Edrengiyn Nuruu mts Mongolia
204 G5 Edrosa Port.
204 G5 Edroso Port.
165 O2 Edsbro Sweden
165 M3 Edsbruk Sweden
163 M6 Edsbyn Sweden
162 N5 Edsele Sweden
246 G4 Edson Alta Can.
284 E4 Eduardo Castex Arg.
245 O2 Eduni, Mount N.W.T. Can.
105 J6 Edward r. N.S.W. Austr.
107 H3 Edward r. Qld Austr.
230 F5 Edward, Lake Dem. Rep. Congo/Uganda
286 T1 Edward, Mount Antarctica
108 K7 Edward, Mount N.T. Austr.
Edwardesabad Pak. see Bannu
106 E3 Edward Island N.T. Austr.
250 F1 Edward Island Ont. Can.
107 H3 Edward River Aboriginal Reserve Qld Austr.
257 J4 Edwards NY U.S.A.
103 A12 Edwardson Sound inlet South I. N.Z.
261 E10 Edwards Plateau TX U.S.A.
260 K6 Edwardsville IL U.S.A.
287 D2 Edward VIII Bay Antarctica
286 N1 Edward VII Peninsula Antarctica
259 G5 Edwin B. Forsythe National Wildlife Refuge nature res. NJ U.S.A.
171 O7 Edwinstowe Nottinghamshire, England U.K.
245 O4 Edziza, Mount B.C. Can.
Edzo N.W.T. Can. see Behchokô
230 B5 Edzouga Congo
186 J4 Eefde Neth.
244 G3 Eek AK U.S.A.
244 G3 Eek r. AK U.S.A.
187 E6 Eeklo Belgium
264 H1 Eel r. CA U.S.A.
264 I1 Eel, South Fork r. CA U.S.A.
186 K2 Eelde-Paterswolde Neth.
186 H4 Eem r. Neth.
186 H4 Eemnes Neth.
186 K2 Eemshaven pt Neth.
186 K2 Eemskanaal canal Neth.
236 C8 Eendekuil S. Africa
186 J2 Eenrum Neth.
236 E3 Eenzamheid Pan salt pan S. Africa
186 J4 Eerbeek Neth.
187 D6 Eernegem Belgium
187 H6 Eersel Neth.
Eesti country Europe see Estonia
100 □5 Éfaté i. Vanuatu
201 J3 Eferding Austria
195 K2 Effeltrich Ger.
250 A2 Effie MN U.S.A.
173 L5 Effingham Surrey, England U.K.
260 K6 Effingham IL U.S.A.
258 E3 Effort PA U.S.A.
212 F1 Effretikon Switz.
148 F3 Eflâni Turkey
194 D6 Efringen-Kirchen Ger.
Efsus Turkey see Afşin
219 K6 Eftimie Murgu Romania
115 F4 Eftorobi i. Papua Indon.
Eg Mongolia see Batshireet
205 Q4 Ega r. Spain
216 C7 Egadi, Isole is Sicilia Italy
285 H5 Egana Arg.
265 R3 Egan Range mts NV U.S.A.
251 Q4 Eganville Ont. Can.
244 G2 Egavik AK U.S.A.
229 G4 Egbe Nigeria
209 D10 Egea hill Spain
Egedesminde Greenland see Aasiaat
244 H4 Egegik AK U.S.A.
244 H4 Egegik Bay AK U.S.A.
193 D7 Egeln Ger.
195 K5 Egenhofen Ger.
247 K3 Egenolf Lake Man. Can.
Egentliga Finland reg. Fin. see Varsinais-Suomi
193 F10 Eger r. Ger.
195 J4 Eger r. Ger.
199 J4 Eger Hungary
199 J4 Egerbakta Hungary
199 J3 Egercsehi Hungary
108 □1 Egeria Point Christmas I.
190 I1 Egernsund Denmark
164 C3 Egersund Norway
109 D8 Egerton, Mount hill W.A. Austr.
198 F5 Egervár Hungary
190 J4 Egestorf Ger.
200 A5 Egg Austria
190 H1 Eggebek Ger.
164 F2 Eggedøla r. Norway
191 G7 Eggegebirge hills Ger.
201 M2 Eggenburg Austria
195 N5 Eggenfelden Ger.
194 E3 Eggenstein-Leopoldshafen Ger.
190 E5 Eggermühlen Ger.
193 E7 Eggersdorf Ger.
201 M5 Eggersdorf bei Graz Austria
192 I5 Eggersdorf bei Strausberg Ger.
192 J3 Eggesin Ger.
250 G4 Egg Harbor WI U.S.A.
258 F5 Egg Harbor City NJ U.S.A.
194 E6 Eggingen Ger.
238 □2b Egg Island St Helena
244 G3 Egg Island AK U.S.A.
258 E6 Egg Island Point NJ U.S.A.
212 D2 Eggiwil Switz.
247 J4 Egg Lake Sask. Can.
195 O4 Egglham Ger.
195 K2 Eggolsheim Ger.
195 M6 Eggstätt Ger.
162 L2 Eggum Norway
173 K5 Egham Surrey, England U.K.
187 G7 Eghezée Belgium
205 Q3 Egiarreta Spain
168 K4 Egilsay i. Scotland U.K.
162 □F1 Egilsstaðir Iceland
Eğin Turkey see Kemaliye
108 E6 Eginbah W.A. Austr.
Egindibulaq Kazakh. see Yegindybulak
195 O4 Eging am See Ger.
221 L5 Eğirdir Turkey
221 L5 Eğirdir Gölü l. Turkey
128 H2 Egiyn Gol r. Mongolia
184 I5 Égletons France
195 L6 Egling Ger.
195 J5 Egling an der Paar Ger.
171 N3 Eglingham Northumberland, England U.K.
169 H2 Eglinton Northern Ireland U.K.
242 G2 Eglinton Island N.W.T. Can.
194 F6 Eglisau Switz.
170 D5 Eglish Northern Ireland U.K.
195 K2 Egloffstein Ger.
172 E2 Eglwys Fach Ceredigion, Wales U.K.
172 C3 Eglwyswrw Pembrokeshire, Wales U.K.
186 G3 Egmond aan Zee Neth.
186 G3 Egmond-Binnen Neth.
102 H6 Egmont, Cape North I. N.Z.
Egmont, Mount vol. North I. N.Z. see Taranaki, Mount
102 I6 Egmont National Park North I. N.Z.
102 I6 Egmont Village North I. N.Z.
213 K3 Egna Italy
171 J5 Egremont Cumbria, England U.K.
221 K3 Eğrigöz Dağı mts Turkey
178 F7 Égriselles-le-Bocage France
171 P5 Egton North Yorkshire, England U.K.
164 F6 Egtved Denmark
274 E3 Egua Col.
278 D5 Éguas r. Brazil
114 C8 Eguet Point Phil.
Eguiarreta Spain see Egiarreta
183 G9 Éguilles France
178 I7 Éguilly-sous-Bois France
179 N7 Eguisheim France
184 H3 Éguzon, Barrage d' dam France
184 H3 Éguzon-Chantôme France
153 T3 Egvekinot Rus. Fed.
199 J4 Egyek Hungary
201 O5 Egyházasfalu Hungary
199 H5 Egyházaskozár Hungary
198 F4 Egyházasrádóc Hungary
225 F2 Egypt country Africa
258 D3 Egypt PA U.S.A.
Ehcel well Mali see Agous-n-Ehsel
150 D4 Ehden Lebanon
195 J2 Ehebach r. Ger.
195 K4 Ehekirchen Ger.
128 G7 Ehen Hudag Nei Mongol China
125 J13 Ehime pref. Japan
195 J3 Ehingen Ger.
194 H5 Ehingen (Donau) Ger.
193 E6 Ehle r. Ger.
191 H8 Ehlen (Habichtswald) Ger.
194 F4 Ehningen Ger.
190 K5 Ehra-Lessien Ger.
265 R8 Ehrenberg AZ U.S.A.
106 C7 Ehrenberg Range hills N.T. Austr.
191 J10 Ehrenberg-Wüstensachsen Ger.
190 G5 Ehrenburg Ger.
201 M6 Ehrenhausen Austria
191 F9 Ehringshausen Ger.
200 C5 Ehrwald Austria
125 H15 Ei Japan
101 □9 Eiao i. Fr. Polynesia
205 P2 Eibar Spain
195 I2 Eibelstadt Ger.
193 G10 Eibenstock Ger.
186 K4 Eibergen Neth.
201 L6 Eibiswald Austria
195 K7 Eibsee l. Ger.
194 E2 Eich Ger.
195 K5 Eichenau Ger.
193 D6 Eichenbarleben Ger.
191 I10 Eichenberg hill Ger.
194 G2 Eichenbühl Ger.
195 N4 Eichendorf Ger.
191 I10 Eichenzell Ger.
201 M3 Eichgraben Austria
193 F10 Eichigt Ger.
191 J8 Eichsfeld reg. Ger.
195 K4 Eichstätt Ger.
194 D5 Eichstetten Ger.
193 I6 Eichwalde Ger.
193 E7 Eickendorf Ger.
190 J5 Eicklingen Ger.
162 I5 Eide Norway
190 G2 Eider r. Ger.
164 D1 Eidfjord Norway
166 D1 Eiði Faroe Is
162 J5 Eidsvåg Norway
107 M8 Eidsvold Qld Austr.
164 H1 Eidsvoll Norway
162 □ Eidsvollfjellet mt. Svalbard
191 C10 Eifel hills Ger.
194 F6 Eigeltingen Ger.
126 D5 Eigenji Japan
212 E2 Eiger mt. Switz.
164 B3 Eigerøya i. Norway
168 D9 Eigg i. Scotland U.K.
168 D9 Eigg, Sound of sea chan. Scotland U.K.
136 C9 Eight Degree Channel India/Maldives
286 R2 Eights Coast Antarctica
108 F5 Eighty Mile Beach W.A. Austr.
126 D3 Eiheiji Japan
187 I7 Eijsden Neth.
164 B1 Eikelandsosen Norway
164 D3 Eiken Norway
164 F2 Eikeren l. Norway
168 F9 Eil, Loch inlet Scotland U.K.
Eilat Israel see Elat
105 J7 Eildon Vic. Austr.
105 K7 Eildon, Lake Vic. Austr.
247 J2 Eileen Lake N.W.T. Can.
193 G8 Eilenburg Ger.
193 D7 Eilenstedt Ger.
275 G4 Eilerts de Haan, Natuurreservaat nature res. Suriname
275 G4 Eilerts de Haan Gebergte mts Suriname
114 □ Eil Malk i. Palau
193 D6 Eilsleben Ger.
191 I6 Eime Ger.
191 I7 Eimen Ger.
Eimeo i. Fr. Polynesia see Moorea
190 J5 Eimke Ger.
164 G1 Eina Norway
168 C6 Einacleit Western Isles, Scotland U.K.
107 J5 Einasleigh Qld Austr.
107 I4 Einasleigh r. Qld Austr.
164 G1 Einavatnet l. Norway
191 I7 Einbeck Ger.
187 H6 Eindhoven Neth.
236 D1 Eindpaal Namibia
193 E7 Eine r. Ger.
194 F2 Einhausen Ger.
168 G7 Einig r. Scotland U.K.
118 B6 Einme Myanmar
193 G9 Einsiedel Ger.
212 F1 Einsiedeln Switz.
179 L6 Einville-au-Jard France
238 □1c Eiras, Ponta das pt São Jorge Azores
288 G2 Eirik Ridge sea feature N. Atlantic Ocean
Eiriosgaigh i. Scotland U.K. see Eriskay
274 D6 Eiru r. Brazil
274 D6 Eirunepé Brazil
191 I8 Eisberg hill Ger.
187 J9 Eisch r. Lux.
187 I7 Eisden Belgium
191 J7 Eisdorf Ger.
234 D3 Eiseb watercourse Namibia
195 M5 Eiselfing Ger.
191 J9 Eisenach Ger.
194 E6 Eisenbach (Hochschwarzwald) Ger.
193 E9 Eisenberg Ger.
194 E2 Eisenberg (Pfalz) Ger.
201 K4 Eisenerz Austria
201 J4 Eisenerzer Alpen mts Austria
Eisenhower, Mount Alta Can. see Castle Mountain
201 I6 Eisenhut mt. Austria
193 K6 Eisenhüttenstadt Ger.
201 K7 Eisenkappel Austria
201 O4 Eisenstadt Austria
201 K4 Eisenwurzen reg. Austria
191 K10 Eisfeld Ger.
168 E8 Eishort, Loch inlet Scotland U.K.
160 H7 Eišiškės Lith.
166 J1 Eislandet Norway
193 E7 Eisleben Lutherstadt Ger.
194 H4 Eislingen (Fils) Ger.
102 J4 Eistow North I. N.Z.
Eitape P.N.G. see Aitape
195 K4 Eitensheim Ger.
191 I9 Eiterfeld Ger.
191 D9 Eitorf Ger.
191 I6 Eitzum (Despetal) Ger.
163 H6 Eivinvik Norway
209 H10 Eivissa Spain
209 I9 Eivissa i. Spain
204 F4 Eixe, Serra do mts Spain
204 C7 Eixo Port.
204 D6 Eja Port.
208 C3 Ejea de los Caballeros Spain
235 □J5 Ejeda Madag.
Ejin Horo Qi Nei Mongol China see Altan Shiret
Ejin Qi Nei Mongol China see Dalain Hob
226 B5 Ej Jill, Sebkhet salt flat Maur.
Ejmiadzin Armenia see Ejmiatsin
151 F5 Ejmiatsin Armenia
208 D6 Ejulve Spain
228 E5 Ejura Ghana
269 K9 Ejutla Mex.
262 L4 Ekalaka MT U.S.A.
229 H5 Ekang Nigeria
237 M1 Ekangala S. Africa
230 B4 Ékata Gabon
125 J13 Ekawasaki Japan
163 Q7 Ekenäs Fin.
164 J3 Ekenäs Sweden
163 Q7 Ekenäskärgårds nationalpark nat. park Fin.
144 F2 Ekerem Turkm.
187 F6 Ekeren Belgium
165 N2 Ekerö Sweden
229 G5 Eket Nigeria
102 J7 Eketahuna North I. N.Z.
Ekhínos Greece see Echinos
Ekhmîm Egypt see Akhmīm
122 H2 Ekimchan Rus. Fed.
150 H2 Ekinyazı Turkey
229 G5 Ekiti state Nigeria
245 Q2 Ekka Island N.W.T. Can.
165 M4 Eknö i. Sweden
230 E5 Ekoli Dem. Rep. Congo
165 N2 Ekoln l. Sweden
153 L3 Ekonda Rus. Fed.
229 H5 Ekondo Titi Cameroon
162 V3 Ekostrovskaya Imandra, Ozero l. Rus. Fed.
230 C4 Ekouamou Congo
229 G5 Ekpoma Nigeria
187 E6 Eksaarde Belgium
187 H6 Eksel Belgium
Eksere Turkey see Gündoğmuş
164 J1 Ekshärad Sweden
221 L5 Ekşili Turkey
165 K4 Eksjö Sweden
122 C1 Ekskavatornyy Rus. Fed.
236 B4 Eksteenfontein S. Africa
286 X2 Ekström Ice Shelf Antarctica
162 O4 Ekträsk Sweden
244 H4 Ekuk AK U.S.A.
230 D5 Ekuku Dem. Rep. Congo
248 D2 Ekwan r. Ont. Can.
248 D2 Ekwan Point Ont. Can.
244 H4 Ekwok AK U.S.A.
118 C5 Ela Myanmar
El Aaiún Western Sahara see Laâyoune
284 B5 El Abanico Chile
225 F6 El Abbasiya Sudan
220 D6 Elafonisos i. Greece
220 D6 Elafonisou, Steno sea chan. Greece
228 D2 El Aghlâf well Maur.
268 E7 El Aguaje Mex.
150 C3 Elaia, Cape Cyprus
225 G5 El Aiadia well Sudan
220 F2 Elaiochori Greece
226 A5 El 'Aïouej well Maur.
El 'Alamein Egypt see Al 'Alamayn
269 H2 El Alamito Mex.
266 A2 El Alamo Mex.
268 C6 El Alcihuatl Mex.
209 D12 El Algar Spain
227 G2 El Alia Alg.
211 B7 El Alia Tunisia
206 G6 El Aljarafe reg. Spain
206 E5 El Almendro Spain
207 O7 El Alquián Spain
282 D3 El Alto Catamarca Arg.
284 D2 El Alto La Rioja Arg.
274 A6 El Alto Peru
178 C6 Élancourt France
206 E5 El Andévalo reg. Spain
237 O1 Elands r. S. Africa
235 F5 Elands r. S. Africa
237 K8 Elandsberg mt. S. Africa
237 N1 Elandsdoorn S. Africa
237 J8 Elandsdrif S. Africa
237 O4 Elandskraal S. Africa
237 N4 Elandslaagte S. Africa
237 K1 Elandsputte S. Africa
172 E3 Elan Village Powys, Wales U.K.
Elar Armenia see Abovyan
206 H6 El Arahal Spain
El Araïche Morocco see Larache
266 C3 El Arco Mex.
205 J8 El Arenal Castilla y León Spain
El Arenal Illes Balears Spain see S'Arenal
227 E2 El Aricha Alg.
107 K4 El Arish Qld Austr.
227 G1 El Arrouch Alg.
221 H7 Elasa i. Greece
El Asnam Alg. see Chlef
220 D3 Elassona Greece
205 M2 El Astillero Spain
150 C9 Elat Israel
205 N7 El Atazar, Embalse de resr Spain
226 B5 El 'Aţf reg. Western Sahara
113 K5 Elato atoll Micronesia
148 I4 Elazığ Turkey
151 A7 Elazığ prov. Turkey
255 D10 Elba AL U.S.A.
214 E2 Elba, Isola d' i. Italy
207 O3 El Ballestero Spain
122 J3 El'ban Rus. Fed.
274 C2 El Banco Col.
228 D2 El Bânoûn well Maur.
204 I8 El Barco de Ávila Spain
El Barco de Valdeorras Spain see O Barco
205 K8 El Barraco Spain
269 I1 El Barranco Tamaulipas Mex.
269 I3 El Barranco Tamaulipas Mex.
266 F2 El Barreal salt l. Mex.
268 E2 El Barril Mex.
232 B2 El Barun Sudan
218 I9 Elbasan Albania
148 G4 Elbaşı Turkey
225 G5 El Bauga Sudan
274 D2 El Baúl Venez.
227 F2 El Bayadh Alg.
190 H3 Elbe r. Ger. alt. Labe (Czech Rep.)
262 C3 Elbe WA U.S.A.
193 E6 Elbe-Havel-Kanal canal Ger.
228 C2 'Elb el Fçâl des. Maur.
284 B3 El Belloto airport Chile
190 K3 Elbe-Lübeck-Kanal canal Ger.
150 E4 El Béqaa val. Lebanon
191 D6 Elbergen Ger.
228 C2 El Berié well Maur.
205 M7 El Berrueco Spain
263 K7 Elbert, Mount CO U.S.A.
250 H5 Elberta MI U.S.A.
265 U2 Elberta UT U.S.A.
255 F8 Elberton GA U.S.A.
232 D4 El Beru Hagia Somalia
232 C4 El Bes well Kenya
178 B5 Elbeuf France
150 F2 Elbeyli Turkey
228 C2 El Beyyeḍ well Maur.
226 C5 El Beyyeḍ well Maur.
204 F4 El Bierzo reg. Spain
200 B5 Elbigenalp Austria
268 F7 El Billete, Cerro mt. Mex.
Elbing Pol. see Elbląg
191 K7 Elbingerode (Harz) Ger.
148 H4 Elbistan Turkey
206 I9 El Biutz Morocco
165 P7 Elbląg Pol.
197 H1 Elbląski, Kanał canal Pol.
266 □R11 El Bluff Nic.
204 G8 El Bodón Spain
284 A4 El Boldo Chile
El Bollo Spain see O Bolo
283 C6 El Bolsón Arg.
207 N3 El Bonillo Spain
268 E3 El Bordo Mex.
206 H9 El Borj Morocco
227 H3 El Borma Tunisia
207 I7 El Bosque Spain
El Boulaïda Alg. see Blida
247 J5 Elbow Sask. Can.
255 I12 Elbow Cay i. Bahamas
260 G2 Elbow Lake MN U.S.A.
268 F2 El Bozal Mex.
267 I4 El Brasil Mex.
151 D2 El'brus Rus. Fed.
151 D2 El'brus mt. Rus. Fed.
151 D2 El'brusskiy Rus. Fed.
193 J9 Elbsandstein Gebirge hills Ger.
230 F3 El Buheyrat state Sudan
207 K2 El Bullaque Spain
186 I4 Elburg Neth.
207 J7 El Burgo Spain
205 O3 Elburgo Spain
208 D4 El Burgo de Ebro Spain
205 N5 El Burgo de Osma Spain
205 J4 El Burgo Ranero Spain
230 E2 El Burma well Sudan
268 E2 El Burrito Mex.
Elburz Mountains Iran see Alborz, Reshteh-ye
205 Q5 El Buste Spain
159 S7 El'buzd r. Rus. Fed.
204 H7 El Cabaco Spain
207 P6 El Cabildo Spain
207 O7 El Cabo de Gata Spain
282 D2 El Cadillal, Embalse resr Arg.
283 C6 El Cain Arg.
264 P9 El Cajon CA U.S.A.
266 □P10 El Cajón, Represa dam Hond.
275 F3 El Callao Venez.
El Caló Spain see Es Caló
269 G8 El Camotal, Sierra mts Mex.
209 E11 El Campello Spain
205 J9 El Campillo de la Jara Spain
El Campo Spain see Campo Lugar
261 G11 El Campo TX U.S.A.
205 J7 El Campo de Peñaranda Spain
205 P9 El Cañavate Spain
268 G1 El Canelo Mex.
285 I4 El Caño Uru.
274 D3 El Cantón Venez.
261 E12 El Capulín r. Mex.
268 F1 El Cardito Mex.
274 D2 El Carmelo Venez.
282 D2 El Carmen Jujuy Arg.
284 C1 El Carmen San Juan Arg.
276 E3 El Carmen Beni Bol.
277 F4 El Carmen Santa Cruz Bol.
284 B5 El Carmen Chile
274 B5 El Carmen Ecuador
274 E4 El Carmen Venez.
269 N7 El Carmen, Laguna l. Mex.
209 D9 El Caroche mt. Spain
207 K5 El Carpio Spain
205 L9 El Carpio de Tajo Spain
268 G9 El Carrizal Mex.
205 N7 El Casar Spain
205 K8 El Casar de Escalona Spain
266 G5 El Casco Mex.
209 D7 El Castellar Spain
208 C4 El Castellar reg. Spain
206 G5 El Castillo de las Guardas Spain
267 M10 El Cebú, Cerro mt. Mex.
207 L4 El Centenillo Spain
265 Q9 El Centro CA U.S.A.
277 E4 El Cerro Bol.
206 F5 El Cerro de Andévalo Spain
284 E2 El Chacho Arg.
285 F6 El Chanco, Salina salt pan Arg.
275 E2 El Chaparro Venez.
269 H3 El Chapulín Mex.
285 F6 El Chara Arg.
209 D11 Elche, Embalse de resr Spain
207 O4 Elche de la Sierra Spain
209 D11 Elche-Elx Spain
269 M8 El Chichón Mex.
267 M9 El Chichónal vol. Mex.
269 I5 El Chico, Parque Nacional nat. park Mex.
266 G3 El Chilicote Mex.
195 I5 Elchingen Ger.
250 E4 Elcho WI U.S.A.
106 E1 Elcho Island N.T. Austr.
205 O3 Elciego Spain
268 G5 El Cimatario, Parque Nacional nat. park Mex.
El Coca Ecuador see Coca
274 C3 El Cocuy, Parque Nacional nat. park Col.
207 K3 El Collado hill Spain
268 C6 El Colomo Mex.
268 G8 El Conejo, Sierra mts Mex.
208 J5 El Congost r. Spain
207 O5 El Contador, Puerto de pass Spain
206 H6 El Coronil Spain
269 M8 El Corte r. Mex.
269 L10 El Coyol Mex.
269 L8 El Coyolito Mex.
204 H7 El Cubo de Don Sancho Spain
204 I6 El Cubo de Tierra del Vino Spain
206 G7 El Cuervo Spain
268 B4 El Custodio, Punta pt Mex.
283 C5 El Cuy Arg.
267 P7 El Cuyo Mex.
209 D11 Elda Spain
209 D10 Elda, Embalse de resr Spain
232 B4 Eldama Ravine Kenya
208 L3 El Daró r. Spain
266 C3 El Dátil Mex.
232 D3 El Debb well Eth.
251 O3 Eldee Ont. Can.
192 D4 Eldena Ger.
250 E8 Eldena IL U.S.A.
104 □3 Elder, Mount hill S. Pacific Ocean
250 E5 Elderon WI U.S.A.
263 H12 El Desemboque Mex.
162 □D2 Eldhraun lava field Iceland
266 H3 El Diamante Mex.
274 C2 El Difícil Col.
153 O3 El'dikan Rus. Fed.
190 J5 Eldingen Ger.
268 C6 El Divisadero Mex.
274 B4 El Diviso Col.
285 G6 El Divisorio Arg.
El Djezair Alg. see Alger
266 B2 El Doctor Mex.
260 I6 Eldon MO U.S.A.
260 I4 Eldora IA U.S.A.
258 F6 Eldora NJ U.S.A.
285 G4 El Dorado Arg.
282 G2 Eldorado Arg.
280 C6 Eldorado Brazil
274 D4 El Dorado Col.
266 F5 El Dorado Mex.
261 I9 El Dorado AR U.S.A.
261 G7 El Dorado KS U.S.A.
261 E10 Eldorado TX U.S.A.
275 F3 El Dorado Venez.
265 R6 Eldorado Mountains NV U.S.A.
232 B4 Eldoret Kenya
258 F1 Eldred NY U.S.A.
245 L2 Eldridge, Mount AK U.S.A.
284 E5 El Durazno Arg.
Elea, Cape Cyprus see Elaia, Cape
256 D10 Eleanor WV U.S.A.
262 I4 Electric Peak MT U.S.A.
220 E4 Elefsina Greece
226 D4 El Eglab plat. Alg.
225 F5 El 'Ein well Sudan
160 G5 Eleja Latvia
207 N7 El Ejido Spain
199 K5 Elek Hungary
Elek r. Rus. Fed. see Ilek
143 V2 Elekmonar Rus. Fed.
160 H7 Elektrėnai Lith.
161 V6 Elektrogorsk Rus. Fed.
161 V6 Elektrostal' Rus. Fed.
161 V6 Elektrougli Rus. Fed.
229 G5 Elele Nigeria
232 B3 Elemi Triangle terr. Africa
219 N8 Elena Bulg.
208 E5 Elena, Planas de plain Spain
274 C5 El Encanto Col.
265 P9 El Encinal Baja California Mex.
269 I1 El Encinal Tamaulipas Mex.
269 H2 El Encino Mex.
191 K7 Elend Ger.
284 D3 Eleodoro Lobos Arg.

220 B3 **Eleousa** Greece
268 G3 **El Epazote** Mex.
136 C3 **Elephanta Caves** tourist site Mahar. India
263 K10 **Elephant Butte Reservoir** NM U.S.A.
286 U2 **Elephant Island** Antarctica
136 G8 **Elephant Pass** Sri Lanka
139 N9 **Elephant Point** Bangl.
244 G2 **Elephant Point** AK U.S.A.
205 L7 **El Escorial** Spain
219 L9 **Eleshnitsa** Bulg.
149 K4 **Eleşkirt** Turkey
206 G5 **El Esparragal, Embalse** resr Spain
205 L7 **El Espinar** Spain
267 O10 **El Estor** Guat.
209 D12 **El Estrecho de San Ginés** Spain
285 I2 **El Eucaliptus** Uru.
270 E1 **Eleuthera** i. Bahamas
250 C5 **Eleva** WI U.S.A.
261 J7 **Eleven Point** r. MO U.S.A.
205 O2 **Elexalde** Spain
211 B7 **El Fahs** Tunisia
El Faiyûm Egypt see **Al Fayyūm**
227 H2 **El Faouar** Tunisia
224 E6 **El Fasher** Sudan
202 D5 **El Fendek** Morocco
El Ferrol Spain see **Ferrol**
El Ferrol del Caudillo Spain see **Ferrol**
191 I10 **Elfershausen** Ger.
208 L3 **El Fluvià** r. Spain
208 H5 **El Francolí** r. Spain
228 B2 **El Freïoua** well Maur.
205 K7 **El Fresno** Spain
265 W10 **Elfrida** AZ U.S.A.
232 D3 **El Fud** Eth.
266 E4 **El Fuerte** Mex.
230 F2 **El Fula** Sudan
163 K5 **Elgå** Norway
227 F4 **El Gaa Taatzebar** basin Alg.
207 O5 **El Gabar** mt. Spain
208 H5 **El Gaià** r. Spain
232 C4 **Elgal** waterhole Kenya
268 G5 **El Gallo** Mex.
206 G5 **El Garrobo** Spain
207 I7 **El Gastor** Spain
269 I1 **El Gavilán** Mex.
226 D5 **El Gçaib** well Mali
140 C6 **El Geili** Sudan
224 D6 **El Geneina** Sudan
191 H8 **Elgershausen (Schauenburg)** Ger.
205 P2 **Elgeta** Spain
225 G6 **El Geteina** Sudan
225 G6 **El Gezira** state Sudan
225 F5 **El Ghaba** Sudan
226 C5 **El Ghallâouîya** well Maur.
228 C2 **El Gheddiya** Maur.
164 H2 **Elgheia** hill Norway
El Ghor plain Jordan/West Bank see **Al Ghawr**
168 J7 **Elgin** Moray, Scotland U.K.
250 F7 **Elgin** IL U.S.A.
260 E2 **Elgin** ND U.S.A.
265 R4 **Elgin** NV U.S.A.
262 F4 **Elgin** OR U.S.A.
261 G10 **Elgin** TX U.S.A.
107 K7 **Elgin Down** Qld Austr.
153 P3 **El'ginskiy** Rus. Fed.
225 F5 **El Gir** well Sudan
El Gîza Egypt see **Al Jīzah**
268 G4 **El Gogorrón, Parque Nacional** nat. park Mex.
205 P2 **Elgoibar** Spain
168 D8 **Elgol** Highland, Scotland U.K.
227 F3 **El Goléa** Alg.
238 □3c **El Golfo** Lanzarote Canary Is
238 □3e **El Golfo** b. El Hierro Canary Is
266 B2 **El Golfo de Santa Clara** Mex.
232 B4 **Elgon, Mount** Uganda
162 U2 **Elgoras, Gora** hill Rus. Fed.
163 K5 **Elgpiggen** mt. Norway
208 F3 **El Grado** Spain
208 F3 **El Grado, Embalse de** resr Spain
206 E5 **El Granado** Spain
209 E8 **El Grau de Borriana** Spain
268 C6 **El Grullo** Jalisco Mex.
267 J5 **El Grullo** Tamaulipas Mex.
269 N8 **El Guanal** Mex.
266 G2 **El Guante** Mex.
227 H2 **El Guetar** Tunisia
226 E5 **El Guettâra** well Mali
153 M3 **El'gyay** Rus. Fed.
211 A7 **El Hadjar** Alg.
227 G2 **El Hadjira** Alg.
227 H2 **El Hamma** Tunisia
226 C5 **El Ḥammâmi** reg. Maur.
226 D4 **El Hank** reg. Alg.
226 C5 **El Ḥank** esc. Mali/Maur.
211 C7 **El Haouaria** Tunisia
146 B9 **El Hasira** Sudan
266 □R13 **El Hato del Volcán** Panama
225 G6 **El Hawata** Sudan
El Hazim Jordan see **Al Hazīm**
238 □3e **El Hierro** i. Canary Is
269 I4 **El Higo** Mex.
224 E6 **El Hilla** Sudan
205 O9 **El Hito** Spain
227 F3 **El Homr** Alg.
225 F6 **El Homra** Sudan
228 C2 **El Houeïtat** well Maur.
205 L7 **El Hoyo de Pinares** Spain
284 B5 **El Huecu** Arg.
225 F5 **El Husheim** well Sudan
229 H3 **Eli** well Niger
115 G8 **Eliase** Maluku Indon.
231 D7 **Elias Garcia** Angola
270 H4 **Elías Piña** Dom. Rep.
215 L2 **Elice** Italy
Elichpur Mahar. India see **Achalpur**
256 A8 **Elida** OH U.S.A.
269 J4 **El Idolo, Isla** i. Mex.
168 K10 **Elie** Fife, Scotland U.K.
136 C7 **Elikalpeni Bank** sea feature India
220 D4 **Elikonas** mts Greece
230 E5 **Elila** Dem. Rep. Congo
231 E5 **Elila** r. Dem. Rep. Congo
236 D10 **Elim** S. Africa
244 G2 **Elim** AK U.S.A.
160 J1 **Elimäki** Fin.
Elimberrum France see **Auch**
258 A2 **Elimsport** PA U.S.A.
268 G6 **El Infiernillo** Mex.
Eling Guizhou China see **Yinjiang**
173 J6 **Eling** Hampshire, England U.K.
230 E5 **Elingampangu** Dem. Rep. Congo
219 L8 **Elin Pelin** Bulg.
151 F2 **Elin-Yurt** Rus. Fed.
215 P4 **Elio, Monte d'** hill Italy
249 I1 **Eliot, Mount** Nfld and Lab. Can.
230 E5 **Elipa** Dem. Rep. Congo
230 D4 **Elisabetha** Dem. Rep. Congo
Élisabethville Dem. Rep. Congo see **Lubumbashi**
278 E4 **Eliseu Martins** Brazil
El Iskandarîya Egypt see **Al Iskandarīyah**
157 I7 **Elista** Rus. Fed.
200 H4 **Elixhausen** Austria
132 C7 **Elixku** Xinjiang China
257 K8 **Elizabeth** NJ U.S.A.
256 D9 **Elizabeth** WV U.S.A.
108 I4 **Elizabeth, Mount** hill W.A. Austr.
257 □S1 **Elizabeth, Mount** hill N.B. Can.
255 I7 **Elizabeth City** NC U.S.A.
106 G5 **Elizabeth Creek** r. Qld Austr.
Elizabeth Island Pitcairn Is see **Henderson Island**
257 O7 **Elizabeth Islands** MA U.S.A.
234 B5 **Elizabeth Point** Namibia
99 F4 **Elizabeth Reef** Austr.
256 C12 **Elizabethton** TN U.S.A.
261 K7 **Elizabethtown** IL U.S.A.
254 E7 **Elizabethtown** KY U.S.A.
255 H8 **Elizabethtown** NC U.S.A.
257 L4 **Elizabethtown** NY U.S.A.
258 B4 **Elizabethtown** PA U.S.A.
251 R9 **Elizabethville** PA U.S.A.
208 B1 **Elizondo** Spain
268 B2 **El Jacuixtle** Mex.
226 C2 **El Jadida** Morocco
266 G4 **El Jaralito** Mex.
204 G8 **Eljas** Spain
269 H5 **El Jazmín** Mex.
225 G6 **El Jebelein** Sudan
227 H2 **El Jem** Tunisia
266 □P11 **El Jícaro** Nic.
268 G8 **El Jilguero** Mex.
269 M8 **El Juile** Mex.
238 □3e **El Julán** slope El Hierro Canary Is
246 H5 **Elk** r. B.C. Can.
197 K2 **Ełk** Pol.
197 K2 **Ełk** r. Pol.
258 D6 **Elk** r. MD U.S.A.
255 D8 **Elk** r. TN U.S.A.
El Kaa Lebanon see **Qaa**
225 G5 **El Kab** Sudan
260 J4 **Elkader** IA U.S.A.
227 H1 **El Kala** Alg.
140 C6 **El Kamlin** Sudan
225 G5 **El Karabi** Sudan
160 I4 **Elkas kalns** hill Latvia
256 B11 **Elkatawa** KY U.S.A.
225 G6 **El Kawa** Sudan
261 F8 **Elk City** OK U.S.A.
264 J2 **Elk Creek** CA U.S.A.
106 E6 **Elkedra** N.T. Austr.
106 F6 **Elkedra** watercourse N.T. Austr.
226 D2 **El Kelaâ des Srarhna** Morocco
191 E9 **Elkenroth** Ger.
232 D3 **Ēl Kerē** Eth.
246 H5 **Elkford** B.C. Can.
264 K3 **Elk Grove** CA U.S.A.
El Khalil West Bank see **Hebron**
225 F5 **El Khandaq** Sudan
El Khârga Egypt see **Al Khārijah**
254 E5 **Elkhart** IN U.S.A.
261 E7 **Elkhart** KS U.S.A.
El Khartûm Sudan see **Khartoum**
El Khenachich esc. Mali see **El Khnâchîch**
226 D5 **El Khnâchîch** esc. Mali
250 F7 **Elkhorn** WI U.S.A.
260 G5 **Elkhorn** r. NE U.S.A.
256 C11 **Elkhorn City** KY U.S.A.
151 F2 **El'khotovo** Rus. Fed.
219 O8 **Elkhovo** Bulg.
Elki Turkey see **Beytüşşebap**
255 G7 **Elkin** NC U.S.A.
256 F10 **Elkins** WV U.S.A.
258 E4 **Elkins Park** PA U.S.A.
247 H4 **Elk Island National Park** Y.T. Can.
248 D4 **Elk Lake** Ont. Can.
250 I5 **Elk Lake** l. MI U.S.A.
256 H7 **Elkland** PA U.S.A.
258 D5 **Elk Mills** MD U.S.A.
262 K6 **Elk Mountain** WY U.S.A.
258 D5 **Elk Neck** MD U.S.A.
246 H5 **Elko** B.C. Can.
262 G6 **Elko** NV U.S.A.
232 E3 **Ēl K'oran** Eth.
247 I4 **Elk Point** Alta Can.
260 G4 **Elk Point** SD U.S.A.
258 B6 **Elkridge** MD U.S.A.
250 A4 **Elk River** MN U.S.A.
El Ksaib Ounane well Mali see **El Gçaib**
265 X1 **Elk Springs** CO U.S.A.
254 D7 **Elkton** KY U.S.A.
258 D5 **Elkton** MD U.S.A.
256 G10 **Elkton** VA U.S.A.
256 D10 **Elkview** WV U.S.A.
269 K9 **El Labrador, Cerro** mt. Mex.
230 F2 **El Lagowa** Sudan
165 O1 **Ellan** Sweden
151 H4 **Ellăryoğu Dağı** hill Azer.
Ellas country Europe see **Greece**
285 G2 **El Laurel** Arg.
109 C8 **Ellavalla** W.A. Austr.
255 E9 **Ellaville** GA U.S.A.
200 D5 **Ellbögen** Austria
180 D6 **Ellé** r. France
193 F10 **Ellefeld** Ger.
243 H2 **Ellef Ringnes Island** Nunavut Can.
232 C4 **Ēl Lēh** Eth.
232 D5 **El Lein** well Kenya
150 E1 **Ellek** Turkey
109 D13 **Elleker** W.A. Austr.
224 C5 **Elléloyé** well Chad
265 V3 **Ellen, Mount** UT U.S.A.
138 E5 **Ellenabad** Haryana India
168 E10 **Ellenabeich** Argyll and Bute, Scotland U.K.
195 I3 **Ellenberg** Ger.
256 D9 **Ellenboro** WV U.S.A.
257 L4 **Ellenburg Depot** NY U.S.A.
257 J10 **Ellendale** DE U.S.A.
260 F2 **Ellendale** ND U.S.A.
262 D3 **Ellensburg** WA U.S.A.
259 G1 **Ellenville** NY U.S.A.
268 B1 **El León, Cerro** mt. Mex.
268 G1 **El Leoncito** Mex.
100 □3a **Eller** i. Kwajalein Marshall Is
190 I3 **Ellerau** Ger.
190 I3 **Ellerbek** Ger.
190 I3 **Ellerhoop** Ger.
103 C11 **Ellery, Lake** South I. N.Z.
103 G10 **Ellesmere** South I. N.Z.
172 G2 **Ellesmere** Shropshire, England U.K.
103 G10 **Ellesmere, Lake** South I. N.Z.
243 J2 **Ellesmere Island** Nunavut Can.
171 L7 **Ellesmere Port** Cheshire, England U.K.
187 E7 **Ellezelles** Belgium
180 D6 **Elliant** France
243 H3 **Ellice** r. Nunavut Can.
245 N1 **Ellice Island** N.W.T. Can.
Ellice Island atoll Tuvalu see **Funafuti**
Ellice Islands country S. Pacific Ocean see **Tuvalu**
258 B6 **Ellicott City** MD U.S.A.
256 G6 **Ellicottville** NY U.S.A.
255 E8 **Ellijay** GA U.S.A.
268 F7 **El Limón** Guerrero Mex.
268 B3 **El Limón** Nayarit Mex.
269 I3 **El Limón** Tamaulipas Mex.
195 J3 **Ellingen** Ger.
171 N2 **Ellingham** Northumberland, England U.K.
Ellington Viti Levu Fiji see **Nakorokula**
171 N3 **Ellington** Northumberland, England U.K.
237 L7 **Elliot** S. Africa
107 K5 **Elliot, Mount** Qld Austr.
237 M7 **Elliotdale** S. Africa
256 F10 **Elliot Knob** mt. VA U.S.A.
248 D4 **Elliot Lake** Ont. Can.
104 F3 **Elliot Price Conservation Park** nature res. S.A. Austr.
104 □3 **Elliot Reef** S. Pacific Ocean
106 D4 **Elliott** N.T. Austr.
245 J2 **Elliott Highway** AK U.S.A.
262 G4 **Ellis** ID U.S.A.
260 F6 **Ellis** KS U.S.A.
104 E5 **Elliston** S.A. Austr.
256 E11 **Elliston** VA U.S.A.
261 K10 **Ellisville** MS U.S.A.
268 G4 **El Llano** Mex.
204 F2 **El Llano** Spain
208 I4 **El Llobregat** r. Spain
200 F4 **Ellmau** Austria
168 L8 **Ellon** Aberdeenshire, Scotland U.K.
138 E9 **Ellora Caves** tourist site Mahar. India
284 D4 **El Loro** Arg.
164 H3 **Ellös** Sweden
204 I8 **El Losar del Barco** Spain
171 P6 **Elloughton** East Riding of Yorkshire, England U.K.
191 K7 **Ellrich** Ger.
285 G2 **Ellsa** Arg.
260 F6 **Ellsworth** KS U.S.A.
257 □Q4 **Ellsworth** ME U.S.A.
260 D4 **Ellsworth** NE U.S.A.
250 B5 **Ellsworth** WI U.S.A.
286 R1 **Ellsworth Land** reg. Antarctica
286 S1 **Ellsworth Mountains** Antarctica
195 I4 **Ellwangen (Jagst)** Ger.
256 E8 **Ellwood City** PA U.S.A.
190 F4 **Ellwürden** Ger.
190 H3 **Elm** Ger.
212 G2 **Elm** Switz.
173 M2 **Elm** Cambridgeshire, England U.K.
197 I1 **Elma** r. Pol.
271 I4 **El Macao** Dom. Rep.
269 H4 **El Madroño** Mex.
El Maestral reg. Spain see **El Maestrazgo**
208 E7 **El Maestrazgo** reg. Spain
226 E5 **El Mahia** reg. Mali
283 C6 **El Maitén** Arg.
151 D6 **Elmakaya** Turkey
150 B2 **Elmakuz Dağı** mt. Turkey
221 K6 **Elmalı** Turkey
263 K9 **El Malpais National Monument** nat. park NM U.S.A.
225 G6 **El Manaqil** Sudan
274 E4 **El Mango** Venez.
El Mansûra Egypt see **Al Manşūrah**
275 F3 **El Manteco** Venez.
202 D5 **El Manzla** Morocco
211 C7 **El Marsa** Tunisia
268 F1 **El Mascarón, Sierra** mts Mex.
208 G5 **El Masroig** Spain
268 F4 **El Mastranto** Mex.
228 C2 **El Mechoual** well Maur.
238 □3a **El Médano** Tenerife Canary Is
266 D5 **El Médano** Mex.
232 D3 **El Medo** Eth.
227 G2 **El Meghaïer** Alg.
230 F2 **El Melemm** Sudan
228 B2 **El Melhes** well Maur.
284 B3 **El Melón** Chile
200 C5 **Elmen** Austria
192 D3 **Elmenhorst** Mecklenburg-Vorpommern Ger.
192 F2 **Elmenhorst** Mecklenburg-Vorpommern Ger.
192 H2 **Elmenhorst** Mecklenburg-Vorpommern Ger.
190 J3 **Elmenhorst** Schleswig-Holstein Ger.
190 K3 **Elmenhorst** Schleswig-Holstein Ger.
258 E5 **Elmer** NJ U.S.A.
225 G6 **El Mesellemiya** Sudan
224 C6 **El Messir** well Chad
268 E2 **El Mezquite** Mex.
258 D2 **Elmhurst** PA U.S.A.
275 F3 **El Miamo** Venez.
268 G2 **El Milagro de Guadalupe** Mex.
228 E5 **Elmina** Ghana
150 D4 **El Mîna** Lebanon
251 N6 **Elmira** Ont. Can.
249 I4 **Elmira** P.E.I. Can.
250 J4 **Elmira** MI U.S.A.
251 R7 **Elmira** NY U.S.A.
268 C5 **El Mirador** Mex.
269 I6 **El Mirador, Cerro** mt. Mex.
265 T8 **El Mirage** AZ U.S.A.
228 C2 **El Moïnane** well Maur.
205 M7 **El Molar** Spain
207 K2 **El Molinillo** Spain
269 I4 **El Molino** Mex.
267 I3 **El Moral** Mex.
207 O5 **El Moral** Spain
105 J7 **Elmore** Vic. Austr.
256 B7 **Elmore** OH U.S.A.
208 H5 **El Morell** Spain
284 E3 **El Morro** mt. Arg.
228 C3 **El Mraïfig** well Maur.
228 E2 **El Mraïti** well Mali
228 D2 **El Mreyyé** reg. Maur.
259 H2 **Elmsford** NY U.S.A.
190 I3 **Elmshorn** Ger.
194 D3 **Elmstein** Ger.
173 N3 **Elmswell** Suffolk, England U.K.
230 E2 **El Muglad** Sudan
209 C10 **El Mugrón** mt. Spain
251 O5 **Elmvale** Ont. Can.
250 E9 **Elmwood** IL U.S.A.
250 B5 **Elmwood** WI U.S.A.
226 D4 **El Mzereb** well Mali
269 H3 **El Naranjo** Mex.
268 D7 **El Naranjo** r. Mex.
185 J10 **Elne** France
162 I5 **Elnesvågen** Norway
114 B6 **El Nido** Palawan Phil.
284 C4 **El Nihuel** Arg.
238 □3f **El Oasis** Gran Canaria Canary Is
265 Q9 **El Oasis** Mex.
225 F6 **El Obeid** Sudan
269 N9 **El Ocote, Parque Natural** nature res. Mex.
269 H8 **El Ocotito** Mex.
225 F6 **El Odaiya** Sudan
284 D5 **El Odre** Arg.
230 B4 **Elogo** Congo
251 N6 **Elora** Ont. Can.
180 C5 **Elorn** r. France
274 B5 **El Oro** prov. Ecuador
266 H4 **El Oro** Coahuila Mex.
268 G6 **El Oro** México Mex.
205 O2 **Elorrio** Spain
285 G3 **Elortondo** Arg.
205 Q3 **Elorz** Spain
220 E7 **Elos** Kriti Greece
205 K7 **El Oso** Spain
199 H5 **Előszállás** Hungary
268 A2 **Elota** Mex.
268 A2 **Elota** r. Mex.
227 G2 **El Oued** Alg.
269 I5 **Eloxochitlán** Mex.
265 U9 **Eloy** AZ U.S.A.
179 M7 **Éloyes** France
275 F3 **El Palmar** Venez.
285 H2 **El Palmar, Parque Nacional** nat. park Arg.
266 G5 **El Palmito** Mex.
238 □3a **El Palm-Mar** Tenerife Canary Is
207 K7 **El Palo** Spain
268 G1 **El Pañuelo** Mex.
275 F2 **El Pao** Bolívar Venez.
274 D2 **El Pao** Cojedes Venez.
268 G8 **El Papayo** Mex.
115 F5 **Elpaputih, Teluk** b. Seram Indon.
266 □P11 **El Paraíso** Hond.
269 L8 **El Paraíso** Mex.
238 □3d **El Paso** La Palma Canary Is
250 F9 **El Paso** IL U.S.A.
El Paso KS U.S.A. see **Derby**
263 K11 **El Paso** TX U.S.A.
204 G8 **El Payo** Spain
207 N2 **El Pedernoso** Spain
269 I3 **El Pedregoso** r. Mex.
206 H5 **El Pedroso** Spain
205 J6 **El Pedroso de la Armuña** Spain
268 G3 **El Peñasco** Mex.
282 D2 **El Peñón** Arg.
284 B3 **El Peñón** mt. Chile
205 Q9 **El Peral** Spain
204 I6 **El Perdigón** Spain
285 F4 **El Peregrino** Arg.
208 G6 **El Perelló** Cataluña Spain
209 E9 **El Perelló** Valencia Spain
190 H2 **Elpersbüttel** Ger.
169 F5 **Elphin** Ireland
168 F6 **Elphin** Highland, Scotland U.K.
Elphinstone i. Myanmar see **Thayawthadangyi Kyun**
207 O2 **El Picazo** Spain
275 F2 **El Pilar** Venez.
Elpin Armenia see **Yelp'in**
269 I4 **El Piñal** Mex.
208 G5 **El Pinell de Bray** Spain
204 I6 **El Piñero** Spain
285 H2 **El Pingo** Arg.
266 H3 **El Pino, Sierra** mts Mex.
282 E2 **El Pintado** Arg.
206 H4 **El Pintado, Embalse** resr Spain
208 H5 **El Pla de Santa María** Spain
284 B3 **El Plomo, Nevado** mt. Chile
283 C7 **El Pluma** Arg.
208 D6 **El Pobo** Spain
205 Q7 **El Pobo de Dueñas** Spain
277 E3 **El Pocito** Bol.
209 E8 **El Port** Spain
264 M4 **El Portal** CA U.S.A.
208 L3 **El Port de la Selva** Spain
274 C1 **El Portele** b. Col.
284 D2 **El Portozuelo** Arg.
274 B7 **El Portugues** Peru
274 D3 **El Porvenir** Col.
264 P9 **El Porvenir** Mex.
266 G2 **El Porvenir** Mex.
266 □T13 **El Porvenir** Panama
269 H4 **El Potosí, Parque Nacional** nat. park Mex.
208 J5 **El Prat de Llobregat** Spain
El Progreso Guat. see **Guastatoya**
266 □P10 **El Progreso** Hond.
207 N2 **El Provencio** Spain
285 H3 **El Pueblito** Arg.
276 D5 **El Puente** Bol.
266 □P11 **El Puente** Nic.
205 N2 **El Puente** Spain
205 J9 **El Puente de Arzobispo** Spain
El Puerto de Andraitx Spain see **Port d'Andratx**
206 G7 **El Puerto de Santa María** Spain
El Qâhira Egypt see **Al Qāhirah**
150 D5 **El Qasimiye** r. Lebanon
El Quds Israel/West Bank see **Jerusalem**
282 D2 **El Quebrachal** Arg.
268 G3 **El Quelital** Mex.
284 B1 **Elqui** r. Chile
284 B3 **El Quisco** Chile
268 D7 **El Ranchito** Michoacán Mex.
269 I1 **El Ranchito** Tamaulipas Mex.
205 O4 **El Rasillo** Spain
266 □U13 **El Real** Panama
206 G5 **El Real de la Jara** Spain
205 K8 **El Real de San Vicente** Spain
205 P7 **El Recuenco** Spain
268 G4 **El Refugio** Mex.
268 B2 **El Regocijo** Mex.
261 G8 **El Reno** OK U.S.A.
284 D3 **El Retamo** Arg.
268 G2 **El Retorno** Mex.
282 D2 **El Rey, Parque Nacional** nat. park Arg.
264 M7 **El Rio** CA U.S.A.
268 A2 **El Roble** Mex.
207 K2 **El Robledo** Spain
206 G6 **El Rocío** Spain
205 N9 **El Romeral** Spain
206 E6 **El Rompido** Spain
206 G5 **El Ronquillo** Spain
269 N8 **El Rosario, Laguna** l. Mex.
247 I5 **Elrose** Sask. Can.
250 D6 **Elroy** WI U.S.A.
205 O5 **El Royo** Spain
207 J6 **El Rubio** Spain
268 G1 **El Rucio** Nuevo León Mex.
268 E2 **El Rucio** Zacatecas Mex.
245 N3 **Elsa** Y.T. Can.
216 H9 **Elsa** r. Sicilia Italy
213 J8 **Elsa** r. Italy
267 J4 **El Sabinal, Parque Nacional** nat. park Mex.
208 C3 **El Sabinar** Aragón Spain
207 O4 **El Sabinar** Murcia Spain
266 C2 **El Sahuaro** Mex.
283 D8 **El Salado** Arg.
268 G1 **El Salado** Mex.
209 E9 **El Saler** Spain
207 P3 **El Salobral** Spain
268 B2 **El Salto** Durango Mex.
268 D5 **El Salto** Jalisco Mex.
267 O11 **El Salvador** country Central America
282 C2 **El Salvador** Chile
268 D5 **El Salvador** Jalisco Mex.
268 G1 **El Salvador** Zacatecas Mex.
114 E7 **El Salvador** Mindanao Phil.
274 D3 **El Samán de Apure** Venez.
208 G4 **Els Arcs** Spain
251 L1 **Elsas** Ont. Can.
Elsass reg. France see **Alsace**
207 I6 **El Saucejo** Spain
204 G8 **El Saugo** Spain
266 F3 **El Sauz** Chihuahua Mex.
268 C4 **El Sauz** Nayarit Mex.
238 □3a **El Sauzal** Tenerife Canary Is
264 P10 **El Sauzal** Mex.
194 G2 **Elsava** r. Ger.
200 H4 **Elsbethen** Austria
171 M3 **Elsdon** Northumberland, England U.K.
190 H4 **Elsdorf** Niedersachsen Ger.
191 C9 **Elsdorf** Nordrhein-Westfalen Ger.
190 I2 **Elsdorf-Westermühlen** Ger.
191 G6 **Else** r. Ger.
271 I4 **El Seibo** Dom. Rep.
187 J8 **Elsenborn** Belgium
195 L4 **Elsendorf** Ger.
194 G2 **Elsenfeld** Ger.
194 F3 **Elsenz** r. Ger.
208 I2 **El Serrat** Andorra
106 D3 **Elsey** N.T. Austr.
106 D3 **Elsey National Park** nat. park Australia
190 F4 **Elsfleth** Ger.
106 D2 **El Sharana** N.T. Austr.
250 J6 **Elsie** MI U.S.A.
Elsinore Denmark see **Helsingør**
264 O8 **Elsinore** CA U.S.A.
265 T3 **Elsinore** UT U.S.A.
264 O8 **Elsinore Lake** CA U.S.A.
187 I7 **Elsloo** Neth.
258 D5 **Elsmere** DE U.S.A.
162 P2 **Elsnes** Norway
193 G7 **Elsnig** Ger.
193 F7 **Elsnigk** Ger.
266 H4 **El Socorro** Mex.
208 G5 **El Soleràs** Spain
244 H1 **Elson Lagoon** AK U.S.A.
284 C4 **El Sosneado** Arg.
186 I4 **Elspeet** Neth.
208 I4 **Els Prats de Rei** Spain
186 I5 **Elst** Gelderland Neth.
186 H5 **Elst** Utrecht Neth.
173 K5 **Elstead** Surrey, England U.K.
193 G7 **Elster** Ger.
193 F9 **Elsterberg** Ger.
193 I8 **Elsterniederung und Westliche Oberlausitzer Heide** park Ger.
193 I8 **Elsterwerda** Ger.
173 L4 **Elstree** Hertfordshire, England U.K.
266 F3 **El Sueco** Mex.
284 B3 **El Tabo** Chile
269 J5 **El Tajín** tourist site Mex.
274 C3 **El Tama, Parque Nacional** nat. park Venez.
227 H1 **El Tarf** Alg.
211 B7 **El Tarf** prov. Alg.
268 F6 **El Tecolote, Cerro** mt. Mex.
268 C2 **El Tecuán, Parque Nacional** nat. park Mex.
285 G4 **El Tejar** Arg.
204 H4 **El Teleno** mt. Spain
269 I1 **El Temascal** Mex.
201 N5 **Eltendorf** Austria
269 H6 **El Tepozteco, Parque Nacional** nat. park Mex.
208 L3 **El Ter** r. Spain
193 G9 **Elterlein** Ger.
102 I6 **Eltham** North I. N.Z.
205 L8 **El Tiemblo** Spain
275 E2 **El Tigre** Venez.
267 N9 **El Tigre, Parque Nacional** nat. park Guat.
195 J2 **Eltmann** Ger.
205 O9 **El Toboso** Spain
274 D2 **El Tocuyo** Venez.
282 C3 **El Tofo** Coquimbo Chile
284 B2 **El Tololo** Chile
169 F8 **Elton** Ireland
142 B3 **El'ton** Rus. Fed.
173 L2 **Elton** Cambridgeshire, England U.K.
171 L7 **Elton** Cheshire, England U.K.
142 B3 **El'ton, Ozero** l. Rus. Fed.
262 E3 **Eltopia** WA U.S.A.
204 I8 **El Torno** Spain
284 B5 **El Toro** Bíobío Chile
274 C2 **El Totumo** Venez.
285 G3 **El Trébol** Arg.
269 H9 **El Treinta** Mex.
266 C2 **El Tren** Mex.
285 H4 **El Trigo** Arg.
207 K2 **El Trincheto** Spain
285 G4 **El Triunfo** Arg.
266 D6 **El Triunfo** Mex.
271 □7 **El Tucuche** hill Trin. and Tob.
268 B5 **El Tuito** Mex.
206 F6 **El Tumbalejo** Spain
282 D2 **El Tunal** Arg.
274 D3 **El Tuparro, Parque Nacional** nat. park Col.
283 B8 **El Turbio** Chile
208 G3 **El Turbón** mt. Spain
191 F10 **Eltville am Rhein** Ger.
228 E5 **Elubo** Ghana
136 G4 **Eluru** Andhra Prad. India
225 G5 **El 'Uteishan** well Sudan
160 J3 **Elva** Estonia
266 E3 **El Vallecillo** Mex.
168 I12 **Elvanfoot** South Lanarkshire, Scotland U.K.
Elvanlı Turkey see **Tömük**
206 E3 **Elvas** Port.
162 Q2 **Elvebakken** Norway
162 N2 **Elvegard** Norway
269 H9 **El Veladero, Parque Nacional** nat. park Mex.
180 F6 **Elven** France
268 C4 **El Venado** Mex.
208 I5 **El Vendrell** Spain
269 J1 **El Verde Chico** Mex.
209 F10 **El Verger** Spain
258 D4 **Elverson** PA U.S.A.
163 K6 **Elverum** Norway
207 L2 **El Vicario, Embalse de** resr Spain
274 C3 **El Viejo** mt. Col.
266 □P11 **El Viejo** Nic.
268 C4 **El Vigía, Cerro** mt. Mex.
205 M7 **El Villar, Embalse de** resr Spain
171 P6 **Elvington** York, England U.K.
274 C6 **Elvira** Brazil
108 J4 **Elvire** r. W.A. Austr.
108 I5 **Elvire Aboriginal Reserve** W.A. Austr.
207 J4 **El Viso** Spain
206 H6 **El Viso del Alcor** Spain
162 U2 **Elvnes** Norway
212 E5 **Elvo** r. Italy
284 D3 **El Volcán** Arg.
284 B3 **El Volcán** Chile
232 D4 **El Wak** Kenya
250 F8 **Elwood** IL U.S.A.
254 E5 **Elwood** IN U.S.A.
260 F5 **Elwood** NE U.S.A.
258 F5 **Elwood** NJ U.S.A.
232 A2 **El Wurl** watercourse Sudan
225 F6 **El Wuz** Sudan
191 K8 **Elxleben** Ger.
173 M3 **Ely** Cambridgeshire, England U.K.
172 F5 **Ely** Cardiff, Wales U.K.
250 C2 **Ely** MN U.S.A.
265 R2 **Ely** NV U.S.A.
173 M3 **Ely, Isle of** reg. England U.K.
274 D3 **El Yagual** Venez.
232 C3 **El Yibo** well Kenya
256 C7 **Elyria** OH U.S.A.
251 R9 **Elysburg** PA U.S.A.
191 F10 **Elz** Ger.
194 D5 **Elz** r. Ger.
269 J9 **El Zacatón, Cerro** mt. Mex.
194 E5 **Elzach** Ger.
266 G5 **El Zape** Mex.
191 I6 **Elze** Ger.
190 I5 **Elze (Wedemark)** Ger.
100 □5 **Émaé** i. Vanuatu
182 H2 **Émagny** France
160 K3 **Emajõgi** r. Estonia
144 H3 **Emāmqolī** Iran
144 F3 **Emāmrūd** Iran
145 M3 **Emām Şaḥēb** Afgh.
144 H3 **Emām Taqī** Iran
165 M4 **Emån** r. Sweden
237 Q2 **Emangusi** S. Africa
100 □5 **Émao** i. Vanuatu
E. Martínez Mex. see **Emiliano Martínez**
280 A3 **Emas, Parque Nacional das** nat. park Brazil
132 F3 **Emazar** Kazakh.
142 H3 **Emba** Kazakh.
237 N2 **Embalenhle** S. Africa
282 D1 **Embarcación** Arg.
247 I3 **Embarras Portage** Alta Can.
250 B2 **Embarrass** MN U.S.A.
Embetsu Japan see **Enbetsu**
Embi Kazakh. see **Emba**
116 □ **Embiah, Mount** hill Sing.
205 Q7 **Embid** Spain
205 Q6 **Embid de Ariza** Spain
Embira r. Brazil see **Envira**
171 N2 **Embleton** Northumberland, England U.K.
168 I7 **Embo** Highland, Scotland U.K.
Émbonas Rodos Greece see **Emponas**
230 C4 **Embondo** Dem. Rep. Congo
280 D3 **Emborcação, Represa de** resr Brazil
Emborion Greece see **Emporeio**
194 F7 **Embrach** Switz.
258 D5 **Embreeville** PA U.S.A.
257 J3 **Embrun** Ont. Can.
183 I7 **Embrun** France
190 J4 **Embsen** Ger.
280 D5 **Embu** Brazil
232 C5 **Embu** Kenya
135 □1 **Embudhu** i. S. Male Maldives
135 □1 **Embudhu Finolhu** i. S. Male Maldives
231 C9 **Embundo** Angola
190 D4 **Emden** Ger.
221 I6 **Emecik** Turkey
Emei Sichuan China see **Emeishan**
130 D4 **Emeishan** Sichuan China
130 D4 **Emei Shan** mt. Sichuan China
107 L7 **Emerald** Qld Austr.
105 J7 **Emerald** Vic. Austr.
258 D3 **Emerald** PA U.S.A.
243 G2 **Emerald Isle** i. N.W.T. Can.
249 H2 **Emeril** Nfld and Lab. Can.
Emerita Augusta Spain see **Mérida**
276 D3 **Emero** r. Bol.
247 L5 **Emerson** Man. Can.
256 B10 **Emerson** KY U.S.A.
265 U3 **Emery** UT U.S.A.
Emesa Syria see **Ḥimş**
221 K3 **Emet** Turkey
237 O1 **eMgwenya** S. Africa
264 M3 **Emigrant Basin Wilderness** nature res. CA U.S.A.
264 L2 **Emigrant Gap** CA U.S.A.
262 F6 **Emigrant Pass** NV U.S.A.
265 Q4 **Emigrant Valley** NV U.S.A.
224 C5 **Emi Koussi** mt. Chad
246 G2 **Emile** r. N.W.T. Can.
285 G2 **Emilia** Arg.
266 G5 **Emiliano Martínez** Mex.
267 N9 **Emiliano Zapata** Chiapas Mex.
268 D1 **Emiliano Zapata** Durango Mex.
268 D2 **Emiliano Zapata** Zacatecas Mex.
212 K7 **Emilia-Romagna** admin. reg. Italy
285 G4 **Emilio Ayarza** Arg.
269 K6 **Emilio Carranza** Veracruz Mex.
268 D1 **Emilio Carranza** Zacatecas Mex.
285 H2 **Emilio R. Coni** Arg.
212 C4 **Emilius, Monte** mt. Italy
132 F3 **Emin** Xinjiang China
145 P5 **Eminabad** Pak.
219 P8 **Emine, Nos** pt Bulg.
261 J7 **Eminence** MO U.S.A.
132 F3 **Emin He** r. China
219 P8 **Eminska Planina** hills Bulg.
221 M3 **Emirdağ** Turkey
221 M4 **Emir Dağı** mt. Turkey
221 K4 **Emirhisar** Turkey
105 K9 **Emita** Tas. Austr.
237 P1 **eMjindini** S. Africa
190 I2 **Emkendorf** Ger.
256 F7 **Emlenton** PA U.S.A.
190 C5 **Emlichheim** Ger.
169 F8 **Emly** Ireland
165 L5 **Emmaboda** Sweden
Emmahaven Sumatera Indon. see **Telukbayur**
271 □10 **Emmastad** Curaçao Neth. Antilles
160 F3 **Emmaste** Estonia
161 T5 **Emmaus** Rus. Fed.
258 E3 **Emmaus** PA U.S.A.
105 M3 **Emmaville** N.S.W. Austr.
212 D1 **Emme** r. Switz.
186 I3 **Emmeloord** Neth.
190 G1 **Emmelsbüll-Horsbüll** Ger.
191 E10 **Emmelshausen** Ger.
186 K3 **Emmen** Neth.
194 E7 **Emmen** Switz.
194 D5 **Emmendingen** Ger.
212 D1 **Emmental** reg. Switz.
191 H6 **Emmer** r. Ger.
186 L3 **Emmer-Compascuum** Neth.
186 K3 **Emmer-Erfscheidenveen** Neth.
191 B7 **Emmerich** Ger.
195 K5 **Emmering** Ger.
195 N5 **Emmerting** Ger.
107 J8 **Emmet** Qld Austr.
260 H4 **Emmetsburg** IA U.S.A.
262 F5 **Emmett** ID U.S.A.
256 C6 **Emmett** MI U.S.A.
136 E5 **Emmiganuru** Andhra Prad. India
256 H9 **Emmitsburg** MD U.S.A.
244 F3 **Emmonak** AK U.S.A.
258 C6 **Emmorton** MD U.S.A.
173 M2 **Emneth** Norfolk, England U.K.
247 M5 **Emo** Ont. Can.
199 J4 **Emőd** Hungary
Emona Slovenia see **Ljubljana**
261 H9 **Emory** TX U.S.A.
261 D11 **Emory Peak** TX U.S.A.
228 B4 **Empada** Guinea-Bissau
266 D4 **Empalme** Mex.
268 G5 **Empalme Escobedo** Mex.
203 E4 **Empanadas** mt. Spain
237 P4 **Empangeni** S. Africa
282 F2 **Empedrado** Arg.
284 A4 **Empedrado** Chile
186 H5 **Empel** Neth.
290 G2 **Emperor Seamount Chain** sea feature N. Pacific Ocean
290 G2 **Emperor Trough** sea feature N. Pacific Ocean
276 C5 **Empexa, Salar de** salt flat Bol.
194 F5 **Empfingen** Ger.
Empingham Reservoir England U.K. see **Rutland Water**
250 H5 **Empire** MI U.S.A.
115 F8 **Emplawas** Maluku Indon.
213 J8 **Empoli** Italy
221 I6 **Emponas** Rodos Greece
221 G6 **Emporeio** Greece
260 G6 **Emporia** KS U.S.A.
256 H12 **Emporia** VA U.S.A.
256 G7 **Emporium** PA U.S.A.
247 I5 **Empress** Alta Can.
235 F3 **Empress Mine** Zimbabwe
187 H8 **Emptinne** Belgium
Empty Quarter des. Saudi Arabia see **Rub' al Khālī**
183 F6 **Empurany** France
190 D4 **Ems** r. Ger.
191 D6 **Emsbüren** Ger.
251 O4 **Emsdale** Ont. Can.
191 E6 **Emsdetten** Ger.
190 E4 **Ems-Jade-Kanal** canal Ger.
195 J2 **Emskirchen** Ger.
190 D5 **Emsland** reg. Ger.
186 I4 **Emst** Neth.
190 F5 **Emstek** Ger.
173 K6 **Emsworth** Hampshire, England U.K.
237 O1 **Emthonjeni** S. Africa
190 G5 **Emtinghausen** Ger.
107 H4 **Emu Creek** r. Qld Austr.
160 J3 **Emumägi** hill Estonia
107 M7 **Emu Park** Qld Austr.
122 D2 **Emur He** r. China
122 C2 **Emur Shan** mts China
169 I4 **Emyvale** Ireland
237 N2 **eMzinoni** S. Africa
126 F5 **Ena** Japan
162 L5 **Enafors** Sweden
274 D4 **Enambú** Col.
275 F3 **Enamuna** Brazil
163 N6 **Enånger** Sweden
113 I7 **Enarotali** Papua Indon.
126 G5 **Ena-san** mt. Japan
124 S2 **Enbetsu** Japan
208 F6 **Encanadé** mt. Spain
279 B9 **Encantadas, Serra das** hills Brazil
269 N9 **Encantado** r. Mex.
114 C4 **Encanto, Cape** Luzon Phil.
268 E4 **Encarnación** Mex.
277 G6 **Encarnación** Para.
184 I5 **Enchanet, Barrage d'** dam France
228 E5 **Enchi** Ghana
207 P2 **Encina** r. Spain
208 C5 **Encinacorba** Spain
261 F11 **Encinal** TX U.S.A.
207 L3 **Encinas** mt. Spain
205 J7 **Encinas de Abajo** Spain
206 F4 **Encinasola** Spain
207 K6 **Encinas Reales** Spain
204 G4 **Encinedo** Spain
264 O8 **Encinitas** CA U.S.A.
263 L9 **Encino** NM U.S.A.
205 P4 **Enciso** Spain
284 D3 **Encón** Arg.
274 C2 **Encontrados** Venez.
104 G6 **Encounter Bay** S.A. Austr.
279 E5 **Encruzilhada** Brazil
279 B9 **Encruzilhada do Sul** Brazil
199 K3 **Encs** Hungary
199 L4 **Encsencs** Hungary
246 E4 **Endako** B.C. Can.
116 E3 **Endau** r. Malaysia
112 B6 **Endau-Rompin National Park** Malaysia
115 B8 **Ende** Flores Indon.
115 B8 **Ende** i. Indon.
107 H1 **Endeavour Strait** Qld Austr.
164 G6 **Endelave** i. Denmark
99 I2 **Enderbury** i. Kiribati
246 G5 **Enderby** B.C. Can.
Enderby atoll Micronesia see **Puluwat**
173 J2 **Enderby** Leicestershire, England U.K.
288 L9 **Enderby Abyssal Plain** sea feature Southern Ocean
108 D6 **Enderby Island** W.A. Austr.
287 D2 **Enderby Land** reg. Antarctica
209 K9 **Enderrocat, Es Cap** c. Spain
244 I2 **Endicott Mountains** AK U.S.A.
276 D2 **Endimari** r. Brazil
212 H4 **Endine, Lago di** l. Italy
194 D5 **Endingen** Ger.
160 J3 **Endla riiklik looduskaitseala** nature res. Estonia
229 I6 **Endom** Cameroon
199 I3 **Endrefalva** Hungary
204 I7 **Endrinal** Spain
185 H10 **Endron, Pique d'** mt. France
251 R7 **Endwell** NY U.S.A.
160 I4 **Endzele** Latvia
276 B2 **Ene** r. Peru
109 C10 **Eneabba** W.A. Austr.
164 H2 **Enebakk** Norway
213 L4 **Enego** Italy
159 R9 **Enem** Rus. Fed.
275 G3 **Enemutu** Brazil
EnenKio N. Pacific Ocean see **Wake Island**
142 H2 **Energetik** Rus. Fed.
285 H6 **Energía** Arg.
Energodar Ukr. see **Enerhodar**
159 N6 **Enerhodar** Ukr.
198 G4 **Enese** Hungary
290 G6 **Enewetak** atoll Marshall Is
221 H2 **Enez** Turkey
150 D4 **Enfe** Lebanon
204 C3 **Enfesta** Spain
231 A8 **Enfião, Ponta do** pt Angola
227 H1 **Enfidaville** Tunisia
249 I4 **Enfield** N.S. Can.
173 L4 **Enfield** Greater London, England U.K.
255 I7 **Enfield** NC U.S.A.
250 I3 **Engadine** MI U.S.A.
162 J5 **Engan** Norway
271 I4 **Engaño, Cabo** c. Dom. Rep.
289 M3 **Engaño, Cape** Luzon Phil.
Engaños, Río de los r. Col. see **Yari**
124 U2 **Engaru** Japan
237 L7 **Engcobo** S. Africa
191 D6 **Engden** Ger.
150 D7 **En Gedi** Israel
212 E2 **Engelberg** Switz.
255 J8 **Engelhard** NC U.S.A.
201 O3 **Engelhartstetten** Austria
201 I2 **Engelhartszell** Austria
190 G5 **Engeln** Ger.
142 B2 **Engel's** Rus. Fed.
195 N5 **Engelsberg** Ger.
186 G2 **Engelschmangat** sea cha
193 F8 **Engelsdorf** Ger.
191 D9 **Engelskirchen** Ger.
186 J2 **Engelsmanplaat** i. Neth
194 F6 **Engen** Ger.
280 A5 **Engenheiro Beltrão** Bra
281 F2 **Engenheiro Navarro** Br
104 E3 **Engenina** watercourse S.
191 G6 **Enger** Ger.
163 K6 **Engerdal** Norway
192 D5 **Engersen** Ger.
190 G1 **Enge-Sande** Ger.
116 E7 **Enggano** i. Indon.
225 H5 **Enghershatu** mt. Eritrea
187 F7 **Enghien** Belgium
246 C3 **Engineer** B.C. Can.
187 H7 **Engis** Belgium
117 I4 **Engkilili** Sarawak Malay
171 O8 **England** admin. div. U.K.
264 K2 **Englebright Reservoir** C
249 K3 **Englee** Nfld and Lab. Ca
178 G3 **Englefontaine** France
248 E4 **Englehart** Ont. Can.
255 F12 **Englewood** FL U.S.A.
259 H3 **Englewood** NJ U.S.A.
256 A9 **Englewood** OH U.S.A.
247 M5 **English** r. Ont. Can.
254 D6 **English** IN U.S.A.
238 □2a **English Bay** Ascension S. Atlantic Ocean
English Bazar W. Bengal **Ingraj Bazar**
258 A2 **English Center** PA U.S.A
167 G7 **English Channel** France
286 S2 **English Coast** Antarctica
258 F6 **English Creek** NJ U.S.A.
271 □2 **English Harbour Town** Antigua and Barbuda
259 G4 **Englishtown** NJ U.S.A.
185 G10 **Engomer** France
156 F2 **Engozero** Rus. Fed.
194 G5 **Engstingen** Ger.
209 D10 **Enguera** Spain
209 D10 **Enguera, Sierra de** mts S
205 Q9 **Enguídanos** Spain
160 G4 **Engure** Latvia
160 G4 **Engures ezers** l. Latvia
151 C3 **Enguri** r. Georgia
150 D8 **'En Hazeva** Israel
237 O5 **Enhlalakahle** S. Africa
261 G7 **Enid** OK U.S.A.
100 □3b **Enigu** i. Majuro Marshal
194 G5 **Eningen unter Achalm** G
220 D3 **Enipeas** r. Greece
124 S4 **Eniwa** Japan
Eniwetok atoll Marshall **Enewetak**
207 N7 **Enix** Spain
Enjiang Jiangxi China se **Yongfeng**
153 P4 **Enkan, Mys** pt Rus. Fed.
Enkeldoorn Zimbabwe s **Chivhu**
179 O5 **Enkenbach** Ger.
186 H3 **Enkhuizen** Neth.
194 C2 **Enkirch** Ger.
160 D1 **Enklinge** Åland Fin.
165 N2 **Enköping** Sweden
Enle Yunnan China see **Z**
269 J4 **Enmedio, Arrecife de** rf
216 G8 **Enna** Sicilia Italy
216 H8 **Enna** prov. Sicilia Italy
212 H4 **Enna** r. Italy
247 K2 **Ennadai Lake** Nunavut C
225 F6 **En Nahud** Sudan
229 H3 **E-n-Nassamé** well Niger
224 C6 **Enné, Ouadi** watercourse
224 D5 **Ennedi, Massif** mts Cha
169 H6 **Ennell, Lough** l. Ireland
191 D8 **Ennepetal** Ger.
237 L2 **Ennerdale** S. Africa
171 K4 **Ennerdale Water** l. Engla
179 L5 **Ennery** France
270 G4 **Ennery** Haiti
182 C5 **Ennezat** France
105 J3 **Enngonia** N.S.W. Austr.
191 F7 **Ennigerloh** Ger.
260 D3 **Enning** SD U.S.A.
169 E7 **Ennis** Ireland
262 I4 **Ennis** MT U.S.A.
261 G9 **Ennis** TX U.S.A.
169 I7 **Enniscorthy** Ireland
169 E9 **Enniskean** Ireland
169 J6 **Enniskerry** Ireland
169 G4 **Enniskillen** Northern Irel
169 D7 **Ennistymon** Ireland
100 □3a **Enniwetak** i. Kwajalein Marshall Is
150 D5 **Enn Nâqoûra** Lebanon
201 J3 **Enns** Austria
201 K3 **Enns** r. Austria
201 J4 **Ennstaler Alpen** mts Aus
100 □3a **Ennubuj** i. Kwajalein Ma
100 □3a **Ennumennet** i. Kwajalein Marshall Is
136 G6 **Ennur** Tamil Nadu India
100 □3a **Ennylabagan** i. Kwajalein Marshall Is
162 U5 **Eno** Fin.
265 S4 **Enoch** UT U.S.A.
116 E5 **Enok** Sumatera Indon.
258 B4 **Enola** PA U.S.A.
162 T5 **Enonkoski** Fin.
162 Q2 **Enontekiö** Fin.
255 G8 **Enoree** r. SC U.S.A.
257 M4 **Enosburg Falls** VT U.S.A
131 I7 **Enping** Guangdong China
115 A5 **Enrekang** Sulawesi Indon
114 C3 **Enrile** Luzon Phil.
270 H5 **Enriquillo** Dom. Rep.
270 H4 **Enriquillo, Lago de** l. Do
186 I3 **Ens** Neth.
105 K7 **Ensay** Vic. Austr.
186 K4 **Enschede** Neth.
195 L3 **Ensdorf** Ger.
191 F8 **Ense** Ger.
285 I4 **Ensenada** Arg.
266 A2 **Ensenada** Baja California
266 E6 **Ensenada** Baja California Mex.
271 □1 **Ensenada** Puerto Rico
274 B3 **Ensenada de Utria** nat. p
194 C3 **Ensheim** Ger.
130 G3 **Enshi** Hubei China
126 G7 **Enshū-nada** g. Japan
179 N8 **Ensisheim** France
255 D10 **Ensley** FL U.S.A.
173 J4 **Enstone** Oxfordshire, Eng
183 G10 **Ensuès-la-Redonne** Fran
238 □3b **Entallada, Punta de la** pt Fuerteventura Canary Is
232 B4 **Entebbe** Uganda
186 K4 **Enter** Neth.
168 I12 **Enterkinfoot** Dumfries an Galloway, Scotland U.K.
246 G2 **Enterprise** N.W.T. Can.
251 R5 **Enterprise** Ont. Can.
255 E10 **Enterprise** AL U.S.A.
262 F4 **Enterprise** OR U.S.A.
265 S4 **Enterprise** UT U.S.A.
114 B6 **Enterprise Point** Palawan
246 E4 **Entiako Provincial Park** B
117 J4 **Entimau, Bukit** hill Malay
212 E2 **Entlebuch** Switz.
206 F6 **Entorno de Doñana, Parc Natural del** nature res. An Spain
212 C7 **Entracque** Italy
206 C5 **Entradas** Port.
183 F8 **Entraigues-sur-la-Sorgue**
182 C2 **Entrains-sur-Nohain** Fra
181 J6 **Entrammes** France
246 G4 **Entrance** Alta Can.
106 B3 **Entrance Island** N.T. Aus
183 J8 **Entraunes** France
183 B7 **Entraygues-sur-Truyère** F
239 □1c **Entre-Deux** Réunion

Entre-deux-Mers reg. France
Entrepeñas, Embalse de resr Spain
Entre Ríos prov. Arg.
Entre Ríos Bol.
Entre Rios Bahia Brazil
Entre Rios Pará Brazil
Entre Rios Moz. see Malema
Entre Rios de Minas Brazil
Entrevaux France
Entroncamento Port.
Entronque San Roberto Mex.
Entuba Zimbabwe
Entumeni S. Africa
Enugu Nigeria
Enugu state Nigeria
Enurmino Rus. Fed.
Envalira, Port d' pass Andorra
Envendos Port.
Envermeu France
Envigado Col.
Envira Brazil
Envira r. Brazil
'En Yahav Israel
Enyamba Dem. Rep. Congo
Enying Hungary
Enys, Mount South I. N.Z.
Enz r. Ger.
Enza r. Italy
Enzan Japan
Enzersdorf an der Fischa Austria
Enzklösterle Ger.
Eo atoll Îles Loyauté New Caledonia
Eo r. Spain
Eochaill Ireland see Youghal
Eoghanacht Ireland
Eolia KY U.S.A.
Eooa i. Tonga see 'Eua
Eoropaidh Western Isles, Scotland U.K.
Épaignes France
Epako Namibia
Epalignes Switz.
Epazoyucan Mex.
Epe Neth.
Epe Nigeria
Epecuén, Lago l. Arg.
Epéna Congo
Eperjes Hungary
Épernay France
Épernon France
Epfendorf Ger.
Ephesus tourist site Turkey
Ephraim UT U.S.A.
Ephrata PA U.S.A.
Ephrata WA U.S.A.
Epi i. Vanuatu
Epidamnus Albania see Durrës
Epidavrou, Asklipieio tourist site Greece
Epidavrou Limiras, Kolpos b. Greece
Épieds-en-Beauce France
Épierre France
Épila Spain
Épinac France
Épinal France
Epira Guyana
Epirus admin. reg. Greece see Ipeiros
Epiry France
Episkopi Cyprus
Episkopi Bay Cyprus
Episkopis, Kolpos b. Cyprus see Episkopi Bay
Epitacio Huerta Mex.
Époisses France
Epomeo, Monte vol. Italy
Eppelborn Ger.
Eppelheim Ger.
Eppenbrunn Ger.
Eppendorf Ger.
Eppertshausen Ger.
Eppeville France
Epping Essex, England U.K.
Epping NH U.S.A.
Eppingen Ger.
Epping Forest National Park Qld Austr.
Eppishausen Ger.
Eppstein Ger.
Eppynt, Mynydd hills Wales U.K.
Epsom Surrey, England U.K.
Epte r. France
Épuisay France
Epu-pel Arg.
Epuyén Arg.
Epworth North Lincolnshire, England U.K.
Eqlīd Iran
Équateur prov. Dem. Rep. Congo
Equatorial Guinea country Africa
Equeipa Venez.
Équeurdreville-Hainneville France
Era r. Italy
Erac Creek watercourse Qld Austr.
Eraclea Italy
Eraclea Mare Italy
Erakchiouene well Mali
Erakurri mt. Spain
Eran Madh. Prad. India
Eran Palawan Phil.
Eran Bay Palawan Phil.
Erandol Mahar. India
Erasmia S. Africa
Erawadi r. Myanmar see Irrawaddy
Erawan National Park Thai.
Erba Italy
Erba, Jebel mt. Sudan
Erbaa Turkey
Erbach Baden-Württemberg Ger.
Erbach Hessen Ger.
Erbendorf Ger.
Erbeskopf hill Ger.
Erbognone r. Italy
Erbray France
Ercan airport Cyprus
Ercé France
Erçek Turkey
Ercilla Chile
Erciş Turkey
Erciyes Dağı mt. Turkey
Ercsi Hungary
Érd Hungary
Erdaobaihe Jilin China see Baihe
Erdaogou Qinghai China
Erdao Jiang r. China
Erdeborn Ger.
Erdek Turkey
Erdemli Turkey
Erdene Dornogovĭ Mongolia
Erdenedalay Mongolia
Erdenemandal Arhangay Mongolia
Erdenesant Mongolia
Erdenet Orhon Mongolia
Erdenet Mongolia see Shine-Ider
Erdenetsagaan Mongolia
Erdenetsogt Bayanhongor Mongolia
Erdenetsogt Mongolia see Bayan-Ovoo
Erdeven France
Erding Ger.
Erdinger Moos marsh Ger.
Erdmannsdorf Ger.
Erdniyevskiy Rus. Fed.
Erdre r. France
Erdweg Ger.
Eré Peru
Eré, Campos hills Brazil
Éréac France
Erebato r. Venez.
Erebus, Mount vol. Antarctica
Erech tourist site Iraq
Erechim Brazil
Ereentsav Mongolia
Ereğli Konya Turkey
Ereğli Zonguldak Turkey
Erego Moz. see Errego
Erei, Monti mts Sicilia Italy
220 A3 Ereikoussa i. Greece
115 C6 Ereke Sulawesi Indon.
Erementaū Kazakh. see Yereymentau
268 G7 Eréndira Mex.
132 G5 Eren Habirga Shan mts China
129 M5 Erenhot Nei Mongol China
151 D7 Erentepe Turkey
144 G5 Eresk Iran
205 K6 Eresma r. Spain
221 G3 Eresos Lesvos Greece
220 E4 Eretria Greece
Erevan Armenia see Yerevan
285 G3 Erézcano Arg.
190 H2 Erfde Ger.
237 K4 Erfenis Dam resr S. Africa
237 K4 Erfenis Dam Nature Reserve S. Africa
226 D3 Erfoud Morocco
191 C9 Erftstadt Ger.
193 D9 Erfurt Ger.
149 I4 Ergani Turkey
226 D5 'Erg Chech des. Alg./Mali
Ergel Mongolia see Hatanbulag
226 D5 'Erg el Aḥmar des. Mali
160 I4 Ērgeme Latvia
221 H2 Ergene r. Turkey
195 I2 Ergersheim Ger.
227 E5 'Erg I-n-Sâkâne des. Mali
160 I5 Ērgļi Latvia
195 M4 Ergolding Ger.
195 M4 Ergoldsbach Ger.
122 F5 Ergu Heilong. China
180 C5 Ergué-Gabéric France
230 B2 Erguig r. Chad
129 Q1 Ergun Nei Mongol China
Ergun He r. China/Rus. Fed. see Argun'
Ergun Youqi Nei Mongol China see Ergun
130 C6 Er Hai l. China
195 N5 Erharting Ger.
225 H5 Erheib Sudan
123 D8 Erhulai Liaoning China
204 I4 Eria r. Spain
168 G6 Eriboll Highland, Scotland U.K.
168 G6 Eriboll, Loch inlet Scotland U.K.
186 K3 Erica Neth.
216 D7 Erice Sicilia Italy
205 Q3 Erice Spain
206 A3 Ericeira Port.
168 J9 Ericht r. Scotland U.K.
168 H9 Ericht, Loch l. Scotland U.K.
247 L5 Erickson Man. Can.
261 H7 Erie KS U.S.A.
256 E6 Erie PA U.S.A.
251 N7 Erie, Lake Can./U.S.A.
Erieddu i. N. Male Maldives see Eriyadhu
228 D2 'Erîgât des. Mali
152 D2 Erik Eriksenstretet sea chan. Svalbard
Erikoússa i. Greece see Ereikoussa
247 L5 Eriksdale Man. Can.
165 L5 Eriksmåla Sweden
207 I4 Erillas hill Spain
Erímanthos Óros mts Greece see Erymanthos
124 U4 Erimo Japan
124 U5 Erimo-misaki c. Japan
251 N6 Erin Ont. Can.
255 D7 Erin TN U.S.A.
195 O5 Ering Ger.
165 L5 Eringsboda Sweden
271 □7 Erin Point Trin. and Tob.
168 B8 Eriskay i. Scotland U.K.
194 H6 Eriskirch Ger.
168 C6 Erisort, Loch inlet Scotland U.K.
173 N3 Eriswell Suffolk, England U.K.
212 D1 Eriswil Switz.
Erithraí Greece see Erythres
Erithropótamos r. Greece see Erythropotamos
225 H6 Eritrea country Africa
135 □1 Eriyadhu i. N. Male Maldives
Eriyadu i. N. Male Maldives see Eriyadhu
143 O8 Erkech-Tam Kyrg.
191 B8 Erkelenz Ger.
178 D2 Erkelsbrugge France
165 O2 Erken l. Sweden
151 C1 Erken-Shakhar Rus. Fed.
195 I5 Erkheim Ger.
221 L4 Erkmen Turkey
193 I6 Erkner Ger.
146 C6 Erkowit Sudan
200 F4 Erl Austria
208 D3 Erla Spain
212 C1 Erlach Switz.
195 K2 Erlangen Ger.
131 H2 Erlangping Henan China
195 P4 Erlau r. Ger.
201 L3 Erlauf Austria
201 L3 Erlauf r. Austria
201 L4 Erlaufsee l. Austria
193 F10 Erlbach Ger.
106 D8 Erldunda N.T. Austr.
194 G2 Erlenbach am Main Ger.
191 G10 Erlensee Ger.
212 E7 Erli Italy
109 F9 Erlistoun watercourse W.A. Austr.
122 F7 Erlong Shan mt. China
258 F7 Erma NJ U.S.A.
Ermak Kazakh. see Aksu
129 M2 Ermana, Khrebet mts Rus. Fed.
186 I4 Ermelo Neth.
204 E6 Ermelo Port.
237 N2 Ermelo S. Africa
148 F5 Ermenek Turkey
150 B2 Ermenek r. Turkey
204 C6 Ermesinde Port.
206 C4 Ermidas do Sado Port.
224 E6 Ermil Sudan
220 E5 Ermioni Greece
268 D3 Ermita de los Correas Mex.
178 D6 Ermont France
220 F5 Ermoupoli Syros Greece
194 G4 Erms r. Ger.
193 D7 Ermsleben Ger.
205 O2 Ermua Spain
104 D2 Ernabella S.A. Austr.
136 E8 Ernakulam Kerala India
191 F9 Erndtebrück Ger.
169 F4 Erne r. Ireland/U.K.
181 J5 Ernée France
181 J5 Ernée r. France
109 G9 Ernest Giles Range hills W.A. Austr.
245 N5 Ernest Sound sea channel AK U.S.A.
201 N2 Ernstbrunn Austria
194 A2 Ernz Noire r. Lux.
136 E7 Erode Tamil Nadu India
100 □3b Eroj i. Majuro Marshall Is
195 I5 Erolzheim Ger.
107 I9 Eromanga Qld Austr.
234 B4 Erongo admin. reg. Namibia
228 E2 'Eroûg well Mali
186 I5 Erp Neth.
199 K4 Érpatak Hungary
191 D9 Erpel Ger.
151 H3 Erpeli Rus. Fed.
128 C5 Erpu Xinjiang China
Erqu Shaanxi China see Zhouzhi
187 F8 Erquelinnes Belgium
180 G4 Erquy France
109 C9 Errabiddy Hills W.A. Austr.
226 D3 Er Rachidia Morocco
225 F6 Er Rahad Sudan
168 D10 Erraid i. Scotland U.K.
136 E5 Erramala Hills India
226 E3 Er Raoui des. Alg.
208 C1 Erratzu Spain
235 H3 Errego Moz.
232 B2 Er Renk Sudan
208 B1 Errenteria Spain
208 A1 Errezil Spain
205 P2 Erribera Spain
169 F2 Errigal hill Ireland
169 G7 Errill Ireland
192 E1 Errindlev Denmark
105 L7 Errinundra National Park Vic. Austr.
169 B4 Erris Head Ireland
212 E6 Erro r. Italy
208 C2 Erro r. Spain
168 H9 Errochty, Loch l. Scotland U.K.
168 I9 Errochty Water r. Scotland U.K.
225 G5 Er Rogel Sudan
168 H8 Errogie Highland, Scotland U.K.
257 □N4 Errol NH U.S.A.
100 □5 Erromango i. Vanuatu
Erronan i. Vanuatu see Futuna
232 B2 Er Roseires Sudan
225 G6 Er Rua'at Sudan
199 H5 Érsekcsanád Hungary
220 B2 Ersekë Albania
199 I3 Érsekvadkert Hungary
191 J8 Ershausen Ger.
122 D2 Ershiyizhan Heilong. China
Ersis Turkey see Kılıçkaya
260 G2 Erskine MN U.S.A.
165 S1 Erstan b. Fin.
179 O7 Erstein France
212 F2 Erstfeld Switz.
232 D1 Erta Ale vol. Eth.
128 B3 Ertai Xinjiang China
157 H6 Ertil' Rus. Fed.
194 G5 Ertingen Ger.
Ertis Kazakh. see Irtyshsk
132 G2 Ertix He r. China/Kazakh.
213 M3 Erto Italy
100 □3a Eru i. Kwajalein Marshall Is
104 G4 Erudina S.A. Austr.
229 G4 Erufu Nigeria
149 K5 Eruh Turkey
214 B6 Erula Sardegna Italy
160 I2 Eru laht b. Estonia
229 F5 Eruwa Nigeria
282 G4 Erval Brazil
281 F4 Ervália Brazil
181 K6 Erve r. France
204 F6 Ervedosa do Douro Port.
206 C5 Ervidel Port.
178 E3 Ervillers France
204 F5 Ervões Port.
178 G7 Ervy-le-Châtel France
255 F7 Erwin TN U.S.A.
191 F7 Erwitte Ger.
192 E5 Erxleben Sachsen-Anhalt Ger.
193 D6 Erxleben Sachsen-Anhalt Ger.
220 C5 Erymanthos mts Greece
220 C5 Erymanthos r. Greece
220 E4 Erythres Greece
221 H1 Erythropotamos r. Greece
130 B5 Eryuan Yunnan China
218 H9 Erzen r. Albania
Erzerum Turkey see Erzurum
193 H9 Erzgebirge mts Czech Rep./Ger.
122 E4 Erzhan Heilong. China
194 F2 Erzhausen Ger.
128 D1 Erzin Rus. Fed.
148 H5 Erzin Turkey
148 I4 Erzincan Turkey
151 A6 Erzincan prov. Turkey
149 J4 Erzurum Turkey
151 C5 Erzurum prov. Turkey
160 F6 Eržvilkas Lith.
113 L8 Esa-ala P.N.G.
213 N9 Esanatoglia Italy
124 S5 Esan-misaki pt Japan
217 M5 Esaro r. Italy
215 Q8 Esaro r. Italy
124 R5 Esashi Hokkaidō Japan
124 T2 Esashi Hokkaidō Japan
124 S7 Esashi Iwate Japan
164 E6 Esbjerg Denmark
164 E6 Esbjerg airport Denmark
178 E6 Esbly France
Esbo Fin. see Espoo
278 G4 Escada Brazil
204 E3 Escairón Spain
114 D6 Escalante Negros Phil.
205 N2 Escalante Spain
265 U4 Escalante UT U.S.A.
265 V4 Escalante r. UT U.S.A.
265 S4 Escalante Desert UT U.S.A.
214 C8 Escalaplano Sardegna Italy
208 G3 Escales, Embassament d' resr Spain
209 E10 Escaleta, Punta de la pt Spain
204 G7 Escalhão Port.
185 B9 Escaliers, Pic des mt. France
208 H2 Escaló Spain
209 I10 Es Caló Spain
266 G4 Escalón Mex.
264 L4 Escalon CA U.S.A.
205 L8 Escalona Spain
205 L6 Escalona del Prado Spain
204 F9 Escalos de Baixo Port.
204 F9 Escalos de Cima Port.
205 O6 Escalote r. Spain
255 D10 Escambia r. FL U.S.A.
205 O7 Escamilla Spain
250 G4 Escanaba MI U.S.A.
209 D7 Escandón, Puerto de pass Spain
183 C9 Escandorgue ridge France
207 K5 Escañuela Spain
103 B13 Escape Reefs South I. N.Z.
267 N8 Escárcega Mex.
205 N8 Escariche Spain
204 F8 Escarigo Port.
208 C2 Escároz Spain
114 D2 Escarpada Point Luzon Phil.
208 □ Es Castell Spain
185 G8 Escatalens France
208 E5 Escatrón Spain
178 F3 Escaudain France
187 D7 Escaut r. Belgium
186 H5 Esch Neth.
195 I6 Eschach r. Ger.
179 O7 Eschau France
194 G2 Eschau Ger.
191 G10 Eschborn Ger.
190 C5 Esche Ger.
190 J4 Escheburg Ger.
190 J5 Eschede Ger.
212 E1 Eschenbach Switz.
195 L2 Eschenbach in der Oberpfalz Ger.
191 F9 Eschenburg-Eibelshausen Ger.
191 I8 Eschenstruth (Helsa) Ger.
191 I7 Eschershausen Ger.
200 D6 Eschio r. Italy
195 N3 Eschlkam Ger.
212 D2 Escholzmatt Switz.
244 G2 Eschscholtz Bay AK U.S.A.
187 I10 Esch-sur-Alzette Lux.
187 I9 Esch-sur-Sûre Lux.
191 J8 Eschwege Ger.
191 B9 Eschweiler Ger.
271 I4 Escocesa, Bahía b. Dom. Rep.
276 C3 Escoma Bol.
209 D12 Escombreras Spain
261 E11 Escondido r. Mex.
266 □R11 Escondido r. Nic.
264 O8 Escondido CA U.S.A.
209 K8 Escorca Spain
208 D6 Escorihuela Spain
185 B9 Escos France
185 I10 Escouloubre France
185 B7 Escource France
185 B7 Escource r. France
183 J9 Escragnolles France
208 D6 Escucha Spain
265 W8 Escudilla mt. AZ U.S.A.
268 B3 Escuinapa Mex.
267 N10 Escuintla Guat.
267 M10 Escuintla Mex.
274 D2 Escuque Venez.
206 H2 Escurial Spain
208 D5 Escuriza r. Spain
182 C4 Escurolles France
280 D2 Escurso r. Brazil
205 K8 Escusa mt. Spain
207 L6 Escúzar Spain
229 H6 Eséka Cameroon
153 O3 Ese-Khayya Rus. Fed.
221 K6 Eşen Turkey
221 K6 Eşen r. Turkey
221 J2 Esence Turkey
151 A6 Esence Dağları mts Turkey
151 F6 Eşengöl Dağı mt. Iran/Turkey
144 E3 Esenguly Turkm.
144 E3 Esenguly Döwlet Gorugy nature res. Turkm.
221 J2 Esenköy Turkey
150 C2 Esenpınar Turkey
190 E3 Esens Ger.
151 B5 Esenyurt Erzurum Turkey
221 J1 Esenyurt İstanbul Turkey
208 F3 Ésera r. Spain
144 D5 Eşfahān Iran
144 E5 Eşfahān prov. Iran
144 G4 Eşfāk Iran
145 J8 Esfandak Iran
144 E6 Esfandārān Iran
144 G3 Esfarayen, Reshteh-ye mts Iran
144 H5 Esfedān Iran
204 E4 Esgos Spain
205 K5 Esgueva r. Spain
205 L5 Esguevillas de Esgueva Spain
144 H8 Es'hak Iran
130 D6 Eshan Yunnan China
168 □M2 Esha Ness hd Scotland U.K.
173 L5 Esher Surrey, England U.K.
151 B2 Eshera Georgia
231 E6 Eshimba Dem. Rep. Congo
145 M3 Eshkamesh Afgh.
144 E8 Eshkanān Iran
237 P4 Eshowe S. Africa
144 D4 Eshtehārd Iran
235 F4 Esigodini Zimbabwe
237 Q4 Esikhawini S. Africa
Esil Kazakh. see Yesil'
Esil r. Kazakh./Rus. Fed. see Ishim
213 O8 Esino r. Italy
151 B5 Esirçölü Tepe mt. Turkey
237 O3 eSizameleni S. Africa
107 N9 Esk Qld Austr.
105 K9 Esk r. Tas. Austr.
171 K5 Esk r. Cumbria, England U.K.
171 K4 Esk r. England/Scotland U.K.
168 J11 Esk r. Midlothian/Scottish Borders, Scotland U.K.
102 K6 Eskdale North I. N.Z.
168 J12 Eskdale val. Scotland U.K.
168 J12 Eskdalemuir Dumfries and Galloway, Scotland U.K.
169 F3 Eske, Lough l. Ireland
Eskene Kazakh. see Iskininskiy
249 H2 Esker Nfld and Lab. Can.
159 P4 Eskhar Ukr.
162 □F1 Eskifjörður Iceland
221 K3 Eski Gediz Turkey
192 E1 Eskilstrup Denmark
165 M2 Eskilstuna Sweden
245 O1 Eskimo Lakes N.W.T. Can.
Eskimo Point Nunavut Can. see Arviat
143 O7 Eski-Nookat Kyrg.
148 F3 Eskipazar Turkey
221 L3 Eskişehir Turkey
221 M3 Eskişehir prov. Turkey
205 N2 Eskutxi mt. Spain
205 H6 Esla r. Spain
Esla, Embalse de resr Spain see Ricobayo, Embalse de
144 B4 Eslāmābād-e Gharb Iran
144 H4 Eslām Qal'eh Iran
195 N2 Eslarn Ger.
205 R3 Eslava Spain
221 K5 Esler Dağı mt. Turkey
191 F8 Eslohe (Sauerland) Ger.
164 J6 Eslöv Sweden
144 G7 Esmā'īlī-ye Soflá Iran
221 J4 Eşme Turkey
151 D5 Eşmeçayır Turkey
151 D6 Esmer Turkey
285 G2 Esmeralda Arg.
284 B3 Esmeralda Chile
270 D3 Esmeralda Cuba
283 B8 Esmeralda, Isla i. Chile
281 E3 Esmeraldas Brazil
274 B4 Esmeraldas Ecuador
274 B4 Esmeraldas prov. Ecuador
276 D3 Esmeraldo r. Bol.
208 □ Es Mercadal Spain
208 □ Es Migjorn Gran Spain
256 G11 Esmont VA U.S.A.
204 C7 Esmoriz Port.
248 C3 Esnagami Lake Ont. Can.
250 J1 Esnagi Lake Ont. Can.
178 F3 Esnes France
187 I7 Esneux Belgium
209 D8 Espada, Serra d' mts Spain
209 E8 Espadán, Pico de mt. Spain
204 H4 Espadañedo Spain
144 I8 Espakeh Iran
Espalha r. Brazil see São Francisco
183 B7 Espalion France
Espalmador, Isla i. Spain see S'Espalmador
183 D6 Espaly-St-Marcel France
España country Europe see Spain
251 M3 Espanola Ont. Can.
263 K8 Espanola NM U.S.A.
274 □ Española, Isla i. Islas Galápagos Ecuador
206 G3 Esparragalejo Spain
207 I3 Esparragosa Spain
208 I4 Esparreguera Spain
183 H9 Esparron France
266 □P10 Esparta Hond.
209 H10 Espartar, Illa s' i. Spain
285 F5 Espartillar Arg.
264 J3 Esparto CA U.S.A.
208 C2 Esparza de Salazar Spain
204 G7 Espeja Spain
205 N5 Espeja de San Marcelino Spain
207 J5 Espejo Spain
205 N5 Espejón Spain
186 I3 Espel Neth.
185 B9 Espelette France
191 G6 Espelkamp Ger.
191 H8 Espenau Ger.
244 G2 Espenberg, Cape AK U.S.A.
206 H7 Espera Spain
206 E2 Esperança Port.
280 B6 Esperança, Serra de mts Brazil
109 F12 Esperance W.A. Austr.
109 F13 Esperance Bay W.A. Austr.
278 D3 Esperantinópolis Brazil
286 U2 Esperanza research stn Antarctica
283 C8 Esperanza Santa Cruz Arg.
285 G2 Esperanza Santa Fé Arg.
269 J7 Esperanza Puebla Mex.
266 E4 Esperanza Sonora Mex.
276 C2 Esperanza Peru
114 E6 Esperanza Masbate Phil.
271 □1 Esperanza Puerto Rico
285 I3 Esperanza Uru.
266 □P10 Esperanza, Sierra de la mts Hond.
185 I10 Espéraza France
215 L5 Esperia Italy
185 I10 Espezel France
206 A4 Espichel, Cabo c. Port.
207 J4 Espiel Spain
279 C8 Espigão, Serra do mts Brazil
285 G5 Espigas Arg.
205 K3 Espigüete mt. Spain
183 E9 Espiguette, Pointe de l' pt France
269 J5 Espina Mex.
205 K2 Espinama Spain
183 I8 Espinasses France
267 I4 Espinazo Mex.
269 M8 Espinazo del Diablo, Sierra mts Mex.
284 B6 Espinazo del Zorro Arg.
281 F2 Espinhaço, Serra do mts Brazil
206 B6 Espinhaço de Cão, Serra do mts Port.
204 D8 Espinhal Port.
231 B9 Espinheira Angola
206 D4 Espinheira hill Port.
204 C6 Espinho Port.
279 B9 Espinilho, Serra do hills Brazil
205 L2 Espinilla Spain
275 E2 Espino Venez.
279 E5 Espinosa Brazil
205 M5 Espinosa de Cerrato Spain
205 N7 Espinosa de Henares Spain
205 M2 Espinosa de los Monteros Spain
205 K9 Espinoso del Rey Spain
183 B9 Espinouse, Monts de l' mts France
185 J10 Espira-de-l'Agly France
Espirito Santo Brazil see Vila Velha
281 G3 Espírito Santo state Brazil
206 D5 Espírito Santo Port.
114 C3 Espiritu Luzon Phil.
276 D4 Espíritu Santo Bol.
268 F3 Espíritu Santo Mex.
100 □5 Espíritu Santo i. Vanuatu
267 P8 Espíritu Santo, Bahía del b. Mex.
266 D5 Espíritu Santo, Isla i. Mex.
267 O7 Espita Mex.
204 C9 Espite Port.
278 F4 Esplanada Brazil
205 P7 Esplegares Spain
208 J5 Esplugues de Llobregat Spain
208 F4 Esplús Spain
208 L3 Espolla Spain
183 C10 Espondeilham France
208 K3 Esponellà Spain
163 R6 Espoo Fin.
209 K8 Esporles Spain
204 C5 Esposende Port.
208 H2 Espot Spain
182 I1 Esprels France
207 P5 Espuña mt. Spain
209 B12 Espuña, Sierra de mts Spain
235 G4 Espungabera Moz.
258 C2 Espy PA U.S.A.
266 E2 Esqueda Mex.
283 C6 Esquel Arg.
246 F5 Esquimalt B.C. Can.
285 H2 Esquina Arg.
267 O10 Esquipulas Guat.
205 M8 Esquivias Spain
162 P3 Esrange Sweden
164 I5 Esrum Sø l. Denmark
232 A1 Es Samalat Sudan
115 E1 Essang Sulawesi Indon.
226 C3 Essaouira Morocco
181 L4 Essay France
229 H5 Essé Cameroon
190 I5 Essel Ger.
226 C4 Es Semara Western Sahara
187 F6 Essen Belgium
191 D8 Essen Ger.
190 E5 Essen (Oldenburg) Ger.
195 M4 Essenbach Ger.
109 F8 Essendon, Mount hill W.A. Austr.
182 J1 Essert France
251 L7 Essex Ont. Can.
173 N4 Essex admin. div. England U.K.
265 Q7 Essex CA U.S.A.
259 K2 Essex CT U.S.A.
257 O6 Essex MA U.S.A.
258 C6 Essex MD U.S.A.
257 L4 Essex NY U.S.A.
259 G3 Essex County county NJ U.S.A.
257 L4 Essex Junction VT U.S.A.
Essexvale Zimbabwe see Esigodini
251 K6 Essexville MI U.S.A.
195 I4 Essingen Ger.
172 H2 Essington Staffordshire, England U.K.
194 G4 Esslingen am Neckar Ger.
153 Q4 Esso Rus. Fed.
178 F5 Essômes-sur-Marne France
178 D6 Essonne dept France
178 D6 Essonne r. France
178 I7 Essoyes France
229 H5 Essu Cameroon
160 J2 Essu Estonia
225 F5 Es Suaifi well Sudan
225 G6 Es Suki Sudan
229 I5 Est prov. Cameroon
179 L7 Est, Canal de l' France
249 I4 Est, Île de l' i. Que. Can.
257 □P1 Est, Lac de l' l. Que. Can.
249 I3 Est, Pointe de l' pt Que. Can.
204 E1 Estaca de Bares, Punta de pt Spain
285 H2 Estacas Arg.
268 G2 Estación Catorce Mex.
265 R9 Estación Coahuila Mex.
207 L4 Estación de Baeza Spain
268 G2 Estación Laguna Seca Mex.
208 F3 Estadilla Spain
283 D9 Estados, Isla de los i. Arg.
185 J10 Estagel France
114 D3 Estagno Point Luzon Phil.
144 F7 Eşţahbān Iran
183 B7 Estaing France
251 N3 Estaire Ont. Can.
178 E2 Estaires France
280 B2 Estância Goiás Brazil
278 F4 Estância Sergipe Brazil
263 K9 Estancia NM U.S.A.
283 C9 Estancia Camerón Chile
283 C9 Estancia Carmen Arg.
207 O5 Estancias, Sierra de las mts Spain
144 I6 Estand, Kūh-e mt. Iran
185 D8 Estang France
144 H7 Estārm Iran
204 C7 Estarreja Port.
208 D2 Estarrón r. Spain
208 H2 Estats, Pic d' mt. France/Spain
212 B2 Estavayer-le-Lac Switz.
237 N5 Estcourt S. Africa
190 I3 Este r. Ger.
213 L5 Este Italy
271 I4 Este, Parque Nacional del nat. park Dom. Rep.
271 □1 Este, Punta pt Puerto Rico
238 □3c Este, Roque del i. Canary Is
208 D4 Esteban hill Spain
285 F5 Esteban A. Gazcón Arg.
282 D1 Esteban de Urizar Arg.
Esteban Echeverria Arg. see Monte Grande
192 D5 Estedt Ger.
204 C6 Estela Port.
266 □P11 Estelí Nic.
205 P3 Estella Spain
258 F6 Estell Manor NJ U.S.A.
206 G2 Estena hill Spain
207 J2 Estena r. Spain
195 I2 Estenfeld Ger.
207 J6 Estepa Spain
205 M4 Estepar Spain
207 I8 Estepona Spain
245 K2 Ester AK U.S.A.
207 J3 Esteras r. Spain
205 P6 Esteras de Medinaceli Spain
208 D6 Estercuel Spain
183 J9 Esterel reg. France
185 B9 Estérençuby France
195 K6 Estergebirge mts Ger.
247 K5 Esterhazy Sask. Can.
230 A4 Esterias, Cap c. Gabon
178 G6 Esternay France
201 I2 Esternberg Austria
269 J3 Estero Mex.
264 K6 Estero Bay CA U.S.A.
212 C8 Esteron r. Italy
269 I3 Esteros Mex.
277 E5 Esteros Para.
208 H2 Esterri d'Aneu Spain
190 E5 Esterwegen Ger.
262 L6 Estes Park CO U.S.A.
274 A1 Este Sudeste, Cayos del is Col.
247 K5 Estevan Sask. Can.
246 D4 Estevan Group is B.C. Can.
260 H4 Estherville IA U.S.A.
183 E6 Estiavreilles France
255 G9 Estill SC U.S.A.
185 F7 Estillac France
187 F8 Estinnes-au-Mont Belgium
178 G7 Estissac France
281 D5 Estiva Brazil
278 D3 Estiva r. Brazil
182 B4 Estivareilles France
209 E8 Estivella Spain
206 D6 Estói Port.
206 C6 Estômbar Port.
247 I5 Eston Sask. Can.
171 O4 Eston Redcar and Cleveland, England U.K.
160 I3 Estonia country Europe
Estonskaya S.S.R. country Europe see Estonia
190 H3 Estorf Niedersachsen Ger.
190 H5 Estorf Niedersachsen Ger.
206 A3 Estoril Port.
183 I9 Estoublon France
182 F5 Estrablin France
178 E5 Estrées-St-Denis France
282 H3 Estreito Brazil
204 E9 Estreito Port.
206 □ Estreito da Calheta Madeira
206 E4 Estrela Port.
204 E8 Estrela, Serra da mts Port.
281 E3 Estrela do Indaiá Brazil
280 D3 Estrela do Sul Brazil
207 L4 Estrella mt. Spain
266 B2 Estrella, Punta pt Mex.
265 T8 Estrella, Sierra mts AZ U.S.A.
100 □6 Estrella Bay Sta Isabel Solomon Is
276 D2 Estrema Brazil
204 B10 Estremadura reg. Port.
205 N8 Estremera Spain
205 N8 Estremera, Canal de Spain
205 O8 Estremera, Embalse de resr Spain
206 D3 Estremoz Port.
205 O6 Estriégala Spain
185 C8 Estrigon r. France
278 C4 Estrondo, Serra hills Brazil
230 A4 Estuaire prov. Gabon
206 B4 Estuário do Sado, Reserva Natural do nature res. Port.
206 B3 Estuário do Tejo, Reserva Natural do nature res. Port.
144 C4 Estūh Iran
Esu Cameroon see Essu
230 D4 Esumba, Île i. Dem. Rep. Congo
181 M7 Esvres France
199 K4 Esztár Hungary
199 H4 Esztergom Hungary
180 F4 Étables-sur-Mer France
104 G3 Etadunna S.A. Austr.
184 F4 Étagnac France
138 G6 Etah Uttar Prad. India
179 K5 Étain France
182 C1 Étais-la-Sauvin France
182 F1 Étalante France
187 I9 Étalle Belgium
249 J3 Étamamiou Que. Can.
178 D7 Étampes France
104 G2 Etamunbanie, Lake salt flat S.A. Austr.
239 □1c Étang-Salé Réunion
182 E3 Étang-sur-Arroux France
178 C2 Étaples France
184 B4 Étaules France
184 C5 Étauliers France
138 F7 Etawah Rajasthan India
138 G6 Etawah Uttar Prad. India
100 □3a Etcharai i. Kwajalein Marshall Is
266 E4 Etchojoa Mex.
230 A5 Étéké Gabon
180 E6 Étel France
163 S6 Etelä-Suomi prov. Fin.
183 I6 Étendard, Pic de l' mt. France
182 I2 Éternoz France
237 O2 Ethandakukhanya S. Africa
187 I9 Ethe Belgium
109 E8 Ethel watercourse W.A. Austr.
247 K5 Ethelbert Man. Can.
108 F7 Ethel Creek W.A. Austr.
107 I3 Ethel Creek r. Qld Austr.
236 G5 E'Thembini S. Africa
107 I4 Etheridge r. Qld Austr.
232 C3 Ethiopia country Africa
93 F4 Ethiopian Highlands plat. Eth.
221 H3 Etili Turkey
148 F4 Etimesğut Turkey
182 H3 Étival France
179 M7 Étival-Clairefontaine France
168 F10 Etive, Loch inlet Scotland U.K.
178 H8 Étivey France
244 H1 Etivluk r. AK U.S.A.
269 K8 Etla Mex.
163 K6 Etna r. Norway
217 I8 Etna, Monte vol. Sicilia Italy
Etna, Mount vol. Sicilia Italy see Etna, Monte
216 H8 Etna, Parco dell' park Italy
164 B2 Etne Norway
251 O6 Etobicoke Ont. Can.
178 G6 Étoges France
183 G10 Étoile, Chaîne de l' hills France
183 F7 Étoile-sur-Rhône France
230 D4 Etoka Dem. Rep. Congo
245 N4 Etolin Island AK U.S.A.
244 F3 Etolin Strait AK U.S.A.
107 L6 Eton Qld Austr.
173 K5 Eton Windsor and Maidenhead, England U.K.
Etorofu-tō i. Kuril'skiye O-va Rus. Fed. see Iturup, Ostrov
234 B3 Etosha National Park Namibia
234 C3 Etosha Pan salt pan Namibia
230 B4 Etoumbi Congo
259 F4 Etra NJ U.S.A.
178 D7 Étréchy France
144 F3 Etrek Iran/Turkm. alt. Atrak (Iran/Turkm.) alt. Atrek (Iran/Turkm.)
178 C5 Étrépagny France
181 L2 Étretat France
178 G4 Étreux France
219 M8 Etropole Bulg.
212 C4 Etroubles Italy
185 C10 Etsaut France
234 D3 Etsha Botswana
187 J9 Ettelbruck Lux.
100 □4a Etten i. Chuuk Micronesia
194 D5 Ettenheim Ger.
186 G5 Etten-Leur Neth.
168 H8 Etteridge Highland, Scotland U.K.
193 D8 Ettersburg Ger.
228 A2 Et Tîdra i. Maur.
173 I3 Ettington Warwickshire, England U.K.
194 E4 Ettlingen Ger.
168 J12 Ettrick Scottish Borders, Scotland U.K.
171 L2 Ettrickbridge Scottish Borders, Scotland U.K.
168 J11 Ettrick Forest reg. Scotland U.K.
168 K11 Ettrick Water r. Scotland U.K.
191 D10 Ettringen Ger.
136 E8 Ettumanur Kerala India
230 E5 Etumba Dem. Rep. Congo
182 H2 Étuz France
173 I2 Etwall Derbyshire, England U.K.
208 B1 Etxalar Spain
Etxarri Spain see Echarri
205 P3 Etxarri-Aranatz Spain
268 C5 Etzatlán Mex.
247 I5 Etzicom Coulee r. Alta Can.
178 B3 Eu France
101 □8a 'Eua i. Tonga
105 K5 Euabalong N.S.W. Austr.
101 □8a 'Euaiki i. Tonga
Eubarca, Cabo c. Spain see Mossons, Cap des
194 H2 Eubigheim Ger.
Euboea i. Greece see Evvoia
109 J11 Eucla W.A. Austr.
256 D7 Euclid OH U.S.A.
278 F4 Euclides da Cunha Brazil
280 A5 Euclides da Cunha Paulista Brazil
105 L7 Eucumbene, Lake N.S.W. Austr.
249 H3 Eudistes, Lac des l. Que. Can.
261 J9 Eudora AR U.S.A.
104 G6 Eudunda S.A. Austr.
'Eueiki i. Tonga see 'Euaiki
191 J10 Euerbach Ger.
191 J10 Euerdorf Ger.
255 E10 Eufaula AL U.S.A.
261 H8 Eufaula OK U.S.A.
261 H8 Eufaula Lake resr OK U.S.A.
285 F1 Eufrasio Loza Arg.
200 H4 Eugendorf Austria
262 C4 Eugene OR U.S.A.
277 F2 Eugênia r. Brazil
266 B4 Eugenia, Punta pt Mex.
185 D8 Eugénie-les-Bains France
185 A10 Eugi, Embalse de resr Spain
105 L5 Eugowra N.S.W. Austr.
205 P3 Eulate Spain
105 J3 Eulo Qld Austr.
204 E2 Eume r. Spain
204 E2 Eume, Encoro do resr Spain
281 H2 Eunápolis Brazil
107 L6 Eungella Qld Austr.
107 L6 Eungella National Park Qld Austr.
261 I10 Eunice LA U.S.A.
261 D9 Eunice NM U.S.A.
187 J7 Eupen Belgium
193 G7 Euper Ger.
140 F3 Euphrates r. Asia alt. Al Furāt (Iraq/Syria), alt. Fırat (Turkey)
151 A6 Euphrates r. Turkey
261 K9 Eupora MS U.S.A.
163 Q6 Eura Fin.
163 P6 Eurajoki Fin.
195 K5 Eurasburg Bayern Ger.
195 K6 Eurasburg Bayern Ger.
201 K3 Euratsfeld Austria
178 B5 Eure dept France
178 B5 Eure r. France
178 B7 Eure-et-Loir dept France
245 J2 Eureka AK U.S.A.
262 B6 Eureka CA U.S.A.
261 G7 Eureka KS U.S.A.
262 G2 Eureka MT U.S.A.
265 Q2 Eureka NV U.S.A.
256 C10 Eureka OH U.S.A.
260 F3 Eureka SD U.S.A.
265 T2 Eureka UT U.S.A.
245 K3 Eureka Roadhouse AK U.S.A.
243 J2 Eureka Sound sea chan. Nunavut Can.
261 I7 Eureka Springs AR U.S.A.
264 O4 Eureka Valley CA U.S.A.
104 H4 Eurinilla watercourse S.A. Austr.
105 H4 Euriowie N.S.W. Austr.
105 J7 Euroa Vic. Austr.
107 L8 Eurombah Qld Austr.
107 L8 Eurombah Creek r. Qld Austr.
223 H6 Europa, Île i. Indian Ocean
205 J2 Europa, Picos de mts Spain
Europa, Punta de pt Gibraltar see Europa Point
207 □ Europa Flats Gibraltar
207 □ Europa Point Gibraltar
154 Europe
186 F5 Europoort reg. Neth.
179 J6 Eurville-Bienville France
191 C9 Euskirchen Ger.
191 I10 Eußenheim Ger.
255 G11 Eustis FL U.S.A.
105 I6 Euston N.S.W. Austr.
255 D9 Eutaw AL U.S.A.
190 K2 Eutin Ger.
194 F5 Eutingen im Gäu Ger.
246 E4 Eutsuk Lake B.C. Can.
193 G7 Eutzsch Ger.
179 K6 Euville France
106 E4 Eva Downs N.T. Austr.
231 B9 Evale Angola
212 D4 Evançon r. Italy
237 N2 Evander S. Africa
248 E3 Evans, Lac l. Que. Can.
260 C6 Evans, Mount CO U.S.A.
246 H4 Evansburg Alta Can.
256 E8 Evans City PA U.S.A.
258 C2 Evans Falls PA U.S.A.
105 N3 Evans Head N.S.W. Austr.
286 S1 Evans Ice Stream Antarctica
243 J3 Evans Strait Nunavut Can.
250 G7 Evanston IL U.S.A.
262 I6 Evanston WY U.S.A.
248 D4 Evansville Ont. Can.
245 J2 Evansville AK U.S.A.
254 D7 Evansville IN U.S.A.
250 E7 Evansville WI U.S.A.
262 K5 Evansville WY U.S.A.
261 F10 Evant TX U.S.A.
168 H7 Evanton Highland, Scotland U.K.
Eva Perón Arg. see La Plata
Eva Perón prov. Arg. see La Pampa
250 I6 Evart MI U.S.A.
237 L2 Evaton S. Africa
182 A4 Évaux-les-Bains France
144 F8 Evaz Iran
151 F6 Evci Turkey
221 K4 Evciler Turkey
150 C1 Evcili Turkey
250 B2 Eveleth MN U.S.A.
261 J7 Evening Shade AR U.S.A.
173 J4 Evenlode r. England U.K.
153 Q3 Evensk Rus. Fed.
162 N2 Evenskjær Norway
104 E4 Everard, Lake salt flat S.A. Austr.
106 D7 Everard, Mount N.T. Austr.
104 D2 Everard, Mount S.A. Austr.
104 D2 Everard Range hills S.A. Austr.
172 G5 Evercreech Somerset, England U.K.
186 H5 Everdingen Neth.
Everek Turkey see Develi
139 K6 Everest, Mount China/Nepal
257 □R1 Everett N.B. Can.
256 G8 Everett PA U.S.A.
262 C3 Everett WA U.S.A.
187 E6 Evergem Belgium
255 G12 Everglades swamp FL U.S.A.
255 G13 Everglades City FL U.S.A.
255 G13 Everglades National Park FL U.S.A.
255 D10 Evergreen AL U.S.A.
252 D7 Everman, Volcán vol. Mex.
262 C2 Everson WA U.S.A.
275 G3 Everton Guyana
163 L6 Evertsberg Sweden
107 I7 Evesham Qld Austr.
173 I3 Evesham Worcestershire, England U.K.
173 I3 Evesham, Vale of val. England U.K.
191 K6 Evessen Ger.
182 J4 Évian-les-Bains France
162 Q5 Evijärvi Fin.
229 H6 Evinayong Equat. Guinea
256 F11 Evington VA U.S.A.
220 C4 Evinos r. Greece
214 B3 Evisa Corse France
164 D3 Evje Norway
212 D3 Evolène Switz.
206 D3 Évora Port.
206 D3 Évora admin. dist. Port.
206 D3 Évora-Monte Port.
122 J3 Evoron, Ozero l. Rus. Fed.
220 D2 Evosmos Greece
144 A2 Evowghlī Iran
180 H5 Évran France
181 I7 Èvre r. France
181 J3 Évrecy France
178 B5 Évreux France
181 K5 Évron France
221 H2 Evros r. Greece alt. Hebros (Greece), alt. Marica (Bulgaria), alt. Maritsa (Europe) alt. Meriç (Turkey),
148 C3 Evros r. Greece/Turkey
220 D6 Evrotas r. Greece
178 D6 Évry France
150 A3 Evrychou Cyprus
Evrykhou Cyprus see Evrychou
122 J3 Evur r. Rus. Fed.
220 F4 Evvoia i. Greece
220 D1 Evzonoi Greece
264 □C12 'Ewa HI U.S.A.
264 □D12 'Ewa Beach HI U.S.A.
107 J5 Ewan Qld Austr.
270 □ Ewarton Jamaica
232 D4 Ewaso Ngiro r. Kenya
236 H2 Ewbank S. Africa
168 E7 Ewe, Loch b. Scotland U.K.
173 L5 Ewell Surrey, England U.K.
250 E3 Ewen MI U.S.A.
Ewenkizu Zizhiqi Nei Mongol China see Bayan Tohoi
173 L5 Ewhurst Surrey, England U.K.
258 F4 Ewing NJ U.S.A.
286 T2 Ewing Island Antarctica
132 H5 Ewirgol Xinjiang China
230 B5 Ewo Congo
276 D3 Exaltación Bol.
220 D5 Examilia Greece
237 L4 Excelsior S. Africa
264 M3 Excelsior Mountain CA U.S.A.
264 N3 Excelsior Mountains NV U.S.A.
260 H6 Excelsior Springs MO U.S.A.
258 B2 Exchange PA U.S.A.
184 G5 Excideuil France

172 F6 **Exe** *r. England* U.K.
172 E5 **Exebridge** *Somerset, England* U.K.
286 P1 **Executive Committee Range** *mts* Antarctica
250 C4 **Exeland** *WI* U.S.A.
105 M6 **Exeter** *N.S.W.* Austr.
251 M6 **Exeter** *Ont.* Can.
172 E6 **Exeter** *Devon, England* U.K.
264 M5 **Exeter** *CA* U.S.A.
257 □O6 **Exeter** *NH* U.S.A.
247 I1 **Exeter Lake** *N.W.T.* Can.
183 J6 **Exilles** Italy
186 K3 **Exloo** Neth.
181 L4 **Exmes** France
172 F6 **Exminster** *Devon, England* U.K.
172 E5 **Exmoor** *hills England* U.K.
172 E5 **Exmoor National Park** *England* U.K.
257 J11 **Exmore** *VA* U.S.A.
108 C6 **Exmouth** *W.A.* Austr.
172 F6 **Exmouth** *Devon, England* U.K.
105 L4 **Exmouth, Mount** *N.S.W.* Austr.
108 C7 **Exmouth Gulf** *W.A.* Austr.
246 H1 **Exmouth Lake** *N.W.T.* Can.
289 L6 **Exmouth Plateau** *sea feature* Indian Ocean
221 H6 **Exo Vathy** *Notio Aigaio* Greece
107 L8 **Expedition National Park** *Qld* Austr.
107 L8 **Expedition Range** *mts Qld* Austr.
249 K3 **Exploits** *r. Nfld and Lab.* Can.
246 H5 **Exshaw** *Alta* Can.
258 D4 **Exton** *PA* U.S.A.
269 H4 **Extoraz** *r.* Mex.
204 N10 **Extremadura** *aut. comm.* Spain
229 I4 **Extrême-Nord** *prov.* Cameroon
204 D5 **Extremo** Port.
270 E1 **Exuma Cays** *is* Bahamas
270 F1 **Exuma Sound** *sea chan.* Bahamas
171 N7 **Eyam** *Derbyshire, England* U.K.
131 L5 **Eyang** *Fujian* China
230 D5 **Eyangu** Dem. Rep. Congo
233 B5 **Eyasi, Lake** *salt l.* Tanz.
Eyawadi *r.* Myanmar *see* **Irrawaddy**
183 H6 **Eybens** France
184 H5 **Eyburie** France
185 G10 **Eycheil** France
164 E3 **Eydehavn** Norway
190 G5 **Eydelstedt** Ger.
173 L2 **Eye** *Peterborough, England* U.K.
173 O3 **Eye** *Suffolk, England* U.K.
247 J2 **Eyeberry Lake** *N.W.T.* Can.
156 M2 **Eyelenoborsk** Rus. Fed.
168 L11 **Eyemouth** *Scottish Borders, Scotland* U.K.
168 D6 **Eye Peninsula** *Scotland* U.K.
169 C9 **Eyeries** Ireland
183 G8 **Eygues** *r.* France
183 H8 **Eyguians** France
183 G9 **Eyguières** France
184 I4 **Eygurande** France
184 E5 **Eygurande-et-Gardedeuil** France
162 □D2 **Eyjafjallajökull** *ice cap* Iceland
162 □D1 **Eyjafjörður** *inlet* Iceland
232 F3 **Eyl** Somalia
Eylau Rus. Fed. *see* **Bagrationovsk**
185 E6 **Eymet** France
221 J5 **Eymir** Turkey
184 H4 **Eymoutiers** France
144 B5 **'Eyn Gazān** Iran
Eynihal Turkey *see* **Kale**
168 B8 **Eynort, Loch** *inlet Scotland* U.K.
173 M5 **Eynsford** *Kent, England* U.K.
173 J4 **Eynsham** *Oxfordshire, England* U.K.
183 F9 **Eyragues** France
184 C5 **Eyrans** France
185 B6 **Eyre** *r.* France
104 F3 **Eyre (North), Lake** *salt flat S.A.* Austr.
169 F6 **Eyrecourt** Ireland
106 G9 **Eyre Creek** *watercourse Qld* Austr.
184 H5 **Eyrein** France
103 C12 **Eyre Mountains** *South I.* N.Z.
103 C12 **Eyre Peak** *South I.* N.Z.
104 E5 **Eyre Peninsula** *S.A.* Austr.
183 F7 **Eyrieux** *r.* France
185 C6 **Eysines** France
190 H5 **Eystrup** Ger.
152 A3 **Eysturoy** *i.* Faroe Is
166 D1 **Eysturoy** *i.* Faroe Is
173 O5 **Eythorne** *Kent, England* U.K.
233 C5 **Eyuku** *waterhole* Kenya
229 H5 **Eyumojok** Cameroon
144 E4 **Eyvānekey** Iran
182 F6 **Eyzin-Pinet** France
237 O4 **Ezakheni** S. Africa
237 N2 **eZamokuhle** S. Africa
205 O4 **Ezcaray** Spain
183 K9 **Èze** France
256 B11 **Ezel** *KY* U.S.A.
237 M3 **Ezenzeleni** S. Africa
284 C6 **Ezequiel Ramos Mexía, Embalse** *resr* Arg.
160 K5 **Ezernieki** Latvia
160 K5 **Ežezers** *l.* Latvia
131 J3 **Ezhou** *Hubei* China
156 J3 **Ezhva** Rus. Fed.
221 J4 **Eziler** Turkey
221 H3 **Ezine** Turkey
148 H3 **Ezinepazar** Turkey
208 B1 **Ezkurra** Spain
Ezo *i.* Japan *see* **Hokkaidō**
150 A4 **Ezousa** *r.* Cyprus
149 M8 **Ezra's Tomb** *tourist site* Iraq
178 B6 **Ézy-sur-Eure** France

F

101 □9a **Faaa** *Tahiti* Fr. Polynesia
164 G6 **Faaborg** Denmark
136 C10 **Faadhippolhu Atoll** Maldives
135 D10 **Faadhippolhu Atoll** Maldives
232 D4 **Faafxadhuun** Somalia
201 I6 **Faaker See** *l.* Austria
101 □9a **Faaone** *Tahiti* Fr. Polynesia
Faarava *atoll Arch. des Tuamotu* Fr. Polynesia *see* **Fakarava**
101 □9a **Faaupo, Pointe** *pt Moorea* Fr. Polynesia
208 F5 **Fabara** Spain
185 G9 **Fabas** France
263 K11 **Fabens** *TX* U.S.A.
116 □ **Faber, Mount** *hill* Sing.
246 G2 **Faber Lake** *N.W.T.* Can.
204 G3 **Fabero** Spain
199 L4 **Fábiánháza** Hungary
197 H3 **Fabianki** Pol.
199 J5 **Fábiánsebestyén** Hungary
199 I3 **Fabova hoľa** *mt.* Slovakia
183 D9 **Fabrègues** France
213 N9 **Fabriano** Italy
215 I3 **Fabrica di Roma** Italy
207 O3 **Fábricas de San Juan de Alcaraz** Spain
217 K7 **Fabrizia** Italy
214 I2 **Fabro** Italy
238 □1c **Faca, Ponta da** *pt Pico* Azores
274 C3 **Facatativá** Col.
231 D6 **Facauma** Angola
204 C5 **Facha** Port.
229 H2 **Fachi** Niger
206 H8 **Facinas** Spain
107 M7 **Facing Island** *Qld* Austr.
100 □1 **Facpi Point** Guam
258 D1 **Factoryville** *PA* U.S.A.
283 C7 **Facundo** Arg.
224 D5 **Fada** Chad
206 E2 **Fadagosa** Port.
144 F7 **Fadāmī** Iran
229 F3 **Fada-N'Gourma** Burkina
199 H5 **Fadd** Hungary
149 J6 **Fadghāmī** Syria
147 J4 **Faḍīlah** *well* Saudi Arabia
146 G9 **Faḍli** *reg.* Yemen
227 H4 **Fadnoun, Plateau du** Alg.
228 C4 **Fadugu** Sierra Leone
213 O3 **Faedis** Italy
213 L7 **Faenza** Italy
Færingehavn Greenland *see* **Kangerluarsoruseq**
Færoerne *terr.* N. Atlantic Ocean *see* **Faroe Islands**
Faeroes *terr.* N. Atlantic Ocean *see* **Faroe Islands**
Faesulae Italy *see* **Fiesole**
214 G2 **Faete, Monte** *hill* Italy
230 C3 **Fafa** *r.* C.A.R.
101 □8a **Fafa** *i.* Tonga
115 G5 **Fafanlap** *Papua* Indon.
204 D6 **Fafe** Port.
232 E3 **Fafen Shet'** *watercourse* Eth.
232 D5 **Fafi** *waterhole* Kenya
229 F3 **Faga** *watercourse* Burkina
213 O3 **Fagagna** Italy
100 □2 **Fagaloa Bay** Samoa
100 □2 **Fagamalo** Samoa
219 M5 **Făgăraş** Romania
Fagatau *atoll Arch. des Tuamotu* Fr. Polynesia *see* **Fangatau**
100 □2 **Fagatogo** American Samoa
162 J5 **Fagerhaug** Norway
163 J6 **Fagernes** Norway
165 L2 **Fagersta** Sweden
219 K5 **Făget** Romania
115 G4 **Fagita** *Papua* Indon.
283 C9 **Fagnano, Lago** *l.* Arg./Chile
215 Q8 **Fagnano Castello** Italy
187 F8 **Fagne** *reg.* Belgium
178 H6 **Fagnières** France
229 G2 **Fagochia** *well* Niger
228 D2 **Faguibine, Lac** *l.* Mali
162 □E2 **Fagurhólsmýri** Iceland
232 A2 **Fagwir** *Jonglei* Sudan
230 F2 **Fagwir** *Wahda* Sudan
170 C3 **Fahan** Ireland
227 G3 **Fahl, Oued el** *watercourse* Alg.
144 D6 **Fahlīān, Rūdkhāneh-ye** *watercourse* Iran
144 F6 **Fahraj** Iran
190 I1 **Fahrdorf** Ger.
190 J3 **Fahrenkrug** Ger.
195 L5 **Fahrenzhausen** Ger.
193 H6 **Fahrland** Ger.
147 M4 **Fahūd, Jabal** *hill* Oman
238 □1c **Faial** *i.* Azores
206 □ **Faial** Madeira
238 □1c **Faial, Canal do** *sea chan.* Azores
215 M5 **Faicchio** Italy
100 □4a **Faichuk** *is Chuuk* Micronesia
225 G2 **Fā'id** Egypt
191 D10 **Faid** Ger.
212 F3 **Faido** Switz.
204 G5 **Failde** Port.
251 R1 **Faillon, Lac** *l. Que.* Can.
187 H7 **Faimes** Belgium
182 E1 **Fain-lès-Montbard** France
179 J6 **Fains-Véel** France
245 K2 **Fairbanks** *AK* U.S.A.
256 A9 **Fairborn** *OH* U.S.A.
260 G5 **Fairbury** *NE* U.S.A.
250 D5 **Fairchild** *WI* U.S.A.
103 C13 **Fairfax** *South I.* N.Z.
256 H10 **Fairfax** *VA* U.S.A.
257 L4 **Fairfax** *VT* U.S.A.
103 E12 **Fairfield** *South I.* N.Z.
264 J3 **Fairfield** *CA* U.S.A.
259 I2 **Fairfield** *CT* U.S.A.
260 J5 **Fairfield** *IA* U.S.A.
262 G5 **Fairfield** *ID* U.S.A.
260 K6 **Fairfield** *IL* U.S.A.
256 A9 **Fairfield** *OH* U.S.A.
261 G10 **Fairfield** *TX* U.S.A.
265 T1 **Fairfield** *UT* U.S.A.
256 F11 **Fairfield** *VA* U.S.A.
259 I2 **Fairfield County** *county CT* U.S.A.
173 I4 **Fairford** *Gloucestershire, England* U.K.
251 K6 **Fairgrove** *MI* U.S.A.
257 O7 **Fairhaven** *MA* U.S.A.
259 G4 **Fair Haven** *NJ* U.S.A.
257 L5 **Fair Haven** *VT* U.S.A.
169 J2 **Fair Head** *Northern Ireland* U.K.
258 D5 **Fair Hill** *MD* U.S.A.
114 A6 **Fairie Queen Shoal** *sea feature* Phil.
168 □M3 **Fair Isle** *i. Scotland* U.K.
259 G3 **Fair Lawn** *NJ* U.S.A.
258 C6 **Fairlee** *MD* U.S.A.
257 M5 **Fairlee** *VT* U.S.A.
258 F4 **Fairless Hills** *PA* U.S.A.
103 E11 **Fairlie** *South I.* N.Z.
168 G11 **Fairlie** *North Ayrshire, Scotland* U.K.
107 J3 **Fairlight** *Qld* Austr.
173 N6 **Fairlight** *East Sussex, England* U.K.
260 H4 **Fairmont** *MN* U.S.A.
256 E9 **Fairmont** *WV* U.S.A.
246 H5 **Fairmont Hot Springs** B.C. Can.
173 J6 **Fair Oak** *Hampshire, England* U.K.
261 J8 **Fair Oaks** *AR* U.S.A.
250 H7 **Fair Plain** *MI* U.S.A.
263 L7 **Fairplay** *CO* U.S.A.
245 L3 **Fairplay, Mount** *AK* U.S.A.
250 H4 **Fairport** *MI* U.S.A.
258 E6 **Fairton** *NJ* U.S.A.
107 J3 **Fairview** *Qld* Austr.
246 G3 **Fairview** *Alta* Can.
250 D9 **Fairview** *IL* U.S.A.
256 B10 **Fairview** *KY* U.S.A.
251 J5 **Fairview** *MI* U.S.A.
259 G4 **Fairview** *NJ* U.S.A.
259 H1 **Fairview** *NY* U.S.A.
261 F7 **Fairview** *OK* U.S.A.
256 E6 **Fairview** *PA* U.S.A.
265 U2 **Fairview** *UT* U.S.A.
250 D6 **Fairview** *WI* U.S.A.
131 □J7 **Fairview Park** *H.K.* China
258 D5 **Fairville** *PA* U.S.A.
245 M4 **Fairweather, Cape** *AK* U.S.A.
245 M4 **Fairweather, Mount** Can./U.S.A.
170 C4 **Fairy Water** *r. Northern Ireland* U.K.
113 J5 **Fais** *i.* Micronesia
145 O6 **Faisalabad** Pak.
178 I4 **Faissault** France
260 D3 **Faith** *SD* U.S.A.
215 M6 **Faito, Monte** *mt.* Italy
Faizabad *Badakhshān* Afgh. *see* **Feyzābād**
138 I6 **Faizabad** *Uttar Prad.* India
206 □ **Fajã da Ovelha** Madeira
238 □1b **Fajã de Cima** *São Miguel* Azores
204 E8 **Fajão** Port.
206 B3 **Fajarda** Port.
271 □1 **Fajardo** Puerto Rico
148 I9 **Fajr, Wādī** *watercourse* Saudi Arabia
197 K4 **Fajsławice** Pol.
199 H5 **Fajsz** Hungary
103 □1 **Fakaofo** *atoll* Tokelau
Fakaofu *atoll* Tokelau *see* **Fakaofo**
101 □9 **Fakarava** *atoll Arch. des Tuamotu* Fr. Polynesia
156 K4 **Fakel** Rus. Fed.
173 N2 **Fakenham** *Norfolk, England* U.K.
162 M5 **Fåker** Sweden
142 C3 **Fakeyevo** Kazakh.
113 H7 **Fakfak** *Papua* Indon.
144 E6 **Fakhrābād** Iran
139 M6 **Fakiragram** *Assam* India
219 P8 **Fakiyska Reka** *r.* Bulg.
164 I6 **Fakse** Denmark
164 I6 **Fakse Bugt** *b.* Denmark
129 R5 **Faku** *Liaoning* China
172 C7 **Fal** *r. England* U.K.
228 C4 **Falaba** Sierra Leone
204 E2 **Faladoira, Serra da** *mts* Spain
229 F3 **Falagountou** Burkina
181 K4 **Falaise** France
246 G2 **Falaise Lake** *N.W.T.* Can.
139 L6 **Falakata** *W. Bengal* India
118 A3 **Falam** Myanmar
213 L3 **Falcade** Italy
Falcarragh Ireland *see* **An Fál Carrach**
205 Q4 **Falces** Spain
219 Q4 **Fălciu** Romania
179 M5 **Falck** France
213 L8 **Falco, Monte** *mt.* Italy
204 B3 **Falcoeira, Punta** *c.* Spain
274 D2 **Falcón** *state* Venez.
216 G9 **Falconara** *Sicilia* Italy
215 Q9 **Falconara Albanese** Italy
213 O8 **Falconara Marittima** Italy
217 I7 **Falcone** *Sicilia* Italy
214 A6 **Falcone, Capo del** *c. Sardegna* Italy
214 C5 **Falcone, Punta** *pt Sardegna* Italy
238 □3a **Falcones, Punta** *pt La Gomera* Canary Is
247 M5 **Falcon Lake** *Man.* Can.
267 J4 **Falcon Lake** *l.* Mex./U.S.A.
284 E2 **Falda del Carmen** Arg.
103 □1 **Fale** Tokelau
100 □2 **Falealupo** Samoa
100 □2 **Falefa** Samoa
100 □2 **Falelatai** Samoa
100 □2 **Falelima** Samoa
228 B3 **Falémé** *r.* Mali/Senegal
156 J4 **Falenki** Rus. Fed.
215 I3 **Faleria** Italy
Falerii Italy *see* **Civita Castellana**
215 Q9 **Falerna** Italy
215 K1 **Falerone** Italy
Faleshty Moldova *see* **Fălești**
158 G6 **Fălești** Moldova
100 □2 **Fale'ula** Samoa
261 F12 **Falfurrias** *TX* U.S.A.
246 G4 **Falher** *Alta* Can.
146 D7 **Falkat** *watercourse* Eritrea
191 J8 **Falken** Ger.
195 M2 **Falkenberg** *Bayern* Ger.
195 N5 **Falkenberg** *Bayern* Ger.
192 I5 **Falkenberg** *Brandenburg* Ger.
193 H7 **Falkenberg** *Brandenburg* Ger.
164 I5 **Falkenberg** Sweden
192 F4 **Falkenhagen** Ger.
193 G8 **Falkenhain** Ger.
192 H5 **Falkensee** Ger.
195 M3 **Falkenstein** *Bayern* Ger.
193 F10 **Falkenstein** *Sachsen* Ger.
192 H5 **Falkenthal** Ger.
168 I11 **Falkirk** *Falkirk, Scotland* U.K.
168 I11 **Falkirk** *admin. div. Scotland* U.K.
168 J10 **Falkland** *Fife, Scotland* U.K.
288 F9 **Falkland Escarpment** *sea feature* S. Atlantic Ocean
283 F8 **Falkland Islands** *terr.* S. Atlantic Ocean
288 F9 **Falkland Plateau** *sea feature* S. Atlantic Ocean
283 E9 **Falkland Sound** *sea chan.* Falkland Is
283 D6 **Falkner** Arg.
220 E6 **Falkonera** *i.* Greece
164 J3 **Falköping** Sweden
197 I4 **Fałków** Pol.
261 H7 **Fall** *r. KS* U.S.A.
256 C12 **Fall Branch** *TN* U.S.A.
264 O8 **Fallbrook** *CA* U.S.A.
250 C5 **Fall Creek** *WI* U.S.A.
212 C4 **Fallère, Monte** *mt.* Italy
180 H8 **Falleron** France
162 P4 **Fällfors** Sweden
286 T2 **Fallieres Coast** Antarctica
168 I10 **Fallin** *Stirling, Scotland* U.K.
190 I5 **Fallingbostel** Ger.
Fallmore Ireland *see* **An Fál Mór**
237 L9 **Fallodon** S. Africa
264 N2 **Fallon** *NV* U.S.A.
257 N7 **Fall River** *MA* U.S.A.
262 L6 **Fall River Pass** *CO* U.S.A.
258 D2 **Falls** *PA* U.S.A.
258 A7 **Falls Church** *VA* U.S.A.
260 H5 **Falls City** *NE* U.S.A.
256 G7 **Falls Creek** *PA* U.S.A.
258 F4 **Fallsington** *PA* U.S.A.
258 C5 **Fallston** *MD* U.S.A.
212 F3 **Falmenta** Italy
271 □2 **Falmouth** Antigua and Barbuda
270 □ **Falmouth** Jamaica
172 B7 **Falmouth** *Cornwall, England* U.K.
256 A10 **Falmouth** *KY* U.S.A.
257 O7 **Falmouth** *MA* U.S.A.
257 □O5 **Falmouth** *ME* U.S.A.
258 B4 **Falmouth** *PA* U.S.A.
256 H10 **Falmouth** *VA* U.S.A.
172 B7 **Falmouth Bay** *England* U.K.
271 □2 **Falmouth Harbour** Antigua and Barbuda
228 D3 **Falo** Mali
228 D3 **Falou** Mali
285 F6 **Falsa, Bahía** *b.* Arg.
276 C5 **Falsa Chipana, Punta** *pt* Chile
249 G1 **False** *r. Que.* Can.
236 C10 **False Bay** S. Africa
237 Q3 **False Bay Park** S. Africa
244 G5 **False Pass** *AK* U.S.A.
139 K9 **False Point** India
208 G5 **Falset** Spain
270 H5 **Falso, Cabo** *c.* Dom. Rep.
266 □R10 **Falso, Cabo** *c.* Hond.
283 C9 **Falso Cabo de Hornos** *c.* Chile
164 H7 **Falster** *i.* Denmark
171 M3 **Falstone** *Northumberland, England* U.K.
219 O3 **Fălticeni** Romania
165 L1 **Falun** Sweden
213 M2 **Falzarego, Passo di** *pass* Italy
115 G4 **Fam, Kepulauan** *is Papua* Indon.
Famagusta Cyprus *see* **Ammochostos**
Famagusta Bay Cyprus *see* **Ammochostos Bay**
204 F8 **Famalicão** Port.
282 D3 **Famatina** Arg.
282 C3 **Famatina, Sierra de** *mts* Arg.
191 J9 **Fambach** Ger.
179 L5 **Fameck** France
144 C4 **Famenin** Iran
187 G8 **Famenne** *val.* Belgium
109 G8 **Fame Range** *hills W.A.* Austr.
247 M5 **Family Lake** *Man.* Can.
108 I7 **Family Well** *W.A.* Austr.
144 D7 **Fāmūr, Daryācheh-ye** *l.* Iran
228 D3 **Fana** Mali
169 G2 **Fanad Head** Ireland
100 □4a **Fanaik** *i. Chuuk* Micronesia
102 J2 **Fanal Island** *North I.* N.Z.
235 □K2 **Fanambana** Madag.
100 □4a **Fanan** *i. Chuuk* Micronesia
100 □4a **Fananani, Mochun** *sea chan. Chuuk* Micronesia
235 □K3 **Fanandrana** Madag.
213 J7 **Fanano** Italy
100 □4a **Fanapanges** *i. Chuuk* Micronesia
221 H5 **Fanari, Akrotirio** *pt Ikaria* Greece
131 L3 **Fanchang** *Anhui* China
235 □J4 **Fandriana** Madag.
169 J5 **Fane** *r.* Ireland
213 M2 **Fanes Sennes Braies, Parco Naturale** *nature res.* Italy
100 □4a **Fanew, Mochun** *sea chan. Chuuk* Micronesia
118 D5 **Fang** Thai.
232 A2 **Fangak** Sudan
208 G6 **Fangar, Punta del** *pt* Spain
101 □9 **Fangatau** *atoll Arch. des Tuamotu* Fr. Polynesia
101 □9 **Fangataufa** *atoll Arch. des Tuamotu* Fr. Polynesia
101 □8a **Fanga Uta** *inlet Tongatapu* Tonga
Fangcheng *Guangxi* China *see* **Fangchenggang**
131 I2 **Fangcheng** *Henan* China
130 G8 **Fangchenggang** *Guangxi* China
130 G3 **Fangdou Shan** *mts* China
131 M7 **Fangliao** Taiwan
214 B3 **Fango** *r. Corse* France
165 M3 **Fångö** *i.* Sweden
131 M7 **Fangshan** Taiwan
130 H2 **Fangxian** *Hubei* China
122 F6 **Fangzheng** *Heilong.* China
218 H9 **Fani i Vogël** *r.* Albania
160 K8 **Fanipal'** Belarus
185 I9 **Fanjeaux** France
130 G3 **Fankuai** *Sichuan* China
Fankuaidian *Sichuan* China *see* **Fankuai**
131 □J7 **Fanling** *H.K.* China
208 E2 **Fanlo** Spain
168 F7 **Fannich, Loch** *l. Scotland* U.K.
Fanning Island *atoll* Kiribati *see* **Tabuaeran**
162 J5 **Fannrem** Norway
144 H8 **Fannūj** Iran
164 E6 **Fanø** *i.* Denmark
213 O8 **Fano** Italy
164 E6 **Fanø Bugt** *b.* Denmark
100 □4a **Fanos** *i. Chuuk* Micronesia
Fanoualie *i.* Tonga *see* **Fonualei**
131 K3 **Fanshan** *Anhui* China
131 M5 **Fanshan** *Zhejiang* China
129 M7 **Fanshi** *Shanxi* China
199 K5 **Fântâna Rece** *hill* Romania
199 K5 **Fântânele** Romania
Fanum Fortunae Italy *see* **Fano**
204 C5 **Fão** Port.
168 B8 **Faoileann, Bagh nam** *b. Scotland* U.K.
144 D7 **Faqīh Aḥmadān** Iran
Farab Turkm. *see* **Farap**
228 C3 **Faraba** Mali
Farab-Pristan' Turkm. *see* **Jeÿhun**
230 F4 **Faradje** Dem. Rep. Congo
Faradofay Madag. *see* **Tôlañaro**
235 □J4 **Farafangana** Madag.
228 B3 **Farafenni** Gambia
215 M3 **Fara Filiorum Petri** Italy
224 F3 **Farāfirah, Wāḥāt al** *oasis* Egypt
Farafra Oasis Egypt *see* **Farāfirah, Wāḥāt al**
144 E6 **Farāgheh** Iran
145 J5 **Farāh** Afgh.
145 I5 **Farāh** *prov.* Afgh.
Faraḥābād Iran *see* **Khezerābād**
235 □K2 **Farahalana** Madag.
145 I6 **Farah Rūd** *watercourse* Afgh.
215 J3 **Fara in Sabina** Italy
145 M4 **Farakhulm** Afgh.
268 B6 **Farallón, Punta** *pt* Mex.
113 K3 **Farallon de Medinilla** *i.* N. Mariana Is
113 J2 **Farallon de Pajaros** *vol.* N. Mariana Is
274 B4 **Farallones de Cali, Parque Nacional** *nat. park* Col.
264 I4 **Farallon National Wildlife Refuge** *nature res. CA* U.S.A.
204 I5 **Faramontanos de Tábara** Spain
230 E2 **Faramuti** *I.* Sudan
228 C4 **Faranah** Guinea
145 P4 **Faranshat** Pak.
219 O4 **Faraoani** Romania
228 B2 **Far'aoun** *well* Maur.
145 J2 **Farap** Turkm.
147 L7 **Fararah** Oman
146 E7 **Farasān** Saudi Arabia
146 E7 **Farasān, Jazā'ir** *is* Saudi Arabia
215 M3 **Fara San Martino** Italy
208 C3 **Farasdues** Spain
235 □J3 **Faratsiho** Madag.
113 J5 **Faraulep** *atoll* Micronesia
219 M3 **Farcău, Vârful** *mt.* Romania
195 K6 **Farchant** Ger.
187 G8 **Farciennes** Belgium
199 L6 **Fărdea** Romania
207 N5 **Fardes** *r.* Spain
169 G6 **Fardrum** Ireland
179 M5 **Farébersviller** France
173 J6 **Fareham** *Hampshire, England* U.K.
178 F6 **Faremoutiers** France
244 I3 **Farewell** *AK* U.S.A.
Farewell, Cape Greenland *see* **Nunap Isua**
102 G7 **Farewell, Cape** *South I.* N.Z.
102 G7 **Farewell Spit** *South I.* N.Z.
215 J3 **Farfa** *r.* Italy
164 I3 **Färgelanda** Sweden
Farghona Uzbek. *see* **Farg'ona**
Farghona Wiloyati *admin. div.* Uzbek. *see* **Farg'ona**
255 F10 **Fargo** *GA* U.S.A.
260 G2 **Fargo** *ND* U.S.A.
143 N7 **Farg'ona** Uzbek.
143 N7 **Farg'ona** *admin. div.* Uzbek.
185 D6 **Fargues-St-Hilaire** France
185 E7 **Fargues-sur-Ourbise** France
190 H1 **Fårhus** Denmark
260 I3 **Faribault** *MN* U.S.A.
249 G1 **Faribault, Lac** *l. Que.* Can.
138 F5 **Faridabad** *Haryana* India
138 E4 **Faridkot** *Punjab* India
139 L8 **Faridpur** Bangl.
138 G5 **Faridpur** *Uttar Prad.* India
224 C2 **Fārigh, Wādī al** *watercourse* Libya
163 M6 **Färila** Sweden
204 A10 **Farilhões** *i.* Port.
228 B3 **Farim** Guinea-Bissau
144 H4 **Farīmān** Iran
173 I4 **Faringdon** *Oxfordshire, England* U.K.
171 L6 **Farington** *Lancashire, England* U.K.
278 D3 **Farinha** *r.* Brazil
212 H6 **Farini** Italy
147 J6 **Fāris, Qalamat** *oasis* Saudi Arabia
204 H6 **Fariza de Sayago** Spain
165 M5 **Färjestaden** *Öland* Sweden
220 D3 **Farkadona** Greece
Farkhar Afgh. *see* **Farkhato**
145 M3 **Farkhato** Afgh.
145 M3 **Farkhor** Tajik.
233 B6 **Farkwa** Tanz.
107 L6 **Farleigh** *Qld* Austr.
173 J5 **Farleigh Wallop** *Hampshire, England* U.K.
208 D4 **Farlete** Spain
214 G1 **Farma** *r.* Italy
144 C4 **Farmahīn** Iran
221 I5 **Farmakonisi** *i.* Greece
172 H5 **Farmborough** *Bath and North East Somerset, England* U.K.
250 F9 **Farmer City** *IL* U.S.A.
248 D1 **Farmer Island** *Nunavut* Can.
261 I9 **Farmerville** *LA* U.S.A.
259 G4 **Farmingdale** *NJ* U.S.A.
246 F4 **Farmington** *B.C.* Can.
259 J1 **Farmington** *CT* U.S.A.
258 D7 **Farmington** *DE* U.S.A.
250 D9 **Farmington** *IL* U.S.A.
257 □O4 **Farmington** *ME* U.S.A.
261 J7 **Farmington** *MO* U.S.A.
257 □N5 **Farmington** *NH* U.S.A.
263 J8 **Farmington** *NM* U.S.A.
262 I6 **Farmington** *UT* U.S.A.
256 B6 **Farmington Hills** *MI* U.S.A.
259 I3 **Farmingville** *NY* U.S.A.
199 I4 **Farmos** Hungary
246 E4 **Far Mountain** *B.C.* Can.
256 G11 **Farmville** *VA* U.S.A.
199 H3 **Farná** Slovakia
173 K5 **Farnborough** *Hampshire, England* U.K.
171 L7 **Farndon** *Cheshire, England* U.K.
171 P7 **Farndon** *Nottinghamshire, England* U.K.
165 M1 **Färnebofjärden** *l.* Sweden
165 M1 **Färnebofjärdens nationalpark** *nat. park* Sweden
171 N2 **Farne Islands** *England* U.K.
214 H2 **Farnese** Italy
257 M3 **Farnham** *Que.* Can.
173 K5 **Farnham** *Surrey, England* U.K.
256 I11 **Farnham** *VA* U.S.A.
109 I8 **Farnham, Lake** *salt flat W.A.* Austr.
246 G5 **Farnham, Mount** *B.C.* Can.
173 K4 **Farnham Royal** *Buckinghamshire, England* U.K.
193 E8 **Farnstädt** Ger.
171 M6 **Farnworth** *Greater Manchester, England* U.K.
285 G6 **Faro** Arg.
275 G5 **Faro** Brazil
229 I4 **Faro** *r.* Cameroon
245 N3 **Faro** *Y.T.* Can.
206 D6 **Faro** Port.
206 C6 **Faro** *admin. dist.* Port.
204 E3 **Faro** *mt.* Spain
165 P4 **Fårö** *Gotland* Sweden
165 P4 **Fårö** *i.* Sweden
270 F8 **Faro, Punta** *pt* Col.
229 I4 **Faro, Réserve du** *nature res.* Cameroon
204 E4 **Faro, Serra do** *mts* Spain
166 D1 **Faroe Islands** *terr.* N. Atlantic Ocean
212 C4 **Faroma, Monte** *mt.* Italy
165 P4 **Fårösund** *Gotland* Sweden
239 □2 **Farquhar Atoll** Seychelles
239 □2 **Farquhar Group** *is* Seychelles
109 G9 **Farquharson Tableland** *hills W.A.* Austr.
168 H8 **Farr** *Highland, Scotland* U.K.
213 M3 **Farra d'Alpago** Italy
256 H7 **Farrandsville** *PA* U.S.A.
169 C8 **Farranfore** Ireland
168 G8 **Farrar** *r. Scotland* U.K.
107 H8 **Farrars Creek** *watercourse Qld* Austr.
144 E7 **Farrāshband** Iran
287 G2 **Farr Bay** Antarctica
251 S4 **Farrellton** *Que.* Can.
284 B3 **Farrelones** Chile
144 H5 **Farrokhī** Iran
Farruch, Cabo *c.* Spain *see* **Ferrutx, Cap**
Farrukhabad *Uttar Prad.* India *see* **Fatehgarh**
144 E7 **Fārs** *prov.* Iran
151 B1 **Fars** *r.* Rus. Fed.
144 F5 **Farsakh** Iran
220 D3 **Farsala** Greece
220 D3 **Farsaliotis** *r.* Greece
145 J5 **Fārsī** Afgh.
144 D8 **Fārsī, Jazīreh-ye** *i. Būshehr* Iran
149 O9 **Fārsī, Jazīreh-ye** *i. Būshehr* Iran
164 F5 **Farsø** Denmark
262 J5 **Farson** *WY* U.S.A.
164 C3 **Farsund** Norway
147 J8 **Fartak, Jabal** *mts* Yemen
147 K8 **Fartak, Ra's** *c.* Yemen
219 P5 **Fărţăneşti** Romania
280 B2 **Fartura** *r.* Brazil
279 B8 **Fartura, Serra da** *mts* Brazil
144 H3 **Fārūj** Iran
164 F5 **Fårvang** Denmark
Farvel, Kap *c.* Greenland *see* **Nunap Isua**
250 J6 **Farwell** *MI* U.S.A.
261 D8 **Farwell** *TX* U.S.A.
145 K3 **Fāryāb** *prov.* Afgh.
144 G8 **Fāryāb** *Hormozgan* Iran
144 G7 **Fāryāb** *Kermān* Iran
160 L6 **Farynava** Belarus
144 E7 **Fasā** Iran
217 M2 **Fasano** Italy
163 K5 **Fåset** Norway
159 R5 **Fashchivka** Ukr.
150 A2 **Faşikan Geçidi** *pass* Turkey
232 C1 **Fasil Ghebbi and Gonder Monuments** *tourist site* Eth.
238 □3a **Fasnia** *Tenerife* Canary Is
190 J5 **Faßberg** Ger.
145 I9 **Fāsteh, Ra's-e** *pt* Iran
158 I3 **Fastiv** Ukr.
Fastov Ukr. *see* **Fastiv**
230 F4 **Fataki** Dem. Rep. Congo
215 K5 **Fate, Monte delle** *mt.* Italy
138 E5 **Fatehabad** *Haryana* India
138 F7 **Fatehgarh** *Madh. Prad.* India
138 G6 **Fatehgarh** *Uttar Prad.* India
138 F4 **Fatehgarh Sahib** *Punjab* India
138 E7 **Fatehnagar** *Rajasthan* India
138 E6 **Fatehpur** *Rajasthan* India
138 H7 **Fatehpur** *Uttar Prad.* India
145 N6 **Fatehpur** Pak.
138 F6 **Fatehpur Sikri** *Uttar Prad.* India
204 F8 **Fatela** Port.
237 L4 **Fateng-Tse-Ntsho** S. Africa
159 N1 **Fateyevka** Rus. Fed.
159 O1 **Fatezh** Rus. Fed.
144 F7 **Fatḥābād** Iran
232 A2 **Fathai** Sudan
251 M4 **Fathom Five National Marine Park** *Ont.* Can.
228 A3 **Fatick** Senegal
204 C9 **Fátima** Port.
Fattoilep *atoll* Micronesia *see* **Faraulep**
Fatuhiva *i.* Fr. Polynesia *see* **Fatu Hiva**
101 □9 **Fatu Hiva** *i.* Fr. Polynesia
231 F6 **Fatuma** Dem. Rep. Congo
231 C6 **Fatundu** Dem. Rep. Congo
100 □6 **Fauabu** *Malaita* Solomon Is
182 I4 **Faucille, Col de la** *pass* France
179 M8 **Faucogney-et-la-Mer** France
183 C9 **Faugères** France
169 H2 **Faughan** *r. Northern Ireland* U.K.
212 J8 **Fauglia** Italy
185 E7 **Fauguerolles** France
194 G2 **Faulbach** Ger.
168 I11 **Fauldhouse** *West Lothian, Scotland* U.K.
192 G3 **Faulenrost** Ger.
260 F3 **Faulkton** *SD* U.S.A.
179 M5 **Faulquemont** France
178 D2 **Fauquembergues** France
246 G5 **Fauquier** *B.C.* Can.
209 E8 **Faura** Spain
109 B8 **Faure Island** *W.A.* Austr.
237 J5 **Fauresmith** S. Africa
100 □6 **Fauro** *i.* Solomon Is
162 M3 **Fauske** Norway
246 H4 **Faust** *Alta* Can.
285 H3 **Faustino M. Parera** Arg.
181 M2 **Fauville-en-Caux** France
185 F6 **Faux** France
184 H4 **Faux-la-Montagne** France
204 F6 **Favaios** Port.
212 G7 **Favale di Malvaro** Italy
213 M9 **Favalto, Monte** *mt.* Italy
216 F9 **Favara** *Sicilia* Italy
209 E9 **Favara** Spain
208 □ **Favàritx, Cap de** *c.* Spain
185 G8 **Faverges** France
179 L8 **Faverney** France
183 C7 **Faverolles** France
173 N5 **Faversham** *Kent, England* U.K.
179 K7 **Favières** France
216 C8 **Favignana** *Sicilia* Italy
216 C8 **Favignana, Isola** *i. Sicilia* Italy
246 H4 **Fawcett** *Alta* Can.
173 J6 **Fawley** *Hampshire, England* U.K.
248 B2 **Fawn** *r. Ont.* Can.
258 B5 **Fawn Grove** *PA* U.S.A.
237 O5 **Fawnleas** S. Africa
146 F2 **Fawwārah** Saudi Arabia
162 □B1 **Faxaflói** *b.* Iceland
162 N5 **Faxälven** *r.* Sweden
258 B2 **Faxon** *PA* U.S.A.
224 C5 **Faya** Chad
100 □5 **Fayaoué** *Îles Loyauté* New Caledonia
178 D8 **Fay-aux-Loges** France
185 H6 **Faycelles** France
146 F2 **Fayd** Saudi Arabia
180 H7 **Fay-de-Bretagne** France
183 J9 **Fayence** France
255 D9 **Fayette** *AL* U.S.A.
250 H4 **Fayette** *MI* U.S.A.
260 I6 **Fayette** *MO* U.S.A.
261 J10 **Fayette** *MS* U.S.A.
256 A7 **Fayette** *OH* U.S.A.
261 H7 **Fayetteville** *AR* U.S.A.
255 E9 **Fayetteville** *GA* U.S.A.
255 H8 **Fayetteville** *NC* U.S.A.
257 I5 **Fayetteville** *NY* U.S.A.
256 H9 **Fayetteville** *PA* U.S.A.
255 D8 **Fayetteville** *TN* U.S.A.
256 D10 **Fayetteville** *WV* U.S.A.
146 F7 **Fayfā** Saudi Arabia
149 N9 **Faylakah** *i.* Kuwait
179 K8 **Fayl-la-Forêt** France
179 M8 **Faymont** France
208 F5 **Fayón** Spain
150 B10 **Fayrān** *well* Egypt
150 B10 **Fayrān, Wādī** *watercourse* Egypt
150 C10 **Fayrānī, Jabal** *mt.* Egypt
183 E7 **Fay-sur-Lignon** France
115 J5 **Fayu** *i.* Micronesia
145 K3 **Fayzābād** *Fāryāb* Afgh.
150 E9 **Fazair al Ghrazi** *watercourse* Saudi Arabia
213 P6 **Fažana** Croatia
229 F4 **Fazao Malfakassa, Parc National de** *nat. park* Togo
229 H2 **Fazeī** *well* Niger
173 I2 **Fazeley** *Staffordshire, England* U.K.
138 E4 **Fazilka** *Punjab* India
145 N7 **Fazilpur** Pak.
147 I2 **Fazrān, Jabal** *hill* Saudi Arabia
226 B5 **Fdérik** Maur.
Fead Group *is* P.N.G. *see* **Nuguria Islands**
169 C8 **Feale** *r.* Ireland
255 I9 **Fear, Cape** *NC* U.S.A.
168 E7 **Fearnmore** *Highland, Scotland* U.K.
185 C9 **Féas** France
258 E4 **Feasterville** *PA* U.S.A.
264 K3 **Feather** *r. CA* U.S.A.
264 K2 **Feather, North Fork** *r. CA* U.S.A.
103 J8 **Featherston** *North I.* N.Z.
172 H2 **Featherstone** *Staffordshire, England* U.K.
171 O6 **Featherstone** *West Yorkshire, England* U.K.
235 F3 **Featherstone** Zimbabwe
181 L2 **Fécamp** France
214 G1 **Feccia** *r.* Italy
179 N7 **Fecht** *r.* France
210 G3 **Federacija Bosna i Hercegovina** *aut. div.* Bos.-Herz.
285 I2 **Federación** Arg.
285 I3 **Federación** Uru.
285 H2 **Federal** Arg.
229 G4 **Federal Capital Territory** *admin. div.* Nigeria
Federal District *admin. dist.* Brazil *see* **Distrito Federal**
Federal District *admin. dist.* Mex. *see* **Distrito Federal**
Federal District *admin. dist.* Venez. *see* **Distrito Capital**
257 J10 **Federalsburg** *MD* U.S.A.
194 H5 **Federsee** *l.* Ger.
166 J1 **Fedje** Norway
159 O7 **Fedorivka** Ukr.
Fedorov Kazakh. *see* **Fedorovka**
142 J1 **Fedorovka** *Kostanayskaya Oblast'* Kazakh.
143 Q1 **Fedorovka** *Pavlodarskaya Oblast'* Kazakh.
142 D2 **Fedorovka** *Zapadnyy Kazakhstan* Kazakh.
142 F1 **Fedorovka** *Respublika Bashkortostan* Rus. Fed.
159 R6 **Fedorovka** *Rostovskaya Oblast'* Rus. Fed.
142 C1 **Fedorovka** *Samarskaya Oblast'* Rus. Fed.
157 I6 **Fedorovka** *Saratovskaya Oblast'* Rus. Fed.
159 R8 **Fedorovskaya** Rus. Fed.
161 W5 **Fedorovskoye** Rus. Fed.
159 O7 **Fedotova Kosa** *spit* Ukr.
161 X6 **Fedotovo** Rus. Fed.
138 D6 **Fedusar** *Rajasthan* India
169 C5 **Fee, Lough** *l.* Ireland
169 C5 **Feeagh, Lough** *l.* Ireland
168 H8 **Feehlin** *r. Scotland* U.K.
169 H3 **Feeny** *Northern Ireland* U.K.
232 E3 **Feerfeer** Somalia
100 □4a **Fefan** *i. Chuuk* Micronesia
180 G6 **Fégréac** France
199 J4 **Fegyvernek** Hungary
199 L4 **Fehérgyarmat** Hungary
199 K5 **Fehér-Körös** *r.* Hungary
199 J5 **Fehér-tó** *l.* Hungary
199 H4 **Fehérvárcsurgó** Hungary
247 M1 **Fehet Lake** *Nunavut* Can.
192 D2 **Fehmarn** *i.* Ger.
Fehmarn Belt *str.* Denmark/Ger. *see* **Femer Bælt**
190 K2 **Fehmarnsund** *sea chan.* Ger.
192 G5 **Fehrbellin** Ger.
201 N6 **Fehring** Austria
281 G4 **Feia, Lagoa** *lag.* Brazil
Feicheng *Shandong* China *see* **Feixian**
131 K3 **Feidong** *Anhui* China
178 G3 **Feignies** France
276 C2 **Feijó** Brazil
206 A3 **Feijó** Port.
194 D2 **Feilbingert** Ger.
102 J7 **Feilding** *North I.* N.Z.
193 E10 **Feilitzsch** Ger.
182 F4 **Feillens** France
160 J5 **Feimaņu ezers** *l.* Latvia
131 □J7 **Fei Ngo Shan** *hill H.K.* China
Feio *r.* Brazil *see* **Aguapeí**
Feira Zambia *see* **Luangwa**
278 F5 **Feira de Santana** Brazil
182 I5 **Feissons-sur-Isère** France
201 J6 **Feistritz im Rosental** Austria
201 K6 **Feistritz ob Bleiburg** Austria
206 D6 **Feiteira** Port.
131 K3 **Feixi** *Anhui* China
129 O9 **Feixian** *Shandong* China
129 N8 **Feixiang** *Hebei* China
227 H2 **Fejaj, Chott el** *salt l.* Tunisia
211 A7 **Fejd el Abiod** *pass* Alg.
199 H4 **Fejér** *county* Hungary
164 H7 **Fejø** *i.* Denmark
148 G5 **Feke** Turkey
199 K5 **Fekete-Körös** *r.* Hungary
209 L9 **Felanitx** Spain
227 G6 **Felaou** *well* Alg.
144 D5 **Felāvarjān** Iran
192 J4 **Felchow** Ger.
191 J9 **Felda** *r.* Ger.
195 K6 **Feldafing** Ger.
201 I6 **Feld am See** Austria
201 M6 **Feldbach** Austria
182 K1 **Feldbach** France
192 H4 **Feldberg** Ger.
194 E6 **Feldberg** *mt.* Ger.
190 I2 **Felde** Ger.
199 J4 **Feldebrő** Hungary
200 A5 **Feldkirch** Austria
194 H7 **Feldkirch** *admin. reg.* Austria
195 L5 **Feldkirchen** Ger.
201 L5 **Feldkirchen bei Graz** Austria
201 J6 **Feldkirchen in Kärnten** Austria
195 L6 **Feldkirchen-Westerham** Ger.
219 M3 **Feldru** Romania
204 G6 **Felgar** Port.
204 D6 **Felgueiras** Port.
199 J5 **Felgyő** Hungary
285 H2 **Feliciano** *r.* Arg.
239 □2a **Félicité** *i. Inner Islands* Seychelles
256 A10 **Felicity** *OH* U.S.A.
135 D11 **Felidhu Atoll** Maldives
135 □1 **Felidhu Channel** Maldives
172 F3 **Felindre** *Powys, Wales* U.K.
183 D6 **Félines** France
212 I6 **Felino** Italy
268 C1 **Felipe Carrillo Puerto** *Durango* Mex.
268 E6 **Felipe Carrillo Puerto** *Michoacán* Mex.
267 O8 **Felipe C. Puerto** Mex.
215 O7 **Felitto** Italy
207 N7 **Félix** Spain
201 N4 **Felixdorf** Austria
281 E3 **Felixlândia** Brazil
173 O4 **Felixstowe** *Suffolk, England* U.K.
237 P4 **Felixton** S. Africa
212 E6 **Felizzano** Italy
194 B2 **Fell** Ger.
168 J12 **Fell, Loch** *hill Scotland* U.K.
213 O3 **Fella** *r.* Italy
194 G4 **Fellbach** Ger.
184 I4 **Felletin** France
171 N4 **Felling** *Tyne and Wear, England* U.K.
270 □ **Fellowship** Jamaica
256 F9 **Fellowsville** *WV* U.S.A.
190 J2 **Felm** Ger.
199 K5 **Felnac** Romania
Fels Lux. *see* **Larochette**
191 H8 **Felsberg** Ger.
Felsina Italy *see* **Bologna**
199 K3 **Felsődobsza** Hungary
199 I4 **Felsőlajos** Hungary
199 H5 **Felsőnyék** Hungary
199 G6 **Felsőszentmárton** Hungary
199 J4 **Felsőtárkány** Hungary
201 O6 **Felső-Válicka** *r.* Hungary
199 J3 **Felsőzsolca** Hungary
190 H1 **Felsted** Denmark
173 M4 **Felsted** *Essex, England* U
171 N3 **Felton** *Northumberland, England* U.K.
258 D6 **Felton** *DE* U.S.A.
258 B5 **Felton** *PA* U.S.A.
213 L3 **Feltre** Italy
173 N3 **Feltwell** *Norfolk, Englan*
215 K2 **Fema, Monte** *mt.* Italy
278 D5 **Femeas** *r.* Brazil
190 K1 **Femer Bælt** *str.* Denma
238 □3c **Femés** *hill Lanzarote* Ca
165 K5 **Femlingen** *l.* Sweden
217 L5 **Femminamorta, Monte** *mt.* Italy
216 H8 **Femmina Morta, Porte** *pass* Italy
164 H7 **Femø** *i.* Denmark
164 H2 **Femsjøen** *l.* Norway
163 K5 **Femunden** *l.* Norway
163 L5 **Femundsmarka Nasjor** *nat. park* Norway
170 B5 **Fenagh** *Leitrim* Ireland
214 F3 **Fenaio, Punta del** *pt* Ital
238 □1b **Fenais da Ajuda** *São Mi* Azores
235 □J5 **Fenambosy, Lohatanjor** Madag.
100 □1 **Fena Valley Reservoir** G
182 G2 **Fénay** France
185 H9 **Fendeille** France
204 D2 **Fene** Spain
251 P5 **Fenelon Falls** *Ont.* Can.
100 □4a **Feneppi** *i. Chuuk* Micro
150 D2 **Fener Burnu** *hd* Turkey
Fenérive Madag. *see* **Fenoarivo Atsinanana**
151 A4 **Fenerköyü** Turkey
212 C5 **Fenestrelle** Italy
179 N6 **Fénétrange** France
181 J6 **Feneu** France
158 J3 **Fenevychi** Ukr.
221 G2 **Fengari** *mt. Samothraki*
Fengcheng *Fujian* Chin **Yongding**
Fengcheng *Fujian* Chin **Lianjiang**
Fengcheng *Fujian* Chin **Anxi**
Fengcheng *Guangdong* **Xinfeng**
Fengcheng *Guangxi* Ch **Fengshan**
Fengcheng *Guizhou* Ch **Tianzhu**
131 J4 **Fengcheng** *Jiangxi* Chir
123 D8 **Fengcheng** *Liaoning* Ch
Fengchuan *Jiangxi* Chir **Fengxin**
130 F4 **Fengdu** *Chongqing* Chir
Fenggang *Fujian* China **Shaxian**
130 F5 **Fenggang** *Guizhou* Chir
Fenggang *Jiangxi* China **Yihuang**
128 J9 **Fenggeling** *Gansu* Chin
131 M4 **Fenghua** *Zhejiang* China
130 G5 **Fenghuang** *Hunan* Chir
Fengjiaba *Sichuan* Chin **Wangcang**
130 G3 **Fengjie** *Chongqing* Chir
131 H7 **Fengkai** *Guangdong* Chi
131 M7 **Fenglin** Taiwan
122 E7 **Fengman** *Jilin* China
Fengming *Shaanxi* Chi **Qishan**
129 P7 **Fengnan** *Hebei* China
129 O6 **Fengning** *Hebei* China
Fengqi *Shaanxi* China s **Luochuan**
130 B6 **Fengqing** *Yunnan* China
129 N9 **Fengqiu** *Henan* China
129 P7 **Fengrun** *Hebei* China
Fengshan *Fujian* China **Luoyuan**
130 F6 **Fengshan** *Guangxi* Chir
Fengshan *Hubei* China **Luotian**
Fengshan *Yunnan* China **Fengqing**
131 J6 **Fengshuba Shuiku** *resr*
131 K2 **Fengtai** *Anhui* China
130 D3 **Fengtongzhai Giant Pa** **Reserve** *nature res.* Chin
130 B7 **Fengwei** *Yunnan* China
Fengweiba *Yunnan* Chir **Fengwei**
129 O9 **Fengxian** *Jiangsu* China
130 F2 **Fengxian** *Shaanxi* China
131 M3 **Fengxian** *Shanghai* Chi
Fengxian *Heilong.* Chi **Luobei**
130 F1 **Fengxiang** *Shaanxi* Chir
Fengxiang *Yunnan* Chin **Lincang**
131 J4 **Fengxin** *Jiangxi* China
131 K2 **Fengyang** *Anhui* China
Fengyi *Guizhou* China s **Zheng'an**
Fengyi *Sichuan* China s **Maoxian**
129 K9 **Fengyuan** *Shaanxi* Chin
131 M6 **Fengyüan** Taiwan
129 M6 **Fengzhen** *Nei Mongol* C
129 L9 **Fen He** *r.* China
129 L7 **Fenhe Shuiku** *resr* Chin
139 M8 **Feni** Bangl.
244 H1 **Feniak Lake** *AK* U.S.A.
113 L7 **Feni Islands** P.N.G.
245 □D5 **Fenimore Pass** *sea chan* *AK* U.S.A.
184 D2 **Fenioux** France
212 C4 **Fenis** Italy
169 C8 **Fenit** Ireland
172 F6 **Feniton** *Devon, England*
169 I7 **Fennagh** *Carlow* Ireland
139 M8 **Fenny** *r.* Bangl./India
214 B4 **Feno, Capo di** *c. Corse* F
214 C5 **Feno, Capo di** *c. Corse* F
235 □K3 **Fenoarivo Atsinanana** M
235 □J3 **Fenoarivo Be** Madag.
185 G8 **Fenouillet** France
185 I10 **Fenouillet** *reg.* France
131 L4 **Fenshui** *Zhejiang* China
173 L3 **Fenstanton** *Cambridges* *England* U.K.
195 M3 **Fensterbach** *r.* Ger.
251 K7 **Fenton** *MI* U.S.A.
103 □1 **Fenua Fale** Tokelau
103 □1 **Fenua Loa** *i.* Tokelau
Fenua Ura *atoll Arch. de* Fr. Polynesia *see* **Manua**
168 H11 **Fenwick** *East Ayrshire, Scotland* U.K.
171 N2 **Fenwick** *Northumberland, England* U.K.
256 E10 **Fenwick** *WV* U.S.A.
129 L8 **Fenyang** *Shanxi* China
199 L3 **Fényeslitke** Hungary
131 J5 **Fenyi** *Jiangxi* China
172 B7 **Feock** *Cornwall, England*
159 O8 **Feodosiya** Ukr.
159 O8 **Feodosiys'ka Zatoka** *b.* U
160 M3 **Feofilova Pustyn'** Rus. F
168 D11 **Feolin Ferry** *Argyll and E* *Scotland* U.K.
169 E8 **Feonanagh** Ireland
227 G1 **Fer, Cap de** *c.* Alg.
100 □6 **Fera** *i.* Solomon Is
182 H3 **Fer-à-Cheval, Cirque du** France
Férai Greece *see* **Feres**
169 G6 **Ferbane** Ireland
193 F6 **Ferchland** Ger.
217 K6 **Ferdinandea** Italy
192 I3 **Ferdinandshof** Ger.
144 H5 **Ferdows** Iran
178 G6 **Fère-Champenoise** Frar
219 N3 **Feredeului, Obcina** *ridge* Romania
178 G5 **Fère-en-Tardenois** France
180 G7 **Férel** France
215 J2 **Ferentillo** Italy
215 K4 **Ferentino** Italy
221 H2 **Feres** Greece

Férez Spain
Fergana Oblast admin. div.
Uzbek. see Farg'ona
Fergana Range mts Kyrg. see
Fergana Too Tizmegi
Fergana Too Tizmegi mts Kyrg.
Ferganskiy Khrebet mts Kyrg. see
Fergana Too Tizmegi
Fergus Ont. Can.
Fergus r. Ireland
Fergus Falls MN U.S.A.
Ferguson Lake Nunavut Can.
Fergusson r. N.T. Austr.
Fergusson Island P.N.G.
Feria, Sierra de hills Spain
Fériana Tunisia
Ferizaj Ferizaj Kosovo
Ferizli Turkey
Ferjukot Iceland
Ferkessédougou Côte d'Ivoire
Ferla Sicilia Italy
Ferlach Austria
Ferlo, Vallée du watercourse
Senegal
Ferlo-Nord, Réserve de Faune du
nature res. Senegal
Ferlo-Sud, Réserve de Faune du
nature res. Senegal
Fermanagh county Northern
Ireland U.K.
Fermelã Port.
Fermentelos Port.
Fermignano Italy
Fermo Italy
Fermo admin. div. Italy
Fermont Que. Can.
Fermoselle Spain
Fermoy Ireland
Fern, Lough l. Ireland
Fernáncaballero Spain
Fernandina, Isla i. Islas Galápagos
Ecuador
Fernandina Beach FL U.S.A.
Fernando de Magallanes, Parque
Nacional nat. park Chile
Fernando de Noronha i. Brazil
Fernandópolis Brazil
Fernando Poó i. Equat. Guinea
see Bioco
Fernán Núñez Spain
Fernão Dias Brazil
Fernão Veloso Moz.
Fernão Veloso, Baía de b. Moz.
Ferndale MD U.S.A.
Ferndale NY U.S.A.
Ferndale WA U.S.A.
Ferndorf Austria
Ferndown Dorset, England U.K.
Ferness Highland, Scotland U.K.
Ferney-Voltaire France
Fernhill North I. N.Z.
Fernhill Heath Worcestershire,
England U.K.
Fernhurst West Sussex, England U.K.
Fernie B.C. Can.
Fernitz Austria
Fernlee Qld Austr.
Fernley NV U.S.A.
Fernpass pass Austria
Fernridge PA U.S.A.
Ferns Ireland
Fernwood ID U.S.A.
Feroleto Antico Italy
Ferozepore Punjab India see
Firozpur
Ferrals-les-Corbières France
Ferrandina Italy
Ferrara Italy
Ferrara prov. Italy
Ferrarese r. Italy
Ferrato, Capo c. Sardegna Italy
Ferrazzano Italy
Ferré Arg.
Ferreira Spain
Ferreira do Alentejo Port.
Ferreira do Zêzere Port.
Ferreira-Gomes Brazil
Ferreiros Brazil
Ferrel Port.
Ferrellsburg WV U.S.A.
Ferreñafe Peru
Ferreras de Abajo Spain
Ferreras de Arriba Spain
Ferrere Italy
Ferreries Spain
Ferreruela de Huerva Spain
Ferreruela de Tábara Spain
Ferrette France
Ferreyra Arg.
Ferriday LA U.S.A.
Ferriere Italy
Ferrière-la-Grande France
Ferrières Belgium
Ferrières France
Ferrières-St-Mary France
Ferrières-sur-Ariège France
Ferro r. Sicilia Italy
Ferro r. Italy
Ferro, Capo c. Sardegna Italy
Ferro, Ilhéu de i. Madeira
Ferro, Porto b. Sardegna Italy
Ferrol Spain
Ferrol, Ría de inlet Spain
Ferron UT U.S.A.
Ferros Brazil
Ferru, Monte hill Sardegna Italy
Ferruccio, Punta di pt Italy
Ferrum VA U.S.A.
Ferrutx, Cap c. Spain
Ferry AK U.S.A.
Ferrycarrig Ireland
Ferryden Angus, Scotland U.K.
Ferryhill Durham, England U.K.
Ferryland Nfld and Lab. Can.
Ferryville Tunisia see
Menzel Bourguiba
Ferschweiler Ger.
Fershampenuaz Rus. Fed.
Fertilia Sardegna Italy
Fertő l. Austria/Hungary
Fertőd Hungary
Fertőrákos Hungary
Fertőszentmiklós Hungary
Fertőszéplak Hungary
Fertő-tavi nat. park Hungary
Fervença Port.
Fervenza, Encoro da resr Spain
Ferwert Neth.
Ferzikovo Rus. Fed.
Fès Morocco
Feshi Dem. Rep. Congo
Feshiebridge Highland,
Scotland U.K.
Fessenden ND U.S.A.
Fessenheim France
Festieux France
Festre, Col du pass France
Fet Dom, Tanjung pt Papua
Indon.
Fété Bowé Senegal
Feteira Faial Azores
Feteiras São Miguel Azores
Fetești Romania
Fetești-Gară Romania
Fethaland, Point of Scotland U.K.
Fethard Tipperary Ireland
Fethard Wexford Ireland
Fethiye Malatya Turkey see
Yazıhan
Fethiye Muğla Turkey
Fetisovo Kazakh.
Fetlar i. Scotland U.K.
Feto, Capo c. Sicilia Italy
Fettercairn Aberdeenshire,
Scotland U.K.
Feucht Ger.
Feuchtwangen Ger.
Feugarolles France
Feuilles, Rivière aux r. Que. Can.
Feuquières France
Feuquières-en-Vimeu France
Feurs France
Fevral'sk Rus. Fed.
Fevzipaşa Turkey

184 G4 Feytiat France
145 N3 Feyzābād Afgh.
144 F6 Feyzābād Kermān Iran
144 H4 Feyzābād Khorāsān Iran
Fez Morocco see Fès
224 B3 Fezzan reg. Libya
172 E2 Ffestiniog Gwynedd, Wales U.K.
172 D3 Ffostrasol Ceredigion, Wales U.K.
Ffynnon Taf Wales U.K. see
Taff's Well
185 H8 Fiac France
282 D2 Fiambalá Arg.
282 D2 Fiambala r. Arg.
215 K3 Fiamignano Italy
228 E4 Fian Ghana
235 □J4 Fianarantsoa Madag.
235 □J4 Fianarantsoa prov. Madag.
230 B2 Fianga Chad
212 D5 Fiano Italy
215 J3 Fiano Romano Italy
213 O9 Fiastra r. Italy
215 K1 Fiastra, Lago di l. Italy
213 J4 Fiavè Italy
206 E5 Ficalho hill Port.
216 E7 Ficarazzi Sicilia Italy
213 K6 Ficarolo Italy
232 C2 Fichē Eth.
195 L2 Fichtelberg Ger.
193 F10 Fichtelgebirge hills Ger.
193 F10 Fichtelgebirge park Ger.
195 M2 Fichtelnaab r. Ger.
194 H4 Fichtenberg Ger.
237 L4 Ficksburg S. Africa
214 I2 Ficulle Italy
216 G9 Ficuzza r. Sicilia Italy
147 M4 Fidā Oman
147 K6 Fidā' oasis Saudi Arabia
168 J8 Fiddich r. Scotland U.K.
169 H8 Fiddown Ireland
212 I6 Fidenza Italy
164 C3 Fidjeland Norway
198 G2 Fidlův kopec hill Czech Rep.
228 C4 Fié r. Guinea
200 E6 Fiè allo Sciliar Italy
200 G5 Fieberbrunn Austria
215 K1 Fiegni, Monte mt. Italy
246 G5 Field B.C. Can.
251 N3 Field Ont. Can.
256 B12 Field KY U.S.A.
106 D2 Field Island N.T. Austr.
160 J5 Fiemanka r. Latvia
219 N5 Fieni Romania
220 A2 Fier Albania
182 H5 Fier r. France
200 E7 Fiera di Primiero Italy
106 G5 Fiery Creek r. Qld Austr.
218 I8 Fierzës, Liqeni i resr Albania
212 E3 Fiesch Switz.
213 K8 Fiesole Italy
213 L6 Fiesso Umbertiano Italy
168 K10 Fife admin. div. Scotland U.K.
250 I5 Fife Lake MI U.S.A.
168 K10 Fife Ness pt Scotland U.K.
105 K5 Fifield N.S.W. Austr.
250 D4 Fifield WI U.S.A.
Fifth Cataract rapids Sudan see
5th Cataract
246 H3 Fifth Meridian Alta Can.
203 F5 Figalo, Cap c. Alg.
183 I9 Figanières France
214 B2 Figarella r. Corse France
214 C5 Figari Corse France
214 D6 Figari, Capo c. Sardegna Italy
185 I6 Figeac France
213 K8 Figline Valdarno Italy
271 □2 Fig Tree St Kitts and Nevis
206 C4 Figueira r. Port.
204 C8 Figueira da Foz Port.
204 G7 Figueira de Castelo Rodrigo Port.
206 C4 Figueira dos Cavaleiros Port.
206 D2 Figueira e Barros Port.
204 E7 Figueiredo de Alva Port.
206 D1 Figueiró r. Port.
204 F7 Figueiró da Granja Port.
204 D9 Figueiró dos Vinhos Port.
Figueras Spain see Figueres
208 K3 Figueres Spain
204 H5 Figueruela de Arriba Spain
227 E2 Figuig Morocco
229 I4 Figuil Cameroon
150 E9 Fiha al 'Inab reg. Saudi Arabia
235 □J3 Fihaonana Madag.
101 □7 Fiji country S. Pacific Ocean
290 G7 Fiji Islands S. Pacific Ocean
186 F5 Fijnaart Neth.
232 D2 Fīk' Eth.
229 H4 Fika Nigeria
207 N6 Filabres, Sierra de los mts Spain
235 F4 Filabusi Zimbabwe
266 □Q12 Filadelfia Costa Rica
217 K6 Filadelfia Italy
277 E5 Filadelfia Para.
199 I3 Fiľakovo Slovakia
228 D4 Filamana Mali
160 L4 Filatova-Gora Rus. Fed.
212 H7 Filattiera Italy
286 V1 Filchner Ice Shelf Antarctica
215 K4 Filettino Italy
171 Q5 Filey North Yorkshire, England U.K.
151 I4 Filfili Azer.
217 □ Filfla i. Malta
215 P6 Filiano Italy
219 L6 Filiaşi Romania
220 B3 Filiates Greece
220 C5 Filiatra Greece
Filibe Bulg. see Plovdiv
216 H6 Filicudi, Isola i. Isole Lipari Italy
216 H6 Filicudi Porto Isole Lipari Italy
229 F3 Filingué Niger
Filipinas country Asia see
Philippines
197 K1 Filipów Pol.
122 J1 Filippa, Mys hd Rus. Fed.
220 B3 Filippiada Greece
220 F1 Filippoi tourist site Greece
165 K2 Filipstad Sweden
212 H2 Filisur Switz.
162 J5 Fillan Norway
178 D3 Fillièvres France
182 I4 Fillinges France
Fillíra Greece see Fillyra
264 N7 Fillmore CA U.S.A.
265 T3 Fillmore UT U.S.A.
173 I3 Fillongley Warwickshire,
England U.K.
221 G1 Fillyra Greece
269 H8 Filo de los Caballos Mex.
269 J5 Filomeno Mata Mex.
221 G5 Filotio Naxos Greece
213 O9 Filottrano Italy
194 G4 Fils r. Ger.
190 E4 Filsum Ger.
172 G4 Filton South Gloucestershire,
England U.K.
232 D3 Fīltu Eth.
201 I5 Filzmoos Austria
171 P5 Fimber East Riding of Yorkshire,
England U.K.
287 A2 Fimbull Ice Shelf Antarctica
144 D5 Fīn Iran
228 C3 Fina, Réserve de nature res. Mali
216 G7 Finale Sicilia Italy
213 K6 Finale Emilia Italy
212 E7 Finale Ligure Italy
207 N6 Fiñana Spain
168 K9 Finavon Angus, Scotland U.K.
256 F11 Fincastle VA U.S.A.
257 J3 Finch Ont. Can.
232 C2 Finch'a'ā Hāyk' l. Eth.
173 K5 Finchampstead Wokingham,
England U.K.
107 L6 Finch Hatton Qld Austr.
173 M4 Finchingfield Essex, England U.K.
173 I2 Findern Derbyshire, England U.K.
168 I7 Findhorn Moray, Scotland U.K.
168 I7 Findhorn r. Scotland U.K.
149 J5 Fındık Turkey
151 C4 Fındıklı Turkey
256 B7 Findlay OH U.S.A.
168 K7 Findochty Moray, Scotland U.K.
173 L6 Findon West Sussex, England U.K.
257 J4 Fine NY U.S.A.
173 K3 Finedon Northamptonshire,
England U.K.

217 L3 Finese, Monte hill Italy
209 E10 Finestrat Spain
208 J3 Finestres, Serra mts Spain
105 L9 Fingal Tas. Austr.
247 M4 Finger Lake Ont. Can.
256 I6 Finger Lakes NY U.S.A.
138 I9 Fingeshwar Chhattisgarh India
235 F2 Fingoè Moz.
185 G8 Finhan France
183 D8 Finiels, Sommet de mt. France
221 L6 Finike Turkey
221 L6 Finike Körfezi b. Turkey
199 L5 Finiş Romania
180 D5 Finistère dept France
Finisterre Spain see Fisterra
Finisterre, Cabo c. Spain see
Fisterra, Cabo
Finisterre, Cape Spain see
Fisterra, Cabo
205 M9 Finisterre, Embalse de resr Spain
244 G2 Fink Creek AK U.S.A.
106 E8 Finke N.T. Austr.
106 E9 Finke watercourse N.T. Austr.
104 E4 Finke, Mount hill S.A. Austr.
106 F8 Finke Aboriginal Land res.
N.T. Austr.
106 C2 Finke Bay N.T. Austr.
104 E2 Finke Flood Flats lowland
S.A. Austr.
106 D8 Finke Gorge National Park
N.T. Austr.
200 E5 Finkenberg Austria
201 I6 Finkenstein Austria
258 B6 Finksburg MD U.S.A.
162 S5 Finland country Europe
250 C2 Finland MN U.S.A.
160 F2 Finland, Gulf of Europe
246 E3 Finlay r. B.C. Can.
246 E3 Finlay, Mount B.C. Can.
246 F4 Finlay Forks B.C. Can.
250 B3 Finlayson MN U.S.A.
105 J6 Finley N.S.W. Austr.
260 G2 Finley ND U.S.A.
250 E1 Finmark Ont. Can.
169 H3 Finn r. Ireland
165 K1 Finnbodarna Sweden
193 D8 Finne ridge Ger.
169 H5 Finnea Ireland
191 E8 Finnentrop Ger.
165 K3 Finnerödja Sweden
107 J3 Finnigan, Mount Qld Austr.
173 O3 Finningham Suffolk, England U.K.
171 P7 Finningley South Yorkshire,
England U.K.
106 C2 Finniss r. N.T. Austr.
104 E5 Finniss, Cape S.A. Austr.
104 F3 Finnis Springs Aboriginal Land
res. S.A. Austr.
162 R1 Finnmark county Norway
162 Q2 Finnmarksvidda reg. Norway
165 N1 Finnsjön Florarna naturreservat
nature res. Sweden
164 I1 Finnskog Norway
162 N2 Finnsnes Norway
192 I5 Finowfurt Ger.
192 I5 Finowkanal canal Ger.
147 N4 Fins Oman
113 K8 Finschhafen P.N.G.
195 L5 Finsing Ger.
165 L3 Finspång Sweden
212 E2 Finsteraarhorn mt. Switz.
193 I7 Finsterwalde Ger.
186 L2 Finsterwolde Neth.
168 J4 Finstown Orkney, Scotland U.K.
163 O6 Finström Åland Fin.
190 I4 Fintel Ger.
199 K2 Fintice Slovakia
Fîntînele Romania see Fântânele
169 H4 Fintona Northern Ireland U.K.
Fintown Ireland see
Baile na Finne
169 E3 Fintragh Bay Ireland
168 H10 Fintry Stirling, Scotland U.K.
107 H7 Finucane Range hills Qld Austr.
169 C8 Finuge Ireland
169 J2 Finvoy Northern Ireland U.K.
215 J2 Fionchi, Monte mt. Italy
168 F7 Fionn Loch l. Scotland U.K.
168 D10 Fionnphort Argyll and Bute,
Scotland U.K.
214 H3 Fiora r. Italy
213 J6 Fiorano Modense Italy
103 B12 Fiordland National Park
South I. N.Z.
246 D4 Fiordland Provincial Recreation
Area park B.C. Can.
212 H6 Fiorenzuola d'Arda Italy
215 L2 Fiori, Montagna dei mt. Italy
146 G1 Fir reg. Saudi Arabia
221 G6 Fira Greece
140 D2 Fırat r. Turkey
alt. Al Furāt (Iraq/Syria),
conv. Euphrates
235 □J3 Firavahana Madag.
150 C9 Fir'awn, Jazīrat i. Egypt
264 L5 Firebaugh CA U.S.A.
247 J2 Firedrake Lake N.W.T. Can.
245 J3 Fire Island AK U.S.A.
259 I3 Fire Island NY U.S.A.
259 I3 Fire Island National Seashore
nature res. NY U.S.A.
213 K8 Firenze Italy
213 K8 Firenze prov. Italy
213 K7 Firenzuola Italy
251 K1 Fire River Ont. Can.
245 P4 Fireside B.C. Can.
260 G4 Firesteel Creek r. SD U.S.A.
238 □3f Firgas Gran Canaria Canary Is
275 E3 Firiña Venez.
149 L8 Firk, Sha'īb watercourse Iraq
229 I3 Firkachi well Niger
197 K4 Firlej Pol.
285 G3 Firmat Arg.
185 I6 Firmi France
280 B2 Firminópolis Brazil
183 E6 Firminy France
215 Q8 Firmo Italy
Firmum Italy see Fermo
Firmum Picenum Italy see Fermo
195 I4 Firngrund reg. Ger.
161 Q4 Firovo Rus. Fed.
145 N7 Firoz Pak.
138 G6 Firozabad Uttar Prad. India
145 K4 Firozkoh reg. Afgh.
138 F6 Firozpur Haryana India
138 E4 Firozpur Punjab India
190 E4 Firrel Ger.
122 M5 Firsovo Rus. Fed.
First Cataract rapids Egypt see
1st Cataract
257 □N3 First Connecticut Lake NH U.S.A.
245 M1 Firth r. Y.T. Can.
168 □N2 Firth Shetland, Scotland U.K.
144 E7 Fīrūzābād Iran
Firuzabad Iran see Rāsk
144 G3 Fīrūzeh Iran
144 E4 Fīrūz Kūh Iran
208 E2 Fiscal Spain
195 J5 Fischach Ger.
201 O3 Fischamend Markt Austria
201 M5 Fischbach Austria
194 C2 Fischbach Ger.
195 L6 Fischbachau Ger.
194 D3 Fischbach bei Dahn Ger.
201 L5 Fischbacher Alpen mts Austria
192 F5 Fischbeck Ger.
195 I7 Fischen im Allgäu Ger.
234 B5 Fischersbrunn Namibia
234 C6 Fish watercourse Namibia
236 E6 Fish r. S. Africa
171 O4 Fishburn Durham, England U.K.
104 C4 Fisher (abandoned) S.A. Austr.
287 J2 Fisher Bay Antarctica
287 E2 Fisher Glacier Antarctica
247 L5 Fisher River Man. Can.
259 L2 Fishers Island NY U.S.A.
243 J3 Fisher Strait Nunavut Can.
256 G10 Fishersville VA U.S.A.
172 C4 Fishguard Pembrokeshire,
Wales U.K.
172 C3 Fishguard Bay Wales U.K.
245 M2 Fishing Branch Game Reserve
nature res. Y.T. Can.
257 I10 Fishing Creek MD U.S.A.

258 C3 Fishing Creek r. PA U.S.A.
247 M4 Fishing Lake Man. Can.
259 H1 Fishkill NY U.S.A.
259 H2 Fishkill Creek r. NY U.S.A.
246 F2 Fish Lake N.W.T. Can.
245 J2 Fish Lake AK U.S.A.
250 B3 Fish Lake MN U.S.A.
265 U3 Fish Lake UT U.S.A.
251 K6 Fish Point MI U.S.A.
173 M2 Fishtoft Lincolnshire, England U.K.
163 H5 Fiskå Norway
286 T2 Fiske, Cape Antarctica
162 M2 Fiskebøl Norway
Fiskenæsset Greenland see
Qeqertarsuatsiaat
178 G5 Fismes France
204 B3 Fisterra Spain
204 B3 Fisterra, Cabo c. Spain
235 □J4 Fitampito Madag.
257 N6 Fitchburg MA U.S.A.
250 E7 Fitchburg WI U.S.A.
259 K1 Fitchville CT U.S.A.
256 C7 Fitchville OH U.S.A.
205 Q4 Fitero Spain
168 □N3 Fitful Head Scotland U.K.
Fitíai Greece see Fyteies
164 B2 Fitjar Norway
100 □2 Fito, Mount vol. Samoa
185 J10 Fitou France
245 M1 Fitton, Mount Y.T. Can.
276 B2 Fitzcarrald Peru
247 I3 Fitzgerald Alta Can.
255 F10 Fitzgerald GA U.S.A.
109 E12 Fitzgerald River National Park
W.A. Austr.
246 D5 Fitz Hugh Sound sea chan.
B.C. Can.
178 D5 Fitz-James France
106 C3 Fitzmaurice r. N.T. Austr.
283 D7 Fitz Roy Arg.
107 M7 Fitzroy r. Qld Austr.
108 G4 Fitzroy r. W.A. Austr.
283 B8 Fitz Roy, Cerro mt. Arg.
106 C3 Fitzroy Aboriginal Land res.
N.T. Austr.
108 H5 Fitzroy Crossing W.A. Austr.
248 D4 Fitzwilliam Island Ont. Can.
215 K4 Fiuggi Italy
213 J7 Fiumalbo Italy
215 O5 Fiumarella r. Italy
Fiume Croatia see Rijeka
215 Q9 Fiumefreddo Bruzio Italy
217 I8 Fiumefreddo di Sicilia
Sicilia Italy
217 M5 Fiume Nicà, Punta pt Italy
213 N4 Fiume Veneto Italy
214 I4 Fiumicino Italy
214 C4 Fium'Orbo r. Corse France
168 E9 Fiunary Highland, Scotland U.K.
103 A12 Five Fingers Peninsula
South I. N.Z.
103 E12 Five Forks South I. N.Z.
169 H4 Fivemiletown Northern Ireland
U.K.
264 L5 Five Points CA U.S.A.
103 C12 Five Rivers South I. N.Z.
212 I7 Fivizzano Italy
183 D6 Fix-St-Geneys France
231 F6 Fizi Dem. Rep. Congo
Fizuli Azer. see Füzuli
162 N4 Fjällsjönäs Sweden
165 M2 Fjärdhundra reg. Sweden
165 O2 Fjärdlångs naturreservat
nature res. Sweden
192 E1 Fjelde Denmark
164 B1 Fjell Norway
162 N2 Fjellbu Norway
164 F4 Fjerritslev Denmark
226 D2 Fkih Ben Salah Morocco
164 F1 Flå Norway
201 H5 Flachau Austria
195 J3 Flachslanden Ger.
190 D4 Flachsmeer Ger.
168 □N2 Fladdabister Shetland,
Scotland U.K.
164 E6 Fladså r. Denmark
191 J9 Fladungen Ger.
162 □D2 Flaga Iceland
185 I6 Flagnac France
237 N7 Flagstaff S. Africa
265 U6 Flagstaff AZ U.S.A.
238 □2b Flagstaff Bay St Helena
257 □O3 Flagstaff Lake ME U.S.A.
258 F3 Flagtown NJ U.S.A.
248 E1 Flaherty Island Nunavut Can.
182 J4 Flaine France
162 P3 Flakaberg Sweden
163 I6 Flåm Norway
239 □1b Flamand, Île i. Mauritius
180 H2 Flamanville France
219 O3 Flămânzi Romania
250 C4 Flambeau r. WI U.S.A.
171 Q5 Flamborough East Riding of
Yorkshire, England U.K.
171 Q5 Flamborough Head England U.K.
283 E6 Flamenco, Isla i. Arg.
238 □1c Flamengos Faial Azores
208 G3 Flamicell r. Spain
193 F6 Fläming hills Ger.
262 J6 Flaming Gorge Reservoir
WY U.S.A.
236 F6 Flaminksvlei salt pan S. Africa
247 M4 Flanagan r. Ont. Can.
271 □7 Flanagin Town Trin. and Tob.
187 C7 Flanders reg. Europe
259 J3 Flanders NY U.S.A.
178 D2 Flandre reg. France
260 G3 Flandreau SD U.S.A.
230 C5 Flandria Dem. Rep. Congo
256 C11 Flannagan Lake VA U.S.A.
168 A6 Flannan Isles Scotland U.K.
165 K4 Flåren l. Sweden
162 M4 Flåsjön l. Sweden
183 I10 Flassans-sur-Issole France
245 P3 Flat r. N.W.T. Can.
244 H3 Flat AK U.S.A.
250 I7 Flat r. MI U.S.A.
258 F2 Flatbrookville NJ U.S.A.
245 M3 Flat Creek Y.T. Can.
162 □E1 Flateyjardalsheiði reg. Iceland
242 G5 Flathead r. MT U.S.A.
262 G3 Flathead Indian Reservation res.
MT U.S.A.
262 G3 Flathead Lake MT U.S.A.
172 F5 Flat Holm i. Wales U.K.
262 H4 Flatiron mt. ID U.S.A.
239 □1b Flat Island Mauritius
112 E4 Flat Island S. China Sea
256 B12 Flat Lick KY U.S.A.
103 B12 Flat Mountain South I. N.Z.
103 J8 Flat Point North I. N.Z.
200 H6 Flattach Austria
107 J3 Flattery, Cape Qld Austr.
262 B2 Flattery, Cape WA U.S.A.
201 J6 Flattnitz Austria
245 M3 Flat Top mt. Y.T. Can.
255 □1 Flatts Village Bermuda
262 K3 Flatwillow Creek r. MT U.S.A.
256 C10 Flatwoods KY U.S.A.
256 E10 Flatwoods WV U.S.A.
200 D5 Flaurling Austria
164 E2 Flåvatnet l. Norway
179 L6 Flavigny-sur-Moselle France
182 F1 Flavigny-sur-Ozerain France
183 B8 Flavin France
212 G1 Flawil Switz.
200 B5 Flaxenpass pass Austria
245 K1 Flaxman Island AK U.S.A.
183 I9 Flayosc France
269 I1 Flechadores Mex.
193 D6 Flechtingen Ger.
193 D6 Flechtinger Höhenzug park Ger.
190 I2 Fleckeby Ger.
192 G4 Flecken Zechlin Ger.
173 J2 Fleckney Leicestershire,
England U.K.
255 □2 Fleeming Point New Prov.
Bahamas
192 F3 Fleesensee l. Ger.
173 K5 Fleet Hampshire, England U.K.
168 H7 Fleet r. Scotland U.K.
168 H7 Fleet, Loch b. Scotland U.K.
192 D5 Fleetmark Ger.
107 J7 Fleetwood Qld Austr.

171 K6 Fleetwood Lancashire,
England U.K.
258 D4 Fleetwood PA U.S.A.
194 G3 Flein Ger.
164 C3 Flekkefjord Norway
164 E3 Flekkerøy i. Norway
187 H7 Flémalle Belgium
256 B10 Flemingsburg KY U.S.A.
258 F3 Flemington NJ U.S.A.
288 G2 Flemish Cap sea feature
N. Atlantic Ocean
173 N3 Flempton Suffolk, England U.K.
165 M2 Flen Sweden
190 I1 Flensborg Fjord inlet
Denmark/Ger.
190 H1 Flensburg Ger.
Flensburger Förde inlet
Denmark/Ger. see
Flensborg Fjord
187 I7 Fléron Belgium
181 J4 Flers France
251 N5 Flesherton Ont. Can.
115 D3 Flesko, Tanjung pt Indon.
192 E5 Flessau Ger.
247 I2 Fletcher Lake N.W.T. Can.
286 S2 Fletcher Peninsula Antarctica
251 K5 Fletcher Pond l. MI U.S.A.
185 F8 Fleurance France
249 J3 Fleur de Lys Nfld and Lab. Can.
249 H3 Fleur-de-May, Lac l. Nfld and Lab.
Can.
184 F3 Fleuré France
182 F4 Fleurie France
212 B2 Fleurier Switz.
187 G8 Fleurus Belgium
183 C10 Fleury France
178 C8 Fleury-les-Aubrais France
178 B5 Fleury-sur-Andelle France
181 K3 Fleury-sur-Orne France
179 K5 Fléville-Lixières France
186 H4 Flevoland prov. Neth.
172 C6 Flexbury Cornwall, England U.K.
191 I10 Flieden Ger.
200 C5 Fließ Austria
171 J4 Flimby Cumbria, England U.K.
212 G2 Flims Switz.
173 M5 Flimwell East Sussex,
England U.K.
107 H4 Flinders r. Qld Austr.
109 C13 Flinders Bay W.A. Austr.
104 F6 Flinders Chase National Park
S.A. Austr.
107 J3 Flinders Group is Qld Austr.
107 J3 Flinders Group National Park
Qld Austr.
104 E5 Flinders Island S.A. Austr.
105 L8 Flinders Island Tas. Austr.
107 L5 Flinders Passage Qld Austr.
104 F5 Flinders Ranges mts S.A. Austr.
104 G4 Flinders Ranges National Park
S.A. Austr.
107 L4 Flinders Reefs Coral Sea Is Terr.
Austr.
178 F3 Flines-lez-Raches France
247 K4 Flin Flon Man. Can.
172 F1 Flint Flintshire, Wales U.K.
251 K6 Flint MI U.S.A.
255 E10 Flint r. GA U.S.A.
251 K6 Flint r. MI U.S.A.
190 J2 Flintbek Ger.
291 I6 Flint Island Kiribati
107 L9 Flinton Qld Austr.
172 F1 Flintshire admin. div. Wales U.K.
256 G9 Flintstone MD U.S.A.
179 K6 Flirey France
200 B5 Flirsch Austria
164 I1 Flisa Norway
163 L6 Flisa r. Norway
164 D2 Fliseggi mt. Norway
173 L3 Flitwick Bedfordshire,
England U.K.
208 G5 Flix Spain
208 G5 Flix, Pantà de resr Spain
178 D3 Flixecourt France
178 I4 Flize France
164 I4 Floda Sweden
171 M2 Flodden Northumberland,
England U.K.
178 G8 Flogny-la-Chapelle France
193 H9 Flöha Ger.
193 H9 Flöha r. Ger.
179 I4 Floing France
185 C6 Floirac France
286 P1 Flood Range mts Antarctica
250 B3 Floodwood MN U.S.A.
171 L5 Flookburgh Cumbria,
England U.K.
106 C3 Flora r. N.T. Austr.
250 H9 Flora IN U.S.A.
183 D8 Florac France
255 D10 Florala AL U.S.A.
179 L5 Florange France
107 K4 Flora Reef Coral Sea Is Terr. Austr.
106 G5 Floraville Qld Austr.
274 C6 Flor de Punga Peru
187 G8 Floreffe Belgium
251 L7 Florence Ont. Can.
Florence Italy see Firenze
255 D8 Florence AL U.S.A.
265 U8 Florence AZ U.S.A.
263 L7 Florence CO U.S.A.
260 G6 Florence KS U.S.A.
258 F4 Florence NJ U.S.A.
262 B5 Florence OR U.S.A.
255 H8 Florence SC U.S.A.
250 F4 Florence WI U.S.A.
265 U8 Florence Junction AZ U.S.A.
257 □R2 Florenceville N.B. Can.
282 E2 Florencia Formosa Arg.
282 F3 Florencia Santa Fé Arg.
274 C4 Florencia Col.
285 I3 Florencio Sánchez Uru.
187 G8 Florennes Belgium
183 C10 Florensac France
Florentia Italy see Firenze
283 D6 Florentino Ameghino Arg.
283 D6 Florentino Ameghino, Embalse
resr Arg.
187 H9 Florenville Belgium
285 H4 Flores r. Arg.
238 □1 Flores i. Azores
278 F3 Flores Pernambuco Brazil
278 E3 Flores Piauí Brazil
267 O9 Flores Guat.
115 B8 Flores i. Indon.
285 I3 Flores dept Uru.
115 A7 Flores, Laut sea Indon.
276 C2 Florescência Brazil
205 J7 Flores de Ávila Spain
278 D5 Flores de Goiás Brazil
Floreshty Moldova see Florești
246 E5 Flores Island B.C. Can.
Flores Sea Indon. see Flores, Laut
278 F4 Floresta Brazil
216 H8 Floresta Sicilia Italy
158 H6 Florești Moldova
280 B5 Florestópolis Brazil
261 F11 Floresville TX U.S.A.
259 G3 Florham Park NJ U.S.A.
278 E3 Floriano Brazil
276 D2 Floriano Peixoto Brazil
279 C8 Florianópolis Brazil
276 E4 Florida Bol.
284 A5 Florida Chile
270 D3 Florida Cuba
271 □1 Florida Puerto Rico
285 I4 Florida Uru.
285 I4 Florida dept Uru.
259 G2 Florida NY U.S.A.
255 F10 Florida state U.S.A.
255 G14 Florida, Straits of
Bahamas/U.S.A.
255 G13 Florida Bay FL U.S.A.
204 I6 Florida de Liébana Spain
100 □6 Florida Islands Solomon Is
255 G13 Florida Keys is FL U.S.A.
283 D8 Florida Negra Arg.
280 B4 Flórida Paulista Brazil
217 I9 Floridia Sicilia Italy
261 C12 Florido r. Mex.
219 L3 Florii, Vârful hill Romania
264 K3 Florin CA U.S.A.
220 C2 Florina Greece
214 B6 Florinas Sardegna Italy

280 B5 Florínia Brazil
236 F9 Floriskraaldam l. S. Africa
260 J6 Florissant MO U.S.A.
163 H6 Florø Norway
191 H10 Flörsbach Ger.
191 F10 Flörsheim am Main Ger.
194 E2 Flörsheim-Dalsheim Ger.
191 G10 Florstadt Ger.
195 M2 Floß Ger.
195 M2 Flossenbürg Ger.
168 J5 Flotta i. Scotland U.K.
185 I9 Floure France
249 H2 Flour Lake Nfld and Lab. Can.
250 B6 Floyd IA U.S.A.
256 E12 Floyd VA U.S.A.
265 T6 Floyd, Mount AZ U.S.A.
261 E9 Floydada TX U.S.A.
200 B6 Fluchthorn mt. Austria/Switz.
212 H2 Flüelapass pass Switz.
212 F2 Flüelen Switz.
186 I3 Fluessen l. Neth.
212 E2 Flühli Switz.
115 E4 Fluk Maluku Indon.
208 E4 Flúmen r. Spain
214 D9 Flumendosa r. Sardegna Italy
215 O5 Flumeri Italy
182 J5 Flumet France
214 D7 Flumineddu r. Sardegna Italy
214 C8 Flumineddu r. Italy
214 B9 Fluminimaggiore Sardegna Italy
212 G1 Flums Switz.
Flushing Neth. see Vlissingen
256 B5 Flushing MI U.S.A.
256 D8 Flushing OH U.S.A.
214 B7 Flussio Sardegna Italy
113 J8 Fly r. P.N.G.
286 R2 Flying Fish, Cape Antarctica
108 □1 Flying Fish Cove Christmas I.
106 E3 Flying Fox Creek r. N.T. Austr.
101 □8 Foa i. Tonga
247 K5 Foam Lake Sask. Can.
212 E4 Fobello Italy
210 G4 Foča Bos.-Herz.
221 H4 Foça Turkey
187 H8 Focant Belgium
213 M5 Focce dell'Adige r. mouth Italy
168 J7 Fochabers Moray, Scotland U.K.
237 L2 Fochville S. Africa
190 I2 Fockbek Ger.
219 P5 Focșani Romania
219 P3 Focuri Romania
230 D3 Fodé C.A.R.
228 C4 Fodékaria Guinea
181 P7 Foëcy France
106 F3 Foelsche r. N.T. Austr.
131 I7 Fogang Guangdong China
106 C2 Fog Bay N.T. Austr.
258 D3 Fogelsville PA U.S.A.
227 F4 Foggâret el Arab Alg.
227 F4 Foggâret ez Zoûa Alg.
215 P5 Foggia Italy
215 P5 Foggia prov. Italy
214 A7 Foghe, Punta di pt Sardegna Italy
115 E5 Fogi Buru Indon.
213 N8 Foglia r. Italy
215 J5 Fogliano, Lago di lag. Italy
163 P6 Föglö Åland Fin.
228 □ Fogo i. Cape Verde
249 K3 Fogo Island Nfld and Lab. Can.
201 K5 Fohnsdorf Austria
190 G1 Föhr i. Ger.
193 F6 Fohrde Ger.
194 B2 Föhren Ger.
206 B6 Fóia hill Port.
213 L9 Foiano della Chiana Italy
199 L4 Foieni Romania
169 B9 Foilclogh hill Ireland
168 G6 Foinaven hill Scotland U.K.
185 H10 Foix France
185 G10 Foix reg. France
208 I5 Foix r. Spain
156 K4 Foki Rus. Fed.
161 R8 Fokino Rus. Fed.
229 G4 Fokku Nigeria
199 H5 Foktő Hungary
164 D1 Folarskarnuten mt. Norway
162 M3 Folda sea chan. Norway
199 J5 Földeák Hungary
162 L4 Foldereid Norway
199 K4 Földes Hungary
162 K4 Foldfjorden sea chan. Norway
220 F6 Folegandros Greece
220 F6 Folegandros i. Greece
235 E4 Foley Botswana
255 D10 Foley AL U.S.A.
260 I3 Foley MN U.S.A.
248 D3 Foleyet Ont. Can.
243 K3 Foley Island Nunavut Can.
107 L7 Foleyvale Qld Austr.
Folgares Angola see Capelongo
213 K4 Folgaria Italy
244 H3 Folger AK U.S.A.
287 H2 Folger, Cape Antarctica
204 F3 Folgoso de Courel Spain
204 H3 Folgoso de la Ribera Spain
215 L2 Folignano Italy
215 J2 Foligno Italy
173 O5 Folkestone Kent, England U.K.
173 L2 Folkingham Lincolnshire,
England U.K.
255 F10 Folkston GA U.S.A.
163 K5 Folldal Norway
213 M4 Follina Italy
162 M5 Föllinge Sweden
214 F2 Follonica Italy
214 F2 Follonica, Golfo di b. Italy
164 F2 Follsjå l. Norway
172 D6 Folly Gate Devon, England U.K.
179 M5 Folschviller France
256 E9 Folsom WV U.S.A.
264 K3 Folsom Lake CA U.S.A.
239 □3 Fomboni Mwali Comoros
270 D2 Fomento Cuba
157 H7 Fomin Rus. Fed.
156 H5 Fominki Rus. Fed.
156 J2 Fominskaya Rus. Fed.
156 J3 Fominskiy Rus. Fed.
156 H4 Fominskoye Rus. Fed.
217 □ Fomm ir-Riħ, Il-Bajja ta' b. Malta
205 N3 Foncea hill Spain
257 K6 Fonda NY U.S.A.
247 J3 Fond-du-Lac Sask. Can.
247 J3 Fond du Lac r. Sask. Can.
250 F6 Fond du Lac WI U.S.A.
250 B3 Fond du Lac Indian Reservation
res. MN U.S.A.
239 □1b Fond du Sac Mauritius
256 B12 Fonde KY U.S.A.
204 D5 Fondevila Spain
215 K5 Fondi Italy
215 K5 Fondi, Lago di l. Italy
207 N7 Fondón Spain
207 M6 Fonelas Spain
208 C5 Fonfría Aragón Spain
204 H5 Fonfría Castilla y León Spain
228 C4 Fon Going ridge Guinea
214 C7 Fonni Sardegna Italy
185 E6 Fonroque France
Fonsagrada Spain see
A Fonsagrada
274 C2 Fonseca Col.
266 □O11 Fonseca, Golfo do b.
Central America
185 G8 Fonsorbes France
179 M8 Fontaine Franche-Comté France
183 H6 Fontaine Rhône-Alpes France
178 E7 Fontainebleau France
182 G1 Fontaine-Française France
247 J3 Fontaine Lake Sask. Can.
178 B4 Fontaine-le-Bourg France
181 M2 Fontaine-le-Dun France
182 G2 Fontaine-lès-Dijon France
179 L8 Fontaine-lès-Luxeuil France
187 F8 Fontaine-l'Évêque Belgium
182 F3 Fontaines Bourgogne France
178 F8 Fontaines Bourgogne France
183 L8 Fontan France
258 C4 Fontana PA U.S.A.
205 N7 Fontanar Spain
207 J2 Fontanarejo Spain
212 I6 Fontanellato Italy
215 L5 Fontanelle r. Italy
183 E9 Fontanès France
249 G2 Fontanges Que. Can.

212 G6 Fontanigorda Italy
183 C6 Fontannes France
207 J3 Fontanosas Spain
246 F3 Fontas B.C. Can.
246 F3 Fontas r. B.C. Can.
Font Blanca, Pic de mt.
France/Spain see Port, Pic du
275 E5 Fonte Boa Brazil
215 L3 Fontecchio Italy
215 K3 Fontecellese, Monte mt. Italy
204 D3 Fonte Díaz Spain
238 □1a Fonte do Bastardo Terceira Azores
277 F3 Fonte do Pau-d'Agua Brazil
229 H5 Fontem Cameroon
184 C3 Fontenay-le-Comte France
178 E6 Fontenay-Trésigny France
249 I3 Fonteneau, Lac l. Que. Can.
182 C1 Fontenoy France
179 L8 Fontenoy-le-Château France
179 K6 Fontenoy-sur-Moselle France
204 D9 Fontes Port.
181 L7 Fontevraud-l'Abbaye France
181 M8 Fontgombault France
213 K4 Fonti, Cima mt. Italy
238 □1a Fontinhas Terceira Azores
205 K7 Fontiveros Spain
179 K5 Fontoy France
185 I10 Font-Romeu-Odeillo-Via France
183 J7 Font Sancte, Pic de la mt. France
169 I6 Fontstown Ireland
162 □F1 Fontur pt Iceland
183 F9 Fontvieille France
Fonuafo'ou i. Tonga see
Fonuafu'u
101 □8 Fonuafu'u i. Tonga
103 □4 Fonuakula Niue
99 I3 Fonualei i. Tonga
100 □4a Fonuchu i. Chuuk Micronesia
199 G5 Fonyód Hungary
208 F3 Fonz Spain
213 L3 Fonzaso Italy
Foochow Fujian China see
Fuzhou
265 T2 Fool Creek Reservoir UT U.S.A.
251 O4 Foot's Bay Ont. Can.
130 G2 Foping Shaanxi China
212 H3 Foppolo Italy
206 □ Fora, Ilhéu de i. Madeira
245 J3 Foraker, Mount AK U.S.A.
215 J3 Forano Italy
144 F4 Forat Iran
209 D9 Forata, Embalse de resr Spain
Foraulep atoll Micronesia see
Faraulep
179 M5 Forbach France
194 E4 Forbach Ger.
105 L5 Forbes N.S.W. Austr.
246 G4 Forbes, Mount Alta Can.
103 A12 Forbes, Mount South I. N.Z.
139 K6 Forbesganj Bihar India
237 P2 Forbes Reef Swaziland
183 I10 Forcalcueiret France
208 E6 Forcall Spain
183 H9 Forcalquier France
204 D3 Forcarei Spain
Forcary Spain see Forcarei
215 K2 Force Italy
194 D5 Forchheim Baden-Württemberg
Ger.
195 K2 Forchheim Bayern Ger.
194 H3 Forchtenberg Ger.
201 N4 Forchtenstein Austria
212 C3 Forclaz, Col de la pass Switz.
249 H1 Ford r. Que. Can.
168 F10 Ford Argyll and Bute, Scotland U.K.
171 M2 Ford Northumberland,
England U.K.
250 G4 Ford r. MI U.S.A.
106 B2 Ford, Cape N.T. Austr.
264 M6 Ford City CA U.S.A.
256 F8 Ford City PA U.S.A.
164 B2 Førde Hordaland Norway
163 H6 Førde Sogn og Fjordane Norway
247 L2 Forde Lake Nunavut Can.
102 J6 Fordell North I. N.Z.
193 E7 Förderstedt Ger.
173 M3 Fordham Cambridgeshire,
England U.K.
173 I6 Fordingbridge Hampshire,
England U.K.
214 B8 Fordongianus Sardegna Italy
168 L9 Fordoun Aberdeenshire,
Scotland U.K.
286 O1 Ford Range mts Antarctica
259 G3 Fords NJ U.S.A.
105 J3 Fords Bridge N.S.W. Austr.
169 I5 Fordstown Ireland
168 K7 Fordyce Aberdeenshire,
Scotland U.K.
261 I9 Fordyce AR U.S.A.
228 B4 Forécariah Guinea
243 O3 Forel, Mont mt. Greenland
173 J6 Foreland hd England U.K.
172 E5 Foreland Point England U.K.
261 H9 Foreman AR U.S.A.
247 I5 Foremost Alta Can.
215 P6 Forenza Italy
246 E4 Foresight Mountain B.C. Can.
248 D5 Forest Ont. Can.
261 K9 Forest MS U.S.A.
256 B8 Forest OH U.S.A.
256 F11 Forest VA U.S.A.
247 H4 Forestburg Alta Can.
258 F1 Forestburg NY U.S.A.
258 E1 Forest City PA U.S.A.
107 H5 Forest Creek r. Qld Austr.
105 K6 Forest Hill N.S.W. Austr.
107 J8 Forest Hill Qld Austr.
264 L2 Foresthill CA U.S.A.
105 L10 Forestier Peninsula Tas. Austr.
250 F5 Forest Junction WI U.S.A.
250 B4 Forest Lake MN U.S.A.
265 V7 Forest Lakes AZ U.S.A.
255 E9 Forest Park GA U.S.A.
264 K2 Forest Ranch CA U.S.A.
173 M5 Forest Row East Sussex,
England U.K.
249 G3 Forestville Que. Can.
264 J3 Forestville CA U.S.A.
258 B7 Forestville MD U.S.A.
251 L6 Forestville MI U.S.A.
256 F6 Forestville NY U.S.A.
164 B2 Føresvik Norway
228 E4 Forêt des Deux Balé nat. park
Burkina
229 F5 Forêt de Togodo nature res. Togo
178 H7 Forêt d'Orient, Parc Naturel
Régional de la nature res. France
182 D5 Forez, Monts du mts France
182 D5 Forez, Plaine du plain France
168 K9 Forfar Angus, Scotland U.K.
261 E7 Forgan OK U.S.A.
178 C4 Forges-les-Eaux France
195 J6 Forggensee l. Ger.
168 J7 Forgie Moray, Scotland U.K.
249 H3 Forillon, Parc National de
nat. park Que. Can.
215 N6 Forino Italy
215 L6 Forio Italy
193 D10 Föritz Ger.
204 C5 Forjães Port.
258 C6 Fork MD U.S.A.
261 K8 Forked Deer r. TN U.S.A.
257 K9 Forked River NJ U.S.A.
169 J4 Forkhill Northern Ireland U.K.
262 B3 Forks WA U.S.A.
258 C1 Forkston PA U.S.A.
258 B1 Forksville PA U.S.A.
256 G11 Fork Union VA U.S.A.
162 Forlandet Nasjonalpark nat. park
Svalbard
162 □ Forlandsundet str. Svalbard
213 M7 Forlì Italy
213 M8 Forlì-Cesena prov. Italy
213 M7 Forlimpopoli Italy
260 G2 Forman ND U.S.A.
212 E3 Formazza Italy
171 K6 Formby Merseyside, England U.K.
209 H10 Formentera i. Spain
209 L8 Formentor, Cap de c. Spain
178 C4 Formerie France
Former Yugoslav Republic of
Macedonia country Europe see
Macedonia

215 L5 **Formia** Italy
209 D7 **Formiche Alto** Spain
214 F2 **Formiche di Grosseto** *is* Italy
215 M5 **Formicola** Italy
281 E4 **Formiga** Brazil
213 J6 **Formigine** Italy
213 L6 **Formignana** Italy
185 I10 **Formiguères** France
282 F2 **Formosa** Arg.
282 F2 **Formosa** *prov.* Arg.
Formosa *country* Asia *see* **Taiwan**
279 D5 **Formosa** Brazil
206 D7 **Formosa, Ria** *lag.* Port.
277 G3 **Formosa, Serra** *hills* Brazil
278 D4 **Formosa do Rio Preto** Brazil
Formosa Strait China/Taiwan *see* **Taiwan Strait**
204 C8 **Formoselha** Port.
280 A4 **Formoso** *Mato Grosso do Sul* Brazil
278 D5 **Formoso** *Minas Gerais* Brazil
278 C4 **Formoso** *Tocantins* Brazil
280 A3 **Formoso** *r.* Brazil
278 C4 **Formoso** *r.* Brazil
278 D5 **Formoso** *r.* Brazil
169 D6 **Formoyle** Ireland
164 G5 **Fornæs** *c.* Denmark
214 A5 **Fornelli** *Sardegna* Italy
208 □ **Fornells** Spain
208 K4 **Fornells de la Selva** Spain
213 N2 **Forni Avoltri** Italy
213 N3 **Forni di Sopra** Italy
213 N3 **Forni di Sotto** Italy
212 C5 **Forno Alpi Graie** Italy
200 F7 **Forno di Zoldo** Italy
235 G4 **Fornos** Moz.
204 G6 **Fornos** Port.
204 E7 **Fornos de Algodres** Port.
212 I6 **Fornovo di Taro** Italy
215 M3 **Foro** *r.* Italy
162 K5 **Forolshogna** *mt.* Norway
159 M9 **Foros** Ukr.
206 C3 **Foros de Vale Figueira** Port.
206 C2 **Foros do Arrão** Port.
Føroyar *terr.* N. Atlantic Ocean *see* **Faroe Islands**
199 I5 **Forráskút** Hungary
168 I7 **Forres** *Moray, Scotland* U.K.
109 J11 **Forrest** *W.A.* Austr.
108 J3 **Forrest** *r. W.A.* Austr.
250 F9 **Forrest** *IL* U.S.A.
286 U1 **Forrestal Range** *mts* Antarctica
261 J8 **Forrest City** *AR* U.S.A.
245 N5 **Forrester Island** *AK* U.S.A.
247 I3 **Forrest Lake** *Sask.* Can.
109 J10 **Forrest Lakes** *salt flat W.A.* Austr.
250 E7 **Forreston** *IL* U.S.A.
Forrest River Mission *W.A.* Austr. *see* **Oombulgurri**
199 K3 **Forró** Hungary
184 D3 **Fors** France
164 C3 **Forsand** Norway
107 I5 **Forsayth** *Qld* Austr.
162 N2 **Forsbakken** Norway
172 H2 **Forsbrook** *Staffordshire, England* U.K.
164 J2 **Forshaga** Sweden
168 I6 **Forsinard** *Highland, Scotland* U.K.
162 O3 **Forsnäs** Sweden
163 Q6 **Forssa** Fin.
194 F3 **Forst** *Baden-Württemberg* Ger.
193 K7 **Forst** *Brandenburg* Ger.
105 N5 **Forster** *N.S.W.* Austr.
195 L5 **Forstern** Ger.
195 L5 **Forstinning** Ger.
255 F9 **Forsyth** *GA* U.S.A.
261 I7 **Forsyth** *MO* U.S.A.
262 K3 **Forsyth** *MT* U.S.A.
251 R1 **Forsythe** *Que.* Can.
103 I7 **Forsyth Island** *South I.* N.Z.
106 G4 **Forsyth Islands** *Qld* Austr.
107 I7 **Forsyth Range** *hills Qld* Austr.
145 O7 **Fort Abbas** Pak.
248 D2 **Fort Albany** *Ont.* Can.
276 D2 **Fortaleza** *Pando* Bol.
276 D3 **Fortaleza** *Pando* Bol.
278 F2 **Fortaleza** Brazil
282 G4 **Fortaleza de Santa Teresa** Uru.
208 D6 **Fortanete** Spain
265 V8 **Fort Apache Indian Reservation** *res. AZ* U.S.A.
Fort Archambault Chad *see* **Sarh**
256 G9 **Fort Ashby** *WV* U.S.A.
246 H4 **Fort Assiniboine** *Alta* Can.
250 F7 **Fort Atkinson** *WI* U.S.A.
168 G8 **Fort Augustus** *Highland, Scotland* U.K.
246 E4 **Fort Babine** B.C. Can.
237 K8 **Fort Beaufort** S. Africa
262 J2 **Fort Belknap Indian Reservation** *res. MT* U.S.A.
262 I3 **Fort Benton** *MT* U.S.A.
260 D2 **Fort Berthold Indian Reservation** *res. ND* U.S.A.
247 J4 **Fort Black** *Sask.* Can.
264 I2 **Fort Bragg** *CA* U.S.A.
Fort Carillon *NY* U.S.A. *see* **Ticonderoga**
Fort Carnot Madag. *see* **Ikongo**
Fort Charlet Alg. *see* **Djanet**
Fort Chimo *Que.* Can. *see* **Kuujjuaq**
247 I3 **Fort Chipewyan** *Alta* Can.
262 L6 **Fort Collins** *CO* U.S.A.
107 H6 **Fort Constantine** *Qld* Austr.
248 E4 **Fort-Coulonge** *Que.* Can.
257 K4 **Fort Covington** *NY* U.S.A.
Fort Crampel C.A.R. *see* **Kaga Bandoro**
Fort-Dauphin Madag. *see* **Tôlañaro**
261 D10 **Fort Davis** *TX* U.S.A.
271 □3 **Fort-de-France** Martinique
271 □3 **Fort-de-France, Baie de** *b.* Martinique
Fort de Kock *Sumatera* Indon. *see* **Bukittinggi**
Fort de Polignac Alg. *see* **Illizi**
255 D9 **Fort Deposit** *AL* U.S.A.
260 H4 **Fort Dodge** *IA* U.S.A.
237 N6 **Fort Donald** S. Africa
265 W1 **Fort Duchesne** *UT* U.S.A.
214 A6 **Forte, Monte** *hill* Italy
257 L5 **Fort Edward** *NY* U.S.A.
231 D6 **Forte Nordeste** Angola
251 P7 **Fort Erie** *Ont.* Can.
108 D6 **Fortescue** *r. W.A.* Austr.
258 E6 **Fortescue** *NJ* U.S.A.
275 H6 **Forte Veneza** Brazil
213 L2 **Fortezza** Italy
214 E3 **Fortezza, Monte della** *hill* Italy
257 □R2 **Fort Fairfield** *ME* U.S.A.
Fort Flatters Alg. *see* **Bordj Omer Driss**
Fort Foureau Cameroon *see* **Kousséri**
250 A1 **Fort Frances** *Ont.* Can.
Fort Franklin *N.W.T.* Can. *see* **Déline**
255 E10 **Fort Gaines** *GA* U.S.A.
Fort Gardel Alg. *see* **Zaouatallaz**
263 L8 **Fort Garland** *CO* U.S.A.
256 C10 **Fort Gay** *WV* U.S.A.
Fort George *Que.* Can. *see* **Chisasibi**
261 H8 **Fort Gibson Lake** *OK* U.S.A.
244 F5 **Fort Glenn** *AK* U.S.A.
245 O2 **Fort Good Hope** *N.W.T.* Can.
Fort Gouraud Maur. *see* **Fdérik**
168 I11 **Forth** *South Lanarkshire, Scotland* U.K.
166 F3 **Forth** *r. Scotland* U.K.
168 J10 **Forth, Firth of** *est. Scotland* U.K.
Fort Hall Kenya *see* **Murang'a**
262 H5 **Fort Hall Indian Reservation** *res. ID* U.S.A.
263 L11 **Fort Hancock** *TX* U.S.A.
237 K8 **Fort Hare** S. Africa
Fort Hertz Myanmar *see* **Putao**
265 R3 **Fortification Range** *mts NV* U.S.A.
269 K7 **Fortín** Mex.
277 E5 **Fortín Aroma** Para.
277 E5 **Fortín Ávalos Sánchez** Para.
277 F5 **Fortín Boquerón** Para.
277 E5 **Fortín Capitán Demattei** Para.
277 F5 **Fortín Carlos Antonio López** Para.
277 F5 **Fortín Coronel Bogado** Para.
277 E5 **Fortín Coronel Eugenio Garay** Para.
168 H9 **Fortingall** *Perth and Kinross, Scotland* U.K.
277 F4 **Fortín Galpón** Para.
277 F6 **Fortín General Caballero** Para.
277 F5 **Fortín General Díaz** Para.
277 E5 **Fortín General Díaz** Para.
277 E5 **Fortín General Mendoza** Para.
277 E5 **Fortín Hernandarías** Para.
277 E5 **Fortín Infante Rivarola** Para.
277 F5 **Fortín Juan de Zalazar** Para.
277 E5 **Fortín Lagerenza** Para.
282 E2 **Fortín Lavalle** Arg.
277 E5 **Fortín Leonardo Britos** Para.
277 E5 **Fortín Leonida Escobar** Para.
277 E5 **Fortín Linares** Para.
277 F5 **Fortín Madrejón** Para.
277 E5 **Fortín May Alberto Gardel** Para.
277 E5 **Fortín Nueva Asunción** Para.
285 F4 **Fortín Olavarría** Arg.
282 E1 **Fortín Pilcomayo** Arg.
277 F5 **Fortín Presidente Ayala** Para.
277 E4 **Fortín Ravelo** Bol.
282 F2 **Fortín Sargento Primero Leyes** Arg.
277 E4 **Fortín Suárez Arana** Bol.
277 E5 **Fortín Teniente Juan Echauri López** Para.
277 F5 **Fortín Teniente Mountania** Para.
277 F4 **Fortín Teniente Primero H. Mendoza** Para.
277 E6 **Fortín Teniente Rojas Silva** Para.
284 E6 **Fortín Uno** Arg.
206 E2 **Fortios** Port.
Fort Jameson Zambia *see* **Chipata**
Fort Johnston Malawi *see* **Mangochi**
257 □Q1 **Fort Kent** *ME* U.S.A.
262 D5 **Fort Klamath** *OR* U.S.A.
Fort Lamy *Chari-Baguirmi* Chad *see* **Ndjamena**
Fort Laperrine Alg. *see* **Tamanrasset**
262 L5 **Fort Laramie** *WY* U.S.A.
255 G12 **Fort Lauderdale** *FL* U.S.A.
259 H3 **Fort Lee** *NJ* U.S.A.
246 F2 **Fort Liard** *N.W.T.* Can.
270 H4 **Fort-Liberté** Haiti
256 H9 **Fort Loudon** *PA* U.S.A.
247 I3 **Fort Mackay** *Alta* Can.
246 H5 **Fort Macleod** *Alta* Can.
250 C9 **Fort Madison** *IA* U.S.A.
178 C3 **Fort-Mahon-Plage** France
Fort Manning Malawi *see* **Mchinji**
250 D5 **Fort McCoy** *WI* U.S.A.
247 I3 **Fort McMurray** *Alta* Can.
245 N2 **Fort McPherson** *N.W.T.* Can.
259 H2 **Fort Montgomery** *NY* U.S.A.
260 D5 **Fort Morgan** *CO* U.S.A.
237 O5 **Fort Mtombeni** S. Africa
145 N7 **Fort Munro** Pak.
255 G12 **Fort Myers** *FL* U.S.A.
246 F3 **Fort Nelson** B.C. Can.
246 F3 **Fort Nelson** *r.* B.C. Can.
245 P2 **Fort Norman** *N.W.T.* Can.
Fort Orange *NY* U.S.A. *see* **Albany**
215 O4 **Fortore** *r.* Italy
255 E8 **Fort Payne** *AL* U.S.A.
262 K2 **Fort Peck** *MT* U.S.A.
262 L2 **Fort Peck Indian Reservation** *res. MT* U.S.A.
262 K3 **Fort Peck Reservoir** *MT* U.S.A.
255 G12 **Fort Pierce** *FL* U.S.A.
260 E3 **Fort Pierre** *SD* U.S.A.
232 A4 **Fort Portal** Uganda
246 G2 **Fort Providence** *N.W.T.* Can.
247 K5 **Fort Qu'Appelle** *Sask.* Can.
256 A8 **Fort Recovery** *OH* U.S.A.
246 H2 **Fort Resolution** *N.W.T.* Can.
235 F3 **Fort Rixon** Zimbabwe
103 C13 **Fortrose** *South I.* N.Z.
168 H7 **Fortrose** *Highland, Scotland* U.K.
Fort Rosebery Zambia *see* **Mansa**
Fort Rousset Congo *see* **Owando**
Fort Rupert *Que.* Can. *see* **Waskaganish**
246 E4 **Fort St James** B.C. Can.
246 F3 **Fort St John** B.C. Can.
Fort Sandeman Pak. *see* **Zhob**
246 H4 **Fort Saskatchewan** *Alta* Can.
261 H7 **Fort Scott** *KS* U.S.A.
248 C1 **Fort Severn** *Ont.* Can.
142 D5 **Fort-Shevchenko** Kazakh.
246 F2 **Fort Simpson** *N.W.T.* Can.
247 H2 **Fort Smith** *N.W.T.* Can.
261 H8 **Fort Smith** *AR* U.S.A.
262 K4 **Fort Smith** *MT* U.S.A.
261 D10 **Fort Stockton** *TX* U.S.A.
263 L9 **Fort Sumner** *NM* U.S.A.
261 F7 **Fort Supply** *OK* U.S.A.
265 W8 **Fort Thomas** *AZ* U.S.A.
260 F2 **Fort Totten (Devils Lake Sioux) Indian Reservation** *res. ND* U.S.A.
Fort Trinquet Maur. *see* **Bîr Mogreïn**
209 C11 **Fortuna** Spain
262 B6 **Fortuna** *CA* U.S.A.
260 D1 **Fortuna** *ND* U.S.A.
249 K4 **Fortune Bay** *Nfld and Lab.* Can.
172 H6 **Fortuneswell** *Dorset, England* U.K.
255 F9 **Fort Valley** *GA* U.S.A.
246 G3 **Fort Vermilion** *Alta* Can.
Fort Victoria Zimbabwe *see* **Masvingo**
Fort Walton *FL* U.S.A. *see* **Fort Walton Beach**
255 D10 **Fort Walton Beach** *FL* U.S.A.
Fort Ware B.C. Can. *see* **Ware**
258 E4 **Fort Washington** *PA* U.S.A.
254 E5 **Fort Wayne** *IN* U.S.A.
275 G3 **Fort Wellington** Guyana
118 A3 **Fort White** Myanmar
168 F9 **Fort William** *Highland, Scotland* U.K.
263 J9 **Fort Wingate** *NM* U.S.A.
261 G9 **Fort Worth** *TX* U.S.A.
260 E2 **Fort Yates** *ND* U.S.A.
258 D2 **Forty Fort** *PA* U.S.A.
245 L2 **Fortymile** *r.* Can./U.S.A.
245 L2 **Fortymile, Middle Fork** *r. AK* U.S.A.
245 L2 **Fortymile, West Fork** *r. AK* U.S.A.
107 J5 **Forty Mile Scrub National Park** *Qld* Austr.
Forty-Second Hill S. Africa *see* **42nd Hill**
245 K2 **Fort Yukon** *AK* U.S.A.
144 G3 **Forūmad** Iran
Forum Iulii France *see* **Fréjus**
144 F8 **Forūr, Jazīreh-ye** *i.* Iran
162 L4 **Forvik** Norway
217 I8 **Forza d'Agrò** *Sicilia* Italy
185 F10 **Fos** France
183 F10 **Fos, Golfe de** *b.* France
212 I7 **Fosdinovo** Italy
131 I7 **Foshan** *Guangdong* China
131 □J7 **Fo Shek Chau** *i. H.K.* China
163 L6 **Foskvallen** Sweden
162 K5 **Fosna** *pen.* Norway
228 E5 **Foso** Ghana
162 □E2 **Foss** Iceland
215 M3 **Fossacesia** Italy
200 G8 **Fossalta di Portogruaro** Italy
212 D6 **Fossano** Italy
213 N9 **Fossato di Vico** Italy
184 F5 **Fossemagne** France
187 G8 **Fosses-la-Ville** Belgium
162 □E1 **Fosshóll** Iceland
182 G4 **Fossiat** France
262 D4 **Fossil** *OR* U.S.A.
108 H5 **Fossil Downs** *W.A.* Austr.
213 N8 **Fossombrone** Italy
183 F10 **Fos-sur-Mer** France
105 K8 **Foster** *Vic.* Austr.
256 A10 **Foster** *KY* U.S.A.
245 N4 **Foster, Mount** Can./U.S.A.
243 P2 **Foster Bugt** *b.* Greenland
258 F1 **Fosterdale** *NY* U.S.A.
247 J3 **Foster Lakes** *Sask.* Can.
257 □R3 **Fosterville** *N.B.* Can.
256 B7 **Fostoria** *OH* U.S.A.
199 I4 **Fót** Hungary
235 □J5 **Fotadrevo** Madag.
171 Q7 **Fotherby** *Lincolnshire, England* U.K.
159 N2 **Fotovyzh** Ukr.
101 □8 **Fotuha'a** *atoll* Tonga
Fotuna *i.* Vanuatu *see* **Futuna**
178 C4 **Foucarmont** France
182 G2 **Foucherans** France
180 C6 **Fouesnant** France
179 K6 **Foug** France
230 A5 **Fougamou** Gabon
180 I5 **Fougères** France
239 □1c **Fougères, Plaine des** *hills* Réunion
179 L8 **Fougerolles** France
181 J5 **Fougerolles-du-Plessis** France
178 E4 **Fouilloy** France
168 □L2 **Foula** *i. Scotland* U.K.
228 D4 **Foulabala** Mali
179 J7 **Foulain** France
228 B3 **Foulamôri** Guinea
185 F7 **Foulayronnes** France
225 G4 **Foul Bay** Egypt
168 L11 **Foulden** *Scottish Borders, Scotland* U.K.
230 A5 **Foulenzem** Gabon
118 B5 **Foul Island** Myanmar
169 I8 **Foulkesmill** Ireland
173 N4 **Foulness Point** *England* U.K.
230 C2 **Foulounga** Chad
136 G8 **Foul Point** Sri Lanka
Foulpointe Madag. *see* **Mahavelona**
171 M6 **Foulridge** *Lancashire, England* U.K.
103 F8 **Foulwind, Cape** *South I.* N.Z.
229 H5 **Foumban** Cameroon
229 H5 **Foumbot** Cameroon
239 □3a **Foumbouni** *Njazidja* Comoros
226 D3 **Foum Zguid** Morocco
286 T1 **Foundation Ice Stream** *glacier* Antarctica
228 A3 **Foundiougne** Senegal
229 F4 **Founougo** Benin
256 B12 **Fount** *KY* U.S.A.
250 B6 **Fountain** *MN* U.S.A.
169 D7 **Fountain Cross** Ireland
265 U2 **Fountain Green** *UT* U.S.A.
258 E3 **Fountain Hill** *PA* U.S.A.
171 N5 **Fountains Abbey and Studley Royal Water Garden** *tourist site England* U.K.
206 E6 **Foupana** *r.* Port.
184 B4 **Fouras** France
185 E8 **Fourcès** France
182 C2 **Fourchambault** France
179 K7 **Fourches, Mont des** *hill* France
264 O7 **Four Corners** *CA* U.S.A.
173 M5 **Four Elms** *Kent, England* U.K.
237 M4 **Fouriesburg** S. Africa
173 J5 **Four Marks** *Hampshire, England* U.K.
178 H3 **Fourmies** France
244 E5 **Four Mountains, Islands of the** *AK* U.S.A.
183 C7 **Fournels** France
102 □ **Fournier, Cape** *Chatham Is* S. Pacific Ocean
249 H3 **Fournier, Lac** *l. Que.* Can.
221 H5 **Fournoi** Greece
221 H5 **Fournoi** *i.* Greece
173 N6 **Four Oaks** *East Sussex, England* U.K.
270 □ **Four Paths** Jamaica
244 I4 **Fourpeaked Mountain** *AK* U.S.A.
183 F9 **Fourques** *Languedoc-Roussillon* France
185 J10 **Fourques** *Languedoc-Roussillon* France
185 E7 **Fourques-sur-Garonne** France
271 □7 **Four Roads** Trin. and Tob.
182 D3 **Fours** France
183 J8 **Fours-St-Laurent** France
250 E3 **Fourteen Mile Point** *MI* U.S.A.
228 B4 **Fouta Djallon** *reg.* Guinea
103 B13 **Foveaux Strait** *South I.* N.Z.
258 B5 **Fowbelsburg** *MD* U.S.A.
172 C7 **Fowey** *Cornwall, England* U.K.
172 C7 **Fowey** *r. England* U.K.
255 I13 **Fowl Cay** *i.* Bahamas
264 M5 **Fowler** *CA* U.S.A.
263 L7 **Fowler** *CO* U.S.A.
254 D5 **Fowler** *IN* U.S.A.
250 J6 **Fowler** *MI* U.S.A.
286 S1 **Fowler Ice Rise** Antarctica
104 D4 **Fowlers Bay** *S.A.* Austr.
104 D5 **Fowlers Bay** *b. S.A.* Austr.
251 J7 **Fowlerville** *MI* U.S.A.
149 N5 **Fowman** Iran
172 G3 **Fownhope** *Herefordshire, England* U.K.
246 E3 **Fox** *r.* B.C. Can.
247 M3 **Fox** *r. Man.* Can.
250 F8 **Fox** *r. IL* U.S.A.
250 E6 **Fox** *r. WI* U.S.A.
107 K7 **Fox Creek** *r. Qld* Austr.
246 G4 **Fox Creek** *Alta* Can.
170 H5 **Foxdale** Isle of Man
243 K3 **Foxe Basin** *g. Nunavut* Can.
243 J3 **Foxe Channel** *Nunavut* Can.
164 H2 **Foxen** *l.* Sweden
243 K3 **Foxe Peninsula** *Nunavut* Can.
169 D5 **Foxford** Ireland
103 E10 **Fox Glacier** *South I.* N.Z.
244 E5 **Fox Islands** *AK* U.S.A.
246 H3 **Fox Lake** *Alta* Can.
250 F7 **Fox Lake** *IL* U.S.A.
245 N3 **Fox Mountain** *Y.T.* Can.
262 K6 **Foxpark** *WY* U.S.A.
102 J7 **Foxton** *North I.* N.Z.
102 J7 **Foxton Beach** *North I.* N.Z.
247 I5 **Fox Valley** *Sask.* Can.
168 H8 **Foyers** *Highland, Scotland* U.K.
170 B6 **Foygh** Ireland
169 H3 **Foyle** *r.* Ireland/U.K.
169 H2 **Foyle, Lough** *b.* Ireland/U.K.
169 D7 **Foynes** Ireland
206 C2 **Foz** Port.
204 F1 **Foz** Spain
279 C8 **Foz de Areia, Represa de** *resr* Brazil
274 D6 **Foz de Gregório** Brazil
206 A2 **Foz do Arelho** Port.
275 F5 **Foz do Copeá** Brazil
231 A9 **Foz do Cunene** Angola
279 B8 **Foz do Iguaçu** Brazil
276 E2 **Foz do Jamari** Brazil
276 C2 **Foz do Jordão** Brazil
274 E5 **Foz do Jutaí** Brazil
274 E5 **Foz do Mamoriá** Brazil
276 C1 **Foz do Riosinho** Brazil
204 E9 **Foz Giraldo** Port.
212 D7 **Frabosa Soprana** Italy
197 L2 **Frącki** Pol.
251 R9 **Frackville** *PA* U.S.A.
204 I7 **Frades de la Sierra** Spain
284 E3 **Fraga** Arg.
208 F4 **Fraga** Spain
217 M3 **Fragagnano** Italy
201 J3 **Fraham** Austria
282 G4 **Fraile Muerto** Uru.
207 L6 **Frailes** Spain
187 G8 **Fraire** Belgium
182 H2 **Fraisans** France
183 B9 **Fraisse-sur-Agout** France
179 N7 **Fraize** France
286 Q1 **Frakes, Mount** Antarctica
187 E8 **Frameries** Belgium
173 M6 **Framfield** *East Sussex, England* U.K.
257 N6 **Framingham** *MA* U.S.A.
173 O3 **Framlingham** *Suffolk, England* U.K.
165 M1 **Främlingshem** Sweden
191 H10 **Frammersbach** Ger.
287 E2 **Framnes Mountains** Antarctica
287 D2 **Fram Peak** Antarctica
197 K5 **Frampol** Pol.
173 L2 **Frampton** *Lincolnshire, England* U.K.
172 H4 **Frampton on Severn** *Gloucestershire, England* U.K.
292 A1 **Fram Strait** *sea chan.* Greenland Sea
280 D4 **Franca** Brazil
100 □5 **Français, Récif des** *rf* New Caledonia
215 M3 **Francavilla al Mare** Italy
217 I8 **Francavilla di Sicilia** *Sicilia* Italy
217 N2 **Francavilla Fontana** Italy
215 Q7 **Francavilla in Sinni** Italy
176 F3 **France** *country* Europe
243 Q2 **France, Île de** *i.* Greenland
208 K3 **France, Roc de** *mt.* France/Spain
104 H7 **Frances** *S.A.* Austr.
245 O3 **Frances** *r. Y.T.* Can.
270 B3 **Francés, Punta** *pt* Cuba
185 E7 **Francescas** France
238 □3d **Franceses** *La Palma* Canary Is
214 C5 **Francesi, Punta di li** *pt Sardegna* Italy
246 D2 **Frances Lake** *Y.T.* Can.
245 O3 **Frances Lake** *Y.T.* Can.
250 H9 **Francesville** *IN* U.S.A.
230 B5 **Franceville** Gabon
179 K8 **Franche-Comté** *admin. reg.* France
285 I3 **Francia** Uru.
204 H7 **Francia, Peña de** *mt.* Spain
247 K5 **Francis** *Sask.* Can.
Francis *atoll Gilbert Is* Kiribati *see* **Beru**
257 N3 **Francis, Lake** *NH* U.S.A.
Francisco de Orellana Ecuador *see* **Coca**
274 C5 **Francisco de Orellana** Peru
269 N9 **Francisco I. Madero** *Chiapas* Mex.
266 H5 **Francisco I. Madero** *Coahuila* Mex.
268 C1 **Francisco I. Madero** *Durango* Mex.
268 C4 **Francisco I. Madero** *Nayarit* Mex.
285 H5 **Francisco Meeks** Arg.
281 F2 **Francisco Sá** Brazil
266 A1 **Francisco Zarco** Mex.
235 E4 **Francistown** Botswana
204 F6 **Franco** Port.
280 D5 **Franco da Rocha** Brazil
216 H9 **Francofonte** *Sicilia* Italy
249 J4 **Francois** *Nfld and Lab.* Can.
246 E4 **François Lake** B.C. Can.
109 B8 **Francois Peron National Park** *W.A.* Austr.
258 A7 **Franconia** *VA* U.S.A.
187 I8 **Francorchamps** Belgium
185 G6 **Francoulès** France
262 J5 **Francs Peak** *WY* U.S.A.
186 I2 **Franeker** Neth.
182 H4 **Frangy** France
191 G8 **Frankenau** Ger.
193 H9 **Frankenberg** Ger.
191 G8 **Frankenberg (Eder)** Ger.
201 H3 **Frankenburg am Hausruck** Austria
201 L4 **Frankenfels** Austria
191 K9 **Frankenhain** Ger.
191 J9 **Frankenheim** Ger.
195 I3 **Frankenhöhe** *park* Ger.
201 H4 **Frankenmarkt** Austria
251 K6 **Frankenmuth** *MI* U.S.A.
194 E2 **Frankenthal (Pfalz)** Ger.
193 E10 **Frankenwald** *mts* Ger.
193 E10 **Frankenwald** *park* Ger.
270 □ **Frankfield** Jamaica
251 Q5 **Frankford** *Ont.* Can.
237 M3 **Frankfort** S. Africa
254 D5 **Frankfort** *IN* U.S.A.
254 E6 **Frankfort** *KY* U.S.A.
250 H5 **Frankfort** *MI* U.S.A.
256 B9 **Frankfort** *OH* U.S.A.
Frankfurt Ger. *see* **Frankfurt am Main**
191 G10 **Frankfurt am Main** Ger.
193 K6 **Frankfurt an der Oder** Ger.
109 F12 **Frank Hann National Park** *W.A.* Austr.
265 Q1 **Frankin Lake** *NV* U.S.A.
195 J4 **Fränkische Alb** *hills* Ger.
195 K3 **Fränkische Rezat** *r.* Ger.
191 I10 **Fränkische Saale** *r.* Ger.
195 K2 **Fränkische Schweiz** *reg.* Ger.
193 D10 **Fränkische Schweiz-Veldensteiner Forst** *park* Ger.
109 D13 **Frankland** *r. W.A.* Austr.
105 K8 **Frankland, Cape** *Tas.* Austr.
172 H3 **Frankley** *Worcestershire, England* U.K.
237 N6 **Franklin** S. Africa
265 W9 **Franklin** *AZ* U.S.A.
255 E9 **Franklin** *GA* U.S.A.
254 D6 **Franklin** *IN* U.S.A.
254 D7 **Franklin** *KY* U.S.A.
261 J11 **Franklin** *LA* U.S.A.
257 N6 **Franklin** *MA* U.S.A.
257 □Q4 **Franklin** *ME* U.S.A.
255 F8 **Franklin** *NC* U.S.A.
260 F5 **Franklin** *NE* U.S.A.
257 N5 **Franklin** *NH* U.S.A.
258 F2 **Franklin** *NJ* U.S.A.
256 A9 **Franklin** *OH* U.S.A.
256 F7 **Franklin** *PA* U.S.A.
255 D8 **Franklin** *TN* U.S.A.
261 G10 **Franklin** *TX* U.S.A.
256 I12 **Franklin** *VA* U.S.A.
250 F7 **Franklin** *WI* U.S.A.
256 F10 **Franklin** *WV* U.S.A.
244 H1 **Franklin, Point** *pt AK* U.S.A.
245 P1 **Franklin Bay** *N.W.T.* Can.
258 A4 **Franklinburg** *PA* U.S.A.
252 C1 **Franklin D. Roosevelt Lake** *resr WA* U.S.A.
256 C10 **Franklin Furnace** *OH* U.S.A.
105 J10 **Franklin-Gordon Wild Rivers National Park** *Tas.* Austr.
250 E8 **Franklin Grove** *IL* U.S.A.
104 F5 **Franklin Harbor** *b. S.A.* Austr.
287 L1 **Franklin Island** Antarctica
245 Q3 **Franklin Mountains** *N.W.T.* Can.
103 B11 **Franklin Mountains** *South I.* N.Z.
245 K1 **Franklin Mountains** *AK* U.S.A.
258 F4 **Franklin Park** *NJ* U.S.A.
105 K9 **Franklin Sound** *sea chan. Tas.* Austr.
259 H3 **Franklin Square** *NY* U.S.A.
243 I2 **Franklin Strait** *Nunavut* Can.
261 J10 **Franklinton** *LA* U.S.A.
258 E5 **Franklinville** *NJ* U.S.A.
256 G6 **Franklinville** *NY* U.S.A.
197 I1 **Frankowo** Pol.
162 L5 **Frankrike** Sweden
105 J8 **Frankston** *Vic.* Austr.
103 C12 **Frankton** *South I.* N.Z.
182 H2 **Franois** France
236 G5 **Fransenhof** S. Africa
234 B4 **Fransfontein** Namibia
243 Q2 **Franske Øer** *is* Greenland
163 N5 **Fränsta** Sweden
198 B1 **Františkovy Lázně** Czech Rep.
152 G2 **Frantsa-Iosifa, Zemlya** *is* Rus. Fed.
248 C3 **Franz** *Ont.* Can.
192 G2 **Franzburg** Ger.
103 E10 **Franz Josef Glacier** *South I.* N.Z.
Franz Josef Land *is* Rus. Fed. *see* **Frantsa-Iosifa, Zemlya**
195 L5 **Franz Josef Strauss** *airport* Ger.
214 A8 **Frasca, Capo della** *c. Sardegna* Italy
216 H9 **Frasca, Monte** *hill* Italy
215 J4 **Frascati** Italy
215 Q8 **Frascineto** Italy
195 M6 **Frasdorf** Ger.
108 G4 **Fraser** *r. W.A.* Austr.
246 F5 **Fraser** *r.* B.C. Can.
249 I1 **Fraser** *r. Nfld and Lab.* Can.
109 E8 **Fraser, Mount** *hill W.A.* Austr.
236 F7 **Fraserburg** S. Africa
168 L7 **Fraserburgh** *Aberdeenshire, Scotland* U.K.
248 D3 **Fraserdale** *Ont.* Can.
107 N8 **Fraser Island** *Qld* Austr.
109 B7 **Fraser Island** *W.A.* Austr.
246 E4 **Fraser Lake** B.C. Can.
246 E4 **Fraser Plateau** B.C. Can.
109 G12 **Fraser Range** *W.A.* Austr.
109 G12 **Fraser Range** *hills W.A.* Austr.
102 L5 **Frasertown** *North I.* N.Z.
182 I3 **Frasne** France
182 I3 **Frasne, Étang de** *lag.* France
187 E7 **Frasnes-lez-Buissenal** Belgium
187 F7 **Frasnes-lez-Gosselies** Belgium
213 J7 **Frassinoro** Italy
215 N5 **Frasso Telesino** Italy
200 A5 **Frastanz** Austria
204 E9 **Fratel** Port.
216 H7 **Fratello** *r. Sicilia* Italy
250 J2 **Frater** *Ont.* Can.
219 N7 **Frătești** Romania
213 L5 **Fratta** *r.* Italy
213 L5 **Fratta Polesine** Italy
215 I2 **Fratta Todina** Italy
212 D1 **Fraubrunnen** Switz.
195 O4 **Frauenau** Ger.
212 F1 **Frauenfeld** Switz.
201 O4 **Frauenkirchen** Austria
193 I9 **Frauenstein** Ger.
201 L6 **Frauental an der Laßnitz** Austria
191 K9 **Frauenwald** Ger.
195 L5 **Fraunberg** Ger.
193 F9 **Fraureuth** Ger.
285 H3 **Fray Bentos** Uru.
284 E6 **Fray Luis Beltrán** *Río Negro* Arg.
285 G3 **Fray Luis Beltrán** *Santa Fé* Arg.
282 G4 **Fray Marcos** Uru.
185 G6 **Frayssinet-le-Gélat** France
258 D4 **Frazer** *PA* U.S.A.
256 C8 **Frazeysburg** *OH* U.S.A.
108 F5 **Frazier Downs Aboriginal Reserve** *W.A.* Austr.
264 N7 **Frazier Park** *CA* U.S.A.
204 D6 **Freamunde** Port.
219 Q6 **Frecăței** Romania
183 C9 **Frech, Mont** *mt.* France
204 F6 **Frechas** Port.
191 C9 **Frechen** Ger.
205 K4 **Frechilla** Spain
171 L6 **Freckleton** *Lancashire, England* U.K.
191 I7 **Freden (Leine)** Ger.
190 H3 **Fredenbeck** Ger.
250 J5 **Frederic** *MI* U.S.A.
250 B4 **Frederic** *WI* U.S.A.
258 E6 **Frederica** *DE* U.S.A.
164 F6 **Fredericia** Denmark
109 D8 **Frederick** *r. W.A.* Austr.
256 H9 **Frederick** *MD* U.S.A.
261 F8 **Frederick** *OK* U.S.A.
243 O1 **Frederick E. Hyde Fjord** *inlet* Greenland
106 E2 **Frederick Hills** *N.T.* Austr.
248 D3 **Frederick House Lake** *Ont.* Can.
250 B7 **Fredericksburg** *IA* U.S.A.
258 C4 **Fredericksburg** *PA* U.S.A.
261 F10 **Fredericksburg** *TX* U.S.A.
256 H10 **Fredericksburg** *VA* U.S.A.
245 N4 **Frederick Sound** *sea channel AK* U.S.A.
261 J7 **Fredericktown** *MO* U.S.A.
256 C8 **Fredericktown** *OH* U.S.A.
249 H4 **Fredericton** *N.B.* Can.
257 □S3 **Fredericton Junction** *N.B.* Can.
Frederikshåb Greenland *see* **Paamiut**
164 G4 **Frederikshavn** Denmark
164 I6 **Frederikssund** Denmark
271 K5 **Frederiksted** Virgin Is (U.S.A.)
164 I6 **Frederiksværk** Denmark
192 I5 **Fredersdorf** Ger.
265 T5 **Fredonia** *AZ* U.S.A.
261 H7 **Fredonia** *KS* U.S.A.
256 F6 **Fredonia** *NY* U.S.A.
256 E7 **Fredonia** *PA* U.S.A.
250 G6 **Fredonia** *WI* U.S.A.
162 O4 **Fredrika** Sweden
165 K1 **Fredriksberg** Sweden
Fredrikshamn Fin. *see* **Hamina**
164 G2 **Fredrikstad** Norway
Fredriksvern Norway *see* **Stavern**
197 K6 **Fredropol** Pol.
258 B3 **Freeburg** *PA* U.S.A.
257 K8 **Freehold** *NJ* U.S.A.
258 D2 **Freeland** *PA* U.S.A.
104 G6 **Freeling** *S.A.* Austr.
106 D7 **Freeling, Mount** *hill N.T.* Austr.
104 G4 **Freeling Heights** *hill S.A.* Austr.
264 M3 **Freel Peak** *CA* U.S.A.
249 K3 **Freels, Cape** *Nfld and Lab.* Can.
260 G4 **Freeman** *SD* U.S.A.
250 H9 **Freeman, Lake** *IN* U.S.A.
258 E3 **Freemansburg** *PA* U.S.A.
162 □ **Freemansundet** *sea chan.* Svalbard
255 D10 **Freeport** *FL* U.S.A.
250 E7 **Freeport** *IL* U.S.A.
257 □O5 **Freeport** *ME* U.S.A.
259 H3 **Freeport** *NY* U.S.A.
256 F8 **Freeport** *PA* U.S.A.
261 H11 **Freeport** *TX* U.S.A.
255 H12 **Freeport City** *Gd Bahama* Bahamas
261 F12 **Freer** *TX* U.S.A.
250 H5 **Freesoil** *MI* U.S.A.
237 K4 **Free State** *prov.* S. Africa
271 □2 **Freetown** Antigua and Barbuda
228 B4 **Freetown** Sierra Leone
259 K3 **Freetown** *NY* U.S.A.
259 G4 **Freewood Acres** *NJ* U.S.A.
239 □2a **Frégate** *i. Inner Islands* Seychelles
248 F2 **Frégate, Lac de la** *l. Que.* Can.
239 □2a **Frégate, L'Îlot** *i. Inner Islands* Seychelles
206 F4 **Fregenal de la Sierra** Spain
214 I4 **Fregene** Italy
208 G6 **Freginals** Spain
104 D2 **Fregon** *S.A.* Austr.
180 G4 **Fréhel** France
180 G4 **Fréhel, Cap** *c.* France
286 U2 **Frei (Chile)** *research stn* Antarctica
193 H9 **Freiberg** Ger.
193 G8 **Freiberger Mulde** *r.* Ger.
194 E6 **Freiburg** *admin. reg.* Ger.
Freiburg Switz. *see* **Fribourg**
190 H3 **Freiburg (Elbe)** Ger.
194 D5 **Freiburg im Breisgau** Ger.
191 H10 **Freiensteinau** Ger.
190 H1 **Freienwill** Ger.
281 G2 **Frei Gonzaga** Brazil
195 L2 **Freihung** Ger.
281 G3 **Frei Inocêncio** Brazil
207 N5 **Freila** Spain
195 N6 **Freilassing** Ger.
194 E2 **Freinsheim** Ger.
284 A6 **Freire** Chile
194 C2 **Freisen** Ger.
195 L5 **Freising** Ger.
183 J7 **Freissinières** France
201 K2 **Freistadt** Austria
179 L5 **Freistroff** France
193 I9 **Freital** Ger.
204 F7 **Freixedas** Port.
204 D9 **Freixianda** Port.
204 F6 **Freixiel** Port.
204 E7 **Freixiosa** Port.
204 C5 **Freixo** Port.
204 G6 **Freixo de Espada à Cinta** Port.
185 I8 **Fréjairolles** France
183 J10 **Fréjus** France
183 J10 **Fréjus, Golfe de** *b.* France
183 J6 **Fréjus Tunnel** France/Italy
164 B1 **Frekhaug** Norway
191 K6 **Frellstedt** Ger.
109 C12 **Fremantle** *W.A.* Austr.
195 I4 **Fremdingen** Ger.
172 D5 **Fremington** *Devon, England* U.K.
264 K4 **Fremont** *CA* U.S.A.
250 J8 **Fremont** *IN* U.S.A.
250 I6 **Fremont** *MI* U.S.A.
260 G5 **Fremont** *NE* U.S.A.
256 B7 **Fremont** *OH* U.S.A.
250 F5 **Fremont** *WI* U.S.A.
265 V3 **Fremont** *r. UT* U.S.A.
265 U3 **Fremont Junction** *UT* U.S.A.
256 B11 **Frenchburg** *KY* U.S.A.
270 G3 **French Cay** *i.* Turks and Caicos Is
French Congo *country* Africa *see* **Congo**
256 F7 **French Creek** *r. PA* U.S.A.
275 H4 **French Guiana** *terr.* S. America
French Guinea *country* Africa *see* **Guinea**
105 J8 **French Island** *Vic.* Austr.
262 K2 **Frenchman** *r. MT* U.S.A.
257 □Q4 **Frenchman Bay** *ME* U.S.A.
260 E5 **Frenchman Creek** *r. NE* U.S.A.
264 L2 **Frenchman Lake** *CA* U.S.A.
265 Q5 **Frenchman Lake** *NV* U.S.A.
103 H7 **French Pass** *South I.* N.Z.
101 □9 **French Polynesia** *terr.* S. Pacific Ocean
French Somaliland *country* Africa *see* **Djibouti**
95 G6 **French Southern and Antarctic Lands** *terr.* Indian Ocean
French Sudan *country* Africa *see* **Mali**
French Territory of the Afars and Issas *country* Africa *see* **Djibouti**
258 E3 **Frenchtown** *NJ* U.S.A.
257 □Q1 **Frenchville** *ME* U.S.A.
178 C2 **Frencq** France
227 F2 **Frenda** Alg.
178 C5 **Freneuse** France
195 J2 **Frensdorf** Ger.
173 K5 **Frensham** *Surrey, England* U.K.
199 H2 **Frenštát pod Radhoštěm** Czech Rep.
215 M4 **Frentani, Monti dei** *mts* Italy
237 N4 **Frere** S. Africa
191 E6 **Freren** Ger.
201 I6 **Fresach** Austria
215 N4 **Fresagrandinaria** Italy
275 I6 **Fresco** *r.* Brazil
228 D5 **Fresco** Côte d'Ivoire
287 K2 **Freshfield, Cape** Antarctica
169 H7 **Freshford** Ireland
173 J6 **Freshwater** *Isle of Wight, England* U.K.
172 C4 **Freshwater East** *Pembrokeshire, Wales* U.K.
178 C7 **Fresnay-l'Évêque** France
181 L5 **Fresnay-sur-Sarthe** France
207 L3 **Fresnedas** *r.* Spain
207 J4 **Fresnedillas** *hill* Spain
182 H1 **Fresne-St-Mamès** France
179 K5 **Fresnes-en-Woëvre** France
179 K8 **Fresnes-sur-Apance** France
178 G3 **Fresnes-sur-Escaut** France
268 E2 **Fresnillo** Mex.
268 G5 **Fresno** Mex.
264 M5 **Fresno** *CA* U.S.A.
264 L5 **Fresno** *r. CA* U.S.A.
204 I7 **Fresno Alhándiga** Spain
204 I5 **Fresno de la Ribera** Spain
204 I6 **Fresno de Sayago** Spain
205 J6 **Fresno el Viejo** Spain
178 B4 **Fresnoy-Folny** France
178 F4 **Fresnoy-le-Grand** France
248 F2 **Fressel, Lac** *l. Que.* Can.
178 C3 **Fressenneville** France
179 M8 **Fresse-sur-Moselle** France
173 O3 **Fressingfield** *Suffolk, England* U.K.
163 I6 **Fresvikbreen** *glacier* Norway
168 J5 **Freswick** *Highland, Scotland* U.K.
182 H2 **Fretigney-et-Velloreille** France
209 L8 **Freu, Cap des** *c.* Spain
194 G2 **Freudenberg** *Baden-Württemberg* Ger.
195 L3 **Freudenberg** *Bayern* Ger.
191 E9 **Freudenberg** *Nordrhein-Westfalen* Ger.
194 B2 **Freudenburg** Ger.
194 E5 **Freudenstadt** Ger.
178 D3 **Frévent** France
106 E6 **Frew** *watercourse N.T.* Austr.
256 F6 **Frewsburg** *NY* U.S.A.
193 E8 **Freyburg (Unstrut)** Ger.
109 B9 **Freycinet Estuary** *inlet W.A.* Austr.
105 L10 **Freycinet Peninsula** *Tas.* Austr.
192 F4 **Freyenstein** Ger.
179 M5 **Freyming-Merlebach** France
285 F2 **Freyre** Arg.
195 K3 **Freystadt** Ger.
195 P4 **Freyung** Ger.
228 B4 **Fria** Guinea
234 B3 **Fria, Cape** Namibia
268 E4 **Fria, Sierra** *mts* Mex.
264 M5 **Friant** *CA* U.S.A.
264 M6 **Friant-Kern Canal** *CA* U.S.A.
282 D3 **Frias** Arg.
205 N3 **Frías** Spain
212 C2 **Fribourg** Switz.
212 C2 **Fribourg** *canton* Switz.
212 E1 **Frick** Switz.
194 G6 **Frickingen** Ger.
262 C2 **Friday Harbor** *WA* U.S.A.
171 P5 **Fridaythorpe** *East Riding of Yorkshire, England* U.K.
194 F5 **Fridingen an der Donau** Ger.
195 N6 **Fridolfing** Ger.
286 M1 **Fridtjof Nansen, Mount** Antarctica
191 J8 **Frieda (Meinhard)** Ger.
201 N5 **Friedberg** Austria
195 J5 **Friedberg** Ger.
191 G10 **Friedberg (Hessen)** Ger.
190 E4 **Friedeburg** Ger.
193 E7 **Friedeburg (Saale)** Ger.
195 M2 **Friedenfels** Ger.
256 G8 **Friedens** *PA* U.S.A.
258 C3 **Friedensburg** *PA* U.S.A.
194 E6 **Friedenweiler** Ger.
193 I6 **Friedersdorf** *Brandenburg* Ger.
193 F7 **Friedersdorf** *Sachsen-Anhalt* Ger.
191 I9 **Friedewald** *Hessen* Ger.
191 E9 **Friedewald** *Rheinland-Pfalz* Ger.
193 J6 **Friedland** *Brandenburg* Ger.
192 I3 **Friedland** *Mecklenburg-Vorpommern* Ger.
191 I8 **Friedland** *Niedersachsen* Ger.
Friedland Rus. Fed. *see* **Pravdinsk**
191 K9 **Friedrichroda** Ger.
193 D7 **Friedrichsbrunn** Ger.
191 G10 **Friedrichsdorf** Ger.
194 H6 **Friedrichshafen** Ger.
193 K7 **Friedrichshain** Ger.
193 D6 **Friedrichskanal** *canal* Ger.
190 G2 **Friedrichskoog** Ger.
192 E3 **Friedrichsruhe** Ger.
190 H2 **Friedrichstadt** Ger.
192 H5 **Friedrichsthal** Ger.
192 I4 **Friedrichswalde** Ger.
191 H9 **Frielendorf** Ger.
191 K9 **Friemar** Ger.
260 G5 **Friend** *NE* U.S.A.
Friendly Islands *country* S. Pacific Ocean *see* **Tonga**
270 □ **Friendship** Jamaica
256 G6 **Friendship** *NY* U.S.A.
248 B5 **Friendship** *WI* U.S.A.
256 E12 **Fries** *VA* U.S.A.
201 J6 **Friesach** Austria
192 G5 **Friesack** Ger.
191 E9 **Friesenhagen** Ger.
194 D5 **Friesenheim** Ger.
195 J6 **Friesenried** Ger.
186 I2 **Friese Wad** *tidal flat* Neth.
186 I2 **Friesland** *prov.* Neth.
190 E4 **Friesoythe** Ger.
Frigate Island *Inner Islands* Seychelles *see* **Frégate**
163 N6 **Friggesund** Sweden
207 L7 **Frigiliana** Spain
213 J7 **Frignano** *reg.* Italy
178 I6 **Frignicourt** France
173 K5 **Frimley** *Surrey, England* U.K.
100 □6 **Frindsbury Reef** Solomon Is
173 O4 **Frinton-on-Sea** *Essex, England* U.K.
261 F11 **Frio** *r. TX* U.S.A.
261 F11 **Frio** *r. TX* U.S.A.
261 D8 **Frio** *watercourse NM/TX* U.S.A.
168 K9 **Friockheim** *Angus, Scotland* U.K.
204 E2 **Friol** Spain
168 D9 **Frisa, Loch** *l. Scotland* U.K.
187 J9 **Frisange** Lux.
263 K7 **Frisco** *CO* U.S.A.
265 S3 **Frisco Mountain** *UT* U.S.
171 R7 **Friskney** *Lincolnshire, England* U.K.
257 L6 **Frissell, Mount** *hill CT* U
172 D6 **Frithelstock Stone** *Devo England* U.K.
164 I4 **Fritsla** Sweden
200 E5 **Fritzens** Austria
191 H8 **Fritzlar** Ger.
213 O3 **Friuli-Venezia Giulia** *ad* Italy
178 C3 **Friville-Escarbotin** Fran
171 K4 **Frizington** *Cumbria, Eng*
258 A5 **Frizzellburg** *MD* U.S.A.
162 J4 **Froan** *nature res.* Norway
162 J5 **Froan** *park* Norway
Frobisher Bay *Nunavut* Iqaluit
243 L3 **Frobisher Bay** *b. Nunav*
247 I3 **Frobisher Lake** *Sask.* Ca
164 G6 **Frøbjerg Bavnehøj** *hill* D
200 B7 **Frodolfo** *r.* Italy
171 L7 **Frodsham** *Cheshire, Engl*
179 O6 **Frœschwiller** France
183 H6 **Froges** France
173 K5 **Frogmore** *Hampshire, England* U.K.
162 J5 **Frohavet** *b.* Norway
193 G8 **Frohburg** Ger.
194 H2 **Frohnberg** *hill* Ger.
201 L5 **Frohnleiten** Austria
179 L8 **Froideconche** France
178 D4 **Froissy** France
157 H6 **Frolovo** Rus. Fed.
156 K3 **Frolovskaya** Rus. Fed.
165 P7 **Frombork** Pol.
104 F3 **Frome** *watercourse S.A.*
270 □ **Frome** Jamaica
172 H5 **Frome** *Somerset, Englan*
172 H6 **Frome** *r. England* U.K.
104 G4 **Frome, Lake** *salt flat S.A*
104 G4 **Frome Downs** *S.A.* Austr
179 I3 **Fromelennes** France
178 G6 **Fromentières** France
180 G8 **Fromentine** France
205 L4 **Frómista** Spain
180 A5 **Fromveur, Passage du** *s*
179 J7 **Froncles** France
191 E8 **Fröndenberg** Ger.
191 G9 **Fronhausen** Ger.
185 D6 **Fronsac** *Aquitaine* France
185 F10 **Fronsac** *Midi-Pyrénées* F
206 D2 **Fronteira** Port.
278 E3 **Fronteiras** Brazil
182 G3 **Frontenard** France
184 C3 **Frontenay-Rohan-Rohan**
195 N4 **Frontenhausen** Ger.
238 □3e **Frontera** *El Hierro* Canar
267 I4 **Frontera** *Coahuila* Mex.
267 M8 **Frontera** *Tabasco* Mex.
267 M8 **Frontera, Punta** *pt* Mex.
266 E2 **Fronteras** Mex.
183 D10 **Frontignan** France
185 G8 **Fronton** France
271 □1 **Frontón de la Brea** *pt* Pu
256 G10 **Front Royal** *VA* U.S.A.
193 D7 **Frose** Ger.
215 K4 **Frosinone** Italy
215 K4 **Frosinone** *prov.* Italy
215 M4 **Frosolone** Italy
162 K5 **Frosta** Norway
256 G9 **Frostburg** *MD* U.S.A.
287 I2 **Frost Glacier** Antarctica
179 L6 **Frouard** France
204 D1 **Frouxeira, Punta da** *pt* S
165 L2 **Frövi** Sweden
162 J5 **Frøya** *i.* Norway
178 E5 **Froyères** France
178 D2 **Fruges** France
265 X2 **Fruita** *CO* U.S.A.
257 J10 **Fruitland** *MD* U.S.A.
265 V1 **Fruitland** *UT* U.S.A.
103 D12 **Fruitlands** *South I.* N.Z.
250 H6 **Fruitport** *MI* U.S.A.
265 X2 **Fruitvale** *CO* U.S.A.
161 W7 **Fruktovaya** Rus. Fed.
205 L6 **Frumales** Spain
143 N7 **Frunze** *Batken* Kyrg.
Frunze *Bishkek* Kyrg. *see*
159 N7 **Frunze** *Khersons'ka Obla*
159 N7 **Frunze** *Khersons'ka Obla*
159 N9 **Frunzens'ke** Ukr.
Frunzenskoye Kyrg. *see*
158 I6 **Frunzivka** Ukr.
Frusino Italy *see* **Frosino**
218 H5 **Fruška Gora** *hills* Serbia
218 H5 **Fruska Gora** *nat. park* Se
280 C4 **Frutal** Brazil
212 D2 **Frutigen** Switz.
283 B6 **Frutillar** Chile
277 E3 **Frutuoso** Brazil
161 V5 **Fryanovo** Rus. Fed.
161 V6 **Fryazino** Rus. Fed.
199 H2 **Frýdek-Místek** Czech Re
198 E1 **Frýdlant** Czech Rep.
257 □O4 **Fryeburg** *ME* U.S.A.
173 M4 **Fryerning** *Essex, England*
197 I2 **Frygnowo** Pol.
198 D3 **Frymburk** Czech Rep.
199 G2 **Fryšták** Czech Rep.
197 J6 **Frysztak** Pol.
101 □8a **Fua'amotu** *Tongatapu* To
131 L5 **Fu'an** *Fujian* China
168 F9 **Fuar Bheinn** *hill Scotland*
212 E6 **Fubine** Italy
213 J8 **Fucecchio** Italy
Fucheng *Anhui* China *see* **Fengyang**
Fucheng *Shaanxi* China **Fuxian**
195 M2 **Fuchsmühl** Ger.
195 J6 **Fuchstal** Ger.
125 K12 **Fuchū** *Hiroshima* Japan
127 J4 **Fuchū** Japan
126 F2 **Fuchū** *Toyama* Japan
131 H6 **Fuchuan** *Guangxi* China
131 M3 **Fuchun Jiang** *r.* China
215 K2 **Fucino** *r.* Italy
215 K3 **Fucino, Piana del** *plain*
124 S6 **Fudai** Japan
168 B8 **Fuday** *i. Scotland* U.K.
131 K6 **Fude** *Fujian* China
131 M5 **Fuding** *Fujian* China
233 C5 **Fudua** *waterhole* Kenya
147 H4 **Fudul** *reg.* Saudi Arabia
238 □3d **Fuencaliente** *La Palma* C
207 K4 **Fuencaliente** Spain
238 □3d **Fuencaliente, Punta de** *Palma* Canary Is
205 R5 **Fuendejalón** Spain
207 J7 **Fuengirola** Spain
205 M8 **Fuenlabrada** Spain
207 J2 **Fuenlabrada de los Mont**
205 O4 **Fuenmayor** Spain
205 L8 **Fuensalida** Spain
207 O2 **Fuensanta** *Castilla-La Ma* Spain
207 O4 **Fuensanta, Embalse de la** Spain
209 C10 **Fuente-Álamo** Spain
209 C12 **Fuente-Álamo de Murcia**
207 P3 **Fuente Albilla, Cerro de**
205 N5 **Fuentearmegil** Spain
205 N5 **Fuentecambrón** Spain
205 M5 **Fuentecén** Spain
206 G4 **Fuente de Cantos** Spain
206 H4 **Fuente del Arco** Spain
206 G3 **Fuente del Maestre** Spain
205 N9 **Fuente de Pedro Naharro**
207 J6 **Fuente de Piedra** Spain
207 J6 **Fuente de Piedra, Laguna** Spain
207 L2 **Fuente el Fresno** Spain
205 K6 **Fuente el Sol** Spain
204 G8 **Fuenteguinaldo** Spain
Fuente la Higuera Spain **La Font de la Figuera**
205 J6 **Fuentelapeña** Spain
205 M5 **Fuentelcésped** Spain
205 O9 **Fuentelespino de Haro**
205 R9 **Fuentelespino de Moya**
205 P6 **Fuentelmonge** Spain
207 I4 **Fuente Obejuna** Spain
207 I5 **Fuente Palmera** Spain

Fuentepelayo Spain
Fuentepinilla Spain
Fuenterodos Spain
Fuenterrabía Spain see Hondarribia
Fuenterrebollo Spain
Fuenterroble de Salvatierra Spain
Fuente Santa mt. Spain
Fuentesaúco Spain
Fuentesaúco de Fuentidueña Spain
Fuentes-Claras Spain
Fuentes de Andalucía Spain
Fuentes de Ebro Spain
Fuentes de Jiloca Spain
Fuentes de León Spain
Fuentes de Nava Spain
Fuentes de Oñoro Spain
Fuentes de Valdepero Spain
Fuentespalda Spain
Fuentestrún r. Spain
Fuente-Tójar Spain
Fuente Vaqueros Spain
Fuentidueña Spain
Fu'er He r. China
Fuerte del Rey Spain
Fuerte Olimpo Para.
Fuertescusa Spain
Fuerteventura i. Canary Is
Fuga i. Phil.
Fügen Austria
Fügenberg Austria
Fugloy i. Faroe Is
Fuglstad Norway
Fugong Yunnan China
Fugou Henan China
Fugu Shaanxi China
Fuguo Shandong China see Zhanhua
Fuhai Xinjiang China
Fuhai Linchang Xinjiang China
Fuḩaymī Iraq
Fuhne r. Ger.
Fuhrberg (Burgwedel) Ger.
Fujairah U.A.E. see Al Fujayrah
Fujeira U.A.E. see Al Fujayrah
Fuji Sichuan China see Xiaoshi
Fuji Sichuan China see Luxian
Fuji Japan
Fujian prov. China
Fu Jiang r. Sichuan China
Fujian Tulou tourist site China
Fujieda Japan
Fuji-Hakone-Izu Kokuritsu-kōen nat. park Japan
Fujihashi Japan
Fujiidera Japan
Fujikawa Japan
Fuji-kawa r. Japan
Fujimi Nagano Japan
Fujimi Saitama Japan
Fujin Heilong. China
Fujino Japan
Fujinomiya Japan
Fujioka Aichi Japan
Fujioka Gunma Japan
Fujioka Tochigi Japan
Fuji-san vol. Japan
Fujisan Shizuoka Kūkō airport Japan
Fujisawa Japan
Fujishiro Japan
Fujiwara Mie Japan
Fujiwara Tochigi Japan
Fujiyoshida Japan
Fukagawa Japan
Fūkah Egypt
Fukang Xinjiang China
Fukaura Japan
Fukave i. Tonga
Fukaya Japan
Fukeshan Heilong. China
Fukiage Japan
Fukien prov. China see Fujian
Fukuchiyama Japan
Fukude Japan
Fukue Japan
Fukue-jima i. Japan
Fukui Japan
Fukui pref. Japan
Fukumitsu Japan
Fukuno Japan
Fukuoka Fukuoka Japan
Fukuoka Gifu Japan
Fukuoka Toyama Japan
Fukuoka pref. Japan
Fukuroi Japan
Fukusaki Japan
Fukushima Fukushima Japan
Fukushima Hokkaidō Japan
Fukushima pref. Japan
Fukuyama Japan
Fūl, Jabal hill Egypt
Fulacunda Guinea-Bissau
Fūlād Maīalleh Iran
Fulayj Oman
Fulbourn Cambridgeshire, England U.K.
Fulchhari Bangl.
Fulda Ger.
Fulda r. Ger.
Fule Yunnan China
Fulford York, England U.K.
Fulham Greater London, England U.K.
Fuli Anhui China
Fuli Heilong. China see Jixian
Fulin Sichuan China see Hanyuan
Fuling Chongqing China
Fulitun Heilong. China see Jixian
Fullarton r. Qld Austr.
Fullarton Trin. and Tob.
Fullerton CA U.S.A.
Fullerton NE U.S.A.
Fullerton, Cape Nunavut Can.
Fulnek Czech Rep.
Fülöp Hungary
Fülöpháza Hungary
Fülöpszállás Hungary
Fulpmes Austria
Fulton Arg.
Fulton IL U.S.A.
Fulton KY U.S.A.
Fulton MD U.S.A.
Fulton MO U.S.A.
Fulton MS U.S.A.
Fulton NY U.S.A.
Fulufjällets nationalpark nature res. Sweden
Fulunäs Sweden
Fumane Moz.
Fumay France
Fumel France
Fumin Yunnan China
Fumone Italy
Funabashi Chiba Japan
Funabashi Toyama Japan
Funafuti atoll Tuvalu
Funan Anhui China
Funan Guangxi China see Fusui
Funan Liaoning China
Funäsdalen Sweden
Funchal Madeira
Fundación Col.
Fundada Port.
Fundão Brazil
Fundão Port.
Fundi Italy see Fondi
Fundición Mex.
Fundo das Figuerias Cape Verde
Fundulea Romania
Fundusfeiler mt. Austria
Fundy, Bay of g. N.B./N.S. Can.
Fünen i. Denmark see Fyn
Funeral Peak CA U.S.A.
Funes Italy
Fünfkirchen Hungary see Pécs
Fung Wong Shan hill H.K. China
Funhalouro Moz.
Funing Jiangsu China
Funing Yunnan China
Funiu Shan mts China
Funnel Creek r. Qld Austr.
Funsi Ghana
245 N4 Funter AK U.S.A.
229 G4 Funtua Nigeria
168 □O1 Funzie Shetland, Scotland U.K.
129 N7 Fuping Hebei China
130 G1 Fuping Shaanxi China
131 L6 Fuqing Fujian China
130 F5 Fuquan Guizhou China
165 L5 Fur Sweden
204 C7 Furadouro Port.
235 G2 Furancungo Moz.
124 T3 Furano Japan
122 F4 Furao Heilong. China
215 N3 Furci Italy
211 E7 Furci Siculo Sicilia Italy
124 W3 Füren-gawa r. Japan
124 W3 Füren-ko l. Japan
164 I6 Furesø l. Denmark
144 G8 Fürgun, Kūh-e mt. Iran
214 C2 Furiani Corse France
212 E2 Furkapass pass Switz.
258 E4 Furlong PA U.S.A.
161 Y4 Furmanov Rus. Fed.
Furmanovka Kazakh. see Moyynkum
Furmanovo Kazakh. see Zhalpaktal
122 I7 Furmanovo Rus. Fed.
168 F10 Furnace Argyll and Bute, Scotland U.K.
258 B6 Furnace Branch MD U.S.A.
238 □[1b] Furnas São Miguel Azores
209 I9 Furnás hill Spain
281 D4 Furnas, Represa resr Brazil
Furneaux atoll Arch. des Tuamotu Fr. Polynesia see Marutea (Nord)
105 L9 Furneaux Group is Tas. Austr.
Furnes Belgium see Veurne
Furong Jiangxi China see Wan'an
150 F4 Furqlus Syria
190 E5 Fürstenau Ger.
192 H4 Fürstenberg Brandenburg Ger.
191 H7 Fürstenberg Niedersachsen Ger.
191 G8 Fürstenberg (Lichtenfels) Ger.
201 N5 Fürstenfeld Austria
195 K5 Fürstenfeldbruck Ger.
195 O4 Fürstenstein Ger.
193 J6 Fürstenwalde Ger.
192 I4 Fürstenwerder Ger.
195 O4 Fürstenzell Ger.
199 K4 Furta Hungary
214 B8 Furtei Sardegna Italy
195 J3 Fürth Bayern Ger.
195 M4 Furth Ger.
194 F2 Fürth Hessen Ger.
201 M3 Furth bei Göttweig Austria
195 N3 Furth im Wald Ger.
194 E5 Furtwangen im Schwarzwald Ger.
124 R3 Furubira Japan
163 M6 Furudal Sweden
127 M1 Furudono Japan
126 F3 Furukawa Gifu Japan
124 R8 Furukawa Miyagi Japan
243 J3 Fury and Hecla Strait Nunavut Can.
274 C3 Fusagasugá Col.
Fusan S. Korea see Pusan
215 Q9 Fuscaldo Italy
200 H4 Fuschlsee l. Austria
130 G9 Fushan Hainan China
129 Q8 Fushan Shandong China
129 L9 Fushan Shanxi China
218 J8 Fushë-Kosovë Fushë-Kosovë Kosovo
218 I8 Fushë Kosovë plain Kosovo
218 H9 Fushë-Krujë Albania
126 C6 Fushimi Japan
Fushun Liaoning China see Funan
129 R6 Fushun Liaoning China
130 E4 Fushun Sichuan China
100 □[2] Fusi Samoa
101 □[8] Fusi, Hakau rf Vava'u Gp Tonga
213 L7 Fusignano Italy
201 I6 Fusine in Valromana Italy
126 E5 Fuso Japan
122 E7 Fusong Jilin China
127 J4 Fussa Japan
212 H1 Fußach Austria
195 J6 Füssen Ger.
181 P7 Fussy France
205 R4 Fustiñana Spain
130 F7 Fusui Guangxi China
127 H4 Futaba Japan
126 F6 Futagawa Japan
125 I13 Futago-san vol. Japan
127 I3 Futago-yama mt. Japan
283 C6 Futaleufú Chile
126 E6 Futami Japan
125 □[3] Futatsu-ne i. Japan
131 □J7 Fu Tau Pun Chau i. H.K. China
179 J5 Futeau France
218 H5 Futog Vojvodina Serbia
127 K5 Futtsu Japan
127 K5 Futtsu-misaki pt Japan
100 □[5] Futuna i. Vanuatu
99 I3 Futuna, Île i. Wallis and Futuna Is
Futuna Islands Wallis and Futuna Is see Hoorn, Îles de
131 K5 Futun Xi r. China
183 H10 Fuveau France
147 J2 Fuwayriţ Qatar
Fuxian Liaoning China see Wafangdian
129 K9 Fuxian Shaanxi China
130 D6 Fuxian Hu l. China
129 Q5 Fuxin Liaoning China
129 Q5 Fuxin Liaoning China
Fuxing Guizhou China see Wangmo
Fuxinzhen Liaoning China see Fuxin
124 Q8 Fuya Japan
131 J2 Fuyang Anhui China
Fuyang Guangxi China see Fuchuan
131 L3 Fuyang Zhejiang China
129 O7 Fuyang He r. China
131 M5 Fuying Dao i. China
Fuyu Anhui China see Susong
129 S3 Fuyu Heilong. China
Fuyu Jilin China see Songyuan
122 E6 Fuyu Jilin China
122 I4 Fuyuan Heilong. China
130 E6 Fuyuan Yunnan China
128 A3 Fuyun Xinjiang China
199 J4 Füzesabony Hungary
199 K4 Füzesgyarmat Hungary
206 D6 Fuzeta Port.
131 L5 Fuzhou Fujian China
131 K5 Fuzhou Jiangxi China
213 R5 Fužine Croatia
151 I6 Füzuli Azer.
231 D6 Fwamba Dem. Rep. Congo
173 M4 Fyfield Essex, England U.K.
171 L6 Fylde lowland England U.K.
164 G6 Fyn i. Denmark
168 G10 Fyne r. Scotland U.K.
168 F11 Fyne, Loch inlet Scotland U.K.
190 I1 Fynshav Denmark
164 G6 Fyns Hoved hd Denmark
164 E2 Fyresdal Norway
164 E2 Fyresvatn l. Norway
165 N2 Fyrisån r. Sweden
F.Y.R.O.M. country Europe see Macedonia
220 C4 Fyteies Greece
168 L8 Fyvie Aberdeenshire, Scotland U.K.
271 □[7] Fyzabad Trin. and Tob.

G

135 □[1] Gaafaru i. N. Male Maldives
135 □[1] Gaafaru Atoll N. Male Maldives
135 □[1] Gaafaru Channel Maldives
211 B7 Gaâfour Tunisia
201 K5 Gaal Austria
232 E3 Gaalkacyo Somalia
117 J4 Gaat r. Malaysia
236 B3 Gab watercourse Namibia
145 J2 Gabakly Turkm.
205 Q9 Gabaldón Spain
232 E3 Gabangab well Eth.
185 E8 Gabarret France
185 C8 Gabas r. France
Gabasumdo Qinghai China see Tongde
232 F2 Gabbac, Raas pt Somalia
264 O3 Gabbs NV U.S.A.
264 N3 Gabbs Valley Range mts NV U.S.A.
199 G4 Gabčíkovo Slovakia
145 I9 Gabd Pak.
231 B7 Gabela Angola
201 K5 Gaberl pass Austria
Gaberones Botswana see Gaborone
198 E5 Gabersdorf Austria
227 H2 Gabès Tunisia
227 H2 Gabès, Golfe de g. Tunisia
225 G4 Gabgaba, Wadi watercourse Sudan
231 C6 Gabia Dem. Rep. Congo
207 L6 Gabia la Grande Spain
183 C9 Gabian France
213 N8 Gabicce Mare Italy
143 O2 Gabiden Mustafin Kazakh.
197 H3 Gąbin Pol.
269 K7 Gabino Barreda Mex.
102 M5 Gable End Foreland hd North I. N.Z.
195 J5 Gablingen Ger.
201 N3 Gablitz Austria
230 A5 Gabon country Africa
230 A4 Gabon, Estuaire du est. Gabon
234 E5 Gaborone Botswana
285 G3 Gaboto Arg.
228 B3 Gabou Senegal
183 B8 Gabriac France
239 □[1b] Gabriel Island Mauritius
276 D4 Gabriel Vera Bol.
204 H8 Gabriel y Galán, Embalse de resr Spain
268 E6 Gabriel Zamora Mex.
144 H9 Gābrīk Iran
144 H9 Gābrīk watercourse Iran
201 M7 Gabrnik Slovenia
219 L7 Gabrovnitsa Bulg.
219 N8 Gabrovo Bulg.
230 E4 Gabu Dem. Rep. Congo
228 B3 Gabú Guinea-Bissau
232 D1 Gabuli vol. Eth.
212 D4 Gaby Italy
197 K5 Gać Pol.
181 L4 Gacé France
195 K5 Gachenbach Ger.
149 O5 Gach Sār Iran
144 D6 Gachsārān Iran
210 G4 Gacko Bos.-Herz.
151 G5 Gädäbäy Azer.
229 G3 Gadabedji, Réserve Totale de Faune de nature res. Niger
136 D5 Gadag Karnataka India
145 L9 Gadap Pak.
138 H9 Gadchiroli Mahar. India
162 M4 Gäddede Sweden
130 B2 Gadê Qinghai China
192 D3 Gadebusch Ger.
191 J6 Gadenstedt (Lahstedt) Ger.
213 L2 Gadera r. Italy
Gades Spain see Cádiz
138 C8 Gadhada Gujarat India
138 C9 Gadhada Gujarat India
138 B8 Gadhka Gujarat India
138 C9 Gadhra Gujarat India
151 K5 Gädi Dağı mt. Azer.
239 □[3a] Gadjou-Lamdjahala depr. Njazidja Comoros
212 E2 Gadmen Switz.
214 C8 Gadoni Sardegna Italy
207 O7 Gádor Spain
207 N7 Gádor, Sierra de mts Spain
199 J5 Gádoros Hungary
145 L8 Gadra Balochistan Pak.
145 N9 Gadra Sindh Pak.
255 D8 Gadsden AL U.S.A.
265 R9 Gadsden AZ U.S.A.
136 E4 Gadwal Andhra Prad. India
Gadyach Ukr. see Hadyach
145 J2 Gadyn Turkm.
230 C3 Gadzi C.A.R.
219 K7 Gadžin Han Gadžin Han Serbia
206 A2 Gaeiras Port.
243 P2 Gael Hamke Bugt b. Greenland
172 F4 Gaer Powys, Wales U.K.
219 N6 Găești Romania
215 L5 Gaeta Italy
215 L5 Gaeta, Golfo di g. Italy
204 C7 Gafanha da Boa Hora Port.
204 C7 Gafanha da Encarnação Port.
204 C7 Gafanha da Nazaré Port.
204 C7 Gafanha do Carmo Port.
206 C3 Gafanhoeira Port.
Gafaru i. N. Male Maldives see Gaafaru
Gafaru Atoll N. Male Maldives see Gaafaru Atoll
Gafaru Channel Maldives see Gaafaru Channel
113 K5 Gaferut i. Micronesia
206 D2 Gáfete Port.
255 G8 Gaffney SC U.S.A.
227 H2 Gafsa Tunisia
115 F4 Gag i. Papua Indon.
230 B2 Gagal Chad
138 E9 Gagaon Madh. Prad. India
161 S6 Gagarin Rus. Fed.
143 M7 Gagarin Uzbek.
219 Q5 Găgăuzia reg. Moldova
192 D3 Gägelow Ger.
229 G3 Gagere watercourse Nigeria
194 E4 Gaggenau Ger.
217 I8 Gaggi Sicilia Italy
213 J7 Gaggio Montano Italy
212 E4 Gaglianico Italy
216 H8 Gagliano Castelferrato Sicilia Italy
217 O4 Gagliano del Capo Italy
183 E8 Gagnières France
228 D5 Gagnoa Côte d'Ivoire
249 G3 Gagnon Que. Can.
Gago Coutinho Angola see Lumbala N'guimbo
151 B2 Gagra Georgia
151 B2 Gagris K'edi hills Georgia
128 E8 Gahai Qinghai China
234 C6 Gaiab watercourse Namibia
139 L7 Gaibandha Bangl.
219 P4 Găiceana Romania
221 G8 Gaïdouronisi i. Greece
194 F6 Gaienhofen Ger.
200 I6 Gail r. Austria
261 E9 Gail TX U.S.A.
194 H4 Gaildorf Ger.
194 F6 Gailingen Ger.
185 H8 Gaillac France
183 B8 Gaillac-d'Aveyron France
259 J2 Gaillard, Lake CT U.S.A.
Gaillimh Ireland see Galway
178 B5 Gaillon France
200 G6 Gailtaler Alpen mts Austria
195 K4 Gaimersheim Ger.
199 L5 Găina mt. Romania
133 J11 Gaindainqoinkor Xizang China
255 E7 Gainesboro TN U.S.A.
169 H6 Gainestown Ireland
255 F11 Gainesville FL U.S.A.
255 F8 Gainesville GA U.S.A.
261 I7 Gainesville MO U.S.A.
261 G9 Gainesville TX U.S.A.
171 N4 Gainford Durham, England U.K.
171 P7 Gainsborough Lincolnshire, England U.K.
213 K9 Gaiole in Chianti Italy
109 E13 Gairdner r. W.A. Austr.
104 E4 Gairdner, Lake salt flat S.A. Austr.
168 E7 Gairloch Highland, Scotland U.K.
168 E7 Gair Loch b. Scotland U.K.
214 D8 Gairo Sardegna Italy
233 C6 Gairo Tanz.
168 K4 Gairsay i. Scotland U.K.
213 L2 Gais Italy
212 G1 Gais Switz.
201 K4 Gaishorn Austria
195 L6 Gaißach Ger.
194 H7 Gaißau Austria
256 H9 Gaithersburg MD U.S.A.
Gaixian Liaoning China see Gaizhou
129 R6 Gaizhou Liaoning China
160 I5 Gaiziņkalns hill Latvia
199 H4 Gaja r. Hungary
116 D1 Gajah Hutan, Bukit hill Malaysia
124 □G17 Gaja-jima i. Nansei-shotō Japan
205 O7 Gajanejos Spain
137 H3 Gajapatinagaram Andhra Prad. India
145 K8 Gajar Pak.
198 F3 Gajary Slovakia
229 H4 Gaji r. Nigeria
229 I3 Gajiram Nigeria
139 L7 Gajol W. Bengal India
236 H3 Gakarosa mt. S. Africa
229 H5 Gakem Nigeria
245 K3 Gakona AK U.S.A.
245 K3 Gakona Junction AK U.S.A.
199 I6 Gakovo Vojvodina Serbia
138 D1 Gakuch Pak.
133 I12 Gala Xizang China
Galaasiya Uzbek. see Galaosiyo
133 I12 Gala Co l. China
197 L1 Gaładuś, Jezioro l. Pol.
198 G5 Galambok Hungary
185 E9 Galan France
282 D2 Galán, Cerro mt. Arg.
233 D5 Galana r. Kenya
219 N3 Gălănești Romania
116 F4 Galang Besar i. Indon.
231 C8 Galangue Angola
162 Q2 Gálaniitu Norway
199 G3 Galanta Slovakia
142 K8 Galaosiyo Uzbek.
205 M7 Galapagar Spain
274 A3 Galápagos prov. Ecuador
274 □ Galápagos, Islas is Pacific Ocean
Galapagos Islands is Pacific Ocean see Galápagos, Islas
291 M6 Galapagos Rise sea feature Pacific Ocean
206 F5 Galaroza Spain
232 C4 Galas well Kenya
168 K11 Galashiels Scottish Borders, Scotland U.K.
219 P7 Galata Bulg.
102 K5 Galatea North I. N.Z.
219 Q5 Galați Romania
217 O3 Galatina Italy
220 C2 Galatini Greece
220 E2 Galatista Greece
217 O3 Galatone Italy
209 K8 Galatzó, Puig de mt. Spain
171 L2 Gala Water r. Scotland U.K.
256 E12 Galax VA U.S.A.
220 D4 Galaxidi Greece
145 J4 Galaýmor Turkm.
Galaymor Turkm. see Galaýmor
169 F8 Galbally Ireland
205 P3 Galbarra Spain
107 H4 Galbraith Qld Austr.
238 □[3f] Gáldar Gran Canaria Canary Is
163 J6 Galdhøpiggen mt. Norway
228 C3 Galé Mali
205 N2 Galea, Punta pt Spain
266 F2 Galeana Chihuahua Mex.
267 I5 Galeana Nuevo León Mex.
213 L8 Galeata Italy
225 G6 Galegu Sudan
144 E8 Galeh Dār Iran
115 E3 Galela Halmahera Indon.
244 H2 Galena AK U.S.A.
260 J4 Galena IL U.S.A.
261 H7 Galena KS U.S.A.
258 D6 Galena MD U.S.A.
261 I7 Galena MO U.S.A.
246 G5 Galena Bay B.C. Can.
192 I3 Galenbecker See l. Ger.
204 G4 Galende Spain
271 □[7] Galeota Point Trin. and Tob.
207 N5 Galera Spain
207 N5 Galera r. Spain
283 B6 Galera, Punta pt Chile
274 A4 Galera, Punta pt Ecuador
269 J10 Galera, Punta pt Mex.
271 □[7] Galera Point Trin. and Tob.
214 B3 Galéria Corse France
214 A3 Galéria, Golfe de b. Corse France
260 J5 Galesburg IL U.S.A.
250 I7 Galesburg MI U.S.A.
259 K2 Gales Ferry CT U.S.A.
237 I4 Galeshewe S. Africa
250 C5 Galesville WI U.S.A.
256 H7 Galeton PA U.S.A.
239 □[1c] Galets, Pointe des pt Réunion
239 □[1c] Galets, Rivière des r. Réunion
196 G4 Galewice Pol.
169 C8 Galey r. Ireland
199 I4 Galga r. Hungary
199 I4 Galgagyörk Hungary
199 I4 Galgamácsa Hungary
184 D6 Galgon France
232 E3 Galguduud admin. reg. Somalia
232 E3 Gal Hareeri Somalia
151 C3 Gali Georgia
280 C5 Gália Brazil
246 F5 Galiano Island B.C. Can.
183 I6 Galibier, Col du pass France
219 L6 Galicea Mare Romania
156 H4 Galich Rus. Fed.
156 H4 Galichskaya Vozvyshennost' hills Rus. Fed.
204 E3 Galicia aut. comm. Spain
218 I9 Galičica nat. park Macedonia
151 C3 Galidzga r. Georgia
107 J7 Galilee, Lake salt flat Qld Austr.
Galilee, Sea of l. Israel see Kinneret, Yam
281 G3 Galiléia Brazil
212 I8 Galileo airport Italy
229 I5 Galim Tignère Cameroon
200 A5 Galinakopf mt. Austria/Liechtenstein
270 □ Galina Point Jamaica
268 G5 Galindo Mex.
204 C4 Galiñeiro hill Spain
197 I1 Galiny Pol.
256 C8 Galion OH U.S.A.
271 □[3] Galion, Baie du b. Martinique
220 F5 Galissas Syros Greece
204 H9 Galisteo Spain
227 H1 Galite, Canal de la sea chan. Tunisia
161 U8 Galitsa Rus. Fed.
265 V9 Galiuro Mountains AZ U.S.A.
106 E2 Galiwinku N.T. Austr.
145 J2 Galkynyş Turkm.
225 H6 Gallabat Sudan
143 L7 G'allaorol Uzbek.
212 F4 Gallarate Italy
178 C6 Gallardon France
183 E9 Gallargues-le-Montueux France
260 I6 Gallatin MO U.S.A.
255 D7 Gallatin TN U.S.A.
262 I4 Gallatin r. MT U.S.A.
136 G9 Galle Sri Lanka
208 D4 Gállego r. Spain
207 N6 Gallegón r. Spain
291 L6 Gallego Rise sea feature Pacific Ocean
283 C8 Gallegos r. Arg.
283 B7 Gallegos, Cabo c. Chile
204 G7 Gallegos de Argañan Spain
205 J7 Gallegos de Solmirón Spain
213 J8 Galleno Italy
215 I3 Gallese Italy
169 E9 Galley Head Ireland
Gallia country Europe see France
184 C5 Gallian-en-Médoc France
212 F5 Galliate Italy
215 J4 Gallicano nel Lazio Italy
192 F3 Gallin Mecklenburg-Vorpommern Ger.
190 K3 Gallin Mecklenburg-Vorpommern Ger.
274 D1 Gallinas, Punta pt Col.
213 L4 Gallio Italy
217 O3 Gallipoli Italy
Gallipoli Turkey see Gelibolu
256 C10 Gallipolis OH U.S.A.
208 E6 Gallipuén, Embalse de resr Spain
162 P3 Gällivare Sweden
201 K6 Gallizien Austria
201 J3 Gallneukirchen Austria
205 P7 Gallo r. Spain
162 M5 Gällö Sweden
216 E7 Gallo, Capo c. Sicilia Italy
212 I2 Gallo, Lago di l. Italy
205 Q7 Gallocanta, Laguna de l. Spain
256 I5 Gallo Island NY U.S.A.
215 L5 Galluccio Italy
256 C10 Gallup KY U.S.A.
263 J9 Gallup NM U.S.A.
205 R5 Gallur Spain
214 B6 Gallura reg. Sardegna Italy
229 G4 Galma watercourse Nigeria
168 D9 Galmisdale Highland, Scotland U.K.
170 B8 Galmoy Ireland
Galne Chechenskaya Respublika Rus. Fed. see Ken'yurt
Galne Chechenskaya Respublika Rus. Fed. see Kalinovskaya
105 L6 Galong N.S.W. Austr.
136 G8 Galoya Sri Lanka
136 G9 Gal Oya National Park Sri Lanka
169 G6 Galros Ireland
129 L3 Galshar Hentiy Mongolia
232 E2 Gal Shiikh Somalia
197 L1 Galstas l. Lith.
168 H11 Galston East Ayrshire, Scotland U.K.
128 F2 Galt Mongolia
264 K3 Galt CA U.S.A.
232 E4 Gal Tardo Somalia
226 B4 Galtat Zemmour Western Sahara
169 F8 Galtee Mountains hills Ireland
214 D7 Galtelli Sardegna Italy
165 M2 Galten l. Sweden
200 B6 Galtür Austria
169 F8 Galtymore hill Ireland
144 F7 Galūgāh, Kūh-e mts Iran
144 H4 Galūgāh-e Āsīyeh Iran
233 B7 Galula Tanz.
128 G3 Galuut Mongolia
250 D8 Galva IL U.S.A.
284 A6 Galvarino Chile
208 D6 Galve Spain
205 N6 Galve de Sorbe Spain
206 D2 Galveias Port.
250 H9 Galveston IN U.S.A.
261 H11 Galveston TX U.S.A.
261 H11 Galveston Bay TX U.S.A.
285 G3 Galvez Arg.
205 L9 Gálvez Spain
138 H5 Galwa Nepal
169 D6 Galway Ireland
169 D6 Galway county Ireland
169 D6 Galway Bay Ireland
271 □[2] Galways Soufrière vol. Montserrat
115 F4 Gam i. Papua Indon.
115 G4 Gam i. Papua Indon.
118 G4 Gâm, Sông r. Vietnam
280 C2 Gamá Brazil
283 E6 Gama, Isla i. Arg.
178 C4 Gamaches France
126 F6 Gamagōri Japan
237 O6 Gamalakhe S. Africa
115 E3 Gamalama vol. Maluku Indon.
185 C8 Gamarde-les-Bains France
274 C2 Gamarra Col.
Gámas Fin. see Kaamanen
199 G5 Gamás Hungary
229 H3 Gamawa Nigeria
284 E5 Gamay Arg.
114 E5 Gamay Bay Samar Phil.
231 C7 Gamba Angola
Gamba Xizang China see Gongbalou
230 A5 Gamba Gabon
228 E4 Gambaga Ghana
212 I5 Gambara Italy
217 J7 Gambarie Italy
213 J8 Gambassi Terme Italy
215 N4 Gambatesa Italy
232 B2 Gambēla Eth.
232 B3 Gambēla Hizboch admin. reg. Eth.
232 B3 Gambēla National Park Eth.
244 E3 Gambell AK U.S.A.
258 B6 Gamber MD U.S.A.
213 M7 Gambettola Italy
Gambia country Africa see The Gambia
228 A3 Gambia r. Gambia
228 B3 Gambie r. Senegal
106 C1 Gambier, Cape N.T. Austr.
Gambier, Île i. Arch. des Tuamotu Fr. Polynesia see Mangareva
101 □[9] Gambier, Îles is Arch. des Tuamotu Fr. Polynesia
104 F6 Gambier Islands S.A. Austr.
Gambier Islands Arch. des Tuamotu Fr. Polynesia see Gambier, Îles
255 □[2] Gambier Village New Prov. Bahamas
249 K3 Gambo Nfld and Lab. Can.
230 D3 Gambo C.A.R.
212 F5 Gambolò Italy
230 B5 Gamboma Congo
107 I4 Gamboola Qld Austr.
230 B3 Gamboula C.A.R.
258 B6 Gambrills MD U.S.A.
179 O6 Gambsheim France
Gamda Sichuan China see Zamtang
Gameti N.W.T. Can. see Gamêtî
246 G1 Gamêtî N.W.T. Can.
201 L4 Gaming Austria
151 H5 Gamış Dağı mt. Azer.
236 F9 Gamka r. S. Africa
115 E3 Gamkunoro, Gunung vol. Halmahera Indon.
Gamlakarleby Fin. see Kokkola
165 M4 Gamleby Sweden
173 L3 Gamlingay Cambridgeshire, England U.K.
201 M6 Gamlitz Austria
225 G5 Gammams well Sudan
195 L4 Gammelsdorf Ger.
162 Q4 Gammelstaden Sweden
194 G5 Gammertingen Ger.
126 D5 Gamō Japan
236 C5 Gamoep S. Africa
204 I2 Gamonal mt. Spain
122 G7 Gamova, Mys pt Rus. Fed.
136 G9 Gampaha Sri Lanka
136 G9 Gampola Sri Lanka
212 G1 Gams Switz.
145 I7 Gamshadzai Kūh mts Iran
130 B3 Gamtog Xizang China
237 J9 Gamtoos r. S. Africa
232 C3 Gamud mt. Eth.
162 T1 Gamvik Norway
185 D9 Gan France
135 □[2] Gan Addu Atoll Maldives
135 □[2] Gan i. Addu Atoll Maldives
130 C2 Gana Sichuan China
265 W6 Ganado AZ U.S.A.
183 H8 Ganagobie France
225 G5 Gananita Sudan
248 E4 Gananoque Ont. Can.
151 H5 Gäncä Azer.
151 H5 Gäncäçay r. Azer.
132 I6 Gancaohu Xinjiang China
130 G9 Gancheng Hainan China
Gand Belgium see Gent
231 B8 Ganda Angola
133 L11 Ganda Xizang China
115 A5 Gandadiwata, Bukit mt. Indon.
138 H9 Gandai Chhattisgarh India
231 D6 Gandajika Dem. Rep. Congo
139 I6 Gandak Barrage dam Nepal
145 I5 Gandalak Afgh.
138 E2 Gandarbal Jammu and Kashmir India
204 D6 Gandarela Port.
145 M7 Gandari Mountain Pak.
145 I5 Gandarra Afgh.
145 L7 Gandava Pak.
212 H4 Gandellino Italy
249 K3 Gander Nfld and Lab. Can.
243 M5 Gander r. Nfld and Lab. Can.
190 G4 Ganderkesee Ger.
249 K3 Gander Lake Nfld and Lab. Can.
208 F5 Gandesa Spain
138 D9 Gandevi Gujarat India
138 C8 Gandhidham Gujarat India
138 D8 Gandhinagar Gujarat India
138 E7 Gandhi Sagar resr India
230 E2 Gandi, Wadi watercourse Sudan
209 E10 Gandia Spain
212 H4 Gandino Italy
238 □[3f] Gando, Punta de pt Gran Canaria Canary Is
144 D6 Gandomān Iran
151 J4 Gändov Azer.
204 C4 Gandra Viana do Castelo Port.
204 D5 Gandra Viana do Castelo Port.
278 F5 Gandu Brazil
128 H9 Gandu Qinghai China
162 T1 Gandvik Norway
Gandzha Azer. see Gäncä
228 C2 Gâneb well Maur.
244 H3 Ganes Creek AK U.S.A.
204 C4 Ganfei Port.
139 L7 Ganga r. Bangl./India alt. Padma (Bangladesh), conv. Ganges
229 G4 Ganga Nigeria
136 G9 Ganga r. Sri Lanka
Ganga Cone sea feature Indian Ocean see Ganges Cone
136 E3 Gangakher Mahar. India
230 F4 Gangala Na Bodia Dem. Rep. Congo
283 C6 Gangán Arg.
283 C6 Gangán, Pampa de plain Arg.
138 D5 Ganganagar Rajasthan India
136 D3 Gangapur Mahar. India
138 E7 Gangapur Rajasthan India
138 F6 Gangapur Rajasthan India
229 H3 Gangara Niger
139 L9 Ganga Sagar W. Bengal India
138 C7 Ganga Sera Rajasthan India
136 D5 Gangavali r. India
118 B3 Gangaw Myanmar
136 E5 Gangawati Karnataka India
118 C3 Gangaw Range mts Myanmar
128 G8 Gangca Qinghai China
138 E8 Gangdhar Rajasthan India
133 F11 Gangdisê Shan mts Xizang China
139 L8 Ganges r. Bangl./India alt. Ganga (India), alt. Padma (Bangladesh)
183 D9 Ganges France
139 L9 Ganges, Mouths of the Bangl./India
289 J3 Ganges Cone sea feature Indian Ocean
216 G8 Gangi Sicilia Italy
216 G8 Gangi r. Sicilia Italy
195 N5 Gangkofen Ger.
228 C5 Ganglota Liberia
128 E7 Gangou Qinghai China
128 I9 Gangouyi Gansu China
Gangra Turkey see Çankırı
138 E7 Gangrar Rajasthan India
139 L6 Gangtok Sikkim India
128 I9 Gangu Gansu China
129 N8 Gangziyao Hebei China
129 S2 Gan He r. China
132 I4 Ganhezi Xinjiang China
115 F4 Gani Halmahera Indon.
228 C4 Ganiakali Guinea
137 I3 Ganjam Orissa India
144 D6 Ganjgūn Iran
129 R5 Ganjig Nei Mongol China
129 L9 Ganjing Shaanxi China
129 N4 Ganjur Sum Nei Mongol China
161 Q2 Gankovo Rus. Fed.
130 D4 Ganluo Sichuan China
129 R3 Gannan Heilong. China
182 C4 Gannat France
249 J2 Gannet Islands Ecological Reserve nature res. Nfld and Lab. Can.
262 J5 Gannett Peak WY U.S.A.
158 F3 Gannopil' Ukr.
260 F3 Gannvalley SD U.S.A.
133 K8 Ganq Qinghai China
129 K8 Ganquan Shaanxi China
236 D10 Gansbaai S. Africa
191 D10 Gänsehals hill Ger.
201 O3 Gänserndorf Austria
187 F7 Ganshoren Belgium
130 F4 Ganshui Chongqing China
128 E6 Gansu prov. China
232 D4 Gantamaa Somalia
128 I8 Gantang Nei Mongol China
139 I9 Gantapara Orissa India
108 G4 Gantheaume Point W.A. Austr.
151 B2 Gant'iadi Ap'khazet'i Georgia
151 F4 Gant'iadi Georgia
Ganting Shaanxi China see Huxian
212 C2 Gantrisch mt. Switz.
Gantsevichi Belarus see Hantsavichy
117 H6 Gantung Indon.
131 J6 Ganxian Jiangxi China
138 F8 Ganyal r. Madh. Prad. India
229 I4 Ganye Nigeria
236 I2 Ganyesa S. Africa
129 P9 Ganyu Jiangsu China
142 C4 Ganyushkino Kazakh.
Ganzhe Fujian China see Minhou
131 J6 Ganzhou Jiangxi China
232 A3 Ganzi Sudan
192 F4 Ganzlin Ger.
229 E2 Gao Mali
229 F2 Gao admin. reg. Mali
131 J4 Gao'an Jiangxi China
128 H8 Gaoba Gansu China
129 N7 Gaocheng Hebei China
Gaocheng Sichuan China see Litang
131 L3 Gaochun Jiangsu China
Gaocun Hunan China see Mayang
131 M4 Gaojian Zhejiang China
128 H8 Gaolan Gansu China
Gaoleshan Hubei China see Xianfeng
Gaoliangjian Jiangsu China see Hongze
130 B6 Gaoligong Shan mts China
129 K9 Gaoling Shaanxi China
129 P8 Gaomi Shandong China
131 H5 Gaomutang Hunan China
129 M9 Gaoping Shanxi China
129 O8 Gaoqing Shandong China
128 F7 Gaotai Gansu China
129 O8 Gaotang Shandong China
Gaotangling Hunan China see Wangcheng
169 F2 Gaoth Dobhair Ireland
Gaoting Zhejiang China see Daishan
129 K7 Gaotouyao Nei Mongol China
228 E4 Gaoua Burkina
228 B4 Gaoual Guinea
Gaoxian Sichuan China see Wenjiang
Gaoxiong Taiwan see Kaohsiung
129 N7 Gaoyang Hebei China
131 I7 Gaoyao Guangdong China
129 N8 Gaoyi Hebei China
131 L2 Gaoyou Jiangsu China
131 L2 Gaoyou Hu l. China
130 H8 Gaozhou Guangdong China
183 I7 Gap France
258 C5 Gap PA U.S.A.
102 □ Gap, Point Chatham Is S. Pacific Ocean
114 C4 Gapan Luzon Phil.
183 I10 Gapeau r. France
230 E3 Gapi Dem. Rep. Congo
106 E2 Gapuwiyak N.T. Austr.
133 F12 Gaqoi Xizang China
139 K5 Gaqung Xizang China
120 D5 Gar Xizang China
145 J8 Gar Pak.
122 F2 Gar' r. Rus. Fed.
199 I5 Gara Hungary
169 F5 Gara, Lough l. Ireland
227 H3 Garaa Tebourt well Tunisia
209 C8 Garaballa Spain
145 K2 Garabekewül Turkm.
145 J3 Garabil Belentligi hills Turkm.
230 B4 Garabinzam Congo
183 C7 Garabit, Viaduc de France
144 E1 Garabogaz Turkm.
144 E1 Garabogazköl Turkm.
144 E1 Garabogazköl Aýlagy b. Turkm.
Garabogazköl Aylagy b. Turkm. see Garabogazköl Aýlagy
144 E1 Garabogazköl Bogazy sea chan. Turkm.
232 F3 Garacad Somalia
238 □[3a] Garachico Tenerife Canary Is
266 □T13 Garachiné Panama
266 □T13 Garachiné, Punta pt Panama
232 E2 Garadag Somalia
170 D7 Garadice Ireland
169 G4 Garadice Lough l. Ireland
227 G6 Gara Ekar hill Alg.
238 □[3d] Garafía La Palma Canary Is
205 P2 Garagarza Spain
144 I6 Garāgheh Iran
274 C3 Garagoa Col.
144 E2 Garagöl Turkm.
Garagum des. Kazakh. see Karakum, Peski
144 I2 Garagum des. Turkm.
145 I3 Garagum Kanaly canal Turkm.
215 Q6 Garaguso Italy
105 L3 Garah N.S.W. Austr.
145 O4 Garai Pak.
238 □[3a] Garajonay, Parque Nacional de nat. park La Gomera Canary Is
228 D4 Garalo Mali
Garamätnyyaz Turkm. see Garamätnyýaz
145 K3 Garamätnyýaz Turkm.
230 F4 Garamba r. Dem. Rep. Congo
230 F3 Garamba, Parc National de la nat. park Dem. Rep. Congo
128 G8 Garang Qinghai China
278 F4 Garanhuns Brazil
237 L1 Ga-Rankuwa S. Africa
278 B5 Garapu Brazil
280 D2 Garapuava Brazil
230 D2 Garar, Plaine de plain Chad
138 G7 Garautha Uttar Prad. India
183 G8 Garaux, Rocher mt. France
106 F4 Garawa Aboriginal Land res. N.T. Austr.
230 D2 Garba C.A.R.
232 D4 Garbahaarrey Somalia
197 J4 Garbatka-Letnisko Pol.
232 C4 Garba Tula Kenya
207 J2 Garbayuela Spain
264 I1 Garberville CA U.S.A.
219 O5 Gârbova, Vârful hill Romania
197 K4 Garbów Pol.
191 I6 Garbsen Ger.
138 H4 Garbyang Uttaranchal India
280 C5 Garça Brazil
280 A1 Garças, Rio das r. Brazil
219 P4 Gârceni Romania
195 N5 Garching an der Alz Ger.
195 L5 Garching bei München Ger.
182 C2 Garchizy France
208 G5 García Spain
268 D5 García, Cerro mt. Mex.
268 D4 García de la Cadena Mex.
280 A4 Garcias Brazil
207 I2 García Sola, Embalse de resr Spain
206 H2 Garcíaz Spain
205 J7 Garcihernández Spain
205 L7 Garcillán Spain
219 O4 Gârcina Romania
205 O8 Garcinarro Spain
183 E8 Gard dept France
183 F9 Gard r. France
213 J4 Garda Italy
213 J5 Garda, Lago di l. Italy
151 G4 Gardabani Georgia
219 K4 Gârda de Sus Romania
183 G10 Gardanne France
211 A7 Garde, Cap de c. Alg.
196 G2 Gardeja Pol.
247 J2 Garde Lake N.W.T. Can.
192 D5 Gardelegen Ger.
213 L2 Gardena r. Italy
260 E7 Garden City KS U.S.A.
259 H3 Garden City NY U.S.A.
261 E10 Garden City TX U.S.A.
250 H4 Garden Corners MI U.S.A.
264 O8 Garden Grove CA U.S.A.
247 M4 Garden Hill Man. Can.
109 C12 Garden Island W.A. Austr.
250 I4 Garden Island MI U.S.A.
256 D11 Garden Mountain VA U.S.A.
258 A2 Garden View PA U.S.A.
186 I4 Garderen Neth.
164 G1 Gardermoen airport Norway
285 H5 Gardey Arg.
145 M5 Gardēz Afgh.
Gardinas Belarus see Hrodna
257 □P4 Gardiner ME U.S.A.
262 I4 Gardiner MT U.S.A.
106 D7 Gardiner, Mount N.T. Austr.
106 B5 Gardiner Range hills N.T. Austr.
259 K2 Gardiners Bay NY U.S.A.
259 K2 Gardiners Island NY U.S.A.
106 D7 Gardiner's Range mts N.T. Austr.
190 G2 Garding Ger.
Gardner atoll Micronesia see Faraulep
250 F8 Gardner IL U.S.A.
257 N6 Gardner MA U.S.A.
286 T1 Gardner Inlet Antarctica
Gardner Island atoll Phoenix Is Kiribati see Nikumaroro
259 K1 Gardner Lake CT U.S.A.
257 □R4 Gardner Lake ME U.S.A.
97 H2 Gardner Pinnacles is HI U.S.A.
264 M3 Gardnerville NV U.S.A.
165 N7 Gardno, Jezioro lag. Pol.
183 E8 Gardon d'Alès r. France
183 D8 Gardon de St-Jean r. France
213 J4 Gardone Riviera Italy
212 I4 Gardone Val Trompia Italy
185 E6 Gardonne France
199 H4 Gárdony Hungary
185 H9 Gardouch France
162 N4 Gardsjönås Sweden
165 M5 Gärdslösa Öland Sweden
Gáregasnjárga Fin. see Karigasniemi
185 C7 Garein France
170 H1 Gare Loch inlet Scotland U.K.
168 G10 Garelochhead Argyll and Bute, Scotland U.K.
245 □C6 Gareloi Island AK U.S.A.
Gares Spain see Puente la Reina
210 F3 Garešnica Croatia
212 E7 Garessio Italy
100 □[5] Garet, Mount vol. Vanuatu
227 G4 Garet el Djenoun mt. Alg.
275 H3 Gare Tigre Fr. Guiana
263 K7 Garfield CO U.S.A.
259 G3 Garfield NJ U.S.A.
171 O6 Garforth West Yorkshire, England U.K.
215 Q8 Garga r. Italy
220 C5 Gargalianoi Greece
206 H2 Gargáligas Spain
207 H2 Gargáligas r. Spain
208 D6 Gargallo Spain
184 H4 Gargan, Mont hill France
215 P4 Gargano, Parco Nazionale del nat. park Italy
204 I8 Garganta la Olla Spain
248 C4 Gargantua, Cape Ont. Can.
149 N8 Gargar Iran
183 G9 Gargas France
213 K2 Gargazzone Italy
200 A6 Gargellen Austria
178 D6 Garges-lès-Gonesse France
184 H2 Gargilesse-Dampierre France
213 J4 Gargnano Italy
183 D8 Gargo mt. France
171 M6 Gargrave North Yorkshire, England U.K.
168 H10 Gargunnock Hills Scotland U.K.
Gargunsa Xizang China see Gar
160 E6 Gargždai Lith.
138 G8 Garhakota Madh. Prad. India
139 K8 Garhbeta W. Bengal India
138 G8 Garhi Madh. Prad. India

138 E8 Garhi Rajasthan India
145 L7 Garhi Khairo Pak.
138 G7 Garhi Malehra Madh. Prad. India
138 G5 Garhmuktesar Uttar Prad. India
138 F4 Garhshankar Punjab India
139 I7 Garhwa Jharkhand India
215 L5 Gari r. Italy
279 C9 Garibaldi Brazil
246 F5 Garibaldi B.C. Can.
246 F5 Garibaldi, Mount B.C. Can.
246 F5 Garibaldi Provincial Park B.C. Can.
237 J6 Gariep Dam resr S. Africa
237 J6 Gariep Dam Nature Reserve S. Africa
236 B6 Garies S. Africa
106 D1 Garig Gunak Barlu National Park N.T. Austr.
215 L5 Garigliano r. Italy
169 B9 Garinish Ireland
205 Q3 Garinoain Spain
232 C5 Garissa Kenya
160 H4 Garkalne Latvia
133 H10 Garkung Caka l. Xizang China
Gârla Mare r. Moldova see Gîrla Mare
261 G9 Garland TX U.S.A.
212 F5 Garlasco Italy
201 K4 Garlenz Austria
160 G7 Garliava Lith.
219 Q6 Gârliciu Romania
168 H13 Garlieston Dumfries and Galloway, Scotland U.K.
185 D8 Garlin France
207 I3 Garlitos Spain
169 I5 Garlowcross Ireland
190 J4 Garlstorf Ger.
Garm Tajik. see Gharm
145 K5 Garmab Afgh.
144 G4 Garmāb Iran
144 H5 Garm Āb, Chashmeh-ye spring Iran
144 C6 Garmdasht Iran
144 F5 Garmeh Eşfahān Iran
144 G3 Garmeh Jājarm Khorāsān Iran
144 C2 Garmī Iran
195 K7 Garmisch-Partenkirchen Ger.
168 E10 Garmony Argyll and Bute, Scotland U.K.
144 E7 Garmosht Iran
144 E4 Garmsār Iran
145 J6 Garmsel reg. Afgh.
145 J6 Garmushki Afgh.
260 I4 Garner IA U.S.A.
256 C11 Garner KY U.S.A.
260 H6 Garnett KS U.S.A.
144 H7 Gārnow Iran
105 I5 Garnpung Lake imp. l. N.S.W. Austr.
139 M7 Garo Hills Meghalaya India
208 G2 Garona r. Spain
185 C6 Garonne r. France
185 E7 Garonne, Canal latéral à la France
183 E9 Garons France
232 F2 Garoowe Somalia
279 C9 Garopaba Brazil
138 F6 Garoth Madh. Prad. India
228 E2 Garou, Lac l. Mali
229 I4 Garoua Cameroon
229 I5 Garoua Boulai Cameroon
165 K2 Garphyttan Sweden
165 K2 Garphyttans nationalpark nat. park Sweden
133 K10 Gar Qu r. Qinghai China
133 K10 Garqu Yan Qinghai China
204 I3 Garrafe de Torío Spain
185 B10 Garralda Spain
205 P5 Garray Spain
285 F5 Garré Arg.
190 F5 Garrel Ger.
114 □ Garreru i. Palau
250 I8 Garrett IN U.S.A.
183 D9 Garrigues reg. France
169 F4 Garrison Northern Ireland U.K.
256 B10 Garrison KY U.S.A.
260 I2 Garrison MN U.S.A.
260 E2 Garrison ND U.S.A.
259 H2 Garrison NY U.S.A.
169 J5 Garristown Ireland
151 E4 Garrnarrich Armenia
269 L7 Garro Mex.
169 K2 Garron Point Northern Ireland U.K.
204 G9 Garrovillas Spain
207 P6 Garrucha Spain
208 D6 Garrucha, Sierra de la mts Spain
145 K7 Garruk Pak.
168 G8 Garry r. Scotland U.K.
168 G8 Garry, Loch l. Highland, Scotland U.K.
144 I3 Garryçyrla Turkm.
245 N1 Garry Island N.W.T. Can.
243 H3 Garry Lake Nunavut Can.
168 C6 Garrynahine Western Isles, Scotland U.K.
237 L7 Garryowen S. Africa
169 F9 Garryvoe Ireland
195 M5 Gars am Inn Ger.
201 M2 Gars am Kamp Austria
171 M5 Garsdale Head Cumbria, England U.K.
232 D5 Garsen Kenya
Garshy Turkm. see Garşy
224 D6 Garsila Sudan
165 K6 Gärsnäs Sweden
171 L6 Garstang Lancashire, England U.K.
190 J4 Garstedt Ger.
201 J3 Garsten Austria
103 C12 Garston South I. N.Z.
144 E1 Garşy Turkm.
Gartar Sichuan China see Qianning
184 F2 Gartempe r. France
172 E3 Garth Powys, Wales U.K.
172 F2 Garthmyl Powys, Wales U.K.
168 G10 Gartocharn West Dunbartonshire, Scotland U.K.
Gartog Xizang China see Markam
Gartok Xizang China see Garyarsa
192 D4 Gartow Ger.
194 F4 Gärtringen Ger.
192 J4 Gartz Ger.
234 C5 Garub Namibia
114 □ Garusuun Palau
117 G8 Garut Jawa Indon.
169 G5 Garvagh Ireland
169 I3 Garvagh Northern Ireland U.K.
169 H4 Garvaghy Northern Ireland U.K.
168 K11 Garvald East Lothian, Scotland U.K.
168 H8 Garvamore Highland, Scotland U.K.
206 C5 Garvão Port.
168 D10 Garvard Argyll and Bute, Scotland U.K.
168 G7 Garve Highland, Scotland U.K.
103 C12 Garvie Mountains South I. N.Z.
197 J4 Garwolin Pol.
133 E10 Gar Xincun Xizang China
254 D7 Gary IN U.S.A.
256 D11 Gary WV U.S.A.
133 E11 Garyarsa Xizang China
130 B3 Garyi Sichuan China
125 J12 Garyū-zan mt. Japan
190 I2 Garz Ger.
282 E3 Garza Arg.
133 D10 Gar Zangbo r. China
269 H1 Garza Valdez Mex.
130 B3 Garzê Sichuan China
274 C4 Garzón Col.
Gasan-Kuli Turkm. see Esenguly
196 F3 Gąsawa Pol.
200 B6 Gaschurn Austria
193 F8 Gaschwitz Ger.
185 C8 Gascogne reg. France
176 C5 Gascogne, Golfe de g. France/Spain
260 J6 Gasconade r. MO U.S.A.
Gascony reg. France see Gascogne
Gascony, Gulf of France/Spain see Gascogne, Golfe de
109 C8 Gascoyne r. W.A. Austr.
109 D8 Gascoyne, Mount hill W.A. Austr.
109 C8 Gascoyne Junction W.A. Austr.
205 O8 Gascueña Spain
Gascuña, Golfo de g. France/Spain see Gascogne, Golfe de
133 H11 Gase Xizang China
135 □ Gasfinolhu i. N. Male Maldives
146 C8 Gash and Setit prov. Eritrea
225 H6 Gash Barka prov. Eritrea
138 F2 Gasherbrum I mt. China/Pak.
145 Q4 Gasherbrum II mt. China/Pak.
225 H6 Gash Setit Wildlife Reserve nature res. Eritrea
133 J7 Gas Hu salt l. China
229 H3 Gashua Nigeria
168 B7 Gasker i. Scotland U.K.
197 K2 Gąski Pol.
185 C5 Gasny France
197 I3 Gąsocin Pol.
270 D3 Gaspar Cuba
116 G6 Gaspar, Selat sea chan. Indon.
249 H3 Gaspé Que. Can.
249 H3 Gaspé, Baie de b. Que. Can.
249 H3 Gaspé, Cap c. Que. Can.
217 L6 Gasperina Italy
249 H3 Gaspésie, Péninsule de la pen. Que. Can.
190 K2 Gaspoltshofen Austria
201 I3 Gassan Burkina
228 E3 Gassan vol. Japan
124 R8 Gassane Senegal
228 B3 Gassaway WV U.S.A.
256 E10 Gasselte Neth.
186 K3 Gasselternijveen Neth.
186 K3 Gasset, Embalse de resr Spain
207 L2 Gassin France
183 J10 Gassol Nigeria
229 H4 Gass Peak NV U.S.A.
265 Q5 Gasteiner Tal val. Austria
200 H5 Gasteiz Spain see Vitoria-Gasteiz
122 M4 Gastello Sakhalin Rus. Fed.
153 P3 Gastello, imeni Rus. Fed.
201 L2 Gastern Austria
185 B7 Gastes France
256 H12 Gaston NC U.S.A.
256 H12 Gaston, Lake NC U.S.A.
255 G8 Gastonia NC U.S.A.
220 C5 Gastouni Greece
283 C6 Gastre Arg.
204 G8 Gata Spain
207 O7 Gata, Cabo de c. Spain
150 B4 Gata, Cape Cyprus
204 G8 Gata, Sierra de mts Spain
209 F10 Gata de Gorgos Spain
245 P4 Gataga r. B.C. Can.
218 J5 Gătaia Romania
Gatas, Akra c. Cyprus see Gata, Cape
161 N2 Gatchina Rus. Fed.
256 C12 Gate City VA U.S.A.
168 H13 Gatehouse of Fleet Dumfries and Galloway, Scotland U.K.
199 I5 Gátér Hungary
193 D7 Gatersleben Ger.
171 N4 Gateshead Tyne and Wear, England U.K.
243 H2 Gateshead Island Nunavut Can.
244 I2 Gates of the Arctic National Park and Preserve AK U.S.A.
255 I7 Gatesville NC U.S.A.
261 G10 Gatesville TX U.S.A.
265 X3 Gateway CO U.S.A.
264 Q5 Gateway National Recreational Area park NJ U.S.A.
276 C5 Gatico Chile
178 E7 Gâtinais reg. France
181 L7 Gâtine reg. France
181 F4 Gatineau Que. Can.
181 F4 Gatineau r. Que. Can.
207 J4 Gato r. Spain
Gatong Xizang China see Jomda
Gatooma Zimbabwe see Kadoma
209 D8 Gátova Spain
201 O3 Gattendorf Austria
213 M7 Gatteo a Mare Italy
183 K9 Gattières France
212 E4 Gattinara Italy
183 N9 Gatton Qld Austr.
274 B2 Gatún Panama
266 □S13 Gatún, Lago l. Panama
144 C5 Gatvand Iran
101 □7 Gau i. Fiji
194 E2 Gau-Algesheim Ger.
278 B5 Gaúcha do Norte Brazil
178 F4 Gauchy France
207 I7 Gaucín Spain
207 J7 Gaudalteba, Embalse de resr Spain
247 L3 Gauer Lake Man. Can.
Gauhati Assam India see Guwahati
160 H4 Gauja r. Latvia
160 I4 Gauja r. Lith.
160 I4 Gaujas nacionālais parks nat. park Latvia
194 H2 Gaukönigshofen Ger.
Gaul country Europe see France
206 □ Gaula Madeira
162 K5 Gaula r. Norway
256 D10 Gauley Bridge WV U.S.A.
187 I9 Gaume reg. Belgium
194 E2 Gau-Odernheim Ger.
163 I6 Gaupne Norway
Gaurdak Turkm. see Gowurdak
136 E6 Gauribidanur Karnataka India
139 M8 Gaurnadi Bangl.
164 E2 Gausta mt. Norway
237 M2 Gauteng prov. S. Africa
195 K5 Gauting Ger.
208 E4 Gautizalema r. Spain
145 K4 Gauzan Afgh.
208 J5 Gavà Spain
149 P9 Gavākān Iran
212 I4 Gavardo Italy
144 H3 Gāvareshg Iran
185 D10 Gavarnie France
185 D10 Gavarnie, Cirque de corrie France/Spain
151 G5 Gavarr Armenia
145 I9 Gavāter Iran
199 K3 Gávavencsellő Hungary
144 E8 Gāvbandī Iran
144 E8 Gāvbūs, Kūh-e mts Iran
220 F8 Gavdopoula i. Greece
220 F8 Gavdos i. Greece
204 D4 Gave Port.
144 B4 Gāveh Rūd r. Iran
187 E7 Gavere Belgium
212 F6 Gavi Italy
215 K6 Gavi, Isola di i. Italy
279 E5 Gavião r. Brazil
206 D2 Gavião Port.
274 D6 Gaviãozinho Brazil
144 B4 Gavīleh Iran
285 F6 Gaviotas Arg.
212 F4 Gavirate Italy
144 E5 Gav Khūnī Iran
165 N1 Gävle Sweden
165 M1 Gävleborg county Sweden
190 H4 Gävlebukten b. Sweden
165 N1 Gavoi Sardegna Italy
214 C7 Gavorrano Italy
212 F4 Gavray France
180 I4 Gavrilovka Vtoraya Rus. Fed.
157 H5 Gavrilov Posad Rus. Fed.
161 X5 Gavrilov-Yam Rus. Fed.
161 W4 Gavrio Andros Greece
220 F5 Gawachab Namibia
234 C5 Gawai Myanmar
118 C1 Gawan Jharkhand India
139 J7 Gawat well Libya
224 B3 Gaweinstal Austria
201 O3 Gāwers Turkm.
144 H3 Gawilgarh Hills India
138 F9 Gawler S.A. Austr.
104 G6 Gawler Ranges hills S.A. Austr.
104 E5 Gawler Ranges National Park nat. park Australia
104 E5 Gawliki Wielkie Pol.
197 K1 Gaworzyce Pol.
196 D4 Gawsworth Cheshire, England U.K.
171 M7 Gawthrop Cumbria, England U.K.
171 M5 Gawu Nigeria
229 G4 Gawür watercourse Turkm.
144 F2 Gawür watercourse Turkm.
128 G5 Gaxun Nur salt l. Nei Mongol China
142 H2 Gay Rus. Fed.
250 F2 Gay MI U.S.A.
139 J7 Gaya Bihar India
117 L1 Gaya i. Malaysia
117 M2 Gaya i. Malaysia
229 F4 Gaya Niger
Gayá r. Spain see El Gaià
122 F7 Gaya He r. China
137 D2 Gayal Gah Pak.
117 K8 Gayam Jawa Indon.
232 A5 Gayaza Uganda
170 C7 Gaybrook Ireland
226 C4 G'Aydat al Jhoucha ridge Western Sahara
159 Q9 Gayduk Rus. Fed.
229 F3 Gayéri Burkina
250 J4 Gaylord MI U.S.A.
260 H3 Gaylord MN U.S.A.
107 M8 Gayndah Qld Austr.
161 T4 Gaynovo Rus. Fed.
156 K3 Gayny Rus. Fed.
Gaysin Ukr. see Haysyn
173 N2 Gayton Norfolk, England U.K.
156 G4 Gayutino Rus. Fed.
Gayvoron Ukr. see Hayvoron
144 D5 Gaz Eşfahān Iran
144 G8 Gaz Hormozgan Iran
150 C7 Gaza terr. Asia
150 C7 Gaza Gaza
235 G4 Gaza prov. Moz.
144 G6 Gazak Iran
143 M7 G'azalkent Uzbek.
145 L7 Gazan Pak.
229 I4 Gazawa Cameroon
100 □5 Gazelle, Récif de la rf New Caledonia
144 F5 Gazestān Iran
230 E4 Gazi Dem. Rep. Congo
148 H5 Gaziantep Turkey
150 F2 Gaziantep prov. Turkey
Gazibenli Turkey see Yahyalı
144 I5 Gazik Iran
151 E5 Gaziler Turkey
Gazimağusa Cyprus see Ammochostos
122 B2 Gazimur r. Rus. Fed.
129 L2 Gazimurо-Ononskiy Khrebet mts Rus. Fed.
122 A3 Gazimurskiy Khrebet mts Rus. Fed.
148 F5 Gazipaşa Turkey
218 I8 Gazivodsko Jezero l. Serbia/Kosovo
142 J7 Gazli Uzbek.
144 H8 Gaz Māhū Iran
144 E3 Gaznāsarā Iran
145 I1 Gazojak Turkm.
Gazojak Turkm. see Gazojak
205 Q3 Gazolaz Spain
213 J5 Gazoldo degli Ippoliti Italy
213 K5 Gazzo Veronese Italy
213 J5 Gazzuolo Italy
228 D5 Gbaaka Liberia
230 D3 Gbadolite Dem. Rep. Congo
228 B5 Gbangbatok Sierra Leone
228 C5 Gbarnga Liberia
228 D5 Gbatala Liberia
199 H4 Gbelce Slovakia
198 G3 Gbely Slovakia
229 F4 Gbéroubouè Benin
229 H5 Gboko Nigeria
230 D4 Gbwado Dem. Rep. Congo
165 O7 Gdańsk Pol.
197 H1 Gdańsk, Gulf of Pol./Rus. Fed.
Gdańska, Zatoka g. Pol./Rus. Fed. see Gdańsk, Gulf of
Gdingen Pol. see Gdynia
160 K3 Gdov Rus. Fed.
197 I6 Gdów Pol.
165 O7 Gdynia Pol.
208 C7 Gea de Albarracín Spain
162 Q2 Geaidnovuohppi Norway
168 H8 Geal Charn hill Highland, Scotland U.K.
168 J8 Geal Charn hill Highland, Scotland U.K.
168 E4 Gealldruig Mhòr i. Scotland U.K.
185 I11 Géant, Pic du mt. France
100 □3a Gea Passage Kwajalein Marshall Is
262 D5 Gearhart Mountain OR U.S.A.
Gearraidh na h-Aibhne Scotland U.K. see Garrynahine
Gearraidh na h-Aibhne Western Isles, Scotland U.K. see Garrynahine
170 C7 Geashill Ireland
258 F6 Geat Sound b. NJ U.S.A.
185 D8 Geaune France
Geavvú Fin. see Kevo
115 F3 Gebe i. Maluku Indon.
225 H5 Gebeit Sudan
225 H4 Gebeit Mine Sudan
191 K8 Gebesee Ger.
192 E8 Gebhardshain Ger.
196 E3 Gębice Pol.
221 L5 Gebiz Turkey
225 H6 Gebre Guracha Eth.
221 K2 Gebze Turkey
232 B3 Gech'a Eth.
Gecheng Chongqing China see Chengkou
194 F4 Gechingen Ger.
151 C6 Geçit Turkey
Geçitkale Cyprus see Lefkonikon
116 D6 Gedang, Gunung mt. Indon.
160 H7 Gedanonių kalnas hill Lith.
225 G6 Gedaref Sudan
225 G6 Gedaref state Sudan
173 K3 Geddington Northamptonshire, England U.K.
199 H5 Géderlak Hungary
191 H10 Gedern Ger.
224 E6 Gedid Ras el Fil Sudan
187 G9 Gedinne Belgium
221 K4 Gediz Turkey
221 H4 Gediz r. Turkey
232 E3 Gedlegubē Eth.
173 M2 Gedney Drove End Lincolnshire, England U.K.
232 C2 Gēdo Eth.
232 D4 Gedo admin. reg. Somalia
117 I4 Gedong Sarawak Malaysia
116 □ Gedong, Tanjong pt Sing.
185 E10 Gèdre France
164 H7 Gedser Denmark
164 H7 Gedser Odde c. Denmark
164 H7 Gedsted Denmark
116 F7 Gedungpakuan Sumatera Indon.
Gedzheti Georgia see Gejet'i
187 H6 Geel Belgium
105 J8 Geelong Vic. Austr.
109 B10 Geelvink Channel W.A. Austr.
236 E5 Geel Vloer salt pan S. Africa
187 I7 Geer r. Belgium
186 I4 Geertruidenberg Neth.
93 G5 Gees Gwardatuy
190 D5 Geeste Ger.
190 G3 Geeste r. Ger.
186 K4 Geesteren Neth.
193 F5 Geestgottberg Ger.
190 J4 Geesthacht Ger.
187 H7 Geetbets Belgium
193 E10 Gefell Ger.
232 C2 Gefersa Eth.
186 H5 Geffen Neth.
193 E10 Gefrees Ger.
160 E6 Gēgē r. Lith.
Gegechkori Georgia see Martvili
129 P1 Gegen He r. China
199 K3 Gégény Hungary
151 F5 Geghadir Armenia
151 F5 Geghama Lermnashght'a mts Armenia
151 G5 Geghamasar Armenia
160 H7 Geguže Lith.
133 E10 Gê'gyai Xizang China
100 □3a Gehh i. Kwajalein Marshall Is
190 F5 Gehrde Ger.
191 I6 Gehrden Ger.
193 D9 Gehren Ger.
131 L3 Ge Hu l. China
229 H3 Geidam Nigeria
194 G2 Geiersberg hill Ger.
195 N3 Geiersthal Ger.
258 D4 Geigertown PA U.S.A.
247 K3 Geikie r. Sask. Can.
248 B3 Geikie Island Ont. Can.
107 I2 Geikie Range hills Qld Austr.
191 B9 Geilenkirchen Ger.
164 E1 Geilo Norway
126 D6 Geinō Japan
163 I5 Geiranger Norway
191 I9 Geisa Ger.
191 H10 Geiselbach Ger.
195 M4 Geiselhöring Ger.
195 J4 Geiselwind Ger.
195 L4 Geisenfeld Ger.
195 M5 Geisenhausen Ger.
194 D2 Geisenheim Ger.
195 N3 Geising Ger.
194 F6 Geisingen Ger.
191 J8 Geisleden Ger.
194 F5 Geislingen Ger.
194 H4 Geislingen an der Steige Ger.
191 J8 Geismar Ger.
179 O6 Geispolsheim France
200 F5 Geißstein mt. Austria
201 L5 Geistthal Austria
Geisûm, Gezâ'ir is Egypt see Qaysūm, Juzur
233 B5 Geita Tanz.
193 G8 Geithain Ger.
162 L4 Geittind mt. Norway
151 D3 Gejet'i Georgia
130 D7 Gejiu Yunnan China
244 B2 Geka, Mys hd Rus. Fed.
144 G2 Gekdepe Turkm.
225 F7 Gel r. Sudan
221 K5 Gel r. Sudan
230 F2 Gel watercourse Sudan
216 G9 Gela Sicilia Italy
216 G9 Gela r. Sicilia Italy
216 G9 Gela, Golfo di g. Sicilia Italy
139 J10 Gêladaindong mt. Qinghai China
233 E3 Geladī Eth.
233 C6 Gelai vol. Tanz.
117 I6 Gelam i. Indon.
183 K8 Gélas, Cime du mt. France/Italy
192 F2 Gelbensande Ger.
195 I2 Gelchsheim Ger.
194 F4 Gelderland prov. Neth.
186 H5 Geldermalsen Neth.
191 B7 Geldern Ger.
191 J10 Geldersheim Ger.
186 G5 Geldrop Neth.
187 I7 Geleen Neth.
221 I3 Gelembe Turkey
232 D2 Gelemso Eth.
193 G9 Gelenau Ger.
221 M4 Gelendost Turkey
157 G7 Gelendzhik Rus. Fed.
232 B2 Gelhak Sudan
232 D2 Gelibolu Turkey
221 H2 Gelibolu Yarımadası pen. Turkey
221 H2 Gelibolu Yarımadası Tarihi Milli Parkı nat. park Turkey
Gelidonya Burnu pt Turkey see Yardımcı Burnu
221 L4 Gelincik Dağı mt. Turkey
232 E3 Gelinsoor Somalia
185 E7 Gelise r. France
199 K3 Gellénháza Hungary
172 F4 Gelligaer Caerphilly, Wales U.K.
100 □3a Gellinam i. Kwajalein Marshall Is
144 G5 Gelmord Iran
191 H10 Gelnhausen Ger.
185 D9 Gelnica Slovakia
191 F7 Gelos France
185 I5 Geloux r. France
164 E6 Gels r. Denmark
208 E5 Gelsa Spain
198 F5 Gelse Hungary
191 D7 Gelsenkirchen Ger.
191 D7 Geltendorf Ger.
195 K5 Gelten-Iffigen nature res. Switz.
212 C3 Gelting Ger.
190 I1 Geltow Ger.
193 G6 Gelumbang Sumatera Indon.
116 F6 Gemas Malaysia
116 D5 Gembloux Belgium
187 G7 Gembu Nigeria
229 H5 Gemeaux France
182 G2 Gemena Dem. Rep. Congo
230 C3 Gemenci park Hungary
199 H5 Géménos France
183 H10 Gemerek Turkey
148 H4 Gemerská Hôrka Slovakia
199 J3 Gemerská Poloma Slovakia
199 J3 Gemert Neth.
186 I5 Geminokağı Cyprus see Karavostasi
221 K5 Gemiş Turkey
221 K2 Gemlik Turkey
221 K2 Gemlik Körfezi b. Turkey
162 □B1 Gemlufall Iceland
219 F4 Gemmingen Ger.
213 O3 Gemona del Friuli Italy
184 C4 Gémozac France
234 D5 Gemsbok National Park Botswana
236 E2 Gemsbokplein well S. Africa
236 I1 Gemsbokvlakte S. Africa
244 H3 Gemuk Mountain AK U.S.A.
194 D3 Gemünden Ger.
191 G9 Gemünden (Wohra) Ger.
191 I10 Gemünden am Main Ger.
207 M8 Genal r. Spain
232 D3 Genalē Wenz r. Eth.
187 F7 Genappe Belgium
207 N4 Génave Spain
207 D7 Genāveh Iran
215 J4 Genazzano Italy
221 M3 Genç Turkey
185 F7 Gençay France
198 F4 Gencsapáti Hungary
146 C9 Gendoa r. Eth.
133 C14 Gendoli Rajasthan India
181 N2 Gendrey France
186 J5 Gendringen Neth.
186 I5 Gendt Neth.
221 H3 Génelard France
182 E1 Genemuiden Neth.
186 J3 General Acha Arg.
284 E5 General Alvear Buenos Aires Arg.
285 G5 General Alvear Mendoza Arg.
284 D4 General Arenales Arg.
285 G3 General Artigas Para.
277 F6 General Belgrano Arg.
285 H4 General Belgrano II research stn Antarctica see Belgrano II
267 I5 General Bravo Mex.
285 F3 General Cabrera Arg.
285 H5 General Campos Arg.
285 H2 General Carneiro Brazil
280 A1 General Carrera, Lago l. Arg./Chile
283 B7 General Conesa Buenos Aires Arg.
283 D6 General Conesa Río Negro Arg.
285 F6 General Daniel Cerri Arg.
285 F3 General Deheza Arg.
189 H2 Generał Dezyderego Chłapowskiego, Park Krajobrazowy imienia Pol.
267 I5 General Escobeda Mex.
General Freire Angola see Muxaluando
285 H3 General Galarza Arg.
285 G2 General Guido Arg.
284 C3 General Gutiérrez Arg.
282 F2 General José de San Martín Arg.
285 G3 General Juan Madariaga Arg.
276 C4 General Lagos Chile
285 G5 General La Madrid Arg.
285 H4 General Las Heras Arg.
285 I4 General Lavalle Arg.
285 G4 General Levalle Arg.
114 F7 General Luna Phil.
114 E6 General MacArthur Samar Phil.
General Machado Angola see Camacupa
285 H4 General Mansilla Arg.
282 D2 General Martín Miguel de Güemes Arg.
285 G4 General O'Brien Arg.
282 F2 General Paz Arg.
285 F4 General Pico Arg.
285 G4 General Pinto Arg.
285 I5 General Pirán Arg.
284 D6 General Roca Arg.
285 H4 General Rodríguez Arg.
285 G3 General Rojo Arg.
277 E4 General Saavedra Bol.
280 B4 General Salgado Brazil
General San Martín research stn Antarctica see San Martín
285 H4 General San Martín Buenos Aires Arg.
285 F5 General San Martín La Pampa Arg.
114 E8 General Santos Mindanao Phil.
268 D1 General Simón Bolívar Mex.
267 J5 General Terán Mex.
219 Q7 General Toshevo Bulg.
266 F3 General Trías Mex.
285 G4 General Viamonte Arg.
285 F4 General Villegas Arg.
256 H7 Genesee PA U.S.A.
256 H5 Genesee r. NY U.S.A.
256 H6 Geneseo NY U.S.A.
204 H2 Genestoso Spain
232 C2 Genet Eth.
180 I4 Genêts France
237 L3 Geneva S. Africa
Geneva Switz. see Genève
255 E10 Geneva AL U.S.A.
250 F8 Geneva IL U.S.A.
260 G5 Geneva NE U.S.A.
256 H6 Geneva NY U.S.A.
256 E7 Geneva OH U.S.A.
Geneva, Lake France/Switz. see Léman, Lac
250 F7 Geneva, Lake WI U.S.A.
212 A3 Genève Switz.
182 I4 Genève canton Switz.
205 P3 Genevilla Spain
182 I4 Genevois mts France
Genf Switz. see Genève
213 N9 Genga Italy
Gengda Sichuan China see Gana
Gengenbach Ger.
Genglou Guangdong China
Gengma Yunnan China
Gengqing Sichuan China see Dêgê
231 D5 Gengwa Dem. Rep. Congo
Gengxuan Yunnan China see Gengma
232 B3 Geni r. Sudan
197 L1 Geniai Lith.
Genichesk Ukr. see Heniches'k
207 I5 Genil r. Spain
220 F1 Genisea Greece
185 D6 Génissac France
182 H4 Génissiat, Barrage de dam France
138 D8 Genji Rajasthan India
187 H7 Genk Belgium
125 H13 Genkai-nada b. Japan
182 G2 Genlis France
214 C8 Gennargentu, Monti del mts Sardegna Italy
214 C9 Genn'Argiolas, Monte hill Italy
186 I5 Gennep Neth.
184 D1 Gennes France
105 L7 Genoa Vic. Austr.
Genoa Italy see Genova
Genoa IL U.S.A.
250 F7 Genoa NE U.S.A.
183 D8 Génolhac France
214 C8 Genoni Sardegna Italy
184 H3 Genouillac France
184 E3 Genouillé France
181 O7 Genouilly France
212 F7 Genova Italy
212 G7 Genova prov. Italy
212 F7 Genova, Golfo di g. Italy
209 E10 Genovés Spain
274 □ Genovesa, Isla i. Islas Galápagos Ecuador
185 E6 Gensac France
187 E6 Gent Belgium
116 G8 Genteng Jawa Indon.
117 J8 Genteng i. Indon.
193 F6 Genthin Ger.
116 D3 Genting Highlands Malaysia
278 E4 Gentio do Ouro Brazil
184 I4 Gentioux, Plateau de France
184 H4 Gentioux-Pigerolles France
Gentsa Italy see Genova
215 Q6 Genzano di Lucania Italy
215 J4 Genzano di Roma Italy
219 L4 Geoagiu r. Romania
168 D10 Geodha, Rubh' a' pt Scotland U.K.
109 C12 Geographe Bay W.A. Austr.
109 B8 Geographe Channel W.A. Austr.
243 P2 Geographical Society Ø i. Greenland
Geok-Tepe Turkm. see Gëkdepe
152 F1 George, Zemlya i. Zemlya Frantsa-Iosifa Rus. Fed.
108 D6 George r. W.A. Austr.
249 H1 George r. Que. Can.
236 G9 George S. Africa
249 I4 George, Cape N.S. Can.
105 L6 George, Lake N.S.W. Austr.
104 G7 George, Lake S.A. Austr.
108 G7 George, Lake salt flat W.A. Austr.
232 A4 George, Lake Uganda
245 K3 George, Lake FL U.S.A.
255 G11 George, Lake NY U.S.A.
257 L5 George Gills Range mts N.T. Austr.
106 C7 Georgeham Devon, England U.K.
172 D5 George Island St Helena
238 □2b George Land i. Zemlya Frantsa-Iosifa Rus. Fed. see
Georga, Zemlya
Georgenberg Ger.
195 M2 Georgensgmünd Ger.
195 K3 Georges Mills NH U.S.A.
257 M5 George Sound inlet South I. N.Z.
103 B11 Georgetown Qld Austr.
107 I5 George Town Tas. Austr.
105 K9 Georgetown Ont. Can.
270 F2 George Town Gt Exuma Bahamas
256 E5 Georgetown Cayman Is
270 C4 George Town Gambia
228 B3 Georgetown Guyana
275 G3 Georgetown Malaysia
116 D2 George Town Malaysia
238 □2a Georgetown Ascension S. Atlantic Ocean
271 □3 Georgetown St Vincent
244 H3 Georgetown AK U.S.A.
258 D7 Georgetown CT U.S.A.
257 J10 Georgetown DE U.S.A.
255 E10 Georgetown GA U.S.A.
254 E6 Georgetown KY U.S.A.
256 B10 Georgetown OH U.S.A.
255 H9 Georgetown SC U.S.A.
261 G10 Georgetown TX U.S.A.
286 T2 George VI Sound sea chan. Antarctica
287 K2 George V Land reg. Antarctica
261 F11 George West TX U.S.A.
151 E4 Georgia country Asia
255 F9 Georgia state U.S.A.
246 E5 Georgia, Strait of B.C. Can.
255 D10 Georgiana AL U.S.A.
248 D4 Georgian Bay Ont. Can.
251 O5 Georgian Bay Islands National Park Ont. Can.
Georgi Dimitrov, Yazovir resr Bulg. see Koprinka, Yazovir
106 G8 Georgina watercourse Qld Austr.
220 F7 Georgioupoli Kriti Greece
Georgi Traykov Bulg. see Dolni Chiflik
Georgiu-Dezh Rus. Fed. see Liski
142 G2 Georgiyevka Aktyubinskaya Oblast' Kazakh.
143 S3 Georgiyevka Vostochnyy Kazakhstan Kazakh.
Georgiyevka Zhambylskaya Oblast' Kazakh. see Korday
151 E1 Georgiyevsk Rus. Fed.
156 I4 Georgiyevskoye Kostromskaya Oblast' Rus. Fed.
151 A1 Georgiyevskoye Krasnodarskiy Kray Rus. Fed.
161 T2 Georgiyevskoye Vologodskaya Oblast' Rus. Fed.
190 D5 Georgsdorf Ger.
190 D4 Georgsheil Ger.
191 F6 Georgsmarienhütte Ger.
Georg von Neumayer research stn Antarctica see Neumayer
200 C6 Gepatsch, Stausee resr Austria
185 D9 Ger Aquitaine France
181 J4 Ger Basse-Normandie France
208 I3 Ger Spain
193 F9 Gera Ger.
187 F2 Geraardsbergen Belgium
191 K9 Geraberg Ger.
194 H3 Gerabronn Ger.
217 K7 Gerace Italy
217 K7 Gerace r. Italy
216 G8 Geraci Siculo Sicilia Italy
169 C9 Gerahies Ireland
220 E2 Gerakarou Greece
220 B5 Gerakas, Akrotirio pt Zakynthos Greece
220 E6 Gerakas, Akrotirio pt Greece
220 D6 Geraki Greece
280 B6 Geral, Serra mts Brazil
278 D4 Geral de Goiás, Serra hills Brazil
103 F11 Geraldine South I. N.Z.
278 D5 Geral do Paraná, Serra hills Brazil
109 C10 Geraldton W.A. Austr.
115 E1 Gerama i. Indon.
220 E5 Geraneia mts Greece
150 C7 Gerar watercourse Israel
179 M7 Gérardmer France
201 M2 Geras Austria
201 N3 Gerasdorf bei Wien Austria
144 F8 Gerāsh Iran
178 H7 Géraudot France
232 B2 Gerba Dima Eth.
264 J1 Gerber CA U.S.A.
179 M7 Gerbéviller France
183 F7 Gerbier de Jonc mt. France
193 E7 Gerbstedt Ger.
198 G4 Gérce Hungary
194 H2 Gerchsheim Ger.
149 J5 Gercüş Turkey
190 J5 Gerdau Ger.
237 K2 Gerdau S. Africa
Gerdauen Rus. Fed. see Zheleznodorozhnyy
244 I3 Gerdine, Mount AK U.S.A.
199 H4 Gerecsei park Hungary
148 F3 Gerede Turkey
148 F3 Gerede r. Turkey
206 G5 Gerena Spain
199 J5 Geréndás Hungary
204 D5 Gerês, Serra do mts Port.
199 H5 Geresdlak Hungary
145 K6 Gereshk Afgh.
200 G3 Geretsberg Austria
201 N3 Geretsried Ger.
207 N6 Gérgal Spain
151 J7 Gergebil' Rus. Fed.
214 C8 Gergei Sardegna Italy
199 K3 Gergely-hegy hill Hungary
182 F3 Gergy France
195 J2 Gerhardshofen Ger.
116 D2 Gerik Malaysia
144 H5 Gerimenj Iran
205 L9 Gerindote Spain
260 D3 Gering NE U.S.A.
193 G8 Geringswalde Ger.
199 J4 Gerje r. Hungary
199 H5 Gerjen Hungary
262 E6 Gerlach NV U.S.A.
199 J2 Gerlachovský štít mt. Slovakia
194 G4 Gerlingen Ger.
201 K5 Gerlos Austria
200 F5 Gerlospass pass Austria
249 H2 Germaine, Lac l. Que. Can.
190 B1 German Bight g. Denmark/Ger.
285 F4 Germania Arg.
Germania country Europe see Germany
243 Q2 Germania Land reg. Greenland
Germanicea Turkey see Kahramanmaraş
246 E4 Germansen Landing B.C. Can.
German South-West Africa country Africa see Namibia
256 H9 Germantown MD U.S.A.
256 A9 Germantown OH U.S.A.
261 K8 Germantown TN U.S.A.
250 F6 Germantown WI U.S.A.
188 E3 Germany country Europe
195 J6 Germaringen Ger.
179 J7 Germay France
221 I5 Germencik Turkey
195 K5 Germering Ger.
194 E3 Germersheim Ger.
178 D8 Germigny-des-Prés France
237 M2 Germiston S. Africa
205 O2 Gernika-Lumo Spain
193 D7 Gernrode Sachsen-Anhalt Ger.
192 D6 Gernrode Thüringen Ger.
191 J8 Gernsbach Ger.
194 E4 Gernsheim Ger.
194 E2 Gero Japan
126 F4 Gero Angeli, Akrotirio pt Greece
220 G4 Gerola Alta Italy
212 H3 Geroldsgrün Ger.
193 E10 Gerolsbach Ger.
195 K5 Gerolstein Ger.
191 C10 Gerolzhofen Ger.
195 I2 Gerona Spain see Girona
220 F7 Geropotamos r. Kriti Greece
213 R4 Gerovo Croatia
187 G8 Gerpinnes Belgium
214 C9 Gerrei reg. Sardegna Italy
Gerri Spain see Guerri de la Sal
Gerrit Denys is P.N.G. see Lihir Group
185 E8 Gers dept France
185 F7 Gers r. France
212 F2 Gersau Switz.
191 I10 Gersfeld (Rhön) Ger.
194 C3 Gersheim Ger.
136 D5 Gersoppa Karnataka India
190 E5 Gersten Ger.
195 K5 Gerstetten Ger.
179 O7 Gerstheim France
195 J5 Gersthofen Ger.
191 J9 Gerstungen Ger.
192 I4 Gerswalde Ger.
183 G7 Gervanne r. France
193 E6 Gerwisch Ger.
Gêryille Alg. see El Bayadh
182 C5 Gerzat France
133 G10 Gêrzê Xizang China
148 G3 Gerze Turkey
195 M4 Gerzen Ger.
191 D7 Gescher Ger.
201 N5 Geschriebenstein hill Austria
191 K9 Geschwenda Ger.
191 F7 Geseke Ger.
214 C8 Gesico Sardegna Italy
Gesoriacum France see Boulogne-sur-Mer
179 I4 Gespunsart France
195 J5 Gessertshausen Ger.
193 F9 Gessler Arg.
212 D7 Gesso r. Italy
209 D8 Gestalgar Spain
181 I7 Gesté France
232 D3 Gestro, Wabē r. Eth.
208 G4 Gestuaden Italy
217 H8 Gesuaden Italy
199 K5 Geszt Hungary
199 K4 Gesztered Hungary
165 K3 Geta Åland Fin.
205 M8 Getafe Spain
187 F7 Gete r. Belgium
219 L6 Getic, Podişul plat. Romania
180 I7 Gétigné France
151 G5 Getik r. Armenia
190 I2 Gettorf Ger.
258 A5 Gettysburg PA U.S.A.
260 F3 Gettysburg SD U.S.A.
256 H9 Gettysburg National Military Park nat. park PA U.S.A.
130 F6 Getu He r. China
280 C4 Getúlina Brazil
279 B8 Getúlio Vargas Brazil
286 P2 Getz Ice Shelf Antarctica
187 I7 Geul r. Neth.
116 B3 Geumapang r. Indon.
116 B2 Geumpang Sumatera Indon.
116 B2 Geureudong, Gunung vol. Indon.
105 L5 Geurie N.S.W. Austr.
144 H8 Gevān-e Ţāleb Khānī Iran
149 K3 Gevaş Turkey
183 C7 Gévaudan reg. France
191 D8 Gevelsberg Ger.
180 H5 Gévezé France
219 K9 Gevgelija Macedonia
206 E2 Gévora r. Spain
136 D3 Gevrai Mahar. India
182 F2 Gevrey-Chambertin France
232 D2 Gewane Wildlife Reserve nature res. Eth.
182 I4 Gex France
Gexianzhuang Hebei China see Qinghe
Gey Iran see Nīkshahr
150 A2 Geydik Dağları mts Turkey
193 G9 Geyer Ger.
221 J3 Geyikli Turkey
116 □ Geylang Sing.
116 □ Geylang r. Sing.
139 M6 Geylegphug Bhutan
237 J2 Geysdorp S. Africa
264 J3 Geyserville CA U.S.A.
221 L2 Geyve Turkey
228 E3 Gezarina Brazil
220 B1 Gezavesh Albania
128 G7 Gezidong Qinghai China
144 F8 Gezīr Iran
201 L2 Gföhl Austria
217 □ Ġgantija Temples Gozo Malta
236 H3 Ghaap Plateau S. Africa
150 E3 Ghabāghib Syria
224 E6 Ghabeish Sudan
149 K7 Ghadaf, Wādī al watercourse Iraq
150 E7 Ghadaf, Wādī al watercourse Jordan
145 N4 Ghadai Pak.
Ghadamés Libya see Ghadāmis
224 A2 Ghadāmis Libya
144 B3 Ghaddūwah Libya
144 E3 Gha'em Shahr Iran
145 L5 Ghāfah, Ramlat al des. Saudi Arabia
139 J7 Ghaghara r. India
100 □6 Ghaghe i. Solomon Is
139 J8 Ghaghra Jharkhand India
217 □ Għagħin, Xrobb l- pt Malta
145 L8 Ghaibi Dero Pak.
217 □ Ghajnsielem Gozo Malta
217 □ Ghajn Tuffieha, Ir-Ramla Malta
145 I6 Ghalend Iran
230 E2 Ghalla, Wadi El watercourse Sudan
Ghallaorol Uzbek. see G'allaorol
217 □ Għallis, Ġebel ta' l- is Malta
228 E4 Ghana country Africa
147 L3 Ghanādah, Rās pt U.A.E.
147 M6 Ghānāh well Oman
147 K6 Ghanīm well Saudi Arabia
138 D6 Ghanliala Rajasthan India
138 C8 Ghantila Gujarat India
138 C9 Ghantwar Gujarat India
147 I2 Ghanwā Saudi Arabia
234 D4 Ghanzi Botswana
234 D4 Ghanzi admin. dist. Botswana
Ghap'an Armenia see Kapan
147 I2 Ghār, Ras al pt Saudi Arabia
Gharakach' Armenia see Lusashogh
146 F5 Gharāmil, Jabal al hill Saudi Arabia
150 D8 Gharandal Jordan
150 A9 Gharandal, Wādī watercourse Egypt
217 □ Gharb Gozo Malta
227 F2 Ghardaïa Alg.
211 B7 Ghardimaou Tunisia
211 C7 Ghar el Melh Tunisia
145 K4 Ghargharib Afgh.
139 I8 Gharghoda Chhattisgarh India
217 □ Għarghur Malta
225 G2 Ghārib, Jabal mt. Egypt
150 B10 Ghārib, Ra's pt Egypt
145 N2 Gharm Tajik.
147 M6 Gharm, Wādī r. Oman
147 L5 Ghār Mihnān Saudi Arabia
145 L9 Gharo Pak.
144 C4 Gharq Ābād Iran
224 B1 Gharyān Libya
148 H7 Gharz, Wādī al watercourse Syria
147 M7 Gharzant i. Oman
224 A3 Ghāt Libya
138 H6 Ghatampur Uttar Prad. India
100 □6 Ghatere Sta Isabel Solomon Is
139 J9 Ghatgan Orissa India
138 E8 Ghatol Rajasthan India
139 K8 Ghatsila Jharkhand India
145 M7 Ghauspur Pak.
Ghawdex i. Malta see Gozo
146 G8 Ghaymān Yemen
224 C6 Ghazal, Bahr el watercourse Chad
230 F2 Ghazal, Bahr el r. Sudan
Ghazalkent Uzbek. see G'azalkent
226 E2 Ghazaouet Alg.
138 F5 Ghaziabad Uttar Prad. India
139 I7 Ghazipur Uttar Prad. India
147 M2 Ghazira, Ghubbat al inlet Oman
145 I6 Ghazluna Pak.
Ghazna Afgh. see Ghaznī
145 M5 Ghaznī Afgh.
145 L5 Ghaznī prov. Afgh.
145 L5 Ghaznī r. Afgh.
145 L5 Ghazoor Afgh.
146 E2 Ghazzālah Saudi Arabia
144 G5 Ghebar Gumbad Iran
138 C9 Ghedi Italy
219 K5 Ghelari Romania
219 O5 Ghelinţa Romania
147 J3 Ghemeis, Ras pt U.A.E.
Ghent Belgium see Gent
256 D11 Ghent WV U.S.A.
Gheorghe Gheorghiu-Dej Romania see Oneşti
219 P6 Gheorghe Lazăr Romania
219 M4 Gheorgheni Romania
136 D4 Gherdi Mahar. India
219 L3 Gherla Romania
212 F4 Ghiffa Italy
Ghijduwon Uzbek. see G'ijduvon
214 B7 Ghilarza Sardegna Italy
145 L6 Ghilzai reg. Afgh.
148 I8 Ghinah, Wādī al watercourse Saudi Arabia
199 K5 Ghiroc Romania
219 L6 Ghioroiu Romania
219 K5 Ghiroda Romania
187 E7 Ghislenghien Belgium
214 C3 Ghisonaccia Corse France
214 C3 Ghisoni Corse France
145 L5 Ghizao Afgh.
138 D1 Ghizar Pak.
199 K6 Ghizela Romania
145 L9 Ghizri Creek inlet Pak.
100 □6 Ghizunabeana Islands Solomon Is
136 C3 Ghod Mahar. India
136 D3 Ghod r. India
138 D9 Ghodsar Mahar. India
145 L9 Ghorabari Pak.
139 L7 Ghoraghat Bangl.
145 K5 Ghorak Afgh.
145 M4 Ghorband r. Afgh.
246 H2 Ghost Lake N.W.T. Can.
138 D7 Ghotaru Rajasthan India
145 L8 Ghotki Pak.
145 K4 Ghowr prov. Afgh.
147 K9 Ghubbah Suquţrā Yemen
Ghudamis Libya see Ghadāmis
145 O2 Ghudara Tajik.
139 K7 Ghugri r. India
136 F3 Ghugus Mahar. India
Ghukasyan Armenia see Ashots'k
145 M9 Ghulam Muhammad Barrage Pak.
150 F4 Ghunthur Syria
150 F7 Ghurayfah hill Saudi Arabia
144 F7 Ghūrī Iran
145 I4 Ghurian Afgh.
146 G3 Ghurrab, Jabal hill Saudi Arabia

Ghurūb, Jabal *hill* Saudi Arabia
Ghutipari *Madh. Prad.* India
Ghuwayṭah, Nafūd al *des.* Saudi Arabia
Ghuzayn Oman
Ghuzayyil, Sabkhat *salt marsh* Libya
Ghuzor Uzbek. *see* **G'uzor**
Ghyvelde France
Giaginskaya Rus. Fed.
Gialias *r.* Cyprus
Gia Nghia Vietnam
Gianh, Sông *r.* Vietnam
Gianisada *i.* Greece
Giannitsa Greece
Giannutri, Isola di *i.* Italy
Giano dell'Umbria Italy
Giant's Castle *mt.* S. Africa
Giant's Causeway *lava field* *Northern Ireland* U.K.
Giant's Neck *CT* U.S.A.
Gianyar *Bali* Indon.
Gia Rai Vietnam
Giardini-Naxos *Sicilia* Italy
Giarmata Romania
Giarratana *Sicilia* Italy
Giarre *Sicilia* Italy
Giat France
Giave *Sardegna* Italy
Giaveno Italy
Giavino, Monte *mt.* Italy
Giba *Sardegna* Italy
Gibalbín *hill* Spain
Gibara Cuba
Gibarrayo *hill* Spain
Gibb *r. W.A.* Austr.
Gibbon *NE* U.S.A.
Gibbonsville *ID* U.S.A.
Gibb River *W.A.* Austr.
Gibb River Aboriginal Reserve *W.A.* Austr.
Gibbsboro *NJ* U.S.A.
Gibb's Hill Bermuda
Gibbstown *NJ* U.S.A.
Gibellina Nuova *Sicilia* Italy
Gibeon Namibia
Giberville France
Gibostad Norway
Giboule *r.* France
Gibraleón Spain
Gibraltar Europe
Gibraltar, Bay of Gibraltar/Spain
Gibraltar, Campo de *reg.* Spain
Gibraltar, Strait of Morocco/Spain
Gibraltar Harbour Gibraltar
Gibraltar Point *England* U.K.
Gibraltar Range National Park *N.S.W.* Austr.
Gibson *W.A.* Austr.
Gibson *GA* U.S.A.
Gibson City *IL* U.S.A.
Gibson Desert *W.A.* Austr.
Gibson Desert Nature Reserve *W.A.* Austr.
Gibson Island *MD* U.S.A.
Gibsons *B.C.* Can.
Giby Pol.
Gicăki Dağı *mt.* Azer.
Gichgeniyn Nuruu *mts* Mongolia
Gīdamī Eth.
Gidar Pak.
Gidayevo Rus. Fed.
Gidda Eth.
Giddalur *Andhra Prad.* India
Giddings *TX* U.S.A.
Giddi Pass *hill* Egypt *see* **Jiddī, Jabal al**
Gideälven *r.* Sweden
Gidle Pol.
Gīdolē Eth.
Giebelstadt Ger.
Gieboldehausen Ger.
Gieczno Pol.
Giekau Ger.
Giełczew *r.* Pol.
Gielniów Pol.
Gielow Ger.
Gien France
Giengen an der Brenz Ger.
Giens, Golfe de *b.* France
Giens, Presqu'île de *pen.* France
Gières France
Gierle Belgium
Giersleben Ger.
Gierstädt Ger.
Gierzwałd Pol.
Giesecke Isfjord *inlet* Greenland *see* **Kangerlussuaq**
Gieselwerder (Oberweser) Ger.
Gießen Ger.
Gießen *admin. reg.* Ger.
Gieten Neth.
Gietrzwałd Pol.
Gièvres France
Gīfan Iran
Gifatin Island Egypt *see* **Jiftūn al Kabīr**
Gifford *East Lothian, Scotland* U.K.
Giffou *r.* France
Giffre *r.* France
Gifhorn Ger.
Gift Lake *Alta* Can.
Gifu Japan
Gifu *pref.* Japan
Gigant Rus. Fed.
Giganta, Cerro *mt.* Mex.
Gigante Col.
Gigante *mt.* Spain
Gigean France
Gigha *i. Scotland* U.K.
Gigha, Sound of *sea chan. Scotland* U.K.
Gighera Romania
Giglio, Isola del *i.* Italy
Giglio Castello Italy
Gignac *Languedoc-Roussillon* France
Gignac *Provence-Alpes-Côte d'Azur* France
Gignod Italy
Gigondas France
G'ijduvon Uzbek.
Gijón-Xixón Spain
Gijou *r.* France
Gikongoro Rwanda
Gila *r. AZ* U.S.A.
Gila, Tanjung *pt Maluku* Indon.
Gila Bend *AZ* U.S.A.
Gila Bend Mountains *AZ* U.S.A.
Gila Mountains *AZ* U.S.A.
Gīlān *prov.* Iran
Gīlān-e Gharb Iran
Gila River Indian Reservation *res. AZ* U.S.A.
Gilău Romania
Gilāzi Azer.
Gilberdyke *East Riding of Yorkshire, England* U.K.
Gilbert Arg.
Gilbert *r. Qld* Austr.
Gilbert *AZ* U.S.A.
Gilbert *MN* U.S.A.
Gilbert *WV* U.S.A.
Gilbert, Mount *AK* U.S.A.
Gilbert Islands *country* Pacific Ocean *see* **Kiribati**
Gilberton *PA* U.S.A.
Gilbert Range *mts Qld* Austr.
Gilbert Ridge *sea feature* Pacific Ocean
Gilbert River *Qld* Austr.
Gilbertsville *PA* U.S.A.
Gilboa *OH* U.S.A.
Gilbués Brazil
Gil Chashmeh Iran
Gilching Ger.
Gildford *MT* U.S.A.
Gilé Moz.
Gilead *reg.* Jordan *see* **Jil'ād**
Gilena Spain
Giles, Lake *salt flat W.A.* Austr.
Giles Creek *r. N.T.* Austr.
109 J8 **Giles Meteorological Station** *W.A.* Austr.
106 D6 **Giles Range** *mts N.T.* Austr.
183 K9 **Gilette** France
Gilf Kebir Plateau Egypt *see* **Jilf al Kabīr, Haḍabat al**
169 J4 **Gilford** *Northern Ireland* U.K.
105 M3 **Gilgai** *N.S.W.* Austr.
105 L4 **Gilgandra** *N.S.W.* Austr.
151 K4 **Gilgilçay** Azer.
105 L3 **Gil Gil Creek** *r. N.S.W.* Austr.
138 E2 **Gilgit** Pak.
138 E2 **Gilgit** *r.* Pak.
105 K5 **Gilgunnia** *N.S.W.* Austr.
117 K8 **Gili Iyang** *i.* Indon.
117 K9 **Gilimanuk** *Bali* Indon.
Gılındire Turkey *see* **Aydıncık**
246 D4 **Gil Island** *B.C.* Can.
169 F4 **Gill, Lough** *l.* Ireland
247 M3 **Gillam** *Man.* Can.
171 P5 **Gillamoor** *North Yorkshire, England* U.K.
164 I5 **Gilleleje** Denmark
106 E7 **Gillen** *watercourse N.T.* Austr.
109 H9 **Gillen, Lake** *salt flat W.A.* Austr.
191 C10 **Gillenfeld** Ger.
104 F5 **Gilles, Lake** *salt flat S.A.* Austr.
103 D10 **Gillespies Point** *South I.* N.Z.
256 I7 **Gillett** *PA* U.S.A.
250 F5 **Gillett** *WI* U.S.A.
262 L4 **Gillette** *WY* U.S.A.
162 M5 **Gillhov** Sweden
107 H6 **Gilliat** *Qld* Austr.
107 H6 **Gilliat** *r. Qld* Austr.
172 H5 **Gillingham** *Dorset, England* U.K.
173 N5 **Gillingham** *Medway, England* U.K.
171 N5 **Gilling West** *North Yorkshire, England* U.K.
244 □A5 **Gillon Point** *pt AK* U.S.A.
238 □2b **Gill Point** St Helena
168 J5 **Gills** *Highland, Scotland* U.K.
250 G4 **Gills Rock** *WI* U.S.A.
182 I5 **Gilly-sur-Isère** France
182 D3 **Gilly-sur-Loire** France
259 K1 **Gilman** *CT* U.S.A.
250 G9 **Gilman** *IL* U.S.A.
250 D4 **Gilman** *WI* U.S.A.
261 H9 **Gilmer** *TX* U.S.A.
168 I10 **Gilmerton** *Perth and Kinross, Scotland* U.K.
243 K4 **Gilmour Island** *Nunavut* Can.
219 L6 **Gilort** *r.* Romania
264 K4 **Gilroy** *CA* U.S.A.
191 H9 **Gilserberg** Ger.
171 L4 **Gilsland** *Northumberland, England* U.K.
168 K11 **Gilston** *Scottish Borders, Scotland* U.K.
190 I5 **Gilten** Ger.
113 J8 **Giluwe, Mount** P.N.G.
172 F4 **Gilwern** *Monmouthshire, Wales* U.K.
186 G5 **Gilze** Neth.
232 B2 **Gīmbī** Eth.
271 □3 **Gimie, Mount** *vol.* St Lucia
217 L6 **Gimigliano** Italy
247 L5 **Gimli** *Man.* Can.
165 O1 **Gimo** Sweden
185 F9 **Gimonde, Barrage de la** *dam* France
185 G8 **Gimone** *r.* France
185 F8 **Gimont** France
182 C3 **Gimouille** France
183 H9 **Ginasservis** France
225 H6 **Ginda** Eritrea
107 L7 **Gindie** *Qld* Austr.
276 D3 **Ginebra, Laguna** *l.* Bol.
214 D7 **Ginepro, Cala** *b. Sardegna* Italy
238 □3c **Ginés, Punta** *pt Lanzarote* Canary Is
183 B10 **Ginestas** France
238 □1b **Ginetes** *São Miguel* Azores
162 □ **Ginevrabotnen** *str.* Svalbard
136 G9 **Gin Ganga** *r.* Sri Lanka
136 F6 **Gingee** *Tamil Nadu* India
187 H7 **Gingelom** Belgium
194 H4 **Gingen an der Fils** Ger.
270 □ **Ginger Hill** Jamaica
107 M8 **Gin Gin** *Qld* Austr.
109 C11 **Gingin** *W.A.* Austr.
237 P5 **Gingindlovu** S. Africa
114 E7 **Gingoog** *Mindanao* Phil.
192 H2 **Gingst** Ger.
232 D3 **Gīnīr** Eth.
160 G6 **Ginkūnai** Lith.
185 I10 **Ginoles** France
217 L2 **Ginosa** Italy
217 I6 **Ginostra** *Isole Lipari* Italy
124 □1 **Ginowan** *Okinawa* Japan
136 G9 **Gintota** Sri Lanka
Ginzo de Limia *Galicia* Spain *see* **Xinzo de Limia**
206 D6 **Giões** Port.
220 G7 **Giofyros** *r. Kriti* Greece
215 O7 **Gioi** Italy
217 J6 **Gioia, Golfo di** *b.* Italy
215 L4 **Gioia dei Marsi** Italy
217 L2 **Gioia del Colle** Italy
215 M5 **Gioia Sannitica** Italy
217 J7 **Gioia Tauro** Italy
217 K7 **Gioiosa Ionica** Italy
216 H7 **Gioiosa Marea** *Sicilia* Italy
Gióna Óros *mts* Greece *see* **Gkiona**
212 F3 **Giornico** Switz.
220 F3 **Gioura** *i.* Greece
215 L3 **Giovenco** *r.* Italy
213 J3 **Gioveretto** *mt.* Italy
200 C7 **Gioveretto, Lago di** *l.* Italy
213 K8 **Giovi, Monte** *hill* Italy
215 R5 **Giovinazzo** Italy
248 F2 **Gipouloux** *r. Que.* Can.
105 J8 **Gippsland** *reg. Vic.* Austr.
135 □1 **Giraavaru** *i. N. Male* Maldives
138 C6 **Girab** *Rajasthan* India
214 C1 **Giraglia, Île de la** *i. Corse* France
199 K2 **Giraltovce** Slovakia
144 H8 **Gīrān** Iran
179 L7 **Girancourt** France
144 H7 **Gīrān Rīg** *mt.* Iran
138 G9 **Girar** *Mahar.* India
261 H7 **Girard** *KS* U.S.A.
256 E7 **Girard** *OH* U.S.A.
256 E6 **Girard** *PA* U.S.A.
249 H1 **Girardin, Lac** *l. Que.* Can.
258 C3 **Girardville** *PA* U.S.A.
214 D8 **Girasole** *Sardegna* Italy
Giravaru *i. N. Male* Maldives *see* **Giraavaru**
144 G4 **Girdab** Iran
145 M6 **Girdao** Pak.
145 K8 **Girdar Dhor** *r.* Pak.
145 I6 **Girdī** Iran
245 J3 **Girdwood** *AK* U.S.A.
229 I4 **Girei** Nigeria
148 I3 **Giresun** Turkey
Girgenti *Sicilia* Italy *see* **Agrigento**
230 C4 **Giri** *r.* Dem. Rep. Congo
232 C4 **Giribabor** *well* Kenya
139 K7 **Giridih** *Jharkhand* India
217 K6 **Girifalco** Italy
105 K4 **Girilambone** *N.S.W.* Austr.
199 K4 **Girişu de Criş** Romania
158 G6 **Gîrla Mare** *r.* Moldova
138 E9 **Girna** *r.* India
138 C9 **Gir National Park** India
Girne Cyprus *see* **Keryneia**
199 K6 **Giroc** Romania
191 E10 **Girod** Ger.
214 A3 **Girolata, Golfe de** *b. Corse* France
179 M8 **Giromagny** France
274 B5 **Girón** Ecuador
Giron Sweden *see* **Kiruna**
208 K4 **Girona** Spain
208 K3 **Girona** *prov.* Spain
185 D6 **Gironde** *dept* France
184 C4 **Gironde** *est.* France
185 D6 **Gironde-sur-Dropt** France
285 G4 **Girondo** Arg.
208 I3 **Gironella** Spain
145 O5 **Girot** Pak.
185 G8 **Girou** *r.* France
185 H8 **Giroussens** France
105 M3 **Girraween National Park** *nat. park Qld* Austr.
107 J4 **Girringun National Park** *nat. park* Australia
173 M3 **Girton** *Cambridgeshire, England* U.K.
279 B9 **Giruá** Brazil
168 G12 **Girvan** *South Ayrshire, Scotland* U.K.
156 F3 **Girvas** Rus. Fed.
138 H7 **Girwan** *Uttar Prad.* India
244 H2 **Gisasa** *r. AK* U.S.A.
102 M5 **Gisborne** *North I.* N.Z.
102 M5 **Gisborne** *admin. reg. North I.* N.Z.
171 M6 **Gisburn** *Lancashire, England* U.K.
246 F4 **Giscome** *B.C.* Can.
233 A5 **Gisenyi** Rwanda
164 J4 **Gislaved** Sweden
178 C5 **Gisors** France
Gisozi Burundi *see* **Kisosi**
Gissar Tajik. *see* **Hisor**
145 L2 **Gissar Range** *mts* Tajik./Uzbek.
Gissarskiy Khrebet *mts* Tajik./Uzbek. *see* **Gissar Range**
215 N3 **Gissi** Italy
187 C6 **Gistel** Belgium
204 H3 **Gistredo, Sierra de** *mts* Spain
212 E2 **Giswil** Switz.
233 A5 **Gitarama** Rwanda
144 E4 **Gītcheh, Kūh-e** *hills* Iran
233 A5 **Gitega** Burundi
191 J7 **Gittelde** Ger.
Giuba *r.* Somalia *see* **Jubba**
219 L6 **Giubega** Romania
212 G3 **Giubiasco** Switz.
213 J4 **Giudicarie, Valli** *val.* Italy
215 M6 **Giugliano in Campania** Italy
215 K4 **Giuliano di Roma** Italy
215 L2 **Giulianova** Italy
212 I7 **Giuncugnano** Italy
219 N4 **Giurgeului, Munţii** *mts* Romania
219 N7 **Giurgiu** Romania
144 G3 **Givar** Iran
164 F6 **Give** Denmark
178 C5 **Giverny** France
179 I3 **Givet** France
182 F5 **Givors** France
187 F8 **Givry** Belgium
182 F3 **Givry** France
179 I6 **Givry-en-Argonne** France
235 F4 **Giyani** S. Africa
232 C2 **Giyon** Eth.
Giza *Al Jīzah* Egypt *see* **Al Jīzah**
196 F3 **Gizałki** Pol.
144 B4 **Gīzeh Rūd** *r.* Iran
151 F2 **Gizel'** Rus. Fed.
181 L7 **Gizeux** France
153 R3 **Gizhiga** Rus. Fed.
215 L3 **Gizio** *r.* Italy
100 □6 **Gizo** *New Georgia Is* Solomon Is
100 □6 **Gizo** *i. New Georgia Is* Solomon Is
197 J1 **Giżycko** Pol.
215 Q10 **Gizzeria** Italy
218 I8 **Gjakovë** *Gjakovë* Kosovo
218 I8 **Gjalicë e Lumës, Mal** *mt.* Albania
218 I8 **Gjeravicë** *mt.* Kosovo
163 I6 **Gjerde** Norway
164 F3 **Gjerstad** Norway
218 J8 **Gjilan** *Gjilan* Kosovo
220 B2 **Gjirokastër** Albania
243 I3 **Gjoa Haven** *Nunavut* Can.
162 □C1 **Gjögur** Iceland
163 K6 **Gjøvik** Norway
220 A2 **Gjuhëzës, Kepi i** *pt* Albania
221 J6 **Gkinas, Akrotirio** *pt Rodos* Greece
220 D4 **Gkiona** *mts* Greece
249 J4 **Glace Bay** *N.S.* Can.
212 D4 **Glacier, Monte** *mt.* Italy
245 N4 **Glacier Bay** *AK* U.S.A.
245 M4 **Glacier Bay National Park and Preserve** *AK* U.S.A.
246 G5 **Glacier National Park** *B.C.* Can.
262 H2 **Glacier National Park** *MT* U.S.A.
262 D2 **Glacier Peak** *vol. WA* U.S.A.
191 C7 **Gladbeck** Ger.
191 G9 **Gladenbach** Ger.
256 D12 **Glade Spring** *VA* U.S.A.
162 K4 **Gladstad** Norway
107 M7 **Gladstone** *Qld* Austr.
104 G5 **Gladstone** *S.A.* Austr.
105 L9 **Gladstone** *Tas.* Austr.
247 L5 **Gladstone** *Man.* Can.
103 J8 **Gladstone** *North I.* N.Z.
250 G4 **Gladstone** *MI* U.S.A.
258 F3 **Gladstone** *NJ* U.S.A.
256 G11 **Gladstone** *VA* U.S.A.
250 J6 **Gladwin** *MI* U.S.A.
256 F11 **Gladys** *VA* U.S.A.
245 N4 **Gladys Lake** *B.C.* Can.
182 J2 **Glainans** France
168 J9 **Glamis** *Angus, Scotland* U.K.
265 Q9 **Glamis** *CA* U.S.A.
210 F3 **Glamoč** Bos.-Herz.
201 J6 **Glan** *r.* Austria
194 D2 **Glan** *r.* Ger.
114 E9 **Glan** *Mindanao* Phil.
165 L3 **Glan** *l.* Sweden
172 E4 **Glanaman** *Carmarthenshire, Wales* U.K.
169 C8 **Glanaruddery Mountains** *hills* Ireland
183 H7 **Glandage** France
184 G5 **Glandon** France
183 I6 **Glandon** *r.* France
191 F6 **Glandorf** Ger.
184 F4 **Glane** *r.* France
191 E6 **Glane** *r.* Ger.
201 J6 **Glanegg** Austria
186 K4 **Glanerbrug** Neth.
169 F9 **Glanmire** Ireland
251 M7 **Glanworth** *Ont.* Can.
212 E2 **Glarner Alpen** *mts* Switz.
194 F8 **Glärnisch** *mts* Switz.
169 J3 **Glarryford** *Northern Ireland* U.K.
212 G1 **Glarus** Switz.
212 G2 **Glarus** *canton* Switz.
168 G6 **Glas Bheinn** *hill Scotland* U.K.
172 F3 **Glasbury** *Powys, Wales* U.K.
168 G7 **Glascarnoch, Loch** *l. Scotland* U.K.
260 G6 **Glasco** *KS* U.S.A.
164 I2 **Glasfjorden** *l.* Sweden
250 E9 **Glasford** *IL* U.S.A.
270 □ **Glasgow** Jamaica
168 H11 **Glasgow** *Glasgow, Scotland* U.K.
168 H11 **Glasgow** *admin. div. Scotland* U.K.
258 D5 **Glasgow** *DE* U.S.A.
254 E7 **Glasgow** *KY* U.S.A.
262 K2 **Glasgow** *MT* U.S.A.
256 F11 **Glasgow** *VA* U.S.A.
193 I9 **Glashütte** Ger.
195 K2 **Glashütten** Ger.
191 F10 **Gläshütten** Ger.
164 I2 **Glaskogens naturreservat** *nature res.* Norway
169 I4 **Glaslough** Ireland
247 I4 **Glaslyn** *Sask.* Can.
168 J9 **Glas Maol** *mt. Scotland* U.K.
168 G7 **Glass, Loch** *l. Scotland* U.K.
169 G6 **Glassan** Ireland
258 E5 **Glassboro** *NJ* U.S.A.
170 I2 **Glassford** *South Lanarkshire, Scotland* U.K.
264 N4 **Glass Mountain** *CA* U.S.A.
171 K4 **Glasson** *Cumbria, England* U.K.
245 N4 **Glass Peninsula** *AK* U.S.A.
172 G5 **Glastonbury** *Somerset, England* U.K.
259 J1 **Glastonbury** *CT* U.S.A.
168 I9 **Glas Tulaichean** *mt. Scotland* U.K.
212 E1 **Glatt** *r.* Switz.
193 H8 **Glaubitz** Ger.
193 G9 **Glauchau** Ger.
219 N6 **Glavacioc** *r.* Romania
219 O8 **Glavan** Bulg.
219 P4 **Glăvăneşti** Romania
219 O7 **Glavinitsa** Bulg.
220 F1 **Glavki** Greece
151 I2 **Glavnyy Kut** Rus. Fed.
161 O6 **Glazomichi** Rus. Fed.
229 F5 **Glazoué** Benin
156 K4 **Glazov** Rus. Fed.
161 T9 **Glazunovka** Rus. Fed.
161 N6 **Glazunovo** Rus. Fed.
169 E3 **Gleann Cholm Cille** Ireland
169 G3 **Gleann Doimhin** Ireland
169 C4 **Gleann na Muaidhe** Ireland
250 E4 **Gleason** *WI* U.S.A.
246 H5 **Gleichen** *Alta* Can.
193 E8 **Gleina** Ger.
201 K5 **Gleinalpe** *mt.* Austria
201 M5 **Gleisdorf** Austria
Gleiwitz Pol. *see* **Gliwice**
182 F5 **Gleizé** France
173 N3 **Glemsford** *Suffolk, England* U.K.
162 L5 **Glen** Sweden
257 □N4 **Glen** *NH* U.S.A.
170 F2 **Glenacardoch Point** *Scotland* U.K.
168 F8 **Glen Affric** *val. Scotland* U.K.
251 N3 **Glen Afton** *Ont.* Can.
102 J4 **Glen Afton** *North I.* N.Z.
256 H11 **Glen Allen** *VA* U.S.A.
169 E5 **Glenamaddy** Ireland
Glenamoy Ireland *see* **Gleann na Muaidhe**
169 C4 **Glenamoy** *r.* Ireland
180 D6 **Glénan, Îles de** *is* France
250 I5 **Glen Arbor** *MI* U.S.A.
169 J2 **Glenariff** *Northern Ireland* U.K.
169 K3 **Glenarm** *Northern Ireland* U.K.
168 H10 **Glen Artney** *val. Scotland* U.K.
168 I8 **Glen Avon** *val. Scotland* U.K.
103 F11 **Glenavy** *South I.* N.Z.
169 J3 **Glenavy** *Northern Ireland* U.K.
168 E11 **Glenbarr** *Argyll and Bute, Scotland* U.K.
168 E9 **Glenbeg** *Highland, Scotland* U.K.
169 C9 **Glenbeg Lough** *l.* Ireland
169 C8 **Glenbeigh** Ireland
247 L5 **Glenboro** *Man.* Can.
168 J12 **Glenbreck** *Scottish Borders, Scotland* U.K.
168 D8 **Glenbrittle** *Highland, Scotland* U.K.
258 D1 **Glenburn** *PA* U.S.A.
258 B6 **Glen Burnie** *MD* U.S.A.
168 F8 **Glen Cannich** *val. Scotland* U.K.
265 U4 **Glen Canyon** *gorge UT* U.S.A.
265 U5 **Glen Canyon Dam** *AZ* U.S.A.
265 V4 **Glen Canyon National Recreation Area** *park UT* U.S.A.
168 I12 **Glencaple** *Dumfries and Galloway, Scotland* U.K.
168 J10 **Glencarse** *Perth and Kinross, Scotland* U.K.
168 G6 **Glen Cassley** *val. Scotland* U.K.
168 J9 **Glen Clova** *val. Scotland* U.K.
248 D5 **Glencoe** *Ont.* Can.
237 O4 **Glencoe** S. Africa
168 F9 **Glencoe** *Highland, Scotland* U.K.
168 F9 **Glen Coe** *val. Scotland* U.K.
260 H3 **Glencoe** *MN* U.S.A.
Glencolumbkille Ireland *see* **Gleann Cholm Cille**
237 J9 **Glenconnor** S. Africa
259 H3 **Glen Cove** *NY* U.S.A.
169 J6 **Glencullen** Ireland
251 J3 **Glendale** *Ont.* Can.
265 T8 **Glendale** *AZ* U.S.A.
264 N7 **Glendale** *CA* U.S.A.
265 T4 **Glendale** *UT* U.S.A.
256 G8 **Glendale Lake** *PA* U.S.A.
104 E4 **Glendambo** *S.A.* Austr.
168 F10 **Glendaruel** *val. Scotland* U.K.
168 I8 **Glen Dee** *val. Scotland* U.K.
107 L6 **Glenden** *Qld* Austr.
262 L3 **Glendive** *MT* U.S.A.
247 I4 **Glendon** *Alta* Can.
258 E3 **Glendon** *PA* U.S.A.
262 L5 **Glendo Reservoir** *WY* U.S.A.
Glendowan Ireland *see* **Gleann Doimhin**
169 F8 **Glenduff** Ireland
169 J2 **Glendun** *r. Northern Ireland* U.K.
168 I10 **Gleneagles** *Perth and Kinross, Scotland* U.K.
170 E8 **Glenealy** Ireland
168 D11 **Glenegedale** *Argyll and Bute, Scotland* U.K.
104 H8 **Glenelg** *r. Vic.* Austr.
168 E8 **Glenelg** *Highland, Scotland* U.K.
168 J10 **Glenfarg** *Perth and Kinross, Scotland* U.K.
169 G4 **Glenfarne** Ireland
168 I8 **Glen Feshie** *val. Scotland* U.K.
173 J2 **Glenfield** *Leicester, England* U.K.
257 J5 **Glenfield** *NY* U.S.A.
168 F9 **Glenfinnan** *Highland, Scotland* U.K.
169 H2 **Glengad Head** Ireland
258 F3 **Glen Gardner** *NJ* U.S.A.
169 C9 **Glengarriff** Ireland
168 F8 **Glen Garry** *val. Highland, Scotland* U.K.
168 H9 **Glen Garry** *val. Perth and Kinross, Scotland* U.K.
109 E9 **Glengarry Range** *hills W.A.* Austr.
170 B5 **Glengavlen** Ireland
270 □ **Glengoffe** Jamaica
106 G8 **Glengyle** *Qld* Austr.
103 C13 **Glenham** *South I.* N.Z.
169 H2 **Glenhead** *Northern Ireland* U.K.
106 D7 **Glen Helen** *N.T.* Austr.
108 J4 **Glen Hill Aboriginal Reserve** *W.A.* Austr.
105 M3 **Glen Innes** *N.S.W.* Austr.
168 K8 **Glenkindie** *Aberdeenshire, Scotland* U.K.
168 G13 **Glenluce** *Dumfries and Galloway, Scotland* U.K.
168 H9 **Glen Lyon** *val. Scotland* U.K.
258 C2 **Glen Lyon** *PA* U.S.A.
245 N3 **Glenlyon Peak** *Y.T.* Can.
102 I4 **Glen Massey** *North I.* N.Z.
258 D4 **Glenmoore** *PA* U.S.A.
168 G8 **Glen More** *val. Scotland* U.K.
107 L9 **Glenmorgan** *Qld* Austr.
168 J9 **Glen Muick** *val. Scotland* U.K.
102 I4 **Glen Murray** *North I.* N.Z.
264 J2 **Glenn** *CA* U.S.A.
265 V10 **Glenn, Mount** *AZ* U.S.A.
169 C5 **Glennagevlagh** Ireland
245 K3 **Glennallen** *AK* U.S.A.
168 F9 **Glen Nevis** *val. Scotland* U.K.
245 K3 **Glenn Highway** *AK* U.S.A.
251 K5 **Glennie** *MI* U.S.A.
256 I11 **Glenns** *VA* U.S.A.
262 G5 **Glenns Ferry** *ID* U.S.A.
170 F4 **Glenoe** *Northern Ireland* U.K.
245 O4 **Glenora** *B.C.* Can.
107 H4 **Glenore** *Qld* Austr.
106 G7 **Glenormiston** *Qld* Austr.
109 F10 **Glenorn Aboriginal Reserve** *W.A.* Austr.
168 G6 **Glen Oykel** *val. Scotland* U.K.
105 N4 **Glenreagh** *N.S.W.* Austr.
257 K3 **Glen Robertson** *Ont.* Can.
258 B5 **Glen Rock** *PA* U.S.A.
256 D11 **Glen Rogers** *WV* U.S.A.
261 G9 **Glen Rose** *TX* U.S.A.
168 J10 **Glenrothes** *Fife, Scotland* U.K.
108 I4 **Glenroy** *W.A.* Austr.
257 L5 **Glens Falls** *NY* U.S.A.
170 D4 **Glenshane Pass** *Northern Ireland* U.K.
168 J9 **Glen Shee** *val. Scotland* U.K.
168 F8 **Glen Shiel** *val. Scotland* U.K.
258 E4 **Glenside** *PA* U.S.A.
168 G9 **Glen Spean** *val. Scotland* U.K.
258 F2 **Glen Spey** *NY* U.S.A.
169 F3 **Glenties** Ireland
169 H2 **Glentogher** Ireland
168 H8 **Glen Tromie** *val. Scotland* U.K.
103 F10 **Glentunnel** *South I.* N.Z.
169 G2 **Glenveagh National Park** Ireland
256 E10 **Glenville** *WV* U.S.A.
170 H5 **Glen Vine** Isle of Man
250 E1 **Glenwater** *Ont.* Can.
256 F11 **Glen Wilton** *VA* U.S.A.
261 I8 **Glenwood** *AR* U.S.A.
264 □F14 **Glenwood** *HI* U.S.A.
260 H5 **Glenwood** *IA* U.S.A.
260 H3 **Glenwood** *MN* U.S.A.
259 G2 **Glenwood** *NJ* U.S.A.
263 J10 **Glenwood** *NM* U.S.A.
265 U3 **Glenwood** *UT* U.S.A.
256 C10 **Glenwood** *WV* U.S.A.
250 B4 **Glenwood City** *WI* U.S.A.
263 K7 **Glenwood Springs** *CO* U.S.A.
182 J2 **Glère** France
193 F8 **Glesien** Ger.
168 □N2 **Gletness** *Shetland, Scotland* U.K.
212 E2 **Gletsch** Switz.
Glevum *Gloucestershire, England* U.K. *see* **Gloucester**
192 G2 **Glewitz** Ger.
250 D3 **Glidden** *WI* U.S.A.
193 J6 **Glienicke** Ger.
Glikí Greece *see* **Glyki**
169 D7 **Glin** Ireland
210 F3 **Glina** *r.* Bos.-Herz./Croatia
210 F3 **Glina** Croatia
190 J3 **Glinde** Ger.
193 G6 **Glindow** Ger.
161 R8 **Glinishchevo** Rus. Fed.
158 G6 **Glinjeni** Moldova
161 P7 **Glinka** Rus. Fed.
197 I3 **Glinojeck** Pol.
173 L2 **Glinton** *Peterborough, England* U.K.
163 J6 **Glittertinden** *mt.* Norway
196 G5 **Gliwice** Pol.
196 G5 **Gliwicki, Kanał** *canal* Pol.
218 J8 **Gllamnik** *Podujevë* Kosovo
218 I8 **Gllogoc** *Gllogoc* Kosovo
201 K6 **Globasnitz** Austria
265 V8 **Globe** *AZ* U.S.A.
199 L6 **Glodea, Vârful** *hill* Romania
219 O6 **Glodeanu-Sărat** Romania
158 G6 **Glodeni** Moldova
219 M4 **Glodeni** Romania
201 J6 **Glödnitz** Austria
196 E2 **Głodowa** Pol.
Glodyany Moldova *see* **Glodeni**
Glogau Pol. *see* **Głogów**
201 M4 **Gloggnitz** Austria
212 G2 **Glogn** *r.* Switz.
Glogovac *Gllogoc* Kosovo *see* **Gllogoc**
196 E4 **Głogów** Pol.
196 F5 **Głogówek** Pol.
197 J5 **Głogów Małopolski** Pol.
196 G2 **Głogowo** Pol.
162 L3 **Glomfjord** Norway
162 O4 **Glommersträsk** Sweden
195 L6 **Glonn** Ger.
195 L5 **Glonn** *r.* Ger.
200 C6 **Glorenza** Italy
278 F4 **Glória** Brazil
206 B2 **Glória do Ribatejo** Port.
239 □2 **Glorieuses, Îles** *is* Indian Ocean
Glorioso Islands Indian Ocean *see* **Glorieuses, Îles**
181 M4 **Glos-la-Ferrière** France
220 E3 **Glossa** Greece
171 N7 **Glossop** *Derbyshire, England* U.K.
193 E7 **Glöthe** Ger.
157 I5 **Glotovka** Rus. Fed.
105 M4 **Gloucester** *N.S.W.* Austr.
113 K8 **Gloucester** *New Britain* P.N.G.
172 H4 **Gloucester** *Gloucestershire, England* U.K.
257 O6 **Gloucester** *MA* U.S.A.
256 I11 **Gloucester** *VA* U.S.A.
172 H4 **Gloucester, Vale of** *val. England* U.K.
258 E5 **Gloucester City** *NJ* U.S.A.
258 E5 **Gloucester County** *county NJ* U.S.A.
107 L6 **Gloucester Island** *Qld* Austr.
256 I11 **Gloucester Point** *VA* U.S.A.
172 H4 **Gloucestershire** *admin. div. England* U.K.
169 F9 **Glounthaune** Ireland
267 P9 **Glover Reef** Belize
257 K5 **Gloversville** *NY* U.S.A.
249 K3 **Glovertown** *Nfld and Lab.* Can.
197 J4 **Głowaczów** Pol.
196 F1 **Główczyce** Pol.
192 H1 **Glowe** Ger.
192 F5 **Glöwen** Ger.
197 H4 **Głowno** Pol.
196 F5 **Głubczyce** Pol.
122 I5 **Glubinnoye** Rus. Fed.
159 T5 **Glubokaya** *r.* Rus. Fed.
157 H6 **Glubokiy** *Rostovskaya Oblast'* Rus. Fed.
157 H7 **Glubokiy** *Rostovskaya Oblast'* Rus. Fed.
Glubokoye Belarus *see* **Hlybokaye**
143 T2 **Glubokoye** Kazakh.
160 M1 **Glubokoye, Ozero** *l.* Rus. Fed.
196 F5 **Głuchołazy** Pol.
197 I4 **Głuchów** Pol.
190 I1 **Glücksburg (Ostsee)** Ger.
190 H3 **Glückstadt** Ger.
166 D1 **Gluggarnir** *hill* Faroe Is
183 F7 **Gluiras** France
Glukhov Ukr. *see* **Hlukhiv**
116 A2 **Glumpangminyeuk** *Sumatera* Indon.
171 N6 **Glusburn** *North Yorkshire, England* U.K.
159 N2 **Glushkovo** Rus. Fed.
196 E5 **Głuszyca** Pol.
196 G3 **Głuszyńskie, Jezioro** *l.* Pol.
172 D1 **Glyder Fawr** *hill Wales* U.K.
220 B3 **Glyki** Greece
172 F2 **Glyn Ceiriog** *Wrexham, Wales* U.K.
172 E4 **Glyncorrwg** *Neath Port Talbot, Wales* U.K.
Glynebwy *Wales* U.K. *see* **Ebbw Vale**
164 E5 **Glyngøre** Denmark
169 K3 **Glynn** *Northern Ireland* U.K.
172 E4 **Glynneath** *Neath Port Talbot, Wales* U.K.
Glyn-Nedd *Wales* U.K. *see* **Glynneath**
142 B2 **Gmelinka** Rus. Fed.
201 I6 **Gmünd** *Kärnten* Austria
201 K2 **Gmünd** *Niederösterreich* Austria
195 L6 **Gmund am Tegernsee** Ger.
201 I4 **Gmunden** Austria
256 D8 **Gnadenhutten** *OH* U.S.A.
163 N5 **Gnarp** Sweden
190 H4 **Gnarrenburg** Ger.
201 M6 **Gnas** Austria
169 D8 **Gneevgullia** Ireland
193 G8 **Gneisenaustadt Schildau** Ger.
217 □ **Ġnejna, Il-Bajja tal-** *b.* Malta
201 I6 **Gnesau** Austria
Gnesen Pol. *see* **Gniezno**
165 N2 **Gnesta** Sweden
164 H5 **Gniben** *pt* Denmark
201 M6 **Gniebing** Austria
196 G2 **Gniew** Pol.
196 G1 **Gniewino** Pol.
196 G3 **Gniewkowo** Pol.
197 I5 **Gnieździska** Pol.
196 F3 **Gniezno** Pol.
165 O4 **Gnisvärd** *Gotland* Sweden
Gnjilane *Gjilan* Kosovo *see* **Gjilan**
213 M6 **Gnocchetta** Italy
192 G3 **Gnoien** Ger.
196 F5 **Gnojna** Pol.
197 I6 **Gnojnik** Pol.
197 I5 **Gnojno** Pol.
172 H2 **Gnosall** *Staffordshire, England* U.K.
195 J3 **Gnotzheim** Ger.
109 D12 **Gnowangerup** *W.A.* Austr.
109 D10 **Gnows Nest Range** *hills W.A.* Austr.
190 I2 **Gnutz** Ger.
136 C5 **Goa** *Goa* India
136 D5 **Goa** *state* India
234 C5 **Goageb** Namibia
105 M7 **Goalen Head** *N.S.W.* Austr.
139 M6 **Goalpara** *Assam* India
115 A8 **Goang** *Flores* Indon.
228 E5 **Goaso** Ghana
168 F11 **Goat Fell** *hill Scotland* U.K.
271 □2 **Goat Point** Antigua and Barbuda
232 D3 **Goba** Eth.
234 C4 **Gobabis** Namibia
Gobannium *Monmouthshire, Wales* U.K. *see* **Abergavenny**
234 C5 **Gobas** Namibia
284 C5 **Gobernador Ayala** Arg.
285 G2 **Gobernador Crespo** Arg.
284 D6 **Gobernador Duval** Arg.
283 C8 **Gobernador Gregores** Arg.
285 H3 **Gobernador Mansilla** Arg.
283 C8 **Gobernador Mayer** Arg.
285 G2 **Gobernador Racedo** Arg.
285 G4 **Gobernador Ugarte** Arg.
282 F3 **Gobernador Virasoro** Arg.
128 J4 **Gobi Desert** China/Mongolia
161 Q8 **Gobiki** Rus. Fed.
201 I3 **Göblberg** *hill* Austria
126 B8 **Gobō** Japan
172 F2 **Gobowen** *Shropshire, England* U.K.
Gobustan Azer. *see* **Qobustan**
221 J6 **Göcek** Turkey
191 B7 **Goch** Ger.
234 C5 **Gochas** Namibia
191 J10 **Gochsheim** Ger.
119 H9 **Go Công** Vietnam
201 O6 **Göcsej** *hills* Hungary
199 I4 **Göd** Hungary
193 J8 **Göda** Ger.
139 L7 **Godagari** Bangl.
164 F2 **Godal** Norway
173 K5 **Godalming** *Surrey, England* U.K.
136 G4 **Godavari** *r.* India
136 H4 **Godavari, Cape** India
136 H4 **Godavari, Mouths of the** India
249 H3 **Godbout** *Que.* Can.
249 H3 **Godbout** *r. Que.* Can.
139 K7 **Godda** *Jharkhand* India
245 N4 **Goddard** *AK* U.S.A.
264 N4 **Goddard, Mount** *CA* U.S.A.
194 F2 **Goddelau** Ger.
191 G8 **Goddelsheim (Lichtenfels)** Ger.
232 D3 **Godē** Eth.
206 C3 **Godeal** *hill* Port.
219 L7 **Godech** Bulg.
258 F2 **Godeffroy** *NY* U.S.A.
200 F8 **Godega di Sant'Urbano** Italy
151 F6 **Gödekli** Turkey
209 D9 **Godelleta** Spain
248 D5 **Goderich** *Ont.* Can.
181 L2 **Goderville** France
Godhavn Greenland *see* **Qeqertarsuaq**
138 D8 **Godhra** *Gujarat* India
138 B8 **Godia Creek** *b. Gujarat* India
212 G6 **Godiasco** Italy
204 E6 **Godim** Port.
232 E3 **Godinlabe** Somalia
197 H1 **Godkowo** Pol.
103 E10 **Godley** *r. South I.* N.Z.
173 L3 **Godmanchester** *Cambridgeshire, England* U.K.
126 E5 **Gōdo** Japan
115 D4 **Godo, Gunung** *mt.* Indon.
206 E4 **Godolín** *r.* Port./Spain
199 I4 **Gödöllő** Hungary
201 J8 **Godovič** Slovenia
285 G3 **Godoy** Arg.
284 C3 **Godoy Cruz** Arg.
199 G5 **Gödre** Hungary
247 M3 **Gods** *r. Man.* Can.
247 M4 **Gods Lake** *Man.* Can.
247 O2 **God's Mercy, Bay of** *Nunavut* Can.
173 L5 **Godstone** *Surrey, England* U.K.
Godthåb Greenland *see* **Nuuk**
162 O2 **Godučohkka** *mt.* Sweden
Godwin-Austen, Mount China/Pak. *see* **K2**
196 G4 **Godziesze Wielkie** Pol.
197 K5 **Godziszów** Pol.
237 K6 **Goedemoed** S. Africa
186 E5 **Goedereede** Neth.
Goedgegun Swaziland *see* **Nhlangano**
236 C5 **Goegap Nature Reserve** S. Africa
248 E3 **Goéland, Lac au** *l. Que.* Can.
249 I2 **Goélands, Lac aux** *l. Que.* Can.
186 E5 **Goes** Neth.
251 J3 **Goetzville** *MI* U.S.A.
257 N5 **Goffstown** *NH* U.S.A.
201 L2 **Göfritz an der Wild** Austria
248 D4 **Gogama** *Ont.* Can.
125 J12 **Gō-gawa** *r.* Japan
250 E3 **Gogebic, Lake** *MI* U.S.A.
250 E3 **Gogebic Range** *hills MI* U.S.A.
150 H2 **Göğeç** Turkey
194 H4 **Göggingen** Ger.
151 G6 **Gogi Lerr** *mt.* Armenia/Azer.
160 J1 **Gogland, Ostrov** *i.* Rus. Fed.
235 G4 **Gogoi** Moz.
161 O7 **Gogolevka** Rus. Fed.
196 G5 **Gogolin** Pol.
219 K6 **Gogoşu** Romania
229 F4 **Gogounou** Benin
Gogra *Jharkhand* India *see* **Ghaghra**
Gogra *r.* India *see* **Ghaghara**
230 F2 **Gogrial** Sudan
138 D7 **Gogunda** *Rajasthan* India
138 G6 **Gohad** *Madh. Prad.* India
138 F5 **Gohana** *Haryana* India
138 F8 **Goharganj** *Madh. Prad.* India
190 K2 **Göhl** Ger.
193 F7 **Gohrau** Ger.
190 K4 **Göhrde** Ger.
192 I2 **Göhren, Ostseebad** Ger.
192 G4 **Göhren-Lebbin** Ger.
278 G3 **Goiana** Brazil
280 C3 **Goiandira** Brazil
279 C5 **Goianésia** Brazil
280 C2 **Goiânia** Brazil
278 G3 **Goianinha** Brazil
280 C2 **Goianira** Brazil
280 B1 **Goiás** Brazil
280 B2 **Goiás** *state* Brazil
280 C3 **Goiatuba** Brazil
133 E10 **Goicangmai** *Xizang* China
114 □ **Goikul** Palau
168 G10 **Goil, Loch** *inlet Scotland* U.K.
130 C2 **Goincang** *Qinghai* China
164 J5 **Göinge** *reg.* Sweden
280 A6 **Goio** *r.* Brazil
280 A6 **Goio-Erê** Brazil
231 E6 **Goi-Pula** Dem. Rep. Congo
186 H5 **Goirle** Neth.
204 D8 **Góis** Port.
180 G8 **Gois, Passage du** France
213 J5 **Goito** Italy
208 B1 **Goizueta** Spain
232 C3 **Gojeb Wenz** *r.* Eth.
126 C7 **Gojō** Japan
124 R7 **Gojōme** Japan
145 O6 **Gojra** Pak.
197 H4 **Gojść** Pol.
127 K3 **Goka** Japan
136 D4 **Gokak** *Karnataka* India
136 D5 **Gokarn** *Karnataka* India
150 A1 **Gök Çay** *r.* Turkey
221 G2 **Gökçeada** *i.* Turkey
221 J3 **Gökçedağ** Turkey
151 A5 **Gökçedere** Turkey
221 L5 **Gökçehüyük** Turkey
221 M2 **Gökçekaya Barajı** *resr* Turkey
221 I4 **Gökçen** Turkey
221 J4 **Gökçeören** Turkey
151 B6 **Gökçeşeyh** Turkey
Gökdepe Turkm. *see* **Gëkdepe**
150 A2 **Gökdere** *r.* Turkey
190 H2 **Gokels** Ger.
148 G3 **Gökirmak** *r.* Turkey
144 G1 **Goklenkuy, Solonchak** *salt l.* Turkm.
151 C6 **Gökoğlan** Turkey
221 J5 **Gökova** *Muğla* Turkey
Gökova *Muğla* Turkey *see* **Ula**
221 I6 **Gökova Körfezi** *b.* Turkey
145 J9 **Gokprosh Hills** Pak.
151 D6 **Göksu** *r.* Turkey
148 H4 **Göksun** Turkey
148 G5 **Göksu Nehri** *r.* Turkey
150 B2 **Göksu Parkı** Turkey
118 C3 **Gokteik** Myanmar
150 A2 **Göktepe** Turkey
235 F3 **Gokwe** Zimbabwe
164 E1 **Gol** Norway
198 G5 **Gola** Croatia
139 J8 **Gola** *Jharkhand* India
138 H5 **Gola** *Uttar Prad.* India
197 J4 **Gołąb** Pol.
213 Q4 **Golac** Slovenia
Golada Spain *see* **Agolada**
139 N6 **Golaghat** *Assam* India
169 F2 **Gola Island** Ireland
201 I8 **Golak** *mt.* Slovenia
139 L6 **Golakganj** *Assam* India
150 D5 **Golan** *hills* Syria
196 F3 **Gołańcz** Pol.
197 K4 **Gołaszyn** Pol.
144 G7 **Golbāf** Iran
145 M4 **Golbahār** Afgh.
148 H5 **Gölbaşı** Turkey
221 K6 **Gölbent** Turkey
179 L7 **Golbey** France
136 F4 **Golconda** *Andhra Prad.* India
261 K7 **Golconda** *IL* U.S.A.
262 F6 **Golconda** *NV* U.S.A.
221 I3 **Gölcük** *Balıkesir* Turkey
Gölçük Turkey *see* **Etili**
221 K2 **Gölcük** *Kocaeli* Turkey
221 J3 **Gölcük** *r.* Turkey
198 E2 **Golčův Jeníkov** Czech Rep.
197 H5 **Gołcza** Pol.
196 C2 **Golczewo** Pol.
256 H7 **Gold** *PA* U.S.A.
194 G7 **Goldach** Switz.
197 K1 **Gołdap** Pol.
197 J1 **Gołdapa** *r.* Pol.
191 H10 **Goldbach** Ger.
262 B5 **Gold Beach** *OR* U.S.A.
192 E5 **Goldbeck** Ger.
192 F3 **Goldberg** Ger.
172 G4 **Goldcliff** *Newport, Wales* U.K.
Gold Coast *country* Africa *see* **Ghana**
105 N3 **Gold Coast** *Qld* Austr.
228 E5 **Gold Coast** *coastal area* Ghana
245 J3 **Gold Creek** *AK* U.S.A.
201 H6 **Goldeck** *mt.* Austria
200 H5 **Goldegg** Austria
190 H1 **Goldelund** Ger.
246 G5 **Golden** *B.C.* Can.
169 G8 **Golden** Ireland
102 G7 **Golden Bay** *South I.* N.Z.
262 D4 **Goldendale** *WA* U.S.A.
103 G8 **Golden Downs** *South I.* N.Z.
246 F5 **Golden Ears Provincial Park** *B.C.* Can.
191 K7 **Goldene Aue** *reg.* Ger.
237 M4 **Golden Gate Highlands National Park** S. Africa
264 J4 **Golden Gate National Recreation Area** *park CA* U.S.A.
270 □ **Golden Grove** Jamaica
246 E5 **Golden Hinde** *mt. B.C.* Can.
248 E4 **Golden Lake** *Ont.* Can.
261 J11 **Golden Meadow** *LA* U.S.A.
173 K5 **Golden Pot** *Hampshire, England* U.K.
247 I5 **Golden Prairie** *Sask.* Can.
271 □2 **Golden Rock** *airport* St Kitts and Nevis
190 F5 **Goldenstedt** Ger.
138 F2 **Golden Throne** *mt.* Pak.
169 F7 **Golden Vale** *lowland* Ireland
237 J8 **Golden Valley** S. Africa
172 G3 **Golden Valley** *val. England* U.K.
235 F3 **Golden Valley** Zimbabwe
264 O4 **Goldfield** *NV* U.S.A.
195 L1 **Goldkronach** Ger.
197 J1 **Goldopiwo, Jezioro** *l.* Pol.
246 E5 **Gold River** *B.C.* Can.
247 K3 **Goldsand Lake** *Man.* Can.
258 D6 **Goldsboro** *MD* U.S.A.
255 I8 **Goldsboro** *NC* U.S.A.
264 P6 **Goldstone Lake** *CA* U.S.A.
108 E6 **Goldsworthy (abandoned)** *W.A.* Austr.
261 F10 **Goldthwaite** *TX* U.S.A.
151 E7 **Göldüzü** Turkey
256 H10 **Goldvein** *VA* U.S.A.
149 K3 **Göle** Turkey
206 C2 **Golegã** Port.
192 K5 **Golenice** Pol.
196 C2 **Goleniów** Pol.
145 J5 **Golestān** Afgh.
144 F3 **Golestān** *prov.* Iran
196 G6 **Goleszów** Pol.
264 M7 **Goleta** *CA* U.S.A.
266 □R13 **Golfito** Costa Rica
214 D6 **Golfo Aranci** *Sardegna* Italy
214 C7 **Golfo di Orosei Gennargentu e Asinara, Parco Nazionale del** *nat. park Sardegna* Italy
221 J6 **Gölgeli Dağları** *mts* Turkey
221 K5 **Gölhisar** Turkey
213 Q5 **Goli** *hill* Croatia
213 R6 **Goli** *i.* Croatia
261 G11 **Goliad** *TX* U.S.A.
218 I7 **Golija** *nat. park* Serbia
218 I7 **Golija Planina** *mts* Serbia
196 G3 **Golina** Pol.
129 Q4 **Golin Baixing** *Nei Mongol* China
183 B7 **Golinhac** France
161 U6 **Golitsyno** Rus. Fed.
148 H3 **Gölköy** Turkey
195 I2 **Gollach** *r.* Ger.
Gollel Swaziland *see* **Lavumisa**
201 N3 **Göllersdorf** Austria
194 E2 **Göllheim** Ger.
192 I4 **Gollin** Ger.
192 E3 **Göllin** Ger.
200 H4 **Golling an der Salzach** Austria
193 D8 **Göllingen** Ger.
192 I4 **Gollmitz** Ger.
193 G6 **Golm** Ger.
221 I4 **Gölmarmara** Turkey
191 I7 **Golmbach** Ger.
193 H6 **Golmberg** *hill* Ger.
208 G4 **Golmes** Spain
128 D8 **Golmud** *Qinghai* China
128 D8 **Golmud He** *r.* China
201 J7 **Golnik** Slovenia
214 D2 **Golo** *r. Corse* France
114 C5 **Golo** *i.* Phil.
161 X6 **Golobino** Rus. Fed.
143 L7 **Golodnaya Step'** *plain* Uzbek.
Gologory *hills* Ukr. *see* **Holohory**
282 E3 **Golondrina** Arg.
207 I2 **Golondrinos, Sierra de los** *mts* Spain
230 C2 **Golongosso** C.A.R.
161 X7 **Golovanovo** Rus. Fed.
150 D2 **Gölovası** Turkey
159 O3 **Golovchino** Rus. Fed.
244 G2 **Golovin** *AK* U.S.A.
244 G2 **Golovin Bay** *AK* U.S.A.
151 A2 **Golovinka** Rus. Fed.
122 N7 **Golovnino** *Kuril'skiye O-va* Rus. Fed.
144 D5 **Golpāyegān** Iran
221 L2 **Gölpazarı** Turkey
204 I6 **Golpejas** Spain
201 O4 **Gols** Austria
201 M3 **Gölsen** *r.* Austria
244 G3 **Golsovia** *AK* U.S.A.
168 I7 **Golspie** *Highland, Scotland* U.K.
193 I7 **Golßen** Ger.
201 K7 **Golte** *mts* Slovenia
193 F9 **Göltzsch** *r.* Ger.
197 H2 **Golub-Dobrzyń** Pol.
159 Q8 **Golubitskaya** Rus. Fed.
143 P1 **Golubovka** Kazakh.
196 F4 **Gołuchów** Pol.
161 U8 **Golun'** Rus. Fed.
231 B7 **Golungo Alto** Angola
232 E4 **Golweyn** Somalia
219 M9 **Golyama Syutkya** *mt.* Bulg.
219 M8 **Golyama Zhelyazna** Bulg.
219 M9 **Golyam Perelik** *mt.* Bulg.
219 M9 **Golyam Persenk** *mt.* Bulg.
151 D7 **Gölyanı** Turkey
Golyashi Belarus *see* **Sasnovy Bor**
221 J2 **Gölyazı** Turkey
197 I3 **Gołymin-Ośrodek** Pol.
161 O7 **Golynki** Rus. Fed.
Golyshi Rus. Fed. *see* **Vetluzhskiy**
151 B5 **Gölyurt Geçidi** *pass* Turkey
192 J5 **Golzow** *Brandenburg* Ger.
193 G6 **Golzow** *Brandenburg* Ger.
230 F5 **Goma** Dem. Rep. Congo
233 A5 **Goma** Uganda
194 G5 **Gomadingen** Ger.
138 F2 **Goma Hanu** *Jammu and Kashmir* India
133 I11 **Gomang Co** *salt l.* China

128 G9 **Gomangxung** Qinghai China
126 C7 **Gomanodan-zan** mt. Japan
205 P5 **Gómara** Spain
205 P5 **Gómara, Campo de** reg. Spain
194 G5 **Gomaringen** Ger.
138 I7 **Gomati** r. India
116 □ **Gombak, Bukit** hill Sing.
230 F4 **Gombari** Dem. Rep. Congo
229 H4 **Gombe** Nigeria
229 H4 **Gombe** state Nigeria
233 A6 **Gombe** r. Tanz.
221 K6 **Gömbe** Turkey
233 A6 **Gombe Stream National Park** Tanz.
229 I4 **Gombi** Nigeria
151 G4 **Gombori** Georgia
228 E4 **Gomboussougou** Burkina
239 □1a **Gombrani Island** Rodrigues I. Mauritius
Gombroon Iran see **Bandar-e 'Abbās**
221 H3 **Gömeç** Turkey
204 I6 **Gomecello** Spain
Gomel' Belarus see **Homyel'**
Gomel Oblast admin. div. Belarus see **Homyel'skaya Voblasts'**
Gomel'skaya Oblast' admin. div. Belarus see **Homyel'skaya Voblasts'**
206 C5 **Gomes Aires** Port.
168 D10 **Gometra** i. Scotland U.K.
269 H2 **Gómez Farías** Mex.
266 H5 **Gómez Palacio** Mex.
274 A5 **Gómez Rendón** Ecuador
144 E3 **Gomīshān** Iran
193 E6 **Gommern** Ger.
133 G10 **Gomo** Xizang China
133 G10 **Gomo Co** salt l. China
161 R1 **Gomorovichi** Rus. Fed.
212 E3 **Goms** reg. Switz.
115 E4 **Gomumu** i. Maluku Indon.
197 H4 **Gomunice** Pol.
Gonabad Iran see **Jūymand**
270 G4 **Gonaïves** Haiti
235 F4 **Gonarezhou National Park** Zimbabwe
270 G4 **Gonâve, Île de la** i. Haiti
144 E5 **Gonbad, Chāh-e** well Iran
144 F3 **Gonbad-e Kāvūs** Iran
199 K3 **Gönc** Hungary
204 F8 **Gonçalo** Port.
183 H6 **Goncelin** France
138 I6 **Gonda** Uttar Prad. India
138 C9 **Gondal** Gujarat India
232 E2 **Gonda Libah** well Eth.
274 C5 **Gondar** Col.
Gondar Eth. see **Gonder**
204 D6 **Gondar** Braga Port.
204 D6 **Gondar** Porto Port.
194 F3 **Gondelsheim** Ger.
232 C1 **Gonder** Eth.
151 E6 **Gönderme Geçidi** pass Turkey
191 D10 **Gondershausen** Ger.
204 G5 **Gondesende** Port.
230 C2 **Gondey** Chad
138 H9 **Gondia** Mahar. India
204 C6 **Gondomar** Port.
204 C4 **Gondomar** Spain
191 D10 **Gondorf** Ger.
204 D5 **Gondoriz** Port.
179 K6 **Gondrecourt-le-Château** France
179 K6 **Gondreville** France
179 M6 **Gondrexange, Étang de** l. France
185 E8 **Gondrin** France
221 I2 **Gönen** Balıkesir Turkey
221 L5 **Gönen** Isparta Turkey
221 I2 **Gönen** r. Turkey
183 I10 **Gonfaron** France
181 L2 **Gonfreville-l'Orcher** France
231 C8 **Gonga** Angola
131 I3 **Gong'an** Hubei China
133 I12 **Gongbalou** Xizang China
133 K12 **Gongbo'gyamda** Xizang China
128 E7 **Gongchakou** Gansu China
Gongchang Gansu China see **Longxi**
130 H6 **Gongcheng** Guangxi China
133 J12 **Gonggar** Xizang China
130 C4 **Gongga Shan** mt. Sichuan China
128 G8 **Gonghe** Qinghai China
Gonghe Yunnan China see **Mouding**
129 N6 **Gonghui** Hebei China
Gongjiang Jiangxi China see **Yudu**
132 F5 **Gongliu** Xinjiang China
229 I4 **Gongola** r. Nigeria
105 K4 **Gongolgon** N.S.W. Austr.
230 A5 **Gongoué** Gabon
130 E4 **Gongquan** Sichuan China
130 B5 **Gongshan** Yunnan China
130 D6 **Gongwang Shan** mts Yunnan China
Gongxian Henan China see **Gongyi**
Gongxian Sichuan China see **Gongquan**
129 M9 **Gongyi** Henan China
122 D7 **Gongzhuling** Jilin China
214 C8 **Goni** Sardegna Italy
285 I3 **Goñi** Uru.
197 K2 **Goniądz** Pol.
229 I4 **Goniri** Nigeria
Gonjo Xizang China see **Kasha**
130 B3 **Gonjo** Xizang China
214 A9 **Gonnesa** Sardegna Italy
214 A9 **Gonnesa, Golfo di** b. Sardegna Italy
220 D3 **Gonnoi** Greece
214 B9 **Gonnosfanadiga** Sardegna Italy
214 B8 **Gonnosnò** Sardegna Italy
124 S6 **Gonohe** Japan
125 G13 **Gōnoura** Japan
182 I2 **Gonsans** France
237 M8 **Gonubie** S. Africa
199 G4 **Gönyű** Hungary
213 J6 **Gonzaga** Italy
269 I3 **Gonzáles** Mex.
264 K5 **Gonzales** CA U.S.A.
261 G11 **Gonzales** TX U.S.A.
285 F4 **González Moreno** Arg.
268 D2 **González Ortega** Mex.
266 □T13 **Gonzalo Vásquez** Panama
122 D2 **Gonzha** Rus. Fed.
105 L8 **Goobang National Park** nat. park Australia
256 H11 **Goochland** VA U.S.A.
256 F11 **Goode** VA U.S.A.
287 I2 **Goodenough, Cape** Antarctica
245 N2 **Goodenough, Mount** hill N.W.T. Can.
113 L8 **Goodenough Island** P.N.G.
251 P5 **Gooderham** Ont. Can.
250 I4 **Good Harbor Bay** MI U.S.A.
250 I4 **Good Hart** MI U.S.A.
237 J1 **Good Hope** Botswana
250 D9 **Good Hope** IL U.S.A.
236 C10 **Good Hope, Cape of** S. Africa
244 G2 **Goodhope Bay** AK U.S.A.
246 E5 **Good Hope Mountain** B.C. Can.
262 G5 **Gooding** ID U.S.A.
260 E6 **Goodland** KS U.S.A.
239 □1b **Goodlands** Mauritius
250 F4 **Goodman** WI U.S.A.
244 G4 **Goodnews** r. AK U.S.A.
244 G4 **Goodnews Bay** AK U.S.A.
244 G4 **Goodnews Bay** AK U.S.A.
105 K3 **Goodooga** N.S.W. Austr.
106 D2 **Goodparla** N.T. Austr.
245 K2 **Goodpaster** r. AK U.S.A.
250 D4 **Goodrich** WI U.S.A.
247 I4 **Goodsoil** Sask. Can.
287 E2 **Goodspeed Nunataks** nunataks Antarctica
172 C3 **Goodwick** Pembrokeshire, Wales U.K.
249 G2 **Goodwood** r. Que. Can.
103 E12 **Goodwood** South I. N.Z.
171 P6 **Goole** East Riding of Yorkshire, England U.K.
105 J6 **Goolgowi** N.S.W. Austr.
104 G6 **Goolwa** S.A. Austr.
106 D1 **Goomadeer** r. N.T. Austr.
109 D11 **Goomalling** W.A. Austr.
105 J3 **Goombalie** N.S.W. Austr.
107 N9 **Goomeri** Qld Austr.
235 G3 **Goonda** Moz.
105 M3 **Goondiwindi** Qld Austr.
109 F10 **Goongarrie, Lake** salt flat W.A. Austr.
109 F10 **Goongarrie National Park** W.A. Austr.
172 B7 **Goonhavern** Cornwall, England U.K.
107 K6 **Goonyella** Qld Austr.
186 K4 **Goor** Neth.
109 D11 **Goorly, Lake** salt flat W.A. Austr.
249 I2 **Goose** r. Nfld and Lab. Can.
260 G2 **Goose** r. ND U.S.A.
Goose Bay Nfld and Lab. Can. see **Happy Valley-Goose Bay**
103 H9 **Goose Bay** South I. N.Z.
255 G9 **Goose Creek** SC U.S.A.
262 H5 **Goose Creek** r. ID/NV U.S.A.
283 F8 **Goose Green** Falkland Is
262 D6 **Goose Lake** CA U.S.A.
264 M6 **Goose Lake Canal** r. CA U.S.A.
136 E5 **Gooty** Andhra Prad. India
137 J3 **Gop** Orissa India
139 L8 **Gopalganj** Bangl.
139 J6 **Gopalganj** Bihar India
137 I3 **Gopalpur** Orissa India
205 O3 **Gopegi** Spain
138 G4 **Gopeshwar** Uttaranchal India
136 E7 **Gopichettipalayam** Tamil Nadu India
138 I7 **Gopiganj** Uttar Prad. India
196 G3 **Gopło, Jezioro** l. Pol.
194 H4 **Göppingen** Ger.
130 A4 **Goqên** Xizang China
207 N6 **Gor** Spain
207 M5 **Gor** r. Spain
196 E4 **Góra** Dolnośląskie Pol.
197 I3 **Góra** Mazowieckie Pol.
Goradiz Azer. see **Horadiz**
207 M6 **Gorafe** Spain
151 G2 **Goragorskiy** Rus. Fed.
197 K5 **Goraj** Pol.
197 J4 **Góra Kalwaria** Pol.
139 I6 **Gorakhpur** Uttar Prad. India
151 H5 **Goranboy** Azer.
197 J4 **Góra Puławska** Pol.
199 H1 **Góra Świętej Anny, Park Krajobrazowy** Pol.
196 D2 **Gorawino** Pol.
210 G4 **Goražde** Bos.-Herz.
161 U8 **Gorbachevo** Rus. Fed.
284 A6 **Gorbea** Chile
199 K4 **Görbeháza** Hungary
205 O2 **Gorbeia** mt. Spain
122 A2 **Gorbitsa** Rus. Fed.
285 H4 **Gorchs** Arg.
156 H4 **Gorchukha** Rus. Fed.
199 H6 **Görcsöny** Hungary
197 I6 **Gorczański Park Narodowy** nat. park Pol.
270 B6 **Gorda, Banco** sea feature Hond.
238 □3d **Gorda, Punta** pt La Palma Canary Is
266 □R10 **Gorda, Punta** pt Nic.
264 H1 **Gorda, Punta** pt CA U.S.A.
207 K6 **Gorda, Sierra** mts Spain
270 E1 **Gorda Cay** i. Bahamas
163 L6 **Gördalen** Sweden
205 J4 **Gordaliza del Pino** Spain
212 H7 **Gordana** r. Italy
183 G9 **Gordes** France
221 J4 **Gördes** Turkey
161 O9 **Gordeyevka** Rus. Fed.
212 F3 **Gordola** Switz.
109 D13 **Gordon** r. W.A. Austr.
168 K11 **Gordon** Scottish Borders, Scotland U.K.
245 L1 **Gordon** AK U.S.A.
260 D4 **Gordon** NE U.S.A.
258 C3 **Gordon** PA U.S.A.
250 C3 **Gordon** WI U.S.A.
283 C9 **Gordon, Isla** i. Chile
105 K10 **Gordon, Lake** Tas. Austr.
212 G3 **Gordona** Italy
106 C1 **Gordon Bay** N.T. Austr.
106 C4 **Gordon Creek** r. N.T. Austr.
108 J5 **Gordon Downs (abandoned)** W.A. Austr.
247 I3 **Gordon Lake** Alta Can.
246 H2 **Gordon Lake** N.W.T. Can.
246 C2 **Gordon Landing** Y.T. Can.
236 C10 **Gordon's Bay** S. Africa
256 G10 **Gordonsville** VA U.S.A.
107 J4 **Gordonvale** Qld Austr.
258 C4 **Gordonville** PA U.S.A.
230 C3 **Goré** Chad
232 B2 **Gorē** Eth.
103 C13 **Gore** South I. N.Z.
256 G9 **Gore** VA U.S.A.
251 L4 **Gore Bay** Ont. Can.
168 J11 **Gorebridge** Midlothian, Scotland U.K.
221 I4 **Görece** Turkey
161 U7 **Gorelki** Rus. Fed.
151 E4 **Gorelovka** Georgia
157 H5 **Goreloye** Rus. Fed.
148 G4 **Göreme Milli Parkı** nat. park Turkey
201 L8 **Gorenja Straža** Slovenia
201 J7 **Gorenja vas** Slovenia
245 J4 **Gore Point** pt AK U.S.A.
169 I7 **Goresbridge** Ireland
161 S6 **Goretovo** Rus. Fed.
169 J7 **Gorey** Ireland
144 H7 **Gorg** Iran
144 F3 **Gorgān** Iran
144 E3 **Gorgān, Khalīj-e** b. Iran
144 E3 **Gorgān, Rūd-e** r. Iran
Gorgany mts Ukr. see **Horhany**
108 E6 **Gorge Range** hills W.A. Austr.
107 J5 **Gorge Range** mts Qld Austr.
103 C13 **Gorge Road** South I. N.Z.
236 B3 **Gorges** Namibia
198 G5 **Gőrgeteg** Hungary
215 Q7 **Gorgoglione** Italy
228 B2 **Gorgol** admin. reg. Maur.
212 H9 **Gorgona, Isola di** i. Italy
212 G4 **Gorgonzola** Italy
232 C1 **Gorgora** Eth.
229 H3 **Gorgoram** Nigeria
209 F10 **Gorgos** r. Spain
219 R5 **Gorgova, Lacul** l. Romania
151 C6 **Görgü** Turkey
257 N4 **Gorham** NH U.S.A.
151 F4 **Gori** Georgia
218 H8 **Gorica** Podgorica Montenegro
201 O7 **Goričan** Croatia
201 N6 **Goričko** reg. Slovenia
186 G5 **Gorinchem** Neth.
173 J4 **Goring** Oxfordshire, England U.K.
213 M6 **Gorino** Italy
151 H6 **Goris** Armenia
195 J6 **Görisried** Ger.
219 P8 **Goritsa** Bulg.
161 T4 **Goritsy** Rus. Fed.
192 I4 **Göritz** Ger.
213 P4 **Gorizia** Italy
213 P4 **Gorizia** prov. Italy
201 L8 **Gorjanci** mts Slovenia
161 V5 **Gorka** Rus. Fed.
151 F1 **Gor'kaya Balka** r. Rus. Fed.
139 J6 **Gorkha** Nepal
Gorki Belarus see **Horki**
156 I4 **Gorki** Rus. Fed.
Gor'kiy Rus. Fed. see **Nizhniy Novgorod**
161 X5 **Gor'kogo, imeni** Rus. Fed.
Gor'kovskaya Oblast' admin. div. Rus. Fed. see **Nizhegorodskaya Oblast'**
161 N4 **Gor'kovskoye Vodokhranilishche** resr Rus. Fed.
143 S1 **Gor'koye, Ozero** salt l. Rus. Fed.
143 S1 **Gor'koye, Ozero** salt l. Rus. Fed.
192 D4 **Gorleben** Ger.
164 H6 **Gørlev** Denmark
197 J6 **Gorlice** Pol.
193 K8 **Görlitz** Ger.
192 D4 **Gorlosen** Ger.
Gorlovka Ukr. see **Horlivka**
161 W8 **Gorlovo** Rus. Fed.
193 I7 **Görlsdorf** Ger.
168 D11 **Gorm, Loch** l. Scotland U.K.
169 J5 **Gormanston** Ireland
205 O5 **Gormaz** Spain
138 G6 **Gormi** Madh. Prad. India
192 H3 **Görmin** Ger.
Gorna Dzhumaya Bulg. see **Blagoevgrad**
216 I9 **Gornalunga** r. Sicilia Italy
219 N7 **Gorna Oryakhovitsa** Bulg.
193 H9 **Gornau** Ger.
219 M7 **Gorni Dŭbnik** Bulg.
210 E2 **Gornja Radgona** Slovenia
219 J7 **Gornja Toponica** Niš Serbia
213 R5 **Gornje Jelenje** Croatia
201 N7 **Gornje Vratno** Croatia
199 J6 **Gornji Breg** Vojvodina Serbia
201 K7 **Gornji Grad** Slovenia
219 J7 **Gornji Matejevac** Niš Serbia
218 I6 **Gornji Milanovac** Gornji Milanovac Serbia
201 N8 **Gornji Tkalec** Croatia
210 F4 **Gornji Vakuf** Bos.-Herz.
197 I5 **Górno** Pol.
219 N7 **Gorno Ablanovo** Bulg.
143 U2 **Gorno-Altaysk** Rus. Fed.
Gorno-Altayskaya Avtonomnaya Oblast' aut. rep. Rus. Fed. see **Altay, Respublika**
Gorno-Badakhshan aut. rep. Tajik. see **Kŭhistoni Badakhshon**
152 H3 **Gornopravdinsk** Rus. Fed.
219 N8 **Gornotrakiyska Nizina** lowland Bulg.
156 L4 **Gornozavodsk** Permskaya Oblast' Rus. Fed.
122 L5 **Gornozavodsk** Sakhalin Rus. Fed.
132 E1 **Gornyak** Altayskiy Kray Rus. Fed.
161 W8 **Gornyak** Ryazanskaya Oblast' Rus. Fed.
Gornyak Ukr. see **Hirnyk**
122 J3 **Gornyy** Khabarovskiy Kray Rus. Fed.
159 T6 **Gornyy** Rostovskaya Oblast' Rus. Fed.
142 C2 **Gornyy** Saratovskaya Oblast' Rus. Fed.
Gornyy Altay aut. rep. Rus. Fed. see **Altay, Respublika**
Gornyy Badakhshan aut. rep. Tajik. see **Kŭhistoni Badakhshon**
157 I6 **Gornyy Balykley** Rus. Fed.
122 H6 **Gornyye Klyuchi** Rus. Fed.
232 D3 **Goro** Eth.
Goro i. Fiji see **Koro**
213 M6 **Goro** Italy
232 C2 **Goroch'an** mt. Eth.
Gorodenka Ukr. see **Horodenka**
156 H4 **Gorodets** Rus. Fed.
159 R2 **Gorodishche** Belgorodskaya Oblast' Rus. Fed.
157 I5 **Gorodishche** Penzenskaya Oblast' Rus. Fed.
157 I6 **Gorodishche** Volgogradskaya Oblast' Rus. Fed.
Gorodishche Ukr. see **Horodyshche**
Gorodok Minskaya Voblasts' Belarus see **Haradok**
Gorodok Vitsyebskaya Voblasts' Belarus see **Haradok**
Gorodok Rus. Fed. see **Zakamensk**
Gorodok Khmel'nyts'ka Oblast' Ukr. see **Horodok**
Gorodok L'vivs'ka Oblast' Ukr. see **Horodok**
157 H7 **Gorodovikovsk** Rus. Fed.
113 K8 **Goroka** P.N.G.
104 H7 **Goroke** Vic. Austr.
156 H4 **Gorokhovets** Rus. Fed.
228 E3 **Gorom Gorom** Burkina
113 H7 **Gorong, Kepulauan** is Indon.
235 G3 **Gorongosa** Moz.
235 G3 **Gorongosa** mt. Moz.
235 G3 **Gorongosa, Parque Nacional de** nat. park Moz.
115 C3 **Gorontalo** Sulawesi Indon.
115 C3 **Gorontalo** prov. Indon.
229 G3 **Goronyo** Nigeria
199 G1 **Gór Opawskich, Park Krajobrazowy** Pol.
285 H4 **Gorostiaga** Arg.
229 F3 **Goroubi** watercourse Niger
229 F3 **Gorouol** r. Burkina/Niger
165 Q7 **Górowo Iławeckie** Pol.
186 J2 **Gorredijk** Neth.
212 G6 **Gorreto** Italy
181 J5 **Gorron** France
191 K8 **Görsbach** Ger.
172 D4 **Gorseinon** Swansea, Wales U.K.
157 G6 **Gorshechnoye** Rus. Fed.
196 G2 **Górsk** Pol.
213 Q5 **Gorski Kotar** reg. Croatia
Gorskoye Ukr. see **Hirs'ke**
198 F1 **Gór Sowich, Park Krajobrazowy** Pol.
186 J4 **Gorssel** Neth.
196 E5 **Gór Stołowych, Park Narodowy** nat. park Pol.
169 E6 **Gort** Ireland
170 C4 **Gortaclare** Northern Ireland U.K.
Gortahork Ireland see **Gort an Choirce**
169 F2 **Gort an Choirce** Ireland
Gorteen Ireland see **An Goirtín**
169 E5 **Gorteen** Galway Ireland
170 C8 **Gorteen** Kilkenny Ireland
169 F6 **Gorteeny** Ireland
169 H3 **Gortin** Northern Ireland U.K.
219 O5 **Goru, Vârful** mt. Romania
221 J2 **Görükle** Turkey
169 C6 **Gorumna Island** Ireland
281 F1 **Gorutuba** r. Brazil
144 G7 **Gorveh** Iran
194 E6 **Görwihl** Ger.
194 F2 **Gorxheimertal** Ger.
151 G2 **Goryacheistochnenskaya** Chechenskaya Respublika Rus. Fed.
Goryacheistochnenskaya Stavropol'skiy Kray Rus. Fed. see **Goryachevodskiy**
151 E1 **Goryachevodskiy** Rus. Fed.
151 A1 **Goryachiy Klyuch** Rus. Fed.
Goryn' r. Ukr. see **Horyn'**
143 P5 **Gory Shu-Ile** mts Kazakh.
122 J3 **Goryun** r. Rus. Fed.
145 J5 **Gorzanak** Afgh.
215 K2 **Gorzano, Monte** mt. Italy
179 L5 **Gorze** France
193 E7 **Görzig** Ger.
193 F6 **Görzke** Ger.
197 H4 **Gorzkowice** Pol.
197 L5 **Gorzków-Osada** Pol.
196 E2 **Górzna** Pol.
189 I2 **Górznieńsko-Lidzbarski Park Krajobrazowy** Pol.
197 H2 **Górzno** Pol.
196 G4 **Gorzów Śląski** Pol.
196 D3 **Gorzów Wielkopolski** Pol.
196 C3 **Górzyca** Lubuskie Pol.
196 D2 **Górzyca** Zachodniopomorskie Pol.
197 J5 **Gorzyce** Podkarpackie Pol.
197 K5 **Gorzyce** Podkarpackie Pol.
196 G6 **Gorzyce** Śląskie Pol.
196 C4 **Górzyn** Pol.
196 D3 **Gorzyń** Pol.
Gosainthan mt. Xizang China see **Xixabangma Feng**
213 L3 **Gosaldo** Italy
201 I4 **Gosau** Austria
173 L2 **Gosberton** Lincolnshire, England U.K.
196 D3 **Gościm** Pol.
196 D1 **Gościno** Pol.
196 D4 **Gósciszów** Pol.
201 M6 **Gosdorf** Austria
126 C7 **Gose** Japan
193 E8 **Goseck** Ger.
198 F5 **Gősfai Hegy** hill Hungary
173 N4 **Gosfield** Essex, England U.K.
105 M5 **Gosford** N.S.W. Austr.
171 K5 **Gosforth** Cumbria, England U.K.
171 N3 **Gosforth** Tyne and Wear, England U.K.
145 K8 **Goshanak** Pak.
194 F5 **Gosheim** Ger.
264 M5 **Goshen** CA U.S.A.
254 E5 **Goshen** IN U.S.A.
257 M5 **Goshen** NH U.S.A.
258 F6 **Goshen** NJ U.S.A.
257 K7 **Goshen** NY U.S.A.
256 F11 **Goshen** VA U.S.A.
126 A7 **Goshiki** Japan
Goshoba Turkm. see **Goşoba**
124 R6 **Goshogawara** Japan
145 I8 **Gosht-e 'Olyā** Iran
191 J7 **Goslar** Ger.
197 H3 **Goślice** Pol.
180 I5 **Gosné** France
144 F1 **Goşoba** Turkm.
210 E3 **Gospić** Croatia
173 J6 **Gosport** Hampshire, England U.K.
228 A3 **Gossas** Senegal
212 G1 **Gossau** St Gallen Switz.
194 F7 **Gossau** Zürich Switz.
106 E5 **Gosse** watercourse N.T. Austr.
201 M6 **Gössendorf** Austria
228 E3 **Gossi** Mali
230 E2 **Gossinga** Sudan
201 I4 **Gößl** Austria
193 F9 **Gößnitz** Ger.
195 K2 **Gößweinstein** Ger.
159 Q8 **Gostagayevskaya** Rus. Fed.
159 P3 **Gostishchevo** Rus. Fed.
218 I9 **Gostivar** Macedonia
201 K4 **Göstling an der Ybbs** Austria
196 F2 **Gostycyn** Pol.
196 F4 **Gostyń** Wielkopolskie Pol.
196 C1 **Gostyń** Zachodniopomorskie Pol.
197 H3 **Gostynin** Pol.
189 I2 **Gostynińsko-Włocławski Park Krajobrazowy** Pol.
130 B2 **Gosu** Sichuan China
196 F4 **Goszcz** Pol.
196 G4 **Goszczanów** Pol.
197 I4 **Goszczyn** Pol.
232 D2 **Gota** Eth.
164 H4 **Götaälven** r. Sweden
165 M3 **Göta Kanal** canal Sweden
165 K5 **Götaland** reg. Sweden
164 H4 **Göteborg** Sweden
164 I4 **Göteborg-Landvetter** airport Sweden
229 H5 **Gotel Mountains** Cameroon/Nigeria
Gotemba Shizuoka Japan see **Gotenba**
127 I5 **Gotenba** Shizuoka Japan
164 J3 **Götene** Sweden
Gotenhafen Pol. see **Gdynia**
213 R4 **Goteniška gora** mts Slovenia
191 K9 **Gotha** Ger.
173 J2 **Gotham** Nottinghamshire, England U.K.
165 O4 **Gothem** Gotland Sweden
165 O4 **Gothemån** r. Gotland Sweden
Gothenburg Sweden see **Göteborg**
260 E5 **Gothenburg** NE U.S.A.
229 F3 **Gothèye** Niger
165 O4 **Gotland** county Sweden
165 O4 **Gotland** i. Gotland Sweden
271 □8 **Goto Meer** Bonaire Neth. Antilles
125 F14 **Gotō-rettō** is Japan
219 L9 **Gotse Delchev** Bulg.
165 P3 **Gotska Sandön** Gotland Sweden
165 P3 **Gotska Sandön** i. Gotland Sweden
165 P3 **Gotska Sandön nationalpark** nat. park Gotland Sweden
125 J12 **Gōtsu** Japan
212 H7 **Gottero, Monte** mt. Italy
195 N4 **Gotteszell** Ger.
195 N4 **Gottfrieding** Ger.
191 I7 **Göttingen** Ger.
194 F6 **Gottmadingen** Ger.
162 O5 **Gottne** Sweden
246 F5 **Gott Peak** B.C. Can.
Gottwaldow Czech Rep. see **Zlín**
144 E2 **Goturdepe** Turkm.
Gotval'd Ukr. see **Zmiyiv**
201 O3 **Götzendorf an der Leitha** Austria
200 A5 **Götzis** Austria
230 D3 **Gouako** C.A.R.
180 E5 **Gouarec** France
186 G4 **Gouda** Neth.
236 D9 **Gouda** S. Africa
183 E8 **Goudargues** France
284 C4 **Goudge** Arg.
173 M5 **Goudhurst** Kent, England U.K.
228 B3 **Goudiri** Senegal
229 H3 **Goudoumaria** Niger
285 F4 **Goudra** Arg.
250 J1 **Goudreau** Ont. Can.
228 C4 **Gouéké** Guinea
180 C5 **Gouesnou** France
180 F4 **Gouet** r. France
229 G2 **Goûgaram** Niger
288 I8 **Gough Island** S. Atlantic Ocean
182 I1 **Gouhenans** France
248 F3 **Gouin, Réservoir** resr Que. Can.
236 G10 **Goukamma Nature Reserve** S. Africa
183 B7 **Goul** r. France
250 J3 **Goulais River** Ont. Can.
105 L6 **Goulburn** N.S.W. Austr.
105 J7 **Goulburn** r. Vic. Austr.
106 D1 **Goulburn Islands** N.T. Austr.
105 M5 **Goulburn River National Park** N.S.W. Austr.
109 D8 **Gould, Mount** hill W.A. Austr.
250 I3 **Gould City** MI U.S.A.
286 O1 **Gould Coast** Antarctica
258 E2 **Gouldsboro** PA U.S.A.
180 B5 **Goulet de Brest** sea chan. France
229 I3 **Goulféy** Cameroon
228 D4 **Goulia** Côte d'Ivoire
Goulou atoll Micronesia see **Ngulu**
183 G9 **Goult** France
228 D3 **Goumbou** Mali
220 D2 **Goumenissa** Greece
182 J2 **Goumois** France
229 I4 **Gouna** Cameroon
230 D2 **Gounda** C.A.R.
228 E2 **Goundam** Mali
230 C2 **Goundi** Chad
230 B2 **Gounou-Gan** Chad
230 B2 **Gounou-Gaya** Chad
249 G2 **Goupil, Lac** l. Que. Can.
228 B3 **Gouraye** Maur.
185 B8 **Gourbera** France
271 □2 **Gourbeyre** Guadeloupe
228 E3 **Gourcy** Burkina
183 J9 **Gourdan, Montagne de** mt. France
185 F9 **Gourdan-Polignan** France
185 G6 **Gourdon** Midi-Pyrénées France
183 J9 **Gourdon** Provence-Alpes-Côte d'Azur France
168 L9 **Gourdon** Aberdeenshire, Scotland U.K.
229 H3 **Gouré** Niger
185 D10 **Gourette** France
178 H6 **Gourgançon** France
180 D5 **Gourin** France
139 M7 **Gouripur** Bangl.
236 F10 **Gourits** r. S. Africa
250 J1 **Gourlay Lake** Ont. Can.
228 E2 **Gourma-Rharous** Mali
228 C2 **Goûrmél** well Maur.
224 D5 **Gourmeur** well Chad
178 C5 **Gournay-en-Bray** France
224 C5 **Gouro** Chad
226 D5 **Goûr Oulad Aḥmed** reg. Mali
224 D5 **Gourouro** well Chad
178 D5 **Goussainville** France
184 E5 **Gout-Rossignol** France
186 I2 **Goutum** Neth.
281 F3 **Gouvêa** Brazil
204 E8 **Gouveia** Port.
257 J4 **Gouverneur** NY U.S.A.
178 D5 **Gouvieux** France
187 I8 **Gouvy** Belgium
271 □6 **Gouyave** Grenada
230 C3 **Gouzé** C.A.R.
184 I3 **Gouzon** France
204 D6 **Gove** Port.
260 E6 **Gove** KS U.S.A.
231 B8 **Gove, Barragem do** resr Angola
219 L8 **Govedartsi** Bulg.
153 R4 **Govena, Mys** hd Rus. Fed.
106 F2 **Gove Peninsula** N.T. Austr.
Goverla, Gora mt. Ukr. see **Hoverla, Hora**
281 G3 **Governador Valadares** Brazil
114 F8 **Governor Generoso** Mindanao Phil.
270 E1 **Governor's Harbour** Eleuthera Bahamas
259 G3 **Governor's Island National Monument** nat. park NY U.S.A.
128 D4 **Govĭ-Altay** prov. Mongolia
128 F4 **Govĭ Altayn Nuruu** mts Mongolia
139 I7 **Govind Ballash Pant Sagar** resr India
138 H7 **Govindgarh** Madh. Prad. India
138 F4 **Govind Sagar** resr India
129 J3 **Govĭ-Ugtaal** Mongolia
256 G6 **Gowanda** NY U.S.A.
107 J8 **Gowan Range** hills Qld Austr.
133 H11 **Gowaqungo** Xizang China
145 K7 **Gowārān** Afgh.
197 I4 **Gowarczów** Pol.
144 F6 **Gowd-e Aḥmar** Iran
144 F8 **Gowdeh, Rūd-e** watercourse Iran
103 G8 **Gowenbridge** South I. N.Z.
258 B3 **Gowen City** PA U.S.A.
172 D4 **Gower** pen. Wales U.K.
104 □2 **Gower, Mount** hill Lord Howe I. Austr.
251 N2 **Gowganda** Ont. Can.
251 N2 **Gowganda Lake** Ont. Can.
196 F1 **Gowidlino** Pol.
196 C2 **Gowienica** r. Pol.
145 M5 **Gowmal Kalay** Afgh.
169 G5 **Gowna, Lough** l. Ireland
197 J3 **Goworowo** Pol.
169 H7 **Gowran** Ireland
145 L3 **Gowurdak** Turkm.
171 L7 **Gowy** r. England U.K.
171 Q6 **Goxhill** North Lincolnshire, England U.K.
282 F3 **Goya** Arg.
271 □2 **Goyave** Guadeloupe
151 I5 **Göyçay** Azer.
151 I5 **Göyçay** r. Azer.
151 I5 **Göyçay Qoruğu** nature res. Azer.
106 E2 **Goyder** r. N.T. Austr.
106 E8 **Goyder** watercourse N.T. Austr.
104 G2 **Goyder Lagoon** salt flat S.A. Austr.
285 F5 **Goyena** Arg.
151 H5 **Göygöl** Azer.
151 H5 **Göygöl Qoruğu** nature res. Azer.
151 J5 **Göylär Çöl** Azer.
144 F1 **Goymatdag** hills Turkm.
221 L6 **Göynük** Antalya Turkey
149 J4 **Göynük** Bingöl Turkey
221 L2 **Göynük** Bolu Turkey
221 L2 **Göynük** r. Turkey
221 K3 **Göynükbelen** Turkey
124 S7 **Goyō-zan** mt. Japan
151 J6 **Göytäpä** Azer.
145 J4 **Gozareh** Afgh.
224 D6 **Goz-Beïda** Chad
150 D2 **Gözcüler** Turkey
197 J4 **Gózd** Pol.
196 D4 **Gozdnica** Pol.
196 C3 **Gozdowice** Pol.
148 I4 **Gözene** Turkey
127 L2 **Gozen-yama** Japan
133 E9 **Gozha Co** salt l. China
150 E2 **Gözkaya** Turkey
217 □ **Gozo** i. Malta
225 G5 **Goz Regeb** Sudan
212 E4 **Gozzano** Italy
236 I8 **Graaff-Reinet** S. Africa
236 C8 **Graafwater** S. Africa
192 F2 **Graal-Müritz, Ostseebad** Ger.
194 E3 **Graben-Neudorf** Ger.
200 H3 **Grabensee** l. Austria
195 N6 **Grabenstätt** Ger.
191 J10 **Grabfeld** plain Ger.
197 G4 **Grabia** r. Pol.
197 H4 **Grabica** Pol.
228 D5 **Grabo** Côte d'Ivoire
236 D10 **Grabouw** S. Africa
219 K6 **Grabovica** Kladovo Serbia
192 E4 **Grabow** Mecklenburg-Vorpommern Ger.
193 E6 **Grabow** Sachsen-Anhalt Ger.
192 G2 **Grabow** inlet Ger.
197 H3 **Grabów** Pol.
165 M7 **Grabowa** r. Pol.
192 G3 **Grabowhöfe** Ger.
197 L5 **Grabowiec** Lubelskie Pol.
197 J4 **Grabowiec** Mazowieckie Pol.
197 J4 **Grabów nad Pilicą** Pol.
196 G4 **Grabów nad Prosną** Pol.
196 F2 **Grabówno** Pol.
196 F4 **Grabowno Wielkie** Pol.
197 K2 **Grabowo** Podlaskie Pol.
197 K1 **Grabowo** Warmińsko-Mazurskie Pol.
212 G1 **Grabs** Switz.
210 E3 **Gračac** Croatia
210 G3 **Gračanica** Bos.-Herz.
218 H8 **Gračanica Jezero** l. Montenegro
184 H1 **Graçay** France
109 E12 **Grace, Lake** salt flat W.A. Austr.
248 E4 **Gracefield** Que. Can.
187 H7 **Grâce-Hollogne** Belgium
107 M7 **Gracemere** Qld Austr.
180 E4 **Grâces** France
161 X9 **Grachevka** Lipetskaya Oblast' Rus. Fed.
142 E1 **Grachevka** Orenburgskaya Oblast' Rus. Fed.
143 R2 **Grachi (abandoned)** Kazakh.
269 I3 **Graciano Sánchez** Mex.
266 □O10 **Gracias** Hond.
238 □1c **Graciosa** i. Azores
238 □3c **Graciosa** i. Canary Is
201 N6 **Grad** Slovenia
210 G3 **Gradačac** Bos.-Herz.
213 N8 **Gradara** Italy
278 C3 **Gradaús** Brazil
278 C4 **Gradaús, Serra dos** hills Brazil
201 N8 **Gradec** Croatia
205 J3 **Gradefes** Spain
219 O8 **Gradets** Bulg.
185 C6 **Gradignan** France
219 O8 **Gradishte** hill Bulg.
Gradiška Bos.-Herz. see **Bosanska Gradiška**
210 G3 **Gradište** Croatia
219 O6 **Grădiştea** Romania
213 O4 **Grado** Italy
204 H2 **Grado** Spain
200 H8 **Grado, Laguna di** lag. Italy
214 H2 **Gradoli** Italy
219 J9 **Gradsko** Gradsko Macedonia
261 D8 **Grady** NM U.S.A.
168 J5 **Graemsay** i. Scotland U.K.
207 M6 **Graena** Spain
195 K5 **Gräfelfing** Ger.
195 K2 **Gräfenberg** Ger.
191 I10 **Gräfendorf** Ger.
201 M5 **Grafendorf bei Hartberg** Austria
193 F7 **Gräfenhainichen** Ger.
194 E6 **Grafenhausen** Ger.
191 K9 **Gräfenroda** Ger.
201 J6 **Grafenstein** Austria
193 D9 **Gräfenthal** Ger.
191 K8 **Gräfentonna** Ger.
195 L2 **Grafenwöhr** Ger.
201 M3 **Grafenworth** Austria
214 I2 **Graffignano** Italy
173 L3 **Grafham Water** resr England U.K.
191 K6 **Grafhorst** Ger.
193 D9 **Gräfinau-Angstedt** Ger.
195 L5 **Grafing bei München** Ger.
164 F1 **Gråfjell** mt. Norway
195 N4 **Grafling** Ger.
195 K5 **Grafrath** Ger.
162 L5 **Gräftåvallen** Sweden
105 N3 **Grafton** N.S.W. Austr.
260 G1 **Grafton** ND U.S.A.
256 C7 **Grafton** OH U.S.A.
250 G6 **Grafton** WI U.S.A.
256 E9 **Grafton** WV U.S.A.
107 J4 **Grafton, Cape** Qld Austr.
265 R3 **Grafton, Mount** NV U.S.A.
107 K4 **Grafton Passage** Qld Austr.
164 F1 **Grågalten** hill Norway
215 N6 **Gragnano** Italy
255 H7 **Graham** NC U.S.A.
261 F9 **Graham** TX U.S.A.
265 W9 **Graham, Mount** AZ U.S.A.
Graham Bell Island Zemlya Frantsa-Iosifa Rus. Fed. see **Greem-Bell, Ostrov**
245 N5 **Graham Island** B.C. Can.
243 I2 **Graham Island** Nunavut Can.
257 □Q4 **Graham Lake** ME U.S.A.
286 T2 **Graham Land** reg. Antarctica
246 F3 **Graham Laurier Provincial Park** B.C. Can.
243 K2 **Graham Moore, Cape** Nunavut Can.
237 K9 **Grahamstown** S. Africa
Grahovo Bos.-Herz. see **Bosansko Grahovo**
201 I7 **Grahovo** Slovenia
170 D8 **Graigue** Ireland
169 I7 **Graiguenamanagh** Ireland
173 N5 **Grain** Medway, England U.K.
173 N5 **Grain, Isle of** pen. England U.K.
195 K7 **Grainau** Ger.
195 P4 **Grainet** Ger.
183 B7 **Graissac** France
183 C9 **Graissessac** France
205 Q9 **Graja de Iniesta** Spain
117 K9 **Grajagan** Jawa Indon.
205 J4 **Grajal de Campos** Spain
278 D3 **Grajaú** Brazil
278 D2 **Grajaú** r. Brazil
197 K2 **Grajewo** Pol.
156 J4 **Grakhovo** Rus. Fed.
168 D4 **Gralisgeir** i. Scotland U.K.
201 M6 **Gralla** Austria
164 F6 **Gram** Denmark
219 K8 **Gramada** mt. Serbia
201 J3 **Gramastettan** Austria
185 H6 **Gramat** France
185 H6 **Gramat, Causse de** hills France
219 P8 **Gramatikovo** Bulg.
201 N3 **Gramatneusiedl** Austria
183 H9 **Grambois** France
192 J4 **Grambow** Ger.
192 D3 **Gramkow** Ger.
192 G2 **Grammendorf** Ger.
216 H9 **Grammichele** Sicilia Italy
Grammont Belgium see **Geraardsbergen**
212 D8 **Grammont, Mont** mt. Italy
220 B2 **Grammos** mt. Greece
256 G8 **Grampian** PA U.S.A.
168 G9 **Grampian Mountains** Scotland U.K.
105 I7 **Grampians National Park** Vic. Austr.
172 C7 **Grampound** Cornwall, England U.K.
186 K3 **Gramsbergen** Neth.
218 I10 **Gramsh** Albania
192 J4 **Gramzow** Ger.
Gran Hungary see **Esztergom**
212 D6 **Grana** r. Italy
212 F5 **Grana** r. Italy
236 D6 **Granaatboskolk** S. Africa
169 J6 **Granabeg** Ireland
274 C4 **Granada** Col.
266 □Q12 **Granada** Nic.
207 L6 **Granada** Spain
207 M6 **Granada** prov. Spain
260 D6 **Granada** CO U.S.A.
238 □3a **Granadilla de Abona** Tenerife Canary Is
206 E5 **Granado** hill Spain
283 C8 **Gran Altiplanicie Central** plain Arg.
169 H5 **Granard** Ireland
213 K6 **Granarolo dell'Emilia** Italy
200 G5 **Granatspitze** mt. Austria
207 L3 **Granátula de Calatrava** Spain
283 D7 **Gran Bajo** depr. Arg.
284 D6 **Gran Bajo Salitroso** salt flat Arg.
283 C8 **Gran Bajo San Julián** val. Arg.
212 B5 **Gran Bosco di Salbertrand, Parco Naturale del** nature res. Italy
261 G9 **Granbury** TX U.S.A.
249 F4 **Granby** Que. Can.
262 K6 **Granby** CO U.S.A.
238 □3f **Gran Canaria** i. Canary Is
179 J8 **Grancey-le-Château-Nouvelle** France
277 E6 **Gran Chaco** reg. Arg./Para.
271 □7 **Gran Couva** Trin. and Tob.
179 J7 **Grand** France
254 D4 **Grand** r. MO U.S.A.
260 E3 **Grand** r. SD U.S.A.
260 D3 **Grand, North Fork** r. SD U.S.A.
260 D3 **Grand, South Fork** r. SD U.S.A.
183 H7 **Grand Armet** mt. France
204 G2 **Grandas** Spain
Grand Atlas mts Morocco see **Haut Atlas**
270 D1 **Grand Bahama** i. Bahamas
179 N8 **Grand Ballon** mt. France
249 K4 **Grand Bank** Nfld and Lab. Can.
288 F3 **Grand Banks of Newfoundland** sea feature N. Atlantic Ocean
228 E5 **Grand-Bassam** Côte d'Ivoire
239 □1c **Grand Bassin** Réunion
271 □2 **Grand Bay** b. Dominica
261 K10 **Grand Bay** AL U.S.A.
249 H4 **Grand Bay-Westfield** N.B. Can.
248 D5 **Grand Bend** Ont. Can.
183 J8 **Grand Bérard** mt. France
228 D5 **Grand-Bérébi** Côte d'Ivoire
256 B6 **Grand Blanc** MI U.S.A.
271 □2 **Grand-Bourg** Guadeloupe
239 □1c **Grand Brûlé** coastal area Réunion
181 I3 **Grandcamp-Maisy** France
Grand Canal China see **Jinghang Yunhe**
169 H6 **Grand Canal** Ireland
Grand Canary i. Canary Is see **Gran Canaria**
265 T5 **Grand Canyon** AZ U.S.A.
265 T5 **Grand Canyon** gorge AZ U.S.A.
265 T5 **Grand Canyon National Park** AZ U.S.A.
265 S5 **Grand Canyon-Parashant National Monument** nat. park AZ U.S.A.
270 C4 **Grand Cayman** i. Cayman Is
247 I4 **Grand Centre** Alta Can.
228 C5 **Grand Cess** Liberia
180 F6 **Grand-Champ** France
182 J1 **Grand-Charmont** France
182 H5 **Grand Colombier** mt. France
212 C4 **Grand Combin** mt. Switz.
262 E3 **Grand Coulee** WA U.S.A.
178 B5 **Grand-Couronne** France
271 □2 **Grand Cul-de-Sac Marin** b. Guadeloupe
250 E8 **Grand Detour** IL U.S.A.
284 C5 **Grande** r. Arg.
276 E4 **Grande** r. Bol.
277 E4 **Grande** r. Bol.
280 B3 **Grande** r. Brazil
278 E4 **Grande** r. Brazil
216 E8 **Grande** r. Sicilia Italy
268 E6 **Grande** r. Jalisco/Michoacán Mex.
269 K8 **Grande** r. Mex.
269 L9 **Grande** r. Mex.
269 N9 **Grande** r. Mex.
266 □R11 **Grande** r. Nic.
276 B3 **Grande** r. Peru
209 D9 **Grande** r. Spain
207 J7 **Grande** r. Spain
207 L4 **Grande** r. Spain
285 I5 **Grande, Arroyo** r. Arg.
283 C8 **Grande, Bahía** b. Arg.
270 D3 **Grande, Cayo** i. Cuba
268 G2 **Grande, Cerro** mt. Mex.
269 J8 **Grande, Cerro** mt. Mex.
274 C2 **Grande, Ciénaga** lag. Col.
180 D4 **Grande, Île** i. France
281 E5 **Grande, Ilha** i. Brazil
216 C8 **Grande, Isola** i. Sicilia Italy
183 K6 **Grande, Lago** l. Italy
216 D8 **Grande, Montagna** hill Italy
284 D5 **Grande, Salina** salt flat Arg.
277 E2 **Grande, Serra** hills Brazil
275 F4 **Grande, Serra** mt. Brazil
284 E2 **Grande, Sierra** mts Arg
271 □2 **Grande-Anse** Guadelo
239 □1b **Grande Baie** Mauritius
239 □2a **Grande Barbe, Pointe** Islands Seychelles
213 M6 **Grande Bonifica Ferra**
180 G7 **Grande Brière** reg. Fra
246 G4 **Grande Cache** Alta Ca
183 J6 **Grande Casse, Pointe** France
Grande Comore i. Cor **Ngazidja**
275 F5 **Grande de Manacapur** Brazil
249 I4 **Grande-Entrée** Que. C
185 C7 **Grande Lande** reg. Fra
185 C7 **Grande Leyre** r. France
181 M3 **Grande Mare** l. France
239 □1a **Grande Passe** Rodrigue Mauritius
246 G4 **Grande Prairie** Alta Ca
227 E3 **Grand Erg Occidental**
227 G3 **Grand Erg Oriental** de
249 H3 **Grande-Rivière** Que. C
271 □3 **Grande Rivière** St Luci
271 □7 **Grande Rivière** Trin. a
239 □1b **Grande Rivière Noire**
239 □1b **Grande Rivière Noire** Mauritius
239 □1b **Grande Rivière South** Mauritius
239 □1b **Grande Rivière Sud-E** Mauritius
239 □1b **Grande Rivière Sud-E** Mauritius
212 C4 **Grande Rochère** mt. It
262 F3 **Grande Ronde** r. OR U
284 E2 **Grandes, Salinas** salt
282 D1 **Grandes, Salinas** salt
182 A2 **Grande Sauldre** r. Frar
266 C2 **Gran Desierto del Pin Parque Natural del** na Mex.
182 K5 **Grandes Jorasses** mts France/Italy
183 I6 **Grandes Rousses** mts
178 D1 **Grande-Synthe** France
271 □6 **Grand Étang** l. Grenad
271 □2 **Grande-Terre** i. Guade
239 □3b **Grande Terre** i. Mayott
183 H7 **Grande Tête de l'Obio** France
180 G8 **Grand Étier** r. France
212 D4 **Grande Tournalin** mt.
185 I6 **Grande-Vabre** France
249 H3 **Grande-Vallée** Que. Ca
271 □2 **Grande Vigie, Pointe d** Guadeloupe
212 C4 **Grand Eyvia** r. Italy
249 H4 **Grand Falls** N.B. Can.
249 K3 **Grand Falls-Windsor** Lab. Can.
246 G5 **Grand Forks** B.C. Can.
260 G2 **Grand Forks** ND U.S.A
178 D1 **Grand-Fort-Philippe**
180 H6 **Grand-Fougeray** Franc
185 D10 **Grand Gabizos** mt. Fra
257 K6 **Grand Gorge** NY U.S.A
270 H4 **Grand-Gosier** Haiti
249 H4 **Grand Harbour** N.B. C
250 H6 **Grand Haven** MI U.S.A
246 G1 **Grandin, Lac** l. N.W.T.
260 F5 **Grand Island** NE U.S.A
250 H3 **Grand Island** i. MI U.S.
261 J11 **Grand Isle** LA U.S.A.
257 □Q1 **Grand Isle** ME U.S.A.
265 X2 **Grand Junction** CO U.S
250 H7 **Grand Junction** MI U.S
228 D5 **Grand-Lahou** Côte d'Iv
249 H4 **Grand Lake** N.B. Can.
249 I2 **Grand Lake** Nfld and L
249 J3 **Grand Lake** Nfld and L
261 I11 **Grand Lake** LA U.S.A.
261 J11 **Grand Lake** LA U.S.A.
251 K4 **Grand Lake** MI U.S.A.
257 □Q2 **Grand Lake Matagamo** ME U.S.A.
256 A8 **Grand Lake St Marys**
257 □Q2 **Grand Lake Seboeis** M
181 I8 **Grand Lay** r. France
250 J7 **Grand Ledge** MI U.S.A.
180 H7 **Grand-Lieu, Lac de** l. F
181 I8 **Grand Maine** r. France
249 H4 **Grand Manan Island**
250 I3 **Grand Marais** MI U.S.A
250 D2 **Grand Marais** MN U.S
250 E6 **Grand Marsh** WI U.S.A
249 F4 **Grand-Mère** Que. Can.
178 E6 **Grand Morin** r. France
206 B4 **Grândola** Port.
206 C4 **Grândola** r. Port.
206 B4 **Grândola, Serra de** mts
245 M4 **Grand Pacific Glacier**
100 □5 **Grand Passage** New C
178 B8 **Grand-Pierre et Vitan, Naturelle** nature res. Fr
250 E2 **Grand Portage** MN U.S
179 I5 **Grandpré** France
178 E6 **Grandpuits-Bailly-Car**
247 L4 **Grand Rapids** Man. Ca
250 I7 **Grand Rapids** MI U.S.A
250 A2 **Grand Rapids** MN U.S
183 F10 **Grand Rhône** r. France
183 D7 **Grandrieu** France
182 E4 **Grandris** France
271 □3 **Grand' Rivière** Martini
183 J6 **Grand Roc Noir** mt. Fr
271 □6 **Grand Roy** Grenada
Grand St Bernard, Col Italy/Switz. see **Great St Bernard Pass**
275 H3 **Grand-Santi** Fr. Guiana
212 B2 **Grandson** Switz.
265 U4 **Grand Staircase-Escala National Monument** n UT U.S.A.
262 I5 **Grand Teton** mt. WY U.
262 I5 **Grand Teton National** WY U.S.A.
250 I5 **Grand Traverse Bay** MI
270 H3 **Grand Turk** Turks and
270 H3 **Grand Turk** i. Turks and
183 C7 **Grandval, Barrage de** d
237 P2 **Grand Valley** Swaziland
182 I1 **Grandvelle-et-le-Perre**
250 C3 **Grand View** WI U.S.A.
182 J1 **Grandvillars** France
250 I7 **Grandville** MI U.S.A.
179 M7 **Grandvillers** France
178 C4 **Grandvilliers** France
265 R5 **Grand Wash** watercours AZ U.S.A.
265 R6 **Grand Wash Cliffs** mts
250 A4 **Grandy** MN U.S.A.
183 F7 **Grane** France
208 E4 **Grañén** Spain
284 B4 **Graneros** Chile
169 E7 **Graney, Lough** l. Irelan
165 M2 **Granfjärden** b. Sweden
169 J5 **Grange** Louth Ireland
169 E4 **Grange** Sligo Ireland
169 G9 **Grange** Waterford Irelar
182 J4 **Grange, Mont de** mt. F
169 J5 **Grangebellow** Ireland
169 I7 **Grangeford** Ireland
270 □ **Grange Hill** Jamaica
168 I10 **Grangemouth** Falkirk, Scotland U.K.
183 E6 **Grangent, Barrage de**
171 L5 **Grange-over-Sands** Cu England U.K.
262 J6 **Granger** WY U.S.A.
165 L1 **Grängesberg** Sweden
179 M7 **Granges-sur-Vologne**
172 F5 **Grangetown** Cardiff, Wa
262 F4 **Grangeville** ID U.S.A.
282 F2 **Gran Guardia** Arg.
162 P3 **Granhult** Sweden
182 H6 **Granier, Col du** pass Fr
183 H6 **Granier, Mont** mt. Fran
246 E4 **Granisle** B.C. Can.
258 B6 **Granite** MD U.S.A.
260 J6 **Granite City** IL U.S.A.
260 H3 **Granite Falls** MN U.S.A.

Granite Mountain hill AK U.S.A.
Granite Mountain hill AK U.S.A.
Granite Mountain NV U.S.A.
Granite Mountains CA U.S.A.
Granite Mountains CA U.S.A.
Granite Peak MT U.S.A.
Granite Peak UT U.S.A.
Granite Point MI U.S.A.
Granite Range mts AK U.S.A.
Granite Reef Aqueduct canal U.S.A.
Granitic Group is Seychelles see Inner Islands
Granitogorsk Kazakh.
Granitola, Capo c. Sicilia Italy
Granitola-Torretta Sicilia Italy
Granity South I. N.Z.
Granja Brazil
Granja Port.
Granja de Moreruela Spain
Granja de Torrehermosa Spain
Granja do Ulmeiro Port.
Gran Laguna Salada l. Arg.
Gran Morelos Mex.
Grann l. Sweden
Gränna Sweden
Granollers Spain
Granowo Pol.
Gran Pajonal plain Peru
Gran Pánfilo Natera Mex.
Gran Paradiso mt. Italy
Gran Paradiso, Parco Nazionale del nat. park Italy
Gran Pilastro mt. Austria/Italy
Gran San Bernardo, Colle del pass Italy/Switz. see Great St Bernard Pass
Gran Sasso d'Italia mts Italy
Gran Sasso e Monti della Laga, Parco Nazionale del nat. park Italy
Granschütz Ger.
Gransee Ger.
Gransha Northern Ireland U.K.
Gransö i. Sweden
Grant NE U.S.A.
Grant, Mount NV U.S.A.
Grant, Mount NV U.S.A.
Gran Tarajal Fuerteventura Canary Is
Grant City MO U.S.A.
Grant Creek AK U.S.A.
Grantham Lincolnshire, England U.K.
Grantham PA U.S.A.
Grant Island Antarctica
Grant Island N.T. Austr.
Grant Lake N.W.T. Can.
Granton WI U.S.A.
Grantown-on-Spey Highland, Scotland U.K.
Grant Park IL U.S.A.
Grant Range mts NV U.S.A.
Grants NM U.S.A.
Grantsburg WI U.S.A.
Grantshouse Scottish Borders, Scotland U.K.
Grants Pass OR U.S.A.
Grantsville WV U.S.A.
Grantville PA U.S.A.
Granville France
Granville AZ U.S.A.
Granville IL U.S.A.
Granville NY U.S.A.
Granville OH U.S.A.
Granville (abandoned) Y.T. Can.
Granville Lake Man. Can.
Granvin Norway
Granzin Ger.
Grão Mogol Brazil
Grapevine Mountains NV U.S.A.
Grappa, Monte mt. Italy
Grappler Bank sea feature Caribbean Sea
Gras, Lac de l. N.W.T. Can.
Grasbakken Norway
Grasberg Ger.
Graskop S. Africa
Grasleben Ger.
Gräsmarken Sweden
Grasmere Cumbria, England U.K.
Gräsö i. Sweden
Grasonville MD U.S.A.
Grasplatz Namibia
Grass r. Man. Can.
Grass r. NY U.S.A.
Grassano Italy
Grassau Ger.
Grasse France
Grassflat PA U.S.A.
Grassington North Yorkshire, England U.K.
Grass Lake MI U.S.A.
Grasslands National Park Sask. Can.
Grassmere, Lake South I. N.Z.
Grass Patch W.A. Austr.
Grassrange MT U.S.A.
Grassridgedam l. S. Africa
Grass River Provincial Park Man. Can.
Grass Valley CA U.S.A.
Grassy Tas. Austr.
Grassy Butte ND U.S.A.
Grassy Creek r. Andros Bahamas
Gråsten Denmark
Grästorp Sweden
Gratallops Spain
Gratangsbotn Norway
Gratens France
Gratentour France
Gratiot WI U.S.A.
Gratkorn Austria
Gråträsk Sweden
Gratteri Sicilia Italy
Gratwein Austria
Graubünden canton Switz.
Graudenz Pol. see Grudziądz
Grauer Kopf hill Ger.
Graulhet France
Graupa Ger.
Graus Spain
Grávalos Spain
Gravata Brazil
Gravatai Brazil
Gravdal Norway
Grave Neth.
Grave, Pointe de pt France
Gravedona Italy
Gravelbourg Sask. Can.
Gravel Hill Lake N.W.T. Can.
Gravelines France
Gravellona Toce Italy
Gravelotte France
Gravenhurst Ont. Can.
Grävenwiesbach Ger.
Grave Peak ID U.S.A.
Grāveri Latvia
Graves reg. France
Gravesend N.S.W. Austr.
Gravesend Kent, England U.K.
Gravette AR U.S.A.
Gravigny France
Gravina r. Italy
Gravina di Matera r. Italy
Gravina in Puglia Italy
Gravina Island AK U.S.A.
Gravois, Pointe-à- pt Haiti
Gravona r. Corse France
Grawn MI U.S.A.
Gray France
Gray GA U.S.A.
Gray KY U.S.A.
Gray ME U.S.A.
Gray TN U.S.A.
Grayan-et-l'Hôpital France
Grayback Mountain OR U.S.A.
Gray Lake N.W.T. Can.
Grayling r. B.C. Can.
Grayling AK U.S.A.
Grayling MI U.S.A.
Grayling Fork r. Can./U.S.A.
Grayrigg Cumbria, England U.K.
Grays Thurrock, England U.K.
262 B3 Grays Harbor inlet WA U.S.A.
173 K5 Grayshott Hampshire, England U.K.
262 I5 Grays Lake ID U.S.A.
256 C10 Grayson KY U.S.A.
254 D6 Grayville IL U.S.A.
159 O3 Grayvoron Rus. Fed.
201 L5 Graz Austria
183 E6 Grazac France
207 I7 Grazalema Spain
197 H2 Grążawy Pol.
216 G1 Grazzanise Italy
219 K8 Grdelica Leskovac Serbia
185 H6 Gréalou France
246 F2 Greasy Lake N.W.T. Can.
270 □ Great r. Jamaica
270 E1 Great Abaco i. Bahamas
Great Ararat mt. Turkey see Büyük Ağrı Dağı
98 C5 Great Australian Bight g. Austr.
171 O5 Great Ayton North Yorkshire, England U.K.
271 □6 Great Bacolet Bay Grenada
173 N4 Great Baddow Essex, England U.K.
270 D1 Great Bahama Bank sea feature Bahamas
102 J3 Great Barrier Island North I. N.Z.
107 J1 Great Barrier Reef Qld Austr.
107 K4 Great Barrier Reef Marine Park (Cairns Section) Qld Austr.
107 M6 Great Barrier Reef Marine Park (Capricorn Section) Qld Austr.
107 L5 Great Barrier Reef Marine Park (Central Section) Qld Austr.
107 J2 Great Barrier Reef Marine Park (Far North Section) Qld Austr.
257 L6 Great Barrington MA U.S.A.
173 N3 Great Barton Suffolk, England U.K.
107 J5 Great Basalt Wall National Park Qld Austr.
265 P2 Great Basin NV U.S.A.
265 R3 Great Basin National Park NV U.S.A.
259 G6 Great Bay NJ U.S.A.
245 P2 Great Bear r. N.W.T. Can.
246 G1 Great Bear Lake N.W.T. Can.
Great Belt sea chan. Denmark see Store Bælt
260 F6 Great Bend KS U.S.A.
257 J7 Great Bend PA U.S.A.
173 O4 Great Bentley Essex, England U.K.
168 C6 Great Bernera i. Scotland U.K.
173 N2 Great Bircham Norfolk, England U.K.
Great Bitter Lake Egypt see Murrah al Kubrá, Al Buḩayrah al
169 A8 Great Blasket Island Ireland
167 G4 Great Britain i. U.K.
171 O5 Great Broughton North Yorkshire, England U.K.
171 K4 Great Clifton Cumbria, England U.K.
119 A7 Great Coco Island Coco Is
173 N3 Great Cornard Suffolk, England U.K.
170 H2 Great Cumbrae i. Scotland U.K.
257 I12 Great Dismal Swamp National Wildlife Refuge nature res. VA U.S.A.
98 E5 Great Dividing Range mts Austr.
171 K4 Great Dodd hill England U.K.
251 L4 Great Duck Island Ont. Can.
173 M4 Great Dunmow Essex, England U.K.
Great Eastern Erg des. Alg. see Grand Erg Oriental
171 L6 Great Eccleston Lancashire, England U.K.
258 F6 Great Egg Harbor r. NJ U.S.A.
258 F6 Great Egg Harbor Inlet NJ U.S.A.
173 N2 Great Ellingham Norfolk, England U.K.
270 C3 Greater Antilles is Caribbean Sea
Greater Khingan Mountains China see Da Hinggan Ling
173 L4 Greater London admin. div. England U.K.
171 M6 Greater Manchester admin. div. England U.K.
112 B8 Greater Sunda Islands Indon.
147 L2 Greater Tunb i. The Gulf
102 H1 Great Exhibition Bay North I. N.Z.
270 F2 Great Exuma i. Bahamas
262 I3 Great Falls MT U.S.A.
237 L9 Great Fish r. S. Africa
235 E7 Great Fish Point S. Africa
102 J7 Greatford North I. N.Z.
139 J7 Great Gandak r. India
Great Ganges atoll Cook Is see Manihiki
173 J2 Great Glen Leicestershire, England U.K.
270 □ Great Goat Island Jamaica
173 K2 Great Gonerby Lincolnshire, England U.K.
173 L3 Great Gransden Cambridgeshire, England U.K.
255 I12 Great Guana Cay i. Bahamas
173 K5 Greatham Hampshire, England U.K.
171 O4 Greatham Hartlepool, England U.K.
270 E1 Great Harbour Cay i. Bahamas
171 M6 Great Harwood Lancashire, England U.K.
173 I2 Great Haywood Staffordshire, England U.K.
173 N4 Great Horkesley Essex, England U.K.
270 G3 Great Inagua i. Bahamas
169 F9 Great Island Ireland
236 H8 Great Karoo plat. S. Africa
237 M8 Great Kei r. S. Africa
107 M7 Great Keppel Island Qld Austr.
105 K9 Great Lake Tas. Austr.
235 F4 Great Limpopo Transfrontier Park nat. park Africa
173 K3 Great Linford Milton Keynes, England U.K.
172 H3 Great Malvern Worcestershire, England U.K.
171 K6 Great Marton Blackpool, England U.K.
258 F3 Great Meadows NJ U.S.A.
102 J3 Great Mercury Island North I. N.Z.
288 H4 Great Meteor Tablemount sea feature N. Atlantic Ocean
256 A9 Great Miami r. OH U.S.A.
173 K4 Great Missenden Buckinghamshire, England U.K.
234 C5 Great Namaqualand reg. Namibia
137 N9 Great Nicobar i. Andaman & Nicobar Is India
113 J8 Great North East Channel Austr./P.N.G.
172 E1 Great Ormes Head Wales U.K.
105 I8 Great Otway National Park Vic. Austr.
173 M2 Great Ouse r. England U.K.
105 L10 Great Oyster Bay Tas. Austr.
107 K5 Great Palm Islands Qld Austr.
259 K3 Great Peconic Bay NY U.S.A.
270 □ Great Pedro Bluff pt Jamaica
260 E4 Great Plains NE U.S.A.
257 O7 Great Point MA U.S.A.
173 K2 Great Ponton Lincolnshire, England U.K.
Great Rann of Kachchh marsh India see Kachchh, Rann of
172 F3 Great Rhos hill Wales U.K.
232 B5 Great Rift Valley Africa
233 C6 Great Ruaha r. Tanz.
257 K5 Great Sacandaga Lake NY U.S.A.
182 K5 Great St Bernard Pass Italy/Switz.
255 H12 Great Sale Cay i. Bahamas
171 L4 Great Salkeld Cumbria, England U.K.
262 H6 Great Salt Lake UT U.S.A.
265 S1 Great Salt Lake Desert UT U.S.A.
271 □2 Great Salt Pond l. St Kitts and Nevis
173 M4 Great Sampford Essex, England U.K.
260 B6 Great Sand Dunes National Park and Preserve CO U.S.A.
247 I5 Great Sand Hills Sask. Can.
224 E2 Great Sand Sea des. Egypt/Libya
108 G6 Great Sandy Desert W.A. Austr.
Great Sandy Island Qld Austr. see Fraser Island
108 C6 Great Sandy Island Nature Reserve W.A. Austr.
107 N9 Great Sandy National Park (Cooloola Section) Qld Austr.
107 N8 Great Sandy National Park (Fraser Island Section) Qld Austr.
101 □7 Great Sea Reef Fiji
173 M3 Great Shelford Cambridgeshire, England U.K.
245 □C5 Great Sitkin Island AK U.S.A.
246 H2 Great Slave Lake N.W.T. Can.
255 E8 Great Smoky Mountains NC/TN U.S.A.
255 F8 Great Smoky Mountains National Park NC/TN U.S.A.
246 E3 Great Snow Mountain B.C. Can.
255 □1 Great Sound b. Bermuda
259 I3 Great South Bay NY U.S.A.
173 O5 Great Stour r. England U.K.
170 E7 Great Sugar Loaf hill Ireland
172 D6 Great Torrington Devon, England U.K.
Great Usutu r. Africa see Usutu
109 J10 Great Victoria Desert W.A. Austr.
109 J10 Great Victoria Desert Nature Reserve W.A. Austr.
173 N4 Great Wakering Essex, England U.K.
286 U2 Great Wall research stn Antarctica
129 P6 Great Wall tourist site China
173 M4 Great Waltham Essex, England U.K.
257 □R4 Great Wass Island ME U.S.A.
Great Western Erg des. Alg. see Grand Erg Occidental
105 K9 Great Western Tiers mts Tas. Austr.
119 C9 Great West Torres Islands Myanmar
171 N5 Great Whernside hill England U.K.
236 D9 Great Winterhoek mt. S. Africa
172 H2 Great Wyrley Staffordshire, England U.K.
173 P2 Great Yarmouth Norfolk, England U.K.
173 N3 Great Yeldham Essex, England U.K.
235 F4 Great Zimbabwe National Monument tourist site Zimbabwe
164 H3 Grebbestad Sweden
191 H9 Grebenau Ger.
191 J8 Grebendorf (Meinhard) Ger.
191 H10 Grebenhain Ger.
Grebenkovskiy Ukr. see Hrebinka
151 H2 Grebenskaya Rus. Fed.
Grebenski Rus. Fed. see Grebenskaya
191 H8 Grebenstein Ger.
190 J2 Grebin Ger.
197 J3 Grębków Pol.
161 W7 Grebnevo Rus. Fed.
196 E4 Grębocice Pol.
196 G2 Grębocin Pol.
197 J5 Grębów Pol.
Grebyonka Ukr. see Hrebinka
215 J3 Greccio Italy
215 O5 Greci Italy
219 Q5 Greci, Vârful hill Romania
Greco, Cape Cyprus see Greko, Cape
211 D5 Greco, Monte mt. Italy
195 K3 Greding Ger.
204 I8 Gredos, Sierra de mts Spain
283 C9 Greec Chile
220 C3 Greece country Europe
256 H5 Greece NY U.S.A.
262 L6 Greeley CO U.S.A.
258 F2 Greeley PA U.S.A.
260 F5 Greely Center NE U.S.A.
243 J1 Greely Fiord inlet Nunavut Can.
152 H1 Greem-Bell, Ostrov i. Zemlya Frantsa-Iosifa Rus. Fed.
253 M1 Green r. N.B. Can.
254 D7 Green r. KY U.S.A.
260 D2 Green r. ND U.S.A.
265 W3 Green r. WY U.S.A.
250 F5 Green Bay WI U.S.A.
250 G4 Green Bay b. WI U.S.A.
258 B6 Greenbelt MD U.S.A.
256 E11 Greenbrier r. WV U.S.A.
109 D12 Greenbushes W.A. Austr.
105 M7 Green Cape N.S.W. Austr.
255 I13 Greencastle Bahamas
169 I2 Greencastle Ireland
169 H3 Greencastle Northern Ireland U.K.
169 J4 Greencastle Northern Ireland U.K.
254 D6 Greencastle IN U.S.A.
256 H9 Greencastle PA U.S.A.
270 E1 Green Cay i. Bahamas
255 G11 Green Cove Springs FL U.S.A.
258 F6 Green Creek NJ U.S.A.
191 I7 Greene Ger.
250 B7 Greene IA U.S.A.
257 □O4 Greene ME U.S.A.
257 J6 Greene NY U.S.A.
255 F7 Greeneville TN U.S.A.
264 K5 Greenfield CA U.S.A.
260 H5 Greenfield IA U.S.A.
254 E6 Greenfield IN U.S.A.
257 M6 Greenfield MA U.S.A.
261 I7 Greenfield MO U.S.A.
256 B9 Greenfield OH U.S.A.
250 F7 Greenfield WI U.S.A.
259 G1 Greenfield Park NY U.S.A.
170 J2 Greengairs North Lanarkshire, Scotland U.K.
173 J5 Greenham West Berkshire, England U.K.
258 B6 Green Haven MD U.S.A.
109 C11 Green Head W.A. Austr.
109 C11 Green Head hd W.A. Austr.
171 L4 Greenhead Northumberland, England U.K.
106 D1 Greenhill Island N.T. Austr.
103 C13 Greenhills South I. N.Z.
270 □ Green Island Jamaica
169 K3 Greenisland Northern Ireland U.K.
114 B6 Green Island Bay Palawan Phil.
113 L7 Green Islands P.N.G.
247 J4 Green Lake Sask. Can.
246 F5 Green Lake l. B.C. Can.
103 B12 Green Lake l. South I. N.Z.
250 F6 Green Lake WI U.S.A.
243 N2 Greenland terr. N. America
250 E3 Greenland MI U.S.A.
292 X2 Greenland Basin sea feature Arctic Ocean
103 D12 Greenland Reservoir South I. N.Z.
240 G1 Greenland Sea Greenland/Svalbard
258 E4 Green Lane PA U.S.A.
258 D4 Green Lane Reservoir PA U.S.A.
168 L11 Greenlaw Scottish Borders, Scotland U.K.
168 I10 Greenloaning Perth and Kinross, Scotland U.K.
168 I12 Green Lowther hill Scotland U.K.
104 E6 Greenly Island S.A. Austr.
258 B5 Greenmount MD U.S.A.
257 M4 Green Mountains VT U.S.A.
168 G11 Greenock Inverclyde, Scotland U.K.
171 K5 Greenodd Cumbria, England U.K.
169 J4 Greenore Ireland
169 J8 Greenore Point Ireland
109 C10 Greenough W.A. Austr.
109 C10 Greenough r. W.A. Austr.
245 L1 Greenough, Mount AK U.S.A.
104 □3 Green Point S. Pacific Ocean
259 G2 Green Pond NJ U.S.A.
257 M7 Greenport NY U.S.A.
265 V3 Green River UT U.S.A.
262 J6 Green River WY U.S.A.
255 D9 Greensboro AL U.S.A.
255 F9 Greensboro GA U.S.A.
258 D7 Greensboro MD U.S.A.
255 H7 Greensboro NC U.S.A.
254 E6 Greensburg IN U.S.A.
261 F7 Greensburg KS U.S.A.
254 E7 Greensburg KY U.S.A.
261 J10 Greensburg LA U.S.A.
256 F8 Greensburg PA U.S.A.
265 W7 Greens Peak NM U.S.A.
168 E7 Greenstone Point Scotland U.K.
255 H8 Green Swamp NC U.S.A.
250 I9 Greentown IN U.S.A.
258 E2 Greentown PA U.S.A.
260 K6 Greenup IL U.S.A.
256 C10 Greenup KY U.S.A.
107 J5 Greenvale Qld Austr.
257 K3 Green Valley Ont. Can.
265 V10 Green Valley AZ U.S.A.
Greenville B.C. Can. see Laxgalts'ap
228 C5 Greenville Liberia
255 D10 Greenville AL U.S.A.
264 L1 Greenville CA U.S.A.
255 F10 Greenville FL U.S.A.
255 E9 Greenville GA U.S.A.
260 K6 Greenville IL U.S.A.
254 D7 Greenville KY U.S.A.
257 □P3 Greenville ME U.S.A.
250 I6 Greenville MI U.S.A.
261 J7 Greenville MO U.S.A.
261 J9 Greenville MS U.S.A.
255 I8 Greenville NC U.S.A.
257 N6 Greenville NH U.S.A.
260 M5 Greenville OH U.S.A.
256 E7 Greenville PA U.S.A.
255 F8 Greenville SC U.S.A.
261 G9 Greenville TX U.S.A.
256 F10 Greenville VA U.S.A.
250 D1 Greenwater Lake Ont. Can.
247 K4 Greenwater Provincial Park Sask. Can.
172 C4 Greenway Pembrokeshire, Wales U.K.
Greenwich atoll Micronesia see Kapingamarangi
173 L5 Greenwich Greater London, England U.K.
259 H2 Greenwich CT U.S.A.
258 E6 Greenwich NJ U.S.A.
257 L5 Greenwich NY U.S.A.
256 C7 Greenwich OH U.S.A.
261 H8 Greenwood AR U.S.A.
258 D7 Greenwood DE U.S.A.
254 D6 Greenwood IN U.S.A.
261 J9 Greenwood MS U.S.A.
255 F8 Greenwood SC U.S.A.
250 D5 Greenwood WI U.S.A.
259 G2 Greenwood Lake NY U.S.A.
259 G2 Greenwood Lake l. NJ U.S.A.
255 F8 Greer SC U.S.A.
261 I8 Greers Ferry Lake AR U.S.A.
170 D8 Greese r. Ireland
190 D3 Greetsiel (Krummhörn) Ger.
274 D6 Gregório r. Brazil
106 G5 Gregory r. Qld Austr.
251 J7 Gregory MI U.S.A.
260 F4 Gregory SD U.S.A.
104 G3 Gregory, Lake salt flat S.A. Austr.
108 I6 Gregory, Lake salt flat W.A. Austr.
109 E8 Gregory, Lake salt flat W.A. Austr.
106 G5 Gregory Downs Qld Austr.
106 C4 Gregory National Park N.T. Austr.
107 I5 Gregory Range hills Qld Austr.
108 F6 Gregory Range hills W.A. Austr.
200 H6 Greifenburg Austria
193 H8 Greifendorf Ger.
212 F1 Greifensee l. Switz.
191 F9 Greifenstein Ger.
192 I4 Greiffenberg Ger.
192 H2 Greifswald Ger.
192 I2 Greifswalder Bodden b. Ger.
192 I2 Greifswalder Oie i. Ger.
201 K3 Grein Austria
193 F9 Greiz Ger.
150 C4 Greko, Cape Cyprus
190 K2 Gremersdorf Ger.
156 G1 Gremikha Rus. Fed.
161 V7 Gremyachev Rus. Fed.
156 L4 Gremyachinsk Permskaya Oblast' Rus. Fed.
120 I1 Gremyachinsk Respublika Buryatiya Rus. Fed.
159 S2 Gremyach'ye Rus. Fed.
164 G5 Grenaa Denmark
261 K9 Grenada MS U.S.A.
271 □6 Grenada country West Indies
261 K9 Grenada Lake resr MS U.S.A.
185 G8 Grenade France
185 D8 Grenade-sur-l'Adour France
179 K8 Grenant France
212 C1 Grenchen Switz.
164 G4 Grenen spit Denmark
105 L5 Grenfell N.S.W. Austr.
247 K5 Grenfell Sask. Can.
183 H6 Grenoble France
162 U2 Grense-Jakobselv Norway
271 □6 Grenville Grenada
107 I1 Grenville, Cape Qld Austr.
Grenville Island Fiji see Rotuma
194 D6 Grenzach-Wyhlen Ger.
183 H9 Gréoux-les-Bains France
192 F2 Gresenhorst Ger.
145 K8 Greshag Pak.
145 L8 Greshak Pak.
262 C4 Gresham OR U.S.A.
185 H7 Grésigne, Forêt de la reg. France
117 J8 Gresik Jawa Indon.
168 D6 Gress Western Isles, Scotland U.K.
162 L4 Gressåmoen Nasjonalpark nat. park Norway
212 C4 Gressan Italy
183 H6 Gresse r. France
190 K4 Gresse Ger.
183 H7 Gresse-en-Vercors France
212 D4 Gressoney-la-Trinite Italy
201 L4 Gresten Austria
182 H5 Grésy-sur-Aix France
182 I5 Grésy-sur-Isère France
171 L5 Greta r. England U.K.
214 G2 Gretano r. Italy
168 J13 Gretna Dumfries and Galloway, Scotland U.K.
261 J11 Gretna LA U.S.A.
256 F12 Gretna VA U.S.A.
195 I2 Grettstadt Ger.
191 K8 Greußen Ger.
179 K7 Greux France
213 K8 Greve r. Italy
213 K8 Greve in Chianti Italy
186 E5 Grevelingen sea chan. Neth.
190 K4 Greven Mecklenburg-Vorpommern Ger.
191 E6 Greven Nordrhein-Westfalen Ger.
220 C2 Grevena Greece
187 I6 Grevenbicht Neth.
191 C8 Grevenbroich Ger.
187 J9 Grevenmacher Lux.
187 J9 Grevenmacher admin. dist. Lux.
192 D3 Grevesmühlen Ger.
249 J4 Grey r. Nfld and Lab. Can.
103 F9 Grey r. South I. N.Z.
106 F2 Grey, Cape N.T. Austr.
169 K3 Greyabbey Northern Ireland U.K.
262 J4 Greybull WY U.S.A.
262 J4 Greybull r. WY U.S.A.
245 N3 Grey Hunter Peak Y.T. Can.
249 K3 Grey Islands Nfld and Lab. Can.
237 M2 Greylingstad S. Africa
257 L6 Greylock, Mount MA U.S.A.
103 F9 Greymouth South I. N.Z.
170 F4 Grey Point Northern Ireland U.K.
105 I3 Grey Range hills Qld Austr.
109 C8 Grey's Plains W.A. Austr.
171 L4 Greystoke Cumbria, England U.K.
235 F4 Greystone Zimbabwe
169 J6 Greystones Ireland
236 D10 Greyton S. Africa
103 J8 Greytown North I. N.Z.
237 O5 Greytown S. Africa
187 G7 Grez-Doiceau Belgium
181 J6 Grez-en-Bouère France
213 K4 Grezzana Italy
201 I7 Grgar Slovenia
220 F5 Gria, Akrotirio pt Andros Greece
Griais Scotland U.K. see Gress
157 H6 Gribanovskiy Rus. Fed.
230 C2 Gribingui r. C.A.R.
230 C3 Gribingui-Bamingui, Réserve de Faune du nature res. C.A.R.
156 F2 Gridino Rus. Fed.
264 K2 Gridley CA U.S.A.
250 F9 Gridley IL U.S.A.
193 E6 Grieben Ger.
205 Q8 Griegos Spain
179 O6 Gries France
200 D5 Gries am Brenner Austria
194 E5 Griesbach Ger.
195 O5 Griesbach im Rottal Ger.
194 F2 Griesheim Ger.
201 I3 Grieskirchen Austria
193 K7 Grießen Ger.
195 M6 Griesstätt Ger.
201 K6 Griffen Austria
255 E9 Griffin GA U.S.A.
245 L1 Griffin Point pt AK U.S.A.
105 K6 Griffith N.S.W. Austr.
251 Q4 Griffith Ont. Can.
242 F2 Griffiths Point N.W.T. Can.
256 D10 Griffithsville WV U.S.A.
Grigan i. N. Mariana Is see Agrihan
214 B8 Grighini, Monte hill Italy
Grigioni canton Switz. see Graubünden
160 I7 Grigiškės Lith.
212 G4 Grigna mt. Italy
212 I4 Grigna r. Italy
183 F8 Grignan France
213 L3 Grigno Italy
213 L3 Grigno r. Italy
185 D7 Grignols France
182 F5 Grigny France
158 I6 Grigoriopol Moldova
205 K4 Grijota Spain
186 J2 Grijpskerk Neth.
Grik Malaysia see Gerik
183 F8 Grillon France
105 J9 Grim, Cape Tas. Austr.
215 Q9 Grimaldi Italy
230 D3 Grimari C.A.R.
183 J10 Grimaud France
168 A7 Griminis Point Scotland U.K.
193 G8 Grimma Ger.
192 H2 Grimmen Ger.
201 I4 Grimming mt. Austria
192 I5 Grimnitzsee l. Ger.
171 R7 Grimoldby Lincolnshire, England U.K.
168 B8 Grimsay i. Scotland U.K.
251 O6 Grimsby Ont. Can.
171 Q6 Grimsby North East Lincolnshire, England U.K.
212 E2 Grimsel nature res. Switz.
162 □E1 Grímsey i. Iceland
246 G3 Grimshaw Alta Can.
162 □E1 Grímsstaðir Iceland
164 E3 Grimstad Norway
173 N2 Grimston Norfolk, England U.K.
164 B2 Grindafjord Norway
163 J6 Grindaheim Norway
162 □B2 Grindavík Iceland
212 E2 Grindelwald Switz.
164 E6 Grindsted Denmark
251 L5 Grind Stone City MI U.S.A.
219 O6 Grindu Ialomița Romania
219 Q5 Grindu Tulcea Romania
219 Q6 Grindul Chituc spit Romania
219 O4 Grindușu, Vârful mt. Romania
161 Q9 Grinevo Rus. Fed.
171 P7 Gringley on the Hill Nottinghamshire, England U.K.
260 I5 Grinnell IA U.S.A.
243 I2 Grinnell Peninsula Nunavut Can.
205 M8 Griñón Spain
200 C5 Grins Austria
219 N3 Grințieș Romania
210 E2 Grintovec mt. Slovenia
200 D5 Grinzens Austria
205 R5 Grío r. Spain
Griomasaigh i. Scotland U.K. see Grimsay
237 N6 Griqualand East reg. S. Africa
236 H4 Griqualand West reg. S. Africa
236 H4 Griquatown S. Africa
Grischun canton Switz. see Graubünden
243 J2 Grise Fiord Nunavut Can.
208 C4 Grisén Spain
Grishino Ukr. see Krasnoarmiys'k
213 L5 Grisignano di Zocco Italy
116 E6 Grisik Sumatera Indon.
178 C2 Gris Nez, Cap c. France
215 P8 Grisolia Italy
185 G8 Grisolles France
Grisons canton Switz. see Graubünden
165 O1 Grisslehamn Sweden
168 K5 Gritley Orkney, Scotland U.K.
159 R8 Grivenskaya Rus. Fed.
171 K5 Grizebeck Cumbria, England U.K.
226 E4 Grizim well Alg.
246 F1 Grizzly Bear Mountain hill N.W.T. Can.
210 F3 Grmeč mts Bos.-Herz.
249 K3 Groais Island Nfld and Lab. Can.
187 G6 Grobbendonk Belgium
195 K5 Gröbenzell Ger.
193 F8 Gröbers Ger.
160 E5 Grobiņa Latvia
237 N1 Groblersdal S. Africa
236 G4 Groblershoop S. Africa
201 I5 Gröbming Austria
193 E7 Gröbzig Ger.
218 I6 Grocka Grocka Serbia
190 G1 Gröde-Appelland i. Ger.
197 K4 Gródek Lubelskie Pol.
197 L2 Gródek Podlaskie Pol.
193 I8 Gröden Ger.
200 H4 Grödig Austria
193 H8 Gröditz Ger.
197 I2 Gródki Pol.
196 F5 Grodków Pol.
Grodnenskaya Oblast' admin. div. Belarus see Hrodzyenskaya Voblasts'
Grodnenskaya Vozvyshennost' hills Belarus see Hrodnyendskaye Wzvyshsha
Grodno Belarus see Hrodna
Grodno Oblast admin. div. Belarus see Hrodzyenskaya Voblasts'
197 H2 Grodziczno Pol.
196 G3 Grodziec Pol.
197 K3 Grodzisk Pol.
197 I3 Grodzisk Mazowiecki Pol.
196 E3 Grodzisk Wielkopolski Pol.
236 H6 Groen watercourse Northern Cape S. Africa
236 B6 Groen watercourse S. Africa
186 K4 Groenlo Neth.
237 O3 Groenvlei S. Africa
261 G10 Groesbeck TX U.S.A.
186 I5 Groesbeek Neth.
162 □B1 Gröf Iceland
107 J4 Groganville Qld Austr.
191 H6 Grohnde (Emmerthal) Ger.
199 L6 Grohot, Vârful hill Romania
193 F8 Groitzsch Ger.
180 E6 Groix France
180 E6 Groix, Île de i. France
197 I4 Grójec Pol.
197 I2 Grom Pol.
196 D4 Gromadka Pol.
211 C7 Grombalia Tunisia
190 K2 Grömitz Ger.
197 I6 Gromnik Pol.
212 H4 Gromo Italy
190 G1 Grønå r. Denmark
191 I6 Gronau (Leine) Ger.
191 D6 Gronau (Westfalen) Ger.
215 Q8 Grondo r. Italy
195 I6 Grönenbach Ger.
162 L4 Grong Norway
193 D7 Gröningen Ger.
186 K2 Groningen Neth.
186 K2 Groningen prov. Neth.
275 H3 Groningen Suriname
186 J2 Groninger Wad tidal flat Neth.
Grønland terr. N. America see Greenland
Grønnedal Greenland see Kangilinnguit
197 H1 Gronowo Pol.
165 L4 Grönskåra Sweden
192 F1 Grønsund sea chan. Denmark
261 E8 Groom TX U.S.A.
265 Q4 Groom Lake NV U.S.A.
169 K3 Groomsport Northern Ireland U.K.
236 I9 Groot r. Eastern Cape S. Africa
236 D8 Groot r. Western Cape S. Africa
236 F9 Groot r. Western Cape S. Africa
236 E3 Groot-Aar Pan salt pan S. Africa
236 C8 Groot Berg r. S. Africa
237 J7 Groot Brak r. S. Africa
236 G10 Groot Brakrivier S. Africa
237 N2 Grootdraaidam dam S. Africa
236 F4 Grootdrink S. Africa
186 H3 Grootebroek Neth.
106 F2 Groote Eylandt i. N.T. Austr.
106 F3 Groote Eylandt Aboriginal Land res. N.T. Austr.
186 J2 Grootegast Neth.
234 C3 Grootfontein Namibia
237 J4 Groot-Grannapan salt pan S. Africa
234 C5 Groot Karas Berg plat. Namibia
234 D4 Groot Laagte watercourse Botswana/Namibia
235 F4 Groot Letaba r. S. Africa
237 K1 Groot Marico S. Africa
236 B5 Grootmis S. Africa
237 K1 Grootpan S. Africa
236 H9 Grootrivierhoogte mts S. Africa
236 F9 Groot Swartberge mts S. Africa
236 C2 Grootvaalgraspan salt pan Namibia
237 M2 Grootvlei S. Africa
236 E5 Grootvloer salt pan S. Africa
237 K8 Groot Winterberg mt. S. Africa
237 I9 Groot-Winterhoekberge mts S. Africa
212 F5 Gropello Cairoli Italy
219 P5 Gropeni Romania
209 D12 Grosa, Isla i. Spain
183 I9 Gros Bessillon hill France
182 F2 Grosbois-en-Montagne France
183 K6 Groscavallo Italy
212 I3 Grosio Italy
271 □3 Gros Islet St Lucia
271 □3 Gros-Morne Martinique
249 J3 Gros Morne National Park Nfld and Lab. Can.
182 F3 Grosne r. France
200 B7 Grosotto Italy
271 □3 Gros Piton mt. St Lucia
209 I9 Grossa, Punta pt Spain
195 J5 Großaitingen Ger.
191 I8 Großalmerode Ger.
193 E6 Groß Ammensleben Ger.
200 H5 Großarl Austria
234 C4 Gross Barmen Namibia
191 J8 Großbartloff Ger.
193 H6 Großbeeren Ger.
190 D5 Groß Berßen Ger.
194 F2 Groß-Bieberau Ger.
191 J8 Großbodungen Ger.
193 G8 Großbothen Ger.
194 G4 Großbottwar Ger.
193 D9 Großbreitenbach Ger.
191 I6 Großburgwedel (Burgwedel) Ger.
191 J8 Großburschla Ger.
192 I5 Groß Dölln Ger.
193 J8 Großdubrau Ger.
191 H5 Große Aue r. Ger.
194 F4 Große Enz r. Ger.
195 N4 Große Laaber r. Ger.
194 H5 Große Lauter r. Ger.
191 J6 Groß Elbe (Elbe) Ger.
194 F5 Grosselfingen Ger.
190 I3 Großenaspe Ger.
192 D2 Großenbrode Ger.
191 G9 Großen-Buseck Ger.
191 K8 Großenehrich Ger.
201 O3 Groß Engersdorf Austria
191 K8 Großengottern Ger.
193 I8 Großenhain Ger.
190 F5 Großenkneten Ger.
191 I9 Großenlüder Ger.
190 J3 Großensee Ger.
193 F9 Großenstein Ger.
190 H1 Großenwiehe Ger.
201 O3 Groß-Enzersdorf Austria
271 □2 Grosse Pointe Guadeloupe
195 O3 Großer Arber mt. Ger.
191 K9 Großer Beerberg hill Ger.
201 J5 Grosser Bösenstein mt. Austria
191 J10 Großer Breitenberg hill Ger.
201 K4 Grosser Buchstein mt. Austria
194 D3 Großer Eyberg hill Ger.
191 K10 Großer Gleichberg hill Ger.
192 H1 Großer Jasmunder Bodden b. Ger.
193 F10 Großer Kornberg hill Ger.
192 H3 Großer Landgraben r. Ger.
200 E5 Grosser Löffler mt. Austria
193 I6 Großer Müggelsee l. Ger.
193 H8 Große Röder r. Ger.
198 C2 Großer Osser mt. Czech Rep./Ger.
190 J2 Großer Plöner See l. Ger.
201 J4 Grosser Priel mt. Austria
195 O4 Großer Rachel mt. Ger.
193 I6 Großer Selchower See l. Ger.
201 I6 Grosser Speikkofel mt. Austria
201 K6 Grosser Speikkogel mt. Austria
193 E10 Großer Waldstein hill Ger.
190 D4 Großes Meer l. Ger.
200 G5 Großes Wiesbachhorn mt. Austria
180 H8 Grosse Terre, Pointe de pt France
214 G2 Grosseto Italy
214 G2 Grosseto prov. Italy
214 B4 Grosseto-Prugna Corse France
122 K5 Grossevichi Rus. Fed.
195 M4 Große Vils r. Ger.
192 I4 Groß Fredenwalde Ger.
191 K8 Großfurra Ger.
192 E5 Groß Garz Ger.
194 E2 Groß-Gerau Ger.
201 K2 Groß-Gerungs Austria
191 I6 Groß Giesen Ger.
193 H6 Groß Glienicke Ger.
200 G5 Großglockner mt. Austria
195 N6 Großgmain Ger.
192 E4 Groß Godems Ger.
201 L2 Großgöttfritz Austria
190 K3 Groß Grönau Ger.
195 J3 Großhabersdorf Ger.
190 J3 Großhansdorf Ger.
201 N2 Großharras Austria
191 J6 Groß Heere (Heere) Ger.
193 K9 Großhennersdorf Ger.
193 E8 Großheringen Ger.
190 D5 Groß-Hesepe Ger.
194 G2 Großheubach Ger.
190 G5 Groß Ippener Ger.
195 M6 Großkarolinenfeld Ger.
193 E8 Großkayna Ger.
192 H2 Groß Kiesow Ger.
201 L6 Großklein Austria
193 F8 Großkorbetha Ger.
193 I6 Groß Köris Ger.
193 J8 Großkoschen Ger.
193 G6 Groß Kreutz Ger.
201 O2 Großkrut Austria
190 J2 Groß Kummerfeld Ger.
192 E4 Groß Laasch Ger.
191 J6 Groß Lafferde (Lahstedt) Ger.
195 I2 Großlangheim Ger.
193 F8 Großlehna Ger.
193 J6 Groß Leine Ger.
193 J6 Groß Leuthen Ger.
193 K6 Groß Lindow Ger.
191 C10 Großlittgen Ger.
191 K8 Großlohra Ger.
193 I8 Großmehlen Ger.
195 L4 Großmehring Ger.
192 I3 Groß Miltzow Ger.
192 G2 Groß Mohrdorf Ger.
193 D8 Großmonra Ger.
193 E7 Groß Mühlingen Ger.
193 I8 Großnaundorf Ger.
193 G7 Groß Naundorf Ger.
192 H4 Groß Nemerow Ger.
190 J5 Groß Oesingen Ger.
193 H9 Großolbersdorf Ger.
193 D7 Großörner Ger.
193 J7 Groß Oßnig Ger.
194 G2 Großostheim Ger.
201 N5 Großpetersdorf Austria
192 G3 Groß Plasten Ger.
193 D7 Groß Quenstedt Ger.
201 K4 Großraming Austria
193 J7 Großräschen Ger.
194 H2 Großrinderfeld Ger.
194 E2 Groß-Rohrheim Ger.
193 J8 Großröhrsdorf Ger.
193 E7 Groß Rosenburg Ger.
194 B3 Großrosseln Ger.
193 D8 Großrudestedt Ger.
201 N3 Großrußbach Austria
201 L6 Groß Sankt Florian Austria
193 J8 Groß Särchen Ger.
193 K7 Groß Schacksdorf Ger.
193 H9 Großschirma Ger.
201 K2 Großschönau Austria
193 K9 Großschönau Ger.
192 I5 Groß Schönebeck Ger.
192 E5 Groß Schwechten Ger.
193 K8 Großschweidnitz Ger.
191 J6 Groß Schwülper (Schwülper) Ger.
201 L2 Groß-Siegharts Austria
190 I1 Großsolt Ger.
190 D5 Groß Stavern Ger.
193 G8 Großsteinberg Ger.
192 D3 Groß Stieten Ger.
193 G7 Großtreben Ger.
191 K6 Groß Twülpstedt Ger.
234 C4 Gross Ums Namibia
194 F2 Groß-Umstadt Ger.
200 F5 Großvenediger mt. Austria
194 G2 Großwallstadt Ger.
212 E1 Grosswangen Switz.
192 E4 Groß Warnow Ger.
191 K8 Großwechsungen Ger.
201 M3 Großweikersdorf Austria
192 F4 Groß Welle Ger.
190 I2 Groß Wittensee Ger.
192 F3 Groß Wokern Ger.
192 F5 Großwudicke Ger.
192 G3 Groß Wüstenfelde Ger.
192 I5 Groß Ziethen Ger.
194 F2 Groß-Zimmern Ger.
179 M6 Grostenquin France
210 E3 Grosuplje Slovenia
287 L1 Grosvenor Mountains Antarctica
262 I5 Gros Ventre Range mts WY U.S.A.
249 J2 Groswater Bay Nfld and Lab. Can.
187 F6 Grote Nete r. Belgium
259 K2 Groton CT U.S.A.
257 I6 Groton NY U.S.A.
260 F3 Groton SD U.S.A.
215 J4 Grottaferrata Italy
217 M2 Grottaglie Italy
215 L2 Grottammare Italy
215 L1 Grottazzolina Italy
216 F9 Grotte Sicilia Italy
214 H2 Grotte di Castro Italy
217 K7 Grotteria Italy
256 G10 Grottoes VA U.S.A.
217 K2 Grottole Italy
186 I2 Grou Neth.
246 G1 Grouard Lake N.W.T. Can.
246 G4 Grouard Mission Alta Can.
180 H4 Grouin, Pointe du pt France
228 E5 Groumania Côte d'Ivoire
248 D3 Groundhog r. Ont. Can.
261 H7 Grove OK U.S.A.
256 B9 Grove City OH U.S.A.
256 E7 Grove City PA U.S.A.
255 D10 Grove Hill AL U.S.A.
163 L5 Grövelsjön Sweden
287 F2 Grove Mountains Antarctica
258 B1 Grover PA U.S.A.
264 L6 Grover Beach CA U.S.A.
257 N4 Groveton NH U.S.A.
261 H10 Groveton TX U.S.A.
258 F4 Groveville NJ U.S.A.
162 N2 Grovfjord Norway
265 S9 Growler Mountains AZ U.S.A.
219 P7 Grozd'ovo Bulg.
151 G2 Groznyy Rus. Fed.
193 D10 Grub am Forst Ger.
164 C3 Grubbåfjellet mt. Norway
187 J6 Grubbenvorst Neth.
192 D2 Grube Ger.
210 F3 Grubišno Polje Croatia
196 G2 Gruczno Pol.
Grudovo Bulg. see Sredets
197 I2 Grudusk Pol.
196 G2 Grudziądz Pol.
212 F6 Grue r. Italy
179 L7 Gruey-lès-Surance France
212 D5 Grugliasco Italy
168 E7 Gruinard Bay Scotland U.K.
168 D11 Gruinart, Loch inlet Scotland U.K.
183 C10 Gruissan France
204 H2 Grullos Spain
162 □ Grumantbyen Svalbard
219 O3 Grumăzești Romania
193 I8 Grumbach Ger.
215 P7 Grumento Nova Italy
217 L1 Grumo Appula Italy
164 J2 Grums Sweden
193 G9 Grüna Ger.
201 M3 Grünau Niederösterreich Austria
201 I4 Grünau Oberösterreich Austria
234 C5 Grünau Namibia
193 I6 Grünau-Grünheider Wald- und Seengebiet park Ger.
201 M4 Grünbach am Schneeberg Austria
191 G9 Grünberg Ger.
Grünberg Pol. see Zielona Góra
201 J4 Grünburg Austria
163 L5 Grundagssätern Sweden
162 □B1 Grundarfjörður Iceland
163 L6 Grundforsen Sweden
201 I4 Grundlsee l. Austria
201 I4 Grundlsee nature res. Austria
236 B1 Grundorner Namibia
162 O5 Grundsuna Sweden
256 C11 Grundy VA U.S.A.
260 I4 Grundy Center IA U.S.A.
192 H5 Grüneberg Ger.
190 I3 Grünendeich Ger.
193 I8 Grünewald Ger.
193 I7 Grünewalde Ger.
193 I6 Grünheide Ger.
268 F1 Gruñidora Mex.
194 H6 Grünkraut Ger.
193 J6 Grunow Ger.
194 H2 Grünsfeld Ger.
194 E2 Grünstadt Ger.
213 K2 Gruppo de Tessa, Parco Naturale nature res. Italy
182 D3 Grury France
196 G2 Gruta Pol.
168 □N3 Grutness Shetland, Scotland U.K.
261 E7 Gruver TX U.S.A.
212 C2 Gruyère, Lac de la l. Switz.
212 C2 Gruyères Switz.
160 G5 Gruzdžiai Lith.
Gruzinskaya S.S.R. country Asia see Georgia
161 W9 Gryazi Rus. Fed.
161 W7 Gryaznoye Rus. Fed.
156 H4 Gryazovets Rus. Fed.
197 I6 Grybów Pol.
165 M1 Grycken l. Sweden
196 D2 Gryfice Pol.
196 C2 Gryfino Pol.
196 D4 Gryfów Śląski Pol.
196 F3 Grylewo Pol.
162 N2 Gryllefjord Norway
164 B2 Grytenuten hill Norway
165 N1 Gryttjom Sweden
283 □ Grytviken S. Georgia
197 I2 Gryźliny Pol.
196 E3 Grzebienisko Pol.
196 G3 Grzegorzew Pol.
196 E2 Grzmiąca Pol.
196 C2 Grzybno Pol.
196 G3 Grzymiszew Pol.

196 G2 **Grzywna** Pol.
200 D5 **Gschnitz** Austria
201 I4 **Gschwandt** Austria
194 H4 **Gschwend** Ger.
212 C3 **Gstaad** Switz.
195 M6 **Gstadt am Chiemsee** Ger.
212 C3 **Gsteig** Switz.
139 J8 **Gua** *Jharkhand* India
213 L5 **Guà** *r.* Italy
266 □R13 **Guabito** Panama
268 C2 **Guacamayita** Mex.
270 E3 **Guacanayabo, Golfo de** *b.* Cuba
271 J8 **Guacara** Venez.
274 D3 **Guacharía** *r.* Col.
268 A1 **Guachimetas de Arriba** Mex.
282 D2 **Guachipas** Arg.
279 B7 **Guaçu** Brazil
281 G4 **Guaçuí** Brazil
207 M5 **Guadahortuna** Spain
207 N5 **Guadahortuna** *r.* Spain
206 G6 **Guadaira** *r.* Spain
206 H6 **Guadairilla** *r.* Spain
206 F3 **Guadajira** *r.* Spain
206 H5 **Guadajoz** Spain
207 J5 **Guadajoz** *r.* Spain
268 D5 **Guadalajara** Mex.
205 N7 **Guadalajara** Spain
205 P7 **Guadalajara** *prov.* Spain
209 C7 **Guadalaviar** *r.* Spain
206 I5 **Guadalbacar** *r.* Spain
207 L5 **Guadalbullón** *r.* Spain
206 H7 **Guadalcacín, Embalse de** *resr* Spain
100 □[6] **Guadalcanal** *i.* Solomon Is
206 H4 **Guadalcanal** Spain
207 J5 **Guadalcázar** Spain
206 H3 **Guadalefra** *r.* Spain
207 L4 **Guadalén** *r.* Spain
207 M4 **Guadalén, Embalse del** *resr* Spain
207 N5 **Guadalentín** *r.* Spain
207 Q5 **Guadalentín** *r.* Spain
284 D4 **Guadales** Arg.
209 E10 **Guadalest, Embalse de** *resr* Spain
206 G7 **Guadalete** *r.* Spain
207 K7 **Guadalhorce** *r.* Spain
207 J7 **Guadalhorce, Embalse de** *resr* Spain
207 L5 **Guadalimar** *r.* Spain
207 I5 **Guadalmazán** *r.* Spain
207 J4 **Guadalmellato, Embalse de** *resr* Spain
207 N4 **Guadalmena** *r.* Spain
207 N4 **Guadalmena, Embalse del** *resr* Spain
207 J3 **Guadalmez** Spain
207 J3 **Guadalmez** *r.* Spain
208 E5 **Guadalope** *r.* Spain
207 G7 **Guadalquivir** *r.* Spain
278 E3 **Guadalupe** Brazil
267 I5 **Guadalupe** *Nuevo León* Mex.
269 J6 **Guadalupe** *Puebla* Mex.
269 H1 **Guadalupe** *Tamaulipas* Mex.
268 E3 **Guadalupe** *Zacatecas* Mex.
269 I9 **Guadalupe** Mex.
266 A3 **Guadalupe** *i.* Mex.
265 P9 **Guadalupe** *watercourse* Mex.
274 B6 **Guadalupe** Peru
207 I2 **Guadalupe** Spain
265 U8 **Guadalupe** *AZ* U.S.A.
264 L7 **Guadalupe** *CA* U.S.A.
261 G11 **Guadalupe** *r. TX* U.S.A.
261 G11 **Guadalupe** *r. TX* U.S.A.
206 H2 **Guadalupe, Sierra de** *mts* Spain
268 C1 **Guadalupe Aguilera** Mex.
263 K11 **Guadalupe Bravos** Mex.
268 A1 **Guadalupe de los Reyes** Mex.
263 L11 **Guadalupe Mountains National Park** *TX* U.S.A.
261 C10 **Guadalupe Peak** *TX* U.S.A.
265 Q9 **Guadalupe Victoria** *Baja California* Mex.
268 C1 **Guadalupe Victoria** *Durango* Mex.
266 F4 **Guadalupe y Calvo** Mex.
207 I5 **Guadalvacarejo** *r.* Spain
205 O8 **Guadamajud** *r.* Spain
207 I3 **Guadamatilla** *r.* Spain
206 H3 **Guadamez** *r.* Spain
205 L9 **Guadamur** Spain
205 L7 **Guadarrama** Spain
205 L9 **Guadarrama** *r.* Spain
274 D2 **Guadarrama** Venez.
205 L7 **Guadarrama, Puerto de** *pass* Spain
205 L7 **Guadarrama, Sierra de** *mts* Spain
205 Q9 **Guadazaón** *r.* Spain
271 □[2] **Guadeloupe** *terr.* West Indies
271 □ **Guadeloupe, Parc National de la** *nat. park* Guadeloupe
271 □[2] **Guadeloupe Passage** Caribbean Sea
206 G7 **Guadiamar** *r.* Spain
207 E6 **Guadiana** *r.* Port./Spain
270 A2 **Guadiana, Bahía de** *b.* Cuba
207 M2 **Guadiana, Canal del** Spain
207 M5 **Guadiana Menor** *r.* Spain
207 I8 **Guadiaro** *r.* Spain
207 I5 **Guadiato** *r.* Spain
205 P8 **Guadiela** *r.* Spain
205 J8 **Guadiervas** *r.* Spain
207 M6 **Guadix** Spain
283 B6 **Guafo, Isla** *i.* Chile
114 C4 **Guagua** *Luzon* Phil.
279 C9 **Guaíba** Brazil
271 □[7] **Guaico** Trin. and Tob.
281 E2 **Guaiçuí** Brazil
277 F5 **Guaicuras** Brazil
274 B4 **Guaillabamba** *r.* Ecuador
270 E3 **Guáimaro** Cuba
275 F3 **Guaina** Venez.
274 D4 **Guainía** *dept* Col.
274 E4 **Guainía** *r.* Col./Venez.
275 F3 **Guaiquinima, Cerro** *mt.* Venez.
279 B8 **Guaíra** Brazil
280 C4 **Guaíra** Brazil
280 A5 **Guairaçá** Brazil
283 B6 **Guaitecas, Islas** *is* Chile
278 C2 **Guajará Açu** Brazil
276 D2 **Guajará Mirim** Brazil
275 F6 **Guajaratuba** Brazil
205 L9 **Guajaraz** *r.* Spain
207 L7 **Guájar-Faraguit** Spain
276 D1 **Guajarraã** Brazil
271 □[1] **Guajataca** *r.* Puerto Rico
271 □[1] **Guajataca, Lago de** *l.* Puerto Rico
266 H3 **Guaje, Laguna de** *l.* Mex.
266 H4 **Guaje, Llano de** *plain* Mex.
274 D2 **Guajira, Península de la** *pen.* Col.
274 B5 **Gualaceo** Ecuador
264 I3 **Gualala** *CA* U.S.A.
267 O10 **Gualán** Guat.
274 B5 **Gualaquiza** Ecuador
215 J2 **Gualdo Cattaneo** Italy
213 N9 **Gualdo Tadino** Italy
285 H3 **Gualeguay** Arg.
285 H3 **Gualeguay** *r.* Arg.
285 H3 **Gualeguaychu** Arg.
283 D6 **Gualicho, Salina** *salt flat* Arg.
283 C6 **Gualjaina** Arg.
276 C4 **Guallatiri** *vol.* Chile
284 B4 **Gualleco** Chile
284 B6 **Gualletue, Lago de** *l.* Chile
268 D2 **Gualterio** Mex.
213 J6 **Gualtieri** Italy
113 J4 **Guam** *terr.* N. Pacific Ocean
271 I8 **Guama** Venez.
283 B7 **Guamblin, Isla** *i.* Chile
285 F5 **Guamini** Arg.
270 E3 **Guamo** Cuba
275 E3 **Guampí, Sierra de** *mts* Venez.
266 E5 **Guamúchil** Mex.
116 D2 **Gua Musang** Malaysia
129 O7 **Gu'an** *Hebei* China
270 B2 **Guanabacoa** Cuba
276 C2 **Guanabara** Brazil
281 F5 **Guanabara, Baía de** *b.* Brazil
266 □Q12 **Guanacaste, Cordillera de** *mts* Costa Rica
266 □Q12 **Guanacaste, Parque Nacional** *nat. park* Costa Rica
266 G5 **Guanacevi** Mex.
285 F5 **Guanaco, Cerro** *hill* Arg.
270 A2 **Guanahacabibes, Península de** *pen.* Cuba
266 □Q9 **Guanaja** Hond.
270 B2 **Guanajay** Cuba
268 F4 **Guanajuato** Mex.
268 G4 **Guanajuato** *state* Mex.
268 F4 **Guanajuato, Sierra de** *mts* Mex.
278 E5 **Guanambi** Brazil
268 F3 **Guaname** Mex.
274 B7 **Guañape, Islas de** *is* Peru
271 □[7] **Guanapo** Trin. and Tob.
284 B2 **Guanaqueros** Chile
274 D2 **Guanare** Venez.
274 E2 **Guanare Viejo** *r.* Venez.
274 D2 **Guanarito** Venez.
274 D2 **Guanarito** *r.* Venez.
238 □[3f] **Guanarteme, Punta de** *pt Gran Canaria* Canary Is
276 D3 **Guanay** Bol.
282 C3 **Guandacol** Arg.
129 L9 **Guandaokou** *Henan* China
129 L8 **Guandi Shan** *mt. Shanxi* China
281 G3 **Guandu** *r.* Brazil
131 I6 **Guandu** *Guangdong* China
270 A2 **Guane** Cuba
130 F3 **Guang'an** *Sichuan* China
131 K5 **Guangchang** *Jiangxi* China
131 L3 **Guangde** *Anhui* China
131 J7 **Guangdong** *prov.* China
131 L4 **Guangfeng** *Jiangxi* China
131 I8 **Guanghai** *Guangdong* China
130 E3 **Guanghan** *Sichuan* China
Guanghua *Hubei* China *see* **Laohekou**
129 N7 **Guangling** *Shanxi* China
130 C5 **Guangmao Shan** *mt. Yunnan* China
Guangming *Sichuan* China *see* **Xide**
131 L3 **Guangming Ding** *mt. Anhui* China
130 E6 **Guangnan** *Yunnan* China
131 I7 **Guangning** *Guangdong* China
Guangning *Liaoning* China *see* **Beizhen**
Guangning China *see* **Beizhen**
129 P8 **Guangrao** *Shandong* China
131 J3 **Guangshan** *Henan* China
131 I3 **Guangshui** *Hubei* China
Guangxi *aut. reg.* China *see* **Guangxi Zhuangzu Zizhiqu**
130 G7 **Guangxi Zhuangzu Zizhiqu** *aut. reg.* China
130 E2 **Guangyuan** *Sichuan* China
131 K5 **Guangze** *Fujian* China
131 I7 **Guangzhou** *Guangdong* China
129 N8 **Guangzong** *Hebei* China
281 F3 **Guanhães** Brazil
281 F3 **Guanhães** *r.* Brazil
129 P9 **Guan He** *r.* China
129 P9 **Guanhe Kou** *r. mouth* China
271 □[1] **Guánica** Puerto Rico
270 A2 **Guaniguanico, Cordillera de** *mts* Cuba
275 F2 **Guanipa** *r.* Venez.
130 E6 **Guanling** *Guizhou* China
130 G3 **Guanmian Shan** *mts* China
275 F2 **Guanoca** Venez.
130 H2 **Guanpo** *Henan* China
123 D8 **Guanshui** *Liaoning* China
Guansuo *Guizhou* China *see* **Guanling**
284 B1 **Guanta** Chile
275 E2 **Guanta** Venez.
270 F3 **Guantánamo** Cuba
270 F4 **Guantánamo Bay Naval Base** *military base* Cuba
129 N8 **Guantao** *Hebei* China
130 E2 **Guanting** *Gansu* China
128 H9 **Guanting** *Qinghai* China
129 N6 **Guanting Shuiku** *resr* China
Guanxian *Sichuan* China *see* **Dujiangyan**
131 H6 **Guanyang** *Guangxi* China
130 C3 **Guanyinqiao** *Sichuan* China
129 P9 **Guanyun** *Jiangsu* China
Guapay *r.* Bol. *see* **Grande**
281 E4 **Guapé** Brazil
274 B4 **Guapí** Col.
280 C6 **Guapiara** Brazil
266 □R12 **Guápiles** Costa Rica
271 □[7] **Guapo Bay** Trin. and Tob.
276 D3 **Guaporé** *r.* Bol./Brazil
279 C9 **Guaporé** Brazil
Guaporé *state* Brazil *see* **Rondônia**
276 C4 **Guaqui** Bol.
280 D4 **Guará** Brazil
278 D5 **Guará** *r.* Brazil
208 E3 **Guara, Sierra de** *mts* Spain
278 G3 **Guarabira** Brazil
281 F4 **Guaraciaba** Brazil
274 B5 **Guaranda** Ecuador
281 F4 **Guarani** Brazil
280 A6 **Guaraniaçu** Brazil
280 C4 **Guarantã** Brazil
281 G4 **Guarapari** Brazil
280 B6 **Guarapuava** Brazil
280 C6 **Guaraqueçaba** Brazil
280 B4 **Guararapes** Brazil
281 H2 **Guaratinga** Brazil
281 E5 **Guaratinguetá** Brazil
279 C8 **Guaratuba** Brazil
276 C3 **Guarayos** Bol.
238 □[3e] **Guarazoca** *El Hierro* Canary Is
215 K4 **Guarcino** Italy
204 F7 **Guarda** Port.
204 F7 **Guarda** *admin. dist.* Port.
Guardafui, Cape Somalia *see* **Gwardafuy, Gees**
207 N5 **Guardal** *r.* Spain
209 D11 **Guardamar del Segura** Spain
280 D2 **Guarda Mor** Brazil
274 E2 **Guardatinajas** Venez.
217 K6 **Guardavalle** Italy
282 E3 **Guardia Escolta** Arg.
215 M3 **Guardiagrele** Italy
215 N4 **Guardialfiera, Lago di** *l.* Italy
265 Q9 **Guardianes de la Patria** Mex.
215 Q7 **Guardia Perticara** Italy
215 Q9 **Guardia Piemontese** Italy
215 N5 **Guardia Sanframondi** Italy
207 N7 **Guardias Viejas** Spain
208 I3 **Guardiola de Berguedà** Spain
205 K3 **Guardo** Spain
204 H6 **Guardramiro** Spain
204 E9 **Guardunha, Serra de** *mts* Port.
206 G3 **Guareña** Spain
205 J6 **Guareña** *r.* Spain
208 E3 **Guarga** *r.* Spain
277 E1 **Guariba** *r.* Brazil
274 E2 **Guárico** *state* Venez.
270 F3 **Guarico, Punta** *pt* Cuba
207 J7 **Guaro** Spain
207 L4 **Guarrizas** *r.* Spain
274 D3 **Guarrojo** *r.* Col.
207 L4 **Guarromán** Spain
280 D5 **Guarujá** Brazil
280 D5 **Guarulhos** Brazil
280 D5 **Guarulhos** *airport* Brazil
270 H8 **Guasare** *r.* Venez.
266 E5 **Guasave** Mex.
274 D3 **Guasdualito** Venez.
214 C8 **Guasila** *Sardegna* Italy
275 F3 **Guasipati** Venez.
213 J6 **Guastalla** Italy
267 O10 **Guastatoya** Guat.
139 L9 **Guasuba** *r.* India
267 N10 **Guatemala** *country* Central America
267 N10 **Guatemala** Guat.
291 M5 **Guatemala Basin** *sea feature* Pacific Ocean
Guatemala City Guat. *see* **Guatemala**
285 F3 **Guatimozin** Arg.
238 □[3c] **Guatiza** *Lanzarote* Canary Is
285 F5 **Guatrache** Arg.
283 D6 **Guatrochi** Arg.
271 □[7] **Guatuaro Point** Trin. and Tob.
274 D4 **Guaviare** *dept* Col.
274 E3 **Guaviare** *r.* Col.
280 D4 **Guaxupé** Brazil
274 D3 **Guayabal** Col.
270 E3 **Guayabal** Cuba
271 □[1] **Guayabal, Lago** *l.* Puerto Rico
284 D2 **Guayaguas, Sierra da** *mts* Arg.
271 □[7] **Guayaguayare** Trin. and Tob.
269 J3 **Guayalejo** *r.* Mex.
271 □[1] **Guayama** Puerto Rico
271 □[1] **Guayanilla** Puerto Rico
271 □[1] **Guayanilla, Punta** *pt* Puerto Rico
274 E3 **Guayapo, Serranía** *mts* Venez.
274 B5 **Guayaquil** Ecuador
274 A5 **Guayaquil, Golfo de** *g.* Ecuador
276 D2 **Guayaramerín** Bol.
274 A5 **Guayas** *prov.* Ecuador
282 D1 **Guayatayoc, Laguna de** *imp. l.* Arg.
266 D4 **Guaymas** Mex.
271 □[1] **Guaynabo** Puerto Rico
285 H2 **Guayquirard** Arg.
285 H2 **Guayquiraró** *r.* Arg.
267 N10 **Guazacapán** Guat.
128 D6 **Guazhou** *Gansu* China
232 B2 **Guba** Eth.
142 H6 **Gubadag** Turkm.
156 L4 **Gubakha** Rus. Fed.
Gûbâl Island Egypt *see* **Jūbāl, Jazīrat**
232 E2 **Guban** *plain* Somalia
114 E5 **Gubat** *Luzon* Phil.
170 B5 **Gubaveeny** Ireland
136 E6 **Gubbi** *Karnataka* India
213 N9 **Gubbio** Italy
151 I3 **Gubden** Rus. Fed.
156 L3 **Gubdor** Rus. Fed.
232 F2 **Gubed Binna** *b.* Somalia
129 O6 **Gubeikou** *Beijing* China
193 K7 **Guben** Ger.
219 N8 **Gŭbene** Bulg.
197 J1 **Guber** *r.* Pol.
196 C4 **Gubin** Pol.
161 S6 **Gubino** Rus. Fed.
229 I3 **Gubio** Nigeria
157 G6 **Gubkin** Rus. Fed.
128 H8 **Gucheng** *Gansu* China
128 F6 **Gucheng** *Gansu* China
129 N8 **Gucheng** *Hebei* China
131 H2 **Gucheng** *Hubei* China
129 L9 **Gucheng** *Shanxi* China
128 H4 **Guchin-Us** Mongolia
136 E7 **Gudalur** *Tamil Nadu* India
151 F3 **Gudamaqris K'edi** *hills* Georgia
208 D7 **Gudar** Spain
209 D7 **Gudar, Sierra de** *mts* Spain
Gudara Tajik. *see* **Ghŭdara**
137 H3 **Gudari** *Orissa* India
151 B2 **Gudaut'a** Georgia
163 J6 **Gudbrandsdalen** *val.* Norway
145 M7 **Guddu Barrage** Pak.
164 G5 **Gudenå** *r.* Denmark
191 H8 **Gudensberg** Ger.
151 H2 **Gudermes** Rus. Fed.
190 I1 **Guderup** Denmark
165 K6 **Gudhjem** *Bornholm* Denmark
229 H4 **Gudi** Nigeria
136 G4 **Gudivada** *Andhra Prad.* India
136 F6 **Gudiyattam** *Tamil Nadu* India
217 □ **Gudja** Malta
164 G6 **Gudme** Denmark
179 J7 **Gudmont-Villiers** France
122 F7 **Gudong He** *r.* China
190 K3 **Gudow** Ger.
145 J8 **Gudri** *r.* Pak.
148 F3 **Güdül** Turkey
136 F5 **Gudur** *Andhra Prad.* India
136 F5 **Gudur** *Andhra Prad.* India
163 I6 **Gudvangen** Norway
122 H4 **Gudzhal** *r.* Rus. Fed.
160 G6 **Gudžiūnai** Lith.
249 G1 **Gué, Rivière du** *r. Que.* Can.
179 N8 **Guebwiller** France
Guecho Spain *see* **Algorta**
228 C4 **Guéckédou** Guinea
180 F6 **Guégon** France
251 Q1 **Guéguen, Lac** *l. Que.* Can.
207 M6 **Güéjar-Sierra** Spain
226 C5 **Guelb er Rîchât** *hill* Maur.
230 B2 **Guélengdeng** Chad
227 G1 **Guelma** Alg.
211 A7 **Guelma** *prov.* Alg.
226 C3 **Guelmine** Morocco
248 D5 **Guelph** *Ont.* Can.
227 E5 **Guem** *waterhole* Mali
227 G2 **Guémar** Alg.
179 N7 **Guémar** France
180 H6 **Guémené-Penfao** France
180 E5 **Guémené-sur-Scorff** France
269 H2 **Guémez** Mex.
179 L5 **Guénange** France
228 C2 **Guendour** *well* Maur.
229 F4 **Guéné** Benin
205 N2 **Güeñes** Spain
180 H6 **Guenrouet** France
228 B3 **Guènt Paté** Senegal
180 G6 **Guer** France
230 C2 **Guéra** *pref.* Chad
230 C2 **Guéra, Massif du** *mts* Chad
180 G7 **Guérande** France
227 G2 **Guerara** Alg.
249 H1 **Guérard, Lac** *l. Que.* Can.
226 E2 **Guercif** Morocco
224 C5 **Guéré** *watercourse* Chad
224 D6 **Guéréda** Chad
224 D4 **Guerende** Libya
184 H3 **Guéret** France
182 C2 **Guérigny** France
229 F4 **Guérin-Kouka** Togo
180 E5 **Guerlédan, Lac de** *l.* France
264 J3 **Guerneville** *CA* U.S.A.
Guernica Spain *see* **Gernika-Lumo**
180 F3 **Guernsey** *terr.* Channel Is
262 L5 **Guernsey** *WY* U.S.A.
228 C2 **Guérou** Maur.
206 E6 **Guerreiros do Rio** Port.
285 I4 **Guerrero** Arg.
261 E11 **Guerrero** *Coahuila* Mex.
267 J4 **Guerrero** *Tamaulipas* Mex.
268 G8 **Guerrero** *state* Mex.
206 F3 **Guerrero** *r.* Spain
269 H8 **Guerrero, Parque Natural de** *nature res.* Mex.
266 B4 **Guerrero Negro** Mex.
185 E10 **Guerreys, Pic de** *mt.* France
208 H3 **Guerri de la Sal** Spain
249 H1 **Guers, Lac** *l. Que.* Can.
226 E3 **Guerzim** Alg.
208 C2 **Güesa** Spain
226 D4 **Guețâțîra** *well* Mali
185 A9 **Guéthary** France
182 E3 **Gueugnon** France
228 D5 **Guéyo** Côte d'Ivoire
Gufeng *Fujian* China *see* **Pingnan**
Gufu *Hubei* China *see* **Xingshan**
151 F5 **Gugark'** Armenia
232 C3 **Gugē** *mt.* Eth.
100 □[3a] **Gugegwe** *i. Kwajalein* Marshall Is
145 O6 **Gugera** Pak.
144 E4 **Gūgerd, Kūh-e** *mts* Iran
172 □ **Gugh** *i. England* U.K.
285 F2 **Guglieri** Arg.
194 F3 **Güglingen** Ger.
215 N4 **Guglionesi** Italy
232 C2 **Gugu** *mts* Eth.
113 K3 **Guguan** *i.* N. Mariana Is
116 F8 **Guhakolak, Tanjung** *pt* Indon.
131 K3 **Guhe** *Anhui* China
144 H8 **Gūh Kūh** *mt.* Iran
192 G4 **Gühlen-Glienicke** Ger.
Guhuai *Henan* China *see* **Pingyu**
277 F3 **Guia** Brazil
204 C9 **Guia** Port.
238 □[3a] **Guía de Isora** *Tenerife* Canary Is
204 G4 **Guiana** *mt.* Spain
288 F5 **Guiana Basin** *sea feature* N. Atlantic Ocean
274 E3 **Guiana Highlands** *mts* S. America
228 D5 **Guibéroua** Côte d'Ivoire
178 B6 **Guichainville** France
180 H6 **Guichen** France
104 G7 **Guichen Bay** *S.A.* Austr.
Guichi *Anhui* China *see* **Chizhou**
269 L8 **Guichicovi** Mex.
285 I3 **Guichón** Uru.
180 D4 **Guiclan** France
229 G3 **Guidan-Roumji** Niger
230 C2 **Guidari** Chad
128 G9 **Guide** *Qinghai* China
180 E6 **Guidel** France
171 N3 **Guide Post** *Northumberland, England* U.K.
229 I4 **Guider** Cameroon
229 H3 **Guidiguir** Niger
229 I4 **Guidiguis** Cameroon
228 B3 **Guidimaka** *admin. reg.* Maur.
130 F5 **Guiding** *Guizhou* China
213 J5 **Guidizzolo** Italy
131 I6 **Guidong** *Hunan* China
215 J4 **Guidonia-Montecelio** Italy
281 F4 **Guidoval** Brazil
269 L9 **Guienagati** Mex.
228 B2 **Guier, Lac de** *l.* Senegal
182 H5 **Guiers** *r.* France
230 A5 **Guietsou** Gabon
130 G7 **Guigang** *Guangxi* China
213 J7 **Guiglia** Italy
228 D5 **Guiglo** Côte d'Ivoire
180 H6 **Guignen** France
178 E6 **Guignes** France
178 G5 **Guignicourt** France
271 J8 **Güigüe** Venez.
235 G5 **Guija** Moz.
130 H7 **Gui Jiang** *r.* China
131 M4 **Guiji Shan** *mts* China
204 H8 **Guijo de Coria** Spain
204 H8 **Guijo de Galisteo** Spain
204 H8 **Guijo de Granadilla** Spain
204 I7 **Guijuelo** Spain
183 J7 **Guil** *r.* France
173 K5 **Guildford** *Surrey, England* U.K.
257 N4 **Guildhall** *VT* U.S.A.
168 J10 **Guildtown** *Perth and Kinross, Scotland* U.K.
180 B5 **Guilers** France
259 J2 **Guilford** *CT* U.S.A.
257 □P3 **Guilford** *ME* U.S.A.
183 F7 **Guilherand** France
Guilherme Capelo Angola *see* **Cacongo**
204 D5 **Guilhofrei** Port.
130 H6 **Guilin** *Guangxi* China
243 K4 **Guillaume-Delisle, Lac** *l. Que.* Can.
183 J8 **Guillaumes** France
206 G5 **Guillena** Spain
183 J7 **Guillestre** France
180 G5 **Guilliers** France
182 E1 **Guillon** France
185 C6 **Guillos** France
180 C6 **Guilvinec** France
238 □[3a] **Güímar** *Tenerife* Canary Is
238 □[3a] **Güimar, Punta de** *pt Tenerife* Canary Is
278 D2 **Guimarães** Brazil
204 D6 **Guimarães** Port.
114 D6 **Guimaras** *i.* Phil.
114 D6 **Guimaras Strait** Phil.
129 O9 **Guimeng Ding** *mt. Shandong* China
229 F4 **Guinagourou** Benin
128 G9 **Guinan** *Qinghai* China
270 D2 **Guinchos Cay** *i.* Cuba
114 E7 **Guindulman** *Bohol* Phil.
228 C4 **Guinea** *country* Africa
229 G6 **Guinea, Gulf of** Africa
288 I5 **Guinea Basin** *sea feature* N. Atlantic Ocean
228 B4 **Guinea-Bissau** *country* Africa
Guinea-Conakry *country* Africa *see* **Guinea**
Guinea Ecuatorial *country* Africa *see* **Equatorial Guinea**
Guiné-Bissau *country* Africa *see* **Guinea-Bissau**
Guinée *country* Africa *see* **Guinea**
228 C4 **Guinée-Forestière** *admin. reg.* Guinea
228 B4 **Guinée-Maritime** *admin. reg.* Guinea
270 B2 **Güines** Cuba
178 C2 **Guînes** France
249 I2 **Guines, Lac** *l. Nfld and Lab.* Can.
180 E4 **Guingamp** France
228 B3 **Guinguinéo** Senegal
266 □Q13 **Guiones, Punta** *pt* Costa Rica
180 C5 **Guipavas** France
130 H7 **Guiping** *Guangxi* China
180 H6 **Guipry** France
208 A1 **Guipúzcoa** *prov.* Spain
228 E2 **Guîr** *well* Mali
270 B2 **Güira de Melena** Cuba
279 B6 **Guiratinga** Brazil
275 F2 **Güiria** Venez.
275 I3 **Guisanbourg** Fr. Guiana
205 J8 **Guisando** Spain
183 J7 **Guisane** *r.* France
171 O4 **Guisborough** *Redcar and Cleveland, England* U.K.
178 F4 **Guiscard** France
180 D5 **Guiscriff** France
178 G4 **Guise** France
171 N6 **Guiseley** *West Yorkshire, England* U.K.
Guishan *Yunnan* China *see* **Xinping**
229 F2 **Guissefa** *well* Mali
180 C4 **Guissény** France
208 H4 **Guissona** Spain
173 N2 **Guist** *Norfolk, England* U.K.
204 E2 **Guitiriz** Spain
184 D5 **Guîtres** France
228 D5 **Guitri** Côte d'Ivoire
114 E6 **Guiuan** *Samar* Phil.
162 S2 **Guivi** *hill* Fin.
Guixi *Chongqing* China *see* **Dianjiang**
130 F5 **Guiyang** *Guizhou* China
131 I5 **Guiyang** *Hunan* China
131 I6 **Guiyang** *Hunan* China
130 F5 **Guizhou** *prov.* China
131 H7 **Guizi** *Guangdong* China
185 B6 **Gujan-Mestras** France
138 D8 **Gujarat** *state* India
151 E4 **Gujaret'i** Georgia
145 O5 **Gujar Khan** Pak.
229 H4 **Gujba** Nigeria
Gujerat *state* India *see* **Gujarat**
129 M8 **Gujiao** *Shanxi* China
145 P5 **Gujranwala** Pak.
145 P5 **Gujrat** Pak.
Gukasyan Armenia *see* **Ashots'k'**
157 G6 **Gukovo** Rus. Fed.
144 A3 **Gūk Tappeh** Iran
138 F3 **Gulabgarh** *Jammu and Kashmir* India
151 H6 **Gülablı** Azer.
128 H8 **Gulang** *Gansu* China
Gulân Islands Egypt *see* **Qul'ān, Jazā'ir**
105 L4 **Gulargambone** *N.S.W.* Austr.
221 H4 **Gülbahçe** Turkey
143 M7 **Gulbahor** Uzbek.
136 E4 **Gulbarga** *Karnataka* India
116 □ **Gul Basin** *dock* Sing.
160 J4 **Gulbene** Latvia
Gul'cha Kyrg. *see* **Gülchö**
143 O7 **Gülchö** Kyrg.
150 D2 **Gülcihan** Turkey
151 C4 **Gül dağı** *mt.* Turkey
192 E1 **Guldborg** Denmark
192 E1 **Guldborg Sund** *str.* Denmark
150 B1 **Güldere** Turkey
151 A6 **Güleç** Turkey
148 G5 **Gülek** Turkey
140 C2 **Gülek Boğazı** *pass* Turkey
Gulf of Chihli China *see* **Bo Hai**
261 K10 **Gulfport** *MS* U.S.A.
255 D10 **Gulf Shores** *AL* U.S.A.
147 J1 **Gulf, The** Asia
105 L5 **Gulgong** *N.S.W.* Austr.
135 □[1] **Gulhi** *i. S. Male* Maldives
122 C2 **Gulian** *Heilong.* China
130 E5 **Gulin** *Sichuan* China
145 L6 **Gulistan** Pak.
Gulistan Uzbek. *see* **Guliston**
143 M7 **Guliston** Uzbek.
114 □ **Gulitel** *hill* Palau
192 E4 **Gülitz** Ger.
129 R2 **Guliya Shan** *mt. Nei Mongol* China
Gulja *Xinjiang* China *see* **Yining**
145 M6 **Gul Kach** Pak.
245 K3 **Gulkana** *AK* U.S.A.
157 H7 **Gul'kevichi** Rus. Fed.
248 B3 **Gull** *r. Ont.* Can.
170 D4 **Gulladuff** *Northern Ireland* U.K.
168 K10 **Gullane** *East Lothian, Scotland* U.K.
163 I6 **Gullbrå** Norway
250 I4 **Gull Island** *MI* U.S.A.
163 Q7 **Gullkrona fjärd** *b.* Fin.
247 I5 **Gull Lake** *Sask.* Can.
164 H3 **Gullmarn** *inlet* Sweden
247 M5 **Gullrock Lake** *Ont.* Can.
165 K3 **Gullspång** Sweden
151 D6 **Güllü** *Erzurum* Turkey
221 K4 **Güllü** *Uşak* Turkey
221 I5 **Güllübahçe** Turkey
151 H4 **Güllük** Azer.
221 I5 **Güllük** Turkey
221 I5 **Güllük Körfezi** *b.* Turkey
148 F5 **Gülnar** Turkey
187 I7 **Gulpen** Neth.
192 F5 **Gülper See** *l.* Ger.
221 H3 **Gülpınar** Turkey
145 I4 **Gulran** Afgh.
151 C3 **Gulrip'shi** Georgia
148 G4 **Gülşehir** Turkey
143 P4 **Gul'shat** Kazakh.
192 H3 **Gültz** Ger.
Gulü *Henan* China *see* **Xincai**
232 B4 **Gulu** Uganda
219 N8 **Gŭlŭbovo** Bulg.
107 M9 **Guluguba** *Qld* Austr.
229 I4 **Gulumba Gana** Nigeria
106 F1 **Guluwuru Island** *N.T.* Austr.
168 F9 **Gulvain** *hill Scotland* U.K.
233 C6 **Gulwe** Tanz.
219 M7 **Gulyantsi** Bulg.
156 K1 **Gulyayevskiye Koshki, Ostrova** *is* Rus. Fed.
192 F3 **Gülzow** *Mecklenburg-Vorpommern* Ger.
190 J4 **Gülzow** *Schleswig-Holstein* Ger.
Guma *Xinjiang* China *see* **Pishan**
145 N6 **Gumal** *r.* Pak.
234 D3 **Gumare** Botswana
145 M6 **Gumbaz** Pak.
Gumbinnen Rus. Fed. *see* **Gusev**
232 A3 **Gumbiri** *mt.* Sudan
144 F2 **Gumdag** Turkm.
229 H3 **Gumel** Nigeria
Gümgüm Turkey *see* **Varto**
205 M5 **Gumiel de Hizán** Spain
205 M5 **Gumiel de Mercado** Spain
151 C2 **Gumist'is Nakrdzali** *nature res.* Georgia
139 J8 **Gumla** *Jharkhand* India
Gumma Japan *see* **Gunma**
Gumma *pref.* Japan *see* **Gunma**
191 E8 **Gummersbach** Ger.
116 B2 **Gumpang** *r.* Indon.
191 J9 **Gumpelstadt** Ger.
229 H3 **Gumsi** Nigeria
192 F5 **Gumtow** Ger.
148 I3 **Gümüşhane** Turkey
151 A5 **Gümüşhane** *prov.* Turkey
221 I4 **Gümüşsuyu** Turkey
221 J1 **Gümüşyaka** Turkey
138 F7 **Guna** *Madh. Prad.* India
Gunan *Chongqing* China *see* **Qijiang**
199 I6 **Gunaroš** *Vojvodina* Serbia
232 C2 **Guna Terara** *mt.* Eth.
105 J6 **Gunbar** *N.S.W.* Austr.
Gund *r.* Tajik. *see* **Gunt**
105 J4 **Gundabooka National Park** *N.S.W.* Austr.
105 L6 **Gundagai** *N.S.W.* Austr.
138 H9 **Gundardehi** *Chhattisgarh* India
194 D5 **Gundelfingen** Ger.
195 I4 **Gundelfingen an der Donau** Ger.
194 G3 **Gundelsheim** *Baden-Württemberg* Ger.
195 J2 **Gundelsheim** *Bayern* Ger.
179 O6 **Gundershoffen** France
230 D4 **Gundji** Dem. Rep. Congo
136 G5 **Gundlakamma** *r.* India
136 E7 **Gundlupet** *Karnataka* India
148 F5 **Gündoğmuş** Turkey
Gundorovka Rus. Fed. *see* **Donetsk**
221 L3 **Gündüzler** Turkey
151 D6 **Gündüzü** Turkey
221 J3 **Güneşli** Turkey
221 K4 **Güney** *Denizli* Turkey
221 J3 **Güney** *Kütahya* Turkey
148 J4 **Güneydoğu Toroslar** *plat.* Turkey
221 L4 **Güneyköy** Turkey
221 H2 **Güneyli** Turkey
151 B5 **Güneysu** Turkey
150 A2 **Güneyyurt** Turkey
118 D1 **Gunglilap** Myanmar
231 C6 **Gungu** Dem. Rep. Congo
231 B8 **Gungue** Angola
151 H3 **Gunib** Rus. Fed.
247 L4 **Gunisao** *r. Man.* Can.
247 L4 **Gunisao Lake** *Man.* Can.
210 G3 **Gunja** Croatia
228 A3 **Gunjur** Gambia
221 K3 **Günlüce** Turkey
127 J3 **Gunma** Japan
127 I2 **Gunma** *pref.* Japan
162 N4 **Gunnarn** Sweden
162 P3 **Gunnarsbyn** Sweden
107 J4 **Gunnawarra** *Qld* Austr.
243 P3 **Gunnbjørn Fjeld** *nunatak* Greenland
105 M4 **Gunnedah** *N.S.W.* Austr.
239 □[1b] **Gunners Quoin** Mauritius
171 P6 **Gunness** *North Lincolnshire, England* U.K.
105 L6 **Gunning** *N.S.W.* Austr.
172 D6 **Gunnislake** *Cornwall, England* U.K.
263 K7 **Gunnison** *CO* U.S.A.
265 U2 **Gunnison** *UT* U.S.A.
263 J7 **Gunnison** *r. CO* U.S.A.
265 U2 **Gunnison Reservoir** *UT* U.S.A.
106 C2 **Gunn Point** *N.T.* Austr.
Gunong Ayer *Sarawak* Malaysia *see* **Gunung Ayer**
271 □[3] **Gun Point** Grenada
106 G5 **Gunpowder Creek** *r. Qld* Austr.
258 C6 **Gunpowder Falls** *r. MD* U.S.A.
Güns Hungary *see* **Kőszeg**
136 E3 **Gun Sangari** *Mahar.* India
201 I3 **Gunskirchen** Austria
193 D8 **Günstedt** Ger.
145 N3 **Gunt** *r.* Tajik.
136 E5 **Guntakal** *Andhra Prad.* India
191 K7 **Güntersberge** Ger.
194 E2 **Guntersblum** Ger.
201 N2 **Guntersdorf** Austria
194 H2 **Güntersleben** Ger.
255 D8 **Guntersville** *AL* U.S.A.
204 E3 **Guntin de Pallares** Spain
201 N3 **Guntramsdorf** Austria
136 G4 **Guntur** *Andhra Prad.* India
106 G4 **Gununa** *Qld* Austr.
115 E7 **Gunungapi** *i. Maluku* Indon.
117 I3 **Gunung Ayer** *Sarawak* Malaysia
117 L6 **Gunungbatubesar** *Kalimantan* Indon.
117 H4 **Gunung Gading National Park** Malaysia
116 G8 **Gunung Gede Pangrango, Taman Nasional** *nat. park* Indon.
116 G8 **Gunung Halimun, Taman Nasional** *nat. park* Indon.
116 B3 **Gunung Leuser, Taman Nasional** *nat. park* Indon.
117 K2 **Gunung Mulu National Park** Malaysia
117 H4 **Gunung Niyut, Suaka Margasatwa** *nature res.* Indon.
117 I5 **Gunung Palung, Taman Nasional** *nat. park* Indon.
117 L9 **Gunung Rinjani, Taman Nasional** *nat. park Lombok* Indon.
116 B4 **Gunungsitoli** Indon.
116 F7 **Gunungsugih** *Sumatera* Indon.
116 C4 **Gunungtua** *Sumatera* Indon.
137 H3 **Gunupur** *Orissa* India
148 E4 **Günyüzü** Turkey
195 I5 **Günz** *r.* Ger.
Gunza Angola *see* **Porto Amboim**
195 I5 **Günzburg** Ger.
195 J3 **Gunzenhausen** Ger.
128 I8 **Guochengyi** *Gansu* China
131 J2 **Guo He** *r.* China
131 K2 **Guo He** *r.* China
128 I9 **Guojia** *Gansu* China
130 H3 **Guojiaba** *Hubei* China
129 O6 **Guojiatun** *Hebei* China
Guoluezhen *Henan* China *see* **Lingbao**
Guovdageaidnu Norway *see* **Kautokeino**
131 K2 **Guoyang** *Anhui* China
Guozhen *Shaanxi* China *see* **Baoji**
138 D1 **Gupis** Pak.
122 J3 **Gur** *r.* Rus. Fed.
219 O5 **Gura Caliţei** Romania
Guradu *i. S. Male* Maldives *see* **Guraidhu**
158 H7 **Gura Galbenei** Moldova
199 L5 **Gurahonţ** Romania
219 N3 **Gura Humorului** Romania
135 □[1] **Guraidhu** *i. S. Male* Maldives
138 E2 **Gurais** *Jammu and Kashmir* India
219 Q6 **Gura Portiţei** *sea chan.* Romania
229 G4 **Gurara** *r.* Nigeria
199 L6 **Gurasada** Romania
219 N6 **Gura şuţii** Romania
219 O5 **Gura Teghii** Romania
230 E4 **Gurba** *r.* Dem. Rep. Congo
129 M5 **Gurban Obo** *Nei Mongol* China
144 H1 **Gurbansoltan Eje** Turkm.
132 H4 **Gurbantünggüt Shamo** *des.* China
151 F6 **Gürbulak** Turkey
151 D5 **Gürbüzler** Turkey
138 E3 **Gurdaspur** *Punjab* India
144 I9 **Gurdim** Iran
261 I9 **Gurdon** *AR* U.S.A.
Gurdzhaani Georgia *see* **Gurjaani**
221 H3 **Güre** *Balıkesir* Turkey
221 K4 **Güre** *Uşak* Turkey
151 L5 **Gürgān** Azer.
Gurgan Iran *see* **Gorgān**
138 F5 **Gurgaon** *Haryana* India
224 E6 **Gurgei, Jebel** *mt.* Sudan
219 M4 **Gurghiu** *r.* Romania
219 M4 **Gurghiului, Munţii** *mts* Romania
278 E3 **Gurgueia** *r.* Brazil
138 C7 **Gurha** *Rajasthan* India
275 F3 **Guri, Embalse de** *resr* Venez.
280 C3 **Gurinhatã** Brazil
151 G4 **Gurjaani** Georgia
201 J6 **Gurk** Austria
201 K6 **Gurk** *r.* Austria
144 H7 **Gur Khar** Iran
201 J6 **Gurktal** *val.* Austria
201 I6 **Gurktaler Alpen** *mts* Austria
142 I7 **Gurlan** Uzbek.
Gurlen Uzbek. *see* **Gurlan**
136 E4 **Gurmatkal** *Karnataka* India
250 G7 **Gurnee** *IL* U.S.A.
172 E4 **Gurnos** *Powys, Wales* U.K.
235 G3 **Guro** Moz.
149 K4 **Gürpınar** Turkey
136 F6 **Gurramkonda** *Andhra Prad.* India
208 D3 **Gurrea de Gállego** Spain
221 K2 **Gürsu** *Bursa* Turkey
151 C4 **Gürsu** *Rize* Turkey
145 L3 **Gurşunmagdan Kärhanasy** Turkm.
169 F5 **Gurteen** *Sligo* Ireland
Gu-ru *i. S. Male* Maldives *see* **Gulhi**
Guru *i. S. Male* Maldives *see* **Gulhi**
235 H2 **Gurué** Moz.
148 H4 **Gürün** Turkey
275 I5 **Gurupá** Brazil
275 I5 **Gurupa, Ilha Grande de** *i.* Brazil
278 C4 **Gurupi** Brazil
278 D2 **Gurupi, Cabo** *c.* Brazil
278 C3 **Gurupi, Serra do** *hills* Brazil
138 D7 **Guru Sikhar** *mt. Rajasthan* India
235 F3 **Guruve** Zimbabwe
Guruwe Zimbabwe *see* **Guruve**
136 F4 **Guruzala** *Andhra Prad.* India
129 N2 **Gurvandzagal** Mongolia
128 H5 **Gurvan Sayan Uul** *mts* Mongolia
129 J4 **Gurvansayhan** Mongolia
128 G5 **Gurvantes** Mongolia
Gur'yev Kazakh. *see* **Atyrau**
160 D7 **Gur'yevsk** Rus. Fed.
Gur'yevskaya Oblast' *admin. div.* Kazakh. *see* **Atyrauskaya Oblast'**
145 K5 **Gurz** Afgh.
161 Y7 **Gus'** *r.* Rus. Fed.
229 G3 **Gusau** Nigeria
192 D4 **Gusborn** Ger.
193 E6 **Güsen** Ger.
160 F7 **Gusev** Rus. Fed.
161 X6 **Gusevskiy** Rus. Fed.
145 J3 **Guşgy** *r.* Turkm.
123 C9 **Gushan** *Liaoning* China
159 Q2 **Gushchino** Rus. Fed.
131 J2 **Gushi** *Henan* China
229 E4 **Gushiegu** Ghana
124 □[1] **Gushikami** *Okinawa* Japan
124 □D20 **Gushikawa** *Nansei-shotō* Japan
124 □[1] **Gushikawa** *Okinawa* Japan
218 H8 **Gusinje** *Plav* Montenegro
161 O7 **Gusino** Rus. Fed.
128 J1 **Gusinoozersk** Rus. Fed.
128 J1 **Gusinoye, Ozero** *l.* Rus. Fed.
139 K8 **Guskara** *W. Bengal* India
161 X6 **Gus'-Khrustal'nyy** Rus. Fed.
192 J5 **Gusow** Ger.
214 B8 **Guspini** *Sardegna* Italy
212 I4 **Gussago** Italy
201 N5 **Güssing** Austria
212 I5 **Gussola** Italy
201 L4 **Gußwerk** Austria
162 □ **Gustav Adolf Land** *reg.* Svalbard
Gustav Holm, Kap *c.* Greenland *see* **Tasiilap Karra**
271 L5 **Gustavia** *St Barthélémy* West Indies
261 F12 **Gustavo Díaz Ordaz** Mex.
269 M8 **Gustavo Díaz Ordaz** Mex.
266 C2 **Gustavo Sotelo** Mex.
165 O2 **Gustavsberg** Sweden
245 N4 **Gustavus** *AK* U.S.A.
162 □ **Gustav V Land** *reg.* Svalbard
193 E7 **Güsten** Ger.
194 B2 **Gusterath** Ger.
264 L4 **Gustine** *CA* U.S.A.
192 F3 **Güstrow** Ger.
124 □C22 **Gusukube** *Nansei-shotō* Japan
194 E5 **Gutach (Schwarzwaldbahn)** Ger.
219 L3 **Gutâiului, Munţii** *mts* Romania
133 L12 **Gutang** *Xizang* China
201 K3 **Gutau** Austria
168 □N1 **Gutcher** *Shetland, Scotland* U.K.
201 M4 **Gutenstein** Austria
193 H6 **Güterfelde** Ger.
193 E7 **Güterglück** Ger.
191 F7 **Gütersloh** Ger.
265 W9 **Guthrie** *AZ* U.S.A.
254 D7 **Guthrie** *KY* U.S.A.
261 G8 **Guthrie** *OK* U.S.A.
261 E9 **Guthrie** *TX* U.S.A.
260 H5 **Guthrie Center** *IA* U.S.A.
258 D4 **Guthriesville** *PA* U.S.A.
131 K6 **Gutian** *Fujian* China
131 L5 **Gutian** *Fujian* China
131 L5 **Gutian Shuiku** *resr* China
276 E4 **Gutiérrez** Bol.
269 N7 **Gutiérrez Gómez** Mex.
269 J5 **Gutiérrez Zamora** Mex.
Guting *Shandong* China *see* **Yutai**
194 A2 **Gutland** *reg.* Ger./Lux.
187 J9 **Gutland** *reg.* Lux.
151 H4 **Guton, Gora** *mt.* Azer./Rus. Fed.
198 F5 **Gutorfölde** Hungary
192 F3 **Gutow** Ger.
212 E2 **Guttannen** Switz.
201 K6 **Guttaring** Austria
260 J4 **Guttenberg** *IA* U.S.A.
235 F3 **Gutu** Zimbabwe
192 H3 **Gützkow** Ger.
151 B7 **Güveçli** Turkey
162 N4 **Guvertfjället** *mts* Sweden
139 M6 **Guwahati** *Assam* India
149 K5 **Guwēr** Iraq
144 E1 **Guwlumaýak** Turkm.
Guwlumaýak Turkm. *se*[e] **Guwlumaýak**
191 H8 **Guxhagen** Ger.
131 J5 **Guxian** *Jiangxi* China
275 G3 **Guyana** *country* S. Ame[rica]
Guyane Française *terr.* … *see* **French Guiana**
Guyang *Hunan* China *s*[ee] **Guzhang**
129 L6 **Guyang** *Nei Mongol* Ch[ina]
182 F3 **Guye** *r.* France
185 C6 **Guyenne** *reg.* France
105 N4 **Guy Fawkes River Nati**[onal Park] *N.S.W.* Austr.
Guyi *Guangxi* China *see* …
261 E7 **Guymon** *OK* U.S.A.
144 E7 **Güyom** Iran
Guyong *Fujian* China *s*[ee] …
245 L3 **Guyot Glacier** Can./U.S[.A.]
105 M4 **Guyra** *N.S.W.* Austr.
249 I4 **Guysborough** *N.S.* Can[.]
235 F4 **Guyu** Zimbabwe
129 N6 **Guyuan** *Hebei* China
128 J9 **Guyuan** *Ningxia* China
151 K5 **Güzdäk** Azer.
151 C6 **Güzelhisar** Turkey
221 I4 **Güzelhisar Barajı** *resr* T[urkey]
151 C6 **Güzelkent** Turkey
150 C2 **Güzeloluk** Turkey
Güzelyurt Cyprus *see* **M**…
130 G4 **Guzhang** *Hunan* China
131 K2 **Guzhen** *Anhui* China
Guzhou *Guizhou* China … **Rongjiang**
266 F2 **Guzmán** Mex.
266 F2 **Guzmán, Lago de** *l.* Me[x.]
143 L8 **G'uzor** Uzbek.
160 E7 **Gvardeysk** Rus. Fed.
Gvardeyskoye Rus. Fed. … **Elin-Yurt**
164 F2 **Gvarv** Norway
122 J5 **Gvasyugi** Rus. Fed.
159 T3 **Gvazda** Rus. Fed.
118 B6 **Gwa** Myanmar
105 L4 **Gwabegar** *N.S.W.* Austr[.]
229 G4 **Gwada** Nigeria
229 G3 **Gwadabawa** Nigeria
145 J9 **Gwadar** Pak.
145 J9 **Gwadar West Bay** Pak.
Gwador Pak. *see* **Gwada**[r]
245 O5 **Gwaii Haanas Nationa**[l Park] **Reserve** B.C. Can.
235 E3 **Gwai River** Zimbabwe
138 G4 **Gwaldam** *Uttaranchal* I[ndia]
145 M6 **Gwal Haidarzai** Pak.
138 E7 **Gwalior** *Madh. Prad.* In[dia]
138 G6 **Gwalior** *Madh. Prad.* In[dia]
235 F4 **Gwanda** Zimbabwe
230 E3 **Gwane** Dem. Rep. Con[go]
232 F2 **Gwardafuy, Gees** *c.* Son[alia]
229 G4 **Gwarzo** Nigeria
145 K7 **Gwash** Pak.
145 I9 **Gwātar Bay** Pak.
172 E4 **Gwaun-Cae-Gurwen** *N*[eath Port] *Talbot, Wales* U.K.
230 F3 **Gwawele** Dem. Rep. Co[ngo]
235 E3 **Gwayi** Zimbabwe
235 E3 **Gwayi** *r.* Zimbabwe
196 E2 **Gwda** *r.* Pol.
196 E2 **Gwda Wielka** Pol.
118 B2 **Gwedaukkon** Myanmar
169 F3 **Gweebarra Bay** Ireland
Gweedore Ireland *see* **Gaoth Dobhair**
Gwelo Zimbabwe *see* **G**[weru]
235 F3 **Gweru** Zimbabwe
234 E4 **Gweta** Botswana
246 F4 **Gwillim Lake Provincia**[l Park] B.C. Can.
250 G3 **Gwinn** *MI* U.S.A.
260 G2 **Gwinner** *ND* U.S.A.
172 B7 **Gwithian** *Cornwall, Eng*[land U.K.]
229 I4 **Gwoza** Nigeria
105 L3 **Gwydir** *r. N.S.W.* Austr.
172 D1 **Gwynedd** *admin. div. W*[ales U.K.]
172 E1 **Gwytherin** *Conwy, Wale*[s U.K.]
182 H2 **Gy** France
133 K11 **Gyablung** *Xizang* China
133 K12 **Gyaca** *Xizang* China
133 F10 **Gyaco** *Xizang* China
Gyaijêpozhanggê *Qing*[hai China] *see* **Zhidoi**
133 L11 **Gyai Qu** *r. Xizang* China
130 A2 **Gyairong** *Qinghai* China
Gyaisi *Sichuan* China *se*[e] …
199 I4 **Gyál** Hungary
221 I6 **Gyali** *i.* Greece
133 E10 **Gyamug** *Xizang* China
Gyandzha Azer. *see* **Gän**[cä]
133 H9 **Gyangnyi Caka** *salt l.* C[hina]
133 G11 **Gyangrang** *Xizang* Chi[na]
Gyangtse *Xizang* China … **Gyangzê**
133 I12 **Gyangzê** *Xizang* China
133 E11 **Gya'nyima** *Xizang* Chin[a]
138 G8 **Gyaraspur** *Madh. Prad.* …
128 E9 **Gyaring** *Qinghai* China
133 I11 **Gyaring Co** *l.* China
128 E9 **Gyaring Hu** *l. Qinghai* …
139 O5 **Gyarishing** *Arun. Prad.* …
198 G4 **Gyarmat** Hungary
220 F5 **Gyaros** Greece
220 F5 **Gyaros** *i.* Greece
Gyaurs Turkm. *see* **Gäw**…
Gydan, Khrebet *mts* Ru[s. Fed. see] **Kolymskiy, Khrebet**
152 I2 **Gydanskiy Poluostrov** *p*[en.] Rus. Fed.
236 D9 **Gydopas** *pass* S. Africa
Gyêgu *Qinghai* China *s*[ee] …
198 G5 **Gyékényes** Hungary
133 K12 **Gyêmdong** *Xizang* Chi[na]
199 H4 **Gyermely** Hungary
133 G11 **Gyêsar Co** *l. Xizang* Chi[na]
178 H7 **Gyé-sur-Seine** France
Gyêwa *Xizang* China *see* …
190 H4 **Gyhum** Ger.
130 A4 **Gyigang** *Xizang* China
133 K11 **Gyimda** *Xizang* China
133 E9 **Gyipug** *Xizang* China
133 G12 **Gyirong** *Xizang* China
133 G12 **Gyirong** *Xizang* China
130 A3 **Gyitang** *Xizang* China
Gyixong *Xizang* China *s*[ee] **Gonggar**
133 L10 **Gyiza** *Qinghai* China
Gyldenløve Fjord *inlet* G[reenland] *see* **Umiiviip Kangertiva**
164 H6 **Gyldenløveshøj** *hill* Den[mark]
169 F9 **Gyleen** Ireland
162 Q3 **Gyljen** Sweden
107 N9 **Gympie** *Qld* Austr.
118 B5 **Gyobingauk** Myanmar
127 J3 **Gyōda** Japan
199 J5 **Gyomaendrőd** Hungary
199 G4 **Gyömöre** Hungary
199 I4 **Gyömrő** Hungary
199 I4 **Gyöngyös** Hungary
198 F4 **Gyöngyös** *r.* Hungary
199 G6 **Gyöngyös** *r.* Romania
199 I4 **Gyöngyöshalász** Hunga[ry]
199 I4 **Gyöngyöspata** Hungary
199 H5 **Gyönk** Hungary
199 G4 **Győr** Hungary
198 G4 **Győr-Moson-Sopron** *co*[unty] Hungary
199 G4 **Győrság** Hungary
Győrszentmárton Hung[ary *see*] **Pannonhalma**
199 L4 **Győrtelek** Hungary
199 G4 **Győrújbarát** Hungary
199 G4 **Győrújfalu** Hungary
246 H2 **Gypsum Point** *N.W.T.* C[an.]
247 L5 **Gypsumville** *Man.* Can.
249 G1 **Gyrfalcon Islands** *Que.* [Can.]
220 D6 **Gytheio** Greece
186 I2 **Gytsjerk** Neth.
199 K5 **Gyula** Hungary
Gyulafehérvár Romania [*see*] **Alba Iulia**
199 L3 **Gyulaháza** Hungary

Gyulaj Hungary
Gyul'gerychay r. Rus. Fed.
Gyümai Qinghai China see Darlag
Gyumri Armenia
Gyungcang Xizang China
Gyurgen Bair hill Turkey
Gyzylaýak Turkm.
Gyzylbaýdak Turkm.
Gyzylbaydak Turkm. see Gyzylbaýdak
Gyzylsuw Turkm.
Gzhat' r. Rus. Fed.
Gzhatsk Rus. Fed. see Gagarin
Gżira Malta
Gzy Pol.

H

Ha Bhutan
Haabneeme Estonia
Haacht Belgium
Häädemeeste Estonia
Haag Austria
Haag am Hausruck Austria
Haag an der Amper Ger.
Haag in Oberbayern Ger.
Haakon VII Land reg. Svalbard
Haaksbergen Neth.
Haaltert Belgium
Haanhöhiy Uul mts Mongolia
Haanja Estonia
Ha'ano i. Tonga
Ha'apai Group is Tonga
Haapajärvi Fin.
Haapavesi Fin.
Haapiti Moorea Fr. Polynesia
Haapsalu Estonia
Haar Ger.
Haarbach Ger.
Haardt hills Ger.
Haardtkopf hill Ger.
Haarlem Neth.
Haarlem S. Africa
Haarstrang ridge Ger.
Haast South I. N.Z.
Haast r. South I. N.Z.
Haast Bluff N.T. Austr.
Haast Range mts South I. N.Z.
Haastrecht Neth.
Haasts Bluff Aboriginal Land res. N.T. Austr.
Ha'atafu Beach b. Tonga
Haaway Somalia
Hab r. Pak.
Habach Ger.
Habahe Xinjiang China
Habai Group is Tonga see Ha'apai Group
Habana Cuba see La Habana
Habarane Sri Lanka
Habarōn well Saudi Arabia
Habartov Czech Rep.
Ḥabarūt Oman
Habas France
Habaswein Kenya
Ḥabawnāh, Wādī watercourse Saudi Arabia
Habay Alta Can.
Habay-la-Neuve Belgium
Ḥabbān Yemen
Ḥabbānīyah, Hawr al l. Iraq
Hab Chauki Pak.
Habhab ash Shaykh, Ḥarrat lava field Saudi Arabia
Habicht mt. Austria
Habichtswald park Ger.
Habiganj Bangl.
Habikino Japan
Habirag Nei Mongol China
Habo Sweden
Haboro Japan
Habovka Slovakia
Habra W. Bengal India
Habry Czech Rep.
Habsheim France
Ḥabshīyah, Jabal mts Yemen
Hacha Col.
Hachado, Paso de pass Arg./Chile
Hachenburg Ger.
Hachibuse-yama mt. Japan
Hachijō-jima i. Japan
Hachikai Japan
Hachiman Japan
Hachiman-misaki c. Japan
Hachimori Japan
Hachimori-yama mt. Japan
Hachinohe Japan
Hachiōji Japan
Hachiryū Japan
Hacıalılı Azer.
Hacıbekir Turkey
Hacıbektaş Turkey
Hacienda de la Mesa Mex.
Hacıhalit Turkey
Hacıköy Turkey see Çekerek
Hacılar Turkey
Hacinas Spain
Hacıömer Turkey
Hacıpaşa Turkey
Hacıqabul Gölü l. Azer.
Hacıqāhrämanlı Azer.
Hacıvelioba Turkey
Hacı Zeynalabdin Azer.
Hack, Mount S.A. Austr.
Hackberry AZ U.S.A.
Hackenheim Ger.
Hackensack NJ U.S.A.
Hacker Valley WV U.S.A.
Hacketstown Ireland
Hackettstown NJ U.S.A.
Hackleton Northamptonshire, England U.K.
Hacklinge Kent, England U.K.
Hackness North Yorkshire, England U.K.
Hack Point MD U.S.A.
Haco Angola
Hacufera Moz.
Haczów Pol.
Hadadong Xinjiang China
Hadagalli Karnataka India
Hadamar Ger.
Hada Mountains Afgh.
Ḥadan, Ḥarrat lava field Saudi Arabia
Hadano Japan
Hadapu Gansu China
Ḥadārah i. Saudi Arabia
Hadârba, Râs pt Sudan
Hadat Nei Mongol China
Hadayang Nei Mongol China
Ḥadd, Ra's al pt Oman
Haddad, Ouadi watercourse Chad
Haddenham Buckinghamshire, England U.K.
Haddington East Lothian, Scotland U.K.
Haddiscoe Norfolk, England U.K.
Haddonfield NJ U.S.A.
Haddon Point Inner Islands Seychelles
Hadejia Nigeria
Hadejia watercourse Nigeria
Hadeland reg. Norway
Ḥadera Israel
Ḥadera r. Israel
Haderslev Denmark
Haderup Denmark
Hadgaon Mahar. India
Ḥādhah Saudi Arabia
Ḥādh Banī Zaynān des. Saudi Arabia
Hadhdhunmathi Atoll Maldives
Hadhramaut reg. Yemen see Ḥaḍramawt
Hādī, Jabal al mts Jordan
Hadīboh Suquṭrā Yemen
Hadilik Xinjiang China
Hadım Turkey
Hadjer Momou mt. Chad

173 N3 Hadleigh Suffolk, England U.K.
172 H2 Hadley Telford and Wrekin, England U.K.
243 H2 Hadley Bay Nunavut Can.
259 K2 Hadlyme CT U.S.A.
193 D7 Hadmersleben Ger.
179 L7 Hadol France
130 E8 Ha Đông Vietnam
148 H8 Ḥadraj, Wādī watercourse Saudi Arabia
147 I7 Ḥaḍramawt governorate Yemen
147 H8 Ḥaḍramawt reg. Yemen
147 I7 Ḥaḍramawt, Wādī watercourse Yemen
Hadranum Sicilia Italy see Adrano
201 N2 Hadres Austria
Hadria Italy see Adria
171 M3 Hadrian's Wall tourist site England U.K.
Hadrumetum Tunisia see Sousse
151 I6 Hadrut Azer.
162 M2 Hadseløy i. Norway
164 G5 Hadsten Denmark
164 G5 Hadsund Denmark
245 K2 Hadweenzic r. AK U.S.A.
159 M3 Hadyach Ukr.
161 N8 Hadzilavichy Belarus
124 □1 Haebaru Okinawa Japan
285 I3 Haedo, Cuchilla de hills Uru.
123 D9 Haeju N. Korea
123 D10 Haeju-man b. N. Korea
187 I6 Haelen Neth.
264 □B11 Hā'ena HI U.S.A.
123 E11 Haenam S. Korea
146 H3 Ḥafar al 'Atk well Saudi Arabia
146 G1 Ḥafar al Bāṭin Saudi Arabia
147 M3 Ḥaffah, Ra's pt Oman
192 J3 Haffküste park Ger.
247 J4 Hafford Sask. Can.
148 H4 Hafik Turkey
150 E7 Ḥafīrah, Qā' al salt pan Jordan
150 D7 Ḥafīrah, Wādī al watercourse Jordan
146 D2 Ḥafīrat al 'Aydā Saudi Arabia
146 H3 Hafirat Nasah Saudi Arabia
147 L4 Ḥafīt Oman
147 L3 Ḥafīt, Jabal mt. U.A.E.
145 O5 Hafizabad Pak.
139 N7 Haflong Assam India
162 □C1 Hafnarfjörður Iceland
201 L3 Hafnerbach Austria
144 C6 Haft Gel Iran
151 J7 Haftoni Azer.
144 E8 Haftvān Iran
162 □B1 Hafursfjörður b. Iceland
Haga Myanmar see Haka
225 G6 Hag Abdullah Sudan
127 I6 Hagachi-zaki pt Japan
237 M8 Haga-Haga S. Africa
201 O8 Haganj Croatia
251 N3 Hagar Ont. Can.
136 E5 Hagari r. India
225 H5 Hagar Nish Plateau Eritrea
100 □1 Hagåtña Guam
165 M5 Hagbyån r. Sweden
190 D3 Hage Ger.
187 G7 Hageland reg. Belgium
193 G6 Hagelberg hill Ger.
244 G4 Hagemeister Island AK U.S.A.
244 G4 Hagemeister Strait AK U.S.A.
191 D8 Hagen Ger.
191 E6 Hagen am Teutoburger Wald Ger.
194 E3 Hagenbach Ger.
191 H6 Hagenburg Ger.
200 H5 Hagengebirge mts Austria
190 G4 Hagen im Bremischen Ger.
192 D4 Hagenow Ger.
246 E4 Hagensborg B.C. Can.
193 K8 Hagenwerder Ger.
232 C2 Hāgere Hiywet Eth.
232 C3 Hāgere Selam Eth.
256 C11 Hagerhill KY U.S.A.
256 H9 Hagerstown MD U.S.A.
185 C8 Hagetaubin France
185 C8 Hagetmau France
165 J1 Hagfors Sweden
165 L1 Haggen l. Sweden
162 M5 Häggenås Sweden
262 H3 Haggin, Mount MT U.S.A.
162 L5 Häggsjön Sweden
162 M5 Häggsjövik Sweden
125 I12 Hagi Japan
118 G3 Ha Giang Vietnam
126 F4 Hagiwara Japan
172 G3 Hagley Herefordshire, England U.K.
172 H3 Hagley Worcestershire, England U.K.
HaGolan hills Syria see Golan
179 L5 Hagondange France
169 D7 Hag's Head Ireland
257 L5 Hague NY U.S.A.
180 H2 Hague, Cap de la c. France
179 O6 Haguenau France
239 □3a Hahaïa Njazidja Comoros
125 □2 Hahajima-rettō is Ogasawara-shotō Japan
191 J7 Hahausen Ger.
195 L2 Hahnbach Ger.
194 F2 Hähnlein Ger.
191 F10 Hahnstätten Ger.
198 F5 Hahót Hungary
233 C5 Hai Tanz.
116 C1 Hai, Ko i. Thai.
130 H8 Hai'an Guangdong China
131 M2 Hai'an Jiangsu China
Haian Shanmo mts Taiwan see T'aitung Shan
234 C6 Haib watercourse Namibia
194 G2 Haibach Bayern Ger.
195 N3 Haibach Bayern Ger.
126 C6 Haibara Nara Japan
127 H6 Haibara Shizuoka Japan
Haibowan Nei Mongol China see Wuhai
Haicheng Guangdong China see Haifeng
129 R6 Haicheng Liaoning China
Haicheng Ningxia China see Haiyuan
138 H6 Haidargarh Uttar Prad. India
195 M2 Haidenaab r. Ger.
201 J3 Haidershofen Austria
128 C9 Haiding Hu salt l. Qinghai China
195 P4 Haidmühle Ger.
118 H4 Hai Dương Vietnam
Haifa Israel see Hefa
131 J7 Haifeng Guangdong China
109 I11 Haig W.A. Austr.
191 F9 Haiger Ger.
194 F5 Haigerloch Ger.
129 O7 Hai He r. China
128 G8 Haihu Qinghai China
Haikakan country Asia see Armenia
Haikang Guangdong China see Leizhou
125 G13 Haiki Japan
130 H8 Haikou Hainan China
146 E2 Ḥā'il Saudi Arabia
146 E2 Ḥā'il prov. Saudi Arabia
146 F2 Ḥā'il, Wādī watercourse Saudi Arabia
139 N7 Hailakandi Assam India
Hailar Nei Mongol China see Hulun Buir
129 O2 Hailar He r. China
262 G5 Hailey ID U.S.A.
248 E4 Haileybury Ont. Can.
122 F6 Hailin Heilong. China
131 H8 Hailing Dao i. Guangdong China
Hailong Jilin China see Meihekou
129 P5 Hails Nei Mongol China
173 M6 Hailsham East Sussex, England U.K.
122 E5 Hailun Heilong. China
162 R4 Hailuoto Fin.
162 R4 Hailuoto i. Fin.
131 M3 Haimen Jiangsu China
195 L5 Haimhausen Ger.
124 □A22 Haimi Nansei-shotō Japan
200 C5 Haiming Austria
195 N5 Haiming Ger.

191 K10 Haina Ger.
191 G8 Haina (Kloster) Ger.
130 H9 Hainan i. China
121 I8 Hainan prov. China
118 C4 Hai-nang Myanmar
Hainan Strait China see Qiongzhou Haixia
187 F8 Hainaut prov. Belgium
178 F3 Hainaut reg. France
201 O3 Hainburg an der Donau Austria
228 C5 Haindi Liberia
245 N4 Haines AK U.S.A.
255 G11 Haines City FL U.S.A.
245 M3 Haines Junction Y.T. Can.
258 F5 Hainesport NJ U.S.A.
245 M3 Haines Road Can./U.S.A.
201 M3 Hainfeld Austria
191 J8 Hainich ridge Ger.
193 H9 Hainichen Ger.
191 K8 Hainleite ridge Ger.
118 H4 Hai Phong Vietnam
Haiphong Vietnam see Hai Phong
122 I5 Haiqing Heilong. China
128 G8 Hairag Qinghai China
179 J6 Haironville France
131 L6 Haitan Dao i. China
194 F4 Haiterbach Ger.
270 G4 Haiti country West Indies
130 G9 Haitou Hainan China
119 I8 Hai Triêu Vietnam
201 M3 Haitzendorf Austria
264 O5 Haiwee Reservoir CA U.S.A.
225 H5 Haiya Sudan
230 E2 Haiyaf l. Sudan
131 I8 Haiyan Guangdong China
128 G8 Haiyan Qinghai China
131 M3 Haiyan Zhejiang China
Haiyang Anhui China see Xiuning
129 Q8 Haiyang Shandong China
Haiyou Zhejiang China see Sanmen
128 I8 Haiyuan Ningxia China
129 P9 Haizhou Wan b. China
131 I7 Haizhu China
239 □3b Hajangoua, Récif rf Mayotte
146 D4 Ḥajar Saudi Arabia
146 D2 Hajar, Jibāl mts Saudi Arabia
228 E2 Ḥajâr, Oued el well Mali
199 K4 Hajdú-Bihar county Hungary
199 K4 Hajdúböszörmény Hungary
199 K4 Hajdúdorog Hungary
199 K4 Hajdúhadház Hungary
199 K4 Hajdúnánás Hungary
199 K4 Hajdúság reg. Hungary
199 K4 Hajdúsámson Hungary
199 K4 Hajdúszoboszló Hungary
199 K4 Hajdúszovát Hungary
147 L9 Ḥajhir mt. Suquṭrā Yemen
144 F4 Haji Abdulla, Chāh well Iran
124 P8 Hajiki-zaki pt Japan
145 L7 Haji Mahesar Pak.
139 J7 Hajipur Bihar India
147 I3 Hajir reg. Saudi Arabia
146 F8 Hājir Yemen
146 F8 Ḥajjah Yemen
146 F7 Ḥajjah governorate Yemen
144 F4 Ḥājj 'Alī Qolī, Kavīr-e salt l. Iran
144 F7 Ḥājjīābād Fārs Iran
144 F3 Ḥājjīābād Iran
144 F7 Ḥājjīābād Hormozgan Iran
144 D4 Ḥājjīābad Iran
144 F5 Ḥājjīābād-e Zarrīn Iran
199 H4 Hajmáskér Hungary
197 L3 Hajnówka Pol.
139 M6 Hajo Assam India
199 I5 Hajós Hungary
147 I8 Ḥājr, Wādī watercourse Yemen
146 E5 Ḥajrah Saudi Arabia
199 G3 Hájske Slovakia
128 F5 Haju Nei Mongol China
Hajuu-Us Mongolia see Govĭ-Ugtaal
118 A3 Haka Myanmar
264 □F14 Hakalau HI U.S.A.
151 H6 Häkäri r. Azer.
125 Q9 Hakase-yama mt. Japan
103 E11 Hakataramea South I. N.Z.
103 F10 Hakatere South I. N.Z.
Hakatere r. South I. N.Z. see Ashburton
164 H4 Hakefjord sea chan. Sweden
283 C6 Hakelhuincul, Altiplanicie de plat. Arg.
102 □ Hakepa, Mount hill Chatham Is S. Pacific Ocean
Hakha Myanmar see Haka
150 D8 Hakippa, Har hill Israel
149 K5 Hakkâri Turkey
162 P3 Hakkas Sweden
126 C7 Hakken-zan mt. Japan
124 R6 Hakkōda-san mt. Japan
127 H6 Hakkō-san hill Japan
124 T2 Hako-dake mt. Japan
124 R5 Hakodate Japan
124 R5 Hakodate-wan b. Japan
127 J5 Hakone Japan
127 J5 Hakone-tōge pass Japan
234 C4 Hakos Mountains Namibia
145 O7 Hakra Right Distributary watercourse Pak.
236 E2 Hakseen Pan salt pan S. Africa
151 C6 Haksever Turkey
127 G2 Hakuba Japan
126 E2 Hakui Japan
103 □4 Hakupu Niue
126 D6 Hakusan Japan
126 E3 Haku-san vol. Japan
126 E3 Haku-san Kokuritsu-kōen nat. park Japan
127 H4 Hakushū Japan
Hal Belgium see Halle
145 M9 Hala Pak.
150 D8 Ḥalā', Jabal al mt. Jordan
150 F2 Ḥalab Syria
150 F2 Ḥalab governorate Syria
146 G4 Halabān Saudi Arabia
149 L6 Ḥalabja Iraq
145 K2 Halaç Turkm.
Halach Turkm. see Halaç
267 N7 Halachó Mex.
103 □4 Halagigie Point Niue
122 D6 Halahai Jilin China
158 G5 Halahora de Sus Moldova
225 H4 Halaib Sudan
225 G4 Halaib Triangle terr. Egypt/Sudan
118 I7 Ha Lam Vietnam
147 M7 Ḥalānīyāt, Juzur al is Oman
147 L7 Ḥalānīyāt, Khalīj al b. Oman
198 G4 Halászi Hungary
148 H9 Ḥālat 'Ammār Saudi Arabia
219 O3 Hălăucești Romania
165 K3 Hålaveden hills Sweden
264 □E12 Hālawa HI U.S.A.
264 □E12 Hālawa, Cape HI U.S.A.
150 E4 Halba Lebanon
Halban Mongolia see Tsetserleg
193 I6 Halbe Ger.
201 M6 Halbenrain Austria
193 D7 Halberstadt Ger.
172 F6 Halberton Devon, England U.K.
195 J6 Halblech Ger.
201 O4 Halbturn Austria
114 C5 Halcon, Mount Mindoro Phil.
237 M6 Halcyon Drift S. Africa
245 Q2 Haldane r. N.W.T. Can.
164 H2 Halden Norway
193 D6 Haldensleben Ger.
195 I6 Haldenwang Ger.
139 L8 Haldi r. W. Bengal India
139 L8 Haldia W. Bengal India
139 L6 Haldibari W. Bengal India
164 F5 Hald Sø l. Denmark
138 G5 Haldwani Uttaranchal India
285 G5 Hale Arg.
106 E8 Hale watercourse N.T. Austr.
129 L6 Hale Nei Mongol China
171 M7 Hale Greater Manchester, England U.K.
251 K5 Hale MI U.S.A.
109 D9 Hale, Mount hill W.A. Austr.
264 □E13 Haleakalā National Park HI U.S.A.
151 E5 Halefoğlu Turkey

144 E8 Hāleh Iran
264 □C12 Hale'iwa HI U.S.A.
187 H7 Halen Belgium
165 K5 Halen l. Sweden
224 D5 Halénia well Chad
199 H2 Halenkov Czech Rep.
Haleparki Deresi r. Syria/Turkey see Quwayq, Nahr
173 P2 Hales Norfolk, England U.K.
172 H3 Halesowen West Midlands, England U.K.
173 O3 Halesworth Suffolk, England U.K.
258 B6 Halethorpe MD U.S.A.
171 L7 Halewood Merseyside, England U.K.
144 D7 Haleyleh Iran
255 D8 Haleyville AL U.S.A.
228 E5 Half Assini Ghana
148 H5 Halfeti Turkey
195 M6 Halfing Ger.
103 C13 Halfmoon Bay Stewart I. N.Z.
104 □3 Half Moon Bay b. S. Pacific Ocean
264 J4 Half Moon Bay CA U.S.A.
104 D4 Half Moon Lake salt flat S.A. Austr.
246 F3 Halfway r. B.C. Can.
256 H9 Halfway MD U.S.A.
244 I3 Halfway Mountain hill AK U.S.A.
186 G4 Halfweg Neth.
236 E6 Halfweg S. Africa
164 J1 Halgån r. Sweden
129 P3 Halhgol Mongolia
129 P3 Halhgol Dornod Mongolia
146 E6 Ḥalī Saudi Arabia
146 E6 Ḥalī, Wādī watercourse Saudi Arabia
149 I6 Ḥalībīyah Syria
251 P4 Haliburton Ont. Can.
248 E4 Haliburton Highlands hills Ont. Can.
199 I3 Halič Slovakia
Halicarnassus Turkey see Bodrum
161 P8 Halichy Rus. Fed.
249 I4 Halifax N.S. Can.
171 N6 Halifax West Yorkshire, England U.K.
255 I7 Halifax NC U.S.A.
258 B4 Halifax PA U.S.A.
256 G12 Halifax VA U.S.A.
107 K5 Halifax, Mount Qld Austr.
107 K5 Halifax Bay Qld Austr.
160 G1 Halikko Fin.
132 E5 Halik Shan mts Xinjiang China
151 C6 Halilçavuş Turkey
144 D7 Halīleh, Ra's-e pt Iran
151 B5 Halilkaya Turkey
115 D8 Halilulik Timor Indon.
150 E4 Ḥalīmah mt. Lebanon/Syria
104 C3 Halinor Lake salt flat S.A. Austr.
150 F2 Ḥalīsah Syria
129 K6 Haliut Nei Mongol China
147 I7 Ḥalīyā well Yemen
136 D5 Haliyal Karnataka India
244 I1 Halkett, Cape AK U.S.A.
168 J5 Halkirk Highland, Scotland U.K.
172 F1 Halkyn Flintshire, Wales U.K.
Hall atoll Gilbert Is Kiribati see Maiana
165 O4 Hall Gotland Sweden
170 H2 Hall East Renfrewshire, Scotland U.K.
258 B7 Hall MD U.S.A.
162 N5 Hälla Sweden
166 F2 Halladale r. Scotland U.K.
258 B4 Hallam PA U.S.A.
164 I4 Halland county Sweden
173 M6 Halland East Sussex, England U.K.
164 I5 Hallandsåsen hills Sweden
164 I5 Hallands Väderö i. Sweden
123 E12 Halla-san mt. S. Korea
123 E12 Halla-san National Park S. Korea
243 J3 Hall Beach Nunavut Can.
195 L5 Hallbergmoos Ger.
187 G6 Halle Antwerpen Belgium
187 F7 Halle Vlaams-Brabant Belgium
191 I7 Halle Ger.
193 E8 Halle (Saale) Ger.
191 F6 Halle (Westfalen) Ger.
165 K2 Hällefors Sweden
165 M2 Hälleforsnäs Sweden
200 H4 Hallein Austria
162 M5 Hallen Sweden
165 N1 Hållen Sweden
191 G8 Hallenberg Ger.
178 C4 Hallencourt France
193 E8 Halle-Neustadt Ger.
195 J2 Hallerndorf Ger.
195 L5 Hallertau reg. Ger.
287 L2 Hallett, Cape Antarctica
261 G11 Hallettsville TX U.S.A.
164 H3 Hälleviksstrand Sweden
286 W1 Halley research stn Antarctica
286 X2 Hallgreen, Mount Antarctica
165 O4 Hall-Hangvars naturreservat nature res. Gotland Sweden
260 D2 Halliday ND U.S.A.
247 I2 Halliday Lake N.W.T. Can.
190 G1 Halligen is Ger.
164 G1 Hallingby Norway
164 E1 Hallingdal val. Norway
164 F2 Hallingdalselva r. Norway
165 M4 Hallingeberg Sweden
200 E5 Hall in Tirol Austria
244 D3 Hall Island AK U.S.A.
290 F5 Hall Islands Micronesia
160 I3 Halliste r. Estonia
162 O4 Hällnäs Sweden
260 G1 Hallock MN U.S.A.
172 H3 Hallow Worcestershire, England U.K.
243 L3 Hall Peninsula Nunavut Can.
108 H3 Hall Point W.A. Austr.
258 B2 Halls PA U.S.A.
165 L2 Hallsberg Sweden
108 I5 Halls Creek W.A. Austr.
251 P4 Halls Lake Ont. Can.
195 J2 Hallstadt Ger.
201 I4 Hallstatt Austria
201 I4 Hallstätter See l. Austria
165 O1 Hallstavik Sweden
257 J7 Hallstead PA U.S.A.
169 I5 Halltown Ireland
187 D7 Halluin Belgium
186 I2 Hallum Neth.
162 N3 Hällvik Sweden
162 M5 Hallviken Sweden
212 E1 Hallwiler See l. Switz.
172 C6 Hallworthy Cornwall, England U.K.
123 F11 Hallyŏ Haesang National Park S. Korea
199 L5 Hălmăgel Romania
199 L5 Hălmagiu Romania
115 F3 Halmahera i. Maluku Indon.
115 F4 Halmahera, Laut sea Maluku Indon.
Halmahera Sea Maluku Indon. see Halmahera, Laut
199 L4 Halmășd Romania
219 L3 Halmeu Romania
164 I5 Halmstad Sweden
164 D1 Halnefjorden l. Norway
138 D8 Halol Gujarat India
118 H4 Ha Long Vietnam
130 F8 Ha Long, Vinh b. Vietnam
197 M3 Halowchytsy Belarus
210 E2 Haloze reg. Slovenia
164 G5 Hals Denmark
217 □ Hal Saflieni Hypogeum tourist site Malta
193 H9 Halsbrücke Ger.
191 E10 Halsenbach Ger.
Hälsingborg Sweden see Helsingborg
173 N4 Halstead Essex, England U.K.
190 I3 Halstenbek Ger.
186 F5 Halsteren Neth.
179 L5 Halstroff France
162 R5 Halsua Fin.
128 D7 Haltang He r. China
191 D7 Haltern Ger.

173 K4 Halton Buckinghamshire, England U.K.
171 L5 Halton Lancashire, England U.K.
171 L7 Halton admin. div. England U.K.
171 M5 Halton Gill North Yorkshire, England U.K.
267 N8 Haltunchén Mex.
171 M4 Haltwhistle Northumberland, England U.K.
147 K3 Ḥālūl i. Qatar
115 B9 Halura i. Indon.
138 C8 Halvad Gujarat India
144 G5 Ḥalvān Iran
165 K2 Halvarsnoren l. Sweden
191 D8 Halver Ger.
152 D2 Halvmåneøya i. Svalbard
172 E7 Halwell Devon, England U.K.
158 D4 Halych Ukr.
197 L2 Halynka Belarus
159 L3 Halytsya Ukr.
198 B2 Halže Czech Rep.
230 B2 Ham Chad
178 F4 Ham France
236 D4 Ham watercourse Namibia
168 □L2 Ham Shetland, Scotland U.K.
236 D4 Hamab Namibia
125 J12 Hamada Japan
144 C4 Hamadān Iran
144 C4 Hamadān prov. Iran
226 E3 Hamaguir Alg.
150 E3 Ḥamāh Syria
150 F3 Ḥamāh governorate Syria
124 □1 Hamahiga-jima i. Okinawa Japan
126 E7 Hamajima Japan
127 G6 Hamakita Japan
239 □3a Hamalengo hill Njazidja Comoros
150 E2 Hamam Turkey
124 S3 Hamamasu Japan
126 G6 Hamamatsu Japan
126 G6 Hamana-ko l. Japan
127 H6 Hamaoka Japan
206 H4 Hamapega hill Spain
162 □B1 Hamar Iceland
163 K6 Hamar Norway
146 H4 Ḥamar, Wādī al watercourse Saudi Arabia
147 M6 Ḥamar Nafūr i. Oman
162 M2 Hamarøy Norway
162 M2 Hamarøy i. Norway
125 L11 Hamasaka Japan
146 D8 Hamasien prov. Eritrea
225 G3 Ḥamāṭah, Jabal mt. Egypt
124 T1 Hamatonbetsu Japan
179 N5 Hambach France
136 G9 Hambantota Sri Lanka
162 □ Hambergbukta b. Svalbard
190 K3 Hamberge Ger.
190 G4 Hambergen Ger.
104 E5 Hambidge Conservation Park nature res. S.A. Austr.
173 K4 Hambleden Buckinghamshire, England U.K.
173 J6 Hamble-le-Rice Hampshire, England U.K.
171 L6 Hambleton Lancashire, England U.K.
256 F9 Hambleton WV U.S.A.
171 O5 Hambleton Hills England U.K.
194 F3 Hambrücken Ger.
190 I5 Hambühren Ger.
190 I3 Hamburg Ger.
190 I3 Hamburg land Ger.
237 L9 Hamburg S. Africa
261 J9 Hamburg AR U.S.A.
259 K2 Hamburg CT U.S.A.
260 H5 Hamburg IA U.S.A.
258 F2 Hamburg NJ U.S.A.
256 G6 Hamburg NY U.S.A.
258 D3 Hamburg PA U.S.A.
190 F3 Hamburgisches Wattenmeer, Nationalpark nat. park Ger.
164 H3 Hamburgsund Sweden
180 I4 Hambye France
146 C3 Ḥamḍ, Wādī al watercourse Saudi Arabia
146 F6 Ḥamḍah Saudi Arabia
229 F3 Hamdallay Niger
146 E6 Ḥamdānah Saudi Arabia
257 M7 Hamden CT U.S.A.
221 I3 Hamdibey Turkey
150 D1 Hamdili Turkey
190 I2 Hamdorf Ger.
163 Q6 Hämeenkangas moorland Fin.
160 I1 Hämeenkoski Etelä-Suomi Fin.
Hämeenkoski Fin. see Koski
163 Q6 Hämeenkyrö Fin.
163 R6 Hämeenlinna Fin.
HaMelaḥ, Yam salt l. Asia see Dead Sea
190 H5 Hämelhausen Ger.
109 C9 Hamelin W.A. Austr.
109 C13 Hamelin, Cape W.A. Austr.
109 C9 Hamelin Pool b. W.A. Austr.
191 H6 Hameln Ger.
232 D3 Hamero Hadad Eth.
193 D6 Hamersleben Ger.
108 D7 Hamersley W.A. Austr.
109 E11 Hamersley Lakes salt flat W.A. Austr.
108 D7 Hamersley Range mts W.A. Austr.
192 E5 Hämerten Ger.
123 F8 Hamgyŏng-sanmaek mts N. Korea
123 E9 Hamhŭng N. Korea
128 C5 Hami Xinjiang China
201 M8 Hamica Croatia
144 C6 Ḥamīd Iran
225 F4 Hamid Sudan
221 H1 Hamidiye Turkey
221 L3 Hamıdiye Turkey
106 H7 Hamilton Qld Austr.
106 E9 Hamilton S.A. Austr.
106 G7 Hamilton watercourse Qld Austr.
104 E2 Hamilton watercourse S.A. Austr.
255 □1 Hamilton Bermuda
248 E5 Hamilton Ont. Can.
Hamilton r. Nfld and Lab. Can. see Churchill
102 J4 Hamilton North I. N.Z.
168 H11 Hamilton South Lanarkshire, Scotland U.K.
244 G3 Hamilton AK U.S.A.
255 D8 Hamilton AL U.S.A.
255 E9 Hamilton GA U.S.A.
250 C9 Hamilton IL U.S.A.
262 G3 Hamilton MT U.S.A.
259 G4 Hamilton NJ U.S.A.
257 J6 Hamilton NY U.S.A.
256 A9 Hamilton OH U.S.A.
261 F10 Hamilton TX U.S.A.
104 □3 Hamilton, Mount hill S. Pacific Ocean
244 H3 Hamilton, Mount AK U.S.A.
264 K4 Hamilton, Mount CA U.S.A.
265 Q2 Hamilton, Mount NV U.S.A.
103 C12 Hamilton Burn South I. N.Z.
264 J2 Hamilton City CA U.S.A.
106 D7 Hamilton Downs N.T. Austr.
249 J2 Hamilton Inlet Nfld and Lab. Can.
257 K5 Hamilton Mountain hill NY U.S.A.
170 D5 Hamilton's Bawn Northern Ireland U.K.
249 K3 Hamilton Sound sea chan. Nfld and Lab. Can.
224 D2 Hamīm, Wādī al watercourse Libya
163 S6 Hamina Fin.
149 J8 Ḥāmir, Wādī al watercourse Saudi Arabia
138 F4 Hamirpur Hima. Prad. India
138 H7 Hamirpur Uttar Prad. India
Hamitabat Turkey see Isparta
164 C1 Hamlagrovatnet l. Norway
255 H8 Hamlet NC U.S.A.
104 G6 Hamley Bridge S.A. Austr.
258 E2 Hamlin PA U.S.A.
261 E9 Hamlin TX U.S.A.
256 C10 Hamlin WV U.S.A.
250 H5 Hamlin Lake MI U.S.A.
119 H10 Ham Luông, Sông r. mouth Vietnam

191 E7 Hamm Nordrhein-Westfalen Ger.
194 E2 Hamm Rheinland-Pfalz Ger.
191 E9 Hamm (Sieg) Ger.
190 H3 Hammah Ger.
149 K5 Ḥammām al 'Alīl Iraq
203 F5 Hammam Boughrara Alg.
211 C7 Hammamet Tunisia
227 H1 Hammamet, Golfe de g. Tunisia
211 C7 Hammam Lif Tunisia
237 M1 Hammanskraal S. Africa
149 M8 Ḥammār, Hawr al imp. l. Iraq
163 O6 Hammarland Åland Fin.
237 O5 Hammarsdale S. Africa
165 K6 Hammarsjön l. Sweden
162 N5 Hammarstrand Sweden
187 F6 Hamme Belgium
164 F5 Hammel Denmark
191 I10 Hammelburg Ger.
192 H4 Hammelspring Ger.
187 G7 Hamme-Mille Belgium
193 F10 Hammerbrücke Ger.
162 M5 Hammerdal Sweden
165 K6 Hammeren pen. Denmark
162 Q1 Hammerfest Norway
173 I2 Hammerwich Staffordshire, England U.K.
191 C7 Hamminkeln Ger.
104 G5 Hammond S.A. Austr.
254 D5 Hammond IN U.S.A.
261 J10 Hammond LA U.S.A.
262 L4 Hammond MT U.S.A.
251 J4 Hammond Bay MI U.S.A.
256 H6 Hammondsport NY U.S.A.
249 J3 Hammone, Lac l. Que. Can.
258 F5 Hammonton NJ U.S.A.
168 □N1 Hamnavoe Shetland, Scotland U.K.
168 □N2 Hamnavoe Shetland, Scotland U.K.
168 □N2 Hamnavoe Shetland, Scotland U.K.
119 G9 Ham Ninh Vietnam
187 I8 Hamoir Belgium
187 H8 Hamois Belgium
187 I6 Hamont Belgium
258 D5 Hamorton PA U.S.A.
103 E12 Hampden South I. N.Z.
257 □Q4 Hampden Highlands ME U.S.A.
256 G11 Hampden Sydney VA U.S.A.
136 E5 Hampi Karnataka India
162 P3 Håmpjåkk Sweden
179 M6 Hampont France
173 I6 Hampreston Dorset, England U.K.
173 J5 Hampshire admin. div. England U.K.
173 I5 Hampshire Downs hills England U.K.
258 B5 Hampstead MD U.S.A.
249 H4 Hampton N.B. Can.
261 I9 Hampton AR U.S.A.
260 I4 Hampton IA U.S.A.
257 □O6 Hampton NH U.S.A.
258 F3 Hampton NJ U.S.A.
255 G9 Hampton SC U.S.A.
257 I11 Hampton VA U.S.A.
259 J3 Hampton Bays NY U.S.A.
109 I12 Hampton Tableland reg. W.A. Austr.
147 M4 Hamrā Oman
230 F2 Hamra Sudan
224 A2 Ḥamrā', Al Ḥamādah al plat. Libya
146 F1 Ḥamrā, Birkat al well Saudi Arabia
Hamra, Vâdii watercourse Syria/Turkey see Ḥimār, Wādī al
147 I3 Hamrā Jūdah plat. Saudi Arabia
224 E6 Hamrat esh Sheikh Sudan
149 L6 Ḥamrīn, Jabal hills Iraq
217 □ Ħamrun Malta
262 J6 Hams Fork r. WY U.S.A.
151 A5 Hamsiköy Turkey
179 M5 Ham-sous-Varsberg France
173 N5 Hamstreet Kent, England U.K.
187 F8 Ham-sur-Heure Belgium
119 H9 Ham Tân Vietnam
138 F3 Hamta Pass Hima. Prad. India
149 K4 Hamur Turkey
127 J4 Hamura Japan
Hamwic Southampton, England U.K. see Southampton
143 N7 Hamza Uzbek.
150 A1 Hamzalar Turkey
187 H8 Han, Grotte de cave Belgium
198 G2 Haná r. Czech Rep.
264 □E13 Hāna HI U.S.A.
270 C2 Hanábana r. Cuba
234 D4 Hanahai watercourse Botswana/Namibia
146 C3 Ḥanak Saudi Arabia
151 D4 Hanak Turkey
Hanakpınar Turkey see Çınar
264 □B11 Hanalei HI U.S.A.
264 □E13 Hanamaioa, Cape HI U.S.A.
124 S7 Hanamaki Japan
264 □B12 Hanamā'ulu HI U.S.A.
127 L4 Hanamigawa Japan
236 B1 Hanam Plateau Namibia
233 B6 Hanang mt. Tanz.
Hananui hill Stewart I. N.Z. see Anglem, Mount
264 □B12 Hanapēpē HI U.S.A.
125 □3 Hanare-iwa i. Japan
191 G10 Hanau Ger.
264 □D12 Hanauma Bay HI U.S.A.
127 L2 Hanawa Japan
129 J5 Hanbogd Mongolia
Hâncești Moldova see Hîncești
Hanchang Hunan China see Pingjiang
160 I8 Hanchary Belarus
129 L9 Hancheng Shaanxi China
178 C6 Hanches France
131 I3 Hanchuan Hubei China
256 G9 Hancock MD U.S.A.
250 F2 Hancock MI U.S.A.
257 J7 Hancock NY U.S.A.
258 E5 Hancocks Bridge NJ U.S.A.
126 E6 Handa Japan
168 F6 Handa Island Scotland U.K.
129 N8 Handan Hebei China
190 I4 Handeloh Ger.
233 C6 Handeni Tanz.
190 H1 Handewitt Ger.
Handian Shanxi China see Changzhi
199 H3 Handlová Slovakia
190 J4 Handorf Ger.
190 E5 Handrup Ger.
104 □3 Handspike Point S. Pacific Ocean
127 K4 Haneda airport Japan
HaNegev des. Israel see Negev
150 D8 HaNeqarot watercourse Israel
190 H2 Hanerau-Hademarschen Ger.
Hanfeng Chongqing China see Kaixian
264 M5 Hanford CA U.S.A.
262 E3 Hanford Reach National Monument nat. park WA U.S.A.
136 D5 Hangal Karnataka India
118 C7 Hangan Myanmar
123 E10 Han-gang r. S. Korea
128 E2 Hangayn Nuruu mts Mongolia
Hangchow Zhejiang China see Hangzhou
Hangchuan Fujian China see Guangze
193 I6 Hangelsberg Ger.
Hanggin Houqi Nei Mongol China see Xamba
Hanggin Qi Nei Mongol China see Xin
Hangö Fin. see Hanko
160 G2 Hangö östra fjärd b. Fin.
160 F2 Hangö västra fjärd b. Fin.
129 O7 Hangu Tianjin China
145 N5 Hangu Pak.
128 E8 Hangya Qinghai China
131 M3 Hangzhou Zhejiang China
131 M3 Hangzhou Wan b. China
172 G5 Hanham South Gloucestershire, England U.K.
149 J4 Hani Turkey
147 I2 Ḥanīdh Saudi Arabia

221 J2 Hanife r. Turkey
199 K3 Haniska Slovakia
Hanji Gansu China see Linxia
Hanjia Chongqing China see Pengshui
131 K7 Han Jiang r. China
128 I8 Hanjiaoshui Ningxia China
122 D2 Hanjiayuanzi Heilong. China
145 I8 Hanjīrak Iran
162 S5 Hankasalmi Fin.
190 K5 Hankensbüttel Ger.
237 I9 Hankey S. Africa
163 Q7 Hanko Fin.
221 L3 Hanköy Turkey
265 V3 Hanksville UT U.S.A.
138 G3 Hanle Jammu and Kashmir India
247 J5 Hanley Sask. Can.
172 H3 Hanley Castle Worcestershire, England U.K.
103 G9 Hanmer Forest Park nature res. South I. N.Z.
103 G9 Hanmer Springs South I. N.Z.
107 J3 Hann r. Qld Austr.
108 I4 Hann r. W.A. Austr.
108 H3 Hann, Mount hill W.A. Austr.
247 I5 Hanna Alta Can.
197 L4 Hanna Pol.
265 W8 Hannagan Meadow AZ U.S.A.
248 D3 Hannah Bay Ont. Can.
260 J6 Hannibal MO U.S.A.
256 I5 Hannibal NY U.S.A.
256 E9 Hannibal OH U.S.A.
225 G5 Hannik well Sudan
159 M5 Hannivka Ukr.
127 J4 Hannō Japan
179 K5 Hannonville-sous-les-Côtes France
191 I6 Hannover Ger.
191 I8 Hannoversch Münden Ger.
106 D7 Hann Range mts N.T. Austr.
187 H7 Hannut Belgium
165 K5 Hanö i. Sweden
165 K6 Hanöbukten b. Sweden
118 G4 Ha Nôi Vietnam
Hanoi Vietnam see Ha Nôi
126 A8 Hanoura Japan
248 D4 Hanover Ont. Can.
Hanover Ger. see Hannover
270 □ Hanover parish Jamaica
236 I7 Hanover S. Africa
259 K1 Hanover CT U.S.A.
257 M5 Hanover NH U.S.A.
256 C8 Hanover OH U.S.A.
258 B5 Hanover PA U.S.A.
256 H11 Hanover VA U.S.A.
283 B8 Hanover, Isla i. Chile
258 B4 Hanoverdale PA U.S.A.
236 I6 Hanover Road S. Africa
255 □2 Hanover Sound sea chan. New Prov. Bahamas
198 G4 Hanság hill Hungary
198 G4 Hansagi park Hungary
187 E6 Hansbeke Belgium
287 D2 Hansen Mountains Antarctica
192 D3 Hanshagen Ger.
131 H4 Hanshou Hunan China
131 J3 Han Shui r. China
138 F5 Hansi Haryana India
173 K3 Hanslope Milton Keynes, England U.K.
162 O2 Hansnes Norway
106 D6 Hanson watercourse N.T. Austr.
104 F4 Hanson, Lake salt flat S.A. Austr.
102 □ Hanson Bay Chatham Is S. Pacific Ocean
256 C12 Hansonville VA U.S.A.
190 J4 Hanstedt Niedersachsen Ger.
190 J4 Hanstedt Niedersachsen Ger.
164 E4 Hanstholm Denmark
129 P4 Han Sum Nei Mongol China
179 L6 Han-sur-Nied France
Hantengri Feng mt. Kazakh./Kyrg. see Khan-Tengri, Pik
199 H5 Hantos Hungary
160 J9 Hantsavichy Belarus
138 I7 Hanumana Madh. Prad. India
138 E5 Hanumangarh Rajasthan India
147 L7 Hanūn well Oman
199 K2 Hanušovce nad Topľou Slovakia
198 F1 Hanušovice Czech Rep.
128 H2 Hanuy Gol r. Mongolia
180 C5 Hanvec France
105 K6 Hanwood N.S.W. Austr.
172 G2 Hanwood Shropshire, England U.K.
128 E7 Hanxia Gansu China
Hanyang Hubei China see Caidian
130 G2 Hanyin Shaanxi China
127 K3 Hanyū Japan
Hanyuan Gansu China see Xihe
130 D4 Hanyuan Sichuan China
144 I9 Hanzaram Iran
130 F2 Hanzhong Shaanxi China
101 □9 Hao atoll Arch. des Tuamotu Fr. Polynesia
Haomen Qinghai China see Menyuan
139 L8 Haora W. Bengal India
227 G2 Haoud el Hamra Alg.
207 I9 Haouz, Jebel el hill Morocco
226 C4 Haouza Western Sahara
162 R4 Haparanda Sweden
162 Q4 Haparanda skärgård nationalpark nat. park Sweden
187 H6 Hapert Neth.
139 N6 Hapoli Arun. Prad. India
195 K3 Happburg Ger.
173 P2 Happisburgh Norfolk, England U.K.
106 F6 Happy Creek watercourse N.T. Austr.
265 U7 Happy Jack AZ U.S.A.
249 I2 Happy Valley-Goose Bay Nfld and Lab. Can.
186 I5 Haps Neth.
123 F8 Hapsu N. Korea
138 F5 Hapur Uttar Prad. India
148 G9 Ḥaql Saudi Arabia
147 J4 Ḥaqshah well Saudi Arabia
225 I5 Ḥaqw Saudi Arabia
127 H4 Hara Japan
147 I3 Ḥaraḍ well Saudi Arabia
146 F7 Ḥaraḍ Yemen
150 D9 Ḥarad, Jabal al mt. Jordan
147 I3 Ḥaraḍh Saudi Arabia
160 J7 Haradok Minskaya Voblasts' Belarus
160 M6 Haradok Vitsyebskaya Voblasts' Belarus
160 M6 Haradotskaye Wzvyshsha hills Belarus
162 P3 Harads Sweden
160 J8 Haradzishcha Brestskaya Voblasts' Belarus
160 M8 Haradzishcha Mahilyowskaya Voblasts' Belarus
197 M3 Haradzyets Belarus
160 J8 Haradzyeya Belarus
139 I6 Haraiya Uttar Prad. India
146 F7 Ḥarajā Saudi Arabia
124 R9 Haramachi Japan
132 H3 Haramgai Xinjiang China
138 E2 Haramukh mt. Jammu and Kashmir India
Haran Turkey see Harran
136 E6 Haranhalli Karnataka India
160 M6 Harany Belarus
145 O6 Harappa Road Pak.
235 F3 Harare Zimbabwe
237 J5 Ha-Rasebei S. Africa
147 L6 Ḥarāsīs, Jiddat al des. Oman
197 K5 Harasiuki Pol.
225 H5 Harat i. Eritrea
144 F6 Harāt Iran
147 K6 Haraym well Saudi Arabia
129 K4 Har-Ayrag Mongolia
224 C6 Haraz-Djombo Chad
230 D2 Haraze-Mangueigne Chad
160 M6 Harbacheva Belarus
191 I7 Harbarnsen Ger.
228 C5 Harbel Liberia
122 E6 Harbin Heilong. China

193 D6 **Harbke** Ger.
193 D6 **Harbke-Allertal** *park* Ger.
173 O5 **Harbledown** *Kent, England* U.K.
145 L7 **Harboi Hills** Pak.
178 E4 **Harbonnières** France
251 L6 **Harbor Beach** *MI* U.S.A.
250 J4 **Harbor Springs** *MI* U.S.A.
168 D6 **Harbost** *Western Isles, Scotland* U.K.
249 K4 **Harbour Breton** *Nfld and Lab.* Can.
195 J4 **Harburg (Schwaben)** Ger.
173 J3 **Harbury** *Warwickshire, England* U.K.
108 G7 **Harbutt Range** *hills W.A.* Austr.
138 H8 **Harchoka** *Chhattisgarh* India
265 S8 **Harcuvar Mountains** *AZ* U.S.A.
200 A5 **Hard** Austria
138 F8 **Harda** *Madh. Prad.* India
147 I7 **Ḩarḑah, Wādī** *r.* Yemen
164 C1 **Hardanger** *reg.* Norway
164 B2 **Hardangerfjorden** *sea chan.* Norway
164 D1 **Hardangervidda Nasjonalpark** *nat. park* Norway
144 D5 **Hardank** Iran
234 C5 **Hardap** *admin. reg.* Namibia
234 C5 **Hardap Dam** Namibia
163 H6 **Hardbakke** Norway
255 G9 **Hardeeville** *SC* U.S.A.
201 M2 **Hardegg** Austria
191 I7 **Hardegsen** Ger.
178 C2 **Hardelot-Plage** France
117 K2 **Harden, Bukit** *mt.* Indon.
186 K3 **Hardenberg** Neth.
186 I4 **Harderwijk** Neth.
236 C7 **Hardeveld** *mts* S. Africa
109 D7 **Hardey** *r. W.A.* Austr.
194 G2 **Hardheim** Ger.
260 J6 **Hardin** *IL* U.S.A.
262 K4 **Hardin** *MT* U.S.A.
108 D6 **Harding** *r. W.A.* Austr.
237 N6 **Harding** S. Africa
245 J3 **Harding Ice Field** *AK* U.S.A.
258 F6 **Harding Lakes** *NJ* U.S.A.
108 H4 **Harding Range** *hills W.A.* Austr.
109 D9 **Harding Range** *hills W.A.* Austr.
173 K3 **Hardingstone** *Northamptonshire, England* U.K.
186 G5 **Hardinxveld-Giessendam** Neth.
247 I4 **Hardisty** *Alta* Can.
246 G1 **Hardisty Lake** *N.W.T.* Can.
138 H6 **Hardoi** *Uttar Prad.* India
194 E5 **Hardt** Ger.
Hardwar *Uttaranchal* India *see* **Haridwar**
255 F9 **Hardwick** *GA* U.S.A.
257 M4 **Hardwick** *VT* U.S.A.
104 F6 **Hardwicke Bay** *S.A.* Austr.
258 E2 **Hardwood Ridge** *PA* U.S.A.
261 J7 **Hardy** *AR* U.S.A.
Hardy, Mount *North I.* N.Z. *see* **Rangipoua**
283 C9 **Hardy, Península** *pen.* Chile
249 K3 **Hare Bay** *Nfld and Lab.* Can.
173 L4 **Harefield** *Greater London, England* U.K.
164 I2 **Harefjorden** *l.* Sweden
171 J2 **Hare Hill** *Scotland* U.K.
162 I5 **Hareid** Norway
245 O2 **Hare Indian** *r. N.W.T.* Can.
187 D7 **Harelbeke** Belgium
186 K2 **Haren** Neth.
190 D5 **Haren (Ems)** Ger.
Hareøen *i.* Greenland *see* **Qeqertarsuatsiaq**
232 D2 **Hārer** Eth.
232 D2 **Hārer Wildlife Sanctuary** *nature res.* Eth.
173 M4 **Hare Street** *Hertfordshire, England* U.K.
232 C2 **Hareto** Eth.
171 N6 **Harewood** *West Yorkshire, England* U.K.
150 D5 **Harf el Mreffi** *mt.* Lebanon
181 L2 **Harfleur** France
258 C5 **Harford County** *county MD* U.S.A.
129 P2 **Hargant** *Nei Mongol* China
Hargeisa Somalia *see* **Hargeysa**
232 D3 **Hargele** Eth.
194 D2 **Hargesheim** Ger.
232 E2 **Hargeysa** Somalia
219 N4 **Harghita, Munţii** *mts* Romania
219 N4 **Harghita-Mădăraş, Vârful** *mt.* Romania
225 H6 **Hargigo** Eritrea
187 H8 **Hargimont** Belgium
179 I3 **Hargnies** France
149 J4 **Harhal Dağları** *mts* Turkey
129 J7 **Harhatan** *Nei Mongol* China
128 H3 **Harhorin** Mongolia
128 E7 **Har Hu** *l. Qinghai* China
238 □3c **Haría** *Lanzarote* Canary Is
146 G8 **Harīb** Yemen
226 D5 **Ḩaricha, Ḩamâda El** *des.* Mali
138 G5 **Haridwar** *Uttaranchal* India
150 C8 **Ḩarif, Har** *mt.* Israel
136 D5 **Harihar** *Karnataka* India
103 E10 **Harihari** *South I.* N.Z.
136 D6 **Hariharpur** *Karnataka* India
138 C8 **Harij** *Gujarat* India
160 F2 **Hari kurk** *sea chan.* Estonia
150 E2 **Ḩārim** Syria
126 A6 **Harima** Japan
126 A6 **Harima-nada** *b.* Japan
139 L9 **Haringhat** *r.* Bangl.
186 F5 **Haringvliet** *est.* Neth.
162 S5 **Harinkaa** Fin.
126 G2 **Harinoki-dake** *mt.* Japan
136 E8 **Haripad** *Kerala* India
145 O5 **Haripur** Pak.
150 E6 **Ḩarīr, Wādī adh** *r.* Syria
145 I3 **Harī Rūd** *r.* Afgh./Iran
146 F6 **Ḩarjab, Wādī** *watercourse* Saudi Arabia
163 M6 **Härjåsjön** Sweden
163 Q6 **Harjavalta** Fin.
163 L5 **Härjedalen** *reg.* Sweden
162 Q4 **Harjufjärden** *b.* Sweden
198 F4 **Harka** Hungary
199 I5 **Harkakötöny** Hungary
162 M5 **Hårkan** *r.* Sweden
199 H6 **Harkány** Hungary
260 H5 **Harlan** *IA* U.S.A.
256 B12 **Harlan** *KY* U.S.A.
260 F5 **Harlan County Lake** *NE* U.S.A.
219 O3 **Hârlău** Romania
172 D2 **Harlech** *Gwynedd, Wales* U.K.
262 J2 **Harlem** *MT* U.S.A.
173 O3 **Harleston** *Norfolk, England* U.K.
258 E4 **Harleysville** *PA* U.S.A.
186 H2 **Harlingen** Neth.
261 G12 **Harlingen** *TX* U.S.A.
190 E3 **Harlinger Land** *reg.* Ger.
173 L4 **Harlington** *Bedfordshire, England* U.K.
173 M4 **Harlow** *Essex, England* U.K.
262 J3 **Harlowton** *MT* U.S.A.
178 F4 **Harly** France
256 F10 **Harman** *WV* U.S.A.
221 K3 **Harmancık** Turkey
221 K5 **Harmanlı** Turkey
201 N3 **Harmannsdorf** Austria
258 B6 **Harmans** *MD* U.S.A.
186 G4 **Harmelen** Neth.
225 I5 **Harmil** *i.* Eritrea
257 □P4 **Harmony** *ME* U.S.A.
250 B6 **Harmony** *MN* U.S.A.
258 E3 **Harmony** *NJ* U.S.A.
190 K2 **Harmsdorf** *Schleswig-Holstein* Ger.
190 K3 **Harmsdorf** *Schleswig-Holstein* Ger.
136 C4 **Harnai** *Mahar.* India
145 L6 **Harnai** Pak.
178 E3 **Harnes** France
262 E5 **Harney Basin** *OR* U.S.A.
262 E5 **Harney Lake** *OR* U.S.A.
162 N5 **Härnösand** Sweden
129 O2 **Har Nuden** *Nei Mongol* China
128 C2 **Har Nuur** *l.* Mongolia
128 E2 **Har Nuur** *l.* Mongolia
205 O3 **Haro** Spain
158 I1 **Harochychy** Belarus
256 C11 **Harold** *KY* U.S.A.
168 □O1 **Haroldswick** *Shetland, Scotland* U.K.
179 L7 **Haroué** France
136 D5 **Harpanahalli** *Karnataka* India
173 L4 **Harpenden** *Hertfordshire, England* U.K.
228 D5 **Harper** Liberia
261 F7 **Harper** *KS* U.S.A.
245 M2 **Harper, Mount** *Y.T.* Can.
245 L2 **Harper, Mount** *AK* U.S.A.
245 J2 **Harper Bend** *reg. AK* U.S.A.
246 H3 **Harper Creek** *r. Alta* Can.
264 O6 **Harper Lake** *CA* U.S.A.
256 H9 **Harpers Ferry** *WV* U.S.A.
249 I2 **Harp Lake** *Nfld and Lab.* Can.
173 K3 **Harpole** *Northamptonshire, England* U.K.
190 G5 **Harpstedt** Ger.
Harqin Qi *Nei Mongol* China *see* **Jinshan**
Harqin Zuoqi Mongolzu Zizhixian *Liaoning* China *see* **Dachengzi**
265 S8 **Harquahala Mountains** *AZ* U.S.A.
138 G8 **Harrai** *Madh. Prad.* India
150 H2 **Harran** Turkey
145 N7 **Harrand** Pak.
146 E4 **Ḩarrāt Kishb** *lava field* Saudi Arabia
168 J4 **Harray, Loch of** *l. Scotland* U.K.
248 E3 **Harricana, Rivière d'** *r. Ont./Que.* Can.
168 I10 **Harrietfield** *Perth and Kinross, Scotland* U.K.
173 N5 **Harrietsham** *Kent, England* U.K.
259 G2 **Harriman** *NY* U.S.A.
257 M6 **Harriman Reservoir** *VT* U.S.A.
105 N4 **Harrington** *N.S.W.* Austr.
258 D7 **Harrington** *DE* U.S.A.
257 □R4 **Harrington** *ME* U.S.A.
249 J3 **Harrington Harbour** *Que.* Can.
255 □1 **Harrington Sound** *inlet* Bermuda
168 C7 **Harris** *reg. Scotland* U.K.
104 E4 **Harris, Lake** *salt flat S.A.* Austr.
106 B8 **Harris, Mount** *N.T.* Austr.
168 B7 **Harris, Sound of** *sea chan. Scotland* U.K.
237 K3 **Harrisburg** S. Africa
261 J8 **Harrisburg** *AR* U.S.A.
261 K7 **Harrisburg** *IL* U.S.A.
260 D5 **Harrisburg** *NE* U.S.A.
256 B9 **Harrisburg** *OH* U.S.A.
251 R9 **Harrisburg** *PA* U.S.A.
190 H1 **Harrislee** Ger.
109 D12 **Harrismith** *W.A.* Austr.
237 N4 **Harrismith** S. Africa
103 C11 **Harris Mountains** *South I.* N.Z.
261 I7 **Harrison** *AR* U.S.A.
250 J5 **Harrison** *MI* U.S.A.
260 D4 **Harrison** *NE* U.S.A.
259 H3 **Harrison** *NY* U.S.A.
249 J2 **Harrison, Cape** *Nfld and Lab.* Can.
245 J1 **Harrison Bay** *AK* U.S.A.
261 J10 **Harrisonburg** *LA* U.S.A.
256 G10 **Harrisonburg** *VA* U.S.A.
246 F5 **Harrison Lake** *B.C.* Can.
258 B6 **Harrisonville** *MD* U.S.A.
260 H6 **Harrisonville** *MO* U.S.A.
251 N6 **Harriston** *Ont.* Can.
251 K5 **Harrisville** *MI* U.S.A.
257 J4 **Harrisville** *NY* U.S.A.
256 D9 **Harrisville** *WV* U.S.A.
Harrodsville *North I.* N.Z. *see* **Otorohanga**
171 N6 **Harrogate** *North Yorkshire, England* U.K.
256 B12 **Harrogate** *TN* U.S.A.
251 R5 **Harrowsmith** *Ont.* Can.
260 I6 **Harry S. Truman Reservoir** *MO* U.S.A.
163 M6 **Harsa** Sweden
128 E9 **Har Sai Shan** *mt. Qinghai* China
199 J4 **Harsány** Hungary
190 I4 **Harsefeld** Ger.
219 M6 **Hârseşti** Romania
191 F7 **Harsewinkel** Ger.
144 B4 **Harsīn** Iran
148 I3 **Harşit** *r.* Turkey
193 D7 **Harsleben** Ger.
219 P6 **Hârşova** Romania
162 O3 **Harsprånget** Sweden
162 N2 **Harstad** Norway
173 M3 **Harston** *Cambridgeshire, England* U.K.
138 F8 **Harsud** *Madh. Prad.* India
191 I6 **Harsum** Ger.
162 K4 **Harsvik** Norway
245 M2 **Hart** *r. Y.T.* Can.
250 H6 **Hart** *MI* U.S.A.
104 F4 **Hart, Lake** *salt flat S.A.* Austr.
108 H4 **Hart, Mount** *hill W.A.* Austr.
199 I5 **Harta** Hungary
129 R5 **Hartao** *Liaoning* China
236 E4 **Hartbees** *watercourse* S. Africa
237 K2 **Hartbeesfontein** S. Africa
237 L1 **Hartbeespoort** S. Africa
201 M5 **Hartberg** Austria
164 D1 **Harteigan** *mt.* Norway
190 J3 **Hartenholm** Ger.
178 F5 **Hartennes-et-Taux** France
193 G9 **Hartenstein** Ger.
171 L5 **Harter Fell** *hill England* U.K.
173 M5 **Hartfield** *East Sussex, England* U.K.
228 C5 **Hartford** Liberia
257 M7 **Hartford** *CT* U.S.A.
254 D7 **Hartford** *KY* U.S.A.
250 H7 **Hartford** *MI* U.S.A.
260 G4 **Hartford** *SD* U.S.A.
250 F6 **Hartford** *WI* U.S.A.
254 E5 **Hartford City** *IN* U.S.A.
193 G8 **Hartha** Ger.
194 E3 **Harthausen** Ger.
194 D6 **Hartheim** Ger.
171 J2 **Harthill** *North Lanarkshire, Scotland* U.K.
219 M5 **Hârtibaciu** *r.* Romania
200 E5 **Hart im Zillertal** Austria
260 G4 **Hartington** *NE* U.S.A.
201 I3 **Hartkirchen** Austria
249 H4 **Hartland** *N.B.* Can.
172 D6 **Hartland** *Devon, England* U.K.
257 □P4 **Hartland** *ME* U.S.A.
172 C5 **Hartland Point** *England* U.K.
172 H3 **Hartlebury** *Worcestershire, England* U.K.
171 O4 **Hartlepool** *Hartlepool, England* U.K.
171 O4 **Hartlepool** *admin. div. England* U.K.
258 A3 **Hartleton** *PA* U.S.A.
173 M5 **Hartley** *Kent, England* U.K.
261 D8 **Hartley** *TX* U.S.A.
Hartley Zimbabwe *see* **Chegutu**
246 D4 **Hartley Bay** *B.C.* Can.
173 K5 **Hartley Wintney** *Hampshire, England* U.K.
258 D6 **Hartly** *DE* U.S.A.
195 O3 **Hartmanice** Czech Rep.
193 E9 **Hartmannsdorf** Ger.
258 C6 **Hart Miller Island** *MD* U.S.A.
262 E5 **Hart Mountain National Wildlife Refuge** *nature res. OR* U.S.A.
163 S6 **Hartola** Fin.
236 I4 **Harts** *r.* S. Africa
259 H2 **Hartsdale** *NY* U.S.A.
234 C4 **Hartseer** Namibia
255 D8 **Hartselle** *AL* U.S.A.
195 I4 **Härtsfeld** *hills* Ger.
173 I2 **Hartshill** *Warwickshire, England* U.K.
173 I2 **Hartshorne** *Derbyshire, England* U.K.
261 H8 **Hartshorne** *OK* U.S.A.
165 N3 **Hartsö naturreservat** *nature res.* Sweden
106 E7 **Harts Range** *N.T.* Austr.
106 E7 **Harts Range** *mts N.T.* Austr.
255 G8 **Hartsville** *SC* U.S.A.
255 D7 **Hartsville** *TN* U.S.A.
237 I3 **Hartswater** S. Africa
261 I7 **Hartville** *MO* U.S.A.
256 D8 **Hartville** *OH* U.S.A.
173 K3 **Hartwell** *Northamptonshire, England* U.K.
255 F8 **Hartwell** *GA* U.S.A.
255 F8 **Hartwell Reservoir** *GA/SC* U.S.A.
105 K10 **Hartz Mountains National Park** *Tas.* Austr.
126 D3 **Harue** Japan
115 F5 **Haruku** *i. Maluku* Indon.
127 I3 **Haruna** Japan
127 G5 **Haruno** Japan
136 F6 **Harur** *Tamil Nadu* India
147 H2 **Ḩarūrī, 'Irq al** *des.* Saudi Arabia
128 C3 **Har Us Nuur** *l.* Mongolia
128 C2 **Har Us Nuur** *salt l.* Mongolia
145 I6 **Harut** *watercourse* Afgh.
147 K7 **Harūt** Yemen
145 I6 **Harut Rud** Afgh.
128 I2 **Haruuhin Gol** *r.* Mongolia
144 G6 **Harūz-e Bālā** Iran
250 F7 **Harvard** *IL* U.S.A.
263 K7 **Harvard, Mount** *CO* U.S.A.
109 C12 **Harvey** *W.A.* Austr.
249 H4 **Harvey** *N.B.* Can.
250 G3 **Harvey** *MI* U.S.A.
260 E2 **Harvey** *ND* U.S.A.
258 C2 **Harveys Lake** *PA* U.S.A.
258 C2 **Harveys Lake** *l. PA* U.S.A.
173 I3 **Harvington** *Worcestershire, England* U.K.
173 J4 **Harwell** *Oxfordshire, England* U.K.
173 O4 **Harwich** *Essex, England* U.K.
257 O7 **Harwich Port** *MA* U.S.A.
259 I1 **Harwington** *CT* U.S.A.
105 N3 **Harwood** *N.S.W.* Austr.
171 O7 **Harworth** *Nottinghamshire, England* U.K.
138 F5 **Haryana** *state* India
158 G1 **Haryn'** *r.* Belarus
Haryn' *r.* Ukr. *see* **Horyn'**
191 J7 **Harz** *hills* Ger.
191 K7 **Harz** *nat. park* Ger.
193 D7 **Harz** *park* Ger.
193 D7 **Harzgerode** Ger.
150 D8 **Har Ẕin** Israel
150 D8 **Ḩaşāh, Wādī al** *watercourse* Jordan
150 F8 **Ḩaşāh, Wādī al** *watercourse* Jordan/Saudi Arabia
133 C8 **Hasalbag** *Xinjiang* China
144 E5 **Ḩasanābād** Iran
150 B8 **Ḩasanah, Wādī** *watercourse* Egypt
151 B5 **Hasan Dağı** *mt.* Turkey
148 G4 **Hasan Dağı** *mts* Turkey
Hasan Guli Turkm. *see* **Esenguly**
149 J5 **Hasankeyf** Turkey
145 J5 **Hasan Kūleh** Afgh.
144 G8 **Ḩasan Langī** Iran
136 F3 **Hasanparti** *Andhra Prad.* India
221 K5 **Hasanpaşa** Turkey
144 B3 **Ḩasan Sālārān** Iran
136 E7 **Hasanur** *Tamil Nadu* India
144 G2 **Hasardag** *mt.* Turkm.
151 B6 **Hasbağlar** Turkey
150 D5 **Hasbaïya** Lebanon
148 G7 **Hasbani** *r.* Lebanon
148 G4 **Hasbek** Turkey
191 E6 **Hasbergen** Ger.
168 □O1 **Hascosay** *i. Scotland* U.K.
138 I9 **Hasdo** *r. Madh. Prad.* India
191 D5 **Hase** *r.* Ger.
127 H4 **Hase** Japan
190 I3 **Haseldorf** Ger.
190 D5 **Haselünne** Ger.
285 H2 **Hasenkamp** Arg.
191 J9 **Hasenkopf** *hill* Ger.
212 C1 **Hasenmatt** *mt.* Switz.
128 H3 **Hashaat** *Arhangay* Mongolia
Hashaat Mongolia *see* **Delgerhangay**
150 C6 **HaSharon** *plain* Israel
126 E5 **Hashima** Japan
126 C7 **Hashimoto** Japan
147 N5 **Ḩashīsh, Ghubbat** *b.* Oman
144 D4 **Hashtgerd** Iran
144 C3 **Hashtpar** *Gīlān* Iran
Hashtpar *Gīlān* Iran *see* **Tālesh**
144 B3 **Hashtrud** Iran
144 G5 **Hasht Tekkeh, Gowd-e** *waterhole* Iran
Hasić Bos.-Herz. *see* **Srnice**
147 L7 **Ḩāsik** Oman
145 O7 **Hasilpur** Pak.
261 F9 **Haskell** *TX* U.S.A.
151 D4 **Hasköy** Turkey
201 J2 **Haslach an der Mühl** Austria
194 E5 **Haslach im Kinzigtal** Ger.
171 O7 **Hasland** *Derbyshire, England* U.K.
165 K6 **Hasle** *Bornholm* Denmark
212 D1 **Hasle** Switz.
173 K5 **Haslemere** *Surrey, England* U.K.
164 H6 **Haslev** Denmark
171 M6 **Haslingden** *Lancashire, England* U.K.
190 I3 **Hasloh** Ger.
199 L5 **Hăşmaş** Romania
219 N4 **Hăşmaşul Mare** *mt.* Romania
185 B9 **Hasparren** France
159 N9 **Haspra** Ukr.
151 I6 **Ḩasratān** Iran
151 D6 **Hasretpınar** Turkey
150 F2 **Ḩaşş, Jabal al** *hills* Syria
150 E2 **Hassa** Turkey
136 E6 **Hassan** *Karnataka* India
265 T8 **Hassayampa** *watercourse AZ* U.S.A.
191 J10 **Haßberge** *hills* Ger.
191 K10 **Haßberge** *park* Ger.
190 H5 **Haßbergen** Ger.
226 C6 **Ḩâsseï Mbârek** *well* Maur.
190 H5 **Hassel (Weser)** Ger.
104 □3 **Hasselborough Bay** S. Pacific Ocean
191 K7 **Hasselfelde** Ger.
165 M4 **Hasselö** *i.* Sweden
187 H7 **Hasselt** Belgium
186 J3 **Hasselt** Neth.
191 K10 **Haßfurt** Ger.
226 B4 **Hassi Aridal** *well* Western Sahara
227 H4 **Hassi Bedjedjene** *well* Alg.
227 G3 **Hassi Bel Guebbour** Alg.
226 E4 **Hassi Bou Bernous** *well* Alg.
227 H4 **Hassi Bourahla** *well* Alg.
227 F3 **Hassi Chebbaba** *well* Alg.
227 F2 **Hassi Dalaa** Alg.
226 B5 **Hassi Doumas** *well* Western Sahara
227 F3 **Hassi el Ahmar** *well* Alg.
227 G3 **Hassi el Hadjar** Alg.
227 F4 **Hassi el Krenig** *well* Alg.
227 F3 **Hassi Fahl** *well* Alg.
228 D2 **Ḩâssi Fouini** *well* Maur.
227 G4 **Hassi Habadra** *well* Alg.
224 A2 **Hassi Ifertas** *well* Libya
227 H4 **Hassi I-n-Akeouet** *well* Alg.
227 F4 **Hassi I-n-Belrem** *well* Alg.
227 F3 **Hassi Inifel** Alg.
227 H4 **Hassi Issendjell** *well* Alg.
228 E2 **Hâssi Karkabane** *well* Mali
227 F3 **Hassi Khanem** *well* Alg.
226 E3 **Hassi Mdakene** *well* Alg.
227 G3 **Hassi Messaoud** Alg.
227 G3 **Hassi Msegguem** *well* Alg.
227 F3 **Hassi Nebka** *well* Alg.
227 G4 **Hassi Ntsel** *well* Alg.
228 B2 **Hâssi Sallâhi** *well* Maur.
227 G3 **Hassi Sebbakh** *well* Alg.
227 G4 **Hassi Tabelbalet** *well* Alg.
227 F4 **Hassi Tiguentourine** *well* Alg.
227 H3 **Hassi Ti-n Fouchaye** *well* Alg.
228 D2 **Hâssi Touîl** *well* Maur.
192 I4 **Haßleben** *Brandenburg* Ger.
193 D8 **Haßleben** *Thüringen* Ger.
165 J5 **Hässleholm** Sweden
194 E3 **Haßloch** Ger.
194 G3 **Haßmersheim** Ger.
165 N1 **Hästbo** Sweden
191 H6 **Haste** Ger.
187 G8 **Hastière-Lavaux** Belgium
105 J8 **Hastings** *Vic.* Austr.
105 N4 **Hastings** *r. N.S.W.* Austr.
271 □4 **Hastings** Barbados
251 Q5 **Hastings** *Ont.* Can.
102 K6 **Hastings** *North I.* N.Z.
173 N6 **Hastings** *East Sussex, England* U.K.
250 I7 **Hastings** *MI* U.S.A.
250 B5 **Hastings** *MN* U.S.A.
260 F5 **Hastings** *NE* U.S.A.
127 K4 **Hasuda** Japan
127 L4 **Hasunuma** Japan
162 Q1 **Hasvik** Norway
147 K8 **Ḩaşwayl** Yemen
224 A3 **Ḩasy Haghe** *well* Libya
199 H2 **Hať** Czech Rep.
199 L3 **Hat'** Ukr.
139 I6 **Hata** *Uttar Prad.* India
127 G3 **Hata** Japan
129 K5 **Hatanbulag** Mongolia
Hatansuudal Mongolia *see* **Bayanlig**
126 D5 **Hatashō** Japan
Hatay Turkey *see* **Antakya**
150 E2 **Hatay** *prov.* Turkey
258 E4 **Hatboro** *PA* U.S.A.
265 T4 **Hatch** *UT* U.S.A.
106 E6 **Hatches Creek (abandoned)** *N.T.* Austr.
247 K3 **Hatchet Lake** *Sask.* Can.
261 K8 **Hatchie** *r. TN* U.S.A.
219 K5 **Haţeg** Romania
102 K5 **Hatepe** *North I.* N.Z.
124 □A22 **Hateruma-jima** *i. Nansei-shotō* Japan
105 I5 **Hatfield** *N.S.W.* Austr.
173 L4 **Hatfield** *Hertfordshire, England* U.K.
171 P6 **Hatfield** *South Yorkshire, England* U.K.
258 E4 **Hatfield** *PA* U.S.A.
173 M4 **Hatfield Broad Oak** *Essex, England* U.K.
173 N4 **Hatfield Peverel** *Essex, England* U.K.
128 G1 **Hatgal** Mongolia
139 I8 **Hath** *Chhattisgarh* India
105 N4 **Hat Head National Park** *N.S.W.* Austr.
172 D6 **Hatherleigh** *Devon, England* U.K.
173 J2 **Hathern** *Leicestershire, England* U.K.
171 N7 **Hathersage** *Derbyshire, England* U.K.
138 G6 **Hathras** *Uttar Prad.* India
139 K6 **Hatia** Nepal
146 D5 **Ḩāţibah, Ra's** *pt* Saudi Arabia
119 G9 **Ha Tiên** Vietnam
118 G5 **Ha Tinh** Vietnam
Hatisar Bhutan *see* **Geylegphug**
271 □8 **Hato** *Bonaire* Neth. Antilles
271 □10 **Hato, Bocht van** *b. Curaçao* Neth. Antilles
274 D3 **Hato Corozal** Col.
Hato Hud East Timor *see* **Hatudo**
275 F3 **Hato la Vergareña** Venez.
271 I4 **Hato Mayor** Dom. Rep.
127 L1 **Hatori-ko** *l.* Japan
138 F8 **Hat Piplia** *Madh. Prad.* India
Hatra Iraq *see* **Al Ḩaḑr**
125 J12 **Hatsukaichi** Japan
127 J5 **Hatsu-shima** *i.* Japan
138 G7 **Hatta** *Madh. Prad.* India
138 H9 **Hatta** *Madh. Prad.* India
105 I6 **Hattah** *Vic.* Austr.
105 I6 **Hattah Kulkyne National Park** *N.S.W.* Austr.
186 J4 **Hattem** Neth.
195 K5 **Hattenhofen** Ger.
255 J8 **Hatteras, Cape** *NC* U.S.A.
288 E4 **Hatteras Abyssal Plain** *sea feature* S. Atlantic Ocean
191 F10 **Hattersheim am Main** Ger.
191 E9 **Hattert** Ger.
162 L4 **Hattfjelldal** Norway
137 H3 **Hatti** *r.* India
261 K10 **Hattiesburg** *MS* U.S.A.
200 D5 **Hatting** Austria
191 D8 **Hattingen** Ger.
168 M8 **Hatton** *Aberdeenshire, Scotland* U.K.
173 I2 **Hatton** *Derbyshire, England* U.K.
117 M2 **Hatton, Gunung** *hill* Malaysia
191 J7 **Hattorf am Harz** Ger.
126 D6 **Hattori-gawa** *r.* Japan
119 C8 **Hattras Passage** Myanmar
190 H1 **Hattstedt** Ger.
163 R6 **Hattula** Fin.
162 U5 **Hattuvaara** Fin.
115 D8 **Hatudo** East Timor
199 I4 **Hatvan** Hungary
119 E11 **Hat Yai** Thai.
194 E3 **Hatzenbühl** Ger.
201 N6 **Hatzendorf** Austria
191 G9 **Hatzfeld (Eder)** Ger.
119 H10 **Hâu, Sông** *r.* Vietnam
Hau Bon Vietnam *see* **A Yun Pa**
178 E2 **Haubourdin** France
232 E2 **Haud** *reg.* Eth.
194 D3 **Hauenstein** Ger.
164 D1 **Haugastøl** Norway
164 C3 **Hauge** Norway
164 B2 **Haugesund** Norway
172 H2 **Haughton** *Staffordshire, England* U.K.
201 N2 **Haugsdorf** Austria
163 R6 **Hauho** Fin.
100 □6 **Hauhui** *Malaita* Solomon Is
102 J5 **Hauhungaroa** *mt. North I.* N.Z.
102 J5 **Hauhungaroa Range** *mts North I.* N.Z.
164 D2 **Haukeligrend** Norway
162 R4 **Haukipudas** Fin.
162 T5 **Haukivesi** *l.* Fin.
163 S5 **Haukivuori** Fin.
186 J2 **Haulerwijk** Neth.
247 J4 **Haultain** *r. Sask.* Can.
102 K6 **Haumoana** *North I.* N.Z.
282 E2 **Haumonia** Arg.
118 C2 **Haungpa** Myanmar
168 B8 **Haunn** *Western Isles, Scotland* U.K.
259 I3 **Hauppauge** *NY* U.S.A.
192 J5 **Hauptgraben** *r.* Ger.
195 K4 **Hauptkanal** *canal* Ger.
237 K2 **Hauptrus** S. Africa
193 I7 **Hauptspree** *r.* Ger.
100 □6 **Hauraha** *San Cristobal* Solomon Is
102 J3 **Hauraki Gulf** *North I.* N.Z.
102 I3 **Hauraki Gulf Maritime Park** *nature res. North I.* N.Z.
103 J8 **Haurangi Forest Park** *nature res. North I.* N.Z.
103 B13 **Hauroko, Lake** *South I.* N.Z.
101 □9a **Hauru, Pointe** *pt Moorea* Fr. Polynesia
201 I5 **Haus** Austria
194 E5 **Hausach** Ger.
193 G8 **Hausdorf** Ger.
195 K2 **Hausen** *Bayern* Ger.
195 M4 **Hausen** *Bayern* Ger.
195 I2 **Hausen bei Würzburg** Ger.
194 D6 **Hausen im Wiesental** Ger.
194 E6 **Häusern** Ger.
195 L6 **Hausham** Ger.
160 H1 **Hausjärvi** Fin.
201 N3 **Hausleiten** Austria
201 M6 **Hausmannstätten** Austria
201 H3 **Hausruck** *mts* Austria
212 G2 **Hausstock** *mt.* Switz.
257 □Q4 **Haut, Isle au** *i. ME* U.S.A.
162 T3 **Hautajärvi** Fin.
226 C3 **Haut Atlas** *mts* Morocco
179 M8 **Haut-du-Them-Château-Lambert** France
179 K8 **Haute-Amance** France
214 C3 **Haute-Corse** *dept Corse* France
182 G4 **Hautecourt-Romanèche** France
184 G5 **Hautefort** France
185 G9 **Haute-Garonne** *dept* France
228 C4 **Haute-Guinée** *admin. reg.* Guinea
230 D3 **Haute-Kotto** *pref.* C.A.R.
183 D6 **Haute-Loire** *dept* France
182 J5 **Hauteluce** France
179 J7 **Haute-Marne** *dept* France
178 B5 **Haute-Normandie** *admin. reg.* France
249 G3 **Hauterive** *Que.* Can.
183 G6 **Hauterives** France
183 I7 **Hautes-Alpes** *dept* France
179 L8 **Haute-Saône** *dept* France
179 K8 **Haute-Saône, Plateaux de la** France
182 I4 **Haute-Savoie** *dept* France
178 G6 **Haute Seine, Canal de la** France
187 J8 **Hautes Fagnes** *moorland* Belgium
187 J7 **Hautes Fagnes-Eifel, Parc Naturel des** *nature res.* Belgium
185 E9 **Hautes-Pyrénées** *dept* France
184 C2 **Hauteurs de la Gâtine** *reg.* France
178 C6 **Haute-Vallée-de-Chevreuse, Parc Naturel Régional de la** *nature res.* France
184 G4 **Haute-Vienne** *dept* France
182 H5 **Hauteville-Lompnes** France
178 G5 **Hautevillers** France
Haute-Volta *country* Africa *see* **Burkina**
187 H8 **Haut-Fays** Belgium
182 E3 **Haut-Folin** *hill* France
182 H4 **Haut Jura, Parc Naturel Régional du** *nature res.* France
231 E7 **Haut-Katanga** *prov.* Dem. Rep. Congo
183 B9 **Haut-Languedoc, Parc Naturel Régional du** *nature res.* France
230 E7 **Haut-Lomami** *prov.* Dem. Rep. Congo
230 E3 **Haut-Mbomou** *pref.* C.A.R.
178 G3 **Hautmont** France
258 D3 **Hauto, Lake** *PA* U.S.A.
230 B5 **Haut-Ogooué** *prov.* Gabon
185 G6 **Haut-Quercy** *reg.* France
179 N8 **Haut-Rhin** *dept* France
181 P4 **Hauts-de-Seine** *dept* France
227 E2 **Hauts Plateaux** Alg.
230 F4 **Haut-Uele** *prov.* Dem. Rep. Congo
264 □D12 **Hau'ula** *HI* U.S.A.
Hauvo Fin. *see* **Nagu**
103 I8 **Hauwai** *South I.* N.Z.
185 C9 **Haux** France
195 P4 **Hauzenberg** Ger.
Havana Cuba *see* **La Habana**
250 D9 **Havana** *IL* U.S.A.
173 K6 **Havant** *Hampshire, England* U.K.
219 O2 **Havârna** Romania
265 R7 **Havasu, Lake** *AZ/CA* U.S.A.
162 R1 **Hávdna** Norway
193 E5 **Havel** *r.* Ger.
187 H8 **Havelange** Belgium
192 F5 **Havelberg** Ger.
145 O4 **Havelian** Pak.
145 O6 **Haveli Bahadur Shah** Pak.
192 F5 **Havelland** *reg.* Ger.
192 F5 **Havelländisches Luch** *marsh* Ger.
251 Q5 **Havelock** *Ont.* Can.
103 H8 **Havelock** *South I.* N.Z.
103 E10 **Havelock** *r. South I.* N.Z.
Havelock Swaziland *see* **Bulembu**
255 I8 **Havelock** *NC* U.S.A.
106 D2 **Havelock Falls** *N.T.* Austr.
137 M7 **Havelock Island** *Andaman & Nicobar Is* India
102 K6 **Havelock North** *North I.* N.Z.
186 J3 **Havelte** Neth.
261 G7 **Haven** *KS* U.S.A.
164 I5 **Haverdal** Sweden
172 C4 **Haverfordwest** *Pembrokeshire, Wales* U.K.
173 M3 **Haverhill** *Suffolk, England* U.K.
257 N6 **Haverhill** *MA* U.S.A.
136 D5 **Haveri** *Karnataka* India
191 J6 **Haverlah** Ger.
163 M5 **Haverö** Sweden
187 H8 **Haversin** Belgium
259 H2 **Haverstraw** *NY* U.S.A.
258 E5 **Havertown** *PA* U.S.A.
Havîrna Romania *see* **Havârna**
199 H2 **Havířov** Czech Rep.
191 D7 **Havixbeck** Ger.
198 E2 **Havlíčkův Brod** Czech Rep.
162 R1 **Havøysund** Norway
199 J2 **Havran** *mt.* Slovakia
221 I3 **Havran** Turkey
221 H3 **Havran** *r.* Turkey
187 F8 **Havré** Belgium
276 C1 **Havre** Brazil
262 J2 **Havre** *MT* U.S.A.
249 I4 **Havre-Aubert** *Que.* Can.
249 I4 **Havre Aubert, Île du** *i. Que.* Can.
258 C5 **Havre de Grace** *MD* U.S.A.
99 I5 **Havre Rock** *i.* N.Z.
249 I3 **Havre-St-Pierre** *Que.* Can.
159 P5 **Havrylivka** *Dnipropetrovs'ka Oblast'* Ukr.
159 P5 **Havrylivka** *Kharkivs'ka Oblast'* Ukr.
158 F5 **Havrylivtsi** Ukr.
219 O9 **Havsa** Turkey
164 H3 **Havstensfjord** *inlet* Sweden
150 D2 **Havutlu** Turkey
148 G3 **Havza** Turkey
139 P6 **Hawai** *Arun. Prad.* India
264 □F13 **Hawai'i** *i. HI* U.S.A.
264 □F14 **Hawaii** *state* U.S.A.
290 H4 **Hawai'ian Islands** N. Pacific Ocean
290 H4 **Hawaiian Ridge** *sea feature* N. Pacific Ocean
264 □F14 **Hawai'i Volcanoes National Park** *HI* U.S.A.
146 E8 **Hawakil** Eritrea
146 E8 **Hawakil Bay** Eritrea
149 N9 **Ḩawallī** Kuwait
Ḩawar *i.* The Gulf *see* **Ḩuwār**
172 F1 **Hawarden** *Flintshire, Wales* U.K.
150 A10 **Ḩawashīyah, Wādī** *watercourse* Egypt
103 D11 **Hawea, Lake** *South I.* N.Z.
103 D11 **Hawea Flat** *South I.* N.Z.
102 I6 **Hawera** *North I.* N.Z.
171 M5 **Hawes** *North Yorkshire, England* U.K.
254 D7 **Hawesville** *KY* U.S.A.
171 L4 **Haweswater Reservoir** *England* U.K.
264 □F13 **Hāwī** *HI* U.S.A.
168 K12 **Hawick** *Scottish Borders, Scotland* U.K.
149 M8 **Ḩawīzah, Hawr al** *imp. l.* Iraq
103 D11 **Hawkdun Range** *mts South I.* N.Z.
102 L6 **Hawke Bay** *North I.* N.Z.
249 K2 **Hawke Island** *Nfld and Lab.* Can.
104 G4 **Hawker** *S.A.* Austr.
104 H3 **Hawkers Gate** *N.S.W.* Austr.
249 J3 **Hawkes Bay** *Nfld and Lab.* Can.
102 K6 **Hawke's Bay** *admin. reg. North I.* N.Z.
257 K3 **Hawkesbury** *Ont.* Can.
172 H4 **Hawkesbury** *South Gloucestershire, England* U.K.
250 C7 **Hawkeye** *IA* U.S.A.
173 N5 **Hawkhurst** *Kent, England* U.K.
245 N4 **Hawk Inlet** *AK* U.S.A.
265 S4 **Hawkins Peak** *UT* U.S.A.
250 J1 **Hawk Junction** *Ont.* Can.
255 E8 **Haw Knob** *mt. NC/TN* U.S.A.
270 E1 **Hawksbill Cay** *i.* Bahamas
257 □R3 **Hawkshaw** *N.B.* Can.
171 L5 **Hawkshead** *Cumbria, England* U.K.
270 F1 **Hawksnest Point** Bahamas
262 L6 **Hawk Springs** *WY* U.S.A.
103 H9 **Hawkswood** *South I.* N.Z.
173 N4 **Hawkwell** *Essex, England* U.K.
107 M8 **Hawkwood** *Qld* Austr.
Hawlēr Iraq *see* **Arbīl**
173 K5 **Hawley** *Hampshire, England* U.K.
258 E2 **Hawley** *PA* U.S.A.
259 I2 **Hawleyville** *CT* U.S.A.
171 O5 **Hawnby** *North Yorkshire, England* U.K.
118 D4 **Hawng Luk** Myanmar
171 N6 **Haworth** *West Yorkshire, England* U.K.
147 I8 **Ḩawrā'** Yemen
149 K7 **Ḩawrān, Wādī** *watercourse* Iraq
150 D10 **Hawşal** *hills* Saudi Arabia
146 G4 **Ḩawshah, Jibāl al** *mts* Saudi Arabia
236 D10 **Hawston** S. Africa
259 G3 **Hawthorne** *NJ* U.S.A.
264 N3 **Hawthorne** *NV* U.S.A.
259 H2 **Hawthorne** *NY* U.S.A.
160 I8 **Hawya** *r.* Belarus
146 D9 **Hawzēn** Eth.
129 M4 **Haxat Hudag** *Nei Mongol* China
171 O5 **Haxby** *York, England* U.K.
171 P7 **Haxey** *North Lincolnshire, England* U.K.
105 J6 **Hay** *N.S.W.* Austr.
106 F8 **Hay** *watercourse N.T.* Austr.
246 H2 **Hay** *r.* Can.
250 C5 **Hay** *r. WI* U.S.A.
106 D7 **Hay, Mount** *N.T.* Austr.
115 F5 **Haya** *Seram* Indon.
124 S7 **Hayachine-san** *mt.* Japan
127 G1 **Haya-gawa** *r.* Japan
127 H5 **Hayakawa** Japan
127 H5 **Haya-kawa** *r.* Japan
124 S4 **Hayakita** Japan
127 K5 **Hayama** Japan
179 L5 **Hayange** France
125 I13 **Hayasui-seto** *sea chan.* Japan
178 I3 **Haybes** France
159 P6 **Haychur** *r.* Ukr.
244 G2 **Haycock** *AK* U.S.A.
250 B5 **Hay Creek** *MN* U.S.A.
150 D7 **Haydān, Wādī al** *r.* Jordan
221 L4 **Haydarlı** Turkey
221 I3 **Haydaroba** Turkey
265 V8 **Hayden** *AZ* U.S.A.
262 K6 **Hayden** *CO* U.S.A.
262 F3 **Hayden** *ID* U.S.A.
171 L7 **Haydock** *Merseyside, England* U.K.
171 M4 **Haydon Bridge** *Northumberland, England* U.K.
173 I4 **Haydon Wick** *Swindon, England* U.K.
247 M3 **Hayes** *r. Man.* Can.
243 I3 **Hayes** *r. Nunavut* Can.
245 K3 **Hayes, Mount** *AK* U.S.A.
260 E5 **Hayes Center** *NE* U.S.A.
106 C2 **Hayes Creek** *N.T.* Austr.
243 M2 **Hayes Halvø** *pen.* Greenland
255 F8 **Hayesville** *NC* U.S.A.
147 L9 **Ḩayf** *Suquţrā* Yemen
171 N7 **Hayfield** *Derbyshire, England* U.K.
250 B6 **Hayfield** *MN* U.S.A.
265 Q8 **Hayfield Reservoir** *CA* U.S.A.
194 G5 **Hayingen** Ger.
147 M3 **Ḩayl** Oman
150 F5 **Hayl, Wādī** *watercourse* Syria
150 H4 **Hayl, Wādī al** *watercourse* Syria
Haylaastay Mongolia *see* **Sühbaatar**
172 B7 **Hayle** *Cornwall, England* U.K.
173 K6 **Hayling Island** *England* U.K.
147 M6 **Haymā'** Oman
148 F4 **Haymana** Turkey
107 L6 **Hayman Island** *Qld* Austr.
256 H10 **Haymarket** *VA* U.S.A.
160 L7 **Hayna** *r.* Belarus
261 I9 **Haynesville** *LA* U.S.A.
255 D9 **Hayneville** *AL* U.S.A.
172 F3 **Hay-on-Wye** *Powys, Wales* U.K.
Hayotboshi Toghi *mt.* Uzbek. *see* **Hayotboshi tog'i**
143 L7 **Hayotboshi tog'i** *mt.* Uzbek.
221 I1 **Hayrabolu** Turkey
151 B5 **Hayrat** Turkey
128 H4 **Hayrhandulaan** Mongolia
246 H2 **Hay River** *N.W.T.* Can.
246 H2 **Hay River Reserve** *N.W.T.* Can.
260 F6 **Hays** *KS* U.S.A.
262 J2 **Hays** *MT* U.S.A.
146 F9 **Ḩays** Yemen
224 B2 **Hayshah, Sabkhat al** *salt pan* Libya
256 C11 **Haysi** *VA* U.S.A.
286 N1 **Hays Mountains** Antarctica
260 D4 **Hay Springs** *NE* U.S.A.
261 G7 **Haysville** *KS* U.S.A.
158 I5 **Haysyn** Ukr.
150 B8 **Ḩayţān, Jabal** *hill* Egypt
260 G3 **Hayti** *SD* U.S.A.
171 L4 **Hayton** *Cumbria, England* U.K.
171 P6 **Hayton** *East Riding of Yorkshire, England* U.K.
139 P5 **Hayutang** *Arun. Prad.* India
158 I5 **Hayvoron** Ukr.
264 J4 **Hayward** *CA* U.S.A.
250 C3 **Hayward** *WI* U.S.A.
173 L6 **Haywards Heath** *West Sussex, England* U.K.
147 N5 **Ḩayy** *well* Oman
144 E2 **Hazar** Turkm.
145 K5 **Hazarajat** *reg.* Afgh.
256 B11 **Hazard** *KY* U.S.A.
139 J8 **Hazaribagh** *Jharkhand* India
139 I8 **Hazaribagh Range** *mts Bihar* India
144 H3 **Hazār Masjed, Kūh-e** *mts* Iran
148 I8 **Ḩazawzā', Qā'** *salt pan* Saudi Arabia
178 E2 **Hazebrouck** France
103 C13 **Hazelburgh Group** *is South I.* N.Z.
171 M7 **Hazel Grove** *Greater Manchester, England* U.K.
250 E4 **Hazelhurst** *WI* U.S.A.
246 E4 **Hazelton** *B.C.* Can.
260 E2 **Hazen** *ND* U.S.A.
243 K1 **Hazen, Lake** *Nunavut* Can.
244 F3 **Hazen Bay** *AK* U.S.A.
243 G2 **Hazen Strait** *N.W.T./Nunavut* Can.
145 L3 **Hazhdanahr** *reg.* Afgh.
255 F10 **Hazlehurst** *GA* U.S.A.
261 J10 **Hazlehurst** *MS* U.S.A.
173 K4 **Hazlemere** *Buckinghamshire, England* U.K.
259 G4 **Hazlet** *NJ* U.S.A.
258 D3 **Hazleton** *PA* U.S.A.
108 J6 **Hazlett, Lake** *salt flat W.A.* Austr.
199 K2 **Hažlín** Slovakia
198 B1 **Hazlov** Czech Rep.
147 M4 **Ḩazm** Oman
142 I7 **Hazorasp** Uzbek.
151 J4 **Häzrä** Azer.
145 L3 **Ḩazrat-e Solţān** Afgh.
145 O5 **Hazro** Pak.
149 J4 **Hazro** Turkey
126 F6 **Hazu** Japan
126 E6 **Hazumi-saki** *pt* Japan
285 F4 **H. Bouchard** Arg.
158 J2 **Hdzyen'** Belarus
173 M2 **Heacham** *Norfolk, England* U.K.
173 N5 **Headcorn** *Kent, England* U.K.
169 D6 **Headford** Ireland
106 G6 **Headingly** *Qld* Austr.
173 K5 **Headley** *Hampshire, England* U.K.
104 C4 **Head of Bight** *b. S.A.* Austr.
108 □1 **Headridge Hill** Christmas I.
168 G12 **Heads of Ayr** *Scotland* U.K.
250 E4 **Heafford Junction** *WI* U.S.A.
168 C8 **Healabhal Bheag** *hill Scotland* U.K.
264 J3 **Healdsburg** *CA* U.S.A.
261 G8 **Healdton** *OK* U.S.A.
105 J7 **Healesville** *Vic.* Austr.
171 Q6 **Healing** *North East Lincolnshire, England* U.K.
256 F11 **Healing Springs** *VA* U.S.A.
245 J3 **Healy** *AK* U.S.A.
245 K3 **Healy Lake** *AK* U.S.A.
171 O7 **Heanor** *Derbyshire, England* U.K.
172 D5 **Heanton Punchardon** *Devon, England* U.K.
289 I8 **Heard Island** Indian Ocean
287 E3 **Heard Island and McDonald Islands** *terr.* Indian Ocean
162 R1 **Heargerášša** *hill* Norway
261 G10 **Hearne** *TX* U.S.A.
246 H2 **Hearne Lake** *N.W.T.* Can.
248 D3 **Hearst** *Ont.* Can.
286 T2 **Hearst Island** Antarctica
260 E2 **Heart** *r. ND* U.S.A.
276 C3 **Heath** *r.* Bol./Peru
171 O7 **Heath** *Derbyshire, England* U.K.
105 J7 **Heathcote** *Vic.* Austr.
173 M6 **Heathfield** *East Sussex, England* U.K.
256 I11 **Heathsville** *VA* U.S.A.
261 H8 **Heavener** *OK* U.S.A.
261 F12 **Hebbronville** *TX* U.S.A.
258 B6 **Hebbville** *MD* U.S.A.
171 M6 **Hebden Bridge** *West Yor*[...] *England* U.K.
129 N7 **Hebei** *prov.* China
105 K3 **Hebel** *Qld* Austr.
265 V7 **Heber** *AZ* U.S.A.
265 Q9 **Heber** *CA* U.S.A.
265 U1 **Heber City** *UT* U.S.A.
261 I8 **Heber Springs** *AR* U.S.A.
195 N5 **Hebertsfelden** Ger.
195 K5 **Hebertshausen** Ger.
262 I4 **Hebgen Lake** *MT* U.S.A.
129 N9 **Hebi** *Henan* China
129 M7 **Hebian** *Shanxi* China
164 B2 **Hebnes** Norway
168 C9 **Hebrides, Sea of the** *Scotland* U.K.
249 I1 **Hebron** *Nfld and Lab.* C[...]
259 K1 **Hebron** *CT* U.S.A.
250 G8 **Hebron** *IN* U.S.A.
257 J10 **Hebron** *MD* U.S.A.
260 D2 **Hebron** *ND* U.S.A.
260 G5 **Hebron** *NE* U.S.A.
150 D7 **Hebron** West Bank
249 I1 **Hebron Fiord** *inlet Nfld* Can.
Hebros *r.* Greece/Turke[...] **Evros**
165 M2 **Heby** Sweden
245 O5 **Hecate Strait** *B.C.* Can.
267 N7 **Hecelchakán** Mex.
245 N5 **Heceta Island** *AK* U.S.A.
Hecheng *Jiangxi* China
Hecheng *Zhejiang* Chin[...] **Qingtian**
130 G6 **Hechi** *Guangxi* China
194 F5 **Hechingen** Ger.
208 D2 **Hecho** Spain
208 D2 **Hecho, Valle de** *val.* Spa[...]
187 H6 **Hechtel** Belgium
190 H3 **Hechthausen** Ger.
130 F3 **Hechuan** *Chongqing* Ch[...]
Hechuan *Jiangxi* China **Yongxin**
Hechuan China *see* **Yon**[...]
130 H8 **Hechun** *Guangdong* Ch[...]
192 I5 **Heckelberg** Ger.
173 L2 **Heckington** *Lincolnshir*[...] *England* U.K.
193 E7 **Hecklingen** Ger.
258 E3 **Hecktown** *PA* U.S.A.
246 L5 **Hecla/Grindstone Provi**[...] **Park** *Man.* Can.
247 L5 **Hecla Island** *Man.* Can.
260 H3 **Hector** *MN* U.S.A.
103 J7 **Hector, Mount** *North I.*
103 C12 **Hector Mountains** *Sou*[...]
270 □ **Hector's River** Jamaica
127 I6 **Heda** Japan
162 O4 **Hedberg** Sweden
164 F2 **Heddalsvatnet** *l.* Norwa[...]
194 F3 **Heddesheim** Ger.
Hede *Jiangsu* China *see*
180 H5 **Hédé** France
163 L5 **Hede** Sweden
164 H3 **Hedekas** Sweden
186 H5 **Hedel** Neth.
165 L1 **Hedemora** Sweden
162 Q3 **Hedenäset** Sweden
164 F6 **Hedensted** Denmark
191 K6 **Hedeper** Ger.
193 E7 **Hedersleben** Ger.
198 G4 **Hédervár** Hungary
165 N1 **Hedesunda** Sweden
165 M1 **Hedesundafjärden** *l.* Sw[...]
262 F4 **He Devil Mountain** *ID*
173 J6 **Hedge End** *Hampshire, England* U.K.
103 C13 **Hedgehope** *South I.* N.Z[...]
267 I5 **Hedionda Grande** Mex.
130 H8 **Hedi Shuiku** *resr* China
164 H1 **Hedmark** *county* Norwa[...]
173 I2 **Hednesford** *Staffordshir*[...] *England* U.K.
124 □1 **Hedo** *Okinawa* Japan
124 □1 **Hedo-misaki** *c. Okinaw*[...]
171 Q6 **Hedon** *East Riding of Yo*[...] *England* U.K.
190 D5 **Heede** Ger.
186 I3 **Heeg** Neth.
191 D6 **Heek** Ger.
187 I6 **Heel** Neth.
190 H5 **Heemsen** Ger.
186 G3 **Heemskerk** Neth.
186 G4 **Heemstede** Neth.
187 G8 **Heer** Belgium
186 J4 **Heerde** Neth.
186 I3 **Heerenveen** Neth.
186 G3 **Heerhugowaard** Neth.
162 □ **Heer Land** *reg.* Svalbar[...]
187 I7 **Heerlen** Neth.
187 H7 **Heers** Belgium
186 I5 **Heesch** Neth.
190 H4 **Heeslingen** Ger.
191 H6 **Heeßen** Ger.
186 H5 **Heeswijk** Neth.
186 J4 **Heeten** Neth.
187 I6 **Heeze** Neth.
150 C6 **Ḩefa** Israel
150 D6 **Ḩefa, Mifraẕ** *b.* Israel
131 K3 **Hefei** *Anhui* China
130 H4 **Hefeng** *Hubei* China
255 E9 **Heflin** *AL* U.S.A.
122 G5 **Hegang** *Heilong.* China
194 F6 **Hegau** *reg.* Ger.
136 E6 **Heggadadevankote** *Kar*[...] India
163 J6 **Heggenes** Norway
258 B3 **Hegins** *PA* U.S.A.
125 O9 **Hegura-jima** *i.* Japan
198 G4 **Hegyeshalom** Hungary
201 O4 **Hegykő** Hungary
191 H7 **Hehlen** Ger.
118 C4 **Heho** Myanmar
232 A2 **Heiban** Sudan
Heidan *r.* Jordan *see* **Haydān, Wādī al**
193 D7 **Heidberg** *hill* Ger.
190 H2 **Heide** Ger.
234 C4 **Heide** Namibia
195 K3 **Heideck** Ger.
194 F3 **Heidelberg** Ger.
237 M2 **Heidelberg** *Gauteng* S. [...]
236 E10 **Heidelberg** *Western Ca*[...]
191 C7 **Heiden** Ger.
212 H1 **Heiden** Switz.
190 I4 **Heidenau** *Niedersachse*[...]
193 I9 **Heidenau** *Sachsen* Ger.
195 J3 **Heidenheim** Ger.
195 I4 **Heidenheim an der Bre**[...]
201 L2 **Heidenreichstein** Austr[...]
258 A5 **Heidlersburg** *PA* U.S.A.
124 S7 **Hei-gawa** *r.* Japan
191 H10 **Heigenbrücken** Ger.
171 N4 **Heighington** *Darlingto*[...] *England* U.K.
171 Q7 **Heighington** *Lincolnshi*[...] *England* U.K.
125 J13 **Heigun-jima** *i.* Japan
122 E3 **Heihe** *Heilong.* China
128 G7 **Hei He** *r. Qinghai* Chin[...]
190 J2 **Heikendorf** Ger.
191 J8 **Heilbad Heiligenstadt**
237 L3 **Heilbron** S. Africa
194 G3 **Heilbronn** Ger.
201 M5 **Heilbrunn** Austria
Heiligenbeil Rus. Fed. [...] **Mamonovo**
194 G6 **Heiligenberg** Ger.
192 D5 **Heiligenfelde** Ger.
192 F4 **Heiligengrabe** Ger.
190 K2 **Heiligenhafen** Ger.
191 C8 **Heiligenhaus** Ger.
201 M6 **Heiligenkreuz am Waa**[...] Austria
201 N6 **Heiligenkreuz im Lafn**[...] Austria
195 K2 **Heiligenstadt in Oberf**[...] Ger.

Heiligenstedten Ger.
Hei Ling Chau i. H.K. China
Heilongjiang prov. China
Heilong Jiang r. China
alt. Amur (Rus. Fed.)
Heiloo Neth.
Heilsbronn Ger.
Heiltz-le-Maurupt France
Heilungkiang prov. China see Heilongjiang
Heimaey i. Iceland
Heimahe Qinghai China
Heimbach Ger.
Heimbuchenthal Ger.
Heimburg Ger.
Heimenkirch Ger.
Heimertingen Ger.
Heimschuh Austria
Heimsheim Ger.
Heinade Ger.
Heinävesi Fin.
Heinebach (Alheim) Ger.
Heinersbrück Ger.
Heinersdorf Ger.
Heinersreuth Ger.
Heiningen Ger.
Heinkenszand Neth.
Heino Neth.
Heinola Fin.
Heinrichswalde Rus. Fed. see Slavsk
Heinsberg Ger.
Heinsen Ger.
Heinz Bay Myanmar
Heinze Islands Myanmar
Heiquan Gansu China
Heishan Liaoning China
Heishantou Nei Mongol China
Heishantou Xinjiang China
Heishi Beihu l. Xizang China
Heishui Sichuan China
Heisker Islands Scotland U.K. see Monach Islands
Heist Ger.
Heist-op-den-Berg Belgium
Heitersheim Ger.
Heituo Shan mt. Shanxi China
Heiwa Japan
Hejaz reg. Saudi Arabia see Hijaz
Hejian Hebei China
Hejiang Sichuan China
He Jiang r. China
Hejiao Nei Mongol China
Hejin Shanxi China
Hejing Xinjiang China
Hejnice Czech Rep.
Hejőbába Hungary
Hekelgem Belgium
Hekimhan Turkey
Hekinan Japan
Hekla vol. Iceland
Heko-san mt. Japan
Hekou Gansu China
Hekou Hubei China
Hekou Jiangxi China see Yanshan
Hekou Sichuan China see Yajiang
Hekou Yunnan China
Hekpoort S. Africa
Hel Pol.
Helagsfjället mt. Sweden
Helam Arun. Prad. India
Helan Shan mts China
Helchteren Belgium
Heldburg Ger.
Helden's Point St Kitts and Nevis
Heldenstein Ger.
Heldrungen Ger.
Helechal Spain
Helechosa de los Montes Spain
Helegiu Romania
Helem Assam India
Helen atoll Palau
Helen, Mount NV U.S.A.
Helena AR U.S.A.
Helena MT U.S.A.
Helena OH U.S.A.
Helengeli i. N. Male Maldives
Helen Reef Palau
Helen's Bay Northern Ireland U.K.
Helensburgh Argyll and Bute, Scotland U.K.
Helen Springs N.T. Austr.
Helensville North I. N.Z.
Ḥelez Israel
Helfenberg Austria
Helfenstein PA U.S.A.
Helgasjön l. Sweden
Helge r. Sweden
Helgenæs pen. Denmark
Helgoland Ger.
Helgoland i. Ger.
Helgoländer Bucht g. Ger.
Helgum Sweden
Helhoughton Norfolk, England U.K.
Heligoland i. Ger. see Helgoland
Heligoland Bight g. Ger. see Helgoländer Bucht
Heixi Anhui China see Ningguo
Hella Iceland
Hellas country Europe see Greece
Hell-Bourg Réunion
Helleh r. Iran
Hellemobotn Norway
Hellendoorn Neth.
Hellenthal Ger.
Hellertown PA U.S.A.
Hellespont str. Turkey see Çanakkale Boğazı
Hellevoetsluis Neth.
Hellhole Gorge National Park Qld Austr.
Hell Hole Reservoir CA U.S.A.
Hellifield North Yorkshire, England U.K.
Helligskogen Norway
Hellín Spain
Hellingly East Sussex, England U.K.
Hells Canyon gorge ID/OR U.S.A.
Hellshire Hills Jamaica
Hell's Mouth b. Wales U.K. see Porth Neigwl
Hellsö Åland Fin.
Hell-Ville Madag. see Andoany
Hellwege Ger.
Helm CA U.S.A.
Helmand prov. Afgh.
Helmand r. Afgh.
Helmand, Hāmūn salt flat Afgh./Iran
Helmantica Spain see Salamanca
Helmbrechts Ger.
Helme r. Ger.
Helmeringhausen Namibia
Helmet Mountain AK U.S.A.
Helmond Neth.
Helmsdale Highland, Scotland U.K.
Helmsdale r. Scotland U.K.
Helmsley North Yorkshire, England U.K.
Helmsley Aboriginal Holding res. Qld Austr.
Helmstadt Ger.
Helmstedt Ger.
Helodrano Antongila b. Madag.
Helong Jilin China
Helpe Majeure r. France
Helper UT U.S.A.
Helpmekaar S. Africa
Helpringham Lincolnshire, England U.K.
Helpsen Ger.
Helpter Berge hills Ger.
Helsby Cheshire, England U.K.
Helse Ger.
Helsingborg Sweden
Helsinge Denmark
Helsingfors Fin. see Helsinki
Helsingør Denmark
Helsinki Fin.
Helska, Mierzeja spit Pol.
Helston Cornwall, England U.K.
160 G3 Heltermaa Estonia
194 D3 Heltersberg Ger.
221 I4 Helvacı Turkey
151 B5 Helvaköy Turkey
285 G2 Helvecia Arg.
281 H2 Helvécia Brazil
171 K4 Helvellyn hill England U.K.
Helvetic Republic country Europe see Switzerland
163 Q5 Helvetinjärven kansallispuisto nat. park Fin.
169 G8 Helvick Head Ireland
186 H5 Helvoirt Neth.
Ḥelwân Egypt see Ḥulwān
178 F2 Hem France
195 L3 Hemau Ger.
Hembudu i. S. Male Maldives see Embudhu
173 L4 Hemel Hempstead Hertfordshire, England U.K.
191 E8 Hemeln Ger.
264 P8 Hemet CA U.S.A.
195 J2 Hemhofen Ger.
260 D4 Hemingford NE U.S.A.
173 L3 Hemingford Grey Cambridgeshire, England U.K.
250 I1 Hemlo Ont. Can.
256 H6 Hemlock Lake NY U.S.A.
190 H2 Hemme Ger.
191 I6 Hemmingen Ger.
257 L3 Hemmingford Que. Can.
190 H2 Hemmingstedt Ger.
190 H3 Hemmoor Ger.
162 L3 Hemnesberget Norway
261 I10 Hemphill TX U.S.A.
173 O2 Hempnall Norfolk, England U.K.
173 M3 Hempstead Essex, England U.K.
259 H3 Hempstead NY U.S.A.
261 G10 Hempstead TX U.S.A.
194 F2 Hemsbach Ger.
190 H4 Hemsbünde Ger.
173 N2 Hemsby Norfolk, England U.K.
165 O4 Hemse Gotland Sweden
163 J6 Hemsedal Norway
163 J6 Hemsedal val. Norway
190 I4 Hemslingen Ger.
190 G5 Hemsloh Ger.
171 O6 Hemsworth West Yorkshire, England U.K.
172 F6 Hemyock Devon, England U.K.
128 G9 Henan Qinghai China
131 I2 Henan prov. China
164 H3 Henån Sweden
180 G4 Hénanbihen France
102 I2 Hen and Chickens Islands North I. N.Z.
205 Q6 Henar r. Spain
205 R9 Henarejos Spain
205 N8 Henares r. Spain
205 Q9 Henares r. Spain
124 Q6 Henashi-zaki pt Japan
106 D8 Henbury N.T. Austr.
199 K4 Hencida Hungary
233 B5 Hendawashi Tanz.
185 A9 Hendaye France
221 L2 Hendek Turkey
285 G5 Henderson Arg.
254 D7 Henderson KY U.S.A.
261 J10 Henderson LA U.S.A.
255 H7 Henderson NC U.S.A.
265 R5 Henderson NV U.S.A.
257 I5 Henderson NY U.S.A.
261 K8 Henderson TN U.S.A.
261 H9 Henderson TX U.S.A.
287 G2 Henderson Island Antarctica
291 K7 Henderson Island Pitcairn Is
255 F8 Hendersonville NC U.S.A.
255 D7 Hendersonville TN U.S.A.
Henderville atoll Gilbert Is Kiribati see Aranuka
144 C6 Hendījān Iran
173 L4 Hendon Greater London, England U.K.
144 E8 Hendorābī i. Iran
186 G5 Hendrik-Ido-Ambacht Neth.
237 O1 Hendriksdal S. Africa
237 N2 Hendrina S. Africa
Hendy-Gwyn Wales U.K. see Whitland
Henegouwen prov. Belgium see Hainaut
173 L6 Henfield West Sussex, England U.K.
144 H9 Hengām Iran
144 F8 Hengām, Jazīreh-ye i. Iran
131 M8 Hengch'un Taiwan
130 E2 Hengdan Gansu China
131 I5 Hengdong Hunan China
130 B4 Hengduan Shan mts Xizang China
186 J4 Hengelo Gelderland Neth.
186 K4 Hengelo Overijssel Neth.
195 O4 Hengersberg Ger.
186 K4 Hengevelde Neth.
212 F1 Henggart Switz.
131 I4 Hengling Hu l. Hunan China
Hengnan Hunan China see Hengyang
172 F4 Hengoed Caerphilly, Wales U.K.
122 G6 Hengshan Heilong. China
131 I5 Hengshan Hunan China
129 K8 Hengshan Shaanxi China
131 I5 Heng Shan mt. Hunan China
129 M7 Heng Shan mts China
129 N8 Hengshui Hebei China
Hengshui Jiangxi China see Chongyi
130 G7 Hengxian Guangxi China
131 I5 Hengyang Hunan China
131 I5 Hengyang Hunan China
Hengzhou Guangxi China see Hengxian
159 N7 Heniches'k Ukr.
159 N7 Heniches'ke, Ozero l. Ukr.
178 E3 Hénin-Beaumont France
Hénin-Liétard France see Hénin-Beaumont
103 E12 Henley South I. N.Z.
173 I3 Henley-in-Arden Warwickshire, England U.K.
173 K4 Henley-on-Thames Oxfordshire, England U.K.
257 J10 Henlopen, Cape DE U.S.A.
173 L3 Henlow Bedfordshire, England U.K.
124 □[1] Henna Okinawa Japan
201 H4 Henndorf am Wallersee Austria
180 E6 Hennebont France
191 D9 Hennef (Sieg) Ger.
237 L3 Hennenman S. Africa
261 G7 Hennessey OK U.S.A.
191 F8 Hennetalsperre resr Ger.
179 L7 Hennezel France
193 H6 Hennickendorf Brandenburg Ger.
193 I5 Hennickendorf Brandenburg Ger.
192 H5 Hennigsdorf Berlin Ger.
257 N5 Henniker NH U.S.A.
190 H2 Hennstedt Ger.
194 C2 Hennweiler Ger.
184 J1 Henrichemont France
261 F9 Henrietta TX U.S.A.
248 D2 Henrietta Maria, Cape Ont. Can.
265 U4 Henrieville UT U.S.A.
Henrique de Carvalho Angola see Saurimo
109 C7 Henry r. W.A. Austr.
250 E8 Henry IL U.S.A.
257 I12 Henry, Cape NC U.S.A.
258 E2 Henry, Lake PA U.S.A.
261 H8 Henryetta OK U.S.A.
286 T1 Henry Ice Rise Antarctica
Henryk Arctowski research stn Antarctica see Arctowski
243 L3 Henry Kater, Cape Nunavut Can.
196 F5 Henryków Pol.
197 I1 Henrykowo Pol.
265 V3 Henry Mountains UT U.S.A.
262 I5 Henrys Fork r. ID U.S.A.
251 M6 Hensall Ont. Can.
264 P8 Henshaw, Lake CA U.S.A.
100 □[6] Hensman, Cape Guadalcanal Solomon Is
108 J4 Hensman, Mount hill W.A. Austr.
190 I3 Henstedt-Ulzburg Ger.
172 H6 Henstridge Somerset, England U.K.
234 B4 Hentiesbaai Namibia
129 L3 Hentiy prov. Mongolia
124 □[1] Hentona Okinawa Japan
Henzada Myanmar see Hinthada
124 □[1] Henza-jima i. Okinawa Japan
Heping Guizhou China see Huishui
Heping Guizhou China see Yanhe
Hepo Guangdong China see Jiexi
187 H6 Heppen Belgium
194 F2 Heppenheim (Bergstraße) Ger.
262 E4 Heppner OR U.S.A.
190 H4 Hepstedt Ger.
Heptanesus is Greece see Ionia Nisia
130 G8 Hepu Guangxi China
128 H8 Heqiao Gansu China
130 C5 Heqing Yunnan China
129 L7 Hequ Shanxi China
Heraclea Turkey see Ereğli
Heraclea Pontica Turkey see Ereğli
Heraklion Kriti Greece see Irakleio
107 L4 Herald Cays atolls Coral Sea Is Terr. Austr.
268 E2 Herández Mex.
102 I5 Herangi hill North I. N.Z.
145 J4 Herāt Afgh.
145 I5 Herāt prov. Afgh.
135 □[2] Heratera i. Addu Atoll Maldives
183 D9 Hérault dept France
183 C10 Hérault r. France
225 H5 Herbagat Sudan
182 I5 Herbasse r. France
180 G7 Herbaudière, Pointe de l' pt France
181 N6 Herbault France
107 K5 Herbert r. Qld Austr.
106 G5 Herbert watercourse N.T. Austr.
247 J5 Herbert Sask. Can.
103 E12 Herbert South I. N.Z.
137 M7 Herbertabad Andaman & Nicobar Is India
106 G7 Herbert Downs Qld Austr.
194 G5 Herbertingen Ger.
244 E5 Herbert Island AK U.S.A.
107 J4 Herberton Qld Austr.
236 F10 Herbertsdale S. Africa
169 F7 Herbertstown Ireland
102 K7 Herbertville North I. N.Z.
109 H8 Herbert Wash salt flat W.A. Austr.
187 H9 Herbeumont Belgium
180 G7 Herbignac France
194 D5 Herbolzheim Ger.
191 F9 Herborn Ger.
195 I4 Herbrechtingen Ger.
191 K8 Herbsleben Ger.
191 H9 Herbstein Ger.
196 G5 Herby Pol.
205 P4 Herce Spain
Hercegfalva Hungary see Mezőfalva
199 H4 Herceghalom Hungary
218 G8 Herceg-Novi Herceg-Novi Montenegro
199 H6 Hercegszántó Hungary
280 B4 Herculândia Brazil
286 Q1 Hercules Dome ice feature Antarctica
191 D8 Herdecke Ger.
191 E9 Herdorf Ger.
199 M4 Hereclean Romania
266 □Q12 Heredia Costa Rica
285 F4 Hereford Arg.
172 G3 Hereford Herefordshire, England U.K.
258 B5 Hereford MD U.S.A.
258 D4 Hereford PA U.S.A.
261 D8 Hereford TX U.S.A.
237 P1 Herefords Swaziland
172 G3 Herefordshire admin. div. England U.K.
101 □[9] Héréhérétué atoll Arch. des Tuamotu Fr. Polynesia
102 H2 Herekino North I. N.Z.
102 H2 Herekino Harbour North I. N.Z.
207 M2 Herencia Spain
199 G4 Herend Hungary
212 C3 Hérens, Val d' val. Switz.
187 G7 Herent Belgium
187 G6 Herentals Belgium
187 G6 Herenthout Belgium
183 C9 Hérépian France
103 D10 Heretaniwha Point South I. N.Z.
191 G6 Herford Ger.
194 H6 Hergatz Ger.
Hergest Island Fr. Polynesia see Motu Iti
212 E2 Hergiswil Switz.
206 H2 Herguijuela Spain
180 H7 Héric France
182 J1 Héricourt France
181 M2 Héricourt-en-Caux France
182 J2 Hérimoncourt France
191 J9 Heringen (Werra) Ger.
192 D2 Heringsdorf Ger.
192 J3 Heringsdorf, Seebad Ger.
260 G6 Herington KS U.S.A.
103 D12 Heriot South I. N.Z.
168 K11 Heriot Scottish Borders, Scotland U.K.
149 M4 Heris Iran
212 G1 Herisau Switz.
182 B3 Hérisson France
286 S1 Heritage Range mts Antarctica
187 H7 Herk r. Belgium
187 H7 Herk-de-Stad Belgium
187 J6 Herkenbosch Neth.
257 K5 Herkimer NY U.S.A.
186 F5 Herkingen Neth.
128 I2 Herlen Mongolia
129 N2 Herlen Gol r. China/Mongolia conv. Kerulen
191 J8 Herleshausen Ger.
264 L1 Herlong CA U.S.A.
180 G3 Herm i. Channel Is
185 B8 Herm France
201 H6 Hermagor Austria
158 F5 Hermakivka Ukr.
267 I4 Hermanas Mex.
168 □O1 Herma Ness hd Scotland U.K.
260 J6 Hermann MO U.S.A.
106 D7 Hermannsburg N.T. Austr.
190 J5 Hermannsburg Ger.
236 D10 Hermanus S. Africa
198 E2 Heřmanův Městec Czech Rep.
195 J3 Hermaringen Ger.
150 E4 Hermel Lebanon
182 B5 Hérment France
194 D3 Hermersberg Ger.
194 B2 Hermeskeil Ger.
105 K4 Hermidale N.S.W. Austr.
238 □[3a] Hermigua La Gomera Canary Is
204 G5 Hermisende Spain
262 E4 Hermiston OR U.S.A.
261 I7 Hermitage MO U.S.A.
256 E7 Hermitage PA U.S.A.
249 J4 Hermitage Bay Nfld and Lab. Can.
283 D9 Hermite, Islas is Chile
113 K7 Hermit Islands P.N.G.
150 D5 Hermon, Mount Lebanon/Syria
Hermonthis Egypt see Armant
178 G5 Hermonville France
Hermopolis Magna Egypt see Al Ashmūnayn
283 C7 Hermosa, Valle val. Arg.
266 D3 Hermosillo Mex.
193 E9 Hermsdorf Ger.
199 J4 Hernád r. Hungary
199 J3 Hernádkak Hungary
277 G6 Hernandarias Para.
285 G3 Hernández Arg.
285 F3 Hernando Arg.
261 K8 Hernando MS U.S.A.
208 B1 Hernani Spain
205 K7 Hernansancho Spain
258 C5 Herndon MD U.S.A.
258 B3 Herndon PA U.S.A.
256 D11 Herndon WV U.S.A.
187 F7 Herne Belgium
191 D7 Herne Ger.
173 O5 Herne Bay Kent, England U.K.
164 E5 Herning Denmark
Heroica Nogales Mex. see Nogales
195 J2 Heroldsbach Ger.
195 K2 Heroldsberg Ger.
187 H7 Héron Belgium
103 F10 Heron, Lake South I. N.Z.
250 H1 Heron Bay Ont. Can.
131 I3 Herong Hubei China
107 M7 Heron Island Qld Austr.
181 K3 Hérouville-St-Clair France
Herowābād Iran see Khalkhāl
159 M8 Heroy'ske Ukr.
201 O5 Herpenyő r. Hungary
191 J9 Herpf Ger.
282 F2 Herradura Arg.
268 F2 Herradura Mex.
238 □[3b] Herradura, Punta de la pt Fuerteventura Canary Is
205 N3 Herramélluri Spain
185 D8 Herré France
260 E3 Herreid SD U.S.A.
194 F4 Herrenberg Ger.
285 H3 Herrera Entre Ríos Arg.
282 E3 Herrera Santiago del Estero Arg.
207 J6 Herrera Spain
208 C5 Herrera mt. Spain
207 I2 Herrera del Duque Spain
208 C5 Herrera de los Navarros Spain
205 L3 Herrera de Pisuerga Spain
285 G5 Herrera Vegas Arg.
205 Q7 Herrería Spain
267 P8 Herrero, Punta pt Mex.
206 F2 Herreruela Spain
195 J3 Herrieden Ger.
260 K7 Herrin IL U.S.A.
194 D6 Herrischried Ger.
179 O6 Herrlisheim France
164 J3 Herrljunga Sweden
195 K6 Herrsching am Ammersee Ger.
165 O4 Herrvik Gotland Sweden
182 B2 Herry France
185 H9 Hers r. France
195 K2 Hersbruck Ger.
191 E9 Herschbach Ger.
191 E8 Herscheid Ger.
245 M1 Herschel Y.T. Can.
237 L6 Herschel S. Africa
245 M1 Herschel Island Y.T. Can.
194 C3 Herschweiler-Pettersheim Ger.
187 G6 Herselt Belgium
179 K4 Herserange France
251 R9 Hershey PA U.S.A.
285 G2 Hersilia Arg.
187 I7 Herstal Belgium
173 M6 Herstmonceux East Sussex, England U.K.
168 J5 Herston Orkney, Scotland U.K.
250 B4 Hertel WI U.S.A.
191 D7 Herten Ger.
173 L4 Hertford Hertfordshire, England U.K.
255 I7 Hertford NC U.S.A.
173 M4 Hertfordshire admin. div. England U.K.
199 K2 Hertník Slovakia
158 F5 Hertsa Ukr.
237 J4 Hertzogville S. Africa
204 I8 Hervás Spain
187 I7 Herve Belgium
249 G2 Hervé, Lac l. Que. Can.
107 N8 Hervey Bay Qld Austr.
107 N8 Hervey Bay b. Qld Austr.
Hervey Island atoll Cook Is see Manuae
103 □[2] Hervey Islands Cook Is
186 H5 Herwijnen Neth.
194 E3 Herxheim bei Landau (Pfalz) Ger.
178 G8 Héry France
192 G5 Herzberg Brandenburg Ger.
193 H7 Herzberg Brandenburg Ger.
192 E3 Herzberg Mecklenburg-Vorpommern Ger.
191 J7 Herzberg am Harz Ger.
191 F7 Herzebrock-Clarholz Ger.
187 E7 Herzele Belgium
193 I6 Herzfelde Ger.
190 H3 Herzhorn Ger.
190 E5 Herzlake Ger.
150 C6 Herzliyya Israel
195 J2 Herzogenaurach Ger.
212 D1 Herzogenbuchsee Switz.
201 M3 Herzogenburg Austria
192 F4 Herzsprung Ger.
144 D7 Ḥeşār Iran
144 H9 Ḥeşār Iran
144 C4 Ḥeşār Iran
145 K4 Ḥeşār, Kūh-e mts Afgh.
187 G7 Hesbaye reg. Belgium
178 D3 Hesdin France
190 E4 Hesel Ger.
130 G7 Heshan Guangxi China
131 J3 Heshengqiao Hubei China
144 E8 Heshnīz Iran
129 K9 Heshui Gansu China
129 M8 Heshun Shanxi China
187 J9 Hespérange Lux.
264 O7 Hesperia CA U.S.A.
250 H6 Hesperia MI U.S.A.
244 I3 Hesperus, Mount AK U.S.A.
246 E5 Hesquiat B.C. Can.
245 N3 Hess r. Y.T. Can.
245 J2 Hess Creek r. AK U.S.A.
195 J2 Heßdorf Ger.
Hesse land Ger. see Hessen
250 J3 Hessel MI U.S.A.
195 J3 Hesselberg hill Ger.
164 H5 Hesselø i. Denmark
164 H5 Hesselø nature res. Denmark
191 K6 Hessen Ger.
191 H9 Hessen land Ger.
195 M2 Hessenreuther und Mantler Wald park Ger.
194 E2 Heßheim Ger.
191 I9 Hessische Rhön, Naturpark nature res. Ger.
191 H10 Hessischer Spessart, Naturpark nature res. Ger.
191 I8 Hessisch Lichtenau Ger.
191 H6 Hessisch Oldendorf Ger.
245 N3 Hess Mountains Y.T. Can.
192 F1 Hestehoved hd Denmark
191 J6 Hestern (Adenbüttel) Ger.
162 J5 Hestvika Norway
171 K7 Heswall Merseyside, England U.K.
118 G4 Het r. Laos
264 J4 Hetch Hetchy Aqueduct canal CA U.S.A.
186 I5 Heteren Neth.
199 G5 Hetés Hungary
198 F5 Hetés hills Hungary
173 O2 Hethersett Norfolk, England U.K.
Hetian Guangdong China see Luhe
190 I3 Hetlingen Ger.
130 G8 Hetou Guangdong China
179 L5 Hettange-Grande France
194 E2 Hettenleidelheim Ger.
195 L4 Hettenshausen Ger.
194 G5 Hettingen Ger.
260 D2 Hettinger ND U.S.A.
171 M5 Hetton North Yorkshire, England U.K.
171 O4 Hetton-le-Hole Tyne and Wear, England U.K.
193 E7 Hettstedt Ger.
194 B2 Hetzerath Ger.
194 H4 Heubach Ger.
191 D7 Heubach r. Ger.
194 F5 Heuberg ridge Ger.
191 G9 Heuchelheim Ger.
178 D3 Heuchin France
191 K7 Heudeber Ger.
186 H5 Heukelum Neth.
236 I5 Heuningneskloof S. Africa
237 L3 Heuningspruit S. Africa
236 H2 Heuningvlei salt pan S. Africa
187 H6 Heusden Belgium
186 H5 Heusden Neth.
191 G10 Heusenstamm Ger.
191 J10 Heustreu Ger.
194 B3 Heusweiler Ger.
257 J4 Heuvelton NY U.S.A.
181 L2 Hève, Cap de la c. France
199 J4 Heves Hungary
199 J4 Heves county Hungary
198 G5 Hévíz Hungary
199 I4 Hévizgyörk Hungary
198 F3 Hevlín Czech Rep.
Ḥevron West Bank see Hebron
259 G2 Hewitt NJ U.S.A.
256 H11 Hewlett VA U.S.A.
200 B5 Hexenkopf mt. Austria
171 M4 Hexham Northumberland, England U.K.
131 L3 Hexian Anhui China
Hexigten Qi Nei Mongol China see Jingpeng
128 H7 Hexipu Gansu China
236 D9 Hexrivierberg mts S. Africa
173 M5 Hextable Kent, England U.K.
Heyang Hebei China see Nanhe
129 L9 Heyang Shaanxi China
173 N4 Heybridge Essex, England U.K.
144 A3 Ḥeydarābād Iran
144 E5 Ḥeydarābād Iran
144 I6 Ḥeydarābād Khorāsān Iran
144 H7 Ḥeydarābād Sīstān va Balūchestān Iran
Heydebreck Pol. see Kędzierzyn-Koźle
236 I7 Heydon S. Africa
191 I6 Heyen Ger.
232 E3 Heygali well Eth.
Heyin Qinghai China see Guide
193 H8 Heynitz Ger.
182 G5 Heyrieux France
171 L5 Heysham Lancashire, England U.K.
237 O2 Heyshope Dam S. Africa
187 I6 Heythuysen Neth.
131 J7 Heyuan Guangdong China
104 H8 Heywood Vic. Austr.
171 M6 Heywood Greater Manchester, England U.K.
250 F9 Heyworth IL U.S.A.
129 N9 Heze Shandong China
130 E5 Hezhang Guizhou China
128 H9 Hezheng Gansu China
131 H6 Hezhou Guangxi China
128 H9 Hezuo Gansu China
237 P2 Hhohho reg. Swaziland
255 G13 Hialeah FL U.S.A.
Hiau i. Fr. Polynesia see Eiao
255 F8 Hiawassee GA U.S.A.
260 H6 Hiawatha KS U.S.A.
171 P6 Hibaldstow North Lincolnshire, England U.K.
146 F7 Hibata reg. Saudi Arabia
237 O6 Hibberdene S. Africa
250 B2 Hibbing MN U.S.A.
105 J10 Hibbs, Point Tas. Austr.
108 G2 Hibernia Reef Ashmore & Cartier Is Austr.
125 H12 Hibiki-nada b. Japan
144 I8 Hīchān Iran
126 F4 Hichisō Japan
261 K7 Hickman KY U.S.A.
255 G8 Hickory NC U.S.A.
258 D5 Hickory Hill PA U.S.A.
105 L7 Hicks, Point c. Vic. Austr.
102 M4 Hicks Bay North I. N.Z.
267 O9 Hicks Cays is Belize
247 K2 Hicks Lake Nunavut Can.
259 H3 Hicksville NY U.S.A.
256 A7 Hicksville OH U.S.A.
261 F9 Hico TX U.S.A.
126 F5 Hida-gawa r. Japan
124 T4 Hidaka Hokkaidō Japan
126 A5 Hidaka Hyōgo Japan
127 J4 Hidaka Saitama Japan
126 B8 Hidaka Wakayama Japan
126 B8 Hidaka-gawa r. Japan
124 T4 Hidaka-sanmyaku mts Japan
126 F4 Hida-Kiso-gawa Kokutei-kōen park Japan
126 E3 Hida-kōchi plat. Japan
267 J4 Hidalgo Coahuila Mex.
268 C1 Hidalgo Durango Mex.
268 G2 Hidalgo San Luis Potosí Mex.
269 H1 Hidalgo Tamaulipas Mex.
268 D2 Hidalgo Zacatecas Mex.
268 E1 Hidalgo Zacatecas Mex.
269 H5 Hidalgo state Mex.
238 □[3a] Hidalgo, Punta del pt Tenerife Canary Is
266 G4 Hidalgo del Parral Mex.
269 M8 Hidalgotitlán Mex.
269 K8 Hidalgo Yalalag Mex.
199 H5 Hidas Hungary
126 G3 Hida-sanmyaku mts Japan
199 K3 Hidasnémeti Hungary
191 G6 Hiddenhausen Ger.
192 H1 Hiddensee Ger.
192 H1 Hiddensee i. Ger.
107 K5 Hidden Valley Qld Austr.
150 D2 Hıdırlı Turkey
219 K4 Hidişelu de Sus Romania
164 C3 Hidra i. Norway
280 C2 Hidrolândia Brazil
278 C5 Hidrolina Brazil
201 K4 Hieflau Austria
205 O6 Hiendelaencina Spain
100 □[5] Hienghène New Caledonia
181 J6 Hière r. France
Hierosolyma Israel/West Bank see Jerusalem
205 M7 Hierro, Cabeza de mt. Spain
184 D4 Hiersac France
162 T3 Hietaniemi Fin.
127 L1 Higashi Japan
125 J12 Higashi-Hiroshima Japan
125 □[3] Higashi-iwa i. Japan
127 J6 Higashiizu Japan
127 J3 Higashi-Matsuyama Japan
127 J4 Higashimurayama Japan
124 R8 Higashine Japan
124 □[1] Higashi-Onna Okinawa Japan
126 C6 Higashi-Ōsaka Japan
126 F4 Higashi-Shirakawa Japan
125 G13 Higashi-suidō sea chan. Japan
126 E6 Higashiura Aichi Japan
126 A6 Higashiura Hyōgo Japan
127 G2 Higashi-yama mt. Japan
208 B1 Higer, Cabo c. Spain
259 J2 Higganum CT U.S.A.
261 E7 Higgins TX U.S.A.
257 K5 Higgins Bay NY U.S.A.
250 J5 Higgins Lake MI U.S.A.
236 H5 Higg's Hope S. Africa
173 M5 Higham Kent, England U.K.
173 K3 Higham Ferrers Northamptonshire, England U.K.
172 D6 Highampton Devon, England U.K.
High Atlas mts Morocco see Haut Atlas
171 L5 High Bentham North Yorkshire, England U.K.
168 H11 High Blantyre South Lanarkshire, Scotland U.K.
172 G5 Highbridge Somerset, England U.K.
258 F3 High Bridge NJ U.S.A.
173 J5 Highclere Hampshire, England U.K.
262 D5 High Desert OR U.S.A.
Higher Bentham England U.K. see High Bentham
171 N4 High Etherley Durham, England U.K.
250 F4 High Falls Reservoir WI U.S.A.
237 O6 Highflats S. Africa
173 N4 High Garrett Essex, England U.K.
270 □ Highgate Jamaica
173 N5 High Halden Kent, England U.K.
171 P5 High Hawsker North Yorkshire, England U.K.
171 L4 High Hesket Cumbria, England U.K.
219 J4 Highiş, Vârful hill Romania
High Island i. H.K. China see Leung Shuen Wan Chau
261 H11 High Island TX U.S.A.
250 I4 High Island i. MI U.S.A.
131 □J7 High Island Reservoir H.K. China
238 □[2b] High Knoll hill St Helena
168 G7 Highland admin. div. Scotland U.K.
264 O7 Highland CA U.S.A.
258 B6 Highland MD U.S.A.
250 C2 Highland MN U.S.A.
259 H1 Highland NY U.S.A.
250 D6 Highland WI U.S.A.
258 C7 Highland Beach MD U.S.A.
259 H2 Highland Falls NY U.S.A.
258 F1 Highland Lake NY U.S.A.
259 G2 Highland Lakes NJ U.S.A.
250 G7 Highland Park IL U.S.A.
256 B6 Highland Park MI U.S.A.
259 G4 Highland Park NJ U.S.A.
264 M3 Highland Peak CA U.S.A.
265 R4 Highland Peak NV U.S.A.
259 H4 Highlands NJ U.S.A.
256 H11 Highland Springs VA U.S.A.
171 M7 High Legh Cheshire, England U.K.
246 G3 High Level Alta Can.
139 K9 High Level Canal India
172 H3 Highley Shropshire, England U.K.
265 Q9 Highline Canal CA U.S.A.
171 K4 High Lorton Cumbria, England U.K.
260 F3 Highmore SD U.S.A.
172 H4 Highnam Gloucestershire, England U.K.
171 N7 High Peak hills England U.K.
255 H8 High Point NC U.S.A.
258 F2 High Point hill NJ U.S.A.
246 G4 High Prairie Alta Can.
246 H5 High River Alta Can.
255 H12 High Rock Gd Bahama Bahamas
247 K4 Highrock Lake Man. Can.
247 J3 Highrock Lake Sask. Can.
255 G8 High Rock Lake resr NC U.S.A.
105 J10 High Rocky Point Tas. Austr.
171 M5 High Seat hill England U.K.
255 F11 High Springs FL U.S.A.
High Tatras mts Pol./Slovakia see Tatry
259 F4 Hightstown NJ U.S.A.
173 I4 Highworth Swindon, England U.K.
173 K4 High Wycombe Buckinghamshire, England U.K.
232 E3 Higlale well Eth.
266 F5 Higuera de Abuya Mex.
207 L5 Higuera de Arjona Spain
206 H3 Higuera de la Serena Spain
206 G5 Higuera de la Sierra Spain
206 F4 Higuera de Vargas Spain
266 E5 Higuera de Zaragoza Mex.
206 F4 Higuera la Real Spain
271 □[1] Higüero, Punta pt Puerto Rico
271 J8 Higuerote Venez.
209 C10 Higueruela Spain
209 D8 Higueruelas Spain
271 I4 Higüey Dom. Rep.
127 K5 Higuri-gawa r. Japan
99 I3 Hihifo Tonga
162 T3 Hihnavaara Fin.
162 T5 Hiidenportin kansallispuisto nat. park Fin.
160 H1 Hiidenvesi l. Fin.
232 E3 Hiiraan Somalia
232 E3 Hiiraan admin. reg. Somalia
160 F3 Hiiumaa i. Estonia
150 E5 Hījānah, Buḥayrat al imp. l. Syria
208 E5 Híjar Spain
116 E6 Hijau, Gunung mt. Indon.
146 C2 Hijaz reg. Saudi Arabia
125 I13 Hiji Japan
127 H5 Hijiri-dake mt. Japan
114 E8 Hijo Mindanao Phil.
205 O2 Hijuela r. Spain
127 I3 Hikabo-yama mt. Japan
126 B5 Hikami Japan
125 I13 Hikari Japan
127 M4 Hikata Japan
125 L12 Hiketa Japan
125 M13 Hikigawa Japan
126 B8 Hiki-gawa r. Japan
224 E2 Ḥikmah, Ra's al pt Egypt
265 Q4 Hiko NV U.S.A.
126 D5 Hikone Japan
125 H13 Hiko-san mt. Japan
102 I2 Hikurangi North I. N.Z.
102 M4 Hikurangi mt. North I. N.Z.
103 □[4] Hikutavake Niue
151 J4 Hil Azer.
115 E7 Hila Maluku Indon.
115 B6 Hilahila Sulawesi Indon.
150 B8 Hilāl, Jabal hill Egypt
276 C5 Hilaricos Chile
287 K1 Hilary Coast Antarctica
193 H9 Hilbersdorf Ger.
191 F9 Hilchenbach Ger.
265 S4 Hildale UT U.S.A.
191 K10 Hildburghausen Ger.
191 C8 Hilden Ger.
173 M5 Hildenborough Kent, England U.K.
191 J9 Hilders Ger.
171 Q5 Hilderthorpe East Riding of Yorkshire, England U.K.
191 I6 Hildesheim Ger.
147 N5 Ḥilf, Ra's c. Oman
173 M2 Hilgay Norfolk, England U.K.
190 H5 Hilgermissen Ger.
195 K5 Hilgertshausen Ger.
139 L7 Hili Bangl.
190 E5 Hilkenbrook Ger.
109 C11 Hill r. W.A. Austr.
271 □[4] Hillaby, Mount Barbados
Hillah Iraq see Al Ḥillah
236 E9 Hillandale S. Africa
256 B8 Hillard OH U.S.A.
267 O9 Hill Bank Belize
260 F6 Hill City KS U.S.A.
260 D4 Hill City SD U.S.A.
265 W2 Hill Creek r. UT U.S.A.
258 B7 Hillcrest Heights MD U.S.A.
191 G6 Hille Ger.
186 G4 Hillegom Neth.
105 L5 Hill End N.S.W. Austr.
164 I6 Hillerød Denmark
103 H8 Hillersden South I. N.Z.
191 J6 Hillerse Ger.
165 J4 Hillerstorp Sweden
191 C10 Hillesheim Ger.
107 J5 Hillgrove Qld Austr.
247 I2 Hill Island Lake N.W.T. Can.
251 K4 Hillman MI U.S.A.
109 D11 Hillman, Lake salt flat W.A. Austr.
260 K6 Hillsboro IL U.S.A.
260 J6 Hillsboro MO U.S.A.
260 G2 Hillsboro ND U.S.A.
257 N5 Hillsboro NH U.S.A.
263 K10 Hillsboro NM U.S.A.
256 B9 Hillsboro OH U.S.A.
262 C4 Hillsboro OR U.S.A.
261 G9 Hillsboro TX U.S.A.
250 D6 Hillsboro WI U.S.A.
255 G12 Hillsboro Canal FL U.S.A.
271 □[3] Hillsborough Grenada
169 J4 Hillsborough Northern Ireland U.K.
255 H7 Hillsborough NC U.S.A.
107 L6 Hillsborough, Cape Qld Austr.
191 E10 Hillscheid Ger.
250 J8 Hillsdale MI U.S.A.
257 L6 Hillsdale NY U.S.A.
251 R8 Hillsgrove PA U.S.A.
108 E6 Hillside W.A. Austr.
168 L9 Hillside Angus, Scotland U.K.
168 □N2 Hillside Shetland, Scotland U.K.
259 G3 Hillside NJ U.S.A.
248 C3 Hillsport Ont. Can.
105 J5 Hillston N.S.W. Austr.
256 E12 Hillsville VA U.S.A.
168 □N2 Hillswick Shetland, Scotland U.K.
169 J4 Hilltown Northern Ireland U.K.
264 □F14 Hilo HI U.S.A.
172 H5 Hilperton Wiltshire, England U.K.
195 K3 Hilpoltstein Ger.
171 K5 Hilpsford Point England U.K.
179 O7 Hilsenheim France
191 F6 Hilter am Teutoburger Wald Ger.
106 G6 Hilton Qld Austr.
237 O5 Hilton S. Africa
173 I2 Hilton Derbyshire, England U.K.
256 H5 Hilton NY U.S.A.
251 K3 Hilton Beach Ont. Can.
255 G9 Hilton Head Island SC U.S.A.
195 K2 Hiltpoltstein Ger.
148 I5 Hilvan Turkey
186 H6 Hilvarenbeek Neth.
186 H4 Hilversum Neth.
194 F6 Hilzingen Ger.
146 G6 Ḥimá well Saudi Arabia
138 F4 Himachal Pradesh state India
146 E3 Ḥimā Ḍarīyah, Jabal mt. Saudi Arabia
126 F6 Himaga-shima i. Japan
138 F3 Himalaya mts Asia
162 Q4 Himanka Fin.
150 H2 Ḥimār, Wādī al watercourse Syria/Turkey
220 A2 Himarë Albania
102 J7 Himatangi North I. N.Z.
102 J7 Himatangi Beach North I. N.Z.
138 D8 Himatnagar Gujarat India
201 N3 Himberg Austria
190 K4 Himbergen Ger.
146 D8 Himbirti Eritrea
127 G1 Hime-gawa r. Japan
125 L12 Himeji Japan
124 S7 Himekami-dake mt. Japan
199 H5 Himesháza Hungary
125 I13 Hime-shima i. Japan
237 N5 Himeville S. Africa
124 P8 Hime-zaki pt Japan
126 E2 Himi Japan
135 □[1] Himmafushi i. N. Male Maldives
201 J6 Himmelberg Austria
164 F5 Himmelbjerget hill Denmark
190 H3 Himmelpforten Ger.
146 C8 Himora Eth.
150 E4 Ḥimş Syria
150 G3 Ḥimş governorate Syria
Ḥimş, Baḥrat resr Syria see Qaţţīnah, Buḥayrat
125 H14 Hinagu Japan
116 B4 Hinako i. Indon.
103 J8 Hinakura North I. N.Z.
114 F7 Hinatuan Mindanao Phil.
114 E7 Hinatuan Passage Phil.
158 H7 Hîncești Moldova
270 G4 Hinche Haiti
245 K3 Hinchinbrook Entrance sea channel AK U.S.A.
107 K5 Hinchinbrook Island Qld Austr.
245 K3 Hinchinbrook Island AK U.S.A.
173 J2 Hinckley Leicestershire, England U.K.
250 F8 Hinckley IL U.S.A.
257 □P4 Hinckley ME U.S.A.
250 B3 Hinckley MN U.S.A.
265 T2 Hinckley UT U.S.A.
257 J5 Hinckley Reservoir NY U.S.A.
150 D9 Hind, Wādī al watercourse Saudi Arabia
231 B6 Hinda Congo
133 C12 Hindan r. India
151 I5 Hindarx Azer.
138 F6 Hindaun Rajasthan India
195 I6 Hindelang Ger.
192 E5 Hindenburg Ger.
Hindenburg Pol. see Zabrze
171 P4 Hinderwell North Yorkshire, England U.K.
173 K5 Hindhead Surrey, England U.K.
171 L6 Hindley Greater Manchester, England U.K.
256 C11 Hindman KY U.S.A.
105 H7 Hindmarsh, Lake dry lake Vic. Austr.
139 J9 Hindola Orissa India
138 E7 Hindoli Rajasthan India
172 H5 Hindon Wiltshire, England U.K.
138 G8 Hindoria Madh. Prad. India
136 F5 Hindri r. India
103 F11 Hinds South I. N.Z.
165 K4 Hindsen l. Sweden
164 G6 Hindsholm pen. Denmark
145 L4 Hindu Kush mts Afgh./Pak.
136 E6 Hindupur Andhra Prad. India
246 G3 Hines Creek Alta Can.
255 G10 Hinesville GA U.S.A.
138 G9 Hinganghat Mahar. India
173 N2 Hingham Norfolk, England U.K.
145 K9 Hinglaj Pak.
Hingol r. Pak. see Girdar Dhor
145 K9 Hingol r. Pak.
136 E3 Hingoli Mahar. India
149 J4 Hınıs Turkey
258 C4 Hinkletown PA U.S.A.
104 F5 Hinks Conservation Park nature res. S.A. Austr.
162 □ Hinlopenstretet str. Svalbard
162 M2 Hinnøya i. Norway
126 D5 Hino Shiga Japan
127 J4 Hino Tōkyō Japan
125 K11 Hino Tottori Japan
114 D7 Hinobaan Negros Phil.
127 J1 Hinoemata Japan
126 D3 Hino-gawa r. Japan
126 D5 Hino-gawa r. Japan
204 H9 Hinojal Spain
206 F4 Hinojales Spain
206 F5 Hinojales, Sierra de hills Spain
207 N5 Hinojares Spain
207 K3 Hinojasas de Calatrava Spain
205 O5 Hinojedo mt. Spain
285 G5 Hinojo Arg.
206 G6 Hinojos Spain
205 Q6 Hinojosa Spain
204 G7 Hinojosa de Duero Spain
208 D6 Hinojosa de Jarque Spain
207 I3 Hinojosa del Duque Spain
202 D2 Hinojosa de San Vicente Spain
125 I14 Hinokage Japan
126 B8 Hino-misaki pt Japan
125 J11 Hino-misaki pt Japan
257 M6 Hinsdale NH U.S.A.
165 M1 Hinsen l. Sweden
190 D4 Hinte Ger.
200 E4 Hinteres Sonnenwendjoch mt. Austria
193 J9 Hinterhermsdorf Ger.
191 K9 Hinternah Ger.
212 G2 Hinterrhein Switz.
212 G2 Hinterrhein r. Switz.
195 P4 Hinterschmiding Ger.
200 H4 Hintersee Austria
192 J3 Hintersee Ger.
194 D3 Hinterweidenthal Ger.
194 E6 Hinterzarten Ger.
118 B6 Hinthada Myanmar
242 G4 Hinton Alta Can.
261 F8 Hinton OK U.S.A.
256 E11 Hinton WV U.S.A.
102 J4 Hinuera North I. N.Z.
127 M3 Hi-numa l. Japan
212 F1 Hinwil Switz.
185 C8 Hinx France
Hiort i. Western Isles, Scotland U.K. see St Kilda
267 I5 Hipólito Mex.
284 D3 Hipólito Yrigoyen Arg.
200 E5 Hippach Austria
186 G3 Hippolytushoef Neth.
Hipponium Italy see Vibo Valentia
231 F6 Hippopotames, Réserve de nature res. Dem. Rep. Congo
231 E5 Hippopotames, Réserve de Faune des nature res. Dem. Rep. Congo
Hippo Regius Alg. see Annaba
Hippo Zarytus Tunisia see Bizerte
190 G4 Hipstedt Ger.
149 L4 Hirabit Dağ mt. Turkey
125 G13 Hirado Japan
125 G13 Hirado-shima i. Japan
172 E1 Hiraethog, Mynydd hills Wales U.K.
227 G5 Hirafok Alg.
127 J1 Hiraga-take mt. Japan
126 C6 Hirakata Japan
139 I9 Hirakud Reservoir India
233 C5 Hiraman watercourse Kenya
124 □C22 Hirara Nansei-shotō Japan
127 M1 Hirata Fukushima Japan

126 E5 Hirata Gifu Japan
125 J11 Hirata Shimane Japan
127 J5 Hiratsuka Japan
126 G5 Hiraya Japan
136 D5 Hirekerur Karnataka India
228 D5 Hiré-Watta Côte d'Ivoire
136 E6 Hiriyur Karnataka India
Hîrlău Romania see Hârlău
232 D2 Hīrna Eth.
159 Q5 Hirnyk Donets'ka Oblast' Ukr.
197 M5 Hirnyk L'vivs'ka Oblast' Ukr.
159 N6 Hirnyts'ke Ukr.
127 I1 Hirogami Japan
126 B7 Hirokawa Japan
127 M1 Hirono Japan
124 U4 Hiroo Japan
124 R6 Hirosaki Japan
125 K11 Hirose Japan
125 J12 Hiroshima Japan
125 J12 Hiroshima airport Japan
125 J12 Hiroshima pref. Japan
124 S8 Hirota-wan b. Japan
194 F5 Hirrlingen Ger.
195 K2 Hirschaid Ger.
195 L2 Hirschau Ger.
193 E10 Hirschberg Ger.
195 L6 Hirschberg mt. Ger.
Hirschberg Pol. see Jelenia Góra
195 N4 Hirschenstein mt. Ger.
193 I8 Hirschfeld Ger.
193 K9 Hirschfelde Ger.
194 F3 Hirschhorn (Neckar) Ger.
164 G4 Hirsholmene nature res. Denmark
182 K1 Hirsingue France
159 O7 Hirsivka Ukr.
159 R5 Hirs'ke Ukr.
158 J5 Hirs'kyy Tikych r. Ukr.
178 H4 Hirson France
Hîrşova Romania see Hârşova
Hirta i. Western Isles, Scotland U.K. see St Kilda
201 N4 Hirtenberg Austria
164 F4 Hirtshals Denmark
127 J5 Hiruga-take mt. Japan
126 F4 Hirukawa Japan
172 E4 Hirwaun Rhondda Cynon Taff, Wales U.K.
191 H10 Hirzenhain Ger.
201 L5 Hirzmannstausee l. Austria
126 D6 Hisai Japan
125 F14 Hisaka-jima i. Japan
138 E5 Hisar Haryana India
149 N5 Hisar Iran
221 K3 Hisarcık Turkey
Hisarköy Turkey see Domaniç
148 F3 Hisarönü Turkey
221 I6 Hisarönü Körfezi b. Turkey
149 L8 Ḩisb, Sha'īb watercourse Iraq
128 H2 Hishig-Öndör Bulgan Mongolia
147 I7 Ḩişn al Fuḑūl Yemen
145 M2 Hisor Tajik.
143 L8 Hisorak qo'riqxonasi nature res. Uzbek.
Hisor Tizmasi mts Tajik./Uzbek. see Gissar Range
Hispalis Spain see Sevilla
Hispania country Europe see Spain
270 G3 Hispaniola i. Caribbean Sea
138 E1 Hispur Glacier Pak.
Hissar Haryana India see Hisar
139 J7 Hisua Bihar India
150 E4 Ḩisyah Syria
149 K7 Hīt Iraq
125 H13 Hita Japan
205 N7 Hita Spain
127 M2 Hitachi Japan
127 M3 Hitachinaka Japan
127 M2 Hitachi-Ōta Japan
135 □2 Hitaddu Addu Atoll Maldives
135 □2 Hitaddu i. Addu Atoll Maldives
173 L4 Hitchin Hertfordshire, England U.K.
107 K5 Hitchinbrook Island National Park nat. park Qld Austr.
Hithadhoo i. Addu Atoll Maldives see Hitaddu
101 □9a Hitiaa Tahiti Fr. Polynesia
125 H14 Hitoyoshi Japan
162 J5 Hitra i. Norway
200 A5 Hittisau Austria
192 D4 Hitzacker Ger.
201 L5 Hitzendorf Austria
195 K4 Hitzhofen Ger.
190 I3 Hitzhusen Ger.
212 E1 Hitzkirch Switz.
100 □5 Hiu i. Vanuatu
127 J2 Hiuchiga-take vol. Japan
125 K12 Hiuchi-nada b. Japan
101 □9 Hiva Oa i. Fr. Polynesia
125 L13 Hiwasa Japan
246 F4 Hixon B.C. Can.
107 N7 Hixson Cay rf Qld Austr.
250 C5 Hixton WI U.S.A.
197 L5 Hiyche Ukr.
126 C5 Hiyoshi Kyōto Japan
126 G4 Hiyoshi Nagano Japan
150 D8 Hiyyon watercourse Israel
149 K4 Hizan Turkey
164 G4 Hjallerup Denmark
165 L2 Hjälmaren l. Sweden
247 I2 Hjalmar Lake N.W.T. Can.
164 F2 Hjartdøld r. Norway
163 I6 Hjelle Norway
164 B1 Hjellestad Norway
192 F1 Hjelm Bugt b. Denmark
164 C2 Hjelmeland Norway
163 J5 Hjerkinn Norway
165 K3 Hjo Sweden
190 H1 Hjordkær Denmark
164 G4 Hjørring Denmark
190 J1 Hjortø i. Denmark
164 H4 Hjuvik Sweden
118 D4 Hka, Nam r. Myanmar
118 C1 Hkakabo Razi mt. Myanmar
118 D4 Hkok r. Myanmar
118 C1 Hkring Bum mt. Myanmar
237 P4 Hlabisa S. Africa
118 C6 Hlaing r. Myanmar
118 C4 Hlaingdet Myanmar
Hlako Kangri mt. Xizang China see Lhagoi Kangri
237 P2 Hlane Royal National Park Swaziland
237 P2 Hlatikulu Swaziland
159 P8 Hlazivka Ukr.
159 M1 Hlazove Ukr.
198 F5 Hlebine Croatia
118 C6 Hlegu Myanmar
158 J3 Hlevakha Ukr.
158 I6 Hlinaia Moldova
199 H3 Hliník nad Hronom Slovakia
199 K3 Hlinné Slovakia
198 E2 Hlinsko Czech Rep.
219 P3 Hlipiceni Romania
213 Q6 Hlm hill Croatia
159 M4 Hlobyne Ukr.
237 L4 Hlohlowane S. Africa
198 F3 Hlohovec Czech Rep.
199 G3 Hlohovec Slovakia
237 M4 Hlotse Lesotho
198 G2 Hlubočky Czech Rep.
198 D2 Hluboká nad Vltavou Czech Rep.
199 H2 Hlučín Czech Rep.
237 Q4 Hluhluwe S. Africa
237 Q4 Hluhluwe Game Reserve nature res. S. Africa
237 P4 Hluhluwe-Umfolozi Park nature res. S. Africa
199 G3 Hluk Czech Rep.
159 M2 Hlukhiv Ukr.
158 H4 Hlukhivtsi Ukr.
118 D3 Hlung-Tan Myanmar
160 L8 Hlusha Belarus
158 G2 Hlushkavichy Belarus
160 L9 Hlusk Belarus
158 E5 Hlyboka Ukr.
160 K6 Hlybokaye Belarus
158 G2 Hlynne Ukr.
159 L5 Hlyns'k Ukr.
158 D4 Hlynyany Ukr.
199 J2 Hniezdné Slovakia
199 J3 Hnilec r. Slovakia
158 H4 Hnivan' Ukr.
197 M6 Hnizdychiv Ukr.
158 E4 Hnizna r. Ukr.
199 I3 Hnúšťa Slovakia
158 D4 Hnyla Lypa r. Ukr.
159 Q3 Hnylytsya Ukr.
158 J5 Hnylyy Tikych r. Ukr.
159 K6 Hnylyy Yelanets' r. Ukr.
229 F5 Ho Ghana
118 G4 Hoa Binh Vietnam
118 G5 Hoa Binh Vietnam
234 C4 Hoachanas Namibia
118 F3 Hoang Liên Sơn mts Vietnam
Hoang Sa is S. China Sea see Paracel Islands
234 B3 Hoanib watercourse Namibia
118 H6 Hoan Lao Vietnam
234 B3 Hoarusib watercourse Namibia
105 K10 Hobart Tas. Austr.
261 F8 Hobart OK U.S.A.
261 D9 Hobbs NM U.S.A.
286 P1 Hobbs Coast Antarctica
151 B6 Höbek Dağı mt. Turkey
255 G12 Hobe Sound FL U.S.A.
237 L5 Hobhouse S. Africa
274 C4 Hobo Col.
259 G3 Hoboken NJ U.S.A.
132 G3 Hoboksar Xinjiang China
199 G5 Hobol Hungary
164 G2 Hobøl Norway
129 M6 Hobor Nei Mongol China
Hobot Xar Qi Nei Mongol China see Xin Bulag
164 F5 Hobro Denmark
187 I9 Hobscheid Lux.
165 O5 Hoburg Gotland Sweden
165 O5 Hoburgen pt Gotland Sweden
232 F3 Hobyo Somalia
221 K4 Hocalar Turkey
244 I2 Hochandochtla Mountain hill AK U.S.A.
200 G5 Hocharn mt. Austria
194 H2 Höchberg Ger.
201 K3 Hochbira hill Austria
190 H2 Hochdonn Ger.
194 H5 Hochdorf Ger.
212 E1 Hochdorf Switz.
194 E6 Höchenschwand Ger.
Hochfeiler mt. Austria/Italy see Gran Pilastro
201 H5 Hochfeind mt. Austria
234 C4 Hochfeld Namibia
179 O6 Hochfelden France
191 G7 Hochfläche reg. Ger.
Hochgall mt. Austria/Italy see Collalto
195 N6 Hochgern mt. Ger.
201 I5 Hochgolling mt. Austria
191 K7 Hochharz nat. park Ger.
191 J10 Höchheim Ger.
191 F10 Hochheim am Main Ger.
119 H9 Hô Chi Minh Vietnam
Ho Chi Minh City Vietnam see Hô Chi Minh
195 N6 Hochkalter mt. Ger.
200 H5 Hochkönig mt. Austria
201 J6 Hochobir mt. Austria
201 L4 Hochschwab mt. Austria
201 K4 Hochschwab mts Austria
194 D3 Hochspeyer Ger.
194 E3 Hochstadt (Pfalz) Ger.
195 J2 Höchstadt an der Aisch Ger.
195 J4 Höchstädt an der Donau Ger.
194 C2 Hochstetten-Dhaun Ger.
194 F2 Höchst im Odenwald Ger.
194 H5 Hochsträß reg. Ger.
200 B5 Hochtannbergpass pass Austria
191 F10 Hochtaunus nature res. Ger.
201 K4 Hochtor mt. Austria
200 E4 Hochunnutz mt. Austria
212 H2 Hochwang mt. Switz.
Hochwilde mt. Austria/Italy see L'Altissima
194 F3 Hockenheim Ger.
256 D9 Hocking r. OH U.S.A.
173 N4 Hockley Essex, England U.K.
173 I3 Hockley Heath West Midlands, England U.K.
197 K6 Hoczew Pol.
197 K6 Hoczewka r. Pol.
228 C2 Ḥôḍ reg. Maur.
138 F6 Hodal Haryana India
199 L4 Hodász Hungary
126 E2 Hödatsu-san hill Japan
232 F2 Hodda mt. Somalia
171 M6 Hodder r. England U.K.
173 L4 Hoddesdon Hertfordshire, England U.K.
Hodeidah Yemen see Al Ḩudaydah
199 J3 Hodejov Slovakia
190 I5 Hodenhagen Ger.
256 E9 Hodgesville WV U.S.A.
106 E3 Hodgson Downs N.T. Austr.
228 D2 Hodh Ech Chargui admin. reg. Maur.
228 C2 Hodh El Gharbi admin. reg. Maur.
199 J5 Hódmezővásárhely Hungary
232 E2 Hodmo watercourse Somalia
227 G2 Hodna, Chott el salt l. Alg.
172 G2 Hodnet Shropshire, England U.K.
199 M4 Hodod Romania
201 N2 Hodonice Czech Rep.
198 G3 Hodonín Czech Rep.
219 M4 Hodoșa Romania
Hödrögö Mongolia see Nömrög
237 N5 Hodsons Peak Lesotho
245 K2 Hodzana r. AK U.S.A.
180 F7 Hœdic, Île de i. France
164 I7 Hoeje Møn nature res. Denmark
187 E6 Hoek Neth.
186 F5 Hoek van Holland Neth.
179 O6 Hœnheim France
187 I7 Hoensbroek Neth.
179 O6 Hœrdt France
122 F7 Hoeryŏng N. Korea
187 H7 Hoeselt Belgium
186 H4 Hoevelaken Neth.
186 G5 Hoeven Neth.
123 E9 Hoeyang N. Korea
193 E10 Hof Bayern Ger.
191 F9 Hof Rheinland-Pfalz Ger.
201 O4 Hof am Leithaberge Austria
200 H4 Hof bei Salzburg Austria
191 I9 Hofbieber Ger.
200 C5 Höfen Austria
190 J5 Höfer Ger.
257 L5 Hoffman Mountain NY U.S.A.
270 E1 Hoffman's Cay i. Bahamas
191 H8 Hofgeismar Ger.
191 F10 Hofheim am Taunus Ger.
191 K10 Hofheim in Unterfranken Ger.
195 O4 Hofkirchen Ger.
237 J7 Hofmeyr S. Africa
162 □F1 Höfn Iceland
165 M1 Hofors Sweden
230 E2 Hofrat en Nahas Sudan
162 □D1 Hofsjökull ice cap Iceland
162 □D1 Hofsós Iceland
125 I12 Hōfu Japan
162 C1 Höfuðborgarsvæði admin. div. Iceland
Hofūf Saudi Arabia see Al Hufūf
164 I5 Höganäs Sweden
105 K8 Hogan Group is Tas. Austr.
257 K4 Hogansburg NY U.S.A.
107 K8 Hoganthulla Creek r. Qld Austr.
106 F6 Hogarth, Mount hill N.T. Austr.
244 I2 Hogatza AK U.S.A.
244 I2 Hogatza r. AK U.S.A.
186 H4 Hoge Vaart canal Neth.
245 N3 Hogg, Mount Y.T. Can.
Hoggar plat. Alg. see Ahaggar
Hog Island New Prov. Bahamas see Paradise Island
250 I4 Hog Island MI U.S.A.
257 J11 Hog Island VA U.S.A.
165 M4 Högsby Sweden
164 C3 Høgsfjorden inlet Norway
165 L2 Högsjö Sweden
163 I6 Høgste Breakulen mt. Norway
171 R7 Hogsthorpe Lincolnshire, England U.K.
270 G3 Hogsty Reef Bahamas
199 H5 Hőgyész Hungary
262 B3 Hoh r. WA U.S.A.
194 D5 Hohberg Ger.
193 G8 Hohburg Ger.
201 H6 Hohe Leier mt. Austria
200 H6 Hohe Leiten mt. Austria
195 J4 Hohen-Altheim Ger.
190 I3 Hohenaspe Ger.
195 P4 Hohenau Ger.
201 O2 Hohenau an der March Austria
201 M4 Hohenberg Austria
193 J8 Hohenbocka Ger.
201 N6 Hohenbrugg-Weinberg Austria
195 L5 Hohenbrunn Ger.
193 H7 Hohenbucko Ger.
195 L3 Hohenburg Ger.
193 E6 Hohendodeleben Ger.
192 I2 Hohendorf Ger.
191 K8 Hohenebra Ger.
201 L2 Hoheneich Austria
200 A5 Hohenems Austria
195 L3 Hohenfels Ger.
195 J6 Hohenfurch Ger.
192 F5 Hohengöhren Ger.
191 J6 Hohenhameln Ger.
195 L5 Hohenkammer Ger.
190 E3 Hohenkirchen Ger.
193 I8 Hohenleipisch Ger.
193 F9 Hohenleuben Ger.
195 L5 Hohenlinden Ger.
190 I3 Hohenlockstedt Ger.
194 H3 Hohenloher Ebene plain Ger.
192 H3 Hohenmocker Ger.
193 F8 Hohenmölsen Ger.
192 F5 Hohennauen Ger.
192 H5 Hohen Neuendorf Berlin Ger.
201 J4 Hohe Nock mt. Austria
191 I9 Hohenroda-Ransbach Ger.
191 J10 Hohenroth Ger.
192 J5 Hohensaaten Ger.
Hohensalza Pol. see Inowrocław
193 F6 Hohenseeden Ger.
193 G9 Hohenstein-Ernstthal Ger.
194 G5 Hohentengen Ger.
194 E6 Hohentengen am Hochrhein Ger.
195 M4 Hohenthann Ger.
193 F7 Hohenthurm Ger.
201 I6 Hohenthurn Austria
255 D8 Hohenwald TN U.S.A.
192 F3 Hohen Wangelin Ger.
195 K4 Hohenwart Ger.
193 E9 Hohenwartetalsperre resr Ger.
195 N3 Hohenwarth Ger.
190 I2 Hohenwestedt Ger.
192 E5 Hohenwulsch Ger.
201 I3 Hohenzell Austria
201 I5 Hoher Dachstein mt. Austria
Hoh Ereg Nei Mongol China see Wuchuan
200 H4 Hoher Göll mt. Austria/Ger.
191 I10 Hohe Rhön mts Ger.
200 B5 Hoher Ifen mt. Austria/Ger.
191 H10 Hoher Vogelsberg, Naturpark nature res. Ger.
200 F5 Hohe Salve mt. Austria
191 H8 Hohes Gras hill Ger.
191 J8 Hohes Kreuz Ger.
200 F5 Hohe Tauern mts Austria
200 G5 Hohe Tauern, Nationalpark nat. park Austria
187 J8 Hohe Venn moorland Belgium
201 M4 Hohe Wand nature res. Austria
212 D2 Hohgant mt. Switz.
129 L6 Hohhot Nei Mongol China
194 E4 Hohloh hill Ger.
128 D3 Höhmorit Mongolia
191 E9 Höhn Ger.
190 I2 Hohn Ger.
190 J5 Hohne Ger.
179 N7 Hohneck mt. France
190 K4 Hohnstorf (Elbe) Ger.
229 F5 Hohoe Ghana
131 □J7 Ho Hok Shan H.K. China
125 H12 Hōhoku Japan
159 M4 Hoholeve Ukr.
244 H3 Hoholitna r. AK U.S.A.
159 K3 Hoholiv Ukr.
159 N7 Hoholivka Ukr.
128 C9 Hoh Sai Hu l. Qinghai China
190 K2 Hohwacht (Ostsee) Ger.
190 K2 Hohwachter Bucht b. Ger.
133 J9 Hoh Xil Hu salt l. China
133 I9 Hoh Xil Shan mts China
128 F8 Hoh Yanhu salt l. Qinghai China
118 I7 Hôi An Vietnam
128 F9 Hoika Qinghai China
232 A4 Hoima Uganda
190 J3 Hoisdorf Ger.
260 F6 Hoisington KS U.S.A.
128 E8 Hoit Taria Qinghai China
144 G2 Hojagala Turkm.
139 N7 Hojai Assam India
145 K2 Hojambaz Turkm.
190 G1 Højer Denmark
125 J13 Hōjo Japan
118 E4 Hok r. Myanmar
165 J4 Hökensås hills Sweden
165 K3 Hokensås naturreservat nature res. Sweden
102 H2 Hokianga Harbour North I. N.Z.
127 L2 Hōki-gawa r. Japan
102 J7 Hokio Beach North I. N.Z.
103 E9 Hokitika South I. N.Z.
122 M7 Hokkaidō i. Japan
124 T3 Hokkaidō pref. Japan
164 F2 Hokksund Norway
144 G3 Ḩokmābād Iran
103 C13 Hokonui South I. N.Z.
103 C12 Hokonui Hills South I. N.Z.
127 M3 Hokota Japan
126 A6 Hokudan Japan
126 E4 Hokunō Japan
127 H1 Hokura-gawa r. Japan
126 E5 Hokusei Japan
164 E1 Hol Buskerud Norway
162 N2 Hol Nordland Norway
233 C5 Hola Kenya
199 J3 Hoľa mt. Slovakia
136 E5 Holalkere Karnataka India
276 D3 Holanda Bol.
159 L7 Hola Prystan' Ukr.
196 F6 Holasovice Czech Rep.
164 H6 Holbæk Denmark
237 O2 Holbank S. Africa
173 M2 Holbeach Lincolnshire, England U.K.
173 M2 Holbeach Marsh England U.K.
246 D5 Holberg B.C. Can.
190 H1 Holbøl Denmark
107 L5 Holborne Island Qld Austr.
105 K6 Holbrook N.S.W. Austr.
173 O4 Holbrook Suffolk, England U.K.
265 V7 Holbrook AZ U.S.A.
259 I3 Holbrook NY U.S.A.
250 C4 Holcombe WI U.S.A.
250 C4 Holcombe Flowage resr WI U.S.A.
247 H4 Holden Alta Can.
171 M6 Holden Lancashire, England U.K.
265 T2 Holden UT U.S.A.
261 G8 Holdenville OK U.S.A.
171 Q6 Holderness pen. England U.K.
283 C7 Holdich Arg.
190 F5 Holdorf Ger.
260 F5 Holdrege NE U.S.A.
190 L1 Holeby Denmark
270 E1 Hole in the Wall pt Gt Abaco Bahamas
136 E6 Hole Narsipur Karnataka India
199 G2 Holešov Czech Rep.
271 □4 Holetown Barbados
236 A4 Holgat watercourse S. Africa
256 A7 Holgate OH U.S.A.
204 H9 Holguera Spain
270 E3 Holguín Cuba
198 G3 Holíč Slovakia
198 E1 Holice Czech Rep.
244 H3 Holikachuk AK U.S.A.
159 M2 Holinka Ukr.
244 H3 Holitna r. AK U.S.A.
163 L6 Höljes Sweden
201 N2 Hollabrunn Austria
191 E6 Hollage (Wallenhorst) Ger.
Holland country Europe see Netherlands
250 H7 Holland MI U.S.A.
256 G6 Holland NY U.S.A.
256 B7 Holland OH U.S.A.
261 J9 Hollandale MS U.S.A.
270 □ Holland Bay Jamaica
173 L2 Holland Fen reg. England U.K.
Hollandia Papua Indon. see Jayapura
173 O4 Holland-on-Sea Essex, England U.K.
186 K3 Hollandscheveld Neth.
186 F5 Hollands Diep est. Neth.
168 L4 Hollandstoun Scotland U.K.
187 I9 Hollange Belgium
191 J6 Holle Ger.
193 E8 Holleben Ger.
195 K5 Hollenbach Ger.
190 K3 Hollenbek Ger.
201 L6 Hollenegg Austria
201 I4 Höllengebirge hills Austria
190 I4 Hollenstedt Ger.
201 K4 Hollenstein an der Ybbs Austria
173 O3 Hollesley Bay England U.K.
256 G5 Holley NY U.S.A.
195 K2 Hollfeld Ger.
286 T2 Hollick-Kenyon Peninsula Antarctica
286 Q1 Hollick-Kenyon Plateau Antarctica
256 G8 Hollidaysburg PA U.S.A.
190 H2 Hollingstedt Ger.
173 N6 Hollington East Sussex, England U.K.
171 N7 Hollingworth Greater Manchester, England U.K.
245 N5 Hollis AK U.S.A.
261 F8 Hollis OK U.S.A.
264 K5 Hollister CA U.S.A.
212 F2 Holloch Karst nature res. Switz.
199 K3 Hollóháza Hungary
199 I3 Hollókő Hungary
163 R6 Hollola Fin.
186 I2 Hollum Neth.
251 K7 Holly MI U.S.A.
170 H3 Hollybush East Ayrshire, Scotland U.K.
172 H3 Hollybush Worcestershire, England U.K.
103 B11 Hollyford r. South I. N.Z.
259 G5 Holly Park NJ U.S.A.
261 K8 Holly Springs MS U.S.A.
169 I6 Hollywood Ireland
264 N7 Hollywood CA U.S.A.
255 G13 Hollywood FL U.S.A.
190 I3 Holm Ger.
162 L4 Holm Norway
158 I6 Hol'ma Ukr.
259 G4 Holmdel NJ U.S.A.
237 N2 Holmdene S. Africa
171 P6 Holme-on-Spalding-Moor East Riding of Yorkshire, England U.K.
259 H1 Holmes NY U.S.A.
171 M7 Holmes Chapel Cheshire, England U.K.
171 N7 Holmesfield Derbyshire, England U.K.
107 K4 Holmes Reef Coral Sea Is Terr. Austr.
164 G2 Holmestrand Norway
256 D8 Holmesville OH U.S.A.
171 N6 Holmfirth West Yorkshire, England U.K.
Holmgard Rus. Fed. see Velikiy Novgorod
Holm Ø i. Greenland see Kiatassuaq
162 P5 Holmöarna naturreservat nature res. Sweden
156 C3 Holmön i. Sweden
162 P5 Holmsund Sweden
163 N6 Holmsveden Sweden
165 P3 Holmudden pt Gotland Sweden
158 E2 Holoby Ukr.
199 L5 Holod Romania
219 K4 Holod r. Romania
197 L5 Hołodowska Pol.
158 D4 Holohory hills Ukr.
244 H3 Holokuk Mountain hill AK U.S.A.
150 C6 Ḩolon Israel
234 C5 Holoog Namibia
108 H2 Holothuria Banks rf W.A. Austr.
195 P2 Holoubkov Czech Rep.
159 N9 Holovanivka Ukr.
158 J5 Holovanivs'k Ukr.
158 B4 Holovets'ko Ukr.
159 L4 Holovkivka Ukr.
197 M4 Holovne Ukr.
158 H3 Holovyne Ukr.
107 H3 Holroyd r. Qld Austr.
109 G9 Holroyd Bluff hills W.A. Austr.
164 I4 Holsljunga Sweden
237 M3 Holspruit r. S. Africa
190 G4 Holste Ger.
164 E5 Holstebro Denmark
164 E6 Holsted Denmark
212 D1 Hölstein Switz.
260 H4 Holstein IA U.S.A.
Holsteinsborg Greenland see Sisimiut
256 B12 Holston r. TN U.S.A.
256 D12 Holston Lake TN U.S.A.
172 D6 Holsworthy Devon, England U.K.
173 O2 Holt Norfolk, England U.K.
172 H5 Holt Wiltshire, England U.K.
172 G1 Holt Wrexham, Wales U.K.
250 J7 Holt MI U.S.A.
186 J4 Holten Neth.
190 E3 Holtgast Ger.
192 D3 Holthusen Ger.
190 E4 Holtland Ger.
260 H6 Holton KS U.S.A.
250 H6 Holton MI U.S.A.
171 Q6 Holton le Clay Lincolnshire, England U.K.
190 E4 Holtrop (Großefehn) Ger.
190 I2 Holtsee Ger.
265 Q9 Holtville CA U.S.A.
258 C5 Holtwood PA U.S.A.
264 □F14 Hōlualoa HI U.S.A.
159 O5 Holubivka Ukr.
159 M9 Holubynka Ukr.
186 I2 Holwerd Neth.
186 K2 Holwierde Neth.
169 G7 Holycross Ireland
244 H3 Holy Cross AK U.S.A.
263 K7 Holy Cross, Mount of the CO U.S.A.
172 C1 Holyhead Isle of Anglesey, Wales U.K.
172 C1 Holyhead Bay Wales U.K.
171 N2 Holy Island England U.K.
168 F11 Holy Island Scotland U.K.
172 C1 Holy Island Wales U.K.
260 D5 Holyoke CO U.S.A.
257 M6 Holyoke MA U.S.A.
Holy See Europe see Vatican City
172 F1 Holywell Flintshire, Wales U.K.
169 G4 Holywell Northern Ireland U.K.
168 I12 Holywood Dumfries and Galloway, Scotland U.K.
169 K3 Holywood Northern Ireland U.K.
191 E10 Holzappel Ger.
193 H7 Holzdorf Ger.
191 I7 Holzen Ger.
194 G4 Holzgerlingen Ger.
193 F8 Holzhausen Ger.
191 E10 Holzhausen an der Haide Ger.
195 I5 Holzheim Bayern Ger.
195 J4 Holzheim Bayern Ger.
195 J4 Holzheim Bayern Ger.
191 G10 Holzheim Hessen Ger.
195 L6 Holzkirchen Ger.
191 H7 Holzminden Ger.
191 K8 Holzthaleben Ger.
193 F7 Holzweißig Ger.
191 E7 Holzwickede Ger.
236 C4 Hom watercourse Namibia
144 C5 Homā Iran
232 B5 Homa Bay Kenya
118 B2 Homalin Myanmar
246 E5 Homathko r. B.C. Can.
Homāyūnshahr Iran see Khomeynīshahr
191 H8 Homberg (Efze) Ger.
191 G9 Homberg (Ohm) Ger.
Hombetsu Japan see Honbetsu
178 E4 Hombleux France
228 E3 Hombori Mali
179 L5 Hombourg-Budange France
179 M5 Hombourg-Haut France
282 D2 Hombre Muerto, Salar del salt flat Arg.
194 C3 Homburg Ger.
204 C4 Home, Cabo de pt Spain
243 L3 Home Bay Nunavut Can.
179 K5 Homécourt France
107 K5 Home Hill Qld Austr.
108 □2 Home Island Cocos Is
204 D5 Homem r. Port.
102 I2 Home Point North I. N.Z.
244 J4 Homer AK U.S.A.
255 F8 Homer GA U.S.A.
261 I9 Homer LA U.S.A.
250 J7 Homer MI U.S.A.
257 I6 Homer NY U.S.A.
256 F8 Homer City PA U.S.A.
173 O3 Homersfield Suffolk, England U.K.
255 F10 Homerville GA U.S.A.
107 J6 Homestead Qld Austr.
255 G13 Homestead FL U.S.A.
258 D3 Hometown PA U.S.A.
258 D5 Homeville PA U.S.A.
103 J8 Homewood North I. N.Z.
255 D9 Homewood AL U.S.A.
162 L4 Hommelstø Norway
162 K5 Hommelvik Norway
136 E4 Homnabad Karnataka India
219 P4 Homocea Romania
229 I2 Homodji well Niger
235 G4 Homoine Moz.
199 I5 Homokmégy Hungary
199 G5 Homokszentgyörgy Hungary
199 M4 Homoroade Romania
199 L3 Homorod r. Romania
Homs Libya see Al Khums
Homs Syria see Ḩimş
159 K1 Homyel' Belarus
Homyel Oblast admin. div. Belarus see Homyel'skaya Voblasts'
161 M9 Homyel'skaya Voblasts' admin. div. Belarus
256 D11 Honaker VA U.S.A.
Honan prov. China see Henan
264 □F14 Hōnaunau HI U.S.A.
136 D5 Honavar Karnataka India
136 D4 Honawad Karnataka India
221 K5 Honaz Turkey
124 U3 Honbetsu Japan
158 J2 Honcharivs'ke Ukr.
159 M9 Honcharne Ukr.
119 G9 Hon Chông Vietnam
274 C3 Honda Col.
139 J9 Honda Orissa India
274 C1 Honda, Bahía b. Col.
114 B7 Honda Bay Palawan Phil.
139 J9 Hondapa Orissa India
208 B1 Hondarribia Spain
235 G3 Honde Moz.
236 I6 Hondeblaf r. S. Africa
236 B6 Hondeklipbaai S. Africa
267 O8 Hondo r. Belize/Mex.
125 H14 Hondo Japan
263 L10 Hondo NM U.S.A.
261 F11 Hondo TX U.S.A.
263 L10 Hondo r. NM U.S.A.
209 D11 Hondón de las Nieves Spain
209 D11 Hondón de los Frailes Spain
178 E2 Hondschoote France
186 K2 Hondsrug reg. Neth.
270 A6 Honduras country Central America
266 □P9 Honduras, Gulf of Belize/Hond.
212 D4 Hône Italy
164 G1 Hønefoss Norway
256 H6 Honeoye Falls NY U.S.A.
258 E1 Honesdale PA U.S.A.
269 I5 Honey Mex.
258 D4 Honey Brook PA U.S.A.
264 L1 Honey Lake salt l. CA U.S.A.
181 L3 Honfleur France
118 H4 Hong, Mouths of the Vietnam
118 H4 Hông, Sông r. Vietnam
131 J3 Hong'an Hubei China
128 H8 Hongchengzi Gansu China
123 E10 Hongch'ŏn S. Korea
129 J8 Hongde Gansu China
129 M4 Honggor Nei Mongol China
132 J7 Honggouzi Qinghai China
128 H8 Honggu Gansu China
131 J7 Honghai Wan b. China
130 D7 Honghe Yunnan China
131 J2 Hong He r. China
131 I4 Honghu Hubei China
131 I4 Hong Hu l. China
Hongjialou Shandong China see Licheng
130 G5 Hongjiang Hunan China
130 G5 Hongjiang Hunan China
Hongjiang Sichuan China see Wangcang
131 □J7 Hong Kong H.K. China
131 J7 Hong Kong special admin. reg. China
131 □J7 Hong Kong Harbour sea chan. H.K. China
131 □J7 Hong Kong Island H.K. China
128 F6 Hongliu Daquan well Nei Mongol China
128 D6 Hongliuhe Gansu China
129 K7 Hongliu He r. China
132 J7 Hongliuquan Qinghai China
Hongliuwan Gansu China see Aksay
128 H7 Hongliuyuan Gansu China
132 L6 Hongliuyuan Gansu China
119 G9 Hông Ngư Vietnam
Hongor Mongolia see Naran
Hongqiao Hunan China see Qidong
Hongqiao Hunan China see Qidong
131 M3 Hongqiao airport China
128 C5 Hongqicun Xinjiang China
Hongqizhen Hainan China see Wuzhishan
130 B4 Hongshan Yunnan China
128 I7 Hongshansi Nei Mongol China
122 E7 Hongshilazi Jilin China
130 H7 Hongshui He r. China
129 L8 Hongtong Shanxi China
126 C8 Hongū Japan
249 H3 Honguedo, Détroit d' sea chan. Que. Can.
Hongwansi Gansu China see Sunan
123 E8 Hongwŏn N. Korea
129 R4 Hongxing Jilin China
128 H7 Hongyashan Shuiku resr Gansu China
130 D2 Hongyuan Sichuan China
131 L2 Hongze Jiangsu China
131 L2 Hongze Hu l. China
100 □6 Honiara Guadalcanal Solomon Is
172 F6 Honiton Devon, England U.K.
124 R7 Honjō Akita Japan
127 G3 Honjo Japan
127 J3 Honjō Saitama Japan
163 Q6 Honkajoki Fin.
127 H5 Honkawane Japan
171 N6 Honley West Yorkshire, England U.K.
136 D5 Honnali Karnataka India
136 E6 Honnavalli Karnataka India
162 R1 Honningsvåg Norway
264 □F13 Honoka'a HI U.S.A.
264 □E13 Honokahua HI U.S.A.
102 L4 Honokawa mt. North I. N.Z.
264 □D12 Honolulu HI U.S.A.
264 □ Honolulu County county HI U.S.A.
264 □F14 Honomū HI U.S.A.
250 H5 Honor MI U.S.A.
196 G3 Honoratka Pol.
264 □C12 Honouliuli HI U.S.A.
196 B3 Hönow Ger.
205 P9 Honrubia Spain
205 M6 Honrubia de la Cuesta Spain
125 K11 Honshū i. Japan
205 P9 Hontacillas Spain
205 L6 Hontalbilla Spain
205 O9 Hontanaya Spain
185 D8 Hontanx France
199 H3 Hontianske Nemce Slovakia
205 M4 Hontoria de la Cantera Spain
205 N5 Hontoria del Pinar Spain
205 M5 Hontoria de Valdearados Spain
264 □F14 Honu'apo HI U.S.A.
173 N5 Hoo Medway, England U.K.
262 D4 Hood, Mount vol. OR U.S.A.
245 N4 Hood Bay AK U.S.A.
Hood Island Islas Galápagos Ecuador see Española, Isla
109 E13 Hood Point W.A. Austr.
262 D4 Hood River OR U.S.A.
186 G4 Hoofddorp Neth.
190 G1 Hooge Ger.
190 G1 Hooge i. Ger.
187 F6 Hoogerheide Neth.
186 J3 Hoogersmilde Neth.
186 J3 Hoogeveen Neth.
186 K2 Hoogezand-Sappemeer Neth.
186 G5 Hooge Zwaluwe Neth.
186 K3 Hooghalen Neth.
Hooghly r. mouth India see Hugli
186 H3 Hoogkarspel Neth.
186 J5 Hoog-Keppel Neth.
186 J2 Hoogkerk Neth.
186 H4 Hoogland Neth.
190 C5 Hoogstede Ger.
187 G6 Hoogstraten Belgium
186 F5 Hoogvliet Neth.
171 P6 Hook East Riding of Yorkshire, England U.K.
173 K5 Hook Hampshire, England U.K.
261 E7 Hooker OK U.S.A.
106 C5 Hooker Creek watercourse N.T. Austr.
106 C4 Hooker Creek Aboriginal Land res. N.T. Austr.
169 I8 Hook Head Ireland
173 J4 Hook Norton Oxfordshire, England U.K.
Hook of Holland Neth. see Hoek van Holland
107 N8 Hook Point Qld Austr.
107 L5 Hook Reef Qld Austr.
190 F3 Hooksiel Ger.
264 □D12 Ho'olehua HI U.S.A.
Hoolt Mongolia see Tögrög
245 N4 Hoonah AK U.S.A.
262 C6 Hoopa Valley Indian Reservation res. CA U.S.A.
244 F3 Hooper Bay AK U.S.A.
244 F3 Hooper Bay AK U.S.A.
257 I10 Hooper Island MD U.S.A.
250 G9 Hoopeston IL U.S.A.
237 J3 Hoopstad S. Africa
164 J6 Höör Sweden
186 H3 Hoorn Neth.
99 I3 Hoorn, Îles de is Wallis and Futuna Is
186 G5 Hoornaar Neth.
127 H4 Hōō-san mt. Japan
257 L6 Hoosick NY U.S.A.
265 R5 Hoover Dam AZ/NV U.S.A.
256 C8 Hoover Memorial Reservoir OH U.S.A.
Höövör Mongolia see Baruunbayan-Ulaan
162 □C1 Hóp lag. Iceland
149 J3 Hopa Turkey
258 F3 Hopatcong NJ U.S.A.
258 F3 Hopatcong, Lake NJ U.S.A.
258 D1 Hop Bottom PA U.S.A.
246 F5 Hope B.C. Can.
103 H8 Hope South I. N.Z.
103 G9 Hope r. South I. N.Z.
172 F1 Hope Flintshire, Wales U.K.
245 J3 Hope AK U.S.A.
261 I9 Hope AR U.S.A.
258 F3 Hope NJ U.S.A.
104 G3 Hope, Lake salt flat S.A. Austr.
109 F12 Hope, Lake salt flat W.A. Austr.
168 G6 Hope, Loch l. Scotland U.K.
244 F1 Hope, Point pt AK U.S.A.
270 □ Hope Bay Jamaica
249 I2 Hopedale Nfld and Lab. Can.
261 K11 Hopedale LA U.S.A.
236 C9 Hopefield S. Africa
Hopei prov. China see Hebei
267 O8 Hopelchén Mex.
168 J7 Hopeman Moray, Scotland U.K.
249 I2 Hope Mountains Nfld and Lab. Can.
162 □ Hopen i. Svalbard
249 G1 Hopes Advance, Baie b. Que. Can.
243 L3 Hopes Advance, Cap c. Que. Can.
Hopes Advance Bay Que. Can. see Aupaluk
105 I6 Hopetoun Vic. Austr.
109 F12 Hopetoun W.A. Austr.
236 I5 Hopetown S. Africa
107 J3 Hope Vale Qld Austr.
107 J3 Hope Vale Aboriginal Reserve Qld Austr.
257 N7 Hope Valley RI U.S.A.
258 F4 Hopewell NJ U.S.A.
256 H11 Hopewell VA U.S.A.
248 E1 Hopewell Islands Nunavut Can.
259 H1 Hopewell Junction NY U.S.A.
200 F5 Hopfgarten im Brixental Austria
200 G6 Hopfgarten in Defereggen Austria
265 V6 Hopi Indian Reservation res. AZ U.S.A.
118 C2 Hopin Myanmar
105 I8 Hopkins r. Vic. Austr.
109 J8 Hopkins, Lake salt flat W.A. Austr.
254 D7 Hopkinsville KY U.S.A.
259 L2 Hopkinton RI U.S.A.
264 I3 Hopland CA U.S.A.
101 □8a Hopohoponga, Mui pt Tongatapu Tonga
118 C4 Hopong Myanmar
194 C2 Hoppstädten Ger.
162 S1 Hopseidet Norway
191 E6 Hopsten Ger.
173 P2 Hopton Norfolk, England U.K.
173 N3 Hopton Suffolk, England U.K.
172 G3 Hoptonheath Shropshire, England U.K.
231 B8 Hoque Angola
262 C3 Hoquiam WA U.S.A.
128 G9 Hor Qinghai China
133 E11 Hor Xizang China
158 J3 Hora Ukr.
232 D2 Hora Califo Eth.
245 J2 Horace Mountain AK U.S.A.
151 I6 Horadiz Azer.
126 E4 Horado Japan
126 G6 Hōrai Japan
126 G6 Hōraiji-san hill Japan
173 M6 Horam East Sussex, England U.K.
149 K3 Horasan Turkey
198 C2 Horažďovice Czech Rep.
194 F5 Horb am Neckar Ger.
192 F1 Horbelev Denmark
173 L2 Horbling Lincolnshire, England U.K.
179 N7 Horbourg-Wihr France
200 A4 Hörbranz Austria
165 J6 Hörby Sweden
205 J6 Horcajo de las Torres Spain
207 J2 Horcajo de los Montes Spain
205 O9 Horcajo de Santiago Spain
205 J7 Horcajo Medianero Spain
266 G3 Horcasitas Mex.
205 N7 Horche Spain
284 B3 Horcón Chile
207 J3 Horcón hill Spain
269 J4 Horconcitos Mex.
282 D2 Horcones r. Arg.
164 C2 Horda Norway
164 C1 Hordaland county Norway
191 J7 Hörden Ger.
173 I6 Hordle Hampshire, England U.K.
172 D3 Horeb Ceredigion, Wales U.K.
102 H2 Horeke North I. N.Z.
219 L5 Horezu Romania
195 J5 Horgau Ger.
212 F1 Horgen Switz.
194 H6 Horgenzell Ger.
Horgo Mongolia see Tari
218 H4 Horgoš Vojvodina Serbia
158 C5 Horhany mts Ukr.
128 I5 Hörh Uul mts Mongolia
219 Q5 Horia Romania
198 E1 Hořice Czech Rep.
250 F6 Horicon WI U.S.A.
127 G3 Horigane Japan
129 L6 Horinger Nei Mongol Ch
127 I1 Horinouchi Japan
201 O4 Horitschon Austria
Horiult Mongolia see Bo
290 H7 Horizon Deep sea featur S. Pacific Ocean
201 J7 Horjul Slovenia
193 K8 Horka Ger.
161 N7 Horki Belarus
173 L5 Horley Surrey, England U
286 Q1 Horlick Mountains Anta
193 I7 Hörlitz Ger.
159 R5 Horlivka Ukr.
144 I7 Hormak Iran
271 □1 Hormigueros Puerto Ric
205 O4 Hormilla Spain
144 G8 Hormoz i. Iran
144 F8 Hormoz, Kūh-e mt. Iran
144 G8 Hormozgān prov. Iran
144 F8 Hormūd-e Bāgh Iran
144 F8 Hormūd-e Mīr Khūnd I
144 G8 Hormuz, Strait of Iran/C
201 M2 Horn Austria
246 G2 Horn r. N.W.T. Can.
162 □B1 Horn c. Iceland
Horn, Cape Chile see Hornos, Cabo de
206 G3 Hornachos Spain
207 I5 Hornachuelos Spain
189 J4 Hornád r. Slovakia
245 Q1 Hornaday r. N.W.T. Can.
199 I2 Horna Orava park Slova
198 G3 Horná Potôň Slovakia
199 H3 Horná Štubňa Slovakia
162 N3 Hornavan l. Sweden
194 C3 Hornbach Ger.
191 G7 Horn-Bad Meinberg Ge
261 I10 Hornbeck LA U.S.A.
194 E5 Hornberg Ger.
164 J3 Hornborgasjöns naturre nature res. Sweden
262 C6 Hornbrook CA U.S.A.
191 K6 Hornburg Ger.
171 L5 Hornby Lancashire, Engl
171 Q7 Horncastle Lincolnshire, England U.K.
165 M1 Horndal Sweden
173 J6 Horndean Hampshire, En
Horne, Îles de is Wallis and Futuna Is see Hoorn, Îles de
190 I3 Horneburg Ger.
162 O5 Hörnefors Sweden
256 H6 Hornell NY U.S.A.
248 C3 Hornepayne Ont. Can.
259 F4 Hornerstown NJ U.S.A.
199 G3 Horné Saliby Slovakia
199 H2 Horné Srnie Slovakia
169 F2 Horn Head Ireland
199 H2 Horní Bečva Czech Rep.
199 G2 Horní Benešov Czech R
193 J10 Horní Beřkovice Czech
198 C2 Horní Bříza Czech Rep.
198 E2 Horní Cerekev Czech R
198 C1 Horní Jiřetín Czech Rep
266 E4 Hornillos Mex.
198 G2 Horní Moštěnice Czech
163 I6 Hornindal Norway
173 O2 Horning Norfolk, Englan
198 D3 Horní Planá Czech Rep.
193 J10 Horní Počaply Czech Re
194 E4 Hornisgrinde mt. Ger.
107 I1 Horn Island Qld Austr.
261 K10 Horn Island MS U.S.A.
198 B1 Horní Slavkov Czech Re
198 D3 Horní Stropnice Czech
234 C4 Hornkranz Namibia
246 F2 Horn Mountains N.W.T.
244 H3 Horn Mountains AK U.S
207 N4 Hornos Spain
283 D9 Hornos, Cabo de c. Chil
283 D9 Hornos, Parque Naciona nat. park Chile
159 K1 Hornostayivka Chernihiv Oblast' Ukr.
159 M6 Hornostayivka Khersons Oblast' Ukr.
159 P8 Hornostayivka Respublik Ukr.
193 K7 Hornow Ger.
178 C4 Hornoy-le-Bourg France
245 O3 Horn Peak Y.T. Can.
105 M5 Hornsby N.S.W. Austr.
171 Q6 Hornsea East Riding of Y England U.K.
163 N6 Hornslandet pen. Swede
164 G5 Hornslet Denmark
192 E3 Hornstorf Ger.
162 □B1 Hornstrandir reg. Icelan
162 □ Hornsund inlet Svalbard
190 F1 Hörnum Ger.
199 I3 Horný Tisovník Slovakia
199 L4 Horoatu Crasnei Roman
158 E5 Horodenka Ukr.
158 F2 Horodets' Ukr.
197 M5 Horodło Pol.
159 K2 Horodnya Ukr.
158 G3 Horodnytsya Ukr.
158 F4 Horodok Khmel'nyts'ka Ukr.
158 C4 Horodok L'vivs'ka Oblast
159 K4 Horodyshche Cherkas'ka Ukr.
159 K2 Horodyshche Chernihivs Oblast' Ukr.
159 S4 Horodyshche Luhans'ka Ukr.
158 E4 Horodyshche Ternopils'k Ukr.
124 T2 Horokanai Japan
158 D3 Horokhiv Ukr.
159 Q4 Horokhuvatka Ukr.
193 J10 Horoměřice Czech Rep.
199 L3 Horonda Ukr.
124 S1 Horonobe Japan
132 F5 Horo Shan mts China
124 T4 Horoshiri-dake mt. Japa
124 T1 Horoshiri-yama hill Japa
198 C2 Hořovice Czech Rep.
129 Q5 Horqin Shadi reg. China
Horqin Youyi Qianqi Ne China see Ulanhot
Horqin Zuoyi Houqi Ne China see Ganjig
Horqin Zuoyi Zhongqi Mongol China see Baoka
277 F5 Horqueta Para.
172 D6 Horrabridge Devon, England U.K.
178 I7 Horre, Étang de la l. Fra
192 E1 Horreby Denmark
164 I4 Horred Sweden
173 N3 Horringer Suffolk, Englar
109 C10 Horrocks W.A. Austr.
133 J11 Horru Xizang China
108 □2 Horsburgh Island Cocos
201 J3 Hörsching Austria
262 L6 Horse Creek r. WY U.S.A
246 F4 Horsefly B.C. Can.
251 R7 Horseheads NY U.S.A.
171 N5 Horsehouse North Yorks England U.K.
249 K3 Horse Islands Nfld and
191 J8 Hörsel r. Ger.
169 E6 Horseleap Galway Irelan
169 G6 Horseleap Westmeath Ire
164 F6 Horsens Denmark
106 E8 Horseshoe Bend N.T. Au
262 F5 Horseshoe Bend ID U.S.
265 U7 Horseshoe Reservoir AZ
288 H3 Horseshoe Seamounts N. Atlantic Ocean

O2 **Horsford** Norfolk, England U.K.
N6 **Horsforth** West Yorkshire, England U.K.
I7 **Horsham** Vic. Austr.
L5 **Horsham** West Sussex, England U.K.
E4 **Horsham** PA U.S.A.
H3 **Horshchyk** Ukr.
D6 **Hörsingen** Ger.
L1 **Horslunde** Denmark
M5 **Horsmonden** Kent, England U.K.
B2 **Horšovský Týn** Czech Rep.
H10 **Horst** hill Ger.
J6 **Horst** Neth.
I3 **Horst (Holstein)** Ger.
O2 **Horstead** Norfolk, England U.K.
H4 **Horstedt** Ger.
E6 **Hörstel** Ger.
D6 **Horstmar** Ger.
J5 **Horsunlu** Turkey
I4 **Hort** Hungary
□1c **Horta** Faial Azores
E11 **Horta, Cap de l'** c. Spain
G2 **Horten** Norway
G4 **Hortensia** Arg.
O6 **Hortezuela** Spain
N4 **Hortigüela** Spain
K4 **Hortobágy** Hungary
J4 **Hortobágy-Berettyó** canal Hungary
K4 **Hortobágyi** nat. park Hungary
P1 **Horton** r. N.W.T. Can.
J6 **Horton Heath** Hampshire, England U.K.
M5 **Horton in Ribblesdale** North Yorkshire, England U.K.
I1 **Høruphav** Denmark
N9 **Horval'** Belarus
E1 **Horw** Switz.
L6 **Horwich** Greater Manchester, England U.K.
D3 **Horwood Lake** Ont. Can.
O8 **Hory** Belarus
F2 **Horyn'** r. Ukr.
L5 **Horyniec-Zdrój** Pol.
L5 **Horyszów** Pol.
C6 **Hōryūji** tourist site Japan
C3 **Hosa'ina** Eth.
H10 **Hösbach** Ger.
E6 **Hosdurga** Karnataka India
3 **Hose, Pegunungan** mts Malaysia
8 **Hosena** Ger.
H9 **Hosenfeld** Ger.
D4 **Hosenofu** well Libya
B4 **Ḩoseynābād** Iran
F4 **Ḩoseynīān, Band-e** mts Iran
C6 **Ḩoseynīyeh** Iran
8 **Hoshab** Pak.
F8 **Hoshangabad** Madh. Prad. India
F3 **Hoshcha** Ukr.
E4 **Hoshiarpur** Punjab India
Höshööt Mongolia see **Tsengel**
Höshööt Mongolia see **Öldziyt**
8 **Hosingen** Lux.
8 **Hoskins** New Britain P.N.G.
2 **Hoşköy** Turkey
G6 **Hosoe** Japan
E5 **Hospet** Karnataka India
F10 **Hospice de France** France
Hospitalet Cataluña Spain see **L'Hospitalet de l'Infant**
Hospitalet Cataluña Spain see **L'Hospitalet de Llobregat**
4 **Hossa** Fin.
8 **Hosseger** France
4 **Hosséré Vokre** mt. Cameroon
D4 **Hossios Luckas** tourist site Greece
6 **Hoßkirch** Ger.
4 **Hosszúpályi** Hungary
4 **Hosszúpereszteg** Hungary
4 **Hostalríc** Spain
Hostalrich Spain see **Hostalríc**
9 **Hoste, Isla** i. Chile
7 **Hostens** France
3 **Hostěradice** Czech Rep.
3 **Hostie** Slovakia
1 **Hostinné** Czech Rep.
1 **Hostivice** Czech Rep.
10 **Hošťka** Czech Rep.
1 **Hostomice** Czech Rep.
2 **Hostouň** Czech Rep.
1 **Hostrupskov** Denmark
6 **Hosur** Tamil Nadu India
15 **Hotagen** r. Sweden
Hotahudo East Timor see **Hatudo**
3 **Hotaka** Japan
3 **Hotaka-dake** mt. Japan
Hotaka-yama mt. Japan
8 **Hotan** Xinjiang China
6 **Hotan He** watercourse China
3 **Hotazel** S. Africa
Hotchkissville CT U.S.A.
3 **Hot Creek** r. NV U.S.A.
3 **Hot Creek Range** mts NV U.S.A.
6 **Hötensleben** Ger.
12 **Hotham** r. W.A. Austr.
2 **Hotham, Cape** N.T. Austr.
2 **Hotham Inlet** AK U.S.A.
5 **Hoti** Seram Indon.
4 **Hoting** Sweden
7 **Hotinja Vas** Slovenia
Hotopuu Tahiti Fr. Polynesia
Hot Springs AR U.S.A.
Hot Springs NM U.S.A. see **Truth or Consequences**
4 **Hot Springs** SD U.S.A.
Hot Sulphur Springs CO U.S.A.
Hottah Lake N.W.T. Can.
Hotte, Massif de la mts Haiti
Hottentots Bay Namibia
Hottentots-Holland Nature Reserve S. Africa
Hottentots Point Namibia
3 **Hotton** Belgium
Hotzenwald reg. Ger.
Houaïlu New Caledonia
Houat, Île d' i. France
Houdain France
Houdan France
Houdelaincourt France
Houécourt France
Houeillès France
Houeydets France
Houffalize Belgium
Hougang Sing.
Houghton r. Qld Austr.
Houghton Cumbria, England U.K.
Houghton MI U.S.A.
Houghton NY U.S.A.
Houghton Lake MI U.S.A.
Houghton Lake l. MI U.S.A.
Houghton le Spring Tyne and Wear, England U.K.
Houghton Regis Bedfordshire, England U.K.
Houie Moc, Phou mt. Laos
Houillères de la Sarre, Canal des France
Houlgate France
2 **Houlton** ME U.S.A.
Houma Shanxi China
Houma Tongatapu Tonga
Houma Tonga
Houma LA U.S.A.
Houmen Guangdong China
Houmt Souk Tunisia
Houndé Burkina
1 **Houndslow** Scottish Borders, Scotland U.K.
Houplines France
Hourdel, Pointe du pt France
Houri Qinghai China
Hourn, Loch inlet Scotland U.K.
Hourtin France
Hourtin-Carcans, Étang d' l. France
Hourtin-Plage France
Housatonic MA U.S.A.
Housatonic r. CT U.S.A.
House Range mts UT U.S.A.
Housesteads tourist site England U.K.
Houston B.C. Can.
Houston AK U.S.A.
258 E7 **Houston** DE U.S.A.
250 C6 **Houston** MN U.S.A.
261 J7 **Houston** MO U.S.A.
261 K9 **Houston** MS U.S.A.
261 H11 **Houston** TX U.S.A.
236 C10 **Hout Bay** S. Africa
236 C10 **Hout Bay** b. S. Africa
186 H4 **Houten** Neth.
187 H6 **Houthalen** Belgium
187 C7 **Houthulst** Belgium
236 I6 **Houtkraal** S. Africa
109 B10 **Houtman Abrolhos** is W.A. Austr.
168 J5 **Houton** Orkney, Scotland U.K.
163 P6 **Houtskär** Fin.
236 H6 **Houwater** S. Africa
132 H5 **Houxia** Xinjiang China
187 H8 **Houyet** Belgium
128 G8 **Houzihe** Qinghai China
164 G6 **Hov** Denmark
164 G1 **Hov** Norway
165 K3 **Hova** Sweden
128 B3 **Hovd** Hovd Mongolia
Hovd Mongolia see **Bogd**
128 C3 **Hovd** prov. Mongolia
164 E3 **Hovdefjell** hill Norway
164 D2 **Hovden** park Norway
128 C2 **Hovd Gol** r. Mongolia
173 L6 **Hove** Brighton and Hove, England U.K.
164 I6 **Hovedstaden** admin. reg. Denmark
191 G7 **Hövelhof** Ger.
158 D5 **Hoverla, Hora** mt. Ukr.
173 O2 **Hoveton** Norfolk, England U.K.
144 C6 **Hoveyzeh** Iran
165 L1 **Hovfjället naturreservat** nature res. Sweden
171 P5 **Hovingham** North Yorkshire, England U.K.
250 E2 **Hovland** MN U.S.A.
165 L5 **Hovmantorp** Sweden
151 L5 **Hövsan** Azer.
129 K5 **Hövsgöl** Mongolia
128 G1 **Hövsgöl** prov. Mongolia
128 G1 **Hövsgöl Nuur** l. Mongolia
159 M4 **Hovtva** Ukr.
159 M4 **Hovtva** r. Ukr.
Hövüün Mongolia see **Noyon**
224 D6 **Howa, Ouadi** watercourse Chad/Sudan
224 E5 **Howar, Wadi** watercourse Sudan
107 N8 **Howard** Qld Austr.
261 G7 **Howard** KS U.S.A.
260 G3 **Howard** SD U.S.A.
250 F5 **Howard** WI U.S.A.
250 I6 **Howard City** MI U.S.A.
258 B6 **Howard County** county MD U.S.A.
171 O5 **Howardian Hills** England U.K.
106 E2 **Howard Island** N.T. Austr.
247 J2 **Howard Lake** N.W.T. Can.
244 H1 **Howard Pass** AK U.S.A.
106 C2 **Howard Springs** N.T. Austr.
171 P6 **Howden** East Riding of Yorkshire, England U.K.
250 I8 **Howe** IN U.S.A.
105 L7 **Howe, Cape** Vic. Austr.
286 O1 **Howe, Mount** Antarctica
251 K7 **Howell** MI U.S.A.
168 K9 **Howe of the Mearns** reg. Scotland U.K.
260 D3 **Howes** SD U.S.A.
257 L3 **Howick** Que. Can.
237 O5 **Howick** S. Africa
104 G2 **Howitt, Lake** salt flat S.A. Austr.
257 □Q3 **Howland** ME U.S.A.
99 I1 **Howland Island** N. Pacific Ocean
105 K6 **Howlong** N.S.W. Austr.
Howrah W. Bengal India see **Haora**
169 J6 **Howth** Ireland
144 H5 **Ḩowz** well Iran
144 F5 **Ḩowz-e Gīvar** Iran
144 G5 **Ḩowz-e Khān** well Iran
144 G6 **Ḩowz-e Panj** Iran
144 F5 **Ḩowz-e Panj** waterhole Iran
144 F5 **Howz i-Mian i-Tak** Iran
118 H6 **Hô Xa** Vietnam
260 E6 **Hoxie** KS U.S.A.
191 H7 **Höxter** Ger.
132 H3 **Hoxtolgay** Xinjiang China
132 H5 **Hoxud** Xinjiang China
168 J5 **Hoy** i. Scotland U.K.
190 H5 **Hoya** Ger.
127 K4 **Hōya** Japan
207 P3 **Hoya Gonzalo** Spain
163 I6 **Høyanger** Norway
193 J8 **Hoyerswerda** Ger.
171 K7 **Hoylake** Merseyside, England U.K.
171 O7 **Hoyland** South Yorkshire, England U.K.
162 L4 **Høylandet** Norway
251 M1 **Hoyle** Ont. Can.
193 D7 **Hoym** Ger.
205 M7 **Hoyo de Manzanares** Spain
128 I6 **Hoyor Amt** Nei Mongol China
204 G8 **Hoyos** Spain
205 J8 **Hoyos del Espino** Spain
162 T5 **Höytiäinen** l. Fin.
148 I4 **Hozat** Turkey
207 I8 **Hozgarganta** r. Spain
160 G8 **Hozha** Belarus
126 C5 **Hozu-gawa** r. Japan
126 E5 **Hozumi** Japan
118 C6 **Hpa-an** Myanmar
118 C5 **Hpapun** Myanmar
158 I5 **Hrabove** Ukr.
159 Q3 **Hrachivka** Ukr.
195 O2 **Hracholusky, Vodní nádrž** resr Czech Rep.
198 E1 **Hradec Králové** Czech Rep.
199 G2 **Hradec nad Moravicí** Czech Rep.
198 F2 **Hradec nad Svitavou** Czech Rep.
195 P2 **Hrádek** Czech Rep.
198 D1 **Hrádek nad Nisou** Czech Rep.
198 C2 **Hradešice** Czech Rep.
198 C1 **Hradiště** hill Czech Rep.
199 H3 **Hradište** Slovakia
159 M4 **Hradyz'k** Ukr.
160 L8 **Hradzyanka** Belarus
197 L2 **Hrandzichy** Belarus
198 B1 **Hranice** Karlovarský kraj Czech Rep.
199 G2 **Hranice** Olomoucký kraj Czech Rep.
159 Q6 **Hranitne** Donets'ka Oblast' Ukr.
158 I3 **Hranitne** Zhytomyrs'ka Oblast' Ukr.
199 J3 **Hranovnica** Slovakia
210 G4 **Hrasnica** Bos.-Herz.
201 L7 **Hrastnik** Slovenia
162 □C1 **Hraun** Iceland
162 □F1 **Hraun** slope Iceland
160 I7 **Hrawzhyshki** Belarus
151 F5 **Hrazdan** Armenia
193 J9 **Hrazený** hill Czech Rep.
159 L3 **Hrebinka** Ukr.
158 J4 **Hrebinky** Ukr.
213 R5 **Hreljin** Croatia
159 M1 **Hrem"yach** Ukr.
159 L6 **Hreyhove** Ukr.
199 J3 **Hrhov** Slovakia
197 L6 **Hrimne** Ukr.
199 I3 **Hriňová** Slovakia
Hristós Ikaria Greece see **Raches**
158 H5 **Hristovaia** Moldova
193 I9 **Hrob** Czech Rep.
199 I3 **Hrochoť** Slovakia
198 E2 **Hrochův Týnec** Czech Rep.
160 G8 **Hrodna** Belarus
Hrodna Oblast admin. div. Belarus see **Hrodzyenskaya Voblasts'**
197 L2 **Hrodnyendskaye Wzvyshsha** hills Belarus
160 I8 **Hrodzyenskaya Voblasts'** admin. div. Belarus
159 N7 **Hromivka** Ukr.
195 O2 **Hromnice** Czech Rep.
199 H4 **Hron** r. Slovakia
199 I3 **Hronec** Slovakia
198 F1 **Hronov** Czech Rep.
199 H3 **Hronský Beňadik** Slovakia
198 F2 **Hrotovice** Czech Rep.
193 G10 **Hroznětín** Czech Rep.
197 L5 **Hrubieszów** Pol.
197 M4 **Hrudky** Ukr.
159 N3 **Hrun'** Ukr.
159 N3 **Hrun'** r. Ukr.
159 P4 **Hrushuvakha** Ukr.
201 J8 **Hrušica** mts Slovenia
198 F3 **Hrušky** Czech Rep.
199 I3 **Hrusov** Slovakia
198 F3 **Hrušovany nad Jevišovkou** Czech Rep.
201 O1 **Hrušovany u Brna** Czech Rep.
199 I2 **Hruštín** Slovakia
197 K3 **Hruszniew** Pol.
Hrvatska country Europe see **Croatia**
210 F3 **Hrvatska Kostajnica** Croatia
Hrvatsko Grahovo Bos.-Herz. see **Bosansko Grahovo**
159 L2 **Hryhorivka** Chernihivs'ka Oblast' Ukr.
159 P5 **Hryhorivka** Dnipropetrovs'ka Oblast' Ukr.
159 M7 **Hryhorivka** Khersons'ka Oblast' Ukr.
158 F4 **Hrymayliv** Ukr.
158 D6 **Hrynyava** Ukr.
158 H4 **Hryshkivtsi** Ukr.
159 M8 **Hryshyne** Ukr.
158 G4 **Hrytsiv** Ukr.
118 C3 **Hsenwi** Myanmar
Hsiang Chang i. H.K. China see **Hong Kong Island**
Hsiang Kang H.K. China see **Hong Kong**
118 C4 **Hsi-hseng** Myanmar
118 D4 **Hsin, Nam** r. Myanmar
Hsin-chia-p'o country Asia see **Singapore**
Hsin-chia-p'o Sing. see **Singapore**
131 M6 **Hsinchu** Taiwan
Hsinking Jilin China see **Changchun**
131 M7 **Hsinying** Taiwan
118 C3 **Hsipaw** Myanmar
Hsi-sha Ch'un-tao is S. China Sea see **Paracel Islands**
131 L7 **Hsiyüp'ing Yü** i. Taiwan
131 M6 **Hsüeh Shan** mt. Taiwan
131 K6 **Hua'an** Fujian China
234 B4 **Huab** watercourse Namibia
129 N8 **Huabei Pingyuan** plain China
276 A2 **Huacaibamba** Peru
276 E3 **Huacaraje** Bol.
276 E5 **Huacaya** Bol.
131 J6 **Huacheng** Guangdong China
276 E3 **Huachi** Bol.
129 K8 **Huachi** Gansu China
266 E2 **Huachinera** Mex.
276 A2 **Huacho** Peru
276 B2 **Huachón** Peru
122 G5 **Huachuan** Heilong. China
265 V10 **Huachuca City** AZ U.S.A.
284 C2 **Huaco** Arg.
276 A2 **Huacrachuco** Peru
276 C4 **Huacullani** Peru
129 M6 **Huade** Nei Mongol China
122 E7 **Huadian** Jilin China
131 I7 **Huadu** Guangdong China
Huafeng Fujian China see **Hua'an**
128 E6 **Huahai** Gansu China
132 L7 **Huahaizi** Qinghai China
119 D8 **Hua Hin** Thai.
101 □9 **Huahine** i. Arch. de la Société Fr. Polynesia
129 N6 **Huai'an** Hebei China
131 L2 **Huai'an** Jiangsu China
131 K2 **Huaibei** Anhui China
131 J2 **Huaibin** Henan China
Huaicheng Guangdong China see **Huaiji**
Huaicheng Jiangsu China see **Chuzhou**
Huaide Jilin China see **Gongzhuling**
122 D7 **Huaide** Jilin China
Huaidian Henan China see **Shenqiu**
118 G6 **Huai Had National Park** Thai.
131 L2 **Huai He** r. China
130 G5 **Huaihua** Hunan China
131 I7 **Huaiji** Guangdong China
118 D7 **Huai Kha Khaeng Wildlife Reserve** nature res. Thai.
129 N6 **Huailai** Hebei China
118 D5 **Huai Nam Dung National Park** Thai.
131 K2 **Huainan** Anhui China
131 K3 **Huaining** Anhui China
Huaining Hubei China see **Wuhan**
129 M7 **Huairen** Shanxi China
129 O6 **Huairou** Beijing China
131 J2 **Huaiyang** Henan China
131 L2 **Huaiyin** Jiangsu China
Huaiyin Jiangsu China see **Huai'an**
131 K2 **Huaiyuan** Anhui China
130 G6 **Huaiyuan** Guangxi China
128 I9 **Huajialing** Gansu China
268 B3 **Huajicori** Mex.
268 C4 **Huajimic** Mex.
269 J8 **Huajuápan de León** Mex.
268 G6 **Huajúmbaro** Mex.
115 E7 **Huaki** Maluku Indon.
267 J5 **Hualahuises** Mex.
265 S6 **Hualapai Indian Reservation** res. AZ U.S.A.
265 S6 **Hualapai Peak** AZ U.S.A.
282 D2 **Hualfín** Arg.
131 M6 **Hualien** Taiwan
276 B3 **Hualla** Peru
274 C6 **Huallaga** r. Peru
128 H8 **Hualong** Qinghai China
284 A5 **Hualqui** Chile
276 A1 **Huamachuco** Peru
276 B3 **Huamani** Peru
269 J6 **Huamantla** Mex.
231 B8 **Huambo** Angola
231 B8 **Huambo** prov. Angola
236 B1 **Huams** watercourse Namibia
269 I8 **Huamuxtitlán** Mex.
122 G5 **Huanan** Heilong. China
274 B6 **Huancabamba** r. Peru
283 C6 **Huancache, Sierra** mts Arg.
276 B3 **Huancapi** Peru
276 B3 **Huancavelica** Peru
276 B3 **Huancavelica** dept Peru
276 B3 **Huancayo** Peru
Huancheng Gansu China see **Huanxian**
285 F3 **Huanchilla** Arg.
131 J5 **Huangbei** Jiangxi China
Huangcaoba Guizhou China see **Xingyi**
128 G8 **Huangcheng** Gansu China
131 J2 **Huangchuan** Henan China
131 J3 **Huanggang** Hubei China
Huang Hai sea N. Pacific Ocean see **Yellow Sea**
129 P8 **Huang He** r. China
129 P8 **Huanghe Kou** r. mouth China
129 O7 **Huanghua** Hebei China
131 M2 **Huangjian** Jiangsu China
130 D5 **Huanglianguan** Sichuan China
129 K9 **Huangling** Shaanxi China
130 G9 **Huangliu** Hainan China
129 K9 **Huanglong** Shaanxi China
129 N9 **Huanglongsi** Henan China
131 L5 **Huangmao Jian** mt. Zhejiang China
131 J3 **Huangmei** Hubei China
122 E7 **Huangnihe** Jilin China
131 J3 **Huangpi** Hubei China
130 F5 **Huangping** Guizhou China
130 H8 **Huangpo** Guangdong China
131 L5 **Huangqi** Fujian China
129 M6 **Huangqi Hai** l. China
131 L4 **Huangshan** Anhui China
131 K3 **Huang Shan** mts Anhui China
130 D2 **Huangshengguan** Sichuan China
131 J3 **Huangshi** Hubei China
128 H8 **Huang Shui** r. China
129 J8 **Huangtu Gaoyuan** plat. China
285 G5 **Huanguelén** Arg.
Huangxian China see **Donglai**
131 M4 **Huangyan** Zhejiang China
128 H8 **Huangyang** Gansu China
128 G8 **Huangyuan** Qinghai China
128 G8 **Huangzhong** Qinghai China
Huangzhou Hubei China see **Huanggang**
130 D6 **Huaning** Yunnan China
128 D6 **Huaniushan** Gansu China
130 G6 **Huanjiang** Guangxi China
129 J8 **Huan Jiang** r. China
269 I9 **Huanjintepec** Mex.
285 G2 **Huanqueros** Arg.
123 D8 **Huanren** Liaoning China
Huanshan Zhejiang China see **Yuhuan**
276 B3 **Huanta** Peru
129 P8 **Huantai** Shandong China
276 A2 **Huánuco** Peru
276 A2 **Huánuco** dept Peru
276 B3 **Huanuhuanu** Peru
276 D4 **Huanuni** Bol.
268 E4 **Huanusco** Mex.
129 J8 **Huanxian** Gansu China
130 C5 **Huaping** Yunnan China
131 N6 **Huap'ing Yü** i. Taiwan
269 I7 **Huaquechula** Mex.
276 D4 **Huar** Bol.
276 A2 **Huaral** Peru
276 A2 **Huaráz** Peru
284 B6 **Huaren Chenque** Arg.
276 A2 **Huari** Peru
276 A2 **Huariaca** Peru
274 B6 **Huarmaca** Peru
276 A2 **Huarmey** Peru
276 A3 **Huarochiri** Peru
276 A2 **Huaron** Peru
131 I4 **Huarong** Hunan China
Huarte-Araquil Spain see **Uharte-Arakil**
274 B5 **Huasaga** r. Peru
276 A2 **Huascarán, Parque Nacional** nat. park Peru
282 C3 **Huasco** Chile
129 L9 **Hua Shan** mt. Shaanxi China
129 N6 **Huashaoying** Hebei China
128 F9 **Huashixia** Qinghai China
Huashugou Gansu China see **Jingtieshan**
266 E4 **Huatabampo** Mex.
129 Q6 **Huatong** Liaoning China
269 K6 **Huatusco** Mex.
269 I5 **Huauchinango** Mex.
276 A2 **Huauru, Islas de** is Peru
269 K7 **Huautla** Mex.
Huaxian Guangdong China see **Huadu**
129 N9 **Huaxian** Henan China
129 K9 **Huaxian** Shaanxi China
269 I5 **Huayacocotla** Mex.
Huayang Anhui China see **Jixi**
276 A2 **Huaylas** Peru
268 C4 **Huaynamota** Mex.
Huayuan Hubei China see **Xiaochang**
130 G4 **Huayuan** Hunan China
118 E4 **Huayxay** Laos
Huazangsi Gansu China see **Tianzhu**
128 G7 **Huazhaizi** Gansu China
130 H8 **Huazhou** Guangdong China
269 J9 **Huazolotitlán** Mex.
245 M3 **Hubbard, Mount** Can./U.S.A.
249 H1 **Hubbard, Pointe** pt Que. Can.
251 K5 **Hubbard Lake** MI U.S.A.
247 M3 **Hubbart Point** Man. Can.
131 I3 **Hubei** prov. China
136 D5 **Hubli** Karnataka India
199 I2 **Hubová** Slovakia
197 M5 **Hubyn** Ukr.
159 O5 **Hubynykha** Ukr.
285 E5 **Hucal** Arg.
123 E8 **Huch'ang** N. Korea
191 B8 **Hückelhoven** Ger.
191 D8 **Hückeswagen** Ger.
171 O7 **Hucknall** Nottinghamshire, England U.K.
178 C2 **Hucqueliers** France
197 L5 **Huczwa** r. Pol.
225 G4 **Ḩudayn, Wādī** watercourse Egypt
146 D2 **Huḑb Ḩumar** mts Saudi Arabia
171 N6 **Huddersfield** West Yorkshire, England U.K.
191 F5 **Hüde** Ger.
190 F4 **Hude (Oldenburg)** Ger.
129 Q2 **Huder** Nei Mongol China
129 J2 **Hüder** Mongolia
219 O2 **Hudești** Romania
135 □1 **Hudhuveli** i. N. Male Maldives
163 N6 **Hudiksvall** Sweden
257 N6 **Hudson** MA U.S.A.
257 I10 **Hudson** MD U.S.A.
257 □Q3 **Hudson** ME U.S.A.
251 J8 **Hudson** MI U.S.A.
257 N6 **Hudson** NH U.S.A.
257 L6 **Hudson** NY U.S.A.
250 B5 **Hudson** WI U.S.A.
257 L8 **Hudson** r. NY U.S.A.
Hudson, Baie d' sea Can. see **Hudson Bay**
283 B7 **Hudson, Cerro** vol. Chile
Hudson, Détroit d' str. Nunavut/Que. Can. see **Hudson Strait**
261 H7 **Hudson, Lake** OK U.S.A.
247 K4 **Hudson Bay** Sask. Can.
243 J4 **Hudson Bay** sea Can.
259 G3 **Hudson County** county NJ U.S.A.
257 L5 **Hudson Falls** NY U.S.A.
Hudson Island Tuvalu see **Nanumanga**
243 P2 **Hudson Land** reg. Greenland
286 R2 **Hudson Mountains** Antarctica
246 F3 **Hudson's Hope** B.C. Can.
243 K3 **Hudson Strait** Nunavut/Que. Can.
118 H6 **Huê** Vietnam
204 H7 **Huebra** r. Spain
205 R5 **Huecha** r. Spain
283 B6 **Huechucuicui, Punta** pt Chile
207 N7 **Huécija** Spain
219 L4 **Huedin** Romania
267 M10 **Huehuetán** Mex.
267 N10 **Huehuetenango** Guat.
269 I7 **Huehuetlán** Mex.
268 B1 **Huehueto, Cerro** mt. Mex.
269 I6 **Huejotzingo** Mex.
268 D3 **Huejúcar** Mex.
268 D3 **Huejuquilla** Mex.
269 I4 **Huejutla** Mex.
207 M6 **Huélago** Spain
180 D5 **Huelgoat** France
207 M5 **Huelma** Spain
206 F6 **Huelva** Spain
206 F5 **Huelva** prov. Spain
206 G6 **Huelva** r. Spain
206 E6 **Huelva, Tierra Llana de** plain Spain
205 O8 **Huelves** Spain
207 N6 **Huéneja** Spain
284 B2 **Huentelauquén** Chile
266 D3 **Huépac** Mex.
284 B5 **Huepil** Chile
284 A5 **Huequén** Chile
207 O7 **Huércal de Almería** Spain
207 P6 **Huércal-Overa** Spain
205 O4 **Huércanos** Spain
263 L7 **Huerfano** r. CO U.S.A.
205 Q8 **Huérguina** Spain
205 M3 **Huérmeces** Spain
284 D2 **Huerta, Sierra de la** mts Arg.
205 N5 **Huerta del Rey** Spain
205 M9 **Huerta de Valdecarábanos** Spain
205 P7 **Huertahernando** Spain
268 F1 **Huertecillas** Mex.
208 E4 **Huerto** Spain
208 D4 **Huerva** r. Spain
207 M5 **Huesa** Spain
208 D5 **Huesa del Común** Spain
208 E3 **Huesca** Spain
208 E3 **Huesca** prov. Spain
207 N5 **Huéscar** Spain
268 G7 **Huétamo** Mex.
205 O8 **Huete** Spain
207 K6 **Huétor-Tájar** Spain
284 A6 **Hueva Toltén** Chile
269 H8 **Hueycantenango** Mex.
269 I6 **Hueyotlipan** Mex.
255 D9 **Hueytown** AL U.S.A.
206 H5 **Huezna** r. Spain
206 H5 **Huezna, Embalse de** resr Spain
101 □8a **Hufangalupe Beach** b. Tonga
194 E6 **Hüfingen** Ger.
164 B1 **Huftarøy** i. Norway
Hufūf Saudi Arabia see **Al Hufūf**
230 E2 **Hugeilig** l. Sudan
171 P6 **Huggate** East Riding of Yorkshire, England U.K.
244 I2 **Huggins Island** AK U.S.A.
106 E8 **Hugh** watercourse N.T. Austr.
107 J6 **Hughenden** Qld Austr.
285 G3 **Hughes** Arg.
247 K3 **Hughes** r. Man. Can.
244 I2 **Hughes** AK U.S.A.
104 B4 **Hughes (abandoned)** S.A. Austr.
286 T2 **Hughes Bay** Antarctica
256 I10 **Hughesville** MD U.S.A.
251 R8 **Hughesville** PA U.S.A.
264 L4 **Hughson** CA U.S.A.
172 □ **Hugh Town** Isles of Scilly, England U.K.
195 K6 **Huglfing** Ger.
139 K9 **Hugli** r. mouth India
139 L8 **Hugli-Chinsurah** W. Bengal India
260 D6 **Hugo** CO U.S.A.
261 H8 **Hugo** OK U.S.A.
261 E7 **Hugoton** KS U.S.A.
199 I3 **Hugyag** Hungary
Huhehot Nei Mongol China see **Hohhot**
Huhhot Nei Mongol China see **Hohhot**
275 E3 **Huhucunya** Venez.
237 I2 **Huhudi** S. Africa
162 U5 **Huhus** Fin.
131 L6 **Hui'an** Fujian China
128 J8 **Hui'anpu** Ningxia China
102 K5 **Huiarau Range** mts North I. N.Z.
234 C5 **Huib-Hoch Plateau** Namibia
131 J6 **Huichang** Jiangxi China
269 H5 **Huichapán** Mex.
Huicheng Anhui China see **Shexian**
Huicheng Guangdong China see **Huilai**
268 C3 **Huicholes, Sierra de los** mts Mex.
123 E8 **Huich'ŏn** N. Korea
131 J7 **Huidong** Guangdong China
130 D5 **Huidong** Sichuan China
122 E7 **Huifa He** r. China
129 P2 **Huihe** Nei Mongol China
187 F6 **Huijbergen** Neth.
131 J2 **Huiji He** r. China
231 B8 **Huíla** Angola
231 B8 **Huíla** prov. Angola
274 C4 **Huila** dept Col.
274 C4 **Huila, Nevado de** vol. Col.
231 B8 **Huíla, Planalto da** plat. Angola
Huíla Plateau plat. Angola see **Huíla, Planalto da**
131 K7 **Huilai** Guangdong China
130 D5 **Huili** Sichuan China
Huilongzhen Jiangsu China see **Qidong**
268 F6 **Huimangaro** Mex.
267 M9 **Huimanguillo** Mex.
268 G5 **Huimilpan** Mex.
129 O8 **Huimin** Shandong China
276 C4 **Huiñaimarca, Lago de** l. Bol./Peru
122 E7 **Huinan** Jilin China
Huinan Shanghai China see **Nanhui**
284 E4 **Huinca Renancó** Arg.
128 I9 **Huining** Gansu China
128 J7 **Huinong** Ningxia China
195 J4 **Huisheim** Ger.
172 G5 **Huish Episcopi** Somerset, England U.K.
Huishi Gansu China see **Huining**
130 F5 **Huishui** Guizhou China
168 B7 **Huisinis** Western Isles, Scotland U.K.
181 L5 **Huisne** r. France
181 N6 **Huisseau-sur-Cosson** France
186 I5 **Huissen** Neth.
128 B9 **Huiten Nur** l. China
130 G5 **Huitong** Hunan China
163 Q6 **Huittinen** Fin.
267 M9 **Huitupan** Mex.
268 D4 **Huitzila** Mex.
269 K8 **Huitzo** Mex.
269 H7 **Huitzuco** Mex.
130 F2 **Huixian** Gansu China
129 M9 **Huixian** Henan China
267 M10 **Huixtla** Mex.
130 D5 **Huize** Yunnan China
186 H4 **Huizen** Neth.
131 J7 **Huizhou** Guangdong China
128 H3 **Hujirt** Övörhangay Mongolia
Hujirt Mongolia see **Tsetserleg**
Hujirt Mongolia see **Delgerhaan**
146 E3 **Hujr** Saudi Arabia
102 J7 **Hukanui** North I. N.Z.
103 F9 **Hukarere** South I. N.Z.
118 C1 **Hukawng Valley** Myanmar
131 K4 **Hukou** Jiangxi China
234 D4 **Hukuntsi** Botswana
245 K1 **Hulahula** r. AK U.S.A.
122 E6 **Hulan** Heilong. China
129 R3 **Hulan Ergi** Heilong. China
122 E6 **Hulan He** r. China
146 E2 **Ḩulayfah** Saudi Arabia
150 G4 **Ḩulayḩilah** well Syria
250 I3 **Hulbert** MI U.S.A.
250 I3 **Hulbert Lake** MI U.S.A.
256 B12 **Hulen** KY U.S.A.
Huliao Guangdong China see **Dabu**
144 B5 **Hulilan** Iran
122 H6 **Hulin** Heilong. China
198 G2 **Hulín** Czech Rep.
129 Q4 **Hulingol** Nei Mongol China
129 S4 **Hulin Gol** r. China
Hulin Rocks is Northern Ireland U.K. see **The Maidens**
248 F4 **Hull** Que. Can.
Hull Kingston upon Hull, England U.K. see **Kingston upon Hull**
257 O6 **Hull** MA U.S.A.
172 H4 **Hullavington** Wiltshire, England U.K.
173 N4 **Hullbridge** Essex, England U.K.
191 G6 **Hüllhorst** Ger.
Hull Island atoll Phoenix Is Kiribati see **Orona**
160 G3 **Hullo** Estonia
187 I7 **Hulsberg** Neth.
191 H6 **Hülsede** Ger.
187 G6 **Hulshout** Belgium
187 F6 **Hulst** Neth.
165 M5 **Hulterstad** Öland Sweden
165 L4 **Hultsfred** Sweden
129 Q6 **Huludao** Liaoning China
129 K9 **Hulu He** r. China
133 J9 **Hulu Hu** salt l. Qinghai China
135 □1 **Huluk** i. N. Male Maldives
Hulumeedhoo i. Addu Atoll Maldives see **Midu**
129 P2 **Hulun Buir** Nei Mongol China
129 O2 **Hulun Nur** l. China
225 F2 **Ḩulwān** Egypt
Ḩulwān Egypt see **Ḩulwān**
159 P6 **Hulyaypole** Ukr.
122 E3 **Huma** Heilong. China
271 □1 **Humacao** Puerto Rico
122 E3 **Huma He** r. China
282 D1 **Humahuaca** Arg.
276 D2 **Humaita** Bol.
277 E1 **Humaitá** Brazil
277 F6 **Humaitá** Para.
205 N7 **Humanes de Mohernando** Spain
237 I10 **Humansdorp** S. Africa
Humåtak Guam see **Umatac**
276 B3 **Humay** Peru
147 L4 **Humaym** well U.A.E.
146 G3 **Humayyān, Jabal** hill Saudi Arabia
231 B9 **Humbe** Angola
231 B8 **Humbe, Serra do** mts Angola
171 R6 **Humber, Mouth of the** England U.K.
171 Q6 **Humberside** airport England U.K.
171 Q6 **Humberston** North East Lincolnshire, England U.K.
276 C5 **Humberstone** Chile
278 E2 **Humberto de Campos** Brazil
171 L2 **Humbie** East Lothian, Scotland U.K.
190 K1 **Humble** Denmark
285 G2 **Humboldt** Arg.
247 J4 **Humboldt** Sask. Can.
265 T7 **Humboldt** AZ U.S.A.
260 H5 **Humboldt** NE U.S.A.
264 N1 **Humboldt** NV U.S.A.
258 C3 **Humboldt** PA U.S.A.
261 K8 **Humboldt** TN U.S.A.
264 N1 **Humboldt** r. NV U.S.A.
100 □5 **Humboldt, Mont** mt. New Caledonia
262 B6 **Humboldt Bay** CA U.S.A.
Humboldt Gletscher glacier Greenland see **Sermersuaq**
264 N1 **Humboldt Lake** NV U.S.A.
103 C11 **Humboldt Mountains** South I. N.Z.
264 N1 **Humboldt Range** mts NV U.S.A.
264 O2 **Humbolt Salt Marsh** NV U.S.A.
245 O2 **Hume** r. N.W.T. Can.
107 J9 **Humeburn** Qld Austr.
285 G5 **Húmeda, Pampa** plain Arg.
131 I7 **Hu Men** sea chan. China
199 G2 **Humenec** hill Czech Rep.
199 K3 **Humenné** Slovakia
105 K6 **Hume Reservoir** N.S.W. Austr.
179 J8 **Humes-Jorquenay** France
207 J6 **Humilladero** Spain
210 F4 **Humina** reg. Bos.-Herz.
210 F3 **Humka, Gora** hill Croatia
165 M4 **Hummeln** l. Sweden
186 J4 **Hummelo** Neth.
258 B4 **Hummelstown** PA U.S.A.
258 B3 **Hummels Wharf** PA U.S.A.
103 E12 **Hummock** hill South I. N.Z.
201 M7 **Hum na Sutli** Croatia
284 A4 **Humos, Cabo** c. Chile
231 B8 **Humpata** Angola
Humphrey Island atoll Cook Is see **Manihiki**
264 N4 **Humphreys, Mount** CA U.S.A.
265 U6 **Humphreys Peak** AZ U.S.A.
198 E2 **Humpolec** Czech Rep.
163 Q6 **Humppila** Fin.
106 C2 **Humpty Doo** N.T. Austr.
171 M3 **Humshaugh** Northumberland, England U.K.
224 B2 **Hūn** Libya
162 □C1 **Húnaflói** b. Iceland
131 H5 **Hunan** prov. China
122 G7 **Hunchun** Jilin China
122 G7 **Hunchun He** r. China
199 J2 **Huncovce** Slovakia
193 F7 **Hundeluft** Ger.
195 N4 **Hunderdorf** Ger.
164 H6 **Hundested** Denmark
145 O6 **Hundewali** Pak.
193 D6 **Hundisburg** Ger.
171 R7 **Hundleby** Lincolnshire, England U.K.
172 C4 **Hundleton** Pembrokeshire, Wales U.K.
163 J6 **Hundorp** Norway
256 E9 **Hundred** WV U.S.A.
193 G9 **Hundshübel** Ger.
190 I1 **Hundslev** Denmark
200 G5 **Hundstein** mt. Austria
219 K5 **Hunedoara** Romania
191 I9 **Hünfeld** Ger.
191 F10 **Hünfelden-Kirberg** Ger.
101 □8 **Hunga** i. Vava'u Gp Tonga
101 □8 **Hunga Ha'apai** i. Tonga
199 H4 **Hungary** country Europe
101 □8 **Hunga Tonga** i. Tonga
191 G10 **Hungen** Ger.
195 J4 **Hungerberg** hill Ger.
105 J3 **Hungerford** Qld Austr.
173 I5 **Hungerford** West Berkshire, England U.K.
131 □J7 **Hung Fa Leng** hill H.K. China
128 C2 **Hüngiy Gol** r. Mongolia
123 E9 **Hŭngnam** N. Korea
255 □1 **Hungry Bay** Bermuda
169 C9 **Hungry Hill** Ireland
262 H2 **Hungry Horse Reservoir** MT U.S.A.
131 □I7 **Hung Shui Kiu** H.K. China
231 C8 **Hungulo** Angola
136 E4 **Hungund** Karnataka India
118 H4 **Hưng Yên** Vietnam
129 R6 **Hun He** r. China
168 D7 **Hunish, Rubha** pt Scotland U.K.
236 D6 **Hunissout Pan** salt pan S. Africa
Hunjiang Jilin China see **Baishan**
123 D8 **Hun Jiang** r. China
171 Q5 **Hunmanby** North Yorkshire, England U.K.
164 H3 **Hunnebostrand** Sweden
187 I6 **Hunsel** Neth.
186 J2 **Hunsingo** reg. Neth.
236 B3 **Huns Mountains** Namibia
179 O6 **Hunspach** France
173 M2 **Hunstanton** Norfolk, England U.K.
136 E6 **Hunsur** Karnataka India
251 M1 **Hunta** Ont. Can.
191 F4 **Hunte** r. Ger.
285 G4 **Hunter** Arg.
105 M5 **Hunter** r. N.S.W. Austr.
103 F11 **Hunter** South I. N.Z.
103 D11 **Hunter** r. South I. N.Z.
245 J3 **Hunter, Mount** AK U.S.A.
104 □1 **Hunter, Point** c. Norfolk I.
258 F3 **Hunterdon County** county NJ U.S.A.
139 J7 **Hunterganj** Jharkhand India
105 J9 **Hunter Island** Tas. Austr.
246 D5 **Hunter Island** B.C. Can.
99 H4 **Hunter Island** S. Pacific Ocean
105 J9 **Hunter Islands** Tas. Austr.
103 B12 **Hunter Mountains** South I. N.Z.
118 A5 **Hunter's Bay** Myanmar
168 G11 **Hunter's Quay** Argyll and Bute, Scotland U.K.
258 A4 **Hunters Run** PA U.S.A.
257 K3 **Huntingdon** Que. Can.
173 L3 **Huntingdon** Cambridgeshire, England U.K.
256 H8 **Huntingdon** PA U.S.A.
261 K7 **Huntingdon** TN U.S.A.
254 E5 **Huntington** IN U.S.A.
262 F4 **Huntington** OR U.S.A.
265 V2 **Huntington** UT U.S.A.
256 C10 **Huntington** WV U.S.A.
264 N8 **Huntington Beach** CA U.S.A.
265 Q1 **Huntington Creek** r. NV U.S.A.
259 I3 **Huntington Station** NY U.S.A.
190 F5 **Huntlosen** Ger.
102 J4 **Huntly** North I. N.Z.
168 K8 **Huntly** Aberdeenshire, Scotland U.K.
262 K4 **Hunt Mountain** WY U.S.A.
104 F3 **Hunt Peninsula** S.A. Austr.
248 E4 **Huntsville** Ont. Can.
255 D8 **Huntsville** AL U.S.A.
261 I7 **Huntsville** AR U.S.A.
260 I6 **Huntsville** MO U.S.A.
261 H10 **Huntsville** TX U.S.A.
225 G2 **Hunū, Kathīb al** des. Egypt
150 A8 **Hunū, Kathīb al** hill Egypt
267 O7 **Hunucmá** Mex.
199 J5 **Hunya** Hungary
Hunyani r. Moz./Zimbabwe see **Manyame**
129 M7 **Hunyuan** Shanxi China
138 E1 **Hunza** Pak.
138 E1 **Hunza** reg. Pak.
145 P4 **Hunza** r. Pak.
186 K2 **Hunze** r. Neth.
132 E4 **Huocheng** Xinjiang China
Huoer Xizang China see **Hor**
129 M9 **Huojia** Henan China
122 D4 **Huolongmen** Heilong. China
Huolu Hebei China see **Luquan**
100 □5 **Huon** i. New Caledonia
118 G5 **Hương Khê** Vietnam
113 K8 **Huon Peninsula** P.N.G.
105 K10 **Huonville** Tas. Austr.
131 K2 **Huoqiu** Anhui China
131 K3 **Huoshan** Anhui China
Huoshao Tao i. Taiwan see **Lü Tao**
234 B4 **Huotsaus** waterhole Namibia
Huoxian Shanxi China see **Huozhou**
129 L8 **Huozhou** Shanxi China
159 N4 **Hupalivka** Ukr.
Hupeh prov. China see **Hubei**
191 J8 **Hüpstedt** Ger.
144 G6 **Ḩūr** Iran
144 B2 **Hurānd** Iran
Huras i. S. Male Maldives see **Embudhu Finolhu**
249 G2 **Hurault, Lac** l. Que. Can.
150 B8 **Ḩuraydīn, Wādī** watercourse Egypt
146 H3 **Ḩuraymilā'** Saudi Arabia
147 H4 **Huraysān** reg. Saudi Arabia
199 H4 **Hurbanovo** Slovakia
248 D4 **Hurd, Cape** Ont. Can.
164 H1 **Hurdalssjøen** l. Norway
Hurd Island Gilbert Is Kiribati see **Arorae**
232 F2 **Hurdiyo** Somalia
104 □3 **Hurd Point** S. Pacific Ocean
129 Q5 **Hure** Nei Mongol China
128 F3 **Hüreemaral** Mongolia
Hüremt Mongolia see **Sayhan**
Hüremt Mongolia see **Taragt**
178 C6 **Hurepoix** reg. France
Hure Qi Nei Mongol China see **Hure**
Hurghada Al Baḩr al Aḩmar Egypt see **Al Ghurdaqah**
232 C4 **Huri** mt. Kenya
182 A4 **Huriel** France
159 M5 **Hurivka** Ukr.
250 F1 **Hurkett** Ont. Can.
128 E8 **Hurleg** Qinghai China
128 E8 **Hurleg Hu** l. Qinghai China
169 E7 **Hurler's Cross** Ireland
257 K7 **Hurley** NY U.S.A.
250 D3 **Hurley** WI U.S.A.
257 J10 **Hurlock** MD U.S.A.
109 E12 **Hurlstone, Lake** salt flat W.A. Austr.
145 K7 **Hurmagai** Pak.
264 L5 **Huron** CA U.S.A.
256 C7 **Huron** OH U.S.A.
260 F3 **Huron** SD U.S.A.
251 L5 **Huron, Lake** Can./U.S.A.
250 F3 **Huron Bay** MI U.S.A.
251 J4 **Huron Beach** MI U.S.A.
206 H7 **Hurones, Embalse de los** resr Spain
250 D1 **Huronian** Ont. Can.
250 G3 **Huron Mountains** hills MI U.S.A.
265 S4 **Hurricane** UT U.S.A.
270 D2 **Hurricane Flats** sea feature Bahamas
173 J5 **Hursley** Hampshire, England U.K.
173 J5 **Hurstbourne Tarrant** Hampshire, England U.K.
173 M5 **Hurst Green** East Sussex, England U.K.
173 L6 **Hurstpierpoint** West Sussex, England U.K.
284 B2 **Hurtado** Chile
284 B2 **Hurtado** r. Chile
205 P4 **Hurteles** Spain
191 C9 **Hürth** Ger.
255 E9 **Hurtsboro** AL U.S.A.
117 J4 **Hurung, Gunung** mt. Indon.
103 H9 **Hurunui** r. South I. N.Z.
164 E5 **Hurup** Denmark
190 I1 **Hürup** Ger.
232 C2 **Huruta** Eth.
171 N5 **Hurworth-on-Tees** Darlington, England U.K.
159 O3 **Hur"yiv Kozachok** Ukr.
145 M6 **Husain Nika** Pak.
159 P6 **Husarka** Ukr.
199 K5 **Husasău de Tinca** Romania
162 □E1 **Húsavík** Norðurland eystra Iceland
162 □C1 **Húsavík** Vestfirðir Iceland
146 G7 **Husayn** reg. Yemen
173 J3 **Husbands Bosworth** Leicestershire, England U.K.
190 I1 **Husby** Ger.
165 M1 **Husby** Sweden
Huseyinabat Turkey see **Alaca**
Huseyınli Turkey see **Kızılırmak**
Hushan Zhejiang China see **Cixi**
158 C2 **Hushcha** Ukr.
225 G6 **Husheib** Sudan
219 Q4 **Huși** Romania
198 C2 **Husinec** Czech Rep.
159 N3 **Huska** r. Ukr.
165 K4 **Huskvarna** Sweden
244 H2 **Huslia** AK U.S.A.
244 H2 **Huslia** r. AK U.S.A.
Husn Jordan see **Al Ḩişn**
147 H7 **Ḩusn Āl 'Abr** Yemen
164 B2 **Husnes** Norway
166 J1 **Husøy** i. Norway
139 J7 **Hussainabad** Jharkhand India
198 F3 **Hustopeče** Czech Rep.
190 H5 **Husum** Niedersachsen Ger.
190 H2 **Husum** Schleswig-Holstein Ger.
162 O5 **Husum** Sweden
283 □ **Husvik** S. Georgia
158 F4 **Husyatyn** Ukr.
159 Q4 **Husynka** Ukr.
197 K3 **Huszlew** Pol.
197 I4 **Huta** Pol.
Hutag Mongolia see **Hutag-Öndör**
128 H2 **Hutag-Öndör** Mongolia
144 G6 **Hūtak** Iran
116 C4 **Hutanopan** Sumatera Indon.
139 J8 **Hutar** Jharkhand India
146 E2 **Hutaym, Ḩarrat** lava field Saudi Arabia
236 H7 **Hutchinson** S. Africa
260 G6 **Hutchinson** KS U.S.A.
260 H3 **Hutchinson** MN U.S.A.
265 U7 **Hutch Mountain** AZ U.S.A.
146 F7 **Ḩūth** Yemen
118 D6 **Huthi** Myanmar
122 H6 **Hutou** Heilong. China
109 C10 **Hutt** r. W.A. Austr.
200 H5 **Hüttau** Austria
201 K6 **Hüttenberg** Austria
192 G3 **Hüttenberg** hill Ger.
191 G9 **Hüttenberg-Hochelheim** Ger.
191 K7 **Hüttenrode** Ger.
195 O4 **Hutthurm** Ger.
195 I4 **Hüttlingen** Ger.
171 R7 **Huttoft** Lincolnshire, England U.K.
172 G5 **Hutton** North Somerset, England U.K.
107 L8 **Hutton, Mount** hill Qld Austr.
171 Q6 **Hutton Cranswick** East Riding of Yorkshire, England U.K.
109 G8 **Hutton Range** hills W.A. Austr.
171 O5 **Hutton Rudby** North Yorkshire, England U.K.
200 H5 **Hüttschlag** Austria
212 D1 **Huttwil** Switz.
132 H4 **Hutubi** Xinjiang China
132 H4 **Hutubi He** r. China
129 O7 **Hutuo He** r. China
159 O3 **Huty** Ukr.
190 J4 **Hützel** Ger.
135 D11 **Huvadhu Atoll** Maldives
145 I8 **Hūvār** Iran
Hüvek Turkey see **Bozova**
190 E5 **Hüven** Ger.
144 H8 **Hūvīān, Kūh-e** mts Iran
147 J3 **Ḩuwār** i. The Gulf
146 G7 **Huwaymil** des. Saudi Arabia
148 H9 **Huwaytat** reg. Saudi Arabia
197 K6 **Huwniki** Pol.
131 J5 **Huxi** Jiangxi China
129 K9 **Huxian** Shaanxi China
108 I5 **Huxley, Mount** hill W.A. Austr.
103 D11 **Huxley, Mount** South I. N.Z.
187 H7 **Huy** Belgium
158 H3 **Huyba** r. Ukr.

171 L7 Huyton Merseyside, England U.K.
122 C3 Huyuan Heilong. China
158 H3 Huyva Ukr.
131 M4 Huzhen Zhejiang China
122 C3 Huzhong Heilong. China
131 M3 Huzhou Zhejiang China
128 G8 Huzhu Qinghai China
136 F4 Huzurnagar Andhra Prad. India
162 □F1 Hvalnes Iceland
162 □B1 Hvammsfjörður inlet Iceland
162 □E1 Hvannadalshnúkur vol. Iceland
210 F4 Hvar Croatia
210 F4 Hvar i. Croatia
159 O5 Hvardiys'ke Dnipropetrovs'ka Oblast' Ukr.
159 N8 Hvardiys'ke Respublika Krym Ukr.
210 F4 Hvarski Kanal sea chan. Croatia
162 □C1 Hveragerði Iceland
164 E5 Hvide Sande Denmark
162 □C2 Hvíta r. Iceland
162 □D1 Hvítárvatn l. Iceland
164 F2 Hvittingfoss Norway
158 E5 Hvizdets' Ukr.
159 M2 Hvyntove Ukr.
123 F8 Hwadae N. Korea
234 E3 Hwange Zimbabwe
234 E3 Hwange National Park Zimbabwe
Hwang Ho r. China see Huang He
123 D9 Hwangju N. Korea
235 F3 Hwedza Zimbabwe
Hwlffordd Pembrokeshire, Wales U.K. see Haverfordwest
126 C5 Hyakuriga-take hill Japan
257 O7 Hyannis MA U.S.A.
260 E4 Hyannis NE U.S.A.
128 C2 Hyargas Nuur salt l. Mongolia
258 B7 Hyattsville MD U.S.A.
256 F12 Hyco Lake NC U.S.A.
245 N5 Hydaburg AK U.S.A.
103 E12 Hyde South I. N.Z.
171 M7 Hyde Greater Manchester, England U.K.
109 E12 Hyden W.A. Austr.
256 B11 Hyden KY U.S.A.
257 M4 Hyde Park VT U.S.A.
245 O5 Hyder AK U.S.A.
136 F4 Hyderabad Andhra Prad. India
145 M9 Hyderabad Pak.
Hydra i. Greece see Ydra
183 I10 Hyères France
183 I11 Hyères, Îles d' is France
183 I10 Hyères, Rade d' g. France
160 K6 Hyermanavichy Belarus
123 F8 Hyesan N. Korea
245 O4 Hyland r. Y.T. Can.
105 N4 Hyland, Mount N.S.W. Austr.
106 B2 Hyland Bay N.T. Austr.
245 O4 Hyland Post B.C. Can.
164 H7 Hyllekrog i. Denmark
163 H6 Hyllestad Norway
164 J4 Hyltebruk Sweden
179 L7 Hymont France
256 G9 Hyndman PA U.S.A.
262 G5 Hyndman Peak ID U.S.A.
168 C10 Hynish Argyll and Bute, Scotland U.K.
126 A5 Hyōgo pref. Japan
125 L11 Hyōno-sen mt. Japan
Hyrcania Iran see Gorgān
Hyrra Banda C.A.R. see Ira Banda
162 T4 Hyrynsalmi Fin.
262 K3 Hysham MT U.S.A.
246 G4 Hythe Alta Can.
173 J6 Hythe Hampshire, England U.K.
173 O5 Hythe Kent, England U.K.
125 I14 Hyūga Japan
163 R6 Hyvinkää Fin.
197 K6 Hyżne Pol.

I

226 E4 Iabès, Erg des. Alg.
280 C4 Iacanga Brazil
278 D5 Iaciara Brazil
276 C2 Iaco r. Brazil
219 M4 Iacobeni Sibiu Romania
219 N3 Iacobeni Suceava Romania
280 B4 Iacri Brazil
278 E5 Iaçu Brazil
Iadera Croatia see Zadar
256 D11 Iaeger WV U.S.A.
235 □J4 Iakora Madag.
Ialbuzi Rus. Fed. see El'brus
158 E9 Ialomiţa r. Romania
219 P6 Ialomiţa r. Romania
219 P6 Ialomiţei, Balta marsh Romania
158 H7 Ialoveni Moldova
158 H7 Ialpug r. Moldova
219 P5 Ianca Romania
219 M6 Iancu Jianu Romania
151 D3 Ianet'i Georgia
281 F3 Iapu Brazil
219 L4 Iara r. Romania
275 F4 Iarauarune, Serra mts Brazil
Iar Connaught reg. Ireland see Connemara
158 H7 Iargara Moldova
219 P3 Iaşi Romania
220 G1 Iasmos Greece
114 B4 Iba Luzon Phil.
229 F5 Ibadan Nigeria
274 C3 Ibagué Col.
206 H2 Ibahernando Spain
280 B5 Ibaiti Brazil
232 A5 Ibanda Uganda
219 M4 Ibăneşti Romania
208 C1 Ibañeta, Puerto de pass Spain
231 D6 Ibanga Kasaï-Occidental Dem. Rep. Congo
230 E5 Ibanga Sud-Kivu Dem. Rep. Congo
265 S1 Ibapah UT U.S.A.
125 K12 Ibara Japan
127 L3 Ibaraki Ibaraki Japan
126 C6 Ibaraki Ōsaka Japan
127 L3 Ibaraki pref. Japan
274 B4 Ibarra Ecuador
208 A1 Ibarra Spain
282 F2 Ibarreta Arg.
280 D4 Ibaté Brazil
146 G8 Ibb Yemen
146 G8 Ibb governorate Yemen
230 F3 Ibba watercourse Sudan
191 E6 Ibbenbüren Ger.
229 F2 Ibdeqqene watercourse Mali
205 Q6 Ibdes Spain
220 A1 Ibë Albania
205 M4 Ibeas de Juarros Spain
218 I7 Ibër r. Serbia/Kosovo
282 F3 Iberá, Esteros del marsh Arg.
282 F3 Iberá, Laguna l. Arg.
274 C6 Iberia Loreto Peru
276 C2 Iberia Madre de Dios Peru
92 E3 Iberian Peninsula pen. Europe
281 F4 Ibertioga Brazil
257 L3 Iberville Que. Can.
249 F2 Iberville, Lac d' l. Que. Can.
162 N2 Ibestad Norway
229 G4 Ibeto Nigeria
116 B2 Ibi Sumatera Indon.
229 H4 Ibi Nigeria
209 D10 Ibi Spain
280 D3 Ibiá Brazil
281 E2 Ibiaí Brazil
278 E2 Ibiapaba, Serra da hills Brazil
204 G2 Ibias r. Spain
279 F5 Ibicaraí Brazil
279 A9 Ibicuí Brazil
279 A9 Ibicuí r. Brazil
183 E8 Ibie r. France
126 E5 Ibigawa Japan
126 E5 Ibi-gawa r. Japan
278 F4 Ibimirim Brazil
230 F4 Ibina r. Dem. Rep. Congo
280 B5 Ibiporã Brazil
280 C4 Ibirá Brazil
281 G3 Ibiraçu Brazil
281 G2 Ibiranhém Brazil
285 I1 Ibirocaí Brazil
126 D5 Ibi-Sekigahara-Yōrō Kokutei-kōen park Japan
278 E5 Ibitiara Brazil
280 C4 Ibitinga Brazil
280 D5 Ibiúna Brazil
Ibiza Illes Balears Spain see Eivissa
Ibiza i. Spain see Eivissa
209 H10 Ibiza/San José airport Spain
216 H9 Iblei, Monti mts Sicilia Italy
221 J6 İblis Burnu pt Turkey
146 G2 Ibn Buşayyiş well Saudi Arabia
146 E6 Ibn Hādī Saudi Arabia
185 D9 Ibos France
278 E5 Ibotirama Brazil
230 A5 Iboundji Gabon
230 A5 Iboundji, Mont hill Gabon
147 N4 Ibrā' Oman
230 E2 Ibra, Wadi watercourse Sudan
Ibrala Turkey see Yeşildere
157 I5 Ibresi Rus. Fed.
147 M4 Ibrī Oman
207 M4 Ibros Spain
173 J2 Ibstock Leicestershire, England U.K.
115 E3 Ibu Halmahera Indon.
124 □1 Ibu Okinawa Japan
114 C1 Ibuhos i. Phil.
126 D5 Ibuki Japan
126 D4 Ibuki-sanchi mts Japan
126 D5 Ibuki-yama mt. Japan
125 H15 Ibusuki Japan
274 E5 Içá r. Brazil
276 B3 Ica Peru
276 B3 Ica dept Peru
275 F3 Icabarú Venez.
271 □7 Icacos Point Trin. and Tob.
267 O8 Icaiché Mex.
274 E4 Içana Brazil
274 E4 Içana r. Brazil
278 F2 Icaraí Brazil
Icaria i. Greece see Ikaria
278 D2 Icatu Brazil
265 R5 Iceberg Canyon gorge NV U.S.A.
İçel İçel Turkey see Mersin
İçel prov. Turkey see Mersin
243 Q3 Iceland country Europe
288 H2 Iceland Basin sea feature N. Atlantic Ocean
288 I1 Icelandic Plateau sea feature N. Atlantic Ocean
280 C4 Icem Brazil
139 J7 Ichak Jharkhand India
136 D4 Ichalkaranji Mahar. India
137 I3 Ichchapuram Andhra Prad. India
195 I5 Ichenhausen Ger.
194 D5 Ichenheim Ger.
125 I14 Ichifusa-yama mt. Japan
127 L5 Ichihara Japan
127 L5 Ichikai Japan
127 K4 Ichikawa Chiba Japan
125 A5 Ichikawa Hyōgo Japan
126 A6 Ichi-kawa r. Japan
127 I4 Ichikawadaimon Japan
276 D4 Ichilo r. Bol.
126 E5 Ichinomiya Aichi Japan
126 F6 Ichinomiya Aichi Japan
127 L5 Ichinomiya Chiba Japan
126 A7 Ichinomiya Hyōgo Japan
127 I4 Ichinomiya Yamanashi Japan
124 S8 Ichinoseki Japan
153 Q4 Ichinskaya Sopka vol. Rus. Fed.
126 D6 Ichishi Japan
Ichkeria aut. rep. Rus. Fed. see Chechenskaya Respublika
211 B7 Ichkeul, Parc National de l' nat. park Tunisia
159 L3 Ichnya Ukr.
123 E9 Ich'ŏn N. Korea
123 E10 Ich'ŏn S. Korea
187 D6 Ichtegem Belgium
191 K9 Ichtershausen Ger.
276 C4 Ichuña Peru
221 J4 İcikler Turkey
195 K6 Icking Ger.
173 N6 Icklesham East Sussex, England U.K.
173 N3 Icklingham Suffolk, England U.K.
221 J6 İçmeler Turkey
271 F3 Icó Brazil
238 □3a Icod de Los Vinos Tenerife Canary Is
144 H1 Içoguz Turkm.
281 G4 Iconha Brazil
Iconium Turkey see Konya
Icosium Alg. see Alger
Iculisma France see Angoulême
245 K4 Icy Bay AK U.S.A.
245 L4 Icy Bay AK U.S.A.
244 G1 Icy Cape AK U.S.A.
245 N4 Icy Strait AK U.S.A.
İd Turkey see Narman
103 E11 Ida, Mount South I. N.Z.
229 H2 Idabdaba well Niger
261 H9 Idabel OK U.S.A.
146 D8 Idaga Hamus Eth.
260 H4 Ida Grove IA U.S.A.
229 G5 Idah Nigeria
262 G4 Idaho state U.S.A.
262 G5 Idaho City ID U.S.A.
262 H5 Idaho Falls ID U.S.A.
107 J8 Idalia National Park Qld Austr.
Idalion Cyprus see Dali
262 C4 Idanha OR U.S.A.
204 F9 Idanha, Barragem da resr Port.
204 F9 Idanha-a-Nova Port.
138 D8 Idar Gujarat India
194 C2 Idar-Oberstein Ger.
194 C2 Idarwald for. Ger.
103 D12 Ida Valley South I. N.Z.
229 H3 Iday well Niger
232 F3 Iddan Somalia
217 □ Id-Dawwara, Ras pt Malta
225 F6 Idd el Asoda well Sudan
230 E2 Idd el Chanam Sudan
225 F5 Idd esh Shurak well Sudan
126 C6 Ide Japan
164 H2 Idefjorden inlet Norway/Sweden
227 G5 Idelès Alg.
192 E5 Iden Ger.
Ider Mongolia see Galt
128 G2 Ideriyn Gol r. Mongolia
192 E1 Idestrup Denmark
225 G3 Idfū Egypt
Idhra i. Greece see Ydra
Ídhras, Kólpos sea chan. Greece see Ydras, Kolpos
Idi Amin Dada, Lake Dem. Rep. Congo/Uganda see Edward, Lake
208 A1 Idiazabal Spain
213 L6 Idice r. Italy
232 D3 Ididole Eth.
231 C6 Idiofa Dem. Rep. Congo
244 H3 Iditarod AK U.S.A.
244 H3 Iditarod r. AK U.S.A.
162 Q2 Idivuoma Sweden
225 F2 Idkū Egypt
171 P7 Idle r. England U.K.
150 E3 Idlib Syria
150 E3 Idlib governorate Syria
173 I5 Idmiston Wiltshire, England U.K.
205 R3 Idocin Spain
233 B6 Idodi Tanz.
199 J6 Iđoš Vojvodina Serbia
Idra i. Greece see Ydra
106 D8 Idracowra N.T. Austr.
163 L6 Idre Sweden
210 E3 Idrija Slovenia
210 D2 Idrijca r. Slovenia
160 L5 Idritsa Rus. Fed.
212 I4 Idro Italy
212 J4 Idro, Lago d' l. Italy
185 D9 Idron-Ousse-Sendets France
190 I1 Idstedt Ger.
191 F10 Idstein Ger.
233 B6 Idugala Tanz.
136 E8 Idukki Kerala India
237 M8 Idutywa S. Africa
264 P8 Idyllwild CA U.S.A.
Idzhevan Armenia see Ijevan
124 □1 Ie Okinawa Japan
160 H5 Iecava Latvia
160 G5 Iecava r. Latvia
124 □1 Ie-jima i. Okinawa Japan
280 B5 Iepê Brazil
187 C7 Ieper Belgium
219 K3 Ier r. Romania
221 G7 Ierapetra Kriti Greece
220 E2 Ierissou, Kolpos b. Greece
162 R2 Iešjávri l. Norway
124 □1 Ie-suidō str. Okinawa Japan
209 F10 Ifac, Penyal d' pt Spain
233 C7 Ifakara Tanz.
146 B1 'Ifāl, Wādī watercourse Saudi Arabia
113 J5 Ifalik atoll Micronesia
Ifaluk atoll Micronesia see Ifalik
235 □J4 Ifanadiana Madag.
235 □J4 Ifanirea Madag.
229 G5 Ife Nigeria
224 C6 Ifenat Chad
229 H2 Iferouâne Niger
227 G4 Ifetesene mt. Alg.
195 K6 Iffeldorf Ger.
180 G5 Iffendic France
194 E4 Iffezheim Ger.
107 H5 Iffley Qld Austr.
162 S1 Ifjord Norway
229 F2 Ifôghas, Adrar des hills Mali
229 G5 Ifon Nigeria
104 D4 Ifould Lake salt flat S.A. Austr.
226 D2 Ifrane Morocco
181 K3 Ifs France
191 J8 Ifta Ger.
230 D5 Ifumo Dem. Rep. Congo
233 B7 Ifunda Tanz.
201 K8 Ig Slovenia
126 D6 Iga Japan
229 G4 Igabi Nigeria
199 G5 Igal Hungary
218 G8 Igalo Herceg-Novi Montenegro
117 I3 Igan Sarawak Malaysia
117 I3 Igan r. Malaysia
232 B4 Iganga Uganda
199 H5 Igar Hungary
280 D4 Igarapava Brazil
278 D2 Igarape Açú Brazil
278 D3 Igarapé Grande Brazil
278 C2 Igarapé Miri Brazil
280 D5 Igaratá Brazil
278 E4 Igarité Brazil
152 J3 Igarka Rus. Fed.
136 C3 Igatpuri Mahar. India
229 G4 Igbetti Nigeria
229 F4 Igboho Nigeria
229 H5 Igbor Nigeria
149 M4 Igdir Iran
149 L4 Iğdır Turkey
151 F6 Iğdır prov. Turkey
181 M5 Igé France
205 P4 Igea Spain
194 B2 Igel Ger.
191 K7 Igensdorf Ger.
194 H3 Igersheim Ger.
194 E3 Iggelheim Ger.
195 O4 Iggensbach Ger.
163 N6 Iggesund Sweden
219 L4 Ighiu Romania
244 I2 Igikpak, Mount AK U.S.A.
212 H2 Igis Switz.
245 □D6 Igitkin Island AK U.S.A.
244 I4 Igiugig AK U.S.A.
284 C2 Iglesia Arg.
214 B9 Iglesias Sardegna Italy
214 A8 Iglesiente reg. Sardegna Italy
226 E3 Igli Alg.
195 J5 Igling Ger.
156 L5 Iglino Rus. Fed.
243 J3 Igloolik Nunavut Can.
Igluligaarjuk Nunavut Can. see Chesterfield Inlet
248 B3 Ignace Ont. Can.
268 C1 Ignacio Allende Mex.
266 L7 Ignacio de la Llave Mex.
266 F3 Ignacio Zaragoza Mex.
269 I2 Ignacio Zaragoza Tamaulipas Mex.
268 D2 Ignacio Zaragoza Zacatecas Mex.
160 J6 Ignalina Lith.
122 C2 Ignashino Rus. Fed.
148 C3 İğneada Turkey
148 D3 İğneada Burnu pt Turkey
199 L5 Ignești Romania
179 L7 Igney France
137 M7 Ignoitijala Andaman & Nicobar Is India
182 G1 Ignon r. France
156 H4 Igodovo Rus. Fed.
115 G4 Igom Papua Indon.
233 B6 Igoma Tanz.
233 A6 Igombe r. Tanz.
161 Q6 Igorevskaya Rus. Fed.
182 E2 Igornay France
220 B3 Igoumenitsa Greece
156 K4 Igra Rus. Fed.
208 E3 Igriés Spain
152 H3 Igrim Rus. Fed.
279 B8 Iguaçu r. Brazil
280 A6 Iguaçu, Parque Nacional do nat. park Brazil
Iguaçu, Saltos do waterfall Arg./Brazil see Iguaçu Falls
282 G2 Iguaçu Falls Arg./Brazil
279 E5 Iguaí Brazil
274 C4 Iguaje, Mesa de hills Col.
269 H7 Iguala Mex.
208 I4 Igualada Spain
207 I7 Igualeja Spain
269 I8 Igualtepec Mex.
280 D6 Iguape Brazil
280 B5 Iguaraçu Brazil
281 E4 Iguarapé Brazil
281 E4 Iguatama Brazil
279 B7 Iguatemi Brazil
279 B7 Iguatemi r. Brazil
278 F3 Iguatu Brazil
Iguazú, Cataratas do waterfall Arg./Brazil see Iguaçu Falls
282 G2 Iguazú, Parque Nacional del nat. park Arg.
230 A5 Iguéla Gabon
204 H3 Igueña Spain
182 E4 Iguerande France
226 C4 Iguetti, Sebkhet salt flat Maur.
226 D4 Iguidi, Erg des. Alg./Maur.
233 B6 Igunga Tanz.
229 G5 Iguobazuwa Nigeria
235 F3 Igusi Zimbabwe
233 B5 Igusule Tanz.
Iguvium Italy see Gubbio
235 □K2 Iharaña Madag.
198 G5 Iharosberény Hungary
136 C9 Ihavandhippolhu Atoll Maldives
Ihbulag Mongolia see Hanbogd
124 □E19 Iheya-jima i. Nansei-shotō Japan
Ihhayrhan Mongolia see Bayan-Önjüül
229 G5 Ihiala Nigeria
227 G5 Ihirène, Oued watercourse Alg.
199 J2 Ihľany Slovakia
190 E4 Ihlowerhörn (Ihlow) Ger.
158 H2 Ihnatpil' Ukr.
185 B9 Iholdy France
235 □J4 Ihosy Madag.
190 D4 Ihrhove Ger.
194 D5 Ihringen Ger.
195 L4 Ihrlerstein Ger.
221 L3 İhsaniye Turkey
129 R5 Ih Tal Nei Mongol China
128 G3 Ihtamir Mongolia
129 Q1 Ih Tol Gol Nei Mongol China
128 G1 Ih-Uul Mongolia
127 G4 Iida Japan
124 Q9 Iide-san mt. Japan
127 G4 Iijima Japan
162 R4 Iijoki r. Fin.
126 D7 Iinan Japan
127 M4 Iioka Japan
162 S5 Iisalmi Fin.
126 D7 Iitaka Japan
160 J1 Iitti Fin.
127 H2 Iiyama Japan
125 H13 Iizuka Japan
226 C5 Ijâfene des. Maur.
233 D5 Ijara Kenya
229 F5 Ijebu-Ode Nigeria
117 K9 Ijen-Merapi-Maelang, Cagar Alam nature res. Jawa Indon.
151 G5 Ijevan Armenia
186 I2 IJlst Neth.
186 G4 IJmuiden Neth.
228 B2 Ijnâouene well Maur.
226 D5 Ijoubbâne des. Mali
186 I3 IJssel r. Neth.
186 H3 IJsselmeer l. Neth.
186 I3 IJsselmuiden Neth.
186 H4 IJsselstein Neth.
279 B9 Ijuí Brazil
277 G6 Ijuí r. Brazil
187 E6 IJzendijke Neth.
187 C7 IJzer r. Belgium alt. Yser (France)
Ikaahuk N.W.T. Can. see Sachs Harbour
163 Q6 Ikaalinen Fin.
237 K1 Ikageleng S. Africa
237 L2 Ikageng S. Africa
235 □J3 Ikahavo hill Madag.
127 I3 Ikaho Japan
235 □J4 Ikalamavony Madag.
Ikaluktutiak Nunavut Can. see Cambridge Bay
103 F9 Ikamatua South I. N.Z.
231 D5 Ikanda-Nord Dem. Rep. Congo
229 H5 Ikang Nigeria
229 H4 Ikara Nigeria
229 G5 Ikare Nigeria
230 C5 Ikari Dem. Rep. Congo
221 H5 Ikaria i. Greece
126 C6 Ikaruga Japan
164 F5 Ikast Denmark
230 C4 Ikau Dem. Rep. Congo
127 H5 Ikawa Japan
103 E11 Ikawai South I. N.Z.
102 K5 Ikawhenua Range mts North I. N.Z.
126 D4 Ikeda Fukui Japan
126 E5 Ikeda Gifu Japan
124 U4 Ikeda Hokkaidō Japan
127 G3 Ikeda Nagano Japan
126 C5 Ikeda Ōsaka Japan
125 K12 Ikeda Tokushima Japan
125 K13 Ikegawa Japan
126 D7 Ikegoya-yama mt. Japan
124 □1 Ikei-jima i. Okinawa Japan
229 F5 Ikeja Nigeria
230 D5 Ikela Dem. Rep. Congo
230 C4 Ikelemba r. Dem. Rep. Congo
231 E7 Ikelenge Zambia
229 G5 Ikem Nigeria
229 C5 Ikengo Dem. Rep. Congo
230 A5 Ikéngue Gabon
229 G5 Ikere Nigeria
Ikerre Nigeria see Ikere
198 F4 Ikervár Hungary
151 I4 Ikhrek Rus. Fed.
219 L8 Ikhtiman Bulg.
237 I4 Ikhutseng S. Africa
150 H1 İkiağiz Turkey
157 I7 Iki-Burul Rus. Fed.
233 A5 Ikimba, Lake Tanz.
229 G5 Ikire Nigeria
125 G13 Iki-shima i. Japan
125 G13 Iki-suidō sea chan. Japan
151 B5 İkizdere Turkey
160 H4 Ikla Estonia
233 A6 Ikola Tanz.
229 H5 Ikom Nigeria
126 C6 Ikoma Japan
233 B5 Ikoma Tanz.
235 □J4 Ikongo Madag.
239 □3a Ikoni Njazidja Comoros
151 C1 Ikon-Khalk Rus. Fed.
235 □J3 Ikopa r. Madag.
159 S3 Ikorets r. Rus. Fed.
229 F5 Ikorodu Nigeria
230 E5 Ikosi Dem. Rep. Congo
229 G5 Ikot-Ekpene Nigeria
227 H4 Ikouhaouene, Adrar mt. Alg.
Ikpiarjuk Nunavut Can. see Arctic Bay
244 I1 Ikpikpuk r. AK U.S.A.
199 G4 Ikrény Hungary
123 E11 Iksan S. Korea
126 F2 Ikuji-hana pt Japan
233 B6 Ikungi Tanz.
233 B6 Ikungu Tanz.
126 A5 Ikuno Japan
127 G3 Ikusaka Japan
158 E3 Ikva r. Ukr.
227 F5 Ilaferh, Oued watercourse Alg.
233 A6 Ilagala Tanz.
114 C3 Ilagan Luzon Phil.
232 C4 Ilaisamis Kenya
136 F8 Ilaiyankudi Tamil Nadu India
235 □K3 Ilaka Atsinanana Madag.
144 B5 Īlām Iran
144 B5 Īlām prov. Iran
139 K6 Ilam Nepal
131 M6 Ilan Taiwan
196 C3 Iłanka r. Pol.
212 G2 Ilanz Switz.
229 G4 Ila Orangun Nigeria
159 O5 Ilarionove Ukr.
229 F5 Ilaro Nigeria
276 C4 Ilave Peru
197 H2 Iława Pol.
229 G5 Ilawe-Ekiti Nigeria
197 H2 Iławskie, Pojezierze reg. Pol.
147 G7 Ilazārān, Kūh-e mt. Iran
217 □ Il-Bajda, Ras pt Gozo Malta
128 F4 Il Bogd Uul mts Mongolia
214 D8 Ilbono Sardegna Italy
172 G6 Ilchester Somerset, England U.K.
221 H5 Ildır Turkey
143 Q5 Ile r. China/Kazakh.
247 J4 Île-à-la-Crosse Sask. Can.
247 J4 Île-à-la-Crosse, Lac l. Sask. Can.
270 G4 Île-à-Vache i. Haiti
231 D6 Ilebo Dem. Rep. Congo
249 I3 Île d'Anticosti, Réserve Faunique de l' nature res. Que. Can.
178 E6 Île-de-France admin. reg. France
233 B7 Ileje Tanz.
142 E2 Ilek Kazakh.
142 E2 Ilek r. Rus. Fed.
159 O3 Ilek-Pen'kovka Rus. Fed.
169 D9 Ilen r. Ireland
Ilerda prov. Spain see Lleida
232 C3 Ileret Kenya
Île Royale i. N.S. Can. see Cape Breton Island
Ilesa Nigeria see Ilesha
229 G5 Ilesha Nigeria
229 F4 Ilesha Ibariba Nigeria
156 J5 Ilet' r. Rus. Fed.
156 H3 Ileza Rus. Fed.
191 K7 Ilfeld Ger.
247 M3 Ilford Man. Can.
173 M4 Ilford Greater London, England U.K.
107 J7 Ilfracombe Qld Austr.
172 D5 Ilfracombe Devon, England U.K.
148 F3 Ilgaz Turkey
148 F3 Ilgaz Dağları mts Turkey
148 E4 Ilgın Turkey
197 M1 Ilgis l. Lith.
217 □ Il-Griebeġ, Ras pt Malta
238 □1c Ilha, Ponta da pt Pico Azores
281 E5 Ilhabela Brazil
281 E5 Ilha Grande Brazil
281 E5 Ilha Grande, Baía da b. Brazil
279 B7 Ilha Grande, Parque Nacional de nat. park Brazil
279 B7 Ilha Grande, Represa resr Brazil
217 □ Il-Ħamrija, Ras pt Malta
237 Q1 Ilhas da Inhaca e dos Portugueses nature res. Moz.
280 B4 Ilha Solteíra, Represa resr Brazil
204 C7 Ílhavo Port.
279 F5 Ilhéus Brazil
Ili r. China/Kazakh. see Ile
Ili Kazakh. see Kapchagay
219 K5 Ilia Romania
244 I4 Iliamna AK U.S.A.
244 I4 Iliamna Lake AK U.S.A.
244 I3 Iliamna Volcano AK U.S.A.
148 I4 İliç Turkey
151 B6 Ilıca Bingöl Turkey
151 C6 Ilıca Erzurum Turkey
151 C1 Il'ich Rus. Fed.
Il'ichevsk Azer. see Şärur
Il'ichevsk Ukr. see Illichivs'k
Ilici Spain see Elche-Elx
232 F3 Ilig, Raas pt Somalia
114 E7 Iligan Mindanao Phil.
114 E7 Iligan Bay Mindanao Phil.
114 D2 Iligan Point Luzon Phil.
Ili He r. China/Kazakh. see Ile
210 G4 Ilijaš Bos.-Herz.
243 P2 Ilimananngip Nunaa i. Greenland
153 L3 Ilimpeya r. Rus. Fed.
219 J9 Ilinden Ilinden Macedonia
142 G3 Il'inka Kazakh.
161 T7 Il'inka Kaluzhskaya Oblast' Rus. Fed.
143 U2 Il'inka Respublika Altay Rus. Fed.
128 D1 Il'inka Respublika Tyva Rus. Fed.
161 O6 Il'ino Rus. Fed.
156 K4 Il'inskiy Permskaya Oblast' Rus. Fed.
161 P1 Il'inskiy Respublika Kareliya Rus. Fed.
122 M5 Il'inskiy Sakhalin Rus. Fed.
156 I3 Il'insko-Podomskoye Rus. Fed.
159 S7 Il'inskoye Krasnodarskiy Kray Rus. Fed.
161 S8 Il'inskoye Orlovskaya Oblast' Rus. Fed.
161 U5 Il'inskoye Tverskaya Oblast' Rus. Fed.
161 V4 Il'inskoye Yaroslavskaya Oblast' Rus. Fed.
161 W5 Il'inskoye-Khovanskoye Rus. Fed.
114 C5 Ilin Strait Phil.
Il'intsy Ukr. see Illintsi
115 E8 Iliomar East Timor
257 J5 Ilion NY U.S.A.
264 □D12 'Ilio Point HI U.S.A.
210 E3 Ilirska Bistrica Slovenia
151 H4 Ilisu Qoruğu nature res. Azer.
Ilium tourist site Turkey see Truva
244 G3 Ilivit Mountains AK U.S.A.
160 K7 Iliya r. Belarus
Iliysk Kazakh. see Kapchagay
199 L3 Ilk Hungary
136 E5 Ilkal Karnataka India
173 J2 Ilkeston Derbyshire, England U.K.
171 N6 Ilkley West Yorkshire, England U.K.
217 □ Il-Kullana pt Malta
179 O6 Ill r. France
205 O8 Illana Spain
114 D8 Illana Bay Mindanao Phil.
284 B2 Illapel Chile
284 B2 Illapel r. Chile
207 N7 Illar Spain
213 K5 Illasi r. Italy
185 D6 Illats France
104 D2 Illbillee, Mount hill S.A. Austr.
180 H5 Ille r. France
180 H5 Ille-et-Rance, Canal d' France
180 H5 Ille-et-Vilaine dept France
229 G3 Illéla Niger
229 G3 Illela Nigeria
195 H5 Iller r. Ger.
195 I5 Illerrieden Ger.
195 I5 Illertissen Ger.
203 G3 Illes Balears aut. comm. Spain
205 M8 Illescas Spain
282 G4 Illescas Uru.
185 J10 Ille-sur-Têt France
159 O8 Illicheve Ukr.
158 J7 Illichivs'k Ukr.
178 B7 Illiers-Combray France
276 D4 Illimani, Nevado de mt. Bol.
194 F4 Illingen Baden-Württemberg Ger.
194 C3 Illingen Saarland Ger.
158 J7 Illinka Odes'ka Oblast' Ukr.
159 M8 Illinka Respublika Krym Ukr.
250 D9 Illinois r. IL U.S.A.
260 K6 Illinois state U.S.A.
250 E8 Illinois and Mississippi Canal IL U.S.A.
158 I4 Illintsi Ukr.
227 H4 Illizi Alg.
179 O6 Illkirch-Graffenstaden France
196 G4 Illmensee Ger.
201 O4 Illmitz Austria
106 E8 Illogwa watercourse N.T. Austr.
207 L6 Íllora Spain
214 B7 Illorai Sardegna Italy
195 L3 Illschwang Ger.
205 Q5 Illueca Spain
179 N8 Illzach France
193 E8 Ilm r. Ger.
195 L4 Ilm r. Ger.
109 I10 Ilma, Lake salt flat W.A. Austr.
146 G6 'Ilmān, Jabal al hill Saudi Arabia
161 O3 Il'men', Ozero l. Rus. Fed.
191 K9 Ilmenau Ger.
190 J4 Ilmenau r. Ger.
217 □ Il-Minkba pt Malta
172 G6 Ilminster Somerset, England U.K.
200 F8 Il Montello mt. Italy
193 D9 Ilmtal park Ger.
244 H4 Ilnik AK U.S.A.
158 C5 Il'nytsya Ukr.
276 C4 Ilo Peru
229 G5 Ilobu Nigeria
114 B6 Iloc i. Phil.
284 A4 Iloca Chile
114 C6 Iloilo Panay Phil.
114 D6 Iloilo Strait Phil.
162 U5 Ilomantsi Fin.
233 B6 Ilongero Tanz.
229 G4 Ilorin Nigeria
210 F3 Ilova r. Croatia
157 I6 Ilovatka Rus. Fed.
159 R6 Ilovays'k Ukr.
219 K9 Ilovica Macedonia
213 R7 Ilovik Croatia
210 E3 Ilovik i. Croatia
159 R3 Ilovka Rus. Fed.
157 H6 Ilovlya Rus. Fed.
157 H6 Ilovlya r. Rus. Fed.
197 I3 Iłów Pol.
196 D4 Iłowa Pol.
197 I2 Iłowo Osada Pol.
186 G4 Ilpendam Neth.
153 R3 Il'pyrskoye Rus. Fed.
217 □ Il-Qala, Ras pt Gozo Malta
164 K2 Ilsbo Sweden
191 J6 Ilse r. Ger.
191 J6 Ilsede Ger.
191 K7 Ilsenburg (Harz) Ger.
191 G8 Ilsfeld Ger.
194 H3 Ilshofen Ger.
172 E6 Ilsington Devon, England U.K.
159 R9 Il'skiy Rus. Fed.
214 A10 Il Toro, Isola i. Sardegna Italy
160 J6 Ilūkste Latvia
243 M3 Ilulissat Greenland
233 B6 Ilunde Tanz.
233 B6 Ilungu Tanz.
Ilva i. Italy see Elba, Isola d'
217 □ Il-Wahx, Ras pt Malta
160 K7 Il'ya Belarus
Il'yaly Turkm. see Gurbansoltan Eje
156 L3 Ilych r. Rus. Fed.
197 K1 Ilyushino Rus. Fed.
201 M5 Ilz Austria
195 O4 Ilz r. Ger.
197 J4 Iłża Pol.
197 J4 Iłżanka r. Pol.
125 J12 Imabari Japan
124 R5 Imabetsu Japan
275 G5 Imabú r. Brazil
126 D4 Imadate Japan
124 R4 Imagane Japan
127 K2 Imaichi Japan
126 D4 Imajō Japan
235 H2 Imala Moz.
149 L8 Imām al Ḩamzah Iraq
145 J3 Imam-baba Turkm.
148 G5 İmamoğlu Turkey
Iman Rus. Fed. see Dal'nerechensk
122 H6 Iman r. Rus. Fed.
156 F2 Imandra Rus. Fed.
143 M1 Imantau, Ozero l. Kazakh.
125 G13 Imari Japan
228 E3 Imasgo Burkina
Imassogo Burkina see Imasgo
276 C3 Imata Peru
275 F3 Imataca, Serranía de mts Venez.
163 T6 Imatra Fin.
160 I3 Imavere Estonia
126 D5 Imazu Japan
274 B4 Imbabura prov. Ecuador
275 F3 Imbaimadai Guyana
Imba-numa l. Japan see Inba-numa
279 C9 Imbituba Brazil
280 B6 Imbituva Brazil
221 L6 İmecik Turkey
199 H4 Imeľ Slovakia
imeni 26 Bakinskikh Komissarov Azer. see Uzboy
imeni Chapayevka Turkm. see S. A. Nyýazow Adyndaky
imeni G. I. Petrovskogo Ukr. see Horodyshche
imeni G. Ya. Sedova Ukr. see Syedove
imeni Kalinina Tajik. see Cheshtebe
imeni Khamzy Khakikmzade Uzbek. see Hamza
imeni Kirova Kazakh. see Kopbirlik
imeni Kirova Donets'ka Oblast' Ukr. see Kirovs'k
imeni Kirova Donets'ka Oblast' Ukr. see Kirove
imeni L. M. Kaganovicha Ukr. see Popasna
imeni Petra Stuchki Latvia see Aizkraukle
imeni Voroshilova Kyrg. see Tash-Bashat
159 O5 Imeny Lenina, Ozero l. Ukr.
213 L3 Imèr Italy
216 G8 Imera r. Sicilia Italy
275 E4 Imeri, Serra mts Brazil
230 C4 Imese Dem. Rep. Congo
232 D3 Īmī Eth.
226 D2 Imilchil Morocco
226 C3 Imi-n-Tanoute Morocco
226 B4 Imirikliy Labyad reg. Western Sahara
Imishli Azer. see İmişli
151 J6 İmişli Azer.
138 D1 Imit Pak.
123 E11 Imja-do i. S. Korea
123 E10 Imjin-gang r. N. Korea/S. Korea
251 K6 Imlay City MI U.S.A.
226 B5 Imlili Western Sahara
191 J9 Immelborn Ger.
165 K5 Immeln l. Sweden
194 F6 Immendingen Ger.
191 H8 Immenhausen Ger.
195 L2 Immenreuth Ger.
194 G6 Immenstaad am Bodensee Ger.
195 I6 Immenstadt im Allgäu Ger.
171 Q6 Immingham North East Lincolnshire, England U.K.
255 G12 Immokalee FL U.S.A.
229 G5 Imo state Nigeria
213 L7 Imola Italy
210 F4 Imotski Croatia
237 N5 Impendle S. Africa
274 E6 Imperatriz Amazonas Brazil
278 D3 Imperatriz Maranhão Brazil
212 E8 Imperia Italy
212 D7 Imperia prov. Italy
284 A6 Imperial r. Chile
276 A3 Imperial Peru
265 Q9 Imperial CA U.S.A.
260 E5 Imperial NE U.S.A.
264 O9 Imperial Beach CA U.S.A.
265 R9 Imperial Dam AZ/CA U.S.A.
265 Q9 Imperial Valley plain CA U.S.A.
108 E4 Imperieuse Reef W.A. Austr.
230 C4 Impfondo Congo
139 N7 Imphal Manipur India
182 C3 Imphy France
173 M3 Impington Cambridgeshire, England U.K.
213 K8 Impruneta Italy
221 J2 İmralı Adası i. Turkey
146 G9 Imrān Yemen
199 I5 Imrehegy Hungary
221 G2 İmroz Gökeada Turkey
İmroz i. Turkey see Gökçeada
İmrun Turkey see Pütürge
123 E11 Imsil S. Korea
200 C5 Imst Austria
150 E6 Imtān Syria
266 D2 Imuris Mex.
114 B6 Imuruan Bay Palawan Phil.
244 F2 Imuruk Basin l. AK U.S.A.
244 G2 Imuruk Lake AK U.S.A.
197 M3 Imyanin Belarus
226 D3 Imzouren Morocco
122 H4 In r. Rus. Fed.
127 K1 Ina Fukushima Japan
127 L4 Ina Ibaraki Japan
127 G4 Ina Nagano Japan
196 C2 Ina r. Pol.
229 F2 I-n-Âbâlene well Mali
229 G2 I-n-Abangharit well Niger
126 E5 Inabe Japan
126 G5 Inabu Japan
238 □2c Inaccessible Island Tristan da Cunha S. Atlantic Ocean
126 D5 Inae Japan
227 H5 In Afaleleh well Alg.
114 B7 Inagauan Palawan Phil.
126 B6 Inagawa Japan
126 B6 Ina-gawa r. Japan
127 L4 Inage Japan
169 D7 Inagh Ireland
127 K4 Inagi Japan
235 H2 Inago Moz.
276 B1 Inahuaya Peru
278 F4 Inajá Brazil
277 H2 Inaja r. Brazil
277 H2 Inaja, Serra do hills Brazil
228 E2 I-n-Akhmed well Mali
228 E5 I-n-Akli well Mali
100 □6 Inakona Guadalcanal Solomon Is
Inalahan Guam see Inarajan
229 F2 I-n-Alakam well Mali
228 F2 I-n-Alchi well Mali
229 F2 I-n-Alchig well Mali
228 E2 I-n-Aleï well Mali
228 C2 I-n-'Amar well Maur.
Inamba-jima i. Japan see Inanba-jima
276 C3 Inambari Peru
276 C3 Inambari r. Peru
228 D2 I-n-Ameddé well Mali
227 H3 In Aménas Alg.
227 G5 In Amguel Alg.
126 A6 Inami Hyōgo Japan
126 E2 Inami Toyama Japan
126 B8 Inami Wakayama Japan
117 L1 Inanam Sabah Malaysia
125 Q13 Inanba-jima i. Japan
199 K3 Ináncs Hungary
237 O5 Inanda S. Africa
103 F8 Inangahua Junction South I. N.Z.
113 H7 Inanwatan Papua Indon.
276 C2 Iñapari Peru
100 □1 Inarajan Guam
229 F2 I-n-Areï well Mali
162 U5 Inari Itä-Suomi Fin.
162 S2 Inari Lappi Fin.
153 L3 Inarigda Rus. Fed.
162 S2 Inarijärvi l. Fin.
162 R2 Inarijoki r. Fin./Norway
229 G2 I-n-Arouinat well Niger
126 G6 Inasa Japan
229 F2 I-n-Atankarer well Mali
276 D2 Inauini r. Brazil
125 R9 Inawashiro-ko l. Japan
227 G4 I-n Azaoua well Alg.
227 G5 In-Azaoua well Alg.
229 G1 I-n-Azaoua watercourse Niger
224 A2 In Azar well Libya
126 E5 Inazawa Japan
224 A3 In Azāwah well Libya
229 F2 I-n-Azerraf well Mali
127 L4 Inba Japan
127 L4 Inba-numa l. Japan
227 F4 In Belbel Alg.
209 K8 Inca Spain
282 C2 Inca de Oro Chile
221 I2 İnce Burnu pt Turkey
148 G2 İnce Burun pt Turkey
221 K5 İnceler Turkey
169 C8 Inch Kerry Ireland
169 J7 Inch Wexford Ireland
168 K9 Inchbare Angus, Scotland
103 F9 Inchbonnie South I. N.Z.
144 G3 Incheh Iran
195 K4 Inchenhofen Ger.
178 B3 Incheville France
169 D9 Inchigeelagh Ireland
232 C3 Inch'īnī Terara mt. Eth.
168 H11 Inchinnan Renfrewshire, Scotland U.K.
226 B5 Inchiri admin. reg. Maur.
169 H2 Inch Island Ireland
171 K1 Inchkeith i. Scotland U.K.
123 E10 Inch'ŏn S. Korea
235 G3 Inchope Moz.
229 F2 I-n-Choumaguene well M
168 J10 Inchture Perth and Kinros Scotland U.K.
205 M3 Incinillas Spain
Incio Spain see A Cruz do
150 D2 Incirli Adana Turkey
Incirli Sakarya Turkey see
235 G5 Incomati r. Moz.
187 G7 Incourt Belgium
214 C4 Incudine, Monte mt. Frar
160 H4 Inčukalns Latvia
168 D11 Indaal, Loch b. Scotland U
226 E5 I-n-Dagouber well Mali
281 E3 Indaiá r. Brazil
280 A3 Indaiá Grande r. Brazil
280 D5 Indaiatuba Brazil
162 N5 Indalsälven r. Sweden
268 G6 Indaparapeo Mex.
138 G7 Indargarh Madh. Prad. In
138 F7 Indargarh Rajasthan Indi
232 C1 Inda Silasē Eth.
118 B3 Indaw Sagaing Myanmar
118 C4 Indaw Shan Myanmar
118 C2 Indawgyi, Lake Myanmar
266 G5 Indé Mex.
Indefatigable Island Islas Galápagos Ecuador see Santa Cruz, Isla
229 F3 I-n-Délimane well Mali
264 N5 Independence CA U.S.A.
260 J4 Independence IA U.S.A.
261 H7 Independence KS U.S.A.
254 E6 Independence KY U.S.A.
250 B3 Independence MN U.S.A.
260 H6 Independence MO U.S.A.
256 D12 Independence VA U.S.A.
250 C5 Independence WI U.S.A.
243 P1 Independence Fjord inlet Greenland
262 F6 Independence Mountain NV U.S.A.
276 D4 Independencia Bol.
278 E3 Independência Brazil
269 K5 Independencia Mex.
219 P6 Independenţa Călăraşi R
219 Q7 Independenţa Constanţa Romania
219 P5 Independenţa Galaţi Ron
129 R3 Inder Nei Mongol China
142 D3 Inder, Ozero salt l. Kazak
232 B3 Inderacha Eth.
142 D3 Inderbor Kazakh.
136 E4 Indi Karnataka India
135 H6 India country Asia
245 M3 Indian r. Y.T. Can.
250 H3 Indian r. MI U.S.A.
256 F8 Indiana PA U.S.A.
254 D5 Indiana state U.S.A.
289 L8 Indian-Antarctic Ridge s Southern Ocean
254 D6 Indianapolis IN U.S.A.
246 G3 Indian Cabins Alta Can.
Indian Desert India/Pak. see Thar Desert
256 B11 Indian Fields KY U.S.A.
249 J2 Indian Harbour Nfld and
247 K5 Indian Head Sask. Can.
257 K5 Indian Lake NY U.S.A.
250 H4 Indian Lake l. MI U.S.A.
257 K5 Indian Lake l. NY U.S.A.
256 B8 Indian Lake l. OH U.S.A.
256 G8 Indian Lake l. PA U.S.A.
244 I2 Indian Mountain AK U.S
259 J2 Indian Neck CT U.S.A.
235 □G5 Indian Ocean
261 I5 Indianola IA U.S.A.
261 J9 Indianola MS U.S.A.
280 D3 Indianópolis Brazil
265 S3 Indian Peak UT U.S.A.
250 J4 Indian River MI U.S.A.
265 Q5 Indian Springs NV U.S.A
265 V6 Indian Wells AZ U.S.A.
280 B2 Indiara Brazil
278 F4 Indiaroba Brazil
232 C2 Indibir Eth.
271 □1 Indiera Alta Puerto Rico
156 J2 Indiga Rus. Fed.
153 P2 Indigirka r. Rus. Fed.
156 J2 Indigskaya Guba b. Rus.
218 I5 Inđija Vojvodina Serbia
118 B3 Indin Myanmar
246 H1 Indin Lake N.W.T. Can.
266 □R12 Indio r. Nic.
265 P8 Indio CA U.S.A.
285 G6 Indio Rico Arg.
137 M9 Indira Point Andaman & Is India
138 G9 Indira Priyadarshini Pen National Park India
99 G3 Indispensable Reefs Solc
100 □6 Indispensable Strait Solc
112 C3 Indo-China reg. Asia
159 O8 Indol r. Ukr.
161 U1 Indomanka r. Rus. Fed.
112 D7 Indonesia country Asia
138 E8 Indore Madh. Prad. India
116 E5 Indragiri r. Indon.
117 H8 Indramayu Jawa Indon.
117 H8 Indramayu, Tanjung pt I
116 D6 Indrapura Sumatera Indo
Indrapura, Gunung vol. I see Kerinci, Gunung
116 D6 Indrapura, Tanjung pt In
137 G3 Indravati r. India
181 O8 Indre dept France
184 E1 Indre r. France
169 D6 Indreabhán Ireland
181 M7 Indre-et-Loire dept Franc
162 U1 Indre Kiberg Norway
164 C1 Indre Samlen b. Norway
104 D2 Indulkana S.A. Austr.
231 C8 Indungo Angola
Indur Andhra Prad. India see Nizamabad
160 G8 Indura Belarus
136 F4 Indurti Andhra Prad. Indi
145 L10 Indus r. China/Pak. alt. Shiquan He (China
145 L9 Indus, Mouths of the Pa
289 I3 Indus Cone sea feature Indian Ocean
237 L7 Indwe S. Africa
237 L8 Indwe r. S. Africa
219 P8 Indzhe Voyvoda Bulg.
126 B4 Ine Japan
227 G5 In Ebeggi well Alg.
148 F3 İnebolu Turkey
229 E5 I-n-Échaï well Mali
221 K2 İnegöl Turkey
227 G4 In Ekker Alg.
115 B8 Inerie vol. Flores Indon.
285 G4 Inés Indart Arg.
219 J4 Ineu Arad Romania
199 L4 Ineu Bihor Romania
Inevi Turkey see Cihanbe
256 C11 Inez KY U.S.A.
226 C3 Inezgane Morocco
227 H5 In Ezzane well Alg.
236 E10 Infanta, Cape S. Africa
274 C3 Infantas Col.
Infantes Spain see Villanueva de los Infante

M9 **Inferior, Laguna** *lag.* Mex.
E2 **Infernão, Cachoeira** *waterfall* Brazil
C2 **Infielés, Punta** *pt* Chile
F7 **Infiernillo, Presa** *resr* Mex.
J2 **Infiesto** Spain
O8 **Infreschi, Punta degli** *pt* Italy
E4 **Ing, Nam Mae** *r.* Thai.
B6 **Inga** Dem. Rep. Congo
R6 **Ingå** Fin.
F2 **Inga** Rus. Fed.
B6 **Ingabu** Myanmar
G2 **Ingal** Niger
D6 **Ingallanna** *watercourse N.T.* Austr.
L2 **Ingalls, Mount** *CA* U.S.A.
J2 **Ingalls Lake** *N.W.T.* Can.
D5 **Inganda** Dem. Rep. Congo
M4 **Ingatestone** *Essex, England* U.K.
H3 **Ingelfingen** Ger.
E2 **Ingelheim am Rhein** Ger.
D7 **Ingelmunster** Belgium
K5 **Ingelstad** Sweden
C5 **Ingende** Dem. Rep. Congo
D4 **Ingeniero Balloffet** Arg.
E1 **Ingeniero Guillermo Nueva Juárez** Arg.
D6 **Ingeniero Huergo** Arg.
C6 **Ingeniero Jacobacci** Arg.
E4 **Ingeniero Luiggi** Arg.
H4 **Ingeniero Maschwitz** Arg.
H4 **Ingeniero Otamendi** Arg.
E3 **Ingenika** *r. B.C.* Can.
□3f **Ingenio** *Gran Canaria* Canary Is
B3 **Ingenio** *r.* Peru
D5 **Ingersoll** *Ont.* Can.
B2 **Ingessana Hills** Sudan
Ingettolgoy Mongolia *see* **Selenge**
Ingezi Zimbabwe *see* **Ngezi**
F3 **Inggelang** *i. Maluku* Indon.
K5 **Ingham** *Qld* Austr.
F4 **In Ghar** Alg.
L8 **Ingichka** Uzbek.
O3 **Inglares** *r.* Spain
M5 **Ingleborough** *hill England* U.K.
K2 **Inglefield Land** *reg.* Greenland
N4 **Ingleton** *Durham, England* U.K.
M5 **Ingleton** *North Yorkshire, England* U.K.
L6 **Inglewhite** *Lancashire, England* U.K.
M3 **Inglewood** *Qld* Austr.
I7 **Inglewood** *Vic.* Austr.
I6 **Inglewood** *North I.* N.Z.
N8 **Inglewood** *CA* U.S.A.
L4 **Inglewood Forest** *England* U.K.
F2 **Inglis Island** *N.T.* Austr.
N1 **Ingoda** *r.* Rus. Fed.
C2 **Ingoka Pum** *mt.* Myanmar
H5 **Ingoldingen** Ger.
R7 **Ingoldmells** *Lincolnshire, England* U.K.
Q1 **Ingolf Fjord** *inlet* Greenland
K4 **Ingolstadt** Ger.
E3 **Ingomar** *S.A.* Austr.
K3 **Ingomar** *MT* U.S.A.
I4 **Ingonish** *N.S.* Can.
L7 **Ingraj Bazar** *W. Bengal* India
M12 **Ingram** *Northumberland, England* U.K.
F12 **Ingram** *VA* U.S.A.
D4 **Ingram** *WI* U.S.A.
I7 **Ingrandes** *Pays de la Loire* France
M8 **Ingrandes** *Poitou-Charentes* France
G1 **Ingray Lake** *N.W.T.* Can.
E5 **Ingre** Bol.
C8 **Ingré** France
F2 **Ingrid Christensen Coast** Antarctica
G6 **I-n-Guezzam** Alg.
E6 **Inguiniel** France
F3 **I-n-Guita** *well* Mali
Ingul *r.* Ukr. *see* **Inhul**
Ingulets Ukr. *see* **Inhulets'**
L4 **Ingulsvatn** Norway
Ingushetia *aut. rep.* Rus. Fed. *see* **Ingushetiya, Respublika**
G3 **Ingushetiya, Respublika** *aut. rep.* Rus. Fed.
Q3 **Ingwavuma** S. Africa
Ingwavuma *r.* Swaziland *see* **Ngwavuma**
E8 **Ingwe** Zambia
N6 **Ingwiller** France
Q1 **Inhaca** Moz.
G5 **Inhaca, Península** *pen.* Moz.
G4 **Inhafenga** Moz.
G4 **Inhambane** Moz.
G4 **Inhambane** *prov.* Moz.
4 **Inhambupe** Brazil
G3 **Inhaminga** Moz.
G3 **Inhamitanga** Moz.
3 **Inhapim** Brazil
G5 **Inharrime** Moz.
G4 **Inhassoro** Moz.
D5 **Inhaúmas** Brazil
5 **I-n-Hihaou, Adrar** *hills* Alg.
2 **İnhisar** Turkey
7 **Inhul** *r.* Ukr.
16 **Inhulets'** Ukr.
7 **Inhulets'** *r.* Ukr.
2 **Inhumas** Brazil
8 **Inielika** *vol. Flores* Indon.
2 **Iniesta** Spain
3 **Inimutaba** Brazil
1 **Iniö** Fin.
4 **Inírida** *r.* Col.
Inis Ireland *see* **Ennis**
Inis Córthaidh Ireland *see* **Enniscorthy**
5 **Inishark** *i.* Ireland
5 **Inishbofin** *i.* Ireland
2 **Inishbofin** *i.* Ireland
6 **Inisheer** *i.* Ireland
4 **Inishkea North** *i.* Ireland
4 **Inishkea South** *i.* Ireland
6 **Inishmaan** *i.* Ireland
6 **Inishmore** *i.* Ireland
4 **Inishmurray** *i.* Ireland
2 **Inishowen** *pen.* Ireland
2 **Inishowen Head** Ireland
2 **Inishtrahull** *i.* Ireland
2 **Inishtrahull Sound** *sea chan.* Ireland
5 **Inishturk** *i.* Ireland
4 **Injgan Sum** *Nei Mongol* China
2 **Injibara** Eth.
1 **Injinoo Aboriginal Reserve** *Qld* Austr.
3 **Injune** *Qld* Austr.
5 **Inkardariya** Kazakh.
Inkberrow *Worcestershire, England* U.K.
5 **Inke** Hungary
2 **I-n-Kerchef** *well* Mali
4 **Inkerman** *Qld* Austr.
9 **Inkerman** Ukr.
3 **Inklin** *B.C.* Can.
4 **Inklin** *r. B.C.* Can.
Inkylap Turkm.
9 **Inland Kaikoura Range** *mts South I.* N.Z.
2 **Inland Lake** *AK* U.S.A.
Inland Sea Japan *see* **Seto-naikai**
5 **Inlet** *NY* U.S.A.
Inman *r. Nunavut* Can.
2 **I-n-Milach** *well* Mali
Inn *r.* Europe
Innaanganeq *c.* Greenland
3 **Innai** Japan
2 **Innamincka** *S.A.* Austr.
2 **Innamincka Regional Reserve** *nature res. S.A.* Austr.
3 **Inndyr** Norway
11 **Innellan** *Argyll and Bute, Scotland* U.K.
Innerbraz Austria
Inner Islands Seychelles
1 **Innerleithen** *Scottish Borders, Scotland* U.K.
Inner Mongolia *aut. reg.* China *see* **Nei Mongol Zizhiqu**
195 O4 **Innernzell** Ger.
Inner Port Shelter *b. H.K.* China *see* **Sai Kung Hoi**
168 E8 **Inner Sound** *sea chan. Scotland* U.K.
212 E2 **Innertkirchen** Switz.
200 F6 **Innervillgraten** Austria
104 F6 **Innes National Park** *S.A.* Austr.
162 M3 **Innhavet** Norway
217 □ **In-Niexfa, Ras** *pt* Malta
195 K5 **Inning am Ammersee** Ger.
107 K4 **Innisfail** *Qld* Austr.
246 H4 **Innisfail** *Alta* Can.
169 E9 **Innishannon** Ireland
169 I4 **Innishkeen** Ireland
122 F4 **Innokent'yevka** Rus. Fed.
244 H3 **Innoko** *r. AK* U.S.A.
244 H3 **Innoko National Wildlife Refuge** *nature res. AK* U.S.A.
125 K12 **Innoshima** Japan
200 D5 **Innsbruck** Austria
213 K1 **Innsbruck** *airport* Austria
248 E1 **Innuksuak** *r. Que.* Can.
201 H3 **Innviertel** *reg.* Austria
169 G5 **Inny** *r.* Ireland
169 B9 **Inny** *r.* Ireland
125 K13 **Ino** Japan
115 D3 **Inobonto** *Sulawesi* Indon.
280 B3 **Inocência** Brazil
126 E2 **Inokuchi** Japan
230 C5 **Inongo** Dem. Rep. Congo
231 B5 **Inoni** Congo
274 C5 **Inonias** Peru
221 L3 **İnönü** Turkey
274 D1 **Inosu** Col.
Inoucdjouac *Que.* Can. *see* **Inukjuak**
228 E2 **I-n-Ouchef** *well* Mali
227 F5 **I-n-Ouzzal, Oued** *watercourse* Alg.
199 H3 **Inovec** *mt.* Slovakia
197 I4 **Inowłódz** Pol.
196 G3 **Inowrocław** Pol.
151 E1 **Inozemtsevo** Rus. Fed.
276 D4 **Inquisivi** Bol.
212 C1 **Ins** Switz.
227 F4 **In Salah** Alg.
157 I5 **Insar** Rus. Fed.
168 K8 **Insch** *Aberdeenshire, Scotland* U.K.
109 B8 **Inscription, Cape** *W.A.* Austr.
118 C6 **Insein** Myanmar
192 J3 **Insel Usedom** *park* Ger.
192 M4 **Iński Park Krajobrazowy** Pol.
196 D2 **Ińsko** Pol.
196 D2 **Ińsko, Jezioro** *l.* Pol.
179 M6 **Insming** France
227 F3 **In Sokki, Oued** *watercourse* Alg.
Insterburg Rus. Fed. *see* **Chernyakhovsk**
151 H5 **İnstitut** Azer.
160 E7 **Instruch** *r.* Rus. Fed.
219 P6 **Însurăţei** Romania
268 G6 **Insurgente José María Morelos y Pavón, Parque Nacional** *nat. park* Mex.
235 E3 **Insuza** *r.* Zimbabwe
156 M2 **Inta** Rus. Fed.
229 G2 **I-n-Tabakat** *well* Niger
229 H1 **I-n-Tadéra** *well* Niger
229 H2 **I-n-Tadrof** *well* Niger
227 G4 **In Takoufi, Oued** *watercourse* Alg.
229 F2 **I-n-Talak** *well* Mali
229 F2 **I-n-Tassit** *well* Mali
229 F2 **I-n-Tebezas** Mali
229 F2 **I-n-Tefiniti** *well* Mali
229 F2 **I-n-Téguift** *well* Mali
229 F3 **I-n-Tékélit** *well* Mali
229 F3 **I-n-Tekoret** *well* Mali
229 F2 **I-n-Telli** *well* Mali
229 F2 **I-n-Témegui** *well* Mali
285 F4 **Intendente Alvear** Arg.
221 H2 **İntepe** Turkey
Interamna Italy *see* **Teramo**
212 D2 **Interlaken** Switz.
250 A1 **International Falls** *MN* U.S.A.
260 E1 **International Peace Garden** *tourist site* Can./U.S.A.
137 M6 **Interview Island** *Andaman & Nicobar Is* India
146 D8 **Intich'o** Eth.
228 E3 **I-n-Tillit** Mali
219 O5 **Întorsura Buzăului** Romania
229 F2 **I-n-Touft** *well* Mali
261 H11 **Intracoastal Waterway** *canal TX* U.S.A.
212 G4 **Introbio** Italy
156 H2 **Intsy** Rus. Fed.
235 E3 **Intundhla** Zimbabwe
274 C5 **Intutu** Peru
127 M4 **Inubō-zaki** *pt* Japan
125 I13 **Inukai** Japan
248 E1 **Inukjuak** *Que.* Can.
283 C9 **Inútil, Bahía** *b.* Chile
245 N1 **Inuvik** *N.W.T.* Can.
276 B2 **Inuya** *r.* Peru
126 E5 **Inuyama** Japan
156 L4 **In'va** *r.* Rus. Fed.
169 F3 **Inver** Ireland
168 E7 **Inveralligin** *Highland, Scotland* U.K.
168 M7 **Inverallochy** *Aberdeenshire, Scotland* U.K.
Inveran Ireland *see* **Indreabhán**
168 F10 **Inveraray** *Argyll and Bute, Scotland* U.K.
168 K9 **Inverarity** *Angus, Scotland* U.K.
168 G10 **Inverarnan** *Argyll and Bute, Scotland* U.K.
169 F3 **Inver Bay** Ireland
168 L9 **Inverbervie** *Aberdeenshire, Scotland* U.K.
103 C13 **Invercargill** *South I.* N.Z.
168 G7 **Invercassley** *Highland, Scotland* U.K.
168 G11 **Inverclyde** *admin. div. Scotland* U.K.
105 M3 **Inverell** *N.S.W.* Austr.
168 I9 **Inverey** *Aberdeenshire, Scotland* U.K.
168 G8 **Invergarry** *Highland, Scotland* U.K.
168 H7 **Invergordon** *Highland, Scotland* U.K.
168 F10 **Inverinan** *Argyll and Bute, Scotland* U.K.
168 K9 **Inverkeilor** *Angus, Scotland* U.K.
168 J10 **Inverkeithing** *Fife, Scotland* U.K.
168 F6 **Inverkirkaig** *Highland, Scotland* U.K.
168 F7 **Inverlael** *Highland, Scotland* U.K.
107 H5 **Inverleigh** *Qld* Austr.
247 K5 **Invermay** *Sask.* Can.
168 G8 **Invermoriston** *Highland, Scotland* U.K.
249 I4 **Inverness** *N.S.* Can.
168 H8 **Inverness** *Highland, Scotland* U.K.
264 J3 **Inverness** *CA* U.S.A.
255 F11 **Inverness** *FL* U.S.A.
168 F10 **Invernoaden** *Argyll and Bute, Scotland* U.K.
168 G10 **Inversnaid** *Stirling, Scotland* U.K.
168 L8 **Inverurie** *Aberdeenshire, Scotland* U.K.
106 B4 **Inverway** *N.T.* Austr.
119 C8 **Investigator Channel** Myanmar
104 E5 **Investigator Group** *is S.A.* Austr.
289 K5 **Investigator Ridge** *sea feature* Indian Ocean
104 F6 **Investigator Strait** *S.A.* Austr.
137 M7 **Invisible Bank** *sea feature Andaman & Nicobar Is* India
256 G9 **Inwood** *WV* U.S.A.
237 M7 **Inxu** *r.* S. Africa
132 H1 **Inya** Rus. Fed.
Inyanga Zimbabwe *see* **Nyanga**
235 G3 **Inyanga Mountains** Zimbabwe
Inyanga National Park Zimbabwe *see* **Nyanga National Park**
235 G3 **Inyangani** *mt.* Zimbabwe
Inyati Zimbabwe *see* **Nyathi**
Inyazura Zimbabwe *see* **Nyazura**
264 O6 **Inyokern** *CA* U.S.A.
264 N4 **Inyo Mountains** *CA* U.S.A.
233 B6 **Inyonga** Tanz.
157 I5 **Inza** Rus. Fed.
127 L4 **Inzai** Japan
195 N6 **Inzell** Ger.
142 G1 **Inzer** Rus. Fed.
156 L5 **Inzer** *r.* Rus. Fed.
157 H5 **Inzhavino** Rus. Fed.
200 D5 **Inzing** Austria
180 E6 **Inzinzac-Lochrist** France
220 B3 **Ioannina** Greece
213 O3 **Iôf di Montasio** *mt.* Italy
124 □H16 **Iō-jima** *i.* Japan
156 G2 **Iokanga** *r.* Rus. Fed.
261 H7 **Iola** *KS* U.S.A.
258 B2 **Iola** *PA* U.S.A.
250 E5 **Iola** *WI* U.S.A.
Iolotan' Turkm. *see* **Ýolöten**
231 B9 **Iona** Angola
249 I4 **Iona** *N.S.* Can.
168 D10 **Iona** *i. Scotland* U.K.
231 B9 **Iona, Parque Nacional do** *nat. park* Angola
168 D10 **Iona, Sound of** *sea chan. Scotland* U.K.
168 D10 **Iona Abbey** *tourist site Scotland* U.K.
264 O3 **Ione** *NV* U.S.A.
262 F2 **Ione** *WA* U.S.A.
219 M6 **Ioneşti** Romania
250 I7 **Ionia** *MI* U.S.A.
220 A3 **Ionia Nisia** *is* Greece
Ionian Islands Greece *see* **Ionia Nisia**
220 A5 **Ionian Sea** Greece/Italy
Ionio *prov.* Italy *see* **Taranto**
127 L2 **Iōno** Japan
153 P4 **Iony, Ostrov** *i.* Rus. Fed.
Iordān Uzbek. *see* **Yordon**
151 H4 **Iori** *r.* Georgia
221 G6 **Ios** *i.* Greece
Iō-shima *i.* Japan *see* **Iō-jima**
125 □2 **Iō-tō** *i. Kazan-rettō* Japan
124 □F19 **Iō-Tori-jima** *i. Nansei-shotō* Japan
228 A2 **Iouîk** Maur.
220 F5 **Ioulis** *Kea* Greece
260 J5 **Iowa** *r. IA* U.S.A.
260 I4 **Iowa** *state* U.S.A.
260 J5 **Iowa City** *IA* U.S.A.
260 I4 **Iowa Falls** *IA* U.S.A.
126 E2 **Iō-zan** *hill* Japan
158 I1 **Ipa** *r.* Belarus
268 B5 **Ipala** Mex.
233 B6 **Ipala** Tanz.
280 C2 **Ipameri** Brazil
281 G3 **Ipanema** Brazil
278 F4 **Ipanema** *r.* Brazil
276 B2 **Iparía** Peru
281 F3 **Ipatinga** Brazil
157 H7 **Ipatovo** Rus. Fed.
280 C5 **Ipauçu** Brazil
250 D9 **Ipava** *IL* U.S.A.
220 B3 **Ipeiros** *admin. reg.* Greece
151 E6 **İpek Geçidi** *pass* Turkey
199 H4 **Ipeľ** *r.* Slovakia
237 J3 **Ipelegeng** S. Africa
199 H4 **Ipeľská pahorkatina** *mts* Slovakia
244 F1 **Ipewik** *r. AK* U.S.A.
195 I2 **Iphofen** Ger.
280 C3 **Ipiaçu** Brazil
274 B4 **Ipiales** Col.
278 F5 **Ipiaú** Brazil
278 F5 **Ipirá** Brazil
274 D5 **Ipiranga** *Amazonas* Brazil
275 F6 **Ipiranga** *Amazonas* Brazil
280 B6 **Ipiranga** *Paraná* Brazil
Ípiros *admin. reg.* Greece *see* **Ipeiros**
100 □4a **Ipis** *i. Chuuk* Micronesia
276 B1 **Ipixuna** Brazil
276 B1 **Ipixuna** *r.* Brazil
275 F6 **Ipixuna** *r.* Brazil
116 D2 **Ipoh** Malaysia
233 B6 **Ipole** Tanz.
199 H4 **Ipoly** *r.* Hungary
237 J5 **Ipopeng** S. Africa
280 B2 **Iporá** Brazil
280 C6 **Iporanga** Brazil
216 G10 **Ippari** *r. Sicilia* Italy
195 I2 **Ippesheim** Ger.
172 E7 **Ipplepen** *Devon, England* U.K.
230 D3 **Ippy** C.A.R.
221 H2 **İpsala** Turkey
195 I2 **Ipsheim** Ger.
171 N7 **Ipstones** *Staffordshire, England* U.K.
107 N9 **Ipswich** *Qld* Austr.
270 □ **Ipswich** Jamaica
173 O3 **Ipswich** *Suffolk, England* U.K.
260 F3 **Ipswich** *SD* U.S.A.
278 E3 **Ipu** Brazil
280 C4 **Ipuã** Brazil
278 E3 **Ipueiras** Brazil
116 D6 **Ipuh** *Sumatera* Indon.
280 D5 **Ipuiúna** Brazil
278 E4 **Ipupiara** Brazil
161 O9 **Iput'** *r.* Rus. Fed.
159 K1 **Iputs'** *r.* Belarus
243 L3 **Iqaluit** *Nunavut* Can.
128 D8 **Iqe** *Qinghai* China
133 L7 **Iqe He** *r.* China
277 F3 **Iquê** *r.* Brazil
276 C5 **Iquique** Chile
Iquiri *r.* Brazil *see* **Ituxi**
274 C5 **Iquitos** Peru
230 D3 **Ira Banda** C.A.R.
124 □C22 **Irabu-jima** *i. Nansei-shotō* Japan
275 H3 **Iracoubo** Fr. Guiana
145 I8 **Īrafshān** Iran
145 J8 **Īrafshān** *reg.* Iran
126 F6 **Irago-misaki** *pt* Japan
126 E6 **Irago-suidō** *str.* Japan
279 B8 **Irai** Brazil
107 M1 **Irai Island** P.N.G.
220 E1 **Irakleia** Greece
221 G6 **Irakleia** *i.* Greece
220 G7 **Irakleio** *Kriti* Greece
220 G7 **Irakleiou, Kolpos** *b. Kriti* Greece
Iráklia *i.* Greece *see* **Irakleia**
Iraklion *Kriti* Greece *see* **Irakleio**
285 G4 **Irala** Arg.
277 G6 **Irala** Para.
278 E5 **Iramaia** Brazil
144 F6 **Iran** *country* Asia
117 K4 **Iran, Pegunungan** *mts* Indon.
151 I6 **Īrānābād** Iran
136 G8 **Iranamadu Tank** *resr* Sri Lanka
178 G8 **Irancy** France
144 B3 **Īrānshāh** Iran
144 I8 **Īrānshahr** Iran
275 F2 **Irapa** Venez.
268 F5 **Irapuato** Mex.
149 K7 **Iraq** *country* Asia
227 G4 **Irarrarene** *reg.* Alg.
257 M4 **Irasville** *VT* U.S.A.
275 H5 **Iratapuru** *r.* Brazil
280 B6 **Irati** Brazil
205 R3 **Irati** *r.* Spain
199 K5 **Iratoşu** Romania
156 K2 **Irayel'** Rus. Fed.
266 □R13 **Irazú, Volcán** *vol.* Costa Rica
160 F4 **Irbe** *r.* Latvia
Irbes šaurums *sea chan.* Estonia/Latvia *see* **Irbe Strait**
160 F4 **Irbe Strait** Estonia/Latvia
Irbe väin *sea chan.* Estonia/Latvia *see* **Irbe Strait**
150 D6 **Irbid** Jordan
Irbil Iraq *see* **Arbīl**
152 H4 **Irbit** Rus. Fed.
173 K3 **Irchester** *Northamptonshire, England* U.K.
201 J4 **Irdning** Austria
159 K4 **Irdyn'** Ukr.
230 C5 **Irebu** Dem. Rep. Congo
278 E4 **Irecê** Brazil
199 H5 **Iregszemcse** Hungary
205 P4 **Iregua** *r.* Spain
230 C5 **Ireko** Dem. Rep. Congo
169 G5 **Ireland** *country* Europe
259 G1 **Ireland Corners** *NY* U.S.A.
255 □1 **Ireland Island** Bermuda
169 J6 **Ireland's Eye** *i.* Ireland
169 E5 **Ireland West Airport Knock** *airport* Ireland
156 L4 **Iren'** *r.* Rus. Fed.
285 G6 **Irene** Arg.
103 B12 **Irene, Mount** *South I.* N.Z.
275 G4 **Ireng** *r.* Guyana/Venez.
280 A6 **Iretama** Brazil
151 F1 **Irgakly** Rus. Fed.
151 F4 **Irganch'ai** Georgia
221 K4 **Irgıllı** Turkey
142 I3 **Irgiz** Kazakh.
214 D7 **Irgoli** *Sardegna* Italy
227 G3 **Irharrhar, Oued** *watercourse Illizi/Tamanrasset* Alg.
227 G5 **Irharrhar, Oued** *watercourse Illizi/Tamanrasset* Alg.
226 C3 **Irherm** Morocco
226 D3 **Irhil M'Goun** *mt.* Morocco
Iri S. Korea *see* **Iksan**
Irian, Teluk *b. Papua* Indon. *see* **Cenderawasih, Teluk**
Irian Barat *prov.* Indon. *see* **Papua Barat**
Irian Jaya *prov.* Indon. *see* **Papua Barat**
113 I7 **Irian Jaya** *reg.* Indon.
224 D6 **Iriba** Chad
275 G4 **Iricoumé, Serra** *hills* Brazil
144 B2 **Īrī Dāgh** *mt.* Iran
218 H5 **Irig** *Vojvodina* Serbia
114 D5 **Iriga** *Luzon* Phil.
182 F5 **Irigny** France
142 H2 **Iriklinskiy** Rus. Fed.
142 H2 **Iriklinskoye Vodokhranilishche** *resr* Rus. Fed.
233 B6 **Iringa** Tanz.
233 B7 **Iringa** *admin. reg.* Tanz.
136 E7 **Irinjalakuda** *Kerala* India
124 □A22 **Iriomote-jima** *i. Nansei-shotō* Japan
124 □A22 **Iriomote Kokuritsu-kōen** *nat. park Nansei-shotō* Japan
275 H5 **Iriri** *r.* Brazil
278 B4 **Iriri Novo** *r.* Brazil
167 E5 **Irish Sea** Ireland/U.K.
185 B9 **Irissarry** France
278 D2 **Irituia** Brazil
147 I2 **'Irj** *well* Saudi Arabia
Irkeshtam Kyrg. *see* **Erkech-Tam**
159 S8 **Irkliyevskaya** Rus. Fed.
159 L4 **Irkliyiv** Ukr.
120 H1 **Irkutsk** Rus. Fed.
120 H1 **Irkutskaya Oblast'** *admin. div.* Rus. Fed.
Irkutsk Oblast *admin. div.* Rus. Fed. *see* **Irkutskaya Oblast'**
195 N4 **Irlbach** Ger.
247 I4 **Irma** *Alta* Can.
250 E4 **Irma** *WI* U.S.A.
148 F4 **Irmak** Turkey
288 G2 **Irminger Basin** *sea feature* N. Atlantic Ocean
216 H10 **Irminio** *r. Sicilia* Italy
255 G8 **Irmo** *SC* U.S.A.
162 T4 **Irnijärvi** *l.* Fin.
230 C2 **Iro, Lac** *l.* Chad
180 H5 **Irodouër** France
180 B5 **Iroise, Mer d'** *g.* France
104 F5 **Iron Baron** *S.A.* Austr.
100 □6 **Iron Bottom Sound** *sea chan.* Solomon Is
251 K3 **Iron Bridge** *Ont.* Can.
172 H2 **Ironbridge** *Telford and Wrekin, England* U.K.
244 F2 **Iron Creek** *AK* U.S.A.
256 H5 **Irondequoit** *NY* U.S.A.
250 B2 **Iron Junction** *MN* U.S.A.
104 F5 **Iron Knob** *S.A.* Austr.
250 F4 **Iron Mountain** *MI* U.S.A.
265 S4 **Iron Mountain** *mt. UT* U.S.A.
169 F4 **Iron Mountains** *hills* Ireland
107 I2 **Iron Range National Park** *Qld* Austr.
250 F3 **Iron River** *MI* U.S.A.
250 C3 **Iron River** *WI* U.S.A.
261 J7 **Ironton** *MO* U.S.A.
256 C10 **Ironton** *OH* U.S.A.
250 D3 **Ironwood** *MI* U.S.A.
265 U9 **Ironwood Forest National Monument** *nat. park AZ* U.S.A.
257 J4 **Iroquois** *Ont.* Can.
245 O1 **Iroquois** *r. N.W.T.* Can.
250 G8 **Iroquois** *r. IN* U.S.A.
248 D3 **Iroquois Falls** *Ont.* Can.
114 E5 **Irosin** *Luzon* Phil.
127 I6 **Irō-zaki** *pt* Japan
Irpen' Ukr. *see* **Irpin'**
158 J3 **Irpin'** Ukr.
158 J3 **Irpin'** *r.* Ukr.
147 H9 **Īrqah** Yemen
217 □ **Irqieqa, Ras i-** *pt* Malta
217 □ **Ir-Raħeb, Ras** *pt* Malta
106 F6 **Irramarne Aboriginal Land** *res. N.T.* Austr.
217 □ **Ir-Ramla** *b. Gozo* Malta
118 B6 **Irrawaddy** *admin. div.* Myanmar
118 B7 **Irrawaddy** *r.* Myanmar
118 B7 **Irrawaddy, Mouths of the** Myanmar
194 A2 **Irrel** Ger.
194 B2 **Irsch** Ger.
200 H6 **Irschen** Austria
195 L6 **Irschenberg** Ger.
195 J6 **Irsee** Ger.
158 I3 **Irsha** *r.* Ukr.
145 P3 **Irshad Pass** Afgh./Pak.
158 H3 **Irshans'k** Ukr.
158 C5 **Irshava** Ukr.
215 Q6 **Irsina** Italy
165 M2 **Irsta** Sweden
156 J3 **Irta** Rus. Fed.
171 L4 **Irthing** *r. England* U.K.
173 K3 **Irthlingborough** *Northamptonshire, England* U.K.
143 P1 **Irtysh** *r.* Kazakh./Rus. Fed.
143 P1 **Irtyshsk** Kazakh.
Irtyshskoye Kazakh. *see* **Irtyshsk**
205 O7 **Irueste** Spain
127 J4 **Iruma** Japan
127 K4 **Iruma-gawa** *r.* Japan
230 F4 **Irumu** Dem. Rep. Congo
208 B1 **Irun** Spain
Iruña Spain *see* **Pamplona**
276 D4 **Irupana** Bol.
208 B1 **Irurita** Spain
205 R3 **Irurozqui** Spain
205 Q3 **Irurtzun** Spain
Irurzun Spain *see* **Irurtzun**
168 G11 **Irvine** *North Ayrshire, Scotland* U.K.
264 O8 **Irvine** *CA* U.S.A.
256 B11 **Irvine** *KY* U.S.A.
107 J4 **Irvinebank** *Qld* Austr.
168 G11 **Irvine Bay** *Scotland* U.K.
286 T2 **Irvine Glacier** Antarctica
169 G4 **Irvinestown** *Northern Ireland* U.K.
261 G9 **Irving** *TX* U.S.A.
109 C10 **Irwin** *r. W.A.* Austr.
255 F9 **Irwinton** *GA* U.S.A.
193 D6 **Irxleben** Ger.
229 G3 **Isa** Nigeria
146 F8 **'Īsá, Ra's** *pt* Yemen
107 L7 **Isaac** *r. Qld* Austr.
246 F4 **Isaac Lake** *B.C.* Can.
208 D2 **Isaba** Spain
260 E3 **Isabel** *SD* U.S.A.
114 D6 **Isabela** *Negros* Phil.
114 C8 **Isabela** Phil.
271 □1 **Isabela** Puerto Rico
270 H4 **Isabela, Cabo** *c.* Dom. Rep.
274 □ **Isabela, Isla** *i. Islas Galápagos* Ecuador
268 B4 **Isabela, Isla** *i.* Mex.
266 □Q11 **Isabelia, Cordillera** *mts* Nic.
250 C2 **Isabella** *MN* U.S.A.
108 I6 **Isabella, Lake** *salt flat W.A.* Austr.
250 J6 **Isabella Indian Reservation** *res. MI* U.S.A.
264 N6 **Isabella Lake** *CA* U.S.A.
250 G2 **Isabelle, Point** *MI* U.S.A.
271 □1 **Isabel Segunda** Puerto Rico
208 F3 **Isábena** *r.* Spain
221 K5 **İsabey** Turkey
151 E7 **İsabey Dağı** *mt.* Turkey
180 G6 **Isac** *r.* France
219 Q5 **Isaccea** Romania
152 J2 **Isachenko, Ostrov** *i.* Rus. Fed.
243 H2 **Isachsen, Cape** *Nunavut* Can.
162 □B1 **Ísafjarðardjúp** *est.* Iceland
162 □B1 **Ísafjörður** Iceland
138 F7 **Isagarh** *Madh. Prad.* India
125 H14 **Isahaya** Japan
145 K8 **Isai Kalat** Pak.
230 C5 **Isaka** Dem. Rep. Congo
145 N5 **Isa Khel** Pak.
156 H2 **Isakogorka** Rus. Fed.
161 Q1 **Isakovo** *Leningradskaya Oblast'* Rus. Fed.
161 R6 **Isakovo** *Smolenskaya Oblast'* Rus. Fed.
214 D7 **Isalle** *r.* Italy
219 L6 **Işalniţa** Romania
235 □J4 **Isalo, Massif de l'** *mts* Madag.
235 □J4 **Isalo, Parc National de l'** *nat. park* Madag.
274 D4 **Isana** *r.* Col.
230 D5 **Isanga** Dem. Rep. Congo
233 A7 **Isangano National Park** Zambia
229 G4 **Isanlu** Nigeria
227 G4 **Isaouane-n-Tifernine** *des.* Alg.
195 N4 **Isar** *r.* Ger.
213 K3 **Isarco** *r.* Italy
114 D5 **Isarog, Mount** Phil.
199 I4 **Isaszeg** Hungary
127 I4 **Isawa** Japan
178 D2 **Isbergues** France
168 □N1 **Isbister** *Shetland, Scotland* U.K.
168 □O2 **Isbister** *Shetland, Scotland* U.K.
Isca *Newport, Wales* U.K. *see* **Caerleon**
205 K6 **Íscar** Spain
276 D5 **Iscayachi** Bol.
221 L4 **İscehisar** Turkey
179 K7 **Isches** France
200 B5 **Ischgl** Austria
215 L6 **Ischia** Italy
215 L6 **Ischia, Isola d'** *i.* Italy
284 C2 **Ischigualasto, Parque Provincial** *nat. park* Arg.
215 P4 **Ischitella** Italy
108 H4 **Isdell** *r. W.A.* Austr.
178 D8 **Isdes** France
126 E7 **Ise** Japan
164 H6 **Isefjord** *b.* Denmark
127 J5 **Isehara** Japan
233 B6 **Iseke** Tanz.
200 G6 **Isel** *r.* Austria
200 G6 **Iseltal** *val.* Austria
195 M5 **Isen** Ger.
195 N5 **Isen** *r.* Ger.
179 J7 **Is-en-Bassigny** France
156 K4 **Isenbayevo** Rus. Fed.
191 K6 **Isenbüttel** Ger.
230 E4 **Isengi** Dem. Rep. Congo
124 □F19 **Isen-zaki** *hd Nansei-shotō* Japan
212 I4 **Iseo** Italy
212 I4 **Iseo, Lago d'** *l.* Italy
183 K6 **Iseran, Col de l'** *pass* France
183 H6 **Isère** *dept* France
183 F7 **Isère** *r.* France
275 H3 **Isère, Pointe** *pt* Fr. Guiana
191 E8 **Iserlohn** Ger.
191 I6 **Isernhagen** Ger.
215 M4 **Isernia** Italy
215 M4 **Isernia** *prov.* Italy
127 J3 **Isesaki** Japan
126 E7 **Ise-shima Kokuritsu-kōen** *nat. park* Japan
126 E6 **Ise-wan** *b.* Japan
229 F5 **Iseyin** Nigeria
Isfahan Iran *see* **Eşfahān**
143 M8 **Isfana** Kyrg.
Isfandaqeh Iran *see* **Sangū'īyeh**
145 N1 **Isfara** Tajik.
162 □ **Isfjorden** *inlet* Svalbard
162 □ **Isfjord Radio** Svalbard
151 G2 **Ishcherskaya** Rus. Fed.
156 L3 **Isherim, Gora** *mt.* Rus. Fed.
275 G4 **Isherton** Guyana
157 J5 **Isheyevka** Rus. Fed.
127 K3 **Ishibashi** Japan
126 D5 **Ishibe** Japan
124 S7 **Ishidoriya** Japan
124 □B22 **Ishigaki** *Nansei-shotō* Japan
124 □B22 **Ishigaki-jima** *i. Nansei-shotō* Japan
127 K3 **Ishige** Japan
124 S3 **Ishikari** Japan
124 S3 **Ishikari-gawa** *r.* Japan
124 R3 **Ishikari-wan** *b.* Japan
127 L1 **Ishikawa** *Fukushima* Japan
124 □1 **Ishikawa** *Okinawa* Japan
126 D3 **Ishikawa** *pref.* Japan
143 N1 **Ishim** *r.* Kazakh./Rus. Fed.
152 H4 **Ishim** Rus. Fed.
126 A8 **I-shima** *i.* Japan
142 G1 **Ishimbay** Rus. Fed.
124 S8 **Ishinomaki** Japan
127 L3 **Ishioka** Japan
125 K13 **Ishizuchi-san** *mt.* Japan
145 N3 **Ishkoshim** Tajik.
138 D1 **Ishkuman** Pak.
161 W4 **Ishnya** Rus. Fed.
250 G3 **Ishpeming** *MI* U.S.A.
Ishtikhon Uzbek. *see* **Ishtixon**
143 L8 **Ishtixon** Uzbek.
145 N3 **Ishtragh** Afgh.
139 L7 **Ishurdi** Bangl.
276 D3 **Isiboro** *r.* Bol.
276 D4 **Isiboro Sécure, Parque Nacional** *nat. park* Bol.
181 I4 **Isigny-le-Buat** France
181 I3 **Isigny-sur-Mer** France
221 L4 **Işıklar** Turkey
221 K4 **Işıklı** Turkey
221 K4 **Işıklı Barajı** *resr* Turkey
214 C8 **Isili** *Sardegna* Italy
152 I4 **Isil'kul'** Rus. Fed.
237 Q3 **iSimangaliso Wetland Park** *nature res.* S. Africa
233 B6 **Isimbira** Tanz.
274 B5 **Isinliví** Ecuador
232 C4 **Isiolo** Kenya
237 O5 **Isipingo** S. Africa
230 E4 **Isiro** Dem. Rep. Congo
107 J8 **Isisford** *Qld* Austr.
162 □ **Isispynten** *pt* Svalbard
201 J8 **Iška** *r.* Slovenia
145 L3 **Iskabad Canal** Afgh.
145 N3 **Iskan** Afgh.
156 K2 **Iskateley** Rus. Fed.
İskele Cyprus *see* **Trikomon**
148 H5 **İskenderun** Turkey
148 G5 **İskenderun Körfezi** *b.* Turkey
148 G3 **İskilip** Turkey
Iski-Naukat Kyrg. *see* **Eski-Nookat**
142 E4 **Iskininskiy** Kazakh.
152 J4 **Iskitim** Rus. Fed.
161 W7 **Iskra** Rus. Fed.
159 M5 **Iskrivka** *Kirovohrads'ka Oblast'* Ukr.
159 O4 **Iskrivka** *Poltavs'ka Oblast'* Ukr.
219 M7 **Iskŭr** *r.* Bulg.
219 L8 **Iskŭr, Yazovir** *resr* Bulg.
232 F2 **Iskushuban** Somalia
245 O4 **Iskut** *r. B.C.* Can.
269 L7 **Isla** Mex.
168 J9 **Isla** *r. Angus/Perth and Kinross, Scotland* U.K.
282 C2 **Isla, Salar de la** *salt flat* Chile
285 I2 **Isla Cabellos** Uru.
206 E6 **Isla Canela** Spain
206 E6 **Isla Cristina** Spain
274 C2 **Isla de Salamanca, Parque Nacional** *nat. park* Col.
107 L8 **Isla Gorge National Park** *Qld* Austr.
148 H5 **İslahiye** Turkey
151 B5 **İslâhiye** Turkey
Islamabad *Jammu and Kashmir* India *see* **Anantnag**
145 O5 **Islamabad** Pak.
283 B7 **Isla Magdalena, Parque Nacional** *nat. park* Chile
206 G6 **Isla Mayor** *marsh* Spain
206 G6 **Isla Menor** *marsh* Spain
145 N8 **Islamgarh** Pak.
145 N9 **Islamkot** Pak.
255 G13 **Islamorada** *FL* U.S.A.
139 J7 **Islampur** *Bihar* India
246 F2 **Island** *r. N.W.T.* Can.
Ísland *country* Europe *see* **Iceland**
114 B7 **Island Bay** *Palawan* Phil.
257 □Q2 **Island Falls** *ME* U.S.A.
104 F4 **Island Lagoon** *salt flat S.A.* Austr.
247 M4 **Island Lake** *Man.* Can.
247 M4 **Island Lake** *l. Man.* Can.
250 B2 **Island Lake** *l. MN* U.S.A.
262 I4 **Island Park** *ID* U.S.A.
257 N4 **Island Pond** *VT* U.S.A.
102 I2 **Islands, Bay of** *North I.* N.Z.
204 C4 **Islas Atlánticas de Galicia, Parque Nacional de las** *nature res.* Spain
266 □Q9 **Islas de Bahá, Parque Nacional** *nat. park* Hond.
285 F3 **Isla Verde** Arg.
168 D11 **Islay** *i. Scotland* U.K.
168 D11 **Islay, Sound of** *sea chan. Scotland* U.K.
219 M7 **Islaz** Romania
184 G4 **Isle** France
184 D6 **Isle** *r.* France
173 M3 **Isleham** *Cambridgeshire, England* U.K.
172 D1 **Isle of Anglesey** *admin. div. Wales* U.K.
170 H5 **Isle of Man** *i.* Irish Sea
168 H13 **Isle of Whithorn** *Dumfries and Galloway, Scotland* U.K.
173 J6 **Isle of Wight** *admin. div. England* U.K.
256 I12 **Isle of Wight** *VA* U.S.A.
250 F2 **Isle Royale National Park** *MI* U.S.A.
178 H5 **Isles-sur-Suippe** France
284 B1 **Islón** Chile
271 □7 **Islote Point** Trin. and Tob.
276 C4 **Isluga, Parque Nacional** *nat. park* Chile
285 I3 **Ismael Cortinas** Uru.
Ismail Ukr. *see* **Izmayil**
Ismâ'ilîya Egypt *see* **Al Ismā'īlīyah**
Ismailly Azer. *see* **İsmayıllı**
195 L5 **Ismaning** Ger.
151 J5 **İsmayıllı** Azer.
151 J5 **İsmayıllı Qoruğu** *nature res.* Azer.
145 N2 **Ismoili Somoní, Qullai** *mt.* Tajik.
225 G3 **Isnā** Egypt
204 E9 **Isna** Port.
216 G8 **Isnello** *Sicilia* Italy
195 I6 **Isny im Allgäu** Ger.
235 □J4 **Isoanala** Madag.
126 E7 **Isobe** Japan
127 K5 **Isogo** Japan
163 P5 **Isojoki** Fin.
233 B7 **Isoka** Zambia
162 S3 **Isokylä** Fin.
162 Q5 **Isokyrö** Fin.
183 K8 **Isola** France
183 K8 **Isola 2000** France
214 C3 **Isolaccio-di-Fiumorbo** *Corse* France
215 L2 **Isola del Gran Sasso d'Italia** Italy
213 K5 **Isola della Scala** Italy
216 E7 **Isola delle Femmine** *Sicilia* Italy
215 L4 **Isola del Liri** Italy
217 M6 **Isola di Capo Rizzuto** Italy
180 D6 **Isole** *r.* France
212 F6 **Isole del Cantone** Italy
208 H3 **Isona** Spain
213 P4 **Isonzo** *r.* Italy
233 A7 **Isopa** Tanz.
238 □3e **Isora** *El Hierro* Canary Is
235 □J4 **Isorana** Madag.
212 I5 **Isorella** Italy
162 S4 **Iso-Syöte** *hill* Fin.
183 D8 **Ispagnac** France
Ispahan Iran *see* **Eşfahān**
221 L5 **Isparta** Turkey
221 L5 **Isparta** *prov.* Turkey
219 O7 **Isperikh** Bulg.
216 H10 **Ispica** *Sicilia* Italy
216 H10 **Ispica** *r. Sicilia* Italy
145 J8 **Ispikan** Pak.
149 J3 **İspir** Turkey
Ispisar Tajik. *see* **Khŭjand**
145 L7 **Isplinji** Pak.
185 B9 **Ispoure** France
212 F4 **Ispra** Italy
151 C1 **Ispravnaya** Rus. Fed.
194 F4 **Ispringen** Ger.
150 C6 **Israel** *country* Asia
280 B2 **Israelândia** Brazil
109 G12 **Israelite Bay** *W.A.* Austr.
Isra'īl *country* Asia *see* **Israel**
Issa Croatia *see* **Vis**
157 I5 **Issa** Rus. Fed.
160 L5 **Issa** *r.* Rus. Fed.
183 J10 **Issambres, Pointe des** *pt* France
229 H5 **Issanguele** Cameroon
275 G3 **Issano** Guyana
227 G4 **Issaouane, Erg** *des.* Alg.
183 E7 **Issarlès** France
224 B6 **Isséirom** Chad
191 B7 **Isselburg** Ger.
179 N8 **Issenheim** France
126 F6 **Isshiki** Japan
228 D5 **Issia** Côte d'Ivoire
185 F6 **Issigeac** France
212 D4 **Issime** Italy
115 C3 **Issimu** *Sulawesi* Indon.
149 L8 **Issin** *tourist site* Iraq
207 P4 **Isso** Spain
212 D4 **Issogne** Italy
182 C5 **Issoire** France
183 I10 **Issole** *r.* France
229 F2 **Issouanka** *well* Mali
184 H2 **Issoudun** France
227 F5 **Issoulane Erareine** *slope* Alg.
191 B7 **Issum** Ger.
233 B6 **Issuna** Tanz.
182 G1 **Is-sur-Tille** France
Issyk-Ata Kyrg. *see* **Ysyk-Ata**
Issyk-Kul' Kyrg. *see* **Balykchy**
Issyk-Kul', Ozero *salt l.* Kyrg. *see* **Ysyk-Köl**
Issyk-Kul Oblast *admin. div.* Kyrg. *see* **Ysyk-Köl**
Issyk-Kul'skaya Oblast' *admin. div.* Kyrg. *see* **Ysyk-Köl**
182 D3 **Issy-l'Évêque** France
213 R7 **Ist** Croatia
213 R7 **Ist** *i.* Croatia
161 T8 **Ista** *r.* Rus. Fed.
146 D3 **Iştabl 'Antar** Saudi Arabia
149 K6 **Iştablāt** *tourist site* Iraq
145 M5 **Īstādeh-ye Moqor, Āb-e** *l.* Afgh.
199 J3 **Istállós-kő** *hill* Hungary
207 J7 **Istán** Spain
221 J1 **İstanbul** Turkey
221 J1 **İstanbul** *prov.* Turkey
221 K1 **İstanbul Boğazı** *str.* Turkey
173 M5 **Istead Rise** *Kent, England* U.K.
196 G6 **Istebna** Pol.
199 I2 **Istebné** Slovakia
198 F5 **Isten dombja** *hill* Hungary
144 C5 **Īstgāh-e Eznā** Iran
282 F3 **Isthilart** Arg.
220 E4 **Istiaia** Greece
145 P3 **Istik** *r.* Tajik.
151 G6 **İstısu** Azer.
274 B3 **Istmina** Col.
159 R2 **Istobnoye** Rus. Fed.
210 F3 **Istočni Drvar** Bos.-Herz.
218 I8 **Istog** *Istog* Kosovo
Istok *Istog* Kosovo *see* **Istog**
255 G12 **Istokpoga, Lake** *FL* U.S.A.
210 D3 **Istra** *pen.* Croatia
161 T6 **Istra** Rus. Fed.
183 F9 **Istres** France
Istria *pen.* Croatia *see* **Istra**
219 Q6 **Istria** Romania
219 O5 **Istriţa, Dealul** *hill* Romania
185 B9 **Isturits** France
161 X7 **Ist'ya** *r.* Rus. Fed.
208 E3 **Isuela** *r. Aragón* Spain
205 R5 **Isuela** *r.* Spain
185 B11 **Isuerre** Spain
127 L5 **Isumi** Japan
127 L5 **Isumi-gawa** *r.* Japan
Isüüj Mongolia *see* **Bayanchandmanĭ**
139 L8 **Iswaripur** Bangl.
237 O2 **Iswepe** S. Africa
142 G1 **Isyangulovo** Rus. Fed.
278 F4 **Itabaianinha** Brazil
281 G4 **Itabapoana** Brazil
281 G4 **Itabapoana** *r.* Brazil
280 C5 **Itaberá** Brazil
278 E5 **Itaberaba** Brazil
280 C2 **Itaberaí** Brazil
281 F3 **Itabira** Brazil
281 F4 **Itabirito** Brazil
275 F6 **Itaboca** Brazil
281 F5 **Itaboraí** Brazil
279 F5 **Itabuna** Brazil
278 C3 **Itacaiuna** *r.* Brazil
278 D4 **Itacajá** Brazil
281 F2 **Itacambira** Brazil
279 D5 **Itacarambi** Brazil
278 F5 **Itacaré** Brazil
277 H1 **Itacayunas, Serra** *hills* Brazil
275 G5 **Itacoatiara** Brazil
274 D6 **Itacuaí** *r.* Brazil
277 F6 **Itacurubí del Rosario** Para.
126 E4 **Itadori** Japan
278 E5 **Itaetê** Brazil
233 B6 **Itaga** Tanz.
Itagmatana Iran *see* **Hamadān**
281 H2 **Itagmirim** Brazil
281 G3 **Itaguaçu** Brazil
281 F5 **Itaguaí** Brazil
280 B5 **Itaguajé** Brazil
281 E4 **Itaguara** Brazil
276 C3 **Itahuania** Peru
280 C5 **Itaí** Brazil
278 E3 **Itaim** *r.* Brazil
279 C8 **Itaiópolis** Brazil
279 B8 **Itaipu, Represa de** *resr* Brazil
163 S6 **Itäisen Suomenlahden kansallispuisto** *nat. park* Fin.
275 G6 **Itaituba** Brazil
280 B3 **Itajá** Brazil
279 C8 **Itajaí** Brazil
280 C4 **Itajobi** Brazil
281 E5 **Itajubá** Brazil
279 F5 **Itajuipe** Brazil
122 A2 **Itaka** Rus. Fed.
139 J8 **Itaki** *Jharkhand* India
127 M4 **Itako** Japan
127 K3 **Itakura** *Gunma* Japan
127 H1 **Itakura** *Niigata* Japan
237 P3 **Itala Game Reserve** *nature res.* S. Africa
Italia *country* Europe *see* **Italy**
285 F4 **Italó** Arg.
210 E5 **Italy** *country* Europe
278 G3 **Itamaracá, Ilha de** *i.* Brazil
281 H2 **Itamaraju** Brazil
281 F2 **Itamarandiba** Brazil
278 D2 **Itamataré** Brazil
281 G3 **Itambacuri** Brazil
281 G3 **Itambacuri** *r.* Brazil
279 E5 **Itambé** Brazil
281 F3 **Itambé, Pico de** *mt.* Brazil
126 B6 **Itami** Japan
126 B6 **Itami** *airport* Japan
235 □I5 **Itampolo** Madag.
134 H6 **Itanagar** *Arun. Prad.* India
278 D5 **Itanguari** *r.* Brazil
280 D6 **Itanhaém** Brazil
281 E5 **Itanhandu** Brazil
275 F6 **Itanhauã** *r.* Brazil
281 G2 **Itanhém** Brazil
281 H2 **Itanhém** *r.* Brazil
281 G3 **Itanhomi** Brazil
Itany *r.* Fr. Guiana/Suriname *see* **Litani**
281 G2 **Itaobím** Brazil
281 F4 **Itaocara** Brazil
278 C5 **Itapaci** Brazil
278 F2 **Itapagé** Brazil
280 C3 **Itapajipe** Brazil
275 F6 **Itaparaná** *r.* Brazil
278 F4 **Itaparica, Represa de** *resr* Brazil
281 H1 **Itapebi** Brazil
285 I2 **Itapebí** Uru.
281 E4 **Itapecerica** Brazil
281 G4 **Itapemirim** Brazil
281 G4 **Itaperuna** Brazil
279 E5 **Itapetinga** Brazil
280 C5 **Itapetininga** Brazil
280 C5 **Itapeva** Brazil
279 C9 **Itapeva, Lago** *l.* Brazil
275 G5 **Itapi** *r.* Brazil
278 E4 **Itapicuru** Brazil
278 F4 **Itapicuru** *r.* Brazil
278 D3 **Itapicuru, Serra de** *hills* Brazil
278 D2 **Itapicuru Mirim** Brazil
278 F4 **Itapicuru Mirim** *r.* Brazil
275 F6 **Itapinima** Brazil
278 F2 **Itapipoca** Brazil
280 D5 **Itapira** Brazil
275 G5 **Itapiranga** Brazil
280 B1 **Itapirapuã** Brazil
285 I1 **Itapitocai** Brazil
278 F3 **Itapiúna** Brazil
280 C4 **Itápolis** Brazil
278 F3 **Itaporanga** *Paraíba* Brazil
280 C5 **Itaporanga** *São Paulo* Brazil
279 C9 **Itapuã** Brazil
279 C5 **Itapuranga** Brazil
280 D5 **Itaquaquecetuba** Brazil
279 A9 **Itaqui** Brazil
281 G3 **Itarana** Brazil
281 G1 **Itarantim** Brazil
280 C6 **Itararé** Brazil
280 C5 **Itararé** *r.* Brazil
138 F8 **Itarsi** *Madh. Prad.* India
280 B3 **Itarumã** Brazil
162 T5 **Itä-Suomi** *prov.* Fin.
284 A5 **Itata** *r.* Chile
277 F7 **Itati, Laguna** *l.* Arg.
280 D5 **Itatiba** Brazil
280 C5 **Itatinga** Brazil
275 F6 **Itatuba** Brazil
275 I5 **Itatupã** Brazil
280 C2 **Itauçu** Brazil
278 E3 **Itaueira** *r.* Brazil
275 E5 **Itaúna** *Amazonas* Brazil
281 E4 **Itaúna** *Minas Gerais* Brazil
281 H3 **Itaúnas** Brazil
281 H3 **Itaúnas** *r.* Brazil
114 C1 **Itbayat** *i.* Phil.
246 E4 **Itcha Ilgachuz Provincial Park** *B.C.* Can.
246 H1 **Itchen Lake** *N.W.T.* Can.
276 C4 **Ite** Peru
220 D4 **Itea** Greece
230 F5 **Itebero** Dem. Rep. Congo
143 N1 **Itemgen, Ozero** *l.* Kazakh.
233 B6 **Itende** Tanz.
205 L4 **Itero de la Vega** Spain
233 C7 **Itete** Tanz.
184 E3 **Iteuil** France
231 E8 **Itezhi-Tezhi Dam** Zambia
Ithaca Greece *see* **Ithaki**
Ithaca *i.* Greece *see* **Ithaki**
250 J6 **Ithaca** *MI* U.S.A.
256 I6 **Ithaca** *NY* U.S.A.
220 B4 **Ithaki** Greece
220 B4 **Ithaki** *i.* Greece
220 B4 **Ithakis, Steno** *sea chan.* Greece
191 H6 **Ith Hils** *ridge* Ger.
150 F7 **Ithrah** Saudi Arabia
233 B6 **Itigi** Tanz.
243 M3 **Itilleq** Greenland
230 D4 **Itimbiri** *r.* Dem. Rep. Congo
281 G2 **Itinga** Brazil
279 B6 **Itiquira** Brazil
277 F4 **Itiquira** *r.* Brazil
280 D5 **Itirapina** Brazil
280 D4 **Itirapuã** Brazil
278 F4 **Itiúba** Brazil
278 F4 **Itiúba, Serra de** *hills* Brazil
282 E1 **Itiyura** *r.* Arg.
139 J7 **Itkhari** *Jharkhand* India
245 J1 **Itkillik** *r. AK* U.S.A.
142 E3 **Itmurinkol', Ozero** *l.* Kazakh.
127 J6 **Itō** Japan
235 I2 **Itoculo** Moz.
127 G1 **Itoigawa** Japan
230 D5 **Itoko** Dem. Rep. Congo
124 □1 **Itoman** *Okinawa* Japan
178 B5 **Iton** *r.* France

235 □J4 Itongafeno mt. Madag.
Iton-Qälla Rus. Fed. see Itum-Kale
126 E5 Itonuki Japan
207 L7 Itrabo Spain
215 L5 Itri Italy
239 □3a Itsandzéni Njazidja Comoros
239 □3a Itsikoudi Njazidja Comoros
125 H14 Itsuki Japan
125 J12 Itsukushima i. Japan
227 G2 Ittel, Oued watercourse Alg.
214 B6 Ittireddu Sardegna Italy
214 B6 Ittiri Sardegna Italy
243 P2 Ittoqqortoormiit Greenland
187 F7 Ittre Belgium
280 D5 Itu Brazil
229 G5 Itu Nigeria
112 D4 Itu Abu Island S. China Sea
278 E5 Ituaçu Brazil
278 F5 Ituberá Brazil
276 C1 Itucumã r. Brazil
204 G8 Ituero de Azaba Spain
274 D6 Ituí r. Brazil
280 C3 Ituiutaba Brazil
231 E5 Itula Dem. Rep. Congo
233 B6 Itumba Tanz.
280 C3 Itumbiara Brazil
280 C3 Itumbiara, Barragem resr Brazil
151 G3 Itum-Kale Rus. Fed.
233 B7 Itungi Port Malawi
275 G3 Ituni Guyana
278 C3 Itupiranga Brazil
280 B3 Iturama Brazil
277 F6 Iturbe Para.
267 O8 Iturbide Campeche Mex.
269 H1 Iturbide Nuevo León Mex.
230 F4 Ituri prov. Dem. Rep. Congo
230 E4 Ituri r. Dem. Rep. Congo
121 Q3 Iturup, Ostrov i. Kuril'skiye O-va Rus. Fed.
281 E4 Itutinga Brazil
280 D4 Ituverava Brazil
276 D1 Ituxi r. Brazil
282 F2 Ituzaingo Arg.
Ityopia country Africa see Ethiopia
191 K11 Itz r. Ger.
190 I3 Itzehoe Ger.
190 J3 Itzstedt Ger.
274 D4 Iuaretê Brazil
216 H8 Iudica, Monte hill Sicilia Italy
261 K8 Iuka MS U.S.A.
153 T3 Iul'tin Rus. Fed.
235 H2 Iuluti Moz.
281 G4 Iúna Brazil
274 D4 Iutica Brazil
280 B6 Ivaí Brazil
280 A5 Ivaí r. Brazil
280 B6 Ivaiporã Brazil
235 □J4 Ivakoany mt. Madag.
162 S2 Ivalo Fin.
162 S2 Ivalojoki r. Fin.
198 F4 Iván Hungary
197 L6 Ivana Franka Ukr.
158 E1 Ivanava Belarus
198 F2 Ivančice Czech Rep.
210 F2 Ivanec Croatia
160 L2 Ivangorod Rus. Fed.
Ivangrad Berane Montenegro see Berane
105 J5 Ivanhoe N.S.W. Austr.
108 J3 Ivanhoe W.A. Austr.
248 D3 Ivanhoe r. Ont. Can.
264 M5 Ivanhoe CA U.S.A.
260 G3 Ivanhoe MN U.S.A.
256 E12 Ivanhoe VA U.S.A.
247 J2 Ivanhoe Lake N.W.T. Can.
251 L1 Ivanhoe Lake Ont. Can.
210 F3 Ivanić-Grad Croatia
159 O2 Ivanino Rus. Fed.
161 X6 Ivanishchi Rus. Fed.
159 Q3 Ivanivka Kharkivs'ka Oblast' Ukr.
159 L7 Ivanivka Khersons'ka Oblast' Ukr.
159 N7 Ivanivka Khersons'ka Oblast' Ukr.
159 K4 Ivanivka Kyivs'ka Oblast' Ukr.
159 R5 Ivanivka Luhans'ka Oblast' Ukr.
158 J7 Ivanivka Odes'ka Oblast' Ukr.
159 M8 Ivanivka Respublika Krym Ukr.
199 L3 Ivanivka Zakarpats'ka Oblast' Ukr.
158 G5 Ivanivtsi Ukr.
218 I7 Ivanjica Ivanjica Serbia
198 G3 Ivanka pri Dunaji Slovakia
158 I3 Ivankiv Ukr.
210 G3 Ivankovo Croatia
161 U7 Ivan'kovo Rus. Fed.
161 X5 Ivan'kovskiy Rus. Fed.
161 T5 Ivan'kovskoye Vodokhranilishche resr Rus. Fed.
122 I4 Ivankovtsy Rus. Fed.
244 H5 Ivanof Bay AK U.S.A.
158 D5 Ivano-Frankivs'k Ukr.
158 D5 Ivano-Frankivs'ka Oblast' admin. div. Ukr.
Ivano-Frankivs'k Oblast admin. div. Ukr. see Ivano-Frankivs'ka Oblast'
158 C4 Ivano-Frankove Ukr.
Ivano-Frankovsk Ukr. see Ivano-Frankivs'k
Ivano-Frankovskaya Oblast' admin. div. Ukr. see Ivano-Frankivs'ka Oblast'
Ivano-Frankovsk Oblast admin. div. Ukr. see Ivano-Frankivs'ka Oblast'
158 H4 Ivanopil' Ukr.
159 O3 Ivano-Shyychyne Ukr.
Ivanovka Kazakh. see Kokzhayyk
122 E3 Ivanovka Amurskaya Oblast' Rus. Fed.
142 E1 Ivanovka Orenburgskaya Oblast' Rus. Fed.
Ivanovo Belarus see Ivanava
219 N7 Ivanovo tourist site Bulg.
161 X5 Ivanovo Ivanovskaya Oblast' Rus. Fed.
161 N5 Ivanovo Pskovskaya Oblast' Rus. Fed.
161 U3 Ivanovo Tverskaya Oblast' Rus. Fed.
Ivanovo Oblast admin. div. Rus. Fed. see Ivanovskaya Oblast'
159 R8 Ivanovskaya Rus. Fed.
161 Y4 Ivanovskaya Oblast' admin. div. Rus. Fed.
143 T2 Ivanovskiy Khrebet mts Kazakh.
159 N2 Ivanovskoye Kurskaya Oblast' Rus. Fed.
161 T8 Ivanovskoye Orlovskaya Oblast' Rus. Fed.
161 W5 Ivanovskoye Yaroslavskaya Oblast' Rus. Fed.
265 Q6 Ivanpah Lake CA U.S.A.
210 E2 Ivanščica mts Croatia
201 O8 Ivanska Croatia
219 P7 Ivanski Bulg.
142 C1 Ivanteyevka Rus. Fed.
Ivantsevichi Belarus see Ivatsevichy
158 D3 Ivanychi Ukr.
159 L3 Ivanytsya Ukr.
235 □J4 Ivato Madag.
160 I9 Ivatsevichy Belarus
219 O9 Ivaylovgrad Bulg.
219 N9 Ivaylovgrad, Yazovir resr Bulg.
156 M3 Ivdel' Rus. Fed.
239 □3a Ivembeni Njazidja Comoros
173 K4 Iver Buckinghamshire, England U.K.
169 C9 Iveragh reg. Ireland
162 □ Iversenfjellet hill Svalbard
219 P5 Ivești Galați Romania
219 P4 Ivești Vaslui Romania
230 B5 Ivindo r. Gabon
230 B4 Ivindo, Parc National d' nat. park Gabon
173 K4 Ivinghoe Buckinghamshire, England U.K.
279 B7 Ivinheima Brazil
280 A5 Ivinheima r. Brazil
161 R1 Ivinskiy Razliv resr Rus. Fed.
245 J1 Ivishak r. AK U.S.A.
277 H1 Iviti Brazil
243 N3 Ivittuut Greenland
Iviza i. Spain see Eivissa
159 P2 Ivnya Rus. Fed.
235 □J4 Ivohibe Madag.
280 B2 Ivolândia Brazil
276 D2 Ivón Bol.
256 I12 Ivor VA U.S.A.
Ivory Coast country Africa see Côte d'Ivoire
165 K5 Ivösjön l. Sweden
161 R8 Ivot Rus. Fed.
159 M2 Ivot Ukr.
159 M2 Ivotka r. Ukr.
212 D5 Ivrea Italy
221 I3 İvrindi Turkey
151 F3 Ivris Ugheltekhili pass Georgia
151 G4 Ivris Zegani plat. Georgia
178 B6 Ivry-la-Bataille France
178 D6 Ivry-sur-Seine France
Ivugivik Que. Can. see Ivujivik
243 K3 Ivujivik Que. Can.
233 B7 Ivuna Tanz.
242 E3 Ivvavik National Park Y.T. Can.
160 J8 Ivyanyets Belarus
172 E7 Ivybridge Devon, England U.K.
256 D10 Ivydale WV U.S.A.
126 B7 Iwade Japan
173 N5 Iwade Kent, England U.K.
127 K3 Iwafune Japan
127 K3 Iwai Japan
125 I13 Iwai-shima i. Japan
124 S7 Iwaizumi Japan
127 M1 Iwaki Japan
124 R6 Iwaki-san vol. Japan
125 J12 Iwakuni Japan
126 E5 Iwakura Japan
127 L3 Iwama Japan
125 J13 Iwamatsu Japan
125 J12 Iwami Ginzan Silver Mine tourist site Japan
124 S3 Iwamizawa Japan
126 F5 Iwamura Japan
127 H3 Iwamurada Japan
117 K4 Iwan r. Indon.
124 R4 Iwanai Japan
233 B7 Iwanda Tanz.
197 J5 Iwaniska Pol.
124 R8 Iwanuma Japan
124 Q6 Iwasaki Japan
127 L3 Iwase Japan
126 F2 Iwasehama Japan
127 I2 Iwasuge-yama vol. Japan
127 G6 Iwata Japan
126 B4 Iwataki Japan
124 S7 Iwate Japan
124 S7 Iwate pref. Japan
124 R7 Iwate-san vol. Japan
127 K4 Iwatsuki Japan
197 I6 Iwkowa Pol.
229 G5 Iwo Nigeria
106 D7 Iwupataka Aboriginal Land res. N.T. Austr.
160 I8 Iwye Belarus
269 L9 Ixaltepec Mex.
269 I7 Ixcamilpa Mex.
269 H7 Ixcateopan Mex.
269 M9 Ixhuatán Mex.
269 I5 Ixhuatlán Veracruz Mex.
269 K6 Ixhuatlán Veracruz Mex.
276 C3 Ixiamas Bol.
269 H5 Ixmiquilpán Mex.
237 O6 Ixopo S. Africa
269 J6 Ixtacamaxtitlán Mex.
267 M9 Ixtacomitán Mex.
268 F8 Ixtapa Guerrero Mex.
268 B5 Ixtapa Jalisco Mex.
268 F8 Ixtapa, Punta pt Mex.
269 H7 Ixtapan de la Sal Mex.
269 H6 Ixtlahuaca Mex.
268 D6 Ixtlahuacán Mex.
268 E5 Ixtlán Michoacán Mex.
268 C4 Ixtlán Nayarit Mex.
269 K8 Ixtlán Oaxaca Mex.
173 N3 Ixworth Suffolk, England U.K.
115 B8 Iya i. Indon.
120 G1 Iya r. Rus. Fed.
225 F6 Iyal Bakhit Sudan
233 B7 Iyayi Tanz.
151 B4 İyidere Turkey
İyirmi Altı Bakı Komissarı Azer. see Uzboy
125 J13 Iyo Japan
125 K13 Iyomishima Japan
125 J13 Iyo-nada b. Japan
219 L3 Iza r. Romania
199 H4 Iža Slovakia
266 □O10 Izabal Guat.
267 O10 Izabal, Lago de l. Guat.
205 R3 Izaga, Peña de mt. Spain
205 N2 Izalde r. Spain
267 O7 Izamal Mex.
267 M10 Izapa tourist site Mex.
124 S4 Izari-dake mt. Japan
205 O3 Izarra Spain
244 G3 Izaviknek r. AK U.S.A.
233 B6 Izazi Tanz.
156 H2 Izba Bol'shaya Bab'ya Rus. Fed.
219 M5 Izbășești hill Romania
151 I3 Izberbash Rus. Fed.
197 L5 Izbica Pol.
196 G3 Izbica Kujawska Pol.
205 Q3 Izco, Sierra de mts Spain
161 Q6 Izdeshkovo Rus. Fed.
183 G6 Izeaux France
204 G5 Izeda Port.
187 D7 Izegem Belgium
144 C6 Īzeh Iran
244 G5 Izembek National Wildlife Refuge nature res. AK U.S.A.
124 □E20 Izena-jima i. Nansei-shotō Japan
182 H4 Izernore France
183 G6 Izeron France
229 H2 Izgagane well Niger
145 O4 Izgal Pak.
156 K4 Izhevsk Rus. Fed.
161 X7 Izhevskoye Rus. Fed.
156 K2 Izhma Respublika Komi Rus. Fed.
Izhma Respublika Komi Rus. Fed. see Sosnogorsk
156 K2 Izhma r. Rus. Fed.
244 F5 Izigan, Cape AK U.S.A.
147 M4 Izkī Oman
Izmail Ukr. see Izmayil
161 U9 Izmalkovo Rus. Fed.
158 H8 Izmayil Ukr.
Izmeny, Proliv sea chan. Japan/Rus. Fed. see Notsuke-suidō
221 I4 İzmir Turkey
221 I4 İzmir prov. Turkey
221 H4 İzmir Körfezi g. Turkey
221 K2 İzmit Turkey
221 K2 İzmit Körfezi b. Turkey
202 E5 Izmorene Morocco
207 K6 Iznájar Spain
207 K6 Iznajar, Embalse de resr Spain
207 L6 Iznalloz Spain
221 K2 İznik Turkey
221 K2 İznik Gölü l. Turkey
161 S7 Iznoski Rus. Fed.
159 O2 Iznoskovo Rus. Fed.
183 J7 Izoard, Col d' pass France
Izobil'noye Rus. Fed. see Izobil'nyy
157 H7 Izobil'nyy Rus. Fed.
210 D3 Izola Slovenia
161 T5 Izoplit Rus. Fed.
277 E4 Izozog Bol.
277 E4 Izozog, Bañados del swamp Bol.
277 E4 Izozog Bajo Bol.
150 E6 Izra' Syria
199 I5 Izsák Hungary
269 I6 Iztaccihuatl, Volcán vol. Mex.
269 I6 Iztaccihuatl-Popocatépetl, Parque Nacional nat. park Mex.
219 N9 Iztochni Rodopi mts Bulg.
269 I7 Izúcar de Matamoros Mex.
127 I6 Izu-hantō pen. Japan
125 G12 Izuhara Japan
126 E4 Izumi Fukui Japan
127 M2 Izumi Fukushima Japan
125 H14 Izumi Kagoshima Japan
127 J5 Izumi Kanagawa Japan
124 R8 Izumi Miyagi Japan
126 B7 Izumi Ōsaka Japan
126 B6 Izumiōtsu Japan
126 B7 Izumisano Japan
127 L1 Izumizaki Japan
125 J11 Izumo Japan
125 P9 Izumozaki Japan
127 I5 Izunagaoka Japan
290 E3 Izu-Ogasawara Trench sea feature N. Pacific Ocean
126 A5 Izushi Japan
127 J7 Izu-shotō is Japan
Izu-tobu vol. Japan see Amagi-san
152 J2 Izvestiy Tsentral'nogo Ispolnitel'nogo Komiteta, Ostrova Rus. Fed.
122 G4 Izvestkovyy Rus. Fed.
219 N6 Izvoarele Giurgiu Romania
219 M6 Izvoarele Olt Romania
219 O5 Izvoarele Prahova Romania
219 N6 Izvoru Romania
158 F3 Izyaslav Ukr.
156 L2 Iz"yayu Rus. Fed.
142 H5 Izyndy Kazakh.
159 Q4 Izyum Ukr.

J

163 S6 Jaala Fin.
160 K2 Jaama Estonia
146 G9 Ja'ar Yemen
162 R3 Jaatila Fin.
144 G4 Jaba watercourse Iran
205 P8 Jabaga Spain
146 F6 Jabal al Farrāsh hill Saudi Arabia
213 R6 Jabalanac Croatia
145 M4 Jabal as Sirāj Afgh.
207 N5 Jabalcón mt. Spain
147 I4 Jabal Dab Saudi Arabia
207 K3 Jabalón r. Spain
209 C7 Jabaloyas Spain
138 G8 Jabalpur Madh. Prad. India
207 L4 Jabalquinto Spain
206 F2 Jabarriega hill Spain
146 E6 Jabbārah Fara Islands Saudi Arabia
187 D6 Jabbeke Belgium
150 F2 Jabbūl Syria
150 F3 Jabbūl, Sabkhat al salt flat Syria
192 G3 Jabel Ger.
106 D2 Jabiluka Aboriginal Land res. N.T. Austr.
147 N4 Jabir reg. Oman
106 D2 Jabiru N.T. Austr.
150 D3 Jablah Syria
213 Q5 Jablanac, Rt pt Croatia
210 F4 Jablanica Bos.-Herz.
219 J7 Jablanica r. Serbia
197 L4 Jabłoń Pol.
198 E1 Jablonec nad Nisou Czech Rep.
198 G3 Jablonica Slovakia
197 H6 Jabłonka Pol.
197 K3 Jabłonka Kościelna Pol.
197 I3 Jabłonna Pol.
197 K3 Jabłonna Lacka Pol.
197 K4 Jabłonna Pierwsza Pol.
198 D1 Jablonné v Podještědí Czech Rep.
197 H2 Jabłonowo Pomorskie Pol.
199 G2 Jablůnka Czech Rep.
199 H2 Jablunkov Czech Rep.
278 G4 Jaboatão Brazil
278 G4 Jaboatão dos Guararapes Pernambuco Brazil
280 C4 Jaboticabal Brazil
281 F3 Jaboticatubas Brazil
183 F7 Jabron r. France
206 F5 Jabugo Spain
210 E4 Jabuka i. Croatia
218 I6 Jabuka Vojvodina Serbia
116 F5 Jabung, Tanjung pt Indon.
275 E6 Jaburu Brazil
275 G6 Jabuti Brazil
208 D2 Jaca Spain
269 H4 Jacala Mex.
267 N10 Jacaltenango Guat.
278 B5 Jacaré Mato Grosso Brazil
276 D2 Jacaré Rondônia Brazil
278 E4 Jacaré r. Brazil
275 F6 Jacaré r. Brazil
275 G6 Jacareacanga Brazil
281 D5 Jacareí Brazil
277 F2 Jacaretinga Brazil
280 C5 Jacarézinho Brazil
281 F4 Jaceaba Brazil
284 D2 Jáchal r. Arg.
195 L6 Jachen r. Ger.
195 K6 Jachenau Ger.
198 B1 Jáchymov Czech Rep.
279 B5 Jaciara Brazil
281 G2 Jacinto Brazil
285 F6 Jacinto Arauz Arg.
279 C9 Jacinto Machado Brazil
276 D2 Jaciparaná Brazil
276 D2 Jaciparaná r. Brazil
107 J3 Jack r. Qld Austr.
250 H1 Jackfish Ont. Can.
247 I4 Jackfish Lake Sask. Can.
251 P5 Jack Lake Ont. Can.
261 I9 Jack Lee, Lake resr AR U.S.A.
257 □O3 Jackman ME U.S.A.
107 J3 Jack River National Park Qld Australia
256 A12 Jacksboro TN U.S.A.
261 F9 Jacksboro TX U.S.A.
107 L9 Jackson Qld Austr.
255 D10 Jackson AL U.S.A.
264 L3 Jackson CA U.S.A.
255 F9 Jackson GA U.S.A.
256 B11 Jackson KY U.S.A.
250 J7 Jackson MI U.S.A.
260 H4 Jackson MN U.S.A.
261 K7 Jackson MO U.S.A.
261 J9 Jackson MS U.S.A.
255 I7 Jackson NC U.S.A.
256 C9 Jackson OH U.S.A.
261 K8 Jackson TN U.S.A.
250 F6 Jackson WI U.S.A.
262 I5 Jackson WY U.S.A.
103 I7 Jackson, Cape South I. N.Z.
286 T2 Jackson, Mount Antarctica
103 C10 Jackson Bay South I. N.Z.
103 C10 Jackson Bay b. South I. N.Z.
103 C10 Jackson Head South I. N.Z.
Jackson Island Zemlya Frantsa-Iosifa Rus. Fed. see Dzheksona, Ostrov
262 I5 Jackson Lake WY U.S.A.
250 G5 Jacksonport WI U.S.A.
103 F9 Jacksons South I. N.Z.
249 J3 Jackson's Arm Nfld and Lab. Can.
255 E9 Jacksonville AL U.S.A.
261 I8 Jacksonville AR U.S.A.
255 G10 Jacksonville FL U.S.A.
260 J6 Jacksonville IL U.S.A.
258 B5 Jacksonville MD U.S.A.
255 I8 Jacksonville NC U.S.A.
256 C9 Jacksonville OH U.S.A.
261 H10 Jacksonville TX U.S.A.
255 G10 Jacksonville Beach FL U.S.A.
270 G4 Jacmel Haiti
115 E8 Jaco i. East Timor
145 M7 Jacobabad Pak.
278 E4 Jacobina Brazil
265 T5 Jacob Lake AZ U.S.A.
237 I5 Jacobsdal S. Africa
250 A2 Jacobson MN U.S.A.
103 D10 Jacobs River South I. N.Z.
258 B6 Jacobsville MD U.S.A.
258 B5 Jacobus PA U.S.A.
268 E6 Jacona Mex.
249 H3 Jacques-Cartier, Détroit de sea chan. Que. Can.
249 H3 Jacques-Cartier, Mont mt. Que. Can.
Jacques Cartier Passage Que. Can. see Jacques-Cartier, Détroit de
249 H4 Jacquet River N.B. Can.
280 A3 Jacuba r. Brazil
280 D4 Jacuí Brazil
279 C9 Jacuí r. Brazil
278 F5 Jacuípe r. Brazil
274 D4 Jacumã r. Brazil
278 C3 Jacunda Brazil
275 I5 Jacundá r. Brazil
281 G3 Jacupemba Brazil
280 D6 Jacupiranga Brazil
274 D2 Jacura Venez.
210 G3 Jadar r. Bos.-Herz.
218 H6 Jadar r. Serbia
136 F4 Jadcherla Andhra Prad. India
136 H4 Jaddangi Andhra Prad. India
145 J9 Jaddi, Ras pt Pak.
190 F4 Jade r. Ger.
190 F3 Jade sea chan. Ger.
190 F4 Jadebusen b. Ger.
146 E6 Jadhdhānah Saudi Arabia
147 K7 Jādib Yemen
243 N3 J. A. D. Jensen Nunatakker nunataks Greenland
Jadotville Dem. Rep. Congo see Likasi
210 E3 Jadova r. Croatia
210 F3 Jadovnik mt. Bos.-Herz.
197 J3 Jadów Pol.
205 O7 Jadraque Spain
274 B6 Jaén Peru
114 C4 Jaen Luzon Phil.
207 L5 Jaén Spain
207 M4 Jaén prov. Spain
164 B3 Jæren reg. Norway
138 C9 Jafarabad Gujarat India
144 C2 Ja'farābād Ardabīl Iran
144 G5 Ja'farābād Iran
144 H3 Ja'farābād Khorāsān Iran
144 C4 Ja'farābād Qazvīn Iran
Jaffa Israel see Tel Aviv-Yafo
104 G7 Jaffa, Cape S.A. Austr.
136 F8 Jaffna Sri Lanka
257 M6 Jaffrey NH U.S.A.
150 E8 Jafr, Qā' al imp. l. Jordan
138 F4 Jagadhri Haryana India
160 I2 Jägala r. Estonia
136 E5 Jagalur Karnataka India
139 K9 Jagatsinghpur Orissa India
145 M4 Jagdalak Afgh.
136 H3 Jagdalpur Chhattisgarh India
129 S1 Jagdaqi Nei Mongol China
133 E13 Jagdishpur Uttar Prad. India
139 J7 Jagdispur Bihar India
201 M6 Jagerberg Austria
237 J5 Jagersfontein S. Africa
133 D10 Jaggang Xizang China
136 G4 Jaggayyapeta Andhra Prad. India
144 G8 Jaghīn Iran
144 H9 Jagīn watercourse Iran
144 H9 Jagīn, Ra's pt Iran
236 E5 Jagkolk Vloer salt pan S. Africa
218 J7 Jagodina Jagodina Serbia
197 J2 Jagodne, Jezioro l. Pol.
196 D4 Jagodzin Pol.
Jagok Tso salt l. China see Urru Co
Jagsamka Sichuan China see Luding
194 G3 Jagst r. Ger.
194 G3 Jagsthausen Ger.
195 I3 Jagstzell Ger.
136 F3 Jagtial Andhra Prad. India
280 B5 Jaguapitã Brazil
282 G4 Jaguarão r. Brazil/Uru.
282 G4 Jaguarão Uru.
278 E4 Jaguarari Brazil
278 F3 Jaguaretama Brazil
279 B9 Jaguari Brazil
280 C6 Jaguariaíva Brazil
278 F3 Jaguaribe Brazil
278 F5 Jaguaripe Brazil
278 F3 Jaguaruana Brazil
282 C3 Jagüe Arg.
270 C2 Jagüey Grande Cuba
147 H2 Jahām, 'Irq des. Saudi Arabia
Jahanabad Bihar India see Jehanabad
144 C3 Jahān Dāgh mt. Iran
150 E9 Jahdānīyah, Wādī al watercourse Jordan
106 C1 Jahleel, Point N.T. Austr.
149 L9 Jahmah well Iraq
193 H8 Jahna r. Ger.
193 J5 Jahnsfelde Ger.
144 E7 Jahrom Iran
229 H3 Jahun Nigeria
144 H8 Jāhyad Iran
278 E3 Jaicós Brazil
136 C4 Jaigarh Mahar. India
115 E3 Jailolo Halmahera Indon.
115 F4 Jailolo, Selat sea chan. Maluku Indon.
Jailolo Gilolo i. Maluku Indon. see Halmahera
276 C4 Jaiña Chile
128 H9 Jainca Qinghai China
139 I6 Jainpur Uttar Prad. India
139 N7 Jaintiapur Bangl.
Jainzhug Xizang China see Gutang
138 E6 Jaipur Rajasthan India
138 H6 Jais Uttar Prad. India
138 C6 Jaisalmer Rajasthan India
138 E7 Jaisamand Lake India
138 H8 Jaisinghnagar Madh. Prad. India
138 E6 Jaitaran Rajasthan India
138 G9 Jaitgarh hill Mahar. India
138 G7 Jaitpur Uttar Prad. India
138 I5 Jajarkot Nepal
210 F3 Jajce Bos.-Herz.
Jajnagar state India see Orissa
139 K9 Jajpur Orissa India
198 F4 Ják Hungary
199 I5 Jakabszállás Hungary
139 M6 Jakar Bhutan
116 G8 Jakarta Jawa Indon.
245 N3 Jakes Corner Y.T. Can.
224 D2 Jakharrah Libya
138 B8 Jakhau Gujarat India
145 L6 Jakin mt. Afgh.
234 C3 Jakkalsberg Namibia
145 I8 Jakkī Kowr Iran
162 N3 Jäkkvik Sweden
138 E5 Jakliat Haryana India
Jako i. East Timor see Jaco
Jakobshavn Greenland see Ilulissat
162 Q5 Jakobstad Fin.
201 M8 Jakovlje Croatia
229 G5 Jakpa Nigeria
197 I3 Jaktorów Pol.
199 J2 Jakubany Slovakia
198 F3 Jakubov Slovakia
218 J9 Jakupica mts Macedonia
261 D9 Jal NM U.S.A.
268 C4 Jala Mex.
269 J6 Jalacingo Mex.
Jalaid Nei Mongol China see Inder
146 G3 Jalājil Saudi Arabia
145 N4 Jalālābād Afgh.
138 E4 Jalalabad Punjab India
138 F5 Jalalabad Uttar Prad. India
138 G6 Jalalabad Uttar Prad. India
143 O7 Jalal-Abad Kyrg.
143 O7 Jalal-Abad admin. div. Kyrg.
Jalal-Abad Oblast admin. div. Kyrg. see Jalal-Abad
225 F2 Jalālah al Baḩrīyah, Jabal plat. Egypt
138 D9 Jalalpur Gujarat India
139 I6 Jalalpur Uttar Prad. India
145 P5 Jalalpur Pak.
145 N7 Jalalpur Pirwala Pak.
225 H2 Jalāmid, Ḩazm al ridge Saudi Arabia
147 N4 Ja'lān, Jabal mts Oman
209 C9 Jalance Spain
138 E4 Jalandhar Punjab India
116 □ Jalan Kayu Sing.
267 O10 Jalapa Guat.
267 M9 Jalapa Mex.
Jalapa Mex. see Xalapa
266 □P11 Jalapa Nic.
269 K7 Jalapa de Díaz Mex.
269 L9 Jalapa del Marqués Mex.
162 Q5 Jalasjärvi Fin.
138 G6 Jalaun Uttar Prad. India
149 L6 Jalawlā' Iraq
106 E3 Jalboi r. N.T. Austr.
268 B4 Jalcocotán Mex.
269 K6 Jalcomulco Mex.
145 L6 Jaldak Afgh.
139 L7 Jaldhaka r. Bangl.
280 B4 Jales Brazil
138 G6 Jalesar Uttar Prad. India
139 K9 Jaleshwar Orissa India
Jaleshwar Nepal see Jaleswar
139 J6 Jaleswar Nepal
138 E9 Jalgaon Mahar. India
187 I7 Jalhay Belgium
149 M8 Jalībah Iraq
182 D4 Jaligny-sur-Besbre France
229 H4 Jalingo Nigeria
268 C4 Jalisco Mex.
268 C6 Jalisco state Mex.
145 O4 Jalkot Pak.
144 G8 Jallābī Iran
181 J7 Jallais France
136 D3 Jalna Mahar. India
145 J8 Jālo Iran
100 □3b Jaloklab i. Majuro Marshall Is
209 E10 Jalón Spain
205 R5 Jalón r. Spain
205 P4 Jalón de Cameros Spain
138 D7 Jalore Rajasthan India
268 E4 Jalostotitlán Mex.
218 H6 Jalovik Vladimirci Serbia
197 L2 Jałówka Pol.
268 F5 Jalpa Guanajuato Mex.
268 D4 Jalpa Zacatecas Mex.
139 L6 Jalpaiguri W. Bengal India
269 H4 Jalpan Mex.
145 M4 Jalrez Afgh.
269 M8 Jaltepec r. Mex.
269 M8 Jaltipan Mex.
269 I4 Jaltocán Mex.
224 D2 Jālū Libya
224 D2 Jālū, Wāḩāt oasis Libya
Jalūlā Iraq see Jalawlā'
144 I4 Jām reg. Iran
274 A5 Jama Ecuador
232 D4 Jamaame Somalia
229 H4 Jama'are Bauchi Nigeria
270 F3 Jamaica Cuba
270 □ Jamaica country West Indies
259 H3 Jamaica Bay NY U.S.A.
270 F4 Jamaica Channel Haiti/Jamaica
160 F3 Jämaja Estonia
145 L9 Jama Jamot Pak.
139 L7 Jamalpur Bangl.
139 K7 Jamalpur Bihar India
271 □9 Jamanota hill Aruba
275 G6 Jamanxim r. Brazil
269 K6 Jamapa r. Mex.
276 E2 Jamari Brazil
229 H4 Jamari Nigeria
132 F4 Jamati Xinjiang China
231 C8 Jamba Angola
116 E5 Jambi Sumatera Indon.
116 E5 Jambi prov. Indon.
237 O1 Jambila S. Africa
107 M8 Jambin Qld Austr.
138 D6 Jambo Rajasthan India
116 B2 Jamboaye r. Indon.
117 L1 Jambongan i. Malaysia
117 L5 Jambu Kalimantan Indon.
116 B2 Jambuair, Tanjung pt Indon.
138 D8 Jambusar Gujarat India
136 F3 Jamekunte Andhra Prad. India
192 D4 Jameln Ger.
106 F6 James watercourse N.T. Austr.
261 I7 James r. MO U.S.A.
260 G4 James r. ND/SD U.S.A.
256 I11 James r. VA U.S.A.
283 B7 James, Isla i. Chile
145 M9 Jamesabad Pak.
248 D2 James Bay Can.
259 G4 Jamesburg NJ U.S.A.
270 E1 James Cistern Eleuthera Bahamas
285 F3 James Craik Arg.
162 □ James I Land reg. Svalbard
James Island Islas Galápagos Ecuador see San Salvador, Isla
243 P2 Jameson Land reg. Greenland
109 I8 Jameson Range hills W.A. Austr.
103 C12 James Peak South I. N.Z.
106 D8 James Ranges mts N.T. Austr.
286 U2 James Ross Island Antarctica
243 I3 James Ross Strait Nunavut Can.
104 G5 Jamestown S.A. Austr.
Jamestown Ont. Can. see Wawa
169 H6 Jamestown Ireland
237 K7 Jamestown S. Africa
238 □2b Jamestown St Helena
264 L4 Jamestown CA U.S.A.
254 E7 Jamestown KY U.S.A.
260 F2 Jamestown ND U.S.A.
256 F6 Jamestown NY U.S.A.
256 B9 Jamestown OH U.S.A.
256 E7 Jamestown PA U.S.A.
255 E7 Jamestown TN U.S.A.
179 J5 Jametz France
197 H2 Jamielnik Pol.
163 Q6 Jämijärvi Fin.
207 L5 Jamilena Spain
269 J9 Jamiltepec Mex.
258 E4 Jamison PA U.S.A.
165 L5 Jämjö Sweden
136 D4 Jamkhandi Karnataka India
136 D3 Jamkhed Mahar. India
147 M4 Jammah Oman
136 F5 Jammalamadugu Andhra Prad. India
164 F4 Jammerbugten b. Denmark
138 E3 Jammu Jammu and Kashmir India
138 F2 Jammu and Kashmir terr. Asia
138 C8 Jamnagar Gujarat India
138 E9 Jamner Mahar. India
138 G7 Jamni r. India
165 M7 Jamno, Jezioro lag. Pol.
187 H9 Jamoigne Belgium
116 G8 Jampang Kulon Jawa Indon.
145 N7 Jampur Pak.
144 I4 Jām Rūd r. Iran
163 R6 Jämsä Fin.
225 G3 Jamsah Egypt
163 R6 Jämsänkoski Fin.
139 K8 Jamshedpur Jharkhand India
132 E6 Jamtai Xinjiang China
139 K8 Jamtara Jharkhand India
229 H5 Jamtari Nigeria
162 L5 Jämtland county Sweden
139 K7 Jamui Bihar India
117 L3 Jamuk, Gunung mt. Indon.
218 J5 Jamu Mare Romania
139 L7 Jamuna r. Bangl.
alt. Dihang (India)
alt. Yarlung Zangbo (China)
conv. Brahmaputra
139 N6 Jamuna r. India
204 I4 Jamuz r. Spain
147 J2 Janā i. Saudi Arabia
232 E4 Janaale Somalia
150 E7 Janāb, Wādī al watercourse Jordan
163 R6 Janakkala Fin.
138 H8 Janakpur Chhattisgarh India
139 J6 Janakpur Nepal
281 F1 Janaúba Brazil
275 I4 Janaucú, Ilha i. Brazil
199 L3 Jánd Hungary
145 O5 Jand Pak.
280 B2 Jandaia Brazil
280 B5 Jandaia do Sul Brazil
106 E4 Jandanku Aboriginal Land res. Australia
144 F4 Jandaq Iran
151 G4 Jandari Georgia
195 P4 Jandelsbrunn Ger.
238 □3b Jandía hill Fuerteventura Canary Is
238 □3b Jandía, Península de pen. Fuerteventura Canary Is
238 □3b Jandía, Punta de pt Fuerteventura Canary Is
138 E4 Jandiala Punjab India
145 P6 Jandiala Pak.
238 □3b Jandía Playa Fuerteventura Canary Is
274 D5 Jandiatuba r. Brazil
145 N5 Jandola Pak.
230 D4 Jandongi Dem. Rep. Congo
107 M9 Jandowae Qld Austr.
207 K4 Jándula r. Spain
207 L4 Jándula, Embalse del resr Spain
207 M5 Jandulilla r. Spain
278 D5 Janeiro r. Brazil
264 L1 Janesville CA U.S.A.
250 E7 Janesville WI U.S.A.
116 F5 Jang, Tanjung pt Indon.
144 H4 Jangal Iran
235 G5 Jangamo Moz.
136 F4 Jangaon Andhra Prad. India
133 J11 Jangco Xizang China
Jangeldi Uzbek. see Jongeldi
138 G4 Jangi Hima. Prad. India
139 L7 Jangipur W. Bengal India
Jangnga Turkm. see Jaňňa
133 H10 Jangngai Ri mts Xizang China
133 H10 Jangngai Zangbo r. Xizang China
277 G5 Jango Brazil
143 N7 Jangy-Bazar Kyrg.
143 O7 Jangy-Jol Kyrg.
144 B2 Jānī Beyglū Iran
193 H6 Jänickendorf Ger.
145 N5 Jani Khel Pak.
196 G3 Janikowo Pol.
280 A6 Janiópolis Brazil
210 G3 Janja Bos.-Herz.
210 G3 Janja r. Bos.-Herz.
218 J8 Janjevë Lipjan Kosovo
162 S3 Jänkälä Fin.
237 I3 Jan Kempdorp S. Africa
199 L4 Jánkmajtis Hungary
218 I7 Jankov Kamen mt. Serbia
197 H3 Janków Pol.
196 F3 Jankowo Dolne Pol.
154 C2 Jan Mayen i. Arctic Ocean
160 I4 Jāņmuiža Latvia
144 E1 Jaňňa Turkm.
149 M7 Jannah Iraq
144 D4 Jannatābād Iran
204 G8 Jañona mt. Spain
266 E2 Janos Mex.
199 I5 Jánoshalma Hungary
198 G4 Jánosháza Hungary
198 G4 Jánossomorja Hungary
195 O3 Janovice nad Úhlavou Czech Rep.
197 L2 Janów Podlaskie Pol.
197 H5 Janów Śląskie Pol.
197 J4 Janowiec Pol.
197 I2 Janowiec Kościelny Pol.
196 F3 Janowiec Wlelkopolski Pol.
197 K5 Janów Lubelski Pol.
197 I2 Janowo Pol.
197 L3 Janów Podlaski Pol.
247 I4 Jans Bay Sask. Can.
193 K7 Jänschwalde Ger.
236 I8 Jansenville S. Africa
275 I5 Jânua Coeli Brazil
279 D5 Januária Brazil
146 G1 Janūbī, Al Fulayj al watercourse Saudi Arabia
238 □3c Janubio, Laguna de l. Lanzarote Canary Is
150 B9 Janūb Sīnā' governorate Egypt
178 C7 Janville France
136 E3 Janwada Karnataka India
145 J9 Janzar mt. Pak.
180 I6 Janzé France
224 B1 Janzūr Libya
145 J8 Jaodar Pak.
138 E8 Jaora Madh. Prad. India
124 K12 Japan country Asia
123 H9 Japan, Sea of N. Pacific Ocean
Japan Alps National Park Japan see Chūbu-Sangaku Kokuritsu-kōen
290 E3 Japan Basin sea feature Sea of Japan
290 E3 Japan Trench sea feature N. Pacific Ocean
151 H4 Jap'aridze Georgia
266 □P10 Japón Hond.
190 F1 Japsand i. Ger.
275 E5 Japurá r. Brazil
139 O7 Japvo Mount Nagaland India
266 □T14 Jaqué Panama
205 Q6 Jaraba Spain
270 H4 Jarabacoa Dom. Rep.
150 G2 Jarābulus Syria
196 F4 Jaraczewo Pol.
146 E6 Jarad Saudi Arabia
209 C9 Jarafuel Spain
280 C1 Jaraguá Brazil
279 C8 Jaraguá do Sul Brazil
279 B7 Jaraguari Brazil
204 I9 Jaraicejo Spain
204 I8 Jaraiz de la Vera Spain
268 F4 Jaral de Berrios Mex.
268 F5 Jaral del Progreso Mex.
139 O5 Jaram Arun. Prad. India
205 N8 Jarama r. Spain
283 D7 Jaramillo Arg.
204 I8 Jarandilla de la Vera Spain
128 I7 Jarantai Nei Mongol China
128 I7 Jarantai Yanchi salt l. Nei Mongol China
150 D6 Jarash Jordan
275 H5 Jarauçu r. Brazil
165 M1 Järbo Sweden
Jarboesville MD U.S.A. see Lexington Park
197 L5 Jarczów Pol.
278 F3 Jardim Ceará Brazil
277 F5 Jardim Mato Grosso do Sul Brazil
207 O3 Jardín r. Spain
107 I1 Jardine River National Park Qld Austr.
270 D3 Jardines de la Reina, Archipiélago de los is Cuba
280 C3 Jardinésia Brazil
280 D4 Jardinópolis Brazil
184 A3 Jard-sur-Mer France
Jares r. Spain see Xares
165 N3 Järflotta naturreservat nature res. Sweden
128 F3 Jargalant Bayanhongor Mongolia
Jargalant Dornod Mongolia see Matad
Jargalant Hovd Mongolia see Hovd
128 F2 Jargalant Mongolia
128 I2 Jargalant Töv Mongolia
Jargalant Mongolia see Bulgan
Jargalant Mongolia see Biger
Jargalant Mongolia see Battsengel
128 C3 Jargalant Hayrhan mt. Mongolia
129 K3 Jargalthaan Mongolia
178 D8 Jargeau France
275 I5 Jari r. Brazil
139 M7 Jaria Jhanjail Bangl.
192 H3 Jarmen Ger.
179 M7 Jarménil France
165 K1 Järna Dalarna Sweden
165 N2 Järna Stockholm Sweden
184 D4 Jarnac France
184 I3 Jarnages France
165 L3 Järnlunden l. Sweden
164 I2 Järnsjön l. Sweden
179 K5 Jarny France
197 K5 Jarocin Podkarpackie Pol.
196 F4 Jarocin Wielkopolskie Pol.
198 E1 Jaroměř Czech Rep.
198 E2 Jaroměřice nad Rokytnou Czech Rep.
198 F3 Jaroslavice Czech Rep.
197 K5 Jarosław Pol.
196 E1 Jarosławiec Pol.
198 E2 Jarošov nad Nežárkou Czech Rep.
199 K2 Jarovnice Slovakia
162 L5 Järpen Sweden
190 H1 Jarplund-Weding Ger.
143 L9 Jarqo'rgo'n Uzbek.
Jarqŭrghon Uzbek. see Jarqo'rgo'n
144 C6 Jarrāhi watercourse Iran
106 D6 Jarra Jarra Range hills N.T. Austr.
256 H12 Jarratt VA U.S.A.
258 C5 Jarrettsville MD U.S.A.
171 O4 Jarrow Tyne and Wear, England U.K.
277 E2 Jarú Brazil
147 K7 Jarūb Yemen
Jarud Nei Mongol China see Lubei
218 I7 Jarut mt. Serbia
160 H3 Järvakandi Estonia
163 R6 Järvenpää Fin.
179 L6 Jarville-la-Malgrange France
97 I4 Jarvis Island terr. N. Pacific Ocean
162 M4 Järvsand Sweden
163 N6 Järvsö Sweden
139 I6 Jarwa Uttar Prad. India
181 K6 Jarzé France
138 C8 Jasdan Gujarat India
183 H10 Jas de Laure hill France
199 I3 Jasenie Slovakia
199 K3 Jasenov Slovakia
139 J8 Jashpurnagar Chhattisgarh India
196 D4 Jasień Lubuskie Pol.
196 F1 Jasień Pomorskie Pol.
197 J3 Jasienica Pol.
197 I4 Jasieniec Pol.
229 F5 Jasikan Ghana
197 J6 Jasiołka r. Pol.
197 K5 Jasionka Pol.
197 I5 Jasionna Pol.
197 L2 Jasionówka Pol.
144 G9 Jāsk Iran
144 G9 Jāsk-e Kohneh Iran
142 G6 Jasliq Uzbek.
197 J6 Jaśliska Pol.
197 J6 Jasło Pol.
199 G3 Jaslovské Bohunice Slovakia
160 I7 Jašlūnai Lith.
192 I1 Jasmund pen. Ger.
192 I1 Jasmund, Nationalpark nature res. Ger.
286 T2 Jason Peninsula Antarctica
199 J3 Jasov Slovakia
199 H4 Jásová Slovakia
246 G4 Jasper Alta Can.
255 D9 Jasper AL U.S.A.
261 I7 Jasper AR U.S.A.
255 F10 Jasper FL U.S.A.
255 E8 Jasper GA U.S.A.
254 D6 Jasper IN U.S.A.
256 H6 Jasper NY U.S.A.
256 B9 Jasper OH U.S.A.
255 E8 Jasper TN U.S.A.
261 I10 Jasper TX U.S.A.
246 G4 Jasper National Park Alta Can.
149 L7 Jaşşān Iraq
182 F5 Jassans-Riottier France
182 G4 Jasseron France
Jassy Romania see Iași
165 O7 Jastarnia Pol.
210 E3 Jastrebarsko Croatia
196 E2 Jastrowie Pol.
197 I4 Jastrząb Pol.
196 G1 Jastrzębia Góra Pol.
196 G6 Jastrzębie-Zdrój Pol.
197 K2 Jaświły Pol.
199 J4 Jászapáti Hungary
199 I4 Jászárokszállás Hungary
199 I4 Jászberény Hungary
199 I4 Jászboldogháza Hungary
199 I4 Jászfényszaru Hungary
199 J4 Jászkarajenő Hungary
199 J4 Jászkisér Hungary
199 J4 Jászladány Hungary
199 J4 Jász-Nagykun-Szolnok county Hungary
199 J4 Jászszentandrás Hungary
199 I5 Jászszentlászló Hungary
199 J4 Jásztelek Hungary
205 O2 Jata, Monte hill Spain
280 B2 Jataí Brazil
275 G5 Jatapu r. Brazil
207 L7 Jatar Spain
138 G7 Jatara Madh. Prad. India
136 D4 Jath Mahar. India
145 M9 Jati Pak.
117 H8 Jatibarang Jawa Indon.
270 D3 Jatibonico Cuba
116 G8 Jatiluhur, Waduk resr Jawa Indon.
Játiva Spain see Xàtiva
117 H8 Jatiwangi Jawa Indon.
216 E7 Jato r. Sicilia Italy
278 B5 Jatobá Brazil
145 N7 Jatoi Janubi Pak.
145 K6 Jat Poti Afgh.
163 N6 Jättendal Sweden
277 E1 Jatuarana Brazil
192 I3 Jatzke Ger.
192 I3 Jatznick Ger.
280 C5 Jaú Brazil
275 F5 Jaú r. Brazil
185 I10 Jau, Col de pass France
275 F5 Jaú, Parque Nacional do nat. park Brazil
275 F5 Jauaperi r. Brazil
275 E3 Jaua Sarisariñama, Parque Nacional nat. park Venez.
270 F3 Jauco Cuba
276 B2 Jauja Peru
208 D5 Jaulín Spain
269 H2 Jaumave Mex.
182 K3 Jaun Switz.
275 F6 Jauna r. Brazil
160 K4 Jaunanna Latvia
180 H8 Jaunay r. France
184 E2 Jaunay-Clan France
160 I5 Jaunjelgava Latvia
160 I5 Jaunkalsnava Latvia
160 F5 Jaunlutriņi Latvia
160 G5 Jaunmārupe Latvia
160 J4 Jaunpiebalga Latvia
160 G5 Jaunpils Latvia
139 I7 Jaunpur Uttar Prad. India
201 K6 Jauntal val. Austria
280 B2 Jaupaci Brazil
183 B9 Jaur r. France
285 H4 Jauregui Arg.
208 C2 Jaurrieta Spain
279 B6 Jauru Brazil
277 F4 Jauru r. Brazil
183 J8 Jausiers France
Java i. Indon. see Jawa
136 F6 Javadi Hills India
Javaés r. Brazil see Formoso
278 C4 Javaés, Serra dos hills Brazil
151 E4 Javakhet'is K'edi hills Armenia/Georgia
209 D7 Javalambre mt. Spain
209 C7 Javalambre, Sierra de mts Spain
205 R8 Javalón mt. Spain
145 K4 Javand Afgh.
274 D6 Javari r. Brazil/Peru
alt. Yavari
289 L5 Java Ridge sea feature Indian Ocean
Javarthushuu Mongolia see Bayan-Uul
Java Sea Indon. see Jawa, Laut
289 K5 Java Trench sea feature Indian Ocean
209 F10 Jávea-Xàbia Spain
192 E5 Jävenitz Ger.
207 K6 Javerero mt. Spain
184 F4 Javerlhac-et-la-Chapelle-St-Robert France
208 C2 Javier Spain
283 B7 Javier, Isla i. Chile
285 I2 Javier de Viana Uru.
218 I7 Javor mts Serbia
198 E2 Javořice hill Czech Rep.
199 I3 Javorie mt. Slovakia
218 H7 Javorje mt. Serbia
198 G1 Javorník Czech Rep.
210 E2 Javornik mt. Slovenia
201 J8 Javorniki mts Slovenia
199 H2 Javorníky mts Slovakia
162 P4 Jävre Sweden
181 K5 Javron-les-Chapelles France
117 G9 Jawa i. Indon.
117 I7 Jawa, Laut sea Indon.
116 G8 Jawa Barat prov. Indon.
138 E7 Jawad Madh. Prad. India
138 C7 Jawai r. India
138 F4 Jawala Mukhi Hima. Prad. India
138 F9 Jawar Madh. Prad. India
117 H8 Jawa Tengah prov. Indon.
117 J8 Jawa Timur prov. Indon.
150 F2 Jawbān Bayk Syria
146 G8 Jawf, Wādī al watercourse Yemen
136 C3 Jawhar Mahar. India
232 E4 Jawhar Somalia
196 E4 Jawor Pol.
197 K6 Jawornik Polski Pol.
197 J4 Jawor Solecki Pol.

Jaworze Pol.
Jaworzno Pol.
Jaworzyna mt. Pol.
Jaworzyna Śląska Pol.
Jawoyn Aboriginal Land res. N.T. Austr.
Jay OK U.S.A.
Jaya, Puncak mt. Papua Indon.
Jayacatlán Mex.
Jayakwadi Sagar l. India
Jayanca Peru
Jayanti W. Bengal India
Jayapura Papua Indon.
Jayb, Wādī al watercourse Israel/Jordan
Jayena Spain
Jāyezān Iran
Jayfī, Wādī al watercourse Egypt
Jaynagar Bihar India
Jaynagar W. Bengal India
Jaypur Orissa India
Jayrūd Syria
Jayton TX U.S.A.
Jayuya Puerto Rico
Jazeneuil France
Jaziewo Pol.
Jazīrat al Hamrā U.A.E.
Jazīreh-ye Shīf Iran
Jazminal Mex.
Jaz Mūrīān, Hāmūn-e salt marsh Iran
Jazvān Iran
Jbail Lebanon
J. C. Murphey Lake IN U.S.A.
Jdaidet Ghazir Lebanon
Jdiriya Western Sahara
Jean NV U.S.A.
Jeanerette LA U.S.A.
Jean Marie River N.W.T. Can.
Jeannin, Lac l. Que. Can.
Jebāl Bārez, Kūh-e mts Iran
Jebba Nigeria
Jebel Libya
Jebel Romania
Jebel Turkm.
Jebel, Bahr el r. Sudan/Uganda alt. Abiad, Bahr el, conv. White Nile
Jebel Abyad Plateau Sudan
Jebel Ali U.A.E. see Mina Jebel Ali
Jebel Dud Sudan
Jeberos Peru
Jebha Morocco
Jebri Pak.
Jebsheim France
Jebus Indon.
Jedburgh Scottish Borders, Scotland U.K.
Jeddah Makkah Saudi Arabia see Jiddah
Jeddore Lake Nfld and Lab. Can.
Jedeida Tunisia
Jedlanka Pol.
Jedlicze Pol.
Jedlina-Zdrój Pol.
Jedlińsk Pol.
Jedlnia-Letnisko Pol.
Jednorożec Pol.
Jędrzejów Pol.
Jédula Spain
Jedwabne Pol.
Jedwabno Pol.
Jeetze r. Ger.
Jefferson GA U.S.A.
Jefferson IA U.S.A.
Jefferson NC U.S.A.
Jefferson OH U.S.A.
Jefferson TX U.S.A.
Jefferson WI U.S.A.
Jefferson r. MT U.S.A.
Jefferson, Mount NV U.S.A.
Jefferson, Mount vol. OR U.S.A.
Jefferson City MO U.S.A.
Jeffersonton VA U.S.A.
Jeffersonville GA U.S.A.
Jeffersonville IN U.S.A.
Jeffersonville KY U.S.A.
Jeffersonville OH U.S.A.
Jeffrey WV U.S.A.
Jeffreys Bay S. Africa
Jega Nigeria
Jegun France
Jegunovtse Macedonia
Jehanabad Bihar India
Jejsing Denmark
Jeju S. Korea see Cheju
Jēkabpils Latvia
Jelbart Ice Shelf Antarctica
Jelcz-Laskowice Pol.
Jeldēsa Eth.
Jelenec Slovakia
Jelenia Góra Pol.
Jeleniewo Pol.
Jeleniowski Park Krajobrazowy Pol.
Jelenje Croatia
Jelep La pass China/India
Jeleśnia Pol.
Jelgava Latvia
Jelka Slovakia
Jellico TN U.S.A.
Jellicoe Ont. Can.
Jellicoe Channel North I. N.Z.
Jelling Denmark
Jelloway OH U.S.A.
Jelmstorf Ger.
Jelondí Kŭhistoni Badakhshon Tajik.
Jelovica mt. Slovenia
Jelow Gīr Iran
Jelšane Slovenia
Jelšava Slovakia
Jelsi Italy
Jemaa Kaduna Nigeria
Jemaja i. Indon.
Jember Jawa Indon.
Jembke Ger.
Jemeppe Belgium
Jemez Pueblo NM U.S.A.
Jemgum Ger.
Jemielnica Pol.
Jemielno Pol.
Jeminay Xinjiang China
Jeminay Kazakh.
Jemnice Czech Rep.
Jempang, Danau l. Indon.
Jena Ger.
Jena LA U.S.A.
Jenbach Austria
Jenda Malawi
Jendouba Tunisia
Jendouba admin. div. Tunisia
Jeneč Czech Rep.
Jengen Ger.
Jengish Chokusu mt. China/Kyrg.
Jenikowo Pol.
Jenīn West Bank
Jenipapo Brazil
Jenkinjones WV U.S.A.
Jenkins KY U.S.A.
Jenkins NJ U.S.A.
Jenkintown PA U.S.A.
Jênlung Xizang China
Jenne Mali see Djenné
Jenner Alta Can.
Jennersdorf Austria
Jennings Antigua and Barbuda
Jennings r. B.C. Can.
Jennings LA U.S.A.
Jenpeg Man. Can.
Jensen UT U.S.A.
Jepara Jawa Indon.
Jeparit Vic. Austr.
Jeppo Fin.
Jequié Brazil
Jequitaí Brazil
Jequitaí r. Brazil
Jequitinhonha Brazil
Jequitinhonha r. Brazil
Jerantut Malaysia
Jerba, Île de i. Tunisia
Jerbar Sudan
Jerchel Ger.
Jerécuaro Mex.
149 O9 Jereh Iran
270 F4 Jérémie Haiti
278 F4 Jeremoabo Brazil
232 D3 Jerer Shet' watercourse Eth.
117 L9 Jereweh Sumbawa Indon.
268 D3 Jerez Mex.
268 D3 Jerez r. Mex.
206 G7 Jerez de la Frontera Spain
207 M6 Jerez del Marquesado Spain
206 F4 Jerez de los Caballeros Spain
162 O4 Jerfojaur Sweden
162 R2 Jergol Norway
220 B3 Jergucat Albania
209 D8 Jérica Spain
107 K7 Jericho Qld Austr.
259 H3 Jericho NY U.S.A.
150 D7 Jericho West Bank
193 F5 Jerichow Ger.
227 H2 Jerid, Chott el salt l. Tunisia
117 I3 Jerijeh, Tanjung pt Malaysia
105 J6 Jerilderie N.S.W. Austr.
196 E4 Jerka Pol.
151 G6 Jermuk Armenia
258 D1 Jermyn PA U.S.A.
277 H3 Jeroaquara Brazil
265 T7 Jerome AZ U.S.A.
262 G5 Jerome ID U.S.A.
256 G8 Jerome PA U.S.A.
268 F7 Jerónimo Mex.
285 G2 Jeronimo Norte Arg.
109 E12 Jerramungup W.A. Austr.
145 M9 Jerruck Pak.
190 J3 Jersbek Ger.
180 G3 Jersey terr. Channel Is
257 K8 Jersey City NJ U.S.A.
251 Q8 Jersey Shore PA U.S.A.
260 J6 Jerseyville IL U.S.A.
204 I8 Jerte Spain
204 H9 Jerte r. Spain
278 E3 Jerumenha Brazil
150 D7 Jerusalem Israel/West Bank
102 J6 Jerusalem North I. N.Z.
105 M6 Jervis Bay Jervis Bay Austr.
105 M6 Jervis Bay b. Jervis Bay Austr.
105 M6 Jervis Bay Territory admin. div. Austr.
246 F5 Jervis Inlet B.C. Can.
106 E7 Jervois Range hills N.T. Austr.
191 K6 Jerxheim Ger.
200 C5 Jerzens Austria
196 E4 Jerzmanowa Pol.
214 D8 Jerzu Sardegna Italy
191 H9 Jesberg Ger.
198 C1 Jesenice Středočeský kraj Czech Rep.
198 D2 Jesenice Středočeský kraj Czech Rep.
210 E2 Jesenice Slovenia
198 B1 Jesenice, Vodní nádrž resr Czech Rep.
198 G1 Jeseník Czech Rep.
198 G1 Jeseníky park Czech Rep.
199 J3 Jesenské Slovakia
193 F6 Jeserig Brandenburg Ger.
193 G6 Jeserig Brandenburg Ger.
193 G8 Jesewitz Ger.
213 O8 Jesi Italy
192 L4 Jesionowo Pol.
246 F5 Jesmond B.C. Can.
213 N4 Jesolo Italy
Jesselton Sabah Malaysia see Kota Kinabalu
193 G7 Jessen Ger.
164 H1 Jessheim Norway
139 L8 Jessore Bangl.
258 B6 Jessup MD U.S.A.
190 I4 Jesteburg Ger.
198 D1 Ještěd mt. Czech Rep.
194 F6 Jestetten Ger.
Jesu Maria Island Admiralty Is P.N.G. see Rambutyo Island
255 G10 Jesup GA U.S.A.
269 M8 Jesús Carranza Mex.
285 E2 Jesús María Arg.
268 E4 Jesús María Aguascalientes Mex.
269 M9 Jesús María Chiapas Mex.
268 C3 Jesús María Mex.
268 C4 Jesús María r. Mex.
269 J1 Jesús María, Barra spit Mex.
268 G1 Jesús María de Aquirre Mex.
228 A4 Jeta, Ilha de i. Guinea-Bissau
138 C9 Jetalsar Gujarat India
Jethro tourist site Saudi Arabia see Maghā'ir Shu'ayb
143 R6 Jeti-Ögüz Kyrg.
260 F6 Jetmore KS U.S.A.
138 C9 Jetpur Gujarat India
195 I5 Jettingen-Scheppach Ger.
195 K5 Jetzendorf Ger.
178 H3 Jeumont France
190 I2 Jevenstedt Ger.
190 E3 Jever Ger.
198 F2 Jevíčko Czech Rep.
198 F3 Jevišovice Czech Rep.
198 F3 Jevišovka r. Czech Rep.
164 G1 Jevnaker Norway
256 A7 Jewell OH U.S.A.
256 D11 Jewell Ridge VA U.S.A.
259 L1 Jewett City CT U.S.A.
Jewish Autonomous Oblast admin. div. Rus. Fed. see Yevreyskaya Avtonomnaya Oblast'
Jeyhun Turkm. see Jeýhun
142 J8 Jeýhun Turkm.
144 C4 Jeyḩunābād Iran
195 O3 Jezerní stěna mt. Ger.
196 G2 Jeżewo Kujawsko-Pomorskie Pol.
197 K2 Jeżewo Podlaskie Pol.
197 H2 Jeziorak, Jezioro l. Pol.
165 Q8 Jeziorany Pol.
197 J3 Jeziorka r. Pol.
196 G4 Jeziorsko, Jezioro l. Pol.
197 K4 Jeziorzany Pol.
197 H4 Jeżów Pol.
197 K5 Jeżowe Pol.
150 D5 Jezzine Lebanon
138 E8 Jhabua Madh. Prad. India
139 K7 Jha Jha Bihar India
138 F5 Jhajjar Haryana India
138 D6 Jhajju Rajasthan India
145 L7 Jhal Pak.
139 M8 Jhalakati Bangl.
138 F7 Jhalawar Rajasthan India
139 J8 Jhalida W. Bengal India
145 K8 Jhal Jhao Pak.
138 F7 Jhalrapatan Rajasthan India
145 O6 Jhang Pak.
139 K6 Jhanjharpur Bihar India
138 G7 Jhansi Uttar Prad. India
133 L13 Jhanzi r. India
139 K6 Jhapa Nepal
138 E8 Jharda Madh. Prad. India
139 K8 Jhargram W. Bengal India
139 K8 Jharia Jharkhand India
139 J8 Jharkhand state India
139 J9 Jharsuguda Orissa India
145 M7 Jhatpat Pak.
139 J6 Jhawani Nepal
138 D4 Jhelum r. India/Pak.
145 O5 Jhelum Pak.
139 L8 Jhenaidah Bangl.
Jhenaidaha Bangl. see Jhenaidah
190 E4 Jheringsfehn (Moormerland) Ger.
145 M9 Jhimpir Pak.
138 C8 Jhinjhuvada Gujarat India
139 J8 Jhinkpani Jharkhand India
145 N6 Jhok Bodo Pak.
145 M9 Jhudo Pak.
139 J7 Jhumritilaiya Jharkhand India
138 E5 Jhunjhunun Rajasthan India
138 H7 Jhusi Uttar Prad. India
130 F2 Jiachuan Sichuan China
Jiachuanzhen Sichuan China see Jiachuan
Jiading Jiangxi China see Xinfeng
131 M3 Jiading Shanghai China
131 I6 Jiahe Hunan China
130 D4 Jiajiang Sichuan China
130 F4 Jialing Jiang r. Sichuan China
Jialu Shaanxi China see Jiaxian
131 J2 Jialu He r. China
122 G5 Jiamusi Heilong. China
131 J5 Ji'an Jiangxi China
131 J5 Ji'an Jiangxi China
123 E8 Ji'an Jilin China
Jianchang Jiangxi China see Nancheng
129 P6 Jianchang Liaoning China
130 B5 Jianchuan Yunnan China
131 L4 Jiande Zhejiang China
130 G9 Jianfeng Hainan China
130 E4 Jiang'an Sichuan China
Jiangbei Chongqing China see Yubei
130 C7 Jiangcheng Yunnan China
130 D6 Jiangchuan Yunnan China
131 H6 Jiangcun Hunan China
131 L2 Jiangdu Jiangsu China
Jiange Sichuan China see Pu'an
130 G8 Jianghong Guangdong China
131 H6 Jianghua Hunan China
129 Q8 Jiangjiapo Shandong China
130 F5 Jiangjiehe Guizhou China
130 F4 Jiangjin Chongqing China
128 A4 Jiangjunmiao Xinjiang China
129 N8 Jiangjunmu Hebei China
128 E6 Jiangjuntai Gansu China
Jiangkou Guangdong China see Fengkai
130 G5 Jiangkou Guizhou China
130 F2 Jiangkou Shaanxi China
Jiangkou Sichuan China see Pingchang
131 K5 Jiangle Fujian China
Jiangling Hubei China see Jingzhou
130 E2 Jiangluozhen Gansu China
131 I7 Jiangmen Guangdong China
Jiangna Yunnan China see Yanshan
131 L3 Jiangning Jiangsu China
131 L4 Jiangshan Zhejiang China
Jiangsi Guizhou China see Dejiang
131 L2 Jiangsu prov. China
128 I9 Jiangtai Ningxia China
131 J5 Jiangxi prov. China
131 J3 Jiangxia Hubei China
129 L9 Jiangxian Shanxi China
128 G8 Jiangxigou Qinghai China
131 M2 Jiangyan Jiangsu China
131 M3 Jiangyin Jiangsu China
131 H6 Jiangyong Hunan China
130 E3 Jiangyou Sichuan China
129 P8 Jiangyu Shandong China
133 G11 Jiangzhesongrong Xizang China
131 L2 Jianhu Jiangsu China
131 H8 Jian Jiang r. China
Jianjun Shaanxi China see Yongshou
130 C5 Jiankang Sichuan China
131 I4 Jianli Hubei China
131 K5 Jianning Fujian China
131 L5 Jian'ou Fujian China
129 P6 Jianping Liaoning China
129 P6 Jianping Liaoning China
129 O8 Jianqiao Hebei China
130 B2 Jianshe Qinghai China
Jianshe Sichuan China see Baiyü
130 G3 Jianshi Hubei China
130 D7 Jianshui Yunnan China
133 F9 Jianshui Hu l. Xizang China
130 E3 Jianxing Sichuan China
131 L5 Jianyang Fujian China
130 E3 Jianyang Sichuan China
130 D2 Jiaochang Sichuan China
Jiaochangba Sichuan China see Jiaochang
Jiaocheng Guangdong China see Jiaoling
129 M8 Jiaocheng Shanxi China
129 O7 Jiaohe Hebei China
122 E7 Jiaohe Jilin China
Jiaojiang Zhejiang China see Taizhou
129 L8 Jiaokou Shanxi China
Jiaokui Yunnan China see Yiliang
129 P8 Jiaolai He r. China
129 R5 Jiaolai He r. China
131 K6 Jiaoling Guangdong China
129 P9 Jiaonan Shandong China
131 L6 Jiaowei Fujian China
129 Q8 Jiaozhou Shandong China
129 Q8 Jiaozhou Wan b. China
129 M9 Jiaozuo Henan China
122 E7 Jiapigou Jilin China
128 D8 Jiarsu Qinghai China
130 C6 Jiasa Yunnan China
Jiashan Anhui China see Mingguang
132 C7 Jiashi Xinjiang China
133 H12 Jia Tsuo La pass Xizang China
131 I2 Jiaxian Henan China
129 L8 Jiaxian Shaanxi China
129 O9 Jiaxiang Shandong China
131 M3 Jiaxing Zhejiang China
Jiayi Taiwan see Chiai
122 G4 Jiayin Heilong. China
131 I4 Jiayu Hubei China
128 F7 Jiayuguan Gansu China
131 K7 Jiazi Guangdong China
219 L3 Jibou Romania
147 N5 Jibsh, Ra's c. Oman
Jībūtī country Africa see Djibouti
Jibuti Djibouti see Djibouti
263 K8 Jicarilla Apache Indian Reservation res. NM U.S.A.
269 I9 Jicayán Mex.
198 E1 Jičín Czech Rep.
146 D5 Jiddah Makkah Saudi Arabia
225 G2 Jiddī, Jabal al hill Egypt
139 O5 Jido Arun. Prad. India
122 G6 Jidong Heilong. China
131 K7 Jiedong Guangdong China
162 O2 Jiehkkevárri mt. Norway
Jiehu Shandong China see Yinan
131 J7 Jieshi Guangdong China
128 I9 Jieshipu Gansu China
131 J7 Jieshi Wan b. China
131 J2 Jieshou Anhui China
160 G7 Jiesia r. Lith.
131 J7 Jiexi Guangdong China
129 L8 Jiexiu Shanxi China
131 K7 Jieyang Guangdong China
160 H7 Jieznas Lith.
225 G3 Jiftūn al Kabīr i. Egypt
109 F7 Jigalong Aboriginal Reserve W.A. Austr.
229 H3 Jigawa state Nigeria
145 J1 Jigerbent Turkm.
109 F7 Jiggalong W.A. Austr.
265 Q1 Jiggs NV U.S.A.
270 E3 Jiguaní Cuba
130 C2 Jigzhi Qinghai China
150 F4 Jiḩār, Wādī al watercourse Syria
198 E2 Jihlava Czech Rep.
198 F3 Jihlava r. Czech Rep.
198 D2 Jihočeský kraj admin. reg. Czech Rep.
198 F2 Jihomoravský kraj admin. reg. Czech Rep.
145 J5 Jija Sarai Afgh.
227 G1 Jijel Alg.
219 Q4 Jijia r. Romania
232 D2 Jijiga Eth.
144 D4 Jījīrud Iran
128 F6 Jijitai Gansu China
209 E10 Jijona-Xixona Spain
130 C4 Jijü Sichuan China
150 D6 Jil'ād reg. Jordan
219 O6 Jilava Romania
109 E11 Jilbadji Nature Reserve W.A. Austr.
198 E1 Jilemnice Czech Rep.
224 E4 Jilf al Kabīr, Haḑabat al plat. Egypt
145 M5 Jilga r. Afgh.
146 G3 Jilh al 'Ishār plain Saudi Arabia
232 D4 Jilib Somalia
132 H3 Jili Hu l. China
122 E7 Jilin Jilin China
129 S5 Jilin prov. China
128 G7 Jiling Gansu China
122 D7 Jilin Hada Ling mts China
122 B3 Jiliu He r. China
138 E6 Jilo Rajasthan India
205 Q6 Jiloca r. Spain
Jilong Taiwan see Chilung
269 H6 Jilotepec Mex.
268 D6 Jilotlán de los Dolores Mex.
198 D1 Jílové Czech Rep.
198 D2 Jílové u Prahy Czech Rep.
232 C3 Jīma Eth.
232 E3 Jima Ali well Eth.
270 H4 Jimaní Haiti
233 C6 Jimbo Tanz.
218 I5 Jimbolia Romania
Jimda Sichuan China see Zindo
207 M5 Jimena Spain
207 I8 Jimena de la Frontera Spain
266 G4 Jiménez Chihuahua Mex.
267 I3 Jiménez Coahuila Mex.
269 I1 Jiménez Tamaulipas Mex.
268 D2 Jiménez del Téul Mex.
128 F8 Jimeng Qinghai China
229 I4 Jimeta Nigeria
113 J7 Jimi r. P.N.G.
106 D2 Jim Jim Creek r. N.T. Austr.
129 Q8 Jimo Shandong China
126 E5 Jimokuji Japan
198 F2 Jimramov Czech Rep.
132 I5 Jimsar Xinjiang China
258 D3 Jim Thorpe PA U.S.A.
219 L5 Jina Romania
129 O8 Jinan Shandong China
Jin'an Sichuan China see Songpan
Jinbi Yunnan China see Dayao
198 C2 Jince Czech Rep.
128 H7 Jinchang Gansu China
129 M9 Jincheng Shanxi China
Jincheng Sichuan China see Leibo
Jincheng Sichuan China see Yilong
Jincheng Yunnan China see Wuding
Jinchengjiang Guangxi China see Hechi
Jinchuan Gansu China see Jinchang
Jinchuan Jiangxi China see Xingan
130 D3 Jinchuan Sichuan China
138 F5 Jind Haryana India
105 L7 Jindabyne N.S.W. Austr.
Jinding Yunnan China see Lanping
199 G1 Jindřichov Czech Rep.
198 E2 Jindřichův Hradec Czech Rep.
Jin'e Sichuan China see Longchang
128 F7 Jinfosi Gansu China
Jing Xinjiang China see Jinghe
Jing'an Guangdong China see Doumen
129 K8 Jingbian Shaanxi China
129 J9 Jingchuan Gansu China
131 L3 Jingde Anhui China
131 K4 Jingdezhen Jiangxi China
130 C6 Jingdong Yunnan China
Jinggangshan China see Ciping
131 J5 Jinggang Shan hill Jiangxi China
131 K4 Jinggongqiao Jiangxi China
128 H9 Jinggu Gansu China
130 C7 Jinggu Yunnan China
129 O7 Jinghai Tianjin China
131 L2 Jinghang Yunhe canal China
129 O9 Jinghang Yunhe canal China
131 L2 Jinghang Yunhe canal China
129 O7 Jinghang Yunhe canal China
132 F4 Jinghe Xinjiang China
129 K9 Jing He r. China
130 C8 Jinghong Yunnan China
Jingjiang Jiangsu China see Zhenjiang
129 M7 Jingle Shanxi China
131 I3 Jingmen Hubei China
128 I9 Jingning Gansu China
129 O5 Jingpeng Nei Mongol China
122 F7 Jingpo Heilong. China
122 F7 Jingpo Hu l. China
Jingsha Hubei China see Jingzhou
131 I3 Jingshan Hubei China
128 H8 Jingtai Gansu China
122 C2 Jingtao Heilong. China
128 E7 Jingtieshan Gansu China
130 F7 Jingxi Guangxi China
131 L3 Jingxian Anhui China
Jingxian Hunan China see Jingzhou
Jingxin Yunnan China see Yongshan
130 E4 Jingyan Sichuan China
Jingyang Anhui China see Jingde
122 E7 Jingyu Jilin China
128 I8 Jingyuan Gansu China
131 I3 Jingzhou Hubei China
131 I3 Jingzhou Hubei China
130 G5 Jingzhou Hunan China
122 B3 Jinhe Nei Mongol China
Jinhe Yunnan China see Jinping
Jinhua Yunnan China see Jianchuan
131 L4 Jinhua Zhejiang China
129 M6 Jining Nei Mongol China
129 O9 Jining Shandong China
232 B4 Jinja Uganda
131 L6 Jinjiang Fujian China
Jinjiang Hainan China see Chengmai
130 C5 Jinjiang Yunnan China
130 H5 Jin Jiang r. China
131 J4 Jin Jiang r. China
232 C3 Jinka Eth.
130 D4 Jinkouhe Sichuan China
Jinmen Taiwan see Chinmen
130 G9 Jinmu Jiao pt China
130 D6 Jinning Yunnan China
266 □Q11 Jinotega Nic.
266 □P12 Jinotepe Nic.
130 G5 Jinping Guizhou China
Jinping Yunnan China see Jingdong
130 D7 Jinping Yunnan China
Jinping Yunnan China see Qiubei
130 C5 Jinping Shan mts Sichuan China
Jinsen S. Korea see Inch'ŏn
130 F5 Jinsha Guizhou China
134 J6 Jinsha Jiang r. China alt. Chang Jiang, alt. Tongtian He, conv. Yangtze, long Yangtze Kiang
129 P6 Jinshan Nei Mongol China
Jinshan Nei Mongol China see Guyang
Jinshan Shanghai China see Zhujing
Jinshan Yunnan China see Lufeng
Jinshi Hunan China see Xinning
131 H4 Jinshi Hunan China
128 F7 Jinta Gansu China
131 L3 Jintan Jiangsu China
130 E3 Jintang Sichuan China
130 H7 Jintiancun Guangxi China
114 D6 Jintotolo i. Phil.
114 D6 Jintotolo Channel Phil.
136 E3 Jintur Mahar. India
Jinxi Anhui China see Taihu
131 K5 Jinxi Jiangxi China
Jinxi Liaoning China see Lianshan
131 L5 Jin Xi r. China
131 K4 Jinxian Jiangxi China
Jinxian Liaoning China see Linghai
129 O9 Jinxiang Shandong China
131 M5 Jinxiang Zhejiang China
130 H6 Jinxiu Guangxi China
130 D5 Jinyang Sichuan China
Jinyuan Sichuan China see Dayi
131 M4 Jinyun Zhejiang China
150 E8 Jinz, Qā' al salt flat Jordan
131 J3 Jinzhai Anhui China
129 M8 Jinzhong Shanxi China
129 Q6 Jinzhou Liaoning China
129 Q7 Jinzhou Liaoning China
129 Q7 Jinzhou Wan b. China
Jinzhu Sichuan China see Daocheng
126 F2 Jinzū-gawa r. Japan
277 E2 Ji-Paraná Brazil
277 E2 Jiparaná r. Brazil
274 A5 Jipijapa Ecuador
133 M11 Ji Qu r. Qinghai China
266 □O11 Jiquilisco El Salvador
268 E6 Jiquilpan de Juárez Mex.
269 N9 Jiquipilas Mex.
281 H2 Jiquitaia Brazil
150 B9 Jirā', Wādī watercourse Egypt
150 G7 Jirānīyāt, Shi'bān al watercourse Saudi Arabia
276 D2 Jírau Brazil
145 N2 Jirgatol Tajik.
139 N7 Jiri r. India
129 O4 Jirin Gol Nei Mongol China
225 F3 Jirjā Egypt
198 C1 Jirkov Czech Rep.
186 I2 Jirnsum Neth.
193 K10 Jirny Czech Rep.
144 G7 Jīroft Iran
232 F3 Jirriiban Somalia
147 J4 Jirwān Saudi Arabia
147 J4 Jirwan well Saudi Arabia
129 L9 Jishan Shanxi China
Jishi Qinghai China see Xunhua
128 H9 Jishishan Gansu China
130 G4 Jishou Hunan China
Jishui Jiangxi China see Yongfeng
150 E3 Jisr ash Shughūr Syria
198 D2 Jistebnice Czech Rep.
Jitian Guangdong China see Lianshan
267 M9 Jitotol Mex.
116 D1 Jitra Malaysia
219 L7 Jiu r. Romania
Jiuchenggong Shaanxi China see Linyou
128 J7 Jiudengkou Nei Mongol China
130 D3 Jiuding Shan mt. Sichuan China
131 J4 Jiugong Shan mt. Hubei China
131 J4 Jiujiang Jiangxi China
131 K4 Jiujiang Jiangxi China
Jiulian Yunnan China see Mojiang
131 J4 Jiuling Shan mts China
Jiulong H.K. China see Kowloon
130 C4 Jiulong Sichuan China
Jiulong Sichuan China see Yuechi
129 Q5 Jiumiao Liaoning China
130 G6 Jiuqian Guizhou China
128 F7 Jiuquan Gansu China
122 D6 Jiutai Jilin China
129 L7 Jiuxian Shanxi China
130 F6 Jiuxu Guangxi China
130 E2 Jiuzhaigou Sichuan China
131 K6 Jiuzhen Fujian China
145 I9 Jiwani Pak.
129 R1 Jiwen Nei Mongol China
131 L3 Jixi Anhui China
122 G6 Jixi Heilong. China
Jixian Hebei China see Jizhou
122 G5 Jixian Heilong. China
Jixian Henan China see Weihui
129 L8 Jixian Shanxi China
129 M9 Jiyuan Henan China
147 K7 Jiz', Wādī al r. Yemen
146 F7 Jīzān Saudi Arabia
146 F7 Jīzān prov. Saudi Arabia
198 D1 Jizera r. Czech Rep.
198 E1 Jizerské hory mts Czech Rep.
198 E1 Jizerské hory park Czech Rep.
129 N8 Jizhou Hebei China
146 D3 Jizl watercourse Saudi Arabia
127 J2 Jizō-dake mt. Japan
125 K11 Jizō-zaki pt Japan
Jizzakh Uzbek. see Jizzax
Jizzakh Wiloyati admin. div. Uzbek. see Jizzax
143 L7 Jizzax Jizzax Uzbek.
143 L7 Jizzax admin. div. Uzbek.
279 C8 Joaçaba Brazil
192 I5 Joachimsthal Ger.
269 K7 Joachín Mex.
281 G2 Joaíma Brazil
228 A3 Joal-Fadiout Senegal
275 I5 Joana Peres Brazil
204 D6 Joane Port.
João Belo Moz. see Xai-Xai
João de Almeida Angola see Chibia
281 F3 João Monlevade Brazil
278 G3 João Pessoa Brazil
280 D2 João Pinheiro Brazil
281 E2 Joaquim Felício Brazil
282 D2 Joaquin V. González Arg.
182 D5 Job France
270 E3 Jobabo Cuba
127 M2 Jōban Japan
138 E8 Jobat Madh. Prad. India
199 I4 Jobbágyi Hungary
114 F7 Jobo Point Mindanao Phil.
271 □[1] Jobos Puerto Rico
264 N2 Job Peak NV U.S.A.
200 F5 Jochberg Austria
193 F9 Jocketa Ger.
162 Q3 Jockfall Sweden
194 E3 Jockgrim Ger.
284 C3 Jocoli Arg.
267 O10 Jocotán Guat.
268 D5 Jocotepec Mex.
269 H6 Jocotitlán, Volcán vol. Mex.
139 J8 Joda Orissa India
207 M5 Jódar Spain
138 D6 Jodhpur Rajasthan India
138 C8 Jodiya Gujarat India
187 G7 Jodoigne Belgium
249 K3 Joe Batt's Arm Nfld and Lab. Can.
162 T5 Joensuu Fin.
162 M4 Joesjö Sweden
265 U2 Joe's Valley Reservoir UT U.S.A.
127 H1 Jōetsu Japan
179 L5 Jœuf France
235 G4 Jofane Moz.
246 H5 Joffre, Mount Alta/B.C. Can.
126 F2 Jōganji-gawa r. Japan
127 K5 Jōga-shima i. Japan
139 K6 Jogbani Bihar India
138 H5 Jogbura Nepal
160 J3 Jõgeva Estonia
249 H4 Joggins N.S. Can.
144 G3 Joghatāy Iran
144 G3 Joghatay, Kūh-ye hill Iran
144 G8 Joghdān Iran
139 M6 Jogighopa Assam India
138 F4 Jogindarnagar Hima. Prad. India
Jogjakarta Indon. see Yogyakarta
126 E2 Jōhana Japan
237 L2 Johannesburg S. Africa
264 O6 Johannesburg CA U.S.A.
193 G10 Johanngeorgenstadt Ger.
195 N4 Johanniskirchen Ger.
243 K2 Johan Peninsula Nunavut Can.
125 J14 Jōhen Japan
138 H8 Johilla r. Madh. Prad. India
245 J2 John r. AK U.S.A.
108 J4 John, Mount hill W.A. Austr.
270 □ John Crow Mountains hills Jamaica
262 E4 John Day OR U.S.A.
262 D4 John Day r. OR U.S.A.
262 E4 John Day, Middle Fork r. OR U.S.A.
262 E4 John Day, North Fork r. OR U.S.A.
246 H3 John D'Or Prairie Alta Can.
257 L8 John F. Kennedy airport NY U.S.A.
256 G12 John H. Kerr Reservoir VA U.S.A.
245 O4 John Jay, Mount Can./U.S.A.
246 F1 Johnny Hoe r. N.W.T. Can.
168 J5 John o'Groats Highland, Scotland U.K.
261 E7 Johnson KS U.S.A.
257 M4 Johnson VT U.S.A.
256 G7 Johnsonburg PA U.S.A.
251 S7 Johnson City NY U.S.A.
255 F7 Johnson City TN U.S.A.
261 F10 Johnson City TX U.S.A.
264 N6 Johnsondale CA U.S.A.
261 E10 Johnson Draw watercourse TX U.S.A.
271 □[3] Johnson Point St Vincent
245 N3 Johnson's Crossing Y.T. Can.
246 C2 Johnson's Crossing Y.T. Can.
271 □[2] Johnsons Point Antigua and Barbuda
255 H9 Johnsonville SC U.S.A.
172 C4 Johnston Pembrokeshire, Wales U.K.
255 G9 Johnston SC U.S.A.
109 F12 Johnston, Lake salt flat W.A. Austr.
Johnston and Sand Islands atoll N. Pacific Ocean see Johnston Atoll
97 H2 Johnston Atoll N. Pacific Ocean
168 G11 Johnstone Renfrewshire, Scotland U.K.
168 J12 Johnstonebridge Dumfries and Galloway, Scotland U.K.
Johnstone Lake Sask. Can. see Old Wives Lake
246 E5 Johnstone Strait B.C. Can.
109 E10 Johnston Range hills W.A. Austr.
169 G7 Johnstown Ireland
257 K5 Johnstown NY U.S.A.
256 C8 Johnstown OH U.S.A.
256 G8 Johnstown PA U.S.A.
169 I6 Johnstown Bridge Ireland
127 L3 Jōhoku Japan
116 E4 Johor state Malaysia
116 □ Johor, Selat str. Malaysia/Sing.
116 □ Johor, Sungai Malaysia
116 □ Johor Bahru Malaysia
193 H9 Jöhstadt Ger.
160 K2 Jõhvi Estonia
178 F8 Joigny France
279 C8 Joinville Brazil
179 J7 Joinville France
286 U2 Joinville Island Antarctica
269 H7 Jojutla Mex.
160 H1 Jokela Fin.
243 P2 Jøkelbugten b. Greenland
163 Q6 Jokioinen Fin.
162 Q5 Jokiperä Fin.
162 O3 Jokkmokk Sweden
162 □B1 Jökulbunga hill Iceland
162 □B1 Jökulfirðir inlet Iceland
162 □F1 Jökulsá á Dál r. Iceland
162 □E1 Jökulsá á Fjöllum r. Iceland
269 I7 Jolalpan Mex.
213 L6 Jolanda di Savoia Italy
136 F6 Jolarpettai Tamil Nadu India
149 L4 Jolfa Iran
250 F8 Joliet IL U.S.A.
258 C3 Joliet PA U.S.A.
248 E3 Joliet, Lac l. Que. Can.
248 F4 Joliette Que. Can.
247 H1 Jolly Lake N.W.T. Can.
114 C8 Jolo Phil.
114 C9 Jolo i. Phil.
182 J5 Joly, Mont mt. France
160 C1 Jomala Åland Fin.
114 D4 Jomalig i. Phil.
107 M1 Jomard Entrance sea chan. P.N.G.
117 J8 Jombang Jawa Indon.
130 B3 Jomda Xizang China
164 F3 Jomfruland i. Norway
127 J3 Jōmine-san mt. Japan
163 K6 Jømna Norway
139 I5 Jomsom Nepal
212 F1 Jona Switz.
144 F8 Jonāḩ Iran
256 C11 Jonancy KY U.S.A.
267 O9 Jonathan Point Belize
160 H6 Jonava Lith.
178 G5 Jonchery-sur-Vesle France
182 F3 Joncy France
164 C1 Jondal Norway
142 K8 Jondor Uzbek.
128 H9 Jonê Gansu China
126 G3 Jōnen-dake mt. Japan
261 J8 Jonesboro AR U.S.A.
261 K7 Jonesboro IL U.S.A.
250 I9 Jonesboro IN U.S.A.
261 I9 Jonesboro LA U.S.A.
257 □R4 Jonesboro ME U.S.A.
256 C12 Jonesboro TN U.S.A.
170 E5 Jonesborough Northern Ireland U.K.
245 J1 Jones Islands AK U.S.A.
256 F8 Jones Mills PA U.S.A.
286 R2 Jones Mountains Antarctica
108 □[1] Jones Point Christmas I.
257 □R4 Jonesport ME U.S.A.
243 J2 Jones Sound sea chan. Nunavut Can.
258 C4 Jonestown PA U.S.A.
261 J10 Jonesville LA U.S.A.
256 B12 Jonesville VA U.S.A.
142 J7 Jongeldi Uzbek.
232 A3 Jonglei Sudan
232 B3 Jonglei state Sudan
232 A3 Jonglei Canal Sudan
197 I3 Joniec Pol.
160 H5 Joniškėlis Lith.
160 G5 Joniškis Lith.
139 I9 Jonk r. India
165 K4 Jönköping Sweden
165 K4 Jönköping county Sweden
197 I2 Jonkowo Pol.
249 G3 Jonquière Que. Can.
183 F8 Jonquières France
267 M8 Jonuta Mex.
184 D5 Jonzac France
232 F2 Joog-Joogto, Raas pt Somalia
261 H7 Joplin MO U.S.A.
269 I3 Jopoy Mex.
Joppa Israel see Tel Aviv-Yafo
258 C6 Joppatowne MD U.S.A.
217 J6 Joppolo Italy
138 F6 Jora Madh. Prad. India
208 D6 Jorcas Spain
150 E7 Jordan country Asia
150 D7 Jordan r. Asia
262 K3 Jordan MT U.S.A.
256 I5 Jordan NY U.S.A.
262 F5 Jordan r. OR U.S.A.
265 T1 Jordan r. UT U.S.A.
107 J7 Jordan Creek watercourse Qld Austr.
281 G1 Jordânia Brazil
183 A7 Jordanne r. France
197 H6 Jordanów Pol.
196 E5 Jordanów Śląski Pol.
262 F5 Jordan Valley OR U.S.A.
192 G3 Jördenstorf Ger.
164 G6 Jordløse Denmark
283 B8 Jorge Montt, Isla i. Chile
139 O6 Jorhat Assam India
132 D7 Jor Hu l. China
151 F4 Jorjiashvili Georgia
276 C5 Jorjino, Punta pt Chile
190 I3 Jork Ger.
164 H4 Jörlanda Sweden
145 N3 Jorm Afgh.
162 M4 Jormvattnet Sweden
162 P4 Jörn Sweden
163 S5 Joroinen Fin.
117 K6 Jorong Kalimantan Indon.
164 C2 Jørpeland Norway
207 P2 Jorquera Spain
229 H4 Jos Nigeria
114 E9 Jose Abad Santos Mindanao Phil.
278 B4 José Bispo r. Brazil
277 E3 José Bonifácio Rondônia Brazil
280 C4 José Bonifácio São Paulo Brazil
269 K6 José Cardel Mex.
278 E3 José de Freitas Brazil
283 C7 José de San Martin Arg.
285 I3 José Enrique Rodó Uru.
285 F2 Josefina Arg.
193 L9 Josefův Důl Czech Rep.
277 F4 Joselândia Brazil
268 A1 José López Portillo, Presa resr Mex.
268 E3 José María Morelos Mex.
114 D4 Jose Pañganiban Luzon Phil.
282 G4 José Pedro Varela Uru.
249 H2 Joseph, Lac l. Nfld and Lab. Can.
108 J3 Joseph Bonaparte Gulf W.A. Austr.
265 V7 Joseph City AZ U.S.A.
207 I5 José Torán, Embalse de resr Spain
138 G4 Joshimath Uttaranchal India
127 H2 Jōshinetsu-kōgen Kokuritsu-kōen nat. park Japan
139 K9 Joshipur Orissa India
259 J2 Joshua Point CT U.S.A.
265 P7 Joshua Tree CA U.S.A.
265 Q8 Joshua Tree National Park CA U.S.A.
178 C8 Josnes France
229 H4 Jos Plateau Nigeria
180 F6 Josselin France
193 F9 Jößnitz Ger.
162 K4 Jossund Norway
163 I6 Jostedalsbreen glacier Norway
163 I6 Jostedalsbreen Nasjonalpark nat. park Norway
160 G6 Josvainiai Lith.
163 J6 Jotunheimen mts Norway
163 J6 Jotunheimen Nasjonalpark nat. park Norway
204 F6 Jou Port.
150 D5 Jouaiya Lebanon
181 J5 Jouanne r. France
178 F6 Jouarre France
236 H9 Joubertina S. Africa
237 K2 Jouberton S. Africa
184 F1 Joué-lès-Tours France
180 I6 Joué-sur-Erdre France
182 B2 Jouet-sur-l'Aubois France
160 K2 Jõuga Estonia
182 I3 Jougne France
162 S4 Joukokylä Fin.
150 D5 Joûnié Lebanon
183 H9 Jouques France
261 F11 Jourdanton TX U.S.A.
186 I3 Joure Neth.
184 F6 Journiac France
246 H4 Joussard Alta Can.
163 S6 Joutsa Fin.
163 T6 Joutseno Fin.
162 S3 Joutsijärvi Fin.
182 H3 Joux, Forêt de la for. France
182 I3 Joux, Lac de l. Switz.
212 A2 Joux, Vallée de val. Switz.
182 D1 Joux-la-Ville France
178 C6 Jouy France
179 L5 Jouy-aux-Arches France
178 D5 Jouy-le-Moutier France
178 C8 Jouy-le-Potier France
178 G5 Jouy-lès-Reims France
270 C2 Jovellanos Cuba
139 N7 Jowai Meghalaya India
144 D3 Jowr Deh Iran
144 I6 Jowzak Iran
144 C4 Jowzān Iran
145 K3 Jowzjān prov. Afgh.
245 N3 Joy, Mount Y.T. Can.
267 O11 Joya de Cerén tourist site El Salvador
169 C5 Joyce's Country reg. Ireland
183 E8 Joyeuse France
126 C6 Jōyō Japan
139 L7 Joypurhat Bangl.
182 C5 Joze France
197 J4 Józefów Lubelskie Pol.
197 L5 Józefów Lubelskie Pol.
197 J3 Józefów Mazowieckie Pol.
237 Q3 Jozini S. Africa
226 B4 Jrayfiya well Western Sahara
228 A2 Jreïda Maur.
274 E5 Juami r. Brazil
271 □[1] Juana Díaz Puerto Rico
268 D1 Juan Aldama Mex.
285 F6 Juan A. Pradere Arg.
285 G4 Juan Bautista Alberdi Arg.
129 N9 Juancheng Shandong China
285 I5 Juancho Arg.
270 □ Juan de Bolas hill Jamaica
246 E5 Juan de Fuca Strait Can./U.S.A.
284 E6 Juan de Garay Arg.
235 □I3 Juan de Nova i. Indian Ocean
269 L7 Juan Díaz Covarrubias Mex.
285 G5 Juan E. Barra Arg.
268 C4 Juan Escutia Mex.
276 □ Juan Fernández, Archipiélago is S. Pacific Ocean
Juan Fernández Islands S. Pacific Ocean see Juan Fernández, Archipiélago
275 F2 Juangriego Venez.
269 L8 Juanita Mex.
284 E3 Juan Jorba Arg.
285 H2 Juan Jorge Arg.
285 F4 Juan José Paso Arg.
276 A1 Juanjuí Peru
162 T5 Juankoski Fin.
183 K9 Juan-les-Pins France
285 I4 Juan L. Lacaze Uru.
284 E3 Juan Llerena Arg.
266 E2 Juan Mata Ortíz Mex.
285 H6 Juan N. Fernández Arg.
269 J4 Juan Ramírez, Isla i. Mex.
269 L7 Juan Rodríguez Clara Mex.
Juanshui Hubei China see Tongcheng
285 I4 Juan Soler Uru.
283 B7 Juan Stuven, Isla i. Chile
229 F5 Juapon Ghana
277 F2 Juara Brazil
267 I4 Juaréz Mex.
269 K8 Juárez, Sierra mts Mex.
266 A1 Juárez, Sierra de mts Mex.
281 E5 Juatinga, Ponta da pt Brazil
278 E4 Juazeiro Brazil
278 F3 Juazeiro do Norte Brazil
228 C5 Juazohn Liberia
Juba r. Somalia see Jubba
232 A3 Juba Sudan
146 A2 Jūbāl, Jazīrat i. Egypt
146 G8 Juban Yemen
286 U2 Jubany research stn Antarctica
232 D5 Jubba r. Somalia
232 D4 Jubbada Dhexe admin. reg. Somalia
232 D4 Jubbada Hoose admin. reg. Somalia
146 E1 Jubbah Saudi Arabia
Jubbulpore Madh. Prad. India see Jabalpur
190 H1 Jübek Ger.
109 I10 Jubilee Lake salt flat W.A. Austr.
249 K3 Jubilee Lake Nfld and Lab. Can.
285 H2 Jubileo Arg.
139 K6 Jubing Nepal
181 K5 Jublains France
226 B4 Juby, Cap c. Morocco
209 E9 Jucar-Turia, Canal r. Spain
278 F3 Jucas Brazil
269 J9 Juchatengo Mex.
191 B8 Jüchen Ger.
268 D4 Juchipila Mex.
268 D4 Juchipila r. Mex.
269 L9 Juchitán Mex.
268 C5 Juchitlán Mex.
197 L2 Juchnowiec Kościelne Pol.
196 E2 Juchowo Pol.
191 K10 Jüchsen Ger.
281 H2 Jucuruçu Brazil
281 H2 Jucuruçu r. Brazil
164 B2 Judaberg Norway
150 C7 Judaea reg. Israel
149 J8 Judaidat al Hamir Iraq
148 I6 Judaydah Syria
150 E5 Judaydat al Wādī Syria
149 J8 Judayyidat 'Ar'ar well Iraq
193 D10 Judenbach Ger.
201 K5 Judenburg Austria
205 P6 Judes mt. Spain
130 B5 Judian Yunnan China
209 C11 Judío, Rambla del r. Spain
262 J3 Judith r. MT U.S.A.
262 J3 Judith Gap MT U.S.A.
Juegang Jiangsu China see Rudong
207 M3 Juego de Bolos mt. Spain
164 G6 Juelsminde Denmark
281 H2 Juerana Brazil
205 Q7 Juez mt. Spain
275 F5 Jufari r. Brazil
180 G5 Jugon-les-Lacs France
Jugoslavija country Europe see Serbia
129 K8 Juh Nei Mongol China
146 F7 Juḩā Saudi Arabia
146 D3 Juhaynah reg. Saudi Arabia
147 J5 Juḩaysh, Qalamat al oasis Saudi Arabia
191 I8 Jühnde Ger.
128 E8 Juhongtu Qinghai China
200 E4 Juifen mt. Austria
266 □Q11 Juigalpa Nic.
181 K7 Juigné-sur-Loire France

184 G5 **Juillac** France
185 E9 **Juillan** France
249 I2 **Juillet, Lac** *l. Que.* Can.
178 E5 **Juilly** France
277 F2 **Juína** Brazil
277 F3 **Juina** *r.* Brazil
178 D6 **Juine** *r.* France
190 C3 **Juist** Ger.
190 D3 **Juist** *i.* Ger.
281 F4 **Juiz de Fora** Brazil
116 D5 **Jujuhan** *r.* Indon.
144 I3 **Ju Ju Klu** Turkm.
182 G4 **Jujurieux** France
282 D1 **Jujuy** *prov.* Arg.
162 P3 **Jukkasjärvi** Sweden
127 I3 **Jukkoku-tōge** *pass* Japan
276 D5 **Julaca** Bol.
201 I2 **Julbach** Austria
195 N5 **Julbach** Ger.
260 D5 **Julesburg** *CO* U.S.A.
276 C4 **Juli** Peru
274 E5 **Julia** Brazil
276 C3 **Juliaca** Peru
107 H6 **Julia Creek** *Qld* Austr.
107 H6 **Julia Creek** *r. Qld* Austr.
264 P8 **Julian** *CA* U.S.A.
248 E2 **Julian, Lac** *l. Que.* Can.
186 G3 **Julianadorp** Neth.
271 □10 **Julianadorp** *Curaçao* Neth. Antilles
187 I6 **Juliana Kanaal** *canal* Neth.
Julian Alps *mts* Slovenia *see* **Julijske Alpe**
Julianatop *mt. Papua* Indon. *see* **Mandala, Puncak**
275 G4 **Juliana Top** *mt.* Suriname
Julianehåb Greenland *see* **Qaqortoq**
169 J5 **Julianstown** Ireland
191 B9 **Jülich** Ger.
182 E3 **Julien, Mont** *hill* France
182 F4 **Juliénas** France
210 D2 **Julijske Alpe** *mts* Slovenia
266 G3 **Julimes** Mex.
279 B9 **Júlio de Castilhos** Brazil
Juliomagus France *see* **Angers**
280 C5 **Júlio Mesquita** Brazil
106 G6 **Julius, Lake** *Qld* Austr.
258 F4 **Juliustown** *NJ* U.S.A.
180 H4 **Jullouville** France
Jullundur *Punjab* India *see* **Jalandhar**
268 D6 **Juluapan** Mex.
275 E6 **Juma** *r.* Brazil
143 L8 **Juma** Uzbek.
129 N7 **Juma He** *r.* China
130 B2 **Jumanggoin** *Sichuan* China
232 D5 **Jumba** Somalia
274 B6 **Jumbilla** Peru
183 C6 **Jumeaux** France
184 G5 **Jumilhac-le-Grand** France
209 C11 **Jumilla** Spain
138 I5 **Jumla** Nepal
190 E4 **Jümme** *r.* Ger.
Jumna *r.* India *see* **Yamuna**
250 C4 **Jump** *r. WI* U.S.A.
160 H5 **Jumprava** Latvia
138 C9 **Junagadh** *Gujarat* India
137 H3 **Junagarh** *Orissa* India
129 P9 **Junan** *Shandong* China
150 A8 **Junayfah** Egypt
150 B9 **Junaynah, Ra's al** *mt.* Egypt
144 H5 **Junbuk** Iran
129 P4 **Jun Bulen** *Nei Mongol* China
284 B3 **Juncal** *mt.* Chile
204 C9 **Juncal** Port.
271 □1 **Juncos** Puerto Rico
208 G5 **Juncosa** Spain
261 F10 **Junction** *TX* U.S.A.
265 T3 **Junction** *UT* U.S.A.
106 D1 **Junction Bay** *N.T.* Austr.
260 G6 **Junction City** *KS* U.S.A.
262 C4 **Junction City** *OR* U.S.A.
107 I8 **Jundah** *Qld* Austr.
280 D5 **Jundiaí** Brazil
245 N4 **Juneau** *AK* U.S.A.
245 N4 **Juneau Icefield** B.C. Can.
208 G4 **Juneda** Spain
105 K6 **Junee** *N.S.W.* Austr.
150 D5 **Jûn el Khudr** *b.* Lebanon
268 G6 **Jungapeo** Mex.
Jungar Qi *Nei Mongol* China *see* **Xuejiawan**
212 D2 **Jungfrau** *mt.* Switz.
132 H4 **Junggar Pendi** *basin* China
194 G5 **Jungingen** Ger.
187 J9 **Junglinster** Lux.
145 L9 **Jungshahi** Pak.
133 J10 **Jungsi** *Xizang* China
232 B2 **Junguls** Sudan
251 Q9 **Juniata** *r. PA* U.S.A.
258 A3 **Juniata County** *county PA* U.S.A.
218 I8 **Junik** *Deçan* Kosovo
285 G4 **Junín** Arg.
284 C3 **Junin** Arg.
276 A2 **Junín** Peru
276 B2 **Junín** *dept* Peru
256 F10 **Junior** *WV* U.S.A.
257 □R2 **Juniper** *N.B.* Can.
265 S6 **Juniper Mountains** *AZ* U.S.A.
264 K5 **Junipero Serro Peak** *CA* U.S.A.
178 H5 **Juniville** France
191 C10 **Jünkerath** Ger.
162 M3 **Junkerdalen Balvatnet** *nature res.* Norway
130 E4 **Junlian** *Sichuan* China
131 J6 **Junmenling** *Jiangxi* China
150 C10 **Junnah, Jabal** *mts* Egypt
136 C3 **Junnar** *Mahar.* India
261 E10 **Juno** *TX* U.S.A.
162 Q3 **Junosuando** Sweden
280 B4 **Junqueirópolis** Brazil
162 N5 **Junsele** Sweden
131 K4 **Junshan Hu** *l.* China
262 E5 **Juntura** *OR* U.S.A.
162 T4 **Juntusranta** Fin.
Junxi *Fujian* China *see* **Datian**
Junxian *Hubei* China *see* **Danjiangkou**
130 B2 **Ju'nyung** *Sichuan* China
Ju'nyunggoin *Sichuan* China *see* **Ju'nyung**
127 M2 **Jūō** Japan
160 E6 **Juodkrantė** Lith.
160 I7 **Juodšiliai** Lith.
160 I5 **Juodupė** Lith.
162 Q3 **Juoksengi** Sweden
160 H6 **Juosta** *r.* Lith.
160 H6 **Juostininkai** Lith.
144 G6 **Jūpār** Iran
281 G3 **Juparanã, Lagoa** *l.* Brazil
280 B4 **Jupiá** Brazil
280 B4 **Jupiá, Represa** *resr* Brazil
181 L6 **Jupilles** France
255 G12 **Jupiter** *FL* U.S.A.
187 I7 **Juprelle** Belgium
280 D6 **Juquiá** Brazil
280 D6 **Juquiá** *r.* Brazil
280 D5 **Juquitiba** Brazil
230 F2 **Jur** *r.* Sudan
182 H3 **Jura** *dept* France
182 G5 **Jura** *mts* France/Switz.
160 F6 **Jūra** *r.* Lith.
212 C1 **Jura** *canton* Switz.
168 E10 **Jura** *i. Scotland* U.K.
146 G2 **Jur'ā, Nafūd al** *des.* Saudi Arabia
168 E11 **Jura, Sound of** *sea chan. Scotland* U.K.
274 B3 **Juradó** Col.
281 F2 **Juramento** Brazil
185 D9 **Jurançon** France
280 A6 **Juranda** Brazil
160 F6 **Jurbarkas** Lith.
187 E7 **Jurbise** Belgium
278 E4 **Juremal** Brazil
150 D8 **Jurf ad Darāwīsh** Jordan
192 E3 **Jürgenshagen** Ger.
192 G3 **Jürgenstorf** Ger.
108 G5 **Jurgurra** *r. W.A.* Austr.
129 Q4 **Jurh** *Nei Mongol* China
129 Q4 **Jurh** *Nei Mongol* China
133 J9 **Jurhen Ul Shan** *mts* China
160 H2 **Jüri** Estonia
109 C11 **Jurien** *W.A.* Austr.
109 C11 **Jurien Bay** *W.A.* Austr.
184 D4 **Jurignac** France
219 Q6 **Jurilovca** Romania
275 G5 **Juriti Velho** Brazil
213 R6 **Jurjevo** Croatia
201 L7 **Jurklošter** Slovenia
160 G5 **Jūrmala** Latvia
163 P7 **Jurmo** Fin.
162 S4 **Jurmu** Fin.
206 E3 **Juromenha** Port.
131 L3 **Jurong** *Jiangsu* China
116 □ **Jurong** Sing.
116 □ **Jurong, Sungai** *r.* Sing.
116 □ **Jurong Island** *reg.* Sing.
Jur pri Bratislave Slovakia *see* **Svätý Jur**
275 E5 **Juruá** Brazil
274 E5 **Juruá** *r.* Brazil
277 F3 **Juruena** Brazil
277 F1 **Juruena** *r.* Brazil
277 F2 **Juruena, Parque Nacional do** *nat. park* Brazil
280 C5 **Jurumirim, Represa de** *resr* Brazil
277 G2 **Juruna** *r.* Brazil
276 C1 **Jurupari** *r.* Brazil
275 G5 **Juruti** Brazil
162 P5 **Jurva** Fin.
124 R5 **Jūsan-ko** *l.* Japan
275 F2 **Jusepín** Venez.
126 E5 **Jūshiyama** Japan
144 G3 **Jūshqān** Iran
150 E4 **Jūsīyah** Syria
184 I6 **Jussac** France
280 B1 **Jussara** Brazil
160 G2 **Jussarö** *i.* Fin.
179 K8 **Jussey** France
256 D11 **Justice** *WV* U.S.A.
285 F3 **Justiniano Posse** Arg.
284 E3 **Justo Daract** Arg.
199 G5 **Juta** Hungary
274 D6 **Jutaí** Brazil
274 E5 **Jutaí** *r.* Brazil
193 H7 **Jüterbog** Ger.
279 B7 **Juti** Brazil
267 O10 **Jutiapa** Guat.
266 □P10 **Jutiapa** Hond.
266 □P10 **Juticalpa** Hond.
Jutland *pen.* Denmark *see* **Jylland**
196 F4 **Jutrosin** Pol.
162 T5 **Juuka** Fin.
163 R6 **Juupajoki** Fin.
160 J1 **Juurikorpi** Fin.
163 S6 **Juva** Fin.
268 G5 **Juventino Rosas** Mex.
270 B3 **Juventud, Isla de la** *i.* Cuba
181 I5 **Juvigné** France
181 I4 **Juvigny-le-Tertre** France
181 J4 **Juvigny-sous-Andaine** France
145 I6 **Juwain** Afgh.
117 I8 **Juwana** *Jawa* Indon.
129 P9 **Juxian** *Shandong* China
129 O9 **Juye** *Shandong* China
144 H4 **Jūymand** Iran
144 E7 **Jūyom** Iran
179 I7 **Juzennecourt** France
185 F10 **Juzet-d'Izaut** France
Južnoukrajinsk Ukr. *see* **Yuzhnoukrayinsk**
234 E5 **Jwaneng** Botswana
164 H6 **Jyderup** Denmark
164 F5 **Jylland** *pen.* Denmark
143 R6 **Jyrgalang** Kyrg.
163 R5 **Jyväskylä** Fin.

K

138 F2 **K2** *mt.* China/Pak.r
229 G4 **Ka** *r.* Nigeria
264 □D12 **Ka'a'awa** *HI* U.S.A.
232 B4 **Kaabong** Uganda
277 E4 **Kaa-Iya del Gran Chaco, Parque Nacional** *nat. park* Bol.
Kaakhka Turkm. *see* **Kaka**
264 □C12 **Ka'ala** *mt. HI* U.S.A.
100 □5 **Kaala-Gomen** New Caledonia
236 I5 **Kaalpan** *salt pan* S. Africa
237 P1 **Kaalrug** S. Africa
162 S2 **Kaamanen** Fin.
160 K4 **Kääpa** Estonia
237 P1 **Kaapamuiden** S. Africa
Kaapstad S. Africa *see* **Cape Town**
163 Q6 **Kaarina** Fin.
192 D4 **Kaarßen** Ger.
191 C8 **Kaarst** Ger.
228 C3 **Kaarta** *reg.* Mali
186 H5 **Kaatsheuvel** Neth.
162 T5 **Kaavi** Fin.
Kaba *Xinjiang* China *see* **Habahe**
143 V4 **Kaba** *r.* China/Kazakh.
199 K4 **Kaba** Hungary
115 B6 **Kabaena** *i.* Indon.
151 D5 **Kabak Tepe** *mt.* Turkey
228 C4 **Kabala** Sierra Leone
233 A5 **Kabale** Uganda
Kabalega Falls National Park Uganda *see* **Murchison Falls National Park**
231 E6 **Kabalo** Dem. Rep. Congo
231 E6 **Kabambare** Dem. Rep. Congo
143 L1 **Kaban'** Kazakh.
143 S5 **Kabanbay** *Almatinskaya Oblast'* Kazakh.
143 L1 **Kabanbay** *Severnyy Kazakhstan* Kazakh.
143 N2 **Kabanbay Batyr** Kazakh.
231 C6 **Kabanga** Dem. Rep. Congo
233 A5 **Kabanga** Tanz.
231 D7 **Kabangu** Dem. Rep. Congo
116 C3 **Kabanjahe** *Sumatera* Indon.
142 D1 **Kabanovka** Rus. Fed.
Kabanye Ukr. *see* **Krasnorichens'ke**
101 □7 **Kabara** *i.* Fiji
115 G4 **Kabarai** *Papua* Indon.
159 Q9 **Kabardinka** Rus. Fed.
Kabardino-Balkarskaya A.S.S.R. *aut. rep.* Rus. Fed. *see* **Kabardino-Balkarskaya Respublika**
151 E2 **Kabardino-Balkarskaya Respublika** *aut. rep.* Rus. Fed.
151 E2 **Kabardino-Balkarskiy Zapovednik** *nature res.* Rus. Fed.
230 F5 **Kabare** Dem. Rep. Congo
Kabarega National Park Uganda *see* **Murchison Falls National Park**
114 D8 **Kabasalan** *Mindanao* Phil.
127 L3 **Kaba-san** *hill* Japan
125 G14 **Kaba-shima** *i.* Japan
118 C5 **Kabaung** *r.* Myanmar
118 B3 **Kabaw Valley** Myanmar
151 B6 **Kabayel** Turkey
229 G5 **Kabba** Nigeria
136 E6 **Kabbani** *r.* India
162 P3 **Kåbdalis** Sweden
229 I3 **Kabélawa** Niger
250 J1 **Kabenung Lake** *Ont.* Can.
232 B4 **Kaberamaido** Uganda
160 I2 **Kaberneeme** Estonia
227 F3 **Kabertene** Alg.
115 B3 **Kabetan** *i.* Indon.
250 B1 **Kabetogama Lake** *MN* U.S.A.
231 E6 **Kabeya** Dem. Rep. Congo
199 G4 **Kab-hegy** *hill* Hungary
248 C3 **Kabinakagami** *r. Ont.* Can.
248 C3 **Kabinakagami Lake** *Ont.* Can.
231 E6 **Kabinda** Dem. Rep. Congo
115 D8 **Kabir** Indon.
150 D3 **Kabīr** *r.* Syria
124 □B22 **Kabira** *Nansei-shotō* Japan
144 B5 **Kabīrkūh** *mts* Iran
151 I6 **Kābirli** Azer.
145 N6 **Kabirwala** Pak.
160 H3 **Kabli** Estonia
138 G9 **Kabneshwar** *Mahar.* India
230 C3 **Kabo** C.A.R.
Kabodiyon Tajik. *see* **Kabutiyon**
231 E8 **Kabompo** Zambia
231 D8 **Kabompo** *r.* Zambia
231 E7 **Kabondo-Dianda** Dem. Rep. Congo
117 I4 **Kabong** *Sarawak* Malaysia
231 E6 **Kabongo** Dem. Rep. Congo
119 C8 **Kabosa Island** Myanmar
230 D3 **Kabou** C.A.R.
229 F4 **Kabou** Togo
161 S3 **Kabozha** Rus. Fed.
228 A3 **Kabrousse** Senegal
146 F3 **Kabshah, Jabal** *hills* Saudi Arabia
144 I5 **Kabūdeh** Iran
144 H3 **Kabūd Gonbad** Iran
144 C4 **Kabūd Rāhang** Iran
114 C3 **Kabugao** *Luzon* Phil.
145 M4 **Kābul** Afgh.
145 M4 **Kābul** *prov.* Afgh.
145 O5 **Kābul** *r.* Afgh.
231 F8 **Kabunda** Dem. Rep. Congo
233 A7 **Kabunda** Zambia
115 A8 **Kabunduk** *Sumba* Indon.
127 J3 **Kabura-gawa** *r.* Japan
115 E2 **Kaburuang** *i.* Indon.
225 G5 **Kabushiya** Sudan
144 G6 **Kabūtar Khān** Iran
145 M3 **Kabutiyon** Tajik.
231 F8 **Kabwe** Zambia
142 J3 **Kabyrga** *r.* Kazakh.
218 J8 **Kaçanik** *Kaçanik* Kosovo
Kačanik *Kaçanik* Kosovo *see* **Kaçanik**
115 F4 **Kacepi** *Maluku* Indon.
159 M9 **Kacha** *r.* Ukr.
145 K8 **Kacha Daman** Pak.
232 B4 **Kachagalau** *mt.* Kenya
Kachagani Georgia *see* **Qach'aghani**
145 I7 **Kāchā Kūh** *mts* Iran/Pak.
157 I6 **Kachalinskaya** Rus. Fed.
145 K9 **Kachari, Ras** *pt* Pak.
138 B8 **Kachchh, Gulf of** *Gujarat* India
138 C8 **Kachchh, Little Rann of** *marsh Gujarat* India
138 C7 **Kachchh, Rann of** *marsh* India
244 J4 **Kachemak Bay** *AK* U.S.A.
138 E7 **Kachhola** *Rajasthan* India
139 I7 **Kachhwa** *Uttar Prad.* India
229 G4 **Kachia** Nigeria
234 E3 **Kachikau** Botswana
118 C1 **Kachin** *state* Myanmar
232 C2 **Kachīsī** Eth.
233 A8 **Kacholola** Zambia
120 I1 **Kachug** Rus. Fed.
232 B4 **Kachung** Uganda
193 I10 **Kačice** Czech Rep.
149 J3 **Kaçkar Dağı** *mt.* Turkey
151 E6 **Kaçmaz** Turkey
189 H3 **Kaczawa** *r.* Pol.
196 E2 **Kaczory** Pol.
126 B7 **Kada** Japan
118 C6 **Kadaingti** Myanmar
136 E8 **Kadaiyanallur** *Tamil Nadu* India
232 B4 **Kadam** *mt.* Uganda
198 C1 **Kadaň** Czech Rep.
224 D6 **Kadana** Chad
145 K6 **Kadanai** *r.* Afgh./Pak.
119 D8 **Kadan Kyun** *i.* Myanmar
117 K7 **Kadapongan** *i.* Indon.
199 G5 **Kadarkút** Hungary
115 C6 **Kadatuang** *i.* Indon.
138 G6 **Kadaura** *Uttar Prad.* India
101 □7 **Kadavu** *i.* Fiji
101 □7a **Kadavu Passage** Fiji
129 P1 **Kadaya** Rus. Fed.
136 F3 **Kaddam** *l.* India
228 E5 **Kade** Ghana
124 □1 **Kadena** *Okinawa* Japan
109 I9 **Kadgo, Lake** *salt flat W.A.* Austr.
225 F4 **Kadhdhāb, Sinn al** *esc.* Egypt
Kādhimain Iraq *see* **Al Kāẓimīyah**
138 D8 **Kadi** *Gujarat* India
228 D4 **Kadiana** Mali
136 E8 **Kadiapattanam** *Tamil Nadu* India
Kadijica *mt.* Bulg. *see* **Kadiytsa**
221 H2 **Kadıköy** *Çanakkale* Turkey
221 K2 **Kadıköy** *İstanbul* Turkey
104 F5 **Kadina** *S.A.* Austr.
118 F5 **Kading** *r.* Laos
148 F4 **Kadınhanı** Turkey
228 D4 **Kadiolo** Mali
228 C4 **Kadiondola, Mont** *mt.* Guinea
136 F5 **Kadiri** *Andhra Prad.* India
148 H5 **Kadirli** Turkey
Kadiyevka Ukr. *see* **Stakhanov**
219 K9 **Kadiytsa** *mt.* Bulg.
229 F5 **Kadjebi** Ghana
136 C7 **Kadmat** *atoll* India
156 H4 **Kadnikov** Rus. Fed.
229 H5 **Kado** Nigeria
123 D9 **Ka-do** *i.* N. Korea
125 I14 **Kadogawa** Japan
116 E2 **Kadok** Malaysia
260 E4 **Kadoka** *SD* U.S.A.
157 H5 **Kadom** Rus. Fed.
235 F3 **Kadoma** Zimbabwe
118 B7 **Kadonkani** Myanmar
160 J2 **Kadrina** Estonia
230 F2 **Kadugli** Sudan
229 G4 **Kaduna** Nigeria
229 G4 **Kaduna** *r.* Nigeria
229 G4 **Kaduna** *state* Nigeria
136 E6 **Kadur** *Karnataka* India
130 A4 **Kadusam** *mt.* China/India
161 U2 **Kaduy** Rus. Fed.
156 H4 **Kadyy** Rus. Fed.
Kadzharan Armenia *see* **K'ajaran**
156 K2 **Kadzherom** Rus. Fed.
Kadzhi-Say Kyrg. *see* **Kajy-Say**
197 J2 **Kadzidło** Pol.
123 D9 **Kaechon** N. Korea
228 B2 **Kaédi** Maur.
249 K3 **Kaegudeck Lake** *Nfld and Lab.* Can.
229 I4 **Kaélé** Cameroon
264 □E13 **Ka'eleku** *HI* U.S.A.
264 □C12 **Ka'ena Point** *HI* U.S.A.
119 D8 **Kaeng Krachan National Park** Thai.
102 H2 **Kaeo** *North I.* N.Z.
190 I1 **Kær** Denmark
123 E10 **Kaesŏng** N. Korea
148 H8 **Kāf** Saudi Arabia
Kafa Ukr. *see* **Feodosiya**
231 D7 **Kafakumba** Dem. Rep. Congo
Kafan Armenia *see* **Kapan**
229 H4 **Kafanchan** Nigeria
Kāfar Qal'eh Iran *see* **Eslām Qal'eh**
243 P1 **Kaffeklubben Ø** *i.* Greenland
237 K5 **Kafferrivier** S. Africa
229 H3 **Kaffin-Hausa** Nigeria
237 J5 **Kaffir** *r.* S. Africa
228 B3 **Kaffrine** Senegal
230 E2 **Kafia Kingi** Sudan
115 F4 **Kafiau** *i. Papua* Indon.
220 F5 **Kafireos, Steno** *sea chan.* Greece
145 N4 **Kafiristan** *reg.* Pak.
Kafirnigan Tajik. *see* **Kofarnihon**
228 D4 **Kafolo** Côte d'Ivoire
225 F2 **Kafr ash Shaykh** Egypt
148 E8 **Kafr ash Shaykh** *governorate* Egypt
150 E3 **Kafr Buhum** Syria
224 E2 **Kafret Rihama** Egypt
150 E4 **Kafrūn Bashūr** Syria
232 B4 **Kafu** *r.* Uganda
231 F8 **Kafue** Zambia
231 F8 **Kafue** *r.* Zambia
231 E8 **Kafue Flats** *marsh* Zambia
231 E8 **Kafue National Park** Zambia
126 D3 **Kaga** Japan
142 G1 **Kaga** Rus. Fed.
230 C3 **Kaga Bandoro** C.A.R.
245 □C6 **Kagalaska Island** *AK* U.S.A.
159 S6 **Kagal'nik** Rus. Fed.
159 S6 **Kagal'nik** *r.* Rus. Fed.
157 H7 **Kagal'nitskaya** Rus. Fed.
127 L1 **Kagamiishi** Japan
145 O4 **Kagan** Pak.
Kagan Uzbek. *see* **Kogon**
128 G9 **Kagang** *Qinghai* China
Kaganovich Rus. Fed. *see* **Tovarkovskiy**
Kaganovichabad Tajik. *see* **Kolkhozobod**
Kaganovichi Pervyye Ukr. *see* **Polis'ke**
Kagarlyk Ukr. *see* **Kaharlyk**
125 L12 **Kagawa** *pref.* Japan
251 L4 **Kagawong** *Ont.* Can.
162 P4 **Kåge** Sweden
233 A5 **Kagera** *admin. reg.* Tanz.
Kagera, Parc National de la *nat. park* Rwanda *see* **Akagera, Parc National de l'**
237 L2 **Kagiso** S. Africa
149 K3 **Kağızman** Turkey
245 O1 **Kaglik Lake** *N.W.T.* Can.
225 F6 **Kagmar** Sudan
116 C5 **Kagologolo** Indon.
230 C2 **Kagopal** Chad
127 I5 **Kagosaka-tōge** *pass* Japan
125 H15 **Kagoshima** Japan
124 □H15 **Kagoshima** *pref.* Japan
125 H15 **Kagoshima-wan** *b.* Japan
Kagul Moldova *see* **Cahul**
244 I4 **Kaguyak** *AK* U.S.A.
144 G3 **Kāhak** Iran
144 C3 **Kahak** *Qazvīn* Iran
264 □E13 **Kahakuloa** *HI* U.S.A.
264 □B11 **Kahala Point** *HI* U.S.A.
264 □D12 **Kahalu'u** *HI* U.S.A.
233 B5 **Kahama** Tanz.
145 M7 **Kahan** Pak.
264 □D12 **Kahana** *HI* U.S.A.
158 J4 **Kaharlyk** Ukr.
115 E3 **Kahatola** *i. Maluku* Indon.
234 B4 **Kahawero** *waterhole* Namibia
117 K6 **Kahayan** *r.* Indon.
231 C6 **Kahemba** Dem. Rep. Congo
264 □C12 **Kahe Point** *HI* U.S.A.
103 B12 **Kaherekoau Mountains** *South I.* N.Z.
144 I8 **Kahīrī** Iran
191 G10 **Kahl** *r.* Ger.
193 E9 **Kahla** Ger.
191 H10 **Kahl am Main** Ger.
246 F3 **Kahntah** *B.C.* Can.
Kahnu Iran *see* **Kahnūj**
144 G8 **Kahnūj** *Kermān* Iran
144 H6 **Kahnūj** *Kermān* Iran
228 C5 **Kahnwia** Liberia
102 H2 **Kahoe** *North I.* N.Z.
260 J5 **Kahoka** *MO* U.S.A.
126 E2 **Kahoku-gata** *l.* Japan
264 □E13 **Kaho'olawe** *i. HI* U.S.A.
152 D3 **Kahperusvaarat** *mts* Fin.
145 I8 **Kahrād** Iran
148 H5 **Kahramanmaraş** Turkey
145 N7 **Kahror Pakka** Pak.
148 I5 **Kâhta** Turkey
264 □F13 **Kahuā** *HI* U.S.A.
144 G4 **Kahugish** *well* Iran
102 □ **Kahuitara Point** *Chatham Is* S. Pacific Ocean
264 □D12 **Kahuku** *HI* U.S.A.
264 □C12 **Kahuku Point** *HI* U.S.A.
158 H8 **Kahul, Ozero** *l.* Ukr.
Kahulaui *i. HI* U.S.A. *see* **Kaho'olawe**
264 □E13 **Kahului** *HI* U.S.A.
144 H7 **Kahūrak** Iran
103 G8 **Kahurangi National Park** *South I.* N.Z.
102 G7 **Kahurangi Point** *South I.* N.Z.
145 O5 **Kahuta** Pak.
230 E5 **Kahuzi-Biega, Parc National du** *nat. park* Dem. Rep. Congo
113 H8 **Kai, Kepulauan** *is* Indon.
232 A3 **Kaia** *r.* Sudan
102 H2 **Kaiaka** *North I.* N.Z.
229 F4 **Kaiama** Nigeria
113 K8 **Kaiapit** P.N.G.
103 G10 **Kaiapoi** *South I.* N.Z.
265 T5 **Kaibab** *AZ* U.S.A.
265 T5 **Kaibab Plateau** *AZ* U.S.A.
128 E7 **Kaibamardang** *Qinghai* China
126 B5 **Kaibara** Japan
113 H8 **Kai Besar** *i.* Indon.
265 U5 **Kaibito Plateau** *AZ* U.S.A.
100 □6 **Kaichui, Mount** *Guadalcanal* Solomon Is
126 G4 **Kaida** Japan
132 H6 **Kaidu He** *r.* China
275 G3 **Kaieteur Falls** Guyana
275 G3 **Kaieteur National Park** *Potaro-Siparuni* Guyana
Kaifeng *Henan* China *see* **Huanglongsi**
102 H2 **Kaihu** *North I.* N.Z.
Kaihua *Yunnan* China *see* **Wenshan**
131 L4 **Kaihua** *Zhejiang* China
236 F5 **Kaiingveld** *reg.* S. Africa
130 F3 **Kaijiang** *Sichuan* China
113 H8 **Kai Kecil** *i.* Indon.
131 □J7 **Kai Keung Leng** *H.K.* China
102 H2 **Kaikohe** *North I.* N.Z.
103 H9 **Kaikoura** *South I.* N.Z.
103 H9 **Kaikoura Peninsula** *South I.* N.Z.
228 C4 **Kailahun** Sierra Leone
138 H5 **Kailali** Nepal
Kailas *mt. Xizang* China *see* **Kangrinboqê Feng**
139 N7 **Kailashahar** *Tripura* India
Kailas Range *mts Xizang* China *see* **Gangdisê Shan**
130 F5 **Kaili** *Guizhou* China
232 B3 **Kailongong** *waterhole* Kenya
129 Q5 **Kailu** *Nei Mongol* China
264 □D12 **Kailua** *HI* U.S.A.
264 □F14 **Kailua-Kona** *HI* U.S.A.
102 J4 **Kaimai** *North I.* N.Z.
102 J4 **Kaimai-Mamaku Forest Park** *nature res. North I.* N.Z.
102 J4 **Kaimai Range** *hills North I.* N.Z.
113 H7 **Kaimana** *Papua* Indon.
102 K5 **Kaimanawa Forest Park** *nature res. North I.* N.Z.
102 J6 **Kaimanawa Mountains** *North I.* N.Z.
130 A2 **Kaimar** *Qinghai* China
103 F9 **Kaimata** *South I.* N.Z.
138 G6 **Kaimganj** *Uttar Prad.* India
125 H15 **Kaimon-dake** *hill* Japan
138 H7 **Kaimur Range** *hills* India
160 F3 **Käina** Estonia
125 L13 **Kainan** *Tokushima* Japan
126 B7 **Kainan** *Wakayama* Japan
Kainda Kyrg. *see* **Kayyngdy**
118 B4 **Kaing** Myanmar
102 K5 **Kaingaroa Forest** *North I.* N.Z.
102 □ **Kaingaroa Harbour** *b. Chatham Is* S. Pacific Ocean
229 F3 **Kaingiwa** Nigeria
229 G4 **Kainji Lake National Park** Nigeria
229 G4 **Kainji Lake National Park** Nigeria
229 G4 **Kainji Reservoir** Nigeria
139 J9 **Kaintaragarh** *Orissa* India
162 Q3 **Kainulasjärvi** Sweden
102 I3 **Kaipara Flats** *North I.* N.Z.
102 I3 **Kaipara Harbour** *North I.* N.Z.
265 U4 **Kaiparowits Plateau** *UT* U.S.A.
131 I7 **Kaiping** *Guangdong* China
Kaiping *Yunnan* China *see* **Dêqên**
131 I7 **Kaiping Diaolou and Villages** *tourist site* China
249 J2 **Kaipokok Bay** *Nfld and Lab.* Can.
Kaira *Gujarat* India *see* **Kheda**
102 K6 **Kairakau Beach** *North I.* N.Z.
162 S3 **Kairala** Fin.
138 F5 **Kairana** *Uttar Prad.* India
115 F5 **Kairatu** *Seram* Indon.
227 H2 **Kairouan** Tunisia
162 O2 **Kaisepakte** Sweden
200 F4 **Kaisergebirge** *mts* Austria
200 F4 **Kaisergebirge** *nature res.* Austria
194 D3 **Kaiserslautern** Ger.
287 F2 **Kaiser Wilhelm II Land** *reg.* Antarctica
122 F7 **Kaishantun** *Jilin* China
195 J4 **Kaisheim** Ger.
160 H7 **Kaišiadorys** Lith.
116 G6 **Kait, Tanjung** *pt* Indon.
125 J12 **Kaita** Japan
102 H2 **Kaitaia** *North I.* N.Z.
103 D13 **Kaitangata** *South I.* N.Z.
102 L5 **Kaitawa** *North I.* N.Z.
138 F8 **Kaitha** *Madh. Prad.* India
138 F5 **Kaithal** *Haryana* India
Kaitong *Jilin* China *see* **Tongyu**
162 P3 **Kaitum** Sweden
162 P3 **Kaitumälven** *r.* Sweden
115 E8 **Kaiwatu** *Maluku* Indon.
264 □D13 **Kaiwi Channel** *HI* U.S.A.
130 G3 **Kaixian** *Chongqing* China
130 F5 **Kaiyang** *Guizhou* China
129 S5 **Kaiyuan** *Liaoning* China
130 D7 **Kaiyuan** *Yunnan* China
244 H3 **Kaiyuh Mountains** *AK* U.S.A.
Kaiyun *Hunan* China *see* **Hengshan**
126 E5 **Kaizu** Japan
126 B7 **Kaizuka** Japan
162 S4 **Kajaani** Fin.
106 H6 **Kajabbi** *Qld* Austr.
145 K5 **Kajaki** Afgh.
116 D3 **Kajang** Malaysia
145 N7 **Kajanpur** Pak.
107 L9 **Kajarabie, Lake** *resr Qld* Austr.
151 H6 **K'ajaran** Armenia
199 H5 **Kajdacs** Hungary
145 I8 **Kajdar** Iran
233 C5 **Kajiado** Kenya
127 H4 **Kajikazawa** Japan
125 H15 **Kajiki** Japan
230 E2 **Kajok** Sudan
232 A4 **Kajo Kaji** Sudan
198 D3 **Kájov** Czech Rep.
145 K5 **Kajrān** Afgh.
144 B3 **Kaju** Iran
105 J5 **Kajuligah Nature Reserve** *N.S.W.* Austr.
229 G4 **Kajuru** Nigeria
143 Q6 **Kajy-Say** Kyrg.
143 L1 **Kak, Ozero** *salt l.* Kazakh.
232 B2 **Kaka** Sudan
144 H3 **Kaka** Turkm.
117 M3 **Kakaban** *i.* Indon.
248 B3 **Kakabeka Falls** *Ont.* Can.
151 G4 **Kakabet'i** Georgia
115 C7 **Kakabia** *i.* Indon.
106 D2 **Kakadu Aboriginal Land** *res. N.T.* Austr.
106 D2 **Kakadu National Park** *N.T.* Austr.
247 M5 **Kakagi Lake** *Ont.* Can.
114 E8 **Kakal** *r. Mindanao* Phil.
115 A4 **Kakali** *Sulawesi Barat* Indon.
236 E4 **Kakamas** S. Africa
232 B4 **Kakamega** Kenya
126 E5 **Kakamigahara** Japan
231 A6 **Kakamoéka** Congo
137 M8 **Kakana** *Andaman & Nicobar Is* India
210 G3 **Kakanj** Bos.-Herz.
103 E12 **Kakanui Mountains** *South I.* N.Z.
145 L8 **Kakar** Pak.
229 H3 **Kakarahil** *well* Niger
102 I6 **Kakaramea** *North I.* N.Z.
102 J5 **Kakaramea** *vol. North I.* N.Z.
199 H5 **Kakasd** Hungary
228 C5 **Kakata** Liberia
102 J6 **Kakatahi** *North I.* N.Z.
139 O7 **Kakching** *Manipur* India
125 J12 **Kake** Japan
245 N4 **Kake** *AK* U.S.A.
127 H6 **Kakegawa** Japan
231 D6 **Kakenge** Dem. Rep. Congo
190 I4 **Kakenstorf** Ger.
192 D5 **Kakerbeck** Ger.
124 □G18 **Kakeroma-jima** *i. Nansei-shotō* Japan
233 B5 **Kakesio** Tanz.
151 C3 **Kakhat'i** Georgia
151 G3 **Kakhet'is K'edi** *hills* Georgia
Kakhi Azer. *see* **Qax**
151 H3 **Kakhib** Rus. Fed.
144 H4 **Kākhk** Iran
244 I4 **Kakhonak** *AK* U.S.A.
159 M7 **Kakhovka** Ukr.
159 M7 **Kakhovs'ke Vodoskhovyshche** *resr* Ukr.
Kakhul Moldova *see* **Cahul**
144 D7 **Kākī** Iran
136 H4 **Kakinada** *Andhra Prad.* India
218 H8 **Kakinjës, Maja e** *mt.* Albania
246 G2 **Kakisa** *N.W.T.* Can.
246 G2 **Kakisa** *r. N.W.T.* Can.
246 G2 **Kakisa Lake** *N.W.T.* Can.
160 E5 **Kākišķe** Latvia
127 H1 **Kakizaki** Japan
231 C6 **Kakobola** Dem. Rep. Congo
126 A6 **Kakogawa** Japan
126 A6 **Kako-gawa** *r.* Japan
197 K4 **Kąkolewnica Wschodnia** Pol.
196 E4 **Kąkolewo** Pol.
233 A5 **Kakonko** Tanz.
128 B4 **Kakpak Kuduk** *well Xinjiang* China
228 E4 **Kakpin** Côte d'Ivoire
138 G6 **Kakrala** *Uttar Prad.* India
228 B4 **Kakrima** *r.* Guinea
141 L1 **Kakshaal-Too** *mts* China/Kyrg.
245 L1 **Kaktovik** *AK* U.S.A.
199 I4 **Kakucs** Hungary
124 R9 **Kakuda** Japan
232 B4 **Kakuma** Kenya
228 E5 **Kakum National Park** *nat. park* Ghana
144 D6 **Kakun** Iran
117 J3 **Kakus** *r.* Malaysia
246 G4 **Kakwa** *r. Alta* Can.
246 F4 **Kakwa Provincial Park** *B.C.* Can.
246 G4 **Kakwa Wildland Provincial Park** *Alta* Can.
210 E3 **Kal** *hill* Croatia
199 J4 **Kál** Hungary
229 I3 **Kala** Nigeria
145 N6 **Kala** Pak.
233 A7 **Kala** Tanz.
227 H2 **Kalaâ Kebira** Tunisia
Kalaallit Nunaat *terr.* N. America *see* **Greenland**
145 N5 **Kalabagh** Pak.
115 D8 **Kalabahi** Indon.
Kalabak *mt.* Bulg./Greece *see* **Radomir**
Kalabáka Greece *see* **Kalampaka**
117 L2 **Kalabakan** *Sabah* Malaysia
Kalabákion Greece *see* **Kalampaki**
232 E2 **Kalabaydh** *Togdheer* Somalia
232 D2 **Kalabaydh** *Woqooyi Galbeed* Somalia
136 F4 **Kalabgur** *Andhra Prad.* India
104 H4 **Kalabity** *S.A.* Austr.
231 D8 **Kalabo** Zambia
157 H6 **Kalach** Rus. Fed.
145 L4 **Kalacha** Afgh.
232 C4 **Kalacha Dida** Kenya
157 H6 **Kalach-na-Donu** Rus. Fed.
118 A4 **Kaladan** *r.* India/Myanmar
248 E4 **Kaladar** *Ont.* Can.
136 D4 **Kaladgi** *Karnataka* India
115 B5 **Kalaena** *r.* Indon.
118 C3 **Kalagwe** Myanmar
234 D4 **Kalahari Desert** Africa
236 E1 **Kalahari Gemsbok National Park** S. Africa
264 □B12 **Kalaheo** *HI* U.S.A.
Kalaikhum Tajik. *see* **Qal'aikhum**
Kalai-Khumb Tajik. *see* **Qal'aikhum**
139 J6 **Kalaiya** Nepal
162 Q4 **Kalajoki** Fin.
162 Q4 **Kalajoki** *r.* Fin.
162 S1 **Kalak** Norway
219 O7 **Kalakoch** *hill* Bulg.
229 F4 **Kalalé** Benin
115 B4 **Kalaliok** *Sulawesi* Indon.
115 D1 **Kalalusu** *i.* Indon.
138 G9 **Kalam** *Mahar.* India
145 O4 **Kalam** Pak.
Kalámai Greece *see* **Kalamata**
220 D3 **Kalamaki** Greece
234 E4 **Kalamare** Botswana
220 D2 **Kalamaria** Greece
220 B3 **Kalamas** *r.* Greece
220 D5 **Kalamata** Greece
250 I7 **Kalamazoo** *MI* U.S.A.
250 H7 **Kalamazoo** *r. MI* U.S.A.
117 K7 **Kalambau** *i.* Indon.
136 E3 **Kalamnuri** *Mahar.* India
220 B4 **Kalamos** *i.* Greece
221 G6 **Kalamos, Akrotirio** *pt* Greece
220 C3 **Kalampaka** Greece
220 F1 **Kalampaki** Greece
159 M8 **Kalamyts'ka Zatoka** *b.* Ukr.
160 F3 **Kalana** Estonia
228 C4 **Kalana** Mali
133 C12 **Kalanaur** *Haryana* India
138 E4 **Kalanaur** *Punjab* India
159 M7 **Kalanchak** Ukr.
145 J7 **Kalandi** Pak.
Kalandula Angola *see* **Calandula**
232 B5 **Kalangala** Uganda
233 B6 **Kalangali** Tanz.
129 O1 **Kalanguy** Rus. Fed.
109 D11 **Kalannie** *W.A.* Austr.
224 D2 **Kalanshiyū ar Ramlī al Kabīr, Sarīr** *des.* Libya
138 E5 **Kalanwali** *Haryana* India
144 H8 **Kālān Zīād** Iran
115 B7 **Kalao** *i.* Indon.
264 □F14 **Kalaoa** *HI* U.S.A.
114 E8 **Kalaong** *Mindanao* Phil.
115 B7 **Kalaotoa** *i.* Indon.
136 F8 **Kala Oya** *r.* Sri Lanka
116 F5 **Kalapa** Indon.
264 □G14 **Kalapana (abandoned)** *HI* U.S.A.
144 I9 **Kalar** *watercourse* Iran
149 L6 **Kalār** Iraq
144 D6 **Kalār, Kūh-e** *mt.* Iran
Kalarash Moldova *see* **Călărași**
161 S4 **Kalashnikovo** Rus. Fed.
118 F6 **Kalasin** Thai.
145 L5 **Kalāt** Afgh.
Kalāt *Khorāsān* Iran *see* **Kabūd Gonbad**
144 H9 **Kalāt** *Sīstān va Balūchestān* Iran
145 K9 **Kalat** *Balochistan* Pak.
145 L7 **Kalat** *Balochistan* Pak.
144 H4 **Kalāt, Kūh-e** *mt.* Iran
145 I5 **Kalata Barangak** Afgh.
144 F3 **Kalāteh-ye Molla** Iran
264 □E12 **Kalaupapa** *HI* U.S.A.
157 I7 **Kalaus** *r.* Rus. Fed.
138 C8 **Kalavad** *Gujarat* India
220 D4 **Kalavryta** Greece
196 D3 **Kaława** Pol.
147 I8 **Kalb, Ra's al** *c.* Yemen
147 M3 **Kalbā** U.A.E.
151 H5 **Kälbäcär** Azer.
109 C9 **Kalbarri** *W.A.* Austr.
109 C9 **Kalbarri National Park** *W.A.* Austr.
236 C9 **Kalbaskraal** S. Africa
192 D5 **Kalbe (Milde)** Ger.
143 T3 **Kalbinskiy Khrebet** *mts* Kazakh.
144 H4 **Kalbū** Iran
201 J8 **Kalce** Slovenia
195 K2 **Kalchreuth** Ger.
159 Q6 **Kal'chyk** Ukr.
159 Q6 **Kal'chyk** *r.* Ukr.
198 G4 **Káld** Hungary
150 D2 **Kaldırım** Turkey
142 E3 **Kaldygayty** *r.* Kazakh.
221 K6 **Kale** *Antalya* Turkey
221 J5 **Kale** *Denizli* Turkey
151 A5 **Kale** *Gümüşhane* Turkey
151 A4 **Kale** *r.* Turkey
148 F3 **Kalecik** Turkey
115 C6 **Kaledupa** *i.* Indon.
191 J7 **Kalefeld** Ger.
118 C7 **Kalegauk Island** Myanmar
144 C3 **Kaleh Sarai** Iran
118 B5 **Kaleindaung** *inlet* Myanmar
232 B4 **Kalekol** Kenya
231 E6 **Kalema** Dem. Rep. Congo
231 F6 **Kalemie** Dem. Rep. Congo
118 B3 **Kalemyo** Myanmar
144 F4 **Kāl-e Namak** Iran
220 B3 **Kalentzi** Greece
144 G3 **Kāl-e Shūr** *r.* Iran
210 G3 **Kalesija** Bos.-Herz.
196 G5 **Kalety** Pol.
162 U4 **Kalevala** Rus. Fed.
118 B3 **Kalewa** Myanmar
168 L11 **Kale Water** *r. Scotland* U.K.
144 B2 **Kaleybar** Iran
129 P1 **Kalga** Rus. Fed.
109 D13 **Kalgan** *r. W.A.* Austr.
Kalgan *Hebei* China *see* **Zhangjiakou**
136 D5 **Kalghatgi** *Karnataka* India
109 F11 **Kalgoorlie** *W.A.* Austr.
229 H3 **Kalguéri** Niger
144 H6 **Kāl Gūsheh** Iran
210 E3 **Kali** Croatia
138 H5 **Kali** *r.* India/Nepal
219 Q7 **Kaliakra, Nos** *pt* Bulg.
116 F7 **Kalianda** *Sumatera* Indon.
114 D6 **Kalibo** *Panay* Phil.
256 A8 **Kalida** *OH* U.S.A.
116 C6 **Kaliet** Indon.
145 M3 **Kalifgan** Afgh.
139 J6 **Kali Gandaki** *r.* Nepal
136 F5 **Kaligiri** *Andhra Prad.* India
Kalikata *W. Bengal* India *see* **Kolkata**
161 W9 **Kalikino** Rus. Fed.
230 E5 **Kalima** Dem. Rep. Congo
117 I6 **Kalimantan** *reg.* Indon.
117 I4 **Kalimantan Barat** *prov.* Indon.
117 K6 **Kalimantan Selatan** *prov.* Indon.
117 J5 **Kalimantan Tengah** *prov.* Indon.
117 L3 **Kalimantan Timur** *prov.* Indon.
199 G5 **Kali-medence** *park* Hungary
Kálimnos *i.* Greece *see* **Kalymnos**
139 L6 **Kalimpang** *W. Bengal* India
136 D5 **Kalinadi** *r.* India
138 H6 **Kali Nadi** *r.* India
233 B7 **Kalinda** Zambia
137 I3 **Kalingapatnam** *Andhra Prad.* India
Kalinin Kyrg. *see* **Tash-Bashat**
Kalinin Rus. Fed. *see* **Tver'**
Kalinin Turkm. *see* **Boldumsaz**
Kalininabad Tajik. *see* **Kalininobod**
Kalinin Adyndaky Tajik. *see* **Cheshtebe**
159 M8 **Kalinine** Ukr.
160 D7 **Kaliningrad** Rus. Fed.
Kaliningrad Oblast *admin. div.* Rus. Fed. *see* **Kaliningradskaya Oblast'**
160 E7 **Kaliningradskaya Oblast'** *admin. div.* Rus. Fed.
160 C7 **Kaliningradskiy Zaliv** *b.* Rus. Fed.
151 G4 **Kalininkänd** Azer.
Kalinino Armenia *see* **Tashir**
197 K1 **Kalinino** *Kaliningradskaya Oblast'* Rus. Fed.
156 H4 **Kalinino** *Kostromskaya Oblast'* Rus. Fed.
159 S8 **Kalinino** *Krasnodarskiy Kray* Rus. Fed.
143 O1 **Kalinino** *Omskaya Oblast'* Rus. Fed.
156 L4 **Kalinino** *Permskaya Oblast'* Rus. Fed.
145 M3 **Kalininobod** Tajik.
Kalininsk Moldova *see* **Cupcina**
157 I6 **Kalininsk** Rus. Fed.
157 G7 **Kalininskaya** Rus. Fed.
Kalininskaya Oblast' *admin. div.* Rus. Fed. *see* **Tverskaya Oblast'**
159 L6 **Kalinins'ke** Ukr.
138 E8 **Kalinjara** *Rajasthan* India
158 I1 **Kalinkavichy** Belarus
Kalinkovichi Belarus *see* **Kalinkavichy**
151 J6 **Kalinovka** Azer.
142 F3 **Kalinovka** Kazakh.
159 N2 **Kalinovka** Rus. Fed.
Kalinovka Ukr. *see* **Kalynivka**
151 G2 **Kalinovskaya** Rus. Fed.
151 H2 **Kalinovskiy** Rus. Fed.
196 G4 **Kalinowa** Pol.
197 K2 **Kalinowo** Pol.
232 B4 **Kaliro** Uganda
232 F2 **Kalis** Somalia
117 J9 **Kalisat** *Jawa* Indon.
Kalisch Pol. *see* **Kalisz**
136 E1 **Kali Sindh** *r.* India
196 G2 **Kaliska** Pol.
262 G2 **Kalispell** *MT* U.S.A.
198 D3 **Kaliště** *hill* Czech Rep.
196 G4 **Kalisz** Pol.
196 D2 **Kalisz Pomorski** Pol.
144 G7 **Kalituyeh** Iran
157 H6 **Kalitva** *r.* Rus. Fed.
233 A6 **Kaliua** Tanz.
138 H7 **Kaliujar** *Uttar Prad.* India
162 Q4 **Kalix** Sweden
162 Q4 **Kalixälven** *r.* Sweden
138 F4 **Kalka** *Haryana* India
159 Q6 **Kalka** *r.* Ukr.
201 J4 **Kalkalpen, Nationalpark** Aus
221 K6 **Kalkan** Turkey
151 B5 **Kalkandere** Turkey
191 B7 **Kalkar** Ger.
106 C4 **Kalkarindji** *N.T.* Austr.
250 I5 **Kalkaska** *MI* U.S.A.
234 C4 **Kalkfeld** Namibia
237 J5 **Kalkfonteindam** *dam* S. Afric
237 J5 **Kalkfontein Dam Nature Re** S. Africa
192 D3 **Kalkhorst** Ger.
136 G9 **Kalkudah** Sri Lanka
275 G3 **Kalkuni** Guyana
236 F4 **Kalkwerf** S. Africa
191 C9 **Kall** Ger.
136 F7 **Kallakkurichchi** *Tamil Nadu*
104 F2 **Kallakoopah Creek** *watercou S.A.* Austr.
162 N3 **Kallaktjåkkå** *mt.* Sweden
136 E3 **Kallam** *Mahar.* India
164 J3 **Kållandsö** *i.* Sweden
116 □ **Kallang** Sing.
116 □ **Kallang** *r.* Sing.
160 K3 **Kallaste** Estonia
162 S5 **Kallavesi** *l.* Fin.
162 L5 **Kållberget** Sweden
162 Q4 **Kallfjärden** *b.* Sweden
201 I3 **Kallham** Austria
220 D4 **Kallidromo** *mts* Greece
220 C3 **Kallifoni** Greece
165 L5 **Kallinge** Sweden
218 H9 **Kallmet i Madh** Albania
195 L3 **Kallmünz** Ger.
220 G5 **Kalloni** *Tinos* Greece
221 H3 **Kallonis, Kolpos** *b. Lesvos* Gr
199 K4 **Kállósemjén** Hungary
162 L5 **Kallsjön** *l.* Sweden
136 E4 **Kallur** *Karnataka* India
142 K4 **Kalmakkyrgan** *watercourse* Kazakh.
199 K4 **Kálmánháza** Hungary
143 T1 **Kalmanka** Rus. Fed.
165 M5 **Kalmar** Sweden
165 M4 **Kalmar** *county* Sweden
165 M4 **Kalmarsund** *sea chan.* Swed
194 E3 **Kalmit** *hill* Ger.
159 Q6 **Kal'mius** *r.* Ukr.
187 F6 **Kalmthout** Belgium
187 F6 **Kalmthoutse Heide Natuurreservaat** *nature res.* Belgium
144 G3 **Kalmūkh Qal'eh** Iran
136 G9 **Kalmunai** Sri Lanka
Kalmykia *aut. rep.* Rus. Fed. *see* **Kalmykiya-Khalm'g-Tangch ublika**
157 I7 **Kalmykiya-Khalm'g-Tangch Respublika** *aut. rep.* Rus. Fe
Kalmykovo Kazakh. *see* **Tay**
Kalmytskaya Avtonomnaya Oblast' *aut. rep.* Rus. Fed. *se* **Kalmykiya-Khalm'g-Tangch ublika**
139 I8 **Kalnai** *Chhattisgarh* India
199 H3 **Kalná nad Hronom** Slovak
160 G5 **Kalnciems** Latvia
139 M7 **Kalni** *r.* Bangl.
210 F2 **Kalnik** *mts* Croatia
199 H5 **Kalocsa** Hungary
158 F2 **Kalodnaye** Belarus
264 □D13 **Kalohi Channel** *HI* U.S.A.
150 A3 **Kalokhorio** Cyprus
231 E6 **Kaloko** Dem. Rep. Congo
138 D8 **Kalol** *Gujarat* India
138 D8 **Kalol** *Gujarat* India
115 D2 **Kaloma** *i.* Indon.
231 E9 **Kalomo** Zambia
118 C3 **Kalon** Myanmar
246 E4 **Kalone Peak** *B.C.* Can.
115 E1 **Kalongan** *Sulawesi* Indon.
150 A4 **Kalopanagiotis** Cyprus
100 □6 **Kalourat, Mount** *Malaita* Solomon Is
144 B2 **Kalow** *r.* Iran
199 H5 **Káloz** Hungary
162 U3 **Kalozhnoye, Ozero** *l.* Rus.
138 G4 **Kalpa** *Hima. Prad.* India
220 B3 **Kalpaki** Greece
136 C7 **Kalpeni** *atoll* India
136 E7 **Kalpetta** *Kerala* India
138 G6 **Kalpi** *Uttar Prad.* India
132 D6 **Kalpin** *Xinjiang* China
136 F8 **Kalpitiya** Sri Lanka
Kalquduq Uzbek. *see* **Ko'lq**
149 M6 **Kal Safīd** Iran
200 G5 **Kals am Großglockner** Aus
201 L6 **Kalsdorf bei Graz** Austria
138 F4 **Kalsi** *Uttaranchal* India
244 H2 **Kaltag** *AK* U.S.A.
160 I6 **Kaltanėnai** Lith.
156 K5 **Kaltasy** Rus. Fed.
212 G1 **Kaltbrunn** Switz.
200 E5 **Kaltenbach** Austria
190 I3 **Kaltenkirchen** Ger.
191 J9 **Kaltennordheim** Ger.
191 J9 **Kaltensundheim** Ger.
191 J9 **Kaltenwestheim** Ger.
160 F6 **Kaltinėnai** Lith.
106 B8 **Kaltukatjara** *N.T.* Austr.
229 H4 **Kaltungo** Nigeria
138 D5 **Kalu** *Rajasthan* India
136 C3 **Kalu** *r.* India
264 □E12 **Kalua'aha** *HI* U.S.A.
218 I6 **Kaluđerica** *Beograd* Serbia
161 T7 **Kaluga** Rus. Fed.
Kaluga Oblast *admin. div.* Rus. Fed. *see* **Kaluzhskaya**
159 L6 **Kaluha** Ukr.
117 L7 **Kalukalukuang** *i.* Indon.
115 A5 **Kaluku** *Sulawesi Barat* Ind
117 K3 **Kalulong, Bukit** *mt.* Malay
231 F8 **Kalulushi** Zambia
108 I3 **Kalumburu** *W.A.* Austr.
108 I3 **Kalumburu Aboriginal Re** *W.A.* Austr.
164 H6 **Kalundborg** Denmark
231 E7 **Kalundwe** Dem. Rep. Con
117 L1 **Kalupis Falls** Malaysia
145 N5 **Kalur Kot** Pak.
158 D4 **Kalush** Ukr.
197 J3 **Kałuszyn** Pol.
136 F9 **Kalutara** Sri Lanka
161 S7 **Kaluzhskaya Oblast'** *adm* Rus. Fed.
163 H6 **Kalvåg** Norway
138 E9 **Kalvan** *Mahar.* India
160 G7 **Kalvarija** Lith.
160 I7 **Kalveliai** Lith.
156 C3 **Kälviä** Fin.
163 S6 **Kalvitsa** Fin.
163 R6 **Kalvola** Fin.
197 I2 **Kalwa, Jezioro** *l.* Pol.
136 F4 **Kalwakurti** *Andhra Prad.* I
201 K5 **Kalwang** Austria
197 H6 **Kalwaria Zebrzydowska** P
156 L3 **Kal'ya** Rus. Fed.
136 C3 **Kalyan** *Mahar.* India
136 E5 **Kalyandurg** *Andhra Prad.*
137 H3 **Kalyansingapuram** *Orissa*
161 U4 **Kalyazin** Rus. Fed.
158 E2 **Kalyena** Belarus
221 H6 **Kalymnos** Greece
221 H5 **Kalymnos** *i.* Greece
158 J3 **Kalynivka** *Kyivs'ka Oblast*
159 O8 **Kalynivka** *Respublika Kryn*
158 H4 **Kalynivka** *Vinnyts'ka Obla*

Kalyshki Belarus
Kalyta Ukr.
Kalythies *Rodos* Greece
Kalyvia Greece
Kalzhat Kazakh.
Kama Dem. Rep. Congo
Kama Myanmar
Kama Rus. Fed.
Kama *r.* Rus. Fed.
Kamagaya Japan
Kamaishi Japan
Kama-iwa *i.* Japan
Kamakura Japan
Kamakusa Guyana
Kamakwie Sierra Leone
Kamal Chad
Kamalapuram *Andhra Prad.* India
Kamalia Pak.
Kamalō *HI* U.S.A.
Kamamaung Myanmar
Kaman *Rajasthan* India
Kaman Turkey
Kamanashi-gawa *r.* Japan
Kamanashi-yama *mt.* Japan
Kamanassie *r.* S. Africa
Kamanassieberg *mts* S. Africa
Kamaniskeg Lake *Ont.* Can.
Kamanjab Namibia
Kamaosi *Sta Isabel* Solomon Is
Kamaran Yemen
Kamarān *i.* Yemen
Kamarang Guyana
Kamaran Island Yemen *see* Kamarān
Kamard *reg.* Afgh.
Kamarde Latvia
Kamareddi *Andhra Prad.* India
Kamares *Dytiki Ellas* Greece
Kamares *Sifnos* Greece
Kamaria Falls Guyana
Kämärli Azer.
Kamarlu Armenia *see* Artashat
Kamaryn Belarus
Kamashi Uzbek. *see* Qamashi
Kamasin *Uttar Prad.* India
Kamativi Zimbabwe
Kamba Nigeria
Kambaiti Myanmar
Kamba Kota C.A.R.
Kambalda *W.A.* Austr.
Kambal'nitskiye Koshki, Ostrova *is* Rus. Fed.
Kambam *Tamil Nadu* India
Kambang *Sumatera* Indon.
Kambangan *i.* Indon.
Kamba-Poko Dem. Rep. Congo
Kambara *i.* Fiji *see* Kabara
Kambara Japan *see* Kanbara
Kambardi *Xinjiang* China
Kambarka Rus. Fed.
Kamber Pak.
Kambia Sierra Leone
Kambing, Pulau *i.* East Timor *see* Ataúro, Ilha de
Kambling Island Cocos Is
Kambo-san *mt.* N. Korea *see* Kwanmo-bong
Kambove Dem. Rep. Congo
Kambuno, Bukit *mt.* Indon.
Kamburovo Bulg.
Kambūt Libya
Kamchatka *r.* Rus. Fed.
Kamchatka, Poluostrov *pen.* Rus. Fed.
Kamchatka Basin *sea feature* Bering Sea
Kamchatka Peninsula Rus. Fed. *see* Kamchatka, Poluostrov
Kamchatskiy Proliv *str.* Rus. Fed.
Kamchatskiy Zaliv *b.* Rus. Fed.
Kamchiya *r.* Bulg.
Kamchiyska Planina *hills* Bulg.
Kamden S. Africa
Kamdesh Afgh.
Kameia, Parque Nacional de *nat. park* Angola *see* Cameia, Parque Nacional da
Kamelik *r.* Rus. Fed.
Kamen Bulg.
Kamen Ger.
Kamen', Gory *mts* Rus. Fed.
Kamende Dem. Rep. Congo
Kamenec *mt.* Czech Rep.
Kamenets-Podol'skiy Ukr. *see* Kam"yanets'-Podil's'kyy
Kamenica Macedonia
Kamenica *Knjaževac* Serbia
Kamenica Slovakia
Kamenicë *Kamenicë* Kosovo
Kamenice nad Lipou Czech Rep.
Kamenický Šenov Czech Rep.
Kameničná Slovakia
Kamenín Slovakia
Kamenitsa *mt.* Bulg.
Kamenitsa *r.* Bulg.
Kamenjak *hill* Croatia
Kamenjak, Rt *pt* Croatia
Kamenka Moldova *see* Camenca
Kamenka *Arkhangel'skaya Oblast'* Rus. Fed.
Kamenka *Kaluzhskaya Oblast'* Rus. Fed.
Kamenka *Leningradskaya Oblast'* Rus. Fed.
Kamenka *Penzenskaya Oblast'* Rus. Fed.
Kamenka *Primorskiy Kray* Rus. Fed.
Kamenka *Smolenskaya Oblast'* Rus. Fed.
Kamenka *Voronezhskaya Oblast'* Rus. Fed.
Kamenka Ukr. *see* Kam"yanka
Kamenka-Bugskaya Ukr. *see* Kam"yanka-Buz'ka
Kamenka-Shevchenkovskaya Ukr. *see* Kam"yanka
Kamen'-Kashirskiy Ukr. *see* Kamin'-Kashyrs'kyy
Kamenka-Strumilovskaya Ukr. *see* Kam"yanka-Buz'ka
Kamenki Rus. Fed.
Kamen'-na-Obi Rus. Fed.
Kamenniki Rus. Fed.
Kamennogorsk Rus. Fed.
Kamennomostskiy Rus. Fed.
Kamennoye, Ozero *l.* Rus. Fed.
Kamenný Přívoz Czech Rep.
Kamenný Újezd Czech Rep.
Kameno Bulg.
Kamenolomni Rus. Fed.
Kamenongue Angola *see* Camanongue
Kamen'-Rybolov Rus. Fed.
Kamenskiy Rus. Fed.
Kamenskoye *Koryakskiy Avtonomnyy Okrug* Rus. Fed.
Kamenskoye *Lipetskaya Oblast'* Rus. Fed.
Kamenskoye Ukr. *see* Dniprodzerzhyns'k
Kamensk-Shakhtinskiy Rus. Fed.
Kamensk-Ural'skiy Rus. Fed.
Kamenz Ger.
Kameoka Japan
Kamern Ger.
Kames *Argyll and Bute, Scotland* U.K.
Kameshkovo Rus. Fed.
Kamet *mt. Xizang* China
Kameyama Japan
Kamëz Albania
Kami *Hyōgo* Japan
Kami *Nagano* Japan
Kamiagata Japan
Kamiah *ID* U.S.A.
Kamichi Japan
Kamień *Lubelskie* Pol.
Kamień *Podkarpackie* Pol.
Kamienica Pol.
Kamieniec Pol.
Kamieniec Ząbkowicki Pol.
Kamień Krajeński Pol.
Kamienna *r.* Pol.
196 E5 Kamienna Gora Pol.
196 F5 Kamiennik Pol.
196 C2 Kamień Pomorski Pol.
197 H4 Kamieńsk Pol.
192 K5 Kamień Wielkie Pol.
236 C6 Kamiesberg S. Africa
236 C6 Kamiesberge *mts* S. Africa
236 B6 Kamieskroon S. Africa
127 K4 Kamifukuoka Japan
124 T3 Kamifurano Japan
126 D5 Kami-ishizu Japan
231 D6 Kamiji Dem. Rep. Congo
126 E6 Kami-jima *i.* Japan
124 T3 Kamikawa *Hokkaidō* Japan
127 J3 Kamikawa *Saitama* Japan
127 K2 Kamikawachi Japan
126 C7 Kamikitayama Japan
125 G15 Kami-Koshiki-jima *i.* Japan
127 I4 Kamikuishiki Japan
106 H5 Kamileroi *Qld* Austr.
247 K2 Kamilukuak Lake *Nunavut* Can.
231 E7 Kamina Dem. Rep. Congo
231 E7 Kamina Base Dem. Rep. Congo
126 C5 Kaminaka Japan
247 M2 Kaminak Lake *Nunavut* Can.
158 D2 Kamin'-Kashyrs'kyy Ukr.
126 F4 Kaminoho Japan
127 K3 Kaminokawa Japan
124 R5 Kaminokuni Japan
124 □G18 Kaminone-jima *i. Nansei-shotō* Japan
124 R8 Kaminoyama Japan
161 Y4 Kaminskiy Rus. Fed.
Kaminuriak Lake *Nunavut* Can. *see* Qamanirjuaq Lake
126 F3 Kamioka Japan
197 I3 Kamion *Mazowieckie* Pol.
197 I4 Kamion *Mazowieckie* Pol.
197 K4 Kamionka Pol.
221 I6 Kamiros *Rodos* Greece
244 I4 Kamishak Bay *AK* U.S.A.
126 D3 Kamishihi Japan
124 U3 Kamishihoro Japan
127 M4 Kamisu Japan
126 E3 Kami-taira Japan
126 F3 Kami-takara Japan
125 G12 Kamitsushima Japan
231 F5 Kamituga Dem. Rep. Congo
126 F5 Kami-yahagi Japan
124 □H16 Kamiyaku Japan
127 H3 Kamiyamada Japan
124 U2 Kamiyūbetsu Japan
139 O7 Kamjong *Manipur* India
139 K6 Kamla *r.* India
139 N6 Kamla *r.* India
143 U2 Kamlak Rus. Fed.
246 F5 Kamloops *B.C.* Can.
246 F5 Kamloops Lake *B.C.* Can.
195 I5 Kammel *r.* Ger.
236 I9 Kammiebos S. Africa
195 I5 Kammlach Ger.
Kammuri-jima *i.* Japan *see* Kanmuri-jima
Kammuri-yama *mt.* Japan *see* Kanmuri-yama
210 E2 Kamnik Slovenia
210 E2 Kamniško-Savinjske Alpe *mts* Slovenia
201 I7 Kamno Slovenia
Kamo Armenia *see* Gavarr
126 C6 Kamo *Kyōto* Japan
127 I6 Kamo *Yamanashi* Japan
102 I2 Kamo *North I.* N.Z.
225 H5 Kamob Sanha Sudan
126 A8 Kamoda-misaki *pt* Japan
124 R3 Kamoenai Japan
127 L5 Kamogawa Japan
125 L12 Kamojima Japan
145 P6 Kamoke Pak.
231 E6 Kamola Dem. Rep. Congo
233 A6 Kamonanira Tanz.
201 M3 Kamp *r.* Austria
191 E10 Kamp Ger.
116 F5 Kampa Indon.
232 B4 Kampala Uganda
220 F4 Kampanos, Akrotirio *pt Andros* Greece
116 E4 Kampar *r.* Indon.
116 D2 Kampar Malaysia
139 I8 Kampara *Chhattisgarh* India
160 F4 Kamparkalns *hill* Latvia
116 D4 Kamparkiri *r.* Indon.
190 F1 Kampen Ger.
186 I3 Kampen Neth.
231 E5 Kampene Dem. Rep. Congo
194 F4 Kämpfelbach Ger.
118 D6 Kamphaeng Phet Thai.
233 B6 Kampi Katoto Tanz.
197 I3 Kampinos Pol.
197 I3 Kampinoski Park Narodowy *nat. park* Pol.
136 E5 Kampli *Karnataka* India
191 C8 Kamp-Lintfort Ger.
125 G11 Kamp'o S. Korea
231 F7 Kampolombo, Lake Zambia
119 G9 Kâmpóng Cham Cambodia
119 G8 Kâmpóng Chhnăng Cambodia
119 G8 Kâmpóng Khleăng Cambodia
Kâmpóng Saôm Cambodia *see* Sihanoukville
119 G9 Kâmpóng Spœ Cambodia
119 G8 Kâmpóng Thum Cambodia
119 G9 Kâmpóng Trâbêk Cambodia
119 G9 Kâmpóng Tranch Cambodia
119 G9 Kâmpôt Cambodia
228 E4 Kampti Burkina
Kampuchea *country* Asia *see* Cambodia
113 H7 Kamrau, Teluk *b. Papua* Indon.
247 K5 Kamsack *Sask.* Can.
228 B4 Kamsar Guinea
193 D9 Kamsdorf Ger.
156 K3 Kamskiy Rus. Fed.
157 J5 Kamskoye Ust'ye Rus. Fed.
156 L4 Kamskoye Vodokhranilishche *resr* Rus. Fed.
232 D4 Kamsuuma Somalia
138 H9 Kamtha *Mahar.* India
247 K3 Kamuchawie Lake *Man./Sask.* Can.
124 T4 Kamui-dake *mt.* Japan
232 B4 Kamuli Uganda
231 E6 Kamungu Dem. Rep. Congo
199 J5 Kamut Hungary
232 A4 Kamwenge Uganda
158 G2 Kam"yane *Rivnens'ka Oblast'* Ukr.
159 N3 Kam"yane *Sums'ka Oblast'* Ukr.
158 F5 Kam"yanets'-Podil's'kyy Ukr.
159 L4 Kam"yanka *Cherkas'ka Oblast'* Ukr.
159 Q4 Kam"yanka *Kharkivs'ka Oblast'* Ukr.
159 L5 Kam"yanka *r.* Ukr.
158 D3 Kam"yanka-Buz'ka Ukr.
159 N6 Kam"yanka-Dniprovs'ka Ukr.
158 I8 Kam"yans'ke *Odes'ka Oblast'* Ukr.
159 O6 Kam"yans'ke *Zaporiz'ka Oblast'* Ukr.
160 G9 Kamyanyets Belarus
160 G9 Kamyanyuki Belarus
144 B4 Kāmyārān Iran
160 L6 Kamyen' Belarus
160 H8 Kamyenka Belarus
157 G7 Kamyshevatskaya Rus. Fed.
157 I6 Kamyshin Rus. Fed.
157 K5 Kamyshla Rus. Fed.
142 I4 Kamyshlybash Kazakh.
Kamyshnaya *r.* Rus. Fed./Ukr. *see* Komyshna
142 C3 Kamysh-Samarskiye Ozera *lakes* Kazakh.
Kamyslybas Kazakh. *see* Kamyshlybash
142 I2 Kamysty Kazakh.
142 I4 Kamystybas, Ozero *l.* Kazakh.
142 C4 Kamyzyak Rus. Fed.
147 M2 Kamzar Oman
153 K4 Kan *r.* Rus. Fed.
232 A2 Kan Sudan
230 F4 Kana Dem. Rep. Congo
235 E3 Kana *r.* Zimbabwe
248 E2 Kanaaupscow *r. Que.* Can.
265 T4 Kanab *UT* U.S.A.
265 T5 Kanab Creek *r. AZ* U.S.A.
101 □7 Kanacea *Taveuni* Fiji
127 G5 Kanae Japan
245 □C6 Kanaga Island *AK* U.S.A.
127 J5 Kanagawa *pref.* Japan
124 R6 Kanagi Japan
275 F3 Kanaima Falls Guyana
249 J2 Kanairiktok *r. Nfld and Lab.* Can.
145 L7 Kanak Pak.
244 H4 Kanakanak *AK* U.S.A.
136 E6 Kanakapura *Karnataka* India
201 I7 Kanal Slovenia
220 F5 Kanala *Kythnos* Greece
220 B3 Kanali Greece
220 B3 Kanallaki Greece
149 L7 Kan'ān Iraq
162 M4 Kanan Sweden
237 K2 Kanana S. Africa
231 D6 Kananga Dem. Rep. Congo
105 M5 Kanangra-Boyd National Park *N.S.W.* Austr.
Kanarak *Orissa* India *see* Konarka
265 S4 Kanarraville *UT* U.S.A.
236 B3 Kanas *watercourse* Namibia
127 L2 Kanasagō Japan
156 I5 Kanash Rus. Fed.
132 H2 Kanas Köl *l.* China
244 H4 Kanatak *AK* U.S.A.
Kanathea *Taveuni* Fiji *see* Kanacea
156 K3 Kanava Rus. Fed.
117 K3 Kanawang, Bukit *mt.* Malaysia
256 C10 Kanawha *r. WV* U.S.A.
127 H6 Kanaya *Shizuoka* Japan
126 B7 Kanaya *Wakayama* Japan
126 F4 Kanayama Japan
126 E2 Kanazawa *Ishikawa* Japan
127 K5 Kanazawa *Kanagawa* Japan
126 D3 Kanazu Japan
118 B3 Kanbalu Myanmar
127 I5 Kanbara Japan
119 D8 Kanchanaburi Thai.
Kanchanjanga *mt.* India/Nepal *see* Kangchenjunga
139 L6 Kanchenjunga Conservation Area *nature res.* Nepal
136 F6 Kanchipuram *Tamil Nadu* India
197 K6 Kańczuga Pol.
145 L6 Kand *mt.* Pak.
145 L7 Kanda Pak.
145 K6 Kandahār Afgh.
145 K6 Kandahār *prov.* Afgh.
136 E3 Kandahar *Mahar.* India
162 V3 Kandalaksha Rus. Fed.
156 F2 Kandalakshskiy Zaliv *g.* Rus. Fed.
231 C6 Kandale Dem. Rep. Congo
116 B3 Kandang *Sumatera* Indon.
117 K6 Kandangan *Kalimantan* Indon.
160 F4 Kandava Latvia
Kandavu *i.* Fiji *see* Kadavu
Kandavu Passage Fiji *see* Kadavu Passage
229 F4 Kandé Togo
194 E3 Kandel Ger.
194 E5 Kandel *mt.* Ger.
192 H2 Kandelin Ger.
212 D2 Kander *r.* Switz.
194 D6 Kandern Ger.
212 D3 Kandersteg Switz.
145 M7 Kandh Kot Pak.
145 N4 Kandhura Pak.
229 F4 Kandi Benin
145 L7 Kandi Pak.
115 B3 Kandi, Tanjung *pt* Indon.
145 M8 Kandiaro Pak.
245 L2 Kandik *r.* Can./U.S.A.
220 B4 Kandila *Dytiki Ellas* Greece
220 D5 Kandila *Peloponnisos* Greece
229 H3 Kandil Bouzou *well* Niger
151 E6 Kandil Dağı *mt.* Turkey
151 B6 Kandilli Turkey
221 L1 Kandıra Turkey
230 D3 Kandja C.A.R.
138 C8 Kandla *Gujarat* India
135 □1 Kandooma Fushi *i. S. Male* Maldives
105 L5 Kandos *N.S.W.* Austr.
137 J1 Kandra *Jharkhand* India
235 □J3 Kandreho Madag.
139 I8 Kandri *Chhattisgarh* India
113 K8 Kandrian *New Britain* P.N.G.
136 F5 Kandukur *Andhra Prad.* India
136 G9 Kandy Sri Lanka
142 G3 Kandyagash Kazakh.
256 G7 Kane *PA* U.S.A.
243 L2 Kane Bassin *b.* Greenland
144 E8 Kaneh *watercourse* Iran
244 G4 Kanektok *r. AK* U.S.A.
224 B6 Kanem *pref.* Chad
264 □D12 Kāne'ohe *HI* U.S.A.
264 □D12 Kāne'ohe Bay *HI* U.S.A.
138 E7 Kanera *Rajasthan* India
145 L7 Kaneti Pak.
Kanev Ukr. *see* Kaniv
156 G2 Kanevka Rus. Fed.
157 G7 Kanevskaya Rus. Fed.
126 F5 Kaneyama *Gifu* Japan
125 R8 Kaneyama *Yamagata* Japan
213 P5 Kanfanar Croatia
228 B4 Kanfarande Guinea
145 I6 Kang Afgh.
234 D4 Kang Botswana
139 L9 Kanga *r.* Bangl.
243 M3 Kangaamiut Greenland
243 K2 Kangaarsussuaq *c.* Greenland
243 M3 Kangaatsiaq Greenland
228 C4 Kangaba Mali
148 H4 Kangal Turkey
153 N3 Kangalassy Rus. Fed.
144 E8 Kangān *Būshehr* Iran
144 G9 Kangān *Hormozgan* Iran
108 E6 Kangan Aboriginal Reserve *W.A.* Austr.
Kangandala, Parque Nacional de *nat. park* Angola *see* Cangandala, Parque Nacional de
116 D1 Kangar Malaysia
228 C4 Kangaré Mali
104 F6 Kangaroo Island *S.A.* Austr.
106 G4 Kangaroo Point *Qld* Austr.
275 G3 Kangaruma Guyana
163 R6 Kangasala Fin.
162 T5 Kangaslampi Fin.
163 S6 Kangasniemi Fin.
144 B4 Kangāvar Iran
136 E7 Kangayam *Tamil Nadu* India
129 N6 Kangbao *Hebei* China
139 L6 Kangchenjunga *mt.* India/Nepal
130 C3 Kangding *Sichuan* China
117 K8 Kangean, Kepulauan *is* Indon.
243 L3 Kangeeak Point *Nunavut* Can.
232 B3 Kangen *r.* Sudan
243 N3 Kangeq *c.* Greenland
243 M3 Kangerluarsoruseq Greenland
243 M3 Kangerlussuaq Greenland
243 M2 Kangerlussuaq *inlet* Greenland
243 M3 Kangerlussuaq *inlet* Greenland
243 O3 Kangerlussuaq *inlet* Greenland
243 N3 Kangerlussuatsiaq *inlet* Greenland
243 M2 Kangersuatsiaq Greenland
243 P2 Kangertittivaq *sea chan.* Greenland
243 O3 Kangertittivatsiaq *inlet* Greenland
232 C4 Kangetet Kenya
123 E8 Kanggye N. Korea
243 P2 Kangikajik *c.* Greenland
243 N3 Kangilinnguit Greenland
Kangiqcliniq *Nunavut* Can. *see* Rankin Inlet
249 H1 Kangiqsualujjuaq *Que.* Can.
243 K3 Kangiqsujuaq *Que.* Can.
Kangiqtugaapik *Nunavut* Can. *see* Clyde River
243 K3 Kangirsuk *Que.* Can.
119 D10 Kang Krung National Park Thai.
128 H9 Kangle *Gansu* China
Kangle *Jiangxi* China *see* Wanzai
133 I12 Kangmar *Xizang* China
123 F10 Kangnŭng S. Korea
230 A4 Kango Gabon
125 □3 Kangoku-iwa *i.* Japan
162 Q3 Kangos Sweden
129 R5 Kangping *Liaoning* China
138 F3 Kangra *Hima. Prad.* India
139 P5 Kangri Karpo Pass China/India
133 E11 Kangrinboqê Feng *mt. Xizang* China
133 G10 Kangro *Xizang* China
Kangsangdobdê *Xizang* China *see* Xainza
114 C9 Kang Tipayan Dakula *i.* Phil.
133 K13 Kangto *mt.* China/India
133 G10 Kangtog *Xizang* China
130 E2 Kangxian *Gansu* China
133 D8 Kangxiwar *Xinjiang* China
118 B6 Kangyidaung Myanmar
138 G9 Kanhan *r.* India
139 I7 Kanhar *r. Jharkhand* India
136 E3 Kanhargaon *Mahar.* India
165 O2 Kanholmsfjärden *b.* Sweden
228 D4 Kani Côte d'Ivoire
144 F8 Kānī Iran
126 F5 Kani Japan
118 B3 Kani Myanmar
231 E6 Kaniama Dem. Rep. Congo
231 E6 Kaniama, Réserve des Éléphants de *nature res.* Dem. Rep. Congo
Kanibadam Tajik. *see* Konibodom
117 L1 Kanibongan *Sabah* Malaysia
126 E5 Kanie Japan
103 F9 Kaniere *South I.* N.Z.
103 F9 Kaniere, Lake *South I.* N.Z.
228 A3 Kanifing Gambia
135 □1 Kanifinolhu *i. N. Male* Maldives
136 F5 Kanigiri *Andhra Prad.* India
145 M5 Kaniguram Pak.
239 □3b Kani-Kéli Mayotte
156 I2 Kanin, Poluostrov *pen.* Rus. Fed.
156 H1 Kanin Nos Rus. Fed.
156 H1 Kanin Nos, Mys *c.* Rus. Fed.
156 H2 Kaninskiy Bereg *coastal area* Rus. Fed.
149 L5 Kānī Rash Iraq
200 A5 Kanisfluh *mt.* Austria
124 R5 Kanita Japan
159 K4 Kaniv Ukr.
104 H7 Kaniva *Vic.* Austr.
159 K3 Kanivs'ke Vodoskhovyshche *resr* Ukr.
138 G8 Kaniwara *Madh. Prad.* India
139 I5 Kanjiroba *mt.* Nepal
218 I4 Kanjiža *Vojvodina* Serbia
163 Q6 Kankaanpää Fin.
250 G8 Kankakee *IL* U.S.A.
250 F8 Kankakee *r. IL* U.S.A.
228 C4 Kankan Guinea
228 C4 Kankan, Réserve Naturelle de *nature res.* Guinea
138 H9 Kanker *Chhattisgarh* India
136 G8 Kankesanturai Sri Lanka
229 G3 Kankiya Nigeria
228 C3 Kankossa Maur.
114 D6 Kanlaon, Mount *vol.* Phil.
119 D9 Kanmaw Kyun *i.* Myanmar
126 B4 Kanmuri-jima *i.* Japan
126 D4 Kanmuri-yama *mt.* Japan
125 J12 Kanmuri-yama *mt.* Japan
138 E9 Kannad *Mahar.* India
127 J3 Kanna-gawa *r.* Japan
127 I5 Kannami Japan
255 G8 Kannapolis *NC* U.S.A.
138 G6 Kannauj *Uttar Prad.* India
193 D8 Kannawurf Ger.
136 E8 Kanniyakumari *Tamil Nadu* India
Kanniya Kumari *c.* India *see* Comorin, Cape
138 F8 Kannod *Madh. Prad.* India
162 R5 Kannonkoski Fin.
126 F1 Kannon-zaki *pt* Japan
136 D7 Kannur *Kerala* India
162 Q5 Kannus Fin.
160 K1 Kannuskoski Fin.
115 D5 Kano *i.* Indon.
229 H3 Kano Nigeria
229 H4 Kano *r.* Nigeria
229 H4 Kano *state* Nigeria
127 I5 Kano-gawa *r.* Japan
271 □10 Kanon, Punt *pt Curaçao* Neth. Antilles
233 A8 Kanona Zambia
143 R2 Kanonerka Kazakh.
125 K12 Kan'onji Japan
236 F10 Kanonpunt *pt* S. Africa
138 E7 Kanor *Rajasthan* India
260 D6 Kanorado *KS* U.S.A.
265 T3 Kanosh *UT* U.S.A.
234 C3 Kanovlei Namibia
117 J3 Kanowit *Sarawak* Malaysia
125 H15 Kanoya Japan
205 O2 Kanpantxua Spain
138 H6 Kanpur *Uttar Prad.* India
127 I3 Kanra Japan
145 L8 Kanrach *reg.* Pak.
126 B7 Kansai *airport* Japan
231 E8 Kansanshi Zambia
260 H6 Kansas *r. KS* U.S.A.
260 F6 Kansas *state* U.S.A.
260 H6 Kansas City *KS* U.S.A.
260 H6 Kansas City *MO* U.S.A.
231 E7 Kansenia Dem. Rep. Congo
153 K4 Kansk Rus. Fed.
132 B7 Kansu *Xinjiang* China
Kansu *prov.* China *see* Gansu
232 B3 Kanta *mt.* Eth.
163 S5 Kantala Fin.
119 D11 Kantang Thai.
150 B3 Kantara *hill* Cyprus
119 G7 Kantaralak Thai.
151 C6 Kantarkaya Turkey
151 B5 Kantarlı Turkey
205 O3 Kantauri Mendilerroa *mts* Spain
Kantavu *i.* Fiji *see* Kadavu
229 F3 Kantchari Burkina
157 G6 Kantemirovka Rus. Fed.
186 K2 Kantens Neth.
138 G5 Kanth *Uttar Prad.* India
139 K9 Kanthi *W. Bengal* India
139 J6 Kanti *Bihar* India
139 J9 Kantilo *Orissa* India
245 J3 Kantishna *AK* U.S.A.
245 J2 Kantishna *r. AK* U.S.A.
133 B12 Kantli *r.* India
127 K4 Kantō-heiya *plain* Japan
99 I2 Kanton *atoll Phoenix Is* Kiribati
Kan-Too, Pik *mt.* Kazakh./Kyrg. *see* Khan-Tengri, Pik
127 H4 Kanto-sanchi *mts* Japan
106 D5 Kanttaji Aboriginal Land *res. N.T.* Austr.
118 C5 Kantulong Myanmar
169 E8 Kanturk Ireland
106 E5 Kanturrpa Aboriginal Land *res. N.T.* Austr.
144 F5 Kanūgar Iran
275 G4 Kanuku Mountains Guyana
127 K2 Kanuma Japan
233 A5 Kanungu Uganda
136 E5 Kanur *Andhra Prad.* India
234 C5 Kanus Namibia
244 I2 Kanuti *r. AK* U.S.A.
245 J2 Kanuti National Wildlife Refuge *nature res. AK* U.S.A.
113 J8 Kanuwe *r.* P.N.G.
Kanyakubja *Uttar Prad.* India *see* Kannauj
237 P1 Kanyamazane S. Africa
234 E5 Kanye Botswana
235 F2 Kanyemba Zimbabwe
161 Q6 Kanyutino Rus. Fed.
126 A5 Kanzaki Japan
115 E3 Kao *Halmahera* Indon.
229 G3 Kao Niger
101 □8 Kao *i.* Tonga
115 E3 Kao, Teluk *b. Halmahera* Indon.
131 M7 Kaohsiung Taiwan
119 F9 Kaôh Tang *i.* Cambodia
234 B3 Kaokoveld *plat.* Namibia
228 A3 Kaolack Senegal
100 □6 Kaolo *Sta Isabel* Solomon Is
231 F7 Kaoma *Northern* Zambia
231 E8 Kaoma *Western* Zambia
224 C5 Kaortchi *well* Chad
230 D3 Kaouadja C.A.R.
101 □8 Kapa *i. Vava'u Gp* Tonga
264 □B11 Kapa'a *HI* U.S.A.
264 □F13 Kapa'au *HI* U.S.A.
143 R5 Kapal Kazakh.
115 E4 Kapalabuaya *Maluku* Indon.
218 H8 Kapa Moračka *mt.* Montenegro
151 H6 Kapan Armenia
231 D7 Kapanga Dem. Rep. Congo
231 F6 Kapangolo Dem. Rep. Congo
Kapara Te Hau *l. South I.* N.Z. *see* Grassmere, Lake
220 E4 Kaparelli Greece
144 C6 Kaparhā Iran
158 H1 Kapatkyevichy Belarus
233 A7 Kapatu Zambia
143 Q6 Kapchagay Kazakh.
143 Q6 Kapchagayskoye Vodokhranilishche *resr* Kazakh.
232 B4 Kapchorwa Uganda
160 G8 Kapčiamiestis Lith.
Kap Dan Greenland *see* Kulusuk
186 E6 Kapelle Neth.
187 F6 Kapellen Belgium
220 E6 Kapello, Akrotirio *pt Kythira* Greece
165 P2 Kapellskär Sweden
Kapelskär Sweden *see* Kapellskär
232 B4 Kapenguria Kenya
201 L5 Kapfenberg Austria
201 M6 Kapfenstein Austria
221 I2 Kapıdağı Yarımadası *pen.* Turkey
139 M6 Kapili *r.* India
99 F1 Kapingamarangi *atoll* Micronesia
290 F5 Kapingamarangi Rise *sea feature* N. Pacific Ocean
221 L2 Kapıorman Dağları *mts* Turkey
145 M6 Kapip Pak.
231 F8 Kapiri Mposhi Zambia
145 M4 Kāpīsā *prov.* Afgh.
243 M3 Kapisillit Greenland
248 D2 Kapiskau *r. Ont.* Can.
251 M2 Kapiskong Lake *Ont.* Can.
117 J3 Kapit *Sarawak* Malaysia
159 K5 Kapitanivka Ukr.
103 I7 Kapiti Island *North I.* N.Z.
275 H4 Kapiting Brazil
224 D5 Kapka *well* Chad
224 D6 Kapka, Massif du *mts* Chad
115 E5 Kaplamada, Gunung *mt. Buru* Indon.
144 F1 Kaplankyr, Chink *esc.* Turkm./Uzbek.
144 G1 Kaplankyr Döwlet Gorugy *nature res.* Turkm.
198 D3 Kaplice Czech Rep.
92 E1 Kap Morris Jesup Macedonia
119 D10 Kapoe Thai.
232 B3 Kapoeta Sudan
199 J4 Kápolna Hungary
115 C8 Kapondai, Tanjung *pt Flores* Indon.
102 I6 Kaponga *North I.* N.Z.
233 B7 Kaporo Malawi
218 G4 Kapos *r.* Romania
199 G5 Kaposfő Hungary
199 H5 Kaposszekcső Hungary
199 G5 Kaposvár Hungary
145 J9 Kappar Pak.
194 C2 Kappel Ger.
201 J6 Kappel am Krappfeld Austria
194 D5 Kappel-Grafenhausen Ger.
190 I1 Kappeln Ger.
194 E4 Kappelrodeck Ger.
200 B5 Kappl Austria
138 F7 Kapren *Rajasthan* India
200 G5 Kaprun Austria
232 B4 Kapsabet Kenya
145 J8 Kap Salt Swamp Pak.
123 F8 Kapsan N. Korea
161 Q2 Kapsha *r.* Rus. Fed.
220 D5 Kapsia Greece
Kapsukas Lith. *see* Marijampolė
139 N8 Kaptai Bangl.
129 P2 Kaptsegaytuy Rus. Fed.
158 H1 Kaptsevichy Belarus
197 L2 Kaptsyowka Belarus
117 H5 Kapuas *r.* Indon.
117 K6 Kapuas *r.* Indon.
117 J4 Kapuas Hulu, Pegunungan *mts* Indon./Malaysia
104 G6 Kapunda *S.A.* Austr.
138 D6 Kapuriya *Rajasthan* India
138 E4 Kapurthala *Punjab* India
199 K2 Kapušany Slovakia
248 D3 Kapuskasing *Ont.* Can.
248 D3 Kapuskasing *r. Ont.* Can.
157 I6 Kapustin Yar Rus. Fed.
159 K3 Kapustyntsi *Kyivs'ka Oblast'* Ukr.
159 N3 Kapustyntsi *Sums'ka Oblast'* Ukr.
231 F7 Kaputa Zambia
144 H9 Kapūtānī Iran
105 M4 Kaputar *mt. N.S.W.* Austr.
232 B4 Kaputir Kenya
198 G4 Kapuvár Hungary
Kapydzhik, Gora *mt.* Armenia/Azer. *see* Qazangödağ
160 K8 Kapyl' Belarus
123 E10 Kap'yŏng S. Korea
161 P6 Kapyrevshchina Rus. Fed.
133 L11 Ka Qu *r. Xizang* China
138 H7 Kara *Uttar Prad.* India
156 N1 Kara *r.* Rus. Fed.
229 F4 Kara Togo
149 J4 Kara *r.* Turkey
221 K2 Kara *r.* Turkey
221 H4 Kara Ada *i.* Turkey
221 I6 Kara Ada *i.* Turkey
221 H3 Karaağaç Turkey
148 F4 Karaali Turkey
132 A7 Kara Art Pass *Xinjiang* China
Karaaul Kazakh. *see* Karaul
143 O6 Kara-Balta Kyrg.
142 J1 Karabalyk Kazakh.
161 V5 Karabanovo Rus. Fed.
143 O3 Karabas Kazakh.
142 E3 Karabau Kazakh.
142 F6 Karabaur, Uval *hills* Uzbek.
Karabekaul Turkm. *see* Garabekewül
151 C7 Karabey Turkey
221 I2 Karabiga Turkey
151 B6 Karaboğa Dağları *mts* Turkey
Kara-Bogaz-Gol Turkm. *see* Garabogazköl
Karaboynak Turkm. *see* Ataýap
151 I3 Karabudakhkent Rus. Fed.
148 F3 Karabük Turkey
143 R5 Karabulak *Almatinskaya Oblast'* Kazakh.
143 U4 Karabulak *Vostochnyy Kazakhstan* Kazakh.
151 F2 Karabulak Rus. Fed.
143 P3 Karabulakskaya (abandoned) Kazakh.
Karabura *Xinjiang* China *see* Yumin
221 J4 Karaburç Turkey
221 H4 Karaburun Turkey
142 I3 Karabutak Kazakh.
221 J2 Karacabey Turkey
148 F5 Karacadağ *mts* Turkey
221 I1 Karacakılavuz Turkey
148 D3 Karacaköy Turkey
149 I5 Karacalı Dağ *mt.* Turkey
150 A2 Karaçal Tepe *mt.* Turkey
221 L5 Karacaören Barajı *resr* Turkey
221 J5 Karacasu Turkey
221 L6 Karaca Yarımadası *pen.* Turkey
Karachay-Cherkess Republic *aut. rep.* Rus. Fed. *see* Karachayevo-Cherkesskaya Respublika
Karachayevo-Cherkesskaya A.S.S.R. *aut. rep.* Rus. Fed. *see* Karachayevo-Cherkesskaya Respublika
151 C2 Karachayevo-Cherkesskaya Respublika *aut. rep.* Rus. Fed.
151 C2 Karachayevsk Rus. Fed.
161 R8 Karachev Rus. Fed.
145 L9 Karachi Pak.
159 M6 Karachunivs'ke Vodoskhovyshche *resr* Ukr.
149 K4 Karaçoban Turkey
221 K6 Karaçulha Turkey
Karacurun Turkey *see* Hilvan
199 G5 Karád Hungary
136 D4 Karad *Mahar.* India
150 G2 Kara Dağ *hill* Turkey
221 H2 Kara Dağ *hill* Turkey
221 J2 Kara Dağ *hills* Turkey
148 F5 Kara Dağ *mt.* Turkey
143 O7 Kara-Darya *r.* Kyrg.
Kara-Dar'ya Uzbek. *see* Payshanba
Kara Deniz *sea* Asia/Europe *see* Black Sea
228 E4 Karaga Ghana
122 B2 Karagan Rus. Fed.
143 O3 Karaganda Kazakh.
143 O3 Karagandinskaya Oblast' *admin. div.* Kazakh.
151 G1 Karagas Rus. Fed.
143 Q5 Karagash Kazakh.
142 D2 Karagay Kazakh.
156 K4 Karagay Rus. Fed.
143 P3 Karagayly Kazakh.
143 U3 Karagaylybulak Kazakh.
144 F2 Karagez Turkm.
153 R4 Karaginskiy, Ostrov *i.* Rus. Fed.
142 D6 Karagiye, Vpadina *depr.* Kazakh.
139 K7 Karagola *Bihar* India
151 B6 Karagöl Dağları *mts* Turkey
143 T2 Karaguzhikha Kazakh.
233 A5 Karagwe Tanz.
219 P9 Karahalil Turkey
221 K4 Karahallı Turkey
148 G4 Karahasanlı Turkey
221 J5 Karahisar Turkey
156 L5 Karaidel' Rus. Fed.
136 F7 Karaikal *Puducherry* India
136 F7 Karaikkudi *Tamil Nadu* India
148 G5 Karaisalı Turkey
117 L4 Karaitan *Kalimantan* Indon.
144 D4 Karaj Iran
Karak Jordan *see* Al Karak
Kara-Kala Turkm. *see* Magtymguly
Karakalli Turkey *see* Özalp
Karakalpakistan, Respublika *aut. rep.* Uzbek. *see* Qoraqalpog'iston Respublikasi
Karakalpakskaya Respublika *aut. rep.* Uzbek. *see* Qoraqalpog'iston Respublikasi
Karakalpakstan *aut. rep.* Uzbek. *see* Qoraqalpog'iston Respublikasi
151 C5 Karakamış Turkey
Karakax *Xinjiang* China *see* Moyu
133 E7 Karakax He *r.* China
133 E9 Karakax Shan *mts Xinjiang* China
151 C5 Karakaya Turkey
151 D6 Karakaya *r.* Turkey
151 C6 Karakaya Tepe *mt.* Turkey
148 I5 Karakeçi Turkey
148 F4 Karakeçili Turkey
115 E1 Karakelong *i.* Indon.
133 E8 Karaki *Xinjiang* China
115 D2 Karakitang *i.* Indon.
Karaklis Armenia *see* Vanadzor
149 J4 Karakoçan Turkey
143 N1 Karakoga Kazakh.
Karakoin *salt l.* Kazakh. *see* Karakoyyn, Ozero
142 E3 Karakol' Kazakh.
143 O7 Kara-Köl Kyrg.
143 Q7 Karakol *Ysyk-Köl* Kyrg.
143 R6 Karakol *Ysyk-Köl* Kyrg.
Karakolka Kyrg. *see* Karakol
Karaköprü Turkey *see* Karaçoban
138 F2 Karakoram Pass China/India
145 P3 Karakoram Range *mts* Asia
232 C2 Kara K'orē Eth.
228 B3 Karakoro *r.* Mali/Maur.
Karaköse *Ağrı* Turkey *see* Ağrı
150 D2 Karaköse *Hatay* Turkey
221 H3 Karaköy Turkey
151 I3 Karakoysu *r.* Rus. Fed.
151 F6 Karakoyunlu Turkey
143 M4 Karakoyyn, Ozero *salt l.* Kazakh.
Karakubbud Ukr. *see* Komsomol's'ke
Kara-Kuga Kazakh. *see* Karakoga
Kara Kul' Kyrg. *see* Kara-Köl
Karakul', Ozero *l.* Tajik. *see* Qarokŭl
Kara-Kul'dzha Kyrg. *see* Kara-Kulja
156 K4 Karakulino Rus. Fed.
143 O7 Kara-Kulja Kyrg.
142 J1 Karakul'skoye Rus. Fed.
143 R4 Karakum Kazakh.
142 E5 Karakum, Peski *des.* Kazakh.
Karakum Desert Kazakh. *see* Karakum, Peski
Karakum Desert Turkm. *see* Garagum
149 K3 Karakurt *Kars* Turkey
221 I3 Karakurt *Manisa* Turkey
221 L4 Karakuş Dağı *ridge* Turkey
234 C3 Karakuwisa Namibia
230 B1 Karal Chad
160 E3 Karala Estonia
109 E8 Karalundi *W.A.* Austr.
115 A5 Karama *r.* Indon.
Karamagay *Xinjiang* China *see* Haramgai
221 J3 Karaman *Balıkesir* Turkey
148 F5 Karaman *Karaman* Turkey
150 B1 Karaman *prov.* Turkey
221 L6 Karamanbeyli Geçidi *pass* Turkey
221 K5 Karamanlı Turkey
132 G4 Karamay *Xinjiang* China
145 O3 Karambar Pass Afgh./Pak.
117 L6 Karambu *Kalimantan* Indon.
103 G8 Karamea *South I.* N.Z.
103 G8 Karamea *r. South I.* N.Z.
103 F8 Karamea Bight *b. South I.* N.Z.
142 K2 Karamendy Kazakh.
117 K7 Karamian *i.* Indon.
221 L4 Karamıkkaracaören Turkey
133 G8 Karamiran *Xinjiang* China
133 G8 Karamiran He *r.* China
133 H8 Karamiran Shankou *pass Xinjiang* China
153 Q3 Karamken Rus. Fed.
221 K2 Karamürsel Turkey
197 K1 Karamyshevo *Kaliningradskaya Oblast'* Rus. Fed.
160 L4 Karamyshevo *Pskovskaya Oblast'* Rus. Fed.
145 N3 Karan *r.* Afgh.
Karan *state* Myanmar *see* Kayin
147 I2 Karān *i.* Saudi Arabia
275 G4 Karanambo Guyana
199 I3 Karancsalja Hungary
199 I3 Karancskeszi Hungary
199 I3 Karancsság Hungary
228 A3 Karang Senegal
115 A4 Karang, Tanjung *pt* Indon.
116 F6 Karangagung *Sumatera* Indon.
116 F7 Karangan *Sumatera* Indon.
103 D10 Karangarua *South I.* N.Z.
117 K9 Karangasem *Bali* Indon.
117 H9 Karangbolong, Tanjung *pt* Indon.
115 D2 Karangetang *vol.* Indon.
230 B4 Karangoua *r.* Congo
138 F9 Karanja *Mahar.* India
136 E3 Karanja *r.* India
138 H8 Karanjia *Madh. Prad.* India
139 J9 Karanjia *Orissa* India
138 D5 Karanpura *Rajasthan* India
143 Q1 Karaoba Kazakh.
221 I5 Karaova Turkey
221 K6 Karaovabeli Geçidi *pass* Turkey
143 P5 Karaoy *Almatinskaya Oblast'* Kazakh.
143 P5 Karaoy *Almatinskaya Oblast'* Kazakh.
219 P7 Karapelit Bulg.
150 E2 Karapınar *Gaziantep* Turkey
148 F5 Karapınar *Konya* Turkey
221 J3 Karapürçek *Balıkesir* Turkey
221 L2 Karapürçek *Sakarya* Turkey
132 C6 Karaqi *Xinjiang* China
234 C5 Karas *admin. reg.* Namibia
236 B3 Karas *mts* Namibia
151 A6 Karasakal Dağları *mts* Turkey
148 E3 Karaşar Turkey
133 F8 Karasay *Xinjiang* China
143 Q7 Kara-Say Kyrg.
234 C6 Karasburg Namibia
Kara Sea Rus. Fed. *see* Karskoye More
161 W5 Karash Rus. Fed.
143 P2 Karashoky Kazakh.
210 G3 Karašica *r.* Croatia
199 H6 Karasica *r.* Hungary/Romania
159 N8 Karasivka *r.* Ukr.
Kárášjohka *Finnmark* Norway *see* Karasjok
162 R2 Kárášjohka *r.* Norway
162 R2 Karasjok *Finnmark* Norway
Karasjokka *r.* Norway *see* Kárášjohka
143 P2 Karasor Kazakh.
143 M1 Karasor, Ozero *l.* Kazakh.
143 P2 Karasor, Ozero *salt l.* Kazakh.
143 P3 Karasor, Ozero *salt l.* Kazakh.
Kara Strait Rus. Fed. *see* Karskiye Vorota, Proliv
126 E6 Karasu Japan
143 P4 Karasu *Karagandinskaya Oblast'* Kazakh.
142 J2 Karasu *Kostanayskaya Oblast'* Kazakh.
142 K1 Karasu *Kostanayskaya Oblast'* Kazakh.
143 P1 Karasu *r.* Kazakh.
150 E2 Karasu *r.* Syria/Turkey
Karasu *Bitlis* Turkey *see* Hizan
221 L1 Karasu *Sakarya* Turkey
149 K4 Karasu *r.* Turkey
Karasubazar Ukr. *see* Bilohirs'k
127 J3 Karasu-gawa *r.* Japan
143 R1 Karasuk Rus. Fed.
158 H8 Karasulak *r.* Ukr.
143 O7 Kara-Suu Kyrg.
127 L2 Karasuyama Japan
158 E2 Karasyn Ukr.
144 I4 Karāt Iran
151 H3 Karata Rus. Fed.
143 U4 Karatal Kazakh.
148 G5 Karataş *Adana* Turkey
150 E2 Karataş *Hatay* Turkey
221 J4 Karatas Turkey
Karataş Burnu *hd* Turkey *see* Fener Burnu
143 N6 Karatau Kazakh.
143 L5 Karatau, Khrebet *mts* Kazakh.
156 M1 Karatayka Rus. Fed.
150 A2 Karatepe Turkey
119 D9 Karathuri Myanmar
136 F8 Karativu *i.* Sri Lanka
162 O3 Karatj *l.* Sweden
142 E3 Karatobe Kazakh.
142 H4 Karatobe, Mys *pt* Kazakh.
142 H3 Karatogay Kazakh.
143 Q4 Karatol *r.* Kazakh.
142 J1 Karatomarskoye Vodokhranilishche *resr* Kazakh.
142 E4 Karaton Kazakh.
162 O3 Karats Sweden
125 G13 Karatsu Japan
115 E1 Karatung *i.* Indon.
128 A3 Karatünggü *Xinjiang* China
142 H4 Karatup, Poluostrov *pen.* Kazakh.
142 K2 Kara-Turgay *r.* Kazakh.
143 R3 Karaul Kazakh.
138 F6 Karauli *Rajasthan* India
Karaulkel'dy Kazakh. *see* Bayganin
149 K3 Karaurgan Turkey
Karavan Kyrg. *see* Kerben
220 D6 Karavas *Kythira* Greece
218 H10 Karavastasë, Gjiri i *b.* Albania
218 H10 Karavastasë, Laguna e *lag.* Albania
158 J1 Karavatsichy Belarus
161 Y4 Karavayevo Rus. Fed.
220 E6 Karavia *i.* Greece
221 H7 Karavonisia *i.* Greece
150 A3 Karavostasi Cyprus
220 E7 Karavoutas, Akrotirio *pt Kriti* Greece
230 D4 Karawa Dem. Rep. Congo
116 G8 Karawang *Jawa* Indon.
201 J6 Karawanken *mts* Austria
Karaxahar *r.* China *see* Kaidu He
151 D6 Karayazı Turkey
143 U4 Kara Yertis *r.* Kazakh.
150 E2 Karayılan Turkey
132 E6 Karayulgan *Xinjiang* China
143 N3 Karazhal Kazakh.
142 D5 Karazhambas Kazakh.
143 O4 Karazhingil (abandoned) Kazakh.
149 L7 Karbalā' Iraq
149 K7 Karbalā' *governorate* Iraq
191 G10 Karben Ger.
219 K9 Karbinci *Karbinci* Macedonia
192 F4 Karbow-Vietlübbe Ger.
144 D5 Karbūsh, Kūh-e *mt.* Iran
190 I1 Karby Ger.
199 J4 Karcag Hungary
199 K3 Karcsa Hungary
197 J3 Karczew Pol.
197 K4 Karczmiska Pol.
219 Q7 Kardam Bulg.
221 I6 Kardamaina *Kos* Greece
220 D6 Kardamyli Greece
201 K1 Kardašova Řečice Czech Rep.
Kardeljevo Croatia *see* Ploče
191 D10 Karden Ger.
Kardhaámaina *Kos* Greece *see* Kardamaina
Kardhítsa Greece *see* Karditsa
220 G6 Kardiotissa *i.* Greece
162 Q3 Kardis Sweden
220 C3 Karditsa Greece
160 F3 Kärdla Estonia
199 J5 Kardos Hungary
201 O4 Kardos-ér *r.* Hungary
199 J5 Kardoskút Hungary
161 P7 Kardymovo Rus. Fed.
151 F2 Kardzhin Rus. Fed.
237 K4 Karee S. Africa
236 F6 Kareeberge *mts* S. Africa
236 G6 Kareebospoort *pass* S. Africa
236 I9 Kareedouw S. Africa
202 D5 Kareha, Jebel *mt.* Morocco
225 F5 Kareima Sudan
151 E4 K'areli Georgia
138 G8 Kareli *Madh. Prad.* India
Karelia *aut. rep.* Rus. Fed. *see* Kareliya, Respublika
160 J8 Karelichy Belarus
156 F3 Kareliya, Respublika *aut. rep.* Rus. Fed.
Karel'skaya A.S.S.R. *aut. rep.* Rus. Fed. *see* Kareliya, Respublika
156 F2 Karel'skiy Bereg *coastal area* Rus. Fed.
233 A6 Karema *Rukwa* Tanz.
Karen *state* Myanmar *see* Kayin
121 K1 Karenga *r.* Rus. Fed.
138 G7 Karera *Madh. Prad.* India
162 Q2 Karesuando Sweden
144 I8 Kārevāndar Iran
102 I4 Karewa *i. North I.* N.Z.
102 K4 Karewa Island *North I.* N.Z.
145 I5 Karez Dasht Afgh.
142 F2 Kargala Rus. Fed.
151 H2 Kargalinskaya Rus. Fed.
Kargalinski Rus. Fed. *see* Kargalinskaya
142 G2 Kargalinskoye Kazakh.
143 P3 Kargaly Kazakh.
149 J4 Kargapazarı Dağları *mts* Turkey
Karghalik *Xinjiang* China *see* Yecheng
148 G3 Kargı Turkey
138 F3 Kargiakh *Jammu and Kashmir* India
138 F2 Kargil *Jammu and Kashmir* India
Kargilik *Xinjiang* China *see* Yecheng
150 C2 Kargıpınarı Turkey
156 G3 Kargopol' Rus. Fed.
196 D3 Kargowa Pol.
144 G8 Kargūshkī Iran
138 G6 Karhal *Uttar Prad.* India
229 H4 Kari Nigeria
226 D2 Karia Ba Mohammed Morocco
144 G8 Karīān Iran
159 U1 Karian Rus. Fed.
220 E2 Kariani Greece

203 E5 **Kariat-Arkmane** Morocco
235 F3 **Kariba** Zimbabwe
231 E9 **Kariba, Lake** *resr* Zambia/Zimbabwe
231 F9 **Kariba Dam** Zambia/Zimbabwe
124 Q4 **Kariba-yama** *vol.* Japan
234 B4 **Karibib** Namibia
236 H9 **Kariega** *r.* S. Africa
147 I7 **Karīf Salāsil** *well* Yemen
162 R2 **Karigasniemi** Fin.
160 J1 **Karijärvi** *l.* Fin.
109 E7 **Karijini National Park** *W.A.* Austr.
102 H1 **Karikari, Cape** *North I.* N.Z.
144 F5 **Karīmābād** Iran
117 H5 **Karimata** *i.* Indon.
117 H5 **Karimata, Pulau-pulau** *is* Indon.
117 H5 **Karimata, Selat** *str.* Indon.
139 N7 **Karimganj** *Assam* India
144 D4 **Karim Khanch** Iran
136 F3 **Karimnagar** *Andhra Prad.* India
116 E4 **Karimun Besar** *i.* Indon.
117 I7 **Karimunjawa** *i.* Indon.
117 I7 **Karimunjawa, Pulau-pulau** *is* Indon.
232 E2 **Karin** Somalia
163 Q6 **Karinainen** Fin.
221 J5 **Karınçalı Dağı** *mts* Turkey
163 L5 **Käringsjön** Sweden
237 P1 **Karino** S. Africa
102 I4 **Karioi** *hill North I.* N.Z.
163 Q6 **Karis** Fin.
233 A5 **Karisimbi, Mont** *vol.* Rwanda
Káristos Greece *see* **Karystos**
220 D2 **Karitsa** Greece
126 E6 **Kariya** Japan
235 E3 **Kariyangwe** Zimbabwe
Karjaa Fin. *see* **Karis**
160 G1 **Karjalohja** Fin.
138 D8 **Karjan** *Gujarat* India
136 D3 **Karjat** *Mahar.* India
139 K8 **Karkai** *r. Jharkhand* India
136 D6 **Karkal** *Karnataka* India
136 D4 **Karkamb** *Mahar.* India
236 B6 **Karkams** S. Africa
143 P3 **Karkaralinsk** Kazakh.
114 E9 **Karkaralong, Kepulauan** *is* Indon.
113 K7 **Karkar Island** P.N.G.
144 D5 **Karkas, Kūh-e** *mts* Iran
145 L8 **Karkh** Pak.
144 B6 **Karkheh, Rūdkhāneh-ye** *r.* Iran
159 L8 **Karkinits'ka Zatoka** *g.* Ukr.
163 R6 **Karkkila** Fin.
163 R6 **Kärkölä** Fin.
Karkonoski Park Narodowy *nat. park* Czech Rep./Pol. *see* **Krkonošský narodní park**
196 D5 **Karkonoski Park Narodowy** *nat. park* Pol.
160 I3 **Karksi-Nuia** Estonia
146 C3 **Karkūmā, Ra's** *hd* Saudi Arabia
145 N5 **Karlachi** Pak.
159 O2 **Karla Libknekhta, imeni** Rus. Fed.
106 D5 **Karlantijpa North Aboriginal Land** *res. N.T.* Austr.
106 D6 **Karlantijpa South Aboriginal Land** *res. N.T.* Austr.
160 D2 **Karlby** *Åland* Fin.
165 N1 **Karlholmsbruk** Sweden
151 C5 **Karlı** Turkey
139 I8 **Karlidi** *Chhattisgarh* India
128 D5 **Karlik Shan** *mts Xinjiang* China
196 D1 **Karlino** Pol.
149 J4 **Karlıova** Turkey
159 O4 **Karlivka** Ukr.
151 E6 **Karlıyayla** Turkey
145 O3 **Karl Marks, Qullai** *mt.* Tajik.
Karl-Marx-Stadt Ger. *see* **Chemnitz**
Karlo-Libknekhtovsk Ukr. *see* **Soledar**
210 E3 **Karlovac** Croatia
198 B1 **Karlovarský kraj** *admin. reg.* Czech Rep.
221 H5 **Karlovasi** *Samos* Greece
198 G1 **Karlovice** Czech Rep.
Karlovka Ukr. *see* **Karlivka**
219 M8 **Karlovo** Bulg.
198 B1 **Karlovy Vary** Czech Rep.
194 F4 **Karlsbad** Ger.
163 M6 **Karlsberg** Sweden
165 K3 **Karlsborg** Sweden
192 I3 **Karlsburg** Ger.
Karlsburg Romania *see* **Alba Iulia**
194 F3 **Karlsdorf-Neuthard** Ger.
195 K5 **Karlsfeld** Ger.
192 I2 **Karlshagen** Ger.
165 K5 **Karlshamn** Sweden
190 H4 **Karlshöfen** Ger.
195 K4 **Karlshuld** Ger.
165 K2 **Karlskoga** Sweden
195 K4 **Karlskron** Ger.
165 L5 **Karlskrona** Sweden
165 N4 **Karlsöarna** *i.* Sweden
194 E3 **Karlsruhe** Ger.
194 F4 **Karlsruhe** *admin. reg.* Ger.
164 J2 **Karlstad** Sweden
260 G1 **Karlstad** *MN* U.S.A.
194 H2 **Karlstadt** Ger.
191 H10 **Karlstein am Main** Ger.
201 L2 **Karlstein an der Thaya** Austria
201 M3 **Karlstetten** Austria
244 I4 **Karluk** *AK* U.S.A.
162 □ **Karl XII Øyane** *i.* Svalbard
145 L3 **Karlyk** Turkm.
161 N8 **Karma** Belarus
229 F3 **Karma** Niger
224 C6 **Karma, Ouadi** *watercourse* Chad
151 F3 **Karmadon** Rus. Fed.
136 D3 **Karmala** *Mahar.* India
161 R6 **Karmanovo** Rus. Fed.
162 O3 **Karmas** Sweden
150 D6 **Karmel, Har** *hill* Israel
Karmir Armenia *see* **Chambarak**
Karmona Spain *see* **Córdoba**
164 B2 **Karmøy** *i.* Norway
145 O7 **Karmpur** Pak.
139 N8 **Karnafuli Reservoir** Bangl.
138 F5 **Karnal** *Haryana* India
138 H5 **Karnali** *r.* Nepal
158 J7 **Karnaliyivka** Ukr.
139 M8 **Karnaphuli** *r.* Bangl.
138 G4 **Karnaprayag** *Uttaranchal* India
136 D5 **Karnataka** *state* India
159 N5 **Karnaukhivka** Ukr.
261 G11 **Karnes City** *TX* U.S.A.
196 D1 **Karnice** Pol.
197 I3 **Karniewo** Pol.
219 O8 **Karnobat** Bulg.
201 I6 **Kärnten** *land* Austria
145 K8 **Karodi** Pak.
235 F3 **Karoi** Zimbabwe
213 P5 **Karojba** Croatia
118 C7 **Karokpi** Myanmar
133 J12 **Karo La** *pass Xizang* China
199 H2 **Karolinka** Czech Rep.
115 B7 **Karompalompo** *i.* Indon.
139 O7 **Karong** *Manipur* India
233 B7 **Karonga** Malawi
109 G11 **Karonie** *W.A.* Austr.
143 Q7 **Karool-Döbö** Kyrg.
Karool-Tëbë Kyrg. *see* **Karool-Döbö**
236 G8 **Karoo National Park** S. Africa
104 G6 **Karoonda** *S.A.* Austr.
145 N6 **Karor** Pak.
225 H5 **Karora** Eritrea
Káros *i.* Greece *see* **Keros**
115 A4 **Karossa** *Sulawesi Barat* Indon.
117 M9 **Karossa, Tanjung** *pt Sumba* Indon.
221 H1 **Karoti** Greece
228 E2 **Karouassa** *well* Mali
224 D6 **Karoub** Chad
220 A3 **Karousades** *Kerkyra* Greece
192 F3 **Karow** *Mecklenburg-Vorpommern* Ger.
193 F6 **Karow** *Sachsen-Anhalt* Ger.
196 D5 **Karpacz** Pol.
150 C3 **Karpasia** *pen.* Cyprus
Karpas Peninsula Cyprus *see* **Karpasia**
221 I7 **Karpathos** *Karpathos* Greece
221 I7 **Karpathos** *i.* Greece
221 I6 **Karpathou, Steno** *sea chan.* Greece
158 D5 **Karpats'kyy Natsional'nyy Park** *nat. park* Ukr.
Karpaty *mts* Europe *see* **Carpathian Mountains**
220 C4 **Karpenisi** Greece
Karpilovka Belarus *see* **Aktsyabrski**
156 M4 **Karpinsk** Rus. Fed.
156 I2 **Karpogory** Rus. Fed.
159 L1 **Karpovychi** Ukr.
221 I5 **Karpuzlu** *Aydın* Turkey
221 H2 **Karpuzlu** *Edirne* Turkey
158 J3 **Karpylivka** *Chernihivs'ka Oblast'* Ukr.
159 M3 **Karpylivka** *Chernihivs'ka Oblast'* Ukr.
158 G2 **Karpylivka** *Rivnens'ka Oblast'* Ukr.
108 D6 **Karratha** *W.A.* Austr.
Karrats Fjord *inlet* Greenland *see* **Nuugaatsiaap Imaa**
192 E4 **Karrenzin** Ger.
144 D7 **Karrī** Iran
237 L6 **Karringmelkspruit** S. Africa
Karroo *plat.* S. Africa *see* **Great Karoo**
109 E10 **Karroun Hill Nature Reserve** *W.A.* Austr.
145 J4 **Karrukh** Afgh.
Karrychirla Turkm. *see* **Garryçyrla**
149 K3 **Kars** Turkey
151 E5 **Kars** *prov.* Turkey
151 E5 **Kars** *r.* Turkey
143 L4 **Karsakpay** Kazakh.
162 R5 **Kärsämäki** Fin.
160 K5 **Kārsava** Latvia
193 E8 **Karsdorf** Ger.
Karshi *Qashqadaryo* Uzbek. *see* **Qarshi**
151 C4 **Karşıköy** Turkey
196 F2 **Karsin** Pol.
221 J2 **Karşıyaka** *Balıkesir* Turkey
221 I4 **Karşıyaka** *İzmir* Turkey
139 L6 **Karsiyang** *W. Bengal* India
152 G3 **Karskiye Vorota, Proliv** *str.* Rus. Fed.
192 L5 **Karsko** Pol.
152 I2 **Karskoye More** *sea* Rus. Fed.
192 E4 **Karstädt** *Brandenburg* Ger.
192 D4 **Karstädt** *Mecklenburg-Vorpommern* Ger.
156 D3 **Karstula** Fin.
157 I5 **Karsun** Rus. Fed.
199 I4 **Kartal** Hungary
221 K2 **Kartal** Turkey
239 □3a **Kartala** *vol. Njazidja* Comoros
239 □3a **Kartala, Forêt du** *for. Njazidja* Comoros
142 I1 **Kartaly** Rus. Fed.
138 E4 **Kartarpur** *Punjab* India
161 O6 **Kartashevichi** Rus. Fed.
161 O6 **Kartavshchina** Rus. Fed.
156 K2 **Kartayel'** Rus. Fed.
160 E6 **Kartena** Lith.
256 G7 **Karthaus** *PA* U.S.A.
200 G6 **Kartitsch** Austria
200 G6 **Kartitscher Sattel** *pass* Austria
151 F3 **K'art'lis K'edi** *hills* Georgia
Kartsa Rus. Fed. *see* **Oktyabr'skoye**
161 N5 **Kartsevo** Rus. Fed.
220 F4 **Kartsino, Akrotirio** *pt Skyros* Greece
162 S5 **Karttula** Fin.
275 G3 **Kartuni** Guyana
165 O7 **Kartuzy** Pol.
231 F8 **Karubwe** Zambia
127 I3 **Karuizawa** Japan
144 H7 **Karūk** Iran
124 S6 **Karumai** Japan
107 H4 **Karumba** *Qld* Austr.
144 D6 **Kārūn, Kūh-e** *hill* Iran
144 C6 **Kārūn, Rūd-e** *r.* Iran
136 E8 **Karunagapalli** *Kerala* India
162 Q3 **Karungi** Sweden
232 B5 **Karungu** Kenya
115 A8 **Karuni** *Sumba* Indon.
108 I4 **Karunjie (abandoned)** *W.A.* Austr.
164 F5 **Karup** Denmark
164 F5 **Karup** *r.* Denmark
136 F7 **Karur** *Tamil Nadu* India
233 A5 **Karuzi** Burundi
136 F6 **Karvetnagar** *Andhra Prad.* India
163 Q5 **Karvia** Fin.
199 H2 **Karviná** Czech Rep.
158 H3 **Karvynivka** Ukr.
136 D5 **Karwar** *Karnataka* India
200 D5 **Karwendelgebirge** *mts* Austria
200 D5 **Karwendelgebirge** *nature res.* Austria
138 H7 **Karwi** *Uttar Prad.* India
197 J2 **Karwica** Pol.
192 D4 **Karwitz** Ger.
220 B4 **Karya** *Lefkada* Greece
Karyagino Azer. *see* **Füzuli**
220 F2 **Karyes** Greece
121 J1 **Karymskoye** Rus. Fed.
142 E6 **Karynzharyk, Peski** *des.* Kazakh.
220 F4 **Karystos** Greece
159 N2 **Karyzh** Rus. Fed.
224 E6 **Kas** Sudan
221 K6 **Kaş** Turkey
136 C3 **Kasa** *Mahar.* India
Kasaba Turkey *see* **Turgutlu**
233 A7 **Kasaba Lodge** Zambia
248 B2 **Kasabonika** *Ont.* Can.
248 B2 **Kasabonika Lake** *Ont.* Can.
233 A6 **Kasacasia** Tanz.
126 G3 **Kasaga-dake** *mt.* Japan
126 C6 **Kasagi** Japan
126 F4 **Kasagi-yama** *mt.* Japan
126 F5 **Kasahara** Japan
231 D6 **Kasaï** *prov.* Dem. Rep. Congo
231 C5 **Kasaï** *r.* Dem. Rep. Congo
126 A6 **Kasai** Japan
231 D6 **Kasaï, Plateau du** Dem. Rep. Congo
231 D6 **Kasaï-Oriental** *prov.* Dem. Rep. Congo
231 D7 **Kasaji** Dem. Rep. Congo
127 J3 **Kasakake** Japan
127 L3 **Kasama** Japan
233 A7 **Kasama** Zambia
126 E5 **Kasamatsu** Japan
Kasan Uzbek. *see* **Koson**
233 A5 **Kasana** Tanz.
234 E3 **Kasane** Botswana
233 A7 **Kasanga** Tanz.
231 B6 **Kasangulu** Dem. Rep. Congo
231 F8 **Kasanka National Park** Zambia
126 D3 **Kasano-misaki** *pt* Japan
Kasansay Uzbek. *see* **Kosonsoy**
231 C6 **Kasanza** Dem. Rep. Congo
225 H5 **Kasar, Ras** *pt* Sudan
136 D6 **Kasaragod** *Kerala* India
124 □G18 **Kasarai-zaki** *hd Nansei-shotō* Japan
160 G3 **Kasari** *r.* Estonia
160 L6 **Kasary** Belarus
122 G4 **Kasatkino** Rus. Fed.
126 D6 **Kasatori-yama** *hill* Japan
247 K2 **Kasba Lake** Can.
226 D2 **Kasba Tadla** Morocco
164 E5 **Kås Bredning** *b.* Denmark
125 H15 **Kaseda** Japan
244 G1 **Kasegaluk Lagoon** *AK* U.S.A.
198 C2 **Kasejovice** Czech Rep.
231 E8 **Kasempa** Zambia
193 D10 **Kasendorf** Ger.
231 D7 **Kasenga** *Katanga* Dem. Rep. Congo
231 F7 **Kasenga** *Katanga* Dem. Rep. Congo
230 F4 **Kasenye** Dem. Rep. Congo
230 E5 **Kasese** Dem. Rep. Congo
232 A4 **Kasese** Uganda
Kasevo Rus. Fed. *see* **Neftekamsk**
138 G6 **Kasganj** *Uttar Prad.* India
130 B3 **Kasha** *Xizang* China
232 D5 **Kasha** *waterhole* Kenya
248 B3 **Kashabowie** *Ont.* Can.
263 K9 **Kasha-Katuwe Tent Rocks National Monument** *nat. park NM* U.S.A.
144 D5 **Kāshān** Iran
157 H6 **Kashary** Rus. Fed.
248 D2 **Kashechewan** *Ont.* Can.
244 F5 **Kashega** *AK* U.S.A.
244 H3 **Kashegelok** *AK* U.S.A.
Kashgar *Xinjiang* China *see* **Kashi**
132 C7 **Kashi** *Xinjiang* China
126 C6 **Kashiba** Japan
126 C7 **Kashihara** Japan
127 M4 **Kashima** *Ibaraki* Japan
126 E2 **Kashima** *Ishikawa* Japan
125 H13 **Kashima** *Saga* Japan
127 M3 **Kashima-nada** *b.* Japan
126 G2 **Kashimayaria-dake** *mt.* Japan
126 F4 **Kashimo** Japan
161 U4 **Kashin** Rus. Fed.
161 U4 **Kashinka** *r.* Rus. Fed.
231 F7 **Kashiobwe** Dem. Rep. Congo
138 G5 **Kashipur** *Uttaranchal* India
161 V7 **Kashira** Rus. Fed.
161 V7 **Kashirka** *r.* Rus. Fed.
159 S2 **Kashirskoye** Rus. Fed.
231 F8 **Kashitu** Zambia
127 K4 **Kashiwa** Japan
126 C6 **Kashiwara** Japan
125 P9 **Kashiwazaki** Japan
Kashkadar'ya *r.* Uzbek. *see* **Qashqadaryo**
Kashkadarya Oblast *admin. div.* Uzbek. *see* **Qashqadaryo**
143 O5 **Kashkanteniz** Kazakh.
156 G2 **Kashkarantsy** Rus. Fed.
Kashken-Teniz Kazakh. *see* **Kashkanteniz**
151 E2 **Kashkhatau** Rus. Fed.
144 F6 **Kashku'iyeh** Iran
161 O6 **Kashkurino** Rus. Fed.
159 P6 **Kashlahach** *r.* Ukr.
144 H4 **Kāshmar** Iran
Kashmir *terr.* Asia *see* **Jammu and Kashmir**
138 E2 **Kashmir, Vale of** *reg.* India
145 M7 **Kashmore** Pak.
145 N4 **Kashmund** *reg.* Afgh.
159 M9 **Kashtany** Ukr.
244 F3 **Kashunuk** *r. AK* U.S.A.
143 Q1 **Kashyr** Kazakh.
231 E6 **Kashyukulu** Dem. Rep. Congo
Kasi *Uttar Prad.* India *see* **Varanasi**
139 I6 **Kasia** *Uttar Prad.* India
145 N4 **Kasigar** Afgh.
244 G3 **Kasigluk** *AK* U.S.A.
161 Q8 **Kasilovo** Rus. Fed.
115 A4 **Kasimbar** *Sulawesi* Indon.
221 M5 **Kasımlar** Turkey
157 H5 **Kasimov** Rus. Fed.
201 N8 **Kašina** Croatia
230 F4 **Kasingi** Dem. Rep. Congo
115 E4 **Kasiruta** *i. Maluku* Indon.
199 I5 **Kaskantyú** Hungary
260 K7 **Kaskaskia** *r. IL* U.S.A.
247 N3 **Kaskattama** *r. Man.* Can.
143 Q6 **Kaskelen** Kazakh.
163 P5 **Kaskinen** Fin.
Kas Klong *i.* Cambodia *see* **Kŏng, Kaôh**
Kaskö Fin. *see* **Kaskinen**
144 E1 **Kaskyrbulak Yuzhnyy, Gora** *hill* Turkm.
246 G5 **Kaslo** *B.C.* Can.
247 K3 **Kasmere Lake** *Man.* Can.
161 R6 **Kasnya** *r.* Rus. Fed.
231 F7 **Kasomeno** Dem. Rep. Congo
117 J5 **Kasongan** *Kalimantan* Indon.
231 E6 **Kasongo** Dem. Rep. Congo
231 C6 **Kasongo-Lunda** Dem. Rep. Congo
231 C6 **Kasongo Lunda Falls** Angola/Dem. Rep. Congo
231 E6 **Kasonguele** Dem. Rep. Congo
221 H7 **Kasos** *i.* Greece
221 I7 **Kasou, Steno** *sea chan.* Greece
198 C2 **Kašperské Hory** Czech Rep.
151 F4 **Kaspi** Georgia
Kaspīy Mangy Oypaty *lowland* Kazakh./Rus. Fed. *see* **Prikaspiyskaya Nizmennost'**
151 I3 **Kaspiysk** Rus. Fed.
Kaspiyskiy Rus. Fed. *see* **Lagan'**
Kaspiyskoye More *l.* Asia/Europe *see* **Caspian Sea**
161 O7 **Kasplya** Rus. Fed.
161 N6 **Kasplya** *r.* Rus. Fed.
138 E8 **Kasrawad** *Madh. Prad.* India
Kasrik Turkey *see* **Gürpınar**
151 H4 **Kasristsqali** Georgia
Kassa Slovakia *see* **Košice**
160 F3 **Kassaare laht** *b.* Estonia
225 H6 **Kassala** Sudan
225 G6 **Kassala** *state* Sudan
220 E3 **Kassandras, Akrotirio** *pt* Greece
220 E2 **Kassandras, Chersonisos** *pen.* Greece
220 E2 **Kassandras, Kolpos** *b.* Greece
220 E2 **Kassandreia** Greece
190 K2 **Kasseedorf** Ger.
191 I8 **Kassel** Ger.
191 H8 **Kassel** *admin. reg.* Ger.
227 H2 **Kasserine** Tunisia
Kassinga Angola *see* **Cassinga**
250 B5 **Kasson** *MN* U.S.A.
229 H3 **Kassouloua** *well* Niger
145 I9 **Kastag** Pak.
148 F3 **Kastamonu** Turkey
191 D10 **Kastellaun** Ger.
221 G7 **Kastelli** *Kriti* Greece
Kastéllion *Kriti* Greece *see* **Kissamos**
Kastellorizon *i.* Greece *see* **Megisti**
221 I7 **Kastelo, Akrotirio** *pt Karpathos* Greece
187 G6 **Kasterlee** Belgium
195 L3 **Kastl** *Bayern* Ger.
195 N5 **Kastl** *Bayern* Ger.
190 K3 **Kastorf** Ger.
220 C2 **Kastoria** Greece
220 C2 **Kastorias, Limni** *l.* Greece
157 G6 **Kastornoye** Rus. Fed.
220 B4 **Kastos** *i.* Greece
220 C4 **Kastrakiou, Techniti Limni** *resr* Greece
160 K3 **Kastre** Estonia
161 P8 **Kastsyukovichy** Belarus
161 N9 **Kastsyukowka** Belarus
126 E5 **Kasuga** *Gifu* Japan
126 B5 **Kasuga** *Hyōgo* Japan
126 E5 **Kasugai** Japan
127 K4 **Kasukabe** Japan
237 K9 **Kasuka Road** S. Africa
127 J3 **Kasukawa** Japan
230 E5 **Kasuku** Dem. Rep. Congo
233 A6 **Kasulu** Tanz.
123 I11 **Kasumi** Japan
127 L3 **Kasumigaura** Japan
127 L3 **Kasumiga-ura** *l.* Japan
151 J4 **Kasumkent** Rus. Fed.
233 B8 **Kasungu** Malawi
233 B8 **Kasungu National Park** Malawi
145 P6 **Kasur** Pak.
199 J5 **Kaszaper** Hungary
196 E4 **Kaszczor** Pol.
196 G1 **Kaszubskie, Pojezierze** *reg.* Pol.
165 O7 **Kaszubski Park Krajobrazowy** Pol.
231 E9 **Kataba** Zambia
229 H3 **Katagum** Nigeria
257 □Q3 **Katahdin, Mount** *ME* U.S.A.
138 G2 **Kataklik** *Jammu and Kashmir* India
231 E5 **Katako-Kombe** Dem. Rep. Congo
220 C5 **Katakolo** Greece
220 C5 **Katakolo, Akrotirio** *pt* Greece
232 B4 **Katakwi** Uganda
245 K3 **Katalla** *AK* U.S.A.
229 I3 **Katalui** Chad
230 F5 **Katana** Dem. Rep. Congo
231 D6 **Katanda** Dem. Rep. Congo
138 G8 **Katangi** *Madh. Prad.* India
138 G9 **Katangi** *Madh. Prad.* India
122 M3 **Katangli** *Sakhalin* Rus. Fed.
109 D12 **Katanning** *W.A.* Austr.
126 C6 **Katano** Japan
230 E5 **Katanti** Dem. Rep. Congo
144 D3 **Kata Pusht** Iran
161 P9 **Katashin** Rus. Fed.
127 J2 **Katashina** Japan
127 J2 **Katashina-gawa** *r.* Japan
220 B5 **Katastari** *Zakynthos* Greece
126 C5 **Katata** Japan
233 A6 **Katavi National Park** Tanz.
145 M5 **Katawaz** Afgh.
145 L5 **Katawaz** *reg.* Afgh.
137 M9 **Katchall** *i. Andaman & Nicobar Is* India
229 F4 **Katchamba** Togo
231 C8 **Katchiungo** Angola
231 E6 **Katea** Dem. Rep. Congo
244 H2 **Kateel** *r. AK* U.S.A.
231 D6 **Katende** Dem. Rep. Congo
220 D2 **Katerini** Greece
158 J5 **Katerynopil'** Ukr.
169 J4 **Katesbridge** *Northern Ireland* U.K.
233 B6 **Katesh** Tanz.
245 N4 **Kate's Needle** *mt.* Can./U.S.A.
233 B8 **Katete** Zambia
151 H4 **Katex** Azer.
139 I8 **Katghora** *Chhattisgarh* India
118 C2 **Katha** Myanmar
106 D3 **Katherine** *N.T.* Austr.
106 C3 **Katherine** *r. N.T.* Austr.
107 I7 **Katherine Creek** *watercourse Qld* Austr.
Katherine Gorge National Park *N.T.* Austr. *see* **Nitmiluk National Park**
138 E9 **Kathi** *Mahar.* India
138 C8 **Kathiawar** *pen. Gujarat* India
146 F8 **Kathīb, Ra's al** *pt* Yemen
136 G8 **Kathiraveli** Sri Lanka
106 C3 **Kathleen Falls** *N.T.* Austr.
193 J7 **Kathlow** Ger.
139 J6 **Kathmandu** Nepal
236 H3 **Kathu** S. Africa
138 E3 **Kathua** *Jammu and Kashmir* India
233 C5 **Kathua** *watercourse* Kenya
228 C3 **Kati** Mali
117 J3 **Katibas** *r.* Malaysia
199 K4 **Kati-ér** *r.* Hungary
139 K7 **Katihar** *Bihar* India
102 J4 **Katikati** *North I.* N.Z.
237 L8 **Katikati** S. Africa
102 J4 **Katikati Entrance** *sea chan. North I.* N.Z.
234 E3 **Katima Mulilo** Namibia
247 L4 **Katimik Lake** *Man.* Can.
161 W8 **Katino** Rus. Fed.
228 D4 **Katiola** Côte d'Ivoire
Kā Tiritiri o te Moana *mts South I.* N.Z. *see* **Southern Alps**
106 C8 **Katiti Aboriginal Land** *res. N.T.* Austr.
236 E6 **Katkop Hills** S. Africa
158 H8 **Katlabuh, Ozero** *l.* Ukr.
237 M2 **Katlehong** S. Africa
191 J7 **Katlenburg-Lindau** Ger.
199 G3 **Kátlovce** Slovakia
133 G7 **Katma** *Xinjiang* China
244 I4 **Katmai National Park and Preserve** *AK* U.S.A.
Katmandu Nepal *see* **Kathmandu**
220 C4 **Kato Achaïa** Greece
131 □J7 **Kat O Chau** *i. H.K.* China
220 C4 **Katochi** Greece
221 G7 **Kato Chorio** *Kriti* Greece
220 D5 **Kato Doliana** Greece
220 D6 **Kato Glykovrysi** Greece
131 □J7 **Kat O Hoi** *b. H.K.* China
138 G9 **Katol** *Mahar.* India
162 Q5 **Kåtölandet** *i.* Fin.
231 D6 **Katombe** Dem. Rep. Congo
221 G6 **Katomeri, Akrotirio** *pt Naxos* Greece
231 E6 **Katompi** Dem. Rep. Congo
259 H2 **Katonah** *NY* U.S.A.
231 F8 **Katondwe** Zambia
220 E1 **Kato Nevrokopi** Greece
116 □ **Katong** Sing.
232 A4 **Katonga** *r.* Uganda
143 U3 **Katon-Karagay** Kazakh.
Katonqaraghay Kazakh. *see* **Katon-Karagay**
105 M5 **Katoomba** *N.S.W.* Austr.
115 B4 **Katoposa, Gunung** *mt.* Indon.
138 D8 **Katosan** *Gujarat* India
220 D4 **Kato Tithorea** Greece
Kåtotjåkka *mt.* Sweden *see* **Godučohkka**
198 C2 **Katovice** Czech Rep.
197 H5 **Katowice** Pol.
139 L8 **Katoya** *W. Bengal* India
138 D9 **Katpur** *Gujarat* India
221 K5 **Katrancık Dağı** *mts* Turkey
225 G2 **Kātrīnā, Jabal** *mt.* Egypt
168 G10 **Katrine, Loch** *l. Scotland* U.K.
165 M3 **Katrineholm** Sweden
201 I5 **Katschberghöhe** *pass* Austria
201 J3 **Katsdorf** Austria
237 M5 **Katse Dam** Lesotho
235 □J2 **Katsepy** Madag.
220 B3 **Katsikas** Greece
229 G3 **Katsina** Nigeria
229 G4 **Katsina** *state* Nigeria
229 H5 **Katsina-Ala** Nigeria
125 G13 **Katsumoto** Japan
127 I4 **Katsunuma** Japan
127 J4 **Katsura-gawa** *r.* Japan
126 C7 **Katsuragi** Japan
126 B7 **Katsuragi-san** *hill* Japan
124 □1 **Katsuren-zaki** *c. Okinawa* Japan
127 L5 **Katsuura** Japan
126 E3 **Katsuyama** *Fukui* Japan
125 K11 **Katsuyama** *Okayama* Japan
249 H1 **Kattaktoc, Cap** *c. Que.* Can.
108 I6 **Kattamudda Well** *W.A.* Austr.
147 K9 **Kattānahan, Ra's** *pt Suquţrā* Yemen
143 L8 **Kattaqo'rg'on** Uzbek.
Kattaqŭrghon Uzbek. *see* **Kattaqo'rg'on**
145 L5 **Kattasang Hills** Afgh.
221 I7 **Kattavia** *Rodos* Greece
164 H5 **Kattegat** *str.* Denmark/Sweden
162 O4 **Kattisavan** Sweden
Kattowitz Pol. *see* **Katowice**
136 F7 **Kattuputtur** *Tamil Nadu* India
231 E6 **Katumba** Dem. Rep. Congo
233 B7 **Katumbi** Malawi
132 G1 **Katun'** *r.* Rus. Fed.
156 I4 **Katunino** Rus. Fed.
132 G1 **Katunskiy Khrebet** *mts* Rus. Fed.
145 M7 **Katuri** Pak.
Katwa *W. Bengal* India *see* **Katoya**
186 F4 **Katwijk aan Zee** Neth.
197 J2 **Kąty** Pol.
Katyk Ukr. *see* **Shakhtars'k**
199 I5 **Katymár** Hungary
161 O7 **Katyn'** Rus. Fed.
196 E4 **Kąty Wrocławskie** Pol.
195 M3 **Katzbach** *r.* Ger.
201 N4 **Katzelsdorf** Austria
194 G3 **Katzenbuckel** *hill* Ger.
191 E10 **Katzenelnbogen** Ger.
193 D9 **Katzhütte** Ger.
194 D2 **Katzweiler** Ger.
264 □B11 **Kaua'i** *i. HI* U.S.A.
264 □B12 **Kaua'i Channel** *HI* U.S.A.
191 E10 **Kaub** Ger.
234 D3 **Kaudom National Park** *nature res.* Namibia
195 J6 **Kaufbeuren** Ger.
195 J5 **Kaufering** Ger.
261 G9 **Kaufman** *TX* U.S.A.
191 I8 **Kaufungen** Ger.
163 Q5 **Kauhajoki** Fin.
163 Q5 **Kauhanevan-Pohjankankaan kansallispuisto** *nat. park* Fin.
162 Q5 **Kauhava** Fin.
250 F5 **Kaukauna** *WI* U.S.A.
118 C2 **Kaukkwè Hills** Myanmar
162 R3 **Kaukonen** Fin.
160 K2 **Kauksi** Estonia
264 □B12 **Kaulakahi Channel** *HI* U.S.A.
187 I6 **Kaulille** Belgium
162 Q3 **Kaulinranta** Fin.
193 D9 **Kaulsdorf** Ger.
102 J7 **Kaumai** *North I.* N.Z.
249 I1 **Kaumajet Mountains** *Nfld and Lab.* Can.
264 □B12 **Kaumakani** *HI* U.S.A.
264 □E13 **Kaumalapau** *HI* U.S.A.
264 □D12 **Kaunakakai** *HI* U.S.A.
160 G7 **Kaunas** Lith.
160 K5 **Kaunata** Latvia
142 E6 **Kaundy, Vpadina** *depr.* Kazakh.
258 F1 **Kauneonga Lake** *NY* U.S.A.
200 C6 **Kaunertal** *val.* Austria
139 L7 **Kaunia** Bangl.
162 Q3 **Kaunisvaara** Sweden
160 H7 **Kauno marios** *l.* Lith.
103 F9 **Kaupiri** *South I.* N.Z.
197 K1 **Kaupiškiai** Lith.
264 □E13 **Kaupō** *HI* U.S.A.
229 G3 **Kaura-Namoda** Nigeria
131 □J7 **Kau Sai Chau** *i. H.K.* China
Kaushany Moldova *see* **Căușeni**
162 Q5 **Kaustinen** Fin.
187 J9 **Kautenbach** Lux.
162 Q2 **Kautokeino** Norway
201 L2 **Kautzen** Austria
119 D9 **Kau-ye Kyun** *i.* Myanmar
153 R3 **Kavacha** Rus. Fed.
219 K9 **Kavadarci** Macedonia
218 H9 **Kavajë** Albania
221 H2 **Kavak** *Çanakkale* Turkey
148 H3 **Kavak** *Samsun* Turkey
221 H3 **Kavak Dağı** *hill* Turkey
221 J4 **Kavaklıdere** *Manisa* Turkey
221 J5 **Kavaklıdere** *Muğla* Turkey
220 F2 **Kavala** Greece
220 F2 **Kavalas, Kolpos** *b.* Greece
122 I6 **Kavalerovo** Rus. Fed.
245 □C6 **Kavalga Island** *AK* U.S.A.
136 G5 **Kavali** *Andhra Prad.* India
161 N6 **Kavalyova** Belarus
275 F3 **Kavanayen** Venez.
144 E7 **Kavār** Iran
136 C7 **Kavaratti** *Lakshadweep* India
136 C7 **Kavaratti** *atoll* India
219 Q7 **Kavarna** Bulg.
160 H6 **Kavarskas** Lith.
161 Q6 **Kavel'shchino** Rus. Fed.
192 F3 **Kavelstorf** Ger.
228 B4 **Kavendou, Mont** *mt.* Guinea
136 F7 **Kaveri** *r.* India
136 F6 **Kaveripatnam** *Tamil Nadu* India
138 D8 **Kavi** *Gujarat* India
113 L7 **Kavieng** *New Ireland* P.N.G.
144 D4 **Kavīr** Iran
144 G4 **Kavīr, Chāh-e** *well* Iran
144 F4 **Kavīr, Dasht-e** *des.* Iran
144 G4 **Kavīr Kūshk** *well* Iran
Kavirondo Gulf Kenya *see* **Winam Gulf**
151 D1 **Kavkazskiy** Rus. Fed.
151 B2 **Kavkazskiy Zapovednik** *nature res.* Rus. Fed.
197 L6 **Kavs'ke** Ukr.
275 H3 **Kaw** Fr. Guiana
115 F5 **Kawa** *Seram* Indon.
124 R7 **Kawabe** *Akita* Japan
126 F5 **Kawabe** *Gifu* Japan
126 B8 **Kawabe** *Wakayama* Japan
127 L4 **Kawachi** *Ibaraki* Japan
126 E3 **Kawachi** *Ishikawa* Japan
127 K2 **Kawachi** *Tochigi* Japan
126 E1 **Kawachi-dake** *hill* Japan
126 C7 **Kawachi-Nagano** Japan
248 E4 **Kawagama Lake** *Ont.* Can.
126 E6 **Kawage** Japan
127 J4 **Kawagoe** Japan
127 I1 **Kawaguchi** *Niigata* Japan
127 K4 **Kawaguchi** *Saitama* Japan
127 I4 **Kawaguchiko** Japan
127 I4 **Kawaguchi-ko** *l.* Japan
125 L11 **Kawahara** Japan
126 F3 **Kawai** *Gifu* Japan
124 S7 **Kawai** *Iwate* Japan
264 □F13 **Kawaihae** *HI* U.S.A.
264 □A12 **Kawaihoa Point** *HI* U.S.A.
264 □B11 **Kawaikini** *mt. HI* U.S.A.
264 □C12 **Kawailoa Beach** *HI* U.S.A.
125 J12 **Kawajiri** Japan
127 I4 **Kawakami** *Nagano* Japan
126 C7 **Kawakami** *Nara* Japan
102 I2 **Kawakawa** *North I.* N.Z.
126 E3 **Kawakita** Japan
124 R9 **Kawamata** Japan
231 F7 **Kawambwa** Zambia
125 I14 **Kawaminami** Japan
127 J3 **Kawamoto** Japan
231 E8 **Kawana** Zambia
127 H2 **Kawanakajima** Japan
127 J6 **Kawana-zaki** *pt* Japan
127 H6 **Kawane** Japan
115 D3 **Kawangkoan** *Sulawesi* Indon.
126 C5 **Kawanishi** *Hyōgo* Japan
127 I1 **Kawanishi** *Niigata* Japan
124 R9 **Kawanishi** *Yamagata* Japan
127 J3 **Kawarazawa-gawa** *r.* Japan
138 H8 **Kawardha** *Chhattisgarh* India
248 E4 **Kawartha Lakes** *Ont.* Can.
231 F7 **Kawasa** Dem. Rep. Congo
127 K4 **Kawasaki** Japan
126 E5 **Kawashima** Japan
125 I12 **Kawashiri-misaki** *pt* Japan
115 C4 **Kawato** *Sulawesi* Indon.
124 R5 **Kawauchi** Japan
126 G4 **Kawaue** Japan
102 I3 **Kawau Island** *North I.* N.Z.
125 H14 **Kawaura** Japan
249 H2 **Kawawachikamach** *Que.* Can.
127 I6 **Kawazu** Japan
118 C7 **Kawdut** Myanmar
115 G3 **Kawe** *i. Papua* Indon.
264 N5 **Kaweah, Lake** *CA* U.S.A.
Kawege *i.* Tonga *see* **'Euaiki**
102 K6 **Kaweka** *mt. North I.* N.Z.
102 K6 **Kaweka Forest Park** *nature res. North I.* N.Z.
102 K6 **Kaweka Range** *mts North I.* N.Z.
264 □C12 **Kawela Bay** *HI* U.S.A.
250 C1 **Kawene** *Ont.* Can.
102 K5 **Kawerau** *North I.* N.Z.
102 I5 **Kawhia** *North I.* N.Z.
102 I5 **Kawhia Harbour** *North I.* N.Z.
265 P4 **Kawich Peak** *NV* U.S.A.
265 P4 **Kawich Range** *mts NV* U.S.A.
247 L4 **Kawinaw Lake** *Man.* Can.
117 M9 **Kawinda** *Sumbawa* Indon.
115 D1 **Kawio** *i.* Indon.
146 F8 **Kawkabān** Yemen
118 D6 **Kawkareik** Myanmar
261 G7 **Kaw Lake** *OK* U.S.A.
118 B3 **Kawlin** Myanmar
118 C5 **Kawludo** Myanmar
119 D8 **Kawmapyin** Myanmar
225 G3 **Kawm Umbū** Egypt
118 D3 **Kawngmeum** Myanmar
119 D9 **Kawthaung** Myanmar
Kawthoolei *state* Myanmar *see* **Kayin**
Kawthule *state* Myanmar *see* **Kayin**
Kaxgar *Xinjiang* China *see* **Kashi**
132 C7 **Kaxgar He** *r.* China
132 E5 **Kax He** *r.* China
133 F8 **Kaxtax Shan** *mts* China
156 K4 **Kay** Rus. Fed.
228 E3 **Kaya** Burkina
151 D5 **Kayaaltı** Turkey
221 J5 **Kayabaşı** Turkey
221 H3 **Kayacı Dağı** *hill* Turkey
148 H4 **Kayadibi** Turkey
127 I4 **Kayaga-take** *mt.* Japan
118 C5 **Kayah** *state* Myanmar
151 I3 **Kayakent** Rus. Fed.
245 K4 **Kayak Island** *AK* U.S.A.
136 F8 **Kayalpatnam** *Tamil Nadu* India
233 A7 **Kayambi** Zambia
117 I5 **Kayan** *r.* Indon.
117 L3 **Kayan** *r.* Indon.
118 C6 **Kayan** Myanmar
233 A5 **Kayanaza** Burundi
114 □ **Kayangel Atoll** Palau
114 □ **Kayangel Passage** Palau
136 E8 **Kayankulam** *Kerala* India
117 K3 **Kayan Mentarang, Taman Nasional** *nat. park* Indon.
136 F3 **Kayar** *Mahar.* India
115 E3 **Kayasa** *Halmahera* Indon.
151 G1 **Kayasula** Rus. Fed.
Kaybagar, Ozero *l.* Kazakh. *see* **Koybagar, Ozero**
262 K5 **Kaycee** *WY* U.S.A.
142 E5 **Kaydak, Sor** *dry lake* Kazakh.
Kaydanovo Belarus *see* **Dzyarzhynsk**
231 D7 **Kayembe-Mukulu** Dem. Rep. Congo
265 V5 **Kayenta** *AZ* U.S.A.
231 B6 **Kayes** Congo
228 C3 **Kayes** Mali
228 C3 **Kayes** *admin. reg.* Mali
142 K2 **Kayga** Kazakh.
Kaygy Kazakh. *see* **Kayga**
244 G3 **Kayigyalik Lake** *AK* U.S.A.
228 C4 **Kayima** Sierra Leone
118 C5 **Kayin** *state* Myanmar
187 J10 **Kayl** Lux.
221 J4 **Kaymakçı** Turkey
143 P1 **Kaymanachikha** Kazakh.
221 M3 **Kaymaz** Turkey
193 F9 **Kayna** Ger.
151 B6 **Kaynakdüzü** Turkey
143 Q3 **Kaynar** Kazakh.
143 P6 **Kaynar** *Zhambylskaya Oblast'* Kazakh.
148 H4 **Kaynar** Turkey
221 L1 **Kaynarca** Turkey
219 P9 **Kaynarlı** *r.* Turkey
221 M2 **Kaynaşlı** Turkey
126 B4 **Kayo** Japan
124 □1 **Kayō** *Okinawa* Japan
115 E3 **Kayoa** *i. Maluku* Indon.
245 M1 **Kay Point** *pt Y.T.* Can.
Kayrakkum Tajik. *see* **Qayroqqum**
Kayrakkumskoye Vodokhranilishche *resr* Tajik. *see* **Qayroqqum, Obanbori**
142 B3 **Kaysatskoye** Rus. Fed.
148 G4 **Kayseri** Turkey
179 N7 **Kaysersberg** France
115 B7 **Kayuadi** *i.* Indon.
116 F6 **Kayuagung** *Sumatera* Indon.
232 B4 **Kayunga** Uganda
231 E5 **Kayuyu** Dem. Rep. Congo
152 J3 **Kayyerkan** Rus. Fed.
142 C2 **Kayyndy** Kazakh.
143 O6 **Kayyngdy** Kyrg.
161 V8 **Kazachka** Rus. Fed.
153 O2 **Kazach'ye** Rus. Fed.
Kazakh Azer. *see* **Qazax**
Kazakhdar'ya Uzbek. *see* **Qozoqdaryo**
Kazakhskaya S.S.R. *country* Asia *see* **Kazakhstan**
142 E6 **Kazakhskiy Zaliv** *b.* Kazakh.
142 T3 **Kazakhstan** *country* Asia
Kazakhstan Kazakh. *see* **Aksay**
Kazakh Steppe *plain* Kazakh. *see* **Saryarka**
161 V9 **Kazaki** Rus. Fed.
Kazakstan *country* Asia *see* **Kazakhstan**
142 J5 **Kazalinsk** Kazakh.
247 M2 **Kazan** *r. Nunavut* Can.
156 J5 **Kazan'** Rus. Fed.
151 D6 **Kazan** Turkey
148 F5 **Kazancı** Turkey
Kazandzhik Turkm. *see* **Bereket**
220 B3 **Kazanje, Mal** *mt.* Albania
156 J5 **Kazanka** *r.* Rus. Fed.
159 L6 **Kazanka** Ukr.
Kazanketken Uzbek. *see* **Qozonketkan**
150 C2 **Kazanlı** Turkey
219 N8 **Kazanlŭk** Bulg.
161 V8 **Kazanovka** Rus. Fed.
197 J4 **Kazanów** Pol.
125 □2 **Kazan-rettō** *is* N. Pacific Ocean
143 S3 **Kazanshunkyr** Kazakh.
157 H6 **Kazanskaya** Rus. Fed.
159 O8 **Kazantyp, Mys** *pt* Ukr.
159 O8 **Kazantyps'ka Zatoka** *b.* Ukr.
Kazatin Ukr. *see* **Kozyatyn**
142 H3 **Kazatskiy** Kazakh.
229 H3 **Kazaure** Nigeria
232 C1 **Kaza Wenz** *r.* Eth.
Kazbegi Georgia *see* **Qazbegi**
151 F3 **Kazbek** *mt.* Georgia/Rus. Fed.
221 H3 **Kaz Dağı** *mts* Turkey
144 D7 **Kāzerūn** Iran
143 N1 **Kazgorodok** Kazakh.
156 J3 **Kazhim** Rus. Fed.
145 J8 **Kazhmak** *r.* Pak.
159 N7 **Kazhovs'kyy Mahistral'nyy Kanal** *canal* Ukr.
Kazidi *Kŭhistoni Badakhshon* Tajik. *see* **Qozideh**
221 K5 **Kazıkbelı Geçidi** *pass* Turkey
Kazi Magomed Azer. *see* **Qazımämmäd**
158 B2 **Kazimierski Park Krajobrazowy** Pol.
197 I5 **Kazimierza Wielka** Pol.
196 G3 **Kazimierz Biskupi** Pol.
197 J4 **Kazimierz Dolne** Pol.
Kāẓimīyah Iraq *see* **Al Kāẓimīyah**
199 J3 **Kazincbarcika** Hungary
159 Q3 **Kazinka** *Belgorodskaya Oblast'* Rus. Fed.
161 W9 **Kazinka** *Lipetskaya Oblast'* Rus. Fed.
161 W8 **Kazinka** *Ryazanskaya Oblast'* Rus. Fed.
159 T3 **Kazinka** *Voronezhskaya Oblast'* Rus. Fed.
139 N6 **Kaziranga National Park** India
160 I8 **Kazlowshchyna** *Hrodzyenskaya Voblasts'* Belarus
160 L6 **Kazlowshchyna** *Vitsyebskaya Voblasts'* Belarus
160 G7 **Kazlų Rūda** Lith.
196 E3 **Kaźmierz** Pol.
198 C2 **Kazněјov** Czech Rep.
127 K3 **Kazo** Japan
142 C3 **Kaztalovka** Kazakh.
234 E3 **Kazuma Pan National Park** Zimbabwe
231 D6 **Kazumba** Dem. Rep. Congo
231 E9 **Kazungula** Zambia
124 R6 **Kazuno** Japan
127 L5 **Kazusa** Japan
144 G2 **Kazy** Turkm.
160 M6 **Kaz'yany** Belarus
143 M7 **Kazygurt** Kazakh.
152 H3 **Kazym** *r.* Rus. Fed.
152 H3 **Kazymskiy Mys** Rus. Fed.
218 H8 **Kçirë** Albania
196 F3 **Kcynia** Pol.
198 C2 **Kdyně** Czech Rep.
264 □F14 **Kea'au** *HI* U.S.A.
100 □6 **Kea'auloa Reef** Solomon Is
169 I4 **Keady** *Northern Ireland* U.K.
264 □E14 **Keahole Point** *HI* U.S.A.
168 D10 **Keal, Loch na** *b. Scotland* U.K.
264 □D13 **Kealaikahiki Channel** *HI* U.S.A.
264 □F14 **Kealakekua** *HI* U.S.A.
264 □F14 **Kealakekua Bay** *HI* U.S.A.
264 □F14 **Keālia** *HI* U.S.A.
169 D9 **Kealkill** Ireland
265 V6 **Keams Canyon** *AZ* U.S.A.
Kéamu *i.* Vanuatu *see* **Anatom**
259 G4 **Keansburg** *NJ* U.S.A.
169 L4 **Kearney** *Northern Ireland* U.K.
260 F5 **Kearney** *NE* U.S.A.
256 H9 **Kearneysville** *WV* U.S.A.
265 V8 **Kearny** *AZ* U.S.A.
259 G3 **Kearny** *NJ* U.S.A.
220 F5 **Keas, Steno** *sea chan.* Greece
237 O4 **Keate's Drift** S. Africa
264 □F14 **Keauhou** *HI* U.S.A.
264 □E13 **Keawakapu** *HI* U.S.A.
148 I4 **Keban** Turkey
148 I4 **Keban Barajı** *resr* Turkey
230 B5 **Kébara** Congo
117 H6 **Kebatu** *i.* Indon.
229 F3 **Kebbi** *state* Nigeria
228 A3 **Kébémèr** Senegal
229 I4 **Kébi** *r.* Cameroon
228 D4 **Kébi** Côte d'Ivoire
227 H2 **Kebili** Tunisia
150 D4 **Kebīr, Nahr al** *r.* Lebanon/
224 E6 **Kebkabiya** Sudan
162 O3 **Kebnekaise** *mt.* Sweden
168 D6 **Kebock Head** *Scotland* U.K
232 E3 **K'ebrī Dehar** Eth.
117 H8 **Kebumen** *Jawa* Indon.
116 E6 **Kebur** *Sumatera* Indon.
199 I5 **Kecel** Hungary
145 L6 **Kech** Pak.
145 J8 **Kech** *reg.* Pak.
232 C3 **K'ech'a Terara** *mt.* Eth.
230 D2 **Kéché** C.A.R.
128 E8 **Kecheng** *Qinghai* China
245 P4 **Kechika** *r. B.C.* Can.
145 M7 **Kechi Kalat** Pak.
221 G1 **Kechros** Greece
221 L5 **Keçiborlu** Turkey
199 I5 **Kecskemét** Hungary
116 D1 **Kedah** *state* Malaysia
160 G6 **Kėdainiai** Lith.
Kedairu Passage Fiji *see* **Kadavu Passage**
133 D11 **Kedarnath Peak** *Uttaranch*
230 C2 **Kédédéssé** Chad
249 H4 **Kedgwick** *N.B.* Can.
131 I3 **Kedian** *Hubei* China
173 M3 **Kedington** *Suffolk, England*
117 J8 **Kediri** *Jawa* Indon.
122 E5 **Kedong** *Heilong.* China
228 B3 **Kédougou** Senegal
117 I4 **Kedukul** *Kalimantan* Indon
156 K2 **Kedva** *r.* Rus. Fed.
196 G5 **Kędzierzyn-Koźle** Pol.
171 Q6 **Keelby** *Lincolnshire, Englan*
245 P2 **Keele** *r. Y.T.* Can.
171 M7 **Keele** *Staffordshire, Englan*
245 O3 **Keele Peak** *Y.T.* Can.
264 O5 **Keeler** *CA* U.S.A.
247 I4 **Keeley Lake** *Sask.* Can.
Keeling Islands *terr.* Indian Ocean *see* **Cocos Is**
Keelung Taiwan *see* **Chilur**
168 K9 **Keen, Mount** *hill Scotland*
169 G5 **Keenagh** Ireland
114 B8 **Keenapusan** *i.* Phil.
264 N6 **Keene** *CA* U.S.A.
257 M6 **Keene** *NH* U.S.A.
256 D8 **Keene** *OH* U.S.A.
106 B3 **Keep** *r. N.T.* Austr.
169 F7 **Keeper Hill** *hill* Ireland
105 M4 **Keepit, Lake** *resr N.S.W.* Au
106 B3 **Keep River National Park** Austr.
187 G7 **Keerbergen** Belgium
237 K4 **Keeromsberg** *mt. Free Stat* S. Africa
236 D9 **Keeromsberg** *mt. Western* S. Africa
107 H2 **Keer-weer, Cape** *Qld* Austr
234 C5 **Keetmanshoop** Namibia
247 M5 **Keewatin** *Ont.* Can.
250 A2 **Keewatin** *MN* U.S.A.
Kefallinía *i.* Greece *see* **Kef**
220 B4 **Kefallonia** *i.* Greece
221 H6 **Kefalos** *Kos* Greece
220 F5 **Kefalos, Akrotirio** *pt Kythn* Greece
115 D8 **Kefamenanu** *Timor* Indon.
Kefe Ukr. *see* **Feodosiya**
191 H10 **Kefenrod** Ger.
201 K3 **Kefermarkt** Austria
229 G4 **Keffi** Nigeria
221 L1 **Kefken** Turkey
162 □B1 **Keflavík** Iceland
119 I9 **Kê Ga, Mui** *pt* Vietnam
136 G9 **Kegalla** Sri Lanka
Kegayli Uzbek. *see* **Kegeyli**
143 R6 **Kegen** Kazakh.
143 P6 **Kegeti** Kyrg.
142 H6 **Kegeyli** Uzbek.
249 H1 **Keglo, Baie de** *b. Que.* Can
246 G3 **Keg River** *Alta* Can.
157 I7 **Kegul'ta** Rus. Fed.
160 H5 **Ķegums** Latvia
173 J2 **Kegworth** *Leicestershire, En* U.K.
225 G5 **Keheili** Sudan
194 D4 **Kehl** Ger.
187 J9 **Kehlen** Lux.
228 C2 **Kehoula** *well* Maur.
160 I2 **Kehra** Estonia
191 D10 **Kehrig** Ger.
118 C4 **Kehsi Mansam** Myanmar
160 H3 **Kehtna** Estonia
159 O4 **Kehychivka** Ukr.
171 N6 **Keighley** *West Yorkshire, En* U.K.
126 C5 **Keihoku** Japan
160 H2 **Keila** Estonia
160 H2 **Keila** *r.* Estonia
230 F2 **Keilak** Sudan
232 B2 **Keili** Sudan
131 □J7 **Kei Ling Ha Hoi** *b. H.K.* C
105 J7 **Keilor** *Vic.* Austr.
236 E4 **Keimoes** S. Africa
237 M8 **Kei Mouth** S. Africa
237 L8 **Kei Road** S. Africa
237 L9 **Keiskama** *r.* S. Africa
237 L8 **Keiskammahoek** S. Africa
168 J5 **Keiss** *Highland, Scotland* U
229 G3 **Keïta** Niger
230 C2 **Kéita, Bahr** *r.* Chad
162 S5 **Keitele** Fin.
162 S5 **Keitele** *l.* Fin.
104 H7 **Keith** *S.A.* Austr.
168 K7 **Keith** *Moray, Scotland* U.K.
106 C1 **Keith, Cape** *N.T.* Austr.
245 Q2 **Keith Arm** *b. N.W.T.* Can.
246 F4 **Keithley Creek** *B.C.* Can.
101 □7a **Keiyasi** *Viti Levu* Fiji
249 H4 **Kejimkujik National Park** Can.
126 G2 **Kekachi-yama** *mt.* Japan
264 □B12 **Kekaha** *HI* U.S.A.
Këk-Art Kyrg. *see* **Kök-Art**
160 H5 **Ķekava** Latvia
Këkaygyr Kyrg. *see* **Kök-Ayg**
199 L3 **Kékcse** Hungary
103 H9 **Kekerengu** *South I.* N.Z.
199 J4 **Kékes** *mt.* Hungary
115 F4 **Kekik** *i. Maluku* Indon.
136 G8 **Kekirawa** Sri Lanka
114 □ **Keklau** Palau
221 K6 **Kekova Adası** *i.* Turkey
153 P4 **Kekra** Rus. Fed.
138 E7 **Kekri** *Rajasthan* India
Kök-Tash Kyrg. *see* **Kök-Tas**
232 E3 **K'elafo** Eth.
136 C9 **Kelai** *i.* Maldives
129 L7 **Kelan** *Shanxi* China
115 E5 **Kelang** *i. Maluku* Indon.
Kelang Malaysia *see* **Klang**
116 E1 **Kelantan** *r.* Malaysia
116 D2 **Kelantan** *state* Malaysia
115 F8 **Kelapa** *i. Maluku* Indon.
115 A6 **Kelara** *r.* Indon.
144 D3 **Kelārdasht** Iran
117 H5 **Kelawar** *i.* Indon.
191 C10 **Kelberg** Ger.
193 D8 **Kelbra (Kyffhäuser)** Ger.
199 G2 **Kelč** Czech Rep.
220 B2 **Këlcyrë** Albania
151 E4 **Kel Dağı** *mt.* Turkey
143 T4 **Kel'demurat** Kazakh.
232 B4 **Kele** Uganda
199 I5 **Kelebia** Hungary
221 K5 **Kelekçi** Turkey
233 B6 **Kelema** *Dodoma* Tanz.
221 K3 **Keles** Turkey
143 M7 **Keles** Uzbek.
199 K4 **Keleti-főcsatorna** *canal* Hu
199 H5 **Kelet-Mecsek** *park* Hunga
195 L4 **Kelheim** Ger.
227 H1 **Kelibia** Tunisia
145 L3 **Kelif** Turkm.
145 J2 **Kelif Uzboýy** *marsh* Turkm
122 F4 **Kelin** *Heilong.* China
144 H9 **Kelīrī** Iran
191 F10 **Kelkheim (Taunus)** Ger.
148 I3 **Kelkit** Turkey
148 H3 **Kelkit** *r.* Turkey
194 B2 **Kell** Ger.
103 A12 **Kellard, Mount** *South I.* N
168 J7 **Kellas** *Moray, Scotland* U.K

Kellavere hill Estonia
Kéllé Congo
Kellenhusen Ger.
Kellerberrin W.A. Austr.
Keller Lake N.W.T. Can.
Kellerovka Kazakh.
Kellett, Cape N.W.T. Can.
Kelleys Island OH U.S.A.
Kelliher Sask. Can.
Kellinghusen Ger.
Kellmünz an der Iller Ger.
Kellogg ID U.S.A.
Kelloselkä Fin.
Kells Kerry Ireland
Kells Kilkenny Ireland
Kells Meath Ireland
Kells Northern Ireland U.K.
Kells r. Northern Ireland U.K.
Kelly r. AK U.S.A.
Kelly, Mount hill AK U.S.A.
Kelly Creek watercourse Qld Austr.
Kelly Lake N.W.T. Can.
Kelly Range hills W.A. Austr.
Kellysgrove Ireland
Kelmė Lith.
Kel'mentsi Ukr.
Kelmis Belgium
Kélo Chad
Keloma i. Solomon Is
Kelowna B.C. Can.
Kelp Head B.C. Can.
Kelsall Cheshire, England U.K.
Kelsey MN U.S.A.
Kelseyville CA U.S.A.
Kelso South I. N.Z.
Kelso Scottish Borders, Scotland U.K.
Kelso CA U.S.A.
Kelso WA U.S.A.
Kelsterbach Ger.
Kelti, Jebel mt. Morocco
Kelty Fife, Scotland U.K.
Keluang Malaysia
Kelujärvi Fin.
Kelvedon Essex, England U.K.
Kelvedon Hatch Essex, England U.K.
Kelvington Sask. Can.
Kelvin Island Ont. Can.
Kelwara Rajasthan India
Kem' Rus. Fed.
Kem' r. Rus. Fed.
Kema r. Rus. Fed.
Kemabung Sabah Malaysia
Ke Macina Mali see Massina
Kemah Turkey
Kemal Turkey
Kemaliye Turkey
Kemalpaşa Artvin Turkey
Kemalpaşa İzmir Turkey
Kemalu i. Solomon Is
Kemano (abandoned) B.C. Can.
Kemasik Malaysia
Kematen in Tirol Austria
Kemba C.A.R.
Kembayan Kalimantan Indon.
Kembé C.A.R.
Kemberg Ger.
Kemblesville PA U.S.A.
Kembolcha Eth.
Kembs France
Kemeneshát hills Hungary
Kemenesmagasi Hungary
Kemenessömjén Hungary
Kemer Antalya Turkey
Kemer Antalya Turkey
Kemer Burdur Turkey
Kemer Muğla Turkey
Kemer Barajı resr Turkey
Kemerovo Rus. Fed.
Kemerovo Oblast admin. div. Rus. Fed. see Kemerovskaya Oblast'
Kemerovskaya Oblast' admin. div. Rus. Fed.
Kémes Hungary
Kemeten Austria
Kemi Fin.
Kemihaara Fin.
Kemijärvi Fin.
Kemijärvi l. Fin.
Kemijoki r. Fin.
Kemin Kyrg.
Keminmaa Fin.
Kemiö Fin. see Kimito
Kemir Turkm. see Keymir
Kemlya Rus. Fed.
Kemmel Belgium
Kemmelberg hill Belgium
Kemmerer WY U.S.A.
Kemmern Ger.
Kemmuna i. Malta
Kemmunett i. Malta
Kemnath Ger.
Kemnay Aberdeenshire, Scotland U.K.
Kemnitz Mecklenburg-Vorpommern Ger.
Kemnitz Sachsen Ger.
Kémo pref. C.A.R.
Kemp, Lake TX U.S.A.
Kempazh r. Rus. Fed.
Kempele Fin.
Kempen Ger.
Kempendyay Rus. Fed.
Kempenich Ger.
Kempisch Kanaal canal Belgium
Kemp Land reg. Antarctica
Kemp Peninsula Antarctica
Kemp's Bay Andros Bahamas
Kempsey N.S.W. Austr.
Kempsey Worcestershire, England U.K.
Kempston Bedfordshire, England U.K.
Kempt, Lac l. Que. Can.
Kempten (Allgäu) Ger.
Kempton Tas. Austr.
Kempton Park S. Africa
Kemptville Ont. Can.
Kemsing Kent, England U.K.
Kemujan i. Indon.
Kemulta Georgia see Qemult'a
Ken r. India
Ken, Loch l. Scotland U.K.
Kenabeek Ont. Can.
Kenai AK U.S.A.
Kenai Fiords National Park AK U.S.A.
Kenai Lake AK U.S.A.
Kenai Mountains AK U.S.A.
Kenai National Wildlife Refuge nature res. AK U.S.A.
Kenai Peninsula AK U.S.A.
Kenam, Tanjung pt Indon.
Kenamu r. Nfld and Lab. Can.
Kenamuke Swamp Sudan
Kenansville NC U.S.A.
Kenar-e Kapeh Afgh.
Kenaston Sask. Can.
Kenbridge VA U.S.A.
Kencong Jawa Indon.
Kenda Chhattisgarh India
Kendal Jawa Indon.
Kendal Jamaica
Kendal S. Africa
Kendal Cumbria, England U.K.
Kendall N.S.W. Austr.
Kendall r. Qld Austr.
Kendall FL U.S.A.
Kendall, Cape Nunavut Can.
Kendall, Mount South I. N.Z.
Kendall Island Bird Sanctuary nature res. N.W.T. Can.
Kendallville IN U.S.A.
Kendari Sulawesi Indon.
Kendawangan Kalimantan Indon.
Kendawangan r. Indon.
Kendégué Chad
Kenderes Hungary
Kendhrikí Makedhonía admin. reg. Greece see Kentriki Makedonia
Kendice Slovakia
142 E6 Kendirli-Kiyasan, Plato plat. Kazakh.
139 K9 Kendrapara Orissa India
236 I8 Kendrew S. Africa
262 F3 Kendrick ID U.S.A.
265 U6 Kendrick Peak AZ U.S.A.
139 L7 Kendua Bangl.
143 P6 Kendyktas mts Kazakh.
142 F6 Kendyrlisor, Solonchak salt l. Kazakh.
105 L4 Kenebri N.S.W. Austr.
261 G11 Kenedy TX U.S.A.
237 N6 Keneka r. S. Africa
228 C5 Kenema Sierra Leone
117 I4 Kenepai, Gunung mt. Indon.
199 K3 Kenézlő Hungary
172 E4 Kenfig Bridgend, Wales U.K.
231 C6 Kenge Dem. Rep. Congo
231 E7 Kengere Dem. Rep. Congo
118 D4 Keng Hkam Myanmar
162 Q3 Kengis Sweden
139 M6 Kengkhar Bhutan
118 E4 Keng Lap Myanmar
118 D4 Keng Lon Myanmar
118 D4 Keng Tawng Myanmar
118 D4 Kengtung Myanmar
231 B5 Kengué Congo
199 J4 Kengyet Hungary
Kengzharyq Kazakh. see Kenzharyk
236 F5 Kenhardt S. Africa
258 D4 Kenhorst PA U.S.A.
228 C3 Kéniéba Mali
228 C3 Kéniébaoulé, Réserve de nature res. Mali
173 I3 Kenilworth Warwickshire, England U.K.
258 D4 Kenilworth PA U.S.A.
226 D2 Kénitra Morocco
151 G3 Kenkhi Rus. Fed.
129 P8 Kenli Shandong China
169 C9 Kenmare Ireland
260 E1 Kenmare ND U.S.A.
169 B9 Kenmare River inlet Ireland
235 F3 Kenmaur Zimbabwe
168 I9 Kenmore Perth and Kinross, Scotland U.K.
256 G6 Kenmore NY U.S.A.
194 B2 Kenn Ger.
261 D9 Kenna NM U.S.A.
168 F11 Kennacraig Argyll and Bute, Scotland U.K.
260 F4 Kennebec SD U.S.A.
257 □P4 Kennebec r. ME U.S.A.
257 □O5 Kennebunk ME U.S.A.
257 □O5 Kennebunkport ME U.S.A.
107 J5 Kennedy Qld Austr.
107 J3 Kennedy r. Qld Austr.
Kennedy, Cape FL U.S.A. see Canaveral, Cape
244 I4 Kennedy Entrance sea channel AK U.S.A.
109 C8 Kennedy Range hills W.A. Austr.
109 C8 Kennedy Range National Park W.A. Austr.
131 □J7 Kennedy Town H.K. China
258 D6 Kennedyville MD U.S.A.
261 J11 Kenner LA U.S.A.
173 K5 Kennet r. England U.K.
168 K8 Kennethmont Aberdeenshire, Scotland U.K.
109 D7 Kenneth Range hills W.A. Austr.
261 J7 Kennett MO U.S.A.
258 D5 Kennett Square PA U.S.A.
262 E3 Kennewick WA U.S.A.
245 L3 Kennicott AK U.S.A.
173 J4 Kennington Oxfordshire, England U.K.
168 J10 Kennoway Fife, Scotland U.K.
245 K3 Kenny Lake AK U.S.A.
248 C3 Kenogami r. Ont. Can.
251 N1 Kenogami Lake Ont. Can.
251 M1 Kenogamissi Lake Ont. Can.
245 N3 Keno Hill Y.T. Can.
247 M5 Kenora Ont. Can.
250 G7 Kenosha WI U.S.A.
256 C10 Kenova WV U.S.A.
156 G3 Kenozero, Ozero l. Rus. Fed.
168 D8 Kensaleyre Highland, Scotland U.K.
259 H2 Kensico Reservoir NY U.S.A.
249 I4 Kensington P.E.I. Can.
259 J1 Kensington CT U.S.A.
173 L4 Kensworth Bedfordshire, England U.K.
173 N5 Kent admin. div. England U.K.
171 L5 Kent r. England U.K.
259 I1 Kent CT U.S.A.
256 D7 Kent OH U.S.A.
263 L11 Kent TX U.S.A.
256 D12 Kent VA U.S.A.
262 C3 Kent WA U.S.A.
173 M5 Kent, Vale of val. England U.K.
258 D6 Kent Acres DE U.S.A.
237 M8 Kentani S. Africa
143 M6 Kentau Kazakh.
258 D6 Kent County county DE U.S.A.
258 C6 Kent County county MD U.S.A.
105 K8 Kent Group is Tas. Austr.
258 C7 Kent Island MD U.S.A.
254 D5 Kentland IN U.S.A.
172 F6 Kenton Devon, England U.K.
258 D6 Kenton DE U.S.A.
250 F3 Kenton MI U.S.A.
256 B8 Kenton OH U.S.A.
237 K9 Kenton-on-Sea S. Africa
242 H3 Kent Peninsula Nunavut Can.
258 C7 Kent Point MD U.S.A.
220 E2 Kentriki Makedonia admin. reg. Greece
256 B11 Kentucky r. KY U.S.A.
256 A11 Kentucky state U.S.A.
261 K7 Kentucky Lake KY U.S.A.
261 J10 Kentwood LA U.S.A.
250 I7 Kentwood MI U.S.A.
Kenxa Rus. Fed. see Kenkhi
232 C4 Kenya country Africa
Kenya, Mount Kenya see Kirinyaga
198 G4 Kenyeri Hungary
116 E2 Kenyir, Tasik resr Malaysia
250 B5 Kenyon MN U.S.A.
151 G2 Ken'yurt Rus. Fed.
127 K5 Ken-zaki pt Japan
143 N3 Kenzharyk Kazakh.
151 E2 Kenzhe Rus. Fed.
194 D5 Kenzingen Ger.
264 □E13 Kēōkea HI U.S.A.
250 C9 Keokuk IA U.S.A.
138 F6 Keoladeo National Park India
264 □D12 Keolu Hills HI U.S.A.
139 J9 Keonjhar Orissa India
260 J5 Keosauqua IA U.S.A.
168 D6 Keose Western Isles, Scotland U.K.
255 F8 Keowee, Lake resr SC U.S.A.
116 E6 Kepahiang Sumatera Indon.
165 M7 Kępice Pol.
100 □4b Kepidau en Pohnahtik sea chan. Pohnpei Micronesia
156 H2 Kepina Rus. Fed.
156 H2 Kepina r. Rus. Fed.
103 B12 Kepler Mountains South I. N.Z.
196 F4 Kępno Pol.
107 M7 Keppel Bay Qld Austr.
116 □ Keppel Harbour sea chan. Sing.
Keppel Island Tonga see Tafahi
221 J3 Kepsut Turkey
Kepulauan Bangka-Belitung prov. Indon. see Bangka-Belitung
136 D7 Kerala state India
124 □E20 Kerama-rettō is Nansei-shotō Japan
220 F2 Keramoti Greece
229 F4 Kéran, Parc National de la nat. park Togo
105 I6 Kerang Vic. Austr.
220 B3 Kerasona Greece
220 E5 Keratea Greece
108 E5 Keraudren, Cape W.A. Austr.
163 R6 Kerava Fin.
228 B3 Kerbatch and Wassu Stone Circles tourist site Gambia
116 E6 Kerbau, Tanjung pt Indon.
Kerbela Iraq see Karbalā'
143 N7 Kerben Kyrg.
122 J2 Kerbi r. Rus. Fed.
249 H2 Kerbodot, Lac l. Que. Can.
217 □ Kercem Gozo Malta
159 P8 Kerch Ukr.
156 K3 Kerchem'ya Rus. Fed.
Kerchens'ka Protoka str. Rus. Fed./Ukr. see Kerch Strait
Kerchenskiy Proliv str. Rus. Fed./Ukr. see Kerch Strait
159 O8 Kerchens'kyy Pivostriv pen. Ukr.
156 L4 Kerchevskiy Rus. Fed.
Kerch Peninsula Ukr. see Kerchens'kyy Pivostriv
159 P8 Kerch Strait Rus. Fed./Ukr.
230 E3 Kéré C.A.R.
232 C3 Kere Eth.
199 J4 Kerecsend Hungary
149 P9 Kereft Iran
230 E2 Kereidila l. Sudan
199 I5 Kerekegyháza Hungary
113 K8 Kerema P.N.G.
246 G5 Keremeos B.C. Can.
148 F2 Kerempe Burun pt Turkey
225 H6 Keren Eritrea
144 B4 Kerend Iran
102 J4 Kerepehi North I. N.Z.
199 I4 Kerepestarcsa Hungary
161 O2 Kerest' r. Rus. Fed.
158 C5 Kerets'ky Ukr.
228 A3 Kerewan Gambia
143 M2 Kerey watercourse Kazakh.
143 M2 Kerey, Ozero salt l. Kazakh.
144 G2 Kergeli Turkm.
289 I8 Kerguélen, Îles is Indian Ocean
Kerguelen Islands Indian Ocean see Kerguélen, Îles
289 I8 Kerguelen Plateau sea feature Indian Ocean
232 B5 Kericho Kenya
117 J4 Kerihun mt. Indon.
102 H2 Kerikeri North I. N.Z.
163 T6 Kerimäki Fin.
116 D6 Kerinci, Danau l. Indon.
116 D5 Kerinci, Gunung vol. Indon.
116 D6 Kerinci Seblat, Taman Nasional nat. park Indon.
Kerintji vol. Indon. see Kerinci, Gunung
232 C4 Kerio watercourse Kenya
Keriya Xinjiang China see Yutian
133 F7 Keriya He watercourse China
133 E9 Keriya Shankou pass Xinjiang China
218 E4 Kerka r. Romania
186 H5 Kerkdriel Neth.
225 H5 Kerkebet Eritrea
191 B8 Kerken Ger.
227 H2 Kerkennah, Îles is Tunisia
145 K3 Kerkiçi Turkm.
220 E1 Kerkini, Limni l. Greece
Kerkini Oros mts Europe see Belasitsa
Kérkira i. Greece see Kerkyra
227 H1 Kerkouane tourist site Tunisia
187 J7 Kerkrade Neth.
186 H5 Kerkwijk Neth.
220 A3 Kerkyra Kerkyra Greece
220 A3 Kerkyra i. Greece
180 C4 Kerlouan France
225 F5 Kerma Sudan
99 I5 Kermadec Islands S. Pacific Ocean
290 H8 Kermadec Trench sea feature S. Pacific Ocean
144 G6 Kermān Iran
144 G7 Kermān prov. Iran
264 L5 Kerman CA U.S.A.
144 H7 Kermān, Bīābān-e des. Iran
144 B4 Kermānshāh Iran
144 F6 Kermānshāh Iran
144 B4 Kermānshāh prov. Iran
Kermānshāhān prov. Iran see Kermānshāh
Kermine Uzbek. see Navoiy
261 D10 Kermit TX U.S.A.
264 M6 Kern r. CA U.S.A.
264 N6 Kern, South Fork r. CA U.S.A.
180 E5 Kernascléden France
249 H1 Kernertut, Cap c. Que. Can.
201 M4 Kernhof Austria
106 D8 Kernot Range hills N.T. Austr.
212 E2 Kerns Switz.
264 N6 Kernville CA U.S.A.
Keroh Malaysia see Pengkalan Hulu
221 G6 Keros i. Greece
156 K3 Keros Rus. Fed.
229 F4 Kérou Benin
228 C4 Kérouané Guinea
191 C9 Kerpen Ger.
287 K1 Kerr, Cape Antarctica
168 E10 Kerrera i. Scotland U.K.
247 I5 Kerrobert Sask. Can.
261 F10 Kerrville TX U.S.A.
169 D8 Kerry county Ireland
169 C8 Kerry Head Ireland
232 C3 Kersa Dek Eth.
255 G8 Kershaw SC U.S.A.
171 L3 Kershopefoot Cumbria, England U.K.
193 D8 Kerspleben Ger.
165 M1 Kerstinbo Sweden
202 E5 Kert, Oued r. Morocco
116 E2 Kerteh Malaysia
164 G6 Kerteminde Denmark
199 K4 Kertészsziget Hungary
117 J8 Kertosono Jawa Indon.
117 L9 Keruak Lombok Indon.
Kerulen r. China/Mongolia see Herlen Gol
116 E5 Kerumutan, Suaka Margasatwa nature res. Indon.
136 D4 Kerur Karnataka India
161 W6 Kerva Rus. Fed.
180 E6 Kervignac France
150 B3 Keryneia Cyprus
227 E3 Kerzaz Alg.
212 C2 Kerzers Switz.
156 I4 Kerzhenets r. Rus. Fed.
248 E3 Kesagami r. Ont. Can.
248 D3 Kesagami Lake Ont. Can.
163 T6 Kesälahti Fin.
221 H2 Keşan Turkey
148 I3 Keşap Turkey
219 N7 Kesarevo Bulg.
139 J6 Kesariya Bihar India
231 C5 Kese Dem. Rep. Congo
124 S8 Kesennuma Japan
173 O3 Kesgrave Suffolk, England U.K.
169 F4 Kesh Ireland
169 G3 Kesh Northern Ireland U.K.
122 D4 Keshan Heilong. China
151 E3 K'eshelt'a Georgia
145 N3 Keshem Afgh.
250 F5 Keshena WI U.S.A.
145 L3 Keshendeh-ye Bala Afgh.
144 H7 Keshīt Iran
138 C9 Keshod Gujarat India
138 F7 Keshorai Patan Rajasthan India
149 N7 Keshvar Iran
148 F4 Keskin Turkey
156 F3 Keskozero Rus. Fed.
161 U3 Kes'ma Rus. Fed.
221 M5 Kesme Turkey
161 U4 Kesova Gora Rus. Fed.
196 F2 Kęsowo Pol.
187 G6 Kessel Belgium
195 J4 Kessel r. Ger.
187 J6 Kessel Neth.
173 P3 Kessingland Suffolk, England U.K.
221 K2 Kestel Bursa Turkey
Kestel Bursa Turkey see Gürsu
221 L5 Kestel Gölü l. Turkey
237 M4 Kestell S. Africa
162 U4 Kesten'ga Rus. Fed.
162 S4 Kestilä Fin.
251 O5 Keswick Ont. Can.
171 K4 Keswick Cumbria, England U.K.
198 G5 Keszthely Hungary
198 G5 Keszthelyihegység park Hungary
152 J4 Ket' r. Rus. Fed.
229 F5 Keta Ghana
116 D6 Ketahun Sumatera Indon.
116 □ Ketam, Pulau i. Sing.
117 J8 Ketapang Jawa Indon.
117 I5 Ketapang Kalimantan Indon.
245 O5 Ketchikan AK U.S.A.
262 G5 Ketchum ID U.S.A.
286 T2 Ketchum Glacier Antarctica
199 K5 Kétegyháza Hungary
229 E5 Kete Krachi Ghana
186 I3 Ketelmeer l. Neth.
198 G5 Kéthely Hungary
133 J10 Ketian Qinghai China
145 L9 Keti Bandar Pak.
244 H1 Ketik r. AK U.S.A.
244 H2 Ketlkede Mountain hill AK U.S.A.
143 S6 Ketmen', Khrebet mts China/Kazakh.
229 F5 Kétou Benin
159 L6 Ketrysanivka Ukr.
165 R7 Kętrzyn Pol.
199 J5 Kétsoprony Hungary
230 B4 Ketta Congo
229 I5 Kétté Cameroon
190 E5 Kettenkamp Ger.
173 K3 Kettering Northamptonshire, England U.K.
256 A9 Kettering OH U.S.A.
195 I5 Kettershausen Ger.
192 E1 Kettinge Denmark
246 G5 Kettle r. B.C. Can.
250 B4 Kettle r. MN U.S.A.
256 H7 Kettle Creek r. PA U.S.A.
262 E2 Kettle Falls WA U.S.A.
264 M5 Kettleman City CA U.S.A.
250 B3 Kettle River MN U.S.A.
262 E2 Kettle River Range mts WA U.S.A.
168 K4 Kettletoft Orkney, Scotland U.K.
171 M5 Kettlewell North Yorkshire, England U.K.
117 I4 Ketungau r. Indon.
197 H6 Kęty Pol.
193 H8 Ketzerbach r. Ger.
193 G6 Ketzin Ger.
256 H6 Keuka NY U.S.A.
256 H6 Keuka Lake NY U.S.A.
191 K8 Keula Ger.
Keumgang, Mount N. Korea see Kumgang-san
Keumsang, Mount N. Korea see Kumgang-san
228 A2 Keur Massène Maur.
163 R5 Keurusselkä l. Fin.
163 R5 Keuruu Fin.
201 J6 Keutschach am See Austria
201 J6 Keutscharcher See l. Austria
191 B7 Kevelaer Ger.
199 K5 Kevermes Hungary
162 S2 Kevo Fin.
162 S2 Kevon luonnonpuisto nature res. Fin.
270 G3 Kew Turks and Caicos Is
250 E8 Kewanee IL U.S.A.
115 C8 Kewapante Flores Indon.
250 F6 Kewaskum WI U.S.A.
250 G5 Kewaunee WI U.S.A.
250 F3 Keweenaw Bay MI U.S.A.
250 F3 Keweenaw Bay b. MI U.S.A.
250 F2 Keweenaw Peninsula MI U.S.A.
250 G2 Keweenaw Point MI U.S.A.
172 G5 Kewstoke North Somerset, England U.K.
169 F4 Key, Lough l. Ireland
232 B3 Keyala Sudan
260 F4 Keya Paha r. NE U.S.A.
248 D4 Key Harbour Ont. Can.
132 F5 Keyi Xinjiang China
129 R1 Keyihe Nei Mongol China
171 Q6 Keyingham East Riding of Yorkshire, England U.K.
255 G13 Key Largo FL U.S.A.
255 G13 Key Largo National Marine Sanctuary nature res. FL U.S.A.
106 B3 Keyling Inlet N.T. Austr.
144 E3 Keymir Turkm.
172 G5 Keynsham Bath and North East Somerset, England U.K.
256 G9 Keyser WV U.S.A.
256 F9 Keysers Ridge MD U.S.A.
261 G7 Keystone Lake OK U.S.A.
251 O9 Keystone Lake PA U.S.A.
265 U10 Keystone Peak AZ U.S.A.
256 G11 Keysville VA U.S.A.
260 I6 Keytesville MO U.S.A.
144 C4 Keytū Iran
156 G2 Keyvy, Vozvyshennost' hills Rus. Fed.
255 G13 Key West FL U.S.A.
173 J2 Keyworth Nottinghamshire, England U.K.
156 K4 Kez Rus. Fed.
257 □O5 Kezar Falls ME U.S.A.
235 F4 Kezi Zimbabwe
199 J2 Kežmarok Slovakia
237 K3 Kgakala S. Africa
234 D5 Kgalagadi admin. dist. Botswana
236 F1 Kgalagadi Transfrontier National Park nat. park Botswana/S. Africa
234 E5 Kgatleng admin. dist. Botswana
237 K3 Kgotsong S. Africa
237 M4 Kgubetswana S. Africa
244 G3 Kgun Lake AK U.S.A.
150 E5 Khabab Syria
144 F6 Khabar Iran
156 K2 Khabarikha Rus. Fed.
122 I4 Khabarovsk Rus. Fed.
122 I3 Khabarovskiy Kray admin. div. Rus. Fed.
Khabarovsk Kray admin. div. Rus. Fed. see Khabarovskiy Kray
143 R1 Khabary Rus. Fed.
146 G7 Khabb, Wādī watercourse Yemen
147 N4 Khabbah, Ra's al pt Oman
151 C1 Khabez Rus. Fed.
Khabis Iran see Shahdād
145 J4 Khabody Pass Afgh.
197 M3 Khabovichy Belarus
144 G7 Khabr Iran
146 E4 Khabrā al'Arn salt pan Saudi Arabia
150 H7 Khabrah Sāfiyah hill Saudi Arabia
140 E2 Khābūr, Nahr al r. Syria
Khachmas Azer. see Xaçmaz
138 E8 Khachrod Madh. Prad. India
147 N4 Khadar, Jabal mt. Oman
146 F7 Khaḑāran Saudi Arabia
230 E2 Khadari watercourse Sudan
146 F1 Khadd, Wādī al watercourse Saudi Arabia
149 N8 Khādeyn Iran
161 O8 Khadun' Belarus
151 A1 Khadyzhensk Rus. Fed.
151 I3 Khadzhalmakhi Rus. Fed.
219 L9 Khadzhidimovo Bulg.
144 G2 Khadzhiolen Turkm.
158 J7 Khadzhybeys'kyy Lyman l. Ukr.
197 M2 Khadziloni Belarus
146 H3 Khafs Banbān well Saudi Arabia
147 H4 Khafs Daghrah Saudi Arabia
144 E7 Khāftar Iran
138 H7 Khaga Uttar Prad. India
139 K7 Khagaria Bihar India
139 J7 Khagaul Bihar India
139 M8 Khagrachari Bangl.
Khagrachchari Bangl. see Khagrachari
138 H9 Khairagarh Chhattisgarh India
133 C13 Khairagarh Uttar Prad. India
145 N7 Khairgarh Pak.
138 H5 Khairigarh Uttar Prad. India
145 O7 Khairpur Pak.
145 M8 Khairpur Pak.
138 D8 Khairwara Rajasthan India
151 D3 Khaishi Georgia
144 D6 Khāīz, Kūh-e mt. Iran
145 K3 Khaja Du Koh hill Afgh.
145 M5 Khajuri Kach Pak.
120 F1 Khakasiya, Respublika aut. rep. Rus. Fed.
Khakassia aut. rep. Rus. Fed. see Khakasiya, Respublika
Khakasskaya A.S.S.R. aut. rep. Rus. Fed. see Khakasiya, Respublika
145 M4 Khāk-e Jabbar Afgh.
151 G3 Khakhalgi, Gora mt. Rus. Fed.
234 D5 Khakhea Botswana
145 K6 Khak-rēz Afgh.
145 K6 Khakriz reg. Afgh.
151 I3 Khalagork r. Rus. Fed.
144 D4 Khalajestan reg. Iran
151 H4 Khalakhurkats, Pereval pass Rus. Fed.
160 M6 Khalamyer"ye Belarus
151 E3 Khalatsa, Mt'a Georgia/Rus. Fed.
138 F2 Khalatse Jammu and Kashmir India
144 E5 Khālidābād Iran
145 L6 Khalifat mt. Pak.
139 I6 Khalilabad Uttar Prad. India
144 H4 Khalīlābād Iran
144 E8 Khalīlī Iran
142 H2 Khalilovo Rus. Fed.
145 J1 Khalkabad Turkm.
144 C3 Khalkhāl Iran
Khálki i. Greece see Chalki
151 G3 Khal-Kiloy Rus. Fed.
Khalkís Greece see Chalkida
137 I3 Khallikot Orissa India
156 N2 Khal'mer"yu Rus. Fed.
160 L7 Khalopyenichy Belarus
Khalqobod Uzbek. see Xalqobod
139 J6 Khalte Nepal
Khalturin Rus. Fed. see Orlov
151 H2 Khamamatyurt Rus. Fed.
128 H1 Khamar-Daban, Khrebet mts Rus. Fed.
138 H8 Khamaria Madh. Prad. India
138 B8 Khambhalia Gujarat India
138 D8 Khambhat Gujarat India
136 B3 Khambhat, Gulf of India
138 F9 Khamgaon Mahar. India
144 F8 Khamīr Iran
146 F7 Khamir Yemen
235 F4 Khami Ruins National Monument tourist site Zimbabwe
146 F6 Khamis Mushayţ Saudi Arabia
142 D4 Khamit Yergaliyev Kazakh.
118 G5 Khamkkeut Laos
146 H2 Khamma well Saudi Arabia
136 G4 Khammam Andhra Prad. India
153 N3 Khampa Rus. Fed.
118 B3 Khampat Myanmar
153 M3 Khamra Rus. Fed.
150 A8 Khamsah Egypt
144 C4 Khamseh reg. Iran
151 B1 Khamyshki Rus. Fed.
Khamza Uzbek. see Hamza
145 M5 Khan Afgh.
118 F5 Khan, Nam r. Laos
145 M3 Khānābād Afgh.
149 K7 Khān al Baghdādī Iraq
149 L7 Khān al Maḩāwīl Iraq
149 L7 Khān al Mashāhidah Iraq
149 L7 Khān al Muşallá Iraq
136 D5 Khanapur Karnataka India
136 D4 Khanapur Mahar. India
144 A3 Khānaqāh Iran
149 L8 Khān ar Raḩbah Iraq
149 L4 Khanasur Pass Iran/Turkey
144 F3 Khān Bāgh Iran
Khanbalik Beijing China see Beijing
144 A3 Khānch Iran
105 L7 Khancoban N.S.W. Austr.
128 C1 Khandagayty Rus. Fed.
136 D4 Khandala Mahar. India
138 E6 Khandela Rajasthan India
145 O3 Khandud Afgh.
138 F9 Khandwa Madh. Prad. India
153 O3 Khandyga Rus. Fed.
144 E6 Khāneh Khowreh Iran
145 N6 Khanewal Pak.
145 N7 Khangarh Pak.
Khan Hung Vietnam see Soc Trăng
153 N4 Khani Rus. Fed.
Khaniá Kriti Greece see Chania
138 G7 Khaniadhana Madh. Prad. India
161 T7 Khanino Rus. Fed.
144 E7 Khānī Yek Iran
149 L7 Khān Jadwal Iraq
122 H6 Khanka, Lake China/Rus. Fed.
Khanka, Ozero l. China/Rus. Fed. see Khanka, Lake
Khankendi Azer. see Xankändi
Khanki Uzbek. see Xonqa
138 F4 Khanna Punjab India
150 E6 Khannā, Qā' salt pan Jordan
227 G4 Khannfoussa hill Alg.
156 M2 Khanovey Rus. Fed.
145 M7 Khanpur Pak.
145 N7 Khanpur Pak.
Khān Ruḩābah Iraq see Khān ar Raḩbah
150 E3 Khān Shaykhūn Syria
232 E2 Khansiir, Raas pt Somalia
151 A1 Khanskaya Rus. Fed.
159 R7 Khanskoye, Ozero salt l. Rus. Fed.
143 O5 Khantau Kazakh.
153 K3 Khantayskoye, Ozero l. Rus. Fed.
152 J3 Khantayskoye Vodokhranilishche resr Rus. Fed.
143 S6 Khan-Tengri, Pik mt. Kazakh./Kyrg.
152 H3 Khanty-Mansiysk Rus. Fed.
156 M3 Khanty-Mansiyskiy Avtonomnyy Okrug-Yugra admin. div. Rus. Fed.
150 C7 Khān Yūnis Gaza
119 E8 Khao Ang Rua Nai Wildlife Reserve nature res. Thai.
119 D11 Khao Banthat Wildlife Reserve nature res. Thai.
119 D10 Khao Chum Thong Thai.
119 D7 Khaoen Si Nakarin National Park Thai.
118 D7 Khao Laem, Ang Kep Nam Thai.
119 D7 Khao Laem National Park Thai.
119 D10 Khao Luang National Park Thai.
119 D11 Khao Pu-Khao Ya National Park Thai.
119 F8 Khao Soi Dao Wildlife Reserve nature res. Thai.
119 D10 Khao Sok National Park Thai.
119 E7 Khao Yai National Park Thai.
138 G9 Khapa Mahar. India
138 F2 Khapalu Pak.
129 M2 Khapcheranga Rus. Fed.
138 H5 Khaptad National Park Nepal
142 B4 Kharabali Rus. Fed.
151 E3 Kharagauli Georgia
139 K7 Kharagdiha Jharkhand India
138 C8 Kharaghoda Gujarat India
139 K7 Kharagpur Bihar India
139 K8 Kharagpur W. Bengal India
144 G3 Kharakī Iran
144 H8 Khārān r. Iran
145 K7 Kharan Pak.
144 F5 Kharānaq, Kūh-e mt. Iran
129 O2 Kharanor Rus. Fed.
Kharari Rajasthan India see Abu Road
197 M3 Kharava Belarus
136 D3 Kharda Mahar. India
136 C3 Khardi Mahar. India
138 F2 Khardung La pass Jammu and Kashmir India
145 I4 Kharez Ilias Afgh.
149 M8 Kharfiyah Iraq
122 H2 Kharga r. Rus. Fed.
Kharga Oasis Egypt see Khārijah, Wāḩāt al
138 G7 Khargapur Madh. Prad. India
Khārg Island Iran see Khārk
138 E9 Khargon Madh. Prad. India
138 E7 Khari r. Rajasthan India
145 O9 Khari r. Rajasthan India
145 O5 Kharian Pak.
139 I9 Khariar Orissa India
225 F3 Khārijah, Wāḩāt al oasis Egypt
150 B8 Kharīm, Jabal hill Egypt
151 E3 Kharist'vala Georgia
144 D7 Khārk i. Iran
138 H9 Kharkhara r. India
138 F5 Kharkhauda Haryana India
Kharkiv r. Rus. Fed./Ukr. see Khar'kov
159 P4 Kharkiv Ukr.
Kharkiv Oblast admin. div. Ukr. see Kharkivs'ka Oblast'
159 P4 Kharkivs'ka Oblast' admin. div. Ukr.
159 P3 Khar'kov r. Rus. Fed./Ukr.
Khar'kov Ukr. see Kharkiv
Kharkov Oblast admin. div. Ukr. see Kharkivs'ka Oblast'
Khar'kovskaya Oblast' admin. div. Ukr. see Kharkivs'ka Oblast'
156 G1 Kharlovka Rus. Fed.
156 E3 Kharlu Rus. Fed.
147 K9 Kharmah, Ghubbat b. Suquţrā Yemen
138 F2 Kharmang Pak.
219 N9 Kharmanli Bulg.
138 H9 Kharora Chhattisgarh India
145 M5 Kharoti reg. Afgh.
156 H4 Kharovsk Rus. Fed.
122 J3 Kharpin r. Rus. Fed.
144 D4 Khar Rūd r. Iran
139 J8 Kharsawan Jharkhand India
139 I8 Kharsia Chhattisgarh India
139 M6 Kharteng Arun. Prad. India
225 G6 Khartoum Sudan
225 G6 Khartoum state Sudan
225 G6 Khartoum North Sudan
159 R5 Khartsyz'k Ukr.
Kharuf, Ra's mt. Israel see Ḩarif, Har
156 L2 Kharutoyuvom Rus. Fed.
145 M5 Kharwar reg. Afgh.
147 L2 Khasab, Khor b. Oman
151 E2 Khasan'ya Rus. Fed.
151 D2 Khasaut Rus. Fed.
151 H2 Khasavyurt Rus. Fed.
145 J6 Khash Afgh.
145 I7 Khāsh Iran
145 J6 Khāsh, Dasht-e des. Afgh.
152 H3 Khashgort Rus. Fed.
225 G6 Khashm el Girba Sudan
232 B1 Khashm el Girba Dam Sudan
146 C2 Khashm Şana' Saudi Arabia
145 I6 Khash Rūd r. Afgh.
151 B2 Khashup'sa Georgia
151 E4 Khashuri Georgia
139 M7 Khasi Hills Meghalaya India
219 N9 Khaskovo Bulg.
146 D2 Khatam, Jabal al hill Saudi Arabia
153 L2 Khatanga Rus. Fed.
153 L2 Khatanga r. Rus. Fed.
Khatanga, Gulf of Rus. Fed. see Khatangskiy Zaliv
153 L2 Khatangskiy Zaliv b. Rus. Fed.
156 L2 Khatayakha Rus. Fed.
138 F8 Khategaon Madh. Prad. India
145 N3 Khatinza Pass Pak.
145 M3 Khatlon admin. div. Tajik.
Khatlon Oblast admin. div. Tajik. see Khatlon
146 G6 Khaţmah, Banī reg. Saudi Arabia
147 M3 Khatmat al Malāha Oman
147 M3 Khatt U.A.E.
151 F2 Khatuley Rus. Fed.
144 F6 Khātūnābād Iran
153 S3 Khatyrka Rus. Fed.
145 O5 Khaur Pak.
159 S2 Khava r. Rus. Fed.
145 M4 Khāvāk, Khowtal-e pass Afgh.
138 B8 Khavda Gujarat India
151 E4 Khavet'i Georgia
147 L9 Khawlaf, Ra's pt Suquţrā Yemen
147 M3 Khawr Fakkan U.A.E.
147 K6 Khawr Shiban well Saudi Arabia
118 C7 Khawsa Myanmar
146 E6 Khawsh Saudi Arabia
237 J7 Khayamnandi S. Africa
146 D3 Khaybar Al Madīnah Saudi Arabia
146 F6 Khaybar 'Asīr Saudi Arabia
143 N8 Khaydarken Kyrg.
236 C10 Khayelitsha S. Africa
156 L1 Khaypudyrskaya Guba b. Rus. Fed.
Khazarasp Uzbek. see Hazorasp
151 H3 Khebda Rus. Fed.
136 C3 Khed Mahar. India
136 C4 Khed Mahar. India
138 D8 Kheda Gujarat India
138 D7 Khedbrahma Gujarat India
144 H4 Khedrī Iran
Khefa Israel see Ḩefa
235 G4 Khehuene, Ponta pt Moz.
118 B1 Khela Arun. Prad. India
138 H5 Khela Uttaranchal India
139 J8 Khelari Jharkhand India
163 U6 Khelyulya Rus. Fed.
202 D5 Khemis Anjra Morocco
202 D5 Khemis Beni Arous Morocco
227 F1 Khemis Miliana Alg.
226 D2 Khemisset Morocco
226 C2 Khemis Zemamra Morocco
118 G6 Khemmarat Thai.
227 G2 Khenchela Alg.
226 D2 Khenifra Morocco
145 M4 Khenjan Afgh.
138 D8 Kheralu Gujarat India
144 E7 Kherāmeh Iran
144 E8 Kherreh Iran
144 D6 Khersan r. Iran
159 L7 Kherson Ukr.
159 M9 Khersones, Mys pt Ukr.
Kherson Oblast admin. div. Ukr. see Khersons'ka Oblast'
159 M7 Khersons'ka Oblast' admin. div. Ukr.
Khersonskaya Oblast' admin. div. Ukr. see Khersons'ka Oblast'
118 H6 Khe Sanh Vietnam
145 M4 Khesh Afgh.
144 D7 Khesht Iran
153 L2 Kheta r. Rus. Fed.
161 N1 Kheynyasensari, Ostrov i. Rus. Fed.
144 F7 Kheyrābād Iran
144 E3 Khezerābād Iran
119 E7 Khiaw, Khao mt. Thai.
139 J9 Khiching Orissa India
146 G5 Khidā, Jabal hill Saudi Arabia
151 F4 Khidist'avi Georgia
138 F7 Khilchipur Madh. Prad. India
Khiliomódhion Greece see Chiliomodi
129 L1 Khilok Rus. Fed.
129 J1 Khilok r. Rus. Fed.
Khimadhítis, Límni l. Greece see Cheimaditida, Limni
161 U6 Khimki Rus. Fed.
122 G4 Khingansk Rus. Fed.
122 F4 Khinganskiy Zapovednik nature res. Rus. Fed.
145 N9 Khinsar Pak.
138 C6 Khinyan Rajasthan India
Khíos i. Greece see Chios
Khios Strait Greece see Chios Strait
145 M9 Khipro Pak.
150 F3 Khirbat Isrīyah Syria
138 F8 Khirkiya Madh. Prad. India
219 M8 Khisarya Bulg.
161 P7 Khislavichi Rus. Fed.
133 D9 Khitai Dawan pass Aksai Chin
151 I4 Khiv Rus. Fed.
Khiwa Uzbek. see Xiva
144 B2 Khīyāv Iran
160 M1 Khiytola Rus. Fed.
161 R6 Khlepen' Rus. Fed.
161 W9 Khlevnoye Rus. Fed.
197 L5 Khlivchany Ukr.
119 E8 Khlong, Mae r. Thai.
119 D10 Khlong Saeng Wildlife Reserve nature res. Thai.
118 D6 Khlong Wang Chao National Park Thai.
119 F8 Khlung Thai.
161 R1 Khmelezero Rus. Fed.
161 V9 Khmelinets Rus. Fed.
161 Q6 Khmelita Rus. Fed.
159 M3 Khmeliv Ukr.
Khmel'nik Ukr. see Khmil'nyk
Khmel'nitskaya Oblast' admin. div. Ukr. see Khmel'nyts'ka Oblast'
Khmel'nitskiy Ukr. see Khmel'nyts'kyy
Khmelnitskiy Oblast admin. div. Ukr. see Khmel'nyts'ka Oblast'
158 G4 Khmel'nyts'ka Oblast' admin. div. Ukr.
158 F4 Khmel'nyts'kyy Ukr.
Khmelnytskyy Oblast admin. div. Ukr. see Khmel'nyts'ka Oblast'
159 K5 Khmel'ove Ukr.
Khmer Republic country Asia see Cambodia
202 D5 Khmes, Jebel mt. Morocco
158 G4 Khmil'nyk Ukr.
197 L3 Khmyelyeva Belarus
151 G6 Khndzorut Armenia
119 G10 Khoai, Hon i. Vietnam
142 F2 Khobda Kazakh.
151 C3 Khobi r. Georgia
161 X8 Khobotovo Rus. Fed.
197 M5 Khobultova Ukr.
144 G5 Khodā Āfarīd spring Iran
151 H6 Khodā Āfarīn Iran
160 I8 Khodarawtsy Belarus
161 O8 Khodasy Belarus
158 D4 Khodoriv Ukr.
158 I3 Khodorkiv Ukr.
151 B1 Khodz' Rus. Fed.
Khodzhal, Gora mt. Georgia see Khojali, Mt'a
Khodzhavend Azer. see Xocavänd
Khodzhent Tajik. see Khŭjand
Khodzheyli Qoraqalpog'iston Respublikasi Uzbek. see Xo'jayli
Khodzhorni Georgia see Khojorni
158 I8 Khodzhyder r. Ukr.
230 E3 Khogali Sudan
151 C3 Khojali, Mt'a Georgia
Khojand Tajik. see Khŭjand
151 F4 Khojorni Georgia
161 U2 Khokhlovo Rus. Fed.
157 G6 Khokhol'skiy Rus. Fed.
145 N9 Khokhropar Pak.
138 F3 Khoksar Hima. Prad. India
138 F9 Kholapur Mahar. India
159 R3 Kholkhol-Trostyanka Rus. Fed.
145 L3 Kholm Afgh.
Kholm Pol. see Chełm
161 O4 Kholm Novgorodskaya Oblast' Rus. Fed.
161 O6 Kholm Smolenskaya Oblast' Rus. Fed.
161 O6 Kholm Smolenskaya Oblast' Rus. Fed.
161 R9 Kholmechi Rus. Fed.
199 L3 Kholmets' Ukr.
156 H2 Kholmogory Rus. Fed.
122 L5 Kholmsk Sakhalin Rus. Fed.
159 R9 Kholmskiy Rus. Fed.
159 L2 Kholmy Ukr.
158 J1 Kholmyech Belarus
161 Q6 Kholm-Zhirkovskiy Rus. Fed.
Kholon Israel see Ḩolon
161 P3 Kholova r. Rus. Fed.
128 H1 Kholtoson Rus. Fed.
143 U2 Kholzun, Khrebet mts Kazakh./Rus. Fed.
144 C3 Khoman Iran
151 I6 Khomārlū Iran
234 C4 Khomas admin. reg. Namibia
234 B4 Khomas Highland hills Namibia
144 D5 Khomeyn Iran
144 D5 Khomeynīshahr Iran
158 G3 Khomora r. Ukr.
197 N3 Khomsk Belarus
159 M3 Khomutets' Ukr.
159 R6 Khomutove Ukr.
159 N2 Khomutovka Rus. Fed.
161 U9 Khomutovo Rus. Fed.
Khong, Mae Nam r. Myanmar see Salween
151 D3 Khoni Georgia
144 E8 Khonj Iran
144 E8 Khonj, Kūh-e mts Iran
118 F6 Khon Kaen Thai.
Khon Kriel Cambodia see Phumĭ Kon Kriel
Khonobod Uzbek. see Xonobod
Khonqa Uzbek. see Xonqa
139 O6 Khonsa Arun. Prad. India
153 P3 Khonuu Rus. Fed.
157 H6 Khoper r. Rus. Fed.
151 D3 Khop'uri Georgia
122 I5 Khor Rus. Fed.
122 I5 Khor r. Rus. Fed.
Khóra Greece see Chora
146 F9 Khôr 'Angar Djibouti
144 F4 Khorāsān, Chāh-e well Iran
144 H5 Khorāsān-e Jonūbī prov. Iran
144 G4 Khorāsān-e Razavī prov. Iran
144 G3 Khorāsān-e Shomālī prov. Iran
118 F6 Khorat Plateau Thai.
Khorazm Wiloyati admin. div. Uzbek. see Xorazm
139 J9 Khordha Orissa India
156 L2 Khoreyver Rus. Fed.
Khorezm Oblast admin. div. Uzbek. see Xorazm
121 I1 Khorinsk Rus. Fed.
234 B4 Khorixas Namibia
159 M7 Khorly Ukr.
144 D7 Khormūj, Kūh-e mt. Iran
Khorog Tajik. see Khorugh
122 H6 Khorol Rus. Fed.
159 M4 Khorol Ukr.
159 M4 Khorol r. Ukr.
159 P5 Khoroshe Ukr.
143 R1 Khorosheye Rus. Fed.
144 B2 Khoroslū Dāgh hills Iran
158 E4 Khorostkiv Ukr.
144 C5 Khorramābād Iran
144 C3 Khorram Darreh Iran
144 C6 Khorramshahr Iran
145 N3 Khorugh Tajik.
159 M3 Khoruzhivka Ukr.
156 L2 Khosedayu r. Rus. Fed.
157 I7 Khosheutovo Rus. Fed.
144 H6 Khoshkrūd Iran
144 C6 Khosravī Iran
151 F5 Khosrovi Argelanots' nature res. Armenia
144 C6 Khosrowābād Iran
149 L6 Khosrowvī Iran
145 M5 Khōst Afgh.
Khost prov. Afgh. see Khōst
145 M5 Khōst prov. Afgh.
145 M5 Khōst reg. Afgh./Pak.
145 L6 Khost Pak.
151 A2 Khosta Rus. Fed.
144 F7 Khosūyeh Iran
138 F5 Khot Haryana India
Khotan Xinjiang China see Hotan
139 K6 Khotang Nepal
197 M4 Khoteshiv Ukr.
161 T9 Khotetovo Rus. Fed.
159 P4 Khotimlya r. Ukr.
159 N2 Khotin' Ukr.
161 S8 Khot'kovo Kaluzhskaya Oblast' Rus. Fed.
161 U5 Khot'kovo Moskovskaya Oblast' Rus. Fed.
159 O3 Khotmyzhsk Rus. Fed.
244 H2 Khotol Mountain hill AK U.S.A.
161 Q8 Khotsimsk Belarus
159 K4 Khots'ky Ukr.
158 F5 Khotyn Ukr.
161 S8 Khotynets Rus. Fed.
226 D2 Khouribga Morocco
145 M2 Khovaling Tajik.
139 M7 Khowai Tripura India
Khowos Uzbek. see Xovos
144 E6 Khowrjān Iran
138 B2 Khowt-e Ashrow Afgh.
122 M3 Khoye Rus. Fed.
158 I2 Khoyniki Belarus
119 E8 Khram, Ko i. Thai.
143 U3 Khrebet Naryn mts Kazakh.
143 U4 Khrebet Sauyr mts China/Kazakh.
159 T2 Khrenovoye Rus. Fed.
159 L4 Khrestyteleve Ukr.
118 A4 Khreum Myanmar
139 M6 Khri r. India
Khrisoúpolis Greece see Chrysoupoli
156 I3 Khristoforovo Rus. Fed.
153 P2 Khroma r. Rus. Fed.
142 H2 Khromtau Kazakh.

139 O6 **Khru** *r.* India
Khrushchev Ukr. *see* **Svitlovods'k**
161 X7 **Khrushchevo** Rus. Fed.
122 I6 **Khrustalnyy** Rus. Fed.
Khrysokhou Bay Cyprus *see* **Chrysochou Bay**
159 M6 **Khrystoforivka** *Dnipropetrovs'ka Oblast'* Ukr.
159 L6 **Khrystoforivka** *Mykolayivs'ka Oblast'* Ukr.
158 I5 **Khrystynivka** Ukr.
237 M5 **Khubelu** *r.* Lesotho
151 I4 **Khuchni** Rus. Fed.
Khudat Azer. *see* **Xudat**
144 F2 **Khudayberdy** Turkm.
145 P6 **Khudian** Pak.
145 L8 **Khudo Range** Pak.
147 I7 **Khuḑrah, Wādī** *r.* Yemen
234 E4 **Khudumelapye** Botswana
Khudzhand Tajik. *see* **Khŭjand**
146 H4 **Khufaysah, Khashm al** *hill* Saudi Arabia
146 G3 **Khuff** Saudi Arabia
Khugiana Afgh. *see* **Pirzada**
145 L6 **Khugiani** Afgh.
144 I9 **Khūh Lab, Ra's** *pt* Iran
236 F2 **Khuis** Botswana
145 M1 **Khŭjand** Tajik.
Khŭjand *admin. div.* Tajik. *see* **Soghd**
Khŭjayli Uzbek. *see* **Xo'jayli**
119 G7 **Khu Khan** Thai.
159 N3 **Khukhra** Ukr.
146 D4 **Khulays** Saudi Arabia
138 E9 **Khuldabad** *Mahar.* India
156 M2 **Khulga** *r.* Rus. Fed.
156 M3 **Khulimsunt** Rus. Fed.
145 L3 **Khulm** *r.* Afgh.
139 L8 **Khulna** Bangl.
139 L8 **Khulna** *admin. div.* Bangl.
237 K2 **Khuma** S. Africa
151 F2 **Khumalag** Rus. Fed.
119 G9 **Khŭm Batheay** Cambodia
150 F4 **Khunayzīr, Jabal al** *mts* Syria
225 F6 **Khuneiqa** *watercourse* Sudan
144 H5 **Khūnīk Bālā** Iran
Khūnīnshahr Iran *see* **Khorramshahr**
138 E1 **Khunjerab National Park** Pak.
138 E1 **Khunjerab Pass** China/Pak.
139 J8 **Khunti** *Jharkhand* India
118 C5 **Khun Yuam** Thai.
151 H3 **Khunzakh** Rus. Fed.
161 X8 **Khupta** *r.* Rus. Fed.
144 H4 **Khūr** Iran
144 H5 **Khūr** Iran
138 G7 **Khurai** *Madh. Prad.* India
144 F8 **Khūran** *sea chan.* Iran
147 I3 **Khurayş** Saudi Arabia
146 G6 **Khurb, Banī** *hills* Saudi Arabia
224 E6 **Khureit** Sudan
Khuria Tank *resr Chhattisgarh* India *see* **Maniari Tank**
138 F5 **Khurja** *Uttar Prad.* India
145 J5 **Khurmalik** Afgh.
122 J3 **Khurmuli** Rus. Fed.
149 K8 **Khurr, Wādī al** *watercourse* Saudi Arabia
144 E7 **Khūrrāb** Iran
151 D2 **Khurzuk** Rus. Fed.
144 H5 **Khūsf** Iran
145 O5 **Khushab** Pak.
145 N5 **Khushalgarh** Pak.
144 C3 **Khūshāvar** Iran
150 E9 **Khushshah, Wādī al** *watercourse* Jordan/Saudi Arabia
144 F3 **Khush Yailaq** *hill* Iran
145 J5 **Khuspas** Afgh.
158 C5 **Khust** Ukr.
160 L8 **Khutar** Belarus
138 H9 **Khutgaon** *Mahar.* India
150 A8 **Khutmīyah, Mamarr al** *pass* Egypt
157 H7 **Khutorskoy** Rus. Fed.
234 E4 **Khutse Game Reserve** *nature res.* Botswana
237 L2 **Khutsong** S. Africa
122 K4 **Khutu** *r.* Rus. Fed.
225 F6 **Khuwei** Sudan
145 L8 **Khuzdar** Pak.
144 C6 **Khūzestān** *prov.* Iran
144 I4 **Khvāf** *reg.* Iran
144 B2 **Khvājeh** Iran
144 I6 **Khvājeh Dow Chāhī** Iran
145 M3 **Khvājeh Ghār** Afgh.
142 C1 **Khvalynsk** Rus. Fed.
151 E3 **Khvanchkara** Georgia
144 D5 **Khvānsār** Iran
144 F7 **Khvānsār** Iran
161 S6 **Khvashchevka** Rus. Fed.
161 S8 **Khvastovichi** Rus. Fed.
144 F6 **Khvodrān** Iran
144 F5 **Khvor** Iran
144 G4 **Khvord Nārvan** Iran
144 D7 **Khvormūj** Iran
161 X9 **Khvorostyanka** *Lipetskaya Oblast'* Rus. Fed.
142 C1 **Khvorostyanka** *Samarskaya Oblast'* Rus. Fed.
144 F4 **Khvors** Iran
144 B3 **Khvosh Maqām** Iran
161 N6 **Khvoshna** Belarus
144 A2 **Khvoy** Iran
161 R3 **Khvoynaya** Rus. Fed.
122 E1 **Khvoynyy** Rus. Fed.
119 D8 **Khwae Noi** *r.* Thai.
145 N3 **Khwahan** Afgh.
145 J6 **Khwaja Ali** Afgh.
145 L6 **Khwaja Amran** *mt.* Pak.
145 N3 **Khwaja Muhammad Range** *mts* Afgh.
145 N4 **Khyber Pass** Afgh./Pak.
Khynchest' Moldova *see* **Hînceşti**
Khynchesty Moldova *see* **Hînceşti**
197 K6 **Khyriv** Ukr.
Khyrov Ukr. *see* **Khyriv**
Khyzy Azer. *see* **Xızı**
151 H3 **Khzanor** *r.* Rus. Fed.
100 □6 **Kia** *Sta Isabel* Solomon Is
144 H9 **Kīā'ī** Iran
105 M6 **Kiama** *N.S.W.* Austr.
114 E8 **Kiamba** *Mindanao* Phil.
231 F6 **Kiambi** Dem. Rep. Congo
258 F1 **Kiamesha Lake** *NY* U.S.A.
261 H9 **Kiamichi** *r. OK* U.S.A.
244 G2 **Kiana** *AK* U.S.A.
Kiangsi *prov.* China *see* **Jiangxi**
Kiangsu *prov.* China *see* **Jiangsu**
228 B3 **Kiang West National Park** Gambia
Kianly Turkm. *see* **Tarta**
162 T4 **Kiantajärvi** *l.* Fin.
138 G3 **Kiari** *Jammu and Kashmir* India
144 E3 **Kīāsar** Iran
243 M2 **Kiatassuaq** *i.* Greenland
220 D4 **Kiato** Greece
164 E5 **Kibæk** Denmark
233 C6 **Kibaha** Tanz.
231 B6 **Kibala** Angola
232 A4 **Kibale** Uganda
230 F4 **Kibali** *r.* Dem. Rep. Congo
231 B6 **Kibambi** Dem. Rep. Congo
231 B5 **Kibangou** Congo
233 B5 **Kibara** Tanz.
231 E7 **Kibara, Monts** *mts* Dem. Rep. Congo
233 B7 **Kibau** Tanz.
114 E8 **Kibawe** *Mindanao* Phil.
233 C6 **Kibaya** Tanz.
233 C6 **Kiberashi** Tanz.
233 C6 **Kiberege** Tanz.
126 B7 **Kibi** Japan
231 C6 **Kibinga** Dem. Rep. Congo
232 A4 **Kiboga** Uganda
231 E5 **Kibombo** Dem. Rep. Congo
233 A5 **Kibondo** Tanz.
Kibray Uzbek. *see* **Qibray**
232 C3 **Kibre Mengist** Eth.
Kibris *country* Asia *see* **Cyprus**
233 A5 **Kibungo** Rwanda
233 A5 **Kibuye** Rwanda
233 A6 **Kibwesa** Tanz.
173 K2 **Kibworth Harcourt** *Leicestershire, England* U.K.
218 I9 **Kičevo** Macedonia
224 C5 **Kichi-Kichi** *well* Chad
156 I4 **Kichmengskiy Gorodok** Rus. Fed.
232 A5 **Kichwamba** Uganda
144 F2 **Kiçi Balkan Daglary** *hill* Turkm.
151 I5 **Kiçik Dähnä** Azer.
246 G5 **Kicking Horse Pass** *Alta/B.C.* Can.
229 F2 **Kidal** Mali
229 F2 **Kidal** *admin. reg.* Mali
233 C6 **Kidatu** Tanz.
233 C6 **Kidayi** Tanz.
172 H3 **Kidderminster** *Worcestershire, England* U.K.
237 L9 **Kidd's Beach** S. Africa
232 B4 **Kidepo Valley National Park** Uganda
233 C6 **Kidete** Tanz.
228 B3 **Kidira** Senegal
173 J4 **Kidlington** *Oxfordshire, England* U.K.
138 G3 **Kidmang** *Jammu and Kashmir* India
102 L6 **Kidnappers, Cape** *North I.* N.Z.
201 M7 **Kidričevo** Slovenia
171 M7 **Kidsgrove** *Staffordshire, England* U.K.
233 C6 **Kidugallo** Tanz.
117 J3 **Kidurong, Tanjung** *pt* Malaysia
146 E6 **Kidwat at A'waj** Saudi Arabia
172 D4 **Kidwelly** *Carmarthenshire, Wales* U.K.
191 F10 **Kiedrich** Ger.
195 M6 **Kiefersfelden** Ger.
196 E3 **Kiekrz** Pol.
190 J2 **Kiel** Ger.
250 F6 **Kiel** *WI* U.S.A.
Kiel Canal Ger. *see* **Nord-Ostsee-Kanal**
197 I5 **Kielce** Pol.
197 J3 **Kiełczew** Pol.
196 G4 **Kiełczygłów** Pol.
171 L3 **Kielder Water** *resr England* U.K.
187 F6 **Kieldrecht** Belgium
190 K2 **Kieler Bucht** *b.* Ger.
190 J2 **Kieler Förde** *g.* Ger.
228 E3 **Kiembara** Burkina
197 H3 **Kiemozia** Pol.
195 M5 **Kienberg** Ger.
231 E7 **Kienge** Dem. Rep. Congo
191 E8 **Kierspe** Ger.
191 J9 **Kieselbach** Ger.
100 □6 **Kieta** P.N.G.
196 G5 **Kietrz** Pol.
192 K5 **Kietz** Ger.
Kīev Kazakh. *see* **Kiyevka**
Kiev Ukr. *see* **Kyiv**
Kiev Oblast *admin. div.* Ukr. *see* **Kyivs'ka Oblast'**
228 C2 **Kiffa** Maur.
220 E4 **Kifisia** Greece
220 E4 **Kifisos** *r.* Greece
149 L6 **Kifrī** Iraq
231 C6 **Kifwanzondo** Dem. Rep. Congo
233 A5 **Kigali** Rwanda
244 I1 **Kigalik** *r. AK* U.S.A.
149 J4 **Kiğı** Turkey
249 I1 **Kiglapait Mountains** *Nfld and Lab.* Can.
244 F2 **Kigluaik Mountains** *AK* U.S.A.
228 D4 **Kignan** Mali
233 A6 **Kigoma** Tanz.
233 A6 **Kigoma** *admin. reg.* Tanz.
233 A6 **Kigosi** *r.* Tanz.
233 A6 **Kigosi Game Reserve** *res.* Tanzania
233 B6 **Kigwe** Tanz.
117 J5 **Kihambatang** *Kalimantan* Indon.
264 □E13 **Kīhei** *HI* U.S.A.
102 J5 **Kihikihi** *North I.* N.Z.
162 Q3 **Kihlanki** Fin.
163 Q5 **Kihniö** Fin.
160 G3 **Kihnu** *i.* Estonia
264 □F14 **Kīholo** *HI* U.S.A.
126 C8 **Kii-hantō** *pen.* Japan
162 U5 **Kiihtelysvaara** Fin.
143 O4 **Kiik** Kazakh.
160 G1 **Kiikala** Fin.
163 Q6 **Kiikoinen** Fin.
162 R4 **Kiiminki** Fin.
126 D7 **Kii-Nagashima** Japan
125 H15 **Kiire** Japan
126 C8 **Kii-sanchi** *mts* Japan
162 R3 **Kiistala** Fin.
126 A8 **Kii-suidō** *sea chan.* Japan
213 Q6 **Kijac, Rt** *pt* Croatia
197 I5 **Kije** Pol.
196 G2 **Kijewo Królewskie** Pol.
127 H2 **Kijimadaira** Japan
125 I14 **Kijo** Japan
233 C6 **Kijungu Well** Tanz.
124 □G18 **Kikai** *Nansei-shotō* Japan
124 □H18 **Kikai-jima** *i. Nansei-shotō* Japan
160 M2 **Kikerino** Rus. Fed.
245 J1 **Kikiakrorak** *r. AK* U.S.A.
218 I5 **Kikinda** *Vojvodina* Serbia
145 J9 **Kikki** Pak.
Kikládhes *is* Greece *see* **Kyklades**
244 F3 **Kikmiktalikamiut** *AK* U.S.A.
156 I4 **Kiknur** Rus. Fed.
197 H3 **Kikół** Pol.
124 R5 **Kikonai** Japan
231 E7 **Kikondja** Dem. Rep. Congo
231 C6 **Kikongo** Dem. Rep. Congo
113 J8 **Kikori** P.N.G.
113 J8 **Kikori** *r.* P.N.G.
196 D2 **Kikorze** Pol.
125 H14 **Kikuchi** Japan
127 H6 **Kikugawa** Japan
157 H6 **Kikvidze** Rus. Fed.
231 C6 **Kikwit** Dem. Rep. Congo
164 F3 **Kil** Norway
164 J2 **Kil** Sweden
165 N3 **Kilaån** *r.* Sweden
163 N6 **Kilafors** Sweden
136 F8 **Kilakkarai** *Tamil Nadu* India
144 E4 **Kīlān** Iran
138 F3 **Kilar** *Hima. Prad.* India
264 □B11 **Kilauea** *HI* U.S.A.
264 □F14 **Kilauea Crater** *HI* U.S.A.
201 L3 **Kilb** Austria
169 C7 **Kilbaha** Ireland
169 H6 **Kilbeggan** Ireland
169 F8 **Kilbeheny** Ireland
169 H6 **Kilberry** *Kildare* Ireland
169 I5 **Kilberry** *Meath* Ireland
168 E11 **Kilberry** *Argyll and Bute, Scotland* U.K.
170 H2 **Kilbirnie** *North Ayrshire, Scotland* U.K.
162 L3 **Kilboghamn** Norway
115 G5 **Kilbon** *Seram* Indon.
162 N2 **Kilbotn** Norway
168 F12 **Kilbrannan Sound** *sea chan. Scotland* U.K.
169 J6 **Kilbride** *Meath* Ireland
170 E7 **Kilbride** *Wicklow* Ireland
169 J7 **Kilbride** *Wicklow* Ireland
168 F10 **Kilbride** *Argyll and Bute, Scotland* U.K.
169 E9 **Kilbrittain** Ireland
244 H3 **Kilbuck Mountains** *AK* U.S.A.
Kilcar Ireland *see* **Cill Charthaigh**
169 H6 **Kilcavan** Ireland
194 F7 **Kilchberg** Switz.
159 O5 **Kil'chen'** *r.* Ukr.
168 E12 **Kilchenzie** *Argyll and Bute, Scotland* U.K.
168 D9 **Kilchoan** *Highland, Scotland* U.K.
168 F10 **Kilchrenan** *Argyll and Bute, Scotland* U.K.
123 F8 **Kilchu** N. Korea
169 I6 **Kilcock** Ireland
169 E6 **Kilcolgan** Ireland
169 E9 **Kilcolman** Ireland
169 G8 **Kilcommon** Ireland
169 F6 **Kilconnell** Ireland
169 H4 **Kilconney** Ireland
169 J6 **Kilcoole** Ireland
169 G6 **Kilcormac** Ireland
107 N9 **Kilcoy** *Qld* Austr.
168 G11 **Kilcreggan** *Argyll and Bute, Scotland* U.K.
169 F6 **Kilcrow** *r.* Ireland
169 I6 **Kilcullen** Ireland
169 I5 **Kildalkey** Ireland
169 I6 **Kildare** Ireland
169 I6 **Kildare** *county* Ireland
169 E7 **Kildimo New** Ireland
162 V2 **Kil'dinstroy** Rus. Fed.
168 F12 **Kildonan** *North Ayrshire, Scotland* U.K.
235 F3 **Kildonan** Zimbabwe
169 F8 **Kildorrery** Ireland
169 I3 **Kildress** *Northern Ireland* U.K.
245 Q2 **Kilekale Lake** *N.W.T.* Can.
156 I4 **Kilemary** Rus. Fed.
231 C6 **Kilembe** Dem. Rep. Congo
231 E6 **Kileo** Dem. Rep. Congo
169 D7 **Kilfenora** Ireland
168 F11 **Kilfinan** *Argyll and Bute, Scotland* U.K.
169 F8 **Kilfinnane** Ireland
172 C4 **Kilgetty** *Pembrokeshire, Wales* U.K.
169 F6 **Kilglass** *Galway* Ireland
169 F5 **Kilglass** *Roscommon* Ireland
169 F5 **Kilglass Lough** *l.* Ireland
169 C8 **Kilgobnet** Ireland
261 H9 **Kilgore** *TX* U.S.A.
106 E4 **Kilgour** *r. N.T.* Austr.
171 Q5 **Kilham** *East Riding of Yorkshire, England* U.K.
171 M2 **Kilham** *Northumberland, England* U.K.
Kilia Ukr. *see* **Kiliya**
227 H5 **Kilian, Erg** *des.* Alg.
231 F5 **Kiliba** Dem. Rep. Congo
229 F4 **Kilibo** Benin
221 L5 **Kılıç** Turkey
151 C5 **Kılıçkaya** Turkey
151 A5 **Kılıçlı** Turkey
233 C5 **Kilifi** Kenya
133 B8 **Kilik Pass** *Xinjiang* China
233 C5 **Kilimanjaro** *admin. reg.* Tanz.
233 C5 **Kilimanjaro** *vol.* Tanz.
233 C5 **Kilimanjaro National Park** Tanz.
233 B6 **Kilimatinde** Tanz.
99 F2 **Kilinailau Islands** P.N.G.
233 C6 **Kilindoni** Tanz.
160 H3 **Kilingi-Nõmme** Estonia
148 H5 **Kilis** Turkey
150 F2 **Kilis** *prov.* Turkey
158 I8 **Kiliya** Ukr.
170 D8 **Kilkea** Ireland
169 C7 **Kilkee** Ireland
169 K4 **Kilkeel** *Northern Ireland* U.K.
169 E5 **Kilkelly** Ireland
169 H7 **Kilkenny** Ireland
169 H7 **Kilkenny** *county* Ireland
169 E5 **Kilkerrin** Ireland
172 D6 **Kilkhampton** *Cornwall, England* U.K.
169 D8 **Kilkinlea** Ireland
220 D2 **Kilkis** Greece
107 N9 **Kilkivan** *Qld* Austr.
169 I6 **Kill** *Kildare* Ireland
169 H8 **Kill** *Waterford* Ireland
169 C9 **Killabunane** Ireland
170 B5 **Killadeas** *Northern Ireland* U.K.
169 D7 **Killadysert** Ireland
170 E3 **Killagan Bridge** *Northern Ireland* U.K.
169 D4 **Killala** Ireland
169 D4 **Killala Bay** Ireland
250 H1 **Killala Lake** *Ont.* Can.
169 F7 **Killaloe** Ireland
251 Q4 **Killaloe Station** *Ont.* Can.
247 I4 **Killam** *Alta* Can.
169 H8 **Killamerry** Ireland
169 I7 **Killann** Ireland
169 C7 **Killard** Ireland
106 C4 **Killarney** *N.T.* Austr.
105 N3 **Killarney** *Qld* Austr.
248 D4 **Killarney** *Ont.* Can.
169 D8 **Killarney** Ireland
255 □2 **Killarney, Lake** *New Prov.* Bahamas
169 C9 **Killarney National Park** Ireland
251 M3 **Killarney Provincial Park** *Ont.* Can.
169 D6 **Killarone** Ireland
169 C5 **Killary Harbour** *b.* Ireland
170 C7 **Killaskillen** Ireland
169 E8 **Killavullen** Ireland
169 G9 **Killeagh** *Cork* Ireland
168 E11 **Killean** *Argyll and Bute, Scotland* U.K.
Killeany Ireland *see* **Cill Éinne**
168 H10 **Killearn** *Stirling, Scotland* U.K.
261 G10 **Killeen** *TX* U.S.A.
169 H6 **Killeigh** Ireland
169 G3 **Killen** *Northern Ireland* U.K.
169 I7 **Killerrig** Ireland
169 G4 **Killeshandra** Ireland
151 D5 **Killı Dağ** *mt.* Turkey
168 I9 **Killiecrankie** *Perth and Kinross, Scotland* U.K.
221 J4 **Killik** Turkey
244 I1 **Killik** *r. AK* U.S.A.
169 D7 **Killimer** Ireland
169 F6 **Killimor** Ireland
168 H10 **Killin** *Stirling, Scotland* U.K.
169 K4 **Killinchy** *Northern Ireland* U.K.
Killinek Island *Nfld and Lab./Nunavut* Can. *see* **Killiniq Island**
162 P3 **Killinge** Sweden
171 N3 **Killingworth** *Tyne and Wear, England* U.K.
259 J2 **Killingworth** *CT* U.S.A.
Killíni *mt.* Greece *see* **Kyllini**
249 H1 **Killiniq** *Que.* Can.
249 H1 **Killiniq Island** *Nfld and Lab./Nunavut* Can.
163 Q5 **Killinkoski** Fin.
169 C8 **Killorglin** Ireland
169 J6 **Killough** Ireland
169 K4 **Killough** *Northern Ireland* U.K.
170 C6 **Killucan** Ireland
168 E9 **Killundine** *Highland, Scotland* U.K.
169 I8 **Killurin** Ireland
169 F3 **Killybegs** Ireland
169 H3 **Killyclogher** *Northern Ireland* U.K.
169 H5 **Killyconnan** Ireland
169 G3 **Killygordon** Ireland
169 I4 **Killylea** *Northern Ireland* U.K.
170 E7 **Kilmacanogue** Ireland
170 H2 **Kilmacolm** *Inverclyde, Scotland* U.K.
169 G2 **Kilmacrenan** Ireland
169 H8 **Kilmacthomas** Ireland
169 H8 **Kilmaganny** Ireland
169 D5 **Kilmaine** Ireland
169 D7 **Kilmaley** Ireland
168 F9 **Kilmalieu** *Highland, Scotland* U.K.
169 E8 **Kilmallock** Ireland
168 D7 **Kilmaluag** *Highland, Scotland* U.K.
169 H7 **Kilmanagh** Ireland
168 H11 **Kilmarnock** *East Ayrshire, Scotland* U.K.
257 I11 **Kilmarnock** *VA* U.S.A.
168 F10 **Kilmartin** *Argyll and Bute, Scotland* U.K.
170 H2 **Kilmaurs** *East Ayrshire, Scotland* U.K.
170 D7 **Kilmeague** Ireland
169 C5 **Kilmeena** Ireland
168 F10 **Kilmelford** *Argyll and Bute, Scotland* U.K.
156 J4 **Kil'mez'** Rus. Fed.
156 J4 **Kil'mez'** *r.* Rus. Fed.
169 J7 **Kilmichael Point** Ireland
172 F6 **Kilmington** *Devon, England* U.K.
169 E9 **Kilmona** Ireland
105 J7 **Kilmore** *Vic.* Austr.
169 E7 **Kilmore** *Clare* Ireland
169 I8 **Kilmore** *Wexford* Ireland
169 I8 **Kilmore Quay** Ireland
169 D8 **Kilmorna** Ireland
168 E11 **Kilmory** *Argyll and Bute, Scotland* U.K.
168 D8 **Kilmory** *Highland, Scotland* U.K.
169 E7 **Kilmurry** Ireland
170 D8 **Kilmyshall** Ireland
169 D7 **Kilnaboy** Ireland
169 H5 **Kilnaleck** Ireland
169 J7 **Kilnamanagh** Ireland
168 D9 **Kilninian** *Argyll and Bute, Scotland* U.K.
168 E10 **Kilninver** *Argyll and Bute, Scotland* U.K.
169 E5 **Kilnock** Ireland
168 D10 **Kiloran** *Argyll and Bute, Scotland* U.K.
233 C6 **Kilosa** Tanz.
162 P2 **Kilpisjärvi** Fin.
162 R4 **Kilpua** Fin.
169 I7 **Kilquiggin** Ireland
169 I3 **Kilrea** *Northern Ireland* U.K.
169 F3 **Kilrean** Ireland
169 F6 **Kilreekill** Ireland
Kilronan Ireland *see* **Cill Rónáin**
169 G3 **Kilross** *Donegal* Ireland
169 F8 **Kilross** *Tipperary* Ireland
169 D7 **Kilrush** Ireland
169 E5 **Kilsallagh** Ireland
170 E6 **Kilsaran** Ireland
169 I5 **Kilskeer** Ireland
170 B5 **Kilskeery** *Northern Ireland* U.K.
168 H11 **Kilsyth** *North Lanarkshire, Scotland* U.K.
136 C7 **Kiltan** *atoll* India
169 E6 **Kiltartan** Ireland
169 I7 **Kiltealy** Ireland
170 D7 **Kilteel** Ireland
169 I7 **Kiltegan** Ireland
169 E5 **Kiltimagh** Ireland
169 F6 **Kiltoom** Ireland
169 E6 **Kiltullagh** Ireland
159 P7 **Kil'tychchya** *r.* Ukr.
170 A5 **Kiltyclogher** Ireland
231 F7 **Kilwa** Dem. Rep. Congo
233 C7 **Kilwa Kivinje** Tanz.
233 C7 **Kilwa Masoko** Tanz.
169 K3 **Kilwaughter** *Northern Ireland* U.K.
168 G11 **Kilwinning** *North Ayrshire, Scotland* U.K.
169 F8 **Kilworth** Ireland
Kilyazi Azer. *see* **Giläzi**
230 B2 **Kim** Chad
138 D9 **Kim** *r.* India
261 D7 **Kim** *CO* U.S.A.
233 C7 **Kimambi** Tanz.
117 K2 **Kimanis, Teluk** *b.* Malaysia
104 F5 **Kimba** *S.A.* Austr.
231 B5 **Kimba** Congo
260 D5 **Kimball** *NE* U.S.A.
256 C7 **Kimball** *OH* U.S.A.
245 K3 **Kimball, Mount** *AK* U.S.A.
113 L8 **Kimbe** *New Britain* P.N.G.
246 H5 **Kimberley** *B.C.* Can.
237 I4 **Kimberley** S. Africa
173 O2 **Kimberley** *Norfolk, England* U.K.
108 H4 **Kimberley Downs** *W.A.* Austr.
108 I4 **Kimberley Plateau** *W.A.* Austr.
109 E9 **Kimberley Range** *hills W.A.* Austr.
258 D4 **Kimberton** *PA* U.S.A.
228 D4 **Kimbirila-Sud** Côte d'Ivoire
173 L3 **Kimbolton** *Cambridgeshire, England* U.K.
123 F8 **Kimch'aek** N. Korea
123 F10 **Kimch'ŏn** S. Korea
123 F11 **Kimhae** S. Korea
Kími Greece *see* **Kymi**
163 Q6 **Kimito** Fin.
127 K5 **Kimitsu** Japan
123 E11 **Kimje** S. Korea
243 L3 **Kimmirut** *Nunavut* Can.
124 R4 **Kimobetsu** Japan
220 F6 **Kimolos** *i.* Greece
220 F6 **Kimolou-Sifnou, Steno** *sea chan.* Greece
231 B6 **Kimongo** Congo
161 V8 **Kimovsk** Rus. Fed.
231 E6 **Kimpanga** Dem. Rep. Congo
231 B6 **Kimpangu** Dem. Rep. Congo
228 D3 **Kimparana** Mali
256 C11 **Kimper** *KY* U.S.A.
231 B6 **Kimpese** Dem. Rep. Congo
231 B6 **Kimpila** Congo
231 B6 **Kimpoko** Dem. Rep. Congo
Kimpoku-san *mt.* Japan *see* **Kinpoku-san**
173 L4 **Kimpton** *Hertfordshire, England* U.K.
161 U5 **Kimry** Rus. Fed.
246 E4 **Kimsquit** *B.C.* Can.
165 L3 **Kimstad** Sweden
231 B6 **Kimvula** Dem. Rep. Congo
156 I2 **Kimzha** Rus. Fed.
124 □1 **Kin** *Okinawa* Japan
124 □1 **Kina** *Okinawa* Japan
117 L1 **Kinabalu, Gunung** *mt. Sabah* Malaysia
117 L1 **Kinabalu National Park** Malaysia
117 L2 **Kinabatangan** *r.* Malaysia
117 M2 **Kinabatangan, Kuala** *r. mouth* Malaysia
221 K2 **Kınalıada** *i.* Turkey
233 C6 **Kinango** Kenya
221 H6 **Kinaros** *i.* Greece
117 L2 **Kinarut** *Sabah* Malaysia
127 H2 **Kinasa** Japan
197 M6 **Kinashiv** Ukr.
245 O4 **Kinaskan Lake** *B.C.* Can.
246 G4 **Kinbasket Lake** *B.C.* Can.
Kinbirila Côte d'Ivoire *see* **Kimbirila-Sud**
168 I6 **Kinbrace** *Highland, Scotland* U.K.
159 K7 **Kinburns'ka Kosa** *spit* Ukr.
247 J5 **Kincaid** *Sask.* Can.
248 D4 **Kincardine** *Ont.* Can.
171 J1 **Kincardine** *Fife, Scotland* U.K.
168 K8 **Kincardine O'Neil** *Aberdeenshire, Scotland* U.K.
118 D1 **Kinchang** Myanmar
105 I5 **Kinchega National Park** *N.S.W.* Austr.
245 O5 **Kincolith** *B.C.* Can.
168 I8 **Kincraig** *Highland, Scotland* U.K.
199 H4 **Kincses** Hungary
231 E7 **Kinda** Dem. Rep. Congo
231 B5 **Kindamba** Congo
118 B3 **Kindat** Myanmar
201 L4 **Kindberg** Austria
251 L6 **Kinde** *MI* U.S.A.
231 B6 **Kindeje** Angola
193 D8 **Kindelbrück** Ger.
231 E7 **Kindele** Dem. Rep. Congo
231 C6 **Kindembe** Dem. Rep. Congo
261 I10 **Kinder** *LA* U.S.A.
191 D10 **Kinderbeuern** Ger.
186 G5 **Kinderdijk** Neth.
171 N7 **Kinder Scout** *hill England* U.K.
247 I5 **Kindersley** *Sask.* Can.
228 B4 **Kindia** Guinea
195 K4 **Kinding** Ger.
231 C5 **Kindongo-Mbe** Dem. Rep. Congo
159 N2 **Kindrativka** Ukr.
194 D3 **Kindsbach** Ger.
231 E5 **Kindu** Dem. Rep. Congo
244 G4 **Kinegnak** *AK* U.S.A.
157 J5 **Kinel'** Rus. Fed.
142 D1 **Kinel'-Cherkasy** Rus. Fed.
156 H4 **Kineshma** Rus. Fed.
173 I4 **Kineton** *Gloucestershire, England* U.K.
106 D1 **King** *r. N.T.* Austr.
106 D3 **King** *r. N.T.* Austr.
108 J3 **King** *r. W.A.* Austr.
283 B7 **King, Canal** *sea chan.* Chile
109 F8 **King, Lake** *salt flat W.A.* Austr.
256 I11 **King and Queen Courthouse** *VA* U.S.A.
231 B6 **Kinganga** Dem. Rep. Congo
107 M9 **Kingaroy** *Qld* Austr.
169 F3 **Kingarrow** Ireland
168 F11 **Kingarth** *Argyll and Bute, Scotland* U.K.
243 H2 **King Christian Island** *Nunavut* Can.
264 K5 **King City** *CA* U.S.A.
246 E5 **Kingcome** *r. B.C.* Can.
244 G5 **King Cove** *AK* U.S.A.
106 G8 **King Creek** *watercourse Qld* Austr.
108 I3 **King Edward** *r. W.A.* Austr.
179 N8 **Kingersheim** France
257 □O4 **Kingfield** *ME* U.S.A.
261 G8 **Kingfisher** *OK* U.S.A.
256 H10 **King George** *VA* U.S.A.
283 E8 **King George Bay** Falkland Is
286 U2 **King George Island** Antarctica
248 E1 **King George Islands** *Nunavut* Can.
King George Islands *Arch. des Tuamotu* Fr. Polynesia *see* **Roi Georges, Îles du**
109 E13 **King George Sound** *b. W.A.* Austr.
275 F3 **King George VI Falls** Guyana
287 A2 **King Haakon VII Sea** Southern Ocean
108 G7 **King Hill** *W.A.* Austr.
168 J10 **Kinghorn** *Fife, Scotland* U.K.
168 F8 **Kingie** *r. Scotland* U.K.
231 B6 **Kingimbi** Dem. Rep. Congo
160 L2 **Kingisepp** Rus. Fed.
105 I8 **King Island** *Tas.* Austr.
246 E4 **King Island** *B.C.* Can.
King Island Myanmar *see* **Kadan Kyun**
244 E2 **King Island** *AK* U.S.A.
Kingisseppa Estonia *see* **Kuressaare**
251 O1 **King Kirkland** *Ont.* Can.
105 J7 **Kinglake National Park** *Vic.* Austr.
287 F2 **King Leopold and Queen Astrid Coast** Antarctica
108 H4 **King Leopold Range National Park** *W.A.* Austr.
108 H4 **King Leopold Ranges** *hills W.A.* Austr.
265 R6 **Kingman** *AZ* U.S.A.
261 F7 **Kingman** *KS* U.S.A.
257 □Q3 **Kingman** *ME* U.S.A.
97 I3 **Kingman Reef** N. Pacific Ocean
245 O4 **King Mountain** *B.C.* Can.
261 D10 **King Mountain** *hill TX* U.S.A.
Kingnait *Nunavut* Can. *see* **Cape Dorset**
258 E4 **King of Prussia** *PA* U.S.A.
231 E5 **Kingombe Mbali** Dem. Rep. Congo
231 C6 **Kingondji** Dem. Rep. Congo
104 E4 **Kingoonya** *S.A.* Austr.
286 S1 **King Peak** Antarctica
286 R2 **King Peninsula** Antarctica
104 □2 **King Point** *Lord Howe I.* Austr.
145 M6 **Kingri** Pak.
169 H7 **Kings** *r.* Ireland
264 L5 **Kings** *r. CA* U.S.A.
262 E6 **Kings** *r. NV* U.S.A.
244 H4 **King Salmon** *AK* U.S.A.
244 H4 **King Salmon** *r. AK* U.S.A.
168 K10 **Kingsbarns** *Fife, Scotland* U.K.
172 E7 **Kingsbridge** *Devon, England* U.K.
264 M5 **Kingsburg** *CA* U.S.A.
173 I2 **Kingsbury** *Warwickshire, England* U.K.
172 G6 **Kingsbury Episcopi** *Somerset, England* U.K.
106 C8 **Kings Canyon** *N.T.* Austr.
264 N5 **Kings Canyon National Park** *CA* U.S.A.
173 J5 **Kingsclere** *Hampshire, England* U.K.
104 F6 **Kingscote** *S.A.* Austr.
259 H3 **Kings County** *county NY* U.S.A.
169 I5 **Kingscourt** Ireland
173 O5 **Kingsdown** *Kent, England* U.K.
102 I4 **Kingseat** *North I.* N.Z.
286 U2 **King Sejong** *research stn* Antarctica
250 F4 **Kingsford** *MI* U.S.A.
168 H10 **Kingshouse** *Stirling, Scotland* U.K.
172 E7 **Kingskerswell** *Devon, England* U.K.
255 G10 **Kingsland** *GA* U.S.A.
250 I9 **Kingsland** *IN* U.S.A.
173 L4 **Kings Langley** *Hertfordshire, England* U.K.
237 O3 **Kingsley** S. Africa
171 N7 **Kingsley** *Staffordshire, England* U.K.
250 I5 **Kingsley** *MI* U.S.A.
173 M2 **King's Lynn** *Norfolk, England* U.K.
99 H2 **Kingsmill Group** *is* Gilbert Is Kiribati
173 N5 **Kingsnorth** *Kent, England* U.K.
108 G4 **King Sound** *b. W.A.* Austr.
259 I3 **Kings Park** *NY* U.S.A.
262 I6 **Kings Peak** *UT* U.S.A.
256 C12 **Kingsport** *TN* U.S.A.
173 J3 **King's Sutton** *Northamptonshire, England* U.K.
172 E6 **Kingsteignton** *Devon, England* U.K.
172 G4 **Kingsthorne** *Herefordshire, England* U.K.
105 K10 **Kingston** *Tas.* Austr.
248 E4 **Kingston** *Ont.* Can.
270 □ **Kingston** Jamaica
104 □1 **Kingston** Norfolk I.
103 C12 **Kingston** *South I.* N.Z.
168 J7 **Kingston** *Moray, Scotland* U.K.
257 O7 **Kingston** *MA* U.S.A.
260 H6 **Kingston** *MO* U.S.A.
257 K7 **Kingston** *NY* U.S.A.
256 C9 **Kingston** *OH* U.S.A.
258 D2 **Kingston** *PA* U.S.A.
255 E8 **Kingston** *TN* U.S.A.
256 D11 **Kingston** *WV* U.S.A.
173 J4 **Kingston Bagpuize** *Oxfordshire, England* U.K.
172 G3 **Kingstone** *Herefordshire, England* U.K.
104 H5 **Kingston-on-Murray** *S.A.* Australia
265 Q6 **Kingston Peak** *CA* U.S.A.
172 G5 **Kingston Seymour** *North Somerset, England* U.K.
104 G7 **Kingston South East** *S.A.* Austr.
171 Q6 **Kingston upon Hull** *Kingston upon Hull, England* U.K.
171 Q6 **Kingston upon Hull** *admin. div. England* U.K.
173 L5 **Kingston upon Thames** *Greater London, England* U.K.
271 □3 **Kingstown** St Vincent
255 H9 **Kingstree** *SC* U.S.A.
258 C6 **Kingsville** *MD* U.S.A.
261 G12 **Kingsville** *TX* U.S.A.
172 E7 **Kingswear** *Devon, England* U.K.
172 G5 **Kingswood** *South Gloucestershire, England* U.K.
173 L5 **Kingswood** *Surrey, England* U.K.
173 J5 **Kings Worthy** *Hampshire, England* U.K.
172 F3 **Kington** *Herefordshire, England* U.K.
231 C6 **Kingungi** Dem. Rep. Congo
249 I1 **Kingurutik** *r. Nfld and Lab.* Can.
168 H8 **Kingussie** *Highland, Scotland* U.K.
256 H11 **King William** *VA* U.S.A.
243 I3 **King William Island** *Nunavut* Can.
228 C5 **King William's Town** Liberia
Kingwilliamstown Ireland *see* **Ballydesmond**
237 L8 **King William's Town** S. Africa
261 H11 **Kingwood** *TX* U.S.A.
256 F9 **Kingwood** *WV* U.S.A.
231 F7 **Kiniama** Dem. Rep. Congo
221 K6 **Kınık** *Antalya* Turkey
221 I3 **Kınık** *İzmir* Turkey
237 M6 **Kinirapoort** S. Africa
247 J4 **Kinistino** *Sask.* Can.
159 O6 **Kinka** *r.* Ukr.
231 B6 **Kinkala** Congo
124 S8 **Kinka-san** *i.* Japan
102 J5 **Kinleith** *North I.* N.Z.
103 C11 **Kinloch** *South I.* N.Z.
168 D8 **Kinloch** *Highland, Scotland* U.K.
168 F6 **Kinlochbervie** *Highland, Scotland* U.K.
168 F9 **Kinlocheil** *Highland, Scotland* U.K.
168 F7 **Kinlochewe** *Highland, Scotland* U.K.
168 F8 **Kinloch Hourn** *Highland, Scotland* U.K.
168 G9 **Kinlochleven** *Highland, Scotland* U.K.
168 H9 **Kinloch Rannoch** *Perth and Kinross, Scotland* U.K.
168 I7 **Kinloss** *Moray, Scotland* U.K.
169 F4 **Kinlough** Ireland
118 B5 **Kinmaw** Myanmar
172 E1 **Kinmel Bay** *Conwy, Wales* U.K.
Kinmen Taiwan *see* **Chinmen**
124 □1 **Kin-misaki** *pt Okinawa* Japan
251 P5 **Kinmount** *Ont.* Can.
164 I4 **Kinna** Sweden
169 C5 **Kinnadoohy** Ireland
103 D10 **Kinnaird, Mount** *South I.* N.Z.
136 G4 **Kinnarasani** *r.* India
162 S1 **Kinnarodden** *pt* Norway
169 H6 **Kinnegad** Ireland
259 G2 **Kinnelon** *NJ* U.S.A.
150 D6 **Kinneret, Yam** *l.* Israel
164 J3 **Kinneviken** *b.* Sweden
169 G6 **Kinnitty** Ireland
136 G8 **Kinniyai** Sri Lanka
162 R5 **Kinnula** Fin.
248 D2 **Kinoje** *r. Ont.* Can.
126 B7 **Kino-kawa** *r.* Japan
126 D5 **Kinomoto** Japan
247 K3 **Kinoosao** *Sask.* Can.
126 A4 **Kinosaki** Japan
124 P8 **Kinpoku-san** *mt.* Japan
187 I6 **Kinrooi** Belgium
237 N2 **Kinross** S. Africa
168 J10 **Kinross** *Perth and Kinross, Scotland* U.K.
169 E9 **Kinsale** Ireland
256 I10 **Kinsale** *VA* U.S.A.
164 C1 **Kinsarvik** Norway
231 C6 **Kinsele** Dem. Rep. Congo
231 B6 **Kinshasa** Dem. Rep. Congo
231 C6 **Kinshasa** *mun.* Dem. Rep. Congo
159 P6 **Kins'ki Rozdory** Ukr.
261 F7 **Kinsley** *KS* U.S.A.
256 E7 **Kinsman** *OH* U.S.A.
255 I8 **Kinston** *NC* U.S.A.
160 E6 **Kintai** Lith.
228 E4 **Kintampo** Ghana
231 B6 **Kintata** Dem. Rep. Congo
173 J5 **Kintbury** *West Berkshire, England* U.K.
258 E3 **Kintersville** *PA* U.S.A.
228 C4 **Kintinian** Guinea
115 C4 **Kintom** *Sulawesi* Indon.
117 K6 **Kintop** *Kalimantan* Indon.
106 B7 **Kintore** *N.T.* Austr.
168 L8 **Kintore** *Aberdeenshire, Scotland* U.K.
104 C2 **Kintore, Mount** *S.A.* Austr.
108 J7 **Kintore Range** *hills N.T.* Austr.
168 D11 **Kintour** *Argyll and Bute, Scotland* U.K.
151 D4 **Kintrishis Nakrdzali** *nature res.* Georgia
168 E11 **Kintyre** *pen. Scotland* U.K.
118 B3 **Kin-U** Myanmar
127 L4 **Kinu-gawa** *r.* Japan
127 J2 **Kinunuma-yama** *mt.* Japan
248 D2 **Kinushseo** *r. Ont.* Can.
246 H4 **Kinuso** *Alta* Can.
169 E6 **Kinvara** Ireland
Kinvarra Ireland *see* **Cinn Mhara**
172 H3 **Kinver** *Staffordshire, England* U.K.
124 □1 **Kin-wan** *b. Okinawa* Japan
136 F3 **Kinwat** *Mahar.* India
233 B6 **Kinyangiri** Tanz.
232 B4 **Kinyeti** *mt.* Sudan
142 G3 **Kinzhaly** Kazakh.
194 D4 **Kinzig** *r.* Ger.
191 G10 **Kinzig** *r.* Ger.
233 B6 **Kiomboi** Tanz.
151 E3 **Kion-Khokh, Gora** *mt.* Rus. Fed.
251 P3 **Kiosk** *Ont.* Can.
263 L7 **Kiowa** *CO* U.S.A.
261 F7 **Kiowa** *KS* U.S.A.
262 L6 **Kiowa Creek** *r. CO* U.S.A.
247 K4 **Kipahigan Lake** *Man./Sask.* Can.
264 □E13 **Kīpahulu** *HI* U.S.A.
Kiparissía Greece *see* **Kyparissia**
248 E4 **Kipawa, Lac** *l. Que.* Can.
132 C6 **Kipchak Pass** *Xinjiang* China
156 G4 **Kipelovo** Rus. Fed.
233 B6 **Kipembawe** Tanz.
160 M2 **Kipen'** Rus. Fed.
233 B7 **Kipengere Range** *mts* Tanz.
195 K4 **Kipfenberg** Ger.
233 A6 **Kipili** Tanz.
233 D5 **Kipini** Kenya
247 K5 **Kipling** *Sask.* Can.
Kipling Station *Sask.* Can. *see* **Kipling**
244 F4 **Kipnuk** *AK* U.S.A.
171 O6 **Kippax** *West Yorkshire, England* U.K.
212 D3 **Kippel** Switz.
168 H10 **Kippen** *Stirling, Scotland* U.K.
194 D5 **Kippenheim** Ger.
169 J6 **Kippure** *hill* Ireland
143 T1 **Kiprino** Rus. Fed.
156 I4 **Kipshenga** Rus. Fed.
159 K2 **Kipti** Ukr.
257 J11 **Kiptopeke** *VA* U.S.A.
Kipungo Angola *see* **Quipungo**
231 E7 **Kipushi** Dem. Rep. Congo
231 F8 **Kipushia** Dem. Rep. Congo
126 F6 **Kira** Japan
151 B6 **Kıraçtepe** Turkey
139 I7 **Kirakat** *Uttar Prad.* India
100 □6 **Kirakira** *San Cristobal* Solomon Is
162 T2 **Kirakkajärvi** Fin.
199 J3 **Királd** Hungary
199 G5 **Királyegyháza** Hungary
199 J5 **Királyhegyes** Hungary
221 H4 **Kiran Dağları** *hills* Turkey
136 G3 **Kirandul** *Chhattisgarh* India
228 C3 **Kirané** Mali
235 □J3 **Kiranomena** Madag.
150 B2 **Kıravga** Turkey
160 M8 **Kirawsk** Belarus
221 J4 **Kiraz** Turkey
160 G3 **Kirbla** Estonia
261 I10 **Kirbyville** *TX* U.S.A.
195 N6 **Kirchanschöring** Ger.
194 F3 **Kirchardt** Ger.
200 H6 **Kirchbach** Austria
201 M6 **Kirchbach in Steiermark** Austria
195 O4 **Kirchberg** *Bayern* Ger.
193 G9 **Kirchberg** *Sachsen* Ger.
212 D1 **Kirchberg** *Bern* Switz.
212 G1 **Kirchberg** *St Gallen* Switz.
194 C2 **Kirchberg (Hunsrück)** Ger.
201 M3 **Kirchberg am Wagram** Austria
201 L2 **Kirchberg am Walde** Austria
201 M4 **Kirchberg am Wechsel** Austria
195 I5 **Kirchberg an der Iller** Ger.
194 H3 **Kirchberg an der Jagst** Ger.
201 L3 **Kirchberg an der Pielach** Austria
201 M6 **Kirchberg an der Raab** Austria
200 F5 **Kirchberg in Tirol** Austria
200 F4 **Kirchbichl** Austria
191 I7 **Kirchbrak** Ger.
192 D3 **Kirchdorf** *Mecklenburg-Vorpommern* Ger.
190 G5 **Kirchdorf** *Niedersachsen* Ger.
195 N5 **Kirchdorf am Inn** Ger.
195 L5 **Kirchdorf an der Amper** Ger.
201 J4 **Kirchdorf an der Krems** Austria
195 O4 **Kirchdorf im Wald** Ger.
200 F4 **Kirchdorf in Tirol** Austria
195 K2 **Kirchehrenbach** Ger.
191 E9 **Kirchen (Sieg)** Ger.
193 E10 **Kirchenlamitz** Ger.
195 L2 **Kirchenpingarten** Ger.
195 K2 **Kirchensittenbach** Ger.
194 G4 **Kirchentellinsfurt** Ger.
195 L2 **Kirchenthumbach** Ger.
191 G9 **Kirchhain** Ger.
191 K8 **Kirchheilingen** Ger.
194 H2 **Kirchheim** *Bayern* Ger.
191 I9 **Kirchheim** *Hessen* Ger.
194 G3 **Kirchheim am Neckar** Ger.
195 L5 **Kirchheim bei München** Ger.
194 E2 **Kirchheim-Bolanden** Ger.
195 I5 **Kirchheim in Schwaben** Ger.
194 G4 **Kirchheim unter Teck** Ger.
191 F8 **Kirchhundem** Ger.
192 D4 **Kirch Jesar** Ger.
191 K10 **Kirchlauter** Ger.
190 H5 **Kirchlinteln** Ger.
192 E3 **Kirch Mulsow** Ger.
191 H6 **Kirchohsen (Emmerthal)** Ger.
195 N4 **Kirchroth** Ger.
201 N4 **Kirchschlag in der Buckligen Welt** Austria
190 G5 **Kirchseelte** Ger.
190 H4 **Kirchtimke** Ger.
190 H4 **Kirchwalsede** Ger.
195 N5 **Kirchweidach** Ger.
190 G4 **Kirchwistedt** Ger.
191 J8 **Kirchworbis** Ger.
194 D6 **Kirchzarten** Ger.
194 G2 **Kirchzell** Ger.
169 K4 **Kircubbin** *Northern Irela*
151 E5 **Kırdamı** Turkey
224 C5 **Kirdimi** Chad
151 C5 **Kireçli Geçidi** *pass* Turke
Kirehesjävri Fin. *see* **Kira**
153 L4 **Kirensk** Rus. Fed.
Kirey *watercourse* Kazakh **Kerey**
Kirey, Ozero *salt l.* Kazak **Kerey, Ozero**
161 U8 **Kireyevsk** Rus. Fed.
161 S8 **Kireykovo** Rus. Fed.
Kirghizia *country* Asia *se* **Kyrgyzstan**
143 O6 **Kirghiz Range** *mts* Asia
142 F1 **Kirgiz-Miyaki** Rus. Fed.
Kirgizskaya S.S.R. *count* **Kyrgyzstan**
Kirgizskiy Khrebet *mts* **Kirghiz Range**
Kirgizstan *country* Asia *s* **Kyrgyzstan**
230 C5 **Kiri** Dem. Rep. Congo
Kíria Greece *see* **Kyrgia**
Kiriákion Greece *see* **Kyr**
99 J2 **Kiribati** *country* Pacific C
232 E2 **Kiridh** Somalia
127 H3 **Kiriga-mine** *mt.* Japan
149 J3 **Kırık** Turkey
148 H5 **Kırıkhan** Turkey
148 F4 **Kırıkkale** Turkey
128 B4 **Kirikkuduk** *Xinjiang* Chi
102 I2 **Kirikopuni** *North I.* N.Z.
161 V2 **Kirillov** Rus. Fed.
122 M5 **Kirillovo** *Sakhalin* Rus. F
160 M1 **Kirillovskoye** Rus. Fed.
Kirin *Jilin* China *see* **Jilin**
Kirin *prov.* China *see* **Jilin**
136 G9 **Kirinda** Sri Lanka
232 C5 **Kirinyaga** *mt.* Kenya
161 P2 **Kirishi** Rus. Fed.
124 □H15 **Kirishima-Yaku Kokurits** *nat. park* Japan
125 H15 **Kirishima-yama** *vol.* Japa
291 I5 **Kiritimati** *atoll* Kiribati
Kiriwina Islands P.N.G. *s* **Trobriand Islands**
221 L3 **Kırka** Turkey
221 I3 **Kırkağaç** Turkey
168 I13 **Kirkbean** *Dumfries and G* *Scotland* U.K.
171 K4 **Kirkbride** *Cumbria, Englc*
144 B3 **Kirk Bulāg Dāgi** *mt.* Iran
171 N6 **Kirkburton** *West Yorkshir* *England* U.K.
171 L7 **Kirkby** *Merseyside, Englar*
171 O7 **Kirkby in Ashfield** *Nottinghamshire, England*
171 L5 **Kirkby Lonsdale** *Cumbri* *England* U.K.
171 N5 **Kirkby Malzeard** *North Y* *England* U.K.
171 P5 **Kirkbymoorside** *North Yc* *England* U.K.
171 M5 **Kirkby Stephen** *Cumbria* *England* U.K.
171 L4 **Kirkby Thore** *Cumbria, England* U.K.
168 J10 **Kirkcaldy** *Fife, Scotland* U
168 F13 **Kirkcolm** *Dumfries and G* *Scotland* U.K.
168 I12 **Kirkconnel** *Dumfries and Galloway, Scotland* U.K.
168 G13 **Kirkcowan** *Dumfries and Galloway, Scotland* U.K.
168 H13 **Kirkcudbright** *Dumfries a* *Galloway, Scotland* U.K.
170 I4 **Kirkcudbright Bay** *Scotla*
194 C3 **Kirkel-Neuhäusel** Ger.
164 I1 **Kirkenær** Norway
162 U2 **Kirkenes** Norway
251 P5 **Kirkfield** *Ont.* Can.
171 L6 **Kirkham** *Lancashire, Eng*
168 H13 **Kirkinner** *Dumfries and* *Scotland* U.K.
168 H11 **Kirkintilloch** *East Dunba* *Scotland* U.K.
163 R6 **Kirkkonummi** Fin.
265 T7 **Kirkland** *AZ* U.S.A.
250 F7 **Kirkland** *IL* U.S.A.
248 D3 **Kirkland Lake** *Ont.* Can.
151 A6 **Kırklar Dağı** *mt.* Turkey
151 B5 **Kırklar Dağı** *mt.* Turkey
148 C3 **Kırklareli** Turkey
221 I1 **Kırklareli** *prov.* Turkey
219 P9 **Kırklareli Barajı** *resr* Turk
171 O5 **Kirklevington** *Stockton-o* *England* U.K.
168 J11 **Kirkliston** *Edinburgh, Scotland* U.K.
103 E11 **Kirkliston Range** *mts South I.* N.Z.
170 H5 **Kirk Michael** Isle of Man
168 I9 **Kirkmichael** *Perth and Ki* *Scotland* U.K.
168 G12 **Kirkmichael** *South Ayrshi* *Scotland* U.K.
168 I11 **Kirkmuirhill** *South Lana* *Scotland* U.K.
160 K1 **Kirkonmaanselkä** *b.* Fin.
217 □ **Kirkop** Malta
171 L4 **Kirkoswald** *Cumbria, England* U.K.
168 G12 **Kirkoswald** *South Ayrshire* *Scotland* U.K.
219 N9 **Kirkovo** Bulg.
151 C7 **Kırköy** Turkey
287 L1 **Kirkpatrick, Mount** Antar
168 J12 **Kirkpatrick-Fleming** *Dur* *and Galloway, Scotland* U.
171 O6 **Kirk Sandall** *South Yorksh* *England* U.K.
260 I5 **Kirksville** *MO* U.S.A.
170 F1 **Kirkton** *Argyll and Bute, Scotland* U.K.
168 L8 **Kirkton of Durris** *Aberde* *Scotland* U.K.
168 K9 **Kirkton of Menmuir** *Ang* *Scotland* U.K.
168 L8 **Kirktown of Auchterless** *Aberdeenshire, Scotland* U.
168 K7 **Kirktown of Deskford** *M* *Scotland* U.K.
149 L6 **Kirkūk** Iraq
168 K5 **Kirkwall** *Orkney, Scotland*
237 J9 **Kirkwood** S. Africa
258 D5 **Kirkwood** *DE* U.S.A.
258 C5 **Kirkwood** *PA* U.S.A.
171 M2 **Kirk Yetholm** *Scottish Bor* *Scotland* U.K.
Kirman Iran *see* **Kermān**
148 E3 **Kırmır** *r.* Turkey
151 A6 **Kırmızıköprü** Turkey
194 C2 **Kirn** Ger.
Kırobası Turkey *see* **Mağa**
Kīrov Kazakh. *see* **Balpyk**
Kirov Kyrg. *see* **Kyzyl-Adyr**
161 R7 **Kirov** *Kaluzhskaya Oblast'* Rus. Fed.
156 J4 **Kirov** *Kirovskaya Oblast'* R
Kirova, Zaliv *b.* Azer. *see* **Qızılağac Körfäzi**
Kirovabad Azer. *see* **Gäncä**
Kirovabad Tajik. *see* **Panj**
Kirovakan Armenia *see* **Va**
159 Q5 **Kirove** *Donets'ka Oblast'* U
159 M5 **Kirove** *Kirovohrads'ka Obl*
159 O6 **Kirove** *Zaporiz'ka Oblast'*
142 E2 **Kirovo** Kazakh.
Kirovo *Donets'ka Oblast'* U **Kirove**
Kirovo *Kirovohrads'ka Obl* *see* **Kirovohrad**
Kirovo Uzbek. *see* **Beshar**
Kirov Oblast *admin. div.* R *see* **Kirovskaya Oblast'**

Kirovo-Chepetsk Rus. Fed.
Kirovo-Chepetskiy Rus. Fed. see Kirovo-Chepetsk
Kirovograd Ukr. see Kirovohrad
Kirovograd Oblast admin. div. Ukr. see Kirovohrads'ka Oblast'
Kirovogradskaya Oblast' admin. div. Ukr. see Kirovohrads'ka Oblast'
Kirovohrad Ukr.
Kirovohrad Oblast admin. div. Ukr. see Kirovohrads'ka Oblast'
Kirovohrads'ka Oblast' admin. div. Ukr.
Kirovsk Azer.
Kirovsk Leningradskaya Oblast' Rus. Fed.
Kirovsk Murmanskaya Oblast' Rus. Fed.
Kirovs'k Donets'ka Oblast' Ukr.
Kirovs'k Luhans'ka Oblast' Ukr.
Kirovskaya Rus. Fed.
Kirovskaya Oblast' admin. div. Rus. Fed.
Kirovs'ke Dnipropetrovs'ka Oblast' Ukr.
Kirovs'ke Donets'ka Oblast' Ukr.
Kirovs'ke Respublika Krym Ukr.
Kirovs'ke Respublika Krym Ukr.
Kirovskiy Kazakh. see Balpyk Bi
Kirovskiy Astrakhanskaya Oblast' Rus. Fed.
Kirovskiy Kurskaya Oblast' Rus. Fed.
Kirovskiy Primorskiy Kray Rus. Fed.
Kirovskoye Kyrg. see Kyzyl-Adyr
Kirovskoye Dnipropetrovs'ka Oblast' Ukr. see Kirovs'ke
Kirovskoye Donets'ka Oblast' Ukr. see Kirovs'ke
Kirovskoye Respublika Krym Ukr. see Kirovs'ke
Kırpaşa pen. Cyprus see Karpasia
Kirpili r. Rus. Fed.
Kirpili Turkm.
Kirpil'skaya Rus. Fed.
Kirpil'skiy Liman marsh Rus. Fed.
Kirriemuir Angus, Scotland U.K.
Kirri Shamozai Pak.
Kirs Rus. Fed.
Kirsanov Rus. Fed.
Kirsanovo Kazakh.
Kirschweiler Ger.
Kırşehir Turkey
Kirsna r. Lith.
Kirtachi Niger
Kirthar National Park Pak.
Kirthar Range mts Pak.
Kirtlington Oxfordshire, England U.K.
Kirton Lincolnshire, England U.K.
Kirton Suffolk, England U.K.
Kirton in Lindsey North Lincolnshire, England U.K.
Kirtorf Ger.
Kirts'khi Georgia
Kiruna Sweden
Kirundo Burundi
Kirundu Dem. Rep. Congo
Kirwan Escarpment Antarctica
Kirya Rus. Fed.
Kiryū Japan
Kirzhach Rus. Fed.
Kisa Sweden
Kisakata Japan
Kisaki Tanz.
Kisama, Parque Nacional de nat. park Angola see Quiçama, Parque Nacional do
Kisangani Dem. Rep. Congo
Kisangire Tanz.
Kisantete Dem. Rep. Congo
Kisar Hungary
Kisar i. Maluku Indon.
Kisaralik r. AK U.S.A.
Kisaran Sumatera Indon.
Kisarawe Tanz.
Kisarazu Japan
Kısas Turkey
Kis-Balaton park Hungary
Kisbér Hungary
Kisei Japan
Kiselevsk Rus. Fed.
Kiseljak Bos.-Herz.
Kisel'nya Rus. Fed.
Kisel'ovka Rus. Fed.
Kisere Tanz.
Kisgyőr Hungary
Kish i. Iran
Kishanganj Bihar India
Kishangarh Madh. Prad. India
Kishangarh Rajasthan India
Kishangarh Rajasthan India
Kishen Ganga r. India/Pak.
Kishi Nigeria
Kishigawa Japan
Kishi-gawa r. Japan
Kishi Kamkaly Kazakh.
Kishi-Karoy, Ozero salt l. Kazakh.
Kishika-zaki pt Japan
Kishinev Moldova see Chişinău
Kishiözen r. Kazakh./Rus. Fed. see Malyy Uzen'
Kishiwada Japan
Kishkenekol' Kazakh.
Kishoreganj Bangl.
Kishorn, Loch inlet Scotland U.K.
Kishtwar Jammu and Kashmir India
Kisi Tanz.
Kisielice Pol.
Kisielnica Pol.
Kisigo r. Tanz.
Kisiguru Rwanda
Kisii Kenya
Kisiju Tanz.
Kısır Dağı mt. Turkey
Kiska Island AK U.S.A.
Kiskittogisu Lake Man. Can.
Kiskitto Lake Man. Can.
Kisko Fin.
Kisköre Hungary
Kiskörei-Víztároló resr Hungary
Kiskőrös Hungary
Kiskunfélegyháza Hungary
Kiskunhalas Hungary
Kiskunlacháza Hungary
Kiskunmajsa Hungary
Kiskunság reg. Hungary
Kiskunsági nat. park Hungary
Kisláng Hungary
Kisléta Hungary
Kislőd Hungary
Kislovodsk Rus. Fed.
Kislyakovskaya Rus. Fed.
Kismaayo Somalia
Kismarja Hungary
Kismayu Somalia see Kismaayo
Kiso Japan
Kisofukushima Japan
Kisogawa Japan
Kiso-gawa r. Japan
Kiso-gawa r. Japan
Kisogle Mountain hill AK U.S.A.
Kisoro Uganda
Kisosaki Japan
Kiso-sanmyaku mts Japan
Kisosi Burundi
Kisovec Slovenia
Kispiox B.C. Can.
Kispiox r. B.C. Can.
Kissamos Kriti Greece
Kissamou, Kolpos b. Kriti Greece
Kisseraing Island Myanmar see Kanmaw Kyun
Kissidougou Guinea
Kissimmee FL U.S.A.
Kissimmee r. FL U.S.A.
Kissimmee, Lake FL U.S.A.
Kissing Ger.
Kississing Lake Man. Can.
Kißlegg Ger.
Kissu, Jebel mt. Sudan
199 I5 Kisszállás Hungary
194 H2 Kist Ger.
210 E4 Kistanje Croatia
199 I5 Kistelek Hungary
157 H5 Kistendey Rus. Fed.
247 M4 Kistigan Lake Man. Can.
Kistna r. India see Krishna
199 J3 Kistokaj Hungary
162 R1 Kistrand Norway
199 J4 Kisújszállás Hungary
125 J11 Kisuki Japan
232 B5 Kisumu Kenya
199 L3 Kisvárda Hungary
Kisykkamys Kazakh. see Dzhangala
196 F3 Kiszkowo Pol.
199 J5 Kiszombor Hungary
232 A3 Kit r. Sudan
126 B6 Kita Hyōgo Japan
126 C5 Kita Kyōto Japan
228 C3 Kita Mali
Kitab Uzbek. see Kitob
121 N6 Kita-Daitō-jima i. Japan
126 E5 Kitagata Japan
125 I14 Kitagawa Japan
124 Q4 Kitahiyama Japan
127 M2 Kitaibaraki Japan
125 □2 Kita-Iō-jima vol. Kazan-rettō Japan
126 A7 Kitajima Japan
124 S7 Kitakami Japan
124 S7 Kitakami-gawa r. Japan
124 Q9 Kitakata Fukushima Japan
125 I14 Kitakata Miyazaki Japan
125 H13 Kita-Kyūshū Japan
232 B4 Kitale Kenya
124 U3 Kitami Japan
127 H3 Kitamimaki Japan
124 T2 Kitami-sanchi mts Japan
127 K3 Kitamoto Japan
231 E6 Kitanda Dem. Rep. Congo
125 □3 Kitano-hana c. Iō-jima Japan
127 J3 Kitatachibana Japan
127 M3 Kitaura Ibaraki Japan
125 I14 Kitaura Miyazaki Japan
127 M4 Kita-ura l. Japan
126 C8 Kitayama Japan
126 C8 Kitayama-gawa r. Japan
260 D6 Kit Carson CO U.S.A.
248 D5 Kitchener Ont. Can.
248 E3 Kitchigama r. Que. Can.
231 E6 Kiteba Dem. Rep. Congo
162 U5 Kitee Fin.
231 F6 Kitendwe Dem. Rep. Congo
232 B4 Kitgum Uganda
Kíthira i. Greece see Kythira
Kíthnos i. Greece see Kythnos
Kíthnou, Stenón sea chan. Greece see Kythnou, Steno
Kiti, Cape Cyprus see Kition, Cape
246 D4 Kitimat B.C. Can.
162 S3 Kitinen r. Fin.
150 B4 Kition, Cape Cyprus
Kitiou, Akra c. Cyprus see Kition, Cape
245 O5 Kitkatla B.C. Can.
246 E4 Kitlope Heritage Conservancy Provincial Park B.C. Can.
143 L8 Kitob Uzbek.
161 Y5 Kitovo Rus. Fed.
220 F6 Kitriani i. Greece
162 V2 Kitsa Rus. Fed.
245 O5 Kitsault B.C. Can.
247 I4 Kitscoty Alta Can.
158 E5 Kitsman' Ukr.
125 I13 Kitsuki Japan
127 L2 Kitsuregawa Japan
256 F8 Kittanning PA U.S.A.
258 F3 Kittatinny Mountains hills NJ U.S.A.
257 □O5 Kittery ME U.S.A.
162 R3 Kittilä Fin.
127 M1 Kittoya-yama hill Japan
201 P3 Kittsee Austria
136 D5 Kittur Karnataka India
255 J7 Kitty Hawk NC U.S.A.
233 C5 Kitui Kenya
233 C5 Kitumbeine vol. Tanz.
233 C7 Kitumbini Tanz.
233 B6 Kitunda Tanz.
246 D4 Kitwanga B.C. Can.
231 F8 Kitwe Zambia
200 F5 Kitzbühel Austria
200 F5 Kitzbüheler Alpen mts Austria
200 F5 Kitzbüheler Horn mt. Austria
201 L6 Kitzeck im Sausal Austria
193 F8 Kitzen Ger.
195 I2 Kitzingen Ger.
193 G8 Kitzscher Ger.
200 G5 Kitzsteinhorn mt. Austria
233 C5 Kiu Kenya
197 H5 Kiucze Pol.
163 Q6 Kiukainen Fin.
118 D5 Kiu Lom, Ang Kep Nam Thai.
113 J8 Kiunga P.N.G.
233 D5 Kiunga Marine National Reserve nature res. Kenya
162 S5 Kiuruvesi Fin.
244 F2 Kivalina AK U.S.A.
162 R4 Kivalo ridge Fin.
220 D5 Kiveri Greece
161 T4 Kiverichi Rus. Fed.
158 E3 Kivertsi Ukr.
244 F2 Kividlo AK U.S.A.
162 R5 Kivijärvi Fin.
160 K1 Kivijärvi l. Fin.
162 R5 Kivijärvi l. Fin.
165 K6 Kivik Sweden
162 Q2 Kivilompolo Norway
160 J2 Kiviõli Estonia
162 U5 Kivivaara Fin.
160 H3 Kivi-Vigala Estonia
159 Q4 Kivsharivka Ukr.
230 F5 Kivu, Lake Dem. Rep. Congo/Rwanda
126 C8 Kiwa Japan
231 C7 Kiwaba N'zogi Angola
113 J8 Kiwai Island P.N.G.
244 G2 Kiwalik AK U.S.A.
244 G2 Kiwalik r. AK U.S.A.
233 C7 Kiwawa Tanz.
108 I7 Kiwirrkurra Aboriginal Reserve W.A. Austr.
197 I1 Kiwity Pol.
124 □1 Kiyan Okinawa Japan
124 □1 Kiyan-zaki c. Okinawa Japan
146 E6 Kiyāt Saudi Arabia
Kiyev Ukr. see Kyiv
143 N2 Kiyevka Kazakh.
Kiyevskaya Oblast' admin. div. Ukr. see Kyivs'ka Oblast'
161 T6 Kiyevskiy Rus. Fed.
Kiyevskoye Vodokhranilishche resr Ukr. see Kyyivs'ke Vodoskhovyshche
219 Q9 Kıyıköy Turkey
143 L2 Kiyma Kazakh.
126 F3 Kiyomi Japan
127 L5 Kiyosumi-yama hill Japan
127 I1 Kiyotsu-gawa r. Japan
156 L4 Kizel Rus. Fed.
156 I3 Kizema Rus. Fed.
129 K1 Kizha Rus. Fed.
156 F3 Kizhi, Ostrov i. Rus. Fed.
231 E7 Kiziba-Baluba, Réserve de nature res. Dem. Rep. Congo
233 B6 Kizigo Game Reserve nature res. Tanz.
221 L4 Kızık Turkey
132 F6 Kizil Xinjiang China
150 B2 Kızılalan Turkey
132 C7 Kizilawat Xinjiang China
150 B2 Kızılca Turkey
221 K5 Kızılcadağ Turkey
221 K6 Kızılca Dağ mt. Turkey
148 F3 Kızılcahamam Turkey
221 L3 Kızılcaören Turkey
221 K4 Kızılcasöğüt Turkey
151 E6 Kızılcaziyaret Dağı mt. Turkey
151 A7 Kızılcık Turkey
151 B6 Kızılçubuk Turkey
150 C1 Kızıldağ mt. Turkey
150 B2 Kızıldağ mt. Turkey
148 I4 Kızıl Dağı mt. Turkey
148 F3 Kızılırmak Turkey
148 G3 Kızılırmak r. Turkey
221 L5 Kızılkaya Turkey
221 L4 Kızılören Afyon Turkey
148 F5 Kızılören Konya Turkey
142 H1 Kizil'skoye Rus. Fed.
159 Q8 Kiziltashskiy Liman lag. Rus. Fed.
149 J5 Kızıltepe Turkey
150 A1 Kızılyaka Karaman Turkey
221 J5 Kızılyaka Muğla Turkey
151 H2 Kizilyurt Rus. Fed.
233 C6 Kizimkazi, Ras pt Tanz.
150 C2 Kızkalesi Turkey
151 H2 Kizlyar Respublika Dagestan Rus. Fed.
151 F2 Kizlyar Respublika Severnaya Osetiya-Alaniya Rus. Fed.
151 H1 Kizlyarskiy Zaliv b. Rus. Fed.
156 J4 Kizner Rus. Fed.
126 C6 Kizu Japan
126 C6 Kizu-gawa r. Japan
Kizyl-Arbat Turkm. see Serdar
Kizyl-Atrek Turkm. see Etrek
133 D9 Kizyl Jilga Aksai Chin
164 F5 Kjellerup Denmark
163 K6 Kjemmoen Norway
162 M3 Kjerringøy Norway
162 S1 Kjøllefjord Norway
162 N2 Kjøpsvik Norway
236 G9 Klaarstroom S. Africa
186 F5 Klaaswaal Neth.
198 C2 Klabava r. Czech Rep.
165 J1 Klacken hill Sweden
199 H3 Kľačno Slovakia
210 G3 Kladanj Bos.-Herz.
192 E5 Kläden Ger.
198 D1 Kladno Czech Rep.
219 K6 Kladovo Kladovo Serbia
198 B2 Kladruby Czech Rep.
117 L2 Klagan Sabah Malaysia
201 J6 Klagenfurt Austria
213 Q2 Klagenfurt airport Austria
265 W6 Klagetoh AZ U.S.A.
160 E6 Klaipėda Lith.
197 I6 Kłaj Pol.
199 H3 Kľak mt. Slovakia
199 I2 Kľak mt. Slovakia
Klaksvig Faroe Is see Klaksvík
166 D1 Klaksvík Faroe Is
262 B6 Klamath CA U.S.A.
262 B6 Klamath r. CA U.S.A.
262 D5 Klamath Falls OR U.S.A.
262 C6 Klamath Mountains CA U.S.A.
165 N2 Klämmingen l. Sweden
117 L4 Klampo Kalimantan Indon.
213 Q5 Klana Croatia
116 D3 Klang Malaysia
196 E1 Kłanino Pol.
201 M7 Klanjec Croatia
190 G1 Klanxbüll Ger.
245 O4 Klappan r. B.C. Can.
164 J2 Klarälven r. Sweden
162 N5 Klärke Sweden
199 H3 Klasov Slovakia
164 I2 Klässbol Sweden
198 C1 Klášterec nad Ohří Czech Rep.
117 I8 Klaten Jawa Indon.
198 C2 Klatovy Czech Rep.
201 J4 Klaus an der Pyhrnbahn Austria
193 H6 Klausdorf Brandenburg Ger.
192 H2 Klausdorf Mecklenburg-Vorpommern Ger.
190 J2 Klausdorf Schleswig-Holstein Ger.
194 B2 Klausen Ger.
201 N3 Klausen Leopoldsdorf Austria
158 J3 Klavdiyevo-Tarasove Ukr.
164 H4 Klåverön naturreservat nature res. Sweden
236 C7 Klawer S. Africa
245 N5 Klawock AK U.S.A.
186 K3 Klazienaveen Neth.
228 C5 Kle Liberia
201 H6 Kleblach-Lind Austria
196 E2 Kłębowiec Pol.
258 E3 Klecknersville PA U.S.A.
196 F3 Kłecko Pol.
196 G3 Kleczew Pol.
246 E5 Kleena Kleene B.C. Can.
150 C3 Kleides Islands Cyprus
201 H5 Kleinarl Austria
236 F4 Kleinbegin S. Africa
190 D5 Klein Berßen Ger.
194 C3 Kleinblittersdorf Ger.
271 □8 Klein Bonaire i. Neth. Antilles
192 I3 Klein Bünzow Ger.
271 □10 Klein Curaçao i. Neth. Antilles
236 D7 Klein Doring r. S. Africa
193 H7 Kleine Elster r. Ger.
162 J5 Kleinegga mt. Norway
195 N4 Kleine Laaber r. Ger.
195 K4 Kleine Paar r. Ger.
192 I2 Kleiner Jasmunder Bodden b. Ger.
200 D5 Kleiner Solstein mt. Austria
193 J7 Kleine Spree r. Ger.
195 M4 Kleine Vils r. Ger.
258 C4 Kleinfeltersville PA U.S.A.
194 G2 Kleinheubach Ger.
193 E8 Kleinjena Ger.
234 C5 Klein Karas Namibia
193 G6 Klein Kreutz Ger.
201 K5 Kleinlobming Austria
193 H6 Kleinmachnow Ger.
236 D10 Kleinmond S. Africa
190 I3 Klein Nordende Ger.
194 G1 Kleinostheim Ger.
193 E7 Kleinpaschleben Ger.
237 I9 Kleinpoort S. Africa
201 K4 Kleinreifling Austria
194 H2 Kleinrinderfeld Ger.
236 E9 Klein Roggeveldberge mts S. Africa
190 J3 Klein Rönnau Ger.
201 K6 Klein Sankt Paul Austria
236 B5 Kleinsee S. Africa
192 G4 Kleinseenplatte Neustrelitz park Ger.
236 F9 Klein Swartberg mt. S. Africa
237 K4 Klein-Vet r. S. Africa
194 G2 Kleinwallstadt Ger.
193 D6 Klein Wanzleben Ger.
191 K6 Kleinwinnigstedt (Winnigstedt) Ger.
201 M4 Kleinzell Austria
220 D5 Kleitoria Greece
197 L3 Klejniki Pol.
210 F3 Klekovača mt. Bos.-Herz.
158 H5 Klembivka Ukr.
246 D4 Klemtu B.C. Can.
198 B2 Klenčí pod Čerchovem Czech Rep.
196 D4 Klenica Pol.
199 I3 Klenovec Slovakia
198 G2 Klenovice na Hané Czech Rep.
199 I3 Klenovský Vepor mt. Slovakia
197 L2 Kleosin Pol.
197 L2 Klepacze Pol.
159 T3 Klepovka Rus. Fed.
164 B3 Kleppe Norway
164 B1 Kleppestø Norway
196 D3 Klępsk Pol.
159 N8 Klepynine Ukr.
237 K2 Klerksdorp S. Africa
237 L2 Klerkskraal S. Africa
244 G2 Klery Creek AK U.S.A.
158 F2 Klesiv Ukr.
197 L3 Kleszczele Pol.
196 F3 Kleszczewo Pol.
197 H4 Kleszczów Pol.
161 Q8 Kletnya Rus. Fed.
Kletsk Belarus see Klyetsk
157 H6 Kletskaya Rus. Fed.
Kletskiy Rus. Fed. see Kletskaya
194 E6 Klettgau reg. Ger./Switz.
193 I7 Klettwitz Ger.
158 E3 Klevan' Ukr.
191 B7 Kleve Ger.
159 M2 Kleven' r. Rus. Fed.
160 M8 Klichaw Belarus
129 O1 Klichka Rus. Fed.
Klidhes Islands Cyprus see Kleides Islands
193 F7 Klieken Ger.
192 F5 Klietz Ger.
161 U4 Klimatino Rus. Fed.
161 O8 Klimavichy Belarus
159 K1 Klimawka Belarus
219 P7 Kliment Bulg.
199 H2 Klimkovice Czech Rep.
156 J4 Klimkovka Rus. Fed.
197 I5 Klimontów Małopolskie Pol.
197 J5 Klimontów Świętokrzyskie Pol.
Klimovichi Belarus see Klimavichy
157 F5 Klimovo Rus. Fed.
161 U6 Klimovsk Rus. Fed.
161 W1 Klimovskaya Rus. Fed.
161 R7 Klimov Zavod Rus. Fed.
162 M4 Klimpfjäll Sweden
161 T5 Klin Rus. Fed.
199 I2 Klin Slovakia
Klina Klinë Kosovo see Klinë
246 E5 Klinaklini r. B.C. Can.
218 I8 Klinë Klinë Kosovo
114 E9 Kling Mindanao Phil.
193 I9 Klingenberg Ger.
194 G2 Klingenberg am Main Ger.
193 F10 Klingenthal Ger.
258 B3 Klingerstown PA U.S.A.
117 I4 Klingkang, Banjaran mts Indon./Malaysia
192 G4 Klink Ger.
198 C1 Klínovec mt. Czech Rep.
161 T5 Klinsko-Dmitrovskaya Gryada ridge Rus. Fed.
165 O4 Klintehamn Gotland Sweden
142 C2 Klintsovka Rus. Fed.
161 P9 Klintsy Rus. Fed.
237 N3 Klip r. S. Africa
236 D10 Klipdale S. Africa
237 J9 Klipfontein S. Africa
190 H1 Kliplev Denmark
164 J5 Klippan Sweden
236 I9 Klipplaat S. Africa
236 C6 Kliprand S. Africa
237 O1 Klipskool S. Africa
210 F4 Klis Croatia
161 V7 Klishino Moskovskaya Oblast' Rus. Fed.
161 Q2 Klishino Novgorodskaya Oblast' Rus. Fed.
219 K8 Klisura Surdulica Serbia
164 E4 Klitmøller Denmark
Klitória Greece see Kleitoria
193 K8 Klitten Ger.
190 G1 Klixbüll Ger.
199 I6 Kljajićevo Vojvodina Serbia
210 F3 Ključ Bos.-Herz.
198 F3 Klobouky Czech Rep.
196 G5 Kłobuck Pol.
201 M6 Klöch Austria
197 J4 Kłoczew Pol.
192 L5 Kłodawa Lubuskie Pol.
196 G3 Kłodawa Wielkopolskie Pol.
196 E5 Kłodzko Pol.
164 H1 Kløfta Norway
197 H5 Kłomnice Pol.
245 M2 Klondike r. Y.T. Can.
245 N4 Klondike Gold Rush National Historical Park nat. park AK U.S.A.
196 G4 Klonowa Pol.
160 H2 Klooga Estonia
186 K4 Kloosterhaar Neth.
187 F6 Kloosterzande Neth.
199 J3 Kloptaň mt. Slovakia
218 I9 Klos Albania
201 N8 Kloštar Ivanić Croatia
198 G6 Kloštar Podravski Croatia
192 H5 Klosterfelde Ger.
193 E8 Klosterhäseler Ger.
200 B5 Klösterle Austria
195 J5 Klosterlechfeld Ger.
193 D7 Klostermansfeld Ger.
201 N3 Klosterneuburg Austria
212 H2 Klosters Switz.
193 J8 Klosterwasser r. Ger.
193 H6 Kloster Zinna Ger.
194 F7 Kloten Switz.
191 D10 Klotten Ger.
245 L2 Klotz, Mount Y.T. Can.
192 D5 Klötze (Altmark) Ger.
245 M3 Kluane r. Y.T. Can.
245 L3 Kluane Game Sanctuary nature res. Y.T. Can.
245 M3 Kluane Lake Y.T. Can.
245 M3 Kluane National Park Y.T. Can.
Kluang Malaysia see Keluang
117 I6 Kluang, Tanjung pt Indon.
196 G5 Kluczbork Pol.
197 H5 Kluczewsko Pol.
Klukhori Rus. Fed. see Karachayevsk
151 C2 Klukhorskiy, Pereval pass Georgia/Rus. Fed.
151 C2 Klukhorskiy, Pereval pass Rus. Fed.
197 H4 Kluki Pol.
197 K3 Klukowo Pol.
245 N4 Klukwan AK U.S.A.
117 L6 Klumpang, Teluk b. Indon.
186 G5 Klundert Neth.
117 K9 Klungkung Bali Indon.
190 D5 Kluse Ger.
199 K2 Kľušov Slovakia
197 K2 Klusy Pol.
245 K3 Klutina Lake AK U.S.A.
192 D3 Klütz Ger.
197 I4 Klwów Pol.
160 L6 Klyastsitsy Belarus
160 L8 Klyava r. Belarus
157 K5 Klyavlino Rus. Fed.
161 Z5 Klyaz'ma r. Rus. Fed.
160 J8 Klyetsk Belarus
159 O4 Klymivka Ukr.
127 H1 Klyosato Japan
159 M2 Klyshky Ukr.
153 R4 Klyuchevskaya, Sopka vol. Rus. Fed.
143 R1 Klyuchi Altayskiy Kray Rus. Fed.
122 E4 Klyuchi Amurskaya Oblast' Rus. Fed.
153 R4 Klyuchi Kamchatskaya Oblast' Rus. Fed.
100 □6 Kmagha Sta Isabel Solomon Is
164 D3 Knaben Norway
237 K6 Knapdaar S. Africa
103 C13 Knapdale South I. N.Z.
168 E11 Knapdale reg. Scotland U.K.
250 D5 Knapp Mound hill WI U.S.A.
164 J5 Knäred Sweden
171 O5 Knaresborough North Yorkshire, England U.K.
165 K1 Knästen hill Sweden
171 O5 Knayton North Yorkshire, England U.K.
173 L4 Knebworth Hertfordshire, England U.K.
247 M4 Knee Lake Man. Can.
247 J4 Knee Lake Sask. Can.
190 K5 Knesebeck Ger.
187 D6 Knesselare Belgium
191 K11 Knetzgau Ger.
213 Q4 Knežak Slovenia
210 G3 Kneževi Vinogradi Croatia
199 H6 Kneževo Croatia
219 M7 Knezha Bulg.
193 L10 Kněžmost Czech Rep.
218 I7 Knić Knić Serbia
260 E2 Knife r. ND U.S.A.
250 C3 Knife River MN U.S.A.
246 E5 Knight Inlet B.C. Can.
172 F3 Knighton Powys, Wales U.K.
264 K3 Knights Landing CA U.S.A.
210 F3 Knin Croatia
165 K5 Knislinge Sweden
201 K5 Knittelfeld Austria
194 F3 Knittlingen Ger.
165 N2 Knivsta Sweden
198 D3 Knížecí stolec mt. Czech Rep.
219 N9 Knizhovnik Bulg.
219 K7 Knjaževac Knjaževac Serbia
109 C10 Knobby Head W.A. Austr.
Knob Lake Nfld and Lab. Can. see Schefferville
108 J3 Knob Peak hill W.A. Austr.
169 D7 Knock Clare Ireland
169 E5 Knock Mayo Ireland
168 E10 Knock Argyll and Bute, Scotland U.K.
169 D8 Knockacummer hill Ireland
169 G9 Knockadoon Head Ireland
169 E4 Knockalongy hill Ireland
169 D7 Knockalough Ireland
170 E8 Knockananna Ireland
170 D8 Knockanarrigan Ireland
168 J8 Knockandhu Moray, Scotland U.K.
169 D8 Knockanefune hill Ireland
168 G7 Knockban Highland, Scotland U.K.
169 D9 Knockboy hill Ireland
169 J7 Knockbrandon Ireland
169 J5 Knockbridge Ireland
169 G7 Knockbrit Ireland
169 F5 Knockcroghery Ireland
168 K7 Knock Hill Scotland U.K.
169 J2 Knocklayd hill Northern Ireland U.K.
169 F8 Knocklong Ireland
169 F8 Knockmealdown Mountains hills Ireland
169 D4 Knockmore Ireland
169 F6 Knockmoyle Ireland
169 D8 Knocknaboul Ireland
170 E3 Knocknacarry Northern Ireland U.K.
169 D8 Knocknagree Ireland
169 F8 Knocknaskagh hill Ireland
169 F9 Knockraha Ireland
169 E9 Knocks Ireland
187 D6 Knokke-Heist Belgium
192 H3 Knorrendorf Ger.
220 G7 Knosos tourist site Greece
Knossós tourist site Greece see Knosos
171 O6 Knottingley West Yorkshire, England U.K.
173 I3 Knowle West Midlands, England U.K.
286 T2 Knowles, Cape Antarctica
257 □Q2 Knowles Corner ME U.S.A.
257 M3 Knowlton Que. Can.
254 D5 Knox IN U.S.A.
256 F7 Knox PA U.S.A.
245 N5 Knox, Cape B.C. Can.
Knox Atoll Kiribati see Tarawa
250 B9 Knox City MO U.S.A.
287 G2 Knox Coast Antarctica
255 F9 Knoxville GA U.S.A.
260 I5 Knoxville IA U.S.A.
255 F8 Knoxville TN U.S.A.
168 E8 Knoydart mts Scotland U.K.
172 F3 Knucklas Powys, Wales U.K.
243 L2 Knud Rasmussen Land reg. Greenland
191 H9 Knüllgebirge hills Ger.
191 H8 Knüllwald-Remsfeld Ger.
196 G5 Knurów Pol.
171 M7 Knutsford Cheshire, England U.K.
156 I5 Knyaginino Rus. Fed.
160 K7 Knyahinin Belarus
122 I4 Knyaze-Bolkonskaye Rus. Fed.
159 M6 Knyaze-Hryhorivka Ukr.
160 L5 Knyazevo Rus. Fed.
197 M5 Knyazhe Ukr.
161 T4 Knyazhikha Rus. Fed.
160 L3 Knyazhitsy Rus. Fed.
161 N7 Knyazhytsy Belarus
236 H10 Knysna S. Africa
197 K2 Knyszyn Pol.
122 J5 Ko, Gora mt. Rus. Fed.
230 F2 Koalib, Jebel mt. Sudan
103 I8 Koamaru, Cape South I. N.Z.
233 C6 Koani Tanz.
Koartac Que. Can. see Quaqtaq
236 D5 Koa Valley watercourse S. Africa
116 G6 Koba Indon.
201 L6 Kobansko mts Slovenia
201 I7 Kobarid Slovenia
125 H15 Kobayashi Japan
162 T2 Kobbfoss Norway
115 E3 Kobe Halmahera Indon.
126 B6 Kōbe Japan
159 N4 Kobelyaky Ukr.
228 C3 Kobenni Maur.
201 K5 Kobenz Austria
200 H3 Kobernaußer Wald for. Austria
201 N4 Kobersdorf Austria
115 F5 Kobi Seram Indon.
229 I4 Kobi Nigeria
197 H4 Kobiele Wielkie Pol.
196 E5 Kobierzyce Pol.
196 G5 Kobiór Pol.
124 □A21 Kōbi-sho i. Nansei-shotō Japan
230 C2 Koblagué Chad
191 E10 Koblenz Ger.
159 K7 Kobleve Ukr.
232 C1 K'obo Eth.
139 O6 Kobo Assam India
232 A4 Koboko Uganda
122 H2 Koboldo Rus. Fed.
161 T3 Kobozha r. Rus. Fed.
156 J4 Kobra Rus. Fed.
Kobrin Belarus see Kobryn
113 H8 Kobroör i. Indon.
192 E3 Kobrow Ger.
158 D1 Kobryn Belarus
127 H4 Kobuchizawa Japan
244 H2 Kobuk AK U.S.A.
244 G2 Kobuk r. AK U.S.A.
244 H2 Kobuk Valley National Park AK U.S.A.
151 C4 K'obulet'i Georgia
127 I4 Kobushiga-take mt. Japan
153 N3 Kobyay Rus. Fed.
196 F4 Kobyla Góra Pol.
196 C2 Kobylanka Pol.
158 D5 Kobylets'ka Polyana Ukr.
198 F3 Kobylí Czech Rep.
196 F4 Kobylin Pol.
197 K2 Kobylin-Borzymy Pol.
197 J3 Kobyłka Pol.
196 F1 Kobylnica Pol.
197 I3 Kobylniki Pol.
221 J2 Kocaafşar r. Turkey
221 L1 Kocaali Turkey
221 L5 Kocaaliler Turkey
221 I3 Kocaavşar Turkey
221 K5 Kocabaş Turkey
221 K4 Koca Dag mt. Turkey
Kocaeli Turkey see İzmit
221 K2 Kocaeli prov. Turkey
221 K1 Kocaeli Yarımadası pen. Turkey
151 E5 Kocaköy Turkey
219 K9 Kočani Macedonia
151 E6 Kocapınar Turkey
221 I5 Koçarlı Turkey
151 D6 Kocasu r. Turkey
221 J2 Kocasu r. Turkey
150 F1 Kocatepe Turkey
151 E6 Koçbaşı Tepe mt. Turkey
128 H9 Kocê Gansu China
218 H6 Koceljevo Koceljevo Serbia
210 E3 Kočevje Slovenia
213 R4 Kočevska Reka Slovenia
123 E11 Koch'ang S. Korea
196 G5 Kochanowice Pol.
139 L6 Koch Bihar W. Bengal India
195 K6 Kochel am See Ger.
195 K6 Kochelsee l. Ger.
194 G3 Kocher r. Ger.
159 O5 Kocherezhky Ukr.
219 L8 Kocherinovo Bulg.
158 I3 Kocheriv Ukr.
159 P2 Kochetovka Rus. Fed.
156 K4 Kochevo Rus. Fed.
136 E8 Kochi Kerala India
125 K13 Kōchi Japan
125 K13 Kōchi pref. Japan
269 I8 Kochihuehuetlán Mex.
124 □1 Kochinda Okinawa Japan
Koçhisar Turkey see Kızıltepe
142 I1 Kochkar' Rus. Fed.
143 P6 Kochkor Kyrg.
Kochkorka Kyrg. see Kochkor
157 I5 Kochkurovo Rus. Fed.
156 M2 Kochmes Rus. Fed.
151 H1 Kochubey Rus. Fed.
151 C1 Kochubeyevskoye Rus. Fed.
220 F4 Kochylas hill Skyros Greece
197 K4 Kock Pol.
151 C5 Koçkaya Turkey
150 F1 Köçke Turkey
151 F5 Koçkıran Turkey
151 E5 Koçköyü Turkey
192 D5 Köckte Ger.
199 G3 Kočovce Slovakia
199 H4 Kocs Hungary
199 I4 Kocsér Hungary
199 H5 Kocsola Hungary
196 F2 Koczała Pol.
136 D5 Kod Karnataka India
156 K3 Kodachdikost Rus. Fed.
136 E7 Kodaikanal Tamil Nadu India
127 J4 Kodaira Japan
124 □G17 Kodakara-jima i. Nansei-shotō Japan
158 J3 Kodaky Ukr.
137 I3 Kodala Orissa India
127 J3 Kodama Japan
139 J6 Kodari Nepal
139 J7 Kodarma Jharkhand India
160 K3 Kodavere Estonia
197 L4 Kodeń Pol.
159 S3 Kodentsovo Rus. Fed.
126 A6 Kōdera Japan
193 K8 Kodersdorf Ger.
244 I4 Kodiak AK U.S.A.
244 I4 Kodiak Island AK U.S.A.
244 I4 Kodiak National Wildlife Refuge nature res. AK U.S.A.
138 C9 Kodinar Gujarat India
156 G3 Kodino Rus. Fed.
160 E1 Kodisjoki Fin.
193 E10 Köditz Ger.
136 F7 Kodiyakkarai Tamil Nadu India
198 G4 Kodó r. Hungary
232 B2 Kodok Sudan
124 R5 Kodomari Japan
124 R5 Kodomari-misaki pt Japan
151 C3 Kodori r. Georgia
151 C3 Kodoris K'edi hills Georgia
158 I3 Kodra Ukr.
197 H4 Kodrąb Pol.
136 E5 Kodumuru Andhra Prad. India
158 I5 Kodyma Ukr.
158 J5 Kodyma r. Ukr.
219 N9 Kodzhaele mt. Bulg./Greece
Kodzhori Georgia see Kojori
236 E8 Koedoesberg mts S. Africa
236 G5 Koegas S. Africa
236 F5 Koegrabie S. Africa
186 J3 Koekange Neth.
187 C6 Koekelare Belgium
236 C7 Koekenaap S. Africa
234 C5 Koës Namibia
187 E6 Koewacht Neth.
265 S8 Kofa Mountains AZ U.S.A.
265 R8 Kofa National Wildlife Refuge nature res. AZ U.S.A.
145 M2 Kofarnihon Tajik.
145 M3 Kofarnihon r. Tajik.
219 P9 Kofçaz Turkey
195 M4 Köfering Ger.
237 J5 Koffiefontein S. Africa
220 G8 Kofinas mt. Kriti Greece
201 L5 Köflach Austria
228 E5 Koforidua Ghana
125 K11 Kōfu Tottori Japan
127 I4 Kōfu Yamanashi Japan
201 N7 Kog Slovenia
127 K3 Koga Japan
219 Q6 Kogălniceanu airport Romania
248 E1 Kogaluc r. Que. Can.
248 E1 Kogaluc, Baie de b. Que. Can.
249 I1 Kogaluk r. Nfld and Lab. Can.
107 M9 Kogan Qld Austr.
127 K4 Koganei Japan
Kögart Kyrg. see Kök-Art
164 I6 Køge Denmark
164 I6 Køge Bugt b. Denmark
156 L3 Kogel' r. Rus. Fed.
229 G4 Kogi state Nigeria
201 M5 Koglhof Austria
142 K8 Kogon Uzbek.
228 D3 Kogoni Mali
125 H12 Kogushi Japan
Kogyl'nicheny Moldova see Cogîlniceni
Kōhaihai pt South I. N.Z. see Gillespies Point
145 K9 Kohaliuen Pak.
145 L8 Kohan Pak.
145 N5 Kohat Pak.
145 K4 Kohestānāt Afgh.
144 D6 Kohgīlūyeh va Būyer Aḩmad prov. Iran
160 H2 Kohila Estonia
139 O7 Kohima Nagaland India
100 □6 Kohinggo i. New Georgia Is Solomon Is
145 O4 Kohistan reg. Pak.
195 M2 Kohlberg Ger.
190 G3 Köhlen Ger.
286 Q2 Kohler Range mts Antarctica
265 U7 Kohls Ranch AZ U.S.A.
145 M7 Kohlu Pak.
144 F4 Kohneh 'Omar Iran
224 D5 Kohouro well Chad
193 G8 Kohrener Land park Ger.
145 I4 Kohsan Afgh.
160 K2 Kohtla-Järve Estonia
102 J4 Kohukohunui hill North I. N.Z.
123 E11 Kohŭng S. Korea
103 E11 Kohurau mt. South I. N.Z.
158 I8 Kohyl'nyk r. Ukr.
127 I1 Koide Japan
245 L3 Koidern Y.T. Can.
245 L3 Koidern Mountain Y.T. Can.
Koidu Sierra Leone see Sefadu
160 I3 Koigi Estonia
137 M8 Koihoa Andaman & Nicobar Is India
133 L9 Koikyim Qu r. Qinghai China
220 B5 Koiliomeno Zakynthos Greece
136 E4 Koilkonda Andhra Prad. India
136 F5 Koilkuntla Andhra Prad. India
239 □3a Koimbani Njazidja Comoros
123 E8 Koin N. Korea
156 J3 Koin r. Rus. Fed.
236 B6 Koingnaas S. Africa
149 L5 Koi Sanjaq Iraq
162 U5 Koitere l. Fin.
127 K5 Koito-gawa r. Japan
162 R3 Koivu Fin.
144 I9 Koja, Kowr-e watercourse Iran
123 F11 Kŏje-do i. S. Korea
198 G2 Kojetín Czech Rep.
124 Q5 Ko-jima i. Japan
125 Q13 Ko-jima i. Japan
109 D12 Kojonup W.A. Austr.
151 F4 Kojori Georgia
144 D3 Kojūr Iran
118 E4 Kok, Nam Mae r. Thai.
199 I4 Kóka Hungary
126 D6 Kōka Japan
257 □P3 Kokadjo ME U.S.A.
127 L4 Kokai-gawa r. Japan
142 K3 Kokalaat Kazakh.
Kokand Farg'ona Uzbek. see Qo'qon
Kokankishlak Uzbek. see Paxtaobod
163 P7 Kökar Åland Fin.
160 D2 Kökar i. Åland Fin.
142 I4 Kokaral (abandoned) Kazakh.
160 D2 Kökarsfjärden b. Fin.
143 P7 Kök-Art Osh Kyrg.
103 F9 Kokatahi South I. N.Z.
126 A8 Kokatsu-shima i. Japan
199 I3 Kokava nad Rimavicou Slovakia
126 B7 Kokawa Japan
143 P7 Kök-Aygyr Kyrg.
145 M3 Kokcha r. Afgh.
Kokchetav Kazakh. see Kokshetau
163 Q6 Kokemäki Fin.
234 C6 Kokerboom Namibia
118 D5 Ko Kha Thai.
160 M7 Kokhanava Belarus
161 Y5 Kokhma Rus. Fed.
228 B3 Koki Senegal
143 O7 Kök-Janggak Kyrg.
136 G8 Kokkilai Sri Lanka
150 A3 Kokkina Cyprus
220 D3 Kokkino Nero Greece
162 Q5 Kokkola Fin.
132 H4 Kok Kuduk well Xinjiang China
160 I5 Koknese Latvia
229 G5 Koko Edo Nigeria
229 G4 Koko Kebbi Nigeria
113 K8 Kokoda Northern P.N.G.
228 C3 Kokofata Mali
264 □D12 Koko Head HI U.S.A.
244 G1 Kokolik r. AK U.S.A.
228 D5 Kokolo-Pozo Côte d'Ivoire
254 D5 Kokomo IN U.S.A.
234 D5 Kokong Botswana
125 I13 Kokonoe Japan
160 K3 Kokora Estonia
161 R9 Kokorevka Rus. Fed.
160 M4 Kokorevo Rus. Fed.
229 F4 Kokoro Benin
232 C3 Kokosa Eth.
161 U6 Kokoshkino Rus. Fed.
237 L2 Kokosi S. Africa
228 B4 Kokou mt. Guinea
143 T3 Kokpekty Kazakh.
201 J7 Kokra r. Slovenia
201 J7 Kokrica Slovenia
244 I2 Kokrines AK U.S.A.
244 I2 Kokrines Hills AK U.S.A.
244 I1 Kokruagarok AK U.S.A.
123 E9 Koksan N. Korea
143 M6 Koksaray Kazakh.
Kokshaal-Tau, Khrebet mts China/Kyrg. see Kakshaal-Too
156 I4 Koksharka Rus. Fed.
143 M1 Kokshetau Kazakh.
187 C6 Koksijde Belgium
249 G1 Koksoak r. Que. Can.
237 N6 Kokstad S. Africa
143 Q5 Koksu Almatinskaya Oblast' Kazakh.
143 R5 Koksu Kazakh.
143 M7 Koksu Yuzhnyy Kazakhstan Kazakh.
143 R5 Koktal Kazakh.
143 P3 Koktas Kazakh.
143 O7 Kök-Tash Kyrg.
143 R4 Kokterek Almatinskaya Oblast' Kazakh.
142 C3 Kokterek Zapadnyy Kazakhstan Kazakh.
143 Q2 Koktobe Kazakh.
128 A3 Koktokay Xinjiang China
Koktokay Xinjiang China see Fuyun
142 G3 Koktubek Kazakh.
143 S5 Koktuma Kazakh.
115 B6 Koku, Tanjung pt Indon.
125 H15 Kokubu Japan
127 K3 Kokubunji Japan
126 F3 Kokufu Japan
127 I4 Kokushiga-take mt. Japan
128 B3 Koküy Xinjiang China
Kok-Yangak Kyrg. see Kök-Janggak
133 C8 Kokyar Xinjiang China
143 T3 Kokzhayyk Kazakh.
162 V2 Kola Rus. Fed.
162 V2 Kola r. Rus. Fed.
Kolab r. India see Sabari
139 J9 Kolabira Orissa India
145 L8 Kolachi r. Pak.
197 H4 Kołacin Pol.
196 E2 Kołacz Pol.
197 L4 Kołacze Pol.
196 F3 Kołaczkowo Pol.
197 J6 Kołaczyce Pol.
146 C9 Kola Diba Eth.
139 K8 Kolaghat W. Bengal India
138 E2 Kolahoi mt. Jammu and Kashmir India
228 C4 Kolahun Liberia
115 B6 Kolaka Sulawesi Indon.
197 K2 Kołaki Kościelne Pol.
114 D7 Kolambugan Mindanao Phil.
115 D8 Kolana Indon.
160 I9 Kolansk Belarus
119 D11 Ko Lanta Thai.
Kola Peninsula Rus. Fed. see Kol'skiy Poluostrov
136 G3 Kolar Chhattisgarh India
136 F6 Kolar Karnataka India
144 D6 Kolār, Kūh-e hill Iran
138 F7 Kolaras Madh. Prad. India
199 I3 Koláre Slovakia
136 F6 Kolar Gold Fields Karnataka India
162 Q3 Kolari Fin.
Kolarovgrad Bulg. see Shumen
199 G4 Kolárovo Slovakia
162 L5 Kolåsen Sweden
139 N7 Kolasib Mizoram India
218 H8 Kolašin Kolašin Montenegro
138 D6 Kolayat Rajasthan India
165 M2 Kolbäck Sweden
192 K4 Kołbacz Pol.
115 D9 Kolbano Timor Indon.
196 C2 Kołbaskowo Pol.
Kolberg Pol. see Kołobrzeg
195 M6 Kolbermoor Ger.
197 J3 Kołbiel Pol.
233 D5 Kolbio Kenya
164 G2 Kolbotn Norway
196 G1 Kolbudy Górne Pol.
197 J5 Kolbuszowa Pol.
161 P1 Kolchanovo Rus. Fed.
161 W5 Kol'chugino Rus. Fed.
159 M9 Kol'chuhyne Ukr.
158 B5 Kol'chyne Ukr.
199 L3 Kölcse Hungary
196 F1 Kołczygłowy Pol.
196 D3 Kołczyn Pol.
228 B3 Kolda Senegal
230 C3 Koldaga Chad
221 I4 Koldere Turkey
164 F6 Kolding Denmark
231 D5 Kole Kasaï-Oriental Dem. Rep. Congo
230 E4 Kole Orientale Dem. Rep. Congo
264 □E13 Kolekole mt. HI U.S.A.
122 M1 Kolendo Sakhalin Rus. Fed.
162 P4 Koler Sweden
199 H5 Kölesd Hungary
160 I3 Kolga-Jaani Estonia
156 J1 Kolguyev, Ostrov i. Rus. Fed.
139 J8 Kolhan reg. Jharkhand India
136 D4 Kolhapur Mahar. India
163 R5 Kolho Fin.
135 D11 Kolhumadulu Atoll Maldives
228 B3 Koliba r. Guinea/Guinea-Bissau
244 H4 Koliganek AK U.S.A.
Kolikata W. Bengal India see Kolkata
162 R5 Kolima l. Fin.
198 E1 Kolín Czech Rep.
198 C2 Kolinec Czech Rep.
162 T5 Kolin kansallispuisto nat. park Fin.
232 C3 K'olīto Eth.
195 I2 Kolitzheim Ger.
160 F3 Kõljala Estonia
160 F4 Kolkasrags pt Latvia
139 L8 Kolkata W. Bengal India
199 H6 Kölked Hungary
151 C3 Kolkhet'is Nakrdzali nature res. Georgia
Kolkhozabad Tajik. see Kolkhozobod
145 M3 Kolkhozobod Tajik.
193 J7 Kolkwitz Ger.
158 E2 Kolky Ukr.
136 E8 Kollam Kerala India
195 O4 Kollbach r. Ger.
193 D8 Kölleda Ger.
136 E6 Kollegal Karnataka India
136 G4 Kolleru Lake India
136 F7 Kollidam r. India
195 N3 Kollnburg Ger.
190 I3 Kölln-Reisiek Ger.
229 F3 Kollo Niger
186 J2 Kollum Neth.
190 H1 Kollund Denmark
191 C9 Köln Ger.
191 B9 Köln admin. reg. Ger.
191 D9 Köln-Bonn airport Ger.
197 L2 Kolnica Pol.
197 J2 Kolno Podlaskie Pol.
197 I2 Kolno Warmińsko-Mazurskie Pol.
231 B6 Kolo Dem. Rep. Congo

196 G3 **Koło** Pol.
233 B6 **Kolo** Tanz.
264 □B12 **Kōloa** *HI* U.S.A.
161 Y5 **Kolobovo** Rus. Fed.
165 L7 **Kołobrzeg** Pol.
193 H7 **Kolochau** Ger.
158 C5 **Kolochava** Ukr.
161 U2 **Kolodenskoye, Ozero** *l.* Rus. Fed.
159 S2 **Kolodeznyy** Rus. Fed.
158 E4 **Kolodne** Ukr.
159 Q3 **Kolodyazne** Ukr.
140 C7 **Kologi** Sudan
156 I4 **Kologriv** Rus. Fed.
228 C3 **Kolokani** Mali
156 K1 **Kolokolkova, Guba** *b.* Rus. Fed.
161 X5 **Koloksha** *r.* Rus. Fed.
159 O4 **Kolomak** Ukr.
159 N4 **Kolomak** *r.* Ukr.
100 □[6] **Kolombangara** *i. New Georgia Is* Solomon Is
Kolomea Ukr. *see* **Kolomyya**
161 V6 **Kolomna** Rus. Fed.
231 D6 **Kolomonyi** Dem. Rep. Congo
Kołomyja Ukr. *see* **Kolomyya**
158 E5 **Kolomyya** Ukr.
228 D4 **Kolondiéba** Mali
115 B5 **Kolonedale** *Sulawesi* Indon.
101 □[8a] **Kolonga** *Tongatapu* Tonga
150 A4 **Koloni** Cyprus
100 □[4b] **Kolonia** *Pohnpei* Micronesia
218 H10 **Kolonjë** Albania
234 D5 **Kolonkwaneng** Botswana
115 C6 **Kolono** *Sulawesi* Indon.
196 G5 **Kolonowskie** Pol.
159 O2 **Kolontayevka** Rus. Fed.
159 N4 **Kolontayiv** Ukr.
133 K13 **Koloriang** *Arun. Prad.* India
161 S1 **Koloshma** *r.* Rus. Fed.
101 □[8a] **Kolovai** *Tongatapu* Tonga
142 D2 **Kolovertnoye** Kazakh.
115 C6 **Kolowana Watobo, Teluk** *b.* Indon.
162 V2 **Kolozero, Ozero** *l.* Rus. Fed.
Kolozsvár Romania *see* **Cluj-Napoca**
161 T2 **Kolp'** *r.* Rus. Fed.
161 Y6 **Kolp'** *r.* Rus. Fed.
152 J4 **Kolpashevo** Rus. Fed.
161 N2 **Kolpino** Rus. Fed.
157 G5 **Kolpny** Rus. Fed.
142 J6 **Ko'lquduq** Uzbek.
200 E5 **Kolsass** Austria
161 Y4 **Kolshevo** Rus. Fed.
156 F2 **Kol'skiy Poluostrov** *pen.* Rus. Fed.
196 D4 **Kolsko** Pol.
165 M2 **Kolsnaren** *l.* Sweden
165 L2 **Kolsva** Sweden
163 M6 **Kölsvallen** Sweden
199 H3 **Kolta** Slovakia
159 M8 **Kol'tsove** Ukr.
142 D1 **Koltubanovskiy** Rus. Fed.
218 I6 **Kolubara** *r.* Serbia
Kölük Turkey *see* **Kâhta**
225 I6 **Koluli** Eritrea
197 H4 **Koluszki** Pol.
143 M2 **Koluton** Kazakh.
156 L2 **Kolva** *r.* Rus. Fed.
156 L3 **Kolva** *r.* Rus. Fed.
136 C3 **Kolvan** *Mahar.* India
162 K4 **Kolvereid** Norway
162 R1 **Kolvik** Norway
156 F2 **Kolvitskoye, Ozero** *l.* Rus. Fed.
145 K8 **Kolwa** *reg.* Pak.
231 E7 **Kolwezi** Dem. Rep. Congo
136 D4 **Kolya** *r.* India
161 W8 **Kolybel'skoye** Rus. Fed.
153 R3 **Kolyma** *r.* Rus. Fed.
Kolyma Lowland Rus. Fed. *see* **Kolymskaya Nizmennost'**
Kolyma Range *mts* Rus. Fed. *see* **Kolymskiy, Khrebet**
153 Q3 **Kolymskaya Nizmennost'** *lowland* Rus. Fed.
153 R3 **Kolymskiy, Khrebet** *mts* Rus. Fed.
153 P3 **Kolymskoye Vodokhranilishche** *resr* Rus. Fed.
157 I5 **Kolyshley** Rus. Fed.
153 T3 **Kolyuchinskaya Guba** *b.* Rus. Fed.
161 O8 **Kolyudy** Rus. Fed.
143 T2 **Kolyvan'** Rus. Fed.
219 L7 **Kom** *mt.* Bulg.
132 H2 **Kom** *Xinjiang* China
118 D7 **Koma** Myanmar
199 K4 **Komádi** Hungary
229 I3 **Komadugu-Gana** *watercourse* Nigeria
127 K4 **Komae** Japan
127 G4 **Komaga-dake** *mt.* Japan
127 G4 **Komagane** Japan
127 J1 **Komaga-take** *mt.* Japan
124 R4 **Komaga-take** *vol.* Japan
162 Q1 **Komagfjord** Norway
236 B5 **Komaggas** S. Africa
236 B5 **Komaggas Mountains** S. Africa
162 U1 **Komagvær** Norway
126 E5 **Komaki** Japan
197 K6 **Komańcza** Pol.
122 K3 **Komandnaya, Gora** *mt.* Rus. Fed.
153 R4 **Komandorskiye Ostrova** *is* Rus. Fed.
161 R9 **Komarichi** Rus. Fed.
218 G7 **Komarnica** *r.* Montenegro
199 H4 **Komárno** Slovakia
158 C4 **Komarno** Ukr.
199 H4 **Komárom** Hungary
199 H4 **Komárom-Esztergom** *county* Hungary
198 C2 **Komárov** Czech Rep.
158 E2 **Komarove** Ukr.
160 M1 **Komarovo** *Leningradskaya Oblast'* Rus. Fed.
161 Q3 **Komarovo** *Novgorodskaya Oblast'* Rus. Fed.
197 K4 **Komarówka Podlaska** Pol.
197 L5 **Komarów Osada** Pol.
161 Q6 **Komary** Rus. Fed.
237 P1 **Komati** *r.* Swaziland
237 P1 **Komatipoort** S. Africa
126 D3 **Komatsu** Japan
126 A7 **Komatsushima** Japan
230 E4 **Komba** Dem. Rep. Congo
115 C7 **Komba** *i.* Indon.
115 C4 **Kombakomba** *Sulawesi* Indon.
234 C3 **Kombat** Namibia
231 E6 **Kombe** Dem. Rep. Congo
233 A6 **Kombe** Tanz.
228 E3 **Kombissiri** Burkina
Kombótion Greece *see* **Kompoti**
114 □ **Komebail Lagoon** Palau
201 I8 **Komen** Slovenia
116 F6 **Komering** *r.* Indon.
237 L8 **Komga** S. Africa
156 J3 **Komi, Respublika** *aut. rep.* Rus. Fed.
Komi A.S.S.R. *aut. rep.* Rus. Fed. *see* **Komi, Respublika**
201 N7 **Komin** Croatia
124 R6 **Kominato** Japan
Komintern Ukr. *see* **Marhanets'**
158 J7 **Kominternivs'ke** Ukr.
210 F4 **Komiža** Croatia
199 H3 **Komjatice** Slovakia
199 I2 **Komjatná** Slovakia
236 C7 **Komkans** S. Africa
199 H5 **Komló** Hungary
199 J4 **Kömlő** Hungary
236 G9 **Kommandokraal** S. Africa
236 C10 **Kommetjie** S. Africa
237 L5 **Kommissiepoort** S. Africa
Kommuna Turkm. *see* **Badabaýhan**
156 H4 **Kommunar** *Kostromskaya Oblast'* Rus. Fed.
161 N2 **Kommunar** *Leningradskaya Oblast'* Rus. Fed.
161 X5 **Kommunar** *Vladimirskaya Oblast'* Rus. Fed.
Kommunarsk Ukr. *see* **Alchevs'k**
Kommunizm, Qullai *mt.* Tajik. *see* **Ismoili Somoní, Qullai**
Kommunizma, Pik *mt.* Tajik. *see* **Ismoili Somoní, Qullai**
201 I7 **Komna** *slope* Slovenia
115 A8 **Komodo** *i.* Indon.
115 A8 **Komodo, Taman Nasional** *nat. park* Indon.
228 C4 **Komodou** Guinea
228 E5 **Komoé** *r.* Côte d'Ivoire
231 B5 **Komono** Congo
126 E5 **Komono** Japan
113 I8 **Komoran** *i. Papua* Indon.
196 E3 **Komorniki** Pol.
199 L3 **Komoró** Hungary
127 H3 **Komoro** Japan
197 J3 **Komorowo** Pol.
196 E2 **Komorze, Jezioro** *l.* Pol.
196 G4 **Komorzno** Pol.
165 J4 **Komosse SNF-reservat** *nature res.* Sweden
221 G1 **Komotini** Greece
159 L5 **Kompaniyivka** Ukr.
199 I5 **Kömpöc** Hungary
Kompong Cham Cambodia *see* **Kâmpóng Cham**
Kompong Chhnang Cambodia *see* **Kâmpóng Chhnăng**
Kompong Kleang Cambodia *see* **Kâmpóng Khleăng**
Kompong Som Cambodia *see* **Sihanoukville**
Kompong Som Bay Cambodia *see* **Sihanoukville, Chhâk**
Kompong Speu Cambodia *see* **Kâmpóng Spœ**
Kompong Thom Cambodia *see* **Kâmpóng Thum**
Kompong Trach Cambodia *see* **Kâmpóng Tranch**
220 C3 **Kompoti** Greece
196 F5 **Komprachcice** Pol.
220 G1 **Kompsatos** *r.* Greece
Komrat Moldova *see* **Comrat**
236 F8 **Komsberg** *mt.* S. Africa
236 E8 **Komsberg** *mts* S. Africa
Komsomol *Atyrauskaya Oblast'* Kazakh. *see* **Komsomol'skiy**
Komsomol *Kostanayskaya Oblast'* Kazakh. *see* **Karabalyk**
142 J8 **Komsomol** Turkm.
153 K1 **Komsomolets, Ostrov** *i. Severnaya Zemlya* Rus. Fed.
142 E5 **Komsomolets, Zaliv** *b.* Kazakh.
161 X4 **Komsomol'sk** *Ivanovskaya Oblast'* Rus. Fed.
197 I1 **Komsomol'sk** Rus. Fed.
160 D7 **Komsomol'sk** *Kaliningradskaya Oblast'* Rus. Fed.
Komsomol'sk Turkm. *see* **Komsomol**
159 M4 **Komsomol's'k** Ukr.
159 R6 **Komsomol's'ke** *Donets'ka Oblast'* Ukr.
159 P4 **Komsomol's'ke** *Kharkivs'ka Oblast'* Ukr.
142 E4 **Komsomol'skiy** Kazakh.
153 S3 **Komsomol'skiy** *Chukotskiy Avtonomnyy Okrug* Rus. Fed.
Komsomol'skiy *Khanty-Mansiyskiy Avtonomnyy Okrug* Rus. Fed. *see* **Yugorsk**
151 H2 **Komsomol'skiy** *Respublika Dagestan* Rus. Fed.
157 I7 **Komsomol'skiy** *Respublika Kalmykiya-Khalm'g-Tangch* Rus. Fed.
157 I5 **Komsomol'skiy** *Respublika Mordoviya* Rus. Fed.
122 J3 **Komsomol'sk-na-Amure** Rus. Fed.
142 I2 **Komsomol'skoye** Kazakh.
142 B2 **Komsomol'skoye** Rus. Fed.
219 N9 **Komuniga** Bulg.
150 E2 **Kömürçukuru** Turkey
149 K3 **Kömürlü** Turkey
159 L7 **Komyshany** Ukr.
159 S5 **Komyshna** *r.* Rus. Fed./Ukr.
159 M3 **Komyshnya** Ukr.
159 O6 **Komyshuvakha** Ukr.
159 K5 **Komyshuvate** Ukr.
159 P6 **Komysh-Zorya** Ukr.
139 I7 **Kon** *Uttar Prad.* India
150 D2 **Konacık** Turkey
137 H3 **Konada** *Andhra Prad.* India
244 I4 **Konaig Peak** *AK* U.S.A.
151 D6 **Konakkuran** Turkey
161 T5 **Konakovo** Rus. Fed.
126 E5 **Kōnan** *Aichi* Japan
126 D6 **Kōnan** *Shiga* Japan
Konarak *Orissa* India *see* **Konarka**
137 J3 **Konarka** *Orissa* India
197 K2 **Konarzyce** Pol.
196 F2 **Konarzyny** Pol.
219 K9 **Konče** *Konče* Macedonia
138 G7 **Konch** *Uttar Prad.* India
161 R3 **Konchanskoye-Suvorovskoye** Rus. Fed.
156 F3 **Konchezero** Rus. Fed.
158 E1 **Konchytsy** Belarus
126 B5 **Konda** Japan
136 G3 **Kondagaon** *Chhattisgarh* India
151 I6 **Köndälänçay** *r.* Azer.
136 G4 **Kondapalle** *Andhra Prad.* India
107 J4 **Kondaparinga Aboriginal Holding** *res. Qld* Austr.
136 G4 **Kondavid** *Andhra Prad.* India
251 R3 **Kondiaronk, Lac** *l. Que.* Can.
109 E12 **Kondinin** *W.A.* Austr.
Kondinskoye *Khanty-Mansiyskiy Avtonomnyy Okrug* Rus. Fed. *see* **Oktyabr'skoye**
152 H3 **Kondinskoye** *Khanty-Mansiyskiy Avtonomnyy Okrug* Rus. Fed.
233 B6 **Kondoa** Tanz.
157 I5 **Kondol'** Rus. Fed.
151 G4 **Kondoli** Georgia
156 F3 **Kondopoga** Rus. Fed.
199 J5 **Kondoros** Hungary
196 E5 **Kondratowice** Pol.
160 L1 **Kondrat'yevo** Rus. Fed.
161 S7 **Kondrovo** Rus. Fed.
Kondūz Afgh. *see* **Kunduz**
100 □[5] **Kone** New Caledonia
219 K9 **Konečka Planina** *mts* Macedonia
156 L2 **Konetsbor** Rus. Fed.
144 H1 **Köneürgenç** Turkm.
Köneürgench Turkm. *see* **Köneürgenç**
161 N1 **Konevits, Ostrov** *i.* Rus. Fed.
229 I5 **Kong** Cameroon
228 D4 **Kong** Côte d'Ivoire
119 F9 **Kŏng, Kaôh** *i.* Cambodia
119 H8 **Kông, Tônlé** *r.* Cambodia
118 H7 **Kong, Xé** *r.* Laos
245 L1 **Kongakut** *r. AK* U.S.A.
228 C3 **Kongassambougou, Réserve de** *nature res.* Mali
114 □ **Kongauru** *i.* Palau
230 D3 **Kongbo** C.A.R.
243 O3 **Kong Christian IX Land** *reg.* Greenland
243 P2 **Kong Christian X Land** *reg.* Greenland
164 E6 **Kongeå** *r.* Denmark
Kongelab *atoll* Marshall Is *see* **Rongelap**
164 I6 **Kongens Lyngby** Denmark
232 B3 **Kongettit** Sudan
243 M3 **Kong Frederik IX Land** *reg.* Greenland
243 P2 **Kong Frederik VIII Land** *reg.* Greenland
243 N3 **Kong Frederik VI Kyst** *coastal area* Greenland
244 G4 **Kongiganak** *AK* U.S.A.
162 □ **Kong Karls Land** *is* Svalbard
117 L4 **Kong Kat** *hill* Indon.
117 L4 **Kongkemul** *mt.* Indon.
126 F3 **Kongōdo-san** *mt.* Japan
126 C6 **Kongō-Ikoma Kokutei-kōen** *park* Japan
234 D3 **Kongola** Namibia
231 E6 **Kongolo** Dem. Rep. Congo
232 A3 **Kongor** Sudan
243 P2 **Kong Oscars Fjord** *inlet* Greenland
228 E3 **Kongoussi** Burkina
164 F2 **Kongsberg** Norway
162 T1 **Kongsfjord** Norway
162 □ **Kongsøya** *i.* Svalbard
164 I1 **Kongsvinger** Norway
132 B7 **Kongur Shan** *mt. Xinjiang* China
233 C6 **Kongwa** Tanz.
243 P2 **Kong Wilhelm Land** *reg.* Greenland
145 N1 **Konibodom** Tajik.
198 F2 **Konice** Czech Rep.
197 H5 **Koniecpol** Pol.
194 H2 **Königheim** Ger.
Königsberg Rus. Fed. *see* **Kaliningrad**
191 K10 **Königsberg in Bayern** Ger.
193 E6 **Königsborn** Ger.
195 I4 **Königsbronn** Ger.
193 I8 **Königsbrück** Ger.
195 J5 **Königsbrunn** Ger.
195 K6 **Königsdorf** Ger.
193 D9 **Königsee** Ger.
195 K2 **Königsfeld** Ger.
194 E5 **Königsfeld im Schwarzwald** Ger.
193 H6 **Königsgraben** *r.* Ger.
193 K8 **Königshain** Ger.
193 E8 **Königshofen** Ger.
Königshütte Pol. *see* **Chorzów**
191 K6 **Königslutter am Elm** Ger.
195 K4 **Königsmoos** Ger.
195 N6 **Königssee** Ger.
195 N6 **Königssee** *l.* Ger.
195 L2 **Königstein** *Bayern* Ger.
193 J9 **Königstein** *Sachsen* Ger.
194 F3 **Königstuhl** *hill* Ger.
193 H9 **Königswalde** Ger.
193 J8 **Königswartha** Ger.
201 K3 **Königswiesen** Austria
191 D9 **Königswinter** Ger.
193 I6 **Königs Wusterhausen** Ger.
Konimekh Uzbek. *see* **Konimex**
142 K7 **Konimex** Uzbek.
196 G3 **Konin** Pol.
122 J2 **Konin** *r.* Rus. Fed.
220 B2 **Konitsa** Greece
193 E9 **Könitz** Ger.
212 C2 **Köniz** Switz.
210 F4 **Konj** *mt.* Bos.-Herz.
210 F4 **Konjic** Bos.-Herz.
210 G3 **Konjuh** *mts* Bos.-Herz.
162 Q2 **Könkämäeno** *r.* Fin./Sweden
234 C6 **Konkiep** *watercourse* Namibia
161 W9 **Kon'-Kolodez'** Rus. Fed.
229 G4 **Konkwesso** Nigeria
228 E3 **Konna** Mali
256 D12 **Konnarock** *VA* U.S.A.
193 E7 **Könnern** Ger.
193 F10 **Konnersreuth** Ger.
162 S5 **Konnevesi** Fin.
163 S6 **Konnivesi** *l.* Fin.
126 D4 **Kōno** Japan
159 K4 **Kononcha** Ukr.
228 E5 **Konongo** Ghana
159 L3 **Kononivka** Ukr.
199 I1 **Konopiska** Pol.
197 I2 **Konopki** Pol.
158 J6 **Konoplyane** Ukr.
156 H3 **Konosha** Rus. Fed.
127 K3 **Kōnosu** Japan
196 D4 **Konotop** Pol.
159 M2 **Konotop** Ukr.
139 I8 **Konpara** *Chhattisgarh* India
119 I7 **Kon Plông** Vietnam
132 I6 **Konqi He** *r.* China
193 E10 **Konradsreuth** Ger.
114 □ **Konrei** Palau
127 J2 **Konsei-tōge** *pass* Japan
197 I4 **Końskie** Pol.
189 K3 **Końskowola** Pol.
232 C3 **Konso** Eth.
197 J3 **Konstancin-Jeziorna** Pol.
Konstantinograd Ukr. *see* **Krasnohrad**
122 E4 **Konstantinovka** Rus. Fed.
Konstantinovka *Donets'ka Oblast'* Ukr. *see* **Kostyantynivka**
Konstantinovka *Kharkivs'ka Oblast'* Ukr. *see* **Kostyantynivka**
Konstantinovka *Khersons'ka Oblast'* Ukr. *see* **Kostyantynivka**
Konstantinovka *Zaporiz'ka Oblast'* Ukr. *see* **Kostyantynivka**
161 V5 **Konstantinovo** Rus. Fed.
157 H7 **Konstantinovsk** Rus. Fed.
161 W4 **Konstantinovskiy** Rus. Fed.
198 B2 **Konstantinovy Lázně** Czech Rep.
197 L3 **Konstantynów** Pol.
197 H4 **Konstantynów Łódzki** Pol.
194 G6 **Konstanz** Ger.
145 I8 **Kont** Iran
229 G4 **Kontagora** Nigeria
229 I5 **Kontcha** Cameroon
118 C4 **Kontha** Myanmar
162 T5 **Kontiolahti** Fin.
162 T4 **Kontiomäki** Fin.
162 S4 **Konttila** Fin.
119 H7 **Kon Tum** Vietnam
119 I8 **Kon Tum, Cao Nguyên** *plat.* Vietnam
Könugard Ukr. *see* **Kyiv**
221 M2 **Konuralp** Turkey
156 H2 **Konushin, Mys** *pt* Rus. Fed.
148 F5 **Konya** Turkey
199 K4 **Konyár** Hungary
143 P4 **Konyrat** Kazakh.
143 R5 **Konyrolen** Kazakh.
159 O2 **Konyshevka** Rus. Fed.
142 E3 **Konystanu** Kazakh.
143 N1 **Konyukhovo** Kazakh.
194 B2 **Konz** Ger.
195 N3 **Konzell** Ger.
156 L4 **Konzhakovskiy Kamen', Gora** *mt.* Rus. Fed.
246 H5 **Koocanusa, Lake** *resr* Can./U.S.A.
109 F10 **Kookynie** *W.A.* Austr.
108 G3 **Koolan Island** *W.A.* Austr.
264 □D12 **Ko'olau Range** *mts HI* U.S.A.
104 E5 **Koolgera Conservation Reserve** *res. S.A.* Austr.
109 D7 **Kooline** *W.A.* Austr.
106 G8 **Koolivoo, Lake** *salt flat Qld* Austr.
104 F3 **Koolkootinnie, Lake** *salt flat S.A.* Austr.
104 G5 **Koolunga** *S.A.* Austr.
109 E11 **Koolyanobbing** *W.A.* Austr.
105 J6 **Koondrook** *Vic.* Austr.
160 H3 **Koonga** Estonia
108 I5 **Koongie Park Aboriginal Reserve** *W.A.* Austr.
104 D4 **Koonibba** *S.A.* Austr.
256 G9 **Koon Lake** *PA* U.S.A.
236 E3 **Koopan-Suid** S. Africa
105 L6 **Koorawatha** *N.S.W.* Austr.
109 D11 **Koorda** *W.A.* Austr.
108 C7 **Koordarrie** *W.A.* Austr.
160 I4 **Koorküla** Estonia
192 H2 **Koos** *i.* Ger.
160 K3 **Koosa** Estonia
265 U3 **Koosharem** *UT* U.S.A.
262 F3 **Kooskia** *ID* U.S.A.
246 G5 **Kootenay** *r.* B.C. Can.
246 G5 **Kootenay Bay** B.C. Can.
246 G5 **Kootenay Lake** B.C. Can.
246 G5 **Kootenay National Park** B.C. Can.
105 M4 **Kootingal** *N.S.W.* Austr.
236 E7 **Kootjieskolk** S. Africa
186 I4 **Kootwijkerbroek** Neth.
244 E3 **Koozata Lagoon** *AK* U.S.A.
143 P6 **Kopa** *Almatinskaya Oblast'* Kazakh.
143 R4 **Kopa** *Vostochnyy Kazakhstan* Kazakh.
199 I2 **Kopa** *mt.* Slovakia
233 A7 **Kopa** Zambia
151 D6 **Kopal** Turkey
196 E1 **Kopań, Jezioro** *lag.* Pol.
159 O6 **Kopani** Ukr.
196 D3 **Kopanica** Pol.
157 I7 **Kopanovka** Rus. Fed.
159 R7 **Kopanskaya** Rus. Fed.
218 I7 **Kopaonik** *nat. park* Serbia
218 I7 **Kopaonik** *mts* Serbia/Kosovo
136 D3 **Kopargaon** *Mahar.* India
162 □E1 **Kópasker** Iceland
158 G5 **Kopayhorod** Ukr.
143 Q4 **Kopbirlik** Kazakh.
198 G3 **Kopčany** Slovakia
210 D3 **Koper** Slovenia
164 B2 **Kopervik** Norway
144 G2 **Kopet Dag** *mts* Iran/Turkm.
Kopet-Dag, Khrebet *mts* Iran/Turkm. *see* **Kopet Dag**
151 B5 **Kop Geçidi** *pass* Turkey
198 F4 **Kópháza** Hungary
196 F5 **Kopice** Pol.
198 E1 **Kopidlno** Czech Rep.
165 M2 **Köping** Sweden
218 H8 **Koplik** Albania
162 O5 **Köpmanholmen** Sweden
161 R6 **Koporikha** Rus. Fed.
136 D6 **Koppa** *Karnataka* India
136 E5 **Koppal** *Karnataka* India
163 K6 **Koppang** Norway
218 G4 **Koppány** *r.* Romania
165 L2 **Kopparberg** Sweden
Kopparberg *county* Sweden *see* **Dalarna**
Koppeh Dāgh *mts* Iran/Turkm. *see* **Kopet Dag**
191 E10 **Köppel** *hill* Ger.
122 L4 **Koppi** *r.* Rus. Fed.
237 L3 **Koppies** S. Africa
237 L3 **Koppies Dam Nature Reserve** S. Africa
236 E3 **Koppieskraal Pan** *salt pan* S. Africa
200 H4 **Koppl** Austria
219 N8 **Koprinka, Yazovir** *resr* Bulg.
210 F2 **Koprivnica** Croatia
148 E5 **Köprü** *r.* Turkey
221 J4 **Köprübaşı** *Manisa* Turkey
151 B5 **Köprübaşı** *Trabzon* Turkey
151 C6 **Köprüköy** Turkey
148 F5 **Köprülü** Turkey
221 M5 **Köprülü Kanyon Milli Parkı** *nat. park* Turkey
197 J5 **Koprzywianka** *r.* Pol.
197 J5 **Koprzywnica** Pol.
237 L7 **Kopshorn** *mt.* S. Africa
187 J9 **Kopstal** Lux.
161 N6 **Koptsi** Belarus
160 I3 **Kõpu** Estonia
160 I3 **Kõpu** *r.* Estonia
102 J4 **Kopu** *North I.* N.Z.
102 L6 **Kopuawhara** *North I.* N.Z.
158 E4 **Kopychyntsi** Ukr.
Kopyl' Belarus *see* **Kapyl'**
159 U2 **Kopyl** Rus. Fed.
144 E7 **Kor, Rūd-e** *watercourse* Iran
138 H6 **Kora** *Uttar Prad.* India
126 D5 **Kōra** Japan
218 I9 **Korab** *mts* Albania/Macedonia
161 X8 **Korablino** Rus. Fed.
138 H9 **Koracha** *Chhattisgarh* India
232 E3 **Koraf** *well* Eth.
232 E3 **K'orahē** Eth.
145 K8 **Korak** Pak.
114 □ **Korak** *i.* Palau
221 H3 **Korakas, Akrotirio** *pt Lesvos* Greece
201 K6 **Koralpe** *mts* Austria
133 G8 **Koramlik** *Xinjiang* China
210 E3 **Korana** *r.* Bos.-Herz./Croatia
136 E4 **Korangal** *Andhra Prad.* India
145 L9 **Korangi** Pak.
145 N3 **Korān va Monjan** Afgh.
137 H3 **Koraput** *Orissa* India
Korat Thai. *see* **Nakhon Ratchasima**
136 F3 **Koratla** *Andhra Prad.* India
139 I8 **Korba** *Chhattisgarh* India
227 H1 **Korba** Tunisia
191 G8 **Korbach** Ger.
161 R1 **Korbenichi** Rus. Fed.
230 C2 **Korbol** Chad
151 E3 **Korbouli** Georgia
211 C7 **Korbous** Tunisia
116 D2 **Korbu, Gunung** *mt.* Malaysia
220 B2 **Korçë** Albania
143 S1 **Korchino** Rus. Fed.
197 L5 **Korchiv** Ukr.
158 F4 **Korchivka** Ukr.
192 D4 **Körchow** Ger.
158 G3 **Korchyk** *r.* Ukr.
210 F4 **Korčula** Croatia
210 F4 **Korčula** *i.* Croatia
210 F4 **Korčulanski Kanal** *sea chan.* Croatia
197 K3 **Korczew** Pol.
197 J6 **Korczyna** Pol.
143 P6 **Korday** Kazakh.
194 B2 **Kordel** Ger.
158 H4 **Kordelivka** Ukr.
144 B4 **Kordestān** *prov.* Iran
224 D5 **Kordi, Ouadi** *watercourse* Chad
149 N6 **Kord Khvord** Iran
144 F3 **Kord Kūy** Iran
156 L4 **Kordon** Rus. Fed.
144 I8 **Kords** *reg.* Iran
123 D9 **Korea Bay** *g.* China/N. Korea
123 E2 **Korea, North** *country* Asia
123 F11 **Korea, South** *country* Asia
125 F12 **Korea Strait** Japan/S. Korea
136 D4 **Koregaon** *Mahar.* India
158 D4 **Korelychi** Ukr.
232 C1 **Korem** Eth.
159 P3 **Koren'** *r.* Rus. Fed.
159 N2 **Korenevo** Rus. Fed.
198 E1 **Kořenov** Czech Rep.
157 G7 **Korenovsk** Rus. Fed.
Korenovskaya Rus. Fed. *see* **Korenovsk**
156 L3 **Korepino** Rus. Fed.
228 C3 **Koréra-Koré** Mali
158 G3 **Korets'** Ukr.
153 R3 **Korf** Rus. Fed.
196 F5 **Korfantów** Pol.
221 K2 **Körfez** Turkey
286 T1 **Korff Ice Rise** Antarctica
122 I4 **Korfovskiy** Rus. Fed.
143 N2 **Korgalzhyn** Kazakh.
143 M2 **Korgalzhyn Nature Reserve** *res.* Kazakhstan
132 E4 **Korgas** *Xinjiang* China
143 L3 **Korgasyn** Kazakh.
162 L3 **Korgen** Norway
151 K5 **Korgöz** Azer.
221 M3 **Körhasan** Turkey
228 D4 **Korhogo** Côte d'Ivoire
124 R9 **Kōri** Japan
275 G3 **Koriabo** Guyana
228 C5 **Koribundu** Sierra Leone
138 B8 **Kori Creek** *inlet Gujarat* India
236 C9 **Koringberg** S. Africa
236 E8 **Koringplaas** S. Africa
102 J6 **Koriniti** *North I.* N.Z.
220 D2 **Korinos** Greece
164 G6 **Korinth** Denmark
220 D4 **Korinthiakos Kolpos** *sea chan.* Greece
220 D5 **Korinthos** Greece
220 E5 **Korinthou, Dioryga** *b.* Greece
199 G4 **Kőris-hegy** *hill* Hungary
220 F5 **Korisia** *Kea* Greece
144 G5 **Korīt** Iran
220 B5 **Korithi** *Zakynthos* Greece
218 I8 **Koritnik** *mt.* Albania
Koritsa Albania *see* **Korçë**
125 R9 **Kōriyama** Japan
162 U4 **Korkana** Fin.
144 G3 **Korkī** Iran
145 K8 **Korkian** Pak.
152 H4 **Korkino** Rus. Fed.
153 Q3 **Korkodon** *r.* Rus. Fed.
221 M4 **Körküler** Turkey
221 L5 **Korkuteli** Turkey
160 G3 **Kõrkvere** Estonia
142 J5 **Korkyt** Kazakh.
132 H6 **Korla** *Xinjiang* China
191 I8 **Körle** Ger.
150 A3 **Kormakitis, Cape** Cyprus
218 H7 **Korman** *mt.* Montenegro
198 F4 **Körmend** Hungary
159 M8 **Kormove** Ukr.
197 L6 **Kornalovychi** Ukr.
210 E4 **Kornat** *i.* Croatia
210 E4 **Kornat** *nat. park* Croatia
191 K8 **Körner** Ger.
Korneshty Moldova *see* **Cornești**
201 N3 **Korneuburg** Austria
197 I1 **Kornevo** Rus. Fed.
143 P2 **Korneyevka** *Karagandinskaya Oblast'* Kazakh.
143 M1 **Korneyevka** *Severnyy Kazakhstan* Kazakh.
142 C2 **Korneyevka** Rus. Fed.
196 F3 **Kórnik** Pol.
143 S1 **Kornilovo** Rus. Fed.
Kornisi Georgia *see* **Qornisi**
164 H3 **Kornsjø** Norway
194 G4 **Kornwestheim** Ger.
199 H4 **Környe** Hungary
158 I3 **Kornyn** Ukr.
228 D4 **Koro** Côte d'Ivoire
101 □[7] **Koro** *i.* Fiji
115 B4 **Koro** *r.* Indon.
228 E3 **Koro** Mali
101 □[7a] **Koroba** *mt. Viti Levu* Fiji
161 Q7 **Korobets** Rus. Fed.
249 H1 **Koroc** *r. Que.* Can.
157 G6 **Korocha** Rus. Fed.
159 P3 **Korocha** *r.* Rus. Fed.
148 F3 **Köroğlu Dağları** *mts* Turkey
148 F3 **Köroğlu Tepesi** *mt.* Turkey
232 D3 **Korogo** *well* Eth.
233 C6 **Korogwe** Tanz.
158 C5 **Korolevo** Ukr.
101 □[7a] **Korolevu** *Viti Levu* Fiji
101 □[7a] **Korolevu** *Viti Levu* Fiji
230 C2 **Korom, Bahr** *watercourse* Chad
213 Q6 **Koromačno** Croatia
Koromba *mt. Viti Levu* Fiji *see* **Koroba**
103 □[3] **Koromiri** *i. Rarotonga* Cook Is
220 E2 **Koroneia, Limni** *l.* Greece
220 C6 **Koroni** Greece
220 B3 **Koronisia** Greece
196 F2 **Koronowo** Pol.
196 F2 **Koronowskie, Jezioro** *l.* Pol.
159 L2 **Korop** Ukr.
220 E5 **Koropi** Greece
114 □ **Koror** Palau
114 □ **Koror** *i.* Palau
218 I4 **Körös** *r.* Romania
101 □[7] **Koro Sea** *b.* Fiji
199 I5 **Kőrös-ér** *r.* Hungary
199 K5 **Körösladány** Hungary
199 K4 **Körösszakál** Hungary
199 K5 **Köröstarcsa** Hungary
161 T6 **Korostelevo** Rus. Fed.
158 H3 **Korosten'** Ukr.
158 I3 **Korostyshiv** Ukr.
199 K5 **Körös-vidék** *reg.* Hungary
156 M1 **Korotaikha** *r.* Rus. Fed.
224 C5 **Koro Toro** Chad
157 G6 **Korotoyak** Rus. Fed.
245 □D5 **Korovin Bay** *AK* U.S.A.
Korovino *Kurskaya Oblast'* Rus. Fed. *see* **Solntsevo**
142 E1 **Korovino** *Orenburgskaya Oblast'* Rus. Fed.
245 □D5 **Korovin Volcano** *AK* U.S.A.
101 □[7a] **Korovou** *Viti Levu* Fiji
100 □[6] **Korovou** Solomon Is
159 M3 **Korovyntsi** Ukr.
101 □[7a] **Koroyanitu** *Viti Levu* Fiji
161 V4 **Korozhechna** *r.* Rus. Fed.
194 A2 **Körperich** Ger.
160 K1 **Korpijärvi** *l.* Fin.
163 R5 **Korpilahti** Fin.
162 Q3 **Korpilombolo** Sweden
162 U5 **Korpisel'kya** Rus. Fed.
162 T5 **Korpivaara** Fin.
163 P6 **Korpo** Fin.
Korppoo Fin. *see* **Korpo**
130 A3 **Korra** *Xizang* China
151 H6 **Kornidzor** Armenia
142 E4 **Korsak** Kazakh.
159 O7 **Korsak** *r.* Ukr.
122 M5 **Korsakov** *Sakhalin* Rus. Fed.
161 U8 **Korsakovo** Rus. Fed.
165 L4 **Korsberga** Sweden
159 T2 **Korshevo** Rus. Fed.
161 P8 **Korsiki** Rus. Fed.
163 M6 **Korskrogen** Sweden
162 P5 **Korsnäs** Fin.
160 I1 **Korso** Fin.
164 H6 **Korsør** Denmark
151 C6 **Körsu** Turkey
159 K4 **Korsun'-Shevchenkivs'kyy** Ukr.
Korsun'-Shevchenkovskiy Ukr. *see* **Korsun'-Shevchenkivs'kyy**
165 R7 **Korsze** Pol.
225 F6 **Kortala** Sudan
158 D2 **Kortelisy** Ukr.
187 D6 **Kortemark** Belgium
162 Q5 **Kortesjärvi** Fin.
187 H7 **Kortessem** Belgium
186 E5 **Kortgene** Neth.
225 F5 **Korti** Sudan
156 J3 **Kortkeros** Rus. Fed.
187 D7 **Kortrijk** Belgium
156 H4 **Kortsovo** Rus. Fed.
150 A1 **Korualan** Turkey
221 I3 **Korucu** Turkey
105 J8 **Korumburra** *Vic.* Austr.
229 H5 **Korup, Parc National de** *nat. park* Cameroon
162 S3 **Korvala** Fin.
138 G7 **Korwai** *Madh. Prad.* India
153 Q4 **Koryakskaya, Sopka** *vol.* Rus. Fed.
153 S3 **Koryakskoye Nagor'ye** *mts* Rus. Fed.
156 I3 **Koryazhma** Rus. Fed.
198 G2 **Koryčany** Czech Rep.
197 L2 **Korycin** Pol.
126 C6 **Kōryō** Japan
125 J11 **Koryō** Japan
123 F11 **Koryŏng** S. Korea
197 J3 **Korytnica** Pol.
159 L2 **Koryukivka** Ukr.
197 I6 **Korzenna** Pol.
196 E4 **Korzeńsko** Pol.
161 P9 **Korzhovka Golubovka** Rus. Fed.
142 E3 **Korzhyn** Kazakh.
196 E1 **Korzybie** Pol.
221 I6 **Kos** *Kos* Greece
221 I6 **Kos** *i.* Greece
156 K4 **Kosa** Rus. Fed.
156 K3 **Kosa** *r.* Rus. Fed.
159 O7 **Kosa Biryuchyy Ostriv** *i.* Ukr.
158 J2 **Kosachivka** Ukr.
142 J2 **Kosagal** Kazakh.
143 P1 **Kosagash** Kazakh.
126 G6 **Kosai** Japan
124 R6 **Kosaka** Japan
196 G1 **Kosakowo** Pol.
138 H7 **Kosam** *Uttar Prad.* India
123 E9 **Kosan** N. Korea
151 B6 **Koşan Dağı** *mts* Turkey
160 I9 **Kosava** Belarus
143 L3 **Kosay** Kazakh.
161 U7 **Kosaya Gora** Rus. Fed.
142 E4 **Koschagyl** Kazakh.
195 L4 **Kösching** Ger.
201 J7 **Koschutnikturm** *mt.* Austria/Slovenia
196 E3 **Kościan** Pol.
196 G3 **Kościelec** Pol.
196 G4 **Kościelna Wieś** Pol.
196 E1 **Kościernica** Pol.
165 N7 **Kościerzyna** Pol.
261 K9 **Kosciusko** *MS* U.S.A.
Kosciusko, Mount *N.S.W.* Austr. *see* **Kosciuszko, Mount**
245 N4 **Kosciusko Island** *AK* U.S.A.
105 L7 **Kosciuszko, Mount** *N.S.W.* Austr.
105 L7 **Kosciuszko National Park** *N.S.W.* Austr.
160 I2 **Kose** Estonia
151 A5 **Köse** Turkey
199 H2 **Košeca** Slovakia
150 B2 **Köseçobanlı** Turkey
151 D6 **Köse Dağı** *mt.* Turkey
148 H3 **Köse Dağı** *mt.* Turkey
151 A5 **Kösedağı Geçidi** *pass* Turkey
221 H3 **Kösedere** Turkey
126 D5 **Kōsei** Japan
190 I1 **Kosel** Ger.
199 K4 **Kösély** *r.* Hungary
165 J5 **Kösen** *l.* Sweden
192 J2 **Koserow** Ger.
136 E4 **Kosgi** *Andhra Prad.* India
225 F4 **Kosha** Sudan
128 A2 **Kosh-Agach** Rus. Fed.
142 C3 **Koshankol'** Kazakh.
145 I1 **Koshbulakskoye Vodokhranilishche** *resr* Turkm.
143 P7 **Kosh-Döbö** Kyrg.
127 K4 **Koshigaya** Japan
125 G15 **Koshikijima-rettō** *is* Japan
125 G15 **Koshiki-kaikyō** *sea chan.* Japan
142 D2 **Koshim** Kazakh.
142 D3 **Koshim** *r.* Kazakh.
124 V3 **Koshimizu** Japan
126 D3 **Koshino** Japan
145 J4 **Koshk** Afgh.
144 I4 **Koshkak** Iran
142 E4 **Koshkar** Kazakh.
151 M2 **Koshkar-Ata, Ozero** *l.* Kazakh.
143 S4 **Koshkarkol', Ozero** *l.* Kazakh.
145 J4 **Koshk-e Kohneh** Afgh.
157 J5 **Koshki** Rus. Fed.
250 F7 **Koshkonong, Lake** *WI* U.S.A.
158 F4 **Koshlyaky** Ukr.
159 N4 **Koshmanivka** Ukr.
127 H2 **Kōshoku** Japan
Koshtëbë Kyrg. *see* **Kosh-Döbö**
138 F6 **Kosi** *Uttar Prad.* India
138 G5 **Kosi** *r.* India
237 Q2 **Kosi Bay** S. Africa
237 Q3 **Kosi Bay Nature Reserve** S. Africa
199 K3 **Košice** Slovakia
199 K3 **Košický kraj** *admin. reg.* Slovakia
136 E5 **Kosigi** *Andhra Prad.* India
139 K6 **Kosi Reservoir** Nepal
142 G2 **Kosistek** Kazakh.
158 E5 **Kosiv** Ukr.
159 M5 **Kosivka** Ukr.
218 H7 **Kosjerić** *Kosjerić* Serbia
221 J5 **Köşk** Turkey
163 Q6 **Koski** *Länsi-Suomi* Fin.
161 Q7 **Koski** Rus. Fed.
143 L3 **Koskol'** Kazakh.
199 K2 **Koškovce** Slovakia
161 Q1 **Kos'kovo** Rus. Fed.
143 Q5 **Koskudyk** Kazakh.
162 P3 **Koskullskulle** Sweden
156 J3 **Koslan** Rus. Fed.
Köslin Pol. *see* **Koszalin**
156 J2 **Kosma** *r.* Rus. Fed.
193 K10 **Kosmonosy** Czech Rep.
161 X4 **Kosmynino** Rus. Fed.
210 G3 **Košnica** *r.* Croatia
196 F2 **Kosobudy** Pol.
142 K8 **Koson** Uzbek.
123 F8 **Kosŏng** *Hamgyŏng-namdo* N. Korea
123 F9 **Kosŏng** *Kangwŏn-do* N. Korea
143 N7 **Kosonsoy** Uzbek.
159 P1 **Kosorzha** Rus. Fed.
Kosova *prov.* Europe *see* **Kosovo**
218 I8 **Kosovo** *country* Europe
Kosovo-Metohija *prov.* Europe *see* **Kosovo**
Kosovo Polje *Fushë-Kosovë* Kosovo *see* **Fushë-Kosovë**
Kosovska Kamenica *Kamenicë* Kosovo *see* **Kamenicë**
Kosovska Mitrovica *Mitrovicë* Kosovo *see* **Mitrovicë**
197 K3 **Kosów Lacki** Pol.
290 F5 **Kosrae** *atoll* Micronesia
133 C8 **Kosrap** *Xinjiang* China
150 D1 **Kösreli** Turkey
228 D3 **Kossa** *well* Maur.
229 I3 **Kossatori** *well* Niger
193 H8 **Koßdorf** Ger.
195 L2 **Kösseine** *hill* Ger.
200 F4 **Kössen** Austria
195 O5 **Kößlar** *r.* Ger.
114 □ **Kossol Passage** Palau
114 □ **Kossol Reef** Palau
228 D5 **Kossou, Lac de** *l.* Côte d'Ivoire
Kosta-Khetagurovo Rus. Fed. *see* **Nazran'**
142 J1 **Kostanay** Kazakh.
142 J1 **Kostanayskaya Oblast'** *admin. div.* Kazakh.
201 L8 **Kostanjevica** *Krško* Slovenia
201 I8 **Kostanjevica** *Nova Gorica* Slovenia
213 R4 **Kostel** Slovenia
198 D2 **Kostelec nad Černými Lesy** Czech Rep.
193 K10 **Kostelec nad Labem** Czech Rep.
198 F1 **Kostelec nad Orlicí** Czech Rep.
219 L8 **Kostenets** Bulg.
237 K1 **Koster** S. Africa
161 W6 **Kosterevo** Rus. Fed.
164 H3 **Kosteroarna naturreservat** *nature res.* Sweden
225 G6 **Kosti** Sudan
201 O2 **Kostice** Czech Rep.
219 L8 **Kostinbrod** Bulg.
152 J3 **Kostino** Rus. Fed.
159 L1 **Kostobobriv** Ukr.
218 J6 **Kostolac** *Pozarevac* Serbia
196 E4 **Kostomłoty** Pol.
162 U4 **Kostomuksha** Rus. Fed.
162 U4 **Kostomukshskiy Zapovednik** *nature res.* Rus. Fed.
158 F3 **Kostopil'** Ukr.
Kostopol' Ukr. *see* **Kostopil'**
161 X4 **Kostroma** Rus. Fed.
156 H4 **Kostroma** *r.* Rus. Fed.
Kostroma Oblast *admin. div.* Rus. Fed. *see* **Kostromskaya Oblast'**
156 H4 **Kostromskaya Oblast'** *admin. div.* Rus. Fed.
196 C3 **Kostrzyn** *Lubuskie* Pol.
196 F3 **Kostrzyn** *Wielkopolskie* Pol.
197 K3 **Kostrzyń** *r.* Pol.
159 Q5 **Kostyantynivka** *Donets'ka Oblast'* Ukr.
159 O4 **Kostyantynivka** *Kharkivs'ka Oblast'* Ukr.
159 M7 **Kostyantynivka** *Khersons'ka Oblast'* Ukr.
159 O7 **Kostyantynivka** *Zaporiz'ka Oblast'* Ukr.
161 Q7 **Kostyri** Rus. Fed.
Kostyukovichi Belarus *see* **Kastsyukovichy**
160 M4 **Kostyzhitsy** Rus. Fed.
229 F4 **Kosubosu** Nigeria
127 I4 **Kosuge** Japan
126 F2 **Kosugi** Japan
199 L3 **Kosyny** Ukr.
156 L2 **Kos'yu** Rus. Fed.
156 L2 **Kos'yu** *r.* Rus. Fed.
156 L2 **Kos'yuvom** Rus. Fed.
165 M7 **Koszalin** Pol.
196 G5 **Koszęcin** Pol.
198 F4 **Kőszeg** Hungary
198 F4 **Kőszegi** *park* Hungary
201 N5 **Kőszegi-hegység** *hill* Hungary
197 I5 **Koszyce** Pol.
136 G5 **Kota** *Andhra Prad.* India
138 I8 **Kota** *Chhattisgarh* India
138 E7 **Kota** *Rajasthan* India
126 F6 **Kōta** Japan
116 F7 **Kotaagung** *Sumatera* Indon.
Kota Baharu Malaysia *see* **Kota Bharu**
117 I5 **Kotabaru** *Kalimantan* Indon.
117 L6 **Kotabaru** *Kalimantan* Indon.
116 B3 **Kotabaru** *Sumatera* Indon.
117 L1 **Kota Belud** *Sabah* Malaysia
117 J6 **Kotabesi** *Kalimantan* Indon.
116 E1 **Kota Bharu** Malaysia
116 F7 **Kotabumi** *Sumatera* Indon.
115 D3 **Kotabunan** *Sulawesi* Indon.
145 N6 **Kot Addu** Pak.
117 L2 **Kota Kinabalu** *Sabah* Malaysia
162 T3 **Kotala** Fin.
115 D3 **Kotamobagu** *Sulawesi* Indon.
246 E2 **Kotaneelee Range** *mts N.W.T./Y.T.* Can.
143 Q4 **Kotanemel', Gora** *mt.* Kazakh.
136 H3 **Kotaparh** *Orissa* India
116 D4 **Kotapinang** *Sumatera* Indon.
138 H7 **Kotar** *Madh. Prad.* India
138 E7 **Kotari** *r.* India
117 I4 **Kota Samarahan** *Sarawak* Malaysia
116 D4 **Kotatengah** *Sumatera* Indon.
116 E4 **Kota Tinggi** Malaysia
117 I6 **Kotawaringin** *Kalimant*
139 L8 **Kotchandpur** Bangl.
246 F3 **Kotcho** *r.* B.C. Can.
246 F3 **Kotcho Lake** B.C. Can.
145 M8 **Kot Diji** Pak.
138 G5 **Kotdwara** *Uttaranchal* In
199 K5 **Kötegyán** Hungary
219 O8 **Kotel** Bulg.
199 J4 **Kőtelek** Hungary
156 J4 **Kotel'nich** Rus. Fed.
157 H7 **Kotel'nikovo** Rus. Fed.
153 O2 **Kotel'nyy, Ostrov** *i. Nov O-va* Rus. Fed.
192 I3 **Kotelow** Ger.
159 N3 **Kotel'va** Ukr.
102 L6 **Kotemaori** *North I.* N.Z.
145 O4 **Kotgala** Pak.
137 H3 **Kotgar** *Orissa* India
138 F4 **Kotgarh** *Hima. Prad.* Inc
Kothagudem *Andhra Pr* *see* **Kottagudem**
193 E7 **Köthen (Anhalt)** Ger.
138 H7 **Kothi** *Madh. Prad.* India
228 B3 **Kotiari Naoude** Senegal
232 B4 **Kotido** Uganda
122 I5 **Kotikovo** Rus. Fed.
145 M8 **Kot Imamgarh** Pak.
163 S6 **Kotka** Fin.
138 E4 **Kot Kapura** *Punjab* India
156 J2 **Kotkino** Rus. Fed.
196 E4 **Kotla** Pol.
156 I3 **Kotlas** Rus. Fed.
145 O5 **Kotli** Pak.
244 G3 **Kotlik** *AK* U.S.A.
196 F4 **Kotlin** Pol.
161 R3 **Kotlovan** Rus. Fed.
162 □D2 **Kötlutangi** *pt* Iceland
160 L2 **Kotly** Rus. Fed.
126 D5 **Kotō** Japan
229 G4 **Koton-Karifi** Nigeria
124 R6 **Kotooka** Japan
218 G8 **Kotor** *Kotor* Montenegro
201 O7 **Kotoriba** Croatia
161 W4 **Kotorosl'** *r.* Rus. Fed.
210 G3 **Kotorsko** Bos.-Herz.
210 F3 **Kotor Varoš** Bos.-Herz.
228 E4 **Kotouba** Côte d'Ivoire
159 N4 **Kotovka** Ukr.
157 I6 **Kotovo** Rus. Fed.
Kotovsk Moldova *see* **Hî**
157 H5 **Kotovsk** Rus. Fed.
158 I6 **Kotovs'k** Ukr.
138 F6 **Kot Putli** *Rajasthan* Ind
160 H8 **Kotra** *r.* Belarus
138 D7 **Kotra** *Rajasthan* India
145 L7 **Kotra** Pak.
136 G3 **Kotri** *r.* India
145 M9 **Kotri** Pak.
145 L9 **Kotri Allahrakhio Shah**
220 D6 **Kotronas** Greece
145 L10 **Kot Sarae** Pak.
200 H6 **Kötschach** Austria
136 G4 **Kottagudem** *Andhra Pra*
136 E8 **Kottayam** *Kerala* India
136 D7 **Kottayam** *Puducherry* Inc
Kotte Sri Lanka *see* **Sri Jayewardenepura Ko**
191 D10 **Kottenheim** Ger.
201 L3 **Kottes** Austria
201 J6 **Köttmannsdorf** Austria
230 D3 **Kotto** *r.* C.A.R.
136 E5 **Kotturu** *Karnataka* India
101 □[8] **Kotu Group** *is* Tonga
197 K3 **Kotuń** Pol.
153 L2 **Kotuy** *r.* Rus. Fed.
139 I8 **Kotwar Peak** *Chhattisgar*
142 H3 **Kotyrtas** Kazakh.
Kotyuzhany Moldova *se* **Cotiujeni**
195 I5 **Kötz** Ger.
244 G2 **Kotzebue** *AK* U.S.A.
244 G2 **Kotzebue Sound** *sea cha* U.S.A.
236 B4 **Kotzehoop** S. Africa
236 B6 **Kotzesrus** S. Africa
195 N3 **Kötzting** Ger.
230 D3 **Kouango** C.A.R.
224 C6 **Kouba Olanga** Chad
228 C4 **Koubia** Guinea
249 H4 **Kouchibouguac Nationa** N.B. Can.
188 A3 **Koudekerke** Neth.
228 E3 **Koudougou** Burkina
186 H3 **Koudum** Neth.
236 D8 **Kouebokkeveld** *mts* S. A
228 E4 **Kouéré** Burkina
236 H8 **Koueveldberge** *mts* S. Af
220 D2 **Koufalia** Greece
229 I3 **Koufey** Niger
221 H8 **Koufonisi** *i. Kriti* Greece
221 G6 **Koufonisi** *i.* Greece
236 I9 **Kouga** *r.* S. Africa
236 H9 **Kougaberge** *mts* S. Africa
230 B3 **Koui** C.A.R.
228 D5 **Kouibli** Côte d'Ivoire
231 A6 **Kouilou** *admin. reg.* Cong
228 D4 **Kouka** Burkina
243 K3 **Koukdjuak, Great Plain c** *Nunavut* Can.
230 C3 **Kouki** C.A.R.
230 D3 **Koukourou** C.A.R.
230 C3 **Koukourou** *r.* C.A.R.
230 C3 **Koukourou-Bamingui, R de Faune du** *nature res.* C
230 B5 **Koulamoutou** Gabon
224 D6 **Koulbo** Chad
Koulen Cambodia *see* **Ku**
228 D3 **Koulikoro** Mali
228 D3 **Koulikoro** *admin. reg.* Ma
229 F3 **Koulou** Niger
224 B6 **Kouloudia** Chad
229 I4 **Koum** Cameroon
230 C3 **Kouma** *r.* C.A.R.
100 □[5] **Koumac** New Caledonia
107 L6 **Koumala** *Qld* Austr.
230 A4 **Koumameyong** Gabon
230 D2 **Koumbala** C.A.R.
228 E4 **Koumbia** Burkina
228 B4 **Koumbia** Guinea
128 C5 **Koumenzi** *Xinjiang* Chin
127 H3 **Koumi** Japan
230 C2 **Koumra** Chad
228 B3 **Koundâra** Guinea
228 C3 **Koundian** Mali
228 D4 **Koundougou** Burkina
228 B3 **Koungheul** Senegal
239 □[3b] **Koungou** Mayotte
228 B3 **Kounkané** Senegal
221 H6 **Kounoupoi** *i.* Greece
Kounradskiy *Karagandin Oblast'* Kazakh. *see* **Kony**
228 B4 **Kounsitél** Guinea
229 H3 **Kountchi** *well* Niger
261 H10 **Kountze** *TX* U.S.A.
236 F9 **Koup** S. Africa
228 E3 **Koupéla** Burkina
Kouqian *Jilin* China *see* **Y**
239 □[3a] **Kourani** *Njazidja* Comor
230 B2 **Kourayadjé** Chad
229 I3 **Kouridinga** *well* Niger
124 □[1] **Kouri-jima** *i. Okinawa* Jap
198 D2 **Kouřim** Czech Rep.
220 F7 **Kournas** *Kriti* Greece
275 H3 **Kourou** Fr. Guiana
228 C2 **Koûroudjél** Maur.
228 C4 **Kouroussa** Guinea
228 B3 **Koussanar** Senegal
228 C3 **Koussané** Mali
229 I3 **Kousséri** Cameroon
229 F4 **Koussountou** Togo
228 D3 **Koutiala** Mali
195 N3 **Kout na Šumav** Czech Re
228 D4 **Kouto** Côte d'Ivoire
100 □[5] **Koutouma** *i.* New Caledo
220 D5 **Koutsopodi** Greece
102 M5 **Koutunui Head** *North I.*
163 S6 **Kouvola** Fin.
230 C5 **Kouyou** *r.* Congo
218 I5 **Kovačica** *Vojvodina* Serbia
221 L5 **Kovada Gölü Milli Parkı** Turkey
199 H5 **Kővágószőlős** Hungary
158 J4 **Kovalivka** Ukr.
156 B2 **Kovallberget** Sweden

Kovarce Slovakia
Kovářská Czech Rep.
Kovchyn Ukr.
Kovdor Rus. Fed.
Kovdozero Rus. Fed.
Kovdozero, Ozero l. Rus. Fed.
Kovel' Ukr.
Kovernino Rus. Fed.
Kovilj Vojvodina Serbia
Kovilpatti Tamil Nadu India
Kovin Vojvodina Serbia
Kovno Lith. see Kaunas
Kovriga, Gora hill Rus. Fed.
Kovrov Rus. Fed.
Kovsuh r. Ukr.
Kov"yahy Ukr.
Kovylkino Rus. Fed.
Kovyl'ne Ukr.
Kovzha canal Rus. Fed.
Kovzhskoye, Ozero l. Rus. Fed.
Kowal Pol.
Kowale Pol.
Kowale Oleckie Pol.
Kowale-Pańskie Pol.
Kowalewo Pomorskie Pol.
Kowalów Pol.
Kowangge Sumbawa Indon.
Kowanyama Qld Austr.
Kowanyama Aboriginal Reserve Qld Austr.
Kowares waterhole Namibia
Kowary Pol.
Kowbcha Belarus
Kowe Dem. Rep. Congo
Kowhitirangi South I. N.Z.
Kowiesy Pol.
Kowlī Kosh, Gardaneh-ye pass Iran
Kowloon H.K. China
Kowloon Peak hill H.K. China see Fei Ngo Shan
Kowloon Peninsula H.K. China
Kowloon Peninsula pen. H.K. China
Kowloon Reservoirs H.K. China
Kowŏn N. Korea
Kox Kuduk well Xinjiang China
Koxlax Xinjiang China
Koxtag Xinjiang China
Kōya Japan
Kōyaguchi Japan
Koyama Guinea
Kōyama-misaki pt Japan
Kōya-Ryūjin Kokutei-kōen park Japan
Koybagar, Ozero l. Kazakh.
Köyceğiz Turkey
Köyceğiz Gölü l. Turkey
Koyda Rus. Fed.
Koygorodok Rus. Fed.
Koyilandi Kerala India
Koynare Bulg.
Koyna Reservoir India
Koyp, Gora mt. Rus. Fed.
Köýtendag Turkm.
Koyuk AK U.S.A.
Koyuk r. AK U.S.A.
Koyukuk AK U.S.A.
Koyukuk r. AK U.S.A.
Koyukuk, Middle Fork r. AK U.S.A.
Koyukuk, North Fork r. AK U.S.A.
Koyukuk, South Fork r. AK U.S.A.
Koyukuk Island AK U.S.A.
Koyukuk National Wildlife Refuge nature res. AK U.S.A.
Koyulhisar Turkey
Koyunören Turkey
Koza Cameroon
Koza Rus. Fed.
Kozacha Lopan' Ukr.
Kozachi Laheri Ukr.
Kozağacı Turkey see Günyüzü
Kozakai Japan
Kōzaki Japan
Kō-zaki pt Japan
Kozan Turkey
Kozani Greece
Kozar, Ras pt Eritrea
Kozara mts Bos.-Herz.
Kozara nat. park Bos.-Herz.
Kozármisleny Hungary
Kozárovce Slovakia
Kozarska Dubica Bos.-Herz. see Bosanska Dubica
Kozary Ukr.
Kozats'ke Khersons'ka Oblast' Ukr.
Kozats'ke Sums'ka Oblast' Ukr.
Kozelets' Ukr.
Kozel'shchyna Ukr.
Kozel'sk Rus. Fed.
Kozen well Chad
Közép-tiszai park Hungary
Kozhabaky Kazakh.
Kozhakol', Ozero l. Kazakh.
Kozhanka Ukr.
Kozhevnikovo Rus. Fed.
Kozhikode Kerala India
Kozhim-Iz, Gora mt. Rus. Fed.
Kozhukiv Ukr.
Kozhva Rus. Fed.
Kozhva r. Rus. Fed.
Kozhym r. Rus. Fed.
Koziegłowy Pol.
Kozielice Pol.
Kozienice Pol.
Kozienicki Park Krajobrazowy Pol.
Kozina Slovenia
Koziyivka Ukr.
Kožlany Czech Rep.
Kozloduy Bulg.
Kozlovice Czech Rep.
Kozlovka Chuvashskaya Respublika Rus. Fed.
Kozlovka Respublika Mordoviya Rus. Fed.
Kozlovka Voronezhskaya Oblast' Rus. Fed.
Kozlovka Voronezhskaya Oblast' Rus. Fed.
Kozlovo Rus. Fed.
Kozłów Pol.
Kozłów Biskupi Pol.
Kozłowo Pol.
Kozlu Turkey
Kozluca Turkey
Kozluk Bos.-Herz.
Kozły Pol.
Koz'maaul Rus. Fed.
Koźminek Pol.
Koźmin Wielkopowski Pol.
Koz'modem'yansk Rus. Fed.
Kozmoldak Kazakh.
Koznitsa mt. Bulg.
Kozova Ukr.
Kozubowski Park Krajobrazowy Pol.
Kozubszczyzna Pol.
Kożuchów Pol.
Kožuf mts Greece/Macedonia
Kōzu-shima i. Japan
Kozyatyn Ukr.
Kozylivka Ukr.
Kozyn Kyivs'ka Oblast' Ukr.
Kozyn Kyivs'ka Oblast' Ukr.
Kozyörük Turkey
Kozyrka Ukr.
Kpalimé Togo
Kpandae Ghana
Kpandu Ghana
Kpedze Ghana
Kpèssi Togo
Kpungan Pass India/Myanmar
Kra, Isthmus of Thai.
Kraai r. S. Africa
Kraankuil S. Africa
Krabbé Arg.
Krabbendijke Neth.
Krabi Estonia
Krabi Thai.
Kra Buri Thai.
Krâchéh Cambodia
Kräckelbäcken Sweden
192 J4 Krackow Ger.
161 R4 Kraftino, Ozero l. Rus. Fed.
193 E9 Kraftsdorf Ger.
196 E1 Krąg Pol.
117 I8 Kragan Jawa Indon.
164 F3 Kragerø Norway
186 I3 Kraggenburg Neth.
196 E2 Krągi Pol.
218 I6 Kragujevac Kragujevac Serbia
195 M5 Kraiburg am Inn Ger.
194 E3 Kraichbach r. Ger.
194 F3 Kraichgau reg. Ger.
195 K5 Krailling Ger.
196 F2 Krajenka Pol.
196 F2 Krajeńskie, Pojezierze reg. Pol.
196 C2 Krajnik Dolny Pol.
116 F8 Krakatau i. Indon.
116 F8 Krakatau, Taman Nasional nat. park Indon.
Krakau Pol. see Kraków
Krak des Chevaliers tourist site Syria see Crac des Chevaliers
162 K5 Kråklivollen Norway
119 G8 Krâkôr Cambodia
158 C4 Krakovets' Ukr.
197 H5 Kraków Pol.
250 F5 Krakow WI U.S.A.
192 F3 Krakow am See Ger.
192 F3 Krakower See l. Ger.
197 G4 Krakowsko-Częstochowska, Wyżyna plat. Pol.
119 F8 Krâlănh Cambodia
271 □8 Kralendijk Bonaire Neth. Antilles
119 D9 Kra Lenya r. Myanmar
198 F1 Králíky Czech Rep.
210 E3 Kraljevića Croatia
218 I7 Kraljevo Kraljevo Serbia
199 G3 Kráľová, Vodná nádrž resr Slovakia
199 J3 Kráľova hoľa mt. Slovakia
199 G3 Kráľová nad Váhom Slovakia
199 G3 Kráľov Brod Slovakia
198 E1 Královéhradecký kraj admin. reg. Czech Rep.
198 C2 Kralovice Czech Rep.
199 K3 Kráľovský Chlmec Slovakia
198 D1 Kralupy nad Vltavou Czech Rep.
198 D2 Králův Dvůr Czech Rep.
196 F1 Kramarzyny Pol.
159 Q5 Kramators'k Ukr.
162 N5 Kramfors Sweden
186 F5 Krammer est. Neth.
162 U1 Krampenes Norway
200 E5 Kramsach Austria
196 G3 Kramsk Pol.
191 B7 Kranenburg Ger.
220 C3 Krania Greece
220 E5 Kranidi Greece
210 E2 Kranj Slovenia
116 □ Kranji Reservoir Sing.
201 I7 Kranjska Gora Slovenia
237 M4 Kransfontein S. Africa
237 O4 Kranskop S. Africa
237 N3 Kranskop mt. S. Africa
195 L5 Kranzberg Ger.
210 E4 Krapanj Croatia
196 D2 Krąpiel Pol.
210 E2 Krapina Croatia
210 E2 Krapinske Toplice Croatia
161 S8 Krapivna Kaluzhskaya Oblast' Rus. Fed.
161 Q7 Krapivna Smolenskaya Oblast' Rus. Fed.
196 F5 Krapkowice Pol.
201 I8 Kras plat. Slovenia
156 I3 Krasavino Rus. Fed.
159 L4 Krasenivka Ukr.
197 K6 Krasiczyn Pol.
Krasilov Ukr. see Krasyliv
Krasilovka Chernihivs'ka Oblast' Ukr. see Krasylivka
Krasilovka Zhytomyrs'ka Oblast' Ukr. see Krasylivka
152 G2 Krasino Novaya Zemlya Rus. Fed.
197 L6 Krasiv Ukr.
158 E4 Krasiyiv Ukr.
122 G7 Kraskino Rus. Fed.
160 K6 Krāslava Latvia
198 B1 Kraslice Czech Rep.
159 R4 Krasna r. Ukr.
193 K9 Krásná Lípa Czech Rep.
161 O8 Krasnapollye Mahilyowskaya Voblasts' Belarus
160 M6 Krasnapollye Vitsyebskaya Voblasts' Belarus
159 Q6 Krasna Polyana Donets'ka Oblast' Ukr.
159 L8 Krasna Polyana Respublika Krym Ukr.
158 J4 Krasna Slobidka Ukr.
160 H8 Krasnasyel'ski Belarus
161 O8 Krasnaya Gora Rus. Fed.
156 H5 Krasnaya Gorbatka Rus. Fed.
143 O3 Krasnaya Polyana Kazakh.
151 B2 Krasnaya Polyana Rus. Fed.
159 O3 Krasnaya Yaruga Rus. Fed.
161 U9 Krasnaya Zarya Rus. Fed.
197 I3 Krasne Mazowieckie Pol.
197 K5 Krasne Podkarpackie Pol.
159 K2 Krasne Chernihivs'ka Oblast' Ukr.
159 L2 Krasne Chernihivs'ka Oblast' Ukr.
158 D5 Krasne Ivano-Frankivs'ka Oblast' Ukr.
159 L7 Krasne Khersons'ka Oblast' Ukr.
158 D4 Krasne L'vivs'ka Oblast' Ukr.
158 F4 Krasne Ternopils'ka Oblast' Ukr.
158 H5 Krasne Vinnyts'ka Oblast' Ukr.
197 L5 Kraśniczyn Pol.
197 K5 Kraśnik Pol.
158 I6 Krasni Okny Ukr.
Krasnoarmeysk Kazakh. see Tayynsha
161 V5 Krasnoarmeysk Moskovskaya Oblast' Rus. Fed.
157 I6 Krasnoarmeysk Saratovskaya Oblast' Rus. Fed.
Krasnoarmeysk Ukr. see Krasnoarmiys'k
Krasnoarmeyskaya Rus. Fed. see Poltavskaya
153 S3 Krasnoarmeyskiy Chukotskiy Avtonomnyy Okrug Rus. Fed.
157 H7 Krasnoarmeyskiy Rostovskaya Oblast' Rus. Fed.
Krasnoarmeyskoye Rus. Fed. see Urus-Martan
159 Q5 Krasnoarmiys'k Ukr.
159 Q6 Krasnoarmiys'ke Ukr.
161 S2 Krasnobarskiy Rus. Fed.
156 I3 Krasnoborsk Rus. Fed.
197 L5 Krasnobród Pol.
199 M1 Krasnobrodzki Park Krajobrazowy Pol.
157 G7 Krasnodar Rus. Fed.
Krasnodar Kray admin. div. Rus. Fed. see Krasnodarskiy Kray
151 B1 Krasnodarskiy Kray admin. div. Rus. Fed.
159 S5 Krasnodon Luhans'ka Oblast' Ukr.
159 S5 Krasnodon Luhans'ka Oblast' Ukr.
161 O2 Krasnofarfornyy Rus. Fed.
159 N8 Krasnoflots'ke Ukr.
Krasnogorka Kazakh. see Ul'ken Sulutor
160 L5 Krasnogorodskoye Rus. Fed.
161 U6 Krasnogorsk Moskovskaya Oblast' Rus. Fed.
122 M4 Krasnogorsk Sakhalin Rus. Fed.
143 V1 Krasnogorskoye Altayskiy Kray Rus. Fed.
156 K4 Krasnogorskoye Udmurtskaya Respublika Rus. Fed.
Krasnograd Ukr. see Krasnohrad
Krasnogvardeysk Uzbek. see Bulung'ur
161 X5 Krasnogvardeyskiy Rus. Fed.
159 R3 Krasnogvardeyskoye Belgorodskaya Oblast' Rus. Fed.
159 S8 Krasnogvardeyskoye Respublika Adygeya Rus. Fed.
157 H7 Krasnogvardeyskoye Stavropol'skiy Kray Rus. Fed.
159 O8 Krasnohirka Ukr.
159 Q5 Krasnohorivka Ukr.
159 O4 Krasnohrad Ukr.
159 N8 Krasnohvardiys'ke Ukr.
129 P2 Krasnokamensk Rus. Fed.
156 K4 Krasnokamsk Rus. Fed.
142 F2 Krasnokholm Rus. Fed.
Krasnokutsk Kazakh. see Aktogay
159 O3 Krasnokuts'k Ukr.
Krasnokutskoye Kazakh. see Aktogay
157 G6 Krasnolesnyy Rus. Fed.
160 F7 Krasnoles'ye Rus. Fed.
159 R2 Krasnolip'ye Rus. Fed.
159 N9 Krasnolissya Ukr.
161 R4 Krasnomayskiy Rus. Fed.
199 H2 Krásno nad Kysucou Slovakia
160 L1 Krasnoostrovskiy Rus. Fed.
159 P4 Krasnopavivs'ke Vodoskhovyshche l. Ukr.
159 P4 Krasnopavlivka Ukr.
159 M8 Krasnoperekops'k Ukr.
158 H4 Krasnopil' Ukr.
158 J5 Krasnopilka Ukr.
159 O3 Krasnopillya Ukr.
197 L1 Krasnopol Pol.
122 M4 Krasnopol'ye Sakhalin Rus. Fed.
122 I6 Krasnorechenskiy Rus. Fed.
Krasnorechenskoye Ukr. see Krasnorichens'ke
159 R4 Krasnorichens'ke Ukr.
152 J3 Krasnosel'kup Rus. Fed.
Krasnoselsk Armenia see Chambarak
160 M1 Krasnosel'skoye Rus. Fed.
143 T2 Krasnoshchekovo Rus. Fed.
156 G2 Krasnoshchel'ye Rus. Fed.
197 J2 Krasnosielc Pol.
158 I5 Krasnosilka Vinnyts'ka Oblast' Ukr.
158 G4 Krasnosilka Zhytomyrs'ka Oblast' Ukr.
159 L5 Krasnosillya Ukr.
157 H5 Krasnoslobodsk Rus. Fed.
159 U1 Krasnosvobodnoye Rus. Fed.
152 H4 Krasnotur'insk Rus. Fed.
156 L4 Krasnoufimsk Rus. Fed.
142 G1 Krasnousol'skiy Rus. Fed.
156 L3 Krasnovishersk Rus. Fed.
Krasnovodsk Turkm. see Türkmenbaşy
144 E2 Krasnovodsk, Mys pt Turkm.
Krasnovodskaya Oblast' admin. div. Turkm. see Balkan
144 E1 Krasnovodskoye Plato plat. Turkm.
122 F3 Krasnoyarovo Rus. Fed.
153 K4 Krasnoyarsk Rus. Fed.
142 H2 Krasnoyarskiy Rus. Fed.
120 F1 Krasnoyarskiy Kray admin. div. Rus. Fed.
Krasnoyarsk Kray admin. div. Rus. Fed. see Krasnoyarskiy Kray
157 G6 Krasnoye Belgorodskaya Oblast' Rus. Fed.
159 R3 Krasnoye Belgorodskaya Oblast' Rus. Fed.
161 Q8 Krasnoye Bryanskaya Oblast' Rus. Fed.
156 I4 Krasnoye Kirovskaya Oblast' Rus. Fed.
159 S7 Krasnoye Krasnodarskiy Kray Rus. Fed.
161 V9 Krasnoye Lipetskaya Oblast' Rus. Fed.
160 M5 Krasnoye Pskovskaya Oblast' Rus. Fed.
Krasnoye Respublika Kalmykiya-Khalm'g-Tangch Rus. Fed. see Ulan Erge
161 O7 Krasnoye Smolenskaya Oblast' Rus. Fed.
153 S3 Krasnoye, Ozero l. Rus. Fed.
161 X6 Krasnoye Ekho Rus. Fed.
161 Y4 Krasnoye-na-Volge Rus. Fed.
161 V5 Krasnoye Plamya Rus. Fed.
161 S4 Krasnoye Znamya Rus. Fed.
158 E5 Krasnoyil's'k Ukr.
156 J3 Krasnozatonskiy Rus. Fed.
161 V5 Krasnozavodsk Rus. Fed.
160 F7 Krasnoznamensk Rus. Fed.
Krasnoznamenskiy Kazakh. see Yegindykol'
159 L7 Krasnoznam"yanka Ukr.
159 L7 Krasnoznam"yans'kyy Kanal canal Ukr.
197 L5 Krasnystaw Pol.
161 O7 Krasnyy Rus. Fed.
129 K1 Krasnyy Chikoy Rus. Fed.
156 I4 Krasnyye Baki Rus. Fed.
157 I7 Krasnyye Barrikady Rus. Fed.
161 W4 Krasnyye Tkachi Rus. Fed.
161 Q4 Krasnyy Gorodok Rus. Fed.
Krasnyy Kamyshanik Rus. Fed. see Komsomol'skiy
161 U3 Krasnyy Kholm Rus. Fed.
142 B2 Krasnyy Kut Rus. Fed.
159 S2 Krasnyy Liman Rus. Fed.
161 N4 Krasnyy Luch Rus. Fed.
159 R5 Krasnyy Luch Ukr.
159 Q5 Krasnyy Lyman Ukr.
159 M9 Krasnyy Mak Ukr.
143 Q4 Krasnyy Oktyabr' Kazakh.
161 V5 Krasnyy Oktyabr' Rus. Fed.
161 X4 Krasnyy Profintern Rus. Fed.
161 Q8 Krasnyy Rog Bryanskaya Oblast' Rus. Fed.
161 Q9 Krasnyy Rog Bryanskaya Oblast' Rus. Fed.
159 T6 Krasnyy Sulin Rus. Fed.
157 I6 Krasnyy Tekstil'shchik Rus. Fed.
143 M1 Krasnyy Yar Kazakh.
142 C4 Krasnyy Yar Astrakhanskaya Oblast' Rus. Fed.
142 D1 Krasnyy Yar Samarskaya Oblast' Rus. Fed.
157 I6 Krasnyy Yar Volgogradskaya Oblast' Rus. Fed.
197 I5 Krasocin Pol.
158 I2 Krasyatychi Ukr.
158 F4 Krasyliv Ukr.
159 K2 Krasylivka Chernihivs'ka Oblast' Ukr.
158 H2 Krasylivka Zhytomyrs'ka Oblast' Ukr.
196 G4 Kraszcwice Pol.
197 I1 Kraszewo Pol.
Kratie Cambodia see Krâchéh
219 K8 Kratovo Macedonia
194 G5 Krauchenwies Ger.
160 J6 Krauja Latvia
286 X2 Kraul Mountains Antarctica
Kraulshavn Greenland see Nuussuaq
193 K7 Krauschwitz Ger.
201 K4 Kräuterin mts Austria
194 H3 Krautheim Ger.
Krâvanh, Chuŏr Phnum mts Cambodia see Cardamom Range
199 H2 Kravaře Czech Rep.
159 K1 Krawtsowka Belarus
151 I2 Kraynovka Rus. Fed.
193 K8 Kreba-Neudorf Ger.
191 J7 Krebeck Ger.
227 E4 Krebs, Erg el des. Alg.
161 O3 Krechevitsy Rus. Fed.
191 C8 Krefeld Ger.
191 I7 Kreiensen Ger.
186 H3 Kreileroord Neth.
193 I9 Kreischa Ger.
244 F3 Krekatok Island AK U.S.A.
160 H6 Krekenava Lith.
220 C4 Kremaston, Techniti Limni resr Greece
210 E3 Kremen mt. Croatia
Kremenchug Ukr. see Kremenchuk
159 M4 Kremenchuk Ukr.
159 L4 Kremenchuts'ke Vodoskhovyshche resr Ukr.
158 E3 Kremenets' Ukr.
161 U7 Kremenki Rus. Fed.
157 H6 Kremenskaya Rus. Fed.
161 S6 Kremenskoye Rus. Fed.
198 E2 Křemešník hill Czech Rep.
Kremges Ukr. see Svitlovods'k
159 R4 Kreminna Ukr.
158 D5 Kremintsi Ukr.
Kreml' Rus. Fed. see Solovetskiy
192 H5 Kremmen Ger.
262 K6 Kremmling CO U.S.A.
220 E6 Kremmydi, Akrotirio pt Greece
199 H3 Kremnica Slovakia
190 I3 Krempe Ger.
197 J6 Krempna Pol.
201 L3 Krems r. Austria
201 M3 Krems an der Donau Austria
201 I6 Kremsbrücke Austria
201 J3 Kremsmünster Austria
198 D3 Křemže Czech Rep.
244 F5 Krenitzin Islands AK U.S.A.
201 O2 Křepice Czech Rep.
159 S6 Krepkaya r. Rus. Fed./Ukr.
219 J6 Krepoljin Žagubica Serbia
258 E3 Kresgeville PA U.S.A.
193 J9 Křešice Czech Rep.
219 L9 Kresna Bulg.
201 K7 Kresnice Slovenia
194 H6 Kressbronn am Bodensee Ger.
153 T3 Kresta, Zaliv g. Rus. Fed.
220 C5 Krestena Greece
153 O3 Krest-Khal'dzhay Rus. Fed.
156 K2 Krestovka Rus. Fed.
161 P3 Kresttsy Rus. Fed.
161 U6 Kresty Moskovskaya Oblast' Rus. Fed.
161 O6 Kresty Pskovskaya Oblast' Rus. Fed.
161 V8 Kresty Tul'skaya Oblast' Rus. Fed.
153 M3 Krestyakh Rus. Fed.
160 E6 Kretinga Lith.
193 F8 Kretzschau Ger.
195 L6 Kreuth Ger.
191 B9 Kreuzau Ger.
200 H6 Kreuzeck mt. Austria
200 G6 Kreuzeck Gruppe mts Austria
200 E5 Kreuzjoch mt. Austria
212 G1 Kreuzlingen Switz.
191 E9 Kreuztal Ger.
194 H2 Kreuzwertheim Ger.
160 J7 Kreva Belarus
229 H6 Kribi Cameroon
Krichev Belarus see Krychaw
219 M8 Krichim Bulg.
201 M4 Krieglach Austria
212 D1 Kriegstetten Switz.
237 N2 Kriel S. Africa
192 H3 Krien Ger.
212 E1 Kriens Switz.
160 E5 Krievukalns hill Latvia
220 F4 Krieza Greece
220 C4 Krikellos Greece
Krikovo Moldova see Cricova
122 M6 Kril'on, Mys c. Sakhalin Rus. Fed.
201 J8 Krim mt. Slovenia
230 B2 Krim-Krim Chad
200 F5 Krimmler Wasserfälle waterfall Austria
186 G5 Krimpen aan de IJssel Neth.
198 E1 Křinec Czech Rep.
220 F1 Krinides Greece
220 E7 Krios, Akrotirio pt Kriti Greece
Kripka r. Rus. Fed./Ukr. see Krepkaya
201 I4 Krippenstein mt. Austria
136 E4 Krishna Andhra Prad. India
136 G4 Krishna r. India
136 G5 Krishna, Mouths of the India
136 F6 Krishnagiri Tamil Nadu India
139 M6 Krishnai r. India
139 L8 Krishnanagar W. Bengal India
136 G5 Krishnapatnam Andhra Prad. India
136 E6 Krishnarajanagara Karnataka India
136 E6 Krishnaraja Sagara l. India
136 E6 Krishnarajpet Karnataka India
165 M4 Kristdala Sweden
Kristiania Norway see Oslo
164 D3 Kristiansand Norway
165 K5 Kristianstad Sweden
162 I5 Kristiansund Norway
Kristiinankaupunki Länsi-Suomi Fin. see Kristinestad
165 K2 Kristinehamn Sweden
163 P5 Kristinestad Fin.
Kristinopol' Ukr. see Chervonohrad
220 F8 Kriti admin. reg. Greece
220 F7 Kriti i. Kriti Greece
220 G6 Kritiko Pelagos sea Greece
192 F2 Kritzmow Ger.
160 G6 Kriūkai Lith.
Kriulyany Moldova see Criuleni
161 W7 Kriusha Rus. Fed.
Kriushi Kazakh. see Arshaly
218 I7 Krivača mt. Serbia
210 G3 Krivaja r. Bos.-Herz.
199 I6 Krivaja r. Serbia
161 W6 Krivandino Rus. Fed.
219 K8 Kriva Palanka Macedonia
219 J8 Kriva Reka r. Macedonia
159 S3 Krivaya Polyana Rus. Fed.
159 Q2 Krivets Rus. Fed.
213 R5 Krivi Put Croatia
218 J9 Krivogaštani Macedonia
198 C2 Křivoklátská vrchovina hills Czech Rep.
161 P8 Krivoles Rus. Fed.
161 W8 Krivopolyan'ye Rus. Fed.
157 H6 Krivorozh'ye Rus. Fed.
156 F2 Krivoy Porog Rus. Fed.
Krivoy Rog Ukr. see Kryvyy Rih
213 P5 Križ, Rt pt Croatia
198 F2 Křižanov Czech Rep.
210 F2 Križevci Croatia
210 G3 Krk mt. Bos.-Herz.
210 E3 Krk Croatia
210 E3 Krk i. Croatia
210 E4 Krka r. Croatia
201 K8 Krka Slovenia
210 E3 Krka r. Slovenia
198 E1 Krkonoše mts Czech Rep.
196 D5 Krkonošský narodní park nat. park Czech Rep./Pol.
201 I7 Krn mt. Slovenia
213 Q6 Krnica Croatia
218 I6 Krnjača Beograd Serbia
199 G1 Krnov Czech Rep.
196 E4 Krobia Pol.
197 H5 Kroczyce Pol.
164 F1 Krøderen Norway
164 F1 Krøderen l. Norway
193 H8 Krögis Ger.
228 D5 Krohnwodoke Liberia
Krokeaí Greece see Krokees
220 D6 Krokees Greece
165 M3 Krokek Sweden
162 U1 Kroknes Norway
162 M5 Krokom Sweden
119 J14 Krokong Sarawak Malaysia
228 E5 Krokosua National Park nat. park Ghana
165 O7 Krokowa Pol.
162 □C1 Króksfjarðarnes Iceland
162 J5 Krokstadøra Norway
162 M3 Krokstranda Norway
159 M2 Krolevets' Ukr.
Królewska Huta Pol. see Chorzów
197 L2 Królowy Most Pol.
193 E9 Krölpa Ger.
237 I10 Krom r. S. Africa
161 S9 Kroma r. Rus. Fed.
237 N1 Kromdraai S. Africa
198 G2 Kroměříž Czech Rep.
186 G3 Krommenie Neth.
199 J3 Krompachy Slovakia
193 D9 Kromsdorf Ger.
161 S9 Kromy Rus. Fed.
193 D10 Kronach Ger.
194 F3 Kronau Ger.
191 F10 Kronberg im Taunus Ger.
164 E2 Kronfjell hill Norway
119 F9 Krŏng Kaôh Kŏng Cambodia
139 O5 Kronli Arun. Prad. India
165 K5 Kronoberg county Sweden
162 Q5 Kronoby Fin.
153 R4 Kronotskiy Poluostrov pen. Rus. Fed.
153 R4 Kronotskiy Zaliv b. Rus. Fed.
153 R4 Kronotskoye Ozero l. Rus. Fed.
243 P1 Kronprins Christian Land reg. Greenland
243 O3 Kronprins Frederik Bjerge nunataks Greenland
190 G3 Kronprinzenkoog Ger.
190 J2 Kronshagen Ger.
160 M2 Kronshtadt Rus. Fed.
Kronstadt Romania see Brașov
Kronstadt Rus. Fed. see Kronshtadt
201 J3 Kronstorf Austria
118 D7 Kronwa Myanmar
237 L3 Kroonstad S. Africa
201 J7 Kropa Slovenia
192 E2 Kröpelin Ger.
157 H7 Kropotkin Rus. Fed.
190 I2 Kropp Ger.
164 I3 Kroppefjäll hills Sweden
193 D7 Kroppenstedt Ger.
193 G7 Kropstädt Ger.
158 I3 Kropyvnya Ukr.
197 I6 Krościenko nad Dunajcem Pol.
192 I2 Kröslin Ger.
197 L1 Krosna Lith.
196 F4 Krośnice Pol.
197 H3 Krośniewice Pol.
197 J6 Krosno Pol.
196 D3 Krosno Odrzańskie Pol.
193 E9 Krossen Ger.
164 E2 Krossen Norway
193 F8 Krostitz Ger.
196 E4 Krotoszyce Pol.
196 F4 Krotoszyn Pol.
201 M5 Krottendorf Austria
261 J10 Krotz Springs LA U.S.A.
198 F2 Krouna Czech Rep.
220 F7 Krousonas Kriti Greece
194 C2 Kröv Ger.
117 H8 Kroya Jawa Indon.
213 Q5 Kršan Croatia
210 E3 Krško Slovenia
218 I8 Krstača mt. Montenegro
196 F3 Kruchowo Pol.
192 E5 Krüden Ger.
191 D10 Kruft Ger.
237 K4 Krugerdrifdam resr S. Africa
237 P1 Kruger Mpumalanga airport S. Africa
237 P1 Kruger National Park S. Africa
237 L2 Krugersdorp S. Africa
122 I4 Kruglikovo Rus. Fed.
244 □A5 Krugloi Point pt AK U.S.A.
151 D1 Kruglolesskoye Rus. Fed.
Kruglyakov Rus. Fed. see Oktyabr'skiy
160 M7 Kruhlaye Belarus
116 E7 Krui Sumatera Indon.
236 F8 Kruidfontein S. Africa
187 F6 Kruiningen Neth.
237 I10 Kruisfontein S. Africa
187 E7 Kruishoutem Belgium
218 H9 Krujë Albania
197 L6 Krukenychi Ukr.
197 J1 Kruklanki Pol.
197 J2 Krukowo Pol.
201 N4 Krumbach Austria
195 I5 Krumbach (Schwaben) Ger.
218 I8 Krumë Albania
190 K3 Krummesse Ger.
219 N9 Krumovgrad Bulg.
193 E8 Krumpa (Geiseltal) Ger.
201 J6 Krumpendorf am Wörther See Austria
195 K6 Krün Ger.
Krungkao Thai. see Ayutthaya
Krung Thep Thai. see Bangkok
160 G5 Kruoja r. Lith.
Krupa Bos.-Herz. see Bosanska Krupa
Krupa na Uni Bos.-Herz. see Bosanska Krupa
218 H6 Krupanj Krupanj Serbia
197 N2 Krupava Belarus
197 L4 Krupe Pol.
159 N2 Krupets Rus. Fed.
199 I3 Krupina Slovakia
199 H3 Krupinica r. Slovakia
199 I3 Krupinská planina plat. Slovakia
198 C1 Krupka Czech Rep.
160 M7 Krupki Belarus
159 L4 Krupoderyntsi Ukr.
159 L5 Krups'ke Ukr.
196 G5 Krupski Młyn Pol.
190 H1 Kruså Denmark
244 G2 Krusenstern, Cape AK U.S.A.
218 J7 Kruševac Kruševac Serbia
218 J9 Kruševo Macedonia
198 B1 Krušné hory mts Czech Rep.
199 H3 Krušovce Slovakia
160 J5 Krustkalnu rezervāts nature res. Latvia
196 E3 Kruszewo Pol.
196 G3 Kruszwica Pol.
196 F1 Kruszyna Pomorskie Pol.
197 H5 Kruszyna Śląskie Pol.
196 F2 Kruszyńskie, Jezioro l. Pol.
159 S2 Krutchenskaya Baygora Rus. Fed.
159 K7 Krutoyarka Ukr.
161 U9 Krutoye Orlovskaya Oblast' Rus. Fed.
161 O6 Krutoye Smolenskaya Oblast' Rus. Fed.
159 L2 Kruty Ukr.
199 K2 Kružlov Slovakia
245 N4 Kruzof Island AK U.S.A.
160 M6 Krybinka r. Belarus
161 O8 Krychaw Belarus
218 I8 Kryezi Albania
221 H6 Krykello, Akrotirio pt Greece
158 F3 Kryliv Ukr.
288 H4 Krylov Seamount sea feature N. Atlantic Ocean
159 S7 Krylovskaya Krasnodarskiy Kray Rus. Fed.
159 S7 Krylovskaya Krasnodarskiy Kray Rus. Fed.
197 M5 Krylów Pol.
Krym' aut. rep. Ukr. see Krym, Respublika
Krym' pen. Ukr. see Kryms'kyy Pivostriv
159 N8 Krym, Respublika aut. rep. Ukr.
151 D1 Krymgireyevskoye Rus. Fed.
197 M4 Krymne Ukr.
157 G7 Krymsk Rus. Fed.
Krymskaya Rus. Fed. see Krymsk
159 R5 Kryms'ke Ukr.
159 N9 Kryms'ki Hori mts Ukr.
159 N8 Kryms'kyy Pivostriv pen. Ukr.
159 N9 Kryms'kyy Zapovidnyk nature res. Ukr.
197 I6 Krynica Pol.
165 P7 Krynica Morska Pol.
196 F5 Krynka r. Pol.
159 R6 Krynka r. Ukr.
161 N6 Krynki Belarus
197 L2 Krynki Pol.
159 N5 Krynychky Dnipropetrovs'ka Oblast' Ukr.
159 K6 Krynychky Mykolayivs'ka Oblast' Ukr.
159 R5 Krynychna Ukr.
159 N6 Krynychuvate Ukr.
197 K2 Krypno Kościelne Pol.
143 P5 Krypsalo (abandoned) Kazakh.
193 H10 Kryry Czech Rep.
159 L2 Krysky Ukr.
Krystynopol Ukr. see Chervonohrad
159 R9 Kryukovskoye Vodokhranilishche resr Rus. Fed.
159 R6 Kryva Kosa spit Ukr.
159 L4 Kryva Ruda Ukr.
158 I4 Kryvchunka Ukr.
158 J6 Kryve Ozero Ukr.
160 K7 Kryvichy Belarus
159 M6 Kryvyy Rih Ukr.
158 H5 Kryzhopil' Ukr.
196 G5 Krzanowice Pol.
197 K4 Krzczonów-Wójtostwo Pol.
196 D2 Krzęcin Pol.
196 E4 Krzelów Pol.
196 G5 Krzepice Pol.
196 E4 Krzepielów Pol.
197 K3 Krzesk-Królowa Niwa Pol.
197 K5 Krzeszów Pol.
197 H5 Krzeszowice Pol.
196 D3 Krzeszyce Pol.
197 H5 Krzętów Pol.
197 L3 Krzna r. Pol.
197 K4 Krzna Południowa r. Pol.
196 G3 Krzymów Wielkopolskie Pol.
192 J5 Krzymów Zachodniopomorskie Pol.
197 I2 Krzynowłoga Mała Pol.
196 D4 Krzystkowice Pol.
197 K6 Krzywcza Pol.
197 K4 Krzywda Pol.
196 E4 Krzywiń Pol.
192 J4 Krzywin Pol.
197 L4 Krzywowierzba Pol.
197 H3 Krzyżanów Pol.
196 G6 Krzyżanowice Pol.
196 E3 Krzyż Wielkopolski Pol.
227 E3 Ksabi Alg.
151 F4 Ksani r. Georgia
227 F2 Ksar Chellala Alg.
227 F2 Ksar el Boukhari Alg.
227 F2 Ksar el Hirane Alg.
226 D2 Ksar el Kebir Morocco
Ksar-es-Souk Morocco see Er Rachidia
202 D5 Ksar Sghir Morocco
158 J3 Ksaverivka Ukr.
156 K3 Ksenofontova Rus. Fed.
161 U9 Kshen' r. Rus. Fed.
157 G6 Kshenskiy Rus. Fed.
198 F1 Książański Park Krajobrazowy Pol.
197 H2 Książki Pol.
197 I5 Książ Wielki Pol.
196 F3 Książ Wielkopolski Pol.
197 K5 Księżpol Pol.
227 E2 Ksour, Monts des mts Alg.
227 H2 Ksour, Monts des mts Tunisia
227 H2 Ksour Essaf Tunisia
156 I4 Kstovo Rus. Fed.
161 S8 Ktsyn' Rus. Fed.
147 H2 Kū', Jabal al hill Saudi Arabia
224 E6 Ku, Wadi el watercourse Sudan
116 C1 Kuah Malaysia
Kuaidamao Jilin China see Tonghua
117 K2 Kuala Belait Brunei
Kuala Dungun Malaysia see Dungun
117 I6 Kualajelai Kalimantan Indon.
116 D2 Kuala Kangsar Malaysia
117 K6 Kualakapuas Kalimantan Indon.
116 E2 Kuala Kerai Malaysia
117 J5 Kualakuayan Kalimantan Indon.
116 D3 Kuala Kubu Baharu Malaysia
117 J5 Kualakurun Kalimantan Indon.
116 B2 Kualalangsa Sumatera Indon.
116 D2 Kuala Lipis Malaysia
116 D3 Kuala Lumpur Malaysia
116 D1 Kuala Nerang Malaysia
117 J6 Kualapembuang Kalimantan Indon.
117 K2 Kuala Penyu Sabah Malaysia
116 E3 Kuala Pilah Malaysia
264 □D12 Kualapu'u HI U.S.A.
116 E3 Kuala Rompin Malaysia
117 J6 Kualasampit Indon.
116 D3 Kuala Selangor Malaysia
116 D2 Kuala Sepetang Malaysia
116 C2 Kualasimpang Sumatera Indon.
116 E2 Kuala Terengganu Malaysia
116 E5 Kualatungal Sumatera Indon.
117 L2 Kuamut Sabah Malaysia
117 L2 Kuamut r. Malaysia
129 P6 Kuancheng Hebei China
123 D8 Kuandian Liaoning China
Kuangyuan Yunnan China see Yiliang
131 M7 Kuanshan Taiwan
116 E3 Kuantan Malaysia
102 J3 Kuaotunu North I. N.Z.
Kuba Azer. see Quba
151 E2 Kuba Rus. Fed.
151 I3 Kubachi Rus. Fed.
151 C2 Kuban' r. Rus. Fed.
151 A1 Kubanskaya Rus. Fed.
151 D1 Kubanskoye Vodokhranilishche resr Rus. Fed.
149 I6 Kubār Dayr az Zawr Syria
149 I6 Kubār Dayr az Zawr Syria
147 M4 Kubārah Oman
160 G3 Kübassaare poolsaar pen. Estonia
150 F3 Kubaybāt Syria
149 K7 Kubaysah Iraq
162 O5 Kubbe Sweden
230 D2 Kubbum Sudan
199 J5 Kübekháza Hungary
156 G4 Kubenskoye, Ozero l. Rus. Fed.
Kuberle Rus. Fed. see Krasnoarmeyskiy
127 H1 Kubiki Japan
161 T6 Kubinka Rus. Fed.
192 H2 Kubitzer Bodden b. Ger.
212 H2 Küblis Switz.
158 I5 Kublych r. Ukr.
156 J5 Kubnya r. Rus. Fed.
125 K13 Kubokawa Japan
219 O7 Kubrat Bulg.
161 V5 Kubrinsk Rus. Fed.
117 K9 Kubu Bali Indon.
117 H5 Kubu Kalimantan Indon.
117 K3 Kubuang Kalimantan Indon.
129 N1 Kubukhay Rus. Fed.
117 K4 Kubumesaäi Kalimantan Indon.
124 □22 Kubura Nansei-shotō Japan
219 J6 Kučevo Kučevo Serbia
138 E6 Kuchaman Rajasthan India
156 H2 Kuchema Rus. Fed.
194 H4 Kuchen Ger.
138 E6 Kuchera Rajasthan India
159 N2 Kucherivka Ukr.
117 I4 Kuching Sarawak Malaysia
124 □H16 Kuchino-Erabu-shima i. Japan
124 □G17 Kuchino-shima i. Nansei-shotō Japan
125 H14 Kuchinotsu Japan
200 H4 Kuchl Austria
143 R1 Kuchukskoye, Ozero salt l. Rus. Fed.
158 I7 Kuchurhan r. Ukr.
Kucing Sarawak Malaysia see Kuching
197 H4 Kuciny Pol.
197 L1 Kučiūnai Lith.
192 J3 Kückelsberg hill Ger.
220 A2 Kuçovë Albania
151 F6 Küçük Ağrı Dağı mt. Turkey
150 E2 Küçükdalyan Turkey
221 L5 Küçükköy Antalya Turkey
221 H3 Küçükköy Balıkesir Turkey
221 H3 Küçükkuyu Turkey
221 H2 Küçükmenderes r. Turkey
221 I5 Küçükmenderes r. Turkey
197 I2 Kuczbork-Osada Pol.
138 C8 Kuda Gujarat India
135 □1 Kuda Finolhu i. S. Male Maldives
124 □1 Kudaka-jima i. Okinawa Japan
136 C5 Kudal Mahar. India
135 □1 Kudalhi i. N. Male Maldives
125 I13 Kudamatsu Japan
117 I5 Kudangan Kalimantan Indon.
116 E4 Kudap Sumatera Indon.
129 J1 Kudara-Somon Rus. Fed.
Kudarebe pt Aruba see Cudarebe
117 L1 Kudat Sabah Malaysia
146 E6 Kudayd Saudi Arabia
136 D4 Kudchi Karnataka India
190 J3 Kuddewörde Ger.
160 L4 Kudev r. Rus. Fed.
160 M5 Kudever' Rus. Fed.
244 G5 Kudiakof Islands AK U.S.A.
160 F7 Kudirkos Naumiestis Lith.
136 E5 Kudligi Karnataka India
244 G4 Kudobin Islands AK U.S.A.
196 E5 Kudowa-Zdrój Pol.
126 C7 Kudoyama Japan
136 D6 Kudremukh mt. Karnataka India
161 S7 Kudrinskaya Rus. Fed.
161 S8 Kudryavets Rus. Fed.
159 K6 Kudryavtsivka Ukr.
229 G4 Kudu Nigeria
117 I8 Kudus Jawa Indon.
156 K4 Kudymkar Rus. Fed.
131 N6 Kueishan Tao i. Taiwan
Kūfah Iraq see Al Kūfah
115 G5 Kufar Seram Indon.
200 F4 Kufstein Austria
243 J3 Kugaaruk Nunavut Can.
245 O1 Kugaluk r. N.W.T. Can.
143 R5 Kugaly Kazakh.
156 I4 Kugesi Rus. Fed.
159 S7 Kugey Rus. Fed.
133 I11 Kugka Lhai Xizang China
242 G3 Kugluktuk Nunavut Can.
245 N1 Kugmallit Bay N.W.T. Can.
159 S7 Kugo-Yeya r. Rus. Fed.
128 F9 Kugri Qinghai China
157 H7 Kugul'ta Rus. Fed.
126 F3 Kuguno Japan
144 E6 Kūh, Khār mt. Iran
144 G9 Kūh, Ra's-al- pt Iran
144 F6 Kūh, Shīr mt. Iran
144 E4 Kūh, Sīāh mts Iran
145 J8 Kūhak Iran
195 K5 Kühbach Ger.
144 G6 Kūh Baneh Iran
192 F4 Kuhbier Ger.
144 B5 Kūhdasht Iran
144 G8 Kūhestak Iran
192 D5 Kuhfelde Ger.
144 C3 Kūhīn Iran
145 O3 Kŭhistoni Badakhshon aut. rep. Tajik.
192 E3 Kuhlen Ger.
192 E2 Kühlung park Ger.
192 E2 Kühlungsborn, Ostseebad Ger.
162 T4 Kuhmo Fin.
163 R6 Kuhmoinen Fin.
191 J9 Kühndorf Ger.
144 E5 Kūhpāyeh Iran
144 G6 Kūhpāyeh mt. Iran
144 H8 Kūhrān, Kūh-e mt. Iran
144 D6 Kūhrang r. Iran
193 G8 Kühren Ger.
190 G3 Kührstedt Ger.
192 F3 Kuhs Ger.
190 G4 Kuhstedt Ger.
119 D8 Kui Buri Thai.
149 P5 Kuidzhuk Turkm.
129 S2 Kuile He r. China
160 I2 Kuimetsa Estonia
186 I3 Kuinre Neth.
234 C5 Kuis Namibia
234 B4 Kuiseb watercourse Namibia
131 J7 Kuitan Guangdong China
231 C8 Kuito Angola
Kuitun Xinjiang China see Kuytun
245 N4 Kuiu Island AK U.S.A.
162 R4 Kuivaniemi Fin.
160 G3 Kuivastu Estonia
160 J5 Kuja r. Latvia
196 G4 Kujakowice Dolne Pol.
139 K9 Kujang Orissa India
123 E9 Kujang N. Korea
196 G2 Kujawsko-Pomorskie prov. Pol.
124 S6 Kuji Japan
127 M3 Kuji-gawa r. Japan
127 L4 Kujikuri Japan
124 S6 Kuji-wan b. Japan
127 L5 Kujūkuri-hama coastal area Japan
125 I13 Kujū-san vol. Japan
244 G1 Kuk r. AK U.S.A.
244 I4 Kukaklek Lake AK U.S.A.
122 H4 Kukan Rus. Fed.
122 H4 Kukan r. Rus. Fed.
251 L1 Kukatush Ont. Can.
229 I3 Kukawa Nigeria
109 E12 Kukerin W.A. Austr.
218 I8 Kukës Albania
158 E2 Kukhits'ka Volya Ukr.
127 K3 Kuki Japan
127 L4 Kukizaki Japan
126 D7 Kuki-zaki pt Japan
162 R4 Kukkola Fin.
197 I2 Kuklin Pol.
196 F4 Kuklinów Pol.
201 N5 Kukmirn Austria
156 J4 Kukmor Rus. Fed.
156 G4 Kukoboy Rus. Fed.
244 G1 Kukpowruk r. AK U.S.A.
244 F1 Kukpuk r. AK U.S.A.
160 K2 Kukruse Estonia
138 E8 Kukshi Madh. Prad. India
100 □6 Kukudu New Georgia Is Solomon Is
264 □F13 Kukuihaele HI U.S.A.
228 B4 Kukuna Sierra Leone
136 G4 Kukunuru Andhra Prad. India
116 E4 Kukup Malaysia
144 H2 Kükürtli Turkm.
117 K6 Kukusan, Gunung hill Indon.
156 L4 Kukushtan Rus. Fed.
144 F8 Kūl r. Iran
219 K7 Kula Bulg.
Kula r. Moldova see Cula
218 H8 Kula mt. Montenegro
229 G5 Kula Nigeria
218 H5 Kula Vojvodina Serbia
221 J4 Kula Turkey
116 C4 Kulabu, Gunung mt. Indon.
145 N6 Kulachi Pak.
161 P9 Kulagi Rus. Fed.
139 M5 Kula Kangri mt. Bhutan
146 E5 Kulākh Saudi Arabia
232 C4 Kulal, Mount Kenya
142 D5 Kulaly, Ostrov i. Kazakh.
143 O6 Kulan Kazakh.
143 P7 Kulanak Kyrg.
145 J9 Kulanch reg. Pak.
142 H4 Kulandy Kazakh.
143 M2 Kulanotpes watercourse Kazakh.
145 K7 Kulao r. Pak.
153 O2 Kular Rus. Fed.
114 C8 Kulassein i. Phil.
117 L4 Kulat, Gunung mt. Indon.
160 G7 Kulautuva Lith.
115 A4 Kulawi Sulawesi Indon.
225 F4 Kulb Sudan
159 N2 Kul'baki Rus. Fed.
160 E5 Kuldīga Latvia
Kuldja Xinjiang China see Yining
122 G4 Kul'dur Rus. Fed.
234 D4 Kule Botswana
157 H5 Kulebaki Rus. Fed.
119 G8 Kulen Cambodia
221 L5 Kuleönü Turkey
161 U9 Kuleshi Rus. Fed.
159 S6 Kuleshovka Rus. Fed.
197 K2 Kulesze Pol.
197 K2 Kulesze Kościelne Pol.
142 I1 Kulevchinskoye Rus. Fed.
Kulevi Georgia see Qulevi
106 D8 Kulgera N.T. Austr.
142 G1 Kulgunino Rus. Fed.
151 I3 Kuli Rus. Fed.
160 E6 Kuliai Lith.
156 K4 Kuligi Rus. Fed.
143 R6 Kulikovka Kazakh.
156 I3 Kulikovo Arkhangel'skaya Oblast' Rus. Fed.
161 W9 Kulikovo Lipetskaya Oblast' Rus. Fed.
116 D2 Kulim Malaysia
109 E12 Kulin W.A. Austr.
136 F7 Kulittalai Tamil Nadu India
109 D11 Kulja W.A. Austr.
105 J4 Kulkyne watercourse N.S.W. Austr.
163 Q6 Kullaa Fin.
107 I2 Kulla Aboriginal Reserve res. Australia
160 H3 Kullamaa Estonia
164 I5 Kullen pt Sweden
191 J8 Küllstedt Ger.
138 F4 Kullu Hima. Prad. India
195 L2 Kulmain Ger.
193 D10 Kulmbach Ger.
145 M3 Kŭlob Tajik.
161 Q3 Kulotino Rus. Fed.
156 H3 Kuloy Rus. Fed.
156 H2 Kuloy r. Rus. Fed.
149 J4 Kulp Turkey
104 F6 Kulpara S.A. Austr.
258 C3 Kulpmont PA U.S.A.
142 F4 Kul'sary Kazakh.
230 F2 Kulshabi Sudan

194 H2 Külsheim Ger.
199 G5 Kűlső-Somogy reg. Hungary
148 F4 Kulu Turkey
221 L5 Kulübe Tepe mt. Turkey
143 R1 Kulunda Rus. Fed.
143 R1 Kulunda r. Rus. Fed.
143 P1 Kulundinskaya Step' plain Kazakh./Rus. Fed.
143 R1 Kulundinskoye, Ozero salt l. Rus. Fed.
243 O3 Kulusuk Greenland
129 N1 Kulusutay Rus. Fed.
144 F6 Kūlvand Iran
105 I6 Kulwin Vic. Austr.
Kulyab Tajik. see Kŭlob
158 D4 Kulykiv Ukr.
159 K2 Kulykivka Ukr.
143 O1 Kulykol' Kazakh.
125 J13 Kuma Japan
151 H1 Kuma r. Rus. Fed.
162 U3 Kuma r. Rus. Fed.
197 I1 Kumachevo Rus. Fed.
159 R6 Kumachove Ukr.
127 J3 Kumagaya Japan
117 I6 Kumai Kalimantan Indon.
117 I6 Kumai, Teluk b. Indon.
124 Q4 Kumaishi Japan
142 I2 Kumak Rus. Fed.
142 H2 Kumak r. Rus. Fed.
275 G4 Kumaka Guyana
129 M1 Kumakhta Rus. Fed.
221 L4 Kumalar Dağı mts Turkey
125 H14 Kumamoto Japan
125 H14 Kumamoto pref. Japan
126 D8 Kumano Japan
126 C8 Kumanogawa Japan
219 J8 Kumanovo Macedonia
103 F9 Kumara South I. N.Z.
122 E3 Kumara Rus. Fed.
103 F9 Kumara Junction South I. N.Z.
139 L8 Kumarkhali Bangl.
228 E5 Kumasi Ghana
237 M7 Ku-Mayima S. Africa
Kumayri Armenia see Gyumri
229 H5 Kumba Cameroon
221 I2 Kumbağ Turkey
136 F7 Kumbakonam Tamil Nadu India
201 M5 Kumberg Austria
221 L3 Kümbet Turkey
136 C4 Kumbharli Ghat mt. Mahar. India
138 H5 Kumbher Nepal
136 D6 Kumbla Kerala India
229 H5 Kumbo Cameroon
160 F5 Kumbri Latvia
234 D4 Kumchuru Botswana
Kum-Dag Turkm. see Gumdag
146 G5 Kumdah Saudi Arabia
221 L4 Kumdanlı Turkey
125 K11 Kume Japan
124 □D20 Kume-jima i. Nansei-shotō Japan
144 E4 Kumel well Iran
156 J4 Kumeny Rus. Fed.
142 F1 Kumertau Rus. Fed.
123 E11 Kŭm-gang r. S. Korea
123 F9 Kumgang-san mt. N. Korea
139 M6 Kumguri Assam India
133 C11 Kumharsain Hima. Prad. India
195 M4 Kumhausen Ger.
138 F6 Kumher Rajasthan India
123 F11 Kŭmho-gang r. S. Korea
123 F10 Kumi S. Korea
232 B4 Kumi Uganda
126 A4 Kumihama Japan
126 A4 Kumihama-wan l. Japan
126 C6 Kumiyama Japan
221 H3 Kumkale Turkey
132 J6 Kum Kuduk well Xinjiang China
165 L2 Kumla Sweden
163 P6 Kumlinge Åland Fin.
150 E2 Kumlu Turkey
221 L6 Kumluca Turkey
192 D4 Kummer Ger.
192 G3 Kummerow Ger.
192 G3 Kummerower See l. Ger.
195 L3 Kümmersbruck Ger.
193 H6 Kummersdorf-Alexanderdorf Ger.
193 H6 Kummersdorf Gut Ger.
229 H4 Kumo Nigeria
123 E11 Kŭmŏ-do i. S. Korea
143 L4 Kumola watercourse Kazakh.
118 C2 Kumon Range mts Myanmar
127 I4 Kumotori-yama mt. Japan
126 E6 Kumozu-gawa r. Japan
213 P6 Kumpare, Rt pt Croatia
118 F6 Kumphawapi Thai.
162 R3 Kumputunturi hill Fin.
201 M7 Kumrovec Croatia
236 D4 Kums Namibia
229 I4 Kumshe Nigeria
136 D5 Kumta Karnataka India
151 I2 Kumtorkala Rus. Fed.
230 E4 Kumu Dem. Rep. Congo
264 □G14 Kumukahi, Cape HI U.S.A.
151 I3 Kumukh Rus. Fed.
Kumul Xinjiang China see Hami
139 I9 Kumund Orissa India
151 E4 Kumurdo Georgia
132 I5 Kümüx Xinjiang China
Kumylzhenskaya Rus. Fed. see Kumylzhenskiy
157 H6 Kumylzhenskiy Rus. Fed.
143 N6 Kumyshtag, Pik mt. Kyrg.
118 C5 Kun r. Myanmar
244 H1 Kuna r. AK U.S.A.
199 I5 Kunadacs Hungary
199 K5 Kunágota Hungary
109 G7 Kunanaggi Well W.A. Austr.
145 N4 Kunar prov. Afgh.
145 N4 Kunar r. Afgh.
122 O6 Kunashir, Ostrov i. Kuril'skiye O-va Rus. Fed.
Kunashirskiy Proliv sea chan. Japan/Rus. Fed. see Nemuro-kaikyō
199 I5 Kunbaja Hungary
199 I5 Kunbaracs Hungary
151 G1 Kun'bator Rus. Fed.
118 C3 Kunchaung Myanmar
231 E5 Kunda Dem. Rep. Congo
160 J2 Kunda Estonia
160 J2 Kunda r. Estonia
138 H7 Kunda Uttar Prad. India
231 C7 Kunda-dia-Baze Angola
160 J2 Kunda laht b. Estonia
136 D6 Kundapura Karnataka India
145 M5 Kundar r. Afgh./Pak.
231 E7 Kundelungu, Parc National de nat. park Dem. Rep. Congo
231 E7 Kundelungu Ouest, Parc National de nat. park Dem. Rep. Congo
136 D5 Kundgol Karnataka India
145 N5 Kundian Pak.
200 E5 Kundl Austria
138 C9 Kundla Gujarat India
159 T6 Kundryuch'ya r. Rus. Fed./Ukr.
116 E4 Kundur i. Indon.
145 M3 Kunduz Afgh.
145 M3 Kunduz prov. Afgh.
143 P2 Kundykol' Pavlodarskaya Oblast' Kazakh.
231 A9 Kunene r. Angola/Namibia alt. Cunene
234 B3 Kunene admin. reg. Namibia
Künes Xinjiang China see Xinyuan
132 F5 Künes Chang Xinjiang China
132 E5 Künes He r. China
132 G5 Künes Linchang Xinjiang China
199 I5 Kunfehértó Hungary
164 H4 Kungälv Sweden
128 E1 Kungar-Tuk Rus. Fed.
143 Q6 Kungei Alatau mts Kazakh./Kyrg.
Kunggar Xizang China see Maizhokunggar
245 O5 Kunghit Island B.C. Can.
Küngöy Ala-Too mts Kazakh./Kyrg. see Kungei Alatau
165 N2 Kungsängen Sweden
164 I4 Kungsbacka Sweden
164 H3 Kungshamn Sweden
165 M2 Kungsör Sweden
230 C4 Kungu Dem. Rep. Congo
Kungur mt. Xinjiang China see Kongur Shan
156 L4 Kungur Rus. Fed.
118 B6 Kungyangon Myanmar
199 J4 Kunhegyes Hungary
179 O7 Kunheim France
130 B8 Kunhing Myanmar
136 F3 Kuni r. India
127 I2 Kuni Japan
196 E4 Kunice Pol.
144 H8 Kūnīch Iran
Kunicha Moldova see Cunicea
Kunié i. New Caledonia see Pins, Île des
136 E6 Kunigal Karnataka India
126 D3 Kunimi-dake hill Japan
125 I14 Kunimi-dake mt. Japan
199 G2 Kunín Czech Rep.
160 K2 Kuningaküla Estonia
117 H8 Kuningan Jawa Indon.
196 G5 Kuniów Pol.
125 I13 Kunisaki Japan
139 J9 Kunjabar Orissa India
138 C9 Kunkavav Gujarat India
258 E3 Kunkletown PA U.S.A.
118 D3 Kunlong Myanmar
139 L7 Kunlui r. India/Nepal
128 C9 Kunlun Shan mts China
128 D9 Kunlun Shankou pass Qinghai China
199 J4 Kunmadaras Hungary
130 D6 Kunming Yunnan China
108 H3 Kunmunya Aboriginal Reserve W.A. Austr.
138 F6 Kuno r. India
198 G2 Kunovice Czech Rep.
197 J5 Kunów Pol.
193 K6 Kunowice Pol.
196 F4 Kunowo Pol.
166 D1 Kunoy i. Faroe Is
199 I4 Kunpeszér Hungary
192 D5 Kunrau Ger.
123 E11 Kunsan S. Korea
131 M3 Kunshan Jiangsu China
198 F2 Kunštát Czech Rep.
199 I5 Kunszállás Hungary
199 J5 Kunszentmárton Hungary
199 I4 Kunszentmiklós Hungary
231 D5 Kuntshankoie Dem. Rep. Congo
108 J3 Kununurra W.A. Austr.
247 L2 Kunwak r. Nunavut Can.
138 G6 Kunwari r. India
161 N5 Kun'ya Rus. Fed.
161 O4 Kun'ya r. Rus. Fed.
Kunyang Henan China see Yexian
Kunyang Yunnan China see Jinning
Kunyang Zhejiang China see Pingyang
Kunya-Urgench Turkm. see Köneürgenç
159 Q4 Kun'ye Ukr.
129 Q8 Kunyu Shan mts China
198 E2 Kunžak Czech Rep.
191 I9 Künzell Ger.
194 H3 Künzelsau Ger.
193 D8 Künzels-Berg hill Ger.
195 O4 Künzing Ger.
231 C5 Kunzulu Dem. Rep. Congo
131 M4 Kuocang Shan mts China
162 T3 Kuolayarvi Rus. Fed.
163 S6 Kuolimo l. Fin.
162 S5 Kuopio Fin.
163 R6 Kuorevesi Fin.
162 T3 Kuosku Fin.
196 F5 Kup Pol.
210 F3 Kupa r. Croatia/Slovenia
115 C9 Kupang Timor Indon.
115 C9 Kupang, Teluk b. Timor Indon.
161 V5 Kupanskoye Rus. Fed.
139 K9 Kupari Orissa India
245 J1 Kuparuk r. AK U.S.A.
Kupchino Moldova see Cupcina
193 E10 Kupferberg Ger.
194 H3 Kupferzell Ger.
159 Q3 Kupino Rus. Fed.
160 H6 Kupiškis Lith.
213 R5 Kupjak Croatia
221 K2 Küplü Turkey
194 E4 Kuppenheim Ger.
160 K4 Kuprava Latvia
245 N4 Kupreanof AK U.S.A.
245 N4 Kupreanof Island AK U.S.A.
244 H5 Kupreanof Point pt AK U.S.A.
244 I4 Kupreanof Strait AK U.S.A.
161 Y6 Kupreyevo Rus. Fed.
193 D10 Küps Ger.
161 N5 Kupuy Rus. Fed.
138 E2 Kupwara Jammu and Kashmir India
159 Q4 Kup"yans'k Ukr.
159 Q4 Kup"yans'k-Vuzlovyy Ukr.
158 D3 Kupychiv Ukr.
132 F6 Kuqa Xinjiang China
151 H5 Kür Azer.
151 K6 Kür r. Azer.
122 I4 Kur r. Rus. Fed.
149 L3 Kura r. Georgia
151 G1 Kura r. Rus. Fed.
151 G4 Kura r. Turkey/Georgia
109 D8 Kurabuka r. W.A. Austr.
143 O6 Kuragaty Kazakh.
229 H4 Kuragwi Nigeria
125 J12 Kurahashi-jima i. Japan
126 F3 Kurai-yama mt. Japan
151 H5 Küräkçay r. Azer.
151 I4 Kurakh Rus. Fed.
159 Q6 Kurakhove Ukr.
Kurakhovo Ukr. see Kurakhove
Kurakhovstroy Ukr. see Kurakhove
Kura kurk sea chan. Estonia/Latvia see Irbe Strait
146 E3 Kuramā, Ḩarrat lava field Saudi Arabia
126 C5 Kurama-yama hill Japan
107 J4 Kuranda Qld Austr.
144 H8 Kūrān Dap Iran
142 G2 Kurashasayskiy Kazakh.
125 K12 Kurashiki Japan
138 I8 Kurasia Chhattisgarh India
108 I5 Kura Soak well W.A. Austr.
147 I2 Kurayn i. Saudi Arabia
125 K11 Kurayoshi Japan
128 A1 Kurayskiy Khrebet mts Rus. Fed.
161 W4 Kurba Rus. Fed.
221 K2 Kurban Dağı mt. Turkey
159 R2 Kurbatovo Rus. Fed.
122 F4 Kurbin He r. China
218 I4 Kurca r. Romania
151 H2 Kurchaloy Rus. Fed.
159 Q8 Kurchanskiy Liman salt l. Rus. Fed.
157 F6 Kurchatov Rus. Fed.
143 T3 Kurchum Kazakh.
151 I5 Kürd Azer.
199 H5 Kurd Hungary
151 J5 Kürdämir Azer.
143 P6 Kurday Kazakh.
144 E7 Kür Deh Iran
144 F8 Kürdeh Iran
151 K7 Kür Dili pt Azer.
136 D3 Kurduvadi Mahar. India
219 N9 Kŭrdzhali Bulg.
151 B2 Kurdzhinovo Rus. Fed.
125 J12 Kure Japan
148 F3 Küre Turkey
97 G1 Kure Atoll HI U.S.A.
160 F3 Kuressaare Estonia
160 M3 Kureya r. Rus. Fed.
152 J3 Kureyskoye Vodokhranilishche resr Rus. Fed.
Kurgal'dzhino Kazakh. see Korgalzhyn
152 H4 Kurgan Rus. Fed.
157 H7 Kurganinsk Rus. Fed.
Kurgannaya Rus. Fed. see Kurganinsk
Kurgantyube Tajik. see Qŭrghonteppa
Kurgasyn Kazakh. see Korgasyn
138 G9 Kurhad Mahar. India
145 N3 Kuri Afgh.
138 C6 Kuri Rajasthan India
99 H1 Kuria is Gilbert Is Kiribati
Kuria Muria Bay Oman see Ḩalāniyāt, Khalīj al
Kuria Muria Islands Oman see Ḩalāniyāt, Juzur al
106 H6 Kuridala Qld Austr.
139 L7 Kurigram Bangl.
127 K5 Kurihama Japan
127 K3 Kurihashi Japan
162 Q5 Kurikka Fin.
124 R8 Kurikoma-yama vol. Japan
290 E2 Kuril Basin sea feature Sea of Okhotsk
218 H8 Kurile, Mal mt. Albania
Kuril Islands Rus. Fed. see Kuril'skiye Ostrova
142 C2 Kurilovka Rus. Fed.
121 Q2 Kuril'sk Kuril'skiye O-va Rus. Fed.
121 Q2 Kuril'skiye Ostrova is Rus. Fed.
290 E3 Kuril Trench sea feature N. Pacific Ocean
198 F2 Kuřim Czech Rep.
199 K2 Kurima Slovakia
127 L4 Kurimoto Japan
125 H15 Kurino Japan
151 A1 Kurinskaya Rus. Fed.
124 S3 Kuriyama Hokkaidō Japan
127 K2 Kuriyama Tochigi Japan
Kurkçü Turkey see Sarıkavak
161 V8 Kurkino Rus. Fed.
109 I7 Kurlkuta Aboriginal Reserve W.A. Austr.
161 X6 Kurlovskiy Rus. Fed.
142 D1 Kurmanayevka Rus. Fed.
142 G2 Kurmansay Kazakh.
Kurmashkino Kazakh. see Kurchum
160 H5 Kurmene Latvia
232 B2 Kurmuk Sudan
195 I2 Kürnach Ger.
194 F3 Kürnbach Ger.
158 H3 Kurne Ukr.
136 E5 Kurnool Andhra Prad. India
127 L2 Kurobane Japan
126 F2 Kurobe Japan
126 F2 Kurobe-gawa r. Japan
126 G2 Kurobe-ko resr Japan
126 B5 Kurodashō Japan
127 G2 Kurohime-yama mt. Japan
127 J3 Kurohone Japan
127 I1 Kurohume-yama hill Japan
124 R6 Kuroishi Japan
127 L2 Kuroiso Japan
124 R4 Kuromatsunai Japan
225 F4 Kuror, Jebel mt. Sudan
159 P8 Kurortne Ukr.
159 O6 Kuroshany r. Ukr.
124 □B22 Kuro-shima i. Nansei-shotō Japan
126 B7 Kuro-shima i. Japan
124 □G16 Kuro-shima i. Japan
126 D6 Kuroso-yama mt. Japan
122 E1 Kurovskiy Rus. Fed.
161 T7 Kurovskoy Rus. Fed.
161 V6 Kurovskoye Rus. Fed.
197 M6 Kurovychi Ukr.
103 E11 Kurow South I. N.Z.
197 K4 Kurów Pol.
197 H4 Kurowice Pol.
145 N5 Kurram r. Afgh./Pak.
145 N5 Kurram Pak.
105 M5 Kurri Kurri N.S.W. Austr.
151 D1 Kursavka Rus. Fed.
139 K7 Kursela Bihar India
160 F5 Kuršėnai Lith.
146 F4 Kursh, Jabal hill Saudi Arabia
Kürshim Kazakh. see Kurchum
143 T3 Kurshim r. Kazakh.
Kurshskiy Zaliv b. Lith./Rus. Fed. see Courland Lagoon
160 J9 Kurshynavichy Belarus
160 F5 Kursīši Latvia
Kuršių marios b. Lith./Rus. Fed. see Courland Lagoon
160 D6 Kuršių neringos nacionalinis parkas nat. park Lith.
157 G6 Kursk Rus. Fed.
151 F1 Kurskaya Rus. Fed.
157 G6 Kurskaya Oblast' admin. div. Rus. Fed.
Kurskiy Zaliv b. Lith./Rus. Fed. see Courland Lagoon
Kursk Oblast admin. div. Rus. Fed. see Kurskaya Oblast'
159 O2 Kurskoye Vodokhranilishche resr Rus. Fed.
218 J7 Kuršumlija Kuršumlija Serbia
148 F3 Kurşunlu Turkey
149 J5 Kurtalan Turkey
221 H1 Kurtbey Turkey
Kürti r. Kazakh. see Kurtty
264 □F14 Kurtistown HI U.S.A.
151 F4 K'urt'lari Georgia
221 J6 Kurtoğlu Burnu pt Turkey
150 D2 Kurtpınar Turkey
150 D1 Kurttepe Turkey
143 Q5 Kurtty r. Kazakh.
Kurty r. Kazakh. see Kurtty
205 O2 Kurtzea Spain
163 Q6 Kuru Fin.
Kurú r. Greece see Kompsatos
139 J8 Kuru Jharkhand India
230 E2 Kuru watercourse Sudan
228 C4 Kurubonla Sierra Leone
148 F3 Kurucaşile Turkey
151 B7 Kurucu Geçidi pass Turkey
138 H9 Kurud Chhattisgarh India
221 L2 Kurudere Turkey
138 F5 Kurukshetra Haryana India
132 H6 Kuruktag mts China
236 H3 Kuruman S. Africa
236 E2 Kuruman watercourse S. Africa
236 H3 Kuruman Hills S. Africa
125 H13 Kurume Japan
121 J1 Kurumkan Rus. Fed.
232 B3 Kurun r. Sudan
106 E6 Kurundi watercourse N.T. Austr.
136 D4 Kurundvad Mahar. India
136 G9 Kurunegala Sri Lanka
129 O1 Kurunzulay Rus. Fed.
244 I1 Kurupa r. AK U.S.A.
137 H3 Kurupam Andhra Prad. India
275 G3 Kurupukari Guyana
225 F4 Kurush, Jebel hills Sudan
143 T2 Kur'ya Altayskiy Kray Rus. Fed.
156 L3 Kur'ya Respublika Komi Rus. Fed.
159 R4 Kuryachivka Ukr.
142 D6 Kuryk Kazakh.
197 M2 Kurylavichy Belarus
159 N5 Kurylivka Ukr.
197 K5 Kuryłówka Pol.
125 G11 Kuryongp'o S. Korea
197 H5 Kurzelów Pol.
197 I4 Kurzeszyn Pol.
197 H2 Kurzętnik Pol.
221 I5 Kuşadası Turkey
221 I5 Kuşadası Körfezi b. Turkey
Kusaie atoll Micronesia see Kosrae
150 E2 Kuşalanı Turkey
Kusary Azer. see Qusar
127 I2 Kusatsu Gunma Japan
126 C5 Kusatsu Shiga Japan
245 M3 Kusawa Lake Y.T. Can.
150 D2 Kuşcenneti nature res. Turkey
221 I2 Kuşcenneti Milli Parkı nat. park Turkey
125 K11 Kuse Japan
194 C2 Kusel Ger.
192 D5 Kusey Ger.
221 I2 Kuş Gölü l. Turkey
138 E8 Kushalgarh Rajasthan India
161 T4 Kushalino Rus. Fed.
144 G4 Kūshang Iran
157 G7 Kushchevskaya Rus. Fed.
229 G4 Kusheriki Nigeria
124 □1 Kushi Okinawa Japan
126 E6 Kushida-gawa r. Japan
127 H4 Kushigata Japan
126 F5 Kushihara Japan
125 H15 Kushikino Japan
125 I15 Kushima Japan
125 M13 Kushimoto Japan
124 V4 Kushiro Japan
124 V3 Kushiro-Shitsugen Kokuritsu-kōen nat. park Japan
Kushka Turkm. see Serhetabat
144 B5 Kūshkī Iran
156 I3 Kushkopola Rus. Fed.
142 K1 Kushmurun Kazakh.
142 K1 Kushmurun, Ozero salt l. Kazakh.
156 K5 Kushnarenkovo Rus. Fed.
136 E5 Kushtagi Karnataka India
139 L8 Kushtia Bangl.
144 H7 Kushtih Iran
161 T1 Kushtozero, Ozero l. Rus. Fed.
159 O6 Kushuhum Ukr.
128 J7 Kushui He r. China
150 B2 Kuskan Turkey
244 G3 Kuskokwim r. AK U.S.A.
244 I3 Kuskokwim, North Fork r. AK U.S.A.
244 I3 Kuskokwim, South Fork r. AK U.S.A.
244 G4 Kuskokwim Bay AK U.S.A.
244 I2 Kuskokwim Mountains AK U.S.A.
161 S6 Kuskovo Rus. Fed.
Kuşluyan Turkey see Gölköy
212 F1 Küsnacht Switz.
123 D9 Kusŏng N. Korea
151 E2 Kusparty Rus. Fed.
124 V3 Kussharo-ko l. Japan
212 E1 Küssnacht Switz.
Kustanay Kazakh. see Kostanay
Kustanay Oblast admin. div. Kazakh. see Kostanayskaya Oblast'
163 P6 Kustavi Fin.
192 D5 Küsten Ger.
Küstence Romania see Constanța
190 E4 Küstenkanal canal Ger.
194 G4 Kusterdingen Ger.
Kustia Bangl. see Kushtia
158 G4 Kustivtsi Ukr.
115 E3 Kusu Halmahera Indon.
126 E6 Kusu Japan
221 K4 Kuşu Turkey
151 H4 Kusur Rus. Fed.
144 C6 Kut Iran
119 F9 Kut, Ko i. Thai.
117 K9 Kuta Bali Indon.
116 B2 Kutabagok Sumatera Indon.
144 C6 Kūt 'Abdollāh Iran
116 B3 Kutacane Sumatera Indon.
221 K3 Kütahya Turkey
221 K3 Kütahya prov. Turkey
117 L4 Kutai, Taman Nasional nat. park Indon.
151 A1 Kutais Rus. Fed.
151 D3 K'ut'aisi Georgia
Kut-al-Imara Iraq see Al Kūt
151 H1 Kutan Rus. Fed.
Kutaraja Sumatera Indon. see Banda Aceh
102 L5 Kutarere North I. N.Z.
199 K4 Kutas-főcsatorna canal Hungary
Kutch, Gulf of Gujarat India see Kachchh, Gulf of
Kutch, Rann of marsh India see Kachchh, Rann of
124 R4 Kutchan Japan
149 N7 Kūt-e Gapu tourist site Iran
190 H4 Kutenholz Ger.
159 R6 Kuteynykove Ukr.
210 F3 Kutina Croatia
210 F3 Kutjevo Croatia
118 C3 Kutkai Myanmar
237 K3 Kutlwanong S. Africa
198 E2 Kutná Hora Czech Rep.
197 H3 Kutno Pol.
136 G3 Kutru Chhattisgarh India
126 C5 Kutsuki Japan
162 Q2 Kuttainen Sweden
230 C5 Kutu Dem. Rep. Congo
139 M9 Kutubdia Channel inlet Bangl.
139 M9 Kutubdia Island Bangl.
232 D4 Kutulo, Lagh watercourse Kenya/Somalia
224 E6 Kutum Sudan
Kutuzov Moldova see Ialoveni
198 G3 Kúty Slovakia
158 F3 Kuty Ukr.
195 J5 Kutzenhausen Ger.
258 D3 Kutztown PA U.S.A.
242 G2 Kuujjua r. N.W.T. Can.
249 G1 Kuujjuaq Que. Can.
248 E2 Kuujjuarapik Que. Can.
187 D7 Kuurne Belgium
162 R3 Kuusajoki Fin.
160 I2 Kuusalu Estonia
162 T4 Kuusamo Fin.
163 S6 Kuusankoski Fin.
160 G1 Kuusjoki Fin.
160 J3 Kuutse mägi hill Estonia
156 K4 Kuva Rus. Fed.
142 G2 Kuvandyk Rus. Fed.
231 C8 Kuvango Angola
161 R4 Kuvshinovo Rus. Fed.
Kuwaé i. Vanuatu see Tongoa
149 M9 Kuwait country Asia
Kuwait Kuwait see Al Kuwayt
149 M9 Kuwait Jun b. Kuwait
Kuwajleen atoll Marshall Is see Kwajalein
126 E5 Kuwana Japan
156 H2 Kuya Rus. Fed.
144 E6 Kuyān Iran
Kūybyshev Kazakh. see Novoishimskiy
152 I4 Kuybyshev Novosibirskaya Oblast' Rus. Fed.
Kuybyshev Respublika Tatarstan Rus. Fed. see Bolgar
Kuybyshev Samarskaya Oblast' Rus. Fed. see Samara
159 Q6 Kuybysheve Donets'ka Oblast' Ukr.
159 P6 Kuybysheve Zaporiz'ka Oblast' Ukr.
Kuybyshevka-Vostochnaya Rus. Fed. see Belogorsk
Kuybyshevo Kazakh. see Zhyngyldy
159 R6 Kuybyshevo Rus. Fed.
Kuybyshevskaya Oblast' admin. div. Rus. Fed. see Samarskaya Oblast'
157 J5 Kuybyshevskoye Vodokhranilishche resr Rus. Fed.
145 J3 Kuybyshew Adyndaky Turkm.
156 K4 Kuyeda Rus. Fed.
144 B2 Kūyeh Iran
129 L7 Kuye He r. China
143 P5 Kuygan Kazakh.
128 C5 Küysu Xinjiang China
132 G4 Kuytun Xinjiang China
132 F4 Kuytun He r. China
221 J5 Kuyucak Turkey
142 K2 Kuyukkol', Ozero salt l. Kazakh.
159 N7 Kuyuktuk, Ostriv i. Ukr.
150 C2 Kuyuluk Turkey
132 H1 Kuyus Rus. Fed.
142 G5 Kuyushe Kazakh.
266 □R10 Kuyu Tingni Nic.
275 G4 Kuyuwini r. Guyana
161 N1 Kuyvozi Rus. Fed.
126 E4 Kuze Japan
159 Q4 Kuzemivka Ukr.
159 N3 Kuzemyn Ukr.
156 J4 Kuzhener Rus. Fed.
161 Q4 Kuzhenkino Rus. Fed.
151 B1 Kuzhorskaya Rus. Fed.
160 G6 Kužiai Lith.
Kuzik'end Armenia see Garrnarrich
161 V2 Kuzino Rus. Fed.
199 K3 Kuzmice Slovakia
197 K6 Kuźmina Pol.
161 Q7 Kuz'minichi Rus. Fed.
161 W7 Kuz'minskoye Rus. Fed.
161 N1 Kuz'molovskiy Rus. Fed.
160 M1 Kuznechnoye Rus. Fed.
142 B1 Kuznetsk Rus. Fed.
122 K5 Kuznetsovo Rus. Fed.
158 E2 Kuznetsovs'k Ukr.
196 G5 Kuźnia Raciborska Pol.
197 L2 Kuźnica Pol.
196 E3 Kuźnica Czarnkowska Pol.
156 G2 Kuzomen' Rus. Fed.
157 I5 Kuzovatovo Rus. Fed.
161 V8 Kuzovka Rus. Fed.
124 S6 Kuzumaki Japan
126 D3 Kuzuryū-gawa r. Japan
126 E4 Kuzuryū-ko resr Japan
127 K3 Kuzuu Japan
162 P1 Kvænangen sea chan. Norway
164 G6 Kværndrup Denmark
190 H1 Kværs Denmark
162 O2 Kvaløya i. Norway
162 Q1 Kvaløya i. Norway
162 Q1 Kvalsund Norway
162 □ Kvalvågen b. Svalbard
Kvareli Georgia see Qvareli
142 H1 Kvarkeno Rus. Fed.
163 M6 Kvarnberg Sweden
210 E3 Kvarner g. Croatia
210 E3 Kvarnerić sea chan. Croatia
198 G2 Kvasice Czech Rep.
158 D5 Kvasy Ukr.
197 N3 Kvasyevichy Belarus
158 F3 Kvasyliv Ukr.
151 D2 K'veda Marghi Georgia
151 D4 K'veda Nasakirali Georgia
160 E6 Kvėdarna Lith.
164 F2 Kvelde Norway
151 G3 K'vemo Alvani Georgia
151 C2 K'vemo Azhara Georgia
151 G4 K'vemo Bodbe Georgia
151 F4 K'vemo Bolnisi Georgia
151 E4 K'vemo Boshuri Georgia
K'vemo-Marghi Georgia see K'veda Marghi
162 J5 Kvenvær Norway
244 H4 Kvichak AK U.S.A.
244 H4 Kvichak r. AK U.S.A.
244 H4 Kvichak Bay AK U.S.A.
164 D3 Kvifjorden l. Norway
162 N3 Kvikkjokk Sweden
165 L4 Kvillsfors Sweden
164 C3 Kvinesdal Norway
164 C3 Kvinlog Norway
163 N5 Kvissleby Sweden
163 I6 Kvitanosi mt. Norway
163 I5 Kvitegga mt. Norway
164 E2 Kviteseid Norway
162 □ Kvitøya i. Svalbard
164 B2 Kvitsøy Norway
231 C5 Kwa r. Dem. Rep. Congo
187 H6 Kwaadmechelen Belgium
Kwabhaca S. Africa see Mount Frere
237 O2 Kwachibukhulu S. Africa
246 E3 Kwadacha Wilderness Provincial Park B.C. Can.
237 N2 KwaDela S. Africa
Kwadelen atoll Marshall Is see Kwajalein
233 A6 Kwaga Tanz.
237 N1 KwaGuqa S. Africa
131 □J7 Kwai Tau Leng hill H.K. China
100 □3a Kwajalein atoll Marshall Is
100 □3a Kwajalein i. Marshall Is
100 □3a Kwajalein Lagoon Kwajalein Marshall Is
275 H3 Kwakoegron Suriname
275 G3 Kwakwani Guyana
237 L3 Kwakwatsi S. Africa
116 C3 Kwala Sumatera Indon.
233 C6 Kwale Kenya
229 G5 Kwale Nigeria
237 O5 KwaMashu S. Africa
237 Q4 KwaMbonambi S. Africa
228 E5 Kwame Danso Ghana
237 M1 KwaMhlanga S. Africa
231 C5 Kwamouth Dem. Rep. Congo
233 B6 Kwa Mtoro Tanz.
115 C3 Kwandang Sulawesi Indon.
231 E6 Kwanga Dem. Rep. Congo
Kwangchow Guangdong China see Guangzhou
123 E11 Kwangju S. Korea
230 C6 Kwango prov. Dem. Rep. Congo
231 C6 Kwango r. Dem. Rep. Congo alt. Cuango (Angola)
Kwangsi Chuang Autonomous Region aut. reg. China see Guangxi Zhuangzu Zizhiqu
Kwangtung prov. China see Guangdong
233 C6 Kwangwazi Tanz.
232 B4 Kwania, Lake Uganda
123 F8 Kwanmo-bong mt. N. Korea
237 J9 Kwanobuhle S. Africa
237 J8 KwaNojoli S. Africa
237 K9 Kwanonqubela S. Africa
237 I7 KwaNonzame S. Africa
Kwanza r. Angola see Cuanza
237 L8 Kwa-Pita S. Africa
229 F4 Kwara state Nigeria
229 G3 Kwatarkwashi Nigeria
237 O2 KwaThandeka S. Africa
237 K8 Kwatinidubu S. Africa
237 N2 KwaZamokuhle S. Africa
236 I8 KwaZamukucinga S. Africa
237 I7 Kwazamuxolo S. Africa
237 N2 KwaZanele S. Africa
237 O4 KwaZulu-Natal prov. S. Africa
Kweichow prov. China see Guizhou
Kweiyang Guizhou China see Guiyang
235 F3 Kwekwe Zimbabwe
237 O1 Kwena Dam S. Africa
234 E4 Kweneng admin. dist. Botswana
231 C6 Kwenge r. Dem. Rep. Congo
248 D3 Kwetabohigan r. Ont. Can.
244 G3 Kwethluk AK U.S.A.
244 G3 Kwethluk r. AK U.S.A.
237 L6 Kwezi-Naledi S. Africa
229 G4 Kwiambana Nigeria
196 G2 Kwidzyn Pol.
244 G4 Kwigillingok AK U.S.A.
244 F3 Kwiguk AK U.S.A.
146 D9 Kwīhā Eth.
113 K8 Kwikila P.N.G.
196 E3 Kwilcz Pol.
231 C5 Kwilu r. Angola/Dem. Rep. Congo
231 C6 Kwilu prov. Dem. Rep. Congo
109 C12 Kwinana W.A. Austr.
196 D4 Kwisa r. Pol.
275 G4 Kwitaro r. Guyana
131 □J7 Kwo Chau Kwan To is H.K. China
113 H7 Kwoka mt. Papua Indon.
230 E3 Kwoungo, Mont mt. C.A.R.
131 □J7 Kwun Tong H.K. China
230 C2 Kyabé Chad
118 B3 Kyabin Myanmar
107 I9 Kyabra Qld Austr.
107 I8 Kyabra watercourse Qld Austr.
105 J7 Kyabram Vic. Austr.
118 B4 Kyadet Myanmar
118 B6 Kyaiklat Myanmar
118 C6 Kyaikto Myanmar
118 D6 Kya-in Seikkyi Myanmar
128 J1 Kyakhta Rus. Fed.
105 I6 Kyalite N.S.W. Austr.
104 E5 Kyancutta S.A. Austr.
156 G2 Kyanda Rus. Fed.
118 B5 Kyangin Irrawaddy Myanmar
118 C5 Kyangin Mandalay Myanmar
133 L11 Kyangngoin Xizang China
118 C5 Kyaukhnyat Myanmar
118 C5 Kyaukkyi Myanmar
118 C3 Kyaukmaw Myanmar
118 C3 Kyaukme Myanmar
118 B3 Kyaukmyaung Myanmar
118 B4 Kyaukpadaung Myanmar
118 A5 Kyaukpyu Myanmar
118 C4 Kyaukse Myanmar
118 C6 Kyauktan Myanmar
118 A4 Kyauktaw Myanmar
118 B4 Kyaukyit Myanmar
118 B6 Kyaunggon Myanmar
160 F7 Kybartai Lith.
105 L7 Kybeyan Range mts N.S.W. Austr.
104 H7 Kybybolite S.A. Austr.
118 H3 Ky Cung, Sông r. Vietnam
103 E12 Kyeburn South I. N.Z.
118 D6 Kyeikdon Myanmar
118 B6 Kyeintali Myanmar
233 B7 Kyela Tanz.
138 F3 Kyelang Hima. Prad. India
232 A4 Kyenjojo Uganda
228 E5 Kyeraa Ghana
118 C5 Kyidaunggan Myanmar
128 G8 Kyikug Qinghai China
229 E4 Kyinderi Ghana
158 J3 Kyiv Ukr.
158 J3 Kyivs'ka Oblast' admin. div. Ukr.
198 G2 Kyjov Czech Rep.
220 G5 Kyklades dept Greece
148 B5 Kyklades is Greece
247 I5 Kyle Sask. Can.
171 O5 Kyle r. England U.K.
168 E8 Kyleakin Highland, Scotland U.K.
168 E8 Kyle of Lochalsh Highland, Scotland U.K.
168 H6 Kyle of Tongue inlet Scotland U.K.
168 E8 Kylerhea Highland, Scotland U.K.
168 F11 Kyles of Bute sea chan. Scotland U.K.
168 C7 Kyles Scalpay Western Isles, Scotland U.K.
168 F6 Kylestrome Highland, Scotland U.K.
191 C11 Kyll r. Ger.
191 C10 Kyllburg Ger.
220 C5 Kyllini Greece
220 D5 Kyllini mt. Greece
220 C5 Kyllinis, Akrotirio pt Greece
163 Q6 Kylmäkoski Fin.
220 F4 Kymi Greece
160 J1 Kymijoki r. Fin.
220 F4 Kymis, Akrotirio pt Greece
164 I2 Kymmen l. Sweden
105 J7 Kyneton Vic. Austr.
164 I1 Kynna r. Norway
198 B1 Kynšperk nad Ohří Czech Rep.
107 H6 Kynuna Qld Austr.
124 □1 Kyoda Okinawa Japan
232 B4 Kyoga, Lake Uganda
126 E3 Kyōga-dake mt. Japan
127 G4 Kyōga-dake mt. Japan
126 B4 Kyōga-misaki pt Japan
105 N3 Kyogle N.S.W. Austr.
230 F2 Kyom watercourse Sudan
127 K5 Kyonan Japan
118 D6 Kyondo Myanmar
107 J6 Kyong Qld Austr.
118 C4 Kyong Myanmar
123 D10 Kyŏnggi-man b. S. Korea
123 F11 Kyŏngju S. Korea
123 F11 Kyongju National Park S. Korea
118 B6 Kyonpyaw Myanmar
126 C6 Kyōtanabe Japan
126 C6 Kyōto Japan
126 B5 Kyōto pref. Japan
124 R7 Kyōwa Akita Japan
127 L3 Kyōwa Ibaraki Japan
220 C5 Kyparissia Greece
220 C5 Kyparissiakos Kolpos b. Greece
Kypros country Asia see Cyprus
143 M2 Kypshak, Ozero salt l. Kazakh.
129 M2 Kyra Rus. Fed.
220 F3 Kyra Panagia i. Greece
Kyrenia Cyprus see Keryneia
Kyrenia Mountains Cyprus see Pentadaktylos Range
220 F1 Kyrgia Greece
143 P7 Kyrgyzstan country Asia
158 I8 Kyrhyzh-Kytay r. Ukr.
220 D4 Kyriaki Greece
192 F5 Kyritz Ger.
192 G4 Kyritz-Ruppiner Heide park Ger.
164 C2 Kyrkjenuten mt. Norway
142 D3 Kyrkopa Kazakh.
162 J5 Kyrksæterøra Norway
158 H5 Kyrnasivka Ukr.
158 I8 Kyrnychky Ukr.
156 L2 Kyrta Rus. Fed.
156 L4 Kyr'ya Rus. Fed.
159 O3 Kyrykivka Ukr.
159 O7 Kyrylivka Ukr.
159 P4 Kyseli Ukr.
158 E5 Kyseliv Ukr.
159 K2 Kyselivka Ukr.
158 G2 Kyshyy Ukr.
156 I2 Kyssa Rus. Fed.
199 I2 Kysuce park Slovakia
199 H2 Kysucké Nové Mesto Slovakia
153 O3 Kytalyktakh Rus. Fed.
158 I8 Kytay, Ozero l. Ukr.
159 N5 Kytayhorod Ukr.
220 D6 Kythira Kythira Greece
220 D6 Kythira i. Greece
220 F5 Kythnos i. Greece
220 F5 Kythnou, Steno sea chan. Greece
150 B3 Kythrea Cyprus
156 L4 Kytlym Rus. Fed.
Kyumyush-Tak, Pik mt. Kyrg. see Kumyshtag, Pik
133 E11 Kyunglung Xizang China
118 D7 Kyungyaung Myanmar
118 B3 Kyunhla Myanmar
246 E5 Kyuquot B.C. Can.
Kyurdamir Azer. see Kürdämir
125 I15 Kyūshū i. Japan
290 E4 Kyushu-Palau Ridge sea feature N. Pacific Ocean
125 I14 Kyūshū-sanchi mts Japan
219 K8 Kyustendil Bulg.
118 C5 Kywebwe Myanmar
105 K6 Kywong N.S.W. Austr.
Kyyev Ukr. see Kyiv
Kyyiv Ukr. see Kyiv
158 J3 Kyyivs'ke Vodoskhovyshche resr Ukr.
162 R5 Kyyjärvi Fin.
163 S6 Kyyvesi l. Fin.
142 E5 Kyzan Kazakh.
151 E2 Kyzburun Tretiy Rus. Fed.
Kyzyl Moldova see Ștefan Vodă
120 F1 Kyzyl Rus. Fed.
143 N6 Kyzyl-Adyr Kyrg.
143 R5 Kyzylagash Kazakh.
Kyzyl-Art, Pereval pass Kyrg./Tajik. see Kyzylart Pass
145 O2 Kyzylart Pass Kyrg./Tajik.
143 O5 Kyzylbelen, Gora hill Kazakh.
Kyzyl-Burun Azer. see Siyäzän
143 M3 Kyzyldikan Kazakh.
143 T4 Kyzylkesek Kazakh.
Kyzylkesken Kazakh. see Kyzylkesek
128 A1 Kyzyl-Khaya Rus. Fed.
Kyzyl-Kiya Kyrg. see Kyzyl-Kyya
142 E3 Kyzylkoga Kazakh.
142 I3 Kyzylkol', Ozero l. Kazakh.
Kyzylkum, Peski des. Kazakh./Uzbek. see Kyzylkum Desert
142 K6 Kyzylkum Desert Kazakh./Uzbek.
143 O7 Kyzyl-Kyya Kyrg.
120 F1 Kyzyl-Mazhalyk Rus. Fed.
142 K5 Kyzylorda Kazakh.
Kyzyl-Orda Oblast admin. div. Kazakh. see Kyzylordinskaya Oblast'
142 J5 Kyzylordinskaya Oblast' admin. div. Kazakh.
142 K5 Kyzylordinskoye Vodokhranilishche resr Kazakh.
Kyzylrabot Tajik. see Qizilrabot
142 E6 Kyzylsay Kazakh.
143 Q6 Kyzyl-Suu Kyrg.
143 N8 Kyzyl-Suu r. Kyrg.
143 P2 Kyzyltas Kazakh.
143 O4 Kyzyltau Kazakh.
142 K3 Kyzyluy Kazakh.
142 D5 Kyzylysor Kazakh.
142 F2 Kyzylzhar Kazakh.
143 M3 Kyzylzhar Kazakh.
Kzyl-Dzhar Kazakh. see Kyzylzhar
Kzyl-Orda Kazakh. see Kyzylorda
Kzyltu Kazakh. see Kishkenekol'
151 L1 Kzyl-Uzen Kazakh.

L

201 N2 Laa an der Thaya Austria
195 L3 Laaber Ger.
191 D10 Laacher See l. Ger.
285 E6 La Adela Arg.
192 F3 Laage Ger.
160 H2 Laagri Estonia
266 D6 La Aguja Mex.
204 H7 La Alberca Castilla y Leó
205 P9 La Alberca de Záncara S
204 G8 La Alberguería de Argañ
206 F3 La Albuera Spain
205 O7 La Alcarria reg. Spain
205 J8 La Aldehuela Spain
206 G6 La Algaba Spain
205 J8 La Aliseda de Tormes Sp
209 C12 La Aljorra Spain
205 P9 La Almarcha Spain
208 E4 La Almolda Spain
207 P4 La Almudema Spain
205 R6 La Almunia de Doña Go Spain
284 E6 La Amarga, Laguna l. Ar
266 □R13 La Amistad, Parque Internacional nat. park Costa Rica/Panama
238 □3b La Ampuyenta Fuerteven Canary Is
267 M10 La Angostura, Presa de
156 D1 Laanila Fin.
160 K3 Lääniste Estonia
232 F2 Laanle well Somalia
284 D1 La Antigua, Salina salt p
206 E6 La Antilla Spain
268 E3 La Ardilla, Cerro mt. Me
285 I5 La Argentina, Laguna l.
201 I4 Laarkirchen Austria
204 J6 La Armuña reg. Spain
187 E6 Laarne Belgium
232 F3 Laas Aano Somalia
232 E2 Laascaanood Somalia
232 F2 Laas Dawaco Somalia
232 F2 Laasgoray Somalia
192 E4 Laaslich Ger.
284 E5 La Asturiana Arg.
275 F2 La Asunción Venez.
204 F9 La Atalaya de Santiago
191 I6 Laatzen Ger.
264 □D12 La'au Point HI U.S.A.
212 G2 Laax Switz.
226 B4 Laâyoune Western Sahar
209 C12 La Azohía Spain
151 B2 Laba r. Rus. Fed.
266 H3 La Babia Mex.
181 J5 La Baconnière France
249 G3 La Baie Que. Can.
205 K7 Labajos Spain
115 C8 Labala Indon.
182 I5 La Balme-de-Sillingy Fr
282 D2 La Banda Arg.
268 B1 La Bandera, Cerro mt. M
204 I4 La Bañeza Spain
117 J3 Labang Sarawak Malaysi
160 I6 Labanoras Lith.
Labao Guangxi China see
268 E5 La Barca Mex.
262 I5 La Barge WY U.S.A.
180 G8 La Barre-de-Monts Fran
181 M4 La Barre-en-Ouche Fran
185 E9 La Barthe-de-Neste Fra
185 F9 Labarthe-Rivière France
101 □7 Labasa Vanua Levu Fiji
178 E2 La Bassée France
185 B9 La Bastide-Clairence Fr
185 H9 Labastide-d'Anjou Franc
185 D8 Labastide-d'Armagnac F
185 H9 La Bastide-de Bousigna
185 G9 La Bastide-de-Sérou Fra
183 H9 La Bastide-des-Jourdans
185 I7 La Bastide-l'Évêque Fra
185 H6 Labastide-Murat France
183 D7 La Bastide-Puylaurent F
183 B10 Labastide-Rouairoux Fra
185 G8 Labastide-St-Pierre Fran
185 H10 La Bastide-sur-l'Hers Fr
182 I5 La Bâthie France
183 I7 La Bâtie-Neuve France
239 □3b Labattoir Mayotte
185 C8 Labatut France
185 E8 Labatut-Rivière France
180 G7 La Baule-Escoublac Fran
153 K2 Labaz, Ozero l. Rus. Fed.
156 K2 Labazhskoye Rus. Fed.
181 M5 La Bazoche-Gouet Franc
181 L5 La Bazoge France
212 A2 L'Abbaye Switz.
198 D1 Labe r. Czech Rep. alt. Elbe (Germany)
228 B4 Labé Guinea
183 F7 La Bégude-de-Mazenc F
185 E8 Labéjan France
248 F4 Labelle Que. Can.
255 G12 La Belle FL U.S.A.
115 C5 Labengke i. Indon.
185 B8 Labenne France
183 I7 La Bérarde France
245 N3 Laberge, Lake Y.T. Can.
182 G2 Labergement-lès-Seurre
285 F6 Laberinto, Punta pt Arg.
183 J9 La Bernarde mt. France
180 G7 La Bernerie-en-Retz Fra
212 C2 La Berra mt. Switz.
195 M4 Laberweinting Ger.
212 E5 La Bessa, Riserva Natura nature res. Italy
117 K2 Labi Brunei
205 R3 Labia, Sierra de mts Spai
117 M2 Labian, Tanjung pt Mala
246 F3 La Biche r. N.W.T. Can.
247 H4 La Biche, Lac l. Alta Can.
210 E3 Labin Croatia
151 B1 Labinsk Rus. Fed.
182 H5 La Biolle France
116 E3 Labis Malaysia
208 G5 La Bisbal de Falset Spain
208 H5 La Bisbal del Penedès Sp
208 L4 La Bisbal d'Empordà Sp
196 F3 Łabiszyn Pol.
266 D3 La Biznaga Mex.
183 E8 Lablachère France
285 G2 La Blanca, Laguna l. Arg
285 F6 La Blanca Grande Lagun
114 D4 Labo Luzon Phil.
115 C4 Labobo i. Indon.
151 E3 Laboda, Gora mt. Georgia/Rus. Fed.
205 O6 La Bodera mt. Spain
190 J2 Laboe Ger.
269 H2 La Bolsa Mex.
285 I2 La Bolsa Uru.
178 B6 La Bonneville-sur-Iton F
266 G4 La Boquilla Mex.
234 C4 Labora Namibia
285 F3 Laborde Arg.
199 K3 Laborec r. Slovakia
271 □3 Laborie St Lucia
109 E8 Labouchere, Mount hill W Austr.
150 E4 Laboué Lebanon
180 I5 La Bouëxière France
285 I2 Labougle Arg.
185 C7 Labouheyre France
183 H10 La Bouilladisse France
285 F4 Laboulaye Arg.
182 B5 La Bourboule France
185 A9 Labourd reg. France
180 H4 La Boussac France
185 I8 Laboutarie France
205 J6 La Bóveda de Toro Spain
197 I6 Łabowa Pol.
249 I2 Labrador reg. Nfld and La
249 H2 Labrador City Nfld and L
243 M3 Labrador Sea Can./Green
Labrang Gansu China see
274 C3 Labranzagrande Col.
285 G2 La Brava Arg.
285 F3 La Brava, Laguna l. Arg.
276 D1 Lábrea Brazil
274 A6 La Brea Peru
271 □7 La Brea Trin. and Tob.
185 C6 La Brède France
183 I8 La Bréole France
179 M7 La Bresse France
182 H5 La Bridoire France
185 C7 Labrit France
179 N7 La Broque France
180 I7 La Bruffière France

Labruguière France
Labrujeira Port.
L'Absie France
Labuan Malaysia
Labuan i. Malaysia
Labuan state Malaysia
Labuanbajo Sulawesi Indon.
Labudalin Nei Mongol China see Ergun
La Bufa, Cerro mt. Mex.
Labuhan Jawa Indon.
Labuhanbajo Flores Indon.
Labuhanbilik Sumatera Indon.
Labuhanhaji Sumatera Indon.
Labuhanmeringgai Sumatera Indon.
Labuhanruku Sumatera Indon.
La Buisse France
Labuk r. Malaysia
Labuk, Teluk b. Malaysia
Labuna Maluku Indon.
Łabunie Pol.
La Bureba reg. Spain
La Bussière France
Labutta Myanmar
Läby Sweden
Labyrinth, Lake salt flat S.A. Austr.
Labyrinth Lake N.W.T. Can.
Labytnangi Rus. Fed.
Laç Albania
Lac pref. Chad
La Cabaneta Spain
La Cabral Arg.
La Cabrera Spain
La Cadena Mex.
La Cadière-d'Azur France
La Caillère-St-Hilaire France
Lacalahorra Spain
La Calandria Arg.
La Calderina mt. Spain
La Calera Arg.
La Calera La Gomera Canary Is
La Calera Chile
La Caleta Lanzarote Canary Is
La Caletta Sardegna Italy
Lac-Allard Que. Can.
La Calle Alg. see El Kala
Lacalm France
La Calmette France
La Calzada de Oropesa Spain
La Campa Spain
La Campana Spain
La Campana, Parque Nacional nat. park Chile
La Cañada de San Urbano Spain
La Cañada de Verich Spain
Lacanau France
Lacanau, Étang de l. France
Lacanau-Océan France
Lacanche France
Lacandón, Parque Nacional nat. park Guat.
La Cañiza Spain see A Cañiza
La Canourgue France
Lacantún r. Mex.
La Capelle France
Lacapelle-Barrès France
Lacapelle-Marival France
Lacapelle-Viescamp France
La Capila Arg.
Lácara r. Spain
Laćarak Vojvodina Serbia
La Caridad Spain
La Carlota Arg.
La Carlota Negros Phil.
La Carlota Spain
La Carolina Spain
Lacarre France
Lacaune France
Lacaune, Monts de mts France
La Cavada Spain
La Cavalerie France
Lacave France
Lacaze France
Lac-Baker N.B. Can.
Laccadive, Minicoy and Amindivi Islands union terr. India see Lakshadweep
Laccadive Islands India
Lacco Ameno Italy
Lac du Bonnet Man. Can.
Lac du Flambeau WI U.S.A.
Laceby North East Lincolnshire, England U.K.
Lacedaemon Greece see Sparti
Lacedonia Italy
La Ceiba Hond.
La Cellera de Ter Spain
La Celle-St-Avant France
La Celle-St-Cloud France
La Cenia Spain see La Sènia
Lacepede Bay S.A. Austr.
Lacepede Islands W.A. Austr.
La Cerca Spain
La Cerdaña reg. Spain see Cerdanya
La Cerollera Spain
Laces Italy
La Cesira Arg.
Lac-Etchemin Que. Can.
Laceyville PA U.S.A.
Lac-Frontière Que. Can.
Lacha, Ozero l. Rus. Fed.
La Chaise-Dieu France
La Chaize-le-Vicomte France
La Chambre France
La Chapelaude France
La Chapelle France
La Chapelle-Aubareil France
La Chapelle-aux-Bois France
La Chapelle-aux-Saints France
La Chapelle-d'Abondance France
La Chapelle-d'Aligné France
La Chapelle-d'Andaine France
La Chapelle-d'Angillon France
La Chapelle-des-Fougeretz France
La-Chapelle-des-Marais France
La Chapelle-en-Valgaudémar France
La Chapelle-en-Vercors France
La Chapelle-la-Reine France
La Chapelle-Laurent France
La Chapelle-St-André France
La Chapelle-St-Laurent France
La Chapelle-St-Luc France
La Chapelle-St-Mesmin France
La Chapelle-St-Quillain France
La Chapelle-St-Ursin France
Lachapelle-sous-Aubenas France
La Chapelle-sur-Erdre France
La Charité-sur-Loire France
La Chartre-sur-le-Loir France
La Châtaigneraie France
La Châtre France
La Châtre-Langlin France
La Chaume France
Lachaussée, Étang de l. France
La Chaussée-St-Victor France
La Chaussée-sur-Marne France
La Chaux-de-Fonds Switz.
La Chaux-du-Dombief France
Lachen Sikkim India
Lachen Switz.
Lachendorf Ger.
Lachens, Montagne de mt. France
Lachen-Speyerdorf Ger.
La Cheppe France
La Chevrolière France
La Chèze France
Lachine MI U.S.A.
Lachinovo Rus. Fed.
Lachlan r. N.S.W. Austr.
La Chorrera Col.
La Chorrera Panama
Lachowo Pol.
Lachte r. Ger.
Lachung Sikkim India
Lachute Que. Can.
La Cierva Spain
Laçın Azer.
La Ciotat France
205 K5 La Cisterniga Spain
268 B2 La Ciudad Mex.
249 I2 Lac Joseph-Atikonak Wilderness Reserve Nfld and Lab. Can.
197 H3 Łąck Pol.
170 B4 Lack Northern Ireland U.K.
165 N3 Lacka naturreservat nature res. Sweden
256 G6 Lackawanna NY U.S.A.
258 D2 Lackawanna r. PA U.S.A.
258 D2 Lackawanna County county PA U.S.A.
258 F2 Lackawaxen r. PA U.S.A.
197 I6 Łącko Pol.
247 I4 Lac La Biche Alta Can.
Lac la Martre Can. see Whatî
247 J4 Lac La Ronge Provincial Park Sask. Can.
182 E4 La Clayette France
230 B4 Lac Lobeke, Réserve du res. Cameroon
182 I5 La Clusaz France
183 H7 La Cluse France
182 I3 La Cluse-et-Mijoux France
249 G4 Lac-Mégantic Que. Can.
282 D2 La Cocha Arg.
172 H5 Lacock Wiltshire, England U.K.
206 E2 La Codosera Spain
208 G5 La Cogulla mt. Spain
285 G5 La Colina Arg.
205 J3 La Collada pass Spain
257 L3 Lacolle Que. Can.
183 K9 La Colle-sur-Loup France
269 H3 La Colmena, Sierra mts Mex.
266 D3 La Colorada Sonora Mex.
268 E2 La Colorada Zacatecas Mex.
246 H4 Lacombe Alta Can.
250 E8 Lacon IL U.S.A.
269 I2 La Concepción Mex.
266 □R13 La Concepción Panama
205 M2 La Concha Spain
267 M9 La Concordia Mex.
183 J8 La Condamine-Châtelard France
214 C8 Laconi Sardegna Italy
257 N5 Laconia NH U.S.A.
284 C3 La Consulta Arg.
285 G5 La Copeta Arg.
183 C9 La Coquillade hill France
184 F4 La Coquille France
247 I4 La Corey Alta Can.
251 Q1 La Corne Que. Can.
207 I4 La Coronada Andalucía Spain
206 H3 La Coronada Extremadura Spain
La Coruña Spain see A Coruña
La Coruña prov. Spain see A Coruña
183 G9 Lacoste France
183 G6 La Côte-St-André France
184 B3 La-Couarde-sur-Mer France
184 E4 La Couronne France
185 G10 Lacourt France
184 I4 La Courtine France
178 B6 La Couture-Boussey France
183 C9 La Couvertoirade France
270 □ Lacovia Jamaica
185 C9 Lacq France
183 I10 La Crau France
184 D3 La Crèche France
271 □8 Lacre Punt pt Bonaire Neth. Antilles
250 C6 La Crescent MN U.S.A.
246 G3 La Crete Alta Can.
208 G6 La Creu de Santos hill Spain
285 H2 La Criolla Entre Ríos Arg.
285 G2 La Criolla Santa Fé Arg.
250 C1 La Croix, Lac l. Can./U.S.A.
183 B7 Lacroix-Barrez France
181 I5 La Croixille France
178 E5 Lacroix-St-Ouen France
183 J10 La Croix-Valmer France
260 F6 La Crosse KS U.S.A.
256 G12 La Crosse VA U.S.A.
250 C6 La Crosse WI U.S.A.
185 I8 Lacrouzette France
284 E3 La Cruz Córdoba Arg.
282 F3 La Cruz Corrientes Arg.
274 B4 La Cruz Col.
266 □Q12 La Cruz Costa Rica
266 G4 La Cruz Chihuahua Mex.
266 F6 La Cruz Sinaloa Mex.
269 H1 La Cruz Tamaulipas Mex.
269 J2 La Cruz Tamaulipas Mex.
266 □Q11 La Cruz Nic.
285 I3 La Cruz Uru.
268 F8 La Cruz, Cerro mt. Mex.
268 B6 La Cruz de Loreto Mex.
266 H3 La Cuesta Coahuila Mex.
268 C5 La Cuesta Jalisco Mex.
284 E2 La Cumbre Arg.
206 H2 La Cumbre Spain
Lacunza Spain see Lakuntza
263 K11 La Curva Mex.
260 H6 La Cygne KS U.S.A.
197 J4 Łączany Pol.
197 I5 Łączna Pol.
196 F5 Łącznik Pol.
197 K5 Łada r. Pol.
116 F8 Lada, Teluk b. Indon.
281 G2 Ladainha Brazil
138 F2 Ladakh reg. India/Pak.
138 F2 Ladakh Range mts India
159 L3 Ladan Ukr.
116 C1 Ladang, Ko i. Thai.
199 I4 Ladánybene Hungary
191 E6 Ladbergen Ger.
199 H2 Ladce Slovakia
250 E8 Ladd IL U.S.A.
196 F3 Lądek Pol.
196 E5 Lądek-Zdrój Pol.
190 H1 Ladelund Ger.
270 B3 La Demajagua Cuba
267 N10 La Democracia Guat.
194 F3 Ladenburg Ger.
271 □2 La Désirade i. Guadeloupe
168 E8 Ladhar Bheinn mt. Scotland U.K.
184 G4 Ladignac-le-Long France
239 □2a La Digue i. Inner Islands Seychelles
148 G3 Ladik Turkey
201 K6 Ladinger Spitz mt. Austria
185 J6 Ladinhac France
236 F9 Ladismith S. Africa
214 I4 Ladispoli Italy
284 B3 La Disputada Chile
145 I7 Lādīz Iran
138 E6 Ladnun Rajasthan India
204 F9 Ladoeiro Port.
Ladoga, Lake Rus. Fed. see Ladozhskoye Ozero
212 A3 La Dôle mt. Switz.
178 E7 Ladon France
220 C5 Ladonas r. Greece
130 G6 Ladong Guangxi China
284 D3 La Dormida Arg.
161 O1 Ladozhskoye Ozero l. Rus. Fed.
204 E2 Ladra r. Spain
283 A8 Ladrillero, Canal sea chan. Chile
Ladrones terr. N. Pacific Ocean see Northern Mariana Islands
266 □R14 Ladrones, Islas is Panama
139 N6 Ladu mt. Arun. Prad. India
245 L3 Ladue r. Can./U.S.A.
284 D6 La Dulce, Laguna l. Arg.
266 E3 La Dura Mex.
160 D7 Ladushkin Rus. Fed.
156 F3 Ladva Rus. Fed.
156 F3 Ladva-Vetka Rus. Fed.
138 F5 Ladwa Haryana India
243 J2 Lady Ann Strait Nunavut Can.
168 J10 Ladybank Fife, Scotland U.K.
105 L9 Lady Barron Tas. Austr.
171 N7 Ladybower Reservoir England U.K.
237 L5 Ladybrand S. Africa
251 N2 Lady Evelyn Lake Ont. Can.
237 L7 Lady Frere S. Africa
237 L6 Lady Grey S. Africa
158 G4 Ladyhy Ukr.
170 H2 Lady Isle i. Scotland U.K.
168 L11 Ladykirk Scottish Borders, Scotland U.K.
287 L2 Lady Newnes Bay Antarctica
168 L7 Ladysford Aberdeenshire, Scotland U.K.
246 F5 Ladysmith B.C. Can.
237 N4 Ladysmith S. Africa
250 C4 Ladysmith WI U.S.A.
158 I5 Ladyzhyn Ukr.
158 J5 Ladyzhynka Ukr.
Ladzhanurges Georgia see Lajanurpekhi
197 H4 Ładzice Pol.
192 K3 Ładzin Pol.
113 K8 Lae P.N.G.
285 G3 La Emilia Arg.
119 F8 Laem Ngop Thai.
165 L5 Läen l. Sweden
269 H5 La Encarnación Mex.
209 D10 La Encina Spain
274 E2 La Encrucijada Venez.
191 D6 Laer Ger.
205 J3 La Ercina Spain
163 I6 Lærdalsøyri Norway
214 B6 Laerru Sardegna Italy
La Escala Spain see L'Escala
268 E1 La Escalera Mex.
269 H1 La Escondida Mex.
285 H2 La Esmeralda Entre Ríos Arg.
282 D3 La Esmeralda Santiago del Estero Arg.
277 E5 La Esmeralda Bol.
275 E4 La Esmeralda Venez.
164 H4 Læsø i. Denmark
164 G4 Læsø Rende sea chan. Denmark
284 D5 La Esperanza Arg.
276 D3 La Esperanza Beni Bol.
277 E3 La Esperanza Santa Cruz Bol.
238 □3a La Esperanza Tenerife Canary Is
266 □O10 La Esperanza Hond.
204 H2 La Espina Spain
284 E3 La Esquina Arg.
269 H5 La Estancia, Cerro mt. Mex.
284 D5 La Estrella Arg.
276 E4 La Estrella Bol.
284 B4 La Estrella Chile
205 J9 La Estrella Spain
160 J3 Laeva Estonia
183 C6 La Fageolle, Col de pass France
284 E2 La Falda Arg.
183 G9 La Fare-les-Oliviers France
250 D6 La Farge WI U.S.A.
257 J4 La Fargeville NY U.S.A.
183 I10 La Farlède France
232 E2 Lafaruug Somalia
208 F5 La Fatarrella Spain
183 H7 La Faurie France
184 B3 La Faute-sur-Mer France
Lafayette Alg. see Bougaa
255 E9 La Fayette AL U.S.A.
264 J4 Lafayette CA U.S.A.
262 L7 Lafayette CO U.S.A.
255 E8 La Fayette GA U.S.A.
254 D5 Lafayette IN U.S.A.
261 I10 Lafayette LA U.S.A.
258 F2 Lafayette NJ U.S.A.
256 B9 Lafayette OH U.S.A.
255 D7 Lafayette TN U.S.A.
239 □1b Lafayette, Pointe pt Mauritius
270 A2 Lafé Cuba
269 I1 La Fe del Golfo Mex.
207 P2 La Felipa Spain
178 F4 La Fère France
239 □1a La Ferme Rodrigues I. Mauritius
180 I8 La Ferrière France
181 J4 La Ferrière-aux-Étangs France
251 P1 Laferté Que. Can.
246 G2 Laferte r. N.W.T. Can.
178 D7 La Ferté-Alais France
181 M5 La Ferté-Bernard France
181 M4 La Ferté-Frênel France
178 F6 La Ferté-Gaucher France
181 O7 La Ferté-Imbault France
178 F8 La Ferté-Loupièrre France
181 K4 La Ferté-Macé France
178 F5 La-Ferté-Milon France
178 C8 La Ferté-St-Aubin France
178 C8 La Ferté-St-Cyr France
178 F6 La Ferté-sous-Jouarre France
179 K8 Laferté-sur-Amance France
179 I7 Laferté-sur-Aube France
181 M4 La Férte-Vidame France
178 B8 La Ferté-Villeneuil France
147 J3 Laffān, Ra's pt Qatar
229 H4 Lafia Nigeria
229 G4 Lafiagi Nigeria
185 E9 Lafitole France
248 E3 Laflamme r. Que. Can.
247 J5 Lafleche Sask. Can.
181 K6 La Flèche France
269 H4 La Florida Mex.
184 B3 La Flotte France
201 N5 Lafnitz Austria
201 N6 Lafnitz r. Austria
100 □5 La Foa New Caledonia
256 A12 La Follette TN U.S.A.
239 □1c La Fontaine Réunion
250 I9 La Fontaine IN U.S.A.
181 L6 La Fontaine-St-Martin France
209 D10 La Font de la Figuera Spain
251 P2 Laforce Que. Can.
185 E6 La Force France
251 M2 Laforest Ont. Can.
249 G2 La Forest, Lac l. Que. Can.
180 D6 La Forêt-Fouesnant France
181 J8 La Forêt-sur-Sèvre France
249 F2 Laforge Que. Can.
249 F2 Laforge r. Que. Can.
179 M7 La Forge France
208 F2 Lafortunada Spain
La Fouce, Pointe pt Rodrigues I. Mauritius see La Fouche, Pointe
239 □1a La Fouche, Pointe pt Rodrigues I. Mauritius
185 I7 La Fouillade France
182 E5 La Fouillouse France
261 J11 Lafourche, Bayou r. LA U.S.A.
183 J8 La Foux-d'Allos France
185 G7 Lafrançaise France
178 I4 La Francheville France
285 F2 La Francia Arg.
204 G7 La Fregeneda Spain
181 L5 La Fresnaye-sur-Chédouat France
179 N6 Lafrimbolle France
205 P8 La Frontera Spain
144 F8 Lāft Iran
207 P5 La Fuensanta Murcia Spain
204 H7 La Fuente de San Esteban Spain
137 M9 Laful Andaman & Nicobar Is India
208 H4 La Fuliola Spain
180 G6 La Gacilly France
208 F6 La Galera Spain
227 H1 La Galite i. Tunisia
282 E3 La Gallareta Arg.
266 G5 La Gallega Mex.
280 D3 Lagamar Brazil
142 B5 Lagan' Rus. Fed.
165 I5 Lagan r. Sweden
169 K3 Lagan r. Northern Ireland U.K.
220 B5 Lagana, Kolpos b. Zakynthos Greece
229 I3 Lagané well Niger
183 I10 La Garde France
183 F8 La Garde-Adhémar France
183 I10 La Garde-Freinet France
185 G9 Lagardelle-sur-Lèze France
204 F5 Lagarelhos Port.
204 E8 Lagares da Beira Port.
207 K4 La Garganta Spain
269 I4 La Garita Mex.
180 H8 La Garnache France
208 J4 La Garriga Spain
185 I8 Lagarrigue France
206 G3 La Garrovilla Spain
205 J9 Lagartera Spain
278 F4 Lagarto Brazil
280 A5 Lagarto, Serra do hills Brazil
181 I8 La Gaubretière France
170 E3 Lagavara Northern Ireland U.K.
228 B3 Lagbar Senegal
229 I4 Lagdo, Lac de l. Cameroon
191 C6 Lage Niedersachsen Ger.
191 G7 Lage Nordrhein-Westfalen Ger.
187 H6 Lage Mierde Neth.
164 E1 Lågen r. Norway
164 G2 Lågen r. Norway
190 I3 Lägerdorf Ger.
186 H4 Lage Vaart canal Neth.
168 F12 Lagg North Ayrshire, Scotland U.K.
168 G8 Laggan Highland, Scotland U.K.
168 H8 Laggan Highland, Scotland U.K.
168 G9 Laggan, Loch l. Scotland U.K.
170 E2 Laggan Bay Scotland U.K.
168 D10 Lagganulva Argyll and Bute, Scotland U.K.
169 F3 Laghey Ireland
145 N4 Laghmān prov. Afgh.
227 F2 Laghouat Alg.
Laghtgeorge Ireland see Leacht Seoirse
196 E5 Łagiewniki Pol.
284 E3 La Gilda Arg.
207 P2 La Gineta Spain
220 E2 Lagkadas Greece
133 G10 Lagkor Co salt l. China
180 H2 La Glacerie France
274 C2 La Gloria Col.
269 M9 La Gloria Chiapas Mex.
261 F12 La Gloria Nuevo León Mex.
182 G5 Lagnieu France
178 E6 Lagny-sur-Marne France
215 Q9 Lago Italy
Lago prov. Moz. see Niassa
238 □1b Lagoa São Miguel Azores
204 G6 Lagoa Bragança Port.
206 C6 Lagoa Faro Port.
204 G6 Lagoaça Port.
281 E4 Lagoa da Prata Brazil
238 □1b Lagoa do Fogo nature res. São Miguel Azores
281 E4 Lagoa Dourada Brazil
280 D3 Lagoa Formosa Brazil
281 F3 Lagoa Santa Brazil
279 C9 Lagoa Vermelha Brazil
283 B7 Lago Belgrano Arg.
283 C8 Lago Cardiel Arg.
278 D3 Lago da Pedra Brazil
151 H4 Lagodekhi Georgia
151 H4 Lagodekhis Nakrdzali nature res. Georgia
204 G4 Lago del Sanabria, Parque Natural del nature res. Spain
214 I3 Lago di Vico, Riserva Naturale nature res. Italy
209 L8 Lago Menor Spain
238 □3a La Gomera i. Canary Is
267 N10 La Gomera Guat.
215 P7 Lagonegro Italy
117 H3 Lagong i. Indon.
114 D5 Lagonoy Gulf Luzon Phil.
106 G4 Lagoon Creek r. Qld Austr.
Lagoon Island atoll Arch. des Tuamotu Fr. Polynesia see Tematangi
283 C7 Lago Posadas Arg.
185 C9 Lagor France
184 D5 Lagorce Aquitaine France
183 E8 Lagorce Rhône-Alpes France
286 O1 La Gorce Mountains Antarctica
184 B3 Lagord France
208 I5 La Gornal Spain
220 G1 Lagos Greece
268 E4 Lagos r. Mex.
229 F5 Lagos Nigeria
229 F5 Lagos state Nigeria
206 B6 Lagos Port.
233 A6 Lagosa Tanz.
213 M6 Lagosanto Italy
268 F4 Lagos de Moreno Mex.
277 E2 Lago Verde Brazil
283 B8 Lago Viedma Arg.
196 D3 Łagów Lubuskie Pol.
197 J5 Łagów Świętokrzyskie Pol.
193 L6 Łagowski Park Krajobrazowy Pol.
162 □ Lågøya i. Svalbard
205 O3 Lagrán Spain
206 G5 La Granada de Riotinto Spain
208 G5 La Granadella Spain
182 F5 La Grand-Croix France
248 E2 La Grande r. Que. Can.
262 E4 La Grande OR U.S.A.
248 F2 La Grande 3, Réservoir resr Que. Can.
248 F2 La Grande 4, Réservoir resr Que. Can.
183 E8 La Grande-Combe France
249 I3 La Grande Île i. Que. Can.
183 E9 La Grande-Motte France
108 F5 La Grange W.A. Austr.
264 L4 La Grange CA U.S.A.
255 E9 La Grange GA U.S.A.
254 E5 Lagrange IN U.S.A.
254 E6 La Grange KY U.S.A.
257 □Q3 La Grange ME U.S.A.
261 G11 La Grange TX U.S.A.
108 F5 Lagrange Bay W.A. Austr.
259 H1 Lagrangeville NY U.S.A.
208 F5 La Granja d'Escarp Spain
207 I4 La Granjuela Spain
275 F3 La Gran Sabana plat. Venez.
183 B10 Lagrasse France
183 I6 La Grave France
274 D2 La Grita Venez.
249 G4 La Guadeloupe Que. Can.
274 E2 La Guaira Venez.
274 C2 La Guajira dept Col.
238 □3a La Guancha Tenerife Canary Is
206 H3 La Guarda Spain
282 D3 La Guardia Arg.
282 C2 La Guardia Chile
205 N9 La Guardia Castilla-La Mancha Spain
La Guardia Galicia Spain see A Guarda
205 O3 Laguardia Spain
207 L5 La Guardia de Jaén Spain
208 E3 Laguarta Spain
La Gudiña Spain see A Gudiña
184 H5 Laguenne France
185 H7 Laguépie France
180 I6 La Guerche-de-Bretagne France
182 B3 La Guerche-sur-l'Aubois France
180 G8 La Guérinière France
182 E3 La Guiche France
183 B7 Laguiole France
268 B1 La Guitarra Mex.
271 □10 Lagún Curaçao Neth. Antilles
279 C9 Laguna Brazil
263 K9 Laguna NM U.S.A.
275 I5 Laguna, Ilha da i. Brazil
266 D6 Laguna, Picacho de la mt. Mex.
285 F5 Laguna Alsina Arg.
264 O8 Laguna Beach CA U.S.A.
284 B6 Laguna Blanca, Parque Nacional nat. park Arg.
204 I4 Laguna Dalga Spain
265 R9 Laguna Dam AZ/CA U.S.A.
205 K5 Laguna de Duero Spain
284 B5 Laguna de Laja, Parque Nacional nat. park Chile
204 I4 Laguna de Negrillos Spain
266 □R11 Laguna de Perlas Nic.
269 K7 Laguna de Temascal, Parque Natural nature res. Mex.
283 C8 Laguna Grande Arg.
267 N10 Laguna Lachua, Parque Nacional nat. park Guat.
265 P9 Laguna Mountains CA U.S.A.
266 B4 Laguna Ojo de Liebre, Parque Natural de la nature res. Mex.
285 G2 Laguna Paiva Arg.
276 C5 Lagunas Chile
274 C6 Lagunas Peru
283 B7 Laguna San Rafael, Parque Nacional nat. park Chile
269 L7 Lagunas de Catemaco, Parque Natural nature res. Mex.
269 J10 Lagunas de Chacahua, Parque Nacional nat. park Mex.
267 N9 Lagunas de Montebello, Parque Nacional nat. park Mex.
207 N2 Lagunas de Ruidera park Spain
269 H6 Lagunas de Zempoala, Parque Nacional nat. park Mex.
282 E2 Laguna Yema Arg.
213 K2 Lagundo Italy
269 H5 Lagunilla Mex.
204 I8 Lagunilla Spain
276 E4 Lagunillas Bol.
268 F8 Lagunillas Guerrero Mex.
269 H4 Lagunillas San Luis Potosí Mex.
274 D2 Lagunillas Venez.
129 S2 Laha Heilong. China
206 H3 La Haba Spain
270 B2 La Habana Cuba
264 O8 La Habra CA U.S.A.
117 M2 Lahad Datu Sabah Malaysia
117 M2 Lahad Datu, Teluk b. Malaysia
264 □E13 Lahaina HI U.S.A.
138 G6 Lahar Madh. Prad. India
169 D4 Lahardaun Ireland
250 D9 La Harpe IL U.S.A.
138 H6 Laharpur Uttar Prad. India
258 E4 Lahaska PA U.S.A.
116 E6 Lahat Sumatera Indon.
180 H3 La Haye-du-Puits France
180 I4 La Haye-Pesnel France
190 E5 Lähden Ger.
118 B1 Lahe Myanmar
160 I2 Lahemaa rahvuspark nat. park Estonia
160 H2 Lahepera laht b. Estonia
284 D4 La Herradura Arg.
284 B2 La Herradura Chile
269 J8 La Herradura Mex.
207 O3 La Herrera Spain
116 B4 Lahewa Indon.
179 J6 Laheycourt France
151 J5 Lahıc Azer.
285 H2 La Hierra Arg.
284 E2 La Higuera Arg.
209 C10 La Higuera Spain
146 G9 Laḩij Yemen
146 G9 Laḩij governorate Yemen
140 F2 Lāhījān Iran
264 □C12 Lahilahi Point HI U.S.A.
169 D7 Lahinch Ireland
204 I5 La Hiniesta Spain
158 E1 Lahishyn Belarus
190 E5 Lahn Ger.
191 E10 Lahn r. Ger.
191 G9 Lahnau Ger.
201 L4 Lahnsattel pass Austria
191 E10 Lahnstein Ger.
191 G9 Lahntal-Goßfelden Ger.
164 J5 Laholm Sweden
164 I5 Laholmsbukten b. Sweden
201 N7 Lahonci Slovenia
268 D1 La Honda Mex.
264 M2 Lahontan Reservoir NV U.S.A.
205 J8 La Horcajada Spain
145 P6 Lahore Pak.
269 M8 La Horqueta Mex.
275 F3 La Horqueta Venez.
205 M5 La Horra Spain
239 □1c La Houssaye, Cap c. Réunion
160 K7 Lahoysk Belarus
194 D5 Lahr (Schwarzwald) Ger.
145 M7 Lahri Pak.
163 R6 Lahti Fin.
274 A6 La Huaca Peru
268 F7 La Huacana Mex.
268 C6 La Huerta Mex.
230 C2 Laï Chad
131 L2 Lai'an Anhui China
Laibach Slovenia see Ljubljana
130 G7 Laibin Guangxi China
139 K9 Laichanpur Orissa India
194 H5 Laichingen Ger.
168 E7 Laide Highland, Scotland U.K.
107 N9 Laidley Qld Austr.
168 G9 Laidon, Loch l. Scotland U.K.
264 □D12 Lā'ie HI U.S.A.
264 □D12 Lā'ie Point HI U.S.A.
130 G4 Laifeng Hubei China
178 I4 Laifour France
181 M4 L'Aigle France
205 K8 La Iglesuela Spain
208 E7 La Iglesuela del Cid Spain
178 H8 Laignes France
212 E8 Laigueglia Italy
184 B3 L'Aiguillon-sur-Mer France
162 Q5 Laihia Fin.
118 C4 Lai-hka Myanmar
118 C4 Lai-Hsak Myanmar
163 T6 Laikko Fin.
151 D3 Laila, Mt'a Georgia
178 C8 Lailly-en-Val France
100 □5 Laimbélé, Mount hill Vanuatu
179 J6 Laimont France
220 E3 Laimos, Akrotirio pt Greece
212 G4 Lainate Italy
236 E9 Laingsburg S. Africa
251 J7 Laingsburg MI U.S.A.
162 Q3 Lainioälven r. Sweden
201 L2 Lainsitz r. Austria
256 A10 Lair KY U.S.A.
258 B2 Lairdsville PA U.S.A.
168 H6 Lairg Highland, Scotland U.K.
207 N5 La Iruela Spain
116 E6 Lais Sumatera Indon.
114 E8 Lais Mindanao Phil.
270 C2 La Isabela Cuba
162 N4 Laisälven r. Sweden
156 J5 Laishevo Rus. Fed.
129 O7 Laishui Hebei China
274 B3 La Isla Col.
238 □3f La Isleta pen. Gran Canaria Canary Is
183 B8 Laissac France
162 N3 Laisvall Sweden
163 P6 Laitila Fin.
151 C4 Lait'uri Georgia
233 C6 Laivera well Tanz.
213 K3 Laives Italy
129 O8 Laiwu Shandong China
115 E4 Laiwui Maluku Indon.
129 Q8 Laixi Shandong China
129 Q8 Laiyang Shandong China
129 N7 Laiyuan Hebei China
181 K3 Laize r. France
129 P8 Laizhou Shandong China
129 P8 Laizhou Wan b. China
181 K3 Laizon r. France
284 B5 Laja, Laguna de l. Chile
269 I5 La Jabonera Mex.
274 C2 La Jagua Col.
106 C5 Lajamanu N.T. Austr.
208 F6 La Jana Spain
151 D3 Lajanurpekhi Georgia
205 K9 La Jara reg. Spain
238 □3b Lajares Fuerteventura Canary Is
184 B3 La Jarrie France
213 J9 Lajatico Italy
183 I8 La Javie France
279 B9 Lajeado Brazil
278 F4 Lajedo Brazil
280 D6 Laje dos Santos i. Brazil
204 G8 Lajeosa Guarda Port.
204 E7 Lajeosa Viseu Port.
204 F7 Lajeosa do Mondego Port.
238 □1a Lajes Terceira Azores
279 C8 Lajes Brazil
238 □1c Lajes do Pico Pico Azores
281 G4 Lajinha Brazil
218 I6 Lajkovac Lajkovac Serbia
184 G3 La Jonchère-St-Maurice France
208 K3 La Jonquera Spain
199 H5 Lajoskomárom Hungary
199 I4 Lajosmizse Hungary
269 N10 La Jova, Laguna l. Mex.
266 F4 La Joya Chihuahua Mex.
268 D2 La Joya Durango Mex.
276 C4 La Joya Peru
274 B5 La Joya de los Sachas Ecuador
198 G4 Lajta r. Austria/Hungary
181 J7 La Jumellière France
La Junquera Spain see La Jonquera
277 E3 La Junta Bol.
266 F3 La Junta Mex.
260 D7 La Junta CO U.S.A.
138 C8 Lakadiya Gujarat India
161 X7 Lakash Rus. Fed.
146 E6 Lakathah Saudi Arabia
235 □K3 Lakato Madag.
162 P3 Lakaträsk Sweden
256 B11 Lake KY U.S.A.
262 I4 Lake WY U.S.A.
102 J7 Lake Alice North I. N.Z.
106 C8 Lake Amadeus Aboriginal Land res. N.T. Austr.
260 F4 Lake Andes SD U.S.A.
258 E2 Lake Ariel PA U.S.A.
261 I10 Lake Arthur LA U.S.A.
105 I7 Lake Bolac Vic. Austr.
255 F10 Lake Butler FL U.S.A.
105 K5 Lake Cargelligo N.S.W. Austr.
259 H2 Lake Carmel NY U.S.A.
261 I10 Lake Charles LA U.S.A.
261 J8 Lake City AR U.S.A.
263 K8 Lake City CO U.S.A.
255 F10 Lake City FL U.S.A.
260 H4 Lake City IA U.S.A.
250 I5 Lake City MI U.S.A.
250 B5 Lake City MN U.S.A.
255 H9 Lake City SC U.S.A.
244 I3 Lake Clark National Park and Preserve AK U.S.A.
257 K4 Lake Clear NY U.S.A.
103 F10 Lake Coleridge South I. N.Z.
246 E5 Lake Cowichan B.C. Can.
159 R6 Lakedemonovka Rus. Fed.
171 K5 Lake District National Park England U.K.
105 J7 Lake Eildon National Park Vic. Austr.
251 M2 Lake Evelyn-Smoothwater Provincial Park Ont. Can.
104 F3 Lake Eyre National Park S.A. Austr.
103 J8 Lake Ferry North I. N.Z.
107 J3 Lakefield Qld Austr.
248 E4 Lakefield Ont. Can.
107 J3 Lakefield National Park Qld Austr.
265 W1 Lake Fork r. CO U.S.A.
104 G4 Lake Frome Regional Reserve nature res. S.A. Austr.
104 E4 Lake Gardner National Park S.A. Austr.
250 F7 Lake Geneva WI U.S.A.
257 L5 Lake George NY U.S.A.
104 F5 Lake Gilles Conservation Park nature res. S.A. Austr.
109 E12 Lake Grace W.A. Austr.
108 I6 Lake Gregory Aboriginal Reserve W.A. Austr.
Lake Harbour Nunavut Can. see Kimmirut
265 R7 Lake Havasu City AZ U.S.A.
259 G3 Lake Hiawatha NJ U.S.A.
258 F3 Lake Hopatcong NJ U.S.A.
259 G4 Lakehurst NJ U.S.A.
264 N6 Lake Isabella CA U.S.A.
261 H11 Lake Jackson TX U.S.A.
109 E12 Lake King W.A. Austr.
109 E12 Lake King Nature Reserve W.A. Austr.
107 J3 Lakeland Qld Austr.
255 G12 Lakeland FL U.S.A.
255 F10 Lakeland GA U.S.A.
258 F3 Lake Lenape NJ U.S.A.
250 F2 Lake Linden MI U.S.A.
246 G5 Lake Louise Alta Can.
106 B6 Lake Mackay Aboriginal Land res. N.T. Austr.
109 E12 Lake Magenta Nature Reserve W.A. Austr.
233 B5 Lake Manyara National Park Tanz.
232 A5 Lake Mburo National Park Uganda
265 R5 Lake Mead National Recreation Area park AZ U.S.A.
260 I4 Lake Mills IA U.S.A.
244 I3 Lake Minchumina AK U.S.A.
106 F6 Lake Nash N.T. Austr.
173 N3 Lakenheath Suffolk, England U.K.
262 C4 Lake Oswego OR U.S.A.
103 □4 Lakepa Niue
103 D10 Lake Paringa South I. N.Z.
258 F5 Lake Pine NJ U.S.A.
255 G12 Lake Placid FL U.S.A.
257 L4 Lake Placid NY U.S.A.
257 K5 Lake Pleasant NY U.S.A.
264 J2 Lakeport CA U.S.A.
251 L6 Lakeport MI U.S.A.
261 J9 Lake Providence LA U.S.A.
264 M1 Lake Range mts NV U.S.A.
248 D2 Lake River Ont. Can.
259 G4 Lake Riviera NJ U.S.A.
251 P4 Lake St Peter Ont. Can.
105 L7 Lakes Entrance Vic. Austr.
264 M4 Lakeshore CA U.S.A.
258 C6 Lake Shore MD U.S.A.
265 W7 Lakeside AZ U.S.A.
264 P9 Lakeside CA U.S.A.
259 I1 Lakeside CT U.S.A.
259 G2 Lakeside NJ U.S.A.
259 H3 Lake Success NY U.S.A.
103 G9 Lake Sumner Forest Park nature res. South I. N.Z.
250 J2 Lake Superior Provincial Park Ont. Can.
105 M6 Lake Tabourie N.S.W. Austr.
103 E11 Lake Tekapo South I. N.Z.
259 G3 Lake Telemark NJ U.S.A.
104 F4 Lake Torrens National Park S.A. Austr.
260 G3 Lake Traverse (Sisseton) Indian Reservation res. ND/SD U.S.A.
256 G6 Lake View NY U.S.A.
256 B8 Lakeview OH U.S.A.
262 D5 Lakeview OR U.S.A.
261 J9 Lake Village AR U.S.A.
250 A5 Lakeville MN U.S.A.
255 G12 Lake Wales FL U.S.A.
262 L7 Lakewood CO U.S.A.
259 G4 Lakewood NJ U.S.A.
256 F6 Lakewood NY U.S.A.
256 D7 Lakewood OH U.S.A.
250 F4 Lakewood WI U.S.A.
138 C6 Lakha Rajasthan India
Lakha Nevre Rus. Fed. see Meken-Yurt
163 U6 Lakhdenpokh'ya Rus. Fed.
138 F7 Lakheri Rajasthan India
138 H6 Lakhimpur Uttar Prad. India
139 N7 Lakhipur Assam India
139 K7 Lakhisarai Bihar India
150 C7 Lakhish r. Israel
138 G8 Lakhnadon Madh. Prad. India
138 B8 Lakhpat Gujarat India
138 C8 Lakhtar Gujarat India
139 O6 Lakhuti Nagaland India
161 N8 Lakhva r. Belarus
151 I5 Läki Azer.
196 F2 Łąkie Pol.
260 E7 Lakin KS U.S.A.
161 W5 Lakinsk Rus. Fed.
Lakinskiy Rus. Fed. see Lakinsk
199 I5 Lakitelek Hungary
248 D2 Lakitusaki r. Ont. Can.
151 G2 Lakkha-Nevre Rus. Fed.
145 N5 Lakki Marwat Pak.
221 G2 Lakkoma Samothraki Greece
115 B8 Lakohembi Sumba Indon.
220 D6 Lakonikos Kolpos b. Greece
115 F8 Lakor i. Maluku Indon.
197 H2 Łąkorz Pol.
228 D5 Lakota Côte d'Ivoire
260 F1 Lakota ND U.S.A.
162 S1 Laksefjorden sea chan. Norway
162 R1 Lakselv Norway
162 L4 Laksfors Norway
Lakshadweep is India see Laccadive Islands
136 C7 Lakshadweep union terr. India
139 M8 Laksham Bangl.
136 F3 Lakshettipet Andhra Prad. India
136 D5 Lakshmeshvar Karnataka India
139 L8 Lakshmikantapur W. Bengal India
160 J9 Laktyshy, Vodaskhovishcha resr Belarus
205 P3 Lakuntza Spain
114 D8 Lala Mindanao Phil.
139 N7 Lalaghat Assam India
233 B5 Lalago Tanz.
285 F3 La Laguna Arg.
268 B3 La Lagunita Mex.
284 A5 La Laja Chile
269 J4 La Laja Mex.
268 F5 La Laja r. Mex.
145 P5 Lala Musa Pak.
269 L8 Lalana r. Mex.
207 I6 La Lantejuela Spain
206 F4 La Lapa Spain
235 F3 Lalapanzi Zimbabwe
219 O9 Lalapaşa Turkey
230 A4 Lalara Gabon
235 H2 Lalaua Moz.
208 G5 L'Albagés Spain
138 H9 Lalbara Madh. Prad. India
183 K6 L'Albaron mt. France
185 H7 Lalbenque France
209 E9 L'Albufera l. Spain
209 E7 L'Alcora Spain
209 D9 L'Alcudia Spain
100 □6 Lale New Georgia Is Solomon Is
182 I5 La Léchère France
107 L7 Laleham Qld Austr.
144 G7 Lāleh Zār, Kūh-e mt. Iran
192 F3 Lalendorf Ger.
275 F2 La Leona Venez.
172 E4 Laleston Bridgend, Wales U.K.
183 E7 Lalevade-d'Ardèche France
209 E10 L'Alfàs del Pi Spain
139 J7 Lalganj Bihar India
138 I7 Lalganj Uttar Prad. India
136 F7 Lalgudi Tamil Nadu India
144 C5 Lālī Iran
232 C1 Lalībela Eth.
274 A5 La Libertad Ecuador
267 O11 La Libertad El Salvador
267 N9 La Libertad Guat.
269 I1 La Libertad Mex.
266 □Q11 La Libertad Nic.
276 A2 La Libertad dept Peru
284 B3 La Ligua Chile
Laligyugh Armenia see Vazashen
115 E7 Laliki Maluku Indon.
115 C5 Lalimboee Sulawesi Indon.
122 E6 Lalin Heilong. China
204 D3 Lalín Spain
185 F6 Lalinde France
207 I8 La Línea de la Concepción Spain
122 D6 Lalin He r. China
138 G7 Lalitpur Uttar Prad. India
Lalitpur Nepal see Patan
183 B10 La Livinière France
285 H3 La Llave Arg.
183 H7 Lalley France
114 C2 Lal-Lo Luzon Phil.
209 D9 La Llosa de Ranes Spain
143 L9 Lalmikor Uzbek.
139 L7 Lalmonirhat Bangl.
115 B6 Laloa Sulawesi Indon.
247 I3 La Loche Sask. Can.
247 I3 La Loche, Lac l. Sask. Can.
276 D5 La Loma Bol.
100 □2 Lalomanu Samoa
183 I10 La Londe-les-Maures France
205 M3 La Lora reg. Spain
205 N3 La Losa reg. Spain
185 E9 Laloubère France
285 H4 La Louisa Arg.
178 B7 La Loupe France
183 F6 Lalouvesc France
187 F8 La Louvière Belgium
199 L3 Lalove Ukr.
182 H2 La Loye France
183 I6 L'Alpe-d'Huez France
138 B8 Lalpur Gujarat India
209 E10 L'Alquería de la Comtessa Spain
156 I3 Lal'sk Rus. Fed.
138 F6 Lalsot Rajasthan India
200 D6 L'Altissima mt. Austria/Italy
208 E4 Lalueza Spain
115 E4 Laluin i. Maluku Indon.
207 I5 La Luisiana Spain
133 H12 Lalung La pass Xizang China
185 C8 Laluque France
268 E2 La Luz Mex.
195 O3 Lam Ger.
139 N9 Lama Bangl.
215 M3 Lama Italy
274 C4 La Macarena, Parque Nacional nat. park Col.
182 C3 La Machine France
214 C5 La Maddalena Sardegna Italy
129 S3 Lamadian Heilong. China
Lamadianzi Heilong. China see Lamadian
117 L2 Lamag Sabah Malaysia
204 I3 La Magdalena Spain
185 F7 Lamagistère France
118 C7 Lamaing Myanmar
115 C8 Lamakera Indon.
249 G4 La Malbaie Que. Can.
183 C8 La Malène France
269 I6 La Malinche, Parque Nacional nat. park Mex.
269 I6 La Malinche, Volcán vol. Mex.
183 C9 Lamalou-les-Bains France
213 J7 Lama Mocogno Italy
266 H5 La Mancha Mex.
207 N2 La Mancha reg. Spain
La Manche str. France/U.K. see English Channel
212 C5 La Mandria, Parco Regionale park Italy
209 D12 La Manga del Mar Menor Spain
207 P5 La Manilla hill Spain
183 G9 Lamanon France
100 □5 Lamap Vanuatu
266 G2 La Máquina Mex.
260 D6 Lamar CO U.S.A.
261 H7 Lamar MO U.S.A.
182 C2 La Marche France
179 K7 Lamarche France
182 G2 Lamarche-sur-Saône France
144 E8 Lamard Iran
182 F1 Lamargelle France
214 C8 La Marmora, Punta mt. Sardegna Italy
284 D4 La Maroma Arg.
284 E6 Lamarque Arg.
261 H11 La Marque TX U.S.A.
246 G2 La Martre, Lac l. N.W.T. Can.
284 E4 La Maruja Arg.
204 C7 Lamas Port.
150 C2 Lamas r. Turkey
204 E6 Lamas de Olo Port.
266 □P10 La Masica Hond.
208 I2 La Massana Andorra
183 F7 Lamastre France
205 L9 La Mata Spain
208 E6 La Mata de los Olmos Spain
238 □3a La Matanza de Acentejo Tenerife Canary Is
205 M6 La Matilla Spain
249 F4 La Mauricie, Parc National de nat. park Que. Can.
129 L6 Lamawan Nei Mongol China
270 F3 La Maya Cuba
201 I3 Lambach Austria
180 F5 Lamballe France
230 A5 Lambaréné Gabon
281 E4 Lambari Brazil
Lambasa Fiji see Labasa
115 B6 Lambasina i. Indon.
274 B6 Lambayeque Peru
274 B6 Lambayeque dept Peru
169 K6 Lambay Island Ireland
117 K5 Lambeng Kalimantan Indon.
173 M5 Lamberhurst Kent, England U.K.
178 F2 Lambersart France
284 B1 Lambert Chile
Lambert atoll Marshall Is see Ailinglaplap
108 D6 Lambert, Cape W.A. Austr.
287 E2 Lambert Glacier Antarctica
236 C8 Lambert's Bay S. Africa
258 F4 Lambertville NJ U.S.A.
183 G9 Lambesc France
251 M7 Lambeth Ont. Can.
138 E4 Lambi Punjab India
100 □6 Lambi Guadalcanal Solomon Is
104 E2 Lambina S.A. Austr.
196 F5 Łambinowice Pol.
163 M6 Lamborn Sweden
173 I4 Lambourn West Berkshire, England U.K.
173 I4 Lambourn Downs hills England U.K.
194 E3 Lambrecht (Pfalz) Ger.
178 F3 Lambres-lez-Douai France
212 H5 Lambro r. Italy
169 B9 Lamb's Head Ireland
194 E2 Lambsheim Ger.
116 B3 Lame Sumatera Indon.

262 K4 **Lame Deer** *MT* U.S.A.
212 E5 **Lame del Sesia, Parco Naturale** *nature res.* Italy
204 E6 **Lamego** Port.
183 I6 **La Meije** *mt.* France
180 I6 **La Meilleraye-de-Bretagne** France
204 F7 **Lameiras** Port.
276 B3 **La Mejorada** Peru
100 □[5] **Lamen Bay** Vanuatu
271 □[2] **Lamentin** Guadeloupe
249 H4 **Lamèque, Île** *i. N.B.* Can.
282 D3 **La Merced** Arg.
276 B2 **La Merced** Peru
195 J5 **Lamerdingen** Ger.
104 H6 **Lameroo** *S.A.* Austr.
215 L4 **La Merta** *mt.* Italy
274 C3 **La Mesa** Col.
269 H9 **La Mesa** Mex.
264 O9 **La Mesa** *CA* U.S.A.
261 E9 **Lamesa** *TX* U.S.A.
171 N4 **Lamesley** *Tyne and Wear, England* U.K.
208 G6 **L'Ametlla de Mar** Spain
215 Q10 **Lamezia** Italy
226 A5 **Lamhar Touil, Sabkhet** *imp. l.* Western Sahara
220 D4 **Lamia** Greece
205 O2 **Lamiako** Spain
114 F8 **Lamigan Point** *Mindanao* Phil.
181 L5 **La Milesse** France
201 L5 **Laming** *r.* Austria
105 N3 **Lamington National Park** *Qld* Austr.
144 C2 **Lamir** Iran
268 E7 **La Mira** Mex.
264 N8 **La Mirada** *CA* U.S.A.
266 D3 **La Misa** Mex.
264 P9 **La Misión** Mex.
114 D8 **Lamitan** Phil.
115 G4 **Lamlam** *Papua* Indon.
100 □[1] **Lamlam, Mount** *hill* Guam
168 F11 **Lamlash** *North Ayrshire, Scotland* U.K.
131 □J7 **Lamma Island** *H.K.* China
237 N1 **Lammerkop** S. Africa
168 K11 **Lammer Law** *hill Scotland* U.K.
103 D12 **Lammerlaw Range** *mts South I.* N.Z.
103 D12 **Lammerlaw Top** *mt. South I.* N.Z.
168 K11 **Lammermuir Hills** *Scotland* U.K.
165 K4 **Lammhult** Sweden
163 R6 **Lammi** Fin.
160 K3 **Lammijärv** *lake channel* Estonia/Rus. Fed.
119 F7 **Lam Nang Rong, Ang Kep Nam** Thai.
250 E8 **La Moille** *IL* U.S.A.
257 L4 **Lamoille** *r. VT* U.S.A.
250 D9 **La Moine** *r. IL* U.S.A.
207 N7 **La Mojonera** Spain
183 I10 **La Môle** France
213 L3 **Lamon** Italy
114 C4 **Lamon Bay** Phil.
213 M6 **Lamone** *r.* Italy
117 J8 **Lamongan** *Jawa* Indon.
185 E10 **La Mongie** France
260 I5 **Lamoni** *IA* U.S.A.
182 D5 **La Monnerie-le-Montel** France
264 N6 **Lamont** *CA* U.S.A.
262 K5 **Lamont** *WY* U.S.A.
216 H9 **La Montagna** *hill* Italy
180 H7 **La Montagne** France
239 □[1c] **La Montagne** Réunion
185 F7 **Lamontjoie** France
185 E6 **Lamonzie-St-Martin** France
284 D4 **La Mora** Arg.
266 H4 **La Mora** Mex.
269 H4 **La Morena** Mex.
266 G3 **La Morita** *Chihuahua* Mex.
261 D11 **La Morita** *Coahuila* Mex.
178 D5 **Lamorlaye** France
284 B3 **La Mostaza** Chile
183 C6 **Lamothe** France
184 A2 **La Mothe-Achard** France
185 G7 **Lamothe-Capdeville** France
185 G6 **Lamothe-Cassel** France
185 E6 **Lamothe-Landerron** France
184 D3 **La Mothe-St-Héray** France
113 K5 **Lamotrek** *atoll* Micronesia
251 P1 **La Motte** *Que.* Can.
183 J9 **La Motte** France
181 P6 **Lamotte-Beuvron** France
183 G8 **La Motte-Chalancon** France
183 H7 **La Motte-d'Aveillans** France
183 I8 **La Motte-du-Caire** France
182 H5 **La Motte-Servolex** France
260 F2 **La Moure** *ND* U.S.A.
284 B3 **Lampa** Chile
276 C3 **Lampa** Peru
269 H1 **Lampacitos** Mex.
118 D5 **Lampang** Thai.
118 F6 **Lam Pao, Ang Kep Nam** Thai.
261 F10 **Lampasas** *TX* U.S.A.
261 G10 **Lampasas** *r. TX* U.S.A.
180 A5 **Lampaul** France
180 C5 **Lampaul-Guimilau** France
180 B5 **Lampaul-Plouarzel** France
267 I4 **Lampazos** Mex.
211 D8 **Lampedusa, Isola di** *i. Sicilia* Italy
164 F2 **Lampeland** Norway
194 E2 **Lampertheim** Ger.
193 I8 **Lampertswalde** Ger.
172 D3 **Lampeter** *Ceredigion, Wales* U.K.
258 C5 **Lampeter** *PA* U.S.A.
139 N7 **Lamphelpat** *Manipur* India
118 D5 **Lamphun** Thai.
173 K3 **Lamport** *Northamptonshire, England* U.K.
156 I2 **Lampozhnya** Rus. Fed.
200 G4 **Lamprechtshausen** Austria
Lampsacus Turkey *see* **Lâpseki**
116 F7 **Lampung** *prov.* Indon.
116 F7 **Lampung, Teluk** *b.* Indon.
193 J7 **Lamsfeld-Groß Liebitz** Ger.
161 V9 **Lamskoye** Rus. Fed.
191 J7 **Lamspringe** Ger.
190 H3 **Lamstedt** Ger.
138 H8 **Lamta** *Madh. Prad.* India
131 □J7 **Lam Tin** *H.K.* China
233 D5 **Lamu** Kenya
118 B5 **Lamu** Myanmar
205 K5 **La Mudarra** Spain
208 C4 **La Muela** Spain
207 M4 **La Muela** *hill* Spain
209 C8 **La Muela** *mt.* Spain
208 L3 **La Muga** *r.* Spain
205 L7 **La Mujer Muerta** *hill* Spain
183 H7 **La Mure** France
182 E4 **Lamure-sur-Azergues** France
107 I7 **Lana** *Qld* Austr.
213 K2 **Lana** Italy
284 E4 **La Nacional** Arg.
264 □D13 **Lāna'i** *i. HI* U.S.A.
264 □E13 **Lāna'i City** *HI* U.S.A.
208 E4 **Lanaja** Spain
187 I7 **Lanaken** Belgium
114 E8 **Lanao, Lake** *Mindanao* Phil.
183 E7 **Lanarce** France
251 R4 **Lanark** *Ont.* Can.
168 I11 **Lanark** *South Lanarkshire, Scotland* U.K.
250 E7 **Lanark** *IL* U.S.A.
117 L2 **Lanas** *Sabah* Malaysia
206 F5 **La Nava** Spain
205 K9 **La Nava de Ricomalillo** Spain
206 G2 **La Nava de Santiago** Spain
151 I5 **Länbäran** Azer.
119 D9 **Lanbi Kyun** *i.* Myanmar
114 D7 **Lanboyan Point** *Mindanao* Phil.
130 B7 **Lancang** *Yunnan* China
112 A1 **Lancang Jiang** *r. Xizang* China
130 C8 **Lancang Jiang** *r.* China *alt.* **Mènam Khong (Laos/Thai.),** *conv.* **Mekong**
171 L6 **Lancashire** *admin. div. England* U.K.
171 K7 **Lancashire Plain** *England* U.K.
257 K3 **Lancaster** *Ont.* Can.
171 L5 **Lancaster** *Lancashire, England* U.K.
264 N7 **Lancaster** *CA* U.S.A.
254 E7 **Lancaster** *KY* U.S.A.
260 I5 **Lancaster** *MO* U.S.A.
257 N4 **Lancaster** *NH* U.S.A.
256 G6 **Lancaster** *NY* U.S.A.
256 C9 **Lancaster** *OH* U.S.A.
258 C4 **Lancaster** *PA* U.S.A.
255 G8 **Lancaster** *SC* U.S.A.
256 I11 **Lancaster** *VA* U.S.A.
260 J4 **Lancaster** *WI* U.S.A.
171 L6 **Lancaster Canal** *England* U.K.
258 C4 **Lancaster County** *county PA* U.S.A.
243 J2 **Lancaster Sound** *str. Nunavut* Can.
271 □[6] **Lance aux Épines** Grenada
109 C11 **Lancelin** *W.A.* Austr.
109 C11 **Lancelin Island** *W.A.* Austr.
171 N4 **Lanchester** *Durham, England* U.K.
151 D3 **Lanch'khut'i** Georgia
215 M3 **Lanciano** Italy
205 P3 **Lanciego** Spain
283 B5 **Lanco** Chile
129 Q8 **Lancun** *Shandong* China
197 K5 **Łańcut** Pol.
212 A3 **Lancy** Switz.
269 H4 **Landa de Matamoros** Mex.
117 H5 **Landak** *r.* Indon.
Landana Angola *see* **Cacongo**
195 N4 **Landau an der Isar** Ger.
194 E3 **Landau in der Pfalz** Ger.
200 C5 **Landeck** Austria
180 B4 **Landéda** France
144 D6 **Landeh** Iran
206 B3 **Landeira** Port.
180 D5 **Landeleau** France
187 H7 **Landen** Belgium
106 C6 **Lander** *watercourse N.T.* Austr.
262 J5 **Lander** *WY* U.S.A.
180 C5 **Landerneau** France
179 N6 **Landersheim** France
185 C8 **Landes** *dept* France
185 C6 **Landes** *reg.* France
190 H5 **Landesbergen** Ger.
185 C7 **Landes de Gascogne, Parc Naturel Régional des** *nature res.* France
180 F6 **Landes de Lanvaux** *reg.* France
180 F5 **Landes du Mené** *reg.* France
285 F3 **Landeta** Arg.
209 C8 **Landete** Spain
180 E6 **Landévant** France
180 C5 **Landévennec** France
137 M6 **Landfall Island** *Andaman & Nicobar Is* India
187 J7 **Landgraaf** Neth.
173 O4 **Landguard Point** *England* U.K.
190 G3 **Land Hadeln** *reg.* Ger.
145 L9 **Landhi** Pak.
145 J6 **Landi Barechi** Afgh.
116 D5 **Landik, Gunung** *mt.* Indon.
145 N4 **Landi Kotal** Pak.
204 D6 **Landim** Port.
258 F3 **Landing** *NJ* U.S.A.
178 H7 **Landion** *r.* France
185 D6 **Landiras** France
247 I4 **Landis** *Sask.* Can.
258 C4 **Landisville** *PA* U.S.A.
180 C4 **Landivisiau** France
181 I5 **Landivy** France
190 H3 **Land Kehdingen** *reg.* Ger.
192 D2 **Landkirchen auf Fehmarn** Ger.
231 F8 **Landless Corner** Zambia
162 M5 **Landögssjön** *l.* Sweden
250 E3 **Land O' Lakes** *WI* U.S.A.
191 J7 **Landolfshausen** Ger.
162 M5 **Landön** Sweden
109 D8 **Landor** *W.A.* Austr.
172 E4 **Landore** *Swansea, Wales* U.K.
183 D7 **Landos** France
212 H2 **Landquart** Switz.
212 H2 **Landquart** *r.* Switz.
178 G3 **Landrecies** France
179 K5 **Landres** France
179 J5 **Landres-et-St-Georges** France
251 Q1 **Landrienne** *Que.* Can.
204 E1 **Landro** *r.* Spain
Landrove *r.* Spain *see* **Landro**
255 F8 **Landrum** *SC* U.S.A.
182 J5 **Landry** France
193 F7 **Landsberg** Ger.
Landsberg Pol. *see* **Gorzów Wielkopolski**
195 J5 **Landsberg am Lech** Ger.
103 D10 **Landsborough** *r. South I.* N.Z.
107 J7 **Landsborough Creek** *watercourse Qld* Austr.
191 C11 **Landscheid** Ger.
172 □ **Land's End** *pt England* U.K.
195 M4 **Landshut** Ger.
165 K4 **Landsjön** *l.* Sweden
164 I6 **Landskrona** Sweden
186 G4 **Landsmeer** Neth.
194 D3 **Landstuhl** Ger.
180 C5 **Landudec** France
190 G3 **Land Wursten** *reg.* Ger.
219 L5 **La Nedei** *mt.* Romania
285 H5 **La Negra** Arg.
276 C5 **La Negra** Chile
109 D12 **Lane Pool Reserve** *nature res. W.A.* Austr.
169 G5 **Lanesborough** Ireland
180 E6 **Lanester** France
255 E9 **Lanett** *AL* U.S.A.
181 M4 **La Neuve-Lyre** France
212 C1 **La Neuveville** Switz.
179 I5 **La Neuville-au-Pont** France
179 J5 **Laneuville-sur-Meuse** France
Lanfeng *Henan* China *see* **Lankao**
118 C1 **Lang, Nam** *r.* Myanmar
164 F5 **Langå** Denmark
205 K6 **Langa** Spain
119 H9 **La Nga, Sông** *r.* Vietnam
151 J5 **Längäbiz Silsiläsi** *hills* Azer.
133 E11 **La'nga Co** *l.* China
205 N5 **Langa de Duero** Spain
Langadhás Greece *see* **Lagkadas**
139 N7 **Langai** *r.* India
162 M5 **Långan** *r.* Sweden
130 G2 **Langao** *Shaanxi* China
145 O3 **Langar** *Badakhshān* Afgh.
145 I5 **Langar** *Farāh* Afgh.
145 M4 **Langar** *Parwān* Afgh.
143 L7 **Langar** *Navoiy* Uzbek.
143 L8 **Langar** *Qashqadaryo* Uzbek.
115 C6 **Langara** *Sulawesi* Indon.
245 N5 **Langara Island** *B.C.* Can.
165 L5 **Långasjö** Sweden
201 M2 **Langau** Austria
168 C6 **Langavat, Loch** *l. Western Isles, Scotland* U.K.
190 I1 **Langballig** Ger.
236 G4 **Langberg** *mts* S. Africa
260 F1 **Langdon** *ND* U.S.A.
104 □[3] **Langdon Point** S. Pacific Ocean
195 O3 **Langdorf** Ger.
183 C6 **Langeac** France
184 E1 **Langeais** France
236 C9 **Langebaan** S. Africa
192 F1 **Langebæk** Denmark
236 D9 **Langeberg** *mts* S. Africa
186 G3 **Langedijk** Neth.
236 I2 **Langehorn** S. Africa
164 G6 **Langeland** *i.* Denmark
164 G7 **Langelands Bælt** *str.* Denmark
163 R6 **Längelmäki** Fin.
156 D3 **Längelmävesi** *l.* Fin.
191 K7 **Langeln** Ger.
191 J7 **Langelsheim** Ger.
187 C7 **Langemark** Belgium
194 F2 **Langen** *Hessen* Ger.
190 D5 **Langen** *Niedersachsen* Ger.
190 G3 **Langen** *Niedersachsen* Ger.
195 J4 **Langenaltheim** Ger.
194 H6 **Langenargen** Ger.
195 I5 **Langenau** Ger.
191 F9 **Langenaubach** Ger.
195 L5 **Langenbach** Ger.
200 A4 **Langen bei Bregenz** Austria
191 F7 **Langenberg** Ger.
193 F9 **Langenbernsdorf** Ger.
247 K5 **Langenburg** *Sask.* Can.
194 H3 **Langenburg** Ger.
193 E8 **Langendorf** Ger.
200 A5 **Langenegg** Austria
193 E8 **Langeneichstädt** Ger.
194 G5 **Langenenslingen** Ger.
200 C5 **Längenfeld** Austria
191 C8 **Langenfeld (Rheinland)** Ger.
191 I6 **Langenhagen** Ger.
191 E9 **Langenhahn** Ger.
190 G1 **Langenhorn** Ger.
193 G9 **Langenleuba-Niederhain** Ger.
201 M3 **Langenlois** Austria
194 D2 **Langenlonsheim** Ger.
195 K4 **Langenmosen** Ger.
193 H7 **Langennaundorf** Ger.
195 J5 **Langenneufnach** Ger.
193 E9 **Langenorla** Ger.
195 L5 **Langenpreising** Ger.
191 H10 **Langenselbold** Ger.
195 K2 **Langensendelbach** Ger.
191 K7 **Langenstein** Ger.
212 D1 **Langenthal** Switz.
201 M4 **Langenwang** Austria
193 E6 **Langenweddingen** Ger.
193 F9 **Langenwetzendorf** Ger.
195 J3 **Langenzenn** Ger.
201 N3 **Langenzersdorf** Austria
190 D3 **Langeoog** Ger.
190 E3 **Langeoog** *i.* Ger.
152 I3 **Langepas** Rus. Fed.
164 G4 **Langerak** *sea chan.* Denmark
192 I5 **Langer Berg** *hill* Ger.
195 J5 **Langerringen** Ger.
193 H6 **Langerwisch** Ger.
164 G6 **Langeskov** Denmark
164 F2 **Langesund** Norway
164 B2 **Langevåg** Norway
239 □[1c] **Langevin, Pointe de** *pt* Réunion
191 K9 **Langewiesen** Ger.
129 O7 **Langfang** *Hebei* China
163 L5 **Långfjallets naturreservat** *nature res.* Sweden
173 L3 **Langford** *Bedfordshire, England* U.K.
195 I3 **Langfurth** Ger.
116 D4 **Langgam** *Sumatera* Indon.
116 D4 **Langgapayung** *Sumatera* Indon.
133 K12 **Langgar** *Xizang* China
191 G10 **Langgöns** Ger.
192 F3 **Langhagen** Ger.
247 J4 **Langham** *Sask.* Can.
173 K2 **Langham** *Rutland, England* U.K.
164 J4 **Länghem** Sweden
212 I6 **Langhirano** Italy
237 K9 **Langholm** S. Africa
168 K12 **Langholm** *Dumfries and Galloway, Scotland* U.K.
164 H1 **Langholsberget** *hill* Norway
258 F4 **Langhorne** *PA* U.S.A.
162 □C1 **Langjökull** *ice cap* Iceland
116 B2 **Langka** *Sumatera* Indon.
116 C1 **Langkawi** *i.* Malaysia
115 D6 **Langkesi, Kepulauan** *is* Indon.
119 D10 **Lang Kha Toek, Khao** *mt.* Thai.
118 C4 **Langkho** Myanmar
236 E4 **Langklip** S. Africa
117 L1 **Langkon** *Sabah* Malaysia
251 S1 **Langlade** *Que.* Can.
250 F4 **Langlade** *WI* U.S.A.
246 F5 **Langley** *B.C.* Can.
256 C11 **Langley** *KY* U.S.A.
190 J5 **Langlingen** Ger.
107 K9 **Langlo** *watercourse Qld* Austr.
107 J9 **Langlo Crossing** *Qld* Austr.
Langmusi *Gansu* China *see* **Dagcanglhamo**
212 D2 **Langnau** Switz.
190 L1 **Langø** Denmark
183 D7 **Langogne** France
185 D6 **Langoiran** France
185 D6 **Langon** France
118 H6 **Langong, Xé** *r.* Laos
180 D5 **Langonnet** France
162 M2 **Langøya** *i.* Norway
172 G5 **Langport** *Somerset, England* U.K.
133 D11 **Langqên Zangbo** *r.* China
131 L5 **Langqi** *Fujian* China
195 M4 **Langquaid** Ger.
204 I2 **Langreo** Spain
179 J8 **Langres** France
179 I8 **Langres, Plateau de** France
133 D8 **Langru** *Xinjiang* China
116 B2 **Langsa** *Sumatera* Indon.
116 C2 **Langsa, Teluk** *b.* Indon.
201 K2 **Langschlag** Austria
162 N5 **Långsele** Sweden
129 J6 **Langshan** *Nei Mongol* China
129 J6 **Lang Shan** *mts* China
165 M1 **Långshyttan** Sweden
162 P2 **Langslett** Norway
118 H4 **Lang Sơn** Vietnam
171 M5 **Langstrothdale Chase** *hills England* U.K.
194 B2 **Langsur** Ger.
229 H4 **Langtang** Nigeria
139 J5 **Langtang National Park** Nepal
118 C1 **Langtao** Myanmar
139 N7 **Langting** *Assam* India
171 Q5 **Langtoft** *East Riding of Yorkshire, England* U.K.
129 Q3 **Langtoutun** *Nei Mongol* China
162 P4 **Långträsk** Sweden
261 E11 **Langtry** *TX* U.S.A.
Languan *Shaanxi* China *see* **Lantian**
185 H9 **Languedoc** *reg.* France
183 A11 **Languedoc-Roussillon** *admin. reg.* France
180 F5 **Langueux** France
285 H5 **Langueyú** Arg.
Languiaru *r.* Brazil *see* **Iquê**
180 E6 **Languidic** France
205 N6 **Languilla** Spain
283 C6 **Languiñeo** Arg.
191 J8 **Langula** Ger.
117 M9 **Langundu, Tanjung** *pt Sumbawa* Indon.
156 C2 **Långvattnet** Sweden
165 L2 **Långvattnet** *l.* Sweden
163 N6 **Långvinds bruk** Sweden
190 F3 **Langwarden (Butjadingen)** Ger.
171 L4 **Langwathby** *Cumbria, England* U.K.
190 H5 **Langwedel** *Niedersachsen* Ger.
190 I2 **Langwedel** *Schleswig-Holstein* Ger.
195 J5 **Langweid am Lech** Ger.
129 N7 **Langya Shan** *mt. Hebei* China
130 F3 **Langzhong** *Sichuan* China
204 C5 **Lanheses** Port.
180 C4 **Lanhouarneau** France
179 L5 **La Nied Française** *r.* France
251 O2 **Laniel** *Que.* Can.
197 H3 **Łanięta** Pol.
247 J5 **Lanigan** *Sask.* Can.
264 □D12 **Lanikai** *HI* U.S.A.
283 C5 **Lanín, Parque Nacional** *nat. park* Arg.
283 C5 **Lanín, Volcán** *vol.* Arg./Chile
172 C7 **Lanivet** *Cornwall, England* U.K.
158 F4 **Lanivtsi** Ukr.
117 I4 **Lanjak, Bukit** *mt.* Malaysia
207 M7 **Lanjarón** Spain
138 H9 **Lanji** *Madh. Prad.* India
Lanka *country* Asia *see* **Sri Lanka**
135 □[1] **Lankanfinolhu** *i. N. Male* Maldives
Lankanfushifinolu *i. N. Male* Maldives *see* **Lankanfinolhu**
129 N9 **Lankao** *Henan* China
151 J7 **Länkäran** Azer.
151 J7 **Länkäran** *r.* Azer.
131 □I7 **Lan Kok Tsui** *pt H.K.* China
276 C3 **Lanlacuni Bajo** Peru
180 F4 **Lanloup** France
180 D4 **Lanmeur** France
201 L6 **Lannach** Austria
185 E9 **Lannemezan** France
185 E9 **Lannemezan, Plateau de** France
185 E8 **Lannepax** France
180 B4 **Lannilis** France
180 E4 **Lannion** France
180 D4 **Lannion, Baie de** *b.* France
248 F4 **L'Annonciation** *Que.* Can.
178 F2 **Lannoy** France
183 B6 **Lanobre** France
182 D3 **La Nocle-Maulaix** France
208 I5 **L'Anoia** *r.* Spain
259 G5 **Lanoka Harbor** *NJ* U.S.A.
277 E3 **La Noria** Bol.
268 A2 **La Noria** Mex.
184 G5 **Lanouaille** France
130 B5 **Lanping** *Yunnan* China
200 D5 **Lans** Austria
183 H7 **Lans, Montagne de** *mts* France
183 E9 **Lansargues** France
258 E4 **Lansdale** *PA* U.S.A.
258 B6 **Lansdowne** *MD* U.S.A.
250 F3 **L'Anse** *MI* U.S.A.
192 G3 **Lansen** Ger.
249 G3 **L'Anse-St-Jean** *Que.* Can.
258 D3 **Lansford** *PA* U.S.A.
245 N3 **Lansing** *r. Y.T.* Can.
250 C6 **Lansing** *IA* U.S.A.
250 J7 **Lansing** *MI* U.S.A.
250 B6 **Lansing** *MN* U.S.A.
162 Q5 **Länsi-Suomi** *prov.* Fin.
162 Q3 **Lansjärv** Sweden
197 I2 **Łańskie, Jezioro** *l.* Pol.
198 F2 **Lanškroun** Czech Rep.
183 J6 **Lanslebourg-Mont-Cenis** France
185 H8 **Lanta** France
119 D11 **Lanta, Ko** *i.* Thai.
205 L4 **Lantadilla** Spain
131 □I7 **Lantau Island** *H.K.* China
Lantau Peak *hill H.K.* China *see* **Fung Wong Shan**
179 L8 **Lanterne** *r.* France
Lantian *Hunan* China *see* **Lianyuan**
129 K9 **Lantian** *Shaanxi* China
185 B6 **Lanton** France
183 K9 **Lantosque** France
159 R4 **Lantratívka** Ukr.
183 E6 **Lantriac** France
182 D3 **Lanty** France
209 E10 **La Nucía** Spain
183 C8 **Lanuéjols** France
185 I7 **Lanuéjouls** France
214 A6 **La Nurra** *reg. Sardegna* Italy
285 H4 **Lanús** Arg.
214 D8 **Lanusei** *Sardegna* Italy
114 F7 **Lanuza** *Mindanao* Phil.
114 F7 **Lanuza Bay** *Mindanao* Phil.
180 G5 **Lanvallay** France
180 C5 **Lanvéoc** France
180 F4 **Lanvollon** France
122 E5 **Lanxi** *Heilong.* China
131 L4 **Lanxi** *Zhejiang* China
129 L7 **Lanxian** *Shanxi* China
193 I10 **Lány** Czech Rep.
196 G5 **Łany** Pol.
232 A3 **Lanya** Sudan
129 L7 **Lanyi He** *r.* China
131 M7 **Lan Yü** *i.* Taiwan
192 E4 **Lanz** Ger.
230 C4 **Lanza** Congo
205 K8 **Lanzahita** Spain
238 □[3c] **Lanzarote** *i.* Canary Is
201 N4 **Lanzenkirchen** Austria
198 F3 **Lanžhot** Czech Rep.
128 H8 **Lanzhou** *Gansu* China
129 R4 **Lanzijing** *Jilin* China
212 C5 **Lanzo Torinese** Italy
215 P8 **Lao** *r.* Italy
118 D5 **Lao, Nam Mae** *r.* Thai.
114 C2 **Laoag** *Luzon* Phil.
114 E5 **Laoang** Phil.
130 B7 **Laobie Shan** *mts Yunnan* China
205 O9 **La Obispalía** *reg.* Spain
130 G6 **Laobukou** *Guangxi* China
118 F3 **Lao Cai** Vietnam
122 E3 **Laodaodian** *Heilong.* China
Laodicea Syria *see* **Al Lādhiqīyah**
Laodicea Turkey *see* **Denizli**
Laodicea ad Lycum Turkey *see* **Denizli**
Laodicea ad Mare Syria *see* **Al Lādhiqīyah**
132 F3 **Laofengkou** *Xinjiang* China
129 Q5 **Laoha He** *r.* China
122 G7 **Laoheishan** *Heilong.* China
131 H2 **Laohekou** *Hubei* China
129 Q7 **Laohutun** *Liaoning* China
169 H7 **Laois** *county* Ireland
Laojie *Yunnan* China *see* **Yongping**
128 E7 **Laojunmiao** *Gansu* China
123 E8 **Laoling** *Jilin* China
123 E8 **Lao Ling** *mts* China
238 □[3b] **La Oliva** *Fuerteventura* Canary Is
Laolong *Guangdong* China *see* **Longchuan**
178 G4 **Laon** France
250 F4 **Laona** *WI* U.S.A.
178 G4 **Laonnois** *reg.* France
178 B6 **Laons** France
128 A5 **Laoqitai** *Xinjiang* China
238 □[3a] **La Orotava** *Tenerife* Canary Is
276 B2 **La Oroya** Peru
118 F5 **Laos** *country* Asia
129 Q8 **Laoshan** *Shandong* China
132 G4 **Laoshawan** *Xinjiang* China
Laotieshan Shuidao *sea chan.* China *see* **Bohai Haixia**
122 F7 **Laotougou** *Jilin* China
123 D8 **Laotuding Shan** *hill Liaoning* China
202 D5 **Laou, Oued** *r.* Morocco
228 E4 **Laoudi-Ba** Côte d'Ivoire
227 G5 **Laouni, Oued** *watercourse* Alg.
183 B9 **Laouzas, Lac de** *l.* France
Laowohi *pass Jammu and Kashmir* India *see* **Khardung La**
128 G6 **Laoximiao** *Nei Mongol* China
128 H8 **Laoyacheng** *Qinghai* China
122 E7 **Laoye Ling** *mts* China
122 F7 **Laoye Ling** *mts* China
128 D4 **Laoyemiao** *Xinjiang* China
279 C8 **Lapa** Brazil
114 C9 **Lapac** *i.* Phil.
207 P5 **La Paca** Spain
182 D4 **La Pacaudière** France
282 F2 **Lapachito** Arg.
229 G4 **Lapai** Nigeria
182 D4 **Lapalisse** France
184 B3 **La Pallice** France
238 □[3d] **La Palma** *i.* Canary Is
284 B4 **La Palma** Chile
274 C3 **La Palma** Col.
267 O9 **La Palma** Guat.
266 □T13 **La Palma** Panama
209 D12 **La Palma** Spain
265 U9 **La Palma** *AZ* U.S.A.
206 F6 **La Palma del Condado** Spain
183 B11 **La Palme** France
183 C11 **Lapalme, Étang de** *lag.* France
182 G4 **La Paloma** Uru.
274 C2 **La Paloma** Venez.
183 F8 **Lapalud** France
183 I9 **La Palud-sur-Verdon** France
284 E5 **La Pampa** *prov.* Arg.
197 I6 **Łapanów** Pol.
264 L6 **La Panza Range** *mts CA* U.S.A.
285 F2 **La Para** Arg.
275 F3 **La Paragua** Venez.
114 B9 **Laparan** *i.* Phil.
268 F1 **La Pardita** Mex.
238 □[3b] **La Pared** *Fuerteventura* Canary Is
285 G3 **La Parejas** Arg.
268 C2 **La Parilla** Mex.
206 F3 **La Parra** Spain
205 P9 **La Parra de Las Vegas** Spain
206 G2 **La Parrilla** *hill* Spain
220 C4 **Lapas** Greece
204 C9 **Lapas** Port.
274 C4 **La Paya, Parque Nacional** *nat. park* Col.
284 E3 **La Paz** *Córdoba* Arg.
285 H2 **La Paz** *Entre Ríos* Arg.
284 D3 **La Paz** *Mendoza* Arg.
276 C4 **La Paz** Bol.
276 C3 **La Paz** *dept* Bol.
266 □P10 **La Paz** Hond.
266 D5 **La Paz** Mex.
266 □P11 **La Paz** Nic.
285 I4 **La Paz** Uru.
250 H8 **Lapaz** *IN* U.S.A.
274 C2 **La Paz** Venez.
266 D5 **La Paz, Bahía** *b.* Mex.
274 D5 **La Pedrera** Col.
251 K6 **Lapeer** *MI* U.S.A.
206 □ **Lapeiras** Madeira
285 G2 **La Pelada** Arg.
181 I5 **La Pellerine** France
269 I2 **La Peña** *Tamaulipas* Mex.
269 L8 **La Peña** *Veracruz* Mex.
266 □S13 **La Peña** Panama
183 J9 **La Penne** France
183 H10 **La Penne-sur-Huveaune** France
205 O8 **La Peraleja** Spain
266 G3 **La Perla** Mex.
124 S1 **La Pérouse Strait** Japan/Rus. Fed.
269 J2 **La Pesca** Mex.
204 H8 **La Pesga** Spain
179 N6 **La Petite-Pierre** France
207 M6 **La Peza** Spain
172 E6 **Lapford** *Devon, England* U.K.
285 G2 **La Picada** Arg.
268 E5 **La Piedad** Mex.
262 D5 **La Pine** *OR* U.S.A.
114 E5 **Lapinig** *Samar* Phil.
209 C12 **La Pinilla** Spain
163 S6 **Lapinjärvi** Fin.
162 S5 **Lapinlahti** Fin.
266 □S13 **La Pintada** Panama
150 B3 **Lapithos** Cyprus
216 E8 **La Pizzuta** *mt. Sicilia* Italy
261 J10 **Laplace** *LA* U.S.A.
118 E6 **Lap Lae** Thai.
182 J5 **La Plagne** France
239 □[1c] **La Plaine-des-Cafres** Réunion
239 □[1c] **La Plaine-des-Palmistes** Réunion
180 G7 **La-Plaine-sur-Mer** France
162 V3 **Laplandskiy Zapovednik** *nature res.* Rus. Fed.
260 E3 **La Plant** *SD* U.S.A.
285 I4 **La Plata** Arg.
256 I10 **La Plata** *MD* U.S.A.
260 I5 **La Plata** *MO* U.S.A.
285 I4 **La Plata, Río de** *sea chan.* Arg./Uru.
284 E2 **La Playa** Arg.
238 □[3f] **La Playa de Mogán** *Gran Canaria* Canary Is
285 F3 **La Playosa** Arg.
204 H2 **La Plaza** Spain
268 B1 **La Plazuela** Mex.
184 I5 **Lapleau** France
247 J4 **La Plonge, Lac** *l. Sask.* Can.
185 F7 **Laplume** France
160 G4 **Lapmežciems** Latvia
208 F6 **La Pobla de Benifassá** Spain
208 I3 **La Pobla de Lillet** Spain
208 G3 **La Pobla de Segur** Spain
204 I3 **La Pola de Gordón** Spain
282 D2 **La Poma** Arg.
156 H2 **Lapominka** Rus. Fed.
181 J7 **La Pommeraye** France
214 C3 **La Porta** *Corse* France
254 D5 **La Porte** *IN* U.S.A.
251 R8 **Laporte** *PA* U.S.A.
245 P3 **Laporte, Mount** *Y.T.* Can.
208 F6 **La Portellada** Spain
209 C9 **La Portera** Spain
115 A6 **Laposo, Bukit** *mt.* Indon.
239 □[1c] **La Possession** Réunion
285 F2 **La Posta** Arg.
249 F1 **La Potherie, Lac** *l. Que.* Can.
181 J6 **La Pouëze** France
179 N7 **Lapoutroie** France
274 C3 **La Poyata** Col.
266 C5 **La Poza Grande** Mex.
162 Q5 **Lappajärvi** *l.* Fin.
165 L2 **Lappe** Sweden
163 T6 **Lappeenranta** Fin.
195 M3 **Lappersdorf** Ger.
163 P6 **Lappi** Fin.
162 S3 **Lappi** *prov.* Fin.
162 O3 **Lappland** *reg.* Europe
160 E1 **Lappo** *Åland* Fin.
160 G2 **Lappohja** Fin.
162 Q3 **Lappträsk** Sweden
257 L3 **La Prairie** *Que.* Can.
269 H2 **La Presa** Mex.
185 I11 **La Preste** France
285 G5 **Laprida** Arg.
285 G5 **La Primavera** Arg.
205 P4 **La Proveda de Soria** Spain
261 F11 **La Pryor** *TX* U.S.A.
221 H2 **Lâpseki** Turkey
183 E6 **Lapte** France
160 L5 **Laptevo** *Pskovskaya Oblast'* Rus. Fed.
Laptevo *Tul'skaya Oblast'* Rus. Fed. *see* **Yasnogorsk**
Laptev Sea Rus. Fed. *see* **Laptevykh, More**
153 N2 **Laptevykh, More** *sea* Rus. Fed.
162 Q5 **Lapua** Fin.
162 Q5 **Lapuanjoki** *r.* Fin.
La Puebla Spain *see* **Sa Pobla**
205 N9 **La Puebla de Almoradiel** Spain
205 O3 **La Puebla de Arganzón** Spain
207 I6 **La Puebla de Cazalla** Spain
208 E5 **La Puebla de Híjar** Spain
207 I5 **La Puebla de los Infantes** Spain
206 G6 **La Puebla del Río** Spain
205 L9 **La Puebla de Montalbán** Spain
205 K3 **La Puebla de Valdavia** Spain
209 D7 **La Puebla de Valverde** Spain
205 K9 **La Pueblanueva** Spain
282 D3 **La Puerta** *Catamarca* Arg.
285 F2 **La Puerta** *Córdoba* Arg.
274 D2 **La Puerta** Venez.
207 N4 **La Puerta de Segura** Spain
199 L6 **Lăpugiu de Jos** Romania
115 C6 **Lapuko** *Sulawesi* Indon.
114 D6 **Lapu-Lapu** Phil.
284 E3 **La Punilla** Arg.
212 H2 **La Punt** Switz.
282 D3 **La Punta** Arg.
Lapurdum France *see* **Bayonne**
266 C4 **La Purísima** Mex.
219 M3 **Lăpuș** Romania
219 L3 **Lăpuș** *r.* Romania
219 J6 **Lăpușnicu Mare** Romania
173 I3 **Lapworth** *Warwickshire, England* U.K.
197 K3 **Łapy** Pol.
224 F4 **Laqiya Arbain** *well* Sudan
224 F5 **Laqiya 'Umran** *well* Sudan
282 D1 **La Quiaca** Arg.
215 K3 **L'Aquila** Italy
215 L3 **L'Aquila** *prov.* Italy
265 P8 **La Quinta** *CA* U.S.A.
144 F8 **Lār** Iran
105 J8 **Lara** *Vic.* Austr.
274 D2 **Lara** *state* Venez.
204 C2 **Laracha** Spain
226 D2 **Larache** Morocco
202 C5 **Larache** *prov.* Morocco
170 D6 **Laracor** Ireland
170 E7 **Laragh** Ireland
183 H8 **Laragne-Montéglin** France
238 □[3a] **La Rajita** *La Gomera* Canary Is
144 G8 **Lārak** *i.* Iran
230 B2 **Laramanay** Chad
207 J5 **La Rambla** Spain
262 L6 **Laramie** *WY* U.S.A.
262 L5 **Laramie** *r. WY* U.S.A.
262 L5 **Laramie Mountains** *WY* U.S.A.
Laranda Turkey *see* **Karaman**
275 G6 **Laranjal** Brazil
280 D5 **Laranjal Paulista** Brazil
278 F4 **Laranjeiras** Brazil
280 C6 **Laranjeiras, Baía das** *b.* Brazil
280 A6 **Laranjeiras do Sul** Brazil
202 B3 **Laranjeiro** Port.
280 B5 **Laranjinha** *r.* Brazil
115 C8 **Larantuka** *Flores* Indon.
205 O7 **Laranueva** Spain
205 N5 **La Rasa** Spain
113 H8 **Larat** *i.* Indon.
182 H5 **La Ravoire** France
183 G7 **La Raye** *mt.* France
226 B5 **La Raygat** *reg.* Western Sahara
168 I10 **Larbert** *Falkirk, Scotland* U.K.
208 I5 **L'Arboç** Spain
182 F5 **L'Arbresle** France
165 O4 **Lärbro** *Gotland* Sweden
185 B9 **Lárceveau-Arros-Cibits** France
181 I5 **Larchamp** France
178 E7 **Larchant** France
184 G5 **Larche** *Limousin* France
183 J8 **Larche** *Provence-Alpes-Côte d'Azur* France
212 B7 **Larche, Col de** *pass* Italy
259 H3 **Larchmont** *NY* U.S.A.
251 M3 **Larchwood** *Ont.* Can.
213 J4 **Lardaro** Italy
213 J9 **Larderello** Italy
251 O1 **Larder Lake** *Ont.* Can.
251 O1 **Larder Lake** *l. Ont.* Can.
204 F9 **Lardosa** Port.
205 N2 **Laredo** Spain
261 F12 **Laredo** *TX* U.S.A.
183 B10 **La Redorte** France
284 D5 **La Reforma** Arg.
269 J9 **La Reforma** *Oaxaca* Mex.
263 I12 **La Reforma** *Sonora* Mex.
269 J5 **La Reforma** *Veracruz* Mex.
251 O1 **La Reine** *Que.* Can.
186 J4 **Laren** *Gelderland* Neth.
186 H4 **Laren** *Noord-Holland* Neth.
185 D6 **La Réole** France
271 □[1] **Lares** Puerto Rico
144 F4 **Lārestān** Iran
238 □[3e] **La Restinga** *El Hierro* Canary Is
169 E4 **Largan** Ireland
Largeau Chad *see* **Faya**
183 E7 **Largentière** France
183 J7 **L'Argentière-la-Bessée** France
255 F12 **Largo** *FL* U.S.A.
270 C3 **Largo, Cayo** *i.* Cuba
168 K10 **Largo Bay** *Scotland* U.K.
168 K10 **Largoward** *Fife, Scotland* U.K.
168 G11 **Largs** *North Ayrshire, Scotland* U.K.
208 B1 **La Rhune** *hill* Spain
144 B2 **Lārī** Iran
213 J8 **Lari** Italy
227 H1 **L'Ariana** Tunisia
211 C7 **L'Ariana** *admin. div.* Tunisia
115 A4 **Lariang** *Sulawesi Barat* Indon.
115 A4 **Lariang** *r.* Indon.
205 O6 **La Riba de Escalote** Spain
285 H4 **La Rica** Arg.
183 E6 **La Ricamarie** France
144 B2 **Lārījān** Iran
260 G1 **Larimore** *ND* U.S.A.
285 F2 **La Rinconada** Arg.
206 H6 **La Rinconada** Spain
215 N4 **Larino** Italy
282 D3 **La Rioja** Arg.
284 D1 **La Rioja** *prov.* Arg.
205 P4 **La Rioja** *aut. comm.* Spain
161 N1 **Larionovo** Rus. Fed.
220 D3 **Larisa** Greece
Larissa Greece *see* **Larisa**
144 G8 **Laristan** *reg.* Iran
239 □[1c] **La Rivière** Réunion
145 M8 **Larkana** Pak.
168 I11 **Larkhall** *South Lanarkshire, Scotland* U.K.
249 J3 **Lark Harbour** *Nfld and Lab.* Can.
173 I5 **Larkhill** *Wiltshire, England* U.K.
145 J5 **Lar Koh** *mt.* Afgh.
107 J3 **Lark Passage** *Qld* Austr.
173 N3 **Larling** *Norfolk, England* U.K.
182 I3 **Larmont** *mt.* France/Switz.
180 E6 **Larmor-Plage** France
Larnaca Cyprus *see* **Larnaka**
150 B4 **Larnaka** Cyprus
169 K3 **Larne** *Northern Ireland* U.K.
260 F6 **Larned** *KS* U.S.A.
169 K3 **Larne Lough** *inlet Northern Ireland* U.K.
229 I4 **Laro** Cameroon
204 I3 **La Robla** Spain
206 F2 **La Roca de la Sierra** Spain
212 C2 **La Roche** Switz.
184 E5 **La Rochebeaucourt-et-Argentine** France
180 G6 **La Roche-Bernard** France
184 H5 **La Roche-Canillac** France
184 E5 **La Roche-Chalais** France
183 J7 **La Roche-de-Rame** France
180 E4 **La Roche-Derrien** France
183 H7 **La Roche-des-Arnauds** France
187 I8 **La Roche-en-Ardenne** Belgium
184 E4 **La Rochefoucauld** France
178 C5 **La Roche-Guyon** France
184 B3 **La Rochelle** France
182 E3 **Larochemillay** France
181 M8 **La Roche-Posay** France
182 F3 **La Rochepot** France
178 F8 **Laroche-St-Cydroine** France
182 I4 **La Roche-sur-Foron** France
180 I8 **La Roche-sur-Yon** France
183 I6 **La Rochette** France
187 J9 **Larochette** Lux.
207 O2 **La Roda** Spain
207 J6 **La Roda de Andalucía** Spain
181 I6 **La Roë** France
207 N6 **Laroles** Spain
271 I4 **La Romana** Dom. Rep.
209 D11 **La Romana** Spain
185 E8 **La Romieu** France
247 J4 **La Ronge** *Sask.* Can.
247 J4 **La Ronge, Lac** *l. Sask.* Can.
184 I6 **Laroquebrou** France
183 H10 **La Roquebrussanne** France
183 G9 **La Roque-d'Anthéron** France
185 H10 **Laroque-d'Olmes** France
183 C8 **La Roque-Ste-Marguerite** France
185 F7 **Laroque-Timbaut** France
267 I5 **La Rosa** Mex.
265 P9 **La Rosa de Castilla** Mex.
267 I3 **La Rosita** Mex.
204 E5 **Larouco, Serra do** *mts* Spain
185 H7 **La Rouquette** France
205 Q3 **Larraga** Spain
208 B2 **Larrainzar** Spain
205 Q3 **Larrasoaina** Spain
185 C9 **Larrau** France
185 G8 **Larrazet** France
185 E8 **Larressingle** France
185 B9 **Larressore** France
108 E5 **Larrey Point** *W.A.* Austr.
106 D3 **Larrimah** *N.T.* Austr.
205 P3 **Larrión** Spain
285 H3 **Larroque** Arg.
287 E2 **Lars Christensen Coast** Antarctica
244 I4 **Larsen Bay** *AK* U.S.A.
286 T2 **Larsen Ice Shelf** Antarctica
162 Q5 **Larsmo** Fin.
162 H5 **Larsnes** Norway
217 □ **L-Artal, Ras** *pt* Malta
La Rúa Spain *see* **A Rúa**
285 G2 **La Rubia** Arg.
185 D10 **Laruns** France
184 D5 **Laruscade** France
207 M5 **Larva** Spain
164 G2 **Larvik** Norway
152 J3 **Lar'yak** Rus. Fed.
159 Q6 **Laryne** Ukr.
183 C8 **Larzac, Causse du** *plat.* France
213 J2 **Lasà** Italy
282 F2 **La Sabana** Arg.
274 D4 **La Sabana** Col.
205 M8 **La Sagra** *reg.* Spain
238 □[3c] **Las Agujas** *hill* Canary Is
115 C6 **Lasahau** *Sulawesi* Indon.
265 W3 **La Sal** *UT* U.S.A.
285 I5 **La Salada Grande, Laguna** *l.* Arg.
268 G2 **Las Albercas** Mex.
284 C2 **La Salina** *salt pan* Arg.
239 □[1c] **La Saline** Réunion
265 W3 **La Sal Junction** *UT* U.S.A.
248 F4 **LaSalle** *Que.* Can.
183 D8 **Lasalle** France
212 C4 **La Salle** Italy
250 E8 **La Salle** *IL* U.S.A.
183 J7 **La Salle les Alpes** France
185 I7 **La Salvetat-Peyralès** France
185 G8 **La Salvetat-St-Gilles** France
183 B9 **La Salvetat-sur-Agout** France
208 F7 **La Salzadella** Spain
117 K4 **Lasan** *Kalimantan* Indon.
260 D6 **Las Animas** *CO* U.S.A.
266 C3 **Las Ánimas, Punta** *pt* Mex.
Las Anod Somalia *see* **Laascaanood**
238 □[3c] **La Santa** *Lanzarote* Canary Is
205 K2 **Las Arenas** Spain
285 I5 **Las Armas** Arg.
248 E3 **La Sarre** *Que.* Can.
285 E3 **Las Asequias** Arg.
268 G4 **La Sauceda** Mex.
185 F8 **La Sauvetat** France
185 E6 **La Sauvetat-du-Dropt**
183 I10 **La Sauvette** *hill* France
271 J8 **Las Aves, Islas** *is* West
209 H10 **La Savina** Spain
285 G1 **Las Avispas** Arg.
266 D3 **Las Avispas** Mex.
249 F2 **La Savonnière, Lac** *l.* Q
285 G3 **Las Bandurrias** Arg.
201 K3 **Lasberg** Austria
205 K7 **Las Berlanas** Spain
275 E3 **Las Bonitas** Venez.
282 E2 **Las Breñas** Arg.
164 F5 **Låsby** Denmark
206 H7 **Las Cabezas de San Ju**
284 B4 **Las Cabras** Chile
268 B3 **Las Cabras** Mex.
207 O4 **Las Cabras** *mt.* Spain
238 □[3d] **Las Caletas** *La Palma*
238 □[3a] **Las Cañadas** *vol. crater* Canary Is
284 A4 **Las Cañas** Chile
285 H3 **Las Cañas** Uru.
216 F8 **Lascari** *Sicilia* Italy
209 E8 **Las Casas** Spain
284 C2 **Las Casuarinas** Arg.
284 C3 **Las Catitas** Arg.
268 B1 **Las Cebollas** Mex.
284 E3 **Las Chacras** Arg.
283 D6 **Las Chapas** Arg.
269 M8 **Las Choapas** Mex.
249 K3 **La Scie** *Nfld and Lab.* C
277 F4 **Las Conchas** Bol.
266 F3 **Las Cruces** Mex.
264 L7 **Las Cruces** *CA* U.S.A.
263 K10 **Las Cruces** *NM* U.S.A.
269 H2 **Las Crucitas** Mex.
208 G3 **Lascuarre** Spain
205 K6 **La Seca** Spain
181 J7 **La Séguinière** France
270 H4 **La Selle, Pic** *mt.* Haiti
208 H5 **La Selva del Camp** Spa
185 J7 **La Selve** France
208 F6 **La Sènia** Spain
284 B1 **La Serena** Chile
206 H3 **La Serena** *reg.* Spain
267 I4 **Las Esperanças** Mex.
183 H10 **La Seyne-sur-Mer** Frar
285 H5 **Las Flores** *Buenos Aires*
282 E2 **Las Flores** *Salta* Arg.
284 C2 **Las Flores** *San Juan* Ar
269 J3 **Las Flores** Mex.
284 B2 **Las Galenas** Chile
284 B4 **Las Garzas** Chile
285 H3 **Las Golas** Arg.
263 J11 **Las Guacamatas, Cerro**
268 E7 **Las Guacamayas** Mex.
145 I8 **Lāshār, Rūd-e** *r.* Iran
247 I4 **Lashburn** *Sask.* Can.
284 C3 **Las Heras** Arg.
205 K9 **Las Herencias** Spain
274 C4 **Las Hermosas, Parque** *nat. park* Col.
266 G5 **Las Herreras** Mex.
285 E3 **Las Higueras** Arg.
118 C3 **Lashio** Myanmar
145 K6 **Lashkar Gāh** Afgh.
283 C8 **Las Horquetas** Arg.
284 A6 **Las Hortensias** Chile
268 F1 **Las Huertas** Mex.
204 H8 **Las Hurdes** *reg.* Spain
217 L5 **La Sila** *reg.* Italy
197 H2 **Łasin** Pol.
238 □[3d] **Las Indias** *La Palma* C
269 K9 **La Sirena, Cerro** *mt.* M
284 E3 **Las Isletas** Arg.
158 F2 **Lasitsk** Belarus
144 E4 **Lāsjerd** Iran
268 F5 **Las Jicamas** Mex.
284 C4 **Las Juntas** Arg.
282 C3 **Las Juntas** Chile
268 G6 **Las Juntas** Mex.
285 F2 **Las Junturas** Arg.
197 H4 **Łask** Pol.
149 O6 **Laskarak** Iran
197 J4 **Łaskarzew** Pol.
158 E4 **Laskivtsi** Ukr.
201 L7 **Laško** Slovenia
197 I6 **Laskowa** Pol.
196 G2 **Laskowice** Pol.
207 L2 **Las Labores** Spain
284 B6 **Las Lajas** Arg.
275 E3 **Las Lajitas** Venez.
269 I2 **Las Lavaderos** Mex.
284 B4 **Las Leñas** Arg.
274 A6 **Las Lomas** Peru
282 E2 **Las Lomitas** Arg.
205 P8 **Las Majadas** Spain
284 C4 **Las Malvinas** Arg.
206 F6 **Las Marismas** *marsh* S
285 G5 **Las Martinetas** Arg.
283 D7 **Las Martinetas** Arg.
204 G4 **Las Médulas** *tourist site*
207 O6 **Las Menas** Spain
274 E2 **Las Mercedes** Venez.
207 N2 **Las Mesas** Spain
266 G3 **Las Mesteñas** Mex.
197 K2 **Łaśmiady, Jezioro** *l.* Pol
275 E2 **Las Minas** Venez.
267 O10 **Las Minas, Cerro de** *m*
284 C4 **Las Molles** Arg.
Las Mulatas *is* Panama **San Blas, Archipiélago**
269 H6 **Las Navajas, Cerro** *mt.*
207 I5 **Las Navas de la Conce** Spain
205 L7 **Las Navas del Marqués**
187 F7 **Lasne** Belgium
207 P7 **Las Negras** Spain
266 G4 **Las Nieves** Mex.
266 H5 **Las Nopaleras, Cerro** *r*
207 M3 **La Solana** Spain
115 C5 **Lasolo, Teluk** *b.* Indon.
204 H3 **Las Omañas** *reg.* Spain
268 G8 **La Sombra** Mex.
274 B3 **Las Orquideas, Parque** *nat. park* Col.
184 G3 **La Souterraine** France
284 B5 **Las Ovejas** Arg.
196 G5 **Lasowice Małe** Pol.
282 F2 **Las Palmas** Arg.
268 E2 **Las Palmas** Mex.
265 O9 **Las Palmas** *watercourse*
266 □S13 **Las Palmas** Panama
238 □[3f] **Las Palmas de Gran Ca** *Gran Canaria* Canary Is
284 C4 **Las Paredes** Arg.
268 G7 **Las Parotas** *r.* Mex.
207 N2 **Las Pedroñeras** Spain
285 F2 **Las Peñas** Arg.
268 B5 **Las Peñitas, Punta** *pt* M
285 F3 **Las Perdices** Arg.
277 F4 **Las Petas** Bol.
212 H7 **La Spezia** Italy
212 H7 **La Spezia** *prov.* Italy
285 I4 **Las Piedras** Uru.
215 P7 **La Spina, Monte** *mt.* Ita
285 I4 **Las Pipinas** Arg.
266 □Q10 **Las Planchas** Hond.
214 B8 **Las Plassas** *Sardegna* It
283 D6 **Las Plumas** Arg.
268 G1 **Las Presas** Mex.
208 F2 **Laspuña** Spain
145 O3 **Laspur** Pak.
285 G3 **Las Rosas** Arg.
205 M7 **Las Rozas de Madrid** S
190 K3 **Lassahn** Ger.
238 □[3b] **Las Salinas** *Fuerteventu* Canary Is
192 I3 **Lassan** Ger.
281 E2 **Lassance** Brazil
181 K5 **Lassay-les-Châteaux** Fr
264 K1 **Lassen Peak** *vol. CA* U.S
264 K1 **Lassen Volcanic Nation** *CA* U.S.A.
185 D9 **Lasseube** France
178 E4 **Lassigny** France
201 K4 **Lassing** *Niederösterreich*
201 J4 **Lassing** *Steiermark* Aust
201 M5 **Laßnitzhöhe** Austria
284 B3 **Las Tablas** Chile
269 H3 **Las Tablas** Mex.

Las Tablas Panama
Lastarria, Parque Nacional de nat. park Chile
Last Chance CO U.S.A.
Lastebasse Italy
Lastè delle Sute mt. Italy
Las Termas Arg.
Las Terreras Spain
Last Mountain Lake Sask. Can.
Las Torres de Cotillas Spain
Las Tórtolas, Cerro mt. Chile
Lastours France
Lastoursville Gabon
Lastovo i. Croatia
Lastovski Kanal sea chan. Croatia
Lastra Arg.
Lastra, Sierra de mts Spain
Lastra a Signa Italy
Lastras de Cuéllar Spain
Lastres, Cabo c. Spain
Las Tres Vírgenes, Volcán vol. Mex.
Las Trincheras Venez.
Lastrup Ger.
Las Tunas Cuba
Las Tunas Grandes, Laguna l. Arg.
La Suze-sur-Sarthe France
Lasva Estonia
Las Vacas Chile
Las Varas Col.
Las Varas Chihuahua Mex.
Las Varas Nayarit Mex.
Las Varas Venez.
Las Varillas Arg.
Las Vegas Mex.
Las Vegas NM U.S.A.
Las Vegas NV U.S.A.
Las Veguillas Spain
Las Ventas con Peña Aguilera Spain
Las Ventas de San Julián Spain
Las Vertientes Arg.
Las Vigas de Ramirez Mex.
Las Villuercas mt. Spain
Las Yaras Peru
Lasy Janowskie, Park Krajobrazowy Pol.
Łaszczów Pol.
Laszki Pol.
Lászláfalva Hungary see Szentkirály
Lata Santa Cruz Is Solomon Is
La Tabatière Que. Can.
Latacunga Ecuador
Latady Island Antarctica
La Tagnière France
La Tagua Col.
Latakia Syria see Al Lādhiqīyah
Latalata i. Maluku Indon.
La Talaudière France
La Tannière France
La Tapona Mex.
Latchford Ont. Can.
Latchingdon Essex, England U.K.
Late i. Vava'u Gp Tonga
Latehar Jharkhand India
Latemar mt. Italy
Laterza Italy
La Teste-de-Buch France
La Tetilla, Cerro mt. Mex.
Latgales augstiene hills Latvia
Latham W.A. Austr.
Lathen Ger.
Latheron Highland, Scotland U.K.
Lathi Gujarat India
Lathi Rajasthan India
Latho Jammu and Kashmir India
Lathrop CA U.S.A.
La Thuile Italy
Lathus France
Latiano Italy
Lātīdān Iran
Latikberg Sweden
Latina Italy
Latina prov. Italy
La Tinaja Mex.
Latisana Italy
Latnaya Rus. Fed.
Lato r. Italy
La Toma Arg.
Latorica r. Slovakia
La Tornette mt. Switz.
La Torre de Cabdella Spain
La Tortuga, Isla i. Venez.
Latorytsya r. Ukr.
Latouche AK U.S.A.
Latouche Island AK U.S.A.
Latouche Treville, Cape W.A. Austr.
Latouma well Niger
La Tour-Blanche France
La Tour-d'Aigues France
La Tour-d'Auvergne France
Latour-de-Carol France
Latour-de-France France
La Tour-du-Crieu France
La Tour-du-Pin France
La Tournette mt. France
La Tour-sur-Orb France
La Toussuire France
Latowicz Pol.
La Tranca Arg.
La Tranche-sur-Mer France
Latrape France
Latrecey-Ormoy-sur-Aube France
La Tremblade France
La Trimouille France
La Trinidad Nic.
La Trinidad Luzon Phil.
La Trinitaria Mex.
La Trinité France
La Trinité Martinique
La Trinité-de-Réville France
La Trinité-Porhoët France
La Trinité-sur-Mer France
Latrobe Tas. Austr.
Latrobe PA U.S.A.
La Tronche France
Latronico Italy
Latronquière France
La Troya r. Arg.
Latrun West Bank
Latskoye Rus. Fed.
Lattaquié Syria see Al Lādhiqīyah
Lattarico Italy
Latte Island Vava'u Gp Tonga see Late
Lattes France
Lattrop Neth.
Latulipe Que. Can.
La Tuque Que. Can.
Latur Mahar. India
La Turballe France
Latvia country Europe
Latvija country Europe see Latvia
Latviyskaya S.S.R. country Europe see Latvia
Lau Nigeria
Lau r. Sudan
Laua r. Chhattisgarh India
Laubach Hessen Ger.
Laubach Rheinland-Pfalz Ger.
Lauban waterhole Namibia
Lauben Bayern Ger.
Lauben Bayern Ger.
Laubusch Ger.
Lauca, Parque Nacional nat. park Chile
Laucha (Unstrut) Ger.
Lauchert r. Ger.
Lauchhammer Ger.
Lauchheim Ger.
Lauchringen Ger.
Lauda-Königshofen Ger.
Laudenbach Ger.
Lauder Scottish Borders, Scotland U.K.
Lauderdale NJ U.S.A.
Laudio Spain see Llodio
Laudun France
Lauenau Ger.
Lauenbrück Ger.
Lauenburg (Elbe) Ger.
191 H7 Lauenförde Ger.
191 J10 Lauer r. Ger.
194 E4 Lauf Ger.
191 H10 Laufach Ger.
195 K2 Lauf an der Pegnitz Ger.
195 N6 Laufen Ger.
212 D1 Laufen Switz.
212 E1 Laufenberg Switz.
194 E6 Laufenburg (Baden) Ger.
162 □C1 Laugarbakki Iceland
243 L2 Lauge Koch Kyst reg. Greenland
172 D4 Laugharne Carmarthenshire, Wales U.K.
106 E7 Laughlen, Mount N.T. Austr.
263 L8 Laughlin Peak NM U.S.A.
185 F7 Laugnac France
163 Q5 Lauhanvuoren kansallispuisto nat. park Fin.
195 I4 Lauingen (Donau) Ger.
207 N7 Laujar de Andarax Spain
160 F3 Lauka Estonia
162 R5 Laukaa Fin.
160 F6 Laukuva Lith.
101 □[8a] Laulea Beach Tongatapu Tonga
100 □[2] Lauli'i Samoa
119 D9 Laun Thai.
185 G8 Launac France
251 P1 Launay Que. Can.
105 K9 Launceston Tas. Austr.
172 D6 Launceston Cornwall, England U.K.
169 C8 Laune r. Ireland
118 D2 Launggyaung Myanmar
119 D8 Launglon Myanmar
119 C8 Launglon Bok Islands Myanmar
267 M10 La Unidad Mex.
277 E3 La Unión Bol.
283 B6 La Unión Chile
274 B4 La Unión Col.
266 □P11 La Unión El Salvador
266 □P10 La Unión Hond.
268 F8 La Unión Mex.
276 A2 La Unión Huánuco Peru
274 A6 La Unión Piura Peru
209 D12 La Unión Spain
178 I4 Launois-sur-Vence France
212 C2 Laupen Switz.
194 H5 Laupheim Ger.
114 C4 Laur Luzon Phil.
107 J3 Laura Qld Austr.
104 G5 Laura S.A. Austr.
185 H9 Lauragais reg. France
185 I9 Lauraguel France
274 E3 La Urbana Venez.
217 K7 Laureana di Borrello Italy
257 J10 Laurel DE U.S.A.
261 K10 Laurel MS U.S.A.
262 J4 Laurel MT U.S.A.
260 G4 Laurel NE U.S.A.
258 D4 Laureldale PA U.S.A.
277 F6 Laureles Para.
256 F9 Laurel Hill hills PA U.S.A.
258 E5 Laurel Springs NJ U.S.A.
258 A3 Laurelton PA U.S.A.
168 L9 Laurencekirk Aberdeenshire, Scotland U.K.
169 F6 Laurencetown Ireland
183 C9 Laurens France
260 H4 Laurens IA U.S.A.
255 G8 Laurens SC U.S.A.
92 D2 Laurentian Plateau Can.
249 G4 Laurentides, Réserve Faunique des nature res. Que. Can.
215 P7 Laurenzana Italy
185 B9 Laurhibar r. France
138 H7 Lauri Madh. Prad. India
215 P7 Lauria Italy
286 V2 Laurie Island S. Orkney Is Antarctica
184 G3 Laurière France
168 H13 Laurieston Dumfries and Galloway, Scotland U.K.
105 N4 Laurieton N.S.W. Austr.
255 H8 Laurinburg NC U.S.A.
215 O7 Laurino Italy
183 G9 Lauris France
103 F10 Lauriston South I. N.Z.
250 F2 Laurium MI U.S.A.
216 H2 Lauro Italy
Lauru i. Solomon Is see Choiseul
212 B2 Lausanne Switz.
193 D7 Lausehügel hill Ger.
193 K8 Lausitzer Gebirge hills Ger.
193 I7 Lausitzer Grenzwall park Ger.
193 G7 Laußig Ger.
193 I8 Laußnitz Ger.
183 E7 Laussonne France
185 F6 Laussou France
117 H2 Laut i. Indon.
117 H5 Laut i. Indon.
117 L6 Laut i. Indon.
117 K6 Laut, Selat sea chan. Indon.
193 J8 Lauta Ger.
183 I6 Lautaret, Col du pass France
284 A6 Lautaro Chile
283 B8 Lautaro, Volcán vol. Chile
115 E8 Lautem East Timor
194 E4 Lautenbach Ger.
179 P6 Lauter r. France/Ger.
193 G9 Lauter Ger.
200 A5 Lauterach Austria
195 L3 Lauterach r. Ger.
179 P6 Lauterbourg France
212 D2 Lauterbrunnen Switz.
194 D2 Lauterecken Ger.
195 L3 Lauterhofen Ger.
191 H9 Lautersbach (Hessen) Ger.
194 H4 Lauterstein Ger.
191 K10 Lautertal Ger.
117 K7 Laut Kecil, Kepulauan is Indon.
101 □[7a] Lautoka Viti Levu Fiji
185 I8 Lautrec France
116 B2 Lauttawar, Danau l. Indon.
162 K4 Lauvsnes Norway
162 T5 Lauvuskylä Fin.
186 J2 Lauwersmeer l. Neth.
185 G7 Lauzerte France
185 H6 Lauzès France
197 J1 Lava r. Rus. Fed.
258 E1 Lava NY U.S.A.
262 D6 Lava Beds National Monument nat. park CA U.S.A.
261 G11 Lavaca r. TX U.S.A.
214 A10 La Vacca, Isola i. Sardegna Italy
204 D1 Lavadoiro, Punta pt Spain
212 G7 Lavagna Italy
212 G7 Lavagne r. Italy
248 F4 Laval Que. Can.
181 J5 Laval France
185 I9 Lavalette France
256 C10 Lavalette WV U.S.A.
183 H10 La Valette-du-Var France
209 E8 La Vall d'Uixó Spain
284 C3 Lavalle Arg.
213 L2 La Valle Italy
201 K6 Lavamünd Austria
144 E8 Lāvān Iran
144 E8 Lāvān i. Iran
100 □[6] Lavanggu Rennell Solomon Is
208 H3 Lavansa r. Spain
182 H4 Lavans-lès-St-Claude France
201 K6 Lavant r. Austria/Slovenia
201 K5 Lavanttal val. Austria
282 B5 Lavapié, Punta pt Chile
144 D7 Lāvar Iran
221 H1 Lavara Greece
235 □J4 Lavaraty Madag.
185 E7 Lavardac France
185 F8 Lavardens France
144 F6 Lāvar Meydān salt marsh Iran
183 C6 Lavaudieu France
185 H8 Lavaur France
212 B3 Lavaux Vineyard Terraces tourist site Switzerland
184 I3 Lavaveix-les-Mines France
264 K5 Laveaga Peak CA U.S.A.
205 J3 La Vecilla Spain
185 D10 Lavedan reg. France
270 H4 La Vega Dom. Rep.
268 D5 La Vega Mex.
204 I2 La Vega Asturias Spain
204 I2 La Vega Asturias Spain
205 K2 La Vega Cantabria Spain
La Vega Galicia Spain see A Veiga
274 D2 La Vela Venez.
185 H10 Lavelanet France
204 I6 La Vellés Spain
215 P5 Lavello Italy
261 D11 La Venada r. Mex.
212 F4 Lavena Ponte Tresa Italy
173 N3 Lavenham Suffolk, England U.K.
212 F4 Laveno Italy
266 □P10 La Venta Hond.
269 N8 La Venta r. Mex.
178 E2 Laventie France
205 P8 La Ventosa Spain
274 D3 La Venturosa Col.
204 I9 La Vera reg. Spain
284 E4 La Verde Arg.
217 K7 La Verde r. Italy
183 H9 La Verdière France
183 D8 La Vernarède France
261 F7 Laverne OK U.S.A.
172 F5 Lavernock Point Wales U.K.
182 G5 La Verpillière France
181 J8 La Verrie France
109 G10 Laverton W.A. Austr.
178 H5 La Veuve France
214 C5 Lavezzi, Îles i. Corse France
214 C5 Lavezzi, Réserve Naturelle des Îles nature res. Corse France
163 Q6 Lavia Fin.
215 O6 Laviano Italy
266 H4 La Víbora Mex.
268 G1 La Victoria Mex.
207 J5 La Victoria Spain
271 J8 La Victoria Venez.
203 □ La Victoria de Acentejo Tenerife Canary Is
205 N5 La Vid Spain
251 P4 Lavieille, Lake Ont. Can.
251 N3 Lavigne Ont. Can.
214 E3 La Villa Italy
205 N9 La Villa de Don Fadrique Spain
178 B8 La Ville-aux-Clercs France
183 D7 La Villedieu France
183 E7 Lavilledieu France
184 E3 La Villedieu-du-Clain France
179 L8 La Villedieu-en-Fontenette France
269 I2 Lavin Mex.
282 D2 La Viña Arg.
274 B6 La Viña Peru
262 J3 Lavina MT U.S.A.
215 J5 Lavinio-Lido di Enea Italy
285 G3 La Violeta Arg.
182 J2 Laviron France
213 K3 Lavìs Italy
185 F8 Lavit France
285 F6 La Vitícola Arg.
179 L7 La Vôge reg. France
Lavongal i. P.N.G. see New Hanover
160 I7 Lavoriškės Lith.
204 C8 Lavos Port.
183 F7 La Voulte-sur-Rhône France
183 C6 Lavoûte-Chilhac France
183 D6 Lavoûte-sur-Loire France
281 E4 Lavras Brazil
279 B9 Lavras do Sul Brazil
206 C3 Lavre Port.
206 B3 Lavre r. Port.
142 K1 Lavrent'yevka Kazakh.
220 F5 Lavrio Greece
161 T9 Lavrovo Orlovskaya Oblast' Rus. Fed.
161 U2 Lavrovo Vologodskaya Oblast' Rus. Fed.
237 P3 Lavumisa Swaziland
233 A8 Lavushi-Manda National Park Zambia
228 C5 Lawa r. Liberia
118 C2 Lawa Myanmar
145 N5 Lawa Pak.
248 E3 Lawagamau r. Ont. Can.
138 I9 Lawan Chhattisgarh India
117 L9 Lawang i. Indon.
179 O6 La Wantzenau France
117 K2 Lawas Sarawak Malaysia
248 D2 Lawashi r. Ont. Can.
146 G9 Lawdar Yemen
287 H2 Law Dome ice feature Antarctica
115 C6 Lawele Sulawesi Indon.
168 H9 Lawers Perth and Kinross, Scotland U.K.
173 O4 Lawford Essex, England U.K.
115 F4 Lawin i. Maluku Indon.
117 J4 Lawit, Gunung mt. Indon./Malaysia
116 E2 Lawit, Gunung mt. Malaysia
118 C4 Lawksawk Myanmar
250 B6 Lawler IA U.S.A.
108 H3 Lawley r. W.A. Austr.
258 B4 Lawn PA U.S.A.
139 N8 Lawngtlai Mizoram India
106 G5 Lawn Hill Qld Austr.
106 G5 Lawn Hill Creek r. Qld Austr.
106 G5 Lawn Hill National Park Qld Austr.
149 K9 Lawqah Saudi Arabia
228 E4 Lawra Ghana
103 D12 Lawrence South I. N.Z.
103 E10 Lawrence r. South I. N.Z.
260 H6 Lawrence KS U.S.A.
257 N6 Lawrence MA U.S.A.
255 D8 Lawrenceburg TN U.S.A.
257 □R3 Lawrence Station N.B. Can.
169 J4 Lawrencetown Northern Ireland U.K.
254 D6 Lawrenceville IL U.S.A.
258 F4 Lawrenceville NJ U.S.A.
256 H7 Lawrenceville PA U.S.A.
256 H12 Lawrenceville VA U.S.A.
109 F9 Lawrence Wells, Mount hill W.A. Austr.
197 K2 Ławsk Pol.
261 F8 Lawton OK U.S.A.
117 I8 Lawu, Gunung vol. Indon.
192 K5 Ławy Pol.
146 B1 Lawz, Jabal al mt. Saudi Arabia
165 K3 Laxå Sweden
204 C2 Laxe Spain
204 C2 Laxe, Cabo de c. Spain
170 I5 Laxey Isle of Man
236 H2 Laxey S. Africa
170 I5 Laxey Bay Isle of Man
168 F6 Laxford, Loch inlet Scotland U.K.
168 F6 Laxford Bridge Highland, Scotland U.K.
245 O5 Laxgalts'ap B.C. Can.
245 O5 Lax Kw'alaams B.C. Can.
168 □N2 Laxo Shetland, Scotland U.K.
133 G9 Laxong Co l. Xizang China
179 L6 Laxou France
162 M5 Laxsjö Sweden
165 K3 Laxsjön l. Sweden
184 B3 Lay r. France
156 L2 Laya r. Rus. Fed.
208 C3 Layana Spain
117 L7 Layar, Tanjung pt Indon.
276 C4 La Yarada Peru
156 I1 Laydennyy, Mys c. Rus. Fed.
115 F7 Layeni Maluku Indon.
268 C4 La Yesca Mex.
146 H4 Laylá Saudi Arabia
150 G7 Layla salt pan Saudi Arabia
184 C1 Layon r. France
205 L9 Layos Spain
271 □[3] Layou St Vincent
185 F7 Layrac France
183 B9 Layre, Roc de mt. France
97 H2 Laysan Island HI U.S.A.
132 F5 Laysu Xinjiang China
258 F2 Layton NJ U.S.A.
264 I2 Laytonville CA U.S.A.
Layturi Georgia see Lait'uri
145 N6 Layyah Pak.
201 N8 Laz Croatia
130 A5 Laza Myanmar
204 F4 Laza Spain
266 E6 La Zacatosa, Picacho mt. Mex.
205 P4 Lazagurría Spain
285 F5 La Zanja Arg.
239 □[2b] Lazare, Pointe pt Mahé Seychelles
199 L5 Lăzăreni Romania
122 L2 Lazarev Rus. Fed.
218 I6 Lazarevac Lazarevac Serbia
161 U8 Lazarevo Rus. Fed.
151 A2 Lazarevskoye Rus. Fed.
266 B2 Lázaro Cárdenas Baja California Mex.
266 B2 Lázaro Cárdenas Baja California Mex.
269 N9 Lázaro Cárdenas Chiapas Mex.
268 E8 Lázaro Cárdenas Michoacán Mex.
199 J3 Lazberci park Hungary
282 G4 Lazcano Uru.
160 G7 Lazdijai Lith.
133 E9 Lazhuglung Xizang China
161 R7 Lazinki Rus. Fed.
215 J3 Lazio admin. reg. Italy
213 J5 Lazise Italy
197 J4 Łaziska Pol.
198 E1 Lázně Bělohrad Czech Rep.
198 E1 Lázně Bohdaneč Czech Rep.
198 B1 Lázně Kynžvart Czech Rep.
285 H3 Lazo Arg.
122 H7 Lazo Primorskiy Kray Rus. Fed.
153 O3 Lazo Respublika Sakha (Yakutiya) Rus. Fed.
171 L4 Lazonby Cumbria, England U.K.
261 E11 La Zorra watercourse Mex.
Lazovsk Moldova see Sîngerei
199 L4 Lazuri Romania
199 L5 Lazuri de Beiuș Romania
159 L7 Lazurne Ukr.
197 H5 Łazy Pol.
285 H5 Lazzarino Arg.
212 G6 Lazzaro, Monte hill Italy
170 E2 Leacan, Rubha nan pt Scotland U.K.
119 F8 Leach Cambodia
250 J2 Leach Island Ont. Can.
169 E6 Leacht Seoirse Ireland
258 C4 Leacock PA U.S.A.
242 H5 Lead SD U.S.A.
168 J11 Leadburn Midlothian, Scotland U.K.
171 P7 Leadenham Lincolnshire, England U.K.
247 I5 Leader Sask. Can.
258 B5 Leader Heights PA U.S.A.
168 K11 Leader Water r. Scotland U.K.
171 N4 Leadgate Durham, England U.K.
168 I12 Leadhills South Lanarkshire, Scotland U.K.
105 L5 Leadville N.S.W. Austr.
263 K7 Leadville CO U.S.A.
261 K10 Leaf r. MS U.S.A.
Leaf Bay Que. Can. see Tasiujaq
247 K3 Leaf Rapids Man. Can.
286 Q2 Leahy, Cape Antarctica
108 I4 Leake, Mount hill W.A. Austr.
261 K10 Leakesville MS U.S.A.
261 F11 Leakey TX U.S.A.
Leaksville NC U.S.A. see Eden
108 D6 Leal, Mount hill W.A. Austr.
282 D2 Leales Arg.
248 D5 Leamington Ont. Can.
173 I3 Leamington Spa, Royal Warwickshire, England U.K.
131 J5 Le'an Jiangxi China
237 M2 Leandra S. Africa
285 G4 Leandro N. Alem Buenos Aires Arg.
282 G2 Leandro N. Alem Misiones Arg.
169 C8 Leane, Lough l. Ireland
235 □J2 Leanja Madag.
199 I4 Leányfalu Hungary
169 D9 Leap Ireland
108 C7 Learmonth W.A. Austr.
171 Q7 Leasingham Lincolnshire, England U.K.
173 L5 Leatherhead Surrey, England U.K.
187 F8 L'Eau d'Heure l. Belgium
187 F8 L'Eau d'Heure r. Belgium
Leava Wallis and Futuna Is see Sigave
171 P5 Leavening North Yorkshire, England U.K.
260 H6 Leavenworth KS U.S.A.
262 D3 Leavenworth WA U.S.A.
264 M3 Leavitt Peak CA U.S.A.
162 S2 Leavvajohka Norway
165 N7 Łeba Pol.
196 F1 Łeba r. Pol.
196 G1 Łeba r. Pol.
194 B3 Lebach Ger.
114 E8 Lebak Mindanao Phil.
237 J3 Lebaleng S. Africa
230 A5 Lébamba Gabon
219 J8 Lebane Lebane Serbia
150 D5 Lebanon country Asia
254 D5 Lebanon IN U.S.A.
260 F6 Lebanon KS U.S.A.
254 E7 Lebanon KY U.S.A.
261 I7 Lebanon MO U.S.A.
257 M5 Lebanon NH U.S.A.
258 F3 Lebanon NJ U.S.A.
256 A9 Lebanon OH U.S.A.
262 C4 Lebanon OR U.S.A.
251 R9 Lebanon PA U.S.A.
255 D7 Lebanon TN U.S.A.
256 C12 Lebanon VA U.S.A.
258 C4 Lebanon County county PA U.S.A.
179 L5 Le Ban-St-Martin France
145 I1 Lebap Turkm.
145 J2 Lebap admin. div. Turkm.
Lebap Oblast admin. div. Turkm. see Lebap
185 K10 Le Barcarès France
185 C6 Le Barp France
187 F6 Lebbeke Belgium
Lebda tourist site Libya see Leptis Magna
183 E7 Le Béage France
183 H10 Le Beausset France
264 N7 Lebec CA U.S.A.
181 M3 Le Bec-Hellouin France
Lebedin Ukr. see Lebedyn
161 W8 Lebedyan' Rus. Fed.
159 N3 Lebedyn Ukr.
248 E3 Lebel-sur-Quévillon Que. Can.
193 E7 Lebendorf Ger.
181 J4 Le Bény-Bocage France
198 G4 Lébénymiklós Hungary
185 I8 Le Bez France
178 C3 Lebiez France
232 E3 Lebiolali well Eth.
182 J4 Le Biot France
184 G2 Le Blanc France
183 D8 Le Bleymard France
196 G1 Łebno Pol.
230 D3 Lebo Dem. Rep. Congo
115 C6 Lebo Sulawesi Indon.
237 M2 Lebohang S. Africa
182 F5 Le Bois-d'Oingt France
184 B3 Le Bois-Plage-en-Ré France
Lebomboberge hills Moz. see Lebombo Mountains
237 Q2 Lebombo Mountains hills Moz.
139 L6 Lebong W. Bengal India
183 K8 Le Boréon France
165 N7 Lębork Pol.
185 J10 Le Boulou France
181 J8 Le Boupère France
185 H6 Le Bourg France
183 I6 Le Bourg-d'Oisans France
182 H5 Le Bourget-du-Lac France
181 J5 Le Bourgneuf-la-Forêt France
185 C6 Le Bouscat France
183 C9 Le Bousquet-d'Orb France
235 F5 Lebowakgomo S. Africa
190 J2 Lebrade Ger.
182 E3 Le Breuil Bourgogne France
178 G6 Le Breuil Champagne-Ardenne France
182 J5 Le Brévent mt. France
206 G7 Lebrija Spain
201 M6 Lebring-Sankt Margarethen Austria
185 E8 Le Brouilh-Monbert France
239 □[1c] Le Brûlé Réunion
183 I8 Le Brusquet France
165 N7 Łebsko, Jezioro lag. Pol.
282 B5 Lebu Chile
204 F5 Lebução Port.
185 F6 Le Bugue France
183 C7 Le Buisson France
185 F6 Le Buisson-de-Cadouin France
193 K6 Lebus Ger.
193 H7 Lebusa Ger.
184 C2 Le Busseau France
159 O4 Leb"yazhe Ukr.
159 R8 Lebyazhiy, Liman l. Rus. Fed.
Lebyazh'ye Kazakh. see Akku
156 J4 Lebyazh'ye Kirovskaya Oblast' Rus. Fed.
160 M2 Lebyazh'ye Leningradskaya Oblast' Rus. Fed.
161 V9 Lebyazh'ye Lipetskaya Oblast' Rus. Fed.
204 C6 Leça da Palmeira Port.
204 C6 Leça do Bailio Port.
Le Caire Egypt see Al Qāhirah
185 I10 Lecamp, Plateau de France
183 K9 Le Cannet France
183 I10 Le Cannet-des-Maures France
180 B5 Le Cap c. France
271 □[3] Le Carbet Martinique
169 F5 Lecarrow Ireland
183 H10 Le Castellet France
178 G3 Le Cateau-Cambrésis France
178 F3 Le Catelet France
183 C9 Le Caylar France
183 B7 Le Cayrol France
217 O3 Lecce Italy
217 O3 Lecce prov. Italy
212 G4 Lecco Italy
212 G4 Lecco prov. Italy
212 G4 Lecco, Lago di l. Italy
260 I3 Le Center MN U.S.A.
208 D5 Lécera Spain
200 B5 Lech Austria
200 C4 Lech r. Austria/Ger.
220 C5 Lechaina Greece
183 E6 Le Chambon-Feugerolles France
183 E6 Le Chambon-sur-Lignon France
131 I6 Lechang Guangdong China
200 C5 Lechaschau Austria
212 B2 Le Chasseron mt. Switz.
184 B4 Le Château-d'Oléron France
182 I5 Le Châtelard France
181 P8 Le Châtelet France
178 E6 Le Châtelet-en-Brie France
195 J6 Lechbruck Ger.
178 H6 Le Chêne France
178 I4 Le Chesne France
182 J4 Le Cheval Blanc mt. France
183 I6 Le Cheval Noir mt. France
183 E7 Le Cheylard France
183 H6 Le Cheylas France
219 M3 Lechința Romania
219 M4 Lechința r. Romania
151 D3 Lech'khumis K'edi hills Georgia
173 I4 Lechlade-on-Thames Gloucestershire, England U.K.
200 B5 Lechtal val. Austria
200 B5 Lechtaler Alpen mts Austria
191 F6 Lechtingen (Wallenhorst) Ger.
208 D4 Leciñena Spain
190 G1 Leck Ger.
169 F4 Leckaun Ireland
168 F7 Leckmelm Highland, Scotland U.K.
183 C9 Le Clapier France
183 D8 Le Collet-de-Dèze France
261 I10 Lecompte LA U.S.A.
180 B5 Le Conquet France
183 I6 Le Corbier France
182 E4 Le Coteau France
178 C5 Le Coudray-St-Germer France
180 I5 Lécousse France
183 D9 Le Crès France
182 E3 Le Creusot France
207 L7 Lecrín Spain
180 F7 Le Croisic France
178 C3 Le Crotoy France
185 F8 Lectoure France
197 K4 Łęczna Pol.
197 H3 Łęczyca Pol.
196 F1 Łęczyce Pol.
190 D4 Leda r. Ger.
168 F10 Ledaig Argyll and Bute, Scotland U.K.
207 P2 Ledaña Spain
205 O7 Ledanca Spain
116 E3 Ledang, Gunung mt. Malaysia
210 F2 Ledava r. Slovenia
173 K4 Ledburn Buckinghamshire, England U.K.
172 H3 Ledbury Herefordshire, England U.K.
187 E7 Lede Belgium
185 F7 Lède r. France
198 E2 Ledeč nad Sázavou Czech Rep.
187 D7 Ledegem Belgium
156 I4 Ledengskoye Rus. Fed.
198 D3 Ledenice Czech Rep.
185 I7 Lédergues France
204 I6 Ledesma Spain
185 C9 Ledeuix France
183 D7 Le Devès mt. France
271 □[3] Le Diamant Martinique
231 C5 Lediba Dem. Rep. Congo
183 E9 Lédignan France
205 K4 Ledigos Spain
105 K3 Ledknapper Nature Reserve res. Australia
156 J2 Ledkovo Rus. Fed.
168 G6 Ledmore Highland, Scotland U.K.
156 F2 Ledmozero Rus. Fed.
199 H2 Lednica Slovakia
198 F3 Lednice Czech Rep.
117 H4 Ledo Kalimantan Indon.
130 G9 Ledong Hainan China
118 I5 Ledong Hainan China
182 D4 Le Donjon France
184 G3 Le Dorat France
Ledosus France see Lezoux
204 I8 Ledrada Spain
200 C8 Ledro, Lago di l. Italy
128 H8 Ledu Qinghai China
246 H4 Leduc Alta Can.
183 H8 Le Duffre mt. France
153 S3 Ledyanaya, Gora mt. Rus. Fed.
196 E2 Lędyczek Pol.
196 D1 Lędzin Pol.
197 H5 Lędziny Pol.
169 F9 Lee r. Ireland
171 L6 Lee Lancashire, England U.K.
257 L6 Lee MA U.S.A.
257 □Q3 Lee ME U.S.A.
256 F8 Leechburg PA U.S.A.
260 H2 Leech Lake MN U.S.A.
260 H2 Leech Lake Indian Reservation res. MN U.S.A.
171 N6 Leeds West Yorkshire, England U.K.
171 N6 Leeds Bradford International airport England U.K.
172 B7 Leedstown Cornwall, England U.K.
186 J2 Leek Neth.
171 M7 Leek Staffordshire, England U.K.
109 C10 Leeman W.A. Austr.
171 N5 Leeming North Yorkshire, England U.K.
172 D7 Lee Moor Devon, England U.K.
169 C5 Leenane Ireland
187 I6 Leende Neth.
186 J2 Leens Neth.
173 J6 Lee-on-the-Solent Hampshire, England U.K.
256 F7 Leeper PA U.S.A.
190 D4 Leer (Ostfriesland) Ger.
186 H5 Leerdam Neth.
186 H4 Leersum Neth.
185 C10 Lées-Athas France
255 G11 Leesburg FL U.S.A.
255 E10 Leesburg GA U.S.A.
256 A10 Leesburg KY U.S.A.
258 F6 Leesburg NJ U.S.A.
256 B9 Leesburg OH U.S.A.
256 H9 Leesburg VA U.S.A.
191 H5 Leese Ger.
258 D4 Leesport PA U.S.A.
260 H6 Lees Summit MO U.S.A.
109 F8 Lee Steere Range hills W.A. Austr.
103 G10 Leeston South I. N.Z.
261 I10 Leesville LA U.S.A.
256 F11 Leesville Lake VA U.S.A.
105 K6 Leeton N.S.W. Austr.
237 K3 Leeudoringstad S. Africa
236 F8 Leeu-Gamka S. Africa
237 J4 Leeukop mt. S. Africa
237 L5 Leeurivierdam l. S. Africa
236 F8 Leeuw r. S. Africa
186 I2 Leeuwarden Neth.
109 C13 Leeuwin, Cape W.A. Austr.
109 C12 Leeuwin-Naturaliste National Park W.A. Austr.
264 M4 Lee Vining CA U.S.A.
271 K4 Leeward Islands Caribbean Sea
Leeward Islands Arch. de la Société Fr. Polynesia see Sous le Vent, Îles
192 D3 Leezen Mecklenburg-Vorpommern Ger.
190 J3 Leezen Schleswig-Holstein Ger.
180 C5 Le Faou France
180 E5 Le Faouët France
185 G9 Le Fauga France
219 N7 Lefedzha r. Bulg.
180 H8 Le Fenouiller France
178 D1 Leffrinckoucke France
230 B5 Léfini, Réserve de Chasse de la nature res. Congo
150 A3 Lefka Cyprus
220 B4 Lefkada Lefkada Greece
220 B4 Lefkada i. Greece
220 E7 Lefka Ori mts Kriti Greece
Lefkás Lefkada Greece see Lefkada
Lefke Cyprus see Lefka
220 B3 Lefkimmi Kerkyra Greece
Lefkoniko Cyprus see Lefkonikon
150 B3 Lefkonikon Cyprus
220 E4 Lefkonisia i. Greece
Lefkoșa Cyprus see Lefkosia
150 B3 Lefkosia Cyprus
185 E6 Le Fleix France
180 C4 Le Folgoët France
178 F3 Leforest France
185 G9 Le Fossat France
185 G9 Le Fousseret France
271 □[3] Le François Martinique
249 G1 Lefroy r. Que. Can.
109 G11 Lefroy, Lake salt flat W.A. Austr.
183 J8 Le Fugeret France
181 I7 Le Fuilet France
197 J5 Łęg r. Pol.
100 □[3a] Legan i. Kwajalein Marshall Is
205 M8 Leganés Spain
205 O8 Leganiel Spain
248 C3 Legarde r. Ont. Can.
114 D5 Legaspi Luzon Phil.
195 I6 Legau Ger.
178 B7 Le Gault-St-Denis France
178 G6 Le Gault-Soigny France
208 A1 Legazpi Spain
192 E5 Legde Ger.
191 D6 Legden Ger.
180 H8 Legé France
185 B6 Lège-Cap-Ferret France
108 D6 Legendre Island W.A. Austr.
181 J5 Le Genest-St-Isle France
105 K9 Legges Tor mt. Tas. Austr.
264 I2 Leggett CA U.S.A.
169 G3 Leggs Northern Ireland U.K.
Leghorn Italy see Livorno
197 I3 Legionowo Pol.
187 I9 Léglise Belgium
213 K5 Legnago Italy
212 F4 Legnano Italy
196 E4 Legnica Pol.
196 E4 Legnickie Pole Pol.
212 G3 Legnone, Monte mt. Italy
Legohli N.W.T. Can. see Norman Wells
184 E4 Le Gond-Pontouvre France
271 □[2] Le Gosier Guadeloupe
196 G1 Łęgowo Pol.
201 O7 Legrad Croatia
264 L4 Le Grand CA U.S.A.
109 F13 Le Grand, Cape W.A. Austr.
239 □[1c] Le Grand Bénare mt. Réunion
182 I5 Le Grand-Bornand France
184 H3 Le Grand-Bourg France
183 J8 Le Grand Coyer mt. France
182 H4 Le Grand Crêt d'Eau mt. France
183 G6 Le Grand-Lemps France
181 L6 Le Grand-Lucé France
182 J5 Le Grand Mont mt. France
181 M8 Le Grand-Pressigny France
178 B5 Le Grand-Quevilly France
183 G6 Le Grand-Serre France
182 I3 Le Grand Taureau mt. France
183 H7 Le Grand Veymont mt. France
183 E9 Le Grau-du-Roi France
239 □[1c] Le Gros Morne mt. Réunion
181 M3 Le Gros Theil France
183 H6 Le Gua France
276 C5 Leguena Chile
180 E4 Léguer r. France
185 G8 Léguevin France
230 E4 Leguga Dem. Rep. Congo
285 H2 Leguizamón Arg.
106 B3 Legune N.T. Austr.
205 O3 Legutiano Spain
230 E4 Legwe r. Dem. Rep. Congo
118 C4 Le-gya Myanmar
138 F2 Leh Jammu and Kashmir India
179 J8 Le Haut-du-Sec hill France
181 L2 Le Havre France
190 H2 Lehe Ger.
193 D10 Lehesten Ger.
265 U1 Lehi UT U.S.A.
258 E3 Lehigh r. PA U.S.A.
258 D3 Lehigh County county PA U.S.A.
258 D3 Lehighton PA U.S.A.
219 O6 Lehliu-Gară Romania
237 M6 Lehlohonolo S. Africa
285 G2 Lehmann Arg.
191 D10 Lehmen Ger.
190 J2 Lehmkuhlen Ger.
193 F9 Lehndorf Ger.
198 G3 Lehnice Slovakia
193 G6 Lehnin Ger.
192 H5 Lehnitz Ger.
179 N7 Le Hohwald France
180 G5 Léhon France
181 K5 Le Horps France
199 G3 Lehota Slovakia
185 D8 Le Houga France
195 J3 Lehrberg Ger.
191 K6 Lehre Ger.
191 I6 Lehrte Ger.
192 D4 Lehsen Ger.
162 Q5 Lehtimäki Fin.
264 □A11 Lehua i. HI U.S.A.
234 D4 Lehututu Botswana
214 B7 Lei Sardegna Italy
220 D4 Leianokladi Greece
194 G5 Leibertingen Ger.
195 M4 Leiblfing Ger.
201 M6 Leibnitz Austria
130 D4 Leibo Sichuan China
193 I6 Leibsch Ger.
173 J2 Leicester Leicester, England U.K.
173 J2 Leicester admin. div. England U.K.
173 K2 Leicestershire admin. div. England U.K.
106 G4 Leichhardt r. Qld Austr.
106 G5 Leichhardt Falls Qld Austr.
107 K6 Leichhardt Range mts Qld Austr.
191 D8 Leichlingen (Rheinland) Ger.
186 G4 Leiden Neth.
186 G4 Leiderdorp Neth.
186 F4 Leidschendam Neth.
187 E6 Leie r. Belgium
160 J3 Leie Estonia
191 J6 Leiferde Ger.
104 G3 Leigh watercourse S.A. Austr.
102 I3 Leigh North I. N.Z.
171 L7 Leigh Greater Manchester, England U.K.
172 H3 Leigh Worcestershire, England U.K.
104 G4 Leigh Creek S.A. Austr.
169 I7 Leighlinbridge Ireland
173 K4 Leighton Buzzard Bedfordshire, England U.K.
163 I6 Leikanger Norway
118 C5 Leiktho Myanmar
194 F3 Leimen Ger.
186 G4 Leimuiden Neth.
195 K3 Leinburg Ger.
191 I5 Leine r. Ger.
191 J8 Leinefelde Ger.
194 G4 Leinfelden-Echterdingen Ger.
212 D5 Leinì Italy
109 F10 Leinster W.A. Austr.
169 I6 Leinster reg. Ireland
169 I7 Leinster, Mount hill Ireland
194 H4 Leinzell Ger.
205 O2 Leioa Spain
160 G7 Leipalingis Lith.
195 I5 Leipheim Ger.
162 P3 Leipojärvi Sweden
258 D6 Leipsic DE U.S.A.
256 B7 Leipsic OH U.S.A.
258 E6 Leipsic r. DE U.S.A.
221 H5 Leipsoi i. Greece
193 F8 Leipzig Ger.
193 G8 Leipzig admin. reg. Ger.
193 F8 Leipzig-Halle airport Ger.
162 J5 Leira Møre og Romsdal Norway
163 J6 Leira Oppland Norway
162 M3 Leiranger Norway
182 C6 Leiranoux mt. France
162 Q1 Leirbotn Norway
204 C9 Leiria Port.
204 C9 Leiria admin. dist. Port.
204 D4 Leiro Spain
204 C8 Leirosa Port.
164 B2 Leirvik Norway
200 G6 Leisach Austria
201 N2 Leiser Berge park Austria
130 G5 Leishan Guizhou China
131 I5 Lei Shui r. China
160 F3 Leisi Estonia
106 B7 Leisler, Mount hill N.T. Austr.
104 C3 Leisler Hills S.A. Austr.
193 G8 Leisnig Ger.
173 P3 Leiston Suffolk, England U.K.
204 H3 Leitariegos, Puerto de pass Spain
254 D7 Leitchfield KY U.S.A.
171 K2 Leith Edinburgh, Scotland U.K.
201 O4 Leithagebirge hills Austria
103 G10 Leithfield South I. N.Z.
173 L5 Leith Hill England U.K.
169 F4 Leitrim county Ireland
208 B1 Leitza Spain
195 L6 Leitzach r. Ger.
193 E6 Leitzkau Ger.
163 S6 Leivonmäki Fin.
194 B2 Leiwen Ger.
169 J6 Leixlip Ireland
Leiyang Anhui China see Wangjiang
131 I5 Leiyang Hunan China
130 H8 Leizhou Guangdong China
130 G8 Leizhou Bandao pen. China
130 H8 Leizhou Wan b. China
165 K1 Lejberget hill Sweden
186 G5 Lek r. Neth.
162 K4 Leka Norway
162 K4 Leka i. Norway
230 B5 Lékana Congo
199 L3 Lekárovce Slovakia
230 D5 Lekatero Dem. Rep. Congo
197 H6 Łękawica Pol.
227 H1 Le Kef Tunisia
211 B8 Le Kef admin. div. Tunisia
205 P2 Lekeitio Spain
230 B5 Lékéti r. Congo
237 K9 Lekfontein S. Africa
Lekhainá Greece see Lechaina
228 C2 Lekhcheb Maur.
161 N6 Lekhovo Rus. Fed.
230 B5 Lékila Gabon
115 D4 Lekitobi Maluku Indon.
236 B5 Lekkersing S. Africa
196 C4 Łęknica Pol.
228 C3 Léko Mali
162 L2 Lekoes Norway
229 I6 Lékoli-Pandaka, Réserve de Faune de la nature res. Congo
230 B5 Lékoni Gabon
231 B5 Lékoumou admin. reg. Congo
196 D2 Lekowo Pol.
165 L1 Leksand Sweden
Lek'suiri Georgia see Lentekhi
115 E5 Leksula Buru Indon.
Leksura Georgia see Lentekhi
162 K5 Leksvik Norway
208 B1 Lekunberri Spain
115 F3 Lelai, Tanjung pt Halmahera Indon.
271 □[3] Le Lamentin Martinique
162 L3 Leland Norway
250 F8 Leland IL U.S.A.
250 I4 Leland MI U.S.A.
261 J9 Leland MS U.S.A.
164 I2 Lelång l. Sweden
184 C3 Le Langon France
184 G5 Le Lardin-St-Lazare France
183 I8 Le Lauzet-Ubaye France
183 I10 Le Lavandou France
283 C6 Leleque Arg.
199 L3 Leles Slovakia
199 L6 Lelese Romania
158 H2 Leleta Ukr.
185 C8 Le Leuy France
Leli Guangxi China see Tianlin
100 □[6] Leli i. Solomon Is
197 H3 Lelice Pol.
210 G4 Lelija mt. Bos.-Herz.
129 O8 Leling Shandong China
115 G5 Lelinta Papua Indon.
181 J6 Le Lion-d'Angers France
197 J2 Lelis Pol.
197 I1 Lelkowo Pol.
212 B1 Le Locle Switz.
115 C8 Lelogama Timor Indon.
180 I7 Le Loroux-Bottereau France
271 □[3] Le Lorrain Martinique
228 B4 Lélouma Guinea
181 J6 Le Louroux-Béconnais France
197 H5 Lelów Pol.
183 I10 Le Luc France
181 L6 Le Lude France
183 B6 Le Luguet mt. France
275 H3 Lelydorp Suriname
186 H3 Lelystad Neth.
283 D9 Le Maire, Estrecho de sea chan. Arg.
183 C7 Le Malzieu-Ville France
212 A3 Léman, Lac l. France/Switz.
181 L5 Le Mans France
271 □[3] Le Marin Martinique
179 N8 Le Markstein France
260 G4 Le Mars IA U.S.A.
183 E8 Le Martinet France
185 E7 Le Mas-d'Agenais France
185 G9 Le Mas-d'Azil France
232 D3 Lema Shilindi Eth.
185 J8 Le Masnau-Massuguiès France
183 C8 Le Massegros France
182 D4 Le Mayet-de-Montagne France
286 T2 LeMay Range mts Antarctica
181 J7 Le May-sur-Èvre France
201 I2 Lembach im Mühlkreis Austria
233 C6 Lembai well Tanz.
117 L9 Lembar Lombok Indon.
115 D3 Lembeh i. Indon.
187 E6 Lembeke Belgium
179 N5 Lemberg France
194 D3 Lemberg Ger.
194 F5 Lemberg mt. Ger.
Lemberg Ukr. see L'viv
185 D9 Lembeye France
185 G7 Lemboulas r. France
185 F6 Lembras France
190 F5 Lembruch Ger.
117 L3 Lembu Kalimantan Indon.
116 B2 Lembu, Gunung mt. Indon.
117 L2 Lembubut Kalimantan Indon.
Lemdiyya Alg. see Médéa
280 D5 Leme Brazil
186 J4 Lemele Neth.
186 J4 Lemelerveld Neth.
181 L4 Le Mêle-sur-Sarthe France
232 E3 Lemem Bar YeWha Gudgwad well Eth.
181 L4 Le Merlerault France
183 G7 Le Merlu Rocher mt. France
199 K3 Lemešany Slovakia
161 O6 Lemeshi Rus. Fed.
159 K1 Lemeshivka Ukr.
178 H6 Le Mesnil-sur-Oger France
150 B4 Lemesos Cyprus
191 F6 Lemförde Ger.
191 G6 Lemgo Ger.
262 H4 Lemhi r. ID U.S.A.

262 H4 **Lemhi Range** *mts ID* U.S.A.
163 S6 **Lemi** Fin.
196 C3 **Lemierzyce** Pol.
243 L3 **Lemieux Islands** *Nunavut* Can.
163 P6 **Lemland** *Åland* Fin.
162 R2 **Lemmenjoen kansallispuisto** *nat. park* Fin.
186 I3 **Lemmer** Neth.
260 D3 **Lemmon** *SD* U.S.A.
265 V9 **Lemmon, Mount** *AZ* U.S.A.
Lemnos *i.* Greece *see* **Limnos**
236 E9 **Lemoenshoek** S. Africa
181 J3 **Le Molay-Littry** France
182 I4 **Le Môle** *mt.* France
212 C2 **Le Moleson** *mt.* Switz.
270 G4 **Le Môle St-Nicolas** Haiti
183 C7 **Le Monastier** France
183 D7 **Le Monastier-sur-Gazeille** France
264 M5 **Lemoncove** *CA* U.S.A.
183 J7 **Le Monêtier-les-Bains** France
264 O9 **Lemon Grove** *CA* U.S.A.
250 F8 **Lemont** *IL* U.S.A.
100 □5 **Le Mont-Dore** New Caledonia
182 C4 **Le Montet** France
180 H4 **Le Mont-St-Michel** *tourist site* France
264 M5 **Lemoore** *CA* U.S.A.
239 □1b **Le Morne Brabant** *pen.* Mauritius
271 □3 **Le Morne-Rouge** Martinique
100 □4a **Lemotol Bay** *Chuuk* Micronesia
271 □2 **Le Moule** Guadeloupe
183 D7 **Le Moure de la Gardille** *mt.* France
183 I7 **Le Mourre Froid** *mt.* France
249 G1 **Le Moyne, Lac** *l. Que.* Can.
163 Q6 **Lempäälä** Fin.
182 C5 **Lempdes** *Auvergne* France
183 C6 **Lempdes** *Auvergne* France
118 A4 **Lemro** *r.* Myanmar
156 L3 **Lemtybozh** Rus. Fed.
117 H4 **Lemukutan** *i.* Indon.
215 Q5 **Le Murge** *hills* Italy
183 J10 **Le Muy** France
156 M2 **Lemva** *r.* Rus. Fed.
164 E5 **Lemvig** Denmark
190 G4 **Lemwerder** Ger.
169 G8 **Lemybrien** Ireland
118 B6 **Lemyethna** Myanmar
156 L3 **Lem"yu** *r.* Rus. Fed.
164 G1 **Lena** Norway
204 C9 **Lena** *r.* Port.
153 N3 **Lena** *r.* Rus. Fed.
250 E7 **Lena** *IL* U.S.A.
250 F5 **Lena** *WI* U.S.A.
169 D4 **Lenadoon Point** Ireland
100 □5 **Lénakel** Vanuatu
117 L9 **Lenangguar** *Sumbawa* Indon.
201 M6 **Lenart** Slovenia
160 E5 **Lēnas** Latvia
199 J6 **Lenauheim** Romania
184 E2 **Lencloître** France
278 E2 **Lençóis Maranhenses, Parque Nacional dos** *nat. park* Brazil
280 C5 **Lençóis Paulista** Brazil
185 D7 **Lencouacq** France
200 H5 **Lend** Austria
230 F4 **Lenda** *r.* Dem. Rep. Congo
199 J2 **Lendak** Slovakia
210 F2 **Lendava** Slovenia
187 D7 **Lendelede** Belgium
156 E3 **Lendery** Rus. Fed.
213 L5 **Lendinara** Italy
201 H6 **Lendorf** Austria
170 C6 **Lene, Lough** *l.* Ireland
198 C1 **Lenešice** Czech Rep.
181 M3 **Le Neubourg** France
144 I4 **Lengar** Iran
200 H3 **Lengau** *Oberösterreich* Austria
200 G5 **Lengau** *Salzburg* Austria
144 H7 **Lengbarūt** Iran
195 M5 **Lengdorf** Ger.
191 J6 **Lengede** Ger.
193 H9 **Lengefeld** Ger.
193 F9 **Lengenfeld** Ger.
191 J8 **Lengenfeld unterm Stein** Ger.
195 J6 **Lengenwang** Ger.
143 M6 **Lenger** Kazakh.
190 E5 **Lengerich** *Niedersachsen* Ger.
191 E6 **Lengerich** *Nordrhein-Westfalen* Ger.
195 L6 **Lenggries** Ger.
132 K7 **Lenghuzhen** *Qinghai* China
128 G7 **Lenglong Ling** *mts* China
212 C1 **Lengnau** Switz.
230 C5 **Lengoué** *r.* Congo
131 H5 **Lengshuijiang** *Hunan* China
131 H5 **Lengshuitan** *Hunan* China
284 B2 **Lengua de Vaca, Punta** *pt* Chile
233 B8 **Lengwe National Park** Malawi
199 G5 **Lengyeltóti** Hungary
173 N5 **Lenham** *Kent, England* U.K.
258 D3 **Lenhartsville** *PA* U.S.A.
165 L5 **Lenhovda** Sweden
214 B9 **Leni** *r.* Italy
151 H5 **Lenin** Azer.
Lenīn Kazakh. *see* **Kazygurt**
145 M2 **Lenin** Tajik.
Lenin, Qullai *mt.* Kyrg./Tajik. *see* **Lenin Peak**
151 F2 **Lenina, Kanal** *canal* Rus. Fed.
Lenina, Pik *mt.* Kyrg./Tajik. *see* **Lenin Peak**
Leninabad Tajik. *see* **Khŭjand**
Leninabad Oblast *admin. div.* Tajik. *see* **Soghd**
Leninakan Armenia *see* **Gyumri**
Lenin Atyndagy Choku *mt.* Kyrg./Tajik. *see* **Lenin Peak**
159 L6 **Lenine** *Mykolayivs'ka Oblast'* Ukr.
159 O8 **Lenine** *Respublika Krym* Ukr.
179 M6 **Léning** France
Leningori Georgia *see* **Akhalgori**
Leningrad Rus. Fed. *see* **Sankt-Peterburg**
145 N2 **Leningrad** Tajik.
Leningrad Oblast *admin. div.* Rus. Fed. *see* **Leningradskaya Oblast'**
157 G7 **Leningradskaya** Rus. Fed.
161 P2 **Leningradskaya Oblast'** *admin. div.* Rus. Fed.
153 S3 **Leningradskiy** Rus. Fed.
Leningradskiy Tajik. *see* **Leningrad**
159 K2 **Leninivka** Ukr.
151 I3 **Leninkent** Rus. Fed.
122 I6 **Lenino** Rus. Fed.
Lenino Ukr. *see* **Lenine**
Leninobod Tajik. *see* **Khŭjand**
Leninobod Uzbek. *see* **Qanliko'l**
Leninogor Kazakh. *see* **Leninogorsk**
143 T2 **Leninogorsk** Kazakh.
157 K5 **Leninogorsk** Rus. Fed.
143 O8 **Lenin Peak** Kyrg./Tajik.
143 N6 **Leninpol'** Kyrg.
Leninsk Kazakh. *see* **Baykonyr**
157 I6 **Leninsk** Rus. Fed.
Leninsk Turkm. *see* **Akdepe**
Leninsk Uzbek. *see* **Asaka**
159 N6 **Lenins'ke** *Dnipropetrovs'ka Oblast'* Ukr.
159 N8 **Lenins'ke** *Respublika Krym* Ukr.
159 O8 **Lenins'ke** *Respublika Krym* Ukr.
161 U7 **Leninskiy** Rus. Fed.
152 J4 **Leninsk-Kuznetskiy** Rus. Fed.
142 G3 **Leninskoye** Kazakh.
Leninskoye *Yuzhnyy Kazakhstan* Kazakh. *see* **Kazygurt**
156 I4 **Leninskoye** *Kirovskaya Oblast'* Rus. Fed.
122 H5 **Leninskoye** *Yevreyskaya Avtonomnaya Oblast'* Rus. Fed.
185 D7 **Le Nizan** France
212 C3 **Lenk** Switz.
158 G4 **Lenkivtsi** Ukr.
Lenkoran' Azer. *see* **Länkäran**
108 H4 **Lennard** *r. W.A.* Austr.
191 I7 **Lenne** Ger.
191 D8 **Lenne** *r.* Ger.
191 F8 **Lennestadt** Ger.
194 G4 **Lenningen** Ger.
283 D9 **Lennox, Isla** *i.* Chile
287 L1 **Lennox-King Glacier** Antarctica
168 H11 **Lennoxtown** *East Dunbartonshire, Scotland* U.K.
212 I5 **Leno** Italy
255 G8 **Lenoir** *NC* U.S.A.
255 E8 **Lenoir City** *TN* U.S.A.
212 B1 **Le Noirmont** Switz.
215 K5 **Lenola** Italy
256 C11 **Lenore** *WV* U.S.A.
247 J4 **Lenore Lake** *Sask.* Can.
178 G3 **Le Nouvion-en-Thiérache** France
257 L6 **Lenox** *MA* U.S.A.
187 E7 **Lens** Belgium
178 E3 **Lens** France
190 K2 **Lensahn** Ger.
153 M3 **Lensk** Rus. Fed.
182 G4 **Lent** France
186 I5 **Lent** Neth.
151 D3 **Lentekhi** Georgia
190 I3 **Lentföhrden** Ger.
198 F5 **Lenti** Hungary
213 M3 **Lentiai** Italy
195 K4 **Lenting** Ger.
217 I9 **Lentini** *Sicilia* Italy
217 I9 **Lentini** *r. Sicilia* Italy
162 T4 **Lentua** *l.* Fin.
Lentvaravas Lith. *see* **Lentvaris**
160 I7 **Lentvaris** Lith.
161 T3 **Lent'yevo** Rus. Fed.
264 O7 **Lenwood** *CA* U.S.A.
119 D9 **Lenya** Myanmar
212 E1 **Lenzburg** Switz.
192 D4 **Lenzen** Ger.
201 I4 **Lenzing** Austria
194 E6 **Lenzkirch** Ger.
228 E4 **Léo** Burkina
213 J7 **Leo** *r.* Italy
201 I6 **Leoben** *Kärnten* Austria
201 L5 **Leoben** *Steiermark* Austria
201 N3 **Leobendorf** Austria
201 N4 **Leobersdorf** Austria
Leodhais, Eilean *i. Scotland* U.K. *see* **Lewis, Isle of**
270 G4 **Léogane** Haiti
200 G5 **Leogang** Austria
200 G5 **Leoganger Steinberge** *mts* Austria
185 C6 **Léognan** France
115 B3 **Leok** *Sulawesi* Indon.
260 F3 **Leola** *SD* U.S.A.
172 G3 **Leominster** *Herefordshire, England* U.K.
257 N6 **Leominster** *MA* U.S.A.
185 B8 **Léon** France
268 F4 **León** Mex.
266 □P11 **León** Nic.
204 I3 **León** Spain
204 I3 **León** *prov.* Spain
260 I5 **Leon** *IA* U.S.A.
261 G10 **Leon** *r. TX* U.S.A.
185 B8 **Léon, Étang de** *l.* France
206 G8 **León, Isla de** *i.* Spain
204 G4 **León, Montes de** *mts* Spain
261 G9 **Leonard** *TX* U.S.A.
215 I4 **Leonardo da Vinci** *airport* Italy
256 I10 **Leonardtown** *MD* U.S.A.
234 C4 **Leonardville** Namibia
Leonarisso Cyprus *see* **Leonarisson**
150 C3 **Leonarisson** Cyprus
267 P7 **Leona Vicario** Mex.
194 G4 **Leonberg** Ger.
183 G7 **Léoncel** France
Leondárion Greece *see* **Leontari**
201 J3 **Leonding** Austria
100 □2 **Leone** American Samoa
212 E3 **Leone, Monte** *mt.* Italy/Switz.
285 F3 **Leones** Arg.
215 J2 **Leonessa** Italy
216 G8 **Leonforte** *Sicilia* Italy
105 J8 **Leongatha** *Vic.* Austr.
214 G2 **Leoni, Monte** *hill* Italy
220 D5 **Leonidio** Greece
122 M4 **Leonidovo** *Sakhalin* Rus. Fed.
109 F10 **Leonora** *W.A.* Austr.
220 D3 **Leontari** Greece
244 G5 **Leontovich, Cape** *AK* U.S.A.
139 M6 **Leopani** Bhutan
108 I5 **Leopold** *r. W.A.* Austr.
256 E9 **Leopold** *WV* U.S.A.
108 H5 **Leopold Downs** *W.A.* Austr.
108 H4 **Leopold Downs Aboriginal Reserve** *W.A.* Austr.
Léopold II, Lac *l.* Dem. Rep. Congo *see* **Mai-Ndombe, Lac**
281 F4 **Leopoldina** Brazil
280 C2 **Leopoldo de Bulhões** Brazil
187 H6 **Leopoldsburg** Belgium
201 O3 **Leopoldsdorf im Marchfelde** Austria
192 I3 **Leopoldshagen** Ger.
191 G6 **Leopoldshöhe** Ger.
194 D5 **Leopoldskanal** *canal* Ger.
Léopoldville Dem. Rep. Congo *see* **Kinshasa**
260 E6 **Leoti** *KS* U.S.A.
158 H7 **Leova** Moldova
247 J4 **Leoville** *Sask.* Can.
Leovo Moldova *see* **Leova**
180 E7 **Le Palais** France
184 G4 **Le Palais-sur-Vienne** France
180 I7 **Le Pallet** France
116 G6 **Lepar** *i.* Indon.
178 D3 **Le Parcq** France
185 F7 **Le Passage** France
178 G7 **Le Pavillon-Ste-Julie** France
284 B3 **Lepe** Chile
206 E6 **Lepe** Spain
183 F6 **Le Péage-de-Roussillon** France
184 H2 **Le Pêchereau** France
Lepel' Belarus *see* **Lyepyel'**
180 H7 **Le Pellerin** France
220 C4 **Lepenou** Greece
183 H7 **Le Périer** France
185 J11 **Le Perthus** France
181 I5 **Le Pertre** France
178 B5 **Le Petit-Quevilly** France
235 E4 **Lephalale** S. Africa
234 E4 **Lephepe** Botswana
237 J6 **Lephoi** S. Africa
184 C6 **Le Pian-Médoc** France
181 L4 **Le Pin-au-Haras** France
178 H6 **L'Épine** *Champagne-Ardenne* France
183 H8 **L'Épine** *Provence-Alpes-Côte d'Azur* France
131 K4 **Leping** *Jiangxi* China
181 M5 **Le Pin-la-Garenne** France
239 □1c **Le Piton** Réunion
184 E5 **Le Pizou** France
185 G9 **Le Plan** France
178 E5 **Le Plessis-Belleville** France
156 M3 **Lep'lya** *r.* Rus. Fed.
183 H8 **Le Poët** France
210 F2 **Lepoglava** Croatia
181 O8 **Le Poinçonnet** France
180 H8 **Le Poiré-sur-Vie** France
182 H5 **Le Pont-de-Beauvoisin** France
183 H6 **Le Pont-de-Claix** France
183 D8 **Le Pont-de-Monvert** France
183 F9 **Le Pontet** France
212 E3 **Lepontine, Alpi** *mts* Italy/Switz.
217 M3 **Leporano** Italy
185 B6 **Le Porge** France
185 B6 **Le Porge-Océan** France
239 □1c **Le Port** Réunion
178 C2 **Le Portel** France
Leposavić *Leposaviq* Kosovo *see* **Leposaviq**
218 I7 **Leposaviq** *Leposaviq* Kosovo
239 □1b **Le Pouce** *hill* Mauritius
183 D9 **Le Pouget** France
180 D6 **Le Pouldu** France
180 G7 **Le Pouliguen** France
183 F7 **Le Pouzin** France
162 R5 **Leppävesi** Fin.
162 S5 **Leppävirta** Fin.
183 I10 **Le Pradet** France
249 H4 **Lepreau, Point** *N.B.* Can.
271 □3 **Le Prêcheur** Martinique
Lepsa Kazakh. *see* **Lepsy**
Lepsa *r.* Kazakh. *see* **Lepsy**
199 H4 **Lepsény** Hungary
Lepsi Kazakh. *see* **Lepsinsk**
143 S5 **Lepsinsk** Kazakh.
143 R4 **Lepsy** Kazakh.
143 R4 **Lepsy** *r.* Kazakh.
224 B1 **Leptis Magna** *tourist site* Libya
220 D2 **Leptokarya** Greece
178 C7 **Le Puiset** France
183 D6 **Le Puy-en-Velay** France
181 K7 **Le Puy-Notre-Dame** France
183 G9 **Le Puy-Ste-Réparade** France
228 B2 **Leqçeïba** Maur.
178 G3 **Le Quesnoy** France
228 D4 **Léraba** *r.* Burkina/Côte d'Ivoire
178 E6 **Le Raincy** France
235 E4 **Lerala** Botswana
185 H10 **Léran** France
237 L4 **Leratswana** S. Africa
216 F8 **Lercara Friddi** *Sicilia* Italy
105 J7 **Lerderderg State Park** *nature res. Vic.* Austr.
269 L7 **Lerdo** Mex.
230 B2 **Léré** Chad
182 B2 **Léré** France
228 D3 **Léré** Mali
229 H4 **Lere** Nigeria
115 A4 **Lereh, Tanjung** *pt* Indon.
180 C5 **Le Relecq-Kerhuon** France
204 C4 **Lérez** *r.* Spain
180 H5 **Le Rheu** France
212 H7 **Lerici** Italy
274 D5 **Lérida** Col.
Lérida Spain *see* **Lleida**
Lérida *prov. Cataluña* Spain *see* **Lleida**
151 J7 **Lerik** Azer.
205 Q4 **Lerín** Spain
183 K9 **Lérins, Îles de** *is* France
267 N8 **Lerma** Mex.
268 E5 **Lerma** *r.* Mex.
205 M4 **Lerma** Spain
269 H6 **Lerma de Vilada** Mex.
185 D7 **Lerm-et Musset** France
151 D1 **Lermontov** Rus. Fed.
122 I5 **Lermontovka** Rus. Fed.
Lermontovskiy Rus. Fed. *see* **Lermontov**
200 C5 **Lermoos** Austria
214 C6 **Lerno, Monte** *mt.* Italy
271 □3 **Le Robert** Martinique
182 J5 **Le Roignais** *mt.* France
221 H5 **Leros** *i.* Greece
185 I6 **Le Rouget** France
179 K6 **Lérouville** France
250 F9 **Le Roy** *IL* U.S.A.
250 B6 **Le Roy** *MN* U.S.A.
256 H6 **Le Roy** *NY* U.S.A.
258 B1 **Leroy** *PA* U.S.A.
248 F1 **Le Roy, Lac** *l. Que.* Can.
183 C8 **Le Rozier** France
179 L7 **Lerrain** France
212 E7 **Lerrone** *r.* Italy
164 I4 **Lerum** Sweden
182 J2 **Le Russey** France
168 □N2 **Lerwick** *Shetland, Scotland* U.K.
230 E2 **Ler Zerai** *well* Sudan
185 F10 **Lés** Spain
212 F4 **Lesa** Italy
182 H5 **Les Abrets** France
271 □2 **Les Abymes** Guadeloupe
200 G6 **Lesachtal** *val.* Austria
183 J9 **Les Adrets-de-l'Estérel** France
208 J4 **Les Agudes** *mt.* Spain
182 B2 **Les Aix-d'Angillon** France
208 B1 **Lesaka** Spain
185 J11 **Les Albères** *reg.* France
182 B5 **Les Ancizes-Comps** France
178 B5 **Les Andelys** France
183 F9 **Les Angles** *Languedoc-Roussillon* France
185 I10 **Les Angles** *Languedoc-Roussillon* France
271 □3 **Les Anses-d'Arlets** Martinique
181 L4 **Le Sap** France
183 I10 **Les Arcs** *Provence-Alpes-Côte d'Azur* France
182 J5 **Les Arcs** *Rhône-Alpes* France
181 J8 **Les Aubiers** France
183 J8 **Le Sauze-Super-Sauze** France
208 G4 **Les Avellanes** Spain
182 H5 **Les Avenières** France
239 □1c **Les Avirons** Réunion
183 D8 **Les Bondons** France
178 D8 **Les Bordes** France
185 G9 **Les Bordes-sur-Arize** France
208 G4 **Les Borges Blanques** Spain
208 H5 **Les Borges del Camp** Spain
Lesbos *i.* Greece *see* **Lesvos**
182 H4 **Les Bouchoux** France
212 B1 **Les Brenets** Switz.
171 N3 **Lesbury** *Northumberland, England* U.K.
185 H10 **Les Cabannes** France
208 L3 **L'Escala** Spain
183 I8 **L'Escale** France
239 □1b **L'Escalier** Mauritius
185 I9 **Les Cammazes** France
185 D9 **Lescar** France
183 K9 **L'Escarène** France
182 J4 **Les Carroz-d'Arâches** France
208 G6 **Les Cases d'Alcanar** Spain
270 G4 **Les Cayes** Haiti
201 J7 **Lesce** Slovenia
181 K5 **Les Coëvrons** *hills* France
180 C6 **Lesconil** France
182 J5 **Les Contamines-Montjoie** France
182 J4 **Les Cornettes de Bise** *mts* France/Switz.
209 F7 **Les Coves de Vinromà** Spain
185 I8 **Lescure-d'Albigeois** France
183 I6 **Les Deux-Alpes** France
212 C3 **Les Diablerets** Switz.
212 C3 **Les Diablerets** *mts* Switz.
230 D4 **Lese** *r.* Dem. Rep. Congo
217 L5 **Lese** *r.* Italy
183 H6 **Les Échelles** France
180 H3 **Les Écréhou** *is* Channel Is
184 D5 **Les Églisottes-et-Chalaures** France
183 J8 **Le Seignus-d'Allos** France
180 H6 **Le Sel-de-Bretagne** France
185 C7 **Le Sen** France
198 G5 **Lesencetomaj** Hungary
212 A2 **Le Sentier** Switz.
179 K5 **Les Éparges** France
181 J8 **Les Epesses** France
208 I2 **Les Escaldes** Andorra
249 G3 **Les Escoumins** *Que.* Can.
182 G3 **Les Essards-Taignevaux** France
180 I8 **Les Essarts** France
257 □Q1 **Les Étroits** *Que.* Can.
208 H3 **Le Seu d'Urgell** Spain
185 G6 **Les Eyzies-de-Tayac-Sireuil** France
182 J2 **Les Fins** France
179 L7 **Les Forges** France
182 I3 **Les Fourgs** France
182 J4 **Les Gets** France
130 D4 **Leshan** *Sichuan* China
179 I4 **Les Hautes-Rivières** France
159 P2 **Leshchinka** *r.* Rus. Fed.
184 B2 **Les Herbiers** France
Leshou *Hebei* China *see* **Xianxian**
182 J5 **Les Houches** France
156 I2 **Leshukonskoye** Rus. Fed.
151 D3 **Lesichine** Georgia
201 M7 **Lesično** Slovenia
178 E6 **Lésigny** France
212 G6 **Lesima, Monte** *mt.* Italy
215 O4 **Lesina** Italy
215 O4 **Lesina, Lago di** *lag.* Italy
183 J10 **Les Issambres** France
163 J5 **Lesja** Norway
165 K2 **Lesjöfors** Sweden
185 G6 **Les Junies** France
183 I6 **Les Karellis** France
151 E2 **Lesken** Rus. Fed.
Leskhimstroy Ukr. *see* **Syeverodonets'k**
197 K6 **Lesko** Pol.
219 J8 **Leskovac** *Leskovac* Serbia
220 B2 **Leskovik** Albania
287 F2 **Leskov Island** Antarctica
159 L4 **Les'ky** Ukr.
181 I8 **Les Landes-Genusson** France
184 E5 **Les Lèches** France
183 H10 **Les Lecques** France
168 J10 **Leslie** *Fife, Scotland* U.K.
250 J7 **Leslie** *MI* U.S.A.
180 I8 **Les Lucs-sur-Boulogne** France
168 I11 **Lesmahagow** *South Lanarkshire, Scotland* U.K.
182 G2 **Les Maillys** France
271 □2 **Les Mangles** Guadeloupe
182 I6 **Les Marches** France
182 C5 **Les Martres-de-Veyre** France
183 D9 **Les Matelles** France
181 J7 **Les Mauges** *reg.* France
178 I4 **Les Mazures** France
249 H3 **Les Méchins** *Que.* Can.
208 L3 **Les Medes** *is* Spain
183 H8 **Les Mées** France
183 J6 **Les Menuires** France
180 G4 **Les Minquiers** *is* Channel Is
183 I8 **Les Monges** *mt.* France
178 H7 **Lesmont** France
178 C6 **Les Mureaux** France
199 G2 **Lešná** Czech Rep.
196 D4 **Leśna** Pol.
197 L3 **Leśna** *r.* Pol.
180 C4 **Lesneven** France
196 G5 **Leśnica** Pol.
196 D4 **Leśniów Wielki** Pol.
178 H7 **Les Noës-près-Troyes** France
156 K4 **Lesnoy** *Kirovskaya Oblast'* Rus. Fed.
Lesnoy *Murmanskaya Oblast'* Rus. Fed. *see* **Umba**
161 X7 **Lesnoy** *Ryazanskaya Oblast'* Rus. Fed.
161 O6 **Lesnoy** *Smolenskaya Oblast'* Rus. Fed.
160 L1 **Lesnoy, Ostrov** *i.* Rus. Fed.
161 S3 **Lesnoye** Rus. Fed.
156 K4 **Lesnyye Polyany** Rus. Fed.
122 M4 **Lesogorsk** *Sakhalin* Rus. Fed.
160 L1 **Lesogorskiy** Rus. Fed.
183 F7 **Les Ollières-sur-Eyrieux** France
122 I5 **Lesopil'noye** Rus. Fed.
183 J7 **Les Orres** France
153 K4 **Lesosibirsk** Rus. Fed.
237 M5 **Lesotho** *country* Africa
237 M5 **Lesotho Highlands Water Project** Lesotho
122 H6 **Lesozavodsk** Rus. Fed.
184 C5 **Lesparre-Médoc** France
184 D5 **Les Peintures** France
183 G10 **Les Pennes-Mirabeau** France
239 □2b **L'Espérance** *Mahé* Seychelles
99 I5 **L'Espérance Rock** *i.* N.Z.
185 B8 **Lesperon** France
178 H5 **Les Petites-Loges** France
219 L3 **Lespezi** *hill* Romania
180 H2 **Les Pieux** France
183 C10 **Lespignan** France
208 F6 **L'Espina** *mt.* Spain
185 J9 **Lespinassière** France
182 I3 **Les Planches-en-Montagne** France
208 H5 **L'Espluga Calba** Spain
208 H5 **L'Espluga de Francolí** Spain
184 C1 **Les Ponts-de-Cé** France
212 B1 **Les Ponts-de-Martel** Switz.
208 J3 **Les Preses** Spain
185 F9 **Lespugue** France
178 H8 **Les Riceys** France
181 K7 **Les Rosiers-sur-Loire** France
209 F10 **Les Rotes** Spain
182 I4 **Les Rousses** France
184 A3 **Les Sables-d'Olonne** France
201 I5 **Lessach** Austria
183 E8 **Les Salles-du-Gardon** France
180 H3 **Lessay** France
187 G8 **Lesse** *r.* Belgium
187 H8 **Lesse et Lomme, Parc Naturel de** *nature res.* Belgium
180 E4 **Les Sept-Îles** *is* France
271 J7 **Lesser Antilles** *is* Caribbean Sea
151 D4 **Lesser Caucasus** *mts* Asia
138 F4 **Lesser Himalaya** *mts* India/Nepal
Lesser Khingan Mountains China *see* **Xiao Hinggan Ling**
246 H4 **Lesser Slave Lake** *Alta* Can.
246 H4 **Lesser Slave Lake Provincial Park** *Alta* Can.
112 E8 **Lesser Sunda Islands** Indon.
147 L2 **Lesser Tunb** *i.* The Gulf
178 G7 **Les Sièges** France
187 E7 **Lessines** Belgium
237 K5 **Lessingskop** *mt.* S. Africa
213 J4 **Lessini, Monti** *mts* Italy
239 □2a **Les Sœurs** *is Inner Islands* Seychelles
180 H7 **Les Sorinières** France
185 D9 **Lestelle-Bétharram** France
256 D11 **Lester** *WV* U.S.A.
183 C6 **Les Ternes** France
178 C5 **Les Thilliers-en-Vexin** France
183 J8 **Les Thuiles** France
162 R5 **Lestijärvi** Fin.
162 Q4 **Lestijoki** *r.* Fin.
183 B8 **Lestrade** France
180 D4 **Les Triagoz** *is* France
239 □1c **Les Trois Bassins** Réunion
271 □3 **Les Trois-Îlets** Martinique
181 L7 **Les Trois-Moutiers** France
230 E3 **Les Trois Rivières** C.A.R.
183 B7 **Les Trucs d'Aubrac** *mt.* France
199 L5 **Leşu, Lacul** *l.* Romania
108 I2 **Lesueur Island** *W.A.* Austr.
178 D6 **Les Ulis** France
117 K4 **Lesung, Bukit** *mt.* Indon.
183 E8 **Les Vans** France
183 C8 **Les Vignes** France
221 G3 **Lesvos** *i.* Greece
196 D2 **Leszczyn** Pol.
197 K4 **Leszkowice** Pol.
197 I3 **Leszno** *Mazowieckie* Pol.
196 E4 **Leszno** *Wielkopolskie* Pol.
196 D4 **Leszno Górne** Pol.
183 H6 **Le Taillefer** *mt.* France
208 E2 **Le Taillon** *mt.* Spain
181 K8 **Le Tallud** France
165 K2 **Letälven** *r.* Sweden
239 □1c **Le Tampon** Réunion
183 E7 **Le Tanargue** *mt.* France
199 K4 **Létavértes** Hungary
173 L4 **Letchworth Garden City** *Hertfordshire, England* U.K.
185 B6 **Le Teich** France
183 F7 **Le Teil** France
181 J4 **Le Teilleul** France
182 E2 **Le Télégraphe** *hill* France
185 C6 **Le Temple** France
198 F5 **Letenye** Hungary
138 F7 **Leteri** *Madh. Prad.* India
118 A3 **Letha Range** *mts* Myanmar
246 H5 **Lethbridge** *Alta* Can.
249 K3 **Lethbridge** *Nfld and Lab.* Can.
190 F4 **Lethe** *r.* Ger.
181 M5 **Le Theil** France
180 I6 **Le-Theil-de-Bretagne** France
275 G4 **Lethem** Guyana
173 O2 **Letheringsett** *Norfolk, England* U.K.
179 M8 **Le Thillot** France
179 M7 **Le Tholy** France
183 I10 **Le Thoronet** France
115 E8 **Leti** *i. Maluku* Indon.
115 E8 **Leti, Kepulauan** *is Maluku* Indon.
274 D6 **Leticia** Col.
129 P7 **Leting** *Hebei* China
215 M5 **Letino** Italy
236 G8 **Letjiesbos** S. Africa
199 H4 **Letkés** Hungary
237 L1 **Letlhabile** S. Africa
234 E4 **Letlhakane** Botswana
234 E5 **Letlhakeng** Botswana
156 F2 **Letnerechenskiy** Rus. Fed.
156 G2 **Letniy Navolok** Rus. Fed.
115 F8 **Letoda** *Maluku* Indon.
213 M2 **Le Tofane** *mt.* Italy
217 I8 **Letoianni** *Sicilia* Italy
201 O1 **Letonice** Czech Rep.
178 C2 **Le Touquet-Paris-Plage** France
183 C9 **Le Tour d'Arre** *hill* France
183 H6 **Le Touvet** France
198 F2 **Letovice** Czech Rep.
118 B6 **Letpadan** Myanmar
178 B3 **Le Tréport** France
183 B8 **Le Truel** France
163 M6 **Letsbo** Sweden
192 J5 **Letschin** Ger.
119 D9 **Letsok-aw Kyun** *i.* Myanmar
237 J2 **Letsopa** S. Africa
229 I5 **Letta** Cameroon
Lette Island *Vava'u Gp* Tonga *see* **Late**
164 I1 **Letten** *l.* Sweden
170 B5 **Letterbreen** *Northern Ireland* U.K.
169 C6 **Lettercallow** Ireland
169 C9 **Letterfinish** Ireland
169 C5 **Letterfrack** Ireland
169 G3 **Letterkenny** Ireland
172 C4 **Letterston** *Pembrokeshire, Wales* U.K.
116 F3 **Letung** Indon.
207 O4 **Letur** Spain
185 C7 **Le Tuzan** France
115 F7 **Letwurung** *Maluku* Indon.
157 H6 **Letyazhevka** Rus. Fed.
158 G4 **Letychiv** Ukr.
Lëtzebuerg *country* Europe *see* **Luxembourg**
193 D6 **Letzlingen** Ger.
219 M6 **Leu** Romania
231 D7 **Léua** Angola
193 H8 **Leuben** Ger.
193 D8 **Leubingen** Ger.
185 I9 **Leuc** France
Leucas *Lefkada* Greece *see* **Lefkada**
185 K10 **Leucate** France
185 K10 **Leucate, Cap** *c.* France
185 K10 **Leucate, Étang de** *l.* France
168 K10 **Leuchars** *Fife, Scotland* U.K.
195 M2 **Leuchtenberg** Ger.
192 I5 **Leuenberg** Ger.
179 I8 **Leuglay** France
212 D3 **Leuk** Switz.
Leukas *Lefkada* Greece *see* **Lefkada**
212 D3 **Leukerbad** Switz.
168 D6 **Leumrabhagh** *Western Isles, Scotland* U.K.
191 F9 **Leun** Ger.
131 □J7 **Leung Shuen Wan Chau** *i. H.K.* China
156 H2 **Leunovo** Rus. Fed.
265 V6 **Leupp** *AZ* U.S.A.
107 L7 **Leura** *Qld* Austr.
186 H4 **Leusden** Neth.
116 B3 **Leuser, Gunung** *mt.* Indon.
200 D5 **Leutasch** Austria
195 K7 **Leutascher Dreitorspitze** *mt.* Ger.
193 D9 **Leutenberg** Ger.
195 I3 **Leutershausen** Ger.
191 D10 **Leutesdorf** Ger.
195 I6 **Leutkirch im Allgäu** Ger.
201 L6 **Leutschach** Austria
187 G7 **Leuven** Belgium
187 E7 **Leuze-en-Hainaut** Belgium
183 I10 **Le Val** France
179 L8 **Le Val-d'Ajol** France
179 J8 **Le Vallinot-Longeau-Percey** France
180 I4 **Le Val-St-Père** France
220 A2 **Levan** Albania
265 U2 **Levan** *UT* U.S.A.
162 K5 **Levanger** Norway
183 I10 **Levant, Île du** *i.* France
212 F7 **Levante, Riviera di** *coastal area* Italy
212 H7 **Levanto** Italy
216 C8 **Levanzo** *Sicilia* Italy
216 C7 **Levanzo, Isola di** *i. Sicilia* Italy
151 I3 **Levashi** Rus. Fed.
271 □3 **Le Vauclin** Martinique
159 S2 **Levaya Rossosh'** Rus. Fed.
198 G4 **Levél** Hungary
261 D9 **Levelland** *TX* U.S.A.
244 H4 **Levelock** *AK* U.S.A.
103 F11 **Levels** *South I.* N.Z.
171 Q6 **Leven** *East Riding of Yorkshire, England* U.K.
168 K10 **Leven** *Fife, Scotland* U.K.
168 F9 **Leven, Loch** *inlet Scotland* U.K.
168 J10 **Leven, Loch** *l. Scotland* U.K.
183 K9 **Levens** France
171 L5 **Levens** *Cumbria, England* U.K.
212 F3 **Leventina, Valle** *val.* Switz.
168 □N3 **Levenwick** *Shetland, Scotland* U.K.
108 G4 **Lévêque, Cape** *W.A.* Austr.
102 □ **L'Eveque, Cape** *Chatham Is* S. Pacific Ocean
217 O3 **Leverano** Italy
168 B7 **Leverburgh** *Western Isles, Scotland* U.K.
184 B4 **Le Verdon-sur-Mer** France
250 J4 **Levering** *MI* U.S.A.
191 C8 **Leverkusen** Ger.
246 G1 **Lever Lake** *N.W.T.* Can.
185 H9 **Le Vernet** France
Leverville Dem. Rep. Congo *see* **Lusanga**
178 B7 **Lèves** France
181 P8 **Levet** France
183 B8 **Lévézou** *mts* France
199 H3 **Levice** Slovakia
213 K3 **Levico Terme** Italy
220 D5 **Levidi** Greece
214 C4 **Levie** *Corse* France
182 I3 **Levier** France
183 D9 **Le Vigan** France
185 G8 **Lévignac** France
185 E6 **Lévignac-de-Guyanne** France
185 B7 **Lévignacq** France
213 M9 **Le Ville** Italy
102 J7 **Levin** *North I.* N.Z.
249 G4 **Lévis** *Que.* Can.
221 H6 **Levitha** *i.* Greece
Levittown *NJ* U.S.A. *see* **Willingboro**
259 H3 **Levittown** *NY* U.S.A.
258 F4 **Levittown** *PA* U.S.A.
180 H4 **Le-Vivier-sur-Mer** France
219 O9 **Levka** Bulg.
Levkás *i.* Greece *see* **Lefkada**
Levkímmi *Kerkyra* Greece *see* **Lefkimmi**
199 J2 **Levoča** Slovakia
199 J2 **Levočské vrchy** *mts* Slovakia
184 H2 **Levroux** France
219 N7 **Levski** Bulg.
Levskigrad Bulg. *see* **Karlovo**
161 W8 **Lev Tolstoy** Rus. Fed.
101 □7a **Levuka** *Ovalau* Fiji
160 H6 **Lėvuo** *r.* Lith.
180 I2 **Lévy, Cap** *c.* France
115 A8 **Lewa** *Sumba* Indon.
118 C5 **Lewe** Myanmar
173 M6 **Lewes** *East Sussex, England* U.K.
257 J10 **Lewes** *DE* U.S.A.
196 F5 **Lewin Brzeski** Pol.
265 X4 **Lewis** *CO* U.S.A.
261 F7 **Lewis** *KS* U.S.A.
262 C4 **Lewis** *r. WA* U.S.A.
168 C6 **Lewis, Isle of** *i. Scotland* U.K.
106 D7 **Lewis, Lake** *salt flat N.T.* Austr.
258 B4 **Lewisberry** *PA* U.S.A.
256 A9 **Lewisburg** *OH* U.S.A.
251 R9 **Lewisburg** *PA* U.S.A.
255 D8 **Lewisburg** *TN* U.S.A.
256 E11 **Lewisburg** *WV* U.S.A.
245 O4 **Lewis Cass, Mount** Can./U.S.A.
249 J3 **Lewis Hills** *Nfld and Lab.* Can.
137 M6 **Lewis Inlet** *Andaman & Nicobar Is* India
103 G9 **Lewis Pass** *South I.* N.Z.
103 G9 **Lewis Pass National Reserve** *nature res. South I.* N.Z.
249 K3 **Lewisporte** *Nfld and Lab.* Can.
108 J6 **Lewis Range** *hills W.A.* Austr.
262 G2 **Lewis Range** *mts MT* U.S.A.
255 D8 **Lewis Smith, Lake** *AL* U.S.A.
262 F3 **Lewiston** *ID* U.S.A.
257 □O4 **Lewiston** *ME* U.S.A.
251 J5 **Lewiston** *MI* U.S.A.
250 C6 **Lewiston** *MN* U.S.A.
256 F5 **Lewiston** *NY* U.S.A.
250 D9 **Lewistown** *IL* U.S.A.
250 C9 **Lewistown** *MO* U.S.A.
262 J3 **Lewistown** *MT* U.S.A.
256 H8 **Lewistown** *PA* U.S.A.
261 I9 **Lewisville** *AR* U.S.A.
256 D9 **Lewisville** *OH* U.S.A.
192 E4 **Lewitz** *park* Ger.
115 C8 **Lewoleba** Indon.
115 C8 **Lewotobi, Gunung** *vol. Flores* Indon.
255 F9 **Lexington** *GA* U.S.A.
250 F9 **Lexington** *IL* U.S.A.
254 E6 **Lexington** *KY* U.S.A.
251 L6 **Lexington** *MI* U.S.A.
260 I6 **Lexington** *MO* U.S.A.
261 J9 **Lexington** *MS* U.S.A.
255 G8 **Lexington** *NC* U.S.A.
260 F5 **Lexington** *NE* U.S.A.
256 C8 **Lexington** *OH* U.S.A.
255 G9 **Lexington** *SC* U.S.A.
261 K8 **Lexington** *TN* U.S.A.
256 F11 **Lexington** *VA* U.S.A.
256 I10 **Lexington Park** *MD* U.S.A.
171 N5 **Leyburn** *North Yorkshire, England* U.K.
Leyden Neth. *see* **Leiden**
130 F6 **Leye** *Guangxi* China
144 B3 **Leyla Dāgh** *mt.* Iran
171 L6 **Leyland** *Lancashire, England* U.K.
185 H6 **Leyme** France
173 N5 **Leysdown-on-Sea** *Kent, England* U.K.
212 C3 **Leysin** Switz.
114 E6 **Leyte** *i.* Phil.
114 E6 **Leyte Gulf** Phil.
212 C3 **Leytron** Switz.
185 G10 **Lez** *r.* France
205 P4 **Leza** *r.* Spain
197 K5 **Leżajsk** Pol.
274 E2 **Lezama** Venez.
183 E8 **Lézan** France
180 E4 **Lézardrieux** France
185 G9 **Lézat-sur-Lèze** France
184 D3 **Lezay** France
185 G9 **Lèze** *r.* France
218 H9 **Lezhë** Albania
130 E3 **Lezhi** *Sichuan* China
161 X5 **Lezhnevo** Rus. Fed.
183 B10 **Lézignan-Corbières** France
197 H2 **Leźno** Pol.
182 C5 **Lezoux** France
207 O3 **Lezuza** Spain
207 O2 **Lezuza** *r.* Spain
197 H4 **Lgota Wielka** Pol.
157 F6 **L'gov** Rus. Fed.
133 H12 **Lhagoi Kangri** *mt. Xizang* China
168 J7 **Lhanbryde** *Moray, Scotland* U.K.
Lhari *Xizang* China *see* **Si'erdingka**
133 K11 **Lhari** *Xizang* China
109 B8 **Lharidon Bight** *b. W.A.* Austr.
133 J10 **Lharigarbo** *Xizang* China
133 J12 **Lhasa** *Xizang* China
133 J12 **Lhasa He** *r.* China
133 K12 **Lhasoi** *Xizang* China
130 A3 **Lhatog** *Xizang* China
178 D6 **L'Hay-les-Roses** France
133 H12 **Lhazê** *Xizang* China
133 L11 **Lhazê** *Xizang* China
201 J1 **Lhenice** Czech Rep.
185 G9 **Lherm** France
184 C2 **L'Hermenault** France
180 H5 **L'Hermitage** France
135 □1 **Lhohifushi** *i. N. Male* Maldives
116 A2 **Lhokkruet** *Sumatera* Indon.
116 B2 **Lhokseumawe** *Sumatera* Indon.
116 B2 **Lhoksukon** *Sumatera* Indon.
133 J11 **Lhomar** *Xizang* China
185 G7 **L'Honor-de-Cos** France
133 L11 **Lhorong** *Xizang* China
185 G7 **Lhospitalet** France
208 G6 **L'Hospitalet de l'Infant** Spain
208 J5 **L'Hospitalet de Llobregat** Spain
183 C9 **L'Hospitalet-du-Larzac** France
185 H10 **L'Hospitalet-près-l'Andorre** France
208 G6 **L'Hostal del Alls** Spain
184 B3 **L'Houmeau** France
159 N8 **L'hovs'ke** Ukr.
133 J12 **Lhozhag** *Xizang* China
182 H5 **Lhuis** France
181 J5 **L'Huisserie** France
178 H6 **Lhuître** France
139 M6 **Lhuntshi** Bhutan
133 K12 **Lhünzê** *Xizang* China
133 K12 **Lhünzê** *Xizang* China
118 D5 **Li, Mae** *r.* Thai.
221 H6 **Liadi** *i.* Greece
151 F3 **Liakhvis Nakrdzali** *nature res.* Georgia
220 D4 **Liakoura** *mt.* Greece
214 B3 **Liamone** *r. Corse* France
271 □2 **Liamuiga, Mount** *vol.* St Kitts and Nevis
131 K6 **Liancheng** *Fujian* China
Liancheng *Guizhou* China *see* **Qinglong**
Liancheng *Yunnan* China *see* **Guangnan**
178 D5 **Liancourt** France
123 G10 **Liancourt Rocks** *i.* N. Pacific Ocean
178 C2 **Liane** *r.* France
Lianfeng *Fujian* China *see* **Liancheng**
115 C4 **Liang** *Sulawesi* Indon.
114 F7 **Lianga** *Mindanao* Phil.
114 F7 **Lianga Bay** *Mindanao* Phil.
129 M6 **Liangcheng** *Nei Mongol* China
130 F2 **Liangdang** *Gansu* China
133 J11 **Liangdaohe** *Xizang* China
130 H6 **Liangfeng** *Guangxi* China
130 G4 **Lianghe** *Chongqing* China
130 D3 **Lianghe** *Sichuan* China
130 B6 **Lianghe** *Yunnan* China
Lianghekou *Chongqing* China *see* **Lianghe**
130 E2 **Lianghekou** *Gansu* China
Liangjiayoufang *Shanxi* China *see* **Youyu**
130 F3 **Liangping** *Chongqing* China
117 K4 **Liangpran, Bukit** *mt.* Indon.
Liangshan *Chongqing* China *see* **Liangping**
118 D2 **Liang Shan** *mt.* Myanmar
Liangshi *Hunan* China *see* **Shaodong**
130 H8 **Liangtian** *Guangxi* China
116 D3 **Liang Timur, Gunung** *mt.* Malaysia
130 D6 **Liangwang Shan** *mts Yunnan* China
129 K8 **Liangzhen** *Shaanxi* China
Liangzhou *Gansu* China *see* **Wuwei**
131 J3 **Liangzi Hu** *l.* China
Lianhe *Chongqing* China *see* **Qianjiang**
131 I5 **Lianhua** *Jiangxi* China
131 J7 **Lianhua Shan** *mts* China
131 L5 **Lianjiang** *Fujian* China
130 H8 **Lianjiang** *Guangdong* China
Lianjiang *Jiangxi* China *see* **Xingguo**
130 F6 **Lian Jiang** *r.* China
131 I6 **Lianjiangkou** *Guangdong* China
131 I6 **Liannan** *Guangdong* China
131 J6 **Lianping** *Guangdong* China
Lianran *Yunnan* China *see* **Anning**
131 I6 **Lianshan** *Guangdong* China
129 Q6 **Lianshan** *Liaoning* China
Liant, Cape *i.* Thai. *see* **Samae San, Laem**
Liantang *Jiangxi* China *see* **Nanchang**
131 H3 **Liantuo** *Hubei* China
Lianxian *Guangdong* China *see* **Lianzhou**
122 C2 **Lianyin** *Heilong.* China
131 H5 **Lianyuan** *Hunan* China
129 P9 **Lianyun** *Jiangsu* China
129 P9 **Lianyungang** *Jiangsu* China
131 I6 **Lianzhou** *Guangdong* China
Lianzhou *Guangxi* China *see* **Hepu**
122 G6 **Lianzhushan** *Heilong.* China
129 N8 **Liaocheng** *Shandong* Ch
129 R6 **Liaodong Bandao** *pen.* C
129 Q6 **Liaodong Wan** *b.* China
128 C5 **Liaodun** *Xinjiang* China
128 C5 **Liaodunzhan** *Xinjiang* C
Liaogao *Guizhou* China
Songtao
129 R6 **Liao He** *r.* China
129 R6 **Liaoning** *prov.* China
129 R6 **Liaoyang** *Liaoning* Chin
122 D7 **Liaoyuan** *Jilin* China
129 R6 **Liaozhong** *Liaoning* Chi
220 A3 **Liapades** *Kerkyra* Greece
246 F2 **Liard** *r.* Can.
246 F2 **Liard Highway** *N.W.T.* C
245 P3 **Liard Plateau** *B.C./Y.T.* C
245 P4 **Liard River** *B.C.* Can.
145 L9 **Liari** Pak.
178 H4 **Liart** France
116 G6 **Liat** *i.* Indon.
168 F7 **Liathach** *mt. Scotland* U.
165 K5 **Liatorp** Sweden
Liban *country* Asia *see* **Le**
198 E1 **Libáň** Czech Rep.
150 E4 **Liban, Jebel** *mts* Lebano
285 G5 **Líbano** Arg.
274 C3 **Libano** Col.
207 I7 **Líbar, Sierra de** *mts* Spa
Libau Latvia *see* **Liepāja**
168 I11 **Libberton** *South Lanark*
Scotland U.K.
262 G2 **Libby** *MT* U.S.A.
198 C1 **Libčeves** Czech Rep.
193 J10 **Libčice nad Vltavou** Cze
230 C4 **Libenge** Dem. Rep. Con
197 I2 **Liberadz** Pol.
261 E7 **Liberal** *KS* U.S.A.
281 E5 **Liberdade** Brazil
278 B4 **Liberdade** *r.* Brazil
276 C1 **Liberdade** *r.* Brazil
198 E1 **Liberec** Czech Rep.
198 E1 **Liberecký kraj** *admin. re*
Czech Rep.
228 C5 **Liberia** *country* Africa
266 □Q12 **Liberia** Costa Rica
271 □2 **Liberta** Antigua and Bar
285 I2 **Libertad** Arg.
285 I4 **Libertad** Uru.
274 D2 **Libertad** Venez.
282 D1 **Libertador General San**
Arg.
284 E3 **Libertador General San**
Arg.
237 L4 **Libertase** S. Africa
245 L2 **Liberty** *AK* U.S.A.
254 E6 **Liberty** *IN* U.S.A.
254 E7 **Liberty** *KY* U.S.A.
257 □P4 **Liberty** *ME* U.S.A.
260 H6 **Liberty** *MO* U.S.A.
257 K7 **Liberty** *NY* U.S.A.
258 A1 **Liberty** *PA* U.S.A.
261 H10 **Liberty** *TX* U.S.A.
256 A7 **Liberty Center** *OH* U.S.A
258 B6 **Liberty Lake** *MD* U.S.A.
250 G7 **Libertyville** *IL* U.S.A.
193 J9 **Liběšice** Czech Rep.
197 H5 **Libiąż** Pol.
198 E1 **Libice nad Cidlinou** Cz
187 H9 **Libin** Belgium
198 D3 **Libín** *mt.* Czech Rep.
198 G2 **Libina** Czech Rep.
114 D5 **Libmanan** *Luzon* Phil.
150 B8 **Libnī, Jabal** *hill* Egypt
130 F6 **Libo** *Guizhou* China
115 F4 **Libobo, Tanjung** *pt Halm*
Indon.
193 J10 **Libochovice** Czech Rep.
237 N7 **Libode** S. Africa
220 B2 **Libohovë** Albania
232 D4 **Liboi** Kenya
231 D8 **Libonda** Zambia
119 D11 **Libong, Ko** *i.* Thai.
237 M4 **Libono** Lesotho
284 E3 **Liborio Luna** Arg.
193 J9 **Libouchec** Czech Rep.
185 D6 **Libourne** France
108 H7 **Libral Well** *W.A.* Austr.
187 H9 **Libramont** Belgium
218 I9 **Librazhd** Albania
266 D3 **Libre, Sierra** *mts* Mex.
269 J6 **Libres** Mex.
230 A4 **Libreville** Gabon
209 C12 **Librilla** Spain
209 C7 **Libros** Spain
114 E8 **Libuganon** *r. Mindanao*
224 C3 **Libya** *country* Africa
224 E3 **Libyan Desert** Egypt/Lib
224 E2 **Libyan Plateau** Egypt
284 A4 **Licantén** Chile
216 F9 **Licata** *Sicilia* Italy
212 I7 **Licciana Nardi** Italy
149 J4 **Lice** Turkey
215 J3 **Licenza** Italy
205 N6 **Liceras** Spain
191 G9 **Lich** Ger.
220 D4 **Lichas** *pen.* Greece
Licheng *Fujian* China *se*
Licheng *Guangxi* China
129 O8 **Licheng** *Shandong* Chin
129 M8 **Licheng** *Shanxi* China
102 J5 **Lichfield** *North I.* N.Z.
173 I2 **Lichfield** *Staffordshire, E*
U.K.
233 B8 **Lichinga** Moz.
199 G1 **Lichnov** Czech Rep.
196 G1 **Lichnowy** Pol.
193 D9 **Lichte** Ger.
194 E4 **Lichtenau** *Baden-Württe*
Ger.
195 J3 **Lichtenau** *Bayern* Ger.
191 G7 **Lichtenau** *Nordrhein-We*
Ger.
201 L2 **Lichtenau im Waldvierte**
193 E10 **Lichtenberg** *Bayern* Ger.
193 H9 **Lichtenberg** *Sachsen* Ge
237 K2 **Lichtenburg** S. Africa
193 D10 **Lichtenfels** Ger.
193 G9 **Lichtenstein** Ger.
186 K5 **Lichtenvoorde** Neth.
201 N4 **Lichtenwörth** Austria
192 I5 **Lichterfelde** Ger.
187 D6 **Lichtervelde** Belgium
130 G3 **Lichuan** *Hubei* China
131 K5 **Lichuan** *Jiangxi* China
235 H3 **Liciro** Moz.
256 A9 **Licking** *r. KY* U.S.A.
210 E3 **Lički Osik** Croatia
216 H9 **Licodia Eubea** *Sicilia* Ital
215 N7 **Licosa, Isola** *i.* Italy
185 C9 **Licq-Athérey** France
178 C2 **Licques** France
Licun *Shandong* China *s*
Laoshan
161 S2 **Lid'** *r.* Rus. Fed.
160 I8 **Lida** Belarus
164 J3 **Lidan** *r.* Sweden
171 L3 **Liddel Water** *r. England/*
U.K.
168 K12 **Liddesdale** *val. Scotland*
237 K8 **Liddleton** S. Africa
199 H2 **Lidečko** Czech Rep.
164 J5 **Lidhult** Sweden
165 O2 **Lidingö** Sweden
230 C4 **Lidjombo** C.A.R.
164 J3 **Lidköping** Sweden
213 M5 **Lido** Italy
213 M7 **Lido Adriano** Italy
213 M7 **Lido di Classe** Italy
215 J5 **Lido di Foce Verde** Italy
213 N4 **Lido di Jesolo** Italy
217 L3 **Lido di Metaponto** Italy
215 I4 **Lido di Ostia** Italy
215 P4 **Lido di Siponto** Italy
213 M6 **Lido di Spina** Italy
162 M4 **Lidsjöberg** Sweden
160 K5 **Līdumnieki** Latvia
197 H2 **Lidzbark** Pol.
165 Q7 **Lidzbark Warmiński** Pol
201 K2 **Liebenau** Austria
191 H8 **Liebenau** *Hessen* Ger.
190 H5 **Liebenau** *Niedersachsen*
237 M3 **Liebenbergs Vlei** *r.* S. Af
191 J6 **Liebenburg** Ger.
201 J6 **Liebenfels** Austria

Liebenwalde Ger.
Lieberose Ger.
Liebertwolkwitz Ger.
Liebig, Mount N.T. Austr.
Liebling Romania
Lieboch Austria
Liebstadt Ger.
Liechtenstein country Europe
Liédena Spain
Liège Belgium
Liège prov. Belgium
Liegnitz Pol. see Legnica
Lieksa Fin.
Lielais Ludzas l. Latvia
Lielupe r. Latvia
Lielvārde Latvia
Liempde Neth.
Lien Sweden
Lienden Neth.
Lienen Ger.
Liên Nghia Vietnam
Liên Sơn Vietnam
Lienz Austria
Liepāja Latvia
Liepaya Latvia see Liepāja
Liepe Ger.
Liepen Ger.
Liepgarten Ger.
Liepna Latvia
Lieponys Lith.
Lier Belgium
Liernais France
Lierneux Belgium
Lierre Belgium see Lier
Liesek Slovakia
Lieser Ger.
Lieshout Neth.
Liesing r. Austria
Liesjärven kansallispuisto nat. park Fin.
Liessel Neth.
Liesse-Notre-Dame France
Liestal Switz.
Liešťany Slovakia
Lieto Fin.
Liétor Spain
Lietuva country Europe see Lithuania
Lietvesi l. Fin.
Lieurey France
Lieuvin reg. France
Lievestuore Fin.
Liévin France
Lièvre, Rivière du r. Que. Can.
Liezen Austria
Lifamatola i. Indon.
Lifanga Dem. Rep. Congo
Liffey r. Ireland
Liffol-le-Grand France
Lifford Ireland
Liffré France
Lifi Mahuida mt. Arg.
Lifou i. Îles Loyauté New Caledonia
Lifton Devon, England U.K.
Lifu i. Îles Loyauté New Caledonia see Lifou
Lifudzin Rus. Fed. see Rudnyy
Lifuka i. Tonga
Ligao Luzon Phil.
Ligardes France
Ligasa Dem. Rep. Congo
Līgatne Latvia
Lightfoot Lake salt flat W.A. Austr.
Lighthouse Reef Belize
Lightning Ridge N.S.W. Austr.
Lightstreet PA U.S.A.
Ligist Austria
Lignano Pineta Italy
Lignano Sabbiadoro Italy
Ligné France
Ligneron r. France
Ligneuville Belgium
Lignières France
Lignon r. France
Lignon r. France
Ligny-en-Barrois France
Ligny-le-Châtel France
Ligny-le-Ribault France
Ligonchio Italy
Ligonha r. Moz.
Ligonier IN U.S.A.
Ligonier PA U.S.A.
Ligoúrion Greece see Asklipieio
Ligowo Pol.
Ligua, Bahía de la b. Chile
Liguanea Island S.A. Austr.
Ligueil France
Ligugé France
Ligui Mex.
Ligure, Mar sea France/Italy see Ligurian Sea
Liguria admin. reg. Italy
Ligurian Sea France/Italy
Ligurienne, Mer sea France/Italy see Ligurian Sea
Ligurta AZ U.S.A.
Liha Point Niue
Lihir Group is P.N.G.
Lihme Denmark
Lihou Reef and Cays Coral Sea Is Terr. Austr.
1 Līhu'e HI U.S.A.
Lihuel Calel, Parque Nacional nat. park Arg.
Lihula Estonia
Liidli Kue N.W.T. Can. see Fort Simpson
Liivi laht b. Estonia/Latvia see Riga, Gulf of
Lija Malta
Lijar Spain
Líjar, Sierra de mts Spain
Lijiang Yunnan China
Lijiang Yunnan China see Yuanjiang
Li Jiang r. China
Lijiazhai Henan China
Lik, Nam r. Laos
Lika reg. Croatia
Līkak Iran
Likala Dem. Rep. Congo
Likasi Dem. Rep. Congo
Likati Dem. Rep. Congo
Likati r. Dem. Rep. Congo
Likely B.C. Can.
Likhachevo Ukr. see Pervomays'kyy
Likhachyovo Ukr. see Pervomays'kyy
Likhás pen. Greece see Lichas
Likhoslavl' Rus. Fed.
Likhovskoy Rus. Fed.
Likimi Dem. Rep. Congo
Likino-Dulevo Rus. Fed.
Likisia East Timor see Liquiçá
Likma Chhattisgarh India
Likolia Dem. Rep. Congo
Likouala admin. reg. Congo
Likouala r. Congo
Likouala aux Herbes r. Congo
Likstammen l. Sweden
Liku Kalimantan Indon.
Liku Sarawak Malaysia
Liku Niue
Likupang Sulawesi Indon.
Likurga Rus. Fed.
Likuri Harbour b. Viti Levu Fiji
L'Île-Bouchard France
L'Île-Rousse Corse France
Lilienfeld Austria
Lilienthal Ger.
Liling Hunan China
Liljendal Fin.
Lilla Pak.
Lilla Edet Sweden
Lilla Luleälven r. Sweden
Lillblaiken hill Sweden
Lille Belgium
Lille France
Lille Bælt sea chan. Denmark
Lillebonne France
Lillehammer Norway
Lillers France

164 E3 Lillesand Norway
172 H2 Lilleshall Telford and Wrekin, England U.K.
164 H2 Lillestrøm Norway
250 I6 Lilley MI U.S.A.
109 I9 Lillian, Point hill W.A. Austr.
287 L2 Lillie Glacier Antarctica
168 K11 Lilliesleaf Scottish Borders, Scotland U.K.
255 H8 Lillington NC U.S.A.
205 N9 Lillo Spain
246 F5 Lillooet B.C. Can.
246 F5 Lillooet r. B.C. Can.
246 F5 Lillooet Range mts B.C. Can.
230 E5 Lilo r. Dem. Rep. Congo
139 N7 Lilong Manipur India
233 B8 Lilongwe Malawi
282 E2 Lilo Viejo Arg.
114 D7 Liloy Mindanao Phil.
250 F4 Lily WI U.S.A.
104 G5 Lilydale S.A. Austr.
105 K9 Lilydale Tas. Austr.
218 H7 Lim r. Montenegro/Serbia
285 H4 Lima Arg.
213 J7 Lima r. Italy
277 F5 Lima Para.
276 A3 Lima Peru
276 A2 Lima dept Peru
250 C9 Lima IL U.S.A.
262 H4 Lima MT U.S.A.
256 H6 Lima NY U.S.A.
256 A8 Lima OH U.S.A.
275 F4 Limaão Brazil
284 B3 Limache Chile
281 F4 Lima Duarte Brazil
182 C5 Limagne reg. France
147 M3 Līmah Oman
Lima Islands Guangdong China see Wanshan Qundao
142 B5 Liman Rus. Fed.
200 F7 Limana Italy
197 I6 Limanowa Pol.
115 E7 Limar Maluku Indon.
284 B2 Limarí r. Chile
116 F4 Limas Indon.
114 E7 Limasawa i. Phil.
Limassol Cyprus see Lemesos
169 I2 Limavady Northern Ireland U.K.
284 D6 Limay r. Arg.
178 C5 Limay France
284 D5 Limay Mahuida Arg.
194 G3 Limbach Baden-Württemberg Ger.
194 B3 Limbach Saarland Ger.
193 F9 Limbach Sachsen Ger.
193 G9 Limbach-Oberfrohna Ger.
217 J6 Limbadi Italy
117 K2 Limbang Sarawak Malaysia
117 K2 Limbang r. Sarawak Malaysia
276 C3 Limbani Peru
214 C6 Limbara, Monte mts Sardegna Italy
160 H4 Limbaži Latvia
138 C8 Limbdi Gujarat India
229 H5 Limbe Cameroon
233 B8 Limbe Malawi
115 C3 Limboto Sulawesi Indon.
115 C3 Limboto, Danau l. Indon.
187 I7 Limbourg Belgium
235 H3 Limbuè Moz.
115 A6 Limbung Sulawesi Indon.
117 K6 Limbungan Kalimantan Indon.
106 B4 Limbunya N.T. Austr.
187 H6 Limburg prov. Belgium
187 I6 Limburg prov. Neth.
191 F10 Limburg an der Lahn Ger.
194 E3 Limburgerhof Ger.
116 □ Lim Chu Kang Sing.
116 □ Lim Chu Kang hill Sing.
236 H4 Lime Acres S. Africa
163 L6 Limedsforsen Sweden
103 C13 Limehills South I. N.Z.
244 I3 Lime Hills AK U.S.A.
280 D5 Limeira Brazil
171 K1 Limekilns Fife, Scotland U.K.
220 F2 Limenaria Thasos Greece
221 G7 Limenas Chersonisou Kriti Greece
169 E7 Limerick Ireland
169 E8 Limerick county Ireland
250 B6 Lime Springs IA U.S.A.
257 □R2 Limestone ME U.S.A.
247 L4 Limestone Point Man. Can.
244 I3 Lime Village AK U.S.A.
164 E5 Limfjorden sea chan. Denmark
204 D5 Limia r. Spain
162 L4 Limingen Norway
162 L4 Limingen l. Norway
257 □O5 Limington ME U.S.A.
162 R4 Liminka Fin.
164 J4 Limmared Sweden
186 G3 Limmen Neth.
106 F3 Limmen Bight b. N.T. Austr.
106 E3 Limmen Bight River r. N.T. Austr.
106 E3 Limmen National Park nat. park Australia
220 E4 Limni Greece
221 G3 Limnos i. Greece
278 G3 Limoeiro Brazil
257 J3 Limoges Ont. Can.
184 G4 Limoges France
185 H7 Limogne, Causse de hills France
185 H7 Limogne-en-Quercy France
266 □Q10 Limón Hond.
260 D6 Limon CO U.S.A.
239 □1a Limon, Mount hill Rodrigues I. Mauritius
212 D7 Limone Piemonte Italy
274 B4 Limones Ecuador
182 F5 Limonest France
213 J4 Limone sul Garda Italy
206 F3 Limonetes r. Spain
148 G5 Limonlu Turkey
Limonum France see Poitiers
276 D3 Limoquije Bol.
215 N4 Limosano Italy
184 H4 Limousin admin. reg. France
184 H4 Limousin, Monts du hills France
184 G4 Limousin, Plateaux du France
185 I9 Limoux France
235 F4 Limpopo prov. S. Africa
235 G5 Limpopo r. S. Africa/Zimbabwe
235 F4 Limpopo National Park S. Africa
130 H6 Limu Guangxi China
101 □8 Limu atoll Tonga
103 □4 Limufuafua Point Niue
231 D8 Limulunga Zambia
162 Q3 Linaälven r. Sweden
146 F1 Līnah Saudi Arabia
237 M5 Linakeng Lesotho
162 U2 Linakhamari Rus. Fed.
Lin'an Yunnan China see Jianshui
131 L3 Lin'an Zhejiang China
114 E8 Linao Bay Mindanao Phil.
114 B6 Linapacan i. Phil.
114 B6 Linapacan Strait Phil.
184 H4 Linards France
284 B4 Linares Chile
267 J5 Linares Mex.
207 L4 Linares Spain
205 M5 Linares, Embalse de resr Spain
209 D7 Linares de Mora Spain
204 I7 Linares de Riofrío Spain
214 B9 Linas, Monte mt. Sardegna Italy
212 G5 Linate airport Italy
117 K3 Linau Balui plat. Malaysia
130 C7 Lincang Yunnan China
187 H7 Lincent Belgium
Lincheng Hainan China see Lingao
Lincheng Hunan China see Huitong
Linchuan Jiangxi China see Fuzhou
286 R1 Linck Nunataks nunataks Antarctica
285 G4 Lincoln Arg.
103 G10 Lincoln South I. N.Z.
171 P7 Lincoln Lincolnshire, England U.K.
264 K3 Lincoln CA U.S.A.
258 E7 Lincoln DE U.S.A.
254 C5 Lincoln IL U.S.A.
260 F6 Lincoln KS U.S.A.
257 □Q3 Lincoln ME U.S.A.
251 K5 Lincoln MI U.S.A.

260 G5 Lincoln NE U.S.A.
257 N4 Lincoln NH U.S.A.
258 C4 Lincoln PA U.S.A.
262 B4 Lincoln City OR U.S.A.
112 D3 Lincoln Island Paracel Is
104 E6 Lincoln National Park S.A. Austr.
256 B6 Lincoln Park MI U.S.A.
243 N1 Lincoln Sea Can./Greenland
171 Q7 Lincolnshire admin. div. England U.K.
171 Q7 Lincolnshire Wolds hills England U.K.
255 F9 Lincolnton GA U.S.A.
258 D5 Lincoln University PA U.S.A.
259 G4 Lincroft NJ U.S.A.
278 E5 Linda, Serra hills Brazil
106 G7 Linda Creek watercourse Qld Austr.
166 J1 Lindas Norway
193 F6 Lindau Sachsen-Anhalt Ger.
190 I1 Lindau Schleswig-Holstein Ger.
194 H6 Lindau (Bodensee) Ger.
186 I3 Linde r. Neth.
190 K1 Lindelse Denmark
107 L6 Lindeman Group is Qld Austr.
246 H5 Linden Alta Can.
191 G9 Linden Hessen Ger.
190 H2 Linden Schleswig-Holstein Ger.
275 G3 Linden Guyana
255 D9 Linden AL U.S.A.
264 K3 Linden CA U.S.A.
256 B6 Linden MI U.S.A.
259 G3 Linden NJ U.S.A.
255 D8 Linden TN U.S.A.
261 H9 Linden TX U.S.A.
192 F4 Lindenberg Brandenburg Ger.
192 I5 Lindenberg Brandenburg Ger.
193 J6 Lindenberg Brandenburg Ger.
194 H6 Lindenberg im Allgäu Ger.
194 F2 Lindenfels Ger.
250 B2 Linden Grove MN U.S.A.
Lindenow Fjord inlet Greenland see Kangerlussuatsiaq
258 F5 Lindenwold NJ U.S.A.
190 E5 Lindern (Oldenburg) Ger.
165 L2 Lindesberg Sweden
164 D3 Lindesnes c. Norway
190 H1 Lindewitt Ger.
173 L5 Lindfield West Sussex, England U.K.
191 H6 Lindhorst Ger.
Líndhos Rodos Greece see Lindos
230 E4 Lindi r. Dem. Rep. Congo
233 C7 Lindi Tanz.
233 C7 Lindi admin. reg. Tanz.
129 S3 Lindian Heilong. China
Lindisfarne i. England U.K. see Holy Island
103 D11 Lindis Peak South I. N.Z.
191 D8 Lindlar Ger.
237 L3 Lindley S. Africa
280 D5 Lindóia Brazil
164 I4 Lindome Sweden
129 P5 Lindong Nei Mongol China
221 J6 Lindos Rodos Greece
204 D5 Lindoso Port.
192 G5 Lindow Ger.
179 M6 Lindre, Étang de l. France
257 □R2 Lindsay N.B. Can.
248 E4 Lindsay Ont. Can.
264 M5 Lindsay CA U.S.A.
262 L3 Lindsay MT U.S.A.
109 F9 Lindsay Gordon Lagoon salt flat W.A. Austr.
260 G6 Lindsborg KS U.S.A.
165 M5 Lindsdal Sweden
256 E11 Lindside WV U.S.A.
192 E5 Lindstedt Ger.
Lindum Lincolnshire, England U.K. see Lincoln
190 I5 Lindwedel Ger.
198 C2 Líně Czech Rep.
258 B5 Lineboro MD U.S.A.
290 I5 Line Islands S. Pacific Ocean
258 E4 Line Lexington PA U.S.A.
159 O1 Linets Rus. Fed.
129 L8 Linfen Shanxi China
258 D4 Linfield PA U.S.A.
173 M5 Linford Thurrock, England U.K.
168 F8 Ling r. Scotland U.K.
136 H4 Lingamparti Andhra Prad. India
136 D6 Linganamakki Reservoir India
130 G9 Lingao Hainan China
183 D8 Lingas, Montagne du mt. France
114 C3 Lingayen Luzon Phil.
114 C3 Lingayen Gulf Luzon Phil.
129 L9 Lingbao Henan China
131 K2 Lingbi Anhui China
Lingcheng Anhui China see Lingbi
Lingcheng Guangxi China see Lingshan
Lingcheng Hainan China see Lingshui
Lingcheng Shandong China see Lingxian
130 H6 Lingchuan Guangxi China
129 M9 Lingchuan Shanxi China
237 K8 Lingelethu S. Africa
237 J8 Lingelihle S. Africa
190 D5 Lingen (Ems) Ger.
200 A5 Lingenau Austria
194 E3 Lingenfeld Ger.
173 L5 Lingfield Surrey, England U.K.
116 F5 Lingga i. Indon.
117 I4 Lingga Sarawak Malaysia
116 F5 Lingga, Kepulauan is Indon.
133 I10 Linggo Co l. Xizang China
129 Q6 Linghai Liaoning China
114 F8 Lingig Mindanao Phil.
117 L1 Lingkabau Sabah Malaysia
117 L3 Lingkas Kalimantan Indon.
262 L5 Lingle WY U.S.A.
258 B4 Linglestown PA U.S.A.
106 G4 Lingnoonganee Island Qld Austr.
179 O6 Lingolsheim France
230 D4 Lingomo Dem. Rep. Congo
129 N7 Lingqiu Shanxi China
130 G7 Lingshan Guangxi China
129 Q9 Lingshan Wan b. China
139 L6 Lingshi Bhutan
129 L8 Lingshi Shanxi China
130 G9 Lingshui Hainan China
130 G9 Lingshui Wan b. China
136 E4 Lingsugur Karnataka India
129 J9 Lingtai Gansu China
217 I8 Linguaglossa Sicilia Italy
228 B3 Linguère Senegal
130 H6 Lingui Guangxi China
214 C3 Linguizzetta Corse France
173 O2 Lingwood Norfolk, England U.K.
Lingxi Hunan China see Yongshun
129 R4 Lingxia Jilin China
Lingxian Hunan China see Yanling
129 O8 Lingxian Shandong China
131 J3 Lingxiang Hubei China
Lingyang Hunan China see Cili
129 P6 Lingyuan Liaoning China
130 F6 Lingyun Guangxi China
130 A4 Lingza Xizang China
Lingzhi Bhutan see Lingshi
133 D9 Lingzi Tang reg. Aksai Chin
131 M4 Linhai Zhejiang China
281 G3 Linhares Brazil
204 F7 Linhares Port.
129 J6 Linhe Nei Mongol China
118 B2 Linhpa Myanmar
196 F1 Linia Pol.
103 D11 Linidis Valley South I. N.Z.
257 □O2 Linière Que. Can.
196 G1 Liniewo Pol.
Linjiang Fujian China see Shanghang
130 E2 Linjiang Gansu China
123 E8 Linjiang Jilin China
Linjiang Sichuan China see Cangxi
194 E3 Linkenheim-Hochstetten Ger.
165 L3 Linköping Sweden
122 G6 Linkou Heilong. China
168 J5 Linksness Orkney, Scotland U.K.
160 G5 Linkuva Lith.

131 H4 Linli Hunan China
168 I11 Linlithgow West Lothian, Scotland U.K.
129 M8 Linlü Shan mt. Henan China
Linmingguan Hebei China see Yongnian
260 J6 Linn MO U.S.A.
261 F12 Linn TX U.S.A.
264 J1 Linn, Mount CA U.S.A.
163 T5 Linnansaaren kansallispuisto nat. park Fin.
164 H2 Linnekleppen hill Norway
257 □R2 Linneus ME U.S.A.
172 B4 Linney Head Wales U.K.
168 E9 Linnhe, Loch inlet Scotland U.K.
191 B9 Linnich Ger.
211 D8 Linosa, Isola di i. Sicilia Italy
160 H9 Linova Belarus
160 K4 Linovo Rus. Fed.
192 G4 Linow Ger.
118 C4 Linpo Myanmar
129 N8 Linqing Shandong China
Linru Henan China see Ruzhou
129 M9 Linruzhen Henan China
280 C4 Lins Brazil
228 B4 Linsan Guinea
190 H5 Linsburg Ger.
130 F3 Linshui Sichuan China
270 □ Linstead Jamaica
235 □J5 Linta r. Madag.
115 A8 Lintah, Selat sea chan. Indon.
128 H9 Lintan Gansu China
128 H9 Lintao Gansu China
212 G1 Linth r. Switz.
212 G2 Linthal Switz.
193 G6 Linthe Ger.
258 B6 Linthicum Heights MD U.S.A.
190 G3 Lintig Ger.
102 J7 Linton North I. N.Z.
173 M3 Linton Cambridgeshire, England U.K.
260 E2 Linton ND U.S.A.
129 K9 Lintong Shaanxi China
208 C2 Lintzoain Spain
192 G5 Linum Ger.
258 F6 Linwood NJ U.S.A.
131 I6 Linwu Hunan China
185 B8 Linxe France
129 P5 Linxi Nei Mongol China
128 H9 Linxia Gansu China
128 H9 Linxia Gansu China
Linxian Henan China see Linzhou
129 L8 Linxian Shanxi China
131 I4 Linxiang Hunan China
234 E3 Linyanti r. Botswana/Namibia
234 D3 Linyanti Swamp Namibia
129 O8 Linyi Shandong China
129 P9 Linyi Shandong China
129 L9 Linyi Shanxi China
131 J2 Linying Henan China
208 G4 Linyola Spain
130 F1 Linyou Shaanxi China
201 J3 Linz Austria
191 D9 Linz am Rhein Ger.
128 G7 Linze Gansu China
194 G6 Linzgau reg. Ger.
129 M8 Linzhou Henan China
235 H2 Lioma Moz.
117 K3 Lio Matoh Sarawak Malaysia
183 D11 Lion, Golfe du g. France
270 □ Lionel Town Jamaica
215 O6 Lioni Italy
Lions, Gulf of France see Lion, Golfe du
246 F5 Lions Bay B.C. Can.
235 F3 Lions Den Zimbabwe
251 M5 Lion's Head Ont. Can.
181 K3 Lion-sur-Mer France
115 E7 Lioppa Maluku Indon.
185 F6 Liorac-sur-Louyre France
169 B8 Lios Póil Ireland
224 B6 Lioua Chad
230 B4 Liouesso Congo
114 C5 Lipa Luzon Phil.
197 I2 Lipa Pol.
115 D2 Lipang i. Indon.
199 J2 Lipany Slovakia
216 H7 Lipari Isole Lipari Italy
216 H7 Lipari, Isola i. Isole Lipari Italy
216 H6 Lipari, Isole is Italy
116 D4 Lipatkain Sumatera Indon.
160 K6 Lipawki Belarus
158 F5 Lipcani Moldova
197 H4 Lipce Reymontowskie Pol.
162 T5 Liperi Fin.
161 W9 Lipetsk Rus. Fed.
161 V9 Lipetskaya Oblast' admin. div. Rus. Fed.
Lipetsk Oblast admin. div. Rus. Fed. see Lipetskaya Oblast'
276 D5 Lipez, Cordillera de mts Bol.
173 K5 Liphook Hampshire, England U.K.
196 C2 Lipiany Pol.
161 U1 Lipin Bor Rus. Fed.
130 G5 Liping Guizhou China
197 J6 Lipinki Pol.
196 D4 Lipinki Łużyckie Pol.
161 U8 Lipitsy Rus. Fed.
218 J8 Lipjan Lipjan Kosovo
196 F2 Lipka Pol.
Lipkany Moldova see Lipcani
161 U8 Lipki Rus. Fed.
196 D3 Lipki Wielkie Pol.
219 J8 Lipkovo Lipkovo Macedonia
Lipljan Lipjan Kosovo see Lipjan
161 Q2 Lipnaya Gorka Rus. Fed.
197 H2 Lipnica Kujawsko-Pomorskie Pol.
196 F2 Lipnica Pomorskie Pol.
197 I6 Lipnica Murowana Pol.
197 J5 Lipnik Pol.
197 H6 Lipnika Wielka Pol.
199 G2 Lipník nad Bečvou Czech Rep.
197 H3 Lipno Kujawsko-Pomorskie Pol.
196 E4 Lipno Wielkopolskie Pol.
198 D3 Lipno, Vodní nádrž resr Czech Rep.
185 C7 Liposthey France
219 J4 Lipova Romania
199 L6 Lipovei, Dealurile hills Romania
157 I6 Lipovka Volgogradskaya Oblast' Rus. Fed.
159 T3 Lipovka Voronezhskaya Oblast' Rus. Fed.
219 L6 Lipovu Romania
197 J2 Lipowiec Pol.
191 C7 Lippe r. Ger.
186 J2 Lippenhuizen Neth.
191 I7 Lippoldsberg (Wahlsburg) Ger.
191 F7 Lippstadt Ger.
261 E7 Lipscomb TX U.S.A.
197 L2 Lipsk Pol.
197 J4 Lipsko Pol.
Lipsoí i. Greece see Leipsoi
199 G2 Liptál Czech Rep.
138 H4 Lipti Lekh pass Nepal
229 F3 Liptougou Burkina
199 I2 Liptovská Kokava Slovakia
199 I2 Liptovská Mara, Vodná nádrž resr Slovakia
199 I3 Liptovská Osada Slovakia
199 J3 Liptovská Teplička Slovakia
199 I2 Liptovský Hrádok Slovakia
199 I2 Liptovský Mikuláš Slovakia
105 J8 Liptrap, Cape Vic. Austr.
161 R6 Liptsy Rus. Fed.
130 H6 Lipu Guangxi China
217 M5 Lipuda r. Italy
196 F1 Lipusz Pol.
115 D8 Liquiçá East Timor
Liquissa East Timor see Liquiçá
232 B4 Lira Uganda
115 D7 Liran i. Maluku Indon.
230 C5 Liranga Congo
181 I7 Liré France
204 B3 Lires, Ría de b. Spain
215 L5 Liri r. Italy
232 A2 Liri, Jebel el mt. Sudan
212 G3 Liro r. Italy
115 E2 Lirung Sulawesi Indon.
218 I9 Lis Albania
219 M5 Lisa Romania
169 E5 Lisacul Ireland
142 J1 Lisakovsk Kazakh.
230 D4 Lisala Dem. Rep. Congo

271 □7 Lisas Bay Trin. and Tob.
170 F4 Lisbane Northern Ireland U.K.
169 G4 Lisbellaw Northern Ireland U.K.
206 A3 Lisboa Port.
206 A2 Lisboa admin. dist. Port.
Lisbon Port. see Lisboa
250 F8 Lisbon IL U.S.A.
258 A6 Lisbon MD U.S.A.
257 □O4 Lisbon ME U.S.A.
260 G2 Lisbon ND U.S.A.
257 N4 Lisbon NH U.S.A.
256 E8 Lisbon OH U.S.A.
257 □O5 Lisbon Falls ME U.S.A.
169 J3 Lisburn Northern Ireland U.K.
244 F1 Lisburne, Cape AK U.S.A.
217 I6 Lisca Blanca, Isola i. Isole Lipari Italy
169 D7 Liscannor Ireland
169 D7 Liscannor Bay Ireland
169 C5 Liscarney Ireland
169 E8 Liscarroll Ireland
214 C5 Liscia r. Sardegna Italy
214 C5 Liscia, Lago di l. Sardegna Italy
214 C7 Liscoi r. Italy
249 I4 Liscomb Game Sanctuary nature res. N.S. Can.
169 D6 Lisdoonvarna Ireland
169 H5 Lisduff Ireland
219 K9 Lisec mt. Macedonia
164 H5 Liseleje Denmark
169 F7 Lisgarode Ireland
169 F9 Lisgoold Ireland
Lishan Shaanxi China see Lintong
131 M6 Lishan Taiwan
158 H3 Lishchyn Ukr.
130 C6 Lishe Jiang r. Yunnan China
Lishi Jiangxi China see Dingnan
144 D6 Līshtar-e Bālā Iran
122 D7 Lishu Jilin China
131 L3 Lishui Jiangsu China
131 L4 Lishui Zhejiang China
130 H4 Li Shui r. China
197 J5 Lisia Góra Pol.
97 H2 Lisianski Island HI U.S.A.
Lisichansk Ukr. see Lysychans'k
196 F5 Lisięcice Pol.
181 L3 Lisieux France
161 N1 Lisiy Nos Rus. Fed.
165 K1 Lisjön l. Sweden
172 D7 Liskeard Cornwall, England U.K.
157 G6 Liski Rus. Fed.
199 I2 Lisková Slovakia
184 F5 Lisle France
169 I3 Lislea Northern Ireland U.K.
178 D5 L'Isle-Adam France
182 G5 L'Isle-d'Abeau France
185 E8 L'Isle-de-Noé France
184 E4 L'Isle-d'Espagnac France
185 F9 L'Isle-en-Dodon France
185 G8 L'Isle-Jourdain Midi-Pyrénées France
184 F3 L'Isle-Jourdain Poitou-Charentes France
183 G9 L'Isle-sur-la-Sorgue France
182 J2 L'Isle-sur-le-Doubs France
182 E1 L'Isle-sur-Serein France
185 H8 Lisle-sur-Tarn France
105 N3 Lismore N.S.W. Austr.
103 F10 Lismore South I. N.Z.
169 G8 Lismore Ireland
168 E10 Lismore i. Scotland U.K.
169 E7 Lisnagry Ireland
169 H8 Lisnakill Ireland
169 I3 Lisnamuck Northern Ireland U.K.
169 G4 Lisnarrick Northern Ireland U.K.
169 H4 Lisnaskea Northern Ireland U.K.
158 I7 Lisne Ukr.
214 G3 L'Isolotto i. Italy
182 H2 Lison r. France
198 D2 Lišov Czech Rep.
169 E9 Lispatrick Ireland
Lispole Ireland see Lios Póil
169 G8 Lisronagh Ireland
170 C6 Lisryan Ireland
150 G7 Liss mt. Saudi Arabia
173 K5 Liss Hampshire, England U.K.
Lissa Croatia see Vis
Lissa Pol. see Leszno
185 H6 Lissac-et-Mouret France
170 D4 Lissan Northern Ireland U.K.
186 G4 Lisse Neth.
169 C8 Lisselton Ireland
191 C10 Lissendorf Ger.
227 H2 Lisseri, Oued watercourse Tunisia
164 J1 Lisskogsbrändan Sweden
212 G4 Lissone Italy
221 G2 Lissos r. Greece
169 D7 Lissycasey Ireland
190 F1 List Ger.
164 C3 Lista pen. Norway
164 C3 Listafjorden b. Norway
165 L6 Listed Bornholm Denmark
287 K1 Lister, Mount Antarctica
169 H8 Listerlin Ireland
170 F5 Listooder Northern Ireland U.K.
106 G8 Listore watercourse Qld Austr.
248 D5 Listowel Ont. Can.
169 D8 Listowel Ireland
107 J8 Listowel Downs Qld Austr.
184 C5 Listrac-Médoc France
143 U3 Listvyaga, Khrebet mts Kazakh./Rus. Fed.
196 H4 Liswarta r. Pol.
172 G4 Liswerry Newport, Wales U.K.
197 H5 Liszki Pol.
196 F2 Liszkowo Pol.
162 M5 Lit Sweden
130 G7 Litang Guangxi China
130 C3 Litang Sichuan China
130 C4 Litang Qu r. Sichuan China
275 H4 Litani r. Fr. Guiana/Suriname
275 H4 Litani r. Fr. Guiana/Suriname
150 D5 Lîtâni, Nahr el r. Lebanon
199 I3 Litava Slovakia
198 D2 Litavka r. Czech Rep.
264 L1 Litchfield CA U.S.A.
259 I1 Litchfield CT U.S.A.
260 K6 Litchfield IL U.S.A.
250 J7 Litchfield MI U.S.A.
260 H3 Litchfield MN U.S.A.
256 C7 Litchfield OH U.S.A.
258 I1 Litchfield County CT U.S.A.
233 D7 Litembe Tanz.
160 K4 Litene Latvia
199 G4 Litér Hungary
185 B7 Lit-et-Mixe France
186 H5 Lith Neth.
146 E5 Līth, Wādī al watercourse Saudi Arabia
171 L7 Litherland Merseyside, England U.K.
105 M5 Lithgow N.S.W. Austr.
220 F8 Lithino, Akrotirio pt Kriti Greece
160 G6 Lithuania country Europe
210 E2 Litija Slovenia
251 R9 Lititz PA U.S.A.
199 I3 Litke Hungary
153 T2 Litke, Mys c. Rus. Fed.
220 D2 Litochoro Greece
198 D1 Litoměřice Czech Rep.
198 F2 Litomyšl Czech Rep.
206 B1 Litoral reg. Port.
198 G2 Litovel Czech Rep.
122 I4 Litovko Rus. Fed.
Litovskaya S.S.R. country Europe see Lithuania
201 L2 Litschau Austria
212 E1 Littau Switz.
261 I10 Little r. LA U.S.A.
261 I9 Little r. OK U.S.A.
261 G10 Little r. TX U.S.A.
255 I12 Little Abaco i. Bahamas
248 D3 Little Abitibi r. Ont. Can.
248 D3 Little Abitibi Lake Ont. Can.
Little Aden Yemen see 'Adan aş Şughrá
137 M7 Little Andaman i. Andaman & Nicobar Is India
Little Ararat mt. Turkey see Küçük Ağrı Dağı
260 G7 Little Arkansas r. KS U.S.A.
255 H12 Little Bahama Bank sea feature Bahamas

102 J3 Little Barrier i. North I. N.Z.
207 □ Little Bay Gibraltar
250 G4 Little Bay de Noc MI U.S.A.
Little Belt sea chan. Denmark see Lille Bælt
262 I3 Little Belt Mountains MT U.S.A.
262 K4 Little Bighorn r. MT U.S.A.
Little Bitter Lake Egypt see Murrah aş Şughrá, Al Buḩayrah al
245 K2 Little Black r. AK U.S.A.
260 G6 Little Blue r. KS U.S.A.
171 M6 Littleborough Greater Manchester, England U.K.
246 H5 Little Bow r. Alta Can.
246 H2 Little Buffalo r. N.W.T. Can.
270 C4 Little Cayman i. Cayman Is
247 M3 Little Churchill r. Man. Can.
173 O4 Little Clacton Essex, England U.K.
119 A8 Little Coco Island Coco Is
168 D10 Little Colonsay i. Scotland U.K.
265 U5 Little Colorado r. AZ U.S.A.
173 M6 Little Common East Sussex, England U.K.
258 E6 Little Creek DE U.S.A.
265 T4 Little Creek Peak UT U.S.A.
170 H2 Little Cumbrae i. Scotland U.K.
248 D4 Little Current Ont. Can.
248 C3 Little Current r. Ont. Can.
172 E6 Little Dart r. England U.K.
172 H4 Littledean Gloucestershire, England U.K.
104 H7 Little Desert National Park Vic. Austr.
173 M3 Little Downham Cambridgeshire, England U.K.
259 G5 Little Egg Harbor inlet NJ U.S.A.
270 F2 Little Exuma i. Bahamas
260 H3 Little Falls MN U.S.A.
257 K5 Little Falls NY U.S.A.
168 H7 Littleferry Highland, Scotland U.K.
265 S5 Littlefield AZ U.S.A.
261 D9 Littlefield TX U.S.A.
237 K9 Little Fish r. S. Africa
250 A1 Little Fork MN U.S.A.
250 A1 Little Fork r. MN U.S.A.
246 F5 Little Fort B.C. Can.
Little Ganges atoll Cook Is see Rakahanga
258 D3 Little Gap PA U.S.A.
247 M4 Little Grand Rapids Man. Can.
264 K2 Little Grass Valley Reservoir CA U.S.A.
173 K6 Littlehampton West Sussex, England U.K.
270 G3 Little Inagua Island Bahamas
256 D9 Little Kanawha r. WV U.S.A.
236 C3 Little Karas Berg plat. Namibia
236 E9 Little Karoo plat. S. Africa
244 H5 Little Koniuji Island AK U.S.A.
264 O6 Little Lake CA U.S.A.
168 F7 Little Loch Broom inlet Scotland U.K.
Little Mecatina r. Nfld and Lab./Que. Can. see Petit Mécatina
Little Mecatina Island Que. Can. see Petit Mécatina, Île du
256 A9 Little Miami r. OH U.S.A.
168 I7 Littlemill Highland, Scotland U.K.
168 B7 Little Minch sea chan. Scotland U.K.
173 K4 Little Missenden Buckinghamshire, England U.K.
260 D2 Little Missouri r. ND U.S.A.
173 J4 Littlemore Oxfordshire, England U.K.
256 D9 Little Muskingum r. OH U.S.A.
137 M9 Little Nicobar i. Andaman & Nicobar Is India
173 O4 Little Oakley Essex, England U.K.
237 N1 Little Olifants r. S. Africa
173 M3 Little Ouse r. England U.K.
145 P3 Little Pamir mts Afgh.
259 K2 Little Peconic Bay NY U.S.A.
250 H1 Little Pic r. Ont. Can.
258 A2 Little Pine Creek r. PA U.S.A.
258 A5 Little Pipe Creek r. MD U.S.A.
173 M3 Littleport Cambridgeshire, England U.K.
262 L4 Little Powder r. MT U.S.A.
246 D2 Little Rancheria r. B.C. Can.
261 J8 Little Red r. AR U.S.A.
246 H3 Little Red River Alta Can.
103 G10 Little River South I. N.Z.
255 H9 Little River SC U.S.A.
261 I8 Little Rock AR U.S.A.
264 O7 Littlerock CA U.S.A.
250 H6 Little Sable Point MI U.S.A.
247 M4 Little Sachigo Lake Ont. Can.
245 N3 Little Salmon Lake Y.T. Can.
265 T4 Little Salt Lake UT U.S.A.
109 E7 Little Sandy Desert W.A. Austr.
270 F1 Little San Salvador i. Bahamas
260 G5 Little Sioux r. IA U.S.A.
245 □B6 Little Sitkin Island AK U.S.A.
246 G4 Little Smoky Alta Can.
246 G4 Little Smoky r. Alta Can.
262 J6 Little Snake r. CO U.S.A.
255 □1 Little Sound b. Bermuda
173 N6 Littlestone-on-Sea Kent, England U.K.
258 A5 Littlestown PA U.S.A.
245 □C6 Little Tanaga Island AK U.S.A.
Little Tibet reg. India/Pak. see Ladakh
271 □5 Little Tobago i. Trin. and Tob.
170 B8 Littleton Ireland
173 J5 Littleton Hampshire, England U.K.
250 D9 Littleton IL U.S.A.
257 N4 Littleton NH U.S.A.
256 E9 Littleton WV U.S.A.
250 I4 Little Traverse Bay MI U.S.A.
257 K4 Little Tupper Lake NY U.S.A.
250 B1 Little Turtle Lake Ont. Can.
256 G6 Little Valley NY U.S.A.
260 K7 Little Wabash r. IL U.S.A.
103 G8 Little Wanganui South I. N.Z.
260 E4 Little White r. SD U.S.A.
261 G9 Little Wichita r. TX U.S.A.
262 J5 Little Wind r. WY U.S.A.
262 G5 Little Wood r. ID U.S.A.
Little Zab r. Iraq see Zāb aş Şaghīr, Nahr az
165 S1 Littoinen Fin.
229 H5 Littoral prov. Cameroon
284 B4 Litueche Chile
233 B8 Litunde Moz.
245 M4 Lituya Bay AK U.S.A.
198 C1 Litvínov Czech Rep.
158 H4 Lityn Ukr.
195 K2 Litzendorf Ger.
160 H3 Liu Estonia
Liu'an Anhui China see Lu'an
130 F2 Liuba Shaanxi China
197 L1 Liubavas Lith.
118 I2 Liucheng Guangxi China
131 L4 Liucheng Zhejiang China
131 M7 Liuchiu Yü i. Taiwan
130 F5 Liuchong He r. Guizhou China
Liuchow Guangxi China see Liuzhou
Liudu Guangdong China see Yun'an
197 L1 Liudvinavas Lith.
129 R8 Liugong Dao i. China
129 Q6 Liugu He r. China
122 D7 Liuhe Jilin China
129 P6 Liu He r. China
129 R6 Liu He r. China
131 N4 Liuheng Dao i. China
131 H3 Liujiachang Hubei China
130 G6 Liujiang Guangxi China
Liujiaxia Gansu China see Yongjing
128 H9 Liujiaxia Shuiku resr Gansu China
122 E5 Liukesong Heilong. China
Liuku Yunnan China see Lushui
Liuku China see Lushui
Liulin Gansu China see Jonê
129 L8 Liulin Shanxi China
Liupai Guangxi China see Tian'e
128 J9 Liupan Shan mts China
Liupanshui Guizhou China see Lupanshui
235 H2 Liupo Moz.

129 O9 Liuquan Jiangsu China
266 □P11 Liure Hond.
128 C5 Liushuquan Xinjiang China
231 D8 Liuwa Plain Zambia
231 D8 Liuwa Plain National Park Zambia
131 I4 Liuyang Hunan China
131 I4 Liuyang He r. China
132 L6 Liuyuan Gansu China
129 S1 Liuzhan Heilong. China
Liuzhangzhen Shanxi China see Yuanqu
130 G6 Liuzhou Guangxi China
199 K5 Livada Arad Romania
219 L3 Livada Satu Mare Romania
221 G5 Livada, Akrotirio pt Tinos Greece
220 D4 Livadeia Greece
220 C2 Livadero Greece
220 D2 Livadi Greece
220 E1 Livadia Greece
122 H7 Livadiya Rus. Fed.
220 E4 Livanates Greece
160 J5 Līvāni Latvia
210 F3 Livanjsko Polje plain Bos.-Herz.
181 L3 Livarot France
160 G5 Līvbērze Latvia
245 J2 Livengood AK U.S.A.
159 R3 Livenka Rus. Fed.
213 M4 Livenza r. Italy
264 K2 Live Oak CA U.S.A.
255 F10 Live Oak FL U.S.A.
179 L6 Liverdun France
108 H5 Liveringa W.A. Austr.
264 K4 Livermore CA U.S.A.
263 L11 Livermore, Mount TX U.S.A.
257 □O4 Livermore Falls ME U.S.A.
185 H6 Livernon France
105 M5 Liverpool N.S.W. Austr.
106 E2 Liverpool r. N.T. Austr.
249 H4 Liverpool N.S. Can.
171 L7 Liverpool Merseyside, England U.K.
257 I5 Liverpool NY U.S.A.
258 B3 Liverpool PA U.S.A.
243 K2 Liverpool, Cape Nunavut Can.
245 O1 Liverpool Bay N.W.T. Can.
171 K7 Liverpool Bay England U.K.
105 M4 Liverpool Plains N.S.W. Austr.
105 L4 Liverpool Range mts N.S.W. Austr.
171 N6 Liversedge West Yorkshire, England U.K.
214 G3 Lividonia, Punta pt Italy
212 I2 Livigno Italy
267 O10 Livingston Guat.
168 I11 Livingston West Lothian, Scotland U.K.
261 K9 Livingston AL U.S.A.
264 L4 Livingston CA U.S.A.
256 A11 Livingston KY U.S.A.
261 J10 Livingston LA U.S.A.
262 I4 Livingston MT U.S.A.
259 G3 Livingston NJ U.S.A.
261 H10 Livingston TX U.S.A.
261 H10 Livingston, Lake TX U.S.A.
231 E9 Livingstone Zambia
233 B7 Livingstone Mountains Tanz.
233 B7 Livingstonia Malawi
286 T2 Livingston Island Antarctica
257 K7 Livingston Manor NY U.S.A.
103 C11 Livingston Mountains South I. N.Z.
210 F4 Livno Bos.-Herz.
161 U9 Livny Rus. Fed.
162 U4 Livo r. Rus. Fed.
213 R4 Livold Slovenia
251 K7 Livonia MI U.S.A.
256 H6 Livonia NY U.S.A.
212 I8 Livorno Italy
212 J9 Livorno prov. Italy
212 E5 Livorno Ferraris Italy
182 D6 Livradois, Monts du mts France
182 D5 Livradois Forez, Parc Naturel Régional du nature res. France
238 □1b Livramento São Miguel Azores
278 E5 Livramento do Brumado Brazil
183 F7 Livron-sur-Drôme France
197 J3 Liw Pol.
147 M3 Liwā Oman
150 E6 Liwā', Wādī al watercourse Syria
233 C7 Liwale Tanz.
233 C7 Liwale Juu Tanz.
197 J3 Liwiec r. Pol.
233 B8 Liwonde Malawi
233 B8 Liwonde National Park Malawi
Liwu Hebei China see Lixian
128 I9 Lixian Gansu China
129 N7 Lixian Hebei China
131 H4 Lixian Hunan China
130 D3 Lixian Sichuan China
131 K2 Lixin Anhui China
179 M5 Lixing-lès-St-Avold France
220 B4 Lixouri Kefallonia Greece
Lixus Morocco see Larache
Liyang Anhui China see Hexian
Liyang Hunan China see Lixian
131 L3 Liyang Jiangsu China
Liyuan Hunan China see Sangzhi
204 C9 Liz r. Port.
172 B8 Lizard Cornwall, England U.K.
278 D4 Lizarda Brazil
107 J3 Lizard Island Qld Austr.
172 B8 Lizard Point England U.K.
Lizarra Spain see Estella
205 P3 Lizarraga Spain
256 D10 Lizemores WV U.S.A.
159 S3 Lizinovka Rus. Fed.
130 D4 Liziping Sichuan China
184 E5 Lizonne r. France
178 F5 Lizy-sur-Ourcq France
217 O3 Lizzanello Italy
217 M3 Lizzano Italy
218 I6 Ljig Ljig Serbia
164 D2 Ljomsnuten mt. Norway
210 F3 Ljubija Bos.-Herz.
218 H7 Ljubišnja mts Bos.-Herz./Montenegro
210 E2 Ljubljana Slovenia
201 J7 Ljubljana airport Slovenia
201 K7 Ljubljanica r. Slovenia
218 H6 Ljubovija Ljubovija Serbia
210 F4 Ljubuški Bos.-Herz.
165 O4 Ljugarn Gotland Sweden
162 N5 Ljungå Sweden
163 N5 Ljungan r. Sweden
163 N5 Ljungaverk Sweden
165 J5 Ljungby Sweden
165 M5 Ljungbyån r. Sweden
162 L5 Ljungdalen Sweden
165 L3 Ljungsbro Sweden
164 H3 Ljungskile Sweden
163 N6 Ljusdal Sweden
165 L3 Ljusfallshammar Sweden
164 J1 Ljusnan r. Sweden
163 N6 Ljusnan r. Sweden
163 N6 Ljusne Sweden
210 F2 Ljutomer Slovenia
208 K4 Llagostera Spain
284 B6 Llaima, Volcán vol. Chile
285 G2 Llambí Campbell Arg.
172 D2 Llanaelhaearn Gwynedd, Wales U.K.
Llanandras Wales U.K. see Presteigne
172 F2 Llanarmon Dyffryn Ceiriog Wrexham, Wales U.K.
172 D3 Llanarth Ceredigion, Wales U.K.
172 D4 Llanarthney Carmarthenshire, Wales U.K.
172 F1 Llanasa Flintshire, Wales U.K.
172 D3 Llanbadarn Fawr Ceredigion, Wales U.K.
172 D1 Llanbadrig Isle of Anglesey, Wales U.K.
Llanbedr Ceredigion, Wales U.K. see Lampeter
172 D2 Llanbedr Gwynedd, Wales U.K.
172 D2 Llanbedrog Gwynedd, Wales U.K.
Llanbedr Pont Steffan Wales U.K. see Lampeter
172 D1 Llanberis Gwynedd, Wales U.K.
172 F3 Llanbister Powys, Wales U.K.
172 E2 Llanbryn-mair Powys, Wales U.K.
208 L3 Llançà Spain

284 C4 **Llancanelo, Laguna** l. Arg.
284 C4 **Llancanelo, Salina** salt flat Arg.
172 D2 **Llandanwg** Gwynedd, Wales U.K.
172 D4 **Llanddarog** Carmarthenshire, Wales U.K.
172 D1 **Llanddeiniolen** Gwynedd, Wales U.K.
172 E2 **Llandderfel** Gwynedd, Wales U.K.
172 C4 **Llanddowror** Carmarthenshire, Wales U.K.
172 E4 **Llandeilo** Carmarthenshire, Wales U.K.
172 G4 **Llandinabo** Herefordshire, England U.K.
172 F3 **Llandinam** Powys, Wales U.K.
172 C4 **Llandissilio** Pembrokeshire, Wales U.K.
172 E4 **Llandovery** Carmarthenshire, Wales U.K.
172 F2 **Llandrillo** Denbighshire, Wales U.K.
172 F3 **Llandrindod Wells** Powys, Wales U.K.
172 E1 **Llandudno** Conwy, Wales U.K.
Llandudoch Wales U.K. see **St Dogmaels**
172 D1 **Llandwrog** Gwynedd, Wales U.K.
172 D4 **Llandybie** Carmarthenshire, Wales U.K.
172 D3 **Llandysul** Ceredigion, Wales U.K.
172 D4 **Llanegwad** Carmarthenshire, Wales U.K.
172 D1 **Llaneilian** Isle of Anglesey, Wales U.K.
172 D4 **Llanelli** Carmarthenshire, Wales U.K.
172 E2 **Llanelltyd** Gwynedd, Wales U.K.
172 F4 **Llanelly** Monmouthshire, Wales U.K.
Llanelwy Denbighshire, Wales U.K. see **St Asaph**
205 K2 **Llanes** Spain
172 D1 **Llanfaelog** Isle of Anglesey, Wales U.K.
172 F2 **Llanfair Caereinion** Powys, Wales U.K.
172 E1 **Llanfairfechan** Conwy, Wales U.K.
172 D1 **Llanfairpwllgwyngyll** Isle of Anglesey, Wales U.K.
172 E1 **Llanfair Talhaiarn** Conwy, Wales U.K.
Llanfair-ym-Muallt Wales U.K. see **Builth Wells**
172 C1 **Llanfair-yn-neubwll** Isle of Anglesey, Wales U.K.
172 D3 **Llanfarian** Ceredigion, Wales U.K.
172 D3 **Llanfihangel-ar-arth** Carmarthenshire, Wales U.K.
172 F2 **Llanfyllin** Powys, Wales U.K.
172 F1 **Llanfynydd** Flintshire, Wales U.K.
172 F2 **Llangadfan** Powys, Wales U.K.
172 E4 **Llangadog** Carmarthenshire, Wales U.K.
172 D1 **Llangefni** Isle of Anglesey, Wales U.K.
172 D3 **Llangeler** Carmarthenshire, Wales U.K.
172 D2 **Llangelynin** Gwynedd, Wales U.K.
172 D4 **Llangendeirne** Carmarthenshire, Wales U.K.
172 E1 **Llangernyw** Conwy, Wales U.K.
172 D1 **Llangoed** Isle of Anglesey, Wales U.K.
172 F2 **Llangollen** Denbighshire, Wales U.K.
172 D3 **Llangrannog** Ceredigion, Wales U.K.
172 D1 **Llangristiolus** Isle of Anglesey, Wales U.K.
172 D4 **Llangunnor** Carmarthenshire, Wales U.K.
172 E3 **Llangurig** Powys, Wales U.K.
172 C4 **Llangwm** Pembrokeshire, Wales U.K.
172 F4 **Llangynidr** Powys, Wales U.K.
172 F4 **Llanharan** Rhondda Cynon Taff, Wales U.K.
172 E3 **Llanidloes** Powys, Wales U.K.
172 D3 **Llanilar** Ceredigion, Wales U.K.
172 F4 **Llanishen** Cardiff, Wales U.K.
172 F2 **Llanllwchaiarn** Powys, Wales U.K.
172 D1 **Llanllyfni** Gwynedd, Wales U.K.
172 D1 **Llannerch-y-medd** Isle of Anglesey, Wales U.K.
172 D4 **Llannon** Carmarthenshire, Wales U.K.
172 D3 **Llan-non** Ceredigion, Wales U.K.
172 D2 **Llannor** Gwynedd, Wales U.K.
266 D2 **Llano** Mex.
261 F10 **Llano** TX U.S.A.
261 F10 **Llano** r. TX U.S.A.
261 D9 **Llano Estacado** plain NM/TX U.S.A.
268 B2 **Llano Grande** Durango Mex.
268 B3 **Llano Grande** Nayarit Mex.
274 D3 **Llanos** plain Col./Venez.
284 D2 **Llanos, Sierra de los** mts Arg.
283 B6 **Llanquihue, Lago** l. Chile
172 F2 **Llanrhaeadr-ym-Mochnant** Powys, Wales U.K.
172 D4 **Llanrhidian** Swansea, Wales U.K.
172 D3 **Llanrhystud** Ceredigion, Wales U.K.
172 D1 **Llanrug** Gwynedd, Wales U.K.
172 F4 **Llanrumney** Cardiff, Wales U.K.
172 E1 **Llanrwst** Conwy, Wales U.K.
Llansá Spain see **Llançà**
172 E1 **Llansanffraid Glan Conwy** Conwy, Wales U.K.
172 E1 **Llansannan** Conwy, Wales U.K.
172 D3 **Llansawel** Carmarthenshire, Wales U.K.
172 D4 **Llansteffan** Carmarthenshire, Wales U.K.
Llanstephan Carmarthenshire, Wales U.K. see **Llansteffan**
172 F4 **Llanthony** Monmouthshire, Wales U.K.
172 F4 **Llantilio Pertholey** Monmouthshire, Wales U.K.
172 G4 **Llantrisant** Monmouthshire, Wales U.K.
172 F4 **Llantrisant** Rhondda Cynon Taff, Wales U.K.
172 F5 **Llantwit Major** Vale of Glamorgan, Wales U.K.
172 E2 **Llanuwchllyn** Gwynedd, Wales U.K.
172 F2 **Llanwddyn** Powys, Wales U.K.
172 D3 **Llanwenog** Ceredigion, Wales U.K.
172 D1 **Llanwnda** Gwynedd, Wales U.K.
172 F2 **Llanwnog** Powys, Wales U.K.
172 E4 **Llanwrda** Carmarthenshire, Wales U.K.
172 E3 **Llanwrtyd Wells** Powys, Wales U.K.
172 D3 **Llanybydder** Carmarthenshire, Wales U.K.
Llanymddyfri Carmarthenshire, Wales U.K. see **Llandovery**
172 C1 **Llanynghenedl** Isle of Anglesey, Wales U.K.
172 D2 **Llanystumdwy** Gwynedd, Wales U.K.
218 J8 **Llap** r. Kosovo
218 I8 **Llapushnik** Gllogoc Kosovo
208 G5 **Llardecans** Spain
276 A2 **Llata** Peru
209 E9 **Llaurí** Spain
208 H2 **Llavorsí** Spain
172 F1 **Llay** Wrexham, Wales U.K.
284 B3 **Llay-Llay** Chile
209 K9 **Llebeig, Es Cap des** c. Spain
172 E3 **Lledrod** Ceredigion, Wales U.K.
208 G4 **Lleida** Spain
208 H3 **Lleida** prov. Cataluña Spain
209 H10 **Llentrisca, Cap** c. Spain
206 G4 **Llera** Spain
269 H2 **Llera de Canales** Mex.
206 G4 **Llerena** Spain
172 C2 **Lleyn Peninsula** Wales U.K.
276 C4 **Llica** Bol.
209 D8 **Llíria** Spain
208 I3 **Llívia** Spain
208 H4 **Llobregós** r. Spain
205 O2 **Llodio** Spain
284 B3 **Llolleo** Chile
208 I5 **Llorenç del Penedès** Spain
208 K4 **Lloret de Mar** Spain
220 A2 **Llorgara** nat. park Albania
209 K8 **Lloseta** Spain
107 I2 **Lloyd Bay** Qld Austr.
246 E3 **Lloyd George, Mount** B.C. Can.
259 I3 **Lloyd Harbor** NY U.S.A.
247 I3 **Lloyd Lake** Sask. Can.
247 I4 **Lloydminster** Alta Can.
209 L8 **Llubí** Spain
Lluchmayor Spain see **Llucmajor**
209 K9 **Llucmajor** Spain
270 □ **Lluidas Vale** Jamaica
276 C6 **Llullaillaco, Parque Nacional** nat. park Chile
276 C6 **Llullaillaco, Volcán** vol. Chile
172 E3 **Llyn Clywedog Reservoir** Wales U.K.
Llyn Tegid l. Wales U.K. see **Bala Lake**
172 F3 **Llyswen** Powys, Wales U.K.
196 G2 **Lniano** Pol.
187 C7 **Lo** Belgium
Lo i. Vanuatu see **Loh**
118 G4 **Lô, Sông** r. China/Vietnam
276 C5 **Loa** r. Chile
265 U3 **Loa** UT U.S.A.
117 K3 **Loagan Bunut National Park** Malaysia
117 L5 **Loakulu** Kalimantan Indon.
280 A5 **Loanda** Brazil
230 A5 **Loango, Parc National de** nature res. Gabon
168 J11 **Loanhead** Midlothian, Scotland U.K.
212 E7 **Loano** Italy
168 G11 **Loans** South Ayrshire, Scotland U.K.
208 D3 **Loarre** Spain
114 E7 **Loay** Bohol Phil.
161 S5 **Lob'** r. Rus. Fed.
197 M5 **Lobachivka** Ukr.
237 P2 **Lobamba** Swaziland
156 J4 **Loban'** r. Rus. Fed.
161 V8 **Lobanovo** Rus. Fed.
115 C5 **Lobata** Sulawesi Indon.
207 K6 **Lobatejo** mt. Spain
234 E5 **Lobatse** Botswana
193 K8 **Löbau** Ger.
230 C3 **Lobaye** pref. C.A.R.
230 C4 **Lobaye** r. C.A.R.
183 K7 **Lobbie, Cima delle** mt. Italy
193 E7 **Löbejün** Ger.
193 G8 **Löbenberg** hill Ger.
208 C3 **Lobera de Onsella** Spain
285 H6 **Loberia** Arg.
196 D2 **Łobez** Pol.
114 E6 **Lobi, Mount** vol. Phil.
100 □3b **Lobikaere** i. Majuro Marshall Is
186 J5 **Lobith** Neth.
231 B8 **Lobito** Angola
274 A6 **Lobitos** Peru
192 G2 **Löbnitz** Mecklenburg-Vorpommern Ger.
193 F7 **Löbnitz** Sachsen Ger.
161 U5 **Lobnya** Rus. Fed.
230 C5 **Loboko** Congo
202 C3 **Lobón** Spain
285 H4 **Lobos** Arg.
238 □3b **Lobos** i. Canary Is
207 O5 **Lobos** mt. Spain
266 C3 **Lobos, Cabo** c. Mex.
266 D4 **Lobos, Isla** i. Mex.
269 J4 **Lobos, Isla de** i. Mex.
284 A4 **Lobos, Punta de** pt Chile
270 E2 **Lobos Cay** i. Cuba
274 A6 **Lobos de Afuera, Islas** is Peru
274 A6 **Lobos de Tierra, Isla** i. Peru
Lobositz Czech Rep. see **Lovosice**
159 N5 **Loboykivka** Ukr.
193 F8 **Lobstädt** Ger.
193 F6 **Loburg** Ger.
103 G10 **Loburn** South I. N.Z.
196 F2 **Łobżenica** Pol.
212 C5 **Locana** Italy
212 F3 **Locarno** Switz.
118 H4 **Lôc Binh** Vietnam
191 H6 **Loccum (Rehburg-Loccum)** Ger.
214 D8 **Loceri** Sardegna Italy
168 G9 **Lochaber** reg. Scotland U.K.
168 E9 **Lochailort** Highland, Scotland U.K.
168 E9 **Lochaline** Highland, Scotland U.K.
251 J1 **Lochalsh** Ont. Can.
169 F2 **Loch an Iúir** Ireland
168 F13 **Lochans** Dumfries and Galloway, Scotland U.K.
168 I12 **Locharbriggs** Dumfries and Galloway, Scotland U.K.
200 A4 **Lochau** Austria
131 □J7 **Lo Chau** i. H.K. China
168 F10 **Lochawe** Argyll and Bute, Scotland U.K.
168 H10 **Lochay** r. Scotland U.K.
Loch Baghasdail Western Isles, Scotland U.K. see **Lochboisdale**
168 B8 **Lochboisdale** Western Isles, Scotland U.K.
168 E10 **Lochbuie** Argyll and Bute, Scotland U.K.
168 E8 **Lochcarron** Highland, Scotland U.K.
168 E10 **Lochdon** Argyll and Bute, Scotland U.K.
168 H10 **Lochearnhead** Stirling, Scotland U.K.
186 J4 **Lochem** Neth.
200 H3 **Lochen** Austria
168 H8 **Lochend** Highland, Scotland U.K.
107 I8 **Lochern National Park** Qld Austr.
184 F1 **Loches** France
Loch Garman Ireland see **Wexford**
168 J10 **Lochgelly** Fife, Scotland U.K.
168 F10 **Lochgilphead** Argyll and Bute, Scotland U.K.
168 G10 **Lochgoilhead** Argyll and Bute, Scotland U.K.
103 C13 **Lochiel** South I. N.Z.
237 O2 **Lochiel** S. Africa
231 E8 **Lochinvar National Park** Zambia
168 F6 **Lochinver** Highland, Scotland U.K.
168 G10 **Loch Lomond and the Trossachs National Park** Scotland U.K.
168 J12 **Lochmaben** Dumfries and Galloway, Scotland U.K.
168 B7 **Lochmaddy** Western Isles, Scotland U.K.
103 C11 **Lochnagar** l. South I. N.Z.
168 J9 **Lochnagar** mt. Scotland U.K.
Loch na Madadh Western Isles, Scotland U.K. see **Lochmaddy**
198 C2 **Lochovice** Czech Rep.
197 J3 **Łochów** Pol.
168 F11 **Lochranza** North Ayrshire, Scotland U.K.
258 B6 **Loch Raven Reservoir** MD U.S.A.
187 E6 **Lochristi** Belgium
262 G3 **Lochsa** r. ID U.S.A.
168 B8 **Loch Sgioport** Western Isles, Scotland U.K.
168 G11 **Lochwinnoch** Renfrewshire, Scotland U.K.
168 G9 **Lochy, Loch** l. Scotland U.K.
160 J6 **Lociki** Latvia
104 E5 **Lock** S.A. Austr.
256 C9 **Lockbourne** OH U.S.A.
256 I6 **Locke** NY U.S.A.
264 K3 **Lockeford** CA U.S.A.
201 N5 **Lockenhaus** Austria
168 J12 **Lockerbie** Dumfries and Galloway, Scotland U.K.
108 C6 **Locker Point** W.A. Austr.
105 K6 **Lockhart** N.S.W. Austr.
261 G11 **Lockhart** TX U.S.A.
107 I2 **Lockhart River** Qld Austr.
107 I2 **Lockhart River Aboriginal Reserve** Qld Austr.
256 H7 **Lock Haven** PA U.S.A.
172 G5 **Locking** North Somerset, England U.K.
192 J4 **Löcknitz** Ger.
192 D4 **Löcknitz** r. Ger.
256 G5 **Lockport** NY U.S.A.
173 J6 **Locks Heath** Hampshire, England U.K.
171 P5 **Lockton** North Yorkshire, England U.K.
244 H2 **Lockwood Hills** AK U.S.A.
180 E7 **Locmaria** France
180 B5 **Locmaria-Plouzané** France
180 F6 **Locmariaquer** France
180 F6 **Locminé** France
180 E6 **Locmiquélic** France
119 H9 **Lôc Ninh** Vietnam
180 E6 **Locoal-Mendon** France
215 P5 **Locone** r. Italy
217 M2 **Locorotondo** Italy
180 D4 **Locquirec** France
217 K7 **Locri** Italy
180 C5 **Locronan** France
180 C6 **Loctudy** France
214 D7 **Loculi** Sardegna Italy
276 C4 **Locumba** r. Peru
259 G4 **Locust** NJ U.S.A.
259 H3 **Locust Valley** NY U.S.A.
150 C7 **Lod** Israel
193 E7 **Lödderitz** Ger.
192 J2 **Loddin** Ger.
172 E7 **Loddiswell** Devon, England U.K.
105 I6 **Loddon** r. Vic. Austr.
173 O2 **Loddon** Norfolk, England U.K.
214 D6 **Lodè** Sardegna Italy
160 I4 **Lode** Latvia
268 B5 **Lo de Marcos** Mex.
198 D1 **Loděnice** Czech Rep.
193 E8 **Lodersleben** Ger.
183 C9 **Lodève** France
161 Q1 **Lodeynoye Pole** Rus. Fed.
245 M4 **Lodge, Mount** Can./U.S.A.
247 I5 **Lodge Creek** r. Can./U.S.A.
262 K4 **Lodge Grass** MT U.S.A.
260 D5 **Lodgepole Creek** r. WY U.S.A.
138 G9 **Lodhikheda** Madh. Prad. India
145 N7 **Lodhran** Pak.
212 H5 **Lodi** Italy
212 H5 **Lodi** prov. Italy
264 K3 **Lodi** CA U.S.A.
259 G3 **Lodi** NJ U.S.A.
256 C7 **Lodi** OH U.S.A.
250 E6 **Lodi** WI U.S.A.
162 M3 **Løding** Norway
162 M2 **Lødingen** Norway
212 G5 **Lodi Vecchio** Italy
231 D5 **Lodja** Dem. Rep. Congo
Lodomeria Rus. Fed. see **Vladimir**
101 □7a **Lodoni** Viti Levu Fiji
205 P4 **Lodosa** Spain
205 Q5 **Lodosa, Canal de** Spain
138 C8 **Lodrani** Gujarat India
232 B4 **Lodwar** Kenya
197 H6 **Łodygowice** Pol.
197 H4 **Łódź** Pol.
197 H4 **Łódzkie** prov. Pol.
205 N8 **Loeches** Spain
118 E6 **Loei** Thai.
186 J4 **Loenen** Gelderland Neth.
186 H4 **Loenen** Utrecht Neth.
237 J9 **Loerie** S. Africa
236 D6 **Loeriesfontein** S. Africa
191 D10 **Löf** Ger.
200 G4 **Lofer** Austria
194 E6 **Löffingen** Ger.
162 L2 **Lofoten** is Norway
163 L5 **Lofsdalen** Sweden
237 J6 **Lofter** S. Africa
171 P4 **Loftus** Redcar and Cleveland, England U.K.
109 E8 **Lofty Range** hills W.A. Austr.
232 B4 **Lofusa** Sudan
157 H6 **Log** Rus. Fed.
201 I7 **Log** Slovenia
229 F3 **Loga** Niger
236 I1 **Logageng** S. Africa
168 H12 **Logan** East Ayrshire, Scotland U.K.
260 H5 **Logan** IA U.S.A.
261 D8 **Logan** NM U.S.A.
256 C9 **Logan** OH U.S.A.
262 I6 **Logan** UT U.S.A.
256 D11 **Logan** WV U.S.A.
245 L3 **Logan, Mount** Y.T. Can.
262 D2 **Logan, Mount** WA U.S.A.
107 K6 **Logan Creek** r. Qld Austr.
260 G5 **Logan Creek** r. NE U.S.A.
265 R5 **Logandale** NV U.S.A.
245 L3 **Logan Glacier** Can./U.S.A.
246 F5 **Logan Lake** B.C. Can.
245 O3 **Logan Mountains** N.W.T./Y.T. Can.
254 D5 **Logansport** IN U.S.A.
261 I10 **Logansport** LA U.S.A.
258 B5 **Loganville** PA U.S.A.
210 E3 **Logatec** Slovenia
162 O4 **Lögda** Sweden
162 O5 **Lögdeälven** r. Sweden
231 B6 **Loge** r. Angola
172 H2 **Loggerheads** Staffordshire, England U.K.
164 D3 **Logna** r. Norway
180 H7 **Logne** r. France
230 B1 **Logone** r. Africa
229 I4 **Logone Birni** Cameroon
230 B2 **Logone Occidental** pref. Chad
230 C2 **Logone Oriental** pref. Chad
228 D5 **Logoualé** Côte d'Ivoire
128 G9 **Logpung** Qinghai China
219 L6 **Logrești** Romania
178 B7 **Logron** France
205 P4 **Logroño** Spain
207 I2 **Logrosán** Spain
164 F5 **Løgstør** Denmark
139 N7 **Logtak Lake** India
214 B6 **Logudoro** reg. Sardegna Italy
164 E6 **Løgumkloster** Denmark
100 □5 **Loh** i. Vanuatu
164 G6 **Lohals** Denmark
139 J8 **Lohardaga** Jharkhand India
138 E5 **Loharu** Haryana India
236 H4 **Lohatlha** S. Africa
138 D6 **Lohawat** Rajasthan India
195 O3 **Lohberg** Ger.
180 H6 **Lohéac** France
190 H2 **Lohe-Rickelshof** Ger.
191 I8 **Lohfelden** Ger.
Lohifushi i. N. Male Maldives see **Lhohifushi**
Lohil r. China/India see **Zayü Qu**
163 T6 **Lohilahti** Fin.
162 R3 **Lohiniva** Fin.
163 R6 **Lohja** Fin.
160 G1 **Lohjanjärvi** l. Fin.
191 D9 **Lohmar** Ger.
192 I1 **Lohme** Ger.
192 F3 **Lohmen** Mecklenburg-Vorpommern Ger.
193 J9 **Lohmen** Sachsen Ger.
191 F9 **Löhnberg** Ger.
191 G6 **Löhne** Ger.
190 F5 **Lohne (Oldenburg)** Ger.
201 H3 **Lohnsburg am Kobernaußerwald** Austria
194 H2 **Lohr** r. Ger.
191 G9 **Lohra** Ger.
194 H2 **Lohr am Main** Ger.
193 J8 **Lohsa** Ger.
162 Q4 **Lohtaja** Fin.
160 K3 **Lohusuu** Estonia
118 E4 **Loi, Nam** r. Myanmar alt. **Nanlei He (China)**
213 K7 **Loiano** Italy
195 M4 **Loiching** Ger.
181 J6 **Loigné-sur-Mayenne** France
178 C7 **Loigny-la-Bataille** France
118 C5 **Loikaw** Myanmar
118 C5 **Loi Lan** mt. Myanmar/Thai.
230 D5 **Loile** r. Dem. Rep. Congo
118 C4 **Loi-lem** Myanmar
118 D3 **Loi Lun** Myanmar
163 Q6 **Loimaa** Fin.
160 F1 **Loimaan kunta** Fin.
160 F1 **Loimijoki** r. Fin.
178 E7 **Loing** r. France
118 C2 **Loipyet Hills** Myanmar
178 B7 **Loir** r. France
181 L6 **Loir, Les Vaux du** val. France
181 J6 **Loiré** France
182 E5 **Loire** dept France
181 G7 **Loire** r. France
182 C3 **Loire, Canal latéral à la** France
182 E5 **Loire, Gorges de la** France
178 C8 **Loire, Val de** val. France
180 G7 **Loire-Atlantique** dept France
182 C3 **Loire et de l'Allier, Plaines de la** plain France
Loire-Inférieure dept France see **Loire-Atlantique**
182 F5 **Loire-sur-Rhône** France
178 D8 **Loiret** dept France
178 C8 **Loiret** r. France
178 B8 **Loir-et-Cher** dept France
214 C6 **Loiri-Porto San Paolo** Sardegna Italy
181 J5 **Loiron** France
195 K6 **Loisach** r. Ger.
118 C4 **Loi Sang** mt. Myanmar
182 E5 **Loise** r. France
179 J5 **Loison** r. France
118 C3 **Loi Song** mt. Myanmar
178 I6 **Loisy-sur-Marne** France
233 B5 **Loita Plains** Kenya
192 H3 **Loitz** Ger.
204 F5 **Loivos** Port.
204 E6 **Loivos do Monte** Port.
271 □1 **Loiza Aldea** Puerto Rico
274 B6 **Loja** Ecuador
274 B6 **Loja** prov. Ecuador
207 K6 **Loja** Spain
199 H3 **Lok** Slovakia
158 D3 **Lokachi** Ukr.
117 L2 **Lokan** r. Malaysia
230 E5 **Lokandu** Dem. Rep. Congo
162 S3 **Lokan tekojärvi** l. Fin.
201 I8 **Lokavec** Slovenia
151 K5 **Lökbatan** Azer.
199 I2 **Lokca** Slovakia
156 J3 **Lokchim** r. Rus. Fed.
164 H2 **Løken** Norway
187 F6 **Lokeren** Belgium
198 B1 **Loket** Czech Rep.
201 I8 **Lokev** Slovenia
234 D5 **Lokgwabe** Botswana
159 M3 **Lokhvytsya** Ukr.
232 B4 **Lokichar** Kenya
232 B3 **Lokichokio** Kenya
115 B4 **Lokilalaki, Gunung** mt. Indon.
235 □K3 **Lokintsy** Madag.
232 B3 **Lokitaung** Kenya
162 S3 **Lokka** Fin.
164 F4 **Løkken** Denmark
162 J5 **Løkken** Norway
161 N5 **Loknya** Rus. Fed.
158 E2 **Loknytsya** Ukr.
229 G4 **Loko** Nigeria
230 D5 **Lokofe** Dem. Rep. Congo
229 G5 **Lokoja** Nigeria
230 C5 **Lokolama** Dem. Rep. Congo
230 C5 **Lokolo** r. Dem. Rep. Congo
229 I6 **Lokomo** Cameroon
230 D5 **Lokona** Dem. Rep. Congo
230 C5 **Lokoro** r. Dem. Rep. Congo
230 C4 **Lokosafa** C.A.R.
199 K5 **Lőkösháza** Hungary
229 F5 **Lokossa** Benin
161 R9 **Lokot'** Rus. Fed.
160 I2 **Loksa** Estonia
162 N2 **Løksebotn** Norway
243 L3 **Loks Land** i. Nunavut Can.
100 □6 **Lokuru** New Georgia Is Solomon Is
Lokutu Dem. Rep. Congo see **Elisabetha**
213 R5 **Lokve** Croatia
201 I7 **Lokve** Slovenia
230 F3 **Lol** Sudan
230 F2 **Lol** watercourse Sudan
231 B8 **Lola** Angola
228 C5 **Lola** Guinea
264 L2 **Lola, Mount** CA U.S.A.
158 E5 **Lolishniy Shepit** Ukr.
164 H7 **Lolland** i. Denmark
191 G9 **Lollar** Ger.
232 A2 **Lolle** watercourse Sudan
209 D10 **L'Olleriia** Spain
233 B5 **Lollondo** Tanz.
230 D4 **Lolo** Dem. Rep. Congo
262 G3 **Lolo** MT U.S.A.
115 F3 **Lolobata** Halmahera Indon.
115 E3 **Loloda** Halmahera Indon.
115 E2 **Loloda Utara, Kepulauan** is Maluku Indon.
229 H6 **Lolodorf** Cameroon
284 B4 **Lolol** Chile
262 G3 **Lolo Pass** MT U.S.A.
115 D8 **Lolotoi** East Timor
116 B4 **Lolowau** Indon.
100 □5 **Lolvavana, Passage** Vanuatu
236 H2 **Lolwane** S. Africa
219 L7 **Lom** Bulg.
219 L7 **Lom** r. Bulg.
193 I9 **Lom** Czech Rep.
163 J6 **Lom** Norway
161 W4 **Lom** Rus. Fed.
265 X2 **Loma** CO U.S.A.
276 D2 **Loma Alta** Bol.
269 L7 **Loma Bonita** Mex.
207 M4 **Loma de Chiclana** reg. Spain
284 C5 **Loma del Jaguel Moro** mt. Arg.
207 M5 **Loma de Úbeda** reg. Spain
185 F8 **Lomagne** reg. France
230 D4 **Lomako** r. Dem. Rep. Congo
264 O7 **Loma Linda** CA U.S.A.
99 I3 **Lomaloma** Fiji
231 E6 **Lomami** prov. Dem. Rep. Congo
231 E4 **Lomami** r. Dem. Rep. Congo
228 C4 **Loma Mountains** Sierra Leone
285 G5 **Loma Negra** Arg.
284 E5 **Loma Negra, Planicie de la** plain Arg.
145 L5 **Lomar Pass** Afgh.
276 B3 **Lomas** Peru
286 T3 **Lomas, Bahía de** b. Chile
283 D6 **Lomas Coloradas** hills Arg.
285 H4 **Lomas de Zamora** Arg.
Lomati r. S. Africa see **Mlumati**
285 H4 **Loma Verde** Arg.
101 □7a **Lomawai** Viti Levu Fiji
197 L4 **Łomazy** Pol.
231 D8 **Lomba** r. Angola
238 □1b **Lomba da Fazenda** São Miguel Azores
238 □1b **Lomba da Maia** São Miguel Azores
275 H4 **Lombarda, Serra** hills Brazil
212 H5 **Lombardia** admin. reg. Italy
108 G4 **Lombardina** W.A. Austr.
185 I8 **Lombers** France
185 F9 **Lombez** France
115 C8 **Lomblen** i. Indon.
117 L9 **Lombok** Lombok Indon.
117 L9 **Lombok** i. Indon.
117 K9 **Lombok, Selat** sea chan. Indon.
181 L5 **Lombron** France
229 F5 **Lomé** Togo
230 D5 **Lomela** Dem. Rep. Congo
230 D5 **Lomela** r. Dem. Rep. Congo
212 F5 **Lomello** Italy
197 I3 **Łomianki** Pol.
229 I6 **Lomié** Cameroon
250 F6 **Lomira** WI U.S.A.
193 H8 **Lommatzsch** Ger.
178 E2 **Lomme** France
187 H6 **Lommel** Belgium
196 D3 **Łomnica** Pol.
198 F2 **Lomnice** Czech Rep.
198 D2 **Lomnice** r. Czech Rep.
201 K1 **Lomnice nad Lužnicí** Czech Rep.
198 E1 **Lomnice nad Popelkou** Czech Rep.
199 I2 **Lomno** mt. Slovakia
249 J3 **Lomond** Nfld and Lab. Can.
168 G10 **Lomond, Loch** l. Scotland U.K.
160 M2 **Lomonosov** Rus. Fed.
292 M1 **Lomonosov Ridge** sea feature Arctic Ocean
182 J2 **Lomont** hills France
156 H2 **Lomovoye** Rus. Fed.
Lomphat Cambodia see **Lumphăt**
117 M7 **Lompobatang, Hutan Lindung** nature res. Sulawesi Indon.
115 A6 **Lompobattang, Gunung** mt. Indon.
264 L7 **Lompoc** CA U.S.A.
118 E6 **Lom Sak** Thai.
162 N4 **Lomsjö** Sweden
197 K2 **Łomża** Pol.
119 I8 **Lơn, Hon** i. Vietnam
136 E3 **Lonar** Mahar. India
212 I5 **Lonato** Italy
136 C3 **Lonavale** Mahar. India
198 G6 **Lončarica** Croatia
122 I5 **Lonchakovo** Rus. Fed.
284 A6 **Loncoche** Chile
284 B5 **Loncopangue** Chile
284 B6 **Loncopue** Arg.
139 M8 **Londa** Bangl.
136 D5 **Londa** Karnataka India
213 L8 **Londa** Italy
231 B6 **Londéla-Kayes** Congo
187 F7 **Londerzeel** Belgium
178 B4 **Londinières** France
Londinium Greater London, England U.K. see **London**
229 H6 **Londji** Cameroon
122 H4 **Londoko** Rus. Fed.
248 D5 **London** Ont. Can.
173 L4 **London** Greater London, England U.K.
256 A11 **London** KY U.S.A.
256 B9 **London** OH U.S.A.
174 **London area map** U.K.
271 □6 **London Bridge** i. Grenada
173 M4 **London City** airport England U.K.
169 H3 **Londonderry** Northern Ireland U.K.
169 I3 **Londonderry** county Northern Ireland U.K.
257 M5 **Londonderry** VT U.S.A.
108 I2 **Londonderry, Cape** W.A. Austr.
283 C9 **Londonderry, Isla** i. Chile
173 L5 **London Gatwick** airport England U.K.
173 L5 **London Heathrow** airport England U.K.
Londoni Fiji see **Lodoni**
173 M4 **London Stansted** airport England U.K.
282 D2 **Londres** Arg.
280 B5 **Londrina** Brazil
231 B8 **Londuimbali** Angola
251 M4 **Lonely Island** Ont. Can.
235 F3 **Lonely Mine** Zimbabwe
259 I3 **Lonelyville** NY U.S.A.
264 N5 **Lone Pine** CA U.S.A.
178 C3 **Long** France
118 D5 **Long** Thai.
244 I2 **Long** AK U.S.A.
271 □3 **Long, Îlet** i. Martinique
168 G10 **Long, Loch** inlet Argyll and Bute, Scotland U.K.
185 E10 **Long, Pic** mt. France
231 C8 **Longa** Angola
231 C9 **Longa** r. Cuando Cubango Angola
231 B7 **Longa** r. Angola
220 C6 **Longa** Greece
153 S2 **Longa, Proliv** sea chan. Rus. Fed.
185 G9 **Longages** France
117 K3 **Longagung** Kalimantan Indon.
232 B3 **Longairo** Sudan
117 K3 **Long Akah** Sarawak Malaysia
231 D9 **Longa-Mavinga, Coutada Pública do** nature res. Angola
130 F7 **Long'an** Guangxi China
Long'an Sichuan China see **Pingwu**
239 □3b **Longani, Baie de** b. Mayotte
122 D5 **Long'anqiao** Heilong. China
213 L5 **Longare** Italy
208 C5 **Longares** Spain
213 M3 **Longarone** Italy
172 G5 **Long Ashton** North Somerset, England U.K.
284 B4 **Longaví** Chile
284 B4 **Longaví** r. Chile
284 B5 **Longaví, Nevado de** mt. Chile
117 K3 **Longbawan** Kalimantan Indon.
270 □ **Long Bay** Jamaica
270 □ **Long Bay** b. Jamaica
270 □ **Long Bay** b. Jamaica
255 H9 **Long Bay** b. NC U.S.A.
103 F11 **Longbeach** South I. N.Z.
264 N8 **Long Beach** CA U.S.A.
259 H3 **Long Beach** NY U.S.A.
262 B3 **Long Beach** WA U.S.A.
259 G5 **Long Beach** coastal area NJ U.S.A.
173 K2 **Long Bennington** Lincolnshire, England U.K.
171 N3 **Longbenton** Tyne and Wear, England U.K.
117 K3 **Longberini** Kalimantan Indon.
117 L3 **Longbia** Kalimantan Indon.
Longbo Hunan China see **Shuangpai**
117 K4 **Longboh** Kalimantan Indon.
257 L8 **Long Branch** NJ U.S.A.
172 H5 **Longbridge Deverill** Wiltshire, England U.K.
131 J6 **Longbu** Jiangxi China
173 J3 **Long Buckby** Northamptonshire, England U.K.
102 J7 **Longburn** North I. N.Z.
270 F2 **Long Cay** i. Bahamas
130 E4 **Longchang** Sichuan China
182 H4 **Longchaumois** France
Longcheng Anhui China see **Xiaoxian**
Longcheng Guangdong China see **Longmen**
Longcheng Jiangxi China see **Pengze**
Longcheng Yunnan China see **Chenggong**
131 J6 **Longchuan** Guangdong China
Longchuan Yunnan China see **Chengzi**
Longchuan Yunnan China see **Nanhua**
130 A6 **Longchuan** Yunnan China
130 A7 **Longchuan Jiang** r. China
173 I4 **Long Compton** Warwickshire, England U.K.
104 E3 **Long Creek** watercourse S.A. Austr.
247 K5 **Long Creek** r. Sask. Can.
262 E4 **Long Creek** OR U.S.A.
173 J4 **Long Crendon** Buckinghamshire, England U.K.
128 J9 **Longde** Ningxia China
173 I2 **Longdon** Staffordshire, England U.K.
173 J2 **Long Eaton** Derbyshire, England U.K.
182 G2 **Longecourt-en-Plaine** France
179 J6 **Longeville-en-Barrois** France
179 M5 **Longeville-lès-St-Avold** France
184 B3 **Longeville-sur-Mer** France
103 G9 **Longfellow, Mount** South I. N.Z.
169 G5 **Longford** Ireland
169 G5 **Longford** county Ireland
168 J10 **Longforgan** Perth and Kinross, Scotland U.K.
171 N3 **Longframlington** Northumberland, England U.K.
Longgang Chongqing China see **Dazu**
131 J7 **Longgang** Guangdong China
117 L3 **Longgi** r. Indon.
173 J4 **Long Hanborough** Oxfordshire, England U.K.
Long Harbour H.K. China see **Tai Tan Hoi Hap**
172 H4 **Longhope** Gloucestershire, England U.K.
168 J5 **Longhope** Orkney, Scotland U.K.
171 N3 **Longhorsley** Northumberland, England U.K.
171 N3 **Longhoughton** Northumberland, England U.K.
129 O6 **Longhua** Hebei China
131 H5 **Longhui** Hunan China
287 K1 **Longhurst, Mount** Antarctica
216 H7 **Longi** Sicilia Italy
117 L3 **Longibau** Kalimantan Indon.
233 C5 **Longido** Tanz.
117 L5 **Longikis** Kalimantan Indon.
286 U2 **Longing, Cape** Antarctica
117 K5 **Longiram** Kalimantan Indon.
107 L7 **Long Island** Qld Austr.
270 F2 **Long Island** Bahamas
249 H4 **Long Island** N.S. Can.
248 E2 **Long Island** Nunavut Can.
137 M6 **Long Island** Andaman & Nicobar Is India
103 A12 **Long Island** South I. N.Z.
113 K8 **Long Island** P.N.G.
Long Island Inner Islands Seychelles see **Longue, Île**
257 M8 **Long Island** NY U.S.A.
257 L7 **Long Island Sound** sea chan. CT/NY U.S.A.
173 J3 **Long Itchington** Warwickshire, England U.K.
129 R3 **Longjiang** Heilong. China
130 G6 **Long Jiang** r. China
Longjin Fujian China see **Qingliu**
Longjin Jiangxi China see **Anyi**
Longjuzhai Shaanxi China see **Danfeng**
129 Q8 **Longkou** Shandong China
129 Q8 **Longkou Gang** b. China
248 C3 **Longlac** Ont. Can.
257 □S1 **Long Lake** l. N.B. Can.
248 C3 **Long Lake** l. Ont. Can.
257 K5 **Long Lake** NY U.S.A.
257 □Q1 **Long Lake** l. ME U.S.A.
250 I5 **Long Lake** l. MI U.S.A.
251 K4 **Long Lake** l. MI U.S.A.
257 K4 **Long Lake** l. NY U.S.A.
117 K3 **Long Lama** Sarawak Malaysia
236 I4 **Longlands** S. Africa
173 J3 **Long Lawford** Warwickshire, England U.K.
130 F5 **Longli** Guizhou China
187 H9 **Longlier** Belgium
130 E6 **Longlin** Guangxi China
130 B6 **Longling** Yunnan China
168 L7 **Longmanhill** Aberdeenshire, Scotland U.K.
130 E4 **Longmatan** Sichuan China
257 M6 **Longmeadow** MA U.S.A.
173 N3 **Long Melford** Suffolk, England U.K.
131 J7 **Longmen** Guangdong China
122 E4 **Longmen** Heilong. China
130 E2 **Longmen Shan** mts Sichuan China
130 F7 **Longming** Guangxi China
262 L6 **Longmont** CO U.S.A.
168 J7 **Longmorn** Moray, Scotland U.K.
117 K3 **Long Murum** Sarawak Malaysia
130 E2 **Longnan** Gansu China
131 J6 **Longnan** Jiangxi China
117 K4 **Longnawan** Kalimantan Indon.
168 K11 **Longniddry** East Lothian, Scotland U.K.
181 M4 **Longny-au-Perche** France
215 Q9 **Longobardi** Italy
217 L5 **Longobucco** Italy
206 D2 **Longomel** Port.
231 B8 **Longonjo** Angola
204 D4 **Longos Vales** Port.
284 B3 **Longotoma** Chile
117 K4 **Longpahangai** Kalimantan Indon.
119 H10 **Long Phu** Vietnam
Longping Guizhou China see **Luodian**
255 □2 **Long Point** pt New Prov. Bahamas
248 D5 **Long Point** Ont. Can.
247 L4 **Long Point** pt Man. Can.
248 D5 **Long Point** pt Ont. Can.
102 L6 **Long Point** pt North I. N.Z.
103 B13 **Long Point** pt South I. N.Z.
103 D13 **Long Point** pt South I. N.Z.
251 N7 **Long Point Bay** Ont. Can.
258 F6 **Longport** NJ U.S.A.
260 H3 **Long Prairie** MN U.S.A.
178 C3 **Longpré-les-Corps-Saints** France
171 M5 **Long Preston** North Yorkshire, England U.K.
117 K3 **Longpujungan** Kalimantan Indon.
Longquan Guizhou China see **Fenggang**
Longquan Guizhou China see **Danzhai**
Longquan Hunan China see **Xintian**
Longquan Yunnan China see **Yimen**
131 L4 **Longquan** Zhejiang China
131 M4 **Longquan Xi** r. China
249 J3 **Long Range Mountains** Nfld and Lab. Can.
249 J4 **Long Range Mountains** Nfld and Lab. Can.
184 D3 **Longré** France
107 J7 **Longreach** Qld Austr.
108 H2 **Long Reef** W.A. Austr.
107 M1 **Long Reef** P.N.G.
130 D2 **Longriba** Sichuan China
171 L6 **Longridge** Lancashire, England U.K.
204 F7 **Longroiva** Port.
Longshan Guizhou China see **Longli**
130 G4 **Longshan** Hunan China
Longshan Yunnan China see **Longling**
128 J9 **Long Shan** mts China
130 H6 **Longsheng** Guangxi China
172 □ **Longships** is England U.K.
128 G7 **Longshou Shan** mts China
103 A13 **Long Sound** inlet South I. N.Z.
262 L6 **Longs Peak** CO U.S.A.
173 O3 **Long Stratton** Norfolk, England U.K.
173 M2 **Long Sutton** Lincolnshire, England U.K.
172 G5 **Long Sutton** Somerset, England U.K.
117 K3 **Long Teru** Sarawak Malaysia
131 H4 **Longtian** Hunan China
246 G1 **Longtom Lake** N.W.T. Can.
237 O1 **Long Tompas** pass S. Africa
107 J6 **Longton** Qld Austr.
171 L6 **Longton** Lancashire, England U.K.
172 H2 **Longton** Stoke-on-Trent, England U.K.
129 R2 **Longtou** Nei Mongol China
171 L3 **Longtown** Cumbria, England U.K.
239 □2b **Longue, Île** i. Inner Islands Seychelles
178 D4 **Longueau** France
184 D1 **Longué-Jumelles** France
178 D2 **Longuenesse** France
249 H3 **Longue-Pointe-de-Mingan** Que. Can.
257 L3 **Longueuil** Que. Can.
178 F6 **Longueville** France
178 B4 **Longueville-sur-Scie** France
179 K5 **Longuyon** France
264 I2 **Longvale** CA U.S.A.
265 U7 **Long Valley** AZ U.S.A.
258 F3 **Long Valley** NJ U.S.A.
182 G2 **Longvic** France
182 G2 **Longvic** airport France
246 H5 **Longview** Alta Can.
261 H9 **Longview** TX U.S.A.
262 C3 **Longview** WA U.S.A.
117 L4 **Longwai** Kalimantan Indon.
122 H6 **Longwangmiao** Heilong. China
133 I10 **Longwei Co** l. Xizang China
170 D7 **Longwood** Ireland
238 □2b **Longwood** St Helena
179 K4 **Longwy** France
128 I9 **Longxi** Gansu China
Longxian Guangdong China see **Wengyuan**
128 J9 **Longxian** Shaanxi China
Longxingchang Nei Mongol China see **Wuyuan**
131 K5 **Longxi Shan** mt. Fujian China
Longxun Fujian China see **Dehua**
119 G9 **Long Xuyên** Vietnam
131 K6 **Longyan** Fujian China
129 N8 **Longyao** Hebei China
162 □ **Longyearbyen** Svalbard
122 E4 **Longzhen** Heilong. China
130 F7 **Longzhou** Guangxi China
Longzhouping Hubei China see **Changyang**
213 K5 **Lonigo** Italy
190 E5 **Löningen** Ger.
210 F3 **Lonja** r. Croatia
201 N8 **Lonjica** Croatia
210 F3 **Lonjsko Polje** plain Cro…
181 J4 **Lonlay-l'Abbaye** France
186 K4 **Lonneker** Neth.
178 I4 **Lonny** France
261 J8 **Lonoke** AR U.S.A.
285 F5 **Lonquimay** Arg.
284 B6 **Lonquimay** Chile
284 B6 **Lonquimay, Volcán** vol.
185 D9 **Lons** France
165 K5 **Lönsboda** Sweden
162 M3 **Lønsdalen** val. Norway
182 H3 **Lons-le-Saunier** France
164 F4 **Lønstrup** Denmark
115 F6 **Lontar** i. Maluku Indon.
118 C2 **Lonton** Myanmar
275 I6 **Lontra** Brazil
279 B7 **Lontra** r. Brazil
278 C3 **Lontra** r. Brazil
284 B4 **Lontué** Chile
187 J7 **Lontzen** Belgium
199 L3 **Lónya** Hungary
160 H2 **Loo** Estonia
151 A2 **Loo** Rus. Fed.
114 D5 **Looc** Phil.
Loochoo Islands Japan **Nansei-shotō**
250 J7 **Looking Glass** r. MI U.S…
248 D2 **Lookout, Cape** Ont. Can…
255 I8 **Lookout, Cape** NC U.S.…
251 K5 **Lookout, Point** MI U.S.…
264 N5 **Lookout Mountain** CA…
107 J3 **Lookout Point** Qld Aust…
109 E13 **Lookout Point** W.A. Aus…
244 H1 **Lookout Ridge** AK U.S.…
233 B5 **Loolmalasin** vol. crater…
108 H5 **Looma** W.A. Austr.
248 B3 **Loon** Ont. Can.
246 H3 **Loon** r. Alta Can.
109 I11 **Loongana** W.A. Austr.
247 I4 **Loon Lake** Sask. Can.
257 □P2 **Loon Lake** l. ME U.S.A.
186 H5 **Loon op Zand** Neth.
178 D2 **Loon-Plage** France
186 H5 **Loonse en Drunense D…** nature res. Neth.
169 C7 **Loop Head** Ireland
178 F2 **Loos** France
201 L3 **Loosdorf** Austria
173 N5 **Loose** Kent, England U.K…
237 I7 **Lootsberg Pass** S. Afric…
133 E8 **Lop** Xinjiang China
159 P4 **Lopan** r. Ukr.
161 R9 **Lopandino** Rus. Fed.
213 R6 **Lopar** Croatia
235 □J4 **Lopary** Madag.
Lopasnya Rus. Fed. see …
161 U7 **Lopasnya** r. Rus. Fed.
151 I2 **Lopatin** Rus. Fed.
122 M3 **Lopatina, Gora** mt. Sakh… Rus. Fed.
142 A1 **Lopatino** Rus. Fed.
161 V6 **Lopatinskiy** Rus. Fed.
Lopatka, Cape Rus. Fed… **Lopatka, Mys**
153 Q2 **Lopatka, Mys** c. Rus. Fe…
153 Q4 **Lopatka, Mys** c. Rus. Fe…
161 P9 **Lopatni** Rus. Fed.
158 G5 **Lopatnic** Moldova
160 L4 **Lopatovo** Rus. Fed.
158 D3 **Lopatyn** Ukr.
161 P8 **Lopazna** Rus. Fed.
119 E7 **Lop Buri** Thai.
173 I5 **Lopcombe Corner** Wilts… England U.K.
230 A5 **Lopé, Parc National de…** nat. park Gabon
180 C5 **Loperhet** France
100 □5 **Lopévi** i. Vanuatu
285 H5 **López** Buenos Aires Arg.
285 G2 **López** Santa Fé Arg.
114 D5 **Lopez** Luzon Phil.
258 C2 **Lopez** PA U.S.A.
230 A5 **Lopez, Cap** c. Gabon
285 F6 **López Lecube** Arg.
197 L4 **Łopiennik Górny** Pol.
214 B3 **Lopigna** Corse France
186 G5 **Lopik** Neth.
Lopnur Xinjiang China …
132 J6 **Lop Nur** salt flat China
230 C4 **Lopori** r. Dem. Rep. Co…
186 K2 **Loppersum** Neth.
162 P1 **Lopphavet** b. Norway
163 R6 **Loppi** Fin.
156 J3 **Loptyuga** Rus. Fed.
197 I5 **Łopuszno** Pol.
205 P3 **Lóquiz, Sierra de** mts S…
204 F4 **Lor** r. Spain
145 L6 **Lora** r. Afgh.
104 E3 **Lora** watercourse S.A. Au…
163 J5 **Lora** Norway
145 K8 **Lora** Pak.
145 K7 **Lora, Hamun-i-** dry lake
284 A4 **Lora, Punta** pt Chile
206 H5 **Lora del Río** Spain
256 C7 **Lorain** OH U.S.A.
250 C9 **Loraine** IL U.S.A.
145 M6 **Loralai** Pak.
145 M6 **Loralai** r. Pak.
115 B5 **Lorana** Sulawesi Indon.
205 N8 **Loranca de Tajuña** Spai…
258 D4 **Lorane** PA U.S.A.
207 P5 **Lorca** Spain
194 H4 **Lorch** Baden-Württembe…
191 E10 **Lorch** Hessen Ger.
209 E10 **Lorcha** Spain
114 A6 **Lord Auckland Shoal** se… Phil.
204 D6 **Lordelo** Port.
Lord Hood atoll Arch. de… Tuamotu Fr. Polynesia s… **Marutea (Sud)**
Lord Howe Atoll Solom… **Ontong Java Atoll**
104 □2 **Lord Howe Island** Austr…
290 F7 **Lord Howe Rise** sea feat… S. Pacific Ocean
119 C9 **Lord Loughborough Isl…** Myanmar
204 E7 **Lordosa** Port.
263 J10 **Lordsburg** NM U.S.A.
258 E2 **Lords Valley** PA U.S.A.
115 E8 **Lore** East Timor
115 B4 **Lore Lindu, Taman Nas…** nat. park Indon.
281 E5 **Lorena** Brazil
113 K7 **Lorengau** Admiralty Is P…
113 I8 **Lorentz** r. Papua Indon.
113 I7 **Lorentz, Taman Nasion…** nat. park Papua Indon.
269 J3 **Lorenzo del Real** Mex.
285 I3 **Lorenzo Geyres** Uru.
213 M5 **Loreo** Italy
144 C5 **Lorestān** prov. Iran
282 F2 **Loreto** Arg.
278 D3 **Loreto** Brazil
213 P9 **Loreto** Italy
266 D4 **Loreto** Baja California S…
268 E3 **Loreto** Zacatecas Mex.
277 F5 **Loreto** Para.
274 C5 **Loreto** dept Peru
114 E6 **Loreto** Phil.
215 L3 **Loreto Aprutino** Italy
250 D4 **Loretta** WI U.S.A.
183 I9 **Lorgues** France
232 C4 **Lorian Swamp** Kenya
274 C2 **Lorica** Col.
180 E6 **Lorient** France
204 E8 **Loriga** Port.
184 C5 **Lorignac** France
257 K3 **L'Orignal** Ont. Can.
209 D8 **Loriguilla** Spain
209 D8 **Loriguilla, Embalse de…**
145 J8 **Lorikand** Pak.
243 I3 **Lorillard** r. Nunavut Can…
199 I4 **Lőrinci** Hungary
262 K2 **Loring** MT U.S.A.
183 F7 **Loriol-sur-Drôme** Franc…
182 D2 **Lormes** France
138 H8 **Lormi** Chhattisgarh Indi…
185 C6 **Lormont** France
168 E10 **Lorn, Firth of** est. Scotla…

Lorne Qld Austr.
Lorne Vic. Austr.
Lorne watercourse N.T. Austr.
Loro r. China
Loro Ciuffenna Italy
Loropéni Burkina
Loro Piceno Italy
Lorp-Sentaraille France
Lorquin France
Lörrach Ger.
Lorrain, Plateau France
Lorraine Qld Austr.
Lorraine admin. reg. France
Lorraine reg. France
Lorraine, Parc Naturel Régional de nature res. France
Lorraine, Plaine plain France
Lorrez-le-Bocage-Préaux France
Lorris France
Lorsch Ger.
Lort r. W.A. Austr.
Lörudden Sweden
Lorup Ger.
Lorzot Tunisia
Los, Îles de is Guinea
Los', Ostrov i. Azer. see Qarasu Adası
Losa Mex.
Losa r. Spain
Losacino Spain
Losa del Obispo Spain
Losai National Reserve nature res. Kenya
Losal Rajasthan India
Los Alamos CA U.S.A.
Los Alamos NM U.S.A.
Los Alcázares Spain
Los Alcornocales, Parque Natural de nature res. Spain
Los Aldamas Mex.
Los Alerces, Parque Nacional nat. park Arg.
Los Altos Mex.
Los Amoles Mex.
Los Amores Arg.
Los Andes Chile
Los Ángeles Chile
Los Angeles CA U.S.A.
Los Angeles Aqueduct canal CA U.S.A.
Los Antiguos Arg.
Los Arabos Cuba
Los Árboles Arg.
Los Arcos Spain
Los Arenales del Sol Spain
Losares mt. Spain
Los Arroyos Mex.
Los Ayala Mex.
Los Azufres, Parque Natural nature res. Mex.
Los Baños Mex.
Los Banos CA U.S.A.
Los Barreros mt. Spain
Los Barrios Spain
Los Barrios de Luna Spain
Los Belones Spain
Los Blancos Arg.
Los Cantareros Spain
Los Cardos Arg.
Los Cerrillos Arg.
Los Charrúas Arg.
Los Chilenos, Laguna l. Arg.
Los Chiles Costa Rica
Los Colorados Arg.
Los Condores Arg.
Los Conquistadores Arg.
Los Corales del Rosario, Parque Nacional nat. park Col.
Los Coronados, Islas is Mex.
Los Corrales de Buelna Spain
Loscos Spain
Los Cristianos Tenerife Canary Is
Los Cusis Beni Bol.
Los Cusis Beni Bol.
Los Difuntios, Lago de l. Uru. see Negra, Lago
Los Dolores Spain
Losevo Rus. Fed.
Loseya well Tanz.
Los Gallardos Spain
Los Gatos r. Mex.
Los Gatos CA U.S.A.
Los Gigantes Tenerife Canary Is
Los Gigantes, Cerro mt. Arg.
Los Glaciares, Parque Nacional nat. park Arg.
Los Haitises nat. park Dom. Rep.
Losheim Ger.
Los Hinojosos Spain
Los Hoyos Mex.
Los Huemules, Parque Nacional nat. park Chile
Łosice Pol.
Los Idolos Mex.
Lošinj i. Croatia
Łosinka Pol.
Los Juríes Arg.
Los Katios, Parque Nacional nat. park Col.
Loskop S. Africa
Loskop Dam Nature Reserve S. Africa
Los Lagos Chile
Los Lagos admin. reg. Chile
Loslau Pol. see Wodzisław Śląski
Los Laureles Chile
Los Leones Mex.
Los Llanos de Aridane La Palma Canary Is
Los Lunas NM U.S.A.
Los Maitenes Santiago Chile
Los Maitenes Valparaíso Chile
Los Maldonados Spain
Los Manatiales Arg.
Los Mármoles, Parque Nacional nat. park Mex.
Los Martínez del Puerto Spain
Los Menucos Arg.
Los'mino Rus. Fed.
Los Mochis Mex.
Los Molares Spain
Los Molinos Fuerteventura Canary Is
Los Molinos Spain
Los Molinos CA U.S.A.
Los Molles r. Chile
Los Monegros reg. Spain
Los Morales Mex.
Los Naranjos Mex.
Los Navalmorales Spain
Los Navalucillos Spain
Los Nevados, Parque Nacional nat. park Col.
Los Obispos mt. Spain
Los Olímpicos Mex.
Losone Switz.
Łososina Dolna Pol.
Los Palacios Cuba
Los Palacios y Villafranca Spain
Los Pandos Spain
Lospatos East Timor
Los Pedroches plat. Spain
Los Pedrones Spain
Los Peladeros Chile
Los Pericos Mex.
Los Placeres del Oro Mex.
Los Pozuelos de Calatrava Spain
Los Rábanos Spain
Los Ralos Arg.
Los Realejos Tenerife Canary Is
Los Remedios r. Mex.
Los Reyes Mex.
Los Ríos admin. reg. Chile
Los Ríos prov. Ecuador
Los Rodríguez Mex.
Los Roques, Islas is Venez.
Los Royos Spain
Lossa r. Ger.
Lossa (Finne) Ger.
Los Santos Spain
Los Santos de Maimona Spain
Los Sauces La Palma Canary Is
Los Sauces Chile
Los Sauces Mex.
194 E5 Loßburg Ger.
185 D7 Losse France
186 K4 Losser Neth.
168 J7 Lossie r. Scotland U.K.
168 J7 Lossiemouth Moray, Scotland U.K.
238 □3a Los Silos Tenerife Canary Is
193 G9 Lößnitz Ger.
212 G3 Lostallo Switz.
274 D2 Los Taques Venez.
193 E6 Lostau Ger.
256 B11 Lost Creek KY U.S.A.
282 E3 Los Telares Arg.
268 D6 Los Tepames Mex.
274 E2 Los Teques Venez.
275 F2 Los Testigos is Venez.
264 M6 Lost Hills CA U.S.A.
282 E2 Los Tigres Arg.
269 L8 Los Tigres Mex.
171 M7 Lostock Gralam Cheshire, England U.K.
205 L2 Los Tojos Spain
262 H4 Lost Trail Pass ID U.S.A.
172 C7 Lostwithiel Cornwall, England U.K.
161 N6 Losvida, Vozyera l. Belarus
265 S10 Los Vidrios Mex.
276 C6 Los Vientos Chile
207 L5 Los Villares Spain
284 B2 Los Vilos Chile
268 C5 Los Volcanes Mex.
205 M9 Los Yébenes Spain
159 K3 Losynivka Ukr.
185 H6 Lot dept France
183 C8 Lot r. France
282 B5 Lota Chile
232 B3 Lotagipi Swamp Kenya
163 I6 Lote Norway
163 K6 Løten Norway
185 F7 Lot-et-Garonne dept France
144 H3 Loṭfābād Turkm.
168 K4 Loth Orkney, Scotland U.K.
232 B3 Lothagum Hills Sudan
237 O2 Lothair S. Africa
168 I6 Lothmore Highland, Scotland U.K.
Lothringen reg. France see Lorraine
232 B3 Lotikipi Plain Kenya
230 D5 Loto Dem. Rep. Congo
230 C5 Lotoi r. Dem. Rep. Congo
161 S5 Lotoshino Rus. Fed.
159 L6 Lotskyne Ukr.
Lot's Wife i. Japan see Sōfu-gan
162 U2 Lotta r. Fin./Rus. Fed.
191 E6 Lotte Ger.
102 M4 Lottin Point North I. N.Z.
194 F6 Lottstetten Ger.
232 B3 Lotuke mt. Sudan
196 E2 Lotyń Pol.
214 D8 Lotzorai Sardegna Italy
181 K6 Louailles France
118 E4 Louangnamtha Laos
118 F5 Louangphabang Laos
180 E4 Louannec France
180 E4 Louargat France
231 B6 Loubomo Congo
193 L10 Loučeň Czech Rep.
198 C1 Loučná hill Czech Rep.
198 D3 Loučovice Czech Rep.
180 F5 Loudéac France
183 D6 Loudes France
131 H5 Loudi Hunan China
231 B6 Loudima Congo
255 E8 Loudon TN U.S.A.
256 C8 Loudonville OH U.S.A.
184 E1 Loudun France
181 K6 Loué France
182 G2 Loue r. France
231 B5 Louéssé r. Congo
129 L7 Loufan Shanxi China
228 A3 Louga Senegal
285 G5 Louge Arg.
185 G9 Louge r. France
Loughanure Ireland see Loch an Iúir
173 J2 Loughborough Leicestershire, England U.K.
169 J4 Loughbrickland Northern Ireland U.K.
243 H2 Lougheed Island Nunavut Can.
169 C8 Lougher Ireland
169 I4 Loughgall Northern Ireland U.K.
169 G5 Lough Gowna Ireland
169 K4 Loughinisland Northern Ireland U.K.
169 G7 Loughmoe Ireland
172 D4 Loughor Swansea, Wales U.K.
172 D4 Loughor r. Wales U.K.
169 E6 Loughrea Ireland
169 E3 Loughros More Bay Ireland
173 M4 Loughton Essex, England U.K.
185 F6 Lougratte France
182 G3 Louhans France
256 C10 Louisa KY U.S.A.
256 H10 Louisa VA U.S.A.
108 I5 Louisa Downs Aboriginal Reserve W.A. Austr.
249 J4 Louisbourg N.S. Can.
Louisburg N.S. Can. see Louisbourg
255 H7 Louisburg NC U.S.A.
245 K3 Louise, Lake AK U.S.A.
246 G2 Louise Falls N.W.T. Can.
Louis-Gentil Morocco see Youssoufia
113 L9 Louisiade Archipelago is P.N.G.
260 J6 Louisiana MO U.S.A.
261 J10 Louisiana state U.S.A.
235 F4 Louis Trichardt S. Africa
236 F4 Louisvale S. Africa
255 F9 Louisville GA U.S.A.
260 K6 Louisville IL U.S.A.
254 E6 Louisville KY U.S.A.
261 K9 Louisville MS U.S.A.
256 D8 Louisville OH U.S.A.
290 H8 Louisville Ridge sea feature S. Pacific Ocean
248 E2 Louis-XIV, Pointe pt Que. Can.
156 F2 Loukhi Rus. Fed.
230 C5 Loukoléla Congo
231 B5 Loukouo Congo
182 I2 Loulans France
184 C3 Loulay France
206 C6 Loulé Port.
228 D4 Loulouni Mali
229 H5 Loum Cameroon
198 C1 Louny Czech Rep.
183 K9 Loup r. France
260 G5 Loup r. NE U.S.A.
260 F5 Loup City NE U.S.A.
249 F1 Loups Marins, Lacs des lakes Que. Can.
249 F1 Loups Marins, Petit lac des l. Que. Can.
249 J3 Lourdes Nfld and Lab. Can.
185 D9 Lourdes France
250 B6 Lourdes IA U.S.A.
184 H3 Lourdoueix-St-Pierre France
275 I4 Lourenço Brazil
Lourenço Marques Moz. see Maputo
206 A3 Loures Port.
204 C8 Louriçal Port.
206 A2 Lourinhã Port.
183 G9 Lourmarin France
220 B3 Louros Greece
204 C7 Lourosa Port.
178 D8 Loury France
204 D8 Lousã Port.
206 A3 Lousa Port.
204 D8 Lousã, Serra da mts Port.
204 D6 Lousada Port.
Loushanguan Guizhou China see Tongzi
236 H9 Louterwater S. Africa
105 J4 Louth N.S.W. Austr.
169 I5 Louth Ireland
169 I5 Louth county Ireland
171 Q7 Louth Lincolnshire, England U.K.
220 F5 Loutra Kythnos Greece
220 E4 Loutra Aidipsou Greece
220 D5 Loutraki Greece
220 D2 Loutro Greece
Louvain Belgium see Leuven
187 I7 Louveigné Belgium
181 J5 Louverné France
185 D9 Louvie-Juzon France
178 B5 Louviers France
180 I5 Louvigné-de-Bais France
181 I5 Louvigné-du-Désert France
178 E5 Louvres France
178 G3 Louvroil France
236 I2 Louwna S. Africa
237 P3 Louwsburg S. Africa
178 I7 Louze France
162 P4 Lövånger Sweden
199 H4 Lovasberény Hungary
198 F5 Lovászi Hungary
199 G4 Lovászpatona Hungary
161 O3 Lovat' r. Rus. Fed.
162 M5 Lövberga Sweden
218 G8 Lovćen nat. park Montenegro
218 H5 Lovćenac Vojvodina Serbia
219 M7 Lovech Bulg.
262 L6 Loveland CO U.S.A.
257 □O4 Lovell ME U.S.A.
262 J4 Lovell WY U.S.A.
Lovello, Monte mt. Austria see Grosser Löffler
103 D13 Lovells Flat South I. N.Z.
271 □3 Lovell Village St Vincent
264 N1 Lovelock NV U.S.A.
258 C1 Lovelton PA U.S.A.
187 E6 Lovendegem Belgium
212 I4 Lovere Italy
212 I3 Lovero Italy
256 E12 Lovers' Leap mt. VA U.S.A.
250 E7 Loves Park IL U.S.A.
163 S6 Loviisa Fin.
162 Q3 Lovikka Sweden
256 G11 Lovingston VA U.S.A.
261 D9 Lovington NM U.S.A.
199 I3 Lovinobaňa Slovakia
163 L6 Lövnäsvallen Sweden
164 F5 Lovns Bredning b. Denmark
198 F4 Lövő Hungary
193 J9 Lovosice Czech Rep.
156 F1 Lovozero Rus. Fed.
210 E3 Lovran Croatia
213 P5 Lovreč Croatia
201 L6 Lovrenc Slovenia
218 I5 Lovrin Romania
165 K1 Lövsjön Sweden
165 N1 Lövstabukten b. Sweden
161 W6 Lovtsy Rus. Fed.
231 D6 Lóvua Angola
231 D7 Lóvua Angola
251 S4 Low Que. Can.
247 O2 Low, Cape Nunavut Can.
230 E5 Lowa Dem. Rep. Congo
230 E5 Lowa r. Dem. Rep. Congo
145 N4 Lowarai Pass Pak.
197 L4 Łowcza Pol.
171 O7 Lowdham Nottinghamshire, England U.K.
250 G8 Lowell IN U.S.A.
257 N6 Lowell MA U.S.A.
250 I7 Lowell MI U.S.A.
262 C5 Lowell OR U.S.A.
257 M4 Lowell VT U.S.A.
232 B3 Lowelli Sudan
257 □O3 Lowelltown ME U.S.A.
236 B3 Löwen watercourse Namibia
192 H5 Löwenberg Ger.
194 G3 Löwenstein Ger.
246 G5 Lower Arrow Lake B.C. Can.
Lower Austria land Austria see Niederösterreich
169 J3 Lower Ballinderry Northern Ireland U.K.
173 L5 Lower Beeding West Sussex, England U.K.
260 F3 Lower Brule Indian Reservation res. SD U.S.A.
Lower California pen. Mex. see Baja California
172 H4 Lower Cam Gloucestershire, England U.K.
168 E7 Lower Diabaig Highland, Scotland U.K.
104 H8 Lower Glenelg National Park Vic. Austr.
265 S6 Lower Granite Gorge AZ U.S.A.
103 I8 Lower Hutt North I. N.Z.
244 G3 Lower Kalskag AK U.S.A.
168 D10 Lower Kilchattan Argyll and Bute, Scotland U.K.
168 D11 Lower Killeyan Argyll and Bute, Scotland U.K.
262 D5 Lower Klamath National Wildlife Refuge nature res. OR U.S.A.
245 N3 Lower Laberge Y.T. Can.
264 J3 Lower Lake CA U.S.A.
237 N5 Lower Loteni S. Africa
169 G4 Lower Lough Erne l. Northern Ireland U.K.
248 A3 Lower Manitou Lake Ont. Can.
259 G3 Lower New York Bay NY U.S.A.
116 □ Lower Peirce Reservoir Sing.
237 M6 Lower Pitseng S. Africa
245 O4 Lower Post B.C. Can.
260 H2 Lower Red Lake MN U.S.A.
237 P1 Lower Sabie S. Africa
Lower Saxony land Ger. see Niedersachsen
Lower Tunguska r. Rus. Fed. see Nizhnyaya Tunguska
231 F8 Lower Zambezi National Park Zambia
173 P3 Lowestoft Suffolk, England U.K.
145 M4 Lowgar prov. Afgh.
171 N2 Lowick Northumberland, England U.K.
197 H3 Łowicz Pol.
Low Island Kiribati see Starbuck Island
145 J6 Lowkhi Afgh.
256 F11 Lowmoor VA U.S.A.
108 □1 Low Point Christmas I.
105 J10 Low Rocky Point Tas. Austr.
173 O2 Low Street Norfolk, England U.K.
256 E9 Lowsville WV U.S.A.
168 I12 Lowther Hills Scotland U.K.
243 I2 Lowther Island Nunavut Can.
257 J5 Lowville NY U.S.A.
196 D3 Łowyń Pol.
269 K9 Loxicha Mex.
190 G4 Loxstedt Ger.
104 H6 Loxton S.A. Austr.
236 G7 Loxton S. Africa
168 H6 Loyal, Loch l. Scotland U.K.
251 R8 Loyalsock Creek r. PA U.S.A.
264 L2 Loyalton CA U.S.A.
258 B3 Loyalton PA U.S.A.
Loyalty Islands New Caledonia see Loyauté, Îles
Loyang Henan China see Luoyang
100 □5 Loyauté, Îles is New Caledonia
250 D6 Loyd WI U.S.A.
237 P2 Loyengo Swaziland
182 G5 Loyettes France
Loyev Belarus see Loyew
158 J2 Loyew Belarus
168 F8 Loyne, Loch l. Scotland U.K.
156 K4 Loyno Rus. Fed.
283 C8 Loyola, Punta pt Arg.
162 L4 Løypskardtinden mt. Norway
183 D7 Lozère dept France
183 D8 Lozère, Mont mt. France
218 H6 Loznica Loznica Serbia
219 O7 Loznitsa Bulg.
159 R4 Lozno-Oleksandrivka Ukr.
159 Q3 Loznoye Rus. Fed.
198 G3 Lozorno Slovakia
159 O4 Lozova Kharkivs'ka Oblast' Ukr.
159 P5 Lozova Kharkivs'ka Oblast' Ukr.
Lozovaya Kazakh. see Lozovoye
Lozovaya Ukr. see Lozova
158 G4 Lozove Ukr.
159 P4 Lozoven'ka Ukr.
218 J6 Lozovik Velika Plana Serbia
219 J9 Lozovo Lozovo Macedonia
143 Q1 Lozovoye Kazakh.
159 T3 Lozovoye Rus. Fed.
205 M7 Lozoya Spain
205 N7 Lozoya r. Spain
205 M7 Lozoya, Canal de Spain
205 M7 Lozoyuela Spain
159 O7 Lozuvatka r. Ukr.
156 M3 Loz'va r. Rus. Fed.
213 M3 Lozzo di Cadore Italy
106 E8 Ltyentye Apurte Aboriginal Land res. N.T. Austr.
231 E7 Luabo Dem. Rep. Congo
235 H3 Luabo Moz.
231 D7 Luacano Angola
231 D7 Luachimo Angola
231 D6 Luachimo r. Angola/Dem. Rep. Congo
231 D6 Luaco Angola
230 C4 Lua Dekere r. Dem. Rep. Congo
231 E6 Luakila Dem. Rep. Congo
235 H3 Luala r. Moz.
231 D7 Lualaba prov. Dem. Rep. Congo
231 B6 Luali Dem. Rep. Congo
264 □C12 Lualualei HI U.S.A.
233 B8 Luambe National Park Zambia
231 E8 Luampa Zambia
231 E8 Luampa r. Zambia
131 K3 Lu'an Anhui China
270 □ Luana Point Jamaica
118 F4 Luân Châu Vietnam
131 H2 Luanchuan Henan China
204 I1 Luanco Spain
231 B7 Luanda Angola
231 B7 Luanda prov. Angola
231 C7 Luando Angola
231 C7 Luando r. Angola
231 C7 Luando, Reserva Natural Integral do nature res. Angola
115 F8 Luang i. Maluku Indon.
118 F6 Luang, Huai r. Thai.
119 D10 Luang, Khao mt. Thai.
119 E11 Luang, Thale lag. Thai.
231 D8 Luanginga r. Zambia
100 □6 Luangiua i. Solomon Is
Luang Nam Tha Laos see Louangnamtha
Luang Phrabang, Thiu Khao mts Laos/Thai. see Luang Prabang Range
Luang Prabang Laos see Louangphabang
130 C10 Luang Prabang Range mts Laos/Thai.
231 C7 Luangue Angola
231 D8 Luanguinga r. Angola
231 F8 Luangwa Zambia
233 A8 Luangwa r. Zambia
128 C9 Luanhaizi Qinghai China
129 P7 Luan He r. China
129 P7 Luannan Hebei China
275 G6 Lua Nova Brazil
129 O6 Luanping Hebei China
231 F8 Luanshya Zambia
284 E5 Luan Toro Arg.
129 P7 Luanxian Hebei China
231 F7 Luanza Dem. Rep. Congo
Luanzhou Hebei China see Luanxian
Luao Angola see Luau
231 F7 Luapula r. Dem. Rep. Congo/Zambia
231 F7 Luapula prov. Zambia
Luar i. Cocos Is see Horsburgh Island
117 J4 Luar, Danau l. Indon.
204 G1 Luarca Spain
231 D7 Luashi Dem. Rep. Congo
231 D8 Luatamba Angola
233 C8 Luatize r. Moz.
231 D7 Luau Angola
229 H6 Luba Equat. Guinea
197 L5 Lubaczów Pol.
197 K5 Lubaczówka r. Pol.
231 C7 Lubalo Angola
196 D4 Lubań Pol.
160 J5 Lubāna Latvia
160 J5 Lubānas ezers l. Latvia
114 C5 Lubang Phil.
114 C5 Lubang i. Phil.
114 B5 Lubang Islands Phil.
231 B8 Lubango Angola
196 C2 Lubanowo Pol.
231 E6 Lubao Dem. Rep. Congo
193 F6 Lübars Ger.
197 K4 Lubartów Pol.
196 E3 Lubasz Pol.
197 H2 Lubawa Pol.
196 E5 Lubawka Pol.
191 G6 Lübbecke Ger.
187 G7 Lubbeek Belgium
193 I7 Lübben Ger.
193 I7 Lübbenau Ger.
236 D5 Lubbeskolk salt pan S. Africa
261 E9 Lubbock TX U.S.A.
192 D5 Lübbow Ger.
196 C2 Lubczyna Pol.
257 □S4 Lubec ME U.S.A.
190 K3 Lübeck Ger.
256 D9 Lubeck WV U.S.A.
190 K2 Lübecker Bucht b. Ger.
231 E6 Lubefu Dem. Rep. Congo
129 Q4 Lubei Nei Mongol China
199 I2 Ľubeľa Slovakia
197 K4 Lubelska, Wyżyna hills Pol.
197 K4 Lubelskie prov. Pol.
Lüben Pol. see Lubin
198 C1 Lubenec Czech Rep.
197 J6 Lubenia Pol.
199 J3 Lubeník Slovakia
142 F2 Lubenka Kazakh.
230 F5 Lubero Dem. Rep. Congo
183 G9 Lubéron, Montagne du ridge France
183 G9 Lubéron, Parc Naturel Régional du nature res. France
184 G5 Lubersac France
192 D4 Lübesse Ger.
204 G4 Lubián Spain
196 G2 Łubianka Pol.
196 E4 Lubiąż Pol.
114 C6 Lubic i. Phil.
199 J2 Ľubica r. Slovakia
196 G2 Lubichowo Pol.
196 G2 Lubicz Dolny Pol.
196 D2 Lubie, Jezioro l. Pol.
196 D4 Lubięcin Pol.
197 H6 Lubień Pol.
197 G3 Lubienka r. Pol.
197 H3 Lubień Kujawski Pol.
196 D2 Lubieszewo Pol.
196 G2 Lubiewo Pol.
196 E4 Lubin Pol.
189 H3 Lubiń Pol.
231 F5 Lubirizi Dem. Rep. Congo
237 L7 Lubisi Dam resr S. Africa
196 C3 Lubiszyn Pol.
197 K4 Lublin Pol.
196 G5 Lubliniec Pol.
192 I2 Lubmin Ger.
Lubnān country Asia see Lebanon
196 F2 Lubnia Pol.
196 G5 Łubniany Pol.
196 G4 Łubnice Łódzkie Pol.
197 J5 Łubnice Świętokrzyskie Pol.
196 D3 Lubniewice Pol.
197 H3 Łubno Łódzkie Pol.
196 F1 Łubno Pomorskie Pol.
196 E2 Lubno Pol.
159 M3 Lubny Ukr.
117 I4 Lubok Antu Sarawak Malaysia
237 P2 Lubombo admin. dist. Swaziland
197 I1 Lubomino Pol.
196 E3 Luboń Pol.
162 U5 Lubosalma Rus. Fed.
199 K2 Ľubotice Slovakia
199 J2 Ľubotín Slovakia
192 E3 Lübow Ger.
197 H2 Lubowidz Pol.
196 F3 Łubowo Wielkopolskie Pol.
196 E2 Łubowo Zachodniopomorskie Pol.
196 G3 Lubraniec Pol.
207 O6 Lubrín Spain
196 D3 Lubrza Lubuskie Pol.
196 F5 Lubrza Opolskie Pol.
196 C4 Lubsko Pol.
192 D3 Lübstorf Ger.
196 G3 Lubstów Pol.
196 F5 Lubsza Pol.
196 C4 Lubsza r. Pol.
192 D4 Lübtheen Ger.
114 C3 Lubuagan Luzon Phil.
231 E6 Lububu Dem. Rep. Congo
231 E7 Lubudi Dem. Rep. Congo
231 E7 Lubudi r. Dem. Rep. Congo
116 F6 Lubukbalang Sumatera Indon.
116 E6 Lubuklinggau Sumatera Indon.
116 C3 Lubukpakam Sumatera Indon.
116 D4 Lubuksikaping Sumatera Indon.
231 E7 Lubumbashi Dem. Rep. Congo
231 E6 Lubunda Dem. Rep. Congo
231 E8 Lubungu Zambia
196 D3 Lubuskie prov. Pol.
196 C3 Lubuskie, Pojezierze reg. Pol.
231 D9 Lubuta Zambia
230 E5 Lubutu Dem. Rep. Congo
230 E5 Lubutu r. Dem. Rep. Congo
231 F7 Lubwe Zambia
198 B1 Luby Czech Rep.
161 S9 Lubyanki Rus. Fed.
197 L5 Lubycza Królewska Pol.
192 F4 Lübz Ger.
183 D7 Luc Languedoc-Roussillon France
185 J7 Luc Midi-Pyrénées France
207 O6 Lucainena de las Torres Spain
231 B7 Lucala Angola
251 M6 Lucan Ont. Can.
169 J6 Lucan Ireland
276 B3 Lucanas Peru
199 L5 Lucani Romania
218 I7 Lučani Lučani Serbia
245 L3 Lucania, Mount Y.T. Can.
133 L8 Lücaoshan Qinghai China
231 D7 Lucapa Angola
207 O6 Lúcar Spain
207 O6 Lúcar mt. Spain
207 N6 Lúcar, Sierra de mts Spain
285 H2 Lucas r. Arg.
277 G3 Lucas Brazil
285 H3 Lucas González Arg.
285 H2 Lucas Sur Arg.
256 C10 Lucasville OH U.S.A.
255 H12 Lucaya Gd Bahama Bahamas
181 N7 Luçay-le-Mâle France
212 J8 Lucca Italy
212 J8 Lucca prov. Italy
260 G2 Lucca ND U.S.A.
216 E8 Lucca Sicula Sicilia Italy
214 C2 Lucciana Corse France
178 B7 Lucé France
201 K7 Luče Slovenia
270 □ Lucea Jamaica
168 G13 Luce Bay Scotland U.K.
261 K10 Lucedale MS U.S.A.
280 B4 Lucélia Brazil
114 C5 Lucena Luzon Phil.
207 K6 Lucena Spain
209 E7 Lucena, Riu r. Spain
207 L5 Lucena, Sierra de mts Spain
208 C4 Lucena de Jalón Spain
209 E7 Lucena del Cid Spain
182 C3 Lucenay-lès-Aix France
182 E2 Lucenay-l'Évêque France
183 G7 Luc-en-Diois France
199 I3 Lučenec Slovakia
208 C4 Luceni Spain
215 O4 Lucera Italy
183 K9 Lucéram France
276 C3 Lucerna Peru
Lucerne Switz. see Luzern
264 J2 Lucerne CA U.S.A.
264 P7 Lucerne Valley CA U.S.A.
266 F2 Lucero Mex.
179 K6 Lucey France
199 I3 Lucfalva Hungary
158 H2 Luchanky Ukr.
160 K6 Luchay Belarus
122 I5 Luchegorsk Rus. Fed.
151 I4 Luchek Rus. Fed.
130 H7 Lucheng Guangxi China
129 M8 Lucheng Shanxi China
Lucheng Sichuan China see Kangding
181 L6 Luché-Pringé France
233 C7 Lucheringo r. Moz.
178 D3 Lucheux France
161 W5 Luchki Rus. Fed.
161 N7 Luchosa r. Belarus
192 D5 Lüchow Ger.
130 D7 Lüchun Yunnan China
178 D4 Luchy France
207 K3 Luciana Spain
197 H4 Luciąża r. Pol.
197 H3 Lucień Pol.
213 L9 Lucignano Italy
210 D3 Lucija Slovenia
204 H4 Lucillo de Somoza Spain
107 K5 Lucinda Qld Austr.
104 H7 Lucindale S.A. Austr.
201 J7 Lučine Slovenia
269 H3 Lucio Vázquez Mex.
115 E6 Lucipara, Kepulauan is Maluku Indon.
231 B8 Lucira Angola
215 N4 Lucito Italy
219 P6 Luciu Romania
Łuck Ukr. see Luts'k
250 B4 Luck WI U.S.A.
193 F8 Lucka Ger.
193 I7 Luckau Ger.
Luckeesarai Bihar India see Lakhisarai
193 H6 Luckenwalde Ger.
237 I5 Luckhoff S. Africa
251 M6 Lucknow Ont. Can.
138 H6 Lucknow Uttar Prad. India
192 E5 Lückstedt Ger.
213 K2 Luco, Monte mt. Italy
215 K4 Luco dei Marsi Italy
184 B3 Luçon France
130 H3 Lücongpo Hubei China
185 C9 Lucq-de-Béarn France
270 F3 Lucrecia, Cabo c. Cuba
181 K3 Luc-sur-Mer France
231 B6 Lucunga Angola
231 D8 Lucusse Angola
106 F7 Lucy Creek N.T. Austr.
182 D1 Lucy-le-Bois France
Lüda Liaoning China see Dalian
156 G2 Luda Rus. Fed.
168 B8 Ludag Western Isles, Scotland U.K.
219 P7 Luda Kamchiya r. Bulg.
210 F2 Ludbreg Croatia
191 E8 Lüdenscheid Ger.
190 K5 Lüder Ger.
193 E5 Lüderitz Ger.
234 B5 Lüderitz Namibia
190 K3 Lüdersdorf Ger.
200 A5 Ludesch Austria
233 B7 Ludewa Tanz.
173 I5 Ludgershall Wiltshire, England U.K.
172 A7 Ludgvan Cornwall, England U.K.
138 E4 Ludhiana Punjab India
130 D5 Ludian Yunnan China
130 D4 Luding Sichuan China
191 D7 Lüdinghausen Ger.
250 H6 Ludington MI U.S.A.
259 H1 Ludingtonville NY U.S.A.
258 F6 Ludlam Bay NJ U.S.A.
172 G3 Ludlow Shropshire, England U.K.
265 P7 Ludlow CA U.S.A.
257 M5 Ludlow VT U.S.A.
201 J6 Ludmannsdorf Austria
219 O7 Ludogorie reg. Bulg.
219 O7 Ludogorsko Plato plat. Bulg.
160 M3 Ludoni Rus. Fed.
184 C6 Ludon-Médoc France
255 G10 Ludowici GA U.S.A.
179 L6 Ludres France
219 M4 Luduş Romania
165 L1 Ludvika Sweden
195 K3 Ludwig-Donau-Main-Kanal canal Ger.
191 I9 Ludwigsau-Friedlos Ger.
194 G4 Ludwigsburg Ger.
193 L8 Ludwigsdorf Ger.
193 H6 Ludwigsfelde Ger.
194 G6 Ludwigshafen Ger.
194 E3 Ludwigshafen am Rhein Ger.
192 D4 Ludwigslust Ger.
192 D4 Ludwigsluster Kanal canal Ger.
Ludwigsort Rus. Fed. see Ladushkin
193 D10 Ludwigsstadt Ger.
197 K4 Ludwin Pol.
160 K5 Ludza Latvia
185 C7 Lüe France
231 D6 Luebo Dem. Rep. Congo
231 E5 Lueki Dem. Rep. Congo
231 E5 Lueki r. Dem. Rep. Congo
204 H6 Luelmo Spain
231 F5 Luemba Dem. Rep. Congo
231 F8 Luembe Zambia
231 C7 Luena Angola
231 E7 Luena Dem. Rep. Congo
231 F7 Luena Zambia
231 D8 Luena r. Zambia
231 D8 Luena Flats plain Zambia
231 D9 Luengé, Coutada Pública do nature res. Angola
231 D9 Luengue r. Angola
235 G3 Luenha r. Moz./Zimbabwe
275 F3 Luepa Venez.
191 I7 Lüerdissen Ger.
208 C3 Luesia Spain
130 F2 Lüeyang Shaanxi China
131 J7 Lufeng Guangdong China
Lufeng Hunan China see Xupu
130 D6 Lufeng Yunnan China
231 B6 Lufico Angola
231 E7 Lufira r. Dem. Rep. Congo
231 E7 Lufira, Lac de retenue de la resr Dem. Rep. Congo
261 H10 Lufkin TX U.S.A.
Lufu Yunnan China see Shilin
233 A7 Lufubu r. Zambia
218 J6 Lug r. Serbia
160 M3 Luga Rus. Fed.
160 L2 Luga r. Rus. Fed.
212 F3 Lugano Switz.
212 F4 Lugano, Lago di l. Italy/Switz.
Lugano, Lake Italy/Switz. see Lugano, Lago di
Lugansk Ukr. see Luhans'k
Luganskaya Oblast' admin. div. Ukr. see Luhans'ka Oblast'
Lugansk Oblast admin. div. Ukr. see Luhans'ka Oblast'
100 □5 Luganville Vanuatu
199 L4 Lugaşu de Jos Romania
193 G9 Lugau Ger.
191 H7 Lügde Ger.
Lugdunum France see Lyon
235 H3 Lugela Moz.
235 H3 Lugela r. Moz.
235 H1 Lugenda r. Moz.
172 G3 Lugg r. Wales U.K.
103 D11 Luggate South I. N.Z.
133 J11 Luggudontsen mt. Xizang China
232 D2 Lughaye Somalia
185 C7 Luglon France
215 I2 Lugnano in Teverina Italy
169 J7 Lugnaquilla hill Ireland
182 F4 Lugny France
182 E4 Lugny-lès-Charolles France
213 L7 Lugo Italy
204 E2 Lugo Spain
204 F3 Lugo prov. Spain
214 C3 Lugo-di-Nazza Corse France
219 J5 Lugoj Romania
204 I2 Lugones Spain
184 D6 Lugon-et-l'Île-du-Carnay France
185 C7 Lugos France
161 U5 Lugovaya Rus. Fed.
Lugovaya Proleyka Rus. Fed. see Primorsk
143 O6 Lugovoy Kazakh.
182 J4 Lugrin France
207 M6 Lugros Spain
130 D4 Lugu Sichuan China
133 G10 Lugu Xizang China
114 C9 Lugus i. Phil.
158 D3 Luha r. Ukr.
199 G2 Luhačovice Czech Rep.
159 S5 Luhan' r. Ukr.
159 S5 Luhanchyk r. Ukr.
163 R6 Luhanka Fin.
159 S5 Luhans'k Ukr.
159 S4 Luhans'ka Oblast' admin. div. Ukr.
159 N8 Luhans'ke Ukr.
Luhansk Oblast admin. div. Ukr. see Luhans'ka Oblast'
161 N6 Luhawskiya Belarus
191 H6 Luhden Ger.
131 J7 Luhe Guangdong China
131 L2 Luhe Jiangsu China
129 K8 Lu He r. China
190 J4 Luhe r. Ger.
195 M2 Luhe-Wildenau Ger.
150 E6 Luḥfī, Wādī watercourse Jordan
129 P3 Luhin Sum Nei Mongol China
Luhit r. China/India see Zayü Qu
118 B1 Luhit r. India
192 I2 Lühmannsdorf Ger.
233 C7 Luhombero Tanz.
159 O8 Luhove Ukr.
162 U5 Luhtapohja Fin.
Luhua Sichuan China see Heishui
130 C3 Luhuo Sichuan China
158 H2 Luhyny Ukr.
231 D7 Luia Angola
231 D6 Luia r. Angola
235 G3 Luia r. Moz.
231 D9 Luiana Angola
231 D9 Luiana r. Angola
231 D9 Luiana, Coutada Pública do nature res. Angola
219 O6 Luica Romania
168 G7 Luichart, Loch l. Scotland U.K.
Luichow Peninsula China see Leizhou Bandao
235 G4 Luido Moz.
Luik Belgium see Liège
230 D5 Luilaka r. Dem. Rep. Congo
Luimbale Angola see Londuimbali
Luimneach Ireland see Limerick
168 E10 Luing i. Scotland U.K.
168 E10 Luing, Sound of sea chan. Scotland U.K.
212 F4 Luino Italy
204 E4 Luíntra Spain
231 D8 Luio r. Angola
162 S3 Luiro r. Fin.
178 B7 Luisant France
278 E2 Luís Correia Brazil
265 P9 Luis Echeverría Álvarez Mex.
278 F3 Luís Gomes Brazil
231 E7 Luishia Dem. Rep. Congo
266 G3 Luis L. León, Presa resr Mex.
268 D1 Luis Moya Durango Mex.
268 E3 Luis Moya Zacatecas Mex.
271 □1 Luis Peña, Cayo de i. Puerto Rico
286 V1 Luitpold Coast Antarctica
268 G7 Luivanos Mex.
231 D6 Luiza Dem. Rep. Congo
231 E6 Luizi Dem. Rep. Congo
285 H4 Luján Buenos Aires Arg.
284 E3 Luján San Luis Arg.
285 H4 Lujan r. Arg.
284 C3 Luján de Cuyo Arg.
131 K3 Lujiang Anhui China
128 I9 Lüjing Gansu China
159 M3 Luka Ukr.
122 H2 Lukachek Rus. Fed.
199 G3 Lukáčovce Slovakia
198 F4 Lukácsháza Hungary
231 B6 Lukala Dem. Rep. Congo
231 C6 Lukanga Dem. Rep. Congo
231 E8 Lukanga Swamps Zambia
Lukapa Angola see Lucapa
159 N6 Lukasheve Ukr.
210 G3 Lukavac Bos.-Herz.
197 L5 Łukawiec Pol.
109 D9 Luke, Mount hill W.A. Austr.
231 E7 Lukenga, Lac l. Dem. Rep. Congo
231 C5 Lukenie r. Dem. Rep. Congo
169 H8 Lukeswell Ireland
265 T10 Lukeville AZ U.S.A.
156 H4 Lukh Rus. Fed.
156 H4 Lukh r. Rus. Fed.
161 W7 Lukhovitsy Rus. Fed.
219 M9 Lŭki Bulg.
161 R1 Lukinskaya Rus. Fed.
158 D2 Lukiv Ukr.
131 □J7 Luk Keng H.K. China
230 C5 Lukolela Équateur Dem. Rep. Congo
231 E6 Lukolela Kasaï-Oriental Dem. Rep. Congo
160 M7 Lukomskaye, Vozyera l. Belarus
Lukou Hunan China see Zhuzhou
210 G3 Lukovac r. Bos.-Herz.
220 A3 Lukovë Albania
219 M7 Lukovit Bulg.
161 R5 Lukovnikovo Rus. Fed.
213 R6 Lukovo Croatia
197 K4 Łuków Pol.
197 K3 Łukowisko Pol.
157 I5 Lukoyanov Rus. Fed.
132 I5 Lükqün Xinjiang China
115 C4 Luksagu Sulawesi Indon.
160 G7 Lukšiai Lith.
231 E6 Lukuga r. Dem. Rep. Congo
231 B6 Lukula Dem. Rep. Congo
233 C7 Lukuledi Tanz.
231 D8 Lukulu Zambia
233 B7 Lukumburu Tanz.
231 C6 Lukuni Dem. Rep. Congo
231 F8 Lukusashi r. Zambia
233 B8 Lukusuzi National Park Zambia
158 C4 Luky Ukr.
231 D5 Lula r. Dem. Rep. Congo
214 C7 Lula Sardegna Italy
162 Q4 Luleå Sweden
162 Q4 Luleälven r. Sweden
221 I1 Lüleburgaz Turkey
282 D2 Lules Arg.
129 L8 Lüliang Shanxi China
130 D6 Luliang Yunnan China
129 L8 Lüliang Shan mts China
231 F6 Lulimba Dem. Rep. Congo
261 G11 Luling TX U.S.A.
169 I6 Lullymore Ireland
129 P7 Lulong Hebei China
230 C4 Lulonga Dem. Rep. Congo
230 C4 Lulonga r. Dem. Rep. Congo
230 D4 Lulu r. Dem. Rep. Congo
231 D6 Lulua prov. Dem. Rep. Congo
Luluabourg Dem. Rep. Congo see Kananga
133 G12 Lülung Xizang China
109 D9 Lulworth, Mount hill W.A. Austr.
100 □2 Luma American Samoa
231 C7 Luma Cassai Angola
133 H11 Lumachomo Xizang China
284 A6 Lumaco Chile
231 D8 Lumai Angola
117 J9 Lumajang Jawa Indon.
133 E9 Lumajangdong Co salt l. China
231 E5 Lumana Dem. Rep. Congo
160 F3 Lümanda Estonia
149 M7 Lūmār Iran
Lumbala Moxico Angola see Lumbala Kaquengue
Lumbala Moxico Angola see Lumbala N'guimbo
231 D8 Lumbala Kaquengue Angola
231 D8 Lumbala N'guimbo Angola
233 A6 Lumbe Tanz.
231 D9 Lumbe r. Zambia
255 H8 Lumber r. SC U.S.A.
255 H8 Lumberton NC U.S.A.
231 C6 Lumbi Dem. Rep. Congo
205 R3 Lumbier Spain
117 L2 Lumbis Kalimantan Indon.
235 I2 Lumbo Moz.
204 G7 Lumbrales Spain
205 O4 Lumbreras Spain
178 D2 Lumbres France
139 N7 Lumding Assam India
233 B7 Lumecha Tanz.
212 I4 Lumezzane Italy
113 J7 Lumi P.N.G.
162 R4 Lumijoki Fin.
219 Q6 Lumina Romania
281 E4 Luminárias Brazil
214 B2 Lumio Corse France
165 O4 Lummelunda Gotland Sweden
187 H7 Lummen Belgium
118 D5 Lum Nam Pai Wildlife Reserve nature res. Thai.
163 P6 Lumparland Åland Fin.
160 D1 Lumparn b. Fin.
168 K8 Lumphanan Aberdeenshire, Scotland U.K.
119 H8 Lumphăt Cambodia
208 C4 Lumpiaque Spain
255 E9 Lumpkin GA U.S.A.
247 J5 Lumsden Sask. Can.
103 C12 Lumsden South I. N.Z.
116 D2 Lumut Malaysia
117 K5 Lumut, Gunung mt. Indon.
116 F6 Lumut, Tanjung pt Indon.
231 E7 Lumwana Zambia
213 R6 Lun Croatia
128 I3 Lün Mongolia
213 R6 Lun, Rt pt Croatia
114 C3 Luna Luzon Phil.
208 D3 Luna Spain
206 H8 Luna hill Spain
204 I4 Luna r. Spain
265 X8 Luna NM U.S.A.
231 D8 Lunache Angola
178 E7 Lunain r. France
214 B8 Lunamatrona Sardegna Italy
168 L9 Lunan Bay Scotland U.K.
130 D5 Lunan Shan mts Sichuan China
251 K8 Luna Pier MI U.S.A.
183 C9 Lunas France
138 D8 Lunavada Gujarat India
146 C3 Lunayyir, Ḥarrat lava field Saudi Arabia
199 L5 Lunca Bihor Romania
219 M7 Lunca Teleorman Romania
219 N4 Lunca Bradului Romania
199 L6 Lunca Cernii de Jos Romania
219 M3 Lunca Ilvei Romania
168 J10 Luncarty Perth and Kinross, Scotland U.K.
219 M6 Luncavăț r. Romania
199 L5 Luncoiu de Jos Romania
145 M8 Lund Pak.
164 J6 Lund Sweden
265 Q3 Lund NV U.S.A.
265 S3 Lund UT U.S.A.
231 C7 Lunda Norte prov. Angola
247 L5 Lundar Man. Can.
231 D7 Lunda Sul prov. Angola
233 B8 Lundazi Zambia
246 H5 Lundbreck Alta Can.
190 K1 Lundby Denmark
164 E6 Lunde Denmark
190 H2 Lunden Ger.
164 C3 Lundevatn l. Norway
Lundi r. Zimbabwe see Runde
168 K10 Lundin Links Fife, Scotland U.K.
250 F5 Lunds WI U.S.A.
165 K2 Lundsfjärden l. Sweden
117 H4 Lundu Sarawak Malaysia
233 B7 Lundu Tanz.
172 C5 Lundy i. England U.K.
190 G3 Lune r. Ger.
171 L5 Lune r. England U.K.
191 B10 Lünebach Ger.
237 O3 Luneberg S. Africa
190 J4 Lüneburg Ger.
190 J4 Lüneburger Heide reg. Ger.
190 I4 Lüneburger Heide, Naturpark nature res. Ger.
183 E9 Lunel France
183 K6 Lunella, Punta mt. Italy
183 E9 Lunel-Viel France
191 E7 Lünen Ger.
256 G12 Lunenburg VA U.S.A.
200 A5 Lünersee l. Austria
181 P8 Lunery France
190 G4 Lunestedt Ger.
179 L6 Lunéville France
235 I2 Lunga Moz.
231 E8 Lunga r. Zambia
201 H5 Lungau r. source Austria
212 E2 Lungern Switz.
100 □6 Lungga Guadalcanal Solomon Is
133 F11 Lunggar Xizang China
133 F11 Lunggar Shan mts Xizang China
228 B4 Lungi Sierra Leone
131 □I7 Lung Kwu Chau i. H.K. China
Lungleh Mizoram India see Lunglei

139 N8 **Lunglei** *Mizoram* India
133 H11 **Lungmari** *mt. Xizang* China
133 E9 **Lungmu Co** *salt l.* China
215 J3 **Lungo, Lago** *l.* Italy
215 Q8 **Lungro** Italy
231 D8 **Lungué-Bungo** *r.* Angola
231 D8 **Lungwebungu** *r.* Zambia
139 I5 **Lunh** Nepal
138 D6 **Luni** *Rajasthan* India
138 C7 **Luni** *r.* India
145 N6 **Luni** *r.* Pak.
Luninets Belarus *see* **Luninyets**
264 N3 **Luning** *NV* U.S.A.
157 I5 **Lunino** Rus. Fed.
158 F1 **Luninyets** Belarus
185 G8 **L'Union** France
138 D5 **Lunkaransar** *Rajasthan* India
138 D5 **Lunkha** *Rajasthan* India
145 O3 **Lunkho** *mt.* Afgh./Pak.
162 S3 **Lunkkaus** Fin.
160 H8 **Lunna** Belarus
168 □N2 **Lunna Ness** *hd Scotland* U.K.
191 D6 **Lünne** Ger.
107 M1 **Lunn Island** P.N.G.
192 J5 **Lunow** Ger.
228 B4 **Lunsar** Sierra Leone
231 F8 **Lunsemfwa** *r.* Zambia
235 F5 **Lunsklip** S. Africa
132 G6 **Luntai** *Xinjiang* China
186 I4 **Lunteren** Neth.
220 B2 **Lunxhërisë, Mali i** *ridge* Albania
117 L9 **Lunyuk** *Sumbawa* Indon.
193 G9 **Lunzenau** Ger.
233 A7 **Lunzua** Zambia
122 G5 **Luobei** *Heilong.* China
132 I7 **Luobuzhuang** *Xinjiang* China
Luocheng *Fujian* China *see* **Hui'an**
128 F7 **Luocheng** *Gansu* China
130 G6 **Luocheng** *Guangxi* China
129 K9 **Luochuan** *Shaanxi* China
130 F6 **Luodian** *Guizhou* China
131 H7 **Luoding** *Guangdong* China
162 R4 **Luodonselkä** *sea chan.* Fin.
130 H8 **Luodou Sha** *i.* China
214 C5 **Luogosanto** *Sardegna* Italy
131 J2 **Luohe** *Henan* China
129 M9 **Luo He** *r. Henan* China
129 L9 **Luo He** *r. Shaanxi* China
130 E3 **Luojiang** *Sichuan* China
130 H8 **Luo Jiang** *r.* China
129 P9 **Luoma Hu** *l.* China
129 L9 **Luonan** *Shaanxi* China
129 L9 **Luoning** *Henan* China
163 S6 **Luonteri** *l.* Fin.
130 E6 **Luoping** *Yunnan* China
163 R6 **Luopioinen** Fin.
131 J2 **Luoshan** *Henan* China
131 J3 **Luotian** *Hubei* China
Luoto Fin. *see* **Larsmo**
128 E6 **Luotuoquan** *Gansu* China
162 T1 **Luovttejohka** Norway
131 I5 **Luoxiao Shan** *mts* China
Luoxiong *Yunnan* China *see* **Luoping**
Luoyang *Guangdong* China *see* **Boluo**
129 M9 **Luoyang** *Henan* China
Luoyang *Zhejiang* China *see* **Taishun**
131 L5 **Luoyuan** *Fujian* China
231 B6 **Luozi** Dem. Rep. Congo
122 G7 **Luozigou** *Jilin* China
233 B7 **Lupa Market** Tanz.
235 E3 **Lupane** Zimbabwe
130 E5 **Lupanshui** *Guizhou* China
117 I4 **Lupar** *r.* Malaysia
165 N7 **Łupawa** *r.* Pol.
195 L3 **Lupburg** Ger.
206 D2 **Lupe** *r.* Port.
219 N4 **Lupeni** *Harghita* Romania
219 L5 **Lupeni** *Hunedoara* Romania
270 H4 **Luperón** Dom. Rep.
194 F5 **Lupfen** *hill* Ger.
185 E8 **Lupiac** France
233 B7 **Lupilichi** Moz.
208 D3 **Lupiñén** Spain
207 L5 **Lupión** Spain
231 C8 **Lupire** Angola
233 C7 **Lupiro** Tanz.
197 K6 **Łupków** Pol.
213 Q5 **Lupoglav** Croatia
114 F8 **Lupon** *Mindanao* Phil.
192 L5 **Łupowo** Pol.
193 G8 **Luppa** Ger.
179 L6 **Luppy** France
265 W6 **Lupton** *AZ* U.S.A.
156 K3 **Lup'ya** *r.* Rus. Fed.
Luqiao *Sichuan* China *see* **Luding**
128 H9 **Luqu** *Gansu* China
Lu Qu *r.* China *see* **Tao He**
129 N7 **Luquan** *Hebei* China
130 D6 **Luquan** *Yunnan* China
207 K5 **Luque** Spain
231 C7 **Luquembo** Angola
271 □1 **Luquillo** Puerto Rico
271 □1 **Luquillo, Sierra de** *mts* Puerto Rico
214 C6 **Luras** *Sardegna* Italy
144 A3 **Lūrā Shīrīn** Iran
250 C9 **Luray** *MO* U.S.A.
256 G10 **Luray** *VA* U.S.A.
185 C9 **Lurbe-St-Christau** France
182 B3 **Lurcy-Lévis** France
179 L8 **Lure** France
183 H8 **Lure, Montagne de** *mt.* France
183 H8 **Lure, Sommet de** *mt.* France
233 C8 **Lureco** *r.* Moz.
231 C7 **Luremo** Angola
168 F6 **Lurgainn, Loch** *l. Scotland* U.K.
169 J4 **Lurgan** *Northern Ireland* U.K.
144 H5 **Lūrg-e Shotorān** *salt pan* Iran
214 C2 **Luri** *Corse* France
232 A3 **Luri** *r.* Sudan
276 D4 **Luribay** Bol.
276 A3 **Lurín** Peru
235 I2 **Lúrio** Moz.
235 I2 **Lurio** *r.* Moz.
235 I2 **Lúrio, Baía do** *b.* Moz.
162 L3 **Lurøy** Norway
183 H9 **Lurs** France
181 P7 **Lury-sur-Arnon** France
164 C2 **Lusaheia** *park* Norway
233 A5 **Lusahunga** Tanz.
231 F6 **Lusaka** Dem. Rep. Congo
231 F8 **Lusaka** Zambia
231 F8 **Lusaka** *prov.* Zambia
231 D6 **Lusambo** Dem. Rep. Congo
113 L8 **Lusancay Islands and Reefs** P.N.G.
231 C6 **Lusanga** Dem. Rep. Congo
231 E6 **Lusangi** Dem. Rep. Congo
151 F6 **Lusashogh** Armenia
216 G2 **Lusciano** Italy
247 I4 **Luseland** *Sask.* Can.
231 F7 **Lusenga Plain National Park** Zambia
212 C6 **Luserna San Giovanni** Italy
233 C7 **Lusewa** Tanz.
108 I4 **Lush, Mount** *hill W.A.* Austr.
130 D3 **Lushan** *Sichuan* China
Lushar *Qinghai* China *see* **Huangzhong**
129 L9 **Lushi** *Henan* China
218 H10 **Lushnjë** Albania
233 C6 **Lushoto** Tanz.
118 D2 **Lushui** *Yunnan* China
122 E7 **Lushuihe** *Jilin* China
129 Q7 **Lüshun** *Liaoning* China
131 M2 **Lüsi** *Jiangsu* China
117 I8 **Lusi** *r.* Indon.
184 E3 **Lusignan** France
182 C3 **Lusigny** France
178 H7 **Lusigny-sur-Barse** France
237 N7 **Lusikisiki** S. Africa
104 □3 **Lusitania Bay** S. Pacific Ocean
233 A8 **Lusiwasi** Zambia
169 J5 **Lusk** Ireland
262 L5 **Lusk** *WY* U.S.A.
183 H7 **Lus-la-Croix-Haute** France
Luso Angola *see* **Luena**
204 D8 **Luso** Port.
168 G10 **Luss** *Argyll and Bute, Scotland* U.K.
184 D6 **Lussac** France
184 F3 **Lussac-les-Châteaux** France
184 G3 **Lussac-les-Églises** France
170 F2 **Lussa Loch** *l. Scotland* U.K.
183 E8 **Lussan** France
280 B4 **Lussanvira** Brazil
190 J5 **Lüßberg** *hill* Ger.
192 F3 **Lüssow** Ger.
231 B7 **Lussusso** Angola
168 C7 **Lusta** *Highland, Scotland* U.K.
194 E3 **Lustadt** Ger.
212 H1 **Lustenau** Austria
237 P2 **Lusushwana** *r.* Swaziland
Lusutufu *r.* Africa *see* **Usutu**
197 H3 **Luszyn** Pol.
Lut, Bahrat *salt l.* Asia *see* **Dead Sea**
144 H6 **Lūt, Kavīr-ye** *des.* Iran
213 L2 **Lutago** Italy
Lutai *Tianjin* China *see* **Ninghe**
131 M7 **Lü Tao** *i.* Taiwan
190 K4 **Lütau** Ger.
280 B5 **Lutécia** Brazil
231 D8 **Lutembo** Angola
165 Q8 **Luterskie, Jezioro** *l.* Pol.
Lutetia France *see* **Paris**
144 H7 **Lūt-e Zangī Aḥmad** *des.* Iran
250 I5 **Luther** *MI* U.S.A.
251 N6 **Luther Lake** *Ont.* Can.
256 G7 **Luthersburg** *PA* U.S.A.
193 G7 **Lutherstadt Wittenberg** Ger.
230 F5 **Lutiba** Dem. Rep. Congo
198 G2 **Lutín** Czech Rep.
190 K2 **Lütjenburg** Ger.
190 J3 **Lütjensee** Ger.
197 H3 **Lutocin** Pol.
197 H4 **Lutomiersk** Pol.
173 L4 **Luton** *Luton, England* U.K.
173 L4 **Luton** *admin. div. England* U.K.
117 K2 **Lutong** *Sarawak* Malaysia
235 F3 **Lutope** *r.* Zimbabwe
197 K6 **Lutowiska** Pol.
197 I1 **Lutry** Pol.
247 I2 **Łutselk'e** *N.W.T.* Can.
231 E6 **Lutshi** Dem. Rep. Congo
158 E3 **Luts'k** Ukr.
191 J7 **Lutter am Barenberge** Ger.
179 N8 **Lutterbach** France
173 J3 **Lutterworth** *Leicestershire, England* U.K.
236 G8 **Luttig** S. Africa
Lutto *r.* Fin./Rus. Fed. *see* **Lotta**
231 D8 **Lutuai** Angola
159 S5 **Lutuhyne** Ukr.
196 G4 **Lututów** Pol.
196 F3 **Lutynia** *r.* Pol.
255 F11 **Lutz** *FL* U.S.A.
193 F8 **Lützen** Ger.
191 D10 **Lutzerath** Ger.
195 J4 **Lutzingen** Ger.
201 O5 **Lutzmannsburg** Austria
192 D3 **Lützow** Ger.
287 C2 **Lützow-Holm Bay** Antarctica
236 E4 **Lutzputs** S. Africa
193 F8 **Lützschena** Ger.
236 C7 **Lutzville** S. Africa
114 C9 **Luuk** Phil.
163 S6 **Luumäki** Fin.
232 D4 **Luuq** Somalia
162 S3 **Luusua** Fin.
231 B6 **Luvaka** Dem. Rep. Congo
237 P2 **Luve** Swaziland
255 D10 **Luverne** *AL* U.S.A.
260 G4 **Luverne** *MN* U.S.A.
163 P6 **Luvia** Fin.
231 B6 **Luvo** Angola
162 U4 **Luvozero** Rus. Fed.
231 E6 **Luvua** *r.* Dem. Rep. Congo
231 D8 **Luvuei** Angola
235 F4 **Luvuvhu** *r.* S. Africa
233 B8 **Luwawa** Malawi
233 C7 **Luwegu** *r.* Tanz.
232 B4 **Luwero** Uganda
231 F7 **Luwingu** Zambia
115 F3 **Luwo** *i. Maluku* Indon.
117 I5 **Luwuhuyu** *Kalimantan* Indon.
115 C4 **Luwuk** *Sulawesi* Indon.
182 G2 **Lux** France
187 H8 **Luxembourg** *prov.* Belgium
187 J9 **Luxembourg** *country* Europe
187 J9 **Luxembourg** Lux.
187 J9 **Luxembourg** *admin. dist.* Lux.
Luxemburg *country* Europe *see* **Luxembourg**
250 G5 **Luxemburg** *WI* U.S.A.
185 B9 **Luxe-Sumberraute** France
179 L8 **Luxeuil-les-Bains** France
185 C7 **Luxey** France
131 J5 **Luxi** *Jiangxi* China
130 B6 **Luxi** *Yunnan* China
130 D6 **Luxi** *Yunnan* China
130 E4 **Luxian** *Sichuan* China
237 J7 **Luxolweni** S. Africa
Luxor Egypt *see* **Al Uqşur**
172 C7 **Luxulyan** *Cornwall, England* U.K.
185 B8 **Luy** *r.* France
Luyang *Sichuan* China *see* **Lushan**
129 L7 **Luya Shan** *mts* China
185 C8 **Luy de Béarn** *r.* France
185 C8 **Luy de France** *r.* France
204 H4 **Luyego de Somoza** Spain
131 J2 **Luyi** *Henan* China
187 H6 **Luyksgestel** Neth.
181 M7 **Luynes** France
Luyuan *Shaanxi* China *see* **Gaoling**
Lu Yunhe *canal* China *see* **Jinghang Yunhe**
281 E3 **Luz** Brazil
206 E4 **Luz** *Évora* Port.
206 B6 **Luz** *Faro* Port.
206 D6 **Luz** *Faro* Port.
204 H5 **Luz** *hill* Port.
156 I3 **Luza** Rus. Fed.
156 I3 **Luza** *r.* Rus. Fed.
156 L2 **Luza** *r.* Rus. Fed.
205 P7 **Luzaga** Spain
178 D5 **Luzarches** France
185 D10 **Luz-Ardiden** France
198 F2 **Luže** Czech Rep.
185 G7 **Luzech** France
198 D1 **Lužec nad Vltavou** Czech Rep.
212 E1 **Luzern** Switz.
212 E1 **Luzern** *canton* Switz.
258 D2 **Luzerne** *PA* U.S.A.
258 C2 **Luzerne County** *county PA* U.S.A.
161 T7 **Luzha** *r.* Rus. Fed.
130 G6 **Luzhai** *Guangxi* China
130 B6 **Luzhang** *Yunnan* China
130 E5 **Luzhi** *Guizhou* China
130 E4 **Luzhou** *Sichuan* China
206 C5 **Luzianes** Port.
280 D2 **Luziânia** Brazil
198 D1 **Lužické hory** *mts* Czech Rep.
278 E2 **Luzilândia** Brazil
196 G1 **Luzino** Pol.
205 L2 **Luzmela** Spain
198 C1 **Lužná** Czech Rep.
160 E4 **Lūžņa** Latvia
197 J6 **Łużna** Pol.
198 D2 **Lužnice** *r.* Czech Rep.
114 D4 **Luzon** *i.* Phil.
205 P6 **Luzón** Spain
114 C1 **Luzon Strait** Phil.
185 E10 **Luz-St-Sauveur** France
182 D3 **Luzy** France
196 G4 **Łużyca** *r.* Pol.
213 J6 **Luzzara** Italy
215 Q9 **Luzzi** Italy
158 G1 **L'va** *r.* Ukr.
158 D4 **L'viv** Ukr.
Lviv Oblast *admin. div.* Ukr. *see* **L'vivs'ka Oblast'**
158 D3 **L'vivs'ka Oblast'** *admin. div.* Ukr.
L'vov Ukr. *see* **L'viv**
Lvov Oblast *admin. div.* Ukr. *see* **L'vivs'ka Oblast'**
L'vovskaya Oblast' *admin. div.* Ukr. *see* **L'vivs'ka Oblast'**
161 U6 **L'vovskiy** Rus. Fed.
151 I2 **L'vovskiy Pervyy** Rus. Fed.
Lwów Ukr. *see* **L'viv**
196 E3 **Lwówek** Pol.
196 D4 **Lwówek Śląski** Pol.
158 G5 **Lyadova** *r.* Ukr.
161 O7 **Lyady** Belarus
160 L3 **Lyady** Rus. Fed.
160 J8 **Lyakhavichy** Belarus
Lyakhovichi Belarus *see* **Lyakhavichy**
153 P2 **Lyakhovskiye Ostrova** *is Novosibirskiye O-va* Rus. Fed.
159 L1 **Lyalichi** Rus. Fed.
103 B12 **Lyall, Mount** *South I.* N.Z.
Lyallpur Pak. *see* **Faisalabad**
Lyal'mikar Uzbek. *see* **Lalmikor**
157 I5 **Lyambir'** Rus. Fed.
156 L4 **Lyamino** Rus. Fed.
156 G2 **Lyamtsa** Rus. Fed.
Lyangar *Navoiy* Uzbek. *see* **Langar**
Lyangar *Qashqadaryo* Uzbek. *see* **Langar**
156 M3 **Lyapin** *r.* Rus. Fed.
159 L4 **Lyashchivka** Ukr.
163 U6 **Lyaskelya** Rus. Fed.
219 N7 **Lyaskovets** Bulg.
160 I9 **Lyasnaya** Belarus
160 G9 **Lyasnaya** *r.* Belarus
199 L3 **Lybokhora** Ukr.
168 J6 **Lybster** *Highland, Scotland* U.K.
197 M4 **Lybytiv** Ukr.
192 H4 **Lychen** Ger.
192 H4 **Lychen-Boitzenberg** *park* Ger.
159 O4 **Lychkove** Ukr.
161 P4 **Lychkovo** Rus. Fed.
Lyck Pol. *see* **Ełk**
162 O4 **Lycksele** Sweden
258 A2 **Lycoming County** *county PA* U.S.A.
258 A2 **Lycoming Creek** *r. PA* U.S.A.
Lycopolis Egypt *see* **Asyūţ**
173 N6 **Lydd** *Kent, England* U.K.
Lydda Israel *see* **Lod**
286 W2 **Lyddan Island** Antarctica
Lydenburg S. Africa *see* **Mashishing**
172 D6 **Lydford** *Devon, England* U.K.
221 I4 **Lydia** *reg.* Turkey
172 G4 **Lydney** *Gloucestershire, England* U.K.
197 I3 **Łydynia** *r.* Pol.
160 I8 **Lyebyada** *r.* Belarus
158 H2 **Lyel'chytsy** Belarus
264 M4 **Lyell, Mount** *CA* U.S.A.
106 C7 **Lyell Brown, Mount** *hill N.T.* Austr.
245 O5 **Lyell Island** *B.C.* Can.
103 G8 **Lyell Range** *mts South I.* N.Z.
159 K1 **Lyenina** Belarus
197 M3 **Lyeninski** Belarus
160 L7 **Lyepyel'** Belarus
197 L3 **Lyevaya Lyasnaya** *r.* Belarus
255 □2 **Lyford Cay** *New Prov.* Bahamas
164 I4 **Lygnern** *l.* Sweden
160 G5 **Lygumai** Lith.
159 P4 **Lyhivka** Ukr.
251 R9 **Lykens** *PA* U.S.A.
159 K2 **Lykhachiv** Ukr.
159 M5 **Lykhivka** Ukr.
161 Q3 **Lykoshino** Rus. Fed.
236 I3 **Lykso** S. Africa
250 B6 **Lyle** *MN* U.S.A.
158 I8 **Lyman** Ukr.
262 I6 **Lyman** *WY* U.S.A.
159 P4 **Lyman, Ozero** *l.* Ukr.
158 I7 **Lymans'ke** Ukr.
172 G6 **Lyme Bay** *England* U.K.
172 G6 **Lyme Regis** *Dorset, England* U.K.
173 O5 **Lyminge** *Kent, England* U.K.
173 I6 **Lymington** *Hampshire, England* U.K.
171 M7 **Lymm** *Warrington, England* U.K.
173 O5 **Lympne** *Kent, England* U.K.
172 F6 **Lympstone** *Devon, England* U.K.
165 R7 **Łyna** *r.* Pol.
256 C12 **Lynch** *KY* U.S.A.
255 D8 **Lynchburg** *TN* U.S.A.
256 F11 **Lynchburg** *VA* U.S.A.
255 H9 **Lynches** *r. SC* U.S.A.
256 F11 **Lynch Station** *VA* U.S.A.
257 □O4 **Lynchville** *ME* U.S.A.
107 I4 **Lynd** *r. Qld* Austr.
262 C2 **Lynden** *WA* U.S.A.
107 J5 **Lyndhurst** *Qld* Austr.
104 G4 **Lyndhurst** *S.A.* Austr.
173 I6 **Lyndhurst** *Hampshire, England* U.K.
109 C7 **Lyndon** *W.A.* Austr.
109 B7 **Lyndon** *r. W.A.* Austr.
260 H6 **Lyndon** *KS* U.S.A.
250 E6 **Lyndon Station** *WI* U.S.A.
256 G5 **Lyndonville** *NY* U.S.A.
257 M4 **Lyndonville** *VT* U.S.A.
171 K4 **Lyne** *r. England* U.K.
173 I4 **Lyneham** *Wiltshire, England* U.K.
171 N3 **Lynemouth** *Northumberland, England* U.K.
168 J5 **Lyness** *Orkney, Scotland* U.K.
164 E5 **Lyngby** *nature res.* Denmark
164 D3 **Lyngdal** Norway
162 P2 **Lyngen** *sea chan.* Norway
162 P2 **Lyngseidet** Norway
172 D7 **Lynher** *r. England* U.K.
108 F3 **Lynher Reef** *W.A.* Austr.
172 E5 **Lynmouth** *Devon, England* U.K.
Lynn *Norfolk, England* U.K. *see* **King's Lynn**
257 O6 **Lynn** *MA* U.S.A.
245 N4 **Lynn Canal** *sea channel AK* U.S.A.
265 T2 **Lynndyl** *UT* U.S.A.
255 E10 **Lynn Haven** *FL* U.S.A.
247 K3 **Lynn Lake** *Man.* Can.
159 N2 **Lynove** Ukr.
159 L3 **Lynovytsya** Ukr.
109 C10 **Lynton** *W.A.* Austr.
172 E5 **Lynton** *Devon, England* U.K.
160 J6 **Lyntupy** Belarus
247 J2 **Lynx Lake** *N.W.T.* Can.
250 C6 **Lynxville** *WI* U.S.A.
182 F5 **Lyon** France
Lyon *airport* France *see* **Satolas**
168 I9 **Lyon** *r. Scotland* U.K.
168 G9 **Lyon, Loch** *l. Scotland* U.K.
257 L4 **Lyon Mountain** *NY* U.S.A.
182 F5 **Lyonnais, Monts du** *hills* France
104 D4 **Lyons** *S.A.* Austr.
109 C8 **Lyons** *r. W.A.* Austr.
Lyons France *see* **Lyon**
255 F9 **Lyons** *GA* U.S.A.
260 F6 **Lyons** *KS* U.S.A.
256 I5 **Lyons** *NY* U.S.A.
257 J5 **Lyons Falls** *NY* U.S.A.
178 B5 **Lyons-la-Forêt** France
259 I2 **Lyons Plain** *CT* U.S.A.
258 D4 **Lyon Station** *PA* U.S.A.
161 N6 **Lyozna** Belarus
158 E3 **Lypa** *r.* Ukr.
158 H2 **Lypnyky** Ukr.
159 M3 **Lypova Dolyna** Ukr.
158 I4 **Lypovets'** Ukr.
159 P3 **Lyptsi** Ukr.
99 F2 **Lyra Reef** P.N.G.
178 F2 **Lys** *r.* France
212 D4 **Lys** *r.* Italy
190 J1 **Lysabild** Denmark
199 H2 **Lysá hora** *mt.* Czech Rep.
159 K5 **Lysa Hora** Ukr.
193 K10 **Lysá nad Labem** Czech Rep.
199 H2 **Lysá pod Makytou** Slovakia
197 J2 **Łyse** Pol.
164 C2 **Lysefjorden** *inlet* Norway
164 C2 **Lysekammen** *mt.* Norway
164 H3 **Lysekil** Sweden
161 P9 **Lyshchichi** Rus. Fed.
197 L3 **Lyshchytsy** Belarus
150 B3 **Lysi** Cyprus
197 I5 **Łysica** *hill* Pol.
198 F2 **Lysice** Czech Rep.
220 C4 **Lysimacheia, Limni** *l.* Greece
197 M3 **Lyskava** Belarus
161 N6 **Lys'kava** Belarus
196 G5 **Lyski** Pol.
156 I4 **Lyskovo** Rus. Fed.
159 S6 **Lysogorka** Rus. Fed.
196 G2 **Łysomice** Pol.
118 I7 **Ly Sơn, Đao** *i.* Vietnam
212 C1 **Lyss** Switz.
164 G5 **Lystrup** Denmark
156 L4 **Lys'va** Rus. Fed.
164 J1 **Lysvik** Sweden
158 J4 **Lysyanka** Ukr.
159 R5 **Lysychans'k** Ukr.
157 I6 **Lysyye Gory** Rus. Fed.
197 H4 **Łyszkowice** Pol.
172 H6 **Lytchett Matravers** *Dorset, England* U.K.
172 H6 **Lytchett Minster** *Dorset, England* U.K.
168 J5 **Lyth** *Highland, Scotland* U.K.
171 K6 **Lytham St Anne's** *Lancashire, England* U.K.
161 U6 **Lytkarino** Rus. Fed.
197 M5 **Lytovezh** Ukr.
103 G10 **Lyttelton** *South I.* N.Z.
103 G10 **Lyttelton Harbour** *South I.* N.Z.
246 F5 **Lytton** *B.C.* Can.
160 L9 **Lyuban'** Belarus
161 O2 **Lyuban'** Rus. Fed.
160 L9 **Lyubanskaye Vodaskhovishcha** *resr* Belarus
158 G4 **Lyubar** Ukr.
158 J6 **Lyubashivka** Ukr.
161 N7 **Lyubavichi** Rus. Fed.
159 O1 **Lyubazh** Rus. Fed.
160 J8 **Lyubcha** Belarus
158 J2 **Lyubech** Ukr.
161 U6 **Lyubertsy** Rus. Fed.
158 E2 **Lyubeshiv** Ukr.
156 H4 **Lyubim** Rus. Fed.
219 O9 **Lyubimets** Bulg.
159 O2 **Lyubimovka** *Kurskaya Oblast'* Rus. Fed.
161 V8 **Lyubimovka** *Tul'skaya Oblast'* Rus. Fed.
160 I9 **Lyubishchytsy** Belarus
161 R3 **Lyubitovo** Rus. Fed.
197 I1 **Lyublino** Rus. Fed.
197 M4 **Lyublynets'** Ukr.
161 R8 **Lyubokhna** Rus. Fed.
197 M4 **Lyubokhyny** Ukr.
158 D2 **Lyuboml'** Ukr.
159 L6 **Lyubomyrivka** Ukr.
159 O2 **Lyubostan'** Rus. Fed.
Lyubotin Ukr. *see* **Lyubotyn**
159 O4 **Lyubotyn** Ukr.
160 K8 **Lyubyacha** Belarus
159 P6 **Lyubymivka** Ukr.
197 L6 **Lyubyntsi** Ukr.
161 Q3 **Lyubytino** Rus. Fed.
161 R8 **Lyudinovo** Rus. Fed.
161 Q1 **Lyugovichi** Rus. Fed.
219 P8 **Lyulyakovo** Bulg.
156 I4 **Lyunda** *r.* Rus. Fed.
160 J9 **Lyusina** Belarus
159 O3 **Lyutivka** Ukr.
156 L2 **Lyzha** *r.* Rus. Fed.
159 R4 **Lyzyne** Ukr.
160 L4 **Lzha** *r.* Rus. Fed.

M

118 D3 **Ma** *r.* Myanmar
118 E4 **Ma, Nam** *r.* Laos
118 G5 **Ma, Sông** *r.* Vietnam
135 □1 **Maabadi** *i. N. Male* Maldives
Maafushi *i. S. Male* Maldives *see* **Mafushi**
225 H6 **Ma'ākel** *prov.* Eritrea
264 □E13 **Ma'alaea** *HI* U.S.A.
136 C10 **Maalhosmadulu Atoll** Maldives
Maamakundhoo *i. N. Male* Maldives *see* **Makunudhoo**
231 E9 **Maamba** Zambia
Maam Cross Ireland *see* **An Teach Dóite**
229 H6 **Ma'an** Cameroon
150 D8 **Ma'ān** Jordan
Maan Turkey *see* **Nusratiye**
162 S5 **Maaninka** Fin.
162 T3 **Maaninkavaara** Fin.
Maanĭt Mongolia *see* **Hishig-Öndör**
Maanĭt Mongolia *see* **Bayan**
162 T5 **Maanselkä** Fin.
131 L3 **Ma'anshan** *Anhui* China
160 I2 **Maardu** Estonia
187 I6 **Maarheeze** Neth.
Maarianhamina *Åland* Fin. *see* **Mariehamn**
146 G6 **Ma'āriḍ, Banī** *des.* Saudi Arabia
186 H4 **Maarn** Neth.
150 E2 **Ma'arrat al Ikhwān** Syria
150 E3 **Ma'arrat an Nu'mān** Syria
186 H4 **Maarssen** Neth.
186 H4 **Maarssenbroek** Neth.
186 H4 **Maartensdijk** Neth.
186 G5 **Maas** *r.* Neth. *alt.* **Meuse (Belgium/France)**
169 F3 **Maas** Ireland
187 I6 **Maasbracht** Neth.
187 J6 **Maasbree** Neth.
186 G5 **Maasdam** Neth.
187 I6 **Maaseik** Belgium
114 E6 **Maasin** *Leyte* Phil.
186 F5 **Maasland** Neth.
187 I7 **Maasmechelen** Belgium
191 A8 **Maas-Schwalm-Nette, Naturpark** *nat. park* Ger./Neth.
186 F5 **Maassluis** Neth.
187 I7 **Maastricht** Neth.
105 K10 **Maatsuyker Group** *is Tas.* Austr.
Maba *Guangdong* China *see* **Qujiang**
131 L2 **Maba** *Jiangsu* China
115 F3 **Maba** *Halmahera* Indon.
224 D6 **Maba, Ouadi** *watercourse* Chad
237 K1 **Mabaalstad** *North West* S. Africa
237 K1 **Mabaalstad** *North West* S. Africa
234 E3 **Mababe Depression** Botswana
114 C4 **Mabalacat** *Luzon* Phil.
235 G4 **Mabalane** Moz.
230 F4 **Mabana** Dem. Rep. Congo
230 A5 **Mabanda** Gabon
146 G8 **Ma'bar** Yemen
275 G2 **Mabaruma** Guyana
Mabating *Yunnan* China *see* **Hongshan**
118 C3 **Mabein** Myanmar
104 E3 **Mabel Creek** *S.A.* Austr.
108 I4 **Mabel Downs** *W.A.* Austr.
248 B3 **Mabella** *Ont.* Can.
246 G5 **Mabel Lake** *B.C.* Can.
251 R5 **Maberly** *Ont.* Can.
130 D4 **Mabian** *Sichuan* China
133 H12 **Mabja** *Xizang* China
171 R7 **Mablethorpe** *Lincolnshire, England* U.K.
182 E4 **Mably** France
237 M1 **Mabopane** S. Africa
235 G4 **Mabote** Moz.
249 I4 **Mabou** *N.S.* Can.
150 D8 **Mabrak, Jabal** *mt.* Jordan
228 E2 **Mabroûk** *well* Mali
224 B4 **Mabrous** *well* Niger
234 D5 **Mabuasehube Game Reserve** *nature res.* Botswana
114 C1 **Mabudis** *i.* Phil.
236 I1 **Mabule** Botswana
124 □1 **Mabuni** *Okinawa* Japan
224 D3 **Ma'būs Yūsuf** *oasis* Libya
234 D5 **Mabutsane** Botswana
283 B7 **Macá, Monte** *mt.* Chile
285 F5 **Macachín** Arg.
109 D8 **Macadam Plains** *W.A.* Austr.
106 B3 **Macadam Range** *hills N.T.* Austr.
281 G5 **Macaé** Brazil
207 O6 **Macael** Spain
151 C4 **Maçahel Geçidi** *pass* Turkey
278 G3 **Macaíba** Brazil
114 E7 **Macajalar Bay** *Mindanao* Phil.
278 E5 **Macajuba** Brazil
233 B8 **Macaloge** Moz.
243 H3 **MacAlpine Lake** *Nunavut* Can.
248 E3 **Macamic** *Que.* Can.
Macan, Kepulauan *atolls* Indon. *see* **Taka'Bonerate, Kepulauan**
235 G4 **Macandze** Moz.
237 Q1 **Macaneta, Ponta de** *pt* Moz.
208 K3 **Maçanet de Cabrenys** Spain
131 I7 **Macao** *Macao* China
204 E9 **Mação** Port.
275 I4 **Macapá** *Amapá* Brazil
276 D2 **Macapá** *Amazonas* Brazil
Macar Turkey *see* **Gebiz**
274 B6 **Macará** Ecuador
266 □S14 **Macaracas** Panama
279 E5 **Macarani** Brazil
274 C4 **Macarena, Cordillera** *mts* Col.
275 F2 **Macareo, Caño** *r.* Venez.
105 I8 **Macarthur** *Vic.* Austr.
274 B5 **Macas** Ecuador
204 G6 **Maçãs** *r.* Port./Spain
Macassar *Sulawesi* Indon. *see* **Makassar**
Macassar Strait Indon. *see* **Makassar, Selat**
209 D9 **Macastre** Spain
235 H3 **Macatanja** Moz.
278 F3 **Macau** Brazil
184 C5 **Macau** France
276 C2 **Macauã** *r.* Brazil
278 C4 **Macaúba** Brazil
278 E5 **Macaúbas** Brazil
99 I5 **Macauley Island** N.Z.
274 C4 **Macayari** Col.
232 F2 **Macbar, Raas** *pt* Somalia
283 F8 **Macbride Head** Falkland Is
212 F3 **Maccagno** Italy
235 G5 **Maccaretane** Moz.
217 I8 **Macchia** *r. Sicilia* Italy
215 M4 **Macchiagodena** Italy
255 F10 **Macclenny** *FL* U.S.A.
171 M7 **Macclesfield** *Cheshire, England* U.K.
112 D3 **Macclesfield Bank** *sea feature* S. China Sea
248 B3 **Macdiarmid** *Ont.* Can.
108 J7 **Macdonald, Lake** *salt flat W.A.* Austr.
106 C7 **Macdonnell Ranges** *mts N.T.* Austr.
247 M4 **MacDowell Lake** *Ont.* Can.
168 L7 **Macduff** *Aberdeenshire, Scotland* U.K.
199 K5 **Macea** Romania
204 E4 **Maceda** Spain
285 I5 **Macedo** Arg.
204 G5 **Macedo de Cavaleiros** Port.
Macedon *country* Europe *see* **Macedonia**
219 J9 **Macedonia** *country* Europe
259 I1 **Macedonia** *CT* U.S.A.
278 G4 **Maceió** Brazil
278 F3 **Maceio, Ponta da** *pt* Brazil
204 F7 **Maceira** *Guarda* Port.
204 C9 **Maceira** *Leiria* Port.
201 M7 **Macelj** Croatia
228 C4 **Macenta** Guinea
213 O9 **Macerata** Italy
213 O9 **Macerata** *prov.* Italy
213 M8 **Macerata Feltria** Italy
104 F5 **Macfarlane, Lake** *salt flat S.A.* Austr.
169 C9 **Macgillycuddy's Reeks** *mts* Ireland
145 L7 **Mach** Pak.
153 M3 **Macha** Rus. Fed.
281 G2 **Machacalis** Brazil
276 D4 **Machacamarca** Bol.
274 B5 **Machachi** Ecuador
277 E2 **Machadinho** *r.* Brazil
281 E4 **Machado** Brazil
237 O1 **Machadodorp** S. Africa
206 E4 **Machados** Port.
231 E8 **Machai** Zambia
235 G4 **Machaila** Moz.
233 C5 **Machakos** Kenya
274 B5 **Machala** Ecuador
284 B4 **Machali** Chile
Machali *Qinghai* China *see* **Madoi**
117 J4 **Machan** *Sarawak* Malaysia
100 □1 **Machanao, Mount** *hill* Guam
235 G4 **Machanga** Moz.
277 E5 **Macharetí** Bol.
232 B2 **Machar Marshes** Sudan
106 G8 **Machattie, Lake** *salt flat Qld* Austr.
237 Q1 **Machatuine** Moz.
178 I5 **Machault** France
Machaze Moz. *see* **Chitobe**
180 H8 **Machecoul** France
187 F7 **Machelen** Belgium
172 F4 **Machen** *Caerphilly, Wales* U.K.
131 J3 **Macheng** *Hubei* China
179 M5 **Macheren** France
136 F4 **Macherla** *Andhra Prad.* India
193 G8 **Machern** Ger.
207 K2 **Machero** *mt.* Spain
250 E7 **Machesney Park** *IL* U.S.A.
139 K9 **Machhagan** *Orissa* India
138 F4 **Machhiwara** *Punjab* India
138 I7 **Machhlishahr** *Uttar Prad.* India
257 □R4 **Machias** *ME* U.S.A.
256 G6 **Machias** *NY* U.S.A.
257 □Q2 **Machias** *r. ME* U.S.A.
257 □R4 **Machias Bay** *ME* U.S.A.
206 □ **Machico** Madeira
127 J4 **Machida** Japan
136 G4 **Machilipatnam** *Andhra Prad.* India
233 B8 **Machinga** Malawi
274 C2 **Machiques** Venez.
168 D11 **Machir Bay** *Scotland* U.K.
Machiwara *Punjab* India *see* **Machhiwara**
145 I9 **Māch Kowr** Iran
263 L10 **Macho, Arroyo del** *watercourse NM* U.S.A.
269 N7 **Machona, Laguna** *lag.* Mex.
168 E12 **Machrihanish** *Argyll and Bute, Scotland* U.K.
159 N4 **Machukhy** Ukr.
276 B3 **Machu Picchu** *tourist site* Peru
276 D3 **Machupo** *r.* Bol.
172 E2 **Machynlleth** *Powys, Wales* U.K.
235 G5 **Macia** Moz.
Macias Nguema *i.* Equat. Guinea *see* **Bioco**
197 J4 **Maciejowice** Pol.
285 G3 **Maciel** Arg.
219 Q5 **Măcin** Romania
214 C2 **Macinaggio** *Corse* France
105 M3 **Macintyre** *r. N.S.W.* Austr.
105 M3 **Macintyre Brook** *r. Qld* Austr.
276 B3 **Macizo de Tocate** *mts* Peru
265 X2 **Mack** *CO* U.S.A.
151 A5 **Maçka** Turkey
107 L6 **Mackay** *Qld* Austr.
247 I3 **MacKay** *r. Alta* Can.
262 H4 **Mackay** *ID* U.S.A.
108 J7 **Mackay, Lake** *salt flat W.A.* Austr.
247 I2 **MacKay Lake** *N.W.T.* Can.
286 O1 **Mackay Mountains** Antarctica
194 D3 **Mackenbach** Ger.
191 K7 **Mackenrode** Ger.
107 L7 **Mackenzie** *r. Qld* Austr.
246 F4 **Mackenzie** *B.C.* Can.
250 F1 **Mackenzie** *Ont.* Can.
245 N1 **Mackenzie** *r. N.W.T.* Can.
Mackenzie Guyana *see* **Linden**
Mackenzie *atoll* Micronesia *see* **Ulithi**
287 E2 **Mackenzie Bay** Antarctica
245 M1 **Mackenzie Bay** *N.W.T./Y.T.* Can.
246 G2 **Mackenzie Bison Sanctuary** *nature res. N.W.T.* Can.
246 G2 **Mackenzie Highway** *N.W.T.* Can.
243 G2 **Mackenzie King Island** *N.W.T.* Can.
245 N2 **Mackenzie Mountains** *N.W.T./Y.T.* Can.
Mackillop, Lake *salt flat Qld* Austr. *see* **Yamma Yamma, Lake**
250 I4 **Mackinac, Straits of** *lake channel MI* U.S.A.
250 J4 **Mackinac Island** *MI* U.S.A.
250 E9 **Mackinaw** *r. IL* U.S.A.
250 J4 **Mackinaw City** *MI* U.S.A.
247 I4 **Macklin** *Sask.* Can.
201 N6 **Mačkovci** Slovenia
105 N4 **Macksville** *N.S.W.* Austr.
107 H7 **Mackunda Creek** *watercourse Qld* Austr.
105 N3 **Maclean** *N.S.W.* Austr.
237 L8 **Macleantown** S. Africa
237 M7 **Maclear** S. Africa
105 N4 **Macleay** *r. N.S.W.* Austr.
MacLeod *Alta* Can. *see* **Fort Macleod**
109 B8 **MacLeod, Lake** *imp. l. W.A.* Austr.
Macleod's Table South *hill Scotland* U.K. *see* **Healabhal Bheag**
245 N3 **Macmillan** *r. Y.T.* Can.
245 O3 **Macmillan Pass** *Y.T.* Can.
169 G4 **Macnean Lower, Lough** *l. Northern Ireland* U.K.
169 G4 **Macnean Upper, Lough** *l.* Ireland/U.K.
235 G4 **Maçobere** Moz.
231 C6 **Macocola** Angola
250 D9 **Macomb** *IL* U.S.A.
214 B7 **Macomer** *Sardegna* Italy
233 D8 **Macomia** Moz.
182 F4 **Mâcon** France
255 F9 **Macon** *GA* U.S.A.
260 I6 **Macon** *MO* U.S.A.
261 K9 **Macon** *MS* U.S.A.
256 B10 **Macon** *OH* U.S.A.
261 J10 **Macon, Bayou** *r. LA* U.S.A.
231 D8 **Macondo** Angola
182 F4 **Mâconnais** *reg.* France
259 G2 **Macopin** *NJ* U.S.A.
235 G3 **Macossa** Moz.
205 J7 **Macotera** Spain
247 K3 **Macoun Lake** *Sask.* Can.
235 G4 **Macovane** Moz.
Macpherson Robertson Land *reg.* Antarctica *see* **Mac. Robertson Land**
105 K4 **Macquarie** *r. N.S.W.* Austr.
105 K9 **Macquarie** *r. Tas.* Austr.
105 M5 **Macquarie, Lake** *b. N.S.W.* Austr.
105 J10 **Macquarie Harbour** *Tas.* Austr.
104 □3 **Macquarie Island** S. Pacific Ocean
105 K4 **Macquarie Marshes** *N.S.W.* Austr.
105 L5 **Macquarie Mountain** *N.S.W.* Austr.
290 F9 **Macquarie Ridge** *sea feature* S. Pacific Ocean
103 E12 **Macraes Flat** *South I.* N.Z.
116 □ **MacRitchie Reservoir** Sing.
287 E2 **Mac. Robertson Land** *reg.* Antarctica
169 E9 **Macroom** Ireland
267 N9 **Mactún** Mex.
274 D4 **Macú** Brazil
212 D4 **Macugnaga** Italy
269 K8 **Macuiltianguis** Mex.
274 D1 **Macuira, Parque Nacional** *nat. park* Col.
274 C4 **Macuje** Col.
218 I9 **Macukull** Albania
104 E2 **Macumba** *S.A.* Austr.
104 F2 **Macumba** *watercourse S.A.* Austr.
258 D3 **Macungie** *PA* U.S.A.
278 F4 **Macururé** Brazil
276 C3 **Macusani** Peru
267 M9 **Macuspana** Mex.
266 E4 **Macuzari, Presa** *resr* Mex.
235 H3 **Macuze** Moz.
257 □Q3 **Macwahoc** *ME* U.S.A.
199 K3 **Mád** Hungary
150 D7 **Mādabā** Jordan
237 O3 **Madadeni** S. Africa
229 I4 **Madagali** Nigeria
145 K7 **Madagan** Pak.
235 □ **Madagascar** *i.* Africa
289 H6 **Madagascar Basin** *sea feature* Indian Ocean
289 G7 **Madagascar Ridge** *sea feature* Indian Ocean
151 H5 **Madagiz** Azer.
146 C2 **Madā'in Şāliḩ** Saudi Arabia
146 D2 **Madā'in Şāliḩ** *tourist site* Saudi Arabia
136 E6 **Madakasira** *Andhra Prad.* India
114 □ **Madalai** Palau
238 □1c **Madalena** *Pico* Azores
278 F3 **Madalena** Brazil
224 B4 **Madama** Niger
219 M9 **Madan** Bulg.
144 H3 **Ma'dan** Iran
230 C2 **Madana** Chad
224 C5 **Madana** *well* Chad
136 F6 **Madanapalle** *Andhra Prad.* India
113 K8 **Madang** P.N.G.
138 G7 **Madaora** *Uttar Prad.* India
229 G3 **Madaoua** Niger
219 P7 **Madara** Bulg.
199 I5 **Madaras** Hungary
219 J4 **Mădăraş** Romania
139 M8 **Madaripur** Bangl.
229 G3 **Madarounfa** Niger
Madau Turkm. *see* **Madaw**
144 F2 **Madaw** Turkm.
251 Q4 **Madawaska** *Ont.* Can.
248 E4 **Madawaska** *r. Ont.* Can.
257 □Q1 **Madawaska** *ME* U.S.A.
118 C3 **Madaya** Myanmar
214 C5 **Maddalena, Isola** *i. Sardegna* Italy
217 I9 **Maddalena, Penisola della** *pen. Sicilia* Italy
214 C9 **Maddalena Spiaggia** *Sardegna* Italy
215 M5 **Maddaloni** Italy
136 G3 **Madded** *Chhattisgarh* India
136 E6 **Maddur** *Karnataka* India
186 G5 **Made** Neth.
230 F3 **Madeir** Sudan
275 G5 **Madeira** *r.* Brazil
206 □ **Madeira** *terr.* N. Atlantic Ocean
206 □ **Madeira, Arquipélago da** *is* N. Atlantic Ocean
Madeira, Arquipélago da *terr.* N. Atlantic Ocean *see* **Madeira**
206 □ **Madeira, Ilha da** *i.* Madeira
206 □ **Madeira, Parque Natural de** *nature res.* Madeira
Madeira Islands N. Atlantic Ocean *see* **Madeira, Arquipélago da**
277 E2 **Madeirinha** *r.* Brazil
249 I4 **Madeleine, Îles de la** *is Que.* Can.
182 D4 **Madeleine, Monts de la** *mts* France
172 H2 **Madeley** *Staffordshire, England* U.K.
172 H2 **Madeley** *Telford and Wrekin, England* U.K.
260 H3 **Madelia** *MN* U.S.A.
250 D3 **Madeline Island** *WI* U.S.A.
230 C2 **Madel Ouèï** Chad
148 I4 **Maden** Turkey
143 R4 **Madeniyet** Kazakh.
210 B2 **Mäder** Austria
266 E3 **Madera** Mex.
207 N4 **Madera** *r.* Spain
264 L5 **Madera** *CA* U.S.A.
205 K5 **Maderano** *r.* Spain
200 B5 **Madererspitze** *mt.* Austria
205 M6 **Maderuelo** Spain
162 S3 **Madetkoski** Fin.
136 C5 **Madgaon** *Goa* India
239 □2a **Madge Rocks** *is Inner Islands* Seychelles
232 D1 **Madgoul** Djibouti
138 C9 **Madhavpur** *Gujarat* India
139 K7 **Madhepura** *Bihar* India
133 E13 **Madhoganj** *Uttar Prad.* India
139 K6 **Madhubani** *Bihar* India
136 E6 **Madhugiri** *Karnataka* India
139 K7 **Madhupur** *Jharkhand* India
138 G8 **Madhya Pradesh** *state* India
117 J4 **Madi, Dataran Tinggi** *plat.* Indon.
233 B7 **Madibira** Tanz.
237 J2 **Madibogo** S. Africa
276 D3 **Madidi** *r.* Bol.
104 F3 **Madigan Gulf** *salt flat S.A.* Austr.
136 D6 **Madikeri** *Karnataka* India
261 G8 **Madill** *OK* U.S.A.
231 B6 **Madimba** Angola
231 B6 **Madimba** Dem. Rep. Congo
228 D4 **Madinani** Côte d'Ivoire
146 F8 **Madīnat al 'Abīd** Yemen
146 G9 **Madīnat ash Sha'b** Yemen
150 G3 **Madīnat ath Thawrah**
179 K6 **Madine, Lac de** *l.* France
231 A6 **Madingo-Kayes** Congo
231 B6 **Madingou** Congo
229 I4 **Madingrin** Cameroon
185 D8 **Madiran** France
235 □J3 **Madirovalo** Madag.
255 D8 **Madison** *AL* U.S.A.
259 J2 **Madison** *CT* U.S.A.
255 F10 **Madison** *FL* U.S.A.
255 F9 **Madison** *GA* U.S.A.
254 E6 **Madison** *IN* U.S.A.
257 □P4 **Madison** *ME* U.S.A.
260 G3 **Madison** *MN* U.S.A.
260 G5 **Madison** *NE* U.S.A.
259 G3 **Madison** *NJ* U.S.A.
256 D7 **Madison** *OH* U.S.A.
260 G3 **Madison** *SD* U.S.A.
256 G10 **Madison** *VA* U.S.A.
250 E6 **Madison** *WI* U.S.A.
256 D10 **Madison** *WV* U.S.A.
262 I4 **Madison** *r. MT* U.S.A.
256 F11 **Madison Heights** *VA* U
254 D7 **Madisonville** *KY* U.S.A.
255 E8 **Madisonville** *TN* U.S.A.
261 H10 **Madisonville** *TX* U.S.A.
115 B9 **Madita** *Sumba* Indon.
117 I8 **Madiun** *Jawa* Indon.
230 B4 **Madjingo** Gabon
227 I4 **Madjūl** Libya
172 G3 **Madley** *Herefordshire, England* U.K.
109 G8 **Madley, Mount** *hill W.A*
160 I5 **Madliena** Latvia
Madnishkevi Rus. Fed. **Uchkulan**
230 F4 **Mado** Dem. Rep. Cong
248 E4 **Madoc** *Ont.* Can.
199 H5 **Madocsa** Hungary
232 C4 **Mado Gashi** Kenya
128 F9 **Madoi** *Qinghai* China
179 L6 **Madon** *r.* France
160 J5 **Madona** Latvia
234 D4 **Madongo Pan** *salt pan*
216 F8 **Madonie** *mts Sicilia* Ita
258 B5 **Madonna** *MD* U.S.A.
213 J3 **Madonna di Campiglio**
138 C7 **Madpura** *Rajasthan* In
221 H3 **Madra Dağı** *mts* Turke
146 D5 **Madrakah** Saudi Arabi
147 M6 **Madrakah, Ra's** *c.* Oma
Madras *Tamil Nadu* In **Chennai**
Madras *state* India *see* **Tamil Nadu**
262 D4 **Madras** *OR* U.S.A.
151 J5 **Mädräsä** Azer.
269 J1 **Madre, Laguna** *lag.* Me
261 G12 **Madre, Laguna** *lag. TX*
Madre, Sierra *mts* Mex
Madre de Chiapas, Sie
114 C3 **Madre, Sierra** *mt. Luzo*
269 N9 **Madre de Chiapas, Sie** Mex.
281 E4 **Madre de Deus de Mi**
276 C2 **Madre de Dios** *dept* Pe
283 B8 **Madre de Dios, Isla** *i.*
268 F7 **Madre del Sur, Sierra**
230 F3 **Madreggi** Sudan
268 B1 **Madre Occidental, Sie** Mex.
268 F1 **Madre Oriental, Sierra**
185 I10 **Madrès, Pic de** *mt.* Fra
114 E7 **Madrid** *Mindanao* Phil.
205 M8 **Madrid** Spain
205 M7 **Madrid** *aut. comm.* Spa
114 D6 **Madridejos** Phil.
207 L2 **Madridejos** Spain
205 K6 **Madrigal de las Altas T** Spain
205 J8 **Madrigal de la Vera** Sp
205 M4 **Madrigal del Monte** Sp
206 H2 **Madrigalejo** Spain
207 P2 **Madrigueras** Spain
200 A6 **Madrisahorn** *mt.* Austr
165 L4 **Madroken** *l.* Sweden
172 □ **Madron** *Cornwall, Engl*
207 K4 **Madrona, Sierra** *mts* S
206 H2 **Madroñera** Spain
207 P3 **Madroño** *mt.* Spain
270 C2 **Madruga** Cuba
224 B3 **Madrūsah** Libya
115 B7 **Madu** *i.* Indon.
135 □1 **Madu** *i. S. Male* Maldiv
231 B6 **Maduda** Dem. Rep. Co
137 H4 **Madugula** *Andhra Prad*
109 I11 **Madura** *W.A.* Austr.
117 J8 **Madura** *i.* Indon.
117 J8 **Madura, Selat** *sea chan*
136 F8 **Madurai** *Tamil Nadu* In
136 F6 **Madurantakam** *Tamil*
144 F6 **Madvār, Kūh-e** *mt.* Iran
138 H7 **Madwas** *Madh. Prad.* In
145 O4 **Madyan** Pak.
233 B6 **Madyo** Tanz.
151 I3 **Madzhalis** Rus. Fed.
219 N9 **Madzharovo** Bulg.
235 F3 **Madziwadzido** Zimbab
235 F3 **Madziwa Mine** Zimbab
213 M3 **Maè** *r.* Italy
Maé *i.* Vanuatu *see* **Éma**
127 J3 **Maebashi** Japan
118 D5 **Mae Chang, Ang Kep** Thai.
118 C5 **Mae Hong Son** Thai.
124 □1 **Mae-jima** *i. Okinawa* Ja
115 C3 **Maelang** *Sulawesi* Indo
180 E5 **Maël-Carhaix** France
164 E2 **Mælefjell** *mt.* Norway
208 F5 **Maella** Spain
205 K7 **Maello** Spain
172 C4 **Maenclochog** *Pembroke* *Wales* U.K.
118 D5 **Mae Ngat, Ang Kep Na** Thai.
172 E2 **Maentwrog** *Gwynedd, W*
215 K4 **Maenza** Italy
118 D6 **Mae Ping National Pa**
118 D6 **Mae Ramat** Thai.
118 D5 **Mae Rim** Thai.
219 K3 **Măerişte** Romania
118 D4 **Mae Sai** Thai.
118 C5 **Mae Sariang** Thai.
118 D6 **Mae Sot** Thai.
172 E4 **Maesteg** *Bridgend, Wale*
270 E4 **Maestra, Sierra** *mts* Cu
207 I6 **Maestre** *hill* Spain
114 C5 **Maestre de Campo** *i.* P
213 L9 **Maestro, Canale** *canal*
118 D5 **Mae Suai** Thai.
118 D6 **Mae Tuen Wildlife Res** *nature res.* Thai.
235 □J3 **Maevatanana** Madag.
100 □5 **Maéwo** *i.* Vanuatu
118 D7 **Mae Wong National Pa**
118 E5 **Mae Yom National Par**
205 P3 **Maeztu** Spain
115 E3 **Mafa** *Halmahera* Indon
239 □1c **Mafaté, Cirque de** *vol.* Réunion
247 K4 **Mafeking** *Man.* Can.
Mafeking S. Africa *see*
237 L5 **Mafeteng** Lesotho
105 K7 **Maffra** *Vic.* Austr.
233 C7 **Mafia Channel** Tanz.
233 C6 **Mafia Island** Tanz.
237 J1 **Mafikeng** S. Africa
233 B7 **Mafinga** Tanz.
279 C8 **Mafra** Brazil
206 A3 **Mafra** Port.
Mafraq Jordan *see* **Al M**
278 E4 **Mafrense** Brazil
235 F3 **Mafungabusi Plateau**
135 □1 **Mafushi** *i. S. Male* Mal
237 O6 **Magabeni** S. Africa
206 H3 **Magacela** *hill* Spain
153 Q4 **Magadan** Rus. Fed.
233 C5 **Magadi** Kenya
235 G4 **Magaiza** Moz.
183 C10 **Magalas** France
237 L1 **Magaliesberg** *mts* S. Af
237 L1 **Magaliesburg** S. Africa
Magallanes Chile *see* **Punta Arenas**

Magallanes Luzon Phil.
Magallanes, Estrecho de sea chan. Chile
Magallanes Bank sea feature Bahamas
Magallanes y Antártica Chilena admin. reg. Chile
Magallón Spain
Magalluf Spain
Magaña Spain
Maganey Ireland
Magangue Col.
Mağara Turkey
Mağara tourist site Turkey
Mağara Dağı mt. Turkey
Mağarali Turkey
Magaramkent Rus. Fed.
Magaria Niger
Magari-zaki pt Okinawa Japan
Magas Iran see Zābolī
Magas Rus. Fed.
Magat r. Luzon Phil.
Magaz Spain
Magazine Mountain hill AR U.S.A.
Magazzolo r. Sicilia Italy
Magbakele Dem. Rep. Congo
Magburaka Sierra Leone
Magdagachi Rus. Fed.
Magdala Ger.
Magdalena Arg.
Magdalena Bol.
Magdalena dept Col.
Magdalena r. Col.
Magdalena Baja California Sur Mex.
Magdalena Sonora Mex.
Magdalena r. Mex.
Magdalena NM U.S.A.
Magdalena, Bahía b. Col.
Magdalena, Bahía b. Mex.
Magdalena, Isla i. Chile
Magdalena, Isla i. Mex.
Magdalena, Sierra de la mts Spain
Magdalena Cuayucatepec Mex.
Magdalena Island Fr. Polynesia see Fatu Hiva
Magdaline, Gunung mt. Malaysia
Magdeburg Ger.
Magdeburgerforth Ger.
Magdelaine Cays atoll Coral Sea Is Terr. Austr.
Magé Brazil
Magee MS U.S.A.
Magee, Island pen. Northern Ireland U.K.
Mageik Volcano AK U.S.A.
Magelang Jawa Indon.
Magellan, Strait of Chile see Magallanes, Estrecho de
Magellan Seamounts sea feature N. Pacific Ocean
Magenta Italy
Magenta, Lake salt flat W.A. Austr.
Magerøya i. Norway
Magescq France
16 Mage-shima i. Japan
Măgești Romania
Maggia Switz.
Maggia r. Switz.
Maggiolo Arg.
Maggiorasca, Monte mt. Italy
Maggiore, Isola i. Italy
Maggiore, Lago l. Italy
Maggiore, Lake Italy see Maggiore, Lago
Maggiore, Monte hill Sardegna Italy
Maggiore, Monte mt. Italy
Maggotty Jamaica
Maghāghah Egypt
Maghā'ir Shu'ayb tourist site Saudi Arabia
Maghama Maur.
Maghanlawaun Ireland
Maghārah, Jabal hill Egypt
Magharee Islands Ireland see The Seven Hogs
Maghera Ireland see An Machaire
Maghera Northern Ireland U.K.
Magherafelt Northern Ireland U.K.
Magheralin Northern Ireland U.K.
Magheramason Northern Ireland U.K.
Maghery Northern Ireland U.K.
Maghnia Alg.
Maghor Afgh.
Maghull Merseyside, England U.K.
Magilligan Northern Ireland U.K.
Magilligan Point Northern Ireland U.K.
Mágina mt. Spain
Mágina, Sierra mts Spain
Magingo Tanz.
Magione Italy
Magisano Italy
Magiscatzín Mex.
Magitang Qinghai China see Jainca
Magiyan Tajik. see Moghiyon
Maglaj Bos.-Herz.
Magland France
Maglavit Romania
Magliano de'Marsi Italy
Magliano in Toscana Italy
Magliano Sabina Italy
Maglie Italy
Maglód Hungary
Magma AZ U.S.A.
Magnac-Laval France
Magnac-sur-Touvre France
Magna Grande hill Italy
Magna Grande mt. Sicilia Italy
Magné France
Magnet Bay Antarctica
Magnetic Island Qld Austr.
Magnetic Passage Qld Austr.
Magnetity Rus. Fed.
Magnières France
Magnisi, Penisola pen. Sicilia Italy
Magnitnyy Rus. Fed.
Magnitogorsk Rus. Fed.
Magnolia AR U.S.A.
Magnolia DE U.S.A.
Magnolia MD U.S.A.
Magnolia MS U.S.A.
Magnor Norway
Magnuszew Pol.
Magny-Cours France
Magny-en-Vexin France
Mago Rus. Fed.
Mágocs Hungary
Mágocs-ér r. Hungary
Màgoé Moz.
Magog Que. Can.
Magole Tanz.
Magomadas Sardegna Italy
Mago National Park Eth.
Magosa Cyprus see Ammochostos
Magoye Zambia
Magozal Mex.
Magpie Que. Can.
Magpie r. Ont. Can.
Magpie r. Que. Can.
Magpie, Lac l. Que. Can.
Magpie Ouest r. Que. Can.
Magra r. Italy
Magrath Alta Can.
Magre r. Spain
Magruder Mountain NV U.S.A.
Magrur Sudan
Magrur, Wadi watercourse Sudan
Magṭa' Laḥjar Maur.
Magtymguly Turkm.
Magu Tanz.
Magu, Chashmeh-ye well Iran
Magu, Khrebet mts Rus. Fed.
Maguan Yunnan China
Maguarinho, Cabo c. Brazil
Magude Moz.
Magudu S. Africa

204 E6 Magueija Port.
266 H4 Magueyal Mex.
238 □[3c] Máguez Lanzarote Canary Is
206 H4 Maguilla Spain
169 H4 Maguiresbridge Northern Ireland U.K.
229 I3 Magumeri Nigeria
257 □R3 Magundy N.B. Can.
235 F3 Magunge Zimbabwe
139 L8 Magura Bangl.
199 H3 Magura mt. Slovakia
158 G6 Măgura, Dealul hill Moldova
219 K3 Măgura Mare, Vârful hill Romania
219 K5 Măgurii, Vârful mt. Romania
247 M2 Maguse Lake Nunavut Can.
237 L8 Magwali S. Africa
Magway Myanmar see Magwe
Magway admin. div. Myanmar see Magwe
118 B4 Magwe Myanmar
118 B4 Magwe admin. div. Myanmar
232 B3 Magwe Sudan
234 D3 Magwegqana watercourse Botswana
199 K4 Magy Hungary
199 G5 Magyaratád Hungary
199 H6 Magyarbóly Hungary
Magyarkanizsa Vojvodina Serbia see Kanjiža
Magyar Köztársaság country Europe see Hungary
199 H5 Magyarszék Hungary
118 A4 Magyichaung Myanmar
144 A3 Mahābād Iran
136 C4 Mahabaleshwar Mahar. India
235 □J3 Mahabe Madag.
138 J6 Mahabharat Range mts Nepal
235 □J4 Mahabo Toliara Madag.
235 □J4 Mahabo Toliara Madag.
235 □J4 Mahaboboka Madag.
136 C3 Mahad Mahar. India
232 E4 Mahaddayweyne Somalia
138 F8 Mahadeo Hills Madh. Prad. India
136 G3 Mahadeopur Andhra Prad. India
101 □[9a] Mahaena Tahiti Fr. Polynesia
256 G8 Mahaffey PA U.S.A.
230 F4 Mahagi Dem. Rep. Congo
230 F4 Mahagi Port Dem. Rep. Congo
133 L7 Mahai Qinghai China
275 G3 Mahaicony Guyana
235 □J2 Mahajamba r. Madag.
138 D5 Mahajan Rajasthan India
235 □J2 Mahajanga Madag.
235 □J3 Mahajanga prov. Madag.
117 L5 Mahakam r. Indon.
235 E4 Mahalapye Botswana
233 A6 Mahale Mountains National Park Tanz.
235 □K2 Mahalevona Madag.
144 D5 Maḥallāt-e Bālā Iran
138 F5 Maham Haryana India
144 G6 Māhān Iran
139 K9 Mahanadi r. India
235 □K3 Mahanoro Madag.
258 C3 Mahanoy City PA U.S.A.
258 B3 Mahanoy Creek r. PA U.S.A.
258 B3 Mahantango Creek r. PA U.S.A.
136 G9 Maha Oya Sri Lanka
139 J6 Maharajganj Bihar India
138 H6 Maharajganj Uttar Prad. India
139 I6 Maharajganj Uttar Prad. India
138 G7 Maharajpur Madh. Prad. India
136 D3 Maharashtra state India
146 B2 Mahārish, Ra's pt Saudi Arabia
144 E7 Mahārlū, Daryācheh-ye salt l. Iran
138 I9 Mahasamund Chhattisgarh India
118 F6 Maha Sarakham Thai.
235 □J5 Mahatalaky Madag.
150 E7 Maḥaṭṭat Ḍab'ah Jordan
271 □[2] Mahaut Dominica
235 □J2 Mahavavy r. Madag.
235 □K3 Mahavelona Madag.
136 G8 Mahaweli Ganga r. Sri Lanka
235 □J3 Mahazoma Madag.
225 F6 Mahbub Sudan
136 G4 Mahbubabad Andhra Prad. India
136 E4 Mahbubnagar Andhra Prad. India
146 E4 Mahd adh Dhahab Saudi Arabia
147 L3 Maḥḍah Oman
159 N5 Mahdalynivka Dnipropetrovs'ka Oblast' Ukr.
159 M7 Mahdalynivka Khersons'ka Oblast' Ukr.
227 F2 Mahdia Alg.
275 G3 Mahdia Guyana
227 H2 Mahdia Tunisia
128 I9 Mahe Gansu China
136 D7 Mahe Puducherry India
239 □[2b] Mahé i. Inner Islands Seychelles
239 □[1b] Mahébourg Mauritius
170 F5 Mahee Island Northern Ireland U.K.
139 L7 Mahendraganj Meghalaya India
138 F5 Mahendragarh Haryana India
137 I3 Mahendragiri mt. Orissa India
233 C7 Mahenge Tanz.
103 E12 Maheno South I. N.Z.
197 L5 Maheriv Ukr.
138 D8 Mahesana Gujarat India
138 E8 Maheshwar Madh. Prad. India
147 L9 Maḥfirhīn Suquṭrā Yemen
138 G6 Mahgawan Madh. Prad. India
138 D8 Mahi r. Rajasthan India
144 H7 Māhī watercourse Iran
102 L6 Mahia North I. N.Z.
102 L6 Mahia Peninsula North I. N.Z.
204 H5 Mahíde Spain
100 □[6] Mahige Island Solomon Is
161 N8 Mahilyow Belarus
Mahilyow Oblast admin. div. Belarus see Mahilyowskaya Voblasts'
161 N8 Mahilyowskaya Voblasts' admin. div. Belarus
136 C3 Mahim Mahar. India
229 G5 Mahin Nigeria
101 □[9a] Mahina Tahiti Fr. Polynesia
228 C3 Mahina Mali
103 E9 Mahinapua, Lake South I. N.Z.
103 D12 Mahinerangi, Lake South I. N.Z.
138 G3 Mahiya Jammu and Kashmir India
136 G9 Mahiyangana Sri Lanka
144 E6 Mah Jān Iran
162 L4 Mahkene mt. Sweden
237 P4 Mahlabatini S. Africa
118 B4 Mahlaing Myanmar
237 P3 Mahlangasi S. Africa
237 L4 Mahlatswetsa S. Africa
194 D5 Mahlberg Ger.
193 H6 Mahlow Ger.
192 D5 Mahlsdorf Ger.
193 E6 Mahlwinkel Ger.
138 H6 Mahmudabad Uttar Prad. India
144 E3 Maḥmūdābād Iran
145 M4 Maḥmūd-e Rāqī Afgh.
219 R5 Mahmudia Romania
221 H3 Mahmudiye Çanakkale Turkey
221 L3 Mahmudiye Eskişehir Turkey
150 A2 Mahmutlar Turkey
221 K1 Mahmutşevketpaşa Turkey
144 C4 Mahniān Iran
260 G2 Mahnomen MN U.S.A.
136 G9 Maho Sri Lanka
138 G7 Mahoba Uttar Prad. India
102 I5 Mahoenui North I. N.Z.
138 H6 Maholi Uttar Prad. India
208 □ Mahón Spain
249 H4 Mahone Bay N.S. Can.
234 D3 Mahongo Game Park nature res. Namibia
245 P2 Mahony Lake N.W.T. Can.
259 H2 Mahopac NY U.S.A.
259 H2 Mahopac Lake NY U.S.A.
207 P2 Mahora Spain
228 D3 Mahou Mali
230 C2 Mahoua Chad
147 J7 Mahrāt, Jabal mt. Yemen
147 J7 Mahrāt, Wādī r. Yemen
138 G7 Mahrauni Uttar Prad. India
Mähren reg. Czech Rep. see Morava
227 H2 Mahrès Tunisia

195 N2 Mähring Ger.
144 I5 Mahrūd Iran
Mahsana Gujarat India see Mahesana
133 L8 Mahuanggou Qinghai China
139 O8 Mahudaung mts Myanmar
264 □F13 Māhukona HI U.S.A.
139 N7 Mahur Assam India
136 E3 Mahur Mahar. India
229 G4 Mahuta Nigeria
233 C7 Mahuta Tanz.
138 C9 Mahuva Gujarat India
138 F6 Mahwa Rajasthan India
219 P9 Mahya Dağı mt. Turkey
144 D5 Mahyār Iran
115 E6 Mai i. Maluku Indon.
Mai i. Vanuatu see Émaé
100 □[2] Maia American Samoa
238 □[1b] Maia São Miguel Azores
204 C6 Maia Port.
Maiaia Moz. see Nacala
208 G5 Maials Spain
99 H1 Maiana atoll Gilbert Is Kiribati
139 N7 Maibang Assam India
274 C2 Maicao Col.
248 E3 Maicasagi r. Que. Can.
248 E3 Maicasagi, Lac l. Que. Can.
182 J2 Maîche France
130 G8 Maichen Guangdong China
275 F6 Maici r. Brazil
275 H5 Maicuru r. Brazil
217 K6 Maida Italy
145 M4 Maīdān Shahr Afgh.
172 H5 Maiden Bradley Wiltshire, England U.K.
258 D4 Maiden Creek r. PA U.S.A.
173 K4 Maidenhead Windsor and Maidenhead, England U.K.
172 G6 Maiden Newton Dorset, England U.K.
250 B5 Maiden Rock WI U.S.A.
168 G12 Maidens South Ayrshire, Scotland U.K.
115 E3 Maidi Halmahera Indon.
247 I4 Maidstone Sask. Can.
173 N5 Maidstone Kent, England U.K.
229 I4 Maiduguri Nigeria
215 M3 Maiella, Parco Nazionale della nat. park Italy
212 H1 Maienfeld Switz.
217 K6 Maierato Italy
195 I6 Maierhöfen Ger.
219 M3 Maieru Romania
169 D6 Maigh Cuilinn Ireland
209 D10 Maigmó mt. Spain
178 E4 Maignelay-Montigny France
232 C3 Mai Gudo mt. Eth.
169 E7 Maigue r. Ireland
138 H7 Maihar Madh. Prad. India
126 D5 Maihara Japan
102 J5 Maihiihi North I. N.Z.
139 M8 Maijdi Bangl.
130 E1 Maiji Gansu China
130 F2 Maiji Shan mt. Gansu China
138 H8 Maikala Range hills Madh. Prad. India
194 E3 Maikammer Ger.
230 E4 Maiko r. Dem. Rep. Congo
230 E5 Maiko, Parc National de la nat. park Dem. Rep. Congo
139 I8 Mailan Hill mt. Chhattisgarh India
138 H5 Mailani Uttar Prad. India
230 B2 Maïlao Chad
116 C6 Maileppe Indon.
264 □C12 Mā'ili HI U.S.A.
185 D7 Maillas France
178 B6 Maillebois France
184 C3 Maillezais France
178 H6 Mailly-le-Camp France
182 D1 Mailly-le-Château France
178 E3 Mailly-Maillet France
145 O7 Mailsi Pak.
130 D2 Maima Gansu China
191 F10 Main r. Ger.
146 G7 Ma'īn tourist site Yemen
139 L6 Mainaguri W. Bengal India
220 D5 Mainalo mts Greece
194 G2 Mainaschaff Ger.
195 I2 Mainbernheim Ger.
249 K3 Main Brook Nfld and Lab. Can.
195 L4 Mainburg Ger.
248 D4 Main Channel lake channel Ont. Can.
136 E4 Maindargi Mahar. India
230 C5 Mai-Ndombe prov. Dem. Rep. Congo
230 C5 Mai-Ndombe, Lac l. Dem. Rep. Congo
195 J2 Main-Donau-Kanal canal Ger.
251 R6 Main Duck Island Ont. Can.
181 J7 Maine r. France
181 K5 Maine reg. France
257 □P3 Maine state U.S.A.
257 □P5 Maine, Gulf of U.S.A.
181 K7 Maine-et-Loire dept France
274 C5 Mainé Hanari, Cerro hill Col.
229 I3 Maïné-Soroa Niger
118 C1 Maingkwan Myanmar
119 D8 Maingy Island Myanmar
169 I6 Mainham Ireland
194 H3 Mainhardt Ger.
114 E7 Mainit Mindanao Phil.
114 E7 Mainit, Lake Mindanao Phil.
130 B4 Mainkung Xizang China
168 J4 Mainland i. Orkney, Scotland U.K.
168 □N2 Mainland i. Shetland, Scotland U.K.
193 D10 Mainleus Ger.
133 L12 Mainling Xizang China
106 E3 Mainoru N.T. Austr.
106 E3 Mainoru r. N.T. Austr.
139 I8 Mainpat reg. Chhattisgarh India
138 G6 Mainpuri Uttar Prad. India
105 N3 Main Range National Park Qld Austr.
184 I3 Mainsat France
178 C6 Maintenon France
235 □J3 Maintirano Madag.
162 S4 Mainua Fin.
178 B7 Mainvilliers France
118 B3 Mainyaung Myanmar
191 F10 Mainz Ger.
228 □ Maio i. Cape Verde
213 O9 Maiolati Spontini Italy
206 B2 Maior r. Port.
204 C8 Maiorca Port.
204 C9 Maiorga Port.
216 H2 Maiori Italy
284 B3 Maipó r. Chile
284 C4 Maipó, Volcán vol. Chile
285 I5 Maipú Buenos Aires Arg.
284 C3 Maipú Mendoza Arg.
284 B3 Maipú Chile
274 E3 Maipures Col.
275 G3 Maipuri Landing Guyana
274 E2 Maiquetía Venez.
133 H12 Maiqu Zangbo r. Xizang China
212 D6 Maira r. Italy
206 H6 Mairena del Alcor Spain
278 E4 Mairi Brazil
280 D5 Mairiporã Brazil
280 C2 Mairipotaba Brazil
204 F5 Mairos mt. Spain
195 K5 Maisach Ger.
195 K5 Maisach r. Ger.
126 G6 Maisaka Japan
200 G5 Maishofen Austria
270 F3 Maisí Cuba
160 I7 Maišiagala Lith.
139 M9 Maiskhal Channel inlet Bangl.
139 M9 Maiskhal Island Bangl.
178 D6 Maisons-Laffitte France
201 M2 Maissau Austria
178 D7 Maisse France
187 H9 Maissin Belgium
Maitea i. Arch. de la Société Fr. Polynesia see Mehetia
195 M5 Maitenbeth Ger.
282 C3 Maitencillo Chile
235 E4 Maitengwe Botswana
139 K8 Maithon W. Bengal India
105 M5 Maitland N.S.W. Austr.
104 F6 Maitland S.A. Austr.

108 D6 Maitland r. W.A. Austr.
117 L2 Maitland, Banjaran mts Malaysia
109 F9 Maitland, Lake salt flat W.A. Austr.
245 O1 Maitland Point pt N.W.T. Can.
287 A2 Maitri research stn Antarctica
Maiwo i. Vanuatu see Maéwo
106 E3 Maiwok r. N.T. Austr.
106 B4 Maiyu, Mount hill N.T. Austr.
266 □R11 Maíz, Islas del is Nic.
133 J12 Maizhokunggar Xizang China
178 G6 Maizières-la-Grande-Paroisse France
179 L5 Maizières-lès-Metz France
126 B5 Maizuru Japan
206 H7 Majaceite r. Spain
205 M8 Majadahonda Spain
204 I9 Majadas de Tiétar Spain
218 H8 Maja Jezercë mt. Albania
136 E3 Majalgaon Mahar. India
275 F4 Majari r. Brazil
147 I8 Majdaḥah Yemen
197 J5 Majdan Królewski Pol.
197 L5 Majdan Niepryski Pol.
219 J6 Majdanpek Majdanpek Serbia
150 D5 Majdel Aanjar tourist site Lebanon
115 A5 Majene Sulawesi Barat Indon.
210 G3 Majevica mts Bos.-Herz.
138 H7 Majhgawan Madh. Prad. India
138 G8 Majholi Madh. Prad. India
147 J4 Majḥūd well Saudi Arabia
129 O7 Majia He r. China
131 H7 Majiang Guangxi China
130 F5 Majiang Guizhou China
Majiawan Ningxia China see Huinong
122 D3 Majiazi Nei Mongol China
229 F3 Majibo well Mali
144 I4 Majnābād Iran
Majōl country N. Pacific Ocean see Marshall Islands
268 F2 Majoma Mex.
238 □[3a] Majona, Punta pt La Gomera Canary Is
209 K8 Major, Puig mt. Spain
Majorca i. Spain see Mallorca
104 □[3] Major Lake S. Pacific Ocean
Mājro atoll Marshall Is see Majuro
199 H6 Majs Hungary
201 M7 Majšperk Slovenia
139 N6 Majuli Island India
Majunga Madag. see Mahajanga
276 D1 Majuriã Brazil
100 □[3b] Majuro atoll Marshall Is
100 □[3b] Majuro Lagoon Majuro Marshall Is
237 K4 Majwemasweu S. Africa
228 B3 Maka Senegal
100 □[6] Maka Malaita Solomon Is
231 B5 Makabana Congo
127 L3 Makabe Japan
199 H4 Makád Hungary
151 H3 Makadzhoy Rus. Fed.
264 □C12 Mākaha HI U.S.A.
264 □B12 Makahū'ena Point HI U.S.A.
229 H6 Makak Cameroon
231 B5 Makaka Congo
230 E5 Makalado Dem. Rep. Congo
115 A5 Makale Sulawesi Indon.
115 D2 Makalehi i. Indon.
139 K6 Makalu mt. China/Nepal
139 K6 Makalu Barun National Park Nepal
233 A6 Makamba Burundi
143 T4 Makanchi Kazakh.
Makane Rus. Fed. see Meken-Yurt
233 B8 Makanjila Malawi
138 H6 Makanpur Uttar Prad. India
233 C6 Makanya Tanz.
230 C4 Makanza Dem. Rep. Congo
264 □D12 Makapu'u Head HI U.S.A.
235 □J3 Makaraingo Madag.
103 C13 Makarewa South I. N.Z.
229 I3 Makari Cameroon
156 J3 Makar-Ib Rus. Fed.
156 L2 Makarikha Rus. Fed.
Makari Mountain National Park Tanz. see Mahale Mountains National Park
158 I3 Makariv Ukr.
103 D11 Makarora r. South I. N.Z.
122 M4 Makarov Sakhalin Rus. Fed.
292 M1 Makarov Basin sea feature Arctic Ocean
158 B5 Makarove Ukr.
157 H5 Makarovo Rus. Fed.
210 F4 Makarska Croatia
145 N5 Makarwal Pak.
156 J4 Makar'ye Rus. Fed.
156 H4 Makar'yev Rus. Fed.
233 A7 Makasa Zambia
115 A6 Makassar Sulawesi Indon.
115 A3 Makassar, Selat str. Indon.
142 E4 Makat Kazakh.
237 Q3 Makatini Flats lowland S. Africa
118 C1 Makaw Myanmar
264 □E13 Makawao HI U.S.A.
235 □J4 Makay, Massif du mts Madag.
Makedonija country Europe see Macedonia
220 C2 Makedonski Brod Macedonia
218 J9 Makedonski Brod Macedonia
103 □[4] Makefu Niue
237 K4 Makeleketla S. Africa
114 □ Makelulu hill Palau
101 □[9] Makemo atoll Arch. des Tuamotu Fr. Polynesia
228 B4 Makeni Sierra Leone
233 B7 Makete Tanz.
Makeyevka Ukr. see Makiyivka
234 E4 Makgadikgadi depr. Botswana
234 E4 Makgadikgadi Pans National Park Botswana
151 I3 Makhachkala Rus. Fed.
145 N5 Makhad Pak.
237 L6 Makhaleng r. Lesotho
142 D4 Makhambet Kazakh.
146 F3 Makhāmīr, Jabal al hill Saudi Arabia
Makharadze Georgia see Ozurget'i
150 A8 Makhāzin, Kathīb al des. Egypt
237 N5 Makheka mt. Lesotho
150 G3 Makhfar al Ḩammām Syria
144 I3 Makhmaldepe Turkm.
151 G1 Makhmud-Mekteb Rus. Fed.
149 K6 Makhmūr Iraq
160 M4 Makhnovka Rus. Fed.
143 M1 Makhorovka Kazakh.
136 E4 Makhtal Andhra Prad. India
127 H1 Maki Japan
115 E3 Makian vol. Maluku Indon.
127 I2 Makihata-yama mt. Japan
103 F11 Makikihi South I. N.Z.
Makima atoll Arch. des Tuamotu Fr. Polynesia see Makemo
Makin atoll Kiribati see Butaritari
233 C5 Makindu Kenya
126 D5 Makino Japan
143 N1 Makinsk Kazakh.
243 J2 Makinson Inlet Nunavut Can.
127 I4 Makioka Japan
Makira i. Solomon Is see San Cristobal
158 F5 Makiv Ukr.
159 K3 Makiyivka Chernihivs'ka Oblast' Ukr.
159 Q5 Makiyivka Donets'ka Oblast' Ukr.
146 D5 Makkah Saudi Arabia
146 E5 Makkah prov. Saudi Arabia
162 U1 Makkaurhalvøya Naturreservat nature res. Norway
249 J2 Makkovik Nfld and Lab. Can.
249 J2 Makkovik, Cape Nfld and Lab. Can.
186 H2 Makkum Neth.
161 R7 Maklaki Rus. Fed.
210 F4 Makljen pass Bos.-Herz.
199 J5 Makó Hungary
228 B3 Mako Senegal
275 G4 Makoa, Serra hills Brazil

101 □[7] Makogai i. Fiji
230 B4 Makokou Gabon
237 K2 Makokskraal S. Africa
233 C7 Makonde Plateau Tanz.
Makongai i. Fiji see Makogai
233 B7 Makongolosi Tanz.
234 D5 Makopong Botswana
151 A2 Makopse Rus. Fed.
230 F4 Makoro Dem. Rep. Congo
235 G3 Makosa Zimbabwe
230 C5 Makotipoko Congo
102 K7 Makotuku North I. N.Z.
230 B5 Makoua Congo
231 B5 Makoubi Congo
199 H2 Makov Slovakia
210 E3 Makovnik mt. Croatia
197 I4 Maków Pol.
196 F2 Mąkowarsko Pol.
197 J3 Maków Mazowiecki Pol.
197 H6 Maków Podhalański Pol.
221 G6 Makra i. Greece
220 D4 Makrakomi Greece
144 I8 Makran reg. Iran/Pak.
138 E6 Makrana Rajasthan India
145 J9 Makran Coast Range mts Pak.
197 M4 Makrany Belarus
136 G3 Makri Chhattisgarh India
221 H5 Makronisi i. Greece
220 F5 Makronisos i. Greece
220 D2 Makrygialos Kentriki Makedonia Greece
221 G7 Makrygialos Kriti Greece
161 S4 Maksatikha Rus. Fed.
138 F8 Maksi Madh. Prad. India
122 J5 Maksimovka Rus. Fed.
145 J7 Maksotag Iran
138 F8 Maksudangarh Madh. Prad. India
151 H5 Maksudlu Azer.
196 G2 Maksymilianowo Pol.
144 A2 Mākū Iran
124 U4 Makubetsu Japan
139 O6 Makum Assam India
233 B7 Makumbako Tanz.
231 D6 Makumbi Dem. Rep. Congo
Makundu i. N. Male Maldives see Makunudhoo
233 C6 Makunduchi Tanz.
131 L7 Makung Taiwan
233 B7 Makungu Tanz.
233 C7 Makunguwiro Tanz.
135 □[1] Makunudhoo i. N. Male Maldives
125 H15 Makurazaki Japan
229 H5 Makurdi Nigeria
102 J7 Makuri North I. N.Z.
244 F5 Makushin Bay AK U.S.A.
244 F5 Makushin Volcano AK U.S.A.
232 D4 Makuungo Somalia
144 E7 Makūyeh Iran
233 C5 Makuyuni Tanz.
237 J3 Makwassie S. Africa
235 F3 Makwiro Zimbabwe
139 L6 Mal W. Bengal India
276 A3 Mala Peru
Mala Ireland see Mallow
Mala i. Solomon Is see Malaita
207 L6 Malá Spain
162 O4 Malå Sweden
266 □S14 Mala, Punta pt Panama
207 I8 Mala, Punta pt Spain
106 C6 Mala Aboriginal Land res. N.T. Austr.
150 A9 Mal'ab, Ra's pt Egypt
114 E8 Malabang Mindanao Phil.
104 □[2] Malabar b. Lord Howe I. Austr.
136 D6 Malabar Coast India
159 N6 Mala Bilozerka Ukr.
229 H6 Malabo Equat. Guinea
199 I5 Mala Bosna Vojvodina Serbia
285 I4 Mal Abrigo Uru.
114 A7 Malabuñgan Palawan Phil.
Malaca Spain see Málaga
281 F2 Malacacheta Brazil
Malacca Malaysia see Melaka
Malacca state Malaysia see Melaka
116 C2 Malacca, Strait of Indon./Malaysia
198 G3 Malacky Slovakia
262 H6 Malad r. ID U.S.A.
262 H5 Malad City ID U.S.A.
159 L3 Mala Divytsya Ukr.
160 J7 Maladzyechna Belarus
199 H2 Malá Fatra mts Slovakia
199 I2 Malá Fatra nat. park Slovakia
207 K7 Málaga Spain
207 J7 Málaga prov. Spain
258 E5 Malaga NJ U.S.A.
263 L10 Malaga NM U.S.A.
256 D9 Malaga OH U.S.A.
207 J7 Málaga, Montes de mts Spain
233 A6 Malagarasi r. Burundi/Tanz.
233 A6 Malagarasi Tanz.
207 L2 Malagón Spain
206 E5 Malagon r. Spain
205 L7 Malagón, Sierra de mts Spain
115 B8 Malahar Sumba Indon.
169 J6 Malahide Ireland
235 □J4 Malaimbandy Madag.
196 D2 Mała Ina r. Pol.
169 E3 Málainn Bhig Ireland
169 E3 Málainn Mhóir Ireland
100 □[6] Malaita i. Solomon Is
117 M9 Malaka mt. Sumbawa Indon.
114 □ Malakal Palau
232 A2 Malakal Sudan
114 □ Malakal Passage Palau
210 E3 Mala Kapela mts Croatia
101 □[7a] Malake i. Fiji
138 H5 Malakheti Nepal
210 E3 Mala Kladuša Bos.-Herz.
106 C2 Malak Malak Aboriginal Land res. N.T. Austr.
100 □[6] Malakobi Island Solomon Is
100 □[5] Malakula i. Vanuatu
145 O5 Malakwal Pak.
213 L6 Malalbergo Italy
159 M6 Mala Lepetykha Ukr.
275 G3 Malali Guyana
115 B5 Malamala Sulawesi Indon.
114 C8 Malamaui i. Phil.
213 M5 Malamocco Italy
158 E3 Mala Moshchanytsya Ukr.
114 B6 Malampaya Sound sea chan. Palawan Phil.
145 K9 Malan, Ras pt Pak.
114 B7 Malanao i. Phil.
179 J5 Malancourt France
206 G7 Malandar, Punta de pt Spain
117 J8 Malang Jawa Indon.
235 H2 Malanga Moz.
233 B7 Malangali Tanz.
Malangana Nepal see Malangwa
Malange Angola see Malanje
162 O2 Malangseidet Norway
139 J6 Malangwa Nepal
114 D8 Malanipa i. Phil.
231 C7 Malanje Angola
231 C7 Malanje prov. Angola
196 G4 Malanów Pol.
180 G6 Malansac France
114 B7 Malanut Bay Palawan Phil.
229 F4 Malanville Benin
284 D2 Malanzán Arg.
284 D2 Malanzán, Sierra de mts Arg.
159 N4 Mala Pereshchepyna Ukr.
136 E7 Malappuram Kerala India
165 N2 Mälaren l. Sweden
284 C4 Malargüe Arg.
275 H4 Malaripo Brazil
248 E3 Malartic Que. Can.
251 P1 Malartic, Lac l. Que. Can.
158 D2 Malaryta Belarus
198 E1 Malá Skála Czech Rep.
115 A6 Malasoro, Teluk b. Indon.
283 D7 Malaspina Arg.
245 L4 Malaspina Glacier AK U.S.A.
246 E5 Malaspina Strait B.C. Can.
201 O7 Mala Subotica Croatia
117 J6 Malatayur, Tanjung pt Indon.
159 O5 Mala Ternivka r. Ukr.
148 I4 Malatya Turkey
183 G8 Malaucène France
178 B4 Malaunay France
185 D8 Malaussanne France

138 E4 Malaut Punjab India
136 E6 Malavalli Karnataka India
275 H4 Malavate Fr. Guiana
144 B5 Malāvī Iran
158 J4 Mala Vil'shanka Ukr.
159 K5 Mala Vyska Ukr.
229 H3 Malawa Niger
117 L1 Malawali i. Malaysia
196 F3 Mała Wełna r. Pol.
233 B7 Malawi country Africa
Malawi, Lake Africa see Nyasa, Lake
Malawi National Park Zambia see Nyika National Park
225 H6 Malawiya Sudan
162 P5 Malax Fin.
Malaya pen. Malaysia see Malaysia, Semenanjung
151 H1 Malaya Areshevka Rus. Fed.
160 G8 Malaya Byerastavitsa Belarus
156 K2 Malaya Pera Rus. Fed.
161 P3 Malaya Vishera Rus. Fed.
114 E7 Malaybalay Mindanao Phil.
144 C4 Malāyer Iran
178 F7 Malay-le-Grand France
107 L4 Malay Reef Coral Sea Is Terr. Austr.
143 Q5 Malaysary Kazakh.
116 H3 Malaysia country Asia
116 E3 Malaysia, Semenanjung pen. Malaysia
149 K4 Malazgirt Turkey
249 G4 Malbaie r. Que. Can.
284 B5 Malbarco, Laguna l. Arg.
229 G3 Malbaza Niger
106 H6 Malbon Qld Austr.
197 H1 Malbork Pol.
194 B2 Malborn Ger.
183 C7 Malbouzon France
282 E3 Malbrán Arg.
182 I3 Malbuisson France
204 F8 Malcata, Serra de mts Port.
213 J4 Malcesine Italy
159 T4 Mal'chevskaya Rus. Fed.
192 G3 Malchin Ger.
192 G3 Malchiner See l. Ger.
192 F4 Malchow Ger.
199 K3 Malčice Slovakia
206 H4 Malcocinado Spain
109 F10 Malcolm W.A. Austr.
109 G12 Malcolm, Point W.A. Austr.
Malcolm Inlet Oman see Ghazira, Ghubbat al
168 D10 Malcolm's Point Scotland U.K.
199 K2 Malcov Slovakia
196 E4 Malczyce Pol.
139 L7 Maldah W. Bengal India
187 D6 Maldegem Belgium
186 I5 Malden Neth.
261 K7 Malden MO U.S.A.
291 I6 Malden Island Kiribati
208 G2 Malditos, Montes mts Spain
214 A8 Mal di Ventre, Isola di i. Sardegna Italy
135 D10 Maldives country Indian Ocean
105 J7 Maldon Vic. Austr.
173 N4 Maldon Essex, England U.K.
282 G4 Maldonado Uru.
269 I9 Maldonado, Punta pt Mex.
197 H2 Małdyty Pol.
239 □[3a] Male Njazidja Comoros
213 J3 Malè Italy
135 □[1] Male N. Male Maldives
118 C3 Male Myanmar
228 C4 Maléa Guinea
220 E6 Maleas, Akrotirio pt Greece
135 □[1] Male Atoll Maldives
237 J4 Malebogo S. Africa
196 E1 Malechowo Pol.
136 E3 Malegaon Mahar. India
138 E9 Malegaon Mahar. India
235 H3 Malei Moz.
205 Q5 Maleján Spain
232 A3 Malek Sudan
144 E5 Malek, Chāh-e well Iran
198 G3 Malé Karpaty hills Slovakia
198 G3 Malé Karpaty park Slovakia
237 M6 Malekgonyane Wildlife Reserve nature res. S. Africa
144 D6 Māl-e Khalīfeh Iran
144 F6 Malek Mīrzā, Chāh-e well Iran
144 I7 Malek Sīāh Kūh mt. Afgh.
230 E5 Malela Maniema Dem. Rep. Congo
231 E6 Malela Maniema Dem. Rep. Congo
231 B6 Malélé Congo
231 B6 Malele Dem. Rep. Congo
235 H2 Malema Moz.
231 E7 Malemba Nkulu Dem. Rep. Congo
183 G8 Malemort-du-Comtat France
184 H5 Malemort-sur-Corrèze France
229 G4 Malendo watercourse Nigeria
190 K2 Malente Ger.
237 N1 Maleoskop S. Africa
165 L5 Målerås Sweden
138 E4 Maler Kotla Punjab India
212 F3 Malesco Italy
219 K9 Maleševske Planine mts Bulg./Macedonia
178 D7 Malesherbes France
220 E4 Malesina Greece
Malesso' Guam see Merizo
145 L5 Mālestān Afgh.
180 G6 Malestroit France
129 K1 Maleta Rus. Fed.
216 H8 Maletto Sicilia Italy
100 □[6] Malevangga Choiseul Solomon Is
161 V8 Malevka Rus. Fed.
216 H6 Malfa Isole Lipari Italy
236 E10 Malgas S. Africa
195 N4 Malgersdorf Ger.
151 F2 Malgobek Rus. Fed.
162 N4 Malgomaj l. Sweden
208 K4 Malgrat de Mar Spain
224 E6 Malha Sudan
278 E5 Malhada Brazil
204 H5 Malhadas Port.
146 H3 Malham Saudi Arabia
138 E7 Malhargarh Madh. Prad. India
262 F4 Malheur r. OR U.S.A.
239 □[1b] Malheureux, Cape Mauritius
262 E5 Malheur Lake OR U.S.A.
262 E5 Malheur National Wildlife Refuge nature res. OR U.S.A.
228 D3 Mali country Africa
230 E5 Mali Dem. Rep. Congo
228 B3 Mali Guinea
221 G7 Malia Kriti Greece
220 D4 Maliakos Kolpos b. Greece
122 G4 Malian Heilong. China
115 D8 Maliana East Timor
129 J9 Malian He r. China
128 D6 Malianjing Gansu China
128 G7 Malianjing Gansu China
237 M5 Malibamatso r. Lesotho
264 N7 Malibu CA U.S.A.
181 K6 Malicorne-sur-Sarthe France
114 D8 Maligay Bay Mindanao Phil.
178 G8 Maligny France
133 E13 Malihabad Uttar Prad. India
118 C2 Mali Hka r. Myanmar
199 I6 Mali Iđoš Vojvodina Serbia
183 I8 Malijai France
145 M5 Malikdin Afgh.
145 J7 Malik Naro mt. Pak.
115 C4 Maliku Sulawesi Indon.
119 D8 Mali Kyun i. Myanmar
115 B5 Malili Sulawesi Indon.
165 L4 Målilla Sweden
210 E3 Mali Lošinj Croatia
284 C1 Malimán de Abajo Arg.
231 F6 Malimba, Monts mts Dem. Rep. Congo
197 L6 Mali Mokryany Ukr.
116 G8 Malimping Jawa Indon.
169 H2 Malin Ireland
Malin Ukr. see Malyn
158 E1 Malinawka Belarus
Malin Beg Ireland see Málainn Bhig
233 D5 Malindi Kenya
235 E3 Malindi Zimbabwe

199 I3 Málinec Slovakia
Malines Belgium see Mechelen
129 J8 Maling Gansu China
230 B5 Malinga Gabon
169 H2 Malin Head Ireland
219 O3 Mălini Romania
Malin More Ireland see Málainn Mhóir
115 A6 Malino Sulawesi Indon.
161 V6 Malino Rus. Fed.
115 B3 Malino, Gunung mt. Indon.
101 □[8a] Malinoa i. Tonga
143 N2 Malinovka Kazakh.
122 H6 Malinovka r. Rus. Fed.
143 R2 Malinovoye Ozero Rus. Fed.
213 R5 Malinska Croatia
233 C7 Malinyi Tanz.
221 G7 Malion, Kolpos b. Kriti Greece
130 E7 Malipo Yunnan China
220 B2 Maliq Albania
210 E3 Mali Raginac mt. Croatia
218 I8 Malit, Qafa e pass Albania
114 E8 Malita Mindanao Phil.
114 E6 Malitbog Leyte Phil.
119 D9 Maliwun Myanmar
138 C8 Maliya Gujarat India
159 L6 Maliyivka Ukr.
218 H6 Mali Zvornik Mali Zvornik Serbia
151 E2 Malka Rus. Fed.
151 F2 Malka r. Rus. Fed.
144 B5 Malkaili Iran
232 D3 Malka Mari Kenya
136 G3 Malkangiri Orissa India
136 C4 Malkapur Mahar. India
138 F9 Malkapur Mahar. India
221 H2 Malkara Turkey
160 J9 Mal'kavichy Belarus
129 K1 Malkhanskiy Khrebet mts Rus. Fed.
197 K3 Małkinia Górna Pol.
219 P9 Malko Tŭrnovo Bulg.
105 L7 Mallacoota Vic. Austr.
105 L7 Mallacoota Inlet b. Vic. Austr.
168 E9 Mallaig Highland, Scotland U.K.
224 D5 Mallanga well Chad
138 C7 Mallani reg. India
225 F3 Mallawī Egypt
105 I6 Mallee Cliffs National Park N.S.W. Austr.
183 G9 Mallemort France
205 R5 Mallén Spain
192 D3 Mallentin Ger.
212 H3 Mallero r. Italy
195 M4 Mallersdorf Ger.
247 L1 Mallery Lake Nunavut Can.
213 J2 Malles Venosta Italy
279 C8 Mallét Brazil
Mallia Kriti Greece see Malia
192 D4 Mallíß Ger.
200 H6 Mallnitz Austria
284 B4 Malloa Chile
209 K8 Mallorca i. Spain
169 E8 Mallow Ireland
108 H7 Mallowa Well W.A. Austr.
172 D1 Malltraeth Bay Wales U.K.
172 E2 Mallwyd Gwynedd, Wales U.K.
162 K4 Malm Norway
145 J5 Malman Rūd r. Afgh.
162 P3 Malmberget Sweden
187 J8 Malmédy Belgium
236 C9 Malmesbury S. Africa
172 H4 Malmesbury Wiltshire, England U.K.
165 M2 Malmköping Sweden
164 J6 Malmö Sweden
271 □[8] Malmok hd Bonaire Neth. Antilles
164 J6 Malmö-Sturup airport Sweden
165 L3 Malmslätt Sweden
156 J4 Malmyzh Rus. Fed.
212 F4 Malnate Italy
108 J4 Malngin Aboriginal Land res. Australia
115 E1 Malo i. Indon.
213 K4 Malo Italy
100 □[5] Malo i. Vanuatu
161 T9 Maloarkhangel'sk Rus. Fed.
275 F5 Maloca Amazonas Brazil
275 H4 Maloca Pará Brazil
277 E3 Maloca Salamaim Brazil
218 J6 Malo Crniće Malo Crniće Serbia
197 I5 Małogoszcz Pol.
101 □[7a] Malolo Barrier Reef Fiji
101 □[7a] Malolo Lailai i. Fiji
114 C4 Malolos Luzon Phil.
237 P2 Malolotja Nature Reserve Swaziland
237 P3 Maloma Swaziland
233 B8 Malombe, Lake Malawi
196 D4 Małomice Pol.
233 B8 Malomo Malawi
159 N5 Malomykhaylivka Dnipropetrovs'ka Oblast' Ukr.
159 P5 Malomykhaylivka Dnipropetrovs'ka Oblast' Ukr.
205 Q5 Malón Spain
212 D5 Malone r. Italy
257 K4 Malone NY U.S.A.
130 D6 Malong Yunnan China
231 D7 Malonga Dem. Rep. Congo
234 B2 Malongo Angola
212 I3 Malonno Italy
198 D3 Malonty Czech Rep.
197 I5 Małopolska, Wyżyna hills Pol.
197 I6 Małopolskie prov. Pol.
159 N9 Malorichens'ke Ukr.
Malorita Belarus see Malaryta
156 G3 Maloshuyka Rus. Fed.
210 F4 Malovan pass Bos.-Herz.
219 K6 Malovăț Romania
Malovata Moldova see Molovata
143 Q6 Malovodnoye Kazakh.
235 F2 Malowera Moz.
163 H6 Måløy Norway
161 T6 Maloyaroslavets Rus. Fed.
161 S9 Maloye Bobrovo Rus. Fed.
161 T2 Maloye Borisovo Rus. Fed.
197 I1 Maloye-Lugovoye Rus. Fed.
156 J2 Malozemel'skaya Tundra lowland Rus. Fed.
238 □[3d] Malpaises La Palma Canary Is
204 G7 Malpartida Port.
206 G2 Malpartida de Cáceres Spain
206 H3 Malpartida de la Serena Spain
204 H9 Malpartida de Plasencia Spain
171 L7 Malpas Cheshire, England U.K.
172 F4 Malpas Newport, Wales U.K.
238 □[3e] Malpaso mt. El Hierro Canary Is
268 E3 Malpaso Mex.
291 N5 Malpelo, Isla de i. N. Pacific Ocean
204 H1 Mal Perro, Punta pt Spain
204 C2 Malpica Spain
205 K9 Malpica de Tajo Spain
204 F9 Malpica do Tejo Port.
160 H4 Mālpils Latvia
136 E4 Malprabha r. India
138 E6 Malpura Rajasthan India
194 E4 Malsch Ger.
198 D3 Malše r. Czech Rep.
191 I8 Malsfeld Ger.
136 D4 Malsiras Mahar. India
201 I6 Malta Austria
211 E8 Malta country Europe
160 K5 Malta Latvia
160 K5 Malta r. Latvia
217 □ Malta i. Malta
204 F7 Malta Port.
262 H5 Malta ID U.S.A.
262 K2 Malta MT U.S.A.
234 C5 Maltahöhe Namibia
229 I3 Maltam Cameroon
171 O7 Maltby South Yorkshire, England U.K.
171 R7 Maltby le Marsh Lincolnshire, England U.K.
194 D5 Malterdingen Ger.
194 E7 Malters Switz.
162 T3 Maltion luonnonpuisto nature res. Fin.
171 P5 Malton North Yorkshire, England U.K.
100 □[2] Malua Samoa
205 Q6 Maluenda Spain
Maluera Moz. see Malowera
Malukken is Indon. see Maluku

231 B6 **Maluku** Dem. Rep. Congo
115 E4 **Maluku** *is* Indon.
115 E3 **Maluku** *is* Indon.
115 F5 **Maluku** *prov.* Indon.
115 D4 **Maluku, Laut** *sea* Indon.
115 E4 **Maluku Utara** *prov.* Indon.
150 E5 **Ma'lūlā, Jabal** *mts* Syria
219 K4 **Malului, Vârful** *hill* Romania
229 G4 **Malumfashi** Nigeria
231 E9 **Malundano** Zambia
231 D8 **Malundo** Angola
165 J1 **Malung** Sweden
196 D3 **Małuszów** Pol.
197 H5 **Maluszyn** Pol.
237 M5 **Maluti Mountains** Lesotho
100 □[6] **Malu'u** *Malaita* Solomon Is
228 E4 **Maluwe** Ghana
205 J5 **Malva** Spain
212 F3 **Malvaglia** Switz.
136 C4 **Malvan** *Mahar.* India
Malvasia Greece *see* **Monemvasia**
206 A3 **Malveira** Port.
270 □ **Malvern** Jamaica
270 □ **Malvern** *hill* Jamaica
Malvern *Worcestershire, England* U.K. *see* **Great Malvern**
261 I8 **Malvern** *AR* U.S.A.
256 D8 **Malvern** *OH* U.S.A.
Malvérnia Moz. *see* **Chicualacuala**
172 H3 **Malvern Link** *Worcestershire, England* U.K.
Malvinas, Islas *terr.* S. Atlantic Ocean *see* **Falkland Islands**
138 F8 **Malwa** *reg. Madh. Prad.* India
232 A2 **Malwal** Sudan
193 J7 **Malxe** *r.* Ger.
199 H4 **Malý Dunaj** *r.* Slovakia
197 M3 **Malyech** Belarus
199 K3 **Malý Horeš** Slovakia
199 J3 **Mályi** Hungary
153 M3 **Malykay** Rus. Fed.
158 I3 **Malyn** Ukr.
159 P4 **Malynivka** Ukr.
158 F2 **Malyns'k** Ukr.
197 K2 **Mały Płock** Pol.
160 L1 **Malyy, Ostrov** *i.* Rus. Fed.
153 R3 **Malyy Anyuy** *r.* Rus. Fed.
199 L3 **Malyy Bereznyy** Ukr.
157 I7 **Malyye Derbety** Rus. Fed.
Malyye Kotyuzhany Moldova *see* **Cotiujenii Mici**
161 X4 **Malyye Soli** Rus. Fed.
157 J5 **Malyy Irgiz** *r.* Rus. Fed.
Malyy Kavkaz *mts* Asia *see* **Lesser Caucasus**
129 J1 **Malyy Kunaley** Rus. Fed.
153 P2 **Malyy Lyakhovskiy, Ostrov** *i. Novosibirskiye O-va* Rus. Fed.
158 F2 **Malyy Stydyn** Ukr.
153 L2 **Malyy Taymyr, Ostrov** *i.* Rus. Fed.
160 J2 **Malyy Tyuters, Ostrov** *i.* Estonia
142 C3 **Malyy Uzen'** *r.* Kazakh./Rus. Fed.
151 C1 **Malyy Zelenchuk** *r.* Rus. Fed.
156 J5 **Mamadysh** Rus. Fed.
237 M3 **Mamafubedu** S. Africa
237 L4 **Mamahabane** S. Africa
101 □[7] **Mamanuca-i-Cake Group** *is* Fiji
Mamanutha-i-Thake Group *is* Fiji *see* **Mamanuca-i-Cake Group**
102 H2 **Mamaranui** *North I.* N.Z.
259 H3 **Mamaroneck** *NY* U.S.A.
115 A5 **Mamasa** *Sulawesi Barat* Indon.
145 K6 **Mamatān Nāvar** *l.* Afgh.
144 C6 **Māmātīn** Iran
133 K11 **Mamba** *Xizang* China
Mamba Japan *see* **Manba**
114 B8 **Mambahenauhan** *i.* Phil.
278 D5 **Mambai** Brazil
114 E7 **Mambajao** Phil.
229 I5 **Mambal** Cameroon
233 B6 **Mambali** Tanz.
106 E4 **Mambaliya-Rrumburriya Wuyaliya Aboriginal Land** *res. N.T.* Australia
230 F4 **Mambasa** Dem. Rep. Congo
230 C4 **Mambéré** *r.* C.A.R.
230 B3 **Mambéré-Kadéï** *pref.* C.A.R.
115 A5 **Mambi** *Sulawesi Barat* Indon.
229 H5 **Mambila Mountains** Cameroon/Nigeria
230 C4 **Mambili** *r.* Congo
228 B4 **Mambolo** Sierra Leone
280 A6 **Mamborê** Brazil
205 M5 **Mambrilla de Castejón** Spain
233 D5 **Mambrui** Kenya
114 C5 **Mamburao** *Mindoro* Phil.
151 J3 **Mamedkala** Rus. Fed.
239 □[2a] **Mamelle** *i. Inner Islands* Seychelles
237 M1 **Mamelodi** S. Africa
181 L5 **Mamers** France
229 H5 **Mamfe** Cameroon
275 F6 **Mamiá** Brazil
275 F6 **Mamiá, Lago** *l.* Brazil
234 D3 **Mamili National Park** Namibia
276 C5 **Mamiña** Chile
274 E5 **Mamirauá, Reserve de Desenvolvimento Sustentával** *nature res.* Brazil
182 I2 **Mamirolle** France
151 E3 **Mamison Pass** Georgia/Rus. Fed.
139 N8 **Mamit** *Mizoram* India
143 M1 **Mamlyutka** Kazakh.
151 H6 **Mämmädbäyli** Azer.
195 K5 **Mammendorf** Ger.
195 N4 **Mamming** Ger.
217 K7 **Mammola** Italy
265 V9 **Mammoth** *AZ* U.S.A.
254 D7 **Mammoth Cave National Park** *KY* U.S.A.
264 N4 **Mammoth Lakes** *CA* U.S.A.
264 M4 **Mammoth Reservoir** *CA* U.S.A.
214 C7 **Mamoiada** *Sardegna* Italy
270 F8 **Mamonal** Col.
214 C6 **Mamone** *Sardegna* Italy
160 C7 **Mamonovo** *Kaliningradskaya Oblast'* Rus. Fed.
161 W8 **Mamonovo** *Ryazanskaya Oblast'* Rus. Fed.
143 S1 **Mamontovo** Rus. Fed.
258 F6 **Mamora** *NJ* U.S.A.
276 D2 **Mamoré** *r.* Bol./Brazil
274 E5 **Mamori** Brazil
275 F5 **Mamori, Lago** *l.* Brazil
276 D1 **Mamoriá** Brazil
228 B4 **Mamou** Guinea
239 □[3b] **Mamoudzou** Mayotte
Mamoutsou Mayotte *see* **Mamoudzou**
235 □J3 **Mampikony** Madag.
228 E5 **Mampong** Ghana
236 C9 **Mamre** S. Africa
197 J1 **Mamry, Jezioro** *l.* Pol.
115 A5 **Mamuju** *Sulawesi Barat* Indon.
147 L6 **Ma'mūl** Oman
104 B3 **Mamungari Conservation Park** *nature res. S.A.* Austr.
144 D4 **Māmūnīyeh** Iran
234 D4 **Mamuno** Botswana
218 H9 **Mamuras** Albania
124 R8 **Mamurogawa** Japan
Mamutzu Mayotte *see* **Mamoudzou**
142 H2 **Mamyt** Kazakh.
228 D5 **Man** Côte d'Ivoire
136 D4 **Man** *r.* India
138 G3 **Man** *Jammu and Kashmir* India
256 D11 **Man** *WV* U.S.A.
170 H5 **Man, Isle of** *i.* Irish Sea
101 □[7a] **Mana** *i.* Fiji
275 H3 **Mana** Fr. Guiana
199 H3 **Maňa** Slovakia
264 □B11 **Mānā** *HI* U.S.A.
274 C2 **Mana Bárbara** Venez.
274 B5 **Manabí** *prov.* Ecuador
274 C3 **Manacacias** *r.* Col.
275 F5 **Manacapuru** Brazil
209 L8 **Manacor** Spain
238 □[1c] **Manadas** *São Jorge* Azores
115 D3 **Manado** *Sulawesi* Indon.
115 D3 **Manadotua** *i.* Indon.
187 F8 **Manage** Belgium
266 □P11 **Managua** Nic.
266 □P11 **Managua, Lago de** *l.* Nic.
147 M4 **Manaḩ** Oman
259 G5 **Manahawkin Bay** *NJ* U.S.A.
102 I6 **Manaia** *North I.* N.Z.
235 □J4 **Manakara** Madag.
102 J7 **Manakau** *North I.* N.Z.
103 H9 **Manakau** *mt. South I.* N.Z.
146 F8 **Manākhah** Yemen
138 F3 **Manali** *Hima. Prad.* India
Manama Bahrain *see* **Al Manāmah**
136 F8 **Manamadurai** *Tamil Nadu* India
235 □J3 **Manambaho** *r.* Madag.
235 □J4 **Manambondro** Madag.
136 F7 **Manamelkudi** *Tamil Nadu* India
113 K7 **Manam Island** P.N.G.
275 F2 **Manamo, Caño** *r.* Venez.
114 C6 **Manamoc** *i.* Phil.
264 □D12 **Mānana** *i. HI* U.S.A.
235 □J4 **Mananantañana** *r.* Madag.
235 □J4 **Mananara** *r.* Madag.
235 □K3 **Mananara, Parc National de** *nat. park* Madag.
235 □K3 **Mananara Avaratra** Madag.
105 I6 **Manangatang** *Vic.* Austr.
106 F4 **Manangoora** *N.T.* Austr.
235 □K4 **Mananjary** Madag.
235 □J5 **Manankoliva** Madag.
228 D4 **Manankoro** Mali
228 C3 **Manantali, Lac de** *l.* Mali
235 □J5 **Manantenina** Madag.
136 E7 **Mananthavady** *Kerala* India
268 C6 **Manantlán, Sierra** *mts* Mex.
136 F4 **Mananur** *Andhra Prad.* India
100 □[6] **Manaoba Island** Solomon Is
133 D11 **Mana Pass** China/India
235 F3 **Mana Pools National Park** Zimbabwe
103 B12 **Manapouri** *South I.* N.Z.
103 B12 **Manapouri, Lake** *South I.* N.Z.
136 F7 **Manapparai** *Tamil Nadu* India
235 □J3 **Manarantsandry** Madag.
205 O2 **Mañaria** Spain
132 H4 **Manas** *Xinjiang* China
139 M6 **Manas** *r.* India
164 J1 **Månäs** Sweden
143 N6 **Manas, Gora** *mt.* Uzbek.
138 E7 **Manasa** *Madh. Prad.* India
151 I3 **Manasaul** Rus. Fed.
132 G4 **Manas He** *r.* China
132 H4 **Manas Hu** *l.* China
147 K4 **Manāşīr** *reg.* U.A.E.
151 I3 **Manaskent** Rus. Fed.
139 J5 **Manaslu** *mt.* Nepal
139 J5 **Manaslu Conservation Area** *nature res.* Nepal
259 G4 **Manasquan** *NJ* U.S.A.
259 G4 **Manasquan** *r. NJ* U.S.A.
256 H10 **Manassas** *VA* U.S.A.
Manastir Macedonia *see* **Bitola**
199 L6 **Mănăștiur** Romania
139 M6 **Manas Wildlife Sanctuary** *nature res.* Bhutan
115 D8 **Manatang** Indon.
271 □[1] **Manatí** Puerto Rico
271 □[1] **Manati, Río Grande de** *r.* Puerto Rico
238 □[2b] **Manati Bay** St Helena
127 J5 **Manatsuru** Japan
115 D8 **Manatuto** East Timor
118 A5 **Man-aung** Myanmar
118 A5 **Man-aung Kyun** *i.* Myanmar
275 F5 **Manaus** Brazil
148 E5 **Manavgat** Turkey
250 F5 **Manawa** *WI* U.S.A.
138 E8 **Manawar** *Madh. Prad.* India
102 J4 **Manawaru** *North I.* N.Z.
224 E6 **Manawashei** Sudan
102 J7 **Manawatu** *r. North I.* N.Z.
102 J6 **Manawatu-Wanganui** *admin. reg. North I.* N.Z.
114 F8 **Manay** *Mindanao* Phil.
161 T8 **Manayenki** Rus. Fed.
127 J5 **Manazuru-misaki** *pt* Japan
127 I3 **Manba** Japan
139 K8 **Manbazar** *W. Bengal* India
150 F2 **Manbij** Syria
171 R7 **Manby** *Lincolnshire, England* U.K.
181 K5 **Mancelles, Alpes** *hills* France
250 I5 **Mancelona** *MI* U.S.A.
205 J7 **Mancera de Abajo** Spain
136 C3 **Manchar** *Mahar.* India
207 L5 **Mancha Real** Spain
180 I4 **Manche** *dept* France
270 □ **Manchester** *parish* Jamaica
171 M7 **Manchester** *Greater Manchester, England* U.K.
257 M7 **Manchester** *CT* U.S.A.
260 J4 **Manchester** *IA* U.S.A.
256 B11 **Manchester** *KY* U.S.A.
258 B5 **Manchester** *MD* U.S.A.
251 J7 **Manchester** *MI* U.S.A.
257 N6 **Manchester** *NH* U.S.A.
256 B10 **Manchester** *OH* U.S.A.
258 B4 **Manchester** *PA* U.S.A.
255 D8 **Manchester** *TN* U.S.A.
257 L5 **Manchester** *VT* U.S.A.
145 L8 **Manchhar Lake** Pak.
195 K4 **Manching** Ger.
270 □ **Manchioneal** Jamaica
206 G3 **Manchita** Spain
Manchuria *reg. Heilong.* China *see* **Dongbei**
214 H2 **Manciano** Italy
185 E8 **Manciet** France
148 H4 **Mancılık** Turkey
221 I3 **Mancınık Dağı** *mts* Turkey
263 J8 **Mancos** *CO* U.S.A.
265 X5 **Mancos** *r. CO* U.S.A.
145 J8 **Mand** Pak.
144 D7 **Mand, Rūd-e** *r.* Iran
139 L7 **Manda** Bangl.
233 B7 **Manda** Malawi
233 B6 **Manda** Tanz.
230 E2 **Manda, Jebel** *mt.* Sudan
230 C2 **Manda, Parc National de** *nat. park* Chad
235 □J4 **Mandabe** Madag.
280 A5 **Mandaguaçu** Brazil
280 B5 **Mandaguari** Brazil
116 E5 **Mandah** *Sumatera* Indon.
129 K4 **Mandah** Mongolia
116 □ **Mandai** Sing.
138 C8 **Mandal** *Gujarat* India
138 E7 **Mandal** *Rajasthan* India
Mandal Mongolia *see* **Orhon**
Mandal Mongolia *see* **Batsümber**
164 D3 **Mandal** Norway
113 J7 **Mandala, Puncak** *mt. Papua* Indon.
118 C4 **Mandalay** Myanmar
118 B4 **Mandalay** *admin. div.* Myanmar
Mandale Myanmar *see* **Mandalay**
Mandale *admin. div.* Myanmar *see* **Mandalay**
114 D6 **Mandalgan, Mount** *vol.* Phil.
138 E7 **Mandalgarh** *Rajasthan* India
128 J4 **Mandalgovĭ** Mongolia
149 L7 **Mandalī** Iraq
128 I4 **Mandal-Ovoo** Mongolia
164 D3 **Mandalselva** *r.* Norway
129 M5 **Mandalt** *Nei Mongol* China
129 M4 **Mandalt Sum** *Nei Mongol* China
260 E2 **Mandan** *ND* U.S.A.
217 I7 **Mandanici** *Sicilia* Italy
114 D5 **Mandaon** *Masbate* Phil.
229 H3 **Mandaoua Soumounti** *well* Niger
136 F8 **Mandapam** *Tamil Nadu* India
115 A5 **Mandar, Teluk** *b.* Indon.
214 C8 **Mandas** *Sardegna* Italy
217 L5 **Mandatoriccio** Italy
138 C8 **Mandav Hills** *Gujarat* India
145 P7 **Mandawa** *Rajasthan* India
205 O7 **Mandayona** Spain
182 F4 **Mandé, Mont de** *hill* France
Mandeghughusu *i. New Georgia Is* Solomon Is *see* **Simbo**
145 I5 **Mandel** Afgh.
194 C3 **Mandelbachtal-Ormesheim** Ger.
183 J9 **Mandelieu-la-Napoule** France
212 G4 **Mandello del Lario** Italy
204 D2 **Mandeo** *r.* Spain
232 D4 **Mandera** Kenya
265 T3 **Manderfield** *UT* U.S.A.
191 C10 **Manderscheid** Ger.
182 J2 **Mandeure** France
270 □ **Mandeville** Jamaica
103 C12 **Mandeville** *South I.* N.Z.
138 C6 **Mandha** *Rajasthan* India
232 E2 **Mandheera** Somalia
Mandhoúdhíon Greece *see* **Mantoudi**
138 F4 **Mandi** *Hima. Prad.* India
228 D3 **Mandiakui** Mali
228 C4 **Mandiana** Guinea
116 E2 **Mandi Angin, Gunung** *mt.* Malaysia
Mandidzuzure Zimbabwe *see* **Chimanimani**
235 G3 **Mandié** Moz.
235 G2 **Mandimba** Moz.
269 K6 **Mandinga Grande, Laguna** *l.* Mex.
228 C3 **Mandingues, Monts** *mts* Mali
115 E4 **Mandioli** *i. Maluku* Indon.
285 H2 **Mandisoví** Arg.
230 A5 **Mandji** Gabon
138 H8 **Mandla** *Madh. Prad.* India
199 L3 **Mándok** Hungary
138 D6 **Mandor** *Rajasthan* India
117 H4 **Mandor** *Kalimantan* Indon.
117 H4 **Mandor, Cagar Alam** *nature res.* Indon.
108 F5 **Mandora** *W.A.* Austr.
106 C2 **Mandorah** *N.T.* Austr.
230 F3 **Mandoro** Dem. Rep. Congo
235 □J3 **Mandoro** Madag.
229 F4 **Mandouri** Togo
220 E4 **Mandra** Greece
138 F6 **Mandrael** *Rajasthan* India
221 I6 **Mandraki** Greece
235 □J5 **Mandrare** *r.* Madag.
Mandrenska *r.* Bulg. *see* **Sredetska Reka**
179 J7 **Mandres-en-Barrois** France
235 □K2 **Mandritsara** Madag.
235 □J4 **Mandrosonoro** Madag.
159 R3 **Mandrovo** Rus. Fed.
138 E7 **Mandsaur** *Madh. Prad.* India
183 E9 **Manduel** France
117 L3 **Mandul** *i.* Indon.
109 C12 **Mandurah** *W.A.* Austr.
217 N3 **Manduria** Italy
138 B8 **Mandvi** *Gujarat* India
138 D9 **Mandvi** *Gujarat* India
136 E6 **Mandya** *Karnataka* India
239 □[3a] **Mandza** *Njazidja* Comoros
185 F9 **Mane** *Midi-Pyrénées* France
183 H9 **Mane** *Provence-Alpes-Côte d'Azur* France
164 E2 **Måne** *r.* Norway
173 M3 **Manea** *Cambridgeshire, England* U.K.
191 K9 **Manebach** Ger.
138 C9 **Manekwara** *Gujarat* India
144 G3 **Maneli** Iran
100 □[1] **Manell Point** Guam
138 I8 **Manendragarh** *Chhattisgarh* India
139 J7 **Maner** *Bihar* India
136 F3 **Maner** *r.* India
212 I5 **Manerbio** Italy
233 C6 **Maneromango** Tanz.
205 Q3 **Mañeru** Spain
144 B5 **Manesht Kūh** *mt.* Iran
219 N6 **Mănești** Romania
198 C2 **Manětín** Czech Rep.
Maneva Madag. *see* **Mahaboboka**
158 E2 **Manevychi** Ukr.
225 F3 **Manfalūţ** Egypt
215 P4 **Manfredonia** Italy
215 Q4 **Manfredonia, Golfo di** *g.* Italy
278 E5 **Manga** Brazil
228 E4 **Manga** Burkina
278 D4 **Mangabeiras, Serra das** *hills* Brazil
231 B6 **Manga Grande** Angola
231 C6 **Mangai** Dem. Rep. Congo
231 C5 **Mangai, Réserve de Faune des Hippopotames de** *nature res.* Dem. Rep. Congo
103 □[2] **Mangaia** *i.* Cook Is
102 J5 **Mangakino** *North I.* N.Z.
136 G4 **Mangalagiri** *Andhra Prad.* India
139 N6 **Mangaldai** *Assam* India
219 Q7 **Mangalia** Romania
224 C6 **Mangalmé** Chad
136 D6 **Mangalore** *Karnataka* India
145 M4 **Mangalpur** Afgh.
136 D4 **Mangalvedha** *Mahar.* India
103 H9 **Mangamaunu** *South I.* N.Z.
102 I6 **Mangamingi** *North I.* N.Z.
102 H2 **Mangamuka** *North I.* N.Z.
204 I5 **Manganeses de la Lampreana** Spain
204 I4 **Manganeses de la Polvorosa** Spain
230 D4 **Mangania** Dem. Rep. Congo
102 H2 **Manganui** *r. North I.* N.Z.
136 C3 **Mangaon** *Mahar.* India
136 G3 **Mangapet** *Andhra Prad.* India
102 G7 **Mangarakau** *South I.* N.Z.
281 E5 **Mangaratiba** Brazil
101 □[9] **Mangareva** *i. Arch. des Tuamotu* Fr. Polynesia
Mangareva Islands *Arch. des Tuamotu* Fr. Polynesia *see* **Gambier, Îles**
106 D3 **Mangarrayi Aboriginal Land** *res.* Australia
102 J7 **Mangatainoka** *North I.* N.Z.
102 J4 **Mangatawhiri** *North I.* N.Z.
237 K5 **Mangaung** S. Africa
138 H7 **Mangawan** *Madh. Prad.* India
102 J6 **Mangaweka** *North I.* N.Z.
102 K6 **Mangaweka** *mt. North I.* N.Z.
102 I3 **Mangawhai** *North I.* N.Z.
Mangde Chhu *r.* Bhutan *see* **Trongsa Chhu**
Ma'ngê *Gansu* China *see* **Luqu**
Mangea *i.* Cook Is *see* **Mangaia**
231 E6 **Mangembe** Dem. Rep. Congo
163 H6 **Manger** Norway
102 □ **Mangere Island** *Chatham Is* S. Pacific Ocean
169 D9 **Mangerton Mountain** *hill* Ireland
195 M6 **Mangfall** *r.* Ger.
195 L6 **Mangfallgebirge** *mts* Ger.
117 H6 **Manggar** Indon.
100 □[6] **Manggautu** *Rennell* Solomon Is
Mangghyshlaq Kazakh. *see* **Mangystau**
Mangghystaū Kazakh. *see* **Mangystau**
Mangghystaū Oblysy *admin. div.* Kazakh. *see* **Mangistauskaya Oblast'**
Mangghyt Uzbek. *see* **Mang'it**
Manghit Uzbek. *see* **Mang'it**
179 K5 **Mangiennes** France
100 □[1] **Mangilao** Guam
142 F6 **Mangistauskaya Oblast'** *admin. div.* Kazakh.
142 I6 **Mang'it** Uzbek.
117 M4 **Mangkalihat, Tanjung** *pt* Indon.
106 B6 **Mangkururrpa Aboriginal Land** *res. N.T.* Austr.
117 K6 **Mangkutup** *r.* Indon.
118 D1 **Mangkyi** Myanmar
145 O5 **Mangla** Pak.
274 B4 **Manglares, Punta** *pt* Col.
151 F4 **Manglisi** Georgia
133 J8 **Mangnai** *Qinghai* China
133 J7 **Mangnai Zhen** *Qinghai* China
235 □K2 **Mangoaka** Madag.
233 B8 **Mangochi** Malawi
228 D4 **Mangodara** Burkina
235 □I4 **Mangoky** *r. Toliara* Madag.
235 □J4 **Mangoky** *r. Toliara* Madag.
115 D4 **Mangole** *i.* Indon.
115 D5 **Mangole, Selat** *sea chan.* Indon.
136 D4 **Mangoli** *Karnataka* India
235 □I4 **Mangolovolo** Madag.
230 E5 **Mangombe** Dem. Rep. Congo
102 H2 **Mangonui** *North I.* N.Z.
235 □K3 **Mangoro** *r.* Madag.
172 G5 **Mangotsfield** *South Gloucestershire, England* U.K.
Mangqystaū Shyghanaghy *b.* Kazakh. *see* **Mangyshlakskiy Zaliv**
Mangra *Qinghai* China *see* **Guinan**
138 C9 **Mangrol** *Gujarat* India
138 F7 **Mangrol** *Rajasthan* India
255 H12 **Mangrove Cay** *i.* Bahamas
138 F9 **Mangrul** *Mahar.* India
204 E7 **Mangualde** Port.
274 D5 **Manguari** Brazil
145 L7 **Manguchar** Pak.
230 D2 **Mangueigne** Chad
282 G4 **Mangueira, Lago** *l.* Brazil
279 B8 **Mangueirinha** Brazil
227 H5 **Manguéni, Plateau du** Niger
122 C3 **Mangui** *Nei Mongol* China
278 F4 **Manguinha, Pontal do** *pt* Brazil
Mangula Zimbabwe *see* **Mhangura**
266 □P10 **Mangulile** Hond.
261 F8 **Mangum** *OK* U.S.A.
278 D2 **Mangunça, Ilha** *i.* Brazil
115 E1 **Mangupung** *i.* Indon.
230 F4 **Manguredjipa** Dem. Rep. Congo
129 M2 **Mangut** Rus. Fed.
Mangyshlak Kazakh. *see* **Mangystau**
142 D5 **Mangyshlak, Poluostrov** *pen.* Kazakh.
Mangyshlak Oblast *admin. div.* Kazakh. *see* **Mangistauskaya Oblast'**
Mangyshlakskaya Oblast' *admin. div.* Kazakh. *see* **Mangistauskaya Oblast'**
142 D5 **Mangyshlakskiy Zaliv** *b.* Kazakh.
142 D6 **Mangystau** Kazakh.
142 D5 **Mangystau, Gory** *hills* Kazakh.
128 C3 **Manhan** Mongolia
Manhan Mongolia *see* **Alag-Erdene**
201 M2 **Manhartsberg** *hill* Austria
260 G6 **Manhattan** *KS* U.S.A.
264 N8 **Manhattan Beach** *CA* U.S.A.
187 I8 **Manhay** Belgium
258 C4 **Manheim** *PA* U.S.A.
235 G5 **Manhica** Moz.
237 Q2 **Manhoca** Moz.
281 F4 **Manhuaçu** Brazil
281 G3 **Manhuaçu** *r.* Brazil
179 K5 **Manhuelles** France
281 G4 **Manhumirim** Brazil
224 B6 **Mani** Chad
224 C5 **Mani** *well* Chad
133 H9 **Mani** *Xizang* China
274 C3 **Mani** Col.
220 D6 **Mani** *pen.* Greece
229 G3 **Mani** Nigeria
138 F6 **Mania** *Rajasthan* India
235 □J3 **Mania** *r.* Madag.
216 H8 **Maniace** *Sicilia* Italy
213 N3 **Maniago** Italy
220 C2 **Maniakoi** Greece
231 D7 **Mania-Muna** Dem. Rep. Congo
138 H8 **Maniari Tank** *resr Chhattisgarh* India
235 G3 **Manica** Moz.
235 G3 **Manica** *prov.* Moz.
235 G3 **Manicaland** *prov.* Zimbabwe
275 F6 **Manicoré** Brazil
275 F6 **Manicoré** *r.* Brazil
249 G3 **Manicouagan** *Que.* Can.
249 G3 **Manicouagan** *r. Que.* Can.
249 H2 **Manicouagan, Petit Lac** *l. Que.* Can.
249 G3 **Manicouagan, Réservoir** *resr Que.* Can.
249 G3 **Manic Trois, Réservoir** *resr Que.* Can.
230 E5 **Maniema** *prov.* Dem. Rep. Congo
147 I2 **Manīfah** Saudi Arabia
107 M7 **Manifold, Cape** *Qld* Austr.
130 B3 **Maniganggo** *Sichuan* China
247 L5 **Manigotagan** *Man.* Can.
139 K7 **Manihari** *Bihar* India
101 □[9] **Manihi** *atoll Arch. des Tuamotu* Fr. Polynesia
103 □[2] **Manihiki** *atoll* Cook Is
243 M3 **Maniitsoq** Greenland
145 K9 **Maniji** *r.* Pak.
231 E7 **Manika** Dem. Rep. Congo
231 E7 **Manika, Plateau de la** Dem. Rep. Congo
139 N8 **Manikchhari** Bangl.
139 M8 **Manikganj** Bangl.
Manikgarh *Mahar.* India *see* **Rajura**
138 H7 **Manikpur** *Uttar Prad.* India
114 C4 **Manila** *Luzon* Phil.
262 J6 **Manila** *UT* U.S.A.
114 C4 **Manila Bay** *Luzon* Phil.
160 H3 **Manilaid** *i.* Estonia
105 L5 **Manildra** *N.S.W.* Austr.
105 M4 **Manilla** *N.S.W.* Austr.
207 I8 **Manilva** Spain
153 R3 **Manily** Rus. Fed.
115 A4 **Manimbaya, Tanjung** *pt* Indon.
106 E2 **Maningrida** *N.T.* Austr.
116 D5 **Maninjau, Danau** *l.* Indon.
115 E5 **Manipa** *i. Maluku* Indon.
115 E5 **Manipa, Selat** *sea chan. Maluku* Indon.
Manipur *Manipur* India *see* **Imphal**
139 N7 **Manipur** *state* India
118 B3 **Manipur** *r.* India/Myanmar
221 I4 **Manisa** Turkey
221 J4 **Manisa** *prov.* Turkey
209 E8 **Manises** Spain
117 I6 **Manismata** *Kalimantan* Indon.
278 B4 **Manissauá Missu** *r.* Brazil
250 H5 **Manistee** *MI* U.S.A.
250 H5 **Manistee** *r. MI* U.S.A.
250 H4 **Manistique** *MI* U.S.A.
250 I3 **Manistique Lake** *MI* U.S.A.
247 L4 **Manitoba** *prov.* Can.
247 L5 **Manitoba, Lake** *Man.* Can.
247 I4 **Manito Lake** *Sask.* Can.
247 L5 **Manitou** *Man.* Can.
249 H3 **Manitou** *r. Que.* Can.
248 D4 **Manitou, Lake** *Ont.* Can.
256 H5 **Manitou Beach** *NY* U.S.A.
247 M5 **Manitou Falls** *Ont.* Can.
250 G2 **Manitou Island** *MI* U.S.A.
250 H4 **Manitou Islands** *MI* U.S.A.
248 D4 **Manitoulin Island** *Ont.* Can.
248 C3 **Manitouwadge** *Ont.* Can.
251 M4 **Manitowaning** *Ont.* Can.
250 J1 **Manitowik Lake** *Ont.* Can.
250 E3 **Manitowish Waters** *WI* U.S.A.
250 G5 **Manitowoc** *WI* U.S.A.
248 F4 **Maniwaki** *Que.* Can.
135 □[1] **Maniyafushi** *i. S. Male* Maldives
274 C3 **Manizales** Col.
235 □J4 **Manja** Madag.
235 G5 **Manjacaze** Moz.
235 □J3 **Manjak** Madag.
146 A4 **Manjam Umm Qurayyāt** *waterhole* Egypt
136 E7 **Manjeri** *Kerala* India
145 M9 **Manjhand** Pak.
123 E7 **Man Jiang** *r.* China
144 C3 **Manjil** Iran
109 D13 **Manjimup** *W.A.* Austr.
229 H5 **Manjo** Cameroon
136 E3 **Manjra** *r.* India
201 L3 **Mank** Austria
118 C1 **Man Kabat** Myanmar
139 L7 **Mankachar** *Assam* India
Mankanza Dem. Rep. Congo *see* **Makanza**
260 F6 **Mankato** *KS* U.S.A.
260 H3 **Mankato** *MN* U.S.A.
145 N6 **Mankera** Pak.
229 I5 **Mankim** Cameroon
158 J5 **Man'kivka** *Cherkas'ka Oblast'* Ukr.
159 R4 **Man'kivka** *Luhans'ka Oblast'* Ukr.
158 I5 **Man'kivka** *Vinnyts'ka Oblast'* Ukr.
228 D4 **Mankono** Côte d'Ivoire
247 J5 **Mankota** *Sask.* Can.
136 G8 **Mankulam** Sri Lanka
182 E2 **Manlay** France
128 J4 **Manlay** Mongolia
245 J2 **Manley Hot Springs** *AK* U.S.A.
208 J4 **Manlleu** Spain
260 I4 **Manly** *IA* U.S.A.
138 E9 **Manmad** *Mahar.* India
106 E2 **Mann** *r. N.T.* Austr.
100 □[3a] **Mann** *i. Kwajalein* Marshall Is
106 B8 **Mann, Mount** *N.T.* Austr.
116 E7 **Manna** *Sumatera* Indon.
118 C3 **Man Na** Myanmar
104 G5 **Mannahill** *S.A.* Austr.
136 F8 **Mannar** Sri Lanka
136 F8 **Mannar, Gulf of** India/Sri Lanka
136 F7 **Mannargudi** *Tamil Nadu* India
194 F7 **Männedorf** Switz.
106 F7 **Manners** *watercourse N.T.* Austr.
201 O4 **Mannersdorf am Leithagebirge** Austria
201 O5 **Mannersdorf an der Rabnitz** Austria
136 G5 **Manneru** *r.* India
249 G2 **Mannessier, Lac** *l. Que.* Can.
194 E3 **Mannheim** Ger.
Mannicolo Islands *Santa Cruz Is* Solomon Is *see* **Vanikoro Islands**
160 H3 **Männikuste** Estonia
246 G3 **Manning** *Alta* Can.
260 D2 **Manning** *ND* U.S.A.
255 G9 **Manning** *SC* U.S.A.
246 F5 **Manning Provincial Park** *B.C.* Can.
100 □[6] **Manning Strait** Solomon Is
256 E9 **Mannington** *WV* U.S.A.
173 O4 **Manningtree** *Essex, England* U.K.
169 E5 **Mannin Lake** Ireland
212 D2 **Männlifluh** *mt.* Switz.
106 B8 **Mann Ranges** *mts S.A.* Austr.
257 I5 **Mannsville** *NY* U.S.A.
214 A6 **Mannu** *r. Sardegna* Italy
214 B8 **Mannu** *r. Sardegna* Italy
214 C9 **Mannu** *r. Sardegna* Italy
214 D6 **Mannu** *r. Sardegna* Italy
214 A6 **Mannu, Capo** *c. Sardegna* Italy
214 A7 **Mannu, Capo** *c. Sardegna* Italy
214 A7 **Mannu, Monte** *hill* Italy
247 I4 **Mannville** *Alta* Can.
228 C5 **Mano** *r.* Liberia/Sierra Leone
228 B5 **Mano** Sierra Leone
276 D2 **Manoa** Bol.
276 C2 **Manoel Urbano** Brazil
271 □[5] **Man of War Bay** Trin. and Tob.
Man-of-War Rocks *is HI* U.S.A. *see* **Gardner Pinnacles**
133 C13 **Manoharpur** *Rajasthan* India
138 F7 **Manohar Thana** *Rajasthan* India
244 H4 **Manokotak** *AK* U.S.A.
113 H7 **Manokwari** *Papua* Indon.
208 L3 **Manol** *r.* Spain
219 P3 **Manoleasa** Romania
235 □I4 **Manombo Atsimo** Madag.
235 □K3 **Manompana** Madag.
231 E6 **Manono** Dem. Rep. Congo
145 L9 **Manora Head** Pak.
172 C4 **Manorbier** *Pembrokeshire, Wales* U.K.
259 H3 **Manorhaven** *NY* U.S.A.
228 C5 **Mano River** Liberia
119 D9 **Manoron** Myanmar
259 J3 **Manorville** *NY* U.S.A.
283 C7 **Manos, Cueva de las** *cave* Arg.
183 H9 **Manosque** France
249 G3 **Manouane, Lac** *l. Que.* Can.
125 P9 **Mano-wan** *b.* Japan
196 E1 **Manowo** Pol.
118 C3 **Man Pan** Myanmar
123 E8 **Manp'o** N. Korea
138 E8 **Manpur** *Madh. Prad.* India
99 I2 **Manra** *i. Phoenix Is* Kiribati
208 I4 **Manresa** Spain
138 D8 **Mansa** *Gujarat* India
138 E5 **Mansa** *Punjab* India
231 F7 **Mansa** Zambia
228 B3 **Mansabá** Guinea-Bissau
228 B3 **Mansa Konko** Gambia
114 C5 **Mansalay Bay** *Mindoro* Phil.
115 C4 **Mansalean** *Sulawesi* Indon.
118 C3 **Man Sam** Myanmar
192 K5 **Manschnow** Ger.
145 O4 **Mansehra** Pak.
243 K3 **Mansel Island** *Nunavut* Can.
162 T3 **Mansel'kya** *ridge* Fin./Rus. Fed.
193 D7 **Mansfeld** Ger.
105 K7 **Mansfield** *Vic.* Austr.
171 O7 **Mansfield** *Nottinghamshire, England* U.K.
261 H8 **Mansfield** *AR* U.S.A.
261 I9 **Mansfield** *LA* U.S.A.
257 N6 **Mansfield** *MA* U.S.A.
256 C8 **Mansfield** *OH* U.S.A.
256 H7 **Mansfield** *PA* U.S.A.
257 M4 **Mansfield, Mount** *VT* U.S.A.
259 K1 **Mansfield Center** *CT* U.S.A.
171 O7 **Mansfield Woodhouse** *Nottinghamshire, England* U.K.
118 C2 **Man Si** Myanmar
118 B2 **Mansi** Myanmar
278 E4 **Mansidão** Brazil
205 O4 **Mansilla** Spain
205 O4 **Mansilla, Embalse de** *resr* Spain
205 J4 **Mansilla de las Mulas** Spain
184 E4 **Mansle** France
Manso *r.* Brazil *see* **Mortes, Rio das**
214 B3 **Manso** *Corse* France
228 E5 **Manso-Nkwanta** Ghana
185 F7 **Mansonville** France
204 D7 **Mansores** Port.
172 H6 **Manston** *Dorset, England* U.K.
115 F5 **Mansuela** *Seram* Indon.
149 N8 **Manşūrī** Iran
148 G5 **Mansurlu** Turkey
274 A5 **Manta** Ecuador
114 A7 **Mantalingajan, Mount** *Palawan* Phil.
230 D5 **Mantantale** Dem. Rep. Congo
115 D4 **Mantarara** *Maluku* Indon.
276 B3 **Mantaro** *r.* Peru
264 K4 **Manteca** *CA* U.S.A.
274 D3 **Mantecal** Venez.
115 D3 **Mantehage** *i.* Indon.
204 E8 **Manteigas** Port.
195 M2 **Mantel** Ger.
281 G3 **Mantena** Brazil
250 G8 **Manteno** *IL* U.S.A.
255 J8 **Manteo** *NC* U.S.A.
187 J9 **Manternach** Lux.
178 C6 **Mantes-la-Jolie** France
178 C6 **Mantes-la-Ville** France
185 I11 **Mantet, Réserve Naturelle de** *nature res.* France
136 F3 **Manthani** *Andhra Prad.* India
181 M7 **Manthelan** France
265 U2 **Manti** *UT* U.S.A.
281 D5 **Mantiqueira, Serra da** *mts* Brazil
266 □P10 **Manto** Hond.
182 H2 **Mantoche** France
259 G4 **Mantoloking** *NJ* U.S.A.
250 I5 **Manton** *MI* U.S.A.
276 C5 **Mantos Blancos** Chile
220 E4 **Mantoudi** Greece
213 J5 **Mantova** Italy
213 J5 **Mantova** *prov.* Italy
163 R6 **Mäntsälä** Fin.
237 M5 **Mantsonyane** Lesotho
163 R5 **Mänttä** Fin.
270 A2 **Mantua** Cuba
Mantua Italy *see* **Mantova**
258 E5 **Mantua** *NJ* U.S.A.
256 D7 **Mantua** *OH* U.S.A.
107 K8 **Mantuan Downs** *Qld* Austr.
156 I4 **Manturovo** *Kostromskaya Oblast'* Rus. Fed.
159 Q2 **Manturovo** *Kurskaya Oblast'* Rus. Fed.
163 S6 **Mäntyharju** Fin.
162 S3 **Mäntyjärvi** Fin.
Manu *r.* Bol. *see* **Mapiri**
276 C3 **Manú** *r.* Peru
276 B3 **Manu, Parque Nacional** *nat. park* Peru
103 □[2] **Manuae** *atoll* Cook Is
101 □[9] **Manuae** *atoll Arch. de la Société* Fr. Polynesia
100 □[2] **Manu'a Islands** American Samoa
237 M8 **Manubi** S. Africa
269 I3 **Manuel** Mex.
209 E9 **Manuel** Spain
278 C4 **Manuel Alves** *r.* Brazil
269 I7 **Manuel Ávila Camacho, Presa** *resr* Mex.
285 I4 **Manuel J. Cobo** Arg.
268 E6 **Manuel M. Diéguez** Mex.
285 G3 **Manuel Ocampo** Arg.
280 B6 **Manuel Ribas** Brazil
283 B9 **Manuel Rodríguez, Isla** *i.* Chile
278 E5 **Manuel Vitorino** Brazil
278 B3 **Manuelzinho** Brazil
115 C5 **Manui** *i.* Indon.
144 G8 **Manūjān** Iran
115 G6 **Manuk** *i. Maluku* Indon.
114 D7 **Manukan** *Mindanao* Phil.
102 I3 **Manukau** *North I.* N.Z.
102 I4 **Manukau Harbour** *North I.* N.Z.
102 □ **Manukau Point** *Chatham Is* S. Pacific Ocean
114 B9 **Manuk Manka** *i.* Phil.
169 D5 **Manulla** Ireland
104 G5 **Manunda** *watercourse S.A.* Austr.
276 D2 **Manupari** *r.* Bol.
276 D2 **Manurimi** *r.* Bol.
276 D2 **Manuripi** *r.* Bol.
115 F5 **Manusela, Taman Nasional** *nat. park Seram* Indon.
113 K7 **Manus Island** *Admiralty Is* P.N.G.
102 L5 **Manutuke** *North I.* N.Z.
136 E5 **Manvi** *Karnataka* India
258 F3 **Manville** *NJ* U.S.A.
136 E3 **Manwat** *Mahar.* India
261 I10 **Many** *LA* U.S.A.
106 D3 **Manyallaluk Aboriginal Reserve** *N.T.* Austr.
235 F2 **Manyame** *r.* Moz./Zimbabwe
233 C6 **Manyara** *admin. reg.* Tanz.
233 B5 **Manyara, Lake** *salt l.* Tanz.
221 I2 **Manyas** Turkey
Manyas Gölü *l.* Turkey *see* **Kuş Gölü**
219 L7 **Manyashki Vrŭkh** *hill* Bulg.
237 L5 **Manyatseng** S. Africa
247 I5 **Manyberries** *Alta* Can.
157 H7 **Manych-Gudilo, Ozero** *l.* Rus. Fed.
159 T6 **Manychskaya** Rus. Fed.
265 W5 **Many Farms** *AZ* U.S.A.
231 E8 **Manyinga** Zambia
247 I5 **Many Island Lake** *Alta/Sask.* Can.
158 G4 **Manykivtsi** Ukr.
233 B6 **Manyoni** Tanz.
107 M8 **Many Peaks** *Qld* Austr.
109 E13 **Many Peaks, Mount** *hill W.A.* Austr.
184 F5 **Manzac-sur-Vern** France
145 N5 **Manzai** Pak.
Manzala, Lake *lag.* Egypt *see* **Manzilah, Buḩayrat al**
204 H3 **Manzanal, Puerto del** *pass* Spain
204 H5 **Manzanal de Arriba** Spain
204 H3 **Manzanal del Puerto** Spain
207 M2 **Manzanares** Spain
205 M8 **Manzanares** *r.* Spain
205 M7 **Manzanares el Real** Spain
204 F4 **Manzaneda** Spain
204 F4 **Manzaneda, Cabeza de** *mt.* Spain
205 M3 **Manzanedo** Spain
205 M9 **Manzaneque** Spain
209 D7 **Manzanera** Spain
271 □[7] **Manzanilla Bay** Trin. and Tob.
271 □[7] **Manzanilla Point** Trin. and Tob.
270 E3 **Manzanillo** Cuba
268 C6 **Manzanillo** Mex.
266 □T13 **Manzanillo, Punta** *pt* Panama
213 O4 **Manzano** Italy
268 F4 **Manzano** Mex.
231 F6 **Manzanza** Dem. Rep. Congo
144 D4 **Manẕārīyeh** Iran
182 B5 **Manzat** France
231 C6 **Manzengele** Dem. Rep. Congo
159 M4 **Manzheliya** Ukr.
129 O2 **Manzhouli** *Nei Mongol* China
214 I3 **Manziana** Italy
182 F4 **Manziat** France
150 A7 **Manzilah, Buḩayrat al** *lag.* Egypt
237 P2 **Manzini** Swaziland
237 P2 **Manzini** *admin. dist.* Swaziland
Manzovka Rus. Fed. *see* **Sibirtsevo**
224 B6 **Mao** Chad
270 H4 **Mao** Dom. Rep.
Maó Spain *see* **Mahón**
Mao, Nam *r.* Myanmar *see* **Shweli**
130 F5 **Maoba** *Guizhou* China
130 G3 **Maoba** *Hubei* China
131 I3 **Maocifan** *Hubei* China
130 D2 **Mao'ergai** *Sichuan* China
128 J8 **Maojiachuan** *Gansu* China
128 J8 **Maojing** *Gansu* China
113 I7 **Maoke, Pegunungan** *mts Papua* Indon.
237 L3 **Maokeng** S. Africa
123 C8 **Maokui Shan** *mt. Liaoning* China
129 R5 **Maolin** *Jilin* China
128 H8 **Maomao Shan** *mt. Gansu* China
130 H8 **Maoming** *Guangdong* China
133 H9 **Maoniupo** *Xizang* China
128 E8 **Maoniushan** *Qinghai* China
131 □J7 **Ma On Shan** *hill H.K.* China
Maoping *Hubei* China *see* **Zigui**
131 M8 **Maopi T'ou** *c.* Taiwan
115 E7 **Maopora** *i. Maluku* Indon.
130 C6 **Maotou Shan** *mt. Yunnan* China
Maowen *Sichuan* China *see* **Maoxian**
130 D3 **Maoxian** *Sichuan* China
235 F4 **Mapai** Moz.
133 E11 **Mapam Yumco** *l.* China
115 B4 **Mapane** *Sulawesi* Indon.
231 E9 **Mapanza** Zambia
274 D2 **Maparari** Venez.
267 M10 **Mapastepec** Mex.
237 Q4 **Mapelane Nature Reserve** S. Africa
237 J6 **Maphodi** S. Africa
113 I8 **Mapi** *r. Papua* Indon.
274 E3 **Mapiche, Serranía** *mts* Venez.
266 H5 **Mapimí** Mex.
235 G4 **Mapinhane** Moz.
275 E3 **Mapire** Venez.
275 H4 **Mapireme** Brazil
276 C3 **Mapiri** Bol.
276 D2 **Mapiri** *r.* Bol.
274 C4 **Mapirpán** Col.
102 J5 **Mapiu** *North I.* N.Z.
260 H5 **Maple** *r. IA* U.S.A.
250 J7 **Maple** *r. MI* U.S.A.
260 F3 **Maple** *r. ND* U.S.A.
260 G2 **Maple** *r. ND* U.S.A.
247 I5 **Maple Creek** *Sask.* Can.
265 W8 **Maple Peak** *AZ* U.S.A.
260 H4 **Mapleton** *IA* U.S.A.
265 U1 **Mapleton** *UT* U.S.A.
250 G5 **Maplewood** *WI* U.S.A.
290 G4 **Mapmakers Seamounts** *sea feature* N. Pacific Ocean
107 H1 **Mapoon** *Qld* Austr.
107 H2 **Mapoon Aboriginal Reserve** *Qld* Austr.
116 F4 **Mapor** *i.* Indon.
237 L5 **Mapoteng** Lesotho
103 E10 **Mapourika, Lake** *South I.* N.Z.
113 J7 **Maprik** P.N.G.
136 C5 **Mapuca** *Goa* India
275 G5 **Mapuera** *r.* Brazil
235 G5 **Mapulanguene** Moz.
237 P5 **Mapumulo** S. Africa
231 E7 **Mapunda** Dem. Rep. Congo
235 F4 **Mapungubwe National Park** *nature res.* S. Africa
235 G5 **Maputo** Moz.
235 G5 **Maputo** *prov.* Moz.
235 G5 **Maputo** *r.* Moz./S. Africa
237 Q2 **Maputo, Baía de** *b.* Moz.
237 Q2 **Maputo, Reserva de Elefantes de** *nature res.* Moz.
237 L4 **Maputsoe** Lesotho
Maqanshy Kazakh. *see* **Makanchi**
149 J8 **Maqar an Na'am** *well* Iraq
Maqat Kazakh. *see* **Makat**
128 G9 **Maqên** *Qinghai* China
133 J11 **Maqên** *Xizang* China
128 F9 **Maqên Kangri** *mt. Qingh*
132 H4 **Maqiao** *Xinjiang* China
150 D10 **Maqla, Jabal al** *mt.* Saud
146 B1 **Maqnā** Saudi Arabia
147 J8 **Maqrat** Yemen
151 I6 **Maqşūdlū** Iran
226 C5 **Maqteïr** *reg.* Maur.
130 D2 **Maqu** *Gansu* China
Ma Qu *r.* China *see* **Hua**
133 G12 **Maquan He** *r. Xizang* Ch
205 L8 **Maqueda** Spain
114 D5 **Maqueda Channel** Phil.
231 B6 **Maquela do Zombo** Ang
283 C6 **Maquinchao** Arg.
284 D3 **Maquinista Levet** Arg.
260 J4 **Maquoketa** *IA* U.S.A.
260 J4 **Maquoketa** *r. IA* U.S.A.
164 E1 **Mår** *l.* Norway
164 E2 **Mår** *r.* Norway
145 K9 **Mar** *r.* Pak.
204 C5 **Mar** Port.
280 C6 **Mar, Serra do** *mts* Brazil
281 E5 **Mar, Serra do** *mts* Brazil
281 F5 **Mar, Serra do** *mts* Brazil
279 C9 **Mar, Serra do** *mts* Brazil
275 G3 **Mara** Guyana
139 O5 **Mara** *Arun. Prad.* India
139 I8 **Mara** *Madh. Prad.* India
214 B7 **Mara** *Sardegna* Italy
233 B5 **Mara** *admin. reg.* Tanz.
275 E5 **Maraã** Brazil
101 □[9a] **Maraa** *Tahiti* Fr. Polynes
278 C3 **Marabá** Brazil
117 K6 **Marabahan** *Kalimantan*
280 B5 **Marabá Paulista** Brazil
117 K7 **Marabatua** *i.* Indon.
274 E4 **Marabitanas** Brazil
107 L7 **Maraboon, Lake** *resr Qld*
179 J8 **Marac** France
275 I5 **Maracá** *r.* Brazil
275 F4 **Maracá, Ilha** *reg.* Brazil
275 I4 **Maracá, Ilha de** *i.* Brazil
280 B5 **Maracaí** Brazil
274 D2 **Maracaibo** Venez.
274 D2 **Maracaibo, Lago de** *l.* Ve
Maracaibo, Lake Venez. **Maracaibo, Lago de**
277 G5 **Maracaju** Brazil
277 G5 **Maracaju, Serra de** *hills*
214 C9 **Maracalagonis** *Sardegna*
278 D2 **Maracanã** Brazil
275 H5 **Maracanaquará, Planalt** Brazil
Maracanda Uzbek. *see* **Samarqand**
278 E5 **Maracás** Brazil
278 E5 **Maracás, Chapada de** *hi*
271 □[7] **Maracas Bay** Trin. and T
274 E2 **Maracay** Venez.
224 C2 **Marādah** Libya
Maradhoo *i. Addu Atoll* *see* **Maradu**
229 G3 **Maradi** Niger
229 G3 **Maradi** *dept* Niger
145 M5 **Maradin** Pak.
135 □[2] **Maradu** *i. Addu Atoll* Ma
101 □[9a] **Maraetiria, Pointe** *pt Ta* Fr. Polynesia
151 J4 **Maraga** Rus. Fed.
204 H4 **Maragatería** *reg.* Spain
144 F8 **Marāgh** Iran
144 B3 **Marāgheh** Iran
278 G4 **Maragogi** Brazil
114 C4 **Maragondon** *Luzon* Phil
146 G3 **Marah** Saudi Arabia
228 D5 **Marahoué** *r.* Côte d'Ivoi
228 D5 **Marahoué, Parc Nationa** *nat. park* Côte d'Ivoire
275 E4 **Marahuaca, Cerro** *mt.* V
260 H6 **Marais des Cygnes** *r. KS*
180 I3 **Marais du Cotentin et d Parc Naturel Régional d** *nature res.* France
184 C3 **Marais Poitevin, Val de Vendée, Parc Naturel Ré du** *nature res.* France
278 C2 **Marajó, Baía de** *est.* Bra
275 I5 **Marajó, Ilha de** *i.* Brazil
237 M5 **Marakabeis** Lesotho
99 H1 **Marakei** *atoll Gilbert Is* K
144 H8 **Marākī** Iran
Maraki *atoll Gilbert Is* Ki **Marakei**
136 F6 **Marakkanam** *Tamil Nad*
Maralaba *i.* Vanuatu *see* **Mere Lava**
232 C4 **Maralal** Kenya
Maralbashi *Xinjiang* Chi **Bachu**
143 Q1 **Maraldy** Kazakh.
143 Q1 **Maraldy, Ozero** *salt l.* Ka
230 C3 **Marali** C.A.R.
151 E5 **Maralik** Armenia
104 C4 **Maralinga** *S.A.* Austr.
104 C3 **Maralinga-Tjarutja Abo Lands** *res. S.A.* Austr.
Maralwexi *Xinjiang* Chir **Bachu**
100 □[6] **Maramasike** *i.* Solomon
Maramba Zambia *see* **Livingstone**
286 U2 **Marambio** *research stn* A
115 E1 **Marampit** *i.* Indon.
219 M3 **Maramureşului, Munţii** Romania
116 E3 **Maran** Malaysia
144 A4 **Marāna** Iraq
265 U9 **Marana** *AZ* U.S.A.
205 P6 **Maranchón** Spain
205 P6 **Maranchóon, Puerto de** Spain
144 A2 **Marand** Iran
Marandellas Zimbabwe **Marondera**
213 J6 **Maranello** Italy
116 E2 **Marang** Malaysia
119 D9 **Marang** Myanmar
179 L5 **Marange-Silvange** Franc
278 F2 **Maranguape** Brazil
278 C5 **Maranhão** *r.* Brazil
278 D3 **Maranhão** *state* Brazil
206 D2 **Maranhão** Port.
206 D2 **Maranhão, Barragem do** Port.
213 K7 **Marano** Italy
213 O4 **Marano, Laguna di** *lag.* I
107 L9 **Maranoa** *r. Qld* Austr.
216 G2 **Marano di Napoli** Italy
274 C6 **Marañón** *r.* Peru
213 J7 **Marano sul Panaro** Italy
184 C3 **Marans** France
179 I7 **Maranville** France
235 G5 **Marão** Moz.
204 E6 **Marão** *mt.* Port.
204 D6 **Marão, Serra do** *mts* Por
100 □[6] **Marapa** *i.* Solomon Is
278 D2 **Marapanim** Brazil
277 F3 **Marape** Brazil
116 D5 **Marapi, Gunung** *vol. Sur* Indon.
214 A7 **Marargiu, Capo** *c. Sarde*
274 E6 **Marari** Brazil
103 B12 **Mararoa** *r. South I.* N.Z.
278 C5 **Mara Rosa** Brazil
Maraş Cyprus *see* **Varosia**
Maraş Turkey *see* **Kahramanmaraş**
117 M7 **Marasende** *i.* Indon.
219 P5 **Mărășești** Romania
219 P6 **Mărașu** Romania
215 P8 **Maratea** Italy
206 B3 **Marateca** Port.
220 B5 **Marathia, Akrotirio** *pt Z* Greece
220 D4 **Marathias** Greece
221 H5 **Marathokampos** *Samos*
248 C3 **Marathon** *Ont.* Can.
Marathón Greece *see* **Ma**
255 G13 **Marathon** *FL* U.S.A.
257 I6 **Marathon** *NY* U.S.A.
261 D10 **Marathon** *TX* U.S.A.
250 E5 **Marathon** *WI* U.S.A.
220 E4 **Marathonas** Greece

Maratua i. Indon.
Marau Kalimantan Indon.
Marauá Brazil
Marauiá r. Brazil
Maraussan France
Maraval Trin. and Tob.
Maravatío Mex.
Marāveh Tappeh Iran
Maravillas Creek watercourse TX U.S.A.
Maravovo Guadalcanal Solomon Is
Marāwah Libya
Marawi Mindanao Phil.
Marawwaḩ, Jazīrat i. U.A.E.
Maraye-en-Othe France
Marayes Arg.
Maray Lake Pak.
Mar'ayt Yemen
Märäzä Azer.
Marazion Cornwall, England U.K.
Marbach Ger.
Marbach Switz.
Marbach am Neckar Ger.
Marbella Spain
Marbella, Ensenada de b. Spain
Marble Bar W.A. Austr.
Marble Canyon AZ U.S.A.
Marble Canyon gorge AZ U.S.A.
Marble Hall S. Africa
Marble Hill MO U.S.A.
Marble Island Nunavut Can.
Marboz France
Marbul Pass Jammu and Kashmir India
Marburg S. Africa
Marburg Slovenia see Maribor
Marburg, Lake PA U.S.A.
Marburg an der Lahn Ger.
Marca Peru
Marca Romania
Marca, Ponta do pt Angola
Marcal r. Hungary
Marcala Hond.
Marcali Hungary
Marcaltő Hungary
Marčana Croatia
Marcanzotta r. Sicilia Italy
Marcapata Peru
Marcaria Italy
Marcelino Brazil
Marcelino Escalada Arg.
Marcellina Italy
Marcellus MI U.S.A.
Marcellus NY U.S.A.
Marcelo Brazil
Marcelová Slovakia
Marcenais France
Marcenat France
March r. Austria alt. Morava
March Cambridgeshire, England U.K.
Marcha Uttaranchal India
Marchand S. Africa
Marchant, Lake South I. N.Z.
Marchant Hill S.A. Austr.
Marche reg. France
Marche admin. reg. Italy
Marche, Plateaux de la France
Marche-en-Famenne Belgium
Marchegg Austria
Marchena Spain
Marchena, Isla i. Islas Galápagos Ecuador
Marchenoir France
Marcheprime France
Marchese, Punta del pt Italy
Marchfeld reg. Austria
Marchiennes France
Marchihue Chile
Marchin Belgium
Marchinbar Island N.T. Austr.
Marchington Staffordshire, England U.K.
Mar Chiquita Arg.
Mar Chiquita, Laguna l. Arg.
Mar Chiquita, Laguna l. Arg.
Marchtrenk Austria
Marchwiel Wrexham, Wales U.K.
Marchykhyna Buda Ukr.
Marciac France
Marciana Italy
Marciana Marina Italy
Marcianise Italy
Marciano della Chiana Italy
Mārciena Latvia
Marcigny France
Marcilhac-sur-Célé France
Marcillac France
Marcillac-la-Croisille France
Marcillac-Vallon France
Marcillat-en-Combraille France
Marcilly-en-Gault France
Marcilly-en-Villette France
Marcilly-le-Hayer France
Marcilly-sur-Eure France
Marcinkonys Lith.
Marcinkowice Małopolskie Pol.
Marcinkowice Zachodniopomorskie Pol.
Marciszów Pol.
Marck France
Marckolsheim France
Marco de Canaveses Port.
Marcoing France
Marcolino r. Brazil
Marcòn Italy
Marcona Peru
Marcopeet Islands Que. Can.
Marco Polo airport Italy
Marcos Juárez Arg.
Marcos Paz Arg.
Marcoux France
Marcq-en-Barœul France
Marcus Baker, Mount AK U.S.A.
Marcy, Mount NY U.S.A.
Märdäkan Azer.
Mardan Pak.
Mardarivka Ukr.
Mar de Ajó Arg.
Mar del Plata Arg.
Marden Herefordshire, England U.K.
Marden Kent, England U.K.
Mardeuil France
Mardīān Afgh.
Mardie W.A. Austr.
Mardın Turkey
Mårdsele Sweden
Mårdudden Sweden
Mardzad Mongolia see Hayrhandulaan
Mare r. France
Mare i. Maluku Indon.
Maré i. Îles Loyauté New Caledonia
Mare aux Vacoas Reservoir Mauritius
Marebbe Italy
Marecchia r. Italy
Mare de Déu del Toro hill Spain
Maree, Loch l. Scotland U.K.
Mareeba Qld Austr.
Marèges, Barrage de dam France
Mareh Iran
Mareham le Fen Lincolnshire, England U.K.
Maremma, Parco Naturale della nature res. Italy
Maréna Mali
Marendet Niger
Marengo IA U.S.A.
Marengo IL U.S.A.
Marengo WI U.S.A.
Marenisco MI U.S.A.
Marenjān Iran
Marennes France
Marensin reg. France
Mare Piccolo b. Italy
Marepotamo r. Italy
Marerano Madag.
Maresfield East Sussex, England U.K.
108 H3 Maret Islands W.A. Austr.
216 C8 Marettimo Sicilia Italy
216 C8 Marettimo, Isola i. Sicilia Italy
184 E5 Mareuil France
181 P8 Mareuil-sur-Arnon France
178 H5 Mareuil-sur-Ay France
184 B2 Mareuil-sur-Lay-Dissais France
161 P4 Marevo Rus. Fed.
182 G1 Marey-sur-Tille France
263 L11 Marfa TX U.S.A.
Marfa Point Malta see Cirkewwa, Il-Ponta tac-
217 □ Marfa Ridge Malta
133 H9 Margai Caka l. Xizang China
172 E4 Margam Neath Port Talbot, Wales U.K.
133 G10 Margam Ri mts Xizang China
Marganets Kazakh. see Zhezdy
Marganets Ukr. see Marhanets'
Margao Goa India see Madgaon
108 H5 Margaret r. W.A. Austr.
104 F3 Margaret watercourse S.A. Austr.
108 D7 Margaret, Mount hill W.A. Austr.
246 E5 Margaret Bay B.C. Can.
246 H3 Margaret Lake Alta Can.
246 G1 Margaret Lake N.W.T. Can.
109 C12 Margaret River W.A. Austr.
257 K6 Margaretville NY U.S.A.
282 E3 Margarita Arg.
275 F2 Margarita, Isla de i. Venez.
122 I7 Margaritovo Primorskiy Kray Rus. Fed.
159 R7 Margaritovo Rostovskaya Oblast' Rus. Fed.
237 O6 Margate S. Africa
173 O5 Margate Kent, England U.K.
259 F6 Margate City NJ U.S.A.
219 K4 Mărgău Romania
184 C5 Margaux France
199 K3 Margecany Slovakia
183 C6 Margeride, Monts de la mts France
178 I6 Margerie-Hancourt France
171 N7 Margery Hill England U.K.
194 H2 Margetshöchheim Ger.
139 O6 Margherita Assam India
Margherita, Lake Eth. see Ābaya Hāyk'
215 Q5 Margherita di Savoia Italy
230 F4 Margherita Peak Dem. Rep. Congo/Uganda
Marghilon Uzbek. see Marg'ilon
219 K3 Marghita Romania
143 N7 Marg'ilon Uzbek.
199 L6 Margina Romania
219 N3 Marginea Romania
160 H8 Margionys Lith.
178 E5 Margny-lès-Compiègne France
133 H10 Margog Caka l. Xizang China
212 C5 Margone Italy
196 F3 Margonin Pol.
276 A2 Margos Peru
114 D8 Margosatubig Mindanao Phil.
145 J6 Māgow, Dasht-e des. Afgh.
187 I7 Margraten Neth.
246 F4 Marguerite B.C. Can.
Marguerite, Pic mt. Dem. Rep. Congo/Uganda see Margherita Peak
286 T2 Marguerite Bay Antarctica
183 E9 Marguerittes France
179 J4 Margut France
133 J12 Margyang Xizang China
149 M7 Marhaj Khalīl Iraq
173 N2 Marham Norfolk, England U.K.
143 O7 Marhamat Uzbek.
199 K2 Marhaň Slovakia
149 K5 Marhan Dāgh hill Iraq
159 N6 Marhanets' Ukr.
227 E2 Marhoum Alg.
276 D1 Mari r. Brazil
118 D1 Mari Myanmar
113 J8 Mari P.N.G.
279 B7 Maria r. Brazil
101 □9 Maria atoll Arch. des Tuamotu Fr. Polynesia
101 □9 Maria atoll Îs Australes Fr. Polynesia
207 O5 María Spain
207 O5 María, Sierra de mts Spain
201 M3 Maria Anzbach Austria
183 E7 Mariac France
268 A4 María Cleofas, Isla i. Mex.
209 E7 María Cristina, Embalse de resr Spain
276 C5 María Elena Chile
285 G2 Mariá Eugenia Arg.
164 F5 Mariager Denmark
285 H5 María Ignacia Arg.
106 E3 Maria Island N.T. Austr.
105 L10 Maria Island Tas. Austr.
105 L10 Maria Island National Park nat. park Tas. Austr.
107 J8 Mariala National Park Qld Austr.
201 L5 Maria Lankowitz Austria
269 L8 María Lombardo de Casso Mex.
200 G6 Maria Luggau Austria
285 G2 María Luisa Arg.
204 F7 Marialva Port.
268 A4 María Madre, Isla i. Mex.
268 A4 María Magdelena, Isla i. Mex.
107 L6 Marian Qld Austr.
281 F4 Mariana Brazil
205 P8 Mariana Spain
270 B2 Marianao Cuba
290 E4 Mariana Ridge sea feature N. Pacific Ocean
290 E5 Mariana Trench sea feature N. Pacific Ocean
139 O6 Mariani Assam India
Mariánica, Cordillera mts Spain see Morena, Sierra
246 G2 Marian Lake N.W.T. Can.
261 J8 Marianna AR U.S.A.
255 E10 Marianna FL U.S.A.
239 □2a Marianne i. Inner Islands Seychelles
165 L4 Mariannelund Sweden
212 G4 Mariano Comense Italy
282 F3 Mariano Loza Arg.
Mariano Machado Angola see Ganda
284 B6 Mariano Moreno Arg.
216 F8 Marianopoli Sicilia Italy
285 G5 Mariano Unzué Arg.
196 D2 Marianowo Pol.
198 B2 Mariánské Lázně Czech Rep.
201 I5 Mariapfarr Austria
274 D4 Mariapirí, Mesa de hills Col.
280 B4 Mariápolis Brazil
201 J6 Maria Rain Austria
262 I3 Marias r. MT U.S.A.
268 A4 Marías, Islas is Mex.
201 J6 Maria Saal Austria
285 G4 María Teresa Arg.
266 □S14 Mariato, Punta pt Panama
102 G1 Maria van Diemen, Cape North I. N.Z.
201 J6 Maria Wörth Austria
201 L4 Mariazell Austria
146 G8 Ma'rib Yemen
146 G8 Ma'rib governorate Yemen
250 G5 Maribel WI U.S.A.
164 H7 Maribo Denmark
210 E2 Maribor Slovenia
281 F5 Maricá Brazil
Marica r. Bulg. see Maritsa
271 □1 Maricao Puerto Rico
136 F8 Marichchukkaddi Sri Lanka
237 K1 Marico Bosveld Nature Reserve S. Africa
265 T8 Maricopa AZ U.S.A.
264 M6 Maricopa CA U.S.A.
265 T8 Maricopa Mountains AZ U.S.A.
Maricourt Que. Can. see Kangiqsujuaq
230 F3 Maridi Sudan
230 F3 Maridi watercourse Sudan
274 E5 Marié r. Brazil
Marie Anne Island Inner Islands Seychelles see Marianne
286 P1 Marie Byrd Land reg. Antarctica
165 N2 Mariefred Sweden
271 □2 Marie-Galante i. Guadeloupe
163 O6 Mariehamn Åland Fin.
Mari El aut. rep. Rus. Fed. see Mariy El, Respublika
278 C5 Mariembero r. Brazil
187 G8 Mariembourg Belgium
Marienbad Czech Rep. see Mariánské Lázně
193 H9 Marienberg Ger.
Marienburg Pol. see Malbork
190 D3 Marienhafe Ger.
191 I6 Marienhagen Ger.
191 E8 Marienheide Ger.
191 K6 Mariental Ger.
234 C5 Mariental Namibia
256 F7 Marienville PA U.S.A.
Marienwerder Pol. see Kwidzyn
165 J3 Mariestad Sweden
248 E1 Mariet r. Que. Can.
255 E9 Marietta GA U.S.A.
256 D9 Marietta OH U.S.A.
261 G9 Marietta OK U.S.A.
258 B4 Marietta PA U.S.A.
257 L3 Marieville Que. Can.
229 G4 Mariga r. Nigeria
215 M6 Marigliano Italy
214 B3 Marignana Corse France
183 G10 Marignane France
181 L6 Marigné-Laillé France
182 J4 Marignier France
180 I3 Marigny France
178 G7 Marigny-le-Châtel France
182 D2 Marigny-l'Église France
271 □2 Marigot Dominica
271 L4 Marigot West Indies
122 M1 Marii, Mys pt Sakhalin Rus. Fed.
142 I1 Mariinskoye Rus. Fed.
160 G7 Marijampolė Lith.
237 L1 Marikana S. Africa
219 L9 Marikostinovo Bulg.
280 C5 Marília Brazil
108 E7 Marillana W.A. Austr.
280 A6 Mariluz Brazil
231 C7 Marimba Angola
117 K5 Marimun Kalimantan Indon.
267 I5 Marín Mex.
145 K7 Marin mt. Pak.
204 C4 Marín Spain
264 K5 Marina CA U.S.A.
214 G2 Marina di Alberese Italy
217 L4 Marina di Amendolara Italy
214 A8 Marina di Arbus Sardegna Italy
215 O7 Marina di Camerota Italy
214 E2 Marina di Campo Italy
214 F1 Marina di Castagneto Donoratico Italy
212 I9 Marina di Cecina Italy
215 O4 Marina di Chieuti Italy
217 L3 Marina di Ginosa Italy
217 K7 Marina di Gioiosa Ionica Italy
214 F2 Marina di Grosseto Italy
217 O4 Marina di Leuca Italy
212 I7 Marina di Massa Italy
216 F9 Marina di Palma Sicilia Italy
217 M3 Marina di Pulsano Italy
216 H10 Marina di Ragusa Sicilia Italy
213 M6 Marina di Ravenna Italy
Mar'ina Gorka Belarus see Mar"ina Horka
160 L8 Mar"ina Horka Belarus
207 J6 Marinaleda Spain
215 L1 Marina Palmense Italy
213 M6 Marina Romea Italy
217 L4 Marina Schiavonea Italy
114 C5 Marinduque i. Phil.
251 L7 Marine City MI U.S.A.
216 D8 Marinella Sicilia Italy
214 D5 Marinella, Golfo di b. Sardegna Italy
216 E8 Marineo Sicilia Italy
287 L2 Mariner Glacier Antarctica
178 C5 Marines France
209 D8 Marines Spain
250 G4 Marinette WI U.S.A.
280 B5 Maringá Brazil
230 C4 Maringa r. Dem. Rep. Congo
256 C8 Maringo OH U.S.A.
235 G3 Maringué Moz.
182 C5 Maringues France
204 C8 Marinha das Ondas Port.
204 C9 Marinha Grande Port.
206 B2 Marinhais Port.
204 C5 Marinhas Port.
213 Q5 Marinići Croatia
215 J4 Marino Italy
151 A2 Marino Rus. Fed.
Marino Alejandro Selkirk, Isla i. S. Pacific Ocean see Alejandro Selkirk, Isla
160 L3 Mar'insko Rus. Fed.
151 E1 Mar'iny Kolodtsy Rus. Fed.
255 D9 Marion AL U.S.A.
261 J8 Marion AR U.S.A.
259 J1 Marion CT U.S.A.
261 K7 Marion IL U.S.A.
254 E5 Marion IN U.S.A.
260 G6 Marion KS U.S.A.
261 K7 Marion KY U.S.A.
250 I5 Marion MI U.S.A.
255 F8 Marion NC U.S.A.
256 B8 Marion OH U.S.A.
255 H8 Marion SC U.S.A.
256 D12 Marion VA U.S.A.
250 F5 Marion WI U.S.A.
255 G9 Marion, Lake SC U.S.A.
104 F6 Marion Bay S.A. Austr.
106 G7 Marion Downs Qld Austr.
260 G6 Marion Lake KS U.S.A.
107 N5 Marion Reef Coral Sea Is Terr. Austr.
215 R5 Mariotto Italy
227 H5 Mariou, Adrar mt. Alg.
275 E3 Maripa Venez.
275 H4 Maripasoula Fr. Guiana
114 E6 Maripipi i. Phil.
264 M4 Mariposa CA U.S.A.
264 L4 Mariposa r. CA U.S.A.
268 G6 Mariposa Monarca, Reserva de la Biosfera res. Mexico
274 C3 Mariquita Col.
115 B3 Marisa Sulawesi Indon.
269 I8 Mariscala Mex.
277 E5 Mariscal José Félix Estigarribia Para.
219 L4 Mărișel Romania
219 M3 Mărișelu Romania
183 J8 Maritime Alps mts France/Italy
Maritime Kray admin. div. Rus. Fed. see Primorskiy Kray
Maritsa Bulg. see Simeonovgrad
219 O9 Maritsa r. Europe.
alt. Evros (Greece),
alt. Hebros (Greece),
alt. Marica (Bulgaria),
alt. Meriç (Turkey)
156 J4 Mari-Turek Rus. Fed.
159 Q6 Mariupol' Ukr.
275 F2 Mariusa nat. park Venez.
275 F2 Mariusa, Isla i. Venez.
149 M6 Marīvān Iran
156 J4 Mariy El, Respublika aut. rep. Rus. Fed.
Mariyskaya A.S.S.R. aut. rep. Rus. Fed. see Mariy El, Respublika
182 E3 Marizy France
205 M9 Marjaliza Spain
160 H3 Märjamaa Estonia
Marjan Afgh. see Wazi Khwa
144 E7 Marjān Iran
150 D5 Marjayoûn Lebanon
145 L2 Marjonbuloq Uzbek.
247 L1 Marjorie Lake Nunavut Can.
172 G5 Mark Somerset, England U.K.
150 E7 Mārkā Jordan
146 E6 Markā i. Saudi Arabia
232 E4 Marka Somalia
143 U3 Markakol', Ozero l. Kazakh.
228 D3 Markala Mali
156 L3 Markalasta Rus. Fed.
130 B4 Markam Xizang China
130 B4 Markam Shan mts Xizang China
151 G7 Mārkān Iran
136 F5 Markapur Andhra Prad. India
165 J5 Markaryd Sweden
232 E3 Markawene well Eth.
147 M6 Markaz, Ra's c. Oman
144 D4 Markazī prov. Iran
251 N5 Markdale Ont. Can.
194 G6 Markdorf Ger.
186 K4 Markelo Neth.
192 D1 Markelsdorfer Huk pt Ger.
186 H4 Marken i. Neth.
235 F4 Marken S. Africa
186 H3 Markermeer l. Neth.
193 G9 Markersdorf bei Burgstädt Ger.
173 J2 Market Bosworth Leicestershire, England U.K.
173 L2 Market Deeping Lincolnshire, England U.K.
172 H2 Market Drayton Shropshire, England U.K.
173 K3 Market Harborough Leicestershire, England U.K.
169 I4 Markethill Northern Ireland U.K.
173 I5 Market Lavington Wiltshire, England U.K.
171 Q7 Market Rasen Lincolnshire, England U.K.
171 O7 Market Warsop Nottinghamshire, England U.K.
171 P6 Market Weighton East Riding of Yorkshire, England U.K.
173 J2 Markfield Leicestershire, England U.K.
194 G4 Markgröningen Ger.
153 M3 Markha r. Rus. Fed.
248 E5 Markham Ont. Can.
287 K1 Markham, Mount Antarctica
247 K2 Markham Lake N.W.T. Can.
197 J3 Marki Pol.
159 S3 Marki Rus. Fed.
205 P2 Markina-Xemein Spain
168 J10 Markinch Fife, Scotland U.K.
193 I6 Märkisch Buchholz Ger.
132 C7 Markit Xinjiang China
162 P3 Markitta Sweden
159 S4 Markivka Ukr.
158 H5 Markivka r. Ukr.
193 F8 Markkleeberg Ger.
264 M3 Markleeville CA U.S.A.
256 F9 Markleysburg PA U.S.A.
195 N4 Marklkofen Ger.
190 H5 Marklohe Ger.
186 I3 Marknesse Neth.
193 F10 Markneukirchen Ger.
199 G4 Márkó Hungary
130 C2 Markog Qu r. Sichuan China
220 E5 Markopoulo Greece
230 C3 Markounda C.A.R.
201 O8 Markovac Trojstveni Croatia
153 S3 Markovo Chukotskiy Avtonomnyy Okrug Rus. Fed.
161 X4 Markovo Ivanovskaya Oblast' Rus. Fed.
159 N2 Markovo Kurskaya Oblast' Rus. Fed.
229 F3 Markoye Burkina
193 F8 Markranstädt Ger.
142 B2 Marks Rus. Fed.
261 J8 Marks MS U.S.A.
258 F3 Marksboro NJ U.S.A.
173 N4 Marks Tey Essex, England U.K.
191 J9 Marksuhl Ger.
261 I10 Marksville LA U.S.A.
201 N5 Markt Allhau Austria
195 I3 Marktbergel Ger.
195 J3 Markt Berolzheim Ger.
195 I2 Markt Bibart Ger.
195 I2 Marktbreit Ger.
195 J3 Markt Erlbach Ger.
201 M5 Markt Hartmannsdorf Austria
194 H2 Marktheidenfeld Ger.
195 K5 Markt Indersdorf Ger.
195 N5 Marktl Ger.
193 E10 Marktleugast Ger.
193 F10 Marktleuthen Ger.
195 J6 Marktoberdorf Ger.
195 I4 Marktoffingen Ger.
246 E5 Marktosis B.C. Can.
201 N4 Markt Piesting Austria
195 M1 Marktredwitz Ger.
195 I6 Markt Rettenbach Ger.
193 D10 Marktrodach Ger.
201 J3 Markt Sankt Florian Austria
201 N4 Markt Sankt Martin Austria
195 O6 Marktschellenberg Ger.
195 L5 Markt Schwaben Ger.
195 I2 Marktseft Ger.
195 J5 Markt Wald Ger.
201 N8 Markusevec Croatia
197 K4 Markuszów Pol.
173 L4 Markyate Hertfordshire, England U.K.
191 D7 Marl Ger.
104 D2 Marla S.A. Austr.
109 D10 Marlandy Hill W.A. Austr.
258 E6 Marlboro NJ U.S.A.
259 G4 Marlboro NJ U.S.A.
259 H1 Marlboro NY U.S.A.
107 L7 Marlborough Qld Austr.
103 H8 Marlborough admin. reg. South I. N.Z.
173 I5 Marlborough Wiltshire, England U.K.
259 K1 Marlborough CT U.S.A.
257 N6 Marlborough MA U.S.A.
257 M6 Marlborough NH U.S.A.
173 I5 Marlborough Downs hills England U.K.
172 E7 Marldon Devon, England U.K.
178 G4 Marle France
213 K2 Marlengo Italy
179 O6 Marlenheim France
213 P6 Marlera, Rt pt Croatia
251 K6 Marlette MI U.S.A.
183 E6 Marlhes France
182 G4 Marlieux France
261 G10 Marlin TX U.S.A.
256 E10 Marlinton WV U.S.A.
193 D9 Marlishausen Ger.
105 L7 Marlo Vic. Austr.
236 E10 Marloth Nature Reserve S. Africa
192 G2 Marlow Ger.
173 K4 Marlow Buckinghamshire, England U.K.
258 F5 Marlton NJ U.S.A.
179 L5 Marly Lorraine France
178 G3 Marly Nord-Pas-de-Calais France
212 C2 Marly Switz.
178 E5 Marly-la-Ville France
136 C5 Marmagao Goa India
182 E3 Marmagne Bourgogne France
181 P7 Marmagne Centre France
185 E6 Marmande France
221 I2 Marmara Turkey
Marmara, Sea of g. Turkey see Marmara Denizi
221 I2 Marmara Adası i. Turkey
221 J2 Marmara Denizi g. Turkey
221 I2 Marmaraereğlisi Turkey
221 J4 Marmara Gölü l. Turkey
224 E2 Marmarica reg. Libya
221 J6 Marmaris Turkey
221 H4 Marmaro Chios Greece
260 D2 Marmarth ND U.S.A.
133 F10 Marmê Xizang China
206 D4 Marmelar Port.
206 B2 Marmeleira Port.
206 B6 Marmelete Port.
275 F6 Marmelos r. Brazil
256 D10 Marmet WV U.S.A.
109 F10 Marmion, Lake salt l. W.A. Austr.
248 B3 Marmion Lake Ont. Can.
213 J5 Marmirolo Italy
268 A2 Mármol Mex.
213 L3 Marmolada mt. Italy
207 K4 Marmolejo Spain
212 D4 Marmore r. Italy
244 I4 Marmot Bay AK U.S.A.
244 J4 Marmot Island AK U.S.A.
179 N6 Marmoutier France
182 H2 Marnay France
182 J4 Marnaz France
178 H5 Marne dept France
178 D6 Marne r. France
190 H3 Marne Ger.
179 J8 Marne, Source de la France
179 J7 Marne à la Saône, Canal de la France
179 M6 Marne au Rhin, Canal de la France
178 E6 Marne-la-Vallée France
151 F4 Marneuli Georgia
194 E2 Marnheim Ger.
172 H6 Marnhull Dorset, England U.K.
192 E4 Marnitz Ger.
139 O6 Marniu Arun. Prad. India
105 I7 Marnoo Vic. Austr.
230 C2 Maro Chad
224 C5 Maro, Enneri watercourse Chad
235 □K2 Maroambihy Madag.
235 □K2 Maroantsetra Madag.
281 H2 Maroba r. Brazil
235 □J4 Marofandilia Madag.
216 G9 Maroglio r. Sicilia Italy
235 K2 Marojejy, Parc National de nat. park Madag.
101 □9 Marokau atoll Arch. des Tuamotu Fr. Polynesia
102 I5 Marokopa North I. N.Z.
138 F2 Marol Pak.
235 □K4 Marolambo Madag.
191 K10 Maroldsweisach Ger.
181 L5 Marolles-les-Braults France
235 □K2 Maromandia Madag.
178 B5 Maromme France
235 □K2 Maromokotro mt. Madag.
235 F3 Marondera Zimbabwe
275 H3 Maroni r. Fr. Guiana
184 H5 Maronne r. France
107 N9 Maroochydore Qld Austr.
109 C7 Maroonah W.A. Austr.
263 K7 Maroon Peak CO U.S.A.
270 □ Maroon Town Jamaica
218 I4 Maros r. Hungary
115 A6 Maros Sulawesi Indon.
115 A6 Maros r. Indon.
235 □K3 Maroseranana Madag.
199 J5 Maros-Körös Köze plain Hungary
199 J5 Maroslele Hungary
213 L4 Marostica Italy
Marosvásárhely Romania see Târgu Mureș
145 O7 Marot Pak.
235 □K3 Marotandrano Madag.
101 □9 Marotiri is Îs Australes Fr. Polynesia
102 I2 Marotiri Islands North I. N.Z.
235 □K2 Marotolana Madag.
229 I4 Maroua Cameroon
180 F5 Maroué France
275 F5 Marova Brazil
235 □K2 Marovato Antsirañana Madag.
235 □J5 Marovato Toliara Madag.
235 □J3 Marovoay Mahajanga Madag.
235 □K3 Marovoay Toamasina Madag.
235 □J3 Marovoay Atsimo Madag.
115 B4 Marowali Sulawesi Indon.
275 H3 Marowijne r. Suriname
197 I2 Maróz, Jezioro l. Pol.
194 C3 Marpingen Ger.
171 M7 Marple Greater Manchester, England U.K.
150 D3 Marqab, Qal'at al tourist site Syria
149 J6 Marqādah Syria
Marqaköl l. Kazakh. see Markakol', Ozero
237 L4 Marquard S. Africa
195 M6 Marquartstein Ger.
269 I9 Marquelia Mex.
178 C3 Marquenterre reg. France
205 O6 Marquesado de Berlanga reg. Spain
Marquesas Islands Fr. Polynesia see Marquises, Îles
255 F13 Marquesas Keys is FL U.S.A.
281 F5 Marquês de Valença Brazil
250 G3 Marquette MI U.S.A.
261 G10 Marquez TX U.S.A.
280 A6 Marquinho Brazil
178 F3 Marquion France
271 □3 Marquis, Cap c. St Lucia
178 C2 Marquise France
101 □9 Marquises, Îles is Fr. Polynesia
185 I10 Marquixanes France
105 I4 Marra N.S.W. Austr.
105 K4 Marra r. N.S.W. Austr.
224 E6 Marra, Jebel mt. Sudan
224 E6 Marra, Jebel plat. Sudan
106 E3 Marra Aboriginal Land res. N.T. Austr.
235 H3 Marracua Moz.
235 G5 Marracuene Moz.
213 L7 Marradi Italy
146 E7 Marrāk i. Saudi Arabia
226 D3 Marrakech Morocco
Marrakesh Morocco see Marrakech
146 E6 Marrān Saudi Arabia
Marra Plateau Sudan see Marra, Jebel
162 R3 Marraskoski Fin.
105 J9 Marrawah Tas. Austr.
104 G3 Marree S.A. Austr.
261 J11 Marrero LA U.S.A.
235 G3 Marromeu Moz.
235 G3 Marromeu, Reserva de nature res. Moz.
269 H1 Marroquin Mex.
214 B8 Marrubiu Sardegna Italy
186 I2 Marrum Neth.
233 C8 Marrupa Moz.
104 D2 Marryat S.A. Austr.
183 A6 Mars r. France
256 E8 Mars PA U.S.A.
225 G3 Marsá al 'Alam Egypt
224 C2 Marsa al Burayqah Libya
203 E5 Marsa Ben Mehidi Alg.
232 C4 Marsabit Kenya
232 C4 Marsabit National Reserve nature res. Kenya
182 D6 Marsac-en-Livradois France
180 H6 Marsac-sur-Don France
225 H5 Marsa Darur Sudan
225 H4 Marsa Delwein Sudan
212 G6 Marsaglia Italy
146 B3 Marsá Ijlī Egypt
179 M6 Marsal France
216 C8 Marsala Sicilia Italy
217 □ Marsalforn Gozo Malta
146 C5 Marsa Mar'ob Sudan
224 E2 Marsá Maţrūḩ Egypt
182 F2 Marsannay-la-Côte France
183 F7 Marsanne France
225 H4 Marsa Oseif Sudan
146 C5 Marsa Salak Sudan
146 C5 Marsa Shin'ab Sudan
Marsaskala Malta see Wied Il-Għajn
228 B3 Marsassoum Senegal
146 B3 Marsá Ţunḑubah Egypt
217 □ Marsaxlokk Malta
217 □ Marsaxlokk, Il-Bajja ta' b. Malta
270 E2 Mars Bay Andros Bahamas
238 □2a Mars Bay b. Ascension S. Atlantic Ocean
191 G8 Marsberg Ger.
190 J4 Marschacht Ger.
215 I2 Marsciano Italy
105 K5 Marsden N.S.W. Austr.
247 I4 Marsden Sask. Can.
171 N6 Marsden West Yorkshire, England U.K.
102 I2 Marsden Point N.Z.
186 G3 Marsdiep sea chan. Neth.
183 D10 Marseillan France
183 G10 Marseille France
Marseille airport France see Provence
183 F9 Marseille au Rhône, Canal de France
178 C4 Marseille-en-Beauvaisis France
Marseilles France see Marseille
250 F8 Marseilles IL U.S.A.
276 D3 Marsella Bol.
162 M4 Marsfjället mt. Sweden
150 C10 Marshah, Jabal mt. Saudi Arabia
106 F7 Marshall watercourse N.T. Austr.
247 I4 Marshall Sask. Can.
244 G3 Marshall AK U.S.A.
261 I8 Marshall AR U.S.A.
254 D6 Marshall IL U.S.A.
250 J7 Marshall MI U.S.A.
260 H3 Marshall MN U.S.A.
260 I6 Marshall MO U.S.A.
255 F8 Marshall NC U.S.A.
261 H9 Marshall TX U.S.A.
256 H10 Marshall VA U.S.A.
290 F5 Marshall Islands country N. Pacific Ocean
258 E2 Marshalls Creek PA U.S.A.
258 D5 Marshallton DE U.S.A.
260 I4 Marshalltown IA U.S.A.
258 D4 Marsh Creek Lake PA U.S.A.
172 H5 Marshfield South Gloucestershire, England U.K.
261 I7 Marshfield MO U.S.A.
250 D5 Marshfield WI U.S.A.
255 I12 Marsh Harbour Bahamas
257 □R2 Mars Hill ME U.S.A.
261 J11 Marsh Island LA U.S.A.
245 N3 Marsh Lake Y.T. Can.
245 N3 Marsh Lake Y.T. Can.
247 M3 Marsh Point Man. Can.
144 C3 Marshūn Iran
183 E9 Marsillargues France
262 F5 Marsing ID U.S.A.
171 O4 Marske-by-the-Sea Redcar and Cleveland, England U.K.
179 K5 Mars-la-Tour France
178 I6 Marson France
185 I8 Marssac-sur-Tarn France
165 N2 Märsta Sweden
164 G7 Marstal Denmark
190 K1 Marstal Bugt b. Denmark
212 G1 Märstetten Switz.
173 J4 Marston Oxfordshire, England U.K.
172 G6 Marston Magna Somerset, England U.K.
173 K3 Marston Moretaine Bedfordshire, England U.K.
100 □3a Marsugalt i. Kwajalein Marshall Is
139 J6 Marsyangdi r. Nepal
258 D7 Marsyhope r. MD U.S.A.
214 H2 Marta Italy
214 H3 Marta r. Italy
Martaban, Gulf of Myanmar see Mottama, Gulf of
214 H2 Martana, Isola i. Italy
117 L1 Martanai Besar i. Malaysia
217 O3 Martano Italy
215 J2 Martano, Monte mt. Italy
229 I5 Martap Cameroon
117 K6 Martapura Kalimantan Indon.
116 F7 Martapura Sumatera Indon.
229 I3 Marte Nigeria
184 H6 Martel France
256 C8 Martel OH U.S.A.
184 G6 Martel, Causse de hills France
187 I9 Martelange Belgium
213 M4 Martellago Italy
213 J2 Martello Italy
199 J5 Mártély Hungary
199 J5 Mártélyi park Hungary
248 E4 Marten River Ont. Can.
247 J4 Martensville Sask. Can.
267 J4 Marte R. Gómez, Presa resr Mex.
209 D9 Martés mt. Spain
209 C9 Martés, Sierra de mts Spain
190 H5 Martfeld Ger.
199 J4 Martfű Hungary
173 P2 Martham Norfolk, England U.K.
257 O7 Martha's Vineyard i. MA U.S.A.
184 E4 Marthon France
270 E3 Martí Cuba
204 H8 Martiago Spain
213 O3 Martignacco Italy
215 I3 Martignano, Lago di l. Italy
185 C6 Martignas-sur-Jalle France
181 K7 Martigné-Briand France
180 I6 Martigné-Ferchaud France
181 J5 Martigné-sur-Mayenne France
212 C3 Martigny Switz.
182 E3 Martigny-le-Comte France
179 K7 Martigny-les-Bains France
179 K7 Martigny-les-Gerbonvaux France
183 G10 Martigues France
205 K7 Martiherrero Spain
207 I9 Martil Morocco
185 C6 Martillac France
206 D6 Martim Longo Port.
Martim Vaz, Ilhas is S. Atlantic Ocean see Martin Vaz, Ilhas
246 F2 Martin r. N.W.T. Can.
199 H2 Martin Slovakia
208 E5 Martín r. Spain
260 E4 Martin SD U.S.A.
168 F7 Martin, Isle i. Scotland U.K.
255 E9 Martin, Lake AL U.S.A.
217 M2 Martina Franca Italy
103 J8 Martinborough North I. N.Z.
204 D9 Martinchel Port.
285 H4 Martín Chico Uru.
285 H5 Martín Colman Arg.
207 J6 Martín de la Jara Spain
284 D4 Martín de Loyola Arg.
204 H7 Martín de Yeltes Spain
212 H4 Martinengo Italy
208 I3 Martinet Spain
269 J5 Martínez Mex.
264 J3 Martinez CA U.S.A.
255 F9 Martinez GA U.S.A.
265 R9 Martinez Lake AZ U.S.A.
191 J8 Martinfeld Ger.
204 C9 Martingança Port.
285 H4 Martín García, Isla i. Arg.
207 K4 Martín Gonzalo, Embalse de resr Spain
281 E3 Martinho Campos Brazil
271 □3 Martinique terr. West Indies
271 □2 Martinique Passage Dominica/Martinique
205 K6 Martín Muñoz de las Posadas Spain
220 E4 Martino Greece
280 B5 Martinópolis Brazil
286 Q2 Martin Peninsula Antarctica
245 L1 Martin Point pt AK U.S.A.
204 I2 Martinporra Spain
103 B11 Martins Bay South I. N.Z.
201 L3 Martinsberg Austria
256 C8 Martinsburg OH U.S.A.
256 G8 Martinsburg PA U.S.A.
256 H9 Martinsburg WV U.S.A.
213 Q6 Martinšćica Croatia
258 E3 Martins Creek PA U.S.A.
258 D1 Martins Creek r. PA U.S.A.
256 E8 Martins Ferry OH U.S.A.
215 L2 Martinsicuro Italy
169 F8 Martinstown Ireland
254 D6 Martinsville IN U.S.A.
256 F12 Martinsville VA U.S.A.
288 H7 Martin Vaz, Ilhas is S. Atlantic Ocean
Martin Vaz Islands S. Atlantic Ocean see Martin Vaz, Ilhas
214 B6 Martis Sardegna Italy
181 N8 Martizay France
173 O3 Martlesham Suffolk, England U.K.
172 H3 Martley Worcestershire, England U.K.
172 G6 Martock Somerset, England U.K.
Martök Kazakh. see Martuk
133 E11 Martoli Uttaranchal India
102 J7 Marton North I. N.Z.
199 H4 Martonvásar Hungary
208 I5 Martorell Spain
207 L5 Martos Spain
185 G9 Martres-Tolosane France
162 T3 Martti Fin.
163 Q6 Marttila Fin.
142 G2 Martuk Kazakh.
151 G5 Martuni Armenia
151 D3 Martvili Georgia
159 L3 Martynivka Ukr.
158 I2 Martynovychi Ukr.
128 H9 Maru Gansu China
229 G3 Maru Nigeria
145 J4 Maruchak Afgh.
117 K2 Marudi Sarawak Malaysia
117 L1 Marudu, Teluk b. Malaysia
145 L6 Maruf Afgh.
125 K12 Marugame Japan
205 L7 Marugán Spain
217 N3 Maruggio Italy
103 G8 Maruia r. South I. N.Z.
278 F4 Maruim Brazil
151 C2 Marukhis Ugheltekhili pass Georgia/Rus. Fed.
127 H3 Maruko Japan
105 L6 Marulan N.S.W. Austr.
285 F2 Marull Arg.
186 J2 Marum Neth.
100 □5 Marum, Mount vol. Vanuatu
144 C6 Mārūn r. Iran
231 D9 Marunga Angola
126 D3 Maruoka Japan
143 U1 Marushka Rus. Fed.
138 C6 Marusthali reg. India
197 J4 Maruszów Mazowieckie Pol.
197 J5 Maruszów Świętokrzyskie Pol.
101 □9 Marutea (Nord) atoll Arch. des Tuamotu Fr. Polynesia
101 □9 Marutea (Sud) atoll Arch. des Tuamotu Fr. Polynesia
108 I7 Maruwa Aboriginal Reserve W.A. Austr.
232 B3 Maruwa Hills Sudan
127 K5 Maruyama Japan
126 A4 Maruyama-gawa r. Japan
206 E2 Marvão Port.
144 F6 Marvast Iran
144 E7 Marv Dasht Iran
183 C7 Marvejols France
109 E11 Marvel Loch W.A. Austr.
179 J5 Marville France
265 U3 Marvine, Mount UT U.S.A.
138 D7 Marwar Junction Rajasthan India
247 I4 Marwayne Alta Can.
195 J4 Marxheim Ger.
Marxwalde Ger. see Neuhardenberg
194 E4 Marxzell Ger.
106 C2 Mary r. N.T. Austr.
107 N8 Mary r. Qld Austr.
108 I5 Mary r. W.A. Austr.
145 I3 Mary Turkm.
144 J3 Mary admin. div. Turkm.
230 E2 Maryal Bai Sudan
159 N8 Mar"yanivka Respublika Krym Ukr.
197 M5 Mar"yanivka Volyns'ka Oblast' Ukr.
159 P6 Mar"yanivka Zaporiz'ka Oblast' Ukr.
158 G3 Mar"yanivka Zhytomyrs'ka Oblast' Ukr.
159 R8 Mar'yanskaya Rus. Fed.
Mary A.S.S.R. aut. rep. Rus. Fed. see Mariy El, Respublika
168 G7 Marybank Highland, Scotland U.K.
107 N8 Maryborough Qld Austr.
105 I7 Maryborough Vic. Austr.
236 G5 Marydale S. Africa
258 D6 Marydel MD U.S.A.
142 C1 Mar'yevka Rus. Fed.
168 □N2 Maryfield Shetland, Scotland U.K.
247 J2 Mary Frances Lake N.W.T. Can.
159 Q6 Mar"yinka Ukr.
Maryino Rus. Fed. see Pristen'
159 P8 Mar"yivka Respublika Krym Ukr.
159 N6 Mar"yivka Zaporiz'ka Oblast' Ukr.
168 K9 Marykirk Aberdeenshire, Scotland U.K.
247 K2 Mary Lake N.W.T. Can.
258 B7 Maryland state U.S.A.
258 B5 Maryland Line MD U.S.A.
158 E5 Marynychi Ukr.
Mary Oblast admin. div. Turkm. see Mary
168 J8 Marypark Moray, Scotland U.K.
171 K4 Maryport Cumbria, England U.K.
249 K2 Mary's Harbour Nfld and Lab. Can.
244 F2 Marys Igloo AK U.S.A.
249 K4 Marystown Nfld and Lab. Can.
265 T3 Marysvale UT U.S.A.
105 J7 Marysville Vic. Austr.
249 H4 Marysville N.B. Can.
264 K2 Marysville CA U.S.A.
260 G6 Marysville KS U.S.A.
251 L7 Marysville MI U.S.A.
256 B8 Marysville OH U.S.A.
258 B4 Marysville PA U.S.A.
262 C2 Marysville WA U.S.A.
106 E8 Maryvale N.T. Austr.
107 J5 Maryvale Qld Austr.
260 H5 Maryville MO U.S.A.
255 F8 Maryville TN U.S.A.
168 K8 Marywell Aberdeenshire, Scotland U.K.
213 K7 Marzabotto Italy
280 C2 Marzagão Brazil
193 G6 Marzahna Ger.
193 G5 Marzahne Ger.
217 I10 Marzamemi Sicilia Italy
180 G6 Marzan France
213 L7 Marzeno r. Italy
195 L5 Marzling Ger.
274 B3 Marzo, Cabo c. Col.
182 C3 Marzy France
205 M3 Masa Spain
266 □P12 Masachapa Nic.
150 D7 Masada tourist site Israel
Más Afuera i. S. Pacific Ocean see Alejandro Selkirk, Isla
232 E4 Masagaweyn Somalia
267 N10 Masagua Guat.
233 C7 Masaguro Tanz.
144 F6 Masāhūn, Kūh-e mt. Iran
233 B5 Masai Mara National Reserve nature res. Kenya
214 B9 Masainas Sardegna Italy
233 C6 Masai Steppe plain Tanz.
232 A5 Masaka Uganda
237 K7 Masakhane S. Africa
233 C6 Masaki Tanz.
234 D4 Masalanyane Pan salt pan Botswana
209 D9 Masalavés Spain
117 K7 Masalembu Besar i. Indon.
117 K7 Masalembu Kecil i. Indon.
151 J6 Masallı Azer.
115 B5 Masamba Sulawesi Indon.
115 B5 Masamba mt. Indon.
123 F11 Masan S. Korea
159 N9 Masandra Ukr.
115 E7 Masapun Maluku Indon.
146 F7 Masāqif i. Saudi Arabia
233 C7 Masasi Tanz.
266 □P12 Masatepe Nic.
Más á Tierra i. S. Pacific Ocean see Robinson Crusoe, Isla
277 E4 Masavi Bol.
266 □P12 Masaya Nic.
266 □P12 Masaya, Volcán vol. Nic.
114 D5 Masbate Masbate Phil.
114 D5 Masbate i. Phil.
185 I9 Mas-Cabardès France
217 I8 Mascali Sicilia Italy
217 I8 Mascalucia Sicilia Italy
227 F2 Mascara Alg.
205 M9 Mascaraque Spain
289 H6 Mascarene Basin sea feature Indian Ocean
289 H6 Mascarene Plain sea feature Indian Ocean
289 H5 Mascarene Ridge sea feature Indian Ocean
204 F5 Mascarenhas Port.
269 J4 Mascareõs Mex.
284 D2 Mascasín Arg.
284 D2 Mascasín, Salinas de salt pan Arg.
215 P6 Maschito Italy
185 G6 Masclat France
268 C5 Mascota Mex.
268 B5 Mascota r. Mex.
254 K3 Mascouche Que. Can.
208 E3 Mascún r. Spain
208 F6 Mas de Barberans Spain
208 E6 Mas de las Matas Spain
205 P7 Masegosa Spain
207 O3 Masegoso Spain
205 O7 Masegoso de Tajuña Spain
118 B3 Masein Myanmar
117 L3 Ma Sekatok b. Indon.
115 F8 Masela Maluku Indon.

115 F8 Masela i. Maluku Indon.
194 H5 Maselheim Ger.
232 B4 Maseno Kenya
115 C5 Masepe i. Indon.
212 E3 Masera Italy
200 F8 Maserada sul Piave Italy
251 R1 Masères, Lac l. Que. Can.
237 L5 Maseru Lesotho
179 M8 Masevaux France
163 H6 Masfjorden Norway
185 G8 Mas-Grenier France
Mashaba Zimbabwe see Mashava
146 C3 Mashābih i. Saudi Arabia
237 M5 Mashai Lesotho
231 D6 Mashala Dem. Rep. Congo
171 N5 Masham North Yorkshire, England U.K.
130 G7 Mashan Guangxi China
235 F4 Mashava Zimbabwe
138 F2 Masherbrum mt. Pak.
159 L1 Masheve Ukr.
144 H3 Mashhad Iran
138 E6 Mashi r. India
124 S3 Mashike Japan
127 L3 Mashiko Japan
144 B2 Mashīrān Iran
235 F5 Mashishing S. Africa
159 N4 Mashivka Ukr.
145 J7 Mashkel, Hamun-i- salt flat Pak.
145 J8 Mashkel, Rudi-i r. Pak.
145 J7 Mashki Chah Pak.
145 J8 Māshkīd, Rūdkhāneh-ye r. Iran
235 F3 Mashonaland Central prov. Zimbabwe
235 F3 Mashonaland East prov. Zimbabwe
235 F3 Mashonaland West prov. Zimbabwe
Mashtagi Azer. see Maştağa
162 Q2 Masi Norway
266 E4 Masiáca Mex.
231 C5 Masia-Mbia Dem. Rep. Congo
237 L7 Masibambane S. Africa
204 D4 Maside Spain
147 J8 Masīlah, Wādī al watercourse Yemen
237 K4 Masilo S. Africa
231 C6 Masi-Manimba Dem. Rep. Congo
115 A4 Masimbu Sulawesi Barat Indon.
232 A4 Masindi Uganda
114 B4 Masinloc Luzon Phil.
212 H3 Masino r. Italy
236 H7 Masinyusane S. Africa
Masira, Gulf of Oman see Maşīrah, Khalīj
Masira Channel Oman see Maşīrah, Tur'at
147 N5 Maşīrah, Jazīrat i. Oman
147 N6 Maşīrah, Khalīj b. Oman
147 N5 Maşīrah, Tur'at sea chan. Oman
Masira Island Oman see Maşīrah, Jazīrat
151 F5 Masis Armenia
276 B2 Masisea Peru
230 F5 Masisi Dem. Rep. Congo
213 L6 Masi Torello Italy
115 G5 Masiwang r. Seram Indon.
237 M4 Masjaing S. Africa
144 C6 Masjed-e Soleymān Iran
169 D5 Mask, Lough l. Ireland
147 I1 Maskān i. Kuwait
140 E7 Maskan, Raas pt Somalia
150 G2 Maskanah Syria
144 H8 Maskūtān Iran
185 C9 Maslacq France
199 K5 Maşloc Romania
159 P3 Maslova Pristan' Rus. Fed.
159 S2 Maslovka Rus. Fed.
197 H4 Masłowice Pol.
145 K7 Maslti Pak.
204 F1 Masma r. Spain
147 I8 Maşna'ah Yemen
213 L3 Maso r. Italy
235 □K2 Masoala, Parc National de nat. park Madag.
235 □K2 Masoala, Saikanosy pen. Madag.
235 □K2 Masoala, Tanjona c. Madag.
115 F5 Masohi Seram Indon.
250 J7 Mason MI U.S.A.
256 A9 Mason OH U.S.A.
261 F10 Mason TX U.S.A.
250 C3 Mason WI U.S.A.
256 C9 Mason WV U.S.A.
109 E9 Mason, Lake salt flat W.A. Austr.
103 B13 Mason Bay Stewart I. N.Z.
260 I4 Mason City IA U.S.A.
250 E9 Mason City IL U.S.A.
212 F6 Masone Italy
271 □5 Mason Hall Trin. and Tob.
115 D4 Masoni i. Indon.
103 G9 Masons Flat South I. N.Z.
256 F9 Masontown PA U.S.A.
256 F9 Masontown WV U.S.A.
238 □3f Maspalomas Gran Canaria Canary Is
238 □3f Maspalomas, Punta de pt Gran Canaria Canary Is
147 N4 Masqaţ Oman
147 N4 Masqaţ governorate Oman
147 M3 Masqaţ reg. Oman
231 B5 Massa Congo
212 I7 Massa Italy
257 M6 Massachusetts state U.S.A.
257 O6 Massachusetts Bay MA U.S.A.
212 I8 Massaciuccoli, Lago di l. Italy
265 X1 Massadona CO U.S.A.
212 H7 Massa e Carrara prov. Italy
213 M6 Massa Fiscaglia Italy
217 M2 Massafra Italy
224 B6 Massaguet Chad
183 C8 Mas-St-Chély France
224 B6 Massakory Chad
230 C2 Massalassef Chad
213 L7 Massa Lombarda Italy
215 M6 Massa Lubrense Italy
209 E8 Massamagrell Spain
214 F1 Massa Marittimo Italy
215 J2 Massa Martana Italy
235 G2 Massamba Moz.
279 B9 Massambará Brazil
230 A5 Massana Gabon
235 G4 Massangena Moz.
231 C7 Massango Angola
235 G2 Massangulo Moz.
259 I3 Massapequa NY U.S.A.
278 E4 Massaroca Brazil
212 I8 Massarosa Italy
185 G10 Massat France
231 C6 Massau Angola
225 H6 Massawa Eritrea
225 H5 Massawa Channel Eritrea
181 O7 Massay France
191 J10 Maßbach Ger.
193 I7 Massen Ger.
257 K4 Massena NY U.S.A.
230 C2 Massenya Chad
184 H4 Masseret France
217 M2 Masseria Risana hill Italy
245 N5 Masset B.C. Can.
246 C4 Masset Inlet B.C. Can.
185 F9 Masseube France
248 D4 Massey Ont. Can.
258 D6 Massey MD U.S.A.
183 C6 Massiac France
231 D7 Massibi Angola
215 L5 Massico, Monte hill Italy
256 C9 Massieville OH U.S.A.
183 C6 Massif Central mts France
228 D4 Massigui Mali
Massilia France see Marseille
256 D8 Massillon OH U.S.A.
212 E7 Massimino Italy
228 D3 Massina Mali
195 N5 Massing Ger.
235 G4 Massinga Moz.
235 G4 Massingir Moz.
251 S4 Masson-Angers Que. Can.
214 F2 Massoncello, Monte hill Italy
287 G2 Masson Island Antarctica
178 D6 Massy France
151 K5 Maştağa Azer.
212 E4 Mastallone, Parco Naturale nature res. Italy
145 M2 Mastchoh Tajik.
142 C3 Masteksay Zapadnyy Kazakhstan Kazakh.
191 D10 Mastershausen Ger.
103 J7 Masterton North I. N.Z.
259 J3 Mastic NY U.S.A.
259 J3 Mastic Beach NY U.S.A.
270 E1 Mastic Point Andros Bahamas
248 F4 Mastigouche, Réserve Faunique de nature res. Que. Can.
214 D8 Mastixi, Punta su pt Sardegna Italy
166 J1 Mastrevik Norway
145 O3 Mastuj Pak.
145 L7 Mastung Pak.
146 D4 Mastūrah Saudi Arabia
160 H8 Masty Belarus
214 A9 Masua Sardegna Italy
125 I12 Masuda Japan
127 H4 Masuho Japan
231 D6 Masuika Dem. Rep. Congo
Masuku Gabon see Franceville
144 C3 Masuleh Iran
Masulipatam Andhra Prad. India see Machilipatnam
214 B8 Masullas Sardegna Italy
Masuna i. American Samoa see Tutuila
116 D6 Masurai, Bukit mt. Indon.
235 F4 Masvingo Zimbabwe
235 F4 Masvingo prov. Zimbabwe
233 B5 Maswa Tanz.
233 B5 Maswe Game Reserve nature res. Tanz.
150 E3 Maşyāf Syria
158 C2 Masyevichy Belarus
196 C3 Maszewo Lubuskie Pol.
196 F1 Maszewo Pomorskie Pol.
196 D2 Maszewo Zachodniopomorskie Pol.
218 H9 Mat r. Albania
118 G5 Mat, Nam r. Laos
239 □1c Mât, Rivière du r. Réunion
118 C1 Mata Myanmar
102 M4 Mata r. North I. N.Z.
275 E3 Mata, Serranía de mts Venez.
283 C8 Mata Amarilla Arg.
231 D8 Mataba Zambia
232 E3 Matabaan Somalia
235 E3 Matabeleland North prov. Zimbabwe
235 F4 Matabeleland South prov. Zimbabwe
139 L6 Matabhanga W. Bengal India
205 M6 Matabuena Spain
206 G3 Matachel r. Spain
248 D4 Matachewan Ont. Can.
266 F3 Matachic Mex.
129 N3 Matad Dornod Mongolia
231 B6 Matadi Dem. Rep. Congo
261 E8 Matador TX U.S.A.
208 J4 Matagalls mt. Spain
266 □Q11 Matagalpa Nic.
248 E3 Matagami Que. Can.
248 E3 Matagami, Lac l. Que. Can.
261 G11 Matagorda TX U.S.A.
261 G11 Matagorda Island TX U.S.A.
278 F4 Mata Grande Brazil
102 J6 Matahiwi North I. N.Z.
101 □9a Mataiea Tahiti Fr. Polynesia
Mataigou Ningxia China see Taole
116 G3 Matak i. Indon.
143 P3 Matak Kazakh.
102 K4 Matakana Island North I. N.Z.
102 M4 Matakaoa Point North I. N.Z.
103 G8 Matakitaki South I. N.Z.
231 B8 Matala Angola
206 F6 Matalascañas Spain
136 G9 Matale Sri Lanka
205 P5 Matalebreras Spain
236 I4 Mataleng S. Africa
146 E2 Maţāli', Jabal hill Saudi Arabia
205 J4 Matallana de Valmadrigal Spain
228 B3 Matam Senegal
205 O5 Matamala de Almazán Spain
102 J4 Matamata North I. N.Z.
236 E1 Mata-Mata S. Africa
102 K7 Matamau North I. N.Z.
229 H3 Matamey Niger
258 F2 Matamoras PA U.S.A.
267 N8 Matamoros Campeche Mex.
261 C12 Matamoros Chihuahua Mex.
266 H5 Matamoros Coahuila Mex.
269 L8 Matamoros Oaxaca Mex.
267 K5 Matamoros Tamaulipas Mex.
205 L3 Matamorosa Spain
228 B2 Ma'ta Moûlana well Maur.
204 C9 Mata Mourisca Port.
115 B5 Matana, Danau l. Indon.
114 D8 Matanal Point Phil.
224 D4 Ma'ţan as Sārah well Libya
224 D4 Ma'ţan Bishrah well Libya
284 B2 Matancilla Chile
233 C7 Matandu r. Tanz.
249 H3 Matane Que. Can.
249 H3 Matane, Réserve Faunique de nature res. Que. Can.
275 F2 Mata Negra Venez.
235 □J4 Matanga Madag.
102 J4 Matangi North I. N.Z.
229 G3 Matankari Niger
145 N5 Matanni Pak.
245 J3 Matanuska AK U.S.A.
270 C2 Matanzas Cuba
284 C5 Matanzilla, Pampa de la plain Arg.
280 C4 Matão Brazil
278 C4 Matão, Serra do hills Brazil
285 I2 Mataojo Uru.
266 □R13 Matapalo, Cabo c. Costa Rica
Matapan, Cape pt Greece see Tainaro, Akrotirio
196 G5 Mata Panew r. Pol.
249 H3 Matapédia, Lac l. Que. Can.
103 □4 Mata Point Niue
205 L3 Mataporquera Spain
205 K6 Matapozuelos Spain
284 A4 Mataquito r. Chile
147 H2 Maţār well Saudi Arabia
282 E3 Matará Arg.
136 G10 Matara Sri Lanka
220 C4 Mataragka Greece
117 L9 Mataram Lombok Indon.
Matarānga Greece see Mataragka
276 B4 Matarani Peru
106 D3 Mataranka N.T. Austr.
115 C5 Matarape, Teluk b. Indon.
150 A9 Matārimah, Ra's pt Egypt
114 E6 Matarinao Bay Samar Phil.
226 E2 Matarka Morocco
208 J4 Mataró Spain
102 J6 Mataroa North I. N.Z.
115 C5 Matarombea r. Indon.
218 I7 Mataruška Banja Kraljevo Serbia
238 □3b Matas Blancas Fuerteventura Canary Is
117 K7 Matasiri i. Indon.
225 F5 Matassi well Sudan
233 C6 Matassi Tanz.
237 M6 Matatiele S. Africa
138 G7 Matatila Reservoir India
100 □2 Matatula, Cape American Samoa
102 I6 Matau North I. N.Z.
103 C13 Mataura South I. N.Z.
103 C13 Mataura r. South I. N.Z.
100 □2 Matautu Samoa
99 I3 Matā'utu Wallis and Futuna Is
101 □9a Matavai, Baie de b. Tahiti Fr. Polynesia
100 □2 Matavanu, Mount vol. crater Samoa
103 □3 Matavera Rarotonga Cook Is
102 L5 Matawai North I. N.Z.
102 H2 Matawaia North I. N.Z.
259 G4 Matawan NJ U.S.A.
254 K2 Matawin r. Que. Can.
143 R5 Matay Kazakh.
147 J3 Maţbakh, Ra's al pt Qatar
Matcha Tajik. see Mastchoh
251 Q1 Matchi-Manitou, Lac l. Que. Can.
118 G5 Mat Con, Hon i. Vietnam
277 E3 Mategua Bol.
268 G2 Matehuala Mex.
219 M4 Matei Romania
230 C2 Matékaga Chad
235 F4 Mateke Hills Zimbabwe
213 O9 Matelica Italy
271 □7 Matelot Trin. and Tob.
233 C7 Matemanga Tanz.
102 I6 Matemateaonga Range hills North I. N.Z.
231 C9 Matende Angola
235 G2 Matenge Moz.
217 L2 Matera Italy
215 R7 Matera prov. Italy
213 Q4 Materija Slovenia
215 M5 Matese, Lago del l. Italy
215 M5 Matese, Monti del mts Italy
199 L4 Mátészalka Hungary
234 E3 Matetsi Zimbabwe
227 H1 Mateur Tunisia
281 E3 Mateus Leme Brazil
256 C11 Matewan WV U.S.A.
184 D4 Matha France
138 C6 Mathaji Rajasthan India
182 J2 Mathay France
248 D3 Matheson Ont. Can.
257 I11 Mathews VA U.S.A.
212 D5 Mathi Italy
256 G10 Mathias WV U.S.A.
135 □1 Mathidahura i. N. Male Maldives
261 G11 Mathis TX U.S.A.
105 J6 Mathoura N.S.W. Austr.
220 A3 Mathraki i. Greece
138 F6 Mathura Uttar Prad. India
239 □1a Mathurin Bay Rodrigues I. Mauritius
138 E8 Mathwar Madh. Prad. India
114 F8 Mati Mindanao Phil.
229 F3 Matiacoali Burkina
139 L6 Matiali W. Bengal India
131 I5 Matianxu Hunan China
145 M9 Matiari Pak.
281 F4 Matias Barbosa Brazil
278 E5 Matias Cardoso Brazil
269 L9 Matías Romero Mex.
235 I2 Matibane Moz.
180 G4 Matignon France
178 F4 Matigny France
249 H2 Matimekosh Que. Can.
138 I8 Matin Chhattisgarh India
266 □R12 Matina Costa Rica
248 D4 Matinenda Lake Ont. Can.
257 □Q5 Matinicus Island ME U.S.A.
217 O3 Matino Italy
101 □9a Matiti Tahiti Fr. Polynesia
130 D2 Matizi Sichuan China
236 E9 Matjiesfontein S. Africa
151 D3 Mat'khoji Georgia
139 L9 Matla r. India
145 M9 Matli Pak.
171 N7 Matlock Derbyshire, England U.K.
171 N7 Matlock Bath Derbyshire, England U.K.
237 L3 Matlwangtlwang S. Africa
225 G6 Matna Sudan
275 E3 Mato r. Venez.
275 E3 Mato, Cerro mt. Venez.
256 D11 Matoaka WV U.S.A.
235 F4 Matobo Hills Zimbabwe
235 F4 Matobo National Park Zimbabwe
277 F3 Mato Grosso Brazil
280 A2 Mato Grosso state Brazil
278 B5 Mato Grosso, Planalto do plat. Brazil
280 A4 Mato Grosso do Sul state Brazil
235 G5 Matola Moz.
235 G3 Matondo Moz.
233 B8 Matope Malawi
Matopo Hills Zimbabwe see Matobo Hills
Matoriki i. Fiji see Moturiki
238 □3b Matorral, Punta del pt Fuerteventura Canary Is
276 D3 Matos r. Bol.
204 C6 Matosinhos Port.
Matou Guangxi China see Pingguo
182 E4 Matour France
281 E3 Matozinhos Brazil
199 I4 Mátra mts Hungary
199 J4 Mátraballa Hungary
147 N4 Maţraḩ Oman
199 J4 Matrai park Hungary
164 I1 Matrand Norway
199 I3 Mátraterenye Hungary
199 I4 Mátraverebély Hungary
200 D5 Matrei am Brenner Austria
200 G5 Matrei in Osttirol Austria
236 D9 Matroosberg S. Africa
236 D9 Matroosberg mt. S. Africa
237 K1 Matrooster S. Africa
228 B5 Matru Sierra Leone
148 C8 Maţrūḩ governorate Egypt
169 I5 Matry Ireland
160 G3 Matsalu laht b. Estonia
160 G3 Matsalu rahvuspark nature res. Estonia
236 G4 Matsap S. Africa
151 A2 Matsesta Rus. Fed.
235 □J4 Matsiatra r. Madag.
237 L5 Matsieng Lesotho
234 E4 Matsitama Botswana
233 F8 Matsoandakana Madag.
126 C6 Matsubara Japan
127 J5 Matsuda Japan
127 I1 Matsudai Japan
127 K4 Matsudo Japan
125 K11 Matsue Japan
127 I3 Matsuida Japan
127 G3 Matsukawa Nagano Japan
127 G4 Matsukawa Nagano Japan
124 R5 Matsumae Japan
127 G3 Matsumoto Japan
125 J13 Matsuno Japan
127 I1 Matsunoyama Japan
127 L4 Matsuo Japan
126 D3 Matsuoka Japan
126 E6 Matsusaka Japan
127 H2 Matsushiro Japan
131 M5 Matsu Tao i. Taiwan
125 G13 Matsuura Japan
125 J13 Matsuyama Japan
127 I6 Matsuzaki Japan
212 G2 Matt Switz.
248 D3 Mattagami r. Ont. Can.
179 L7 Mattaincourt France
285 E4 Mattaldi Arg.
255 I8 Mattamuskeet, Lake NC U.S.A.
248 E4 Mattawa Ont. Can.
257 □Q3 Mattawamkeag ME U.S.A.
212 D4 Matterhorn mt. Italy/Switz.
262 G6 Matterhorn mt. NV U.S.A.
201 N4 Mattersburg Austria
212 D3 Mattertal val. Switz.
Matthew atoll Gilbert Is Kiribati see Marakei
99 H4 Matthew Island S. Pacific Ocean
255 G8 Matthews NC U.S.A.
232 C4 Matthews Peak Kenya
275 F3 Matthews Ridge Guyana
270 G3 Matthew Town Gt Inagua Bahamas
147 K4 Maţţī, Sabkhat salt pan Saudi Arabia
200 H3 Mattighofen Austria
215 Q4 Mattinata Italy
173 O2 Mattishall Norfolk, England U.K.
259 J3 Mattituck NY U.S.A.
162 L5 Mattmar Sweden
126 E2 Mattō Japan
260 K6 Mattoon IL U.S.A.
200 H4 Mattsee Austria
200 H4 Mattsee l. Austria
163 M6 Mattsmyra Sweden
162 P4 Måttsund Sweden
Matturai Sri Lanka see Matara
117 I3 Matu Sarawak Malaysia
276 A2 Matucana Peru
136 G9 Matugama Sri Lanka
197 M1 Matuizos Lith.
101 □7 Matuku i. Fiji
213 Q5 Matulji Croatia
231 C8 Matumbo Angola
Matun Afgh. see Khōst
271 □7 Matura Trin. and Tob.
271 □7 Matura Bay Trin. and Tob.
275 F2 Maturín Venez.
275 F3 Maturuca Brazil
235 F3 Matusadona National Park Zimbabwe
205 P5 Matute mt. Spain
281 E3 Matutina Brazil
115 D1 Matutuang i. Indon.
114 E8 Matutum, Mount vol. Phil.
156 L1 Matveyev, Ostrov i. Rus. Fed.
142 E1 Matveyevka Rus. Fed.
159 R6 Matveyev Kurgan Rus. Fed.
159 K6 Matviyivka Mykolayivs'ka Oblast' Ukr.
159 O6 Matviyivka Zaporiz'ka Oblast' Ukr.
237 L4 Matwabeng S. Africa
205 O2 Matxitxako, Cabo c. Spain
Maty Island P.N.G. see Wuvulu Island
159 S1 Matyra r. Rus. Fed.
161 W9 Matyrskiy Rus. Fed.
161 W9 Matyrskoye Vodokhranilishche resr Rus. Fed.
160 L6 Matyryna Belarus
157 I6 Matyshevo Rus. Fed.
138 G6 Mau Madh. Prad. India
138 H7 Mau Uttar Prad. India
235 H2 Maúa Moz.
138 H7 Mau Aimma Uttar Prad. India
208 G2 Maubermé, Pic de mt. France/Spain
178 H4 Maubert-Fontaine France
178 G3 Maubeuge France
137 N4 Maubin Myanmar
118 C2 Ma-ubin Myanmar
185 E9 Maubourguet France
184 B5 Maubuisson France
168 H11 Mauchline East Ayrshire, Scotland U.K.
168 L7 Maud Aberdeenshire, Scotland U.K.
109 B7 Maud, Point W.A. Austr.
138 H7 Maudaha Uttar Prad. India
105 J6 Maude N.S.W. Austr.
288 J10 Maud Seamount sea feature S. Atlantic Ocean
Mau-é-ele Moz. see Marão
201 N3 Mauerbach Austria
200 H3 Mauerkirchen Austria
195 L4 Mauern Ger.
195 J6 Mauerstetten Ger.
275 G5 Maués Brazil
275 G5 Maués r. Brazil
Mauga Afi mt. Samoa see Afi, Mount
138 H7 Mauganj Madh. Prad. India
170 I5 Maughold Isle of Man
170 I5 Maughold Head Isle of Man
113 K2 Maug Islands N. Mariana Is
183 E9 Mauguio France
264 □E13 Maui i. HI U.S.A.
103 □2 Mauke i. Cook Is
118 B3 Maukkadaw Myanmar
194 F4 Maulbronn Ger.
179 O8 Maulburg Ger.
184 H4 Maulde r. France
173 L3 Maulden Bedfordshire, England U.K.
284 B4 Maule Chile
284 A4 Maule admin. reg. Chile
284 A4 Maule r. Chile
284 B5 Maule, Lago del l. Chile
184 C2 Mauléon France
185 F10 Mauléon-Barousse France
185 D8 Mauléon-d'Armagnac France
185 C9 Mauléon-Licharre France
181 J7 Maulévrier France
283 B6 Maullín Chile
Maum Ireland see An Mám
169 D4 Maumakeogh hill Ireland
102 J4 Maumaupaki hill North I. N.Z.
256 B7 Maumee OH U.S.A.
256 B7 Maumee r. OH U.S.A.
256 B7 Maumee Bay MI/OH U.S.A.
115 C8 Maumere Flores Indon.
169 C5 Maumtrasna hill Ireland
169 C5 Maumturk Mountains hills Ireland
234 D3 Maun Botswana
271 □1 Maunabo Puerto Rico
264 □F14 Mauna Kea vol. HI U.S.A.
264 □D12 Mauna Loa HI U.S.A.
264 □F14 Mauna Loa vol. HI U.S.A.
264 □D12 Maunalua Bay HI U.S.A.
139 I7 Maunath Bhanjan Uttar Prad. India
235 E4 Maunatlala Botswana
138 G9 Maunda Mahar. India
244 H2 Mauneluk r. AK U.S.A.
102 K6 Maungaharuru Range mts North I. N.Z.
102 L5 Maungahaumi mt. North I. N.Z.
102 L5 Maungapohatu mt. North I. N.Z.
102 I6 Maungarau hill North I. N.Z.
102 K5 Maungataniwha mt. North I. N.Z.
102 I2 Maungatapere North I. N.Z.
102 I3 Maungaturoto North I. N.Z.
118 A4 Maungdaw Myanmar
119 C7 Maungmagan Islands Myanmar
119 D7 Maungmagon Myanmar
245 P2 Maunoir, Lac l. N.W.T. Can.
101 □9 Maupihaa atoll Arch. de la Société Fr. Polynesia
262 D4 Maupin OR U.S.A.
164 G1 Maura Norway
138 G7 Mau Ranipur Uttar Prad. India
138 H6 Maurawan Uttar Prad. India
183 I8 Maure, Col de pass France
180 H6 Maure-de-Bretagne France
185 J11 Maureillas-las-Illas France
184 E6 Maurens France
261 J10 Maurepas, Lake LA U.S.A.
183 I10 Maures, Massif des hills France
276 C4 Mauri r. Bol.
185 D6 Mauriac Aquitaine France
184 I5 Mauriac Auvergne France
Maurice country Indian Ocean see Mauritius
258 E6 Maurice r. NJ U.S.A.
104 C3 Maurice, Lake salt flat S.A. Austr.
258 F6 Mauricetown NJ U.S.A.
183 I6 Maurienne reg. France
186 H5 Maurik Neth.
226 C6 Mauritania country Africa
Mauritanie country Africa see Mauritania
239 □1b Mauritius country Indian Ocean
215 N4 Mauro, Monte mt. Italy
180 G5 Mauron France
185 G7 Mauroux France
185 I6 Maurs France
185 J10 Maury France
258 B3 Mausdale PA U.S.A.
183 F9 Maussanne-les-Alpilles France
250 D6 Mauston WI U.S.A.
196 F1 Mausz, Jezioro l. Pol.
201 M3 Mautern an der Donau Austria
201 I5 Mauterndorf Austria
201 K5 Mautern in Steiermark Austria
195 P4 Mauth Ger.
201 K3 Mauthausen Austria
200 H6 Mauthen Austria
Mauti i. Cook Is see Mauke
179 K6 Mauvages France
183 F6 Mauves France
185 F8 Mauvezin France
212 C3 Mauvoisin Switz.
184 C3 Mauzé-sur-le-Mignon France
230 E4 Mava Dem. Rep. Congo
275 E4 Mavaca r. Venez.
233 C8 Mavago Moz.
99 I3 Mavana Fiji
235 G4 Mavanza Moz.
162 N3 Mavasjaure l. Sweden
231 C9 Mavengue Angola
221 L6 Mavikent Turkey
231 D8 Mavinga Angola
270 □ Mavis Bank Jamaica
256 C11 Mavisdale VA U.S.A.
168 □N2 Mavis Grind isth. Scotland U.K.
235 G3 Mavita Moz.
215 L2 Mavone r. Italy
221 H6 Mavria i. Greece
220 C2 Mavrodendri Greece
221 G6 Mavropetra, Akrotirio pt Greece
220 E2 Mavrothalassa Greece
218 I9 Mavrovo nat. park Macedonia
235 G4 Mavume Moz.
237 L7 Mavuya S. Africa
117 J4 Mawa, Bukit mt. Indon.
131 □J7 Ma Wan i. H.K. China
146 H4 Māwān, Khashm hill Saudi Arabia
138 F5 Mawana Uttar Prad. India
231 C6 Mawanga Dem. Rep. Congo
115 C6 Mawasangka Sulawesi Indon.
118 C5 Mawchi Myanmar
119 D9 Mawdaung Pass Myanmar/Thai.
131 L5 Mawei Fujian China
102 M5 Mawhai Point North I. N.Z.
103 F9 Mawheraiti South I. N.Z.
Māwheranui r. South I. N.Z. see Grey
118 C2 Mawhun Myanmar
146 G9 Māwiyah Yemen
150 D7 Mawjib, Wādī al r. Jordan
118 D6 Mawkhi Myanmar
118 C4 Mawkmai Myanmar
118 B3 Mawlaik Myanmar
118 C6 Mawlamyaing Myanmar
118 B6 Mawlamyainggyun Myanmar
Mawlamyine Myanmar see Mawlamyaing
172 B7 Mawnan Cornwall, England U.K.
139 M7 Mawphlang Meghalaya India
146 E2 Mawqaq Saudi Arabia
225 I6 Mawshij Yemen
287 E2 Mawson research stn Antarctica
287 E2 Mawson Coast Antarctica
287 E2 Mawson Escarpment Antarctica
287 K2 Mawson Peninsula Antarctica
119 D9 Maw Taung mt. Myanmar
146 F9 Mawza Yemen
260 E2 Max ND U.S.A.
232 E3 Maxaas Somalia
282 D3 Maxán Arg.
258 D3 Maxatawny PA U.S.A.
267 O7 Maxcanú Mex.
180 G6 Maxent France
246 F3 Maxhamish Lake B.C. Can.
195 M3 Maxhütte-Haidhof Ger.
214 B9 Maxia, Punta mt. Sardegna Italy
204 E9 Maxieira Port.
285 G3 Máximo Paz Arg.
219 P5 Măxineni Romania
235 G4 Maxixe Moz.
162 Q5 Maxmo Fin.
191 E9 Maxsain Ger.
257 K3 Maxville Ont. Can.
102 I6 Maxwell North I. N.Z.
107 I6 Maxwelton Qld Austr.
108 G4 May r. W.A. Austr.
168 K10 May, Isle of i. Scotland U.K.
230 C3 Maya Chad
130 D2 Maya Gansu China
117 H5 Maya i. Indon.
153 O3 Maya r. Rus. Fed.
159 N4 Mayachka Ukr.
157 K5 Mayachnyy Rus. Fed.
270 G2 Mayaguana i. Bahamas
270 G2 Mayaguana Passage Bahamas
271 □1 Mayagüez Puerto Rico
271 □1 Mayagüez, Bahía de b. Puerto Rico
229 G3 Mayahi Niger
122 J4 Mayak Rus. Fed.
142 F2 Mayak Rus. Fed.
Mayakovskiy Georgia see Baghdat'i
145 N3 Mayakovskiy, Qullai mt. Tajik.
Mayakovskogo, Pik mt. Tajik. see Mayakovskiy, Qullai
197 K1 Mayakovskoye Rus. Fed.
143 M6 Mayakum Kazakh.
158 H5 Mayaky Ukr.
231 C6 Mayala Dem. Rep. Congo
115 G4 Mayalibit, Teluk b. Papua Indon.
Mayals Spain see Maials
231 B5 Mayama Congo
231 C6 Mayamba Dem. Rep. Congo
144 F3 Mayāmey Iran
267 O9 Maya Mountains Belize/Guat.
Mayan Gansu China see Mayanhe
130 G5 Mayang Hunan China
128 I9 Mayanhe Gansu China
Mayaqum Kazakh. see Mayakum
168 J9 Mayar hill Scotland U.K.
270 F3 Mayarí Cuba
271 □7 Mayaro county Trin. and Tob.
271 □7 Mayaro Bay Trin. and Tob.
126 B6 Maya-san hill Japan
124 Q8 Maya-san mt. Japan
262 J6 Maybell CO U.S.A.
256 D11 Maybeury WV U.S.A.
168 G12 Maybole South Ayrshire, Scotland U.K.
259 G2 Maybrook NY U.S.A.
232 C1 Maych'ew Eth.
270 □ May Day Mountains hills Jamaica
105 K10 Maydena Tas. Austr.
232 E2 Maydh Somalia
Maydos Turkey see Eceabat
191 D10 Mayen Ger.
181 J5 Mayenne France
181 J5 Mayenne dept France
181 J7 Mayenne r. France
265 T7 Mayer AZ U.S.A.
133 H10 Mayêr Kangri mt. Xizang China
261 J9 Mayersville MS U.S.A.
246 H4 Mayerthorpe Alta Can.
181 L6 Mayet France
147 H8 Mayfa'ah Yemen
103 F10 Mayfield South I. N.Z.
171 N7 Mayfield Staffordshire, England U.K.
261 K7 Mayfield KY U.S.A.
258 D1 Mayfield PA U.S.A.
265 U2 Mayfield UT U.S.A.
Mayhan Mongolia see Sant
263 L10 Mayhill NM U.S.A.
122 F6 Mayi He r. China
143 P2 Maykain Kazakh.
132 C3 Maykamys Kazakh.
145 M2 Maykhura Tajik.
151 B1 Maykop Rus. Fed.
156 K4 Maykor Rus. Fed.
Maylibash Kazakh. see Maylybas
143 O7 Mayluu-Suu Kyrg.
142 J5 Maylybas Kazakh.
Mayly-Say Kyrg. see Mayluu-Suu
143 U1 Mayma Rus. Fed.
143 N6 Maymak Kazakh.
145 K4 Maymanah Afgh.
268 B1 Maymorita Mex.
120 F1 Mayna Respublika Khakasiya Rus. Fed.
157 I5 Mayna Ul'yanovskaya Oblast' Rus. Fed.
255 F7 Maynardville TN U.S.A.
107 H7 Mayne watercourse Qld Austr.
136 D4 Mayni Mahar. India
251 Q4 Maynooth Ont. Can.
169 I6 Maynooth Ireland
245 N3 Mayo Y.T. Can.
263 J13 Mayo r. Mex.
276 A1 Mayo r. Peru
169 D5 Mayo Ireland
169 D5 Mayo county Ireland
255 F10 Mayo FL U.S.A.
258 B7 Mayo MD U.S.A.
229 I4 Mayo Alim Cameroon
229 I4 Mayo Belwa Nigeria
169 J4 Mayobridge Northern Ireland U.K.
229 H5 Mayo Darlé Cameroon
229 H4 Mayo Kam Nigeria
230 B2 Mayo-Kebbi pref. Chad
230 B5 Mayoko Congo
230 D5 Mayoko Dem. Rep. Congo
245 N3 Mayo Lake Y.T. Can.
230 B3 Mayo Lara C.A.R.
114 D5 Mayon vol. Luzon Phil.
205 O8 Mayor r. Spain
205 Q4 Mayor r. Spain
205 M2 Mayor, Cabo c. Spain
Mayor, Puig mt. Spain see Major, Puig
285 F6 Mayor Buratovich Arg.
205 J4 Mayorga Spain
102 K4 Mayor Island North I. N.Z.
277 E4 Mayor Pablo Lagerenza Para.
239 □3b Mayotte terr. Africa
270 □ May Pen Jamaica
Mayqayyng Kazakh. see Maykain
114 C2 Mayraira Point Luzon Phil.
271 □3 Mayreau i. St Vincent
183 E7 Mayres France
185 H9 Mayreville France
200 E5 Mayrhofen Austria
150 D7 Maysah, Tall al mt. Jordan
149 M8 Maysān governorate Iraq
191 D9 Mayschoss Ger.
197 I1 Mayskaya r. Rus. Fed.
159 N8 Mays'ke Ukr.
122 F2 Mayskiy Amurskaya Oblast' Rus. Fed.
159 P3 Mayskiy Belgorodskaya Oblast' Rus. Fed.
151 F2 Mayskiy Kabardino-Balkarskaya Respublika Rus. Fed.
156 K4 Mayskiy Permskaya Oblast' Rus. Fed.
159 T6 Mayskiy Rostovskaya Oblast' Rus. Fed.
143 R2 Mayskoye Kazakh.
258 F6 Mays Landing NJ U.S.A.
247 J3 Mayson Lake Sask. Can.
256 B10 Maysville KY U.S.A.
260 H6 Maysville MO U.S.A.
Maytag Xinjiang China see Dushanzi
115 E3 Mayu i. Maluku Indon.
118 A4 Mayu r. Myanmar
232 B4 Mayuge Uganda
231 A5 Mayumba Gabon
231 A5 Mayumba, Parc National de nat. park Nyanga Gabon
133 F11 Mayum La pass Xizang China
136 F7 Mayuram Tamil Nadu India
251 K6 Mayville MI U.S.A.
260 G2 Mayville ND U.S.A.
256 F6 Mayville NY U.S.A.
260 E5 Maywood NE U.S.A.
153 O3 Mayya Rus. Fed.
285 F5 Maza Arg.
161 T2 Maza Rus. Fed.
231 E8 Mazabuka Zambia
Mazaca Turkey see Kayseri
Mazagan Morocco see El Jadida
275 I5 Mazagão Brazil
275 I5 Mazagão Velho Brazil
206 F6 Mazagón Spain
178 I5 Mazagran France
160 H5 Maza Jugla r. Latvia
208 F5 Mazaleón Spain
185 I9 Mazamet France
268 D6 Mazamitla Mex.
183 G8 Mazan France
274 C5 Mazán Peru
144 D3 Māzandarān prov. Iran
183 E7 Mazan-l'Abbaye France
231 D7 Mazao Dem. Rep. Congo
268 F1 Mazapil Mex.
133 C8 Mazar Xinjiang China
150 D7 Mazār Jordan
147 N4 Mazāra Oman
216 D8 Mazara, Val di reg. Sicilia Italy
216 D8 Mazara del Vallo Sicilia Italy
205 L9 Mazarambroz Spain
145 L3 Mazār-e Sharīf Afgh.
205 P7 Mazarete Spain
216 D8 Mazaro r. Sicilia Italy
283 D7 Mazarredo Arg.
209 C12 Mazarrón Spain
209 C13 Mazarrón, Golfo de b. Spain
132 E7 Mazartag Xinjiang China
132 D7 Mazartag mt. Xinjiang China
275 G3 Mazaruni r. Guyana
266 D3 Mazatán Mex.
269 K7 Mazateca, Sierra mts Mex.
267 N10 Mazatenango Guat.
268 A2 Mazatlán Mex.
265 U7 Mazatzal Peak AZ U.S.A.
144 G8 Mazāvī watercourse Iran
144 I3 Mazdāvand Iran
181 K7 Mazé France
126 F4 Maze Japan
126 F4 Maze-gawa r. Japan
160 F5 Mažeikiai Lith.
229 H2 Mazelet well Niger
258 B3 Mazeppa PA U.S.A.
237 M8 Mazeppa Bay S. Africa
233 C5 Mazeras Kenya
185 H9 Mazères France
185 D9 Mazerolles France
183 E6 Mazet-St-Voy France
185 G6 Mazeyrolles France
151 A6 Mazgirt Turkey
146 F2 Mazhūr, 'Irq al des. Saudi Arabia
221 I5 Mazı Turkey
160 K5 Mazīča r. Latvia
256 C10 Mazie KY U.S.A.
184 D2 Mazières-en-Gâtine France
147 M4 Mazīm Oman
231 C6 Mazinda Dem. Rep. Congo
160 F4 Mazirbe Latvia
238 □3d Mazo La Palma Canary Is
266 D3 Mazocahui Mex.
276 C4 Mazocruz Peru
Mazoe Zimbabwe see Mazowe
250 E6 Mazomanie WI U.S.A.
231 E6 Mazomeno Dem. Rep. Congo
233 C6 Mazomora Tanz.
128 E6 Mazongshan Gansu China
128 E6 Mazong Shan mt. Gansu China
128 D6 Mazong Shan mts China
205 M3 Mazorra, Puerto de la pass Spain
235 F3 Mazowe Zimbabwe
235 G3 Mazowe r. Zimbabwe
197 I3 Mazowiecka, Nizina reg. Pol.
197 J3 Mazowieckie prov. Pol.
158 A1 Mazowiecki Park Krajobrazowy Pol.
144 C3 Mazr'eh Iran
225 F6 Mazrub well Sudan
160 I4 Mazsalaca Latvia
144 C5 Māzū Iran
235 F4 Mazunga Zimbabwe
197 I2 Mazurskie, Pojezierze reg. Pol.
189 J2 Mazurski Park Krajobrazowy Pol.
197 J1 Mazurskiy Kanal canal Pol./Rus. Fed.
158 I1 Mazyr Belarus
158 I1 Mazyrskaye Hrada ridge Belarus
212 I4 Mazzano Italy
215 I3 Mazzano Romano Italy
216 G9 Mazzarino Sicilia Italy
216 H9 Mazzarrone Sicilia Italy
200 B7 Mazzo di Valtellina Italy
227 H2 Mazzouna Tunisia
229 H5 Mba Cameroon
Mba Viti Levu Fiji see Ba
237 P2 Mbabane Swaziland
228 B3 Mbacké Senegal
230 C4 Mbaéré r. C.A.R.
228 B2 Mbagne Maur.
228 D5 Mbahiakro Côte d'Ivoire
230 C4 Mbaïki C.A.R.
229 I5 Mbakaou Cameroon
229 I5 Mbakaou, Lac de l. Cameroon
231 C5 Mbala Dem. Rep. Congo
233 A7 Mbala Zambia
235 F4 Mbalabala Zimbabwe
229 I6 Mbalam Cameroon
232 B4 Mbale Uganda
229 H6 Mbalmayo Cameroon
100 □6 Mbalo Guadalcanal Solomon Is
229 H5 Mbam r. Cameroon
229 I7 Mbama Congo
233 B7 Mbamba Bay Tanz.
230 C5 Mbandaka Dem. Rep. Congo
229 H5 Mbandjok Cameroon
230 B4 Mbandza Congo
229 I5 Mbang Adamaoua Cameroon
229 I6 Mbang Est Cameroon
229 H5 Mbanga Cameroon
100 □6 Mbanika i. Solomon Is
231 B6 M'banza Congo Angola
231 B6 Mbanza-Ngungu Dem. Rep. Congo
228 B3 Mbar Senegal
233 C7 Mbarangandu Tanz.
232 A5 Mbarara Uganda
230 D3 Mbari r. C.A.R.
233 C7 Mbarika Mountains Tan
237 Q3 Mbaswana S. Africa
230 C4 Mbata C.A.R.
233 A7 Mbati Zambia
Mbatiki i. Fiji see Batiki
Mbau i. Fiji see Bau
100 □6 Mbava i. New Georgia Is Solomon Is
229 I5 Mbé Cameroon
231 B5 Mbé Congo
233 B8 Mbemba Moz.
235 F3 Mbembesi Zimbabwe
233 C7 Mbemkuru r. Tanz.
Mbengga i. Fiji see Beqa
229 H5 Mbengwi Cameroon
239 □3a Mbéni Njazidja Comoros
228 D4 Mbenqué Côte d'Ivoire
235 F4 Mberengwa Zimbabwe
231 F7 Mbereshi Zambia
233 B7 Mbeya Tanz.
233 B7 Mbeya admin. reg. Tanz.
229 I5 Mbi r. Cameroon
230 C3 Mbi r. C.A.R.
230 A5 Mbigou Gabon
230 A5 Mbilapé Gabon
230 F3 Mbili Sudan
218 H8 Mbilqethit, Maja e mt. A
230 B5 Mbinda Congo
233 B7 Mbinga Tanz.
229 H6 Mbini Equat. Guinea
229 H6 Mbini r. Equat. Guinea
100 □6 Mbita'ama Malaita Solo
230 D3 Mbiyi C.A.R.
235 F4 Mbizi Zimbabwe
233 A7 Mbizi Mountains Tanz.
230 C2 Mbo C.A.R.
230 E3 Mboki C.A.R.
230 D3 Mboli Dem. Rep. Congo
Mbolompo Point S. Afric Mncwasa Point
230 B4 Mbomo Congo
230 D3 Mbomou pref. C.A.R.
230 D3 Mbomou r. C.A.R./Dem. Rep. Congo
230 B5 Mbon Congo
228 A3 Mboro Senegal
100 □6 Mborokua i. Solomon Is
229 H5 Mbouda Cameroon
228 B3 Mboun Senegal
228 A3 Mbour Senegal
228 B2 Mbout Maur.
231 E8 Mbowela Zambia
233 B7 Mbozi Tanz.
230 C3 Mbrès C.A.R.
220 A2 Mbrostar Albania
Mbua Vanua Levu Fiji see
231 D6 Mbuji-Mayi Dem. Rep. C
100 □6 Mbulo i. New Georgia Is Solomon Is
233 B5 Mbulu Tanz.
237 P2 Mbuluzana r. Swaziland
237 Q2 Mbuluzi r. Swaziland
233 B7 Mbura Tanz.
282 F3 Mburucuyá Arg.
100 □6 Mburuku New Georgia Is Solomon Is
Mbutha Vanua Levu Fiji
237 P2 Mbutini Hills Swaziland
233 C6 Mbuyuni Tanz.
233 C6 Mbwewe Tanz.
249 H4 McAdam N.B. Can.
258 D3 McAdoo PA U.S.A.
258 F2 McAfee NJ U.S.A.
261 H8 McAlester OK U.S.A.
258 A3 McAlisterville PA U.S.A.
261 F12 McAllen TX U.S.A.
250 G4 McAllister WI U.S.A.
106 F3 McArthur r. N.T. Austr.
256 C9 McArthur OH U.S.A.
251 Q4 McArthur Mills Ont. Car
250 I5 McBain MI U.S.A.
246 F4 McBride B.C. Can.
262 F4 McCall ID U.S.A.
261 D10 McCamey TX U.S.A.
262 H5 McCammon ID U.S.A.
247 J2 McCann Lake N.W.T. Ca
245 L3 McCarthy AK U.S.A.
250 F4 McCaslin Mountain hill
245 O5 McCauley Island B.C. Ca
287 K1 McClintock, Mount Ant
243 H2 McClintock Channel Nu Can.
108 I5 McClintock Range hills W Austr.
106 D1 McCluer Island N.T. Aus
256 B7 McClure OH U.S.A.
256 H8 McClure PA U.S.A.
264 L4 McClure, Lake CA U.S.A.
242 G2 McClure Strait N.W.T. C
260 E2 McClusky ND U.S.A.
261 J10 McComb MS U.S.A.
256 B7 McComb OH U.S.A.
260 E5 McConaughy, Lake NE U
256 H9 McConnellsburg PA U.S
256 D9 McConnelsville OH U.S.
260 E5 McCook NE U.S.A.
255 F9 McCormick SC U.S.A.
256 E11 McCoy VA U.S.A.
246 H2 McCrea r. N.W.T. Can.
247 L5 McCreary Man. Can.
265 Q6 McCullough Range mts U.S.A.
245 M2 McCullum, Mount Y.T. C
256 B8 McCutchenville OH U.S.
245 O4 McDame B.C. Can.
262 F6 McDermitt NV U.S.A.
256 B10 McDermott OH U.S.A.
289 I8 McDonald Islands India
262 H3 McDonald Peak MT U.S.
104 G3 McDonnell Creek waterc S.A. Austr.
255 E9 McDonough GA U.S.A.
106 E5 McDouall Range hills N.
245 J3 McDougall AK U.S.A.
236 A5 McDougall's Bay S. Afric
265 U8 McDowell Peak AZ U.S.A
258 B2 McEwensville PA U.S.A.
264 M6 McFarland CA U.S.A.
250 E6 McFarland WI U.S.A.
247 J3 McFarlane r. Sask. Can.
103 D10 McFarlane, Mount South
265 R2 McGill NV U.S.A.
249 H4 McGivney N.B. Can.
244 I3 McGrath AK U.S.A.
250 A3 McGrath MN U.S.A.
246 F4 McGregor r. B.C. Can.
236 D9 McGregor S. Africa
250 A3 McGregor MN U.S.A.
246 H5 McGregor, Lake Alta Car
251 M3 McGregor Bay Ont. Can.
107 I9 McGregor Range hills Ql
170 E4 McGregor's Corner Nort Ireland U.K.
262 G4 McGuire, Mount ID U.S.
151 F3 Mchadijvari Georgia
226 D4 Mcherrah reg. Alg.
233 C7 Mchinga Tanz.
233 B8 Mchinji Malawi
107 I3 McIlwraith Range hills Q
247 M4 McInnes Lake Ont. Can.
260 E3 McIntosh SD U.S.A.
108 G7 McKay Range hills W.A. A
99 I2 McKean i. Phoenix Is Kiri
256 A11 McKee KY U.S.A.
258 F6 McKee NJ U.S.A.
256 F8 McKeesport PA U.S.A.
256 E8 McKees Rocks PA U.S.A.
256 H12 McKenney VA U.S.A.
261 K7 McKenzie TN U.S.A.
262 C4 McKenzie r. OR U.S.A.
103 C11 McKerrow, Lake South I.
107 H6 McKinlay Qld Austr.
107 H6 McKinlay r. Qld Austr.
245 J3 McKinley, Mount AK U.S
245 J3 McKinley Park AK U.S.A.
261 G9 McKinney TX U.S.A.
264 M6 McKittrick CA U.S.A.
260 E3 McLaughlin SD U.S.A.
250 E9 McLean IL U.S.A.
258 A7 McLean VA U.S.A.
260 K6 McLeansboro IL U.S.A.
246 G4 McLennan Alta Can.
246 H4 McLeod r. Alta Can.
247 I2 McLeod Bay N.W.T. Can.

F4 McLeod Lake B.C. Can.
D9 McLeod's Island Myanmar
□1 McMicken Point Christmas I.
D8 McMinns Creek watercourse N.T. Austr.
C4 McMinnville OR U.S.A.
E8 McMinnville TN U.S.A.
L1 McMurdo research stn Antarctica
L1 McMurdo Sound b. Antarctica
W7 McNary AZ U.S.A.
E4 McNaughton WI U.S.A.
McNaughton Lake B.C. Can. see Kinbasket Lake
W10 McNeal AZ U.S.A.
H2 McPhadyen r. Nfld and Lab. Can.
G6 McPherson KS U.S.A.
N3 McPherson Range mts N.S.W. Austr.
M3 McQuesten r. Y.T. Can.
F9 McRae GA U.S.A.
C11 McRoberts KY U.S.A.
A5 McSherrystown PA U.S.A.
E3 McSwynes Bay Ireland
G3 McTavish Arm b. N.W.T. Can.
H8 McVeytown PA U.S.A.
F1 McVicar Arm b. N.W.T. Can.
E9 McWhorter WV U.S.A.
P3 Mda r. Rus. Fed.
L8 Mdantsane S. Africa
G1 M'Daourouch Alg.
□3a Mde Njazidja Comoros
□ Mdina Malta
D5 Mdiq Morocco
I8 M'Đrak Vietnam
G5 Mê, Hon i. Vietnam
R5 Mead, Lake resr NV U.S.A.
H2 Mead Corners NY U.S.A.
E7 Meade KS U.S.A.
C2 Meade r. AK U.S.A.
H1 Meade r. AK U.S.A.
H1 Meade r. AK U.S.A.
C9 Meadow W.A. Austr.
D3 Meadow SD U.S.A.
T3 Meadow UT U.S.A.
E11 Meadow Bridge WV U.S.A.
4 Meadow Lake Sask. Can.
4 Meadow Lake Provincial Park Sask. Can.
R5 Meadow Valley Wash r. NV U.S.A.
D12 Meadowview VA U.S.A.
10 Meadville MS U.S.A.
E7 Meadville PA U.S.A.
N5 Meaford Ont. Can.
V3 Meaken-dake vol. Japan
B6 Mealasta Island Scotland U.K.
G8 Meal Fuar-mhonaidh hill Scotland U.K.
D8 Mealhada Port.
B6 Mealisval hill Scotland U.K.
H9 Meall Chuaich hill Scotland U.K.
G8 Meall Dubh hill Scotland U.K.
K4 Mealsgate Cumbria, England U.K.
2 Mealy Mountains Nfld and Lab. Can.
C8 Meana Sardo Sardegna Italy
L9 Meandarra Qld Austr.
G3 Meander River Alta Can.
G5 Meare Somerset, England U.K.
D1 Meares i. Indon.
2 Mease r. England U.K.
2 Measham Leicestershire, England U.K.
5 Meath county Ireland
H6 Méaudre, Roche de mt. France
B3 Meaulne France
E4 Méaulte France
E6 Meaux France
G7 Meauzac France
B6 Mebridege r. Angola
D5 Mebu Arun. Prad. India
K9 Mebulu, Tanjung pt Indon.
G2 Mecanhelas Moz.
B4 Mecatán Mex.
Mecca Saudi Arabia see Makkah
8 Mecca CA U.S.A.
E7 Mecca OH U.S.A.
O4 Mechanic Falls ME U.S.A.
B8 Mechanicsburg OH U.S.A.
4 Mechanicsburg PA U.S.A.
E11 Mechanicsburg VA U.S.A.
H11 Mechanicsville VA U.S.A.
6 Mechanicville NY U.S.A.
2 Mechāra Eth.
6 Mechelen Belgium
7 Mechelen Neth.
Mecherchar i. Palau see Eil Malk
2 Mecheria Alg.
9 Mechernich Ger.
7 Mechetinskaya Rus. Fed.
6 Mechiméré Chad
4 Mechita Arg.
8 Mechka r. Bulg.
6 Mechongue Arg.
2 Mechowo Pol.
4 Mechtersen Ger.
9 Mechterstädt Ger.
2 Mecidiye Edirne Turkey
4 Mecidiye Manisa Turkey
2 Měčín Czech Rep.
7 Mecina-Bombarón Spain
4 Męcinka Pol.
3 Mecitözü Turkey
6 Meckenbeuren Ger.
9 Meckenheim Ger.
3 Meckesheim Ger.
2 Mecklenburger Bucht b. Ger.
3 Mecklenburgische Seenplatte reg. Ger.
3 Mecklenburg-Vorpommern land Ger.
Mecklenburg - West Pomerania land Ger. see Mecklenburg-Vorpommern
7 Meco Spain
2 Meconta Moz.
3 Mecox Bay NY U.S.A.
5 Mecsek mts Hungary
5 Mecseknádasd Hungary
2 Mecubúri Moz.
2 Mecubúri r. Moz.
2 Mecúfi Moz.
8 Mecula Moz.
4 Meda r. W.A. Austr.
7 Meda Port.
4 Meda mt. Spain
3 Medak Andhra Prad. India
3 Medan Sumatera Indon.
9 Medang i. Indon.
2 Medano Arg.
6 Médanos Buenos Aires Arg.
3 Médanos Entre Ríos Arg.
8 Medanosa, Punta pt Arg.
2 Médanos de Coro, Parque Nacional nat. park Venez.
8 Medaryville IN U.S.A.
6 Medas Port.
8 Medawachchiya Sri Lanka
4 Medchal Andhra Prad. India
2 Meddersheim Ger.
4 Meddo Neth.
R3 Meddybemps Lake ME U.S.A.
5 Mede Italy
1 Médéa Alg.
8 Medebach Ger.
2 Medeiros Neto Brazil
3 Medelim Port.
3 Medellín Col.
3 Medellín Spain
3 Medem r. Ger.
3 Medemblik Neth.
7 Meden r. England U.K.
2 Medenine Tunisia
Medenitsa Ukr. see Medenychi
4 Medenychi Ukr.
3 Meder Eritrea
2 Mederdra Maur.
Medesano Italy
8 Medford NY U.S.A.
7 Medford OK U.S.A.
5 Medford OR U.S.A.
4 Medford WI U.S.A.
Medford Lakes NJ U.S.A.
Medfra AK U.S.A.
6 Medgidia Romania

199 J5 Medgyesbodzás Hungary
199 K5 Medgyesegyháza Hungary
135 □1 Medhufinolhu i. N. Male Maldives
258 E5 Media PA U.S.A.
228 E2 Mediadilet well Mali
284 D4 Media Luna Arg.
266 □R10 Media Luna, Arrecife de la rf Hond.
208 D5 Mediana Spain
207 P7 Media Naranja, Punta de la pt Spain
208 F3 Mediano, Embalse de resr Spain
219 M4 Mediaş Romania
262 F3 Medical Lake WA U.S.A.
213 L7 Medicina Italy
262 K6 Medicine Bow WY U.S.A.
262 K6 Medicine Bow r. WY U.S.A.
262 K6 Medicine Bow Mountains WY U.S.A.
262 K6 Medicine Bow Peak WY U.S.A.
247 I5 Medicine Hat Alta Can.
262 L2 Medicine Lake MT U.S.A.
261 F7 Medicine Lodge KS U.S.A.
281 G2 Medina Brazil
274 C3 Medina Col.
Medina Al Madīnah Saudi Arabia see Al Madīnah
260 F2 Medina ND U.S.A.
256 G5 Medina NY U.S.A.
256 D7 Medina OH U.S.A.
261 G11 Medina r. TX U.S.A.
205 P6 Medinaceli Spain
206 G4 Medina de las Torres Spain
205 K6 Medina del Campo Spain
205 N3 Medina de Pomar Spain
205 J5 Medina de Rioseco Spain
228 B3 Medina Gounas Senegal
261 F11 Medina Lake TX U.S.A.
206 H8 Medina-Sidonia Spain
239 □1b Medine Mauritius
139 K8 Medinipur W. Bengal India
214 B8 Medio Campidano prov. Italy
Mediolanum Italy see Milano
184 C4 Médis France
154 F7 Mediterranean Sea World
183 D9 Méditerranée airport France
230 E4 Medje Dem. Rep. Congo
227 F2 Medjedel Alg.
211 A7 Medjerda, Monts de la mts Alg.
198 G2 Medlov Czech Rep.
142 G2 Mednogorsk Rus. Fed.
161 S5 Mednoye Rus. Fed.
153 R4 Mednyy, Ostrov i. Rus. Fed.
184 B5 Médoc reg. France
133 L12 Mêdog Xizang China
213 K6 Medolla Italy
260 D2 Medora ND U.S.A.
230 A4 Médouneu Gabon
197 I1 Medovoye Rus. Fed.
284 C3 Medrano Arg.
197 I5 Mędrzechów Pol.
247 I4 Medstead Sask. Can.
173 J5 Medstead Hampshire, England U.K.
Medu Kongkar Xizang China see Maizhokunggar
213 P6 Medulin Croatia
201 N7 Međumurje reg. Croatia
213 N4 Meduna r. Italy
213 N3 Meduno Italy
Meduro atoll Marshall Is see Majuro
219 J8 Medveđa Medveđa Serbia
159 M8 Medvedeve Ukr.
156 I4 Medvedevo Rus. Fed.
157 H6 Medveditsa r. Rus. Fed.
159 N8 Medvedivka Ukr.
210 E3 Medvednica mts Croatia
156 J4 Medvedok Rus. Fed.
159 S8 Medvedovskaya Rus. Fed.
160 F6 Medvėgalio kalnas hill Lith.
159 P2 Medvenka Rus. Fed.
153 R2 Medvezh'i, Ostrova is Rus. Fed.
156 F3 Medvezh'yegorsk Rus. Fed.
201 J7 Medvode Slovenia
173 N5 Medway admin. div. England U.K.
173 M5 Medway r. England U.K.
108 □1 Medwin Point Christmas I.
197 K6 Medyka Pol.
161 S7 Medyn' Rus. Fed.
158 G4 Medzhybizh Ukr.
199 K2 Medzilaborce Slovakia
109 C9 Meeberrie W.A. Austr.
186 K2 Meeden Neth.
191 K10 Meeder Ger.
109 E9 Meekatharra W.A. Austr.
262 K6 Meeker CO U.S.A.
256 B8 Meeker OH U.S.A.
264 L2 Meeks Bay CA U.S.A.
232 F2 Meeladeen Somalia
236 I8 Meelberg mt. S. Africa
169 F6 Meelick Ireland
249 J3 Meelpaeg Reservoir Nfld and Lab. Can.
Meenacross Ireland see Mín na Croise
169 F3 Meenanarwa Ireland
169 F3 Meentullynagarn Ireland
187 G6 Meer Belgium
193 F9 Meerane Ger.
160 K3 Meerapalu Estonia
191 H6 Meerbeck Ger.
191 C8 Meerbusch Ger.
187 H6 Meerhout Belgium
186 G5 Meerkerk Neth.
187 G6 Meerle Belgium
186 J5 Meerlo Neth.
194 G6 Meersburg Ger.
187 I7 Meerssen Neth.
135 □1 Meerufenfushi i. N. Male Maldives
138 F5 Meerut Uttar Prad. India
185 B8 Mées France
262 J4 Meeteetse WY U.S.A.
Me'etia i. Arch. de la Société Fr. Polynesia see Mehetia
187 D6 Meetkerke Belgium
187 I6 Meeuwen Belgium
162 N2 Mefjordvær Norway
232 C3 Mēga Eth.
116 D6 Mega i. Indon.
232 C3 Mega Escarpment Eth./Kenya
220 C3 Megala Kalyvia Greece
220 E2 Megali Panagia Greece
232 D3 Megalo Eth.
221 I6 Megalo Chorio Greece
220 D5 Megalopoli Greece
221 H5 Megalos Anthropofagos i. Greece
220 B4 Meganisi i. Greece
249 G4 Mégantic, Lac l. Que. Can.
220 E4 Megara Greece
186 I5 Megen Neth.
182 J5 Megève France
232 C2 Megezez mt. Eth.
139 M7 Meghalaya state India
139 K9 Meghasani mt. Orissa India
139 M8 Meghna r. Bangl.
151 H7 Meghri Armenia
Meghrut Armenia see Gugark'
144 G2 Megin Turkm.
152 I3 Megion Rus. Fed.
251 S1 Mégiscane, Lac l. Que. Can.
221 K6 Megisti i. Greece
161 R3 Megletsy Rus. Fed.
161 S3 Meglino, Ozero l. Rus. Fed.
161 S1 Megra r. Rus. Fed.
161 Q1 Megrega Rus. Fed.
Megri Armenia see Meghri
161 Q1 Megrozero Rus. Fed.
Megrut Armenia see Gugark'
219 K5 Mehadica Romania
187 H7 Mehaigne r. Belgium
227 F2 Mehaïguène, Oued watercourse Alg.
162 S1 Mehamn Norway
159 O9 Mehanom, Mys pt Ukr.
145 L8 Mehar Pak.
109 E7 Meharry, Mount W.A. Austr.
Mehdia Tunisia see Mahdia
144 B4 Mehdīkhān Iran
144 E4 Mehdīshahr Iran
190 H3 Mehe r. Ger.
165 N1 Mehedeby Sweden

227 F4 Mehedjibat, Erg des. Alg.
138 F9 Mehekar Mahar. India
139 L8 Meherpur Bangl.
256 G11 Meherrin VA U.S.A.
256 I12 Meherrin r. VA U.S.A.
101 □9 Mehetia i. Arch. de la Société Fr. Polynesia
138 E8 Mehidpur Madh. Prad. India
189 J5 Méhkerék Hungary
193 F9 Mehltheuer Ger.
260 J6 Mehlville MO U.S.A.
138 D8 Mehmadabad Gujarat India
139 I6 Mehndawal Uttar Prad. India
258 C1 Mehoopany PA U.S.A.
144 B2 Mehrābān Iran
144 F8 Mehrān Iran
144 F8 Mehrān watercourse Iran
149 M7 Mehrān Iraq
191 C10 Mehren Ger.
194 B2 Mehring Ger.
193 E7 Mehringen Ger.
201 H3 Mehrnbach Austria
194 H5 Mehrstetten Ger.
145 N4 Mehtar Lām Afgh.
184 I1 Mehun-sur-Yèvre France
280 C3 Meia Ponte r. Brazil
Meicheng Anhui China see Qianshan
Meicheng Fujian China see Minqing
131 H4 Meichengzhen Hunan China
130 E1 Meichuan Gansu China
229 I5 Meidougou Cameroon
172 D4 Meidrim Carmarthenshire, Wales U.K.
229 I5 Meiganga Cameroon
170 E5 Meigh Northern Ireland U.K.
243 I2 Meighen Island Nunavut Can.
168 J9 Meigle Perth and Kinross, Scotland U.K.
130 D4 Meigu Sichuan China
122 D7 Meihekou Jilin China
126 F4 Meihō Japan
187 I6 Meijel Neth.
186 F4 Meijendel nature res. Neth.
Meijiang Jiangxi China see Ningdu
131 J6 Mei Jiang r. China
131 J6 Meikeng Guangdong China
246 G3 Meikle r. Alta Can.
170 I1 Meikle Bin hill Scotland U.K.
170 G2 Meikle Kilmory Argyll and Bute, Scotland U.K.
168 J9 Meikleour Perth and Kinross, Scotland U.K.
168 K11 Meikle Says Law hill Scotland U.K.
118 B4 Meiktila Myanmar
212 F1 Meilen Switz.
185 C8 Meilhan France
185 E6 Meilhan-sur-Garonne France
Meilin Jiangxi China see Ganxian
180 H5 Meillac France
182 A3 Meillant France
182 J4 Meillerie France
246 E2 Meilleur r. N.W.T. Can.
Meilu China see Wuchuan
204 F8 Meimoa Port.
212 F4 Meina Italy
191 K6 Meine Ger.
191 J6 Meinersen Ger.
191 E8 Meinerzhagen Ger.
200 A5 Meiningen Austria
191 J9 Meiningen Ger.
204 F2 Meira Spain
204 F2 Meira, Serra de mts Spain
212 E2 Meiringen Switz.
236 G9 Meiringspoort pass S. Africa
168 D9 Meirleach, Rubha nam pt Scotland U.K.
193 D7 Meisdorf Ger.
194 D2 Meisenheim Ger.
Meishan Anhui China see Jinzhai
130 D3 Meishan Sichuan China
193 H8 Meißen Ger.
190 I5 Meißendorf Ger.
194 D5 Meißenheim Ger.
191 I8 Meißner hill Ger.
191 I8 Meißner-Kaufunger Wald, Naturpark nature res. Ger.
245 O3 Meister r. Y.T. Can.
130 F5 Meitan Guizhou China
195 J4 Meitingen Ger.
127 K3 Meiwa Gunma Japan
126 E6 Meiwa Mie Japan
187 H9 Meix-devant-Virton Belgium
122 F5 Meixi Heilong. China
Meixian Guangdong China see Meizhou
131 J6 Meixian Guangdong China
129 J9 Meixian Shaanxi China
Meixing Sichuan China see Xiaojin
131 K6 Meizhou Guangdong China
138 F7 Mej r. India
138 I7 Meja Uttar Prad. India
183 E7 Méjan, Sommet de mt. France
226 D5 Mejaouda well Maur.
100 □3a Mejatto i. Kwajalein Marshall Is
183 C8 Méjean, Causse plat. France
211 B7 Mejez el Bab Tunisia
282 D3 Mejicana mt. Arg.
276 C5 Mejillones Chile
276 C5 Mejillones del Sur, Bahía de b. Chile
205 K8 Mejorada Spain
205 N8 Mejorada del Campo Spain
225 G5 Mekadio well Sudan
230 B4 Mékambo Gabon
221 L2 Mekece Turkey
232 C1 Mek'elē Eth.
151 G2 Meken-Yurt Rus. Fed.
227 F4 Mekerrhane, Sebkha salt pan Alg.
161 Q1 Mekhbaza Rus. Fed.
228 A3 Mékhé Senegal
151 H3 Mekhel'ta Rus. Fed.
145 M6 Mekhtar Pak.
232 C2 Mekī Eth.
201 K7 Mekinje Slovenia
226 D2 Meknès Morocco
229 F5 Meko Nigeria
119 G9 Mekong r. Asia alt. Lancang Jiang (China), alt. Mènam Khong (Laos/Thail.)
119 H10 Mekong, Mouths of the Vietnam
244 F3 Mekoryuk AK U.S.A.
151 D3 Mek'vena Georgia
213 M3 Mel Italy
230 D2 Méla, Mont hill C.A.R.
284 B4 Melado r. Chile
227 G3 Melah, Oued el watercourse Alg.
116 E3 Melaka Malaysia
116 E3 Melaka state Malaysia
117 K2 Melalap Sabah Malaysia
116 F5 Melalo, Tanjung pt Indon.
215 O6 Melandro r. Italy
290 F6 Melanesia is Oceania
290 F5 Melanesian Basin sea feature Pacific Ocean
162 □B1 Melar Iceland
213 K5 Melara Italy
117 I4 Melawi r. Indon.
182 E4 Melay Bourgogne France
179 K8 Melay Champagne-Ardenne France
181 J7 Melay Pays de la Loire France
212 E6 Melazzo Italy
190 J4 Melbeck Ger.
173 M3 Melbourn Cambridgeshire, England U.K.
105 J7 Melbourne Vic. Austr.
173 J2 Melbourne Derbyshire, England U.K.
261 J7 Melbourne AR U.S.A.
255 G11 Melbourne FL U.S.A.
162 M2 Melbu Norway
168 □M2 Melby Shetland, Scotland U.K.
162 □ Melchers, Kapp c. Svalbard
283 B7 Melchor, Isla i. Chile
267 O9 Melchor de Mencos Guat.
267 I5 Melchor Ocampo Mex.
192 I5 Melchow Ger.
162 J5 Meldal Norway
213 M7 Meldola Italy

190 H2 Meldorf Ger.
256 B12 Meldrum KY U.S.A.
248 D4 Meldrum Bay Ont. Can.
212 F7 Mele Italy
212 E8 Mele, Capo c. Italy
161 T4 Melech r. Rus. Fed.
212 G5 Melegnano Italy
198 G4 Meleg-víz r. Hungary
114 □ Melekeok Palau
Melekess Rus. Fed. see Dimitrovgrad
156 K4 Melekhina Rus. Fed.
161 Y5 Melekhovo Rus. Fed.
159 Q7 Melekyne Ukr.
238 □3f Melenara Gran Canaria Canary Is
218 I5 Melenci Vojvodina Serbia
148 G4 Melendiz Dağı mt. Turkey
217 O3 Melendugno Italy
157 H5 Melenki Rus. Fed.
180 H5 Melesse France
Melet Turkey see Mesudiye
142 F1 Meleuz Rus. Fed.
249 G1 Mélèzes, Rivière aux r. Que. Can.
215 L4 Melfa r. Italy
257 J11 Melfa VA U.S.A.
230 C2 Melfi Chad
215 P6 Melfi Italy
247 J4 Melfort Sask. Can.
275 I5 Melgaço Brazil
204 D4 Melgaço Port.
205 M9 Melgar r. Spain
205 J4 Melgar de Arriba Spain
205 L4 Melgar de Fernamental Spain
204 H5 Melgar de Tera Spain
180 D6 Melgven France
162 K5 Melhus Norway
247 M2 Meliadine Lake Nunavut Can.
117 I5 Meliau Kalimantan Indon.
187 J6 Melick Neth.
217 K7 Melicucco Italy
204 E3 Melide Spain
206 B4 Melides Port.
220 C5 Meligalas Greece
151 E5 Melikköyü Turkey
115 C4 Melilis i. Indon.
203 E5 Melilla N. Africa
217 I9 Melilli Sicilia Italy
283 B7 Melimoyu, Monte mt. Chile
103 D11 Melina, Mount South I. N.Z.
285 G3 Melincué Arg.
285 G3 Melincué, Laguna l. Arg.
117 L5 Melintang, Danau l. Indon.
159 O5 Melioratyvne Ukr.
100 □5 Melip Vanuatu
284 B6 Melipeuco Chile
284 B3 Melipilla Chile
179 M8 Mélisey France
186 E5 Meliskerke Neth.
217 M5 Melissa Italy
247 K5 Melita Man. Can.
Melitene Turkey see Malatya
220 C2 Meliti Greece
217 J8 Melito r. Italy
217 J8 Melito di Porto Salvo Italy
159 O7 Melitopol' Ukr.
201 L3 Melk Austria
201 L3 Melk r. Austria
237 I8 Melk r. S. Africa
232 C3 Melka Guba Eth.
236 B5 Melkbospunt pt S. Africa
236 C9 Melkbosstrand S. Africa
172 H5 Melksham Wiltshire, England U.K.
212 I5 Mella r. Italy
180 D6 Mellac France
162 R3 Mellakoski Fin.
164 J2 Mellanfryken l. Sweden
162 O5 Mellansel Sweden
163 M5 Mellansjö Sweden
162 O4 Mellanström Sweden
200 A5 Mellau Austria
187 E6 Melle Belgium
184 D3 Melle France
191 F6 Melle Ger.
192 E4 Mellen Ger.
250 D3 Mellen WI U.S.A.
190 I5 Mellendorf (Wedemark) Ger.
193 H6 Mellensee Ger.
164 I3 Mellerud Sweden
260 F3 Mellette SD U.S.A.
Mellid Spain see Melide
217 □ Mellieħa Malta
217 □ Mellieħa, Il-Bajja tal- b. Malta
190 K5 Mellin Ger.
193 D9 Mellingen Ger.
190 G5 Mellinghausen Ger.
224 E6 Mellit Sudan
283 B8 Mellizo Sur, Cerro mt. Chile
287 E2 Mellor Glacier Antarctica
202 D5 Mellousa Morocco
191 J10 Mellrichstadt Ger.
172 E4 Mellte r. Wales U.K.
100 □3a Mellu i. Kwajalein Marshall Is
190 F3 Mellum i. Ger.
100 □3a Mellu Passage Kwajalein Marshall Is
224 C6 Melmele watercourse Chad
171 L4 Melmerby Cumbria, England U.K.
237 P4 Melmoth S. Africa
122 I6 Mel'nichoye Rus. Fed.
198 D1 Mělník Czech Rep.
160 M1 Mel'nikovo Rus. Fed.
159 N8 Mel'nychne Ukr.
159 O4 Mel'nykove Ukr.
158 F5 Mel'nytsya-Podil's'ka Ukr.
285 F4 Melo Arg.
230 A4 Melo Gabon
282 G4 Melo Uru.
235 H2 Meloco Moz.
237 K4 Meloding S. Africa
115 B8 Melolo Sumba Indon.
204 D4 Melón Spain
229 H5 Mélong Cameroon
151 M2 Melovoy, Mys pt Kazakh.
Melovoye Ukr. see Milove
244 I2 Melozitna r. AK U.S.A.
180 E6 Melrand France
204 D6 Melres Port.
227 G2 Melrhir, Chott salt l. Alg.
109 F9 Melrose W.A. Austr.
168 K11 Melrose Scottish Borders, Scotland U.K.
260 H3 Melrose MN U.S.A.
212 G1 Mels Switz.
191 D10 Melsbach Ger.
190 J2 Melsdorf Ger.
Melsetter Zimbabwe see Chimanimani
171 N5 Melsonby North Yorkshire, England U.K.
191 I8 Melsungen Ger.
Melta, Mount Malaysia see Tawai, Bukit
162 R3 Meltaus Fin.
171 N6 Meltham West Yorkshire, England U.K.
105 J7 Melton Vic. Austr.
173 O3 Melton Suffolk, England U.K.
173 K2 Melton Mowbray Leicestershire, England U.K.
117 I4 Meluan Sarawak Malaysia
233 C8 Meluco Moz.
178 E6 Melun France
136 F7 Melur Tamil Nadu India
232 B2 Melut Sudan
168 E7 Melvaig Highland, Scotland U.K.
168 I5 Melvich Highland, Scotland U.K.
247 K5 Melville Sask. Can.
107 J3 Melville, Cape Qld Austr.
Melville, Cape Dominica see Capucin, Cape
114 A8 Melville, Cape Phil.
249 J2 Melville, Lake Nfld and Lab. Can.
106 F2 Melville Bay N.T. Austr.
Melville Bugt b. Greenland see Qimusseriarsuaq
245 Q1 Melville Hills Nunavut Can.
106 C1 Melville Island N.T. Austr.
243 H2 Melville Island N.W.T./Nunavut Can.
243 J3 Melville Peninsula Nunavut Can.
250 F9 Melvin IL U.S.A.
169 F4 Melvin, Lough l. Ireland/U.K.
199 I5 Mélykút Hungary
212 G5 Melzo Italy

220 A2 Memaliaj Albania
133 F9 Mêmar Co salt l. China
235 I2 Memba Moz.
235 I2 Memba, Baía de b. Moz.
113 I7 Memberamo r. Papua Indon.
115 A8 Memboro Sumba Indon.
182 H1 Membrey France
207 M3 Membrilla Spain
204 F9 Membrío Spain
Memel Lith. see Klaipėda
237 N3 Memel S. Africa
160 H5 Mēmele r. Latvia
160 J6 Memiakalnis hill Lith.
195 J2 Memmelsdorf Ger.
195 I6 Memmingen Ger.
195 I6 Memmingerberg Ger.
178 I5 Mémorial Américain tourist site France
117 H4 Mempawah Kalimantan Indon.
148 E9 Memphis tourist site Egypt
251 L7 Memphis MI U.S.A.
260 I5 Memphis MO U.S.A.
261 J8 Memphis TN U.S.A.
261 E8 Memphis TX U.S.A.
257 M3 Memphrémagog, Lac l. Que. Can.
168 L7 Memsie Aberdeenshire, Scotland U.K.
124 T4 Memuro-dake mt. Japan
232 C3 Mena Eth.
115 D8 Mena Timor Indon.
159 L2 Mena Ukr.
159 L2 Mena r. Ukr.
261 H8 Mena AR U.S.A.
232 D3 Mena, Wabē r. Eth.
235 □J4 Menabe mts Madag.
285 I3 Menafra Uru.
212 G3 Menaggio Italy
213 K5 Menago r. Italy
172 D1 Menai Bridge Isle of Anglesey, Wales U.K.
172 D1 Menai Strait Wales U.K.
229 F3 Ménaka Mali
186 I2 Menaldum Neth.
119 G7 Mènam Khong r. Laos/Thai. alt. Lancang Jiang (China) conv. Mekong
115 D4 Menanga Maluku Indon.
235 □J5 Menarandra r. Madag.
261 F10 Menard TX U.S.A.
178 B8 Menars France
205 L9 Menasalbas Spain
248 B4 Menasha WI U.S.A.
182 B4 Menat France
213 M6 Menata Italy
179 J6 Menaucourt France
207 M5 Mencal mt. Spain
283 C6 Mencué Arg.
125 H14 Menda Japan
116 G6 Mendanau i. Indon.
281 F3 Mendanha Brazil
138 C9 Mendarda Gujarat India
116 G4 Mendarik i. Indon.
208 B1 Mendaur mt. Spain
205 P4 Mendavia Spain
117 J6 Mendawai Kalimantan Indon.
117 J6 Mendawai r. Indon.
183 D7 Mende France
232 C3 Mendebo mts Eth.
225 H6 Mendefera Eritrea
144 C3 Mendejīn Iran
292 M1 Mendeleyev Ridge sea feature Arctic Ocean
156 K5 Mendeleyevsk Rus. Fed.
191 E8 Menden (Sauerland) Ger.
261 K10 Mendenhall MS U.S.A.
244 F4 Mendenhall, Cape AK U.S.A.
245 N4 Mendenhall Glacier AK U.S.A.
221 I4 Menderes Turkey
143 L2 Mendesh (abandoned) Kazakh.
267 J5 Méndez Tamaulipas Mex.
269 I3 Méndez Veracruz Mex.
114 C4 Mendez-Nuñez Luzon Phil.
258 F3 Mendham NJ U.S.A.
232 B2 Mendī Eth.
113 J8 Mendi P.N.G.
205 Q3 Mendigorría Spain
172 G5 Mendip Hills England U.K.
185 C9 Menditte France
264 I2 Mendocino CA U.S.A.
262 B6 Mendocino, Cape CA U.S.A.
264 I2 Mendocino, Lake CA U.S.A.
216 F8 Mendola r. Sicilia Italy
216 F9 Mendola r. Sicilia Italy
250 I7 Mendon MI U.S.A.
105 L4 Mendooran N.S.W. Austr.
264 L5 Mendota CA U.S.A.
250 E8 Mendota IL U.S.A.
250 E6 Mendota, Lake WI U.S.A.
284 C3 Mendoza Arg.
284 C4 Mendoza prov. Arg.
284 C3 Mendoza r. Arg.
276 D4 Mendoza Bol.
285 I4 Mendoza Uru.
212 F4 Mendrisio Switz.
109 F12 Mends, Lake salt flat W.A. Austr.
180 G5 Ménéac France
274 D2 Mene de Mauroa Venez.
212 H6 Menegosa, Monte mt. Italy
270 H9 Mene Grande Venez.
221 I4 Menemen Turkey
187 D7 Menen Belgium
183 G9 Ménerbes France
184 E5 Ménesplet France
182 E2 Ménessaire France
183 B6 Menet France
181 P7 Menetou-Salon France
180 E4 Menez Bré hill France
180 C5 Menez Hom hill France
216 D8 Menfi Sicilia Italy
205 J8 Menga, Puerto de pass Spain
214 B10 Menga, Punta pt Sardegna Italy
117 K1 Mengalum i. Malaysia
129 J9 Mengba Gansu China
130 C7 Mengban Yunnan China
131 K2 Mengcheng Anhui China
Mengdong Yunnan China see Cangyuan
194 G5 Mengen Ger.
148 F3 Mengen Turkey
191 F9 Mengerskirchen Ger.
201 K7 Mengeš Slovenia
258 B5 Menges Mills PA U.S.A.
116 F7 Menggala Sumatera Indon.
130 C8 Menghai Yunnan China
207 L5 Mengíbar Spain
143 L1 Mengisor, Ozero salt l. Kazakh.
117 K6 Mengkatip Kalimantan Indon.
117 I4 Mengkiang r. Indon.
195 M4 Mengkofen Ger.
115 B5 Mengkoka, Gunung mt. Indon.
130 C8 Mengla Yunnan China
Menglang Yunnan China see Lancang
130 B7 Menglian Yunnan China
Menglie Yunnan China see Jiangcheng
Mengmeng Yunnan China see Shuangjiang
229 H6 Mengong Cameroon
130 H6 Mengshan Guangxi China
Mengsuo Yunnan China see Ximeng
Mengxian Henan China see Mengzhou
Mengyang Sichuan China see Mingshan
129 O9 Mengyin Shandong China
129 M9 Mengzhou Henan China
130 D7 Mengzi Yunnan China
172 D7 Menheniot Cornwall, England U.K.
184 D3 Ménigoute France
249 H2 Menihek Nfld and Lab. Can.
249 H2 Menihek Lakes Nfld and Lab. Can.
179 K6 Ménil-la-Tour France
179 M7 Ménil-sur-Belvitte France
Menin Belgium see Menen
201 O1 Měnín Czech Rep.
201 K7 Menina mts Slovenia
105 I5 Menindee N.S.W. Austr.
105 I5 Menindee, Lake N.S.W. Austr.
105 I5 Menindee Aboriginal Reserve N.S.W. Austr.

104 G6 Meningie S.A. Austr.
144 C4 Menjān Iran
153 N3 Menkere Rus. Fed.
Menlough Ireland see Mionlach
146 D9 Menna r. Eth.
178 D6 Mennecy France
181 O7 Mennetou-sur-Cher France
106 C3 Menngen Aboriginal Land res. N.T. Austr.
277 F5 Mennonite Colony res. Para.
250 G4 Menominee MI U.S.A.
250 G4 Menominee r. WI U.S.A.
250 F4 Menominee Indian Reservation res. WI U.S.A.
250 F6 Menomonee Falls WI U.S.A.
250 C5 Menomonie WI U.S.A.
231 C8 Menongue Angola
209 D12 Menor, Mar lag. Spain
208 □ Menorca i. Spain
208 □ Menorca, Cap c. Spain
182 C2 Menou France
226 E3 Menouarar Alg.
183 H7 Mens France
117 L3 Mensalong Kalimantan Indon.
184 F5 Mensignac France
190 E5 Menslage Ger.
171 N6 Menston West Yorkshire, England U.K.
Mentakab Malaysia see Mentekab
215 J3 Mentana Italy
114 A9 Mentapok mt. Malaysia
117 L3 Mentarang r. Indon.
245 L3 Mentasta Lake AK U.S.A.
245 K3 Mentasta Mountains AK U.S.A.
116 C6 Mentawai, Kepulauan is Indon.
116 D6 Mentawai, Selat sea chan. Indon.
117 J6 Mentaya r. Indon.
204 F5 Mente r. Port./Spain
168 H10 Menteith, Lake of Scotland U.K.
116 E3 Mentekab Malaysia
109 C12 Mentelle, Cape W.A. Austr.
191 K8 Menteroda Ger.
221 L4 Menteş Turkey
182 I5 Menthon-St-Bernard France
206 E4 Mentiras hill Port.
207 O4 Mentiras mt. Spain
265 X6 Mentmore NM U.S.A.
116 F6 Mentok Indon.
183 L9 Menton France
261 D10 Mentone TX U.S.A.
256 D7 Mentor OH U.S.A.
205 L8 Méntrida Spain
117 J6 Mentuba r. Indon.
Menufia governorate Egypt see Minūfīyah
117 J5 Menukung Kalimantan Indon.
127 J3 Menuma Japan
117 K2 Menumbok Sabah Malaysia
115 B3 Menunu Sulawesi Indon.
117 L4 Menyapa, Gunung mt. Indon.
128 G8 Menyuan Qinghai China
129 K2 Menza Rus. Fed.
129 K1 Menza r. Rus. Fed.
227 H1 Menzel Bourguiba Tunisia
148 H5 Menzelet Barajı resr Turkey
156 K5 Menzelinsk Rus. Fed.
211 C7 Menzel Temime Tunisia
109 F10 Menzies W.A. Austr.
287 E2 Menzies, Mount Antarctica
212 E1 Menznau Switz.
234 B5 Meobbaai b. Namibia
181 N8 Méobecq France
213 M4 Meolo Italy
266 G3 Meoqui Mex.
183 H10 Méounes-les-Montrieux France
231 B6 Mepala Angola
151 D4 Mep'istsqaro, Mt'a Georgia
233 B8 Meponda Moz.
186 J3 Meppel Neth.
190 D5 Meppen Ger.
235 G4 Mepuze Moz.
237 L4 Meqheleng S. Africa
277 E3 Mequéns r. Brazil
208 F5 Mequinenza Spain
208 F5 Mequinenza, Embalse de resr Spain
250 G6 Mequon WI U.S.A.
178 C8 Mer France
212 G3 Mera r. Italy
210 E3 Merag Croatia
117 L4 Merah Kalimantan Indon.
116 G7 Merak Jawa Indon.
162 K5 Meråker Norway
104 D3 Meramangye, Lake salt flat S.A. Austr.
260 J6 Meramec r. MO U.S.A.
213 K2 Merano Italy
117 I8 Merapi, Gunung vol. Jawa Indon.
117 K9 Merapi, Gunung vol. Jawa Indon.
185 D8 Méraq France
275 F3 Merari, Serra mt. Brazil
249 K4 Merasheen Nfld and Lab. Can.
162 P3 Merasjärvi Sweden
212 G4 Merate Italy
234 E4 Meratswe r. Botswana
117 K6 Meratus, Pegunungan mts Indon.
113 J8 Merauke Papua Indon.
116 E4 Merbau Sumatera Indon.
105 I6 Merbein Vic. Austr.
187 F8 Merbes-le-Château Belgium
Merca Somalia see Marka
205 N2 Mercadillo Spain
151 B6 Mercan Turkey
151 A6 Mercan Dağları mts Turkey
183 J8 Mercantour, Parc National du nat. park France
213 M9 Mercatale Italy
213 M8 Mercatello sul Metauro Italy
213 N8 Mercatino Conca Italy
215 N6 Mercato San Severino Italy
213 M8 Mercato Saraceno Italy
264 L4 Merced CA U.S.A.
264 L4 Merced r. CA U.S.A.
284 B2 Mercedario, Cerro mt. Arg.
269 K9 Merced del Potrero Mex.
285 H4 Mercedes Buenos Aires Arg.
282 F3 Mercedes Corrientes Arg.
285 H3 Mercedes Uru.
238 □3a Mercedes, Monte de las hill Tenerife Canary Is
282 C3 Merceditas Chile
257 □P4 Mercer ME U.S.A.
256 A8 Mercer OH U.S.A.
256 E7 Mercer PA U.S.A.
250 D3 Mercer WI U.S.A.
258 F4 Mercer County county NJ U.S.A.
256 H9 Mercersburg PA U.S.A.
258 F4 Mercerville NJ U.S.A.
276 C2 Mercês Acre Brazil
281 F4 Mercês Minas Gerais Brazil
195 J5 Merching Ger.
187 F7 Merchtem Belgium
276 C2 Mercier Bol.
150 D1 Mercimek Turkey
184 H5 Mercœur France
215 N6 Mercogliano Italy
185 G7 Mercuès France
182 F3 Mercurey France
182 I5 Mercury France
265 Q5 Mercury NV U.S.A.
102 J3 Mercury Bay North I. N.Z.
102 J3 Mercury Islands North I. N.Z.
185 H10 Mercus-Garrabet France
243 L3 Mercy, Cape Nunavut Can.
Merdenik Turkey see Göle
194 D5 Merdingen Ger.
226 D2 Merdja Zerga, Réserve de nature res. Morocco
180 G5 Merdrignac France
187 E7 Mere Belgium
172 H5 Mere Wiltshire, England U.K.
181 P7 Méreau France
257 N5 Meredith NH U.S.A.
283 E9 Meredith, Cape Falkland Is
261 E8 Meredith, Lake TX U.S.A.
227 F4 Meredoua Alg.
232 E4 Mereeg Somalia
159 P4 Merefa Ukr.
100 □5 Mere Lava i. Vanuatu
187 E7 Merelbeke Belgium
160 K4 Meremäe Estonia
102 J4 Meremere North I. N.Z.
162 P5 Merenkurkku str. Fin./Sweden
185 H10 Mérens-les-Vals France

107 I2 Merepah Aboriginal Holding res. Qld Austr.
178 D7 Méréville France
161 T2 Merezha Rus. Fed.
224 E5 Merga Oasis Sudan
142 D3 Mergen Kazakh.
212 E4 Mergozzo Italy
Mergui Myanmar see Myeik
Mergui Archipelago is Myanmar see Myeik Kyunzu
219 R5 Merhei, Lacul l. Romania
214 C2 Meria Corse France
104 H6 Meribah S.A. Austr.
183 J6 Méribel-les-Allues France
221 H1 Meriç Turkey
Meriç r. see Maritsa
220 F5 Merichas Kythnos Greece
178 E3 Méricourt France
267 O7 Mérida Mex.
206 G3 Mérida Spain
274 D2 Mérida Venez.
274 D2 Mérida state Venez.
274 D3 Mérida, Cordillera de mts Venez.
173 I3 Meriden West Midlands, England U.K.
257 M7 Meriden CT U.S.A.
261 K9 Meridian MS U.S.A.
261 G10 Meridian TX U.S.A.
285 F4 Meridiano Arg.
185 C6 Mérignac France
162 R4 Merijärvi Fin.
163 P6 Merikarvia Fin.
105 L7 Merimbula N.S.W. Austr.
198 E2 Měřín Czech Rep.
Merín, Laguna l. Brazil/Uru. see Mirim, Lagoa
182 A5 Mérinchal France
107 L6 Merinda Qld Austr.
183 G9 Mérindol France
237 L2 Merindol S. Africa
195 J5 Mering Ger.
229 I4 Meringa Nigeria
104 H6 Meringur Vic. Austr.
285 I3 Merinos Uru.
113 H6 Merir i. Palau
275 H4 Merirumã Brazil
117 J3 Merit Sarawak Malaysia
107 K8 Merivale r. Qld Austr.
100 □1 Merizo Guam
199 L4 Mérk Hungary
261 E9 Merkel TX U.S.A.
201 M6 Merkendorf Austria
195 J3 Merkendorf Ger.
143 O6 Merki Kazakh.
160 H7 Merkinė Lith.
198 C2 Merklín Czech Rep.
194 H4 Merklingen Ger.
187 G6 Merksplas Belgium
197 M1 Merkys r. Lith.
213 K5 Merlara Italy
Merlav i. Vanuatu see Mere Lava
180 E6 Merlevenez France
116 □ Merlimau, Pulau reg. Sing.
184 I4 Merlines France
284 E3 Merlo Arg.
159 N4 Merlo r. Ukr.
107 I2 Merluna Qld Austr.
108 E4 Mermaid Reef W.A. Austr.
199 G5 Mernye Hungary
204 D2 Mero r. Spain
109 G10 Merolia W.A. Austr.
208 J3 Merolla, Coll de pass Spain
150 D6 Meron, Har mt. Israel
219 J7 Merošina Merošina Serbia
225 F5 Merowe Sudan
109 E11 Merredin W.A. Austr.
179 K7 Merrey France
250 I8 Merriam IN U.S.A.
168 H12 Merrick hill Scotland U.K.
251 S5 Merrickville Ont. Can.
251 J6 Merrill MI U.S.A.
250 E4 Merrill WI U.S.A.
246 E2 Merrill, Mount Y.T. Can.
250 D5 Merrillan WI U.S.A.
254 D5 Merrillville IN U.S.A.
236 H7 Merriman S. Africa
260 E4 Merriman NE U.S.A.
172 G6 Merriott Somerset, England U.K.
246 F5 Merritt B.C. Can.
255 G11 Merritt Island FL U.S.A.
255 G11 Merritt Island National Wildlife Refuge nature res. FL U.S.A.
105 M5 Merriwa N.S.W. Austr.
105 L4 Merrygoen N.S.W. Austr.
225 I6 Mersa Fatma Eritrea
225 H5 Mersa Gulbub Eritrea
225 H5 Mersa Teklay Eritrea
187 J9 Mersch Lux.
193 H8 Merschwitz Ger.
214 G1 Merse r. Italy
173 N4 Mersea Island England U.K.
193 E8 Merseburg (Saale) Ger.
171 L7 Mersey est. England U.K.
171 K6 Merseyside admin. div. England U.K.
150 C2 Mersin admin. div. Turkey
151 A4 Mersin Trabzon Turkey
150 B2 Mersin prov. Turkey
221 I5 Mersinbeleni Turkey
116 E3 Mersing Malaysia
117 J3 Mersing, Bukit mt. Malaysia
232 E3 Mersin Galgalo Eth.
178 B3 Mers-les-Bains France
160 G4 Mērsrags Latvia
160 G4 Mērsrags pt Latvia
138 E6 Merta Rajasthan India
138 D6 Merta Road Rajasthan India
187 J9 Mertert Lux.
194 B2 Mertesdorf Ger.
172 F4 Merthyr Tydfil Merthyr Tydfil, Wales U.K.
172 F4 Merthyr Tydfil admin. div. Wales U.K.
232 C4 Merti Kenya
195 J4 Mertingen Ger.
232 C4 Merti Plateau Kenya
191 D10 Mertloch Ger.
206 D5 Mértola Port.
206 D5 Mértola, Serra de hills Port.
227 G4 Mertoutek Alg.
142 E5 Mertvyy Kultuk, Sor dry lake Kazakh.
287 J2 Mertz Glacier Antarctica
287 J2 Mertz Glacier Tongue Antarctica
261 E10 Mertzon TX U.S.A.
258 D3 Mertztown PA U.S.A.
179 O6 Mertzwiller France
178 D5 Méru France
232 C4 Meru Kenya
233 C5 Meru vol. Tanz.
117 J9 Meru Betiri, Taman Nasional nat. park Indon.
204 D4 Merufe Port.
145 J7 Merui Pak.
232 C4 Meru National Park Kenya
117 L2 Merutai Sabah Malaysia
Merv Turkm. see Mary
182 G3 Mervans France
184 C2 Mervent France
185 G8 Merville Midi-Pyrénées France
178 E2 Merville Nord-Pas-de-Calais France
181 K3 Merville-Franceville-Plage France
236 F8 Merweville S. Africa
Merya Turkey see Veliköy
178 G6 Méry-sur-Seine France
191 E6 Merzen Ger.
148 G3 Merzifon Turkey
194 B3 Merzig Ger.
286 T2 Merz Peninsula Antarctica
115 F3 Mesa Halmahera Indon.
237 K2 Mesa S. Africa
205 Q6 Mesa r. Spain
265 U8 Mesa AZ U.S.A.
263 L10 Mesa NM U.S.A.
250 B2 Mesabi Range hills MN U.S.A.
274 D2 Mesa Bolívar Venez.
217 N2 Mesagne Italy
246 H1 Mesa Lake N.W.T. Can.
244 I3 Mesa Mountain hill AK U.S.A.
116 F4 Mesanak i. Indon.
180 I7 Mésanger France
204 E6 Mesão Frio Port.

263 J8 Mesa Verde National Park CO U.S.A.
263 L10 Mescalero Apache Indian Reservation res. NM U.S.A.
191 F8 Meschede Ger.
184 C4 Meschers-sur-Gironde France
151 B5 Mescit Dağları mts Turkey
162 N4 Meselefors Sweden
100 □4a Meseong i. Chuuk Micronesia
232 C1 Mesfinto Eth.
248 F3 Mesgouez, Lac l. Que. Can.
178 G7 Mesgrigny France
156 J5 Mesha r. Rus. Fed.
161 S7 Meshchovsk Rus. Fed.
Meshed Iran see Mashhad
144 H3 Meshkān Iran
144 F2 Meshkhed Turkm.
157 H6 Meshkovskaya Rus. Fed.
258 C1 Meshoppen PA U.S.A.
258 C1 Meshoppen Creek r. PA U.S.A.
230 F2 Meshra'er Req Sudan
250 I5 Mesick MI U.S.A.
210 F4 Mesihovina Bos.-Herz.
217 J6 Mesima r. Italy
220 E2 Mesimeri Greece
151 C4 Meskhet'is K'edi hills Georgia
226 D3 Meski Morocco
181 J6 Meslay-du-Maine France
182 H3 Mesnay France
212 G3 Mesocco Switz.
213 M6 Mesola Italy
220 C4 Mesolongi Greece
Mesolóngion Greece see Mesolongi
220 C4 Mesolongiou, Limnothalassa lag. Greece
Mesón del Viente Spain see O Mesón do Vento
217 L5 Mesoraca Italy
194 G2 Mespelbrunn Ger.
180 G7 Mesquer France
281 F3 Mesquita Brazil
265 R5 Mesquite NV U.S.A.
261 G9 Mesquite TX U.S.A.
265 Q6 Mesquite Lake CA U.S.A.
227 F2 Messaad Alg.
180 H6 Messac France
224 A3 Messak Mellet hills Libya
233 D7 Messalo r. Moz.
229 I6 Messaména Cameroon
Messana Sicilia Italy see Messina
187 I9 Messancy Belgium
185 B8 Messanges France
227 E4 Messaoud, Oued watercourse Alg.
220 F7 Messaras, Kolpos b. Kriti Greece
192 E5 Meßdorf Ger.
181 J4 Messei France
182 B5 Messeix France
206 C5 Messejana Port.
194 F2 Messel Ger.
283 B8 Messier, Canal sea chan. Chile
217 J7 Messina Sicilia Italy
216 G8 Messina prov. Sicilia Italy
Messina, Strait of Italy see Messina, Stretta di
217 J7 Messina, Stretta di str. Italy
179 J4 Messincourt France
251 R3 Messines Que. Can.
191 D6 Messingen Ger.
171 P6 Messingham North Lincolnshire, England U.K.
220 D5 Messini Greece
220 D6 Messiniakos Kolpos b. Greece
194 G6 Meßkirch Ger.
162 L5 Messlingen Sweden
194 F5 Meßstetten Ger.
219 M9 Mesta r. Bulg.
207 N3 Mesta r. Spain
221 G4 Mesta, Akrotirio pt Chios Greece
207 K3 Mestanza Spain
219 N3 Mestecănișului, Obcina ridge Romania
198 E1 Městec Králové Czech Rep.
Mestghanem Alg. see Mostaganem
151 D2 Mestia Georgia
192 E3 Mestlin Ger.
199 G1 Město Albrechtice Czech Rep.
195 O2 Město Touškov Czech Rep.
213 M5 Mestre Italy
148 H3 Mesudiye Turkey
116 F7 Mesuji r. Indon.
182 B2 Mesves-sur-Loire France
182 E3 Mesvres France
182 E3 Mesvrin r. France
274 C4 Meta dept Col.
274 E3 Meta r. Col./Venez.
215 M6 Meta Italy
249 G3 Métabetchouan Que. Can.
182 I3 Métabief France
251 M2 Metagama Ont. Can.
243 L3 Meta Incognita Peninsula Nunavut Can.
261 J11 Metairie LA U.S.A.
219 K4 Metaliferi, Munții mts Romania
218 H7 Metalika pass Bos.-Herz./Montenegro
213 J9 Metallifere, Colline mts Italy
161 N2 Metallostroy Rus. Fed.
250 E9 Metamora IL U.S.A.
282 D2 Metán Arg.
232 C2 Metanara Eth.
117 K6 Metangai Kalimantan Indon.
233 B8 Metangula Moz.
267 O10 Metapán El Salvador
235 H2 Metarica Moz.
213 O8 Metauro r. Italy
249 H4 Meteghan N.S. Can.
191 D6 Metelen Ger.
160 G7 Metelys l. Lith.
232 C1 Metema Eth.
235 G2 Metengobalame Moz.
220 C3 Meteora tourist site Greece
107 L8 Meteor Creek r. Qld Austr.
173 O3 Metfield Suffolk, England U.K.
220 E5 Methanon, Chersonisos pen. Greece
220 E5 Methanon, Steno sea chan. Greece
171 Q7 Metheringham Lincolnshire, England U.K.
168 L8 Methlick Aberdeenshire, Scotland U.K.
220 C6 Methoni Greece
257 N6 Methuen MA U.S.A.
108 H3 Methuen, Mount hill W.A. Austr.
103 F10 Methven South I. N.Z.
168 I10 Methven Perth and Kinross, Scotland U.K.
173 N2 Methwold Norfolk, England U.K.
285 F4 Metileo Arg.
248 B3 Metionga Lake Ont. Can.
101 □8 Metis Shoal sea feature Tonga
210 F4 Metković Croatia
245 O5 Metlakatla AK U.S.A.
269 J5 Metlaltoyuca Mex.
227 H2 Metlaoui Tunisia
269 I8 Metlatonoc Mex.
210 E3 Metlika Slovenia
227 G2 Metlili, Oued watercourse Alg.
201 J6 Metnitz Austria
201 J6 Metnitz r. Austria
235 H2 Metoro Moz.
217 K6 Metramo r. Italy
116 F7 Metro Sumatera Indon.
261 K7 Metropolis IL U.S.A.
Metsada tourist site Israel see Masada
162 T4 Metsäkylä Fin.
192 G3 Metschow Ger.
186 J2 Metslawier Neth.
220 C3 Metsovo Greece
195 N4 Metten Ger.
194 A2 Mettendorf Ger.
195 M5 Mettenheim Ger.
255 F9 Metter GA U.S.A.
201 M6 Mettersdorf am Saßbach Austria
187 G8 Mettet Belgium
191 E6 Mettingen Ger.
194 B3 Mettlach Ger.
264 N6 Mettler CA U.S.A.
201 H3 Mettmach Austria
191 C8 Mettmann Ger.
181 M7 Mettray France
136 E7 Mettuppalaiyam Tamil Nadu India
136 E7 Mettur Tamil Nadu India
232 B2 Metu Eth.
259 G3 Metuchen NJ U.S.A.
198 E1 Metuje r. Czech Rep.
233 D7 Metundo, Ilha i. Moz.
179 L5 Metz France
179 N7 Metzeral France
179 L5 Metzervisse France
194 G4 Metzingen Ger.
269 I5 Metzquititlán Mex.
180 H5 Meu r. France
191 E10 Meudt Ger.
116 B2 Meulaboh Sumatera Indon.
178 C5 Meulan France
187 D7 Meulebeke Belgium
178 C8 Meung-sur-Loire France
116 B2 Meureudu Sumatera Indon.
182 F3 Meursault France
179 L6 Meurthe r. France
179 L6 Meurthe-et-Moselle dept France
187 I6 Meuse r. Belgium/France alt. Maas (Neth.)
179 J5 Meuse dept France
193 F8 Meuselwitz Ger.
184 G4 Meuzac France
182 G3 Meuzin r. France
172 C7 Mevagissey Cornwall, England U.K.
130 D2 Mêwa Sichuan China
171 O7 Mexborough South Yorkshire, England U.K.
269 H8 Mexcala Mex.
268 B4 Mexcaltitán Mex.
261 G10 Mexia TX U.S.A.
275 I4 Mexiana, Ilha i. Brazil
266 B1 Mexicali Mex.
265 W4 Mexican Hat UT U.S.A.
266 F3 Mexicanos, Lago de los l. Mex.
265 W5 Mexican Water AZ U.S.A.
266 B2 Mexico country Central America
269 H6 México Mex.
269 H6 México state Mex.
257 □O4 Mexico ME U.S.A.
260 J6 Mexico MO U.S.A.
257 I5 Mexico NY U.S.A.
253 G6 Mexico, Gulf of Mex./U.S.A.
Mexico City Mex. see México
206 B6 Mexilhoeira Grande Port.
182 G5 Meximieux France
268 F3 Mexquitic Mex.
168 J5 Mey Highland, Scotland U.K.
144 E5 Meybod Iran
144 F7 Meydān Eyn ol Baqar-e Gel Iran
144 H9 Meydanī, Ra's-e pt Iran
192 F4 Meyenburg Ger.
245 N5 Meyers Chuck AK U.S.A.
256 F9 Meyersdale PA U.S.A.
237 M2 Meyerton S. Africa
221 L2 Meyitler Geçidi pass Turkey
183 H6 Meylan France
184 I4 Meymac France
144 D5 Meymeh Iran
153 S3 Meynypil'gyno Rus. Fed.
229 H6 Meyo Centre Cameroon
183 H9 Meyrargues France
183 H10 Meyreuil France
183 J8 Meyronnes France
183 C8 Meyrueis France
184 H5 Meyssac France
183 F7 Meysse France
182 I5 Meythet France
182 F5 Meyzieu France
118 C2 Meza Myanmar
Mezada tourist site Israel see Masada
208 C5 Mezalocha, Embalse de resr Spain
204 G8 Mezas mt. Spain
269 H8 Mezcala r. Mex.
267 M9 Mezcalapa Mex.
267 M8 Mezcalapa r. Mex.
219 L7 Mezdra Bulg.
183 D10 Mèze France
183 I9 Mézel France
156 I2 Mezen' Rus. Fed.
156 I2 Mezen' r. Rus. Fed.
183 E7 Mézenc, Mont mt. France
156 H2 Mezenskaya Guba b. Rus. Fed.
182 G4 Mézériat France
161 O6 Mezha r. Rus. Fed.
120 E1 Mezhdurechensk Kemerovskaya Oblast' Rus. Fed.
156 J3 Mezhdurechensk Respublika Komi Rus. Fed.
152 H4 Mezhdurechenskiy Rus. Fed.
Mezhdurechnye Rus. Fed. see Shali
152 G2 Mezhdusharskiy, Ostrov i. Novaya Zemlya Rus. Fed.
159 P5 Mezhova Ukr.
142 H1 Mezhozernyy Rus. Fed.
159 N3 Mezhyrich Ukr.
198 C1 Meziboří Czech Rep.
201 K6 Mežica Slovenia
181 K3 Mézidon-Canon France
181 N8 Mézières-en-Brenne France
184 F3 Mézières-sur-Issoire France
183 E7 Mézilhac France
178 F8 Mézilles France
198 F1 Meziměstí Czech Rep.
185 E7 Mézin France
161 X6 Mezinovskiy Rus. Fed.
204 E7 Mezio Port.
150 C2 Mezitli Turkey
199 K5 Mezőberény Hungary
199 J4 Mezőcsát Hungary
199 H5 Mezőfalva Hungary
199 K5 Mezőgyán Hungary
199 J5 Mezőhegyes Hungary
199 J4 Mezőkeresztes Hungary
199 H5 Mezőkomárom Hungary
199 J5 Mezőkovácsháza Hungary
199 J4 Mezőkövesd Hungary
199 G4 Mezőörs Hungary
185 B7 Mézos France
199 J4 Mezőszemere Hungary
199 H5 Mezőszilas Hungary
199 J4 Mezőtárkány Hungary
199 J5 Mezőtúr Hungary
208 D6 Mezquita de Jarque Spain
268 C2 Mezquital Mex.
268 B4 Mezquital r. Mex.
268 D4 Mezquital del Oro Mex.
268 D3 Mezquitic Mex.
150 F2 Mezraaköy Turkey
160 K5 Mežvidi Latvia
213 J3 Mezzana Italy
212 G7 Mezzanego Italy
213 L3 Mezzano Italy
213 K3 Mezzocorona Italy
216 E8 Mezzojuso Sicilia Italy
212 G3 Mezzola, Lago di l. Italy
212 H3 Mezzoldo Italy
213 K3 Mezzolombardo Italy
229 H6 Mfou Cameroon
231 B6 Mfouati Congo
233 A8 Mfuwe Zambia
122 M3 Mgachi Sakhalin Rus. Fed.
217 □ Mġarr Gozo Malta
217 □ Mġarr Malta
229 G5 Mgbidi Nigeria
161 P8 Mglin Rus. Fed.
237 M7 Mgwali r. S. Africa
168 D11 Mhàil, Rubh' a' pt Scotland U.K.
235 F3 Mhangura Zimbabwe
206 H9 Mharhar, Oued r. Morocco
136 D4 Mhasvad Mahar. India
237 P2 Mhlambanyatsi Swaziland
237 P3 Mhlosheni Swaziland
237 P2 Mhlume Swaziland
237 N1 Mhluzi S. Africa
168 H8 Mhòr, Loch l. Scotland U.K.
138 E8 Mhow Madh. Prad. India
118 A4 Mi r. Myanmar
Miabhaig Scotland U.K. see Miavaig
269 H7 Miacatlan Mex.
197 L5 Miączyn Pol.
269 K9 Miahuatlán Mex.
269 K9 Miahuatlán, Sierra de mts Mex.
206 H2 Miajadas Spain
184 F4 Mialet France
196 E3 Miały Pol.
230 C2 Miaméré C.A.R.
265 V8 Miami AZ U.S.A.
255 G13 Miami FL U.S.A.
261 H7 Miami OK U.S.A.
261 E8 Miami TX U.S.A.
Miami Zimbabwe see Mwami
255 G13 Miami Beach FL U.S.A.
256 A9 Miamisburg OH U.S.A.
144 G3 Miānābād Iran
145 J8 Mianaz Pak.
128 F9 Miancaowan Qinghai China
145 O6 Mian Channun Pak.
129 L9 Mianchi Henan China
144 E4 Mīān Darreh Iran
144 G3 Mīāndasht Iran
144 H4 Mīāndehī Iran
144 B3 Mīāndowāb Iran
235 □J3 Miandrivazo Madag.
129 Q2 Mianduhe Nei Mongol China
144 B3 Mīāneh Iran
114 F9 Miangas i. Phil.
145 L9 Miani Hor b. Pak.
145 K5 Mianjoi Afgh.
145 N4 Mian Kalai Pak.
144 E3 Mīān Kāleh, Shebh-e Jazīreh-ye pen. Iran
130 C5 Mianmian Shan mts Sichuan/Yunnan China
130 D4 Mianning Sichuan China
145 N5 Mianwali Pak.
130 F2 Mianxian Shaanxi China
Mianyang Hubei China see Xiantao
Mianyang Shaanxi China see Mianxian
130 E3 Mianyang Sichuan China
130 E3 Mianzhu Sichuan China
123 B10 Miao Dao i. China
129 Q8 Miaodao Liedao is China
132 F4 Miao'ergou Xinjiang China
Miaogao Zhejiang China see Suichang
131 M6 Miaoli Taiwan
235 □J3 Miarinarivo Madag.
127 G2 Miasa Japan
152 H4 Miass Rus. Fed.
196 F2 Miasteckzo Krajeńskie Pol.
196 E1 Miastko Pol.
197 J4 Miastków Kościelny Pol.
197 J2 Miastkowo Pol.
168 C6 Miavaig Western Isles, Scotland U.K.
126 E3 Miboro-ko l. Japan
127 K3 Mibu Japan
127 G4 Mibu-gawa r. Japan
276 C5 Mica, Cerro de mt. Chile
246 G4 Mica Creek B.C. Can.
285 G6 Micaela Cascallares Arg.
265 V9 Mica Mountain AZ U.S.A.
130 F2 Micang Shan mts China
235 H3 Micaune Moz.
156 J2 Michaichmon' Rus. Fed.
199 K3 Michal'any Slovakia
199 I3 Michalová Slovakia
199 K3 Michalovce Slovakia
197 I5 Michałów Pol.
197 J4 Michałów Górny Pol.
197 H5 Michałowice Małopolskie Pol.
196 F5 Michałowice Opolskie Pol.
197 L2 Michałowo Pol.
247 I4 Michel Sask. Can.
193 D10 Michelau in Oberfranken Ger.
194 H3 Michelbach an der Bilz Ger.
201 J6 Micheldorf Austria
201 J4 Micheldorf in Oberösterreich Austria
194 H3 Michelfeld Ger.
245 K1 Michelson, Mount AK U.S.A.
194 G2 Michelstadt Ger.
193 H6 Michendorf Ger.
Micheng Yunnan China see Midu
271 I4 Miches Dom. Rep.
250 F3 Michigamme Lake MI U.S.A.
250 F3 Michigamme Reservoir MI U.S.A.
260 K2 Michigan state U.S.A.
250 G6 Michigan, Lake MI/WI U.S.A.
254 D5 Michigan City IN U.S.A.
230 B2 Michika Nigeria
136 G3 Michinberi Chhattisgarh India
248 C4 Michipicoten Bay Ont. Can.
248 C4 Michipicoten Island Ont. Can.
248 C4 Michipicoten River Ont. Can.
268 E7 Michoacán state Mex.
197 K4 Michów Pol.
Michurin Bulg. see Tsarevo
157 H5 Michurinsk Rus. Fed.
171 M4 Mickleton Durham, England U.K.
173 I3 Mickleton Gloucestershire, England U.K.
266 □Q11 Mico r. Nic.
269 H3 Micos Mex.
271 □3 Micoud St Lucia
290 E5 Micronesia is Pacific Ocean
113 L6 Micronesia, Federated States of country N. Pacific Ocean
219 K3 Micula Romania
117 G3 Midai i. Indon.
229 G2 Midal well Niger
247 K5 Midale Sask. Can.
288 F4 Mid-Atlantic Ridge sea feature Atlantic Ocean
168 K4 Midbea Orkney, Scotland U.K.
187 H6 Middelbeers Neth.
236 D8 Middelberg Pass S. Africa
186 E5 Middelburg Neth.
237 J7 Middelburg Eastern Cape S. Africa
237 N1 Middelburg Mpumalanga S. Africa
164 F6 Middelfart Denmark
186 F5 Middelharnis Neth.
187 C6 Middelkerke Belgium
236 E7 Middelpos S. Africa
186 K2 Middelstum Neth.
235 E5 Middelwit S. Africa
186 G3 Middenbeemster Neth.
186 H3 Middenmeer Neth.
262 D6 Middle Alkali Lake CA U.S.A.
291 M5 Middle America Trench sea feature N. Pacific Ocean
137 M6 Middle Andaman i. Andaman & Nicobar Is India
Middle Atlas mts Morocco see Moyen Atlas
173 J4 Middle Barton Oxfordshire, England U.K.
249 J3 Middle Bay Que. Can.
104 □2 Middle Beach b. Lord Howe I. Austr.
257 O7 Middleboro MA U.S.A.
254 G6 Middlebourne WV U.S.A.
251 Q9 Middleburg PA U.S.A.
256 H10 Middleburg VA U.S.A.
257 K6 Middleburgh NY U.S.A.
259 I1 Middlebury CT U.S.A.
250 I8 Middlebury IN U.S.A.
257 L4 Middlebury VT U.S.A.
270 H3 Middle Caicos i. Turks and Caicos Is
245 N1 Middle Channel watercourse N.W.T. Can.
261 E10 Middle Concho r. TX U.S.A.
Middle Congo country Africa see Congo
107 H4 Middle Creek r. Qld Austr.
258 E2 Middle Creek r. PA U.S.A.
259 J1 Middlefield CT U.S.A.
259 J1 Middle Haddam CT U.S.A.
171 N5 Middleham North Yorkshire, England U.K.
207 □ Middle Hill Gibraltar
259 G1 Middle Hope NY U.S.A.
238 □2c Middle Island i. Tristan da Cunha S. Atlantic Ocean
259 J3 Middle Island NY U.S.A.
260 G5 Middle Loup r. NE U.S.A.
172 H6 Middlemarsh Dorset, England U.K.
107 L7 Middlemount Qld Austr.
108 □1 Middle Point Christmas I.
256 C9 Middleport OH U.S.A.
258 C3 Middleport PA U.S.A.
260 I5 Middle Raccoon r. IA U.S.A.
171 Q7 Middle Rasen Lincolnshire, England U.K.
249 K3 Middle Ridge Wildlife Reserve nature res. Nfld and Lab. Can.
258 C6 Middle River MD U.S.A.
256 B12 Middlesboro KY U.S.A.
171 O4 Middlesbrough Middlesbrough, England U.K.
171 O4 Middlesbrough admin. div. England U.K.
267 O9 Middlesex Belize
270 □ Middlesex reg. Jamaica
256 H6 Middlesex NY U.S.A.
258 A4 Middlesex PA U.S.A.
259 J1 Middlesex County county CT U.S.A.
259 G4 Middlesex County county NJ U.S.A.
171 N5 Middlesmoor North Yorkshire, England U.K.
Middle Strait Andaman & Nicobar Is India see Andaman Strait
107 H7 Middleton Qld Austr.
249 H4 Middleton N.S. Can.
237 J8 Middleton S. Africa
171 M6 Middleton Greater Manchester, England U.K.
173 M2 Middleton Norfolk, England U.K.
256 A5 Middleton MI U.S.A.
250 E6 Middleton WI U.S.A.
173 J3 Middleton Cheney Northamptonshire, England U.K.
171 M4 Middleton in Teesdale Durham, England U.K.
245 K4 Middleton Island AK U.S.A.
173 K6 Middleton-on-Sea West Sussex, England U.K.
171 P6 Middleton-on-the-Wolds East Riding of Yorkshire, England U.K.
99 F4 Middleton Reef Austr.
173 J4 Middleton Stoney Oxfordshire, England U.K.
169 I4 Middletown Northern Ireland U.K.
264 J3 Middletown CA U.S.A.
259 J1 Middletown CT U.S.A.
258 D6 Middletown DE U.S.A.
256 H9 Middletown MD U.S.A.
259 G4 Middletown NJ U.S.A.
257 K7 Middletown NY U.S.A.
256 A9 Middletown OH U.S.A.
251 R9 Middletown PA U.S.A.
256 G9 Middletown VA U.S.A.
250 I7 Middleville MI U.S.A.
257 K5 Middleville NY U.S.A.
171 M7 Middlewich Cheshire, England U.K.
103 C12 Mid Dome mt. South I. N.Z.
226 D2 Midelt Morocco
102 I6 Midhirst North I. N.Z.
232 E2 Midhisho well Somalia
173 K6 Midhurst West Sussex, England U.K.
146 F7 Mīdī Yemen
185 I9 Midi, Canal du France
185 E10 Midi de Bigorre, Pic du mt. France
185 D10 Midi d'Ossau, Pic du mt. France
289 J5 Mid-Indian Basin sea feature Indian Ocean
289 I6 Mid-Indian Ridge sea feature Indian Ocean
183 A8 Midi-Pyrénées admin. reg. France
248 E4 Midland Ont. Can.
265 R8 Midland CA U.S.A.
251 J6 Midland MI U.S.A.
260 E3 Midland SD U.S.A.
261 E9 Midland TX U.S.A.
109 C11 Midland Junction W.A. Austr.
235 F3 Midlands prov. Zimbabwe
169 F9 Midleton Ireland
168 J11 Midlothian admin. div. Scotland U.K.
261 G9 Midlothian TX U.S.A.
256 H11 Midlothian VA U.S.A.
190 G3 Midlum Ger.
237 O5 Midmar Nature Reserve S. Africa
251 M5 Midmay Ont. Can.
Midnapore W. Bengal India see Medinipur
235 □J4 Midongy Atsimo Madag.
127 K4 Midori Japan
125 H14 Midori-gawa r. Japan
185 C8 Midou r. France
185 C8 Midouze r. France
290 F4 Mid-Pacific Mountains sea feature N. Pacific Ocean
237 M1 Midrand S. Africa
114 E8 Midsayap Mindanao Phil.
172 H5 Midsomer Norton Bath and North East Somerset, England U.K.
162 I5 Midsund Norway
164 F5 Midtjylland admin. reg. Denmark
130 C6 Midu Yunnan China
135 □2 Midu i. Addu Atoll Maldives
262 F4 Midvale ID U.S.A.
Midway Oman see Thamarīt
265 U1 Midway UT U.S.A.
97 H2 Midway Islands N. Pacific Ocean
245 J1 Midway Islands AK U.S.A.
109 G7 Midway Well W.A. Austr.
262 K5 Midwest WY U.S.A.
261 G8 Midwest City OK U.S.A.
186 L2 Midwolda Neth.
146 B2 Midyan reg. Saudi Arabia
149 J5 Midyat Turkey
Midye Turkey see Kıyıköy
168 □N1 Mid Yell Shetland, Scotland U.K.
219 K7 Midzhur mt. Bulg./Yugo.
125 I14 Mie Japan
126 D7 Mie pref. Japan
197 I5 Miechów Pol.
199 L1 Mieczka r. Pol.
200 D5 Mieders Austria
205 R6 Miedes Spain
196 C2 Miedwie, Jezioro l. Pol.
197 I5 Miedziana Góra Pol.
196 D3 Miedzichowo Pol.
197 K3 Miedzna Pol.
197 H6 Miedźna Pol.
196 G5 Miedźno Pol.
196 F4 Międzybórz Pol.
196 D3 Międzychód Pol.
196 E5 Międzylesie Pol.
197 K4 Międzyrzec Podlaski Pol.
196 D3 Międzyrzecz Pol.
189 I3 Międzyrzecza Warty i Widawki, Park Krajobrazowy Pol.
196 C2 Międzyzdroje Pol.
163 S6 Miehikkälä Fin.
191 E10 Miehlen Ger.
197 J6 Miejsce Piastowe Pol.
196 E4 Miejska Górka Pol.
196 E4 Miękinia Pol.
185 E9 Miélan France
183 G8 Miélandre, Montagne de mt. France
197 J5 Mielec Pol.
192 K4 Mielęcin Pol.
196 F3 Mieleszyn Pol.
190 J2 Mielkendorf Ger.
197 L3 Mielnik Pol.
196 E1 Mielno Pol.
233 C7 Miembwe Tanz.
200 D5 Mieming Austria
200 C5 Mieminger Gebirge mts Austria
197 G3 Mień r. Pol.
165 K5 Mien l. Sweden
105 K9 Miena Tas. Austr.
231 C9 Mienga Angola
231 F8 Miengwe Zambia
131 N6 Mienhua Yü i. Taiwan
205 M2 Miera r. Spain
162 S2 Mieraslompolo Fin.
Mierašluoppal Fin. see Mieraslompolo
219 N4 Miercurea-Ciuc Romania
204 I2 Mieres Spain
Mieres del Camín Spain see Mieres
Mieres del Camino Spain see Mieres
187 I6 Mierlo Neth.
162 Q2 Mierojávri Norway
196 E5 Mieroszów Pol.
185 H6 Miers France
268 G2 Mier y Noriaga Mex.
197 I5 Mierzawa r. Pol.
192 J4 Mierzyn Pol.
194 C3 Miesau Ger.
195 L6 Miesbach Ger.
196 F3 Mieścisko Pol.
194 D3 Miesenbach Ger.
232 D2 Mī'ēso Eth.
193 D6 Mieste Ger.
193 D6 Miesterhorst Ger.
196 F3 Mieszków Pol.
196 C3 Mieszkowice Pol.
194 H5 Mietingen Ger.
163 P6 Mietoinen Fin.
182 J4 Mieussy France
204 G6 Mieza Spain
146 E6 Mīfah Saudi Arabia
256 C8 Mifflin OH U.S.A.
251 Q9 Mifflinburg PA U.S.A.
256 H8 Mifflintown PA U.S.A.
258 C2 Mifflinville PA U.S.A.
126 F1 Mifune-zaki pt Japan
128 J9 Migang Shan mt. Gansu/Ningxia China
237 J2 Migdol S. Africa
178 G8 Migennes France
144 H6 Mīghān Iran
226 C3 Mighert, Tizi pass Morocco
139 O5 Miging Arun. Prad. India
213 L6 Migliarino Italy
212 I8 Migliarino-San Rossore-Massaciuccoli, Parco Naturale di nature res. Italy
213 L6 Migliaro Italy
217 K2 Miglionica Italy
184 E2 Mignaloux-Beauvoir France
215 L5 Mignano Monte Lungo Italy
214 H3 Mignone r. Italy
182 I3 Mignovillard France
133 J10 Migriggyangzham Co l. Qinghai China
249 H3 Miguasha, Parc de nature res. N.B. Can.
269 K7 Miguel Alemán Mex.
269 K7 Miguel Alemán, Presa resr Mex.
278 E3 Miguel Alves Brazil
268 D1 Miguel Auza Mex.
278 E4 Miguel Calmon Brazil
266 □S13 Miguel de la Borda Panama
269 K8 Miguel de la Madrid, Presa resr Mex.
205 N9 Miguel Esteban Spain
285 I4 Miguelete Uru.
269 H3 Miguel Hidalgo Mex.
266 E4 Miguel Hidalgo, Presa resr Mex.
281 F5 Miguel Pereira Brazil
285 F5 Miguel Riglos Arg.
207 L3 Miguelturra Spain
160 M6 Migushino Rus. Fed.
118 B5 Migyaunye Myanmar
219 N6 Mihăilești Romania
198 G5 Miháld Hungary
221 L2 Mihalgazi Turkey
148 E4 Mihalıççık Turkey
198 G4 Mihályi Hungary
126 E6 Mihama Aichi Japan
126 C4 Mihama Fukui Japan
126 D8 Mihama Mie Japan
126 B8 Mihama Wakayama Japan
125 K12 Mihara Hiroshima Japan
126 A7 Mihara Hyōgo Japan
127 J6 Mihara-yama vol. Japan
129 P8 Mi He r. China
Mihidjan W. Bengal India see Chittaranjan
139 K8 Mihijam Jharkhand India
136 G8 Mihintale Sri Lanka
191 J8 Mihla Ger.
127 L4 Mihō Japan
125 K11 Miho-wan b. Japan
233 C7 Mihumo Chini Tanz.
205 K8 Mijares Spain
209 D7 Mijares r. Spain
207 J7 Mijas Spain
207 J7 Mijas mt. Spain
186 G4 Mijdrecht Neth.
127 J1 Mijōga-take mt. Japan
182 I4 Mijoux France
156 I4 M. I. Kalinina, imeni Rus. Fed.
124 S3 Mikasa Japan
158 G1 Mikashevichy Belarus
126 C4 Mikata Japan
126 C4 Mikata-ko l. Japan
126 D3 Mikawa Japan
126 F6 Mikawa-wan b. Japan
126 F6 Mikawa-wan Kokutei-kōen park Japan
199 K4 Mikepércs Hungary
Mikhalevo Rus. Fed. see Paneyevo
161 W6 Mikhali Rus. Fed.
160 J7 Mikhalishki Belarus
160 K8 Mikhanavichy Belarus
Mikha Tskhakaia Georgia see Senaki
Mikhaykovskiy Rus. Fed. see Prozorovo
161 W7 Mikhaylov Rus. Fed.
Mikhaylovgrad Bulg. see Montana
287 F2 Mikhaylov Island Antarctica
143 Q1 Mikhaylovka Pavlodarskaya Oblast' Kazakh.
Mikhaylovka Zhambylskaya Oblast' Kazakh. see Sarykemer
122 F4 Mikhaylovka Amurskaya Oblast' Rus. Fed.
122 A3 Mikhaylovka Chitinskaya Oblast' Rus. Fed.
159 O1 Mikhaylovka Kurskaya Oblast' Rus. Fed.
122 H7 Mikhaylovka Primorskiy Kray Rus. Fed.
Mikhaylovka Tul'skaya Oblast' Rus. Fed. see Kimovsk
157 H6 Mikhaylovka Volgogradskaya Oblast' Rus. Fed.
219 L7 Mikhaylovo Bulg.
159 T4 Mikhaylovo-Aleksandrovskiy Rus. Fed.
143 R2 Mikhaylovskiy Altayskiy Kray Rus. Fed.
Mikhaylovskiy Altayskiy Kray Rus. Fed. see Malinovoye Ozero
Mikhaylovskoye Rus. Fed. see Shpakovskoye
161 U6 Mikhnevo Rus. Fed.
150 C9 Mikhrot Timna Israel
146 E6 Mikhwa Saudi Arabia
126 A6 Miki Japan
Mikínes tourist site Greece see Mycenae
139 N6 Mikir Hills India
126 D8 Miki-zaki pt Japan
126 G6 Mikkabi Japan
163 S6 Mikkeli Fin.
163 S6 Mikkelin mlk Fin.
246 H3 Mikkwa r. Alta Can.
201 M6 Miklavž Slovenia
197 J2 Mikołajki Pol.
197 H2 Mikołajki Pomorskie Pol.
196 G5 Mikołów Pol.
Míkonos i. Greece see Mykonos
196 G1 Mikoszewo Pol.
Mikoyan Armenia see Yeghegnadzor
Mikoyanovka Rus. Fed. see Oktyabr'skiy
220 E1 Mikropoli Greece
196 F4 Mikstat Pol.
193 J9 Mikulasovice Czech Rep.
198 G3 Mikulčice Czech Rep.
156 I2 Mikulkin, Mys c. Rus. Fed.
198 F3 Mikulov Czech Rep.
198 G1 Mikulovice Czech Rep.
233 C6 Mikumi Tanz.
233 C6 Mikumi National Park Tanz.
126 E6 Mikumo Japan
156 J3 Mikun' Rus. Fed.
126 D3 Mikuni Japan
127 I2 Mikuni-sanmyaku mts Japan
127 I4 Mikuni-yama mt. Japan
127 K8 Mikura-jima i. Japan
227 G1 Mila Alg.
260 I3 Milaca MN U.S.A.
136 C9 Miladhunmadulu Atoll Maldives
278 F3 Milagres Brazil
284 E2 Milagro Arg.
274 B5 Milagro Ecuador
205 Q4 Milagro Spain
205 M5 Milagros Spain
197 I1 Miłakowo Pol.
138 H4 Milam Uttaranchal India
Milan Italy see Milano
251 K7 Milan MI U.S.A.
260 I5 Milan MO U.S.A.
256 C7 Milan OH U.S.A.
231 C7 Milando Angola
231 C7 Milando, Reserva Especial do nature res. Angola
104 G6 Milang S.A. Austr.
235 G3 Milange Moz.
212 G5 Milano Italy
212 G5 Milano prov. Italy
212 F4 Milano (Malpensa) airport Italy
235 □K2 Milanoa Madag.
213 M7 Milano Marittima Italy
Milanovce Slovakia see Veľký Kýr
197 K4 Milanów Pol.
197 I3 Milanówek Pol.
258 E1 Milanville PA U.S.A.
219 M4 Milaș Romania
221 I5 Milas Turkey
158 G2 Milashavichy Belarus
161 P8 Milaslavichy Rus. Fed.
160 I9 Milavidy Belarus
217 I7 Milazzo Sicilia Italy
217 I7 Milazzo, Capo di c. Sicilia Italy
217 I7 Milazzo, Golfo di b. Sicilia Italy
260 G3 Milbank SD U.S.A.
172 H6 Milborne Port Somerset, England U.K.
172 H6 Milborne St Andrew Dorset, England U.K.
257 □R4 Milbridge ME U.S.A.
192 E5 Milde r. Ger.
173 N3 Mildenhall Suffolk, England U.K.
251 R8 Mildred PA U.S.A.
190 H2 Mildstedt Ger.
105 I6 Mildura Vic. Austr.
151 I5 Mil Düzü lowland Azer.
130 D6 Mile Yunnan China
232 D2 Mīlē Eth.
170 F4 Milebush Northern Ireland U.K.
173 N4 Mile End Essex, England U.K.
270 □ Mile Gully Jamaica
197 L3 Milejczyce Pol.
197 H1 Milejewo Pol.
197 K4 Milejów Pol.
216 F9 Milena Sicilia Italy
107 M9 Miles Qld Austr.
256 H8 Milesburg PA U.S.A.
262 L3 Miles City MT U.S.A.
232 D2 Mīlē Serdo Reserve nature res. Eth.
198 C1 Milešovka hill Czech Rep.
169 F7 Milestone Ireland
219 P3 Miletin r. Romania
217 K6 Mileto Italy
215 M5 Miletto, Monte mt. Italy
109 D9 Mileura W.A. Austr.
198 D2 Mílevsko Czech Rep.
161 S8 Mileyevo Rus. Fed.
171 M2 Milfield Northumberland, England U.K.
206 B5 Milfontes Port.
169 E8 Milford Cork Ireland
169 G2 Milford Donegal Ireland
173 K5 Milford Surrey, England U.K.
259 I2 Milford CT U.S.A.
258 E7 Milford DE U.S.A.
250 G9 Milford IL U.S.A.
257 N6 Milford MA U.S.A.
258 B6 Milford MD U.S.A.
257 □Q4 Milford ME U.S.A.
256 B6 Milford MI U.S.A.
260 G5 Milford NE U.S.A.
257 N6 Milford NH U.S.A.
258 E3 Milford NJ U.S.A.
258 F2 Milford PA U.S.A.
265 S3 Milford UT U.S.A.
256 H10 Milford VA U.S.A.
172 B4 Milford Haven Pembrokeshire, Wales U.K.
260 G6 Milford Lake KS U.S.A.
173 I6 Milford on Sea Hampshire, England U.K.
103 B11 Milford Sound South I. N.Z.
103 B11 Milford Sound inlet South I. N.Z.
258 E4 Milford Square PA U.S.A.
107 H5 Milgarra Qld Austr.
109 E8 Milgun W.A. Austr.
Milḥ, Baḥr al l. Iraq see Razāzah, Buḥayrat ar
204 G5 Milhão Port.
183 E9 Milhaud France
196 F4 Milicz Pol.
Milid Turkey see Malatya
106 C1 Milikapiti N.T. Austr.
109 D11 Miling W.A. Austr.
106 E2 Milingimbi N.T. Austr.
214 B7 Milis Sardegna Italy
142 I3 Milisay Kazakh.
216 H9 Militello in Val di Catania Sicilia Italy
180 B5 Milizac France
201 M7 Miljana Croatia
262 K2 Milk r. MT U.S.A.
225 F5 Milk, Wadi el watercourse Sudan
193 J8 Milkel Ger.
197 J2 Miłki Pol.
153 Q4 Mil'kovo Rus. Fed.
196 E4 Miłkowice Pol.
247 H5 Milk River Alta Can.
186 I5 Mill Neth.
107 J4 Millaa Millaa Qld Austr.
250 B9 Millard MO U.S.A.
209 D9 Millares Spain
255 □2 Millars New Prov. Bahamas
183 C8 Millau France
182 E3 Millay France
256 F11 Millboro VA U.S.A.
251 P5 Millbrook Ont. Can.
172 D7 Millbrook Cornwall, England U.K.
255 D9 Millbrook AL U.S.A.
257 L7 Millbrook NY U.S.A.
168 I7 Mill Buie hill Scotland U.K.
262 C4 Mill City OR U.S.A.
256 F10 Mill Creek WV U.S.A.
264 J1 Mill Creek r. CA U.S.A.
258 C5 Mill Creek r. PA U.S.A.
259 J1 Milldale CT U.S.A.
255 F9 Milledgeville GA U.S.A.
250 E8 Milledgeville IL U.S.A.
260 I2 Mille Lacs lakes MN U.S.A.
248 B3 Mille Lacs, Lac des l. Ont. Can.
255 G9 Millen GA U.S.A.
Millennium Island atoll Kiribati see Caroline Island
104 E4 Miller watercourse S.A. Austr.
236 H9 Miller S. Africa
260 F3 Miller SD U.S.A.
245 L3 Miller, Mount AK U.S.A.
250 D4 Miller Dam Flowage resr WI U.S.A.
251 M4 Miller Lake Ont. Can.
157 H6 Millerovo Rus. Fed.
265 V10 Miller Peak AZ U.S.A.
251 J4 Millersburg MI U.S.A.
256 D8 Millersburg OH U.S.A.
251 R9 Millersburg PA U.S.A.
104 F4 Millers Creek S.A. Austr.
256 B11 Millers Creek KY U.S.A.
257 M6 Millers Falls MA U.S.A.
103 D12 Millers Flat South I. N.Z.
256 C9 Millersport OH U.S.A.
258 A3 Millerstown PA U.S.A.
258 B6 Millersville MD U.S.A.
258 C5 Millersville PA U.S.A.
257 L7 Millerton NY U.S.A.
264 M4 Millerton Lake CA U.S.A.
168 F12 Milleur Point Scotland U.K.
184 I4 Millevaches France
184 H4 Millevaches, Plateau de France
169 I4 Millford Northern Ireland U.K.
287 L1 Mill Glacier Antarctica
256 H7 Mill Hall PA U.S.A.
259 G4 Millhurst NJ U.S.A.
104 H7 Millicent S.A. Austr.
179 J7 Millières France
108 H5 Millijiddie Aboriginal Re W.A. Austr.
186 J5 Millingen aan de Rijn N
258 D6 Millington MD U.S.A.
251 K6 Millington MI U.S.A.
261 K8 Millington TN U.S.A.
286 T2 Mill Inlet Antarctica
257 □Q3 Millinocket ME U.S.A.
276 C5 Milliri, Cerro mt. Bol.
287 G2 Mill Island Antarctica
243 K3 Mill Island Nunavut Can
169 K3 Millisle Northern Ireland
107 M9 Millmerran Qld Austr.
258 A3 Millmont PA U.S.A.
171 K5 Millom Cumbria, Englanc
168 G11 Millport North Ayrshire, S U.K.
258 F2 Millrift PA U.S.A.
257 J10 Millsboro DE U.S.A.
107 I7 Mills Creek watercourse C
246 G2 Mills Lake N.W.T. Can.
201 I6 Millstatt Austria
201 I6 Millstätter See l. Austria
250 D5 Millston WI U.S.A.
256 C11 Millstone KY U.S.A.
256 D10 Millstone WV U.S.A.
258 F3 Millstone r. NJ U.S.A.
108 D6 Millstream W.A. Austr.
108 D6 Millstream-Chichester N Park W.A. Austr.
169 D8 Millstreet Ireland
249 H4 Milltown N.B. Can.
170 C5 Milltown Cavan Ireland
169 E5 Milltown Galway Ireland
169 C8 Milltown Kerry Ireland
170 D7 Milltown Kildare Ireland
170 E5 Milltown Northern Irelan
262 H3 Milltown MT U.S.A.
250 B4 Milltown WI U.S.A.
169 D7 Milltown Malbay Ireland
168 K8 Milltown of Kildrummy Aberdeenshire, Scotland U.
168 K7 Milltown of Rothiemay M Scotland U.K.
107 H5 Millungera Qld Austr.
237 K1 Millvale S. Africa
264 J4 Mill Valley CA U.S.A.
257 □R2 Millville N.B. Can.
258 E6 Millville NJ U.S.A.
258 B2 Millville PA U.S.A.
259 H2 Millwood NY U.S.A.
261 I9 Millwood Lake AR U.S.A.
178 D7 Milly-la-Forêt France
182 F4 Milly-Lamartine France
109 D9 Milly Milly W.A. Austr.
205 Q6 Milmarcos Spain
192 I4 Milmersdorf Ger.
187 I7 Milmort Belgium
168 J10 Milnathort Perth and Kin Scotland U.K.
Milne Land i. Greenland Ilimananngip Nunaa
168 H11 Milngavie East Dunbarto Scotland U.K.
171 M6 Milnrow Greater Manches England U.K.
171 L5 Milnthorpe Cumbria, Eng U.K.
228 C4 Milo r. Guinea
217 I8 Milo Sicilia Italy
257 □Q3 Milo ME U.S.A.
196 E2 Miłocice Pol.
122 I7 Milogradovo Rus. Fed.
213 Q5 Milohnić Croatia
264 □F14 Miloli'i HI U.S.A.
197 H2 Miłomłyn Pol.
196 G1 Miłoradz Pol.
220 F6 Milos i. Greece
161 W8 Miloslavskoye Rus. Fed.
196 F3 Miłosław Pol.
226 D4 Miloud well Alg.
168 C8 Milovaig Highland, Scotla
159 Q3 Milove Kharkivs'ka Oblas
159 T4 Milove Luhans'ka Oblast'
193 K10 Milovice Czech Rep.
193 F5 Milow Brandenburg Ger.
192 E4 Milow Mecklenburg-Vorpo Ger.
197 H6 Milówka Pol.
105 H3 Milparinka N.S.W. Austr.
264 K4 Milpitas CA U.S.A.
256 H8 Milroy PA U.S.A.
195 N3 Miltach Ger.
194 G2 Miltenberg Ger.
105 M6 Milton N.S.W. Austr.
251 O6 Milton Ont. Can.
103 D13 Milton South I. N.Z.
168 G8 Milton Highland, Scotlan
168 I9 Milton Perth and Kinross, Scotland U.K.
257 J10 Milton DE U.S.A.
255 D10 Milton FL U.S.A.
257 □O5 Milton NH U.S.A.
259 H1 Milton NY U.S.A.
258 B2 Milton PA U.S.A.
257 L4 Milton VT U.S.A.
256 C10 Milton WV U.S.A.
172 D6 Milton Abbot Devon, Engl
262 E4 Milton-Freewater OR U.S
173 K3 Milton Keynes Milton Ke England U.K.
173 K3 Milton Keynes admin. div England U.K.
192 H2 Miltzow Ger.
131 I4 Miluo Hunan China
251 N6 Milverton Ont. Can.
172 F5 Milverton Somerset, Engl
250 G6 Milwaukee WI U.S.A.
288 E4 Milwaukee Deep sea feat Caribbean Sea
143 P3 Milybulabk Kazakh.
157 H6 Milyutinskaya Rus. Fed.
191 K10 Milz Ger.
185 C8 Mimbaste France
230 C4 Mimbelly Congo
263 K10 Mimbres watercourse NM
205 N2 Mimetiz Spain
104 D2 Mimili S.A. Austr.
136 F8 Mimisal Tamil Nadu Indi
125 I14 Mimitsu Japan
185 B7 Mimizan France
185 B7 Mimizan-Plage France
198 D1 Mimoň Czech Rep.
230 A5 Mimongo Gabon
105 L7 Mimosa Rocks National N.S.W. Austr.
281 G4 Mimoso do Sul Brazil
125 L11 Mimuro-yama mt. Japan
267 I4 Mina Mex.
264 N3 Mina NV U.S.A.
276 C3 Mina, Nevado mt. Peru
147 I1 Mīnā' 'Abd Allāh Kuwait
144 G8 Mīnāb Iran
144 G8 Mīnāb r. Iran
145 M6 Mina Bazar Pak.
126 B8 Minabe Japan
126 B8 Minabegawa Japan
284 E2 Mina Clavero Arg.
278 C5 Minaçu Brazil
206 E5 Mina de São Domingos
247 L4 Minago r. Man. Can.
115 B3 Minahasa, Semenanjung Indon.
Minahassa Peninsula Inc Minahasa, Semenanjung
147 L3 Mina Jebel Ali U.A.E.
127 I2 Minakami Japan
Minaker B.C. Can. see Prophet River
150 F2 Mīnakh Syria
247 M5 Minaki Ont. Can.
126 D6 Minakuchi Japan
125 H14 Minamata Japan
126 E4 Minami Japan
106 E3 Minamia N.T. Austr.
127 H4 Minami-arupusu Kokuri nat. park Japan
127 J5 Minamiashigara Japan
127 K6 Minami-Bōsō Kokutei-kō Japan
126 E6 Minamichita Japan
121 N6 Minami-Daitō-jima i. Jap

Minami-gawa r. Japan
Minami-Iō-jima vol. Kazan-rettō Japan
Minamiizu Japan
Minami-kawara Japan
Minamimaki Japan
Minamiminowa Japan
Minaminasu Japan
Minamishinano Japan
Min'an Hunan China see Longshan
Minano Japan
Minard Argyll and Bute, Scotland U.K.
Minaret Peaks South I. N.Z.
Minas Cuba
Minas Sumatera Indon.
Minas Uru.
Minā' Sa'ūd Kuwait
Minas Basin b. N.S. Can.
Minas Channel N.S. Can.
Minas de Corrales Uru.
Minas de Matahambre Cuba
Minas de Riotinto Spain
Minas Gerais state Brazil
Minas Novas Brazil
Minateda Spain
Minatitlán Colima Mex.
Minatitlán Veracruz Mex.
Minaya Spain
Minbu Myanmar
Minbya Myanmar
Minchinabad Pak.
Minchinmávida vol. Chile
Minch Moor hill Scotland U.K.
Minchumina, Lake AK U.S.A.
Mincio r. Italy
Mincivan Azer.
Mindanao i. Phil.
Mindanao r. Mindanao Phil.
Mindarie S.A. Austr.
Mindat Sakan Myanmar
Minde Port.
Mindel r. Ger.
Mindelheim Ger.
Mindelo Cape Verde
Mindelo Port.
Mindelstetten Ger.
Minden Ont. Can.
Minden Ger.
Minden LA U.S.A.
Minden NE U.S.A.
Minden NV U.S.A.
Minden City MI U.S.A.
Mindenhout Belgium
Minderoo W.A. Austr.
Mindon Myanmar
Mindona Lake imp. l. N.S.W. Austr.
Mindoro i. Phil.
Mindoro Strait Phil.
Mindouli Congo
Mindszent Hungary
Mindszentgodisa Hungary
Minduri Brazil
Mindyak Rus. Fed.
Mindzhivan Azer. see Mincivan
Mine Japan
Mine Centre Ont. Can.
Mine Head hd Ireland
Mine Head hd Ireland
Minehead Somerset, England U.K.
Mineiros Brazil
Mineo Sicilia Italy
Mineola NY U.S.A.
Mineola TX U.S.A.
Miner r. N.W.T. Can.
Miner r. Y.T. Can.
Minera Wrexham, Wales U.K.
Mineral VA U.S.A.
Mineral del Monte Mex.
Mineral del Refugio Mex.
Minerales de la Pampa Arg.
Mineral'nyye Vody Rus. Fed.
Mineral Point WI U.S.A.
Mineral Wells TX U.S.A.
Mineralwells WV U.S.A.
Minerbio Italy
Minersville PA U.S.A.
Minersville UT U.S.A.
Minerva atoll Arch. des Tuamotu Fr. Polynesia see Reao
Minerva OH U.S.A.
Minerva Reefs Fiji
Minervino Murge Italy
Minervois reg. France
Minervois, Monts du hills France
Mineyama Japan
Minfeld Ger.
Minfeng Xinjiang China
Minga Dem. Rep. Congo
Minga Zambia
Mingäçevir Azer.
Mingäçevir Su Anbarı resr Azer.
Mingala C.A.R.
Mingan Que. Can.
Mingan, Îles de is Que. Can.
Mingardo r. Italy
Mingary S.A. Austr.
Mingbuloq Uzbek.
Mingechaur Azer. see Mingäçevir
Mingechaurskoye Vodokhranilishche resr Azer. see Mingäçevir Su Anbarı
Mingela Qld Austr.
Mingenew W.A. Austr.
Mingera Creek watercourse Qld Austr.
Mingfeng Hubei China see Yuan'an
Minggang Henan China
Mingguang Anhui China
Mingin Myanmar
Mingin Range mts Myanmar
Ming-Kush Kyrg.
Minglanilla Spain
Mingo Junction OH U.S.A.
Mingorría Spain
Mingoyo Tanz.
Mingshan Chongqing China see Fengdu
Mingshan Sichuan China
Mingshui Gansu China
Mingshui Heilong. China
Mingteke Xinjiang China
Minguez, Puerto de pass Spain
Mingulay i. Scotland U.K.
Mingun Myanmar
Minguri Moz.
Mingxi Fujian China
Mingzhou Hebei China see Weixian
Mingzhou Shaanxi China see Suide
Minhe Jiangxi China see Jinxian
Minhe Qinghai China
Minhla Magwe Myanmar
Minhla Pegu Myanmar
Minho reg. Port.
Minhou Fujian China
Miniac-Morvan France
Minico, Parco del park Italy
Minicoy atoll India
Minidoka Internment National Monument nat. park ID U.S.A.
Minigwal, Lake salt flat W.A. Austr.
Minihof-Liebau Austria
Minija r. Lith.
Minilla, Embalse de la resr Spain
Minilya W.A. Austr.
Minilya r. W.A. Austr.
Miñimiñe Chile
Mininco Chile
Mininian Côte d'Ivoire
Minipi Lake Nfld and Lab. Can.
Miniss Lake Ont. Can.
Ministra mt. Spain
Ministra, Sierra mts Spain
Minitonas Man. Can.
Minitskaya Rus. Fed.
Minjian Sichuan China see Mabian

130 E4 Min Jiang r. Sichuan China
131 L5 Min Jiang r. China
106 D1 Minjilang N.T. Austr.
151 H6 Minkänd Azer.
230 B4 Minkébé, Parc National de nat. park Woleu-Ntem Gabon
Min-Kush Kyrg. see Ming-Kush
104 F6 Minlaton S.A. Austr.
128 G7 Minle Gansu China
229 G4 Minna Nigeria
287 L1 Minna Bluff pt Antarctica
169 F3 Mín na Croise Ireland
124 □[3] Minna-jima i. Okinawa Japan
124 □B22 Minna-shima i. Okinawa Japan
163 M5 Minne Sweden
260 G6 Minneapolis KS U.S.A.
250 A5 Minneapolis MN U.S.A.
247 L5 Minnedosa Man. Can.
256 F10 Minnehaha Springs WV U.S.A.
261 E7 Minneola KS U.S.A.
260 I3 Minnesota r. MN U.S.A.
260 I2 Minnesota state U.S.A.
250 C5 Minnesota City MN U.S.A.
260 F1 Minnewaukan ND U.S.A.
119 O8 Min-ngaw Myanmar
109 C7 Minnie Creek W.A. Austr.
168 H13 Minnigaff Dumfries and Galloway, Scotland U.K.
104 E5 Minnipa S.A. Austr.
248 B3 Minnitaki Lake Ont. Can.
126 E4 Mino Japan
204 C5 Miño r. Port./Spain
127 H5 Minobu Japan
127 H5 Minobu-san mt. Japan
127 H6 Minobu-sanchi mts Japan
126 F5 Minokamo Japan
126 F5 Mino-Mikawa-kōgen reg. Japan
285 H2 Miñones Arg.
250 C3 Minong WI U.S.A.
250 E9 Minonk IL U.S.A.
126 B6 Minoo Japan
Minorca i. Spain see Menorca
214 I1 Minore, Isola i. Italy
127 L3 Minori Japan
182 F1 Minot France
260 E1 Minot ND U.S.A.
127 G4 Minowa Japan
150 F6 Minqār, Ghadīr imp. l. Syria
128 H7 Minqin Gansu China
131 L5 Minqing Fujian China
258 D5 Minquadale DE U.S.A.
129 N9 Minquan Henan China
129 E3 Minsen Ger.
130 D2 Min Shan mts Sichuan China
118 B2 Minsin Myanmar
160 K8 Minsk Belarus
Minskaya Oblast' admin. div. Belarus see Minskaya Voblasts'
160 K8 Minskaya Voblasts' admin. div. Belarus
197 J3 Mińsk Mazowiecki Pol.
Minsk Oblast admin. div. Belarus see Minskaya Voblasts'
173 N5 Minster Kent, England U.K.
173 O5 Minster Kent, England U.K.
256 A8 Minster OH U.S.A.
172 G2 Minsterley Shropshire, England U.K.
229 I5 Minta Cameroon
143 P9 Mintaka Pass China/Pak.
130 C2 Mintang Qinghai China
168 M7 Mintlaw Aberdeenshire, Scotland U.K.
249 H4 Minto N.B. Can.
Minto atoll Arch. des Tuamotu Fr. Polynesia see Tenarunga
245 J2 Minto AK U.S.A.
248 F1 Minto, Lac l. Que. Can.
287 L2 Minto, Mount Antarctica
242 G2 Minto Inlet N.W.T. Can.
216 H8 Mintom Cameroon
247 J5 Minton Sask. Can.
195 M4 Mintraching Ger.
263 K7 Minturn CO U.S.A.
Minturnae Italy see Minturno
215 L5 Minturno Italy
212 I7 Minucciano Italy
144 F3 Mīnū Dasht Iran
225 F2 Minūf Egypt
148 E8 Minūfiyah governorate Egypt
151 F10 Minusinsk Rus. Fed.
212 F3 Minusio Switz.
130 A4 Minutang Arun. Prad. India
206 C3 Minutos, Barragem dos resr Port.
230 B4 Minvoul Gabon
128 I9 Minxian Gansu China
Minya Konka mt. Sichuan China see Gongga Shan
156 L5 Minyar Rus. Fed.
105 I7 Minyip Vic. Austr.
118 B3 Minywa Myanmar
139 P6 Minzong Arun. Prad. India
229 H2 Mio well Niger
251 J5 Mio MI U.S.A.
216 D3 Mionica Mionica Serbia
169 D6 Mionlach Ireland
182 F5 Mionnay France
182 F5 Mions France
126 G8 Mipia, Lake salt flat Qld Austr.
136 H3 Miquan Xinjiang China
183 E2 Miquelon Que. Can.
249 J4 Miquelon i. St Pierre and Miquelon
269 H2 Miquihuana Mex.
160 J8 Mir Belarus
274 B4 Mira r. Col.
213 M5 Mira Italy
204 C8 Mira Port.
206 B5 Mira r. Port.
205 R9 Mira Spain
205 Q9 Mira r. Spain
204 H5 Mira, Sierra de mt. Spain
209 C6 Mira, Sierra de mts Spain
183 H9 Mirabeau France
257 K3 Mirabel Que. Can.
185 G7 Mirabel France
204 H9 Mirabel Spain
281 E2 Mirabela Brazil
183 G8 Mirabel-aux-Baronnies France
216 G9 Mirabella Imbaccari Sicilia Italy
281 F4 Miracema Brazil
Miracema do Norte Brazil see Miracema do Tocantins
278 C4 Miracema do Tocantins Brazil
Mirada Hills CA U.S.A. see La Mirada
204 C9 Mira de Aire Port.
281 G4 Miradouro Brazil
267 O9 Mirador-Dos Lagunos-Río Azul, Parque Nacional nat. park Guat.
281 F4 Miradouro Brazil
185 F8 Miradoux France
274 C3 Miraflores Boyaca Col.
274 C4 Miraflores Guaviare Col.
266 E6 Miraflores Mex.
205 M7 Miraflores de la Sierra Spain
149 J7 Mirah, Wādī al watercourse Iraq/Saudi Arabia
281 F4 Miraí Brazil
136 D4 Miraj Mahar. India
281 F2 Miralta Brazil
285 I6 Miramar Buenos Aires Arg.
285 F2 Miramar Córdoba Arg.
283 B8 Miramar, Canal sea chan. Chile
284 E2 Miramar, Lago l. Mex.
213 N7 Miramare Italy
183 G9 Miramas France
184 C5 Mirambeau France
208 E6 Mirambel Spain
249 H4 Miramichi N.B. Can.
249 H4 Miramichi Bay N.B. Can.
185 E6 Miramont-de-Guyenne France
185 D8 Miramont-Sensacq France
132 I7 Miran Xinjiang China
274 D5 Miraña Col.
185 H5 Miranda Arg.
277 F5 Miranda Brazil
277 F6 Miranda r. Brazil
Miranda Moz. see Macaloge
264 I1 Miranda CA U.S.A.
274 E2 Miranda state Venez.
109 F9 Miranda, Lake salt flat W.A. Austr.

205 Q4 Miranda de Arga Spain
205 O3 Miranda de Ebro Spain
204 I8 Miranda del Castañar Spain
204 D8 Miranda do Corvo Port.
204 H5 Miranda do Douro Port.
185 E8 Mirande France
204 F6 Mirandela Port.
206 G2 Mirandilla Spain
268 E5 Mirandillas Mex.
213 K6 Mirandola Italy
183 H8 Mirandol-Bourgnounac France
280 B4 Mirandópolis Brazil
213 M5 Mirano Italy
145 N5 Miran Shah Pak.
280 B5 Mirante, Serra do hills Brazil
280 B5 Mirante do Paranapanema Brazil
285 F4 Mira Pampa Arg.
275 F5 Mirapinima Brazil
220 B2 Miras Albania
125 J12 Mirasaka Japan
280 C4 Mirassol Brazil
204 G3 Miravalles mt. Spain
204 I9 Miravete hill Spain
145 M4 Mir Bacheh Kowt Afgh.
Mir-Bashir Azer. see Tärtär
147 L7 Mirbāṭ Oman
147 L7 Mirbāṭ, Ra's c. Oman
151 J6 Mircälal Azer.
197 L5 Mircze Pol.
Mirear Island Egypt see Murayr, Jazīrat
270 G4 Mirebalais Haiti
182 G2 Mirebeau Bourgogne France
184 E2 Mirebeau Poitou-Charentes France
179 L7 Mirecourt France
224 B6 Miréméné Chad
185 G9 Miremont France
201 I8 Miren Slovenia
185 H9 Mirepoix France
183 D9 Mireval France
139 J6 Mirganj Bihar India
Mirgorod Ukr. see Myrhorod
117 K2 Miri Sarawak Malaysia
145 J7 Miri mt. Pak.
229 H3 Miria Niger
136 F4 Mirialguda Andhra Prad. India
107 M8 Miriam Vale Qld Austr.
139 O6 Mirik Hills India
282 G4 Mirim, Lagoa l. Brazil/Uru.
279 C9 Mirim, Lagoa do l. Brazil
274 D2 Mirimire Venez.
Mírina Limnos Greece see Myrina
105 I3 Mirintu watercourse Qld Austr.
136 D5 Mirjan Karnataka India
145 I7 Mirjāveh Iran
219 M8 Mirkovo Bulg.
210 D3 Mirna r. Croatia
201 L8 Mirna Slovenia
201 L8 Mirna r. Slovenia
201 L8 Mirna Peč Slovenia
287 G2 Mirny research stn Antarctica
156 H3 Mirnyy Arkhangel'skaya Oblast' Rus. Fed.
161 O9 Mirnyy Bryanskaya Oblast' Rus. Fed.
153 M3 Mirnyy Respublika Sakha (Yakutiya) Rus. Fed.
151 F1 Mirnyy Stavropol'skiy Kray Rus. Fed.
219 K6 Miroč hills Serbia
196 D4 Mirocin Górny Pol.
109 G3 Miromiro mt. South I. N.Z.
247 K4 Mirond Lake Sask. Can.
Mironovka Kharkivs'ka Oblast' Ukr. see Myronivka
Mironovka Kyïvs'ka Oblast' Ukr. see Myronivka
201 N2 Miroslav Czech Rep.
196 E2 Mirosławiec Pol.
198 C2 Mirošov Czech Rep.
173 L7 Mirostowice Dolne Pol.
198 D2 Mirovice Czech Rep.
192 G4 Mirow Ger.
145 O5 Mirpur Pak.
145 M9 Mirpur Batoro Pak.
145 M9 Mirpur Khas Pak.
145 L9 Mirpur Sakro Pak.
246 H4 Mirror Alta Can.
232 E3 Mirsale Somalia
132 G6 Mirsali Xinjiang China
Mirs Bay Guangdong/H.K. China see Dapeng Wan
196 D5 Mirsk Pol.
105 I8 Mirtna Qld Austr.
107 K6 Mirtoan Sea Greece see Myrtoo Pelagos
217 L4 Mirto Crosia Italy
205 J7 Miruena de los Infanzones Spain
235 F2 Miruro Moz.
Miryalaguda Andhra Prad. India see Mirialguda
123 F11 Miryang S. Korea
144 E5 Mirzā, Chāh-e well Iran
Mirzachirla Turkm. see Murzechirla
Mirzachul Uzbek. see Guliston
139 I7 Mirzapur Uttar Prad. India
197 J4 Mirzec Pol.
213 M5 Mis, Lago del l. Italy
213 O8 Misa r. Italy
126 I1 Misaka Japan
127 L4 Misaki Chiba Japan
125 J13 Misaki Ehime Japan
126 B7 Misaki Ōsaka Japan
127 G5 Misakubo Japan
133 E7 Misalay Xinjiang China
213 N8 Misano Adriatico Italy
145 O5 Misantla Mex.
127 K3 Misato Gunma Japan
126 D6 Misato Mie Japan
126 D7 Misato Nagano Japan
124 □[2] Misato Okinawa Japan
127 J3 Misato Saitama Japan
127 K4 Misato Saitama Japan
126 B7 Misato Wakayama Japan
229 H4 Misau Nigeria
124 S6 Misawa Japan
124 K3 Misaw Lake Sask. Can.
199 K5 Mișca Romania
215 N5 Miscano r. Italy
212 D3 Mischabel mt. Switz.
201 N3 Mischendorf Austria
249 H4 Miscou Island N.B. Can.
269 K9 Misehkow r. Ont. Can.
126 F6 Miseno, Capo c. Italy
125 I12 Miserey-Salines France
182 H2 Misery, Mount hill Gibraltar
207 □ Misgar Pak.
138 E1 Misgund S. Africa
236 H9 Mish, Kūh-e hill Iran
144 G4 Misha Andaman & Nicobar Is India
137 M9 Mishamattawa r. Ont. Can.
248 C2 Mishamo Tanz.
233 A6 Mishan Heilong. China
122 G6 Mishash al Ashāwī well Saudi Arabia
147 I3 Mishāsh al Hādī well Saudi Arabia
147 I2 Mishāsh az Zuayyinī well Saudi Arabia
147 I3 Mishāsh 'Uwayr well Saudi Arabia
147 I3 Mishawaka IN U.S.A.
250 H8 Mishoguk Mountain AK U.S.A.
244 G1 Mishevsky Rus. Fed.
161 W6 Mishibishu Lake Ont. Can.
250 G5 Mishicot WI U.S.A.
127 I5 Mishima Japan
125 I12 Mi-shima i. Japan
156 L5 Mishkino Rus. Fed.
146 G5 Mishlah, Khashm hill Saudi Arabia
151 I4 Mishlesh Rus. Fed.
139 O5 Mishmi Hills India
161 N6 Mishutki Belarus
156 K2 Mishvan' Rus. Fed.
216 E7 Misilmeri Sicilia Italy
107 N1 Misima Island P.N.G.
282 G2 Misiones prov. Arg.
151 D4 Misırlı Turkey
146 G3 Misis Dağ hills Turkey
150 D2 Miskah Saudi Arabia
146 F3 Miske Hungary
199 I5

147 M4 Miskin Oman
266 □R10 Miskitos, Cayos is Nic.
Miskitos, Costa de coastal area Nic. see Costa de Mosquitos
199 J3 Miskolc Hungary
201 L7 Mislinja Slovenia
210 E2 Mislinja r. Slovenia
146 E2 Mismā, Jibāl al mts Saudi Arabia
150 F6 Mismā, Tall al hill Jordan
276 C3 Mismi, Nevado mt. Peru
183 H8 Mison France
115 G4 Misoöl i. Papua Indon.
258 E7 Mispillion r. DE U.S.A.
250 C2 Misquah Hills MN U.S.A.
259 L2 Misquamicut RI U.S.A.
Misr country Africa see Egypt
Misraç Turkey see Kurtalan
224 B1 Miṣrātah Libya
138 H6 Misrikh Uttar Prad. India
251 J1 Missanabie Ont. Can.
215 Q7 Missanello Italy
180 G7 Missillac France
248 D3 Missinaibi r. Ont. Can.
251 K1 Missinaibi Lake Ont. Can.
247 J4 Missinipe Sask. Can.
107 H2 Mission r. Qld Austr.
261 F12 Mission SD U.S.A.
261 F12 Mission TX U.S.A.
107 K4 Mission Beach Qld Austr.
264 O8 Mission Viejo CA U.S.A.
228 B3 Missira Senegal
248 C2 Missisa r. Ont. Can.
248 C2 Missisa Lake Ont. Can.
248 E3 Missisicabi r. Que. Can.
248 D4 Missisagi r. Ont. Can.
248 E5 Mississauga Ont. Can.
250 I9 Mississinewa Lake IN U.S.A.
248 E4 Mississippi r. Ont. Can.
261 K11 Mississippi r. U.S.A.
261 K9 Mississippi state U.S.A.
261 K11 Mississippi Delta LA U.S.A.
251 R4 Mississippi Lake Ont. Can.
261 K10 Mississippi Sound sea chan. MS U.S.A.
Missolonghi Greece see Mesolongi
262 H3 Missoula MT U.S.A.
226 E2 Missour Morocco
260 J6 Missouri r. U.S.A.
260 I6 Missouri state U.S.A.
260 H5 Missouri Valley IA U.S.A.
106 B4 Mistake Creek N.T. Austr.
107 K6 Mistake Creek r. Qld Austr.
249 I3 Mistanipisipou r. Que. Can.
249 F3 Mistassibi r. Que. Can.
249 F3 Mistassini Que. Can.
249 F3 Mistassini r. Que. Can.
248 F3 Mistassini, Lac l. Que. Can.
249 I2 Mistastin Lake Nfld and Lab. Can.
201 O2 Mistelbach Austria
195 K2 Mistelgau Ger.
217 I8 Misterbianco Sicilia Italy
165 M4 Misterhults nature res. Sweden
270 B4 Misteriosa Bank sea feature Caribbean Sea
171 P7 Misterton Nottinghamshire, England U.K.
248 I1 Mistinibi, Lac l. Que. Can.
248 F3 Mistissini Que. Can.
159 R4 Mistky Ukr.
285 F2 Mistolar, Laguna del l. Arg.
220 D5 Mistras tourist site Greece
216 G8 Mistretta Sicilia Italy
245 O5 Misty Fiords National Monument Wilderness nat. park AK U.S.A.
247 K3 Misty Lake Man. Can.
126 D6 Misugi Japan
125 I12 Misumi Japan
Misuratah Libya see Miṣrātah
213 M2 Misurina Italy
162 M3 Misvær Norway
268 G5 Mita, Punta de pt Mex.
127 K4 Mitaka Japan
126 F5 Mitake Gifu Japan
126 F4 Mitake Nagano Japan
235 G2 Mitande Moz.
275 H4 Mitaraca hill Suriname
274 D2 Mitare Venez.
225 H6 Mitatib Sudan
172 H4 Mitcheldean Gloucestershire, England U.K.
107 K9 Mitchell Qld Austr.
105 N3 Mitchell r. N.S.W. Austr.
107 H3 Mitchell r. Qld Austr.
105 K7 Mitchell r. Vic. Austr.
251 M6 Mitchell Ont. Can.
262 D4 Mitchell OR U.S.A.
260 F4 Mitchell SD U.S.A.
107 J4 Mitchell, Lake Qld Austr.
250 I5 Mitchell, Lake MI U.S.A.
255 I8 Mitchell, Mount NC U.S.A.
107 I3 Mitchell and Alice Rivers National Park Qld Austr.
Mitchell Island Cook Is see Nassau
Mitchell Island atoll Tuvalu see Nukulaelae
106 C1 Mitchell Point N.T. Austr.
106 E2 Mitchell Range hills N.T. Austr.
105 K7 Mitchell River National Park Vic. Austr.
236 D9 Mitchells Pass S. Africa
256 F10 Mitchelltown VA U.S.A.
169 F8 Mitchelstown Ireland
225 F2 Mit Ghamr Egypt
138 B8 Mithapur Gujarat India
145 O5 Mitha Tiwana Pak.
145 M9 Mithi Pak.
Mithimna Greece see Mithymna
145 M8 Mithrani Canal canal Pak.
145 M8 Mithrau Pak.
220 F3 Mithymna Greece
221 H3 Mithymna Greece
115 F3 Miti i. Maluku Indon.
103 □[2] Mitiaro i. Cook Is
Mitiero i. Cook Is see Mitiaro
Mitilini Lesvos Greece see Mytilini
161 Q7 Mitishkino Rus. Fed.
102 H3 Mititai North I. N.Z.
245 N4 Mitkof Island AK U.S.A.
221 H5 Mitla Mex.
126 F6 Mito Aichi Japan
127 L3 Mito Ibaraki Japan
125 I12 Mitō Japan
233 C7 Mitole Tanz.
127 I4 Mitomi Japan
233 B7 Mitomoni Tanz.
162 □ Mitra, Kapp c. Svalbard
102 J7 Mitre mt. North I. N.Z.
283 D9 Mitre, Península pen. Arg.
99 H3 Mitre Island Solomon Is
103 B11 Mitre Peak South I. N.Z.
244 H5 Mitrofania Island AK U.S.A.
157 G6 Mitrofanovka Rus. Fed.
218 I8 Mitrovicë Mitrovicë Kosovo
189 □ Mitry-Mory France
239 □[3a] Mitsamiouli Njazidja Comoros
220 B3 Mitsikeli mt. Greece
235 □J3 Mitsinjo Madag.
Mits'iwa Eritrea see Massawa
239 □[3a] Mitsoudjé Njazidja Comoros
126 D7 Mitsue Japan
124 T4 Mitsuishi Japan
127 K5 Mitsukaidō Japan
125 P9 Mitsuke Japan
126 G3 Mitsumatarenge-dake mt. Japan
125 G12 Mitsushima Japan
127 I4 Mitsutōge-yama mt. Japan
105 M6 Mittagong N.S.W. Austr.
105 K7 Mitta Mitta Vic. Austr.
200 C6 Mittelberg Tirol Austria
200 B5 Mittelberg Vorarlberg Austria
195 J3 Mittelberg hill Ger.
195 H5 Mittelbiberach Ger.
193 E7 Mittelelbe park Ger.
193 J8 Mittelfranken admin. reg. Ger.
193 D8 Mittelhausen Ger.
191 I10 Mittelkalbach Ger.
212 C2 Mittelland reg. Switz.
191 F6 Mittellandkanal canal Ger.
191 I10 Mittelsinn Ger.

195 N6 Mittelspitze mt. Ger.
195 K7 Mittenwald Ger.
192 I4 Mittenwalde Brandenburg Ger.
193 I6 Mittenwalde Brandenburg Ger.
201 L4 Mitterbach am Erlaufsee Austria
201 H3 Mitterding Austria
201 M4 Mitterdorf im Mürztal Austria
195 N4 Mitterfels Ger.
179 M6 Mittersheim France
200 F5 Mittersill Austria
195 N5 Mitterskirchen Ger.
195 M2 Mitterteich Ger.
162 I5 Mittet Norway
Mittimatalik Nunavut Can. see Pond Inlet
165 M5 Mittlands skogen reg. Öland Sweden
193 E9 Mittleres Saaletal park Ger.
193 G9 Mittweida Ger.
274 D4 Mitú Col.
274 D4 Mituas Col.
231 E7 Mitumba, Chaîne des mts Dem. Rep. Congo
230 F5 Mitumba, Monts mts Dem. Rep. Congo
231 E7 Mitwaba Dem. Rep. Congo
193 D10 Mitwitz Ger.
230 A4 Mitzic Gabon
Miughalaigh i. Scotland U.K. see Mingulay
127 K5 Miura Japan
127 K5 Miura-hantō pen. Japan
159 R5 Mius r. Rus. Fed.
159 R6 Miusskiy Liman est. Rus. Fed.
159 R5 Miusyns'k Ukr.
127 M1 Miwa Fukushima Japan
127 L2 Miwa Ibaraki Japan
126 B5 Miwa Kyōto Japan
Mixian Henan China see Xinmi
269 I7 Mixteco r. Mex.
268 C5 Mixtlán Mex.
126 F3 Miya Japan
229 H4 Miya Nigeria
127 G4 Miyada Japan
127 J5 Miyagase-ko resr Japan
126 F3 Miyagawa Gifu Japan
126 D7 Miyagawa Mie Japan
126 E6 Miya-gawa r. Japan
126 F3 Miya-gawa r. Japan
124 □[1] Miyagi Okinawa Japan
124 R8 Miyagi pref. Japan
124 □[3] Miyagusuku-jima i. Okinawa Japan
146 F3 Miyah, Wādī al watercourse Saudi Arabia
148 I6 Miyāh, Wādī al watercourse Syria
125 J12 Miyajima Japan
127 K7 Miyake-jima i. Japan
124 S5 Miyako Japan
124 R9 Miyakoji Japan
124 □C22 Miyako-jima i. Nansei-shotō Japan
125 I15 Miyakonojō Japan
124 □B22 Miyako-rettō is Japan
124 S7 Miyako-wan b. Japan
130 D3 Miyaluo Sichuan China
142 E3 Miyaly Kazakh.
126 D3 Miyama Fukui Japan
126 E4 Miyama Gifu Japan
126 C5 Miyama Kyōto Japan
126 D7 Miyama Mie Japan
126 B8 Miyama Wakayama Japan
127 K4 Miyamae Japan
Miyang Yunnan China see Mile
138 B9 Miyani Gujarat India
125 H15 Miyanojō Japan
124 □H16 Miyanoura-dake mt. Japan
126 D4 Miyazaki Fukui Japan
125 I15 Miyazaki Miyazaki Japan
125 I14 Miyazaki pref. Japan
126 B4 Miyazu Japan
126 B4 Miyazu-wan b. Japan
130 D5 Miyi Sichuan China
126 F5 Miyoshi Aichi Japan
127 K5 Miyoshi Chiba Japan
125 J12 Miyoshi Hiroshima Japan
129 O6 Miyota Japan
129 O6 Miyun Beijing China
129 O6 Miyun Shuiku resr China
145 L5 Mīzāni Afgh.
232 B3 Mīzan Teferī Eth.
Mizar Turkey see Karakeçi
224 B2 Mizdah Libya
169 C10 Mizen Head Ireland
169 J7 Mizen Head Ireland
160 I9 Mizhevichy Belarus
158 C5 Mizhhir"ya Ukr.
129 L8 Mizhi Shaanxi China
219 O5 Mizil Romania
219 L7 Miziya Bulg.
158 F3 Mizoch Ukr.
217 L4 Mizofato r. Italy
Mizo Hills state India see Mizoram
139 N8 Mizoram state India
258 F6 Mizpah NJ U.S.A.
150 C8 Mizpé Ramon Israel
276 D4 Mizque Bol.
276 D4 Mizque r. Bol.
127 I4 Mizugaki-yama mt. Japan
126 D4 Mizuhashi Japan
126 F5 Mizuho Kyōto Japan
127 J4 Mizuho Tōkyō Japan
126 F4 Mizunami Japan
127 K3 Mizuno-gawa r. Japan
124 S7 Mizusawa Japan
163 H3 Mjällom Sweden
165 L3 Mjölby Sweden
165 I3 Mjølfell Norway
164 G2 Mjøndalen Norway
164 H2 Mjörn l. Sweden
164 G1 Mjøsa l. Norway
237 N7 Mkambati S. Africa
237 O7 Mkambati Nature Reserve S. Africa
233 C6 Mkata Tanz.
233 C6 Mkata Plain Tanz.
237 P2 Mkhaya Game Reserve nature res. Swaziland
237 P2 Mkhondvo r. Swaziland
233 C6 Mkoani Tanz.
233 C6 Mkokotoni Tanz.
233 C6 Mkomazi Tanz.
233 C5 Mkomazi Game Reserve nature res. Tanz.
233 C6 Mkujani Tanz.
233 C6 Mkumbi, Ras pt Tanz.
Mkumvura Zimbabwe see Mukumbura
233 C7 Mkunja Tanz.
233 C6 Mkuranga Tanz.
233 B6 Mkurusi Tanz.
231 F8 Mkushi Zambia
237 Q3 Mkuze S. Africa
237 Q3 Mkuze r. S. Africa
237 Q3 Mkuzi Game Reserve nature res. S. Africa
198 D1 Mladá Boleslav Czech Rep.
198 D2 Mladá Vožice Czech Rep.
198 E1 Mladé Buky Czech Rep.
218 I6 Mladenovac Mladenovac Serbia
233 A6 Mlala Hills Tanz.
233 C6 Mlandizi Tanz.
233 B7 Mlangali Tanz.
237 Q2 Mlaula r. Swaziland
219 J6 Mlava r. Serbia
197 I2 Mława Pol.
197 I3 Mławka r. Pol.
237 Q2 Mlawula Nature Reserve Swaziland
237 P2 Mlilwane Nature Reserve Swaziland
239 □[3b] Mlima Bénara hill Mayotte
239 □[3b] Mlima Chougui hill Mayotte
210 F4 Mljet i. Croatia
210 F4 Mljet nat. park Croatia
210 F4 Mljetski Kanal sea chan. Croatia
159 P2 Mlodat' r. Rus. Fed.
197 I3 Młodzieszyn Pol.
233 C7 Mlowoka Tanz.
237 M1 Mlungisi S. Africa
237 K7 Mlungisi S. Africa
197 H1 Młynary Pol.
197 J3 Młynarze Pol.

158 E3 Mlyniv Ukr.
197 M6 Mlynys'ka Ukr.
237 J1 Mmabatho S. Africa
235 E4 Mmadinare Botswana
234 E4 Mmamabula Botswana
234 E4 Mmashoro Botswana
234 E5 Mmathethe Botswana
237 N8 Mncwasa Point S. Africa
198 D2 Mnichovice Czech Rep.
198 D1 Mnichovo Hradiště Czech Rep.
197 I5 Mniów Pol.
220 B4 Mnimati mt. Lefkada Greece
197 I4 Mniów Pol.
199 J3 Mníšek nad Hnilcom Slovakia
197 J4 Mniszew Pol.
197 I4 Mniszków Pol.
237 P2 Mnjoli Dam Swaziland
122 K1 Mnogovershinnyy Rus. Fed.
163 H6 Mo Norway
276 B1 Moa r. Brazil
270 F3 Moa Cuba
115 F8 Moa i. Maluku Indon.
150 D7 Moab reg. Jordan
265 W3 Moab UT U.S.A.
230 A5 Moabi Gabon
276 C1 Moaco r. Brazil
113 J9 Moa Island Qld Austr.
101 □[7] Moala i. Fiji
144 F4 Mo'allemān Iran
235 G5 Moamba Moz.
103 F9 Moana South I. N.Z.
204 C4 Moaña Spain
230 B5 Moanda Gabon
265 R5 Moapa NV U.S.A.
169 G6 Moate Ireland
235 G3 Moatize Moz.
231 F6 Moba Dem. Rep. Congo
127 L5 Mobara Japan
144 E7 Mobārakābād Iran
144 D5 Mobārakeh Eșfahān Iran
144 F7 Mobārakeh Yazd Iran
230 D3 Mobaye C.A.R.
Mobayembongo Dem. Rep. Congo see Mobayi-Mbongo
230 D3 Mobayi-Mbongo Dem. Rep. Congo
171 M7 Mobberley Cheshire, England U.K.
230 C4 Mobeka Dem. Rep. Congo
260 I6 Moberly MO U.S.A.
246 F4 Moberly Lake B.C. Can.
250 I1 Mobert Ont. Can.
255 C10 Mobile AL U.S.A.
265 T8 Mobile AZ U.S.A.
261 K10 Mobile Bay AL U.S.A.
255 D10 Mobile Point AL U.S.A.
107 J9 Mobile watercourse Qld Austr.
114 D5 Mobo Masbate Phil.
260 E3 Mobridge SD U.S.A.
Mobutu, Lake Dem. Rep. Congo/Uganda see Albert, Lake
Mobutu Sese Seko, Lake Dem. Rep. Congo/Uganda see Albert, Lake
270 H4 Moca Dom. Rep.
150 B2 Moca Geçidi pass Turkey
278 C2 Mocajuba Brazil
235 H2 Moçambicano, Planalto plat. Moz.
Moçambique country Africa see Mozambique
235 I2 Moçambique Moz.
235 I2 Mocambo, Porto b. Moz.
Moçâmedes Angola see Namibe
238 □[3e] Mocanal El Hierro Canary Is
258 C2 Mocanaqua PA U.S.A.
206 B2 Moçarria Port.
264 L4 Moccasin CA U.S.A.
256 C12 Moccasin Gap VA U.S.A.
118 G4 Môc Châu Vietnam
204 G2 Mocejón Spain
199 G3 Močenok Slovakia
161 U6 Mocha r. Rus. Fed.
Mocha Yemen see Al Mukhā
282 B5 Mocha, Isla i. Chile
205 Q6 Mochales Spain
100 □[4a] Mochenap sea chan. Chuuk Micronesia
266 E5 Mochicahui Mex.
161 V7 Mochily Rus. Fed.
275 E2 Mochirma, Parque Nacional nat. park Venez.
127 H3 Mochizuki Japan
270 □ Mocho Mountains Jamaica
100 □[4a] Mochonap sea chan. Chuuk Micronesia
197 H3 Mochowo Pol.
234 E5 Mochudi Botswana
196 E3 Mochy Pol.
233 D7 Mocimboa da Praia Moz.
233 C7 Mocimboa do Rovuma Moz.
219 M4 Mociu Romania
165 K2 Möckeln l. Sweden
165 K5 Möckeln l. Sweden
193 E6 Möckern Ger.
193 F6 Möckern-Magdeburger Forst park Ger.
194 G3 Möckmühl Ger.
193 G7 Mockrehna Ger.
255 G8 Mocksville NC U.S.A.
207 L6 Moclín Spain
207 K7 Moclinejo Spain
276 C1 Mocó r. Brazil
274 B4 Mocoa Col.
280 D4 Mococa Brazil
235 G3 Mocodoene Moz.
285 I2 Mocoretá r. Arg.
266 F5 Mocorito Mex.
266 F2 Moctezuma Chihuahua Mex.
268 F3 Moctezuma San Luis Potosí Mex.
266 E3 Moctezuma Sonora Mex.
269 I4 Moctezuma r. Mex.
263 J12 Moctezuma r. Mex.
235 H3 Mocuba Moz.
131 I7 Mocun Guangdong China
183 J6 Modane France
138 D8 Modasa Gujarat India
187 H8 Modave Belgium
172 F7 Modbury Devon, England U.K.
237 I5 Modder r. S. Africa
236 I5 Modderrivier S. Africa
145 P6 Model Town Pak.
213 J6 Modena Italy
213 J7 Modena prov. Italy
259 G1 Modena NY U.S.A.
258 D5 Modena PA U.S.A.
265 S4 Modena UT U.S.A.
179 O6 Moder r. France
284 E4 Modestino Pizarro Arg.
264 L4 Modesto CA U.S.A.
216 H10 Modica Sicilia Italy
213 L7 Modigliana Italy
235 F5 Modimolle S. Africa
216 D8 Modione r. Sicilia Italy
197 K5 Modliborzyce Pol.
201 N3 Mödling Austria
197 I4 Modliszewice Pol.
214 B7 Modolo Sardegna Italy
Modot Mongolia see Tsenhermandal
198 G3 Modra Slovakia
201 L6 Modriach Austria
210 G3 Modriča Bos.-Herz.
198 F2 Modřice Czech Rep.
201 M2 Modringberg mt. Austria
199 I3 Modrý Kameň Slovakia
217 L1 Modugno Italy
105 K8 Moe Vic. Austr.
235 H3 Moebase Moz.
102 J3 Moehau hill North I. N.Z.
180 D6 Moëlan-sur-Mer France
172 F1 Moel Famau hill Wales U.K.
172 D1 Moelfre Isle of Anglesey, Wales U.K.
172 F2 Moel Sych hill Wales U.K.
163 K6 Moelv Norway
162 K4 Moemaneng S. Africa
237 L4 Moemaneng S. Africa
231 D6 Moembe Dem. Rep. Congo
Moen i. Chuuk Micronesia see Weno
162 O2 Moen Norway
213 L3 Moena Italy
275 H3 Moengo Suriname

265 U5 Moenkopi AZ U.S.A.
265 U6 Moenkopi Wash r. AZ U.S.A.
103 E12 Moeraki Point South I. N.Z.
187 E6 Moerbeke Belgium
102 I2 Moerewa North I. N.Z.
186 H5 Moergestel Neth.
187 D6 Moerkerke Belgium
Moero, Lake Dem. Rep. Congo/Zambia see Mweru, Lake
191 C8 Moers Ger.
212 G3 Moesa r. Switz.
236 G3 Moeswal S. Africa
100 □[6] Moetambe, Mount Choiseul Solomon Is
168 J12 Moffat Dumfries and Galloway, Scotland U.K.
204 G5 Mofreita Port.
199 L4 Moftin Romania
138 E4 Moga Punjab India
Mogadishu Somalia see Muqdisho
Mogador Morocco see Essaouira
204 G6 Mogadouro Port.
204 G6 Mogadouro, Serra de mts Port.
235 F4 Mogalakwena r. S. Africa
230 C4 Mogalo Dem. Rep. Congo
136 G4 Mogalturra Andhra Prad. India
124 Q8 Mogami-gawa r. Japan
238 □[3f] Mogán Gran Canaria Canary Is
230 E4 Mogandjo Dem. Rep. Congo
235 F5 Moganyaka S. Africa
132 L7 Mogao Ku Gansu China
146 C8 Mogareb watercourse Eritrea
118 C2 Mogaung Myanmar
122 H3 Mogdy Rus. Fed.
169 F9 Mogeely Ireland
192 F5 Mögelin Ger.
190 G1 Møgeltønder Denmark
209 D10 Mogente Spain
201 N6 Mogersdorf Austria
227 G2 Moggar Alg.
213 O3 Moggio Udinese Italy
194 H4 Mögglingen Ger.
145 L2 Moghiyon Tajik.
227 E2 Moghrar Foukani Alg.
197 I4 Mogielnica Pol.
197 I6 Mogielnica mt. Pol.
280 D5 Mogi-Guaçu Brazil
218 J9 Mogila Macedonia
197 H6 Mogilany Pol.
Mogilev Belarus see Mahilyow
Mogilev Oblast admin. div. Belarus see Mahilyowskaya Voblasts'
Mogilev Podol'skiy Ukr. see Mohyliv Podil's'kyy
Mogilevskaya Oblast' admin. div. Belarus see Mahilyowskaya Voblasts'
196 E3 Mogilnica r. Pol.
196 F3 Mogilno Pol.
280 D5 Mogi-Mirim Brazil
235 I2 Mogincual Moz.
281 H2 Mogiquiçaba Brazil
213 J6 Moglia Italy
213 O9 Mogliano Italy
213 M4 Mogliano Veneto Italy
194 G4 Möglingen Ger.
284 C2 Mogna Arg.
122 A2 Mogocha Rus. Fed.
161 T4 Mogocha r. Rus. Fed.
227 H1 Mogod mts Tunisia
234 E5 Mogoditshane Botswana
204 D8 Mogofores Port.
232 A2 Mogogh Sudan
118 C3 Mogok Myanmar
265 U7 Mogollon Plateau AZ U.S.A.
207 M4 Mogón Spain
Mogontiacum Ger. see Mainz
232 D3 Mogor Eth.
214 B8 Mogorella Sardegna Italy
214 B8 Mogoro Sardegna Italy
214 B8 Mogoro r. Sardegna Italy
219 P3 Mogoşeşti Romania
285 I6 Mogotes, Punta pt Arg.
197 I3 Mogowo Pol.
129 N1 Mogoytuy Rus. Fed.
230 B2 Mogroum Chad
206 F6 Moguer Spain
129 R3 Moguqi Nei Mongol China
235 F4 Mogwadi S. Africa
237 L1 Mogwase S. Africa
199 I4 Mogyoród Hungary
199 H6 Mohács Hungary
102 L6 Mohaka r. North I. N.Z.
138 H9 Mohala Chhattisgarh India
237 M5 Mohale Dam Lesotho
237 L6 Mohale's Hoek Lesotho
133 C11 Mohali Punjab India
260 E1 Mohall ND U.S.A.
144 H4 Mohammad Iran
Mohammadābād Iran see Darreh Gaz
227 F2 Mohammadia Alg.
Mohammad Reza Shah Pahlavi Dam resr Iran see Dez, Sadd-e
138 H5 Mohan r. India/Nepal
138 F7 Mohana Madh. Prad. India
139 M7 Mohanganj Bangl.
138 G9 Mohari Mahar. India
207 P4 Moharque Spain
265 R6 Mohave, Lake NV U.S.A.
265 R7 Mohave Mountains AZ U.S.A.
250 F2 Mohawk MI U.S.A.
257 L6 Mohawk r. NY U.S.A.
265 S9 Mohawk Mountains AZ U.S.A.
138 H7 Mohdra Madh. Prad. India
122 C2 Mohe Heilong. China
165 N3 Moheda Sweden
165 K4 Moheda Sweden
204 H8 Mohedas de Granadilla Spain
259 K2 Mohegan CT U.S.A.
259 H2 Mohegan Lake NY U.S.A.
Mohéli i. Comoros see Mwali
198 F2 Mohelnice Czech Rep.
198 F2 Mohelno Czech Rep.
234 D3 Mohembo Botswana
145 M8 Mohenjo Daro tourist site Pak.
169 D7 Moher, Cliffs of Ireland
205 N7 Mohernando Spain
244 F3 Mohican, Cape AK U.S.A.
169 H7 Mohill Ireland
169 H7 Mohill Ireland
162 U5 Möhkö Fin.
237 L2 Mohlakeng S. Africa
193 F7 Möhlau Ger.
162 □ Mohn, Kapp c. Svalbard
191 E8 Möhne r. Ger.
191 F8 Möhnetalsperre resr Ger.
258 C4 Mohnton PA U.S.A.
118 C2 Mohnyin Myanmar
276 C3 Moho Peru
136 D4 Mohol Mahar. India
265 S7 Mohon Peak AZ U.S.A.
199 I4 Mohora Hungary
193 H9 Mohorn Ger.
239 □[3a] Mohoro Njazidja Comoros
233 C7 Mohoro Tanz.
138 G8 Mohpani Madh. Prad. India
195 J2 Möhrendorf Ger.
190 I1 Mohrkirch Ger.
258 D4 Mohrsville PA U.S.A.
211 P6 Mohyla-Bel'mak, Hora hill Ukr.
158 G5 Mohyliv Podil's'kyy Ukr.
158 F3 Mohyliany Ukr.
164 C3 Moi Rogaland Norway
164 D3 Moi Vest-Agder Norway
208 J4 Moià Spain
216 H1 Moiano Italy
168 E9 Moidart reg. Scotland U.K.
234 E4 Moijabana Botswana
204 E7 Moimenta da Beira Port.
133 E11 Moincêr Xizang China
133 J12 Moinda Xizang China
139 M6 Moindawang Arun. Prad. India
100 □[5] Moindou New Caledonia
181 I7 Moine r. France
235 G5 Moine Moz.
219 O4 Moineşti Romania
182 E5 Moingt France
Moyynkum, Peski
Mointy Kazakh. see Moyynty

169 J4 **Moira** *Northern Ireland* U.K.
275 I5 **Moiraba** Brazil
Moírai *Kriti* Greece *see* **Moires**
162 M3 **Mo i Rana** Norway
139 N7 **Moirang** *Manipur* India
182 H4 **Moirans-en-Montagne** France
185 F7 **Moirax** France
220 F7 **Moires** *Kriti* Greece
160 I3 **Mõisaküla** Estonia
190 I4 **Moisburg** Ger.
180 I6 **Moisdon-la-Rivière** France
219 M3 **Moisei** Romania
285 G2 **Moisés Ville** Arg.
249 H3 **Moisie** *Que.* Can.
249 H3 **Moisie** *r. Que.* Can.
178 E4 **Moislains** France
185 G7 **Moissac** France
183 I9 **Moissac-Bellevue** France
230 C2 **Moïssala** Chad
182 H2 **Moissey** France
214 C3 **Moïta** *Corse* France
204 D8 **Moita** *Aveiro* Port.
206 B3 **Moita** *Setúbal* Port.
275 E3 **Moitaco** Venez.
165 O2 **Möja** *i.* Sweden
207 P6 **Mojácar** Spain
205 K6 **Mojados** Spain
264 N6 **Mojave** *CA* U.S.A.
264 O7 **Mojave** *r. CA* U.S.A.
264 O6 **Mojave Desert** *CA* U.S.A.
130 C7 **Mojiang** *Yunnan* China
280 D5 **Moji das Cruzes** Brazil
280 C4 **Moji-Guaçu** *r.* Brazil
125 H13 **Mojikō** Japan
207 L3 **Mojina** *mt.* Spain
218 H8 **Mojkovac** *Mojkovac* Montenegro
276 D5 **Mojo** Bol.
232 C2 **Mojo** Eth.
117 J8 **Mojokerto** *Jawa* Indon.
207 M6 **Mojón Alto** *mt.* Spain
205 P9 **Mojón Alto** *mt.* Spain
282 D2 **Mojones, Cerro** *mt.* Arg.
276 D3 **Mojos, Llanos de** *plain* Bol.
232 D3 **Mojo Shet'** *r.* Eth.
276 D4 **Mojotoro** Bol.
201 I7 **Mojstrana** Slovenia
278 C2 **Moju** Brazil
127 L3 **Mōka** Japan
239 □1b **Moka** Mauritius
102 J5 **Mokai** *North I.* N.Z.
139 J7 **Mokama** *Bihar* India
231 F8 **Mokambo** Dem. Rep. Congo
264 □D12 **Mōkapu Peninsula** *HI* U.S.A.
230 D4 **Mokaria** Dem. Rep. Congo
102 I5 **Mokau** *North I.* N.Z.
102 I5 **Mokau** *r. North I.* N.Z.
230 B4 **Mokéko** Congo
264 K3 **Mokelumne** *r. CA* U.S.A.
264 K3 **Mokelumne Aqueduct** *canal* CA U.S.A.
144 F7 **Mokh, Gowd-e** *l.* Iran
237 M5 **Mokhoabong Pass** Lesotho
237 N5 **Mokhotlong** Lesotho
161 T9 **Mokhovoye** Rus. Fed.
153 N3 **Mokhsogollokh** Rus. Fed.
144 H5 **Mokhtārān** Iran
231 F6 **Mokimbo** Dem. Rep. Congo
103 B14 **Mokinui Island** *Stewart I.* N.Z.
158 G3 **Mokiyivtsi** Ukr.
227 H2 **Moknine** Tunisia
197 K3 **Mokobody** Pol.
Mokogai *i.* Fiji *see* **Makogai**
102 J2 **Mokohinau Islands** *North I.* N.Z.
139 O6 **Mokokchung** *Nagaland* India
229 I4 **Mokolo** Cameroon
235 E4 **Mokolo** *r.* S. Africa
235 F5 **Mokopane** S. Africa
103 D13 **Mokoreta** *South I.* N.Z.
103 D13 **Mokoreta** *hill South I.* N.Z.
103 C13 **Mokotua** *South I.* N.Z.
123 E11 **Mokp'o** S. Korea
218 I8 **Mokra Gora** *mts* Montenegro/Serbia
159 K5 **Mokra Kalyhirka** Ukr.
199 K3 **Mokrance** Slovakia
197 J2 **Mokre, Jezioro** *l.* Pol.
218 I5 **Mokrin** *Vojvodina* Serbia
159 P6 **Mokri Yaly** *r.* Ukr.
201 L8 **Mokronog** Slovenia
142 B2 **Mokrous** Rus. Fed.
161 S6 **Mokroye** *Moskovskaya Oblast'* Rus. Fed.
161 T8 **Mokroye** *Tul'skaya Oblast'* Rus. Fed.
157 H5 **Moksha** *r.* Rus. Fed.
157 I5 **Mokshan** Rus. Fed.
Môktama Myanmar *see* **Mottama**
264 □D12 **Moku 'Āuia** *i. HI* U.S.A.
264 □C12 **Mokulē'ia** *HI* U.S.A.
264 □D12 **Moku Lua** *is HI* U.S.A.
Mokundurra *Rajasthan* India *see* **Mukandwara**
Mokvin Pershotravnevoye Ukr. *see* **Mokvyn**
158 F3 **Mokvyn** Ukr.
229 G4 **Mokwa** Nigeria
237 L3 **Mokwallo** S. Africa
187 H6 **Mol** Belgium
199 J6 **Mol** *Vojvodina* Serbia
209 J8 **Mola, Cap de sa** *c.* Spain
208 E7 **Mola de Ares** *mt.* Spain
217 M1 **Mola di Bari** Italy
Molaly Kazakh. *see* **Mulaly**
185 H9 **Molandier** France
269 I5 **Molango** Mex.
220 D6 **Molaoi** Greece
214 D6 **Molara, Isola** *i. Sardegna* Italy
212 F6 **Molare** Italy
213 R7 **Molat** Croatia
210 E3 **Molat** *i.* Croatia
209 C10 **Molatón** *mt.* Spain
190 E5 **Molbergen** Ger.
201 J6 **Mölbling** Austria
172 F1 **Mold** *Flintshire, Wales* U.K.
199 J3 **Moldava nad Bodvou** Slovakia
Moldavia *country* Europe *see* **Moldova**
Moldavskaya S.S.R. *country* Europe *see* **Moldova**
162 I5 **Molde** Norway
162 I5 **Moldefjorden** *inlet* Norway
162 M3 **Moldjord** Norway
158 H7 **Moldova** *country* Europe
219 O4 **Moldova** *r.* Romania
219 J6 **Moldova Nouă** Romania
219 M5 **Moldoveanu, Vârful** *mt.* Romania
219 M2 **Moldovei, Podișul** *plat.* Romania
158 G6 **Moldovei Centrale, Podișul** *plat.* Moldova
158 G6 **Moldovei de Nord, Cîmpia** *lowland* Moldova
158 G5 **Moldovei de Nord, Podișul** *plat.* Moldova
158 H7 **Moldovei de Sud, Cîmpia** *plain* Moldova
219 N3 **Moldovița** Romania
151 A2 **Moldovka** Rus. Fed.
143 R2 **Mol'dyr** Kazakh.
233 B7 **Mole** Tanz.
172 E6 **Mole** *r. England* U.K.
130 A6 **Mole Chaung** *r.* Myanmar
204 C5 **Moledo** *Viana do Castelo* Port.
204 E7 **Moledo** *Viseu* Port.
249 H4 **Molega Lake** *N.S.* Can.
230 D3 **Molegbe** Dem. Rep. Congo
204 D7 **Molelos** Port.
237 M3 **Molen** *r.* S. Africa
228 E4 **Mole National Park** Ghana
187 F7 **Molenbeek-St-Jean** Belgium
180 B5 **Molène, Île de** *i.* France
234 E5 **Molepolole** Botswana
171 Q6 **Molescroft** *East Riding of Yorkshire, England* U.K.
178 H8 **Molesmes** France
160 I6 **Molėtai** Lith.
215 R5 **Molfetta** Italy
190 J2 **Molfsee** Ger.
162 O5 **Moliden** Sweden
185 G7 **Molières** *Midi-Pyrénées* France
185 H6 **Molières** *Midi-Pyrénées* France
183 E8 **Molières-sur-Cèze** France
185 B8 **Moliets-et-Maa** France
284 C3 **Molina** Arg.
284 B4 **Molina** Chile
215 L3 **Molina Aterno** Italy
205 Q7 **Molina de Aragón** Spain
209 C11 **Molina de Segura** Spain
213 J4 **Molina di Ledro** Italy
215 N5 **Molinara** Italy
204 H3 **Molinaseca** Spain
260 J5 **Moline** *IL* U.S.A.
261 G7 **Moline** *KS* U.S.A.
213 L6 **Molinella** Italy
183 J7 **Molines-en-Queyras** France
182 D4 **Molinet** France
182 H4 **Molinges** France
207 O4 **Molinicos** Spain
213 L2 **Molini di Tures** Italy
255 D10 **Molino** *FL* U.S.A.
258 C3 **Molino** *PA* U.S.A.
208 E3 **Molino de Villobas** Spain
285 G3 **Molino Doll** Arg.
282 D2 **Molinos** Arg.
208 E6 **Molinos** Spain
206 G3 **Molinos de Matachel, Embalse de los** *resr* Spain
208 J5 **Molins de Rei** Spain
231 F7 **Moliro** Dem. Rep. Congo
215 N4 **Molise** *admin. reg.* Italy
215 P7 **Moliterno** Italy
185 I10 **Molitg-les-Bains** France
199 L5 **Moliviș** *mt.* Romania
193 F8 **Mölkau** Ger.
165 J2 **Molkom** Sweden
200 H6 **Möll** *r.* Austria
214 A5 **Molla, Capo** *c. Sardegna* Italy
144 C4 **Mollā Bodāgh** Iran
142 F8 **Mollagara** Turkm.
151 J5 **Mollakänd** Azer.
151 B6 **Mollaömer** Turkey
164 F6 **Møllebjerg** *hill* Denmark
205 L2 **Molledo** Spain
164 F6 **Mollehøj** *hill* Denmark
162 Q2 **Mollejos** *hill* Norway
139 O7 **Mol Len** *mt. Nagaland* India
192 H4 **Möllenbeck** Ger.
276 C4 **Mollendo** Peru
192 G3 **Möllenhagen** Ger.
109 D11 **Mollerin, Lake** *salt flat* W.A. Austr.
208 G4 **Mollerussa** Spain
182 D4 **Molles** France
208 J4 **Mollet del Vallès** Spain
178 D4 **Molliens-Dreuil** France
207 J6 **Mollina** Spain
212 G1 **Mollis** Switz.
201 J4 **Molln** Austria
192 H3 **Mölln** *Mecklenburg-Vorpommern* Ger.
190 K3 **Mölln** *Schleswig-Holstein* Ger.
208 J3 **Molló** Spain
200 G5 **Mölltal** *val.* Austria
165 K3 **Mölltorp** Sweden
164 I4 **Mölnlycke** Sweden
264 □B11 **Moloa'a** *HI* U.S.A.
159 O6 **Molochans'k** Ukr.
159 O7 **Molochna** *r.* Ukr.
159 M8 **Molochne** Ukr.
156 G4 **Molochnoye** Rus. Fed.
156 F1 **Molochnyy** Rus. Fed.
159 O7 **Molochnyy Lyman** *inlet* Ukr.
Molodechno Belarus *see* **Maladzyechna**
159 L5 **Molodizhne** *Kirovohrads'ka Oblast'* Ukr.
159 N9 **Molodizhne** *Respublika Krym* Ukr.
161 P8 **Molod'kovo** Rus. Fed.
228 D3 **Molodo** Mali
143 N1 **Molodogvardeyskoye** Kazakh.
161 Q5 **Molodoy Tud** Rus. Fed.
161 U3 **Mologa** *r.* Rus. Fed.
264 □D12 **Moloka'i** *i. HI* U.S.A.
161 T3 **Molokovo** Rus. Fed.
156 J4 **Moloma** *r.* Rus. Fed.
183 C6 **Molompize** France
105 L5 **Molong** *N.S.W.* Austr.
234 D6 **Molopo** *watercourse* Botswana/S. Africa
236 I1 **Moloporivier** Botswana
220 D4 **Molos** Greece
Molotov Rus. Fed. *see* **Perm'**
Molotovo Rus. Fed. *see* **Oktyabr'skoye**
Molotovsk Kyrg. *see* **Kayyngdy**
Molotovsk *Arkhangel'skaya Oblast'* Rus. Fed. *see* **Severodvinsk**
Molotovsk *Kirovskaya Oblast'* Rus. Fed. *see* **Nolinsk**
229 I6 **Moloundou** Cameroon
158 I6 **Molovata** Moldova
231 D6 **Molowaie** Dem. Rep. Congo
182 F1 **Moloy** France
191 K8 **Molschleben** Ger.
179 N6 **Molsheim** France
247 L5 **Molson** *Man.* Can.
247 L4 **Molson Lake** *Man.* Can.
237 K7 **Molteno** S. Africa
236 G8 **Moltenopass** *pass* S. Africa
214 C3 **Moltifao** *Corse* France
113 H8 **Molu** *i.* Indon.
Moluccas *is* Indon. *see* **Maluku**
Molucca Sea Indon. *see* **Maluku, Laut**
205 R10 **Moluengo** *mt.* Spain
235 H2 **Molumbo** Moz.
213 J3 **Molveno** Italy
213 J3 **Molveno, Lago di** *l.* Italy
161 P4 **Molvotitsy** Rus. Fed.
231 E7 **Molwe** Dem. Rep. Congo
230 D5 **Moma** Dem. Rep. Congo
235 H3 **Moma** Moz.
153 P3 **Moma** *r.* Rus. Fed.
268 D4 **Momax** Mex.
105 I4 **Momba** *N.S.W.* Austr.
278 F3 **Mombaça** Brazil
212 E6 **Mombaldone** Italy
233 C5 **Mombasa** Kenya
206 C4 **Mombeja** Port.
205 J8 **Mombeltrán** Spain
230 C4 **Mombenzélé** Dem. Rep. Congo
212 E6 **Mombercelli** Italy
Mombetsu *Hokkaidō* Japan *see* **Monbetsu**
139 N7 **Mombi New** *Manipur* India
230 C5 **Momboyo** *r.* Dem. Rep. Congo
191 H10 **Mömbris** Ger.
280 A3 **Mombuca, Serra da** *hills* Brazil
204 H4 **Mombuey** Spain
219 N9 **Momchilgrad** Bulg.
146 E7 **Momed** *i.* Saudi Arabia
Momeik Myanmar *see* **Mong Mit**
250 G8 **Momence** *IL* U.S.A.
147 L9 **Momi, Ra's** *pt Suquṭrā* Yemen
206 H8 **Momia, Sierra** *mts* Spain
187 F8 **Momignies** Belgium
266 □P11 **Momotombo, Volcán** *vol.* Nic.
126 B7 **Momoyama** Japan
114 D5 **Mompog Passage** Phil.
230 D4 **Mompono** Dem. Rep. Congo
274 C2 **Mompós** Col.
153 P3 **Momskiy Khrebet** *mts* Rus. Fed.
185 C8 **Momuy** France
164 I6 **Møn** *i.* Denmark
139 O6 **Mon** *Nagaland* India
118 C6 **Mon** *state* Myanmar
265 U2 **Mona** *UT* U.S.A.
271 J4 **Mona, Isla** *i.* Puerto Rico
207 L7 **Mona, Punta de la** *pt* Spain
256 E8 **Monaca** *PA* U.S.A.
168 A7 **Monach, Sound of** *sea chan.* Scotland U.K.
207 L6 **Monachil** Spain
207 L6 **Monachil** *r.* Spain
168 A7 **Monach Islands** *Scotland* U.K.
214 C4 **Monacia-d'Aullène** *Corse* France
183 K9 **Monaco** *country* Europe
288 H4 **Monaco Basin** *sea feature* N. Atlantic Ocean
168 G8 **Monadhliath Mountains** *S cotland* U.K.
275 F2 **Monagas** *state* Venez.
169 I4 **Monaghan** Ireland
169 I4 **Monaghan** *county* Ireland
261 D10 **Monahans** *TX* U.S.A.
169 J7 **Monamolin** Ireland
271 I4 **Mona Passage** Dom. Rep./Puerto Rico
235 I2 **Monapo** Moz.
231 C7 **Mona Quimbundo** Angola
168 F8 **Monar, Loch** *l. Scotland* U.K.
246 E5 **Monarch Mountain** B.C. Can.
263 K7 **Monarch Pass** *CO* U.S.A.
265 U2 **Mona Reservoir** *UT* U.S.A.
246 G5 **Monashee Mountains** B.C. Can.
217 L7 **Monasterace** Italy
169 H6 **Monasterevin** Ireland
214 C9 **Monastir** *Sardegna* Italy
Monastir Macedonia *see* **Bitola**
227 H2 **Monastir** Tunisia
197 M6 **Monastyrets'** Ukr.
Monastyrishche Ukr. *see* **Monastyryshche**
161 O7 **Monastyrshchina** Rus. Fed.
158 I5 **Monastyryshche** Ukr.
158 E4 **Monastyrys'ka** Ukr.
229 H5 **Monatélé** Cameroon
103 E11 **Monavale** *South I.* N.Z.
101 □7a **Monavatu** *mt. Viti Levu* Fiji
169 G8 **Monavullagh Mountains** *hills* Ireland
185 F6 **Monbahus** France
185 E6 **Monbazillac** France
185 G8 **Monbéqui** France
124 T4 **Monbetsu** *Hokkaidō* Japan
124 U2 **Monbetsu** *Hokkaidō* Japan
229 I4 **Monboré** Cameroon
185 G8 **Monbrun** France
209 E8 **Moncada** Spain
212 D5 **Moncalieri** Italy
212 E5 **Moncalvo** Italy
204 G4 **Moncalvo** *mt.* Spain
204 D4 **Monção** Port.
206 D6 **Moncarapacho** Port.
185 E7 **Moncaut** France
205 Q5 **Moncayo, Sierra del** *mts* Spain
181 L6 **Moncé-en-Belin** France
179 L6 **Moncel-sur-Seille** France
212 E2 **Mönch** *mt.* Switz.
162 V3 **Monchegorsk** Rus. Fed.
191 B8 **Mönchengladbach** Ger.
201 O4 **Mönchhof** Austria
212 I7 **Monchio delle Corti** Italy
206 B6 **Monchique** Port.
206 B6 **Monchique, Serra de** *mts* Port.
195 J4 **Mönchsdeggingen** Ger.
271 □3 **Monchy** St Lucia
255 G9 **Moncks Corner** *SC* U.S.A.
185 F7 **Monclar** France
185 H8 **Monclar-de-Quercy** France
267 I4 **Monclova** Mex.
209 E8 **Moncofa** Spain
180 F5 **Moncontour** *Bretagne* France
181 K8 **Moncontour** *Poitou-Charentes* France
249 G3 **Moncouche, Lac** *l. Que.* Can.
181 J8 **Moncoutant** France
185 E7 **Moncrabeau** France
249 H4 **Moncton** *N.B.* Can.
207 J7 **Monda** Spain
279 B8 **Mondai** Brazil
204 D4 **Mondariz** Spain
204 D4 **Mondariz-Balneario** Spain
185 G9 **Mondavezan** France
213 N8 **Mondavio** Italy
204 C8 **Mondego** *r.* Port.
204 C8 **Mondego, Cabo** *c.* Port.
205 N8 **Mondéjar** Spain
216 E7 **Mondello** *Sicilia* Italy
181 K3 **Mondeville** France
230 D4 **Mondimbi** Dem. Rep. Congo
204 E6 **Mondim de Basto** Port.
230 D4 **Mondjamboli** Dem. Rep. Congo
237 O3 **Mondlo** S. Africa
224 B6 **Mondo** Chad
213 O8 **Mondolfo** Italy
204 F2 **Mondoñedo** Spain
187 J9 **Mondorf-les-Bains** Lux.
181 M6 **Mondoubleau** France
212 D7 **Mondovì** Italy
250 C5 **Mondovi** *WI* U.S.A.
183 F8 **Mondragon** France
Mondragón Spain *see* **Arrasate**
215 L5 **Mondragone** Italy
201 H4 **Mondsee** Austria
201 H4 **Mondsee** *l.* Austria
233 C5 **Monduli** Tanz.
209 E9 **Mondúver** *hill* Spain
270 □ **Moneague** Jamaica
199 L5 **Moneasa** Romania
184 H4 **Monédières, Massif des** *hills* France
250 G8 **Monee** *IL* U.S.A.
169 E6 **Moneen** Ireland
212 G7 **Moneglia** Italy
208 E4 **Monegrillo** Spain
208 D4 **Monegros, Canal de** Spain
185 C9 **Monein** France
220 E6 **Monemvasia** Greece
122 L5 **Moneron, Ostrov** *i.* Rus. Fed.
256 F8 **Monessen** *PA* U.S.A.
206 G4 **Monesterio** Spain
183 H7 **Monestier-de-Clermont** France
185 I7 **Monestiés** France
251 S1 **Monet** *Que.* Can.
256 F11 **Moneta** *VA* U.S.A.
262 K5 **Moneta** *WY* U.S.A.
178 G8 **Monéteau** France
261 I7 **Monett** *MO* U.S.A.
208 D5 **Moneva, Embalse de** *resr* Spain
169 G7 **Moneygall** Ireland
168 D13 **Moneyglass** *Northern Ireland* U.K.
169 I3 **Moneymore** *Northern Ireland* U.K.
170 D4 **Moneyneany** *Northern Ireland* U.K.
170 F4 **Moneyreagh** *Northern Ireland* U.K.
213 P4 **Monfalcone** Italy
215 N6 **Monfecorvino Rovella** Italy
185 F6 **Monflanquin** France
274 D4 **Monfort** Col.
185 F8 **Monfort** France
206 E2 **Monforte** Port.
204 F9 **Monforte da Beira** Port.
212 D6 **Monforte d'Alba** Italy
209 D11 **Monforte del Cid** Spain
204 E3 **Monforte de Lemos** Spain
208 D5 **Monforte de Moyuela** Spain
204 G8 **Monfortinho** Port.
206 C3 **Monfurado** *hill* Port.
206 C3 **Monfurado, Serra de** *mts* Port.
231 E7 **Monga** *Katanga* Dem. Rep. Congo
230 D3 **Monga** *Orientale* Dem. Rep. Congo
280 D6 **Mongaguá** Brazil
230 D4 **Mongala** *prov.* Dem. Rep. Congo
230 C4 **Mongala** *r.* Dem. Rep. Congo
232 A3 **Mongalla** Sudan
105 L6 **Monga National Park** *N.S.W.* Austr.
139 M6 **Mongar** Bhutan
258 F2 **Mongaup** *r. NY* U.S.A.
258 F1 **Mongaup Valley** *NY* U.S.A.
230 F4 **Mongbwalu** Dem. Rep. Congo
118 H4 **Mông Cai** Vietnam
231 D5 **Mongemputu** Dem. Rep. Congo
109 D10 **Mongers Lake** *salt flat* W.A. Austr.
100 □6 **Mongga** *New Georgia Is* Solomon Is
129 P2 **Monggon Qulu** *Nei Mongol* China
118 D4 **Mong Hai** Myanmar
118 D4 **Mong Hang** Myanmar
213 K7 **Monghidoro** Italy
130 C8 **Mong Hkan** Myanmar
118 D4 **Mong Hkok** Myanmar
118 D4 **Mong Hpayak** Myanmar
118 D4 **Mong Hsat** Myanmar
118 C4 **Mong Hsawk** Myanmar
118 D4 **Mong Hsu** Myanmar
Monghyr *Bihar* India *see* **Munger**
118 C4 **Mong Kung** Myanmar
118 D5 **Mong Kyawt** Myanmar
139 L8 **Mongla** Bangl.
118 E4 **Mong La** Myanmar
118 C4 **Mong Lang** Myanmar
118 E4 **Mong Lin** Myanmar
118 E4 **Mong Loi** Myanmar
118 C3 **Mong Long** Myanmar
118 D4 **Mong Ma** Myanmar
118 C5 **Mong Mau** Myanmar
118 C3 **Mong Mit** Myanmar
118 C4 **Mong Nai** Myanmar
118 D4 **Mong Nawng** Myanmar
224 C6 **Mongo** Chad
Mongó *hill* Spain *see* **Montgó**
128 H3 **Mongolia** *country* Asia
Mongolküre *Xinjiang* China *see* **Zhaosu**
Mongol Uls *country* Asia *see* **Mongolia**
229 H6 **Mongomo** Equat. Guinea
108 I3 **Mongona, Mount** *hill* W.A. Austr.
129 K2 **Möngönmorĭt** Mongolia
145 O4 **Mongora** Pak.
224 D6 **Mongororo** Chad
230 C4 **Mongoumba** C.A.R.
168 L9 **Mongour** *hill Scotland* U.K.
118 D4 **Mong Pan** Myanmar
118 D3 **Mong Pat** Myanmar
118 D3 **Mong Pawk** Myanmar
118 D4 **Mong Ping** Myanmar
118 D4 **Mong Pu** Myanmar
118 D4 **Mong Pu-awn** Myanmar
212 E4 **Mongrando** Italy
268 E8 **Mongrove, Punta** *pt* Mex.
118 D3 **Mong Si** Myanmar
130 B8 **Mong Ton** Myanmar
118 D4 **Mong Tum** Myanmar
130 A7 **Mong Tung** Myanmar
231 D8 **Mongu** Zambia
231 B9 **Mongua** Angola
228 B2 **Mônguel** Maur.
213 M2 **Monguelfo** Italy
118 E4 **Mong Un** Myanmar
229 I3 **Monguno** Nigeria
118 D3 **Mong Yai** Myanmar
118 D4 **Mong Yang** Myanmar
118 D4 **Mong Yawn** Myanmar
118 E4 **Mong Yawng** Myanmar
118 C3 **Mong Yu** Myanmar
129 M3 **Mönhaan** Mongolia
Mönhbulag Mongolia *see* **Yösöndzüyl**
257 □P5 **Monhegan Island** *ME* U.S.A.
195 J4 **Monheim** Ger.
128 B3 **Mönh Hayrhan Uul** *mt.* Mongolia
168 I12 **Moniaive** *Dumfries and Galloway, Scotland* U.K.
250 E4 **Monico** *WI* U.S.A.
183 G8 **Monieux** France
168 K10 **Monifieth** *Angus, Scotland* U.K.
285 G2 **Monigotes** Arg.
170 C6 **Monilea** Ireland
274 C3 **Moniquirá** Col.
183 D7 **Monistrol-d'Allier** France
208 I4 **Monistrol de Montserrat** Spain
183 E6 **Monistrol-sur-Loire** France
264 P3 **Monitor Mountain** *NV* U.S.A.
264 P3 **Monitor Range** *mts NV* U.S.A.
274 B2 **Moñitos** Col.
144 E6 **Monj** Iran
205 P9 **Monje, Sierra del** *mts* Spain
281 E3 **Monjolos** Brazil
144 F2 **Monjukly** Turkm.
190 J2 **Mönkeberg** Ger.
233 B8 **Monkey Bay** Malawi
109 B8 **Monkey Mia** W.A. Austr.
197 K2 **Mońki** Pol.
106 H8 **Monkira** *Qld* Austr.
246 F4 **Monkman Provincial Park** B.C. Can.
172 D6 **Monkokehampton** *Devon, England* U.K.
230 D5 **Monkoto** Dem. Rep. Congo
173 N3 **Monks Eleigh** *Suffolk, England* U.K.
251 M6 **Monkton** *Ont.* Can.
258 B5 **Monkton** *MD* U.S.A.
185 F9 **Monléon-Magnoac** France
209 E7 **Monlleó, Riu** *r.* Spain
172 G4 **Monmouth** *Monmouthshire, Wales* U.K.
264 M5 **Monmouth** *CA* U.S.A.
260 J5 **Monmouth** *IL* U.S.A.
259 G4 **Monmouth County** *county NJ* U.S.A.
258 F4 **Monmouth Junction** *NJ* U.S.A.
246 F5 **Monmouth Mountain** B.C. Can.
172 G4 **Monmouthshire** *admin. div.* Wales U.K.
181 M6 **Monnaie** France
256 B8 **Monnett** *OH* U.S.A.
186 H4 **Monnickendam** Neth.
172 G4 **Monnow** *r. England/Wales* U.K.
229 F5 **Mono** *r.* Togo
266 □R12 **Mono, Punta del** *pt* Nic.
100 □6 **Mono Island** Solomon Is
199 K3 **Monok** Hungary
264 N3 **Mono Lake** *CA* U.S.A.
221 I6 **Monolithos** *Rodos* Greece
257 P7 **Monomoy Island** *MA* U.S.A.
250 H9 **Monon** *IN* U.S.A.
250 C6 **Monona** *IA* U.S.A.
256 F8 **Monongahela** *r. PA* U.S.A.
217 M2 **Monopoli** Italy
199 I4 **Monor** Hungary
271 □7 **Monos Island** Trin. and Tob.
199 K4 **Monostorpályi** Hungary
224 D5 **Monou** Chad
209 D11 **Monóvar** Spain
Monover Spain *see* **Monóvar**
103 B12 **Monowai, Lake** *South I.* N.Z.
185 F6 **Monpazier** France
205 R3 **Monreal** Spain
207 N2 **Monreal** *r.* Spain
208 C6 **Monreal del Campo** Spain
216 E7 **Monreale** *Sicilia* Italy
168 G13 **Monreith** *Dumfries and Galloway, Scotland* U.K.
255 F9 **Monroe** *GA* U.S.A.
260 I5 **Monroe** *IA* U.S.A.
261 I9 **Monroe** *LA* U.S.A.
251 K8 **Monroe** *MI* U.S.A.
255 G8 **Monroe** *NC* U.S.A.
258 F2 **Monroe** *NJ* U.S.A.
259 G2 **Monroe** *NY* U.S.A.
265 T3 **Monroe** *UT* U.S.A.
256 F11 **Monroe** *VA* U.S.A.
262 D3 **Monroe** *WA* U.S.A.
250 E7 **Monroe** *WI* U.S.A.
250 E5 **Monroe Center** *WI* U.S.A.
260 J6 **Monroe City** *MO* U.S.A.
258 E2 **Monroe County** *county PA* U.S.A.
254 D6 **Monroe Lake** *IN* U.S.A.
251 R8 **Monroeton** *PA* U.S.A.
255 D10 **Monroeville** *AL* U.S.A.
250 J9 **Monroeville** *IN* U.S.A.
258 E5 **Monroeville** *NJ* U.S.A.
256 C7 **Monroeville** *OH* U.S.A.
228 C5 **Monrovia** Liberia
204 H9 **Monroy** Spain
208 E6 **Monroyo** Spain
187 E8 **Mons** Belgium
183 B9 **Mons** *Languedoc-Roussillon* France
183 J9 **Mons** *Provence-Alpes-Côte d'Azur* France
285 I5 **Monsalvo** Arg.
215 L2 **Monsampolo del Tronto** Italy
204 F8 **Monsanto** Port.
281 H3 **Monsarás, Ponta de** *pt* Brazil
206 E4 **Monsaraz** Port.
191 B9 **Monschau** Ger.
184 F5 **Monsec** France
185 D9 **Monségur** *Aquitaine* France
185 E6 **Monségur** *Aquitaine* France
213 L5 **Monselice** Italy
185 F7 **Monsempron-Libos** France
178 F2 **Mons-en-Barœul** France
259 G2 **Monsey** *NY* U.S.A.
194 F4 **Mönsheim** Ger.
194 E2 **Monsheim** Ger.
164 I7 **Møns Klint** *cliff* Denmark
182 F4 **Monsols** France
257 □P3 **Monson** *ME* U.S.A.
186 F4 **Monster** Neth.
165 M4 **Mönsterås** Sweden
213 J8 **Monsummano Terme** Italy
212 D6 **Monta** Italy
191 E10 **Montabaur** Ger.
185 K9 **Montady** France
200 A5 **Montafon** *val.* Austria
183 C10 **Montagnac** France
213 K5 **Montagnana** Italy
184 D6 **Montagne** France
235 □K2 **Montagne d'Ambre, Parc National de la** *nat. park* Madag.
178 G5 **Montagne de Reims, Parc Naturel Régional de la** *nature res.* France
182 H2 **Montagney** France
183 C9 **Montagnol** France
182 E4 **Montagny** France
184 E5 **Montagrier** France
236 E9 **Montagu** S. Africa
249 I4 **Montague** *P.E.I.* Can.
258 F2 **Montague** *NJ* U.S.A.
261 G9 **Montague** *TX* U.S.A.
245 K3 **Montague Island** *AK* U.S.A.
109 E9 **Montague Range** *hills* W.A. Austr.
108 H3 **Montague Sound** *b.* W.A. Austr.
245 J4 **Montague Strait** *AK* U.S.A.
273 G7 **Montagu Island** S. Sandwich Is
Montagu Island Vanuatu *see* **Nguna**
180 I8 **Montaigu** France
185 G7 **Montaigu-de-Quercy** France
182 B4 **Montaigut** France
185 G8 **Montaigut-sur-Save** France
213 J8 **Montaione** Italy
117 K5 **Montalat** *r.* Indon.
208 D6 **Montalbán** Spain
207 J5 **Montalbán de Córdoba** Spain
217 I7 **Montalbano Elicona** *Sicilia* Italy
217 L3 **Montalbano Jonico** Italy
205 O9 **Montalbo** Spain
214 G1 **Montalcino** Italy
213 K8 **Montale** Italy
204 E5 **Montalegre** Port.
183 B9 **Montalet, Roc de** *mt.* France
182 G5 **Montalieu-Vercieu** France
184 B5 **Montalivet-les-Bains** France
216 E9 **Montallegro** *Sicilia* Italy
217 J7 **Montalto** *mt.* Italy
215 L2 **Montalto delle Marche** Italy
214 H3 **Montalto di Castro** Italy
214 H3 **Montalto Marina** Italy
215 Q9 **Montalto Uffugo** Italy
204 E9 **Montalvão** Port.
274 B5 **Montalvo** Ecuador
264 M7 **Montalvo** *CA* U.S.A.
204 I5 **Montamarta** Spain
219 L7 **Montana** Bulg.
212 C3 **Montana** Switz.
245 J3 **Montana** *AK* U.S.A.
262 J3 **Montana** *state* U.S.A.
238 □3c **Montaña Clara** *i.* Canary Is
266 □P10 **Montaña de Comayagua, Parque Nacional** *nat. park* Hond.
267 O10 **Montaña de Cusuco, Parque Nacional** *nat. park* Hond.
266 □P10 **Montaña de Yoro** *nat. park* Hond.
Montañana Spain *see* **Puente de Montañana**
266 □Q10 **Montañas de Colón** *mts* Hond.
206 G2 **Montánchez** *hill* Spain
206 G2 **Montánchez, Sierra de** *mts* Spain
258 B3 **Montandon** *PA* U.S.A.
209 D7 **Montanejos** Spain
185 D9 **Montaner** France
281 G3 **Montanha** Brazil
275 H4 **Montanhas do Tumucumaque, Parque Nacional** *nat. park* Brazil
215 O7 **Montano Antilia** Italy
185 H8 **Montans** France
215 M4 **Montaquila** Italy
206 C2 **Montargil** Port.
206 C2 **Montargil, Barragem de** *resr* Port.
178 E8 **Montargis** France
185 H8 **Montastruc-la-Conseillère** France
178 D5 **Montataire** France
185 G7 **Montauban** France
180 G5 **Montauban-de-Bretagne** France
185 I9 **Montaud, Pic de** *mt.* France
181 J5 **Montaudin** France
257 N7 **Montauk** *NY* U.S.A.
259 L2 **Montauk, Lake** *b. NY* U.S.A.
257 N7 **Montauk Point** *NY* U.S.A.
185 F6 **Montauriol** France
183 J9 **Montauroux** France
185 C8 **Montaut** *Aquitaine* France
185 D9 **Montaut** *Aquitaine* France
185 H9 **Montaut** *Midi-Pyrénées* France
185 F8 **Montaut-les-Créneaux** France
237 M4 **Mont-aux-Sources** *mt.* Lesotho
209 E10 **Montaverner** Spain
185 F7 **Montayral** France
215 M4 **Montazzoli** Italy
182 E1 **Montbard** France
182 H2 **Montbarrey** France
185 G8 **Montbartier** France
185 I7 **Montbazens** France
183 D9 **Montbazin** France
181 M7 **Montbazon** France
182 J1 **Montbéliard** France
182 I3 **Montbenoît** France
185 F9 **Montbernard** France
185 G7 **Montbeton** France
182 J5 **Mont Blanc** *mt.* France/Italy
183 C10 **Montblanc** France
208 H5 **Montblanc** Spain
Montblanch Spain *see* **Montblanc**
239 □1b **Mont Blanche** Mauritius
182 J5 **Mont Blanc Tunnel** France/Italy
183 F7 **Montboucher-sur-Jabron** France
182 I2 **Montbozon** France
208 H5 **Montbrió del Camp** Spain
182 E5 **Montbrison** France
184 F4 **Montbron** France
185 H6 **Montbrun** France
183 G8 **Montbrun-les-Bains** France
256 D11 **Montcalm** *WV* U.S.A.
185 E6 **Montcaret** France
178 C2 **Montcavrel** France
182 E3 **Montceau-les-Mines** France
182 E3 **Montcenis** France
183 J6 **Mont Cenis, Lac du** *l.* France
182 E3 **Montchanin** France
259 G3 **Montclair** *NJ* U.S.A.
178 H4 **Montcornet** France
178 E8 **Montcresson** France
185 G7 **Montcuq** France
178 I4 **Montcy-Notre-Dame** France
183 D9 **Montdardier** France
183 J7 **Mont-Dauphin** France
185 D8 **Mont-de-Marsan** France
178 E4 **Montdidier** France
182 B5 **Mont-Dore** France
285 F5 **Monte, Laguna del** *l.* Arg.
215 P8 **Montea** *mt.* Italy
276 D4 **Monteagudo** Bol.
205 Q5 **Monteagudo** Spain
205 Q9 **Monteagudo de las Salinas** Spain
205 P6 **Monteagudo de las Vicarías** Spain
284 A5 **Monte Águila** Chile
269 K8 **Monte Alban** *tourist site* Mex.
275 H5 **Monte Alegre** Brazil
280 B2 **Monte Alegre** *r.* Brazil
278 D5 **Monte Alegre de Goiás** Brazil
209 C10 **Montealegre del Castillo** Spain
280 C3 **Monte Alegre de Minas** Brazil
280 C4 **Monte Alto** Brazil
280 C4 **Monte Aprazível** Brazil
279 E5 **Monte Azul** Brazil
280 C4 **Monte Azul Paulista** Brazil
248 F4 **Montebello** *Que.* Can.
274 C6 **Monte Bello** Peru
217 J8 **Montebello Ionico** Italy
108 C6 **Montebello Islands** W.A. Austr.
213 K5 **Montebello Vicentino** Italy
213 M4 **Montebelluna** Italy
180 I3 **Montebourg** France
212 G6 **Montebruno** Italy
285 F3 **Monte Buey** Arg.
213 N8 **Montecalvo in Foglia** Italy
282 G2 **Montecarlo** Arg.
183 K9 **Monte-Carlo** Monaco
280 D3 **Monte Carmelo** Brazil
285 I2 **Monte Caseros** Arg.
213 O9 **Montecassiano** Italy
215 I2 **Monte Castello di Vibio** Italy
215 I2 **Montecastrilli** Italy
213 J8 **Montecatini Terme** Italy
213 J9 **Montecatini Val di Cecina** Italy
213 N8 **Montecchio** Italy
212 I6 **Montecchio Emilia** Italy
213 K4 **Montecchio Maggiore** Italy
185 G8 **Montech** France
212 E5 **Montechiaro d'Asti** Italy
206 C6 **Montechoro** Port.
215 N4 **Montecilfone** Italy
264 M7 **Montecito** *CA* U.S.A.
204 E9 **Monte Claro** Port.
284 D4 **Monte Comán** Arg.
204 D6 **Monte Córdova** Port.
215 N7 **Montecorice** Italy
213 K3 **Monte Corno, Parco Naturale** *nature res.* Italy
215 Q7 **Monte Cotugna, Lago di** *l.* Italy
213 N3 **Montecreale Valcellina** Italy
213 J7 **Montecreto** Italy
270 H4 **Monte Cristi** Dom. Rep.
270 H4 **Monte Cristi** *nat. park* Dom. Rep.
274 A5 **Montecristi** Ecuador
285 F2 **Monte Cristo** Arg.
277 E3 **Monte Cristo** Bol.
235 E4 **Monte Cristo** S. Africa
214 E3 **Montecristo, Isola di** *i.* Italy
213 N9 **Monte Cucco, Parco Naturale Regionale del** *park* Italy
206 D2 **Monte da Pedra** Port.
206 C5 **Monte da Rocha, Barragem do** *resr* Port.
204 F4 **Montederramo** Spain
283 C9 **Monte Dinero** Arg.
215 M6 **Monte di Procida** Italy
213 M8 **Montedoglio, Lago di** *l.* Italy
206 D4 **Monte do Trigo** Port.
275 H5 **Monte Dourado** Brazil
268 D3 **Monte Escobedo** Mex.
215 N6 **Montefalcione** Italy
215 J2 **Montefalco** Italy
215 N4 **Montefalcone** Italy
215 O5 **Montefalcone di Val Fortore** Italy
213 L8 **Monte Falterona, Campigna e delle Foreste Casentinesi, Parco Nazionale del** *nat. park* Italy
213 O9 **Montefano** Italy
213 N8 **Montefelcino** Italy
213 M8 **Montefeltro** *reg.* Italy
214 I2 **Montefiascone** Italy
206 C6 **Monte Figo, Serra de** *mts* Port.
215 L1 **Montefiore dell'Aso** Italy
213 J7 **Montefiorino** Italy
215 N6 **Monteforte Irpino** Italy
215 K2 **Montefortino** Italy
215 J2 **Montefranco** Italy
207 K6 **Montefrío** Spain
217 L3 **Montegiordano** Italy
215 L1 **Montegiorgio** Italy
270 □ **Montego Bay** Jamaica
270 □ **Montego Bay** *b.* Jamaica
206 E6 **Monte Gordo** Port.
213 P9 **Montegranaro** Italy
285 H4 **Monte Grande** Arg.
185 E9 **Montégut-Arros** France
285 G6 **Monte Hermoso** Arg.
204 H8 **Montehermoso** Spain
217 M3 **Monteiasi** Italy
185 H7 **Monteils** France
278 F3 **Monteiro** Brazil
238 □1c **Monteiros, Ponta dos** *pt São Jorge* Azores
200 B8 **Monte Isola** *i.* Italy
207 I7 **Montejaque** Spain
207 M5 **Montejícar** Spain
106 C4 **Montejinnie** *N.T.* Austr.
205 M6 **Montejo de la Sierra** Spain
206 A2 **Montejunto, Serra de** *hill* Port.
213 N8 **Montelabbate** Italy
215 K4 **Montelanico** Italy
206 A3 **Montelavar** Port.
182 B5 **Montel-de-Gelat** France
283 C8 **Monte León** Arg.
215 O5 **Monteleone di Puglia** Italy
215 J2 **Monteleone di Spoleto** Italy
214 I2 **Monteleone d'Orvieto** Italy
214 B7 **Monteleone Rocca Doria** *Sardegna* Italy
215 J3 **Monteleone Sabino** Italy
216 E7 **Montelepre** *Sicilia* Italy
274 C2 **Monte Libano** Col.
215 J3 **Montelibretti** Italy
183 G7 **Montélier** France
183 F7 **Montélimar** France
277 F5 **Monte Lindo** *r.* Para.
215 O6 **Montella** Italy
206 H6 **Montellano** Spain
250 E6 **Montello** *WI* U.S.A.
185 G9 **Montels** France
213 K8 **Montelupo Fiorentino** Italy
213 P9 **Montelupone** Italy
216 F8 **Montemaggiore Belsito** *Sicilia* Italy
285 F3 **Monte Maíz** Arg.
215 O6 **Montemarano** Italy
213 O8 **Montemarciano** Italy
207 O3 **Montemayon** *r.* Spain
207 J5 **Montemayor** Spain
283 D7 **Montemayor, Meseta de** *plat.* Arg.
205 L5 **Montemayor de Pililla** Spain
184 F4 **Montemboeuf** France
217 M2 **Montemesola** Italy
215 P5 **Montemilone** Italy
206 G4 **Montemolín** Spain
215 K2 **Montemonaco** Italy
267 J5 **Montemorelos** Mex.
206 C3 **Montemor-o-Novo** Port.
204 C8 **Montemor-o-Velho** Port.
213 K8 **Montemurlo** Italy
204 D6 **Montemuro, Serra de** *mts* Port.
215 P7 **Montemurro** Italy
181 J5 **Montenay** France
184 D5 **Montendre** France
218 H8 **Montenegro** *country* Europe
205 O4 **Montenegro de Cameros** Spain
215 N4 **Montenero di Bisaccia** Italy
215 M3 **Montenerodomo** Italy
217 M3 **Monteparano** Italy
281 H2 **Monte Pascoal, Parque Nacional de** *nat. park* Brazil
284 B2 **Monte Patria** Chile
271 I4 **Monte Plata** Dom. Rep.
213 O8 **Monte Porzio** Italy
215 L2 **Monteprandone** Italy
233 C8 **Montepuez** Moz.
233 D8 **Montepuez** *r.* Moz.
214 H1 **Montepulciano** Italy
214 H1 **Montepulciano, Lago di** *l.* Italy
282 E2 **Monte Quemado** Arg.
180 F6 **Monterblanc** France
213 M9 **Monterchi** Italy
204 C9 **Monte Real** Port.
215 K2 **Montereale** Italy
178 E7 **Montereau-Fault-Yonne** France
204 C9 **Monte Redondo** Port.
213 K7 **Monterenzio** Italy
Monterey Mex. *see* **Monterrey**
264 K5 **Monterey** *CA* U.S.A.
256 F10 **Monterey** *VA* U.S.A.
264 J5 **Monterey Bay** *CA* U.S.A.
264 J5 **Monterey Bay National Marine Sanctuary** *nature res. CA* U.S.A.
274 C2 **Montería** Col.
213 K9 **Monteriggioni** Italy
277 E4 **Montero** Bol.
215 M4 **Monteroduni** Italy
214 H3 **Monte Romano** Italy
213 K9 **Monteroni d'Arbia** Italy
217 O3 **Monteroni di Lecce** Italy
275 F3 **Monte Roraima, Parque Nacional do** *nat. park* Brazil
282 D2 **Monteros** Arg.
215 I3 **Monterosi** Italy
212 H7 **Monterosso al Mare** Italy
216 H9 **Monterosso Almo** *Sicilia* Italy
217 K6 **Monterosso Calabro** Italy
215 J3 **Monterotondo** Italy
214 F1 **Monterotondo Marittimo** Italy
204 F5 **Monterrei** Spain
265 Q9 **Monterrey** *Baja California* Mex.
267 I5 **Monterrey** *Nuevo León* Mex.
204 E3 **Monterroso** Spain
207 I3 **Monterrubio de la Serena** Spain
215 L1 **Monterubbiano** Italy
209 D10 **Montesa** Spain
278 D3 **Montes Altos** Brazil
215 K5 **Monte San Biagio** Italy
215 L4 **Monte San Giovanni Campano** Italy
262 C3 **Montesano** *WA* U.S.A.
217 O4 **Montesano Salentino** Ital
215 P7 **Montesano sulla Marcella** Italy
213 L9 **Monte San Savino** Italy
213 M9 **Monte Santa Maria Tiber** Italy
215 P4 **Monte Sant'Angelo** Italy
278 F4 **Monte Santo** Brazil
280 D4 **Monte Santo de Minas** B
214 D7 **Monte Santu, Capo di** *c. Sardegna* Italy
215 N5 **Montesarchio** Italy
217 L2 **Montescaglioso** Italy
281 F2 **Montes Claros** Brazil
205 K8 **Montesclaros** Spain
213 J9 **Montescudaio** Italy
285 F6 **Montes de Oca** Arg.
213 J7 **Montese** Italy
215 M2 **Montesilvano** Italy
185 G7 **Montesquieu** France
185 G9 **Montesquieu-Volvestre** F
185 E8 **Montesquiou** France
185 F8 **Montestruc-sur-Gers** Fra
215 J1 **Monte Subasio, Parco Na Regionale del** *park* Italy
206 C5 **Montes Velhos** Port.
183 F8 **Monteux** France
216 D8 **Montevago** *Sicilia* Italy
213 L8 **Montevarchi** Italy
214 B8 **Montevecchia** *Sardegna* It
285 G2 **Monte Vera** Arg.
215 P5 **Monteverde** Italy
285 I4 **Montevideo** Uru.
285 I4 **Montevideo** *dept* Uru.
260 H3 **Montevideo** *MN* U.S.A.
206 B4 **Montevil** Port.
263 K8 **Monte Vista** *CO* U.S.A.
204 G5 **Montezinho, Parque Natu** *nature res.* Port.
260 I5 **Montezuma** *IA* U.S.A.
261 E7 **Montezuma** *KS* U.S.A.
265 W4 **Montezuma Creek** *UT* U.S
265 W4 **Montezuma Creek** *r. CO*
264 O4 **Montezuma Peak** *NV* U.S
185 H6 **Montfaucon** *Midi-Pyrénée* France
181 I7 **Montfaucon** *Pays de la Lo* France
179 J5 **Montfaucon-d'Argonne** F
183 E6 **Montfaucon-en-Velay** Fra
185 F8 **Montferran-Savès** France
183 I9 **Montferrat** France
185 H10 **Montferrier** France
186 G4 **Montfoort** Neth.
185 C9 **Montfort** *Aquitaine* Franc
180 H5 **Montfort** *Bretagne* France
185 C8 **Montfort-en-Chalosse** Fr
178 C6 **Montfort-l'Amaury** Franc
181 L5 **Montfort-le-Gesnois** Fran
181 M3 **Montfort-sur-Risle** Franc
204 H9 **Montfragüe, Parque Naci** *nat. park.* Spain
208 G4 **Montgai** Spain
185 E9 **Montgaillard** *Midi-Pyréné* France
185 F8 **Montgaillard** *Midi-Pyréné* France
185 H10 **Montgaillard** *Midi-Pyréné* France
183 J7 **Montgenèvre** France
183 J7 **Montgenèvre, Col de** *pass*
178 D6 **Montgeron** France
185 H9 **Montgiscard** France
181 O8 **Montgivray** France
209 F10 **Montgó** *hill* Spain
208 L3 **Montgó, Cala** *b.* Spain
172 F2 **Montgomery** *Powys, Wales*
255 D9 **Montgomery** *AL* U.S.A.
259 G1 **Montgomery** *NY* U.S.A.
256 A9 **Montgomery** *OH* U.S.A.
251 R8 **Montgomery** *PA* U.S.A.
256 D10 **Montgomery** *WV* U.S.A.
260 J6 **Montgomery City** *MO* U.S
258 A6 **Montgomery County** *cour* U.S.A.
258 E4 **Montgomery County** *cour* U.S.A.
108 G3 **Montgomery Islands** *W.A*
184 D5 **Montguyon** France
178 I4 **Monthermé** France
212 B3 **Monthey** Switz.
178 I5 **Monthois** France
179 K7 **Monthureux-sur-Saône** F
214 C6 **Monti** *Sardegna* Italy
213 N4 **Monticano** *r.* Italy
212 H5 **Monticelli d'Ongina** Italy
214 B2 **Monticello** *Corse* France
261 J9 **Monticello** *AR* U.S.A.
255 F10 **Monticello** *FL* U.S.A.
255 F9 **Monticello** *GA* U.S.A.
260 K5 **Monticello** *IL* U.S.A.
254 D5 **Monticello** *IN* U.S.A.
254 E7 **Monticello** *KY* U.S.A.
257 □R2 **Monticello** *ME* U.S.A.
260 I3 **Monticello** *MN* U.S.A.
260 J5 **Monticello** *MO* U.S.A.
261 J10 **Monticello** *MS* U.S.A.
258 F1 **Monticello** *NY* U.S.A.
265 W4 **Monticello** *UT* U.S.A.
250 E7 **Monticello** *WI* U.S.A.
212 I5 **Montichiari** Italy
214 G1 **Monticiano** Italy
207 N3 **Montiel** Spain
285 H2 **Montiel, Cuchilla de** *hills*
181 O8 **Montierchaume** France
178 I7 **Montier-en-Der** France
214 G1 **Montieri** Italy
179 J6 **Montiers-sur-Saulx** Franc
184 G5 **Montignac** France
187 F8 **Montignies-le-Tilleul** Belg
212 I7 **Montignoso** Italy
179 M6 **Montigny** France
251 Q1 **Montigny, Lac de** *l. Que.* C
178 G8 **Montigny-la-Resie** France
179 J7 **Montigny-le-Roi** France
179 L5 **Montigny-lès-Metz** Franc
182 G1 **Montigny-Mornay-Villene sur-Vingeanne** France
179 I8 **Montigny-sur-Aube** Franc
206 B3 **Montijo** Port.
206 F3 **Montijo** Spain
207 J5 **Montilla** Spain
207 L5 **Montillana** Spain
231 B8 **Montipa** Angola
185 I7 **Montirat** France
215 K2 **Monti Sibillini, Parco Naz dei** *nat. park* Italy
215 K4 **Monti Simbruini, Parco N Regionale dei** *nature res.* It
280 B2 **Montividiu** Brazil
181 L2 **Montivilliers** France
207 M4 **Montizón** Spain
207 M4 **Montizón** *r.* Spain
183 B8 **Montjaux** France
181 J5 **Montjean** France
181 J7 **Montjean-sur-Loire** Franc
249 G3 **Mont-Joli** *Que.* Can.
212 D4 **Montjovet** Italy
185 J9 **Montlaur** France
248 F4 **Mont-Laurier** *Que.* Can.
178 D6 **Montlhéry** France
184 D5 **Montlieu-la-Garde** France
249 H3 **Mont-Louis** *Que.* Can.
185 I10 **Mont-Louis** France
181 M7 **Montlouis-sur-Loire** Fran
182 B4 **Montluçon** France
182 G5 **Montluel** France
243 K5 **Montmagny** *Que.* Can.
182 B4 **Montmarault** France
180 H4 **Montmartin-sur-Mer** Frar
179 J4 **Montmédy** France
182 I5 **Montmélian** France
182 F4 **Montmerle-sur-Saône** Fra
183 F7 **Montmeyran** France
183 I9 **Montmeyan** France
178 G6 **Montmirail** *Champagne-A* France
181 M5 **Montmirail** *Pays de la Loir* France
182 H2 **Montmirey-le-Château** Fr
184 E5 **Montmoreau-St-Cybard** F
250 G9 **Montmorenci** *IN* U.S.A.
254 L2 **Montmorency** *Que.* Can.

Montmorillon France
Montmorin France
Montmorot France
Montmort-Lucy France
Montnegre de Llevant hill Spain
Monto Qld Austr.
Montoir-de-Bretagne France
Montoire-sur-le-Loir France
Montois slope France
Montoison France
Montoito Port.
Montolieu France
Montón Spain
Montone Italy
Montone r. Italy
Montopoli di Sabina Italy
Montorio al Vomano Italy
Montoro Spain
Montoro r. Spain
Montoro, Embalse de resr Spain
Montory France
Montour County county PA U.S.A.
Montour Falls NY U.S.A.
Montournais France
Montoursville PA U.S.A.
Mont Peko, Parc National du nat. park Côte d'Ivoire
Montpelier Jamaica
Montpelier ID U.S.A.
Montpelier IN U.S.A.
Montpelier OH U.S.A.
Montpelier VT U.S.A.
Montpellier France
Montpeyroux France
Montpezat France
Montpézat France
Montpezat-de-Quercy France
Montpezat-sous-Bauzon France
Montpon-Ménestérol France
Montpont-en-Bresse France
Mont-près-Chambord France
Montréal Que. Can.
Montreal Que. Can. see Montréal
Montreal r. Ont. Can.
Montreal r. Ont. Can.
Montréal Bourgogne France
Montréal Languedoc-Roussillon France
Montréal Midi-Pyrénées France
Montreal WI U.S.A.
Montreal Island Ont. Can.
Montréal-la-Cluse France
Montreal Lake Sask. Can.
Montreal Lake l. Sask. Can.
Montréal-Mirabel airport Que. Can.
Montreal River Ont. Can.
Montréal-Trudeau airport Que. Can.
Montredon-Labessonnié France
Montregard France
Montréjeau France
Montrésor France
Montresta Sardegna Italy
Montret France
Montreuil Île-de-France France
Montreuil Nord-Pas-de-Calais France
Montreuil-Bellay France
Montreuil-Juigné France
Montreux Switz.
Montrevault France
Montrevel-en-Bresse France
Montrichard France
Montricoux France
Montriond France
Montrodat France
Montrodre mt. France
Mont-roig del Camp Spain
Montrond France
Montrond-les-Bains France
Montrose well S. Africa
Montrose Angus, Scotland U.K.
Montrose CO U.S.A.
Montrose MI U.S.A.
Montrose NY U.S.A.
Montrose PA U.S.A.
Montrose WV U.S.A.
Montross VA U.S.A.
Montroy Spain
Montrozier France
Monts France
Mont-St-Aignan France
Mont-St-Jean France
Mont-St-Martin France
Mont-St-Michel, Baie du b. France
Mont-St-Sulpice France
Mont-St-Vincent France
Montsalvy France
Mont Sangbé, Parc National du nat. park Côte d'Ivoire
Montsant r. Spain
Montsauche-les-Settons France
Montsaunès France
Monts de Cristal, Parc National de nat. park Estuaire Gabon
Montsec, Serra del mts Spain
Montségur France
Montseny Spain
Montseny, Parc Natural de nature res. Spain
Montserrat terr. West Indies
Montsoreau France
Montsoué France
Mont-sous-Vaudrey France
Monts-sur-Guesnes France
Mont St-Michel tourist site France see Le Mont-St-Michel
Montsûrs France
Montsuzain France
Montuïri Spain
Montuosa, Isla i. Panama
Monturque Spain
Montvale VA U.S.A.
Montvalent France
Montviel, Lac l. Que. Can.
Montville France
Montville CT U.S.A.
Montzen Belgium
Montzéville France
Monument Draw watercourse NM/TX U.S.A.
Monument Mountain hill AK U.S.A.
Monument Valley reg. AZ U.S.A.
Monveda Dem. Rep. Congo
Monyakeng S. Africa
Monywa Myanmar
Monza Italy
Monza e Brianza admin. div. Italy
Monze Zambia
Monze, Cape pt Pak. see Muari, Ras
Monzelfeld Ger.
Monzen Japan
Monzingen Ger.
Monzón Peru
Monzón Spain
Monzón de Campos Spain
Moodus CT U.S.A.
Moodus Reservoir CT U.S.A.
Mooi r. KwaZulu-Natal S. Africa
Mooi r. North West S. Africa
Mooirivier S. Africa
Mook Neth.
Mookane Botswana
Moolawatana S.A. Austr.
Moomba S.A. Austr.
Moomin Creek r. N.S.W. Austr.
Moonah Creek watercourse Qld Austr.
Moonaree S.A. Austr.
Moonbi Range mts N.S.W. Austr.
Mooncoin Ireland
Moonda Lake salt flat Qld Austr.
Moone Ireland
Moonie Qld Austr.
Moonie r. N.S.W./Qld Austr.
Moonta S.A. Austr.
Moora W.A. Austr.
Mooraberree Qld Austr.
Moorbad Lobenstein Ger.
Moorcroft WY U.S.A.
237 M6 Moordenaarsnek pass S. Africa
190 D4 Moordorf (Südbrookmerland) Ger.
186 G5 Moordrecht Neth.
109 C11 Moore r. W.A. Austr.
262 J3 Moore MT U.S.A.
109 D10 Moore, Lake salt flat W.A. Austr.
101 □[9a] Moorea i. Fr. Polynesia
244 H3 Moore Creek AK U.S.A.
287 K1 Moore Embayment b. Antarctica
256 G9 Moorefield WV U.S.A.
255 G12 Moore Haven FL U.S.A.
171 P6 Moorends South Yorkshire, England U.K.
195 K5 Moorenweis Ger.
107 L4 Moore Reef Coral Sea Is Terr. Austr.
257 N4 Moore Reservoir NH/VT U.S.A.
109 C11 Moore River National Park W.A. Austr.
285 F4 Moores Arg.
258 B3 Mooresburg PA U.S.A.
270 E1 Moores Island Bahamas
257 □R3 Moores Mills N.B. Can.
258 F5 Moorestown NJ U.S.A.
270 □ Moore Town Jamaica
170 E4 Moorfields Northern Ireland U.K.
168 J11 Moorfoot Hills Scotland U.K.
260 G2 Moorhead MN U.S.A.
105 I5 Moornanyah Lake imp. l. N.S.W. Austr.
104 H6 Moorook S.A. Austr.
106 E1 Mooroongga Island N.T. Austr.
105 J7 Mooroopna Vic. Austr.
264 N7 Moorpark CA U.S.A.
236 C9 Moorreesburg S. Africa
107 J6 Moorrinya National Park Qld Austr.
187 D7 Moorslede Belgium
169 I3 Moortown Northern Ireland U.K.
190 E3 Moorweg Ger.
194 F6 Moos Baden-Württemberg Ger.
195 N4 Moos Bayern Ger.
195 M2 Moosbach Ger.
201 J6 Moosburg Austria
195 L5 Moosburg an der Isar Ger.
248 D3 Moose r. Ont. Can.
245 K2 Moose Creek AK U.S.A.
248 D3 Moose Factory Ont. Can.
257 □P3 Moosehead Lake ME U.S.A.
247 J5 Moose Jaw Sask. Can.
247 J5 Moose Jaw r. Sask. Can.
250 B3 Moose Lake MN U.S.A.
257 □O4 Mooselookmeguntic Lake ME U.S.A.
247 K5 Moose Mountain Creek r. Sask. Can.
245 J3 Moose Pass AK U.S.A.
200 G5 Mooserboden, Stausee resr Austria
248 D3 Moose River Ont. Can.
257 N4 Moosilauke, Mount NH U.S.A.
195 L5 Moosinning Ger.
201 L6 Mooskirchen Austria
247 K5 Moosomin Sask. Can.
248 D3 Moosonee Ont. Can.
195 N4 Moosthenning Ger.
105 I4 Mootwingee National Park N.S.W. Austr.
235 F4 Mopane S. Africa
235 G3 Mopeia Moz.
Mopelia atoll Arch. de la Société Fr. Polynesia see Maupihaa
234 E4 Mopipi Botswana
228 D3 Mopti Mali
228 E3 Mopti admin. reg. Mali
232 B1 Moqatta Sudan
145 L5 Moqor Afgh.
276 C4 Moquegua Peru
276 C4 Moquegua dept Peru
285 H4 Moquehuá Arg.
199 H4 Mór Hungary
229 I4 Mora Cameroon
206 C3 Mora Port.
205 M9 Mora Spain
163 M6 Mora Sweden
250 A4 Mora MN U.S.A.
263 L9 Mora NM U.S.A.
263 L9 Mora r. NM U.S.A.
284 B4 Mora, Cerro mt. Arg./Chile
218 H8 Morača r. Montenegro
160 K9 Morach r. Belarus
145 L7 Morad r. Pak.
138 G5 Moradabad Uttar Prad. India
276 C1 Morada Nova Amazonas Brazil
278 F3 Morada Nova Ceará Brazil
281 E3 Morada Nova de Minas Brazil
208 G5 Móra d'Ebre Spain
209 D7 Mora de Rubielos Spain
205 M5 Moradillo de Roa Spain
151 J6 Morādlū Iran
235 □J3 Morafenobe Madag.
197 H2 Morąg Pol.
199 I5 Mórahalom Hungary
247 J1 Moraine Lake N.W.T. Can.
209 F10 Moraira, Punta de pt Spain
204 G5 Morais Port.
208 G5 Móra la Nova Spain
207 L3 Moral de Calatrava Spain
283 B7 Moraleda, Canal sea chan. Chile
207 L6 Moraleda de Zafayona Spain
204 G8 Moraleja Spain
204 I6 Moraleja del Vino Spain
204 I6 Moraleja de Sayago Spain
266 □O10 Morales Guat.
207 O7 Morales r. Spain
204 I6 Morales del Vino Spain
205 J5 Morales de Toro Spain
204 I5 Morales de Valverde Spain
204 H6 Moralina Spain
136 E4 Moram Mahar. India
235 □K3 Moramanga Madag.
250 J4 Moran MI U.S.A.
262 I5 Moran WY U.S.A.
107 L6 Moranbah Qld Austr.
138 G4 Morang Hima. Prad. India
Morang Nepal see Biratnagar
280 A3 Morangas Brazil
139 O6 Moranhat Assam India
151 J6 Moranlı Azer.
215 Q8 Morano Calabro Italy
212 E5 Morano sul Po Italy
270 □ Morant Bay Jamaica
270 F5 Morant Cays is Jamaica
270 □ Morant Point Jamaica
136 F6 Morappur Tamil Nadu India
168 E9 Morar Highland, Scotland U.K.
168 E9 Morar hills Scotland U.K.
168 E9 Morar, Loch l. Scotland U.K.
138 G3 Morari, Tso l. Jammu and Kashmir India
164 I5 Mörarp Sweden
204 F1 Morás, Punta de pt Spain
204 H7 Morasverdes Spain
205 R6 Morata de Jalón Spain
205 N8 Morata de Tajuña Spain
207 P4 Moratalla Spain
136 F9 Moratuwa Sri Lanka
198 F2 Morava reg. Czech Rep.
201 O3 Morava r. Europe alt. March (Austria)
213 R4 Morava Slovenia
201 O1 Moravany Czech Rep.
199 K3 Moravany Slovakia
235 □K2 Moravato Madag.
201 K8 Moravče Slovenia
Moravia reg. Czech Rep. see Morava
256 I6 Moravia NY U.S.A.
218 I7 Moravica r. Serbia
219 J7 Moravica r. Serbia
199 G2 Moravice r. Czech Rep.
199 H2 Morávka Czech Rep.
198 E3 Moravská Dyje r. Czech Rep.
201 P2 Moravská Nová Ves Czech Rep.
198 F2 Moravská Třebová Czech Rep.
198 E2 Moravské Budějovice Czech Rep.
199 H2 Moravskoslezské Beskydy mts Czech Rep.
199 H2 Moravskoslezský kraj admin. reg. Czech Rep.
198 G2 Moravský Beroun Czech Rep.
Moravský Ján Slovakia see Moravský Svätý Ján
201 N1 Moravský Krumlov Czech Rep.
198 G3 Moravský Písek Czech Rep.
198 G3 Moravský Svätý Ján Slovakia
109 C10 Morawa W.A. Austr.
275 G2 Morawhanna Guyana
197 I5 Morawica Pol.
168 J7 Moray admin. div. Scotland U.K.
107 K6 Moray Downs Qld Austr.
168 H7 Moray Firth b. Scotland U.K.
106 C3 Moray Range hills N.T. Austr.
194 C2 Morbach Ger.
212 H3 Morbegno Italy
138 C8 Morbi Gujarat India
182 I3 Morbier France
180 F6 Morbihan dept France
201 O4 Mörbisch am See Austria
165 M5 Mörbylånga Öland Sweden
185 C7 Morcenx France
217 O4 Morciano di Leuca Italy
213 N8 Morciano di Romagna Italy
268 C1 Morcillo Mex.
215 N5 Morcone Italy
122 B3 Mordaga Nei Mongol China
149 L5 Mor Dağı mt. Turkey
180 H5 Mordelles France
247 L5 Morden Man. Can.
221 H4 Mordoğan Turkey
Mordovia aut. rep. Rus. Fed. see Mordoviya, Respublika
157 I5 Mordoviya, Respublika aut. rep. Rus. Fed.
157 H5 Mordoviya Zapovednik nature res. Rus. Fed.
157 H5 Mordovo Rus. Fed.
Mordovskaya A.S.S.R. aut. rep. Rus. Fed. see Mordoviya, Respublika
161 V7 Mordves Rus. Fed.
Mordvinia aut. rep. Rus. Fed. see Mordoviya, Respublika
244 F5 Mordvinof, Cape AK U.S.A.
159 O7 Mordvynivka Ukr.
197 K3 Mordy Pol.
168 G6 More, Loch l. Highland, Scotland U.K.
168 I6 More, Loch l. Highland, Scotland U.K.
180 F6 Moréac France
206 D5 Moreanes Port.
260 E3 Moreau r. SD U.S.A.
260 D3 Moreau, South Fork r. SD U.S.A.
168 L11 Morebattle Scottish Borders, Scotland U.K.
171 L5 Morecambe Lancashire, England U.K.
171 K5 Morecambe Bay England U.K.
204 I2 Moreda Asturias Spain
205 P3 Moreda País Vasco Spain
105 L3 Moree N.S.W. Austr.
178 B8 Morée France
113 J8 Morehead P.N.G.
256 B10 Morehead KY U.S.A.
255 I8 Morehead City NC U.S.A.
275 F5 Moreira Brazil
204 D6 Moreira do Rei Port.
138 F6 Morel r. India
212 E3 Mörel Switz.
274 C4 Morelia Col.
268 F6 Morelia Mex.
107 I7 Morella Qld Austr.
208 E6 Morella Spain
216 G9 Morello r. Sicilia Italy
268 E3 Morelos Mex.
269 I7 Morelos state Mex.
269 J7 Morelos Cañada Mex.
234 D3 Moremi Wildlife Reserve nature res. Botswana
138 G6 Morena Madh. Prad. India
206 G5 Morena, Sierra mts Spain
265 W8 Morenci AZ U.S.A.
251 J8 Morenci MI U.S.A.
219 N6 Moreni Romania
285 H4 Moreno Arg.
266 D3 Moreno Mex.
264 O8 Moreno Valley CA U.S.A.
205 P3 Morentín Spain
162 I5 Møre og Romsdal county Norway
277 F2 Morerú r. Brazil
204 I5 Moreruela de Tábara Spain
214 B6 Mores Sardegna Italy
245 N5 Moresby, Mount B.C. Can.
245 N5 Moresby Island B.C. Can.
171 J4 Moresby Parks Cumbria, England U.K.
182 G5 Morestel France
107 N9 Moreton Bay Qld Austr.
172 E6 Moretonhampstead Devon, England U.K.
173 I4 Moreton-in-Marsh Gloucestershire, England U.K.
107 N9 Moreton Island Qld Austr.
107 N9 Moreton Island National Park Qld Austr.
172 G2 Moreton Say Shropshire, England U.K.
178 E7 Moret-sur-Loing France
212 D6 Moretta Italy
178 D4 Moreuil France
156 L1 Moreyu r. Rus. Fed.
182 I3 Morez France
172 C2 Morfa Nefyn Gwynedd, Wales U.K.
212 H6 Morfasso Italy
194 F2 Mörfelden Ger.
220 C2 Morfi Greece
150 A3 Morfou Cyprus
150 A3 Morfou Bay Cyprus
162 R2 Morgam-Viibus hill Fin.
104 G6 Morgan S.A. Austr.
255 E10 Morgan GA U.S.A.
256 A10 Morgan KY U.S.A.
264 N4 Morgan, Mount CA U.S.A.
261 J11 Morgan City LA U.S.A.
254 D7 Morganfield KY U.S.A.
264 K4 Morgan Hill CA U.S.A.
255 G8 Morganton NC U.S.A.
254 D7 Morgantown KY U.S.A.
258 D4 Morgantown PA U.S.A.
256 F9 Morgantown WV U.S.A.
259 G4 Morganville NJ U.S.A.
180 B5 Morgat France
206 B5 Morgavel, Barragem de resr Port.
237 N2 Morgenzon S. Africa
212 B2 Morges Switz.
212 C4 Morgex Italy
145 M4 Morgh, Kowtal-e pass Afgh.
145 J4 Morghāb Afgh.
145 J4 Morghāb r. Afgh.
145 J4 Morghāb reg. Afgh.
144 E6 Morghāb Iran
179 M6 Morhange France
139 J7 Morhar r. India
128 B5 Mori Xinjiang China
213 J4 Mori Italy
124 R4 Mori Hokkaidō Japan
127 G6 Mori Shizuoka Japan
271 □[5] Moriah Trin. and Tob.
265 R2 Moriah, Mount NV U.S.A.
263 L9 Moriarty NM U.S.A.
105 J3 Moriarty's Range hills Qld Austr.
228 C4 Moribaya Guinea
171 K4 Moricambe b. England U.K.
246 E4 Morice Lake B.C. Can.
246 E4 Moricetown B.C. Can.
145 O3 Morich Pak.
274 D4 Morichal Col.
259 J3 Moriches Bay NY U.S.A.
215 J3 Moricone Italy
160 F4 Moricsalas rezervāts nature res. Latvia
178 E5 Morienval France
139 N6 Morigaon Assam India
126 C6 Moriguchi Japan
237 L5 Morija Lesotho
229 G3 Moriki Nigeria
207 J6 Moriles Spain
Morin Dawa Nei Mongol China see Nirji
210 G4 Morine pass Bos.-Herz.
191 I7 Moringen Ger.
215 K4 Morino Italy
161 N4 Morino Rus. Fed.
124 S7 Morioka Japan
235 G3 Morire Moz.
266 E3 Moris Mex.
219 O3 Morișca r. Romania
105 M5 Morisset N.S.W. Austr.
168 G8 Moriston r. Scotland U.K.
269 H3 Morita Mex.
193 I8 Moritzburg Ger.
127 K4 Moriya Japan
126 D5 Moriyama Japan
124 R6 Moriyoshi Japan
124 R7 Moriyoshi-zan vol. Japan
162 Q3 Morjärv Sweden
145 J7 Morjen r. Pak.
156 J4 Morki Rus. Fed.
161 T4 Morkiny Gory Rus. Fed.
185 D9 Morlaàs France
180 D4 Morlaix France
180 D4 Morlaix, Baie de b. France
185 C8 Morlanne France
187 F8 Morlanwelz Belgium
194 F2 Mörlenbach Ger.
246 H5 Morley Alta Can.
179 J6 Morley France
171 N6 Morley West Yorkshire, England U.K.
160 M9 Mormal' Belarus
215 Q8 Mormanno Italy
178 E6 Mormant France
183 G8 Mormoiron France
265 U7 Mormon Lake AZ U.S.A.
Mormugao Goa India see Marmagao
182 E5 Mornand France
182 F5 Mornant France
183 F8 Mornas France
271 □[2] Morne-à-l'Eau Guadeloupe
271 □[2] Morne Constant hill Guadeloupe
271 □ Morne Diablotin National Park Dominica
271 □[2] Morne Diablotins vol. Dominica
271 □[2] Morne Macaque vol. Dominica
212 F6 Mornese Italy
239 □[2b] Morne Seychellois hill Mahé Seychelles
271 □[2] Morne Trois Pitons National Park Dominica
107 H8 Morney Qld Austr.
107 H8 Morney watercourse Qld Austr.
283 B8 Mornington, Isla i. Chile
288 D9 Mornington Abyssal Plain sea feature S. Atlantic Ocean
106 G4 Mornington Island Qld Austr.
105 J8 Mornington Peninsula National Park Vic. Austr.
220 C4 Mornos r. Greece
195 K4 Mörnsheim Ger.
145 L8 Moro Pak.
262 D4 Moro OR U.S.A.
205 P9 Moro, Cerro mts Spain
209 C11 Moro, Rambla del r. Spain
113 K8 Morobe P.N.G.
226 D3 Morocco country Africa
250 G9 Morocco IN U.S.A.
158 E2 Morochne Ukr.
261 I9 Moro Creek r. AR U.S.A.
233 C6 Morogoro Tanz.
233 C7 Morogoro admin. reg. Tanz.
114 D8 Moro Gulf Phil.
237 K5 Morojaneng S. Africa
236 H2 Morokweng S. Africa
268 F5 Moroleón Mex.
215 K4 Morolo Italy
115 D7 Moromaho i. Indon.
235 □I4 Morombe Madag.
276 D4 Moromoro Bol.
283 E6 Morón Arg.
270 D2 Morón Cuba
269 J3 Morón Mex.
128 G2 Mörön Mongolia
212 C1 Moron mt. Switz.
271 I8 Morón Venez.
274 B5 Morona Ecuador
274 B6 Morona r. Peru
274 B5 Morona-Santiago prov. Ecuador
235 □J4 Morondava Madag.
205 P6 Morón de Almazán Spain
207 I6 Morón de la Frontera Spain
228 D4 Morondo Côte d'Ivoire
268 D4 Morone, Sierra mts Mex.
128 G5 Moron Gol watercourse China
264 P7 Morongo Valley CA U.S.A.
239 □[3a] Moroni Njazidja Comoros
265 U2 Moroni UT U.S.A.
Moron Us He r. Qinghai China see Tongtian He
205 Q6 Moros Spain
205 L6 Moros r. Spain
214 C3 Morosaglia Corse France
115 F2 Morotai i. Maluku Indon.
115 E2 Morotai, Selat sea chan. Maluku Indon.
232 B4 Moroto Uganda
232 B4 Moroto, Mount Uganda
125 I14 Morotsuka Japan
218 H5 Morović Vojvodina Serbia
271 □[1] Morovis Puerto Rico
103 B12 Morowai South I. N.Z.
115 B4 Morowali, Cagar Alam nature res. Indon.
161 N2 Morozova Rus. Fed.
159 S3 Morozovka Rus. Fed.
161 X5 Morozovo Rus. Fed.
157 H6 Morozovsk Rus. Fed.
212 D7 Morozzo Italy
278 E4 Morpara Brazil
251 M7 Morpeth Ont. Can.
171 N3 Morpeth Northumberland, England U.K.
Morphou Cyprus see Morfou
194 G2 Morre r. Ger.
208 I3 Morreres, Puig de les mt. Spain
280 C6 Morretes Brazil
256 A11 Morrill KY U.S.A.
260 D4 Morrill NE U.S.A.
261 I8 Morrilton AR U.S.A.
246 H5 Morrin Alta Can.
280 C2 Morrinhos Brazil
102 J4 Morrinsville North I. N.Z.
247 L5 Morris Man. Can.
250 F8 Morris IL U.S.A.
260 H3 Morris MN U.S.A.
251 Q8 Morris PA U.S.A.
257 J4 Morrisburg Ont. Can.
258 F3 Morris County county NJ U.S.A.
243 O1 Morris Jesup, Kap c. Greenland
285 F3 Morrison Arg.
250 E8 Morrison IL U.S.A.
103 E12 Morrisons South I. N.Z.
259 G3 Morris Plains NJ U.S.A.
258 B1 Morris Run PA U.S.A.
172 E4 Morriston Swansea, Wales U.K.
265 T8 Morristown AZ U.S.A.
259 G3 Morristown NJ U.S.A.
257 J4 Morristown NY U.S.A.
255 F7 Morristown TN U.S.A.
257 J6 Morrisville NY U.S.A.
258 F4 Morrisville PA U.S.A.
257 M4 Morrisville VT U.S.A.
107 H4 Morr Morr Aboriginal Holding res. Qld Austr.
281 E2 Morro Brazil
214 D5 Morro, Monte hill Italy
282 C2 Morro, Punta pt Chile
280 C4 Morro Agudo Brazil
264 L6 Morro Bay CA U.S.A.
281 H3 Morro d'Anta Brazil
207 J3 Morro del Águila hill Spain
268 F8 Morro de Papanoa hd Mex.
268 F8 Morro de Petatlán hd Mex.
278 E4 Morro do Chapéu Brazil
281 G4 Morro do Coco Brazil
277 G2 Morro do Sinal hills Brazil
269 L9 Morro Mazatán Mex.
215 L3 Morrone, Monte mt. Italy
278 D2 Morros Brazil
274 C2 Morrosquillo, Golfo de b. Col.
213 P9 Morrovalle Italy
235 G3 Morrumbala Moz.
235 G4 Morrumbene Moz.
164 E5 Mors reg. Denmark
191 E9 Morsbach Ger.
194 F2 Morsberg hill Ger.
191 I8 Morschen Ger.
247 J5 Morse Sask. Can.
261 E7 Morse TX U.S.A.
250 D3 Morse WI U.S.A.
287 I2 Morse, Cape Antarctica
157 H5 Morshanka Rus. Fed.
Morshansk Rus. Fed. see Morshanka
158 C4 Morshyn Ukr.
138 G9 Morsi Mahar. India
151 I1 Morskaya Chapura, Ostrov i. Rus. Fed.
156 F3 Morskaya Masel'ga Rus. Fed.
159 N9 Mors'ke Ukr.
193 D6 Morsleben Ger.
190 H5 Morsum Ger.
162 M3 Mørsvikbotn Norway
106 H7 Mort watercourse Qld Austr.
247 I2 Mort, Lac du l. N.W.T. Can.
179 L6 Mortagne r. France
181 M4 Mortagne-au-Perche France
184 C5 Mortagne-sur-Gironde France
184 C1 Mortagne-sur-Sèvre France
204 D8 Mortágua Port.
181 J4 Mortain France
212 F5 Mortara Italy
182 H2 Morte r. France
182 J2 Morteau France
181 K4 Morteaux-Coulibœuf France
172 D5 Morte Bay England U.K.
178 E5 Mortefontaine France
213 O4 Mortegliano Italy
172 D5 Mortehoe Devon, England U.K.
217 J7 Mortelle Sicilia Italy
285 G2 Morteros Arg.
268 E1 Morteros Mex.
281 E4 Mortes, Rio das r. Brazil
278 C4 Mortes, Rio das r. Brazil
237 J8 Mortimer S. Africa
173 J5 Mortimer West Berkshire, England U.K.
270 F2 Mortimer's Long I. Bahamas
172 G3 Mortimer's Cross Herefordshire, England U.K.
247 J5 Mortlach Sask. Can.
105 I8 Mortlake Vic. Austr.
290 F5 Mortlock Islands Micronesia
Mortlock Islands P.N.G. see Takuu Islands
173 L2 Morton Lincolnshire, England U.K.
171 P7 Morton Lincolnshire, England U.K.
250 E9 Morton IL U.S.A.
261 D9 Morton TX U.S.A.
262 C3 Morton WA U.S.A.
105 M6 Morton National Park N.S.W. Austr.
214 D5 Mortorio, Isola i. Sardegna Italy
181 L4 Mortrée France
200 G6 Mörtschach Austria
187 F6 Mortsel Belgium
271 □[7] Moruga Trin. and Tob.
271 □[7] Moruga Point Trin. and Tob.
105 K6 Morundah N.S.W. Austr.
232 B4 Morungole mt. Uganda
235 E4 Morupule Botswana
Moruroa atoll Arch. des Tuamotu Fr. Polynesia see Mururoa
105 M6 Moruya N.S.W. Austr.
182 D2 Morvan hills France
182 E2 Morvan, Parc Naturel Régional du nature res. France
107 K9 Morven Qld Austr.
103 F11 Morven South I. N.Z.
168 J8 Morven hill Aberdeenshire, Scotland U.K.
168 I6 Morven hill Highland, Scotland U.K.
168 E9 Morvern reg. Scotland U.K.
Morvi Gujarat India see Morbi
172 H2 Morville Shropshire, England U.K.
105 K8 Morwell Vic. Austr.
172 C6 Morwenstow Cornwall, England U.K.
161 O1 Mor'ye Rus. Fed.
196 C3 Moryń Pol.
196 G2 Morzeszczyn Pol.
156 H2 Morzhovets, Ostrov i. Rus. Fed.
244 G5 Morzhovoi Bay AK U.S.A.
182 J4 Morzine France
161 R7 Mosal'sk Rus. Fed.
158 G5 Moșana Moldova
194 G3 Mosbach Ger.
171 O7 Mosborough South Yorkshire, England U.K.
262 K3 Mosby MT U.S.A.
209 I9 Moscarter, Punta des pt Spain
206 A3 Moscavide Port.
213 Q5 Mošćenička Draga Croatia
213 L8 Moscia r. Italy
215 L2 Mosciano Sant'Angelo Italy
Moscow Rus. Fed. see Moskva
262 F3 Moscow ID U.S.A.
258 D2 Moscow PA U.S.A.
Moscow Oblast admin. div. Rus. Fed. see Moskovskaya Oblast'
287 I2 Moscow University Ice Shelf Antarctica
193 F9 Mosel Ger.
191 E10 Mosel r. Ger.
234 D5 Moselebe watercourse Botswana
256 H11 Moseley VA U.S.A.
179 M5 Moselle dept France
179 L5 Moselle r. France
193 E6 Möser Ger.
264 O1 Moses, Mount NV U.S.A.
262 E3 Moses Lake WA U.S.A.
244 G2 Moses Point AK U.S.A.
234 E4 Mosetse Botswana
156 I2 Moseyevo Rus. Fed.
103 E12 Mosgiel South I. N.Z.
256 G7 Moshannon PA U.S.A.
236 G2 Moshaweng watercourse S. Africa
160 K2 Moshchnyy, Ostrov i. Rus. Fed.
161 R3 Moshenskoye Rus. Fed.
251 J1 Mosher Ont. Can.
144 F7 Moshgān Iran
229 G4 Moshi r. Nigeria
233 C5 Moshi Tanz.
159 K4 Moshny Ukr.
156 K2 Mosh'yuga Rus. Fed.
196 E3 Mosina Pol.
250 E5 Mosinee WI U.S.A.
Mosi-oa-Tunya National Park Zimbabwe see Victoria Falls National Park
237 I2 Mosita S. Africa
162 L4 Mosjøen Norway
122 M2 Moskal'vo Sakhalin Rus. Fed.
162 P2 Moskángáisi mt. Norway
162 L3 Moskenesøy i. Norway
162 L3 Moskenestraumen sea chan. Norway
197 H5 Moskorzew Pol.
162 O4 Moskosel Sweden
161 V6 Moskovskaya Oblast' admin. div. Rus. Fed.
Moskovskiy Uzbek. see Shahrihon
159 S2 Moskovskoye Rus. Fed.
161 U6 Moskva Rus. Fed.
161 V6 Moskva r. Rus. Fed.
145 M3 Moskva Tajik.
161 U5 Moskvy, Kanal imeni canal Rus. Fed.
199 G6 Moslavna Podravska Croatia
284 D3 Mosmota Arg.
219 P4 Moșna Romania
199 K6 Moșnița Nouă Romania
100 □[5] Moso i. Vanuatu
213 K2 Moso in Passiria Italy
198 G4 Mosonmagyaróvár Hungary
210 F4 Mosor mts Croatia
199 H3 Mošovce Slovakia
159 P4 Mos'panove Ukr.
159 R6 Mospyne Ukr.
274 B4 Mosquera Col.
263 L9 Mosquero NM U.S.A.
209 E7 Mosqueruela Spain
266 □R10 Mosquitia reg. Hond.
271 □[1] Mosquito Puerto Rico
256 E7 Mosquito Creek Lake OH U.S.A.
247 K2 Mosquito Lake N.W.T. Can.
244 H3 Mosquito Mountain hill AK U.S.A.
266 □S13 Mosquitos, Golfo de los b. Panama
164 G2 Moss Norway
230 C5 Mossaka Congo
Mossâmedes Angola see Namibe
280 B2 Mossâmedes Brazil
168 K8 Mossat Aberdeenshire, Scotland U.K.
103 C12 Mossburn South I. N.Z.
Mosselbaai S. Africa see Mossel Bay
236 G10 Mossel Bay S. Africa
236 G10 Mossel Bay b. S. Africa
231 B5 Mossendjo Congo
185 I10 Mosset France
105 J5 Mossgiel N.S.W. Austr.
237 N1 Mossiesdal S. Africa
194 G5 Mössingen Ger.
170 F4 Mossley Northern Ireland U.K.
107 J4 Mossman Qld Austr.
164 F5 Mossø l. Denmark
209 H9 Mossons, Cap des c. Spain
278 F3 Mossoró Brazil
169 J2 Moss-side Northern Ireland U.K.
168 J7 Mosstodloch Moray, Scotland U.K.
235 I2 Mossuril Moz.
105 M6 Moss Vale N.S.W. Austr.
247 K4 Mossy r. Sask. Can.
219 N9 Most Bulg.
198 C1 Most Czech Rep.
217 □ Mosta Malta
144 F5 Moșṭafáābād Iran
227 F2 Mostaganem Alg.
210 F4 Mostar Bos.-Herz.
279 C9 Mostardas Brazil
206 D5 Mosteiro Beja Port.
204 E9 Mosteiro Castelo Branco Port.
204 F2 Mosteiro Galicia Spain
238 □[1b] Mosteiros São Miguel Azores
219 N6 Moșteni Romania
219 O6 Mostiștea r. Romania
197 I2 Mostkowo Warmińsko-Mazurskie Pol.
196 D3 Mostkowo Zachodniopomorskie Pol.
201 I7 Most na Soči Slovenia
205 M8 Móstoles Spain
247 I4 Mostoos Hills Sask. Can.
158 J6 Mostove Ukr.
151 B1 Mostovskoy Rus. Fed.
197 J3 Mostówka Pol.
Mosty Belarus see Masty
197 L4 Mosty Pol.
117 M2 Mostyn Sabah Malaysia
158 C4 Mostys'ka Ukr.
197 L6 Mostys'ka Druha Ukr.
234 E4 Mosu Botswana
Mosul Iraq see Al Mawṣil
132 H4 Mosuowan Xinjiang China
164 E2 Møsvatn Austfjell park Norway
164 E2 Møsvatnet l. Norway
162 K5 Mosvik Norway
197 M4 Mosyr Ukr.
197 H4 Moszczenica Pol.
232 C2 Mot'a Eth.
100 □[5] Mota i. Vanuatu
230 C4 Motaba r. Congo
207 N2 Mota del Cuervo Spain
205 J5 Mota del Marqués Spain
267 O10 Motagua r. Guat.
130 B6 Motai Myanmar
158 E1 Motal' Belarus
165 L3 Motala Sweden
100 □[5] Mota Lava i. Vanuatu
196 F1 Motarzyno Pol.
235 G5 Motaze Moz.
219 O3 Moțca Romania
127 L2 Motegi Japan
230 C4 Motenge-Boma Dem. Rep. Congo
237 M4 Moteng Pass Lesotho
235 F5 Motetema S. Africa
138 G7 Moth Uttar Prad. India
244 H4 Mother Goose Lake AK U.S.A.
168 I11 Motherwell North Lanarkshire, Scotland U.K.
236 H3 Mothibistad S. Africa
220 E6 Mothonaio, Akrotirio pt Kythira Greece
115 E3 Moti i. Maluku Indon.
123 C8 Motian Ling hill Liaoning China
212 B2 Môtiers Switz.
139 J6 Motihari Bihar India
207 I3 Motilla hill Spain
205 Q9 Motilla del Palancar Spain
102 K4 Motiti Island North I. N.Z.
165 J2 Motjärnshyttan Sweden
235 F4 Motloutse r. Botswana
124 □[1] Motobu Okinawa Japan
124 □[1] Motobu-hantō pen. Okinawa Japan
275 E3 Motocurunya Venez.
234 D5 Motokwe Botswana
127 L4 Motono Japan
205 Q7 Motos Spain
126 E5 Motosu Japan
127 I5 Motosu-ko l. Japan
162 V2 Motovskiy Zaliv sea chan. Rus. Fed.
213 P5 Motovun Croatia
125 □[3] Moto-yama hill Iō-jima Japan
124 S8 Motoyoshi Japan
267 M10 Motozintla Mex.
207 L7 Motril Spain
219 K6 Motru Romania
219 L6 Motru r. Romania
237 L1 Motshikiri S. Africa
236 I5 Motswedimosa S. Africa
260 D2 Mott ND U.S.A.
118 C6 Mottama Myanmar
118 C6 Mottama, Gulf of Myanmar
215 O4 Motta Montecorvino Italy
217 J7 Motta San Giovanni Italy
212 F5 Motta Visconti Italy
191 I10 Motten Ger.
195 J4 Möttingen Ger.
276 D7 Motto Botello Arg.
217 M2 Mottola Italy
103 H8 Motueka South I. N.Z.
103 □[1] Motu Fakataga i. Tokelau
Motuhora Island North I. N.Z. see Moutohora Island
Motu Ihupuku i. N.Z. see Campbell Island
Motuiti i. Fr. Polynesia see Motu Iti
101 □[9] Motu Iti i. Fr. Polynesia
103 G10 Motukarara South I. N.Z.
267 O7 Motul Mex.
103 H10 Motunau Island South I. N.Z.
101 □[9] Motu One atoll Arch. de la Société Fr. Polynesia
101 □[9] Motu One i. Fr. Polynesia
103 G8 Motupiko South I. N.Z.
102 G7 Motupipi South I. N.Z.
101 □[7a] Moturiki i. Fiji
102 H1 Motutangi North I. N.Z.
103 □[3] Motutapu i. Rarotonga Cook Is
200 C5 Mötz Austria
164 G5 Mou Denmark
230 C4 Mouali Gbangba Congo
118 G5 Mouan, Nam r. Laos
229 H6 Mouanko Cameroon
183 J9 Mouans-Sartoux France
Mouaskar Alg. see Mascara
287 L2 Moubray Bay Antarctica
249 G3 Mouchalagane r. Que. Can.
181 I8 Mouchamps France
185 E8 Mouchan France
182 H3 Mouchard France
183 C7 Mouchet, Mont mt. France
270 H3 Mouchoir Bank sea feature Turks and Caicos Is
270 H3 Mouchoir Passage Turks and Caicos Is
204 E6 Mouçós Port.
130 C6 Mouding Yunnan China
228 B2 Moudjéria Maur.
212 B2 Moudon Switz.
220 G3 Moudros Limnos Greece
230 C2 Moufa Chad
183 K9 Mougins France
228 B2 Mougri well Maur.
163 Q6 Mouhijärvi Fin.
228 E4 Mouhoun r. Africa alt. Volta Noire, conv. Black Volta
230 A5 Mouila Gabon
227 E4 Mouilah well Alg.
181 J8 Mouilleron-en-Pareds France
230 D3 Mouka C.A.R.
229 I3 Moul well Niger
105 J6 Moulamein N.S.W. Austr.
105 I6 Moulamein Creek r. N.S.W. Austr.
185 I7 Moularès France
Moulavibazar Bangl. see Moulvibazar
181 J5 Moulay France
271 □[3] Moule à Chique, Cape St Lucia
231 A5 Moulèngui Binza Gabon
228 D2 Moulentâr well Mali
185 F6 Mouleydier France
232 D1 Moulhoulé Djibouti
181 L7 Mouliherne France
185 H9 Moulin-Neuf France
182 C3 Moulins France
182 D3 Moulins-Engilbert France
181 L4 Moulins-la-Marche France
185 G10 Moulis France
184 C5 Moulis-en-Médoc France
184 F3 Moulismes France
185 D9 Moulle de Jaut, Pic du mt. France
Moulmein Myanmar see Mawlamyaing
226 E2 Moulouya r. Morocco
173 L6 Moulsecoomb Brighton and Hove, England U.K.
181 K3 Moult France
173 L2 Moulton Lincolnshire, England U.K.
173 K3 Moulton Northamptonshire, England U.K.
173 M3 Moulton Suffolk, England U.K.
255 D8 Moulton AL U.S.A.
286 P1 Moulton, Mount Antarctica
257 N5 Moultonborough NH U.S.A.
255 F10 Moultrie GA U.S.A.
255 H9 Moultrie, Lake SC U.S.A.
139 M7 Moulvibazar Bangl.
Moumolu-Naunitu i. Solomon Is see San Jorge
230 B5 Mounana Gabon
261 K7 Mound City IL U.S.A.
260 H6 Mound City KS U.S.A.
260 H5 Mound City MO U.S.A.
260 E3 Mound City SD U.S.A.
230 C2 Moundou Chad
256 E9 Moundsville WV U.S.A.
255 D9 Moundville AL U.S.A.
230 B5 Moungoundou-Sud Congo
183 J8 Mounier, Mont mt. France
220 B4 Mounta, Akrotirio pt Kefallonia Greece
220 B4 Mounta, Akrotirio pt Greece
138 D7 Mount Abu Rajasthan India
258 C4 Mount Aetna PA U.S.A.
245 O2 Mountain r. N.W.T. Can.
263 K9 Mountainair NM U.S.A.
172 F4 Mountain Ash Rhondda Cynon Taff, Wales U.K.
255 D9 Mountain Brook AL U.S.A.
256 D12 Mountain City TN U.S.A.
261 I7 Mountain Grove MO U.S.A.
261 I7 Mountain Home AR U.S.A.
262 G5 Mountain Home ID U.S.A.
258 E2 Mountainhome PA U.S.A.
265 V1 Mountain Home UT U.S.A.
250 B2 Mountain Iron MN U.S.A.
256 F9 Mountain Lake Park MD U.S.A.
259 G3 Mountain Lakes NJ U.S.A.
265 Q6 Mountain Pass CA U.S.A.
258 D2 Mountain Top PA U.S.A.
261 I8 Mountain View AR U.S.A.
264 J4 Mountain View CA U.S.A.
264 □F14 Mountain View HI U.S.A.
244 G3 Mountain Village AK U.S.A.
237 J8 Mountain Zebra National Park S. Africa
258 A6 Mount Airy MD U.S.A.
256 E12 Mount Airy NC U.S.A.
108 G4 Mount Anderson Aboriginal Reserve W.A. Austr.
104 H7 Mount Arapiles-Tooan State Park nature res. Vic. Austr.
258 F3 Mount Arlington NJ U.S.A.
103 C11 Mount Aspiring National Park South I. N.Z.
246 H5 Mount Assiniboine Provincial Park B.C. Can.
109 D8 Mount Augustus W.A. Austr.
237 N6 Mount Ayliff S. Africa
260 H5 Mount Ayr IA U.S.A.
264 O7 Mount Baldy CA U.S.A.
104 G6 Mount Barker S.A. Austr.
109 D13 Mount Barker W.A. Austr.
108 H4 Mount Barnett W.A. Austr.
108 I4 Mount Barnett Aboriginal Reserve W.A. Austr.
105 K7 Mount Beauty Vic. Austr.
169 F6 Mountbellew Ireland
168 J11 Mountbenger Scottish Borders, Scotland U.K.
102 J7 Mount Bruce North I. N.Z.
251 M7 Mount Brydges Ont. Can.
105 K7 Mount Buffalo National Park Vic. Austr.
107 J4 Mount Carbine Qld Austr.
257 □S1 Mount Carleton Provincial Park N.B. Can.
254 D6 Mount Carmel IL U.S.A.
258 C3 Mount Carmel PA U.S.A.
256 C12 Mount Carmel TN U.S.A.
265 T4 Mount Carmel Junction UT U.S.A.
250 E7 Mount Carroll IL U.S.A.
106 D8 Mount Cavenagh N.T. Austr.
169 F3 Mountcharles Ireland
109 D8 Mount Clere W.A. Austr.
169 D8 Mountcollins Ireland
Mount Cook South I. N.Z. see Aoraki
107 K6 Mount Coolon Qld Austr.
237 N6 Mount Currie Nature Reserve S. Africa
235 F3 Mount Darwin Zimbabwe
106 D7 Mount Denison N.T. Austr.
257 □Q4 Mount Desert Island ME U.S.A.
104 E4 Mount Eba S.A. Austr.
106 D8 Mount Ebenezer N.T. Austr.
104 H8 Mount Eccles National Park Vic. Austr.
246 C3 Mount Edgecumbe AK U.S.A.
246 D3 Mount Edziza Provincial Park B.C. Can.
261 H10 Mount Enterprise TX U.S.A.
250 I9 Mount Etna IN U.S.A.
170 C4 Mountfield Northern Ireland U.K.
105 K10 Mount Field National Park Tas. Austr.
237 M6 Mount Fletcher S. Africa
248 D5 Mount Forest Ont. Can.
109 D13 Mount Frankland National Park W.A. Austr.
237 M6 Mount Frere S. Africa
104 H7 Mount Gambier S.A. Austr.
107 J4 Mount Garnet Qld Austr.
256 C11 Mount Gay WV U.S.A.
256 C8 Mount Gilead OH U.S.A.
113 J8 Mount Hagen P.N.G.
170 C4 Mount Hamilton Northern Ireland U.K.
258 F5 Mount Holly NJ U.S.A.
258 A4 Mount Holly Springs PA U.S.A.
105 J5 Mount Hope N.S.W. Austr.
104 E6 Mount Hope S.A. Austr.
256 D11 Mount Hope WV U.S.A.
250 E6 Mount Horeb WI U.S.A.
108 H4 Mount House W.A. Austr.
107 I9 Mount Howitt Qld Austr.
103 F10 Mount Hutt South I. N.Z.
261 I8 Mount Ida AR U.S.A.
105 L7 Mount Imlay National Park N.S.W. Austr.
106 G6 Mount Isa Qld Austr.
256 G10 Mount Jackson VA U.S.A.
109 D8 Mount James Aboriginal Reserve W.A. Austr.
256 G7 Mount Jewett PA U.S.A.
169 H3 Mountjoy Northern Ireland U.K.
169 I3 Mountjoy Northern Ireland U.K.
258 B4 Mount Joy PA U.S.A.

105 M4 Mount Kaputar National Park N.S.W. Austr.
109 F9 Mount Keith W.A. Austr.
232 C5 Mount Kenya National Park Kenya
259 H2 Mount Kisco NY U.S.A.
107 M7 Mount Larcom Qld Austr.
256 E8 Mount Lebanon PA U.S.A.
104 G6 Mount Lofty Range mts S.A. Austr.
251 N2 Mount MacDonald Ont. Can.
109 D10 Mount Magnet W.A. Austr.
105 I5 Mount Manara N.S.W. Austr.
109 E10 Mount Manning Nature Reserve W.A. Austr.
102 K4 Mount Maunganui North I. N.Z.
Mount McKinley National Park U.S.A. see Denali National Park and Preserve
264 L1 Mount Meadows Reservoir CA U.S.A.
169 H6 Mountmellick Ireland
107 J4 Mount Molloy Qld Austr.
237 L6 Mount Moorosi Lesotho
107 M7 Mount Morgan Qld Austr.
250 E7 Mount Morris IL U.S.A.
251 K6 Mount Morris MI U.S.A.
256 H6 Mount Morris NY U.S.A.
105 I4 Mount Murchison N.S.W. Austr.
256 E10 Mount Nebo WV U.S.A.
169 J4 Mount Norris Northern Ireland U.K.
169 H5 Mount Nugent Ireland
256 A10 Mount Olivet KY U.S.A.
256 B9 Mount Orab OH U.S.A.
249 K4 Mount Pearl Nfld and Lab. Can.
258 D4 Mount Penn PA U.S.A.
107 M8 Mount Perry Qld Austr.
108 I5 Mount Pierre Aboriginal Reserve W.A. Austr.
103 D11 Mount Pisa South I. N.Z.
104 G6 Mount Pleasant S.A. Austr.
255 □² Mount Pleasant New Prov. Bahamas
249 H4 Mount Pleasant P.E.I. Can.
260 J5 Mount Pleasant IA U.S.A.
250 J6 Mount Pleasant MI U.S.A.
256 F8 Mount Pleasant PA U.S.A.
255 H9 Mount Pleasant SC U.S.A.
261 H9 Mount Pleasant TX U.S.A.
265 U2 Mount Pleasant UT U.S.A.
258 A3 Mount Pleasant Mills PA U.S.A.
258 E2 Mount Pocono PA U.S.A.
258 B7 Mount Rainier MD U.S.A.
262 D3 Mount Rainier National Park WA U.S.A.
169 H6 Mountrath Ireland
104 G5 Mount Remarkable National Park S.A. Austr.
246 G5 Mount Revelstoke National Park B.C. Can.
103 H8 Mount Richmond Forest Park nature res. South I. N.Z.
246 G4 Mount Robson Provincial Park B.C. Can.
256 D12 Mount Rogers National Recreation Area park VA U.S.A.
236 I4 Mount Rupert S. Africa
262 C3 Mount St Helens National Volcanic Monument nat. park WA U.S.A.
258 F3 Mount Salem NJ U.S.A.
106 C4 Mount Sanford N.T. Austr.
172 B7 Mount's Bay England U.K.
104 G5 Mount Searle Aboriginal Land res. Australia
169 F7 Mountshannon Ireland
262 C6 Mount Shasta CA U.S.A.
103 F10 Mount Somers South I. N.Z.
173 J2 Mountsorrel Leicestershire, England U.K.
260 J6 Mount Sterling IL U.S.A.
256 B10 Mount Sterling KY U.S.A.
256 B9 Mount Sterling OH U.S.A.
236 I9 Mount Stewart S. Africa
256 F9 Mount Storm WV U.S.A.
107 J5 Mount Surprise Qld Austr.
106 E7 Mount Swan N.T. Austr.
169 F5 Mount Talbot Ireland
256 H8 Mount Union PA U.S.A.
257 J6 Mount Upton NY U.S.A.
109 E8 Mount Vernon W.A. Austr.
261 K10 Mount Vernon AL U.S.A.
255 F9 Mount Vernon GA U.S.A.
260 K6 Mount Vernon IL U.S.A.
254 D7 Mount Vernon IN U.S.A.
256 A11 Mount Vernon KY U.S.A.
261 I7 Mount Vernon MO U.S.A.
259 H3 Mount Vernon NY U.S.A.
256 C8 Mount Vernon OH U.S.A.
261 H9 Mount Vernon TX U.S.A.
262 C2 Mount Vernon WA U.S.A.
258 C4 Mountville PA U.S.A.
106 D7 Mount Wedge N.T. Austr.
104 E5 Mount Wedge S.A. Austr.
108 D6 Mount Welcome Aboriginal Reserve W.A. Austr.
105 L9 Mount William National Park Tas. Austr.
104 E2 Mount Willoughby S.A. Austr.
258 B4 Mount Wolf PA U.S.A.
258 B7 Mount Zion MD U.S.A.
107 L8 Moura Qld Austr.
275 F5 Moura Brazil
276 B1 Moura r. Brazil
206 E4 Moura Port.
206 E4 Mourão Port.
230 D2 Mouraya Chad
224 D5 Mourdi, Dépression du depr. Chad
228 D3 Mourdiah Mali
204 D5 Moure Port.
185 C9 Mourenx France
183 F9 Mouriès France
204 D7 Mourisca do Vouga Port.
204 D9 Mouriscas Port.
178 H5 Mourmelon-le-Grand France
170 C4 Mourne r. Northern Ireland U.K.
169 J4 Mourne Mountains hills Northern Ireland U.K.
239 □1c Mourouvin, Forêt reg. Réunion
183 I9 Mourre de Chanier mt. France
183 G9 Mourre Nègre mt. France
220 G3 Mourtzeflos, Akrotirio pt Limnos Greece
168 □N2 Mousa i. Scotland U.K.
187 D7 Mouscron Belgium
187 D7 Mouscron dept Belgium
230 C2 Mousgougou Chad
256 C11 Mousie KY U.S.A.
183 E9 Moussac France
230 C2 Moussafoyo Chad
183 B10 Moussan France
179 N7 Moussey France
224 C5 Mousso well Chad
224 C6 Moussoro Chad
185 I9 Moussoulens France
182 C2 Moussy France
180 E4 Moustéru France
185 C7 Moustey France
183 I9 Moustiers-Ste-Marie France
231 B5 Moutamba Congo
182 I3 Mouthe France
182 G3 Mouthier-en-Bresse France
182 I2 Mouthier-Haute-Pierre France
184 E4 Mouthiers-sur-Boëme France
256 D12 Mouth of Wilson VA U.S.A.
185 J10 Mouthoumet France
212 C1 Moutier Switz.
184 I3 Moutier-d'Ahun France
182 J6 Moûtiers France
184 B3 Moutiers-les-Mauxfaits France
201 O1 Moutnice Czech Rep.
102 K4 Moutohora Island North I. N.Z.
115 B3 Moutong Sulawesi Indon.
229 I4 Moutourwa Cameroon
183 B10 Moux France
182 E2 Moux-en-Morvan France
178 D5 Mouy France
227 F4 Mouydir, Monts du plat. Alg.
231 B5 Mouyondzi Congo
220 C3 Mouzaki Greece
224 B6 Mouzarak Chad
179 J5 Mouzay France
179 J4 Mouzon France
179 K7 Mouzon r. France
266 E3 Movas Mex.
144 C6 Moveyleh Iran
219 P5 Movila Miresii Romania
219 M6 Movileni Romania
169 H2 Moville Ireland
108 G4 Mowanjum Aboriginal Reserve W.A. Austr.
107 M9 Mowbullan, Mount Qld Austr.
160 I8 Mowchadz' Belarus
168 L9 Mowtie Aberdeenshire, Scotland U.K.
256 C9 Moxahala OH U.S.A.
270 E1 Moxey Town Andros Bahamas
231 C8 Moxico prov. Angola
257 □P3 Moxie, Lake ME U.S.A.
169 D4 Moy r. Ireland
168 H8 Moy Highland, Scotland U.K.
169 I4 Moy Northern Ireland U.K.
238 □3f Moya Gran Canaria Canary Is
239 □3 Moya Nzwani Comoros
209 C8 Moya Castilla-La Mancha Spain
Moya Cataluña Spain see Moià
268 D4 Moyahua Mex.
232 C4 Moyale Eth.
228 B4 Moyamba Sierra Leone
169 B5 Moyard Ireland
Moycullen Ireland see Maigh Cuilinn
178 F4 Moy-de-l'Aisne France
226 D2 Moyen Atlas mts Morocco
230 C2 Moyen-Chari pref. Chad
Moyen Congo country Africa see Congo
237 L6 Moyeni Lesotho
179 M7 Moyenmoutier France
239 □2b Moyenne, Île i. Inner Islands Seychelles
228 B4 Moyenne-Guinée admin. reg. Guinea
178 C3 Moyenneville France
230 A5 Moyen-Ogooué prov. Gabon
169 I5 Moyer hill Ireland
179 L5 Moyeuvre-Grande France
169 I4 Moygashel Northern Ireland U.K.
169 D4 Moylaw Ireland
170 C6 Moylett Ireland
169 E6 Moylough Ireland
161 S8 Moylovo Rus. Fed.
169 I5 Moynalty Ireland
Moynaq Uzbek. see Mo'ynoq
169 G5 Moyne Ireland
142 H6 Mo'ynoq Uzbek.
231 E5 Moyo Dem. Rep. Congo
117 L9 Moyo i. Indon.
232 A4 Moyo Uganda
274 B6 Moyobamba Peru
170 D4 Moyola r. Northern Ireland U.K.
233 A6 Moyowosi r. Tanz.
233 A5 Moyowosi Game Reserve res. Tanzania
162 M2 Møysalen mt. Norway
224 C6 Moyto Chad
133 D8 Moyu Xinjiang China
232 C4 Moyum waterhole Kenya
169 I6 Moyvalley Ireland
169 D7 Moyvane Ireland
170 B6 Moyvore Ireland
170 B7 Moyvoughly Ireland
143 O5 Moyynkum Kazakh.
143 O6 Moyynkum Kazakh.
143 L4 Moyynkum, Peski des. Kazakh.
143 M5 Moyynkum, Peski des. Kazakh.
143 O4 Moyynty Kazakh.
182 C5 Mozac France
235 G4 Mozambique country Africa
235 I4 Mozambique Channel Africa
289 G6 Mozambique Ridge sea feature Indian Ocean
204 I7 Mozárbez Spain
151 F2 Mozdok Rus. Fed.
256 B11 Mozelle KY U.S.A.
204 E7 Mozelos Port.
159 P4 Mozh r. Ukr.
160 M7 Mozha r. Belarus
159 S5 Mozhayevka Rus. Fed.
161 T6 Mozhaysk Rus. Fed.
156 K4 Mozhga Rus. Fed.
130 A2 Mozhong Qinghai China
201 K7 Mozirje Slovenia
201 K7 Mozirske planine mts Slovenia
118 B3 Mozo Myanmar
159 L4 Mozoliyivka Ukr.
205 L6 Mozoncillo Spain
199 G5 Mozsgó Hungary
Mozyr' Belarus see Mazyr
197 J1 Mozyr' Rus. Fed.
228 A3 Mpal Senegal
233 A6 Mpanda Tanz.
234 E3 Mpandamatenga Botswana
233 A7 Mpande Zambia
230 B5 Mpé Congo
237 O3 Mpemvana S. Africa
228 D3 Mpessoba Mali
237 M8 Mpetu S. Africa
232 B4 Mpigi Uganda
233 A7 Mpika Zambia
237 K8 Mpofu Game Reserve nature res. S. Africa
230 C3 Mpoko r. C.A.R.
237 O5 Mpolweni S. Africa
231 F8 Mpongwe Zambia
231 F7 Mporokoso Zambia
237 Q4 Mposa S. Africa
230 C5 Mpouya Congo
233 A7 Mpui Tanz.
233 A7 Mpulungu Zambia
237 O5 Mpumalanga S. Africa
237 N2 Mpumalanga prov. S. Africa
233 C6 Mpwapwa Tanz.
217 □ Mqabba Malta
237 M7 Mqanduli S. Africa
Mqinvartsveri mt. Georgia/Rus. Fed. see Kazbek
197 J2 Mrągowo Pol.
195 N3 Mrákov Czech Rep.
157 L5 Mrakovo Rus. Fed.
118 A4 Mrauk-U Myanmar
Mrewa Zimbabwe see Murehwa
210 E3 Mrežnica r. Croatia
210 F3 Mrkonjić-Grad Bos.-Herz.
213 R5 Mrkopalj Croatia
196 F2 Mrocza Pol.
196 F4 Mroczeń Pol.
197 I4 Mroczków Pol.
197 H2 Mroczno Pol.
197 H3 Mroga r. Pol.
197 J3 Mrozy Pol.
159 K2 Mryn Ukr.
227 H2 M'Saken Tunisia
233 C6 Msambweni Kenya
233 C6 Msata Tanz.
196 E1 Mścice Pol.
198 D1 Mšeno Czech Rep.
160 M2 Mshinskaya Rus. Fed.
227 G2 M'Sila Alg.
161 R4 Msta Rus. Fed.
161 O3 Msta r. Rus. Fed.
161 P3 Mstinskiy Most Rus. Fed.
Mstislavl' Belarus see Mstsislaw
197 H5 Mstów Pol.
161 O7 Mstsislaw Belarus
237 Q3 Msunduze r. S. Africa
197 I6 Mszana Dolna Pol.
197 I4 Mszczonów Pol.
233 A6 Mtakuja Tanz.
233 C7 Mtama Tanz.
151 G3 Mt'at'ushet'is Nakrdzali nature res. Georgia
232 B4 Mtelo Kenya
233 B6 Mtera Reservoir Tanz.
237 M7 Mthatha S. Africa
237 N7 Mthatha r. S. Africa
237 M7 Mthatha Dam resr S. Africa
Mtoko Zimbabwe see Mutoko
237 P4 Mtonjaneni S. Africa
Mtorashanga Zimbabwe see Mutorashanga
239 □3b Mtsamboro Mayotte
239 □3b Mtsangamouji Mayotte
161 T8 Mtsensk Rus. Fed.
151 F4 Mts'khet'a Georgia
235 G6 Mtubatuba S. Africa
233 C7 Mtukula Tanz.
237 P4 Mtunzini S. Africa
233 D7 Mtwara Tanz.
233 C7 Mtwara admin. reg. Tanz.
118 B4 Mu r. Myanmar
206 C6 Mu hill Port.
101 □8a Mu'a Tongatapu Tonga
Mu'āb, Jibāl reg. Jordan see Moab
233 C8 Muaguide Moz.
235 G2 Mualadzi Moz.
235 H3 Mualama Moz.
278 C2 Muana Brazil
231 B6 Muanda Dem. Rep. Congo
118 G4 Muang Ham Laos
118 F4 Muang Hiam Laos
118 G6 Muang Hinboun Laos
118 E5 Muang Hôngsa Laos
130 D8 Muang Hounxianghoung Laos
118 F5 Muang Kao Laos
118 E5 Muang Khi Laos
119 G7 Muang Không Laos
118 G7 Muang Khôngxédôn Laos
118 F4 Muang Khoua Laos
118 G5 Muang Mok Laos
118 F4 Muang Ngoy Laos
118 H6 Muang Nong Laos
118 E3 Muang Ou Nua Laos
118 E5 Muang Pakbeng Laos
118 E4 Muang Paktha Laos
118 G6 Muang Phalan Laos
118 E5 Muang Phiang Laos
118 H6 Muang Phin Laos
118 G7 Muang Sam Sip Thai.
118 E4 Muang Sing Laos
118 G6 Muang Songkhon Laos
118 F5 Muang Soum Laos
118 F5 Muang Souy Laos
118 E5 Muang Thadua Laos
Muang Thai country Asia see Thailand
118 F4 Muang Va Laos
118 F5 Muang Vangviang Laos
118 F4 Muang Xon Laos
235 G3 Muanza Moz.
116 E3 Muar Malaysia
116 E3 Muar r. Malaysia
117 K2 Muara Brunei
117 L4 Muaraancalong Kalimantan Indon.
117 L4 Muaraatap Kalimantan Indon.
116 E6 Muarabeliti Sumatera Indon.
116 E5 Muarabulian Sumatera Indon.
116 E5 Muarabungo Sumatera Indon.
116 F7 Muaradua Sumatera Indon.
116 E6 Muaraenim Sumatera Indon.
117 K5 Muarainu Kalimantan Indon.
117 L5 Muarajawa Kalimantan Indon.
117 L5 Muarakaman Kalimantan Indon.
117 L4 Muara Kaman Sedulang, Cagar Alam nature res. Kalimantan Indon.
116 D5 Muaralabuh Sumatera Indon.
116 E6 Muaralakitan Sumatera Indon.
117 K5 Muaralaung Kalimantan Indon.
117 L4 Muaralesan Kalimantan Indon.
117 L4 Muaramayang Kalimantan Indon.
117 L4 Muaranawai Kalimantan Indon.
116 E6 Muararupit Sumatera Indon.
116 E5 Muarasabak Sumatera Indon.
116 C5 Muarasiberut Indon.
116 C4 Muarasipongi Sumatera Indon.
116 C4 Muarasoma Sumatera Indon.
117 M4 Muaras Reef Indon.
116 E5 Muaratebo Sumatera Indon.
116 E5 Muaratembesi Sumatera Indon.
117 K5 Muarateweh Kalimantan Indon.
Muara Tuang Sarawak Malaysia see Kota Samarahan
117 L4 Muarawahau Kalimantan Indon.
115 E4 Muari i. Maluku Indon.
145 L9 Muari, Ras pt Pak.
235 H2 Muatua Moz.
147 I2 Mu'ayqil, Khashm al hill Saudi Arabia
138 E4 Muazzam Punjab India
150 D9 Mubārak, Jabal mt. Jordan/Saudi Arabia
139 I6 Mubarakpur Uttar Prad. India
Mubarek Uzbek. see Muborak
149 J9 Mubarraz well Saudi Arabia
232 A4 Mubende Uganda
229 I4 Mubi Nigeria
142 K8 Muborak Uzbek.
116 G3 Mubur i. Indon.
231 B6 Mucaba Angola
231 B6 Mucaba, Serra mts Angola
275 G5 Mucajá Brazil
275 F4 Mucajaí r. Brazil
275 F4 Mucajaí, Serra do mts Brazil
249 H1 Mucalic r. Que. Can.
235 F2 Mucanha r. Moz.
218 I7 Mučanj mt. Serbia
108 F6 Muccan W.A. Austr.
215 K1 Muccia Italy
191 D9 Much Ger.
238 □3d Muchachos, Roque de los vol. La Palma Canary Is
197 H6 Mucharz Pol.
109 C11 Muchea W.A. Austr.
193 E8 Mücheln (Geiseltal) Ger.
Mucheng Henan China see Wuzhi
122 B2 Muchikan Rus. Fed.
233 A8 Muchinga Escarpment Zambia
277 E4 Muchiri Bol.
157 H6 Muchkapskiy Rus. Fed.
156 J2 Muchkas Rus. Fed.
192 E4 Muchow Ger.
197 I6 Muchówka Pol.
130 D4 Muchuan Sichuan China
172 G2 Much Wenlock Shropshire, England U.K.
205 K5 Mucientes Spain
168 D9 Muck i. Scotland U.K.
193 K8 Mücka Ger.
107 L9 Muckadilla Qld Austr.
106 D5 Muckaty Aboriginal Land res. N.T. Austr.
191 H9 Mücke Große-Eichen Ger.
191 H9 Mücke-Nieder-Ohmen Ger.
169 F2 Muckish Mountain hill Ireland
168 □O1 Muckle Flugga i. Scotland U.K.
168 □N2 Muckle Roe i. Scotland U.K.
170 D5 Muckno Lake Ireland
274 D3 Muco r. Col.
233 D8 Mucojo Moz.
231 D7 Muconda Angola
217 K5 Mucone r. Italy
231 B9 Mucope Angola
199 H5 Mucsi-hegy hill Hungary
199 J3 Múcsony Hungary
235 H3 Mucubela Moz.
235 H3 Mucúbi Moz.
275 F5 Mucucuaú r. Brazil
275 E6 Mucuim r. Brazil
235 F3 Mucumbura Moz.
231 C9 Mucundi Angola
231 C8 Mucunha Angola
235 H3 Mucupia Moz.
148 G4 Mucur Turkey
275 F5 Mucura Brazil
281 H3 Mucuri Brazil
281 H3 Mucuri r. Brazil
281 G3 Mucurici Brazil
274 D5 Mucuripe Brazil
278 F2 Mucuripe, Ponta de pt Brazil
231 D9 Mucusso, Coutada Pública do nature res. Angola
231 D7 Mucussueje Angola
238 □3b Muda hill Fuerteventura Canary Is
116 D2 Muda r. Malaysia
136 D6 Mudabidri Karnataka India
Mudan Shandong China see Heze
122 F6 Mudanjiang Heilong. China
122 F5 Mudan Jiang r. China
122 E7 Mudan Ling mts China
221 J2 Mudanya Turkey
194 G2 Mudau Ger.
149 M9 Mudayrah Kuwait
150 E7 Mudaysīsāt, Jabal al hill Jordan
136 E4 Muddebihal Karnataka India
162 O3 Muddus nationalpark nat. park Sweden
265 R5 Muddy r. NV U.S.A.
261 H9 Muddy Boggy Creek r. OK U.S.A.
258 C5 Muddy Creek r. PA U.S.A.
265 V3 Muddy Creek r. UT U.S.A.
262 K5 Muddy Gap pass WY U.S.A.
265 R5 Muddy Peak NV U.S.A.
258 C5 Muddy Run Reservoir PA U.S.A.
144 H5 Mūd-e Dahanāb Iran
237 O4 Muden S. Africa
190 J5 Müden (Aller) Ger.
190 J5 Müden (Örtze) Ger.
191 E9 Mudersbach Ger.
136 E5 Mudgal Karnataka India
105 L5 Mudgee N.S.W. Austr.
136 D4 Mudhol Karnataka India
136 D6 Mudigere Karnataka India
247 J3 Mudjatik r. Sask. Can.
136 E3 Mudkhed Mahar. India
138 E4 Mudki Punjab India
264 O4 Mud Lake NV U.S.A.
118 C6 Mudon Myanmar
Mudraya country Africa see Egypt
232 E3 Mudug admin. reg. Somalia
233 B5 Mudukani Tanz.
234 D3 Mudumu National Park Namibia
221 M2 Mudurnu Turkey
221 L2 Mudurnu r. Turkey
156 G3 Mud'yuga Rus. Fed.
235 H2 Muecate Moz.
233 C7 Mueda Moz.
208 C5 Muel Spain
205 M4 Muela de Quintanilla hill Spain
204 I5 Muelas del Pan Spain
108 I5 Mueller Range hills W.A. Austr.
235 G2 Muende Moz.
269 M9 Muerto, Mar lag. Mex.
270 C1 Muertos Cays is Bahamas
147 I1 Mufattah, Khawr b. Saudi Arabia
169 H2 Muff Ireland
225 G4 Muftah well Sudan
156 I2 Muftyuga Rus. Fed.
231 F8 Mufulira Zambia
231 E8 Mufumbwe Zambia
131 J4 Mufu Shan mts China
204 H6 Muga de Sayago Spain
249 H4 Mugaguadavic Lake N.B. Can.
142 H3 Mugalzhar Kazakh.
151 J5 Muğan Azer.
151 J6 Muğan Düzü lowland Azer.
151 H4 Muğanlı Azer.
204 D2 Mugardos Spain
206 B2 Muge Port.
206 B2 Muge r. Port.
235 H3 Mugeba Moz.
126 E4 Mugegawa Japan
193 H8 Mügeln Sachsen Ger.
193 H7 Mügeln Sachsen-Anhalt Ger.
194 E4 Muggensturm Ger.
213 P4 Muggia Italy
Mughalbhin Pak. see Jati
139 I7 Mughal Sarai Uttar Prad. India
144 E5 Mūghār Iran
148 H9 Mughayrā' Saudi Arabia
146 G3 Mughayrā' well Saudi Arabia
147 L6 Mughshin Oman
147 K6 Mughshin, Wādī r. Oman
145 N2 Mughsu r. Tajik.
126 F4 Mugi Gifu Japan
125 L13 Mugi Tokushima Japan
Mugia Spain see Muxía
231 F6 Mugila, Monts mts Dem. Rep. Congo
221 J5 Muğla Turkey
221 J5 Muğla prov. Turkey
142 H4 Mugodzhary, Gory mts Kazakh.
128 C9 Mug Qu r. Qinghai China
185 C8 Mugron France
204 E5 Mugueimes Spain
233 C8 Muguia Moz.
138 H5 Mugu Karnali r. Nepal
233 B5 Mugumu Tanz.
128 B1 Mugur-Aksy Rus. Fed.
133 L10 Mugxung Qinghai China
150 G4 Mūḩ, Sabkhat imp. l. Syria
230 E2 Muhagiriya Sudan
Muhala Xinjiang China see Yutian
231 F6 Muhala Dem. Rep. Congo
225 G3 Muḩammad, Ra's pt Egypt
139 I7 Muhammadabad Uttar Prad. India
145 M8 Muhammad Ashraf Pak.
225 H4 Muhammad Qol Sudan
Muhammarah Iran see Khorramshahr
128 F8 Muhar Qinghai China
150 C8 Muhashsham, Wādī al watercourse Egypt
146 G4 Muḩayriqah Saudi Arabia
150 E9 Muḩaysh, Wādī al watercourse Jordan
150 H2 Muhaysin Syria
233 B6 Muhesi Game Reserve nature res. Tanz.
233 C6 Muheza Tanz.
194 F4 Mühlacker Ger.
193 G7 Mühlanger Ger.
192 I3 Mühlbach r. Ger.
193 H8 Mühlberg Brandenburg Ger.
191 K9 Mühlberg Thüringen Ger.
201 H6 Mühldorf Austria
195 N5 Mühldorf am Inn Ger.
201 K5 Mühlen Austria
192 G2 Mühlen hill Ger.
192 H5 Mühlenbeck Ger.
192 D3 Mühlen-Eichsen Ger.
194 F3 Mühlhausen Baden-Württemberg Ger.
195 K3 Mühlhausen Bayern Ger.
191 J8 Mühlhausen (Thüringen) Ger.
191 G10 Mühlheim am Main Ger.
194 F5 Mühlheim an der Donau Ger.
287 A2 Mühlig-Hofmann Mountains Antarctica
194 G6 Mühlingen Ger.
193 E9 Mühltroff Ger.
201 J2 Mühlviertel reg. Austria
162 R4 Muhos Fin.
150 E3 Muḩradah Syria
195 J3 Muhr am See Ger.
160 G3 Muhu i. Estonia
233 B7 Muhukuru Tanz.
235 H2 Muhula Moz.
230 E5 Muhulu Dem. Rep. Congo
232 B3 Mui Eth.
Mui Bai Bung c. Vietnam see Ca Mau, Mui
186 H4 Muiden Neth.
178 B5 Muids France
233 C7 Muidumbe Moz.
231 D8 Muié Angola
127 I1 Muika Japan
115 F4 Muiliyk i. Maluku Indon.
Muineachán Ireland see Monaghan
250 J7 Muir MI U.S.A.
258 B3 Muir PA U.S.A.
168 K9 Muirdrum Angus, Scotland U.K.
245 M4 Muir Glacier Can./U.S.A.
168 J10 Muirhead Angus, Scotland U.K.
168 H11 Muirkirk East Ayrshire, Scotland U.K.
168 D6 Muirneag hill Scotland U.K.
168 K8 Muir of Fowlis Aberdeenshire, Scotland U.K.
168 H7 Muir of Ord Highland, Scotland U.K.
274 B4 Muisne Ecuador
235 H2 Muite Moz.
178 G5 Muizon France
144 F4 Mūjān, Chāh-e well Iran
267 P7 Mujeres, Isla i. Mex.
133 D8 Muji Xinjiang China
117 J3 Mujong r. Malaysia
123 E10 Muju S. Korea
275 H5 Mujuí Joboti Brazil
144 B2 Mujūmbar Iran
Mukačevo Ukr. see Mukacheve
158 B5 Mukacheve Ukr.
Mukachevo Ukr. see Mukacheve
117 J3 Mukah Sarawak Malaysia
117 J3 Mukah r. Malaysia
Mukalla Yemen see Al Mukallā
138 E6 Mukandgarh Rajasthan India
138 F7 Mukandwara Rajasthan India
231 D6 Mukanga Dem. Rep. Congo
147 I5 Mukassir, Banī des. Saudi Arabia
124 S4 Mukawa Hokkaidō Japan
127 H4 Mukawa Yamanashi Japan
124 S4 Mu-kawa r. Japan
225 H4 Mukawwar, Gezirat i. Sudan
118 G6 Mukdahan Thai.
Mukden Liaoning China see Shenyang
138 E4 Mukerian Punjab India
114 □ Mukeru Palau
248 C2 Muketei r. Ont. Can.
232 C2 Muke T'urī Eth.
197 L3 Mukhavyets Belarus
197 M3 Mukhavyets, Kanal r. Belarus
122 J4 Mukhen Rus. Fed.
122 E2 Mukhino Rus. Fed.
129 K1 Mukhorshibir' Rus. Fed.
Mukhtuya Rus. Fed. see Lensk
151 F6 Mūkhvor Iran
144 G5 Mūkīk, Chashmeh-ye spring Iran
109 E11 Mukinbudin W.A. Austr.
126 C6 Mukō Japan
119 F9 Mu Ko Chang Marine National Park Thai.
125 □2 Muko-jima i. Japan
125 □2 Mukojima-rettō is Japan
116 D6 Mukomuko Sumatera Indon.
232 B4 Mukono Uganda
231 F7 Mukoshi Zambia
145 K3 Mukry Turkm.
Muksu r. Tajik. see Mughsu
139 I5 Muktinath Nepal
138 E4 Muktsar Punjab India
231 F8 Mukuku Zambia
235 F3 Mukumbura Zimbabwe
231 F7 Mukunsa Zambia
142 F4 Mukur Atyrauskaya Oblast' Kazakh.
247 L4 Mukutawa r. Man. Can.
250 F7 Mukwonago WI U.S.A.
143 S2 Mukyr Vostochnyy Kazakhstan Kazakh.
138 G9 Mul Mahar. India
136 D3 Mula r. India
145 L7 Mula r. Pak.
209 C11 Mula Spain
207 Q4 Mula r. Spain
Mulaku atoll Maldives see Mulaku Atoll
135 D11 Mulaku Atoll Maldives
143 R5 Mulaly Kazakh.
122 F6 Mulan Heilong. China
114 D5 Mulanay Luzon Phil.
233 B8 Mulanje Malawi
235 G2 Mulanje, Mount Malawi
104 F3 Mulapula, Lake salt flat S.A. Austr.
214 C8 Mulargia, Lago l. Sardegna Italy
266 E3 Mulatos Mex.
266 □U13 Mula-tupo Panama
146 G2 Mulayḩ Saudi Arabia
150 G9 Mulayḩ salt pan Saudi Arabia
147 I2 Mulayjah Saudi Arabia
150 B8 Mulayz, Wādī al watercourse Egypt
212 H7 Mulazzo Italy
136 F6 Mulbagal Karnataka India
173 O2 Mulbarton Norfolk, England U.K.
138 F2 Mulbekh Jammu and Kashmir India
168 J7 Mulben Moray, Scotland U.K.
261 H8 Mulberry AR U.S.A.
244 H3 Mulchatna r. AK U.S.A.
284 A5 Mulchén Chile
193 H9 Mulda Ger.
193 F7 Mulde r. Ger.
193 F7 Muldenstein Ger.
233 A5 Muleba Tanz.
262 L5 Mule Creek WY U.S.A.
266 C4 Mulegé Mex.
233 B7 Mulekatembo Zambia
115 B8 Mules i. Indon.
261 D8 Muleshoe TX U.S.A.
235 H3 Mulevala Moz.
194 H3 Mulfingen Ger.
108 E7 Mulga Downs W.A. Austr.
106 C8 Mulga Park N.T. Austr.
104 E4 Mulgathing S.A. Austr.
244 G2 Mulgrave Hills AK U.S.A.
207 M6 Mulhacén mt. Spain
Mülhausen France see Mulhouse
191 C8 Mülheim an der Ruhr Ger.
191 D10 Mülheim-Kärlich Ger.
179 N8 Mulhouse France
130 C5 Muli Sichuan China
Muli Rus. Fed. see Vysokogorniy
100 □2 Mulifanua Samoa
135 □2 Mulikadu i. Addu Atoll Maldives
138 C8 Mulila Gujarat India
233 B7 Mulilansolo Zambia
122 G6 Muling Heilong. China
122 G6 Muling Heilong. China
122 H6 Muling He r. China
100 □2 Mulitapu'ili, Cape Samoa
201 K8 Muljava Slovenia
168 E10 Mull i. Scotland U.K.
168 D9 Mull, Sound of sea chan. Scotland U.K.
144 C3 Mulla Ali Iran
232 E2 Mullaaxe Beyle Somalia
170 D6 Mullagh Cavan Ireland
169 D7 Mullagh Clare Ireland
169 C5 Mullagh Mayo Ireland
169 I6 Mullagh Meath Ireland
169 D8 Mullaghareirk hill Ireland
169 D8 Mullaghareirk Mountains hills Ireland
169 H3 Mullaghcarn hill Northern Ireland U.K.
169 J6 Mullaghcleevaun hill Ireland
169 H3 Mullaghcloga hill Northern Ireland U.K.
169 F4 Mullaghmore Ireland
136 G8 Mullaittivu Sri Lanka
105 L4 Mullaley N.S.W. Austr.
169 I4 Mullan Ireland
169 G4 Mullan Northern Ireland U.K.
168 F8 Mullardoch, Loch l. Scotland U.K.
169 K4 Mullartown Northern Ireland U.K.
260 E4 Mullen NE U.S.A.
105 K4 Mullengudgery N.S.W. Austr.
256 D11 Mullens WV U.S.A.
106 E7 Muller watercourse N.T. Austr.
117 J4 Muller, Pegunungan mts Indon.
250 J4 Mullett Lake MI U.S.A.
109 C10 Mullewa W.A. Austr.
168 K5 Mull Head Orkney, Scotland U.K.
194 D6 Müllheim Ger.
258 G5 Mullica r. NJ U.S.A.
258 E5 Mullica Hill NJ U.S.A.
106 G8 Mulligan watercourse Qld Austr.
169 H8 Mullinavat Ireland
169 H5 Mullingar Ireland
255 H8 Mullins SC U.S.A.
172 B7 Mullion Cornwall, England U.K.
105 L5 Mullion Creek N.S.W. Austr.
167 E4 Mull of Galloway c. Scotland U.K.
168 E12 Mull of Kintyre hd Scotland U.K.
168 D11 Mull of Oa hd Scotland U.K.
157 J5 Mullovka Rus. Fed.
193 J6 Müllrose Ger.
165 J4 Mullsjö Sweden
160 F3 Mullutu laht l. Estonia
231 E9 Mulobezi Zambia
231 B8 Mulondo Angola
231 D9 Mulonga Plain Zambia
231 E6 Mulongo Dem. Rep. Congo
169 C5 Mulrany Ireland
169 G2 Mulroy Bay Ireland
181 L6 Mulsanne France
136 C3 Mulshi Lake India
138 G9 Multai Madh. Prad. India
145 I8 Mūltān Iran
145 N6 Multan Pak.
162 R5 Multia Fin.
178 E6 Multien reg. France
117 K2 Mulu, Gunung mt. Malaysia
136 F3 Mulug Andhra Prad. India
231 E7 Mulumbe, Monts mts Dem. Rep. Congo
105 I5 Mulurulu Lake N.S.W. Austr.
230 D4 Muma Dem. Rep. Congo
230 E2 Mumallah Sudan
144 I9 Mūmān Iran
136 C3 Mumbai Mahar. India
231 D8 Mumbeji Zambia
105 L5 Mumbil N.S.W. Austr.
172 E4 Mumbles Head Wales U.K.
231 B7 Mumbondo Angola
231 C8 Mumbué Angola
231 E8 Mumbwa Zambia
233 C6 Mumbwi Tanz.
231 E7 Mume Dem. Rep. Congo
Muminabad Tajik. see Leningrad
Mŭ'minobod Tajik. see Leningrad
212 D1 Mümliswil Switz.
119 D11 Mum Nok, Laem pt Thai.
231 D6 Mumoma Dem. Rep. Congo
142 B5 Mumra Rus. Fed.
214 A9 Mumullonis, Punta hill Italy
118 G7 Mun, Mae Nam r. Thai.
115 C6 Muna i. Indon.
267 O7 Muna Mex.
153 N3 Muna r. Rus. Fed.
145 N9 Munabao Pak.
162 □C1 Munaðarnes Iceland
136 F4 Munagala Andhra Prad. India
125 H13 Munakata Japan
205 J7 Muñana Spain
146 B4 Munayjah, Jabal mts Egypt/Sudan
142 F4 Munayly Kazakh.
142 E6 Munayshy Kazakh.
193 E10 Münchberg Ger.
193 J5 Müncheberg Ger.
195 L5 München Ger.
München airport Ger. see Franz Josef Strauss
193 E9 Münchenbernsdorf Ger.
212 C1 Münchenbuchsee Switz.
München-Gladbach Ger. see Mönchengladbach
191 G9 Münchhausen Ger.
274 B4 Munchique, Parque Nacional nat. park Col.
246 E3 Muncho Lake B.C. Can.
246 E3 Muncho Lake Provincial Park B.C. Can.
123 E9 Munch'ŏn N. Korea
195 L4 Münchsmünster Ger.
195 J2 Münchsteinach Ger.
194 D3 Münchweiler an der Rodalb Ger.
212 G1 Münchwilen Switz.
254 E5 Muncie IN U.S.A.
106 G8 Muncoonie West, Lake salt flat Qld Austr.
251 R8 Muncy PA U.S.A.
258 B2 Muncy Creek r. PA U.S.A.
258 B2 Muncy Valley PA U.S.A.
231 B9 Munda Angola
230 D4 Munda Dem. Rep. Congo
145 N6 Munda Pak.
100 □6 Munda New Georgia Is Solomon Is
205 O2 Mundaka Spain
136 F9 Mundel Lake Sri Lanka
229 H5 Mundemba Cameroon
200 H3 Munderfing Austria
194 H5 Munderkingen Ger.
173 O2 Mundesley Norfolk, England U.K.
173 N2 Mundford Norfolk, England U.K.
109 F7 Mundiwindi W.A. Austr.
107 H5 Mundjura Creek r. Qld Austr.
207 P4 Mundo r. Spain
179 O6 Mundolsheim France
278 E4 Mundo Novo Brazil
138 B8 Mundra Gujarat India
109 I11 Mundrabilla W.A. Austr.
265 U7 Munds Park AZ U.S.A.
107 M8 Mundubbera Qld Austr.
138 D6 Mundwa Rajasthan India
205 Q6 Munebrega Spain
207 O2 Munera Spain
136 G4 Muneru r. India
254 E7 Munfordville KY U.S.A.
107 K9 Mungallala Qld Austr.
105 K3 Mungallala Creek r. Qld Austr.
107 J4 Mungana Qld Austr.
138 G7 Mungaoli Madh. Prad. India
235 G3 Mungári Moz.
108 E6 Mungaroona Range Nature Reserve W.A. Austr.
230 F4 Mungbere Dem. Rep. Congo
138 H8 Mungeli Chhattisgarh India
139 K7 Munger Bihar India
251 K6 Munger MI U.S.A.
104 G3 Mungeranie S.A. Austr.
Mu Nggava i. Solomon Is see Rennell
117 H4 Mungguresak, Tanjung pt Indon.
205 O2 Mungia Spain
Mu Ngiki i. Solomon Is see Bellona
109 H8 Mungilli Aboriginal Reserve W.A. Austr.
105 L3 Mungindi N.S.W. Austr.
106 E6 Mungkarta Aboriginal Land res. N.T. Austr.
231 C7 Mungo Angola
105 I5 Mungo, Lake N.S.W. Austr.
105 I5 Mungo National Park N.S.W. Austr.
169 E7 Mungret Ireland
Munguía Spain see Mungia
233 A7 Mungwi Zambia
123 E10 Mun'gyŏng S. Korea
231 C8 Munhango Angola
231 B8 Munhino Angola
280 D5 Munhoz Brazil
Munich Ger. see München
205 J7 Muñico Spain
204 G2 Muniellos, Reserva Natural Integral de nature res. Spain
208 D5 Muniesa Spain
205 P4 Munilla Spain
250 H3 Munising MI U.S.A.
281 G4 Muniz Freire Brazil
138 C8 Munjpur Gujarat India
Munkács Ukr. see Mukacheve
156 E1 Munkebakken Norway
164 H3 Munkedal Sweden
162 M5 Munkflohögen Sweden
164 J2 Munkfors Sweden
128 G1 Munku-Sardyk, Gora mt. Mongolia/Rus. Fed.
187 E7 Munkzwalm Belgium
168 H7 Munlochy Highland, Scotland U.K.
191 J10 Münnerstadt Ger.
195 J4 Munningen Ger.
102 □ Munning Point Chatham Is S. Pacific Ocean
205 K7 Muñogalindo Spain
105 L9 Munro, Mount Tas. Austr.
247 L3 Munroe Lake Man. Can.
115 C6 Munse Sulawesi Indon.
139 M8 Munshiganj Bangl.
195 K6 Münsing Ger.
194 G5 Münsingen Ger.
212 D2 Münsingen Switz.
200 E5 Münster Austria
179 N7 Munster France
194 F2 Münster Hessen Ger.
190 J5 Münster Niedersachsen Ger.
191 E7 Münster Nordrhein-Westfalen Ger.
191 E7 Münster admin. reg. Ger.
169 E8 Munster reg. Ireland
212 E3 Münster Switz.
190 I3 Münsterdorf Ger.
195 I5 Münsterhausen Ger.
191 E7 Münsterland reg. Ger.
191 D10 Münstermaifeld Ger.
191 E6 Münster-Osnabrück airport Ger.
109 E11 Muntadgin W.A. Austr.
200 G5 Muntanitz mt. Austria
115 A3 Munte Sulawesi Indon.
219 L4 Muntele Mare, Vârful mt. Romania
186 K2 Muntendam Neth.
219 P5 Munteni Romania
232 B4 Muntu Uganda
231 F7 Mununga Zambia
217 □ Munxar Gozo Malta
Munyal-Par sea feature India see Bassas de Pedro Padua Bank
235 F3 Munyati r. Zimbabwe
237 M7 Munyu S. Africa
191 G10 Münzenberg Ger.
201 I3 Münzkirchen Austria
148 I4 Munzur Vadisi Milli Par[k] nat. park Turkey
162 Q3 Muodoslompolo Sweder
162 T4 Muojärvi l. Fin.
118 F3 Mường Nhe Vietnam
Muong Sai Laos see Xay
118 F3 Mường Te Vietnam
162 Q3 Muonio Fin.
162 Q3 Muonioälven r. Fin./Swe
162 Q3 Muonionalusta Sweden
Muonionjoki r. Fin./Swe Muonioälven
115 F3 Muor i. Maluku Indon.
212 F2 Muotathal Switz.
231 B9 Mupa Angola
231 B8 Mupa, Parque Nacional nat. park Angola
235 F3 Mupfure r. Zimbabwe
129 Q8 Muping Shandong China
225 F5 Muqaddam watercourse
232 E3 Muqakoori Somalia
146 H9 Muqaybirah Yemen
147 I4 Muqaynimah well Saudi
232 E4 Muqdisho Somalia
147 M4 Muqnīyāt Oman
151 J4 Müqtädır Azer.
278 C5 Muquem Brazil
281 G4 Muqui Brazil
Muqyr Kazakh. see Muku
201 L5 Mur r. Austria alt. Mura (Croatia/Slov
150 B10 Mu'r, Wādī watercourse E
201 O7 Mura r. Croatia/Slovenia alt. Mur (Austria)
195 M3 Murach r. Ger.
204 E9 Muradal, Serra do mts P
221 I4 Muradiye Manisa Turkey
149 K4 Muradiye Van Turkey
158 H5 Murafa r. Ukr.
116 □ Murai, Tanjong pt Sing.
116 □ Murai Reservoir Sing.
124 Q8 Murakami Japan
198 F5 Murakeresztúr Hungary
283 B8 Murallón, Cerro mt. Chi
233 A5 Muramvya Burundi
199 J3 Muráň Slovakia
199 J3 Muráň r. Slovakia
232 C5 Murang'a Kenya
213 M5 Murano Italy
199 I3 Muránska planina park S
125 L11 Muraoka Japan
204 E2 Muras Spain
156 J4 Murashi Rus. Fed.
183 B9 Murasson France
198 F5 Muraszemenye Hungary
183 B6 Murat France
151 C7 Murat r. Turkey
149 I4 Murat r. Turkey
151 C7 Muratgören Turkey
221 I1 Muratlı Turkey
214 C2 Murato Corse France
183 B9 Murat-sur-Vèbre France
201 J5 Murau Austria
197 M3 Murava Belarus
214 D9 Muravera Sardegna Italy
124 R8 Murayama Japan
146 E3 Murayr, Jabal hill Saudi A
225 G4 Murayr, Jazīrat i. Egypt
224 E2 Muraysah, Ra's al pt Liby
212 E7 Murazzano Italy
179 N8 Murbach France
204 F6 Murça Port.
205 Q4 Murchante Spain
144 D5 Mūrcheh Khvort Iran
192 I3 Murchin Ger.
105 J7 Murchison Vic. Austr.
109 C9 Murchison watercourse W Austr.
103 G8 Murchison South I. N.Z.
287 L2 Murchison, Mount Anta
109 D9 Murchison, Mount hill W
103 F10 Murchison, Mount South
232 A4 Murchison Falls Nationa Uganda
248 B3 Murchison Island Ont. C
103 B12 Murchison Mountains S N.Z.
106 E6 Murchison Range hills N
209 C12 Murcia Spain
207 Q5 Murcia aut. comm. Spain
114 D7 Murcielagos Bay Mindan
196 F3 Murczyn Pol.
183 B7 Mur-de-Barrez France
180 F5 Mûr-de-Bretagne France
258 E6 Murderkill r. DE U.S.A.
181 O7 Mur-de-Sologne France
260 E4 Murdo SD U.S.A.
249 H3 Murdochville Que. Can.
127 H2 Mure Japan
201 M6 Mureck Austria
221 I2 Mürefte Turkey
229 G4 Muregi Nigeria
235 F3 Murehwa Zimbabwe
206 E3 Mures r. Port.
218 I4 Mureşul r. Romania
185 G9 Muret France
Murewa Zimbabwe see M
162 M4 Murfjället mt. Norway
261 I8 Murfreesboro AR U.S.A.
255 I7 Murfreesboro NC U.S.A.
255 D8 Murfreesboro TN U.S.A.
194 E6 Murg Ger.
194 E4 Murg r. Ger.
Murgab Tajik. see Murgh
Murgab Turkm. see Murg
Murgab r. Turkm. see Mu
145 J3 Murgap Turkm.
145 J3 Murgap r. Turkm.
106 D1 Murgenella Creek r. N.T.
219 Q4 Murgeni Romania
212 D1 Murgenthal Switz.
217 M3 Murge Tarantine hills Ital
145 M6 Murgha Kibzai Pak.
145 L6 Murgha Mehterzai Pak.
145 P2 Murghob Tajik.
145 O2 Murghob r. Tajik.
151 G5 Murghuz Lerr mt. Armen
205 O3 Murgia Spain
215 R6 Murgia Sant'Elia hill Italy
107 M9 Murgon Qld Austr.
109 D9 Murgoo W.A. Austr.
151 C4 Murgul Turkey
128 F8 Muri Qinghai China
128 G8 Muri Qinghai China
139 J8 Muri Jharkhand India
144 G3 Mūrī Iran
212 E1 Muri Aargau Switz.
212 C2 Muri Bern Switz.
117 I8 Muria, Gunung mt. Indon
281 F4 Muriaé Brazil
204 H3 Murias de Paredes Spain
145 L7 Murid Pak.
205 M2 Muriedas Spain
231 D7 Muriege Angola
117 H4 Murih, Pulau i. Indon.
124 U3 Murii-dake mt. Japan
250 E1 Murillo Ont. Can.
205 R4 Murillo el Fruto Spain
212 E5 Murisengo Italy
192 G4 Müritz l. Ger.
192 H4 Müritz, Nationalpark nat. Ger.
192 D4 Müritz-Elde-Wasserstraß
192 G4 Müritz Seenpark nature r
102 L5 Muriwai North I. N.Z.
162 P3 Murjek Sweden
139 O6 Murkong Selek Assam In
170 C5 Murley Northern Ireland U
214 G1 Murlo Italy
162 V2 Murmansk Rus. Fed.
162 W2 Murmanskaya Oblast' ad Rus. Fed.
156 F1 Murmanskiy Bereg coast Rus. Fed.
Murmansk Oblast admin. Rus. Fed. see Murmanskaya Oblast'
162 V2 Murmashi Rus. Fed.
161 X7 Murmino Rus. Fed.
195 M6 Murn r. Ger.
195 K6 Murnau am Staffelsee Ge
169 I8 Murntown Ireland
126 D6 Muro Japan

Muro Port.
Muro Spain
Muro r. Spain
Muro, Capo di c. Corse France
Murō-Akame-Aoyama Kokutei-kōen park Japan
Muro de Alcoy Spain
Murol France
Muro Leccese Italy
Muro Lucano Italy
Murom Rus. Fed.
Muromagi-gawa r. Japan
Muron France
Murongo Tanz.
Murony Hungary
Muroran Japan
Muros Sardegna Italy
Muros Asturias Spain
Muros Galicia Spain
Muros e Noia, Ría de est. Spain
Muroto Japan
Muroto-Anan-kaigan Kokutei-kōen park Japan
Muroto-zaki pt Japan
Murovane Ukr.
Murovani Kurylivtsi Ukr.
Murovdağ Silsiläsi hills Azer.
Murów Pol.
Murowana Goślina Pol.
Murphy ID U.S.A.
Murphy NC U.S.A.
Murphys CA U.S.A.
Murrah reg. Saudi Arabia
Murrah, Wādī watercourse Egypt
Murrah al Kubrá, Al Buḥayrah al l. Egypt
Murrah aş Şughrá, Al Buḥayrah al l. Egypt
Murramarang National Park N.S.W. Austr.
Murra Murra Qld Austr.
Murranji Aboriginal Land res. N.T. Austr.
Murray r. S.A. Austr.
Murray r. W.A. Austr.
Murray r. B.C. Can.
Murray KY U.S.A.
Murray, Lake P.N.G.
Murray, Lake SC U.S.A.
Murray, Mount Y.T. Can.
Murray Bridge S.A. Austr.
Murray City OH U.S.A.
Murray Downs N.T. Austr.
Murray Harbour P.E.I. Can.
Murray Hill Christmas I.
Murray Range hills W.A. Austr.
Murraysburg S. Africa
Murray Sunset National Park Vic. Austr.
Murrayville Vic. Austr.
Murree Pak.
Mürren Switz.
Murrhardt Ger.
Murrieta CA U.S.A.
Murringo N.S.W. Austr.
Murrisk reg. Ireland
Murroa Moz.
Murroogh Ireland
Murrumbateman N.S.W. Austr.
Murrumbidgee r. N.S.W. Austr.
Murrupula Moz.
Murrurundi N.S.W. Austr.
Mûrs-Erigné France
Murshidabad W. Bengal India
Murska Sobota Slovenia
Mursko Središće Croatia
Murtajapur Mahar. India
Murtas Spain
Murtede Port.
Murten Switz.
Murtensee l. Switz.
Murter Croatia
Murter i. Croatia
Murtoa Vic. Austr.
Murtosa Port.
Murtovaara Fin.
Muru r. Brazil
Murua i. P.N.G. see Woodlark Island
Murua Ngithigerr mts Kenya
Murud Mahar. India
Murud, Gunung mt. Indon.
Murui r. Indon.
Muruin Sum Shuiku resr China
Murung r. Indon.
Murung r. Indon.
Murunkan Sri Lanka
Muruntov Uzbek.
Murupara North I. N.Z.
Mururoa atoll Arch. des Tuamotu Fr. Polynesia
Muruti, Ilha i. Brazil
Murutinga Brazil
Murviedro Spain see Sagunto
Murviel-lès-Béziers France
Murwānī, Wādī watercourse Saudi Arabia
Murwara Madh. Prad. India
Murwillumbah N.S.W. Austr.
Murygino Kirovskaya Oblast' Rus. Fed.
Murygino Smolenskaya Oblast' Rus. Fed.
Mürz r. Austria
Murzechirla Turkm.
Mürzsteg Austria
Murzūq Libya
Murzuq, Ḥamādat plat. Libya
Murzūq, Idhān des. Libya
Murzynowo Pol.
Mürzzuschlag Austria
Muş Turkey
Muş prov. Turkey
Musa Dem. Rep. Congo
Mūsa r. Latvia/Lith.
Mūsá, Jabal mt. Egypt
Mūsā, Khowr-e b. Iran
Musa Āli Terara vol. Africa
Musabani Jharkhand India
Musabeyli Turkey
Muşabih Saudi Arabia
Musakhel Pak.
Musala mt. Bulg.
Musala i. Indon.
Musalı Turkey
Musan N. Korea
Musandam admin. reg. Oman
Musandam Peninsula Oman/U.A.E.
Musa Qala Afgh.
Mūsá Qal'eh, Rūd-e r. Afgh.
Musashino Japan
Musay'īd Qatar see Umm Sa'id
Musaymir Yemen
Musbat well Sudan
Musbury Devon, England U.K.
Muscat Oman see Masqaţ
Muscat reg. Oman see Masqaţ
Muscat and Oman country Asia see Oman
Muscatine IA U.S.A.
Muschwitz Ger.
Muscoda WI U.S.A.
Musconetcong r. NJ U.S.A.
Muscongus Bay ME U.S.A.
Musė r. Lith.
Musei Sardegna Italy
Musgrave Qld Austr.
Musgrave, Mount South I. N.Z.
Musgrave Harbour Nfld and Lab. Can.
Musgrave Ranges mts S.A. Austr.
Mūshakī Afgh.
Mushāsh al Kabid well Jordan
Mushash Dabl well Saudi Arabia
Mushāsh Ḥadraj Jordan
Mushāsh Muḍayyān well Saudi Arabia
Mushaynīqah well Yemen
Mushayyish, Wādī al watercourse Jordan
Mushenge Dem. Rep. Congo
Mushie Dem. Rep. Congo
Mushin Nigeria
159 M5 Mushuryn Rig Ukr.
136 F4 Musi r. India
116 F6 Musi r. Indon.
218 J9 Musica mt. Macedonia
265 S6 Music Mountain AZ U.S.A.
139 I5 Musikot Nepal
213 N4 Musile di Piave Italy
235 F4 Musina S. Africa
265 U2 Musinia Peak UT U.S.A.
159 L4 Musiyivka Ukr.
246 F2 Muskeg r. N.W.T. Can.
257 O7 Muskeget Channel MA U.S.A.
250 H6 Muskegon MI U.S.A.
250 H6 Muskegon r. MI U.S.A.
250 H6 Muskegon Heights MI U.S.A.
246 G4 Muskeg River Alta Can.
256 D9 Muskingum r. OH U.S.A.
261 H8 Muskogee OK U.S.A.
251 O5 Muskoka Ont. Can.
248 E4 Muskoka, Lake Ont. Can.
247 N4 Muskrat Dam Lake Ont. Can.
246 F3 Muskwa r. B.C. Can.
145 L6 Muslimbagh Pak.
Muslim-Croat Federation aut. div. Bos.-Herz. see Federacija Bosna i Hercegovina
150 F2 Muslimīyah Syria
156 K5 Muslyumovo Rus. Fed.
225 G5 Musmar Sudan
231 F8 Musofu Zambia
233 B5 Musoma Tanz.
233 B6 Musombe Tanz.
213 P9 Musone r. Italy
220 D1 Mušov Grob pass Macedonia
249 I3 Musquanousse, Lac l. Que. Can.
249 I3 Musquaro Que. Can.
249 I3 Musquaro, Lac l. Que. Can.
231 D8 Mussaca Angola
113 K7 Mussau Island P.N.G.
168 J11 Musselburgh East Lothian, Scotland U.K.
186 L3 Musselkanaal Neth.
262 K3 Musselshell r. MT U.S.A.
231 C7 Mussende Angola
151 B2 Mussera Georgia
231 B6 Musserra Angola
184 E5 Mussidan France
231 C7 Mussolo Angola
216 F8 Mussomeli Sicilia Italy
187 I9 Musson Belgium
138 G4 Mussoorie Uttaranchal India
231 D8 Mussuma Angola
231 D8 Mussuma r. Angola
178 I8 Mussy-sur-Seine France
138 G6 Mustafabad Uttar Prad. India
138 H7 Mustafabad Uttar Prad. India
221 J2 Mustafakemalpaşa Turkey
232 E3 Mustahīl Eth.
212 I2 Müstair Switz.
160 K1 Mustamaa i. Fin.
261 E10 Mustang Draw watercourse TX U.S.A.
132 G3 Mustau, Gora mt. Xinjiang China
142 E2 Mustayevo Rus. Fed.
283 C7 Musters, Lago l. Arg.
271 □3 Mustique i. St Vincent
160 F3 Mustjala Estonia
160 J4 Mustjõgi r. Estonia
160 I3 Mustla Estonia
162 T2 Mustola Fin.
160 J3 Mustvee Estonia
123 F8 Musu-dan pt N. Korea
151 I5 Müsüslü Azer.
105 M5 Muswellbrook N.S.W. Austr.
197 I2 Muszaki Pol.
197 I6 Muszyna Pol.
225 F3 Mūţ Egypt
148 F5 Mut Turkey
201 L6 Muta Slovenia
200 C6 Muta, Lago di l. Italy
278 F5 Mutá, Ponta do pt Brazil
103 □4 Mutalau Niue
231 E8 Mutanda Zambia
235 G3 Mutare Zimbabwe
146 G5 Mutarjim, Khashm hill Saudi Arabia
146 H2 Mutayr reg. Saudi Arabia
231 E6 Mutengwa Dem. Rep. Congo
201 P2 Mutěnice Czech Rep.
231 F7 Muteta Dem. Rep. Congo
168 I10 Muthill Perth and Kinross, Scotland U.K.
147 M4 Mutī Oman
205 Q3 Mutilva Baja Spain
Mutina Italy see Modena
146 A2 Mu'tiq, Jabal mts Egypt
274 B3 Mutis Col.
115 D8 Mutis, Gunung mt. Timor Indon.
156 K2 Mutnyy Materik Rus. Fed.
235 G3 Mutoko Zimbabwe
231 D6 Mutombo Dem. Rep. Congo
104 H5 Mutooroo S.A. Austr.
235 F3 Mutorashanga Zimbabwe
231 D6 Mutoto Dem. Rep. Congo
215 N5 Mutria, Monte mt. Italy
239 □3 Mutsamudu Nzwani Comoros
231 E7 Mutshatsha Dem. Rep. Congo
124 S5 Mutsu Japan
124 S5 Mutsu-wan b. Japan
127 L5 Mutsuzawa Japan
107 J7 Muttaburra Qld Austr.
221 L3 Muttalip Turkey
200 C5 Muttekopf mt. Austria
212 D1 Muttenz Switz.
200 D5 Mutters Austria
194 E3 Mutterstadt Ger.
104 □2 Mutton Bird Island Lord Howe I. Austr.
103 C13 Muttonbird Islands Stewart I. N.Z.
Muttonbird Islands N.Z. see Titi Islands
169 C7 Mutton Island Ireland
136 G5 Muttukuru Andhra Prad. India
136 F7 Muttupet Tamil Nadu India
235 H2 Mutuali Moz.
281 G3 Mutum Brazil
274 D6 Mutum r. Brazil
233 A5 Mutumba Burundi
229 H4 Mutum Biyu Nigeria
276 D2 Mutumparaná Brazil
231 C6 Mutungu-Tari Dem. Rep. Congo
278 C5 Mutunópolis Brazil
136 G8 Mutur Sri Lanka
209 E11 Mutxamel Spain
159 M2 Mutyn Ukr.
179 N6 Mutzig France
193 G8 Mutzschen Ger.
160 J2 Muuga Estonia
163 R5 Muurame Fin.
163 Q6 Muurla Fin.
162 R3 Muurola Fin.
129 K7 Mu Us Shamo des. China
231 B7 Muxaluando Angola
151 H4 Muxax Azer.
Muxi Sichuan China see Muchuan
204 B2 Muxía Spain
231 B7 Muxima Angola
156 F3 Muyezerskiy Rus. Fed.
233 A5 Muyinga Burundi
Muynoq Uzbek. see Mo'ynoq
233 B7 Muyombe Zambia
229 H5 Muyuka Cameroon
231 E6 Muyumba Dem. Rep. Congo
130 H3 Muyuping Hubei China
145 O4 Muzaffarabad Pak.
145 N6 Muzaffargarh Pak.
138 F5 Muzaffarnagar Uttar Prad. India
139 J6 Muzaffarpur Bihar India
235 G4 Muzamane Moz.
280 D4 Muzambinho Brazil
132 F6 Muzat He r. China
150 E3 Muzayri'ah tourist site Syria
142 F6 Muzbel', Uval hills Kazakh.
235 F2 Muze Moz.
151 F2 Muzhichi Rus. Fed.
180 G6 Muzillac France
145 I8 Mūzin Iran
274 C3 Muzo Col.
245 N5 Muzon, Cape AK U.S.A.
267 I4 Múzquiz Mex.
133 E9 Muztag mt. Xinjiang China
133 H8 Muz Tag mt. Xinjiang China
132 B7 Muztagata mt. Xinjiang China
Muztor Kyrg. see Toktogul
212 G5 Muzza, Canale canal Italy
213 O4 Muzzana del Turgnano Italy
230 B4 Mvadi Gabon
229 H6 Mvangan Cameroon
230 F3 Mvolo Sudan
233 C6 Mvomero Tanz.
230 B4 Mvoung r. Gabon
239 □3a Mvouni Njazidja Comoros
231 B6 Mvouti Congo
235 F3 Mvuma Zimbabwe
235 F3 Mvurwi Zimbabwe
230 B4 Mwagné, Parc National de nat. park Ogooué-Ivindo Gabon
239 □3 Mwali i. Comoros
235 F3 Mwami Zimbabwe
231 E9 Mwandi Zambia
233 C5 Mwanga Tanz.
233 B6 Mwanisenga Tanz.
100 □6 Mwaniwowo San Cristobal Solomon Is
233 B8 Mwanjawira Zambia
233 B8 Mwanya Zambia
233 B8 Mwanza Malawi
233 B5 Mwanza Tanz.
233 B5 Mwanza admin. reg. Tanz.
233 A8 Mwape Zambia
233 A5 Mwaro Burundi
231 E6 Mweho Dem. Rep. Congo
231 D6 Mweka Dem. Rep. Congo
233 C6 Mwele Tanz.
231 F7 Mwenda Zambia
231 D7 Mwene-Biji Dem. Rep. Congo
231 D6 Mwene-Ditu Dem. Rep. Congo
235 F4 Mwenezi Zimbabwe
235 F4 Mwenezi r. Zimbabwe
231 F5 Mwenga Dem. Rep. Congo
231 F7 Mwense Zambia
233 C6 Mwereni Kenya
231 F7 Mweru, Lake Dem. Rep. Congo/Zambia
233 C7 Mweru Plateau Tanz.
231 F7 Mweru Wantipa, Lake Zambia
231 F7 Mweru Wantipa National Park Zambia
233 A7 Mwewa Zambia
231 D7 Mwimba Dem. Rep. Congo
233 C5 Mwingi Kenya
231 E7 Mwinilunga Zambia
227 G3 Mya, Oued watercourse Alg.
118 C3 Myadaung Myanmar
160 J7 Myadzyel Belarus
160 J7 Myadzyel, Vozyera l. Belarus
118 B4 Myaing Myanmar
138 C6 Myajlar Rajasthan India
160 L5 Myakishevo Rus. Fed.
153 Q3 Myakit Rus. Fed.
158 F3 M"yakoty Ukr.
105 N5 Myall Lakes National Park N.S.W. Austr.
118 B5 Myanaung Myanmar
118 B3 Myanmar country Asia
160 K6 Myaretskiya Belarus
161 S7 Myatlevo Rus. Fed.
153 P3 Myaundzha Rus. Fed.
118 B6 Myaungmya Myanmar
118 D6 Myawadi Thai.
168 J6 Mybster Highland, Scotland U.K.
220 D5 Mycenae tourist site Greece
165 L4 Mycklaflon l. Sweden
118 A4 Myebon Myanmar
158 C2 Myedna Belarus
119 D8 Myeik Myanmar
119 C9 Myeik Kyunzu is Myanmar
161 N9 Myerkulavichy Belarus
256 B10 Myers KY U.S.A.
258 C4 Myerstown PA U.S.A.
118 B4 Myingyan Myanmar
119 D8 Myinmoletkat mt. Myanmar
118 B4 Myinmu Myanmar
118 C2 Myitkyina Myanmar
118 C3 Myitson Myanmar
119 D7 Myitta Myanmar
118 C4 Myittha Myanmar
137 N1 Myittha r. Myanmar
199 G3 Myjava Slovakia
198 F3 Myjava r. Slovakia
159 L4 Mykhaylivka Cherkas'ka Oblast' Ukr.
159 O5 Mykhaylivka Dnipropetrovs'ka Oblast' Ukr.
159 R6 Mykhaylivka Donets'ka Oblast' Ukr.
159 P4 Mykhaylivka Kharkivs'ka Oblast' Ukr.
159 N4 Mykhaylivka Poltavs'ka Oblast' Ukr.
159 O6 Mykhaylivka Zaporiz'ka Oblast' Ukr.
159 O6 Mykhaylivka Zaporiz'ka Oblast' Ukr.
159 K2 Mykhaylo-Kotsyubyns'ke Ukr.
158 G3 Mykhaylyuchka Ukr.
166 D1 Mykines i. Faroe Is
162 M3 Myklebostad Norway
158 C4 Mykolayiv L'vivs'ka Oblast' Ukr.
197 M5 Mykolayiv L'vivs'ka Oblast' Ukr.
159 L7 Mykolayiv Mykolayivs'ka Oblast' Ukr.
159 L1 Mykolayivka Chernihivs'ka Oblast' Ukr.
159 N6 Mykolayivka Dnipropetrovs'ka Oblast' Ukr.
159 P5 Mykolayivka Dnipropetrovs'ka Oblast' Ukr.
159 Q5 Mykolayivka Donets'ka Oblast' Ukr.
159 P5 Mykolayivka Kharkivs'ka Oblast' Ukr.
159 N6 Mykolayivka Khersons'ka Oblast' Ukr.
158 J6 Mykolayivka Odes'ka Oblast' Ukr.
158 J8 Mykolayivka Odes'ka Oblast' Ukr.
159 P6 Mykolayivka Zaporiz'ka Oblast' Ukr.
158 I7 Mykolayivka-Novorosiys'ka Ukr.
Mykolayiv Oblast admin. div. Ukr. see Mykolayivs'ka Oblast'
159 L6 Mykolayivs'ka Oblast' admin. div. Ukr.
159 L6 Mykolo-Hulak Ukr.
221 G5 Mykonos Mykonos Greece
221 G5 Mykonos i. Greece
158 E4 Mykulyntsi Ukr.
197 M5 Mykytychi Ukr.
156 J2 Myla Rus. Fed.
156 J2 Myla r. Rus. Fed.
Mylae Sicilia Italy see Milazzo
Mylasa Turkey see Milas
193 F9 Mylau Ger.
160 J1 Myllykoski Fin.
172 B7 Mylor Cornwall, England U.K.
Mymensing Bangl. see Mymensingh
139 M7 Mymensingh Bangl.
160 E1 Mynäjoki r. Fin.
163 Q6 Mynämäki Fin.
143 O5 Mynaral Kazakh.
236 H6 Mynfontein S. Africa
Myngaral Kazakh. see Mynaral
127 I3 Myōgi Japan
127 I3 Myōgi-Arafune-Saku-kōgen Kokutei-kōen park Japan
127 I3 Myōgi-san mt. Japan
126 A6 Myōken-yama hill Japan
127 H2 Myōkō Japan
127 H2 Myōkō-kōgen Japan
182 H2 Myon France
123 F8 Myŏnggan N. Korea
160 K6 Myory Belarus
118 B4 Myotha Myanmar
118 B4 Myothit Myanmar
125 Q15 Myozin-sho i. Japan
125 R15 Myozin-sho i. Japan
119 H9 My Phước Vietnam
162 □D2 Mýrdalsjökull ice cap Iceland
162 □D2 Mýrdalssandur sand area Iceland
162 M2 Myre Nordland Norway
162 M2 Myre Nordland Norway
162 P4 Myrheden Sweden
159 M4 Myrhorod Ukr.
220 G3 Myrina Limnos Greece
159 M5 Myrivs'ke Ukr.
162 N2 Myrlandshaugen Norway
247 I4 Myrnam Alta Can.
159 Q6 Myrne Donets'ka Oblast' Ukr.
159 M7 Myrne Khersons'ka Oblast' Ukr.
159 K3 Myrne Kyivs'ka Oblast' Ukr.
197 M5 Myrne Volyns'ka Oblast' Ukr.
159 O7 Myrne Zaporiz'ka Oblast' Ukr.
158 I7 Myrnopillya Ukr.
159 M8 Myrnyy Ukr.
159 P4 Myronivka Kharkivs'ka Oblast' Ukr.
158 J4 Myronivka Kyivs'ka Oblast' Ukr.
158 G3 Myropil' Ukr.
159 O2 Myropillya Ukr.
159 N6 Myrove Ukr.
163 R6 Myrskylä Fin.
255 H9 Myrtle Beach SC U.S.A.
262 C5 Myrtle Creek OR U.S.A.
105 K7 Myrtleford Vic. Austr.
262 B5 Myrtle Point OR U.S.A.
220 E6 Myrtoo Pelagos sea Greece
143 M7 Myrzakent Kazakh.
164 H2 Mysen Norway
170 D8 Myshall Ireland
160 I9 Myshanka r. Belarus
161 V4 Myshkin Rus. Fed.
Myshkino Rus. Fed. see Myshkin
159 Q9 Myskhako Rus. Fed.
196 C3 Myśla r. Pol.
Mys Lazareva Rus. Fed. see Lazarev
197 H6 Myślenice Pol.
196 C3 Myśliborskie, Jezioro l. Pol.
196 C3 Myślibórz Pol.
197 H2 Myślice Pol.
197 H5 Mysłowice Pol.
Myslowitz Pol. see Mysłowice
118 I7 My Son tourist site Vietnam
136 E6 Mysore Karnataka India
Mysore state India see Karnataka
159 N8 Mysove Ukr.
Mysovsk Rus. Fed. see Babushkin
153 T3 Mys Shmidta Rus. Fed.
259 L2 Mystic CT U.S.A.
259 G5 Mystic Islands NJ U.S.A.
156 K3 Mysy Rus. Fed.
197 H1 Myszewo Pol.
197 H5 Myszków Pol.
197 J2 Myszyniec Pol.
156 H4 Myt Rus. Fed.
119 H9 My Tho Vietnam
220 D2 Mytikas mt. Greece
Mytilene i. Greece see Lesvos
221 H3 Mytilini Lesvos Greece
221 H5 Mytilinioi Samos Greece
148 C4 Mytilini Strait Greece/Turkey
161 U6 Mytishchi Rus. Fed.
199 I3 Mýtna Slovakia
198 C2 Mýto Czech Rep.
265 V1 Myton UT U.S.A.
159 L5 Mytrofanivka Ukr.
151 I3 Myurego Rus. Fed.
162 □E1 Mývatn l. Iceland
162 □E1 Mývatn-Laxá nature res. Iceland
162 □E1 Mývatnsöræfi lava field Iceland
156 K3 Myyeldino Rus. Fed.
Myylybulak Kazakh. see Milybulabk
158 D2 Myzove Ukr.
227 F2 M'zab, Vallée du tourist site Alg.
237 K7 Mzamomhle S. Africa
198 B2 Mže r. Czech Rep.
233 C6 Mziha Tanz.
233 B7 Mzimba Malawi
235 F4 Mzingwani r. Zimbabwe
233 B7 Mzuzu Malawi
151 A2 Mzymta r. Rus. Fed.

N

118 F3 Na, Nam r. China/Vietnam
195 M3 Naab r. Ger.
186 F5 Naaldwijk Neth.
264 □F14 Nā'ālehu HI U.S.A.
230 F2 Naam Sudan
227 E2 Naama Alg.
163 Q6 Naantali Fin.
186 H4 Naarden Neth.
201 K3 Naarn im Machlande Austria
169 I6 Naas Ireland
162 T2 Näätämö Fin.
162 T5 Näätänmaa Fin.
118 C2 Naba Myanmar
236 B5 Nababeep S. Africa
Nabadwip W. Bengal India see Navadwip
151 C3 Nabakevi Georgia
204 D9 Nabão r. Port.
137 H3 Nabarangapur Orissa India
126 D6 Nabari Japan
126 D6 Nabari-gawa r. Japan
114 D6 Nabas Panay Phil.
150 D5 Nabatîyé et Tahta Lebanon
109 F8 Nabberu, Lake salt flat W.A. Austr.
195 M3 Nabburg Ger.
228 E4 Nabéré, Réserve Partielle de nature res. Burkina
233 C6 Naberera Tanz.
159 R2 Naberezhnoye Rus. Fed.
156 K5 Naberezhnyye Chelny Rus. Fed.
142 A2 Naberezhnyy Uvekh Rus. Fed.
245 L3 Nabesna AK U.S.A.
245 L3 Nabesna r. AK U.S.A.
244 I3 Nabesna Glacier AK U.S.A.
245 L3 Nabesna Village AK U.S.A.
227 H1 Nabeul Tunisia
211 C7 Nabeul admin. div. Tunisia
138 F4 Nabha Punjab India
151 H5 Nābiağalı Azer.
277 F5 Nabileque r. Brazil
139 J7 Nabinagar Bihar India
113 I7 Nabire Papua Indon.
150 D5 Nabi Younés, Ras en pt Lebanon
150 D6 Nāblus West Bank
228 E4 Nabolo Ghana
235 F5 Naboomspruit S. Africa
101 □7a Naboutini Viti Levu Fiji
101 □7 Nabouwalu Vanua Levu Fiji
199 L3 Nábrád Hungary
119 D7 Nabule Myanmar
267 M8 Nacajuca Mex.
235 I2 Nacala Moz.
269 K8 Nacaltepec Mex.
266 □P11 Nacaome Hond.
235 H2 Nacaroa Moz.
276 D2 Nacebe Bol.
198 D2 Načeradec Czech Rep.
160 H7 Nacha Belarus
160 L7 Nacha r. Belarus
142 C4 Nachalovo Rus. Fed.
262 D3 Naches WA U.S.A.
249 H1 Nachicapau, Lac l. Que. Can.
233 C7 Nachingwea Tanz.
138 C6 Nachna Rajasthan India
198 F1 Náchod Czech Rep.
137 M7 Nachuge Andaman & Nicobar Is India
101 □7a Nacilau Point Viti Levu Fiji
284 A5 Nacimiento Chile
207 N6 Nacimiento Spain
207 N7 Nacimiento r. Spain
264 L6 Nacimiento Reservoir CA U.S.A.
192 G5 Nackel Ger.
194 E2 Nackenheim Ger.
261 H10 Nacogdoches TX U.S.A.
266 E2 Nacozari de García Mex.
197 I3 Nacpolsk Pol.
284 D4 Nacuñan Arg.
Nada Hainan China see Danzhou
127 H1 Nadachi Japan
245 N3 Nadaleen r. Y.T. Can.
101 □7a Nadarivatu Viti Levu Fiji
196 E2 Nadarzyce Pol.
198 F5 Nádasd Hungary
199 H4 Nádasdladány Hungary
138 F6 Nadbai Rajasthan India
173 I5 Nadder r. England U.K.
159 L7 Naddnipryans'ke Ukr.
Nådendal Fin. see Naantali
142 J1 Nadezhdinka Kazakh.
Nadezhdinskiy Kazakh. see Nadezhdinka
122 H4 Nadezhdinskoye Rus. Fed.
105 M7 Nadgee Nature Reserve Vic. Austr.
101 □7a Nadi Viti Levu Fiji
146 A6 Nadi Sudan
138 D8 Nadiad Gujarat India
101 □7a Nadi Bay Viti Levu Fiji
144 F6 Nadīk Iran
218 I4 Nădlac Romania
165 O7 Nadmorski Park Krajobrazowy Pol.
199 J1 Nadnidziański Park Krajobrazowy Pol.
138 D7 Nadol Rajasthan India
226 E2 Nador Morocco
202 E5 Nador prov. Morocco
161 R1 Nadporozh'ye Rus. Fed.
147 J4 Nadqān, Qalamat well Saudi Arabia
219 K5 Nădrag Romania
101 □7a Nadrau Plateau Viti Levu Fiji
151 G2 Nadterechnaya Rus. Fed.
199 K4 Nádudvar Hungary
217 □ Nadur Gozo Malta
217 □ Nadur hill Malta
101 □7 Naduri Vanua Levu Fiji
144 E5 Nadūshan Iran
158 D5 Nadvirna Ukr.
Nadvornaya Ukr. see Nadvirna
152 I3 Nadym Rus. Fed.
138 E7 Naenwa Rajasthan India
164 H6 Næstved Denmark
139 N9 Naf r. Bangl./Myanmar
150 C9 Nafas, Ra's an mt. Egypt
212 G1 Näfels Switz.
171 Q5 Nafferton East Riding of Yorkshire, England U.K.
150 C8 Nafḥa, Har hill Israel
220 C4 Nafpaktos Greece
220 D5 Nafplio Greece
Naft r. Iraq see Naft, Āb
149 L7 Naft, Āb r. Iraq
151 H5 Naftalan Azer.
144 C6 Naft-e Sefīd Iran
Naft-e Shāh Iran see Naft Shahr
144 A4 Naft Shahr Iran
224 A2 Nafūsah, Jabal hills Libya
146 F3 Nafy Saudi Arabia
133 J10 Nag, Co l. China
126 B7 Naga Japan
114 D5 Naga Luzon Phil.
248 C3 Nagagami r. Ont. Can.
248 C3 Nagagami Lake Ont. Can.
125 J13 Nagahama Ehime Japan
126 D5 Nagahama Shiga Japan
139 O6 Naga Hills India
Naga Hills state India see Nagaland
124 R8 Nagai Japan
244 G5 Nagai Island AK U.S.A.
127 I5 Nagaizumi Japan
126 F5 Nagakute Japan
139 O6 Nagaland state India
105 J7 Nagambie Vic. Austr.
124 □1 Nagannu-jima i. Okinawa Japan
127 H2 Nagano Japan
127 G3 Nagano pref. Japan
127 I2 Naganohara Japan
127 L1 Naganuma Japan
125 P9 Nagaoka Japan
126 C6 Nagaokakyō Japan
139 N6 Nagaon Assam India
Nagapatam Tamil Nadu India see Nagapattinam
136 F7 Nagapattinam Tamil Nadu India
139 L7 Nagar r. Bangl./India
138 F3 Nagar Hima. Prad. India
136 D6 Nagar Karnataka India
138 F6 Nagar Rajasthan India
127 L5 Nagara Japan
228 C3 Nagara Mali
126 E5 Nagara-gawa r. Japan
136 G3 Nagaram Andhra Prad. India
127 K4 Nagareyama Japan
136 F4 Nagarjuna Sagar Reservoir India
136 F4 Nagar Karnul Andhra Prad. India
266 □P11 Nagarote Nic.
145 N9 Nagar Parkar Pak.
139 I7 Nagar Untari Jharkhand India
133 J12 Nagarzê Xizang China
127 H4 Nagasaka Japan
125 G14 Nagasaki Japan
125 G13 Nagasaki pref. Japan
125 H14 Nagashima Kagoshima Japan
126 E5 Nagashima Mie Japan
125 H14 Naga-shima i. Japan
125 J13 Naga-shima i. Japan
127 H3 Nagato Nagano Japan
125 I12 Nagato Yamaguchi Japan
127 J3 Nagatoro Japan
138 D6 Nagaur Rajasthan India
137 H3 Nagavali r. India
126 G3 Nagawa Japan
138 G9 Nagbhir Mahar. India
138 E8 Nagda Madh. Prad. India
195 L2 Nagel Ger.
186 I3 Nagele Neth.
136 E8 Nagercoil Tamil Nadu India
145 K8 Nagha Kalat Pak.
138 G5 Nagina Uttar Prad. India
144 G4 Nagineh Iran
133 L13 Naginimara Nagaland India
126 G4 Nagiso Japan
133 M11 Nagjog Xizang China
169 E8 Nagles Mountains hills Ireland
197 I5 Nagłowice Pol.
138 H5 Nagma Nepal
124 □1 Nago Okinawa Japan
138 H7 Nagod Madh. Prad. India
194 F4 Nagold Ger.
194 F4 Nagold r. Ger.
Nagong Chu r. China see Parlung Zangbo
205 R3 Nagore Spain
Nagorno-Karabakh aut. reg. Azer. see Dağlıq Qarabağ
153 N4 Nagornyy Rus. Fed.
Nagornyy Karabakh aut. reg. Azer. see Dağlıq Qarabağ
156 J4 Nagorsk Rus. Fed.
161 V5 Nagor'ye Rus. Fed.
213 J4 Nago-Torbole Italy
124 □1 Nago-wan b. Okinawa Japan
126 E5 Nagoya Japan
138 G9 Nagpur Mahar. India
133 K11 Nagqu Xizang China
133 K11 Nag Qu r. Xizang China
271 □2 Nag's Head pt St Kitts and Nevis
163 P6 Nagu Fin.
271 I4 Nagua Dom. Rep.
271 □1 Naguabo Puerto Rico
114 E5 Nagumbuaya Point Phil.
152 F1 Nagurskoye Zemlya Frantsa-Iosifa Rus. Fed.
106 B4 Nagurunguru Aboriginal Land res. N.T. Austr.
151 D1 Nagutskoye Rus. Fed.
198 G5 Nagyatád Hungary
199 G5 Nagybajom Hungary
199 J5 Nagybánhegyes Hungary
199 H5 Nagybaracska Hungary
Nagybecskerek Vojvodina Serbia see Zrenjanin
199 G5 Nagybereki Fehérvíz nature res. Hungary
199 H5 Nagyberény Hungary
199 H5 Nagyberki Hungary
198 F4 Nagycenk Hungary
199 J4 Nagycsécs Hungary
199 K4 Nagycserkesz Hungary
199 L3 Nagydobos Hungary
199 H5 Nagydorog Hungary
199 L4 Nagyecsed Hungary
Nagyenyed Romania see Aiud
199 J4 Nagyfüged Hungary
199 K3 Nagyhalász Hungary
199 H6 Nagyharsány Hungary
199 K4 Nagyhegyes Hungary
199 H4 Nagyigmánd Hungary
199 J4 Nagyiván Hungary
199 K4 Nagykálló Hungary
199 K5 Nagykamarás Hungary
198 F5 Nagykanizsa Hungary
198 F5 Nagykapornak Hungary
199 H5 Nagykarácsony Hungary
199 I4 Nagykáta Hungary
199 K4 Nagykereki Hungary
199 H5 Nagykónyi Hungary
199 I4 Nagykőrös Hungary
199 H4 Nagykovácsi Hungary
199 J5 Nagykunság reg. Hungary
199 J4 Nagykunsági Öntöző Főcsatorna canal Hungary
199 J5 Nagylak Hungary
199 I3 Nagylóc Hungary
198 F4 Nagylózs Hungary
199 J5 Nagymágocs Hungary
199 H5 Nagymányok Hungary
199 H4 Nagymaros Hungary
199 K3 Nagy-Milic hill Hungary/Slovakia
199 H6 Nagynyárád Hungary
199 I4 Nagyoroszi Hungary
199 K4 Nagyrábé Hungary
198 G5 Nagyrécse Hungary
199 K5 Nagy-sárrét reg. Hungary
198 G4 Nagysimonyi Hungary
199 J5 Nagyszénás Hungary
199 G4 Nagyszentjános Hungary
199 H5 Nagyszokoly Hungary
199 I4 Nagytarcsa Hungary
199 J5 Nagytőke Hungary
199 K4 Nagy-Vadas-tó l. Hungary
Nagyvárad Romania see Oradea
199 L3 Nagyvarsány Hungary
199 G5 Nagyvázsony Hungary
199 H5 Nagyvenyim Hungary
160 K3 Naha Estonia
124 □1 Naha Okinawa Japan
138 F4 Nahan Hima. Prad. India
145 J8 Nahang r. Iran/Pak.
246 F2 Nahanni Butte N.W.T. Can.
245 P3 Nahanni National Park Reserve N.W.T. Can.
246 F2 Nahanni Range mts N.W.T. Can.
150 D6 Naharāyim Jordan
125 L13 Nahari Japan
150 D5 Nahariyya Israel
205 P8 Naharros Spain
144 C4 Nahāvand Iran
190 J3 Nahe Ger.
194 D2 Nahe r. Ger.
Na h-Eileanan an Iar admin. div. Scotland U.K. see Western Isles
227 F4 N'Ahnet, Adrar mts Alg.
100 □5 Nahoï, Cap c. Vanuatu
181 O7 Nahon r. France
146 D2 Nahr, Jabal hill Saudi Arabia
190 K4 Nahrendorf Ger.
268 F6 Nahuatzen Mex.
283 C6 Nahuel Huapí Arg.
283 C6 Nahuel Huapí, Parque Nacional nat. park Arg.
284 D4 Nahuel Mapá Arg.
283 D6 Nahuel Niyeu Arg.
285 I5 Nahuel Rucá Arg.
145 J8 Nāhūg Iran
255 F10 Nahunta GA U.S.A.
145 L3 Nāībābād Afgh.
114 C4 Naic Luzon Phil.
266 G4 Naica Mex.
284 E5 Naicó Arg.
233 C6 Naidor well Tanz.
118 C1 Nai Ga Myanmar
101 □7a Naigani i. Fiji
128 D9 Naij Tal Qinghai China
224 C3 Nā'ikah, Qarārat an depr. Libya
115 C8 Naikliu Timor Indon.
246 C4 Naikoon Provincial Park B.C. Can.
193 E10 Naila Ger.
185 H9 Nailloux France
172 G5 Nailsea North Somerset, England U.K.
172 H4 Nailsworth Gloucestershire, England U.K.
133 K12 Nailung Xizang China
225 G6 Na'ima Sudan
Naiman Qi Nei Mongol China see Daqin Tal
128 B4 Naimin Shuiquan well Xinjiang China
249 I1 Nain Nfld and Lab. Can.
144 E5 Nā'īn Iran
138 H7 Naina Uttar Prad. India
Naingani i. Fiji see Naigani
138 G5 Nainital Uttaranchal India
138 H8 Nainpur Madh. Prad. India
181 L8 Naintré France
235 H3 Naiopué Moz.
101 □7 Nairai i. Fiji
107 K6 Nairana National Park nat. park Australia
101 □9a Nairiri Tahiti Fr. Polynesia
168 I7 Nairn Highland, Scotland U.K.
168 I7 Nairn r. Scotland U.K.
251 M3 Nairn Centre Ont. Can.
233 C5 Nairobi Kenya
160 H2 Naissaar i. Estonia
Naissus Niš Serbia see Niš
232 C5 Naivasha Kenya
179 J6 Naives-Rosières France
180 F6 Naizin France
122 E7 Naizishan Jilin China
185 H7 Najac France
Najaf Iraq see An Najaf
144 D5 Najafābād Iran
147 H3 Na'jān Saudi Arabia
270 E3 Najasa r. Cuba
146 E2 Najd reg. Saudi Arabia
205 O4 Nájera Spain
205 O3 Najerilla r. Spain
225 G3 Naj' Ḥammādī Egypt
129 R2 Naji Nei Mongol China
138 G5 Najibabad Uttar Prad. India
205 P6 Nájima r. Spain
123 G7 Najin N. Korea
Najitun Nei Mongol China see Naji
147 J2 Najmah Saudi Arabia
146 G7 Najrān Saudi Arabia
146 G6 Najrān prov. Saudi Arabia
146 G7 Najrān, Wādī watercourse Saudi Arabia
126 A5 Naka Hyōgo Japan
127 L3 Naka Ibaraki Japan
135 □1 Nakachchaafushi i. N. Male Maldives
125 G14 Nakadōri-shima i. Japan
118 G6 Na Kae Thai.
127 G4 Nakagawa Nagano Japan
126 A8 Nakagawa Tokushima Japan
125 L13 Naka-gawa r. Japan
127 M3 Naka-gawa r. Japan
127 H2 Nakagō Japan
124 □1 Nakagusuku Okinawa Japan
124 □1 Nakagusuku-wan b. Okinawa Japan
Nakahchaafushi i. N. Male Maldives see Nakachchaafushi
126 C8 Nakahechi Japan
127 J5 Nakai Japan
127 J6 Nakaizu Japan
127 L1 Nakajima Fukushima Japan
126 E1 Nakajima Ishikawa Japan
125 J13 Naka-jima i. Japan
127 H2 Nakajō Japan
127 H5 Nakakawane Japan
264 □E12 Nākālele Point HI U.S.A.
125 H13 Nakama Japan
228 E4 Nakambé watercourse Burkina alt. Nakanbe, alt. Volta Blanche, conv. White Volta
127 I4 Nakamichi Japan
127 M3 Nakaminato Japan
125 J14 Nakamura Japan
Nakanbe r. see White Volta
153 L3 Nakanno Rus. Fed.
127 H2 Nakano Japan
127 I2 Nakanojō Japan
124 □G17 Nakano-shima i. Nansei-shotō Japan
125 K10 Nakano-shima i. Japan
127 J1 Nakano-take mt. Japan
124 □1 Nakaoshi Okinawa Japan
233 C7 Nakapanya Tanz.
232 B4 Nakapiripirit Uganda
124 R6 Nakasato Aomori Japan
127 I3 Nakasato Gunma Japan
127 I1 Nakasato Niigata Japan
124 U4 Nakasatsunai Japan
124 R7 Nakasen Japan
124 V3 Nakashibetsu Japan
232 B4 Nakasongola Uganda
Nakatchafushi i. N. Male Maldives see Nakachchaafushi
127 H5 Nakatomi Japan
124 T2 Nakatonbetsu-chō hill Japan
125 I13 Nakatsu Ōita Japan
126 B8 Nakatsu Wakayama Japan
126 G5 Nakatsugawa Japan
127 I2 Nakatsu-gawa r. Japan
135 □1 Nakatuku Fushi i. N. Male Maldives
244 H4 Nakchamik Island AK U.S.A.
225 H5 Nakfa Eritrea
225 H5 Nakfa Wildlife Reserve nature res. Eritrea
Nakhichevan' Azer. see Naxçıvan
Nakhichevan' aut. reg. Azer. see Naxçıvan
225 G2 Nakhl Egypt
144 E8 Nakhl-e Taqī Iran
122 H7 Nakhodka Rus. Fed.
139 N6 Nakhola Assam India
119 E7 Nakhon Nayok Thai.
119 E8 Nakhon Pathom Thai.
118 G6 Nakhon Phanom Thai.
119 F7 Nakhon Ratchasima (Korat) Thai.
118 E7 Nakhon Sawan Thai.
119 D10 Nakhon Si Thammarat Thai.
118 E6 Nakhon Thai Thai.
Nakhrachi Rus. Fed. see Kondinskoye
138 B8 Nakhtarana Gujarat India
248 C3 Nakina Ont. Can.
245 N4 Nakina r. B.C. Can.
151 D3 Nakip'u Georgia
196 F1 Nakla Pol.
146 E5 Nakl an Nīlah Saudi Arabia
198 G2 Náklo Czech Rep.
197 H5 Nakło Pol.
201 J7 Naklo Slovenia
196 F2 Nakło nad Notecią Pol.
244 H4 Naknek AK U.S.A.
244 H4 Naknek Lake AK U.S.A.
138 E4 Nakodar Punjab India
125 □2 Nakōdo-jima i. Japan
197 J1 Nakomiady Pol.
233 B7 Nakonde Zambia
236 D4 Nakop Namibia
101 □7a Nakorokula Viti Levu Fiji
127 M2 Nakoso Japan
160 G5 Nākotne Latvia
199 J6 Nakovo Vojvodina Serbia
229 E4 Nakpanduri Ghana
151 D2 Nakra, Ugheltekhili pass Georgia/Rus. Fed.
164 H7 Nakskov Denmark
190 L1 Nakskov Fjord inlet Denmark
162 M5 Näkten l. Sweden
123 F11 Naktong-gang r. S. Korea
232 C5 Nakuru Kenya
246 G5 Nakusp B.C. Can.
145 L8 Nal Pak.
145 K8 Nal r. Pak.
230 E4 Nala Dem. Rep. Congo
118 C3 Na-lang Myanmar
129 J3 Nalayh Mongolia
235 G5 Nalázi Moz.
194 B3 Nalbach Ger.
139 M6 Nalbari Assam India
151 E2 Nal'chik Rus. Fed.
205 P4 Nalda Spain
136 E4 Naldurg Mahar. India
197 K4 Nałęczów Pol.
199 J3 Nálepkovo Slovakia
228 E4 Nalerigu Ghana
136 F4 Nalgonda Andhra Prad. India
139 K7 Nalhati W. Bengal India
139 M7 Nalitabari Bangl.
138 B8 Naliya Gujarat India
138 F8 Nalkhera Madh. Prad. India
136 F5 Nallamala Hills India
184 B3 Nalliers France
221 M2 Nallıhan Turkey
143 M1 Nalobino Kazakh.
231 D8 Nalolo Zambia
204 H2 Nalón r. Spain
232 B4 Nalubaale Dam Uganda
224 A2 Nālūt Libya
198 C2 Nalžovské Hory Czech Rep.
115 F5 Namaa, Tanjung pt Seram Indon.
235 G5 Namaacha Moz.
235 H2 Namacala Moz.
101 □7 Namacu Fiji
231 B9 Namacunde Angola
235 H3 Namacurra Moz.
105 L6 Namadgi National Park N.S.W. Austr.
237 M3 Namahadi S. Africa
114 □ Namai Bay Palau
144 D4 Namak, Daryācheh-ye salt flat Iran
144 G4 Namak, Kavīr-e salt flat Iran
144 C4 Namak-e Mīqhān, Kavīr-e salt flat Iran
144 F6 Nāmakī watercourse Iran
136 F7 Namakkal Tamil Nadu India
144 I5 Namakzar Afgh.
144 H6 Namakzar-e Shadad salt flat Iran
116 G6 Namang Indon.
233 C5 Namanga Kenya
143 N7 Namangan Uzbek.
143 N7 Namangan admin. div. Uzbek.
Namangan Oblast admin. div. Uzbek. see Namangan
Namangan Wiloyati admin. div. Uzbek. see Namangan
233 A6 Namanyere Tanz.
235 H2 Namapa Moz.
235 H2 Namaponda Moz.
236 A4 Namaqualand reg. S. Africa
236 B6 Namaqua National Park S. Africa
235 H2 Namarrói Moz.
232 B4 Namasale Uganda
144 A3 Namashīr Iran
113 L7 Namatanai New Ireland P.N.G.
Namathu Fiji see Namacu
231 B7 Namba Angola
231 E8 Nambala Zambia
233 C7 Nambiranji Tanz.
139 N7 Nambol Manipur India
194 C2 Namborn Ger.
107 N9 Nambour Qld Austr.
Namboutini Viti Levu Fiji see Naboutini
Nambouwalu Vanua Levu Fiji see Nabouwalu
205 M9 Nambroca Spain
Nambu Japan see Nanbu
105 N4 Nambucca Heads N.S.W. Austr.
109 C11 Nambung National Park W.A. Austr.
119 G10 Năm Căn Vietnam
Namcha Barwa mt. Xizang China see Namjagbarwa Feng
139 K6 Namche Bazar Nepal
133 J11 Namco Xizang China
133 J11 Nam Co salt l. China
144 D6 Namdagūn Iran
162 L4 Namdalen val. Norway
162 K4 Namdalseid Norway
118 H4 Nam Đinh Vietnam
165 O2 Nämdö i. Sweden
165 O2 Nämdöfjärden b. Sweden
119 G10 Nam Du, Quân Đao i. Vietnam
127 J3 Namegawa Japan
250 C4 Namekagon r. WI U.S.A.
114 □ Namelakl Passage Palau
Namen Belgium see Namur
126 F2 Namerikawa Japan
198 F2 Náměšť nad Oslavou Czech Rep.
199 I2 Námestovo Slovakia
235 H2 Nametil Moz.
247 K4 Namew Lake Man./Sask. Can.
123 D9 Nam-gang r. N. Korea
123 E11 Namhae-do i. S. Korea
118 C3 Namhkan Myanmar
118 C3 Namhsan Myanmar
126 G5 Namiai Japan
235 H2 Namialo Moz.

234 B5 **Namib Desert** Namibia
231 B8 **Namibe** Angola
231 B8 **Namibe** prov. Angola
231 B8 **Namibe, Reserva de** nature res. Angola
234 B4 **Namibia** country Africa
288 J8 **Namibia Abyssal Plain** sea feature N. Atlantic Ocean
234 B5 **Namib-Naukluft National Park** Namibia
233 C7 **Namichiga** Tanz.
235 H2 **Namicunde** Moz.
235 H3 **Namidobe** Moz.
124 R9 **Namie** Japan
236 D5 **Namies** S. Africa
144 C2 **Namīn** Iran
235 H2 **Namina** Moz.
233 B8 **Namitete** Malawi
133 L12 **Namjagbarwa Feng** mt. Xizang China
133 J12 **Namka** Xizang China
118 C3 **Namlan** Myanmar
118 C3 **Namlang** r. Myanmar
115 E5 **Namlea** Buru Indon.
133 I12 **Namling** Xizang China
118 E6 **Nam Nao National Park** Thai.
118 F5 **Nam Ngum Reservoir** Laos
133 H11 **Namoding** Xizang China
105 L4 **Namoi** r. N.S.W. Austr.
127 I3 **Namoku** Japan
113 K5 **Namonuito** atoll Micronesia
227 E3 **Namous, Oued en** watercourse Alg.
231 E5 **Namoya** Dem. Rep. Congo
246 G3 **Nampa** Alta Can.
138 H4 **Nampa** mt. Nepal
262 F5 **Nampa** ID U.S.A.
228 D3 **Nampala** Mali
118 E6 **Nam Pat** Thai.
235 H3 **Nampevo** Moz.
118 F6 **Nam Phong** Thai.
118 F6 **Nam Phung, Ang Kep Nam** Thai.
123 D9 **Namp'o** N. Korea
235 I2 **Nampuecha** Moz.
235 H2 **Nampula** Moz.
235 H2 **Nampula** prov. Moz.
115 E5 **Namrole** Buru Indon.
139 O6 **Namrup** Assam India
139 O6 **Namsai** Arun. Prad. India
118 C2 **Namsai** Myanmar
118 C4 **Namsang** Myanmar
162 K4 **Namsfjorden** sea chan. Norway
131 □J7 **Nam She Tsim** hill H.K. China
162 K4 **Namsos** Norway
162 L4 **Namsskogan** Norway
229 I4 **Namtari** Nigeria
118 C2 **Namti** Myanmar
118 C5 **Namtok** Myanmar
119 D7 **Nam Tok** Thai.
118 E6 **Nam Tok Chattakan National Park** Thai.
118 D5 **Nam Tok Mae Surin National Park** Thai.
118 D3 **Namton** Myanmar
153 N3 **Namtsy** Rus. Fed.
118 C3 **Namtu** Myanmar
246 E5 **Namu** B.C. Can.
Namuka i. Tonga see **Nomuka**
103 □4 **Namukulu** Niue
235 H2 **Namuli, Monte** mt. Moz.
235 H2 **Namuno** Moz.
187 G8 **Namur** Belgium
187 G8 **Namur** prov. Belgium
234 C3 **Namutoni** Namibia
231 E8 **Namwala** Zambia
233 B8 **Namwera** Malawi
123 E11 **Namwŏn** S. Korea
118 C1 **Namya Ra** Myanmar
112 D4 **Namyit Island** S. China Sea
196 F4 **Namysłów** Pol.
118 E5 **Nan** Thai.
118 E7 **Nan, Mae Nam** r. Thai.
229 I5 **Nana** Cameroon
230 B3 **Nana** r. C.A.R.
199 H4 **Nána** Slovakia
230 C3 **Nana Bakassa** C.A.R.
230 C3 **Nana Barya** r. C.A.R./Chad
230 C3 **Nana-Grébizi** pref. C.A.R.
246 F5 **Nanaimo** B.C. Can.
127 L3 **Nanakai** Japan
264 □C12 **Nānākuli** HI U.S.A.
230 B3 **Nana-Mambéré** pref. C.A.R.
131 L6 **Nan'an** Fujian China
Nan'an Jiangxi China see **Dayu**
107 N9 **Nanango** Qld Austr.
234 C5 **Nananib Plateau** Namibia
101 □7a **Nananu-i-Ra** i. Fiji
126 E1 **Nanao** Japan
126 E1 **Nanao-wan** b. Japan
126 E2 **Nanatsuka** Japan
125 N9 **Nanatsu-shima** i. Japan
274 C5 **Nanay** r. Peru
Nanbai Guizhou China see **Zunyi**
133 L8 **Nanbaxian** Qinghai China
Nanbin Chongqing China see **Shizhu**
130 F3 **Nanbu** Sichuan China
127 H5 **Nanbu** Japan
284 B4 **Nancagua** Chile
181 P7 **Nançay** France
122 F5 **Nancha** Heilong. China
131 J4 **Nanchang** Jiangxi China
131 J4 **Nanchang** Jiangxi China
Nanchangshan Shandong China see **Changdao**
131 K5 **Nancheng** Jiangxi China
269 M7 **Nanchital** Mex.
130 F3 **Nanchong** Sichuan China
130 F4 **Nanchuan** Chongqing China
205 O3 **Nanclares de la Oca** Spain
277 E5 **Ñancorainza** Bol.
137 M9 **Nancowry** i. Andaman & Nicobar Is India
129 M9 **Nancun** Henan China
Nancun Shanxi China see **Zezhou**
246 E4 **Nancut** B.C. Can.
179 L6 **Nancy** France
103 B12 **Nancy Sound** inlet South I. N.Z.
138 H4 **Nanda Devi** mt. Uttaranchal India
138 H4 **Nanda Kot** mt. Uttaranchal India
130 F6 **Nandan** Guangxi China
126 A7 **Nandan** Japan
Nandarivatu Viti Levu Fiji see **Nadarivatu**
136 E3 **Nanded** Mahar. India
Nander Mahar. India see **Nanded**
105 M4 **Nandewar Range** mts N.S.W. Austr.
138 E9 **Nandgaon** Mahar. India
Nandi Fiji see **Nadi**
235 F4 **Nandi** Zimbabwe
Nandi Bay Viti Levu Fiji see **Nadi Bay**
136 G4 **Nandigama** Andhra Prad. India
136 F5 **Nandikotkur** Andhra Prad. India
130 B7 **Nanding He** r. Yunnan China
138 D9 **Nandod** Gujarat India
Nandrau Plateau Viti Levu Fiji see **Nadrau Plateau**
187 H7 **Nandrin** Belgium
285 G2 **Ñanducita** Arg.
130 H8 **Nandu Jiang** r. China
138 F9 **Nandura** Mahar. India
138 E9 **Nandurbar** Mahar. India
Nanduri Vanua Levu Fiji see **Naduri**
136 F5 **Nandyal** Andhra Prad. India
219 P5 **Nănești** Romania
131 H7 **Nanfeng** Guangdong China
131 K5 **Nanfeng** Jiangxi China
133 K12 **Nang** Xizang China
233 C7 **Nangade** Moz.
229 I5 **Nanga Eboko** Cameroon
117 J4 **Nangahbunut** Kalimantan Indon.
117 I5 **Nangah Dedai** Kalimantan Indon.
117 J4 **Nangahembaloh** Kalimantan Indon.
117 I4 **Nangahkantuk** Kalimantan Indon.
117 J5 **Nangahkemangai** Kalimantan Indon.
117 I4 **Nangahketungau** Kalimantan Indon.
117 I5 **Nangahmau** Kalimantan Indon.
117 I4 **Nangah Merakai** Kalimantan Indon.
117 I5 **Nangahpinoh** Kalimantan Indon.
117 J4 **Nangahsuruk** Kalimantan Indon.
117 J4 **Nangahtempuai** Kalimantan Indon.
106 E2 **Nangalala** N.T. Austr.
114 C6 **Nangalao** i. Phil.
233 C7 **Nanganga** Tanz.
122 F7 **Nangang Shan** mts China
138 E2 **Nanga Parbat** mt. Pak.
145 N4 **Nangarhār** prov. Afgh.
105 L7 **Nangar National Park** N.S.W. Austr.
117 I5 **Nangataman** Kalimantan Indon.
117 I5 **Nangatayap** Kalimantan Indon.
229 F5 **Nangbéto, Retenue de** resr Togo
128 G8 **Nangdoi** Qinghai China
119 D9 **Nangin** Myanmar
178 F6 **Nangis** France
138 H4 **Nangling** Uttaranchal India
123 E8 **Nangnim** N. Korea
123 E8 **Nangnim-sanmaek** mts N. Korea
127 K1 **Nangō** Fukushima Japan
125 I15 **Nangō** Miyazaki Japan
129 N8 **Nangong** Hebei China
130 A2 **Nangqên** Qinghai China
129 K7 **Nangsin Sum** Nei Mongol China
233 C7 **Nangulangwa** Tanz.
136 E8 **Nanguneri** Tamil Nadu India
129 N8 **Nanhe** Hebei China
132 L7 **Nanhu** Gansu China
128 C5 **Nanhu** Xinjiang China
128 F7 **Nanhua** Gansu China
130 C6 **Nanhua** Yunnan China
131 M3 **Nanhui** Shanghai China
145 M5 **Nani** Afgh.
243 J2 **Nanisivik (abandoned)** Nunavut Can.
136 E6 **Nanjangud** Karnataka India
130 G5 **Nanjia** Guizhou China
130 C6 **Nanjian** Yunnan China
130 F2 **Nanjiang** Sichuan China
Nanjie Guangdong China see **Guangning**
131 K6 **Nanjing** Fujian China
131 L2 **Nanjing** Jiangsu China
131 M5 **Nanji Shan** i. China
126 D4 **Nanjō** Japan
130 B7 **Nanka Jiang** r. Yunnan China
131 J6 **Nankang** Jiangxi China
Nankang Jiangxi China see **Xingzi**
Nanking Jiangsu China see **Nanjing**
125 K13 **Nankoku** Japan
231 C9 **Nankova** Angola
130 B8 **Nanlan He** r. Yunnan China
100 □4b **Nanlaud** hill Pohnpei Micronesia
129 N8 **Nanle** Henan China
130 B8 **Nanlei He** r. Yunnan China alt. **Loi, Nam**
131 L3 **Nanling** Anhui China
131 H6 **Nan Ling** mts China
130 G8 **Nanliu Jiang** r. China
Nanlong Sichuan China see **Nanbu**
Nanma Shandong China see **Yiyuan**
Nanmulingzue Xizang China see **Namling**
109 E9 **Nannine** W.A. Austr.
130 G7 **Nanning** Guangxi China
129 K8 **Nanniwan** Shaanxi China
126 E5 **Nannō** Japan
109 C12 **Nannup** W.A. Austr.
118 E5 **Na Noi** Thai.
243 N3 **Nanortalik** Greenland
Nanouki atoll Gilbert Is Kiribati see **Nonouti**
Nanouti atoll Gilbert Is Kiribati see **Nonouti**
130 F6 **Nanpan Jiang** r. China
138 H6 **Nanpara** Uttar Prad. India
129 O7 **Nanpi** Hebei China
129 Q6 **Nanpiao** Liaoning China
131 L5 **Nanping** Fujian China
Nanpu Fujian China see **Pucheng**
131 L5 **Nanpu Xi** r. China
Nanqiao Shanghai China see **Fengxian**
131 L6 **Nanri Dao** i. China
205 L2 **Nansa** r. Spain
232 C3 **Nansebo** Eth.
126 E7 **Nansei** Japan
124 □B22 **Nansei-shotō** is Japan
Nansei-shotō Trench sea feature N. Pacific Ocean see **Ryukyu Trench**
292 B1 **Nansen Basin** sea feature Arctic Ocean
231 E8 **Nansenga** Zambia
243 N1 **Nansen Land** reg. Greenland
243 I1 **Nansen Sound** sea chan. Nunavut Can.
Nansha Yunnan China see **Yuanyang**
131 □I7 **Nanshan** Guangdong China
112 E4 **Nanshan Island** S. China Sea
128 D8 **Nanshankou** Qinghai China
128 C5 **Nanshankou** Xinjiang China
Nansha Qundao is S. China Sea see **Spratly Islands**
233 B5 **Nansio** Tanz.
183 H10 **Nans-les-Pins** France
183 C8 **Nant** France
138 E7 **Nanta** Rajasthan India
127 L2 **Nantai-san** hill Japan
127 J2 **Nantai-san** mt. Japan
104 G4 **Nantawarrina Aboriginal Land** res. S.A. Austr.
172 F4 **Nant Bran** r. Wales U.K.
235 H3 **Nante** Moz.
178 D6 **Nanterre** France
180 H7 **Nantes** France
180 G6 **Nantes à Brest, Canal de** France
184 A1 **Nantes Atlantique** airport France
178 E5 **Nanteuil-le-Haudouin** France
136 G8 **Nanthi Kadal** lag. Sri Lanka
184 G3 **Nantiat** France
248 D5 **Nanticoke** Ont. Can.
257 J10 **Nanticoke** MD U.S.A.
258 C2 **Nanticoke** PA U.S.A.
257 J10 **Nanticoke** r. MD U.S.A.
126 E7 **Nantō** Japan
246 H5 **Nanton** Alta Can.
131 M3 **Nantong** Jiangsu China
Nantong Jiangsu China see **Tongzhou**
131 M7 **Nant'ou** Taiwan
182 H4 **Nantua** France
257 O7 **Nantucket** MA U.S.A.
257 P7 **Nantucket Island** MA U.S.A.
257 O7 **Nantucket Sound** g. MA U.S.A.
233 C8 **Nantulo** Moz.
171 L7 **Nantwich** Cheshire, England U.K.
172 F4 **Nantyglo** Blaenau Gwent, Wales U.K.
256 G8 **Nanty Glo** PA U.S.A.
172 E3 **Nant-y-moch Reservoir** Wales U.K.
259 G2 **Nanuet** NY U.S.A.
101 □7a **Nanukuloa** Viti Levu Fiji
Nanumaga i. Tuvalu see **Nanumanga**
99 H2 **Nanumanga** i. Tuvalu
99 H2 **Nanumea** atoll Tuvalu
281 G2 **Nanuque** Brazil
115 E1 **Nanusa, Kepulauan** is Indon.
245 J1 **Nanushuk** r. AK U.S.A.
109 C7 **Nanutarra Roadhouse** W.A. Austr.
Nanwai Sichuan China see **Daxian**
130 E4 **Nanxi** Sichuan China
131 I4 **Nanxian** Hunan China
131 J6 **Nanxiong** Guangdong China
131 M5 **Nanyandang Shan** mt. Zhejiang China
131 I2 **Nanyang** Henan China
124 R8 **Nanyō** Japan
232 C5 **Nanyuki** Kenya
Nan Yunhe canal China see **Jinghang Yunhe**
129 S6 **Nanzamu** Liaoning China
131 H3 **Nanzhang** Hubei China
Nanzhao Fujian China see **Zhao'an**
131 I2 **Nanzhao** Henan China
Nanzheng Shaanxi China see **Zhoujiaping**
Nanzhou Hunan China see **Nanxian**
145 N4 **Nao** Afgh.
209 F10 **Nao, Cabo de la** c. Spain
249 G2 **Naococane, Lac** l. Que. Can.
139 L7 **Naogaon** Bangl.
122 I5 **Naoli He** r. China
269 K6 **Naolinco** Mex.
144 I5 **Naomid, Dasht-e** des. Afgh./Iran
117 J3 **Naong, Bukit** mt. Malaysia
138 E3 **Naoshera** Jammu and Kashmir India
220 D2 **Naousa** Kentriki Makedonia Greece
220 G5 **Naousa** Paros Greece
264 J3 **Napa** CA U.S.A.
257 □S2 **Napadogan** N.B. Can.
235 H2 **Napaha** Moz.
244 H3 **Napaimiut** AK U.S.A.
232 B4 **Napak** mt. Uganda
244 G3 **Napakiak** AK U.S.A.
242 G3 **Napaktulik Lake** Nunavut Can.
285 H5 **Napaleofú** Arg.
248 E4 **Napanee** Ont. Can.
259 G1 **Napanoch** NY U.S.A.
138 D6 **Napasar** Rajasthan India
244 G3 **Napaskiak** AK U.S.A.
243 M3 **Napasoq** Greenland
250 F8 **Naperville** IL U.S.A.
212 D1 **Napf** mt. Switz.
102 K6 **Napier** North I. N.Z.
236 D10 **Napier** S. Africa
108 I2 **Napier Broome Bay** W.A. Austr.
287 D2 **Napier Mountains** Antarctica
106 E2 **Napier Peninsula** N.T. Austr.
108 H4 **Napier Range** hills W.A. Austr.
257 L3 **Napierville** Que. Can.
197 I2 **Napiwoda** Pol.
199 K4 **Napkor** Hungary
Naples Italy see **Napoli**
255 G12 **Naples** FL U.S.A.
257 □O5 **Naples** ME U.S.A.
256 H6 **Naples** NY U.S.A.
265 W1 **Naples** UT U.S.A.
130 E7 **Napo** Guangxi China
274 B5 **Napo** prov. Ecuador
274 C5 **Napo** r. Ecuador
216 D8 **Napola** Sicilia Italy
260 F2 **Napoleon** ND U.S.A.
256 A7 **Napoleon** OH U.S.A.
238 □2b **Napoleon's Tomb** tourist site St Helena
261 J11 **Napoleonville** LA U.S.A.
215 M6 **Napoli** Italy
215 M6 **Napoli** prov. Italy
215 M6 **Napoli, Golfo di** b. Italy
285 F6 **Naposta** Arg.
285 F6 **Naposta** r. Arg.
183 J9 **Napoule, Golfe de la** b. France
250 I8 **Nappanee** IN U.S.A.
106 D7 **Napperby** N.T. Austr.
107 I2 **Napranum Aboriginal Reserve** Qld Austr.
144 A3 **Naqadeh** Iran
150 A9 **Naqb Māliḥah** mt. Egypt
150 H3 **Naqīb Mustajidd** Syria
144 C4 **Naqqash** Iran
146 G8 **Naqūb** Yemen
209 E8 **Náquera** Spain
138 B8 **Nara** Gujarat India
126 C6 **Nara** Japan
126 C7 **Nara** pref. Japan
228 D3 **Nara** Mali
161 U7 **Nara** r. Rus. Fed.
160 J7 **Narach** Belarus
160 J7 **Narach** r. Belarus
160 J7 **Narach, Vozyera** l. Belarus
104 H7 **Naracoorte** S.A. Austr.
105 K5 **Naradhan** N.S.W. Austr.
198 F4 **Nárai** Hungary
127 G3 **Narai-gawa** r. Japan
139 L8 **Narail** Bangl.
138 E6 **Naraina** Rajasthan India
136 G3 **Narainpur** Chhattisgarh India
127 G4 **Narakawa** Japan
139 K6 **Naralua** Bihar India
129 M4 **Naran** Mongolia
128 C2 **Naranbulag** Uvs Mongolia
Naranbulag Mongolia see **Bayandun**
145 N4 **Narang** Afgh.
274 B5 **Naranjal** Ecuador
274 C6 **Naranjal** Peru
271 □1 **Naranjito** Puerto Rico
269 J4 **Naranjos** Mex.
128 E5 **Naran Sebstein Bulag** spring Gansu China
125 G14 **Narao** Japan
144 D5 **Narāq** Iran
137 I3 **Narasannapeta** Andhra Prad. India
136 G4 **Narasapatnam, Point** India
136 G4 **Narasapur** Andhra Prad. India
136 G4 **Narasaraopet** Andhra Prad. India
127 L4 **Narashino** Japan
139 J9 **Narasinghapur** Orissa India
129 M2 **Narasun** Rus. Fed.
132 G5 **Narat** Xinjiang China
119 E11 **Narathiwat** Thai.
132 F5 **Narat Shan** mts China
261 D8 **Nara Visa** NM U.S.A.
139 M8 **Narayanganj** Bangl.
138 H8 **Narayanganj** Madh. Prad. India
136 D3 **Narayangaon** Mahar. India
136 E4 **Narayanpet** Andhra Prad. India
197 M6 **Narayiv** Ukr.
197 M6 **Narayivka** r. Ukr.
145 N4 **Naray Kelay** Afgh.
Narbada r. India see **Narmada**
172 C4 **Narberth** Pembrokeshire, Wales U.K.
Narbo France see **Narbonne**
214 B7 **Narbolia** Sardegna Italy
183 C10 **Narbonne** France
183 C10 **Narbonne-Plage** France
173 J2 **Narborough** Leicestershire, England U.K.
173 N2 **Narborough** Norfolk, England U.K.
Narborough Island Islas Galápagos Ecuador see **Fernandina, Isla**
163 K5 **Narbuvoll** Norway
214 B9 **Narcao** Sardegna Italy
204 H1 **Narcea** r. Spain
137 N6 **Narcondam Island** Andaman & Nicobar Is India
182 C2 **Narcy** France
144 F3 **Nardin** Iran
217 O3 **Nardò** Italy
285 G2 **Nare** Arg.
145 M6 **Narechi** r. Pak.
136 D5 **Naregal** Karnataka India
109 E12 **Narembeen** W.A. Austr.
138 G4 **Narendranagar** Uttaranchal India
288 E4 **Nares Abyssal Plain** sea feature S. Atlantic Ocean
288 E4 **Nares Deep** sea feature N. Atlantic Ocean
243 K2 **Nares Strait** Can./Greenland
151 H5 **Nareştar** Azer.
109 H11 **Naretha** W.A. Austr.
197 L3 **Narew** Pol.
197 I3 **Narew** r. Pol.
197 L3 **Narewka** Pol.
197 L3 **Narewka** r. Pol.
145 L7 **Nari** r. Pak.
139 M8 **Naria** Bangl.
234 C5 **Narib** Namibia
197 I2 **Narie, Jezioro** l. Pol.
236 B6 **Nariep** S. Africa
204 C2 **Nariga, Punta** pt Spain
151 J7 **Närimanabad** Azer.
151 J5 **Närimankänd** Azer.
142 B4 **Narimanov** Rus. Fed.
145 M3 **Narin** Afgh.
145 M3 **Narin** reg. Afgh.
129 L7 **Narin** Nei Mongol China
148 I5 **Narince** Turkey
133 K8 **Narin Gol** watercourse China
274 B4 **Nariño** dept Col.
127 L4 **Narita** Japan
127 L4 **Narita** airport Japan
126 B4 **Nariu-misaki** pt Japan
271 □7 **Nariva** county Trin. and Tob.
271 □7 **Nariva Swamp** Trin. and Tob.
125 K12 **Nariwa** Japan
128 G4 **Nariynteel** Mongolia
266 D4 **Narizon, Punta** pt Mex.
138 F4 **Narkanda** Hima. Prad. India
133 G13 **Narkatiaganj** Bihar India
162 S3 **Narkaus** Fin.
162 Q3 **Narken** Sweden
138 G9 **Narkher** Mahar. India
161 Y6 **Narma** r. Rus. Fed.
138 D9 **Narmada** r. India
151 C5 **Narman** Turkey
138 F5 **Narnaul** Haryana India
215 J2 **Narni** Italy
Narnia Italy see **Narni**
216 F9 **Naro** Sicilia Italy
216 F9 **Naro** r. Sicilia Italy
156 M2 **Narodnaya, Gora** mt. Rus. Fed.
158 I2 **Narodychi** Ukr.
161 T6 **Naro-Fominsk** Rus. Fed.
101 □7 **Naroi** Fiji
233 B5 **Narok** Kenya
105 M7 **Narooma** N.S.W. Austr.
157 H5 **Narovchat** Rus. Fed.
158 I2 **Narowlya** Belarus
163 P5 **Närpes** Fin.
105 L4 **Narrabri** N.S.W. Austr.
257 N7 **Narragansett Bay** RI U.S.A.
105 K3 **Narran** r. N.S.W. Austr.
105 K6 **Narrandera** N.S.W. Austr.
105 K3 **Narran Lake** N.S.W. Austr.
109 D12 **Narrogin** W.A. Austr.
105 L5 **Narromine** N.S.W. Austr.
185 B8 **Narrosse** France
247 J4 **Narrow Hills Provincial Park** Sask. Can.
256 E11 **Narrows** VA U.S.A.
258 E1 **Narrowsburg** NY U.S.A.
243 N3 **Narsalik** Greenland
136 F3 **Narsapur** Andhra Prad. India
243 N3 **Narsaq** Greenland
243 N3 **Narsarsuaq** Greenland
193 G8 **Narsdorf** Ger.
139 M8 **Narsingdi** Bangl.
138 F8 **Narsinghgarh** Madh. Prad. India
138 G8 **Narsinghpur** Madh. Prad. India
137 H4 **Narsipatnam** Andhra Prad. India
129 N5 **Nart** Nei Mongol China
Nart Mongolia see **Orhon**
201 O8 **Narta** Croatia
220 A2 **Nartë** Albania
151 E2 **Nartkala** Rus. Fed.
183 J10 **Nartuby** r. France
124 R8 **Naruko** Japan
127 I5 **Narusawa** Japan
125 F14 **Naru-shima** i. Japan
197 I3 **Naruszewo** Pol.
127 L4 **Narutō** Japan
126 A7 **Naruto** Japan
126 A7 **Naruto-kaikyō** sea chan. Japan
160 L2 **Narva** Estonia
160 L2 **Narva** r. Estonia/Rus. Fed.
160 K2 **Narva Bay** Estonia/Rus. Fed.
114 C3 **Narvacan** Luzon Phil.
160 L2 **Narva-Jõesuu** Estonia
Narva laht b. Estonia/Rus. Fed. see **Narva Bay**
160 L2 **Narva Reservoir** Estonia/Rus. Fed.
162 N2 **Narvik** Norway
Narvskiy Zaliv b. Estonia/Rus. Fed. see **Narva Bay**
Narvskoye Vodokhranilishche resr Estonia/Rus. Fed. see **Narva Reservoir**
138 F5 **Narwana** Haryana India
138 F7 **Narwar** Madh. Prad. India
189 K2 **Narwiański Park Narodowy** Pol.
106 D7 **Narwietooma** N.T. Austr.
106 F4 **Narwinbi Aboriginal Land** res. N.T. Austr.
156 K2 **Nar'yan-Mar** Rus. Fed.
143 P7 **Naryn** Kyrg.
143 P7 **Naryn** admin. div. Kyrg.
143 O7 **Naryn** r. Kyrg./Uzbek.
128 D1 **Naryn** Rus. Fed.
143 S6 **Narynkol** Kazakh.
Naryn Oblast admin. div. Kyrg. see **Naryn**
Narynqol Kazakh. see **Narynkol**
Narynskaya Oblast' admin. div. Kyrg. see **Naryn**
161 S9 **Naryshkino** Rus. Fed.
212 D6 **Narzole** Italy
162 N5 **Näsåker** Sweden
219 M3 **Năsăud** Romania
198 E2 **Nasavrky** Czech Rep.
183 C7 **Nasbinals** France
165 M5 **Näsby** Öland Sweden
Na Scealaga is Ireland see **The Skelligs**
278 D4 **Nascentes do Rio Parnaíba, Parque Nacional das** nat. park Brazil
284 E3 **Naschel** Arg.
103 E12 **Naseby** South I. N.Z.
244 F3 **Nash Harbor** AK U.S.A.
138 D9 **Nashik** Mahar. India
224 B3 **Nashū, Wādī an** watercourse Libya
250 B7 **Nashua** IA U.S.A.
257 N6 **Nashua** NH U.S.A.
165 M2 **Näshultasjön** l. Sweden
261 I9 **Nashville** AR U.S.A.
255 F10 **Nashville** GA U.S.A.
260 K6 **Nashville** IL U.S.A.
255 I8 **Nashville** NC U.S.A.
256 C8 **Nashville** OH U.S.A.
258 B5 **Nashville** PA U.S.A.
255 D7 **Nashville** TN U.S.A.
250 A2 **Nashwauk** MN U.S.A.
228 E4 **Nasia** Ghana
148 H7 **Naşīb** Syria
210 G3 **Našice** Croatia
197 I3 **Nasielsk** Pol.
163 Q6 **Näsijärvi** l. Fin.
Nasik Mahar. India see **Nashik**
101 □7a **Nasilai Reef** Fiji
117 I4 **Nasilat** Kalimantan Indon.
98 H3 **Nasinu** Fiji
101 □7 **Nasinu** Fiji
145 M7 **Nasir** Pak.
232 B2 **Nasir** Sudan
225 G4 **Nāşir, Buḥayrat** resr Egypt
Nasirabad Bangl. see **Mymensingh**
138 E6 **Nasirabad** Rajasthan India
145 M7 **Nasirabad** Pak.
Nāşirīyah Iraq see **An Nāşirīyah**
249 I2 **Naskaupi** r. Nfld and Lab. Can.
224 B2 **Nasmah** Libya
139 J7 **Nasmganj** Bihar India
165 M3 **Näsnaren** l. Sweden
216 H7 **Naso** Sicilia Italy
216 H7 **Naso** r. Sicilia Italy
231 E7 **Nasondoye** Dem. Rep. Congo
250 D5 **Nasonville** WI U.S.A.
101 □7 **Nasorolevu** mt. Vanua Levu Fiji
Nasosnyy Azer. see **Hacı Zeynalabdin**
144 G5 **Nasqenj** Iran
225 F2 **Naşr** Egypt
144 H4 **Naşrābād** Khorāsān Iran
150 F5 **Naşrānī, Jabal an** mts Syria
Nasratabad Iran see **Zābol**
144 H8 **Naşrī** Iran
144 B5 **Naşrīān-e Pā'īn** Iran
245 O5 **Nass** r. B.C. Can.
229 G4 **Nassarawa** Nigeria
229 H4 **Nassarawa** state Nigeria
107 H3 **Nassau** r. Qld Austr.
270 E1 **Nassau** New Prov. Bahamas
103 □2 **Nassau** i. Cook Is
191 E10 **Nassau** Rheinland-Pfalz Ger.
193 I9 **Nassau** Sachsen Ger.
257 L6 **Nassau** NY U.S.A.
191 E10 **Nassau, Naturpark** nature res. Ger.
259 H3 **Nassau County** county NY U.S.A.
257 J11 **Nassawadox** VA U.S.A.
192 H5 **Nassenheide** Ger.
Nasser, Lake resr Egypt see **Nāşir, Buḥayrat**
200 C5 **Nassereith** Austria
228 E4 **Nassian** Côte d'Ivoire
165 K4 **Nässjö** Sweden
187 H8 **Nassogne** Belgium
243 M3 **Nassuttooq** inlet Greenland
248 E1 **Nastapoca** r. Que. Can.
248 E1 **Nastapoka Islands** Nunavut Can.
191 E10 **Nastätten** Ger.
160 I1 **Nastola** Fin.
127 L1 **Nasu** Japan
127 K1 **Nasu-dake** vol. Japan
114 C4 **Nasugbu** Luzon Phil.
197 K4 **Nasutów** Pol.
161 N5 **Nasva** Rus. Fed.
161 N5 **Nasva** r. Rus. Fed.
163 N6 **Näsviken** Sweden
199 H4 **Naszály** Hungary
234 E4 **Nata** Botswana
234 E4 **Nata** watercourse Botswana/Zimbabwe
115 E5 **Nataboti** Buru Indon.
277 E1 **Natal** Amazonas Brazil
278 G3 **Natal** Rio Grande do Norte Brazil
116 C4 **Natal** Sumatera Indon.
Natal prov. S. Africa see **KwaZulu-Natal**
289 G7 **Natal Basin** sea feature Indian Ocean
258 C3 **Natalie** PA U.S.A.
144 D5 **Naţanz** Iran
126 C5 **Natashō** Japan
249 I3 **Natashquan** Que. Can.
249 I3 **Natashquan** r. Nfld and Lab./Que. Can.
103 □1 **Na Taulaga** i. Tokelau
245 L3 **Natazhat, Mount** AK U.S.A.
261 J10 **Natchez** MS U.S.A.
261 I10 **Natchitoches** LA U.S.A.
171 M5 **Nateby** Cumbria, England U.K.
196 D3 **Natecka, Puszcza** for. Pol.
212 D3 **Naters** Switz.
101 □7 **Natewa Bay** Vanua Levu Fiji
105 J7 **Nathalia** Vic. Austr.
138 E4 **Nathana** Punjab India
106 E3 **Nathan River** N.T. Austr.
138 D7 **Nathdwara** Rajasthan India
Nathilau Point Viti Levu Fiji see **Nacilau Point**
162 □ **Nathorst Land** reg. Svalbard
208 □ **Nati, Punta** pt Spain
229 F4 **Natiaboani** Burkina
267 I5 **Natillas** Mex.
245 L2 **Nation** AK U.S.A.
264 O9 **National City** CA U.S.A.
102 J6 **National Park** North I. N.Z.
234 B4 **National West Coast Tourist Recreation Area** park Namibia
213 O4 **Natisone** r. Italy
229 F4 **Natitingou** Benin
266 B4 **Natividad, Isla** i. Mex.
281 G4 **Natividade** Rio de Janeiro Brazil
278 D4 **Natividade** Tocantins Brazil
119 C7 **Natkyizin** Myanmar
245 O3 **Natla** r. N.W.T. Can.
118 B4 **Natmauk** Myanmar
118 B4 **Natogyi** Myanmar
263 J12 **Nátora** Mex.
139 L7 **Natore** Bangl.
124 R8 **Natori** Japan
233 C5 **Natron, Lake** salt l. Tanz.
127 M1 **Natsui-gawa** r. Japan
105 M6 **Nattai National Park** N.S.W. Austr.
118 B5 **Nattalin** Myanmar
136 F7 **Nattam** Tamil Nadu India
165 O3 **Nåttarö** i. Sweden
118 C5 **Nattaung** mt. Myanmar
162 P3 **Nattavaara** Sweden
162 P3 **Nattavaara by** Sweden
201 I3 **Natternback** Austria
195 I4 **Nattheim** Ger.
144 I4 **Na'tū** Iran
101 □7 **Natua** Vanua Levu Fiji
249 I2 **Natuashish** Nfld and Lab. Can.
159 Q9 **Natukhayevskaya** Rus. Fed.
117 G2 **Natuna, Kepulauan** is Indon.
117 H2 **Natuna Besar** i. Indon.
256 F11 **Natural Bridge** VA U.S.A.
265 V4 **Natural Bridges National Monument** nat. park UT U.S.A.
109 C12 **Naturaliste, Cape** W.A. Austr.
109 A8 **Naturaliste Channel** W.A. Austr.
289 L7 **Naturaliste Plateau** sea feature Indian Ocean
236 H9 **Nature's Valley** S. Africa
265 X3 **Naturita** CO U.S.A.
213 J2 **Naturno** Italy
244 I2 **Natuvukti Lake** AK U.S.A.
Nau Tajik. see **Nov**
250 I3 **Naubinway** MI U.S.A.
185 I7 **Naucelle** France
184 I6 **Naucelles** France
234 C4 **Nauchas** Namibia
133 F10 **Nau Co** l. Xizang China
200 C6 **Nauders** Austria
236 I8 **Naudesberg Pass** S. Africa
235 H2 **Nauela** Moz.
192 G5 **Nauen** Ger.
193 E7 **Nauendorf** Ger.
259 I2 **Naugatuck** CT U.S.A.
259 I2 **Naugatuck** r. CT U.S.A.
194 E2 **Nauheim** Ger.
145 L6 **Nau Hissar** Pak.
Naujaat Nunavut Can. see **Repulse Bay**
184 B5 **Naujac-sur-Mer** France
114 C5 **Naujan** Mindoro Phil.
160 F5 **Naujoji Akmenė** Lith.
138 D6 **Naukh** Rajasthan India
145 M9 **Naukot** Pak.
169 J5 **Naul** Ireland
231 B9 **Naulila** Angola
191 H8 **Naumburg (Hessen)** Ger.
193 E8 **Naumburg (Saale)** Ger.
193 H8 **Naundorf** Sachsen Ger.
193 H9 **Naundorf** Sachsen Ger.
118 C6 **Naunglon** Myanmar
118 C5 **Naungpale** Myanmar
150 D7 **Na'ūr** Jordan
191 E9 **Nauroth** Ger.
145 K7 **Nauroz Kalat** Pak.
151 G2 **Naurskaya** Rus. Fed.
99 G2 **Nauru** i. Nauru
99 G2 **Nauru** country S. Pacific Ocean
142 J2 **Naurzum Nature Reserve** res. Kazakhstan
145 M8 **Naushahro Feroze** Pak.
145 M8 **Naushara** Pak.
128 J1 **Naushki** Rus. Fed.
183 D7 **Naussac, Barrage de** dam France
163 H6 **Naustdal** Norway
274 C6 **Nauta** Peru
Nautaca Uzbek. see **Qarshi**
139 I6 **Nautanwa** Uttar Prad. India
236 B2 **Naute Dam** Namibia
269 K5 **Nautla** Mex.
162 T2 **Nautsi** Rus. Fed.
250 C9 **Nauvoo** IL U.S.A.
145 K5 **Nauzad** Afgh.
230 E4 **Nava** r. Dem. Rep. Congo
267 I3 **Nava** Mex.
205 J2 **Nava** Spain
Navabad Tajik. see **Novobod**
205 J8 **Navacepeda de Tormes** Spain
205 M7 **Navacerrada, Puerto de** pass Spain
205 L7 **Navacerreda** Spain
207 L7 **Navachica** mt. Spain
204 I8 **Navaconcejo** Spain
205 K7 **Nava de Arévalo** Spain
205 L6 **Nava de la Asunción** Spain
205 J6 **Nava del Rey** Spain
205 J7 **Nava de Sotrobal** Spain
160 K6 **Navadrutsk** Belarus
139 L8 **Navadwip** W. Bengal India
205 M6 **Navafría** Spain
205 L9 **Navahermosa** Spain
151 K5 **Navahı** Azer.
160 I8 **Navahrudak** Belarus
160 I8 **Navahrudskaye Wzvyshsha** hills Belarus
209 E8 **Navajas** Spain
263 K8 **Navajo** r. CO U.S.A.
265 W6 **Navajo Indian Reservation** res. AZ U.S.A.
263 K8 **Navajo Lake** NM U.S.A.
265 V4 **Navajo Mountain** UT U.S.A.
205 J4 **Navajos** hill Spain
114 E6 **Naval** Phil.
208 F3 **Naval** Spain
205 L8 **Navalagamella** Spain
205 O5 **Navalcaballo** Spain
205 J8 **Navalcán** Spain
205 J8 **Navalcán, Embalse de** resr Spain
205 L8 **Navalcarnero** Spain
205 O5 **Navalero** Spain
205 L6 **Navalmanzano** Spain
205 K8 **Navalmoral** Spain
205 K7 **Navalmoral, Puerto de** pass Spain
204 I9 **Navalmoral de la Mata** Spain
205 J8 **Navalonguilla** Spain
205 K8 **Navalosa** Spain
205 L7 **Navalperal de Pinares** Spain
207 J2 **Navalpino** Spain
205 K8 **Navaluenga** Spain
205 J9 **Navalvillar de Ibor** Spain
207 I2 **Navalvillar de Pela** Spain
205 K8 **Navamorcuende** Spain
169 I5 **Navan** Ireland
Navangar Gujarat India see **Jamnagar**
160 L6 **Navapolatsk** Belarus
145 L5 **Nāvar, Dasht-e** depr. Afgh.
208 I4 **Navarcles** Spain
208 C2 **Navardún** Spain
153 S3 **Navarin, Mys** c. Rus. Fed.
283 D9 **Navarino, Isla** i. Chile
205 Q3 **Navarra** aut. comm. Spain
105 I7 **Navarre** Vic. Austr.
Navarre aut. comm. Spain see **Navarra**
204 H7 **Navarredonda de la Rinconada** Spain
185 C9 **Navarrenx** France
209 D9 **Navarrés** Spain
205 O4 **Navarrete** Spain
285 H4 **Navarro** Arg.
274 C6 **Navarro** Peru
264 I2 **Navarro** r. CA U.S.A.
208 I4 **Navàs** Spain
185 D10 **Navasa** Spain
208 C2 **Navascués** Spain
207 J1 **Navas de Estrena** Spain
204 G9 **Navas del Madroño** Spain
205 L8 **Navas del Rey** Spain
205 L6 **Navas de Oro** Spain
207 M4 **Navas de San Juan** Spain
204 G8 **Navasfrías** Spain
156 H5 **Navashino** Rus. Fed.
261 G10 **Navasota** TX U.S.A.
261 G10 **Navasota** r. TX U.S.A.
270 F4 **Navassa Island** terr. West Indies
158 H1 **Navasyolki** Belarus
208 K3 **Navata** Spain
205 K8 **Navatalgordo** Spain
160 I8 **Navayel'nya** Belarus
212 I4 **Nave** Italy
206 B6 **Nave** Port.
204 B3 **Nave, Cabo da** c. Spain
204 F4 **Navea** r. Spain
204 G7 **Nave de Haver** Port.
170 E2 **Nave Island** Scotland U.K.
215 L3 **Navelli** Italy
182 I1 **Navenne** France
168 H5 **Naver** r. Scotland U.K.
168 H6 **Naver, Loch** l. Scotland U.K.
206 C6 **Nave Redonda** Port.
164 H3 **Naverstad** Sweden
184 H5 **Naves** France
208 I4 **Navès** Spain
161 U9 **Navesnoye** Rus. Fed.
160 H3 **Navesti** r. Estonia
271 □7 **Navet** Trin. and Tob.
207 I1 **Navezuelas** Spain
284 D4 **Navia** Arg.
204 G1 **Navia** Spain
204 G1 **Navia** r. Spain
204 G1 **Navia, Ría de** inlet Spain
138 B9 **Navibandar** Gujarat India
284 B3 **Navidad** Chile
261 G11 **Navidad** r. TX U.S.A.
271 I3 **Navidad Bank** sea feature Caribbean Sea
212 G5 **Naviglio di Pavia** canal Italy
212 G5 **Naviglio Grande** canal Italy
182 G3 **Navilly** France
136 C3 **Navi Mumbai** Mahar. India
279 B7 **Naviraí** Brazil
101 □7 **Naviti** i. Fiji
158 E2 **Naviz** Ukr.
138 C8 **Navlakhi** Gujarat India
161 R9 **Navlya** Rus. Fed.
161 R9 **Navlya** r. Rus. Fed.
219 Q6 **Năvodari** Romania
142 K7 **Navoiy** Uzbek.
142 J7 **Navoiy** admin. div. Uzbek.
266 E4 **Navojoa** Mex.
266 F5 **Navolato** Mex.
101 □7 **Navotuvotu** hill Vanua Levu Fiji
Navoy Oblast admin. div. Uzbek. see **Navoiy**
Návpaktos Greece see **Nafpaktos**
Návplion Greece see **Nafplio**
165 L5 **Nävragöl** Sweden
164 C3 **Navrestad** hill Norway
228 E4 **Navrongo** Ghana
Navşar Turkey see **Şemdinli**
138 D9 **Navsari** Gujarat India
101 □7a **Navua** Viti Levu Fiji
101 □7a **Navua** r. Viti Levu Fiji
101 □7a **Navula Reef** rf Fiji
244 □A5 **Navy Town** AK U.S.A.
138 E6 **Nawa** Rajasthan India
150 E6 **Nawá** Syria
139 L7 **Nawabganj** Bangl.
120 D6 **Nawabganj** Uttar Prad. India
133 F13 **Nawabganj** Uttar Prad. India
145 M8 **Nawabshah** Pak.
139 J7 **Nawada** Bihar India
139 I9 **Nawagaon** Chhattisgarh India
145 L5 **Nāwah** Afgh.
139 J6 **Nawakot** Nepal
145 N7 **Nawa Kot** Pak.
138 E6 **Nawalgarh** Rajasthan India
145 N6 **Nawan Kot** Pak.
133 C11 **Nawanshahr** Punjab India
146 F5 **Nawāşīf, Ḥarrat** lava field Saudi Arabia
118 C3 **Nawnghkio** Myanmar
118 D3 **Nawngleng** Myanmar
Nawoiy Uzbek. see **Navoiy**
Nawoiy Wiloyati admin. div. Uzbek. see **Navoiy**
197 I6 **Nawojowa** Pol.
147 L7 **Naws, Ra's** c. Oman
151 G6 **Naxçıvan** Azer.
151 G6 **Naxçıvan** aut. reg. Azer.
151 G6 **Naxçıvançay** r. Azer.
130 E4 **Naxi** Sichuan China
221 G5 **Naxos** Naxos Greece
221 G5 **Naxos** i. Greece
274 B4 **Naya** Col.
133 K10 **Nayag** Xizang China
139 J9 **Nayagarh** Orissa India
145 L4 **Nayak** Afgh.
268 C3 **Nayar** Mex.
268 C3 **Nayarit** state Mex.
144 G5 **Nāy Band** Iran
144 G5 **Nāy Band, Kūh-e** mt. Iran
185 D9 **Nay-Bourdettes** France
159 N8 **Nayd'onivka** Ukr.
147 J6 **Nayfah** oasis Saudi Arabia
130 E5 **Nayong** Guizhou China
124 T2 **Nayoro** Japan
118 C5 **Nay Pyi Taw** Myanmar
147 K9 **Nayt** Suquṭrā Yemen
233 B8 **Nayuchi** Malawi
136 F6 **Nayudupeta** Andhra Prad. India
146 D1 **Nayyāl, Wādī** watercourse Saudi Arabia
138 F8 **Nazarabad** Madh. Prad. India
274 E4 **Nazare** Amazonas Brazil
275 H6 **Nazaré** Brazil
278 E3 **Nazare** Piauí Brazil
204 B9 **Nazaré** Port.
266 H5 **Nazareno** Mex.
136 E8 **Nazareth** Tamil Nadu Ind
Nazareth Israel see **Nazer**
258 E3 **Nazareth** PA U.S.A.
280 C2 **Nazário** Brazil
266 G5 **Nazas** Mex.
266 G5 **Nazas** r. Mex.
276 B3 **Nazca** Peru
291 N7 **Nazca Ridge** sea feature S. Pacific Ocean
124 □G18 **Naze** Nansei-shotō Japan
173 M4 **Nazeing** Essex, England U
181 M7 **Nazelles-Négron** France
150 D6 **Nazerat** Israel
144 C5 **Nazian** Iran
144 A2 **Nāzīk** Iran
144 I7 **Nāzīl** Iran
221 J5 **Nazilli** Turkey
145 L9 **Nazimabad** Pak.
149 I4 **Nazımiye** Turkey
228 E4 **Nazinon** r. Burkina alt. **Volta Rouge** conv. **Red Volta**
139 O6 **Nazira** Assam India
139 M8 **Nazir Hat** Bangl.
151 I5 **Nāzirli** Azer.
161 O2 **Naziya** Rus. Fed.
246 F4 **Nazko** B.C. Can.
246 F4 **Nazko** r. B.C. Can.
144 A3 **Nāzlū** r. Iran
151 F2 **Nazran'** Rus. Fed.
232 C2 **Nazrēt** Eth.
147 M4 **Nazwá** Oman
152 I4 **Nazyvayevsk** Rus. Fed.
228 B2 **Nbâk** Maur.
228 D2 **Nbeïket Dlîm** well Maur.
237 J9 **Ncanaha** S. Africa
231 F7 **Nchelenge** Zambia
Ncheu Malawi see **Ntcheu**
234 D4 **Ncojane** Botswana
237 L7 **Ncora** S. Africa
229 H6 **Ncue** Equat. Guinea
228 C2 **Ndaghma Barké** well Mau
233 B6 **Ndala** Tanz.
231 B7 **N'dalatando** Angola
229 F4 **Ndali** Benin
230 D3 **Ndanda** C.A.R.
235 F4 **Ndanga** Zimbabwe
115 C9 **Ndao** i. Indon.
233 B6 **Ndareda** Tanz.
230 B5 **Ndekabalandji** Gabon
230 D2 **Ndélé** C.A.R.
229 I5 **Ndélélé** Cameroon
230 A5 **Ndendé** Gabon
Ndende i. Santa Cruz Is Solomon Is see **Ndeni**
100 □6 **Ndeni** i. Santa Cruz Is Sol
229 H5 **Ndikiniméki** Cameroon
230 B3 **Ndim** C.A.R.
231 A5 **Ndindi** Gabon
228 B3 **Ndioum Guènt** Senegal
N'Djamena Chad see **Ndja**
224 B6 **Ndjamena** Chad
230 D3 **Ndji** r. C.A.R.
229 H5 **Ndjim** r. Cameroon
230 A5 **Ndjolé** Gabon
Ndjouani i. Comoros see **N**
230 B5 **Ndjounou** Gabon
228 B3 **Ndofane** Senegal
230 A5 **Ndogo, Lagune** lag. Gabo
Ndoi i. Fiji see **Doi**
229 I5 **Ndok** Cameroon
231 F8 **Ndola** Zambia
228 D4 **Ndorola** Burkina
232 C4 **Ndoto** mt. Kenya
230 A5 **Ndougou** Gabon
230 D3 **Ndoukou** C.A.R.
230 C3 **Ndoumbou** C.A.R.
100 □6 **Ndovele** New Georgia Is Solomon Is
100 □6 **Nduindui** Solomon Is
Nduke i. New Georgia Is Solomon Is see **Kolomban**
233 C7 **Ndumbwe** Tanz.
237 Q2 **Ndumu** S. Africa
237 Q2 **Ndumu Game Reserve** na Moz.
230 F4 **Nduye** Dem. Rep. Congo
237 O5 **Ndwedwe** S. Africa
184 D4 **Né** r. France
118 G5 **Ne, Hon** i. Vietnam
185 E10 **Né, Mont** mt. France
220 G7 **Nea Alikarnassos** Kriti Gre
220 D3 **Nea Anchialos** Greece
220 E4 **Nea Apollonia** Greece
220 E4 **Nea Artaki** Greece
107 K9 **Neabul Creek** r. Qld Austr.
220 E5 **Nea Epidavros** Greece
220 C5 **Nea Figaleia** Greece
126 D3 **Neagari** Japan
169 J3 **Neagh, Lough** l. Northern U.K.
262 B2 **Neah Bay** WA U.S.A.
219 N6 **Neajlov** r. Romania
220 E2 **Nea Kallikrateia** Greece
220 F2 **Nea Karvali** Greece
169 D5 **Neale** Ireland
106 C8 **Neale, Lake** salt flat N.T. A
109 H10 **Neale Junction Nature Re** W.A. Austr.
104 F3 **Neales** watercourse S.A. Au
220 E4 **Nea Liosia** Greece
220 E4 **Nea Makri** Greece
221 H4 **Nea Monu** tourist site Gree
220 E2 **Nea Moudania** Greece
219 O3 **Neamț** r. Romania
220 F2 **Nea Peramos** Greece
220 C2 **Neapoli** Dytiki Makedonia
221 G7 **Neapoli** Kriti Greece
220 E6 **Neapoli** Peloponnisos Gree
Neapolis Italy see **Napoli**
244 □A5 **Near Islands** AK U.S.A.
220 E2 **Nea Roda** Greece
171 L5 **Near Sawrey** Cumbria, Eng U.K.
220 D2 **Nea Santa** Greece
Néa Stíra Greece see **Nea S**
220 F4 **Nea Styra** Greece
172 E4 **Neath** Neath Port Talbot, W
172 E4 **Neath** r. Wales U.K.
172 E4 **Neath Port Talbot** admin. d Wales U.K.
220 E1 **Nea Zichni** Greece
126 G5 **Neba** Japan
232 A4 **Nebbi** Uganda
214 C2 **Nebbio** reg. Corse France
228 E4 **Nebbou** Burkina
190 F1 **Nebel** Ger.
195 I7 **Nebelhorn** mt. Ger.
132 E5 **Nebesnaya, Gora** mt. Xinji China
185 I10 **Nébias** France
105 K3 **Nebine Creek** r. Qld Austr.
107 L6 **Nebo** Qld Austr.
265 U2 **Nebo, Mount** UT U.S.A.
161 Q2 **Nebolchi** Rus. Fed.
185 F9 **Nébouzan** reg. France
193 E8 **Nebra (Unstrut)** Ger.
260 E5 **Nebraska** state U.S.A.
260 H5 **Nebraska City** NE U.S.A.
205 M5 **Nebreda** Spain
216 G8 **Nebrodi, Monti** mts Sicilia
161 W5 **Nebylove** Rus. Fed.
269 J5 **Necaxa** r. Mex.
250 D5 **Necedah** WI U.S.A.
250 D5 **Necedah National Wildlife Refuge** nature res. WI U.S.A.
198 E1 **Nechanice** Czech Rep.
159 K7 **Nechayane** Ukr.
161 X6 **Nechayevskaya** Rus. Fed.
159 L5 **Nechayivka** Ukr.
261 I11 **Neches** r. TX U.S.A.
274 C2 **Nechí** r. Col.
232 C3 **Nechisar National Park** Et
207 M7 **Nechite** r. Spain
193 H10 **Nechranice, Vodní nádrž** r Czech Rep.
194 E2 **Neckar** r. Ger.
194 F3 **Neckarbischofsheim** Ger.
194 F3 **Neckargemünd** Ger.
194 F3 **Neckarsteinach** Ger.
194 G3 **Neckarsulm** Ger.
194 G3 **Neckartal-Odenwald, Natu** nature res. Ger.

H2 Necker Island HI U.S.A.
H6 Necochea Arg.
B2 Necoclí Col.
N2 Necton Norfolk, England U.K.
C5 Neda r. Greece
D2 Neda Spain
J2 Nedanchychi Ukr.
H2 Nedašov Czech Rep.
H3 Neddemin Ger.
C6 Nédéley Chad
N9 Nedelino Bulg.
F2 Nedelišće Croatia
T7 Nedel'noye Rus. Fed.
Nederland country Europe see Netherlands
Nederlandse Antillen terr. West Indies see Netherlands Antilles
H4 Nederlangbroek Neth.
H5 Neder Rijn r. Neth.
E1 Neder Vindinge Denmark
I6 Nederweert Neth.
Nédha r. Greece see Neda
M1 Nedingis l. Lith.
F6 Nedlitz Ger.
F1 Nedlouc, Lac l. Que. Can.
Nedluk Lake Que. Can. see Nedlouc, Lac
F5 Nedoboyivtsi Ukr.
J12 Nêdong Xizang China
P2 Nedre Soppero Sweden
F2 Nedre Tokke l. Norway
M3 Nedryhayliv Ukr.
B2 Nedstrand Norway
B2 Nedstrandsfjorden sea chan. Norway
F4 Neduka r. Dem. Rep. Congo
F2 Nedvědice Czech Rep.
G5 Nędza Pol.
I2 Neeba-san mt. Japan
K4 Neede Neth.
N6 Needham MA U.S.A.
O3 Needham Market Suffolk, England U.K.
L3 Needingworth Cambridgeshire, England U.K.
R7 Needles CA U.S.A.
G9 Needmore PA U.S.A.
E7 Neemuch Madh. Prad. India
F5 Neenah WI U.S.A.
L5 Neepawa Man. Can.
Neer Neth.
Neergaard Lake Nunavut Can.
H5 Neerijnen Neth.
D4 Neermoor Ger.
Neeroeteren Belgium
H6 Neerpelt Belgium
E5 Nees Sund sea chan. Denmark
K4 Neetze Ger.
C2 Nefas Mewch'a Eth.
D3 Neffs PA U.S.A.
C4 Neffsville PA U.S.A.
G2 Nefta Tunisia
K6 Neftçala Azer.
L5 Neft Daşları Azer.
Neftechala Azer. see Uzboy
Neftechala Azer. see Neftçala
A1 Neftegorsk Krasnodarskiy Kray Rus. Fed.
M2 Neftegorsk Sakhalin Rus. Fed.
O1 Neftegorsk Samarskaya Oblast' Rus. Fed.
K4 Neftekamsk Rus. Fed.
F1 Neftekumsk Rus. Fed.
F1 Neftenbach Switz.
Nefteyugansk Rus. Fed.
Neftezavodsk Turkm. see Seýdi
Neftyanyye Kamni Azer. see Neft Daşları
Nefyn Gwynedd, Wales U.K.
Nefza Tunisia
Negada Weyn well Eth.
Negage Angola
Négala Mali
Negār Iran
Negara Bali Indon.
Negara Kalimantan Indon.
Negara r. Indon.
Negaunee MI U.S.A.
Negēlē Oromīya Eth.
Negēlē Oromīya Eth.
Negeri Sembilan state Malaysia
Negev des. Israel
Negola Angola
Negomane Moz.
Negombo Sri Lanka
Negotin Negotin Serbia
Negotino Macedonia
Negotino Macedonia
Negra, Cordillera mts Peru
Negra, Lago l. Uru.
Negra, Peña mt. Spain
Negra, Punta pt Peru
Negra, Serra mts Brazil
Negra, Serranía de mts Bol.
Negrais, Cape Myanmar
Negrar Italy
Negratín, Embalse de resr Spain
Negre, Pic mt. Andorra
Negredo Spain
Negreira Spain
Negreiros Chile
Nègrepelisse France
Negrești Romania
Negrești-Oaș Romania
Negrete Chile
Negrete, Cabo c. Spain
Negri r. N.T. Austr.
Negri Romania
Negribreen glacier Svalbard
Negril Jamaica
Négrine Alg.
Negri Sembilan state Malaysia see Negeri Sembilan
Negritos Peru
Negro r. Arg.
Negro r. Brazil
Negro r. Para.
Negro r. S. America
Negro r. Spain
Negro r. Uru.
Negro r. Uru.
Negro, Cabo c. Morocco
Negroponte i. Greece see Evvoia
Negros i. Phil.
Negru Vodă Romania
Nehalem r. OR U.S.A.
Nehavand Iran
Nehbandān Iran
Nehe Heilong. China
Nehoiu Romania
Nehone Angola
Neiafu Vava'u Gp Tonga
Neiba Dom. Rep.
Neiguanying Gansu China
Neijiang Sichuan China
Neila, Sierra de mts Spain
Neilburg Sask. Can.
Neilersdrif S. Africa
Neill Island Andaman & Nicobar Is India
Neillsville WI U.S.A.
Nei Mongol Zizhiqu aut. reg. China
Neinstedt Ger.
Neiqiu Hebei China
Neiße r. Ger./Pol.
Neiva Col.
Neiva r. Port.
Neive Italy
Neixiang Henan China
Neixpa r. Mex.
Nejanilini Lake Man. Can.
Nejapa Mex.
Nejd reg. Saudi Arabia see Najd
Nejdek Czech Rep.
Nekā Iran
Nekā, Rūdkhāneh-ye r. Iran
Nek'emtē Eth.
Nekhayevskaya Rus. Fed.
Nekhayevskiy Rus. Fed. see Nekhayevskaya
Nekhayivka Ukr.
Nekla Pol.
161 X6 Neklyudovo Rus. Fed.
139 L7 Nekmarad Bangl.
126 A4 Neko-zaki pt Japan
158 H4 Nekrasove Ukr.
157 I6 Nekrasovo Rus. Fed.
161 U5 Nekrasovskiy Rus. Fed.
161 X4 Nekrasovskoye Rus. Fed.
164 H6 Nekselø i. Denmark
165 L6 Neksø Bornholm Denmark
205 N3 Nela r. Spain
136 E6 Nelamangala Karnataka India
138 G4 Nelang Hima. Prad. India
204 E7 Nelas Port.
164 E3 Nelaug l. Norway
161 U2 Nelazskoye Rus. Fed.
107 I6 Nelia Qld Austr.
161 P5 Nelidovo Rus. Fed.
260 G4 Neligh NE U.S.A.
153 O4 Nel'kan Khabarovskiy Kray Rus. Fed.
153 P3 Nel'kan Respublika Sakha (Yakutiya) Rus. Fed.
100 □3a Nell i. Kwajalein Marshall Is
251 N1 Nellie Lake Ont. Can.
136 E6 Nelligere Karnataka India
162 T2 Nellim Fin.
194 H4 Nellingen Ger.
136 F5 Nellore Andhra Prad. India
100 □3a Nell Passage Kwajalein Marshall Is
150 H2 Nelluz watercourse Turkey
122 K5 Nel'ma Rus. Fed.
237 O1 Nelshoogte pass S. Africa
285 G2 Nelson Arg.
246 G5 Nelson B.C. Can.
247 M3 Nelson r. Man. Can.
103 H8 Nelson South I. N.Z.
103 H8 Nelson admin. reg. South I. N.Z.
171 M6 Nelson Lancashire, England U.K.
265 S6 Nelson AZ U.S.A.
260 F5 Nelson NE U.S.A.
265 R6 Nelson NV U.S.A.
250 B5 Nelson WI U.S.A.
104 H8 Nelson, Cape Vic. Austr.
283 B8 Nelson, Estrecho str. Chile
105 N5 Nelson Bay N.S.W. Austr.
103 F9 Nelson Creek South I. N.Z.
246 F3 Nelson Forks B.C. Can.
247 L4 Nelson House Man. Can.
257 J11 Nelsonia VA U.S.A.
244 F3 Nelson Island AK U.S.A.
244 G5 Nelson Lagoon AK U.S.A.
103 G9 Nelson Lakes National Park South I. N.Z.
259 H2 Nelsonville NY U.S.A.
236 H8 Nelspoort S. Africa
237 O1 Nelspruit S. Africa
156 K3 Nem r. Rus. Fed.
228 D2 Néma Maur.
156 J4 Nema Rus. Fed.
250 B3 Nemadji r. MN U.S.A.
Neman r. Belarus/Lith. see Nyoman
160 F6 Neman Rus. Fed.
160 F6 Neman r. Rus. Fed. alt. Nemunas (Lith.), alt. Nyoman (Belarus)
144 H7 Ne'matābād Iran
Nemausus France see Nîmes
100 □6 Nembao Santa Cruz Is Solomon Is
229 G5 Nembe Nigeria
212 H4 Nembro Italy
199 I3 Nemce Slovakia
156 H4 Nemda r. Rus. Fed.
220 D5 Nemea Greece
156 K3 Nemed Rus. Fed.
251 K2 Nemegos Ont. Can.
251 K1 Nemegosenda Lake Ont. Can.
160 I7 Nemenčinė Lith.
227 G2 Nementcha, Monts des mts Alg.
220 B2 Nëmerçkë, Mal ridge Albania
198 G4 Nemesszalók Hungary
198 G5 Nemesvid Hungary
199 H5 Németkér Hungary
Nemetocenna France see Arras
162 U2 Nemetskiy, Mys c. Rus. Fed.
Nemirov Ukr. see Nemyriv
248 E3 Nemiscau r. Que. Can.
248 E3 Nemiscau, Lac l. Que. Can.
158 J3 Nemishayeve Ukr.
129 S2 Nemor He r. China
Nemours Alg. see Ghazaouet
178 E7 Nemours France
149 K4 Nemrut Dağı mt. Turkey
193 E8 Nemsdorf-Göhrendorf Ger.
199 H3 Nemšová Slovakia
122 I4 Nemta r. Rus. Fed.
197 M1 Nemunaitis Lith.
160 E6 Nemunas r. Lith. alt. Neman (Rus. Fed.), alt. Nyoman (Belarus)
160 H5 Nemunėlio Radviliškis Lith.
160 I5 Nemunėlis r. Lith.
124 W3 Nemuro Japan
124 W3 Nemuro-hantō pen. Japan
124 W3 Nemuro-kaikyō sea chan. Japan/Rus. Fed.
124 W3 Nemuro-wan b. Japan
158 C3 Nemyriv L'vivs'ka Oblast' Ukr.
158 H5 Nemyriv Vinnyts'ka Oblast' Ukr.
158 G4 Nemyryntsi Ukr.
169 F7 Nenagh Ireland
122 D4 Nenan Heilong. China
245 J2 Nenana AK U.S.A.
245 J2 Nenana r. AK U.S.A.
161 U7 Nenashevo Rus. Fed.
212 C3 Nendaz Switz.
173 M2 Nene r. England U.K.
Nenets Autonomous Okrug admin. div. Rus. Fed. see Nenetskiy Avtonomnyy Okrug
156 K2 Nenetskiy Avtonomnyy Okrug admin. div. Rus. Fed.
199 I3 Nenince Slovakia
129 S2 Nenjiang Heilong. China
129 S4 Nen Jiang r. China
190 D3 Nenndorf Ger.
192 G5 Nennhausen Ger.
195 K3 Nennslingen Ger.
156 G2 Nenoksa Rus. Fed.
191 I8 Nentershausen Hessen Ger.
191 E10 Nentershausen Rheinland-Pfalz Ger.
171 M4 Nenthead Cumbria, England U.K.
200 A5 Nenzing Austria
126 E4 Neo Japan
220 D2 Neo Agioneri Greece
100 □4a Neoch atoll Chuuk Micronesia
220 F2 Neo Erasmio Greece
126 E5 Neo-gawa r. Japan
Neokhórion Greece see Oichalia
265 V1 Neola UT U.S.A.
168 J4 Neolithic Orkney tourist site Scotland U.K.
220 D3 Neo Monastiri Greece
214 B7 Neoneli Sardegna Italy
Néon Karlovásion Samos Greece see Karlovasi
250 F5 Neopit WI U.S.A.
261 H7 Neosho MO U.S.A.
261 H7 Neosho r. KS U.S.A.
220 E2 Neos Marmaras Greece
183 I10 Néoules France
208 F2 Néouvielle, Pic de mt. France
185 E10 Néouvielle, Réserve Naturelle de nature res. France
138 I5 Nepal country Asia
138 H5 Nepalganj Nepal
138 H6 Nepalganj Road Uttar Prad. India
138 F9 Nepanagar Madh. Prad. India
248 F4 Nepean Ont. Can.
104 □1 Nepean Island Norfolk I.
265 U2 Nephi UT U.S.A.
169 D4 Nephin hill Ireland
169 C4 Nephin Beg Range hills Ireland
215 I3 Nepi Italy
243 L5 Nepisiguit r. N.B. Can.
198 C2 Nepomuk Czech Rep.
161 V8 Nepryadva r. Rus. Fed.
259 G4 Neptune City NJ U.S.A.
104 F6 Neptune Islands S.A. Austr.
197 G3 Ner r. Pol.
215 I3 Nera r. Italy
185 E7 Nérac France
244 F3 Neragon Island AK U.S.A.
136 C3 Neral Mahar. India
107 N9 Nerang Qld Austr.
198 D1 Neratovice Czech Rep.
199 J6 Nerău Romania
160 H7 Neravai Lith.
193 G8 Nerchau Ger.
121 K1 Nerchinsk Rus. Fed.
122 A3 Nerchinskiy Zavod Rus. Fed.
184 D4 Nercillac France
214 D7 Nercone, Monte su mt. Italy
156 K4 Nerdva Rus. Fed.
184 D4 Néré France
219 O5 Nereju Romania
161 X4 Nerekhta Rus. Fed.
195 I4 Neresheim Ger.
249 G2 Néret, Lac l. Que. Can.
160 I5 Nereta Latvia
215 L2 Nereto Italy
210 F4 Neretva r. Bos.-Herz./Croatia
197 L4 Neretva r. Ukr.
210 F4 Neretvanski Kanal sea chan. Croatia
213 Q6 Nerezine Croatia
138 G9 Neri Mahar. India
160 D6 Neringa admin. div. Lithuania
133 J11 Nêri Pünco l. Xizang China
231 D8 Neriquinha Angola
160 G7 Neris r. Lith.
182 B4 Néris-les-Bains France
207 L7 Nerja Spain
242 C4 Nerka, Lake AK U.S.A.
161 X5 Nerl' Ivanovskaya Oblast' Rus. Fed.
161 V4 Nerl' Tverskaya Oblast' Rus. Fed.
161 U4 Nerl' r. Rus. Fed.
161 W4 Nero, Ozero l. Rus. Fed.
156 M3 Nerokhi Rus. Fed.
182 E5 Néronde France
182 B3 Nérondes France
280 C2 Nerópolis Brazil
191 C10 Neroth Ger.
159 S3 Nerovnovka Rus. Fed.
156 L2 Neroyka, Gora mt. Rus. Fed.
138 F9 Ner Pinglai Mahar. India
207 O4 Nerpio Spain
184 E4 Nersac France
195 I5 Nersingen Ger.
158 J7 Nerubays'ke Ukr.
161 T9 Neruch' r. Rus. Fed.
161 Q9 Nerussa r. Rus. Fed.
206 F5 Nerva Spain
213 M4 Nervesa della Battaglia Italy
182 E5 Nervieux France
205 O2 Nervión r. Spain
212 D4 Nery, Monte mt. Italy
153 N4 Neryungri Rus. Fed.
186 I2 Nes Neth.
164 F1 Nes Norway
156 I2 Nes' Rus. Fed.
156 I2 Nes' r. Rus. Fed.
144 G7 Nesā' Iran
144 D3 Nesa' Iran
164 F1 Nesbyen Norway
193 J8 Neschwitz Ger.
258 F5 Nesco NJ U.S.A.
258 C2 Nescopeck PA U.S.A.
258 C2 Nescopeck Creek r. PA U.S.A.
219 P8 Nesebŭr Bulg.
271 □4 Nesfield Barbados
164 C2 Nes Flaten Norway
258 F4 Neshaminy Creek r. PA U.S.A.
162 □G1 Neskaupstaður Iceland
178 E4 Nesle France
199 H2 Nesluša Slovakia
162 L3 Nesna Norway
158 G3 Nesolon' Ukr.
198 G2 Nesovice Czech Rep.
183 F8 Nesque r. France
258 D3 Nesquehoning PA U.S.A.
136 D4 Nesri Mahar. India
168 H8 Ness r. Scotland U.K.
168 G8 Ness, Loch l. Scotland U.K.
214 B2 Nessa Corse France
260 F6 Ness City KS U.S.A.
190 D3 Nesse Ger.
191 J9 Nesse r. Ger.
245 N4 Nesselrode, Mount Can./U.S.A.
195 J6 Nesselwang Ger.
212 G1 Nesslau Switz.
185 F9 Neste r. France
160 F7 Nesterov Rus. Fed.
Nesterov Ukr. see Zhovkva
161 Q7 Nestery Rus. Fed.
171 K7 Neston Cheshire, England U.K.
271 □7 Nestor Trin. and Tob.
215 I2 Nestore r. Italy
213 M9 Nestore r. Italy
247 M5 Nestor Falls Ont. Can.
250 F3 Nestoria MI U.S.A.
220 F2 Nestos r. Greece
164 E2 Nesvatn l. Norway
Nesvizh Belarus see Nyasvizh
150 C6 Netanya Israel
139 J8 Netarhat Jharkhand India
258 F3 Netcong NJ U.S.A.
191 H7 Nethe r. Ger.
186 I3 Netherlands country Europe
271 I7 Netherlands Antilles terr. West Indies
168 L8 Netherley Aberdeenshire, Scotland U.K.
172 F5 Nether Stowey Somerset, England U.K.
171 M3 Netherton Northumberland, England U.K.
168 I8 Nethy Bridge Highland, Scotland U.K.
235 H2 Netia Moz.
158 F3 Netishyn Ukr.
217 M5 Neto r. Italy
198 D2 Netolice Czech Rep.
191 F9 Netphen Ger.
191 J8 Netra (Ringgau) Ger.
139 M7 Netrakona Bangl.
138 D9 Netrang Gujarat India
212 G1 Netstal Switz.
179 I6 Nettancourt France
191 C10 Nettersheim Ger.
191 B8 Nettetal Ger.
243 K3 Nettilling Lake Nunavut Can.
250 A1 Nett Lake MN U.S.A.
171 Q7 Nettleham Lincolnshire, England U.K.
215 J5 Nettuno Italy
193 F9 Netzschkau Ger.
195 M2 Neualbenreuth Ger.
191 G10 Neu-Anspach Ger.
232 B3 Neubari r. Sudan
190 I1 Neuberend Ger.
201 M4 Neuberg an der Mürz Austria
195 M6 Neubeuern Ger.
195 L5 Neubiberg Ger.
190 D5 Neubörger Ger.
181 M3 Neubourg, Campagne du reg. France
192 H3 Neubrandenburg Ger.
190 G5 Neubruchhausen Ger.
194 H2 Neubrunn Ger.
192 E2 Neubukow Ger.
194 F4 Neubulach Ger.
195 O4 Neuburg am Inn Ger.
194 E4 Neuburg am Rhein Ger.
195 K4 Neuburg an der Donau Ger.
195 I5 Neuburg an der Kammel Ger.
192 E3 Neuburg-Steinhausen Ger.
193 H8 Neuburxdorf Ger.
212 B2 Neuchâtel Switz.
212 B1 Neuchâtel canton Switz.
212 B2 Neuchâtel, Lac de l. Switz.
190 K4 Neu Darchau Ger.
191 K9 Neudietendorf Ger.
201 N4 Neudorf Austria
193 G10 Neudorf Ger.
193 E10 Neudrossenfeld Ger.
194 F4 Neuenbürg Ger.
194 D6 Neuenburg am Rhein Ger.
195 J3 Neuendettelsau Ger.
193 I6 Neuendorfer See l. Ger.
192 J5 Neuenhagen Ger.
192 I5 Neuenhagen Berlin Ger.
191 C6 Neuenhaus Ger.
194 E7 Neuenhof Switz.
212 E1 Neuenkirch Switz.
192 H1 Neuenkirchen Mecklenburg-Vorpommern Ger.
192 H2 Neuenkirchen Mecklenburg-Vorpommern Ger.
190 G3 Neuenkirchen Niedersachsen Ger.
190 G4 Neuenkirchen Niedersachsen Ger.
190 G5 Neuenkirchen Niedersachsen Ger.
190 I4 Neuenkirchen Niedersachsen Ger.
191 E6 Neuenkirchen Niedersachsen Ger.
191 D6 Neuenkirchen Nordrhein-Westfalen Ger.
190 H2 Neuenkirchen Schleswig-Holstein Ger.
191 F5 Neuenkirchen (Oldenburg) Ger.
191 D9 Neuenkirchen-Seelscheid Ger.
191 E8 Neuenrade Ger.
194 G3 Neuenstadt am Kocher Ger.
194 H3 Neuenstein Ger.
190 G3 Neuenwalde Ger.
191 B10 Neuerburg Ger.
195 L5 Neufahrn bei Freising Ger.
195 M4 Neufahrn in Niederbayern Ger.
179 O7 Neuf-Brisach France
187 H9 Neufchâteau Belgium
179 K7 Neufchâteau France
178 B4 Neufchâtel-en-Bray France
181 L5 Neufchâtel-en-Saosnois France
178 C2 Neufchâtel-Hardelot France
178 H5 Neufchâtel-sur-Aisne France
190 H3 Neufeld Ger.
201 N4 Neufeld an der Leitha Austria
201 J3 Neufelden Austria
194 G4 Neuffen Ger.
179 I4 Neufmanil France
194 G5 Neufra Ger.
193 E7 Neugattersleben Ger.
193 K9 Neugersdorf Ger.
192 H4 Neuglobsow Ger.
192 J5 Neuhardenberg Ger.
190 E3 Neuharlingersiel Ger.
201 K6 Neuhaus Kärnten Austria
201 L4 Neuhaus Niederösterreich Austria
190 K4 Neuhaus (Elbe) Ger.
190 H3 Neuhaus (Oste) Ger.
195 O5 Neuhaus am Inn Ger.
201 N6 Neuhaus am Klausenbach Austria
193 D9 Neuhaus am Rennweg Ger.
195 L2 Neuhaus an der Pegnitz Ger.
194 F4 Neuhausen Baden-Württemberg Ger.
193 H9 Neuhausen Sachsen Ger.
Neuhausen Rus. Fed. see Gur'yevsk
212 F1 Neuhausen Switz.
194 F6 Neuhausen ob Eck Ger.
193 D10 Neuhaus-Schierschnitz Ger.
191 I10 Neuhof Ger.
195 J3 Neuhof an der Zenn Ger.
201 J3 Neuhofen an der Krems Austria
201 K3 Neuhofen an der Ybbs Austria
181 M6 Neuillé-Pont-Pierre France
182 D2 Neuilly France
178 D5 Neuilly-en-Thelle France
182 C4 Neuilly-le-Réal France
179 J8 Neuilly-l'Évêque France
178 F5 Neuilly-St-Front France
178 D6 Neuilly-sur-Seine France
191 G10 Neu-Isenburg Ger.
192 G3 Neukalen Ger.
192 D4 Neu Kaliß Ger.
190 E4 Neukamperfehn Ger.
193 F8 Neukieritzsch Ger.
194 H6 Neukirch Baden-Württemberg Ger.
193 J8 Neukirch Sachsen Ger.
191 H9 Neukirchen Hessen Ger.
193 F9 Neukirchen Sachsen Ger.
193 G9 Neukirchen Sachsen Ger.
192 D2 Neukirchen Schleswig-Holstein Ger.
190 G1 Neukirchen Schleswig-Holstein Ger.
200 F5 Neukirchen am Großvenediger Austria
200 H3 Neukirchen an der Enknach Austria
201 I3 Neukirchen an der Vöckla Austria
195 M3 Neukirchen-Balbini Ger.
195 L2 Neukirchen bei Sulzbach-Rosenberg Ger.
195 O4 Neukirchen vorm Wald Ger.
192 E3 Neukloster Ger.
Neukuhren Rus. Fed. see Pionerskiy
190 D4 Neulehe Ger.
201 M3 Neulengbach Austria
195 I4 Neuler Ger.
192 J5 Neulewin Ger.
182 E5 Neulise France
208 K3 Neulos, Pic mt. Spain
193 I6 Neu Lübbenau Ger.
194 B2 Neumagen Ger.
193 F9 Neumark Sachsen Ger.
193 D8 Neumark Thüringen Ger.
200 H4 Neumarkt am Wallersee Austria
201 J3 Neumarkt im Mühlkreis Austria
195 K3 Neumarkt in der Oberpfalz Ger.
201 J5 Neumarkt in Steiermark Austria
195 N5 Neumarkt-Sankt Veit Ger.
286 X2 Neumayer research stn Antarctica
190 I2 Neumünster Ger.
118 G5 Neun, Nam r. Laos
195 M3 Neunburg vorm Wald Ger.
193 F9 Neundorf Ger.
181 O6 Neung-sur-Beuvron France
212 F1 Neunkirch Switz.
201 N4 Neunkirchen Austria
191 F9 Neunkirchen Nordrhein-Westfalen Ger.
194 C3 Neunkirchen Saarland Ger.
195 K2 Neunkirchen am Sand Ger.
195 N5 Neuötting Ger.
193 J7 Neupetershain Ger.
201 L2 Neupölla Austria
284 C6 Neuquén Arg.
284 C6 Neuquén prov. Arg.
284 D6 Neuquén r. Arg.
195 P4 Neureichenau Ger.
195 K5 Neuried Ger.
192 G5 Neuruppin Ger.
193 K8 Neusalza-Spremberg Ger.
Neu Sandez Pol. see Nowy Sącz
195 J5 Neusäß Ger.
195 O4 Neuschönau Ger.
255 I8 Neuse r. NC U.S.A.
193 G6 Neuseddin Ger.
201 O4 Neusiedl am See Austria
201 O4 Neusiedler See l. Austria/Hungary
201 O4 Neusiedler See Seewinkel, Nationalpark nat. park Austria
195 L2 Neusorg Ger.
191 C8 Neuss Ger.
183 B6 Neussargues-Moissac France
194 E6 Neustadt Baden-Württemberg Ger.
192 F5 Neustadt Brandenburg Ger.
193 E9 Neustadt Thüringen Ger.
191 K7 Neustadt (Harz) Ger.
191 H9 Neustadt (Hessen) Ger.
191 D9 Neustadt (Wied) Ger.
195 L2 Neustadt am Kulm Ger.
191 K9 Neustadt am Rennsteig Ger.
191 H5 Neustadt am Rübenberge Ger.
195 J2 Neustadt an der Aisch Ger.
195 L4 Neustadt an der Donau Ger.
Neustadt an der Hardt Ger. see Neustadt an der Weinstraße
195 M2 Neustadt an der Waldnaab Ger.
194 E3 Neustadt an der Weinstraße Ger.
193 D10 Neustadt bei Coburg Ger.
192 E4 Neustadt-Glewe Ger.
190 K2 Neustadt in Holstein Ger.
193 J8 Neustadt in Sachsen Ger.
200 D5 Neustift im Stubaital Austria
192 H4 Neustrelitz Ger.
195 M4 Neutraubling Ger.
192 J5 Neutrebbin Ger.
195 I5 Neu-Ulm Ger.
183 B7 Neuvéglise France
179 L6 Neuves-Maisons France
184 E5 Neuvic Aquitaine France
184 I5 Neuvic Limousin France
184 I5 Neuvic, Barrage de dam France
178 D7 Neuville-aux-Bois France
181 L8 Neuville-de-Poitou France
182 G4 Neuville-les-Dames France
178 B4 Neuville-lès-Dieppe France
182 F5 Neuville-sur-Saône France
181 L5 Neuville-sur-Sarthe France
179 J5 Neuvilly-en-Argonne France
182 D3 Neuvy-Grandchamp France
181 M6 Neuvy-le-Roi France
181 O8 Neuvy-Pailloux France
181 O8 Neuvy-St-Sépulchre France
178 G7 Neuvy-Sautour France
181 P7 Neuvy-sur-Barangeon France
193 D6 Neuwegersleben Ger.
194 F4 Neuweiler Ger.
190 G3 Neuwerk i. Ger.
191 D10 Neuwied Ger.
190 J2 Neuwittenbek Ger.
190 I4 Neu Wulmstorf Ger.
193 G9 Neuwürschnitz Ger.
193 J7 Neu Zauche Ger.
193 K6 Neuzelle Ger.
193 I6 Neu Zittau Ger.
161 N2 Neva r. Rus. Fed.
183 J6 Névache France
260 I4 Nevada IA U.S.A.
261 H7 Nevada MO U.S.A.
264 O2 Nevada state U.S.A.
282 C2 Nevada, Sierra mt. Arg.
207 M6 Nevada, Sierra mts Spain
264 K1 Nevada, Sierra mts CA U.S.A.
264 K2 Nevada City CA U.S.A.
284 C4 Nevado, Cerro mt. Arg.
284 C5 Nevado, Sierra del mts Arg.
268 D6 Nevado de Colima, Parque Nacional nat. park Mex.
269 H6 Nevado de Tolúca, Parque Nacional nat. park Mex.
269 H6 Nevado de Toluca, Volcán vol. Mex.
207 I4 Névalo r. Spain
136 D3 Nevasa Mahar. India
150 C7 Nevatim Israel
159 N1 Nevdol'sk Rus. Fed.
Nevdubstroy Rus. Fed. see Kirovsk
231 B8 Neve, Serra da mts Angola
198 D2 Neveklov Czech Rep.
160 M5 Nevel' Rus. Fed.
161 M6 Nevel', Ozero l. Rus. Fed.
187 E6 Nevele Belgium
122 L5 Nevel'sk Sakhalin Rus. Fed.
205 Q7 Nevera mt. Spain
142 B1 Neverkino Rus. Fed.
172 C3 Nevern Pembrokeshire, Wales U.K.
160 H7 Neveronys Lith.
182 C2 Nevers France
258 F2 Neversink r. NY U.S.A.
105 K4 Nevertire N.S.W. Austr.
281 F5 Neves Brazil
213 L2 Neves, Lago di l. Italy
210 G4 Nevesinje Bos.-Herz.
180 D6 Névez France
160 G7 Nevėžis r. Lith.
183 B10 Névian France
217 O3 Neviano Italy
181 M2 Néville France
151 C1 Nevinnomyssk Rus. Fed.
271 □2 Nevis i. St Kitts and Nevis
168 E8 Nevis, Loch inlet Scotland U.K.
271 □2 Nevis Peak hill St Kitts and Nevis
148 G4 Nevşehir Turkey
122 H6 Nevskoye Rus. Fed.
265 Q8 New r. CA U.S.A.
256 D11 New r. WV U.S.A.
168 I13 New Abbey Dumfries and Galloway, Scotland U.K.
168 L7 New Aberdour Aberdeenshire, Scotland U.K.
173 L5 New Addington Greater London, England U.K.
245 O5 New Aiyansh B.C. Can.
233 C7 Newala Tanz.
254 E6 New Albany IN U.S.A.
261 K8 New Albany MS U.S.A.
258 C1 New Albany PA U.S.A.
250 F4 Newald WI U.S.A.
173 J5 New Alresford Hampshire, England U.K.
275 G3 New Amsterdam Guyana
105 K3 New Angledool N.S.W. Austr.
237 P5 Newark S. Africa
264 J4 Newark CA U.S.A.
258 D5 Newark DE U.S.A.
257 K8 Newark NJ U.S.A.
256 H5 Newark NY U.S.A.
256 C8 Newark OH U.S.A.
257 K8 Newark airport NJ U.S.A.
265 Q2 Newark Lake NV U.S.A.
171 P7 Newark-on-Trent Nottinghamshire, England U.K.
251 R7 Newark Valley NY U.S.A.
173 M5 New Ash Green Kent, England U.K.
261 K10 New Augusta MS U.S.A.
250 I6 Newaygo MI U.S.A.
257 O7 New Bedford MA U.S.A.
262 C4 Newberg OR U.S.A.
257 J6 New Berlin NY U.S.A.
258 B3 New Berlin PA U.S.A.
258 D4 New Berlinville PA U.S.A.
255 I8 New Bern NC U.S.A.
250 I3 Newberry MI U.S.A.
255 G8 Newberry SC U.S.A.
262 D5 Newberry National Volcanic Monument nat. park OR U.S.A.
264 P7 Newberry Springs CA U.S.A.
258 B4 Newberrytown PA U.S.A.
256 F7 New Bethlehem PA U.S.A.
171 N3 Newbiggin-by-the-Sea Northumberland, England U.K.
168 I11 Newbigging South Lanarkshire, Scotland U.K.
270 F1 New Bight Cat I. Bahamas
169 H4 Newbliss Ireland
251 Q9 New Bloomfield PA U.S.A.
248 E4 Newboro Ont. Can.
256 C10 New Boston OH U.S.A.
261 H9 New Boston TX U.S.A.
261 F11 New Braunfels TX U.S.A.
169 F5 Newbridge Galway Ireland
169 I6 Newbridge Kildare Ireland
169 E7 Newbridge Limerick Ireland
172 F4 Newbridge Caerphilly, Wales U.K.
172 F3 Newbridge on Wye Powys, Wales U.K.
256 E8 New Brighton PA U.S.A.
113 K8 New Britain i. P.N.G.
259 J1 New Britain CT U.S.A.
258 E4 New Britain PA U.S.A.
290 F6 New Britain Trench sea feature Pacific Ocean
270 □ New Broughton Jamaica
249 H4 New Brunswick prov. Can.
257 K8 New Brunswick NJ U.S.A.
250 H8 New Buffalo MI U.S.A.
258 B4 New Buffalo PA U.S.A.
169 H3 New Buildings Northern Ireland U.K.
256 H8 Newburg PA U.S.A.
251 R5 Newburgh Ont. Can.
168 L8 Newburgh Aberdeenshire, Scotland U.K.
168 J10 Newburgh Fife, Scotland U.K.
168 J12 Newburgh Scottish Borders, Scotland U.K.
257 K7 Newburgh NY U.S.A.
173 J5 Newbury West Berkshire, England U.K.
Newbury admin. div. England U.K. see West Berkshire
257 O6 Newburyport MA U.S.A.
229 G4 New Bussa Nigeria
171 L5 Newby Bridge Cumbria, England U.K.
168 L7 New Byth Aberdeenshire, Scotland U.K.
New Caledonia i. S. Pacific Ocean see Nouvelle-Calédonie
100 □5 New Caledonia terr. S. Pacific Ocean
290 F7 New Caledonia Trough sea feature Tasman Sea
259 I2 New Canaan CT U.S.A.
249 H3 New Carlisle Que. Can.
256 A9 New Carlisle OH U.S.A.
258 B7 New Carrollton MD U.S.A.
105 M5 Newcastle N.S.W. Austr.
248 E5 Newcastle Ont. Can.
270 □ Newcastle Jamaica
169 J6 Newcastle Dublin Ireland
169 E6 Newcastle Galway Ireland
169 G8 Newcastle Tipperary Ireland
169 J6 Newcastle Wicklow Ireland
237 N3 Newcastle S. Africa
271 □2 Newcastle St Kitts and Nevis
169 K4 Newcastle Northern Ireland U.K.
172 F3 Newcastle Shropshire, England U.K.
264 K3 Newcastle CA U.S.A.
258 D5 New Castle DE U.S.A.
254 E6 New Castle IN U.S.A.
254 E6 New Castle KY U.S.A.
257 □P4 Newcastle ME U.S.A.
256 E7 New Castle PA U.S.A.
265 S4 Newcastle UT U.S.A.
256 E11 New Castle VA U.S.A.
262 L5 Newcastle WY U.S.A.
258 D5 New Castle County county DE U.S.A.
106 D4 Newcastle Creek r. N.T. Austr.
172 D3 Newcastle Emlyn Ceredigion, Wales U.K.
107 I5 Newcastle Range hills Qld Austr.
168 K12 Newcastleton Scottish Borders, Scotland U.K.
171 M7 Newcastle-under-Lyme Staffordshire, England U.K.
171 N4 Newcastle upon Tyne Tyne and Wear, England U.K.
106 D4 Newcastle Waters N.T. Austr.
169 D8 Newcastle West Ireland
169 E9 Newcestown Ireland
257 J11 New Church VA U.S.A.
Newchwang Liaoning China see Yingkou
259 H2 New City NY U.S.A.
258 B2 New Columbia PA U.S.A.
258 C2 New Columbus PA U.S.A.
265 X5 Newcomb NM U.S.A.
256 D8 Newcomerstown OH U.S.A.
256 D9 New Concord OH U.S.A.
259 H2 New Croton Reservoir NY U.S.A.
258 B4 New Cumberland PA U.S.A.
168 H12 New Cumnock East Ayrshire, Scotland U.K.
168 L7 New Deer Aberdeenshire, Scotland U.K.
109 E12 Newdegate W.A. Austr.
138 F5 New Delhi Delhi India
257 □R1 New Denmark N.B. Can.
264 L4 New Don Pedro Reservoir CA U.S.A.
171 O6 New Earswick York, England U.K.
258 F4 New Egypt NJ U.S.A.
194 B2 Newel Ger.
107 J4 Newell Qld Austr.
260 D3 Newell SD U.S.A.
256 E8 Newell WV U.S.A.
109 I8 Newell, Lake salt flat W.A. Austr.
247 I5 Newell, Lake Alta Can.
105 N4 New England National Park N.S.W. Austr.
105 M4 New England Range mts N.S.W. Austr.
288 F3 New England Seamounts sea feature N. Atlantic Ocean
244 G4 Newenham, Cape AK U.S.A.
172 H4 Newent Gloucestershire, England U.K.
250 H6 New Era MI U.S.A.
256 G5 Newfane NY U.S.A.
257 M6 Newfane VT U.S.A.
258 E5 Newfield NJ U.S.A.
173 I6 New Forest National Park England U.K.
257 N5 Newfound Lake NH U.S.A.
249 J3 Newfoundland i. Nfld and Lab. Can.
259 G2 Newfoundland NJ U.S.A.
258 E2 Newfoundland PA U.S.A.
249 J2 Newfoundland and Labrador prov. Can.
262 H6 Newfoundland Evaporation Basin salt l. UT U.S.A.
258 B5 New Freedom PA U.S.A.
168 H12 New Galloway Dumfries and Galloway, Scotland U.K.
100 □6 New Georgia i. New Georgia Is Solomon Is
100 □6 New Georgia Islands Solomon Is
100 □6 New Georgia Sound sea chan. Solomon Is
250 E7 New Glarus WI U.S.A.
249 I4 New Glasgow N.S. Can.
169 J5 Newgrange Ireland
167 D5 Newgrange Tomb tourist site Ireland
271 □7 New Grant Trin. and Tob.
259 G5 New Gretna NJ U.S.A.
113 J8 New Guinea i. Indon./P.N.G.
244 I4 Newhalen AK U.S.A.
225 G6 New Halfa Sudan
264 N7 Newhall CA U.S.A.
259 H1 New Hamburg NY U.S.A.
244 G3 New Hamilton AK U.S.A.
257 N4 New Hampshire state U.S.A.
250 B6 New Hampton IA U.S.A.
259 G2 New Hampton NY U.S.A.
113 L7 New Hanover i. P.N.G.
237 O5 New Hanover S. Africa
257 J5 New Hartford NY U.S.A.
173 M6 Newhaven East Sussex, England U.K.
257 M7 New Haven CT U.S.A.
250 B6 New Haven IA U.S.A.
250 I8 New Haven IN U.S.A.
251 L7 New Haven MI U.S.A.
256 D10 New Haven WV U.S.A.
259 J2 New Haven County county CT U.S.A.
246 E4 New Hazelton B.C. Can.
New Hebrides country S. Pacific Ocean see Vanuatu
290 G7 New Hebrides Trench sea feature Pacific Ocean
264 L3 New Hogan Reservoir CA U.S.A.
New Holland country Oceania see Australia
258 C4 New Holland PA U.S.A.
250 F6 New Holstein WI U.S.A.
258 F4 New Hope PA U.S.A.
261 J10 New Iberia LA U.S.A.
173 M6 Newick East Sussex, England U.K.
173 N5 Newington Kent, England U.K.
259 J1 Newington CT U.S.A.
170 C6 New Inn Cavan Ireland
169 H6 New Inn Laois Ireland
169 G8 Newinn Ireland
113 L7 New Ireland i. P.N.G.
258 G5 New Jersey state U.S.A.
138 C8 New Kandla Gujarat India
256 F8 New Kensington PA U.S.A.
256 H11 New Kent VA U.S.A.
263 L9 Newkirk NM U.S.A.
261 G7 Newkirk OK U.S.A.
168 I11 New Lanark Scotland U.K.
168 I11 New Lanark World Heritage Site tourist site Scotland U.K.
255 G7 Newland NC U.S.A.
109 G10 Newland Range hills W.A. Austr.
168 L7 New Leeds Aberdeenshire, Scotland U.K.
256 C9 New Lexington OH U.S.A.
250 D6 New Lisbon WI U.S.A.
248 E4 New Liskeard Ont. Can.
257 M7 New London CT U.S.A.
256 C7 New London OH U.S.A.
250 F5 New London WI U.S.A.
259 K1 New London County county CT U.S.A.
168 G13 New Luce Dumfries and Galloway, Scotland U.K.
172 □ Newlyn Cornwall, England U.K.
168 L8 Newmachar Aberdeenshire, Scotland U.K.
261 K7 New Madrid MO U.S.A.
109 E7 Newman W.A. Austr.
264 K4 Newman CA U.S.A.
109 E7 Newman, Mount W.A. Austr.
286 O1 Newman Island Antarctica
258 C4 Newmanstown PA U.S.A.
248 E4 Newmarket Ont. Can.
270 □ Newmarket Jamaica
169 D8 Newmarket Cork Ireland
169 H8 Newmarket Kilkenny Ireland
173 M3 Newmarket Suffolk, England U.K.
168 D6 Newmarket Western Isles, Scotland U.K.
257 □O5 Newmarket NH U.S.A.
256 G10 New Market VA U.S.A.
169 E7 Newmarket-on-Fergus Ireland
256 E9 New Martinsville WV U.S.A.
262 F4 New Meadows ID U.S.A.
263 L9 New Mexico state U.S.A.
256 A9 New Miami OH U.S.A.
259 I1 New Milford CT U.S.A.
257 J7 New Milford PA U.S.A.
168 K7 Newmill Moray, Scotland U.K.
171 M7 New Mills Derbyshire, England U.K.
168 H11 Newmilns East Ayrshire, Scotland U.K.
173 I6 New Milton Hampshire, England U.K.
173 O4 New Mistley Essex, England U.K.
256 B9 New Moorefield OH U.S.A.
255 E9 Newnan GA U.S.A.
172 H4 Newnham Gloucestershire, England U.K.
109 D11 New Norcia W.A. Austr.
105 K10 New Norfolk Tas. Austr.
261 J11 New Orleans LA U.S.A.
258 A5 New Oxford PA U.S.A.
257 K7 New Paltz NY U.S.A.
250 I8 New Paris IN U.S.A.
256 A9 New Paris OH U.S.A.
256 D8 New Philadelphia OH U.S.A.
258 C3 New Philadelphia PA U.S.A.
168 L7 New Pitsligo Aberdeenshire, Scotland U.K.
102 I6 New Plymouth North I. N.Z.
172 C6 New Polzeath Cornwall, England U.K.
270 □ Newport Jamaica
169 C5 Newport Mayo Ireland
169 F7 Newport Tipperary Ireland
173 M4 Newport Essex, England U.K.
168 J6 Newport Highland, Scotland U.K.
173 J6 Newport Isle of Wight, England U.K.
172 F4 Newport Newport, Wales U.K.
172 C3 Newport Pembrokeshire, Wales U.K.
172 H2 Newport Telford and Wrekin, England U.K.
172 G4 Newport admin. div. Wales U.K.
261 J8 Newport AR U.S.A.
258 D5 Newport DE U.S.A.
254 D6 Newport IN U.S.A.
257 □P4 Newport ME U.S.A.
251 K8 Newport MI U.S.A.
257 M5 Newport NH U.S.A.
258 E6 Newport NJ U.S.A.
262 B4 Newport OR U.S.A.
258 A4 Newport PA U.S.A.
257 N7 Newport RI U.S.A.
255 F8 Newport TN U.S.A.
257 M4 Newport VT U.S.A.
262 F2 Newport WA U.S.A.
172 C3 Newport Bay Wales U.K.
264 O8 Newport Beach CA U.S.A.
256 I11 Newport News VA U.S.A.
168 K10 Newport-on-Tay Fife, Scotland U.K.
173 K3 Newport Pagnell Milton Keynes, England U.K.
255 F11 New Port Richey FL U.S.A.
259 I1 New Preston CT U.S.A.
270 E1 New Providence i. Bahamas
259 G3 New Providence NJ U.S.A.
258 C5 New Providence PA U.S.A.
172 D3 New Quay Ceredigion, Wales U.K.
172 B7 Newquay Cornwall, England U.K.
172 F3 New Radnor Powys, Wales U.K.
249 H3 New Richmond Que. Can.
256 A10 New Richmond OH U.S.A.
250 B4 New Richmond WI U.S.A.
258 D3 New Ringgold PA U.S.A.
265 T8 New River AZ U.S.A.
103 C13 New River Estuary South I. N.Z.
261 J10 New Roads LA U.S.A.
259 H3 New Rochelle NY U.S.A.
260 F2 New Rockford ND U.S.A.
173 N6 New Romney Kent, England U.K.
249 H4 New Ross N.S. Can.
169 I8 New Ross Ireland
106 B4 Newry N.T. Austr.
169 J4 Newry Northern Ireland U.K.
250 D6 Newry WI U.S.A.
169 J4 Newry Canal Northern Ireland U.K.
New Siberia Islands Rus. Fed. see Novosibirskiye Ostrova
255 G11 New Smyrna Beach FL U.S.A.
105 K5 New South Wales state Austr.
256 F8 New Stanton PA U.S.A.
244 H4 New Stuyahok AK U.S.A.
259 K3 New Suffolk NY U.S.A.
256 B12 New Tazewell TN U.S.A.
138 G4 New Tehri Uttaranchal India
244 F3 Newtok AK U.S.A.
285 H4 Newton Arg.
168 F10 Newton Argyll and Bute, Scotland U.K.
171 M6 Newton Lancashire, England U.K.
255 E10 Newton GA U.S.A.
260 I5 Newton IA U.S.A.
260 K6 Newton IL U.S.A.
260 G6 Newton KS U.S.A.
257 N6 Newton MA U.S.A.
261 K9 Newton MS U.S.A.
255 G8 Newton NC U.S.A.
258 F2 Newton NJ U.S.A.
261 I10 Newton TX U.S.A.
172 E6 Newton Abbot Devon, England U.K.
171 N4 Newton Aycliffe Durham, England U.K.
257 K4 Newton Falls NY U.S.A.
172 D7 Newton Ferrers Devon, England U.K.
168 L8 Newtonhill Aberdeenshire, Scotland U.K.
171 L7 Newton-le-Willows Merseyside, England U.K.
173 K4 Newton Longville Buckinghamshire, England U.K.
168 H11 Newton Mearns East Renfrewshire, Scotland U.K.
168 H8 Newtonmore Highland, Scotland U.K.
172 F6 Newton Poppleford Devon, England U.K.
172 E6 Newton St Cyres Devon, England U.K.
168 H13 Newton Stewart Dumfries and Galloway, Scotland U.K.
162 □ Newtontoppen mt. Svalbard
169 E8 Newtown Cork Ireland
169 H7 Newtown Laois Ireland
169 F6 Newtown Roscommon Ireland
169 F8 Newtown Tipperary Ireland
169 H8 Newtown Waterford Ireland
172 G3 Newtown Herefordshire, England U.K.
172 F2 Newtown Powys, Wales U.K.
259 I2 Newtown CT U.S.A.
260 D1 New Town ND U.S.A.
258 C3 Newtown PA U.S.A.
258 F4 Newtown PA U.S.A.
169 K3 Newtownabbey Northern Ireland U.K.
169 K3 Newtownards Northern Ireland U.K.
Newtownbarry Ireland see Bunclody
169 H4 Newtownbutler Northern Ireland U.K.
170 E4 Newtown Crommelin Northern Ireland U.K.
169 G3 Newtowncunningham Ireland

169 G5 **Newtown Forbes** Ireland
169 G4 **Newtown Gore** Ireland
169 I4 **Newtownhamilton** Northern Ireland U.K.
169 H6 **Newtownlow** Ireland
169 J6 **Newtown Mount Kennedy** Ireland
168 K11 **Newtown St Boswells** Scottish Borders, Scotland U.K.
258 E5 **Newtown Square** PA U.S.A.
169 H3 **Newtownstewart** Northern Ireland U.K.
172 F4 **New Tredegar** Caerphilly, Wales U.K.
258 D3 **New Tripoli** PA U.S.A.
168 J9 **Newtyle** Angus, Scotland U.K.
260 H3 **New Ulm** MN U.S.A.
256 B9 **New Vienna** OH U.S.A.
256 H8 **Newville** PA U.S.A.
257 □O4 **New Vineyard** ME U.S.A.
171 Q6 **New Waltham** North East Lincolnshire, England U.K.
258 A5 **New Windsor** MD U.S.A.
259 G2 **New Windsor** NY U.S.A.
257 J6 **New Woodstock** NY U.S.A.
257 L8 **New York** NY U.S.A.
257 J6 **New York** state U.S.A.
259 H3 **New York County** county NY U.S.A.
265 Q6 **New York Mountains** CA U.S.A.
102 I9 **New Zealand** country Oceania
269 I7 **Nexapa** r. Mex.
184 G4 **Nexon** France
156 H4 **Neya** Rus. Fed.
156 H4 **Neya** r. Rus. Fed.
126 C6 **Neyagawa** Japan
144 I5 **Neybasteh** Afgh.
144 G7 **Ney Bīd** Iran
144 E5 **Neyestānak** Iran
172 C4 **Neyland** Pembrokeshire, Wales U.K.
144 F7 **Neyrīz** Iran
144 H3 **Neyshābūr** Iran
136 E8 **Neyyattinkara** Kerala India
269 H6 **Nezahualcóyotl** Mex.
269 N8 **Nezahualcóyotl, Presa** resr Mex.
198 G2 **Nezamyslice** Czech Rep.
198 D2 **Nežárka** r. Czech Rep.
239 □[1c] **Nez de Bœuf** mt. Réunion
159 P3 **Nezhegol'** r. Rus. Fed.
Nezhin Ukr. see **Nizhyn**
151 E1 **Nezlobnaya** Rus. Fed.
262 F3 **Nezperce** ID U.S.A.
262 F3 **Nez Perce Indian Reservation** res. ID U.S.A.
199 I4 **Nézsa** Hungary
198 C2 **Nezvěstice** Czech Rep.
158 E5 **Nezvys'ko** Ukr.
108 H9 **Ngaanyatjarra Aboriginal Land** res. Australia
117 H4 **Ngabang** Kalimantan Indon.
231 C5 **Ngabé** Congo
119 D7 **Nga Chong, Khao** mt. Myanmar/Thai.
229 I3 **Ngadda** watercourse Nigeria
115 A8 **Ngadubolu** Sumba Indon.
118 C2 **Ngagahtawng** Myanmar
102 I2 **Ngaiotonga** North I. N.Z.
114 □ **Ngajangel** i. Palau
233 B6 **Ngajira** Tanz.
230 D4 **Ngala** Dem. Rep. Congo
229 I3 **Ngala** Nigeria
115 D2 **Ngalipaëng** Sulawesi Indon.
106 C3 **Ngaliwurru/Nungali Aboriginal Land** res. N.T. Austr.
115 B9 **Ngalu** Sumba Indon.
106 D7 **Ngalurrtja Aboriginal Land** res. Australia
230 C2 **Ngam** Chad
230 C2 **Ngama** Chad
234 D3 **Ngamaseri** watercourse Botswana
102 I6 **Ngamatapouri** North I. N.Z.
229 H5 **Ngambé** Cameroon
130 A3 **Ngamda** Xizang China
114 □ **Ngamegei Passage** Palau
234 D3 **Ngamiland** admin. dist. Botswana
133 H12 **Ngamring** Xizang China
232 A3 **Ngangala** Sudan
133 F11 **Ngangla Ringco** salt l. China
133 E10 **Nganglong Kangri** mt. Xizang China
133 E10 **Nganglong Kangri** mts Xizang China
231 B7 **N'gangula** Angola
133 H11 **Ngangzê Co** salt l. China
133 H11 **Ngangzê Shan** mts Xizang China
131 □J7 **Ngan Hei Shui Tong** resr H.K. China
117 I8 **Nganjuk** Jawa Indon.
130 E9 **Ngan Sâu, Sông** r. Vietnam
118 G3 **Ngân Sơn** Vietnam
118 D5 **Ngao** Thai.
229 I5 **Ngaoundal** Cameroon
229 I5 **Ngaoundéré** Cameroon
102 J5 **Ngapuke** North I. N.Z.
233 B7 **Ngara** Malawi
233 A5 **Ngara** Tanz.
116 F7 **Ngaras** Sumatera Indon.
114 □ **Ngardmau** Palau
114 □ **Ngardmau Bay** Palau
114 □ **Ngaregur** i. Palau
233 C7 **Ngarimbi** Tanz.
114 □ **Ngariungs** i. Palau
104 H6 **Ngarkat Conservation Park** nature res. S.A. Austr.
102 J4 **Ngaruawahia** North I. N.Z.
102 K6 **Ngaruroro** r. North I. N.Z.
102 H1 **Ngataki** North I. N.Z.
103 □[3] **Ngatangiia** Rarotonga Cook Is
102 L5 **Ngatapa** North I. N.Z.
102 J4 **Ngatea** North I. N.Z.
114 □ **Ngateguil, Point** Palau
118 B6 **Ngathainggyaung** Myanmar
229 I6 **Ngato** Cameroon
Ngau i. Fiji see **Gau**
131 □J7 **Ngau Mei Hoi** b. H.K. China
Ngawa Sichuan China see **Aba**
119 D8 **Ngawan Chaung** r. Myanmar
117 I8 **Ngawi** Jawa Indon.
118 B6 **Ngayok Bay** Myanmar
239 □[3a] **Ngazidja** i. Comoros
230 B4 **Ngbala** Congo
Ngcheangel atoll Palau see **Kayangel Atoll**
Ngeaur i. Palau see **Angaur**
233 A6 **Ngegera** Tanz.
Ngemelachel Palau see **Malakal**
114 □ **Ngemelis Islands** Palau
114 □ **Ngergoi** i. Palau
113 H5 **Ngeruangel** i. Palau
114 □ **Ngesebus** i. Palau
235 F4 **Ngezi** Zimbabwe
Nggamea i. Fiji see **Qamea**
100 □[6] **Nggatokae** i. New Georgia Is Solomon Is
100 □[6] **Nggela Sule** i. Solomon Is
234 D4 **Nghabe** r. Botswana
119 G9 **Nghê, Hon** i. Vietnam
118 F5 **Ngiap** r. Laos
115 D8 **Ngilmina** Timor Indon.
117 J8 **Ngimbang** Jawa Indon.
Ngiva Angola see **Ondjiva**
230 B5 **Ngo** Congo
114 □ **Ngobasangel** i. Palau
115 E3 **Ngofakiaha** Maluku Indon.
133 L11 **Ngoichogê** Xizang China
229 I6 **Ngoïla** Cameroon
133 I11 **Ngoin, Co** salt l. China
118 H7 **Ngok Linh** mt. Vietnam
229 6 **Ngoko** r. Cameroon/Congo
230 B5 **Ngoko** Congo
128 F8 **Ngola Shan** mts Qinghai China
128 F9 **Ngola Shankou** pass Qinghai China
229 H4 **Ngol Bembo** Nigeria
231 E8 **Ngoma** Zambia
234 E3 **Ngoma Bridge** Botswana
231 B6 **Ngoma Tsé-Tsé** Congo
233 B7 **Ngomba** Tanz.
237 P3 **Ngome** S. Africa
133 M11 **Ngom Qu** r. Xizang China
229 I4 **Ngong** Cameroon
231 C8 **Ngongola** Angola
102 K5 **Ngongotaha** North I. N.Z.
131 □J7 **Ngong Shuen Chau** pen. H.K. China
133 H10 **Ngoqumaima** Xizang China
128 E9 **Ngoring** Qinghai China
128 E9 **Ngoring Hu** l. Qinghai China
233 B5 **Ngorongoro Conservation Area** nature res. Tanz.
233 B5 **Ngorongoro Crater** Tanz.
230 C3 **Ngoto** C.A.R.
229 H6 **Ngoulémakong** Cameroon
229 H6 **Ngoumou** Centre Cameroon
229 I5 **Ngoumou** Est Cameroon
230 A5 **Ngounié** prov. Gabon
230 A5 **Ngounié** r. Gabon
230 B5 **Ngouoni** Gabon
224 C6 **Ngoura** Chad
224 B6 **Ngouri** Chad
229 I3 **Ngourti** Niger
224 C5 **Ngoutchey** well Chad
230 E3 **Ngouyo** C.A.R.
233 A5 **Ngozi** Burundi
237 N7 **Ngqeleni** S. Africa
237 M7 **Ngqungqu** S. Africa
230 B3 **Nguia Bouar** C.A.R.
229 I3 **Nguigmi** Niger
229 H3 **Nguini** well Niger
106 C1 **Nguiu** N.T. Austr.
133 K11 **Ngükang** Xizang China
106 E3 **Ngukurr** N.T. Austr.
113 I5 **Ngulu** atoll Micronesia
118 F5 **Ngum, Nam** r. Laos
100 □[5] **Nguna** i. Vanuatu
235 F4 **Ngundu** Zimbabwe
231 B7 **N'gungo** Angola
102 I2 **Ngunguru Bay** North I. N.Z.
115 B9 **Ngunju, Tanjung** pt Sumba Indon.
Ngunza Angola see **Sumbe**
Ngunza-Kabolu Angola see **Sumbe**
130 C1 **Ngura** Gansu China
229 H3 **Nguru** Nigeria
233 C6 **Nguru Mountains** Tanz.
234 D4 **Ngwako Pan** salt pan Botswana
Ngwane country Africa see **Swaziland**
237 L3 **Ngwathe** S. Africa
237 Q2 **Ngwavuma** r. Swaziland
237 P4 **Ngwelezana** S. Africa
237 P2 **Ngwempisi** r. S. Africa
231 E9 **Ngwezi** r. Zambia
235 G4 **Nhachengue** Moz.
235 G3 **Nhamassonge** Moz.
235 G3 **Nhamatanda** Moz.
275 G5 **Nhamundá** Brazil
275 G5 **Nhamundá** r. Brazil
280 B4 **Nhandeara** Brazil
231 C7 **N'harea** Angola
119 I8 **Nha Trang** Vietnam
277 F4 **Nhecolândia** Brazil
104 H7 **Nhill** Vic. Austr.
237 P3 **Nhlangano** Swaziland
237 P4 **Nhlazatshe** S. Africa
234 D3 **Nhoma** Namibia
118 G4 **Nho Quan** Vietnam
Nhow i. Fiji see **Gau**
106 F2 **Nhulunbuy** N.T. Austr.
277 G7 **Nhu Pora** Brazil
230 E5 **Niabembe** Dem. Rep. Congo
228 E5 **Niablé** Ghana
247 J4 **Niacam** Sask. Can.
228 E3 **Niafounké** Mali
250 G4 **Niagara** WI U.S.A.
248 E5 **Niagara Falls** Ont. Can.
256 F5 **Niagara Falls** NY U.S.A.
251 O6 **Niagara-on-the-Lake** Ont. Can.
228 C3 **Niagassola** Guinea
228 C4 **Niagouelé, Mont du** hill Guinea
133 D9 **Niagzu** Aksai Chin
117 J3 **Niah** Sarawak Malaysia
139 J5 **Niak** Nepal
228 D4 **Niakaramandougou** Côte d'Ivoire
229 F3 **Niamey** Niger
228 D3 **Niamina** Mali
144 H8 **Nīām Kand** Iran
229 F4 **Niamtougou** Togo
Nianbai Qinghai China see **Ledu**
228 C4 **Niandan** r. Guinea
228 C4 **Niandankoro** Guinea
233 C6 **Niangandu** Tanz.
230 E4 **Niangara** Dem. Rep. Congo
228 E3 **Niangay, Lac** l. Mali
228 D4 **Niangoloko** Burkina
261 I7 **Niangua** r. MO U.S.A.
Niangxi Hunan China see **Xinshao**
230 E4 **Nia-Nia** Dem. Rep. Congo
228 D4 **Niankorodougou** Burkina
259 K2 **Niantic** CT U.S.A.
Nianyuwan Liaoning China see **Xingangzhen**
129 R3 **Nianzishan** Heilong. China
230 E4 **Niapu** Dem. Rep. Congo
231 B5 **Niari** admin. reg. Congo
116 B4 **Nias** i. Indon.
235 H2 **Niassa** prov. Moz.
Niassa, Lago l. Africa see **Nyasa, Lake**
233 C8 **Niassa, Reserva do** nature res. Moz.
220 D6 **Niata** Greece
Niaur i. Palau see **Angaur**
185 H10 **Niaux** France
144 I4 **Niāzābād** Iran
212 G6 **Nibbiano** Italy
108 H7 **Nibil Well** W.A. Austr.
151 I5 **Nic** Azer.
217 M5 **Nicà** r. Italy
160 E5 **Nīca** Latvia
Nicaea Turkey see **İznik**
270 A7 **Nicaragua** country Central America
266 □Q12 **Nicaragua, Lago de** l. Nic.
Nicaragua, Lake Nic. see **Nicaragua, Lago de**
270 F3 **Nicaro** Cuba
217 K6 **Nicastro** Italy
183 K9 **Nice** France
Nice airport France see **Côte d'Azur**
264 J2 **Nice** CA U.S.A.
Nicephorium Syria see **Ar Raqqah**
255 D10 **Niceville** FL U.S.A.
145 L7 **Nichara** Pak.
212 D5 **Nichelino** Italy
249 G2 **Nichicun, Lac** l. Que. Can.
125 I12 **Nichihara** Japan
125 I15 **Nichinan** Japan
139 I6 **Nichlaul** Uttar Prad. India
270 C2 **Nicholas Channel** Bahamas/Cuba
254 E7 **Nicholasville** KY U.S.A.
270 D1 **Nicholl's Town** Andros Bahamas
257 I6 **Nichols** NY U.S.A.
108 J5 **Nicholson** W.A. Austr.
106 G4 **Nicholson** r. Qld Austr.
251 K2 **Nicholson** Ont. Can.
258 D1 **Nicholson** PA U.S.A.
247 K2 **Nicholson Lake** N.W.T. Can.
109 D9 **Nicholson Range** hills W.A. Austr.
257 K4 **Nicholville** NY U.S.A.
201 P4 **Nickelsdorf** Austria
256 C12 **Nickelsville** VA U.S.A.
108 D6 **Nickol Bay** W.A. Austr.
137 M8 **Nicobar Islands** Andaman & Nicobar Is India
219 Q6 **Nicolae Bălcescu** Romania
267 O8 **Nicolás Bravo** Mex.
284 E4 **Nicolás Bruzzone** Arg.
285 F6 **Nicolás Levalle** Arg.
269 H6 **Nicolás Romero** Mex.
264 K3 **Nicolaus** CA U.S.A.
216 G8 **Nicoletti, Lago** l. Sicilia Italy
239 □[1b] **Nicolière, Lac** l. Mauritius
217 I8 **Nicolosi** Sicilia Italy
Nicomedia Turkey see **İzmit**
282 G4 **Nico Pérez** Uru.
Nicopolis Bulg. see **Nikopol**
Nicosia Cyprus see **Lefkosia**
216 G8 **Nicosia** Sicilia Italy
217 J6 **Nicotera** Italy
266 □Q12 **Nicoya** Costa Rica
266 □Q13 **Nicoya, Golfo de** b. Costa Rica
266 □Q13 **Nicoya, Península de** pen. Costa Rica
257 □R1 **Nictau** N.B. Can.
235 H3 **Nicuadala** Moz.
219 Q5 **Niculițel** Romania
160 D6 **Nida** Lith.
197 I2 **Nida** r. Pol.
197 I5 **Nida** r. Pol.
136 G4 **Nidadavole** Andhra Prad. India
136 F4 **Nidagunda** Andhra Prad. India
212 C1 **Nidau** Switz.
171 O5 **Nidd** r. England U.K.
191 H10 **Nidda** Ger.
191 G10 **Nidda** r. Ger.
191 G10 **Nidder** r. Ger.
171 N5 **Nidderdale** val. England U.K.
164 E3 **Nidelva** r. Norway
212 E2 **Nidwalden** canton Switz.
153 K3 **Nidym** Rus. Fed.
219 J10 **Nidže** mt. Greece/Macedonia
197 I2 **Nidzica** Pol.
197 I5 **Nidzica** r. Pol.
197 J2 **Nidzkie, Jezioro** l. Pol.
186 J2 **Niebert** Neth.
206 F6 **Niebla** Spain
197 I3 **Nieborów** Pol.
190 G1 **Niebüll** Ger.
197 J6 **Niebylec** Pol.
196 F3 **Niechanowo** Pol.
197 H4 **Niechcice** Pol.
197 I2 **Niechłonin** Pol.
196 E4 **Niechlów** Pol.
196 D1 **Niechorze** Pol.
179 M5 **Nied** r. France
179 L5 **Nied Allemande** r. France
191 H8 **Niedenstein** Ger.
195 M4 **Niederaichbach** Ger.
187 J9 **Niederanven** Lux.
191 I9 **Niederaula** Ger.
195 N4 **Niederbayern** admin. reg. Ger.
212 D1 **Niederbipp** Switz.
191 F10 **Niederbrechen** Ger.
179 O6 **Niederbronn-les-Bains** France
193 F6 **Niederer Fläming** park Ger.
194 F5 **Niedereschach** Ger.
201 I5 **Niedere Tauern** mts Austria
192 I5 **Niederfinow** Ger.
191 E9 **Niederfischbach** Ger.
191 H9 **Nieder-Gemünden** Ger.
193 G7 **Niedergörsdorf** Ger.
191 D9 **Niederkassel** Ger.
194 D2 **Niederkirchen** Ger.
191 B8 **Niederkrüchten** Ger.
190 D5 **Niederlangen** Ger.
193 I7 **Niederlausitz** reg. Ger.
193 I6 **Niederlehme** Ger.
193 D6 **Niederndodeleben** Ger.
200 F4 **Niederndorf** Austria
191 F10 **Niederneisen** Ger.
194 H3 **Niedernhall** Ger.
191 F10 **Niedernhausen** Ger.
200 G5 **Niedernsill** Austria
191 H6 **Niedernwöhren** Ger.
194 E2 **Nieder-Olm** Ger.
191 J8 **Niederorschel** Ger.
201 M3 **Niederösterreich** land Austria
191 H10 **Nieder-Rodenbach** Ger.
193 D8 **Niederroßla** Ger.
190 G5 **Niedersachsen** land Ger.
187 K1 **Niedersächsisches Wattenmeer, Nationalpark** nat. park Ger.
191 K7 **Niedersachswerfen** Ger.
191 F10 **Niederselters** Ger.
194 H3 **Niederstetten** Ger.
195 I4 **Niederstotzingen** Ger.
193 E8 **Niedertrebra** Ger.
212 G1 **Niederurnen** Switz.
195 M4 **Niederviehbach** Ger.
191 J10 **Niederwerrn** Ger.
193 H9 **Niederwiesa** Ger.
195 N4 **Niederwinkling** Ger.
194 C2 **Niederwörresbach** Ger.
191 D10 **Niederzissen** Ger.
197 K4 **Niedrzwica Duża** Pol.
197 K2 **Niedźwiadna** Pol.
197 I6 **Niedźwiedź** Pol.
229 H6 **Niefang** Equat. Guinea
194 F4 **Niefern-Öschelbronn** Ger.
197 J1 **Niegocin, Jezioro** l. Pol.
196 D3 **Niegosław** Pol.
196 D4 **Niegosławice** Pol.
197 H5 **Niegowa** Pol.
193 E6 **Niegripp** Ger.
191 H7 **Nieheim** Ger.
186 J2 **Niekerk** Neth.
236 G5 **Niekerkshoop** S. Africa
197 I4 **Niekłań Wielki** Pol.
196 E2 **Niekursko** Pol.
187 F6 **Niel** Belgium
197 L5 **Nielisz** Pol.
228 D4 **Niellé** Côte d'Ivoire
230 B3 **Niem** C.A.R.
231 F6 **Niemba** Dem. Rep. Congo
193 F7 **Niemberg** Ger.
197 K4 **Niemce** Pol.
196 E5 **Niemcza** Pol.
193 G6 **Niemegk** Ger.
162 P3 **Niemisel** Sweden
196 F5 **Niemodlin** Pol.
196 G4 **Niemysłów** Pol.
228 D4 **Niéna** Mali
197 K5 **Nienadówka** Pol.
190 I2 **Nienborstel** Ger.
193 E7 **Nienburg (Saale)** Ger.
190 H5 **Nienburg (Weser)** Ger.
190 J5 **Nienhagen** Ger.
192 E2 **Nienhagen, Ostseebad** Ger.
191 H6 **Nienstädt** Ger.
192 G2 **Niepars** Ger.
197 I5 **Niepołomice** Pol.
197 J3 **Nieporęt** Pol.
178 E2 **Nieppe** France
228 B3 **Niéri Ko** watercourse Senegal
191 A7 **Niers** r. Ger.
194 E2 **Nierstein** Ger.
193 K8 **Niesky** Ger.
191 I8 **Nieste** Ger.
197 I4 **Nieświń** Pol.
196 G3 **Nieszawa** Pol.
197 J5 **Nietulisko Duże** Pol.
184 G4 **Nieul** France
184 A2 **Nieul-le-Dolent** France
184 B3 **Nieul-sur-Mer** France
275 H3 **Nieuw Amsterdam** Suriname
186 J5 **Nieuw-Bergen** Neth.
186 H4 **Nieuwegein** Neth.
186 G3 **Nieuwe-Niedorp** Neth.
186 K2 **Nieuwe Pekela** Neth.
186 F5 **Nieuwerkerk** Neth.
186 G5 **Nieuwerkerk aan de IJssel** Neth.
187 H7 **Nieuwerkerken** Belgium
186 L2 **Nieuweschans** Neth.
186 F5 **Nieuwe-Tonge** Neth.
186 J4 **Nieuw-Heeten** Neth.
275 H3 **Nieuw-Jacobkondre** Suriname
186 G4 **Nieuwkoop** Neth.
186 K3 **Nieuwlande** Neth.
186 J3 **Nieuwleusen** Neth.
186 H4 **Nieuw-Loosdrecht** Neth.
186 I4 **Nieuw-Milligen** Neth.
187 F6 **Nieuw-Namen** Neth.
275 G3 **Nieuw Nickerie** Suriname
186 K2 **Nieuwolda** Neth.
236 D7 **Nieuwoudtville** S. Africa
187 C6 **Nieuwpoort** Belgium
271 □[10] **Nieuwpoort** Curaçao Neth. Antilles
186 G4 **Nieuwveen** Neth.
186 G4 **Nieuw-Vennep** Neth.
186 F5 **Nieuw-Vossemeer** Neth.
186 K3 **Nieuw-Weerdinge** Neth.
191 E10 **Nievern** Ger.
268 D2 **Nieves** Mex.
Nieves Spain see **As Neves**
238 □[3f] **Nieves, Pico de las** mt. Gran Canaria Canary Is
182 D2 **Nièvre** dept France
182 C2 **Nièvre** r. France
182 C3 **Nièvre de Champlemy** r. France
197 K4 **Niewęgłosz** Pol.
115 G5 **Nif** Seram Indon.
148 G5 **Niğde** Turkey
237 M2 **Nigel** S. Africa
229 H2 **Niger** country Africa
229 G5 **Niger** r. Africa
229 G4 **Niger** state Nigeria
229 G5 **Niger, Mouths of the** Nigeria
228 C4 **Niger, Source of the** Guinea
288 J5 **Niger Cone** sea feature S. Atlantic Ocean
229 G4 **Nigeria** country Africa
168 H7 **Nigg Bay** Scotland U.K.
138 H5 **Nighasan** Uttar Prad. India
103 C12 **Nightcaps** South I. N.Z.
248 D3 **Nighthawk Lake** Ont. Can.
238 □[2c] **Nightingale Island** Tristan da Cunha S. Atlantic Ocean
107 I2 **Night Island** Qld Austr.
244 F3 **Nightmute** AK U.S.A.
204 C4 **Nigrán** Spain
160 F5 **Nīgrande** Latvia
220 E2 **Nigrita** Greece
268 F3 **Nigromante** Mex.
207 L7 **Nigüelas** Spain
160 H3 **Nigula looduskaitseala** nature res. Estonia
181 O8 **Niherne** France
145 K7 **Nihing** Pak.
Nihommatsu Japan see **Nihonmatsu**
Nihon country Asia see **Japan**
124 R9 **Nihonmatsu** Japan
284 C4 **Nihuil, Embalse del** resr Arg.
124 Q9 **Niigata** Japan
127 H1 **Niigata** pref. Japan
127 H2 **Niigata-yake-yama** vol. Japan
125 K13 **Niihama** Japan
127 I2 **Niihari** Japan
264 □A12 **Ni'ihau** i. HI U.S.A.
127 J7 **Nii-jima** i. Japan
124 T4 **Niikappu** Japan
125 K12 **Niimi** Japan
124 Q9 **Niitsu** Japan
207 O7 **Níjar** Spain
228 C2 **Nijerâne** well Maur.
186 J3 **Nijeveen** Neth.
150 D8 **Nijil** Jordan
150 D8 **Nijil, Wādī** watercourse Jordan
186 H4 **Nijkerk** Neth.
187 G6 **Nijlen** Belgium
186 I5 **Nijmegen** Neth.
186 J4 **Nijverdal** Neth.
220 D3 **Nikaia** Greece
103 □[3] **Nikao** Rarotonga Cook Is
162 U2 **Nikel'** Rus. Fed.
142 H2 **Nikel'tau** Kazakh.
146 E5 **Nikhb** Saudi Arabia
115 D8 **Nikiniki** Timor Indon.
244 J3 **Nikiski** AK U.S.A.
159 R3 **Nikitovka** Rus. Fed.
162 O3 **Nikkaluokta** Sweden
229 F4 **Nikki** Benin
127 K2 **Nikkō** Japan
127 K2 **Nikkō Kokuritsu-kōen** nat. park Japan
201 L5 **Niklasdorf** Austria
156 I4 **Nikola** Rus. Fed.
219 N8 **Nikolaevo** Bulg.
244 J4 **Nikolaevsk** AK U.S.A.
244 I3 **Nikolai** AK U.S.A.
Nikolayev Ukr. see **Mykolayiv**
143 L1 **Nikolayevka** Kazakh.
161 O8 **Nikolayevka** Bryanskaya Oblast' Rus. Fed.
142 J1 **Nikolayevka** Chelyabinskaya Oblast' Rus. Fed.
122 I4 **Nikolayevka** Khabarovskiy Kray Rus. Fed.
159 R6 **Nikolayevka** Rostovskaya Oblast' Rus. Fed.
157 I5 **Nikolayevka** Ul'yanovskaya Oblast' Rus. Fed.
Nikolayev Oblast admin. div. Ukr. see **Mykolayivs'ka Oblast'**
157 I6 **Nikolayevsk** Rus. Fed.
Nikolayevskaya Oblast' admin. div. Ukr. see **Mykolayivs'ka Oblast'**
Nikolayevskiy Rus. Fed. see **Nikolayevsk**
122 L2 **Nikolayevsk-na-Amure** Rus. Fed.
Nikolayevskoye Rus. Fed. see **Krasnogvardeyskoye**
161 U5 **Nikolo-Kropotki** Rus. Fed.
200 G6 **Nikolsdorf** Austria
157 I5 **Nikol'sk** Penzenskaya Oblast' Rus. Fed.
156 I4 **Nikol'sk** Vologodskaya Oblast' Rus. Fed.
Nikol'skaya Pestravka Rus. Fed. see **Nikol'sk**
244 E5 **Nikolski** AK U.S.A.
Nikol'skiy Kazakh. see **Satpayev**
161 R1 **Nikol'skiy** Rus. Fed.
153 R4 **Nikol'skoye** Kamchatskaya Oblast' Rus. Fed.
161 Y4 **Nikol'skoye** Kostromskaya Oblast' Rus. Fed.
161 W9 **Nikol'skoye** Lipetskaya Oblast' Rus. Fed.
142 F1 **Nikol'skoye** Orenburgskaya Oblast' Rus. Fed.
161 T9 **Nikol'skoye** Orlovskaya Oblast' Rus. Fed.
151 F1 **Nikol'skoye** Stavropol'skiy Kray Rus. Fed.
Nikol'skoye Vologodskaya Oblast' Rus. Fed. see **Sheksna**
161 U2 **Nikol'skoye** Vologodskaya Oblast' Rus. Fed.
219 M7 **Nikopol** Bulg.
159 N6 **Nikopol'** Ukr.
220 B3 **Nikopoli** Greece
144 C3 **Nīk Pey** Iran
148 H3 **Niksar** Turkey
144 I8 **Nīkshahr** Iran
218 G8 **Nikšić** Nikšić Montenegro
144 I8 **Nīkū Jahān** Iran
161 X6 **Nikulino** Rus. Fed.
99 I2 **Nikumaroro** atoll Phoenix Is Kiribati
99 H2 **Nikunau** i. Gilbert Is Kiribati
Nīl, Nahr an r. Africa see **Nile**
115 F7 **Nila** vol. Maluku Indon.
145 O5 **Nila** Pak.
139 K9 **Nilagiri** Orissa India
162 S5 **Nilakka** l. Fin.
136 E7 **Nilakkottai** Tamil Nadu India
136 E7 **Nilambur** Kerala India
265 Q8 **Niland** CA U.S.A.
135 D11 **Nilandhoo Atoll** Maldives
Nilang Hima. Prad. India see **Nelang**
136 E3 **Nilanga** Mahar. India
136 G8 **Nilaveli** Sri Lanka
225 F2 **Nile** r. Africa
225 G5 **Nile** state Sudan
250 H8 **Niles** MI U.S.A.
256 E7 **Niles** OH U.S.A.
136 D6 **Nileshwar** Kerala India
136 E7 **Nilgiri Hills** India
145 L5 **Nīlī** Afgh.
146 D9 **Nili** r. Eth.
162 P3 **Nilivaara** Sweden
132 F5 **Nilka** Xinjiang China
145 L4 **Nīl Kowtal** pass Afgh.
281 F5 **Nilópolis** Brazil
139 L7 **Nilphamari** Bangl.
162 T5 **Nilsiä** Fin.
269 M9 **Niltepec** Mex.
221 J2 **Nilüfer** r. Turkey
179 L5 **Nilvange** France
164 F6 **Nim** Denmark
125 J11 **Nima** Japan
Nimach Madh. Prad. India see **Neemuch**
138 E6 **Nimaj** Rajasthan India
122 H3 **Niman** r. Rus. Fed.
Nimba, Monts mts Africa see **Nimba, Mount**
228 C5 **Nimba, Mount** mts Africa
138 E7 **Nimbahera** Rajasthan India
136 D4 **Nimbal** Karnataka India
108 G7 **Nimberra Well** W.A. Austr.
Nimbhera Rajasthan India see **Nimbahera**
122 J2 **Nimelen** r. Rus. Fed.
183 E9 **Nîmes** France
213 O3 **Nimis** Italy
138 E6 **Nimka Thana** Rajasthan India
105 L7 **Nimmitabel** N.S.W. Austr.
221 I6 **Nimos** i. Greece
246 E5 **Nimpkish** r. B.C. Can.
287 K1 **Nimrod Glacier** Antarctica
145 J6 **Nīmrūz** prov. Afgh.
138 F2 **Nimu** Jammu and Kashmir India
232 B4 **Nimule** Sudan
232 B4 **Nimule National Park** Sudan
Nimwegen Neth. see **Nijmegen**
160 K3 **Nina** Estonia
100 □[3a] **Ninai** i. Kwajalein Marshall Is
149 K6 **Nīnawá** governorate Iraq
149 K5 **Nīnawá** tourist site Iraq
231 D8 **Ninda** Angola
233 B7 **Nindai** Tanz.
105 L3 **Nindigully** Qld Austr.
190 H2 **Nindorf** Ger.
136 C8 **Nine Degree Channel** India
Nine Islands P.N.G. see **Kilinailau Islands**
Ninemile Bar Dumfries and Galloway, Scotland U.K. see **Crocketford**
105 I4 **Nine Mile Lake** salt flat N.S.W. Austr.
265 P2 **Ninemile Peak** NV U.S.A.
Ninepin Group is H.K. China see **Kwo Chau Kwan To**
289 J7 **Ninetyeast Ridge** sea feature Indian Ocean
105 K8 **Ninety Mile Beach** Vic. Austr.
102 G1 **Ninety Mile Beach** North I. N.Z.
Nineveh tourist site Iraq see **Nīnawá**
283 D6 **Ninfas, Punta** pt Arg.
173 M6 **Ninfield** East Sussex, England U.K.
109 B7 **Ningaloo Marine Park** nature res. W.A. Austr.
122 F6 **Ning'an** Heilong. China
131 M4 **Ningbo** Zhejiang China
129 P6 **Ningcheng** Nei Mongol China
131 L5 **Ningde** Fujian China
131 J5 **Ningdu** Jiangxi China
Ning'er Yunnan China see **Pu'er**
131 L3 **Ningguo** Anhui China
131 M4 **Ninghai** Zhejiang China
129 O7 **Ninghe** Tianjin China
Ninghsia Hui Autonomous Region aut. reg. China see **Ningxia Huizu Zizhiqu**
131 K5 **Ninghua** Fujian China
229 H4 **Ningi** Nigeria
130 B3 **Ningjing Shan** mts Xizang China
130 C5 **Ninglang** Yunnan China
129 N9 **Ningling** Henan China
130 F7 **Ningming** Guangxi China
130 D5 **Ningnan** Sichuan China
130 F2 **Ningqiang** Shaanxi China
130 G2 **Ningshan** Shaanxi China
129 M7 **Ningwu** Shanxi China
Ningxia aut. reg. China see **Ningxia Huizu Zizhiqu**
128 I8 **Ningxia Huizu Zizhiqu** aut. reg. China
129 J9 **Ningxian** Gansu China
131 I4 **Ningxiang** Hunan China
129 O9 **Ningyang** Shandong China
131 H6 **Ningyuan** Hunan China
Ningzhou Yunnan China see **Huaning**
118 H4 **Ninh Binh** Vietnam
119 I8 **Ninh Hoa** Vietnam
119 I9 **Ninh Sơn** Vietnam
284 A5 **Ninhue** Chile
113 J7 **Ninigo Group** atolls P.N.G.
244 J3 **Ninilchik** AK U.S.A.
287 J2 **Ninnis Glacier** Antarctica
287 K2 **Ninnis Glacier Tongue** Antarctica
206 H8 **Niño, Sierra del** mts Spain
124 S6 **Ninohe** Japan
127 J5 **Ninomiya** Kanagawa Japan
127 K3 **Ninomiya** Tochigi Japan
151 E4 **Ninotsminda** Georgia
187 F7 **Ninove** Belgium
283 B7 **Ninualac, Canal** sea chan. Chile
151 E1 **Niny** Rus. Fed.
277 G5 **Nioaque** Brazil
260 F4 **Niobrara** r. NE U.S.A.
243 Q2 **Nioghalvfjerdsfjorden** inlet Greenland
230 F4 **Nioka** Dem. Rep. Congo
230 C5 **Nioki** Dem. Rep. Congo
139 O6 **Nioko** Arun. Prad. India
228 B3 **Niokolo Koba, Parc National du** nat. park Senegal
228 D3 **Niono** Mali
228 C3 **Nioro** Mali
228 B3 **Nioro du Rip** Senegal
184 D3 **Niort** France
228 D3 **Nioût** well Maur.
113 J8 **Nipa** P.N.G.
136 D4 **Nipani** Karnataka India
115 C5 **Nipanipa, Tanjung** pt Indon.
284 A5 **Ñipas** Chile
247 J4 **Nipawin** Sask. Can.
138 E9 **Niphad** Mahar. India
248 B3 **Nipigon** Ont. Can.
260 K1 **Nipigon** r. Ont. Can.
248 B3 **Nipigon, Lake** Ont. Can.
248 C3 **Nipigon Bay** Ont. Can.
235 H3 **Nipiodi** Moz.
249 I2 **Nipishish Lake** Nfld and Lab. Can.
251 O3 **Nipissing** Ont. Can.
248 E4 **Nipissing, Lake** Ont. Can.
264 L6 **Nipomo** CA U.S.A.
Nippon country Asia see **Japan**
Nippon Hai sea N. Pacific Ocean see **Japan, Sea of**
149 L7 **Nippur** tourist site Iraq
265 Q6 **Nipton** CA U.S.A.
278 C5 **Niquelândia** Brazil
284 B5 **Niquen** Chile
270 E3 **Niquero** Cuba
284 C2 **NIquivil** Arg.
144 B2 **Nīr** Ardabīl Iran
144 F6 **Nir** Yazd Iran
144 F6 **Nīr** Iran
146 F3 **Nīr, Jabal an** hills Saudi Arabia
136 D4 **Nira** r. India
127 H4 **Nirasaki** Japan
127 I5 **Nirayama** Japan
284 A4 **Nirivilo** Chile
129 S2 **Nirji** Nei Mongol China
136 F3 **Nirmal** Andhra Prad. India
139 K6 **Nirmali** Bihar India
136 E3 **Nirmal Range** hills India
160 K5 **Nirzas** l. Latvia
219 J7 **Niš** Niš Serbia
204 E9 **Nisa** Port.
204 E9 **Nisa** r. Port.
144 H3 **Nisa** tourist site Turkm.
146 H8 **Nişāb** Yemen
146 H3 **Nisah, Wādī** watercourse Saudi Arabia
219 J7 **Nišava** r. Serbia
168 K11 **Nisbet** Scottish Borders, Scotland U.K.
216 G9 **Niscemi** Sicilia Italy
124 R4 **Niseko** Japan
133 G10 **Nishan** Xizang China
Nîshāpūr Iran see **Neyshābūr**
160 L6 **Nishcha** r. Belarus
130 H4 **Nishi** Hunan China
126 D5 **Nishiazai** Japan
124 W3 **Nishibetsu-gawa** r. Japan
127 L1 **Nishigō** Japan
127 I6 **Nishiizu** Japan
125 H15 **Nishikata** Kagoshima Japan
127 K3 **Nishikata** Tochigi Japan
127 I4 **Nishikatsura** Japan
124 R8 **Nishikawa** Japan
126 B5 **Nishi-maizuru** Japan
127 K2 **Nishinasuno** Japan
126 B6 **Nishinomiya** Japan
124 □H16 **Nishino-omote** Japan
125 K10 **Nishino-shima** i. Japan
125 □[2] **Nishino-shima** vol. Japan
126 F6 **Nishio** Japan
125 G14 **Nishi-Sonogi-hantō** pen. Japan
125 G12 **Nishi-suidō** sea chan. Japan/S. Korea
126 A6 **Nishiwaki** Japan
126 C7 **Nishiyoshino** Japan
278 G3 **Nísia Floresta** Brazil
Nisibis Turkey see **Nusaybin**
126 E5 **Nisiharu** Japan
125 I14 **Nisi-mera** Japan
Nísiros i. Greece see **Nisyros**
162 S4 **Niskanselkä** l. Fin.
257 L6 **Niskayuna** NY U.S.A.
248 B1 **Niskibi** r. Ont. Can.
197 K5 **Nisko** Pol.
245 M3 **Nisling** r. Y.T. Can.
187 G8 **Nismes** Belgium
187 G8 **Nismes, Forêt de** for. Belgium
158 H6 **Nisporeni** Moldova
164 I5 **Nissan** r. Sweden
183 C10 **Nissan-lez-Enserune** France
164 E2 **Nisser** l. Norway
126 F5 **Nisshin** Japan
216 G8 **Nissoria** Sicilia Italy
164 E5 **Nissum Bredning** b. Denmark
186 I5 **Nistelrode** Neth.
158 J7 **Nistru** r. Moldova alt. **Dnister (Ukraine)**, conv. **Dniester**
158 I6 **Nistrului Inferior, Cîmpia** lowland Moldova
245 N3 **Nisutlin** r. Y.T. Can.
221 I6 **Nisyros** i. Greece
125 K11 **Nita** Japan
147 I2 **Niţā** Saudi Arabia
125 G12 **Nita-wan** b. Japan
249 G2 **Nitchequon** Que. Can.
Nitendi i. Santa Cruz Is Solomon Is see **Ndeni**
281 F5 **Niterói** Brazil
168 I12 **Nith** r. Scotland U.K.
168 I12 **Nithsdale** val. Scotland U.K.
115 D8 **Nitibe** East Timor
141 L3 **Niti Pass** Xizang China
106 D3 **Nitmiluk National Park** N.T. Austr.
199 H3 **Nitra** Slovakia
199 H4 **Nitra** r. Slovakia
199 H3 **Nitrianske Pravno** Slovakia
199 H3 **Nitriansky kraj** admin. reg. Slovakia
256 D10 **Nitro** WV U.S.A.
178 G8 **Nitry** France
127 J3 **Nitta** Japan
164 G1 **Nittedal** Norway
194 A2 **Nittel** Ger.
195 M3 **Nittenau** Ger.
195 L3 **Nittendorf** Ger.
Niua i. Vanuatu see **Aniwa**
99 I3 **Niuafo'ou** i. Tonga
Niuafu i. Tonga see **Niuafo'ou**
99 I3 **Niuatoputopu** i. Tonga
101 □[8a] **Niu 'Aunofo** cliff Tongatapu Tonga
132 K7 **Niubiziliang** Qinghai China
103 □[4] **Niue** terr. S. Pacific Ocean
Niujing Yunnan China see **Binchuan**
99 H3 **Niulakita** i. Tuvalu
130 D5 **Niulan Jiang** r. Yunnan China
264 □F13 **Niuli'i** HI U.S.A.
116 E5 **Niur, Pulau** i. Indon.
Niushan Jiangsu China see **Donghai**
99 H2 **Niutao** i. Tuvalu
131 L3 **Niutoushan** Anhui China
129 R6 **Niuzhuang** Liaoning China
162 R5 **Nivala** Fin.
162 V3 **Nivastroy** Rus. Fed.
107 K8 **Nive** watercourse Qld Austr.
185 B9 **Nive** r. France
107 K8 **Nive Downs** Qld Austr.
187 F7 **Nivelles** Belgium
197 I1 **Nivenskoye** Rus. Fed.
182 C2 **Nivernais** reg. France
182 D2 **Nivernais, Canal du** France
180 G6 **Nivillac** France
178 D5 **Nivillers** France
161 P8 **Nivnoye** Rus. Fed.
182 G5 **Nivolas-Vermelle** France
156 K3 **Nivshera** Rus. Fed.
162 V3 **Nivskiy** Rus. Fed.
138 E6 **Niwai** Rajasthan India
138 G7 **Niwari** Madh. Prad. India
138 H8 **Niwas** Madh. Prad. India
197 J5 **Niwiska** Pol.
179 J5 **Nixéville-Blercourt** France
Nixia Sichuan China see **Sêrxü**
264 M2 **Nixon** NV U.S.A.
Niya Xinjiang China see **Minfeng**
133 F8 **Niya He** r. China
151 J4 **Niyazoba** Azer.
117 H4 **Niyut, Gunung** mt. Indon.
161 S2 **Niz** Rus. Fed.
127 K4 **Niza** Japan
136 F3 **Nizamabad** Andhra Prad. India
136 G5 **Nizampatnam** Andhra Prad. India
136 E3 **Nizam Sagar** l. India
198 D2 **Nižbor** Czech Rep.
156 I4 **Nizhegorodskaya Oblast'** admin. div. Rus. Fed.
153 L4 **Nizhneangarsk** Rus. Fed.
159 Q9 **Nizhnebakanskiy** Rus. Fed.
157 G6 **Nizhnedevitsk** Rus. Fed.
143 U1 **Nizhnekamenka** Rus. Fed.
156 J5 **Nizhnekamsk** Rus. Fed.
156 K5 **Nizhnekamskoye Vodokhranilishche** resr Rus. Fed.
153 R3 **Nizhnekolymsk** Rus. Fed.
161 Q1 **Nizhne-Svirskiy Zapovednik** nature res. Rus. Fed.
122 K3 **Nizhnetambovskoye** Rus. Fed.
120 G1 **Nizhneudinsk** Rus. Fed.
152 I3 **Nizhnevartovsk** Rus. Fed.
Nizhnevolzhsk Rus. Fed. see **Narimanov**
153 O2 **Nizhneyansk** Rus. Fed.
161 P9 **Nizhneye** Rus. Fed.
129 O1 **Nizhneye Giryunino** Rus. Fed.
156 L4 **Nizhni Irginski** Rus. Fed.
157 I6 **Nizhniy Baskunchak** Rus. Fed.
156 K2 **Nizhniy Bugayevo** Rus. Fed.
151 E2 **Nizhniy Chegem** Rus. Fed.
157 H6 **Nizhniy Chir** Rus. Fed.
151 I3 **Nizhniy Dzhengutay** Rus. Fed.
143 O3 **Nizhniye Kayrakty** Kazakh.
Nizhniye Kresty Rus. Fed. see **Cherskiy**
Nizhniye Ustriki Pol. see **Ustrzyki Dolne**
159 S3 **Nizhniy Karabut** Rus. Fed.
159 T3 **Nizhniy Kislyay** Rus. Fed.
151 F2 **Nizhniy Kurp** Rus. Fed.
157 H5 **Nizhniy Lomov** Rus. Fed.
159 T3 **Nizhniy Mamon** Rus. Fed.
156 H4 **Nizhniy Novgorod** Rus. Fed.
Nizhniy Novgorod Oblast admin. div. Rus. Fed. see **Nizhegorodskaya Oblast'**
156 K3 **Nizhniy Odes** Rus. Fed.
159 R3 **Nizhniy Ol'shan** Rus. Fed.
Nizhniy Pyandzh Tajik. see **Panji Poyon**
152 G4 **Nizhniy Tagil** Rus. Fed.
129 N1 **Nizhniy Tsasuchey** Rus. Fed.
156 I4 **Nizhniy Yenansk** Rus. Fed.
156 J2 **Nizhnyaya Kamenka** Rus. Fed.
156 I2 **Nizhnyaya Mola** Rus. Fed.
156 K3 **Nizhnyaya Omra** Rus. Fed.
156 I2 **Nizhnyaya Pesha** Rus. Fed.
162 V3 **Nizhnyaya Pirenga, Ozero** l. Rus. Fed.
153 K4 **Nizhnyaya Poyma** Rus. Fed.
143 R1 **Nizhnyaya Suyetka** Rus. Fed.
151 C2 **Nizhnyaya Teberda** Rus. Fed.
153 J3 **Nizhnyaya Tunguska** r. Rus. Fed.
152 G4 **Nizhnyaya Tura** Rus. Fed.
159 R2 **Nizhnyaya Veduga** Rus. Fed.
156 H2 **Nizhnyaya Zolotitsa** Rus. Fed.
159 K2 **Nizhyn** Ukr.
148 H5 **Nizip** Turkey
161 N6 **Nizkabor"ye** Belarus
199 K2 **Nízke Beskydy** hills Slovakia
199 I3 **Nízke Tatry** mts Slovakia
199 I3 **Nízke Tatry** nat. park Slovakia
122 I7 **Nizmennyy, Mys** pt Rus. Fed.
199 J3 **Nižná Slaná** Slovakia
199 K3 **Nižný Hrušov** Slovakia
199 K3 **Nižný Žipov** Slovakia
Nizwā Oman see **Nazwá…**
Nizza France see **Nice**
217 I8 **Nizza di Sicilia** Sicilia It…
212 E6 **Nizza Monferrato** Italy
218 G8 **Njegoš** mts Montenegro…
Njellim Fin. see **Nellim**
235 F4 **Njesuthi** mt. Lesotho/S. …
233 C7 **Njinjo** Tanz.
213 R5 **Njivice** Croatia
231 E9 **Njoko** r. Zambia
233 B7 **Njombe** Tanz.
233 B6 **Njombe** r. Tanz.
100 □[6] **Njoroveto** New Georgia … Solomon Is
163 N5 **Njurundabommen** Swe…
163 N6 **Njutånger** Sweden
Nkai Zimbabwe see **Nka…**
229 H5 **Nkambe** Cameroon
237 P4 **Nkandla** S. Africa
233 A6 **Nkasi** Tanz.
228 E5 **Nkawkaw** Ghana
235 F3 **Nkayi** Zimbabwe
228 D2 **Nkhaïlé** well Maur.
233 B7 **Nkhata Bay** Malawi
233 B8 **Nkhotakota** Malawi
233 B8 **Nkhotakota Game Rese…** nature res. Malawi
230 A4 **Nkolabona** Gabon
230 A5 **Nkomi, Lagune** lag. Gab…
233 A6 **Nkondwe** Tanz.
229 H5 **Nkonfap** Nigeria
229 H5 **Nkongsamba** Cameroon
228 E5 **Nkoranza** Ghana
229 I5 **Nkoteng** Cameroon
237 L6 **Nkululeko** S. Africa
233 A6 **Nkundi** Tanz.
233 A6 **Nkungwi** Tanz.
234 C3 **Nkurenkuru** Namibia
232 A4 **Nkusi** r. Uganda
237 P4 **Nkwalini** S. Africa
229 F4 **Nkwanta** Ghana
237 K9 **Nkwenkwezi** S. Africa
118 C2 **Nmai Hka** r. Myanmar
139 P6 **Noa Dihing** r. India
185 D7 **Noaillan** France
178 D5 **Noailles** France
185 A10 **Noain** Spain
139 M8 **Noakhali** Bangl.
213 M4 **Noale** Italy
207 L5 **Noalejo** Spain
139 J8 **Noamundi** Jharkhand In…
186 J2 **Noardburgum** Neth.
212 C5 **Noasca** Italy
244 G2 **Noatak** AK U.S.A.
244 G2 **Noatak** r. AK U.S.A.
244 H1 **Noatak National Preser…** nature res. AK U.S.A.
170 D6 **Nobber** Ireland
125 I14 **Nobeoka** Japan
193 F9 **Nobitz** Ger.
205 N9 **Noblejas** Spain
254 D5 **Noblesville** IN U.S.A.
237 L7 **Nobokwe** S. Africa
124 S4 **Noboribetsu** Japan
277 F3 **Nobres** Brazil
107 I9 **Noccundra** Qld Austr.
181 M5 **Nocé** France
213 K3 **Noce** r. Italy
215 P8 **Noce** r. Italy
204 H3 **Noceda** Spain
215 N6 **Nocera Inferiore** Italy
215 Q9 **Nocera Terinese** Italy
215 J1 **Nocera Umbra** Italy
212 I6 **Noceto** Italy
268 E4 **Nochistlán** Mex.
269 J8 **Nochixtlán** Mex.
201 K3 **Nöchling** Austria
217 M2 **Noci** Italy
197 M1 **Nočia** r. Belarus/Lith.
217 O3 **Nociglia** Italy
258 E4 **Nockamixon Lake** PA U…
107 I9 **Nockatunga** Qld Austr.
105 J3 **Nocoleche Nature Rese…** N.S.W. Austr.
261 G9 **Nocona** TX U.S.A.
127 K4 **Noda** Japan
126 B4 **Nodagawa** Japan
283 D8 **Nodales, Bahía de los** b. …
260 H6 **Nodaway** r. MO U.S.A.
164 D3 **Nodeland** Norway
182 I2 **Nods** France
185 G9 **Noé** France
277 E3 **Noel Kempff Mercado, …** **Nacional** nat. park Bol.
248 D4 **Noelville** Ont. Can.
236 E3 **Noenieput** S. Africa
215 Q7 **Noepoli** Italy
190 J2 **Noer** Ger.
285 F3 **Noetinger** Arg.
178 E3 **Nœux-les-Mines** France
205 L9 **Noez** Spain
205 L9 **Noez, Pico de** mt. Spain
205 N3 **Nofuentes** Spain
266 D2 **Nogales** Mex.
206 F3 **Nogales** Spain
263 I11 **Nogales** AZ U.S.A.
151 F2 **Nogamirzin-Yurt** Rus. F…
213 K5 **Nogara** Italy
185 D8 **Nogaro** France
196 H1 **Nogat** r. Pol.
125 H13 **Nōgata** Japan
Nogaysk Ukr. see **Prymo…**
151 H1 **Nogayskaya Step'** reg. Ru…
142 F3 **Nogayty** Kazakh.
179 J7 **Nogent** France
181 L5 **Nogent-le-Bernard** Fran…
178 C6 **Nogent-le-Roi** France
181 M5 **Nogent-le-Rotrou** France
178 H7 **Nogent-sur-Aube** France
178 D6 **Nogent-sur-Marne** Fran…
178 D5 **Nogent-sur-Oise** France
178 G7 **Nogent-sur-Seine** France
178 E8 **Nogent-sur-Vernisson** F…
127 K3 **Nogi** Japan
153 K3 **Noginsk** Evenkiyskiy Avto… Okrug Rus. Fed.
161 V6 **Noginsk** Moskovskaya O… Rus. Fed.
122 M3 **Nogliki** Sakhalin Rus. Fe…
107 M8 **Nogo** r. Qld Austr.
107 L7 **Nogoa** r. Qld Austr.
126 E4 **Nōgōhaku-san** mt. Japan
128 I7 **Nogon Toli** Nei Mongol …
285 H3 **Nogoyá** Arg.
285 H3 **Nogoya** r. Arg.
199 I4 **Nógrád** Hungary
199 I4 **Nógrád** county Hungary
205 O6 **Nograles** Spain
126 G3 **Noguchigorō-dake** mt. J…
204 G5 **Nogueira, Serra de** mts P…
208 G4 **Noguera** reg. Spain
205 Q8 **Noguera de Albarracín** S…
185 C9 **Noguères** France
209 D7 **Nogueruelas** Spain
182 B2 **Nohain** r. France
267 O8 **Nohalal** Mex.
181 O8 **Nohant-Vic** France
138 E5 **Nohar** Rajasthan India
185 I10 **Nohèdes, Réserve Natur…** nature res. France
124 S6 **Noheji** Japan
194 C2 **Nohfelden** Ger.
185 G8 **Nohic** France
264 □B11 **Nohili Point** HI U.S.A.
128 D7 **Nohoit** Qinghai China
144 G2 **Nohur** Turkm.
204 C3 **Noia** Spain
217 L1 **Noicattaro** Italy
138 F5 **Noida** Uttar Prad. India
182 I1 **Noidans-lès-Vesoul** Fran…
185 F8 **Noilhan** France
183 C8 **Noir, Causse** plat. France
251 R4 **Noire** r. Que. Can.
185 I9 **Noire, Montagne** mts Fra…
202 E5 **Noire, Pointe** pt Morocco
180 D5 **Noires, Montagnes** hills …
182 D5 **Noirétable** France
180 G8 **Noirmoutier, Île de** i. Fra…
180 G7 **Noirmoutier-en-l'Île** Fra…
179 L5 **Noisseville** France
205 M2 **Noja** Spain
127 K6 **Nojima-zaki** c. Japan
127 H2 **Nojiri-ko** l. Japan

B7 Nokami Japan
H10 Nokesville VA U.S.A.
D6 Nokha Rajasthan India
J9 Nokhbur Pak.
I8 Nokhowch, Kūh-e mt. Iran
Q6 Nokia Fin.
Nōkis Uzbek. see Nukus
J7 Nok Kundi Pak.
J5 Nokomis Sask. Can.
K3 Nokomis Lake Sask. Can.
B6 Nokou Chad
M7 Nokrek Peak Meghalaya India
I4 Nol Sweden
C4 Nola C.A.R.
H2 Nola Italy
F3 Nolay France
E7 Noli Italy
E7 Noli, Capo di c. Italy
F7 Nolichuky r. TN U.S.A.
J4 Nolinsk Rus. Fed.
G9 Noll S. Africa
D1 Nólsoy i. Faroe Is
H15 Noma-misaki pt Japan
O7 No Mans Land i. MA U.S.A.
L8 Nombela Spain
C2 Nombre de Dios Mex.
F2 Nome AK U.S.A.
F2 Nome, Cape AK U.S.A.
J7 Nomenj Slovenia
L6 Nomeny France
F7 Nomexy France
I5 Nomgon Mongolia
E8 Nomhon Qinghai China
D8 Nomhon He r. Qinghai China
S2 Nomin Gol r. China
Nomoi Islands Micronesia see Mortlock Islands
K7 Nomonde S. Africa
Nomoneas is Chuuk Micronesia
G14 Nomo-zaki pt Japan
E2 Nömrög Mongolia
I1 Nomto Rus. Fed.
G3 Nomugi-tōge pass Japan
Nomuka Tonga
Nomuka i. Tonga
Nomuka Group is Tonga
Nomuka Iki i. Tonga
Nomwin atoll Micronesia
Nomzha Rus. Fed.
Nonacho Lake N.W.T. Can.
Nonancourt France
Nonant-le-Pin France
Nonantola Italy
Nonaspe Spain
Nondalton AK U.S.A.
Nondweni S. Africa
Nonette r. France
Nong'an Jilin China
Nông Hêt Laos
Nong Hong Thai.
Nonghui Sichuan China see Guang'an
Nongkha Meghalaya India
Nong Khai Thai.
Nongoma S. Africa
Nongpoh Meghalaya India
Nongstoin Meghalaya India
Nonières France
Nonnenweier Ger.
Nonni r. China see Nen Jiang
Nonning S.A. Austr.
Nonnweiler Ger.
Nono Ecuador
Nonoai Brazil
Nonoava Mex.
Nonoichi Japan
Nonouti atoll Gilbert Is Kiribati
Nonquén Chile
Nonsan S. Korea
Nonsuch Island Bermuda
Nonthaburi Thai.
Nontron France
Nonvianuk Lake AK U.S.A.
Nonza Corse France
Nonzwakazi S. Africa
Nõo Estonia
Nookawarra W.A. Austr.
Nooleyanna Lake salt flat S.A. Austr.
Noonamah N.T. Austr.
Noondie, Lake salt flat W.A. Austr.
Noonkanbah W.A. Austr.
Noonkanbah Aboriginal Reserve W.A. Austr.
Noonthorangee Range hills N.S.W. Austr.
Noorama Creek watercourse Qld Austr.
Noordbeveland i. Neth.
Noord-Brabant prov. Neth.
Noordbroek-Uiterburen Neth.
Noorderhaaks i. Neth.
Noord-Holland prov. Neth.
Noordhollands Duinreservaat nature res. Neth.
Noordkaap S. Africa
Noordkuil S. Africa
Noordoewer Namibia
Noordoost Polder Neth.
Noordpunt pt Curaçao Neth. Antilles
Noordwijk aan Zee Neth.
Noordwijk-Binnen Neth.
Noordwijkerhout Neth.
Noordwolde Neth.
Noormarkku Fin.
Noorvik AK U.S.A.
Noosa Heads Qld Austr.
Nootdorp Neth.
Nootka Island B.C. Can.
Nopala Mex.
Nopaltepec Mex.
Nopiming Provincial Park Man. Can.
Noqueves Arg.
Nóqui Angola
Nora r. Italy
Nora r. Rus. Fed.
Nora Sweden
Noragugume Sardegna Italy
Norak Tajik.
Norak, Obanbori resr Tajik.
Norakert Armenia see Baghramyan
Norala Mindanao Phil.
Noranda Que. Can.
Nor-Bayazet Armenia see Gavarr
Norberg Sweden
Norberto de la Riestra Arg.
Norcang Xizang China
Norcia Italy
Norcross ME U.S.A.
Nord prov. Cameroon
Nord dept France
Nord Greenland see Station Nord
Nord, Canal du France
Nord, Pointe pt Njazidja Comoros
Nord, Récif du rf Mayotte
Nordaustlandet i. Svalbard
Nordborg Denmark
Nord-Bornholm nature res. Bornholm Denmark
Nordborn Norway
Nordby Denmark
Norddeich Ger.
Nordegg Alta Can.
Norden Ger.
Nordendorf Ger.
Nordenham Ger.
Nordenshel'da, Arkhipelag is Rus. Fed.
Nordenskiöld r. Y.T. Can.
Nordenskiöld Land reg. Svalbard
Nordenskjold Archipelago is Rus. Fed. see Nordenshel'da, Arkhipelag
Norder Hever sea chan. Ger.
Norderland reg. Ger.
Norderney Ger.
Norderney i. Ger.
Norderoogsand i. Ger.
Norderstedt Ger.
239 Nord Est, Grand Récif du rf Mayotte
238 Nordeste São Miguel Azores
238 Nordestinho São Miguel Azores
162 U1 Nordfjord Norway
163 H6 Nordfjord reg. Norway
163 H6 Nordfjordeid Norway
162 Nordfjorden inlet Svalbard
162 M3 Nordfold Norway
190 F1 Nordfriesische Inseln is Ger.
190 G1 Nordfriesland reg. Ger.
193 D6 Nordgermersleben Ger.
193 E10 Nordhalben Ger.
190 H2 Nordhastedt Ger.
191 K8 Nordhausen Ger.
194 G3 Nordheim Ger.
190 G3 Nordholz Ger.
191 D6 Nordhorn Ger.
164 B2 Nordhuglo Norway
162 O5 Nordingrå naturreservat nature res. Sweden
164 F5 Nordjylland county Denmark
Nord Kap c. Iceland see Horn
162 R1 Nordkapp c. Norway
162 S1 Nordkinnhalvøya i. Norway
191 E7 Nordkirchen Ger.
230 F5 Nord-Kivu prov. Dem. Rep. Congo
162 O1 Nordkvaløy i. Norway
162 M3 Nordland county Norway
190 G3 Nordleda Ger.
162 L4 Nordli Norway
195 M2 Nördlicher Oberpfälzer Wald park Ger.
191 K7 Nördliches Harzvorland park Ger.
195 I4 Nördlingen Ger.
162 O5 Nordmaling Sweden
164 D1 Nordmannslågen l. Norway
162 P2 Nordmannvik Norway
190 G1 Nordmarsch-Langeness i. Ger.
243 O2 Nord- og Østgrønland, Nationalparken i nat. park Greenland
190 H2 Nord-Ostsee-Kanal canal Ger.
229 H5 Nord-Ouest prov. Cameroon
152 A3 Norðoyar i. Faroe Is
178 E3 Nord-Pas-de-Calais admin. reg. France
178 F3 Nord-Pas-de-Calais, Parc Naturel Régional du nature res. France
194 D2 Nordpfälzer Bergland reg. Ger.
Nordre Strømfjord inlet Greenland see Nassuttooq
191 D8 Nordrhein-Westfalen land Ger.
191 I6 Nordstemmen Ger.
190 G1 Nordstrand pen. Ger.
190 G1 Nordstrandischmoor i. Ger.
162 L4 Nord-Trøndelag county Norway
230 D4 Nord-Ubangi prov. Dem. Rep. Congo
162 D1 Norðurland eystra constituency Iceland
162 C1 Norðurland vestra constituency Iceland
162 Nordvest-Spitsbergen Nasjonalpark nat. park Svalbard
153 M2 Nordvik Rus. Fed.
162 J5 Nordvika Norway
191 D6 Nordwalde Ger.
169 I8 Nore r. Ireland
185 I9 Nore, Pic de mt. France
Noreg country Europe see Norway
160 G7 Noreikiškės Lith.
204 I2 Noreña Spain
162 N4 Noresund Norway
208 L3 Norfeu, Cap de c. Spain
190 J2 Norfolk admin. div. England U.K.
260 G4 Norfolk NE U.S.A.
257 K4 Norfolk NY U.S.A.
257 I12 Norfolk VA U.S.A.
104 Norfolk Island terr. S. Pacific Ocean
290 G7 Norfolk Island Ridge sea feature Tasman Sea
261 I7 Norfolk Lake AR U.S.A.
186 J2 Norg Neth.
Norge country Europe see Norway
171 M2 Norham Northumberland, England U.K.
164 C1 Norheimsund Norway
276 C5 Noria Chile
268 F3 Noria de Ángeles Mex.
266 E1 Norias Mex.
126 G3 Norikura-dake vol. Japan
152 J3 Noril'sk Rus. Fed.
159 M1 Norino Rus. Fed.
133 I12 Norkyung Xizang China
251 P5 Norland Ont. Can.
215 J4 Norma Italy
257 K6 Norma NJ U.S.A.
133 I10 Norma Co l. Xizang China
250 F9 Normal IL U.S.A.
107 H4 Norman r. Qld Austr.
261 G8 Norman OK U.S.A.
255 G8 Norman, Lake resr NC U.S.A.
107 J3 Normanby r. Qld Austr.
102 J6 Normanby North I. N.Z.
113 L8 Normanby Island P.N.G.
107 M7 Normanby Range hills Qld Austr.
Normandes, Îles is English Chan. see Channel Islands
275 G4 Normandia Brazil
181 J4 Normandie reg. France
181 J4 Normandie, Collines de hills France
181 K5 Normandie-Maine, Parc Naturel Régional nature res. France
237 N3 Normandien S. Africa
Normandy reg. France see Normandie
107 H4 Normanton Qld Austr.
171 O6 Normanton West Yorkshire, England U.K.
104 G6 Normanville S.A. Austr.
245 P2 Norman Wells N.W.T. Can.
251 O1 Normétal Que. Can.
109 D13 Normalup W.A. Austr.
100 Noro New Georgia Is Solomon Is
266 F4 Norogachic Mex.
129 L2 Norovlin Mongolia
182 I1 Noroy-le-Bourg France
245 K5 Norquay Sask. Can.
284 B5 Norquín Arg.
283 C6 Norquinco Arg.
165 L1 Norra Barken l. Sweden
165 N2 Norra Björkfjärden b. Sweden
162 M4 Norra Bredåker Sweden
162 P5 Norra gloppet b. Fin.
163 M2 Norråker Sweden
162 P5 Norra Kvarken str. Fin./Sweden
165 O2 Norra Ljusterö i. Sweden
162 O3 Norrbotten county Sweden
164 F5 Nørreå r. Denmark
164 H7 Nørre Alslev Denmark
164 I1 Nørreballe Denmark
164 G6 Nørre Lyndelse Denmark
164 E6 Nørre Nebel Denmark
178 D2 Nørrent-Fontes France
164 F6 Nørre Snede Denmark
162 P4 Norrfjärden Sweden
165 K1 Norr Hörken l. Sweden
165 K5 Norrhult-Klavreström Sweden
256 B12 Norris Lake TN U.S.A.
258 E4 Norristown PA U.S.A.
165 M3 Norrköping Sweden
165 N2 Norrsundet Sweden
165 O2 Norrtälje Sweden
109 F12 Norseman W.A. Austr.
102 K7 Norsewood North I. N.Z.
164 F2 Norsjø l. Norway
162 O4 Norsjö Sweden
122 F2 Norsk Rus. Fed.
243 Q2 Norske Øer is Greenland
100 Norsup Vanuatu
275 I4 Norte, Cabo c. Brazil
275 I4 Norte, Canal do sea chan. Brazil
271 Norte, Cayo i. Puerto Rico
285 I5 Norte, Punta pt Arg.
283 C8 Norte, Punta pt Arg.
283 E6 Norte, Punta pt Arg.
238 Norte, Punta pt El Hierro Canary Is
277 F2 Norte, Serra do hills Brazil
285 E2 Norte, Sierra de mts Arg.
274 C2 Norte de Santander dept Col.
238 Norte Grande São Jorge Azores
277 F3 Nortelândia Brazil
191 I7 Nörten-Hardenberg Ger.
238 Norte Pequeno São Jorge Azores
287 L2 North, Cape Antarctica
253 J2 North, Cape N.S. Can.
249 I4 North Adams MA U.S.A.
257 L6 North Adams MA U.S.A.
171 O5 Northallerton North Yorkshire, England U.K.
109 D11 Northam W.A. Austr.
172 D5 Northam Devon, England U.K.
240 North America
257 R3 North Amity ME U.S.A.
109 C10 Northampton W.A. Austr.
173 K3 Northampton Northamptonshire, England U.K.
257 M6 Northampton MA U.S.A.
258 E3 Northampton PA U.S.A.
258 E3 Northampton County county PA U.S.A.
107 J8 Northampton Downs Qld Austr.
173 K3 Northamptonshire admin. div. England U.K.
137 M6 North Andaman i. Andaman & Nicobar Is India
256 H11 North Anna r. VA U.S.A.
257 P4 North Anson ME U.S.A.
246 H2 North Arm b. N.W.T. Can.
249 I1 North Aulatsivik Island Nfld and Lab. Can.
289 L5 North Australian Basin sea feature Indian Ocean
168 G11 North Ayrshire admin. div. Scotland U.K.
173 J6 North Baddesley Hampshire, England U.K.
114 A7 North Balabac Strait Phil.
256 B7 North Baltimore OH U.S.A.
247 I4 North Battleford Sask. Can.
248 E4 North Bay Ont. Can.
248 E1 North Belcher Islands Nunavut Can.
262 B5 North Bend OR U.S.A.
256 H7 North Bend PA U.S.A.
257 L6 North Bennington VT U.S.A.
259 G3 North Bergen NJ U.S.A.
168 K10 North Berwick East Lothian, Scotland U.K.
257 O5 North Berwick ME U.S.A.
North Borneo state Malaysia see Sabah
261 G10 North Bosque r. TX U.S.A.
105 J4 North Bourke N.S.W. Austr.
261 K6 North Branch MI U.S.A.
250 B4 North Branch MN U.S.A.
258 F3 North Branch NJ U.S.A.
259 J2 North Branford CT U.S.A.
270 H3 North Caicos i. Turks and Caicos Is
261 H8 North Canadian r. OK U.S.A.
249 H4 North Cape c. P.E.I. Can.
North Cape c. Norway see Nordkapp
102 H1 North Cape c. North I. N.Z.
283 North Cape c. S. Georgia
250 F7 North Cape WI U.S.A.
245 D5 North Cape AK U.S.A.
245 F7 North Cape May NJ U.S.A.
248 B2 North Caribou Lake Ont. Can.
255 H7 North Carolina state U.S.A.
262 D2 North Cascades National Park WA U.S.A.
258 E3 North Catasauqua PA U.S.A.
171 P6 North Cave East Riding of Yorkshire, England U.K.
255 North Cay i. New Prov. Bahamas
108 I7 North Central Aboriginal Reserve W.A. Austr.
248 D4 North Channel lake channel Ont. Can.
168 D12 North Channel Northern Ireland/Scotland U.K.
255 H9 North Charleston SC U.S.A.
172 H5 North Cheriton Somerset, England U.K.
262 K4 North Cheyenne Indian Reservation res. MT U.S.A.
109 D13 Northcliffe W.A. Austr.
287 G2 Northcliffe Glacier Antarctica
256 G6 North Collins NY U.S.A.
261 E10 North Concho r. TX U.S.A.
257 N4 North Conway NH U.S.A.
North Cousin Islet i. Inner Islands Seychelles see Cousin
246 F5 North Cowichan B.C. Can.
171 N5 North Cowton North Yorkshire, England U.K.
257 L5 North Creek NY U.S.A.
260 E2 North Dakota state U.S.A.
168 C6 North Dell Western Isles, Scotland U.K.
172 G6 North Dorset Downs hills England U.K.
173 K5 North Downs hills England U.K.
171 P6 North Duffield North Yorkshire, England U.K.
235 E4 North-East admin. dist. Botswana
258 D5 North East MD U.S.A.
256 F6 North East PA U.S.A.
238 North East Bay Ascension S. Atlantic Ocean
244 E3 Northeast Cape AK U.S.A.
107 N6 North East Cay rf Coral Sea Is Terr. Austr.
232 D4 North Eastern prov. Kenya
North-East Frontier Agency state India see Arunachal Pradesh
171 Q6 North East Lincolnshire admin. div. England U.K.
291 I4 Northeast Pacific Basin sea feature Pacific Ocean
270 G2 Northeast Point Acklins I. Bahamas
270 G3 Northeast Point Gt Inagua Bahamas
108 North East Point Christmas I.
270 Northeast Point Jamaica
270 E1 Northeast Providence Channel Bahamas
264 O6 North Edwards CA U.S.A.
191 I7 Northeim Ger.
173 N2 North Elmham Norfolk, England U.K.
255 J13 North End Point Bahamas
114 North Entrance sea chan. Palau
228 E4 Northern admin. reg. Ghana
233 B7 Northern admin. reg. Malawi
228 C4 Northern prov. Sierra Leone
225 F4 Northern state Sudan
231 F7 Northern prov. Zambia
Northern Aegean admin. reg. Greece see Voreio Aigaio
145 O3 Northern Areas admin. div. Pak.
227 G1 Northern Bahr el Ghazal state Sudan
236 D5 Northern Cape prov. S. Africa
103 Northern Cook Islands Cook Is
224 E5 Northern Darfur state Sudan
Northern Donets r. Rus. Fed. see Severskiy Donets
Northern Dvina r. Rus. Fed. see Severnaya Dvina
247 L3 Northern Indian Lake Man. Can.
169 I3 Northern Ireland prov. U.K.
225 F6 Northern Kordofan state Sudan
99 I3 Northern Lau Group is Fiji
248 B3 Northern Light Lake Ont. Can.
113 J3 Northern Mariana Islands terr. N. Pacific Ocean
Northern Pindus Mountains Greece see Voreia Pindos
108 Northern Plateau Christmas I.
271 Northern Range hills Trin. and Tob.
Northern Rhodesia country Africa see Zambia
246 E3 Northern Rocky Mountains Provincial Park nat. park B.C. Can.
Northern Sporades is Greece see Voreies Sporades
106 D4 Northern Territory admin. div. Austr.
Northern Transvaal prov. S. Africa see Limpopo
168 L9 North Esk r. Angus, Scotland U.K.
93 F2 North European Plain Europe
260 J6 North Fabius r. MO U.S.A.
171 P6 North Ferriby East Riding of Yorkshire, England U.K.
257 M6 Northfield MA U.S.A.
250 A5 Northfield MN U.S.A.
258 F6 Northfield NJ U.S.A.
257 M4 Northfield VT U.S.A.
250 C5 Northfield WI U.S.A.
173 M5 Northfleet Kent, England U.K.
259 J2 Northford CT U.S.A.
173 O5 North Foreland c. England U.K.
264 M4 North Fork CA U.S.A.
245 M2 North Fork Pass Y.T. Can.
250 I4 North Fox Island MI U.S.A.
259 K1 North Franklin CT U.S.A.
248 D3 North French r. Ont. Can.
271 North Friar's Bay St Kitts and Nevis
North Frisian Islands Ger. see Nordfriesische Inseln
243 K2 North Geomagnetic Pole Nunavut Can.
171 P5 North Grimston North Yorkshire, England U.K.
259 J2 North Haven CT U.S.A.
252 S4 North Head N.B. Can.
102 I3 North Head hd North I. N.Z.
104 North Head hd S. Pacific Ocean
247 L2 North Henik Lake Nunavut Can.
257 L4 North Hero VT U.S.A.
264 K3 North Highlands CA U.S.A.
232 C4 North Horr Kenya
257 L5 North Hudson NY U.S.A.
171 P7 North Hykeham Lincolnshire, England U.K.
173 L3 Northill Bedfordshire, England U.K.
106 F3 North Island N.T. Austr.
109 B10 North Island W.A. Austr.
136 C7 North Island India
102 H5 North Island N.Z.
114 C1 North Island Phil.
239 North Island Inner Islands Seychelles
114 C7 North Islet rf Phil.
265 V6 North Jadito Canyon gorge AZ U.S.A.
250 H8 North Judson IN U.S.A.
North Kazakhstan Oblast admin. div. Kazakh. see Severnyy Kazakhstan
108 North Keeling Island Cocos Is
107 J3 North Kennedy r. Qld Austr.
168 H7 North Kessock Highland, Scotland U.K.
256 E7 North Kingsville OH U.S.A.
247 M3 North Knife r. Man. Can.
247 L3 North Knife Lake Man. Can.
139 I7 North Koel r. Jharkhand India
265 U9 North Komelik AZ U.S.A.
123 E8 North Korea country Asia
139 O6 North Lakhimpur Assam India
168 I11 North Lanarkshire admin. div. Scotland U.K.
102 I2 Northland admin. reg. North I. N.Z.
North Land is Rus. Fed. see Severnaya Zemlya
102 H2 Northland Forest Park nature res. North I. N.Z.
265 Q5 North Las Vegas NV U.S.A.
173 I4 Northleach Gloucestershire, England U.K.
250 H8 North Liberty IN U.S.A.
256 E8 North Lima OH U.S.A.
171 P6 North Lincolnshire admin. div. England U.K.
261 I8 North Little Rock AR U.S.A.
260 F5 North Loup r. NE U.S.A.
233 B7 North Luangwa National Park Zambia
245 N3 North Macmillan r. Y.T. Can.
259 J2 North Madison CT U.S.A.
292 R1 North Magnetic Pole Arctic Ocean
135 North Malé Atoll Maldives
263 K7 North Mam Peak CO U.S.A.
256 A7 North Manchester IN U.S.A.
250 I9 North Manitou Island MI U.S.A.
250 H4 North Middletown KY U.S.A.
256 A10 North Molton Devon, England U.K.
172 E5 North Moose Lake Man. Can.
247 K4 North Mountain mts PA U.S.A.
258 C2 North Muiron Island W.A. Austr.
108 C6 North Nahanni r. N.W.T. Can.
246 F2 North Negril Point Jamaica
270 North Olmsted OH U.S.A.
251 M8 Northome MN U.S.A.
260 H2 North Ossetia aut. rep. Rus. Fed. see Severnaya Osetiya-Alaniya, Respublika
264 N4 North Palisade mt. CA U.S.A.
260 E5 North Platte NE U.S.A.
260 E5 North Platte r. NE U.S.A.
109 C11 North Point W.A. Austr.
271 North Point Barbados
North Point H.K. China see Tsat Tsze Mui
238 North Point Ascension S. Atlantic Ocean
238 North Point Tristan da Cunha S. Atlantic Ocean
239 North Point Mahé Seychelles
292 A1 North Pole Arctic Ocean
245 K2 North Pole AK U.S.A.
255 D9 Northport AL U.S.A.
255 F12 North Port FL U.S.A.
250 I4 Northport MI U.S.A.
171 K1 North Queensferry Fife, Scotland U.K.
137 M6 North Reef Island Andaman & Nicobar Is India
North Rhine - Westphalia land Ger. see Nordrhein-Westfalen
265 T5 North Rim AZ U.S.A.
249 I4 North River Bridge N.S. Can.
104 North Rock i. Lord Howe I. Austr.
168 N1 North Roe Shetland, Scotland U.K.
North Rona i. Western Isles, Scotland U.K. see Rona
168 L4 North Ronaldsay i. Scotland U.K.
168 L4 North Ronaldsay Firth sea chan. Scotland U.K.
262 C4 North Santiam r. OR U.S.A.
246 J4 North Saskatchewan r. Alta/Sask. Can.
265 R2 North Schell Peak NV U.S.A.
166 H3 North Sea sea Europe
259 K3 North Sea NY U.S.A.
247 L3 North Seal r. Man. Can.
137 M7 North Sentinel Island Andaman & Nicobar Is India
171 O3 North Shields Tyne and Wear, England U.K.
247 L5 North Shoal Lake Man. Can.
264 O2 North Shoshone Peak NV U.S.A.
North Siberian Lowland Rus. Fed. see Severo-Sibirskaya Nizmennost'
North Sinai governorate Egypt see Shamāl Sīnā'
245 J1 North Slope plain AK U.S.A.
171 R7 North Somercotes Lincolnshire, England U.K.
172 G5 North Somerset admin. div. England U.K.
169 C6 North Sound sea chan. Ireland
247 M4 North Spirit Lake Ont. Can.
107 N9 North Stradbroke Island Qld Austr.
257 N4 North Stratford NH U.S.A.
171 N2 North Sunderland Northumberland, England U.K.
102 I5 North Taranaki Bight b. North I. N.Z.
246 F5 North Thompson r. B.C. Can.
171 Q7 North Thoresby Lincolnshire, England U.K.
168 B7 Northton Western Isles, Scotland U.K.
256 G5 North Tonawanda NY U.S.A.
103 B14 North Trap rf South I. N.Z.
257 M4 North Troy VT U.S.A.
257 O6 North Truro MA U.S.A.
116 North Tuas Basin dock Sing.
248 E2 North Twin Island Nunavut Can.
249 K3 North Twin Lake Nfld and Lab. Can.
171 M4 North Tyne r. England U.K.
114 C8 North Ubian i. Phil.
168 M7 North Ugie r. Scotland U.K.
168 B7 North Uist i. Scotland U.K.
171 L3 Northumberland admin. div. England U.K.
258 B3 Northumberland PA U.S.A.
258 B3 Northumberland County county PA U.S.A.
107 M6 Northumberland Isles Qld Austr.
171 M3 Northumberland National Park England U.K.
249 H4 Northumberland Strait Can.
262 C5 North Umpqua r. OR U.S.A.
246 F5 North Vancouver B.C. Can.
114 B6 North Verde i. Phil.
257 K5 Northville NY U.S.A.
246 H3 North Wabasca Lake Alta Can.
258 E4 North Wales PA U.S.A.
173 O2 North Walsham Norfolk, England U.K.
257 O4 Northwaterford ME U.S.A.
245 L3 Northway Junction AK U.S.A.
173 M4 North Weald Bassett Essex, England U.K.
237 J2 North West prov. S. Africa
288 F1 Northwest Atlantic Mid-Ocean Channel N. Atlantic Ocean
North West Bay Mahé Seychelles see Beau Vallon, Baie
271 North West Bluff c. Montserrat
108 C6 North West Cape W.A. Austr.
244 E3 Northwest Cape AK U.S.A.
259 K1 North Westchester CT U.S.A.
231 D8 North-Western prov. Zambia
145 N5 North West Frontier prov. Pak.
North West Nelson Forest Park nat. park South I. N.Z. see Kahurangi National Park
290 F3 Northwest Pacific Basin sea feature N. Pacific Ocean
108 North West Point Christmas I.
270 D1 Northwest Providence Channel Bahamas
249 J2 North West River Nfld and Lab. Can.
246 J2 Northwest Territories admin. div. Can.
171 L7 Northwich Cheshire, England U.K.
261 F9 North Wichita r. TX U.S.A.
258 F6 North Wildwood NJ U.S.A.
259 K1 North Windham CT U.S.A.
257 O5 North Windham ME U.S.A.
292 N1 Northwind Ridge sea feature Arctic Ocean
171 O7 North Wingfield Derbyshire, England U.K.
173 J6 Northwood Isle of Wight, England U.K.
260 I4 Northwood IA U.S.A.
260 G2 Northwood ND U.S.A.
257 N5 Northwood NH U.S.A.
250 C4 Northwoods Beach WI U.S.A.
251 O6 North York Ont. Can.
171 P5 North York Moors moorland England U.K.
171 P5 North York Moors National Park England U.K.
171 N5 North Yorkshire admin. div. England U.K.
190 E4 Nortmoor Ger.
249 H4 Norton N.B. Can.
171 P5 Norton North Yorkshire, England U.K.
173 N3 Norton Suffolk, England U.K.
260 F6 Norton KS U.S.A.
256 C12 Norton VA U.S.A.
257 N4 Norton VT U.S.A.
235 F3 Norton Zimbabwe
244 G2 Norton Bay AK U.S.A.
171 N8 Norton Canes Staffordshire, England U.K.
Norton de Matos Angola see Balombo
172 F5 Norton Fitzwarren Somerset, England U.K.
250 H6 Norton Shores MI U.S.A.
244 G3 Norton Sound sea channel AK U.S.A.
190 I2 Nortorf Ger.
190 E5 Nortrup Ger.
180 H7 Nort-sur-Erdre France
285 G4 Norumbega Arg.
244 I2 Norutak Lake AK U.S.A.
286 X2 Norvegia, Cape Antarctica
259 I2 Norwalk CT U.S.A.
256 C7 Norwalk OH U.S.A.
250 D6 Norwalk WI U.S.A.
259 I2 Norwalk r. CT U.S.A.
163 K5 Norway country Europe
257 O4 Norway ME U.S.A.
251 R4 Norway Bay Que. Can.
247 L4 Norway House Man. Can.
288 I1 Norwegian Basin sea feature N. Atlantic Ocean
243 I2 Norwegian Bay Nunavut Can.
288 J1 Norwegian Sea N. Atlantic Ocean
251 N7 Norwich Ont. Can.
173 O2 Norwich Norfolk, England U.K.
257 M7 Norwich CT U.S.A.
257 J6 Norwich NY U.S.A.
168 O1 Norwick Shetland, Scotland U.K.
257 N6 Norwood MA U.S.A.
255 G8 Norwood NC U.S.A.
257 K4 Norwood NY U.S.A.
256 A9 Norwood OH U.S.A.
114 C4 Norzagaray Luzon Phil.
127 M4 Nosaka Japan
124 W3 Nosapu-misaki pt Japan
126 B6 Nose Japan
126 C7 Nosegawa Japan
147 I1 Nose Lake Nunavut Can.
124 S1 Noshappu-misaki hd Japan
124 R6 Noshiro Japan
156 J3 Noshul' Rus. Fed.
159 K3 Nosivka Ukr.
158 G5 Noskivtsi Ukr.
159 N4 Noskovo Rus. Fed.
236 E2 Nosop watercourse Botswana alt. Nossob (Namibia/S. Africa)
156 K1 Nosovaya Rus. Fed.
Nosovka Ukr. see Nosivka
144 H7 Noşratābād Iran
168 N2 Noss, Isle of i. Scotland U.K.
164 I3 Nossan r. Sweden
206 C3 Nossa Senhora da Boa Fé Port.
276 B1 Nossa Senhora da Glória Brazil
206 B1 Nossa Senhora da Graça de Póvoa e Meadas Port.
206 D3 Nossa Senhora da Graça do Divor Port.
206 D4 Nossa Senhora das Neves Port.
206 C4 Nossa Senhora da Torega Port.
206 C3 Nossa Senhora de Machede Port.
277 F3 Nossa Senhora do Livramento Brazil
238 Nossa Senhora dos Remédios São Miguel Azores
164 I3 Nossebro Sweden
193 H8 Nossen Ger.
192 G3 Nossendorf Ger.
192 F3 Nossentiner Hütte Ger.
168 J6 Noss Head Scotland U.K.
236 E2 Nossob watercourse Namibia/S. Africa alt. Nosop (Botswana)
236 E1 Nossob Camp S. Africa
228 D3 Nossombougou Mali
235 K4 Nosy Varika Madag.
198 G4 Noszlop Hungary
199 J4 Noszvaj Hungary
162 U2 Nota r. Fin./Rus. Fed.
Notabile Malta see Mdina
249 I1 Notakwanon r. Nfld and Lab. Can.
215 L2 Notaresco Italy
265 S2 Notch Peak UT U.S.A.
196 D3 Noteć r. Pol.
196 F2 Notecki, Kanał canal Pol.
220 C3 Notia Pindos mts Greece
246 G3 Notikewin r. Alta Can.
199 I4 Nótincs Hungary
220 H6 Notio Aigaio admin. reg. Greece
Nótion Aiyaíon admin. reg. Greece see Notio Aigaio
220 E4 Notios Evvoïkos Kolpos sea chan. Greece
220 B3 Notio Steno Kerkyras sea chan. Greece
160 E2 Nõtö Fin.
217 I10 Noto Sicilia Italy
126 F1 Noto Japan
217 I10 Noto, Golfo di g. Sicilia Italy
216 G9 Noto, Val di reg. Sicilia Italy
164 F2 Notodden Norway
126 D5 Notogawa Japan
126 E1 Noto-hantō pen. Japan
126 E1 Noto-hantō Kokutei-kōen park Japan
126 F1 Notojima Japan
126 F1 Noto-jima i. Japan
124 V2 Notoro-ko l. Japan
201 J8 Notranje Gorice Slovenia
249 G4 Notre-Dame, Monts mts Que. Can.
249 K3 Notre Dame Bay Nfld and Lab. Can.
181 M3 Notre-Dame-de-Gravenchon France
Notre-Dame-de-Koartac Que. Can. see Quaqtaq
251 S4 Notre-Dame-de-la-Salette Que. Can.
180 G8 Notre-Dame-de-Monts France
180 H8 Notre-Dame-de-Riez France
184 F5 Notre-Dame-de-Sanilhac France
257 N3 Notre-Dame-des-Bois Que. Can.
181 M7 Notre-Dame-d'Oé France
251 S3 Notre-Dame-du-Laus Que. Can.
251 O2 Notre-Dame-du-Nord Que. Can.
201 I6 Nötsch im Gailtal Austria
229 F5 Notsé Togo
125 I13 Notsu Japan
124 W3 Notsuke-saki pt Japan
124 W3 Notsuke-suidō sea chan. Japan/Rus. Fed.
251 N5 Nottawasaga Bay Ont. Can.
248 E3 Nottaway r. Que. Can.
190 I4 Nottensdorf Ger.
173 J2 Nottingham Nottingham, England U.K.
173 J2 Nottingham admin. div. England U.K.
258 C5 Nottingham PA U.S.A.
243 K3 Nottingham Island Nunavut Can.
237 O5 Nottingham Road S. Africa
171 P7 Nottinghamshire admin. div. England U.K.
256 G11 Nottoway VA U.S.A.
256 I12 Nottoway r. VA U.S.A.
191 D7 Nottuln Ger.
247 J5 Notukeu Creek r. Sask. Can.
127 G1 Nou Japan
230 C4 Nouabalé-Ndoki, Parc National nat. park Congo
226 A5 Nouâdhibou Maur.
226 A5 Nouâdhibou, Râs c. Maur.
228 B2 Nouakchott Maur.
228 D2 Noual well Maur.
228 A2 Nouâmghâr Maur.
181 P6 Nouan-le-Fuzelier France
181 N7 Nouans-les-Fontaines France
179 J5 Nouart France
118 H7 Nouei Vietnam
228 B2 Nouekch well Maur.
100 Nouméa New Caledonia
229 H5 Noun r. Cameroon
228 E3 Nouna Burkina
168 J4 Noup Head Scotland U.K.
237 I7 Noupoort S. Africa
237 M4 Nouportsnek pass S. Africa
162 T3 Nousu Fin.
Nouveau-Comptoir Que. Can. see Wemindji
Nouvelle Anvers Dem. Rep. Congo see Makanza
100 Nouvelle-Calédonie i. S. Pacific Ocean
Nouvelle Calédonie terr. S. Pacific Ocean see New Caledonia
Nouvelles Hébrides country S. Pacific Ocean see Vanuatu
178 C3 Nouvion France
180 H5 Nouvoitou France
181 M6 Nouzilly France
178 I4 Nouzonville France
145 M1 Nov Tajik.
160 H3 Nõva Estonia
198 F5 Nova Hungary
281 G4 Nova Almeida Brazil
281 E3 Nova América Brazil
280 A5 Nova Andradina Brazil
159 R4 Nova Astrakhan' Ukr.
280 C3 Nova Aurora Brazil
Novabad Tajik. see Novobod
199 H3 Nová Baňa Slovakia
158 H3 Nova Borova Ukr.
198 E2 Nová Bystřice Czech Rep.
231 B6 Nova Caipemba Angola
280 A6 Nova Cantu Brazil
Nova Chaves Angola see Muconda
218 J10 Novaci Novaci Macedonia
219 L5 Novaci Romania
218 J10 Novaci Macedonia
218 I5 Nova Crnja Vojvodina Serbia
278 G3 Nova Cruz Brazil
199 H3 Nová Dubnica Slovakia
281 F3 Nova Era Brazil
Nova Esperança Angola see Buengas
280 A5 Nova Esperança Brazil
213 M8 Novafeltria Italy
Nova Freixa Moz. see Cuamba
281 F5 Nova Friburgo Brazil
Nova Gaia Angola see Cambundi-Catembo
Nova Goa Goa India see Panaji
235 G4 Nova Golegã Moz.
210 D3 Nova Gorica Slovenia
210 F3 Nova Gradiška Croatia
280 C4 Nova Granada Brazil
159 M4 Nova Haleshchyna Ukr.
281 F5 Nova Iguaçu Brazil
159 M7 Nova Kakhovka Ukr.
159 M6 Nova Kam"yanka Ukr.
199 H3 Nováky Slovakia
182 H5 Novalaise France
208 E3 Novales Spain
213 L3 Nova Levante Italy
281 F3 Nova Lima Brazil
Nova Lisboa Angola see Huambo
213 R6 Novalja Croatia
280 A5 Nova Londrina Brazil
199 J2 Nová Ľubovňa Slovakia
160 M7 Novalukoml' Belarus
235 G4 Nova Mambone Moz.
159 M7 Nova Mayachka Ukr.
235 H3 Nova Nabúri Moz.
159 N5 Nova Odesa Ukr.
198 E1 Nová Paka Czech Rep.
159 O4 Nova Parafiyivka Ukr.
275 F4 Nova Paraiso Brazil
218 I6 Nova Pazova Vojvodina Serbia
278 E4 Nova Pilão Arcado Brazil
280 D3 Nova Ponte Brazil
280 D3 Nova Ponte, Represa resr Minas Gerais Brazil
279 D6 Nova Ponte, Represa resr Brazil
159 L5 Nova Praha Ukr.
212 F5 Novara Italy
212 E3 Novara prov. Italy
217 I7 Novara di Sicilia Sicilia Italy
278 E4 Nova Remanso Brazil
280 D4 Nova Resende Brazil
193 G10 Nová Role Czech Rep.
278 D5 Nova Roma Brazil
278 E3 Nova Russas Brazil
249 H5 Nova Scotia prov. Can.
278 E4 Nova Sento Sé Brazil
281 E3 Nova Serrana Brazil
Nova Sintra Angola see Catabola
217 L3 Nova Siri Italy
159 O4 Nova Sloboda Ukr.
278 F4 Nova Soure Brazil
212 G3 Novate Mezzola Italy
264 J3 Novato CA U.S.A.
210 F3 Nova Topola Bos.-Herz.
156 I3 Novator Rus. Fed.
158 G5 Nova Ushytsya Ukr.
235 G3 Nova Vandúzi Moz.
218 H7 Nova Varoš Nova Varoš Serbia
201 J8 Nova Vas Slovenia
201 L1 Nová Včelnice Czech Rep.
281 G3 Nova Venécia Brazil
193 I5 Nová Ves Czech Rep.
281 H2 Nova Viçosa Brazil
275 E4 Nova Vida Amazonas Brazil
277 E2 Nova Vida Rondônia Brazil
159 O4 Nova Vodolaha Ukr.
278 B5 Nova Xavantino Brazil
159 T2 Novaya Chigla Rus. Fed.
Novaya Kakhovka Ukr. see Nova Kakhovka
159 T3 Novaya Kalitva Rus. Fed.
142 C3 Novaya Kazanka Kazakh.
161 P1 Novaya Ladoga Rus. Fed.
Novaya Odessa Ukr. see Nova Odesa
Novaya Pismyanka Rus. Fed. see Leninogorsk
153 P2 Novaya Sibir', Ostrov i. Novosibirskiye O-va Rus. Fed.
159 S2 Novaya Usman' Rus. Fed.
122 J4 Novaya Ussura Rus. Fed.
Novaya Vodolaga Ukr. see Nova Vodolaha
158 J2 Novaya Yolcha Belarus
152 G2 Novaya Zemlya is Rus. Fed.
Novaya Zhizn Rus. Fed. see Kazinka
219 O8 Nova Zagora Bulg.
159 L7 Nova Zbur"yivka Ukr.
159 L5 Nove Ukr.
198 D3 Nové Hrady Czech Rep.
209 D11 Novelda Spain
213 J6 Novellara Italy
198 F1 Nové Město nad Metují Czech Rep.
199 G3 Nové Mesto nad Váhom Slovakia
198 F2 Nové Město na Moravě Czech Rep.
197 K6 Nove Misto Ukr.
198 F3 Nové Mlýny, Vodní nádrž resr Czech Rep.
198 B6 Noventa di Piave Italy
213 L5 Noventa Vicentina Italy
183 F9 Noves France
205 L8 Novés Spain
193 G10 Nové Sedlo Czech Rep.
193 I10 Nové Strašecí Czech Rep.
199 H4 Nové Zámky Slovakia
Novgorod Rus. Fed. see Velikiy Novgorod
160 L4 Novgorodka Rus. Fed.
Novgorod Oblast admin. div. Rus. Fed. see Novgorodskaya Oblast'
Novgorod-Severskiy Ukr. see Novhorod-Sivers'kyy
161 P3 Novgorodskaya Oblast' admin. div. Rus. Fed.
Novgorod-Volynskiy Ukr. see Novohrad-Volyns'kyy
Novgradets Bulg. see Suvorovo
159 L5 Novhorodka Ukr.
159 O7 Novhorodkivka Ukr.
159 M2 Novhorod-Sivers'kyy Ukr.
159 Q5 Novhorods'ke Ukr.
251 K7 Novi MI U.S.A.
218 I5 Novi Bečej Vojvodina Serbia
158 H2 Novi Bilokorovychi Ukr.
159 K2 Novi Borovychi Ukr.
159 K2 Novi Chervyshcha Ukr.
143 S1 Novichikha Rus. Fed.
213 J6 Novi di Modena Italy
205 P5 Noviergas Spain
Novi Grad Bos.-Herz. see Bosanski Novi
213 P5 Novigrad Croatia
198 F5 Novigrad Podravski Croatia
219 L8 Novi Iskŭr Bulg.
199 J5 Novi Kneževac Vojvodina Serbia
122 M5 Novikovo Sakhalin Rus. Fed.
218 I5 Novi Kozarci Vojvodina Serbia
Novi Kritsim Bulg. see Stamboliyski
212 F6 Novi Ligure Italy
182 F2 Novillars France
187 G7 Noville Belgium
268 B3 Novillero Mex.
210 F2 Novi Marof Croatia
159 L2 Novi Mlyny Ukr.
178 H4 Novion-Porcien France
219 P7 Novi Pazar Bulg.
218 I7 Novi Pazar Novi Pazar Serbia
218 H5 Novi Sad Vojvodina Serbia
159 K2 Novi Sanzhary Ukr.
197 M6 Novi Strilyshcha Ukr.
210 F3 Novi Travnik Bos.-Herz.
210 E3 Novi Vinodolski Croatia
161 Y5 Novki Rus. Fed.
275 I4 Novo, Lago l. Brazil
122 M5 Novoaleksandropov Sakhalin Rus. Fed.
159 R3 Novoaleksandrovka Rus. Fed.
157 H7 Novoaleksandrovsk Rus. Fed.
161 R7 Novoaleksandrovskiy Rus. Fed.
Novoalekseyevka Kazakh. see Khobda
120 D1 Novoaltaysk Rus. Fed.
159 R6 Novoamvrosiyivs'ke Ukr.
159 N8 Novoandriyivka Ukr.
157 H6 Novoanninskiy Rus. Fed.
275 F6 Novo Aripuanã Brazil
159 J5 Novoarkhanhel's'k Ukr.
159 S5 Novoaydar Ukr.
159 R6 Novoazovs'k Ukr.
159 S7 Novobataysk Rus. Fed.
159 S4 Novobelaya Rus. Fed.
218 I6 Novo Beograd Beograd Serbia
159 S8 Novobeysugskaya Rus. Fed.
159 S4 Novobila Ukr.
151 I2 Novobiryuzyak Rus. Fed.
145 M2 Novobod Tajik.
145 N2 Novobod Tajik.
Novobogatinsk Kazakh. see Khamit Yergaliyev
159 O6 Novobohdanivka Ukr.
159 M5 Novoborove Ukr.
122 F4 Novobureyskiy Rus. Fed.
156 I4 Novocheboksarsk Rus. Fed.
157 J5 Novocheremshansk Rus. Fed.
157 H7 Novocherkassk Rus. Fed.
122 H6 Novochuguyevka Rus. Fed.
281 G2 Novo Cruzeiro Brazil
159 N7 Novodanylivka Ukr.
159 R7 Novoderevyankovskaya Rus. Fed.
161 P8 Novodmitrovs'k Ukr.
158 G5 Novodnistrovs'k Ukr.
143 O2 Novodolinka Kazakh.
159 Q5 Novodonets'ke Ukr.
129 M1 Novodoroninskoye Rus. Fed.
159 R5 Novodruzhes'k Ukr.
159 O4 Novodugino Rus. Fed.
161 R6 Novodvinsk Rus. Fed.
156 H2 Novoekonomicheskoye Ukr. see Dymytrov
158 I4 Novofastiv Ukr.
159 K7 Novofedorivka Ukr.
122 E3 Novogeorgiyevka Rus. Fed.
161 S9 Novogoroznenskiy Rus. Fed. see Oyskhara
Novogrudok Belarus see Navahrudak
161 U7 Novogurovskiy Rus. Fed.
279 C9 Novo Hamburgo Brazil
159 O6 Novohorivka Ukr.
280 C4 Novo Horizonte Brazil

159 L6 Novohradivka Ukr.
198 D3 Novohradské hory mts Czech Rep.
158 G3 Novohrad-Volyns'kyy Ukr.
159 Q5 Novohrodivka Ukr.
159 N7 Novohryhorivka Ukr.
143 L1 Novoishimskiy Kazakh.
159 N6 Novoivanivka Dnipropetrovs'ka Oblast' Ukr.
159 R6 Novoivanivka Donets'ka Oblast' Ukr.
159 M8 Novoivanivka Respublika Krym Ukr.
159 O5 Novoivankivka Ukr.
151 G5 Novoivanovka Azer.
142 H1 Novokaolinovyy Rus. Fed.
151 I3 Novokayakent Rus. Fed.
Novokazalinsk Kazakh. see Ayteke Bi
157 H6 Novokhopersk Rus. Fed.
160 M6 Novokhovansk Rus. Fed.
122 F3 Novokiyevskiy Uval Rus. Fed.
159 K6 Novokostyantynivka Mykolayivs'ka Oblast' Ukr.
159 O7 Novokostyantynivka Zaporiz'ka Oblast' Ukr.
159 K5 Novokrasne Ukr.
159 R4 Novokrasnyanka Ukr.
159 N8 Novokryms'ke Ukr.
157 H7 Novokubansk Rus. Fed.
Novokubanskiy Rus. Fed. see Novokubansk
142 C1 Novokuybyshevsk Rus. Fed.
152 J4 Novokuznetsk Rus. Fed.
159 M7 Novokyivka Ukr.
151 H2 Novolakskoye Rus. Fed.
287 A2 Novolazarevskaya research stn Antarctica
159 S8 Novoleushkovskaya Rus. Fed.
Novolukoml' Belarus see Navalukoml'
161 V8 Novol'vovsk Rus. Fed.
159 S8 Novomalorossiyskaya Rus. Fed.
275 E5 Novo Marapi Brazil
143 O2 Novomarkovka Kazakh.
159 N5 Novomar"yivka Ukr.
159 T3 Novomelovatka Rus. Fed.
210 E3 Novo Mesto Slovenia
161 W7 Novomichurinsk Rus. Fed.
157 G7 Novomikhaylovskiy Rus. Fed.
218 I5 Novo Miloševo Vojvodina Serbia
159 R7 Novominskaya Rus. Fed.
Novomirgorod Ukr. see Novomyrhorod
161 V7 Novomoskovsk Rus. Fed.
159 O5 Novomoskovs'k Ukr.
197 I1 Novomoskovskiy Rus. Fed.
276 C1 Novo Mundo Brazil
159 N7 Novomykhaylivka Ukr.
159 R4 Novomykil's'ke Ukr.
159 N5 Novomykolayivka Dnipropetrovs'ka Oblast' Ukr.
159 L7 Novomykolayivka Khersons'ka Oblast' Ukr.
159 N7 Novomykolayivka Khersons'ka Oblast' Ukr.
158 I8 Novomykolayivka Odes'ka Oblast' Ukr.
159 O6 Novomykolayivka Zaporiz'ka Oblast' Ukr.
159 K5 Novomyrhorod Ukr.
159 M7 Novonatalivka Ukr.
Novonazyvayevka Rus. Fed. see Nazyvayevsk
143 N6 Novonikolayevka (abandoned) Kazakh.
Novonikolayevsk Rus. Fed. see Novosibirsk
159 R8 Novonikolayevskaya Rus. Fed.
157 H6 Novonikolayevskiy Rus. Fed.
157 I6 Novonikol'skoye Rus. Fed.
159 N7 Novooleksandrivka Ukr.
159 N7 Novooleksiyivka Ukr.
275 G5 Novo Olinda do Norte Brazil
199 I6 Novo Orahovo Vojvodina Serbia
278 E3 Novo Oriente Brazil
142 H2 Novoorsk Rus. Fed.
159 L3 Novoorzhyts'ke Ukr.
159 M8 Novoozerne Ukr.
158 H2 Novoozeryanka Ukr.
278 E3 Novo Parnarama Brazil
Novopashiyskiy Rus. Fed. see Gornozavodsk
159 P5 Novopavlivka Dnipropetrovs'ka Oblast' Ukr.
158 J6 Novopavlivka Mykolayivs'ka Oblast' Ukr.
129 K1 Novopavlovka Rus. Fed.
151 E2 Novopavlovsk Rus. Fed.
Novopavlovskaya Rus. Fed. see Novopavlovsk
159 N4 Novopetrivka Ukr.
159 N5 Novopidkryazh Ukr.
142 K1 Novopokrovka Kostanayskaya Oblast' Kazakh.
143 L1 Novopokrovka Severnyy Kazakhstan Kazakh.
143 S2 Novopokrovka Vostochnyy Kazakhstan Kazakh.
122 I6 Novopokrovka Primorskiy Kray Rus. Fed.
159 T1 Novopokrovka Tambovskaya Oblast' Rus. Fed.
159 N5 Novopokrovka Ukr.
157 H7 Novopokrovskaya Rus. Fed.
Novopolotsk Belarus see Navapolatsk
159 L6 Novopoltavka Mykolayivs'ka Oblast' Ukr.
159 P6 Novopoltavka Zaporiz'ka Oblast' Ukr.
161 W8 Novopolyan'ye Rus. Fed.
159 S4 Novopskov Ukr.
Novo Redondo Angola see Sumbe
142 C2 Novorepnoye Rus. Fed.
122 F2 Novorossiyka Rus. Fed.
157 G7 Novorossiysk Rus. Fed.
Novorossiyskiy Kazakh. see Akzhar
159 S8 Novorozhdestvenskaya Rus. Fed.
143 N2 Novorybinka Akmolinskaya Oblast' Kazakh.
143 L1 Novorybinka Severnyy Kazakhstan Kazakh.
153 L2 Novorybnaya Rus. Fed.
160 M4 Novorzhev Rus. Fed.
158 I6 Novosamarka Ukr.
151 G5 Novosaratovka Azer.
193 I9 Novosedlice Czech Rep.
198 F3 Novosedly Czech Rep.
128 J1 Novoselenginsk Rus. Fed.
151 E1 Novoselitskoye Rus. Fed.
158 I6 Novoselivka Ukr.
159 M8 Novoselivs'ke Ukr.
161 V7 Novoselki Moskovskaya Oblast' Rus. Fed.
161 O6 Novoselki Tverskaya Oblast' Rus. Fed.
219 K9 Novo Selo Macedonia
197 I1 Novoselovo Kaliningradskaya Oblast' Rus. Fed.
161 W5 Novoselovo Vladimirskaya Oblast' Rus. Fed.
Novoselskoye Rus. Fed. see Achkhoy-Martan
160 L3 Novosel'ye Rus. Fed.
158 F5 Novoselytsya Ukr.
142 E1 Novosergiyevka Rus. Fed.
157 G7 Novoshakhtinsk Rus. Fed.
122 H6 Novoshakhtinskiy Rus. Fed.
159 R7 Novoshcherbinovskaya Rus. Fed.
157 J5 Novosheshminsk Rus. Fed.
152 J4 Novosibirsk Rus. Fed.
153 P2 Novosibirskiye Ostrova is Rus. Fed.
161 U9 Novosil' Rus. Fed.
159 L8 Novosil's'ke Ukr.
159 R2 Novosil'skoye Rus. Fed.
159 L7 Novosofiyivka Ukr.
161 N5 Novosokol'niki Rus. Fed.
159 P7 Novospas'ke Ukr.
142 B1 Novospasskoye Rus. Fed.
197 J1 Novostroyevo Rus. Fed.
159 S5 Novosvitlivka Ukr.
199 I2 Novoť Slovakia
151 I1 Novoterechnoye Rus. Fed.
159 R8 Novotitarovskaya Rus. Fed.
142 H2 Novotroitsk Rus. Fed.
Novotroitskoye Kazakh. see Tole Bi
161 Q8 Novotroitskoye Rus. Fed.
122 G4 Novotroitskoye Rus. Fed.
159 Q5 Novotroyits'ke Donets'ka Oblast' Ukr.
159 Q6 Novotroyits'ke Donets'ka Oblast' Ukr.
159 N7 Novotroyits'ke Khersons'ka Oblast' Ukr.
159 O6 Novotroyits'ke Zaporiz'ka Oblast' Ukr.
Novoukrainka Kirovohrads'ka Oblast' Ukr. see Novoukrayinka
Novoukrainka Rivnens'ka Oblast' Ukr. see Novoukrayinka
159 K5 Novoukrayinka Kirovohrads'ka Oblast' Ukr.
158 E3 Novoukrayinka Rivnens'ka Oblast' Ukr.
142 G2 Novoural'sk Rus. Fed.
142 C2 Novouzensk Rus. Fed.
143 P1 Novovarshavka Rus. Fed.
159 O7 Novovasylivka Zaporiz'ka Oblast' Ukr.
159 P7 Novovasylivka Zaporiz'ka Oblast' Ukr.
210 F2 Novo Virje Croatia
158 D3 Novovolyns'k Ukr.
157 G6 Novovoronezh Rus. Fed.
Novovoronezhskiy Rus. Fed. see Novovoronezh
159 M6 Novovorontsovka Ukr.
122 E2 Novovoskresenovka Rus. Fed.
159 M6 Novovoskresens'ke Ukr.
143 R6 Novovoznesenovka Kyrg.
159 O5 Novov"yazivs'ke Ukr.
159 N1 Novoyamskoye Rus. Fed.
158 C4 Novoyavorivs'ke Ukr.
161 W9 Novoye Dubovoye Rus. Fed.
143 S2 Novoyegor'yevskoye Rus. Fed.
161 X5 Novoye Leushino Rus. Fed.
161 T5 Novozavidovskiy Rus. Fed.
156 J2 Novozhilovskaya Rus. Fed.
158 I4 Novozhyvotiv Ukr.
161 O9 Novozybkov Rus. Fed.
210 F3 Novska Croatia
158 J1 Novy Barsuk Belarus
161 N6 Novy Bolyetsk Belarus
198 D1 Nový Bor Czech Rep.
198 E1 Nový Bydžov Czech Rep.
161 N8 Novy Bykhaw Belarus
178 H4 Novy-Chevrières France
197 M2 Novy Dvor Hrodzyenskaya Voblasts' Belarus
160 H9 Novy Dvor Hrodzyenskaya Voblasts' Belarus
Novyj Cholmogory Rus. Fed. see Arkhangel'sk
Novyj Holmogory Rus. Fed. see Arkhangel'sk
199 G2 Nový Jičín Czech Rep.
198 G2 Nový Malín Czech Rep.
Novyy Afon Georgia see Akhali Ap'oni
160 K6 Novyya Kruki Belarus
160 L7 Novyya Valosavichy Belarus
161 N8 Novyya Zhuravichy Belarus
156 K2 Novyy Bor Rus. Fed.
Novyy Bug Ukr. see Novyy Buh
159 L6 Novyy Buh Ukr.
159 K3 Novyy Bykiv Ukr.
Novyy Donbass Ukr. see Dymytrov
197 M5 Novyy Dvir Ukr.
Novyye Aneny Moldova see Anenii Noi
Novyye Belokorovichi Ukr. see Novi Bilokorovychi
142 B1 Novyye Burasy Rus. Fed.
161 Q9 Novyye Ivaytenki Rus. Fed.
Novyye Petushki Rus. Fed. see Petushki
160 K4 Novyy Izborsk Rus. Fed.
Novyy Kholmogory Rus. Fed. see Arkhangel'sk
Novyy Margelan Uzbek. see Farg'ona
159 O4 Novyy Merchyk Ukr.
161 V4 Novyy Nekouz Rus. Fed.
157 G6 Novyy Oskol Rus. Fed.
152 I3 Novyy Port Rus. Fed.
159 L1 Novyy Ropsk Rus. Fed.
158 D4 Novyy Rozdil Ukr.
161 T8 Novyy Sinets Rus. Fed.
159 M5 Novyystarodub Ukr.
159 R6 Novyy Svit Donets'ka Oblast' Ukr.
159 N9 Novyy Svit Respublika Krym Ukr.
151 I2 Novyy Terek r. Rus. Fed.
156 J4 Novyy Tor'yal Rus. Fed.
152 I3 Novyy Urengoy Rus. Fed.
122 H3 Novyy Urgal Rus. Fed.
Novyy Uzen' Kazakh. see Zhanaozen
197 M5 Novyy Vytkiv Ukr.
197 M6 Novyy Yarychiv Ukr.
156 K5 Novyy Zay Rus. Fed.
198 G3 Nový Život Slovakia
144 F6 Now Iran
197 H4 Nowa Brzeźnica Pol.
197 L2 Nowa Chodorówka Pol.
197 J5 Nowa Dęba Pol.
196 G1 Nowa Karczma Pol.
196 E5 Nowa Ruda Pol.
197 K5 Nowa Sarzyna Pol.
197 J5 Nowa Słupia Pol.
196 D4 Nowa Sól Pol.
261 H7 Nowata OK U.S.A.
193 L6 Nowa Wieś Pol.
197 K2 Nowa Wieś Ełcka Pol.
196 F1 Nowa Wieś Lęborskie Pol.
196 G3 Nowa Wieś Wielka Pol.
197 L2 Nowa Wola Pol.
197 J4 Nowa Wola Gołębiowska Pol.
144 C4 Nowbarān Iran
144 H5 Now Deh Iran
144 H4 Now Deh-e Pashang Iran
144 D4 Now Dezh Iran
144 C3 Nowdī Iran
196 G2 Nowe Pol.
197 I5 Nowe Brzesko Pol.
196 C2 Nowe Czarnowo Pol.
196 D4 Nowe Miasteczko Pol.
197 I3 Nowe Miasto Pol.
197 H2 Nowe Miasto Lubawskie Pol.
197 I4 Nowe Miasto nad Pilicą Pol.
169 D9 Nowen Hill Ireland
197 H3 Nowe Ostrowy Pol.
197 K3 Nowe Piekuty Pol.
196 F4 Nowe Skalmierzyce Pol.
196 C2 Nowe Warpno Pol.
144 D4 Nowfel low Shātow Qom Iran
144 E5 Now Gonbad Iran
Nowgong Assam India see Nagaon
138 G7 Nowgong Madh. Prad. India
197 K2 Nowinka Pol.
244 I2 Nowitna r. AK U.S.A.
244 I2 Nowitna National Wildlife Refuge nature res. AK U.S.A.
149 N4 Nowjeh Deh Iran
144 F3 Now Kharegan Iran
247 K2 Nowleye Lake Nunavut Can.
197 K4 Nowodwór Pol.
196 D2 Nowogard Pol.
197 J2 Nowogród Pol.
196 D4 Nowogród Bobrzański Pol.
196 D3 Nowogródek Pomorski Pol.
196 D4 Nowogrodziec Pol.
262 K4 Nowood r. WY U.S.A.
Noworadomsk Pol. see Radomsko
197 L3 Nowosady Pol.
197 K6 Nowosielce Pol.
197 K5 Nowosielec Pol.
197 H4 Nowosolna Pol.
105 M6 Nowra N.S.W. Austr.
144 C2 Nowshahr Iran
144 D3 Nowshahr Iran
145 O4 Nowshera Pak.
144 B4 Nowsūd Iran
247 L2 Nowyak Lake Nunavut Can.
197 K3 Nowy Bartków Pol.
197 H3 Nowy Duninów Pol.
196 F2 Nowy Dwór Kujawsko-Pomorskie Pol.
197 L2 Nowy Dwór Podlaskie Pol.
165 P7 Nowy Dwór Gdański Pol.
197 I3 Nowy Dwór Mazowiecki Pol.
197 I5 Nowy Korczyn Pol.
197 L5 Nowy Lubliniec Pol.
197 I6 Nowy Sącz Pol.
165 P7 Nowy Staw Pol.
197 I6 Nowy Targ Pol.
196 E3 Nowy Tomyśl Pol.
197 J6 Nowy Żmigród Pol.
251 R8 Noxen PA U.S.A.
261 K9 Noxubee National Wildlife Refuge nature res. MS U.S.A.
118 G6 Noy, Xé r. Laos
Noya Cataluña Spain see Sant Sadurní d'Anoia
Noya Galicia Spain see Noia
152 I3 Noyabr'sk Rus. Fed.
180 G6 Noyal-Muzillac France
180 F6 Noyalo France
180 F5 Noyal-Pontivy France
181 L6 Noyant France
181 K7 Noyant-la-Plaine France
183 H6 Noyarey France
149 Q5 Noyek Iran
151 G4 Noyemberyan Armenia
181 K6 Noyen-sur-Sarthe France
178 G8 Noyers France
181 N7 Noyers-sur-Cher France
183 H8 Noyers-sur-Jabron France
245 N5 Noyes Island AK U.S.A.
136 E7 Noyil r. India
178 E4 Noyon France
128 H5 Noyon Mongolia
127 H2 Nozawaonsen-mura Japan
180 H6 Nozay France
197 K6 Nozdrzec Pol.
182 I3 Nozeroy France
151 H2 Nozhay-Yurt Rus. Fed.
237 J6 Nozizwe S. Africa
200 B8 Nozza r. Italy
232 B4 Npitamaiong mt. Kenya
237 O6 Nqabeni S. Africa
237 L8 Nqamakwe S. Africa
237 O4 Nqutu S. Africa
151 H7 Nrnadzor Armenia
144 E3 Nūr Rūd r. Iran
230 B5 Nsa Congo
233 A8 Nsalamu Zambia
230 C5 Nsambi Dem. Rep. Congo
233 B8 Nsanje Malawi
228 E5 Nsawam Ghana
233 A7 Nseluka Zambia
229 H6 Nsoc Equat. Guinea
237 P3 Nsoko Swaziland
231 F7 Nsombo Zambia
230 C5 Nsondia Dem. Rep. Congo
229 G5 Nsukka Nigeria
Nsumbu National Park Zambia see Sumbu National Park
226 B5 Ntalfa well Maur.
231 E8 Ntambu Zambia
230 C5 Ntandembele Dem. Rep. Congo
233 B8 Ntcheu Malawi
233 B8 Ntchisi Malawi
229 H6 Ntem r. Cameroon
237 L3 Ntha S. Africa
237 M2 Nthorwane S. Africa
237 M7 Ntibane S. Africa
224 B6 Ntiona Chad
220 F4 Ntoro, Kavo pt Greece
232 A4 Ntoroko Uganda
230 A4 Ntoum Gabon
239 □3a Ntsamouéni Njazidja Comoros
237 N3 Ntshingwayo Dam S. Africa
239 □3a Ntsoudjini Njazidja Comoros
229 H5 Ntui Cameroon
233 A5 Ntungamo Uganda
234 E4 Ntwetwe Pan salt pan Botswana
237 M7 Ntywenka S. Africa
181 J7 Nuaillé France
184 C3 Nuaillé-d'Aunis France
Nuanetsi r. Zimbabwe see Mwenezi
115 D3 Nuangan Sulawesi Indon.
258 D2 Nuangola PA U.S.A.
139 I9 Nuapara Orissa India
147 L4 Nu'aym reg. Oman
225 F4 Nuba, Lake resr Sudan
232 A2 Nuba Mountains Sudan
190 I2 Nübbel Ger.
269 K9 Nube Flan, Cerro mt. Mex.
190 I1 Nübel Ger.
225 G4 Nubian Desert Sudan
162 Q2 Nubivarri hill Norway
284 A5 Ñuble r. Chile
204 I1 Nubledo Spain
138 F2 Nubra r. India
101 □7 Nubu Vanua Levu Fiji
219 K4 Nucet Romania
265 X3 Nucla CO U.S.A.
Nüden Mongolia see Ulaanbadrah
193 G7 Nudersdorf Ger.
191 J10 Nüdlingen Ger.
161 T5 Nudol' Rus. Fed.
197 M4 Nudyzhe Ukr.
261 G12 Nueces r. TX U.S.A.
181 J8 Nueil-sur-Argent France
247 L2 Nueltin Lake Man./Nunavut Can.
187 I6 Nuenen Neth.
208 E3 Nueno Spain
205 K2 Nueva Spain
283 D9 Nueva, Isla i. Chile
274 C6 Nueva Alejandría Peru
266 □O10 Nueva Arcadia Hond.
284 C3 Nueva California Arg.
207 K5 Nueva-Carteya Spain
261 F12 Nueva Ciudad Guerrero Mex.
284 D4 Nueva Constitución Arg.
284 E3 Nueva Escocia Arg.
275 E2 Nueva Esparta state Venez.
274 D2 Nueva Florida Venez.
284 E4 Nueva Galia Arg.
277 F5 Nueva Germania Para.
270 B3 Nueva Gerona Cuba
283 D9 Nueva Harberton Arg.
285 I4 Nueva Helvecia Uru.
284 A6 Nueva Imperial Chile
268 E6 Nueva Italia de Ruiz Mex.
206 G7 Nueva Jarilla Spain
274 B4 Nueva Loja Ecuador
283 C7 Nueva Lubecka Arg.
266 □O10 Nueva Ocotepeque Hond.
285 H3 Nueva Palmira Uru.
282 E2 Nueva Población Arg.
269 I3 Nueva Polonia Mex.
267 I4 Nueva Rosita Mex.
267 O11 Nueva San Salvador El Salvador
Nueva Tabarca i. Spain see Plana, Isla
269 I1 Nueva Villa de Padilla Mex.
Nueve de Julio Arg. see 9 de Julio
270 E3 Nuevitas Cuba
267 N7 Nuevo, Cayo i. Mex.
283 D6 Nuevo, Golfo g. Arg.
285 I3 Nuevo Berlín Uru.
266 F2 Nuevo Casas Grandes Mex.
266 G5 Nuevo Ideal Mex.
267 J4 Nuevo Laredo Mex.
265 Q9 Nuevo León Mex.
268 G1 Nuevo León state Mex.
275 F2 Nuevo Mamo Venez.
269 H3 Nuevo-Morelos Mex.
268 C2 Nuevo Pilares Mex.
274 C5 Nuevo Rocafuerte Ecuador
268 F4 Nuevo Valle de Moreno Mex.
146 G4 Nufayyid Şabḩah des. Saudi Arabia
Nuga Mongolia see Dzavhanmandal
232 F2 Nugaal admin. reg. Somalia
232 F3 Nugaal watercourse Somalia
107 L8 Nuga Nuga, Lake Qld Austr.
103 D13 Nugget Point South I. N.Z.
104 □3 Nuggets Point S. Pacific Ocean
214 C6 Nughedu di San Nicolò Sardegna Italy
161 T8 Nugr' r. Rus. Fed.
136 E6 Nugu r. India
99 F2 Nuguria Islands P.N.G.
145 J9 Nuh, Ras pt Pak.
102 L6 Nuhaka North I. N.Z.
221 L4 Nuhköy Turkey
99 H2 Nui atoll Tuvalu
Nui Con Voi r. Vietnam see Hông, Sông
160 L1 Nuijamaa Fin.
181 J6 Nuillé-sur-Vicoin France
245 J1 Nuiqsut AK U.S.A.
118 I7 Nui Thanh Vietnam
118 H7 Nui Ti On mt. Vietnam
178 H8 Nuits France
182 F2 Nuits-St-Georges France
Nu Jiang r. Myanmar see Salween
245 J4 Nuka Island AK U.S.A.
126 F6 Nukata Japan
104 E5 Nukey Bluff hill S.A. Austr.
Nukha Azer. see Şäki
100 □6 Nukiki Choiseul Solomon Is
144 E5 Nūklok, Chāh-e well Iran
101 □8a Nuku i. Tonga
101 □8a Nuku'alofa Tongatapu Tonga
99 H2 Nukufetau atoll Tuvalu
101 □9 Nuku Hiva i. Fr. Polynesia
Nukuhiva i. Fr. Polynesia see Nuku Hiva
99 H2 Nukulaelae atoll Tuvalu
Nukulailai atoll Tuvalu see Nukulaelae
99 F2 Nukumanu Islands P.N.G.
Nukunau i. Gilbert Is Kiribati see Nikunau
Nukunono atoll Tokelau see Nukunonu
103 □1 Nukunonu Tokelau
103 □1 Nukunonu atoll Tokelau
142 H6 Nukus Uzbek.
186 H5 Nuland Neth.
244 H2 Nulato AK U.S.A.
214 C7 Nule Sardegna Italy
209 E8 Nules Spain
108 F6 Nullagine W.A. Austr.
108 F6 Nullagine r. W.A. Austr.
104 C4 Nullarbor S.A. Austr.
104 C4 Nullarbor National Park S.A. Austr.
104 B4 Nullarbor Plain S.A. Austr.
104 C4 Nullarbor Regional Reserve park S.A. Austr.
248 E1 Nuluarniavik, Lac l. Que. Can.
129 P6 Nulu'erhu Shan mts China
214 B6 Nulvi Sardegna Italy
113 I7 Num i. Papua Indon.
139 K6 Num Nepal
105 J3 Numalla, Lake salt flat Qld Austr.
229 I4 Numan Nigeria
146 B2 Nu'mān i. Saudi Arabia
213 P8 Numana Italy
114 E7 Numancia Phil.
186 F5 Numansdorp Neth.
127 J2 Numata Gunma Japan
124 S3 Numata Hokkaidō Japan
230 E3 Numatinna watercourse Sudan
127 I5 Numazu Japan
237 P1 Numbi Gate S. Africa
Numbu Vanua Levu Fiji see Nubu
106 E3 Numbulwar N.T. Austr.
164 F1 Numedal val. Norway
113 H7 Numfoor i. Papua Indon.
122 E5 Numin He r. China
234 C3 Numkaub Namibia
163 Q6 Nummi Fin.
105 J7 Numurkah Vic. Austr.
244 H4 Nunachuak AK U.S.A.
249 I2 Nunaksaluk Island Nfld and Lab. Can.
243 N3 Nunakuluut i. Greenland
243 N3 Nunap Isua c. Greenland
244 G3 Nunapitchuk AK U.S.A.
Nunarsuit i. Greenland see Nunakuluut
244 H4 Nunavaugaluk, Lake AK U.S.A.
248 E1 Nunavik reg. Que. Can.
247 L2 Nunavut admin. div. Can.
274 C3 Nunchía Col.
193 H8 Nünchritz Ger.
231 F5 Nunda Dem. Rep. Congo
256 H6 Nunda NY U.S.A.
105 M4 Nundle N.S.W. Austr.
173 J2 Nuneaton Warwickshire, England U.K.
109 E11 Nungarin W.A. Austr.
139 N7 Nungba Manipur India
247 M5 Nungesser Lake Ont. Can.
129 P4 Nungnain Sum Nei Mongol China
235 H2 Nungo Moz.
233 C6 Nungwi, Ras pt Tanz.
244 F4 Nunivak Island AK U.S.A.
139 J9 Nunkapasi Orissa India
194 B3 Nunkirchen Ger.
138 F3 Nunkun mt. Jammu and Kashmir India
153 T3 Nunligran Rus. Fed.
209 H9 Nunó, Cap c. Spain
276 C3 Nuñoa Peru
204 H8 Nuñomoral Spain
193 H6 Nunsdorf Ger.
186 I4 Nunspeet Neth.
117 L3 Nunukan i. Indon.
244 E2 Nunyamo Rus. Fed.
Nuojiang Sichuan China see Tongjiang
214 C7 Nuoro Sardegna Italy
214 C7 Nuoro prov. Sardegna Italy
Nuorttijoki r. Fin./Rus. Fed. see Nota
100 □6 Nupani i. Santa Cruz Is Solomon Is
144 F6 Nūq Iran
224 C4 Nuqayy, Jabal mts Libya
146 E3 Nuqrah Saudi Arabia
225 G3 Nuqruş, Jabal mt. Egypt
274 B3 Nuquí Col.
133 E8 Nur Xinjiang China
197 K3 Nur Pol.
143 Q6 Nura Almatinskaya Oblast' Kazakh.
143 P3 Nura Kazakh.
143 M2 Nura r. Kazakh.
144 D6 Nūrābād Iran
144 C4 Nūrābād Iran
214 C8 Nuragus Sardegna Italy
Nurakita i. Tuvalu see Niulakita
214 C8 Nurallao Sardegna Italy
214 C9 Nuraminis Sardegna Italy
Nurata Uzbek. see Nurota
150 E1 Nurdağı Turkey
148 G5 Nur Dağları mts Turkey
212 H5 Nure r. Italy
214 B8 Nureci Sardegna Italy
Nurek Tajik. see Norak
Nurek Reservoir Tajik. see Norak, Obanbori
Nurekskoye Vodokhranilishche resr Tajik. see Norak, Obanbori
Nuremberg Ger. see Nürnberg
258 C3 Nuremberg PA U.S.A.
145 N4 Nūrestān prov. Afgh.
145 N4 Nūrestān reg. Afgh.
145 N4 Nūr Gal Afgh.
266 E3 Nuri Mex.
225 G5 Nuri Sudan
117 H5 Nuri, Teluk b. Indon.
215 K3 Nuria, Monte mt. Italy
Nuristan prov. Afgh. see Nūrestān
138 F2 Nurla Jammu and Kashmir India
157 J5 Nurlat Rus. Fed.
156 J5 Nurlaty Rus. Fed.
162 T5 Nurmes Fin.
163 R6 Nurmijärvi Fin.
162 Q5 Nurmo Fin.
195 K3 Nürnberg Ger.
170 D8 Nurney Carlow Ireland
170 D7 Nurney Kildare Ireland
143 L8 Nurobad Uzbek.
142 K7 Nurota Uzbek.
143 L7 Nurota tizmasi mts Uzbek.
145 N6 Nurpur Pak.
104 C3 Nurrai Lakes salt flat S.A. Austr.
214 C8 Nurri Sardegna Italy
105 K4 Nurri, Mount hill N.S.W. Austr.
162 L4 Nursfjellet mt. Norway
Nursia Italy see Norcia
160 F3 Nurste Estonia
194 G4 Nürtingen Ger.
133 K8 Nur Turu Qinghai China
197 K3 Nurzec r. Pol.
197 L3 Nurzec-Stacja Pol.
212 C4 Nus Italy
117 H8 Nusa Kambangan, Cagar Alam nature res. Jawa Indon.
115 F5 Nusa Laut i. Maluku Indon.
117 L9 Nusa Tenggara Barat prov. Indon.
115 B8 Nusa Tenggara Timur prov. Indon.
149 J5 Nusaybin Turkey
148 H6 Nuşayrīyah, Jabal an mts Syria
215 O6 Nusco Italy
115 G4 Nusela, Kepulauan is Papua Indon.
219 K3 Nuşfalău Romania
144 D4 Nūshābād Eşfahān Iran
244 H4 Nushagak r. AK U.S.A.
244 H4 Nushagak Bay AK U.S.A.
244 H4 Nushagak Peninsula AK U.S.A.
130 B5 Nu Shan mts China
126 A7 Nu-shima i. Japan
145 L7 Nushki Pak.
194 F5 Nusplingen Ger.
150 G2 Nusratiye Turkey
201 J4 Nußbach Austria
195 N6 Nußdorf Ger.
195 M6 Nußdorf am Inn Ger.
200 G6 Nußdorf-Debant Austria
190 K3 Nusse Ger.
249 I1 Nutak Nfld and Lab. Can.
247 L2 Nutarawit Lake Nunavut Can.
187 I7 Nuth Neth.
193 H6 Nuthe r. Ger.
173 L5 Nuthurst West Sussex, England U.K.
259 G3 Nutley NJ U.S.A.
265 W8 Nutrioso AZ U.S.A.
145 M7 Nuttal Pak.
169 J3 Nutt's Corner Northern Ireland U.K.
106 E3 Nutwood Downs N.T. Austr.
245 K2 Nutzotin Mountains AK U.S.A.
243 M2 Nuugaatsiaap Imaa inlet Greenland
243 M2 Nuugaatsiaq Greenland
243 M3 Nuuk Greenland
160 H1 Nuuksion kansallispuisto nat. park Fin.
162 S3 Nuupas Fin.
101 □9a Nuupere, Pointe pt Moorea Fr. Polynesia
243 M2 Nuussuaq Greenland
243 M2 Nuussuaq pen. Greenland
100 □2 Nu'uuli American Samoa
139 I5 Nuwakot Nepal
147 L3 Nuway Oman
225 G2 Nuwaybi' al Muzayyinah Egypt
236 H9 Nuwekloof pass S. Africa
236 C7 Nuwerus S. Africa
236 F8 Nuweveldberge mts S. Africa
244 H1 Nuwuk AK U.S.A.
268 G8 Nuxco Mex.
214 B9 Nuxis Sardegna Italy
244 H4 Nuyakuk Lake AK U.S.A.
197 M4 Nuyno Ukr.
109 D13 Nuyts, Point W.A. Austr.
104 D5 Nuyts Archipelago is S.A. Austr.
104 D5 Nuyts Archipelago Conservation Park nature res. S.A. Austr.
109 H12 Nuytsland Nature Reserve W.A. Austr.
150 H3 Nuzayzah reg. Syria
200 A5 Nüziders Austria
136 G4 Nuzvid Andhra Prad. India
229 H5 Nwa Cameroon
234 E3 Nxai Pan National Park Botswana
234 D3 Nxaunxau Botswana
117 K4 Nyaän, Bukit hill Indon.
229 H6 Nyabessan Cameroon
109 E12 Nyabing W.A. Austr.
244 H3 Nyac AK U.S.A.
257 L7 Nyack NY U.S.A.
152 H3 Nyagan' Rus. Fed.
Nyagquka Sichuan China see Yajiang
Nyagrong Sichuan China see Xinlong
233 B6 Nyahua Tanz.
232 C4 Nyahururu Kenya
105 I6 Nyah West Vic. Austr.
133 K12 Nyaimai Xizang China
133 J11 Nyainqêntanglha Feng mt. Xizang China
133 J12 Nyainqêntanglha Shan mts Xizang China
133 K10 Nyainrong Xizang China
233 A5 Nyakahanga Tanz.
233 A5 Nyakahura Kagera Tanz.
233 A6 Nyaka Kangaga Tanz.
233 B5 Nyakaliro Tanz.
237 K3 Nyakallong S. Africa
233 A5 Nyakanazi Tanz.
162 O5 Nyåker Sweden
Nyakh Rus. Fed. see Nyagan'
160 I9 Nyakhachava Belarus
228 E5 Nyakrom Ghana
156 M3 Nyaksimvol' Rus. Fed.
224 E6 Nyala Sudan
Nyalam Xizang China see Congdü
162 □ Ny-Ålesund Svalbard
231 F8 Nyama Zambia
235 F3 Nyamandhiovu Zimbabwe
235 G3 Nyamapanda Zimbabwe
233 B5 Nyambiti Tanz.
233 A5 Nyamirembe Kagera Tanz.
230 E2 Nyamlell Sudan
233 C7 Nyamtumbo Tanz.
197 N3 Nyamyerzha Belarus
Nyande Zimbabwe see Masvingo
156 H3 Nyandoma Rus. Fed.
156 G3 Nyandomskiy Vozvyshennost' hills Rus. Fed.
230 A5 Nyanga Congo
231 A5 Nyanga Gabon
231 A5 Nyanga prov. Gabon
235 G3 Nyanga Zimbabwe
235 G3 Nyanga National Park Zimbabwe
133 K11 Nyangbo Xizang China
133 I12 Nyang Qu r. China
133 L12 Nyang Qu r. China
228 E4 Nyankpala Ghana
233 A5 Nyanza Rwanda
233 A6 Nyanza-Lac Burundi
117 L4 Nyapa, Gunung mt. Indon.
232 B3 Nyapongeth Sudan
138 G4 Nyar r. India
198 G4 Nyárád Hungary
246 H2 Nyarling r. N.W.T. Can.
199 I5 Nyárlőrinc Hungary
199 I4 Nyársapát Hungary
233 A5 Nyarugumba Rwanda
233 B7 Nyasa, Lake Africa
Nyasaland country Africa see Malawi
156 K2 Nyashabozh Rus. Fed.
160 J8 Nyasvizh Belarus
235 F3 Nyathi Zimbabwe
118 C6 Nyaunglebin Myanmar
118 B4 Nyaungu Myanmar
156 M3 Nyays r. Rus. Fed.
235 G3 Nyazura Zimbabwe
190 I1 Nybøl Nor b. Denmark
164 G6 Nyborg Denmark
156 E1 Nyborg Norway
162 Q4 Nyborg Sweden
165 L5 Nybro Sweden
199 H2 Nýdek Czech Rep.
243 M1 Nyeboe Land reg. Greenland
160 K8 Nyeharelaye Belarus
133 J12 Nyêmo Xizang China
Nyenchen Tanglha Range mts Xizang China see Nyainqêntanglha Shan
232 C5 Nyeri Kenya
232 B2 Nyerol Sudan
160 M6 Nyeshcharda, Vozyera l. Belarus
162 □ Ny-Friesland reg. Svalbard
165 K1 Nyhammar Sweden
133 H9 Nyi, Co l. Xizang China
233 B7 Nyika National Park Zambia
233 B7 Nyika Plateau Malawi
133 K11 Nyima Xizang China
233 A8 Nyimba Zambia
133 L12 Nyingchi Xizang China
133 L12 Nyingchi Xizang China
133 J11 Nyingzhong Xizang China
Nyinma Gansu China see Maqu
199 L4 Nyírábrány Hungary
199 K4 Nyíracsád Hungary
198 G4 Nyirád Hungary
199 K4 Nyíradony Hungary
233 A5 Nyiragongo vol. Dem. Rep. Congo
199 L4 Nyírbátor Hungary
199 L4 Nyírbéltek Hungary
199 L4 Nyírbogát Hungary
199 K3 Nyírbogdány Hungary
199 L4 Nyírcsászári Hungary
199 K4 Nyíregyháza Hungary
199 K4 Nyírgelse Hungary
233 C5 Nyiri Desert Kenya
199 L4 Nyírlugos Hungary
199 K4 Nyírmártonfalva Hungary
199 K4 Nyírmihálydi Hungary
199 K3 Nyírtelek Hungary
199 K3 Nyírtét Hungary
199 K3 Nyírtura Hungary
232 C4 Nyiru, Mount Kenya
199 L4 Nyírvasvári Hungary
162 Q5 Nykarleby Fin.
164 H7 Nykøbing Denmark
164 E5 Nykøbing Mors Denmark
164 H6 Nykøbing Sjælland Denmark
165 N3 Nyköping Sweden
165 K2 Nykroppa Sweden
165 N2 Nykvarn Sweden
156 B3 Nyland Sweden
105 K5 Nymagee N.S.W. Austr.
105 N3 Nymboida N.S.W. Austr.
105 N3 Nymboida National Park N.S.W. Austr.
198 E1 Nymburk Czech Rep.
164 E6 Nymindegab Denmark
165 N3 Nynäshamn Sweden
105 K4 Nyngan N.S.W. Austr.
133 F11 Nyogzê Xizang China
127 K2 Nyohō-san mt. Japan
181 J6 Nyoiseau France
237 M8 Nyokana S. Africa
160 G8 Nyoman r. Belarus alt. Neman (Rus. Fed.), alt. Nemunas (Lith.)
160 I8 Nyomanskaya Nizina lowland Belarus
212 A3 Nyon Switz.
229 H6 Nyong r. Cameroon
183 G8 Nyons France
192 F1 Nyord i. Denmark
192 E1 Nyråd Denmark
198 C2 Nýřany Czech Rep.
156 L3 Nyrob Rus. Fed.
198 C2 Nýrsko Czech Rep.
162 T2 Nyrud Norway
196 F5 Nysa Pol.
196 F5 Nysa Kłodzka r. Pol.
164 I2 Nysäter Sweden
162 L5 Nysätern Sweden
122 M3 Nysh Sakhalin Rus. Fed.
164 I2 Nysockensjön l. Sweden
262 F5 Nyssa OR U.S.A.
Nystad Fin. see Uusikaupunki
164 H7 Nysted Denmark
156 J3 Nyuchpas Rus. Fed.
124 Q7 Nyūdō-zaki pt Japan
127 H4 Nyūgasa-yama mt. Japan
199 K4 Nyugati-főcsatorna canal Hungary
126 F3 Nyūkawa Japan
156 I3 Nyukhcha Rus. Fed.
156 I3 Nyuksenitsa Rus. Fed.
199 G4 Nyúl Hungary
231 F6 Nyunzu Dem. Rep. Congo
153 M3 Nyurba Rus. Fed.
156 J3 Nyuvchim Rus. Fed.
153 M3 Nyuya Rus. Fed.
153 M3 Nyuya r. Rus. Fed.
126 G2 Nyūzen Japan
159 M8 Nyva Ukr.
122 M1 Nyvrovo Rus. Fed.
197 M5 Nyvytsi Ukr.
122 M2 Nyyskiy Zaliv lag. Sakhalin Rus. Fed.
158 B4 Nyzhankovychi Ukr.
159 N7 Nyzhni Sirohozy Ukr.
159 N7 Nyzhni Torhayi Ukr.
158 C5 Nyzhni Vorota Ukr.
158 C5 Nyzhniy Bystryy Ukr.
159 S5 Nyzhniy Nahol'chyk Ukr.
159 N8 Nyzhn'ohirs'kyy Ukr.
159 R4 Nyzhnya Duvanka Ukr.
159 N3 Nyzhnya Syrovatka Ukr.
159 O5 Nyzhnya Tersa r. Ukr.
199 M2 Nyzhnya Vysots'ke Ukr.
199 L2 Nyzhnya Yablun'ka Ukr.
159 N3 Nyzy Ukr.
230 D3 Nzako C.A.R.
231 A5 Nzambi Congo
230 F3 Nzara Sudan
228 C4 Nzébéla Guinea
233 B6 Nzega Tanz.
228 C5 Nzérékoré Guinea
231 B6 N'zeto Angola
228 D5 Nzi r. Côte d'Ivoire
231 E7 Nzilo, Lac l. Dem. Rep. Congo
231 E5 Nzingu Dem. Rep. Congo
228 D5 Nzo r. Côte d'Ivoire
228 D5 N'Zo, Réserve de Faune du nature res. Côte d'Ivoire
231 B6 Nzobe Dem. Rep. Congo
232 B4 Nzoia r. Kenya
230 F4 Nzoro r. Dem. Rep. Congo
239 □3 Nzwani i. Comoros

O

260 F4 Oacoma SD U.S.A.
173 J2 Oadby Leicestershire, England U.K.
260 E3 Oahe, Lake SD U.S.A.
264 □D12 O'ahu i. HI U.S.A.
Oaitupu i. Tuvalu see Vaitupu
104 H5 Oakbank S.A. Austr.
257 O7 Oak Bluffs MA U.S.A.
265 T2 Oak City UT U.S.A.
250 G7 Oak Creek WI U.S.A.
264 L4 Oakdale CA U.S.A.
259 K2 Oakdale CT U.S.A.
261 I10 Oakdale LA U.S.A.
259 I3 Oakdale NY U.S.A.
172 H2 Oakengates Telford and Wrekin, England U.K.
260 F2 Oakes ND U.S.A.
107 M9 Oakey Qld Austr.
256 G5 Oakfield NY U.S.A.
258 F4 Oakford PA U.S.A.
261 J9 Oak Grove LA U.S.A.
250 J5 Oak Grove MI U.S.A.
173 K2 Oakham Rutland, England U.K.
256 B7 Oak Harbor OH U.S.A.
262 C2 Oak Harbor WA U.S.A.
256 C10 Oak Hill OH U.S.A.
256 D11 Oak Hill WV U.S.A.
264 M4 Oakhurst CA U.S.A.
259 G4 Oakhurst NJ U.S.A.
250 D3 Oak Island WI U.S.A.
264 L7 Oak Knolls CA U.S.A.
247 K5 Oak Lake Man. Can.
264 J4 Oakland CA U.S.A.
256 F9 Oakland MD U.S.A.
257 □P4 Oakland ME U.S.A.
260 G5 Oakland NE U.S.A.
259 G2 Oakland NJ U.S.A.
262 C5 Oakland OR U.S.A.
264 J4 Oakland airport CA U.S.A.
254 D6 Oakland City IN U.S.A.
105 K6 Oaklands N.S.W. Austr.
250 G8 Oak Lawn IL U.S.A.
173 K3 Oakley Bedfordshire, England U.K.
173 J4 Oakley Buckinghamshire, England U.K.
168 I10 Oakley Fife, Scotland U.K.
173 J5 Oakley Hampshire, Engla
260 E6 Oakley KS U.S.A.
251 J6 Oakley MI U.S.A.
256 F8 Oakmont PA U.S.A.
108 F6 Oakover r. W.A. Austr.
250 G8 Oak Park IL U.S.A.
259 G2 Oak Ridge NJ U.S.A.
262 C5 Oakridge OR U.S.A.
255 E7 Oak Ridge TN U.S.A.
258 E4 Oaks PA U.S.A.
258 F5 Oak Shade NJ U.S.A.
102 H6 Oakura North I. N.Z.
104 H5 Oakvale S.A. Austr.
264 M7 Oak View CA U.S.A.
248 E5 Oakville Ont. Can.
259 I1 Oakville CT U.S.A.
256 A7 Oakwood OH U.S.A.
256 A9 Oakwood OH U.S.A.
258 D5 Oakwood Beach NJ U.S.A.
103 E12 Oamaru South I. N.Z.
127 L4 Ōamishirasato Japan
102 H6 Oaonui North I. N.Z.
127 M3 Ōarai Japan
103 H9 Oaro South I. N.Z.
204 C4 O Arrabal Spain
125 J12 Ōasa Japan
127 K3 Ōashi-gawa r. Japan
264 O4 Oasis CA U.S.A.
262 G6 Oasis NV U.S.A.
219 L2 Oaşului, Munţii mts Ron
Oates Coast reg. Antarcti
Oates Land
287 K2 Oates Land reg. Antarctic
105 K10 Oatlands Tas. Austr.
236 I8 Oatlands S. Africa
269 K8 Oaxaca Mex.
269 K8 Oaxaca state Mex.
143 M1 Ob' r. Rus. Fed.
Ob, Gulf of sea chan. Rus
Obskaya Guba
248 C3 Oba Ont. Can.
143 S2 Oba r. Kazakh.
Oba i. Vanuatu see Aoba
Obaghan r. Kazakh. see U
126 C7 Obako-dake mt. Japan
150 A2 Obaköy Turkey
160 M6 Obal' Vitsyebskaya Voblas Belarus
160 M6 Obal' Vitsyebskaya Voblas Belarus
160 M6 Obal' canal Belarus
229 H5 Obala Cameroon
251 J1 Oba Lake Ont. Can.
126 C5 Obama Japan
126 C4 Obama-wan b. Japan
229 H5 Oban Nigeria
168 F10 Oban Argyll and Bute, Sco U.K.
124 R8 Obanazawa Japan
229 H5 Oban Hills mt. Nigeria
126 F5 Obara Japan
204 G4 O Barco Spain
205 N3 Obarenes, Montes mts S
219 P4 Obârşeni, Dealul hill Ror
126 E6 Obata Japan
151 D5 Obayayla Turkey
Obbia Somalia see Hoby
162 P5 Obbola Sweden
219 N3 Obcina Mare ridge Roma
201 K5 Obdach Austria
186 G3 Obdam Neth.
Obdorsk Rus. Fed. see Sal
198 C2 Obecnice Czech Rep.
Óbecse Vojvodina Serbia
246 G4 Obed Alta Can.
207 J4 Obejo Spain
151 A5 Öbektaş Turkey
160 I6 Obeliai Lith.
197 L1 Obelija l. Lith.
103 D12 Obelisk mt. South I. N.Z.
282 G2 Oberá Arg.
201 L5 Oberaich Austria
200 H4 Oberalm Austria
212 F2 Oberalpstock mt. Switz.
195 K6 Oberammergau Ger.
195 J3 Oberasbach Ger.
195 K6 Oberau Ger.
195 M6 Oberaudorf Ger.
191 H9 Oberaula Ger.
195 L6 Oberbayern admin. reg. G
194 F3 Oberderdingen Ger.
195 L5 Oberding Ger.
191 J8 Oberdorla Ger.
200 G6 Oberdrauburg Austria
194 F5 Obere Donau park Ger.
212 H1 Oberegg Switz.
191 J10 Oberelsbach Ger.
212 H2 Ober Engadin reg. Switz.
212 E1 Oberentfelden Switz.
195 N3 Oberer Bayerischer Wald Ger.
193 E9 Obere Saale park Ger.
194 H6 Oberessendorf Ger.
193 G10 Oberes Westerzgebirge
191 D10 Oberfell Ger.
193 D11 Oberfranken admin. reg.
191 J6 Oberg (Lahstedt) Ger.
212 D1 Obergösgen Switz.
201 M3 Ober-Grafendorf Austria
195 K5 Obergriesbach Ger.
195 I6 Obergünzburg Ger.
200 D6 Obergurgl Austria
193 J8 Obergurig Ger.
201 L6 Oberhaag Austria
195 L5 Oberhaching Ger.
195 J2 Oberhaid Ger.
194 E5 Oberharmersbach Ger.
195 K4 Oberhausen Bayern Ger.
191 C8 Oberhausen Nordrhein-W Ger.
191 K9 Oberhof Ger.
212 D2 Oberhofen Switz.
200 D5 Oberhofen im Inntal Aus
179 O6 Oberhoffen-sur-Moder F
200 B4 Oberjochpass pass Austri
194 E4 Oberkirch Ger.
195 I4 Oberkochen Ger.
193 E10 Oberkotzau Ger.
190 D5 Oberlangen Ger.
193 J8 Oberlausitz reg. Ger.
193 J8 Oberlausitzer Bergland
193 J8 Oberlichtenau Ger.
200 G6 Oberlienz Austria
260 E6 Oberlin KS U.S.A.
261 I10 Oberlin LA U.S.A.
256 C7 Oberlin OH U.S.A.
194 H5 Obermarchtal Ger.
191 J9 Obermaßfeld-Grimment
194 D2 Obermoschel Ger.
179 N7 Obernai France
201 H3 Obernberg am Inn Austr
194 G2 Obernburg am Main Ger
195 J4 Oberndorf am Lech Ger.
194 F5 Oberndorf am Neckar Ge
201 L3 Oberndorf an der Melk A
200 G4 Oberndorf bei Salzburg
201 J3 Oberneukirchen Austria
191 J7 Obernfeld Ger.
194 F5 Obernheim Ger.
194 D3 Obernheim-Kirchenarnb
191 H6 Obernkirchen Ger.
195 P4 Obernzell Ger.
195 I3 Obernzenn Ger.
193 K9 Oberoderwitz Ger.
194 E2 Ober-Olm Ger.
105 L5 Oberon N.S.W. Austr.
195 J6 Oberostendorf Ger.
201 I3 Oberösterreich land Aust
195 L2 Oberpfalz admin. reg. Ger.
195 M2 Oberpfälzer Wald mts Ge
198 B2 Oberpfälzer Wald park Ge
195 L5 Oberpframmern Ger.
201 O4 Oberpullendorf Austria
194 F2 Ober-Ramstadt Ger.
194 H6 Oberreute Ger.
194 D6 Oberried Ger.
195 I5 Oberrieden Ger.
212 H1 Oberriet Switz.
193 D8 Oberröblingen Ger.
194 F2 Ober-Roden Ger.
193 D8 Oberroßla Ger.
194 H3 Oberrot Ger.
194 D5 Oberrotweil Ger.
195 L5 Oberschleißheim Ger.

N4 Oberschneiding Ger.
H9 Oberschöna Ger.
N5 Oberschützen Austria
O3 Obersiebenbrunn Austria
E1 Obersiggenthal Switz.
I10 Obersinn Ger.
H3 Obersontheim Ger.
K8 Oberspier Ger.
H5 Oberstadion Ger.
I6 Oberstaufen Ger.
I7 Oberstdorf Ger.
G3 Oberstenfeld Ger.
M5 Obertaufkirchen Ger.
G6 Oberteuringen Ger.
C2 Oberthal Ger.
I10 Oberthulba Ger.
G6 Obertilliach Austria
M4 Obertraubling Ger.
K2 Obertrubach Ger.
H4 Obertrum am See Austria
H4 Obertrumer See l. Austria
G10 Obertshausen Ger.
E5 Obertyn Ukr.
I4 Oberueckersee l. Ger.
G10 Oberursel (Taunus) Ger.
H6 Obervellach Austria
M3 Oberviechtach Ger.
E2 Oberwald Switz.
H7 Oberwälder Land reg. Ger.
N4 Oberwaltersdorf Austria
N5 Oberwart Austria
E10 Oberwesel Ger.
G10 Oberwiesenthal, Kurort Ger.
M3 Oberwölbling Austria
E5 Oberwolfach Ger.
J5 Oberwölz Austria
N2 Obesta r. Rus. Fed.
E8 Obhausen Ger.
E4 Obi i. Maluku Indon.
H4 Obi Nigeria
E4 Obi, Kepulauan is Maluku Indon.
E4 Obi, Selat sea chan. Maluku Indon.
H5 Óbidos Brazil
A2 Óbidos Port.
A2 Óbidos, Lagoa de lag. Port.
M2 Obigarm Tajik.
U4 Obihiro Japan
E4 Obilatu i. Maluku Indon.
Obilić Obiliq Kosovo see Obiliq
8 Obiliq Obiliq Kosovo
7 Obil'noye Rus. Fed.
M5 Obing Ger.
K7 Obion r. TN U.S.A.
S2 Obira Japan
D2 Obispos Venez.
F2 Obispo Trejo Arg.
Obitochnaya Kosa spit Ukr. see Obytichna Kosa
K5 Obitsu-gawa r. Japan
G5 Objat France
F1 Objazda Pol.
M4 Oblapy Ukr.
5 Öblarn Austria
K9 Obleševo Češinovo-Obleševo Macedonia
H6 Oblivskaya Rus. Fed.
G4 Obluch'ye Rus. Fed.
I6 Obninsk Rus. Fed.
E3 Obo C.A.R.
G8 Obo Qinghai China
E3 Obobogorap S. Africa
D2 Obock Djibouti
5 Obodivka Ukr.
F8 Ŏbŏk N. Korea
E5 Obokote Dem. Rep. Congo
K7 Obo Liang Qinghai China
G5 Obolo Nigeria
F4 O Bolo Spain
L4 Obolon' Ukr.
D6 Obón Spain
K2 Obong, Gunung mt. Malaysia
K3 Oborín Slovakia
E3 Oborniki Pol.
E4 Oborniki Śląskie Pol.
B5 Obouya Congo
G6 Oboyan' Rus. Fed.
H3 Obozerskiy Rus. Fed.
7 Obra Uttar Prad. India
D3 Obra r. Pol.
F3 Obrage Arg.
E4 Obregón, Presa resr Mex.
K2 Obre Lake N.W.T. Can.
6 Obrenovac Obrenovac Serbia
E5 O'Brien OR U.S.A.
G3 Obrigheim Ger.
E2 Obrigheim (Pfalz) Ger.
Obringa r. Switz. see Aare
C1 Obrnice Czech Rep.
Q7 Obrochishte Bulg.
D4 Obrov Slovenia
G3 Obrowo Pol.
4 Obruk Turkey
4 Obry, Kanał canal Pol.
3 Obryte Pol.
3 Obrzycko Pol.
3 Observatory Hill S.A. Austr.
D5 Observatory Inlet B.C. Can.
2 Observatory Rock i. Lord Howe I. Austr.
6 Obsha r. Rus. Fed.
D2 Obshchiy Syrt hills Rus. Fed.
3 Obskaya Guba sea chan. Rus. Fed.
5 Obsza Pol.
12 Obtove Ukr.
5 Ōbu Japan
5 Obuasi Ghana
H5 Obubra Nigeria
G3 Obudovac Bos.-Herz.
H5 Obudu Nigeria
3 Obukhiv Ukr.
Obukhov Ukr. see Obukhiv
6 Obukhovo Rus. Fed.
12 Obuse Japan
4 Obva r. Rus. Fed.
2 Obwalden canton Switz.
3 Ob"yachevo Rus. Fed.
7 Obytichna Kosa spit Ukr.
7 Obytichna Zatoka b. Ukr.
2 O Cádavo Spain
11 Ocala FL U.S.A.
5 O Calvario Spain
3 Ocampo Chihuahua Mex.
4 Ocampo Coahuila Mex.
4 Ocampo Guanajuato Mex.
3 Ocampo Tamaulipas Mex.
2 O Campo da Feira Spain
2 Ocaña Col.
4 Ocana Corse France
3 Ocaña Peru
9 Ocaña Spain
9 Ocaña, Mesa de plat. Spain
4 O Carballiño Spain
4 O Castelo Spain
3 O Castro Spain
4 O Castro de Caldelas Spain
3 O Castro de Ferreira Spain
6 Occhiobello Italy
4 Occhito, Lago di l. Italy
4 Occidental, Cordillera mts Chile
4 Occidental, Cordillera mts Col.
4 Occidental, Cordillera mts Peru
5 Occimiano Italy
10 Occoquan VA U.S.A.
11 Oceana WV U.S.A.
3 Ocean Beach NY U.S.A.
4 Ocean Cape AK U.S.A.
1 Ocean Cay i. Bahamas
0 Ocean City MD U.S.A.
5 Ocean City NJ U.S.A.
5 Ocean County county NJ U.S.A.
4 Ocean Falls B.C. Can.
5 Ocean Gate NJ U.S.A.
4 Ocean Grove NJ U.S.A.
Oceania
Ocean Island Kiribati see Banaba
Ocean Island atoll HI U.S.A. see Kure Atoll
5 Oceano CA U.S.A.
8 Oceanside CA U.S.A.
10 Ocean Springs MS U.S.A.
5 Ocean View NJ U.S.A.
6 Oceanville NJ U.S.A.
6 Ocejón mt. Spain

100 □4a Ocha i. Chuuk Micronesia
100 □4a Ocha, Mochun sea chan. Chuuk Micronesia
208 C2 Ochagavía Spain
159 K7 Ochakiv Ukr.
151 C3 Och'amch'ire Georgia
204 E2 O Chao Spain
156 K4 Ocher Rus. Fed.
158 I4 Ocheretnya Ukr.
159 O6 Ocheretuvate Ukr.
179 K6 Ochey France
220 F4 Ochi mt. Greece
125 J11 Ōchi Japan
124 W3 Ochiishi-misaki pt Japan
168 I10 Ochil Hills Scotland U.K.
168 H12 Ochiltree East Ayrshire, Scotland U.K.
145 L9 Ochito r. Pak.
159 M1 Ochkyne Ukr.
255 E11 Ochlockonee r. GA U.S.A.
197 H3 Ochnia r. Pol.
190 E4 Ocholt Ger.
270 □ Ocho Rios Jamaica
Ochrida, Lake Albania/Macedonia see Ohrid, Lake
195 I2 Ochsenfurt Ger.
194 H5 Ochsenhausen Ger.
191 D10 Ochtendung Ger.
193 D6 Ochtmersleben Ger.
191 D6 Ochtrup Ger.
255 F10 Ocilla GA U.S.A.
163 N6 Ockelbo Sweden
190 G1 Ockholm Ger.
168 E9 Ockle Highland, Scotland U.K.
219 N4 Ocland Romania
255 F10 Ocmulgee r. GA U.S.A.
219 L4 Ocna Mureş Romania
219 M5 Ocna Sibiului Romania
158 G5 Ocniţa Moldova
219 N4 Ocolaşul Mare, Vârful mt. Romania
276 B4 Ocoña Peru
255 F9 Oconee, Lake resr GA U.S.A.
107 I6 O'Connell Creek r. Qld Austr.
250 F6 Oconomowoc WI U.S.A.
250 G5 Oconto WI U.S.A.
250 F5 Oconto Falls WI U.S.A.
204 C4 O Convento Spain
204 F3 O Corgo Spain
266 E5 Ocoroni Mex.
276 C3 Ocoruro Peru
267 M10 Ocos Guat.
267 M9 Ocosingo Mex.
266 □P11 Ocotal Nic.
269 K9 Ocotepec Mex.
268 E5 Ocotlán Jalisco Mex.
269 K9 Ocotlán Oaxaca Mex.
199 I3 Očová Slovakia
267 M9 Ocozocoautla Mex.
204 E9 Ocreza r. Port.
199 I4 Ócsa Hungary
199 I4 Ócsai park Hungary
199 H5 Öcsény Hungary
199 J5 Öcsöd Hungary
181 L2 Octeville-sur-Mer France
October Revolution Island Severnaya Zemlya Rus. Fed. see Oktyabr'skoy Revolyutsii, Ostrov
258 C5 Octoraro Creek r. MD U.S.A.
258 C5 Octoraro Lake PA U.S.A.
266 □S14 Ocú Panama
235 H2 Ocua Moz.
269 H7 Ocuilan de Arteaga Mex.
271 J8 Ocumare del Tuy Venez.
276 D4 Ocurí Bol.
196 G2 Ocypel Pol.
228 E5 Oda Ghana
125 J11 Ōda Japan
225 H4 Oda, Jebel mt. Sudan
150 E2 Odabaşı Turkey
162 □E1 Ódáðahraun lava field Iceland
123 F8 Ŏdaejin N. Korea
123 F10 Odae-san National Park S. Korea
126 D7 Ōdai Japan
126 D7 Ōdaigahara-zan mt. Japan
126 G4 Odaira-tōge pass Japan
124 R9 Odaka Japan
250 D3 Odanah WI U.S.A.
124 R6 Ōdate Japan
127 J5 Odawara Japan
164 C1 Odda Norway
164 G6 Odder Denmark
168 □O1 Oddsta Shetland, Scotland U.K.
206 D4 Odearce r. Port.
206 B6 Odeceixe Port.
247 L3 Odei r. Man. Can.
206 E6 Odeleite Port.
206 E6 Odeleite r. Port.
250 F8 Odell IL U.S.A.
206 C6 Odelouca r. Port.
195 K5 Odelzhausen Ger.
261 G12 Odem TX U.S.A.
206 B5 Odemira Port.
221 I4 Ödemiş Turkey
208 I4 Òdena Spain
Ödenburg Hungary see Sopron
237 K3 Odendaalsrus S. Africa
165 L2 Odensbacken Sweden
164 G6 Odense Denmark
164 G6 Odense Fjord b. Denmark
258 B6 Odenton MD U.S.A.
194 F2 Odenwald reg. Ger.
196 C2 Oder r. Ger.
alt. Odra (Poland)
191 I7 Oder r. Ger.
192 J5 Oderberg Ger.
192 J5 Oderbruch reg. Ger.
192 J2 Oderbucht b. Ger.
192 J3 Oderhaff b. Ger.
192 H5 Oder-Havel-Kanal canal Ger.
193 I6 Oderin Ger.
194 D2 Odernheim am Glan Ger.
213 M4 Oderzo Italy
158 J7 Odesa Ukr.
156 K3 Odesdino Rus. Fed.
165 K3 Ödeshog Sweden
158 I6 Odes'ka Oblast' admin. div. Ukr.
Odessa Ukr. see Odesa
258 D6 Odessa DE U.S.A.
261 D10 Odessa TX U.S.A.
262 E3 Odessa WA U.S.A.
Odessa Oblast admin. div. Ukr. see Odes'ka Oblast'
Odesskaya Oblast' admin. div. Ukr. see Odes'ka Oblast'
143 O1 Odesskoye Rus. Fed.
Odessus Bulg. see Varna
180 C6 Odet r. France
225 H5 Odi watercourse Sudan
206 B6 Odiáxere Port.
206 F6 Odiel r. Spain
228 D4 Odienné Côte d'Ivoire
173 K5 Odiham Hampshire, England U.K.
186 H4 Odijk Neth.
230 A5 Odimba Gabon
161 U6 Odintsovo Rus. Fed.
206 C4 Odivelas Beja Port.
206 A3 Odivelas Lisboa Port.
206 C4 Odivelas r. Port.
206 C4 Odivelas, Barragem de resr Port.
219 P5 Odobeşti Romania
219 O5 Odobeştilor, Măgura hill Romania
196 F4 Odolanów Pol.
193 J10 Odolena Voda Czech Rep.
286 T2 Odom Inlet Antarctica
181 K3 Odon r. France
205 Q7 Odón Spain
119 G9 Ôdôngk Cambodia
186 K3 Odoorn Neth.
219 N4 Odorheiu Secuiesc Romania
161 T8 Odoyev Rus. Fed.
196 C2 Odra r. Pol.
alt. Oder (Germany)
205 L4 Odra r. Spain
159 N7 Odradivka Ukr.
199 G2 Odry Czech Rep.
197 I4 Odrzywół Pol.
218 H5 Odžaci Vojvodina Serbia
230 B4 Odzala, Parc National d' nat. park Congo
235 G3 Odzi Zimbabwe
235 G3 Odzi r. Zimbabwe

126 B5 Ōe Japan
Oea Libya see Ţarābulus
191 K6 Oebisfelde Ger.
191 I7 Oedelsheim (Oberweser) Ger.
193 H9 Oederan Ger.
190 H3 Oederquart Ger.
125 G11 Oedong S. Korea
186 I5 Oeffelt Neth.
186 G4 Oegstgeest Neth.
278 E3 Oeiras Brazil
206 A3 Oeiras Port.
206 D5 Oeiras r. Port.
191 F7 Oelde Ger.
190 I3 Oelixdorf Ger.
260 D4 Oelrichs SD U.S.A.
193 F10 Oelsnitz Sachsen Ger.
193 G9 Oelsnitz Sachsen Ger.
260 J4 Oelwein IA U.S.A.
186 J4 Oene Neth.
106 D2 Oenpelli N.T. Austr.
212 D1 Oensingen Switz.
190 H4 Oerel Ger.
190 J3 Oering Ger.
191 J10 Oerlenbach Ger.
191 G7 Oerlinghausen Ger.
Oesel i. Estonia see Hiiumaa
187 I9 Oesling hills Lux.
187 F6 Oesterdam barrage Neth.
282 E2 Oetling Arg.
193 E9 Oettersdorf Ger.
195 J4 Oettingen in Bayern Ger.
200 C5 Oetz Austria
190 K4 Oetzen Ger.
249 F2 Oeufs, Lac des l. Que. Can.
190 H1 Oeversee Ger.
126 B5 Ōe-yama hill Japan
185 B8 Œyreluy France
149 J3 Of Turkey
262 L3 O'Fallon r. MT U.S.A.
215 Q5 Ofanto r. Italy
150 C7 Ofaqim Israel
215 L3 Ofena Italy
229 G4 Offa Nigeria
169 G6 Offaly county Ireland
212 H5 Offanengo Italy
179 M8 Offemont France
191 G10 Offenbach am Main Ger.
194 E3 Offenbach an der Queich Ger.
195 N4 Offenberg Ger.
194 D5 Offenburg Ger.
201 I4 Offensee l. Austria
162 M5 Offerdal Sweden
215 L2 Offida Italy
195 I5 Offingen Ger.
178 B4 Offranville France
221 H6 Ofidoussa i. Greece
101 □8 Ofolanga atoll Tonga
204 D3 O Forte Spain
162 N2 Ofotfjorden sea chan. Norway
194 G5 Ofterdingen Ger.
100 □2 Ofu i. American Samoa
124 S7 Ōfunato Japan
117 K4 Oga r. Indon.
124 Q7 Oga Japan
124 R7 Ogachi Japan
127 K1 Oga-dake mt. Japan
232 E3 Ogadēn reg. Eth.
124 Q7 Oga-hantō pen. Japan
126 E5 Ōgaki Japan
260 E5 Ogallala NE U.S.A.
116 F6 Ogan r. Indon.
127 J3 Ogano Japan
127 H6 Ogasa Japan
125 □2 Ogasawara-shotō is N. Pacific Ocean
251 P2 Ogascanane, Lac l. Que. Can.
127 H1 Ōgata Japan
127 H3 Ōga-tō mt. Japan
127 M1 Ogawa Fukushima Japan
127 L3 Ogawa Ibaraki Japan
127 L2 Ogawa Ibaraki Japan
127 G2 Ogawa Nagano Japan
127 J3 Ogawa Saitama Japan
127 L2 Ōgawa Japan
124 R8 Ōgawara Japan
124 S6 Ogawara-ko l. Japan
229 G4 Ogbomosho Nigeria
Ogbomoso Nigeria see Ogbomosho
260 H4 Ogden IA U.S.A.
262 I6 Ogden UT U.S.A.
245 N4 Ogden, Mount B.C. Can.
258 F2 Ogdensburg NJ U.S.A.
257 J4 Ogdensburg NY U.S.A.
255 G10 Ogeechee r. GA U.S.A.
250 D4 Ogema WI U.S.A.
190 E3 Ogenbargen Ger.
178 H6 Oger France
185 C9 Ogeu-les-Bains France
179 M6 Ogéviller France
212 G4 Oggiono Italy
138 D7 Oghna Rajasthan India
100 □6 Ogho Choiseul Solomon Is
125 P9 Ogi Japan
248 C4 Ogidaki Ont. Can.
245 M2 Ogilvie r. Y.T. Can.
245 L2 Ogilvie Mountains Y.T. Can.
124 □1 Ogimi Okinawa Japan
128 H3 Ögiynuur Mongolia
151 D6 Oğlaksuyu Turkey
245 □B6 Oglala Pass sea channel AK U.S.A.
144 F2 Oglanly Turkm.
226 E5 'Oglât el Khnâchîch well Mali
226 D4 Oglat Sbot well Alg.
214 D8 Ogliastra prov. Sardegna Italy
214 D8 Ogliastra reg. Sardegna Italy
214 D8 Ogliastra, Isola dell' i. Sardegna Italy
214 C2 Ogliastro Corse France
216 H9 Ogliastro, Lago di l. Sicilia Italy
212 J5 Oglio r. Italy
122 K2 Oglongi Rus. Fed.
107 L7 Ogmore Qld Austr.
172 E5 Ogmore Vale of Glamorgan, Wales U.K.
172 E4 Ogmore Vale Bridgend, Wales U.K.
182 G2 Ognon r. France
Oğnut Turkey see Göynük
127 J3 Ōgo Japan
115 B3 Ogoamas, Gunung mt. Indon.
127 J4 Ogōchi-damu dam Japan
122 H2 Ogodzha Rus. Fed.
229 H5 Ogoja Nigeria
248 C3 Ogoki r. Ont. Can.
248 C3 Ogoki Lake Ont. Can.
248 B3 Ogoki Reservoir Ont. Can.
122 M5 Ogon'ki Rus. Fed.
205 O2 Ogoño, Cabo c. Spain
230 A5 Ogooué r. Gabon
230 B5 Ogooué-Ivindo prov. Gabon
230 B5 Ogooué-Lolo prov. Gabon
230 A5 Ogooué-Maritime prov. Gabon
125 I12 Ogōri Japan
122 F1 Ogoron Rus. Fed.
127 J4 Ogose Japan
219 L7 Ogosta r. Bulg.
229 F5 Ogou r. Togo
109 D11 O'Grady, Lake salt flat W.A. Austr.
219 K9 Ogražden mts Bulg./Macedonia
Ograzhden mts Bulg./Macedonia see Ogražden
160 H5 Ogre Latvia
160 H5 Ogre r. Latvia
197 J3 Ogrodniki Pol.
197 H5 Ogrodzieniec Pol.
193 J7 Ogrosen Ger.
204 C4 O Grove Spain
126 E5 Ōguchi Japan
161 V5 Ogudnevo Rus. Fed.
226 E4 Oguïlet Merzoug well Mali
210 E3 Ogulin Croatia
229 F5 Ogun state Nigeria
127 I1 Oguni Japan
257 □O5 Ogunquit ME U.S.A.
144 E2 Ogurjaly Adasy i. Turkm.
151 I4 Oğuz Azer.
151 I1 Oguzer Rus. Fed.
199 K6 Ohaba Lungă Romania
229 G5 Ohafia Nigeria
103 B12 Ohai South I. N.Z.
102 J6 Ohakune North I. N.Z.
232 E3 Ohale well Somalia
207 N6 Ohanes Spain
227 H3 Ohanet Alg.

234 C3 Ohangwena admin. reg. Namibia
127 L5 Ōhara Japan
124 S5 Ōhata Japan
102 J7 Ohau North I. N.Z.
103 E11 Ohau r. South I. N.Z.
103 D11 Ohau, Lake South I. N.Z.
102 J4 Ohaupo North I. N.Z.
Ohcejohka Fin. see Utsjoki
190 E4 Ohe r. Ger.
195 O4 Ohe r. Ger.
Ohétéroah i. Îs Australes Fr. Polynesia see Rurutu
187 H8 Ohey Belgium
276 C5 O'Higgins Chile
284 B4 O'Higgins admin. reg. Chile
286 U2 O'Higgins (Chile) research stn Antarctica
283 B8 O'Higgins, Lago l. Chile
102 J4 Ohinewai North I. N.Z.
250 E8 Ohio IL U.S.A.
260 K7 Ohio r. OH/WV U.S.A.
256 C8 Ohio state U.S.A.
256 A8 Ohio City OH U.S.A.
286 Q1 Ohio Range mts Antarctica
259 G1 Ohioville NY U.S.A.
127 K3 Ōhira Japan
127 I5 Ōhito Japan
102 L4 Ohiwa Harbour North I. N.Z.
159 O4 Ohiyivka Ukr.
194 D5 Ohlsbach Ger.
201 I4 Ohlsdorf Austria
195 K6 Ohlstadt Ger.
191 G9 Ohm r. Ger.
160 J3 Õhne r. Estonia
191 D6 Ohne Ger.
194 F6 Öhningen Ger.
244 G3 Ohogamiut AK U.S.A.
101 □8 'Ohonua Tonga
102 L4 Ohope North I. N.Z.
199 G3 Ohrady Slovakia
191 K9 Ohrdruf Ger.
198 D1 Ohře r. Czech Rep.
193 E6 Ohre r. Ger.
218 I9 Ohrid Macedonia
218 I9 Ohrid, Lake Albania/Macedonia
Ohridsko Ezero l. Albania/Macedonia see Ohrid, Lake
235 F5 Ohrigstad S. Africa
194 G3 Öhringen Ger.
Ohrit, Liqeni i l. Albania/Macedonia see Ohrid, Lake
191 K6 Ohrum Ger.
102 I5 Ohura North I. N.Z.
126 C5 Ōi Fukui Japan
127 J5 Ōi Kanagawa Japan
204 C7 Oiã Port.
275 I4 Oiapoque Brazil
208 B1 Oiartzun Spain
274 C3 Oiba Col.
168 G8 Oich r. Scotland U.K.
168 G8 Oich, Loch l. Scotland U.K.
220 C3 Oichalia Greece
135 □1 Oidhuni i. S. Male Maldives
133 K12 Oiga Xizang China
127 H6 Ōigawa Japan
126 C5 Ōi-gawa r. Japan
127 H6 Ōi-gawa r. Japan
168 C9 Oigh-sgeir is Scotland U.K.
178 E3 Oignies France
182 H4 Oignin r. France
204 D4 O Igrexario Spain
162 R4 Oijärvi Fin.
186 H5 Oijen Neth.
Oik Kazakh. see Uyuk
256 F7 Oil City PA U.S.A.
264 M6 Oildale CA U.S.A.
130 C4 Oilê Sichuan China
169 I8 Oilgate Ireland
169 F3 Oily r. Ireland
204 F5 Oímbra Spain
205 P3 Oion Spain
130 B4 Oi Qu r. Xizang China
124 S6 Oirase-gawa r. Japan
204 D3 O Irixo Spain
181 K8 Oiron France
186 H5 Oirschot Neth.
183 H6 Oisans reg. France
178 D5 Oise dept France
178 D6 Oise r. France
178 F5 Oise à l'Aisne, Canal de l' France
185 B6 Oiseaux, Île aux i. France
228 A2 Oiseaux du Djoudj, Parc National des nat. park Senegal
182 H2 Oiselay-et-Grachaux France
178 C4 Oisemont France
127 J5 Ōiso Japan
181 J5 Oisseau France
178 B5 Oissel France
186 H5 Oisterwijk Neth.
271 □4 Oistins Barbados
125 I13 Ōita Japan
125 I13 Ōita pref. Japan
204 C4 Oitavén r. Spain
220 D4 Oiti mt. Greece
220 D4 Oitis, Ethnikos Drymos nat. park Greece
219 O4 Oituz r. Romania
220 D6 Oitylo Greece
224 C4 Oiuru well Libya
124 S4 Oiwake Japan
181 Q7 Oizon France
127 J3 Ōizumi Gunma Japan
127 H4 Ōizumi Yamanashi Japan
126 E3 Oizuruga-dake mt. Japan
165 N3 Öja i. Sweden
264 M7 Ojai CA U.S.A.
207 L3 Ojailén r. Spain
Ojalava i. Samoa see 'Upolu
160 K2 Ojamaa r. Estonia
165 M1 Öjaren l. Sweden
197 H5 Ojcowski Park Narodowy nat. park Pol.
163 L6 Öje Sweden
285 E4 Ojeda Arg.
207 J7 Ojén Spain
126 C6 Ōji Japan
125 F13 Ojika-jima i. Japan
266 G3 Ojinaga Mex.
269 K7 Ojitlán Mex.
127 I1 Ojiya Japan
229 G5 Ojobo Nigeria
268 E3 Ojocaliente Mex.
263 K8 Ojo Caliente NM U.S.A.
284 E2 Ojo de Agua Arg.
268 G5 Ojo de Agua Mex.
266 F3 Ojo de Laguna Mex.
266 B4 Ojo de Liebre, Lago b. Mex.
207 L2 Ojos del Guadiana lakes Spain
282 C2 Ojos del Salado, Nevado mt. Arg./Chile
205 R7 Ojos Negros Spain
197 I3 Ojrzeń Pol.
229 H5 Oju Nigeria
268 F4 Ojuelos de Jalisco Mex.
163 M6 Öjung Sweden
229 G5 Oka Nigeria
161 W7 Oka r. Rus. Fed.
127 J3 Okabe Saitama Japan
127 H6 Okabe Shizuoka Japan
234 C4 Okahandja Namibia
Okahu b. South I. N.Z. see Jackson Bay
102 J5 Okahukura North I. N.Z.
102 H2 Okaihau North I. N.Z.
103 H10 Okains Bay South I. N.Z.
103 H10 Okains Bay b. South I. N.Z.
229 F4 Okaka Nigeria
234 C4 Okakarara Namibia
249 I1 Okak Islands Nfld and Lab. Can.
197 H2 Okalewo Pol.
246 G5 Okanagan Falls B.C. Can.
246 G5 Okanagan Lake B.C. Can.
136 G9 Okanda Sri Lanka
262 E2 Okanogan WA U.S.A.
262 E2 Okanogan r. WA U.S.A.
262 D2 Okanogan Range mts WA U.S.A.
199 K5 Okány Hungary
230 E4 Okapi, Parc National de la nat. park Dem. Rep. Congo
234 C4 Okaputa Namibia
145 O6 Okara Pak.
103 E10 Okarito Lagoon South I. N.Z.

102 H6 Okato North I. N.Z.
234 B3 Okaukuejo Namibia
234 D3 Okavango r. Botswana/Namibia
234 C3 Okavango admin. reg. Namibia
234 D3 Okavango Delta swamp Botswana
125 H13 Ōkawa Japan
126 A5 Ōkawachi Japan
102 □ Okawa Point Chatham Is S. Pacific Ocean
127 H3 Okaya Japan
125 K12 Okayama Japan
125 K12 Okayama pref. Japan
126 F6 Okazaki Japan
151 B5 Okçular Dağı mt. Turkey
255 G12 Okeechobee FL U.S.A.
255 G12 Okeechobee, Lake FL U.S.A.
261 F7 Okeene OK U.S.A.
255 F10 Okefenokee National Wildlife Refuge and Wilderness nature res. GA U.S.A.
255 F10 Okefenokee Swamp GA U.S.A.
127 K3 Okegawa Japan
172 D6 Okehampton Devon, England U.K.
229 F4 Oke-Iho Nigeria
261 G8 Okemah OK U.S.A.
172 D6 Okement r. England U.K.
229 G5 Okene Nigeria
191 J5 Oker r. Ger.
124 U3 Oketo Japan
138 B8 Okha Gujarat India
122 M2 Okha Sakhalin Rus. Fed.
Okhadunga Nepal see Okhaldhunga
139 K6 Okhaldhunga Nepal
156 K4 Okhansk Rus. Fed.
138 G4 Okhimath Uttaranchal India
122 M1 Okhinskiy Peresheyek isth. Rus. Fed.
Ókhi Óros mt. Greece see Ochi
159 P2 Okhochevka Rus. Fed.
161 V4 Okhotino Rus. Fed.
153 P4 Okhotka r. Rus. Fed.
159 M8 Okhotnykove Ukr.
153 P4 Okhotsk Rus. Fed.
124 V2 Okhotsk, Sea of Japan/Rus. Fed.
Okhotskoye More sea Japan/Rus. Fed. see Okhotsk, Sea of
159 O7 Okhrimivka Ukr.
Okhthoniá Greece see Oktonia
159 N3 Okhtyrka Ukr.
161 P5 Okhvat Rus. Fed.
236 B5 Okiep S. Africa
124 □1 Okinawa Okinawa Japan
124 □1 Okinawa i. Japan
124 □ Okinawa pref. Japan
Okinawa-guntō is Japan see Okinawa-shotō
124 □D20 Okinawa-shotō is Japan
121 N7 Okino-Daitō-jima i. Japan
124 □F19 Okinoerabu-jima i. Nansei-shotō Japan
126 B7 Okino-shima i. Japan
125 H12 Okino-shima i. Japan
125 J14 Okino-shima i. Japan
121 O7 Okino-Tori-shima i. Japan
125 J10 Oki-shotō is Japan
229 G5 Okitipupa Nigeria
118 B6 Okkan Myanmar
261 G8 Oklahoma state U.S.A.
261 G8 Oklahoma City OK U.S.A.
255 G11 Oklawaha r. FL U.S.A.
244 E5 Okmok sea feature N. Pacific Ocean
261 G8 Okmulgee OK U.S.A.
199 L3 Okna r. Slovakia
Oknitsa Moldova see Ocniţa
225 H4 Oko, Wadi watercourse Sudan
199 G4 Okoč Slovakia
229 H5 Okola Cameroon
261 K8 Okolona MS U.S.A.
256 A7 Okolona OH U.S.A.
234 B4 Okombache Namibia
230 B5 Okondja Gabon
196 E2 Okonek Pol.
197 L4 Okopy Pol.
199 G6 Okor r. Hungary
246 H5 Okotoks Alta Can.
234 A3 Okotusu well Namibia
161 P7 Okovskiy Les for. Rus. Fed.
230 B5 Okoyo Congo
142 D5 Okpan, Gora hill Kazakh.
143 S4 Okpekty, Gora mt. Kazakh.
198 E2 Okříšky Czech Rep.
198 E2 Okrouhlice Czech Rep.
197 K4 Okrzeja Pol.
197 I5 Oksa Pol.
164 E6 Oksbøl Denmark
162 Q1 Øksfjord Norway
161 X7 Okskiy Zapovednik nature res. Rus. Fed.
156 G3 Oksovskiy Rus. Fed.
162 M3 Oksskolten mt. Norway
Oktemberyan Armenia see Armavir
220 F4 Oktonia Greece
144 E1 Oktumgum des. Turkm.
118 C5 Oktwin Myanmar
Oktyabr' Aktyubinskaya Oblast' Kazakh. see Kandyagash
161 U4 Oktyabr' Rus. Fed.
Oktyabr'sk Kazakh. see Kandyagash
142 C1 Oktyabr'sk Rus. Fed.
Oktyabr'skaya Belarus see Aktsyabrskaya
159 S7 Oktyabr'skaya Rus. Fed.
Oktyabr'skiy Homyel'skaya Voblasts' Belarus see Aktsyabrski
Oktyabr'skiy Vitsyebskaya Voblasts' Belarus see Aktsyabrski
142 J1 Oktyabr'skiy Kazakh.
122 F2 Oktyabr'skiy Amurskaya Oblast' Rus. Fed.
122 F2 Oktyabr'skiy Amurskaya Oblast' Rus. Fed.
156 H3 Oktyabr'skiy Arkhangel'skaya Oblast' Rus. Fed.
159 P3 Oktyabr'skiy Belgorodskaya Oblast' Rus. Fed.
161 X4 Oktyabr'skiy Ivanovskaya Oblast' Rus. Fed.
161 T7 Oktyabr'skiy Kaluzhskaya Oblast' Rus. Fed.
153 Q4 Oktyabr'skiy Kamchatskaya Oblast' Rus. Fed.
159 R8 Oktyabr'skiy Krasnodarskiy Kray Rus. Fed.
156 F2 Oktyabr'skiy Murmanskaya Oblast' Rus. Fed.
Oktyabr'skiy Respublika Adygeya Rus. Fed. see Takhtamukay
157 K5 Oktyabr'skiy Respublika Bashkortostan Rus. Fed.
159 S6 Oktyabr'skiy Rostovskaya Oblast' Rus. Fed.
161 V7 Oktyabr'skiy Ryazanskaya Oblast' Rus. Fed.
161 W8 Oktyabr'skiy Ryazanskaya Oblast' Rus. Fed.
156 L4 Oktyabr'skiy Sverdlovskaya Oblast' Rus. Fed.
157 H7 Oktyabr'skiy Volgogradskaya Oblast' Rus. Fed.
142 K1 Oktyabr'skoye Kazakh.
142 J1 Oktyabr'skoye Chelyabinskaya Oblast' Rus. Fed.
152 H3 Oktyabr'skoye Khanty-Mansiyskiy Avtonomnyy Okrug Rus. Fed.
161 W9 Oktyabr'skoye Lipetskaya Oblast' Rus. Fed.
142 F1 Oktyabr'skoye Orenburgskaya Oblast' Rus. Fed.
151 F2 Oktyabr'skoye Respublika Severnaya Osetiya-Alaniya Rus. Fed.
122 G5 Oktyabr'skoye Yevreyskaya Avtonomnaya Oblast' Rus. Fed.
153 K2 Oktyabr'skoy Revolyutsii, Ostrov i. Severnaya Zemlya Rus. Fed.
124 □1 Oku Okinawa Japan
210 F3 Okučani Croatia

126 E3 Okuchi Japan
125 H14 Ōkuchi Japan
161 Q3 Okulovka Rus. Fed.
151 C3 Ok'umi Georgia
Okureshi Georgia see Oqureshi
103 C10 Okuru South I. N.Z.
126 G4 Oku-sangai-dake mt. Japan
124 Q4 Okushiri-kaikyō sea chan. Japan
124 Q4 Okushiri-tō i. Japan
229 F4 Okuta Nigeria
127 J1 Okutadami-ko resr Japan
127 J4 Okutama Japan
127 J4 Okutama-ko l. Japan
126 B4 Okutango-hantō pen. Japan
127 J2 Okutone-ko resr Japan
126 G4 Ōkuwa Japan
234 E4 Okwa watercourse Botswana
153 Q4 Ola Rus. Fed.
261 I8 Ola AR U.S.A.
285 F3 Olaeta Arg.
162 □B1 Ólafsvík Iceland
208 B2 Olague Spain
135 □1 Olahali i. N. Male Maldives
160 G5 Olaine Latvia
136 F6 Olakkur Tamil Nadu India
204 D9 Olalhas Port.
183 I7 Olan, Pic d' mt. France
264 N5 Olancha CA U.S.A.
264 N5 Olancha Peak CA U.S.A.
266 □P10 Olanchito Hond.
165 N5 Öland i. Sweden
165 N4 Ölands norra udde pt Öland Sweden
165 M5 Ölands sodra udde pt Öland Sweden
162 U3 Olanga Rus. Fed.
183 B9 Olargues France
199 K5 Olari Romania
104 H5 Olary S.A. Austr.
104 H5 Olary watercourse S.A. Austr.
285 G4 Olascoaga Arg.
199 K3 Olaszliszka Hungary
260 H6 Olathe KS U.S.A.
136 E7 Olavakod Kerala India
285 G5 Olavarría Arg.
205 Q3 Olave Spain
162 □ Olav V Land reg. Svalbard
196 F5 Oława Pol.
205 P3 Olazti Spain
209 D7 Olba Spain
201 N5 Olbendorf Austria
193 H9 Olbernhau Ger.
193 K9 Olbersdorf Ger.
193 D8 Olbersleben Ger.
214 C6 Olbia Sardegna Italy
214 D6 Olbia, Golfo di b. Sardegna Italy
197 K5 Olbięcin Pol.
214 C6 Olbio-Tempio prov. Sardegna Italy
198 D2 Olbramovice Czech Rep.
199 K5 Olcea Romania
151 D4 Ölçek Turkey
151 C6 Ölçekli Turkey
153 P3 Ol'chan Rus. Fed.
195 K5 Olching Ger.
256 G5 Olcott NY U.S.A.
151 E5 Ölçülü Turkey
270 D2 Old Bahama Channel Bahamas/Cuba
173 J5 Old Basing Hampshire, England U.K.
136 G3 Old Bastar Chhattisgarh India
259 G4 Old Bridge NJ U.S.A.
172 H2 Oldbury West Midlands, England U.K.
169 H5 Oldcastle Ireland
108 H5 Old Cherrabun W.A. Austr.
172 E1 Old Colwyn Conwy, Wales U.K.
107 H7 Old Cork Qld Austr.
245 M2 Old Crow Y.T. Can.
245 M2 Old Crow r. Y.T. Can.
168 G12 Old Dailly South Ayrshire, Scotland U.K.
225 F5 Old Dongola Sudan
186 J3 Oldeberkoop Neth.
186 I4 Oldebroek Neth.
186 J2 Oldehove Neth.
163 H6 Oldeide Norway
186 I3 Oldemarkt Neth.
190 F4 Oldenbrok Ger.
190 F4 Oldenburg Ger.
190 K2 Oldenburg in Holstein Ger.
190 H3 Oldendorf Ger.
190 K4 Oldendorf (Luhe) Ger.
190 G2 Oldenswort Ger.
186 K4 Oldenzaal Neth.
162 P2 Olderdalen Norway
173 O4 Old Felixstowe Suffolk, England U.K.
109 F12 Oldfield r. W.A. Austr.
257 K5 Old Forge NY U.S.A.
258 D2 Old Forge PA U.S.A.
256 B7 Old Fort OH U.S.A.
255 □2 Old Fort Point New Prov. Bahamas
271 □2 Old Fort Point Montserrat
109 E9 Old Gidgee W.A. Austr.
171 M6 Oldham Greater Manchester, England U.K.
244 I4 Old Harbor AK U.S.A.
270 □ Old Harbour Jamaica
270 □ Old Harbour Bay Jamaica
169 E9 Old Head of Kinsale Ireland
193 D8 Oldisleben Ger.
245 K1 Old John Lake AK U.S.A.
172 H5 Oldland South Gloucestershire, England U.K.
171 R7 Old Leake Lincolnshire, England U.K.
259 K2 Old Lyme CT U.S.A.
242 G5 Oldman r. Alta Can.
258 E5 Oldman's Creek r. NJ U.S.A.
168 L8 Oldmeldrum Aberdeenshire, Scotland U.K.
231 F8 Old Mkushi Zambia
237 N7 Old Morley S. Africa
259 L2 Old Mystic CT U.S.A.
257 □O5 Old Orchard Beach ME U.S.A.
249 K4 Old Perlican Nfld and Lab. Can.
245 L2 Old Rampart AK U.S.A.
264 M6 Old River CA U.S.A.
271 □2 Old Road Antigua and Barbuda
169 I8 Old Ross Ireland
246 H5 Olds Alta Can.
259 K2 Old Saybrook CT U.S.A.
257 □O4 Old Speck Mountain ME U.S.A.
190 F1 Oldsum Ger.
169 J5 Oldtown Ireland
171 L5 Old Town Cumbria, England U.K.
256 C10 Oldtown KY U.S.A.
257 □Q4 Old Town ME U.S.A.
233 B5 Olduvai Gorge tourist site Tanz.
256 D8 Old Washington OH U.S.A.
258 F3 Oldwick NJ U.S.A.
247 J5 Old Wives Lake Sask. Can.
265 Q7 Old Woman Mountains CA U.S.A.
128 H2 Öldziyt Arhangay Mongolia
128 G3 Öldziyt Bayanhongor Mongolia
128 J4 Öldziyt Dundgovĭ Mongolia
Öldziyt Mongolia see Erdenemandal
Öldziyt Mongolia see Sayhandulaan
256 G6 Olean NY U.S.A.
197 K1 Olecko Pol.
204 F9 Oledo Port.
212 F4 Oleggio Italy
204 E9 Oleiros Port.
153 N3 Olekma r. Rus. Fed.
153 N3 Olekminsk Rus. Fed.
159 L2 Oleksandrivka Chernihivs'ka Oblast' Ukr.
159 P6 Oleksandrivka Dnipropetrovs'ka Oblast' Ukr.
159 P5 Oleksandrivka Donets'ka Oblast' Ukr.
159 O3 Oleksandrivka Kharkivs'ka Oblast' Ukr.
159 K5 Oleksandrivka Kirovohrads'ka Oblast' Ukr.
159 L5 Oleksandrivka Kirovohrads'ka Oblast' Ukr.
159 K6 Oleksandrivka Mykolayivs'ka Oblast' Ukr.

159 L7 Oleksandrivka Mykolayivs'ka Oblast' Ukr.
159 N8 Oleksandrivka Respublika Krym Ukr.
159 O7 Oleksandrivka Zaporiz'ka Oblast' Ukr.
Oleksandrivs'k Ukr. see Zaporizhzhya
159 M5 Oleksandriya Kirovohrads'ka Oblast' Ukr.
158 F3 Oleksandriya Rivnens'ka Oblast' Ukr.
159 Q5 Oleksiyevo-Druzhkivka Ukr.
159 M7 Oleksiyivka Khersons'ka Oblast' Ukr.
159 R4 Oleksiyivka Luhans'ka Oblast' Ukr.
159 M8 Oleksiyivka Respublika Krym Ukr.
156 I2 Olema Rus. Fed.
187 G6 Olen Belgium
164 B2 Ølen Norway
156 F1 Olenegorsk Rus. Fed.
153 M3 Olenek Rus. Fed.
153 M2 Olenek r. Rus. Fed.
Olenek Bay Rus. Fed. see Olenekskiy Zaliv
153 N2 Olenekskiy Zaliv b. Rus. Fed.
Ölengti r. Kazakh. see Olenti
161 Q5 Olenino Rus. Fed.
156 F2 Olenitsa Rus. Fed.
159 Q6 Olenivka Ukr.
Olenivs'ki Kar"yery Ukr. see Dokuchayevs'k
152 I2 Oleniy, Ostrov i. Rus. Fed.
142 E3 Olenti r. Kazakh.
129 N1 Olentuy Rus. Fed.
143 P1 Olenty r. Kazakh.
Olenya Rus. Fed. see Olenegorsk
184 B4 Oléron, Île d' i. France
208 I4 Olesa de Montserrat Spain
Oleshky Ukr. see Tsyurupyns'k
159 K2 Oleshnya Chernihivs'ka Oblast' Ukr.
159 N3 Oleshnya Sums'ka Oblast' Ukr.
158 D4 Oles'ko Ukr.
196 F4 Oleśnica Dolnośląskie Pol.
197 J5 Oleśnica Świętokrzyskie Pol.
197 I5 Olesno Małopolskie Pol.
196 G5 Olesno Opolskie Pol.
197 L5 Oleszyce Pol.
214 C2 Oletta Corse France
185 I10 Olette France
117 L9 Olet Tongo mt. Sumbawa Indon.
158 G2 Olevs'k Ukr.
258 D4 Oley PA U.S.A.
191 D7 Olfen Ger.
162 M3 Ølfjellet mt. Norway
122 I7 Ol'ga Rus. Fed.
248 E3 Olga, Lac l. Que. Can.
106 C8 Olga, Mount N.T. Austr.
162 □ Olgastretet str. Svalbard
212 G4 Olginate Italy
159 R9 Ol'ginka Rus. Fed.
122 H2 Ol'ginsk Rus. Fed.
159 R8 Ol'ginskaya Krasnodarskiy Kray Rus. Fed.
159 S6 Ol'ginskaya Rostovskaya Oblast' Rus. Fed.
Olginskoye Rus. Fed. see Kochubeyevskoye
128 A2 Ölgiy Mongolia
168 I6 Olgrinmore Highland, Scotland U.K.
206 A2 Olhalvo Port.
206 D6 Olhão Port.
162 R4 Olhava Fin.
206 A2 Olho Marinho Port.
281 F2 Olhos d'Agua Brazil
135 □1 Olhuveli i. S. Male Maldives
106 C8 Olia Chain mts N.T. Austr.
208 H3 Oliana Spain
208 H3 Oliana, Embassament d' resr Spain
205 M9 Olías del Rey Spain
213 R7 Olib Croatia
210 E3 Olib i. Croatia
214 C7 Oliena Sardegna Italy
214 C7 Oliena r. Sardegna Italy
208 D5 Oliete Spain
234 C5 Olifants watercourse Namibia
236 C7 Olifants r. Western Cape S. Africa
236 G9 Olifants r. Western Cape S. Africa
235 F5 Olifants r. S. Africa
236 G3 Olifantshoek S. Africa
236 C8 Olifantsrivierberge mts S. Africa
215 N7 Oligastro Marina Italy
113 K5 Olimarao atoll Micronesia
Olimbos hill Cyprus see Olympos
Olimbos mt. Greece see Mytikas
280 C4 Olímpia Brazil
221 L6 Olimpos Beydağları Milli Parkı nat. park Turkey
269 I8 Olinalá Mex.
278 G3 Olinda Brazil
235 H3 Olinda, Ponta pt Moz.
107 J1 Olinda Entrance sea chan. Qld Austr.
235 H3 Olinga Moz.
163 M6 Olingsjövallen Sweden
107 I6 Olio Qld Austr.
208 H4 Oliola Spain
Öli Qoltyq Sory dry lake Kazakh. see Mertvyy Kultuk, Sor
Olisipo Port. see Lisboa
205 Q4 Olite Spain
285 F3 Oliva Arg.
215 Q9 Oliva r. Italy
209 E10 Oliva Spain
206 G3 Oliva hill Spain
282 C3 Oliva, Cordillera de mts Arg./Chile
206 F4 Oliva de la Frontera Spain
206 G3 Oliva de Mérida Spain
204 C6 Olival Port.
284 C2 Olivares, Cerro de mt. Arg./Chile
205 P9 Olivares de Júcar Spain
256 B10 Olive Hill KY U.S.A.
264 K2 Olivehurst CA U.S.A.
281 E4 Oliveira Brazil
204 D7 Oliveira de Azeméis Port.
204 D7 Oliveira de Frades Port.
204 D7 Oliveira do Bairro Port.
204 E8 Oliveira do Conde Port.
204 C6 Oliveira do Douro Port.
204 E8 Oliveira do Hospital Port.
278 E5 Oliveira dos Brejinhos Brazil
Olivença Moz. see Lupilichi
Olivença-a-Nova Angola see Capunda Cavilongo
215 P5 Olivento r. Italy
206 E3 Olivenza r. Port./Spain
206 E3 Olivenza Spain
206 E3 Olivenza, Llanos de plain Spain
246 G5 Oliver B.C. Can.
217 I7 Oliveri Sicilia Italy
247 K3 Oliver Lake Sask. Can.
285 G3 Oliveros Arg.
178 C8 Olivet France
250 J7 Olivet MI U.S.A.
260 G4 Olivet SD U.S.A.
215 O6 Oliveto Citra Italy
215 Q6 Oliveto Lucano Italy
260 H3 Olivia MN U.S.A.
103 C11 Olivine Range mts South I. N.Z.
212 F2 Olivone Switz.
158 E4 Oliyiv Ukr.
129 J7 Oljoq Nei Mongol China
233 C6 Oljoro Wells Tanz.
163 I6 Øljuvatnet l. Norway
199 K2 Oľka Slovakia
199 K3 Oľka r. Slovakia
232 C5 Ol Kalou Kenya
Ölkeyek r. Kazakh. see Ul'kayak
157 H5 Ol'khi Rus. Fed.
157 G6 Ol'khovatka Rus. Fed.
161 W8 Ol'khovets Rus. Fed.
157 I6 Ol'khovka Rus. Fed.
197 H5 Olkusz Pol.
168 □N1 Ollaberry Shetland, Scotland U.K.
276 C3 Ollachea Peru
276 C5 Ollagüe Chile
276 C5 Ollagüe, Volcán vol. Bol.
214 C9 Ollastu r. Italy

171 O7 Ollerton Nottinghamshire, England U.K.
182 D5 Olliergues France
183 H10 Ollioules France
284 B2 Ollita, Cordillera de mts Arg./Chile
284 B2 Ollitas mt. Arg.
205 Q3 Ollo Spain
162 U5 Öllölä Fin.
214 C7 Ollolai Sardegna Italy
230 B5 Ollombo Congo
212 B3 Ollon Switz.
143 M7 Olmaliq Uzbek.
205 M5 Olmedilla de Roa Spain
214 A6 Olmedo Sardegna Italy
205 K6 Olmedo Spain
214 C2 Olmeta-di-Tuda Corse France
214 B4 Olmeto Corse France
285 F3 Olmos Arg.
274 B6 Olmos Peru
205 L3 Olmos de Ojeda Spain
Olmütz Czech Rep. see Olomouc
173 K3 Olney Milton Keynes, England U.K.
260 K6 Olney IL U.S.A.
258 A6 Olney MD U.S.A.
261 F9 Olney TX U.S.A.
209 D8 Olocau Spain
208 E6 Olocau del Rey Spain
122 A3 Olochi Rus. Fed.
165 K5 Olofström Sweden
143 L1 Ol'oinka Kazakh.
249 I3 Olomane r. Que. Can.
100 □6 Olomburi Malaita Solomon Is
198 G2 Olomouc Czech Rep.
198 G2 Olomoucký kraj admin. reg. Czech Rep.
212 G5 Olona r. Italy
161 P1 Olonets Rus. Fed.
161 Q1 Olonetskaya Vozvyshennost' hills Rus. Fed.
114 C4 Olongapo Luzon Phil.
117 K5 Olongliko Kalimantan Indon.
161 P1 Olonka r. Rus. Fed.
184 A2 Olonne-sur-Mer France
183 B10 Olonzac France
185 B8 Oloron, Gave d' r. France
185 C9 Oloron-Ste-Marie France
100 □2 Olosega i. American Samoa
Olosenga atoll American Samoa see Swains Island
208 J3 Olot Spain
142 J8 Olot Uzbek.
193 G10 Oloví Czech Rep.
210 G3 Olovo Bos.-Herz.
129 N1 Olovyannaya Rus. Fed.
264 □E13 Olowalu HI U.S.A.
153 Q3 Oloy r. Rus. Fed.
Oloy, Qatorkŭhi mts Asia see Alai Range
138 D9 Olpad Gujarat India
284 D2 Olpas Arg.
191 E8 Olpe Ger.
200 E5 Olperer mt. Austria
160 M8 Ol'sa r. Belarus
198 F2 Olšany Czech Rep.
198 G2 Olšany u Prostějova Czech Rep.
164 J2 Olsätter Sweden
199 G2 Olšava r. Czech Rep.
199 K3 Olšava r. Slovakia
191 F8 Olsberg Ger.
199 H2 Olše r. Czech Rep.
161 O7 Ol'sha Rus. Fed.
159 Q2 Ol'shanka Rus. Fed.
159 K6 Ol'shans'ke Ukr.
186 J4 Olst Neth.
197 K3 Olszanka Mazowieckie Pol.
196 F5 Olszanka Opolskie Pol.
197 K6 Olszany Pol.
197 J2 Olszewka Pol.
197 J2 Olszewo-Borki Pol.
196 G3 Olszówka Pol.
197 H5 Olsztyn Śląskie Pol.
197 I2 Olsztyn Warmińsko-Mazurskie Pol.
197 I2 Olsztynek Pol.
197 L3 Olszyn Pol.
196 D4 Olszyna Pol.
219 M7 Olt r. Romania
284 D2 Olta Arg.
283 C6 Olte, Sierra de mts Arg.
164 C3 Oltedal Norway
212 D1 Olten Switz.
219 O6 Oltenița Romania
219 M6 Olteț r. Romania
219 P6 Oltina Romania
142 H6 Oltinko'l Uzbek.
Oltinkŭl Uzbek. see Oltinko'l
145 M1 Oltintopkan Tajik.
149 J3 Oltu Turkey
151 C5 Oltu r. Turkey
131 M8 Oluan Pi c. Taiwan
135 □1 Olugiri i. N. Male Maldives
151 D5 Oluklu Turkey
207 O6 Olula del Río Spain
151 D5 Olur Turkey
114 D8 Olutanga i. Phil.
205 Q5 Ólvega Spain
208 F3 Olvena Spain
207 I7 Olvera Spain
172 G4 Olveston South Gloucestershire, England U.K.
Ol'viopol' Ukr. see Pervomays'k
158 E3 Olyka Ukr.
161 V9 Olym r. Rus. Fed.
Olymbos hill Cyprus see Olympos
220 C5 Olympia tourist site Greece
262 C3 Olympia WA U.S.A.
220 E2 Olympiada Greece
262 C3 Olympic National Park WA U.S.A.
150 B3 Olympos hill Cyprus
221 L6 Olympos tourist site Turkey
220 D2 Olympou, Ethnikos Drymos nat. park Greece
Olympus, Mount Greece see Mytikas
262 C3 Olympus, Mount WA U.S.A.
159 R2 Olymskiy Rus. Fed.
258 D2 Olyphant PA U.S.A.
159 K2 Olyshivka Ukr.
153 R3 Olyutorskiy Rus. Fed.
153 S4 Olyutorskiy, Mys c. Rus. Fed.
153 R4 Olyutorskiy Zaliv b. Rus. Fed.
214 C7 Olzai Sardegna Italy
143 O2 Olzhabay Batyr Kazakh.
Olzheras Rus. Fed. see Mezhdurechensk
133 F10 Oma Xizang China
124 R5 Ōma Japan
156 I2 Oma r. Rus. Fed.
127 G3 Ōmachi Japan
127 H6 Omaezaki Japan
127 H6 Omae-zaki pt Japan
124 R7 Ōmagari Japan
169 H3 Omagh Northern Ireland U.K.
274 C6 Omaguas Peru
260 H5 Omaha NE U.S.A.
260 G4 Omaha Indian Reservation res. NE U.S.A.
234 C4 Omaheke admin. reg. Namibia
102 K7 Omakere North I. N.Z.
151 G3 Omalo Georgia
151 G3 Omalo Georgia
122 J2 Omal'skiy Khrebet mts Rus. Fed.
136 F7 Omalur Tamil Nadu India
127 J3 Ōmama Japan
147 K6 Oman country Asia
147 M3 Oman, Gulf of Asia
234 B4 Omangambo Namibia
102 H2 Omapere, Lake North I. N.Z.
103 D11 Omarama South I. N.Z.
219 O8 Omarchevo Bulg.
210 F3 Omarska Bos.-Herz.
234 B4 Omaruru Namibia
276 A3 Omas Peru
234 D3 Omatako watercourse Namibia
276 C4 Omate Peru
234 B4 Omatjette Namibia
236 G1 Omaweneno Botswana
124 R5 Ōma-zaki c. Japan
Omba i. Vanuatu see Aoba
115 D8 Ombai, Selat sea chan. Indon.
Ombalantu Namibia see Uutapi
230 C3 Ombella-Mpoko pref. C.A.R.
172 H3 Ombersley Worcestershire, England U.K.
229 H5 Ombessa Cameroon
Ombetsu Japan see Onbetsu
234 B3 Ombika waterhole Namibia
116 B4 Ombolata Indon.
230 A5 Omboué Gabon
214 G2 Ombrone r. Italy
133 H11 Ombu Xizang China
285 I3 Ombúes de Lavalle Uru.
151 C6 Omcalı Turkey
236 H6 Omdraaisvlei S. Africa
225 G6 Omdurman Sudan
127 J4 Ōme Japan
269 K7 Omealca Mex.
169 J4 Omeath Ireland
160 K3 Omedu Estonia
212 E4 Omegna Italy
159 M4 Omel'nyk Poltavs'ka Oblast' Ukr.
159 O6 Omel'nyk Zaporiz'ka Oblast' Ukr.
159 N8 Omelyanivka Ukr.
224 D5 Omena well Chad
105 K7 Omeo Vic. Austr.
256 B4 Omer MI U.S.A.
221 K3 Ömerler Turkey
204 D2 O Mesón do Vento Spain
214 C3 Omessa Corse France
266 □Q12 Ometepe, Isla de i. Nic.
269 I9 Ometepec Mex.
169 B5 Omey Island Ireland
118 D6 Omgoy Wildlife Reserve nature res. Thai.
225 H6 Om Hajēr Eritrea
127 H3 Omi Japan
127 G1 Ōmi Niigata Japan
126 D5 Ōmi Shiga Japan
144 C6 Omīdīyeh Iran
127 M4 Omigawa Japan
126 D5 Ōmihachiman Japan
103 G10 Omihi South I. N.Z.
Omilo Georgia see Omalo
246 E3 Omineca Mountains B.C. Can.
246 E4 Omineca Provincial Park B.C. Can.
142 D6 Omirzak Kazakh.
210 F4 Omiš Croatia
213 R5 Omišalj Croatia
125 I12 Ōmi-shima i. Japan
234 C4 Omitara Namibia
269 H8 Omitlán r. Mex.
127 L2 Ōmiya Ibaraki Japan
126 B4 Ōmiya Kyōto Japan
126 D7 Ōmiya Mie Japan
127 K4 Ōmiya Saitama Japan
245 N4 Ommaney, Cape AK U.S.A.
164 E6 Omme r. Denmark
190 J1 Ommel Denmark
186 J3 Ommen Neth.
129 K3 Ömnödelger Hentiy Mongolia
128 I5 Ömnögovĭ prov. Mongolia
214 C7 Omodeo, Lago l. Sardegna Italy
127 K3 Omōi-gawa r. Japan
229 G5 Omoko Nigeria
220 D3 Omolio Greece
153 R3 Omolon Rus. Fed.
153 Q3 Omolon r. Rus. Fed.
232 B3 Omo National Park Eth.
128 G5 Omon Gol watercourse China
124 R7 Omono-gawa r. Japan
178 I4 Omont France
124 R7 Ōmori Japan
204 C3 O Mosteiro Galicia Spain
127 L1 Omotegō Japan
232 C3 Omo Wenz r. Eth.
231 B9 Ompupa Angola
144 H4 'Omrānī Iran
250 F5 Omro WI U.S.A.
152 I4 Omsk Rus. Fed.
153 Q3 Omsukchan Rus. Fed.
124 T2 Ōmū Japan
118 D3 O-mu Myanmar
219 N5 Omu, Vârful mt. Romania
229 G4 Omu-Aran Nigeria
197 J2 Omulew r. Pol.
197 I2 Omulew, Jezioro l. Pol.
229 G5 Omuo Nigeria
125 G14 Ōmura Japan
125 G14 Ōmura-wan b. Japan
127 J6 Ōmuro-yama hill Japan
127 I5 Ōmuro-yama mt. Japan
127 J4 Ōmuro-yama mt. Japan
219 O7 Omurtag Bulg.
234 B3 Omusati admin. reg. Namibia
125 H13 Ōmuta Japan
156 K4 Omutninsk Rus. Fed.
205 N3 Oña Spain
124 S8 Onagawa Japan
Onaght Ireland see Eoghanacht
102 K5 Onakuri, Lake North I. N.Z.
250 C6 Onalaska WI U.S.A.
248 C3 Onaman Lake Ont. Can.
260 I2 Onamia MN U.S.A.
100 □4a Onamue i. Chuuk Micronesia
257 J11 Onancock VA U.S.A.
115 A5 Onang Sulawesi Barat Indon.
230 A5 Onangué, Lac l. Gabon
214 C7 Onani Sardegna Italy
214 H2 Onano Italy
248 D4 Onaping Lake Ont. Can.
250 F9 Onarga IL U.S.A.
249 G3 Onatchiway, Lac l. Que. Can.
205 P2 Oñati Spain
266 E3 Onavas Mex.
260 G4 Onawa IA U.S.A.
251 J4 Onaway MI U.S.A.
124 U4 Onbetsu Japan
119 C7 Onbingwin Myanmar
205 P5 Oncala Spain
205 P5 Oncala, Puerto de pass Spain
285 F2 Oncativo Arg.
170 I5 Onchan Isle of Man
231 B9 Oncócua Angola
150 H2 Öncül Turkey
209 E8 Onda Spain
Ondal W. Bengal India see Andal
234 B3 Ondangwa Namibia
209 F10 Ondara Spain
205 P2 Ondarroa Spain
199 K3 Ondava r. Slovakia
236 E6 Onderstedorings S. Africa
231 B9 Ondjiva Angola
229 G5 Ondo Nigeria
229 G5 Ondo state Nigeria
129 L3 Öndörhaan Mongolia
129 Q4 Ondor Had Nei Mongol China
Öndörhushuu Mongolia see Bulgan
128 A3 Ondorkara Xinjiang China
128 I6 Ondor Mod Nei Mongol China
129 K4 Öndörshil Mongolia
129 M5 Ondor Sum Nei Mongol China
128 G2 Öndör-Ulaan Mongolia
156 F3 Ondozero Rus. Fed.
185 B8 Ondres France
234 D4 One Botswana
135 D11 One and a Half Degree Channel Maldives
107 J3 One and a Half Mile Opening sea chan. Qld Austr.
One Arm Point W.A. Austr. see Bardi
259 L1 Oneco CT U.S.A.
156 G3 Onega Rus. Fed.
156 G3 Onega r. Rus. Fed.
Onega, Lake Rus. Fed. see Onezhskoye Ozero
Onega Bay g. Rus. Fed. see Onezhskaya Guba
212 E8 Oneglia Italy
One Hundred and Fifty Mile House B.C. Can. see 150 Mile House
One Hundred Mile House B.C. Can. see 100 Mile House
257 J5 Oneida NY U.S.A.
258 C3 Oneida PA U.S.A.
257 J5 Oneida Lake NY U.S.A.
260 F4 O'Neill NE U.S.A.
102 G7 Onekaka South I. N.Z.
250 H5 Onekama MI U.S.A.
153 Q5 Onekotan, Ostrov i. Kuril'skiye O-va Rus. Fed.
100 □3a Onemak i. Kwajalein Marshall Is
255 D9 Oneonta AL U.S.A.
257 J6 Oneonta NY U.S.A.
100 □6 Onepusu Malaita Solomon Is
103 □3 Oneroa i. Rarotonga Cook Is
102 J3 Oneroa North I. N.Z.
185 B7 Onesse-et-Laharie France
219 O4 Onești Romania
183 B8 Onet-le-Château France
101 □8a Onevai i. Tonga
156 F2 Onezhskaya Guba g. Rus. Fed.
161 S1 Onezhskiy Kanal canal Rus. Fed.
152 E3 Onezhskoye Ozero l. Rus. Fed.
156 F3 Onezhskoye Ozero l. Rus. Fed.
139 I9 Ong r. India
230 B5 Onga Gabon
234 B3 Ongandjera Namibia
102 K6 Ongaonga North I. N.Z.
119 G10 Ông Đốc, Sông r. Vietnam
231 E6 Ongeri Dem. Rep. Congo
236 H5 Ongers watercourse S. Africa
109 E12 Ongerup W.A. Austr.
122 C4 Onggot Nei Mongol China
Ongi Mongolia see Uyanga
Ongi Mongolia see Sayhan-Ovoo
128 H4 Ongiyn Gol r. Mongolia
123 D10 Ongjin N. Korea
183 H8 Ongles France
Ongniud Qi Nei Mongol China see Wudan
136 G5 Ongole Andhra Prad. India
Ongon Mongolia see Bürd
230 C5 Ongonyi Congo
128 H6 Ongt Gol Nei Mongol China
Ongtüstik Qazaqstan Oblysy admin. div. Kazakh. see Yuzhnyy Kazakhstan
132 H1 Onguday Rus. Fed.
151 E3 Oni Georgia
168 F9 Onich Highland, Scotland U.K.
260 E3 Onida SD U.S.A.
214 D7 Onifai Sardegna Italy
214 C7 Oniferi Sardegna Italy
127 J3 Oniishi Japan
209 D10 Onil Spain
235 □I4 Onilahy r. Madag.
249 G3 Onistagane, Lac l. Que. Can.
229 G5 Onitsha Nigeria
234 C4 Onjati Mountain Namibia
Onjiva Angola see Ondjiva
127 L5 Onjuku Japan
162 U5 Onkamo Fin.
162 S5 Onkivesi l. Fin.
124 □1 Onna Okinawa Japan
124 □1 Onna-dake hill Okinawa Japan
178 G3 Onnaing France
100 □4a Onnang i. Chuuk Micronesia
153 O3 Onnes Rus. Fed.
101 □7 Ono i. Fiji
126 D4 Ōno Fukui Japan
127 M1 Ono Fukushima Japan
126 E5 Ōno Gifu Japan
124 R5 Ōno Hokkaidō Japan
126 A6 Ono Hyōgo Japan
258 B4 Ono PA U.S.A.
125 I13 Onoda Japan
127 J7 Ōnohara-jima i. Japan
125 Q12 Ōnohara-jima i. Japan
99 I4 Ono-i-Lau i. Fiji
125 H13 Ōnojō Japan
125 K12 Onomichi Japan
Onon atoll Micronesia see Namonuito
Onon Mongolia see Binder
129 N1 Onon r. Rus. Fed.
129 M2 Onon Gol r. Mongolia
122 M3 Onor Rus. Fed.
122 M3 Onor, Gora mt. Sakhalin Rus. Fed.
99 H2 Onotoa atoll Gilbert Is Kiribati
204 C4 Ons, Illa de i. Spain
125 G11 Onsan S. Korea
236 D4 Onseepkans S. Africa
208 C2 Onsella r. Spain
192 E1 Ønslev Denmark
108 C6 Onslow W.A. Austr.
103 D12 Onslow, Lake South I. N.Z.
255 I8 Onslow Bay NC U.S.A.
122 F7 Onsŏng N. Korea
194 F5 Onstmettingen Ger.
186 L2 Onstwedde Neth.
126 F4 Ontake-san vol. Japan
207 P3 Ontalafia, Laguna de l. Spain
245 O2 Ontaratue r. N.W.T. Can.
247 N5 Ontario prov. Can.
264 O7 Ontario CA U.S.A.
262 F4 Ontario OR U.S.A.
250 D6 Ontario WI U.S.A.
251 Q6 Ontario, Lake Can./U.S.A.
258 D4 Ontelaunee, Lake PA U.S.A.
Onteniente Spain see Ontinyent
208 F4 Ontiñena Spain
209 D10 Ontinyent Spain
162 T4 Ontojärvi l. Fin.
250 E3 Ontonagon MI U.S.A.
100 □6 Ontong Java Atoll Solomon Is
209 C10 Ontur Spain
159 M5 Onufriyivka Ukr.
197 M1 Onuškis Lith.
Onutu atoll Gilbert Is Kiribati see Onotoa
275 H3 Onverwacht Suriname
264 N6 Onyx CA U.S.A.
181 N6 Onzain France
204 I3 Onzonilla Spain
185 E10 Oô, Lac d' l. France
104 E2 Oodnadatta S.A. Austr.
232 E2 Oodweyne Somalia
127 G2 Ōoka Japan
264 □F13 'Ō'ōkala HI U.S.A.
169 F7 Oola Ireland
104 C4 Ooldea S.A. Austr.
104 C4 Ooldea Range hills S.A. Austr.
261 H7 Oologah Lake resr OK U.S.A.
186 F5 Ooltgensplaat Neth.
108 I3 Oombulg Aboriginal Reserve W.A. Austr.
108 I3 Oombulgurri W.A. Austr.
106 F6 Ooratippra r. N.T. Austr.
107 H6 Oorindi Qld Austr.
Oos-Londen S. Africa see East London
187 E6 Oostakker Belgium
255 E8 Oostanaula r. GA U.S.A.
187 D6 Oostburg Neth.
187 C6 Oostende Belgium
186 I4 Oostendorp Neth.
186 I5 Oosterbeek Neth.
186 G2 Oosterend Neth.
186 K3 Oosterhesselen Neth.
186 G5 Oosterhout Neth.
186 F5 Oosterland Neth.
186 E5 Oosterschelde est. Neth.
186 E5 Oosterscheldekering barrage Neth.
186 J3 Oosterwolde Neth.
187 E7 Oosterzele Belgium
179 J1 Oostham Belgium
186 G3 Oosthuizen Neth.
187 D6 Oostkamp Belgium
187 G6 Oostmalle Belgium
187 E6 Oost-Souburg Neth.
186 H4 Oostvaardersplassen nature res. Neth.
187 E7 Oost-Vlaanderen prov. Belgium
187 C7 Oostvleteren Belgium
186 H2 Oost-Vlieland Neth.
186 F5 Oostvoorne Neth.
186 G4 Oostzaan Neth.
Ootacamund Tamil Nadu India see Udagamandalam
186 K4 Ootmarsum Neth.
246 E4 Ootsa Lake B.C. Can.
246 E4 Ootsa Lake l. B.C. Can.
264 □C12 'Ōpae'ula r. HI U.S.A.
268 E1 Opal Mex.
230 E5 Opala Dem. Rep. Congo
196 E3 Opalenica Pol.
196 G2 Opalenie Pol.
199 L4 Ópályi Hungary
102 I5 Oparau North I. N.Z.
103 J7 Opari North I. N.Z.
232 B4 Opari Sudan
156 J4 Oparino Rus. Fed.
Oparo i. Îs Australes Fr. Polynesia see Rapa
248 D3 Opasatika r. Ont. Can.
248 D3 Opasatika Lake Ont. Can.
247 M4 Opasquia Ont. Can.
247 M4 Opasquia Provincial Park Ont. Can.
248 F3 Opataca, Lac l. Que. Can.
210 E3 Opatija Croatia
198 F2 Opatov Czech Rep.
198 E1 Opatovice nad Labem Czech Rep.
196 G5 Opatów Śląskie Pol.
197 J5 Opatów Świętokrzyskie Pol.
196 G4 Opatów Wielkopolskie Pol.
196 G4 Opatówek Pol.
197 I5 Opatowiec Pol.
197 J5 Opatówka r. Pol.
199 G2 Opava Czech Rep.
199 G1 Opava r. Czech Rep.
204 D4 O Pazo Spain
204 D2 O Pazo de Irixoa Spain
161 R3 Opechenskiy Posad Rus. Fed.
204 D3 O Pedrouzo Spain
186 J2 Opeinde Neth.
194 D2 Opel hill Ger.
255 E9 Opelika AL U.S.A.
261 I10 Opelousas LA U.S.A.
186 J2 Opende Neth.
285 H4 Open Door Arg.
248 E4 Opeongo Lake Ont. Can.
204 E4 O Pereiro de Aguiar Spain
194 H6 Opfenbach Ger.
194 F7 Opfikon Switz.
187 I6 Opglabbeek Belgium
262 K2 Opheim MT U.S.A.
186 I5 Opheusden Neth.
251 K3 Ophir Ont. Can.
103 D12 Ophir South I. N.Z.
116 D4 Ophir, Gunung vol. Indon.
215 L4 Opi Italy
230 E4 Opienge Dem. Rep. Congo
103 F11 Opihi r. South I. N.Z.
264 □G14 Opihikao HI U.S.A.
102 J7 Opiki North I. N.Z.
115 F5 Opin Seram Indon.
248 E2 Opinaca r. Que. Can.
248 E2 Opinaca, Réservoir resr Que. Can.
248 D2 Opinnagau r. Ont. Can.
183 J9 Opio France
149 L7 Opis tourist site Iraq
249 G2 Opiscotéo, Lac l. Que. Can.
159 N4 Opishnya Ukr.
186 I5 Oploo Neth.
201 L7 Oplotnica Slovenia
201 L7 Oplotnica r. Slovenia
118 D5 Op Luang National Park Thai.
186 G3 Opmeer Neth.
229 G5 Opobo Nigeria
160 L5 Opochka Rus. Fed.
198 F1 Opočno Czech Rep.
276 D4 Opoco Bol.
249 H2 Opocopa, Lac l. Que. Can.
197 I4 Opoczno Pol.
266 D3 Opodepe Mex.
187 I6 Opoeteren Belgium
196 F5 Opole Pol.
197 J4 Opole Lubelskie Pol.
196 F5 Opolskie prov. Pol.
102 H2 Opononi North I. N.Z.
158 C5 Oporets' Ukr.
204 C4 O Porriño Spain
Oporto Port. see Porto
102 L5 Opotiki North I. N.Z.
185 J10 Opoul-Périllos France
218 I5 Opovo Vojvodina Serbia
255 D10 Opp AL U.S.A.
193 K8 Oppach Ger.
124 S8 Oppa-wan b. Japan
162 J5 Oppdal Norway
213 K5 Oppeano Italy
163 H6 Oppedal Norway
Oppeln Pol. see Opole
194 E5 Oppenau Ger.
194 E2 Oppenheim Ger.
194 G4 Oppenweiler Ger.
215 P6 Oppido Lucano Italy
217 J7 Oppido Mamertina Italy
193 F7 Oppin Ger.
164 G1 Oppkuven hill Norway
163 J6 Oppland county Norway
201 K4 Opponitz Austria
262 F3 Opportunity WA U.S.A.
193 E9 Oppurg Ger.
219 L6 Oprișor Romania
213 P5 Oprtalj Croatia
219 M6 Optași-Măgura Romania
261 E7 Optima Lake OK U.S.A.
102 I2 Opua North I. N.Z.
102 I4 Opuatia North I. N.Z.
102 H6 Opunake North I. N.Z.
101 □9a Opunoho, Baie d' b. Moorea Fr. Polynesia
199 J5 Ópusztaszer Hungary
234 B3 Opuwo Namibia
187 F7 Opwijk Belgium
142 D4 Opytnoye Kazakh.
142 K6 Oqbaytal Uzbek.
Oqqal"a Uzbek. see Oqqal'a
142 H6 Oqqal'a Uzbek.
145 P2 Oqsu r. Tajik.
142 K8 Oqtosh Uzbek.
260 J5 Oquawka IL U.S.A.
266 D2 Oquitoa Mex.
257 □O4 Oquossoc ME U.S.A.
151 D3 Oqureshi Georgia
199 L4 Őr Hungary
142 H2 Or' r. Rus. Fed.
182 I3 Or, Le Mont d' mt. France
213 K3 Ora Italy
127 J3 Ōra Japan
162 P1 Øra Norway
164 G2 Øra nature res. Norway
185 C9 Oraàs France
270 □ Oracabessa Jamaica
265 V9 Oracle AZ U.S.A.
206 E3 Orada Port.
219 J3 Oradea Romania
184 G4 Oradour-sur-Glane France
184 F4 Oradour-sur-Vayres France
Orahovac Rahovec Kosovo see Rahovec
210 F3 Orahovica Croatia
138 G7 Orai Uttar Prad. India
265 V6 Oraibi AZ U.S.A.
265 V6 Oraibi Wash watercourse AZ U.S.A.
182 G3 Orain r. France
183 H9 Oraison France
162 R3 Orajärvi Fin.
Oral Kazakh. see Ural'sk
227 E2 Oran Alg.
282 D1 Orán Arg.
158 J2 Orane Ukr.
119 H8 O Rang Cambodia
139 N6 Orang Assam India
123 F8 Ŏrang N. Korea
105 L5 Orange N.S.W. Austr.
183 F8 Orange France
234 C6 Orange r. Namibia/S. Africa
264 O8 Orange CA U.S.A.
259 I2 Orange CT U.S.A.
261 I10 Orange TX U.S.A.
256 G10 Orange VA U.S.A.
275 I3 Orange, Cabo c. Brazil
259 H2 Orangeburg NY U.S.A.
255 G9 Orangeburg SC U.S.A.
270 D1 Orange Cay i. Bahamas
260 G4 Orange City IA U.S.A.
288 J8 Orange Cone sea feature S. Atlantic Ocean
259 G2 Orange County county NY U.S.A.
264 M5 Orange Cove CA U.S.A.
Orange Free State prov. S. Africa see Free State
259 G1 Orange Lake NY U.S.A.
255 G10 Orange Park FL U.S.A.
264 K3 Orangevale CA U.S.A.
248 D5 Orangeville Ont. Can.
258 C2 Orangeville PA U.S.A.
265 U2 Orangeville UT U.S.A.
267 O8 Orange Walk Belize
228 A4 Orango, Ilha de i. Guinea-Bissau
214 C7 Orani Sardegna Italy
114 C4 Orani Luzon Phil.
193 F7 Oranienbaum Ger.
192 H5 Oranienburg Ger.
Oranje r. Namibia/S. Africa see Orange
275 H4 Oranje Gebergte hills Suriname
186 K3 Oranjekanaal canal Neth.
234 C6 Oranjemund Namibia
236 I5 Oranjerivier S. Africa
271 □9 Oranjestad Aruba
271 □2 Oranjestad St Eustatius Neth. Antilles
237 M2 Oranjeville S. Africa
169 E6 Oranmore Ireland
109 J7 Orantjugurr, Lake salt flat W.A. Austr.
157 I7 Oranzherei Rus. Fed.
234 E4 Orapa Botswana
206 F6 Oraque r. Spain
103 F11 Orari r. South I. N.Z.
114 E5 Oras Samar Phil.
210 F3 Orašac Bos.-Herz.
114 E5 Oras Bay Samar Phil.
219 L5 Orăștie Romania
219 L5 Orăștioara de Sus Romania
Orașul Stalin Romania see Brașov
244 G4 Oratia, Mount AK U.S.A.
158 I4 Orativ Ukr.
100 □6 Orava P.N.G.
199 I2 Orava r. Slovakia
199 I2 Orava, Vodná nádrž resr Slovakia
162 Q5 Oravais Fin.
219 J5 Oravița Romania
199 I2 Oravská Lesná Slovakia
199 I2 Oravská Magura mts Slovakia
199 I2 Oravská Polhora Slovakia
103 B13 Orawia South I. N.Z.
183 B9 Orb r. France
212 F6 Orba r. Italy
209 E10 Orba Spain
204 C5 Orbacém Port.
133 E9 Orba Co l. China
164 G6 Ørbæk Denmark
178 G6 Orbais-l'Abbaye France
208 C2 Orbara Spain
212 D5 Orbassano Italy
212 B2 Orbe Switz.
212 B2 Orbe r. Switz.
219 N6 Orbeasca Romania
181 L3 Orbec France
214 G3 Orbetello Italy
214 G3 Orbetello, Laguna di lag. Italy
179 N7 Orbey France
185 J9 Orbieu r. France
204 I5 Orbigo r. Spain
256 H8 Orbisonia PA U.S.A.
105 L7 Orbost Vic. Austr.
165 N1 Örbyhus Sweden
204 F8 Orca Port.
245 K3 Orca Bay AK U.S.A.
286 V2 Orcadas research stn S. Orkney Is Antarctica
207 O5 Orce Spain
207 N4 Orcera Spain
182 J2 Orchamps-Vennes France
258 B6 Orchard Beach MD U.S.A.
265 X2 Orchard Mesa CO U.S.A.
138 G7 Orchha Madh. Prad. India
178 F3 Orchies France
275 E2 Orchila, Isla i. Venez.
238 □3e Orchilla, Punta pt El Hierro Canary Is
220 D4 Orchomenos Greece
197 H4 Orchów Pol.
196 G3 Orchowo Pol.
168 F10 Orchy r. Scotland U.K.
214 G2 Orcia r. Italy
213 N8 Orciano di Pesaro Italy
183 I7 Orcières France
182 B5 Orcival France
212 D5 Orco r. Italy
151 I5 Orconikidze Azer.
151 I6 Orconikidze Azer.
276 B2 Orcotuna Peru
264 L7 Orcutt CA U.S.A.
108 J3 Ord r. W.A. Austr.
260 F5 Ord NE U.S.A.
108 H4 Ord, Mount hill W.A. Austr.
Orda Kazakh. see Urda
156 L4 Orda Rus. Fed.
185 E8 Ordan-Larroque France
Órdenes Spain see Ordes
265 T4 Orderville UT U.S.A.
204 D2 Ordes Spain
208 F2 Ordesa y Monte Perdido, Parque Nacional de nat. park Spain
208 I2 Ordino Andorra
264 P7 Ord Mountain CA U.S.A.
215 P5 Ordona Italy
205 P3 Ordoñana Spain
285 F3 Ordoñez Arg.
129 L7 Ordos Nei Mongol China
108 J4 Ord River Dam W.A. Austr.
108 J3 Ord River Nature Reserve W.A. Austr.
Ordu Hatay Turkey see Yayladağı
148 H3 Ordu Ordu Turkey
151 H7 Ordubad Azer.
207 L6 Orduña mt. Spain
205 N2 Ordunte, Montes de mts Spain
260 D6 Ordway CO U.S.A.
Ordzhonikidze Georgia see Kharagauli
Ordzhonikidze Kazakh. see Denisovka
Ordzhonikidze Rus. Fed. see Vladikavkaz
159 M5 Ordzhonikidze Dnipropetrovs'ka Oblast' Ukr.
159 N6 Ordzhonikidze Dnipropetrovs'ka Oblast' Ukr.
Ordzhonikidzeabad Tajik. see Kofarnihon
Ordzhonikidzevskaya Rus. Fed. see Sleptsovskaya
151 C2 Ordzhonikidzevskiy Rus. Fed.
229 G5 Ore Nigeria
205 Q7 Orea Spain
204 D2 O Real Spain
275 G3 Orealla Guyana
163 M6 Oreälven r. Sweden
162 O5 Öreälven r. Sweden
264 N1 Oreana NV U.S.A.
100 □3a Oreba i. Kwajalein Marshall Is
163 L6 Örebäcken Sweden
165 L2 Örebro Sweden
165 K2 Örebro county Sweden
198 F2 Ořechov Czech Rep.
161 M3 Oredezh r. Rus. Fed.
258 D3 Orefield PA U.S.A.
199 H4 Öreg-Futóné hill Hungary
199 G5 Öreglak Hungary
250 E7 Oregon IL U.S.A.
260 H6 Oregon MO U.S.A.
256 B7 Oregon OH U.S.A.
250 E7 Oregon WI U.S.A.
262 D5 Oregon state U.S.A.
262 C4 Oregon City OR U.S.A.
165 O1 Öregrund Sweden
165 O1 Öregrundsgrepen b. Sweden
192 E1 Orehoved Denmark
Orekhi-Vydritsa Belarus see Arekhawsk
Orekhov Ukr. see Orikhiv
Orekhova Belarus see Arekhava
161 V6 Orekhovo-Zuyevo Rus. Fed.
Orekhovsk Belarus see Arekhawsk
143 V3 Orel' Kazakh.
161 T9 Orel Orlovskaya Oblast' Rus. Fed.
156 L4 Orel Permskaya Oblast' Rus. Fed.
159 N5 Orel' r. Ukr.
122 K1 Orel, Gora mt. Rus. Fed.
122 K2 Orel', Ozero l. Rus. Fed.
219 L9 Orelek mt. Bulg.
274 B5 Orellana prov. Ecuador
274 C6 Orellana Peru
207 I2 Orellana, Embalse de resr Spain
206 H2 Orellana la Vieja Spain
Orel Oblast admin. div. Rus. Fed. see Orlovskaya Oblast'
265 U1 Orem UT U.S.A.
Ore Mountains Czech Rep./Ger. see Erzgebirge
221 I5 Ören Muğla Turkey
221 K6 Ören Muğla Turkey
142 F2 Orenburg Rus. Fed.
Orenburg Oblast admin. div. Rus. Fed. see Orenburgskaya Oblast'
142 D2 Orenburgskaya Oblast' admin. div. Rus. Fed.
151 B5 Örence Turkey
221 K3 Örencik Turkey
194 B2 Orenhofen Ger.
285 H6 Orense Arg.
Orense Spain see Ourense
Orense prov. Galicia Spain see Ourense
Oreón, Dhíavlos sea chan. Greece see Oreon, Diavlos
220 D4 Oreon, Diavlos sea chan. Greece
Oreor Palau see Koror
Oreor i. Palau see Koror
103 B13 Orepuki South I. N.Z.
158 G3 Orepy Ukr.
208 C3 Orés Spain
219 N7 Oresh Bulg.
164 I4 Öresjön l. Sweden
164 H3 Öreskilsälven r. Sweden
221 H1 Orestiada Greece
Orestiás Greece see Orestiada
164 I6 Öresund str. Denmark/Sweden
Oretana, Cordillera mts Spain see Toledo, Montes de
103 C13 Oreti r. South I. N.Z.
102 I3 Orewa North I. N.Z.
187 H7 Oreye Belgium
229 G2 Orfane well Niger
220 E2 Orfanou, Kolpos b. Greece
105 K10 Orford Tas. Austr.
173 P3 Orford Suffolk, England U.K.
107 I1 Orford Bay Qld Austr.
173 P3 Orford Ness hd England U.K.
Orgañá Spain see Organyà
275 H3 Organabo Fr. Guiana
238 □3a Órganos, Punta de los pt La Gomera Canary Is
265 T9 Organ Pipe Cactus National Monument nat. park AZ U.S.A.
208 H3 Organyà Spain
205 M9 Orgaz Spain
178 D6 Orge r. France
182 H3 Orgelet France
178 C7 Orgères-en-Beauce France
Orgeyev Moldova see Orhei
213 K5 Orgiano Italy
Orgil Mongolia see Jargalant
207 M7 Orgiva Spain
183 G9 Orgon France
129 M5 Orgon Tal Nei Mongol China
214 C7 Orgosolo Sardegna Italy
199 I5 Orgovány Hungary
199 I5 Orgoványi park Hungary
161 X5 Orgtrud Rus. Fed.
145 M5 Orgūn Afgh.
199 I3 Őrhalom Hungary
221 J3 Orhaneli Turkey
221 K2 Orhangazi Turkey
221 J6 Orhaniye Turkey
221 I3 Orhanlar Turkey
158 H6 Orhei Moldova
128 H2 Orhon Bulgan Mongolia
128 I2 Orhon Mongolia
128 J1 Orhon Gol r. Mongolia
128 I2 Orhontuul Mongolia
208 C2 Orhy, Pic d' mt. France/Spain
217 N3 Oria Italy
207 O6 Oria Spain
208 A1 Oria r. Spain
204 C4 O Rial Spain
204 D4 O Ribeiro reg. Spain
237 O6 Oribi Gorge Nature Reserve S. Africa
156 J4 Orichi Rus. Fed.
257 □R3 Orient ME U.S.A.
259 K2 Orient NY U.S.A.
178 H7 Orient, Lac d' resr France
269 J6 Oriental Mex.
203 E5 Oriental prov. Morocco
276 D4 Oriental, Cordillera mts Bol.
274 C3 Oriental, Cordillera mts Col.
276 C3 Oriental, Cordillera mts Peru
285 G6 Oriente Arg.
276 D2 Oriente Rondônia Brazil
280 B5 Oriente São Paulo Brazil
259 K2 Orient Island NY U.S.A.
178 H4 Origny-en-Thiérache France
178 G7 Origny-le-Sec France
178 F4 Origny-Ste-Benoîte France
209 D11 Orihuela Spain
159 O6 Orikhiv Ukr.
220 A2 Orikum Albania
159 O4 Oril' r. Ukr.
159 P5 Oril'ka Ukr.
159 O5 Oril'ka r. Ukr.
248 E4 Orillia Ont. Can.
163 R6 Orimattila Fin.
262 L5 Orin WY U.S.A.
275 F3 Orinduik Falls Brazil/Guyana
275 F2 Orinoco r. Col./Venez.
275 F2 Orinoco Delta Venez.
208 A1 Orio Spain
206 D4 Oriola Port.
258 A2 Oriole PA U.S.A.
217 K3 Oriolo Italy
214 I3 Oriolo Romano Italy
163 Q6 Oripää Fin.
257 J5 Oriskany NY U.S.A.
139 J9 Orissa state India
160 G3 Orissaare Estonia
208 J4 Oristà Spain
214 B8 Oristano Sardegna Italy
214 B8 Oristano prov. Sardegna Italy
214 B8 Oristano, Golfo di b. Sardegna Italy
Oristown Ireland see Baile Órthaí
198 F5 Őriszentpéter Hungary
197 L6 Oriv Ukr.
163 R6 Orivesi Fin.
162 T5 Orivesi l. Fin.
275 H5 Oriximiná Brazil
269 J7 Orizaba Mex.
269 J6 Orizaba, Pico de vol. Mex.
269 I4 Orizatlán Mex.
280 C2 Orizona Brazil
Orjonikidze Georgia see Kharagauli
Orjonikidzeobod Tajik. see Kofarnihon
164 J5 Örkelljunga Sweden
199 I4 Örkény Hungary
Orkhey Moldova see Orhei
Orkhomenós Greece see Orchomenos
128 H3 Orkhon Valley tourist site Mongolia
237 K2 Orkney S. Africa
168 K5 Orkney admin. div. Scotland U.K.
166 F2 Orkney Islands Scotland U.K.
197 L3 Orla Pol.
196 E4 Orla r. Pol.
196 F2 Orla r. Pol.
261 D10 Orla TX U.S.A.
193 E9 Orlamünde Ger.
264 J2 Orland CA U.S.A.
280 D4 Orlândia Brazil
255 G11 Orlando FL U.S.A.
197 L3 Orlanka r. Pol.
279 C9 Orleaes Brazil
178 C7 Orléanais reg. France
178 C8 Orléans France
257 P7 Orleans MA U.S.A.
257 M4 Orleans VT U.S.A.
178 E7 Orléans, Canal d' France
249 G4 Orléans, Île d' i. Que. Can.
178 D8 Orléans, Val d' val. France
Orléansville Alg. see Chlef
185 E9 Orleix France
165 K3 Orlen l. Sweden
198 E1 Orlice r. Czech Rep.
199 I1 Orlich Gniazd, Park Krajobrazowy Pol.
198 F1 Orlické hory mts Czech Rep.
198 F1 Orlické hory park Czech Rep.
121 G1 Orlik Rus. Fed.
198 D2 Orlik, Vodní nádrž resr Czech Rep.
159 L2 Orlivka Chernihivs'ka Oblast' Ukr.
159 P7 Orlivka Zaporiz'ka Oblast' Ukr.
159 M8 Orlivs'ke Ukr.
210 F3 Orljava r. Croatia
156 J4 Orlov Rus. Fed.
199 H2 Orlová Czech Rep.
142 C2 Orlov Gay Rus. Fed.
159 T2 Orlovka Rus. Fed.
157 G6 Orlovo Rus. Fed.
161 T9 Orlovskaya Oblast' admin. Rus. Fed.
157 H7 Orlovskiy Rus. Fed.
159 O6 Orlyans'ke Ukr.
159 N5 Orlyk Ukr.
159 M9 Orlyne Ukr.
160 I5 Ormankalns hill Latvia
199 G6 Ormánság reg. Hungary
145 K9 Ormara Pak.
145 K9 Ormara, Ras hd Pak.
212 D7 Ormea Italy
199 J5 Örménykút Hungary
173 P2 Ormesby St Margaret Nor England U.K.
Ormília Greece see Ormyl
247 J5 Ormiston Sask. Can.
171 L2 Ormiston East Lothian, Scotland U.K.
114 E6 Ormoc Leyte Phil.
102 L5 Ormond North I. N.Z.
255 G11 Ormond Beach FL U.S.A.
201 N7 Ormož Slovenia
171 L6 Ormskirk Lancashire, Engl U.K.
257 L3 Ormstown Que. Can.
220 E2 Ormylia Greece
145 L8 Ornach Pak.
208 E3 Orna de Gállego Spain
179 I6 Ornain r. France
183 B10 Ornaisons France
182 I2 Ornans France
212 E4 Ornavasso Italy
195 J3 Ornbau Ger.
181 L4 Orne dept France
181 K3 Orne r. France
181 L5 Orne r. France
162 L3 Ørnes Norway
165 Q7 Orneta Pol.
165 O2 Ornö i. Sweden
185 H10 Ornolac-Ussat-les-Bains F
162 O5 Örnsköldsvik Sweden
160 F2 Örö i. Fin.
123 E8 Oro N. Korea
Oro r. Spain see Ouro
214 C3 Oro, Monte d' mt. Corse Fr
276 E3 Orobayaya Bol.
212 H3 Orobie, Alpi mts Italy
278 F4 Orocó Brazil
274 D3 Orocué Col.
228 D4 Orodara Burkina
Orodzholari Georgia see Orojolari
208 D2 Oroel, Peña de mt. Spain
262 F3 Orofino ID U.S.A.
128 G4 Orog Nuur salt l. Mongoli
264 O7 Oro Grande CA U.S.A.
263 K10 Orogrande NM U.S.A.
101 □9a Orohena mt. Tahiti Fr. Pol
151 E4 Orojolari Georgia
Orol Dengizi salt l. Kazakh./Uzbek. see Aral Se
213 L5 Orolo r. Italy
218 H5 Orom Vojvodina Serbia
232 C2 Oromīya admin. reg. Eth.
249 H4 Oromocto N.B. Can.
249 H4 Oromocto Lake N.B. Can.
150 D8 Oron Israel
229 H5 Oron Nigeria
99 I2 Orona atoll Phoenix Is Kiri
212 B2 Oron-la-Ville Switz.
257 □Q4 Orono ME U.S.A.
275 G4 Oronoque Guyana
275 G4 Oronoque r. Guyana
208 B1 Oronoz Spain
168 D10 Oronsay i. Scotland U.K.
197 I4 Orońsko Pol.
150 E4 Orontes r. Asia
alt. 'Āṣī (Lebanon),
alt. Asi (Turkey),
alt. 'Āṣī, Nahr al (Syria)
212 D4 Oropa Italy
274 C2 Orope Venez.
268 F7 Oropeo Mex.
205 J9 Oropesa Castilla-La Manch Spain
209 F7 Oropesa, Cabo de c. Spain
209 F7 Oropesa del Mar Valencia
271 □7 Oropuche r. Trin. and Tob.
Oroqen Zizhiqi Nei Mong China see Alihe
114 D7 Oroquieta Mindanao Phil.
205 Q3 Ororbia Spain
278 F3 Orós Brazil
278 F3 Orós, Açude resr Brazil
214 D7 Orosei Sardegna Italy
214 D7 Orosei, Golfo di b. Sardegr
199 J5 Orosháza Hungary
201 M8 Oroslavje Croatia
199 H4 Oroszlány Hungary
214 C7 Orotelli Sardegna Italy
100 □1 Orote Peninsula Guam
153 Q3 Orotukan Rus. Fed.
265 V9 Oro Valley AZ U.S.A.
264 K2 Oroville CA U.S.A.
262 E2 Oroville WA U.S.A.
264 K2 Oroville, Lake resr CA U.S.
183 H8 Orpierre France
129 Q2 Orqohan Nei Mongol Chin
250 B1 Orr MN U.S.A.
208 C1 Orreaga Navarra Spain
171 L6 Orrell Greater Manchester, England U.K.
214 B9 Orri, Monte hill Italy
208 H3 Orri, Tossal de l' mt. Spain
168 H7 Orrin r. Scotland U.K.
168 G7 Orrin Reservoir Scotland U
208 D6 Orrios Spain
164 H1 Orrkjølen hill Norway
214 C8 Orroli Sardegna Italy
104 G5 Orroroo S.A. Austr.
256 D8 Orrville OH U.S.A.
163 M6 Orsa Sweden
215 O5 Orsara di Puglia Italy
178 D6 Orsay France
198 F5 Őrség reg. Hungary
198 F5 Őrségi Tájvédelmi Körzet nature res. Hungary
184 H3 Orsennes France
161 N7 Orsha Belarus
161 T5 Orsha Rus. Fed.
156 I4 Orshanka Rus. Fed.
212 C5 Orsiera-Rocciavrè, Parco Naturale nature res. Italy
212 C3 Orsières Switz.
163 N6 Orsjön l. Sweden
142 H2 Orsk Rus. Fed.
192 E1 Ørslev Denmark
215 M3 Orsogna Italy
215 P8 Orsomarso Italy
219 K6 Orșova Romania
162 I5 Ørsta Norway
165 N2 Örsundaän r. Sweden
165 N2 Örsundsbro Sweden
212 E4 Orta, Lago d' l. Italy
221 J6 Ortaca Turkey
151 B4 Ortaköy Turkey
215 P5 Orta Nova Italy
150 B2 Orta Toroslar plat. Turkey
151 G1 Orta-Tyube Rus. Fed.
215 I3 Orte Italy
204 E1 Ortegal, Cabo c. Spain
274 C4 Orteguaza r. Col.
194 D5 Ortenau reg. Ger.
194 D5 Ortenberg Baden-Württem Ger.
191 H10 Ortenberg Hessen Ger.
195 O4 Ortenburg Ger.
201 O3 Orth an der Donau Austri
185 C9 Orthez France
163 L5 Ortholmen Sweden
206 H3 Ortiga r. Spain
205 O4 Ortigosa Spain
280 B6 Ortigueira Brazil
204 E1 Ortigueira Spain
204 E1 Ortigueira, Ría de inlet Sp
213 L2 Ortisei Italy
218 J5 Orţişoara Romania

Ortíz Mex.
Ortíz Venez.
Ortles *mt.* Italy
Ortoire *r.* Trin. and Tob.
Ortolo *r. Corse* France
Orton *Cumbria, England* U.K.
Ortona Italy
Orton Longueville *Peterborough, England* U.K.
Ortonville *MI* U.S.A.
Ortonville *MN* U.S.A.
Ortospana Afgh. *see* **Kābul**
Orto-Tokoy Kyrg.
Ortovera Italy
Ortrand Ger.
Örträsk Sweden
Ortucchio Italy
Ortueri *Sardegna* Italy
Örtülü Turkey *see* **Şenkaya**
Örtze *r.* Ger.
Oru Estonia
Orukuizu *i.* Palau
Orulgan, Khrebet *mts* Rus. Fed.
Orumbo Namibia
Orumbo Boka *hill* Côte d'Ivoire
Orūmīyeh Iran
Orūmīyeh, Daryācheh-ye *salt l.* Iran
Orune *Sardegna* Italy
Oruro Bol.
Oruro *dept* Bol.
Orusco Spain
Orust *i.* Sweden
Orūzgān Afgh.
Orval France
Orvalho Port.
Orvault France
Orvieto Italy
Orville Coast Antarctica
Orvilos *mts* Greece
Orvinio Italy
Orvin Land *reg.* Svalbard
Orwell *l. England* U.K.
Orwell *OH* U.S.A.
Orwell *VT* U.S.A.
Orwigsburg *PA* U.S.A.
Orxon Gol *r.* China
Oryakhovo Bulg.
Orynyn Ukr.
Oryol Rus. Fed. *see* **Orel**
Orz *r.* Pol.
Orzechowo Pol.
Orzesze Pol.
Orzeszkowo Pol.
Orzhiv Ukr.
Orzhytsya Ukr.
Orzhytsya *r.* Ukr.
Orzinuovi Italy
Orzola *Lanzarote* Canary Is
Orzyc *r.* Pol.
Orzyny Pol.
Orzysz Pol.
Orzysz, Jezioro *l.* Pol.
Os Norway
Oša *r.* Latvia
Osa *r.* Pol.
Osa Rus. Fed.
Osa, Península de *pen.* Costa Rica
Osa de Vega Spain
Osage *IA* U.S.A.
Osage *WV* U.S.A.
Osage *WY* U.S.A.
Osage *r. MO* U.S.A.
Osage City *KS* U.S.A.
Osaka Japan
Ōsaka Japan
Ōsaka *pref.* Japan
Osakarovka Kazakh.
Ōsakasayama Japan
Ōsaka-wan *b.* Japan
Osaro, Monte *mt.* Italy
Osasco Brazil
Ōsawano Japan
Osawatomie *KS* U.S.A.
Osawin *r. Ont.* Can.
Osbaldwick *York, England* U.K.
Os Blancos Spain
Osborn S. Africa
Osborn, Mount *AK* U.S.A.
Osborne *KS* U.S.A.
Osburg Ger.
Osburger Hochwald *mts* Ger.
Øsby Denmark
Osby Sweden
Oščadnica Slovakia
Oscar Fr. Guiana
Oscar II Land *reg.* Svalbard
Oscar Range *hills W.A.* Austr.
Oscawana Corners *NY* U.S.A.
Osceola *AR* U.S.A.
Osceola *IA* U.S.A.
Osceola *MO* U.S.A.
Osceola *NE* U.S.A.
Osceola *WI* U.S.A.
Oschatz Ger.
Oschersleben (Bode) Ger.
Oschiri *Sardegna* Italy
Oscoda *MI* U.S.A.
Os Dices Spain
Osdorf Ger.
Osečina *Osečina* Serbia
O Seixo Spain
Oseja de Sajambre Spain
Osek *Plzeňský kraj* Czech Rep.
Osek *Ústecký kraj* Czech Rep.
Ösel *i.* Estonia *see* **Hiiumaa**
Osensjøen *l.* Norway
Osera Spain
Osered' *r.* Rus. Fed.
Osetno Pol.
Ōseto Japan
Osetr *r.* Rus. Fed.
Ōse-zaki *pt* Japan
Ōse-zaki *pt* Japan
Osgoode *Ont.* Can.
Osgood Mountains *NV* U.S.A.
Osh Kyrg.
Osh *admin. div.* Kyrg.
Oshakati Namibia
Oshamambe Japan *see* **Oshamanbe**
Oshamanbe Japan
Oshana *admin. reg.* Namibia
Oshawa *Ont.* Can.
Oshika Japan
Ōshika Japan
Oshika-hantō *pen.* Japan
Oshikango Namibia
Oshikoto *admin. reg.* Namibia
Oshikuku Namibia
Ōshima *Niigata* Japan
Ōshima *Tōkyō* Japan
Ōshima *Toyama* Japan
Ō-shima *i.* Japan
Ō-shima *i.* Japan
Ō-shima *i.* Japan
Ō-shima *i.* Japan
Oshima-hantō *pen.* Japan
Oshimizu Japan
Oshin *r.* Nigeria
Oshino Japan
Oshivelo Namibia
Oshkosh *NE* U.S.A.
Oshkosh *WI* U.S.A.
Oshkur'ya Rus. Fed.
Oshmyany Belarus *see* **Ashmyany**
Oshnovīyeh Iran
Osh Oblast *admin. div.* Kyrg. *see* **Osh**
Oshogbo Nigeria
Oshper Rus. Fed.
Oshskaya Oblast' *admin. div.* Kyrg. *see* **Osh**
Oshtorān Kūh *mt.* Iran
Oshtorīnān Iran
Oshtro Kople *mt.* Kosovo
Oshun *state* Nigeria
Oshvor Rus. Fed.
Oshwe Dem. Rep. Congo
Ősi Hungary
Osica de Sus Romania
Osidda *Sardegna* Italy
Osie Pol.
Osięciny Pol.
196 G2 **Osieczna** *Pomorskie* Pol.
196 E4 **Osieczna** *Wielkopolskie* Pol.
196 D4 **Osiecznica** Pol.
197 H2 **Osiek** *Kujawsko-Pomorskie* Pol.
196 G2 **Osiek** *Pomorskie* Pol.
197 J5 **Osiek** *Świętokrzyskie* Pol.
197 J6 **Osiek Jasielski** Pol.
212 E7 **Osiglia** Italy
210 G3 **Osijek** Croatia
219 M8 **Osikovitsa** Bulg.
246 E3 **Osilinka** *r. B.C.* Can.
214 B6 **Osilo** *Sardegna* Italy
213 O9 **Osimo** Italy
196 D2 **Osina** Pol.
214 C8 **Osini** *Sardegna* Italy
129 K1 **Osinovka** Rus. Fed.
197 K4 **Osiny** Pol.
218 J6 **Osipaonica** *Smederevo* Serbia
Osipenko Ukr. *see* **Berdyans'k**
Osipovichi Belarus *see* **Asipovichy**
234 C4 **Osire** Namibia
138 D6 **Osiyan** *Rajasthan* India
237 O3 **Osizweni** S. Africa
196 G4 **Osjaków** Pol.
210 F3 **Osječenica** *mts* Bos.-Herz.
156 A3 **Ösjön** *l.* Sweden
260 I5 **Oskaloosa** *IA* U.S.A.
260 H6 **Oskaloosa** *KS* U.S.A.
165 M4 **Oskarshamn** Sweden
164 I5 **Oskarström** Sweden
251 S1 **Oskélanéo** *Que.* Can.
Öskemen Kazakh. *see* **Ust'-Kamenogorsk**
159 Q4 **Oskil** *r.* Ukr. *alt.* **Oskol (Rus. Fed.)**
157 G6 **Oskol** *r.* Rus. Fed. *alt.* **Oskil (Ukraine)**
193 L10 **Oskořínek** Czech Rep.
199 H4 **Öskü** Hungary
161 O2 **Oskuya** *r.* Rus. Fed.
199 H3 **Osľany** Slovakia
198 F2 **Oslava** *r.* Czech Rep.
198 F2 **Oslavany** Czech Rep.
197 K6 **Osława** *r.* Pol.
198 G4 **Osli** Hungary
164 G2 **Oslo** Norway
Oslo *airport* Norway *see* **Gardermoen**
164 G2 **Oslo** *county* Norway
114 D7 **Oslob** *Cebu* Phil.
164 G2 **Oslofjorden** *sea chan.* Norway
218 J9 **Oslomej** *Oslomej* Macedonia
191 K6 **Osloß** Ger.
205 N3 **Osma** Spain
136 E3 **Osmanabad** *Mahar.* India
148 G3 **Osmancık** Turkey
221 K2 **Osmaneli** Turkey
148 H5 **Osmaniye** Turkey
150 E1 **Osmaniye** *prov.* Turkey
136 F3 **Osmannagar** *Andhra Prad.* India
160 M2 **Os'mino** Rus. Fed.
165 N3 **Ösmo** Sweden
197 H3 **Osmolin** Pol.
160 G2 **Osmussaar** *i.* Estonia
191 F6 **Osnabrück** Ger.
Osnaburg *atoll Arch. des Tuamotu* Fr. Polynesia *see* **Mururoa**
Osnaburgh *Fife, Scotland* U.K. *see* **Dairsie**
196 C3 **Osno Lubuskie** Pol.
178 D5 **Osny** France
230 E5 **Oso** *r.* Dem. Rep. Congo
205 L7 **Oso** *mt.* Spain
199 G1 **Osoblaha** Czech Rep.
Osogbo Nigeria *see* **Oshogbo**
212 F3 **Osogna** Switz.
219 K8 **Osogovska Planina** *mts* Bulg./Macedonia
159 M6 **Osokorivka** Ukr.
213 O3 **Osoppo** Italy
213 Q6 **Osor** Croatia
210 E3 **Osor** *hill* Croatia
213 Q6 **Osor, Rt** *pt* Croatia
199 L4 **Oşorhei** Romania
279 C9 **Osório** Brazil
283 B6 **Osorno** Chile
205 L4 **Osorno** Spain
159 M2 **Osota** *r.* Ukr.
197 K1 **Osowa** Pol.
197 J3 **Osownica** *r.* Pol.
246 G5 **Osoyoos** *B.C.* Can.
164 B1 **Osøyri** Norway
214 C4 **Ospédale, Forêt de l'** *for. Corse* France
274 D2 **Ospino** Venez.
107 K2 **Osprey Reef** *Coral Sea Is Terr.* Austr.
186 I5 **Oss** Neth.
202 C3 **Ossa** *hill* Port.
105 K9 **Ossa, Mount** *Tas.* Austr.
206 D3 **Ossa, Serra de** *hills* Port.
207 N3 **Ossa de Montiel** Spain
213 J3 **Ossana** Italy
185 C9 **Ossau, Gave d'** *r.* France
185 D10 **Ossau, Vallée d'** *val.* France
185 E7 **Osse** *r.* France
229 G5 **Osse** *r.* Nigeria
185 C9 **Osse-en-Aspe** France
185 H11 **Osséja** France
187 F6 **Ossendrecht** Neth.
250 C5 **Osseo** *WI* U.S.A.
185 B9 **Ossès** France
171 N6 **Ossett** *West Yorkshire, England* U.K.
214 B6 **Ossi** *Sardegna* Italy
201 I6 **Ossiach** Austria
201 I6 **Ossiacher See** *l.* Austria
250 C6 **Ossian** *IA* U.S.A.
251 K5 **Ossineke** *MI* U.S.A.
259 H2 **Ossining** *NY* U.S.A.
257 □N5 **Ossipee** *NH* U.S.A.
257 □N5 **Ossipee Lake** *NH* U.S.A.
249 H2 **Ossokmanuan Lake** *Nfld and Lab.* Can.
153 R4 **Ossora** Rus. Fed.
115 E8 **Ossu** East Timor
185 D9 **Ossun** France
159 M4 **Ostap"ye** Ukr.
161 S6 **Ostashevo** Rus. Fed.
161 Q4 **Ostashkov** Rus. Fed.
196 G1 **Ostaszewo** Pol.
191 E6 **Ostbevern** Ger.
163 L6 **Østby** Norway
190 H3 **Oste** *r.* Ger.
190 D3 **Osteel** Ger.
213 L6 **Ostellato** Italy
190 H3 **Osten** Ger.
Ostend Belgium *see* **Oostende**
285 I5 **Ostende** Arg.
Ostende Belgium *see* **Oostende**
190 H2 **Ostenfeld (Husum)** Ger.
161 P7 **Oster** Rus. Fed.
161 P8 **Oster** *r.* Rus. Fed.
158 J3 **Oster** Ukr.
164 E5 **Øster Agger** Denmark
195 O4 **Osterbach** *r.* Ger.
192 E5 **Osterburg (Altmark)** Ger.
194 G3 **Osterburken** Ger.
190 I2 **Osterby** Ger.
165 N1 **Österbybruk** Sweden
165 L4 **Österbymo** Sweden
191 F6 **Ostercappeln** Ger.
163 L6 **Österdalälven** *l.* Sweden
165 M1 **Österfärnebo** Sweden
193 E8 **Osterfeld** Ger.
165 L3 **Östergotland** *county* Sweden
193 E8 **Osterhausen** Ger.
190 G2 **Osterhever** Ger.
195 O4 **Osterhofen** Ger.
190 H1 **Øster Højst** Denmark
190 G4 **Osterholz-Scharmbeck** Ger.
164 G5 **Øster Hurup** Denmark
200 G3 **Ostermiething** Austria
212 C2 **Ostermundigen** Switz.
193 F7 **Osternienburg** Ger.
201 I6 **Osternig** *mt.* Austria/Italy
191 J7 **Osterode am Harz** Ger.
Österreich *country* Europe *see* **Austria**
190 I2 **Osterrönfeld** Ger.
162 M5 **Östersund** Sweden
192 E1 **Øster Ulslev** Denmark
165 N1 **Östervåla** Sweden
164 G4 **Østervrå** Denmark
190 D5 **Osterwald** Ger.
193 E6 **Osterweddingen** Ger.
191 K7 **Osterwieck** Ger.
193 I9 **Osterzgebirge** *park* Ger.
164 C1 **Østese** Norway
194 G4 **Ostfildern** Ger.
164 H2 **Østfold** *county* Norway
190 D3 **Ostfriesische Inseln** *is* Ger.
190 E4 **Ostfriesland** *reg.* Ger.
190 E4 **Ostgroßefehn (Großefehn)** Ger.
165 O1 **Östhammar** Sweden
191 J10 **Ostheim vor der Rhön** Ger.
194 E2 **Osthofen** Ger.
215 I4 **Ostia** Italy
212 I5 **Ostiano** Italy
213 K5 **Ostiglia** Italy
205 Q3 **Ostiz** Spain
158 G2 **Ostky** Ukr.
195 N6 **Östliche Chiemgauer Alpen** *nature res.* Ger.
200 D5 **Östliche Karwendelspitze** *mt.* Austria/Ger.
164 I1 **Östmark** Sweden
199 J6 **Ostojićevo** *Vojvodina* Serbia
201 O1 **Ostopovice** Czech Rep.
194 G6 **Ostrach** Ger.
194 G5 **Ostrach** *r.* Ger.
162 P5 **Östra gloppet** *b.* Fin.
162 P5 **Östra Kvarken** *str.* Fin./Sweden
165 L4 **Östra Lägern** *l.* Sweden
164 I4 **Östra Nedsjön** *l.* Sweden
164 J6 **Östra Ringsjön** *l.* Sweden
164 I2 **Östra Silen** *l.* Sweden
193 H8 **Ostrau** *Sachsen* Ger.
193 F7 **Ostrau** *Sachsen-Anhalt* Ger.
199 H2 **Ostrava** Czech Rep.
199 H2 **Ostravice** Czech Rep.
199 I3 **Ostredok** *mt.* Slovakia
190 E4 **Ostrhauderfehn** Ger.
194 F3 **Östringen** Ger.
193 K8 **Ostritz** Ger.
197 H2 **Ostróda** Pol.
157 G6 **Ostrogozhsk** Rus. Fed.
158 F3 **Ostroh** Ukr.
197 J2 **Ostrołęka** Pol.
196 G2 **Ostromecko** Pol.
198 E1 **Ostroměř** Czech Rep.
196 E3 **Ostroróg** Pol.
198 B1 **Ostrov** Czech Rep.
219 P6 **Ostrov** *Constanța* Romania
219 Q6 **Ostrov** *Tulcea* Romania
160 L4 **Ostrov** Rus. Fed.
142 C5 **Ostrova Tyulen'i** *is* Kazakh.
Ostrovets Pol. *see* **Ostrowiec Świętokrzyski**
159 N8 **Ostrovs'ke** Ukr.
156 H4 **Ostrovskoye** Rus. Fed.
197 J5 **Ostrów** Pol.
Ostrow Pol. *see* **Ostrów Wielkopolski**
196 G4 **Ostrówek** *Łódzkie* Pol.
197 K4 **Ostrówek** *Lubelskie* Pol.
196 D2 **Ostrowice** Pol.
Ostrowiec *Świętokrzyskie* Pol. *see* **Ostrowiec Świętokrzyski**
196 E1 **Ostrowiec** *Zachodniopomorskie* Pol.
197 J5 **Ostrowiec Świętokrzyski** Pol.
197 H2 **Ostrowite** *Kujawsko-Pomorskie* Pol.
196 G3 **Ostrowite** *Wielkopolskie* Pol.
197 K4 **Ostrów Lubelski** Pol.
197 J3 **Ostrów Mazowiecka** Pol.
196 G3 **Ostrowo** *Kujawsko-Pomorskie* Pol.
Ostrowo *Wielkopolskie* Pol. *see* **Ostrów Wielkopolski**
196 F4 **Ostrów Wielkopolski** Pol.
197 H5 **Ostrowy nad Okszą** Pol.
197 J4 **Ostrożeń** Pol.
196 F4 **Ostrzeszów** Pol.
190 J3 **Oststeinbek** Ger.
200 F6 **Osttirol** *reg.* Austria
268 D7 **Ostula** Mex.
217 N2 **Ostuni** Italy
179 O6 **Ostwald** France
161 R4 **Osuga** *r.* Rus. Fed.
161 R5 **Osuga** *r.* Rus. Fed.
127 G6 **Ōsuka** Japan
251 S2 **O'Sullivan, Lac** *l. Que.* Can.
248 C3 **O'Sullivan Lake** *Ont.* Can.
220 A2 **Osum** *r.* Albania
219 M7 **Osŭm** *r.* Bulg.
125 H16 **Ōsumi-hantō** *pen.* Japan
125 H16 **Ōsumi-kaikyō** *sea chan.* Japan
124 □H16 **Ōsumi-shotō** *is* Japan
Osun *state* Nigeria *see* **Oshun**
207 I6 **Osuna** Spain
280 B4 **Osvaldo Cruz** Brazil
171 O5 **Oswaldkirk** *North Yorkshire, England* U.K.
171 M6 **Oswaldtwistle** *Lancashire, England* U.K.
250 F8 **Oswego** *IL* U.S.A.
261 H7 **Oswego** *KS* U.S.A.
256 I5 **Oswego** *NY* U.S.A.
259 F5 **Oswego** *r. NJ* U.S.A.
256 I5 **Oswego** *r. NY* U.S.A.
172 F2 **Oswestry** *Shropshire, England* U.K.
197 H5 **Oświęcim** Pol.
160 L5 **Osyno** Rus. Fed.
159 P7 **Osypenko** Ukr.
214 B3 **Ota** *Corse* France
126 D4 **Ota** Japan
127 J3 **Ōta** Japan
206 B2 **Ota** Port.
206 B2 **Ota** *r.* Port.
103 D12 **Otago** *admin. reg. South I.* N.Z.
103 E12 **Otago Peninsula** *South I.* N.Z.
Otahiti *i.* Fr. Polynesia *see* **Tahiti**
102 J6 **Otairi** *North I.* N.Z.
126 G4 **Ōtake** Japan
124 □G17 **O-take** *vol. Nansei-shotō* Japan
127 J4 **Ōtake-san** *mt.* Japan
127 L5 **Ōtaki** *Chiba* Japan
127 I4 **Ōtaki** *Saitama* Japan
102 J7 **Otaki** *North I.* N.Z.
103 C12 **Otama** *South I.* N.Z.
102 K6 **Otamauri** *North I.* N.Z.
142 K6 **O'tamurot** Uzbek.
143 P6 **Otar** Kazakh.
127 G2 **Otari** Japan
124 R3 **Otaru** Japan
198 G2 **Otaslavice** Czech Rep.
103 C13 **Otatara** *South I.* N.Z.
269 K7 **Otatitlán** Mex.
103 B13 **Otautau** *South I.* N.Z.
198 D2 **Otava** *r.* Czech Rep.
163 S6 **Otava** Fin.
274 B4 **Otavalo** Ecuador
234 C3 **Otavi** Namibia
127 L2 **Ōtawara** Japan
231 B9 **Otchinjau** Angola
Otdia *atoll* Marshall Is *see* **Wotje**
143 Q6 **Otegen Batyr** Kazakh.
205 Q3 **Oteiza** Spain
103 E11 **Otekaieke** *South I.* N.Z.
249 G1 **Otelnuc, Lac** *l. Que.* Can.
219 K5 **Oțelu Roșu** Romania
103 E11 **Otematata** *South I.* N.Z.
150 E2 **Ötençay** Turkey
160 J3 **Otepää** Estonia
160 J3 **Otepää kõrgustik** *hills* Estonia
162 O2 **Oteren** Norway
204 H5 **Otero de Bodas** Spain
205 L7 **Otero de Herreros** Spain
263 J13 **Oteros** *r.* Mex.
220 B2 **Oteševo** Macedonia
197 I5 **Otfinów** Pol.
173 M5 **Otford** *Kent, England* U.K.
128 E3 **Otgon Tenger Uul** *mt.* Mongolia
179 J4 **Othain** *r.* France
178 F7 **Othe, Forêt d'** *for.* France
262 E3 **Othello** *WA* U.S.A.
220 A3 **Othonoi** *i.* Greece
220 D3 **Othrys** *mt.* Greece
229 F4 **Oti** *r.* Ghana/Togo
115 A4 **Oti** *Sulawesi* Indon.
229 F4 **Oti, Réserve de Faune de l'** *nature res.* Togo
199 G2 **Otice** Czech Rep.
194 E4 **Ötigheim** Ger.
237 P5 **Otimati** S. Africa
268 B1 **Otinapa** Mex.
103 F9 **Otira** *South I.* N.Z.
260 D5 **Otis** *CO* U.S.A.
257 I6 **Otisco Lake** *NY* U.S.A.
249 G3 **Otish, Monts** *hills Que.* Can.
194 F4 **Ötisheim** Ger.
276 B2 **Otishi, Parque Nacional** *nat. park* Peru
258 F2 **Otisville** *NY* U.S.A.
207 L7 **Otívar** Spain
234 C4 **Otjinene** Namibia
234 B3 **Otjitambi** Namibia
234 C4 **Otjiwarongo** Namibia
234 C4 **Otjosondu** Namibia
234 B3 **Otjovasandu** *waterhole* Namibia
234 C4 **Otjozondjupa** *admin. reg.* Namibia
173 O3 **Otley** *Suffolk, England* U.K.
171 N6 **Otley** *West Yorkshire, England* U.K.
151 A6 **Otlukbeli** Turkey
151 A6 **Otlukbeli Dağları** *mts* Turkey
196 F5 **Otmuchów** Pol.
163 K6 **Otnes** Norway
201 O1 **Otnice** Czech Rep.
126 C7 **Ōto** Japan
124 R5 **Otobe** Japan
124 R4 **Otobe-dake** *mt.* Japan
210 E3 **Otočac** Croatia
124 U4 **Otofuke** Japan
Otog Qi *Nei Mongol* China *see* **Ulan**
124 T2 **Otoineppu** Japan
210 G3 **Otok** Croatia
210 F3 **Otoka** Bos.-Herz.
102 L5 **Otoko** *North I.* N.Z.
229 F4 **Otola** Benin
102 I2 **Otonga** *North I.* N.Z.
232 A2 **Otoro, Jebel** *mt.* Sudan
102 J5 **Otorohanga** *North I.* N.Z.
196 E3 **Otorowo** Pol.
248 B3 **Otoskwin** *r. Ont.* Can.
125 □2 **Otōto-jima** *i. Ogasawara-shotō* Japan
204 C4 **O Toural** Spain
126 F6 **Otowa** Japan
125 K13 **Ōtoyo** Japan
Otpor Rus. Fed. *see* **Zabaykal'sk**
164 E3 **Otra** *r.* Norway
271 □10 **Otrabanda** *Curaçao* Neth. Antilles
161 T8 **Otradinskiy** Rus. Fed.
151 C1 **Otradnaya** Rus. Fed.
161 N2 **Otradnoye** *Leningradskaya Oblast'* Rus. Fed.
Otradnoye *Samarskaya Oblast'* Rus. Fed. *see* **Otradnyy**
161 N1 **Otradnoye, Ozero** *l.* Rus. Fed.
142 D1 **Otradnyy** Rus. Fed.
217 O3 **Otranto** Italy
217 P2 **Otranto, Strait of** Albania/Italy
215 I3 **Otricoli** Italy
Otrogovo Rus. Fed. *see* **Stepnoye**
199 G2 **Otrokovice** Czech Rep.
153 S3 **Otrozhnyy** Rus. Fed.
201 L4 **Ötscher-Tormäuer** *nature res.* Austria
250 I7 **Otsego** *MI* U.S.A.
257 K6 **Otsego Lake** *NY* U.S.A.
127 M2 **Ōtsu** *Ibaraki* Japan
126 C5 **Ōtsu** *Shiga* Japan
124 S7 **Ōtsuchi** Japan
127 I4 **Ōtsuki** Japan
163 J6 **Otta** Norway
214 C7 **Ottana** *Sardegna* Italy
179 L5 **Ottange** France
248 F4 **Ottawa** *Ont.* Can.
248 F4 **Ottawa** *r. Ont./Que.* Can.
250 F8 **Ottawa** *IL* U.S.A.
260 H6 **Ottawa** *KS* U.S.A.
256 A7 **Ottawa** *OH* U.S.A.
248 D1 **Ottawa Islands** *Nunavut* Can.
193 I8 **Ottendorf-Okrilla** Ger.
194 D5 **Ottenheim** Ger.
194 E4 **Ottenhöfen im Schwarzwald** Ger.
201 L3 **Ottenschlag** Austria
201 J3 **Ottensheim** Austria
191 H7 **Ottenstein** Ger.
201 L2 **Ottenstein Stausee** *resr* Austria
190 I4 **Otter** Ger.
172 F6 **Otter** *r. England* U.K.
194 D3 **Otterbach** Ger.
194 D2 **Otterberg** Ger.
171 M3 **Otterburn** *Northumberland, England* U.K.
168 F10 **Otter Ferry** *Argyll and Bute, Scotland* U.K.
195 L6 **Otterfing** Ger.
250 H1 **Otter Island** *Ont.* Can.
244 E4 **Otter Island** *AK* U.S.A.
247 J4 **Otter Lake** *Sask.* Can.
186 I4 **Otterlo** Neth.
190 G3 **Otterndorf** Ger.
248 D3 **Otter Rapids** *Ont.* Can.
190 H4 **Ottersberg** Ger.
164 J3 **Otterstad** Sweden
194 E4 **Ottersweier** Ger.
168 □N1 **Otterswick** *Shetland, Scotland* U.K.
164 G6 **Otterup** Denmark
193 G8 **Otterwisch** Ger.
172 D6 **Ottery** *r. England* U.K.
172 F6 **Ottery St Mary** *Devon, England* U.K.
199 G4 **Öttevény** Hungary
187 G7 **Ottignies** Belgium
214 D6 **Ottiolo, Punta d'** *pt Sardegna* Italy
179 O8 **Ottmarsheim** France
201 I3 **Ottnang am Hausruck** Austria
165 M1 **Ottnaren** *l.* Sweden
195 I6 **Ottobeuren** Ger.
195 L5 **Ottobrunn** Ger.
243 J1 **Otto Fiord** *inlet Nunavut* Can.
199 I5 **Öttömös** Hungary
212 G6 **Ottone** Italy
237 J2 **Ottosdal** S. Africa
237 J1 **Ottoshoop** S. Africa
191 H9 **Ottrau** Ger.
143 P7 **Ottuk** Kyrg.
260 I5 **Ottumwa** *IA* U.S.A.
194 C3 **Ottweiler** Ger.
229 G5 **Otukpa** Nigeria
229 H5 **Otukpo** Nigeria
269 I6 **Otumba** Mex.
277 F4 **Otuquis, Bañados de** *marsh* Bol.
277 F4 **Otuquis, Parque Nacional** *nat. park* Bolivia
276 D4 **Otuyo** Bol.
274 B6 **Otuzco** Peru
Otvazhniy Rus. Fed. *see* **Zhigulevsk**
256 B10 **Otway** *OH* U.S.A.
283 B9 **Otway, Bahía** *b.* Chile
105 I8 **Otway, Cape** *Vic.* Austr.
283 C9 **Otway, Seno** *b.* Chile
105 I8 **Otway Range** *mts Vic.* Austr.
197 J3 **Otwock** Pol.
205 O2 **Otxandio** Spain
196 D4 **Otyń** Pol.
158 D5 **Otyniya** Ukr.
195 N4 **Otzing** Ger.
200 C5 **Ötztal** *val.* Austria
200 C6 **Ötztaler Alpen** *mts* Austria
118 F4 **Ou, Nam** *r.* Laos
229 H3 **Ouacha** Niger
261 J10 **Ouachita** *r. AR* U.S.A.
261 I8 **Ouachita, Lake** *AR* U.S.A.
261 H8 **Ouachita Mountains** *AR/OK* U.S.A.
226 C5 **Ouadâne** Maur.
230 D2 **Ouadda** C.A.R.
224 D6 **Ouaddaï** *pref.* Chad
229 G1 **Ouadjinkarem** *well* Niger
228 B2 **Ouâd Nâga** Maur.
228 C3 **Ouadou** *watercourse* Maur.
228 E3 **Ouagadougou** Burkina
228 E3 **Ouahigouya** Burkina
Ouahran Alg. *see* **Oran**
230 D3 **Ouaka** *pref.* C.A.R.
230 C3 **Ouaka** *r.* C.A.R.
228 D2 **Oualâta** Maur.
228 D2 **Oualâta, Dhar** *hills* Maur.
229 F4 **Oualé** *r.* Burkina
228 C3 **Oualia** Mali
229 F3 **Ouallam** Niger
227 F4 **Ouallene** Alg.
275 I3 **Ouanary** Fr. Guiana
224 C5 **Ouanazein** *well* Chad
230 D2 **Ouanda-Djailé** C.A.R.
230 C3 **Ouandago** C.A.R.
230 D2 **Ouandja** *Haute-Kotto* C.A.R.
230 D2 **Ouandja** *Vakaga* C.A.R.
230 D2 **Ouandja-Vakaga, Réserve de Faune de la** *nature res.* C.A.R.
230 E3 **Ouando** C.A.R.
230 D3 **Ouango** C.A.R.
228 D4 **Ouangolodougou** Côte d'Ivoire
229 G3 **Ouani Kalaoua** *well* Niger
182 C1 **Ouanne** France
178 E8 **Ouanne** *r.* France
275 H4 **Ouaqui** Fr. Guiana
230 E3 **Ouara** *r.* C.A.R.
229 F4 **Ouargaye** Burkina
227 G3 **Ouargla** Alg.
229 F2 **Ouarissibitil** *well* Mali
229 F2 **Ouaritoufoulout** *well* Mali
226 C3 **Ouarkziz, Jbel** *ridge* Alg./Morocco
Ouarogou Burkina *see* **Ouargaye**
178 C7 **Ouarville** France
226 D3 **Ouarzazate** Morocco
249 F3 **Ouasiemsca** *r. Que.* Can.
229 F3 **Ouatagouna** Mali
Oubangui *r.* C.A.R./Dem. Rep. Congo *see* **Ubangi**
234 E7 **Oubergpas** *pass* S. Africa
204 C7 **Ouca** Port.
182 G2 **Ouche** *r.* France
126 D7 **Ōuchiyama** Japan
178 B8 **Oucques** France
126 C7 **Ouda** Japan
186 F5 **Oud-Beijerland** Neth.
186 E5 **Ouddorp** Neth.
186 J2 **Oudega** Neth.
186 I3 **Oudehaske** Neth.
228 E2 **Oudeïka** *well* Mali
186 I3 **Oudemirdum** Neth.
187 E7 **Oudenaarde** Belgium
186 G5 **Oudenbosch** Neth.
187 D6 **Oudenburg** Belgium
186 L2 **Oude Pekela** Neth.
186 G4 **Oude Rijn** *r.* Neth.
186 G4 **Ouderkerk aan de Amstel** Neth.
186 G2 **Oudeschild** Neth.
186 F5 **Oude-Tonge** Neth.
186 G4 **Oudewater** Neth.
186 F5 **Oud-Gastel** Neth.
180 I7 **Oudon** France
181 J6 **Oudon** *r.* France
236 G9 **Oudtshoorn** S. Africa
187 G6 **Oud-Turnhout** Belgium
187 D6 **Oudzele** Belgium
202 D5 **Oued Laou** Morocco
226 D2 **Oued Zem** Morocco
100 □5 **Ouegoa** New Caledonia
239 □3a **Ouela** *Njazidja* Comoros
228 D4 **Ouéléssébougou** Mali
229 F3 **Ouella** Niger
229 F5 **Ouémé** *r.* Benin
100 □5 **Ouen** *i.* New Caledonia
228 E4 **Ouessa** Burkina
180 A5 **Ouessant, Île d'** *i.* France
229 F4 **Ouèssè** Benin
230 C4 **Ouesso** Congo
229 H5 **Ouest** *prov.* Cameroon
249 H3 **Ouest, Pointe de l'** *pt Que.* Can.
226 D2 **Ouezzane** Morocco
187 H8 **Ouffet** Belgium
169 H4 **Oughter, Lough** *l.* Ireland
169 D6 **Oughterard** Ireland
226 D3 **Ougnat, Jbel** *mt.* Morocco
182 H2 **Ougney** France
126 A6 **Ougo-gawa** *r.* Japan
206 E2 **Ouguela** Port.
127 I3 **Ougura-yama** *mt.* Japan
230 C3 **Ouham** *pref.* C.A.R.
230 C2 **Ouham** *r.* C.A.R./Chad
230 C3 **Ouham-Pendé** *pref.* C.A.R.
229 F5 **Ouidah** Benin
228 E2 **Ouinardene** Mali
266 E4 **Ouiriego** Mex.
181 K3 **Ouistreham** France
228 D2 **Oujâf** *well* Maur.
226 E2 **Oujda** Morocco
228 B2 **Oujeft** Maur.
226 C3 **Oulad Teïma** Morocco
162 R4 **Oulainen** Fin.
162 T3 **Oulangan kansallispuisto** *nat. park* Fin.
178 F5 **Oulchy-le-Château** France
187 J8 **Oulder** Belgium
228 C3 **Ould Yenjé** Maur.
227 G2 **Ouled Djellal** Alg.
227 F2 **Ouled Naïl, Monts des** *mts* Alg.
227 F3 **Ouled Saïd** *well* Alg.
229 I5 **Ouli** Cameroon
182 F5 **Oullins** France
226 D2 **Oulmès** Morocco
173 P3 **Oulton** *Suffolk, England* U.K.
162 R4 **Oulu** Fin.
162 S4 **Oulu** *prov.* Fin.
162 S4 **Oulujärvi** *l.* Fin.
162 R4 **Oulujoki** *r.* Fin.
162 R4 **Oulunsalo** Fin.
212 B5 **Oulx** Italy
224 D6 **Oum-Chalouba** Chad
228 D5 **Oumé** Côte d'Ivoire
227 G2 **Oum el Bouaghi** Alg.
224 C6 **Oum-Hadjer** Chad
226 C5 **Oumm ed Droûs Guebli, Sebkhet** *salt flat* Maur.
226 C4 **Oumm ed Droûs Telli, Sebkha** *salt flat* Maur.
226 D5 **Oumm el A'sel** *well* Mali
227 G4 **Ounane, Djebel** *mt.* Alg.
226 C3 **Ounara** Morocco
162 R3 **Ounasjoki** *r.* Fin.
173 L3 **Oundle** *Northamptonshire, England* U.K.
247 K5 **Oungre** *Sask.* Can.
224 D5 **Ounianga Kébir** Chad
224 D5 **Ounianga Sérir** Chad
229 I2 **Ounissoui** *well* Niger
230 C3 **Ouogo** C.A.R.
187 I7 **Oupeye** Belgium
187 J9 **Our** *r.* Lux.
221 H4 **Oura, Akrotirio** *pt Chios* Greece
220 E2 **Ouranoupoli** Greece
124 □1 **Ōura-wan** *b. Okinawa* Japan
263 K7 **Ouray** *CO* U.S.A.
265 W1 **Ouray** *UT* U.S.A.
178 H7 **Ource** *r.* France
178 F5 **Ourcq** *r.* France
228 C4 **Ouré Kaba** Guinea
278 D2 **Ourém** Brazil
204 E4 **Ourense** Spain
204 F4 **Ourense** *prov. Galicia* Spain
224 B4 **Ouri, Enneri** *watercourse* Chad
278 E3 **Ouricurí** Brazil
280 C5 **Ourinhos** Brazil
224 D5 **Ourini** Chad
206 C5 **Ourique** Port.
278 D4 **Ouro** Brazil
278 D4 **Ouro** *r.* Brazil
204 F1 **Ouro** *r.* Spain
237 Q2 **Ouro, Ponta do** *pt* Moz.
281 F4 **Ouro Branco** Brazil
280 D5 **Ouro Fino** Brazil
204 E1 **Ourol** Spain
281 F4 **Ouro Preto** Brazil
182 D2 **Ouroux-en-Morvan** France
182 F3 **Ouroux-sur-Saône** France
187 I7 **Ourthe** *r.* Belgium
181 M2 **Ourville-en-Caux** France
173 M6 **Ouse** *r. East Sussex, England* U.K.
171 P6 **Ouse** *r. England* U.K.
185 G10 **Oust** France
180 G6 **Oust** *r.* France
228 B4 **Outamba Kilimi National Park** Sierra Leone
206 B4 **Outão** Port.
Outaouais, Rivère *r. see* **Ottawa**
249 G3 **Outardes, Rivière aux** *r. Que.* Can.
249 G3 **Outardes Quatre, Réservoir** *resr Que.* Can.
178 D7 **Outarville** France
226 E2 **Outat Oulad el Haj** Morocco
228 D2 **Outeïd Arkâs** *well* Mali
204 G5 **Outeiro** *Bragança* Port.
204 C5 **Outeiro** *Viana do Castelo* Port.
204 E2 **Outeiro de Rei** Spain
204 F5 **Outeiro Seco** Port.
236 G9 **Outeniekwaberge** *mts* S. Africa
168 B7 **Outer Hebrides** *is Scotland* U.K.
250 D2 **Outer Island** *WI* U.S.A.
Outer Mongolia *country* Asia *see* **Mongolia**
264 N8 **Outer Santa Barbara Channel** *CA* U.S.A.
228 C2 **Outfene** *well* Maur.
234 C4 **Outjo** Namibia
247 J5 **Outlook** *Sask.* Can.
156 E3 **Outokumpu** Fin.
204 E4 **Outomuro** Spain
227 G5 **Outoul** Alg.
103 E12 **Outram** *South I.* N.Z.
178 C2 **Outreau** France
168 □O2 **Out Skerries** *is Scotland* U.K.
173 M2 **Outwell** *Norfolk, England* U.K.
100 □5 **Ouvéa** *atoll Îles Loyauté* New Caledonia
183 B10 **Ouveillan** France
183 F8 **Ouvèze** *r.* France
131 I6 **Ouyanghai Shuiku** *resr* China
105 I6 **Ouyen** *Vic.* Austr.
173 K3 **Ouzel** *r. England* U.K.
244 I4 **Ouzinkie** *AK* U.S.A.
178 C8 **Ouzouer-le-Marché** France
178 D8 **Ouzouer-sur-Loire** France
221 I1 **Ova** *r.* Turkey
214 C4 **Ovace, Punta d'** *mt. Corse* France
148 F5 **Ovacık** *İçel* Turkey
148 I4 **Ovacık** *Tunceli* Turkey
221 M5 **Ovacık Dağı** *mt.* Turkey
212 F6 **Ovada** Italy
221 I5 **Ovaeymiri** Turkey
221 K6 **Ova Gölü** *l.* Turkey
221 J4 **Ovakent** Turkey
151 D7 **Ovakışla** Turkey
221 I5 **Ovakışlacık** Turkey
221 K6 **Ovaköy** Turkey
258 A2 **Oval** *PA* U.S.A.
101 □7a **Ovalau** *i.* Fiji
284 B2 **Ovalle** Chile
234 B3 **Ovamboland** *reg.* Namibia
230 B4 **Ovan** Gabon
204 C7 **Ovar** Port.
213 N3 **Ovaro** Italy
100 □6 **Ovau** *i.* Solomon Is
284 E3 **Oveja** *mt.* Arg.
274 C2 **Ovejas** Col.
284 D4 **Ovejería** Arg.
190 F4 **Ovelgönne** Ger.
229 I6 **Oveng** Cameroon
229 H6 **Oveng** Equat. Guinea
105 K7 **Ovens** *r. Vic.* Austr.
169 E9 **Ovens** Ireland
191 D9 **Overath** Ger.
168 K4 **Overbister** *Orkney, Scotland* U.K.
186 L4 **Overdinkel** Neth.
162 O2 **Øvergard** Norway
162 K4 **Overhalla** Norway
187 G7 **Overijse** Belgium
186 K4 **Overijssel** *prov.* Neth.
186 J4 **Overijssels Kanaal** *canal* Neth.
162 Q3 **Överkalix** Sweden
109 C9 **Overlander Roadhouse** *W.A.* Austr.
260 H6 **Overland Park** *KS* U.S.A.
258 B6 **Overlea** *MD* U.S.A.
186 I5 **Overloon** Neth.
162 P5 **Övermark** Fin.
284 B4 **Overo, Volcán** *vol.* Arg.
187 H6 **Overpelt** Belgium
173 I2 **Overseal** *Derbyshire, England* U.K.
173 J5 **Overton** *Hampshire, England* U.K.
172 G2 **Overton** *Wrexham, Wales* U.K.
265 R5 **Overton** *NV* U.S.A.
261 H9 **Overton** *TX* U.S.A.
162 Q3 **Övertorneå** Sweden
168 I11 **Overtown** *North Lanarkshire, Scotland* U.K.
165 M4 **Överum** Sweden
162 M3 **Överuman** *l.* Sweden
186 G4 **Overveen** Neth.
173 I5 **Over Wallop** *Hampshire, England* U.K.
212 E3 **Ovesca** *r.* Italy
187 E6 **Ovezande** Neth.
Övgödiy Mongolia *see* **Telmen**
204 E1 **O Vicedo** Spain
260 D5 **Ovid** *CO* U.S.A.
250 J6 **Ovid** *MI* U.S.A.
256 I6 **Ovid** *NY* U.S.A.
158 J7 **Ovidiopol'** Ukr.
219 Q6 **Ovidiu** Romania
204 I2 **Oviedo** Spain
204 H2 **Oviedo** *prov.* Spain
212 E6 **Oviglio** Italy
215 L3 **Ovindoli** Italy
161 T3 **Ovinishchenskaya Vozvyshennost'** *hills* Rus. Fed.
160 E4 **Ovišrags** *hd* Latvia
237 J6 **Oviston Nature Reserve** S. Africa
142 J7 **Ovminzatov tog'lari** *hills* Uzbek.
217 N3 **Ovo, Punta dell'** *pt* Italy
214 C7 **Ovodda** *Sardegna* Italy
Ovolau *i.* Fiji *see* **Ovalau**
Ovoot Mongolia *see* **Darīganga**
128 H4 **Övörhangay** *prov.* Mongolia
162 R2 **Øvre Anárjohka Nasjonalpark** *nat. park* Norway
163 I6 **Øvre Årdal** Norway
162 O2 **Øvre Dividal Nasjonalpark** *nat. park* Norway
162 K5 **Øvre Forra** *nature res.* Norway
164 J2 **Övre Fryken** *l.* Sweden
164 I2 **Övre Gla** *l.* Sweden
164 D1 **Øvre Hein** *l.* Norway
162 T2 **Øvre Pasvik Nasjonalpark** *nat. park* Norway
163 K6 **Øvre Rendal** Norway
162 P2 **Övre Soppero** Sweden
158 H2 **Ovruch** Ukr.
122 E2 **Ovsyanka** Rus. Fed.
Övt Mongolia *see* **Bat-Öldziy**
102 K7 **Owahanga** *North I.* N.Z.
103 D13 **Owaka** *South I.* N.Z.
250 D1 **Owakonze** *Ont.* Can.
230 B5 **Owando** Congo
124 R6 **Ōwani** Japan
Owa Rafa *i.* Solomon Is *see* **Santa Ana**
126 F5 **Owariasahi** Japan
Owa Riki *i.* Solomon Is *see* **Santa Catalina**
256 I6 **Owasco Lake** *NY* U.S.A.
126 D7 **Owase** Japan
126 D7 **Owase-wan** *b.* Japan
261 H7 **Owasso** *OK* U.S.A.
260 I3 **Owatonna** *MN* U.S.A.
145 J4 **Owbeh** Afgh.
197 J4 **Owczarnia** Pol.
257 I6 **Owego** *NY* U.S.A.
169 H5 **Owel, Lough** *l.* Ireland
194 G4 **Owen** Ger.
103 G8 **Owen, Mount** *South I.* N.Z.
229 G5 **Owena** Nigeria
169 E4 **Owenbeg** Ireland
236 H4 **Owendale** S. Africa
169 C4 **Owenduff** *r.* Ireland
102 □ **Owenga** *Chatham Is* S. Pacific Ocean
169 C4 **Oweniny** *r.* Ireland
119 D9 **Owen Island** Myanmar
169 C4 **Owenmore** *r.* Ireland
169 H3 **Owenreagh** *r. Northern Ireland* U.K.
103 G8 **Owen River** *South I.* N.Z.
264 O5 **Owens** *r. CA* U.S.A.
254 D7 **Owensboro** *KY* U.S.A.
264 O5 **Owens Lake** *CA* U.S.A.
248 D4 **Owen Sound** *Ont.* Can.
251 N5 **Owen Sound** *inlet Ont.* Can.
106 D7 **Owen Springs** *N.T.* Austr.
113 K8 **Owen Stanley Range** *mts* P.N.G.
260 J6 **Owensville** *MO* U.S.A.
256 A9 **Owensville** *OH* U.S.A.
254 E6 **Owenton** *KY* U.S.A.
229 G5 **Owerri** Nigeria
169 F2 **Owey Island** Ireland
102 J6 **Owhango** *North I.* N.Z.
246 E5 **Owikeno Lake** *B.C.* Can.
194 G6 **Owingen** Ger.
256 I10 **Owings** *MD* U.S.A.
258 B6 **Owings Mills** *MD* U.S.A.
256 B10 **Owingsville** *KY* U.S.A.
247 M3 **Owl** *r. Man.* Can.
262 J5 **Owl Creek** *r. WY* U.S.A.
257 □P4 **Owls Head** *ME* U.S.A.
Owminzatow Toghi *hills* Uzbek. *see* **Ovminzatov tog'lari**
229 G5 **Owo** Nigeria
251 J7 **Owosso** *MI* U.S.A.
Owrtyn *Wales* U.K. *see* **Overton**
190 I2 **Owschlag** Ger.
262 F6 **Owyhee** *NV* U.S.A.
262 F5 **Owyhee** *r. OR* U.S.A.
262 F5 **Owyhee Mountains** *ID* U.S.A.
262 F5 **Owyhee North Fork** *r. ID* U.S.A.
262 F5 **Owyhee South Fork** *r. ID* U.S.A.
276 B2 **Oxapampa** Peru
162 □E1 **Öxarfjörður** *b.* Iceland
247 K5 **Oxbow** *Sask.* Can.
260 E1 **Ox Creek** *r. ND* U.S.A.
165 N3 **Oxelösund** Sweden
171 N6 **Oxenhope** *West Yorkshire, England* U.K.
103 G10 **Oxford** *South I.* N.Z.
173 J4 **Oxford** *Oxfordshire, England* U.K.
259 I2 **Oxford** *CT* U.S.A.
257 N6 **Oxford** *MA* U.S.A.
257 □O4 **Oxford** *ME* U.S.A.
251 K7 **Oxford** *MI* U.S.A.
261 K8 **Oxford** *MS* U.S.A.
255 H7 **Oxford** *NC* U.S.A.
258 F3 **Oxford** *NJ* U.S.A.
257 J6 **Oxford** *NY* U.S.A.
256 A9 **Oxford** *OH* U.S.A.
258 D5 **Oxford** *PA* U.S.A.
250 E6 **Oxford** *WI* U.S.A.
107 L6 **Oxford Downs** *Qld* Austr.
247 M4 **Oxford House** *Man.* Can.
247 M4 **Oxford Lake** *Man.* Can.
173 J4 **Oxfordshire** *admin. div. England* U.K.
164 J6 **Oxie** Sweden
267 O7 **Oxkutzcab** Mex.
105 J6 **Oxley** *N.S.W.* Austr.
105 M4 **Oxleys Peak** *N.S.W.* Austr.
105 N4 **Oxley Wild Rivers National Park** *N.S.W.* Austr.
169 D5 **Ox Mountains** *hills* Ireland
264 M7 **Oxnard** *CA* U.S.A.
173 L5 **Oxshott** *Surrey, England* U.K.
173 M5 **Oxted** *Surrey, England* U.K.
168 K11 **Oxton** *Scottish Borders, Scotland* U.K.
251 P4 **Oxtongue Lake** *Ont.* Can.
Oxus *r.* Asia *see* **Amudar'ya**
220 F4 **Oxylithos** Greece
117 I3 **Oya** *Sarawak* Malaysia
117 I3 **Oya** *r.* Malaysia
126 E2 **Oyabe** Japan
126 F2 **Oyabe-gawa** *r.* Japan
127 I5 **Oyama** *Shizuoka* Japan
127 K3 **Oyama** *Tochigi* Japan
126 F2 **Ōyama** Japan
127 J5 **Ō-yama** *mt.* Japan
127 K7 **Ō-yama** *vol.* Japan
126 D6 **Ōyamada** Japan
126 C6 **Ōyamazaki** Japan
205 L2 **Oyambre, Cabo de** *c.* Spain
275 I3 **Oyapock** *r.* Brazil/Fr. Guiana
275 I3 **Oyapock, Baie d'** *b.* Fr. Guiana
143 T4 **Oychilik** Kazakh.
230 A4 **Oyem** Gabon
247 I5 **Oyen** *Alta* Can.
178 D2 **Oye-Plage** France
164 H2 **Øyeren** *l.* Norway
Oygon Mongolia *see* **Tüdevtey**
168 H7 **Oykel** *r. Scotland* U.K.
168 G7 **Oykel Bridge** *Highland, Scotland* U.K.
195 I6 **Oy-Mittelberg** Ger.
153 P3 **Oymyakon** Rus. Fed.
230 B5 **Oyo** Congo
229 F5 **Oyo** Nigeria
229 F4 **Oyo** *state* Nigeria
225 H4 **Oyo** Sudan
126 C7 **Ōyodo** Japan
276 A2 **Oyón** Peru
182 H4 **Oyonnax** France
142 K7 **Oyoqog'itma botig'i** *depr.* Uzbek.
142 K7 **Oyoqquduq** Uzbek.
Oysangur Rus. Fed. *see* **Oyskhara**
Oyshilik Kazakh. *see* **Oychilik**
151 H2 **Oyskhara** Rus. Fed.
236 I10 **Oyster Bay** S. Africa
259 H3 **Oyster Bay** *NY* U.S.A.
259 G6 **Oyster Creek** *NJ* U.S.A.
118 A4 **Oyster Island** Myanmar
136 D5 **Oyster Rocks** *is* India
143 O6 **Oytal** Kazakh.
143 P7 **Oy-Tal** Kyrg.
190 H4 **Oyten** Ger.
133 E8 **Oytograk** *Xinjiang* China
150 A2 **Oyukludağı** *mt.* Turkey
Oyyl Kazakh. *see* **Uil**
142 E3 **Oyyl** *r.* Kazakh.
Oyyq Kazakh. *see* **Uyuk**
204 D2 **Oza** Spain
205 P3 **Ozaeta** Spain
124 T7 **Ō-zaki** *pt* Japan
149 L4 **Özalp** Turkey
114 D7 **Ozamiz** *Mindanao* Phil.
178 B7 **Ozanne** *r.* France
255 E10 **Ozark** *AL* U.S.A.
261 I8 **Ozark** *AR* U.S.A.
261 I7 **Ozark** *MO* U.S.A.
261 I7 **Ozark Plateau** *MO* U.S.A.
260 I6 **Ozarks, Lake of the** *MO* U.S.A.
197 J5 **Ożarów** Pol.
197 H5 **Ożarowice** Pol.
197 I3 **Ożarów Mazowiecki** Pol.
144 G4 **Ozbakūh** Iran
201 L6 **Ožbalt** Slovenia
221 I5 **Özbaşı** Turkey
Ozbekiston *country* Asia *see* **Uzbekistan**
199 J3 **Ózd** Hungary
199 I3 **Ožďany** Slovakia
151 C5 **Özdere** *Erzurum* Turkey
221 I5 **Özdere** *İzmir* Turkey
151 C7 **Özdilek** Turkey
Özen Kazakh. *see* **Kyzylsay**
197 J6 **Ożenna** Pol.
161 R2 **Ozerevo** Rus. Fed.
161 Q7 **Ozerishche** Rus. Fed.
158 H8 **Ozerne** *Odes'ka Oblast'* Ukr.
158 E2 **Ozerne** *Volyns'ka Oblast'* Ukr.
158 H3 **Ozerne** *Zhytomyrs'ka Oblast'* Ukr.
161 T6 **Ozerninskoye Vodokhranilishche** *resr* Rus. Fed.
153 Q4 **Ozernovskiy** Rus. Fed.
142 J1 **Ozernoye** Kazakh.
142 D2 **Ozernoye** Rus. Fed.
Ozernyy *Karagandinskaya Oblast'* Kazakh. *see* **Shashubay**
Ozernyy *Kostanayskaya Oblast'* Kazakh. *see* **Ozernoye**
161 X4 **Ozernyy** *Ivanovskaya Oblast'* Rus. Fed.
142 I2 **Ozernyy** *Orenburgskaya Oblast'* Rus. Fed.
161 P6 **Ozernyy** *Smolenskaya Oblast'* Rus. Fed.
143 U1 **Ozero-Petrovskoye** Rus. Fed.
220 C4 **Ozeros, Limni** *l.* Greece
122 L2 **Ozerpakh** Rus. Fed.
160 F7 **Ozersk** Rus. Fed.
122 M5 **Ozerskiy** *Sakhalin* Rus. Fed.
161 V7 **Ozery** Rus. Fed.
122 F3 **Ozeryane** Rus. Fed.
159 L3 **Ozeryany** Ukr.
143 O7 **Özgön** Kyrg.
161 V7 **Ozherel'ye** Rus. Fed.
153 Q3 **Ozhogina** *r.* Rus. Fed.
214 C6 **Ozieri** *Sardegna* Italy
196 G5 **Ozimek** Pol.
142 C2 **Ozinki** Rus. Fed.
151 B6 **Özlüce Barajı** *resr* Turkey
178 E6 **Ozoir-la-Ferrière** France
160 G5 **Ozolnieki** Latvia
261 E10 **Ozona** *TX* U.S.A.
199 H5 **Ozora** Hungary

197 H4 Ozorków Pol.
229 G5 Ozoro Nigeria
125 J13 Ōzu Ehime Japan
125 H14 Ōzu Kumamoto Japan
125 I12 Ozuki Japan
269 J4 Ozuluama Mex.
269 I6 Ozumba de Alzate Mex.
151 D4 Ozurget'i Georgia
150 A1 Özyurt Dağı mts Turkey
197 M5 Ozyutychi Ukr.
213 K7 Ozzano dell'Emilia Italy
212 E5 Ozzano Monferrato Italy

P

228 E4 Pâ Burkina
162 R4 Paakkola Fin.
187 H6 Paal Belgium
100 □5 Paama i. Vanuatu
243 N3 Paamiut Greenland
Pa-an Myanmar see Hpa-an
Paanopa i. Kiribati see Banaba
236 C9 Paarl S. Africa
160 J2 Paasvere Estonia
100 □4a Paata i. Chuuk Micronesia
Paatsjoki r. Europe see Patsoyoki
264 □F13 Pa'auilo HI U.S.A.
Pabaigh i. Western Isles, Scotland U.K. see Pabbay
Pabail Uarach Scotland U.K. see Upper Bayble
236 F4 Paballelo S. Africa
123 F8 P'abal-li N. Korea
168 B7 Pabbay i. Western Isles, Scotland U.K.
168 A9 Pabbay i. Western Isles, Scotland U.K.
268 E3 Pabellón de Arteaga Mex.
284 B2 Pabellón Chile
197 H4 Pabianice Pol.
Pabianitz Pol. see Pabianice
214 B8 Pabillonis Sardegna Italy
269 H1 Pablillo r. Mex.
285 H5 Pablo Acosta Arg.
139 L7 Pabna Bangl.
201 K3 Pabneukirchen Austria
160 I7 Pabradė Lith.
145 L8 Pab Range mts Pak.
180 E4 Pabu France
276 D2 Pacaás, Serra dos hills Brazil
277 E2 Pacaás Novos, Parque Nacional nat. park Brazil
280 B4 Pacaembu Brazil
276 D2 Pacahuaras r. Bol.
278 F3 Pacajus Brazil
236 G10 Pacaltsdorp S. Africa
197 J5 Pacanów Pol.
276 B3 Pacapausa Peru
Pacaraimã, Serra mts S. America see Pakaraima Mountains
276 B3 Pacarán Peru
274 B6 Pacasmayo Peru
278 F2 Pacatuba Brazil
274 C6 Pacaya r. Peru
267 N10 Pacaya, Volcán de vol. Guat.
274 C6 Pacaya Samiria, Reserva Nacional nature res. Peru
180 H5 Pacé France
216 D8 Paceco Sicilia Italy
284 C2 Pachaco Arg.
136 F7 Pachaimalai Hills India
259 L1 Pachaug Pond l. CT U.S.A.
266 E2 Pacheco Chihuahua Mex.
268 E1 Pacheco Zacatecas Mex.
221 G6 Pacheia i. Greece
157 H5 Pachelma Rus. Fed.
276 C4 Pachía Peru
156 I3 Pachikha Rus. Fed.
217 I10 Pachino Sicilia Italy
276 B2 Pachitea r. Peru
276 A1 Pachiza Peru
138 G8 Pachmarhi Madh. Prad. India
220 F1 Pachni Greece
138 F8 Pachor Madh. Prad. India
138 E9 Pachora Mahar. India
138 D7 Pachpadra Rajasthan India
138 D7 Pachpadra Salt Depot Rajasthan India
269 I5 Pachuca Mex.
214 I1 Paciano Italy
264 J4 Pacifica CA U.S.A.
291 I9 Pacific-Antarctic Ridge sea feature Pacific Ocean
264 K5 Pacific Grove CA U.S.A.
290 Pacific Ocean
246 E5 Pacific Rim National Park B.C. Can.
114 E6 Pacijan i. Phil.
199 K3 Pácin Hungary
117 K8 Pacinan, Tanjung pt Indon.
218 H5 Pačir Vojvodina Serbia
117 I9 Pacitan Jawa Indon.
201 K6 Pack Austria
105 H4 Packsaddle N.S.W. Austr.
201 K6 Packsattel pass Austria
204 D6 Pacos de Ferreira Port.
198 E2 Pacov Czech Rep.
275 H5 Pacoval Brazil
198 G5 Pacsa Hungary
281 E2 Pacuí r. Brazil
199 K2 Pacutová hill Slovakia
197 H3 Pacyna Pol.
178 B5 Pacy-sur-Eure France
196 F5 Paczków Pol.
114 E8 Padada Mindanao Phil.
115 C5 Padalere Sulawesi Indon.
Padali Rus. Fed. see Amursk
115 B6 Padamarang i. Indon.
138 D5 Padampur Rajasthan India
138 B8 Padana Gujarat India
117 H5 Padang Kalimantan Indon.
115 B7 Padang Sulawesi Indon.
116 D5 Padang Sumatera Indon.
116 E4 Padang i. Indon.
116 E3 Padang Endau Malaysia
117 L5 Padang Luwai, Cagar Alam nature res. Kalimantan Indon.
116 D5 Padangpanjang Sumatera Indon.
116 C4 Padangsidimpuan Sumatera Indon.
117 H5 Padangtikar Kalimantan Indon.
117 H5 Padangtikar i. Indon.
156 F3 Padany Rus. Fed.
160 H9 Padarosk Belarus
151 J5 Padarqışlaq Azer.
117 K2 Padas r. Malaysia
163 R6 Padasjoki Fin.
144 C5 Padatha, Kūh-e mt. Iran
275 E5 Padauiri r. Brazil
118 B5 Padaung Myanmar
190 H1 Padborg Denmark
173 K4 Padbury Buckinghamshire, England U.K.
276 D5 Padcaya Bol.
105 J5 Paddington N.S.W. Austr.
237 O6 Paddock S. Africa
173 M5 Paddock Wood Kent, England U.K.
115 C5 Padeabesar i. Indon.
199 J6 Padej Vojvodina Serbia
256 E9 Paden City WV U.S.A.
191 G7 Paderborn Ger.
206 C6 Paderne Faro Port.
204 D4 Paderne Viana do Castelo Port.
232 B4 Pader Palwo Uganda
219 K5 Padeşu, Vârful mt. Romania
197 J5 Padew Narodowa Pol.
118 C3 Padibyu Myanmar
171 M6 Padiham Lancashire, England U.K.
276 D4 Padilla Bol.
219 P6 Padina Romania
218 I5 Padina Vojvodina Serbia
218 I6 Padinska Skela Beograd Serbia
185 H6 Padirac France
162 N3 Padjelanta nationalpark nat. park Sweden
161 O8 Padluzhzha Belarus
139 L8 Padma r. Bangl. alt. Ganga, conv. Ganges
136 E8 Padmanabhapuram Tamil Nadu India
138 H9 Padmapur Mahar. India
204 G4 Padornelo, Portilla del pass Spain
179 M7 Padoux France
213 L5 Padova Italy
213 L5 Padova prov. Italy
138 D8 Padra Gujarat India
139 J6 Padrauna Uttar Prad. India
206 F5 Padre Caro hill Spain
261 G12 Padre Island TX U.S.A.
261 G12 Padre Island National Seashore nature res. TX U.S.A.
281 G2 Padre Paraíso Brazil
214 B7 Padria Sardegna Italy
214 B3 Padro, Monte mt. Corse France
204 C3 Padrón Spain
237 K9 Padrone, Cape S. Africa
214 D6 Padru Sardegna Italy
172 C6 Padstow Cornwall, England U.K.
160 K6 Padsvillye Belarus
104 H7 Padthaway S.A. Austr.
137 H3 Padua Orissa India
Padua Italy see Padova
261 K7 Paducah KY U.S.A.
261 E8 Paducah TX U.S.A.
207 L6 Padul Spain
215 P7 Padula Italy
215 N5 Paduli Italy
138 F3 Padum Jammu and Kashmir India
219 K4 Pădurea Craiului, Munții mts Romania
101 □9a Paea Tahiti Fr. Polynesia
123 F8 Paegam N. Korea
103 I7 Paekakariki North I. N.Z.
Paektu-san mt. China/N. Korea see Baitou Shan
123 D10 Paengnyŏng-do i. S. Korea
103 D12 Paerau South I. N.Z.
102 J4 Paeroa North I. N.Z.
102 K5 Paeroa hill North I. N.Z.
212 C6 Paesana Italy
213 M4 Paese Italy
217 H3 Paestum tourist site Italy
114 C4 Paete Luzon Phil.
150 A4 Pafos Cyprus
150 A4 Pafos airport Cyprus
235 F4 Pafuri Moz.
210 E3 Pag Croatia
210 E3 Pag i. Croatia
115 C8 Paga Flores Indon.
156 M2 Paga r. Rus. Fed.
275 H6 Paga Conta Brazil
117 G8 Pagadenbaru Jawa Indon.
114 D8 Pagadian Mindanao Phil.
116 D6 Pagai Selatan i. Indon.
116 D6 Pagai Utara i. Indon.
Pagalu i. Equat. Guinea see Annobón
113 K3 Pagan i. N. Mariana Is
213 K3 Paganella mt. Italy
215 K3 Paganica Italy
214 G2 Paganico Italy
284 D2 Paganzo Arg.
116 E6 Pagaralam Sumatera Indon.
220 D3 Pagasitikos Kolpos b. Greece
117 J6 Pagatan Kalimantan Indon.
117 K6 Pagatan Kalimantan Indon.
265 U5 Page AZ U.S.A.
108 H4 Page, Mount hill W.A. Austr.
245 L1 Page, Mount Y.T. Can.
160 E6 Pagėgiai Lith.
116 F6 Pagerdewa Sumatera Indon.
283 □ Paget, Mount S. Georgia
107 N5 Paget Cay rf Coral Sea Is Terr. Austr.
173 K6 Pagham West Sussex, England U.K.
145 M4 Paghman mt. Afgh.
160 H6 Pagiriai Kaunas Lith.
160 I7 Pagiriai Vilnius Lith.
214 I2 Paglia r. Italy
215 M3 Paglieta Italy
179 L6 Pagny-sur-Moselle France
100 □1 Pago Bay Guam
285 H1 Pago Largo Arg.
Pagon i. N. Mariana Is see Pagan
100 □2 Pago Pago American Samoa
263 K8 Pagosa Springs CO U.S.A.
229 F4 Pagouda Togo
Pagqên Qinghai China see Gadê
133 I13 Pagri Xizang China
271 □2 Pagua Bay Dominica
248 C3 Pagwachuan r. Ont. Can.
248 C3 Pagwa River Ont. Can.
244 H2 Pah r. AK U.S.A.
264 □F14 Pāhala HI U.S.A.
116 E3 Pahang r. Malaysia
116 E3 Pahang state Malaysia
138 F6 Pahari Rajasthan India
139 L7 Paharpur tourist site Bangl.
145 N5 Paharpur Pak.
117 H4 Pahauman Kalimantan Indon.
103 B13 Pahia Point South I. N.Z.
102 J7 Pahiatua North I. N.Z.
195 K6 Pähl Ger.
Pahlavī Dezh Iran see Āq Qal'eh
190 H2 Pahlen Ger.
138 E2 Pahlgam Jammu and Kashmir India
264 □G14 Pāhoa HI U.S.A.
255 G12 Pahokee FL U.S.A.
158 F1 Pahost, Vodaskhovishcha resr Belarus
138 H7 Pahra Uttar Prad. India
145 I4 Pahra Kariz Afgh.
265 Q4 Pahranagat Range mts NV U.S.A.
160 G8 Pahranichny Belarus
265 Q5 Pahrump NV U.S.A.
138 G6 Pahuj r. India
264 P4 Pahute Mesa plat. NV U.S.A.
118 D5 Pai Thai.
264 □E13 Paia HI U.S.A.
277 F4 Paiaguás Brazil
204 C8 Paião Port.
264 K5 Paicines CA U.S.A.
160 I3 Paide Estonia
172 E7 Paignton Torbay, England U.K.
102 I2 Paihia North I. N.Z.
284 B2 Paihuano Chile
274 B6 Paiján Peru
163 R6 Päijänne l. Fin.
229 G4 Paiko Nigeria
133 G12 Paikü Co l. China
276 D4 Paila r. Bol.
284 A6 Pailahueque Chile
138 H7 Pailani Uttar Prad. India
185 I10 Pailhères, Port de pass France
185 G9 Pailhès France
119 F8 Pailin Cambodia
283 B6 Paillaco Chile
264 □E13 Pailolo Channel HI U.S.A.
180 G7 Paimbœuf France
163 Q6 Paimio Fin.
160 F1 Paimionselkä b. Fin.
244 F3 Paimiut AK U.S.A.
244 G3 Paimiut AK U.S.A.
180 E4 Paimpol France
180 G5 Paimpont France
180 G6 Paimpont, Forêt de for. France
116 D5 Painan Sumatera Indon.
136 E8 Painavu Kerala India
284 B3 Paine Chile
283 B8 Paine, Cerro mt. Chile
281 E3 Paineiras Brazil
279 C8 Painel Brazil
250 F2 Painesdale MI U.S.A.
256 D7 Painesville OH U.S.A.
281 E4 Pains Brazil
172 H4 Painswick Gloucestershire, England U.K.
265 U5 Painted Desert AZ U.S.A.
265 S8 Painted Rock Dam AZ U.S.A.
195 L4 Painten Ger.
Paint Hills Que. Can. see Wemindji
247 L4 Paint Lake Man. Can.
247 L4 Paint Lake Provincial Recreation Park Man. Can.
261 F10 Paint Rock TX U.S.A.
256 C11 Paintsville KY U.S.A.
274 C3 Paipa Col.
138 H9 Pairi r. India
251 M5 Paisley Ont. Can.
168 H11 Paisley Renfrewshire, Scotland U.K.
205 P2 País Vasco aut. comm. Spain
100 □5 Paita New Caledonia
274 A6 Paita Peru
117 L1 Paitan, Teluk b. Malaysia
136 D3 Paithan Mahar. India
145 L9 Paitiani Creek inlet Pak.
131 M4 Paitou Zhejiang China
204 D6 Paiva r. Port.
Paiva Couceiro Angola see Quipungo
267 N9 Paixban Mex.
131 I3 Paizhou Hubei China
162 Q3 Pajala Sweden
274 A5 Paján Ecuador
269 M7 Pajapan Mex.
238 □3b Pájara Fuerteventura Canary Is
204 I2 Pajares, Puerto de pass Spain
274 C3 Pajarito Col.
205 Q9 Pajarón Spain
205 Q9 Pajaroncillo Spain
282 C3 Pájaros, Islotes Chile
196 G4 Pajęczno Pol.
198 F5 Páka Hungary
116 E2 Paka Malaysia
115 F3 Pakal i. Maluku Indon.
136 F6 Pakala Andhra Prad. India
Pakanbaru Sumatera Indon. see Pekanbaru
137 N2 Pakangyi Myanmar
160 G6 Pakapė Lith.
275 F4 Pakaraima Mountains S. America
248 B3 Pakashkan Lake Ont. Can.
139 K7 Pakaur Jharkhand India
102 G7 Pakawau South I. N.Z.
123 D9 Pakch'ŏn N. Korea
248 D4 Pakesley Ont. Can.
153 R3 Pakhachi Rus. Fed.
142 G3 Pakhar' Kazakh.
Pakhiá i. Greece see Pacheia
Pákhni Greece see Pachni
Pakhoi Guangxi China see Beihai
161 U7 Pakhomovo Rus. Fed.
145 K7 Pakistan country Asia
131 □J7 Pak Ka Shan hill H.K. China
116 C3 Pakkat Sumatera Indon.
210 E3 Paklenica nat. park Croatia
215 Q1 Pakleni Otoci is Croatia
Paknampho Thai. see Nakhon Sawan
198 G5 Pakod Hungary
118 B4 Pakokku Myanmar
196 G3 Pakość Pol.
196 G3 Pakoskie, Jezioro l. Pol.
196 F4 Pakosław Pol.
210 E4 Pakoštane Croatia
102 H2 Pakotai North I. N.Z.
247 I5 Pakowki Lake imp. l. Alta Can.
199 H4 Pákozd Hungary
145 O6 Pakpattan Pak.
119 E10 Pak Phanang Thai.
119 E11 Pak Phayun Thai.
210 F3 Pakra r. Croatia
210 F3 Pakrac Croatia
160 G6 Pakruojis Lith.
199 H5 Paks Hungary
Pakse Laos see Pakxé
131 □J7 Pak Tai To Yan mt. H.K. China
131 □J7 Pak Tam Chung H.K. China
119 F7 Pak Thong Chai Thai.
145 M5 Paktīā prov. Afgh.
145 M5 Paktīkā prov. Afgh.
117 J3 Paku r. Malaysia
116 G6 Paku, Tanjung pt Indon.
115 B5 Pakue Sulawesi Indon.
158 J2 Pakul' Ukr.
247 M5 Pakwash Lake Ont. Can.
118 F5 Pakxan Laos
118 G7 Pakxé Laos
118 F4 Pakxeng Laos
Pal Senegal see Mpal
230 B2 Pala Chad
119 D8 Pala Myanmar
116 G8 Palabuhanratu Jawa Indon.
116 F8 Palabuhanratu, Teluk b. Indon.
285 G2 Palacios Arg.
276 D3 Palacios Bol.
205 K6 Palacios de Goda Spain
205 N5 Palacios de la Sierra Spain
204 H3 Palacios del Sil Spain
204 G4 Palacios de Sanabria Spain
200 E7 Pala di San Martino mt. Italy
183 H6 Paladru, Lac de l. France
Palaestinia reg. Asia see Palestine
208 L4 Palafrugell Spain
217 L2 Palagianello Italy
217 M2 Palagiano Italy
216 H9 Palagonia Sicilia Italy
210 F4 Palagruža i. Croatia
213 J8 Palaia Italy
220 E5 Palaia Fokaia Greece
150 B4 Palaichori Cyprus
221 H7 Palaikastro Kriti Greece
220 E7 Palaiochora Kriti Greece
Palaiókastron Kriti Greece see Palaikastro
220 B4 Palairos Greece
178 D6 Palaiseau France
136 E7 Palakkad Kerala India
Palakkat Kerala India see Palakkad
139 J9 Pala Laharha Orissa India
137 M7 Palalankwe Andaman & Nicobar Is India
234 D4 Palamakoloi Botswana
220 D3 Palamas Greece
115 E4 Palamea Maluku Indon.
208 L4 Palamós Spain
138 F3 Palam Pur Hima. Prad. India
139 J8 Palamu Jharkhand India
138 D6 Palana Rajasthan India
153 Q4 Palana Rus. Fed.
114 D3 Palanan Luzon Phil.
114 D3 Palanan Point Luzon Phil.
209 E8 Palancia, Riu r. Spain
151 B6 Palandöken Dağları mts Turkey
138 H9 Palandur Mahar. India
160 E6 Palanga Lith.
149 M6 Palangān Iran
144 I6 Palangān, Kūh-e mts Iran
183 B8 Palanges, Montagne des mts France
117 J6 Palangkaraya Kalimantan Indon.
136 E7 Palani Tamil Nadu India
138 D7 Palanpur Gujarat India
115 A6 Palanro Sulawesi Indon.
145 K8 Palantak Pak.
212 I7 Palanzano Italy
114 E5 Palapag Samar Phil.
235 E4 Palapye Botswana
136 G6 Palar r. India
145 O4 Palas Pak.
115 B3 Palasa Sulawesi Indon.
139 M6 Palasbari Assam India
204 E3 Palas de Rei Spain
160 L6 Palata r. Belarus
215 N4 Palata Italy
153 Q3 Palatka Rus. Fed.
255 G11 Palatka FL U.S.A.
214 C5 Palau Sardegna Italy
114 □ Palau country N. Pacific Ocean
115 G6 Palau Hatta i. Maluku Indon.
114 D2 Palaui i. Phil.
114 B4 Palauig Luzon Phil.
113 H5 Palau Islands Palau
119 D8 Palauk Myanmar
100 □2 Palauli Bay Samoa
116 F7 Palausekopong, Tanjung pt Indon.
290 D5 Palau Trench sea feature N. Pacific Ocean
198 F3 Pálava park Czech Rep.
183 D9 Palavas-les-Flots France
119 D8 Palaw Myanmar
114 A7 Palawan i. Phil.
114 A7 Palawan Passage str. Phil.
290 C5 Palawan Trough sea feature N. Pacific Ocean
114 C4 Palayan Luzon Phil.
136 E8 Palayankottai Tamil Nadu India
205 L7 Palazuelos de Eresma Spain
214 B3 Palazzo, Punta pt Corse France
216 E8 Palazzo Adriano Sicilia Italy
216 H9 Palazzolo Acreide Sicilia Italy
212 H4 Palazzolo sull'Oglio Italy
215 Q6 Palazzo San Gervasio Italy
136 G4 Palchal Lake India
201 M6 Paldau Austria
160 H2 Paldiski Estonia
210 G4 Pale Bos.-Herz.
118 B4 Pale Myanmar
156 H4 Palekh Rus. Fed.
Palekhori Cyprus see Palaichori
115 B3 Paleleh Sulawesi Indon.
116 F6 Palembang Sumatera Indon.
285 G4 Palemón Huergo Arg.
283 B6 Palena Aisén Chile
283 C6 Palena Los Lagos Chile
215 M4 Palena Italy
205 K4 Palencia Spain
205 K4 Palencia prov. Spain
207 J6 Palenciana Spain
267 M9 Palenque Mex.
205 L4 Palenzuela Spain
282 D2 Palermo Arg.
216 E7 Palermo Sicilia Italy
216 F8 Palermo prov. Sicilia Italy
216 E7 Palermo, Golfo di b. Sicilia Italy
150 D6 Palestine reg. Asia
261 H10 Palestine TX U.S.A.
215 J4 Palestrina Italy
118 A4 Paletwa Myanmar
122 M3 Palevo Rus. Fed.
145 M6 Palezgir Chauki Pak.
199 H5 Pálfa Hungary
136 C3 Palghar Mahar. India
Palghat India see Palakkad
109 C7 Palgrave, Mount hill W.A. Austr.
234 B4 Palgrave Point Namibia
204 C7 Palhaça Port.
199 K3 Pálháza Hungary
279 C8 Palhoca Brazil
138 H8 Pali Madh. Prad. India
136 C3 Pali Mahar. India
138 D7 Pali Rajasthan India
215 K4 Paliano Italy
117 K8 Paliat i. Indon.
199 I5 Palić Vojvodina Serbia
218 H4 Palićko Jezero l. Serbia
160 L7 Palik Belarus
100 □4b Palikir Pohnpei Micronesia
100 □4b Palikir Passage Pohnpei Micronesia
114 E8 Palimbang Mindanao Phil.
182 E3 Palinges France
215 O7 Palinuro Italy
215 O7 Palinuro, Capo c. Italy
220 E3 Paliouri Greece
220 E3 Paliouri, Akrotirio pt Greece
178 G7 Palis France
263 J7 Palisade CO U.S.A.
187 H9 Paliseul Belgium
138 C9 Palitana Gujarat India
160 G3 Palivere Estonia
217 K8 Palizzi Italy
162 O3 Palja hill Sweden
162 T4 Paljakka hill Fin.
163 R6 Pälkäne Fin.
136 F8 Palk Bay Sri Lanka
160 L4 Palkino Rus. Fed.
162 S2 Palkisoja Fin.
137 H3 Palkohda Andhra Prad. India
136 F6 Palkonda Range mts India
139 J8 Palkot Jharkhand India
199 H2 Palkovice Czech Rep.
136 F8 Palk Strait India/Sri Lanka
Palla Bianca mt. Austria/Italy see Weißkugel
136 E7 Palladani Tamil Nadu India
217 L5 Pallagorio Italy
276 B3 Pallapalla mt. Peru
206 G4 Pallarés Spain
208 H3 Pallaresa r. Spain
208 G3 Pallaresa, Noguera r. Spain
169 F7 Pallas Grean New Ireland
169 E7 Pallaskenry Ireland
142 B2 Pallasovka Rus. Fed.
162 Q2 Pallas-Yllästunturin kansallispuisto nat. park Fin.
136 G6 Pallavaram Tamil Nadu India
136 G4 Palleru r. India
218 H9 Pallës, Bishti i pt Albania
195 N5 Palling Ger.
109 E13 Pallinup r. W.A. Austr.
232 B4 Pallisa Uganda
103 J8 Palliser, Cape North I. N.Z.
101 □9 Palliser, Îles is Arch. des Tuamotu Fr. Polynesia
103 J8 Palliser Bay North I. N.Z.
214 A7 Pallosu, Cala su b. Sardegna Italy
138 E5 Pallu Rajasthan India
180 H8 Palluau France
181 N8 Palluau-sur-Indre France
278 D5 Palma r. Brazil
139 K8 Palma W. Bengal India
233 D7 Palma Moz.
206 B4 Palma Port.
209 K8 Palma, Badia de b. Spain
214 A8 Palma, Porto b. Sardegna Italy
215 N6 Palma Campania Italy
205 O6 Pálmaces, Embalse de resr Spain
207 I5 Palma del Río Spain
209 K8 Palma de Mallorca Spain
216 F9 Palma di Montechiaro Sicilia Italy
214 A6 Palmadula Sardegna Italy
136 F6 Palmaner Andhra Prad. India
213 O4 Palmanova Italy
209 K8 Palmanova Spain
268 F3 Palma Pegada Mex.
282 G4 Palmar, Punta del pt Uru.
268 G7 Palmar Chico Mex.
276 D2 Palmares Acre Brazil
278 G4 Palmares Pernambuco Brazil
279 C9 Palmares do Sul Brazil
212 H7 Palmaria, Isola i. Italy
274 D3 Palmarito Venez.
215 J6 Palmarola, Isola i. Italy
251 O1 Palmarolle Que. Can.
266 □R13 Palmar Sur Costa Rica
279 C8 Palmas Paraná Brazil
278 C4 Palmas Tocantins Brazil
228 D5 Palmas, Cape Liberia
214 B10 Palmas, Golfo di b. Sardegna Italy
269 K6 Palma Sola Mex.
271 I8 Palma Sola Venez.
270 F3 Palma Soriano Cuba
204 D7 Palmaz Port.
255 G12 Palm Bay FL U.S.A.
255 G11 Palm Coast FL U.S.A.
264 N7 Palmdale CA U.S.A.
265 P8 Palm Desert CA U.S.A.
280 C6 Palmeira Brazil
204 D5 Palmeira Port.
279 B8 Palmeira das Missões Brazil
278 F4 Palmeira dos Índios Brazil
278 E3 Palmeirais Brazil
278 D5 Palmeiras r. Brazil
280 C2 Palmeiras de Goiás Brazil
231 B7 Palmeirinhas, Ponta das pt Angola
206 B3 Palmela Port.
286 T2 Palmer research stn Antarctica
107 I4 Palmer r. Qld Austr.
106 D8 Palmer watercourse N.T. Austr.
245 J3 Palmer AK U.S.A.
286 T2 Palmer Land reg. Antarctica
258 B7 Palmer Park MD U.S.A.
106 C2 Palmerston N.T. Austr.
Palmerston N.T. Austr. see Darwin
251 N6 Palmerston Ont. Can.
103 □2 Palmerston atoll Cook Is
103 E12 Palmerston South I. N.Z.
169 J6 Palmerston Ireland
107 L6 Palmerston, Cape Qld Austr.
102 J7 Palmerston North North I. N.Z.
258 D3 Palmerton PA U.S.A.
107 J3 Palmerville Qld Austr.
255 F12 Palmetto FL U.S.A.
271 □2 Palmetto Point Antigua and Barbuda
255 I13 Palmetto Point Bahamas
217 J7 Palmi Italy
269 H2 Palmillas Mex.
284 C3 Palmira Arg.
274 B4 Palmira Col.
270 C2 Palmira Cuba
147 L3 Palm Islands tourist site U.A.E.
280 A6 Palmital Paraná Brazil
280 B5 Palmital São Paulo Brazil
285 I3 Palmitas Uru.
Palmnicken Rus. Fed. see Yantarnyy
206 I8 Palmones r. Spain
199 I5 Pálmonostora Hungary
264 P8 Palm Springs CA U.S.A.
107 L8 Palm Tree Creek r. Qld Austr.
106 D8 Palm Valley N.T. Austr.
Palmyra Syria see Tadmur
260 J6 Palmyra MO U.S.A.
258 E4 Palmyra NJ U.S.A.
256 H5 Palmyra NY U.S.A.
251 R9 Palmyra PA U.S.A.
256 G11 Palmyra VA U.S.A.
97 I3 Palmyra Atoll N. Pacific Ocean
139 K9 Palmyras Point India
168 I13 Palnackie Dumfries and Galloway, Scotland U.K.
214 C4 Palneca Corse France
136 E7 Palni Hills India
156 K3 Pal'niki Rus. Fed.
114 E6 Palo Leyte Phil.
214 C4 Palo, Étang de lag. Corse France
204 G2 Palo, Puerto del pass Spain
268 E4 Palo Alto Aguascalientes Mex.
269 H1 Palo Alto Tamaulipas Mex.
264 J4 Palo Alto CA U.S.A.
282 D2 Palo Blanco Arg.
267 I4 Palo Blanco Mex.
274 B3 Palo de las Letras Col.
217 L1 Palo del Colle Italy
261 E8 Palo Duro watercourse TX U.S.A.
117 I3 Paloh Sarawak Malaysia
232 B2 Paloich Sudan
162 Q2 Palojärvi Fin.
162 Q2 Palojoensuu Fin.
162 S2 Palomaa Fin.
276 C3 Palomani mt. Peru
208 D6 Palomar de Arroyos Spain
269 L8 Palomares Mex.
206 G6 Palomares del Río Spain
264 P8 Palomar Mountain CA U.S.A.
206 G3 Palomas Spain
206 H8 Palomas, Punta pt Spain
215 M3 Palombaro Italy
205 L2 Palombera, Embalse de mts Spain
205 L2 Palombera, Puerto de pass Spain
216 I10 Palombieri r. Sicilia Italy
205 P8 Palomera Spain
208 C6 Palomera, Sierra mts Spain
205 O9 Palomeras del Campo Spain
206 G3 Palomilas r. Spain
274 C2 Palomino Col.
282 D2 Palomitas Arg.
215 O6 Palomonte Italy
213 K4 Palòn, Cima mt. Italy
136 G4 Paloncha Andhra Prad. India
261 F9 Palo Pinto TX U.S.A.
115 B5 Palopo Sulawesi Indon.
209 D12 Palos, Cabo de c. Spain
282 F2 Palo Santo Arg.
206 F6 Palos de la Frontera Spain
271 □7 Palo Seco Trin. and Tob.
145 O4 Palosi Pak.
262 F3 Palouse r. WA U.S.A.
265 R8 Palo Verde CA U.S.A.
266 □Q12 Palo Verde, Parque Nacional nat. park Costa Rica
163 Q6 Palovesi l. Fin.
276 B3 Palpa Ica Peru
276 A2 Palpa Lima Peru
107 H8 Palparara Qld Austr.
115 E5 Palpetu, Tanjung pt Buru Indon.
284 B3 Palquico Chile
208 L4 Pals Spain
138 D9 Palsana Gujarat India
162 S4 Paltamo Fin.
162 S4 Paltaselkä l. Fin.
160 L1 Pal'tsevo Rus. Fed.
161 R8 Pal'tso Rus. Fed.
115 A4 Palu Sulawesi Indon.
115 B8 Palu i. Indon.
115 A4 Palu r. Indon.
149 I4 Palu Turkey
114 C5 Paluan Mindoro Phil.
114 C5 Paluan Bay Mindoro Phil.
217 L4 Paludi Italy
185 B8 Palue r. France
181 M2 Paluel France
213 O2 Paluzza Italy
145 K2 Pal'vart Turkm.
138 F5 Palwal Haryana India
Palwancha Andhra Prad. India see Paloncha
152 H3 Pal'yanovo Rus. Fed.
160 I7 Palyatskishki Belarus
153 S3 Palyavaam r. Rus. Fed.
Palyeskaya Nizina marsh Belarus/Ukr. see Pripet Marshes
160 M9 Palyessye Homyel'skaya Voblasts' Belarus
161 O8 Palyessye Homyel'skaya Voblasts' Belarus
194 A2 Palzem Ger.
201 P3 Pama Austria
229 F4 Pama Burkina
230 C3 Pama r. C.A.R.
229 F4 Pama, Réserve Partielle de nature res. Burkina
105 I5 Pamamaroo Lake N.S.W. Austr.
115 C9 Pamana i. Indon.
115 C8 Pamana Besar i. Indon.
239 □3b Pamandzi Mayotte
117 G8 Pamanukan Jawa Indon.
239 □3b Pamanzi, Récif rf Mayotte
274 D5 Pamar Col.
151 F5 P'ambaki Lernnashghht'a mts Armenia
136 F8 Pamban Channel India
235 G4 Pambarra Moz.
115 A3 Pambero Sulawesi Indon.
105 L7 Pambula N.S.W. Austr.
201 L6 Pameče Slovenia
117 J8 Pamekasan Jawa Indon.
117 G8 Pameungpeuk Jawa Indon.
221 H3 Pamfylla Lesvos Greece
201 O4 Pamhagen Austria
196 E3 Pamiątkowo Pol.
136 E5 Pamidi Andhra Prad. India
185 H9 Pamiers France
145 O3 Pamir r. Afgh./Tajik.
143 O8 Pamir mts Asia
255 I8 Pamlico r. NC U.S.A.
255 I8 Pamlico Sound sea chan. NC U.S.A.
249 G3 Pamouscachiou, Lac l. Que. Can.
276 C5 Pampa Chile
261 E8 Pampa TX U.S.A.
283 C7 Pampa Chica Arg.
276 B3 Pampachiri Peru
282 E2 Pampa de Infierno Arg.
276 D4 Pampa Grande Bol.
115 B6 Pampanua Sulawesi Indon.
212 D7 Pamparato Italy
285 E5 Pampas reg. Arg.
276 B3 Pampas Peru
276 B3 Pampas r. Peru
185 I7 Pampelonne France
Pampeluna Spain see Pamplona
236 I3 Pampierstad S. Africa
204 D8 Pampilhosa Port.
204 E8 Pampilhosa da Serra Port.
239 □1b Pamplemousses Mauritius
205 M4 Pampliega Spain
256 G11 Pamplin VA U.S.A.
274 C3 Pamplona Col.
114 D7 Pamplona Negros Phil.
205 Q3 Pamplona Spain
192 D3 Pampow Ger.
184 D3 Pamproux France
117 L6 Pamukan, Teluk b. Indon.
221 I3 Pamukçu Turkey
148 D5 Pamukkale Turkey
221 L2 Pamukova Turkey
256 I11 Pamunkey r. VA U.S.A.
220 B3 Pamvotida, Limni l. Greece
138 G2 Pamzal Jammu and Kashmir India
204 I5 Pan, Tierra del reg. Spain
230 B5 Pana Gabon
260 K6 Pana IL U.S.A.
267 O7 Panabá Mex.
114 E8 Panabo Mindanao Phil.
114 D8 Panabutan Bay Mindanao Phil.
265 R4 Panaca NV U.S.A.
220 C4 Panachaïko mts Greece
248 D4 Panache, Lake Ont. Can.
219 N3 Panaci Romania
107 N1 Panaeati Island P.N.G.
138 H8 Panagar Madh. Prad. India
220 F2 Panagia i. Thasos Greece
136 F4 Panagiri Andhra Prad. India
114 B7 Panagtaran Point Palawan Phil.
219 M8 Panagyurishte Bulg.
116 F8 Panaitan i. Indon.
220 C4 Panaitolio Greece
136 C5 Panaji Goa India
270 C9 Panama country Central America
266 □T13 Panamá Panama
266 □T13 Panamá, Bahía de b. Panama
266 □T13 Panamá, Canal de Panama
266 □T14 Panamá, Golfo de g. Panama
Panama, Gulf of Panama see Panamá, Golfo de
Panama City Panama see Panamá
255 E10 Panama City FL U.S.A.
138 F2 Panamik Jammu and Kashmir India
264 O5 Panamint Range mts CA U.S.A.
264 O5 Panamint Valley CA U.S.A.
117 H8 Pananjung Pangandaran, Taman Wisata nat. park Indon.
276 A2 Panao Peru
114 E7 Panaon i. Phil.
107 N1 Panapompom Island P.N.G.
139 L7 Panar r. India
217 I6 Panarea, Isola i. Isole Lipari Italy
117 H3 Panarik Indon.
213 K6 Panaro r. Italy
117 J8 Panarukan Jawa Indon.
185 F9 Panassac France
114 D6 Panay i. Phil.
162 T3 Panayarvi Natsional'nyy Park nat. park Rus. Fed.
114 D6 Panay Gulf Phil.
Panayía i. Thasos Greece see Panagia
184 G4 Panazol France
237 O2 Panbult S. Africa
265 Q3 Pancake Range mts NV U.S.A.
212 D6 Pancalieri Italy
281 G3 Pancas Brazil
218 I6 Pančevo Vojvodina Serbia
139 L6 Panchagarh Bangl.
138 G7 Panchamnagar Madh. Prad. India
159 K5 Pancheve Ukr.
131 M6 Panch'iao Taiwan
138 F4 Panchkula Haryana India
117 K4 Pancingapan, Bukit mt. Indon.
219 P5 Panciu Romania
205 N3 Pancorbo Spain
219 J4 Pâncota Romania
208 C6 Pancrudo Spain
208 C6 Pancrudo r. Spain
Pancsova Vojvodina Serbia see Pančevo
116 C3 Pancurbatu Sumatera Indon.
235 G5 Panda Moz.
138 H9 Pandada Chhattisgarh India
114 D6 Pandan Panay Phil.
114 E4 Pandan Phil.
116 □ Pandan, Selat str. Sing.
114 C6 Pandan Bay Panay Phil.
117 K5 Pandang Kalimantan Indon.
108 □2 Pandang, Pulu i. Cocos Is
116 □ Pandan Reservoir Sing.
138 H8 Pandaria Chhattisgarh India
138 H8 Pandatarai Chhattisgarh India
136 E6 Pandavapura Karnataka India
282 C2 Pan de Azúcar Chile
114 D6 Pan de Azucar i. Phil.
282 C2 Pan de Azúcar, Parque Nacional nat. park Chile
116 G8 Pandeglang Jawa Indon.
279 D5 Pandeiros r. Brazil
160 I5 Pandėlys Lith.
138 F9 Pandhana Madh. Prad. India
136 D4 Pandharpur Mahar. India
138 G9 Pandhurna Madh. Prad. India
104 G2 Pandie Pandie S.A. Austr.
212 H5 Pandino Italy
276 D2 Pando dept Bol.
285 J4 Pando Uru.
Pandokrátor hill Kerkyra Greece see Pantokratoras
266 □R13 Pandora Costa Rica
256 B8 Pandora OH U.S.A.
107 J1 Pandora Entrance sea chan. Qld Austr.
164 F4 Pandrup Denmark
172 G4 Pandy Monmouthshire, Wales U.K.
199 G4 Pándzsa r. Hungary
100 □5 Pané, Mont mt. New Caledonia
Paneas Syria see Bāniyās
216 I9 Panebianco r. Sicilia Italy
277 E2 Panelas Brazil
205 K2 Panes Spain
213 L3 Paneveggio-Pale di San Martino, Parco Naturale nature res. Italy
160 H6 Panevėžys Lith.
161 X5 Paneyevo Rus. Fed.
Panfilov Kazakh. see Zharkent
161 Y5 Panfilovo Ivanovskaya Oblast' Rus. Fed.
157 H6 Panfilovo Volgogradskaya Oblast' Rus. Fed.
159 K3 Panfyly Ukr.
118 D4 Pang, Nam r. Myanmar
230 E4 Panga Dem. Rep. Congo
160 F3 Panga Estonia
101 □8 Pangai Tonga
136 F4 Pangal Andhra Prad. India
231 B5 Pangala Congo
117 H8 Pangandaran Jawa Indon.
233 C6 Pangani Tanz.
233 C6 Pangani r. Tanz.
114 E5 Pañganiban Phil.
229 I5 Pangar r. Cameroon
229 I5 Pangar Djerem, Réserve du nature res. Cameroon
173 J5 Pangbourne West Berkshire, England U.K.
179 L5 Pange France
115 A4 Pangean Sulawesi Barat Indon.
100 □6 Panggoe Choiseul Solomon Is
118 D3 Panghsang Myanmar
231 E5 Pangi Dem. Rep. Congo
145 P4 Pangi Range mts Pak.
129 N6 Pangjiabu Hebei China
117 J8 Pangkah, Tanjung pt Indon.
115 A6 Pangkajene Sulawesi Indon.
117 I6 Pangkalanbuun Kalimantan Indon.
116 C3 Pangkalanlunang Sumatera Indon.
116 C2 Pangkalansusu Sumatera Indon.
116 E2 Pangkal Kalong Malaysia
116 G6 Pangkalpinang Indon.
115 C4 Pangkalsiang, Tanjung pt Indon.
118 C2 Panglang Myanmar
114 D7 Panglao i. Phil.
247 J5 Pangman Sask. Can.
243 L3 Pangnirtung Nunavut Can.
231 B7 Pango Aluquém Angola
152 I3 Pangody Rus. Fed.
230 D3 Pangonda C.A.R.
Pangong Tso salt l. China/India see Bangong Co
116 G8 Pangrango vol. Indon.
119 F7 Pang Sida National Park Thai.
116 □ Pang Sua, Sungai r. Sing.
118 C4 Pangtara Myanmar
122 D2 Pangu He r. China
283 B5 Panguipulli Chile
265 T4 Panguitch UT U.S.A.
117 I6 Pangujon, Tanjung pt Indon.
100 □6 Panguna P.N.G.
102 H2 Panguru North I. N.Z.
116 C3 Pangururan Sumatera Indon.
114 C8 Pangutaran i. Phil.
114 C8 Pangutaran Group is Phil.
261 E8 Panhandle TX U.S.A.
284 B4 Paniahue Chile
231 F6 Pania-Mwanga Dem. Re
214 I1 Panicale Italy
284 B4 Panimávida Chile
138 D8 Pani Mines Gujarat Indi
268 F6 Paníndicuaro Mex.
161 R5 Panino Tverskaya Oblast'
157 H6 Panino Voronezhskaya Ob Rus. Fed.
161 T1 Paninskaya Rus. Fed.
138 F5 Panipat Haryana India
145 L7 Panir Pak.
182 E5 Panissières France
114 B7 Panitan Palawan Phil.
269 J9 Panixtlahuaca Mex.
208 C5 Paniza Spain
161 N7 Panizowye Belarus
145 M3 Panj r. Afgh./Tajik.
145 M3 Panj Tajik.
145 L4 Panjāb Afgh.
145 L2 Panjakent Tajik.
116 F7 Panjang Sumatera Indon
117 H3 Panjang i. Indon.
117 M3 Panjang i. Indon.
116 □ Panjang, Bukit Sing.
116 E4 Panjang, Selat sea chan.
185 D8 Panjas France
144 B5 Panjbarār Iran
145 K8 Panjgur Pak.
138 E9 Panjhra r. India
Panjim Goa India see Pa
Panjin Liaoning China se Panshan
145 M3 Panji Poyon Tajik.
145 N4 Panjkora r. Pak.
145 N7 Panjnad r. Pak.
145 N7 Panjnad Barrage Pak.
145 M4 Panjshīr prov. Afgh.
162 U5 Pankakoski Fin.
190 K2 Panker Ger.
196 G5 Panki Pol.
244 G5 Pankof, Cape AK U.S.A.
161 O3 Pankovka Rus. Fed.
229 H4 Pankshin Nigeria
Panlian Sichuan China se
122 G7 Pan Ling mts China
Panlong Henan China se Queshan
120 D7 Panna Madh. Prad. India
108 D6 Pannawonica W.A. Austr.
178 E7 Pannes France
182 D2 Pannesière-Chaumard, de dam France
215 O5 Panni Italy
187 I6 Panningen Neth.
199 G4 Pannonhalma Hungary
145 M8 Pano Aqil Pak.
206 C5 Panóias Port.
150 B4 Pano Lefkara Cyprus
117 I5 Panopah Kalimantan Ind
Panoplis Egypt see Akhm
280 B4 Panorama Brazil
Panormus Sicilia Italy see Palermo
136 F7 Panruti Tamil Nadu India
193 J8 Panschwitz-Kuckau Ger.
129 R6 Panshan Liaoning China
122 E7 Panshi Jilin China
Panshui Guizhou China s
144 F4 Pansu, Chāh-e well Iran
173 N4 Pant r. England U.K.
117 L6 Pantai Kalimantan Indon
116 D5 Pantaicermin, Gunung m Indon.
277 F4 Pantanal reg. S. America
277 F4 Pantanal Matogrossense Nacional do nat. park Bra
118 B6 Pantanaw Myanmar
265 V10 Pantano AZ U.S.A.
115 D8 Pantar i. Indon.
159 L5 Pantayivka Ukr.
Pantelaria Sicilia Italy see Pantelleria
159 Q5 Panteleymonivka Ukr.
216 B10 Pantelleria Sicilia Italy
216 C10 Pantelleria, Isola di i. Sic
115 D8 Pante Macassar East Tim
Pantemakassar East Tim Pante Macassar
269 J5 Pantepec r. Mex.
118 B3 Pantha Myanmar
138 E8 Panth Piploda Madh. Pra
Panticapaeum Ukr. see K
208 E2 Panticosa Spain
108 H4 Pantijan Aboriginal Rese Austr.
205 M8 Pantoja Spain
220 A3 Pantokratoras hill Kerkyra
108 J4 Panton r. W.A. Austr.
116 B2 Pantonlabu Sumatera Ind
104 F2 Pantoowarinna, Lake salt Austr.
208 F5 Pantorrillas hill Spain
114 E8 Pantukan Mindanao Phil.
172 F3 Pant-y-dwr Powys, Wales
231 C5 Panu Dem. Rep. Congo
115 B3 Panua, Cagar Alam natur Indon.
268 B2 Pánuco Sinaloa Mex.
269 I3 Pánuco Veracruz Mex.
269 J3 Pánuco r. Mex.
268 C1 Pánuco de Coronado Me
138 G7 Panwari Uttar Prad. India
130 E6 Panxian Guizhou China
118 G2 Panxian Guizhou China
131 I7 Panyu Guangdong China
159 P5 Panyutyne Ukr.
201 I8 Panzaro, Golfo di b. Italy
130 C5 Panzhihua Sichuan China
231 C6 Panzi Dem. Rep. Congo
267 O10 Panzos Guat.
275 E2 Pao r. Venez.
102 K7 Paoanui Point North I. N
278 F4 Pão de Açúcar Brazil
215 Q9 Paola Italy
260 H6 Paola KS U.S.A.
254 D6 Paoli IN U.S.A.
258 E4 Paoli PA U.S.A.
214 C5 Paoloni, Serra hill Italy
115 F5 Paoni Seram Indon.
263 K7 Paonia CO U.S.A.
101 □9a Paopao Moorea Fr. Polyne
Paopao, Baie de b. Moore Fr. Polynesia see Cook, Ba
230 C3 Paoua C.A.R.
119 F8 Paôy Pêt Cambodia
Pap Uzbek. see Pop
198 G4 Pápa Hungary
264 □F14 Pāpā HI U.S.A.
215 P7 Papa, Monte del mt. Italy
264 □F14 Pāpa'aloa HI U.S.A.
220 D6 Papadianika Greece
Papagaio r. Brazil see Sau
281 E3 Papagaios Minas Gerais B
277 E2 Papagaios Rondônia Braz
269 H9 Papagayo r. Mex.
238 □3c Papagayo, Punta del pt La Canary Is
284 D2 Papagayos Arg.
136 F5 Papagni r. India
264 □F14 Pāpa'ikou HI U.S.A.
102 I4 Papakura North I. N.Z.
274 B5 Papallacta Ecuador
269 L7 Papaloapan r. Mex.
102 K4 Papamoa Beach North I.
136 E8 Papanasam Tamil Nadu I
136 F7 Papanasam Tamil Nadu I
268 F8 Papanoa Mex.
269 J5 Papantla Mex.
274 C6 Papa Playa Peru
117 K2 Papar Sabah Malaysia
101 □9a Papara Tahiti Fr. Polynesi
137 H3 Paparhahandi Orissa Indi
102 I3 Paparoa North I. N.Z.
103 F9 Paparoa National Park So N.Z.
103 F9 Paparoa Range mts South
221 G5 Papas, Akrotirio pt Ikaria
215 P8 Papasidero Italy
168 □M2 Papa Stour i. Scotland U.K
168 K4 Papa Stronsay i. Scotland
199 G4 Pápateszér Hungary
102 I3 Papatoetoe North I. N.Z.
103 D13 Papatowai South I. N.Z.
101 □9a Papawa Tahiti Fr. Polynesi

Papa Westray *i. Scotland* U.K.
Papay *i. Scotland* U.K. *see* **Papa Westray**
Papeete *Tahiti* Fr. Polynesia
Papenburg Ger.
Papendorf Ger.
Papendorp S. Africa
Papendrecht Neth.
Papenoo *Tahiti* Fr. Polynesia
Papenoo *r. Tahiti* Fr. Polynesia
Papetoai *Moorea* Fr. Polynesia
Papetoai, Baie de *b. Moorea* Fr. Polynesia *see* **Opunoho, Baie d'**
Paphos Cyprus *see* **Pafos**
Paphus Cyprus *see* **Pafos**
Papigochic *r.* Mex.
Papikio *mt.* Bulg./Greece
Papilė Lith.
Papillion *NE* U.S.A.
Papín Slovakia
Papineau-Labelle, Réserve Faunique de *nature res. Que.* Can.
Papineauville *Que.* Can.
Papiya *hill* Bulg.
Papkeszi Hungary
Papoose Lake *NV* U.S.A.
Paposo Chile
Papowo Biskupie Pol.
Pappenheim Ger.
Paprotnia Pol.
Paps of Jura *hills Scotland* U.K.
Papua, Gulf of P.N.G.
Papua Barat *prov.* Indon.
Papua New Guinea *country* Oceania
Papudo Chile
Papunya *N.T.* Austr.
Papworth Everard *Cambridgeshire, England* U.K.
Par *Cornwall, England* U.K.
Pará *r.* Brazil
Pará *state* Brazil
Para *i.* Indon.
Para *r.* Rus. Fed.
Pará, Rio do *r.* Brazil
Paraburdoo *W.A.* Austr.
Paráč *mt.* Slovakia
Paracale *Luzon* Phil.
Paracambi Brazil
Paracas Peru
Paracas, Península *pen.* Peru
Paracatu Brazil
Paracatu *r.* Brazil
Paracatu *r.* Brazil
Paracel Islands S. China Sea
Parachany Belarus
Parachilna *S.A.* Austr.
Parachinar Pak.
Paracho Mex.
Paraćin *Paracin* Serbia
Parácuaro *Guanajuato* Mex.
Parácuaro *Michoacán* Mex.
Paracuellos Spain
Paracuru Brazil
Parád Hungary
Parada Port.
Parada, Punta *pt* Peru
Parada de Ester Port.
Parada de Pinhão Port.
Parada de Rubiales Spain
Parada de Sil Spain
Paradas Spain
Paradeisia Greece
Paradela *Vila Real* Port.
Paradela *Viseu* Port.
Paradela Spain
Paradela de Guiães Port.
Pará de Minas Brazil
Paradera Aruba
Paradis *Que.* Can.
Paradise *r. Nfld and Lab.* Can.
Paradise Guyana
Paradise *AK* U.S.A.
Paradise *CA* U.S.A.
Paradise *MI* U.S.A.
Paradise *NV* U.S.A.
Paradise Gardens *N.W.T.* Can.
Paradise Hill *Sask.* Can.
Paradise Island *New Prov.* Bahamas
Paradise Peak *NV* U.S.A.
Paradise River *Nfld and Lab.* Can.
Paradise Valley *AZ* U.S.A.
Paradise Valley *NV* U.S.A.
Parado *Sumbawa* Indon.
Paradwip *Orissa* India
Paradyż Pol.
Paraetonium Egypt *see* **Marsá Maţrūḩ**
Parafiyivka Ukr.
Paraf"yanava Belarus
Parağaçay Azer.
Paragominas Brazil
Paragould *AR* U.S.A.
Paragua *r.* Bol.
Paragua *i.* Phil. *see* **Palawan**
Paragua *r.* Venez.
Paraguaçu Brazil
Paraguaçu Paulista Brazil
Paraguai *r.* Brazil
Paraguáipoa Venez.
Paraguaná, Península de *pen.* Venez.
Paraguarí Para.
Paraguay *r.* Arg./Para.
Paraguay *country* S. America
Parahadab Pak.
Paraíba *r.* Brazil
Paraíba *state* Brazil
Paraíba do Sul Brazil
Paraíba do Sul *r.* Brazil
Paraibuna Brazil
Parainen Fin. *see* **Pargas**
Paraíso Brazil
Paraíso *Campeche* Mex.
Paraíso *Tabasco* Mex.
Paraíso *Tabasco* Mex.
Paraíso do Norte Brazil
Paraisópolis Brazil
Parakka Sweden
Parakou Benin
Parakylia *S.A.* Austr.
Paralakhemundi *Orissa* India
Paralia *Peloponnisos* Greece
Paralia Saranti *Sterea Ellas* Greece
Paralkot *Chhattisgarh* India
Paramagudi *Tamil Nadu* India *see* **Paramakkudi**
Paramakkudi *Tamil Nadu* India
Paramaribo Suriname
Paramé France
Paramera, Puerto de la *pass* Spain
Paramera, Sierra de la *mts* Spain
Paramillo *mt.* Col.
Paramillo, Parque Nacional *nat. park* Col.
Paramillos, Sierra de los *mts* Arg.
Parâmio Port.
Paramirim Brazil
Paramirim *r.* Brazil
Páramo *hill* Spain
Páramo del Sil Spain
Páramo de Masa, Puerto del *pass* Spain
Páramo Leonés *reg.* Spain
Paramonga Peru
Paramonovo Rus. Fed.
Paramos Port.
Paramus *NJ* U.S.A.
Paramushir, Ostrov *i. Kuril'skiye O-va* Rus. Fed.
Paramythia Greece
Paran *watercourse* Israel
Paraná Arg.
Paranã Brazil
Paraná *r.* Brazil
Paraná *state* Brazil
Paraná *r.* S. America
Paraná, Delta del Arg.
Paranaguá Brazil
Paranaguá, Baía de *b.* Brazil
280 B3 **Paranaíba** Brazil
280 B4 **Paranaíba** *r.* Brazil
285 H3 **Paraná Ibicuy** *r.* Arg.
280 B3 **Paranaiguara** Brazil
277 F2 **Paranaita** *r.* Brazil
280 A5 **Paranapanema** *r.* Brazil
280 B6 **Paranapiacaba, Serra** *mts* Brazil
274 B6 **Paranapura** Peru
275 E5 **Paranari** Brazil
280 A5 **Paranavaí** Brazil
144 D4 **Parandak** Iran
117 I7 **Parang** *i.* Indon.
114 C9 **Parang** Phil.
136 G8 **Parangi Aru** *r.* Sri Lanka
136 F7 **Parangipettai** *Tamil Nadu* India
138 F3 **Parang Pass** *Hima. Prad.* India
219 L5 **Parângul Mare, Vârful** *mt.* Romania
204 E8 **Paranhos** Port.
136 G8 **Paranthan** Sri Lanka
281 E3 **Paraopeba** Brazil
281 E3 **Paraopeba** *r.* Brazil
207 L6 **Parapanda** *mt.* Spain
115 E3 **Parapara** *Halmahera* Indon.
149 L6 **Pārapāra** Iraq
103 I7 **Paraparaumu** *North I.* N.Z.
220 E6 **Parapola** *i.* Greece
280 B4 **Parapuã** Brazil
274 E3 **Paraque, Cerro** *mt.* Venez.
162 P2 **Paras** Norway
145 O4 **Paras** Pak.
221 I7 **Paraspori, Akrotirio** *pt* Greece
214 B4 **Parata, Pointe de la** *pt Corse* France
281 E5 **Parati** Brazil
278 E5 **Paratinga** Brazil
104 G5 **Paratoo** *S.A.* Austr.
149 M6 **Parāū, Kūh-e** *mt.* Iraq
278 C3 **Parauapebas** *r.* Brazil
275 H5 **Parauaquara, Serra** *hill* Brazil
275 G6 **Parauari** *r.* Brazil
151 I3 **Paraulozen'** *r.* Rus. Fed.
280 B2 **Paraúna** Brazil
136 E7 **Paravur** *Kerala* India
182 E4 **Paray-le-Monial** France
138 F7 **Parbati** *r.* India
139 L7 **Parbatipur** Bangl.
136 E3 **Parbhani** *Mahar.* India
171 L6 **Parbold** *Lancashire, England* U.K.
271 □1 **Parcelas Martorell** Puerto Rico
209 E10 **Parcent** Spain
181 K6 **Parcé-sur-Sarthe** France
238 □3f **Parchel, Punta del** *pt Gran Canaria* Canary Is
193 F6 **Parchen** Ger.
143 L1 **Parchevka** Kazakh.
192 E4 **Parchim** Ger.
149 O6 **Parchīn** Iran
250 I7 **Parchment** *MI* U.S.A.
199 K3 **Parchovany** Slovakia
196 D4 **Parchów** Pol.
196 F1 **Parchowo** Pol.
197 J2 **Parciaki** Pol.
184 E5 **Parcoul** France
197 K4 **Parczew** Pol.
206 E3 **Pardais** Port.
264 L3 **Pardee Reservoir** *CA* U.S.A.
250 E6 **Pardeeville** *WI* U.S.A.
185 C9 **Pardies** France
204 C7 **Pardilhó** Port.
219 Q5 **Pardina** Romania
285 H5 **Pardo** Arg.
280 A4 **Pardo** *r.* Brazil
280 C4 **Pardo** *r.* Brazil
280 C6 **Pardo** *r.* Brazil
279 D5 **Pardo** *r.* Brazil
279 F5 **Pardo** *r.* Brazil
108 E6 **Pardoo** *W.A.* Austr.
205 Q6 **Pardos, Sierra de** *mts* Spain
198 E1 **Pardubice** Czech Rep.
198 F2 **Pardubický kraj** *admin. reg.* Czech Rep.
117 J8 **Pare** *Jawa* Indon.
Parece Vela *i.* Japan *see* **Okino-Tori-shima**
160 H8 **Parechcha** Belarus
133 D10 **Pare Chu** *r.* China
277 F3 **Parecis** Brazil
277 F3 **Parecis** *r.* Brazil
277 E2 **Parecis, Serra dos** *hills* Brazil
204 D6 **Paredes** Port.
204 C5 **Paredes de Coura** Port.
205 K4 **Paredes de Nava** Spain
284 C3 **Pareditas** Arg.
269 N9 **Paredón** *Chiapas* Mex.
267 I5 **Paredón** *Coahuila* Mex.
284 B4 **Paredones** Chile
144 A2 **Pareh** Iran
205 O7 **Pareja** Spain
183 B8 **Pareloup, Lac de** *l.* France
100 □4a **Parem** *i. Chuuk* Micronesia
103 I8 **Paremata** *North I.* N.Z.
100 □4b **Parempei** *i. Pohnpei* Micronesia
184 C6 **Parempuyre** France
136 D3 **Parenda** *Mahar.* India
102 G1 **Parengarenga Harbour** *North I.* N.Z.
117 J6 **Parenggean** *Kalimantan* Indon.
248 F4 **Parent** *Que.* Can.
248 E3 **Parent, Lac** *l. Que.* Can.
217 K5 **Parenti** Italy
185 B7 **Parentis-en-Born** France
103 F11 **Pareora** *South I.* N.Z.
115 A6 **Parepare** *Sulawesi* Indon.
284 E4 **Parera** Arg.
208 J4 **Parets del Vallès** Spain
193 E6 **Parey** Ger.
156 H4 **Parfen'yevo** Rus. Fed.
161 O4 **Parfino** Rus. Fed.
220 B3 **Parga** Greece
163 Q6 **Pargas** Fin.
217 J6 **Parghelia** Italy
136 E4 **Pargi** *Andhra Prad.* India
179 I6 **Pargny-sur-Saulx** France
206 □ **Pargo, Ponta do** *pt* Madeira
161 N1 **Pargolovo** Rus. Fed.
271 □2 **Parham** Antigua and Barbuda
276 D4 **Paria** Bol.
265 U5 **Paria** *r. AZ/UT* U.S.A.
271 □7 **Paria, Gulf of** Trin. and Tob./Venez.
275 F2 **Paria, Península de** *pen.* Venez.
116 D5 **Pariaman** *Sumatera* Indon.
265 T5 **Paria Plateau** *AZ* U.S.A.
275 F6 **Paricatuba** Brazil
268 E6 **Paricutín, Volcán** *vol.* Mex.
266 □R13 **Parida, Isla** *i.* Panama
115 B4 **Parigi** *Sulawesi* Indon.
181 L6 **Parigné-l'Évêque** France
199 H5 **Pári-hegy** *hill* Hungary
163 T6 **Parikkala** Fin.
137 I3 **Parikud Islands** India
Parima *r.* Brazil *see* **Uatatás**
275 E4 **Parima, Serra** *mts* Brazil
275 E4 **Parima-Tapirapecó, Parque Nacional** *nat. park* Venez.
274 C6 **Parinari** Peru
274 A6 **Pariñas, Punta** *pt* Peru
104 H6 **Paringa** *S.A.* Austr.
200 A8 **Parino** *r.* Italy
275 G5 **Parintins** Brazil
251 N6 **Paris** *Ont.* Can.
178 D6 **Paris** France
261 I8 **Paris** *AR* U.S.A.
262 I5 **Paris** *ID* U.S.A.
254 D6 **Paris** *IL* U.S.A.
256 A10 **Paris** *KY* U.S.A.
257 □O4 **Paris** *ME* U.S.A.
260 I6 **Paris** *MO* U.S.A.
261 K7 **Paris** *TN* U.S.A.
261 H9 **Paris** *TX* U.S.A.
178 E5 **Paris (Charles de Gaulle)** *airport* France
178 D6 **Paris (Orly)** *airport* France
175 **Paris area map** France
257 I5 **Parish** *NY* U.S.A.
250 J3 **Parisienne, Île** *i. Ont.* Can.
185 H7 **Parisot** *Midi-Pyrénées* France
185 H8 **Parisot** *Midi-Pyrénées* France
116 D2 **Parit Buntar** Malaysia
144 F7 **Pārīz** Iran
142 I1 **Parizh** Rus. Fed.
144 I9 **Pārk** Iran
260 G1 **Park** *r. ND* U.S.A.
230 E3 **Parka** Dem. Rep. Congo
162 Q3 **Parkajoki** Sweden
136 F3 **Parkal** *Andhra Prad.* India
163 Q5 **Parkano** Fin.
249 J2 **Parke Lake** *Nfld and Lab.* Can.
143 M7 **Parkent** Uzbek.
265 R7 **Parker** *AZ* U.S.A.
260 C6 **Parker** *CO* U.S.A.
260 G4 **Parker** *SD* U.S.A.
Parker, Mount *hill H.K.* China *see* **Pak Ka Shan**
265 R7 **Parker Dam** *CA* U.S.A.
247 M2 **Parker Lake** *Nunavut* Can.
109 E12 **Parker Range** *hills W.A.* Austr.
256 D9 **Parkersburg** *WV* U.S.A.
105 L5 **Parkes** *N.S.W.* Austr.
258 D5 **Parkesburg** *PA* U.S.A.
250 D4 **Park Falls** *WI* U.S.A.
250 G8 **Park Forest** *IL* U.S.A.
Parkhar Tajik. *see* **Farkhor**
251 M6 **Parkhill** *Ont.* Can.
159 S5 **Parkhomenko** Ukr.
159 O3 **Parkhomivka** Ukr.
251 K3 **Parkinson** *Ont.* Can.
256 D7 **Parkman** *OH* U.S.A.
169 C9 **Parknasilla** Ireland
260 H2 **Park Rapids** *MN* U.S.A.
257 J11 **Parksley** *VA* U.S.A.
195 M2 **Parkstein** Ger.
195 N4 **Parkstetten** Ger.
260 G4 **Parkston** *SD* U.S.A.
246 E5 **Parksville** *B.C.* Can.
138 F2 **Parkutta** Pak.
262 H6 **Park Valley** *UT* U.S.A.
258 B6 **Parkville** *MD* U.S.A.
205 M8 **Parla** Spain
Parlakimedi *Orissa* India *see* **Paralakhemundi**
137 I3 **Parla Kimedi** *Orissa* India
185 I6 **Parlan** France
271 □5 **Parlatuvier** Trin. and Tob.
136 E3 **Parli Vaijnath** *Mahar.* India
130 A3 **Parlung Zangbo** *r.* China
212 I6 **Parma** Italy
212 I6 **Parma** *prov.* Italy
212 I6 **Parma** *r.* Italy
156 L2 **Parma** Rus. Fed.
262 F5 **Parma** *ID* U.S.A.
250 J7 **Parma** *MI* U.S.A.
256 D7 **Parma** *OH* U.S.A.
275 E3 **Parmana** Venez.
185 A9 **Parme** *airport* France
278 D4 **Parnaguá** Brazil
278 E2 **Parnaíba** Brazil
278 B4 **Parnaíba** *r.* Brazil
278 D4 **Parnaibinha** *r.* Brazil
278 E3 **Parnarama** Brazil
220 D4 **Parnassou, Ethnikos Drymos** *nat. park* Greece
103 H9 **Parnassus** *South I.* N.Z.
Parnassus, Mount Greece *see* **Liakoura**
104 F6 **Parndana** *S.A.* Austr.
201 O4 **Parndorf** Austria
136 D3 **Parner** *Mahar.* India
220 E4 **Parnithas, Ethnikos Drymos** *nat. park* Greece
220 D5 **Parnonas** *mts* Greece
160 H3 **Pärnu** Estonia
160 H3 **Pärnu** *r.* Estonia
160 H3 **Pärnu-Jaagupi** Estonia
160 H3 **Pärnu laht** *b.* Estonia
139 L6 **Paro** Bhutan
103 F9 **Paroa** *South I.* N.Z.
220 G5 **Paroikia** *Paros* Greece
160 H1 **Parola** Fin.
178 F7 **Paron** France
Parona Turkey *see* **Fındık**
105 I4 **Paroo** *watercourse Qld* Austr.
105 I4 **Paroo Channel** *watercourse N.S.W.* Austr.
105 I4 **Paroo-Darling National Park** *N.S.W.* Austr.
Paropamisus *mts* Afgh. *see* **Safīd Kūh**
115 A5 **Paroreang, Bukit** *mt.* Indon.
220 G5 **Paros** *i.* Greece
270 □ **Parottee Point** Jamaica
236 C9 **Parow** S. Africa
193 L8 **Parowa** Pol.
265 T4 **Parowan** *UT* U.S.A.
183 J8 **Parpaillon** *mts* France
104 H6 **Parrakie** *S.A.* Austr.
284 B5 **Parral** Chile
261 C12 **Parral** *r.* Mex.
105 M5 **Parramatta** *N.S.W.* Austr.
257 J11 **Parramore Island** *VA* U.S.A.
266 H5 **Parras** Mex.
285 I5 **Parravicini** Arg.
172 F5 **Parrett** *r. England* U.K.
205 J8 **Parrillas** Spain
250 E4 **Parrish** *WI* U.S.A.
266 □Q13 **Parrita** Costa Rica
249 H4 **Parrsboro** *N.S.* Can.
245 P1 **Parry, Cape** *N.W.T.* Can.
Parry, Kap *c.* Greenland *see* **Kangaarsussuaq**
248 F1 **Parry, Lac** *l. Que.* Can.
243 J3 **Parry Bay** *Nunavut* Can.
243 H2 **Parry Channel** *Nunavut* Can.
Parry Island Cook Is *see* **Mauke**
243 G2 **Parry Islands** *Nunavut* Can.
108 J3 **Parry Lagoons Nature Reserve** *W.A.* Austr.
271 □7 **Parrylands** Trin. and Tob.
245 P1 **Parry Peninsula** *N.W.T.* Can.
108 C7 **Parry Range** *hills W.A.* Austr.
248 D4 **Parry Sound** *Ont.* Can.
258 D3 **Parryville** *PA* U.S.A.
Pars *prov.* Iran *see* **Fārs**
139 J7 **Parsa** *Bihar* India
Parsa *prov.* Iran *see* **Fārs**
151 I6 **Pārsābād** Iran
190 K5 **Parsau** Ger.
139 J6 **Parsa Wildlife Reserve** *nature res.* Nepal
195 L3 **Parsberg** Ger.
196 E2 **Parsęcko** Pol.
200 B5 **Parseierspitze** *mt.* Austria
196 D1 **Parsęta** *r.* Pol.
260 D2 **Parshall** *ND* U.S.A.
259 G3 **Parsippany** *NJ* U.S.A.
265 R3 **Parsnip Peak** *NV* U.S.A.
261 H7 **Parsons** *KS* U.S.A.
256 F9 **Parsons** *WV* U.S.A.
245 N1 **Parsons Lake** *N.W.T.* Can.
106 E2 **Parsons Range** *hills N.T.* Austr.
192 J5 **Parstein** Ger.
192 I5 **Parsteiner See** *l.* Ger.
133 J11 **Parta** *Xizang* China
136 C4 **Partabgarh** *Mahar.* India
136 G3 **Partabpur** *Chhattisgarh* India
139 I8 **Partabpur** *Chhattisgarh* India
162 S2 **Partakko** Fin.
207 O6 **Partaloa** Spain
151 I6 **Par Talū** Iran
216 D8 **Partanna** *Sicilia* Italy
162 N3 **Pårte** *mt.* Sweden
200 B6 **Partenen** Austria
191 I10 **Partenstein** Ger.
184 D2 **Parthenay** France
266 D5 **Partida, Isla** *i.* Mex.
214 B3 **Partinello** *Corse* France
171 M7 **Partington** *Greater Manchester, England* U.K.
216 E7 **Partinico** *Sicilia* Italy
122 H7 **Partizansk** Rus. Fed.
199 I2 **Partizánska Ľupča** Slovakia
199 H3 **Partizánske** Slovakia
171 R7 **Partney** *Lincolnshire, England* U.K.
171 J4 **Parton** *Cumbria, England* U.K.
248 D3 **Partridge** *r. Ont.* Can.
169 D5 **Partry** Ireland
160 K3 **Partsi** Estonia
151 D3 **P'arts'khanaqanevi** Georgia
159 N7 **Partyzany** Ukr.
275 H5 **Paru** *r.* Brazil
275 E3 **Parú, Serranía** *mts* Venez.
145 I8 **Pārūd** Iran
275 G5 **Paru de Oeste** *r.* Brazil
159 K7 **Parutyne** Ukr.
144 G5 **Parvādeh** Iran
137 H3 **Parvatipuram** *Andhra Prad.* India
138 E6 **Parvatsar** *Rajasthan* India
145 M4 **Parwān** *prov.* Afgh.
133 F11 **Paryang** *Xizang* China
160 M9 **Parychy** Belarus
165 L5 **Påryd** Sweden
143 U3 **Parygino** Kazakh.
237 L2 **Parys** S. Africa
197 J4 **Parysów** Pol.
197 H4 **Parzęczew** Pol.
205 M2 **Pas** *r.* Spain
144 E5 **Pās, Chāh** *well* Iran
148 F4 **Pasa Dağı** *mt.* Turkey
264 N7 **Pasadena** *CA* U.S.A.
258 B6 **Pasadena** *MD* U.S.A.
261 H11 **Pasadena** *TX* U.S.A.
274 A5 **Pasado, Cabo** *c.* Ecuador
208 B1 **Pasai Donibane** Spain
274 B5 **Pasaje** Ecuador
Pasajes de San Juan Spain *see* **Pasai Donibane**
118 E7 **Pa Sak, Mae Nam** *r.* Thai.
151 D5 **Paşalı** Turkey
221 I2 **Paşalimanı Adası** *i.* Turkey
138 I8 **Pasan** *Chhattisgarh* India
151 F3 **P'asanauri** Georgia
118 D5 **Pa Sang** Thai.
115 A4 **Pasangkayu** *Sulawesi Barat* Indon.
116 D6 **Pasarbantal** *Sumatera* Indon.
149 P8 **Pasargadae** *tourist site* Iran
116 D6 **Pasarseblat** *Sumatera* Indon.
116 E7 **Pasarseluma** *Sumatera* Indon.
115 C6 **Pasarwajo** *Sulawesi* Indon.
118 C5 **Pasawng** Myanmar
248 F3 **Pascagama** *r. Que.* Can.
261 K10 **Pascagoula** *MS* U.S.A.
261 K10 **Pascagoula** *r. MS* U.S.A.
251 Q1 **Pascalis** *Que.* Can.
219 O3 **Paşcani** Romania
201 J3 **Pasching** Austria
276 B2 **Pasco** *dept* Peru
262 E3 **Pasco** *WA* U.S.A.
257 N7 **Pascoag** *RI* U.S.A.
281 H2 **Pascoal, Monte** *hill* Brazil
107 I2 **Pascoe** *r. Qld* Austr.
106 G4 **Pascoe Inlet** *Qld* Austr.
272 C5 **Pascua, Isla de** *i.* S. Pacific Ocean
114 D5 **Pascual** Phil.
178 D2 **Pas-de-Calais** *dept* France
Pas de Calais *str.* France/U.K. *see* **Dover, Strait of**
178 D3 **Pas-en-Artois** France
192 J3 **Pasewalk** Ger.
247 J3 **Pasfield Lake** *Sask.* Can.
144 I5 **Pāsgāh-e Gol Vardeh** Iran
161 Q1 **Pasha** Rus. Fed.
161 P1 **Pasha** *r.* Rus. Fed.
122 G4 **Pashkovo** Rus. Fed.
159 S8 **Pashkovskiy** Rus. Fed.
161 R1 **Pashozero** Rus. Fed.
145 J4 **Pashtun Zarghun** Afgh.
144 H7 **Pashū'īyeh** Iran
213 O3 **Pasiàn di Prato** Italy
200 G8 **Pasiano di Pordenone** Italy
197 J3 **Pasieki** Pol.
114 C4 **Pasig** *Luzon* Phil.
118 C1 **Pasi Ga** Myanmar
115 D2 **Pasige** *i.* Indon.
139 O5 **Pasighat** *Arun. Prad.* India
149 J4 **Pasinler** Turkey
116 □ **Pasir Gudang** Malaysia
117 J9 **Pasirian** *Jawa* Indon.
116 □ **Pasir Laba, Tanjong** *pt* Sing.
116 E1 **Pasir Mas** Malaysia
116 D4 **Pasirpangarayan** *Sumatera* Indon.
116 □ **Pasir Panjang** Sing.
116 □ **Pasir Panjang** *hill* Sing.
116 E2 **Pasir Putih** Malaysia
115 B7 **Pasitelu, Pulau-pulau** *is* Indon.
165 M4 **Påskallavik** Sweden
Paskevicha, Zaliv *l.* Kazakh. *see* **Shevchenko, Zaliv**
213 R6 **Paški Kanal** *sea chan.* Croatia
199 H2 **Paskov** Czech Rep.
145 I8 **Paskūh** Iran
165 P7 **Pasłęk** Pol.
165 P7 **Pasłęka** *r.* Pol.
109 G12 **Pasley, Cape** *W.A.* Austr.
151 D5 **Paslı Geçidi** *pass* Turkey
210 E4 **Pašman** *i.* Croatia
104 G4 **Pasmore** *watercourse S.A.* Austr.
145 J9 **Pasni** Pak.
267 N9 **Paso Caballos** Guat.
274 E2 **Paso de Caballo** Venez.
283 C6 **Paso de Indios** Arg.
285 H2 **Paso de la Laguna** Arg.
269 J5 **Paso del Correo** Mex.
283 C6 **Paso del Limay** Arg.
269 K6 **Paso del Macho** Mex.
284 D5 **Paso de los Algarrobos** Arg.
284 C6 **Paso de los Indios** Arg.
285 I1 **Paso de los Libres** Arg.
285 I3 **Paso de los Toros** Uru.
285 I3 **Paso del Palmar, Lago Artificial de** *resr* Uru.
269 N8 **Paso del Rosario** Mex.
283 C6 **Paso del Sapo** Arg.
269 K6 **Paso de Ovejas** Mex.
277 F6 **Paso de Patria** Para.
261 D11 **Paso de San Antonio** *Chihuahua* Mex.
268 G3 **Paso de San Antonio** *San Luis Potosí* Mex.
284 E3 **Paso Grande** Arg.
118 B4 **Pasok** Myanmar
266 □Q10 **Paso Real** Hond.
283 C7 **Paso Río Mayo** Arg.
264 L6 **Paso Robles** *CA* U.S.A.
247 K4 **Pasquia Hills** *Sask.* Can.
145 P5 **Pasrur** Pak.
257 □Q3 **Passadumkeag** *ME* U.S.A.
250 F1 **Passage Island** *MI* U.S.A.
278 E3 **Passagem Franca** Brazil
169 F9 **Passage West** Ireland
259 G3 **Passaic** *NJ* U.S.A.
259 G3 **Passaic** *r. NJ* U.S.A.
259 G2 **Passaic County** *county NJ* U.S.A.
201 M5 **Passail** Austria
181 J4 **Passais** France
239 □3b **Passamaïnti** Mayotte
281 E5 **Passa Quatro** Brazil
281 E4 **Passa Tempo** Brazil
195 O4 **Passau** Ger.
179 L8 **Passavant-la-Rochère** France
114 D6 **Passi** *Panay* Phil.
214 I1 **Passignano sul Trasimeno** Italy
213 K2 **Passirio** *r.* Italy
279 B9 **Passo Fundo** Brazil
282 G2 **Passo Fundo, Barragem do** *resr* Brazil
279 B9 **Passo Real, Barragem** *resr* Brazil
280 D4 **Passos** Brazil
192 J4 **Passow** Ger.
182 J5 **Passy** France
160 J6 **Pastavy** Belarus
274 B5 **Pastaza** *prov.* Ecuador
274 B6 **Pastaza** *r.* Peru
285 F4 **Pasteur** Arg.
274 B4 **Pasto** Col.
277 E1 **Pasto Grande** Brazil
244 G3 **Pastol Bay** *AK* U.S.A.
265 W5 **Pastora Peak** *AZ* U.S.A.
269 I4 **Pastoría** Mex.
269 J10 **Pastoria, Laguna** *l.* Mex.
204 F2 **Pastoriza** Spain
268 F5 **Pastor Ortíz** Mex.
278 D3 **Pastos Bons** Brazil
205 O8 **Pastrana** Spain
138 E1 **Pasu** Pak.
114 C2 **Pasuquin** *Luzon* Phil.
Pasur Turkey *see* **Kulp**
117 J8 **Pasuruan** *Jawa* Indon.
160 H5 **Pasvalys** Lith.
Pasvikelva *r.* Europe *see* **Patsoyoki**
197 I2 **Pasym** Pol.
196 E4 **Paszowice** Pol.
199 I4 **Pásztó** Hungary
276 C3 **Pata** Bol.
230 D2 **Pata** C.A.R.
114 C9 **Pata** *i.* Phil.
228 B3 **Pata** Senegal
199 G3 **Pata** Slovakia
283 C8 **Patagonia** *reg.* Arg.
265 V10 **Patagonia** *AZ* U.S.A.
204 C9 **Pataias** Port.
133 J14 **Patakata** *Assam* India
Pataliputra *Bihar* India *see* **Patna**
268 E6 **Patambán** Mex.
Patan *Gujarat* India *see* **Somnath**
138 D8 **Patan** *Gujarat* India
139 J7 **Patan** *Jharkhand* India
138 G8 **Patan** *Madh. Prad.* India
136 C4 **Patan** *Mahar.* India
139 J6 **Patan** Nepal
145 O4 **Patan** Pak.
136 F4 **Patancheru** *Andhra Prad.* India
145 K8 **Patandar, Koh-i-** *mt.* Pak.
115 F3 **Patani** *Halmahera* Indon.
229 G5 **Patani** Nigeria
138 G9 **Patan Saongi** *Mahar.* India
258 B6 **Patapsco** *r. MD* U.S.A.
258 B6 **Patapsco, South Branch** *r. MD* U.S.A.
144 I5 **Patargān, Daqq-e** *salt flat* Iran
138 F5 **Pataudi** *Haryana* India
Patavium Italy *see* **Padova**
282 E2 **Patay** Arg.
178 C7 **Patay** France
105 I6 **Patchewollock** *Vic.* Austr.
259 I3 **Patchogue** *NY* U.S.A.
172 G4 **Patchway** *South Gloucestershire, England* U.K.
102 I6 **Patea** *North I.* N.Z.
Patea *inlet South I.* N.Z. *see* **Doubtful Sound**
102 I6 **Patea** *r. North I.* N.Z.
229 G4 **Pategi** Nigeria
233 D5 **Pate Island** Kenya
171 N5 **Pateley Bridge** *North Yorkshire, England* U.K.
237 I9 **Patensie** S. Africa
201 I6 **Patergassen** Austria
209 E8 **Paterna** Spain
206 G6 **Paterna del Campo** Spain
206 H7 **Paterna de Rivera** Spain
201 I6 **Paternion** Austria
215 P7 **Paterno** Italy
216 H8 **Paternò** *Sicilia* Italy
215 O6 **Paternopoli** Italy
236 B8 **Paternoster** S. Africa
195 N3 **Patersdorf** Ger.
105 M5 **Paterson** *N.S.W.* Austr.
105 K3 **Paterson** *r. Qld* Austr.
237 J9 **Paterson** S. Africa
257 K8 **Paterson** *NJ* U.S.A.
103 B13 **Paterson Inlet** *Stewart I.* N.Z.
108 G6 **Paterson Range** *hills W.A.* Austr.
139 I8 **Pathalgaon** *Chhattisgarh* India
133 L13 **Pathalipam** *Assam* India
144 G8 **Pathān** Iran
136 E8 **Pathanamthitta** *Kerala* India
138 E3 **Pathankot** *Punjab* India
138 G8 **Pathari** *Madh. Prad.* India
138 G8 **Patharia** *Madh. Prad.* India
Pathein Myanmar *see* **Bassein**
138 F6 **Pathena** *Rajasthan* India
262 K5 **Pathfinder Reservoir** *WY* U.S.A.
119 D9 **Pathiu** Thai.
136 E3 **Pathri** *Mahar.* India
119 E8 **Pathum Thani** Thai.
274 E5 **Pati** *r.* Brazil
138 E9 **Pati** *Madh. Prad.* India
117 I8 **Pati** *Jawa* Indon.
274 B4 **Patía** *r.* Col.
138 F4 **Patiala** *Punjab* India
271 □1 **Patillas** Puerto Rico
271 □1 **Patillas, Puerto** *b.* Puerto Rico
115 E4 **Patinti, Selat** *sea chan. Maluku* Indon.
100 □1 **Pati Point** Guam
115 B6 **Patiro, Tanjung** *pt* Indon.
220 E3 **Patitiri** Greece
276 A2 **Pativilca** *r.* Peru
118 B1 **Patkai Bum** *mts* India/Myanmar
133 H8 **Patkaklik** *Xinjiang* China
221 K6 **Patlangıç** Turkey
221 H5 **Patmos** *i.* Greece
139 J7 **Patna** *Bihar* India
168 H12 **Patna** *East Ayrshire, Scotland* U.K.
139 I9 **Patnagarh** *Orissa* India
114 D4 **Patnanongan** *i.* Phil.
149 K4 **Patnos** Turkey
196 G4 **Pątnów** Pol.
283 B7 **Pato, Cerro** *mt.* Chile
279 B8 **Pato Branco** Brazil
136 D3 **Patoda** *Mahar.* India
254 D6 **Patoka** *r. IN* U.S.A.
153 M4 **Patomskoye Nagor'ye** *mts* Rus. Fed.
138 H4 **Paton** *Uttaranchal* India
162 S2 **Patoniva** Fin.
220 A2 **Patos** Albania
278 F3 **Patos** *Paraíba* Brazil
278 E3 **Patos** *Piauí* Brazil
271 □7 **Patos, Isla** *i.* Venez.
279 C9 **Patos, Lagoa dos** *l.* Brazil
285 F2 **Patos, Laguna de los** *l.* Arg.
284 C2 **Patos, Río de los** *r.* Arg.
280 D3 **Patos de Minas** Brazil
284 D2 **Patquía** Arg.
220 C4 **Patra** Greece
Patrae Greece *see* **Patra**
Pátrai Greece *see* **Patra**
220 C4 **Patraïkos Kolpos** *b.* Greece
156 H2 **Patrakeyevka** Rus. Fed.
Patras Greece *see* **Patra**
139 K8 **Patrasaer** *W. Bengal* India
139 J8 **Patratu** *Jharkhand* India
162 □B1 **Patreksfjörður** Iceland
138 C8 **Patri** *Gujarat* India
217 I7 **Patri** *r. Sicilia* Italy
103 H8 **Patriarch, Mount** *South I.* N.Z.
215 K4 **Patrica** Italy
106 C6 **Patricia, Mount** *hill N.T.* Austr.
283 B8 **Patricio Lynch, Isla** *i.* Chile
170 H5 **Patrick** Isle of Man
107 J7 **Patrick Creek** *watercourse Qld* Austr.
256 E12 **Patrick Springs** *VA* U.S.A.
169 E7 **Patrickswell** Ireland
280 C3 **Patrimônio** Brazil
214 C2 **Patrimonio** *Corse* France
171 R6 **Patrington** *East Riding of Yorkshire, England* U.K.
280 D3 **Patrocínio** Brazil
199 K3 **Pátroha** Hungary
144 H4 **Paţrū** Iran
200 D5 **Patscherkofel** *mt.* Austria
156 E1 **Patsoyoki** *r.* Europe
214 C6 **Pattada** *Sardegna* Italy
136 D4 **Pattadakal** *tourist site Karnataka* India
136 E8 **Pattanapuram** *Kerala* India
119 E11 **Pattani** Thai.
119 E11 **Pattani, Mae Nam** *r.* Thai.
119 E8 **Pattaya** Thai.
257 □Q3 **Patten** *ME* U.S.A.
258 E3 **Pattenburg** *NJ* U.S.A.
191 I6 **Pattensen** Ger.
171 L4 **Patterdale** *Cumbria, England* U.K.
264 K4 **Patterson** *CA* U.S.A.
261 J11 **Patterson** *LA* U.S.A.
259 H1 **Patterson** *NY* U.S.A.
256 G9 **Patterson** *r. WV* U.S.A.
245 N2 **Patterson, Mount** *Y.T.* Can.
250 I4 **Patterson, Point** *MI* U.S.A.
264 M5 **Patterson Mountain** *CA* U.S.A.
Patteson Passage Vanuatu *see* **Lolvavana, Passage**
138 I7 **Patti** *Uttar Prad.* India
115 E8 **Patti** *Maluku* Indon.
216 H7 **Patti** *Sicilia* Italy
162 R4 **Pattijoki** Fin.
162 P2 **Pättikkä** Fin.
136 E5 **Pattikonda** *Andhra Prad.* India
172 H2 **Pattingham** *Staffordshire, England* U.K.
102 □ **Pattisson, Cape** *Chatham Is* S. Pacific Ocean
136 F7 **Pattukkottai** *Tamil Nadu* India
245 O4 **Pattullo, Mount** *B.C.* Can.
278 F3 **Patu** Brazil
139 M8 **Patuakhali** Bangl.
247 J4 **Patuanak** *Sask.* Can.
266 □Q10 **Patuca** *r.* Hond.
266 □Q10 **Patuca, Punta** *pt* Hond.
266 □Q10 **Patucas, Parque Nacional** *nat. park* Hond.
219 K6 **Pătulele** Romania
138 F9 **Patur** *Mahar.* India
187 E8 **Pâturages** Belgium
102 J6 **Patutu** *mt. North I.* N.Z.
256 I10 **Patuxent** *r. MD* U.S.A.
286 S1 **Patuxent Range** *mts* Antarctica
162 U5 **Patvinsuon kansallispuisto** *nat. park* Fin.
199 H4 **Páty** Hungary
268 F6 **Pátzcuaro** Mex.
268 F6 **Patzcuaro, Laguna de** *l.* Mex.
185 D9 **Pau** France
Pau *airport* France *see* **Pyrénées**
185 C9 **Pau, Gave de** *r.* France
281 H2 **Pau Brasil, Parque Nacional do** *nat. park* Brazil
276 B3 **Paucarbamba** Peru
276 B2 **Paucartambo** Peru
Paucartambo *r.* Peru *see* **Yavero**
278 C3 **Pau d'Arco** Brazil
277 H1 **Pau d'Arco** *r.* Brazil
201 M3 **Paudorf** Austria
139 L6 **Pauhunri** *mt.* China/India
185 F8 **Pauilhac** France
184 C5 **Pauillac** France
276 D1 **Pauini** Brazil
276 D1 **Pauiní** *r.* Brazil
275 F5 **Pauini** *r.* Brazil
118 B4 **Pauk** Myanmar
118 B5 **Paukkaung** Myanmar
118 A4 **Pauktaw** Myanmar
228 □ **Paúl** Cape Verde
204 E8 **Paul** Port.
213 O2 **Paularo** Italy
245 Q1 **Paulatuk** *N.W.T.* Can.
265 T7 **Paulden** *AZ* U.S.A.
261 K9 **Paulding** *MS* U.S.A.
256 A7 **Paulding** *OH* U.S.A.
287 I2 **Paulding Bay** Antarctica
183 B6 **Paulhac** France
183 C7 **Paulhac-en-Margeride** France
183 D6 **Paulhaguet** France
183 C9 **Paulhan** France
280 B4 **Paulicéia** Brazil
214 B7 **Paulilatino** *Sardegna* Italy
192 G5 **Paulinenaue** Ger.
185 I8 **Paulinet** France
258 E3 **Paulins Kill** *r. NJ* U.S.A.
Paulis Dem. Rep. Congo *see* **Isiro**
219 J4 **Păuliş** Romania
249 I1 **Paul Island** *Nfld and Lab.* Can.
278 G3 **Paulista** Brazil
278 E4 **Paulistana** Brazil
260 H4 **Paullina** *IA* U.S.A.
278 F4 **Paulo Afonso** Brazil
280 C4 **Paulo de Faria** Brazil
244 G5 **Pauloff Harbor** *AK* U.S.A.
237 O3 **Paulpietersburg** S. Africa
208 F6 **Paüls** Spain
261 G8 **Pauls Valley** *OK* U.S.A.
172 G5 **Paulton** *Bath and North East Somerset, England* U.K.
180 H8 **Paulx** France
Paum *i.* Vanuatu *see* **Paama**
Paumotu, Îles *is* Fr. Polynesia *see* **Tuamotu, Archipel des**
284 E3 **Paunero** Arg.
219 P4 **Păuneşti** Romania
118 C6 **Paung** Myanmar
118 B2 **Paungbyin** Myanmar
118 B5 **Paungde** Myanmar
138 G9 **Pauni** *Mahar.* India
258 E2 **Paupack** *PA* U.S.A.
138 G4 **Pauri** *Uttaranchal* India
193 F9 **Pausa** Ger.
276 B3 **Pausa** Peru
274 D3 **Pauto** *r.* Col.
162 N4 **Pauträsk** Sweden
178 I5 **Pauvres** France
264 □E13 **Pa'uwela** *HI* U.S.A.
136 E5 **Pavagada** *Karnataka* India
281 G2 **Pavão** Brazil
274 B3 **Pavarandocito** Col.
156 L4 **Pavda** Rus. Fed.
144 B4 **Pāveh** Iran
161 W8 **Pavelets** Rus. Fed.
212 G5 **Pavia** Italy
212 G5 **Pavia** *prov.* Italy
206 C3 **Pavia** Port.
204 D8 **Pavia** *r.* Port.
213 O4 **Pavia di Udine** Italy
209 E8 **Pavías** Spain
185 F8 **Pavie** France
256 G6 **Pavilion** *NY* U.S.A.
178 A4 **Pavilly** France
160 E5 **Pāvilosta** Latvia
156 I4 **Pavino** Rus. Fed.
160 F7 **Pavištyčio kalnas** *hill* Lith.
197 M4 **Pavitstsye** Belarus
219 N7 **Pavlikeni** Bulg.
161 Q7 **Pavlinovo** Rus. Fed.
158 I6 **Pavlivka** *Odes'ka Oblast'* Ukr.
159 N2 **Pavlivka** *Sums'ka Oblast'* Ukr.
158 D3 **Pavlivka** *Volyns'ka Oblast'* Ukr.
143 Q1 **Pavlodar** Kazakh.
Pavlodar Oblast *admin. div.* Kazakh. *see* **Pavlodarskaya Oblast'**
Pavlodar Oblysy *admin. div.* Kazakh. *see* **Pavlodarskaya Oblast'**
143 Q1 **Pavlodarskaya Oblast'** *admin. div.* Kazakh.
244 G5 **Pavlof Bay** *AK* U.S.A.
244 G5 **Pavlof Islands** *AK* U.S.A.
244 G5 **Pavlof Volcano** *AK* U.S.A.
Pavlograd Ukr. *see* **Pavlohrad**
143 O1 **Pavlogradka** Rus. Fed.
159 O5 **Pavlohrad** Ukr.
159 N6 **Pavlopillya** Ukr.
199 L3 **Pavlovce nad Uhom** Slovakia
143 O2 **Pavlovka** *Akmolinskaya Oblast'* Kazakh.
142 J1 **Pavlovka** *Kostanayskaya Oblast'* Kazakh.
156 L5 **Pavlovka** *Respublika Bashkortostan* Rus. Fed.
142 B1 **Pavlovka** *Ul'yanovskaya Oblast'* Rus. Fed.
156 H5 **Pavlovo** Rus. Fed.
143 T1 **Pavlovsk** *Altayskiy Kray* Rus. Fed.
161 N2 **Pavlovsk** *Leningradskaya Oblast'* Rus. Fed.
157 H6 **Pavlovsk** *Voronezhskaya Oblast'* Rus. Fed.
157 G7 **Pavlovskaya** Rus. Fed.
142 J1 **Pavlovskiy** Kazakh.
161 V6 **Pavlovskiy Posad** Rus. Fed.
161 X5 **Pavlovskoye** Rus. Fed.
156 L5 **Pavlovskoye Vodokhranilishche** *resr* Rus. Fed.
159 M5 **Pavlysh** Ukr.
213 J7 **Pavullo nel Frignano** Italy
100 □6 **Pavuvu** *i.* Solomon Is
160 M3 **Pavy** Rus. Fed.
100 □6 **Pawa** Solomon Is
130 B5 **Pawahku** Myanmar
138 H7 **Pawai** *Madh. Prad.* India
117 H5 **Pawan** *r.* Indon.
102 H2 **Pawarenga** *North I.* N.Z.
138 H5 **Pawayan** *Uttar Prad.* India
259 L2 **Pawcatuck** *CT* U.S.A.
193 G5 **Päwesin** Ger.
261 G7 **Pawhuska** *OK* U.S.A.
161 P8 **Pawlavichy** Belarus
259 H1 **Pawling** *NY* U.S.A.
196 F2 **Pawłówek** Pol.
196 G6 **Pawłowice** *Śląskie* Pol.
196 E4 **Pawłowice** *Wielkopolskie* Pol.
196 G5 **Pawłowiczki** Pol.
118 C5 **Pawn** *r.* Myanmar
261 G7 **Pawnee** *OK* U.S.A.
260 F6 **Pawnee** *r. KS* U.S.A.
260 G5 **Pawnee City** *NE* U.S.A.
196 G5 **Pawonków** Pol.
250 I7 **Paw Paw** *MI* U.S.A.
256 G9 **Paw Paw** *WV* U.S.A.
257 N7 **Pawtucket** *RI* U.S.A.
106 D6 **Pawu Aboriginal Land** *res. N.T.* Austr.
119 D8 **Pawut** Myanmar
204 F3 **Paxaro** *mt.* Spain
221 H7 **Paximada** *i.* Greece
220 F7 **Paximadia** *i.* Greece
258 B3 **Paxinos** *PA* U.S.A.
220 B3 **Paxoi** *i.* Greece
245 K3 **Paxson** *AK* U.S.A.
143 O7 **Paxtaobod** Uzbek.
168 L11 **Paxton** *Scottish Borders, Scotland* U.K.
250 F9 **Paxton** *IL* U.S.A.
260 E5 **Paxton** *NE* U.S.A.
258 B4 **Paxtonia** *PA* U.S.A.
258 A3 **Paxtonville** *PA* U.S.A.
115 E3 **Payahe** *Halmahera* Indon.
116 D5 **Payakumbuh** *Sumatera* Indon.
116 □ **Paya Lebar** Sing.
136 D6 **Payaswani** *r.* India
162 □ **Payer, Kapp** *c.* Svalbard
201 M4 **Payerbach** Austria
212 B2 **Payerne** Switz.
262 F4 **Payette** *ID* U.S.A.
262 F4 **Payette** *r. ID* U.S.A.
156 M1 **Pay-Khoy, Khrebet** *hills* Rus. Fed.
206 E5 **Paymogo** Spain
Payne *Que.* Can. *see* **Kangirsuk**
256 A7 **Payne** *OH* U.S.A.
248 F1 **Payne, Lac** *l. Que.* Can.
264 K1 **Paynes Creek** *CA* U.S.A.
109 D10 **Payne's Find** *W.A.* Austr.
105 K7 **Paynesville** *Vic.* Austr.
260 H3 **Paynesville** *MN* U.S.A.
206 F4 **Payo, Sierra** *hills* Spain
185 G6 **Payrac** France
185 I8 **Payrin-Augmontel** France
285 H3 **Paysandú** Uru.
285 I3 **Paysandú** *dept* Uru.
185 A9 **Pays Basque** *reg.* France
181 L3 **Pays d'Auge** *reg.* France
185 B7 **Pays de Born** *reg.* France
178 B4 **Pays de Bray** *reg.* France
181 M2 **Pays de Caux** *reg.* France
184 B1 **Pays de la Loire** *admin. reg.* France
180 B5 **Pays de Léon** *reg.* France
180 G7 **Pays de Retz** *reg.* France
185 I10 **Pays de Sault** *reg.* France
178 G7 **Pays d'Othe** *reg.* France
181 M4 **Pays d'Ouche** *reg.* France
143 L7 **Payshanba** Uzbek.
265 U7 **Payson** *AZ* U.S.A.
284 C5 **Payún, Cerro** *vol.* Arg.
117 J3 **Payung, Tanjung** *pt* Malaysia
284 C5 **Payún Matrú, Altiplanicie del** *plat.* Arg.
282 C5 **Payún Matrú, Volcán** *vol.* Arg.
156 N2 **Payyer, Gora** *mt.* Rus. Fed.
184 G5 **Payzac** France
Payzawat *Xinjiang* China *see* **Jiashi**
278 C4 **Paz, Rio da** *r.* Brazil
149 J3 **Pazar** Turkey
148 H5 **Pazarcık** Turkey
219 M8 **Pazardzhik** Bulg.
221 I3 **Pazarköy** Turkey
221 K4 **Pazarlar** Turkey
221 K3 **Pazaryeri** Turkey
151 B5 **Pazaryolu** Turkey
274 D3 **Paz de Ariporo** Col.
274 C3 **Paz de Rio** Col.
210 D3 **Pazin** Croatia
185 J10 **Paziols** France
276 D4 **Pazña** Bol.
200 B6 **Paznauntal** *val.* Austria
204 C4 **Pazos** Spain
144 G4 **Pazūk** Iran
161 O2 **Pchevzha** *r.* Rus. Fed.
197 H6 **Pcim** Pol.
219 J9 **Pčinja** *r.* Macedonia
119 D8 **Pe** Myanmar
101 □8a **Pea** *Tongatapu* Tonga
280 A5 **Peabiru** Brazil
260 G6 **Peabody** *KS* U.S.A.
257 O6 **Peabody** *MA* U.S.A.
246 I3 **Peace** *r. Alta/B.C.* Can.
255 F12 **Peace** *r. FL* U.S.A.
173 L6 **Peacehaven** *East Sussex, England* U.K.
247 H3 **Peace Point** *Alta* Can.
246 G3 **Peace River** *Alta* Can.
256 D11 **Peach Creek** *WV* U.S.A.
246 G5 **Peachland** *B.C.* Can.
265 S6 **Peach Springs** *AZ* U.S.A.
247 I1 **Peacock Hills** *Nunavut* Can.
275 F3 **Peaima Falls** Guyana
255 J8 **Pea Island National Wildlife Refuge** *nature res. NC* U.S.A.
109 F12 **Peak Charles** *hill W.A.* Austr.
109 F12 **Peak Charles National Park** *W.A.* Austr.
171 N7 **Peak District National Park** *England* U.K.
104 F3 **Peake** *watercourse S.A.* Austr.
257 □Q2 **Peaked Mountain** *hill ME* U.S.A.
105 L5 **Peak Hill** *N.S.W.* Austr.
109 E8 **Peak Hill** *W.A.* Austr.
264 M7 **Peak Mountain** *CA* U.S.A.
107 L7 **Peak Range** *hills Qld* Austr.
207 M5 **Peal de Becerro** Spain
265 W3 **Peale, Mount** *UT* U.S.A.
265 W10 **Pearce** *AZ* U.S.A.
106 B3 **Pearce Point** *N.T.* Austr.
244 H1 **Peard Bay** *AK* U.S.A.
204 E3 **Peares, Encoro dos** *resr* Spain
256 E11 **Pearisburg** *VA* U.S.A.
250 F1 **Pearl** *Ont.* Can.
261 K10 **Pearl** *r. MS* U.S.A.
97 H1 **Pearl and Hermes Atoll** *HI* U.S.A.
264 □D12 **Pearl City** *HI* U.S.A.
264 □C13 **Pearl Harbor** *inlet HI* U.S.A.
Pearl River *r. Guangdong* China *see* **Zhu Jiang**
259 G2 **Pearl River** *NY* U.S.A.
261 F11 **Pearsall** *TX* U.S.A.
285 G3 **Pearson** Arg.
255 F10 **Pearson** *GA* U.S.A.
250 E4 **Pearson** *WI* U.S.A.
104 E5 **Pearson Islands** *S.A.* Austr.
237 J8 **Pearston** S. Africa
243 I2 **Peary Channel** *Nunavut* Can.
243 O1 **Peary Land** *reg.* Greenland
261 F8 **Pease** *r. TX* U.S.A.
172 H5 **Peasedown St John** *Bath and North East Somerset, England* U.K.
180 G6 **Péaule** France
250 F3 **Peavy Falls Reservoir** *MI* U.S.A.
108 D6 **Peawah** *r. W.A.* Austr.
248 C2 **Peawanuck** *Ont.* Can.
235 H3 **Pebane** Moz.
274 D5 **Pebas** Peru
283 F8 **Pebble Island** Falkland Is
231 D6 **Pebeangu** Dem. Rep. Congo
115 B4 **Pebengko** *Sulawesi* Indon.
183 D6 **Pébrac** France
Peć *Pejë* Kosovo *see* **Pejë**
261 F10 **Pecan Bayou** *r. TX* U.S.A.
281 F3 **Peçanha** Brazil
261 I11 **Pecan Island** *LA* U.S.A.
280 C6 **Peças, Ilha das** *i.* Brazil
250 E7 **Pecatonica** *IL* U.S.A.
212 F3 **Peccia** Switz.
213 J8 **Peccioli** Italy
199 I4 **Pécel** Hungary
162 U2 **Pecha** *r.* Rus. Fed.
162 U2 **Pechenga** Rus. Fed.
162 U2 **Pechenga** *r.* Rus. Fed.
159 P4 **Pechenihy** Ukr.
161 R1 **Pechenitsy** Rus. Fed.
159 P4 **Pecheniz'ke Vodoskhovyshche** *resr* Ukr.
161 W7 **Pecherniki** Rus. Fed.
161 P7 **Pechersk** Rus. Fed.
238 □3c **Pechiguera, Punta** *pt Lanzarote* Canary Is
207 O7 **Pechina** Spain
156 L2 **Pechora** Rus. Fed.
156 K1 **Pechora** *r.* Rus. Fed.
Pechora Sea Rus. Fed. *see* **Pechorskoye More**
156 L3 **Pechoro-Ilychskiy Zapovednik** *nature res.* Rus. Fed.
156 K1 **Pechorskaya Guba** *b.* Rus. Fed.
156 K1 **Pechorskoye More** *sea* Rus. Fed.
160 K4 **Pechory** Rus. Fed.
162 □ **Pechuel Løsche, Kapp** *c.* Svalbard
218 J4 **Pecica** Romania
219 Q7 **Pecineaga** Romania
228 A4 **Pecixe, Ilha de** *i.* Guinea-Bissau

251 L6 **Peck** *MI* U.S.A.
246 E3 **Peck, Mount** B.C. Can.
258 E2 **Pecks Pond** *PA* U.S.A.
198 E1 **Pečky** Czech Rep.
196 E4 **Pęcław** Pol.
119 H8 **Pe Cô, Krông** *r.* Vietnam
214 F2 **Pecora** *r.* Italy
214 A9 **Pecora, Capo** *c. Sardegna* Italy
261 D10 **Pecos** *TX* U.S.A.
261 E11 **Pecos** *r. NM/TX* U.S.A.
187 D7 **Pecq** Belgium
199 H5 **Pécs** Hungary
199 H5 **Pécsvárad** Hungary
196 G4 **Pęczniew** Pol.
266 □S14 **Pedasí** Panama
215 L1 **Pedaso** Italy
136 F3 **Pedda Vagu** *r.* India
136 F4 **Peddavagu** *r.* India
105 K10 **Pedder, Lake** *Tas.* Austr.
237 L9 **Peddie** S. Africa
160 K4 **Pededze** Latvia
160 J5 **Pededze** *r.* Latvia
274 A4 **Pedernales** Ecuador
270 H4 **Pedernales** Haiti
263 K12 **Pedernales** Mex.
261 F10 **Pedernales** *r. TX* U.S.A.
275 F2 **Pedernales** Venez.
282 C2 **Pedernales, Salar de** *salt flat* Chile
280 C5 **Pederneiras** Brazil
213 L4 **Pederobba** Italy
162 Q5 **Pedersöre** Fin.
231 B9 **Pediva** Angola
115 E3 **Pediwang** *Halmahera* Indon.
160 J3 **Pedja** *r.* Estonia
281 G1 **Pedra Azul** Brazil
228 □ **Pedra Badejo** *Santiago* Cape Verde
204 D5 **Pedrada** *mt.* Port.
204 F3 **Pedrafita do Cebreiro** Spain
204 C6 **Pedra Furada** Port.
205 K6 **Pedrajas de San Esteban** Spain
209 D8 **Pedralba** Spain
204 G4 **Pedralba de la Pradería** Spain
228 □ **Pedra Lume** Cape Verde
278 C5 **Pedra Preta, Serra da** *mts* Brazil
278 B3 **Pedras** *r.* Brazil
278 D5 **Pedras** *r.* Brazil
204 E8 **Pedras Lavradas** *pass* Port.
277 E3 **Pedras Negras** Brazil
266 □R13 **Pedregal** Panama
274 D2 **Pedregal** Venez.
209 F10 **Pedreguer** Spain
280 D4 **Pedregulho** Brazil
278 D3 **Pedreiras** *Maranhão* Brazil
280 D5 **Pedreiras** *São Paulo* Brazil
207 J6 **Pedrera** Spain
209 D11 **Pedrera, Embalse de la** *resr* Spain
208 J4 **Pedres, Serrat de les** *hill* Spain
266 H5 **Pedriceña** Mex.
258 E5 **Pedricktown** *NJ* U.S.A.
205 N5 **Pedro** *r.* Spain
136 G8 **Pedro, Point** Sri Lanka
207 K5 **Pedro Abad** Spain
278 C4 **Pedro Afonso** Brazil
269 I4 **Pedro Antonio de los Santos** Mex.
278 F3 **Pedro Avelino** Brazil
270 D5 **Pedro Bank** *sea feature* Jamaica
280 D6 **Pedro Barros** Brazil
244 I4 **Pedro Bay** *AK* U.S.A.
205 K8 **Pedro Bernardo** Spain
270 E5 **Pedro Cays** *is* Jamaica
207 J4 **Pedroche** Spain
274 D4 **Pedro Chico** Col.
275 I4 **Pedro de Freitas** Brazil
276 C5 **Pedro de Valdivia** Chile
285 H2 **Pedro Díaz Colodrero** Arg.
268 G5 **Pedro Escobedo** Mex.
206 D4 **Pedrógão** *Beja* Port.
204 F8 **Pedrógão** *Castelo Branco* Port.
204 C9 **Pedrógão** *Leiria* Port.
204 D9 **Pedrógão Grande** Port.
204 D9 **Pedrógão Pequeno** Port.
279 B6 **Pedro Gomes** Brazil
206 H2 **Pedro Gómez** *mt.* Spain
278 E3 **Pedro II** Brazil
274 E4 **Pedro II, Ilha** *reg.* Brazil/Venez.
277 G5 **Pedro Juan Caballero** Para.
281 E3 **Pedro Leopoldo** Brazil
285 F6 **Pedro Luro** Arg.
207 M5 **Pedro-Martínez** Spain
207 N2 **Pedro Muñoz** Spain
282 G3 **Pedro Osório** Brazil
270 □ **Pedro Point** Jamaica
208 I3 **Pedrós, Puig** *mt.* Spain
205 M2 **Pedrosa** Spain
205 L4 **Pedrosa del Príncipe** Spain
204 I7 **Pedrosillo de los Aires** Spain
204 C6 **Pedroso** Port.
205 O4 **Pedroso** Spain
280 D6 **Pedro Toledo** Brazil
185 H10 **Pédrous, Pic** *mt.* France
204 C3 **Pedrouzos** Spain
214 B6 **Pedruso, Monte** *hill* Italy
104 H6 **Peebinga** *S.A.* Austr.
168 J11 **Peebles** *Scottish Borders, Scotland* U.K.
256 B10 **Peebles** *OH* U.S.A.
108 C6 **Peedamulla** *W.A.* Austr.
108 C6 **Peedamulla Aboriginal Reserve** *W.A.* Austr.
255 H9 **Pee Dee** *r. SC* U.S.A.
257 L7 **Peekskill** *NY* U.S.A.
245 N1 **Peel** *r. N.W.T./Y.T.* Can.
170 H5 **Peel** Isle of Man
103 F10 **Peel, Mount** *South I.* N.Z.
109 C12 **Peel Inlet** *W.A.* Austr.
245 N2 **Peel River Game Preserve** *nature res. N.W.T./Y.T.* Can.
192 I3 **Peene** *r.* Ger.
192 I2 **Peenemünde** Ger.
192 I3 **Peenestrom** *sea chan.* Ger.
187 H6 **Peer** Belgium
162 P2 **Peera** Fin.
104 G2 **Peera Peera Poolanna Lake** *salt flat S.A.* Austr.
246 H3 **Peerless Lake** *Alta* Can.
246 H3 **Peerless Lake** *l. Alta* Can.
246 G4 **Peers** *Alta* Can.
204 F8 **Pega** Port.
183 C9 **Pégairolles-de-l'Escalette** France
103 G10 **Pegasus Bay** *South I.* N.Z.
193 F8 **Pegau** Ger.
201 L5 **Peggau** Austria
212 F7 **Pegli** Italy
215 P7 **Peglio** *r.* Italy
195 L2 **Pegnitz** Ger.
195 J3 **Pegnitz** *r.* Ger.
206 C2 **Pego** Port.
209 E10 **Pego** Spain
206 C4 **Pego do Altar, Barragem do** *resr* Port.
206 B3 **Pegões** Port.
196 E4 **Pęgów** Pol.
118 C6 **Pegu** Myanmar
118 B5 **Pegu** *admin. div.* Myanmar
209 J8 **Peguera** Spain
115 B5 **Pegunungan Latimojong** *nature res.* Indon.
115 B5 **Pegunungan Peruhumpenai** *nature res.* Indon.
118 B5 **Pegu Yoma** *mts* Myanmar
173 O5 **Pegwell Bay** *England* U.K.
156 J3 **Pegysh** Rus. Fed.
219 K9 **Pehčevo** *Pehčevo* Macedonia
221 H1 **Pehlivanköy** Turkey
229 F4 **Péhonko** Benin
138 F5 **Pehowa** *Haryana* India
285 G4 **Pehuajó** Arg.
285 G6 **Pehuén-Có** Arg.
131 M7 **Peikang** Taiwan
180 G6 **Peillac** France
183 K9 **Peille** France
168 D8 **Peinchorran** *Highland, Scotland* U.K.
276 C5 **Peine** Chile
191 J6 **Peine** Ger.
283 B8 **Peineta, Cerro** *mt.* Arg.
138 D9 **Peint** *Mahar.* India
213 J3 **Peio** Italy
183 H8 **Peipin** France
Peipsi järv *l.* Estonia/Rus. Fed. *see* **Peipus, Lake**
160 K3 **Peipus, Lake** Estonia/Rus. Fed.
183 K9 **Peïra-Cava** France
220 E5 **Peiraias** Greece
244 G4 **Peirce, Cape** *AK* U.S.A.
182 J5 **Peisey-Nancroix** France
Pei Shan *mts* China *see* **Bei Shan**
193 E7 **Peißen** *Sachsen-Anhalt* Ger.
193 F7 **Peißen** *Sachsen-Anhalt* Ger.
195 K6 **Peißenberg** Ger.
195 J6 **Peiting** Ger.
193 J7 **Peitz** Ger.
278 C5 **Peixe** Brazil
280 B4 **Peixe** *r.* Brazil
280 C2 **Peixe** *r.* Brazil
278 C5 **Peixe** *r.* Brazil
280 A2 **Peixe, Rio do** *r.* Brazil
281 F5 **Peixes** *r.* Brazil
277 F2 **Peixes** *r.* Brazil
129 O9 **Peixian** *Jiangsu* China
Peixian *Jiangsu* China *see* **Pizhou**
280 D4 **Peixoto, Represa** *resr* Brazil
278 B4 **Peixoto de Azevedo** Brazil
277 G2 **Peixoto de Azevedo** *r.* Brazil
186 K2 **Peize** Neth.
116 G4 **Pejantan** *i.* Indon.
218 I8 **Pejë** *Pejë* Kosovo
219 J6 **Pek** *r.* Serbia
237 L4 **Peka** Lesotho
115 A5 **Pekabata** *Sulawesi* Indon.
117 H8 **Pekalongan** *Jawa* Indon.
116 E3 **Pekan** Malaysia
116 D4 **Pekanbaru** *Sumatera* Indon.
249 H2 **Pékans, Rivière aux** *r. Que.* Can.
161 X8 **Pekhlets** Rus. Fed.
229 F5 **Peki** Ghana
250 E9 **Pekin** *IL* U.S.A.
Peking *Beijing* China *see* **Beijing**
161 Q8 **Peklino** Rus. Fed.
205 N6 **Pela, Sierra de** *mts* Spain
116 D3 **Pelabuhan Klang** Malaysia
283 C7 **Pelada, Pampa** *hills* Arg.
209 C8 **Pelado** *mt.* Spain
211 D8 **Pelagie, Isole** *is Sicilia* Italy
213 L8 **Pelago** Italy
218 J9 **Pelagonija** *plain* Macedonia
205 K8 **Pelahustán** Spain
117 K6 **Pelaihari** *Kalimantan* Indon.
116 E4 **Pelalawan** *Sumatera* Indon.
117 H5 **Pelapis** *i.* Indon.
284 B4 **Pelarco** Chile
204 C9 **Pelariga** Port.
204 H7 **Pelarrodríguez** Spain
220 D4 **Pelasgia** Greece
Pelasyía Greece *see* **Pelasgia**
183 J8 **Pelat, Mont** *mt.* France
237 M4 **Pelatsoeu** *mt.* Lesotho
100 □6 **Pelau** *i.* Solomon Is
117 L4 **Pelawanbesar** *Kalimantan* Indon.
196 D2 **Pełczyce** Pol.
219 K5 **Peleaga, Vârful** *mt.* Romania
205 J6 **Peleagonzalo** Spain
276 C3 **Pelechuco** Bol.
160 J5 **Pelēči** Latvia
271 □3 **Pelée, Montagne** *vol.* Martinique
248 D5 **Pelee Island** *Ont.* Can.
248 D5 **Pelee Point** *Ont.* Can.
215 Q1 **Pelegrin, Rt** *pt* Croatia
114 □ **Peleliu** *i.* Palau
115 C4 **Peleng** *i.* Indon.
115 C4 **Peleng, Selat** *sea chan.* Indon.
115 C4 **Peleng, Teluk** *b.* Indon.
156 J3 **Peles** Rus. Fed.
198 E2 **Pelhřimov** Czech Rep.
245 M4 **Pelican** *AK* U.S.A.
107 I4 **Pelican Creek** *r. Qld* Austr.
247 K4 **Pelican Lake** *l. Man.* Can.
250 E4 **Pelican Lake** *WI* U.S.A.
250 B1 **Pelican Lake** *l. MN* U.S.A.
247 K4 **Pelican Narrows** *Sask.* Can.
238 □3a **Peligro, Punta del** *pt La Gomera* Canary Is
207 L6 **Peligros** Spain
158 G6 **Pelinia** Moldova
183 G9 **Pélissanne** France
218 J10 **Pelister** *mt.* Macedonia
218 J10 **Pelister** *nat. park* Macedonia
210 F4 **Pelješac** *pen.* Croatia
162 S3 **Pelkosenniemi** Fin.
235 D5 **Pella** S. Africa
250 A1 **Pelland** *MN* U.S.A.
217 J7 **Pellaro** Italy
247 I1 **Pellatt Lake** *N.W.T.* Can.
255 D9 **Pell City** *AL* U.S.A.
285 F5 **Pellegrini** Arg.
285 F5 **Pellegrini, Lago** *l.* Arg.
212 H6 **Pellegrino Parmense** Italy
185 E6 **Pellegrue** France
113 J7 **Pelleluhu Islands** P.N.G.
199 H5 **Pellérd** Hungary
213 M5 **Pellestrina** Italy
181 N8 **Pellevoisin** France
212 D6 **Pellice** *r.* Italy
200 C7 **Pellizzano** Italy
162 Q3 **Pello** Fin.
250 J4 **Pellston** *MI* U.S.A.
284 A4 **Pelluhue** Chile
190 G1 **Pellworm** *i.* Ger.
245 M3 **Pelly** *r. Y.T.* Can.
Pelly Bay *Nunavut* Can. *see* **Kugaaruk**
245 M3 **Pelly Crossing** *Y.T.* Can.
245 N1 **Pelly Island** *N.W.T.* Can.
245 N3 **Pelly Mountains** *Y.T.* Can.
191 C10 **Pelm** Ger.
200 F7 **Pelmo, Monte** *mt.* Italy
207 I2 **Peloche** Spain
117 M8 **Pelokang** *is* Indon.
Peloponnese *admin. reg.* Greece *see* **Peloponnisos**
Peloponnesus *admin. reg.* Greece *see* **Peloponnisos**
220 D5 **Peloponnisos** *admin. reg.* Greece
220 D5 **Peloponnisos** *pen.* Greece
217 H8 **Peloritani, Monti** *mts Sicilia* Italy
217 J7 **Peloro, Capo** *c. Sicilia* Italy
103 H8 **Pelorus Sound** *sea chan. South I.* N.Z.
282 G3 **Pelotas** Brazil
279 C8 **Pelotas, Rio das** *r.* Brazil
219 M7 **Pelovo** Bulg.
196 G2 **Pelplin** Pol.
173 I2 **Pelsall** *West Midlands, England* U.K.
109 B10 **Pelsart Group** *is W.A.* Austr.
192 I3 **Pelsin** Ger.
162 R2 **Peltovuoma** Fin.
150 A7 **Pelusium** *tourist site* Egypt
Pelusium, Bay of Egypt *see* **Ţînah, Khalīj aţ**
183 F6 **Pélussin** France
183 I7 **Pelvoux** France
183 I7 **Pelvoux, Mont** *mt.* France
199 J4 **Pély** Hungary
172 C7 **Pelynt** *Cornwall, England* U.K.
251 K2 **Pemache** *r. Ont.* Can.
257 □Q3 **Pemadumcook Lake** *ME* U.S.A.
117 H8 **Pemalang** *Jawa* Indon.
117 H4 **Pemangkat** *Kalimantan* Indon.
117 L5 **Pemarung, Pulau** *i.* Indon.
116 C3 **Pematangsiantar** *Sumatera* Indon.
235 I2 **Pemba** Moz.
231 E9 **Pemba** Zambia
233 D8 **Pemba, Baía de** *b.* Moz.
233 C6 **Pemba Channel** Tanz.
233 C6 **Pemba Island** Tanz.
233 C6 **Pemba North** *admin. reg.* Tanz.
233 C6 **Pemba South** *admin. reg.* Tanz.
109 C13 **Pemberton** *W.A.* Austr.
246 F5 **Pemberton** *B.C.* Can.
258 F5 **Pemberton** *NJ* U.S.A.
246 H4 **Pembina** *r. Alta* Can.
260 G1 **Pembina** *ND* U.S.A.
260 G1 **Pembina** *r. ND* U.S.A.
250 G4 **Pembine** *WI* U.S.A.
172 D4 **Pembrey** *Carmarthenshire, Wales* U.K.
172 G3 **Pembridge** *Herefordshire, England* U.K.
248 E4 **Pembroke** *Ont.* Can.
172 C4 **Pembroke** *Pembrokeshire, Wales* U.K.
255 G9 **Pembroke** *GA* U.S.A.
257 □R4 **Pembroke** *ME* U.S.A.
283 F8 **Pembroke, Cape** Falkland Is
103 B11 **Pembroke, Mount** *South I.* N.Z.
172 C4 **Pembroke Dock** *Pembrokeshire, Wales* U.K.
255 G12 **Pembroke Pines** *FL* U.S.A.
172 C4 **Pembrokeshire** *admin. div. Wales* U.K.
172 B4 **Pembrokeshire Coast National Park** *Wales* U.K.
117 J6 **Pembuanghulu** *Kalimantan* Indon.
173 M5 **Pembury** *Kent, England* U.K.
284 B5 **Pemehue, Cordillera de** *mts* Chile
195 N3 **Pemfling** Ger.
117 I5 **Pemuar** *Kalimantan* Indon.
284 A5 **Pemuco** Chile
136 C3 **Pen** *Mahar.* India
118 A4 **Pen** *r.* Myanmar
159 O2 **Pena** *r.* Rus. Fed.
208 D3 **Peña, Embalse de la** *resr* Spain
276 D5 **Pena Barrosa** Bol.
284 B2 **Peña Blanca** Chile
205 O3 **Peñacerrada** Spain
204 D8 **Penacova** Port.
204 H8 **Peña de Francia, Sierra de la** *mts* Spain
206 F2 **Peña del Águila, Embalse de la** *resr* Spain
204 D6 **Penafiel** Port.
205 L5 **Peñafiel** Spain
207 I5 **Peñaflor** Spain
205 K5 **Peñaflor de Hornija** Spain
205 M2 **Peñagos** Spain
271 □7 **Penal** Trin. and Tob.
205 K2 **Peña Labra, Sierra de** *mts* Spain
205 M7 **Peñalara** *mt.* Spain
208 E5 **Peñalba** Spain
204 G4 **Peñalba de Santiago** *tourist site* Spain
205 P7 **Peñalén** Spain
172 C4 **Penally** *Pembrokeshire, Wales* U.K.
207 I3 **Peñalsordo** Spain
204 E7 **Penalva do Castelo** Port.
204 F8 **Penamacor** Port.
Penambo Range *mts* Malaysia *see* **Tama Abu, Banjaran**
269 H4 **Peñamiller** Mex.
117 L2 **Penampang** *Sabah* Malaysia
269 H2 **Peña Nevada, Cerro** *mt.* Mex.
Penang *state* Malaysia *see* **Pinang**
280 B4 **Penápolis** Brazil
205 J7 **Peñaranda de Bracamonte** Spain
205 N5 **Peñaranda de Duero** Spain
258 E3 **Pen Argyl** *PA* U.S.A.
105 I6 **Penarie** *N.S.W.* Austr.
Penarlâg *Wales* U.K. *see* **Hawarden**
208 D7 **Peñarroya** *mt.* Spain
207 M2 **Peñarroya, Embalse de** *resr* Spain
207 I4 **Peñarroya-Pueblonuevo** Spain
207 O4 **Peñarrubia** Spain
172 F5 **Penarth** *Vale of Glamorgan, Wales* U.K.
204 I1 **Peñas, Cabo de** *c.* Spain
283 B7 **Penas, Golfo de** *g.* Chile
271 □7 **Peñas, Punta** *pt* Venez.
205 L2 **Peña Sagra, Sierra** *mts* Spain
284 D5 **Peñas Blancas** Arg.
266 □Q12 **Peñas Blancas** Nic.
263 L10 **Peñasco** *watercourse NM* U.S.A.
207 O3 **Peñascosa** Spain
205 M5 **Peñas de Cervera** *hills* Spain
207 P3 **Peñas de San Pedro** Spain
116 A2 **Penasi, Pulau** *i.* Indon.
204 I6 **Peñausende** Spain
172 D3 **Penbryn** *Ceredigion, Wales* U.K.
199 I4 **Penc** Hungary
172 D3 **Pencader** *Carmarthenshire, Wales* U.K.
168 K11 **Pencaitland** *East Lothian, Scotland* U.K.
138 G9 **Pench** *r.* India
Pencheng *Jiangxi* China *see* **Ruichang**
287 F2 **Penck, Cape** Antarctica
172 F4 **Pencoed** *Bridgend, Wales* U.K.
230 C3 **Pendé** *r.* C.A.R.
172 □ **Pendeen** *Cornwall, England* U.K.
228 C4 **Pendembu** *Eastern* Sierra Leone
228 B4 **Pendembu** *Northern* Sierra Leone
260 G4 **Pender** *NE* U.S.A.
108 G4 **Pender Bay** *W.A.* Austr.
108 G4 **Pender Bay Aboriginal Reserve** *W.A.* Austr.
221 K2 **Pendik** Turkey
204 E7 **Pendilhe** Port.
172 C4 **Pendine** *Carmarthenshire, Wales* U.K.
229 F4 **Pendjari, Parc National de la** *nat. park* Benin
171 M6 **Pendle Hill** *England* U.K.
262 E4 **Pendleton** *OR* U.S.A.
246 E4 **Pendleton Bay** *B.C.* Can.
116 E6 **Pendopo** *Sumatera* Indon.
262 E2 **Pend Oreille** *r. WA* U.S.A.
262 F2 **Pend Oreille Lake** *ID* U.S.A.
138 H8 **Pendra** *Chhattisgarh* India
138 H8 **Pendra Road** *Chhattisgarh* India
136 C4 **Penduv** *Mahar.* India
Pendzhikent Tajik. *see* **Panjakent**
117 H5 **Penebangan** *i.* Indon.
204 D5 **Peneda, Serra da** *mts* Port.
204 D5 **Peneda Gerês, Parque Nacional da** *nat. park* Port.
206 D5 **Penedo Gordo** Port.
204 F7 **Penedono** Port.
204 D8 **Penela** Port.
231 F6 **Pene-Mende** Dem. Rep. Congo
229 F4 **Pénessoulou** Benin
180 G7 **Pénestin** France
199 L4 **Penészlek** Hungary
251 O5 **Penetanguishene** *Ont.* Can.
256 G7 **Penfield** *PA* U.S.A.
Penfro *Pembrokeshire, Wales* U.K. *see* **Pembroke**
130 F3 **Peng'an** *Sichuan* China
136 F3 **Penganga** *r.* India
131 □J7 **Peng Chau** *i. H.K.* China
131 N6 **P'engchia Yü** *i.* Taiwan
231 E6 **Penge** Dem. Rep. Congo
P'enghu Ch'üntao *is* Taiwan *see* **P'enghu Liehtao**
P'enghu Liehtao *is* Taiwan *see* **P'enghu Ch'üntao**
131 L7 **P'enghu Tao** *i.* Taiwan
117 H4 **Pengiki** *i.* Indon.
250 A2 **Pengilly** *MN* U.S.A.
116 D2 **Pengkalan Hulu** Malaysia
116 □ **Peng Kang** *hill* Sing.
129 Q8 **Penglai** *Shandong* China
130 D3 **Pengshan** *Sichuan* China
130 G4 **Pengshui** *Chongqing* China
116 □ **Peng Siang, Sungai** *r.* Sing.
118 A4 **Pengwa** Myanmar
130 E3 **Pengxi** *Sichuan* China
Pengxian *Sichuan* China *see* **Pengzhou**
131 K4 **Pengze** *Jiangxi* China
130 D3 **Pengzhou** *Sichuan* China
279 C8 **Penha** Brazil
204 F8 **Penha Garcia** Port.
235 G3 **Penhalonga** Zimbabwe
204 D9 **Penhascoso** Port.
180 B5 **Penhir, Pointe de** *pt* France
237 K7 **Penhoek Pass** S. Africa
256 F12 **Penhook** *VA* U.S.A.
206 A2 **Peniche** Port.
168 J11 **Penicuik** *Midlothian, Scotland* U.K.
117 K9 **Penida** *i.* Indon.
193 G9 **Penig** Ger.
156 F3 **Peninga** Rus. Fed.
Peninsular Malaysia Malaysia *see* **Malaysia, Semenanjung**
168 E12 **Peninver** *Argyll and Bute, Scotland* U.K.
209 F7 **Peñíscola** Spain
171 N6 **Penistone** *South Yorkshire, England* U.K.
278 D4 **Penitente, Serra do** *hills* Brazil
229 H5 **Penja** Cameroon
268 F5 **Penjamo** Mex.
149 L6 **Penjwin** Iraq
171 L7 **Penketh** *Warrington, England* U.K.
161 X5 **Penkino** Rus. Fed.
172 H2 **Penkridge** *Staffordshire, England* U.K.
192 J4 **Penkun** Ger.
172 G2 **Penley** *Wrexham, Wales* U.K.
178 B4 **Penly** France
180 C6 **Penmarch** France
180 C6 **Penmarch, Pointe de** *pt* France
Penn *PA* U.S.A. *see* **Penn Hills**
215 N3 **Penna, Punta della** *pt* Italy
215 I3 **Penna in Teverina** Italy
185 I9 **Pennautier** France
185 H7 **Penne** France
215 L3 **Penne** Italy
217 N2 **Penne, Punta** *pt* Italy
185 F7 **Penne-d'Agenais** France
287 L2 **Pennell Coast** Antarctica
136 G5 **Penner** *r.* India
104 F6 **Penneshaw** *S.A.* Austr.
257 □S3 **Pennfield** *N.B.* Can.
258 D3 **Penn Forest Reservoir** *PA* U.S.A.
256 F8 **Penn Hills** *PA* U.S.A.
182 K5 **Pennine, Alpi** *mts* Italy/Switz.
Pennine Alps *mts* Italy/Switz. *see* **Pennine, Alpi**
171 M5 **Pennines** *hills England* U.K.
237 O6 **Pennington** S. Africa
258 F4 **Pennington** *NJ* U.S.A.
256 B12 **Pennington Gap** *VA* U.S.A.
215 J1 **Pennino, Monte** *mt.* Italy
256 E9 **Pennsboro** *WV* U.S.A.
258 E4 **Pennsburg** *PA* U.S.A.
258 A3 **Penns Creek** *PA* U.S.A.
258 B3 **Penns Creek** *r. PA* U.S.A.
258 E5 **Penns Grove** *NJ* U.S.A.
258 D5 **Pennsville** *NJ* U.S.A.
251 P8 **Pennsylvania** *state* U.S.A.
271 □2 **Pennville** Dominica
256 H6 **Penn Yan** *NY* U.S.A.
168 D10 **Pennyghael** *Argyll and Bute, Scotland* U.K.
243 L3 **Penny Icecap** *Nunavut* Can.
287 K1 **Penny Point** Antarctica
258 F5 **Penny Pot** *NJ* U.S.A.
161 P5 **Peno** Rus. Fed.
257 □Q4 **Penobscot** *r. ME* U.S.A.
257 □Q4 **Penobscot Bay** *ME* U.S.A.
104 H7 **Penola** *S.A.* Austr.
266 G5 **Peñón Blanco** Mex.
104 D4 **Penong** *S.A.* Austr.
266 □S13 **Penonomé** Panama
172 D3 **Penrhiw-pâl** *Ceredigion, Wales* U.K.
103 □2 **Penrhyn** *atoll* Cook Is
291 I6 **Penrhyn Basin** *sea feature* Pacific Ocean
172 E1 **Penrhyn Bay** *Conwy, Wales* U.K.
172 D2 **Penrhyndeudraeth** *Gwynedd, Wales* U.K.
172 C2 **Penrhyn Mawr** *pt Wales* U.K.
105 M5 **Penrith** *N.S.W.* Austr.
171 L4 **Penrith** *Cumbria, England* U.K.
172 B7 **Penryn** *Cornwall, England* U.K.
255 D10 **Pensacola** *FL* U.S.A.
255 D10 **Pensacola Bay** *FL* U.S.A.
286 T1 **Pensacola Mountains** Antarctica
277 E3 **Pensamiento** Bol.
144 C2 **Pensär** Azer.
250 G5 **Pensaukee** *WI* U.S.A.
105 I7 **Penshurst** *Vic.* Austr.
117 L2 **Pensiangan** *Sabah* Malaysia
138 F3 **Pensi La** *pass Jammu and Kashmir* India
172 D6 **Pensilva** *Cornwall, England* U.K.
150 B3 **Pentadaktylos Range** *mts* Cyprus
214 C3 **Penta-di-Casinca** *Corse* France
137 H4 **Pentakota** *Andhra Prad.* India
220 C2 **Pentalofos** Greece
108 I3 **Pentecost** *r. W.A.* Austr.
100 □5 **Pentecost Island** Vanuatu
249 H3 **Pentecôte** *r. Que.* Can.
Pentecôte, Île *i.* Vanuatu *see* **Pentecost Island**
219 O5 **Penteleu, Vârful** *mt.* Romania
180 F5 **Penthièvre** *reg.* France
246 G5 **Penticton** *B.C.* Can.
208 □ **Pentinat, Punta** *pt* Spain
172 D1 **Pentir** *Gwynedd, Wales* U.K.
172 B6 **Pentire Point** *England* U.K.
107 J6 **Pentland** *Qld* Austr.
168 J5 **Pentland Firth** *sea chan. Scotland* U.K.
168 I11 **Pentland Hills** *Scotland* U.K.
195 M4 **Pentling** Ger.
172 D1 **Pentraeth** *Isle of Anglesey, Wales* U.K.
172 E1 **Pentrefoelas** *Conwy, Wales* U.K.
250 H6 **Pentwater** *MI* U.S.A.
116 F5 **Penuba** Indon.
116 F6 **Penuguan** *Sumatera* Indon.
136 E5 **Penukonda** *Andhra Prad.* India
116 E2 **Penunjuk, Tanjung** *pt* Malaysia
180 E4 **Penvénan** France
118 C5 **Penwegon** Myanmar
171 L6 **Penwortham** *Lancashire, England* U.K.
159 O2 **Peny** Rus. Fed.
209 E7 **Penyagolosa** *mt.* Spain
172 F3 **Penybont** *Powys, Wales* U.K.
Pen-y-Bont ar Ogwr *Bridgend, Wales* U.K. *see* **Bridgend**
172 F2 **Penybontfawr** *Powys, Wales* U.K.
172 E4 **Pen-y-fai** *Bridgend, Wales* U.K.
172 E2 **Penygadair** *hill Wales* U.K.
171 M5 **Pen-y-Ghent** *hill England* U.K.
172 D1 **Penygroes** *Gwynedd, Wales* U.K.
247 J2 **Penylan Lake** *N.W.T.* Can.
115 E6 **Penyu, Kepulauan** *is Maluku* Indon.
172 F4 **Penywaun** *Rhondda Cynon Taff, Wales* U.K.
157 I5 **Penza** Rus. Fed.
172 □ **Penzance** *Cornwall, England* U.K.
Penza Oblast *admin. div.* Rus. Fed. *see* **Penzenskaya Oblast'**
195 K6 **Penzberg** Ger.
157 I5 **Penzenskaya Oblast'** *admin. div.* Rus. Fed.
153 R3 **Penzhinskaya Guba** *b.* Rus. Fed.
195 J5 **Penzing** Ger.
192 H4 **Penzlin** Ger.
183 J8 **Péone** France
262 J2 **Peoples Creek** *r. MT* U.S.A.
265 T8 **Peoria** *AZ* U.S.A.
250 E9 **Peoria** *IL* U.S.A.
250 E9 **Peoria Heights** *IL* U.S.A.
264 □F14 **Pepe'ekeo** *HI* U.S.A.
228 B4 **Pepel** Sierra Leone
192 E2 **Pepelow** Ger.
285 I2 **Pepe Núñez** Uru.
232 B3 **Peper** Sudan
Peper, Teluk *b.* Indon. *see* **Lada, Teluk**
183 B10 **Pépieux** France
187 F7 **Pepingen** Belgium
187 I7 **Pepinster** Belgium
196 F4 **Pępowo** Pol.
237 N4 **Pepworth** S. Africa
218 H9 **Pëqin** Albania
259 G3 **Pequannock** *NJ* U.S.A.
204 H4 **Peque** Spain
258 C5 **Pequea** *PA* U.S.A.
258 C5 **Pequea Creek** *r. PA* U.S.A.
266 C4 **Pequeña, Punta** *pt* Mex.
258 E3 **Pequest** *r. NJ* U.S.A.
281 E3 **Pequi** Brazil
199 G4 **Pér** Hungary
206 C6 **Pêra** Port.
220 D4 **Perachora** Greece
136 G9 **Peradeniya** Sri Lanka
107 H2 **Pera Head** *Qld* Austr.
119 E12 **Perai** Malaysia
204 E9 **Perais** Port.
275 F3 **Peraitepuy** Venez.
116 C2 **Perak** *i.* Malaysia
116 D2 **Perak** *r.* Malaysia
116 D2 **Perak** *state* Malaysia
208 L3 **Peralada** Spain
205 J9 **Peraleda de la Mata** Spain
206 H4 **Peraleda del Zaucejo** Spain
208 C7 **Peralejos** Spain
208 D6 **Perales del Alfambra** Spain
204 G8 **Perales del Puerto** Spain
285 G6 **Peralta** Arg.
205 Q4 **Peralta** Spain
208 E4 **Peralta de Alcofea** Spain
208 F4 **Peralta de la Sal** Spain
208 E3 **Peraltilla** Spain
206 D6 **Peralva** Port.
205 P7 **Peralveche** Spain
220 F7 **Perama** *Kriti* Greece
136 F7 **Perambalur** *Tamil Nadu* India
162 R4 **Perämeren kansallispuisto** *nat. park* Fin.
233 B7 **Peramiho** Tanz.
208 H3 **Peramola** Spain
206 E5 **Peramora** *r.* Spain
116 E5 **Peranap** *Sumatera* Indon.
162 S3 **Perä-Posio** Fin.
200 F7 **Perarolo di Cadore** Italy
249 H3 **Percé** *Que.* Can.
181 L4 **Perche, Collines du** *hills* France
201 N3 **Perchtoldsdorf** Austria
108 H6 **Percival Lakes** *salt flat W.A.* Austr.
180 I4 **Percy** France
257 N4 **Percy** *NH* U.S.A.
107 M6 **Percy Isles** *Qld* Austr.
251 Q5 **Percy Reach** *l. Ont.* Can.
214 C8 **Perdasdefogu** *Sardegna* Italy
214 B9 **Perdaxius** *Sardegna* Italy
237 N3 **Perdekop** S. Africa
236 H9 **Perdepoort** *pass* S. Africa
285 H3 **Perdices** Arg.
205 P5 **Perdices, Sierra de** *mts* Spain
278 D4 **Perdida** *r.* Brazil
285 H5 **Perdido** *r.* Arg.
277 F5 **Perdido** *r.* Brazil
208 F2 **Perdido, Monte** *mt.* Spain
215 O7 **Perdifumo** Italy
208 D4 **Perdiguera** Spain
208 G2 **Perdiguère, Pic** *mt.* France/Spain
220 B3 **Perdika** Greece
258 B4 **Perdix** *PA* U.S.A.
280 D3 **Perdizes** Brazil
281 E4 **Perdões** Brazil
249 G3 **Perdu, Lac** *l. Que.* Can.
207 O5 **Perea** *mt.* Spain
158 F2 **Perebrody** Ukr.
158 B5 **Perechyn** Ukr.
161 S6 **Peredel** *Kaluzhskaya Oblast'* Rus. Fed.
161 X6 **Peredel** *Vladimirskaya Oblast'* Rus. Fed.
204 G6 **Peredo** Port.
152 H3 **Peregrebnoye** Rus. Fed.
199 J5 **Peregu Mare** Romania
158 D5 **Perehins'ke** Ukr.
274 C3 **Pereira** Col.
280 B4 **Pereira Barreto** Brazil
Pereira de Eça Angola *see* **Ondjiva**
206 C6 **Pereiras** Port.
278 F3 **Pereiro** Brazil
202 C4 **Pereiro** Port.
204 E1 **Pereiro** Spain
205 Q6 **Perejiles** *r.* Spain
161 O3 **Perekhoda** *r.* Rus. Fed.
159 M3 **Perekopivka** Ukr.
159 M8 **Perekops'ka Zatoka** *b.* Ukr.
161 H6 **Perelazovskiy** Rus. Fed.
161 O8 **Perelazy** Rus. Fed.
159 T2 **Pereleshinskiy** Rus. Fed.
142 D2 **Perelyub** Rus. Fed.
250 H6 **Pere Marquette** *r. MI* U.S.A.
142 D2 **Peremetnoye** Kazakh.
159 P4 **Peremoha** *Kharkivs'ka Oblast'* Ukr.
159 K3 **Peremoha** *Kyivs'ka Oblast'* Ukr.
136 C7 **Peremul Par** *rf* India
159 T2 **Peremyshl'** Rus. Fed.
158 D4 **Peremyshlyany** Ukr.
276 B2 **Perené** *r.* Peru
109 D10 **Perenjori** *W.A.* Austr.
204 I6 **Pereruela** Spain
158 H6 **Peresecina** Moldova
159 O4 **Pereshchepyne** Ukr.
161 V5 **Pereslavl'-Zalesskiy** Rus. Fed.
161 V5 **Pereslavskiy Natsional'nyy Park** *nat. park* Rus. Fed.
197 M5 **Perespa** Ukr.
201 O4 **Pereszteg** Hungary
213 K8 **Peretola** *airport* Italy
219 N6 **Peretu** Romania
159 R5 **Pereval's'k** Ukr.
159 L3 **Perevid** *r.* Ukr.
142 F2 **Perevolotskiy** Rus. Fed.
156 I5 **Perevoz** Rus. Fed.
122 I5 **Pereyaslavka** Rus. Fed.
Pereyaslav-Khmel'nitskiy Ukr. *see* **Pereyaslav-Khmel'nyts'kyy**
159 K3 **Pereyaslav-Khmel'nyts'kyy** Ukr.
285 G3 **Pérez** Arg.
282 C2 **Pérez** Chile
214 B6 **Perfugas** *Sardegna* Italy
201 K3 **Perg** Austria
285 G3 **Pergamino** Arg.
221 L6 **Perge** *tourist site* Turkey
213 L9 **Pergine Valdarno** Italy
213 K3 **Pergine Valsugana** Italy
213 N8 **Pergola** Italy
158 G2 **Perha** Ukr.
116 E2 **Perhentian Besar, Pulau** *i.* Malaysia
162 R5 **Perho** Fin.
218 I4 **Periam** Romania
207 K7 **Periana** Spain
268 E6 **Peribán de Ramos** Mex.
249 F3 **Péribonka** *r. Que.* Can.
249 G3 **Péribonka, Lac** *l. Que.* Can.
282 D2 **Perico** Arg.
268 B3 **Pericos** *Nayarit* Mex.
266 F5 **Pericos** *Sinaloa* Mex.
265 V8 **Peridot** *AZ* U.S.A.
219 P4 **Perieni** Romania
180 I3 **Périers** France
184 B3 **Périgny** France
184 F4 **Périgord** *reg.* France
184 F5 **Périgord Blanc** *reg.* France
185 F6 **Périgord Noir** *reg.* France
275 I5 **Perigoso, Canal** *sea chan.* Brazil
184 F5 **Périgueux** France
274 C2 **Perijá, Parque Nacional** *nat. park* Venez.
274 C2 **Perija, Sierra de** *mts* Venez.
204 I5 **Perilla de Castro** Spain
Perim Island Yemen *see* **Barīm**
199 K3 **Perín-Chym** Slovakia
116 E1 **Peringat** Malaysia
219 R5 **Periprava** Romania
219 P6 **Perişoru** Romania
220 E3 **Peristera** *i.* Greece
220 E4 **Peristeri** Greece
151 A7 **Peri Suyu** *r.* Turkey
219 R6 **Periteasca-Gura Portiţei** *nature res.* Romania
283 C7 **Perito Moreno** Arg.
283 B7 **Perito Moreno, Parque Nacional** *nat. park* Arg.
220 B3 **Perivoli** *Kerkyra* Greece
220 F7 **Perivolia** *Kriti* Greece
136 E7 **Periyar** *r.* India
199 J4 **Perje** *r.* Hungary
258 E4 **Perkasie** *PA* U.S.A.
116 F5 **Perkat, Tanjung** *pt* Indon.
199 H4 **Perkáta** Hungary
258 E4 **Perkiomen Creek** *r. PA* U.S.A.
194 A3 **Perl** Ger.
266 □T13 **Perlas, Archipiélago de las** *is* Panama
266 □R11 **Perlas, Laguna de** *lag.* Nic.
266 □R11 **Perlas, Punta de** *pt* Nic.
195 M3 **Perlbach** *r.* Ger.
192 E4 **Perleberg** Ger.
197 K3 **Perlejewo** Pol.
195 O4 **Perlesreut** Ger.
159 R2 **Perlevka** Rus. Fed.
116 D1 **Perlis** *state* Malaysia
197 M1 **Perloja** Lith.
197 J1 **Perły** Pol.
156 L4 **Perm'** Rus. Fed.
213 Q5 **Permani** Croatia
156 I4 **Permas** Rus. Fed.
220 B2 **Përmet** Albania
156 K4 **Permskiy Kray** *admin. div.* Rus. Fed.
213 R7 **Permuda** Croatia
210 E3 **Permuda** *i.* Croatia
160 J1 **Pernå** Fin.
Pernambuco Brazil *see* **Recife**
278 F4 **Pernambuco** *state* Brazil
288 H6 **Pernambuco Plain** *sea feature* S. Atlantic Ocean
182 F2 **Pernand-Vergelesses** France
198 C2 **Pernarec** Czech Rep.
206 C5 **Perna Seca, Barragem da** *resr* Port.
213 Q6 **Pernat, Rt** *pt* Croatia
104 F4 **Pernatty Lagoon** *salt flat S.A.* Austr.
201 L5 **Pernegg an der Mur** Austria
136 C5 **Pernem** *Goa* India
201 N2 **Pernersdorf** Austria
206 B2 **Pernes** Port.
183 G9 **Pernes-les-Fontaines** France
220 F1 **Perni** Greece
219 L8 **Pernik** Bulg.
163 Q6 **Perniö** Fin.
201 M4 **Pernitz** Austria
Pernov Estonia *see* **Pärnu**
212 G4 **Pero** Italy
206 C4 **Peroguarda** Port.
280 A2 **Perolândia** Brazil
183 D9 **Pérols** France
182 H4 **Péron** France
109 B8 **Peron, Cape** *W.A.* Austr.
109 C12 **Peron, Point** *W.A.* Austr.
106 C2 **Peron Islands** *N.T.* Austr.
182 G4 **Péronnas** France
178 E4 **Péronne** France
109 B8 **Peron Peninsula** *W.A.* Austr.
212 C6 **Perosa Argentina** Italy
269 J6 **Perote** Mex.
182 G5 **Pérouges** France
204 F8 **Pero Viseu** Port.
105 M6 **Perpendicular, Point** *N.S.W.* Austr.
185 J10 **Perpignan** France
284 A6 **Perquenco** Chile
284 B4 **Perquilauquén** *r.* Chile
284 D5 **Perra, Salitral de la** *salt pan* Arg.
172 B7 **Perranporth** *Cornwall, England* U.K.
172 B7 **Perranzabuloe** *Cornwall, England* U.K.
182 E3 **Perrecy-les-Forges** France
Perrégaux Alg. *see* **Mohammadia**
182 E4 **Perreux** France
182 H3 **Perrigny** France
264 O8 **Perris** *CA* U.S.A.
206 G7 **Perro, Punta del** *pt* Spain
179 J8 **Perrogney-les-Fontaines** France
176 C2 **Perros-Guirec** France
257 L3 **Perrot, Île** *i. Que.* Can.
162 S2 **Perrum-Äbmir** Fin.
250 J2 **Perry** *Ont.* Can.
255 F10 **Perry** *FL* U.S.A.
255 F9 **Perry** *GA* U.S.A.
260 H5 **Perry** *IA* U.S.A.
257 □R4 **Perry** *ME* U.S.A.
251 J7 **Perry** *MI* U.S.A.
261 G7 **Perry** *OK* U.S.A.
258 A4 **Perry County** *county PA* U.S.A.
258 C6 **Perry Hall** *MD* U.S.A.
258 C6 **Perryman** *MD* U.S.A.
287 G2 **Perrymennyy, Cape** Antarctica
256 B7 **Perrysburg** *OH* U.S.A.
261 E7 **Perryton** *TX* U.S.A.
244 H5 **Perryville** *AK* U.S.A.
261 I8 **Perryville** *AR* U.S.A.
258 C5 **Perryville** *MD* U.S.A.
185 I6 **Pers** France
151 E4 **P'ersa** Georgia
178 D5 **Persan** France
151 D3 **P'ersat'i** Georgia
201 L3 **Persenbeug** Austria
144 E7 **Persepolis** *tourist site* Iran
277 E3 **Perseverancia** Bol.
165 N2 **Pershagen** Sweden
159 M5 **Pershe Travnya** *Dnipropetrovs'ka Oblast'* Ukr.
159 O5 **Pershe Travnya** *Dnipropetrovs'ka Oblast'* Ukr.
Pershnotravnevoye Ukr. *see* **Pershotravens'k**
172 H3 **Pershore** *Worcestershire, England* U.K.
159 P5 **Pershotravens'k** Ukr.
159 Q6 **Pershotravneve** *Donets'ka Oblast'* Ukr.
159 Q4 **Pershotravneve** *Kharkivs'ka Oblast'* Ukr.
159 L7 **Pershotravneve** *Mykolayivs'ka Oblast'* Ukr.
158 H2 **Pershotravneve** *Zhytomyrs'ka Oblast'* Ukr.
Pershotravnevoye Ukr. *see* **Mokvyn**
Persia *country* Asia *see* **Iran**
Persian Gulf Asia *see* **The Gulf**
Persis *prov.* Iran *see* **Fārs**
165 M4 **Persnäs** *Öland* Sweden
165 N3 **Persö naturreservat** *nature res.* Sweden
164 J5 **Perstorp** Sweden
148 I4 **Pertek** Turkey
105 K9 **Perth** *Tas.* Austr.
109 C11 **Perth** *W.A.* Austr.
248 E4 **Perth** *Ont.* Can.
168 J10 **Perth** *Perth and Kinross, Scotland* U.K.
259 G3 **Perth Amboy** *NJ* U.S.A.
168 H9 **Perth and Kinross** *admin. div. Scotland* U.K.
249 H4 **Perth-Andover** *N.B.* Can.
289 L6 **Perth Basin** *sea feature* Indian Ocean
178 H5 **Perthes** *Champagne-Ardenne* France
178 E7 **Perthes** *Île-de-France* France
178 I6 **Perthois** *reg.* France
185 J11 **Perthus, Col du** *pass* France/Spain
156 G2 **Pertominsk** Rus. Fed.
163 Q6 **Pertteli** Fin.
183 H9 **Pertuis** France
184 A3 **Pertuis Breton** *sea chan.* France
184 A3 **Pertuis d'Antioche** *sea chan.* France
163 S6 **Pertunmaa** Fin.
208 E3 **Pertusa** Spain
214 C5 **Pertusato, Capo** *c. Corse* France
285 E5 **Perú** Arg.
276 D3 **Perú** Bol.
Peru *atoll Gilbert Is* Kiribati *see* **Beru**
276 B2 **Peru** *country* S. America
250 E8 **Peru** *IL* U.S.A.
254 D5 **Peru** *IN* U.S.A.
257 L4 **Peru** *NY* U.S.A.
291 M7 **Peru Basin** *sea feature* S. Pacific Ocean
193 I10 **Peruc** Czech Rep.
291 N6 **Peru-Chile Trench** *sea feature* S. Pacific Ocean
210 F4 **Perućko Jezero** *l.* Croatia
215 I1 **Perugia** Italy
213 M9 **Perugia** *prov.* Italy
282 F3 **Perugorría** Arg.
280 D6 **Peruíbe** Brazil
136 E5 **Peruru** *Andhra Prad.* India
219 M8 **Perushtitsa** Bulg.
Perusia Italy *see* **Perugia**
187 E7 **Péruwelz** Belgium
151 C1 **Pervaya Sinyukha** Rus. Fed.
181 L5 **Pervenchères** France
187 C6 **Pervijze** Belgium
159 O1 **Pervoavgustovskiy** Rus. Fed.
158 I7 **Pervomaisc** Moldova
143 P6 **Pervomay** Kyrg.
143 N2 **Pervomayka** Kazakh.
157 H5 **Pervomaysk** Rus. Fed.
159 R5 **Pervomays'k** *Luhans'ka Oblast'* Ukr.
158 J5 **Pervomays'k** *Mykolayivs'ka Oblast'* Ukr.
160 L3 **Pervomayskaya** Rus. Fed.
159 L6 **Pervomays'ke** *Mykolayivs'ka Oblast'* Ukr.
159 M8 **Pervomays'ke** *Respublika Krym* Ukr.
143 T2 **Pervomayskiy** Kazakh.
Pervomayskiy Kyrg. *see* **Pervomay**
Pervomayskiy *Arkhangel'skaya Oblast'* Rus. Fed. *see* **Novodvinsk**
142 F2 **Pervomayskiy** *Orenburgskaya Oblast'* Rus. Fed.
161 P7 **Pervomayskiy** *Smolensk[...] Oblast'* Rus. Fed.
161 X8 **Pervomayskiy** *Tambovsk[...] Oblast'* Rus. Fed.
161 U7 **Pervomayskiy** *Tul'skaya [...]* Rus. Fed.
Pervomayskoye Kyrg. *see* **Pervomay**
160 M1 **Pervomayskoye** *Leningr[...] Oblast'* Rus. Fed.
151 I3 **Pervomayskoye** *Respubl[...] Dagestan* Rus. Fed.
122 M4 **Pervomayskoye** *Sakhali[...] Oblast'* Rus. Fed.
159 P4 **Pervomays'kyy** Ukr.
153 R3 **Pervorechenskiy** Rus. Fe[...]
187 G7 **Perwez** Belgium
161 R3 **Pes'** Rus. Fed.
161 S2 **Pes'** *r.* Rus. Fed.
213 K8 **Pesa** *r.* Italy
205 M3 **Pesadas de Burgos** Spai[...]
117 I5 **Pesaguan** *Kalimantan* In[...]
117 I6 **Pesaguan** *r.* Indon.
213 N8 **Pesaro** Italy
213 N8 **Pesaro e Urbino** *prov.* It[...]
264 J4 **Pescadero** *CA* U.S.A.
Pescadores *is* Taiwan *see* **P'enghu Ch'üntao**
276 B4 **Pescadores, Punta** *pt* Pe[...]
212 I8 **Pescaglia** Italy
213 J5 **Pescantina** Italy
215 M3 **Pescara** Italy
215 L3 **Pescara** *prov.* Italy
215 M3 **Pescara** *r.* Italy
219 J6 **Pescari** Romania
215 L4 **Pescasseroli** Italy
182 C5 **Peschadoires** France
157 H7 **Peschanokopskoye** Rus.
Peschanoye Rus. Fed. *see* [...]
142 D6 **Peschanyy, Mys** *pt* Kazak[...]
215 Q4 **Peschici** Italy
213 J8 **Pescia** Italy
215 L3 **Pescina** Italy
215 M4 **Pescocostanzo** Italy
215 M4 **Pescolanciano** Italy
215 O6 **Pescopagano** Italy
215 M4 **Pescopennataro** Italy
215 K3 **Pescorocchiano** Italy
215 N5 **Pesco Sannita** Italy
266 □S14 **Pesé** Panama
238 □3b **Pesebre, Punta** *pt Fuerte[...]* Canary Is
116 □ **Pesek, Pulau** *i.* Sing.
116 □ **Pesek Kechil, Pulau** *i.* Si[...]
212 B2 **Peseux** Switz.
156 I2 **Pesha** *r.* Rus. Fed.
145 I5 **Peshanjan** Afgh.
145 N4 **Peshawar** Pak.
218 I9 **Peshkopi** Albania
159 S7 **Peshkovo** Rus. Fed.
Peshnyye, Ostrova *is* Ka[...] **Bol'shiye Peshnyye, Ost[...]**
219 M8 **Peshtera** Bulg.
250 G4 **Peshtigo** *WI* U.S.A.
250 G5 **Peshtigo** *r. WI* U.S.A.
212 D7 **Pesio** *r.* Italy
143 L1 **Peski** Kazakh.
161 V6 **Peski** *Moskovskaya Oblas[...]* Rus. Fed.
157 H6 **Peski** *Voronezhskaya Obl[...]* Rus. Fed.
145 J2 **Peski** Turkm.
156 K4 **Peskovka** Rus. Fed.
182 H2 **Pesmes** France
210 E2 **Pesnica** Slovenia
161 W3 **Pesochnoye** Rus. Fed.
161 Q8 **Pesochnya** Rus. Fed.
204 E6 **Peso da Régua** Port.
266 □P11 **Pespire** Hond.
278 F4 **Pesqueira** Brazil
266 D3 **Pesqueira** Mex.
205 L5 **Pesquera de Duero** Spai[...]
185 C6 **Pessac** France
185 F8 **Pessan** France
186 J3 **Pesse** Neth.
192 G5 **Pessin** Ger.
199 I4 **Pest** *county* Hungary
161 S3 **Pestovo** Rus. Fed.
142 C1 **Pestravka** Rus. Fed.
156 H4 **Pestyaki** Rus. Fed.
205 L2 **Pesués** Spain
156 L1 **Pesyakov, Ostrov** *i.* Rus.
268 E8 **Petacalco, Bahía de** *b.* M[...]
215 N3 **Petacciato** Italy
150 C6 **Petah Tiqwa** Israel
163 R5 **Petäjävesi** Fin.
115 F3 **Petak, Tanjung** *pt Halma[...]* Indon.
220 C6 **Petalidi** Greece
220 F4 **Petalioi** *i.* Greece
220 F4 **Petalion, Kolpos** *sea cha[...]*
264 J3 **Petaluma** *CA* U.S.A.
187 I9 **Pétange** Lux.
117 K5 **Petangis** *Kalimantan* Ind[...]
274 E2 **Petare** Venez.
220 C3 **Petas** Greece
268 F8 **Petatlán** Mex.
233 A8 **Petauke** Zambia
253 S3 **Petawaga, Lac** *l. Que.* Ca[...]
251 Q4 **Petawawa** *Ont.* Can.
267 O9 **Petén Itzá, Lago** *l.* Guat.
250 E5 **Petenwell Lake** *WI* U.S.A.
201 O7 **Peteranec** Croatia
248 D3 **Peterbell** *Ont.* Can.
104 G5 **Peterborough** *S.A.* Austr.
105 I8 **Peterborough** *Vic.* Austr.
248 E4 **Peterborough** *Ont.* Can.
173 L2 **Peterborough** *Peterborou[...] England* U.K.
173 L2 **Peterborough** *admin. div[...]* U.K.
257 N6 **Peterborough** *NH* U.S.A.
168 L8 **Peterculter** *Aberdeen, Sco[...]* U.K.
168 M7 **Peterhead** *Aberdeenshire, Scotland* U.K.
199 I4 **Péteri** Hungary
286 R2 **Peter I Island** Antarctica
Peter I Øy *i.* Antarctica *s[...]* **Peter I Island**
199 I5 **Péteri-tó** *l.* Hungary
247 M2 **Peter Lake** *Nunavut* Can
171 O4 **Peterlee** *Durham, Englan[...]*
246 H5 **Peter Lougheed Provinc[...]** B.C. Can.
106 C8 **Petermann Aboriginal L[...]** *N.T./W.A.* Austr.
243 P2 **Petermann Bjerg** *nunata[...]* Greenland
106 B8 **Petermann Ranges** *mts [...]* Austr.
284 B4 **Peteroa, Volcán** *vol.* Chil[...]
247 I4 **Peter Pond Lake** *Sask.* C[...]
249 G1 **Peters, Lac** *l. Que.* Can.
195 J3 **Petersaurach** Ger.
191 I9 **Petersberg** Ger.
237 I8 **Petersburg** S. Africa
245 N4 **Petersburg** *AK* U.S.A.
260 K6 **Petersburg** *IL* U.S.A.
254 D6 **Petersburg** *IN* U.S.A.
258 F6 **Petersburg** *NJ* U.S.A.
257 L6 **Petersburg** *NY* U.S.A.
256 B9 **Petersburg** *OH* U.S.A.
256 H11 **Petersburg** *VA* U.S.A.
256 F10 **Petersburg** *WV* U.S.A.
195 K4 **Petersdorf** Ger.
192 D2 **Petersdorf auf Fehmarn[...]**
173 K5 **Petersfield** *Hampshire, England* U.K.
193 J6 **Petershagen** *Brandenbur[...]*
191 G6 **Petershagen** *Nordrhein-W[...]* Ger.
195 K5 **Petershausen** Ger.
275 G3 **Peters Mine** Guyana
256 E11 **Peterstown** *WV* U.S.A.
245 J3 **Petersville** *AK* U.S.A.
169 E6 **Peterswell** Ireland
Peter the Great Bay Rus. **Petra Velikogo, Zaliv**
Pétervárad *Vojvodina* Ser[...] **Petrovaradin**
199 J3 **Pétervására** Hungary
Peterwardein *Vojvodina* [...] **Petrovaradin**

Peth Mahar. India
Petilia Policastro Italy
Petilla de Aragón Spain
Petín Spain
Petit Atlas mts Morocco see Anti Atlas
Petit-Bourg Guadeloupe
Petit-Canal Guadeloupe
Petitcodiac N.B. Can.
Petit-Couronne France
Petit Cul-de-Sac Marin b. Guadeloupe
Petite Camargue reg. France
Petite Creuse r. France
Petite-Île Réunion
Petite Leyre r. France
Petite Maine r. France
Petite Martinique i. Grenada
Petite-Rosselle France
Petite Sauldre r. France
Petite Suisse Luxembourgeoise reg. Lux.
Petite Terre i. Mayotte
Petit-Goâve Haiti
Petitjean Morocco see Sidi Kacem
Petit Lay r. France
Petit Manan Point ME U.S.A.
Petit-Mars France
Petit Mécatina r. Nfld and Lab./Que. Can.
Petit Mécatina r. Que. Can.
Petit Mécatina, Île du i. Que. Can.
Petitmont France
Petit Morin r. France
Petit-Noir France
Petitot r. Alta/B.C. Can.
Petit Rhône r. France
Petit St-Bernard, Col du pass France
Petkino Rus. Fed.
Petkula Fin.
Petkus Ger.
Petlad Gujarat India
Petlalcingo Mex.
Petlawad Madh. Prad. India
Petneháza Hungary
Peto Mex.
Petőfibánya Hungary
Petőfiszállás Hungary
Petorca Chile
Petoskey MI U.S.A.
Petra tourist site Jordan
Petra Spain
Petrace r. Italy
Petralia-Soprana Sicilia Italy
Petralia-Sottana Sicilia Italy
Petras, Mount Antarctica
Petra Velikogo, Zaliv b. Rus. Fed.
Petre, Point Ont. Can.
Petre Bay Chatham Is S. Pacific Ocean
Petrel Valencia Spain see Petrer
Petrella, Monte mt. Italy
Petrella Salto Italy
Petrella Tifernina Italy
Petrer Spain
Petrești Romania
Petreto-Bicchisano Corse France
Petriano Italy
Petrich Bulg.
Petrie, Récif rf New Caledonia
Petrified Forest National Park AZ U.S.A.
Petrijevci Croatia
Petrikau Pol. see Piotrków Trybunalski
Petrikov Belarus see Pyetrykaw
Petrila Romania
Petrinja Croatia
Petriș Romania
Petritoli Italy
Petrivka Khersons'ka Oblast' Ukr.
Petrivka Odes'ka Oblast' Ukr.
Petrivs'ke Ukr.
Petrivtsi Ukr.
Petro, Cerro de mt. Chile
Petroaleksandrovsk Uzbek. see To'rtko'l
Petrodvorets Rus. Fed.
Petrograd Rus. Fed. see Sankt-Peterburg
Petrokov Pol. see Piotrków Trybunalski
Petrokrepost' Rus. Fed. see Shlissel'burg
Petrokrepost', Bukhta b. Rus. Fed.
Pétrola Spain
Petrolândia Brazil
Petrólea Col.
Petrolia Ont. Can.
Petrolia CA U.S.A.
Petrolina Amazonas Brazil
Petrolina Pernambuco Brazil
Petrolina de Goiás Brazil
Petromaryevka Ukr. see Pervomays'k
Petron, Limni l. Greece
Petronà Italy
Petropavl Kazakh. see Petropavlovsk
Petropavlivka Ukr.
Petropavlovka Kazakh.
Petropavlovka Amurskaya Oblast' Rus. Fed.
Petropavlovka Respublika Buryatiya Rus. Fed.
Petropavlovka Voronezhskaya Oblast' Rus. Fed.
Petropavlovsk Kazakh.
Petropavlovsk Rus. Fed. see Petropavlovsk-Kamchatskiy
Petropavlovsk-Kamchatskiy Rus. Fed.
Petropavlovskoye Rus. Fed.
Petrópolis Brazil
Petroșani Romania
Petrosino Sicilia Italy
Petrov Czech Rep.
Petrovac Bos.-Herz. see Bosanski Petrovac
Petrovac Petrovac Serbia
Petrovany Slovakia
Petrovaradin Vojvodina Serbia
Petrove Ukr.
Petrovec Petrovec Macedonia
Petrovice Czech Rep.
Petrovichi Rus. Fed.
Petrovka Kazakh.
Petrovsk Rus. Fed.
Petrovskaya Rus. Fed.
Petrovs'ke Ukr.
Petrovskiy Rus. Fed.
Petrovskoye Moskovskaya Oblast' Rus. Fed.
Petrovskoye Respublika Bashkortostan Rus. Fed.
Petrovskoye Stavropol'skiy Kray Rus. Fed. see Svetlograd
Petrovskoye Tambovskaya Oblast' Rus. Fed.
Petrovskoye Yaroslavskaya Oblast' Rus. Fed.
Petrovsk-Zabaykal'skiy Rus. Fed.
Petrov Val Rus. Fed.
Petrozavodsk Rus. Fed.
Petru Rareș Romania
Petrusburg S. Africa
Petrușeni Moldova
Petrus Steyn S. Africa
Petrusville S. Africa
Petřvald Czech Rep.
Petrykivka Ukr.
Petsamo Rus. Fed. see Pechenga
Petsana S. Africa
Pettau Slovenia see Ptuj
Petten Neth.
Pettendorf Ger.
Pettigo Northern Ireland U.K.
Pettinascura, Monte mt. Italy
Pettineo Sicilia Italy
Petting Ger.
Pettneu am Arlberg Austria
Pettorano sul Gizio Italy
213 L3 Pettorina r. Italy
152 H4 Petukhovo Rus. Fed.
161 W6 Petushki Rus. Fed.
173 K6 Petworth West Sussex, England U.K.
200 G6 Petzeck mt. Austria
201 I3 Peuerbach Austria
116 B2 Peuetsagu, Gunung vol. Indon.
184 D5 Peujard France
244 H4 Peulik Volcano, Mount AK U.S.A.
284 B4 Peumo Chile
162 S3 Peurasuvanto Fin.
116 B2 Peureula Sumatera Indon.
153 S3 Pevek Rus. Fed.
173 M6 Pevensey East Sussex, England U.K.
173 M6 Pevensey Levels lowland England U.K.
212 D7 Peveragno Italy
173 I5 Pewsey Wiltshire, England U.K.
173 I5 Pewsey, Vale of val. England U.K.
190 D4 Pewsum (Krummhörn) Ger.
179 M7 Pexonne France
133 K10 Pêxung Xizang China
144 H9 Pey Beshk Iran
183 J9 Peymeinade France
183 C10 Peyne r. France
183 H10 Peynier France
144 G4 Pey Ostān Iran
183 H10 Peypin France
285 G3 Peyrano Arg.
184 H4 Peyrat-le-Château France
185 B8 Peyrehorade France
183 C8 Peyreleau France
184 I4 Peyrelevade France
185 E10 Peyresourde, Col de pass France
212 D8 Peyrevieille, Mont mt. Italy
183 B10 Peyriac-de-Mer France
185 J9 Peyriac-Minervois France
182 H5 Peyrieu France
183 G6 Peyrins France
183 H9 Peyrolles-en-Provence France
183 H8 Peyruis France
185 E8 Peyrusse-Grande France
185 I6 Peyrusse-le-Roc France
156 I2 Peza r. Rus. Fed.
183 C10 Pézenas France
196 D2 Pęzino Pol.
198 G3 Pezinok Slovakia
145 N5 Pezu Pak.
185 F6 Pezuls France
195 M4 Pfaffenberg Ger.
193 J6 Pfaffendorf Ger.
195 I5 Pfaffenhausen Ger.
195 L4 Pfaffenhofen an der Ilm Ger.
195 I5 Pfaffenhofen an der Roth Ger.
179 O6 Pfaffenhoffen France
201 M4 Pfaffensattel pass Austria
194 D6 Pfaffenweiler Ger.
212 F1 Pfäffikon Schwyz Switz.
212 F1 Pfäffikon Zürich Switz.
195 M5 Pfaffing Ger.
194 D3 Pfälzer Wald hills Ger.
194 D3 Pfälzer Wald park Ger.
191 E10 Pfalzfeld Ger.
194 F4 Pfalzgrafenweiler Ger.
195 N5 Pfarrkirchen Ger.
191 K10 Pfarrweisach Ger.
200 H5 Pfarrwerfen Austria
195 M4 Pfatter Ger.
194 G3 Pfedelbach Ger.
195 L4 Pfeffenhausen Ger.
200 C4 Pflach Austria
200 D5 Pfons Austria
195 L4 Pförring Ger.
195 J6 Pforzen Ger.
194 F4 Pforzheim Ger.
195 M3 Pfreimd Ger.
195 M2 Pfreimd r. Ger.
194 G5 Pfronstetten Ger.
195 J6 Pfronten Ger.
194 G6 Pfullendorf Ger.
194 G5 Pfullingen Ger.
200 C6 Pfunds Austria
194 F2 Pfungstadt Ger.
212 F1 Pfyn Switz.
118 F4 Phac Mo, Phu mt. Vietnam
235 F5 Phagameng Limpopo S. Africa
138 E4 Phagwara Punjab India
237 K4 Phahameng Free State S. Africa
235 F4 Phalaborwa S. Africa
145 O5 Phalia Pak.
138 D6 Phalodi Rajasthan India
179 N6 Phalsbourg France
138 C6 Phalsund Rajasthan India
136 D4 Phaltan Mahar. India
139 L6 Phalut Peak India/Nepal
119 E10 Phangan, Ko i. Thai.
118 E6 Phang Hoei, San Khao mts Thai.
119 D10 Phangnga Thai.
118 F3 Phăng Xi Păng mt. Vietnam
119 G7 Phanom Dong Rak, Thiu Khao mts Cambodia/Thai.
119 I9 Phan Rang-Thap Cham Vietnam
119 I9 Phan Ri Cưa Vietnam
119 I9 Phan Thiêt Vietnam
119 I9 Phan Thiêt, Vinh b. Vietnam
138 G6 Phaphund Uttar Prad. India
139 K6 Phaplu Nepal
170 E3 Pharis Northern Ireland U.K.
118 H4 Phat Diêm Vietnam
119 E11 Phatthalung Thai.
118 D5 Phayao Thai.
118 E7 Phayuhakhiri Thai.
139 O7 Phek Nagaland India
106 E3 Phelp r. N.T. Austr.
256 H6 Phelps NY U.S.A.
250 E3 Phelps WI U.S.A.
247 K3 Phelps Lake Sask. Can.
118 F6 Phen Thai.
256 G11 Phenix VA U.S.A.
255 E9 Phenix City AL U.S.A.
236 G1 Phephane watercourse S. Africa
119 D8 Phet Buri Thai.
118 E6 Phetchabun Thai.
119 G7 Phiafai Laos
118 E6 Phichai Thai.
118 E6 Phichit Thai.
Philadelphia Jordan see 'Ammān
236 C9 Philadelphia S. Africa
Philadelphia Turkey see Alașehir
261 K9 Philadelphia MS U.S.A.
257 J4 Philadelphia NY U.S.A.
258 E5 Philadelphia PA U.S.A.
258 E5 Philadelphia County county PA U.S.A.
225 G4 Philae tourist site Egypt
Philip atoll Arch. des Tuamotu Fr. Polynesia see Makemo
260 E3 Philip SD U.S.A.
Philip Atoll Micronesia see Sorol
104 □[1] Philip Island Norfolk I.
Philippeville Alg. see Skikda
187 G8 Philippeville Belgium
256 E9 Philippi WV U.S.A.
106 G8 Philippi, Lake salt flat Qld Austr.
187 E6 Philippine Neth.
290 D4 Philippine Basin sea feature N. Pacific Ocean
114 D4 Philippines country Asia
112 F3 Philippine Sea N. Pacific Ocean
290 D4 Philippine Trench sea feature N. Pacific Ocean
237 J6 Philippolis S. Africa
237 J6 Philippolis Road S. Africa
Philippopolis Bulg. see Plovdiv
194 E3 Philippsburg Ger.
195 P4 Philippsreut Ger.
191 J9 Philippsthal (Werra) Ger.
271 L4 Philipsburg St Maarten Neth. Antilles
262 H3 Philipsburg MT U.S.A.
256 G8 Philipsburg PA U.S.A.
186 F5 Philipsdam barrage Neth.
245 J2 Philip Smith Mountains AK U.S.A.
236 I6 Philipstown S. Africa
105 J8 Phillip Island Vic. Austr.
104 □[2] Phillip Point Lord Howe I. Austr.
109 F12 Phillips r. W.A. Austr.
257 □O4 Phillips ME U.S.A.
250 D4 Phillips WI U.S.A.
246 E5 Phillips Arm B.C. Can.
260 F6 Phillipsburg KS U.S.A.
258 E3 Phillipsburg NJ U.S.A.
243 J1 Phillips Inlet Nunavut Can.
104 E3 Phillipson, Lake salt flat S.A. Austr.
108 H4 Phillips Range hills W.A. Austr.
256 F8 Phillipston PA U.S.A.
257 L6 Philmont NY U.S.A.
Philomelium Turkey see Akșehir
256 E12 Philpott Reservoir VA U.S.A.
118 G7 Phimun Mangsahan Thai.
237 L3 Phiritona S. Africa
118 E6 Phitsanulok Thai.
250 E4 Phlox WI U.S.A.
Phnom Penh Cambodia see Phnum Pénh
119 G9 Phnum Pénh Cambodia
119 E11 Pho, Laem pt Thai.
118 G5 Phô Châu Vietnam
257 K6 Phoenicia NY U.S.A.
239 □[1b] Phoenix Mauritius
265 T8 Phoenix AZ U.S.A.
257 I5 Phoenix NY U.S.A.
Phoenix Island Phoenix Is Kiribati see Rawaki
99 I2 Phoenix Islands Kiribati
258 D4 Phoenixville PA U.S.A.
237 N2 Phola S. Africa
118 G3 Phô Lu Vietnam
237 L3 Phomolong S. Africa
118 F7 Phon Thai.
118 H6 Phong Nha Vietnam
118 F4 Phôngsali Laos
Phong Saly Laos see Phôngsali
118 F3 Phong Thô Vietnam
118 F5 Phon Phisai Thai.
118 F6 Phon Thong Thai.
105 I8 Phoques Bay Tas. Austr.
106 H6 Phosphate Hill Qld Austr.
138 F2 Photaksur Jammu and Kashmir India
118 E5 Phrae Thai.
Phra Nakhon Si Ayutthaya Thai. see Ayutthaya
118 D5 Phrao Thai.
119 D10 Phra Saeng Thai.
119 D10 Phra Thong, Ko i. Thai.
118 E6 Phrom Phiram Thai.
119 F9 Phsar Ream Cambodia
118 H6 Phu Bai Vietnam
119 G7 Phuchong-Nayoi National Park Thai.
Phu Cuong Vietnam see Thu Dâu Môt
118 G4 Phuc Yên Vietnam
234 E4 Phuduhudu Botswana
139 L6 Phuentsholing Bhutan
119 D11 Phuket Thai.
119 D11 Phuket, Ko i. Thai.
118 E6 Phu Khieo Wildlife Reserve nature res. Thai.
139 J9 Phulbani Orissa India
145 L8 Phulji Pak.
118 H6 Phu Lôc Vietnam
119 G10 Phu Lôc Vietnam
138 I7 Phulpur Uttar Prad. India
118 E6 Phu Luang National Park Thai.
118 G4 Phu Ly Vietnam
119 F8 Phumĭ Bânhchok Kon Cambodia
119 G8 Phumĭ Chhlong Cambodia
119 G9 Phumĭ Chhuk Cambodia
119 G7 Phumĭ Kâmpóng Srâlau Cambodia
119 G8 Phumĭ Kâmpóng Trâlach Cambodia
119 F9 Phumĭ Kaôh Kŏng Cambodia
119 F8 Phumĭ Kiliĕk Cambodia
119 F7 Phumĭ Kon Kriel Cambodia
119 F8 Phumĭ Koŭk Kduŏch Cambodia
119 G8 Phumĭ Mlu Prey Cambodia
118 D6 Phumiphon, Khuan Thai.
119 F8 Phumĭ Prâmaôy Cambodia
119 G8 Phumĭ Prêk Kak Cambodia
119 F7 Phumĭ Sâmraông Cambodia
119 G8 Phumĭ Thalabârĭvăt Cambodia
119 G8 Phumĭ Toêng Cambodia
119 G9 Phumĭ Trâm Kak Cambodia
119 F7 Phumĭ Trom Cambodia
119 F9 Phumĭ Veal Renh Cambodia
119 I7 Phu My Vietnam
119 G10 Phung Hiêp Vietnam
Phuntsholing Bhutan see Phuentsholing
119 H9 Phước Bưu Vietnam
119 H9 Phước Hai Vietnam
119 G10 Phước Long Vietnam
118 F6 Phu Phan National Park Thai.
119 F9 Phu Quôc, Đao i. Vietnam
119 I9 Phu Quy, Đao i. Vietnam
237 M4 Phuthaditjhaba S. Africa
118 G4 Phu Tho Vietnam
Phu Vinh Vietnam see Tra Vinh
118 F6 Phu Wiang Thai.
118 G4 Phu Yên Vietnam
118 C5 Phyu Myanmar
185 J10 Pia France
109 D9 Pia Aboriginal Reserve W.A. Austr.
117 J4 Piabung, Gunung mt. Indon.
278 D3 Piaca Brazil
280 B4 Piacatu Brazil
212 H5 Piacenza Italy
212 H6 Piacenza prov. Italy
249 G3 Piacouadie, Lac l. Que. Can.
212 I5 Piadena Italy
248 E2 Piagochioui r. Que. Can.
116 E4 Piai, Tanjung pt Malaysia
285 G3 Piamonte Arg.
105 L4 Pian r. N.S.W. Austr.
214 B3 Piana Corse France
214 A6 Piana, Isola i. Sardegna Italy
214 A9 Piana, Isola i. Sardegna Italy
212 E7 Piana Crixia Italy
216 E8 Piana degli Albanesi Sicilia Italy
214 H2 Piancastagnaio Italy
213 M8 Piandimeleto Italy
215 M3 Pianella Italy
212 G6 Pianello Val Tidone Italy
105 I6 Piangil Vic. Austr.
129 L7 Pianguan Shanxi China
118 D1 Pianma Yunnan China
213 K7 Piano del Voglio Italy
213 K7 Pianoro Italy
214 E2 Pianosa Italy
214 E2 Pianosa, Isola i. Italy
215 P3 Pianosa, Isole is Italy
214 C5 Pianotolli-Caldarello Corse France
214 H2 Piansano Italy
271 □[7] Piarco airport Trin. and Tob.
206 E4 Pias Port.
204 G4 Pias, Embalse de resr Spain
197 J3 Piaseczno Mazowieckie Pol.
196 C2 Piaseczno Zachodniopomorskie Pol.
196 C3 Piasek Pol.
197 K4 Piaski Lubelskie Pol.
196 F4 Piaski Wielkopolskie Pol.
278 F4 Piassabussu Brazil
197 I3 Piastów Pol.
278 E5 Piatã Brazil
197 H3 Piątek Pol.
197 K2 Piątnica Poduchowna Pol.
219 N7 Piatra Romania
219 O4 Piatra Neamț Romania
219 M6 Piatra Olt Romania
219 O4 Piatra ḑoimului Romania
185 E10 Piau-Engaly France
278 E3 Piauí r. Brazil
278 E3 Piauí state Brazil
278 E4 Piauí, Serra de hills Brazil
213 N4 Piave r. Italy
268 A2 Piaxtla r. Mex.
212 I7 Piazza al Serchio Italy
216 G9 Piazza Armerina Sicilia Italy
212 H4 Piazza Brembana Italy
212 H4 Piazzatorre Italy
212 I3 Piazzi, Cima de' mt. Italy
283 B8 Piazzi, Isla i. Chile
213 L4 Piazzola sul Brenta Italy
232 B2 Pibor r. Sudan
232 B3 Pibor Post Sudan
185 G8 Pibrac France
248 C3 Pic r. Ont. Can.
276 C5 Pica Chile
265 U9 Picacho AZ U.S.A.
268 B3 Picachos Mex.
266 B3 Picachos, Cerro dos mt. Mex.
213 Q5 Pićan Croatia
209 C8 Picaracho mt. Spain
178 E4 Picardie admin. reg. France
178 C4 Picardie reg. France
Picardy reg. France see Picardie
209 E9 Picassent Spain
180 I3 Picauville France
261 K10 Picayune MS U.S.A.
213 L2 Picco della Croce mt. Italy
183 K6 Piccolo, Lago l. Italy
267 N8 Pich Mex.
284 B5 Pichachén, Paso pass Arg./Chile
266 F3 Picháchic Mex.
282 D1 Pichanal Arg.
284 B2 Pichasca Chile
192 D4 Picher Ger.
284 C3 Pichi Ciego Arg.
284 B3 Pichidanguí Chile
284 A4 Pichilemu Chile
266 D5 Pichilingue Mex.
284 E6 Pichi Mahuida Arg.
274 B5 Pichincha prov. Ecuador
201 I3 Pichl bei Wels Austria
138 G7 Pichor Madh. Prad. India
267 M9 Pichucalco Mex.
250 H1 Pic Island Ont. Can.
256 E10 Pickens WV U.S.A.
250 C1 Pickerel Lake Ont. Can.
251 O6 Pickering Ont. Can.
171 P5 Pickering North Yorkshire, England U.K.
171 P5 Pickering, Vale of val. England U.K.
275 G3 Pickersgill Guyana
251 J3 Pickford MI U.S.A.
270 C3 Pickle Bank sea feature Caribbean Sea
248 B3 Pickle Lake Ont. Can.
238 □[1c] Pico i. Azores
238 □[1c] Pico mt. Pico Azores
215 L5 Pico Italy
205 J8 Pico, Puerto del pass Spain
266 □P10 Pico Bonito, Parque Nacional nat. park Hond.
214 D9 Picocca r. Italy
275 E4 Pico da Neblina, Parque Nacional do nat. park Brazil
269 J6 Pico de Orizaba, Parque Nacional nat. park Mex.
268 E6 Pico de Tancítaro, Parque Nacional nat. park Mex.
238 □[1c] Pico Gorda vol. Faial Azores
207 K2 Picón Spain
278 E3 Picos Brazil
204 C5 Picos, Punta dos pt Spain
205 K2 Picos de Europa, Parque Nacional de los nat. park Spain
274 B6 Picota Peru
204 C6 Picoto Port.
283 D7 Pico Truncado Arg.
178 D4 Picquigny France
250 H1 Pic River Ont. Can.
105 M6 Picton N.S.W. Austr.
248 E5 Picton Ont. Can.
103 I8 Picton South I. N.Z.
105 K10 Picton, Mount Tas. Austr.
249 I4 Pictou N.S. Can.
246 H5 Picture Butte Alta Can.
250 H3 Pictured Rocks National Lakeshore nature res. MI U.S.A.
258 B2 Picture Rocks PA U.S.A.
271 □[1] Picua, Punta pt Puerto Rico
278 F3 Picuí Brazil
284 C6 Picún Leufú Arg.
284 C6 Picún Leufú r. Arg.
145 J9 Pidarak Pak.
197 M5 Pidberezzya Ukr.
197 L6 Pidbuzh Ukr.
172 H6 Piddle r. England U.K.
172 H6 Piddletrenthide Dorset, England U.K.
158 E4 Pidhaytsi Ukr.
158 J5 Pidhorodna Ukr.
159 O5 Pidhorodne Ukr.
197 L6 Pidhorodtsi Ukr.
195 N6 Piding Ger.
239 □[3a] Pidjani Njazidja Comoros
158 E4 Pidkamin' Ukr.
159 L5 Pidlisne Ukr.
161 R1 Pid'ma Rus. Fed.
136 G9 Pidurutalagala mt. Sri Lanka
158 F4 Pidvolochys'k Ukr.
158 J5 Pidvysoke Ukr.
196 G3 Piechcin Pol.
196 D5 Piechowice Pol.
197 J2 Piecki Pol.
196 E2 Piecnik Pol.
238 □[1c] Piedade Pico Azores
280 D5 Piedade Brazil
206 B6 Piedade, Ponta da pt Port.
284 C2 Pie de Palo, Sierra mts Arg.
214 C3 Piedicorte-di-Gaggio Corse France
214 C3 Piedicroce Corse France
215 J2 Piediluco, Lago di l. Italy
217 I8 Piedimonte Etneo Sicilia Italy
215 M5 Piedimonte Matese Italy
212 E3 Piedimulera Italy
Piedmont admin. reg. Italy see Piemonte
255 E9 Piedmont AL U.S.A.
261 J7 Piedmont MO U.S.A.
256 D8 Piedmont OH U.S.A.
256 D8 Piedmont Lake OH U.S.A.
205 Q6 Piedra r. Spain
206 F3 Piedra Aguda, Embalse de resr Spain
207 K2 Piedrabuena Spain
283 C6 Piedra de Águila Arg.
269 J8 Piedra de Olla, Cerro mt. Mex.
Piedrafita Spain see Pedrafita do Cebreiro
204 F3 Piedrafita, Porto de pass Spain
204 H3 Piedrafita de Babia Spain
205 J8 Piedrahita Spain
205 K8 Piedralaves Spain
206 E6 Piedras, Embalse de resr Spain
285 I4 Piedras, Punta pt Arg.
276 C3 Piedras, Río de las r. Peru
204 G9 Piedras Albas Spain
204 I1 Piedras Blancas Spain
264 K6 Piedras Blancas Point CA U.S.A.
205 L2 Piedrasluengas, Puerto de pass Spain
267 N9 Piedras Negras Guat.
267 I3 Piedras Negras Coahuila Mex.
269 K7 Piedras Negras Veracruz Mex.
285 I3 Piedra Sola Uru.
285 F4 Piedritas Arg.
214 I2 Piegaro Italy
184 F4 Piégut-Pluviers France
250 E1 Pie Island Ont. Can.
196 G5 Piekary Śląskie Pol.
192 I1 Piekberg hill Ger.
197 I5 Piekoszów Pol.
162 S5 Pieksämäki Fin.
229 E3 Piéla Burkina
201 L3 Pielach r. Austria
162 S5 Pielavesi Fin.
162 S5 Pielavesi l. Fin.
196 D4 Pielgrzymka Pol.
162 T5 Pielinen l. Fin.
162 N3 Pieljekaise nationalpark nat. park Sweden
183 F10 Piémanson, Plage de coastal area France
212 D6 Piemonte admin. reg. Italy
237 M1 Pienaarsrivier S. Africa
196 E2 Pieniężnica Pol.
165 Q7 Pieniężno Pol.
197 I6 Pieniński Park Narodowy nat. park Pol.
199 J2 Pieninský nat. park Slovakia
196 E1 Pieńkowo Pol.
179 K5 Piennes France
196 D4 Pieńsk Pol.
214 H1 Pienza Italy
208 I4 Piera Spain
260 G4 Pierce NE U.S.A.
247 M4 Pierce Lake Man./Ont. Can.
247 I4 Pierceland Sask. Can.
250 I8 Pierceton IN U.S.A.
285 H6 Pieres Arg.
220 D2 Pieria mts Greece
168 K4 Pierowall Orkney, Scotland U.K.
260 E3 Pierre SD U.S.A.
261 J10 Pierre, Bayou r. MS U.S.A.
261 I10 Pierre Bayou r. LA U.S.A.
184 G4 Pierre-Buffière France
183 H7 Pierre-Châtel France
182 G3 Pierre-de-Bresse France
183 I10 Pierrefeu-du-Var France
185 D10 Pierrefitte-Nestalas France
179 J6 Pierrefitte-sur-Aire France
182 D4 Pierrefitte-sur-Loire France
178 E5 Pierrefonds France
182 J2 Pierrefontaine-les-Varans France
183 B7 Pierrefort France
183 F8 Pierrelatte France
179 K5 Pierrepont France
178 C6 Pierres France
182 D5 Pierre-sur-Haute mt. France
183 H9 Pierrevert France
271 □[7] Pierreville Trin. and Tob.
239 □[1a] Pierrot Island Rodrigues I. Mauritius
178 G5 Pierry France
186 F5 Piershil Neth.
197 I5 Pierzchnica Pol.
193 D9 Piesau Ger.
200 G5 Piesendorf Austria
162 N3 Pieskehaure l. Sweden
196 D3 Pieski Pol.
194 B2 Piesport Ger.
199 G3 Piešťany Slovakia
197 I1 Pieszkowo Pol.
196 E5 Pieszyce Pol.
239 □[1b] Pieter Both hill Mauritius
237 O5 Pietermaritzburg S. Africa
Pietersaari Fin. see Jakobstad
Pietersburg Limpopo S. Africa see Polokwane
236 I2 Piet Plessis S. Africa
215 M4 Pietrabbondante Italy
215 N4 Pietracatella Italy
214 C2 Pietracorbara Corse France
214 C3 Pietra-di-Verde Corse France
215 P6 Pietragalla Italy
214 C2 Pietralba Corse France
212 E7 Pietra Ligure Italy
213 M9 Pietralunga Italy
215 M5 Pietramelara Italy
215 O4 Pietramontecorvino Italy
216 G9 Pietraperzia Sicilia Italy
212 C7 Pietraporzio Italy
212 I8 Pietrasanta Italy
217 K6 Pietra Spada, Passo di pass Italy
215 N6 Pietrastornina Italy
215 M5 Pietravairano Italy
215 N5 Pietrelcina Italy
237 O3 Piet Retief S. Africa
199 L5 Pietroasa Bihor Romania
199 L6 Pietroasa Timiș Romania
214 B4 Pietrosella Corse France
219 M3 Pietrosu, Vârful mt. Romania
219 N3 Pietrosu, Vârful mt. Romania
219 M3 Pietrosul Mare nature res. Romania
196 G5 Pietrowice Wielkie Pol.
213 M3 Pieve d'Alpago Italy
212 F5 Pieve del Cairo Italy
200 C8 Pieve di Bono Italy
213 M3 Pieve di Cadore Italy
213 M3 Pieve di Cadore, Lago di l. Italy
213 K6 Pieve di Cento Italy
213 M4 Pieve di Soligo Italy
212 D7 Pieve di Teco Italy
215 K1 Pievefavera, Lago di l. Italy
213 J7 Pievepelago Italy
213 M8 Pieve Santo Stefano Italy
215 K1 Pieve Torina Italy
212 E3 Pieve Vergonte Italy
178 F7 Piffonds France
248 B3 Pigeon r. Can./U.S.A.
251 K6 Pigeon MI U.S.A.
251 L8 Pigeon Bay Ont. Can.
103 G10 Pigeon Bay South I. N.Z.
270 □ Pigeon Island Jamaica
246 H4 Pigeon Lake Alta Can.
271 □[3] Pigeon Point St Lucia
271 □[5] Pigeon Point Trin. and Tob.
250 E1 Pigeon River MN U.S.A.
256 F11 Pigg r. VA U.S.A.
261 J7 Piggott AR U.S.A.
237 P1 Pigg's Peak Swaziland
215 K4 Piglio Italy
212 D8 Pigna Italy
183 D9 Pignan France
183 I10 Pignans France
215 L5 Pignataro Interamna Italy
216 G1 Pignataro Maggiore Italy
215 P6 Pignola Italy
220 C3 Pigon Aoou, Limni l. Greece
Pigs, Bay of Cuba see Cochinos, Bahía de
285 F5 Pigüé Arg.
269 H4 Piguicas mt. Mex.
102 I3 Piha North I. N.Z.
102 H6 Pihama North I. N.Z.
138 H6 Pihani Uttar Prad. India
101 □[8a] Piha Passage Tonga
131 K2 Pi He r. China
Pihkva järv l. Estonia/Rus. Fed. see Pskov, Lake
163 T6 Pihlajavesi l. Fin.
163 P6 Pihlava Fin.
162 R5 Pihtipudas Fin.
268 D6 Pihuamo Mex.
160 F1 Piikkiö Fin.
162 R4 Piippola Fin.
160 K3 Piirissaar i. Estonia
160 H2 Piirsalu Estonia
162 T4 Piispajärvi Fin.
100 □[4a] Piis-Panewu i. Chuuk Micronesia
Piji Sichuan China see Puge
267 M10 Pijijiapan Mex.
186 F4 Pijnacker Neth.
161 R2 Pikalevo Rus. Fed.
160 J3 Pikasilla Estonia
256 G6 Pike NY U.S.A.
256 D9 Pike WV U.S.A.
251 M5 Pike Bay Ont. Can.
258 E2 Pike County county PA U.S.A.
113 K5 Pikelot i. Micronesia
258 C2 Pikes Creek Reservoir PA U.S.A.
263 L7 Pikes Peak CO U.S.A.
258 B6 Pikesville MD U.S.A.
236 C8 Piketberg S. Africa
256 B9 Piketon OH U.S.A.
256 C11 Pikeville KY U.S.A.
255 E8 Pikeville TN U.S.A.
Pikihatiti b. Stewart I. N.Z. see Port Pegasus
Pikirakatahi mt. South I. N.Z. see Earnslaw, Mount
186 I2 Pikmeer l. Neth.
244 G3 Pikmiktalik AK U.S.A.
129 R7 Pikou Liaoning China
230 C4 Pikounda Congo
285 H5 Pila Arg.
213 M6 Pila Italy
196 E2 Piła Pol.
209 C11 Pila mt. Spain
119 C9 Pila, Kyun i. Myanmar
285 I5 Pila, Laguna de l. Arg.
209 C11 Pila, Sierra de la mts Spain
282 F2 Pilagá r. Arg.
237 L1 Pilanesberg National Park S. Africa
138 E5 Pilani Rajasthan India
285 H4 Pilar Buenos Aires Arg.
285 F2 Pilar Córdoba Arg.
285 G2 Pilar Santa Fé Arg.
277 F6 Pilar Para.
114 F7 Pilar Phil.
283 B9 Pilar, Cabo c. Chile
278 C5 Pilar de Goiás Brazil
209 D12 Pilar de la Horadada Spain
209 I10 Pilar de la Mola Spain
280 D5 Pilar do Sul Brazil
114 C8 Pilas i. Phil.
206 G6 Pilas Spain
114 C8 Pilas Channel Phil.
183 F6 Pilat, Mont mt. France
183 F6 Pilat, Parc Naturel Régional du nature res. France
212 E2 Pilatus mt. Switz.
197 J4 Pilawa Pol.
196 E2 Piława r. Pol.
196 E5 Piława Górna Pol.
276 D5 Pilaya r. Bol.
283 C6 Pilcaniyeu Arg.
196 D5 Pilchowicie, Jezioro l. Pol.
192 J3 Pilchowo Pol.
277 F6 Pilcomayo r. Bol./Para.
196 E2 Pile, Jezioro l. Pol.
244 I4 Pile Bay Village AK U.S.A.
Pilenkovo Georgia see Gant'iadi
136 F6 Piler Andhra Prad. India
209 E10 Piles Spain
244 F2 Pilgrim Springs AK U.S.A.
Píli Kos Greece see Pyli
114 D5 Pili Luzon Phil.
276 D5 Pili, Cerro mt. Chile
160 I6 Piliakalnis hill Lith.
138 E5 Pilibangan Rajasthan India
138 G5 Pilibhit Uttar Prad. India
197 H5 Pilica Pol.
197 J4 Pilica r. Pol.
Pilipinas country Asia see Philippines
199 I4 Pilis Hungary
199 H4 Pilis hill Hungary
199 H4 Piliscsév Hungary
199 H4 Pilisi park Hungary
199 H4 Pilisszentiván Hungary
199 H4 Pilisszentkereszt Hungary
199 H4 Pilisvörösvár Hungary
200 E5 Pill Austria
171 K5 Pillar hill England U.K.
238 □[2a] Pillar Bay Ascension S. Atlantic Ocean
Pillau Rus. Fed. see Baltiysk
276 C3 Pillcopata Peru
200 G4 Pillersee l. Austria
105 L4 Pilliga N.S.W. Austr.
171 L6 Pilling Lancashire, England U.K.
285 G3 Pillo, Isla del i. Arg.
258 B3 Pillow PA U.S.A.
264 J2 Pillsbury, Lake CA U.S.A.
156 I5 Pil'na Rus. Fed.
159 P3 Pil'na Ukr.
159 P3 Pil'na r. Ukr.
172 G4 Pilning South Gloucestershire, England U.K.
156 L1 Pil'nya, Ozero l. Rus. Fed.
280 D2 Pilões, Serra dos mts Brazil
270 E4 Pilón Cuba
205 J2 Piloña r. Spain
Pílos Greece see Pylos
247 I2 Pilot Lake N.W.T. Can.
268 B5 Piloto Mex.
285 H2 Piloto Ávila Arg.
Piloto Juan Fernández i. S. Pacific Ocean see Alejandro Selkirk, Isla
264 O3 Pilot Peak NV U.S.A.
244 H4 Pilot Point AK U.S.A.
262 E4 Pilot Rock OR U.S.A.
244 G3 Pilot Station AK U.S.A.
261 K11 Pilottown LA U.S.A.
195 L3 Pilsach Ger.
Pilsen Czech Rep. see Plzeň
250 G5 Pilsen WI U.S.A.
197 H6 Pilsko mt. Pol.
195 N4 Pilsting Ger.
160 E4 Piltene Latvia
145 N9 Pilu Pak.
199 K5 Pilu Romania
118 C5 Pilu, Nam r. Myanmar
160 G7 Pilvė r. Lith.
160 G7 Pilviškiai Lith.
122 M3 Pil'vo Rus. Fed.
197 J6 Pilzno Pol.
265 W9 Pima AZ U.S.A.
277 E2 Pimenta Bueno Brazil
214 C9 Pimentel Sardegna Italy
138 E9 Pimpalner Mahar. India
172 H6 Pimperne Dorset, England U.K.
138 D9 Pimpri Gujarat India
230 D4 Pimu Dem. Rep. Congo
138 G3 Pin r. India
118 B4 Pin r. Myanmar
158 F1 Pina r. Belarus
208 D5 Pina Spain
209 D7 Pina mt. Spain
208 D4 Pina, Embalse de resr Spain
265 S10 Pinacate, Cerro del mt. Mex.
205 L5 Piña de Esgueva Spain
138 G6 Pinahat Uttar Prad. India
265 V9 Pinaleno Mountains AZ U.S.A.
114 C5 Pinamalayan Mindoro Phil.
285 I5 Pinamar Arg.
Pinang Malaysia see George Town
116 D2 Pinang i. Malaysia
116 D2 Pinang state Malaysia
117 L2 Pinangah Sabah Malaysia
207 I7 Pinar mt. Spain
209 L8 Pinar, Cap des c. Spain
207 O4 Pinar, Puerto del pass Spain
148 H4 Pınarbaşı Turkey
270 B2 Pinar del Río Cuba
148 C3 Pinarhisar Turkey
221 I5 Pınarköy Turkey
151 A7 Pınarlar Turkey
151 E6 Pınarlı Turkey
274 B5 Piñas Ecuador
212 C6 Pinasca Italy
112 F3 Pinatubo, Mount vol. Phil.
199 H5 Pincehely Hungary
173 L2 Pinchbeck Lincolnshire, England U.K.
246 H5 Pincher Creek Alta Can.
260 K6 Pinckneyville IL U.S.A.
181 J4 Pinçon, Mont hill France
251 K6 Pinconning MI U.S.A.
Pîncota Romania see Pâncota
197 I5 Pińczów Pol.
278 B5 Pindaíba Brazil
281 E5 Pindamonhangaba Brazil
109 C10 Pindar W.A. Austr.
138 G4 Pindar r. India
278 D2 Pindaré r. Brazil
278 D2 Pindaré Mirim Brazil
145 O5 Pind Dadan Khan Pak.
105 I3 Pindera Downs Aboriginal Land res. Australia
Píndhos Óros mts Greece see Pindos
145 O6 Pindi Bhattian Pak.
145 O5 Pindi Gheb Pak.
278 C2 Pindobal Brazil
220 B3 Pindos mts Greece
220 C3 Pindou, Ethnikos Drymos nat. park Greece
138 H8 Pindrei Madh. Prad. India
Pindus Mountains Greece see Pindos
138 D7 Pindwara Rajasthan India
104 H5 Pine watercourse N.S.W. Austr.
250 I5 Pine r. MI U.S.A.
250 J6 Pine r. MI U.S.A.
250 D6 Pine r. WI U.S.A.
250 F4 Pine r. WI U.S.A.
249 K4 Pine, Cape Nfld and Lab. Can.
261 I8 Pine Bluff AR U.S.A.
262 L6 Pine Bluffs WY U.S.A.
259 G1 Pine Bush NY U.S.A.
250 B4 Pine City MN U.S.A.
106 C2 Pine Creek N.T. Austr.
256 H7 Pine Creek r. PA U.S.A.
265 P1 Pine Creek watercourse NV U.S.A.
264 L3 Pinecrest CA U.S.A.
205 O8 Pineda de Cigüela Spain
205 N4 Pineda de la Sierra Spain
208 K4 Pineda de Mar Spain
262 J5 Pinedale WY U.S.A.
247 L5 Pine Dock Man. Can.
247 L5 Pine Falls Man. Can.
263 E8 Pine Flat Lake CA U.S.A.
156 H2 Pinega Rus. Fed.
156 H2 Pinega r. Rus. Fed.
109 C9 Pinegrove W.A. Austr.
256 A10 Pine Grove KY U.S.A.
251 R9 Pine Grove PA U.S.A.
256 E9 Pine Grove WV U.S.A.
106 D7 Pine Hill N.T. Austr.
258 F5 Pine Hill NJ U.S.A.
255 G11 Pine Hills FL U.S.A.
247 J4 Pinehouse Lake Sask. Can.
247 J4 Pinehouse Lake l. Sask. Can.
258 C6 Pinehurst MD U.S.A.
248 B2 Pineimuta r. Ont. Can.
220 D3 Pineios r. Greece
220 C5 Pineiou, Techniti Limni resr Greece
250 B5 Pine Island MN U.S.A.
259 G2 Pine Island NY U.S.A.
286 R2 Pine Island Bay Antarctica
286 R1 Pine Island Glacier Antarctica
255 F12 Pine Islands FL U.S.A.
255 G13 Pine Islands FL U.S.A.
204 G5 Pinela Port.
261 I10 Pineland TX U.S.A.
205 L5 Piñel de Abajo Spain
246 F4 Pine Le Moray Provincial Park B.C. Can.
103 D12 Pinelheugh mt. South I. N.Z.
255 F12 Pinellas Park FL U.S.A.
264 K6 Pine Mountain CA U.S.A.
265 S7 Pine Peak AZ U.S.A.
246 H2 Pine Point pt N.W.T. Can.
246 H2 Pine Point (abandoned) N.W.T. Can.
285 I3 Piñera Uru.
264 M4 Pineridge CA U.S.A.
260 D4 Pine Ridge SD U.S.A.
260 D4 Pine Ridge Indian Reservation res. SD U.S.A.
212 C6 Pinerolo Italy
220 F2 Pines, Akrotirio pt Greece
Pines, Isle of i. Cuba see Juventud, Isla de la
Pines, Isle of i. New Caledonia see Pins, Île des
261 H9 Pines, Lake o' the TX U.S.A.
212 F4 Pinet di Appiano Tradate, Parco del park Italy
215 M2 Pineto Italy
265 W7 Pinetop AZ U.S.A.
237 O5 Pinetown S. Africa
185 E6 Pineuilh France
251 R7 Pine Valley NY U.S.A.
256 B12 Pineville KY U.S.A.
261 I10 Pineville LA U.S.A.
258 E4 Pineville PA U.S.A.
256 D11 Pineville WV U.S.A.
178 H7 Piney France
118 E7 Ping, Mae Nam r. Thai.
138 D1 Pingal Pak.
128 H8 Ping'an Qinghai China
Ping'anyi Qinghai China see Ping'an
109 E12 Pingaring W.A. Austr.
130 F5 Pingba Guizhou China
130 D7 Pingbian Yunnan China
130 F3 Pingchang Sichuan China
130 C5 Pingchuan Sichuan China
129 P9 Ping Dao i. China
129 M8 Pingding Shanxi China
Pingdingbu Hebei China see Guyuan
131 I2 Pingdingshan Henan China
Pingdong Taiwan see P'ingtung
Pingdu Jiangxi China see Anfu
129 P8 Pingdu Shandong China
109 D12 Pingelly W.A. Austr.
122 D7 Pinggang Liaoning China
201 N5 Pinggau Austria
129 O6 Pinggu Beijing China
130 F7 Pingguo Guangxi China
131 J7 Pinghai Guangdong China
131 K6 Pinghe Fujian China
Pinghu Guizhou China see Pingtang
131 M3 Pinghu Zhejiang China
131 I4 Pingjiang Hunan China
130 H6 Pingle Guangxi China
130 G2 Pingli Shaanxi China
128 J9 Pingliang Gansu China
129 L9 Pinglu Shanxi China
128 J7 Pingluo Ningxia China
128 J7 Pingluozhan Ningxia China
Pingma Guangxi China see Tiandong
131 L5 Pingnan Fujian China
130 H7 Pingnan Guangxi China
129 J9 Pingquan Gansu China
129 P6 Pingquan Hebei China
109 E12 Pingrup W.A. Austr.
Pingshan Guangdong China see Huidong
129 N7 Pingshan Hebei China
130 E4 Pingshan Sichuan China
Pingshan Yunnan China see Luquan
131 I6 Pingshi Guangdong China
Pingshu Hebei China see Daicheng
131 L6 Pingtan Fujian China
Pingtan Dao i. China see Haitan Dao
130 F6 Pingtang Guizhou China
131 M7 P'ingtung Taiwan
130 E2 Pingwu Sichuan China
Pingxi Guizhou China see Yuping
Pingxiang Gansu China see Tongwei
130 F7 Pingxiang Guangxi China
131 I5 Pingxiang Jiangxi China
129 S2 Pingyang Heilong. China
131 M5 Pingyang Zhejiang China
129 M8 Pingyao Shanxi China
129 O9 Pingyi Shandong China
129 O8 Pingyin Shandong China
131 J2 Pingyu Henan China
131 J6 Pingyuan Guangdong China
129 O8 Pingyuan Shandong China
Pingyuan Yunnan China see Yingjiang
130 D7 Pingyuanjie Yunnan China
Pingzhai Guizhou China see Luzhi
130 G6 Pingzhai Guizhou China
280 D5 Pinhal Brazil
206 B3 Pinhal Novo Port.
204 E6 Pinhão Port.
278 D2 Pinheiro Brazil
204 D6 Pinheiro Porto Port.
206 B4 Pinheiro Setúbal Port.
282 G3 Pinheiro Machado Brazil
281 G3 Pinheiros Brazil
204 F7 Pinhel Port.
172 F6 Pinhoe Devon, England U.K.
275 E6 Pinhuã r. Brazil
116 C4 Pini i. Indon.
207 N3 Pinilla r. Spain
205 M7 Pinilla, Embalse de resr Spain
205 Q7 Pinilla de Molina Spain
205 J5 Pinilla de Toro Spain
Piniós r. Greece see Pineios
109 C12 Pinjarra W.A. Austr.
109 G11 Pinjin W.A. Austr.
109 G11 Pinjin Aboriginal Reserve W.A. Austr.
201 N5 Pinkafeld Austria
104 E5 Pinkawilinie Conservation Park nature res. S.A. Austr.
106 B3 Pinkerton Range hills N.T. Austr.
246 F3 Pink Mountain B.C. Can.
118 C4 Pinlaung Myanmar
118 B2 Pinlebu Myanmar
103 H8 Pinnacle mt. South I. N.Z.
256 G9 Pinnacle hill VA/WV U.S.A.
244 D3 Pinnacle Island AK U.S.A.
264 K5 Pinnacles National Monument nat. park CA U.S.A.
104 H6 Pinnaroo S.A. Austr.
190 I3 Pinnau r. Ger.
190 I3 Pinneberg Ger.
193 K7 Pinnow Ger.
214 C2 Pino Corse France
204 H5 Pino Spain
205 K3 Pino del Río Spain
204 H8 Pinofranqueado Spain
117 I5 Pinoh r. Indon.
183 C6 Pinols France
264 O7 Pinon Hills CA U.S.A.
204 D3 Piñor Spain
268 F3 Pinos Mex.
208 I4 Pinós hill Spain
Pinos, Isla de i. Cuba see Juventud, Isla de la
264 M7 Pinos, Mount CA U.S.A.
209 C11 Pinoso Spain

205 O7 **Pinoso** mt. Spain
207 L6 **Pinos-Puente** Spain
269 I9 **Pinotepa Nacional** Mex.
115 A5 **Pinrang** Sulawesi Indon.
115 B5 **Pinrang** Sulawesi Indon.
239 □2b **Pins, Anse aux** b. Mahé Seychelles
100 □5 **Pins, Île des** i. New Caledonia
251 M7 **Pins, Pointe aux** pt Ont. Can.
185 H6 **Pinsac** France
201 I4 **Pinsdorf** Austria
158 F1 **Pinsk** Belarus
205 R4 **Pinsoro** Spain
274 □ **Pinta, Isla** i. Islas Galápagos Ecuador
265 S9 **Pinta, Sierra** hill AZ U.S.A.
263 L9 **Pintada Creek** watercourse NM U.S.A.
285 I2 **Pintado Grande** Uru.
276 C5 **Pintados** Chile
208 C2 **Pintano** Spain
117 L2 **Pintasan** Sabah Malaysia
205 M8 **Pinto** Spain
265 S4 **Pintura** UT U.S.A.
214 C6 **Pinu, Monte** hill Italy
168 G12 **Pinwherry** South Ayrshire, Scotland U.K.
213 N3 **Pinzano al Tagliamento** Italy
200 F5 **Pinzgau** val. Austria
204 F7 **Pinzio** Port.
213 J3 **Pinzolo** Italy
213 N8 **Piobbico** Italy
265 R4 **Pioche** NV U.S.A.
231 E6 **Piodi** Dem. Rep. Congo
100 □6 **Pio Island** Solomon Is
278 E3 **Pio IX** Brazil
183 F8 **Piolenc** France
212 G5 **Pioltello** Italy
215 M2 **Piomba** r. Italy
214 F2 **Piombino** Italy
214 E2 **Piombino, Canale di** sea chan. Italy
213 L4 **Piombino Dese** Italy
256 A7 **Pioneer** OH U.S.A.
262 H4 **Pioneer Mountains** MT U.S.A.
153 K2 **Pioner, Ostrov** i. Severnaya Zemlya Rus. Fed.
160 D7 **Pionerskiy** Kaliningradskaya Oblast' Rus. Fed.
152 H3 **Pionerskiy** Khanty-Mansiyskiy Avtonomnyy Okrug Rus. Fed.
197 J4 **Pionki** Pol.
182 B4 **Pionsat** France
102 J5 **Piopio** North I. N.Z.
Piopiotahi inlet South I. N.Z. see **Milford Sound**
215 J1 **Pioraco** Italy
275 F5 **Piorini** r. Brazil
275 F5 **Piorini, Lago** l. Brazil
212 C6 **Piossasco** Italy
196 E4 **Piotrkowice** Pol.
196 G3 **Piotrków Kujawski** Pol.
197 H4 **Piotrków Trybunalski** Pol.
213 M5 **Piove di Sacco** Italy
213 K4 **Piovene Rocchette** Italy
212 G3 **Pioverna** r. Italy
144 I8 **Pīp** Iran
122 F7 **Pipa Dingzi** mt. China
282 D3 **Pipanaco, Salar de** salt flat Arg.
138 D6 **Pipar** Rajasthan India
138 D6 **Pipar Road** Rajasthan India
220 F3 **Piperi** i. Greece
264 O4 **Piper Peak** NV U.S.A.
258 E4 **Pipersville** PA U.S.A.
265 V4 **Pipe Spring National Monument** nat. park AZ U.S.A.
247 K5 **Pipestone** Man. Can.
248 B2 **Pipestone** r. Ont. Can.
260 G4 **Pipestone** MN U.S.A.
219 O3 **Pipirig** Romania
102 J6 **Pipiriki** North I. N.Z.
145 N5 **Piplan** Pak.
138 E5 **Pipli** Haryana India
249 G3 **Pipmuacan, Réservoir** resr Que. Can.
108 E6 **Pippingarra Aboriginal Reserve** W.A. Austr.
138 H9 **Pipraud** Chhattisgarh India
180 H6 **Pipriac** France
Piqan Xinjiang China see **Shanshan**
132 E6 **Piqanlik** Xinjiang China
256 A8 **Piqua** OH U.S.A.
185 F9 **Pique** r. France
205 O4 **Piqueras, Puerto de** pass Spain
278 F3 **Piquet Carneiro** Brazil
281 E5 **Piquete** Brazil
280 A6 **Piquiri** r. Brazil
277 G4 **Piquiri** r. Brazil
199 L4 **Pir** Romania
280 D5 **Piracaia** Brazil
280 C2 **Piracanjuba** Brazil
280 C3 **Piracanjuba** r. Brazil
280 D5 **Piracicaba** Brazil
280 C5 **Piracicaba** r. Brazil
281 F3 **Piracicaba** r. Brazil
280 D4 **Piraçununga** Brazil
278 E2 **Piracuruca** Brazil
101 □9a **Pirae** Tahiti Fr. Polynesia
Piraeus Greece see **Peiraias**
280 C6 **Piraí do Sul** Brazil
Piráievs Greece see **Peiraias**
216 H7 **Piraino** Sicilia Italy
280 C5 **Piraju** Brazil
280 C3 **Pirajuba** Brazil
280 C4 **Pirajuí** Brazil
151 L5 **Pirallahı Adası** Azer.
213 P4 **Piran** Slovenia
282 F2 **Pirané** Arg.
281 F4 **Piranga** Brazil
281 F4 **Piranga** r. Brazil
281 E5 **Piranguinho** Brazil
278 F4 **Piranhas** Alagoas Brazil
275 F6 **Piranhas** Amazonas Brazil
280 B2 **Piranhas** Goiás Brazil
280 B2 **Piranhas** r. Brazil
278 F3 **Piranhas** r. Brazil
278 D2 **Pirapemas** Brazil
277 E1 **Pirapetinga** Amazonas Brazil
281 F4 **Pirapetinga** Minas Gerais Brazil
280 A5 **Pirapó** r. Brazil
281 E2 **Pirapora** Brazil
280 B5 **Pirapozinho** Brazil
277 F4 **Piraputangas** Brazil
280 C6 **Piraquara** Brazil
275 G4 **Pirara** Guyana
282 G4 **Pirarajá** Uru.
139 J6 **Pirari** Nepal
282 G3 **Piratini** Brazil
280 C5 **Piratininga** Brazil
249 G3 **Piraube, Lac** l. Que. Can.
138 F7 **Pirawa** Rajasthan India
151 I5 **Pirăzä** Azer.
173 K5 **Pirbright** Surrey, England U.K.
Pirchevan Azer. see **Zängilan**
197 M1 **Pirčiupiai** Lith.
283 C6 **Pire Mahuida, Sierra** mts Arg.
280 C1 **Pirenópolis** Brazil
280 C2 **Pires do Rio** Brazil
139 L7 **Pirganj** Bangl.
Pírgos Greece see **Pyrgos**
219 N7 **Pirgovo** Bulg.
180 F7 **Piriac-sur-Mer** France
102 J5 **Piriaka** North I. N.Z.
282 G4 **Piriápolis** Uru.
199 L4 **Piricse** Hungary
219 L9 **Pirin** mts Bulg.
219 L9 **Pirin** nat. park Bulg.
278 E3 **Piripiri** Brazil
160 H2 **Pirita** r. Estonia
274 D2 **Píritu** Falcón Venez.
274 D2 **Píritu** Portuguesa Venez.
277 F4 **Pirizal** Brazil
201 L5 **Pirka** Austria
163 Q6 **Pirkkala** Fin.
145 I6 **Pir Kundil** Afgh.
Pirlerkondu Turkey see **Taşkent**
194 D3 **Pirmasens** Ger.
136 E8 **Pirmed** Kerala India
144 G5 **Pīr Morāl** spring Iran
193 I9 **Pirna** Ger.
168 F11 **Pirnmill** North Ayrshire, Scotland U.K.
139 L8 **Pirojpur** Bangl.
205 K6 **Pirón** r. Spain
102 J4 **Pirongia** North I. N.Z.
102 J4 **Pirongia** vol. North I. N.Z.
102 J4 **Pirongia Forest Park** nature res. North I. N.Z.
161 Q3 **Piros, Ozero** l. Rus. Fed.
219 K7 **Pirot** Pirot Serbia
285 G5 **Pirovano** Arg.
139 K7 **Pirpainti** Bihar India
138 E3 **Pir Panjal Pass** Jammu and Kashmir India
138 D2 **Pir Panjal Range** mts India/Pak.
149 K4 **Pirrasit Dağ** hill Turkey
151 K6 **Pirsaat** Azer.
151 J5 **Pirsaatçay** r. Azer.
199 I5 **Pirtó** Hungary
162 O3 **Pirttivuopio** Sweden
115 F5 **Piru** Seram Indon.
115 F5 **Piru, Teluk** b. Seram Indon.
Pir'yakh, Gora mt. Tajik. see **Piryakh, Kūhi**
145 M2 **Piryakh, Kūhi** mt. Tajik.
Piryatin Ukr. see **Pyryatyn**
Piryetós Greece see **Pyrgetos**
Piryíon Chios Greece see **Pyrgi**
145 K6 **Pirzada** Afgh.
212 I8 **Pisa** Italy
213 J9 **Pisa** prov. Italy
197 J2 **Pisa** r. Pol.
276 C3 **Pisac** Peru
Pisae Italy see **Pisa**
276 C4 **Pisagua** Chile
100 □4a **Pisamwe** i. Chuuk Micronesia
115 F4 **Pisang** i. Maluku Indon.
184 C4 **Pisany** France
100 □4a **Pisar** i. Chuuk Micronesia
103 D11 **Pisa Range** mts South I. N.Z.
117 M1 **Pisau, Tanjung** pt Malaysia
Pisaurum Italy see **Pesaro**
274 C3 **Pisba, Parque Nacional** nat. park Col.
259 F3 **Piscataway** NJ U.S.A.
201 M5 **Pischelsdorf in der Steiermark** Austria
199 K6 **Pişchia** Romania
215 O7 **Pisciotta** Italy
276 A3 **Pisco** Peru
276 A3 **Pisco** r. Peru
284 B2 **Pisco Elqui** Chile
199 L4 **Pişcolt** Romania
201 M7 **Pišece** Slovenia
257 K5 **Piseco Lake** NY U.S.A.
198 D2 **Písek** Czech Rep.
103 B12 **Pisgah, Mount** South I. N.Z.
103 E12 **Pisgah, Mount** South I. N.Z.
Pisha Sichuan China see **Ningnan**
133 D8 **Pishan** Xinjiang China
158 C2 **Pishcha** Ukr.
158 I5 **Pishchana** Ukr.
159 K4 **Pishchane** Ukr.
158 H5 **Pishchanka** Ukr.
159 M8 **Pishchanyy, Mys** pt Ukr.
144 F5 **Pīsh Gāzū** Iran
145 I8 **Pīshīn** Iran
145 L6 **Pishin** Pak.
145 K7 **Pishin Lora** r. Pak.
Pishpek Kyrg. see **Bishkek**
142 G9 **Pīsh Qal'eh** Iran
145 I9 **Pishukan, Ras** pt Pak.
197 I3 **Pisia** r. Pol.
148 E5 **Pisidia** reg. Turkey
115 B6 **Pising** Sulawesi Indon.
265 T9 **Pisinimo** AZ U.S.A.
100 □4a **Pisininin** i. Chuuk Micronesia
143 M7 **Piskent** Uzbek.
158 I3 **Piskivka** Ukr.
159 Q4 **Pisky** Kharkivs'ka Oblast' Ukr.
159 S4 **Pisky** Luhans'ka Oblast' Ukr.
264 L6 **Pismo Beach** CA U.S.A.
277 E3 **Piso Firme** Bol.
212 I4 **Pisogne** Italy
160 E7 **Pissa** r. Rus. Fed.
282 C2 **Pissis, Cerro** mt. Arg.
185 C7 **Pissos** France
162 U4 **Pista** r. Rus. Fed.
267 O7 **Pisté** Mex.
217 L3 **Pisticci** Italy
213 J8 **Pistoia** Italy
213 J8 **Pistoia** prov. Italy
Pistoriae Italy see **Pistoia**
161 X4 **Pistsovo** Rus. Fed.
205 K5 **Pisuerga** r. Spain
197 J2 **Pisz** Pol.
197 L4 **Piszczac** Pol.
262 C6 **Pit** r. CA U.S.A.
228 B4 **Pita** Guinea
249 H2 **Pitaga** Nfld and Lab. Can.
267 N8 **Pital** Mex.
274 B4 **Pitalito** Col.
280 B6 **Pitanga** Brazil
280 C4 **Pitangueiras** Brazil
281 E3 **Pitangui** Brazil
138 C8 **Pitar** Gujarat India
105 I6 **Pitarpunga Lake** imp. l. N.S.W. Austr.
208 D6 **Pitarque** Spain
291 K7 **Pitcairn Island** S. Pacific Ocean
228 B3 **Pitche** Guinea-Bissau
271 □7 **Pitch Lake** Trin. and Tob.
162 P4 **Piteå** Sweden
162 P4 **Piteälven** r. Sweden
213 J7 **Piteglio** Italy
157 H5 **Pitelino** Rus. Fed.
142 B2 **Piterka** Rus. Fed.
219 M6 **Pitești** Romania
109 D11 **Pithara** W.A. Austr.
178 D7 **Pithiviers** France
138 H5 **Pithoragarh** Uttaranchal India
100 □1 **Piti** Guam
214 H2 **Pitigliano** Italy
138 G8 **Pitihra** Madh. Prad. India
205 Q4 **Pitillas** Spain
185 A11 **Pitillas, Laguna de** l. Spain
266 C2 **Pitiquito** Mex.
244 G3 **Pitkas Point** AK U.S.A.
156 E3 **Pitkyaranta** Rus. Fed.
168 I9 **Pitlochry** Perth and Kinross, Scotland U.K.
258 E5 **Pitman** NJ U.S.A.
168 L8 **Pitmedden** Aberdeenshire, Scotland U.K.
172 F6 **Pitminster** Somerset, England U.K.
229 I4 **Pitoa** Cameroon
210 F3 **Pitomača** Croatia
239 □1c **Piton de la Fournaise** vol. Réunion
239 □1b **Piton de la Petite Rivière Noire** hill Mauritius
239 □1c **Piton des Neiges** mt. Réunion
Pitong Sichuan China see **Pixian**
178 B5 **Pîtres** France
207 M7 **Pitres** Spain
284 A6 **Pitrufquén** Chile
237 J1 **Pitsane Siding** Botswana
201 L6 **Pitschgau** Austria
237 M5 **Pitseng** Lesotho
173 K3 **Pitsford Reservoir** England U.K.
173 K4 **Pitstone** Buckinghamshire, England U.K.
Pitsunda Georgia see **Bichvint'a**
173 J5 **Pitt** Hampshire, England U.K.
187 D7 **Pittem** Belgium
201 N4 **Pitten** Austria
168 H7 **Pittentrail** Highland, Scotland U.K.
168 K10 **Pittenweem** Fife, Scotland U.K.
136 C7 **Pitti** i. India
136 C7 **Pitti Sand Bank** sea feature India
245 O5 **Pitt Island** B.C. Can.
102 □ **Pitt Island** Chatham Is S. Pacific Ocean
Pitt Islands Santa Cruz Is Solomon Is see **Vanikoro Islands**
261 K9 **Pittsboro** MS U.S.A.
255 H8 **Pittsboro** NC U.S.A.
264 K3 **Pittsburg** CA U.S.A.
261 H7 **Pittsburg** KS U.S.A.
257 N3 **Pittsburg** NH U.S.A.
261 H9 **Pittsburg** TX U.S.A.
256 F8 **Pittsburgh** PA U.S.A.
260 J6 **Pittsfield** IL U.S.A.
257 L6 **Pittsfield** MA U.S.A.
257 □P4 **Pittsfield** ME U.S.A.
257 N5 **Pittsfield** NH U.S.A.
257 M5 **Pittsfield** VT U.S.A.
258 D2 **Pittston** PA U.S.A.
257 □P3 **Pittston Farm** ME U.S.A.
102 □ **Pitt Strait** Chatham Is S. Pacific Ocean
250 D5 **Pittsville** WI U.S.A.
107 M9 **Pittsworth** Qld Austr.
106 G7 **Pituri Creek** watercourse Qld Austr.
199 J5 **Pitvaros** Hungary
247 L2 **Pitz Lake** Nunavut Can.
200 C5 **Pitztal** val. Austria
278 C4 **Pium** Brazil
281 E4 **Piumhí** Brazil
274 A6 **Piura** Peru
274 A6 **Piura** dept Peru
160 K4 **Piusa** r. Estonia
265 Q7 **Piute Mountains** CA U.S.A.
264 N6 **Piute Peak** CA U.S.A.
139 I5 **Piuthan** Nepal
248 D3 **Pivabiska** r. Ont. Can.
197 M1 **Pivašiūnai** Lith.
158 K7 **Pivdennyy Buh** r. Ukr.
274 C2 **Pivijay** Col.
210 E3 **Pivka** Slovenia
213 Q4 **Pivka** r. Slovenia
159 N8 **Pivnichno-Kryms'kyy Kanal** canal Ukr.
197 I6 **Piwniczna-Zdrój** Pol.
133 D8 **Pixa** Xinjiang China
Pixariá mt. Greece see **Pyxaria**
130 D3 **Pixian** Sichuan China
264 M6 **Pixley** CA U.S.A.
267 N8 **Pixoyal** Mex.
276 C4 **Pizacoma** Peru
207 J7 **Pizarra** Spain
212 H3 **Piz Bernina** mt. Italy/Switz.
200 E6 **Piz Boè** mt. Italy
200 B6 **Piz Buin** mt. Austria/Switz.
212 G2 **Piz d'Anarosa** mt. Switz.
212 H3 **Piz Duan** mt. Switz.
212 H2 **Piz Ela** mt. Switz.
156 J4 **Pizhanka** Rus. Fed.
229 G4 **Pizhi** Nigeria
156 I4 **Pizhma** Rus. Fed.
156 J4 **Pizhma** r. Rus. Fed.
156 K2 **Pizhma** r. Rus. Fed.
129 P9 **Pizhou** Jiangsu China
212 H2 **Piz Kesch** mt. Switz.
212 F2 **Piz Medel** mt. Switz.
212 G2 **Pizol** mt. Switz.
212 I2 **Piz Pisoc** mt. Switz.
212 H3 **Piz Platta** mt. Switz.
212 H3 **Piz Varuna** mt. Italy/Switz.
212 H5 **Pizzighettone** Italy
217 K6 **Pizzo** Italy
215 M4 **Pizzoferrato** Italy
215 K3 **Pizzoli** Italy
215 J3 **Pizzuto, Monte** mt. Italy
114 □ **Pkulagalid Point** Palau
114 □ **Pkulagasemieg** pt Palau
114 □ **Pkulngril** pt Palau
114 □ **Pkurengei** pt Palau
192 F3 **Plaaz** Ger.
180 C4 **Plabennec** France
182 L5 **Place Moulin, Lago di** l. Italy
249 K4 **Placentia** Nfld and Lab. Can.
Placentia Italy see **Piacenza**
249 K4 **Placentia Bay** Nfld and Lab. Can.
114 D6 **Placer** Masbate Phil.
114 E7 **Placer** Mindanao Phil.
264 L3 **Placerville** CA U.S.A.
263 J7 **Placerville** CO U.S.A.
270 D2 **Placetas** Cuba
276 D2 **Plácido de Castro** Brazil
284 B3 **Placilla** Chile
212 C2 **Plaffeien** Switz.
191 D10 **Plaidt** Ger.
119 F7 **Plai Mat, Lam** r. Thai.
181 P7 **Plaimpied-Givaudins** France
261 I9 **Plain Dealing** LA U.S.A.
179 N7 **Plainfaing** France
259 L1 **Plainfield** CT U.S.A.
254 D6 **Plainfield** IN U.S.A.
259 G3 **Plainfield** NJ U.S.A.
257 M4 **Plainfield** VT U.S.A.
250 E5 **Plainfield** WI U.S.A.
261 E7 **Plains** KS U.S.A.
261 D9 **Plains** TX U.S.A.
258 F4 **Plainsboro** NJ U.S.A.
180 F5 **Plaintel** France
250 B5 **Plainview** MN U.S.A.
260 G4 **Plainview** NE U.S.A.
259 I3 **Plainview** NY U.S.A.
261 E8 **Plainview** TX U.S.A.
259 J1 **Plainville** CT U.S.A.
260 F6 **Plainville** KS U.S.A.
250 I7 **Plainwell** MI U.S.A.
185 E8 **Plaisance** France
270 G4 **Plaisance** Haiti
185 G8 **Plaisance-du-Touch** France
178 C6 **Plaisir** France
257 N6 **Plaistow** NH U.S.A.
116 F6 **Plaju** Sumatera Indon.
221 G2 **Plaka** Limnos Greece
221 H7 **Plaka, Akrotirio** pt Kriti Greece
150 C3 **Plakoti, Cape** Cyprus
117 L9 **Plampang** Sumbawa Indon.
198 B2 **Planá** Czech Rep.
209 E11 **Plana, Isla** i. Spain
209 K9 **Plana, Sa Punta** pt Spain
270 G2 **Plana Cays** is Bahamas
264 L4 **Planada** CA U.S.A.
280 D1 **Planaltina** Brazil
193 L10 **Plaňany** Czech Rep.
179 M8 **Plancher-Bas** France
179 M8 **Plancher-les-Mines** France
284 **Planchón, Paso del** pass Arg.
Planchón, Portezuelo del pass Arg. see **Planchón, Paso del**
180 G4 **Plancoët** France
178 G6 **Plancy-l'Abbaye** France
269 J6 **Plan de Arroyos** Mex.
268 F4 **Plan de Ayala** Mex.
268 C4 **Plan de Barrancas** Mex.
183 G7 **Plan-de-Baux** France
183 G10 **Plan-de-Cuques** France
269 K6 **Plan de las Hayas** Mex.
183 J10 **Plan-de-la-Tour** France
218 J5 **Plandište** Vojvodina Serbia
183 F9 **Plan-d'Orgon** France
193 F6 **Plane** r. Ger.
239 □2b **Planeau, Montagne** plat. Mahé Seychelles
195 K5 **Planegg** Ger.
185 I11 **Planès** France
183 B7 **Planèze** reg. France
198 C2 **Plánice** Czech Rep.
183 G10 **Planier, Île de** i. France
213 Q5 **Planik** mt. Croatia
201 J8 **Planina** Postojna Slovenia
201 L7 **Planina** Šentjur pri Celju Slovenia
195 K2 **Plankenfels** Ger.
260 F4 **Plankinton** SD U.S.A.
250 F8 **Plano** IL U.S.A.
261 G9 **Plano** TX U.S.A.
285 I1 **Plano Alto** Brazil
200 C5 **Plansee** l. Austria
270 □ **Plantain Garden** r. Jamaica
284 B3 **Planta Los Queltehues** Chile
238 □2b **Plantation House** St Helena
185 G9 **Plantaurel, Chaîne du** hills France
255 F12 **Plant City** FL U.S.A.
259 J1 **Plantsville** CT U.S.A.
280 C4 **Planura** Brazil
261 J10 **Plaquemine** LA U.S.A.
204 H8 **Plasencia** Spain
208 C4 **Plasencia, Llano de** plain Spain
208 D3 **Plasencia del Monte** Spain
197 L2 **Płaska** Pol.
210 E3 **Plaški** Croatia
142 I1 **Plast** Rus. Fed.
265 Q9 **Plaster City** CA U.S.A.
249 H4 **Plaster Rock** N.B. Can.
237 P1 **Plaston** S. Africa
199 H3 **Plášťovce** Slovakia
122 J6 **Plastun** Rus. Fed.
151 A2 **Plastunka** Rus. Fed.
159 S8 **Plastunovskaya** Rus. Fed.
198 C2 **Plasy** Czech Rep.
218 G8 **Platamon, Rt** pt Montenegro
214 A6 **Platamona Lido** Sardegna Italy
220 D3 **Platamonas** Greece
276 C4 **Platanal** Peru
216 E9 **Platani** r. Sicilia Italy
217 K5 **Platania** Italy
220 E3 **Platanias** Greece
269 L9 **Platanillo** Mex.
220 F4 **Platanistos** Greece
220 C5 **Platanos** Greece
236 C6 **Platbakkies** S. Africa
237 N4 **Platberg** mt. S. Africa
192 E3 **Plate** Ger.
229 G4 **Plateau** state Nigeria
187 I8 **Plateau des Tailles, Réserves Domaniales du** nature res. Belgium
230 B5 **Plateaux** admin. reg. Congo
230 B5 **Plateaux Batéké, Parc National des** nat. park Haut-Ogooué Gabon
160 E5 **Plateliai** Lith.
162 □ **Platen, Kapp** c. Svalbard
190 K5 **Platendorf (Sassenburg)** Ger.
268 E2 **Plateros** Mex.
236 E9 **Plathuis** S. Africa
217 K7 **Platì** Italy
218 H6 **Platičevo** Vojvodina Serbia
Platíkambos Greece see **Platykampos**
264 J1 **Platina** CA U.S.A.
244 G4 **Platinum** AK U.S.A.
208 L4 **Platja d'Aro** Spain
159 S8 **Platnirovskaya** Rus. Fed.
274 C2 **Plato** Col.
282 C2 **Plato de Sopa** Chile
269 I4 **Platón Sánchez** Mex.
237 N3 **Platrand** S. Africa
260 H6 **Platte** r. MO U.S.A.
260 H5 **Platte** r. NE U.S.A.
260 H6 **Platte City** MO U.S.A.
239 □2 **Platte Island** Seychelles
259 G1 **Plattekill** NY U.S.A.
201 K3 **Plattenberg** hill Austria
262 L6 **Platteville** CO U.S.A.
260 J4 **Platteville** WI U.S.A.
195 N4 **Plattling** Ger.
257 L4 **Plattsburgh** NY U.S.A.
260 H5 **Plattsmouth** NE U.S.A.
220 D2 **Platy** Greece
220 D3 **Platykampos** Greece
192 F4 **Plau** Ger.
191 K9 **Plaue** Ger.
193 F9 **Plauen** Ger.
192 F4 **Plauer See** l. Ger.
218 H8 **Plav** Plav Montenegro
158 G2 **Plav** r. Ukr.
161 U8 **Plava** r. Rus. Fed.
198 G3 **Plavecký Mikuláš** Slovakia
201 P3 **Plavecký Štvrtok** Slovakia
160 I5 **Pļaviņas** Latvia
159 T1 **Plavitsa** r. Rus. Fed.
210 E3 **Plavnik** i. Croatia
161 U8 **Plavsk** Rus. Fed.
268 E8 **Playa Azul** Mex.
238 □3c **Playa Blanca** Lanzarote Canary Is
238 □3b **Playa Blanca** coastal area Fuerteventura Canary Is
285 I6 **Playa Chapadmalal** Arg.
268 D7 **Playa Corrida de San Juan, Punta** pt Mex.
238 □3b **Playa de Barlovento** coastal area Fuerteventura Canary Is
206 F6 **Playa de Castilla** coastal area Spain
271 □1 **Playa de Fajardo** Puerto Rico
238 □3a **Playa de las Americas** Tenerife Canary Is
267 P7 **Playa del Carmen** Mex.
203 □ **Playa del Inglés** Gran Canaria Canary Is
238 □3b **Playa de Sotavento** coastal area Fuerteventura Canary Is
269 L7 **Playa Hermosa** Mex.
285 I4 **Playa Pascaul** Uru.
274 A5 **Playas** Ecuador
269 N8 **Playas** r. Mex.
238 □3b **Playas de Corralejo** coastal area Fuerteventura Canary Is
269 L8 **Playa Vicente** Mex.
106 F5 **Playford** watercourse N.T. Austr.
247 L4 **Playgreen Lake** Man. Can.
119 I8 **Plây Ku** Vietnam
266 E5 **Playón** Mex.
274 C2 **Playones de Santa Ana** l. Col.
205 O2 **Plaza** Spain
184 G5 **Plazac** France
207 J3 **Plaza del Judío** mt. Spain
284 C6 **Plaza Huincul** Arg.
197 L5 **Płazów** Pol.
265 T8 **Pleasant, Lake** AZ U.S.A.
257 □S3 **Pleasant, Mount** hill N.B. Can.
257 P7 **Pleasant Bay** MA U.S.A.
258 D3 **Pleasant Corners** PA U.S.A.
259 G4 **Pleasant Grove** NJ U.S.A.
265 U1 **Pleasant Grove** UT U.S.A.
264 J4 **Pleasant Hill** CA U.S.A.
256 A8 **Pleasant Hill** OH U.S.A.
264 K4 **Pleasanton** CA U.S.A.
261 F11 **Pleasanton** TX U.S.A.
103 F11 **Pleasant Point** South I. N.Z.
259 H1 **Pleasant Valley** NY U.S.A.
258 D5 **Pleasantville** DE U.S.A.
258 F6 **Pleasantville** NJ U.S.A.
259 H2 **Pleasantville** NY U.S.A.
258 B5 **Pleaseant Hill** PA U.S.A.
171 O7 **Pleasley** Derbyshire, England U.K.
259 K2 **Pleasure Beach** CT U.S.A.
258 B5 **Pleasureville** PA U.S.A.
184 I5 **Pleaux** France
195 K2 **Plech** Ger.
198 C3 **Plechý** mt. Czech Rep.
197 H3 **Plecka Dąbrowa** Pol.
180 F5 **Plédran** France
180 E4 **Pléhédel** France
119 H7 **Plei Doch** Vietnam
117 K6 **Pleihari Martapura, Suaka Margasatwa** nature res. Indon.
117 K7 **Pleihari Tanah, Suaka Margasatwa** nature res. Kalimantan Indon.
119 H7 **Plei Kân** Vietnam
180 H4 **Pleine-Fougères** France
195 J3 **Pleinfeld** Ger.
195 N5 **Pleiskirchen** Ger.
193 G9 **Pleißa** Ger.
193 F8 **Pleiße** r. Ger.
159 S1 **Plekhanovo** Rus. Fed.
180 G5 **Plélan-le-Grand** France
180 G5 **Plélan-le-Petit** France
180 F4 **Plélo** France
180 F5 **Plémet** France
180 G5 **Plénée-Jugon** France
180 F4 **Pléneuf-Val-André** France
106 F8 **Plenty** watercourse N.T. Austr.
102 K4 **Plenty, Bay of** g. North I. N.Z.
262 L2 **Plentywood** MT U.S.A.
205 O2 **Plentzia** Spain
180 F4 **Plérin** France
161 Y4 **Ples** Rus. Fed.
201 L5 **Pleschkogel** mt. Austria
180 F6 **Plescop** France
199 L5 **Pleşcuţa** Romania
156 H3 **Plesetsk** Rus. Fed.
142 E1 **Pleshanovo** Rus. Fed.
Pleshchentsy Belarus see **Plyeshchanitsy**
161 V5 **Pleshcheyevo, Ozero** l. Rus. Fed.
199 J3 **Plešivec** Slovakia
201 K7 **Plešivec** mt. Slovenia
180 G4 **Pleslin-Trigavou** France
198 B1 **Plesná** Czech Rep.
161 S2 **Pleso** Rus. Fed.
191 J9 **Pleß** hill Ger.
193 I8 **Plessa** Ger.
180 H6 **Plessé** France
180 D4 **Plestin-les-Grèves** France
196 F4 **Pleszew** Pol.
159 K5 **Pletenyy Tashlyk** Ukr.
210 F3 **Pleternica** Croatia
249 G3 **Plétipi, Lac** l. Que. Can.
191 E8 **Plettenberg** Ger.
236 H10 **Plettenberg Bay** S. Africa
201 K5 **Pletzen** mt. Austria
180 E4 **Pleubian** France
180 H4 **Pleudihen-sur-Rance** France
181 M8 **Pleumartin** France
180 D4 **Pleumeur-Bodou** France
178 G6 **Pleurs** France
180 G4 **Pleurtuit** France
180 C6 **Pleuven** France
219 M7 **Pleven** Bulg.
Plevna Bulg. see **Pleven**
199 H2 **Plevník-Drienové** Slovakia
180 D5 **Pleyben** France
180 D4 **Pleyber-Christ** France
195 M2 **Pleystein** Ger.
209 C12 **Pliego** Spain
195 L5 **Pliening** Ger.
117 K3 **Plieran** r. Malaysia
199 I3 **Pliešovce** Slovakia
185 F8 **Plieux** France
213 J2 **Plima** r. Italy
160 F5 **Plinkšių ežeras** l. Lith.
196 C3 **Pliszka** r. Pol.
218 D6 **Plitvička Jezera** nat. park Croatia
210 E3 **Plješevica** mts Croatia
218 H7 **Pljevlja** Pljevlja Montenegro
214 B6 **Ploaghe** Sardegna Italy
180 C6 **Plobannalec** France
179 O7 **Plobsheim** France
210 F4 **Ploče** Croatia
194 G4 **Plochingen** Ger.
197 K1 **Płociczno** Pol.
197 H3 **Płock** Pol.
200 G6 **Plöckenpass** pass Austria/Italy
168 E8 **Plockton** Highland, Scotland U.K.
210 F4 **Pločno** mt. Bos.-Herz.
161 N1 **Plodovoye** Rus. Fed.
180 E6 **Ploemeur** France
180 F6 **Ploeren** France
180 G6 **Ploërmel** France
Ploeşti Romania see **Ploieşti**
180 F5 **Plœuc-sur-Lié** France
180 C6 **Plogastel-St-Germain** France
180 C5 **Plogonnec** France
192 H1 **Plogshagen** Ger.
219 O6 **Ploieşti** Romania
221 H4 **Plomari** Lesvos Greece
183 B6 **Plomb du Cantal** mt. France
179 L8 **Plombières-les-Bains** France
180 C6 **Plomelin** France
180 C6 **Plomeur** France
213 Q5 **Plomin** Croatia
180 C5 **Plomodiern** France
268 B2 **Plomosas** Mex.
190 J2 **Plön** Ger.
196 D2 **Płoń, Jezioro** l. Pol.
180 C6 **Plonéour-Lanvern** France
180 D5 **Plonévez-du-Faou** France
180 C5 **Plonévez-Porzay** France
196 C2 **Płonia** r. Pol.
197 I3 **Płonka** r. Pol.
197 I3 **Płońsk** Pol.
219 K3 **Plopiş** Romania
197 H1 **Płoskinia** Pol.
161 O5 **Ploskosh'** Rus. Fed.
Ploskoye Rus. Fed. see **Stanovoye**
197 I2 **Płośnica** Pol.
195 M2 **Plößberg** Ger.
161 R1 **Plotichino** Rus. Fed.
158 F1 **Plotnitsa** Belarus
196 D2 **Płoty** Pol.
193 G6 **Plötzin** Ger.
193 E6 **Plötzky** Ger.
180 F4 **Plouagat** France
180 E4 **Plouaret** France
180 B5 **Plouarzel** France
180 E6 **Plouay** France
180 G4 **Ploubalay** France
180 E4 **Ploubazlanec** France
180 E4 **Ploubezre** France
198 D1 **Ploučnice** r. Czech Rep.
180 B4 **Ploudalmézeau** France
180 C4 **Ploudaniel** France
180 C5 **Ploudiry** France
180 C5 **Plouédern** France
180 D4 **Plouénan** France
180 C4 **Plouescat** France
180 F4 **Plouézec** France
180 F5 **Ploufragan** France
180 D4 **Plougasnou** France
180 C5 **Plougastel-Daoulas** France
180 B5 **Plougonvelin** France
180 D4 **Plougonven** France
180 E5 **Plougonver** France
180 E4 **Plougrescant** France
180 F5 **Plouguenast** France
180 B4 **Plouguerneau** France
180 E5 **Plouguernével** France
180 E4 **Plouguiel** France
180 B4 **Plouguin** France
180 F4 **Plouha** France
180 E6 **Plouharnel** France
180 C5 **Plouhinec** Bretagne France
180 E6 **Plouhinec** Bretagne France
180 D4 **Plouigneau** France
180 E4 **Ploumagoar** France
180 D4 **Ploumilliau** France
180 C4 **Plounévez-Lochrist** France
180 E4 **Plounévez-Moëdec** France
180 E5 **Plounévez-Quintin** France
180 E5 **Plouray** France
180 D4 **Plourin-lès-Morlaix** France
180 C4 **Plouvien** France
180 C4 **Plouvorn** France
180 D5 **Plouyé** France
180 B5 **Plouzané** France
180 C4 **Plouzévédé** France
219 M8 **Plovdiv** Bulg.
250 E5 **Plover** WI U.S.A.
250 E5 **Plover** r. WI U.S.A.
131 □J7 **Plover Cove Reservoir** H.K. China
244 I1 **Plover Islands** AK U.S.A.
180 C6 **Plozévet** France
Plozk Pol. see **Płock**
169 G3 **Pluck** Ireland
258 F3 **Pluckemin** NJ U.S.A.
194 H4 **Plüderhausen** Ger.
180 C6 **Pluguffan** France
256 F8 **Plum** PA U.S.A.
169 H3 **Plumbridge** Northern Ireland U.K.
247 L5 **Plum Coulee** Man. Can.
180 F6 **Plumelec** France
180 F6 **Pluméliau** France
180 F6 **Plumergat** France
259 K2 **Plum Island** NY U.S.A.
262 F3 **Plummer** ID U.S.A.
109 H10 **Plumridge Lakes** salt flat W.A. Austr.
109 H10 **Plumridge Lakes Nature Reserve** W.A. Austr.
258 E4 **Plumsteadville** PA U.S.A.
235 E4 **Plumtree** Zimbabwe
160 E6 **Plungė** Lith.
197 K1 **Pluszkiejmy** Pol.
197 I2 **Pluszne, Jezioro** l. Pol.
266 E3 **Plutarco Elís Calles, Presa** resr Mex.
249 G2 **Pluto, Lac** l. Que. Can.
180 E6 **Pluvigner** France
218 G7 **Plužine** Plužine Montenegro
196 G2 **Płużnica** Pol.
180 E4 **Pluzunet** France
172 D3 **Plwmp** Ceredigion, Wales U.K.
160 K7 **Plyeshchanitsy** Belarus
118 D6 **Ply Huey Wati, Khao** mt. Myanmar/Thai.
172 D7 **Plym** r. England U.K.
271 □5 **Plymouth** Trin. and Tob.
172 D7 **Plymouth** Plymouth, England U.K.
172 D7 **Plymouth** admin. div. England U.K.
264 L3 **Plymouth** CA U.S.A.
259 I1 **Plymouth** CT U.S.A.
250 D9 **Plymouth** IL U.S.A.
254 D5 **Plymouth** IN U.S.A.
257 O7 **Plymouth** MA U.S.A.
255 I8 **Plymouth** NC U.S.A.
257 N5 **Plymouth** NH U.S.A.
258 D2 **Plymouth** PA U.S.A.
250 G6 **Plymouth** WI U.S.A.
271 □2 **Plymouth (abandoned)** Montserrat
257 O7 **Plymouth Bay** MA U.S.A.
172 D7 **Plympton** Plymouth, England U.K.
172 D7 **Plymstock** Plymouth, England U.K.
172 E3 **Plynlimon** hill Wales U.K.
158 I4 **Plyskiv** Ukr.
159 L2 **Plysky** Ukr.
160 M3 **Plyussa** Rus. Fed.
160 L2 **Plyussa** r. Rus. Fed.
198 C2 **Plzeň** Czech Rep.
198 C2 **Plzeňský kraj** admin. reg. Czech Rep.
106 E8 **Pmere Nyente Aboriginal Land** res. N.T. Austr.
197 J3 **Pniewo** Pol.
197 I4 **Pniewy** Mazowieckie Pol.
196 E3 **Pniewy** Wielkopolskie Pol.
228 E4 **Pô** Burkina
213 M5 **Po** r. Italy
228 E4 **Pô, Parc National de** nat. park Burkina
117 I4 **Po, Tanjung** pt Malaysia
266 □Q12 **Poás, Volcán** vol. Costa Rica
115 C4 **Poat** i. Indon.
229 F5 **Pobè** Benin
153 P3 **Pobeda, Gora** mt. Rus. Fed.
288 P10 **Pobeda Ice Island** Antarctica
Pobeda Peak China/Kyrg. see **Jengish Chokusu**
199 G3 **Pobedím** Slovakia
122 M4 **Pobedino** Sakhalin Rus. Fed.
Pobedinskiy Rus. Fed. see **Zarechnyy**
Pobedy, Pik mt. China/Kyrg. see **Jengish Chokusu**
198 B2 **Poběžovice** Czech Rep.
196 F3 **Pobiedziska** Pol.
192 K2 **Pobierowo** Pol.
197 K3 **Pobikry** Pol.
284 B4 **Población** Chile
209 C7 **Pobla de Sant Miguel** Spain
204 I4 **Pobladura del Valle** Spain
285 H4 **Poblet** Arg.
208 H5 **Poblet** tourist site Spain
207 L3 **Poblete** Spain
196 F1 **Pobłocie** Pol.
208 G5 **Poboleda** Spain
238 □3c **Pobre, Punta de** pt Canary Is
196 D2 **Pobrzeże** reg. Pol.
196 F1 **Pobrzeże Koszalińskie** reg. Pol.
158 J5 **Pobuz'ke** Ukr.
159 N8 **Pobyedne** Ukr.
256 D10 **Poca** WV U.S.A.
261 J7 **Pocahontas** AR U.S.A.
260 H4 **Pocahontas** IA U.S.A.
256 D10 **Pocatalico** r. WV U.S.A.
262 H5 **Pocatello** ID U.S.A.
198 E2 **Počátky** Czech Rep.
206 B3 **Poceirão** Port.
232 B3 **Pochala** Sudan
158 E3 **Pochayiv** Ukr.
161 Q9 **Pochep** Rus. Fed.
157 I5 **Pochinki** Rus. Fed.
161 P7 **Pochinok** Smolenskaya Oblast' Rus. Fed.
161 R4 **Pochinok** Tverskaya Oblast' Rus. Fed.
201 L3 **Pöchlarn** Austria
284 E2 **Pocho, Sierra de** mts Arg.
269 K10 **Pochutla** Mex.
207 O3 **Pocicos, Puerto de los** pass Spain
284 A5 **Pocillas** Chile
117 M2 **Pock, Gunung** hill Malaysia
193 H9 **Pockau** Ger.
195 K6 **Pöcking** Ger.
195 O5 **Pocking** Ger.
171 P6 **Pocklington** East Riding of Yorkshire, England U.K.
278 E5 **Poções** Brazil
281 E4 **Poço Fundo** Brazil
199 L5 **Pocola** Romania
257 J10 **Pocomoke City** MD U.S.A.
257 J11 **Pocomoke Sound** b. MD/VA U.S.A.
276 D4 **Pocona** Bol.
277 F4 **Poconé** Brazil
258 D2 **Pocono Mountains** hills PA U.S.A.
258 E2 **Pocono Pines** PA U.S.A.
258 E2 **Pocono Summit** PA U.S.A.
115 B8 **Poco Ranakah** vol. Flores Indon.
280 D4 **Poços de Caldas** Brazil
281 G3 **Pocrane** Brazil
199 K4 **Pocsaj** Hungary
197 H5 **Poczesna** Pol.
161 N5 **Podberez'ye** Rus. Fed.
199 I2 **Podbiel** Slovakia
198 C1 **Podbořany** Czech Rep.
160 L4 **Podborov'ye** Rus. Fed.
201 I7 **Podbrdo** Slovenia
201 M7 **Podčetrtek** Slovenia
156 L3 **Podcher'ye** Rus. Fed.
156 L3 **Podcher'ye** r. Rus. Fed.
196 G4 **Poddębice** Pol.
161 O4 **Poddor'ye** Rus. Fed.
198 E1 **Poděbrady** Czech Rep.
197 I6 **Podegrodzie** Pol.
193 K6 **Podelzig** Ger.
185 D6 **Podensac** France
212 H7 **Podenzana** Italy
212 H6 **Podenzano** Italy
201 O4 **Podersdorf am See** Austria
196 E2 **Podgaje** Pol.
219 J7 **Podgorac** Boljevac Serbia
157 G6 **Podgorenskiy** Rus. Fed.
218 H8 **Podgorica** Podgorica Montenegro
201 K7 **Podgorica** Slovenia
220 B2 **Podgorie** Albania
151 E1 **Podgornaya** Rus. Fed.
152 J4 **Podgornoye** Rus. Fed.
213 Q4 **Podgrad** Slovenia
199 L3 **Podhoroď** Slovakia
136 F5 **Podile** Andhra Prad. India
213 M5 **Po di Levante** r. Italy
201 O2 **Podivín** Czech Rep.
153 K3 **Podkamennaya Tunguska** Rus. Fed.
153 K3 **Podkamennaya Tunguska** r. Rus. Fed.
197 K6 **Podkarpackie** prov. Pol.
161 V7 **Podkhozheye** Rus. Fed.
219 N9 **Podkova** Bulg.
197 I3 **Podkowa Leśna** Pol.
201 L7 **Podkum** Slovenia
151 E1 **Podkumok** r. Rus. Fed.
197 K2 **Podlaska, Nizina** lowland Pol.
197 K2 **Podlaskie** prov. Pol.
201 M7 **Podlehnik** Slovenia
142 B2 **Podlesnoye** Rus. Fed.
201 K7 **Podlipoglav** Slovenia
201 I8 **Podnanos** Slovenia
274 B6 **Podocarpus, Parque Nacional** nat. park Ecuador
219 O4 **Podoleni** Romania
201 O1 **Podolí** Czech Rep.
161 U6 **Podol'sk** Rus. Fed.
228 B2 **Podor** Senegal
197 M6 **Podorozhnye** Ukr.
161 O6 **Podosinki** Rus. Fed.
159 N7 **Podove** Ukr.
161 X4 **Podozerskiy** Rus. Fed.
161 R1 **Podporozh'ye** Rus. Fed.
198 F5 **Podravina** reg. Croatia
198 G5 **Podravske Sesvete** Croatia
201 M7 **Podsreda** Slovenia
201 K8 **Podtabor** Slovenia
201 O7 **Podturen** Croatia
218 J8 **Podujevë** Podujevë Kosovo
Podujevo Podujevë Kosovo see **Podujevë**
197 H6 **Podwilk** Pol.
156 H3 **Podyuga** Rus. Fed.
159 N1 **Podyvot'ye** Rus. Fed.
156 J3 **Podz'** Rus. Fed.
192 D2 **Poel** i. Ger.
186 F4 **Poeldijk** Neth.
106 F8 **Poeppel Corner** salt flat N.T. Austr.
Poetovio Slovenia see **Ptuj**
236 D5 **Pofadder** S. Africa
215 K4 **Pofi** Italy
251 M3 **Pogamasing** Ont. Can.
161 Q9 **Pogar** Rus. Fed.
192 H2 **Poggendorf** Ger.
201 J6 **Poggersdorf** Austria
217 O3 **Poggiardo** Italy
213 K9 **Poggibonsi** Italy
214 F2 **Poggio Ballone** hill Italy
215 J2 **Poggio Bustone** Italy
214 G3 **Poggio del Leccio** hill Italy
214 G1 **Poggio di Montieri** mt. Italy
215 J2 **Poggiodomo** Italy
215 O4 **Poggio Imperiale** Italy
214 G2 **Poggio Lecci** hill Italy
214 C3 **Poggio-Mezzana** Corse France
215 J3 **Poggio Mirteto** Italy
215 J3 **Poggio Moiano** Italy
214 F2 **Poggio Peroni** hill Italy
215 L3 **Poggio Picenze** Italy
216 E8 **Poggioreale** Sicilia Italy
213 L6 **Poggio Renatico** Italy
215 Q6 **Poggiorsini** Italy
213 K6 **Poggio Rusco** Italy
201 L3 **Pöggstall** Austria
218 I8 **Pogled** mt. Montenegro
214 A7 **Poglina, Punta di** pt Sar[...] Italy
178 H6 **Pogny** France
220 B3 **Pogoniani** Greece
161 R5 **Pogoreloye-Gorodishch[...]** Rus. Fed.
196 F4 **Pogorzela** Pol.
196 F1 **Pogorzelice** Pol.
159 Q2 **Pogozheye** Rus. Fed.
218 I10 **Pogradec** Albania
122 G6 **Pogranichnyy** Rus. Fed.
Pogrebishche Ukr. see **Pohrebyshche**
197 H1 **Pogrodzie** Pol.
244 F5 **Pogromni Volcano** AK U[...]
277 G4 **Poguba** r. Brazil
115 C4 **Poh** Sulawesi Indon.
Po Hai g. China see **Bo** [...]
123 F10 **P'ohang** S. Korea
163 Q6 **Pohja** Fin.
191 H6 **Pohle** Ger.
213 R7 **Pohlibski Kanal** sea char[...]
100 □4b **Pohnpei** atoll Micronesi[...]
199 J3 **Pohorelá** Slovakia
198 F3 **Pohořelice** Czech Rep.
201 L7 **Pohorje** mts Slovenia
199 H3 **Pohranice** Slovakia
158 J3 **Pohreby** Kyivs'ka Oblast'[...]
159 M4 **Pohreby** Poltavs'ka Obla[...]
158 I4 **Pohrebyshche** Ukr.
138 F7 **Pohri** Madh. Prad. India
199 H3 **Pohronská pahorkatina** Slovakia
139 O7 **Poi** Manipur India
212 I3 **Poia** r. Italy
219 L7 **Poiana Mare** Romania
219 K5 **Poiana Ruscă, Munții** m[...] Romania
219 N3 **Poiana Stampei** Roman[...]
199 L5 **Poiana Vadului** Romani[...]
219 P4 **Poienești** Romania
199 L5 **Poieni** Romania
219 M3 **Poienile de Sub Munte** [...]
219 L4 **Poienița, Vârful** mt. Rom[...]
115 D3 **Poigar** Sulawesi Indon.
178 E8 **Poilly-lez-Gien** France
157 H5 **Poim** Rus. Fed.
178 H8 **Poinçon-lès-Larrey** Fran[...]
256 A10 **Poindexter** KY U.S.A.
99 G4 **Poindimié** New Caledon[...]
100 □5 **Poindimié** r. New Caled[...]
195 L5 **Poing** Ger.
287 H2 **Poinsett, Cape** Antarctic[...]
264 I3 **Point Arena** CA U.S.A.
261 J11 **Point au Fer Island** LA U[...]
245 N4 **Point Baker** AK U.S.A.
251 S3 **Point-Comfort** Que. Can[...]
261 K11 **Pointe a la Hache** LA U.[...]
271 □7 **Pointe-à-Pierre** Trin. an[...]
271 □2 **Pointe-à-Pitre** Guadelou[...]
251 N4 **Pointe au Baril Station** [...]
250 J4 **Pointe Aux Pins** MI U.S.[...]
271 □2 **Pointe Michel** Dominic[...]
231 A6 **Pointe-Noire** Congo
271 □2 **Pointe-Noire** Guadelou[...]
182 J5 **Pointe Percée** mt. France
271 □7 **Point Fortin** Trin. and T[...]
244 F1 **Point Hope** AK U.S.A.
208 G1 **Pointis-Inard** France
104 E5 **Point Kenny** S.A. Austr.
246 H1 **Point Lake** N.W.T. Can.
244 G1 **Point Lay** AK U.S.A.
256 F9 **Point Marion** PA U.S.A.
256 H9 **Point of Rocks** MD U.S.[...]
262 J6 **Point of Rocks** WY U.S.A[...]
251 L8 **Point Pelee National Pa[...]** Can.
257 K8 **Point Pleasant** NJ U.S.A.
256 C10 **Point Pleasant** WV U.S.A[...]
259 G4 **Point Pleasant Beach** N[...]
264 J3 **Point Reyes National Se[...]** nature res. CA U.S.A.
109 G10 **Point Salvation Aborigin[...]** Reserve W.A. Austr.
98 B4 **Point Samson** W.A. Aust[...]
212 D6 **Poirino** Italy
182 C2 **Poiseux** France
156 K5 **Poisevo** Rus. Fed.
103 B11 **Poison Bay** South I. N.Z.
251 S4 **Poisson Blanc, Lac du** l. [...] Can.
108 E5 **Poissonnier Point** W.A. [...]
179 J7 **Poissons** France
178 D6 **Poissy** France
182 I5 **Poisy** France
184 E2 **Poitiers** France
184 E2 **Poitou** reg. France
184 E3 **Poitou, Plaines et Seuil** [...] France
184 D3 **Poitou-Charentes** admin[...] France
239 □2 **Poivre Atoll** Seychelles
178 C4 **Poix-de-Picardie** France
178 I4 **Poix-Terron** France
201 M8 **Pojatno** Croatia
189 I2 **Pojezierza Iławskiego, P[...]** Krajobrazowy Pol.
158 C2 **Pojezierze Łęczyńskie, P[...]** Krajobrazowy Pol.
276 D4 **Pojo** Bol.
278 F5 **Pojuca** Brazil
264 □C12 **Pōka'ī Bay** HI U.S.A.
145 O4 **Pokal** Pak.
138 C6 **Pokaran** Rajasthan India
198 F5 **Pókaszepetk** Hungary
105 L3 **Pokataroo** N.S.W. Austr.
161 N9 **Pokats'** r. Belarus
156 L3 **Pokcha** Rus. Fed.
102 J4 **Pokeno** North I. N.Z.
139 I5 **Pokhara** Nepal
145 L9 **Pokhran Landi** Pak.
142 E1 **Pokhvistnevo** Rus. Fed.
275 H3 **Pokigron** Suriname
162 R2 **Pokka** Fin.
Pok Liu Chau i. H.K. Chi[...] **Lamma Island**
201 I7 **Pokljuka** reg. Slovenia
230 E4 **Poko** Dem. Rep. Congo
196 F5 **Pokój** Pol.
244 G1 **Poko Mountain** hill AK U[...]
151 F1 **Pokoynoye** Rus. Fed.
161 S6 **Pokrov** Smolenskaya Obl[...] Rus. Fed.
161 W6 **Pokrov** Vladimirskaya Ob[...] Rus. Fed.
151 J6 **Pokrovka** Azer.
143 M2 **Pokrovka** Kazakh.
143 N6 **Pokrovka** Talas Kyrg.
Pokrovka Ysyk-Köl Kyrg. s[...] **Kyzyl-Suu**
122 B2 **Pokrovka** Chitinskaya Ob[...] Rus. Fed.
161 T5 **Pokrovka** Moskovskaya [...] Rus. Fed.
142 E2 **Pokrovka** Orenburgskaya [...] Rus. Fed.
122 G7 **Pokrovka** Primorskiy Kray[...] Rus. Fed.
Pokrovka Yevreyskaya Avtonomnaya Oblast' Rus[...] **Priamurskiy**
159 K6 **Pokrovka** Mykolayivs'ka [...] Ukr.
159 K7 **Pokrovka** Mykolayivs'ka [...] Ukr.
159 O3 **Pokrovka** Sums'ka Oblast[...]
159 U1 **Pokrovo-Marfino** Rus. F[...]
153 N3 **Pokrovsk** Respublika Sakh[...] (Yakutiya) Rus. Fed.
Pokrovsk Saratovskaya O[...] Rus. Fed. see **Engel's**
159 N6 **Pokrovs'ke** Dnipropetrovs[...] Oblast' Ukr.
159 R4 **Pokrovs'ke** Luhans'ka Ob[...]
161 V9 **Pokrovskoye** Lipetskaya [...] Rus. Fed.

T9 Pokrovskoye Orlovskaya Oblast' Rus. Fed.
G7 Pokrovskoye Rostovskaya Oblast' Rus. Fed.
L3 Pokrovsk-Ural'skiy Rus. Fed.
L4 Pokrówka Pol.
Y4 Poksha r. Rus. Fed.
I3 Pokshen'ga r. Rus. Fed.
D8 Pol Gujarat India
X6 Pol' r. Rus. Fed.
Pola Croatia see Pula
C5 Pola Mindoro Phil.
O4 Pola Rus. Fed.
O4 Pola r. Rus. Fed.
V6 Polacca AZ U.S.A.
V6 Polacca Wash watercourse AZ U.S.A.
P7 Polacra, Punta de la pt Spain
G2 Pola de Allande Spain
I2 Pola de Laviana Spain
I2 Pola de Lena Spain
I2 Pola de Siero Spain
H2 Pola de Somiedo Spain
L8 Polaincourt-et-Clairefontaine France
E3 Połajewo Pol.
I9 Polān Iran
L9 Polán Spain
I3 Poľana mt. Slovakia
I3 Poľana mt. Slovakia
I3 Poľana park Slovakia
H3 Poland country Europe
I5 Poland NY U.S.A.
E7 Poland OH U.S.A.
E5 Polanica-Zdrój Pol.
I5 Połaniec Pol.
E1 Polanów Pol.
D2 Polar Bear Provincial Park Ont. Can.
V1 Polar Plateau Antarctica
E2 Polar Times Glacier Antarctica
F2 Polatbey Turkey
Polathane Turkey see Akçaabat
F4 Polatlı Turkey
L6 Polatsk Belarus
L6 Polatskaya Nizina lowland Belarus
G4 Polavaram Andhra Prad. India
L4 Polazna Rus. Fed.
D10 Polch Ger.
B5 Polcura Chile
G1 Połczyno Pol.
E2 Połczyn Zdrój Pol.
3 Poldarsa Rus. Fed.
A2 Pol Dasht Iran
M5 Pol-e 'Alam Afgh.
G5 Polee i. Papua Indon.
E7 Pol-e Fāsā Iran
M6 Polegate East Sussex, England U.K.
3 Pol-e Khātūn Iran
M4 Pol-e Khomrī Afgh.
4 Poleñino Spain
D1 Polepy Czech Rep.
E3 Pol-e Sefīd Iran
6 Polesella Italy
K6 Polesine reg. Italy
M6 Polesine, Isola di i. Italy
L4 Poleski Park Narodowy nat. park Pol.
E7 Polessk Rus. Fed.
2 Polesworth Warwickshire, England U.K.
Poles'ye marsh Belarus/Ukr. see Pripet Marshes
J2 Poletayevo Rus. Fed.
P2 Polevaya Rus. Fed.
A5 Polewali Sulawesi Barat Indon.
G9 Polgahawela Sri Lanka
K4 Polgár Hungary
7 Polhograjsko hribovje mts Slovenia
4 Poli Cameroon
9 Poli Shandong China
Poli Cyprus see Polis
6 Polia Italy
Políaigos i. Greece see Polyaigos
H6 Polica mt. Pol.
G2 Poliçan Albania
3 Policarpo Arg.
8 Policastro, Golfo di b. Italy
2 Police Pol.
2b Police, Pointe pt Mahé Seychelles
1 Police nad Metuj Czech Rep.
I3 Polichnitos Lesvos Greece
2 Polička Czech Rep.
3 Policoro Italy
4 Policzna Pol.
Polídhrosos Greece see Polydrosos
I3 Polientes Spain
I6 Polignac France
I2 Polignano a Mare Italy
I3 Poligny France
Políkastron Greece see Polykastro
Polikhnítos Lesvos Greece see Polichnitos
I7 Polikraishte Bulg.
4 Polillo i. Phil.
4 Polillo Islands Phil.
4 Polillo Strait Phil.
Poliny Osipenko, imeni Rus. Fed.
3 Polis Cyprus
2 Polis'ke Kyivs'ka Oblast' Ukr.
3 Polis'ke Rivnens'ka Oblast' Ukr.
I3 Polis'ke Zhytomyrs'ka Oblast' Ukr.
I2 Polis'kyy Zapovidnyk nature res. Ukr.
7 Polisot France
I3 Polist' r. Rus. Fed.
7 Polistena Italy
I4 Polisto, Ozero l. Rus. Fed.
5 Politotdel'skoye Rus. Fed.
Politovo Rus. Fed.
Pölitz Ger.
7 Polivanovo Rus. Fed.
Políyiros Greece see Polygyros
8 Polizzi Generosa Sicilia Italy
Poljane Slovenia
I7 Poljčane Slovenia
7 Polk PA U.S.A.
Polkorona Latvia
4 Polkowice Pol.
6 Polla Italy
7 Pollachi Tamil Nadu India
Pollard Islands HI U.S.A. see Gardner Pinnacles
5 Pöllau Austria
5 Pöllauberg Austria
5 Pöllauer Tal nature res. Austria
7 Polle Ger.
7 Polleben Ger.
3 Pollença Spain
3 Pollença, Badia de b. Spain
4 Pollenfeld Ger.
Pollensa Spain see Pollença
6 Pollhagen Ger.
4 Polliat France
7 Pollica Italy
3 Pollina Sicilia Italy
7 Pollina r. Sicilia Italy
5 Polling Bayern Ger.
5 Polling Bayern Ger.
8 Pollino, Monte mt. Italy
8 Pollino, Parco Nazionale del nat. park Italy
5 Pollitz Ger.
9 Polloch Highland, Scotland U.K.
8 Polloc Harbour b. Mindanao Phil.
Pollock Pines CA U.S.A.
13 Pollock Reef W.A. Austr.
Pollok North I. N.Z.
Pollos Spain
1 Pollux mt. South I. N.Z.
Polmak Norway
7 Polminhac France
1 Polmont Falkirk, Scotland U.K.
2 Polná Czech Rep.
2 Polnaya r. Rus. Fed.
Polnica Pol.
3 Polnovat Rus. Fed.
Polo Fin.
Polo IL U.S.A.
101 □8a Polo'a i. Tonga
Poloat atoll Micronesia see Puluwat
Pologi Ukr. see Polohy
159 P6 Polohy Ukr.
235 F4 Polokwane Limpopo S. Africa
156 J4 Polom Rus. Fed.
161 P4 Polomet' r. Rus. Fed.
114 E8 Polomoloc Mindanao Phil.
136 G9 Polonnaruwa Sri Lanka
158 G3 Polonne Ukr.
Polonnoye Ukr. see Polonne
124 X3 Polonskogo i. Kuril'skiye O-va Rus. Fed.
207 M7 Polopos Spain
201 O6 Pölöske Hungary
161 S7 Polotnyanyy Zavod Rus. Fed.
Polotsk Belarus see Polatsk
Polovinka Rus. Fed. see Ugleural'skiy
219 L5 Polovragi Romania
284 B3 Polpaico Chile
172 C7 Polperro Cornwall, England U.K.
201 K5 Pöls Austria
201 K5 Pöls r. Austria
186 G5 Polsbroek Neth.
195 J4 Polsingen Ger.
Polska country Europe see Poland
201 M7 Polskava r. Slovenia
219 N7 Polski Trŭmbesh Bulg.
262 G3 Polson MT U.S.A.
156 H2 Polta r. Rus. Fed.
199 I3 Poltár Slovakia
159 N4 Poltava Ukr.
Poltava Oblast admin. div. Ukr. see Poltavs'ka Oblast'
143 N1 Poltavka Omskaya Oblast' Rus. Fed.
122 G6 Poltavka Primorskiy Kray Rus. Fed.
159 Q5 Poltavka Donets'ka Oblast' Ukr.
159 L5 Poltavka Kirovohrads'ka Oblast' Ukr.
159 P6 Poltavka Zaporiz'ka Oblast' Ukr.
159 M4 Poltavs'ka Oblast' admin. div. Ukr.
157 G7 Poltavskaya Rus. Fed.
Poltavskaya Oblast' admin. div. Ukr. see Poltavs'ka Oblast'
Poltoratsk Turkm. see Aşgabat
160 I3 Põltsamaa Estonia
160 J3 Põltsamaa r. Estonia
143 M1 Poludino Kazakh.
158 C3 Południoworoztoczański Park Krajobrazowy Pol.
196 D3 Połupin Pol.
136 F6 Polur Tamil Nadu India
198 D3 Poluška hill Czech Rep.
160 K3 Põlva Estonia
263 K9 Polvadera NM U.S.A.
284 C3 Polvaredos Arg.
213 O8 Polverigi Italy
214 I1 Polvese, Isola i. Italy
162 T5 Polvijärvi Fin.
267 N8 Polvoxal Mex.
168 L11 Polwarth Scottish Borders, Scotland U.K.
161 W6 Polya r. Rus. Fed.
220 F6 Polyaigos i. Greece
220 F6 Polyaigou-Folegandrou, Steno sea chan. Greece
158 B5 Polyana Ukr.
Polyanovgrad Bulg. see Karnobat
160 M1 Polyany Rus. Fed.
Polyarnoye Rus. Fed. see Russkoye Ust'ye
153 S3 Polyarnyy Chukotskiy Avtonomnyy Okrug Rus. Fed.
162 V2 Polyarnyy Murmanskaya Oblast' Rus. Fed.
162 V3 Polyarnyye Zori Rus. Fed.
156 M2 Polyarnyy Ural mts Rus. Fed.
220 D4 Polydrosos Greece
220 E2 Polygyros Greece
220 D2 Polykastro Greece
290 H6 Polynesia is Oceania
Polynésie Française terr. S. Pacific Ocean see French Polynesia
197 N4 Polytsi Ukr.
201 L7 Polzela Slovenia
193 F9 Pölzig Ger.
216 E8 Poma, Lago l. Sicilia Italy
276 A2 Pomabamba Peru
103 D13 Pomahaka r. South I. N.Z.
274 B6 Pomahuaca Peru
205 M2 Pomaluengo Spain
282 D3 Pomán Arg.
213 J9 Pomarance Italy
206 D5 Pomarão Port.
185 C8 Pomarez France
217 L2 Pomarico Italy
163 Q6 Pomarkku Fin.
199 I4 Pomáz Hungary
281 F4 Pomba r. Brazil
275 H5 Pombal Pará Brazil
278 F3 Pombal Paraíba Brazil
204 F6 Pombal Bragança Port.
204 C9 Pombal Leiria Port.
275 F6 Pombas r. Brazil
280 A4 Pombo r. Brazil
183 G10 Pomègues, Île i. France
235 G4 Pomene Moz.
205 Q5 Pomer Spain
196 C1 Pomeranian Bay Pol.
279 C8 Pomerode Brazil
237 O4 Pomeroy S. Africa
169 I3 Pomeroy Northern Ireland U.K.
256 C9 Pomeroy OH U.S.A.
258 D5 Pomeroy PA U.S.A.
262 F3 Pomeroy WA U.S.A.
199 L5 Pomezeu Romania
198 F2 Pomezí Czech Rep.
215 J4 Pomezia Italy
236 H1 Pomfret S. Africa
159 K5 Pomichna Ukr.
197 I3 Pomiechówek Pol.
113 L8 Pomio New Britain P.N.G.
182 F2 Pommard France
180 E4 Pommerit-Jaudy France
195 J2 Pommersfelden Ger.
162 S3 Pomokaira reg. Fin.
107 N9 Pomona Qld Austr.
267 O9 Pomona Belize
234 B5 Pomona Namibia
264 O7 Pomona CA U.S.A.
258 F6 Pomona NJ U.S.A.
284 E6 Pomono Arg.
219 P8 Pomorie Bulg.
196 F1 Pomorskie prov. Pol.
196 F2 Pomorskie, Pojezierze reg. Pol.
156 F2 Pomorskiy Bereg coastal area Rus. Fed.
156 J1 Pomorskiy Proliv sea chan. Rus. Fed.
196 D3 Pomorsko Pol.
213 L6 Po Morto di Primaro watercourse Italy
150 A3 Pomos Point Cyprus
Pomo Tso l. China see Puma Yumco
Pomou, Akra pt Cyprus see Pomos Point
156 K3 Pomozdino Rus. Fed.
133 K11 Pompain Xizang China
184 D2 Pompaire France
215 N6 Pompei Italy
280 B5 Pompéia Brazil
281 E3 Pompéu Brazil
179 L6 Pompey France
122 G4 Pompeyevka Rus. Fed.
262 K3 Pompeys Pillar National Monument nat. park MT U.S.A.
183 D9 Pompignan France
259 G2 Pompton Lakes NJ U.S.A.
196 F1 Pomysk Mały Pol.
Ponape atoll Micronesia see Pohnpei
247 M4 Ponask Lake Ont. Can.
156 I4 Ponazyrevo Rus. Fed.
260 G4 Ponca NE U.S.A.
261 G7 Ponca City OK U.S.A.
271 □1 Ponce Puerto Rico
255 G13 Ponce de Leon Bay FL U.S.A.
263 K7 Poncha Springs CO U.S.A.
248 E3 Poncheville, Lac l. Que. Can.
182 G4 Poncin France
268 E5 Poncitlán Mex.
108 H3 Pond, Cape W.A. Austr.
136 D5 Ponda Goa India
261 G7 Pond Creek OK U.S.A.
258 F2 Pond Eddy NY U.S.A.
173 L2 Pondersbridge Cambridgeshire, England U.K.
Pondicherry India see Puducherry
Pondichéry Puducherry India see Puducherry
243 K2 Pond Inlet Nunavut Can.
237 N7 Pondoland reg. S. Africa
201 H3 Pöndorf Austria
249 K2 Ponds, Island of Nfld and Lab. Can.
Ponds Bay Nunavut Can. see Pond Inlet
119 H7 Pơ Ne, Đak r. Vietnam
266 □P11 Poneloya Nic.
212 D8 Ponente, Riviera di coastal area Italy
100 □5 Ponérihouen New Caledonia
100 □4a Pones i. Chuuk Micronesia
159 S9 Ponezhukay Rus. Fed.
204 G3 Ponferrada Spain
102 K4 Pongakawa North I. N.Z.
230 A4 Pongara, Parc National de nat. park Estuaire Gabon
230 A4 Pongara, Pointe pt Gabon
102 K7 Pongaroa North I. N.Z.
201 H5 Pongau val. Austria
139 O6 Pong-Chaa Arun. Prad. India
133 L11 Pongda Xizang China
230 E3 Pongo watercourse Sudan
274 B6 Pongo de Manseriche gorge Peru
237 P3 Pongola S. Africa
237 Q2 Pongola r. S. Africa
237 P3 Pongolapoort Dam l. S. Africa
237 P3 Pongolapoort Public Resort Nature Reserve S. Africa
228 E4 Pong Tamale Ghana
197 K4 Poniatowa Pol.
197 H2 Poniatowo Pol.
196 E4 Poniec Pol.
115 C3 Poniki, Gunung mt. Indon.
199 I3 Poniky Slovakia
115 B4 Ponindilisa, Tanjung pt Indon.
158 G3 Poninka Ukr.
199 H3 Ponitrie park Slovakia
193 F9 Ponitz Ger.
161 O6 Ponizov'ye Rus. Fed.
118 A4 Ponnagyun Myanmar
136 F7 Ponnaivar r. India
136 D6 Ponnampet Karnataka India
136 D7 Ponnani Kerala India
136 D7 Ponnani r. India
136 G6 Ponneri Tamil Nadu India
118 B3 Ponnyadaung Range mts Myanmar
246 H4 Ponoka Alta Can.
142 F1 Ponomarevka Rus. Fed.
159 L2 Ponornytsya Ukr.
117 I8 Ponorogo Jawa Indon.
156 H2 Ponoy Rus. Fed.
156 H2 Ponoy r. Rus. Fed.
249 G1 Pons r. Que. Can.
184 C4 Pons France
Pons Spain see Ponts
213 J8 Ponsacco Italy
114 E6 Ponson i. Phil.
204 F9 Ponsul r. Port.
182 E2 Pont, Lac de l. France
206 □ Ponta Madeira
187 F7 Pont-à-Celles Belgium
185 D9 Pontacq France
238 □1b Ponta Delgada São Miguel Azores
206 □ Ponta Delgada Madeira
278 C2 Ponta de Pedras Brazil
206 □ Ponta do Pargo Madeira
228 □ Ponta do Sol Cape Verde
206 □ Ponta do Sol Madeira
238 □1b Ponta Garça São Miguel Azores
280 B6 Ponta Grossa Brazil
182 G2 Pontailler-sur-Saône France
183 G7 Pontaix France
280 C4 Pontal Brazil
281 H3 Pontal do Ipiranga Brazil
280 C2 Pontalina Brazil
178 F2 Pont-à-Marcq France
179 L6 Pont-à-Mousson France
285 G5 Pontant Arg.
278 C3 Pontão Brazil
277 G5 Ponta Porã Brazil
172 E4 Pontardawe Neath Port Talbot, Wales U.K.
172 D4 Pontarddulais Swansea, Wales U.K.
Pontardulais Swansea, Wales U.K. see Pontarddulais
Pontarfynach Ceredigion, Wales U.K. see Devil's Bridge
184 H4 Pontarion France
182 I3 Pontarlier France
213 K8 Pontassieve Italy
180 I4 Pontaubault France
181 M3 Pont-Audemer France
182 B5 Pontaumur France
180 D6 Pont-Aven France
248 E3 Pontax r. Que. Can.
212 D5 Pont-Canavese Italy
183 I6 Pontcharra France
261 J10 Pontchartrain, Lake LA U.S.A.
180 G7 Pontchâteau France
180 C5 Pont-Croix France
182 G4 Pont-d'Ain France
180 C5 Pont-de-Buis-lès-Quimerch France
182 G5 Pont-de-Chéruy France
185 I8 Pont-de-Larn France
183 F6 Pont-de-l'Isère France
187 G8 Pont-de-Loup Belgium
182 H3 Pont-de-Poitte France
182 J2 Pont-de-Roide France
183 B8 Pont-de-Salars France
208 G3 Pont de Suert Spain
182 F4 Pont-de-Vaux France
182 F4 Pont-de-Veyle France
183 D8 Pont-d'Hérault France
181 K4 Pont-d'Ouilly France
185 F7 Pont-du-Casse France
182 C5 Pont-du-Château France
183 F9 Pont du Gard tourist site France
182 H3 Pont-du-Navoy France
215 N5 Ponte Italy
204 D6 Ponte Port.
278 D4 Ponte Alta do Norte Brazil
204 E2 Ponte Aranga Spain
204 D4 Ponteareas Spain
213 O2 Pontebba Italy
280 A2 Ponte Branca Brazil
204 D4 Ponte Caldelas Spain
204 C2 Ponteceso Spain
212 C6 Pontechianale Italy
215 L5 Pontecorvo Italy
212 F6 Pontecurone Italy
204 D5 Ponte da Barca Port.
212 E8 Pontedassio Italy
204 C5 Ponte de Lima Port.
212 H6 Ponte dell'Olio Italy
277 F3 Ponte de Pedra Brazil
213 J8 Pontedera Italy
206 C2 Ponte de Sor Port.
204 D2 Pontedeume Spain
204 C8 Ponte de Vagos Port.
200 C7 Ponte di Legno Italy
213 M4 Ponte di Piave Italy
279 B6 Ponte do Rio Verde Brazil
206 A2 Ponte do Rol Port.
280 D3 Ponte Firme Brazil
171 O6 Pontefract West Yorkshire, England U.K.
213 L2 Ponte Gardena Italy
247 J5 Ponteix Sask. Can.
171 N3 Ponteland Northumberland, England U.K.
215 N5 Pontelandolfo Italy
214 C3 Ponte-Leccia Corse France
213 M5 Pontelongo Italy
213 M3 Ponte nelle Alpi Italy
212 H4 Ponte Nossa Italy
281 F4 Ponte Nova Brazil
213 K3 Ponte Nova Italy
183 G6 Pont-en-Royans France
212 H5 Pontenure Italy
185 B7 Pontenx-les-Forges France
172 E3 Ponterwyd Ceredigion, Wales U.K.
206 B3 Pontes Port.
213 L5 Ponte San Nicolò Italy
212 H4 Ponte San Pietro Italy
172 G2 Pontesbury Shropshire, England U.K.
200 F7 Pontesei, Lago di l. Italy
277 F3 Pontes-e-Lacerda Brazil
204 C3 Ponte Valga Spain
204 C4 Pontevedra Spain
204 D4 Pontevedra prov. Spain
204 C4 Pontevedra, Ría de est. Spain
206 B2 Pontével Port.
182 F5 Pont-Évêque France
212 I5 Pontevico Italy
181 I4 Pont-Farcy France
178 H5 Pontfaverger-Moronvilliers France
182 B5 Pontgibaud France
181 I3 Pont-Hébert France
Ponthierville Dem. Rep. Congo see Ubundu
178 C3 Ponthieu reg. France
250 F9 Pontiac IL U.S.A.
251 K7 Pontiac MI U.S.A.
Pontiae is Italy see Ponziane, Isole
117 H5 Pontianak Kalimantan Indon.
178 G8 Pontigny France
Pontine Islands is Italy see Ponziane, Isole
215 K5 Pontinia Italy
215 J4 Pontino, Agro plain Italy
180 F5 Pontivy France
180 C6 Pont-l'Abbé France
184 C4 Pont-l'Abbé-d'Arnoult France
179 I7 Pont-la-Ville France
182 I2 Pont-les-Moulins France
181 L3 Pont-l'Évêque France
181 N7 Pontlevoy France
181 I5 Pontmain France
281 G3 Pontões Capixabas, Parque Nacional dos nat. park Brazil
275 H4 Pontoetoe Suriname
178 D5 Pontoise France
109 G10 Ponton watercourse W.A. Austr.
247 L4 Ponton Man. Can.
205 J2 Pontón, Puerto del pass Spain
207 N4 Pontones Spain
185 C8 Pontonx-sur-l'Adour France
169 D5 Pontoon Ireland
180 H4 Pontorson France
151 D4 Pontos Mucha Nakrdzali nature res. Georgia
261 K8 Pontotoc MS U.S.A.
180 H5 Pont-Péan France
178 E5 Pontpoint France
212 H7 Pontremoli Italy
212 H3 Pontresina Switz.
172 E3 Pontrhydfendigaid Ceredigion, Wales U.K.
180 E4 Pontrieux France
172 G4 Pontrilas Herefordshire, England U.K.
208 H4 Ponts Spain
178 H7 Pont-Ste-Marie France
178 E5 Pont-Ste-Maxence France
183 F8 Pont-St-Esprit France
212 D4 Pont-St-Martin Italy
180 E6 Pont-Scorff France
172 F4 Pontsticill Reservoir Wales U.K.
178 G6 Pont-sur-Seine France
178 F7 Pont-sur-Yonne France
181 L6 Pontvallain France
172 D4 Pontyberem Carmarthenshire, Wales U.K.
251 P5 Pontypool Ont. Can.
172 F4 Pontypool Torfaen, Wales U.K.
172 F4 Pontypridd Rhondda Cynon Taff, Wales U.K.
102 J3 Ponui Island North I. N.Z.
159 R8 Ponura r. Rus. Fed.
159 L1 Ponurovka Rus. Fed.
161 P8 Ponyatovka Rus. Fed.
161 T9 Ponyri Rus. Fed.
215 J6 Ponza Italy
215 J6 Ponza, Isola di i. Italy
215 J6 Ponziane, Isole is Italy
212 E6 Ponzone Italy
212 E4 Ponzone r. Italy
104 E5 Poochera S.A. Austr.
231 B5 Pool admin. reg. Congo
171 N6 Pool West Yorkshire, England U.K.
103 D12 Poolburn Reservoir South I. N.Z.
271 □7 Poole Trin. and Tob.
173 I6 Poole Poole, England U.K.
173 I6 Poole admin. div. England U.K.
173 I6 Poole Bay England U.K.
168 E7 Poolewe Highland, Scotland U.K.
171 L4 Pooley Bridge Cumbria, England U.K.
104 F2 Poolowanna Lake salt flat S.A. Austr.
Poona Mahar. India see Pune
105 I5 Pooncarie N.S.W. Austr.
109 D9 Poondarrie, Mount hill W.A. Austr.
105 J4 Poopelloe Lake N.S.W. Austr.
276 D4 Poopó Bol.
276 D4 Poopó, Lago de l. Bol.
102 I2 Poor Knights Islands North I. N.Z.
244 I2 Poorman AK U.S.A.
143 N7 Pop Uzbek.
270 B9 Popa, Isla i. Panama
118 B4 Popa Mountain Myanmar
159 R5 Popasna Ukr.
Popasnaya Ukr. see Popasna
159 O5 Popasne Dnipropetrovs'ka Oblast' Ukr.
159 Q4 Popasne Kharkivs'ka Oblast' Ukr.
274 B4 Popayán Col.
160 E4 Pope Latvia
159 M5 Popel'naste Ukr.
187 C7 Poperinge Belgium
256 I10 Popes Creek MD U.S.A.
196 F5 Popielów Pol.
153 L2 Popigay r. Rus. Fed.
158 I4 Popil'nya Ukr.
105 H5 Popilta Lake imp. l. N.S.W. Austr.
105 H5 Popio Lake N.S.W. Austr.
159 M3 Popivka Ukr.
247 L4 Poplar r. Man. Can.
246 G2 Poplar r. N.W.T. Can.
262 L2 Poplar MT U.S.A.
250 C3 Poplar WI U.S.A.
262 L2 Poplar r. MT U.S.A.
262 L2 Poplar, West Fork r. MT U.S.A.
261 J7 Poplar Bluff MO U.S.A.
256 E12 Poplar Camp VA U.S.A.
256 B10 Poplar Plains KY U.S.A.
261 K10 Poplarville MS U.S.A.
161 X8 Poplevino Rus. Fed.
161 W8 Poplevinskiy Rus. Fed.
269 I6 Popocatépetl, Volcán vol. Mex.
117 I9 Popoh Jawa Indon.
231 C6 Popokabaka Dem. Rep. Congo
215 L3 Popoli Italy
100 □6 Popomanaseu, Mount Guadalcanal Solomon Is
113 K8 Popondetta P.N.G.
210 F3 Popovača Croatia
Popovichskaya Rus. Fed. see Kalininskaya
161 U2 Popovka Rus. Fed.
219 O7 Popovo Bulg.
210 F4 Popovo Polje plain Bos.-Herz.
219 O8 Popovska Reka r. Bulg.
197 H3 Popów Łódzkie Pol.
196 G4 Popów Śląskie Pol.
195 L3 Poppberg hill Ger.
191 K7 Poppenberg hill Ger.
191 J10 Poppenhausen Ger.
191 I10 Poppenhausen (Wasserkuppe) Ger.
195 L3 Poppenricht Ger.
213 L8 Poppi Italy
197 I6 Poprad r. Pol.
199 J2 Poprad Slovakia
199 J2 Popradzki Park Krajobrazowy Pol.
199 J3 Poproč Slovakia
267 O9 Poptún Guat.
214 E2 Populonia Italy
151 C1 Poputnaya Rus. Fed.
259 K2 Poquetanuck CT U.S.A.
276 D5 Poquis, Nevado de mt. Chile
259 K2 Poquonock Bridge CT U.S.A.
257 I11 Poquoson VA U.S.A.
197 L5 Por r. Pol.
197 H6 Porąbka Pol.
197 H5 Poraj Pol.
145 L9 Porali r. Pak.
102 K7 Porangahau North I. N.Z.
278 C5 Porangatu Brazil
160 H9 Porazava Belarus
138 B9 Porbandar Gujarat India
213 J8 Porcari Italy
145 J5 Por Chaman Afgh.
245 O5 Porcher Island B.C. Can.
213 N4 Porcia Italy
178 H4 Porcien reg. France
281 F4 Porciúncula Brazil
276 D4 Porco Bol.
199 L4 Porcsalma Hungary
207 K5 Porcuna Spain
245 K2 Porcupine r. Can./U.S.A.
249 J2 Porcupine, Cape Nfld and Lab. Can.
288 H2 Porcupine Abyssal Plain sea feature N. Atlantic Ocean
107 J6 Porcupine Creek r. Qld Austr.
262 K2 Porcupine Creek r. MT U.S.A.
107 J6 Porcupine Gorge National Park Qld Austr.
247 K4 Porcupine Hills Man./Sask. Can.
250 E3 Porcupine Mountains MI U.S.A.
247 K4 Porcupine Plain Sask. Can.
247 K4 Porcupine Provincial Forest nature res. Sask. Can.
213 N4 Pordenone Italy
213 N3 Pordenone prov. Italy
180 F4 Pordic France
219 M7 Pordim Bulg.
274 D3 Pore Col.
210 D3 Poreč Croatia
280 B5 Porecatu Brazil
161 S6 Porech'ye Moskovskaya Oblast' Rus. Fed.
161 N5 Porech'ye Pskovskaya Oblast' Rus. Fed.
161 T3 Porech'ye Tverskaya Oblast' Rus. Fed.
161 W4 Porech'ye-Rybnoye Rus. Fed.
157 I5 Poretskoye Rus. Fed.
214 C2 Poretta airport Corse France
201 I7 Porezen mt. Slovenia
283 D6 Pórfido, Punta pt Arg.
229 F4 Porga Benin
133 F10 Porgyang Xizang China
163 P6 Pori Fin.
193 K10 Poříčany Czech Rep.
103 I8 Porirua North I. N.Z.
162 O3 Porjus Sweden
160 M4 Porkhov Rus. Fed.
160 H2 Porkkalafjärden b. Fin.
275 F2 Porlamar Venez.
212 G3 Porlezza Italy
172 E5 Porlock Somerset, England U.K.
205 J3 Porma r. Spain
205 J3 Porma, Embalse de resr Spain
107 H3 Pormpuraaw Qld Austr.
163 R6 Pornainen Fin.
212 D7 Pornassio Italy
195 K4 Pörnbach Ger.
180 G7 Pornic France
180 G7 Pornichet France
114 E6 Poro i. Phil.
100 □6 Poro Sta Isabel Solomon Is
217 J6 Poro, Monte hill Italy
156 L3 Porog Rus. Fed.
139 N7 Porompat Manipur India
122 M4 Poronaysk Sakhalin Rus. Fed.
133 J11 Porong Xizang China
119 G8 Pôrông, Stœng r. Cambodia
284 D2 Porongo, Cerro mt. Arg.
220 E5 Poros Greece
220 E5 Poros i. Greece
158 B5 Poroshkovo Ukr.
156 F3 Porosozero Rus. Fed.
199 J4 Poroszló Hungary
156 K3 Porozhsk Rus. Fed.
213 Q5 Porozina Croatia
287 I2 Porpoise Bay Antarctica
238 □2a Porpoise Point Ascension S. Atlantic Ocean
208 K3 Porqueres Spain
183 I11 Porquerolles, Île de i. France
251 N1 Porquis Junction Ont. Can.
215 M4 Porrara, Monte mt. Italy
212 C1 Porrentruy Switz.
209 L8 Porreres Spain
213 J7 Porretta Terme Italy
207 P4 Porrón hill Spain
162 R1 Porsangerfjorden sea chan. Norway
162 R1 Porsangerhalvøya pen. Norway
164 F2 Porsgrunn Norway
180 B4 Porspoder France
221 M3 Porsuk r. Turkey
169 E3 Port Ireland
185 H10 Port, Pic du mt. France/Spain
185 H10 Porta France
Portacloy Ireland see Port an Chlóidh
284 B6 Portada Covunco Arg.
104 G6 Port Adelaide S.A. Austr.
169 J4 Portadown Northern Ireland U.K.
103 C14 Port Adventure b. Stewart I. N.Z.
169 K4 Portaferry Northern Ireland U.K.
250 G8 Portage IN U.S.A.
250 I7 Portage MI U.S.A.
256 G8 Portage PA U.S.A.
250 E6 Portage WI U.S.A.
244 H4 Portage Creek AK U.S.A.
256 D8 Portage Lakes OH U.S.A.
247 L5 Portage la Prairie Man. Can.
204 G9 Portaje Spain
260 D1 Portal ND U.S.A.
246 E5 Port Alberni B.C. Can.
105 K8 Port Albert Vic. Austr.
206 E2 Portalegre Port.
206 D2 Portalegre admin. dist. Port.
261 D8 Portales NM U.S.A.
245 N4 Port Alexander AK U.S.A.
Port-Alfred Que. Can. see La Baie
237 K9 Port Alfred S. Africa
246 E5 Port Alice B.C. Can.
256 G7 Port Allegany PA U.S.A.
107 M7 Port Alma Qld Austr.
209 K9 Portals Vells Spain
244 I3 Port Alsworth AK U.S.A.
169 C4 Port an Chlóidh Ireland
262 C2 Port Angeles WA U.S.A.
270 □ Port Antonio Jamaica
270 F4 Port-à-Piment Haiti
168 F9 Port Appin Argyll and Bute, Scotland U.K.
220 E2 Portaria Greece
169 H6 Portarlington Ireland
105 K10 Port Arthur Tas. Austr.
Port Arthur Liaoning China see Lüshun
261 I11 Port Arthur TX U.S.A.
204 F4 Portas, Encoro das resr Spain
168 D11 Port Askaig Argyll and Bute, Scotland U.K.
104 F5 Port Augusta S.A. Austr.
249 J3 Port-au-Port Bay Nfld and Lab. Can.
270 G4 Port-au-Prince Haiti
251 L5 Port Austin MI U.S.A.
249 J3 Port aux Choix Nfld and Lab. Can.
170 G5 Portavogie Northern Ireland U.K.
180 H3 Portbail France
169 I2 Portballintrae Northern Ireland U.K.
168 F11 Port Bannatyne Argyll and Bute, Scotland U.K.
185 K10 Port-Barcarès France
114 B6 Port Barton b. Palawan Phil.
236 E10 Port Beaufort S. Africa
232 B4 Port Bell Uganda
137 M7 Port Blair Andaman & Nicobar Is India
251 O5 Port Bolster Ont. Can.
208 L3 Portbou Spain
106 F2 Port Bradshaw b. N.T. Austr.
181 J5 Port Brillet France
104 F5 Port Broughton S.A. Austr.
251 N7 Port Burwell Ont. Can.
105 I8 Port Campbell Vic. Austr.
105 I8 Port Campbell National Park Vic. Austr.
139 L8 Port Canning W. Bengal India
258 C3 Port Carbon PA U.S.A.
251 O4 Port Carling Ont. Can.
249 H3 Port-Cartier Que. Can.
103 E12 Port Chalmers South I. N.Z.
102 J3 Port Charles North I. N.Z.
255 F12 Port Charlotte FL U.S.A.
173 J6 Portchester Hampshire, England U.K.
259 H2 Port Chester NY U.S.A.
244 F2 Port Clarence b. AK U.S.A.
245 N5 Port Clements B.C. Can.
256 C7 Port Clinton OH U.S.A.
258 C3 Port Clinton PA U.S.A.
257 □P5 Port Clyde ME U.S.A.
248 E5 Port Colborne Ont. Can.
258 F3 Port Colden NJ U.S.A.
251 O6 Port Credit Ont. Can.
183 I10 Port-Cros, Île de i. France
183 I11 Port-Cros, Parc National de nat. park France
208 □ Port d'Addaia Spain
209 J8 Port d'Andratx Spain
106 C2 Port Darwin b. N.T. Austr.
105 J10 Port Davey b. Tas. Austr.
183 F10 Port-de-Bouc France
184 C4 Port-d'Envaux France
270 G4 Port-de-Paix Haiti
181 M7 Port-de-Piles France
209 L8 Port de Pollença Spain
258 C5 Port Deposit MD U.S.A.
184 B4 Port-des-Barques France
209 K8 Port de Sóller Spain
116 D3 Port Dickson Malaysia
107 J4 Port Douglas Qld Austr.
251 N7 Port Dover Ont. Can.
106 C1 Port Easington inlet N.T. Austr.
250 H4 Porte des Morts lake channel WI U.S.A.
245 O5 Port Edward B.C. Can.
237 O7 Port Edward S. Africa
250 E5 Port Edwards WI U.S.A.
275 G5 Porteira Brazil
281 F1 Porteirinha Brazil
275 I5 Portel Brazil
206 D4 Portel Port.
281 G4 Portela Brazil
280 A2 Portelândia Brazil
183 B10 Portel-des-Corbières France
249 H4 Port Elgin N.B. Can.
248 D4 Port Elgin Ont. Can.
237 J9 Port Elizabeth S. Africa
271 □3 Port Elizabeth St Vincent
208 E6 Portell de Morella Spain
168 D11 Port Ellen Argyll and Bute, Scotland U.K.
285 F2 Portena Arg.
181 J3 Port-en-Bessin-Huppain France
170 H5 Port Erin Isle of Man
247 J2 Porter Lake N.W.T. Can.
247 J3 Porter Lake Sask. Can.
245 O4 Porter Landing B.C. Can.
271 □3 Porter Point St Vincent
258 E2 Porters Lake PA U.S.A.
236 C9 Porterville S. Africa
264 M5 Porterville CA U.S.A.
172 G6 Portesham Dorset, England U.K.
183 F7 Portes-lès-Valence France
270 □ Port Esquivel Jamaica
185 F10 Portet d'Aspet, Col de pass France
Port Étienne Maur. see Nouâdhibou
Port Everglades FL U.S.A. see Fort Lauderdale
172 D4 Port Eynon Swansea, Wales U.K.
105 I8 Port Fairy Vic. Austr.
102 J3 Port Fitzroy North I. N.Z.
Port Francqui Dem. Rep. Congo see Ilebo
Port Fuad Egypt see Būr Fu'ād
230 A5 Port-Gentil Gabon
104 G5 Port Germein S.A. Austr.
261 J10 Port Gibson MS U.S.A.
168 G11 Port Glasgow Inverclyde, Scotland U.K.
169 J3 Portglenone Northern Ireland U.K.
103 I8 Port Gore b. South I. N.Z.
244 J4 Port Graham AK U.S.A.
183 J10 Port Grimaud France
237 N7 Port Grosvenor S. Africa
172 F4 Porth Rhondda Cynon Taff, Wales U.K.
Porthaethwy Isle of Anglesey, Wales U.K. see Menai Bridge
229 G5 Port Harcourt Nigeria
246 E5 Port Hardy B.C. Can.
Port Harrison Que. Can. see Inukjuak
249 I4 Port Hawkesbury N.S. Can.
172 E5 Porthcawl Bridgend, Wales U.K.
108 E6 Port Hedland W.A. Austr.
244 H4 Port Heiden AK U.S.A.
270 □ Port Henderson Jamaica
168 E7 Port Henderson Highland, Scotland U.K.
257 L4 Port Henry NY U.S.A.
Port Herald Malawi see Nsanje
172 B7 Porthleven Cornwall, England U.K.
172 D2 Porthmadog Gwynedd, Wales U.K.
172 C2 Porth Neigwl b. Wales U.K.
251 P6 Port Hope Ont. Can.
251 L6 Port Hope MI U.S.A.
249 K2 Port Hope Simpson Nfld and Lab. Can.
264 M7 Port Hueneme CA U.S.A.
251 L7 Port Huron MI U.S.A.
214 B4 Porticcio Corse France
215 M6 Portici Italy
179 L7 Portieux France
151 J7 Port-İliç Azer.
205 P8 Portilla Spain
205 K2 Portilla de la Reina Spain
284 B3 Portillo Chile
270 E4 Portillo Cuba
205 K6 Portillo Spain
205 M2 Portillo de la Sía mt. Spain
205 L8 Portillo de Toledo Spain
185 F10 Portillon, Col du pass France
206 B6 Portimão Port.
162 S3 Portimo Fin.
209 I9 Portinatx Spain
172 C6 Port Isaac Bay England U.K.
172 G5 Portishead North Somerset, England U.K.
Port Island H.K. China see Chek Chau
Port Jackson N.S.W. Austr. see Sydney
105 M5 Port Jackson inlet N.S.W. Austr.
259 I3 Port Jefferson NY U.S.A.
259 I3 Port Jefferson Station NY U.S.A.
258 F2 Port Jervis NY U.S.A.
180 G8 Port-Joinville France
270 □ Port Kaiser Jamaica
275 G3 Port Kaituma Guyana
Port Keats N.T. Austr. see Wadeye
105 M6 Port Kembla N.S.W. Austr.
257 L4 Port Kent NY U.S.A.
Port-Khorly Ukr. see Khorly
Port Klang Malaysia see Pelabuhan Klang
168 K7 Portknockie Moray, Scotland U.K.
Port Láirge Ireland see Waterford
105 L5 Portland N.S.W. Austr.
104 H8 Portland Vic. Austr.
270 □ Portland parish Jamaica
102 I2 Portland North I. N.Z.
169 F6 Portland Ireland
259 J1 Portland CT U.S.A.
254 E5 Portland IN U.S.A.
257 □O5 Portland ME U.S.A.
250 J7 Portland MI U.S.A.
262 C4 Portland OR U.S.A.
172 H6 Portland, Isle of pen. England U.K.
104 H8 Portland Bay Vic. Austr.
270 □ Portland Bight inlet Jamaica
Portland Bill hd England U.K. see Bill of Portland
245 O5 Portland Canal inlet B.C. Can.
249 J3 Portland Creek Pond l. Nfld and Lab. Can.
172 H6 Portland Harbour England U.K.
245 O5 Portland Inlet B.C. Can.
102 L6 Portland Island North I. N.Z.
270 □ Portland Point Jamaica
238 □2a Portland Point Ascension S. Atlantic Ocean
270 □ Portland Ridge hill Jamaica
107 I2 Portland Roads Qld Austr.
270 E5 Portland Rock i. Jamaica
183 C10 Port-la-Nouvelle France
169 H6 Portlaoise Ireland
261 G11 Port Lavaca TX U.S.A.
169 H8 Portlaw Ireland
168 L8 Portlethen Aberdeenshire, Scotland U.K.
185 K10 Port-Leucate France
104 E6 Port Lincoln S.A. Austr.
244 I4 Port Lions AK U.S.A.
244 J4 Portlock AK U.S.A.
168 G13 Port Logan Dumfries and Galloway, Scotland U.K.
228 B4 Port Loko Sierra Leone
180 E6 Port-Louis France
271 □2 Port-Louis Guadeloupe
239 □1b Port Louis Mauritius
Port-Lyautrey Morocco see Kénitra
104 H8 Port MacDonnell S.A. Austr.
105 N4 Port Macquarie N.S.W. Austr.
Portmadoc Gwynedd, Wales U.K. see Porthmadog
169 B9 Portmagee Ireland
168 I7 Portmahomack Highland, Scotland U.K.
258 E6 Port Mahon DE U.S.A.
209 D12 Portman Spain
180 D6 Port-Manec'h France
249 I1 Port Manvers inlet Nfld and Lab. Can.
270 □ Port Maria Jamaica
169 J6 Portmarnock Ireland
239 □1a Port Mathurin Rodrigues I. Mauritius
106 F3 Port McArthur b. N.T. Austr.
246 E5 Port McNeill B.C. Can.
249 H3 Port-Menier Que. Can.
244 G5 Port Moller AK U.S.A.
244 G5 Port Moller b. AK U.S.A.
270 □ Port Morant Jamaica
270 □ Portmore Jamaica
113 K8 Port Moresby P.N.G.
178 B5 Port-Mort France
169 K3 Portmuck Northern Ireland U.K.
107 H1 Port Musgrave b. Qld Austr.
168 F9 Portnacroish Argyll and Bute, Scotland U.K.
168 D6 Portnaguran Western Isles, Scotland U.K.
168 C11 Portnahaven Argyll and Bute, Scotland U.K.
168 D8 Portnalong Highland, Scotland U.K.
Port nan Giúran Western Isles, Scotland U.K. see Portnaguran
168 B7 Port nan Long Western Isles, Scotland U.K.
180 F6 Port-Navalo France
261 I11 Port Neches TX U.S.A.
104 F6 Port Neill S.A. Austr.
270 F2 Port Nelson Rum Cay Bahamas
249 G3 Portneuf r. Que. Can.
262 H5 Portneuf r. ID U.S.A.
249 F4 Portneuf, Réserve Faunique de nature res. Que. Can.
Port Nis Scotland U.K. see Port of Ness
104 G6 Port Noarlunga S.A. Austr.
236 A5 Port Nolloth S. Africa
169 F3 Portnoo Ireland
258 E6 Port Norris NJ U.S.A.
Port-Nouveau-Québec Que. Can. see Kangiqsualujjuaq
278 E2 Porto Brazil
214 B3 Porto Corse France
204 C6 Porto Port.
204 D6 Porto admin. dist. Port.
204 G4 Porto Spain
214 B3 Porto, Golfe de b. Corse France
276 D2 Porto Acre Brazil
276 D2 Porto Alegre Amazonas Brazil
279 B7 Porto Alegre Mato Grosso do Sul Brazil
275 H6 Porto Alegre Pará Brazil
279 C9 Porto Alegre Rio Grande do Sul Brazil
280 B3 Porto Alencastro Brazil
Porto Alexandre Angola see Tombua
206 B3 Porto Alto Port.
277 E3 Porto Amarante Brazil
231 B7 Porto Amboim Angola
Porto Amélia Moz. see Pemba
277 G3 Porto Artur Brazil
214 E2 Porto Azzurro Italy
103 E12 Portobello South I. N.Z.
279 C8 Porto Belo Brazil
266 □T13 Portobelo Panama
266 □T13 Portobelo, Parque Nacional nat. park Panama
214 B9 Porto Botte Sardegna Italy
204 C3 Portobravo Spain
244 I4 Port O'Brien AK U.S.A.
279 B7 Porto Camargo Brazil
278 G4 Porto Cavlo Brazil
214 D5 Porto Cervo Sardegna Italy
217 N3 Porto Cesareo Italy
209 L9 Portocolom Spain
206 B5 Porto Covo da Bandeira Port.
209 L8 Porto Cristo Spain
206 □ Porto da Cruz Madeira
278 F4 Porto da Fôlha Brazil
275 H6 Porto da Lontra Brazil
278 B5 Porto de Meinacos Brazil
204 C9 Porto de Mós Port.
204 D3 Portodemouros, Encoro de resr Spain
275 H5 Porto de Moz Brazil
275 H6 Porto do Barka Brazil
204 E1 Porto do Barqueiro Spain
277 E3 Porto do Massacas Brazil
277 F2 Porto dos Gaúchos Óbidos Brazil
204 B3 Porto do Son Spain
216 F9 Porto Empedocle Sicilia Italy
214 G3 Porto Ercole Italy
277 F4 Porto Esperança Brazil
277 F3 Porto Esperidião Brazil
277 F3 Porto Estrêla Brazil
280 D5 Porto Feliz Brazil
214 E2 Portoferraio Italy
280 D4 Porto Ferreira Brazil
212 G7 Portofino Italy
281 F4 Porto Firme Brazil
168 H10 Port of Menteith Stirling, Scotland U.K.
168 D6 Port of Ness Western Isles, Scotland U.K.
278 D3 Porto Franco Brazil
271 □7 Port of Spain Trin. and Tob.
213 M6 Porto Garibaldi Italy
275 I4 Porto Grande Brazil
213 N4 Portogruaro Italy
279 B7 Porto Guareí Brazil
277 F4 Porto Jofre Brazil
238 □1a Porto Judeu Terceira Azores
220 E3 Porto Koufo Greece
264 L2 Portola CA U.S.A.
216 H7 Porto Levante Isole Lipari Italy
213 M5 Porto Levante Veneto Italy
279 B8 Porto Luceno Brazil
213 L6 Portomaggiore Italy
204 E3 Portomarín Spain
279 B8 Porto Mauá Brazil
206 □ Porto Moniz Madeira
277 F5 Porto Murtinho Brazil
278 C4 Porto Nacional Brazil
229 F5 Porto-Novo Benin

228 □ **Porto Novo** Cape Verde
Porto Novo *Tamil Nadu* India *see* **Parangipettai**
216 D8 **Porto Palo** *Sicilia* Italy
211 E7 **Portopalo di Capo Passero** *Sicilia* Italy
209 L9 **Porto Petro** Spain
214 B10 **Porto Pino** *Sardegna* Italy
280 A5 **Porto Primavera** Brazil
280 A4 **Porto Primavera, Represa** *resr* Brazil
255 G11 **Port Orange** *FL* U.S.A.
262 C3 **Port Orchard** *WA* U.S.A.
213 P9 **Porto Recanati** Italy
262 B5 **Port Orford** *OR* U.S.A.
231 B6 **Porto Rico** Angola
228 □ **Porto Rincão** *Santiago* Cape Verde
214 D5 **Porto Rotondo** *Sardegna* Italy
213 P4 **Portorož** Slovenia
213 P9 **Porto San Giorgio** Italy
214 D6 **Porto San Paolo** *Sardegna* Italy
275 I5 **Porto Santana** Brazil
213 P9 **Porto Sant'Elpidio** Italy
206 □ **Porto Santo, Ilha de** *i.* Madeira
214 G3 **Porto Santo Stefano** Italy
280 A5 **Porto São José** Brazil
214 A9 **Portoscuso** *Sardegna* Italy
281 H2 **Porto Seguro** Brazil
213 M6 **Porto Tolle** Italy
214 A6 **Porto Torres** *Sardegna* Italy
277 E3 **Porto Triunfo** Brazil
279 C8 **Porto União** Brazil
214 C4 **Porto-Vecchio** *Corse* France
214 C4 **Porto-Vecchio, Golfe de** *b. Corse* France
276 E2 **Porto Velho** Brazil
212 H7 **Portovenere** Italy
274 A5 **Portoviejo** Ecuador
276 B2 **Porto Walter** Brazil
168 F13 **Portpatrick** *Dumfries and Galloway, Scotland* U.K.
103 B14 **Port Pegasus** *b. Stewart I.* N.Z.
258 D5 **Port Penn** *DE* U.S.A.
251 P5 **Port Perry** *Ont.* Can.
105 J8 **Port Phillip Bay** *Vic.* Austr.
104 G5 **Port Pirie** *S.A.* Austr.
Port Radium *N.W.T.* Can. *see* **Echo Bay**
169 J6 **Portrane** Ireland
172 B7 **Portreath** *Cornwall, England* U.K.
168 D8 **Portree** *Highland, Scotland* U.K.
246 E5 **Port Renfrew** B.C. Can.
249 K3 **Port Rexton** *Nfld and Lab.* Can.
169 F7 **Portroe** Ireland
106 E3 **Port Roper** *b. N.T.* Austr.
251 N7 **Port Rowan** *Ont.* Can.
270 □ **Port Royal** Jamaica
256 H10 **Port Royal** *VA* U.S.A.
255 G9 **Port Royal Sound** *inlet SC* U.S.A.
169 I2 **Portrush** *Northern Ireland* U.K.
244 F2 **Port Safety** *AK* U.S.A.
Port Said Egypt *see* **Būr Sa'īd**
185 E6 **Port-Ste-Foy-et-Ponchapt** France
185 E7 **Port-Ste-Marie** France
255 E11 **Port St Joe** *FL* U.S.A.
237 N7 **Port St Johns** S. Africa
Port St-Louis Madag. *see* **Antsohimbondrona**
183 F10 **Port-St-Louis-du-Rhône** France
255 G12 **Port St Lucie City** *FL* U.S.A.
170 H5 **Port St Mary** Isle of Man
180 H7 **Port-St-Père** France
180 B4 **Portsall** France
169 G2 **Portsalon** Ireland
283 F8 **Port Salvador** Falkland Is
251 L6 **Port Sanilac** *MI* U.S.A.
201 J6 **Pörtschach am Wörther See** Austria
208 F6 **Ports de Beseit** *mts* Spain
251 O5 **Port Severn** *Ont.* Can.
Port Shelter *b. H.K.* China *see* **Ngau Mei Hoi**
237 O6 **Port Shepstone** S. Africa
Port Simpson Can. *see* **Lax Kw'alaams**
271 □2 **Portsmouth** Dominica
173 J6 **Portsmouth** *Portsmouth, England* U.K.
173 J6 **Portsmouth** *admin. div. England* U.K.
257 □O5 **Portsmouth** *NH* U.S.A.
256 C10 **Portsmouth** *OH* U.S.A.
257 I12 **Portsmouth** *VA* U.S.A.
168 K7 **Portsoy** *Aberdeenshire, Scotland* U.K.
Port Stanley Falkland Is *see* **Stanley**
105 N5 **Port Stephens** *b. N.S.W.* Austr.
283 E9 **Port Stephens** Falkland Is
169 I2 **Portstewart** *Northern Ireland* U.K.
225 H5 **Port Sudan** Sudan
261 K11 **Port Sulphur** *LA* U.S.A.
179 L8 **Port-sur-Saône** France
Port Swettenham Malaysia *see* **Pelabuhan Klang**
172 E4 **Port Talbot** *Neath Port Talbot, Wales* U.K.
114 D5 **Port Tambang** *b. Luzon* Phil.
Port Taufiq Egypt *see* **Būr Tawfīq**
162 S2 **Porttipahdan tekojärvi** *l.* Fin.
262 C2 **Port Townsend** *WA* U.S.A.
258 B3 **Port Trevorton** *PA* U.S.A.
202 C3 **Portugal** *country* Europe
205 N2 **Portugalete** Spain
Portugália Angola *see* **Chitato**
274 D2 **Portuguesa** *state* Venez.
Portuguese East Africa *country* Africa *see* **Mozambique**
Portuguese Guinea *country* Africa *see* **Guinea-Bissau**
Portuguese Timor *country* Asia *see* **East Timor**
Portuguese West Africa *country* Africa *see* **Angola**
169 F6 **Portumna** Ireland
Portus Herculis Monoeci *country* Europe *see* **Monaco**
204 C5 **Portuzelo** Port.
185 K10 **Port-Vendres** France
104 F6 **Port Victoria** *S.A.* Austr.
100 □5 **Port Vila** Vanuatu
256 G6 **Portville** *NY* U.S.A.
104 F6 **Port Vincent** *S.A.* Austr.
162 V2 **Port Vladimir** Rus. Fed.
102 I4 **Port Waikato** *North I.* N.Z.
104 G6 **Port Wakefield** *S.A.* Austr.
108 H3 **Port Warrender** *W.A.* Austr.
259 H3 **Port Washington** *NY* U.S.A.
250 G6 **Port Washington** *WI* U.S.A.
Port Weld Malaysia *see* **Kuala Sepetang**
168 G13 **Port William** *Dumfries and Galloway, Scotland* U.K.
250 C3 **Port Wing** *WI* U.S.A.
136 F5 **Porumamilla** *Andhra Prad.* India
270 □ **Porus** Jamaica
161 O4 **Porus'ya** *r.* Rus. Fed.
285 F4 **Porvenir** Arg.
276 C2 **Porvenir** *Pando* Bol.
277 E3 **Porvenir** *Santa Cruz* Bol.
283 C9 **Porvenir** Chile
285 I3 **Porvenir** Uru.
163 R6 **Porvoo** Fin.
160 I1 **Porvoonjoki** *r.* Fin.
123 E10 **Poryŏng** S. Korea
197 J3 **Porządzie** Pol.
207 K2 **Porzuna** Spain
161 R1 **Posad** Rus. Fed.
214 D6 **Posada** *Sardegna* Italy
214 D6 **Posada** *r. Sardegna* Italy
204 I2 **Posada** Spain
205 K2 **Posada de Valdeón** Spain
282 G2 **Posadas** Arg.
207 I5 **Posadas** Spain
287 G2 **Posadowsky Bay** Antarctica
159 L7 **Posad-Pokrovs'ke** Ukr.
210 F3 **Posavina** *reg.* Bos.-Herz./Croatia
201 K7 **Posavsko hribovje** *reg.* Slovenia
212 I3 **Poschiavo** Switz.
220 F5 **Poseidonia** *Syros* Greece
Poseidonia *tourist site* Italy *see* **Paestum**
Posen Pol. *see* **Poznań**
251 K4 **Posen** *MI* U.S.A.
192 H2 **Poseritz** Ger.
208 F2 **Posets** *mt.* Spain
156 G4 **Poshekhon'ye** Rus. Fed.
Poshekon'ye-Volodarsk Rus. Fed. *see* **Poshekhon'ye**
144 H7 **Posht** *watercourse* Iran
144 G4 **Posht-e Āsemān** *spring* Iran
144 H6 **Poshteh-ye Chaqvīr** *hill* Iran
144 B5 **Posht-e Kūh** *mts* Iran
144 C3 **Posht Kūh** *hill* Iran
159 M9 **Poshtove** Ukr.
200 D8 **Posina** *r.* Italy
195 N3 **Pösing** Ger.
162 T3 **Posio** Fin.
215 M6 **Positano** Italy
Poskam *Xinjiang* China *see* **Zepu**
259 J2 **Posnet** *CT* U.S.A.
115 B4 **Poso** *Sulawesi* Indon.
115 B4 **Poso** *r.* Indon.
115 B4 **Poso, Danau** *l.* Indon.
115 B4 **Poso, Teluk** *b.* Indon.
149 K3 **Posof** Turkey
151 D4 **Posof** *r.* Turkey
123 E11 **Posŏng** S. Korea
274 A5 **Posorja** Ecuador
143 S1 **Pospelikha** Rus. Fed.
200 E8 **Possagno** Italy
278 D5 **Posse** Brazil
230 C3 **Possel** C.A.R.
193 I9 **Possendorf** Ger.
179 I6 **Possesse** France
234 B5 **Possession Island** Namibia
287 L2 **Possession Islands** Antarctica
193 E9 **Pößneck** Ger.
267 J1 **Possum Kingdom Lake** *TX* U.S.A.
261 E9 **Post** *TX* U.S.A.
215 K2 **Posta** Italy
219 O5 **Poşta Câlnău** Romania
Poşta Cîlnău Romania *see* **Poşta Câlnău**
213 K2 **Postal** Italy
215 P5 **Posta Piana** Italy
195 M4 **Postau** Ger.
Postavy Belarus *see* **Pastavy**
195 K3 **Postbauer-Heng** Ger.
237 J8 **Post Chalmers** S. Africa
239 □1b **Poste de Flacq** Mauritius
239 □1b **Poste de Flacq, Rivière du** *r.* Mauritius
Poste-de-la-Baleine *Que.* Can. *see* **Kuujjuarapik**
187 J6 **Posterholt** Neth.
227 F4 **Poste Weygand** Alg.
236 H4 **Postmasburg** S. Africa
Post-Mawr *Wales* U.K. *see* **Synod Inn**
195 N5 **Postmünster** Ger.
210 E3 **Postojna** Slovenia
197 J3 **Postoliska** Pol.
198 C1 **Postoloprty** Czech Rep.
196 C3 **Postomia** *r.* Pol.
196 E1 **Postomino** Pol.
265 R7 **Poston** *AZ* U.S.A.
249 J2 **Postville** *Nfld and Lab.* Can.
250 C6 **Postville** *IA* U.S.A.
Postysheve Ukr. *see* **Krasnoarmiys'k**
210 F4 **Posušje** Bos.-Herz.
197 I4 **Poświętne** *Łódzkie* Pol.
197 J3 **Poświętne** Pol.
197 K3 **Poświętne** *Podlaskie* Pol.
122 G7 **Pos'yet** Rus. Fed.
115 B8 **Pota** *Flores* Indon.
266 D4 **Pótam** Mex.
220 F2 **Potamia** *Thasos* Greece
220 D6 **Potamos** *Kythira* Greece
161 P1 **Potanino** Rus. Fed.
260 E4 **Potato Creek** *SD* U.S.A.
237 L2 **Potchefstroom** S. Africa
219 M6 **Potcoava** Romania
281 G2 **Poté** Brazil
261 H8 **Poteau** *OK* U.S.A.
136 G3 **Potegaon** *Mahar.* India
196 G3 **Potęgowo** Pol.
157 I6 **Potemkino** Rus. Fed.
Potentia Italy *see* **Potenza**
215 P6 **Potenza** Italy
215 P6 **Potenza** *prov.* Italy
213 P9 **Potenza** *r.* Italy
213 P9 **Potenza Picena** Italy
103 B13 **Poteriteri, Lake** *South I.* N.Z.
205 K2 **Potes** Spain
236 I6 **Potfontein** S. Africa
278 E3 **Poti** *r.* Brazil
151 C3 **P'ot'i** Georgia
181 K4 **Potigny** France
136 G3 **Potikal** *Chhattisgarh* India
279 F5 **Potiraguá** Brazil
229 H4 **Potiskum** Nigeria
158 H3 **Potiyivka** Ukr.
262 F3 **Potlatch** *ID* U.S.A.
100 □5 **Potnarvin** Vanuatu
276 C3 **Poto** Peru
131 □J7 **Po Toi** *i. H.K.* China
197 K5 **Potok Górny** Pol.
197 H5 **Potok Złoty** Pol.
256 H9 **Potomac** *MD* U.S.A.
256 I10 **Potomac** *r. MD/VA* U.S.A.
256 G9 **Potomac, South Branch** *r. WV* U.S.A.
256 F10 **Potomac, South Fork South Branch** *r. WV* U.S.A.
115 D8 **Potomana, Gunung** *mt.* Indon.
228 C5 **Potoru** Sierra Leone
276 D4 **Potosí** Bol.
276 D5 **Potosí** *dept* Bol.
254 B7 **Potosi** *MO* U.S.A.
265 Q6 **Potosi Mountain** *NV* U.S.A.
114 D6 **Pototan** *Panay* Phil.
282 C2 **Potrerillos** Chile
266 □P10 **Potrerillos** Hond.
284 C3 **Potrerillos** Arg.
266 G3 **Potrero del Llano** *Chihuahua* Mex.
269 J4 **Potrero del Llano** *Veracruz* Mex.
269 M8 **Potrero Largo** Mex.
274 B6 **Potro** *r.* Peru
193 H6 **Potsdam** Ger.
257 K4 **Potsdam** *NY* U.S.A.
193 G6 **Potsdamer Havelseengebiet** *park* Ger.
199 G2 **Potštát** Czech Rep.
100 □5 **Pott, Île** *i.* New Caledonia
137 H3 **Pottangi** *Orissa* India
201 N4 **Pottendorf** Austria
201 N4 **Pottenstein** Austria
195 K2 **Pottenstein** Ger.
260 D5 **Potter** *NE* U.S.A.
172 H5 **Potterne** *Wiltshire, England* U.K.
173 L4 **Potters Bar** *Hertfordshire, England* U.K.
264 I2 **Potter Valley** *CA* U.S.A.
256 A6 **Potterville** *MI* U.S.A.
195 K4 **Pöttmes** Ger.
173 L3 **Potton** *Bedfordshire, England* U.K.
201 N4 **Pöttsching** Austria
258 B2 **Potts Grove** *PA* U.S.A.
258 D4 **Pottstown** *PA* U.S.A.
258 C3 **Pottsville** *PA* U.S.A.
136 G9 **Pottuvil** Sri Lanka
159 S2 **Potudan'** *r.* Rus. Fed.
145 O5 **Potwar** *reg.* Pak.
197 I4 **Potworów** Pol.
194 C2 **Potzberg** *hill* Ger.
180 I6 **Pouancé** France
246 F4 **Pouce Coupe** B.C. Can.
249 K4 **Pouch Cove** *Nfld and Lab.* Can.
100 □5 **Pouébo** New Caledonia
100 □5 **Pouembout** New Caledonia
257 L7 **Poughkeepsie** *NY* U.S.A.
259 H1 **Poughquag** *NY* U.S.A.
182 C2 **Pougny** France
182 C2 **Pougues-les-Eaux** France
178 H7 **Pougy** France
182 H2 **Pouilley-les-Vignes** France
185 C8 **Pouillon** France
182 F2 **Pouilly-en-Auxois** France
182 E4 **Pouilly-sous-Charlieu** France
182 B2 **Pouilly-sur-Loire** France
182 G2 **Pouilly-sur-Saône** France
181 O7 **Poulaines** France
180 C6 **Pouldreuzic** France
180 D6 **Pouldu, Anse de** *b.* France
182 E4 **Poule-les-Écharmeaux** France
169 D9 **Poulgorm Bridge** Ireland
181 N8 **Pouligny-St-Pierre** France
249 G3 **Poulin de Courval, Lac** *l. Que.* Can.
180 D5 **Poullaouen** France
169 G8 **Poulnamucky** Ireland
257 L5 **Poultney** *VT* U.S.A.
171 L6 **Poulton-le-Fylde** *Lancashire, England* U.K.
100 □5 **Poum** New Caledonia
229 H6 **Pouma** Cameroon
256 C11 **Pound** *VA* U.S.A.
220 F4 **Pountas, Akrotirio** *pt* Greece
236 I6 **Poupan** S. Africa
185 F8 **Poupas** France
182 H3 **Poupet, Mont** *hill* France
183 H10 **Pourcieux** France
102 K7 **Pourerere** *North I.* N.Z.
220 C3 **Pournariou, Techniti Limni** *resr* Greece
178 F8 **Pourrain** France
182 J5 **Pourri, Mont** *mt.* France
183 H9 **Pourrières** France
285 G5 **Pourtalé** Arg.
185 D10 **Pourtalet, Col du** *pass* France
204 F7 **Pousada** Port.
281 E5 **Pouso Alegre** Brazil
280 A2 **Pouso Alto** Brazil
204 C9 **Pousos** Port.
183 D10 **Poussan** France
179 L7 **Poussay** France
162 T4 **Poussu** Fin.
100 □2 **Poutasi** Samoa
119 F8 **Poŭthĭsăt** Cambodia
102 I3 **Pouto** *North I.* N.Z.
179 M7 **Pouxeux** France
118 E5 **Pouy, Nam** *r.* Laos
185 E9 **Pouyastruc** France
185 D8 **Pouydesseaux** France
185 G9 **Pouy-de-Touges** France
184 C2 **Pouzauges** France
181 M7 **Pouzay** France
161 U5 **Povarovo** Rus. Fed.
199 H2 **Považská Bystrica** Slovakia
199 G3 **Považský Inovec** *mts* Slovakia
161 R4 **Poved'** *r.* Rus. Fed.
207 N3 **Povedilla** Spain
156 F3 **Povenets** Rus. Fed.
102 L5 **Poverty Bay** *North I.* N.Z.
213 J6 **Poviglio** Italy
218 H6 **Povlen** *mt.* Serbia
206 D2 **Póvoa, Barragem da** *resr* Port.
238 □1b **Povoação** *São Miguel* Azores
281 H3 **Povoação** Brazil
204 D5 **Póvoa de Lanhoso** Port.
206 E4 **Póvoa de São Miguel** Port.
204 C6 **Póvoa de Varzim** Port.
204 F7 **Póvoa do Concelho** Port.
213 O3 **Povoletto** Italy
157 H6 **Povorino** Rus. Fed.
122 H7 **Povorotnyy, Mys** *hd* Rus. Fed.
158 E2 **Povors'k** Ukr.
193 J9 **Povrly** Czech Rep.
264 O9 **Poway** *CA* U.S.A.
171 N3 **Powburn** *Northumberland, England* U.K.
262 L3 **Powder** *r. MT* U.S.A.
262 F4 **Powder** *r. OR* U.S.A.
262 K5 **Powder, South Fork** *r. WY* U.S.A.
262 K5 **Powder River** *WY* U.S.A.
258 B1 **Powell** *PA* U.S.A.
262 J4 **Powell** *WY* U.S.A.
256 B12 **Powell** *r. TN/VA* U.S.A.
265 V4 **Powell, Lake** *resr UT* U.S.A.
107 I8 **Powell Creek** *watercourse Qld* Austr.
264 N3 **Powell Mountain** *NV* U.S.A.
270 E1 **Powell Point** *Eleuthera* Bahamas
246 E5 **Powell River** B.C. Can.
169 F9 **Power Head** Ireland
250 G4 **Powers** *MI* U.S.A.
169 F6 **Power's Cross** Ireland
261 J7 **Powhatan** *AR* U.S.A.
256 H11 **Powhatan** *VA* U.S.A.
256 E9 **Powhatan Point** *OH* U.S.A.
172 H3 **Powick** *Worcestershire, England* U.K.
196 F3 **Powidz** Pol.
196 F3 **Powidzkie, Jezioro** *l.* Pol.
168 I10 **Powmill** *Perth and Kinross, Scotland* U.K.
130 B2 **Powo** *Sichuan* China
144 H3 **Pöwrize** Turkm.
Pöwrize Turkm. *see* **Pöwrize**
172 F3 **Powys** *admin. div. Wales* U.K.
279 B5 **Poxoréu** Brazil
100 □5 **Poya** New Caledonia
205 J8 **Poyales del Hoyo** Spain
116 □ **Poyan, Sungai** *r.* Sing.
Poyang *Jiangxi* China *see* **Poyang**
131 K4 **Poyang** *Jiangxi* China
131 K4 **Poyang Hu** *l.* China
116 □ **Poyan Reservoir** Sing.
122 F4 **Poyarkovo** Rus. Fed.
205 P8 **Poyatos** Spain
250 F5 **Poygan, Lake** *WI* U.S.A.
151 H4 **Poylu** Azer.
250 E6 **Poynette** *WI* U.S.A.
171 M7 **Poynton** *Cheshire, England* U.K.
169 J4 **Poyntz Pass** *Northern Ireland* U.K.
207 O5 **Poyo, Cerro** *mt.* Spain
221 I3 **Poyrazcık** Turkey
201 O2 **Poysdorf** Austria
163 Q6 **Pöytyä** Fin.
205 N3 **Poza de la Sal** Spain
205 K6 **Pozaldez** Spain
148 G5 **Pozantı** Turkey
218 J6 **Požarevac** *Pozarevac* Serbia
269 J5 **Poza Rica** Mex.
199 K3 **Pozdišovce** Slovakia
210 F3 **Požega** Croatia
218 I7 **Požega** *Požega* Serbia
197 J1 **Pozezdrze** Pol.
161 O5 **Pozhnya** Rus. Fed.
159 O3 **Pozhnya** Ukr.
156 L4 **Pozhva** Rus. Fed.
199 G2 **Pozlovice** Czech Rep.
196 E3 **Poznań** Pol.
207 N5 **Pozo, Sierra del** *mts* Spain
207 N5 **Pozo Alcón** Spain
205 J5 **Pozoantiguo** Spain
282 D2 **Pozo Betbeder** Arg.
207 J4 **Pozoblanco** Spain
207 P3 **Pozo Cañada** Spain
277 F5 **Pozo Colorado** Para.
205 N8 **Pozo de Guadalajara** Spain
285 F3 **Pozo del Molle** Arg.
282 E2 **Pozo del Tigre** Arg.
282 D2 **Pozo Hondo** Arg.
207 P3 **Pozohondo** Spain
207 Q2 **Pozo-Lorente** Spain
205 R7 **Pozondón** Spain
205 R7 **Pozondón, Puerto de** *pass* Spain
238 □3b **Pozo Negro** *Fuerteventura* Canary Is
266 D3 **Pozo Nuevo** Mex.
201 O1 **Pozořice** Czech Rep.
205 O9 **Pozorrubio** Spain
283 D7 **Pozos, Punta** *pt* Arg.
282 E2 **Pozo San Martin** Arg.
196 D2 **Poźrzadło Wielkie** Pol.
Pozsony Slovakia *see* **Bratislava**
207 O3 **Pozuelo** Spain
205 M8 **Pozuelo de Alarcón** Spain
205 R5 **Pozuelo de Aragón** Spain
204 I4 **Pozuelo del Páramo** Spain
205 N8 **Pozuelo del Rey** Spain
204 H8 **Pozuelo de Zarzón** Spain
207 K3 **Pozuelos de Calatrava** Spain
276 B2 **Pozuzo** Peru
213 L3 **Pozza di Fassa** Italy
216 H10 **Pozzallo** *Sicilia* Italy
216 H8 **Pozzillo, Lago di** *l. Sicilia* Italy
212 F6 **Pozzolo Formigaro** Italy
214 B7 **Pozzomaggiore** *Sardegna* Italy
215 M6 **Pozzuoli** Italy
200 H8 **Pozzuolo del Friuli** Italy
228 E5 **Pra** *r.* Ghana
161 Y7 **Pra** *r.* Rus. Fed.
116 F6 **Prabumulih** *Sumatera* Indon.
197 H2 **Prabuty** Pol.
204 E9 **Pracana, Barragem de** *resr* Port.
198 D2 **Prachatice** Czech Rep.
137 J3 **Prachi** *r.* India
119 E7 **Prachin Buri** Thai.
191 E9 **Pracht** Ger.
119 D9 **Prachuap Khiri Khan** Thai.
195 N3 **Prackenbach** Ger.
204 G4 **Prada, Encoro de** *resr* Spain
204 F2 **Pradairo** *mt.* Spain
205 L3 **Prádanos de Ojeda** Spain
198 G1 **Praděd** *mt.* Czech Rep.
205 P4 **Pradejón** Spain
183 D7 **Pradelles** France
185 J9 **Pradelles-en-Val** France
205 M6 **Prádena** Spain
274 B4 **Pradera** Col.
185 I10 **Prades** *Languedoc-Roussillon* France
185 H10 **Prades** *Midi-Pyrénées* France
183 B7 **Prades-d'Aubrac** France
205 O4 **Pradillo** Spain
185 G7 **Pradines** France
281 H2 **Prado** Brazil
204 D5 **Prado** Port.
205 J3 **Prado de la Guzpeña** Spain
206 H7 **Prado del Rey** Spain
205 N4 **Pradoluengo** Spain
280 C4 **Pradópolis** Brazil
183 I8 **Prads-Haute-Bléone** France
Praeneste Italy *see* **Palestrina**
164 I6 **Præstø** Denmark
212 B5 **Pragelato** Italy
201 M7 **Pragersko** Slovenia
200 F5 **Prägraten** Austria
Prague Czech Rep. *see* **Praha**
198 D1 **Praha** Czech Rep.
193 J10 **Praha** *admin. reg.* Czech Rep.
198 C2 **Praha** *hill* Czech Rep.
184 D3 **Prahecq** France
219 O6 **Prahova** *r.* Romania
Prai Malaysia *see* **Perai**
228 □ **Praia** *Santiago* Cape Verde
238 □1c **Praia, Ilhéu da** *i.* Azores
215 P8 **Praia a Mare** Italy
204 C7 **Praia da Barra** Port.
206 B6 **Praia da Rocha** Port.
204 C8 **Praia da Tocha** Port.
204 C7 **Praia de Esmoriz** Port.
204 C8 **Praia de Mira** Port.
238 □1c **Praia do Almoxarife** *Faial* Azores
235 G5 **Praia do Bilene** Moz.
238 □1c **Praia do Norte** *Faial* Azores
280 D6 **Praia Grande** Brazil
216 H2 **Praiano** Italy
277 G3 **Praia Rica** Brazil
206 B3 **Praias do Sado** Port.
238 □1c **Prainha** *Pico* Azores
277 E1 **Prainha** *Amazonas* Brazil
275 H5 **Prainha** *Pará* Brazil
107 J6 **Prairie** *Qld* Austr.
250 A2 **Prairie** *r. MN* U.S.A.
262 E4 **Prairie City** *OR* U.S.A.
261 E8 **Prairie Dog Town Fork** *r. TX* U.S.A.
250 C6 **Prairie du Chien** *WI* U.S.A.
247 K4 **Prairie River** *Sask.* Can.
117 J8 **Prajekan** *Jawa* Indon.
119 F7 **Prakhon Chai** Thai.
199 J3 **Prakovce** Slovakia
183 J6 **Pralognan-la-Vanoise** France
183 J8 **Pra-Loup** France
161 P8 **Pralyetarskaye** Belarus
201 H3 **Pram** *r.* Austria
220 C3 **Pramanta** Greece
201 I3 **Prambachkirchen** Austria
229 F5 **Prampram** Ghana
119 E8 **Pran** *r.* Thai.
119 D8 **Pran Buri** Thai.
228 E5 **Prang** Ghana
160 I2 **Prangli** *i.* Estonia
136 F3 **Pranhita** *r.* India
201 J5 **Prankerhöhe** *mt.* Austria
138 D8 **Prantij** *Gujarat* India
116 C3 **Prapat** *Sumatera* Indon.
199 H3 **Prašice** Slovakia
151 F1 **Praskoveya** Rus. Fed.
198 G2 **Přáslavice** Czech Rep.
179 J8 **Praslay** France
239 □2a **Praslin** *i. Inner Islands* Seychelles
271 □3 **Praslin Bay** St Lucia
221 I7 **Prasonisi, Akrotirio** *pt Rodos* Greece
165 N2 **Prästfjärden** *b.* Sweden
196 G4 **Praszka** Pol.
283 B8 **Prat** *i.* Chile
280 C3 **Prata** Brazil
280 A3 **Prata** *r.* Brazil
280 C3 **Prata** *r.* Brazil
280 D2 **Prata** *r.* Brazil
213 N4 **Prata di Pordenone** Italy
138 E7 **Pratapgarh** *Rajasthan* India
193 G7 **Pratau** Ger.
208 F6 **Prat de Comte** Spain
Prat de Llobregat Spain *see* **El Prat de Llobregat**
208 G5 **Pratdip** Spain
215 M5 **Pratella** Italy
Prathes Thai *country* Asia *see* **Thailand**
280 D3 **Pratinha** Brazil
213 K8 **Prato** Italy
213 K8 **Prato** *prov.* Italy
213 J2 **Prato allo Stelvio** Italy
215 L3 **Pratola Peligna** Italy
216 H2 **Pratola Serra** Italy
213 L8 **Pratovecchio** Italy
208 J3 **Prats de Lluçanès** Spain
185 I11 **Prats-de-Mollo-la-Preste** France
261 F7 **Pratt** *KS* U.S.A.
212 D1 **Pratteln** Switz.
212 H2 **Prättigau** *reg.* Switz.
255 D9 **Prattville** *AL* U.S.A.
179 J8 **Prauthoy** France
136 D3 **Pravara** *r.* India
219 P7 **Pravda** Bulg.
160 E7 **Pravdinsk** Rus. Fed.
159 L7 **Pravdyne** Ukr.
204 H2 **Pravia** Spain
197 M2 **Pravyya Masty** Belarus
172 E7 **Prawle Point** *England* U.K.
117 L9 **Praya** *Lombok* Indon.
185 G6 **Prayssac** France
185 F7 **Prayssas** France
160 L6 **Prazaroki** Belarus
182 J5 **Praz-sur-Arly** France
119 H8 **Preah, Prêk** *r.* Cambodia
119 G8 **Preăh Vihéar** Cambodia
201 I5 **Prebersee** *l.* Austria
257 I6 **Preble** *NY* U.S.A.
201 L7 **Prebold** Slovenia
185 D7 **Préchac** France
185 C8 **Préchacq-les-Bains** France
161 P6 **Prechistoye** *Smolenskaya Oblast'* Rus. Fed.
156 H4 **Prechistoye** *Yaroslavskaya Oblast'* Rus. Fed.
215 K2 **Preci** Italy
181 K6 **Précigné** France
199 H2 **Prečín** Slovakia
107 M8 **Precipice National Park** *Qld* Austr.
182 E2 **Précy-sous-Thil** France
213 L7 **Predappio** Italy
213 L3 **Predazzo** Italy
219 N5 **Predeal** Romania
201 L6 **Preding** Austria
201 I5 **Predlitz** Austria
201 I8 **Predmeja** Slovenia
212 F6 **Predosa** Italy
247 K5 **Preeceville** *Sask.* Can.
181 K5 **Pré-en-Pail** France
172 G2 **Prees** *Shropshire, England* U.K.
171 L6 **Preesall** *Lancashire, England* U.K.
190 J2 **Preetz** Ger.
180 G7 **Préfailles** France
213 M4 **Preganziòl** Italy
201 K3 **Pregarten** Austria
160 D7 **Pregolya** *r.* Rus. Fed.
208 □ **Pregonda, Cala** *b.* Spain
201 M7 **Pregrada** Croatia
151 C2 **Pregradnaya** Rus. Fed.
185 D6 **Preignac** France
185 F8 **Preignan** France
160 J5 **Preiļi** Latvia
251 P1 **Preissac, Lac** *l. Que.* Can.
201 K6 **Preitenegg** Austria
185 I9 **Preixan** France
219 N5 **Prejmer** Romania
218 H8 **Prekornica** *mts* Montenegro
247 I5 **Prelate** *Sask.* Can.
201 O3 **Prellenkirchen** Austria
201 O7 **Prelog** Croatia
198 E1 **Přelouč** Czech Rep.
213 Q4 **Prem** Slovenia
210 D3 **Premantura** Croatia
105 L4 **Premer** *N.S.W.* Austr.
182 C2 **Prémery** France
212 E3 **Premia** Italy
208 J5 **Premià de Mar** Spain
213 L8 **Premilcuore** Italy
182 B4 **Prémilhat** France
192 F5 **Premnitz** Ger.
178 F4 **Prémontré** France
212 E3 **Premosello Chiovenda** Italy
158 H6 **Prenistrului, Dealurile** *hills* Moldova
210 F4 **Prenj** *mts* Bos.-Herz.
250 D4 **Prentice** *WI* U.S.A.
261 K10 **Prentiss** *MS* U.S.A.
192 I4 **Prenzlau** Ger.
122 H7 **Preobrazheniye** Rus. Fed.
159 N6 **Preobrazhenka** Ukr.
151 E1 **Preobrazhenskoye** Rus. Fed.
119 A7 **Preparis Island** Coco Is
118 A7 **Preparis North Channel** Coco Is
119 A7 **Preparis South Channel** Coco Is
182 D3 **Préporché** France
198 G2 **Přerov** Czech Rep.
192 G2 **Prerow am Darß, Ostseebad** Ger.
204 D9 **Presa** Port.
268 G3 **Presa de Guadalupe** Mex.
267 I3 **Presa de la Amistad, Parque Natural** *nature res.* Mex.
183 E7 **Présailles** France
182 J5 **Pre-St-Didier** Italy
213 J3 **Presanella, Cima** *mt.* Italy
267 I5 **Presa San Antonio** Mex.
Prescelly Mts *hills Wales* U.K. *see* **Preseli, Mynydd**
171 L7 **Prescot** *Merseyside, England* U.K.
248 F4 **Prescott** *Ont.* Can.
261 I9 **Prescott** *AR* U.S.A.
265 T7 **Prescott** *AZ* U.S.A.
250 B5 **Prescott** *WI* U.S.A.
265 T7 **Prescott Valley** *AZ* U.S.A.
172 C4 **Preseli, Mynydd** *hills Wales* U.K.
103 A13 **Preservation Inlet** *South I.* N.Z.
219 J8 **Preševo** *Preševo* Serbia
260 E4 **Presho** *SD* U.S.A.
217 O4 **Presicce** Italy
282 F2 **Presidencia Roca** Arg.
282 E2 **Presidencia Roque Sáenz Peña** Arg.
280 C5 **Presidente Alves** Brazil
280 B5 **Presidente Bernardes** Brazil
282 F2 **Presidente de la Plaza** Arg.
278 D3 **Presidente Dutra** Brazil
280 A4 **Presidente Epitácio** Brazil
277 E2 **Presidente Hermes** Brazil
Presidente Juan Perón *prov.* Arg. *see* **Chaco**
281 E3 **Presidente Juscelino** Brazil
280 D3 **Presidente Olegário** Brazil
280 B5 **Presidente Prudente** Brazil
280 B4 **Presidente Venceslau** Brazil
268 A2 **Presidio** *r.* Mex.
263 L12 **Presidio** *TX* U.S.A.
Preslav Bulg. *see* **Veliki Preslav**
143 L1 **Presnovka** Kazakh.
212 I4 **Presolana, Pizzo della** *mt.* Italy
199 K3 **Prešov** Slovakia
199 K2 **Prešovský kraj** *admin. reg.* Slovakia
220 C2 **Prespa, Lake** Europe
Prespansko Ezero *l.* Europe *see* **Prespa, Lake**
220 C2 **Prespes** *nat. park* Greece
Prespës, Liqeni i *l.* Europe *see* **Prespa, Lake**
257 □Q2 **Presque Isle** *ME* U.S.A.
251 K4 **Presque Isle** *MI* U.S.A.
250 E3 **Presque Isle** *WI* U.S.A.
250 G3 **Presque Isle Point** *MI* U.S.A.
184 F3 **Pressac** France
195 L2 **Pressath** Ger.
201 N3 **Pressbaum** Austria
Pressburg Slovakia *see* **Bratislava**
193 E10 **Presseck** Ger.
201 H6 **Pressegger See** *l.* Austria
193 G7 **Pressel** Ger.
193 D10 **Pressig** Ger.
172 F1 **Prestatyn** *Denbighshire, Wales* U.K.
171 M7 **Prestbury** *Cheshire, England* U.K.
172 H4 **Prestbury** *Gloucestershire, England* U.K.
228 E5 **Prestea** Ghana
164 H3 **Prestebakke** Norway
172 F3 **Presteigne** *Powys, Wales* U.K.
198 C2 **Přeštice** Czech Rep.
172 H6 **Preston** *Dorset, England* U.K.
171 Q6 **Preston** *East Riding of Yorkshire, England* U.K.
171 L6 **Preston** *Lancashire, England* U.K.
168 L11 **Preston** *Scottish Borders, Scotland* U.K.
255 E9 **Preston** *GA* U.S.A.
262 I5 **Preston** *ID* U.S.A.
257 J10 **Preston** *MD* U.S.A.
250 B6 **Preston** *MN* U.S.A.
261 I7 **Preston** *MO* U.S.A.
108 D6 **Preston, Cape** *W.A.* Austr.
171 L2 **Prestonpans** *East Lothian, Scotland* U.K.
256 C11 **Prestonsburg** *KY* U.S.A.
286 N1 **Prestrud Inlet** Antarctica
171 M6 **Prestwich** *Greater Manchester, England* U.K.
168 G12 **Prestwick** *South Ayrshire, Scotland* U.K.
280 B3 **Preto** *r.* Brazil
280 C4 **Preto** *r.* Brazil
280 D2 **Preto** *r.* Brazil
277 E2 **Preto** *r.* Brazil
278 E4 **Preto** *r.* Brazil
275 E5 **Preto** *r.* Brazil
275 F5 **Preto** *r.* Brazil
237 M1 **Pretoria** S. Africa
Pretoria-Witwatersrand-Vereeniging *prov.* S. Africa *see* **Gauteng**
193 G7 **Prettin** Ger.
258 B5 **Prettyboy Lake** *MD* U.S.A.
195 K2 **Pretzfeld** Ger.
192 D5 **Pretzier** Ger.
193 G7 **Pretzsch** Ger.
193 I9 **Pretzschendorf** Ger.
181 M8 **Preuilly-sur-Claise** France
Preussisch-Eylau Rus. Fed. *see* **Bagrationovsk**
191 G6 **Preußisch Oldendorf** Ger.
Preußisch Stargard Pol. *see* **Starogard Gdański**
201 K6 **Prevalje** Slovenia
183 D7 **Prévenchères** France
184 I3 **Préveranges** France
220 B4 **Preveza** Greece
119 G9 **Prey Vêng** Cambodia
201 K7 **Prežganje** Slovenia
213 R4 **Prezid** Croatia
179 J7 **Prez-sous-Lafauche** France
200 D8 **Priaforà, Monte** *mt.* Italy
122 I4 **Priamurskiy** Rus. Fed.
142 J4 **Priaral'skiy Karakum** *des.* Kazakh.
204 G3 **Priaranza del Bierzo** Spain
129 P1 **Priargunsk** Rus. Fed.
159 R8 **Priazovskaya** Rus. Fed.
199 H4 **Pribeta** Slovakia
198 F3 **Přibice** Czech Rep.
244 E4 **Pribilof Islands** *AK* U.S.A.
210 F3 **Pribinić** Bos.-Herz.
201 N7 **Pribislavec** Croatia
218 H7 **Priboj** *Priboj* Serbia
199 H2 **Příbor** Czech Rep.
192 G4 **Priborn** Ger.
198 D2 **Příbram** Czech Rep.
197 I1 **Pribrezhnoye** Rus. Fed.
198 E2 **Přibyslav** Czech Rep.
106 C3 **Price** *r. N.T.* Austr.
249 G3 **Price** *Que.* Can.
256 F12 **Price** *NC* U.S.A.
265 V2 **Price** *UT* U.S.A.
265 V2 **Price** *r. UT* U.S.A.
246 D4 **Price Island** B.C. Can.
160 E6 **Prichaly** Rus. Fed.
261 K10 **Prichard** *AL* U.S.A.
256 C10 **Prichard** *WV* U.S.A.
195 I2 **Prichsenstadt** Ger.
271 □6 **Prickly Point** Grenada
205 P8 **Priego** Spain
207 K6 **Priego de Córdoba** Spain
160 E5 **Priekule** Latvia
160 E6 **Priekulė** Lith.
160 I4 **Priekuļi** Latvia
151 D2 **Priel'brus'ye, Natsional'nyy Park** *nat. park* Rus. Fed.
160 G7 **Prienai** *Kaunas* Lith.
160 I7 **Prienai** *Vilnius* Lith.
195 M6 **Prien am Chiemsee** Ger.
193 I6 **Prieros** Ger.
236 G5 **Prieska** S. Africa
236 G5 **Prieskapoort** *pass* S. Africa
193 G8 **Prießnitz** *Sachsen* Ger.
193 E8 **Prießnitz** *Sachsen-Anhalt* Ger.
193 I8 **Priestewitz** Ger.
Priestholm *i. Wales* U.K. *see* **Puffin Island**
262 F2 **Priest Lake** *ID* U.S.A.
270 □ **Priestman's River** Jamaica
205 K2 **Prieta, Peña** *mt.* Spain
207 J7 **Prieta, Sierra** *mt.* Spain
207 M3 **Prieto** *hill* Spain
198 G3 **Prievaly** Slovakia
199 H3 **Prievidza** Slovakia
192 F4 **Prignitz** *reg.* Ger.
161 Q8 **Prigor'ye** Rus. Fed.
210 F3 **Prijedor** Bos.-Herz.
218 H7 **Prijepolje** *Prijepolje* Serbia
142 A5 **Prikaspiyskaya Nizmennost'** *lowland* Kazakh./Rus. Fed.
228 E5 **Prikro** Côte d'Ivoire
159 R8 **Prikubanskaya Nizmennost'** *lowland* Rus. Fed.
219 J9 **Prilep** Macedonia
Priluki Ukr. *see* **Pryluky**
209 H10 **Prima, Punta** *pt* Spain
276 D2 **Primavera** Bol.
278 B5 **Primavera do Leste** Brazil
198 B2 **Přimda** Czech Rep.
278 E2 **Primeira Cruz** Brazil
180 D4 **Primel, Pointe de** *pt* France
285 F2 **Primero** *r.* Arg.
270 D3 **Primero de Enero** Cuba
199 L2 **Primeval Beech Forests** *tourist site* Slovakia
219 M2 **Primeval Beech Forests** *tourist site* Ukraine
260 H4 **Primghar** *IA* U.S.A.
213 L4 **Primolano** Italy
197 I1 **Primorsk** *Kaliningradskaya Oblast'* Rus. Fed.
160 L1 **Primorsk** *Leningradskaya Oblast'* Rus. Fed.
157 I6 **Primorsk** *Volgogradskaya Oblast'* Rus. Fed.
Primorsk Ukr. *see* **Prymors'k**
122 G7 **Primorskiy** Rus. Fed.
122 I6 **Primorskiy Kray** *admin. div.* Rus. Fed.
157 G7 **Primorsko-Akhtarsk** Rus. Fed.
Primorskoye Ukr. *see* **Prymors'ke**
266 A1 **Primo Tapia** Mex.
245 M3 **Primrose** *r. Y.T.* Can.
247 I4 **Primrose Lake** *Alta/Sask.* Can.
194 B3 **Prims** *r.* Ger.
247 J4 **Prince Albert** *Sask.* Can.
236 G9 **Prince Albert** S. Africa
287 K1 **Prince Albert Mountains** Antarctica
247 J4 **Prince Albert National Park** *Sask.* Can.
242 G2 **Prince Albert Peninsula** *N.W.T.* Can.
236 F8 **Prince Albert Road** S. Africa
242 G2 **Prince Albert Sound** *sea chan. N.W.T.* Can.
242 F2 **Prince Alfred, Cape** *N.W.T.* Can.
236 D9 **Prince Alfred Hamlet** S. Africa
243 K3 **Prince Charles Island** *Nunavut* Can.
287 E2 **Prince Charles Mountains** Antarctica
249 I4 **Prince Edward Island** *prov.* Can.
289 G8 **Prince Edward Islands** Indian Ocean
251 R6 **Prince Edward Point** *Ont.* Can.
256 I10 **Prince Frederick** *MD* U.S.A.
108 H3 **Prince Frederick Harbour** *W.A.* Austr.
246 F4 **Prince George** B.C. Can.
258 B7 **Prince George's County** *county MD* U.S.A.
243 H2 **Prince Gustaf Adolf Sea** *Nunavut* Can.
287 C2 **Prince Harald Coast** Antarctica
244 E2 **Prince of Wales, Cape** *AK* U.S.A.
107 I1 **Prince of Wales Island** *Qld* Austr.
243 I2 **Prince of Wales Island** *Nunavut* Can.
245 N5 **Prince of Wales Island** *AK* U.S.A.
242 G2 **Prince of Wales Strait** *N.W.T.* Can.
242 G2 **Prince Patrick Island** *N.W.T.* Can.
108 H3 **Prince Regent** *r. W.A.* Austr.
243 I2 **Prince Regent Inlet** *sea chan. Nunavut* Can.
108 H3 **Prince Regent Nature Reserve** *W.A.* Austr.
245 O5 **Prince Rupert** B.C. Can.
271 □2 **Prince Rupert Bay** Dominica
173 K4 **Princes Risborough** *Buckinghamshire, England* U.K.
257 J10 **Princess Anne** *MD* U.S.A.
287 A2 **Princess Astrid Coast** Antarctica
107 I3 **Princess Charlotte Bay** *Qld* Austr.
287 B2 **Princess Elisabeth** *research stn* Antarctica
287 F2 **Princess Elizabeth Land** *reg.* Antarctica
247 L1 **Princess Mary Lake** *Nunavut* Can.
108 H3 **Princess May Range** *hills W.A.* Austr.
103 B12 **Princess Mountains** *South I.* N.Z.
287 B2 **Princess Ragnhild Coast** Antarctica
109 F8 **Princess Range** *hills W.A.* Austr.
246 D4 **Princess Royal Island** B.C. Can.
271 □7 **Prince's Town** Trin. and Tob.
173 J3 **Princethorpe** *Warwickshire, England* U.K.
246 F5 **Princeton** B.C. Can.
264 J2 **Princeton** *CA* U.S.A.
250 E8 **Princeton** *IL* U.S.A.
254 D6 **Princeton** *IN* U.S.A.
254 D7 **Princeton** *KY* U.S.A.
257 □R3 **Princeton** *ME* U.S.A.
260 I5 **Princeton** *MO* U.S.A.
258 F4 **Princeton** *NJ* U.S.A.
250 E6 **Princeton** *WI* U.S.A.
256 D11 **Princeton** *WV* U.S.A.
258 F4 **Princeton Junction** *NJ* U.S.A.
172 E6 **Princetown** *Devon, England* U.K.
257 □R3 **Prince William** *N.B.* Can.
104 □2 **Prince William Henry Bay** *Lord Howe I.* Austr.
245 K3 **Prince William Sound** *b. AK* U.S.A.
229 G6 **Príncipe** *i.* São Tomé and Príncipe
245 K2 **Prindle, Mount** *AK* U.S.A.
262 D4 **Prineville** *OR* U.S.A.
220 F2 **Prinos** *Thasos* Greece
186 G5 **Prinsenbeek** Neth.
Prins Harald Kyst *coastal area* Antarctica *see* **Prince Harald Coast**
162 □ **Prins Karls Forland** *i.* Svalbard
159 Q3 **Printsevka** Rus. Fed.
266 □R11 **Prinzapolca** Nic.
190 G5 **Prinzhöfte** Ger.
217 I9 **Priolo Gargallo** *Sicilia* Italy
104 □3 **Prion Lake** S. Pacific Ocean
204 D1 **Prior, Cabo** *c.* Spain
204 D2 **Prioriño Grande, Cabo** *c.* Spain
205 K3 **Prioro** Spain
Priozernyy Kazakh. *see* **Tugyl**
161 N1 **Priozersk** Rus. Fed.
Priozyorsk Rus. Fed. *see* **Priozersk**
158 J2 **Pripet** *r.* Belarus/Ukr. *alt.* **Prypʺyat' (Ukraine)**, *alt.* **Prypyats' (Belarus)**
158 D2 **Pripet Marshes** Belarus/Ukr.
133 K14 **Priphema** *Nagaland* India
156 L2 **Pripolyarnyy Ural** *mts* Rus. Fed.
219 P4 **Priponeşti** Romania
162 U2 **Prirechnyy** Rus. Fed.
219 P3 **Prisăcani** Romania
210 F3 **Priseka** *hill* Croatia
218 J8 **Prishtinë** *Prishtinë* Kosovo
219 M3 **Prislop, Pasul** *pass* Romania
198 E1 **Příšovice** Czech Rep.
184 G2 **Prissac** France
182 F4 **Prissé** France
Pristan' Przheval'sk Kyrg. *see* **Przheval'sk Pristany**
159 P2 **Pristen'** Rus. Fed.
Priština *Prishtinë* Kosovo *see* **Prishtinë**
138 G7 **Prithvipur** *Madh. Prad.* India
195 J5 **Prittriching** Ger.
193 F6 **Pritzerbe** Ger.
192 D4 **Pritzier** Ger.
192 F4 **Pritzwalk** Ger.
183 F7 **Privas** France
215 K5 **Priverno** Italy
210 E3 **Privlaka** Croatia
161 S6 **Privokzal'nyy** Rus. Fed.
159 R7 **Privol'naya** Rus. Fed.
161 Y4 **Privolzhsk** Rus. Fed.
157 I6 **Privolzhskaya Vozvyshennost'** *hills* Rus. Fed.
157 I6 **Privolzhskiy** Rus. Fed.
142 A2 **Privolzhskoye** Rus. Fed.
142 C1 **Privolzh'ye** Rus. Fed.
157 H7 **Priyutnoye** Rus. Fed.
218 I8 **Prizren** *Prizren* Kosovo
216 E8 **Prizzi** *Sicilia* Italy
210 F3 **Prnjavor** Bos.-Herz.
204 H2 **Proaza** Spain
219 K8 **Probištip** Macedonia
117 J8 **Probolinggo** *Jawa* Indon.
190 J2 **Probsteierhagen** Ger.
193 D9 **Probstzella** Ger.
172 C7 **Probus** *Cornwall, England* U.K.
214 H2 **Proceno** Italy
196 E4 **Prochowice** Pol.
215 M6 **Procida** Italy
215 M6 **Procida, Isola di** *i.* Italy
250 B3 **Proctor** *MN* U.S.A.
257 L5 **Proctor** *VT* U.S.A.
256 C10 **Proctorville** *OH* U.S.A.
136 F5 **Proddatur** *Andhra Prad.* India
204 E9 **Proença-a-Nova** Port.
204 F8 **Proença-a-Velha** Port.
193 F8 **Profen** Ger.
275 H3 **Professor van Blommestein Meer** *resr* Suriname
187 G8 **Profondeville** Belgium
213 J5 **Progno** *r.* Italy
285 G2 **Progreso** Arg.
267 I4 **Progreso** *Coahuila* Mex.
269 H5 **Progreso** *Hidalgo* Mex.
269 K9 **Progreso** *Oaxaca* Mex.
267 O7 **Progreso** *Yucatán* Mex.
268 D2 **Progreso** *Zacatecas* Mex.
287 F2 **Progress 2** *research stn* Antarctica
122 F4 **Progress** Rus. Fed.
276 C2 **Progresso** Brazil
192 H2 **Prohn** Ger.
262 C6 **Project City** *CA* U.S.A.
197 I1 **Prokhladnaya** *r.* Rus. Fed.
151 F2 **Prokhladnyy** Rus. Fed.
159 P2 **Prokhorovka** Rus. Fed.
159 L2 **Prokhory** Ukr.
218 H8 **Prokletije** *mts* Albania/Yugo.
220 E4 **Prokopi** Greece
152 J4 **Prokop'yevsk** Rus. Fed.
219 J7 **Prokuplje** *Prokuplje* Serbia
161 O3 **Proletariy** Rus. Fed.
157 H7 **Proletarsk** Rus. Fed.
Proletarskaya Rus. Fed. *see* **Proletarsk**
159 O3 **Proletarskiy** Rus. Fed.
Prome Myanmar *see* **Pyè**
258 E2 **Promised Land Lake** *PA* U.S.A.
277 G4 **Promissão** *Mato Grosso do Sul* Brazil
280 C4 **Promissão** *São Paulo* Brazil
280 C4 **Promissão, Represa** *resr* Brazil
197 I4 **Promna** Pol.
215 P4 **Promontorio del Gargano** … Italy
258 E1 **Prompton** *PA* U.S.A.
258 E1 **Prompton Lake** *PA* U.S.A.
156 H4 **Pronino** Rus. Fed.
191 B10 **Pronsfeld** Ger.
161 W7 **Pronsk** Rus. Fed.
190 J3 **Pronstorf** Ger.
161 O8 **Pronya** *r.* Belarus
246 F3 **Prophet** *r.* B.C. Can.
246 F3 **Prophet River** B.C. Can.
250 E8 **Prophetstown** *IL* U.S.A.
278 F4 **Propriá** Brazil
214 B4 **Propriano** *Corse* France
192 I2 **Prorer Wiek** *b.* Ger.
151 H1 **Prorva** *r.* Rus. Fed.
142 K1 **Proryvnoye** Rus. Fed.
198 F2 **Proseč** Czech Rep.
193 I8 **Prösen** Ger.
201 N6 **Prosenjakovci** Slovenia
168 K9 **Prosen Water** *r. Scotland* U.K.
107 L6 **Proserpine** *Qld* Austr.
Proskurov Ukr. *see* **Khmel'nyts'kyy**
221 G2 **Proskynites** Greece
196 F3 **Prosna** *r.* Pol.
220 E1 **Prosotsani** Greece
259 J1 **Prospect** *CT* U.S.A.
257 J5 **Prospect** *NY* U.S.A.
256 B8 **Prospect** *OH* U.S.A.
262 C5 **Prospect** *OR* U.S.A.
256 E8 **Prospect** *PA* U.S.A.
259 G4 **Prospect Plains** *NJ* U.S.A.
270 □ **Prospect Point** Jamaica
114 E7 **Prosperidad** *Mindanao* Phil.
170 D7 **Prosperous** Ireland
238 □2b **Prosperous Bay** St Helena
262 E3 **Prosser** *WA* U.S.A.
198 G2 **Prostějov** Czech Rep.
197 K2 **Prostki** Pol.
107 M9 **Proston** *Qld* Austr.
159 N8 **Prostorne** Ukr.
156 K2 **Prosunduy** Rus. Fed.
159 O4 **Prosyane** Ukr.
196 F5 **Prószków** Pol.
197 I5 **Proszowice** Pol.
197 I5 **Proszówki** Pol.
236 E10 **Protem** S. Africa
220 C5 **Proti** *i.* Greece
198 F2 **Protivanov** Czech Rep.
198 D2 **Protivín** Czech Rep.
159 Q8 **Protoka** *r.* Rus. Fed.
159 P4 **Protopopivka** Ukr.
158 J3 **Protsiv** Ukr.
161 T6 **Protva** Rus. Fed.
161 U7 **Protva** *r.* Rus. Fed.
161 U7 **Protvino** Rus. Fed.
192 I5 **Prötzel** Ger.
219 P7 **Provadiya** Bulg.
Prøven Greenland *see* **Kangersuatsiaq**
206 B5 **Provença** Port.
183 G10 **Provence** *airport* France
183 I9 **Provence-Alpes-Côte d'Azur** *admin. reg.* France
179 N7 **Provenchères-sur-Fave** France
Providence *MD* U.S.A. *see* **Annapolis**
257 N7 **Providence** *RI* U.S.A.
103 A13 **Providence, Cape** *South I.* N.Z.
244 H4 **Providence, Cape** *AK* U.S.A.
239 □2 **Providence Atoll** Seychelles
251 L4 **Providence Bay** *Ont.* Can.
274 B5 **Providencia** Ecuador
270 C7 **Providencia, Isla de** *i.* Caribbean Sea
277 E2 **Providência, Serra de** *hills* …

G3 **Providenciales Island** Turks and Caicos Is
T3 **Provideniya** Rus. Fed.
I2 **Providential Channel** *Qld* Austr.
O6 **Provincetown** *MA* U.S.A.
C3 **Provincia** Col.
F6 **Provins** France
U1 **Provo** *UT* U.S.A.
I4 **Provost** *Alta* Can.
F4 **Prozor** Bos.-Herz.
U3 **Prozorovo** Rus. Fed.
I9 **Prrenjas** Albania
E4 **Pru** *r.* Ghana
K3 **Prub** *r.* Rus. Fed.
L8 **Prubiynyy, Mys** *pt* Ukr.
K6 **Pruchnik** Pol.
B6 **Prudentópolis** Brazil
N4 **Prudhoe** *Northumberland, England* U.K.
J1 **Prudhoe Bay** *AK* U.S.A.
J1 **Prudhoe Bay** *AK* U.S.A.
L6 **Prudhoe Island** *Qld* Austr.
N8 **Prudi** Ukr.
P7 **Prudki** Rus. Fed.
F5 **Prudnik** Pol.
P3 **Prudyanka** Ukr.
L6 **Prudzinki** Belarus
K3 **Prügy** Hungary
K10 **Průhonice** Czech Rep.
B10 **Prüm** Ger.
B11 **Prüm** *r.* Ger.
I7 **Pruna** Spain
M6 **Prundeni** Romania
O6 **Prundu** Romania
M3 **Prundu Bârgăului** Romania
Prundu Bîrgăului Romania *see* **Prundu Bârgăului**
C3 **Prunelli-di-Fiumorbo** *Corse* France
6 **Prunet** France
7 **Prunières** France
O7 **Pruniers-en-Sologne** France
E9 **Pruntytown** *WV* U.S.A.
Prusa Turkey *see* **Bursa**
O2 **Prušánky** Czech Rep.
Prushkov Pol. *see* **Pruszków**
E4 **Prusice** Pol.
G2 **Prusinovice** Czech Rep.
G2 **Pruszcz** Pol.
O7 **Pruszcz Gdański** Pol.
3 **Pruszków** Pol.
H8 **Prut** *r.* Europe
M6 **Prutting** Ger.
C5 **Prutz** Austria
H9 **Pruzhany** Belarus
W9 **Pruzhinki** Rus. Fed.
H2 **Pružina** Slovakia
8 **Prvačina** Slovenia
E3 **Prvić** *i.* Croatia
O2 **Pryamitsyno** Rus. Fed.
O6 **Pryazovs'ka Vysochyna** *hills* Ukr.
O7 **Pryazovs'ke** Ukr.
L6 **Prychornomors'ka Nyzovyna** *lowland* Ukr.
F2 **Prydz Bay** Antarctica
Q3 **Prykolotne** Ukr.
L3 **Pryluky** Ukr.
P7 **Prymors'k** Ukr.
Prymors'ke *Donets'ka Oblast'* Ukr. *see* **Sartana**
M7 **Prymors'ke** *Khersons'ka Oblast'* Ukr.
8 **Prymors'ke** *Odes'ka Oblast'* Ukr.
O6 **Prymors'ke** *Zaporiz'ka Oblast'* Ukr.
O8 **Prymors'kyy** Ukr.
H7 **Pryor** *OK* U.S.A.
2 **Pryp"yat'** *r.* Ukr. *alt.* **Prypyats' (Belarus),** *conv.* **Pripet**
2 **Pryp"yat' (abandoned)** Ukr.
H1 **Prypyats'** *r.* Belarus *alt.* **Pryp"yat' (Ukraine),** *conv.* **Pripet**
G2 **Prypyatski, Natsyyanal'ny Park** *nature res.* Belarus
6 **Prypyernaye** Belarus
4 **Pryvillya** Ukr.
6 **Pryvil'ne** Ukr.
O8 **Pryvitne** *Respublika Krym* Ukr.
O3 **Pryvitne** *Volyns'ka Oblast'* Ukr.
I5 **Pryyutivka** Ukr.
2 **Przasnysz** Pol.
2 **Przechlewo** Pol.
I5 **Przeciszów** Pol.
5 **Przecław** Pol.
1 **Przedborski Park Krajobrazowy** Pol.
I4 **Przedbórz** Pol.
I3 **Przedecz** Pol.
O2 **Przelewice** Pol.
I3 **Przemęcki Park Krajobrazowy** Pol.
I4 **Przemków** Pol.
1 **Przemsza** *r.* Pol.
6 **Przemyśl** Pol.
1 **Przerośl** Pol.
3 **Przesmyki** Pol.
5 **Przewale** Pol.
4 **Przewłoka** Pol.
5 **Przeworno** Pol.
5 **Przeworsk** Pol.
4 **Przewóz** Pol.
3 **Przeździatka** Pol.
2 **Przezdzięk Wielki** Pol.
I2 **Przezmark** Pol.
Przheval'sk Kyrg. *see* **Karakol**
I7 **Przheval'skogo, Gory** *mts* Rus. Fed.
I6 **Przheval'skoye** Rus. Fed.
6 **Przheval'sk Pristany** Kyrg.
I1 **Przodkowo** Pol.
2 **Przybiernów** Pol.
3 **Przyborowice** Pol.
I3 **Przybranowo** Pol.
4 **Przygodzice** Pol.
4 **Przykona** Pol.
5 **Przyrów** Pol.
Przyrwa *r.* Pol.
5 **Przystajń** Pol.
Przysucha Pol.
3 **Przytoczna** Pol.
4 **Przytoczno** Pol.
2 **Przytuły** Pol.
4 **Przytyk** Pol.
1 **Przywidz** Pol.
4 **Psachna** Greece
Psakhná Greece *see* **Psachna**
6 **Psalidi, Akrotirio** *pt Milos* Greece
4 **Psara** Greece
4 **Psara** *i.* Greece
3 **Psathoura** *i.* Greece
1 **Psebay** Rus. Fed.
2 **Psedakh** Rus. Fed.
1 **Psekups** *r.* Rus. Fed.
Psel *r.* Rus. Fed./Ukr. *see* **Ps'ol**
2 **Pselets** Rus. Fed.
5 **Pserimos** *i.* Greece
9 **Pshada** Rus. Fed.
1 **Pshekha** *r.* Rus. Fed.
8 **Pshenychne** Ukr.
1 **Pshish** *r.* Rus. Fed.
Pskent Uzbek. *see* **Piskent**
2 **P'skhu** Georgia
2 **P'skhus Nakrdzali** *nature res.* Georgia
4 **Pskov** Rus. Fed.
3 **Pskov, Lake** Estonia/Rus. Fed.
4 **Pskova** *r.* Rus. Fed.
Pskov Oblast *admin. div.* Rus. Fed. *see* **Pskovskaya Oblast'**
I4 **Pskovskaya Oblast'** *admin. div.* Rus. Fed.
Pskovskoye Ozero *l.* Estonia/Rus. Fed. *see* **Pskov, Lake**
2 **Ps'ol** *r.* Rus. Fed./Ukr.
3 **Psunj** *mts* Croatia
2 **Psynodakh** Rus. Fed.
3 **Pszczew** Pol.
2 **Pszczewski Park Krajobrazowy** Pol.
1 **Pszczółki** Pol.
4 **Pszczonów** Pol.
6 **Pszczyna** Pol.

161 V8 **Ptan'** *r.* Rus. Fed.
220 D3 **Pteleos** Greece
Ptich' Belarus *see* **Ptsich**
220 C2 **Ptolemaïda** Greece
Ptolemais Israel *see* **'Akko**
158 H1 **Ptsich** Belarus
160 L9 **Ptsich** *r.* Belarus
210 E2 **Ptuj** Slovenia
201 M7 **Ptujsko jezero** *l.* Slovenia
158 E3 **Ptycha** Ukr.
116 E6 **Pu** *r.* Indon.
284 A6 **Púa** Chile
118 E5 **Pua** Thai.
116 □ **Puaka** *hill* Sing.
264 □F14 **Puakō** *HI* U.S.A.
285 F5 **Puán** Arg.
130 E6 **Pu'an** *Guizhou* China
130 E3 **Pu'an** *Sichuan* China
100 □2 **Pu'apu'a** Samoa
100 □2 **Puava, Cape** Samoa
118 I3 **Pubei** *Guangxi* China
182 J4 **Publier** France
274 B6 **Pucacaca** Peru
274 C5 **Pucacuro** Peru
274 C5 **Pucacuro** *r.* Peru
274 B6 **Pucalá** Peru
276 B2 **Pucallpa** Peru
276 D4 **Pucará** Bol.
276 C3 **Pucara** Peru
276 C4 **Pucarani** Bol.
Pucarevo Bos.-Herz. *see* **Novi Travnik**
274 D5 **Puca Urco** Peru
200 H4 **Puch bei Hallein** Austria
201 M4 **Puchberg am Schneeberg** Austria
131 L5 **Pucheng** *Fujian* China
129 K9 **Pucheng** *Shaanxi* China
156 H4 **Puchezh** Rus. Fed.
195 K5 **Puchheim** Ger.
123 E10 **Puch'ŏn** S. Korea
199 H2 **Púchov** Slovakia
284 C2 **Puchuzúh** Arg.
219 N5 **Pucioasa** Romania
114 C6 **Pucio Point** *Panay* Phil.
165 O7 **Puck** Pol.
165 O7 **Pucka, Zatoka** *b.* Pol.
169 F7 **Puckaun** Ireland
109 D8 **Puckford, Mount** *hill W.A.* Austr.
209 E8 **Puçol** Spain
284 B6 **Pucón** Chile
Pudai *watercourse* Afgh. *see* **Dor**
144 F5 **Pūdanū** Iran
162 S4 **Pudasjärvi** Fin.
172 H6 **Puddletown** *Dorset, England* U.K.
191 E9 **Puderbach** Ger.
117 L6 **Pudi** *Kalimantan* Indon.
237 I3 **Pudimoe** S. Africa
130 E5 **Puding** *Guizhou* China
131 M3 **Pudong** *Shanghai* China
121 L5 **Pudong** *airport Shanghai* China
131 M3 **Pudong** *airport* China
156 G3 **Pudozh** Rus. Fed.
171 N6 **Pudsey** *West Yorkshire, England* U.K.
Pudu *Hubei* China *see* **Suizhou**
Puduchcheri *Puducherry* India *see* **Puducherry**
136 F7 **Puducherry** *Puducherry* India
136 F7 **Puducherry** *union terr.* India
136 F7 **Pudukkottai** *Tamil Nadu* India
269 J5 **Puebillo** Mex.
265 Q9 **Puebla** *Baja California* Mex.
269 I6 **Puebla** *Puebla* Mex.
269 I7 **Puebla** *state* Mex.
285 G2 **Puebla Brugo** Arg.
208 D5 **Puebla de Albortón** Spain
207 I3 **Puebla de Alcocer** Spain
208 D4 **Puebla de Alfindén** Spain
205 O9 **Puebla de Almenara** Spain
205 N7 **Puebla de Beleña** Spain
207 O5 **Puebla de Don Fadrique** Spain
207 J2 **Puebla de Don Rodrigo** Spain
206 E5 **Puebla de Guzmán** Spain
206 F3 **Puebla de la Calzada** Spain
206 G3 **Puebla de la Reina** Spain
205 J2 **Puebla de Lillo** Spain
206 G4 **Puebla del Maestre** Spain
207 N3 **Puebla del Príncipe** Spain
206 G3 **Puebla del Prior** Spain
206 F2 **Puebla de Obando** Spain
204 G4 **Puebla de Sanabria** Spain
206 G4 **Puebla de Sancho Pérez** Spain
Puebla de San Julián Spain *see* **A Pobra de San Xiao**
204 H7 **Puebla de Yeltes** Spain
Puebla de Zaragoza Mex. *see* **Puebla**
270 F8 **Pueblito** Col.
263 L7 **Pueblo** *CO* U.S.A.
285 H2 **Pueblo Arrúa** Arg.
282 C2 **Pueblo Hundido** Chile
285 F3 **Pueblo Italiano** Arg.
285 H2 **Pueblo Libertador** Arg.
285 G2 **Pueblo Marini** Arg.
268 B2 **Pueblo Nuevo** Mex.
266 □P11 **Pueblo Nuevo** Nic.
274 E4 **Pueblo Viejo** Col.
269 J3 **Pueblo Viejo, Laguna de** *lag.* Mex.
266 D4 **Pueblo Yaqui** Mex.
183 B8 **Puech del Pal** *mt.* France
185 I7 **Puech de Rouet** *hill* France
284 E6 **Puelches** Arg.
284 D5 **Puelén** Arg.
284 B3 **Puente Alto** Chile
Puenteareas Spain *see* **Ponteareas**
Puente Caldelas Spain *see* **Ponte Caldelas**
205 O2 **Puente Colgante** *tourist site* Spain
268 D4 **Puente de Camotlán** Mex.
204 G4 **Puente de Domingo Flórez** Spain
207 N4 **Puente de Génave** Spain
269 H7 **Puente de Ixtla** Mex.
204 I8 **Puente del Congosto** Spain
284 C3 **Puente del Inca** Arg.
208 G3 **Puente de Montañana** Spain
205 L2 **Puente de San Miguel** Spain
207 J6 **Puente-Genil** Spain
205 Q3 **Puente la Reina** Spain
205 L2 **Puentenansa** Spain
207 J4 **Puente Nuevo, Embalse de** *resr* Spain
207 P5 **Puentes, Embalse de** *resr* Spain
Puentes de García Rodríguez Spain *see* **As Pontes de García Rodríguez**
205 M6 **Puentes Viejas, Embalse de** *resr* Spain
274 D2 **Puente Torres** Venez.
205 M2 **Puente Viesgo** Spain
130 C7 **Pu'er** *Yunnan* China
271 □1 **Puerca, Punta** *pt* Puerto Rico
265 V7 **Puerco** *watercourse AZ* U.S.A.
263 K9 **Puerco** *watercourse NM* U.S.A.
276 C3 **Puerto Acosta** Bol.
283 B7 **Puerto Aisén** Chile
277 E3 **Puerto Alegre** Bol.
276 D3 **Puerto Alejandría** Bol.
274 D5 **Puerto Alfonso** Col.
274 B6 **Puerto America** Peru
267 K10 **Puerto Ángel** Mex.
269 K10 **Puerto Angel** Mex.
277 F6 **Puerto Antequera** Para.
269 N10 **Puerto Arista** Mex.
266 □R13 **Puerto Armuelles** Panama
274 B4 **Puerto Asís** Col.
274 E3 **Puerto Ayacucho** Venez.
274 □ **Puerto Ayora** *Islas Galápagos* Ecuador
283 B7 **Puerto Bajo Pisagua** Chile
274 □ **Puerto Baquerizo Moreno** *Islas Galápagos* Ecuador
266 □O10 **Puerto Barrios** Guat.
285 F6 **Puerto Belgrano** Arg.
282 F2 **Puerto Bermejo** Arg.
274 C3 **Puerto Berrío** Col.
274 C3 **Puerto Boyacá** Col.
274 D2 **Puerto Cabello** Venez.
266 □R10 **Puerto Cabezas** Nic.
266 □R10 **Puerto Cabo Gracias á Dios** Nic.
274 E3 **Puerto Carreño** Col.
277 F5 **Puerto Casado** Para.
276 D3 **Puerto Cavinas** Bol.
274 C5 **Puerto Cerpera** Peru
276 C2 **Puerto Ceticayo** Peru

283 B7 **Puerto Chacabuco** Chile
274 B6 **Puerto Chicama** Peru
283 B7 **Puerto Cisnes** Chile
283 C8 **Puerto Coig** Arg.
270 F8 **Puerto Colombia** Col.
285 H3 **Puerto Constanza** Arg.
274 D5 **Puerto Córdoba** Col.
266 □R13 **Puerto Cortés** Costa Rica
266 □P10 **Puerto Cortés** Hond.
266 D5 **Puerto Cortés** Mex.
274 C4 **Puerto Cuemaní** Col.
274 D2 **Puerto Cumarebo** Venez.
204 I8 **Puerto de Béjar** Spain
Puerto de Cabras *Fuerteventura* Canary Is *see* **Puerto del Rosario**
274 A5 **Puerto de Cayo** Ecuador
276 C3 **Puerto Definitivo** Peru
271 L8 **Puerto de Hierro** Venez.
238 □3b **Puerto de la Cruz** *Fuerteventura* Canary Is
238 □3a **Puerto de la Cruz** *Tenerife* Canary Is
238 □3e **Puerto de la Estaca** *El Hierro* Canary Is
268 G2 **Puerto del Aire** Mex.
238 □3b **Puerto de la Peña** *Fuerteventura* Canary Is
Puerto de la Selva Spain *see* **El Port de la Selva**
238 □3c **Puerto del Carmen** *Lanzarote* Canary Is
268 G8 **Puerto del Gallo** Mex.
269 H3 **Puerto del Higuerón** Mex.
266 C2 **Puerto de Lobos** Mex.
268 B2 **Puerto de Los Ángeles, Parque Natural** *nature res.* Mex.
269 I1 **Puerto de los Ébanos** Mex.
238 □3b **Puerto del Rosario** *Fuerteventura* Canary Is
Puerto del Son *Galicia* Spain *see* **Porto do Son**
209 C12 **Puerto de Mazarrón** Spain
267 P7 **Puerto de Morelos** Mex.
274 D2 **Puerto de Nutrias** Venez.
268 G4 **Puerto de Palmas** Mex.
268 G1 **Puerto de Pastores** Mex.
Puerto de Pollensa Spain *see* **Port de Pollença**
207 I1 **Puerto de San Vicente** Spain
Puerto de Sóller Spain *see* **Port de Sóller**
269 J10 **Puerto Escondido** Mex.
274 D1 **Puerto Estrella** Col.
274 B6 **Puerto Eten** Peru
282 C2 **Puerto Flamenco** Chile
Puerto Francisco de Orellana *Orellana* Ecuador *see* **Coca**
277 E3 **Puerto Frey** Bol.
285 F6 **Puerto Galván** Arg.
276 D3 **Puerto Génova** Bol.
276 D4 **Puerto Grether** Bol.
277 F5 **Puerto Guarani** Para.
283 D9 **Puerto Harberton** Arg.
276 C3 **Puerto Heath** Bol.
274 C4 **Puerto Huitoto** Col.
285 H3 **Puerto Ibicuy** Arg.
276 B2 **Puerto Inca** Peru
283 B7 **Puerto Ingeniero Ibáñez** Chile
285 F6 **Puerto Ingeniero White** Arg.
274 E4 **Puerto Inírida** Col.
282 E1 **Puerto Irigoyen** Arg.
277 F4 **Puerto Isabel** Bol.
266 □Q12 **Puerto Jesús** Costa Rica
267 P7 **Puerto Juáres** Mex.
271 K8 **Puerto La Cruz** Venez.
282 E1 **Puerto La Paz** Arg.
207 M2 **Puerto Lápice** Spain
208 F2 **Puértolas** Spain
274 C5 **Puerto Leguizamo** Col.
266 □R10 **Puerto Lempira** Hond.
266 C3 **Puerto Libertad** Mex.
266 □R12 **Puerto Limón** Costa Rica
207 K3 **Puertollano** Spain
283 D6 **Puerto Lobos** Arg.
274 D2 **Puerto Lopez** Col.
274 C3 **Puerto Lopéz** Col.
274 A5 **Puerto López** Ecuador
207 P5 **Puerto Lumbreras** Spain
267 M10 **Puerto Madero** Mex.
283 D6 **Puerto Madryn** Arg.
266 C5 **Puerto Magdalena** Mex.
276 C3 **Puerto Maldonado** Peru
276 D4 **Puerto Mamoré** Bol.
270 E3 **Puerto Manatí** Cuba
274 A6 **Puerto Máncora** Peru
277 F5 **Puerto María Auxiliadora** Para.
Puertomarín Spain *see* **Portomarín**
276 D3 **Puerto Marquez** Bol.
283 B6 **Puerto Melinka** Chile
274 C4 **Puerto Mercedes** Col.
Puerto México Mex. *see* **Coatzacoalcos**
277 F5 **Puerto Mihanovich** Para.
209 E7 **Puertomingalvo** Spain
274 E3 **Puerto Miranda** Venez.
283 B6 **Puerto Montt** Chile
266 □P11 **Puerto Morazán** Nic.
274 B7 **Puerto Morín** Peru
238 □3d **Puerto Naos** *La Palma* Canary Is
283 B8 **Puerto Natales** Chile
274 D3 **Puerto Nuevo** Col.
274 C3 **Puerto Olaya** Col.
275 F2 **Puerto Ordaz** Venez.
274 C4 **Puerto Ospina** Col.
270 E3 **Puerto Padre** Cuba
274 E3 **Puerto Páez** Venez.
276 D3 **Puerto Pando** Bol.
274 B5 **Puerto Pardo** Peru
276 C3 **Puerto Pariamanu** Peru
266 C2 **Puerto Peñasco** Mex.
277 F5 **Puerto Pinasco** Para.
283 D6 **Puerto Pirámides** Arg.
275 E2 **Puerto Píritu** Venez.
274 C5 **Puerto Pizarro** Col.
270 H4 **Puerto Plata** Dom. Rep.
276 B2 **Puerto Portillo** Peru
276 B2 **Puerto Prado** Peru
Puerto Presidente Stroessner Para. *see* **Ciudad del Este**
114 B7 **Puerto Princesa** *Palawan* Phil.
266 □Q13 **Puerto Quepos** Costa Rica
266 N11 **Puerto Quetzal** Guat.
267 N8 **Puerto Real** Mex.
206 G7 **Puerto Real** Spain
282 G2 **Puerto Rico** Arg.
276 D2 **Puerto Rico** Bol.
238 □3f **Puerto Rico** *Gran Canaria* Canary Is
274 C4 **Puerto Rico** Col.
271 □1 **Puerto Rico** *terr.* West Indies
288 E4 **Puerto Rico Trench** *sea feature* Caribbean Sea
285 H3 **Puerto Ruiz** Arg.
283 B5 **Puerto Saavedra** Chile
274 C3 **Puerto Salgar** Col.
Puerto Sama Cuba *see* **Samá**
274 D5 **Puerto San Agustín** Peru
283 B7 **Puerto San Carlos** Chile
266 □P11 **Puerto Sandino** Nic.
267 N11 **Puerto San José** Guat.
283 C8 **Puerto Santa Cruz** Arg.
277 F5 **Puerto Sastre** Para.
277 E3 **Puerto Saucedo** Bol.
Puertos de Beceite *mts* Spain *see* **Ports de Beseit**
204 G7 **Puerto Seguro** Spain
206 H7 **Puerto Serrano** Spain
276 D3 **Puerto Siles** Bol.
274 D5 **Puerto Socorro** Peru
Puerto Somoza Nic. *see* **Puerto Sandino**
277 F4 **Puerto Suárez** Bol.
276 A2 **Puerto Supe** Peru
276 C3 **Puerto Tahuantisuyo** Peru
274 B4 **Puerto Tejado** Col.
274 B5 **Puerto Tunigrama** Peru
274 B4 **Puerto Umbría** Col.
283 E6 **Puerto Valdés** Arg.
268 B5 **Puerto Vallarta** Mex.
283 B6 **Puerto Varas** Chile
274 □ **Puerto Velasco Ibarra** *Islas Galápagos* Ecuador
276 B2 **Puerto Victoria** Peru

274 □ **Puerto Villamil** *Islas Galápagos* Ecuador
277 E3 **Puerto Villazon** Bol.
283 D7 **Puerto Visser** Arg.
274 C3 **Puerto Wilches** Col.
283 D9 **Puerto Williams** *Magallanes* Chile
283 C9 **Puerto Yartou** Chile
285 H2 **Puerto Yerua** Arg.
274 C5 **Puesto Arturo** Peru
284 D6 **Puesto Sánchez** Arg.
101 □9a **Pueu** *Tahiti* Fr. Polynesia
205 Q3 **Pueyo** Spain
213 L2 **Puez-Odle, Parco Naturale** *nature res.* Italy
172 D1 **Puffin Island** *Wales* U.K.
277 F4 **Puga** Brazil
142 C1 **Pugachev** Rus. Fed.
156 K4 **Pugachevo** Rus. Fed.
138 D5 **Pugal** *Rajasthan* India
233 C8 **Puga Puga, Ilha** *i.* Moz.
130 D5 **Puge** *Sichuan* China
117 J9 **Puger** *Jawa* Indon.
183 J10 **Puget-sur-Argens** France
183 J9 **Puget-Théniers** France
183 I10 **Puget-Ville** France
258 D4 **Pughtown** *PA* U.S.A.
215 P5 **Puglia** *admin. reg.* Italy
215 I2 **Puglia** *r.* Italy
184 C5 **Pugnac** France
215 Q4 **Pugnochiuso** Italy
249 I4 **Pugwash** *N.S.* Can.
102 L5 **Puha** *North I.* N.Z.
144 F8 **Pūhāl-e Khamīr, Kūh-e** *mts* Iran
129 J9 **Pu He** *r.* China
Puhiwaero *c. Stewart I.* N.Z. *see* **South West Cape**
160 J3 **Puhja** Estonia
219 L5 **Pui** Romania
183 B10 **Puichéric** France
219 P5 **Puiești** Romania
209 E8 **Puig** Spain
208 I3 **Puigcerdà** Spain
208 J3 **Puigmal** *mt.* France/Spain
208 I4 **Puig-reig** Spain
208 G4 **Puigverd de Lleida** Spain
183 I9 **Puimoisson** France
131 □I7 **Pui O Wan** *b. H.K.* China
182 B2 **Puisaye** *reg.* France
178 D7 **Puiseaux** France
178 E3 **Puisieux** France
185 D6 **Puisseguin** France
183 C10 **Puisserguier** France
178 H6 **Puits** *r.* France
224 C6 **Puits 29** *well* Chad
224 C6 **Puits 30** *well* Chad
185 I10 **Puivert** France
114 F8 **Pujada Bay** *Mindanao* Phil.
183 F8 **Pujaut** France
228 C5 **Pujehun** Sierra Leone
Puji *Shaanxi* China *see* **Wugong**
131 L4 **Pujiang** *Zhejiang* China
185 E9 **Pujo** France
185 D6 **Pujols** *Aquitaine* France
185 F7 **Pujols** *Aquitaine* France
103 E11 **Pukaki, Lake** *South I.* N.Z.
199 H3 **Pukanec** Slovakia
123 E10 **Puk'an-san National Park** S. Korea
103 □2 **Pukapuka** *atoll* Cook Is
101 □9 **Pukapuka** *atoll Arch. des Tuamotu* Fr. Polynesia
101 □9 **Pukarua** *atoll Arch. des Tuamotu* Fr. Polynesia
250 I1 **Pukaskwa** *r. Ont.* Can.
248 C3 **Pukaskwa National Park** *Ont.* Can.
247 K4 **Pukatawagan** *Man.* Can.
123 D8 **Pukchin** N. Korea
123 F8 **Pukch'ŏng** N. Korea
218 H8 **Pukë** Albania
102 M4 **Pukeamaru** *hill North I.* N.Z.
102 I5 **Pukearuhe** *North I.* N.Z.
102 K6 **Pukehoi** *North I.* N.Z.
102 I4 **Pukekohe** *North I.* N.Z.
102 H1 **Pukenui** *North I.* N.Z.
102 J6 **Pukeokahu** *North I.* N.Z.
103 E12 **Pukerangi** *South I.* N.Z.
103 D13 **Pukerau** *South I.* N.Z.
102 J6 **Pukeroa** *North I.* N.Z.
103 I8 **Pukerua Bay** *North I.* N.Z.
103 G10 **Puketeraki Range** *mts South I.* N.Z.
102 K6 **Puketitiri** *North I.* N.Z.
102 L4 **Puketoetoe** *mt. North I.* N.Z.
102 K7 **Puketoi Range** *hills North I.* N.Z.
102 J5 **Puketutu** *North I.* N.Z.
103 F12 **Pukeuri Junction** *South I.* N.Z.
161 O6 **Pukhnovo** Rus. Fed.
159 S3 **Pukhovo** Rus. Fed.
163 R6 **Pukkila** Fin.
156 K4 **Puksib** Rus. Fed.
156 H3 **Puksoozero** Rus. Fed.
123 E8 **Puksubaek-san** *mt.* N. Korea
210 D3 **Pula** Croatia
213 P6 **Pula** *airport* Croatia
214 C9 **Pula** *Sardegna* Italy
214 C10 **Pula, Capo di** *c. Sardegna* Italy
276 D5 **Pulacayo** Bol.
129 R7 **Pulandian** *Liaoning* China
129 Q7 **Pulandian Wan** *b.* China
114 E8 **Pulangi** *r. Mindanao* Phil.
117 K6 **Pulangpisau** *Kalimantan* Indon.
113 K5 **Pulap** *atoll* Micronesia
276 C6 **Pular, Cerro** *mt.* Chile
115 B7 **Pulasi** *i.* Indon.
257 I5 **Pulaski** *NY* U.S.A.
255 D8 **Pulaski** *TN* U.S.A.
256 E11 **Pulaski** *VA* U.S.A.
250 F5 **Pulaski** *WI* U.S.A.
113 I8 **Pulau** *r. Papua* Indon.
116 E5 **Pulaukijang** *Sumatera* Indon.
117 J4 **Pulaumajang** *Kalimantan* Indon.
Pulau Pinang *state* Malaysia *see* **Pinang**
197 J4 **Puławy** Pol.
173 K6 **Pulborough** *West Sussex, England* U.K.
213 O3 **Pulfero** Italy
138 G9 **Pulgaon** *Mahar.* India
205 L9 **Pulgar** Spain
191 C8 **Pulheim** Ger.
136 G6 **Pulicat** *Tamil Nadu* India
136 G6 **Pulicat Lake** *inlet* India
182 F3 **Puligny-Montrachet** France
136 F5 **Pulivendla** *Andhra Prad.* India
162 R2 **Pulju** Fin.
201 M2 **Pulkau** Austria
201 N2 **Pulkau** *r.* Austria
162 R4 **Pulkkila** Fin.
195 L5 **Pullach in Isartal** Ger.
262 F3 **Pullman** *WA* U.S.A.
276 B3 **Pullo** Peru
114 C3 **Pulog, Mount** *Luzon* Phil.
162 V2 **Pulozero** Rus. Fed.
207 P6 **Pulpí** Spain
266 D4 **Púlpito, Punta** *pt* Mex.
217 M3 **Pulsano** Italy
193 H8 **Pulsen** Ger.
193 J8 **Pulsnitz** Ger.
193 I8 **Pulsnitz** *r.* Ger.
197 J3 **Pułtusk** Pol.
133 E8 **Pulu** *Xinjiang* China
149 I4 **Pülümür** Turkey
113 K5 **Pulusuk** *atoll* Micronesia
115 E1 **Pulutan** *Sulawesi* Indon.
113 K5 **Puluwat** *atoll* Micronesia
179 N8 **Pulversheim** France
138 E3 **Pulwama** *Jammu and Kashmir* India
233 B6 **Puma** Tanz.
283 B6 **Pumalin, Parque** *nat. park* Chile
284 B4 **Pumanque** Chile
133 J12 **Puma Yumco** *l.* China
Pumiao *Guangxi* China *see* **Yongning**
262 L3 **Pumpkin Creek** *r. MT* U.S.A.
172 E3 **Pumsaint** *Carmarthenshire, Wales* U.K.
282 E2 **Puna** Arg.
274 A5 **Puná, Isla** *i.* Ecuador
101 □9a **Punaauia** *Tahiti* Fr. Polynesia
101 □9a **Punaauia, Pointe** *pt Tahiti* Fr. Polynesia
103 F9 **Punakaiki** *South I.* N.Z.

139 L6 **Punakha** Bhutan
264 □F14 **Punalu'u** *HI* U.S.A.
101 □9a **Punaruu** *r. Tahiti* Fr. Polynesia
213 R5 **Punat** Croatia
276 D4 **Punata** Bol.
145 P5 **Punch** Pak.
246 F4 **Punchaw** *B.C.* Can.
235 F4 **Punda Maria** S. Africa
138 F5 **Pundri** *Haryana* India
136 C3 **Pune** *Mahar.* India
136 F6 **Punganuru** *Andhra Prad.* India
116 □ **Punggol** Sing.
116 □ **Punggol, Sungai** *r.* Sing.
231 B7 **Pungo Andango** Angola
123 F8 **P'ungsan** N. Korea
235 G3 **Púnguè** *r.* Moz.
213 J2 **Puni** *r.* Italy
230 E5 **Punia** Dem. Rep. Congo
197 M1 **Punia** Lith.
282 C3 **Punilla, Cordillera de la** *mts* Chile
131 K7 **Puning** *Guangdong* China
284 B2 **Punitaqui** Chile
138 E4 **Punjab** *state* India
145 N6 **Punjab** *prov.* Pak.
163 T6 **Punkaharju** Fin.
138 F2 **Punmah Glacier** Pak.
276 C3 **Puno** Peru
276 C3 **Puno** *dept* Peru
139 J7 **Punpun** *r.* India
197 L1 **Puńsk** Pol.
271 □1 **Punta, Cerro de** *mt.* Puerto Rico
214 F2 **Punta Ala** Italy
285 F6 **Punta Alta** Arg.
283 C9 **Punta Arenas** Chile
274 D2 **Punta Cardón** Venez.
276 C4 **Punta de Bombón** Peru
282 C3 **Punta de Díaz** Chile
284 C4 **Punta del Agua** Arg.
282 G4 **Punta del Este** Uru.
283 E6 **Punta Delgada** Arg.
284 D2 **Punta de los Llanos** Arg.
268 B5 **Punta de Mita** Mex.
284 C3 **Punta de Vacas** Arg.
266 □O9 **Punta Gorda** Belize
238 □3d **Puntagorda** *La Palma* Canary Is
266 □R12 **Punta Gorda** Nic.
255 F12 **Punta Gorda** *FL* U.S.A.
285 I4 **Punta Indio** Arg.
213 Q6 **Punta Križa** Croatia
238 □3d **Puntallana** *La Palma* Canary Is
284 D4 **Puntana, Travesía** *des.* Arg.
276 C6 **Punta Negra, Salar** *salt flat* Chile
283 E6 **Punta Norte** Arg.
266 B3 **Punta Prieta** Mex.
266 □Q12 **Puntarenas** Costa Rica
213 M5 **Punta Sabbioni** Italy
271 □1 **Punta Santiago** Puerto Rico
276 D5 **Puntas Negras, Cerro** *mt.* Chile
206 F6 **Punta Umbría** Spain
269 K5 **Puntilla Aldama** Mex.
232 F3 **Puntland** *physical area* Somalia
274 D2 **Punto Fijo** Venez.
208 E3 **Puntón de Guara** *mt.* Spain
244 E3 **Punuk Islands** *AK* U.S.A.
256 G8 **Punxsutawney** *PA* U.S.A.
162 S4 **Puokio** Fin.
162 S4 **Puolanka** Fin.
162 P3 **Puoltikasvaara** Sweden
Puqi *Hubei* China *see* **Chibi**
276 B3 **Puquio** Peru
276 C4 **Puquios** Chile
152 I3 **Pur** *r.* Rus. Fed.
274 B4 **Puracé, Parque Nacional** *nat. park* Col.
136 D3 **Purandhar** *Mahar.* India
138 H5 **Puranpur** *Uttar Prad.* India
113 J8 **Purari** *r.* P.N.G.
201 O4 **Purbach am Neusiedler See** Austria
117 H8 **Purbalingga** *Jawa* Indon.
172 H6 **Purbeck, Isle of** *pen. England* U.K.
261 G8 **Purcell** *OK* U.S.A.
244 H2 **Purcell Mountain** *AK* U.S.A.
246 G5 **Purcell Mountains** *B.C.* Can.
256 H9 **Purcellville** *VA* U.S.A.
207 O6 **Purchena** Spain
207 L6 **Purchil** Spain
133 E9 **Pur Co** *l.* China
104 E4 **Pureba Conservation Park** *nature res. S.A.* Austr.
160 I2 **Purekkari neem** *pt* Estonia
282 B5 **Purén** Chile
102 J5 **Pureora Forest Park** *nature res. North I.* N.Z.
268 E6 **Purépero** Mex.
173 M5 **Purfleet** *Thurrock, England* U.K.
133 G10 **Purgadala** *Xizang* China
261 D6 **Purgatoire** *r. CO* U.S.A.
195 J5 **Pürgen** Ger.
201 L3 **Purgstall an der Erlauf** Austria
231 B6 **Puri** Angola
137 I3 **Puri** *Orissa* India
268 C6 **Purificación** Mex.
269 I2 **Purificación** *r.* Mex.
172 G5 **Puriton** *Somerset, England* U.K.
201 N3 **Purkersdorf** Austria
173 L5 **Purley** *Greater London, England* U.K.
173 J5 **Purley on Thames** *West Berkshire, England* U.K.
186 G3 **Purmerend** Neth.
136 E3 **Purna** *Mahar.* India
136 E3 **Purna** *r. Mahar.* India
138 F9 **Purna** *r. Mahar.* India
139 L7 **Purnabhaba** *r.* India
136 C4 **Purnagad** *Mahar.* India
104 C2 **Purndu Saltpan** *salt flat S.A.* Austr.
Purnea *Bihar* India *see* **Purnia**
139 K7 **Purnia** *Bihar* India
108 J4 **Purnululu National Park** *W.A.* Austr.
283 B6 **Purranque** Chile
Pursat Cambodia *see* **Poŭthĭsăt**
173 I4 **Purton** *Wiltshire, England* U.K.
243 K3 **Purtuniq** *Que.* Can.
268 F5 **Puruandíro** Mex.
268 F6 **Puruarán** Mex.
274 D5 **Puruê** *r.* Brazil
205 Q5 **Purujosa** Spain
117 K5 **Purukcahu** *Kalimantan* Indon.
139 K8 **Puruliya** *W. Bengal* India
207 M6 **Purullena** Spain
275 F5 **Purus** *r.* Peru
163 T6 **Puruvesi** *l.* Fin.
261 K10 **Purvis** *MS* U.S.A.
219 N8 **Pŭrvomay** Bulg.
138 H6 **Purwa** *Uttar Prad.* India
116 G8 **Purwakarta** *Jawa* Indon.
117 I8 **Purwareja** *Jawa* Indon.
117 I8 **Purwodadi** *Jawa* Indon.
117 H8 **Purwokerto** *Jawa* Indon.
123 F7 **Puryŏng** N. Korea
136 E3 **Pus** *r.* India
139 J7 **Pusa** *Bihar* India
160 K5 **Puša** Latvia
117 I4 **Pusa** *Sarawak* Malaysia
205 K9 **Pusa** *r.* Spain
136 E3 **Pusad** *Mahar.* India
123 F11 **Pusan** S. Korea
114 F8 **Pusan Point** *Mindanao* Phil.
117 I4 **Pusatdamai** *Kalimantan* Indon.
195 J2 **Puschendorf** Ger.
193 J8 **Puschwitz** Ger.
257 □Q4 **Pushaw Lake** *ME* U.S.A.
158 J3 **Pushcha-Vodytsya** Ukr.
161 U7 **Pushchino** Rus. Fed.
156 I3 **Pushemskiy** Rus. Fed.
138 E6 **Pushkar** *Rajasthan* India
161 N2 **Pushkin** Rus. Fed.
Pushkino Azer. *see* **Biläsuvar**
142 B2 **Pushkino** Rus. Fed.
122 M5 **Pushkinskaya, Gora** *mt. Sakhalin* Rus. Fed.
160 L4 **Pushkinskiye Gory** Rus. Fed.
208 D3 **Pusilibro** *mt.* Spain
199 K4 **Püspökladány** Hungary
160 K2 **Püssi** Estonia
199 H2 **Pustá Polom** Czech Rep.
213 L2 **Pusteria, Val** *val.* Italy
200 F6 **Pustertal** *val.* Austria
201 J5 **Pusterwald** Austria

199 G3 **Pusté Úľany** Slovakia
218 G8 **Pusti Lisac** *mt.* Montenegro
198 G2 **Pustiměř** Czech Rep.
158 C4 **Pustomyty** Ukr.
160 M5 **Pustoshka** Rus. Fed.
158 J4 **Pustovity** Ukr.
160 G1 **Pusula** Fin.
139 L9 **Pusur** *r.* Bangl.
197 I4 **Puszcza Mariańska** Pol.
189 K2 **Puszczy Knyszyńskiej, Park Krajobrazowy** Pol.
196 E3 **Puszczykowo** Pol.
199 M1 **Puszczy Solskiej, Park Krajobrazowy** Pol.
199 J4 **Pusztakocsi mocsarak** *nature res.* Hungary
199 G5 **Pusztakovácsi** Hungary
199 I5 **Pusztamérges** Hungary
199 I4 **Pusztamonostor** Hungary
199 H4 **Pusztaszabolcs** Hungary
199 I5 **Pusztaszer** Hungary
199 J5 **Pusztaszeri** *park* Hungary
199 I4 **Pusztavacs** Hungary
199 H4 **Pusztavám** Hungary
284 B3 **Putaendo** Chile
247 K3 **Putahow Lake** *Man.* Can.
115 D8 **Putain** *Timor* Indon.
181 K4 **Putanges-Pont-Écrepin** France
118 C1 **Putao** Myanmar
102 J5 **Putaruru** *North I.* N.Z.
192 H2 **Putbus** Ger.
Puteoli Italy *see* **Pozzuoli**
117 K8 **Puteran** *i.* Indon.
102 L5 **Putere** *North I.* N.Z.
156 L2 **Puteyets** Rus. Fed.
144 I8 **Puthak** Iran
Puthein Myanmar *see* **Bassein**
131 L6 **Putian** *Fujian* China
214 A6 **Putifigari** *Sardegna* Italy
217 M2 **Putignano** Italy
156 I4 **Putilovo** Rus. Fed.
161 T9 **Putimets** Rus. Fed.
276 C3 **Putina** Peru
Puting *Jiangxi* China *see* **De'an**
117 I6 **Puting, Tanjung** *pt* Indon.
143 U3 **Putintsevo** Kazakh.
269 J8 **Putla** Mex.
145 L6 **Putla Khan** Afgh.
192 F4 **Putlitz** Ger.
219 O5 **Putna** *r.* Romania
257 N7 **Putnam** *CT* U.S.A.
259 H2 **Putnam County** *county NY* U.S.A.
259 H2 **Putnam Valley** *NY* U.S.A.
257 M6 **Putney** *VT* U.S.A.
199 J3 **Putnok** Hungary
130 B4 **Pütog** *Xizang* China
Putoi *i. H.K.* China *see* **Po Toi**
153 K3 **Putorana, Gory** *mts* Rus. Fed.
116 D3 **Putrajaya** Malaysia
276 C4 **Putre** Chile
236 F5 **Putsonderwater** S. Africa
136 F8 **Puttalam** Sri Lanka
136 F8 **Puttalam Lagoon** Sri Lanka
187 G6 **Putte** Belgium
187 F6 **Putte** Neth.
179 M5 **Puttelange-aux-Lacs** France
186 I4 **Putten** Neth.
192 D1 **Puttgarden** Ger.
194 B3 **Püttlingen** Ger.
136 D6 **Puttur** *Karnataka* India
284 A4 **Putú** Chile
231 C6 **Putubumba** Dem. Rep. Congo
274 C4 **Putumayo** *dept* Col.
274 D5 **Putumayo** *r.* Col.
123 C14 **Putuo** *Zhejiang* China
148 I4 **Pütürge** Turkey
117 J4 **Putusibau** *Kalimantan* Indon.
157 H5 **Putyatino** Rus. Fed.
158 E6 **Putyla** Ukr.
158 H2 **Putylovychi** Ukr.
159 M2 **Putyvl'** Ukr.
192 I3 **Putzar** Ger.
193 J8 **Putzkau** Ger.
264 □F14 **Pu'uanahulu** *HI* U.S.A.
264 □E13 **Pu'ukoli'i** *HI* U.S.A.
163 S6 **Puula** *l.* Fin.
163 T6 **Puumala** Fin.
187 F6 **Puurs** Belgium
264 □A12 **Pu'uwai** *HI* U.S.A.
243 K3 **Puvirnituq** *Que.* Can.
129 L8 **Puxian** *Shanxi* China
262 C3 **Puyallup** *WA* U.S.A.
129 N9 **Puyang** *Henan* China
Puyang *Zhejiang* China *see* **Pujiang**
185 H6 **Puybrun** France
185 F8 **Puycasquier** France
181 J8 **Puy Crapaud** *hill* France
182 C5 **Puy-de-Dôme** *dept* France
182 B5 **Puy de Dôme** *mt.* France
185 H9 **Puy de Faucher** *hill* France
183 G7 **Puy de la Gagère** *mt.* France
182 D5 **Puy de Montoncel** *mt.* France
182 B5 **Puy de Sancy** *mt.* France
184 H3 **Puy des Trois-Cornes** *hill* France
283 C6 **Puyehue, Parque Nacional** *nat. park* Chile
283 C6 **Puyel** Arg.
185 I8 **Puygouzon** France
183 B6 **Puy Griou** *mt.* France
183 I6 **Puy Gris** *mt.* France
182 C5 **Puy-Guillaume** France
185 H7 **Puylaroque** France
185 I8 **Puylaurens** France
185 G6 **Puy-l'Évêque** France
183 B6 **Puy Mary** *mt.* France
185 F9 **Puymaurin** France
185 F7 **Puymirol** France
185 H10 **Puymorens, Col de** *pass* France
184 E4 **Puymoyen** France
274 B5 **Puyo** Ecuador
185 C8 **Puyôo** France
183 I7 **Puy-St-Vincent** France
103 A13 **Puysegur Point** *South I.* N.Z.
145 I6 **Puzak, Hāmūn-e** *marsh* Afgh.
156 K3 **Puzla** Rus. Fed.
Puzol *Valencia* Spain *see* **Puçol**
233 C6 **Pwani** *admin. reg.* Tanz.
100 □4b **Pwel Weite** *Pohnpei* Micronesia
231 F7 **Pweto** Dem. Rep. Congo
172 D2 **Pwllheli** *Gwynedd, Wales* U.K.
100 □4b **Pwok** *Pohnpei* Micronesia
156 G2 **Pyalitsa** Rus. Fed.
156 F3 **Pyal'ma** Rus. Fed.
118 B5 **Pyalo** Myanmar
118 B7 **Pyamalaw** *r.* Myanmar
Pyandzh *r.* Afgh./Tajik. *see* **Panj**
Pyandzh *Khatlon* Tajik. *see* **Dŭstí**
Pyandzh *Khatlon* Tajik. *see* **Panj**
Pyanskiy Perevoz Rus. Fed. *see* **Perevoz**
156 L3 **Pyanteg** Rus. Fed.
162 U3 **Pyaozero, Ozero** *l.* Rus. Fed.
162 U4 **Pyaozerskiy** Rus. Fed.
118 B6 **Pyapon** Myanmar
152 J2 **Pyasina** *r.* Rus. Fed.
152 J3 **Pyasino, Ozero** *l.* Rus. Fed.
152 J2 **Pyasinskiy Zaliv** *b.* Rus. Fed.
160 H8 **Pyaski** Belarus
160 K8 **Pyasochnaye** Belarus
219 M8 **Pyasŭchnik** *r.* Bulg.
197 I1 **Pyatidorozhnoye** Rus. Fed.
151 E1 **Pyatigorsk** Rus. Fed.
Pyatikhatka Ukr. *see* **P"yatykhatka**
Pyatikhatki Ukr. *see* **P"yatykhatky**
Pyatimar Kazakh. *see* **Pyatimarskoye**
142 D3 **Pyatimarskoye** Kazakh.
161 N1 **Pyatirech'ye** Rus. Fed.
158 H3 **P"yatka** Ukr.
159 Q3 **Pyatnitskoye** Rus. Fed.
161 T7 **Pyatovskiy** Rus. Fed.
159 N8 **P"yatykhatka** Ukr.
159 M5 **P"yatykhatky** Ukr.
118 C5 **Pyaunglaung** *r.* Myanmar
118 C4 **Pyawbwe** Myanmar
161 S1 **Pyazhelka** Rus. Fed.
161 S1 **Pyazhozero, Ozero** *l.* Rus. Fed.
156 K4 **Pychas** Rus. Fed.
118 B5 **Pyè** Myanmar
103 D13 **Pye, Mount** *hill South I.* N.Z.
245 J4 **Pye Islands** *AK* U.S.A.
197 L3 **Pyelishcha** Belarus
160 I8 **Pyershamayski** Belarus

102 K4 **Pyes Pa** *North I.* N.Z.
158 H1 **Pyetrykaw** Belarus
160 G1 **Pyhäjärvi** *l.* Fin.
163 Q6 **Pyhäjärvi** *l.* Fin.
162 R5 **Pyhäjärvi** *l.* Fin.
162 R5 **Pyhäjärvi** *l.* Fin.
163 S6 **Pyhäjärvi** *l.* Fin.
163 U6 **Pyhäjärvi** *l.* Fin.
162 R4 **Pyhäjoki** Fin.
162 R4 **Pyhäjoki** *r.* Fin.
162 S3 **Pyhä-Louston kansallispuisto** *nat. park* Fin.
160 K1 **Pyhältö** Fin.
162 S4 **Pyhäntä** Fin.
163 P6 **Pyhäranta** Fin.
162 R5 **Pyhäsalmi** Fin.
162 T5 **Pyhäselkä** Fin.
162 T5 **Pyhäselkä** *l.* Fin.
201 M3 **Pyhra** Austria
163 S6 **Pyhtää** Fin.
Pyin Myanmar *see* **Pyè**
118 B3 **Pyingaing** Myanmar
118 C5 **Pyinmana** Myanmar
118 C3 **Pyin-U-Lwin** Myanmar
185 B6 **Pyla-sur-Mer** France
172 E4 **Pyle** *Bridgend, Wales* U.K.
221 I6 **Pyli** *Kos* Greece
220 C3 **Pyli** *Thessalia* Greece
152 J3 **Pyl'karamo** Rus. Fed.
162 R5 **Pylkönmäki** Fin.
220 C6 **Pylos** Greece
158 G3 **Pylypovychi** Ukr.
256 E7 **Pymatuning Reservoir** *PA* U.S.A.
123 D9 **Pyŏksŏng** N. Korea
123 D8 **Pyŏktong** N. Korea
123 E9 **P'yŏnggang** N. Korea
123 E9 **P'yŏngsan** N. Korea
123 D9 **P'yŏngsong** N. Korea
123 E10 **P'yŏngt'aek** S. Korea
123 D9 **P'yŏngyang** N. Korea
123 E11 **Pyŏnsan Bando National Park** S. Korea
200 F4 **Pyramidenspitze** *mt.* Austria
105 J7 **Pyramid Hill** *Vic.* Austr.
102 □ **Pyramid Island** *Chatham Is* S. Pacific Ocean
109 F12 **Pyramid Lake** *salt flat W.A.* Austr.
264 M1 **Pyramid Lake** *NV* U.S.A.
264 M1 **Pyramid Lake Indian Reservation** *res. NV* U.S.A.
238 □2a **Pyramid Point** *Ascension* S. Atlantic Ocean
250 I5 **Pyramid Point** *MI* U.S.A.
264 M2 **Pyramid Range** *mts NV* U.S.A.
148 E9 **Pyramids of Giza** *tourist site* Egypt
195 K3 **Pyrbaum** Ger.
208 J3 **Pyrenees** *mts* Europe
185 D9 **Pyrénées** *airport* France
208 D2 **Pyrénées, Parc National des** *nat. park* France/Spain
185 C9 **Pyrénées-Atlantiques** *dept* France
185 J10 **Pyrénées-Orientales** *dept* France
245 □D5 **Pyre Peak** *vol. AK* U.S.A.
220 D3 **Pyrgetos** Greece
221 G4 **Pyrgi** *Chios* Greece
220 C5 **Pyrgos** Greece
158 I3 **Pyrizhky** Ukr.
159 M4 **Pyrohy** Ukr.
220 B2 **Pyrsogianni** Greece
108 D6 **Pyrton, Mount** *hill W.A.* Austr.
159 L3 **Pyryatyn** Ukr.
196 C2 **Pyrzyce** Pol.
156 I4 **Pyshchug** Rus. Fed.
159 N8 **Pyshkine** Ukr.
160 L7 **Pyshna** Belarus
196 G5 **Pyskowice** Pol.
159 O5 **Pys'menne** Ukr.
196 G4 **Pyszna** *r.* Pol.
197 K5 **Pysznica** Pol.
160 K4 **Pytalovo** Rus. Fed.
251 R3 **Pythonga, Lac** *l. Que.* Can.
220 E4 **Pyxaria** *mt.* Greece

Q

146 D2 **Qā', Wādī al** *watercourse* Saudi Arabia
148 H6 **Qaa** Lebanon
243 L2 **Qaanaaq** Greenland
151 I5 **Qäbälä** Azer.
150 D6 **Qabātiya** West Bank
147 L4 **Qābil** Oman
151 H4 **Qabırrı** *r.* Azer.
133 L12 **Qabnag** *Xizang* China
Qabqa *Qinghai* China *see* **Gonghe**
147 I7 **Qabr Hūd** Oman
Qabyrgha *r.* Kazakh. *see* **Kabyrga**
Qacentina Alg. *see* **Constantine**
151 F4 **Qach'aghani** Georgia
237 M6 **Qacha's Nek** Lesotho
151 J4 **Qäçräş** Azer.
144 H3 **Qadamgāli** Iran
146 F6 **Qaḍḍā** Saudi Arabia
145 J4 **Qādes** Afgh.
146 D4 **Qaḍīmah** Saudi Arabia
149 L6 **Qādir Karam** Iraq
145 O6 **Qadirpur** Pak.
149 K6 **Qādisīyah, Sadd** *dam* Iraq
Qadisiyah Dam Iraq *see* **Qādisīyah, Sadd**
147 K9 **Qādub** *Suquṭrā* Yemen
144 I6 **Qā'emābād** Iran
144 D7 **Qā'emiyeh** Iran
144 H5 **Qā'en** Iran
220 B2 **Qafzez** Albania
129 P2 **Qagan** *Nei Mongol* China
128 J6 **Qagan Ders** *Nei Mongol* China
129 K7 **Qagan Nur** *Nei Mongol* China
129 M5 **Qagan Nur** *Nei Mongol* China
129 N5 **Qagan Nur** *Nei Mongol* China
128 F8 **Qagan Nur** *Qinghai* China
132 H5 **Qagan Nur** *Xinjiang* China
129 S4 **Qagan Nur** *l.* China
129 N5 **Qagan Nur** *resr* China
129 L4 **Qagan Obo** *Nei Mongol* China
129 P3 **Qagan Qulut** *Nei Mongol* China
129 M5 **Qagan Teg** *Nei Mongol* China
128 D9 **Qagan Tohoi** *Qinghai* China
Qagan Us *Qinghai* China *see* **Dulan**
128 E8 **Qagan Us He** *r.* China
130 B2 **Qagca** *Sichuan* China
Qagchêng *Sichuan* China *see* **Xiangcheng**
Qahar Youyi Houqi *Nei Mongol* China *see* **Bayan Qagan**
Qahar Youyi Qianqi *Nei Mongol* China *see* **Togrog Ul**
Qahar Youyi Zhongqi *Nei Mongol* China *see* **Hobor**
146 F3 **Qahd, Wādī** *watercourse* Saudi Arabia
146 G6 **Qahr, Jibāl al** *hills* Saudi Arabia
151 I6 **Qährämanlı** Azer.
Qahremānshahr Iran *see* **Kermānshāh**
146 F5 **Qaḥṭān** *reg.* Saudi Arabia
145 N5 **Qaidabad** Pak.
128 D8 **Qaidam He** *r.* China
133 K8 **Qaidam Pendi** *basin* China
128 D8 **Qaidam Shan** *mts Qinghai* China
Qaidar *Qinghai* China *see* **Cêtar**
133 I10 **Qainaqangma** *Xizang* China
133 E8 **Qakar** *Xinjiang* China
217 □ **Qala** *Gozo* Malta
237 M3 **Qalabotjha** S. Africa
149 L5 **Qalā Diza** Iraq
225 G6 **Qala'en Nahl** Sudan
145 M4 **Qalagai** Afgh.
145 N2 **Qal'aikhum** Tajik.
145 J5 **Qala Jamal** Afgh.
147 K5 **Qalamat Abū Shafrah** Saudi Arabia
Qalamshia Georgia *see* **Gant'iadi**
147 K9 **Qalansīyah** *Suquṭrā* Yemen
145 L4 **Qala Shinia Takht** Afgh.
149 P9 **Qalāt** Iran
146 B2 **Qal'at al Azlam** Saudi Arabia
150 E4 **Qal'at al Ḥiṣn** Syria

146 C2 Qal'at al Mu'aẓẓam Saudi Arabia
146 F5 Qal'at Bīshah Saudi Arabia
150 G3 Qal'at Muqaybirah, Jabal *mt.* Syria
149 M8 Qal'at Şāliḩ Iraq
149 M8 Qal'at Sukkar Iraq
145 J4 Qala Vali Afgh.
Qalbī Zhotasy *mts* Kazakh. *see* Kalbinskiy Khrebet
144 F3 Qal'eh Iran
144 A2 Qal'eh Dāgh *mt.* Iran
145 I4 Qal'eh Tirpul Afgh.
145 K6 Qal'eh-ye Bost Afgh.
145 I6 Qal'eh-ye Fatḩ Afgh.
144 G8 Qal'eh-ye Ganj Iran
145 J4 Qal'eh-ye Now Afgh.
149 N7 Qal'eh-ye Now Iran
144 H5 Qal'eh-ye Shūrak *well* Iran
128 I8 Qalgar *Nei Mongol* China
147 N4 Qalhāt Oman
149 L9 Qalīb Bāqūr *well* Iraq
248 F1 Qalluviartuuq, Lac *l. Que.* Can.
150 C6 Qalqīlya West Bank
Qalqutan Kazakh. *see* Koluton
225 F2 Qalyūb Egypt
148 E8 Qalyūbīyah *governorate* Egypt
128 F9 Qamalung *Qinghai* China
247 M2 Qamanirjuaq Lake *Nunavut* Can.
Qamanittuaq *Nunavut* Can. *see* Baker Lake
147 K7 Qamar, Ghubbat al *b.* Yemen
147 K7 Qamar, Jabal al *mts* Oman
151 I4 Qämärvan Azer.
143 L8 Qamashi Uzbek.
144 B4 Qāmchīān Iran
130 A3 Qamdo *Xizang* China
101 □[7] Qamea *i.* Fiji
146 E6 Qam Hadīl Saudi Arabia
224 C2 Qamīnis Libya
217 □ Qammieħ, Il-Ponta tal- *pt* Malta
145 M6 Qamruddin Karez Pak.
144 D5 Qamşar Iran
Qamystybas Kazakh. *see* Kamyshlybash
150 E6 Qanawāt Syria
147 L7 Qanawt Oman
Qandahar Afgh. *see* Kandahār
232 F2 Qandala Somalia
144 B2 Qandarānbāshī, Kūh-e *mt.* Iran
Qandyaghash Kazakh. *see* Kandyagash
129 N5 Qangdin Sum *Nei Mongol* China
133 E10 Qangdoi *Xizang* China
133 D11 Qangzê *Xizang* China
142 H6 Qanliko'l Uzbek.
Qapal Kazakh. *see* Kapal
144 F3 Qapan Iran
132 E5 Qapqal *Xinjiang* China
Qapshagay Kazakh. *see* Kapchagay
Qapshagay Bögeni *resr* Kazakh. *see* Kapchagayskoye Vodokhranilishche
Qaq Köli *salt l.* Kazakh. *see* Kak, Ozero
243 N3 Qaqortoq Greenland
147 K7 Qarā', Jabal al *mts* Oman
Qara Āghach *r.* Iran *see* Mand, Rūd-e
150 D5 Qaraaoun Lebanon
145 I4 Qarabagh Afgh.
151 H5 Qarabağ Silsiläsi *hills* Azer.
151 G6 Qarabağ Yaylası *plat.* Armenia/Azer.
Qarabas Kazakh. *see* Karabas
Qarabaū Kazakh. *see* Karabau
Qarabulaq Kazakh. *see* Karabulak
Qarabutaq Kazakh. *see* Karabutak
151 J6 Qaraçala Azer.
149 K6 Qarachōq, Jabal *mts* Iraq
151 J6 Qaradonlu Azer.
Qara Ertis *r.* China/Kazakh. *see* Ertix He
Qaraghandy Kazakh. *see* Karaganda
Qaraghandy Oblysy *admin. div.* Kazakh. *see* Karagandinskaya Oblast'
Qaraghayly Kazakh. *see* Karagayly
148 C9 Qārah Egypt
149 J9 Qārah Saudi Arabia
146 G6 Qārah, Jabal al *hill* Saudi Arabia
145 M5 Qarah Bāgh *Ghaznī* Afgh.
145 M4 Qarah Bāgh *Kābul* Afgh.
Qarah Tappah Iraq *see* Qara Tepe
132 C7 Qarak *Xinjiang* China
Qaraköl Kazakh. *see* Karakol'
151 G5 Qaralar Azer.
151 J5 Qaramäryam Azer.
144 B3 Qaranqu *r.* Iran
Qaraoy Kazakh. *see* Karaoy
Qara Özek Uzbek. *see* Qorao'zak
Qaraqalpaqstan Respublikasy *aut. rep.* Uzbek. *see* Qoraqalpog'iston Respublikasi
Qaraqoyyn Köli *salt l.* Kazakh. *see* Karakoyyn, Ozero
Qaraqozha Kazakh. *see* Karaguzhikha
Qaraqum *des.* Kazakh. *see* Karakum, Peski
Qaraqum *des.* Turkm. *see* Garagum
Qarasor Köli *l.* Kazakh. *see* Karasor, Ozero
151 J5 Qarasu Azer.
151 I5 Qarasu *r.* Azer.
151 I6 Qarasu *r.* Azer.
Qarasū Kazakh. *see* Karasu
151 K6 Qarasu Adası *i.* Azer.
Qara Şū Chāy *r.* Syria/Turkey *see* Karasu
145 K4 Qara Tarai *mt.* Afgh.
Qarataū Kazakh. *see* Karatau
Qarataū Zhotasy *mts* Kazakh. *see* Karatau, Khrebet
149 L6 Qara Tepe Iraq
149 N5 Qara Tikan Iran
Qaratöbe Kazakh. *see* Karatobe
Qaratoghay Kazakh. *see* Karatogay
Qaratomar Bögeni *resr* Kazakh. *see* Karatomarskoye Vodokhranilishche
Qaraton Kazakh. *see* Karaton
Qaraūyl Kazakh. *see* Karaul
151 H5 Qarayeri Azer.
Qarazhal Kazakh. *see* Karazhal
232 F2 Qardho Somalia
230 F2 Qardud Sudan
151 I6 Qareh Āghāj Iran
144 B3 Qar'eh Aqāj Iran
144 D4 Qareh Chāy *r.* Iran
144 A2 Qareh Dāgh *mt.* Iran
144 B2 Qareh Dāgh *mts* Iran
144 B3 Qareh Dāsh, Kūh-e *mt.* Iran
151 F6 Qareh Khāj Iran
144 E4 Qareh Qāch, Kūh-e *mts* Iran
144 F3 Qareh Qūzī-ye Bālā Iran
144 B2 Qareh Sū *r.* Iran
144 I3 Qareh Tīkān Turkm.
151 G7 Qareh Ẕīā' od Dīn Iran
128 D8 Qarhan *Qinghai* China
Qarkilik *Xinjiang* China *see* Ruoqiang
225 G2 Qarn al Kabsh, Jabal *mt.* Egypt
147 K3 Qarnayn *i.* U.A.E.
146 E5 Qarnayţ, Jabal *hill* Saudi Arabia
142 K8 Qarnobcho'l cho'li *plain* Uzbek.
145 O2 Qarokŭl *l.* Tajik.
Qarqan *Xinjiang* China *see* Qiemo
132 H7 Qarqan He *r.* China
Qarqaraly Kazakh. *see* Karkaralinsk
151 I6 Qarqarçay *r.* Azer.
132 E6 Qarqi *Xinjiang* China
132 G6 Qarqi *Xinjiang* China
142 F9 Qārqi Iran
145 L3 Qarqīn Afgh.
220 B2 Qarrit, Qafa e *pass* Albania
Qarsaqbay Kazakh. *see* Karsakpay
142 K8 Qarshi *Qashqadaryo* Uzbek.
142 K8 Qarshi cho'li *plain* Uzbek.
Qarshi Chŭli *plain* Uzbek. *see* Qarshi cho'li
150 D4 Qartaba Lebanon
149 N9 Qārūh, Jazīrat *i.* Kuwait
225 F2 Qārūn, Birkat *l.* Egypt
146 G6 Qaryat al Fāw *tourist site* Saudi Arabia
147 H2 Qaryat al Ulyā Saudi Arabia
147 H2 Qaryat as Sufla Saudi Arabia
144 G5 Qasamī Iran
145 J4 Qasa Murg *mts* Afgh.
139 K7 Qasba *Bihar* India
147 M4 Qaşbīyat al Burayk Oman
144 G4 Qāsemābād *Khorāsān* Iran
144 H3 Qāsemābād *Khorāsān* Iran
143 L8 Qashqadaryo *admin. div.* Uzbek.
145 K2 Qashqadaryo *r.* Uzbek.
Qashqadaryo Wiloyati *admin. div.* Uzbek. *see* Qashqadaryo
144 D6 Qash Qā'ī *reg.* Iran
Qashqantengiz Kazakh. *see* Kashkanteniz
243 M3 Qasigiannguit Greenland
146 F2 Qasīm *reg.* Saudi Arabia
Qaskelen Kazakh. *see* Kaskelen
129 L6 Qasq *Nei Mongol* China
150 D8 Qaşr ad Dayr, Jabal *mt.* Jordan
150 E7 Qaşr al Azraq Jordan
224 E3 Qaşr al Farāfirah Egypt
150 F4 Qasr al Ḩayr *tourist site* Syria
150 E7 Qaşr al Kharānah Jordan
149 K7 Qasr al Khubbāz Iraq
150 E7 Qaşr 'Amrah *tourist site* Jordan
149 N9 Qaşr aş Şabīyah Kuwait
224 C2 Qaşr Bū Hādī Libya
150 F6 Qaşr Burqu' *tourist site* Jordan
144 I8 Qaşr-e Qand Iran
149 L6 Qaşr-e Shīrīn Iran
146 G5 Qaşr Ḩimām Saudi Arabia
224 B3 Qaşr Larocu Libya
243 N3 Qassimiut Greenland
146 G9 Qa'tabah Yemen
150 E5 Qaţanā Syria
147 J3 Qatar *country* Asia
141 H5 Qatār, Jabal *hill* Oman
144 G3 Qatlīsh Iran
150 E2 Qaţmah Syria
225 F2 Qaţrānī, Jabal *esc.* Egypt
144 F7 Qaţrūyeh Iran
150 F7 Qaţţāfī, Wādī al *watercourse* Jordan
Qattara Depression Egypt *see* Qaţţārah, Munkhafaḑ al
224 E2 Qaţţārah, Munkhafaḑ al *depr.* Egypt
224 E2 Qaţţārah, Ra's *esc.* Egypt
150 E4 Qaţţīnah, Buḩayrat *resr* Syria
Qausuittuq *Nunavut* Can. *see* Resolute
144 G6 Qavāmābād Iran
151 H4 Qax Azer.
132 F5 Qaxi *Xinjiang* China
Qayghy Kazakh. *see* Kayga
Qaynar Kazakh. *see* Kaynar
Qayraqty Kazakh. *see* Nizhniye Kayrakty
145 M1 Qayroqqum Tajik.
145 N1 Qayroqqum, Obanbori *resr* Tajik.
151 H4 Qaysa Georgia
145 K4 Qayşār Afgh.
145 K3 Qayşār *r.* Afgh.
150 E7 Qaysīyah, Qā' al *imp. l.* Jordan
146 A2 Qaysūm, Juzur *is* Egypt
133 K12 Qayü *Xizang* China
149 K6 Qayyārah Iraq
Qazaly Kazakh. *see* Kazalinsk
151 H6 Qazangödağ *mt.* Armenia/Azer.
151 H6 Qazanzämi Azer.
Qazaq Shyghanaghy *b.* Kazakh. *see* Kazakhskiy Zaliv
Qazaqstan *country* Asia *see* Kazakhstan
151 G4 Qazax Azer.
151 F3 Qazbegi Georgia
145 M8 Qazi Ahmad Pak.
151 J5 Qazımämmäd Azer.
144 C3 Qazvīn Iran
144 C3 Qazvīn *prov.* Iran
Qazyqurt Kazakh. *see* Kazygurt
132 G6 Qedir *Xinjiang* China
128 G5 Qeh *Nei Mongol* China
144 E5 Qehī Iran
Qeisûm Islands Egypt *see* Qaysūm, Juzur
220 B2 Qelqëzës, Mali i *mt.* Albania
151 E3 Qemult'a Georgia
Qena *Qinā* Egypt *see* Qinā
243 M3 Qeqertarsuaq Greenland
243 M3 Qeqertarsuaq *i.* Greenland
243 M3 Qeqertarsuatsiaat Greenland
243 M2 Qeqertarsuatsiaq *i.* Greenland
243 M3 Qeqertarsuup Tunua *b.* Greenland
144 B4 Qeshlāq Iran
144 D4 Qeshlāq-e Ḩoseyn Iran
144 G8 Qeshm Iran
144 G8 Qeshm *i.* Iran
144 C3 Qeydār Iran
144 F7 Qeyşar, Chāh-e *well* Iran
145 K5 Qeyşār, Kūh-e *mt.* Afgh.
144 C3 Qezel Owzan, Rūdkhāneh-ye *r.* Iran
151 G6 Qezel Qeshlāq Iran
150 C8 Qeẕi'ot Israel
129 P7 Qian'an *Hebei* China
129 S4 Qian'an *Jilin* China
Qiancheng *Hunan* China *see* Hongjiang
Qiandaohu *Zhejiang* China *see* Chun'an
131 L4 Qiandao Hu *resr* China
Qianfo Dong *Gansu* China *see* Mogao Ku
132 F6 Qianfodong *Xinjiang* China
122 D6 Qianguozhen *Jilin* China
129 P9 Qiangwei He *r.* China
129 J9 Qian He *r.* China
130 G4 Qianjiang *Chongqing* China
131 I3 Qianjiang *Hubei* China
122 H5 Qianjin *Heilong.* China
122 F6 Qianjin *Jilin* China
130 C3 Qianning *Sichuan* China
129 R4 Qianqihao *Jilin* China
131 K3 Qianshan *Anhui* China
129 R6 Qian Shan *mts* China
132 G4 Qianshanlaoba *Xinjiang* China
288 R4 Qiansuo *Zhejiang* China
130 D4 Qianwei *Sichuan* China
130 F5 Qianxi *Guizhou* China
129 P6 Qianxi *Hebei* China
129 K9 Qianxian *Shaanxi* China
130 H5 Qianyang *Hunan* China
129 J9 Qianyang *Shaanxi* China
Qianyou *Shaanxi* China *see* Zhashui
Qiaocheng *Anhui* China *see* Bozhou
129 M7 Qiaocun *Shanxi* China
130 D5 Qiaojia *Yunnan* China
Qiaoshan *Shaanxi* China *see* Huangling
Qiaotou *Qinghai* China *see* Datong
Qiaowa *Sichuan* China *see* Muli
128 E6 Qiaowan *Gansu* China
Qiaozhuang *Sichuan* China *see* Qingchuan
144 A2 Qīās Iran
146 G2 Qibā' Saudi Arabia
237 L5 Qibing S. Africa
143 M7 Qibray Uzbek.
131 J3 Qichun *Hubei* China
131 I5 Qidong *Hunan* China
131 M3 Qidong *Jiangsu* China
133 G7 Qiemo *Xinjiang* China
129 O8 Qihe *Shandong* China
129 N9 Qi He *r.* China
130 F4 Qijiang *Chongqing* China
128 B5 Qijiaojing *Xinjiang* China
243 L3 Qikiqtarjuaq *Nunavut* Can.
128 B5 Qiktim *Xinjiang* China
145 L6 Qila Abdullah Pak.
145 J8 Qila Ladgasht Pak.
129 O6 Qilaotu Shan *mts* China
145 I7 Qila Safed Pak.
145 M6 Qila Saifullah Pak.
Qili *Anhui* China *see* Shitai
128 G7 Qilian *Qinghai* China
128 F7 Qilian Shan *mt.* China
128 E7 Qilian Shan *mts* China
132 L6 Qilizhen *Gansu* China
243 O3 Qillak *i.* Greenland
Qīma Kazakh. *see* Kiyma
132 F6 Qiman *Xinjiang* China
133 J8 Qiman Tag *mts* China
131 K4 Qimen *Anhui* China
243 L2 Qimusseriarsuaq *b.* Greenland
225 G3 Qinā *Qinā* Egypt
146 A3 Qinā *governorate* Egypt
225 G3 Qinā, Wādī *watercourse* Egypt
147 I7 Qināb, Wādī *r.* Yemen
128 I9 Qin'an *Gansu* China
Qincheng *Jiangxi* China *see* Nanfeng
128 D5 Qincheng *Xinjiang* China
122 E5 Qing'an *Heilong.* China
Qingaq *Nunavut* Can. *see* Bathurst Inlet (abandoned)
Qingcheng *Gansu* China *see* Qingyang
123 C8 Qingchengzi *Liaoning* China
130 E2 Qingchuan *Sichuan* China
129 Q8 Qingdao *Shandong* China
122 E5 Qinggang *Heilong.* China
Qinggil *Xinjiang* China *see* Qinghe
133 G8 Qinggilik *Xinjiang* China
130 H4 Qingguandu *Hunan* China
128 E8 Qinghai *prov.* China
128 G8 Qinghai Hu *salt l. Qinghai* China
128 F8 Qinghai Nanshan *mts* China
129 N8 Qinghe *Hebei* China
122 F5 Qinghe *Heilong.* China
128 B3 Qinghe *Xinjiang* China
122 C7 Qing He *r.* China
123 D8 Qinghecheng *Liaoning* China
Qinghua *Henan* China *see* Bo'ai
129 L8 Qingjian *Shaanxi* China
Qingjiang *Jiangsu* China *see* Huai'an
Qingjiang *Jiangxi* China *see* Zhangshu
130 H3 Qing Jiang *r.* China
Qingkou *Jiangsu* China *see* Ganyu
130 H9 Qinglan *Hainan* China
131 K5 Qingliu *Fujian* China
130 E6 Qinglong *Guizhou* China
129 P6 Qinglong *Hebei* China
129 P7 Qinglong He *r.* China
133 J11 Qinglung *Xizang* China
118 I4 Qingping *Guangdong* China
131 M3 Qingpu *Shanghai* China
Qingquan *Hubei* China *see* Xishui
Qingshan *Heilong.* China *see* Wudalianchi
130 D4 Qingshen *Sichuan* China
128 G8 Qingshizui *Qinghai* China
Qingshui *Gansu* China *see* Qingshuipu
128 J9 Qingshui *Gansu* China
129 L7 Qingshuihe *Nei Mongol* China
130 A2 Qingshuihe *Qinghai* China
132 H5 Qingshuihe *Xinjiang* China
132 E4 Qingshuihezi *Xinjiang* China
130 B5 Qingshuilang Shan *mts Yunnan* China
128 F7 Qingshuipu *Gansu* China
131 M4 Qingtian *Zhejiang* China
128 J7 Qingtongxia *Ningxia* China
129 O7 Qingxian *Hebei* China
131 I7 Qingxin *Guangdong* China
129 M8 Qingxu *Shanxi* China
131 K3 Qingyang *Anhui* China
129 J8 Qingyang *Gansu* China
129 J9 Qingyang *Gansu* China
Qingyang *Jiangsu* China *see* Sihong
Qingyuan *Gansu* China *see* Weiyuan
131 I7 Qingyuan *Guangdong* China
Qingyuan *Guangxi* China *see* Yizhou
122 D7 Qingyuan *Liaoning* China
Qingyuan *Shanxi* China *see* Qingxu
131 L5 Qingyuan *Zhejiang* China
129 O8 Qingyun *Shandong* China
133 G10 Qingzang Gaoyuan *plat. Xizang* China
130 F5 Qingzhen *Guizhou* China
Qingzhou *Hebei* China *see* Qingxian
131 H3 Qingzhou *Hubei* China
129 P8 Qingzhou *Shandong* China
129 M9 Qin He *r.* China
129 P7 Qinhuangdao *Hebei* China
Qinjiang *Jiangxi* China *see* Shicheng
130 F2 Qin Ling *mts* China
Qinshan *Heilong.* China *see* Wudalianchi
129 M9 Qinshui *Shanxi* China
Qinting *Jiangxi* China *see* Lianhua
129 M8 Qinxian *Shanxi* China
129 M9 Qinyang *Henan* China
129 M8 Qinyuan *Shanxi* China
130 G8 Qinzhou *Guangxi* China
130 G8 Qinzhou Wan *b.* China
130 H9 Qionghai *Hainan* China
Qiongjiexue *Xizang* China *see* Qonggyai
130 D3 Qionglai *Sichuan* China
130 D3 Qionglai Shan *mts Sichuan* China
130 H9 Qiongshan *Hainan* China
Qiongxi *Sichuan* China *see* Hongyuan
130 G9 Qiongzhong *Hainan* China
130 G9 Qiongzhou Haixia *str.* China
151 H4 Qıpçaq Azer.
128 E7 Qiping *Gansu* China
129 R3 Qiqihar *Heilong.* China
132 I5 Qiquanhu *Xinjiang* China
144 E7 Qīr *Fārs* Iran
144 C5 Qīr *Lorestān* Iran
133 E8 Qira *Xinjiang* China
151 H6 Qırmızı Bazar Azer.
151 H5 Qırmızı Samux Azer.
151 J6 Qırmızkänd Azer.
150 C7 Qiryat Gat Israel
150 D5 Qiryat Shemona Israel
130 G8 Qisha *Guangxi* China
Qishan *Anhui* China *see* Qimen
129 J9 Qishan *Shaanxi* China
147 J8 Qishn Yemen
150 D6 Qishon *r.* Israel
146 E5 Qishrān *i.* Saudi Arabia
148 H8 Qitab ash Shāmah *vol. crater* Saudi Arabia
132 I5 Qitai *Xinjiang* China
122 G6 Qitaihe *Heilong.* China
147 L7 Qitbīt, Wādī *r.* Oman
130 E6 Qiubei *Yunnan* China
131 J4 Qiujin *Jiangxi* China
129 Q8 Qixia *Shandong* China
129 N9 Qixian *Henan* China
129 N9 Qixian *Henan* China
129 M8 Qixian *Shanxi* China
122 H5 Qixing He *r.* China
122 D4 Qixingpao *Heilong.* China
131 H5 Qiyang *Hunan* China
128 J8 Qiying *Ningxia* China
130 B4 Qizhong *Xizang* China
131 H9 Qizhou Liedao *i.* China
151 K6 Qızılağac Körfäzi *b.* Azer.
151 K6 Qızılağac Qoruğu *nature res.* Azer.
Qizil-Art, Aghbai *pass* Kyrg./Tajik. *see* Kyzylart Pass
145 I4 Qizil Bulak Afgh.
151 K5 Qızıldaş Azer.
145 P3 Qizilrabot Tajik.
142 J7 Qizilravot Uzbek.
142 H6 Qizketkan Uzbek.
Qizqetkan Uzbek. *see* Qizketkan
144 E4 Qobād, Chāh-e *well* Iran
237 M8 Qoboqobo S. Africa
151 K5 Qobustan Azer.
151 K5 Qobustan Qoruğu *nature res.* Azer.
Qoghaly Kazakh. *see* Kugaly
129 O4 Qog Ul *Nei Mongol* China
128 G9 Qoigargoinba *Qinghai* China
128 F8 Qoijê *Qinghai* China
144 B3 Qojūr Iran
132 F6 Qolawat *Xinjiang* China
237 M8 Qolora Mouth S. Africa
132 I5 Qoltag *mts* China
144 D4 Qom Iran
144 D4 Qom *prov.* Iran
Qomdo *Xizang* China *see* Qumdo
Qomisheh Iran *see* Shahrezā
Qomolangma Feng *mt.* China/Nepal *see* Everest, Mount
151 J4 Qonaqkänd Azer.
133 J12 Qonggyai *Xizang* China
142 H6 Qo'ng'irot Uzbek.
129 K6 Qongj *Nei Mongol* China
132 H6 Qongkol *Xinjiang* China
133 F9 Qong Muztag *mt.* Xinjiang/Xizang China
Qongrat Uzbek. *see* Qo'ng'irot
Qongyrat *Karagandinskaya Oblast'* Kazakh. *see* Konyrat
Qongyröleng Kazakh. *see* Konyrolen
128 F8 Qonj *Qinghai* China
Qonystanū Kazakh. *see* Konystanu
232 F3 Qooriga Neegro *b.* Somalia
243 M3 Qoornoq Greenland
Qoqek *Xinjiang* China *see* Tacheng
237 K7 Qoqodala S. Africa
143 N7 Qo'qon *Farg'ona* Uzbek.
Qoradaryo *r.* Kyrg. *see* Kara-Darya
Qoraghaty Kazakh. *see* Kuragaty
142 H6 Qorajar Uzbek.
142 J8 Qorako'l *Buxoro* Uzbek.
142 J8 Qorako'l *Buxoro* Uzbek.
142 H6 Qorao'zak Uzbek.
Qoraqalpoghiston Uzbek. *see* Qoraqalpog'iston
Qoraqalpoghiston Respublikasi *aut. rep.* Uzbek. *see* Qoraqalpog'iston Respublikasi
142 G5 Qoraqalpog'iston Uzbek.
142 H6 Qoraqalpog'iston Respublikasi *aut. rep.* Uzbek.
142 K7 Qoraqata botig'i *depr.* Uzbek.
Qoraŭzak Uzbek. *see* Qorao'zak
Qorday Kazakh. *see* Kurday
Qorghalzhyn Kazakh. *see* Korgalzhyn
217 □ Qormi Malta
150 E4 Qornet es Saouda *mt.* Lebanon
151 E3 Qornisi Georgia
142 K8 Qorovulbozor Uzbek.
Qorowulbozor Uzbek. *see* Qorovulbozor
144 D3 Qoroy, Gardaneh-ye *pass* Iran
217 □ Qorrot, Daħlet *b. Gozo* Malta
144 B4 Qorveh Iran
151 I5 Qoşaqovaq Azer.
142 I7 Qo'shko'pir Uzbek.
Qoshqar Kazakh. *see* Koshkar
143 L7 Qo'shrabot Uzbek.
149 K5 Qosh Tepe Iraq
151 H5 Qoşqarçay *r.* Azer.
Qosshaghyl Kazakh. *see* Koschagyl
Qostanay Kazakh. *see* Kostanay
Qostanay Oblysy *admin. div.* Kazakh. *see* Kostanayskaya Oblast'
144 G8 Qoţbābād Iran
144 A2 Qoţūr Iran
150 E4 Qoubaiyat Lebanon
151 G5 Qovlar Azer.
Qowowuyag *mt.* China/Nepal *see* Cho Oyu
Qozhaköl *l.* Kazakh. *see* Kozhakol', Ozero
145 N3 Qozideh *Kŭhistoni Badakhshon* Tajik.
142 H6 Qozonketkan Uzbek.
142 H6 Qozoqdaryo Uzbek.
217 □ Qrejten, Il-Ponta tal- *pt* Malta
217 □ Qrendi Malta
257 M6 Quabbin Reservoir *MA* U.S.A.
246 E5 Quadra Island B.C. Can.
204 G8 Quadrazais Port.
215 M4 Quadri Italy
279 C9 Quadros, Lago dos *l.* Brazil
236 E7 Quaggasfontein Poort *pass* S. Africa
168 I9 Quaich *r. Scotland* U.K.
264 O6 Quail Mountains *CA* U.S.A.
109 D12 Quairading *W.A.* Austr.
190 E5 Quakenbrück Ger.
259 K2 Quaker Hill *CT* U.S.A.
258 F3 Quakertown *NJ* U.S.A.
258 E4 Quakertown *PA* U.S.A.
258 C3 Qualake *PA* U.S.A.
147 I2 Qualay'ah, Ra's al *pt* Saudi Arabia
215 M6 Qualiano Italy
105 I6 Quambatook *Vic.* Austr.
105 K4 Quambone *N.S.W.* Austr.
106 H6 Quamby *Qld* Austr.
261 F8 Quanah *TX* U.S.A.
129 L9 Quanbao Shan *mt. Henan* China
Quan Dao Hoang Sa *is* S. China Sea *see* Paracel Islands
Quan Dao Truong Sa *is* S. China Sea *see* Spratly Islands
118 H4 Quang Ha Vietnam
118 I7 Quang Ngai Vietnam
118 H6 Quang Tri Vietnam
118 H4 Quang Yên Vietnam
131 J2 Quan He *r.* China
118 G4 Quan Hoa Vietnam
Quanjiang *Jiangxi* China *see* Suichuan
Quan Long Vietnam *see* Ca Mau
131 J6 Quannan *Jiangxi* China
Quan Phu Quoc *i.* Vietnam *see* Phu Quôc, Đao
131 K5 Quanshang *Fujian* China
138 G2 Quanshuigou Aksai Chin
172 F5 Quantock Hills *England* U.K.
Quanwan *H.K.* China *see* Tsuen Wan
131 L6 Quanzhou *Fujian* China
131 H6 Quanzhou *Guangxi* China
247 K5 Qu'Appelle *Sask.* Can.
247 K5 Qu'Appelle *r. Man./Sask.* Can.
243 L3 Quaqtaq *Que.* Can.
279 A9 Quaraí Brazil
285 I2 Quaraí *r.* Brazil
187 E8 Quaregnon Belgium
231 C7 Quarenta Angola
168 □N2 Quarff *Shetland, Scotland* U.K.
212 F6 Quargnento Italy
164 F7 Quarnbek Ger.
212 E4 Quarona Italy
213 J8 Quarrata Italy
182 D2 Quarré-les-Tombes France
131 □J7 Quarry Bay *H.K.* China
103 D13 Quarry Hills *South I.* N.Z.
258 C5 Quarryville *PA* U.S.A.
206 C6 Quarteira Port.
209 E8 Quartell Spain
212 G1 Quarten Switz.
239 □[1c] Quartier-Français Réunion
239 □[1b] Quartier Militaire Mauritius
213 M8 Quarto, Lago di *l.* Italy
214 C9 Quartu Sant'Elena *Sardegna* Italy
265 P4 Quartzite Mountain *NV* U.S.A.
265 R8 Quartzsite *AZ* U.S.A.
280 B5 Quatá Brazil
271 □[3] Quatre, Isle á *i.* St Vincent
239 □[1b] Quatre Bornes Mauritius
178 I5 Quatre-Champs France
239 □[1b] Quatre Cocos, Pointe *pt* Mauritius
209 E10 Quatretonda Spain
238 □[1a] Quatro Ribeiras *Terceira* Azores
151 J4 Quba Azer.
151 H6 Qubadlı Azer.
151 K5 Qubalıbalaoğlan Azer.
144 H3 Qūchān Iran
150 G3 Qudaym Syria
147 M6 Qudaysah *well* Oman
237 O4 Qudeni S. Africa
151 J4 Qudıyalçay *r.* Azer.
234 B2 Qué Angola
105 L6 Queanbeyan *N.S.W.* Austr.
249 G4 Québec *Que.* Can.
249 F2 Québec *prov.* Can.
280 D3 Quebra Anzol *r.* Brazil
285 I3 Quebracho Uru.
282 E3 Quebrachos Arg.
284 E2 Quebrada del Condorito, Parque Nacional *nat. park* Arg.
271 □[1] Quebradillas Puerto Rico
269 H8 Quechultenango Mex.
283 B6 Quedal, Cabo *c.* Chile
235 G3 Quedas Moz.
172 H4 Quedgeley *Gloucestershire, England* U.K.
193 D7 Quedlinburg Ger.
Queen Adelaide Islands Chile *see* Reina Adelaida, Archipiélago de la
150 D7 Queen Alia *airport* Jordan
258 D7 Queen Anne *MD* U.S.A.
258 C6 Queen Anne's County *county MD* U.S.A.
246 E5 Queen Bess, Mount B.C. Can.
173 N5 Queenborough *Kent, England* U.K.
245 N5 Queen Charlotte B.C. Can.
283 E8 Queen Charlotte Bay Falkland Is
245 N5 Queen Charlotte Islands B.C. Can.
246 D5 Queen Charlotte Sound *sea chan.* B.C. Can.
103 H8 Queen Charlotte Sound *sea chan. South I.* N.Z.
246 E5 Queen Charlotte Strait B.C. Can.
250 B9 Queen City *MO* U.S.A.
265 U8 Queen Creek *AZ* U.S.A.
243 H2 Queen Elizabeth Islands *N.W.T./Nunavut* Can.
232 A5 Queen Elizabeth National Park Uganda
287 K1 Queen Elizabeth Range *mts* Antarctica
287 C2 Queen Fabiola Mountains Antarctica
245 M3 Queen Mary, Mount *Y.T.* Can.
287 G2 Queen Mary Land *reg.* Antarctica
238 □[2c] Queen Mary's Peak *Tristan da Cunha* S. Atlantic Ocean
243 H3 Queen Maud Gulf *Nunavut* Can.
287 A2 Queen Maud Land *reg.* Antarctica
286 O1 Queen Maud Mountains Antarctica
237 O5 Queensburgh S. Africa
171 N6 Queensbury *West Yorkshire, England* U.K.
106 B3 Queens Channel *N.T.* Austr.
243 I2 Queens Channel *Nunavut* Can.
105 J8 Queenscliff *Vic.* Austr.
259 H3 Queens County *county NY* U.S.A.
107 J7 Queensland *state* Austr.
105 J10 Queenstown *Tas.* Austr.
103 C12 Queenstown *South I.* N.Z.
Queenstown Ireland *see* Cobh
237 K7 Queenstown S. Africa
116 □ Queenstown Sing.
258 C7 Queenstown *MD* U.S.A.
109 G11 Queen Victoria Spring Nature Reserve *W.A.* Austr.
262 B3 Queets *WA* U.S.A.
285 H3 Queguay Grande *r.* Uru.
276 D4 Quehua Bol.
284 E5 Quehué Arg.
224 D5 Queiba *well* Chad
182 I5 Queige France
205 M1 Queijo, Cabo *c.* Spain
277 E2 Queimada Brazil
275 I5 Queimada, Ilha *i.* Brazil
238 □[1c] Queimada, Ponta da *pt Pico* Azores
278 F4 Queimadas Brazil
238 □[1a] Queimado, Ponta do *pt Terceira* Azores
204 E7 Queiriga Port.
280 B4 Queiroz Brazil
205 P4 Quel Spain
231 C7 Quela Angola
181 J6 Quelaines-St-Gault France
235 H3 Quelimane Moz.
268 A2 Quelite Mex.
284 A5 Quella Chile
193 F7 Quellendorf Ger.
283 B6 Quellón Chile
231 B6 Quelo Angola
Quelpart Island S. Korea *see* Cheju-do
281 E5 Queluz Brazil
206 A3 Queluz Port.
205 M5 Quemada Spain
280 D6 Quemada Grande, Ilha *i.* Brazil
263 J9 Quemado *NM* U.S.A.
231 D8 Quembo *r.* Angola
283 B6 Quemchi Chile
Quemoy *i.* Taiwan *see* Chinmen Tao
285 F5 Quemú-Quemú Arg.
178 C3 Quend France
191 D6 Quendorf Ger.
193 D7 Quenstedt Ger.
207 M6 Quéntar Spain
258 C4 Quentin *PA* U.S.A.
136 D5 Quepem *Goa* India
Que Que Zimbabwe *see* Kwekwe
285 H6 Quequén Arg.
285 H6 Quequén Grande *r.* Arg.
208 J3 Queralbs Spain
212 I9 Quercianella Italy
185 G7 Quercy *reg.* France
206 D6 Querença Port.
278 B5 Querência Brazil
280 A5 Querência do Norte Brazil
268 G6 Queréndaro Mex.
191 K6 Querenhorst Ger.
268 G5 Querétaro Mex.
269 H5 Querétaro *state* Mex.
193 E8 Querfurt Ger.
185 I10 Quérigut France
190 I1 Quern Ger.
191 F6 Quernheim Ger.
171 L5 Quernmore *Lancashire, England* U.K.
213 L4 Quero Italy
205 N9 Quero Spain
266 D2 Querobabi Mex.
208 H5 Querol Spain
274 B6 Querpon Peru
180 H2 Querqueville France
178 D4 Querrieu France
179 L8 Quers France
209 D9 Quesa Spain
207 M5 Quesada Spain
207 M5 Quesada *r.* Spain
226 C4 Quesat *watercourse* Western Sahara
131 J2 Queshan *Henan* China
246 F4 Quesnel B.C. Can.
246 F4 Quesnel *r.* B.C. Can.
246 F4 Quesnel Lake B.C. Can.
178 F2 Quesnoy-sur-Deûle France
180 F5 Quessoy France
178 F4 Quessy France
180 G6 Questembert France
276 D5 Quetena de Lipez *r.* Bol.
250 C1 Quetico Provincial Park *Ont.* Can.
182 G2 Quetigny France
145 L6 Quetta Pak.
180 I2 Quettehou France
180 I4 Quettreville-sur-Sienne France
269 I9 Quetzala *r.* Mex.
269 H7 Quetzalapa *Guerrero* Mex.
269 H5 Quetzalapa *Hidalgo* Mex.
267 N10 Quetzaltenango Guat.
284 B5 Queuco Chile
283 B7 Queulat, Parque Nacional *nat. park* Chile
283 B5 Queule Chile
283 D6 Queupán Arg.
178 D4 Quevauvillers France
180 E6 Quéven France
180 G5 Quévert France
184 C5 Queyrac France
183 J7 Queyras, Parc Naturel Régional du *nature res.* France
185 I6 Quézac France
267 O11 Quezaltepeque El Salvador
114 D6 Quezon *Negros* Phil.
114 B7 Quezon *Palawan* Phil.
114 C4 Quezon City *Luzon* Phil.
146 E2 Qufār Saudi Arabia
129 O9 Qufu *Shandong* China
204 C8 Quiaios Port.
231 B7 Quibala Angola
231 B7 Quibaxe Angola
274 B3 Quibdó Col.
180 E7 Quiberon France
180 E6 Quiberon, Baie de *b.* France
180 E6 Quiberon, Presqu'île de *pen.* France
274 D2 Quíbor Venez.
231 B7 Quicabo Angola
231 B7 Quiçama, Parque Nacional do *nat. park* Angola
118 G5 Qui Châu Vietnam
190 I3 Quickborn Ger.
231 B7 Quiculungo Angola
179 N5 Quierschied Ger.
178 F4 Quierzy France
245 N3 Quiet Lake *Y.T.* Can.
178 G3 Quiévrechain France
231 B8 Quihita Angola
231 C6 Quihuhu Angola
277 F6 Quiindy Para.
266 F5 Quilá Mex.
284 A5 Quilaco Chile
266 □P11 Quilalí Nic.
283 B6 Quilán, Cabo *c.* Chile
276 B4 Quilca Peru
285 G5 Quilco Arg.
231 B7 Quilenda Angola
231 B8 Quilengues Angola
212 E7 Quiliano Italy
284 B3 Quilimarí Chile
284 E2 Quilino Arg.
276 D4 Quillacollo Bol.
284 B2 Quillaicillo Chile
185 I10 Quillan France
247 J5 Quill Lakes *Sask.* Can.
284 A5 Quillón Chile
284 B3 Quillota Chile
285 H4 Quilmes Arg.
231 B7 Quilombo dos Dembos Angola
Quilon India *see* Kollam
107 J9 Quilpie *Qld* Austr.
284 B3 Quilpué Chile
235 H3 Quilua Moz.
231 C7 Quimbango Angola
231 C6 Quimbele Angola
231 C7 Quimbonge Angola
276 D4 Quime Bol.
268 B3 Quimichis Mex.
282 E2 Quimilí Arg.
277 E4 Quimome Bol.
180 C6 Quimper France
180 D6 Quimperlé France
169 E7 Quin Ireland
168 F6 Quinag *hill Scotland* U.K.
114 D5 Quinalasag *i.* Phil.
262 B3 Quinault *r. WA* U.S.A.
262 B3 Quinault Indian Reservation *res. WA* U.S.A.
276 C3 Quince Mil Peru
212 D4 Quincinetto Italy
264 L2 Quincy *CA* U.S.A.
255 E10 Quincy *FL* U.S.A.
254 B6 Quincy *IL* U.S.A.
257 N6 Quincy *MA* U.S.A.
250 J8 Quincy *MI* U.S.A.
256 B8 Quincy *OH* U.S.A.
178 E6 Quincy-Voisins France
274 C3 Quindío *dept* Col.
284 E3 Quines Arg.
180 I2 Quinéville France
235 I2 Quinga Moz.
182 H2 Quingey France
132 I6 Quinggir *Xinjiang* China
244 G4 Quinhagak *AK* U.S.A.
228 B4 Quinhámel Guinea-Bissau
275 E3 Quinigua, Cerro *mts* Venez.
285 G5 Quiñihual Arg.
114 C6 Quiniluban *i.* Phil.
274 B4 Quinindé Ecuador
107 J3 Quinkan Aboriginal Holding *res. Qld* Austr.
262 E6 Quinn *r. NV* U.S.A.
265 Q4 Quinn Canyon Range *mts NV* U.S.A.
256 D11 Quinnimont *WV* U.S.A.
276 D2 Quiñones Bol.
183 I9 Quinson France
182 B4 Quinssaines France
206 D6 Quintã *hill* Port.
206 B3 Quinta do Anjo Port.
280 B5 Quintana Brazil
206 H3 Quintana de la Serena Spain
204 H3 Quintana del Castillo Spain
205 M3 Quintana del Pino Spain
205 L4 Quintana del Puente Spain
205 J3 Quintana de Rueda Spain
205 M4 Quintanapalla Spain
205 N9 Quintanar de la Orden Spain
205 N5 Quintanar de la Sierra Spain
207 P2 Quintanar del Rey Spain
205 O5 Quintana Redonda Spain
267 O8 Quintana Roo *state* Mex.
204 G5 Quintanilha Port.
Quintanilla de Abajo Spain *see* Quintanilla de Onésimo
205 L5 Quintanilla de Onésimo Spain
204 C7 Quintãs Port.
284 B3 Quintay Chile
204 D4 Quintela de Leirado Spain
183 F6 Quintenas France
260 E6 Quinter *KS* U.S.A.
284 B3 Quintero Chile
180 F5 Quintin France
284 E4 Quinto *r.* Arg.
208 E5 Quinto Spain
212 F2 Quinto Switz.
258 E5 Quinton *NJ* U.S.A.
204 D5 Quinxo, Monte do *mts* Port.
231 B6 Quinzau Angola
251 O2 Quinze, Lac des *l. Que.* Can.
233 D7 Quionga Moz.
269 K8 Quiotepec Mex.
278 G4 Quipapá Brazil
207 P4 Quípar *r.* Spain
231 B8 Quipungo Angola
276 D3 Quiquive *r.* Bol.
266 □O10 Quiriguá *tourist site* Guat.
284 A5 Quirihue Chile
231 C7 Quirima Angola
233 D8 Quirimbas, Parque Nacional das *nat. park* Moz.
105 M4 Quirindi *N.S.W.* Austr.
280 B3 Quirinópolis Brazil
271 L9 Quiriquire Venez.
251 L3 Quirke Lake *Ont.* Can.
285 G4 Quiroga Arg.
276 D4 Quiroga Bol.
268 F6 Quiroga Mex.
204 F4 Quiroga Spain
214 D8 Quirra, Isola di *i. Sardegna* Italy
204 I4 Quiruelas de Vidriales Spain
274 D2 Quisiro Venez.
205 L8 Quismondo Spain
183 E9 Quissac France
281 G5 Quissamã Brazil
233 D8 Quissanga Moz.
235 G5 Quissico Moz.
231 C7 Quitapa Angola
270 C6 Quita Sueño Bank *sea feature* Caribbean Sea
233 D7 Quiterajo Moz.
280 B4 Quitéria *r.* Brazil
231 B9 Quiteve Angola
Quitexe Angola *see* Dange
282 E2 Quitilipi Arg.
255 F10 Quitman *GA* U.S.A.
261 K9 Quitman *MS* U.S.A.
261 H9 Quitman *TX* U.S.A.
274 B5 Quito Ecuador
266 C2 Quitovac Mex.
283 B7 Quitralco, Parque Nacior[…] *nat. park* Chile
178 A5 Quittebeuf France
278 F3 Quixadá Brazil
235 I2 Quixaxe Moz.
278 F3 Quixeramobim Brazil
231 B7 Quixinge Angola
131 I6 Qujiang *Guangdong* Chin[…]
Qujiang *Sichuan* China *s*[…] Quxian
130 F3 Qu Jiang *r.* China
130 H8 Qujie *Guangdong* China
130 D6 Qujing *Yunnan* China
237 M8 Quko S. Africa
Qulaly Araly *i.* Kazakh. *se*[…] Kulaly, Ostrov
225 G3 Qul'ān, Jazā'ir *i.* Egypt
Qulandy Kazakh. *see* Kula[…]
Qulanötpes *watercourse* K[…] *see* Kulanotpes
147 I1 Qulay'ah, Ra's al *pt* Kuwa[…]
149 M9 Qulbān Layyah *well* Iraq
151 C3 Qulevi Georgia
133 G11 Qulho *Xizang* China
142 J7 Quljuqtov tog'lari *hills* U[…]
Quljuqtow Toghi *hills* Uz[…] Quljuqtov tog'lari
Qulsary Kazakh. *see* Kul's[…]
148 E9 Qulūşanā Egypt
150 A9 Qulzum, Baḩr al *b.* Egypt
128 D9 Qumar He *r.* China
128 C9 Qumarheyan *Qinghai* Ch[…]
133 L10 Qumarlêb *Qinghai* China
237 M7 Qumbu S. Africa
133 L11 Qumdo *Xizang* China
133 H11 Qumigxung *Xizang* Chin[…]
Qumola *watercourse* Kaza[…] Kumola
237 L8 Qumrha S. Africa
151 G4 Qünäşli Azer.
146 G3 Qunayfidhah, Nafūd *des.* Saudi Arabia
146 G4 Qunayy *well* Saudi Arabia
224 D2 Qunayyin, Sabkhat al *sal*[…] Libya
147 I7 Qunfudh Yemen
Qŭnghirot Uzbek. *see* Qo[…]
128 G9 Qu'ngoin *r. Qinghai* Chir[…]
133 J10 Quntamari *Xizang* China
130 A3 Qu'nyido *Xizang* China
247 M1 Quoich *r. Nunavut* Can.
168 F8 Quoich, Loch *l. Scotland* […]
169 K4 Quoile *r. Northern Ireland*
239 □[1b] Quoin Channel Mauritiu[…]
106 B3 Quoin Island *N.T.* Austr.
236 D10 Quoin Point S. Africa
104 G5 Quorn *S.A.* Austr.
234 E4 Quoxo *r.* Botswana
Quqên *Sichuan* China *see* Jinchuan
Qŭqon Uzbek. *see* Qo'qo[…]
140 C7 Quraid Sudan
147 N4 Qurayat Oman
150 E10 Qurayyah *tourist site* Sau[…]
150 C8 Qurayyah, Wādī *waterco*[…] Egypt
150 F7 Qurayyat al Milḩ *l.* Jorda[…]
145 M3 Qŭrghonteppa Tajik.
151 H4 Qurmuxçay *r.* Azer.
144 E5 Qūrtān Iran
151 F7 Qūrū Gol *pass* Iran
225 G3 Qūş Egypt
151 J4 Qusar Azer.
151 J4 Qusarçay *r.* Azer.
147 J8 Quşay'ir Saudi Arabia
Qushan *Sichuan* China *s*[…] Beichuan
144 A3 Qūshchī Iran
144 B2 Qūsheh Dāgh *mts* Iran
Qŭshkŭpir Uzbek. *see* Qo'shko'pir
Qŭshrabot Uzbek. *see* Qo[…]
Qusmuryn Kazakh. *see* Kushmurun
Qusmuryn Köli *salt l.* Ka[…] Kushmurun, Ozero
133 D10 Qusum *Xizang* China
133 K12 Qusum *Xizang* China
Quthing Lesotho *see* Moy[…]
237 L6 Quthing *r.* Lesotho
144 C4 Qūtīābād Iran
146 F2 Quţn, Jabal *hill* Saudi Ara[…]
243 K1 Quttinirpaaq National P[…] *Nunavut* Can.
146 E6 Qutū' *i.* Saudi Arabia
150 F3 Quwayq, Nahr *r.* Syria/Tu[…]
147 L6 Qū' Wishām *reg.* Oman
129 L9 Quwo *Shanxi* China
128 I8 Quwu Shan *mts* China
Quxi *Guangdong* China *s*[…] Jiedong
130 F3 Quxian *Sichuan* China
Quxian *Zhejiang* China *se*[…] Quzhou
133 J12 Qüxü *Xizang* China
Quyang *Hunan* China *see* Jingzhou
Quyghan Kazakh. *see* Kuy[…]
118 F4 Quynh Nhai Vietnam
119 I8 Quy Nhơn Vietnam
251 R4 Quyon *Que.* Can.
144 A3 Qūyūn Eshek *i.* Iran
146 E6 Qūz Saudi Arabia
151 I5 Quzanlı Azer.
129 N8 Quzhou *Hebei* China
131 L4 Quzhou *Zhejiang* China
129 J8 Quzi *Gansu* China
151 G4 Qvareli Georgia
151 E3 Qvirila *r.* Georgia
Qypshaq Köli *salt l.* Kaza[…] Kypshak, Ozero
Qyteti Stalin Albania *see* […]
Qyzan Kazakh. *see* Kyzan
Qyzylaghash Kazakh. *see* Kyzylagash
Qyzylkesek Kazakh. *see* Kyzylkesek
Qyzylköl *l.* Kazakh. *see* Kyzylkol', Ozero
Qyzylorda Kazakh. *see* Ky[…]
Qyzylorda Oblysy *admin.* Kazakh. *see* Kyzylordinsk[…] Oblast'
Qyzyltas Kazakh. *see* Kyzy[…]
Qyzyltaū Kazakh. *see* Kyzy[…]
Qyzyltū Kazakh. *see* Kishk[…]
Qyzylzhar Kazakh. *see* Ky[…]

R

201 I3 Raab Austria
201 N6 Raab *r.* Austria
Raab Hungary *see* Győr
201 L2 Raabs an der Thaya Austr[…]
162 R4 Raahe Fin.
162 T5 Rääkkylä Fin.
186 J4 Raalte Neth.
186 G5 Raamsdonksveer Neth.
146 F2 Ra'an, Khashm ar *hill* Saudi Arabia
162 R3 Raanujärvi Fin.
117 K8 Raas *i.* Indon.
168 D8 Raasay *i. Scotland* U.K.
168 D8 Raasay, Sound of *sea char*[…] *Scotland* U.K.
160 I2 Raasiku Estonia
162 T4 Raate Fin.
213 R6 Rab Croatia
210 E3 Rab *i.* Croatia
198 G4 Rába *r.* Hungary
117 M9 Raba *Sumbawa* Indon.
197 I5 Raba *r.* Pol.
232 F2 Rabaale Somalia
213 Q5 Rabac Croatia
204 D8 Rabaçal *Coimbra* Port.
204 F7 Rabaçal *Guarda* Port.
204 F5 Rabaçal *r.* Port./Spain
204 E2 Rábade Spain
199 L5 Răbăgani Romania
198 F4 Rábahidvég Hungary

Rabak Sudan
Rábakecöl Hungary
Rabanales Spain
Rabang *Xizang* China
Rábapaty Hungary
Rábapordány Hungary
Rabastens France
Rabastens-de-Bigorre France
Rabat Kazakh.
Rabat *Gozo* Malta *see* **Victoria**
Rabat Malta
Rabat Morocco
Rabatakbaytal Tajik. *see* **Rabotoqbaytal**
Rabāt-e Kamah Iran
Rabaul *New Britain* P.N.G.
Raba Wyżna Pol.
Rabbath Ammon Jordan *see* **'Ammān**
Rabbi *r.* Italy
Rabbies *r.* Italy
Rabbit *r. B.C.* Can.
Rabbit Flat *N.T.* Austr.
Rabbitskin *r. N.W.T.* Can.
Rábca *r.* Hungary
Rabča Slovakia
Rabčice Slovakia
Rabe *Vojvodina* Serbia
Rabenau Ger.
Rabenstein an der Pielach Austria
Raben Steinfeld Ger.
Rabezha Rus. Fed.
Rabi *i.* Fiji
Rabia *Papua* Indon.
Rabidine *well* Niger
Rābigh Saudi Arabia
Rabinal Guat.
Rąbino Pol.
Rabisca, Punta de *pt La Palma* Canary Is
Rabiusa *r.* Switz.
Rabjerg *nature res.* Denmark
Rabka Pol.
Räbke Ger.
Rabkob *Chhattisgarh* India *see* **Dharmjaygarh**
Rabnabad Islands Bangl.
Râbniţa Moldova *see* **Rîbniţa**
Rabo de Peixe *São Miguel* Azores
Rābor Iran
Raboso *r.* Italy
Rabotoqbaytal *Kŭhistoni Badakhshon* Tajik.
Rabovichi Rus. Fed.
Rabt Sbayta *des.* Western Sahara
Rabyānah *oasis* Libya
Rabyānah, Ramlat *des.* Libya
Rača *Rača* Serbia
Racaka *Xizang* China
Racale Italy
Rácalmás Hungary
Racalmuto *Sicilia* Italy
Racanello *r.* Italy
Raccolana *r.* Italy
Racconigi Italy
Raccoon Cay *i.* Bahamas
Raccoon Creek *r. NJ* U.S.A.
Raccoon Creek *r. OH* U.S.A.
Raccuia *Sicilia* Italy
Rače Slovenia
Race, Cape *Nfld and Lab.* Can.
Raceland *LA* U.S.A.
Race Point *MA* U.S.A.
Rachaïya Lebanon
Rachal *TX* U.S.A.
Rachanie Pol.
Racha Noi, Ko *i.* Thai.
Racha Yai, Ko *i.* Thai.
Rachecourt-sur-Marne France
Rachel *NV* U.S.A.
Raches *Ikaria* Greece
Rachevo Rus. Fed.
Rach Gia Vietnam
Rach Gia, Vinh *b.* Vietnam
Rachis K'edi *hills* Georgia
Raciąż *Kujawsko-Pomorskie* Pol.
Raciąż *Mazowieckie* Pol.
Raciążnica *r.* Pol.
Racibórz Pol.
Raciechowice Pol.
Racimierz Pol.
Racine *WI* U.S.A.
Racine *WV* U.S.A.
Racine Lake *Ont.* Can.
Râciu Romania
Ráckeve Hungary
Rackwick *Orkney, Scotland* U.K.
Rackwitz Ger.
Racławice Pol.
Racoş Romania
Racoviţa *Brăila* Romania
Racoviţa *Timiş* Romania
Raczki Pol.
Rączki Pol.
Radā' Yemen
Radal Chile
Radashkovichy Belarus
Rădăuţi Romania
Radbuza *r.* Czech Rep.
Radchenko Rus. Fed.
Radchenskoye Rus. Fed.
Radcliff *KY* U.S.A.
Radcliffe *Greater Manchester, England* U.K.
Radcliffe on Trent *Nottinghamshire, England* U.K.
Radde Rus. Fed.
Raddusa *Sicilia* Italy
Rade Norway
Radeberg Ger.
Radebeul Ger.
Radeburg Ger.
Radeče Slovenia
Radefeld Ger.
Radegast Ger.
Radekhiv Ukr.
Radenci Slovenia
Radens'k Ukr.
Radensleben Ger.
Radenthein Austria
Radevormwald Ger.
Radew *r.* Pol.
Radfeld Austria
Radford *VA* U.S.A.
Radford Point *N.T.* Austr.
Radford Semele *Warwickshire, England* U.K.
Radhanpur *Gujarat* India
Radibor Ger.
Radicofani Italy
Radicondoli Italy
Radicosa *r.* Italy
Radili Ko *N.W.T.* Can. *see* **Fort Good Hope**
Radis Ger.
Radishchevo Rus. Fed.
Radisson *Que.* Can.
Radisson *Sask.* Can.
Radisson *WI* U.S.A.
Raditsa-Krylovka Rus. Fed.
Radium Hot Springs B.C. Can.
Radizelj Slovenia
Rad'kovka Rus. Fed.
Radków *Dolnośląskie* Pol.
Radków *Świętokrzyskie* Pol.
Radlett *Hertfordshire, England* U.K.
Radlinski, Mount Antarctica
Radlje ob Dravi Slovenia
Radłów *Małopolskie* Pol.
Radłów *Opolskie* Pol.
Radnevo Bulg.
Radnice Czech Rep.
Rado de Tumaco *inlet* Col.
Radogoshcha Rus. Fed.
Radojevo *Vojvodina* Serbia
Radolfzell am Bodensee Ger.
Radom Pol.
Radom Sudan
Radomin Pol.
Radomir Bulg.
Radomir *mt.* Bulg./Greece
Radomka *r.* Pol.
199 K2 **Radomka** *r.* Slovakia
159 L2 **Radomka** Ukr.
230 D2 **Radom National Park** Sudan
197 J4 **Radomska, Równina** *plain* Pol.
197 H4 **Radomsko** Pol.
158 I3 **Radomyshl'** Ukr.
197 J5 **Radomyśl nad Sanem** Pol.
197 J5 **Radomyśl Wielki** Pol.
198 C1 **Radonice** Czech Rep.
Radoshkovichi Belarus *see* **Radashkovichy**
199 G3 **Radošina** Slovakia
198 G3 **Radošovce** Slovakia
197 I4 **Radoszyce** Pol.
196 D3 **Radoszyn** Pol.
219 O9 **Radovets** Bulg.
219 K9 **Radoviš** Macedonia
161 W6 **Radovitskiy** Rus. Fed.
210 E2 **Radovljica** Slovenia
196 D2 **Radowo Małe** Pol.
166 J1 **Radøy** *i.* Norway
201 H5 **Radstadt** Austria
201 H5 **Radstädter Tauern** *mts* Austria
201 I5 **Radstädter Tauern** *pass* Austria
172 H5 **Radstock** *Bath and North East Somerset, England* U.K.
104 E5 **Radstock, Cape** *S.A.* Austr.
219 P4 **Răducăneni** Romania
158 J2 **Radul'** Ukr.
160 H7 **Radun'** Belarus
165 O7 **Radunia** *r.* Pol.
159 M6 **Radushne** Ukr.
199 K2 **Radvaň nad Laborcom** Slovakia
160 G6 **Radviliškis** Lith.
146 D3 **Raḑwá, Jabal** *mt.* Saudi Arabia
196 D4 **Radwanice** Pol.
197 K6 **Radymno** Pol.
159 M4 **Radyvonivka** Ukr.
158 E3 **Radyvyliv** Ukr.
197 I3 **Radzanów** Pol.
197 I4 **Radzice Duże** Pol.
196 F2 **Radzicz** Pol.
197 J1 **Radzieje** Pol.
196 G3 **Radziejów** Pol.
197 I6 **Radziejowa** *mt.* Pol.
197 I3 **Radziejowice** Pol.
197 I5 **Radziemice** Pol.
196 C3 **Radzików** Pol.
197 K2 **Radziłów** Pol.
Radzivilovichi Belarus *see* **Dzyarzhynsk**
199 I3 **Radzovce** Slovakia
197 J3 **Radzymin** Pol.
196 G2 **Radzyń Chełminski** Pol.
197 K4 **Radzyń Podlaski** Pol.
138 H6 **Rae Bareli** *Uttar Prad.* India
245 M2 **Raecreek** *r. Y.T.* Can.
Rae-Edzo Can. *see* **Behchokô**
255 H8 **Raeford** *NC* U.S.A.
Rae Lakes Can. *see* **Gamètì**
187 J7 **Raeren** Belgium
191 C7 **Raesfeld** Ger.
109 F10 **Raeside, Lake** *salt flat W.A.* Austr.
102 H2 **Raetea** *hill North I.* N.Z.
102 J6 **Raetihi** *North I.* N.Z.
149 I9 **Rāf** *hill* Saudi Arabia
284 A5 **Rafael** Chile
285 G2 **Rafaela** Arg.
270 F3 **Rafael Freyre** Cuba
269 J6 **Rafael J. García** Mex.
285 G4 **Rafael Obligado** Arg.
Rafaḩ Gaza *see* **Rafiah**
230 D3 **Rafaï** C.A.R.
158 F2 **Rafalivka** Ukr.
209 E8 **Rafelbuñol** Spain
216 F9 **Raffadali** *Sicilia* Italy
246 K5 **Rafferty Reservoir** Can.
168 I7 **Rafford** *Moray, Scotland* U.K.
169 K4 **Raffrey** *Northern Ireland* U.K.
149 K9 **Rafḩā'** Saudi Arabia
150 C7 **Rafiah** Gaza
230 E3 **Rafili** Sudan
220 F4 **Rafina** Greece
169 E6 **Raford** *r.* Ireland
144 F6 **Rafsanjān** Iran
262 H5 **Raft** *r. ID/NV* U.S.A.
230 E2 **Raga** Sudan
230 E2 **Ragag** Sudan
205 J7 **Rágama** Spain
160 H4 **Ragana** Latvia
217 K4 **Raganello** *r.* Italy
114 E8 **Ragang, Mount** *vol. Mindanao* Phil.
114 D5 **Ragay Gulf** *Luzon* Phil.
192 G4 **Rägelin** Ger.
109 G12 **Ragged, Mount** *hill W.A.* Austr.
270 F2 **Ragged Island** Bahamas
257 □Q5 **Ragged Island** *ME* U.S.A.
271 □4 **Ragged Point** Barbados
145 N3 **Rāgh** Afgh.
138 F7 **Raghogarh** *Madh. Prad.* India
146 G1 **Raghwah** Saudi Arabia
146 G8 **Raghwān, Wādī** *watercourse* Yemen
102 I4 **Raglan** *North I.* N.Z.
172 G4 **Raglan** *Monmouthshire, Wales* U.K.
102 I4 **Raglan Harbour** *North I.* N.Z.
201 M6 **Ragnitz** Austria
162 N3 **Rago Nasjonalpark** *nat. park* Norway
193 G6 **Ragösen** Ger.
207 M6 **Ragua, Puerto de la** *pass* Spain
249 G3 **Ragueneau** *Que.* Can.
193 F7 **Raguhn** Ger.
Ragusa Croatia *see* **Dubrovnik**
216 H10 **Ragusa** *Sicilia* Italy
216 H10 **Ragusa** *prov. Sicilia* Italy
133 K11 **Ragxi** *Xizang* China
128 G9 **Ra'gyagoinba** *Qinghai* China
118 A1 **Raha** *Assam* India
115 C6 **Raha** *Sulawesi* Indon.
161 N8 **Rahachow** Belarus
225 G6 **Rahad** *r.* Sudan
225 G6 **Rahad Canal** Sudan
230 D2 **Rahad el Berdi** Sudan
224 E6 **Rahad Wahal** *well* Sudan
Rahaeng Thai. *see* **Tak**
146 E4 **Rahaţ, Ḩarrat** *lava field* Saudi Arabia
138 F8 **Rahatgaon** *Madh. Prad.* India
191 G6 **Rahden** Ger.
136 D4 **Rahimatpur** *Mahar.* India
145 N7 **Rahimyar Khan** Pak.
179 L8 **Rahin** *r.* France
144 D4 **Rāhjerd** Iran
144 H6 **Raḩmān, Chāh-e** *well* Iran
102 H6 **Rahotu** *North I.* N.Z.
218 I8 **Rahovec** *Rahovec* Kosovo
284 B6 **Rahué** Arg.
284 B6 **Rahue** *mt.* Chile
160 K3 **Rahumäe** Estonia
136 D3 **Rahuri** *Mahar.* India
145 I4 **Rahzanak** Afgh.
119 G10 **Rai, Hon** *i.* Vietnam
215 L3 **Raiano** Italy
101 □9 **Raiatea** *i. Arch. de la Société* Fr. Polynesia
Raibu *i.* Indon. *see* **Air**
285 H2 **Raices** Arg.
136 E4 **Raichur** *Karnataka* India
139 L7 **Raiganj** *W. Bengal* India
139 I9 **Raigarh** *Chhattisgarh* India
136 H3 **Raigarh** *Orissa* India
115 B9 **Raijua** *i.* Indon.
138 E4 **Raikot** *Punjab* India
244 H3 **Railroad City** *AK* U.S.A.
265 Q3 **Railroad Valley** *NV* U.S.A.
139 L9 **Raimangal** *r.* Bangl.
249 G2 **Raimbault, Lac** *l. Que.* Can.
195 J4 **Rain** *Bayern* Ger.
195 M4 **Rain** *Bayern* Ger.
201 J2 **Rainbach im Mühlkreis** Austria
105 I6 **Rainbow** *Vic.* Austr.
107 N8 **Rainbow Beach** *Qld* Austr.
265 V4 **Rainbow Bridge National Monument** *nat. park UT* U.S.A.
246 G3 **Rainbow Lake** *Alta* Can.
107 J1 **Raine Entrance** *sea chan. Qld* Austr.
107 J1 **Raine Island** *Qld* Austr.
256 E11 **Rainelle** *WV* U.S.A.
171 L6 **Rainford** *Merseyside, England* U.K.
145 M7 **Raini** *r.* Pak.
262 D3 **Rainier, Mount** *vol. WA* U.S.A.
115 E1 **Rainis** *Sulawesi* Indon.
171 M7 **Rainow** *Cheshire, England* U.K.
171 O7 **Rainworth** *Nottinghamshire, England* U.K.
260 H1 **Rainy** *r. MN* U.S.A.
247 M5 **Rainy Lake** *Ont.* Can.
244 I3 **Rainy Pass Lodge** *AK* U.S.A.
247 M5 **Rainy River** *Ont.* Can.
162 P5 **Raippaluoto** *i.* Fin.
139 M8 **Raipur** Bangl.
138 H9 **Raipur** *Chhattisgarh* India
138 E6 **Raipur** *Rajasthan* India
139 K8 **Raipur** *W. Bengal* India
139 K8 **Rairangpur** *Orissa* India
100 □3b **Rairik** *i. Majuro* Marshall Is
204 E4 **Rairiz de Veiga** Spain
Rairoa *atoll Arch. des Tuamotu* Fr. Polynesia *see* **Rangiroa**
190 J2 **Raisdorf** Ger.
138 F8 **Raisen** *Madh. Prad.* India
216 E7 **Raisi, Punta** *pt Sicilia* Italy
138 D5 **Raisinghnagar** *Rajasthan* India
163 Q6 **Raisio** Fin.
178 F3 **Raismes** France
162 T3 **Raistakka** Fin.
138 F9 **Raitalai** *Madh. Prad.* India
195 K3 **Raitenbuch** Ger.
250 E1 **Raith** *Ont.* Can.
103 H8 **Rai Valley** *South I.* N.Z.
101 □9 **Raivavae** *i. Îs Australes* Fr. Polynesia
145 P6 **Raiwind** Pak.
160 J3 **Raja** Estonia
117 J8 **Raja** *i.* Indon.
116 B3 **Raja, Ujung** *pt* Indon.
115 F4 **Rajaampat, Kepulauan** *is Papua* Indon.
116 F7 **Rajabasa, Gunung** *vol.* Indon.
208 I4 **Rajadell, Riera de** *r.* Spain
139 J8 **Rajagangapur** *Orissa* India
136 G4 **Rajahmundry** *Andhra Prad.* India
162 T2 **Raja-Jooseppi** Fin.
138 E5 **Rajaldesar** *Rajasthan* India
160 H1 **Rajamäki** Fin.
136 F5 **Rajampet** *Andhra Prad.* India
117 I3 **Rajang** *Sarawak* Malaysia
117 I3 **Rajang** *r.* Malaysia
145 N7 **Rajanpur** Pak.
136 E8 **Rajapalaiyam** *Tamil Nadu* India
136 C4 **Rajapur** *Mahar.* India
138 D6 **Rajasthan** *state* India
138 D5 **Rajasthan Canal** India
139 J7 **Rajauli** *Bihar* India
139 L8 **Rajbari** Bangl.
198 F2 **Rájec** Czech Rep.
199 H2 **Rajec** Slovakia
199 H2 **Rajecká Lesná** Slovakia
138 F7 **Rajgarh** *Madh. Prad.* India
136 C3 **Rajgarh** *Mahar.* India
138 E5 **Rajgarh** *Rajasthan* India
138 F6 **Rajgarh** *Rajasthan* India
139 J7 **Rajgir** *Bihar* India
197 K2 **Rajgród** Pol.
197 K2 **Rajgrodzkie, Jezioro** *l.* Pol.
139 J7 **Rajhara** *Jharkhand* India
201 O1 **Rajhrad** Czech Rep.
198 F2 **Rajhradice** Czech Rep.
Rájijovsset Fin. *see* **Raja-Jooseppi**
116 F6 **Rajik** Indon.
138 H9 **Rajim** *Chhattisgarh* India
219 J8 **Rajince** *Preševo* Serbia
198 G3 **Rajka** Hungary
138 C8 **Rajkot** *Gujarat* India
139 K7 **Rajmahal** *Jharkhand* India
138 E7 **Raj Mahal** *Rajasthan* India
139 J7 **Rajmahal Hills** India
139 K8 **Rajnagar** *W. Bengal* India
138 H9 **Raj Nandgaon** *Chhattisgarh* India
138 E3 **Rajouri** *Jammu and Kashmir* India
138 D9 **Rajpipla** *Gujarat* India
138 E9 **Rajpur** *Madh. Prad.* India
138 F4 **Rajpura** *Punjab* India
Rajputana Agency *state* India *see* **Rajasthan**
138 D7 **Rajsamand** *Rajasthan* India
139 L7 **Rajshahi** Bangl.
139 L7 **Rajshahi** *admin. div.* Bangl.
150 E2 **Rājū** Syria
138 C9 **Rajula** *Gujarat* India
138 G9 **Rajur** *Mahar.* India
Rajura *Mahar.* India *see* **Ahmadpur**
136 F3 **Rajura** *Mahar.* India
133 G12 **Raka** *Xizang* China
201 L8 **Raka** Slovenia
147 K5 **Rakabah, Qalamat ar** *oasis* Saudi Arabia
199 J3 **Rakaca** *r.* Hungary
103 □2 **Rakahanga** *atoll* Cook Is
Rakahuri *r. South I.* N.Z. *see* **Ashley**
232 A5 **Rakai** Uganda
103 G10 **Rakaia** *South I.* N.Z.
103 G10 **Rakaia** *r. South I.* N.Z.
199 K3 **Rakamaz** Hungary
147 J2 **Rakan, Ra's** *pt* Qatar
138 E1 **Rakaposhi** *mt.* Pak.
Raka Zangbo *r. Xizang* China *see* **Dogxung Zangbo**
103 B13 **Rakeahua, Mount** *hill Stewart I.* N.Z.
201 J8 **Rakek** Slovenia
Rakhaing *state* Myanmar *see* **Arakan**
Rakhine *state* Myanmar *see* **Arakan**
158 D5 **Rakhiv** Ukr.
159 M6 **Rakhmanivka** Ukr.
145 M6 **Rakhni** Pak.
145 N6 **Rakhni** *r.* Pak.
145 J8 **Rakhshan** *r.* Pak.
101 □7a **Rakiraki** *Viti Levu* Fiji
117 H7 **Rakit** *i.* Indon.
117 L9 **Rakit** *i.* Indon.
201 J8 **Rakitna** Slovenia
219 N8 **Rakitnitsa** *r.* Bulg.
157 F6 **Rakitnoye** *Belgorodskaya Oblast'* Rus. Fed.
122 I6 **Rakitnoye** *Primorskiy Kray* Rus. Fed.
213 P5 **Rakitovec** Slovenia
102 J3 **Rakitu Island** *North I.* N.Z.
Rakiura *i.* N.Z. *see* **Stewart Island**
160 J3 **Rakke** Estonia
164 H2 **Rakkestad** Norway
132 H2 **Rakmanovskie Klyuchi** Kazakh.
199 J4 **Rákóczifalva** Hungary
199 J4 **Rákócziújfalu** Hungary
196 E3 **Rakoniewice** Pol.
234 E4 **Rakops** Botswana
199 L3 **Rakoshyn** Ukr.
199 H2 **Raková** Slovakia
219 K7 **Rakovitsa** Bulg.
198 C1 **Rakovnická pahorkatina** *hills* Czech Rep.
198 C1 **Rakovník** Czech Rep.
219 M8 **Rakovski** Bulg.
192 H2 **Rakow** Ger.
197 J5 **Raków** Pol.
197 K5 **Rakszawa** Pol.
157 K7 **Rakusha** Kazakh.
142 D6 **Rakushechnyy, Mys** *pt* Kazakh.
160 J2 **Rakvere** Estonia
198 F3 **Rakvice** Czech Rep.
237 M6 **Ralebona** Lesotho
261 K9 **Raleigh** *MS* U.S.A.
255 H8 **Raleigh** *NC* U.S.A.
275 G3 **Raleighvallen Voltsberg, Natuurreservaat** *nature res.* Suriname
194 B2 **Ralingen** Ger.
115 A6 **Ralla** *Sulawesi* Indon.
250 G3 **Ralph** *MI* U.S.A.
247 I5 **Ralston** *Alta* Can.
251 R8 **Ralston** *PA* U.S.A.
135 □1 **Raluara Giri** *i. N. Male* Maldives
246 F2 **Ram** *r. N.W.T.* Can.
150 D6 **Rama** Israel
266 □Q11 **Rama** Nic.
158 D3 **Rama** *r.* Ukr.
216 H9 **Ramacca** *Sicilia* Italy
284 B3 **Ramada, Cerro de la** *mt.* Arg.
Ramādī Iraq *see* **Ar Ramādī**
276 C5 **Ramaditas** Chile
137 I3 **Ramagiri** *Orissa* India
249 I1 **Ramah** *Nfld and Lab.* Can.
205 N2 **Ramales de la Victoria** Spain
206 A2 **Ramalhal** Port.
278 D5 **Ramalho, Serra do** *hills* Brazil
150 D7 **Rāmallāh** West Bank
285 G3 **Ramallo** Arg.
136 E6 **Ramanagaram** *Karnataka* India
136 F8 **Ramanathapuram** *Tamil Nadu* India
139 I8 **Ramanuj Ganj** *Chhattisgarh* India
259 G3 **Ramapo** *r. NJ* U.S.A.
290 E3 **Ramapo Deep** *sea feature* N. Pacific Ocean
139 I9 **Ramapur** *Orissa* India
136 C5 **Ramas, Cape** India
161 Q9 **Ramasukha** Rus. Fed.
237 J1 **Ramatlabama** *watercourse* Botswana/S. Africa
237 J1 **Ramatlabama** S. Africa
183 J10 **Ramatuelle** France
136 F3 **Ramayampet** *Andhra Prad.* India
162 L2 **Ramberg** Norway
179 M7 **Rambervillers** France
138 E8 **Rambhapur** *Madh. Prad.* India
Rambi *i.* Fiji *see* **Rabi**
192 H2 **Rambin** Ger.
209 C11 **Rambla del Judio, Embalse** *resr* Spain
178 C6 **Rambouillet** France
178 C6 **Rambouillet, Forêt de** *for.* France
187 I9 **Rambrouch** Lux.
179 K6 **Rambucourt** France
113 K7 **Rambutyo Island** *Admiralty Is* P.N.G.
136 D5 **Ramdurg** *Karnataka* India
172 D7 **Rame** *Cornwall, England* U.K.
139 K6 **Ramechhap** Nepal
237 N7 **Rame Head** S. Africa
172 D7 **Rame Head** *England* U.K.
169 G2 **Ramelton** Ireland
165 L1 **Rämen** *l.* Sweden
235 □K2 **Ramena** Madag.
161 V6 **Ramenskoye** Rus. Fed.
178 H6 **Ramerupt** France
103 F9 **Rameses, Mount** *South I.* N.Z.
161 T4 **Rameshki** Rus. Fed.
136 F8 **Rameswaram** *Tamil Nadu* India
144 I9 **Ramezān Kalak** Iran
133 D13 **Ramganga** *r.* India
139 M8 **Ramgarh** Bangl.
139 J8 **Ramgarh** *Jharkhand* India
138 C6 **Ramgarh** *Rajasthan* India
138 E6 **Ramgarh** *Rajasthan* India
138 F6 **Ramgarh** *Rajasthan* India
145 N4 **Ramgul** *reg.* Afgh.
144 C6 **Rāmhormoz** Iran
187 G7 **Ramillies** Belgium
106 E2 **Ramingining** *N.T.* Austr.
201 I5 **Ramingstein** Austria
238 □1a **Raminho** *Terceira* Azores
204 E4 **Ramirás** Spain
Ramit Tajik. *see* **Romit**
Ramitan Uzbek. *see* **Romiton**
139 I8 **Ramkola** *Chhattisgarh* India
150 C7 **Ramla** Israel
150 D9 **Ramm** Jordan
150 D9 **Ramm, Jabal** *mts* Jordan
194 C2 **Rammelsbach** Ger.
193 J8 **Rammenau** Ger.
195 I4 **Rammingen** Ger.
237 K3 **Rammulotsi** S. Africa
Ramnad *Tamil Nadu* India *see* **Ramanathapuram**
138 H7 **Ramnagar** *Madh. Prad.* India
138 H8 **Ramnagar** *Madh. Prad.* India
138 G5 **Ramnagar** *Uttaranchal* India
138 E3 **Ramnagar** *Jammu and Kashmir* India
165 M2 **Ramnäs** Sweden
164 G2 **Ramnes** Norway
161 N6 **Ramni** Belarus
219 P5 **Râmnicul Sărat** *r.* Romania
219 P5 **Râmnicu Sărat** Romania
219 M5 **Râmnicu Vâlcea** Romania
232 D3 **Ramo** Eth.
235 E4 **Ramokgwebane** Botswana
159 S2 **Ramon'** Rus. Fed.
264 P8 **Ramona** *CA* U.S.A.
179 M8 **Ramonchamp** France
268 D1 **Ramón Corona** Mex.
283 D7 **Ramón Lista** Arg.
284 C6 **Ramón M. Castro** Arg.
285 H6 **Ramón Santamarina** Arg.
185 G8 **Ramonville-St-Agne** France
169 H5 **Ramor, Lough** *l.* Ireland
251 N1 **Ramore** *Ont.* Can.
282 D1 **Ramos** Arg.
266 G5 **Ramos** Mex.
261 C13 **Ramos** *r.* Mex.
267 I5 **Ramos Arizpe** Mex.
212 I2 **Ramosch** Switz.
234 E5 **Ramotswa** Botswana
245 J2 **Rampart** *AK* U.S.A.
129 M2 **Rampart of Genghis Khan** *tourist site* Asia
245 O2 **Ramparts** *r. N.W.T.* Can.
171 K5 **Rampside** *Cumbria, England* U.K.
133 C11 **Rampur** *Hima. Prad.* India
138 F5 **Rampur** *Uttar Prad.* India
138 G5 **Rampur** *Uttar Prad.* India
138 E7 **Rampura** *Madh. Prad.* India
Rampur Boalia Bangl. *see* **Rajshahi**
139 K7 **Rampur Hat** *W. Bengal* India
118 A5 **Ramree** Myanmar
118 A5 **Ramree Island** Myanmar
144 D3 **Rāmsar** Iran
201 I5 **Ramsau am Dachstein** Austria
195 N6 **Ramsau bei Berchtesgaden** Ger.
200 E5 **Ramsau im Zillertal** Austria
165 L2 **Ramsberg** Sweden
171 M6 **Ramsbottom** *Greater Manchester, England* U.K.
173 I5 **Ramsbury** *Wiltshire, England* U.K.
162 N5 **Ramsele** Sweden
194 F6 **Ramsen** Switz.
251 L2 **Ramsey** *Ont.* Can.
170 I5 **Ramsey** Isle of Man
173 L3 **Ramsey** *Cambridgeshire, England* U.K.
259 G2 **Ramsey** *NJ* U.S.A.
170 I5 **Ramsey Bay** Isle of Man
172 B4 **Ramsey Island** *Wales* U.K.
248 D4 **Ramsey Lake** *Ont.* Can.
173 L3 **Ramsey St Mary's** *Cambridgeshire, England* U.K.
237 O6 **Ramsgate** S. Africa
173 O5 **Ramsgate** *Kent, England* U.K.
139 L6 **Ramshai Hat** *W. Bengal* India
144 C6 **Rāmshir** Iran
139 O5 **Ramsing** *Arun. Prad.* India
139 O5 **Ramsing** *mt. Arun. Prad.* India
163 M5 **Ramsjö** Sweden
190 E4 **Ramsloh (Saterland)** Ger.
194 D3 **Ramstein** Ger.
138 G9 **Ramtek** *Mahar.* India
139 N9 **Ramu** Bangl.
113 J7 **Ramu** *r.* P.N.G.
162 L5 **Ramundberget** Sweden
249 I2 **Ramusio, Lac** *l. Que.* Can.
162 N5 **Ramvik** Sweden
271 □3 **Ramville, Îlet** *i.* Martinique
160 H6 **Ramygala** Lith.
274 D4 **Rana, Cerro** *hill* Col.
204 G3 **Rañadoiro, Puerto de** *pass* Spain
204 G2 **Rañadoiro, Sierra de** *mts* Spain
139 L8 **Ranaghat** *W. Bengal* India
Ranai *i. HI* U.S.A. *see* **Lāna'i**
138 E7 **Rana Pratap Sagar** *resr* India
138 E8 **Ranapur** *Madh. Prad.* India
138 C7 **Ranasar** *Rajasthan* India
164 H1 **Rånåsfoss** Norway
117 L2 **Ranau** *Sabah* Malaysia
116 E7 **Ranau, Danau** *l.* Indon.
284 B4 **Rancagua** Chile
187 F8 **Rance** Belgium
180 G5 **Rance** *r.* France
183 B9 **Rance** *r.* France
280 B5 **Rancharia** Brazil
245 O3 **Rancheria** *Y.T.* Can.
245 O3 **Rancheria** *r. Y.T.* Can.
262 K4 **Ranchester** *WY* U.S.A.
139 J8 **Ranchi** *Jharkhand* India
264 K3 **Rancho Cordova** *CA* U.S.A.
277 F2 **Rancho de Caçados Tapiúnas** Brazil
268 E2 **Rancho Grande** Mex.
269 J2 **Rancho Nuevo** Mex.
285 H4 **Ranchos** Arg.
263 L8 **Ranchos de Taos** *NM* U.S.A.
283 B6 **Ranco, Lago** *l.* Chile
258 F5 **Rancocas Creek, North Branch** *r. NJ* U.S.A.
258 F5 **Rancocas Woods** *NJ* U.S.A.
105 K6 **Rand** *N.S.W.* Austr.
256 D10 **Rand** *WV* U.S.A.
237 P4 **Randalhurst** S. Africa
258 B6 **Randallstown** *MD* U.S.A.
169 J3 **Randalstown** *Northern Ireland* U.K.
182 C4 **Randan** France
216 H8 **Randazzo** *Sicilia* Italy
237 L2 **Randburg** S. Africa
201 K3 **Randegg** Austria
164 G5 **Randers** Denmark
194 H2 **Randersacker** Ger.
237 L2 **Randfontein** S. Africa
162 O3 **Randijaure** *l.* Sweden
257 N6 **Randolph** *MA* U.S.A.
257 □P4 **Randolph** *ME* U.S.A.
256 G6 **Randolph** *NY* U.S.A.
262 I6 **Randolph** *UT* U.S.A.
257 M5 **Randolph** *VT* U.S.A.
181 M4 **Randonnai** France
192 J3 **Randow** *r.* Ger.
264 O6 **Randsburg** *CA* U.S.A.
164 G1 **Randsfjorden** *l.* Norway
163 L5 **Randsjö** Sweden
163 J6 **Randsverk** Norway
237 M2 **Randvaal** S. Africa
162 Q4 **Råneå** Sweden
228 B3 **Ranérou** Senegal
181 K4 **Rânes** France
103 E12 **Ranfurly** *South I.* N.Z.
139 O6 **Ranga** *r.* India
119 E11 **Rangae** Thai.
139 N8 **Rangamati** Bangl.
139 N6 **Rangapara** *Assam* India
115 A5 **Rangas, Tanjung** *pt* Indon.
115 A5 **Rangasa, Tanjung** *pt* Indon.
102 □ **Rangatira Island** *Chatham Is* S. Pacific Ocean
102 H1 **Rangaunu Bay** *North I.* N.Z.
257 □O4 **Rangeley** *ME* U.S.A.
257 □O3 **Rangeley Lake** *ME* U.S.A.
265 X1 **Rangely** *CO* U.S.A.
194 F5 **Rangendingen** Ger.
248 D4 **Ranger Lake** *Ont.* Can.
251 K3 **Ranger Lake** *l. Ont.* Can.
200 G6 **Rangersdorf** Austria
138 H9 **Rangi** *Mahar.* India
139 M6 **Rangia** *Assam* India
Rangiauria *i. Chatham Is* S. Pacific Ocean *see* **Pitt Island**
103 G10 **Rangiora** *South I.* N.Z.
102 L4 **Rangipoua** *mt. North I.* N.Z.
101 □9 **Rangiroa** *atoll Arch. des Tuamotu* Fr. Polynesia
102 K5 **Rangitaiki** *North I.* N.Z.
102 K4 **Rangitaiki** *r. North I.* N.Z.
103 F11 **Rangitata** *South I.* N.Z.
103 F11 **Rangitata** *r. South I.* N.Z.
102 J7 **Rangitikei** *r. North I.* N.Z.
102 H7 **Rangitoto Islands** *South I.* N.Z.
102 J6 **Rangiwaea Junction** *North I.* N.Z.
102 J6 **Rangiwahia** *North I.* N.Z.
116 G8 **Rangkasbitung** *Jawa* Indon.
139 O5 **Rangku** *Arun. Prad.* India
145 P2 **Rangkŭl** Tajik.
Rangôn Myanmar *see* **Yangôn**
Rangôn *admin. div.* Myanmar *see* **Yangôn**
Rangoon Myanmar *see* **Yangôn**
Rangoon *admin. div.* Myanmar *see* **Yangôn**
118 C6 **Rangoon** *r.* Myanmar
139 L7 **Rangpur** Bangl.
145 N6 **Rangpur** Pak.
116 E4 **Rangsang** *i.* Indon.
193 H6 **Rangsdorf** Ger.
118 B1 **Rangse** Myanmar
130 D2 **Rangtag** *Gansu* China
204 E7 **Ranhados** Port.
138 D7 **Rani** *Rajasthan* India
138 E5 **Rania** *Haryana* India
136 D5 **Ranibennur** *Karnataka* India
250 A1 **Ranier City** *MN* U.S.A.
139 K8 **Raniganj** *W. Bengal* India
139 I8 **Ranijula Peak** *Chhattisgarh* India
138 G5 **Ranikhet** *Uttaranchal* India
145 M8 **Ranipur** Pak.
193 E9 **Ranis** Ger.
138 D7 **Raniwara** *Rajasthan* India
197 J5 **Ranizów** Pol.
139 I7 **Ranka Kalan** *Jharkhand* India
106 F6 **Ranken** *watercourse N.T.* Austr.
261 E10 **Rankin** *TX* U.S.A.
247 M2 **Rankin Inlet** *Nunavut* Can.
247 M2 **Rankin Inlet** *inlet Nunavut* Can.
105 K5 **Rankin's Springs** *N.S.W.* Austr.
219 K8 **Rankovce** *Rankovce* Macedonia
Rankovićevo *Kraljevo* Serbia *see* **Kraljevo**
200 A5 **Rankweil** Austria
160 K3 **Ranna** Estonia
107 M8 **Rannes** *Qld* Austr.
142 E2 **Ranneye** Rus. Fed.
168 H9 **Rannoch, Loch** *l. Scotland* U.K.
168 G9 **Rannoch Moor** *moorland Scotland* U.K.
168 G9 **Rannoch Station** *Perth and Kinross, Scotland* U.K.
160 J3 **Rannu** Estonia
229 H4 **Rano** Nigeria
165 O3 **Ränö** *i.* Sweden
100 □6 **Rano, Mount** *New Georgia Is* Solomon Is
235 □J3 **Ranobe** *r.* Madag.
235 □J4 **Ranohira** Madag.
235 □K3 **Ranomafana** Madag.
235 J4 **Ranomafana, Parc National de** *nat. park* Madag.
235 □J5 **Ranomatana** Madag.
235 □J4 **Ranomena** Madag.
100 □5 **Ranon** Vanuatu
119 D10 **Ranong** Thai.
100 □6 **Ranongga** *i. New Georgia Is* Solomon Is
235 □J5 **Ranopiso** Madag.
119 E11 **Ranot** Thai.
235 □J4 **Ranotsara Avaratra** Madag.
161 X7 **Ranova** *r.* Rus. Fed.
138 C8 **Ranpur** *Gujarat* India
284 C5 **Ranquilcó, Salitral** *salt pan* Arg.
284 C5 **Ranquil del Norte** Arg.
149 N7 **Rānsa** Iran
191 E10 **Ransbach-Baumbach** Ger.
164 I1 **Ransby** Sweden
113 H7 **Ransiki** *Papua* Indon.
171 O7 **Ranskill** *Nottinghamshire, England* U.K.
250 F8 **Ransom** *IL* U.S.A.
258 D2 **Ransom** *PA* U.S.A.
187 G6 **Ranst** Belgium
162 S2 **Ranta** Fin.
235 □K2 **Rantabe** Madag.
163 T5 **Rantasalmi** Fin.
117 K6 **Rantau** *Kalimantan* Indon.
116 E4 **Rantau** *i.* Indon.
116 D4 **Rantaukampar** *Sumatera* Indon.
117 J5 **Rantaupanjang** *Kalimantan* Indon.
117 L3 **Rantaupanjang** *Kalimantan* Indon.
116 C3 **Rantauprapat** *Sumatera* Indon.
117 J5 **Rantaupulut** *Kalimantan* Indon.
115 B5 **Rantemario, Gunung** *mt.* Indon.
201 J5 **Ranten** Austria
115 A5 **Rantepao** *Sulawesi* Indon.
250 F9 **Rantoul** *IL* U.S.A.
190 H2 **Rantrum** Ger.
161 R5 **Rantsevo** Rus. Fed.
162 R4 **Rantsila** Fin.
190 F1 **Rantum** Ger.
162 S4 **Ranua** Fin.
164 F5 **Ranum** Denmark
218 H9 **Ranxë** Albania
149 L5 **Rānya** Iraq
146 F5 **Ranyah, Wādī** *watercourse* Saudi Arabia
118 G5 **Rao Go** *mt.* Laos/Vietnam
122 H5 **Raohe** *Heilong.* China
179 M7 **Raon-l'Étape** France
213 K4 **Raossi** Italy
99 I4 **Raoul Island** N.Z.
101 □9 **Rapa** *i. Îs Australes* Fr. Polynesia
162 O3 **Rapaälven** *r.* Sweden
Rapa-iti *i. Îs Australes* Fr. Polynesia *see* **Rapa**
212 G7 **Rapallo** Italy
Rapa Nui *i.* S. Pacific Ocean *see* **Pascua, Isla de**
138 C8 **Rapar** *Gujarat* India
144 H9 **Rapch** *watercourse* Iran
284 B3 **Rapel** Chile
284 B3 **Rapel** *r.* Chile
284 B4 **Rapel, Embalse** *resr* Chile
170 B7 **Rapemills** Ireland
243 L3 **Raper, Cape** *Nunavut* Can.
169 G3 **Raphoe** Ireland
193 K6 **Rapice** Pol.
256 H10 **Rapidan** *r. VA* U.S.A.
104 G6 **Rapid Bay** *S.A.* Austr.
260 D3 **Rapid City** *SD* U.S.A.
251 P2 **Rapide-Deux** *Que.* Can.
251 P2 **Rapide-Sept** *Que.* Can.
215 L4 **Rapido** *r.* Italy
250 H4 **Rapid River** *MI* U.S.A.
160 K3 **Räpina** Estonia
276 D2 **Rapirrān** *r.* Brazil
160 H3 **Rapla** Estonia
213 L9 **Rapolano Terme** Italy
215 P6 **Rapolla** Italy
206 B2 **Raposa** Port.
198 G1 **Rapotín** Czech Rep.
204 F8 **Rapoula do Côa** Port.
256 I11 **Rappahannock** *r. VA* U.S.A.
115 A5 **Rappang** *Sulawesi* Indon.
191 K7 **Rappbodetalstausee** *resr* Ger.
194 F7 **Rapperswil** Switz.
201 L2 **Rappottenstein** Austria
138 I6 **Rapti** *r.* India
103 □3 **Rapua Passage** *Rarotonga* Cook Is
276 D3 **Rapulo** *r.* Bol.
136 F5 **Rapur** *Andhra Prad.* India
138 B8 **Rapur** *Gujarat* India
114 E5 **Rapurapu** *i.* Phil.
Raqqa Syria *see* **Ar Raqqah**
257 K4 **Raquette** *r. NY* U.S.A.
257 K5 **Raquette Lake** *NY* U.S.A.
106 F1 **Raragala Island** *N.T.* Austr.
138 I5 **Rara National Park** Nepal
178 E5 **Raray** France
258 F3 **Raritan, South Branch** *r. NJ* U.S.A.
259 G4 **Raritan Bay** *NJ* U.S.A.
145 M6 **Rarkan** Pak.
101 □9 **Raroia** *atoll Arch. des Tuamotu* Fr. Polynesia
212 D3 **Raron** Switz.
103 □3 **Rarotonga** *i.* Cook Is
138 E6 **Ras** *Rajasthan* India
213 Q5 **Raša** Croatia
210 E3 **Raša** *r.* Croatia
114 B7 **Rasa** *i.* Phil.
283 E6 **Rasa, Punta** *pt* Arg.
147 M6 **Ra's ad Daqm** Oman
147 N4 **Ra's al Ḩadd** Oman
224 E2 **Ra's al Ḩikmah** Egypt
Ras al Khaimah U.A.E. *see* **Ra's al Khaymah**
147 L3 **Ra's al Khaymah** U.A.E.
147 I1 **Ra's al Mish āb** Saudi Arabia
146 F4 **Raşan, Jabal** *hill* Saudi Arabia
150 D8 **Ra's an Naqb** Jordan
150 E4 **Ras Ba'albek** Lebanon
238 □3a **Rasca, Punta de la** *pt Tenerife* Canary Is
205 M7 **Rascafría** Spain
Râşcani Moldova *see* **Rîşcani**
193 G9 **Raschau** Ger.
232 C1 **Ras Dejen** *mt.* Eth.
191 I9 **Rasdorf** Ger.
160 G6 **Raseiniai** Lith.
227 E2 **Râs el Ma** Alg.
228 D2 **Râs el Mâ** Mali
135 □1 **Rasfaree** *i. N. Male* Maldives
225 G2 **Ra's Ghārib** Egypt
Rashaant Mongolia *see* **Delüün**
Rashaant Mongolia *see* **Öldziyt**
232 A2 **Rashad** Sudan
169 J3 **Rasharkin** *Northern Ireland* U.K.
169 G3 **Rashedoge** Ireland
225 F2 **Rashīd** Egypt
147 K4 **Rāshid** *reg.* Saudi Arabia
145 L6 **Rashid Qala** Afgh.
159 M3 **Rashivka** Ukr.
237 L1 **Rashoop** S. Africa
147 H8 **Rashshah** Yemen
144 C3 **Rasht** Iran
201 K8 **Rašica** Slovenia
160 K3 **Rasina** Estonia
218 J7 **Rasina** *r.* Serbia
205 N2 **Rasines** Spain
201 O7 **Rasinja** Croatia
163 M5 **Råsjö** Sweden
145 I8 **Räsk** Iran
218 I7 **Raška** *Raška* Serbia
133 B8 **Raskam** *mts* China
203 E5 **Ras Kebdana** Morocco
145 K7 **Ras Koh** *mt.* Pak.
145 K7 **Raskoh** *mts* Pak.
199 H2 **Raškovice** Czech Rep.
199 K2 **Raslavice** Slovakia
150 A9 **Ra's Matārimah** Egypt
146 B2 **Ra's Muḩammad National Park** Egypt
243 I3 **Rasmussen Basin** *sea feature Nunavut* Can.
161 O7 **Rasna** *Mahilyowskaya Voblasts'* Belarus
160 M7 **Rasna** *Vitsyebskaya Voblasts'* Belarus
219 N5 **Râşnov** Romania
228 □ **Raso** *i.* Cape Verde
283 D7 **Raso, Cabo** *c.* Arg.
278 F4 **Raso da Catarina** *hills* Brazil
109 H10 **Rason Lake** *salt flat W.A.* Austr.
160 L6 **Rasony** Belarus
219 P6 **Rasova** Romania
219 L7 **Rasovo** Bulg.
244 I4 **Raspberry Island** *AK* U.S.A.
193 L9 **Raspenava** Czech Rep.
208 G5 **Rasquera** Spain
139 I7 **Rasra** *Uttar Prad.* India
146 C2 **Ra's Sāq, Jabal** *hill* Saudi Arabia
147 J8 **Ra's Sharwayn** *c.* Yemen
239 □3b **Rassi Douamounyo** *c.* Mayotte
147 M5 **Ra's Şirāb** Oman
211 C7 **Rass Jebel** Tunisia
157 H5 **Rasskazovo** Rus. Fed.
219 L7 **Rast** Romania
161 N8 **Rasta** *r.* Belarus
147 J2 **Ras Tannūrah** Saudi Arabia
194 E4 **Rastatt** Ger.
190 E5 **Rastdorf** Ger.
164 F5 **Råsted** Denmark
190 F4 **Rastede** Ger.
193 D8 **Rastenberg** Ger.
201 L2 **Rastenfeld** Austria
200 E5 **Rastkogel** *mt.* Austria
Rastorguyevo Rus. Fed. *see* **Vidnoye**
192 D4 **Rastow** Ger.
205 J6 **Rasueros** Spain
145 O5 **Rasul** Pak.
164 C3 **Rasvåg** Norway
165 L2 **Råsvalen** *l.* Sweden
196 F4 **Raszków** Pol.
159 P2 **Rat'** *r.* Rus. Fed.
102 J6 **Rata** *North I.* N.Z.
Ratae *Leicester, England* U.K. *see* **Leicester**
116 F7 **Ratai, Gunung** *mt.* Indon.
160 K8 **Ratamka** Belarus
237 M2 **Ratanda** S. Africa
138 E7 **Ratangarh** *Madh. Prad.* India
138 E5 **Ratangarh** *Rajasthan* India
138 I8 **Ratanpur** *Chhattisgarh* India
138 D9 **Ratanpur** *Gujarat* India
163 M5 **Rätansbyn** Sweden
197 L3 **Rataychytsy** Belarus
119 D8 **Rat Buri** Thai.
161 W8 **Ratchino** *Lipetskaya Oblast'* Rus. Fed.
142 F1 **Ratchino** *Orenburgskaya Oblast'* Rus. Fed.
201 I6 **Rateče** Slovenia
190 K3 **Ratekau** Ger.
236 C7 **Ratelfontein** S. Africa
204 C6 **Rates** Port.
138 G7 **Rath** *Uttar Prad.* India
170 B7 **Rath** Ireland
169 I6 **Rathangan** Ireland
260 I5 **Rathbun Lake** *IA* U.S.A.
169 F6 **Rathcabban** Ireland
169 G5 **Rathconrath** Ireland
169 E8 **Rathcool** Ireland
169 J6 **Rathcoole** Ireland
169 F8 **Rathcormac** Ireland
170 D8 **Rathdangan** Ireland
169 G7 **Rathdowney** Ireland
169 J7 **Rathdrum** Ireland
118 A4 **Rathedaung** Myanmar
192 F5 **Rathenow** Ger.
192 F5 **Rathenower Wald- und Seengebiet** *park* Ger.
172 A1 **Rathfarnham** Ireland
169 J4 **Rathfriland** *Northern Ireland* U.K.
168 J10 **Rathillet** *Fife, Scotland* U.K.
169 E7 **Rathkeale** Ireland
169 G8 **Rathkeevin** Ireland
169 D4 **Rathlackan** Ireland
169 D4 **Rathlee** Ireland
169 J2 **Rathlin Island** *Northern Ireland* U.K.
169 E3 **Rathlin O'Birne Island** Ireland
169 I6 **Rathmolyon** Ireland
169 D8 **Rathmore** Ireland
169 G2 **Rathmullan** Ireland
145 L9 **Rath Nath** Pak.
169 J7 **Rathnew** Ireland
168 J11 **Ratho** *Edinburgh, Scotland* U.K.
169 G5 **Rathowen** Ireland
Ratibor Pol. *see* **Racibórz**
191 C8 **Ratingen** Ger.
Ratisbon Ger. *see* **Regensburg**
245 □B6 **Rat Island** *AK* U.S.A.
245 □B6 **Rat Islands** *AK* U.S.A.
210 E2 **Ratitovec** *mt.* Slovenia
138 E5 **Ratiya** *Haryana* India
150 E9 **Raţīyah, Wādī** *watercourse* Jordan
199 K3 **Rátka** Hungary
247 L3 **Rat Lake** *Man.* Can.
138 E8 **Ratlam** *Madh. Prad.* India
244 E2 **Ratmanova, Ostrov** *i.* Rus. Fed.
136 C4 **Ratnagiri** *Mahar.* India
136 G9 **Ratnapura** Sri Lanka
158 D2 **Ratne** Ukr.
Ratno Ukr. *see* **Ratne**
170 E6 **Ratoath** Ireland
145 M8 **Rato Dero** Pak.
263 L8 **Raton** *NM* U.S.A.
183 G10 **Ratonneau, Île** *i.* France
191 K10 **Rattelsdorf** Ger.
201 M5 **Ratten** Austria
162 R3 **Rattosjärvi** Fin.
168 J9 **Rattray** *Perth and Kinross, Scotland* U.K.
168 M7 **Rattray Head** *Scotland* U.K.
163 M6 **Rättvik** Sweden
245 N4 **Ratz, Mount** *B.C.* Can.
190 K3 **Ratzeburg** Ger.
190 K3 **Ratzeburger See** *l.* Ger.
193 D6 **Rätzlingen** Ger.
115 F2 **Rau** *i. Maluku* Indon.
116 D3 **Raub** Malaysia
191 E9 **Raubach** Ger.
195 M6 **Raubling** Ger.
285 H5 **Rauch** Arg.
258 A2 **Rauchtown** *PA* U.S.A.
284 B4 **Rauco** Chile
179 I4 **Raucourt-et-Flaba** France
269 N8 **Raudales de Malpaso** Mex.
162 □B1 **Rauðamýri** Iceland
162 S3 **Raudanjoki** *r.* Fin.
219 K5 **Râu de Mori** Romania
149 M9 **Raudhatain** Kuwait
160 I3 **Raudna** *r.* Estonia
160 G7 **Raudondvaris** Lith.
193 J6 **Rauen** Ger.
194 F3 **Rauenberg** Ger.
193 D10 **Rauenstein** Ger.
162 □F1 **Raufarhöfn** Iceland
160 L1 **Rauha** Fin.
195 J2 **Rauhe Ebrach** *r.* Ger.
102 L4 **Raukokore** *North I.* N.Z.
102 M4 **Raukumara** *mt. North I.* N.Z.
102 L4 **Raukumara Forest Park** *nature res. North I.* N.Z.
102 L5 **Raukumara Range** *mts North I.* N.Z.
139 I9 **Raul** *r.* India
183 B7 **Raulhac** France
281 F4 **Raul Soares** Brazil
163 P6 **Rauma** Fin.
103 I7 **Raumati** *North I.* N.Z.
160 I4 **Rauna** Latvia
173 K3 **Raunds** *Northamptonshire, England* U.K.
102 J6 **Raurimu** *North I.* N.Z.
200 G5 **Rauris** Austria
139 J8 **Raurkela** *Orissa* India
Rauschen Rus. Fed. *see* **Svetlogorsk**
191 G9 **Rauschenberg** Ger.
124 W2 **Rausu** Japan
124 W2 **Rausu-dake** *mt.* Japan
158 I6 **Răut** *r.* Moldova
213 N3 **Raut, Monte** *mt.* Italy
162 S5 **Rautalampi** Fin.
162 T5 **Rautavaara** Fin.
193 F10 **Rautenkranz** Ger.
163 T6 **Rautjärvi** Fin.
Rauza *Mahar.* India *see* **Khuldabad**
185 D6 **Rauzan** France
101 □9 **Ravahere** *atoll Arch. des Tuamotu* Fr. Polynesia
144 I8 **Rāvak** Iran
262 G3 **Ravalli** *MT* U.S.A.
144 G8 **Rāvang** Iran
144 B4 **Ravānsar** Iran
216 F9 **Ravanusa** *Sicilia* Italy
144 G6 **Rāvar** Iran
158 C3 **Rava-Rus'ka** Ukr.
143 N8 **Ravat** Kyrg.
215 N6 **Ravello** Italy
187 G6 **Ravels** Belgium
201 M2 **Ravelsbach** Austria
165 L5 **Rävemåla** Sweden
257 L6 **Ravena** *NY* U.S.A.
171 K5 **Ravenglass** *Cumbria, England* U.K.
213 M7 **Ravenna** Italy
213 M7 **Ravenna** *prov.* Italy
260 F5 **Ravenna** *NE* U.S.A.
256 D7 **Ravenna** *OH* U.S.A.
258 E4 **Raven Rock** *NJ* U.S.A.
107 J8 **Ravensbourne Creek** *watercourse Qld* Austr.
194 H6 **Ravensburg** Ger.
170 E5 **Ravensdale** Ireland
107 J4 **Ravenshoe** *Qld* Austr.
186 I5 **Ravenstein** Neth.
109 F12 **Ravensthorpe** W.A. Austr.
171 M5 **Ravenstonedale** *Cumbria, England* U.K.
107 K6 **Ravenswood** *Qld* Austr.
256 D10 **Ravenswood** *WV* U.S.A.
138 F9 **Raver** *Mahar.* India
145 N6 **Ravi** *r.* Pak.
183 B9 **Raviège, Lac de la** *l.* France
178 H8 **Ravières** France
258 C3 **Ravine** *PA* U.S.A.
210 E3 **Ravna Gora** Croatia
210 F3 **Ravna Gora** *hill* Croatia
201 L7 **Ravne** Slovenia
201 K6 **Ravne na Koroškem** Slovenia
142 H6 **Ravshan** Uzbek.
190 H1 **Ravsted** Denmark
115 B6 **Rawa Aopa Watumohai, Taman Nasional** *nat. park* Indon.
149 J6 **Rāwah** Iraq
150 A10 **Rawāhimī, Ra's** *pt* Egypt
225 G5 **Rawai** *well* Sudan

99 I2 **Rawaki** *i. Phoenix Is* Kiribati
145 O5 **Rawala Kot** Pak.
145 O5 **Rawalpindi** Pak.
246 H1 **Rawalpindi Lake** *N.W.T.* Can.
197 I4 **Rawa Mazowiecka** Pol.
149 L5 **Ŗawāndiz** Iraq
116 E6 **Rawas** *r.* Indon.
138 E5 **Rawatsar** *Rajasthan* India
171 P6 **Rawcliffe** *East Riding of Yorkshire, England* U.K.
171 O6 **Rawcliffe** *York, England* U.K.
146 G8 **Rawḍah** Yemen
150 F10 **Rawghah** *watercourse* Saudi Arabia
251 L3 **Rawhide Lake** *Ont.* Can.
116 C1 **Rawi, Ko** *i.* Thai.
196 E4 **Rawicz** Pol.
197 I3 **Rawka** *r.* Pol.
109 H11 **Rawlinna** *W.A.* Austr.
262 K6 **Rawlins** *WY* U.S.A.
109 I8 **Rawlinson, Mount** *hill W.A.* Austr.
109 J8 **Rawlinson Range** *hills W.A.* Austr.
171 O7 **Rawmarsh** *South Yorkshire, England* U.K.
145 J2 **Rawnina** Turkm.
Rawnina Turkm. *see* **Rawnina**
285 G4 **Rawson** *Buenos Aires* Arg.
283 D6 **Rawson** *Chubut* Arg.
286 N1 **Rawson Mountains** Antarctica
236 D9 **Rawsonville** S. Africa
171 M6 **Rawtenstall** *Lancashire, England* U.K.
130 A4 **Rawu** *Xizang* China
201 M4 **Raxalpe** *mts* Austria
139 J6 **Raxaul** *Bihar* India
250 A1 **Ray** *MN* U.S.A.
249 J4 **Ray, Cape** *Nfld and Lab.* Can.
117 I5 **Raya, Bukit** *mt. Kalimantan* Indon.
117 J5 **Raya, Bukit** *mt. Kalimantan* Indon.
136 F5 **Rayachoti** *Andhra Prad.* India
136 E5 **Rayadurg** *Andhra Prad.* India
137 H3 **Rayagada** *Orissa* India
150 E5 **Rayak** Lebanon
145 O3 **Rayan** Pak.
122 F4 **Raychikhinsk** Rus. Fed.
161 T3 **Rayda** Rus. Fed.
146 G8 **Raydah** Yemen
147 I7 **Raydah, Wādī ar** *r.* Yemen
144 G7 **Rāyen** Iran
264 M7 **Rayes Peak** *CA* U.S.A.
142 F1 **Rayevskiy** Rus. Fed.
159 K4 **Rayhorod** Ukr.
159 S5 **Rayhorodka** Ukr.
159 Q5 **Rayhorodok** Ukr.
173 N4 **Rayleigh** *Essex, England* U.K.
246 H5 **Raymond** *Alta* Can.
257 N5 **Raymond** *NH* U.S.A.
262 C3 **Raymond** *WA* U.S.A.
105 M5 **Raymond Terrace** *N.S.W.* Austr.
261 G12 **Raymondville** *TX* U.S.A.
247 J5 **Raymore** *Sask.* Can.
244 I2 **Ray Mountains** *AK* U.S.A.
139 K8 **Rayna** *W. Bengal* India
173 N4 **Rayne** *Essex, England* U.K.
287 D2 **Rayner Glacier** Antarctica
183 I10 **Rayol-Canadel-sur-Mer** France
269 H4 **Rayón** Mex.
268 G6 **Rayón, Parque Nacional** *nat. park* Mex.
267 I5 **Rayones** Mex.
119 E8 **Rayong** Thai.
159 L4 **Rayozero** Ukr.
261 G9 **Ray Roberts, Lake** *TX* U.S.A.
256 G8 **Raystown Lake** *PA* U.S.A.
147 K7 **Raysūt** Oman
150 F10 **Rayth al Khayl** *watercourse* Saudi Arabia
237 M1 **Rayton** S. Africa
133 L11 **Rayü** *Xizang* China
261 J9 **Rayville** *LA* U.S.A.
146 D4 **Rayyis** Saudi Arabia
180 B5 **Raz, Pointe du** *pt* France
184 F5 **Razac-sur-l'Isle** France
137 H3 **Razam** *Andhra Prad.* India
144 C4 **Razan** Iran
144 C5 **Rāzān** Iran
145 N5 **Razani** Pak.
219 J7 **Ražanj** *Ražanj* Serbia
149 K7 **Razāzah, Buḩayrat ar** *l.* Iraq
Razdan Armenia *see* **Hrazdan**
Razdel'naya Ukr. *see* **Rozdil'na**
122 G7 **Razdol'noye** Rus. Fed.
151 H1 **Razdol'ye** Rus. Fed.
201 J8 **Razdrto** Slovenia
160 J9 **Razdzyalavichy** Belarus
144 C5 **Razeh** Iran
184 G3 **Razès** France
185 I9 **Razès** *reg.* France
219 O7 **Razgrad** Bulg.
197 M2 **Razhanka** Belarus
133 J11 **Razhêng Zangbo** *r. Xizang* China
219 Q6 **Razim, Lacul** *lag.* Romania
219 L9 **Razlog** Bulg.
160 K5 **Rāznas** *l.* Latvia
199 H3 **Ráztočno** Slovakia
159 P3 **Razumnoye** Rus. Fed.
Raz"yezd 3km Rus. Fed. *see* **Novyy Urgal**
214 C5 **Razzoli, Isola** *i. Sardegna* Italy
256 D11 **R. D. Bailey Lake** *WV* U.S.A.
184 B3 **Ré, Île de** *i.* France
169 E6 **Rea, Lough** *l.* Ireland
172 G3 **Rea Brook** *r. England* U.K.
270 □ **Reading** Jamaica
173 K5 **Reading** *Reading, England* U.K.
173 K5 **Reading** *admin. div. England* U.K.
250 J8 **Reading** *MI* U.S.A.
256 A9 **Reading** *OH* U.S.A.
258 D4 **Reading** *PA* U.S.A.
258 F3 **Readington** *NJ* U.S.A.
257 M6 **Readsboro** *VT* U.S.A.
250 D6 **Readstown** *WI* U.S.A.
169 I5 **Reaghstown** Ireland
237 K1 **Reagile** S. Africa
278 F4 **Real** *r.* Brazil
285 H5 **Real Audiencia** Arg.
284 D4 **Real de Padre** Arg.
217 N2 **Reale, Canale** *r.* Italy
214 A5 **Reale, Rada della** *b. Sardegna* Italy
207 I8 **Reales** *mt.* Spain
285 E4 **Realicó** Arg.
185 I8 **Réalmont** France
216 E9 **Realmonte** *Sicilia* Italy
185 G7 **Réalville** France
258 C4 **Reamstown** *PA* U.S.A.
119 F8 **Reăng Kesei** Cambodia
101 □9 **Reao** *atoll Arch. des Tuamotu* Fr. Polynesia
267 I4 **Reata** Mex.
Reate Italy *see* **Rieti**
185 E7 **Réaup** France
258 F4 **Reaville** *NJ* U.S.A.
168 I5 **Reay** *Highland, Scotland* U.K.
227 H3 **Rebaa** Alg.
178 F6 **Rebais** France
162 O1 **Rebbenesøya** *i.* Norway
109 G10 **Rebecca, Lake** *salt flat W.A.* Austr.
187 F7 **Rebecq** Belgium
185 D9 **Rébénacq** France
185 I10 **Rébenty** *r.* France
246 G1 **Rebesca Lake** *N.W.T.* Can.
Rebiana Sand Sea *des.* Libya *see* **Rabyānah, Ramlat**
207 K4 **Rebollera** *mt.* Spain
205 M6 **Rebollo** Spain
205 O6 **Rebollosa de Jadraque** Spain
162 U5 **Reboly** Rus. Fed.
204 F5 **Rebordelo** Port.
204 D2 **Rebordelo** Spain
232 E3 **Rebrebti Dhubo** *well* Eth.
143 T1 **Rebrikha** Rus. Fed.
124 R1 **Rebun-suidō** *sea chan.* Japan
124 R1 **Rebun-tō** *i.* Japan
285 G5 **Recalde** Arg.
216 G1 **Recale** Italy
213 P9 **Recanati** Italy
219 J5 **Recaş** Romania
205 M8 **Recas** Spain
212 G7 **Recco** Italy
158 H6 **Recea** Moldova
Recess Ireland *see* **Sraith Salach**
179 I8 **Recey-sur-Ource** France
161 O5 **Rechane** Rus. Fed.
109 G13 **Recherche, Archipelago of the** *is W.A.* Austr.
109 G13 **Recherche Archipelago Nature Reserve** *W.A.* Austr.
179 M6 **Réchicourt-le-Château** France
Rechitsa Belarus *see* **Rechytsa**
192 G4 **Rechlin** Ger.
145 O6 **Rechna Doab** *lowland* Pak.
201 N5 **Rechnitz** Austria
187 J8 **Recht** Belgium
194 H2 **Rechtenbach** Ger.
190 D3 **Rechtsupweg** Ger.
158 F2 **Rechytsa** *Brestskaya Voblasts'* Belarus
158 J1 **Rechytsa** *Homyel'skaya Voblasts'* Belarus
201 L7 **Rečica** Slovenia
278 G4 **Recife** Brazil
237 J10 **Recife, Cape** S. Africa
239 □2a **Récifs, Île aux** *i. Inner Islands* Seychelles
284 B5 **Recinto** Chile
191 E6 **Recke** Ger.
212 E3 **Reckingen** Switz.
191 D7 **Recklinghausen** Ger.
192 F2 **Recknitz** *r.* Ger.
213 K4 **Recoaro Terme** Italy
282 F3 **Reconquista** Arg.
183 G7 **Recoubeau-Jansac** France
183 B8 **Recoules-Prévinquières** France
286 V1 **Recovery Glacier** Antarctica
277 F2 **Recreio** *Mato Grosso* Brazil
281 F4 **Recreio** *Minas Gerais* Brazil
282 D3 **Recreo** *Catamarca* Arg.
285 G2 **Recreo** *Santa Fé* Arg.
199 J4 **Recsk** Hungary
256 B10 **Rectorville** *KY* U.S.A.
205 O6 **Recuerda** Spain
196 D2 **Recz** Pol.
197 H4 **Ręczno** Pol.
107 I4 **Red** *r. Qld* Austr.
245 P4 **Red** *r. B.C.* Can.
247 L5 **Red** *r.* Can./U.S.A.
261 J10 **Red** *r.* U.S.A.
261 F8 **Red, North Fork** *r. OK* U.S.A.
196 G1 **Reda** Pol.
196 G1 **Reda** *r.* Pol.
116 E2 **Redang** *i.* Malaysia
187 I9 **Redange** Lux.
259 G4 **Red Bank** *NJ* U.S.A.
255 E8 **Red Bank** *TN* U.S.A.
Red Basin *Sichuan* China *see* **Sichuan Pendi**
249 J3 **Red Bay** *Nfld and Lab.* Can.
247 J4 **Redberry Lake** *Sask.* Can.
109 E8 **Red Bluff** *hill W.A.* Austr.
264 J1 **Red Bluff** *CA* U.S.A.
261 D10 **Red Bluff Lake** *TX* U.S.A.
173 L4 **Redbourn** *Hertfordshire, England* U.K.
265 T6 **Red Butte** *mt. AZ* U.S.A.
171 O4 **Redcar** *Redcar and Cleveland, England* U.K.
171 O4 **Redcar and Cleveland** *admin. div. England* U.K.
170 C3 **Redcastle** Ireland
247 I5 **Redcliff** *Alta* Can.
250 D3 **Red Cliff** *WI* U.S.A.
235 F3 **Redcliff** Zimbabwe
172 G5 **Redcliff Bay** *North Somerset, England* U.K.
107 N9 **Redcliffe** *Qld* Austr.
109 F10 **Redcliffe, Mount** *hill W.A.* Austr.
105 I6 **Red Cliffs** *Vic.* Austr.
260 F5 **Red Cloud** *NE* U.S.A.
169 J7 **Redcross** Ireland
246 H4 **Red Deer** *Alta* Can.
246 I5 **Red Deer** *r. Alta/Sask.* Can.
247 K4 **Red Deer** *r. Man./Sask.* Can.
247 K4 **Red Deer Lake** *Man.* Can.
192 E2 **Reddelich** Ger.
237 K5 **Reddersburg** S. Africa
244 H3 **Red Devil** *AK* U.S.A.
262 C6 **Redding** *CA* U.S.A.
259 I2 **Redding** *CT* U.S.A.
259 I2 **Redding Ridge** *CT* U.S.A.
173 I3 **Redditch** *Worcestershire, England* U.K.
171 M3 **Rede** *r. England* U.K.
246 H3 **Red Earth Creek** *Alta* Can.
192 D4 **Redefin** Ger.
236 C8 **Redelinghuys** S. Africa
278 C3 **Redenção** *Pará* Brazil
278 D4 **Redenção** *Piauí* Brazil
180 E6 **Rédené** France
183 E9 **Redessan** France
227 H2 **Redeyef** Tunisia
260 F3 **Redfield** *SD* U.S.A.
168 K9 **Redford** *Angus, Scotland* U.K.
245 M3 **Red Granite Mountain** *Y.T.* Can.
271 □7 **Redhead** Trin. and Tob.
104 G5 **Redhill** *S.A.* Austr.
173 L5 **Redhill** *Surrey, England* U.K.
258 E4 **Red Hill** *PA* U.S.A.
169 H4 **Redhills** Ireland
261 F7 **Red Hills** *KS* U.S.A.
257 L7 **Red Hook** *NY* U.S.A.
198 F5 **Rédics** Hungary
133 I12 **Red Idol Gorge** China
249 J3 **Red Indian Lake** *Nfld and Lab.* Can.
179 N6 **Réding** France
Redingen Lux. *see* **Redange**
204 C8 **Redinha** Port.
254 E5 **Redkey** *IN* U.S.A.
161 T5 **Redkino** Rus. Fed.
246 G2 **Redknife** *r. N.W.T.* Can.
247 M5 **Red Lake** *Ont.* Can.
247 M5 **Red Lake** *l. Ont.* Can.
265 T6 **Red Lake** *AZ* U.S.A.
260 H2 **Red Lake** *MN* U.S.A.
260 G2 **Red Lake** *r. MN* U.S.A.
260 G2 **Red Lake Falls** *MN* U.S.A.
260 H1 **Red Lake Indian Reservation** *res. MN* U.S.A.
260 H1 **Red Lakes** *MN* U.S.A.
264 O7 **Redlands** *CA* U.S.A.
258 F5 **Red Lion** *NJ* U.S.A.
258 B5 **Red Lion** *PA* U.S.A.
262 J4 **Red Lodge** *MT* U.S.A.
173 I6 **Redlynch** *Wiltshire, England* U.K.
102 J3 **Red Mercury Island** *North I.* N.Z.
262 D4 **Redmond** *OR* U.S.A.
265 U2 **Redmond** *UT* U.S.A.
195 J2 **Rednitz** *r.* Ger.
195 K3 **Rednitzhembach** Ger.
260 H5 **Red Oak** *IA* U.S.A.
259 H1 **Red Oaks Mill** *NY* U.S.A.
232 C5 **Redojari** *waterhole* Kenya
180 G6 **Redon** France
271 □2 **Redonda** *i.* Antigua and Barbuda
274 □ **Redonda, Roca** *i. Islas Galápagos* Ecuador
204 C4 **Redondela** Spain
204 E5 **Redondelo** Port.
206 D3 **Redondo** Port.
264 N8 **Redondo Beach** *CA* U.S.A.
244 I3 **Redoubt Volcano** *AK* U.S.A.
262 H3 **Red Peak** *MT* U.S.A.
168 E7 **Red Point** *Highland, Scotland* U.K.
Red River *r.* Vietnam *see* **Hông, Sông**
Red River, Mouths of the Vietnam *see* **Hong, Mouths of the**
248 B3 **Red Rock** *Ont.* Can.
265 U9 **Red Rock** *AZ* U.S.A.
251 R8 **Red Rock** *PA* U.S.A.
262 H4 **Red Rock** *r. MT* U.S.A.
246 H1 **Redrock Lake** *N.W.T.* Can.
109 I12 **Red Rocks Point** *W.A.* Austr.
172 C4 **Red Roses** *Carmarthenshire, Wales* U.K.
172 B7 **Redruth** *Cornwall, England* U.K.
146 B2 **Red Sea** Africa/Asia
225 G5 **Red Sea** *state* Sudan
246 F4 **Redstone** *B.C.* Can.
245 P2 **Redstone** *r. N.W.T.* Can.
251 M1 **Redstone** *r. Ont.* Can.
247 M4 **Red Sucker Lake** *Man.* Can.
186 I2 **Reduzum** Neth.
228 E4 **Red Volta** *r.* Burkina/Ghana *alt.* **Nazinon (Burkina)**
262 L2 **Redwater** *r. MT* U.S.A.
264 I1 **Redway** *CA* U.S.A.
172 D1 **Red Wharf Bay** *Wales* U.K.
260 E5 **Red Willow Creek** *r. NE* U.S.A.
249 J2 **Red Wine** *r. Nfld and Lab.* Can.
250 B5 **Red Wing** *MN* U.S.A.
193 D10 **Redwitz an der Rodach** Ger.
264 J4 **Redwood City** *CA* U.S.A.
260 H3 **Redwood Falls** *MN* U.S.A.
262 B6 **Redwood National Park** *CA* U.S.A.
264 I2 **Redwood Valley** *CA* U.S.A.
197 H5 **Rędziny** Pol.
169 G5 **Ree, Lough** *l.* Ireland
250 I6 **Reed City** *MI* U.S.A.
247 K4 **Reed Lake** *Man.* Can.
264 M5 **Reedley** *CA* U.S.A.
259 G6 **Reeds Bay** *NJ* U.S.A.
250 E6 **Reedsburg** *WI* U.S.A.
262 B5 **Reedsport** *OR* U.S.A.
256 D9 **Reedsville** *OH* U.S.A.
256 H8 **Reedsville** *PA* U.S.A.
257 I11 **Reedville** *VA* U.S.A.
256 D10 **Reedy** *WV* U.S.A.
107 J7 **Reedy Creek** *watercourse Qld* Austr.
286 P1 **Reedy Glacier** Antarctica
Reef Islands Vanuatu *see* **Rowa**
103 F9 **Reefton** *South I.* N.Z.
169 E7 **Reens** Ireland
173 O2 **Reepham** *Norfolk, England* U.K.
191 B7 **Rees** Ger.
251 K6 **Reese** *MI* U.S.A.
264 P1 **Reese** *r. NV* U.S.A.
190 H4 **Reeßum** Ger.
192 E4 **Reetz** *Brandenburg* Ger.
193 F6 **Reetz** *Brandenburg* Ger.
186 G4 **Reeuwijksebrug** Neth.
148 I4 **Refahiye** Turkey
204 C5 **Refóios do Lima** Port.
261 K9 **Reform** *AL* U.S.A.
267 M9 **Reforma** *Chiapas* Mex.
269 M9 **Reforma** *Oaxaca* Mex.
258 C5 **Refton** *PA* U.S.A.
261 G11 **Refugio** *TX* U.S.A.
196 D1 **Rega** *r.* Pol.
204 D6 **Regadas** Port.
268 F8 **Regaditos** Mex.
209 E8 **Regajo, Embalse del** *resr* Spain
216 H8 **Regalbuto** *Sicilia* Italy
208 E5 **Regallo** *r.* Spain
201 I4 **Regau** Austria
195 O4 **Regen** Ger.
195 M3 **Regen** *r.* Ger.
281 H3 **Regência** Brazil
195 M3 **Regensburg** Ger.
212 E1 **Regensdorf** Switz.
195 M3 **Regenstauf** Ger.
280 B5 **Regente Feijó** Brazil
227 F4 **Reggane** Alg.
186 J3 **Regge** *r.* Neth.
213 L8 **Reggello** Italy
Reggio *Calabria* Italy *see* **Reggio di Calabria**
Reggio *Emilia-Romagna* Italy *see* **Reggio nell'Emilia**
217 J7 **Reggio di Calabria** Italy
217 K7 **Reggio di Calabria** *prov.* Italy
Reggio Emilia Italy *see* **Reggio nell'Emilia**
213 J6 **Reggio nell'Emilia** Italy
213 J6 **Reggio nell'Emilia** *prov.* Italy
219 M4 **Reghin** Romania
145 K5 **Regi** Afgh.
215 L6 **Regi Lagni** *canal* Italy
197 I3 **Regimin** Pol.
247 J5 **Regina** *Sask.* Can.
275 H3 **Régina** Fr. Guiana
145 K6 **Registān** *reg.* Afgh.
280 D6 **Registro** Brazil
280 B1 **Registro do Araguaia** Brazil
Regium Lepidum Italy *see* **Reggio nell'Emilia**
193 F10 **Regnitzlosau** Ger.
182 E5 **Régny** France
139 O5 **Regong** *Arun. Prad.* India
162 U4 **Regozero** Rus. Fed.
204 C4 **Reguengo** Spain
206 D4 **Reguengos de Monsaraz** Port.
180 F6 **Réguiny** France
145 L7 **Regwash** Pak.
193 F10 **Rehau** Ger.
191 H6 **Rehburg (Rehburg-Loccum)** Ger.
190 F5 **Rehden** Ger.
138 G8 **Rehli** *Madh. Prad.* India
195 J5 **Rehling** Ger.
194 B3 **Rehlingen-Siersburg** Ger.
193 I9 **Řehlovice** Czech Rep.
192 D3 **Rehna** Ger.
234 C4 **Rehoboth** Namibia
257 J10 **Rehoboth Bay** *DE* U.S.A.
257 J10 **Rehoboth Beach** *DE* U.S.A.
179 K4 **Réhon** France
150 C7 **Reḥovot** Israel
Reïbell Alg. *see* **Ksar Chellala**
193 F7 **Reibitz** Ger.
195 J2 **Reiche Ebrach** *r.* Ger.
194 F2 **Reichelsheim (Odenwald)** Ger.
191 G10 **Reichelsheim (Wetterau)** Ger.
194 G6 **Reichenau** Ger.
201 M4 **Reichenau an der Rax** Austria
194 F2 **Reichenbach** *Hessen* Ger.
193 F9 **Reichenbach** *Sachsen* Ger.
212 D2 **Reichenbach** Switz.
193 K8 **Reichenbach (Oberlausitz)** Ger.
194 H2 **Reichenberg** Ger.
201 K5 **Reichenfels** Austria
191 J8 **Reichensachsen (Wehretal)** Ger.
195 K2 **Reichenschwand** Ger.
200 F5 **Reichenspitze** *mt.* Austria
201 J2 **Reichenthal** Austria
195 L5 **Reichertshausen** Ger.
195 M5 **Reichertsheim** Ger.
195 K4 **Reichertshofen** Ger.
195 J6 **Reichling** Ger.
193 D9 **Reichmannsdorf** Ger.
194 H2 **Reicholzheim** Ger.
201 J4 **Reichraming** Austria
179 O6 **Reichshoffen** France
179 O6 **Reichstett** France
109 J11 **Reid** *W.A.* Austr.
212 D1 **Reiden** Switz.
168 E7 **Reidh, Rubha** *pt Scotland* U.K.
255 F9 **Reidsville** *GA* U.S.A.
255 H7 **Reidsville** *NC* U.S.A.
204 G7 **Reigada** Port.
173 L5 **Reigate** *Surrey, England* U.K.
184 C5 **Reignac** France
182 I4 **Reignier** France
191 D10 **Reil** Ger.
265 V9 **Reiley Peak** *AZ* U.S.A.
185 G6 **Reilhaguet** France
194 F3 **Reilingen** Ger.
183 H9 **Reillanne** France
205 Q9 **Reillo** Spain
178 H5 **Reims** France
206 H4 **Reina** Spain
283 B9 **Reina Adelaida, Archipiélago de la** *is* Chile
212 E1 **Reinach** *Aargau* Switz.
212 D1 **Reinach** *Basellandschaft* Switz.
164 C2 **Reinaknuten** *hill* Norway
190 J3 **Reinbek** Ger.
192 H2 **Reinberg** Ger.
247 K4 **Reindeer** *r. Sask.* Can.
245 O1 **Reindeer Grazing Reserve** *nature res. N.W.T.* Can.
247 L4 **Reindeer Island** *Man.* Can.
247 K3 **Reindeer Lake** *Man./Sask.* Can.
162 L3 **Reine** Norway
256 D9 **Reinersville** *OH* U.S.A.
163 J6 **Reineskarvet** *mt.* Norway
190 J3 **Reinfeld (Holstein)** Ger.
102 G1 **Reinga, Cape** *North I.* N.Z.
191 H7 **Reinhardswald** *mts* Ger.
194 F2 **Reinheim** Ger.
258 C4 **Reinholds** *PA* U.S.A.
205 L3 **Reinosa** Spain
182 E4 **Reins** *r.* France
193 G7 **Reinsdorf** *Sachsen-Anhalt* Ger.
193 D8 **Reinsdorf** *Thüringen* Ger.
194 B2 **Reinsfeld** Ger.
164 C2 **Reinsnosi** *mt.* Norway
162 □B1 **Reipholsfjöll** *hill* Iceland
Reirson Island *atoll* Cook Is *see* **Rakahanga**
162 Q2 **Reisa Nasjonalpark** *nat. park* Norway
195 N4 **Reisbach** Ger.
195 N5 **Reischach** Ger.
162 R5 **Reisjärvi** Fin.
191 G9 **Reiskirchen** Ger.
258 B6 **Reisterstown** *MD* U.S.A.
216 G8 **Reitano** *Sicilia* Italy
186 J2 **Reitdiep** *r.* Neth.
195 M6 **Reit im Winkl** Ger.
237 M3 **Reitz** S. Africa
237 L3 **Reitzburg** S. Africa
160 H3 **Reiu** *r.* Estonia
236 I3 **Reivilo** S. Africa
232 A3 **Rejaf** Sudan
165 L3 **Rejmyre** Sweden
197 L4 **Rejowiec** Pol.
197 L4 **Rejowiec Fabryczny** Pol.
201 O7 **Reka** Croatia
213 Q5 **Reka** *r.* Slovenia
136 G4 **Rekapalle** *Andhra Prad.* India
191 D7 **Reken** Ger.
186 K4 **Rekken** Neth.
197 M5 **Reklynets'** Ukr.
Rekohua *i. Chatham Is* S. Pacific Ocean *see* **Chatham Island**
218 J7 **Rekovac** *Rekovac* Serbia
197 M6 **Rekshyn** Ukr.
164 E1 **Reksjåeggi** *mt.* Norway
160 G6 **Rėkyvos ežeras** *l.* Lith.
247 I2 **Reliance** *N.W.T.* Can.
216 H10 **Religione, Punta** *pt Sicilia* Italy
206 C5 **Relíquias** Port.
227 F2 **Relizane** Alg.
266 G4 **Rellano** Mex.
209 E10 **Relleu** Spain
137 H4 **Relli** *Andhra Prad.* India
190 I3 **Rellingen** Ger.
238 □1b **Relva** *São Miguel* Azores
199 I5 **Rém** Hungary
227 H2 **Remada** Tunisia
191 D9 **Remagen** Ger.
181 M5 **Rémalard** France
104 G5 **Remarkable, Mount** *hill S.A.* Austr.
117 I8 **Rembang** *Jawa* Indon.
179 J6 **Rembercourt-Sommaisne** France
193 D9 **Remda** Ger.
285 F5 **Remecó** Arg.
238 □1b **Remédios** *São Miguel* Azores
274 C3 **Remedios** Col.
270 D2 **Remedios** Cuba
268 A1 **Remedios** Mex.
267 O11 **Remedios, Punta** *pt* El Salvador
204 B3 **Remedios, Punta dos** *pt* Spain
227 H3 **Remel el Abiod** *des.* Tunisia
190 E4 **Remels (Uplengen)** Ger.
160 L5 **Remennikovo** Rus. Fed.
260 I2 **Remer** *MN* U.S.A.
144 H8 **Remeshk** Iran
162 S5 **Remeskylä** Fin.
199 L5 **Remetea** Romania
199 K6 **Remetea Mare** Romania
219 L3 **Remeţi** Romania
201 N7 **Remetinec** Croatia
Remi France *see* **Reims**
187 J9 **Remich** Lux.
187 H7 **Remicourt** Belgium
179 I4 **Remilly-Aillicourt** France
256 H10 **Remington** *VA* U.S.A.
275 H3 **Rémire** Fr. Guiana
239 □2 **Rémire** *i.* Seychelles
179 M7 **Remiremont** France
191 K6 **Remlingen** Ger.
262 D2 **Remmel Mountain** *WA* U.S.A.
208 C4 **Remolinos** Spain
179 L7 **Remoncourt** France
157 H7 **Remontnoye** Rus. Fed.
187 I8 **Remouchamps** Belgium
183 F9 **Remoulins** France
116 F4 **Rempang** *i.* Indon.
239 □1c **Remparts, Rivière des** *r.* Réunion
192 G3 **Remplin** Ger.
193 E9 **Remptendorf** Ger.
194 G4 **Rems** *r.* Ger.
191 D8 **Remscheid** Ger.
200 B7 **Remulo** *r.* Italy
180 F6 **Remungol** France
250 I6 **Remus** *MI* U.S.A.
183 G8 **Rémuzat** France
163 K6 **Rena** Norway
163 K6 **Rena** *r.* Norway
206 H2 **Rena** Spain
251 K1 **Renabie** *Ont.* Can.
183 G6 **Renage** France
284 A5 **Renaico** Chile
182 D4 **Renaison** France
Renaix Belgium *see* **Ronse**
118 D1 **Renam** Myanmar
136 E3 **Renapur** *Mahar.* India
181 I6 **Renazé** France
284 E3 **Renca** Arg.
194 E4 **Renchen** Ger.
128 F1 **Renchinlhümbe** Mongolia
235 F4 **Renco** Zimbabwe
Rende *Yunnan* China *see* **Xundian**
215 Q9 **Rende** Italy
260 K6 **Rend Lake** *IL* U.S.A.
100 □6 **Rendova** *i. New Georgia Is* Solomon Is
190 I2 **Rendsburg** Ger.
205 M2 **Renedo** *Cantabria* Spain
205 K5 **Renedo** *Castilla y León* Spain
205 K4 **Renedo de la Vega** Spain
249 G3 **René-Levasseur, Île** *i. Que.* Can.
212 B2 **Renens** Switz.
186 E5 **Renesse** Neth.
249 K4 **Renews** *Nfld and Lab.* Can.
248 E4 **Renfrew** *Ont.* Can.
168 H11 **Renfrew** *Renfrewshire, Scotland* U.K.
168 G11 **Renfrewshire** *admin. div. Scotland* U.K.
139 J9 **Rengali Reservoir** *Orissa* India
116 E5 **Rengat** *Sumatera* Indon.
284 B4 **Rengo** Chile
191 D9 **Rengsdorf** Ger.
191 I8 **Rengshausen (Knüllwald)** Ger.
130 G2 **Ren He** *r.* China
131 J3 **Renheji** *Henan* China
Renhou *Hebei* China *see* **Tangxian**
131 I6 **Renhua** *Guangdong* China
130 F5 **Renhuai** *Guizhou* China
158 H8 **Reni** Ukr.
256 E11 **Renick** *WV* U.S.A.
136 F6 **Renigunta** *Andhra Prad.* India
168 C7 **Renish Point** *Scotland* U.K.
190 D5 **Renkenberge** Ger.
160 H1 **Renko** Fin.
186 I5 **Renkum** Neth.
Renland *reg.* Greenland *see* **Tuttut Nunaat**
104 H6 **Renmark** *S.A.* Austr.
216 H10 **Renna** *r. Sicilia* Italy
191 K6 **Rennau** Ger.
100 □6 **Rennell** *i.* Solomon Is
283 B8 **Rennell, Islas** *is* Chile
191 F9 **Rennerod** Ger.
106 D5 **Renner Springs** *N.T.* Austr.
195 K4 **Rennertshofen** Ger.
180 H5 **Rennes** France
180 H5 **Rennes, Bassin de** *basin* France
185 I10 **Rennes-les-Bains** France
164 B2 **Rennesøy** *i.* Norway
287 K2 **Rennick Glacier** Antarctica
247 M5 **Rennie** *Man.* Can.
247 J2 **Rennie Lake** *N.W.T.* Can.
194 F4 **Renningen** Ger.
171 N3 **Rennington** *Northumberland, England* U.K.
201 I5 **Rennweg** Austria
213 M6 **Reno** *r.* Italy
250 C6 **Reno** *MN* U.S.A.
264 M2 **Reno** *NV* U.S.A.
213 K2 **Renòn** Italy
214 C3 **Rénoso, Monte** *mt. Corse* France
237 K2 **Renoster** *r.* S. Africa
236 E7 **Renoster** *watercourse* S. Africa
236 G8 **Renosterkop** S. Africa
237 K2 **Renosterspruit** S. Africa
256 H7 **Renovo** *PA* U.S.A.
129 O7 **Renqiu** *Hebei* China
190 H1 **Rens** Denmark
130 E4 **Renshou** *Sichuan* China
196 F5 **Reńska Wieś** *Opolskie* Pol.
196 G5 **Reńska Wieś** *Opolskie* Pol.
254 D5 **Rensselaer** *IN* U.S.A.
257 L6 **Rensselaer** *NY* U.S.A.
186 I4 **Renswoude** Neth.
Rentería Spain *see* **Errenteria**
220 C3 **Rentina** Greece
162 O4 **Rentjärn** Sweden
262 C3 **Renton** *WA* U.S.A.
191 K10 **Rentweinsdorf** Ger.
139 I7 **Renukut** *Uttar Prad.* India
178 I4 **Renwez** France
103 H8 **Renwick** *South I.* N.Z.
161 U3 **Renya** *r.* Rus. Fed.
192 D3 **Renzow** Ger.
228 E3 **Réo** Burkina
115 B8 **Reo** *Flores* Indon.
275 G5 **Repartimento** Brazil
198 F4 **Répce** *r.* Hungary
198 G4 **Répcelak** Hungary
235 G4 **Repembe** *r.* Moz.
145 J2 **Repetek** Turkm.
145 J2 **Repetek Döwlet Gorugy** *nature res.* Turkm.
161 P6 **Repino** Rus. Fed.
197 K3 **Repki** Pol.
182 F4 **Replonges** France
162 R2 **Repokaira** *reg.* Fin.
160 M2 **Repolka** Rus. Fed.
102 K5 **Reporoa** *North I.* N.Z.
163 P6 **Reposaari** Fin.
119 G7 **Repou, Tônle** *r.* Laos
192 F2 **Reppelin** Ger.
190 J4 **Reppenstedt** Ger.
256 B7 **Republic** *OH* U.S.A.
262 E2 **Republic** *WA* U.S.A.
260 G6 **Republican** *r. NE* U.S.A.
260 E5 **Republican, South Fork** *r. NE* U.S.A.
210 F3 **Republika Srpska** *aut. div.* Bos.-Herz.
183 E6 **République, Col de la** *pass* France
107 L6 **Repulse Bay** *b. Qld* Austr.
243 J3 **Repulse Bay** *Nunavut* Can.
162 R1 **Repvåg** Norway
157 G6 **Rep'yevka** Rus. Fed.
217 □ **Reqqa, Il-Ponta ta'** *pt Gozo* Malta
205 L3 **Requejada, Embalse de** *resr* Spain
204 G4 **Requejo** Spain
274 C6 **Requena** Peru
209 C9 **Requena** Spain
284 B4 **Requinoa** Chile
185 J7 **Réquista** France
100 □6 **Rere** *Guadalcanal* Solomon Is
192 E2 **Rerik, Ostseebad** Ger.
278 E3 **Reriutaba** Brazil
149 K4 **Reşadiye** Turkey
Reşadiye *Bolu* Turkey *see* **Yeniçağa**
148 H3 **Reşadiye** *Tokat* Turkey
221 I6 **Reşadiye Yarımadası** *pen.* Turkey
116 F7 **Resag, Gunung** *mt.* Indon.
213 L4 **Resana** Italy
219 J6 **Resava** *r.* Serbia
219 J6 **Resavica** *Despotovac* Serbia
168 K9 **Rescobie** *Angus, Scotland* U.K.
218 J9 **Resen** Macedonia
281 E5 **Resende** Brazil
204 E6 **Resende** Port.
280 B6 **Reserva** Brazil
263 J10 **Reserve** *NM* U.S.A.
161 T5 **Reshetnikovo** Rus. Fed.
159 N4 **Reshetylivka** Ukr.
131 H4 **Reshi** *Hunan* China
144 F4 **Reshm** Iran
128 G8 **Reshui** *Qinghai* China
213 J2 **Resia, Lago di** *l.* Italy
200 C6 **Resia, Passo di** *pass* Austria/Italy
258 E2 **Resica Falls** *PA* U.S.A.
282 F2 **Resistencia** Arg.
219 J5 **Reşiţa** Romania
196 D2 **Resko** Pol.
196 D1 **Resko Przymorskie, Jezioro** *lag.* Pol.
243 I2 **Resolute** *Nunavut* Can.
243 L3 **Resolution Island** *Nunavut* Can.
103 A12 **Resolution Island** *South I.* N.Z.
172 E4 **Resolven** *Neath Port Talbot, Wales* U.K.
168 B6 **Resort, Loch** *inlet Scotland* U.K.
205 K3 **Respenda de la Peña** Spain
281 G3 **Resplendor** Brazil
161 S7 **Ressa** *r.* Rus. Fed.
275 G5 **Ressaca** Brazil
237 P1 **Ressango Garcia** S. Africa
161 S8 **Resseta** *r.* Rus. Fed.
178 E4 **Ressons-sur-Matz** France
276 B2 **Restauração** Brazil
183 J8 **Restefond, Col de** *pass* France
218 I9 **Restelicë** *Gora* Kosovo
257 □S1 **Restigouche** *r. N.B.* Can.
202 D5 **Restinga** Morocco
238 □3e **Restinga, Punta de la** *pt El Hierro* Canary Is
281 E5 **Restinga de Marambaia** *coastal area* Brazil
279 B9 **Restinga Seca** Brazil
274 C3 **Restrepo** Col.
Resülayn Turkey *see* **Ceylanpınar**
216 G8 **Resuttano** *Sicilia* Italy
159 M2 **Ret'** *r.* Ukr.
267 N10 **Retalhuleu** Guat.
206 H3 **Retamal** Spain
284 C3 **Retamito** Arg.
116 □ **Retan Laut, Pulau** *i.* Sing.
204 E9 **Retaxo** Port.
227 G2 **Retem, Oued er** *watercourse* Alg.
284 B3 **Retén Atalaya** Chile
284 A4 **Retén Llico** Chile
219 K5 **Retezat, Parcul Naţional** *nat. park* Romania
171 P7 **Retford** *Nottinghamshire, England* U.K.
178 H4 **Rethel** France
190 H5 **Rethem (Aller)** Ger.
Réthimnon *Kriti* Greece *see* **Rethymno**
178 E5 **Rethondes** France
220 F7 **Rethymno** *Kriti* Greece
187 H6 **Retie** Belgium
205 N7 **Retiendas** Spain
180 I6 **Retiers** France
206 G3 **Retín** *r.* Spain
284 B5 **Retiro** Chile
213 R4 **Retje** Slovenia
199 K3 **Rétköz** *reg.* Hungary
204 H7 **Retortillo** Spain
205 L3 **Retortillo** *tourist site* Spain
207 I5 **Retortillo, Embalse de** *resr* Spain
205 O6 **Retortillo de Soria** Spain
183 E6 **Retournac** France
107 I8 **Retreat** *Qld* Austr.
199 I4 **Rétság** Hungary
195 I6 **Rettenberg** Ger.
208 C6 **Retuerta** *mt.* Spain
207 K2 **Retuerta del Bullaque** Spain
201 M2 **Retz** Austria
193 F6 **Reuden** *Sachsen-Anhalt* Ger.
193 F8 **Reuden** *Sachsen-Anhalt* Ger.
181 P7 **Reuilly** France
284 A5 **Reunión** Chile
239 □1c **Réunion** *terr.* Indian Ocean
191 K10 **Reurieth** Ger.
208 H5 **Reus** Spain
116 B3 **Reusam, Pulau** *i.* Indon.
187 H6 **Reusel** Neth.
187 H5 **Reusel** *r.* Neth.
212 E1 **Reuss** *r.* Switz.
195 N5 **Reut** Ger.
Reut *r.* Moldova *see* **Răut**
159 O2 **Reut** *r.* Rus. Fed.
194 D5 **Reute** Ger.
158 G6 **Reuţel** Moldova
195 M2 **Reuth bei Erbendorf** Ger.
194 G5 **Reutlingen** Ger.
161 U6 **Reutov** Rus. Fed.
200 C5 **Reutte** Austria
187 J6 **Reuver** Neth.
145 N3 **Revak** Afgh.
Reval Estonia *see* **Tallinn**
156 F2 **Revda** Rus. Fed.
265 P4 **Reveille Peak** *NV* U.S.A.
Revel Estonia *see* **Tallinn**
185 I9 **Revel** France
139 J7 **Revelganj** *Bihar* India
214 B2 **Revellata, Pointe de la** *pt Corse* France
212 C6 **Revello** Italy
246 G5 **Revelstoke** *B.C.* Can.
269 I3 **Reventadero** Mex.
274 A6 **Reventazón** Peru
258 E3 **Revere** *PA* U.S.A.
182 G5 **Revermont** *reg.* France
183 H8 **Revest-du-Bion** France
199 G5 **Révfülöp** Hungary
235 H2 **Rèvia** Moz.
219 P6 **Reviga** Romania
219 P6 **Reviga** *r.* Romania
179 I6 **Revigny-sur-Ornain** France
205 L3 **Revilla de Collazos** Spain
205 M4 **Revilla del Campo** Spain
252 D7 **Revillagigedo, Islas** *is* Mex.
245 O5 **Revillagigedo Island** *AK* U.S.A.
178 I4 **Revin** France
213 M4 **Revine-Lago** Italy
150 C7 **Revivim** Israel
161 R9 **Revna** *r.* Rus. Fed.
198 D2 **Řevnice** Czech Rep.
198 C1 **Řevničov** Czech Rep.
213 K3 **Revò** Italy
Revolyutsii, Pik *mt.* Tajik. *see* **Revolyutsiya, Qullai**
145 O2 **Revolyutsiya, Qullai** *mt.* Tajik.
162 N2 **Revsnes** Norway
199 J3 **Revúca** Slovakia
235 G3 **Revuè** *r.* Moz.
161 U7 **Revyakino** Rus. Fed.
101 □7a **Rewa** *r. Viti Levu* Fiji
138 H7 **Rewa** *Madh. Prad.* India
103 J8 **Rewa** *hill North I.* N.Z.
196 D1 **Rewal** Pol.
138 F5 **Rewari** *Haryana* India
245 J2 **Rex** *AK* U.S.A.
286 S2 **Rex, Mount** Antarctica
262 I5 **Rexburg** *ID* U.S.A.
249 H4 **Rexton** *N.B.* Can.
266 □T13 **Rey, Isla del** *i.* Panama
158 H3 **Reya** Ukr.
229 I4 **Rey Bouba** Cameroon
173 P3 **Reydon** *Suffolk, England* U.K.
276 D3 **Reyes** Bol.
238 □3e **Reyes, Bahía de los** *b. El Hierro* Canary Is
264 I3 **Reyes, Point** *CA* U.S.A.
274 B4 **Reyes, Punta** *pt* Col.
150 E2 **Reyhanlı** Turkey
162 □C1 **Reykir** Iceland
288 G2 **Reykjanes Ridge** *sea feature* N. Atlantic Ocean
162 □B2 **Reykjanestá** *pt* Iceland
162 □C1 **Reykjavík** Iceland
106 C2 **Reynolds** *r. N.T.* Austr.
256 C9 **Reynoldsburg** *OH* U.S.A.
106 D7 **Reynolds Range** *mts N.T.* Austr.
267 J4 **Reynosa** Mex.
182 F5 **Reyrieux** France
182 F4 **Reyssouze** *r.* France
144 E5 **Reẕā** Iran
144 D5 **Reẕā, Kūh-e** *hill* Iran
144 E6 **Reẕāābād** Iran
Reẕā'īyeh Iran *see* **Orūmīyeh**
Reẕā'īyeh, Daryācheh-ye *salt l.* Iran *see* **Orūmīyeh, Daryācheh-ye**
180 H7 **Rezé** France
160 K5 **Rēzekne** Latvia
160 K5 **Rēzekne** *r.* Latvia
198 G5 **Rezi** Hungary
158 H6 **Rezina** Moldova
210 E3 **Rezinjski vrh** *mt.* Slovenia
219 Q9 **Rezovska Reka** *r.* Bulg./Turkey
145 I7 **Rezvān** Iran
Reẕvāndeh Iran *see* **Reẕvānshahr**
144 C3 **Reẕvānshahr** Iran
212 I4 **Rezzato** Italy
212 D7 **Rezzo** Italy
212 G6 **Rezzoaglio** Italy
R. F. Magón Mex. *see* **Ricardo Flores Magón**
219 K6 **Rgotina** *Zaječar* Serbia
190 H4 **Rhade** Ger.
Rhaeadr Gwy *Wales* U.K. *see* **Rhayader**
212 H3 **Rhaetian Railway** *tourist Site* Switzerland
227 F3 **Rharbi, Oued el** *watercourse* Alg.
212 H1 **Rhätikon** *mts* Switz.
194 C2 **Rhaunen** Ger.
172 E3 **Rhayader** *Powys, Wales* U.K.
191 F7 **Rheda-Wiedenbrück** Ger.
191 C7 **Rhede** Ger.
190 D4 **Rhede (Ems)** Ger.
191 I6 **Rheden** Ger.
258 B4 **Rheems** *PA* U.S.A.
Rhegium Italy *see* **Reggio di Calabria**
172 D3 **Rheidol** *r. Wales* U.K.
Rheims France *see* **Reims**
190 B7 **Rhein** *r.* Ger. *alt.* **Rhin (France),** *conv.* **Rhine**
194 D4 **Rheinau** Ger.
191 C9 **Rheinbach** Ger.
191 C7 **Rheinberg** Ger.
194 D2 **Rheinböllen** Ger.
191 D9 **Rheinbreitbach** Ger.
191 D10 **Rheinbrohl** Ger.
191 D6 **Rheine** Ger.
212 H1 **Rheineck** Switz.
212 D1 **Rheinfelden** Switz.
194 D6 **Rheinfelden (Baden)** Ger.
191 E10 **Rheingaugebirge** *hills* Ger.
191 B10 **Rheinisches Schiefergebirge** *hills* Ger.
191 D11 **Rheinland-Pfalz** *land* Ger.
191 C8 **Rhein-Ruhr** *airport* Ger.
192 G4 **Rheinsberg** Ger.
194 E4 **Rheinstetten** Ger.
191 F10 **Rhein-Taunus, Naturpark** *nature res.* Ger.
212 G2 **Rheinwaldhorn** *mt.* Switz.
191 D9 **Rhein-Westerwald, Naturpark** *nature res.* Ger.
194 E3 **Rheinzabern** Ger.
212 C4 **Rhêmes-Notre-Dame** Italy
212 C4 **Rhêmes-St-Georges** Italy
226 D3 **Rhemilès** *well* Alg.
186 I5 **Rhenen** Neth.
191 E10 **Rhens** Ger.
226 D3 **Rheris, Oued** *watercourse* Morocco
168 G6 **Rhiconich** *Highland, Scotland* U.K.
179 P6 **Rhin** *r.* France *alt.* **Rhein (Germany),** *conv.* **Rhine**
192 G4 **Rhin** *r.* Ger.
179 O7 **Rhinau** France
190 B7 **Rhine** *r.* Europe *alt.* **Rhein (Germany),** *alt.* **Rhin (France)**
257 L7 **Rhinebeck** *NY* U.S.A.
250 E4 **Rhinelander** *WI* U.S.A.
Rhineland-Palatinate *land* Ger. *see* **Rheinland-Pfalz**
192 G5 **Rhinkanal** *canal* Ger.
192 G5 **Rhinluch** *marsh* Ger.
168 H12 **Rhinns of Kells** *hills Scotland* U.K.
232 A4 **Rhino Camp** Uganda
192 F5 **Rhinow** Ger.
192 F5 **Rhinowes Berge** *hills* Ger.
226 C3 **Rhir, Cap** *c.* Morocco
187 G7 **Rhisnes** Belgium
Rhiwabon *Wales* U.K. *see* **Ruabon**
212 G4 **Rho** Italy
270 □ **Rhoades, Point** Jamaica
169 H6 **Rhode** Ireland
257 N7 **Rhode Island** *state* U.S.A.
191 H8 **Rhoden (Diemelstadt)** Ger.
Rhodes *Rodos* Greece *see* **Rodos**
Rhodes *i.* Greece *see* **Rodos**
Rhodesia *country* Africa *see* **Zimbabwe**
Rhodes Inyanga National Park Zimbabwe *see* **Nyanga National Park**
Rhodes Matopos National Park Zimbabwe *see* **Matobo National Park**
262 G3 **Rhodes Peak** *ID* U.S.A.
219 L9 **Rhodope Mountains** Bulg./Greece
Rhodus *i.* Greece *see* **Rodo**
191 I10 **Rhön** *mts* Ger.
172 F4 **Rhondda** *reg. Wales* U.K.
172 F4 **Rhondda Cynon Taff** *adm* *Wales* U.K.
182 F5 **Rhône** *dept* France
183 F9 **Rhône** *r.* France/Switz.
183 G6 **Rhône-Alpes** *admin. reg.* F
183 E9 **Rhône à Sète, Canal du** F
179 N8 **Rhône au Rhin, Canal du**
172 F5 **Rhoose** *Vale of Glamorgan* U.K.
195 M6 **Rhordorf** Ger.
172 E4 **Rhos** *Neath Port Talbot, W* U.K.
172 F1 **Rhosllanerchrugog** *Wrexh* *Wales* U.K.
172 E1 **Rhôs-on-Sea** *Conwy, Wales*
172 D4 **Rhossili** *Swansea, Wales* U
227 G2 **Rhoufi** Alg.
170 H1 **Rhu** *Argyll and Bute, Scotla*
Rhube, Oasis of Syria *see*
172 F1 **Rhuddlan** *Denbighshire, W* U.K.
183 A6 **Rhue** *r.* France
Rhum *i. Scotland* U.K. *see*
191 J7 **Rhumspringe** Ger.
Rhuthun *Denbighshire, Wa* *see* **Ruthin**
180 F6 **Rhuys, Presqu'île de** *pen.*
Rhydaman *Carmarthenshi* U.K. *see* **Ammanford**
172 F1 **Rhyl** *Denbighshire, Wales* U
172 F4 **Rhymney** *Caerphilly, Wales*
168 K8 **Rhynie** *Aberdeenshire, Scot* U.K.
229 H6 **Riaba** Equat. Guinea
217 K7 **Riace** Italy
278 D3 **Riachão** Brazil
278 D4 **Riachão das Neves** Brazil
281 G3 **Riacho** Brazil
278 E5 **Riacho de Santana** Brazil
281 F1 **Riacho dos Machados** Bra
283 E6 **Riachos, Islas de los** *is* Arg
206 D6 **Ria Formosa, Parque Nat** *nature res.* Port.
205 N6 **Riaguas** *r.* Spain
180 I6 **Riaillé** France
Rialb de Noguera Spain *se*
279 C5 **Rialma** Brazil
208 H3 **Rialp** Spain
208 H4 **Rialp, Pantà de** *resr* Spain
264 O7 **Rialto** *CA* U.S.A.
117 I5 **Riam** *Kalimantan* Indon.
139 N6 **Riang** *Arun. Prad.* India
230 F2 **Riangnom** Sudan
Rianjo *Galicia* Spain *see* **Ri**
215 J3 **Riano** Italy
205 K3 **Riaño** Spain
205 J3 **Riaño, Embalse de** *resr* Sp
277 H3 **Rianópolis** Brazil
183 H9 **Rians** France
205 N9 **Riansáres** *r.* Spain
180 E6 **Riantec** France
204 C3 **Rianxo** Spain
138 E3 **Riasi** *Jammu and Kashmir*
116 E4 **Riau** *prov.* Indon.
116 F4 **Riau, Kepulauan** *is* Indon.
212 C2 **Riaz** Switz.
205 N6 **Riaza** Spain
205 M5 **Riaza** *r.* Spain
205 M2 **Riba** Spain
204 D4 **Ribadavia** Spain
204 G4 **Ribadelago** Spain
204 F1 **Ribadeo** Spain
204 F1 **Ribadeo, Ría del** *inlet* Spai
205 P7 **Riba de Saelices** Spain
205 J2 **Ribadesella** Spain
205 Q4 **Ribaforada** Spain
205 P4 **Ribafrecha** Spain
208 G4 **Ribagorçana, Noguera** *r.*
208 F5 **Riba-roja, Pantà de** *resr* Sp
208 F5 **Riba-roja d'Ebre** Spain
Ribas de Fresser Spain *see* **Ribes de Freser**
279 B7 **Ribas do Rio Pardo** Brazil
145 M3 **Ribat** Afgh.
206 C2 **Ribatejo** *reg.* Port.
144 I7 **Ribat Qila** Pak.
235 H2 **Ribáuè** Moz.
191 K6 **Ribbesbüttel** Ger.
171 L6 **Ribble** *r. England* U.K.
171 M5 **Ribblesdale** *val. England* U
164 E6 **Ribe** Denmark
179 N7 **Ribeauvillé** France
178 E4 **Ribécourt-Dreslincourt** F
280 C6 **Ribeira** Brazil
280 D6 **Ribeira** *r.* Brazil
204 E2 **Ribeira, Encoro da** *resr* Sp
206 □ **Ribeira Brava** Madeira
206 □ **Ribeira da Janela** Madeira
204 E5 **Ribeira de Pena** Port.
238 □1b **Ribeira Grande** *São Migue* Azores
276 D2 **Ribeirão** Brazil
204 C6 **Ribeirão** Port.
280 C6 **Ribeirão Branco** Brazil
281 E3 **Ribeirão das Neves** Brazil
280 B5 **Ribeirão do Pinhal** Brazil
280 D4 **Ribeirão Preto** Brazil
238 □1c **Ribeiras** *Pico* Azores
238 □1c **Ribeira Seca** *São Jorge* Azo
238 □1b **Ribeira Seca** *São Miguel* A
238 □1c **Ribeirinha** *Faial* Azores
238 □1c **Ribeirinha** *Pico* Azores
238 □1a **Ribeirinha** *Terceira* Azores
178 F4 **Ribemont** France
216 E8 **Ribera** *Sicilia* Italy
184 E5 **Ribérac** France
206 G3 **Ribera del Fresno** Spain
276 D2 **Riberalta** Bol.
205 Q4 **Ribera Navarra** *reg.* Spain
209 E7 **Ribesalbes** Spain
208 J3 **Ribes de Freser** Spain
183 H8 **Ribiers** France
199 L5 **Ribiţa** Romania
201 L6 **Ribnica** *Radlje Ob Dravi* Sl
210 E3 **Ribnica** *Ribnica* Slovenia
218 I8 **Ribnik** *r.* Kosovo
158 I6 **Rîbniţa** Moldova
192 F2 **Ribnitz-Damgarten** Ger.
219 L9 **Ribnovo** Bulg.
122 L2 **Ribnovsk** Rus. Fed.
205 N6 **Ribota** Spain
276 C5 **Rica Aventura** Chile
217 J6 **Ricadi** Italy
201 N1 **Říčany** *Jihomoravský kraj* Czech Rep.
198 D2 **Říčany** *Středočeský kraj* Czech Rep.
266 F3 **Ricardo Flores Magón** Me
171 P5 **Riccal** *r. England* U.K.
215 N5 **Riccia** Italy
213 M9 **Riccio** Italy
213 N7 **Riccione** Italy
212 H7 **Riccò del Golfo di Spezia**
265 R7 **Rice** *CA* U.S.A.
256 G11 **Rice** *VA* U.S.A.
251 L2 **Rice Lake** *l. Ont.* Can.
248 E4 **Rice Lake** *l. Ont.* Can.
250 C4 **Rice Lake** *WI* U.S.A.
250 A3 **Rice Lake** *l. MN* U.S.A.
250 B6 **Riceville** *IA* U.S.A.
256 C11 **Riceville** *KY* U.S.A.
179 L6 **Richardménil** France
237 Q4 **Richards Bay** S. Africa
287 L1 **Richards Inlet** Antarctica
245 N1 **Richards Island** *N.W.T.* Ca
247 I3 **Richardson** *r. Alta* Can.
245 K2 **Richardson** *AK* U.S.A.
245 K3 **Richardson Highway** *AK* U
246 G1 **Richardson Island** *N.W.T.*
257 □O4 **Richardson Lakes** *ME* U.S
245 N2 **Richardson Mountains** *N.W.T./Y.T.* Can.
103 C11 **Richardson Mountains** *So* N.Z.
228 B2 **Richard Toll** Senegal
258 E4 **Richboro** *PA* U.S.A.
239 □1b **Riche en Eau** Mauritius
186 H2 **Richel** *i.* Neth.

L3 Richelieu Que. Can.
E1 Richelieu France
A3 Richfield PA U.S.A.
T3 Richfield UT U.S.A.
K6 Richfield Springs NY U.S.A.
I6 Richford NY U.S.A.
M4 Richford VT U.S.A.
M6 Richgrove CA U.S.A.
I4 Richhill Northern Ireland U.K.
H4 Richibucto N.B. Can.
I4 Rich Lake Alta Can.
F6 Richland NJ U.S.A.
C4 Richland PA U.S.A.
E3 Richland WA U.S.A.
D6 Richland Center WI U.S.A.
D11 Richlands VA U.S.A.
E4 Richlandtown PA U.S.A.
M5 Richmond N.S.W. Austr.
I6 Richmond Qld Austr.
S4 Richmond Ont. Can.
F4 Richmond Que. Can.
□ Richmond Jamaica
H8 Richmond South I. N.Z.
O5 Richmond KwaZulu-Natal S. Africa
H7 Richmond Northern Cape S. Africa
N5 Richmond North Yorkshire, England U.K.
J4 Richmond CA U.S.A.
F7 Richmond IL U.S.A.
E6 Richmond IN U.S.A.
A11 Richmond KY U.S.A.
□P4 Richmond ME U.S.A.
L7 Richmond MI U.S.A.
H11 Richmond TX U.S.A.
H11 Richmond VA U.S.A.
M4 Richmond VT U.S.A.
H8 Richmond, Mount South I. N.Z.
G3 Richmond County county NY U.S.A.
C9 Richmond Dale OH U.S.A.
E5 Richmond Hill Ont. Can.
G10 Richmond Hill GA U.S.A.
□3 Richmond Peak St Vincent
N3 Richmond Range hills N.S.W. Austr.
H8 Richmond Range mts South I. N.Z.
K6 Richmondville NY U.S.A.
H11 Richoi Xizang China
G2 Richtenberg Ger.
B4 Richtersveld Cultural and Botanical Landscape tourist site S. Africa
B4 Richtersveld National Park S. Africa
F7 Richterswil Switz.
K10 Richton MS U.S.A.
K2 Richvald Slovakia
K2 Richvale CA U.S.A.
B8 Richwood OH U.S.A.
E10 Richwood WV U.S.A.
O6 Ricigliano Italy
D6 Rickenbach Ger.
N3 Rickinghall Suffolk, England U.K.
P4 Rickleån r. Sweden
J2 Rickling Ger.
L4 Rickmansworth Hertfordshire, England U.K.
R5 Ricla Spain
I5 Ricobayo, Embalse de resr Spain
Ricomagus France see Riom
K3 Ricse Hungary
E2 Riddell Nunataks nunataks Antarctica
Ridder Kazakh. see Leninogorsk
G5 Ridderkerk Neth.
C3 Riddes Switz.
G8 Riddlesburg PA U.S.A.
S4 Rideau r. Ont. Can.
E4 Rideau Lakes Ont. Can.
B6 Riderwood MD U.S.A.
C3 Ridge r. Ont. Can.
J3 Ridge NY U.S.A.
O6 Ridgecrest CA U.S.A.
I2 Ridgefield CT U.S.A.
G3 Ridgefield NJ U.S.A.
J9 Ridgeland MS U.S.A.
G9 Ridgeland SC U.S.A.
C4 Ridgeland WI U.S.A.
D7 Ridgely MD U.S.A.
M7 Ridgetown Ont. Can.
C6 Ridgeway IA U.S.A.
G4 Ridgeway NJ U.S.A.
F12 Ridgeway VA U.S.A.
G3 Ridgewood NJ U.S.A.
G7 Ridgway PA U.S.A.
I6 Riđica Vojvodina Serbia
M13 Riding Mill Northumberland, England U.K.
K5 Riding Mountain National Park Man. Can.
E6 Ridley r. W.A. Austr.
K3 Riebeeckstad S. Africa
C9 Riebeek-Kasteel S. Africa
K9 Riebeek-Oos S. Africa
C9 Riebeek-Wes S. Africa
N3 Riebnes l. Sweden
D2 Riecito Venez.
D6 Riec-sur-Belon France
K5 Ried Ger.
E3 Ried Switz.
I7 Riedbergerhorn mt. Ger.
G5 Riede Ger.
L3 Rieden Ger.
L4 Riedenburg Ger.
M6 Riedering Ger.
H3 Ried im Innkreis Austria
C5 Ried im Oberinntal Austria
E5 Ried im Zillertal Austria
K3 Ried in der Riedmark Austria
N8 Riedisheim France
G5 Riedlingen Ger.
B3 Riegelsberg Ger.
M5 Riegersburg Austria
E3 Rieglelsville PA U.S.A.
H7 Riego, Canal de Spain
I4 Riego de la Vega Spain
D1 Riehen Switz.
K1 Riekertsdam S. Africa
F6 Rielasingen-Worblingen Ger.
3 Riello Spain
9 Rielves Spain
7 Riemst Belgium
10 Rieneck Ger.
L5 Rieni Romania
L2 Rienza r. Italy
P2 Rieppesgai'sa mt. Norway
K2 Riepsdorf Ger.
H8 Riesa Ger.
B9 Riesco, Isla i. Chile
1 Rieseby Ger.
G9 Riesi Sicilia Italy
F6 Rieste Ger.
D8 Riestedt Ger.
H5 Riet r. S. Africa
E7 Riet watercourse S. Africa
E6 Rietavas Lith.
F7 Rietberg Ger.
H8 Rietbron S. Africa
E2 Rietfontein S. Africa
3 Rieth Ger.
H6 Riethoven Neth.
F10 Riethuiskraal S. Africa
3 Rieti Italy
3 Rieti prov. Italy
N3 Rietkuil S. Africa
E6 Rietpoort S. Africa
K8 Rietschen Ger.
E6 Riet se Vloer salt pan S. Africa
D5 Rietvlei S. Africa
M1 Rietvlei Nature Reserve S. Africa
D5 Rietz Austria
G9 Rieumes France
7 Rieupeyroux France
E7 Rieutort-de-Randon France
G6 Rieux Bretagne France
G9 Rieux Midi-Pyrénées France
9 Rieux-Minervois France
9 Riez France
6 Rifā'ī, Tall mt. Jordan/Syria
4 Rifaina Brazil
Rifeng Jiangxi China see Lichuan
200 H4 Rifflkopf mt. Austria
213 K2 Rifiano Italy
263 K7 Rifle CO U.S.A.
232 B4 Rift Valley prov. Kenya
Rift Valley Lakes National Park Eth. see Abijatta-Shalla National Park
133 L12 Riga Arun. Prad. India
160 H5 Rīga Latvia
160 G4 Riga, Gulf of Estonia/Latvia
229 G4 Rigacikun Nigeria
133 H10 Rigain Pünco l. Xizang China
220 D3 Rigaio Greece
144 H7 Rīgān Iran
Rīgas jūras līcis b. Estonia/Latvia see Riga, Gulf of
257 K3 Rigaud Que. Can.
183 J9 Rigaud France
262 I5 Rigby ID U.S.A.
262 F4 Riggins ID U.S.A.
182 K3 Riggisberg Switz.
168 E11 Righ Mòr, Loch l. Scotland U.K.
212 F1 Rigi mts Switz.
212 H5 Riglio r. Italy
144 H8 Rīg Matī Iran
185 I7 Rignac France
215 I3 Rignano Flaminio Italy
215 P4 Rignano Garganico Italy
213 K8 Rignano sull'Arno Italy
178 G7 Rigny-le-Ferron France
182 E3 Rigny-sur-Arroux France
181 L7 Rigny-Ussé France
249 J2 Rigolet Nfld and Lab. Can.
224 B6 Rig-Rig Chad
168 I11 Rigside South Lanarkshire, Scotland U.K.
205 R4 Riguel r. Spain
146 D6 Rīh, Gezirat er i. Sudan
135 □1 Rihiveli i. S. Male Maldives
Riia laht b. Estonia/Latvia see Riga, Gulf of
163 R6 Riihimäki Fin.
162 S3 Riipi Fin.
286 W2 Riiser-Larsen Ice Shelf Antarctica
160 H2 Riisipere Estonia
162 T3 Riisitunturin kansallispuisto nat. park Fin.
266 B1 Riito Mex.
229 G4 Rijau Nigeria
210 E3 Riječki Zaliv b. Croatia
210 E3 Rijeka Croatia
213 R5 Rijeka airport Croatia
186 G5 Rijen Neth.
187 G6 Rijkevorsel Belgium
186 G4 Rijnsaterwoude Neth.
186 F4 Rijnsburg Neth.
162 □ Rijpfjorden inlet Svalbard
186 G5 Rijsbergen Neth.
186 K4 Rijssen Neth.
186 F4 Rijswijk Neth.
158 C5 Rika r. Ukr.
146 G4 Rikā, Wādī ar watercourse Saudi Arabia
116 B2 Rikitgaib Sumatera Indon.
139 O5 Rikor Arun. Prad. India
162 O2 Riksgränsen Sweden
124 U3 Rikubetsu Japan
124 T7 Rikuchū-kaigan Kokuritsu-kōen nat. park Japan
124 S7 Rikuzen-takata Japan
219 L8 Rila Bulg.
219 L8 Rila mts Bulg.
133 G12 Rila Xizang China
262 E5 Riley OR U.S.A.
256 G10 Rileyville VA U.S.A.
184 G4 Rilhac-Rancon France
187 F6 Rilland Neth.
181 L7 Rillé France
182 F5 Rillieux-la-Pape France
265 U9 Rillito AZ U.S.A.
208 D6 Rillo Spain
205 Q7 Rillo de Gallo Spain
178 H5 Rilly-la-Montagne France
229 G3 Rima watercourse Niger/Nigeria
146 F2 Rimah, Wādī al watercourse Saudi Arabia
101 □9 Rimatara i. Îs Australes Fr. Polynesia
Rimatera i. Îs Australes Fr. Polynesia see Rimatara
116 F6 Rimau, Pulau i. Indon.
179 J7 Rimaucourt France
199 J3 Rimava r. Slovakia
199 I3 Rimavská Baňa Slovakia
199 J3 Rimavská Seč Slovakia
199 J3 Rimavská Sobota Slovakia
195 N3 Rimbach Bayern Ger.
194 F2 Rimbach Hessen Ger.
246 H4 Rimbey Alta Can.
165 O2 Rimbo Sweden
256 F7 Rimersburg PA U.S.A.
219 L4 Rimetea Romania
165 L3 Rimforsa Sweden
213 N7 Rimini Italy
213 M7 Rimini prov. Italy
Rîmnicu Sărat Romania see Râmnicu Sărat
Rîmnicu Vîlcea Romania see Râmnicu Vâlcea
138 F2 Rimo Glacier Jammu and Kashmir India
178 I4 Rimogne France
185 G10 Rimont France
249 G3 Rimouski Que. Can.
249 G3 Rimouski, Réserve Faunique de nature res. Que. Can.
194 H2 Rimpar Ger.
201 L7 Rimske Toplice Slovenia
195 M6 Rimsting Ger.
103 J8 Rimutaka Forest Park nature res. North I. N.Z.
133 I12 Rinbung Xizang China
115 A8 Rinca i. Indon.
280 C4 Rincão Brazil
195 O4 Rinchnach Ger.
282 D2 Rincón Arg.
Rincon Morocco see Mdiq
271 □8 Rincón Bonaire Neth. Antilles
271 □1 Rincón Puerto Rico
271 □1 Rincón, Bahía de b. Puerto Rico
276 D6 Rincón, Cerro del mt. Chile
282 D1 Rinconada Arg.
269 K6 Rinconada Mex.
207 J2 Rinconada, Sierra de la mts Spain
285 I3 Rincón de Cololó Uru.
284 C4 Rincón del Atuel Arg.
207 K7 Rincón de la Victoria Spain
285 I3 Rincón del Bonete, Lago Artificial de resr Uru.
284 C5 Rincón de los Sauces Arg.
285 I4 Rincón del Pino Uru.
285 I3 Rincón de Palacio Uru.
268 E3 Rincón de Romos Mex.
205 Q4 Rincón de Soto Spain
138 H7 Rind r. India
160 E4 Rinda r. Latvia
162 J5 Rindal Norway
139 L5 Rindü Xizang China
220 G5 Rineia i. Greece
216 H6 Rinella Isole Lipari Italy
256 E11 Riner VA U.S.A.
105 K9 Ringarooma Bay Tas. Austr.
165 M3 Ringarum Sweden
138 E6 Ringas Rajasthan India
169 F9 Ringaskiddy Ireland
164 G6 Ringe Denmark
190 C5 Ringe Ger.
163 K6 Ringebu Norway
212 G2 Ringelspitz mt. Switz.
192 I4 Ringenwalde Ger.
255 E8 Ringgold GA U.S.A.
118 D1 Ringhkung Myanmar
229 H3 Ringim Nigeria
164 E5 Ringkøbing Denmark
164 E6 Ringkøbing Fjord lag. Denmark
173 O2 Ringland Norfolk, England U.K.
193 D8 Ringleben Ger.
173 M6 Ringmer East Sussex, England U.K.
258 F4 Ringoes NJ U.S.A.
170 D3 Ringsend Northern Ireland U.K.
164 H6 Ringsted Denmark
133 F11 Ringtor Xizang China
162 O2 Ringvassøya i. Norway
Ringville Ireland see An Rinn
173 I6 Ringwood Hampshire, England U.K.
257 K7 Ringwood NJ U.S.A.
Rinía i. Greece see Rineia
190 I1 Rinkenæs Denmark
168 J8 Rinloan Aberdeenshire, Scotland U.K.
200 E5 Rinn Austria
168 D11 Rinns of Islay pen. Scotland U.K.
168 D11 Rinns Point Scotland U.K.
280 B4 Rinópolis Brazil
191 H6 Rinteln Ger.
218 F5 Rinya r. Romania
250 E6 Rio WI U.S.A.
276 A1 Río Abiseo, Parque Nacional nat. park Peru
277 F4 Rio Alegre Brazil
279 C8 Rio Azul Brazil
274 B5 Riobamba Ecuador
281 G3 Rio Bananal Brazil
284 B3 Río Blanco Chile
263 K7 Rio Blanco CO U.S.A.
281 F5 Rio Bonito Brazil
276 D2 Rio Branco Brazil
Rio Branco state Brazil see Roraima
275 F4 Rio Branco, Parque Nacional do nat. park Brazil
280 C6 Rio Branco do Sul Brazil
266 H3 Río Bravo, Parque Internacional del nat. park Mex.
279 B7 Rio Brilhante Brazil
283 B6 Río Bueno Chile
270 □ Rio Bueno Jamaica
204 D5 Rio Caldo Port.
275 F2 Río Caribe Venez.
281 F4 Rio Casca Brazil
284 E2 Río Ceballos Arg.
283 C8 Río Chico Arg.
275 E2 Río Chico Venez.
281 E5 Rio Claro Rio de Janeiro Brazil
280 D5 Rio Claro São Paulo Brazil
271 □7 Rio Claro Trin. and Tob.
271 I9 Río Claro Venez.
270 □ Rio Cobre r. Jamaica
285 E6 Río Colorado Arg.
274 B5 Río Corrientes Ecuador
284 E3 Río Cuarto Arg.
235 G4 Rio das Pedras Moz.
281 F5 Rio de Janeiro Brazil
281 F4 Rio de Janeiro state Brazil
266 □S14 Río de Jesús Panama
262 B6 Rio Dell CA U.S.A.
284 E3 Río de Los Sauces Arg.
204 F7 Rio de Mel Port.
206 C5 Rio de Moinhos Beja Port.
206 D3 Rio de Moinhos Évora Port.
206 C4 Rio de Moinhos Setúbal Port.
204 G5 Rio de Onor Port.
226 A5 Río de Oro, Bahía de b. Western Sahara
209 C7 Ríodeva r. Spain
213 L2 Rio di Pusteria Italy
281 F4 Rio Doce Brazil
279 C8 Rio do Sul Brazil
204 E5 Rio Douro Port.
278 G4 Rio Formoso Brazil
266 □R12 Río Frío Costa Rica
205 K7 Riofrío Spain
204 H5 Riofrío de Aliste Spain
205 N6 Riofrío de Riaza Spain
283 C8 Río Gallegos Arg.
207 K7 Ríogordo Spain
283 D9 Río Grande Arg.
276 D5 Río Grande Bol.
282 G4 Rio Grande Brazil
270 □ Rio Grande r. Jamaica
269 J10 Río Grande Oaxaca Mex.
268 D2 Río Grande Zacatecas Mex.
267 K5 Rio Grande r. Mex./U.S.A. alt. Bravo del Norte, Río
271 □1 Río Grande Puerto Rico
258 F6 Rio Grande NJ U.S.A.
282 C2 Río Grande, Salar de salt flat Arg.
261 F12 Rio Grande City TX U.S.A.
271 □1 Río Grande de Loiza, Embalse resr Puerto Rico
278 F3 Rio Grande do Norte state Brazil
279 B9 Rio Grande do Sul state Brazil
288 G8 Rio Grande Rise sea feature S. Atlantic Ocean
274 C2 Ríohacha Col.
266 □S13 Río Hato Panama
282 D2 Río Hondo, Embalse resr Arg.
274 B6 Rioja Peru
207 O7 Rioja Spain
267 O7 Río Lagartos Mex.
278 G4 Rio Largo Brazil
214 B8 Riola Sardo Sardegna Italy
204 H9 Riolobos Spain
269 K7 Río Lodo Mex.
213 L7 Riolo Terme Italy
183 B9 Riols France
182 C5 Riom France
212 H7 Riomaggiore Italy
206 B2 Rio Maior Port.
284 B4 Río Malo Chile
277 G3 Rio Manso, Represa do resr Brazil
214 E2 Rio Marina Italy
204 C6 Rio Mau Port.
183 B6 Riom-ès-Montagnes France
270 □ Rio Minho r. Jamaica
282 E2 Río Muerto Arg.
276 D4 Río Mulatos Bol.
229 H6 Río Muni reg. Equat. Guinea
185 C8 Rion-des-Landes France
284 D6 Río Negro prov. Arg.
279 C8 Rio Negro Brazil
283 B6 Río Negro Chile
285 I3 Río Negro dept Uru.
204 H4 Rionegro del Puente Spain
215 P6 Rionero in Vulture Italy
215 M4 Rionero Sannitico Italy
151 C3 Rioni r. Georgia
281 F4 Rio Novo Brazil
281 G4 Rio Novo do Sul Brazil
185 D6 Rions France
203 E3 Riópar Spain
285 H3 Río Paranacito Arg.
279 E5 Rio Pardo de Minas Brazil
270 □ Rio Pedro r. Jamaica
266 □Q10 Río Plátano, Reserva Biósfera del nature res. Hond.
281 F4 Rio Pomba Brazil
281 F5 Rio Preto Brazil
280 D2 Rio Preto, Serra do hills Brazil
285 F2 Río Primero Arg.
274 D5 Río Puré, Parque Nacional nat. park Colombia
274 D5 Río Puré, Parque Nacional nat. park Peru
263 K9 Rio Rancho NM U.S.A.
182 E4 Riorges France
265 V10 Rio Rico AZ U.S.A.
204 F5 Ríos Spain
204 E4 Rioseco Spain
204 I3 Rioseco de Tapia Spain
285 F2 Río Segundo Arg.
205 M7 Riosequillo, Embalse de resr Spain
274 B3 Ríosucio Col.
285 H3 Río Tala Arg.
285 E3 Río Tercero Arg.
284 E3 Río Tercero, Embalse resr Arg.
274 B5 Río Tigre Ecuador
278 G3 Rio Tinto Brazil
270 I8 Río Tocuyo Venez.
204 F5 Rio Torto Port.
114 A7 Rio Tuba Palawan Phil.
183 G10 Riou, Île de i. France
247 J3 Riou Lake Sask. Can.
280 B2 Rio Verde Brazil
283 C9 Río Verde Chile
274 B4 Rioverde Ecuador
212 D6 Rioverde r. Italy
267 O8 Río Verde Quintana Roo Mex.
269 H4 Río Verde San Luis Potosí Mex.
279 B6 Rio Verde de Mato Grosso Brazil
281 F3 Rio Vermelho Brazil
264 K3 Rio Vista CA U.S.A.
182 I2 Rioz France
276 D2 Riozinho Amazonas Brazil
277 E2 Riozinho Rondônia Brazil
274 E5 Riozinho r. Brazil
277 F4 Riozinho r. Brazil
212 B5 Ripa r. Italy
214 E2 Ripalti, Punta dei pt Italy
218 I6 Ripanj Beograd Serbia
213 J9 Riparbella Italy
215 J3 Ripa Sottile, Lago di l. Italy
215 L2 Ripatransone Italy
162 P3 Ripats Sweden
213 O8 Ripe Italy
215 K4 Ripi Italy
215 O7 Ripiti r. Italy
159 K2 Ripky Ukr.
171 O7 Ripley Derbyshire, England U.K.
171 N5 Ripley North Yorkshire, England U.K.
261 K8 Ripley MS U.S.A.
256 F6 Ripley NY U.S.A.
256 B10 Ripley OH U.S.A.
261 K8 Ripley TN U.S.A.
256 D10 Ripley WV U.S.A.
208 J3 Ripoll Spain
208 J3 Ripolles reg. Spain
171 N5 Ripon North Yorkshire, England U.K.
264 K4 Ripon CA U.S.A.
250 F6 Ripon WI U.S.A.
217 I8 Riposto Sicilia Italy
172 H3 Ripple Worcestershire, England U.K.
171 N6 Ripponden West Yorkshire, England U.K.
186 I5 Rips Neth.
139 M6 Ripu Assam India
179 N7 Riquewihr France
145 O4 Risalpur Pak.
150 B8 Risān 'Unayzah hill Egypt
274 C3 Risaralda dept Col.
163 M6 Risarven Sweden
230 E5 Risasi Dem. Rep. Congo
162 M4 Risbäck Sweden
172 F4 Risca Caerphilly, Wales U.K.
158 G6 Rîşcani Moldova
185 D8 Riscle France
284 C4 Risco Plateado mt. Arg.
162 M4 Risede Sweden
164 F5 Risgårde Bredning b. Denmark
146 G3 Rishā, Wādī ar watercourse Saudi Arabia
138 G4 Rishikesh Uttaranchal India
124 R1 Rishiri-Rebun-Sarobetsu Kokuritsu-kōen nat. park Japan
124 S1 Rishiri-tō i. Japan
122 L6 Rishiri-zan vol. Japan
150 C7 Rishon LeZiyyon Israel
145 J8 Rish Pish Iran
171 M6 Rishton Lancashire, England U.K.
254 E6 Rising Sun IN U.S.A.
258 C5 Rising Sun MD U.S.A.
181 L3 Risle r. France
210 E3 Risnjak nat. park Croatia
Rîşnov Romania see Râşnov
261 I8 Rison AR U.S.A.
164 F3 Risør Norway
178 D6 Ris-Orangis France
182 I3 Risoux, Mont mt. France
162 M2 Risøyhamn Norway
194 H5 Riß r. Ger.
162 J5 Rissa Norway
182 I4 Risse r. France
102 K6 Rissington North I. N.Z.
163 S6 Ristiina Fin.
162 T4 Ristijärvi Fin.
162 U2 Ristikent Rus. Fed.
133 D10 Risum Xizang China
190 G1 Risum-Lindholm Ger.
117 K4 Ritan r. Indon.
133 K12 Ritang Xizang China
160 H5 Rītausmas Latvia
236 I5 Ritchie S. Africa
137 M6 Ritchie's Archipelago is Andaman & Nicobar Is India
245 R2 Ritch Island N.W.T. Can.
100 □1 Ritidian Point Guam
231 C9 Rito Angola
151 B2 Ritsa Georgia
286 X2 Ritscher Upland mts Antarctica
162 N3 Ritsem Sweden
151 B2 Ritsis Nakrdzali nature res. Georgia
264 M4 Ritter, Mount CA U.S.A.
190 G4 Ritterhude Ger.
191 B10 Rittersdorf Ger.
193 G10 Rittersgrün Ger.
126 C5 Rittō Japan
205 P5 Rituerto r. Spain
160 K5 Rītupe r. Latvia
262 E3 Ritzville WA U.S.A.
208 H5 Riudoms Spain
158 H4 Riv r. Ukr.
160 E5 Rīva r. Latvia
181 K3 Riva Bella France
285 F4 Rivadavia Buenos Aires Arg.
284 C3 Rivadavia Mendoza Arg.
282 E2 Rivadavia Salta Arg.
284 B1 Rivadavia Chile
213 J4 Riva del Garda Italy
200 B8 Riva di Solto Italy
213 M2 Riva di Tures Italy
162 □ Rivalensundet str. Svalbard
212 D8 Riva Ligure Italy
212 G6 Rivanazzano Italy
263 K12 Riva Palacio Mex.
212 F7 Rivardo Ligure Italy
212 D5 Rivarolo Canavese Italy
212 I5 Rivarolo Mantovano Italy
285 H4 Rivas Arg.
266 □Q12 Rivas Nic.
285 I2 Rivas Uru.
144 H4 Rīvash Iran
205 N8 Rivas-Vaciamadrid Spain
182 F5 Rive-de-Gier France
184 B3 Rivedoux-Plage France
215 P7 Rivello Italy
285 F5 Rivera Arg.
279 B9 Rivera Uru.
228 C5 River Cess Liberia
264 M5 Riverdale CA U.S.A.
250 B5 River Falls WI U.S.A.
257 M8 Riverhead NY U.S.A.
247 J5 Riverhurst Sask. Can.
109 F10 Riverina W.A. Austr.
105 J6 Riverina reg. N.S.W. Austr.
283 B7 Rivero, Isla i. Chile
229 G5 Rivers state Nigeria
103 C12 Riversdale South I. N.Z.
236 F10 Riversdale S. Africa
103 K8 Riversdale Beach North I. N.Z.
103 F11 Riverside South I. N.Z.
237 N6 Riverside S. Africa
264 O8 Riverside CA U.S.A.
258 F4 Riverside NJ U.S.A.
258 B3 Riverside PA U.S.A.
246 E5 Rivers Inlet B.C. Can.
106 G5 Riversleigh Qld Austr.
169 F4 Riverstown Sligo Ireland
169 G6 Riverstown Tipperary Ireland
247 L5 Riverton Man. Can.
103 C13 Riverton South I. N.Z.
236 I4 Riverton S. Africa
258 E4 Riverton NJ U.S.A.
265 U1 Riverton UT U.S.A.
256 G10 Riverton VA U.S.A.
262 J5 Riverton WY U.S.A.
249 H4 Riverview N.B. Can.
237 Q4 River View S. Africa
259 G4 Riverwood NJ U.S.A.
178 D4 Rivery France
183 H6 Rives France
185 J10 Rivesaltes France
256 E9 Rivesville WV U.S.A.
258 B6 Riviera Beach MD U.S.A.
259 G4 Riviera Beach NJ U.S.A.
249 H3 Rivière-au-Renard Que. Can.
249 G4 Rivière-Bleue Que. Can.
239 □1c Rivière d'Abord, Pointe pt Réunion
239 □1b Rivière des Anguilles Mauritius
249 G4 Rivière-du-Loup Que. Can.
239 □1b Rivière du Rempart Mauritius
249 H3 Rivière-Pentecôte Que. Can.
249 H3 Rivière-Pigou Que. Can.
271 □3 Rivière-Pilote Martinique
271 □3 Rivière-Salée Martinique
183 C8 Rivière-sur-Tarn France
236 D10 Riviersonderend S. Africa
236 D10 Riviersonderend Mountains S. Africa
213 O4 Rivignano Italy
159 K5 Rivne Kirovohrads'ka Oblast' Ukr.
159 N8 Rivne Respublika Krym Ukr.
158 F3 Rivne Rivnens'ka Oblast' Ukr.
158 G5 Rivne Vinnyts'ka Oblast' Ukr.
158 F2 Rivnens'ka Oblast' admin. div. Ukr.
Rivne Oblast admin. div. Ukr. see Rivnens'ka Oblast'
215 J2 Rivodutri Italy
212 D5 Rivoli Italy
237 O1 Rivulets S. Africa
231 D9 Rivungo Angola
103 G8 Riwaka South I. N.Z.
130 A3 Riwoqê Xizang China
187 G7 Rixensart Belgium
179 N8 Rixheim France
Riyadh Saudi Arabia see Ar Riyāḍ
147 I8 Riyan Yemen
128 G8 Riyue Shankou pass Qinghai China
144 F4 Riza well Iran
114 C4 Rizal Luzon Phil.
149 J3 Rize Turkey
151 B4 Rize prov. Turkey
129 P9 Rizhao Shandong China
Rizhao Shandong China see Donggang
269 M9 Rizo de Oro Mex.
Rizokarpaso Cyprus see Rizokarpason
150 C3 Rizokarpason Cyprus
220 D3 Rizomylos Greece
144 G5 Rīzū well Iran
144 G6 Rīzū'īyeh Iran
214 B4 Rizzanese r. Corse France
217 J7 Rizziconi Italy
216 G9 Rizzuto r. Sicilia Italy
217 M6 Rizzuto, Capo c. Italy
164 E2 Rjukan Norway
164 D2 Rjuvbrokkene mt. Norway
228 B2 Rkîz Maur.
255 E9 R. L. Harris Reservoir AL U.S.A.
213 L6 Ro Italy
164 G1 Roa Norway
205 M5 Roa Spain
104 □2 Roach Island Lord Howe I. Austr.
265 Q6 Roach Lake NV U.S.A.
173 K3 Roade Northamptonshire, England U.K.
172 D6 Roadford Reservoir England U.K.
256 C9 Roads OH U.S.A.
168 J5 Roadside Highland, Scotland U.K.
271 K4 Road Town Virgin Is (U.K.)
185 D7 Roaillan France
162 K4 Roan Norway
265 W2 Roan Cliffs ridge UT U.S.A.
168 K12 Roan Fell hill Scotland U.K.
182 E4 Roannais reg. France
182 E4 Roanne France
182 E4 Roanne à Digoin, Canal de France
255 E9 Roanoke AL U.S.A.
250 E9 Roanoke IL U.S.A.
256 F11 Roanoke VA U.S.A.
256 I12 Roanoke r. NC U.S.A.
255 I7 Roanoke Rapids NC U.S.A.
265 W2 Roan Plateau UT U.S.A.
258 B1 Roaring Branch PA U.S.A.
169 C10 Roaringwater Bay Ireland
212 I3 Roasco r. Italy
266 □P9 Roatán Hond.
172 F5 Roath Cardiff, Wales U.K.
156 C3 Röbäck Sweden
145 J6 Robat r. Afgh.
144 G5 Robāṭ Iran
144 G5 Robāt-e Ābgarm Iran
144 G5 Robāṭ-e Khān Iran
144 F5 Robāṭ-e Posht-e Bādām Iran
144 F4 Robāṭ-e Samangān Iran
144 F6 Robāṭ-e Shahr-e Bābak Iran
145 I4 Robāṭ-e Sorkh Afgh.
144 H3 Robāṭ-e Ṭoroq Iran
144 D4 Robāṭ Karīm Iran
144 H4 Robāt Sang Iran
144 D5 Robāṭ Tork Iran
246 G4 Robb Alta Can.
236 C9 Robben Island S. Africa
105 J9 Robbins Island Tas. Austr.
255 F8 Robbinsville NC U.S.A.
258 F4 Robbinsville NJ U.S.A.
212 F5 Robbio Italy
104 G7 Robe S.A. Austr.
108 C6 Robe r. W.A. Austr.
232 C3 Robē Eth.
169 D5 Robe r. Ireland
104 H4 Robe, Mount hill N.S.W. Austr.
212 I5 Robecco d'Oglio Italy
192 G4 Röbel Ger.
249 I3 Robe Noire, Lac de la l. Que. Can.
248 E2 Robert-Bourassa, Réservoir resr Que. Can.
179 J6 Robert-Espagne France
287 D2 Robert Glacier Antarctica
261 E10 Robert Lee TX U.S.A.
168 K12 Roberton Scottish Borders, Scotland U.K.
168 I11 Roberton South Lanarkshire, Scotland U.K.
285 F4 Roberts Arg.
262 H5 Roberts ID U.S.A.
105 N3 Roberts, Mount Qld Austr.
256 D10 Robertsburg WV U.S.A.
287 K2 Roberts Butte mt. Antarctica
265 P2 Roberts Creek Mountain NV U.S.A.
162 P4 Robertsfors Sweden
139 I7 Robertsganj Uttar Prad. India
261 H8 Robert S. Kerr Reservoir OK U.S.A.
244 F3 Roberts Mountain hill AK U.S.A.
107 I5 Robertson r. Qld Austr.
236 D9 Robertson S. Africa
249 J3 Robertson, Lac l. Que. Can.
287 L2 Robertson Bay Antarctica
286 U2 Robertson Island Antarctica
103 I8 Robertson Point South I. N.Z.
109 F7 Robertson Range hills W.A. Austr.
228 C5 Robertsport Liberia
104 G5 Robertstown S.A. Austr.
Robert Williams Angola see Caála
249 F3 Roberval Que. Can.
243 L1 Robeson Channel Can./Greenland
258 C4 Robesonia PA U.S.A.
183 E8 Robiac-Rochessadoule France
171 P5 Robin Hood's Bay North Yorkshire, England U.K.
Robin's Nest hill H.K. China see Hung Fa Leng
106 F4 Robinson r. N.T. Austr.
108 H4 Robinson r. W.A. Austr.
245 N3 Robinson Y.T. Can.
254 D6 Robinson IL U.S.A.
256 A10 Robinson KY U.S.A.
107 L8 Robinson Creek r. Qld Austr.
276 □ Robinson Crusoe, Isla i. S. Pacific Ocean
244 I4 Robinson Mountains AK U.S.A.
245 L3 Robinson Mountains AK U.S.A.
109 E8 Robinson Range hills W.A. Austr.
106 F4 Robinson River N.T. Austr.
105 I6 Robinvale Vic. Austr.
183 G9 Robion France
207 O3 Robledo Spain
205 L7 Robledo de Chavela Spain
205 K9 Robledo del Mazo Spain
204 I9 Robledollano Spain
205 J3 Robles de la Valcueva Spain
274 C2 Robles La Paz Col.
247 K5 Roblin Man. Can.
193 E8 Röblingen am See Ger.
204 I7 Robliza de Cojos Spain
277 F4 Robore Bol.
205 M6 Robregordo Spain
208 E4 Robres Spain
205 P4 Robres del Castillo Spain
100 □6 Rob Roy i. Solomon Is
247 I5 Robsart Sask. Can.
246 G4 Robson, Mount B.C. Can.
261 G12 Robstown TX U.S.A.
261 E9 Roby TX U.S.A.
213 Q5 Roč Croatia
206 A3 Roca, Cabo da c. Port.
Roçadas Angola see Xangongo
208 H5 Rocafort de Queralt Spain
185 H6 Rocamadour France
285 H3 Rocamora Arg.
252 D7 Roca Partida, Isla i. Mex.
269 L7 Roca Partida, Punta pt Mex.
266 B5 Rocas Alijos is Mex.
217 O3 Roca Vecchia Italy
183 I10 Rocbaron France
212 I5 Roccabianca Italy
216 E8 Rocca Busambra mt. Sicilia Italy
215 O7 Roccadaspide Italy
215 L5 Rocca d'Evandro Italy
215 K3 Rocca di Cambio Italy
215 L3 Rocca di Mezzo Italy
217 L5 Rocca di Neto Italy
215 J4 Rocca di Papa Italy
212 H5 Roccafranca Italy
215 O7 Roccagloriosa Italy
217 L3 Rocca Imperiale Italy
212 C7 Rocca la Meia mt. Italy
214 H2 Roccalbegna Italy
217 I8 Roccalumera Sicilia Italy
215 M4 Roccamandolfi Italy
215 J4 Rocca Massima Italy
216 E8 Roccamena Sicilia Italy
215 L5 Roccamonfina Italy
215 M3 Roccamontepiano Italy
215 Q7 Roccanova Italy
216 F8 Roccapalumba Sicilia Italy
215 L4 Rocca Pia Italy
215 M4 Roccaraso Italy
213 L7 Rocca San Casciano Italy
215 M3 Rocca San Giovanni Italy
215 L4 Roccasecca Italy
215 K5 Roccasecca dei Volsci Italy
215 J3 Rocca Sinibalda Italy
214 G1 Roccastrada Italy
212 C7 Roccavione Italy
217 K7 Roccella Ionica Italy
215 O5 Rocchetta Sant'Antonio Italy
182 J4 Roc d'Enfer mt. France
173 I2 Rocester Staffordshire, England U.K.
282 G4 Rocha Uru.
171 M6 Rochdale Greater Manchester, England U.K.
172 C7 Roche Cornwall, England U.K.
206 G8 Roche, Cabo c. Spain
183 J7 Rochebrune, Pic de mt. France
184 F4 Rochechouart France
181 M7 Rochecorbon France
279 B6 Rochedo Brazil
187 H8 Rochefort Belgium
184 C4 Rochefort France
249 F1 Rochefort, Lac l. Que. Can.
180 G6 Rochefort-en-Terre France
182 B5 Rochefort-Montagne France
182 H2 Rochefort-sur-Nenon France
156 H3 Rochegda Rus. Fed.
183 F8 Rochegude France
187 H9 Rochehaut Belgium
183 E6 Roche-la-Molière France
182 I2 Roche-lez-Beaupré France
250 E8 Rochelle IL U.S.A.
183 F7 Rochemaure France
239 □1b Roches, Plaine des plain Mauritius
179 J7 Roches-Bettaincourt France
180 H8 Rocheservière France
105 J7 Rochester Vic. Austr.
173 N5 Rochester Medway, England U.K.
171 M3 Rochester Northumberland, England U.K.
254 D5 Rochester IN U.S.A.
251 K7 Rochester MI U.S.A.
250 B5 Rochester MN U.S.A.
257 □O5 Rochester NH U.S.A.
256 H5 Rochester NY U.S.A.
169 H8 Rochestown Ireland
179 J8 Rochetaillée France
173 N4 Rochford Essex, England U.K.
169 H6 Rochfortbridge Ireland
178 F2 Rochin France
193 G8 Rochlitz Ger.
180 D5 Roc'h Trévezel hill France
206 F6 Rociana del Condado Spain
207 G7 Rocina r. Spain
201 I7 Ročinj Slovenia
245 M2 Rock r. Y.T. Can.
245 P3 Rock r. Y.T. Can.
172 H3 Rock Worcestershire, England U.K.
250 G3 Rock MI U.S.A.
260 G4 Rock r. IA U.S.A.
250 D8 Rock r. IL U.S.A.
166 □ Rockall i. N. Atlantic Ocean
288 H2 Rockall Bank sea feature N. Atlantic Ocean
103 D12 Rock and Pillar Range mts South I. N.Z.
186 F5 Rockanje Neth.
246 E5 Rock Bay B.C. Can.
168 I13 Rockcliffe Dumfries and Galloway, Scotland U.K.
169 H4 Rockcorry Ireland
245 M2 Rock Creek Y.T. Can.
256 E7 Rock Creek OH U.S.A.
262 K2 Rock Creek r. MT U.S.A.
258 A5 Rock Creek r. PA U.S.A.
258 B6 Rockdale MD U.S.A.
261 G10 Rockdale TX U.S.A.
261 I11 Rockefeller National Wildlife Refuge nature res. LA U.S.A.
286 O1 Rockefeller Plateau Antarctica
191 G10 Rockenberg Ger.
194 D2 Rockenhausen Ger.
259 J1 Rockfall CT U.S.A.
255 D9 Rockford AL U.S.A.
250 E7 Rockford IL U.S.A.
250 I6 Rockford MI U.S.A.
256 A8 Rockford OH U.S.A.
247 J5 Rockglen Sask. Can.
258 C3 Rock Glen PA U.S.A.
258 C6 Rock Hall MD U.S.A.
107 M7 Rockhampton Qld Austr.
106 E5 Rockhampton Downs N.T. Austr.
250 F1 Rock Harbor MI U.S.A.
169 E8 Rockhill Ireland
258 F1 Rock Hill NY U.S.A.
255 G8 Rock Hill SC U.S.A.
109 C12 Rockingham W.A. Austr.
173 K2 Rockingham Northamptonshire, England U.K.
255 H8 Rockingham NC U.S.A.
107 K5 Rockingham Bay Qld Austr.
173 K2 Rockingham Forest England U.K.
247 H1 Rockinghorse Lake Nunavut Can.
257 M3 Rock Island Que. Can.
260 J5 Rock Island IL U.S.A.
260 F1 Rocklake ND U.S.A.
257 J3 Rockland Ont. Can.
257 O6 Rockland MA U.S.A.
257 □P4 Rockland ME U.S.A.
250 E3 Rockland MI U.S.A.
259 G2 Rockland County county NY U.S.A.
105 I7 Rocklands Reservoir Vic. Austr.
109 D7 Rocklea W.A. Austr.
264 K3 Rocklin CA U.S.A.
246 H1 Rocknest Lake N.W.T. Can.
193 G8 Röcknitz Ger.
265 W5 Rock Point AZ U.S.A.
254 D7 Rockport IN U.S.A.
257 O6 Rockport MA U.S.A.
261 G12 Rockport TX U.S.A.
262 D2 Rockport WA U.S.A.
256 D9 Rockport WV U.S.A.
260 G4 Rock Rapids IA U.S.A.
262 L6 Rock River WY U.S.A.
270 E1 Rock Sound Eleuthera Bahamas
262 K3 Rock Springs MT U.S.A.
261 E11 Rocksprings TX U.S.A.
262 J6 Rock Springs WY U.S.A.
275 G3 Rockstone Guyana
250 E7 Rockton IL U.S.A.
254 D6 Rockville IN U.S.A.
258 A6 Rockville MD U.S.A.
259 L1 Rockville RI U.S.A.
259 H3 Rockville Centre NY U.S.A.
261 G9 Rockwall TX U.S.A.
260 H4 Rockwell City IA U.S.A.
172 F6 Rockwell Green Somerset, England U.K.
257 □P3 Rockwood ME U.S.A.
251 K7 Rockwood MI U.S.A.
256 F9 Rockwood PA U.S.A.
262 J2 Rocky Boy's Indian Reservation res. MT U.S.A.
246 H5 Rockyford Alta Can.
260 D6 Rocky Ford CO U.S.A.
256 B9 Rocky Fork Lake OH U.S.A.
109 D13 Rocky Gully W.A. Austr.
249 J3 Rocky Harbour Nfld and Lab. Can.
259 J1 Rocky Hill CT U.S.A.
256 C10 Rocky Hill OH U.S.A.
248 D4 Rocky Island Lake Ont. Can.
246 G3 Rocky Lane Alta Can.
255 I8 Rocky Mount NC U.S.A.
256 F12 Rocky Mount VA U.S.A.
246 H4 Rocky Mountain House Alta Can.
262 L6 Rocky Mountain National Park CO U.S.A.
252 E2 Rocky Mountains CO U.S.A.
246 G4 Rocky Mountains Forest Reserve nature res. Alta Can.
270 □ Rocky Point Jamaica
270 □ Rocky Point pt Jamaica
234 B3 Rocky Point pt Namibia
104 □1 Rocky Point pt Norfolk I.
244 G2 Rocky Point pt AK U.S.A.
178 F5 Rocourt-St-Martin France
178 I4 Rocroi France
193 D10 Rodach r. Ger.
191 K10 Rodach r. Ger.
191 K10 Rodach bei Coburg Ger.
208 H5 Roda de Bara Spain
208 J4 Roda de Ter Spain
194 D3 Rodalben Ger.
190 H4 Rodau r. Ger.
164 E1 Rodberg Norway
172 H4 Rodborough Gloucestershire, England U.K.
190 L1 Rødby Denmark
164 H7 Rødbyhavn Denmark
249 K3 Roddickton Nfld and Lab. Can.
164 F6 Rødding Sønderjylland Denmark
164 F5 Rødding Viborg Denmark
237 N6 Rode S. Africa
165 L5 Rödeby Sweden
171 M7 Rode Heath Cheshire, England U.K.
204 E3 Rodeiro Spain
164 F6 Rødekro Denmark
168 C7 Rodel Western Isles, Scotland U.K.
208 E3 Rodellar Spain
183 B7 Rodelle France
186 J2 Roden Neth.
172 G2 Roden r. England U.K.
205 R7 Ródenas Spain
190 F4 Rodenkirchen (Stadland) Ger.
193 D10 Rödental Ger.
284 C2 Rodeo Arg.
266 G5 Rodeo Mex.
263 J11 Rodeo NM U.S.A.
109 D9 Roderick r. W.A. Austr.
190 H5 Rodewald Ger.
193 F9 Rodewisch Ger.
183 B8 Rodez France
191 G9 Rodheim-Bieber Ger.
Rodholívos Greece see Rodolivos
Rodhópolis Greece see Rodopoli
Ródhos i. Greece see Rodos
Rodi i. Greece see Rodos
201 I7 Rodica mt. Slovenia
215 P4 Rodi Garganico Italy
195 N3 Roding Ger.
143 S1 Rodino Rus. Fed.
159 S6 Rodionovo-Nesvetayskaya Rus. Fed.
165 N1 Rödjebro Sweden
145 K8 Rodkhan Pak.
193 F7 Rodleben Ger.
162 M4 Rødlia Norway
219 M3 Rodna Romania
219 M3 Rodnei, Munţii mts Romania
102 I3 Rodney, Cape North I. N.Z.
244 F2 Rodney, Cape AK U.S.A.
172 G5 Rodney Stoke Somerset, England U.K.
258 D6 Rodney Village DE U.S.A.
Rodnichek Rus. Fed. see Rodnichok
157 H6 Rodnichok Rus. Fed.
142 G2 Rodnikovka Kazakh.
161 P8 Rodnya Belarus
161 R5 Rodnya Rus. Fed.
159 L5 Rodnykivka Ukr.
208 J4 Rodó, Puig mt. Spain
266 A2 Rodolfo Sanchez Toboada Mex.
220 E2 Rodolivos Greece
218 H9 Rodonit, Kepi i pt Albania
Rodopi Planina mts Bulg./Greece see Rhodope Mountains
220 E1 Rodopoli Greece
220 E7 Rodopos Kriti Greece
221 J6 Rodos Rodos Greece
221 J6 Rodos i. Greece
Rodosto Turkey see Tekirdağ
160 K4 Rodovoye Rus. Fed.
162 L3 Rodøya i. Norway
274 C6 Rodrigues Peru
239 □1a Rodrigues Island Mauritius
285 I4 Rodríguez Uru.
192 E1 Rødsand sea feature Denmark
162 U2 Rødsand Norway
164 E1 Rødungen l. Norway
108 H3 Roe r. W.A. Austr.
170 D3 Roe r. Northern Ireland U.K.
109 G11 Roe, Lake salt flat W.A. Austr.
258 F4 Roebling NJ U.S.A.
108 D6 Roebourne W.A. Austr.
108 G5 Roebuck Bay W.A. Austr.
235 F5 Roedtan S. Africa
213 K3 Roèn, Monte mt. Italy
109 I11 Roe Plains W.A. Austr.
187 I6 Roermond Neth.
187 C7 Roesbrugge-Haringe Belgium
187 D7 Roeselare Belgium
243 J3 Roes Welcome Sound sea chan. Nunavut Can.
191 B9 Roetgen Ger.
215 O7 Rofrano Italy
Rogachev Belarus see Rahachow
159 S2 Rogachevka Rus. Fed.
161 U5 Rogachevo Rus. Fed.
276 D3 Rogagua, Laguna l. Bol.
164 C2 Rogaland county Norway
210 E2 Rogaška Slatina Slovenia
196 F4 Rogaszyce Pol.
173 K5 Rogate West Sussex, England U.K.
201 M7 Rogatec Slovenia
210 G4 Rogatica Bos.-Herz.
Rogatin Ukr. see Rohatyn
193 E6 Rogätz Ger.
164 I1 Røgden l. Norway
251 P2 Roger, Lac l. Que. Can.
246 G5 Rogers B.C. Can.
261 H7 Rogers AR U.S.A.
256 D12 Rogers, Mount VA U.S.A.
251 K4 Rogers City MI U.S.A.
264 O7 Rogers Lake CA U.S.A.
262 G5 Rogerson ID U.S.A.
256 B12 Rogersville TN U.S.A.
248 E2 Roggan r. Que. Can.
248 E2 Roggan, Lac l. Que. Can.
187 I6 Roggel Neth.
195 I5 Roggenburg Ger.
192 D3 Roggendorf Ger.
192 G4 Roggentin Ger.
291 N8 Roggeveen Basin sea feature S. Pacific Ocean
236 E8 Roggeveld plat. S. Africa
236 E8 Roggeveldberge esc. S. Africa
215 Q8 Roggiano Gravina Italy
Roghadal Scotland U.K. see Rodel
Roghadal Western Isles, Scotland U.K. see Rodel
217 J7 Roghudi Italy
206 B6 Rogil Port.
214 C2 Rogliano Corse France
217 K5 Rogliano Italy

213 J8 **Roglio** r. Italy
183 G10 **Rognac** France
162 M3 **Rognan** Norway
161 Q8 **Rognedino** Rus. Fed.
183 G9 **Rognes** France
190 K4 **Rögnitz** r. Ger.
179 J7 **Rognon** r. France
183 F9 **Rognonas** France
212 B6 **Rognosa, Punta** mt. Italy
159 R2 **Rogovatoye** Rus. Fed.
159 R8 **Rogovskaya** Rus. Fed.
197 H4 **Rogów** Pol.
196 F3 **Rogowo** Kujawsko-Pomorskie Pol.
197 H3 **Rogowo** Kujawsko-Pomorskie Pol.
196 E4 **Rogoźnica** Pol.
197 K3 **Rogoźniczka** Pol.
196 G2 **Rogóźno** Pol.
196 F3 **Rogoźno** Pol.
165 L1 **Rogsjön** l. Sweden
163 N6 **Rogsta** Sweden
262 B5 **Rogue** r. OR U.S.A.
100 □3b **Roguron** i. Majuro Marshall Is
197 J3 **Roguszyn** Pol.
136 C3 **Roha** Mahar. India
158 G3 **Rohachiv** Ukr.
180 F5 **Rohan** France
159 P4 **Rohan'** Ukr.
198 G3 **Rohatec** Czech Rep.
158 D4 **Rohatyn** Ukr.
138 D7 **Rohera** Rajasthan India
100 □6 **Rohinari** Malaita Solomon Is
159 K2 **Rohizky** Ukr.
195 I4 **Röhlingen** Ger.
192 E4 **Rohlsdorf** Brandenburg Ger.
192 F4 **Rohlsdorf** Brandenburg Ger.
264 J3 **Rohnert Park** CA U.S.A.
199 L3 **Rohod** Hungary
198 G3 **Rohovce** Slovakia
201 O3 **Rohrau** Austria
195 L4 **Rohrbach** Ger.
201 I2 **Rohrbach in Oberösterreich** Austria
179 N5 **Rohrbach-lès-Bitche** France
192 D5 **Rohrberg** Ger.
195 L4 **Rohr in Niederbayern** Ger.
145 M8 **Rohri Sangar** Pak.
195 K5 **Röhrmoos** Ger.
195 P4 **Röhrnbach** Ger.
190 H5 **Rohrsen** Ger.
138 F5 **Rohtak** Haryana India
160 G3 **Rohuküla** Estonia
118 F6 **Roi Et** Thai.
183 F6 **Roiffieux** France
209 D12 **Roig, Cabo** c. Spain
209 I9 **Roig, Cap** c. Spain
101 □9 **Roi Georges, Îles du** is Arch. des Tuamotu Fr. Polynesia
100 □3a **Roi-Namur** i. Kwajalein Marshall Is
163 R6 **Roine** l. Fin.
139 O5 **Roing** Arun. Prad. India
168 E9 **Rois-Bheinn** hill Scotland U.K.
178 F4 **Roisel** France
178 E6 **Roissy-en-Brie** France
205 L2 **Roiz** Spain
160 F4 **Roja** Latvia
238 □3a **Roja, Punta** pt Tenerife Canary Is
209 I10 **Roja, Punta** pt Spain
209 D11 **Rojales** Spain
285 G4 **Rojas** Arg.
164 I1 **Röjdåfors** Sweden
196 G3 **Rojewo** Pol.
145 N7 **Rojhan** Pak.
269 J4 **Rojo, Cabo** c. Mex.
271 □1 **Rojo, Cabo** c. Puerto Rico
276 D3 **Rojo Aguado, Laguna** l. Bol.
116 D4 **Rokan** r. Indon.
107 I2 **Rokeby** Qld Austr.
107 I2 **Rokeby National Park** Qld Austr.
100 □6 **Rokera** Solomon Is
197 H4 **Rokiciny** Pol.
197 K6 **Rokietnica** Podkarpackie Pol.
196 E3 **Rokietnica** Wielkopolskie Pol.
160 I6 **Rokiškis** Lith.
197 L3 **Rokitno** Pol.
124 S6 **Rokkasho** Japan
125 O9 **Rokkō-zaki** pt Japan
162 M3 **Røkland** Norway
162 P4 **Roknäs** Sweden
199 H3 **Rokoš** mt. Slovakia
127 H4 **Rokugō** Japan
127 H3 **Rokuriga-hara** plain Japan
126 E2 **Rokusei** Japan
198 C2 **Rokycany** Czech Rep.
158 E3 **Rokyni** Ukr.
198 F2 **Rokytná** r. Czech Rep.
158 J4 **Rokytne** Kyivs'ka Oblast' Ukr.
158 G2 **Rokytne** Rivnens'ka Oblast' Ukr.
198 G2 **Rokytnice** Czech Rep.
133 I9 **Rola Co** l. Xizang China
133 I9 **Rolagang** Xizang China
133 I9 **Rola Kangri** mt. Xizang China
179 J8 **Rolampont** France
280 B5 **Rolândia** Brazil
229 G7 **Rolas, Ilha das** i. São Tomé and Príncipe
285 G3 **Roldan** Arg.
186 K3 **Rolde** Neth.
277 E2 **Rolim de Moura** Brazil
265 S9 **Roll** AZ U.S.A.
260 J7 **Rolla** MO U.S.A.
260 F1 **Rolla** ND U.S.A.
164 F1 **Rollag** Norway
204 I7 **Rollán** Spain
212 A3 **Rolle** Switz.
173 P2 **Rollesby** Norfolk, England U.K.
107 L8 **Rolleston** Qld Austr.
103 G10 **Rolleston** South I. N.Z.
103 F9 **Rolleston, Mount** South I. N.Z.
103 F10 **Rolleston Range** mts South I. N.Z.
251 O2 **Rollet** Que. Can.
270 F2 **Rolleville** Gt Exuma Bahamas
261 J9 **Rolling Fork** MS U.S.A.
262 G3 **Rollins** MT U.S.A.
257 □O5 **Rollinsford** NH U.S.A.
228 E3 **Rollo** Burkina
251 Q3 **Rolphton** Ont. Can.
164 B2 **Rolvsnes** Norway
162 R1 **Rolvsøya** i. Norway
184 E3 **Rom** France
192 E4 **Rom** Ger.
232 B4 **Rom** mt. Uganda
107 L9 **Roma** Qld Austr.
215 J4 **Roma** Italy
215 I3 **Roma** prov. Italy
237 L5 **Roma** Lesotho
219 O3 **Roma** Romania
165 O4 **Roma** Gotland Sweden
261 F12 **Roma** TX U.S.A.
Roma, Pulau i. Maluku Indon. see **Romang, Pulau**
212 E4 **Romagnano Sesia** Italy
180 I5 **Romagné** France
103 D13 **Romahapa** South I. N.Z.
255 H9 **Romain, Cape** SC U.S.A.
249 I3 **Romaine** r. Que. Can.
212 A2 **Romainmôtier** Switz.
219 O4 **Roman** Romania
173 N4 **Roman** r. England U.K.
214 B7 **Romana** Sardegna Italy
219 L6 **Română, Câmpia** plain Romania
219 L6 **Romanaţilor, Câmpia** plain Romania
171 O5 **Romanby** North Yorkshire, England U.K.
183 H6 **Romanche** r. France
288 H6 **Romanche Gap** sea feature S. Atlantic Ocean
258 C7 **Romancoke** MD U.S.A.
182 F4 **Romanèche-Thorins** France
249 H1 **Romanet, Lac** l. Que. Can.
115 E7 **Romang, Pulau** i. Maluku Indon.
219 M4 **Romania** country Europe
205 O6 **Romanillos de Atienza** Spain
197 M6 **Romaniv** Ukr.
159 N9 **Roman-Kosh** mt. Ukr.
168 J11 **Romannobridge** Scottish Borders, Scotland U.K.
270 D2 **Romano, Cayo** i. Cuba
213 L4 **Romano d'Ezzelino** Italy
212 H4 **Romano di Lombardia** Italy
205 O7 **Romanones** Spain
Romanovka Moldova see **Basarabeasca**
121 J1 **Romanovka** Respublika Buryatiya Rus. Fed.
157 H6 **Romanovka** Saratovskaya Oblast' Rus. Fed.
143 S1 **Romanovo** Rus. Fed.
196 E3 **Romanowo** Pol.
212 G1 **Romanshorn** Switz.
183 G6 **Romans-sur-Isère** France
244 F3 **Romanzof, Cape** AK U.S.A.
245 K1 **Romanzof Mountains** AK U.S.A.
275 F5 **Romão** Brazil
180 I5 **Romazy** France
179 L5 **Rombas** France
217 K6 **Rombiolo** Italy
114 D5 **Romblon** Phil.
114 D5 **Romblon** i. Phil.
114 D5 **Romblon Passage** Phil.
Rombo, Ilhéus do is Cape Verde see **Secos, Ilhéus**
Rome Italy see **Roma**
255 E8 **Rome** GA U.S.A.
250 E9 **Rome** IL U.S.A.
257 □P4 **Rome** ME U.S.A.
257 J5 **Rome** NY U.S.A.
182 F3 **Rome Château, Mont de** hill France
250 I8 **Rome City** IN U.S.A.
206 B2 **Romeira** Port.
159 M3 **Romen** r. Ukr.
263 K8 **Romeo** CO U.S.A.
251 K7 **Romeo** MI U.S.A.
194 H4 **Römerstein** hill Ger.
204 F5 **Romeu** Port.
173 M4 **Romford** Greater London, England U.K.
191 K10 **Römhild** Ger.
180 H5 **Romillé** France
178 B5 **Romilly-sur-Andelle** France
178 G6 **Romilly-sur-Seine** France
145 M2 **Romit** Tajik.
268 F5 **Romita** Mex.
142 K8 **Romiton** Uzbek.
191 C8 **Rommerskirchen** Ger.
256 G9 **Romney** WV U.S.A.
173 N5 **Romney Marsh** reg. England U.K.
159 M3 **Romny** Ukr.
164 E6 **Rømø** i. Denmark
159 M4 **Romodan** Ukr.
157 I5 **Romodanovo** Rus. Fed.
212 B2 **Romont** Switz.
100 □4a **Romonum** i. Chuuk Micronesia
184 H1 **Romorantin-Lanthenay** France
116 E3 **Rompin** r. Malaysia
162 T5 **Romppala** Fin.
191 H9 **Romrod** Ger.
173 J6 **Romsey** Hampshire, England U.K.
164 H2 **Rømskog** Norway
172 H3 **Romsley** Worcestershire, England U.K.
117 M9 **Romu** mt. Sumbawa Indon.
219 M3 **Romuli** Romania
251 K7 **Romulus** MI U.S.A.
136 D5 **Ron** Karnataka India
118 H6 **Ron** Vietnam
118 H5 **Ron, Mui** hd Vietnam
168 E7 **Rona** i. Highland, Scotland U.K.
168 E4 **Rona** i. Western Isles, Scotland U.K.
Ronaigh i. Scotland U.K. see **Ronay**
168 □N1 **Ronas Hill** Scotland U.K.
168 B8 **Ronay** i. Scotland U.K.
213 M4 **Roncade** Italy
204 E1 **Roncadoira, Punta** pt Spain
280 A6 **Roncador** Brazil
278 B5 **Roncador, Serra do** hills Brazil
270 C7 **Roncador Cay** i. Caribbean Sea
100 □6 **Roncador Reef** Solomon Is
208 D2 **Roncal** Spain
208 C2 **Roncal, Valle del** val. Spain
200 D7 **Roncegno** Italy
184 B4 **Ronce-les-Bains** France
Roncesvalles Navarra Spain see **Orreaga**
256 E11 **Ronceverte** WV U.S.A.
179 M8 **Ronchamp** France
213 O4 **Ronchi dei Legionari** Italy
214 I3 **Ronciglione** Italy
213 M7 **Ronco** r. Italy
212 D5 **Ronco Canavese** Italy
213 J4 **Roncone** Italy
212 F6 **Ronco Scrivia** Italy
178 F2 **Roncq** France
204 C2 **Roncudo, Punta** pt Spain
207 I7 **Ronda** Spain
207 I7 **Ronda, Serranía de** mts Spain
207 J7 **Ronda, Serranía de** nature res. Spain
277 E3 **Ronda das Salinas** Brazil
163 J6 **Rondane Nasjonalpark** nat. park Norway
164 G5 **Rønde** Denmark
271 □6 **Ronde** i. Grenada
212 D5 **Rondissone** Italy
280 A5 **Rondon** Brazil
274 D3 **Rondón** Col.
276 E2 **Rondônia** state Brazil
279 B6 **Rondonópolis** Brazil
257 K7 **Rondout Reservoir** NY U.S.A.
138 E2 **Rondu** Pak.
130 G6 **Rong'an** Guangxi China
130 B3 **Rongbaca** Sichuan China
130 E4 **Rongchang** Chongqing China
Rongcheng Anhui China see **Qingyang**
Rongcheng Guangxi China see **Rongxian**
Rongcheng Hubei China see **Jianli**
129 R8 **Rongcheng** Shandong China
129 R8 **Rongcheng Wan** b. China
133 I12 **Rong Chu** r. China
290 G6 **Rongelap** atoll Marshall Is
130 G6 **Rongjiang** Guizhou China
Rongjiang Jiangxi China see **Nankang**
130 G7 **Rong Jiang** r. China
Rongjiawan Hunan China see **Yueyang**
118 A3 **Rongklang Range** mts Myanmar
Rongmei Hubei China see **Hefeng**
130 G6 **Rongshui** Guangxi China
Rongwo Qinghai China see **Tongren**
130 H7 **Rongxian** Guangxi China
130 E4 **Rongxian** Sichuan China
Rongzhag Sichuan China see **Danba**
101 □9a **Roniu** mt. Tahiti Fr. Polynesia
Rōnlap atoll Marshall Is see **Rongelap**
165 K6 **Rønne** Bornholm Denmark
193 F9 **Ronneburg** Ger.
165 L5 **Ronneby** Sweden
286 S2 **Ronne Entrance** str. Antarctica
286 T1 **Ronne Ice Shelf** Antarctica
191 I6 **Ronnenberg** Ger.
162 L5 **Rönnöfors** Sweden
108 D6 **Ronsard Island** W.A. Austr.
195 I6 **Ronsberg** Ger.
187 E7 **Ronse** Belgium
191 I9 **Ronshausen** Ger.
278 B5 **Ronuro** r. Brazil
169 F6 **Rooaun** Ireland
237 N2 **Roodebank** S. Africa
186 K2 **Roodeschool** Neth.
237 M4 **Rooiberg** mt. Free State S. Africa
236 F9 **Rooiberg** mt. Western Cape S. Africa
236 F5 **Rooibergdam** l. S. Africa
236 E8 **Rooikloof** pass S. Africa
237 N1 **Rooikraal** S. Africa
237 L3 **Rooiwal** S. Africa
Rooke Island P.N.G. see **Umboi**
238 □2c **Rookery Point** Tristan da Cunha S. Atlantic Ocean
108 E6 **Rookh Aboriginal Reserve** W.A. Austr.
169 C5 **Roonah Quay** Ireland
138 F5 **Roorkee** Uttaranchal India
237 N4 **Roosboom** S. Africa
186 F5 **Roosendaal** Neth.
265 U8 **Roosevelt** AZ U.S.A.
259 G4 **Roosevelt** NJ U.S.A.
265 W1 **Roosevelt** UT U.S.A.
246 E3 **Roosevelt, Mount** B.C. Can.
259 G5 **Roosevelt City** NJ U.S.A.
286 N1 **Roosevelt Island** Antarctica
169 G5 **Roosky** Leitrim Ireland
169 E5 **Roosky** Mayo Ireland
160 I2 **Roosna-Alliku** Estonia
237 N1 **Roossenekal** S. Africa
246 F2 **Root** r. N.W.T. Can.
250 C6 **Root** r. MN U.S.A.
197 J6 **Ropa** Pol.
197 J6 **Ropa** r. Pol.
160 H5 **Ropaži** Latvia
197 J5 **Ropczyce** Pol.
106 E3 **Roper** r. N.T. Austr.
106 E3 **Roper Bar** N.T. Austr.
106 E3 **Roper Bar Aboriginal Land** res. N.T. Austr.
107 L7 **Roper Creek** r. Qld Austr.
204 I4 **Roperuelos del Páramo** Spain
106 E3 **Roper Valley** N.T. Austr.
197 K6 **Ropienka** Pol.
162 P2 **Ropinsalmi** Fin.
200 C5 **Roppen** Austria
183 K8 **Roquebillière** France
183 C9 **Roquebrun** France
183 K9 **Roquebrune-Cap-Martin** France
183 J10 **Roquebrune-sur-Argens** France
185 F7 **Roquecor** France
185 I8 **Roquecourbe** France
185 D7 **Roquefort** France
183 B9 **Roquefort-sur-Soulzon** France
183 F8 **Roquemaure** France
285 H4 **Roque Pérez** Arg.
183 K9 **Roquesteron** France
208 G6 **Roquetas** Spain
207 N7 **Roquetas de Mar** Spain
183 H10 **Roquevaire** France
275 F4 **Roraima** state Brazil
275 F3 **Roraima, Mount** Guyana
164 E3 **Rore** l. Norway
245 O2 **Rorey Lake** N.W.T. Can.
138 E5 **Rori** Punjab India
Ro Ro Reef Fiji see **Malolo Barrier Reef**
162 K5 **Røros** Norway
212 H1 **Rorschach** Switz.
164 H6 **Rørvig** Denmark
162 K4 **Rørvik** Norway
197 M2 **Ros'** Belarus
160 H8 **Ros'** r. Belarus
158 K4 **Ros'** r. Ukr.
197 J2 **Roś, Jezioro** l. Pol.
213 L4 **Rosà** Italy
270 G3 **Rosa, Lake** Gt Inagua Bahamas
212 D4 **Rosa, Monte** mt. Italy/Switz.
266 E4 **Rosa, Punta** pt Mex.
212 C3 **Rosablanche** mt. Switz.
238 □1c **Rosais** São Jorge Azores
238 □1c **Rosais, Ponta dos** pt São Jorge Azores
204 C5 **Rosal, Val do** reg. Spain
206 E5 **Rosal de la Frontera** Spain
266 G3 **Rosales** Mex.
262 F3 **Rosalia** WA U.S.A.
271 □2 **Rosalie Bay** Dominica
270 C5 **Rosalind Bank** sea feature Caribbean Sea
264 N7 **Rosamond** CA U.S.A.
264 N7 **Rosamond Lake** CA U.S.A.
268 B3 **Rosamorada** Mex.
280 A5 **Rosana** Brazil
169 C6 **Ros an Mhíl** Ireland
200 B5 **Rosanna** r. Austria
183 G8 **Rosans** France
169 G2 **Rosapenna** Ireland
282 D1 **Rosario** Jujuy Arg.
285 G3 **Rosario** Santa Fé Arg.
278 D2 **Rosário** Brazil
276 C6 **Rosario** Chile
266 B2 **Rosario** Baja California Mex.
266 H4 **Rosario** Coahuila Mex.
268 B3 **Rosario** Sinaloa Mex.
266 E4 **Rosario** Sonora Mex.
268 F1 **Rosario** Zacatecas Mex.
277 F6 **Rosario** Para.
114 C3 **Rosario** Luzon Phil.
114 C5 **Rosario** Luzon Phil.
206 C5 **Rosário** Port.
285 I4 **Rosario** Uru.
274 C2 **Rosario** Venez.
270 C3 **Rosario, Cayo del** i. Cuba
270 A4 **Rosario Bank** sea feature Caribbean Sea
282 D2 **Rosario de la Frontera** Arg.
282 D2 **Rosario de Lerma** Arg.
285 H3 **Rosario del Tala** Arg.
284 D2 **Rosario del Tama** Arg.
279 B9 **Rosário do Sul** Brazil
277 F3 **Rosário Oeste** Brazil
266 A1 **Rosarito** Baja California Mex.
266 B3 **Rosarito** Baja California Mex.
266 D4 **Rosarito** Baja California Sur Mex.
205 J8 **Rosarito, Embalse de** resr Spain
217 J7 **Rosarno** Italy
Rosas Spain see **Roses**
Rosas, Golfo de b. Spain see **Roses, Golf de**
159 K4 **Rosava** r. Ukr.
191 G10 **Rosbach vor der Höhe** Ger.
169 I8 **Rosbercon** Ireland
180 B5 **Roscanvel** France
169 D6 **Ros Cathail** Ireland
190 K5 **Rosche** Ger.
201 M2 **Röschitz** Austria
197 H3 **Rościszewo** Pol.
245 Q1 **Roscoe** r. N.W.T. Can.
250 E7 **Roscoe** IL U.S.A.
180 D4 **Roscoff** France
169 F5 **Roscommon** Ireland
169 F5 **Roscommon** county Ireland
250 J5 **Roscommon** MI U.S.A.
169 G7 **Roscrea** Ireland
191 I8 **Rosdorf** Ger.
106 E3 **Rose** r. N.T. Austr.
215 Q9 **Rose** Italy
264 M2 **Rose, Mount** NV U.S.A.
271 □2 **Roseau** Dominica
260 H1 **Roseau** MN U.S.A.
260 G1 **Roseau** r. MN U.S.A.
239 □1b **Rose Belle** Mauritius
171 O4 **Roseberry Topping** hill England U.K.
106 G8 **Roseberth** Qld Austr.
105 J9 **Rosebery** Tas. Austr.
249 J4 **Rose Blanche** Nfld and Lab. Can.
246 H5 **Rosebud** r. Alta Can.
262 K3 **Rosebud** MT U.S.A.
262 K3 **Rosebud Creek** r. MT U.S.A.
260 E4 **Rosebud Indian Reservation** res. SD U.S.A.
262 C5 **Roseburg** OR U.S.A.
251 J5 **Rose City** MI U.S.A.
250 B6 **Rose Creek** MN U.S.A.
107 M8 **Rosedale** Qld Austr.
105 K8 **Rosedale** Vic. Austr.
258 B6 **Rosedale** MD U.S.A.
261 J9 **Rosedale** MS U.S.A.
171 P5 **Rosedale Abbey** North Yorkshire, England U.K.
236 G8 **Rosedene** S. Africa
187 G8 **Rosée** Belgium
201 J6 **Rosegg** Austria
275 G3 **Rosehall** Guyana
270 □ **Rose Hall** Jamaica
168 L7 **Rosehearty** Aberdeenshire, Scotland U.K.
239 □1b **Rose Hill** Mauritius
232 B2 **Roseires Reservoir** Sudan
97 H4 **Rose Island** atoll American Samoa
255 □2 **Rose Island** Bahamas
182 J5 **Roselend, Barrage de** dam France
259 G3 **Roselle** NJ U.S.A.
168 H7 **Rosemarkie** Highland, Scotland U.K.
108 D6 **Rosemary Island** W.A. Austr.
169 H6 **Rosenallis** Ireland
261 H11 **Rosenberg** TX U.S.A.
164 C2 **Rosendal** Norway
237 L4 **Rosendal** S. Africa
250 F6 **Rosendale** WI U.S.A.
168 K5 **Rose Ness** hd Scotland U.K.
194 F5 **Rosenfeld** Ger.
190 I4 **Rosengarten** Ger.
258 E6 **Rosenhayn** NJ U.S.A.
195 M6 **Rosenheim** Ger.
201 I6 **Rosennock** mt. Austria
192 H3 **Rosenow** Ger.
201 J6 **Rosental** val. Austria
191 G9 **Rosenthal** Ger.
265 W8 **Rose Peak** AZ U.S.A.
245 O5 **Rose Point** pt B.C. Can.
165 N2 **Roserberg** Sweden
208 L3 **Roses** Spain
208 L3 **Roses, Golf de** b. Spain
258 E3 **Roseto** PA U.S.A.
217 L4 **Roseto Capo Spulico** Italy
215 M2 **Roseto degli Abruzzi** Italy
215 O5 **Roseto Valfortore** Italy
247 J5 **Rosetown** Sask. Can.
Rosetta Egypt see **Rashīd**
107 K6 **Rosetta Creek** r. Qld Austr.
247 K4 **Rose Valley** Sask. Can.
264 K3 **Roseville** CA U.S.A.
260 J5 **Roseville** IL U.S.A.
251 L7 **Roseville** MI U.S.A.
256 C9 **Roseville** OH U.S.A.
168 J11 **Rosewell** Midlothian, Scotland U.K.
107 N9 **Rosewood** Qld Austr.
256 B8 **Rosewood** OH U.S.A.
161 W6 **Roshal'** Rus. Fed.
160 M1 **Roshchino** Leningradskaya Oblast' Rus. Fed.
151 G1 **Roshchino** Stavropol'skiy Kray Rus. Fed.
159 N8 **Roshchyne** Ukr.
179 N6 **Rosheim** France
151 G2 **Roshni-Chu** Rus. Fed.
250 E5 **Rosholt** WI U.S.A.
234 C5 **Rosh Pinah** Namibia
Roshtkala Tajik. see **Roshtqal'a**
144 H4 **Roshtkhvār** Iran
145 N3 **Roshtqal'a** Tajik.
168 E9 **Roshven** Highland, Scotland U.K.
207 □ **Rosia** Gibraltar
199 L5 **Roşia** Romania
207 □ **Rosia Bay** Gibraltar
198 F2 **Rosice** Czech Rep.
183 D6 **Rosières** France
178 E4 **Rosières-en-Santerre** France
178 H7 **Rosières-près-Troyes** France
212 I9 **Rosignano Marittimo** Italy
108 C6 **Rosily Island** W.A. Austr.
199 H2 **Rosina** Slovakia
219 P6 **Roşiori** Romania
219 N6 **Roşiori de Vede** Romania
160 K6 **Rositsa** Belarus
219 P7 **Rositsa** Bulg.
219 N7 **Rositsa** r. Bulg.
193 F8 **Rositz** Ger.
169 E4 **Roskeeragh Point** Ireland
168 C8 **Roskhill** Highland, Scotland U.K.
164 I6 **Roskilde** Denmark
196 E3 **Rosko** Pol.
220 A2 **Roskovec** Albania
193 G6 **Roskow** Ger.
265 U9 **Roskruge Mountains** AZ U.S.A.
193 E10 **Röslau** Ger.
193 F10 **Röslau** r. Ger.
161 P8 **Roslavl'** Rus. Fed.
168 J11 **Roslin** Midlothian, Scotland U.K.
162 V2 **Roslyakovo** Rus. Fed.
156 I4 **Roslyatino** Rus. Fed.
186 H5 **Rosmalen** Neth.
204 F9 **Rosmaninhal** Port.
237 J7 **Rosmead** S. Africa
169 C6 **Ros Muc** Ireland
Rosmuck Ireland see **Ros Muc**
196 E1 **Rosnowo** Pol.
213 M5 **Rosolina** Italy
213 M5 **Rosolina Mare** Italy
216 H10 **Rosolini** Sicilia Italy
219 J9 **Rosoman** Macedonia
178 F7 **Rosoy** France
200 F5 **Röspitze** mt. Austria/Italy
180 D6 **Rosporden** France
191 D9 **Rösrath** Ger.
105 K10 **Ross** Tas. Austr.
245 N3 **Ross** r. Y.T. Can.
103 E9 **Ross** South I. N.Z.
103 J8 **Ross, Mount** hill North I. N.Z.
217 L4 **Rossano** Italy
213 L4 **Rossano Veneto** Italy
169 E3 **Rossan Point** Ireland
204 D5 **Rossas** Port.
Rossaveel Ireland see **Ros an Mhíl**
195 N4 **Roßbach** Bayern Ger.
193 E8 **Roßbach** Sachsen-Anhalt Ger.
261 K9 **Ross Barnett Reservoir** MS U.S.A.
249 H2 **Ross Bay Junction** Nfld and Lab. Can.
169 E3 **Rossbeg** Ireland
169 D9 **Rossbrin** Ireland
Rosscahill Ireland see **Ros Cathail**
169 D9 **Rosscarbery** Ireland
169 F4 **Rosscor** Northern Ireland U.K.
286 N2 **Ross Dependency** Antarctica
194 F2 **Roßdorf** Ger.
251 O4 **Rosseau, Lake** Ont. Can.
113 L9 **Rossel Island** P.N.G.
208 F6 **Rossell** Spain
208 G4 **Rosselló** Spain
213 J7 **Rossenno** r. Italy
169 F2 **Rosses Bay** Ireland
169 E4 **Rosses Point** Ireland
172 G1 **Rossett** Wrexham, Wales U.K.
195 J6 **Roßhaupten** Ger.
108 □1 **Ross Hill** Christmas I.
287 M1 **Ross Ice Shelf** Antarctica
212 F6 **Rossiglione** Italy
187 H9 **Rossignol** Belgium
248 F2 **Rossignol, Lac** l. Que. Can.
249 H4 **Rossignol, Lake** N.S. Can.
234 B4 **Rössing** Namibia
191 I6 **Rössing (Nordstemmen)** Ger.
171 O7 **Rossington** South Yorkshire, England U.K.
169 F4 **Rossinver** Ireland
206 C2 **Rossio ao Sul do Tejo** Port.
287 L1 **Ross Island** Antarctica
Ross Island Myanmar see **Daung Kyun**
109 G12 **Rossiter Bay** W.A. Austr.
Rossiyskaya Sovetskaya Federativnaya Sotsialisticheskaya Respublika country Asia/Europe see **Russian Federation**
164 D2 **Rosskreppfjorden** l. Norway
193 D8 **Roßla** Ger.
246 G5 **Rossland** B.C. Can.
169 J8 **Rosslare** Ireland
169 J8 **Rosslare Harbour** Ireland
169 J8 **Rosslare Point** Ireland
193 F7 **Roßlau** Ger.
169 H4 **Rosslea** Northern Ireland U.K.
193 D8 **Roßleben** Ger.
201 J4 **Roßleithen** Austria
251 Q5 **Rossmore** Ont. Can.
169 F3 **Rossnowlagh** Ireland
228 B2 **Rosso** Maur.
214 B3 **Rosso, Capo** c. Corse France
162 N5 **Rossön** Sweden
172 G4 **Ross-on-Wye** Herefordshire, England U.K.
Rossony Belarus see **Rasony**
157 G6 **Rossosh'** Rus. Fed.
197 L4 **Rossosz** Pol.
196 G4 **Rossoszyca** Pol.
237 L7 **Rossouw** S. Africa
192 G4 **Rossow** Ger.
250 G1 **Rossport** Ont. Can.
106 E7 **Ross River** N.T. Austr.
245 N3 **Ross River** Y.T. Can.
287 L1 **Ross Sea** Antarctica
195 J3 **Roßtal** Ger.
186 H5 **Rossum** Neth.
162 M4 **Røssvatnet** l. Norway
250 C6 **Rossville** IA U.S.A.
250 G9 **Rossville** IL U.S.A.
250 H9 **Rossville** IN U.S.A.
258 B4 **Rossville** PA U.S.A.
193 H8 **Roßwein** Ger.
246 D4 **Rosswood** B.C. Can.
149 L5 **Rōst** Iraq
162 L3 **Røst** Norway
145 M3 **Rostāq** Afgh.
144 F7 **Rostāq** Fārs Iran
144 E8 **Rostāq** Hormozgan Iran
196 E3 **Rostarzewo** Pol.
158 J4 **Rostavytsya** r. Ukr.
162 L3 **Røsthavet** sea chan. Norway
247 J4 **Rosthern** Sask. Can.
192 F2 **Rostock** Ger.
162 P2 **Rostonsölkä** ridge Sweden
159 T2 **Rostoshi** Rus. Fed.
161 W4 **Rostov** Rus. Fed.
157 G7 **Rostov-na-Donu** Rus. Fed.
Rostov Oblast admin. div. Rus. Fed. see **Rostovskaya Oblast'**
Rostov-on-Don Rus. Fed. see **Rostov-na-Donu**
157 H7 **Rostovskaya Oblast'** admin. div. Rus. Fed.
237 J2 **Rostrataville** S. Africa
180 E5 **Rostrenen** France
169 J4 **Rostrevor** Northern Ireland U.K.
162 P2 **Rostujávri** l. Sweden
169 C5 **Rosturk** Ireland
218 I9 **Rostuša** Mavrovo and Rostuša Macedonia
162 M3 **Røsvik** Norway
162 P4 **Rosvik** Sweden
255 E9 **Roswell** GA U.S.A.
263 L10 **Roswell** NM U.S.A.
171 K1 **Rosyth** Fife, Scotland U.K.
199 J5 **Röszke** Hungary
194 H5 **Rot** r. Ger.
113 K4 **Rota** i. N. Mariana Is
206 G7 **Rota** Spain
194 H6 **Rotach** r. Ger.
215 Q9 **Rota Greca** Italy
195 I3 **Rot am See** Ger.
195 I5 **Rot an der Rot** Ger.
193 G10 **Rotava** Czech Rep.
Rotch Island Gilbert Is Kiribati see **Tamana**
115 C9 **Rote** i. Indon.
215 N4 **Rotello** Italy
190 H4 **Rotenburg (Wümme)** Ger.
191 I8 **Rotenburg an der Fulda** Ger.
193 D10 **Roter Main** r. Ger.
200 A5 **Rote Wand** mt. Austria
Rot-Front Ukr. see **Dobropillya**
201 H5 **Rotgülden** Austria
195 K3 **Roth** Ger.
195 I5 **Roth** r. Ger.
195 K3 **Roth** r. Ger.
193 F8 **Rötha** Ger.
191 F9 **Rothaargebirge** hills Ger.
171 N3 **Rothbury** Northumberland, England U.K.
171 N3 **Rothbury Forest** England U.K.
195 K3 **Röthenbach an der Pegnitz** Ger.
194 F2 **Rothenberg** Ger.
194 G2 **Rothenbuch** Ger.
193 E7 **Rothenburg** Ger.
193 K8 **Rothenburg (Oberlausitz)** Ger.
195 I3 **Rothenburg ob der Tauber** Ger.
180 H4 **Rothéneuf** France
194 H2 **Rothenfels** Ger.
193 E9 **Rothenstein** Ger.
173 K6 **Rother** r. England U.K.
286 T2 **Rothera** research stn Antarctica
173 M5 **Rotherfield** East Sussex, England U.K.
103 G9 **Rotherham** South I. N.Z.
171 O7 **Rotherham** South Yorkshire, England U.K.
168 J7 **Rothes** Moray, Scotland U.K.
168 F11 **Rothesay** Argyll and Bute, Scotland U.K.
187 H7 **Rotheux-Rimière** Belgium
168 K4 **Rothiesholm** Orkney, Scotland U.K.
195 I2 **Röthlein** Ger.
194 D7 **Rothrist** Switz.
250 E5 **Rothschild** WI U.S.A.
286 T2 **Rothschild Island** Antarctica
258 C4 **Rothsville** PA U.S.A.
173 K3 **Rothwell** Northamptonshire, England U.K.
171 O6 **Rothwell** West Yorkshire, England U.K.
191 I8 **Rothwesten (Fuldatal)** Ger.
115 C9 **Roti** Indon.
Roti i. Indon. see **Rote**
115 C9 **Roti, Selat** sea chan. Indon.
Rotja, Punta pt Spain see **Roja, Punta**
105 J5 **Roto** N.S.W. Austr.
102 J6 **Rotoaira, Lake** North I. N.Z.
102 K5 **Rotoehu, Lake** North I. N.Z.
102 K5 **Rotoiti, Lake** North I. N.Z.
103 G8 **Rotoiti, Lake** South I. N.Z.
102 K5 **Rotoma, Lake** North I. N.Z.
Rotomagus France see **Rouen**
102 K5 **Rotomahana, Lake** North I. N.Z.
103 F9 **Rotomanu** South I. N.Z.
215 Q8 **Rotonda** Italy
217 L3 **Rotondella** Italy
214 C3 **Rotondo, Monte** mt. Corse France
212 E2 **Rotondo, Pizzo** mt. Switz.
103 G8 **Rotoroa, Lake** South I. N.Z.
102 K5 **Rotorua** North I. N.Z.
102 K5 **Rotorua, Lake** North I. N.Z.
187 G7 **Rotselaar** Belgium
200 G6 **Rotsteinberg** mt. Austria
195 J6 **Rott** Ger.
195 O5 **Rott** r. Ger.
193 G7 **Rotta** Ger.
195 L6 **Rottach-Egern** Ger.
195 M6 **Rott am Inn** Ger.
179 L6 **Rotte** r. France
194 H5 **Rottenacker** Ger.
195 J2 **Röttenbach** Bayern Ger.
195 K3 **Röttenbach** Bayern Ger.
193 D9 **Rottenbach** Ger.
195 J6 **Rottenbuch** Ger.
194 F5 **Rottenburg am Neckar** Ger.
195 M4 **Rottenburg an der Laaber** Ger.
195 I2 **Rottendorf** Ger.
201 J4 **Rottenmann** Austria
201 J5 **Rottenmanner Tauern** mts Austria
186 G5 **Rotterdam** Neth.
257 L6 **Rotterdam** NY U.S.A.
186 J2 **Rottevalle** Neth.
195 O5 **Rotthalmünster** Ger.
173 L6 **Rottingdean** Brighton and Hove, England U.K.
194 H2 **Röttingham** Ger.
191 K7 **Rottleberode** Ger.
164 I2 **Rottnan** r. Sweden
165 L5 **Rottnen** l. Sweden
109 C12 **Rottnest Island** W.A. Austr.
212 H5 **Rottofreno** Italy
186 K1 **Rottumeroog** i. Neth.
186 J1 **Rottumerplaat** i. Neth.
194 F5 **Rottweil** Ger.
99 H3 **Rotuma** i. Fiji
219 M7 **Rotunda** Romania
162 M5 **Rötviken** Sweden
195 L6 **Rotwand** mt. Ger.
195 N3 **Rötz** Ger.
180 H7 **Rouans** France
178 F2 **Roubaix** France
183 F7 **Roubion** r. France
208 H2 **Rouch, Mont** mt. France/Spain
182 D4 **Rouchain, Barrage du** dam France
198 F2 **Rouchovany** Czech Rep.
198 D1 **Roudnice nad Labem** Czech Rep.
178 B5 **Rouen** France
185 I7 **Rouergue** reg. France
179 N8 **Rouffach** France
184 I5 **Rouffiac** France
184 F5 **Rouffignac** France
160 J4 **Rõuge** Estonia
180 I6 **Rougé** France
271 □7 **Rouge, Point** Trin. and Tob.
248 F4 **Rouge-Matawin, Réserve Faunique** nature res. Que. Can.
182 I2 **Rougemont** France
179 M8 **Rougemont-le-Château** France
103 D12 **Rough Ridge** South I. N.Z.
173 O2 **Roughton** Norfolk, England U.K.
169 C9 **Roughty** r. Ireland
184 E4 **Rougnac** France
224 A4 **Roui, Oued er** watercourse Niger
184 D4 **Rouillac** France
184 E3 **Rouillé** France
183 C9 **Roujan** France
182 I2 **Roulans** France
Roulers Belgium see **Roeselare**
256 G7 **Roulette** PA U.S.A.
106 D7 **Roulpmaulpma Aboriginal Land** res. N.T. Austr.
Roumania country Europe see **Romania**
184 F4 **Roumazières-Loubert** France
181 M3 **Roumois** reg. France
183 I9 **Roumoules** France
249 G2 **Roundeyed Lake** Que. Can.
256 B8 **Roundhead** OH U.S.A.
171 O5 **Round Hill** England U.K.
105 K5 **Round Hill Nature Reserve** N.S.W. Austr.
239 □1b **Round Island** Mauritius
248 E4 **Round Lake** Ont. Can.
105 N4 **Round Mountain** mt. N.S.W. Austr.
264 O3 **Round Mountain** NV U.S.A.
265 W5 **Round Rock** AZ U.S.A.
261 G10 **Round Rock** TX U.S.A.
169 C6 **Roundstone** Ireland
258 B3 **Round Top** hill PA U.S.A.
262 J3 **Roundup** MT U.S.A.
258 F3 **Round Valley Reservoir** NJ U.S.A.
173 I5 **Roundway** Wiltshire, England U.K.
170 E7 **Roundwood** Ireland
275 H3 **Roura** Fr. Guiana
212 C5 **Roure** Italy
168 J4 **Rousay** i. Scotland U.K.
257 L4 **Rouses Point** NY U.S.A.
198 F2 **Rousínov** Czech Rep.
170 C4 **Rousky** Northern Ireland U.K.
183 H10 **Rousset** France
183 G7 **Rousset, Col de** pass France
183 G9 **Roussillon** Provence-Alpes-Côte d'Azur France
177 G4 **Roussillon** Rhône-Alpes France
185 J10 **Roussillon** reg. France
183 E8 **Rousson** France
Routh Bank sea feature Phil. see **Seahorse Bank**
181 M3 **Routot** France
186 J3 **Rouveen** Neth.
181 K4 **Rouvre** r. France
178 E3 **Rouvroy** France
178 I4 **Rouvroy-sur-Audry** France
183 J10 **Roux, Cap** c. France
237 K6 **Rouxville** S. Africa
182 D2 **Rouy** France
248 E3 **Rouyn-Noranda** Que. Can.
Rouyuan Gansu China see **Huachi**
Rouyuanchengzi Gansu China see **Huachi**
162 R3 **Rovaniemi** Fin.
212 E5 **Rovasenda** r. Italy
212 I4 **Rovato** Italy
212 G6 **Rovegno** Italy
157 G6 **Roven'ki** Rus. Fed.
Rovenki Ukr. see **Roven'ky**
159 S5 **Roven'ky** Ukr.
Rovenskaya Oblast' admin. div. Ukr. see **Rivnens'ka Oblast'**
213 J5 **Roverbella** Italy
212 G3 **Roveredo** Switz.
213 K4 **Rovereto** Italy
192 F2 **Rövershagen** Ger.
282 E2 **Roversi** Arg.
215 J3 **Roviano** Italy
119 G8 **Rôviĕng Tbong** Cambodia
213 L5 **Rovigo** Italy
213 L5 **Rovigo** prov. Italy
219 L6 **Rovinari** Romania
210 D3 **Rovinj** Croatia
198 G3 **Rovinka** Slovakia
201 O8 **Rovišće** Croatia
Rovno Ukr. see **Rivne**
Rovno Oblast admin. div. Ukr. see **Rivnens'ka Oblast'**
160 L3 **Rovnoye** Pskovskaya Oblast' Rus. Fed.
142 B2 **Rovnoye** Saratovskaya Oblast' Rus. Fed.
196 C3 **Rów** Pol.
100 □5 **Rowa** Vanuatu
172 H5 **Rowde** Wiltshire, England U.K.
105 L3 **Rowena** N.S.W. Austr.
258 F2 **Rowland** PA U.S.A.
256 F9 **Rowlesburg** WV U.S.A.
243 K3 **Rowley Island** Nunavut Can.
108 E4 **Rowley Shoals** sea feature W.A. Austr.
160 M6 **Rownaye** Belarus
Równe Ukr. see **Rivne**
196 E4 **Rów Polski** r. Pol.
256 C8 **Rowsburg** OH U.S.A.
114 C3 **Roxas** Luzon Phil.
114 D7 **Roxas** Mindanao Phil.
114 C5 **Roxas** Mindoro Phil.
114 B6 **Roxas** Palawan Phil.
114 D6 **Roxas** Panay Phil.
255 H7 **Roxboro** NC U.S.A.
271 □5 **Roxborough** Trin. and Tob.
106 G7 **Roxborough Downs** Qld Austr.
103 D12 **Roxburgh** South I. N.Z.
Roxburgh Island Cook Is see **Rarotonga**
259 I1 **Roxbury** CT U.S.A.
259 I1 **Roxbury Falls** CT U.S.A.
104 F4 **Roxby Downs** S.A. Austr.
165 L3 **Roxen** l. Sweden
206 C5 **Roxo** r. Port.
206 C5 **Roxo, Barragem do** resr Port.
173 L3 **Roxton** Bedfordshire, England U.K.
168 G9 **Roy** r. Scotland U.K.
262 J3 **Roy** MT U.S.A.
263 L8 **Roy** NM U.S.A.
183 L9 **Roya** r. France/Italy
169 H6 **Royal Canal** Ireland
250 H9 **Royal Center** IN U.S.A.
139 J6 **Royal Chitwan National Park** Nepal
250 F1 **Royale, Isle** i. MI U.S.A.
237 M4 **Royal Natal National Park** S. Africa
251 K7 **Royal Oak** MI U.S.A.
287 K1 **Royal Society Range** mts Antarctica
138 H5 **Royal Sukla Phanta Wildlife Reserve** nature res. Nepal
258 B4 **Royalton** PA U.S.A.
250 F5 **Royalton** WI U.S.A.
184 B4 **Royan** France
182 C5 **Royat** France
183 G6 **Roybon** France
173 N2 **Roydon** Norfolk, England U.K.
173 O3 **Roydon** Norfolk, England U.K.
178 E4 **Roye** France
184 H4 **Royère-de-Vassivière** France
258 D4 **Royersford** PA U.S.A.
108 E7 **Roy Hill** W.A. Austr.
159 K2 **Royishche** Ukr.
173 L3 **Royston** Hertfordshire, England U.K.
171 O6 **Royston** South Yorkshire, England U.K.
171 M6 **Royton** Greater Manchester, England U.K.
162 R4 **Röyttä** Fin.
205 R8 **Royuela** Spain
218 I8 **Rožaje** Rožaje Montenegro
205 O9 **Rozalén del Monte** Spain
197 J3 **Różan** Pol.
218 H6 **Rožanj** h. Serbia
196 D3 **Różanki** Pol.
204 H3 **Rozas, Embalse de las** resr Spain
178 E6 **Rozay-en-Brie** France
198 E1 **Rožďalovice** Czech Rep.
197 M6 **Rozdil** Ukr.
158 J7 **Rozdil'na** Ukr.
159 R6 **Rozdol'ne** Donets'ka Oblast' Ukr.
159 M8 **Rozdol'ne** Respublika Krym Ukr.
159 O5 **Rozdory** Ukr.
196 F4 **Rozdrażew** Pol.
186 F5 **Rozenburg** Neth.
186 I4 **Rozendaal** Neth.
161 T5 **Rozhdestveno** Tverskaya Oblast' Rus. Fed.
161 U4 **Rozhdestveno** Yaroslavskaya Oblast' Rus. Fed.
156 I4 **Rozhdestvenskoye** Rus. Fed.
161 Q4 **Rozhdestvo** Rus. Fed.
151 B2 **Rozhkao** Rus. Fed.
159 N1 **Rozhkovychi** Rus. Fed.
159 L3 **Rozhnivka** Ukr.
158 J3 **Rozhny** Ukr.
158 D5 **Rozhnyativ** Ukr.
158 E3 **Rozhyshche** Ukr.
219 M8 **Rozino** Bulg.
159 Q6 **Rozivka** Ukr.
198 C2 **Rožmitál pod Třemšínem** Czech Rep.
199 J3 **Rožňava** Slovakia
196 G3 **Rożniatów** Pol.
199 H2 **Rožnov pod Radhoštěm** Czech Rep.
197 I6 **Rożnów** Pol.
196 E3 **Roznowo** Pol.
197 J2 **Rozoga** r. Pol.
197 J2 **Rozogi** Pol.
178 H4 **Rozoy-sur-Serre** France
197 H4 **Rozprza** Pol.
159 R4 **Rozsypne** Ukr.
197 L5 **Roztoczański Park Narodow** nat. park Pol.
197 I6 **Roztoka Wielka** Pol.
193 I10 **Roztoky** Středočeský kraj Czech Rep.
193 J10 **Roztoky** Středočeský kraj Czech Rep.
144 D5 **Rozveh** Iran
212 G5 **Rozzano** Italy
218 H9 **Rrëshen** Albania
218 H9 **Rrogozhinë** Albania
157 H5 **Rtishchevo** Rus. Fed.
204 D2 **Ru** Spain
204 E7 **Rua** Port.
115 A8 **Rua, Tanjung** pt Sumba Ind
172 F2 **Ruabon** Wrexham, Wales U.K
234 B3 **Ruacana** Namibia
233 B6 **Ruaha National Park** Tanz.
102 K6 **Ruahine Forest Park** nature North I. N.Z.
102 K7 **Ruahine Range** mts North I
102 I2 **Ruakaka** North I. N.Z.
169 E7 **Ruan** Ireland
Ruanda country Africa see **Rw**
115 D2 **Ruang** i. Indon.
102 J6 **Ruapehu, Mount** vol. North
103 C13 **Ruapuke Island** South I. N.Z
172 G4 **Ruardean** Gloucestershire, England U.K.
233 B7 **Ruarwe** Malawi
102 I2 **Ruatangata** North I. N.Z.
103 E9 **Ruatapu** South I. N.Z.
102 M4 **Ruatoria** North I. N.Z.
181 L6 **Ruaudin** France
100 □6 **Ruavatu** Guadalcanal Solom
161 N6 **Ruba** Belarus
146 H6 **Rub' al Khālī** des. Saudi Ara
199 H4 **Rúbaň** Slovakia
170 G5 **Rubane** Northern Ireland U.
159 N7 **Rubanivka** Ukr.
213 L5 **Rubano** Italy
160 K6 **Rubashki** Belarus
147 I3 **Rubaydā** reg. Saudi Arabia
205 M2 **Rubayo** Spain
233 C6 **Rubeho Mountains** Tanz.
191 K7 **Rübeland** Ger.
281 F2 **Rubelita** Brazil
205 M4 **Rubena** Spain
193 H9 **Rübenau** Ger.
268 G8 **Rubén Figueroa** Mex.
124 U3 **Rubeshibe** Japan
Rubezhnoye Ukr. see **Rubiz**
Rubha an t-Siumpain hd Sc U.K. see **Tiumpan Head**
Rubha Robhanais hd Scotla U.K. see **Butt of Lewis**
230 E4 **Rubi** r. Dem. Rep. Congo
208 J5 **Rubí** Spain
204 G4 **Rubiá** Spain
280 B4 **Rubiácea** Brazil
209 C8 **Rubial, Serra de** mts Spain
264 K3 **Rubicon** r. CA U.S.A.
213 M7 **Rubicone** r. Italy
205 K6 **Rubí de Bracamonte** Spain
208 C6 **Rubielos de la Cérida** Spain
209 D7 **Rubielos de Mora** Spain
213 J6 **Rubiera** Italy
281 G2 **Rubim** Brazil
280 B4 **Rubinéia** Brazil
205 M6 **Rubio** mt. Spain
159 R4 **Rubizhne** Ukr.
192 I3 **Rubkow** Ger.
205 N3 **Rublacedo de Abajo** Spain
233 A5 **Rubondo National Park** Ta
159 Q4 **Rubtsi** Ukr.
143 S2 **Rubtsovsk** Rus. Fed.
233 B6 **Rubuga** Tanz.
146 F6 **Rubūţ, Jabal ar** hill Saudi A
244 I2 **Ruby** AK U.S.A.
103 H8 **Ruby Bay** South I. N.Z.
262 G6 **Ruby Dome** mt. NV U.S.A.
158 G2 **Rubyel'** Belarus
161 N6 **Rubyezhnitsa** Belarus
265 Q1 **Ruby Lake** NV U.S.A.
265 Q1 **Ruby Lake National Wildlif** Refuge nature res. NV U.S.A
265 Q1 **Ruby Mountains** NV U.S.A.
246 E4 **Rubyrock Lake Provincial** nat. park B.C. Can.
265 T4 **Rubys Inn** UT U.S.A.
107 K7 **Rubyvale** Qld Austr.
265 Q1 **Ruby Valley** NV U.S.A.
284 E5 **Rucanelo** Arg.
219 N5 **Rucăr** Romania
160 K6 **Ruchay** Belarus
Rucheng Guangdong China **Ruyuan**
131 I6 **Rucheng** Hunan China
159 M3 **Ruchky** Ukr.
159 M8 **Ruch"yi** Ukr.
197 J2 **Ruciane-Nida** Pol.
193 I7 **Rückersdorf** Ger.
256 G10 **Ruckersville** VA U.S.A.
186 G5 **Rucphen** Neth.
196 G4 **Ruda** Pol.
199 J3 **Rudabánya** Hungary
197 L4 **Ruda-Huta** Pol.
108 G7 **Rudall** watercourse W.A. Aus
108 G7 **Rudall River National Park** Austr.
109 L7 **Rudalls** watercourse N.T. Au
197 I4 **Ruda Maleniecka** Pol.
197 L1 **Rudamina** Lith.
197 L5 **Ruda Różaniecka** Pol.
139 I6 **Rudarpur** Uttar Prad. India
196 G5 **Ruda Śląska** Pol.
138 H6 **Rudauli** Uttar Prad. India
198 E1 **Rudawski Park Krajobrazo**
145 J6 **Rudbar** Afgh.
149 P9 **Rūdbār** Fārs Iran
144 C3 **Rūdbār** Gīlān Iran
187 D6 **Ruddervoorde** Belgium
173 J2 **Ruddington** Nottinghamsh England U.K.
195 L4 **Rudelzhausen** Ger.
201 K6 **Ruden** Austria
192 I2 **Ruden** i. Ger.
194 H4 **Rudersberg** Ger.
201 N5 **Rudersdorf** Austria
193 I6 **Rüdersdorf Berlin** Ger.
191 J7 **Rüdershausen** Ger.
195 O4 **Ruderting** Ger.
158 I4 **Rude Selo** Ukr.
194 D2 **Rüdesheim** Ger.
194 D2 **Rüdesheim am Rhein** Ger.
173 L5 **Rudgwick** West Sussex, Engl U.K.
218 H7 **Rudina** pass Montenegro
160 H7 **Rūdiškės** Lith.
191 K9 **Rudisleben** Ger.
159 L3 **Rudivka** Chernihivs'ka Obla
159 R4 **Rudivka** Luhans'ka Oblast'
197 K3 **Rudka** Pol.
197 L3 **Rudka** r. Pol.
164 G7 **Rudkøbing** Denmark
197 L6 **Rudky** Ukr.
193 J10 **Rudná** Czech Rep.
196 E4 **Rudna** Pol.
219 K6 **Rudna Glava** Majdanpek Se
196 E4 **Rudna Wielka** Pol.
122 I6 **Rudnaya Pristan'** Primorsk Rus. Fed.
122 I7 **Rudnaya Pristan'** Primorsk Rus. Fed.

C4 **Rudne** Ukr.
I1 **Rudniański, Park Krajobrazowy** Pol.
L5 **Rudnica** Pol.
K4 **Rudnichnyy** Rus. Fed.
G5 **Rudnik** *Śląskie* Pol.
G4 **Rudniki** Pol.
Rudnik Ingichka Uzbek. *see* **Ingichka**
K5 **Rudnik nad Sadem** *Podkarpackie* Pol.
I5 **Rüdnitz** Ger.
M3 **Rudnya** Belarus
O7 **Rudnya** *Smolenskaya Oblast'* Rus. Fed.
O5 **Rudnya** *Tverskaya Oblast'* Rus. Fed.
I6 **Rudnya** *Volgogradskaya Oblast'* Rus. Fed.
G3 **Rudnya-Ivanivs'ka** Ukr.
L6 **Rudnyky** Ukr.
H5 **Rudnytsya** Ukr.
J1 **Rudnyy** Kazakh.
I6 **Rudnyy** Rus. Fed.
Rudolf, Lake *salt l.* Eth./Kenya *see* **Turkana, Lake**
G1 **Rudol'fa, Ostrov** *i. Zemlya Frantsa-Iosifa* Rus. Fed.
C4 **Rudolfo Iselin** Arg.
K2 **Rudolfov** Czech Rep.
Rudolph Island *Zemlya Frantsa-Iosifa* Rus. Fed. *see* **Rudol'fa, Ostrov**
D9 **Rudolstadt** Ger.
M2 **Rudong** *Jiangsu* China
M9 **Rudozem** Bulg.
M3 **Rudrón** *resr* Spain
D3 **Rūdsar** Iran
E2 **Rudsgrendi** Norway
Q5 **Rudston** *East Riding of Yorkshire, England* U.K.
J3 **Rudyard** *MI* U.S.A.
F5 **Rudziczka** Pol.
K8 **Rudzyensk** Belarus
H2 **Rue** France
C3 **Ruecas** *r.* Spain
K6 **Rueda** Spain
D6 **Rueil-Malmaison** France
M2 **Ruel** *Ont.* Can.
Ruen *mt.* Macedonia *see* **Rujen**
L2 **Ruente** Spain
G3 **Ruenya** *r.* Zimbabwe
D5 **Ruetz** *r.* Austria
B6 **Rufa'a** Sudan
O4 **Ruffano** Italy
N8 **Ruffec** *Centre* France
E3 **Ruffec** *Poitou-Charentes* France
G2 **Ruffey-lès-Echirey** France
G3 **Ruffey-sur-Seille** France
G6 **Ruffiac** France
H4 **Ruffieu** France
H5 **Ruffieux** France
L6 **Rufford** *Lancashire, England* U.K.
C7 **Rufiji** *r.* Tanz.
H3 **Rufina** Italy
F4 **Rufino** Arg.
A3 **Rufisque** Senegal
F8 **Rufunsa** Zambia
O1 **Rufus Lake** *N.W.T.* Can.
K4 **Rugāji** Latvia
M2 **Rugao** *Jiangsu* China
E3 **Rugberg** *hill* Ger.
J3 **Rugby** *Warwickshire, England* U.K.
E1 **Rugby** *ND* U.S.A.
F2 **Rugeley** *Staffordshire, England* U.K.
J2 **Rügen** *i.* Ger.
H1 **Rügen, Naturpark** *nature res.* Ger.
E5 **Rugged Mountain** *B.C.* Can.
F5 **Rugheiwa** *well* Sudan
J3 **Rugland** Ger.
M2 **Rugles** France
N8 **Rugvica** Croatia
C5 **Ruhangino** Tanz.
H3 **Ruḩayyat al Ḩamr'ā'** *waterhole* Saudi Arabia
H7 **Ruḩbah** *oasis* Syria
K6 **Rühen** Ger.
A5 **Ruhengeri** Rwanda
J9 **Ruhla** Ger.
I8 **Ruhland** Ger.
N4 **Ruhmannsfelden** Ger.
E3 **Rühn** Ger.
G4 **Ruhnu** *i.* Estonia
N6 **Ruhpolding** Ger.
C8 **Ruhr** *r.* Ger.
O5 **Ruhstorf an der Rott** Ger.
B7 **Ruhudji** *r.* Tanz.
G9 **Ruhuna National Park** Sri Lanka
H6 **Ru'i, Chāh** *well* Iran
M5 **Rui'an** *Zhejiang* China
H2 **Ruichang** *Jiangxi* China
J3 **Ruidera** Spain
L12 **Ruidosa** *TX* U.S.A.
L10 **Ruidoso** *NM* U.S.A.
J6 **Ruijin** *Jiangxi* China
A6 **Ruili** *Yunnan* China
B8 **Ruinas** *Sardegna* Italy
J3 **Ruinen** Neth.
J3 **Ruinerwold** Neth.
C7 **Ruipa** Tanz.
D6 **Ruiselede** Belgium
D5 **Ruivães** Port.
C5 **Ruivo, Pico** *mt.* Madeira
B4 **Ruiz** Mex.
I3 **Ruiz Cortines** Mex.
K8 **Ruj** *mt.* Bulg.
I9 **Rūja** *r.* Latvia
E4 **Ruja** Pol.
F6 **Rujaylah, Ḩarrat ar** *lava field* Jordan
K8 **Rujen** *mt.* Macedonia
I4 **Rūjiena** Latvia
J4 **Rük** Azer.
Ruk *is* Micronesia *see* **Chuuk**
M8 **Ruk** Pak.
P7 **Rukanpur** Pak.
I2 **Rukbah** *well* Saudi Arabia
I2 **Rukel'** Rus. Fed.
C3 **Rukhi** Georgia
C4 **Ruki** *r.* Dem. Rep. Congo
I5 **Rukumkot** Nepal
A5 **Rukungiri** Uganda
A6 **Rukuwa** *Sulawesi* Indon.
A3 **Rukwa** *admin. reg.* Tanz.
B7 **Rukwa, Lake** Tanz.
M6 **Rulbo** Sweden
M3 **Rūl Ḑadnah** U.A.E.
J9 **Ruleville** *MS* U.S.A.
I2 **Rulhieres, Cape** *W.A.* Austr.
Rulin *Hunan* China *see* **Chengbu**
F6 **Rulle (Wallenhorst)** Ger.
K4 **Rullstorf** Ger.
F3 **Rully** France
Rulong *Sichuan* China *see* **Xinlong**
E3 **Rülzheim** Ger.
D5 **Rum** Austria
F4 **Rum** Hungary
H5 **Rūm** Iran
Rum Jordan *see* **Ramm**
D9 **Rum** *i. Scotland* U.K.
I3 **Rum** *r. MN* U.S.A.
Rum, Jebel *mts* Jordan *see* **Ramm, Jabal**
D9 **Rum, Sound of** *sea chan. Scotland* U.K.
G3 **Ruma** Nigeria
H5 **Ruma** *Vojvodina* Serbia
F9 **Rumādah** Yemen
H3 **Rumāh** Saudi Arabia
B5 **Ruma National Park** Kenya
Rumania *country* Europe *see* **Romania**
F7 **Rumayn** *i.* Saudi Arabia
D3 **Rumbai** *Sulawesi* Indon.
F3 **Rumbek** Sudan
L4 **Rumblar** *r.* Spain
L4 **Rumblar, Embalse del** *resr* Spain
D1 **Rumburk** Czech Rep.
F2 **Rum Cay** *i.* Bahamas
J10 **Rumelange** Lux.
D7 **Rumes** Belgium
□O4 **Rumford** *ME* U.S.A.
O7 **Rumia** Pol.
178 H4 **Rumigny** France
182 H5 **Rumilly** France
106 C2 **Rum Jungle** *N.T.* Austr.
146 E2 **Rummān, Jabal ar** *mts* Saudi Arabia
150 G5 **Rummānā** *hill* Syria
172 F4 **Rumney** *Cardiff, Wales* U.K.
124 S3 **Rumoi** Japan
233 A5 **Rumonge** Burundi
179 J6 **Rumont** France
233 B7 **Rumphi** Malawi
259 H4 **Rumson** *NJ* U.S.A.
187 F6 **Rumst** Belgium
107 J4 **Rumula** *Qld* Austr.
232 C4 **Rumuruti** Kenya
115 F6 **Run** *i. Maluku* Indon.
206 A2 **Runa** Port.
269 J2 **Runabay Head** *Northern Ireland* U.K.
131 J2 **Runan** *Henan* China
103 F9 **Runanga** *South I.* N.Z.
103 I9 **Runaway, Cape** *North I.* N.Z.
270 □ **Runaway Bay** Jamaica
171 L7 **Runcorn** *Halton, England* U.K.
219 L5 **Runcu** Romania
199 L6 **Runcu** *r.* Romania
235 G4 **Runde** *r.* Zimbabwe
234 C3 **Rundu** Namibia
115 D6 **Runduma** *i.* Indon.
162 O5 **Rundvik** Sweden
119 F9 **Rŭng, Kaôh** *i.* Cambodia
117 J6 **Rungan** *r.* Indon.
230 E4 **Rungu** Dem. Rep. Congo
233 A6 **Rungwa** *Rukwa* Tanz.
233 B6 **Rungwa** *Singida* Tanz.
233 A6 **Rungwa** *r.* Tanz.
233 B6 **Rungwa Game Reserve** *nature res.* Tanz.
131 K2 **Runhe** *Anhui* China
Runing *Henan* China *see* **Runan**
144 E7 **Rūnīz-e Bālā** Iran
191 F10 **Runkel** Ger.
165 O2 **Runnarö** *i.* Sweden
165 L1 **Runn** *l.* Sweden
264 O7 **Running Springs** *CA* U.S.A.
261 E9 **Running Water** *watercourse NM/TX* U.S.A.
165 M4 **Runnö** *i.* Sweden
109 G7 **Runton Range** *hills W.A.* Austr.
173 N4 **Runwell** *Essex, England* U.K.
100 □[4a] **Ruo** *i. Chuuk* Micronesia
163 T6 **Ruokolahti** Fin.
163 R8 **Ruoms** France
132 I7 **Ruoqiang** *Xinjiang* China
132 I7 **Ruoqiang He** *r.* China
128 G6 **Ruo Shui** *watercourse* China
215 P6 **Ruoti** Italy
163 S6 **Ruotsinpyhtää** Fin.
163 R6 **Ruovesi** Fin.
213 Q5 **Rupa** Croatia
139 N6 **Rupa** *Arun. Prad.* India
116 D4 **Rupat** *i.* Indon.
219 N4 **Rupea** Romania
248 E3 **Rupert** *r. Que.* Can.
262 H5 **Rupert** *ID* U.S.A.
256 E11 **Rupert** *WV* U.S.A.
248 E3 **Rupert Bay** *Que.* Can.
96 B5 **Rupert Coast** Antarctica
107 I6 **Rupert Creek** *r. Qld* Austr.
138 F4 **Rupnagar** *Punjab* India
138 E6 **Rupnagar** *Rajasthan* India
233 C7 **Ruponda** Tanz.
192 G5 **Ruppiner See** *l.* Ger.
201 L3 **Ruprechtshofen** Austria
138 F3 **Rupshu** *reg. Jammu and Kashmir* India
179 M8 **Rupt-sur-Moselle** France
146 F5 **Ruqaytah** Saudi Arabia
150 D6 **Ruqqād, Wādī ar** *watercourse* Israel
256 D12 **Rural Retreat** *VA* U.S.A.
276 D3 **Rurrenabaque** Bol.
201 B9 **Rurstausee** *resr* Ger.
101 □[9] **Rurutu** *i. Îs Australes* Fr. Polynesia
219 Q5 **Rus** Romania
207 M2 **Rus** Spain
207 N4 **Rus** *r.* Spain
Rusaddir *N. Africa* *see* **Melilla**
159 N8 **Rusakivka** Ukr.
159 M3 **Rusanivka** Ukr.
235 G3 **Rusape** Zimbabwe
219 K5 **Rusca Montană** Romania
Ruschuk Bulg. *see* **Ruse**
219 M3 **Ruscova** Romania
219 N7 **Ruse** Bulg.
201 M6 **Ruše** Slovenia
219 O7 **Rusenski Lom** *nat. park* Bulg.
139 K7 **Rusera** *Bihar* India
219 P6 **Ruşeţu** Romania
169 J5 **Rush** Ireland
173 I2 **Rushall** *West Midlands, England* U.K.
129 Q8 **Rushan** *Shandong* China
Rushan Tajik. *see* **Rushon**
Rushanskiy Khrebet *mts* Tajik. *see* **Rushon, Qatorkŭhi**
260 D6 **Rush Creek** *r. CO* U.S.A.
173 K3 **Rushden** *Northamptonshire, England* U.K.
250 C6 **Rushford** *MN* U.S.A.
235 G3 **Rushinga** Zimbabwe
250 E6 **Rush Lake** *WI* U.S.A.
256 F9 **Rushmere** *VA* U.S.A.
173 O3 **Rushmere St Andrew** *Suffolk, England* U.K.
139 O5 **Rushon** *Arun. Prad.* India
145 O2 **Rushon** Tajik.
145 N3 **Rushon, Qatorkŭhi** *mts* Tajik.
128 J9 **Rushui He** *r.* China
260 J5 **Rushville** *IL* U.S.A.
254 E6 **Rushville** *IN* U.S.A.
260 E4 **Rushville** *NE* U.S.A.
256 C9 **Rushville** *OH* U.S.A.
105 J7 **Rushworth** *Vic.* Austr.
196 G4 **Rusiec** Pol.
197 I4 **Rusinów** Pol.
196 E2 **Rusinowo** Pol.
261 H10 **Rusk** *TX* U.S.A.
162 O4 **Ruskele** Sweden
165 K4 **Rusken** *l.* Sweden
218 H5 **Ruski Krstur** *Vojvodina* Serbia
255 F12 **Ruskin** *FL* U.S.A.
171 Q7 **Ruskington** *Lincolnshire, England* U.K.
159 P3 **Rus'ki Tyshky** Ukr.
199 J6 **Rusko Selo** *Vojvodina* Serbia
199 K3 **Ruskov** Slovakia
165 K6 **Rusnė** Lith.
219 P8 **Rusokastro** Bulg.
160 J5 **Rušona** Latvia
160 J5 **Rušonu ezers** *l.* Latvia
158 H5 **Rusova** *r.* Ukr.
172 G4 **Ruspidge** *Gloucestershire, England* U.K.
160 F2 **Russarö** *i.* Fin.
278 F3 **Russas** Brazil
247 K5 **Russell** *Man.* Can.
257 J3 **Russell** *Ont.* Can.
102 I2 **Russell** *North I.* N.Z.
260 F6 **Russell** *KS* U.S.A.
256 F7 **Russell** *PA* U.S.A.
244 J3 **Russell, Mount** *AK* U.S.A.
286 P2 **Russell Bay** Antarctica
243 I2 **Russell Island** *Nunavut* Can.
100 □[6] **Russell Islands** Solomon Is
247 K3 **Russell Lake** *Man.* Can.
246 H2 **Russell Lake** *N.W.T.* Can.
247 J3 **Russell Lake** *Sask.* Can.
255 D8 **Russellville** *AL* U.S.A.
261 I8 **Russellville** *AR* U.S.A.
254 D7 **Russellville** *KY* U.S.A.
256 B10 **Russellville** *OH* U.S.A.
258 D5 **Russellville** *PA* U.S.A.
194 E1 **Rüsselsheim** Ger.
213 M7 **Russi** Italy
Russia *country* Asia/Europe *see* **Russian Federation**
152 F4 **Russian Federation** *country* Asia/Europe
244 G3 **Russian Mission** *AK* U.S.A.
244 H3 **Russian Mountains** *AK* U.S.A.
Russian Soviet Federal Socialist Republic *country* Asia/Europe *see* **Russian Federation**
143 O1 **Russkaya-Polyana** Rus. Fed.
157 H6 **Russkaya Zhuravka** Rus. Fed.
161 U9 **Russkiy Brod** Rus. Fed.
142 B1 **Russkiy Kameshkir** Rus. Fed.
156 K1 **Russkiy Zavorot, Poluostrov** *pen.* Rus. Fed.
161 P8 **Russkoye** *Smolenskaya Oblast'* Rus. Fed.
151 F2 **Russkoye** *Stavropol'skiy Kray* Rus. Fed.
153 P2 **Russkoye Ust'ye** Rus. Fed.
201 O4 **Rust** Austria
151 G5 **Rüstäm Äliyev** Azer.
151 G4 **Rust'avi** Georgia
256 F11 **Rustburg** *VA* U.S.A.
237 M1 **Rust de Winter** S. Africa
237 M1 **Rust de Winter Nature Reserve** S. Africa
191 D6 **Rüstemgedik** Turkey
237 L1 **Rustenburg** S. Africa
237 L1 **Rustenburg Nature Reserve** S. Africa
164 D3 **Rustfjellheii** *mt.* Norway
237 K5 **Rustfontein Dam** *l.* S. Africa
237 L3 **Rustig** S. Africa
173 K6 **Rustington** *West Sussex, England* U.K.
261 I9 **Ruston** *LA* U.S.A.
151 J4 **Rustov** Azer.
183 G9 **Rustrel** France
212 E1 **Ruswil** Switz.
196 F4 **Ruszów** Pol.
161 T4 **Rut'** *r.* Rus. Fed.
115 E4 **Ruta** *Maluku* Indon.
103 □[1] **Rutaki Passage** *Rarotonga* Cook Is
214 C2 **Rutali** *Corse* France
233 A5 **Rutana** Burundi
Rutanzige, Lake Dem. Rep. Congo/Uganda *see* **Edward, Lake**
207 K6 **Rute** Spain
115 B8 **Ruteng** *Flores* Indon.
235 F4 **Rutenga** Zimbabwe
194 F4 **Rutesheim** Ger.
265 Q2 **Rüthen** Ger.
191 F8 **Ruthenia** *admin. div.* Ukr. *see* **Zakarpats'ka Oblast'**
259 G3 **Rutherford** *NJ* U.S.A.
255 F8 **Rutherfordton** *NC* U.S.A.
105 K7 **Rutherglen** *Vic.* Austr.
257 I3 **Rutherglen** *Ont.* Can.
168 H11 **Rutherglen** *South Lanarkshire, Scotland* U.K.
Ruther Glen *VA* U.S.A.
172 F1 **Ruthin** *Denbighshire, Wales* U.K.
138 F7 **Ruthiyai** *Madh. Prad.* India
212 F1 **Rüti** Switz.
217 M1 **Rutigliano** Italy
217 O7 **Rutino** Italy
156 I4 **Rutka** *r.* Rus. Fed.
197 K1 **Rutka-Tartak** Pol.
197 K2 **Rutki-Kossaki** Pol.
173 K2 **Rutland** *admin. div. England* U.K.
257 M5 **Rutland** *VT* U.S.A.
137 M7 **Rutland Island** *Andaman & Nicobar Is* India
107 H3 **Rutland Plains** *Qld* Austr.
173 K2 **Rutland Water** *resr England* U.K.
256 B12 **Rutledge** *TN* U.S.A.
247 I2 **Rutledge Lake** *N.W.T.* Can.
133 H12 **Rutog** *Xizang* China
133 F12 **Rutog** *Xizang* China
133 D10 **Rutog** *Xizang* China
230 F5 **Rutshuru** Dem. Rep. Congo
186 I3 **Rutten** Neth.
251 N3 **Rutter** *Ont.* Can.
151 I4 **Rutul** Rus. Fed.
162 R4 **Ruukki** Fin.
186 J4 **Ruurlo** Neth.
160 K3 **Ruusa** Estonia
162 T5 **Ruvaslahti** Fin.
215 P6 **Ruvo del Monte** Italy
215 Q5 **Ruvo di Puglia** Italy
162 U3 **Ruvozero** Rus. Fed.
162 U3 **Ruvozero, Ozero** *l.* Rus. Fed.
Ruvu Tanz. *see* **Pangani**
233 D7 **Ruvuma** *r.* Moz./Tanz.
233 C7 **Ruvuma** *admin. reg.* Tanz.
146 G3 **Ruwaydah** Saudi Arabia
147 M3 **Ruways, Ra's ar** *c.* Oman
150 F6 **Ruwayshid, Wādī** *watercourse* Jordan
150 E9 **Ruwaytah, Wādī** *watercourse* Jordan
150 C9 **Ruweijil** *pt* Saudi Arabia
147 K3 **Ruweis** U.A.E.
Ruwenzori National Park Uganda *see* **Queen Elizabeth National Park**
182 G5 **Ruy** France
235 G3 **Ruya** *r.* Zimbabwe
149 Q5 **Rūyān** Iran
233 A5 **Ruyigi** Burundi
179 K6 **Ruynes-en-Margeride** France
172 G2 **Ruyton-XI-Towns** *Shropshire, England* U.K.
131 J6 **Ruyuan** *Guangdong* China
161 T6 **Ruza** Rus. Fed.
143 L1 **Ruzayevka** Kazakh.
157 I5 **Ruzayevka** Rus. Fed.
160 I7 **Ruzhany** Belarus
161 R9 **Ruzhnoye** Rus. Fed.
129 M9 **Ruzhou** *Henan* China
158 I4 **Ruzhyn** Ukr.
199 I2 **Ružomberok** Slovakia
199 I5 **Ruzsa** Hungary
230 F5 **Rwamagana** *East* Rwanda
233 A5 **Rwanda** *country* Africa
230 F5 **Rwenzori** *mts* Dem. Rep. Congo/Uganda
232 A4 **Rwenzori Mountains National Park** Uganda
164 F5 **Ry** Denmark
164 F4 **Ryā** *r.* Denmark
144 F3 **Ryābād** Iran
156 H2 **Ryabovo** Rus. Fed.
160 I1 **Ryabovo** Rus. Fed.
103 C11 **Ryal Bush** *South I.* N.Z.
103 F9 **Ryall, Mount** *South I.* N.Z.
168 F12 **Ryan, Loch** *b. Scotland* U.K.
159 N4 **Ryas'ke** Ukr.
159 O2 **Ryasne** Ukr.
159 N3 **Ryasnopil'** Ukr.
157 H5 **Ryazan'** Rus. Fed.
161 W7 **Ryazan Oblast** *admin. div.* Rus. Fed. *see* **Ryazanskaya Oblast'**
161 W6 **Ryazanovskiy** Rus. Fed.
159 S9 **Ryazanskaya** Rus. Fed.
161 X7 **Ryazanskaya Oblast'** *admin. div.* Rus. Fed.
161 W5 **Ryazantsevo** Rus. Fed.
161 X8 **Ryazhsk** Rus. Fed.
162 V2 **Rybachiy, Poluostrov** *pen.* Rus. Fed.
143 S4 **Rybach'ye** Kazakh.
Rybach'ye *Kyrg. see* **Balykchy**
199 H3 **Rybany** Slovakia
159 H3 **Rybinsk** Rus. Fed.
161 V3 **Rybinskoye Vodokhranilishche** *resr* Rus. Fed.
198 E1 **Rybitví** Czech Rep.
196 G5 **Rybnik** Pol.
Rybnitsa Moldova *see* **Rîbniţa**
197 I3 **Rybno** *Mazowieckie* Pol.
197 H2 **Rybno** *Warmińsko-Mazurskie* Pol.
197 J2 **Rybno** *Warmińsko-Mazurskie* Pol.
161 W7 **Rybnoye** Rus. Fed.
197 L3 **Ryboły** Pol.
156 F3 **Rybreka** Rus. Fed.
197 H2 **Rychliki** Pol.
198 F1 **Rychnov nad Kněžnou** Czech Rep.
193 L9 **Rychnov u Jablonce nad Nisou** Czech Rep.
197 I2 **Rychnowo** Pol.
196 F4 **Rychtal** Pol.
196 G3 **Rychwał** Pol.
197 I2 **Ryck** *r.* Ger.
246 G4 **Rycroft** *Alta* Can.
197 J4 **Ryczywół** *Mazowieckie* Pol.
196 E3 **Ryczywół** *Wielkopolskie* Pol.
196 K5 **Ryd** Sweden
286 S2 **Rydberg Peninsula** Antarctica
173 J6 **Ryde** *Isle of Wight, England* U.K.
158 E4 **Rydomyl'** Ukr.
196 G5 **Rydułtowy** Pol.
197 K4 **Rydzyna** Pol.
173 N6 **Rye** *East Sussex, England* U.K.
171 P5 **Rye** *r. England* U.K.
259 H3 **Rye** *NY* U.S.A.
173 N6 **Rye Bay** *England* U.K.
257 □O6 **Rye Beach** *NH* U.S.A.
262 J3 **Ryegate** *MT* U.S.A.
264 N1 **Rye Patch Dam** *NV* U.S.A.
264 N1 **Rye Patch Reservoir** *NV* U.S.A.
181 J3 **Ryes** France
197 J6 **Ryglice** Pol.
173 L2 **Ryhall** *Rutland, England* U.K.
196 G2 **Ryjewo** Pol.
158 G3 **Rykhal's'ke** Ukr.
197 J4 **Ryki** Pol.
Rykovo Ukr. *see* **Yenakiyeve**
197 M5 **Rykovychi** Ukr.
197 M1 **Ryliškiai** Lith.
157 F6 **Ryl'sk** Rus. Fed.
105 L5 **Rylstone** *N.S.W.* Austr.
198 J6 **Rymanów** Pol.
198 G2 **Rýmařov** Czech Rep.
163 Q6 **Rymättylä** Fin.
165 R8 **Ryn** Pol.
196 F2 **Rynarzewo** Pol.
156 G1 **Rynda** Rus. Fed.
142 G4 **Ryn-Peski** *des.* Kazakh.
196 G4 **Ryńsk** Pol.
197 J2 **Ryńskie, Jezioro** *l.* Pol.
127 I3 **Ryōgami-san** *mt.* Japan
126 E4 **Ryōhaku-sanchi** *mts* Japan
Ryojun *Liaoning* China *see* **Lüshun**
127 I3 **Ryōkami** Japan
124 S7 **Ryōri-zaki** *pt* Japan
124 F3 **Ryōtsu** Japan
126 D5 **Ryōzen-zan** *mt.* Japan
197 H2 **Rypin** Pol.
Ryshkany Moldova *see* **Rîşcani**
159 O1 **Ryshkovo** Rus. Fed.
163 H6 **Rysjedal** Norway
190 D4 **Rysum (Krummhörn)** Ger.
199 J2 **Rysy** *mt.* Pol.
196 F2 **Rytel** Pol.
165 K6 **Rytterknægten** *hill Bornholm* Denmark
160 H1 **Ryttylä** Fin.
197 J5 **Rytwiany** Pol.
125 H6 **Ryūga-dake** *mt.* Japan
127 L4 **Ryūgasaki** Japan
126 B8 **Ryūjin** Japan
161 P9 **Ryukhovo** Rus. Fed.
Ryukyu Islands Japan *see* **Nansei-shotō**
Ryūkyū-rettō *is* Japan *see* **Nansei-shotō**
290 D4 **Ryukyu Trench** *sea feature* N. Pacific Ocean
126 D5 **Ryūō** *Shiga* Japan
127 J4 **Ryūō** *Yamanashi* Japan
127 H5 **Ryūsō-san** *mt.* Japan
127 G6 **Ryūyō** Japan
161 O7 **Ryzhikovo** Rus. Fed.
158 N9 **Ryzhkawka** Belarus
161 P2 **Ryzyne** Ukr.
197 J3 **Rządza** *r.* Pol.
197 H4 **Rząśnia** Pol.
197 J3 **Rząśnik** Pol.
210 G4 **Rzav** *r.* Bos.-Herz.
196 E2 **Rzeczenica** Pol.
196 G4 **Rzeczyca** *Łódzkie* Pol.
197 J3 **Rzeczyca** *Łódzkie* Pol.
197 I4 **Rzeczyca** *Łódzkie* Pol.
197 I2 **Rzegnowo** Pol.
197 J4 **Rzejowice** Pol.
196 D2 **Rzepin** Pol.
197 H5 **Rzerzęczyce** Pol.
196 D2 **Rzesznikowo** Pol.
198 K2 **Rzeszów** Pol.
197 H4 **Rzgów** Pol.
196 G3 **Rzgów Pierwszy** Pol.
157 H5 **Rzhaksa** Rus. Fed.
161 Q8 **Rzhanitsa** Rus. Fed.
160 M6 **Rzhawka** Belarus
158 I5 **Rzhawka** *r.* Belarus
161 R5 **Rzhev** Rus. Fed.
159 M3 **Rzhyshchiv** Ukr.
197 I4 **Rzuców** Pol.

S

144 G4 **Sa'ābād** Iran
232 D4 **Saacow** Somalia
150 E9 **Sa'ādah al Barṣā'** *pass* Saudi Arabia
144 E6 **Sa'ādatābād** *Fārs* Iran
144 F7 **Sa'ādatābād** *Hormozgan* Iran
236 F7 **Saaifontein** S. Africa
192 F2 **Saal** Ger.
195 O6 **Saalach** *r.* Ger.
195 L4 **Saal an der Donau** Ger.
191 J10 **Saal an der Saale** Ger.
192 E5 **Saalbach** *r.* Ger.
194 E3 **Saalbach** Ger.
200 G5 **Saalbach-Hinterglemm** Austria
193 E10 **Saalburg** Ger.
195 N6 **Saaldorf** Ger.
193 E7 **Saale** *r.* Ger.
195 K4 **Saaler Bodden** *inlet* Ger.
179 N7 **Saales** France
197 D3 **Saalfeld** Ger.
200 G5 **Saalfelden am Steinernen Meer** Austria
Saamba K'e *N.W.T.* Can. *see* **Trout Lake**
178 A4 **Saâne** *r.* France
212 C2 **Saane** *r.* Switz.
212 C3 **Saanen** Switz.
246 F5 **Saanich** *B.C.* Can.
Saar *land* Ger. *see* **Saarland**
194 B2 **Saar** *r.* Ger.
194 B2 **Saarbrücken** Ger.
194 B2 **Saarburg** Ger.
160 J3 **Saare** Estonia
160 F4 **Sääre** Estonia
160 F3 **Saaremaa** *i.* Estonia
162 R3 **Saarenkylä** Fin.
162 R3 **Saargau** *reg.* Ger.
Saar-Hunsrück, Naturpark *nature res.* Ger.
163 T6 **Saari** Fin.
162 T5 **Saarijärvi** Fin.
162 S3 **Saari-Kämä** Fin.
162 P3 **Saarikoski** Fin.
162 S2 **Saariselkä** Fin.
Saaristomeren Kansallispuisto *nat. park* Fin. *see* **Skärgårdshavets nationalpark**
194 B3 **Saarland** *land* Ger.
194 B3 **Saarlouis** Ger.
194 B3 **Saarwellingen** Ger.
212 H2 **Saas** Switz.
212 D3 **Saas Fee** Switz.
212 D3 **Saas Grund** Switz.
212 D3 **Saastal** *val.* Switz.
225 F6 **Sa'ata** Sudan
151 J6 **Saatlı** Azer.
Saatly Azer. *see* **Saatlı**
160 K4 **Saatse** Estonia
285 F5 **Saavedra** *Buenos Aires* Arg.
285 G2 **Saavedra** *Santa Fé* Arg.
271 L5 **Saba** *i.* Neth. Antilles
146 C1 **Saba, Wādī** *watercourse* Saudi Arabia
150 A8 **Saba'ah** Egypt
150 F5 **Sab' Ābār** Syria
191 I7 **Sababurg** Ger.
218 H6 **Šabac** *Šabac* Serbia
208 J4 **Sabadell** Spain
228 C2 **Sabadou Baranama** Guinea
126 D4 **Sabae** Japan
233 A6 **Sabagusi** Tanz.
117 L2 **Sabah** *state* Malaysia
116 D3 **Sabak** Malaysia
244 □A5 **Sabak, Cape** *AK* U.S.A.
233 D5 **Sabaki** *r.* Kenya
144 B2 **Sabalan, Kūhhā-ye** *mts* Iran
115 A7 **Sabalana** *i.* Indon.
115 A7 **Sabalana, Kepulauan** *is* Indon.
138 F6 **Sabalgarh** *Madh. Prad.* India
225 E2 **Saban** Venez.
270 C2 **Sabana, Archipiélago de** *is* Cuba
271 I4 **Sabana de la Mar** Dom. Rep.
266 □P11 **Sabanagrande** Hond.
271 □[1] **Sabana Grande** Puerto Rico
274 C2 **Sabanalarga** Col.
Sabaneta Aruba *see* **Savaneta**
270 H4 **Sabaneta** Dom. Rep.
270 I8 **Sabaneta** Venez.
116 A2 **Sabang** *Aceh* Indon.
115 A3 **Sabang** *Sulawesi* Indon.
115 B5 **Sabang** *Sulawesi* Indon.
274 C5 **Sabano** Col.
148 F3 **Şabanözü** Turkey
219 O3 **Săbăoani** Romania
281 F3 **Sabará** Brazil
185 G9 **Sabarat** France
136 G4 **Sabari** *r.* India
138 D8 **Sabarmati** *r. Gujarat* India
115 A7 **Sabaru** *i.* Indon.
150 D6 **Sabastiya** West Bank
146 G8 **Sab'atayn, Ramlat as** *des.* Yemen
215 N5 **Sabato** *r.* Italy
215 N5 **Sabaudia** Italy
215 K5 **Sabaudia, Lago di** *lag.* Italy
276 C4 **Sabaya** Bol.
146 E6 **Şabyā** *i.* Saudi Arabia
151 C3 **Sabazho** Georgia
212 I6 **Sabbioneta** Italy
236 H7 **Sabelo** S. Africa
232 C4 **Sabena Desert** Kenya
145 I6 **Şāberī, Hāmūn-e** *marsh* Afgh.
205 J3 **Sabero** Spain
236 C4 **Şabḩā** Jordan
224 B3 **Sabhā** Libya
146 F3 **Şabḩā'** Saudi Arabia
138 B8 **Sabhrai** *Gujarat* India
138 F5 **Sabi** *r.* India
Sabi *r.* Moz./Zimbabwe *see* **Save**
235 G5 **Sabie** Moz.
237 Q1 **Sabie** *r.* Moz./S. Africa
235 F5 **Sabie** S. Africa
233 D3 **Sabiha Gökçen** *airport* Turkey
160 F4 **Sabile** Latvia
256 B9 **Sabina** *OH* U.S.A.
266 F2 **Sabinal** Mex.
270 E3 **Sabinal, Cayo** *i.* Cuba
208 E2 **Sabiñánigo** Spain
207 N7 **Sabinar, Punta del** *pt* Spain
207 N7 **Sabinar, Punta del** *mt.* Spain
267 I4 **Sabinas** Mex.
261 E12 **Sabinas** *r.* Mex.
261 F12 **Sabinas** *r.* Mex.
267 I4 **Sabinas Hidalgo** Mex.
261 I11 **Sabine** *r. LA/TX* U.S.A.
261 I11 **Sabine Lake** *LA/TX* U.S.A.
162 □ **Sabine Land** *reg.* Svalbard
261 I11 **Sabine National Wildlife Refuge** *nature res. LA* U.S.A.
261 I11 **Sabine Pass** *TX* U.S.A.
215 J3 **Sabini, Monti** *mts* Italy
281 F3 **Sabinópolis** Brazil
238 □[3e] **Sabinosa** *El Hierro* Canary Is
199 K2 **Sabinov** Slovakia
206 E3 **Sabiote** Spain
151 J5 **Sabir** Azer.
151 J5 **Sabirabad** Azer.
114 C5 **Sablayan** *Mindoro* Phil.
249 H5 **Sable, Cape** *N.S.* Can.
255 G13 **Sable, Cape** *FL* U.S.A.
100 □[5] **Sable, Île de** *i.* New Caledonia
250 G3 **Sable, Lac du** *l. Que.* Can.
249 G2 **Sable, Rivière du** *r. Que.* Can.
239 □[3b] **Sable Blanc, Récif du** *rf* Mayotte
249 J5 **Sable Island** *N.S.* Can.
239 □[1a] **Sables, Île aux** *i. Rodrigues I.* Mauritius
251 L3 **Sables, River aux** *r. Ont.* Can.
180 G4 **Sables-d'Or-les-Pins** France
181 K6 **Sablé-sur-Sarthe** France
183 G8 **Sablet** France
183 F7 **Sablières** France
151 E1 **Sablinskoye** Rus. Fed.
183 F10 **Sablon, Pointe du** *pt* France
183 F6 **Sablons** France
144 G6 **Sablū'iyeh** Iran
278 F3 **Saboeiro** Brazil
206 C5 **Sabóia** Port.
229 H3 **Sabon Kafi** Niger
204 F6 **Sabor** *r.* Port.
228 E3 **Sabou** Burkina
251 Q2 **Sabourin, Lac** *l. Que.* Can.
224 B1 **Sabrātah** Libya
185 C7 **Sabres** France
286 P2 **Sabrina Coast** Antarctica
204 E5 **Sabrosa** Port.
114 C1 **Sabtang** *i.* Phil.
151 G3 **Sabue** Georgia
126 E6 **Sabugal** Port.
204 F8 **Sabugal** Port.
206 C3 **Sabugueiro** *Évora* Port.
204 E8 **Sabugueiro** *Guarda* Port.
115 B8 **Sabulu** *Sulawesi* Indon.
151 K5 **Sabunçu** Azer.
121 I3 **Sabuncu** Turkey
117 K8 **Sabunten** *i.* Indon.
127 I2 **Saburyū-yama** *mt.* Japan
146 F7 **Şabyā** Saudi Arabia
Sabzawar Afgh. *see* **Shīndand**
Sabzevār Iran
144 G3 **Sabzvārān** Iran *see* **Jīroft**
219 N4 **Saca, Vârful** *mt.* Romania
276 D4 **Sacaba** Bol.
276 D4 **Sacaca** Bol.
199 L4 **Săcădat** Romania
199 L5 **Săcălaz** Romania
219 R6 **Sacalinul Mare, Insula** *i.* Romania
283 C6 **Sacanana, Pampa** *plain* Arg.
257 K5 **Sacandaga** *r. NY* U.S.A.
235 C6 **Sacandica** Angola
209 D8 **Sacañet** Spain
285 F2 **Sacanta** Arg.
199 L4 **Săcăşeni** Romania
125 U8 **Saçavém** Port.
206 A3 **Sacavém** Port.
212 D7 **Saccarel, Mont** *mt.* France/Italy
260 H4 **Sac City** *IA* U.S.A.
215 L4 **Sacco** *r.* Italy
205 P7 **Sacecorbo** Spain
205 O8 **Sacedón** Spain
219 N5 **Săcele** *Braşov* Romania
219 Q7 **Săcele** *Constanţa* Romania
219 N6 **Săceni** Romania
207 J3 **Saceruela** Spain
151 D6 **Saç Geçidi** *pass* Turkey
235 C6 **Sachanga** Angola
247 N4 **Sachigo** *r. Ont.* Can.
247 M4 **Sachigo Lake** *Ont.* Can.
138 D9 **Sachin** *Gujarat* India
123 E10 **Sach'ŏn** S. Korea
138 F3 **Sach Pass** *Hima. Prad.* India
212 E2 **Sachseln** Switz.
193 H8 **Sachsen** *land* Ger.
192 D6 **Sachsen-Anhalt** *land* Ger.
195 J3 **Sachsen bei Ansbach** Ger.
191 G8 **Sachsenberg (Lichtenfels)** Ger.
191 K10 **Sachsenbrunn** Ger.
201 H6 **Sachsenburg** Austria
191 H6 **Sachsenhagen** Ger.
191 H8 **Sachsenhausen (Waldeck)** Ger.
194 G4 **Sachsenheim** Ger.
242 F2 **Sachs Harbour** *N.W.T.* Can.
193 J9 **Sächsische Schweiz** *park* Ger.
193 J9 **Sächsische Schweiz, Nationalpark** *nat. park* Ger.
213 M4 **Sacile** Italy
Sacirsuyu *r.* Syria/Turkey *see* **Sājūr, Nahr**
257 I5 **Sackets Harbor** *NY* U.S.A.
191 G9 **Sackpfeife** *hill* Ger.
249 H4 **Sackville** *N.B.* Can.
257 □O5 **Saco** *ME* U.S.A.
262 K2 **Saco** *MT* U.S.A.
114 D8 **Sacol** *i.* Phil.
219 K5 **Sacoşu Turcesc** Romania
182 G1 **Sacquenay** France
205 M5 **Sacramenia** Spain
280 D3 **Sacramento** Brazil
264 K3 **Sacramento** *CA* U.S.A.
264 K3 **Sacramento** *r. CA* U.S.A.
276 A1 **Sacramento, Pampa del** *plain* Peru
263 K9 **Sacramento Mountains** *NM* U.S.A.
264 J1 **Sacramento Valley** *CA* U.S.A.
207 M7 **Sacratif, Cabo** *c.* Spain
277 F3 **Sacre** *r.* Brazil
233 C6 **Sacred Mijikenda Kaya Forests** *tourist site* Kenya
209 I10 **Sa Creu, Punta de** *pt* Spain
171 N4 **Sacriston** *Durham, England* U.K.
215 I3 **Sacrofano** Italy
219 K3 **Săcueni** Romania
199 L5 **Săcuieu** Romania
277 F3 **Sacuriuiná** *r.* Brazil
267 O8 **Sacxán** Mex.
239 □[3b] **Sada** Mayotte
237 K8 **Sada** S. Africa
204 D2 **Sada** Spain
185 B10 **Sada** Spain
205 R4 **Sádaba** Spain
138 G4 **Sadabad** *Uttar Prad.* India
144 D7 **Sa'dābād** Iran
Sá da Bandeira Angola *see* **Lubango**
150 E4 **Şadad** Syria
146 F7 **Şa'dah** Yemen
146 F7 **Şa'dah** *governorate* Yemen
214 C8 **Sadali** *Sardegna* Italy
125 J13 **Sada-misaki** *pt* Japan
115 A5 **Sadang** *r.* Indon.
233 C6 **Sadani** Tanz.
119 E11 **Sadao** Thai.
147 I8 **Şadārah** Yemen
139 I8 **Sadārāk** Azer.
136 E4 **Sadaseopet** *Andhra Prad.* India
145 N5 **Sadda** Pak.
150 E7 **Sadd as Sultānī** Jordan
149 L7 **Saddat al Hindīyah** Iraq
168 E11 **Saddell** *Argyll and Bute, Scotland* U.K.
237 P1 **Saddleback** *pass* S. Africa
Saddleback *hill England* U.K. *see* **Blencathra**
261 D8 **Saddleback Mesa** *mt. NM* U.S.A.
107 J3 **Saddle Hill** *Qld* Austr.
103 H8 **Saddle Hill** *mt. South I.* N.Z.
Saddle Island Vanuatu *see* **Mota Lava**
137 M6 **Saddle Peak** *hill Andaman & Nicobar Is* India
119 G9 **Sa Dec** Vietnam
147 L7 **Sadḩ** Oman
138 F4 **Sadhaura** *Haryana* India
271 □[7] **Sadhoowa** Trin. and Tob.
232 B2 **Sadi** Eth.
144 H9 **Sadīj** *watercourse* Iran
151 G4 **Sadiqabad** Pak.
139 O6 **Sadıqlı** Azer.
146 D5 **Sadiya** *Assam* India
149 M7 **Sa'diyah** Saudi Arabia
147 J3 **Sa'dīyah, Hawr as** *imp. l.* Iraq
235 □K2 **Sa'dīyyat** *i.* U.A.E.
144 G3 **Sadjoavato** Madag.
196 F2 **Sad Kharv** Iran
197 I4 **Sadki** Pol.
196 E2 **Sadkowice** Pol.
196 G2 **Sadkowo** Pol.
206 B4 **Sadlinki** Pol.
124 P9 **Sado** *r.* Port.
206 B5 **Sadoga-shima** *i.* Japan
149 L2 **Sado Morgavel, Canal do** Port.
117 I4 **Sadon** Rus. Fed.
214 C6 **Sadong** *r.* Malaysia
159 N8 **Sa Donna, Pico** *mt.* Italy
197 J1 **Sadove** Ukr.
Sadovoye *Kaliningradskaya Oblast'* Rus. Fed.
157 I7 **Sadovoye** *Respublika Kalmykiya-Khalm'g-Tangch* Rus. Fed.
159 T2 **Sadovoye** *Voronezhskaya Oblast'* Rus. Fed.
197 J5 **Sadowie** Pol.
196 E3 **Sadowne** Pol.
209 J8 **Sa Dragonera** *i.* Spain
136 G6 **Sadras** *Tamil Nadu* India
138 D7 **Sadri** *Rajasthan* India
258 D5 **Sadsburyville** *PA* U.S.A.
193 K10 **Sadská** Czech Rep.
138 E5 **Sadulshahar** *Rajasthan* India
146 E5 **Sadūs** Saudi Arabia
143 N6 **Sadu Shakirov** Kazakh.
150 C7 **Sadūt (abandoned)** Egypt
164 G4 **Sæby** Denmark
190 G1 **Sæd** Denmark
256 E7 **Saegertown** *PA* U.S.A.
205 O9 **Saelices** Spain
205 P7 **Saelices de la Sal** Spain
205 J3 **Saelices del Rio** Spain
205 J4 **Saelices de Mayorga** Spain
Saena Julia Italy *see* **Siena**
191 E6 **Saerbeck** Ger.
187 I9 **Saeul** Lux.
Safad Israel *see* **Zefat**
Safāga Island Egypt *see* **Safājah, Jazīrat**
225 G3 **Safājah, Jazīrat** *i.* Egypt
228 E3 **Safané** Burkina
206 E4 **Safara** Port.
Šafárikovo Slovakia *see* **Tornaľa**
151 I6 **Şafarlu** Iran
144 E6 **Safāshahr** Iran
100 □[2] **Safata Bay** Samoa
149 M8 **Safayal Maqūf** *well* Iraq
145 N2 **Safed Khirs** *mts* Afgh.
145 K4 **Safed Koh** *mts* Afgh.
145 N4 **Safed Koh** *mts* Afgh./Pak.
147 I1 **Saffānīyah, Ra's as** *pt* Saudi Arabia
164 I2 **Säffle** Sweden
265 W9 **Safford** *AZ* U.S.A.
180 H6 **Saffré** France
173 M3 **Saffron Walden** *Essex, England* U.K.
Safi Jordan *see* **Aş Şāfī**
226 C2 **Safi** Morocco
144 G3 **Safīābād** Iran
144 D3 **Safīd** *r.* Iran
144 G5 **Safīd, Chashmeh-ye** *spring* Iran
145 K3 **Safīd, Daryā-ye** *r.* Afgh.
144 E4 **Safīd Ab** Iran
144 I6 **Safīdabeh** Iran
144 E7 **Safīdār, Kūh-e** *mt.* Iran
144 C5 **Safīd Dasht** Iran
144 E5 **Safīd Kūh** Iran
145 I4 **Safīd Kūh** *mts* Afgh. *see* **Paropamisus**
Safīd Kūh *mts* Afgh.
146 H8 **Sāfir** Yemen
281 G3 **Safiras, Serra das** *mts* Brazil
150 E4 **Şāfītā** Syria
152 J2 **Safonovo** *Arkhangel'skaya Oblast'* Rus. Fed.
156 I1 **Safonovo** *Murmanskaya Oblast'* Rus. Fed.
161 Q6 **Safonovo** *Smolenskaya Oblast'* Rus. Fed.
100 □[2] **Safotu** Samoa
146 F2 **Safrā' al Asyāḩ** *esc.* Saudi Arabia
146 G2 **Safrā' as Sark** *esc.* Saudi Arabia
148 F3 **Safranbolu** Turkey
100 □[2] **Safune** Samoa
147 I2 **Şafwa** Saudi Arabia
149 M8 **Safwān** Iraq
199 L4 **Şag** Romania
218 J5 **Şag** Romania
133 G12 **Saga** *Xizang* China
125 K13 **Saga** *Kōchi* Japan
125 H13 **Saga** *Saga* Japan
142 J3 **Saga** *Kostanayskaya Oblast'* Kazakh.
142 K2 **Saga** *Kostanayskaya Oblast'* Kazakh.
124 R8 **Sagae** Japan
118 B4 **Sagaing** Myanmar
118 B3 **Sagaing** *admin. div.* Myanmar
Sagala Mali *see* **Séguéla**
214 B7 **Sagama** *Sardegna* Italy
127 J4 **Sagamihara** Japan
127 J4 **Sagamiko** Japan
126 J4 **Sagami-nada** *g.* Japan
127 J5 **Sagami-wan** *b.* Japan
256 F8 **Sagamore** *PA* U.S.A.
Sagamu Nigeria *see* **Shagamu**
251 L1 **Saganash Lake** *Ont.* Can.
125 I13 **Saganoseki** Japan
119 D8 **Saganthit Kyun** *i.* Myanmar
136 D5 **Sagar** *Karnataka* India
136 E4 **Sagar** *Karnataka* India
138 G8 **Sagar** *Madh. Prad.* India
127 H6 **Sagara** Japan
192 I1 **Sagard** Ger.
Sagaredzho Georgia *see* **Sagarejo**
151 G4 **Sagarejo** Georgia
139 M8 **Sagaria** Bangl.
139 L9 **Sagar Island** India
Sagarmatha *mt.* China/Nepal *see* **Everest, Mount**
139 K6 **Sagarmatha National Park** Nepal
153 N2 **Sagastyr** Rus. Fed.
139 J6 **Sagauli** *Bihar* India
245 J1 **Sagavanirktok** *r. AK* U.S.A.
190 F5 **Sage** Ger.
262 I6 **Sage** *WY* U.S.A.
262 I2 **Sage Creek** *r. MT* U.S.A.
165 K1 **Sagen** Sweden
169 J6 **Saggart** Ireland
162 M3 **Saggat** *l.* Sweden
150 C8 **Saggi, Har** *mt.* Israel
144 F5 **Saghand** Iran
145 J5 **Saghar** Afgh.
259 K3 **Sag Harbor** *NY* U.S.A.
Saghyz Kazakh. *see* **Sagiz**
136 F5 **Sagileru** *r.* India
251 K6 **Saginaw** *MI* U.S.A.
250 B3 **Saginaw** *MN* U.S.A.
251 K6 **Saginaw Bay** *MI* U.S.A.
221 J3 **Sağırlar** Turkey
215 L3 **Sagittario** *r.* Italy
142 F3 **Sagiz** *Atyrauskaya Oblast'* Kazakh.
Sagiz *r.* Kazakh. *see* **Sagyz**
221 I2 **Sağlamtaş** Turkey
151 J7 **Sağlasār** Azer.
228 C5 **Sagleipie** Liberia
249 I1 **Saglek Bay** *Nfld and Lab.* Can.
Saglouc *Que.* Can. *see* **Salluit**
128 B1 **Saglyy** Rus. Fed.
214 B3 **Sagone** *Corse* France
214 B3 **Sagone, Golfe de** *b. Corse* France
207 N5 **Sagra** *mt.* Spain
284 B4 **Sagrada Familia** Chile
206 B6 **Sagres** Port.
206 B7 **Sagres, Ponta de** *pt* Port.
128 E4 **Sagsay** *watercourse* Mongolia
138 E8 **Sagthale** *Rajasthan* India
115 C8 **Sagu** Indon.
118 B4 **Sagu** Myanmar
199 K5 **Şagu** Romania
263 K7 **Saguache** *CO* U.S.A.
263 L8 **Saguache Creek** *r. CO* U.S.A.
270 F3 **Sagua de Tánamo** Cuba
270 C2 **Sagua la Grande** Cuba
265 V9 **Saguaro National Park** *AZ* U.S.A.
249 G3 **Saguenay** *r. Que.* Can.
249 G3 **Saguenay, Parc de Conservation du** *nature res. Que.* Can.
249 G3 **Saguenay-Saint-Laurent, Parc** *nature res. Que.* Can.
116 G8 **Saguling, Waduk** *resr Jawa* Indon.
Sagunt Spain *see* **Sagunto**
209 E8 **Sagunto** Spain
Saguntum Spain *see* **Sagunto**
159 S3 **Saguny** Rus. Fed.
164 B2 **Sagvåg** Norway
138 E8 **Sagwara** *Rajasthan* India
245 J1 **Sagwon** *AK* U.S.A.
182 G3 **Sagy** France
142 D5 **Sagyndyk, Mys** *pt* Kazakh.
142 E4 **Sagyz** *Atyrauskaya Oblast'* Kazakh.
142 E4 **Sagyz** *r.* Kazakh.
150 E7 **Saḩāb** Jordan
138 G5 **Sahabab** *Uttar Prad.* India
144 C2 **Şahağac** Azer.
269 I6 **Sahagún** Mex.
205 J4 **Sahagún** Spain
163 R6 **Sahalahti** Fin.
173 N2 **Saham Toney** *Norfolk, England* U.K.
144 B3 **Sahand, Kūh-e** *mt.* Iran
151 D5 **Şahandöken** Turkey
226 G6 **Sahara** *des.* Africa
Saharan Atlas *mts* Alg. *see* **Atlas Saharien**
138 F5 **Saharanpur** *Uttar Prad.* India
108 G6 **Sahara Well** *W.A.* Austr.
139 K7 **Saharsa** *Bihar* India
138 G5 **Sahaswan** *Uttar Prad.* India
144 F4 **Sahat, Kūh-e** *hill* Iran
139 J7 **Sahatwar** *Uttar Prad.* India
235 □K4 **Sahavato** Madag.
147 I4 **Sahbā', Wādī as** *watercourse* Saudi Arabia
151 G6 **Şahbuz** Azer.
228 C3 **Sahel** *reg.* Africa
92 E4 **Sahel** *reg.* Africa
146 D7 **Sahel** *prov.* Eritrea
228 E3 **Sahel, Réserve Partielle du** *nature res.* Burkina
139 K7 **Sahibganj** *Jharkhand* India
145 O6 **Sahiwal** *Punjab* Pak.
145 O6 **Sahiwal** *Punjab* Pak.
144 H5 **Sahlābād** Iran
146 D2 **Sahl al Maṭrān** Saudi Arabia
146 E5 **Sahl Rakbah** *plain* Saudi Arabia
147 M3 **Şaḩm** Oman
144 B4 **Şaḩneh** Iran
149 L8 **Şaḩrā al Ḩijārah** *reg.* Iraq
Sahu *Qinghai* China *see* **Zadoi**
115 E3 **Sahu** *Halmahera* Indon.
266 E3 **Sahuaripa** Mex.
265 V10 **Sahuarita** *AZ* U.S.A.
268 E5 **Sahuayo** Mex.
208 F2 **Sahun** Spain
183 G8 **Sahune** France
159 L4 **Sahunivka** Ukr.
146 E3 **Şahūq** *reg.* Saudi Arabia
146 F3 **Şaḩūq, Wādī** *watercourse* Saudi Arabia
119 F7 **Sa Huynh** Vietnam
151 C6 **Şahvelet Dağları** *mts* Turkey
199 H3 **Šahy** Slovakia
Sahyadri *mts* India *see* **Western Ghats**
138 E9 **Sahyadriparvat Range** *hills* India
138 I7 **Sai** *r.* India
113 J8 **Saibai Island** *Qld* Austr.
119 E11 **Sai Buri** Thai.
119 E11 **Sai Buri, Mae Nam** *r.* Thai.
227 F2 **Saïda** Alg.
150 D5 **Saïda** Lebanon
119 F8 **Sai Dao Tai, Khao** *mt.* Thai.
147 M4 **Sa'id Bin Sahrān** Oman
144 J8 **Sa'īdī** Iran
203 E5 **Saïdia** Morocco
Sa'īdīyeh Iran *see* **Solţānīyeh**
139 L7 **Saidpur** Bangl.
139 I7 **Saidpur** *Uttar Prad.* India
145 O4 **Saidu** Pak.
126 C4 **Sai-gawa** *r.* Japan
127 H2 **Sai-gawa** *r.* Japan
168 B7 **Saighdinis** *Western Isles, Scotland* U.K.
184 I5 **Saignes** France
183 G9 **Saignon** France
125 K10 **Saigō** Japan
Saigon Vietnam *see* **Hô Chi Minh**
139 N8 **Saiha** *Mizoram* India
129 M5 **Saihan Tal** *Nei Mongol* China
128 G6 **Saihan Toroi** *Nei Mongol* China
162 T3 **Saija** Fin.
125 K13 **Saijō** Japan
125 G13 **Saikai Kokuritsu-kōen** *nat. park* Japan
125 I14 **Saiki** Japan
125 I14 **Saiki-wan** *b.* Japan
131 □J7 **Sai Kung** *H.K.* China
131 □J7 **Sai Kung Hoi** *b. H.K.* China
138 E8 **Sailana** *Madh. Prad.* India
185 I11 **Saillagouse-Llo** France
183 F7 **Saillans** France
184 F4 **Saillat-sur-Vienne** France
115 G4 **Sailolof** *Papua* Indon.
182 D5 **Sail-sous-Couzan** France
163 T6 **Saimaa** *l.* Fin.
163 T6 **Saimaankanava** *r.* Fin.
148 H4 **Saimbeyli** Turkey
268 D2 **San Alto** Mex.

182 C3 Saincaize-Meauce France
145 I7 Saindak Pak.
144 B3 Sa'indezh Iran
Sa'in Qal'eh Iran see Sa'indezh
228 C3 Saïnsoubou Senegal
178 G4 Sains-Richaumont France
260 K7 Saint r. IL U.S.A.
168 L11 St Abbs Scottish Borders, Scotland U.K.
207 □ St Abb's Head Gibraltar
168 L11 St Abb's Head Scotland U.K.
178 D3 St-Acheul France
183 B9 St-Affrique France
183 B8 St-Affrique, Causse de plat. France
182 D3 St-Agnan Bourgogne France
182 E2 St-Agnan Bourgogne France
183 G7 St-Agnan-en-Vercors France
184 C4 St-Agnant France
184 H3 St-Agnant-de-Versillat France
172 B7 St Agnes Cornwall, England U.K.
172 □ St Agnes i. England U.K.
183 E6 St-Agrève France
184 G1 St-Aignan France
181 I6 St-Aignan-sur-Roë France
184 D5 St-Aigulin France
182 F4 St-Albain France
180 F4 St-Alban France
183 F6 St-Alban-d'Ay France
182 H5 St-Alban-Leysse France
249 K4 St Alban's Nfld and Lab. Can.
173 L4 St Albans Hertfordshire, England U.K.
257 L4 St Albans VT U.S.A.
256 D10 St Albans WV U.S.A.
St Alban's Head England U.K. see St Aldhelm's Head
183 C7 St-Alban-sur-Limagnole France
246 H4 St Albert Alta Can.
172 H6 St Aldhelm's Head England U.K.
181 J3 St-Amand France
182 C1 St-Amand-en-Puisaye France
178 F3 St-Amand-les-Eaux France
181 N6 St-Amand-Longpré France
183 E9 St-Amand-Montrond France
178 I6 St-Amand-sur-Fion France
183 C7 St-Amans France
183 B7 St-Amans-des-Cots France
183 B9 St-Amans-Soult France
184 E4 St-Amant-de-Boixe France
182 D5 St-Amant-Roche-Savine France
182 C5 St-Amant-Tallende France
179 N8 St-Amarin France
249 G3 St-Ambroise Que. Can.
183 E8 St-Ambroix France
182 G4 St-Amour France
183 F9 St-Andiol France
185 J10 St-André Languedoc-Roussillon France
183 K9 St-André Provence-Alpes-Côte d'Azur France
239 □1b St-André Mauritius
239 □1c St-André Réunion
St-André, Cap pt Madag. see Vilanandro, Tanjona
178 B6 St-André, Plaine de plain France
182 F5 St-André-de-Corcy France
183 E8 St-André-de-Cruzières France
184 D6 St-André-de-Cubzac France
178 B6 St-André-de-l'Eure France
183 J7 St-André-d'Embrun France
183 D9 St-André-de-Sangonis France
185 B8 St-André-de-Seignanx France
183 D8 St-André-de-Valborgne France
182 D2 St-André-en-Morvan France
182 H5 St-André-le-Gaz France
183 J9 St-André-les-Alpes France
178 H7 St-André-les-Vergers France
270 □ St Andrew parish Jamaica
271 □7 St Andrew county Trin. and Tob.
257 □R3 St Andrews N.B. Can.
103 F11 St Andrews South I. N.Z.
168 K10 St Andrews Fife, Scotland U.K.
255 G10 St Andrew Sound inlet GA U.S.A.
184 I4 St-Angel France
270 □ St Ann parish Jamaica
180 G2 St Anne Channel Is
250 G8 St Anne IL U.S.A.
270 □ St Ann's Bay Jamaica
172 B4 St Ann's Head Wales U.K.
250 B6 St Ansgar IA U.S.A.
182 D5 St-Anthème France
249 K3 St Anthony Nfld and Lab. Can.
262 I5 St Anthony ID U.S.A.
150 A10 St Anthony, Monastery of tourist site Egypt
185 H7 St-Antonin-Noble-Val France
181 O8 St-Août France
182 G2 St-Apollinaire France
183 D6 St-Arcons-d'Allier France
105 I7 St Arnaud Vic. Austr.
103 G8 St Arnaud South I. N.Z.
103 G9 St Arnaud Range mts South I. N.Z.
105 I7 St Arnaud Range National Park nature res. Vic. Austr.
178 C6 St-Arnoult-en-Yvelines France
172 F1 St Asaph Denbighshire, Wales U.K.
106 C1 St Asaph Bay N.T. Austr.
185 F4 St-Astier Aquitaine France
185 E6 St-Astier Aquitaine France
172 F5 St Athan Vale of Glamorgan, Wales U.K.
183 J9 St-Auban France
183 G8 St-Auban-sur-l'Ouvèze France
182 G2 St-Aubin France
178 F8 St-Aubin-Château-Neuf France
180 H5 St-Aubin-d'Aubigné France
181 O5 St-Aubin-du-Cormier France
178 B5 St-Aubin-lès-Elbeuf France
181 K3 St-Aubin-sur-Mer France
249 J3 St-Augustin Que. Can.
249 J3 St Augustin r. Nfld and Lab./Que. Can.
255 G11 St Augustine FL U.S.A.
184 E5 St-Aulaye France
172 C7 St Austell Cornwall, England U.K.
172 C7 St Austell Bay England U.K.
180 F6 St-Avé France
181 M7 St-Avertin France
179 M5 St-Avold France
178 C8 St-Ay France
183 J10 St-Aygulf France
185 H5 St-Baldoph France
249 J3 St Barbe Nfld and Lab. Can.
249 F4 St-Barthélemy Que. Can.
271 L5 St-Barthélemy terr. West Indies
185 H10 St-Barthélemy, Pic de mt. France
185 F6 St-Barthélemy-d'Agenais France
181 K7 St-Barthélemy-d'Anjou France
184 E5 St-Barthélemy-de-Bellegarde France
183 F6 St-Barthélemy-de-Vals France
103 D11 St Bathans South I. N.Z.
103 D11 St Bathans, Mount South I. N.Z.
183 D9 St-Bauzille-de-Putois France
185 F10 St-Béat France
183 B8 St-Beauzély France
171 J5 St Bees Cumbria, England U.K.
171 I4 St Bees Head England U.K.
182 C2 St-Benin-d'Azy France
185 I9 St-Benoît Languedoc-Roussillon France
184 E2 St-Benoît Poitou-Charentes France
239 □1c St-Benoît Réunion
185 I7 St-Benoît-de-Carmaux France
184 G3 St-Benoît-du-Sault France
178 D8 St-Benoît-sur-Loire France
103 H9 St Bernard mt. South I. N.Z.
182 H5 St-Béron France
181 J5 St-Berthevin France
185 F9 St-Bertrand-de-Comminges France
212 B1 St-Blaise Switz.
179 N7 St-Blaise-la-Roche France
179 J7 St-Blin-Semilly France
182 F3 St-Boil France
184 F3 St-Bonnet-de-Bellac France
182 E4 St-Bonnet-de-Joux France
182 E4 St-Bonnet-des-Bruyères France
183 I7 St-Bonnet-en-Champsaur France
183 E6 St-Bonnet-le-Château France
183 E6 St-Bonnet-le-Froid France
184 C5 St-Bonnet-sur-Gironde France
182 E2 St-Brancher France
181 M7 St-Branchs France
180 G3 St Brelade Channel Is
180 G7 St-Brevin-les-Pins France
180 G4 St-Briac-sur-Mer France
172 G4 St Briavels Gloucestershire, England U.K.
178 H5 St-Brice-Courcelles France
181 I5 St-Brice-en-Coglès France
172 B4 St Brides Pembrokeshire, Wales U.K.
172 B4 St Bride's Bay Wales U.K.
172 E5 St Brides Major Vale of Glamorgan, Wales U.K.
180 F4 St-Brieuc France
180 F4 St-Brieuc, Baie de b. France
178 G8 St-Bris-le-Vineux France
182 E2 St-Brisson France
179 I8 St-Broing-les-Moines France
180 H4 St-Broladre France
172 □ St Buryan Cornwall, England U.K.
181 M6 St-Calais France
183 G9 St-Cannat France
180 G4 St-Cast-le-Guildo France
248 E5 St Catharines Ont. Can.
270 □ St Catherine parish Jamaica
150 B10 St Catherine, Monastery of tourist site Egypt
271 □6 St Catherine, Mount hill Grenada
249 K4 St Catherine's Nfld and Lab. Can.
255 G10 St Catherines Island GA U.S.A.
255 □1 St Catherine's Point Bermuda
173 J6 St Catherine's Point England U.K.
185 H6 St-Céré France
212 A3 St-Cergue Switz.
182 I4 St-Cergues France
184 I5 St-Cernin France
257 L3 St-Césaire Que. Can.
183 J7 St-Chaffrey France
185 G6 St-Chamarand France
183 G9 St-Chamas France
183 F6 St-Chamond France
183 E9 St-Chaptes France
251 N3 St Charles Ont. Can.
262 I5 St Charles ID U.S.A.
256 I10 St Charles MD U.S.A.
251 J6 St Charles MI U.S.A.
250 B6 St Charles MN U.S.A.
260 J6 St Charles MO U.S.A.
182 G5 St-Chef France
183 C7 St-Chély-d'Apcher France
183 B7 St-Chély-d'Aubrac France
183 B10 St-Chinian France
183 G8 St-Christol France
183 E8 St-Christol-lès-Alès France
184 C5 St-Christoly-de-Blaye France
184 C5 St-Christoly-Médoc France
182 K5 St-Christophe Italy
180 H8 St-Christophe-du-Ligneron France
181 O7 St-Christophe-en-Bazelle France
182 E4 St-Christophe-en-Brionnais France
184 C5 St-Ciers-sur-Gironde France
183 E7 St-Cirgues-en-Montagne France
185 H7 St-Cirq-Lapopie France
248 D5 St Clair r. Can./U.S.A.
251 K7 St Clair MI U.S.A.
258 C3 St Clair PA U.S.A.
251 L7 St Clair, Lake Can./U.S.A.
183 F6 St-Clair-du-Rhône France
178 C5 St-Clair-sur-Epte France
181 I3 St-Clair-sur-l'Elle France
256 E8 St Clairsville OH U.S.A.
185 F8 St-Clar France
184 E4 St-Claud France
182 H4 St-Claude France
271 □2 St-Claude Guadeloupe
172 D4 St Clears Carmarthenshire, Wales U.K.
180 G3 St Clement Channel Is
178 F7 St-Clément Bourgogne France
184 H5 St-Clément Limousin France
179 M6 St-Clément Lorraine France
183 D9 St-Clément-de-Rivière France
255 G11 St Cloud FL U.S.A.
260 H3 St Cloud MN U.S.A.
249 G3 St-Coeur-de-Marie Que. Can.
172 C7 St Columb Major Cornwall, England U.K.
168 M7 St Combs Aberdeenshire, Scotland U.K.
185 I6 St-Constant France
181 L5 St-Cosme-en-Vairais France
184 F5 St-Crépin-de-Richemont France
185 C8 St-Cricq-Chalosse France
243 L5 St Croix r. Can./U.S.A.
250 B4 St Croix r. WI U.S.A.
271 K5 St Croix i. Virgin Is (U.S.A.)
250 B4 St Croix Falls WI U.S.A.
185 G6 St-Cyprien Aquitaine France
185 K10 St-Cyprien Languedoc-Roussillon France
185 G7 St-Cyprien Midi-Pyrénées France
178 D6 St-Cyr-l'École France
184 F1 St-Cyr-sur-Loire France
183 H10 St-Cyr-sur-Mer France
178 F6 St-Cyr-sur-Morin France
183 J8 St-Dalmas-le-Selvage France
249 G4 St-Damien-de-Buckland Que. Can.
271 □7 St David county Trin. and Tob.
265 V10 St David AZ U.S.A.
250 D9 St David IL U.S.A.
172 B4 St David's Pembrokeshire, Wales U.K.
172 B4 St David's Head Wales U.K.
255 □1 St David's Island Bermuda
172 D7 St Day Cornwall, England U.K.
178 D6 St-Denis Île-de-France France
183 D10 St-Denis Languedoc-Roussillon France
239 □1c St-Denis Réunion
181 K6 St-Denis-d'Anjou France
181 J5 St-Denis-de-Gastines France
184 H2 St-Denis-de-Jouhet France
184 B3 St-Denis-d'Oléron France
181 K5 St-Denis-d'Orques France
St-Denis-du-Sig Alg. see Sig
182 G5 St-Denis-en-Bugey France
182 F4 St-Denis-lès-Bourg France
172 C7 St Dennis Cornwall, England U.K.
180 G4 St-Denoual France
182 F3 St-Désert France
183 E6 St-Didier-en-Velay France
182 F4 St-Didier-sur-Chalaronne France
182 D5 St-Didier-sur-Rochefort France
179 M7 St-Dié France
182 C5 St-Dier-d'Auvergne France
179 I6 St-Dizier France
184 H3 St-Dizier-Leyrenne France
172 C3 St Dogmaels Pembrokeshire, Wales U.K.
180 G6 St-Dolay France
180 H5 St-Domineuc France
St-Domingue country West Indies see Haiti
183 F6 St-Donat-sur-l'Herbasse France
181 P7 St-Doulchard France
181 L2 Ste-Adresse France
184 F6 Ste-Alvère France
247 L5 Sainte Anne Man. Can.
271 □2 Ste-Anne Guadeloupe
271 □3 Ste-Anne Martinique
239 □1c Ste-Anne Réunion
239 □2b Ste-Anne i. Seychelles
249 I3 Sainte Anne, Lac l. Alta Can.
249 H3 Ste-Anne, Lac l. Que. Can.
180 F6 Ste-Anne-d'Auray France
249 G4 Ste-Anne-de-Beaupré Que. Can.
257 □Q1 Ste-Anne-de-Madawaska N.B. Can.
249 G3 Ste-Anne-de-Portneuf Que. Can.
249 H3 Ste-Anne-des-Monts Que. Can.
251 S3 Ste-Anne-du-Lac Que. Can.
183 H10 Ste-Baume, Chaîne de la mts France
185 E6 Ste-Bazeille France
257 □O2 Ste-Camille-de-Lellis Que. Can.
230 A5 Ste-Catherine, Pointe pt Gabon
183 F8 Ste-Cécile-les-Vignes France
182 G3 Ste-Croix Bourgogne France
183 G7 Ste-Croix Rhône-Alpes France
212 B2 Ste-Croix Switz.
183 I9 Ste-Croix, Barrage de dam France
183 I9 Ste-Croix, Lac de l. France
185 G9 Ste-Croix-Volvestre France
248 F4 Ste-Émélie-de-l'Énergie Que. Can.
185 C9 Ste-Engrâce France
183 C8 Ste-Énimie France
183 B8 Ste-Eulalie d'Olt France
185 B7 Ste-Eulalie-en-Born France
184 H3 Ste-Feyre France
183 C6 Ste-Florine France
184 H5 Ste-Fortunade France
185 G9 Ste-Foy-de-Peyrolières France
185 E6 Ste-Foy-la-Grande France
182 E5 Ste-Foy-l'Argentière France
182 F5 Ste-Foy-lès-Lyon France
182 J5 Ste-Foy-Tarentaise France
181 L4 Ste-Gauburge-Ste-Colombe France
184 B3 Ste-Gemme-la-Plaine France
178 D5 Ste-Geneviève France
260 J7 Sainte Genevieve MO U.S.A.
183 B7 Ste-Geneviève-sur-Argence France
183 H6 St-Égrève France
184 C6 Ste-Hélène France
184 B2 Ste-Hermine France
257 □O2 Ste-Justine Que. Can.
257 □P1 St-Éleuthère Que. Can.
245 K4 St Elias, Cape AK U.S.A.
245 L3 St Elias, Mount AK U.S.A.
245 L3 St Elias Mountains Y.T. Can.
275 H3 St-Élie Fr. Guiana
185 F7 Ste-Livrade-sur-Lot France
185 G9 St-Élix-le-Château France
185 E9 St-Élix-Theux France
270 □ St Elizabeth parish Jamaica
181 P7 Ste-Lizaigne France
182 B4 St-Éloy-les-Mines France
271 □3 Ste-Luce Martinique
214 C4 Ste-Lucie-de-Tallano Corse France
249 H3 Ste-Marguerite r. Que. Can.
179 M7 Ste-Marguerite France
249 H3 Ste-Marguerite 3, Réservoir resr Que. Can.
249 G4 Ste-Marie Que. Can.
183 B7 Ste-Marie Auvergne France
185 K10 Ste-Marie Languedoc-Roussillon France
271 □3 Ste-Marie Martinique
239 □1c Ste-Marie Réunion
Ste-Marie, Cap c. Madag. see Vohimena, Tanjona
Sainte-Marie, Île i. Madag. see Boraha, Nosy
179 N7 Ste-Marie-aux-Mines France
181 M7 Ste-Maure, Plateau de France
185 E7 Ste-Maure-de-Peyriac France
184 F1 Ste-Maure-de-Touraine France
183 J10 Ste-Maxime France
179 I5 Ste-Menehould France
180 I3 Ste-Mère-Église France
182 E3 St-Émiland France
185 D6 St-Émilion France
172 C6 St Endellion Cornwall, England U.K.
172 C7 St Enoder Cornwall, England U.K.
184 G5 Ste-Orse France
180 H7 Ste-Pazanne France
181 K8 Ste-Radegonde France
178 G4 St-Erme-Outre-et-Ramecourt France
271 □2 Ste-Rose Guadeloupe
239 □1c Ste-Rose Réunion
Ste-Rose-du-Dégelé Que. Can. see Dégelis
247 L5 Sainte Rose du Lac Man. Can.
172 B7 St Erth Cornwall, England U.K.
184 C4 Saintes France
271 □2 Saintes, Îles des is Guadeloupe
182 F2 Ste-Sabine France
178 H7 Ste-Savine France
Ste-Scholastique Que. Can. see Mirabel
184 I3 Ste-Sévère-sur-Indre France
183 E6 Ste-Sigolène France
271 □3 St-Esprit Martinique
185 B9 St-Esteben France
184 C5 St-Estèphe France
185 J10 St-Estève France
181 K5 Ste-Suzanne France
239 □1c Ste-Suzanne Réunion
257 P1 Ste-Thérèse Que. Can.
246 F1 Sainte Thérèse, Lac l. N.W.T. Can.
183 E6 St-Étienne France
184 I6 St-Étienne-Cantalès France
185 B9 St-Étienne-de-Baïgorry France
183 H6 St-Étienne-de-Crossey France
183 E7 St-Étienne-de-Fontbellon France
184 H3 St-Étienne-de-Fursac France
183 D7 St-Étienne-de-Lugdarès France
180 H7 St-Étienne-de-Montluc France
183 G6 St-Étienne-de-St-Geoirs France
183 J8 St-Étienne-de-Tinée France
185 G7 St-Étienne-de-Tulmont France
182 G4 St-Étienne-du-Bois France
178 B5 St-Étienne-du-Rouvray France
183 H7 St-Étienne-en-Dévoluy France
183 H8 St-Étienne-les-Orgues France
179 M7 St-Étienne-lès-Remiremont France
183 D8 St-Étienne-Vallée-Française France
183 H9 Ste-Tulle France
257 K3 St Eugene Ont. Can.
257 □Q1 St-Eusèbe Que. Can.
257 L3 St-Eustache Que. Can.
180 C6 St-Évarzec France
178 G8 Ste-Vertu France
183 H9 Ste-Victoire, Montagne mt. France
249 G3 St-Fabien Que. Can.
237 O6 St Faith's S. Africa
182 C1 St-Fargeau France
249 F3 St-Félicien Que. Can.
183 F6 St-Félicien France
251 P1 St-Félix-de-Dalquier Que. Can.
185 H9 St-Félix-Lauragais France
168 M7 St Fergus Aberdeenshire, Scotland U.K.
185 E6 St-Ferme France
169 K4 Saintfield Northern Ireland U.K.
168 H10 St Fillans Perth and Kinross, Scotland U.K.
179 L7 St-Firmin Lorraine France
183 I7 St-Firmin Provence-Alpes-Côte d'Azur France
178 G7 St-Flavy France
214 C2 St-Florent Corse France
214 C2 St-Florent, Golfe de b. Corse France
184 B2 St-Florent-des-Bois France
178 G7 St-Florentin France
181 I7 St-Florent-le-Vieil France
181 P8 St-Florent-sur-Cher France
230 D2 St Floris, Parc National nat. park C.A.R.
183 C6 St-Flour France
181 N8 St-Flovier France
182 F5 St-Fons France
184 C5 St-Fort-sur-Gironde France
185 F9 St-Frajou France
261 J10 St Francesville LA U.S.A.
257 □Q1 St Francis r. Can./U.S.A.
261 E6 St Francis KS U.S.A.
257 □Q1 St Francis ME U.S.A.
261 J8 St Francis r. AR/MO U.S.A.
237 I10 St Francis, Cape S. Africa
237 J10 St Francis Bay S. Africa
104 D5 St Francis Isles S.A. Austr.
249 F2 St-François r. Que. Can.
271 □2 St-François Guadeloupe
239 □2 St François i. Seychelles
249 G4 St-François, Lac l. Que. Can.
183 I6 St-François-Longchamp France
257 □O2 St Froid Lake ME U.S.A.
183 E7 St-Front France
184 E5 St-Front-de-Pradoux France
180 I8 St-Fulgent France
182 E5 St-Galmier France
181 L3 St-Gatien-des-Bois France
185 F9 St-Gaudens France
184 G2 St-Gaultier France
257 □O3 St-Gédéon Que. Can.
185 D8 St-Gein France
183 D9 St-Gély-du-Fesc France
183 D6 St-Genest-Malifaux France
182 F3 St-Gengoux-le-National France
183 E9 St-Geniès-de-Malgoirès France
183 I8 St-Geniez France
183 B8 St-Geniez-d'Olt France
184 C5 St-Genis-de-Saintonge France
185 J10 St-Génis-des-Fontaines France
182 F5 St-Genis-Laval France
182 I4 St-Genis-Pouilly France
182 H5 St-Genix-sur-Guiers France
172 C6 St Gennys Cornwall, England U.K.
181 N8 St-Genou France
183 H6 St-Geoire-en-Valdaine France
105 L3 St George Qld Austr.
107 J4 St George r. Qld Austr.
255 □1 St George Bermuda
249 H4 St George N.B. Can.
271 □7 St George county Trin. and Tob.
244 E4 St George AK U.S.A.
255 G9 St George SC U.S.A.
265 S4 St George UT U.S.A.
113 L7 St George, Cape New Ireland P.N.G.
262 B6 St George, Point CA U.S.A.
244 E4 St George Island AK U.S.A.
255 E11 St George Island FL U.S.A.
108 H5 St George Range hills W.A. Austr.
249 J3 St George's Nfld and Lab. Can.
249 G4 St-Georges Que. Can.
275 G4 St-Georges Fr. Guiana
271 □6 St George's Grenada
258 D5 St Georges DE U.S.A.
249 J3 St George's Bay Nfld and Lab. Can.
249 I4 St George's Bay N.S. Can.
181 J5 St-Georges-Buttavent France
267 P9 St George's Cay i. Belize
127 M9 St George's Channel Andaman & Nicobar Is India
113 L7 St George's Channel P.N.G.
169 J9 St George's Channel Ireland/U.K.
183 D5 St-Georges-d'Aurac France
183 H6 St-Georges-de-Commiers France
184 C4 St-Georges-de-Didonne France
183 B8 St-Georges-de-Luzençon France
182 B5 St-Georges-de-Mons France
180 I8 St-Georges-de-Montaigu France
182 F4 St-Georges-de-Reneins France
181 J4 St-Georges-des-Groseillers France
182 G5 St-Georges-d'Espéranche France
184 B4 St-Georges-d'Oléron France
181 M3 St-Georges-du-Vièvre France
182 D5 St-Georges-en-Couzan France
255 □1 St George's Harbour b. Bermuda
105 M6 St George's Head A.C.T. Austr.
255 □1 St George's Island Bermuda
181 L8 St-Georges-lès-Baillargeaux France
178 G8 St-Georges-sur-Baulche France
181 N7 St-Georges-sur-Cher France
178 B7 St-Georges-sur-Eure France
181 J7 St-Georges-sur-Loire France
185 B8 St-Geours-de-Maremne France
182 D4 St-Gérand-le-Puy France
250 E4 St Germain WI U.S.A.
182 C3 St-Germain-Chassenay France
183 D8 St-Germain-de-Calberte France
181 M5 St-Germain-de-la-Coudre France
182 C4 St-Germain-des-Fossés France
184 C5 St-Germain-d'Esteuil France
185 G6 St-Germain-du-Bel-Air France
182 G3 St-Germain-du-Bois France
181 L5 St-Germain-du-Corbéis France
182 F3 St-Germain-du-Plain France
181 P8 St-Germain-du-Puy France
183 C8 St-Germain-du-Teil France
178 D6 St-Germain-en-Laye France
182 E5 St-Germain-Laval France
182 C5 St-Germain-Lembron France
184 G4 St-Germain-les-Belles France
182 D4 St-Germain-Lespinasse France
184 H5 St-Germain-les-Vergnes France
182 D5 St-Germain-l'Herm France
172 D7 St Germans Cornwall, England U.K.
185 D8 St-Germé France
178 C5 St-Germer-de-Fly France
180 G8 St-Gervais Pays de la Loire France
182 I5 St-Gervais Rhône-Alpes France
182 B4 St-Gervais-d'Auvergne France
181 N6 St-Gervais-la-Forêt France
182 J5 St-Gervais-les-Bains France
181 L8 St-Gervais-les-Trois-Clochers France
183 C9 St-Gervais-sur-Mare France
185 H7 St-Géry France
187 E8 St-Ghislain Belgium
180 G7 St-Gildas, Pointe de pt France
180 G7 St-Gildas-de-Rhuys France
180 G6 St-Gildas-des-Bois France
271 □5 St Giles Islands Trin. and Tob.
183 E9 St-Gilles France
180 H8 St-Gilles-Croix-de-Vie France
239 □1c St-Gilles-les-Bains Réunion
182 I4 St-Gingolph France
185 G10 St-Girons France
185 B8 St-Girons-Plage France
178 F4 St-Gobain France
St Gotthard Pass pass Switz. see San Gottardo, Passo del
172 C4 St Govan's Head Wales U.K.
180 H5 St-Grégoire France
180 E5 St-Guénolé France
183 D8 St-Guilhem-le-Désert France
182 D4 St-Haon-le-Châtel France
182 E5 St-Héand France
250 J5 St Helen MI U.S.A.
238 □2b St Helena terr. S. Atlantic Ocean
264 J3 St Helena CA U.S.A.
236 C8 St Helena Bay S. Africa
236 C8 St Helena Bay b. S. Africa
255 G9 St Helena Sound inlet SC U.S.A.
105 L9 St Helens Tas. Austr.
171 L7 St Helens Merseyside, England U.K.
262 C4 St Helens OR U.S.A.
262 C3 St Helens, Mount vol. WA U.S.A.
105 L9 St Helens Point Tas. Austr.
180 G3 St Helier Channel Is
180 H7 St-Herblain France
185 I9 St-Hilaire France
178 H5 St-Hilaire-au-Temple France
183 E8 St-Hilaire-de-Brethmas France
180 I7 St-Hilaire-de-Loulay France
185 F7 St-Hilaire-de-Lusignan France
180 H8 St-Hilaire-de-Riez France
184 C3 St-Hilaire-des-Loges France
184 C4 St-Hilaire-de-Villefranche France
181 I4 St-Hilaire-du-Harcouët France
183 G6 St-Hilaire-du-Rosier France
182 D3 St-Hilaire-Fontaine France
178 H5 St-Hilaire-le-Grand France
181 K7 St-Hilaire-St-Florent France
179 N7 St-Hippolyte Alsace France
179 L8 St-Hippolyte Franche-Comté France
183 D9 St-Hippolyte-du-Fort France
139 K8 Sainthiya W. Bengal India
183 J8 St-Honorat, Mont mt. France
182 D3 St-Honoré-les-Bains France
183 E6 St-Hostien France
187 H8 St-Hubert Belgium
249 F4 St-Hyacinthe Que. Can.
250 J4 St Ignace MI U.S.A.
248 C3 St Ignace Island Ont. Can.
275 G4 St Ignatius Guyana
212 B1 St-Imier Switz.
212 B1 St-Imier, Vallon de val. Switz.
172 D4 St Ishmael Carmarthenshire, Wales U.K.
183 H6 St-Ismier France
172 D7 St Ive Cornwall, England U.K.
173 L3 St Ives Cambridgeshire, England U.K.
172 □ St Ives Cornwall, England U.K.
172 B7 St Ives Bay England U.K.
183 B9 St-Izaire France
257 □Q1 St-Jacques N.B. Can.
St Jacques, Cap Vietnam see Vung Tau
248 E3 St-Jacques-de-Dupuy Que. Can.
180 H5 St-Jacques-de-la-Lande France
180 G4 St-Jacut-de-la-Mer France
270 □ St James parish Jamaica
251 I3 St James MI U.S.A.
260 H4 St James MN U.S.A.
260 J6 St James MO U.S.A.
259 I3 St James NY U.S.A.
246 D5 St James, Cape B.C. Can.
249 H3 St-Jean r. Que. Can.
249 H3 St-Jean r. Que. Can.
185 G8 St-Jean France
275 H3 St-Jean Fr. Guiana
249 F3 St-Jean, Lac l. Que. Can.
180 F6 St-Jean-Brévelay France
183 K9 St-Jean-Cap-Ferrat France
St-Jean-d'Acre Israel see 'Akko
184 C4 St-Jean-d'Angély France
181 L5 St-Jean-d'Assé France
182 G5 St-Jean-de-Bournay France
178 C8 St-Jean-de-Braye France
181 I3 St-Jean-de-Daye France
182 G3 St-Jean-de-Losne France
185 A9 St-Jean-de-Luz France
183 E8 St-Jean-de-Maurejols-et-Avéjan France
183 I6 St-Jean-de-Maurienne France
180 G8 St-Jean-de-Monts France
183 F6 St-Jean-de-Muzols France
249 G4 St-Jean-de-Port-Joli Que. Can.
181 L8 St-Jean-de-Sauves France
182 I5 St-Jean-de-Sixt France
183 D9 St-Jean-de-Védas France
185 C6 St-Jean-d'Illac France
183 C8 St-Jean-du-Bruel France
185 H9 St-Jean-du-Falga France
183 D8 St-Jean-du-Gard France
183 G6 St-Jean-en-Royans France
185 B9 St-Jean-Pied-de-Port France
185 E8 St-Jean-Poutge France
182 E6 St-Jean-Soleymieux France
181 K5 St-Jean-sur-Erve France
182 G4 St-Jean-sur-Reyssouze France
249 F4 St-Jean-sur-Richelieu Que. Can.
182 I4 St-Jeoire France
248 F4 St-Jérôme Que. Can.
183 F6 St-Jeure-d'Ay France
183 E6 St-Jeures France
180 G7 St-Joachim France
262 F3 St Joe r. ID U.S.A.
249 H4 Saint John N.B. Can.
180 G3 St John Channel Is
232 C5 St John r. Liberia
261 F6 St John KS U.S.A.
257 □S3 St John r. ME U.S.A.
271 K5 St John i. Virgin Is (U.S.A.)
249 K3 St John, Cape Nfld and Lab. Can.
249 J3 St John Bay Nfld and Lab. Can.
249 J3 St John Island Nfld and Lab. Can.
271 □1 St John's Antigua and Barbuda
249 K4 St John's Nfld and Lab. Can.
265 W7 St Johns AZ U.S.A.
251 J7 St Johns MI U.S.A.
256 A8 St Johns OH U.S.A.
255 G10 St Johns r. FL U.S.A.
257 M4 St Johnsbury VT U.S.A.
169 K3 St John's Point Northern Ireland U.K.
170 C4 St Johnstown Ireland
168 H12 St John's Town of Dalry Dumfries and Galloway, Scotland U.K.
257 K6 St Johnsville NY U.S.A.
180 I3 St-Jores France
182 I5 St-Jorioz France
185 G8 St-Jory France
184 F4 St-Jory-de-Chalais France
271 □2 St Joseph Dominica
271 □3 St-Joseph Martinique
239 □1c St-Joseph Réunion
261 J10 St Joseph LA U.S.A.
250 H7 St Joseph MI U.S.A.
260 H6 St Joseph MO U.S.A.
250 H7 St Joseph r. MI U.S.A.
250 I8 St Joseph r. MI U.S.A.
248 B3 St Joseph, Lake Ont. Can.
St-Joseph-d'Alma Que. Can. see Alma
248 D4 St Joseph Island Ont. Can.
261 G12 St Joseph Island TX U.S.A.
180 H4 St-Jouan-des-Guérets France
181 L2 St-Jouin-Bruneval France
181 K8 St-Jouin-de-Marnes France
248 F4 St-Jovité Que. Can.
185 I8 St-Juéry France
St Julian's Malta see San Ġiljan
St Julian's Bay Malta see Spinola, Il-Xatt ta'
182 G4 St-Julien France
182 G4 St-Julien Franche-Comté France
185 G9 St-Julien Midi-Pyrénées France
184 C5 St-Julien-Beychevelle France
183 E7 St-Julien-Boutières France
182 E4 St-Julien-de-Civry France
180 I7 St-Julien-de-Concelles France
181 I6 St-Julien-de-Vouvantes France
178 F7 St-Julien-du-Sault France
183 J9 St-Julien-du-Verdon France
183 H7 St-Julien-en-Beauchêne France
185 B7 St-Julien-en-Born France
182 I4 St-Julien-en-Genevois France
183 G7 St-Julien-en-Quint France
184 F2 St-Julien-l'Ars France
183 E8 St-Julien-les-Rosiers France
178 H7 St-Julien-les-Villas France
182 G4 St-Julien-sur-Reyssouze France
184 F4 St-Junien France
183 F8 St-Just France
172 □ St Just Cornwall, England U.K.
178 D4 St-Just-en-Chaussée France
182 D5 St-Just-en-Chevalet France
185 B9 St-Just-Ibarre France
185 D8 St-Justin France
172 B7 St Just in Roseland Cornwall, England U.K.
182 E5 St-Just-la-Pendue France
184 B4 St-Just-Luzac France
178 G6 St-Just-Sauvage France
182 E5 St-Just-St-Rambert France
172 B7 St Keverne Cornwall, England U.K.
168 □ St Kilda i. Western Isles, Scotland U.K.
168 □ St Kilda is Scotland U.K.
271 □ St Kitts i. St Kitts and Nevis
271 □ St Kitts and Nevis country West Indies
181 K7 St-Lambert-des-Levées France
181 J7 St-Lambert-du-Lattay France
185 E8 St-Lary France
185 E10 St-Lary-Soulan France
St-Laurent, Golfe du g. Que. Can. see St Lawrence, Gulf of
178 E3 St-Laurent-Blangy France
185 D9 St-Laurent-Bretagne France
183 E9 St-Laurent-d'Aigouze France
183 F8 St-Laurent-de-Carnols France
208 K3 St-Laurent-de-Cerdans France
182 E5 St-Laurent-de-Chamousset France
183 B10 St-Laurent-de-la-Cabrerisse France
185 J10 St-Laurent-de-la-Salanque France
185 E9 St-Laurent-de-Neste France
275 H3 St-Laurent-du-Maroni Fr. Guiana
183 H6 St-Laurent-du-Pont France
183 K9 St-Laurent-du-Var France
181 M2 St-Laurent-en-Caux France
182 H3 St-Laurent-en-Grandvaux France
183 D7 St-Laurent-les-Bains France
184 C5 St-Laurent-Médoc France
181 N6 St-Laurent-Nouan France
184 G5 St-Laurent-sur-Gorre France
179 K5 St-Laurent-sur-Othain France
181 I8 St-Laurent-sur-Sèvre France
107 L7 St Lawrence Qld Austr.
249 K4 St Lawrence Nfld and Lab. Can.
249 G3 St Lawrence inlet Que. Can.
258 D4 St Lawrence PA U.S.A.
249 I4 St Lawrence, Cape N.S. Can.
249 I3 St Lawrence, Gulf of Que. Can.
244 E3 St Lawrence Island AK U.S.A.
251 S5 St Lawrence Islands National Park Ont. Can.
248 F4 St Lawrence Seaway sea chan. Can./U.S.A.
247 K5 St Lazare Man. Can.
187 I9 St-Léger Belgium
182 D2 St-Léger-de-Fougeret France
178 C6 St-Léger-en-Yvelines France
182 E3 St-Léger-sous-Beuvray France
182 F3 St-Léger-sur-Dheune France
249 H4 St-Léonard N.B. Can.
249 F4 St-Léonard Que. Can.
179 M7 St-Léonard France
256 I10 St Leonard MD U.S.A.
184 G4 St-Léonard-de-Noblat France
173 I6 St Leonards Dorset, England U.K.
184 F5 St-Léon-sur-l'Isle France
239 □1c St-Leu Réunion
178 D5 St-Leu-d'Esserent France
249 K2 St Lewis Nfld and Lab. Can.
249 J2 St Lewis r. Nfld and Lab. Can.
185 G9 St-Lizier France
181 I3 St-Lô France
185 B8 St-Lon-les-Mines France
182 G3 St-Lothain France
185 D6 St-Loubès France
182 L1 St-Louis France
271 □2 St-Louis Guadeloupe
239 □1c St-Louis Réunion
228 A2 St-Louis Senegal
250 J6 St Louis MI U.S.A.
260 J6 St Louis MO U.S.A.
250 B3 St Louis r. MN U.S.A.
257 L3 St-Louis, Lac l. Que. Can.
270 G4 St-Louis du Nord Haiti
179 N6 St-Louis-lès-Bitche France
183 D9 St-Loup, Pic hill France
182 F3 St-Loup-de-la-Salle France
178 F6 St-Loup-de-Naud France
181 K8 St-Loup-Lamairé France
179 L8 St-Loup-sur-Semouse France
178 B6 St-Lubin-des-Joncherets France
180 I7 St-Luce-sur-Loire France
271 □3 St Lucia country West Indies
237 Q4 St Lucia, Lake S. Africa
271 □3 St Lucia Channel Martinique/St Lucia
237 Q4 St Lucia Estuary S. Africa
237 Q4 St Lucia Game Reserve nature res. S. Africa
237 Q4 St Lucia Park nature res. S. Africa
St Luke's Island Myanmar see Zadetkale Kyun
180 G4 St-Lunaire France
182 H4 St-Lupicin France
178 H7 St-Lyé France
185 G8 St-Lys France
185 D6 St-Macaire France
184 C1 St-Macaire-en-Mauges France
185 C6 St-Magne France
185 D6 St-Magne-de-Castillon France
168 □M2 St Magnus Bay Scotland U.K.
183 H9 St-Maime France
184 D3 St-Maixent-l'École France
180 G4 St-Malo France
180 G4 St-Malo, Golfe de g. France
180 H3 St-Malo-de-la-Lande France
183 E9 St-Mamert-du-Gard France
185 I6 St-Mamet-la-Salvetat France
183 H10 St-Mandrier-sur-Mer France
270 G4 St-Marc Haiti
270 G4 St-Marc, Canal de sea chan. Haiti
182 F3 St-Marcel Bourgogne France
184 H2 St-Marcel Centre France
178 B5 St-Marcel Haute-Normandie France
183 F8 St-Marcel-d'Ardèche France
183 F6 St-Marcel-lès-Annonay France
183 F7 St-Marcel-lès-Sauzet France
183 F7 St-Marcel-lès-Valence France
183 G6 St-Marcellin France
185 F9 St-Marcet France
181 I3 St-Marcouf, Îles is France
178 I8 St-Marc-sur-Seine France
178 G7 St-Mards-en-Othe France
173 O5 St Margaret's at Cliffe Kent, England U.K.
270 □ St Margaret's Bay Jamaica
168 K5 St Margaret's Hope Orkney, Scotland U.K.
262 F3 St Maries ID U.S.A.
St Mark's S. Africa see Cofimvaba
237 L8 St Mark's S. Africa
255 E10 St Marks National Wildlife Refuge nature res. FL U.S.A.
185 J10 St-Marsal France
181 L6 St-Mars-d'Outillé France
180 I7 St-Mars-du-Désert France
181 L5 St-Mars-la-Brière France
180 I6 St-Mars-la-Jaille France
183 D8 St-Martial France
185 G6 St-Martial-de-Nabirat France
184 F4 St-Martial-de-Valette France
180 F3 St Martin Guernsey Channel Is
180 G3 St Martin Jersey Channel Is
183 H9 St-Martin France
271 L4 St-Martin terr. West Indies
271 □3 St-Martin, Cap c. Martinique
236 B8 St Martin, Cape S. Africa
247 L5 St Martin, Lake Man. Can.
178 C2 St-Martin-Boulogne France
178 G5 St-Martin-d'Ablois France
185 B9 St-Martin-d'Arrossa France
181 P7 St-Martin-d'Auxigny France
183 H9 St-Martin-de-Castillon France
183 F9 St-Martin-de-Crau France
183 D7 St-Martin-de-Fugères France
180 I4 St-Martin-de-Landelles France
183 D9 St-Martin-de-Londres France
183 J8 St-Martin-d'Entraunes France
184 B3 St-Martin-de-Ré France
181 J3 St-Martin-des-Besaces France
181 L3 St-Martin-des-Champs Basse-Normandie France
180 D4 St-Martin-des-Champs Bretagne France
185 B8 St-Martin-de-Seignanx France
183 E7 St-Martin-de-Valamas France
183 E8 St-Martin-de-Valgalgues France
183 H6 St-Martin-d'Hères France
185 C8 St-Martin-d'Oney France
182 H4 St-Martin-du-Frêne France
182 G4 St-Martin-du-Mont France
183 K9 St-Martin-du-Var France
182 G3 St-Martin-en-Bresse France
182 F5 St-Martin-en-Haut France
250 H4 St Martin Island MI U.S.A.
182 F5 St-Martin-la-Plaine France
181 M7 St-Martin-le-Beau France
172 F3 St Martin's Shropshire, England U.K.
172 □ St Martin's i. England U.K.
139 N9 St Martin's Island Bangl.
178 F8 St-Martin-sur-Ouanne France
183 E6 St-Martin-Valmeroux France
183 K8 St-Martin-Vésubie France
185 F9 St-Martory France
246 H5 St Mary r. B.C. Can.
270 □ St Mary parish Jamaica
103 D11 St Mary, Mount South I. N.Z.
173 J5 St Mary Bourne Hampshire, England U.K.
173 N5 St Mary in the Marsh Kent, England U.K.
104 G4 St Mary Peak S.A. Austr.
105 L9 St Marys Tas. Austr.
251 M6 St Marys Ont. Can.
271 □7 St Mary's Trin. and Tob.
168 K5 St Mary's Orkney, Scotland U.K.
172 □ St Mary's i. England U.K.
244 G3 St Marys AK U.S.A.
260 G6 St Marys KS U.S.A.
256 A8 St Marys OH U.S.A.
256 G7 St Marys PA U.S.A.
256 D9 St Marys WV U.S.A.
260 M5 St Marys r. OH U.S.A.
249 K4 St Mary's, Cape Nfld and Lab. Can.
249 K4 St Mary's Bay Nfld and Lab. Can.
173 N5 St Mary's Bay Kent, England U.
256 I10 St Marys City MD U.S.A.
168 J12 St Mary's Loch l. Scotland U.
251 P1 St-Mathieu Que. Can.
184 F4 St-Mathieu France
180 B5 St-Mathieu, Pointe de pt Fran
184 A2 St-Mathurin France
244 D3 St Matthew Island AK U.S.A.
255 G9 St Matthews SC U.S.A.
St Matthew's Island Myanma see Zadetkyi Kyun
113 K7 St Matthias Group is P.N.G.
181 O8 St-Maur France
178 E6 St-Maur-des-Fossés France
248 F4 St-Maurice r. Que. Can.
212 B3 St-Maurice Switz.
248 F4 St-Maurice, Réserve Faunique nature res. Que. Can.
182 F5 St-Maurice-de-Beynost Franc
183 E6 St-Maurice-de-Lignon France
184 F4 St-Maurice-des-Lions France
184 G3 St-Maurice-la-Souterraine France
183 F6 St-Maurice-l'Exil France
183 D9 St-Maurice-Navacelles Franc
185 F7 St-Maurin France
172 B7 St Mawes Cornwall, England
179 L6 St-Max France
178 C3 St-Maxent France
178 D5 St-Maximin France
183 H10 St-Maximin-la-Ste-Baume France
184 E5 St-Méard-de-Drône France
184 D5 St-Médard-de-Guizières Fran
185 C6 St-Médard-en-Jalles France
180 G5 St-Méen-le-Grand France
180 H4 St-Méloir-des-Ondes France
184 D4 St-Même-les-Carrières Fran
178 H6 St-Memmie France
179 I4 St-Menges France
182 C3 St-Menoux France
172 C6 St Merryn Cornwall, England
184 G5 St-Mesmin Aquitaine France
178 G5 St-Mesmin Champagne-Arden
181 J8 St-Mesmin Pays de la Loire France
185 F7 St-Mézard France
244 G3 St Michael AK U.S.A.
257 I10 St Michaels MD U.S.A.
249 K2 St Michael's Bay Nfld and La Can.
172 □ St Michael's Mount tourist si England U.K.
185 E9 St-Michel Midi-Pyrénées Fran
178 H4 St-Michel Picardie France
184 E4 St-Michel Poitou-Charentes France
180 D5 St-Michel, Montagne hill Fra
180 D5 St-Michel, Réservoir de resr France
180 G7 St-Michel-Chef-Chef France
185 D7 St-Michel-de-Castelnau Fra
183 I6 St-Michel-de-Maurienne Fra
248 F4 St-Michel-des-Saints Que. C
180 D4 St-Michel-en-Grève France
184 B3 St-Michel-en-l'Herm France
181 J8 St-Michel-Mont-Mercure Fr
179 M7 St-Michel-sur-Meurthe Fra
179 K6 St-Mihiel France
168 K10 St Monans Fife, Scotland U.K.
185 D8 St-Mont France
183 F8 St-Montant France
179 M7 St-Nabord France
185 G8 St-Nauphary France
180 G7 St-Nazaire France
St-Nazaire, Étang de lag. Fra see Canet, Étang de
183 G6 St-Nazaire-en-Royans France
183 G7 St-Nazaire-le-Désert France
182 B5 St-Nectaire France
173 L3 St Neots Cambridgeshire, Eng U.K.
St Nicolas Belgium see Sint-Niklaas
178 E3 St-Nicolas France
187 J9 St-Nicolas, Mont hill Lux.
178 B4 St-Nicolas-d'Aliermont Fran
185 G7 St-Nicolas-de-la-Grave Fran
179 L6 St-Nicolas-de-Port France
180 G6 St-Nicolas-de-Redon France
180 E5 St-Nicolas-du-Pélem France
168 □N3 St Ninian's Isle i. Scotland U.
180 F6 St-Nolff France
186 H5 St-Oedenrode Neth.
178 D2 St-Omer France
184 C4 Saintonge reg. France
185 H8 St-Orens-de-Gameville Fran
185 E9 St-Ost France
173 O4 St Osyth Essex, England U.K.
180 G3 St Ouen Channel Is
178 B8 St-Ouen Centre France
178 D3 St-Ouen Picardie France
181 J5 St-Ouen-des-Toits France
178 H6 St-Ouen-Domprot France
172 G4 St Owen's Cross Herefordshir England U.K.
249 G4 St-Pacôme Que. Can.
180 H4 St-Pair-sur-Mer France
185 B9 St-Palais France
184 B5 St-Palais-sur-Mer France
183 D6 St-Pal-de-Chalancon France
183 E6 St-Pal-de-Mons France
257 □P2 St-Pamphile Que. Can.
182 E3 St-Pantaléon Bourgogne Fran
185 G7 St-Pantaléon Midi-Pyrénées France
184 G5 St-Pantaléon-de-Larche Fra
185 I9 St-Papoul France
184 G3 St-Pardoux, Lac de l. France
185 E6 St-Pardoux-Isaac France
184 F5 St-Pardoux-la-Rivière France
256 B8 St Paris OH U.S.A.
182 C3 St-Parize-le-Châtel France
178 H7 St-Parres-lès-Vaudes France
249 G4 St-Pascal Que. Can.
181 L5 St-Paterne France
181 L6 St-Paterne-Racan France
251 Q3 St-Patrice, Lac l. Que. Can.
271 □7 St Patrick county Trin. and To
247 I4 St Paul Alta Can.
249 J3 St Paul r. Nfld and Lab./Que.
183 J7 St-Paul France
St Paul atoll Arch. des Tuamo Fr. Polynesia see Hérèhérétue
228 C5 St Paul r. Liberia
239 □1c St-Paul Réunion
244 E4 St Paul AK U.S.A.
250 A5 St Paul MN U.S.A.
260 F5 St Paul NE U.S.A.
256 C12 St Paul VA U.S.A.
239 □1c St-Paul, Baie de b. Réunion
229 F5 St Paul, Cape Ghana
289 J7 St Paul, Île i. Indian Ocean
150 A10 St Paul, Monastery of tourist Egypt
185 H8 St-Paul-Cap-de-Joux France
185 J10 St-Paul-de-Fenouillet France
185 H10 St-Paul-de-Jarrat France
184 I6 St-Paul-des-Landes France
185 F7 St-Paul-d'Espis France
185 B7 St-Paul-en-Born France
183 J9 St-Paul-en-Forêt France
183 D9 St-Paul-et-Valmalle France
183 D6 St-Paulien France
249 I4 St Paul Island N.S. Can.
244 D4 St Paul Island AK U.S.A.
183 E8 St-Paul-le-Jeune France
185 B8 St-Paul-lès-Dax France
183 H9 St-Paul-lès-Durance France
183 G6 St-Paul-lès-Romans France
271 □2 St Paul's Bay Malta see San Pawl il-Bahar
St Paul's Bay b. Malta see San Pawl il-Bahar, Il-Bajja ta'
St Paul's Islands Malta see San Pawl, Gżejjer ta'
114 B6 St Paul Subterranean River National Park Phil.
183 F8 St-Paul-Trois-Châteaux France
185 D9 St-Pé-de-Bigorre France
185 A9 St-Pée-sur-Nivelle France
183 F7 St-Péray France

St-Père France
St-Père-en-Retz France
St Peter MN U.S.A.
St Peter and St Paul Rocks is N. Atlantic Ocean see São Pedro e São Paulo
St Peter in the Wood Channel Is
St Peter Port Channel Is
St Peter's N.S. Can.
St Peters P.E.I. Can.
St Peter's Kent, England U.K.
St Petersburg Rus. Fed. see Sankt-Peterburg
St Petersburg FL U.S.A.
St-Phal France
St-Philbert-de-Bouaine France
St-Philbert-de-Grand-Lieu France
St-Philippe Réunion
St-Pierre mt. France
St-Pierre Italy
St-Pierre Martinique
St-Pierre Mauritius
St-Pierre Réunion
St Pierre i. Seychelles
St-Pierre St Pierre and Miquelon
St-Pierre, Lac l. Que. Can.
St Pierre and Miquelon terr. N. America
St-Pierre-d'Albigny France
St-Pierre-d'Allevard France
St-Pierre-d'Aurillac France
St-Pierre-de-Chartreuse France
St-Pierre-de-Chignac France
St-Pierre-de-Côle France
St-Pierre-de-la-Fage France
St-Pierre-de-Maillé France
St-Pierre-de-Plesguen France
St-Pierre-des-Corps France
St-Pierre-des-Échaubrognes France
St-Pierre-des-Landes France
St-Pierre-des-Nids France
St-Pierre-de-Trivisy France
St-Pierre-d'Irube France
St-Pierre-d'Oléron France
St-Pierre-du-Chemin France
St-Pierre-du-Mont France
St-Pierre-Église France
St-Pierre-en-Faucigny France
St-Pierre-en-Port France
St-Pierre-la-Cour France
St-Pierre-le-Moûtier France
St-Pierre-lès-Elbeuf France
St-Pierre-lès-Nemours France
St-Pierre-Quiberon France
St-Pierre-sur-Dives France
St-Pierreville France
St-Plancard France
St-Point, Lac de l. France
St-Pois France
St-Poix France
St-Pol-de-Léon France
St-Pol-sur-Mer France
St-Pol-sur-Ternoise France
St-Pompont France
St-Pons France
St-Pons-de-Thomières France
St-Porchaire France
St-Porquier France
St-Pourçain-sur-Sioule France
St-Prex Switz.
St-Priest France
St-Priest-de-Champs France
St-Priest-Laprugne France
St-Priest-Taurion France
St-Privat France
St-Privat-d'Allier France
St-Privat-des-Vieux France
St-Prix Auvergne France
St-Prix Rhône-Alpes France
St-Projet France
St-Prosper Que. Can.
St-Puy France
St Quentin N.B. Can.
St-Quentin France
St-Quentin, Canal de France
St-Quentin-la-Poterie France
St-Quentin-sur-Isère France
St-Quirin France
St-Rambert-d'Albon France
St-Rambert-en-Bugey France
St-Raphaël France
St Regis MT U.S.A.
St Regis r. NY U.S.A.
St Regis Falls NY U.S.A.
St-Remèze France
St-Rémi Que. Can.
St-Rémy France
St-Rémy-de-Provence France
St-Remy-en-Bouzemont-St-Genest-et-Isson France
St-Rémy-sur-Avre France
St-Rémy-sur-Durolle France
St-Renan France
St-Révérien France
St-Rhemy Italy
St-Rigaud, Mont mt. France
St-Riquier France
St-Romain-de-Colbosc France
St-Romain-de-Jalionas France
St-Romain-en-Gal France
St-Romain-le-Puy France
St-Romain-sous-Versigny France
St-Romain-sur-Cher France
St-Romans France
St-Rome-de-Cernon France
St-Rome-de-Tarn France
St-Saëns France
St Sampson Channel Is
St-Santin France
St-Saturnin France
St-Saturnin-lès-Apt France
St-Saud-Lacoussière France
St-Saulge France
St-Sauves-d'Auvergne France
St-Sauveur Bretagne France
St-Sauveur Franche-Comté France
St-Sauveur-de-Montagut France
St-Sauveur-des-Monts Que. Can.
St-Sauveur-en-Puisaye France
St-Sauveur-Gouvernet France
St-Sauveur-Lendelin France
St-Sauveur-le-Vicomte France
St-Sauveur-sur-Tinée France
St-Sauvy France
St-Savin Aquitaine France
St-Savin Poitou-Charentes France
St-Savinien France
St Saviour Channel Is
St Sebastian Bay S. Africa
St-Sébastien Que. Can.
St-Sébastien-de-Morsent France
St-Sébastien-sur-Loire France
St-Seine-l'Abbaye France
St-Selve France
St-Sernin France
St-Sernin-sur-Rance France
St-Sérotin France
St-Sever France
St-Sever-Calvados France
St-Siméon Que. Can.
St-Siméon-de-Bressieux France
St-Simon Auvergne France
St-Simon Picardie France
St Simons Island GA U.S.A.
St-Sorlin, Mont de mt. France
St-Sorlin-d'Arves France
St-Soupplets France
St Stephen N.B. Can.
St Stephen Cornwall, England U.K.
St Stephen SC U.S.A.
St-Sulpice France
St-Sulpice-de-Royan France
St-Sulpice-des-Landes France
St-Sulpice-Laurière France
St-Sulpice-le-Guérétois France
St-Sulpice-les-Champs France
St-Sulpice-les-Feuilles France
St-Sulpice-sur-Lèze France
St-Sulpice-sur-Risle France
St-Sylvain France
St-Sylvain-d'Anjou France

185 F7 St-Sylvestre-sur-Lot France
185 D7 St-Symphorien France
182 E5 St-Symphorien-de-Lay France
182 F5 St-Symphorien-d'Ozon France
182 E5 St-Symphorien-sur-Coise France
172 C6 St Teath Cornwall, England U.K.
245 N4 St Terese AK U.S.A.
180 D4 St-Thégonnec France
257 □O3 St-Théophile Que. Can.
247 M4 St Theresa Point Man. Can.
183 C10 St-Thibéry France
179 K7 St-Thiébault France
248 D5 St Thomas Ont. Can.
270 □ St Thomas parish Jamaica
271 K4 St Thomas i. Virgin Is (U.S.A.)
St Thomas Bay Malta see San Tumas, Il-Bajja ta'
180 D6 St-Thurien France
249 G4 St-Tite-des-Caps Que. Can.
182 G4 St-Trivier-de-Courtes France
182 F4 St-Trivier-sur-Moignans France
184 B4 St-Trojan-les-Bains France
St Trond Belgium see Sint-Truiden
183 J10 St-Tropez France
183 J10 St-Tropez, Cap de c. France
183 J10 St-Tropez, Golfe de b. France
172 D2 St Tudwal's Road b. Wales U.K.
185 H8 St-Urcisse France
183 C7 St-Urcize France
183 F6 St-Uze France
180 I2 St-Vaast-la-Hougue France
178 F7 St-Valérien France
181 M2 St-Valery-en-Caux France
178 C3 St-Valery-sur-Somme France
182 E3 St-Vallier Bourgogne France
183 F6 St-Vallier Rhône-Alpes France
183 J9 St-Vallier-de-Thiey France
181 K8 St-Varent France
184 H3 St-Vaury France
183 J7 St-Véran France
183 F6 St-Victor France
183 G10 St-Victoret France
183 F8 St-Victor-la-Coste France
181 J3 St-Vigor-le-Grand France
212 D4 St-Vincent Italy
260 G1 St Vincent MN U.S.A.
271 □3 St Vincent i. West Indies
St-Vincent, Cap pt Madag. see Ankaboa, Tanjona
105 J10 St Vincent, Cape Tas. Austr.
St Vincent, Cape Port. see São Vicente, Cabo de
104 F6 St Vincent, Gulf S.A. Austr.
271 □3 St Vincent and the Grenadines country West Indies
184 E5 St-Vincent-de-Connezac France
185 C8 St-Vincent-de-Paul France
185 B8 St-Vincent-de-Tyrosse France
255 E11 St Vincent Island FL U.S.A.
183 I8 St-Vincent-les-Forts France
271 □3 St Vincent Passage St Lucia/St Vincent
182 H2 St-Vit France
185 F7 St-Vite France
187 J8 St-Vith Belgium
184 B5 St-Vivien-de-Médoc France
247 I4 St Walburg Sask. Can.
251 N7 St Williams Ont. Can.
184 B3 St-Xandre France
182 E4 St-Yan France
185 G9 St-Ybars France
182 C4 St-Yorre France
184 G4 St-Yrieix-la-Perche France
184 E4 St-Yrieix-sur-Charente France
180 D6 St-Yvy France
183 H10 St-Zacharie France
129 J6 Sain Us Nei Mongol China
178 C7 Sainville France
208 B1 Saioa mt. Spain
138 H5 Saipal mt. Nepal
113 K3 Saipan i. N. Mariana Is
114 □ Saipan Palau
131 □J7 Sai Pok Liu Hoi Hap sea chan. H.K. China
285 F3 Saira Arg.
180 I2 Saire r. France
185 C9 Saison r. France
185 I9 Saissac France
127 K4 Saitama pref. Japan
Saiteli Turkey see Kadınhanı
118 A3 Saitlai Myanmar
125 I14 Saito Japan
162 Q2 Saivomuotka Sweden
185 I8 Saïx France
119 D7 Sai Yok National Park Thai.
276 C4 Sajama, Nevado mt. Bol.
276 C4 Sajama, Parque Nacional nat. park Chile
146 E7 Sajīd Saudi Arabia
219 K8 Šajince Trgovište Serbia
146 G3 Sājir Saudi Arabia
147 K7 Sājir, Ra's c. Oman
197 J1 Sajna r. Pol.
197 L2 Sajno, Jezioro l. Pol.
199 J4 Sajó r. Hungary
199 J3 Sajóhidvég Hungary
199 J3 Sajókaza Hungary
199 J3 Sajópetri Hungary
199 J3 Sajószentpéter Hungary
199 K4 Sajószöged Hungary
199 J3 Sajóvámos Hungary
150 G2 Sājūr, Nahr r. Syria/Turkey
236 F5 Sak watercourse S. Africa
232 C2 Saka Eth.
226 E2 Saka Morocco
127 J4 Sakado Japan
127 L4 Sakae Chiba Japan
127 I2 Sakae Nagano Japan
126 E5 Sakahogi Japan
126 D3 Sakai Fukui Japan
127 J3 Sakai Gunma Japan
127 K3 Sakai Ibaraki Japan
127 H3 Sakai Nagano Japan
126 B6 Sakai Ōsaka Japan
125 K12 Sakaide Japan
127 I4 Sakaigawa Japan
125 K11 Sakaiminato Japan
149 J9 Sakākah Saudi Arabia
145 K8 Saka Kalat Pak.
260 D2 Sakakawea, Lake ND U.S.A.
127 H3 Sakaki Japan
127 H3 Sakakita Japan
117 L8 Sakala i. Indon.
233 A7 Sakalile Tanz.
248 F2 Sakami Que. Can.
248 E2 Sakami r. Que. Can.
127 J5 Sakami-gawa r. Japan
248 E2 Sakami Lake Que. Can.
145 K9 Sakani, Ras pt Pak.
231 F8 Sakania Dem. Rep. Congo
231 F8 Sakania, Réserve de Hippopotames de nature res. Dem. Rep. Congo
231 F7 Sakania, Réserve Partielle aux, Éléphants de nature res. Dem. Rep. Congo
219 O9 Sakar mts Bulg.
145 J2 Sakar Turkm.
235 □J4 Sakaraha Madag.
145 I3 Sakarçäge Turkm.
Sakartvelo country Asia see Georgia
Sakarya Turkey see Adapazarı
221 L2 Sakarya prov. Turkey
221 L1 Sakarya r. Turkey
126 G4 Sakashita Japan
228 D5 Sakassou Côte d'Ivoire
124 Q8 Sakata Japan
126 D4 Sakauchi Japan
125 K13 Sakawa Japan
123 D8 Sakchu N. Korea
143 O3 Saken Seyfullin Kazakh.
119 E8 Sa Keo r. Thai.
229 F5 Sakété Benin
122 M4 Sakhalin i. Rus. Fed.
Sakhalin Oblast admin. div. Rus. Fed. see Sakhalinskaya Oblast'
122 M3 Sakhalinskaya Oblast' admin. div. Rus. Fed.
122 L2 Sakhalinskiy Zaliv b. Sakhalin Rus. Fed.
161 T5 Sakharovo Rus. Fed.

237 O1 Sakhelwe S. Africa
138 D5 Sakhi Rajasthan India
237 N2 Sakhile S. Africa
145 N7 Sakhi Sarwar Pak.
158 F4 Sakhnivtsi Ukr.
159 O4 Sakhnovshchyna Ukr.
151 I4 Şäki Azer.
Saki Nigeria see Shaki
Saki Ukr. see Saky
160 G7 Šakiai Lith.
211 B7 Sakiet Sidi Youssef Tunisia
145 L6 Sakir mt. Pak.
124 □A22 Sakishima-shotō is Japan
136 D6 Sakleshpur Karnataka India
142 F2 Sakmara Rus. Fed.
118 C5 Sa-koi Myanmar
138 G9 Sakoli Mahar. India
118 G6 Sakon Nakhon Thai.
257 N7 Sakonnet r. RI U.S.A.
116 □ Sakra, Pulau reg. Sing.
145 M8 Sakrand Pak.
236 E6 Sakrivier S. Africa
142 I4 Saksaul'skiy Kazakh.
Saksaul'skoye Kazakh. see Saksaul'skiy
162 K5 Sakshaug Norway
192 E1 Sakskøbing Denmark
139 I8 Sakti Chhattisgarh India
139 I7 Saktisgarh Uttar Prad. India
160 H2 Saku Estonia
127 H3 Saku Nagano Japan
127 H3 Saku Nagano Japan
Sakulia Georgia see Saqulia
127 G5 Sakuma Japan
127 L4 Sakura Japan
127 L4 Sakuragawa Japan
127 L3 Sakura-gawa r. Japan
126 C6 Sakurai Japan
125 H15 Sakura-jima vol. Japan
126 F6 Saku-shima i. Japan
159 M8 Saky Ukr.
163 Q6 Säkylä Fin.
228 □ Sal i. Cape Verde
157 H7 Sal r. Rus. Fed.
276 B2 Sal, Cerros de la mts Peru
266 □P10 Sal, Punta pt Hond.
160 I5 Sala Jēkabpils Latvia
160 G5 Sala Rīga Latvia
199 G3 Šaľa Slovakia
165 M2 Sala Sweden
115 C5 Salabangka, Kepulauan is Indon.
248 F4 Salaberry-de-Valleyfield Que. Can.
160 H4 Salaca r. Latvia
219 K3 Sălacea Romania
199 L4 Sălacea, Lacul l. Romania
160 H4 Salacgrīva Latvia
215 P7 Sala Consilina Italy
282 C2 Salada, Bahía b. Chile
266 B1 Salada, Laguna salt l. Mex.
208 H3 Salada, Ribera r. Spain
209 D11 Salada de la Mata, Laguna l. Spain
209 D11 Salada de Torrevieja, Laguna l. Spain
282 F3 Saladas Arg.
150 D9 Salādīḩ, Wādī watercourse Jordan
285 H4 Saladillo Buenos Aires Arg.
284 E3 Saladillo San Luis Arg.
285 F3 Saladillo r. Arg.
285 G2 Saladillo r. Arg.
285 H4 Saladillo r. Arg.
282 E3 Saladillo r. Arg.
284 D5 Salado r. Arg.
284 E6 Salado r. Arg.
285 G3 Salado r. Arg.
285 I4 Salado r. Arg.
282 C3 Salado r. Arg.
283 D6 Salado r. Arg.
282 F2 Salado r. Arg.
270 E3 Salado r. Cuba
274 B5 Salado Ecuador
268 F2 Salado Mex.
269 H5 Salado r. Hidalgo/México Mex.
269 K8 Salado r. Oaxaca/Puebla Mex.
267 J4 Salado r. Mex.
206 G8 Salado r. Andalucía Spain
206 H7 Salado r. Andalucía Spain
207 K5 Salado r. Andalucía Spain
207 K5 Salado r. Andalucía Spain
263 K9 Salado watercourse NM U.S.A.
228 C4 Saladou Guinea
228 E4 Salaga Ghana
184 G5 Salagnac France
183 C9 Salagou, Lac du l. France
146 E5 Şalāḩ Saudi Arabia
150 G5 Şalāḩ, Tall hill Jordan
149 K6 Şalāḩ ad Dīn governorate Iraq
149 L5 Salahuddin Iraq
100 □2 Sala'ilua Samoa
183 F6 Salaise-sur-Sanne France
199 M4 Sălaj county Romania
234 E4 Salajwe Botswana
147 M4 Salakh, Jabal mt. Oman
224 C6 Salal Chad
225 H4 Salâla Sudan
147 L7 Şalālah Oman
229 I3 Salalé well Niger
267 N10 Salamá Guat.
266 □P10 Salamá Hond.
162 R5 Salamajärven kansallispuisto nat. park Fin.
284 B2 Salamanca Chile
268 F5 Salamanca Mex.
204 I7 Salamanca Spain
204 H7 Salamanca prov. Spain
256 G6 Salamanca NY U.S.A.
235 G5 Salamanga Moz.
Salamantica Spain see Salamanca
230 D2 Salamat pref. Chad
230 C2 Salamat, Bahr r. Chad
144 B4 Salāmatābād Iran
117 K6 Salamban Kalimantan Indon.
144 H4 Salamī Iran
220 E5 Salamina Greece
220 E5 Salamina i. Greece
150 B3 Salamis tourist site Cyprus
Salamís i. Greece see Salamina
150 F3 Salamīyah Syria
250 I9 Salamonie r. IN U.S.A.
250 I9 Salamonie Lake IN U.S.A.
139 K9 Salandi r. India
215 Q6 Salandra Italy
100 □2 Salani Samoa
160 E5 Salantai Lith.
238 □1c Salão Faial Azores
216 D8 Salaparuta Sicilia Italy
129 L6 Salaqi Nei Mongol China
207 K6 Salar Spain
219 K3 Sălard Romania
282 D2 Salar de Pocitos Arg.
208 G2 Salardu Spain
145 K8 Salari Pak.
274 B6 Salas Peru
219 K6 Salaš Zaječar Serbia
204 H2 Salas Spain
204 E5 Salas, Encoro de resr Spain
205 N4 Salas de los Infantes Spain
160 H5 Salaspils Latvia
185 F9 Salat r. France
117 I8 Salatiga Jawa Indon.
199 I3 Salatín nature res. Slovakia
184 C6 Salaunes France
156 K4 Salaush Rus. Fed.
219 M3 Sălăuța r. Romania
118 H7 Salavan Laos
142 F1 Salavat Rus. Fed.
276 A2 Salaverry Peru
115 G4 Salawati i. Papua Indon.
Salawin, Mae Nam r. China/Myanmar see Salween
118 C5 Salawin Wildlife Reserve nature res. Thai.
114 E7 Salay Mindanao Phil.
138 B8 Salaya Gujarat India
115 B7 Salayar i. Indon.
115 B6 Salayar, Selat sea chan. Indon.
291 L7 Sala y Gómez, Isla i. S. Pacific Ocean
Salazar Angola see N'dalatando
285 F5 Salazar Arg.
208 C2 Salazar r. Spain
239 □1c Salazie Réunion

239 □1c Salazie, Cirque de vol. crater Réunion
212 B5 Salbertrand Italy
184 I1 Salbris France
276 B3 Salccantay, Cerro mt. Peru
270 H4 Salcedo Dom. Rep.
245 K2 Salcha r. AK U.S.A.
195 N4 Salching Ger.
160 H7 Šalčia r. Lith.
219 O6 Sălciile Romania
160 I7 Šalčininkai Lith.
197 N1 Šalčininkėliai Lith.
219 O6 Sălcioara Romania
172 E7 Salcombe Devon, England U.K.
Saldae Alg. see Bejaïa
221 K5 Salda Gölü l. Turkey
274 C4 Saldana Col.
205 K3 Saldaña Spain
236 B9 Saldanha S. Africa
236 B9 Saldanha Bay S. Africa
195 O4 Saldenburg Ger.
205 R8 Saldón Spain
205 O5 Salduero Spain
285 G6 Saldungaray Arg.
213 J2 Saldura r. Italy
160 F5 Saldus Latvia
105 K8 Sale Vic. Austr.
108 H4 Sale r. W.A. Austr.
212 F6 Sale Italy
118 B4 Sale Myanmar
171 M7 Sale Greater Manchester, England U.K.
115 B4 Salea Sulawesi Indon.
185 F10 Saléchan France
271 □2 Salée sea chan. Guadeloupe
117 L9 Saleh, Teluk b. Sumbawa Indon.
144 C4 Şāleḩābād Hamadān Iran
144 B5 Şāleḩābād Īlām Iran
144 I4 Şāleḩābād Khorāsān Iran
173 M6 Salehurst East Sussex, England U.K.
152 H3 Salekhard Rus. Fed.
100 □2 Salelologa Samoa
194 G6 Salem Baden-Württemberg Ger.
190 K3 Salem Schleswig-Holstein Ger.
136 F7 Salem Tamil Nadu India
237 K9 Salem S. Africa
261 J7 Salem AR U.S.A.
260 K6 Salem IL U.S.A.
254 D6 Salem IN U.S.A.
257 O6 Salem MA U.S.A.
261 J7 Salem MO U.S.A.
258 E5 Salem NJ U.S.A.
257 L5 Salem NY U.S.A.
256 E8 Salem OH U.S.A.
262 C4 Salem OR U.S.A.
260 G4 Salem SD U.S.A.
265 U1 Salem UT U.S.A.
256 E11 Salem VA U.S.A.
256 E9 Salem WV U.S.A.
258 D5 Salem r. NJ U.S.A.
258 E5 Salem County county NJ U.S.A.
216 D8 Salemi Sicilia Italy
163 L6 Sälen Sweden
165 K5 Salen l. Sweden
168 E9 Salen Argyll and Bute, Scotland U.K.
168 E9 Salen Highland, Scotland U.K.
217 N2 Salentino, Penisola pen. Italy
183 I9 Salernes France
215 N6 Salerno Italy
215 O7 Salerno prov. Italy
215 N7 Salerno, Golfo di g. Italy
Salernum Italy see Salerno
184 I5 Salers France
280 D4 Sales Oliveira Brazil
281 E5 Salesópolis Brazil
173 N4 Sales Point England U.K.
183 D7 Salettes France
178 D4 Saleux France
182 I4 Salève, Mont mt. France
171 M7 Salford Greater Manchester, England U.K.
173 L5 Salfords Surrey, England U.K.
275 F5 Salgada Brazil
278 F4 Salgado Brazil
278 F3 Salgado r. Brazil
199 I3 Salgótarján Hungary
278 F4 Salgueiro Brazil
204 E9 Salgueiro Port.
204 F5 Salgueiros Port.
285 F4 Salguero Arg.
173 O2 Salhouse Norfolk, England U.K.
164 B1 Salhus Norway
159 N8 Salhyr r. Ukr.
227 E4 Sali Alg.
145 I6 Salian Afgh.
115 E2 Salibabu i. Indon.
Salibea Trin. and Tob. see Salybia
217 N3 Salice Salentino Italy
212 E7 Saliceto Italy
216 H8 Salici, Monte mt. Sicilia Italy
263 L7 Salida CO U.S.A.
160 G5 Saliena Latvia
185 C9 Salies-de-Béarn France
185 F9 Salies-du-Salat France
184 G6 Salignac-Eyvignes France
221 J4 Salihli Turkey
160 K9 Salihorsk Belarus
160 K9 Salihorskaye Vodaskhovishcha resr Belarus
228 B3 Salikénié Senegal
208 C4 Salillas de Jalón Spain
233 B8 Salima Malawi
117 L3 Salimbatu Kalimantan Indon.
204 G2 Salime, Encoro de resr Spain
231 D7 Salimi Dem. Rep. Congo
233 C8 Salimo Moz.
118 B4 Salin Myanmar
260 G6 Salina KS U.S.A.
265 U3 Salina UT U.S.A.
217 □ Salina, Il-Bajja tas- b. Malta
216 H6 Salina, Isola i. Isole Lipari Italy
269 L9 Salina Cruz Mex.
270 F2 Salina Point Acklins I. Bahamas
281 F2 Salinas Brazil
274 A5 Salinas Ecuador
268 F3 Salinas San Luis Potosí Mex.
269 L7 Salinas Veracruz Mex.
261 F13 Salinas r. Mex.
271 □1 Salinas Puerto Rico
204 I1 Salinas Asturias Spain
209 D10 Salinas Valencia Spain
264 K5 Salinas CA U.S.A.
264 K5 Salinas r. CA U.S.A.
Salinas, Cabo de c. Spain see Salines, Cap de ses
284 D2 Salinas, Pampa de las salt pan Arg.
231 B8 Salinas, Ponta das pt Angola
238 □3d Salinas, Punta pt La Palma Canary Is
270 H4 Salinas, Punta pt Dom. Rep.
276 D4 Salinas de Garci Mendoza Bol.
205 Q8 Salinas del Manzano Spain
205 Q3 Salinas de Pamplona Spain
205 L3 Salinas de Pisuerga Spain
208 F2 Salinas de Sín Spain
263 K10 Salinas Peak NM U.S.A.
183 F10 Salin-de-Giraud France
183 E8 Salindres France
215 M2 Saline r. Italy
215 Q5 Saline salt marsh Italy
171 J1 Saline Fife, Scotland U.K.
251 K7 Saline MI U.S.A.
261 I9 Saline r. AR U.S.A.
260 G6 Saline r. KS U.S.A.
271 □7 Saline Bay Trin. and Tob.
213 J9 Saline di Volterra Italy
215 L2 Salinello r. Italy
209 L9 Salines, Cap de ses c. Spain
271 □6 Salines, Point Grenada
264 O5 Saline Valley depr. CA U.S.A.
256 E8 Salineville OH U.S.A.
118 B4 Salingyi Myanmar
278 D2 Salinópolis Brazil
276 A2 Salinosó Lachay, Punta pt Peru
184 I5 Salins France
182 H3 Salins-les-Bains France
206 C6 Salir Port.
173 I5 Salisbury Wiltshire, England U.K.
257 J10 Salisbury MD U.S.A.
255 G8 Salisbury NC U.S.A.
256 F9 Salisbury PA U.S.A.
Salisbury Zimbabwe see Harare

245 K1 Salisbury, Mount AK U.S.A.
243 K3 Salisbury Island Nunavut Can.
259 G2 Salisbury Mills NY U.S.A.
173 H5 Salisbury Plain England U.K.
219 L5 Săliște Romania
219 M3 Săliștea de Sus Romania
216 F9 Salito r. Sicilia Italy
268 E3 Salitral de Carrera Mex.
278 E4 Salitre r. Brazil
199 H4 Salka Slovakia
150 E6 Şalkhad Syria
139 J9 Salki r. India
150 F1 Salkım Turkey
158 I5 Sal'kove Ukr.
162 T3 Salla Fin.
258 A2 Salladasburg PA U.S.A.
182 J5 Sallanches France
228 B4 Sallatouk, Pointe pt Guinea
208 I4 Sallent Spain
208 E2 Sallent de Gállego Spain
185 C6 Salles France
183 B8 Salles-Curan France
184 D4 Salles-d'Angles France
183 C10 Salles-d'Aude France
185 J7 Salles-la-Source France
185 H9 Salles-sur-l'Hers France
193 I7 Sallgast Ger.
164 E5 Salling reg. Denmark
201 L3 Sallingberg Austria
169 I6 Sallins Ireland
Salliq Nunavut Can. see Coral Harbour
285 F5 Salliqueló Arg.
261 H8 Sallisaw OK U.S.A.
225 H5 Sallom Sudan
243 K3 Salluit Que. Can.
224 E2 Sallum, Khalīj as b. Egypt
138 I5 Sallyana Nepal
169 F7 Sallypark Ireland
187 I8 Salm r. Belgium
150 E3 Salmá Syria
151 B5 Salmankas Geçidi pass Turkey
144 A2 Salmās Iran
205 P7 Salmerón Spain
205 O7 Salmeroncillos de Abajo Spain
156 E3 Salmi Rus. Fed.
162 T3 Salmivaara Fin.
246 G5 Salmo B.C. Can.
262 H4 Salmon ID U.S.A.
259 K2 Salmon r. CT U.S.A.
262 F4 Salmon r. ID U.S.A.
262 G4 Salmon, Middle Fork r. ID U.S.A.
246 G5 Salmon Arm B.C. Can.
262 G5 Salmon Falls Creek r. ID/NV U.S.A.
245 L2 Salmon Fork r. Can./U.S.A.
109 F12 Salmon Gums W.A. Austr.
Salmonhurst N.B. Can. see New Denmark
257 J5 Salmon Reservoir NY U.S.A.
262 G4 Salmon River Mountains ID U.S.A.
236 D10 Salmonsdam Nature Reserve S. Africa
245 L2 Salmon Village AK U.S.A.
205 J7 Salmoral Spain
194 B2 Salmtal Ger.
162 U2 Sal'nyye Tundry, Khrebet mts Rus. Fed.
230 C4 Salo C.A.R.
163 Q6 Salo Fin.
213 J4 Salò Italy
156 J4 Salobelyak Rus. Fed.
207 N3 Salobre Spain
207 L7 Salobreña Spain
162 R4 Saloinen Fin.
265 S8 Salome AZ U.S.A.
271 □3 Salomon, Cap c. Martinique
178 H6 Salon France
182 H1 Salon r. France
138 H6 Salon Uttar Prad. India
183 G9 Salon-de-Provence France
230 D5 Salonga r. Dem. Rep. Congo
230 D5 Salonga Nord, Parc National de la nat. park Dem. Rep. Congo
230 D5 Salonga Sud, Parc National de la nat. park Dem. Rep. Congo
Salonica Greece see Thessaloniki
Salonika Greece see Thessaloniki
219 J4 Salonta Romania
Salop admin. div. England U.K. see Shropshire
204 F9 Salor r. Spain
206 G2 Salor, Embalse de resr Spain
208 H2 Salòria, Pic de mt. Spain
206 E2 Salorino Spain
182 F3 Salornay-sur-Guye France
213 K3 Salorno Italy
208 H5 Salou Spain
208 H5 Salou, Cap de c. Spain
178 D4 Salouël France
228 A3 Saloum watercourse Senegal
201 N6 Šalovci Slovenia
163 R6 Salpausselkä reg. Fin.
162 □ Salpynten pt Svalbard
150 E2 Salqīn Syria
228 □ Sal Rei Cape Verde
169 C5 Salruck Ireland
284 E2 Salsacate Arg.
162 K4 Salsbruket Norway
Salses, Étang de l. France see Leucate, Étang de
185 J10 Salses-le-Château France
157 H7 Sal'sk Rus. Fed.
216 F9 Salso r. Sicilia Italy
216 H8 Salso r. Sicilia Italy
215 P4 Salsola r. Italy
212 H6 Salsomaggiore Terme Italy
Salt Jordan see As Salţ
236 H9 Salt watercourse S. Africa
208 K4 Salt Spain
265 T8 Salt r. AZ U.S.A.
260 J6 Salt r. MO U.S.A.
262 I5 Salt r. WY U.S.A.
282 D2 Salta Arg.
282 D2 Salta prov. Arg.
171 N6 Saltaire West Yorkshire, England U.K.
259 I3 Saltaire NY U.S.A.
161 R9 Saltanovka Rus. Fed.
213 N8 Saltara Italy
172 D7 Saltash Cornwall, England U.K.
171 P4 Saltburn-by-the-Sea Redcar and Cleveland, England U.K.
255 □2 Salt Cay i. New Prov. Bahamas
168 G11 Saltcoats North Ayrshire, Scotland U.K.
256 C9 Salt Creek r. OH U.S.A.
173 L6 Saltdean Brighton and Hove, England U.K.
169 I8 Saltee Islands Ireland
206 G6 Salteras Spain
246 E5 Saltery Bay B.C. Can.
162 M3 Saltfjellet Svartisen Nasjonalpark nat. park Norway
162 L3 Saltfjorden sea chan. Norway
263 L11 Salt Flat TX U.S.A.
172 H5 Saltford Bath and North East Somerset, England U.K.
261 F7 Salt Fork r. KS U.S.A.
261 G7 Salt Fork Arkansas r. KS U.S.A.
261 E9 Salt Fork Brazos r. TX U.S.A.
256 D8 Salt Fork Lake OH U.S.A.
261 F8 Salt Fork Red r. OK U.S.A.
265 U8 Salt Gila Aqueduct canal U.S.A.
169 D6 Salthill Ireland
267 I5 Saltillo Mex.
Salt Island Vanuatu see Loh
138 E6 Salt Lake salt l. India
236 I5 Salt Lake S. Africa
262 I6 Salt Lake City UT U.S.A.
256 B10 Salt Lick KY U.S.A.
265 S2 Salt Marsh Lake salt l. UT U.S.A.
172 G1 Saltney Flintshire, Wales U.K.
285 G4 Salto Arg.
280 D5 Salto Brazil
215 J3 Salto r. Italy
204 E5 Salto Port.
285 I2 Salto Uru.
285 I2 Salto dept Uru.
215 K3 Salto, Lago del l. Italy
281 H2 Salto da Divisa Brazil
267 M9 Salto de Agua Chiapas Mex.

269 H3 Salto de Agua San Luis Potosí Mex.
284 C4 Saltode Las Rosas Arg.
277 G6 Salto del Guairá Para.
214 C8 Salto di Quirra reg. Sardegna Italy
285 G3 Salto Grande Arg.
280 C5 Salto Grande Brazil
268 A1 Salto Grande Mex.
285 I2 Salto Grande, Embalse de resr Uru.
265 P8 Salton City CA U.S.A.
265 Q8 Salton Sea salt l. CA U.S.A.
228 E5 Saltpond Ghana
247 H2 Salt River N.W.T. Can.
Saltrou Haiti see Belle-Anse
165 O2 Saltsjöbaden Sweden
163 P6 Saltvik Åland Fin.
256 D12 Saltville VA U.S.A.
103 E10 Saltwater Lagoon South I. N.Z.
161 W8 Saltyki Rus. Fed.
100 □2 Saluafata Samoa
255 G8 Saluda SC U.S.A.
256 I11 Saluda VA U.S.A.
255 F8 Saluda r. SC U.S.A.
213 N8 Saludecio Italy
115 C4 Saluebesar i. Indon.
115 C5 Saluekecil i. Indon.
115 C4 Salue Timpaus, Selat sea chan. Indon.
212 E5 Saluggia Italy
144 G3 Sālūk, Kūh-e mt. Iran
138 E7 Salumbar Rajasthan India
137 H3 Salur Andhra Prad. India
212 E5 Salussola Italy
212 C6 Saluzzo Italy
151 H6 Şälvä Azer.
205 R8 Salvacañete Spain
206 D5 Salvada Port.
205 N3 Sálvada, Sierra mts Spain
284 E2 Salvador Arg.
278 F5 Salvador Brazil
204 F8 Salvador Port.
261 J11 Salvador, Lake LA U.S.A.
282 E1 Salvador Mazza Arg.
185 H8 Salvagnac France
206 F3 Salvaleón Spain
278 C2 Salvaterra Brazil
206 B2 Salvaterra de Magos Port.
204 G9 Salvaterra do Extremo Port.
268 G5 Salvatierra Mex.
205 P3 Salvatierra Spain
206 F4 Salvatierra de los Barros Spain
206 G2 Salvatierra de Santiago Spain
265 V3 Salvation Creek r. UT U.S.A.
217 O4 Salve Italy
185 G6 Salviac France
204 B4 Sálvora, Illa de i. Spain
147 J3 Salwah Saudi Arabia
147 J3 Salwah, Dawḩat b. Qatar/Saudi Arabia
130 B6 Salween r. China
118 C6 Salween r. Myanmar
151 D6 Salyamaç Turkey
151 J6 Salyan Azer.
Sal'yany Azer. see Salyan
271 □7 Salybia Trin. and Tob.
256 B11 Salyersville KY U.S.A.
201 K4 Salza r. Austria
200 G3 Salzach r. Austria/Ger.
201 I4 Salza-Stausee resr Austria
191 D6 Salzbergen Ger.
234 C5 Salzbrunn Namibia
200 H4 Salzburg Austria
200 H5 Salzburg land Austria
191 J6 Salzgitter Ger.
190 J4 Salzhausen Ger.
191 I6 Salzhemmendorf Ger.
201 I4 Salzkammergut reg. Austria
191 G7 Salzkotten Ger.
193 E7 Salzmünde Ger.
192 D5 Salzwedel Ger.
190 K5 Salzwedel-Diesdorf park Ger.
195 O4 Salzweg Ger.
230 A4 Sam Gabon
138 C6 Sam Rajasthan India
118 G5 Sam, Nam r. Laos/Vietnam
270 F3 Samá Cuba
196 E3 Sama r. Pol.
Šamac Bos.-Herz. see Bosanski Šamac
147 N4 Şamad Oman
185 D8 Samadet France
119 E8 Samae San, Laem i. Thai.
128 D1 Samagaltay Rus. Fed.
146 G1 Samāh well Saudi Arabia
Samaida Iran see Someydeh
276 E4 Samaipata Bol.
133 F10 Samaixung Xizang China
116 F5 Samak, Tanjung pt Indon.
228 C3 Samakoulou Mali
114 E8 Samal i. Phil.
100 □2 Samalae'ulu Samoa
116 B2 Samalanga Sumatera Indon.
117 H4 Samalantan Kalimantan Indon.
266 F2 Samalayuca Mex.
114 C9 Samales Group is Phil.
244 E5 Samalga Pass sea channel AK U.S.A.
136 H4 Samalkot Andhra Prad. India
225 F2 Samālūţ Egypt
271 I4 Samaná Dom. Rep.
138 F4 Samana Punjab India
271 I4 Samaná, Cabo c. Dom. Rep.
270 G2 Samana Cay i. Bahamas
Samanala mt. Sri Lanka see Sri Pada
148 G5 Samandağı Turkey
145 L3 Samangān prov. Afgh.
124 T4 Samani Japan
274 B4 Samaniego Col.
221 J2 Samanlı Dağları mts Turkey
225 F2 Samannūd Egypt
249 F3 Samaqua r. Que. Can.
Samar Kazakh. see Samarskoye
114 E6 Samar i. Phil.
142 D1 Samara Rus. Fed.
142 D1 Samara r. Rus. Fed.
159 O5 Samara r. Ukr.
Samarahan Sarawak Malaysia see Sri Aman
113 L9 Samarai P.N.G.
Samara Oblast admin. div. Rus. Fed. see Samarskaya Oblast'
212 F4 Samarate Italy
122 K5 Samarga Rus. Fed.
274 E3 Samariapo Venez.
220 E7 Samarias, Ethnikos Drymos nat. park Greece
201 O8 Samarica Croatia
117 L5 Samarinda Kalimantan Indon.
143 O3 Samarka Karagandinskaya Oblast' Kazakh.
122 I6 Samarka Rus. Fed.
Samarkand Uzbek. see Samarqand
Samarkand, Pik mt. Tajik. see Samarqand, Qullai
Samarkand Oblast admin. div. Uzbek. see Samarqand
Samarobriva France see Amiens
143 L8 Samarqand Uzbek.
143 L8 Samarqand admin. div. Uzbek.
145 M2 Samarqand, Qullai mt. Tajik.
Samarqand Wiloyati admin. div. Uzbek. see Samarqand
149 K6 Sāmarrā' Iraq
114 E6 Samar Sea g. Phil.
142 C1 Samarskaya Oblast' admin. div. Rus. Fed.
143 T3 Samarskoye Vostochnyy Kazakhstan Kazakh.
159 S7 Samarskoye Rus. Fed.
158 D2 Samary Ukr.
129 N4 Samarz Nei Mongol China
145 N7 Samasata Pak.
214 B9 Samassi Sardegna Italy
139 J7 Samastipur Bihar India
185 F9 Samatan France
115 G4 Samate Papua Indon.
214 C9 Samatzai Sardegna Italy
275 F6 Samaúma Brazil
151 J5 Şamaxı Azer.
230 D4 Samba Équateur Dem. Rep. Congo

231 E6 Samba Maniema Dem. Rep. Congo
117 J5 Samba r. Indon.
138 E3 Samba Jammu and Kashmir India
231 B7 Samba Cajú Angola
204 G6 Sambade Port.
278 D3 Sambaiba Brazil
228 B3 Sambaïlo Guinea
117 L4 Sambaliung mts Indon.
139 I9 Sambalpur Orissa India
117 I6 Sambar, Tanjung pt Indon.
117 H4 Sambas Kalimantan Indon.
Sambat Ukr. see Kyiv
199 L5 Sâmbăta Romania
235 □K2 Sambava Madag.
159 S6 Sambek Rostovskaya Oblast' Rus. Fed.
159 S6 Sambek Rostovskaya Oblast' Rus. Fed.
Sambe-san vol. Japan see Sanbe-san
139 M6 Sambha Arun. Prad. India
138 G5 Sambhal Uttar Prad. India
138 E6 Sambhar Rajasthan India
138 E6 Sambhar Lake India
215 Q10 Sambiase Italy
115 C4 Sambiat Sulawesi Indon.
158 C4 Sambir Ukr.
117 M4 Sambit i. Indon.
231 C8 Sambo Angola
115 A5 Sambo Sulawesi Barat Indon.
205 L6 Samboal Spain
117 L5 Samboja Kalimantan Indon.
119 H8 Sâmbor Cambodia
Sambor Ukr. see Sambir
119 H8 Sâmbor Dam Cambodia
285 I4 Samborombón r. Arg.
285 I4 Samborombón, Bahía b. Arg.
197 J5 Samborzec Pol.
187 F8 Sambre r. Belgium/France
Sambu Japan see Sanbu
216 E8 Sambuca di Sicilia Sicilia Italy
213 K7 Sambuca Pistoiese Italy
183 K8 Sambuco Italy
216 G8 Sambughetti, Monte mt. Sicilia Italy
123 F10 Samch'ŏk S. Korea
Samch'ŏnp'o S. Korea see Sach'on
140 E2 Samdi Dag mt. Turkey
212 H2 Samedan Switz.
127 M1 Samegawa Japan
118 B4 Sameikkon Myanmar
204 F8 Sameiro Port.
178 C2 Samer France
191 D6 Samern Ger.
151 E3 Samerts'khle, Mt'a Georgia
205 J2 Sames Spain
161 X4 Samet' Rus. Fed.
119 E8 Samet, Ko i. Thai.
231 F7 Samfya Zambia
147 K9 Samḩah i. Yemen
147 L7 Samḩān, Jabal mts Oman
158 I4 Samhorodok Kyivs'ka Oblast' Ukr.
158 H4 Samhorodok Vinnyts'ka Oblast' Ukr.
220 B4 Sami Kefallonia Greece
138 C8 Sami Gujarat India
145 J8 Sami Pak.
115 C3 Samia, Tanjung pt Indon.
204 G5 Samil Port.
146 F2 Samīrah Saudi Arabia
204 H5 Samir de los Caños Spain
274 C6 Samiria r. Peru
Samirum Iran see Yazd-e Khvāst
146 F7 Sāmitah Saudi Arabia
159 N6 Samiylivka Ukr.
127 H2 Samizu Japan
123 F8 Samjiyŏn N. Korea
130 A3 Samka Xizang China
151 F3 Samkhret' Oset'i reg. Georgia
151 H5 Şämkir Azer.
151 H5 Şämkirçay r. Azer.
150 F1 Samköy Turkey
221 I3 Şamlı Turkey
217 L2 Sammichele di Bari Italy
146 C3 Samnah oasis Saudi Arabia
212 I2 Samnaun Switz.
200 B5 Samnaungruppe mts Austria
Sam Neua Laos see Xam Nua
224 B3 Samnū Libya
204 D3 Samo r. Spain
100 □2 Samoa country S. Pacific Ocean
290 H7 Samoa Basin sea feature Pacific Ocean
Samoa i Sisifo country S. Pacific Ocean see Samoa
284 B2 Samo Alto Chile
210 E3 Samobor Croatia
201 M8 Samoborska Gora hills Croatia
156 H3 Samoded Rus. Fed.
182 J4 Samoëns France
213 K6 Samoggia r. Italy
219 L8 Samokov Bulg.
212 G3 Samolaco Italy
158 F4 Samoluskivtsi Ukr.
160 K3 Samolva Rus. Fed.
206 B3 Samora Correia Port.
198 G3 Šamorín Slovakia
221 H5 Samos Samos Greece
221 H5 Samos i. Greece
204 F3 Samos Spain
116 C3 Samosir i. Indon.
Samothrace i. Greece see Samothraki
221 G2 Samothraki Samothraki Greece
221 G2 Samothraki i. Greece
219 N7 Samovodene Bulg.
157 H6 Samoylovka Rus. Fed.
228 E5 Sampa Côte d'Ivoire
284 E3 Sampacho Arg.
115 A5 Sampaga Sulawesi Barat Indon.
117 J8 Sampang Jawa Indon.
208 E5 Samper de Calanda Spain
212 C6 Sampeyre Italy
216 H10 Sampieri Sicilia Italy
179 K6 Sampigny France
117 J6 Sampit Kalimantan Indon.
117 J6 Sampit r. Indon.
117 J6 Sampit, Teluk b. Indon.
115 C6 Sampolawa Sulawesi Indon.
157 H5 Sampur Rus. Fed.
231 E7 Sampwe Dem. Rep. Congo
119 G7 Samran, Huai r. Thai.
261 H10 Sam Rayburn Reservoir TX U.S.A.
228 E5 Samreboe Ghana
160 L3 Samro, Ozero l. Rus. Fed.
Samrong Cambodia see Phumĭ Sâmraông
133 F11 Samsang Xizang China
118 F4 Sam Sao, Phou mts Laos/Vietnam
164 J4 Sämsjön l. Sweden
164 G6 Samsø i. Denmark
164 G6 Samsø Bælt sea chan. Denmark
118 G5 Sâm Sơn Vietnam
199 L4 Şamşud Romania
148 H3 Samsun Turkey
193 E6 Samswegen Ger.
143 Q6 Samsy Kazakh.
192 H2 Samtens Ger.
138 G7 Samthar Uttar Prad. India
151 D3 Samtredia Georgia
106 E5 Samuel, Mount hill N.T. Austr.
214 B8 Samugheo Sardegna Italy
119 E10 Samui, Ko i. Thai.
127 J5 Samukawa Japan
116 □ Samulun, Pulau i. Sing.
145 O6 Samundri Pak.
151 J4 Samur Azer.
151 J4 Samur r. Azer./Rus. Fed.
151 J4 Samur-Abşeron Kanalı canal Azer.
Samutlu Turkey see Temelli
119 E8 Samut Prakan Thai.
119 E8 Samut Sakhon Thai.
119 E8 Samut Songkhram Thai.
133 J12 Samyai Xizang China
228 D3 San Mali
197 J5 San r. Pol.
118 F5 San, Phou mt. Laos
119 H8 San, Tônlé r. Cambodia
210 F3 Sana r. Bos.-Herz.
146 G8 Şan'ā' Yemen
146 G8 Şan'ā' governorate Yemen

232 E2 Sanaag admin. reg. Somalia
204 H4 Sanabria reg. Spain
127 H3 Sanada Japan
205 Q4 San Adrián Spain
204 C2 San Adrián, Cabo c. Spain
286 X2 SANAE IV research stn Antarctica
229 H6 Sanaga r. Cameroon
126 F5 Sanage Japan
138 G7 Sanagir Madh. Prad. India
San Agostín FL U.S.A. see St Augustine
284 E2 San Agustín Arg.
238 □3f San Agustín Gran Canaria Canary Is
274 B4 San Agustín Col.
114 F8 San Agustin, Cape Mindanao Phil.
274 B4 San Agustín, Parque Arqueológico tourist site Col.
205 M7 San Agustín de Guadalix Spain
168 D11 Sanaigmore Argyll and Bute, Scotland U.K.
244 G5 Sanak AK U.S.A.
244 G5 Sanak Island AK U.S.A.
146 G4 Sanām Saudi Arabia
204 D4 San Amaro Spain
276 A6 San Ambrosio, Isla i. Islas de los Desventurados S. Pacific Ocean
115 D5 Sanana Maluku Indon.
144 B4 Sanandaj Iran
228 D3 Sanando Mali
264 L3 San Andreas CA U.S.A.
199 K6 Sânandrei Romania
276 D3 San Andrés Bol.
274 C3 San Andrés Col.
267 O9 San Andrés Guat.
114 E5 San Andres Phil.
270 C7 San Andrés, Isla de i. Caribbean Sea
207 L4 San Andrés, Sierra de mts Spain
285 H4 San Andrés de Giles Arg.
204 I3 San Andrés del Rabanedo Spain
268 D6 San Andrés Ixtlán Mex.
263 K10 San Andres Mountains NM U.S.A.
269 L7 San Andrés Tuxtla Mex.
270 F8 San Ángel Col.
261 E10 San Angelo TX U.S.A.
228 D3 Sanankoroba Mali
264 J4 San Anselmo CA U.S.A.
204 G2 San Antolín Spain
268 G4 San Antón de los Martínez Mex.
282 D3 San Antonio Catamarca Arg.
284 D3 San Antonio San Luis Arg.
266 □O9 San Antonio Belize
276 D3 San Antonio Bol.
282 C2 San Antonio Atacama Chile
284 B3 San Antonio Valparaíso Chile
266 □P10 San Antonio Hond.
268 G2 San Antonio San Luis Potosí Mex.
269 H2 San Antonio Tamaulipas Mex.
274 C5 San Antonio Peru
114 C4 San Antonio Luzon Phil.
209 C8 San Antonio Spain
285 I2 San Antonio Uru.
263 K10 San Antonio NM U.S.A.
261 F11 San Antonio TX U.S.A.
264 L6 San Antonio r. CA U.S.A.
261 G11 San Antonio r. TX U.S.A.
271 L8 San Antonio Venez.
285 I5 San Antonio, Cabo c. Arg.
270 A3 San Antonio, Cabo c. Cuba
209 F10 San Antonio, Cabo de c. Spain
264 O7 San Antonio, Mount CA U.S.A.
205 K2 San Antonio, Punta de pt Spain
114 A7 San Antonio Bay Palawan Phil.
285 H4 San Antonio de Areco Arg.
274 D3 San Antonio de Caparo Venez.
271 L8 San Antonio del Golfo Venez.
266 A2 San Antonio del Mar Mex.
282 D2 San Antón de los Cobres Arg.
266 □P10 San Antonio de Oriente Hond.
229 G7 San Antonio de Palé Equat. Guinea
275 E2 San Antonio de Tamanaco Venez.
269 H5 San Antonio Escabedo Mex.
283 D6 San Antonio Este Arg.
269 I2 San Antonio Nogalar Mex.
283 D6 San Antonio Oeste Arg.
269 I3 San Antonio Rayón Mex.
264 L6 San Antonio Reservoir CA U.S.A.
269 H4 San Antonio Tancoyol Mex.
183 H10 Sanary-sur-Mer France
205 O3 San Asensio Spain
100 □4a Sanat i. Chuuk Micronesia
258 D4 Sanatoga PA U.S.A.
285 H6 San Augustín Arg.
284 D2 San Augustín de Valle Fértil Arg.
261 H10 San Augustine TX U.S.A.
147 N4 Sanāw Oman
147 J7 Sanaw Yemen
138 F8 Sanawad Madh. Prad. India
145 N6 Sanawan Pak.
269 K9 San Baltasar Loxicha Mex.
268 G3 San Bartolo Mex.
238 □3c San Bartolomé Lanzarote Canary Is
205 K9 San Bartolomé de las Abiertas Spain
206 E6 San Bartolomé de la Torre Spain
205 K7 San Bartolomé de Pinares Spain
238 □3f San Bartolomé de Tirajana Gran Canaria Canary Is
215 O5 San Bartolomeo in Galdo Italy
269 H6 San Bartolo Morelos Mex.
269 I5 San Bartolo Tutotepec Mex.
284 E3 San Basilio Arg.
214 C8 San Basilio Sardegna Italy
San Baudillo de Llobregat Cataluña Spain see Sant Boi de Llobregat
215 L2 San Benedetto del Tronto Italy
213 J5 San Benedetto Po Italy
252 D7 San Benedicto, Isla i. Mex.
267 O9 San Benito Guat.
207 J3 San Benito Spain
261 G12 San Benito TX U.S.A.
264 K5 San Benito r. CA U.S.A.
206 E3 San Benito de la Contienda Spain
264 L5 San Benito Mountain CA U.S.A.
264 O7 San Bernardino CA U.S.A.
212 G3 San Bernardino, Passo di pass Switz.
265 O7 San Bernardino Mountains CA U.S.A.
114 E5 San Bernardino Strait Phil.
285 I5 San Bernardo Arg.
284 B3 San Bernardo Chile
266 G5 San Bernardo Mex.
268 B2 San Bernardo de Milipas Chico Mex.
125 J11 Sanbe-san vol. Japan
213 M4 San Biagio di Callalta Italy
216 F8 San Biago Platani Sicilia Italy
282 D3 San Blas Arg.
268 B4 San Blas Nayarit Mex.
266 E4 San Blas Sinaloa Mex.
266 □T13 San Blas, Archipiélago de is Panama
255 E11 San Blas, Cape FL U.S.A.
266 □T13 San Blas, Cordillera de mts Panama
217 □ San Blas, Il-Bajja ta' b. Gozo Malta
213 K5 San Bonifacio Italy
276 D3 San Borja Bol.
260 H4 Sanborn IA U.S.A.
257 □N5 Sanbornville NH U.S.A.
Sanbu Guangdong China see Kaiping
127 L4 Sanbu Japan
267 I4 San Buenaventura Mex.
235 G3 Sança Moz.
213 M2 San Candido Italy
208 E4 San Caprasio hill Spain
284 E2 San Carlos Córdoba Arg.
284 C3 San Carlos Mendoza Arg.
282 D2 San Carlos Salta Arg.
284 B5 San Carlos Chile
San Carlos Equat. Guinea see Luba
267 I3 San Carlos Coahuila Mex.
269 I1 San Carlos Tamaulipas Mex.
266 □Q12 San Carlos Nic.
277 F5 San Carlos Para.
277 F5 San Carlos r. Para.
114 C4 San Carlos Luzon Phil.
114 D6 San Carlos Negros Phil.
282 G4 San Carlos Uru.
265 V8 San Carlos AZ U.S.A.
274 E4 San Carlos Amazonas Venez.
274 E3 San Carlos Apure Venez.
274 D2 San Carlos Cojedes Venez.
285 G2 San Carlos Centro Arg.
283 C6 San Carlos de Bariloche Arg.
285 G5 San Carlos de Bolívar Arg.
San Carlos de la Rápita Spain see Sant Carles de la Ràpita
207 M3 San Carlos del Valle Spain
274 D2 San Carlos del Zulia Venez.
265 V8 San Carlos Indian Reservation res. AZ U.S.A.
265 V8 San Carlos Lake AZ U.S.A.
285 G2 San Carlos Sur Arg.
214 H2 San Casciano dei Bagni Italy
213 K8 San Casciano in Val di Pesa Italy
217 O3 San Cataldo Puglia Italy
216 F9 San Cataldo Sicilia Italy
285 H6 San Cayetano Arg.
204 I5 San Cebrián de Castro Spain
San Celoni Spain see Sant Celoni
182 B2 Sancergues France
182 B2 Sancerre France
182 B2 Sancerrois, Collines du hills France
217 O3 San Cesario di Lecce Italy
182 J2 Sancey-le-Grand France
128 I9 Sancha Gansu China
129 L7 Sancha Shanxi China
Sanchahe Jilin China see Fuyu
130 F5 Sancha He r. Guizhou China
132 D7 Sanchakou Xinjiang China
178 C7 Sancheville France
269 N7 Sánchez Magallanes Mex.
138 F8 Sanchi Madh. Prad. India
205 K7 Sanchidrián Spain
118 F4 San Chien Pau mt. Laos
268 F7 Sanchiqueo Mex.
215 Q6 San Chirico Nuovo Italy
215 Q7 San Chirico Raparo Italy
206 E6 Sancho, Embalse de resr Spain
138 C7 Sanchor Rajasthan India
129 L8 Sanchuan He r. China
156 I4 Sanchursk Rus. Fed.
204 E4 San Cibráo das Viñas Spain
216 E8 San Cipirello Sicilia Italy
215 M6 San Cipriano d'Aversa Italy
269 H4 San Ciro de Acosta Mex.
284 B4 San Clemente Chile
207 O2 San Clemente Spain
264 O8 San Clemente CA U.S.A.
207 N5 San Clemente, Embalse de resr Spain
285 I5 San Clemente del Tuyú Arg.
264 N9 San Clemente Island CA U.S.A.
Sanclêr Wales U.K. see St Clears
204 F4 San Clodio Spain
182 B3 Sancoins France
114 F7 Sanco Point Mindanao Phil.
282 F2 San Cosme Arg.
204 F1 San Cosme Spain
215 Q7 San Costantino Albanese Italy
213 O8 San Costanzo Italy
267 N10 San Crisóbal Verapez Guat.
285 G2 San Cristóbal Arg.
276 D5 San Cristóbal Potosí Bol.
277 E3 San Cristóbal Santa Cruz Bol.
274 C5 San Cristóbal Col.
270 H4 San Cristóbal Dom. Rep.
269 I5 San Cristóbal Hidalgo Mex.
268 F4 San Cristóbal Jalisco Mex.
100 □6 San Cristobal i. Solomon Is
274 C3 San Cristóbal Venez.
274 □ San Cristóbal, Isla i. Islas Galápagos Ecuador
266 □P11 San Cristóbal, Volcán vol. Nic.
San Cristóbal de Cea Spain see Cea
204 I4 San Cristóbal de Entreviñas Spain
268 D4 San Cristóbal de la Barranca Mex.
238 □3a San Cristóbal de la Laguna Tenerife Canary Is
267 M9 San Cristóbal de las Casas Mex.
205 K6 San Cristóbal de la Vega Spain
265 S9 San Cristobal Wash watercourse AZ U.S.A.
215 P6 San Croce, Monte mt. Italy
206 G8 Sancti Petri, Isla i. Spain
285 F3 Sancti Spíritu Arg.
270 D3 Sancti Spíritus Cuba
270 D3 Sancti Spíritus prov. Cuba
204 H7 Sancti-Spíritus Spain
207 I3 Sancti-Spíritus Spain
179 K5 Sancy France
164 C2 Sand Norway
237 K4 Sand r. Free State S. Africa
235 F4 Sand r. Limpopo S. Africa
126 B6 Sanda Japan
122 I7 Sandagou Rus. Fed.
117 I5 Sandai Kalimantan Indon.
168 E12 Sanda Island Scotland U.K.
117 M2 Sandakan Sabah Malaysia
117 M2 Sandakan, Pelabuhan inlet Malaysia
139 L6 Sandakphu Peak Sikkim India
205 N2 Sandamendi Spain
212 E6 San Damiano d'Asti Italy
212 C7 San Damiano Macra Italy
191 K11 Sand am Main Ger.
119 H8 Sândăn Cambodia
163 I6 Sandane Norway
200 H7 San Daniele del Friuli Italy
212 I5 San Daniele Po Italy
219 L9 Sandanski Bulg.
Sandaohezi Xinjiang China see Shawan
228 C3 Sandaré Mali
192 F5 Sandau Ger.
168 L4 Sanday i. Scotland U.K.
168 K4 Sanday Sound sea chan. Scotland U.K.
171 M7 Sandbach Cheshire, England U.K.
191 J10 Sandberg Ger.
236 C8 Sandberg S. Africa
190 L1 Sandby Denmark
136 C7 Sand Cay rf India
162 L4 Sanddøla r. Norway
190 F4 Sande Ger.
163 H6 Sande Sogn og Fjordane Norway
164 G2 Sande Vestfold Norway
204 D6 Sande Port.
164 G2 Sandefjord Norway
164 G2 Sandefjord (Torp) airport Norway
164 B2 Sandeid Norway
104 □3 Sandell Bay S. Pacific Ocean
162 P2 Sandelva Norway
217 K4 San Demetrio Corone Italy
215 L3 San Demetrio ne Vestini Italy
287 D2 Sandercock Nunataks nunataks Antarctica
265 W6 Sanders AZ U.S.A.
193 F7 Sandersdorf Ger.
191 I8 Sandershausen (Niestetal) Ger.
193 E7 Sandersleben Ger.
261 D10 Sanderson TX U.S.A.
255 F9 Sandersville GA U.S.A.
190 J3 Sandesneben Ger.
108 F5 Sandfire Roadhouse W.A. Austr.
164 D2 Sandfloeggi mt. Norway
256 E10 Sand Fork WV U.S.A.
168 K4 Sandgarth Orkney, Scotland U.K.
194 F3 Sandhausen Ger.
168 G13 Sandhead Dumfries and Galloway, Scotland U.K.
260 G2 Sand Hill r. MN U.S.A.
260 D5 Sand Hills NE U.S.A.
162 M3 Sandhornøy i. Norway
173 K5 Sandhurst Bracknell Forest, England U.K.
138 H6 Sandi Uttar Prad. India
276 C3 Sandia Peru
204 E4 Sandiás Spain
266 G3 San Diego Chihuahua Mex.
263 J11 San Diego Chihuahua Mex.
268 G4 San Diego Guanajuato Mex.
264 O9 San Diego CA U.S.A.
261 F12 San Diego TX U.S.A.
283 D9 San Diego, Cabo c. Arg.
266 E2 San Diego, Sierra mts Mex.
269 H6 San Diego Alcalá Mex.
275 E2 San Diego de Cabrutica Venez.
269 H3 San Dieguito Mex.
221 L4 Sandıklı Turkey
138 H6 Sandila Uttar Prad. India
255 □2 Sandilands Village New Prov. Bahamas
178 D8 Sandillon France
109 C8 Sandiman, Mount hill W.A. Austr.
217 □ San Dimitri, Il-Ponta ta' pt Gozo Malta
116 D6 Sanding i. Indon.
269 M9 San Dionisio del Mar Mex.
250 D3 Sand Island WI U.S.A.
244 F3 Sand Islands AK U.S.A.
156 L2 Sandivey r. Rus. Fed.
192 I5 Sandkrug Ger.
201 K2 Sandl Austria
248 C4 Sand Lake Ont. Can.
247 M5 Sand Lake l. Ont. Can.
164 B3 Sandnes Norway
168 □M2 Sandness Shetland, Scotland U.K.
162 L3 Sandnessjøen Norway
Sandø i. Faroe Is see Sandoy
204 H7 Sando Spain
231 D7 Sandoa Dem. Rep. Congo
197 J5 Sandomierska, Kotlina basin Pol.
197 J5 Sandomierz Pol.
219 N4 Sândominic Romania
215 O3 San Domino, Isola i. Italy
274 B4 Sandoná Col.
217 N3 San Donaci Italy
213 N4 San Donà di Piave Italy
217 O3 San Donato di Lecce Italy
215 Q8 San Donato di Ninea Italy
212 G5 San Donato Milanese Italy
215 L4 San Donato Val di Comino Italy
199 J5 Sándorfalva Hungary
106 F6 Sandover watercourse N.T. Austr.
161 T3 Sandovo Rus. Fed.
287 G2 Sandow, Mount Antarctica
Sandoway Myanmar see Thandwè
173 J6 Sandown Isle of Wight, England U.K.
236 C10 Sandown Bay S. Africa
166 D1 Sandoy i. Faroe Is
162 I5 Sandøy Norway
172 D7 Sandplace Cornwall, England U.K.
244 G5 Sand Point AK U.S.A.
262 F2 Sandpoint ID U.S.A.
168 B9 Sandray i. Scotland U.K.
173 L4 Sandridge Hertfordshire, England U.K.
106 G8 Sandringham Qld Austr.
237 P2 Sand River Reservoir Swaziland
198 G6 Šandrovac Croatia
162 N4 Sandsele Sweden
171 P4 Sandsend North Yorkshire, England U.K.
245 O5 Sandspit B.C. Can.
261 G7 Sand Springs OK U.S.A.
264 N2 Sand Springs Salt Flat NV U.S.A.
237 K3 Sandspruit r. S. Africa
190 G4 Sandstedt Ger.
256 H11 Sandston VA U.S.A.
109 E9 Sandstone W.A. Austr.
250 B3 Sandstone MN U.S.A.
264 N7 Sandstone Peak hill CA U.S.A.
265 T9 Sand Tank Mountains AZ U.S.A.
237 M2 Sandton S. Africa
258 E3 Sandts Eddy PA U.S.A.
130 F6 Sandu Guizhou China
131 I6 Sandu Hunan China
136 E5 Sandur Karnataka India
251 L6 Sandusky MI U.S.A.
256 C7 Sandusky OH U.S.A.
256 C7 Sandusky Bay OH U.S.A.
236 C7 Sandveld mts S. Africa
237 J3 Sandveld Nature Reserve S. Africa
236 B2 Sandverhaar Namibia
164 G2 Sandvika Akershus Norway
162 L5 Sandvika Nord-Trøndelag Norway
165 M1 Sandviken Sweden
236 I9 Sandvlakte S. Africa
173 O5 Sandwich Kent, England U.K.
257 O7 Sandwich MA U.S.A.
249 J2 Sandwich Bay Nfld and Lab. Can.
234 B4 Sandwich Bay Namibia
Sandwich Island Vanuatu see Éfaté
Sandwich Islands N. Pacific Ocean see Hawai'ian Islands
139 M8 Sandwip Bangl.
139 M8 Sandwip Channel Bangl.
173 L3 Sandy Bedfordshire, England U.K.
262 I6 Sandy UT U.S.A.
257 □P4 Sandy r. ME U.S.A.
247 K4 Sandy Bay Sask. Can.
207 □ Sandy Bay b. Gibraltar
270 □ Sandy Bay Jamaica
102 I2 Sandy Bay b. North I. N.Z.
104 □3 Sandy Bay b. S. Pacific Ocean
238 □2b Sandy Bay b. St Helena
109 G12 Sandy Bight b. W.A. Austr.
107 N8 Sandy Cape Qld Austr.
105 J9 Sandy Cape Tas. Austr.
106 G5 Sandy Creek r. Qld Austr.
170 H5 Sandygate Isle of Man
259 I2 Sandy Hook CT U.S.A.
256 B10 Sandy Hook KY U.S.A.
259 G4 Sandy Hook pt NJ U.S.A.
108 F3 Sandy Island W.A. Austr.
Sandy Island Rodrigues I. Mauritius see Sables, Île aux
145 J3 Sandykgaçy Turkm.
145 J2 Sandykly Gumy des. Turkm.
246 H4 Sandy Lake Alta Can.
247 M4 Sandy Lake Ont. Can.
247 M4 Sandy Lake l. Ont. Can.
238 □2c Sandy Point Tristan da Cunha S. Atlantic Ocean
271 □2 Sandy Point Town St Kitts and Nevis
255 E9 Sandy Springs GA U.S.A.
256 D10 Sandyville WV U.S.A.
182 G3 Sâne r. France
187 I9 Sanem Lux.
204 I3 San Emiliano Spain
285 G4 San Enrique Arg.
277 F6 San Estanislao Para.
266 □Q10 San Esteban Hond.
269 J3 San Esteban Mex.
266 C3 San Esteban, Isla i. Mex.
269 J6 San Esteban Cuautempan Mex.
205 N5 San Esteban de Gormaz Spain
204 I7 San Esteban de la Sierra Spain
284 B5 San Fabián de Alico Chile
215 P6 San Fele Italy
215 M5 San Felice a Cancello Italy
215 K5 San Felice Circeo Italy
204 G7 San Felices de los Gallegos Spain
213 K6 San Felice sul Panaro Italy
284 B3 San Felipe Chile
266 B2 San Felipe Baja California Mex.
266 F4 San Felipe Chihuahua Mex.
268 F4 San Felipe Guanajuato Mex.
205 Q8 San Felipe mt. Spain
274 D2 San Felipe Venez.
270 B3 San Felipe, Cayos de is Cuba
265 Q8 San Felipe Creek watercourse CA U.S.A.
268 E1 San Felipe de Teyra Mex.
268 E1 San Felipe Nuevo Mercurio Mex.
269 K8 San Felipe Usila Mex.
San Feliú de Guíxols Spain see Sant Feliu de Guíxols
San Feliú de Pallarols Spain see Sant Feliu de Pallerols
San Feliú Sasssera Spain see Sant Feliu Sasserra
276 A6 San Félix, Isla i. Islas de los Desventurados S. Pacific Ocean
217 J7 San Ferdinando Italy
215 Q5 San Ferdinando di Puglia Italy
285 H4 San Fernando Arg.
284 B4 San Fernando Chile
266 B3 San Fernando Baja California Mex.
267 J5 San Fernando Tamaulipas Mex.
114 C3 San Fernando Luzon Phil.
114 C4 San Fernando Luzon Phil.
206 G8 San Fernando Spain
271 □7 San Fernando Trin. and Tob.
264 N7 San Fernando CA U.S.A.
274 E3 San Fernando de Apure Venez.
274 E3 San Fernando de Atabapo Venez.
205 M8 San Fernando de Henares Spain
215 Q9 San Fili Italy
217 I7 San Filippo del Mela Sicilia Italy
204 F6 Sanfins do Douro Port.
163 L5 Sånfjället nationalpark nat. park Sweden
109 C9 Sanford r. W.A. Austr.
255 G11 Sanford FL U.S.A.
257 □O5 Sanford ME U.S.A.
250 J6 Sanford MI U.S.A.
255 H8 Sanford NC U.S.A.
245 K3 Sanford, Mount AK U.S.A.
271 □7 San Francique Trin. and Tob.
285 F2 San Francisco Arg.
276 D3 San Francisco Bol.
268 F2 San Francisco San Luis Potosí Mex.
269 H3 San Francisco San Luis Potosí Mex.
266 C2 San Francisco Sonora Mex.
264 J4 San Francisco CA U.S.A.
263 J10 San Francisco r. NM U.S.A.
270 H8 San Francisco Venez.
274 A4 San Francisco, Cabo de c. Ecuador
282 C2 San Francisco, Paso de pass Arg.
266 C4 San Francisco, Sierra mts Mex.
264 J4 San Francisco Bay inlet CA U.S.A.
269 K10 San Francisco Cozoaltepec Mex.
285 G6 San Francisco de Bellocq Arg.
266 G4 San Francisco de Conchos Mex.
282 E3 San Francisco del Chañar Arg.
284 D3 San Francisco del Monte de Oro Arg.
266 G4 San Francisco del Oro Mex.
277 E5 San Francisco del Parapetí Bol.
268 F4 San Francisco del Rincón Mex.
270 H4 San Francisco de Macorís Dom. Rep.
284 B3 San Francisco de Mostazal Chile
283 D8 San Francisco de Paula, Cabo c. Arg.
269 I2 San Francisco el Alto Mex.
266 □O11 San Francisco Gotera El Salvador
209 H10 San Francisco Javier Spain
216 H7 San Fratello Sicilia Italy
212 C6 Sanfront Italy
231 B7 Sanga Angola
231 F6 Sanga Dem. Rep. Congo
284 B3 San Gabriel Chile
274 B4 San Gabriel Ecuador
266 C3 San Gabriel, Punta pt Mex.
269 J7 San Gabriel Chilac Mex.
264 N7 San Gabriel Mountains CA U.S.A.
151 K5 Sängäçal Burnu pt Azer.
Sangachaly Azer. see Sanqaçal
116 F6 Sangaigerong Sumatera Indon.
130 B3 Sa'ngain Xizang China
204 D8 Sangalhos Port.
276 A3 San Gallan, Isla i. Peru
136 F5 Sangam Andhra Prad. India
136 C4 Sangameshwar Mahar. India
136 D3 Sangamner Mahar. India
260 J5 Sangamon r. IL U.S.A.
145 K5 Sangan Afgh.
144 H4 Sangān Khorāsān Iran
144 I4 Sangān Iran
145 L7 Sangan Pak.
145 K5 Sangān, Kūh-e mt. Afgh.
153 N3 Sangar Rus. Fed.
205 L7 Sangarcía Spain
228 B4 Sangaréa Guinea
136 F4 Sangareddi Andhra Prad. India
228 B4 Sangarédi Guinea
138 E5 Sangaria Rajasthan India
117 L5 Sangasanga Kalimantan Indon.
114 B9 Sanga Sanga i. Phil.
Sangasso Mali see Zangasso
160 J4 Sangaste Estonia
230 A5 Sangatanga Gabon
178 C2 Sangatte France
214 B8 San Gavino Monreale Sardegna Italy
274 B5 Sangay, Parque Nacional nat. park Ecuador
274 B5 Sangay, Volcán vol. Ecuador
133 K11 Sangba Xizang China
163 M5 Sångbäcken Sweden
144 H4 Sang Bast Iran
229 I5 Sangbé Cameroon
114 C8 Sangboy Islands Phil.
145 I5 Sangbur Afgh.
115 A8 Sangeang i. Indon.
128 I6 Sangejing Nei Mongol China
215 J2 San Gemini Italy
285 G3 San Genaro Arg.
Sangenjo Galicia Spain see Sanxenxo
217 O2 San Gennaro, Capo c. Italy
219 M4 Sângeorgiu de Pădure Romania
219 M3 Sângeorz-Băi Romania
128 B5 Sangequanzi Xinjiang China
219 M4 Sânger Romania
264 M5 Sanger CA U.S.A.
Sângera Moldova see Sîngera
Sângerei Moldova see Sîngerei
257 J6 Sangerfield NY U.S.A.
193 D8 Sangerhausen Ger.
285 F6 San German Arg.
271 □1 San Germán Puerto Rico
183 K7 San Germano Chisone Italy
284 D3 San Gerónimo Arg.
Sang-e Sar Iran see Mehdīshahr
129 N6 Sanggan He r. China
117 M9 Sanggar, Teluk b. Sumbawa Indon.
117 I4 Sanggau Kalimantan Indon.
117 H4 Sanggauledo Kalimantan Indon.
115 D2 Sanggeluhang i. Indon.
129 R8 Sanggou Wan b. China
229 F4 Sangha Burkina
230 B4 Sangha admin. reg. Congo
230 C5 Sangha r. Congo
230 C4 Sangha-Mbaéré pref. C.A.R.
145 M8 Sanghar Pak.
145 N6 Sanghar r. Pak.
213 K2 San Giacomo, Cima mt. Italy
212 I2 San Giacomo, Lago di l. Italy
274 C3 San Gil Col.
128 D1 Sangilen, Nagor'ye mts Rus. Fed.
217 □ San Giljan Malta
213 K9 San Gimignano Italy
145 K5 Sangīn Afgh.
205 R7 San Ginés mt. Spain
215 K1 San Ginesio Italy
215 L5 San Giorgio a Liri Italy
213 N3 San Giorgio della Richinvelda Italy
213 O4 San Giorgio di Nogaro Italy
213 K6 San Giorgio di Piano Italy
217 M3 San Giorgio Ionico Italy
215 N5 San Giorgio la Molara Italy
217 K3 San Giorgio Lucano Italy
215 O7 San Giovanni a Piro Italy
212 H4 San Giovanni Bianco Italy
214 H1 San Giovanni d'Asso Italy
216 F8 San Giovanni Gemini Sicilia Italy
215 K4 San Giovanni Incarico Italy
212 I5 San Giovanni in Croce Italy
217 L5 San Giovanni in Fiore Italy
213 K6 San Giovanni in Persiceto Italy
213 K5 San Giovanni Lupatoto Italy
215 P4 San Giovanni Rotondo Italy
214 B9 San Giovanni Suegiu Sardegna Italy
215 M3 San Giovanni Teatino Italy
213 L8 San Giovanni Valdarno Italy
138 E9 Sangir Mahar. India
115 D2 Sangir i. Indon.
115 D2 Sangir, Kepulauan is Indon.
217 K2 San Giuliano, Lago di l. Italy
212 I8 San Giuliano Terme Italy
216 E8 San Giuseppe Jato Sicilia Italy
216 H2 San Giuseppe Vesuviano Italy
213 M8 San Giustino Italy
Sangiyn Dalay Mongolia see Erdenedalay
128 F2 Sangiyn Dalay Nuur salt l. Mongolia
123 F10 Sangju S. Korea
117 J7 Sangkapura Jawa Indon.
115 A6 Sangkarang, Kepulauan is Indon.
119 F8 Sângke, Stœ̆ng r. Cambodia
119 D7 Sangkhla Buri Thai.
117 M4 Sangkulirang Kalimantan Indon.
117 M4 Sangkulirang, Teluk b. Indon.
145 O6 Sangla Pak.
136 D4 Sangli Mahar. India
145 N3 Sanglich Afgh.
205 K2 San Glorio, Puerto de pass Spain
229 H6 Sangmélima Cameroon
138 G4 Sangnam Hima. Prad. India
133 K12 Sangngagqoiling Xizang China
235 F4 Sango Zimbabwe
138 F7 Sangod Rajasthan India
213 L8 San Godenzo Italy
136 D4 Sangole Mahar. India
209 C12 Sangonera r. Spain
264 P7 San Gorgonio Mountain CA U.S.A.
212 F2 San Gottardo, Passo del pass Switz.
115 F2 Sangowo Maluku Indon.
Sangpi Sichuan China see Xiangcheng
130 A4 Sang Qu r. Xizang China
263 K7 Sangre de Cristo Range mts CO U.S.A.
285 F4 San Gregorio Arg.
284 B5 San Gregorio Chile
285 I3 San Gregorio Uru.
282 G4 San Gregorio de Polanca Uru.
215 O6 San Gregorio Magno Italy
215 M5 San Gregorio Matese Italy
271 □7 Sangre Grande Trin. and Tob.
205 K9 Sangrera r. Spain
133 K12 Sangri Xizang China
215 N3 Sangro r. Italy
197 L1 Sangrūda Lith.
130 B2 Sangruma Qinghai China
138 E4 Sangrur Punjab India
133 H12 Sangsang Xizang China
139 M8 Sangu r. Bangl.
246 H4 Sangudo Alta Can.
277 F2 Sangue r. Brazil
205 R3 Sangüesa Spain
212 G5 San Guiliano Milanese Italy
285 G2 San Guillermo Arg.
282 C3 San Guillermo, Parque Nacional nat. park Arg.
208 H4 San Guim de Freixenet Spain
214 B4 Sanguinaires, Îles i. Corse France
185 B7 Sanguinet France
213 K5 Sanguinetto Italy
144 G7 Sangū'īyeh Iran
285 H2 San Gustavo Arg.
145 N2 Sangvor Tajik.
Sangyuan Hebei China see Wuqiao
130 H4 Sangzhi Hunan China
228 D4 Sanhala Côte d'Ivoire
Sanhe Guizhou China see Sandu
129 Q1 Sanhe Nei Mongol China
131 K3 Sanhezhen Anhui China
266 D5 San Hilario Mex.
San Hilario Sacalm Spain see Sant Hilari Sacalm
266 B4 San Hipólito, Punta pt Mex.
225 F2 Sanhūr Egypt
255 F12 Sanibel Island FL U.S.A.
285 H5 San Ignacio Arg.
267 O9 San Ignacio Belize
276 D3 San Ignacio Beni Bol.
276 E4 San Ignacio Santa Cruz Bol.
277 E4 San Ignacio Santa Cruz Bol.
266 C3 San Ignacio Baja California Mex.
266 C4 San Ignacio Baja California Sur Mex.
268 A2 San Ignacio Sinaloa Mex.
266 D2 San Ignacio Sonora Mex.
277 F6 San Ignacio Para.
274 B6 San Ignacio Peru
266 C4 San Ignacio, Laguna l. Mex.
248 E1 Sanikiluaq Nunavut Can.
205 M7 San Ildefonso Spain
114 D3 San Ildefonso Peninsula Luzon Phil.
126 A4 Sanin-kaigan Kokuritsu-kōen nat. park Japan
237 N5 Sanipas pass S. Africa
Sanirajak Nunavut Can. see Hall Beach
284 D3 San Isidro Arg.
269 K10 San Isidro Oaxaca Mex.
269 I1 San Isidro Tamaulipas Mex.
268 E1 San Isidro Zacatecas Mex.
205 J2 San Isidro, Puerto de pass Spain
269 L10 San Isidro Chacalapa Mex.
269 K10 San Isidro del Palmar Mex.
219 K3 Sanislău Romania
192 F2 Sanitz Ger.
224 C3 Sāniyat al Fawākhir well Libya
274 C2 San Jacinto Col.
114 D5 San Jacinto Masbate Phil.
264 P8 San Jacinto CA U.S.A.
264 P8 San Jacinto Peak CA U.S.A.
139 K8 Sanjai r. Jharkhand India
285 H2 San Jaime Arg.
285 H2 San Javier Arg.
276 D3 San Javier Beni Bol.
277 E4 San Javier Santa Cruz Bol.
269 H5 San Javier Mex.
209 D12 San Javier Spain
285 H3 San Javier Uru.
284 B4 San Javier de Loncomilla Chile
145 M6 Sanjawi Pak.
144 C3 Sanjbod Iran
268 G8 San Jerónimo Guerrero Mex.
268 D2 San Jerónimo Zacatecas Mex.
276 B1 San Jerónimo Peru
269 K9 San Jerónimo Taviche Mex.
Sanjiang Guangdong China see Liannan
130 G6 Sanjiang Guangxi China
Sanjiang Guizhou China see Jinping
129 R5 Sanjiangkou Liaoning China
Sanjiaocheng Qinghai China see Haiyan
130 H4 Sanjiaoping Hunan China
131 M4 Sanjie Zhejiang China
125 P9 Sanjō Japan
276 D3 San Joaquín Bol.
269 H5 San Joaquin Mex.
277 F6 San Joaquin Para.
264 L5 San Joaquin CA U.S.A.
264 K3 San Joaquin r. CA U.S.A.
264 L4 San Joaquin Valley CA U.S.A.
261 D8 San Jon NM U.S.A.
208 F6 San Jordi Spain
284 D3 San Jorge San Luis Arg.
285 G2 San Jorge Santa Fé Arg.
100 □6 San Jorge i. Solomon Is
283 D7 San Jorge, Golfo de g. Arg.
San Jorge, Golfo de g. Spain see Sant Jordi, Golf de
206 E3 San Jorge de Alor Spain
284 C3 San José Arg.
274 D4 San José Col.
266 □Q13 San José Costa Rica
268 G1 San José Mex.
114 C4 San Jose Luzon Phil.
114 C5 San Jose Mindoro Phil.
114 C5 San Jose Mindoro Phil.
207 O7 San José Andalucía Spain
285 I4 San José dept Uru.
285 I4 San José r. Uru.
264 K4 San Jose CA U.S.A.
263 L9 San Jose NM U.S.A.
263 K9 San Jose watercourse NM U.S.A.
274 E2 San José Venez.
283 D7 San José, Cabo c. Arg.
285 I2 San José, Cuchilla de hills Uru.
283 D6 San José, Golfo g. Arg.
266 D5 San José, Isla i. Mex.
284 C3 San José, Volcán vol. Chile
268 G6 San José Allende Mex.
267 N8 San José Carpizo Mex.
268 G4 San José de Alburquerque Mex.
275 F2 San José de Amacuro Venez.
266 F3 San José de Bavicora Mex.
114 C6 San Jose de Buenavista Panay Phil.
277 E4 San José de Chiquitos Bol.
266 D4 San José de Comondú Mex.
285 H2 San José de Feliciano Arg.
268 G3 San José de Gallinas Mex.
268 E3 San José de Gracia Mex.
266 C4 San José de Gracia Baja California Sur Mex.
268 D6 San José de Gracia Michoacán Mex.
266 F4 San José de Gracia Sinaloa Mex.
266 D3 San José de Gracia Sonora Mex.
271 K9 San José de Guaribe Venez.
284 C2 San José de Jáchal Arg.
266 E5 San Joséde la Brecha Mex.
285 F2 San José de la Dormida Arg.
285 G3 San José de la Esquina Arg.
283 B5 San José de la Mariquina Chile
268 D7 San José de la Montaña Mex.
284 E2 San José de las Salinas Arg.
282 E2 San José del Boquerón Arg.
266 E6 San José del Cabo Mex.
274 C4 San José del Guaviare Col.
284 E3 San José del Morro Arg.
269 J9 San José del Progreso Mex.
206 H7 San José del Valle Spain
284 B3 San José de Maipó Chile
285 I4 San José de Mayo Uru.
270 H4 San José de Ocoa Dom. Rep.
274 D3 San José de Ocuné Col.
263 I12 San José de Primas Mex.
268 G1 San José de Raíces Mex.
268 D1 San José de Reyes Mex.
268 G4 San José Iturbide Mex.
133 D8 Sanju Xinjiang China
284 C2 San Juan Arg.
284 C2 San Juan prov. Arg.
277 E4 San Juan Bol.
238 □3a San Juan Tenerife Canary Is
274 B2 San Juan Col.
274 B3 San Juan r. Col.
266 □R12 San Juan r. Costa Rica/Nic.
270 C3 San Juan mt. Cuba
270 H4 San Juan Dom. Rep.
266 F4 San Juan Chihuahua Mex.
267 I4 San Juan Coahuila Mex.
268 E2 San Juan Zacatecas Mex.
268 E4 San Juan r. Mex.
269 L7 San Juan r. Mex.
276 B3 San Juan Peru
114 E6 San Juan Leyte Phil.
114 F7 San Juan Mindanao Phil.
271 □1 San Juan Puerto Rico
205 O2 San Juan Spain
206 G3 San Juan r. Spain
271 □7 San Juan Trin. and Tob.
264 L6 San Juan r. CA U.S.A.
265 V4 San Juan r. UT U.S.A.
275 E3 San Juan Venez.
271 □1 San Juan, Bahía de b. Puerto Rico
283 E9 San Juan, Cabo c. Arg.
229 H6 San Juan, Cabo c. Equat. Guinea
205 L8 San Juan, Embalse de resr Spain
266 □O11 San Juan, Punta pt El Salvador
207 I7 San Juan, Sierra de hills Spain
269 J8 San Juan Achiutla Mex.
277 F6 San Juan Bautista Para.
276 □ San Juan Bautista S. Pacific Ocean
264 K5 San Juan Bautista CA U.S.A.
269 I9 San Juan Bautista lo de Soto Mex.
269 J8 San Juan Bautista Suchitepec Mex.
269 K7 San Juan Bautista Tuxtepec Mex.
264 O8 San Juan Capistrano CA U.S.A.
266 □P10 San Juancito Hond.
268 B5 San Juan de Abajo Mex.
206 G6 San Juan de Aznalfarache Spain
274 C2 San Juan de Cesar Col.
268 E1 San Juan de Guadalupe Mex.
270 F8 San Juan de Guía, Cabo de c. Col.
283 B6 San Juan dela Costa Chile
208 D3 San Juan de la Peña, Sierra de mts Spain
269 H6 San Juan de las Huertas Mex.
266 □R12 San Juan del Norte Nic.
266 □R12 San Juan del Norte, Bahía de b. Nic.
274 D2 San Juan de los Cayos Venez.
268 E4 San Juan de los Lagos Mex.
274 E2 San Juan de los Morros Venez.
268 D4 San Juan de los Potreros Mex.
206 F6 San Juan del Puerto Spain
266 G5 San Juan del Río Durango Mex.
269 L8 San Juan del Río Oaxaca Mex.
269 H5 San Juan del Río Querétaro Mex.
266 □Q12 San Juan del Sur Nic.
283 E9 San Juan de Salvamento Arg.
269 L8 San Juan Evangelista Mex.
266 C4 San Juanico, Punta pt Mex.
262 C2 San Juan Islands WA U.S.A.
266 F4 San Juanito Mex.
268 A4 San Juanito, Isla i. Mex.
269 J7 San Juan Ixcaquixtla Mex.
267 N10 San Juan Ixcoy Guat.
269 L9 San Juan Lachixila Mex.
269 L8 San Juan Mazatlán Mex.
269 K9 San Juan Mixtepec Mex.
263 K8 San Juan Mountains CO U.S.A.
269 K8 San Juan Tepeuxila Mex.
270 B2 San Juan y Martínez Cuba
133 D8 Sanju He watercourse China
283 D8 San Julián Arg.
268 E4 San Julian Mex.
208 D6 San Just mt. Spain
285 G2 San Justo Arg.
204 H4 San Justo de la Vega Spain
118 C4 Sanka Myanmar
228 C4 Sankanbiriwa mt. Sierra Leone
228 C4 Sankarani r. Côte d'Ivoire/Guinea
136 E8 Sankarankovil Tamil Nadu India
136 D4 Sankeshwar Karnataka India
139 J8 Sankh r. Jharkhand India
138 E5 Sankhu Rajasthan India
144 G3 Sankhvāst Iran
Sankosh r. Bhutan see Sunkosh Chhu
138 I9 Sankra Chhattisgarh India
138 C6 Sankra Rajasthan India
201 M4 Sankt Aegyd am Neuwalde Austria
201 K6 Sankt Andrä Austria
201 O4 Sankt Andrä am Zicksee Austria
191 K7 Sankt Andreasberg Ger.
201 M6 Sankt Anna am Aigen Austria
200 B5 Sankt Anton am Arlberg Austria
201 L4 Sankt Anton an der Jeßnitz Austria
191 D9 Sankt Augustin Ger.
194 E6 Sankt Blasien Ger.
193 G9 Sankt Egidien Ger.
201 K4 Sankt Gallen Austria
212 G1 Sankt Gallen Switz.
212 G1 Sankt Gallen canton Switz.
200 A5 Sankt Gallenkirch Austria
193 E9 Sankt Gangloff Ger.
201 J6 Sankt Georgen am Längsee Austria
201 K3 Sankt Georgen am Walde Austria
201 J3 Sankt Georgen an der Gusen Austria
201 H4 Sankt Georgen im Attergau Austria
201 K6 Sankt Georgen im Lavanttal Austria
194 E5 Sankt Georgen im Schwarzwald Ger.
201 H4 Sankt Gilgen Austria
191 E10 Sankt Goar Ger.
191 E10 Sankt Goarshausen Ger.
Sankt Gotthard Hungary see Szentgotthárd
194 C3 Sankt Ingbert Ger.
201 J6 Sankt Jakob im Rosental Austria
201 M5 Sankt Jakob im Walde Austria
200 F6 Sankt Jakob in Defereggen Austria
201 J5 Sankt Johann am Tauern Austria
200 H5 Sankt Johann im Pongau Austria
201 L6 Sankt Johann im Saggautal Austria
200 G6 Sankt Johann im Walde Austria
200 F4 Sankt Johann in Tirol Austri
194 D2 Sankt Julian Ger.
201 K6 Sankt Kanzian am Klopeine Austria
201 J5 Sankt Lambrecht Austria
201 L3 Sankt Leonhard am Forst A
201 M2 Sankt Leonhard am Horner Austria
200 C5 Sankt Leonhard im Pitztal Austria
201 H4 Sankt Lorenz Austria
200 H6 Sankt Lorenzen im Gitschta Austria
200 G6 Sankt Lorenzen im Lesacht Austria
201 L5 Sankt Lorenzen im Mürztal Austria
201 J5 Sankt Lorenzen ob Murau Austria
201 L5 Sankt Marein im Mürztal A
201 J6 Sankt Margareten im Roser Austria
190 H3 Sankt Margarethen Ger.
201 M5 Sankt Margarethen an der Austria
201 K5 Sankt Margarethen bei Knittelfeld Austria
201 O4 Sankt Margarethen im Burgenland Austria
194 E5 Sankt Märgen Ger.
201 J3 Sankt Marien Austria
201 I3 Sankt Marienkirchen an de Polsenz Austria
201 K2 Sankt Martin Niederösterrei Austria
201 H5 Sankt Martin Salzburg Austr
201 N6 Sankt Martin an der Raab A
201 J3 Sankt Martin im Mühlkreis Austria
201 L6 Sankt Martin im Sulmtal A
201 N5 Sankt Michael im Burgenla Austria
201 I5 Sankt Michael im Lungau Austria
201 L5 Sankt Michael in Obersteiermark Austria
190 H3 Sankt Michaelisdonn Ger.
212 H2 Sankt Moritz Switz.
212 D3 Sankt Niklaus Switz.
201 L6 Sankt Nikolai im Saustal A
201 J5 Sankt Nikolai im Sölktal Au
201 K2 Sankt Oswald bei Freistadt Austria
201 L6 Sankt Oswald ob Eibiswald Austria
195 O4 Sankt Oswald-Riedlhütte G
201 J4 Sankt Pankraz Austria
200 G3 Sankt Pantaleon Austria
201 K6 Sankt Paul im Lavanttal Au
194 E5 Sankt Peter Ger.
200 H3 Sankt Peter am Hart Austri
201 J5 Sankt Peter am Kammersb Austria
201 M6 Sankt Peter am Ottersbach Austria
161 N2 Sankt-Peterburg Rus. Fed.
201 L5 Sankt Peter-Freienstein Au
201 L6 Sankt Peter im Sulmtal Au
201 K3 Sankt Peter in der Au Austr
190 G2 Sankt Peter-Ording Ger.
Sankt Petersburg Rus. Fed. Sankt-Peterburg
201 M3 Sankt Pölten Austria
200 G3 Sankt Radegund Austria
201 M5 Sankt Ruprecht an der Raal Austria
201 K6 Sankt Stefan Austria
201 I6 Sankt Stefan im Gailtal Au
201 M6 Sankt Stefan im Rosental A
201 K5 Sankt Stefan ob Leoben Au
201 L6 Sankt Stefan ob Stainz Aus
200 G4 Sankt Ulrich am Pillersee A
201 J3 Sankt Ulrich bei Steyr Aust
201 J6 Sankt Urban Austria
201 K3 Sankt Valentin Austria
201 M6 Sankt Veit am Vogau Austri
201 J6 Sankt Veit an der Glan Aust
201 M3 Sankt Veit an der Gölsen A
200 H5 Sankt Veit im Pongau Austr
200 F6 Sankt Veit in Defereggen A
194 C3 Sankt Wendel Ger.
195 M5 Sankt Wolfgang Ger.
201 H4 Sankt Wolfgang im Salzkammergut Austria
138 F2 Sanku Jammu and Kashmir
230 D5 Sankuru prov. Dem. Rep. Co
231 D6 Sankuru r. Dem. Rep. Cong
217 □ San Lawrenz Gozo Malta
277 F5 San Lázaro Para.
266 C5 San Lázaro, Cabo c. Mex.
266 E6 San Lázaro, Sierra de mts M
213 K7 San Lazzaro di Savena Italy
264 J4 San Leandro CA U.S.A.
213 M8 San Leo Italy
216 F8 San Leonardo r. Sicilia Italy
205 N5 San Leonardo de Yagüe Sp
213 K2 San Leonardo in Passiria It
148 I5 Şanlıurfa Turkey
150 H1 Şanlıurfa prov. Turkey
282 F3 San Lorenzo Corrientes Arg.
285 G3 San Lorenzo Santa Fé Arg.
276 D3 San Lorenzo Beni Bol.
276 D2 San Lorenzo Pando Bol.
276 D5 San Lorenzo Tarija Bol.
274 B4 San Lorenzo Ecuador
266 □P11 San Lorenzo Hond.
217 J8 San Lorenzo Italy
266 F3 San Lorenzo Mex.
276 C2 San Lorenzo Peru
205 O4 San Lorenzo mt. Spain
274 A5 San Lorenzo, Cabo c. Ecuad
214 D9 San Lorenzo, Capo c. Sarde Italy
266 C3 San Lorenzo, Isla i. Mex.
276 A3 San Lorenzo, Isla i. Peru
283 B7 San Lorenzo, Monte mt. Arg./Chile
212 D8 San Lorenzo al Mare Italy
215 Q8 San Lorenzo Bellizzi Italy
269 K8 San Lorenzo Cacaotepec M
207 L4 San Lorenzo de Calatrava
205 L7 San Lorenzo de El Escorial
205 P9 San Lorenzo de la Parrilla
San Lorenzo de Morunys see Sant Llorenç de Morun
213 L2 San Lorenzo di Sebato Ital
213 N8 San Lorenzo in Campo Ital
214 H2 San Lorenzo Nuovo Italy
217 K7 San Luca Italy
206 G7 Sanlúcar de Barrameda Sp
206 E6 Sanlúcar de Guadiana Spai
206 G6 Sanlúcar la Mayor Spain
276 D5 San Lucas Bol.
266 C4 San Lucas Baja California Mex.
266 E6 San Lucas Baja California Mex.
268 G7 San Lucas Michoacán Mex.
266 E6 San Lucas, Cabo c. Mex.
274 C3 San Lucas, Serranía de mts
215 Q9 San Lucido Italy
284 D3 San Luis Arg.
284 D3 San Luis prov. Arg.
276 D2 San Luís Brazil
270 F3 San Luis Cuba
267 O9 San Luis Guat.
268 G8 San Luis Guerrero Mex.
269 M8 San Luis Veracruz Mex.
274 C5 San Luis Peru
265 R9 San Luis AZ U.S.A.
265 U9 San Luis AZ U.S.A.
263 L8 San Luis CO U.S.A.
274 D2 San Luis Venez.
266 B3 San Luís, Isla i. Mex.
265 R9 San Luis, Mesa de plat. Me
284 D3 San Luis, Sierra de mts Arg
269 I9 San Luis Acatlán Mex.
269 K9 San Luis Amatlán Mex.
268 G4 San Luis de la Paz Mex.
282 F2 San Luis del Palmar Arg.
266 D5 San Luis Gonzaga Mex.
266 C2 San Luisito Mex.
264 L6 San Luis Obispo CA U.S.A
264 L6 San Luis Obispo Bay CA U

San Luis Pajón Hond.
San Luis Potosí Mex.
San Luis Potosí state Mex.
San Luis Reservoir CA U.S.A.
San Luis Río Colorado Mex.
Sanluri Sardegna Italy
San Maddalena Vallalta Italy
San Mamede, Serra do mts Spain
San Mamés de Campos Spain
San Mango d'Aquino Italy
San Manuel Arg.
San Manuel Chile
San Manuel AZ U.S.A.
San Marcello Italy
San Marcello Pistoiese Italy
San Marcial, Punta pt Mex.
San Marco, Capo c. Sardegna Italy
San Marco, Capo c. Sicilia Italy
San Marco Argentano Italy
San Marco d'Alunzio Sicilia Italy
San Marco dei Cavoti Italy
San Marco in Lamis Italy
San Marcos Chile
San Marcos Col.
San Marcos Guat.
San Marcos Hond.
San Marcos Guerrero Mex.
San Marcos Jalisco Mex.
San Marcos Peru
San Marcos Spain
San Marcos CA U.S.A.
San Marcos TX U.S.A.
San Marcos r. TX U.S.A.
San Marcos, Isla i. Mex.
San Marino country Europe
San Marino San Marino
San Martín research stn Antarctica
San Martín Catamarca Arg.
San Martín Mendoza Arg.
San Martín r. Bol.
San Martín Mex.
San Martín dept Peru
Sânmartin Romania
San Martin Spain
San Martín, Cabo de c. Spain
San Martín, Lago l. Arg./Chile
San Martín, Volcán vol. Mex.
San Martín Chalchicuautla Mex.
San Martín de Bolaños Mex.
San Martín de la Vega Spain
San Martín de la Vega del Alberche Spain
San Martín de los Andes Arg.
San Martin del Pimpollar Spain
San Martín de Montalbán Spain
San Martín de Pusa Spain
San Martin de Unx Spain
San Martín de Valdeiglesias Spain
San Martín Hidalgo Mex.
San Martino Buon Albergo Italy
San Martino di Castrozza Italy
San-Martino-di-Lota Corse France
San Martino di Lupari Italy
San Martino di Venezze Italy
San Martino in Badia Italy
San Martino in Passiria Italy
San Martino in Pensilis Italy
San Mateo Peru
San Mateo Spain see Sant Mateu
San Mateo CA U.S.A.
San Mateo Venez.
San Mateo de Gállego Spain
San Mateo Ixtatán Guat.
San Matías Bol.
San Matías, Golfo g. Arg.
San Mauricio Venez.
San Mauro Castelverde Sicilia Italy
San Mauro Forte Italy
San Mauro Pascoli Italy
San Mauro Torinese Italy
Sanmen Zhejiang China
San Menaio Italy
Sanmen Wan b. China
Sanmenxia Henan China
San Michele al Tagliamento Italy
San Michele Mondovì Italy
San Michele Salentino Italy
San Miguel Corrientes Arg.
San Miguel San Juan Arg.
San Miguel Bol.
San Miguel r. Bol.
San Miguel r. Col.
San Miguel El Salvador
San Miguel Mex.
San Miguel Panama
San Miguel Peru
San Miguel Luzon Phil.
San Miguel Spain see Sant Miquel de Balansat
San Miguel CA U.S.A.
San Miguel r. CO U.S.A.
San Miguel Venez.
San Miguel Bay Luzon Phil.
San Miguel Coatlán Mex.
San Miguel de Abona Tenerife Canary Is
San Miguel de Allende Mex.
San Miguel de Arroyo Spain
San Miguel de Bernuy Spain
San Miguel de Cruces Mex.
San Miguel Deheti Mex.
San Miguel de Horcasitas r. Mex.
San Miguel de Huachi Bol.
San Miguel de la Sierra Mex.
San Miguel del Monte Arg.
San Miguel del Puerto Mex.
San Miguel de Salinas Spain
San Miguel de Tucumán Arg.
San Miguel do Araguaia Brazil
San Miguel el Alto Mex.
San Miguel Island CA U.S.A.
San Miguel Islands Phil.
San Miguelito Mex.
San Miguelito Panama
San Miguel Octopan Mex.
San Miguel Sola de Vega Mex.
San Miguel Tecuixiapan Mex.
San Millán mt. Spain
San Millán de la Cogolla Spain
Sanming Fujian China
San Miniato Italy
Sanna r. Pol.
Sannan Japan
San Narciso Luzon Phil.
Sannaspos S. Africa
Sannat Gozo Malta
Sannazzaro de'Burgondi Italy
Sanndraigh i. Scotland U.K. see Sandray
Sanni Pak.
Sannicandro di Bari Italy
Sannicandro Garganico Italy
Sannicola Italy
San Nicola, Isole is Italy
San Nicola dell'Alto Italy
San-Nicolao Corse France
San Nicolás Chile
San Nicolás Guerrero Mex.
San Nicolás Tamaulipas Mex.
San Nicolás r. Mex.
San Nicolás Peru
San Nicolas Luzon Phil.
San Nicolás, Bahía b. Peru
San Nicolás de los Agustinos Mex.
San Nicolás de los Arroyos Arg.
San Nicolás del Presidio Mex.
San Nicolás del Puerto Spain
San Nicolás de Tolentino Gran Canaria Canary Is
San Nicolas Island CA U.S.A.
San Nicolás Tolentino Mex.
Sânnicolau Mare Romania
San Nicolò Italy
San Nicolò d'Arcidano Sardegna Italy
San Nicolò Gerrei Sardegna Italy
Sannieshof S. Africa
Sanniki Pol.
Sannio, Monti del mts Italy
Sanniquellie Liberia
124 S6 Sannohe Japan
127 K3 Sano Japan
282 D3 Sañogasta, Sierra de mts Arg.
197 K6 Sanok Pol.
274 C2 San Onofre Col.
283 D9 San Pablo Arg.
276 D5 San Pablo Potosí Bol.
277 E3 San Pablo Santa Cruz Bol.
277 E3 San Pablo r. Bol.
274 D3 San Pablo Col.
269 H5 San Pablo Mex.
114 C4 San Pablo Luzon Phil.
264 J4 San Pablo CA U.S.A.
205 L9 San Pablo de los Montes Spain
San Pablo de Manta Ecuador see Manta
213 K2 San Pancrazio Italy
217 N3 San Pancrazio Salentino Italy
215 O4 San Paolo di Civitate Italy
217 □ San Pawl, Gżejjer ta' is Malta
217 □ San Pawl il-Baħar Malta
217 □ San Pawl-il-Baħar, Il-Bajja ta' b. Malta
285 H3 San Pedro Buenos Aires Arg.
282 D2 San Pedro Catamarca Arg.
284 E2 San Pedro Córdoba Arg.
282 D2 San Pedro Jujuy Arg.
282 G2 San Pedro Misiones Arg.
267 P9 San Pedro Belize
276 D3 San Pedro Beni Bol.
277 E4 San Pedro Santa Cruz Bol.
276 D4 San Pedro r. Bol.
284 B3 San Pedro Santiago Chile
284 B3 San Pedro Valparaíso Chile
228 D5 San-Pédro Côte d'Ivoire
270 D3 San Pedro r. Cuba
266 D6 San Pedro Baja California Sur Mex.
266 F3 San Pedro Chihuahua Mex.
268 B4 San Pedro r. Mex.
263 L12 San Pedro r. Mex.
276 C2 San Pedro Peru
114 C5 San Pedro Mindoro Phil.
207 O3 San Pedro Spain
285 I4 San Pedro Uru.
265 V9 San Pedro watercourse AZ U.S.A.
266 □R13 San Pedro, Punta pt Costa Rica
206 E1 San Pedro, Sierra de mts Spain
268 F4 San Pedro Almoloyan Mex.
268 C4 San Pedro Analco Mex.
269 K9 San Pedro Apóstol Mex.
267 N10 San Pedro Carchá Guat.
264 N8 San Pedro Channel CA U.S.A.
207 J8 San Pedro de Alcántara Spain
274 D3 San Pedro de Arimena Col.
276 C5 San Pedro de Atacama Chile
204 H4 San Pedro de Ceque Spain
263 J12 San Pedro de la Cueva Mex.
205 K7 San Pedro del Arroyo Spain
266 H5 San Pedro de las Colonias Mex.
205 J5 San Pedro de Latarce Spain
274 B6 San Pedro de Lloc Peru
277 F6 San Pedro del Paraná Para.
209 D12 San Pedro del Pinatar Spain
205 M2 San Pedro del Romeral Spain
271 I4 San Pedro de Macorís Dom. Rep.
204 I7 San Pedro de Rozados Spain
277 F6 San Pedro de Ycuamandyyú Para.
269 K9 San Pedro el Alto Mex.
266 D3 San Pedro el Saucito Mex.
205 P4 San Pedro Manrique Spain
266 B2 San Pedro Martir, Parque Nacional nat. park Mex.
269 J10 San Pedro Mixtepec Mex.
266 □O10 San Pedro Sula Hond.
199 J5 Sânpetru Mare Romania
213 K8 San Piero a Sieve Italy
217 H7 San Piero Patti Sicilia Italy
217 I6 San Pietro Isole Lipari Italy
214 A9 San Pietro, Isola di i. Sardegna Italy
200 G6 San Pietro di Cadore Italy
213 J4 San Pietro in Cariano Italy
213 K6 San Pietro in Casale Italy
217 O3 San Pietro Vernotico Italy
265 U2 San Pitch r. UT U.S.A.
212 I6 San Polo d'Enza Italy
213 K6 San Prospero Italy
128 G7 Sanpu Gansu China
151 K5 Sanqaçal Azer.
131 L4 Sanqingshan National Park tourist site China
168 I12 Sanquhar Dumfries and Galloway, Scotland U.K.
274 B4 Sanquianga, Parque Nacional nat. park Col.
208 F4 San Quilez mt. Spain
266 A2 San Quintín, Cabo c. Mex.
214 H1 San Quirico d'Orcia Italy
284 C4 San Rafael Arg.
277 E4 San Rafael Bol.
284 B4 San Rafael Chile
274 D3 San Rafael Col.
268 F2 San Rafael San Luis Potosí Mex.
269 K5 San Rafael Veracruz Mex.
264 J4 San Rafael CA U.S.A.
265 V3 San Rafael r. UT U.S.A.
274 D2 San Rafael Venez.
San Rafael del Moján Venez. see San Rafael
266 □P11 San Rafael del Norte Nic.
208 F6 San Rafael del Río Spain
271 I4 San Rafael del Yuma Dom. Rep.
265 V3 San Rafael Knob mt. UT U.S.A.
264 L7 San Rafael Mountains CA U.S.A.
207 J5 San Rafael Navallana, Embalse de resr Spain
284 D2 San Ramón Arg.
276 D3 San Ramón Beni Bol.
277 E4 San Ramón Santa Cruz Bol.
269 I2 San Ramón Mex.
285 J4 San Ramón Uru.
131 K6 Sanrao Guangdong China
212 D8 San Remo Italy
259 I3 San Remo NY U.S.A.
124 S7 Sanriku Japan
261 E11 San Rodrigo watercourse Mex.
285 G6 San Román Arg.
204 F3 San Román Spain
274 D1 San Román, Cabo c. Venez.
205 K4 San Román de la Cuba Spain
205 K8 San Román de los Montes Spain
207 I8 San Roque Andalucía Spain
204 C2 San Roque Galicia Spain
266 B4 San Roque, Punta pt Mex.
204 D4 San Roque de Crespos Galicia Spain
215 O7 San Rufo Italy
261 F10 San Saba TX U.S.A.
261 F10 San Saba r. TX U.S.A.
185 I6 Sansac-de-Marmiesse France
San Sadurniño Spain see Avenida do Marqués de Figueroa
284 E2 San Salano Arg.
269 J6 San Salvador el Seco Mex.
228 B4 Sansalé Guinea
285 H2 San Salvador Arg.
270 F1 San Salvador i. Bahamas
267 O11 San Salvador El Salvador
269 H1 San Salvador Mex.
274 D5 San Salvador Peru
285 H3 San Salvador r. Uru.
274 □ San Salvador, Isla i. Islas Galápagos Ecuador
205 L3 San Salvador de Cantamunda Spain
282 D2 San Salvador de Jujuy Arg.
214 A8 San Salvatore Sardegna Italy
212 F6 San Salvatore Monferrato Italy
215 M5 San Salvatore Telesino Italy
215 N3 San Salvo Italy
229 F3 Sansané Haoussa Niger
229 F4 Sansanné-Mango Togo
283 C9 San Sebastián Arg.
268 C5 San Sebastián Mex.
271 □1 San Sebastián Puerto Rico
204 D3 San Sebastián hill Spain
283 C9 San Sebastián, Bahía de b. Arg.
204 G4 San Sebastián, Embalse de resr Spain
238 □3a San Sebastián de la Gomera La Gomera Canary Is
205 M7 San Sebastián de los Reyes Spain
269 K9 San Sebastián Río Hondo Mex.
269 J7 San Sebastián Zinacatepec Mex.
212 I6 San Secondo Parmense Italy
213 M8 Sansepolcro Italy
214 H3 San Severa Italy
215 Q7 San Severino Lucano Italy
213 O9 San Severino Marche Italy
215 O4 San Severo Italy
131 M5 Sansha Fujian China
276 C2 San Silvestre Bol.
274 D2 San Silvestre Venez.
265 W9 San Simon AZ U.S.A.
210 F3 Sanski Most Bos.-Herz.
205 P3 Sansol Spain
102 J7 Sanson North I. N.Z.
Sansoral Islands Palau see Sonsorol Islands
215 Q8 San Sosti Italy
214 C9 San Sperate Sardegna Italy
217 L1 San Spirito Italy
271 □2 Sans Toucher mt. Guadeloupe
130 G5 Sansui Guizhou China
128 H3 Sant Mongolia
276 A2 Santa Peru
276 A2 Santa r. Peru
280 C4 Santa Adélia Brazil
206 G2 Santa Amalia Spain
267 O9 Santa Amelia Guat.
285 I2 Santa Ana Entre Ríos Arg.
282 D2 Santa Ana Tucumán Arg.
276 D3 Santa Ana La Paz Bol.
277 E4 Santa Ana Santa Cruz Bol.
277 F4 Santa Ana Santa Cruz Bol.
267 O10 Santa Ana El Salvador
100 □1 Santa Ana Guam
269 H6 Santa Ana México Mex.
268 G1 Santa Ana Nuevo León Mex.
266 D2 Santa Ana Sonora Mex.
100 □6 Santa Ana i. Solomon Is
207 P3 Santa Ana Spain
205 L8 Santa Ana hill Spain
264 O8 Santa Ana CA U.S.A.
208 G4 Santa Ana, Embassament de resr Spain
205 K9 Santa Ana de Pusa Spain
276 D3 Santa Ana de Yacuma Bol.
285 H3 Santa Anita Arg.
266 E6 Santa Anita Baja California Sur Mex.
268 D5 Santa Anita Jalisco Mex.
261 F10 Santa Anna TX U.S.A.
238 □1a Santa Bárbara Terceira Azores
277 F3 Santa Bárbara Mato Grosso Brazil
281 F3 Santa Bárbara Minas Gerais Brazil
284 A5 Santa Bárbara Chile
Santa Bárbara Cuba see La Demajagua
266 □O10 Santa Bárbara Hond.
266 G4 Santa Bárbara Chihuahua Mex.
268 E4 Santa Bárbara Jalisco Mex.
208 G6 Santa Bàrbara Spain
209 C10 Santa Bárbara mt. Spain
207 N6 Santa Bárbara mt. Spain
264 M7 Santa Barbara CA U.S.A.
274 E4 Santa Bárbara Amazonas Venez.
274 D3 Santa Bárbara Barinas Venez.
281 H2 Santa Bárbara, Ilha i. Brazil
238 □1a Santa Barbara, Serra de vol. Terceira Azores
279 B7 Santa Bárbara, Serra de hills Brazil
264 L7 Santa Barbara Channel CA U.S.A.
206 E5 Santa Bárbara de Casa Spain
206 D5 Santa Bárbara de Padrões Port.
280 D5 Santa Bárbara d'Oeste Brazil
279 B9 Santa Barbara do Sul Brazil
264 M8 Santa Barbara Island CA U.S.A.
285 I3 Santa Bernardina Uru.
238 □3f Santa Brígida Gran Canaria Canary Is
205 Q4 Santacara Spain
284 E3 Santa Catalina Arg.
282 C2 Santa Catalina Chile
266 □S13 Santa Catalina Panama
100 □6 Santa Catalina i. Solomon Is
275 F2 Santa Catalina Venez.
264 O8 Santa Catalina, Gulf of CA U.S.A.
266 D5 Santa Catalína, Isla i. Mex.
204 C2 Santa Cataliña de Armada Spain
264 N8 Santa Catalina Island CA U.S.A.
279 C8 Santa Catarina state Brazil
266 B3 Santa Catarina Baja California Mex.
267 I5 Santa Catarina Nuevo León Mex.
269 H4 Santa Catarina San Luis Potosí Mex.
269 I9 Santa Catarina r. Mex.
271 □10 Santa Catarina Curaçao Neth. Antilles
206 C4 Santa Catarina Port.
279 C8 Santa Catarina, Ilha de i. Brazil
217 L6 Santa Caterina dello Ionio Italy
214 B7 Santa Caterina di Pittinuri Sardegna Italy
269 J9 Santa Caterina Juquila Mex.
216 G8 Santa Caterina Villarmosa Sicilia Italy
217 O3 Santa Cesarea Terme Italy
208 D2 Santa Cilia de Jaca Spain
284 A5 Santa Clara Chile
274 D5 Santa Clara Col.
270 D2 Santa Clara Cuba
266 F3 Santa Clara Chihuahua Mex.
268 D1 Santa Clara Durango Mex.
265 P10 Santa Clara r. Mex.
263 K12 Santa Clara r. Mex.
264 K4 Santa Clara CA U.S.A.
265 S4 Santa Clara UT U.S.A.
264 M7 Santa Clara r. CA U.S.A.
206 C5 Santa Clara, Barragem de resr Port.
276 □ Santa Clara, Isla i. S. Pacific Ocean
206 C6 Santa Clara-a-Nova Port.
206 C5 Santa Clara-a-Velha Port.
285 G2 Santa Clara de Buena Vista Arg.
206 D5 Santa Clara de Louredo Port.
285 G2 Santa Clara de Saguier Arg.
264 N7 Santa Clarita CA U.S.A.
274 C5 Santa Clotilde Peru
208 K4 Santa Coloma de Farners Spain
208 J5 Santa Coloma de Gramanet Spain
208 H4 Santa Coloma de Queralt Spain
204 H4 Santa Colomba de Somoza Spain
205 J3 Santa Columba de Curueño Spain
Santa Comba Angola see Waku-Kungo
204 D8 Santa Comba Dão Port.
204 G5 Santa Comba de Rossas Port.
208 K4 Santa Cristina d'Aro Spain
204 I4 Santa Cristina de la Polvorosa Spain
217 I9 Santa Croce, Capo c. Sicilia Italy
216 H10 Santa Croce Camerina Sicilia Italy
215 N5 Santa Croce del Sannio Italy
215 O4 Santa Croce di Magliano Italy
213 J8 Santa Croce sull'Arno Italy
285 E2 Santa Cruz Arg.
283 C8 Santa Cruz prov. Arg.
283 C8 Santa Cruz r. Arg.
271 □9 Santa Cruz Aruba
277 E4 Santa Cruz Bol.
277 E4 Santa Cruz dept Bol.
274 D5 Santa Cruz Amazonas Brazil
281 G3 Santa Cruz Espírito Santo Brazil
275 H5 Santa Cruz Pará Brazil
275 I5 Santa Cruz Pará Brazil
278 G3 Santa Cruz Rio Grande do Norte Brazil
284 B4 Santa Cruz Chile
266 □Q12 Santa Cruz Costa Rica
270 □ Santa Cruz Jamaica
206 □ Santa Cruz Madeira
268 B4 Santa Cruz Nayarit Mex.
268 B4 Santa Cruz Nayarit Mex.
266 D2 Santa Cruz Sonora Mex.
274 C6 Santa Cruz Peru
114 B4 Santa Cruz Luzon Phil.
114 C3 Santa Cruz Luzon Phil.
114 C4 Santa Cruz Luzon Phil.
206 A2 Santa Cruz Port.
205 Q6 Santa Cruz mt. Spain
264 J5 Santa Cruz CA U.S.A.
265 T8 Santa Cruz watercourse AZ U.S.A.
274 D2 Santa Cruz Venez.
274 □ Santa Cruz, Isla i. Islas Galápagos Ecuador
266 D5 Santa Cruz, Isla i. Mex.
283 C8 Santa Cruz, Puerto inlet Arg.
205 Q6 Santa Cruz, Sierra de mts Spain
267 N10 Santa Cruz Barillas Guat.
281 H2 Santa Cruz Cabrália Brazil
280 D4 Santa Cruz das Palmeiras Brazil
204 D7 Santa Cruz da Tapa Port.
205 M2 Santa Cruz de Bezana Spain
205 P3 Santa Cruz de Campézo Spain
280 C2 Santa Cruz de Goiás Brazil
238 □3d Santa Cruz de la Palma La Palma Canary Is
185 C10 Santa Cruz de la Serós Spain
268 D5 Santa Cruz de las Flores Mex.
206 H2 Santa Cruz de la Sierra Spain
205 N9 Santa Cruz de la Zarza Spain
267 N10 Santa Cruz del Quiché Guat.
205 L8 Santa Cruz del Retamar Spain
270 E3 Santa Cruz del Sur Cuba
209 C8 Santa Cruz de Moya Spain
207 M3 Santa Cruz de Mudela Spain
238 □3a Santa Cruz de Tenerife Tenerife Canary Is
266 □P10 Santa Cruz de Yojoa Hond.
280 C5 Santa Cruz do Rio Pardo Brazil
279 B9 Santa Cruz do Sul Brazil
269 K10 Santa Cruz Huatulco Mex.
264 M7 Santa Cruz Island CA U.S.A.
100 □6 Santa Cruz Islands Solomon Is
270 □ Santa Cruz Mountains hills Jamaica
205 K2 Santa de Enol, Peña mt. Spain
214 B9 Santadi Sardegna Italy
215 P8 Santa Domenica Talao Italy
216 H8 Santa Domenica Vittoria Sicilia Italy
281 F3 Santa Efigênia de Minas Brazil
285 G5 Santa Elena Buenos Aires Arg.
285 F2 Santa Elena Córdoba Arg.
285 H2 Santa Elena Entre Ríos Arg.
276 D5 Santa Elena Bol.
274 C6 Santa Elena Peru
207 L4 Santa Elena Spain
275 F3 Santa Elena Venez.
266 □Q12 Santa Elena, Cabo c. Costa Rica
274 A5 Santa Elena, Punta pt Ecuador
204 I4 Santa Elena de Jamuz Spain
285 F4 Santa Eleonora Arg.
216 F9 Santa Elisabetta Sicilia Italy
207 J5 Santaella Spain
205 P4 Santa Engracia Spain
280 D4 Santa Eudóxia Brazil
285 F3 Santa Eufemia Arg.
207 J3 Santa Eufemia Spain
215 Q10 Santa Eufemia, Golfo di g. Italy
Santa Eugenia Galicia Spain see Santa Uxía de Ribeira
267 I3 Santa Eulalia Mex.
206 E2 Santa Eulália Port.
208 C6 Santa Eulalia Aragón Spain
204 I2 Santa Eulalia Asturias Spain
205 J2 Santa Eulalia Asturias Spain
209 I10 Santa Eulalia del Río Spain
204 F2 Santa Eulalia de Oscos Spain
208 J4 Santa Eulàlia de Riuprimer Spain
285 G2 Santa Fé Arg.
285 G2 Santa Fé prov. Arg.
270 B3 Santa Fé Cuba
266 □S13 Santa Fé Panama
114 C5 Santa Fe Phil.
207 L6 Santa Fé Spain
263 L9 Santa Fe NM U.S.A.
274 □ Santa Fé, Isla i. Islas Galápagos Ecuador
Santa Fé de Bogotá Col. see Bogotá
281 E2 Santa Fé de Minas Brazil
280 B4 Santa Fé do Sul Brazil
278 D4 Santa Filomena Brazil
214 H2 Santa Fiora Italy
215 N5 Sant'Agata de'Goti Italy
217 K7 Sant'Agata del Bianco Italy
215 P8 Sant'Agata di Esaro Italy
216 H7 Sant'Agata di Militello Sicilia Italy
215 O5 Sant'Agata di Puglia Italy
213 M8 Sant'Agata Feltria Italy
266 G4 Santa Gertrudis Mex.
214 B8 Santa Giusta Sardegna Italy
214 B8 Santa Giusta, Stagno di l. Sardegna Italy
213 M3 Santa Giustina Italy
213 K6 Sant'Agostino Italy
278 D2 Santa Helena Brazil
280 B2 Santa Helena de Goiás Brazil
130 E3 Santai Sichuan China
132 E4 Santai Xinjiang China
132 I4 Santai Xinjiang China
130 C5 Santai Yunnan China
278 F5 Santa Inês Bahia Brazil
278 D2 Santa Inês Maranhão Brazil
269 K9 Santa Ines Mex.
283 B9 Santa Inés, Isla i. Chile
206 D5 Santa Iria Port.
284 D5 Santa Isabel La Pampa Arg.
285 G3 Santa Isabel Santa Fé Arg.
276 D5 Santa Isabel Bol.
277 E3 Santa Isabel Brazil
274 B5 Santa Isabel Ecuador
Santa Isabel Equat. Guinea see Malabo
269 N9 Santa Isabel Mex.
274 C6 Santa Isabel Peru
271 □1 Santa Isabel Puerto Rico
100 □6 Santa Isabel i. Solomon Is
278 E2 Santa Isabel, Ilha Grande de i. Brazil
266 B2 Santa Isabel, Sierra mts Mex.
276 B4 Santa Isabel de Sihuas Peru
280 A5 Santa Isabel do Ivaí Brazil
284 A5 Santa Juana Chile
280 D3 Santa Juliana Brazil
206 C2 Santa Justa Port.
271 □10 Santa Krus Curaçao Neth. Antilles
213 M6 Sant'Alberto Italy
204 F5 Santalha Port.
208 F3 Santa Liestra y San Quílez Spain
138 C8 Santalpur Gujarat India
213 J9 Santa Luce Italy
285 G3 Santa Lucia Arg.
276 C5 Santa Lucia Chile
Santa Lucía Cuba see Rafael Freyre
274 B5 Santa Lucía Ecuador
267 N10 Santa Lucia Guat.
214 D6 Santa Lucia Sardegna Italy
285 I4 Santa Lucia Uru.
285 I4 Santa Lucia r. Uru.
207 K6 Santa Lucía, Cerro de mt. Spain
285 F3 Santa Lucia, Lago l. Arg.
268 C3 Santa Lucia de la Sierra Mex.
217 I7 Santa Lucia del Mela Sicilia Italy
204 C3 Santa Lucía de Moraña Spain
238 □3f Santa Lucía de Tirajana Gran Canaria Canary Is
264 K5 Santa Lucia Range mts CA U.S.A.
285 G5 Santa Luisa Arg.
238 □1c Santa Luzia Pico Azores
278 D3 Santa Luzia Maranhão Brazil
278 F3 Santa Luzia Paraíba Brazil
228 □ Santa Luzia i. Cape Verde
206 C5 Santa Luzia Beja Port.
206 D6 Santa Luzia Faro Port.
285 F4 Santa Magdalena Arg.
209 F7 Santa Magdalena de Pulpís Spain
214 C5 Santa-Manza, Golfe de b. Corse France
219 P3 Santa Mare Romania
209 L8 Santa Margalida Spain
208 I4 Santa Margarida de Montbui Spain
206 C4 Santa Margarida do Sádão Port.
282 E3 Santa Margarita Arg.
264 L6 Santa Margarita CA U.S.A.
266 D5 Santa Margarita, Isla i. Mex.
216 E8 Santa Margherita di Belice Sicilia Italy
212 G7 Santa Margherita Ligure Italy
282 D2 Santa María Arg.
238 □1 Santa Maria i. Azores
276 E3 Santa María Bol.
275 F5 Santa Maria Amazonas Brazil
275 G5 Santa Maria Amazonas Brazil
275 H5 Santa Maria Pará Brazil
279 B9 Santa Maria Rio Grande do Sul Brazil
282 G3 Santa Maria r. Brazil
228 □ Santa Maria Cape Verde
267 N8 Santa María Mex.
266 F2 Santa María r. Mex.
268 H4 Santa María r. Mex.
208 D3 Santa María Spain
209 D8 Santa María mt. Spain
206 G6 Santa María r. Spain
212 I2 Santa Maria Switz.
264 L7 Santa Maria CA U.S.A.
265 S7 Santa Maria r. AZ U.S.A.
274 E3 Santa María Venez.
282 G4 Santa María, Cabo c. Uru.
235 G5 Santa Maria, Cabo de c. Moz.
206 D7 Santa Maria, Cabo de c. Port.
255 J14 Santa Maria, Cape Bahamas
270 D2 Santa María, Cayo i. Cuba
279 D5 Santa Maria, Chapadão de hills Brazil
282 B5 Santa María, Isla i. Chile
274 □ Santa María, Isla i. Islas Galápagos Ecuador
214 C5 Santa Maria, Isola i. Sardegna Italy
276 B3 Santa María, Punta pt Peru
278 D5 Santa Maria, Serra de hills Brazil
284 C5 Santa María, Volcán vol. Arg.
269 H6 Santa María Ajoloapan Mex.
215 M5 Santa Maria Capua Vetere Italy
278 F4 Santa Maria da Boa Vista Brazil
204 C7 Santa Maria da Feira Port.
278 C4 Santa Maria das Barreiras Brazil
280 C5 Santa Maria da Serra Brazil
278 D5 Santa Maria da Vitória Brazil
205 M2 Santa María de Cayón Spain
266 F4 Santa María de Cuevas Mex.
269 H3 Santa María de Guadalupe Mex.
238 □3f Santa María de Guía Gran Canaria Canary Is
268 C3 Santa María de Huazamota Mex.
205 P6 Santa María de Huertas Spain
275 E2 Santa María de Ipire Venez.
205 J7 Santa María del Berrocal Spain
205 M4 Santa María del Campo Spain
205 P9 Santa María del Campo Rus Spain
215 P8 Santa Maria del Cedro Italy
212 G6 Santa Maria della Versa Italy
269 J7 Santa María del Monte Mex.
266 G5 Santa María del Oro Mex.
268 C4 Santa María del Oro Mex.
204 I4 Santa María del Páramo Spain
268 F2 Santa María del Refugio Mex.
268 G4 Santa María del Río Mex.
205 P7 Santa María del Val Spain
207 P6 Santa María de Nieva Spain
207 O5 Santa María de Nieva, Puerto de pass Spain
215 N7 Santa Maria di Castellabate Italy
217 O4 Santa Maria di Leuca, Capo c. Italy
216 H8 Santa Maria di Licodia Sicilia Italy
214 C2 Santa-Maria-di-Lota Corse France
213 M4 Santa Maria di Sala Italy
281 G2 Santa Maria do Salto Brazil
281 F3 Santa Maria do Suaçuí Brazil
269 L9 Santa María Ecatepec Mex.
269 K10 Santa María Huatulco Mex.
100 □5 Santa María Island Vanuatu
269 J8 Santa María Ixcatlán Mex.
205 L6 Santa María la Real de Nieva Spain
281 F4 Santa Maria Madalena Brazil
212 E3 Santa Maria Maggiore Italy
265 T7 Santa Maria Mountains AZ U.S.A.
214 D8 Santa Maria Navarrese Sardegna Italy
212 G3 Santa Maria Rezzonico Italy
214 B4 Santa-Maria-Siché Corse France
269 K8 Santa María Tlalixtac Mex.
269 J9 Santa María Zaniza Mex.
269 K9 Santa María Zoquitlán Mex.
215 P7 Santa Marina Italy
204 I3 Santa Marina del Rey Spain
216 H6 Santa Marina Salina Isole Lipari Italy
214 H3 Santa Marinella Italy
274 C2 Santa Marta Col.
207 O2 Santa Marta Castilla-La Mancha Spain
206 F3 Santa Marta Extremadura Spain
231 B8 Santa Marta, Cabo de c. Angola
Santa Marta, Serra de mts Brazil see Divisões, Serra das
204 I7 Santa Marta de Tormes Spain
279 C9 Santa Marta Grande, Cabo de c. Brazil
269 M7 Santa Martha, Cerro mt. Mex.
Santa Maura i. Greece see Lefkada
214 B2 Sant'Ambroggio Corse France
264 N7 Santa Monica CA U.S.A.
263 H13 Santa Monica, Pico mt. Mex.
264 N8 Santa Monica Bay CA U.S.A.
264 N7 Santa Monica Mountains National Recreation Area park CA U.S.A.
117 L5 Santan Kalimantan Indon.
274 E4 Santana Amazonas Brazil
278 E5 Santana Bahia Brazil
280 B3 Santana r. Brazil
206 □ Santana Madeira
204 C8 Santana Coimbra Port.
206 D4 Santana Évora Port.
206 A4 Santana Setúbal Port.
219 J4 Sântana Romania
279 B9 Santana da Boa Vista Brazil
206 C5 Santana da Serra Port.
206 D5 Santana de Cambas Port.
278 E2 Santana do Acarau Brazil
278 C4 Santana do Araguaia Brazil
206 C3 Santana do Campo Port.
278 F3 Santana do Cariri Brazil
279 B9 Santana do Livramento Brazil
206 C3 Santana do Mato Port.
281 F3 Santana do Paraíso Brazil
216 G2 Sant'Anastasia Italy
215 J2 Sant'Anatolia di Narco Italy
274 B4 Santander Col.
274 C3 Santander dept Col.
205 M2 Santander Spain
205 L2 Santander prov. Spain
205 M2 Santander, Bahía de b. Spain
217 N3 Sant'Andrea, Isola i. Italy
217 L6 Sant'Andrea Apostolo dello Ionio Italy
214 C9 Sant'Andrea Frius Sardegna Italy
199 K4 Sântandrei Romania
264 K4 Santa Nella CA U.S.A.
217 K6 Sant'Angelo Italy
215 N5 Sant'Angelo a Cupola Italy
215 O7 Sant'Angelo a Fasanella Italy
215 O6 Sant'Angelo dei Lombardi Italy
213 N8 Sant'Angelo in Lizzola Italy
213 M8 Sant'Angelo in Vado Italy
212 G5 Sant'Angelo Lodigiano Italy
128 C4 Santanghu Xinjiang China
Santanilla, Islas is Caribbean Sea see Cisne, Islas del
216 D8 Santa Ninfa Sicilia Italy
265 U8 Santan Mountain hill AZ U.S.A.
281 G5 Sant'Anna, Ilha de i. Brazil
214 B9 Sant'Anna Arresi Sardegna Italy
214 A9 Sant'Antioco Sardegna Italy
214 A9 Sant'Antioco, Isola di i. Sardegna Italy
209 H10 Sant Antoni de Portmany Spain
214 C6 Sant'Antonio di Gallura Sardegna Italy
214 A8 Sant'Antonio di Santadi Sardegna Italy
Santañy Spain see Santanyí
209 L9 Santanyí Spain
205 L8 Santa Olalla Spain
204 G8 Santa Olalla hill Spain
208 I5 Santa Oliva Spain
206 G5 Santa Ollala del Cala Spain
217 I9 Santa Panagia, Capo c. Sicilia Italy
208 K3 Santa Pau Spain
264 M7 Santa Paula CA U.S.A.
137 H3 Santapilly Andhra Prad. India
209 D11 Santa Pola Spain
209 E11 Santa Pola, Cabo de c. Spain
265 U2 Santaquin UT U.S.A.
278 E3 Santa Quitéria Brazil
204 E7 Santar Port.
215 Q7 Sant'Arcangelo Italy
213 M7 Santarcangelo di Romagna Italy
285 F4 Santa Regina Arg.
275 H5 Santarém Brazil
206 B2 Santarém Port.
206 B2 Santarém admin. dist. Port.
270 D2 Santaren Channel Bahamas
277 F1 Santa Rita Mato Grosso Brazil
278 G3 Santa Rita Paraíba Brazil
274 C4 Santa Rita Col.
100 □1 Santa Rita Guam
267 I4 Santa Rita Coahuila Mex.
268 G1 Santa Rita Nuevo León Mex.
274 E2 Santa Rita Guárico Venez.
270 H8 Santa Rita Zulia Venez.
278 D4 Santa Rita de Cassia Brazil
280 A2 Santa Rita do Araguaia Brazil
280 A4 Santa Rita do Pardo Brazil
281 E5 Santa Rita do Sapucaí Brazil
274 D5 Santa Rita do Weil Brazil
282 F3 Santa Rosa Corrientes Arg.
285 E5 Santa Rosa La Pampa Arg.
284 C3 Santa Rosa Mendoza Arg.
283 D6 Santa Rosa Río Negro Arg.
282 D2 Santa Rosa Salta Arg.
276 D3 Santa Rosa Bol.
279 B8 Santa Rosa Rio Grande do Sul Brazil
274 D4 Santa Rosa Col.
274 B5 Santa Rosa Ecuador
268 G6 Santa Rosa Michoacán Mex.
268 G1 Santa Rosa Nuevo León Mex.
267 O8 Santa Rosa Quintana Roo Mex.
269 I4 Santa Rosa San Luis Potosí Mex.
269 J1 Santa Rosa Tamaulipas Mex.
277 F6 Santa Rosa Para.
274 C5 Santa Rosa Loreto Peru
276 C3 Santa Rosa Puno Peru
285 I4 Santa Rosa Uru.
264 J3 Santa Rosa CA U.S.A.
263 L9 Santa Rosa NM U.S.A.
274 E4 Santa Rosa Amazonas Venez.
275 E2 Santa Rosa Anzoátegui Venez.
274 E3 Santa Rosa Apure Venez.
100 □1 Santa Rosa, Mount Guam
265 P8 Santa Rosa and San Jacinto Mountains National Monument nat. park CA U.S.A.
266 □O10 Santa Rosa de Copán Hond.
277 E4 Santa Rosa de la Roca Bol.
284 E3 Santa Rosa del Conlara Arg.
277 E4 Santa Rosa del Palmar Bol.
285 F2 Santa Rosa del Río Primero Arg.
274 C3 Santa Rosa de Osos Col.
274 B4 Santa Rosa de Sucumbio Ecuador
276 D3 Santa Rosa de Vigo Bol.
280 D4 Santa Rosa de Viterbo Brazil
276 C2 Santa Rosa do Purus Acre Brazil
264 L8 Santa Rosa Island CA U.S.A.
268 G5 Santa Rosa Jauregui Mex.
266 C4 Santa Rosalía Mex.
265 P8 Santa Rosa Mountains CA U.S.A.
262 F6 Santa Rosa Range mts NV U.S.A.
265 T8 Santa Rosa Wash watercourse AZ U.S.A.
215 O7 Sant'Arsenio Italy
217 L5 Santa Severina Italy
205 J4 Santas Martas Spain
213 L8 Santa Sofia Italy
206 C3 Santa Sofia Port.
206 D3 Santa Susana Évora Port.
206 C4 Santa Susana Setúbal Port.
282 E2 Santa Sylvina Arg.
285 G3 Santa Teresa Arg.
106 E8 Santa Teresa N.T. Austr.
281 G3 Santa Teresa Brazil
278 C4 Santa Teresa r. Brazil
268 C1 Santa Teresa Durango Mex.
268 C3 Santa Teresa Nayarit Mex.
267 K5 Santa Teresa Tamaulipas Mex.
271 J8 Santa Teresa Venez.
204 I7 Santa Teresa, Embalse de resr Spain
Santa Teresa Aboriginal Land res. N.T. Austr. see Ltyentye Apurte Aboriginal Land
214 C5 Santa Teresa di Gallura Sardegna Italy
217 I8 Santa Teresa di Riva Sicilia Italy
285 I5 Santa Teresita Arg.
278 C4 Santa Terezinha Brazil
199 L4 Santău Romania
238 □3a Santa Úrsula Tenerife Canary Is
204 C3 Santa Uxía de Ribeira Galicia Spain
217 I8 Santa Venerina Sicilia Italy
280 B3 Santa Vitória Brazil
206 C5 Santa Vitória Port.
206 D3 Santa Vitória do Ameixial Port.
282 G4 Santa Vitória do Palmar Brazil
214 C8 Santa Vittoria, Monte mt. Sardegna Italy
264 L7 Santa Ynez r. CA U.S.A.
Santa Ysabel i. Solomon Is see Santa Isabel
208 K4 Sant Benet mt. Spain
208 J5 Sant Boi de Llobregat Spain
208 G6 Sant Carles de la Ràpita Spain
208 J4 Sant Celoni Spain
208 J5 Sant Cugat del Vallès Spain
180 C4 Santec France
264 P9 Santee CA U.S.A.
255 H9 Santee r. SC U.S.A.
215 L2 Sant'Egidio alla Vibrata Italy
214 C9 Sant'Elia, Capo c. Sardegna Italy
215 N4 Sant'Elia a Pianisi Italy
215 L4 Sant Elia Fiumerapido Italy
209 J8 Sant Elm Spain
266 A2 San Telmo Mex.
206 F5 San Telmo Spain
213 P9 Sant'Elpidio a Mare Italy
214 D6 San Teodoro Sardegna Italy
211 F5 Santeramo in Colle Italy
213 L6 Santerno r. Italy
178 D4 Santerre reg. France
205 K3 Santervás de la Vega Spain
208 H5 Santes Creus Spain
217 J7 Sant'Eufemia d'Aspromonte Italy
208 L4 Sant Feliu de Guíxols Spain
208 K3 Sant Feliu de Pallerols Spain
208 J4 Sant Feliu Sasserra Spain
212 E5 Santhià Italy
208 K4 Sant Hilari Sacalm Spain
208 J3 Sant Hipòlit de Voltregà Spain
279 B9 Santiago Brazil
228 □ Santiago i. Cape Verde
284 B3 Santiago Chile
284 B3 Santiago admin. reg. Chile
270 H4 Santiago Dom. Rep.
266 E6 Santiago Baja California Sur Mex.
268 C6 Santiago Colima Mex.
267 I5 Santiago Nuevo León Mex.
268 B1 Santiago r. Mex.
266 □S13 Santiago Panama
277 F6 Santiago Para.
276 B3 Santiago Peru
274 B6 Santiago r. Peru
114 C3 Santiago Luzon Phil.
283 B8 Santiago, Cabo c. Chile
266 □S13 Santiago, Cerro mt. Panama
268 B4 Santiago, Río Grande de r. Mex.
277 F4 Santiago, Sierra de hills Bol.
269 L9 Santiago Astata Mex.
204 F9 Santiago de Alcántara Spain
207 K5 Santiago de Calatrava Spain
274 B6 Santiago de Cao Peru
Santiago de Carbajo Spain see Santiago de Alcántara
204 C3 Santiago de Compostela Spain
204 D4 Santiago de Covelo Spain
270 F3 Santiago de Cuba Cuba
207 N4 Santiago de la Espada Spain
269 J5 Santiago de la Peña Mex.
209 D12 Santiago de la Ribera Spain
204 H9 Santiago del Campo Spain
282 D2 Santiago del Estero Arg.
285 F1 Santiago del Estero prov. Arg.
Santiago de los Caballeros Dom. Rep. see Santiago
238 □3a Santiago del Teide Tenerife Canary Is
274 B5 Santiago de Méndez Ecuador
276 C3 Santiago de Pacaguaras Bol.
206 B4 Santiago do Cacém Port.
206 C3 Santiago do Escoural Port.
268 B4 Santiago Ixcuintla Mex.
269 J9 Santiago Ixtayutla Mex.
269 I8 Santiago Juxtlahuaca Mex.
269 J9 Santiago Minas Mex.
269 J8 Santiago Mitlatengo Mex.
264 O8 Santiago Peak CA U.S.A.
285 F2 Santiago Temple Arg.
269 L8 Santiago Tutla Mex.
269 L7 Santiago Tuxtla Mex.
285 I4 Santiago Vazquez Uru.
268 C1 Santiaguillo, Laguna de l. Mex.
204 I8 Santibáñez de Béjar Spain
205 K3 Santibáñez de la Peña Spain
204 I7 Santibáñez de la Sierra Spain
204 H4 Santibáñez de Vidriales Spain
204 H8 Santibáñez el Bajo Spain
205 M4 Santibáñez Zarzaguda Spain
268 F1 San Tiburcio Mex.
115 B3 Santigi Sulawesi Indon.
115 B3 Santiki, Tanjung pt Indon.
212 I6 Sant'Ilario d'Enza Italy
205 L2 Santillana Spain
205 M7 Santillana, Embalse de resr Spain
274 D2 San Timoteo Venez.
206 G6 Santiponce Spain
Santipur W. Bengal India see Shantipur
212 G1 Säntis mt. Switz.
207 M4 Santisteban del Puerto Spain
205 K6 Santiuste de San Juan Bautista Spain
204 I6 Santiz Spain
208 □ Sant Jaime Mediterráneo Spain
208 G6 Sant Jaume d'Enveja Spain
208 □ Sant Joan Spain
209 E11 Sant Joan d'Alacant Spain
209 I9 Sant Joan de Labritja Spain
208 J3 Sant Joan de les Abadesses Spain
208 I4 Sant Joan de Vilatorrada Spain
208 G6 Sant Jordi, Golf de g. Spain
209 H10 Sant Josep de sa Talaia Illes Balears Spain
208 I3 Sant Julià de Lòria Andorra
208 I3 Sant Llorenç de Morunys Spain
208 I4 Sant Llorenç de Munt, Parc Natural del nature res. Spain
209 L8 Sant Llorenç des Cardassar Spain
208 □ Sant Lluís Spain
208 I4 Sant Martí de Tous Spain
208 I5 Sant Martí Sarroca Spain
208 F7 Sant Mateu Spain
209 H9 Sant Miquel de Balansat Spain
126 A5 Santō Hyōgo Japan
126 D5 Santō Shiga Japan
206 E3 Santo Aleixo Port.
206 E4 Santo Aleixo da Restauração Port.
238 □1c Santo Amaro Pico Azores
238 □1c Santo Amaro São Jorge Azores
278 F5 Santo Amaro Brazil
281 G4 Santo Amaro de Campos Brazil
280 B4 Santo Anastácio Brazil
280 A4 Santo Anastácio r. Brazil
280 D5 Santo André Brazil
206 B4 Santo André Port.
206 B4 Santo André, Lagoa de lag. Port.
279 B9 Santo Angelo Brazil
238 □1c Santo Antão São Jorge Azores
228 □ Santo Antão i. Cape Verde
204 C3 Santo Antoniño Spain
238 □1c Santo António Pico Azores
238 □1b Santo António São Miguel Azores
275 F5 Santo Antônio Amazonas Brazil
278 D3 Santo Antônio Maranhão Brazil
278 G3 Santo Antônio Rio Grande do Norte Brazil
281 F3 Santo Antônio r. Brazil
229 G6 Santo António São Tomé and Príncipe
281 H2 Santo Antônio, Ponta pt Brazil
280 B2 Santo Antônio da Barra Brazil
275 H5 Santo Antônio da Cachoeira Brazil
280 B5 Santo Antônio da Platina Brazil
278 F5 Santo Antônio de Jesus Brazil
277 F3 Santo Antônio de Leverger Brazil
281 F4 Santo Antônio de Pádua Brazil
281 E4 Santo Antônio do Amparo Brazil
274 E5 Santo Antônio do Içá Brazil
281 G2 Santo Antônio do Jacinto Brazil
281 E4 Santo Antônio do Monte Brazil
280 D2 Santo Antônio do Rio Verde Brazil
206 A3 Santo António dos Cavaleiros Port.
Santo António do Zaire Angola see Soyo
277 F4 Santo Corazón Bol.
213 M3 Santo Croce, Lago di l. Italy
285 I5 Santo Domingo Arg.
284 B3 Santo Domingo Chile
270 C2 Santo Domíngo Cuba
270 I4 Santo Domingo Dom. Rep.
267 O10 Santo Domingo Guat.
266 B3 Santo Domingo Baja California Mex.
266 D5 Santo Domingo Baja California Sur Mex.
269 M9 Santo Domingo Oaxaca Mex.
268 F2 Santo Domingo San Luis Potosí Mex.
269 K7 Santo Domingo r. Mex.
266 □Q11 Santo Domingo Nic.
276 C3 Santo Domingo Peru
208 D3 Santo Domingo mt. Spain
Santo Domingo country West Indies see Dominican Republic
Santo Domingo de Garafía La Palma Canary Is see Garafía
205 O4 Santo Domingo de la Calzada Spain
269 K10 Santo Domingo de Morelos Mex.
205 N5 Santo Domingo de Silos Spain
269 K9 Santo Domingo Ozolotepec Mex.
269 L9 Santo Domingo Petapa Mex.
263 K9 Santo Domingo Pueblo NM U.S.A.
269 L9 Santo Domingo Tehuantepec Mex.
281 G4 Santo Eduardo Brazil
206 D6 Santo Estêvão Faro Port.
206 B3 Santo Estêvão Santarém Port.
204 F4 Santo Estevo, Encoro de resr Spain
102 J7 Santoft North I. N.Z.
281 E3 Santo Hipólito Brazil
278 E4 Santo Inácio Bahia Brazil
280 B5 Santo Inácio Paraná Brazil
206 B3 Santo Isidro de Pegões Port.
275 E2 San Tomé Venez.
209 C11 Santomera Spain
209 C11 Santomera, Embalse de resr Spain
215 L2 Sant Omero Italy
205 N2 Santoña Spain
122 E7 Santong He r. China
114 E6 Santo Niño i. Phil.
217 K6 Sant'Onofrio Italy
216 H9 Santo Pietro Sicilia Italy
214 C2 Santo-Pietro-di-Tenda Corse France
214 C3 Santo-Pietro-di-Venaco Corse France
221 G6 Santorini i. Greece

280 D5 **Santos** Brazil
207 I4 **Santos, Sierra de los** *hills* Spain
281 F4 **Santos Dumont** Brazil
276 D2 **Santos Mercado** Bol.
288 F7 **Santos Plateau** *sea feature* S. Atlantic Ocean
212 E6 **Santo Stefano Belbo** Italy
213 N2 **Santo Stefano di Cadore** Italy
216 G7 **Santo Stefano di Camastra** *Sicilia* Italy
212 H7 **Santo Stefano di Magra** Italy
216 E8 **Santo Stefano Quisquina** *Sicilia* Italy
213 N4 **Santo Stino di Livenza** Italy
204 D6 **Santo Tirso** Port.
263 K12 **Santo Tomás** *Chihuahua* Mex.
263 H11 **Santo Tomás** *Sonora* Mex.
266 □P11 **Santo Tomás** Nic.
276 B3 **Santo Tomás** Peru
282 F3 **Santo Tomé** *Corrientes* Arg.
285 G2 **Santo Tomé** *Santa Fé* Arg.
207 M4 **Santo Tomé** Spain
204 I5 **Santovenia** Spain
208 I5 **Sant Pere de Ribes** Spain
208 J3 **Sant Pere de Torelló** Spain
208 L3 **Sant Pere Pescador** Spain
186 G4 **Santpoort** Neth.
208 J3 **Sant Privat d'en Bas** Spain
208 I5 **Sant Quintí de Mediona** Spain
138 D8 **Santrampur** *Gujarat* India
208 I5 **Sant Sadurní d'Anoia** Spain
209 L9 **Sant Salvador, Puig de** *hill* Spain
204 I2 **Santullano** Spain
214 B7 **Santu Lussurgiu** *Sardegna* Italy
217 □ **San Tumas, Il-Bajja ta'** *b.* Malta
Santurce *País Vasco* Spain *see* **Santurtzi**
205 O4 **Santurde** Spain
205 N2 **Santurtzi** Spain
208 I4 **Sant Vincenç de Castellet** Spain
265 S5 **Sanup Plateau** *AZ* U.S.A.
283 B7 **San Valentín, Cerro** *mt.* Chile
200 F8 **San Vendemiano** Italy
214 B7 **San Vero Milis** *Sardegna* Italy
285 G2 **San Vicente** Arg.
276 D5 **San Vicente** Bol.
284 B4 **San Vicente** Chile
266 □O11 **San Vicente** El Salvador
266 A2 **San Vicente** *Baja California* Mex.
268 G1 **San Vicente** *San Luis Potosí* Mex.
114 D2 **San Vicente** *Luzon* Phil.
205 K8 **San Vicente, Sierra de** *mts* Spain
206 E2 **San Vicente de Alcántara** Spain
205 P3 **San Vicente de Arana** Spain
276 A3 **San Vicente de Cañete** Peru
San Vicente de Castellet Spain *see* **Sant Vincenç de Castellet**
205 L2 **San Vicente de la Barquera** Spain
205 O3 **San Vicente de la Sonsierra** Spain
274 C4 **San Vicente del Caguán** Col.
209 D11 **San Vicente del Raspeig** Spain
205 K6 **San Vicente de Palacio** Spain
205 M2 **San Vicente de Toranzo** Spain
269 I4 **San Vicente Tancuayalab** Mex.
204 C3 **San Vicenzo** Spain
213 O9 **San Vicino, Monte** *mt.* Italy
285 H2 **San Victor** Arg.
182 E3 **Sanvignes-les-Mines** France
268 G8 **San Vincente de Benitez** Mex.
217 I6 **San Vincenzo** *Isole Lipari* Italy
214 F1 **San Vincenzo** *Toscana* Italy
204 H5 **San Vitero** Spain
214 D9 **San Vito** *Sardegna* Italy
216 D7 **San Vito, Capo** *c. Sicilia* Italy
217 M3 **San Vito, Capo** *c.* Italy
213 N4 **San Vito al Tagliamento** Italy
215 M3 **San Vito Chietino** Italy
217 N2 **San Vito dei Normanni** Italy
213 M3 **San Vito di Cadore** Italy
216 D7 **San Vito lo Capo** *Sicilia* Italy
215 J4 **San Vito Romano** Italy
217 K6 **San Vito sullo Ionio** Italy
127 K3 **Sanwa** *Ibaraki* Japan
127 H1 **Sanwa** *Niigata* Japan
138 E8 **Sanwer** *Madh. Prad.* India
204 C4 **Sanxenxo** Spain
130 G3 **Sanxia Shuiku** *resr* China
130 G9 **Sanya** *Hainan* China
274 D4 **San Yanaro** Col.
235 F3 **Sanyati** *r.* Zimbabwe
129 K9 **Sanyuan** *Shaanxi* China
145 J3 **S. A. Nyýazow Adyndaky** Turkm.
215 P7 **Sanza** Italy
231 C6 **Sanza Pombo** Angola
204 I6 **Sanzoles** Spain
118 F5 **Sao, Phou** *mt.* Laos
206 C6 **São Barnabé** Port.
238 □1a **São Bartolomeu** *Terceira* Azores
280 D2 **São Bartolomeu** *r.* Brazil
206 D2 **São Bartolomeu** Port.
206 B4 **São Bartolomeu da Serra** Port.
206 C6 **São Bartolomeu de Messines** Port.
278 E3 **São Benedito** Brazil
238 □1a **São Bento** *Terceira* Azores
276 D1 **São Bento** *Amazonas* Brazil
278 D2 **São Bento** *Maranhão* Brazil
275 F4 **São Bento** *Roraima* Brazil
280 B6 **São Bento do Amparo** Brazil
278 G3 **São Bento do Norte** Brazil
278 E2 **São Bernardo** Brazil
280 D5 **São Bernardo do Campo** Brazil
277 F7 **São Borja** Brazil
206 D5 **São Brás** Port.
206 D6 **São Brás de Alportel** Port.
206 C4 **São Brás do Regedouro** Port.
238 □1c **São Caetano** *Pico* Azores
276 D2 **São Carlos** *Rondônia* Brazil
277 E2 **São Carlos** *Rondônia* Brazil
279 B8 **São Carlos** *Santa Catarina* Brazil
280 D5 **São Carlos** *São Paulo* Brazil
204 E6 **São Cosmado** Port.
206 C4 **São Cristóvão** Port.
206 B4 **São Cristóvão** *r.* Port.
278 D5 **São Desidério** Brazil
278 D5 **São Domingos** Brazil
280 A4 **São Domingos** *r.* Brazil
280 B3 **São Domingos** *r.* Brazil
206 B5 **São Domingos** Port.
281 G3 **São Domingos do Norte** Brazil
206 C2 **São Facundo** Port.
281 E1 **São Felipe, Serra de** *hills* Brazil
278 F5 **São Félix** *Bahia* Brazil
278 C4 **São Félix** *Mato Grosso* Brazil
275 I6 **São Félix** *Pará* Brazil
204 C6 **São Félix da Marinha** Port.
281 G4 **São Fidélis** Brazil
228 □ **São Filipe** Cape Verde
276 C2 **São Francisco** *Acre* Brazil
275 F6 **São Francisco** *Amazonas* Brazil
281 E1 **São Francisco** *Minas Gerais* Brazil
281 E1 **São Francisco** *r.* Brazil
276 D2 **São Francisco** *r.* Brazil
279 C8 **São Francisco, Ilha de** *i.* Brazil
206 B4 **São Francisco da Serra** Port.
279 B9 **São Francisco de Assis** Brazil
280 C1 **São Francisco de Goiás** Brazil
279 C9 **São Francisco de Paula** Brazil
280 C3 **São Francisco de Sales** Brazil
278 E3 **São Francisco do Maranhão** Brazil
279 C8 **São Francisco do Sul** Brazil
279 B9 **São Gabriel** Brazil
281 G3 **São Gabriel da Palha** Brazil
206 C3 **São Geraldo** Port.
281 F5 **São Gonçalo** Brazil
281 E3 **São Gonçalo do Abaeté** Brazil
281 E3 **São Gonçalo do Pará** Brazil
281 E4 **São Gonçalo do Sapucaí** Brazil
281 E3 **São Gotardo** Brazil
206 D3 **São Gregório** Port.
233 B7 **Sao Hill** Tanz.
204 C7 **São Jacinto** Port.
280 B5 **São Jerônimo da Serra** Brazil
238 □1c **São João** *Pico* Azores
274 E5 **São João** Brazil
278 D2 **São João, Ilhas de** *is* Brazil
277 E2 **São João, Serra de** *hills* Brazil
278 D5 **São João da Aliança** Brazil
281 G4 **São João da Barra** Brazil
280 D4 **São João da Boa Vista** Brazil
204 D7 **São João da Madeira** Port.
204 F6 **São João da Pesqueira** Port.
281 E1 **São João da Ponte** Brazil
280 B4 **São João das Duas Pontas** Brazil
281 E4 **São João del Rei** Brazil
281 F5 **São João de Meriti** Brazil
204 E7 **São João de Tarouca** Port.
278 C3 **São João do Araguaia** Brazil
280 A5 **São João do Caiuá** Brazil
204 D8 **São João do Campo** Port.
278 F3 **São João do Cariri** Brazil
279 E5 **São João do Paraíso** Brazil
278 E4 **São João do Piauí** Brazil
206 D5 **São João dos Caldeireiros** Port.
278 E3 **São João dos Patos** Brazil
231 B8 **São João do Sul** Angola
281 F3 **São João Evangelista** Brazil
281 F4 **São João Nepomuceno** Brazil
274 E4 **São Joaquim** *Amazonas* Brazil
279 C9 **São Joaquim** *Santa Catarina* Brazil
280 D4 **São Joaquim da Barra** Brazil
238 □1c **São Jorge** *i.* Azores
206 □ **São Jorge** Madeira
238 □1c **São Jorge, Canal de** *sea chan.* Azores
São Jorge da Mina Ghana *see* **Elmina**
280 A5 **São Jorge do Ivaí** Brazil
274 E5 **São José** *Amazonas* Brazil
279 C8 **São José** *Santa Catarina* Brazil
280 D4 **São José da Boa Vista** Brazil
206 C2 **São José da Lamarosa** Port.
275 F4 **São José do Anauá** Brazil
281 E5 **São José do Barreiro** Brazil
278 F3 **São José do Belmonte** Brazil
281 G4 **São José do Calçado** Brazil
281 G3 **São José do Divino** Brazil
278 F3 **São José do Egito** Brazil
281 F3 **São José do Jacurí** Brazil
282 G4 **São José do Norte** Brazil
278 E3 **São José do Peixe** Brazil
280 D4 **São José do Rio Pardo** Brazil
280 C4 **São José do Rio Preto** Brazil
281 E5 **São José dos Campos** Brazil
280 B4 **São José dos Dourados** *r.* Brazil
279 C8 **São José dos Pinhais** Brazil
204 F5 **São Julião de Montenegro** Port.
277 G4 **São Lourenço** *Mato Grosso* Brazil
281 E5 **São Lourenço** *Minas Gerais* Brazil
277 F4 **São Lourenço** *r.* Brazil
277 F4 **São Lourenço, Pantanal de** *marsh* Brazil
206 □ **São Lourenço, Ponta de** *pt* Madeira
206 D3 **São Lourenço de Mamporcão** Port.
282 H3 **São Lourenço do Sul** Brazil
231 C7 **São Lucas** Angola
278 D2 **São Luís** Brazil
275 G6 **São Luís** Brazil
206 B5 **São Luís** Port.
276 D1 **São Luís de Cassianã** Brazil
280 B2 **São Luís de Montes Belos** Brazil
281 E5 **São Luís do Paraitinga** Brazil
278 G4 **São Luís do Quitunde** Brazil
279 B9 **São Luís Gonzaga** Brazil
206 E2 **São Mamede, Serra de** *mts* Port.
206 C4 **São Mamede do Sádão** Port.
206 D4 **São Manços** Port.
280 C5 **São Manuel** Brazil
274 E4 **São Marceline** Brazil
280 D3 **São Marcos** *r.* Brazil
278 D2 **São Marcos, Baía de** *b.* Brazil
206 D5 **São Marcos da Ataboeira** Port.
206 C6 **São Marcos da Serra** Port.
206 D4 **São Marcos do Campo** Port.
275 G6 **São Martinho** Brazil
204 D8 **São Martinho da Cortiça** Port.
206 C5 **São Martinho das Amoreiras** Port.
204 H5 **São Martinho de Angueira** Port.
204 B9 **São Martinho do Porto** Port.
238 □1c **São Mateus** *Pico* Azores
238 □1a **São Mateus** *Terceira* Azores
281 H3 **São Mateus** Brazil
281 H3 **São Mateus** *r.* Brazil
279 C8 **São Mateus do Sul** Brazil
206 D4 **São Matias** Port.
238 □1b **São Miguel** *i.* Azores
280 D2 **São Miguel** *r.* Brazil
204 E9 **São Miguel** *hill* Port.
280 D5 **São Miguel Arcanjo** Brazil
279 B9 **São Miguel das Missões** *tourist site* Brazil
204 F8 **São Miguel de Acha** Port.
206 D3 **São Miguel de Machede** Port.
206 C2 **São Miguel de Rio Torto** Port.
206 D5 **São Miguel do Pinheiro** Port.
278 E3 **São Miguel do Tapuio** Brazil
271 I4 **Saona, Isla** *i.* Dom. Rep.
213 N9 **Saonda** *r.* Italy
239 □3a **Saondzou** *mt. Njazidja* Comoros
182 I2 **Saône** France
179 L7 **Saône** *r.* France
182 F3 **Saône-et-Loire** *dept* France
138 G9 **Saoner** *Mahar.* India
São Nicolau Angola *see* **Bentiaba**
277 G7 **São Nicolau** Brazil
228 □ **São Nicolau** *i.* Cape Verde
280 D5 **São Paulo** Brazil
280 C5 **São Paulo** *state* Brazil
274 D5 **São Paulo de Olivença** Brazil
275 G6 **São Pedro** *Amazonas* Brazil
280 B3 **São Pedro** *Mato Grosso do Sul* Brazil
277 E2 **São Pedro** *Rondônia* Brazil
280 D5 **São Pedro** *São Paulo* Brazil
281 F5 **São Pedro da Aldeia** Brazil
206 A2 **São Pedro da Cadeira** Port.
204 F5 **São Pedro de Agostem** Port.
204 B9 **São Pedro de Muel** Port.
206 D6 **São Pedro de Solis** Port.
206 E4 **São Pedro do Corval** Port.
276 D2 **São Pedro do Desterro** Brazil
280 B5 **São Pedro do Ivaí** Brazil
279 B9 **São Pedro do Sul** Brazil
204 D7 **São Pedro do Sul** Port.
288 H5 **São Pedro e São Paulo** *is* N. Atlantic Ocean
São Pires *r.* Brazil *see* **Teles Pires**
278 D3 **São Raimundo das Mangabeiras** Brazil
278 E4 **São Raimundo Nonato** Brazil
183 L9 **Saorge** France
126 E5 **Saori** Japan
274 E6 **São Romão** *Amazonas* Brazil
281 E2 **São Romão** *Minas Gerais* Brazil
206 E3 **São Romão** *Évora* Port.
204 E8 **São Romão** *Guarda* Port.
206 C4 **São Romão do Sado** Port.
238 □1c **São Roque** *Pico* Azores
280 D5 **São Roque** Brazil
280 D4 **São Roque de Minas** Brazil
São Salvador Angola *see* **M'banza Congo**
São Salvador do Congo Angola *see* **M'banza Congo**
238 □1a **São Sebastião** *Terceira* Azores
276 C1 **São Sebastião** *Amazonas* Brazil
275 H6 **São Sebastião** *Pará* Brazil
277 E2 **São Sebastião** *Rondônia* Brazil
281 E5 **São Sebastião** *São Paulo* Brazil
281 E5 **São Sebastião, Ilha do** *i.* Brazil
280 B5 **São Sebastião da Amoreira** Brazil
275 I5 **São Sebastião da Boa Vista** Brazil
275 F6 **São Sebastião de Tapuru** Brazil
280 D4 **São Sebastião do Paraíso** Brazil
279 B9 **São Sepé** Brazil
204 C8 **São Silvestre** Port.
277 F5 **São Simão** *Mato Grosso do Sul* Brazil
280 B3 **São Simão** *Minas Gerais* Brazil
280 D4 **São Simão** *São Paulo* Brazil
280 B3 **São Simão, Barragem de** *resr* Brazil
280 C3 **São Simão, Represa de** *resr* Brazil
115 E3 **Sao-Siu** *Maluku* Indon.
206 B5 **São Teotónio** Port.
281 E4 **São Tiago** Brazil
São Tiago *i.* Cape Verde *see* **Santiago**
229 G6 **São Tomé** São Tomé and Príncipe
229 G6 **São Tomé** *i.* São Tomé and Príncipe
281 G5 **São Tomé, Cabo de** *c.* Brazil
229 G6 **São Tomé, Pico de** *mt.* São Tomé and Príncipe
229 G6 **São Tomé and Príncipe** *country* Africa
206 B3 **São Torcato** *hill* Port.
183 G7 **Saou** France
226 E3 **Saoura, Oued** *watercourse* Alg.
280 D5 **São Vicente** Brazil
228 □ **São Vicente** *i.* Cape Verde
206 □ **São Vicente** Madeira
206 E3 **São Vicente** *Portalegre* Port.
204 F5 **São Vicente** *Vila Real* Port.
206 B6 **São Vicente, Cabo de** *c.* Port.
204 E8 **São Vicente da Beira** Port.
278 D2 **São Vicente Ferrer** Brazil
199 K4 **Sáp** Hungary
Sápai Greece *see* **Sapes**
116 C5 **Sapako** Indon.
206 E6 **Sapal de Castro Marim e Vila Real de Santo António, Reserva Natural do** *nature res.* Spain
276 B3 **Sapallanga** Peru
221 L2 **Sapanca** Turkey
221 L2 **Sapanca Gölü** *l.* Turkey
278 D4 **Sapão** *r.* Brazil
144 H1 **Saparmyrat Türkmenbaşy** Turkm.
115 F5 **Saparua** *Maluku* Indon.
115 F5 **Saparua** *i. Maluku* Indon.
173 J2 **Sapcote** *Leicestershire, England* U.K.
115 A8 **Sape, Selat** *sea chan.* Indon.
117 M9 **Sape, Teluk** *b. Sumbawa* Indon.
229 G5 **Sapele** Nigeria
221 G1 **Sapes** Greece
221 K3 **Şaphane** Turkey
214 C6 **Sa Pianedda, Monte** *hill* Italy
220 C5 **Sapienza** *i.* Greece
266 □T14 **Sapo, Serranía del** *mts* Panama
209 L8 **Sa Pobla** Spain
217 I7 **Saponara** *Sicilia* Italy
228 C5 **Sapo National Park** Liberia
280 B5 **Sapopema** Brazil
160 G8 **Sapotskin** Belarus
228 E4 **Sapouy** Burkina
161 X8 **Sapozhok** Rus. Fed.
260 F5 **Sappa Creek** *r. NE* U.S.A.
213 N2 **Sappada** Italy
255 □1 **Sapphire Bay** Bermuda
124 S3 **Sapporo** Japan
139 L9 **Saptamukhi** *r.* India
280 C4 **Sapucai** *r.* Brazil
281 E4 **Sapucai** *r.* Brazil
275 G5 **Sapucaia** Brazil
117 K8 **Sapudi** *i.* Indon.
261 G7 **Sapulpa** *OK* U.S.A.
117 J8 **Sapulu** *Jawa* Indon.
117 L2 **Sapulut** *Sabah* Malaysia
146 F2 **Sāq, Jabal** *hill* Saudi Arabia
144 H5 **Sāqī** Iran
243 M2 **Saqqaq** Greenland
144 B3 **Saqqez** Iran
146 F7 **Saqr** Saudi Arabia
151 D3 **Saqulia** Georgia
139 L7 **Sara** Bangl.
144 B3 **Sarā** Iran
144 B3 **Sarāb** *Āzarbāyjān-e Sharqī* Iran
144 H5 **Sarāb** *Khorāsān* Iran
149 M7 **Sarābe Meymeh** Iran
150 B9 **Sarābīț al Khādim** *tourist site* Egypt
119 E7 **Sara Buri** Thai.
162 Q1 **Saraby** Norway
275 G5 **Saracá, Lago** *l.* Brazil
217 L4 **Saraceno** *r.* Italy
216 D7 **Saraceno, Punta del** *pt Sicilia* Italy
201 N7 **Saračinec** Croatia
138 C9 **Saradiya** *Gujarat* India
224 C6 **Saraf Doungous** Chad
Saragossa Spain *see* **Zaragoza**
145 I3 **Saragt** Turkm.
274 B5 **Saraguro** Ecuador
145 L5 **Sarai** Afgh.
157 H5 **Sarai** Rus. Fed.
139 J8 **Saraikela** *Jharkhand* India
145 O6 **Sarai Sidhu** Pak.
162 S4 **Säräisniemi** Fin.
210 G4 **Sarajevo** Bos.-Herz.
107 L7 **Saraji** *Qld* Austr.
145 I3 **Sarakhs** Iran
220 E4 **Sarakiniko, Akrotirio** *pt* Greece
220 F4 **Sarakino** *i.* Greece
142 G2 **Saraktash** Rus. Fed.
261 K10 **Saraland** *AL* U.S.A.
142 F3 **Saralzhin** Kazakh.
139 O7 **Saramati** *mt.* India/Myanmar
274 B6 **Samameriza** Peru
185 F8 **Saramon** France
178 C8 **Saran** France
143 O3 **Saran'** Kazakh.
117 I5 **Saran, Gunung** *mt.* Indon.
257 L4 **Saranac** *r. NY* U.S.A.
257 K4 **Saranac Lake** *NY* U.S.A.
199 K4 **Sáránd** Hungary
220 B3 **Sarandë** Albania
280 B5 **Sarandi** *Paraná* Brazil
279 B8 **Sarandi** *Rio Grande do Sul* Brazil
Sarandib *country* Asia *see* **Sri Lanka**
282 G4 **Sarandí del Yí** Uru.
285 I3 **Sarandí de Navarro** Uru.
285 I3 **Sarandí Grande** Uru.
114 E9 **Sarangani** *i.* Phil.
114 E9 **Sarangani Bay** *Mindanao* Phil.
114 E9 **Sarangani Islands** Phil.
114 E9 **Sarangani Strait** Phil.
139 I9 **Sarangarh** *Chhattisgarh* India
138 F8 **Sarangpur** *Madh. Prad.* India
157 I5 **Saransk** Rus. Fed.
Sara-Ostrov Azer. *see* **Närimanabad**
229 H4 **Sara Peak** Nigeria
118 D5 **Saraphi** Thai.
156 K4 **Sarapul** Rus. Fed.
150 E3 **Sarāqib** Syria
255 F12 **Sarasota** *FL* U.S.A.
138 C8 **Saraswati** *r. Gujarat* India
158 H7 **Sărata** *r.* Moldova
219 O6 **Sărata** *r.* Romania
158 I7 **Sarata** Ukr.
158 I8 **Sarata** *r.* Ukr.
158 H6 **Sărătenii Vechi** Moldova
264 J4 **Saratoga** *CA* U.S.A.
262 K6 **Saratoga** *WY* U.S.A.
257 L5 **Saratoga Lake** *NY* U.S.A.
257 L5 **Saratoga Springs** *NY* U.S.A.
117 I4 **Saratok** *Sarawak* Malaysia
142 A2 **Saratov** Rus. Fed.
Saratov Oblast *admin. div.* Rus. Fed. *see* **Saratovskaya Oblast'**
151 A1 **Saratovskaya** Rus. Fed.
142 B2 **Saratovskaya Oblast'** *admin. div.* Rus. Fed.
142 B1 **Saratovskoye Vodokhranilishche** *resr* Rus. Fed.
221 G3 **Saratsina, Akrotirio** *pt Lesvos* Greece
145 J8 **Sarāvān** Iran
114 D6 **Saravia** *Negros* Phil.
119 D8 **Sarawa** *r.* Myanmar
117 I4 **Sarawak** *state* Malaysia
151 K5 **Saray** Azer.
148 C3 **Saray** Turkey
228 C4 **Saraya** Guinea
228 C3 **Saraya** Senegal
150 D3 **Şarāyā** Syria
144 H5 **Sarāyān** Iran
221 K4 **Saraycık** Turkey
221 J5 **Sarayköy** Turkey
221 I2 **Saraylar** Turkey
148 F4 **Sarayönü** Turkey
145 I8 **Sarbāz** Iran
145 I9 **Sarbāz** *r.* Iran
145 I8 **Sarbāz** *reg.* Iran
219 N6 **Sârbeni** Romania
139 M6 **Sarbhang** Bhutan
199 L4 **Sârbi** Romania
144 H5 **Sarbīsheh** Iran
199 H5 **Sárbogárd** Hungary
196 F1 **Sarbsko, Jezioro** *lag.* Pol.
128 A3 **Sarbulak** *Xinjiang* China
213 J4 **Sarca** *r.* Italy
200 C7 **Sarca di Genova** *r.* Italy
178 D6 **Sarcelles** France
144 C3 **Sarcham** Iran
151 F4 **Sarch'apet** Armenia
214 B8 **Sarcidano** *reg. Sardegna* Italy
282 C3 **Sarco** Chile
133 E12 **Sarda** *r.* India/Nepal
138 H5 **Sarda** *r.* Nepal
145 N3 **Sard Āb** *pass* Afgh.
145 I8 **Sardāb** Iran
206 B5 **Sardão, Cabo** *c.* Port.
144 H4 **Sardaq** Iran
214 B8 **Sardara** *Sardegna* Italy
138 E8 **Sardarpur** *Madh. Prad.* India
138 E5 **Sardarshahr** *Rajasthan* India
144 A3 **Sar Dasht** Iran
144 C5 **Sardasht** *Khūzestān* Iran
144 D6 **Sardasht** *Khūzestān* Iran
214 C7 **Sardegna** *admin. reg.* Italy
214 A7 **Sardegna** *i. Sardegna* Italy
Sardica Bulg. *see* **Sofiya**
198 G3 **Šardice** Czech Rep.
238 □3f **Sardina** *Gran Canaria* Canary Is
238 □3f **Sardina, Punta de** *pt Gran Canaria* Canary Is
274 C2 **Sardinata** Col.
266 □Q12 **Sardinia** Costa Rica
Sardinia *i. Sardegna* Italy *see* **Sardegna**
207 L4 **Sardinilla** *r.* Spain
261 K8 **Sardis** *MS* U.S.A.
256 E9 **Sardis** *WV* U.S.A.
261 K8 **Sardis Lake** *resr MS* U.S.A.
204 D9 **Sardoal** Port.
149 M5 **Sardrūd** Iran
185 A9 **Sare** France
147 J3 **Sareb, Rās as** *pt* U.A.E.
145 L4 **Sar-e Būm** Afgh.
162 N3 **Sareks nationalpark** *nat. park* Sweden
162 N3 **Sarektjåkkå** *mt.* Sweden
117 K5 **Sarempaka, Gunung** *mt.* Indon.
209 K8 **S'Arenal** Spain
213 K2 **Sarentino** Italy
145 K3 **Sar-e Pol** Afgh.
145 L4 **Sar-e Pol** Afgh.
145 L3 **Sar-e Pol** *prov.* Afgh.
149 L6 **Sar-e Pol-e Žahāb** Iran
Sar Eskandar Iran *see* **Hashtrud**
212 C4 **Sareva** *r.* Italy
145 O2 **Sarez, Kŭli** *l.* Tajik.
Sarezskoye Ozero *l.* Tajik. *see* **Sarez, Kŭli**
212 G1 **Sargans** Switz.
288 E4 **Sargasso Sea** Atlantic Ocean
274 C5 **Sargentu Loros** Peru
145 O5 **Sargodha** Pak.
230 C2 **Sarh** Chad
144 I7 **Sarhad** *reg.* Iran
228 D4 **Sarhala** Côte d'Ivoire
226 D3 **Sarhro, Jbel** *mt.* Morocco
144 E3 **Sārī** Iran
221 I7 **Saria** *i. Karpathos* Greece
266 D2 **Sáric** Mex.
221 L2 **Sarıcakaya** Turkey
151 B7 **Sarıcan** Turkey
219 Q6 **Sarichioi** Romania
151 E6 **Sarıçiçek Dağı** *mt.* Turkey
214 B3 **Sari-d'Orcino** *Corse* France
204 I3 **Sariegos** Spain
113 K3 **Sarigan** *i.* N. Mariana Is
151 C5 **Sarıgöl** *Artvin* Turkey
221 J4 **Sarıgöl** *Manisa* Turkey
221 M5 **Sarıidris** Turkey
149 K3 **Sarıkamış** Turkey
150 B2 **Sarıkavak** Turkey
117 I3 **Sarikei** *Sarawak* Malaysia
221 I5 **Sarıkemer** Turkey
221 I2 **Sarıköy** Turkey
Sarikŭl, Qatorkŭhi *mts* China/Tajik. *see* **Sarykol Range**
138 G7 **Sarila** *Uttar Prad.* India
116 □ **Sarimbun Reservoir** Sing.
107 L6 **Sarina** *Qld* Austr.
212 C2 **Sarine** *r.* Switz.
208 E4 **Sariñena** Spain
232 D4 **Sarinleev** Somalia
Sarıoğlan Turkey *see* **Belören**
151 D6 **Sarıpınar** Turkey
144 F3 **Sāri Qamīsh** Iran
Sariqamish Kuli *salt l.* Turkm./Uzbek. *see* **Sarykamyshskoye Ozero**
224 C4 **Sarīr Tibesti** *des.* Libya
224 D3 **Sarir Water Wells Field** Libya
139 L7 **Sarishabari** Bangl.
151 B4 **Sarısu** Turkey
151 J5 **Sarısu Gölü** *l.* Azer.
261 G12 **Sarita** *TX* U.S.A.
150 A2 **Sarıveliler** Turkey
123 D9 **Sariwŏn** N. Korea
151 I6 **Sarıxanlı** Azer.
221 M2 **Sarıyar** Turkey
221 K1 **Sarıyer** Turkey
148 H4 **Sarız** Turkey
180 G3 **Sark** *i.* Channel Is
199 K5 **Sarkad** Hungary
199 K5 **Sarkadkeresztúr** Hungary
143 R5 **Sarkand** Kazakh.
138 C6 **Sarkari Tala** *Rajasthan* India
199 H4 **Sárkeresztes** Hungary
199 H4 **Sárkeresztúr** Hungary
148 E4 **Şarkikaraağaç** Turkey
163 Q6 **Särkisalo** Fin.
148 H4 **Şarkışla** Turkey
221 I2 **Şarköy** Turkey
145 L7 **Sarlath Range** *mts* Afgh./Pak.
185 G6 **Sarlat-la-Canéda** France
144 F2 **Şarlawuk** Turkm.
201 I2 **Sarleinsbach** Austria
184 F5 **Sarliac-sur-l'Isle** France
151 E2 **Sarmakovo** Rus. Fed.
145 K5 **Sarmalan** Afgh.
156 K5 **Sarmanovo** Rus. Fed.
219 K3 **Şărmăşag** Romania
219 M4 **Şărmaşu** Romania
217 K3 **Sarmento** *r.* Italy
113 I7 **Sarmi** *Papua* Indon.
283 C7 **Sarmiento** Arg.
163 L6 **Särna** Sweden
204 E9 **Sarnadas do Ródão** Port.
197 K3 **Sarnaki** Pol.
215 K1 **Sarnano** Italy
160 E4 **Sārnate** Latvia
139 I7 **Sarnath** *Uttar Prad.* India
144 B5 **Sarneh** Iran
212 E2 **Sarnen** Switz.
212 E2 **Sarner See** *l.* Switz.
Sarni *Madh. Prad.* India *see* **Amla**
248 D5 **Sarnia** *Ont.* Can.
212 H4 **Sarnico** Italy
215 N6 **Sarno** Italy
196 E4 **Sarnowa** Pol.
158 F2 **Sarny** Ukr.
115 B5 **Saroako** *Sulawesi* Indon.
161 S3 **Sarogozha** *r.* Rus. Fed.
116 E6 **Sarolangun** *Sumatera* Indon.
124 U2 **Saroma-ko** *l.* Japan
250 C4 **Sarona** *WI* U.S.A.
220 E5 **Saronikos Kolpos** *g.* Greece
212 G4 **Saronno** Italy
199 H4 **Sárosd** Hungary
221 H2 **Saros Körfezi** *b.* Turkey
199 K3 **Sárospatak** Hungary
138 D7 **Sarotra** *Gujarat* India
157 H5 **Sarova** Rus. Fed.
199 H3 **Šarovce** Slovakia
192 H3 **Sarow** Ger.
145 M4 **Sarowbī** Afgh.
157 I6 **Sarpa, Ozero** *l.* Rus. Fed.
157 I7 **Sarpa, Ozero** *l.* Rus. Fed.
Sarpan *i.* N. Mariana Is *see* **Rota**
114 □ **Sar Passage** Palau
218 I9 **Šar Planina** *mts* Macedonia/Yugo.
164 H2 **Sarpsborg** Norway
Sarqant Kazakh. *see* **Sarkand**
214 C9 **Sarrabus** *reg. Sardegna* Italy
205 M4 **Sarracín** Spain
208 H5 **Sarral** Spain
179 N6 **Sarralbe** France
185 C9 **Sarrance** France
185 E10 **Sarrancolin** France
183 B7 **Sarrans, Barrage de** *dam* France
204 E5 **Sarraquinhos** Port.
183 F6 **Sarras** France
179 N5 **Sarre** *r.* France
212 C4 **Sarre** Italy
173 O5 **Sarre** *Kent, England* U.K.
Sarreal Spain *see* **Sarral**
204 E4 **Sarreaus** Spain
179 N6 **Sarre Blanche** *r.* France
179 N6 **Sarrebourg** France
179 N5 **Sarreguemines** France
199 H4 **Sarreti** *park* Hungary
199 K4 **Sárrétudvari** Hungary
179 N6 **Sarre-Union** France
204 F3 **Sarria** Spain
208 K3 **Sarrià de Ter** Spain
183 F8 **Sarrians** France
209 D7 **Sarrión** Spain
228 D3 **Sarro** Mali
208 G5 **Sarroca de Lleida** Spain
214 C9 **Sarròch** *Sardegna* Italy
201 O4 **Sarród** Hungary
214 B3 **Sarrola-Carcopino** *Corse* France
185 D8 **Sarron** France
178 H6 **Sarry** France
156 L4 **Sars** Rus. Fed.
213 M8 **Sarsina** Italy
184 I4 **Sarssonne** *r.* France
191 I6 **Sarstedt** Ger.
199 H5 **Sárszentágota** Hungary
199 H4 **Sárszentmihály** Hungary
187 I7 **Sart** Belgium
205 P4 **Sartaguda** Spain
159 Q6 **Sartana** Ukr.
145 N8 **Sartanahu** Pak.
214 H2 **Sarteano** Italy
214 B4 **Sartène** *Corse* France
181 L6 **Sarthe** *dept* France
181 J6 **Sarthe** *r.* France
220 E2 **Sarti** Greece
151 G4 **Sart'ichala** Georgia
180 I4 **Sartilly** France
160 E6 **Sartininkai** Lith.
128 A3 **Sartokay** *Xinjiang* China
Sartu *Heilong.* China *see* **Daqing**
199 J4 **Sarud** Hungary
144 D4 **Sarud, Rūdkhāneh-ye** *r.* Iran
124 T4 **Saru-gawa** *r.* Japan
221 I4 **Saruhanlı** Turkey
214 C7 **Sarule** *Sardegna* Italy
145 L8 **Saruna** Pak.
145 L8 **Saruna** *r.* Pak.
138 D5 **Sarupsar** *Rajasthan* India
144 C4 **Sārūq** Iran
151 F6 **Şarur** Azer.
145 J6 **Saru Tara** *tourist site* Afgh.
147 O2 **Sarvāb** Iran
144 B4 **Sarvābād** Iran
Sarvani Georgia *see* **Marneuli**
198 F4 **Sárvár** Hungary
144 E7 **Sarvestān** Iran
208 E2 **Sarvisé** Spain
218 G4 **Sárvíz** *r.* Romania
199 H5 **Sárvíz-malomcsatorna** *canal* Hungary
138 E6 **Sarwar** *Rajasthan* India
136 C3 **Sarya** *r.* India
143 M7 **Saryagash** Kazakh.
160 K6 **Sar"yanka** *r.* Belarus/Latvia
143 N2 **Saryarka** *plain* Kazakh.
144 F6 **Sar Yazd** Iran
143 O7 **Sary-Bulak** Kyrg.
Sarydhaz *r.* Kyrg. *see* **Sary-Jaz**
Sarydzhas Kazakh. *see* **Saryzhaz**
Sarygamysh Köli *salt l.* Turkm./Uzbek. *see* **Sarykamyshskoye Ozero**
Sary-Ishikotrau, Peski *des.* Kazakh. *see* **Saryyesik-Atyrau, Peski**
143 R6 **Sary-Jaz** *r.* Kyrg.
142 E5 **Sarykamys** *Atyrauskaya Oblast'* Kazakh.
143 L3 **Sarykamys** *Karagandinskaya Oblast'* Kazakh.
144 G1 **Sarykamyshskoye Ozero** *salt l.* Turkm./Uzbek.
143 N6 **Sarykemer** Kazakh.
143 P2 **Sarykiyak** Kazakh.
142 K1 **Sarykol'** Kazakh.
145 P2 **Sarykol Range** *mts* China/Tajik.
143 P5 **Sarykomey** Kazakh.
142 K2 **Sarymoyyn, Ozero** *salt l.* Kazakh.
142 D2 **Saryomir** Kazakh.
143 R5 **Saryozek** Kazakh.
Saryqamys Kazakh. *see* **Sarykamys**
143 O4 **Saryshagan** Kazakh.
143 L5 **Sarysu** *watercourse* Kazakh.
151 H2 **Sarysu** Rus. Fed.
142 D5 **Sarytash** Kazakh.
143 O8 **Sary-Tash** Kyrg.
143 Q7 **Sary-Ter, Gora** *mt.* Kyrg.
145 J3 **Saryýazy Suw Howdany** *resr* Turkm.
143 P5 **Saryyesik-Atyrau, Peski** *des.* Kazakh.
Saryzhal Kazakh. *see* **Sarzhal**
143 R6 **Saryzhaz** Kazakh.
212 H7 **Sarzana** Italy
180 F6 **Sarzeau** France
204 E9 **Sarzedas** Port.
142 D6 **Sarzha** Kazakh.
143 R3 **Sarzhal** Kazakh.
265 U10 **Sasabe** *AZ* U.S.A.
232 D2 **Sasabeneh** Eth.
116 C4 **Sasak** *Sumatera* Indon.
205 L4 **Sasamón** Spain
100 □6 **Sasamungga** *Choiseul* Solomon Is
115 A8 **Sasar, Tanjung** *pt Sumba* Indon.
139 J7 **Sasaram** *Bihar* India
100 □6 **Sasari, Mount** *Sta Isabel* Solomon Is
126 B5 **Sasayama** Japan
194 D5 **Sasbach** *Baden-Württemberg* Ger.
194 E4 **Sasbach** *Baden-Württemberg* Ger.
194 E4 **Sasbachwalden** Ger.
199 H5 **Sásd** Hungary
125 G13 **Sasebo** Japan
197 I2 **Sasek Wielki, Jezioro** *l.* Pol.
127 K3 **Sashima** Japan
159 L5 **Sasivka** Ukr.
247 J4 **Saskatchewan** *prov.* Can.
247 K4 **Saskatchewan** *r. Man./Sask.* Can.
246 J5 **Saskatchewan Landing Provincial Park** *Sask.* Can.
247 J4 **Saskatoon** *Sask.* Can.
153 M2 **Saskylakh** Rus. Fed.
266 □Q11 **Saslaya** *mt.* Nic.
266 □Q11 **Saslaya, Parque Nacional** *nat. park* Nic.
158 I1 **Sasnovy Bor** Belarus
237 L2 **Sasolburg** S. Africa
157 H5 **Sasovo** Rus. Fed.
246 H2 **Sass** *r. N.W.T.* Can.
258 D6 **Sassafras** *MD* U.S.A.
228 D5 **Sassandra** Côte d'Ivoire
228 D5 **Sassandra** *r.* Côte d'Ivoire
215 P7 **Sassano** Italy
214 B6 **Sassari** *Sardegna* Italy
214 B6 **Sassari** *prov. Sardegna* Italy
212 E7 **Sassello** Italy
192 H2 **Sassen** Ger.
183 H6 **Sassenage** France
191 F7 **Sassenberg** Ger.
186 G4 **Sassenheim** Neth.
214 F1 **Sassetta** Italy
192 I1 **Sassnitz** Ger.
213 M8 **Sassocorvaro** Italy
212 G3 **Sasso della Paglia** *mt.* Switz.
213 K7 **Sasso di Castro** *mt.* Italy
213 N9 **Sassoferrato** Italy
213 L2 **Sasso Lungo** *mt.* Italy
213 K7 **Sasso Marconi** Italy
213 L2 **Sass Rigais** *mt.* Italy
228 C5 **Sass Town** Liberia
213 J6 **Sassuolo** Italy
208 E5 **Sástago** Spain
198 G3 **Šaštín-Stráže** Slovakia
143 N6 **Sastobe** Kazakh.
285 G2 **Sastre** Arg.
136 D3 **Sasvad** *Mahar.* India
187 E6 **Sas Van Gent** Neth.
159 K7 **Sasyk** *r.* Ukr.
159 M8 **Sasyk, Ozero** *l.* Ukr.
143 S4 **Sasykkol', Ozero** *l.* Kazakh.
157 I7 **Sasykoli** Rus. Fed.
159 L3 **Sasynivka** Ukr.
Sasyqköl *l.* Kazakh. *see* **Sasykkol', Ozero**
228 C3 **Satadougou** Mali
Satahual *i.* Micronesia *see* **Satawal**
228 D5 **Satama-Sokoura** Côte d'Ivoire
125 H16 **Sata-misaki** *c.* Japan
138 E9 **Satana** *Mahar.* India
158 F4 **Sataniv** Ukr.
204 E7 **Satão** Port.
100 □2 **Satapuala** Samoa
136 D4 **Satara** *Mahar.* India
235 F5 **Satara** S. Africa
100 □2 **Sataua** Samoa
113 K5 **Satawal** *i.* Micronesia
Sätbaev Kazakh. *see* **Satpayev**
218 J5 **Satchinez** Romania
230 D3 **Satéma** C.A.R.
117 L8 **Satengar** *i.* Indon.
165 L1 **Säter** Sweden
266 F4 **Satevó** Mex.
263 K13 **Satevo** *r.* Mex.
264 M7 **Saticoy** *CA* U.S.A.
162 O3 **Satihaure** *l.* Sweden
255 G10 **Satilla** *r. GA* U.S.A.
183 F6 **Satillieu** France
157 H5 **Satinka** Rus. Fed.
276 B2 **Satipo** Peru
228 D4 **Satiri** Burkina
Satırlar Turkey *see* **Yeşilova**
152 G4 **Satka** Rus. Fed.
139 N9 **Satkania** Bangl.
151 E4 **Sat'khe** Georgia
139 L8 **Satkhira** Bangl.
Satluj *r.* India/Pak. *see* **Sutlej**
136 F3 **Satmala Range** *hills* India
138 H7 **Satna** *Madh. Prad.* India
182 G5 **Satolas** *airport* France
127 L2 **Satomi** Japan
117 L9 **Satonda** *i.* Indon.
199 K3 **Sátoraljaújhely** Hungary
210 E3 **Satorina** *mt.* Croatia
192 E3 **Satow** Ger.
143 L3 **Satpayev** *Karagandinskaya Oblast'* Kazakh.
143 L4 **Satpayev** *Karagandinskaya Oblast'* Kazakh.
138 E9 **Satpura Range** *mts* India
215 P6 **Satriano di Lucania** Italy
160 F6 **Šatrijos kalnas** *hill* Lith.
190 I1 **Satrup** Ger.
125 H15 **Satsuma-hantō** *pen.* Japan
124 U4 **Satsunai-gawa** *r.* Japan
119 E8 **Sattahip** Thai.
162 S3 **Sattanen** Fin.
127 K3 **Satte** Japan
200 A5 **Satteins** Austria
195 I3 **Satteldorf** Ger.
136 G4 **Sattenapalle** *Andhra Prad.* India
118 B5 **Satthwa** Myanmar
138 F2 **Satti** *Jammu and Kashmir* India
201 J3 **Sattledt** Austria
201 J6 **Sattnitz** *reg.* Austria
117 K6 **Satui** *Kalimantan* Indon.
219 K3 **Satu Mare** Romania
199 L4 **Satu Mare** *county* Romania
119 E11 **Satun** Thai.
124 □F18 **Satunan-shotō** *is* Japan
100 □2 **Satupa'itea** Samoa
285 F2 **Saturnino M. Laspiur** Arg.
138 F8 **Satwas** *Madh. Prad.* India
208 J4 **Sau, Pantà de** *resr* Spain
201 K6 **Saualpe** *mts* Austria
164 C2 **Sauanuten** *mt.* Norway
117 K8 **Saubi** *i.* Indon.
185 B8 **Saubusse** France
199 L4 **Săuca** Romania
205 O6 **Saúca** Spain
185 C6 **Saucats** France
285 H2 **Sauce** Arg.
285 G6 **Sauce** *r.* Arg.
261 E13 **Sauceda** Mex.
265 T9 **Sauceda Mountains** *AZ* U.S.A.
285 H2 **Sauce de Luna** Arg.
285 I2 **Saucedo** Uru.
204 G6 **Saucelle, Embalse de** *resr* Port./Spain
266 G3 **Saucillo** Mex.
183 C9 **Sauclières** France
164 C2 **Sauda** Norway
143 M6 **Saudakent** Kazakh.
162 □D1 **Sauðárkrókur** Iceland
140 E5 **Saudi Arabia** *country* Asia
160 H2 **Saue** Estonia
190 I4 **Sauensiek** Ger.
179 P6 **Sauer** *r.* France
195 L6 **Sauerlach** Ger.
191 E8 **Sauerland** *reg.* Ger.
277 F3 **Sauêruiná** *r.* Brazil
114 E8 **Saug** *r. Mindanao* Phil.
160 H3 **Sauga** *r.* Estonia
250 H7 **Saugatuck** *MI* U.S.A.
259 I2 **Saugatuck Reservoir** *CT* U.S.A.
248 D4 **Saugeen** *r. Ont.* Can.
257 L6 **Saugerties** *NY* U.S.A.
171 L7 **Saughall** *Cheshire, England* U.K.
185 C7 **Saugnacq-et-Muret** France
183 D7 **Saugues** France
Sāūjbolāgh Iran *see* **Mahābād**
282 D2 **Saujil** Arg.
184 C4 **Saujon** France
160 I5 **Saukas ezers** *l.* Latvia
260 H3 **Sauk Center** *MN* U.S.A.
250 E6 **Sauk City** *WI* U.S.A.
275 H4 **Saül** Fr. Guiana
169 K4 **Saul** *Northern Ireland* U.K.
185 G10 **Saula, Port de** *pass* Spain
164 E2 **Sauland** Norway
183 F7 **Saulce-sur-Rhône** France
179 M7 **Saulcy-sur-Meurthe** France
194 G6 **Sauldorf** Ger.
184 G1 **Sauldre** *r.* France
194 H5 **Saulgau** Ger.
184 F3 **Saulgé** France
195 K6 **Saulgrub** Ger.
194 E2 **Saulheim** Ger.
182 E2 **Saulieu** France
160 H4 **Saulkrasti** Latvia
179 L6 **Saulnois** *reg.* France
183 G8 **Sault** France
185 C8 **Sault-de-Navailles** France
178 H5 **Sault-lès-Rethel** France
248 C4 **Sault Sainte Marie** *Ont.* Can.
251 J3 **Sault Sainte Marie** *MI* U.S.A.
179 L8 **Saulx** France
179 I6 **Saulx** *r.* France
179 M8 **Saulxures-sur-Moselotte** France
182 B3 **Saulzais-le-Potier** France
143 M1 **Saumalkol'** Kazakh.
107 N6 **Saumarez Reef** *Coral Sea Is Terr.* Austr.
113 H8 **Saumlakki** *Maluku* Indon.
185 B6 **Saumos** France
184 D1 **Saumur** France
181 K7 **Saumurois** *reg.* France
162 S3 **Saunavaara** Fin.
136 D5 **Saundatti** *Karnataka* India
106 C2 **Saunders, Mount** *hill N.T.* Austr.
286 O1 **Saunders Coast** Antarctica
172 C4 **Saundersfoot** *Pembrokeshire, Wales* U.K.
283 E8 **Saunders Island** Falkland Is
273 G7 **Saunders Island** S. Sandwich Is
250 F9 **Saunemin** *IL* U.S.A.
119 D10 **Saung** Thai.
118 C2 **Saungka** Myanmar
257 J5 **Sauquoit** *NY* U.S.A.
142 D5 **Saura** Kazakh.
185 H10 **Saurat** France
160 H5 **Saurieši** Latvia
231 D7 **Saurimo** Angola
213 N3 **Sauris** Italy
213 N3 **Sauris, Lago di** *l.* Italy
215 Q7 **Sauro** *r.* Italy
201 L6 **Sausal** *hills* Austria
264 J4 **Sausalito** *CA* U.S.A.
138 G9 **Sausar** *Madh. Prad.* India
183 G10 **Sausset-les-Pins** France
182 F2 **Saussy** France
115 B4 **Sausu** *Sulawesi* Indon.
231 C7 **Sautar** Angola
200 C5 **Sautens** Austria
185 D6 **Sauternes** France
271 □6 **Sauteurs** Grenada
180 H7 **Sautron** France
185 D9 **Sauvagnon** France
183 D9 **Sauve** France
183 C8 **Sauveterre, Causse de** *plat.* France
185 C9 **Sauveterre-de-Béarn** Franc
185 D6 **Sauveterre-de-Guyenne** Fr
185 I7 **Sauveterre-de Rouergue** F
185 G6 **Sauveterre-la-Lémance** Fra
184 H4 **Sauviat-sur-Vige** France
182 C3 **Sauvigny-les-Bois** France
163 Q6 **Sauvo** Fin.
186 K2 **Sauwerd** Neth.
182 C5 **Sauxillanges** France
284 A4 **Sauzal** *Maule* Chile
284 B4 **Sauzal** *O'Higgins* Chile
268 C1 **Sauz de Arriba** Mex.
185 G7 **Sauzet** France
184 E3 **Sauzé-Vaussais** France
180 E7 **Sauzon** France
189 J6 **Sava** *r.* Europe
266 □P10 **Savá** Hond.
217 N3 **Sava** Italy
201 K7 **Sava** Slovenia
258 B6 **Savage** *MD* U.S.A.
105 J9 **Savage River** *Tas.* Austr.
100 □2 **Savai'i** *i.* Samoa
157 H6 **Savala** *r.* Rus. Fed.
229 F5 **Savalou** Benin
Savanat Iran *see* **Eşţahbān**
249 G3 **Savane** *r. Que.* Can.
235 G3 **Savane** Moz.
271 □9 **Savaneta** Aruba
260 J4 **Savanna** *IL* U.S.A.
255 G9 **Savannah** *GA* U.S.A.
260 H6 **Savannah** *MO* U.S.A.
256 C8 **Savannah** *OH* U.S.A.
261 K8 **Savannah** *TN* U.S.A.
255 G9 **Savannah** *r. GA/SC* U.S.A.
270 E1 **Savannah Sound** *Eleuthera* Bahamas
118 G6 **Savannakhét** Laos
270 □ **Savanna-la-Mar** Jamaica
250 D1 **Savanne** *Ont.* Can.
248 B3 **Savant Lake** *Ont.* Can.
248 B3 **Savant Lake** *l. Ont.* Can.
Savantvadi *Mahar.* India *se*
136 D5 **Savanur** *Karnataka* India
162 P5 **Sävar** Sweden
219 K4 **Săvârşin** Romania
162 P4 **Sävast** Sweden
221 I3 **Savaştepe** Turkey
201 N7 **Savci** Slovenia
229 F4 **Savè** Benin
185 G8 **Save** *r.* France
235 G4 **Save** Moz.
235 G4 **Save** *r.* Moz./Zimbabwe
144 D4 **Sāveh** Iran
217 L5 **Savelli** Italy
228 E4 **Savelugu** Ghana
213 K7 **Savena** *r.* Italy
180 H7 **Savenay** France
219 O3 **Săveni** Romania
185 H9 **Saverdun** France
275 G3 **Saveretik** Guyana
179 N6 **Saverne** France
162 T5 **Saviaho** Fin.
178 G7 **Savières** France
212 D6 **Savigliano** Italy
184 F5 **Savignac-les-Églises** Franc
215 O5 **Savignano Irpino** Italy
213 M7 **Savignano sul Rubicone** It
181 L5 **Savigné-l'Évêque** France
182 E5 **Savigneux** France
182 B2 **Savigny-en-Sancerre** Franc
182 F2 **Savigny-lès-Beaune** France
181 M6 **Savigny-sur-Braye** France
178 D6 **Savigny-sur-Orge** France
183 I7 **Savines-le-Lac** France
219 O4 **Săvineşti** Romania
161 O8 **Savinichy** Belarus
210 E2 **Savinja** *r.* Slovenia
142 B2 **Savinka** Rus. Fed.
161 Y5 **Savino** Rus. Fed.
156 L3 **Savinobor** Rus. Fed.
156 H3 **Savinskiy** Rus. Fed.
161 W6 **Savinskoye** Rus. Fed.
213 M7 **Savio** *r.* Italy
163 S6 **Savitaipale** Fin.
136 C3 **Savitri** *r.* India
165 N2 **Sävja** Sweden
221 L5 **Savköy** Turkey
218 H8 **Šavnik** *Šavnik* Montenegro
100 □6 **Savo** *i.* Solomon Is
212 H2 **Savognin** Switz.
215 P6 **Savoia di Lucania** Italy
182 J6 **Savoie** *dept* France
182 I4 **Savoie** *reg.* France
178 H8 **Savoisy** France
212 E7 **Savona** Italy
212 E7 **Savona** *prov.* Italy
215 L5 **Savone** *r.* Italy
163 T6 **Savonlinna** Fin.
162 T5 **Savonranta** Fin.
244 E3 **Savoonga** *AK* U.S.A.
Savoy *reg.* France *see* **Savoie**
161 Q1 **Savozero, Ozero** *l.* Rus. Fed
158 J5 **Savran'** Ukr.
158 J5 **Savranka** *r.* Ukr.
149 K3 **Şavşat** Turkey
165 K4 **Sävsjö** Sweden
115 B9 **Savu** *i.* Indon.
213 O5 **Savudrija** Croatia
210 D3 **Savudrija, Rt** *pt* Croatia
162 T3 **Savukoski** Fin.
149 J5 **Savur** Turkey
101 □7 **Savusavu** *Vanua Levu* Fiji
101 □7 **Savusavu Bay** *Vanua Levu* F
Savu Sea Indon. *see* **Sawu,** I
234 E3 **Savute** *r.* Botswana
234 E3 **Savuti** Botswana
215 Q9 **Savuto** *r.* Italy
129 P1 **Savvo-Borzya** Rus. Fed.
159 L2 **Savynky** Ukr.
159 Q4 **Savyntsi** Ukr.
118 B4 **Saw** Myanmar
116 D5 **Sawahlunto** *Sumatera* Indo
115 F5 **Sawai, Teluk** *b. Seram* Indon
138 F7 **Sawai Madhopur** *Rajasthan*
101 □7 **Sawaleke** Fiji
117 K5 **Sawan** *Kalimantan* Indon.
118 C1 **Sawan** Myanmar
118 D6 **Sawankhalok** Thai.
138 E7 **Sawar** *Rajasthan* India
127 M4 **Sawara** Japan
125 P9 **Sawasaki-bana** *pt* Japan
124 P9 **Sawata** Japan
263 K7 **Sawatch Range** *mts CO* U.S
173 M4 **Sawbridgeworth** *Hertfordsh* *England* U.K.
224 B2 **Sawdā', Jabal as** *hills* Libya
169 H3 **Sawel Mountain** *hill Northe* *Ireland* U.K.
Sawhāj Egypt *see* **Sūhāj**
119 D9 **Sawi, Ao** *b.* Thai.
197 L4 **Sawin** Pol.
228 E4 **Sawla** Ghana
235 F3 **Sawmills** Zimbabwe
118 C3 **Sawn** *Yunnan* China
147 M6 **Şawqirah, Ghubbat** *b.* Oma
147 M6 **Şawqirah, Ra's** *c.* Oman
Şawqirah Bay Oman *see* **Şawqirah, Ghubbat**
173 M3 **Sawston** *Cambridgeshire, En* U.K.
105 N4 **Sawtell** *N.S.W.* Austr.
245 J2 **Sawtooth Mountain** *AK* U.S
250 C2 **Sawtooth Mountains** *hills M* U.S.A.
262 G4 **Sawtooth Range** *mts ID* U.S
262 D2 **Sawtooth Range** *mts WA* U.
173 L3 **Sawtry** *Cambridgeshire, Engl* U.K.
115 B9 **Sawu** Indon.
Sawu *i.* Indon. *see* **Savu**
115 B8 **Sawu, Laut** *sea* Indon.
209 D10 **Sax** Spain
168 □O1 **Saxa Vord** *hill Scotland* U.K.
107 H5 **Saxby** *r. Qld* Austr.
201 K3 **Saxen** Austria
171 P7 **Saxilby** *Lincolnshire, England*
245 O5 **Saxman** *AK* U.S.A.

O3 **Saxmundham** *Suffolk, England* U.K.
M4 **Saxnäs** Sweden
C3 **Saxon** Switz.
Saxony *land* Ger. *see* **Sachsen**
Saxony-Anhalt *land* Ger. *see* **Sachsen-Anhalt**
O2 **Saxthorpe** *Norfolk, England* U.K.
A12 **Saxton** *KY* U.S.A.
G8 **Saxton** *PA* U.S.A.
D3 **Say** Mali
F3 **Say** Niger
C2 **Saya** *Sichuan* China
E5 **Saya** Japan
D3 **Şāyā** Syria
Sayabouri Laos *see* **Xaignabouli**
F3 **Sayafi** *i. Maluku* Indon.
H6 **Sayago** *reg.* Spain
Q4 **Sayak** Kazakh.
F8 **Sayalkudi** *Tamil Nadu* India
I3 **Sayam** *well* Niger
J4 **Sayama** Japan
A2 **Sayán** Peru
F3 **Sayang** *i. Papua* Indon.
F1 **Sayano-Shushenskoye Vodokhranilishche** *resr* Rus. Fed.
Sayaq Kazakh. *see* **Sayak**
J2 **Saýat** Turkm.
O8 **Sayatón** Spain
N9 **Sayaxché** Guat.
H9 **Sayda** Ger.
Sayda Lebanon *see* **Saïda**
D6 **Saye** *r.* France
F6 **Sāyen** Iran
D1 **Saygeçit** Turkey
L4 **Sayghān** Afgh.
G7 **Şayḩ** *well* Yemen
M5 **Sayḩ al Aḩmar** *reg.* Oman
H2 **Sayhan** Mongolia
K4 **Sayhandulaan** *Dornogovĭ* Mongolia
H4 **Sayhan-Ovoo** *Dundgovĭ* Mongolia
J8 **Sayḩūt** Yemen
H6 **Şayıflı** Azer.
D5 **Sayingpan** *Yunnan* China
B3 **Saykhin** Kazakh.
D2 **Saylac** Somalia
Saylan *country* Asia *see* **Sri Lanka**
E3 **Saylorsburg** *PA* U.S.A.
I2 **Saylyugem, Khrebet** *mts* Rus. Fed.
L4 **Saynshand** Mongolia
Sayn-Ust Mongolia *see* **Höhmorĭt**
Sayot Turkm. *see* **Saýat**
Say-Ötesh Kazakh. *see* **Say-Utes**
F5 **Şayqal, Bahr** *imp. l.* Syria
Sayqyn Kazakh. *see* **Saykhin**
E4 **Sayram Hu** *salt l.* China
N6 **Sayramskiy, Pik** *mt.* Uzbek.
F8 **Sayre** *OK* U.S.A.
R8 **Sayre** *PA* U.S.A.
G4 **Sayreville** *NJ* U.S.A.
L3 **Sayrob** Uzbek.
D5 **Saysu** *Xinjiang* China
D6 **Sayula** *Jalisco* Mex.
M8 **Sayula** *Veracruz* Mex.
D6 **Sayula, Laguna de** *imp. l.* Mex.
I7 **Say'ūn** Yemen
E5 **Say-Utes** Kazakh.
I3 **Sayville** *NY* U.S.A.
E5 **Sayward** *B.C.* Can.
M6 **Sayy** *well* Oman
Sayyod Turkm. *see* **Saýat**
A2 **Sazan** *i.* Albania
D2 **Sázava** *r.* Czech Rep.
C4 **Sazdy** Kazakh.
L4 **Sazhino** Rus. Fed.
P3 **Sazhnoye** Rus. Fed.
□3b **Sazile, Pointe** *pt* Mayotte
O4 **Sazin** Pak.
S2 **Sazonovo** Rus. Fed.
Saztöbe Kazakh. *see* **Sastobe**
E3 **Sbaa** Alg.
H2 **Sbeitla** Tunisia
F12 **Scaddan** *W.A.* Austr.
D5 **Scaër** France
M3 **Scafa** Italy
K5 **Scafell Pike** *hill England* U.K.
B6 **Scaggsville** *MD* U.S.A.
G9 **Scala, Monte della** *hill* Italy
D10 **Scalasaig** *Argyll and Bute, Scotland* U.K.
Q5 **Scalby** *North Yorkshire, England* U.K.
K2 **Scald Law** *hill Scotland* U.K.
P8 **Scalea** Italy
P8 **Scalea, Capo** *c.* Italy
I7 **Scaletta Zanclea** *Sicilia* Italy
□N2 **Scalloway** *Shetland, Scotland* U.K.
Scalpaigh, Eilean *i. Western Isles, Scotland* U.K. *see* **Scalpay**
E8 **Scalpay** *i. Highland, Scotland* U.K.
C7 **Scalpay** *i. Western Isles, Scotland* U.K.
H2 **Scalp Mountain** *hill* Ireland
L9 **Scamander** *Tas.* Austr.
E9 **Scamandre, Étang de** *lag.* France
F3 **Scammon Bay** *AK* U.S.A.
P7 **Scampton** *Lincolnshire, England* U.K.
L5 **Scandale** Italy
K2 **Scandarello, Lago di** *l.* Italy
J6 **Scandiano** Italy
K8 **Scandicci** Italy
E2 **Scandinavia** Europe
J3 **Scandriglia** Italy
Scania *reg.* Sweden *see* **Skåne**
L4 **Scanno** Italy
L4 **Scanno, Lago di** *l.* Italy
B7 **Scano di Montiferro** *Sardegna* Italy
G2 **Scansano** Italy
P6 **Scânteia** Romania
L3 **Scanzano Jonico** Italy
K5 **Scapa** *Orkney, Scotland* U.K.
J5 **Scapa Flow** *inlet Scotland* U.K.
I6 **Scaraben** *hill Scotland* U.K.
E10 **Scarba** *i. Scotland* U.K.
E5 **Scarborough** *Ont.* Can.
□5 **Scarborough** Trin. and Tob.
Q5 **Scarborough** *North Yorkshire, England* U.K.
E3 **Scarborough Shoal** *sea feature* S. China Sea
D11 **Scarbro** *WV* U.S.A.
M6 **Scardovari** Italy
G9 **Scargill** *South I.* N.Z.
B9 **Scariff Island** Ireland
C9 **Scarinish** *Argyll and Bute, Scotland* U.K.
L6 **Scarisbrick** *Lancashire, England* U.K.
D4 **Scarlets Mill** *PA* U.S.A.
F2 **Scarlino** Italy
B6 **Scarp** *i. Scotland* U.K.
Scarpanto *i.* Greece *see* **Karpathos**
F2 **Scarpe** *r.* France
K8 **Scarperia** Italy
E7 **Scarriff** Ireland
H2 **Scarsdale** *NY* U.S.A.
4 **Scarva** *Northern Ireland* U.K.
4 **Scaterie Island** *N.S.* Can.
B10 **Scauri** *Sicilia* Italy
D8 **Scavaig, Loch** *b. Scotland* U.K.
N6 **Ščavnica** *r.* Slovenia
G1 **Scawfell Shoal** *sea feature* S. China Sea
E5 **Sceale Bay** *S.A.* Austr.
F4 **Šćedro** *i.* Croatia
N3 **Scerni** Italy
K8 **Scey-sur-Saône-et-St-Albin** France
G2 **Schaafheim** Ger.
1 **Schaalby** Ger.
K4 **Schaale** *r.* Ger.
K3 **Schaalsee** *l.* Ger.
K3 **Schaalsee** *park* Ger.
H7 **Schaan** Liechtenstein
4 **Schaarsbergen** Neth.
2 **Schacht-Audorf** Ger.
C4 **Schaefferstown** *PA* U.S.A.
F7 **Schaerbeek** Belgium
187 J7 **Schaesberg** Neth.
212 F1 **Schaffhausen** Switz.
212 F1 **Schaffhausen** *canton* Switz.
190 H1 **Schafflund** Ger.
190 H2 **Schafstedt** Ger.
195 K6 **Schäftlarn** Ger.
186 G3 **Schagen** Neth.
186 G3 **Schagerbrug** Neth.
186 I5 **Schaijk** Neth.
234 C5 **Schakalskuppe** Namibia
200 H3 **Schalchen** Austria
193 D10 **Schalkau** Ger.
186 J4 **Schalkhaar** Neth.
191 E8 **Schalksmühle** Ger.
194 D6 **Schallstadt** Ger.
212 G1 **Schänis** Switz.
144 I6 **Schao** *watercourse* Afgh./Iran
191 E6 **Schapen** Ger.
192 H1 **Schaprode** Ger.
190 K2 **Scharbeutz** Ger.
201 H2 **Schardenberg** Austria
201 H3 **Schärding** Austria
200 H5 **Schareck** *mt.* Austria
186 E5 **Scharendijke** Neth.
200 E4 **Scharfreiter** *mt.* Austria/Ger.
190 F3 **Scharhörn** *sea feature* Ger.
193 J6 **Scharmützelsee** *l.* Ger.
190 K4 **Scharnebeck** Ger.
186 I2 **Scharnegoutum** Neth.
200 D5 **Scharnitz** Austria
201 I4 **Scharnstein** Austria
190 E4 **Scharrel (Oldenburg)** Ger.
191 C10 **Scharteberg** *hill* Ger.
186 H3 **Scharwoude** Neth.
190 K2 **Schashagen** Ger.
201 O4 **Schattendorf** Austria
250 F7 **Schaumburg** *IL* U.S.A.
195 I2 **Schebheim** Ger.
195 M6 **Schechen** Ger.
191 I8 **Scheden** Ger.
186 K2 **Scheemda** Neth.
194 G5 **Scheer** Ger.
190 H4 **Scheeßel** Ger.
200 H4 **Scheffau am Tennengebirge** Austria
200 F4 **Scheffau am Wilden Kaiser** Austria
249 H2 **Schefferville** *Nfld and Lab.* Can.
194 G3 **Schefflenz** Ger.
213 N9 **Scheggia e Pascelupo** Italy
215 J2 **Scheggino** Italy
201 L3 **Scheibbs** Austria
201 N4 **Scheiblingkirchen** Austria
194 H6 **Scheidegg** Ger.
201 J5 **Scheifling** Austria
195 I2 **Scheinfeld** Ger.
194 H5 **Schelklingen** Ger.
265 R3 **Schell Creek Range** *mts NV* U.S.A.
187 F6 **Schelle** Belgium
191 J6 **Schellerten** Ger.
190 J2 **Schellhorn** Ger.
256 G8 **Schellsburg** *PA* U.S.A.
264 J3 **Schellville** *CA* U.S.A.
194 H5 **Schemmerhofen** Ger.
257 L6 **Schenectady** *NY* U.S.A.
190 H2 **Schenefeld** *Schleswig-Holstein* Ger.
190 I3 **Schenefeld** *Schleswig-Holstein* Ger.
201 J2 **Schenkenfelden** Austria
194 E5 **Schenkenzell** Ger.
191 I9 **Schenklengsfeld** Ger.
191 C7 **Schermbeck** Ger.
193 E6 **Schermen** Ger.
186 G3 **Schermerhorn** Neth.
191 K8 **Schernberg** Ger.
195 K4 **Schernfeld** Ger.
187 G7 **Scherpenheuvel** Belgium
186 H4 **Scherpenzeel** Neth.
261 F11 **Schertz** *TX* U.S.A.
179 N7 **Scherwiller** France
212 G1 **Scherzingen** Switz.
200 A5 **Schesaplana** *mt.* Austria/Switz.
195 K2 **Scheßlitz** Ger.
195 K5 **Scheyern** Ger.
213 M3 **Schiara, Monte** *mt.* Italy
215 M4 **Schiavi di Abruzzo** Italy
186 F5 **Schiedam** Neth.
191 H7 **Schieder-Schwalenberg** Ger.
201 J6 **Schiefling am See** Austria
168 H9 **Schiehallion** *mt. Scotland* U.K.
187 J9 **Schieren** Lux.
191 K7 **Schierke** Ger.
195 M4 **Schierling** Ger.
186 J2 **Schiermonnikoog** Neth.
186 J1 **Schiermonnikoog** *i.* Neth.
186 J1 **Schiermonnikoog Nationaal Park** *nat. park* Neth.
212 H2 **Schiers** Switz.
190 G3 **Schiffdorf** Ger.
194 E3 **Schifferstadt** Ger.
187 J9 **Schifflange** Lux.
194 C3 **Schiffweiler** Ger.
186 H5 **Schijndel** Neth.
187 G6 **Schilde** Belgium
190 K4 **Schilde** *r.* Ger.
186 K2 **Schildmeer** *l.* Neth.
192 H5 **Schildow** Ger.
186 K2 **Schildwolde-Hellum** Neth.
194 B2 **Schillingen** Ger.
195 I3 **Schillingsfürst** Ger.
212 I3 **Schilpario** Italy
194 E5 **Schiltach** Ger.
195 K5 **Schiltberg** Ger.
179 O6 **Schiltigheim** France
220 E4 **Schimatari** Greece
187 I7 **Schinnen** Neth.
187 I7 **Schinveld** Neth.
213 K4 **Schio** Italy
186 J4 **Schipbeek** *r.* Neth.
186 G4 **Schiphol** *airport* Neth.
193 I7 **Schipkau** Ger.
179 N7 **Schirmeck** France
195 M2 **Schirmitz** Ger.
193 F10 **Schirnding** Ger.
219 P3 **Schitu Duca** Romania
220 C6 **Schiza** *i.* Greece
193 F8 **Schkeuditz** Ger.
193 E8 **Schkölen** Ger.
193 G7 **Schköna** Ger.
193 E8 **Schkopau** Ger.
193 I7 **Schlabendorf** Ger.
191 K6 **Schladen** Ger.
201 I5 **Schladming** Austria
201 I5 **Schladminger Tauern** *mts* Austria
190 K3 **Schlagsdorf** Ger.
191 G7 **Schlangen** Ger.
191 F10 **Schlangenbad** Ger.
193 D6 **Schlanstedt** Ger.
195 M6 **Schleching** Ger.
200 E5 **Schlegeisspeicher** *l.* Austria
190 J1 **Schlei** *r.* Ger.
191 B9 **Schleiden** Ger.
193 K7 **Schleife** Ger.
201 N3 **Schleinbach** Austria
212 E1 **Schleitheim** Switz.
193 E9 **Schleiz** Ger.
193 G9 **Schlema** Ger.
193 I6 **Schlepzig** Ger.
Schlesien *reg.* Europe *see* **Silesia**
190 I1 **Schleswig** Ger.
190 I2 **Schleswig-Holstein** *land* Ger.
190 G2 **Schleswig-Holsteinisches Wattenmeer, Nationalpark** *nat. park* Ger.
193 G9 **Schlettau** Ger.
191 K9 **Schleusingen** Ger.
193 H7 **Schlieben** Ger.
194 D6 **Schliengen** Ger.
194 H6 **Schlier** Ger.
201 J4 **Schlierbach** Austria
212 E1 **Schlieren** Switz.
195 L6 **Schliersee** Ger.
195 L6 **Schliersee** *l.* Ger.
200 A5 **Schlins** Austria
200 E5 **Schlitters** Austria
191 I9 **Schlitz** Ger.
191 G7 **Schloss Holte-Stukenbrock** Ger.
212 D2 **Schlosswil** Switz.
191 K8 **Schlotheim** Ger.
194 E6 **Schluchsee** Ger.
194 E6 **Schluchsee** *l.* Ger.
179 N7 **Schlucht, Col de la** *pass* France
191 I10 **Schlüchtern** Ger.
Schlüsselburg Rus. Fed. *see* **Shlissel'burg**
195 J2 **Schlüsselfeld** Ger.
190 I3 **Schmalfeld** Ger.
191 J9 **Schmalkalden, Kurort** Ger.
191 F8 **Schmallenberg** Ger.
194 B3 **Schmelz** Ger.
195 M3 **Schmidgaden** Ger.
195 L3 **Schmidmühlen** Ger.
Schmidt Island Rus. Fed. *see* **Shmidta, Ostrov**
236 I4 **Schmidtsdrif** S. Africa
193 I9 **Schmiedeberg** Ger.
200 E5 **Schmirn** Austria
200 G5 **Schmittenhöhe** *mt.* Austria
192 J4 **Schmölln** *Brandenburg* Ger.
193 F9 **Schmölln** *Thüringen* Ger.
195 L2 **Schnabelwaid** Ger.
192 E4 **Schnackenburg** Ger.
195 M5 **Schnaitsee** Ger.
195 K2 **Schnaittach** Ger.
195 M2 **Schnaittenbach** Ger.
212 F1 **Schnebelhorn** *mt.* Switz.
258 D3 **Schnecksville** *PA* U.S.A.
193 G9 **Schneeberg** Ger.
190 K5 **Schnega** Ger.
Schneidemühl Pol. *see* **Piła**
193 D7 **Schneidlingen** Ger.
191 B10 **Schneifel** *hills* Ger.
195 N6 **Schneizlreuth** Ger.
195 I3 **Schnelldorf** Ger.
190 I4 **Schneverdingen** Ger.
194 H5 **Schnürpflingen** Ger.
190 H1 **Schobüll** Ger.
271 □3 **Schœlcher** Martinique
237 O1 **Schoemanskloof** *pass* S. Africa
187 J8 **Schoenberg** Belgium
250 E5 **Schofield** *WI* U.S.A.
264 □C12 **Schofield Barracks** *military base HI* U.S.A.
257 K6 **Schoharie** *NY* U.S.A.
186 I3 **Schokland** *tourist site* Neth.
190 G5 **Scholen** Ger.
171 O6 **Scholes** *West Yorkshire, England* U.K.
192 F5 **Schollene** Ger.
191 H10 **Schöllkrippen** Ger.
195 O4 **Schöllnach** Ger.
237 J7 **Schombee** S. Africa
194 F4 **Schömberg** *Baden-Württemberg* Ger.
194 F5 **Schömberg** *Baden-Württemberg* Ger.
194 G4 **Schönaich** Ger.
194 F3 **Schönau** *Baden-Württemberg* Ger.
195 N5 **Schönau** *Bayern* Ger.
195 N6 **Schönau am Königssee** Ger.
194 D6 **Schönau im Schwarzwald** Ger.
201 L3 **Schönbach** Austria
195 O4 **Schönberg** *Bayern* Ger.
192 G5 **Schönberg** *Brandenburg* Ger.
190 K3 **Schönberg** *Mecklenburg-Vorpommern* Ger.
190 J3 **Schönberg** *Schleswig-Holstein* Ger.
190 J2 **Schönberg (Holstein)** Ger.
201 M2 **Schönberg am Kamp** Austria
190 J2 **Schönbergerstrand** Ger.
200 D5 **Schönberg im Stubaital** Austria
193 I7 **Schönborn** Ger.
191 K9 **Schönbrunn** Ger.
194 F4 **Schönbuch** *reg.* Ger.
194 G4 **Schönbuch, Naturpark** *nature res.* Ger.
193 E8 **Schönburg** Ger.
191 I10 **Schondra** Ger.
192 F4 **Schönebeck** Ger.
193 E6 **Schönebeck (Elbe)** Ger.
193 F10 **Schöneck** Ger.
191 B10 **Schönecken** Ger.
193 H6 **Schönefeld** Ger.
193 I6 **Schönefeld** *airport* Ger.
193 I6 **Schöneiche Berlin** Ger.
194 C3 **Schönenberg-Kübelberg** Ger.
192 I4 **Schönermark** *Brandenburg* Ger.
192 J4 **Schönermark** *Brandenburg* Ger.
193 H7 **Schönewalde** Ger.
190 K5 **Schönewörde** Ger.
193 I8 **Schönfeld** Ger.
195 J6 **Schongau** Ger.
192 F5 **Schönhausen** Ger.
193 G9 **Schönheide** Ger.
191 K6 **Schöningen** Ger.
190 J2 **Schönkirchen** Ger.
195 N2 **Schönsee** Ger.
191 K8 **Schönstedt** Ger.
194 H3 **Schöntal** Ger.
195 N3 **Schönthal** Ger.
191 J10 **Schonungen** Ger.
193 F10 **Schönwald** Ger.
192 H5 **Schönwalde** *Brandenburg* Ger.
192 H5 **Schönwalde** *Brandenburg* Ger.
193 I7 **Schönwalde** *Brandenburg* Ger.
190 K2 **Schönwalde am Bungsberg** Ger.
200 C5 **Schönwies** Austria
257 □Q3 **Schoodic Lake** *ME* U.S.A.
257 □R4 **Schoodic Point** *ME* U.S.A.
250 I7 **Schoolcraft** *MI* U.S.A.
187 E6 **Schoondijke** Neth.
186 K3 **Schoonebeek** Neth.
186 G5 **Schoonhoven** Neth.
186 K3 **Schoonoord** Neth.
186 G3 **Schoorl** Neth.
194 D6 **Schopfheim** Ger.
201 M3 **Schöpfl** *hill* Austria
195 I3 **Schopfloch** Ger.
191 K6 **Schöppenstedt** Ger.
200 B5 **Schoppernau** Austria
191 D6 **Schöppingen** Ger.
192 I5 **Schorfheide** *reg.* Ger.
201 I4 **Schörfling am Attersee** Austria
194 H4 **Schorndorf** *Baden-Württemberg* Ger.
195 N3 **Schorndorf** *Bayern* Ger.
190 E3 **Schortens** Ger.
187 F6 **Schoten** Belgium
191 H10 **Schotten** Ger.
105 L10 **Schouten Island** *Tas.* Austr.
113 J7 **Schouten Islands** P.N.G.
258 C1 **Schrader** *r. PA* U.S.A.
194 E5 **Schramberg** Ger.
200 D5 **Schrankogel** *mt.* Austria
193 E8 **Schraplau** Ger.
191 H9 **Schrecksbach** Ger.
248 C3 **Schreiber** *Ont.* Can.
201 L2 **Schrems** Austria
192 F5 **Schrepkow** Ger.
194 F3 **Schriesheim** Ger.
195 K4 **Schrobenhausen** Ger.
201 J5 **Schröder** Austria
257 L5 **Schroon Lake** *NY* U.S.A.
257 L5 **Schroon Lake** *l. NY* U.S.A.
Schröttersburg Pol. *see* **Płock**
194 H3 **Schrozberg** Ger.
200 A5 **Schruns** Austria
212 F1 **Schübelbach** Switz.
190 H1 **Schuby** Ger.
191 J7 **Schulenberg im Oberharz** Ger.
261 G11 **Schulenburg** *TX* U.S.A.
247 I5 **Schuler** *Alta* Can.
169 C9 **Schull** Ireland
247 L1 **Schultz Lake** *Nunavut* Can.
192 J5 **Schulzendorf** Ger.
193 I6 **Schulzendorf bei Eichwalde** Ger.
212 E2 **Schüpfheim** Switz.
194 G4 **Schurwald** *for.* Ger.
264 N3 **Schurz** *NV* U.S.A.
194 H6 **Schussen** *r.* Ger.
194 D4 **Schutter** *r.* Ger.
195 K4 **Schutter** *r.* Ger.
194 D5 **Schuttertal** Ger.
194 D5 **Schutterwald** Ger.
191 D6 **Schüttorf** Ger.
260 G5 **Schuyler** *NE* U.S.A.
257 J6 **Schuyler Lake** *NY* U.S.A.
257 L5 **Schuylerville** *NY* U.S.A.
258 E5 **Schuylkill** *r. PA* U.S.A.
258 C3 **Schuylkill County** *county PA* U.S.A.
251 R9 **Schuylkill Haven** *PA* U.S.A.
192 F3 **Schwaan** Ger.
195 K3 **Schwabach** Ger.
195 I5 **Schwaben** *admin. reg.* Ger.
194 F6 **Schwäbische Alb** *mts* Ger.
194 H4 **Schwäbisch-Fränkischer Wald, Naturpark** *nature res.* Ger.
194 H4 **Schwäbisch Gmünd** Ger.
194 H3 **Schwäbisch Hall** Ger.
195 J5 **Schwabmünchen** Ger.
190 H2 **Schwabstedt** Ger.
190 G5 **Schwaförden** Ger.
195 K3 **Schwaig bei Nürnberg** Ger.
194 G3 **Schwaigern** Ger.
194 B3 **Schwalbach** Ger.
191 J9 **Schwallungen** Ger.
191 H8 **Schwalm** *r.* Ger.
191 H9 **Schwalmstadt-Treysa** Ger.
191 H9 **Schwalmstadt-Ziegenhain** Ger.
201 L6 **Schwanberg** Austria
212 G1 **Schwanden** Switz.
195 M3 **Schwandorf** Ger.
192 I5 **Schwanebeck** *Brandenburg* Ger.
193 D7 **Schwanebeck** *Sachsen-Anhalt* Ger.
201 I3 **Schwanenstadt** Austria
117 J5 **Schwaner, Pegunungan** *mts* Indon.
190 G4 **Schwanewede** Ger.
195 J6 **Schwangau** Ger.
190 K4 **Schwanheide** Ger.
190 I1 **Schwansen** *reg.* Ger.
195 K3 **Schwanstetten** Ger.
190 H5 **Schwarme** Ger.
190 I5 **Schwarmstedt** Ger.
287 D2 **Schwartz Range** *mts* Antarctica
192 G4 **Schwarz** Ger.
191 K9 **Schwarza** Ger.
194 E6 **Schwarza** *r.* Ger.
193 D9 **Schwarza** *r.* Ger.
200 A5 **Schwarzach** Austria
195 N4 **Schwarzach** Ger.
195 K4 **Schwarzach** *r.* Ger.
195 M3 **Schwarzach** *r.* Ger.
200 H5 **Schwarzach im Pongau** Austria
201 M4 **Schwarzau im Gebirge** Austria
193 G7 **Schwarze Elster** *r.* Ger.
195 M4 **Schwarze Laber** *r.* Ger.
201 L2 **Schwarzenau** Austria
201 N4 **Schwarzenbach** Austria
193 E10 **Schwarzenbach am Wald** Ger.
193 E10 **Schwarzenbach an der Saale** Ger.
190 J3 **Schwarzenbek** Ger.
193 G9 **Schwarzenberg** Ger.
191 H9 **Schwarzenborn** Ger.
195 K3 **Schwarzenbruck** Ger.
212 C2 **Schwarzenburg** Switz.
195 M3 **Schwarzenfeld** Ger.
200 E5 **Schwarzenstein** *mt.* Austria/Italy
193 J7 **Schwarze Pumpe** Ger.
195 M3 **Schwarzer Bach** *r.* Ger.
191 B10 **Schwarzer Mann** *hill* Ger.
195 N3 **Schwarzer Regen** *r.* Ger.
193 K8 **Schwarzer Schöps** *r.* Ger.
213 P1 **Schwarzersee** *l.* Austria
193 I8 **Schwarzheide** Ger.
195 M3 **Schwarzhofen** Ger.
200 D5 **Schwarzhorn** *mt.* Austria
212 E2 **Schwarzhorn** *mt.* Switz.
234 C5 **Schwarzrand** *mts* Namibia
195 N3 **Schwarzriegel** *mt.* Ger.
194 E6 **Schwarzwald** *mts* Ger.
245 K2 **Schwatka, Mount** *AK* U.S.A.
244 H2 **Schwatka Mountains** *AK* U.S.A.
200 E5 **Schwaz** Austria
201 N3 **Schwechat** Austria
190 J2 **Schwedeneck** Ger.
192 J4 **Schwedt an der Oder** Ger.
194 E3 **Schwegenheim** Ger.
190 F4 **Schwei (Stadland)** Ger.
190 F4 **Schweiburg** Ger.
194 B2 **Schweich** Ger.
194 D3 **Schweigen-Rechtenbach** Ger.
179 O6 **Schweighouse-sur-Moder** France
191 J9 **Schweina** Ger.
191 J10 **Schweinfurt** Ger.
193 H7 **Schweinitz** Ger.
192 G4 **Schweinrich** Ger.
195 L4 **Schweitenkirchen** Ger.
Schweiz *country* Europe *see* **Switzerland**
237 J3 **Schweizer-Reneke** S. Africa
191 D8 **Schwelm** Ger.
200 E5 **Schwendau** Austria
194 H5 **Schwendi** Ger.
194 F5 **Schwenningen** *Baden-Württemberg* Ger.
194 F5 **Schwenningen** *Baden-Württemberg* Ger.
193 I8 **Schwepnitz** Ger.
192 D3 **Schwerin** Ger.
192 D3 **Schweriner See** *l.* Ger.
192 D3 **Schweriner Seenlandschaft** *park* Ger.
190 H5 **Schweringen** Ger.
201 K3 **Schwertberg** Austria
191 E8 **Schwerte** Ger.
194 F3 **Schwetzingen** Ger.
192 I3 **Schwichtenberg** Ger.
194 G4 **Schwieberdingen** Ger.
193 J6 **Schwielochsee** *l.* Ger.
192 D5 **Schwiesau** Ger.
195 M5 **Schwindegg** Ger.
190 H3 **Schwinge** *r.* Ger.
192 G3 **Schwinkendorf** Ger.
200 F4 **Schwoich** Austria
194 D6 **Schwörstadt** Ger.
212 F1 **Schwyz** Switz.
212 F1 **Schwyz** *canton* Switz.
216 E8 **Sciacca** *Sicilia* Italy
216 H10 **Scicli** *Sicilia* Italy
178 B4 **Scie** *r.* France
182 I4 **Sciez** France
217 K5 **Scigliano** Italy
213 L3 **Sciliar, Parco Naturale dello** *nature res.* Italy
217 J7 **Scilla** Italy
Scilly, Île *atoll Arch. de la Société* Fr. Polynesia *see* **Manuae**
172 □ **Scilly, Isles of** *England* U.K.
196 E4 **Ścinawa** Pol.
196 E5 **Ścinawka** *r.* Pol.
256 D8 **Scio** *OH* U.S.A.
182 J4 **Scionzier** France
258 E3 **Sciota** *PA* U.S.A.
256 C10 **Scioto** *r. OH* U.S.A.
265 T2 **Scipio** *UT* U.S.A.
172 C4 **Scleddau** *Pembrokeshire, Wales* U.K.
262 L2 **Scobey** *MT* U.S.A.
Scodra Albania *see* **Shkodër**
265 U2 **Scofield Reservoir** *UT* U.S.A.
214 F2 **Scoglia dello Sparviero** *i.* Italy
216 G10 **Scoglitti** *Sicilia* Italy
217 H7 **Scolaticci** *Isole Lipari* Italy
173 O3 **Scole** *Norfolk, England* U.K.
213 J7 **Scoltenna** *r.* Italy
105 M5 **Scone** *N.S.W.* Austr.
168 J10 **Scone** *Perth and Kinross, Scotland* U.K.
168 D8 **Sconser** *Highland, Scotland* U.K.
212 E4 **Scopello** Italy
215 K3 **Scoppito** Italy
181 L8 **Scorbé-Clairvaux** France
216 H9 **Scordia** *Sicilia* Italy
243 P2 **Scoresby Land** *reg.* Greenland
Scoresbysund Greenland *see* **Ittoqqortoormiit**
Scoresby Sund *sea chan.* Greenland *see* **Kangertittivaq**
180 E6 **Scorff** *r.* France
219 M6 **Scornicești** Romania
Scorno, Punta dello *pt Sardegna* Italy *see* **Caprara, Punta**
109 I12 **Scorpion Bight** *b. W.A.* Austr.
217 O3 **Scorrano** Italy
171 N5 **Scorton** *North Yorkshire, England* U.K.
213 M4 **Scorzè** Italy
170 D5 **Scotch Corner** Ireland
171 N5 **Scotch Corner** *North Yorkshire, England* U.K.
259 G3 **Scotch Plains** *NJ* U.S.A.
288 F9 **Scotia Ridge** *sea feature* S. Atlantic Ocean
289 B9 **Scotia Ridge** *sea feature* S. Atlantic Ocean
288 G9 **Scotia Sea** S. Atlantic Ocean
251 N6 **Scotland** *Ont.* Can.
168 I8 **Scotland** *admin. div.* U.K.
257 I10 **Scotland** *MD* U.S.A.
258 E2 **Scotrun** *PA* U.S.A.
169 H4 **Scotshouse** Ireland
249 G4 **Scotstown** *Que.* Can.
106 B2 **Scott, Cape** *N.T.* Austr.
246 D5 **Scott, Cape** *B.C.* Can.
261 G9 **Scott, Mount** *hill OK* U.S.A.
287 L1 **Scott Base** *research stn* Antarctica
237 O6 **Scottburgh** S. Africa
260 E6 **Scott City** *KS* U.S.A.
287 K1 **Scott Coast** Antarctica
171 P7 **Scotter** *Lincolnshire, England* U.K.
286 N1 **Scott Glacier** Antarctica
287 G2 **Scott Glacier** Antarctica
243 K2 **Scott Inlet** *Nunavut* Can.
168 K11 **Scottish Borders** *admin. div. Scotland* U.K.
287 L2 **Scott Island** Antarctica
246 D5 **Scott Islands** *B.C.* Can.
247 J3 **Scott Lake** *Sask.* Can.
287 D2 **Scott Mountains** Antarctica
171 N5 **Scotton** *North Yorkshire, England* U.K.
173 O2 **Scottow** *Norfolk, England* U.K.
102 G1 **Scott Point** *North I.* N.Z.
108 G3 **Scott Reef** *W.A.* Austr.
260 D5 **Scottsbluff** *NE* U.S.A.
255 D8 **Scottsboro** *AL* U.S.A.
254 E6 **Scottsburg** *IN* U.S.A.
105 K9 **Scottsdale** *Tas.* Austr.
265 U8 **Scottsdale** *AZ* U.S.A.
271 □2 **Scotts Head** Dominica
254 D7 **Scottsville** *KY* U.S.A.
256 G11 **Scottsville** *VA* U.S.A.
250 H6 **Scottville** *MI* U.S.A.
168 F6 **Scourie** *Highland, Scotland* U.K.
168 □N3 **Scousburgh** *Shetland, Scotland* U.K.
168 I5 **Scrabster** *Highland, Scotland* U.K.
258 D2 **Scranton** *PA* U.S.A.
169 C6 **Screeb** Ireland
169 G6 **Screggan** Ireland
169 F4 **Scribbagh** *Northern Ireland* U.K.
168 D10 **Scridain, Loch** *inlet Scotland* U.K.
212 F5 **Scrivia** *r.* Italy
248 E4 **Scugog, Lake** *Ont.* Can.
171 P6 **Scunthorpe** *North Lincolnshire, England* U.K.
212 I2 **Scuol** Switz.
Scupi Macedonia *see* **Skopje**
215 K3 **Scurcola Marsicana** Italy
168 B8 **Scurrival Point** *Scotland* U.K.
Scutari Albania *see* **Shkodër**
218 H8 **Scutari, Lake** Albania/Montenegro
256 H12 **Seaboard** *NC* U.S.A.
258 E5 **Seabrook** *NJ* U.S.A.
109 E11 **Seabrook, Lake** *salt flat W.A.* Austr.
219 M6 **Seaca** Romania
173 M6 **Seaford** *East Sussex, England* U.K.
257 J10 **Seaford** *DE* U.S.A.
251 M6 **Seaforth** *Ont.* Can.
270 □ **Seaforth** Jamaica
168 C7 **Seaforth, Loch** *inlet Scotland* U.K.
171 O4 **Seaham** *Durham, England* U.K.
114 A6 **Seahorse Bank** *sea feature* Phil.
171 N2 **Seahouses** *Northumberland, England* U.K.
258 F6 **Sea Isle City** *NJ* U.S.A.
247 M3 **Seal** *r. Man.* Can.
236 H10 **Seal, Cape** S. Africa
105 I6 **Sea Lake** *Vic.* Austr.
286 X2 **Seal Bay** Antarctica
238 □2c **Seal Bay** *Tristan da Cunha* S. Atlantic Ocean
244 H5 **Seal Cape** *AK* U.S.A.
270 H3 **Seal Cays** *is* Turks and Caicos Is
257 □S4 **Seal Cove** *N.B.* Can.
249 J3 **Seal Cove** *Nfld and Lab.* Can.
168 F7 **Sealga, Loch na** *l. Scotland* U.K.
257 □Q5 **Seal Island** *ME* U.S.A.
249 I2 **Seal Lake** *Nfld and Lab.* Can.
247 I1 **Seal Lake** *N.W.T.* Can.
237 I10 **Seal Point** S. Africa
261 G11 **Sealy** *TX* U.S.A.
256 B10 **Seaman** *OH* U.S.A.
265 Q4 **Seaman Range** *mts NV* U.S.A.
171 Q5 **Seamer** *North Yorkshire, England* U.K.
170 H2 **Seamill** *North Ayrshire, Scotland* U.K.
204 C5 **Seara** Port.
265 R6 **Searchlight** *NV* U.S.A.
261 J8 **Searcy** *AR* U.S.A.
264 O6 **Searles Lake** *CA* U.S.A.
257 □Q4 **Searsport** *ME* U.S.A.
171 K5 **Seascale** *Cumbria, England* U.K.
264 K5 **Seaside** *CA* U.S.A.
262 C4 **Seaside** *OR* U.S.A.
259 G5 **Seaside Park** *NJ* U.S.A.
171 J4 **Seaton** *Cumbria, England* U.K.
172 F6 **Seaton** *Devon, England* U.K.
171 N3 **Seaton Delaval** *Northumberland, England* U.K.
287 D2 **Seaton Glacier** Antarctica
171 O3 **Seaton Sluice** *Northumberland, England* U.K.
262 C3 **Seattle** *WA* U.S.A.
245 M3 **Seattle, Mount** Can./U.S.A.
237 J10 **Sea View** S. Africa
173 J6 **Seaview** *Isle of Wight, England* U.K.
107 J5 **Seaview Range** *mts Qld* Austr.
258 F6 **Seaville** *NJ* U.S.A.
103 H9 **Seaward Kaikoura Range** *mts South I.* N.Z.
115 B9 **Seba** Indon.
266 □P11 **Sebaco** Nic.
257 □O5 **Sebago Lake** *ME* U.S.A.
117 L5 **Sebakung** *Kalimantan* Indon.
204 C8 **Sebal** Port.
117 J6 **Sebangan, Teluk** *b.* Indon.
116 F4 **Sebangka** *i.* Indon.
Sebastea Turkey *see* **Sivas**
255 G12 **Sebastian** *FL* U.S.A.
285 F2 **Sebastián Elcano** Arg.
266 B3 **Sebastián Vizcaíno, Bahía** *b.* Mex.
257 □P4 **Sebasticook** *r. ME* U.S.A.
257 □P4 **Sebasticook Lake** *ME* U.S.A.
Sebastopol Ukr. *see* **Sevastopol'**
264 J3 **Sebastopol** *CA* U.S.A.
117 L2 **Sebatik** *i.* Indon.
117 J3 **Sebauh** *Sarawak* Malaysia
117 I5 **Sebayan, Bukit** *mt.* Indon.
183 B8 **Sébazac-Concourès** France
229 F3 **Sebba** Burkina
164 F5 **Sebbersund** Denmark
225 H6 **Sebderat** Eritrea
227 E2 **Sebdou** Alg.
228 C3 **Sébékoro** Mali
148 E3 **Seben** Turkey
Sebenico Croatia *see* **Šibenik**
Sebennytos Egypt *see* **Samannūd**
219 L5 **Sebeş** Romania
219 L4 **Sebeş** *r.* Romania
116 F7 **Sebesi** *i.* Indon.
199 J5 **Sebes-Körös** *r.* Hungary
251 K6 **Sebewaing** *MI* U.S.A.
160 L5 **Sebezh** Rus. Fed.
148 I3 **Şebinkarahisar** Turkey
219 K4 **Sebiş** Romania
161 U3 **Sebla** *r.* Rus. Fed.
116 E6 **Seblat, Gunung** *mt.* Indon.
193 J9 **Sebnitz** Ger.
257 □Q3 **Seboeis** *ME* U.S.A.
257 □Q3 **Seboeis Lake** *ME* U.S.A.
257 □P3 **Seboomook Lake** *ME* U.S.A.
256 H12 **Sebrell** *VA* U.S.A.
255 G12 **Sebring** *FL* U.S.A.
157 H6 **Sebrovo** Rus. Fed.
117 L6 **Sebuku** *i.* Indon.
117 L2 **Sebuku** *r.* Indon.
117 L3 **Sebuku, Teluk** *b.* Indon.
117 L2 **Sebuku-Sembakung, Taman Nasional** *nat. park Kalimantan* Indon.
117 I4 **Sebuyau** *Sarawak* Malaysia
208 F7 **Sec, Riu** *r.* Spain
284 D5 **Seca, Pampa** *plain* Arg.
218 I5 **Sečanj** *Vojvodina* Serbia
204 D8 **Secarias** Port.
199 K6 **Secaş** Romania
219 L4 **Secaş** *r.* Romania
266 □S14 **Secas, Islas** *is* Panama
213 K5 **Secchia** *r.* Italy
232 C3 **Seccia** *mts* Eth.
197 H5 **Secemin** Pol.
246 F5 **Sechelt** *B.C.* Can.
157 I5 **Sechenovo** Rus. Fed.
274 A6 **Sechura** Peru
274 A6 **Sechura, Bahía de** *b.* Peru
274 A6 **Sechura, Desierto de** *des.* Peru
194 G3 **Seckach** Ger.
201 K5 **Seckau** Austria
201 K5 **Seckauer Alpen** *mts* Austria
178 F2 **Seclin** France
184 D2 **Secondigny** France
257 □N3 **Second Lake** *NH* U.S.A.
265 V6 **Second Mesa** *AZ* U.S.A.
258 B4 **Second Mountain** *ridge PA* U.S.A.
228 □ **Secos, Ilhéus** *is* Cape Verde
199 K3 **Sečovce** Slovakia
103 A12 **Secretary Island** *South I.* N.Z.
237 N2 **Secunda** S. Africa
136 F4 **Secunderabad** *Andhra Prad.* India
276 D3 **Sécure** *r.* Bol.
199 J5 **Secusigiu** Romania
160 I4 **Seda** Latvia
160 I4 **Seda** *r.* Latvia
160 F5 **Seda** Lith.
206 D2 **Seda** Port.
206 C3 **Seda** *r.* Port.
260 I6 **Sedalia** *MO* U.S.A.
136 E4 **Sedam** *Karnataka* India
104 G6 **Sedan** *S.A.* Austr.
179 I4 **Sedan** France
261 G7 **Sedan** *KS* U.S.A.
107 H5 **Sedan Dip** *Qld* Austr.
244 F5 **Sedanka Island** *AK* U.S.A.
205 M3 **Sedano** Spain
171 L5 **Sedbergh** *Cumbria, England* U.K.
103 I8 **Seddon** *South I.* N.Z.
103 F8 **Seddonville** *South I.* N.Z.
221 H2 **Seddülbahir** Turkey
150 C8 **Sedé Boqer** Israel
144 E6 **Sedeh** *Fārs* Iran
144 H5 **Sedeh** *Khorāsān* Iran
183 H8 **Séderon** France
150 C7 **Sederot** Israel
171 O4 **Sedgefield** *Durham, England* U.K.
247 I4 **Sedgewick** *Alta* Can.
172 H2 **Sedgley** *West Midlands, England* U.K.
257 □Q4 **Sedgwick** *ME* U.S.A.
228 B3 **Sédhiou** Senegal
213 M3 **Sedico** Italy
214 B7 **Sedilo** *Sardegna* Italy
214 B6 **Sedini** *Sardegna* Italy
198 G6 **Sedlarica** Croatia
198 D2 **Sedlčany** Czech Rep.
198 D2 **Sedlec Prčice** Czech Rep.
Sedlets Pol. *see* **Siedlce**
199 K3 **Sedlice** Slovakia
193 J7 **Sedlitz** Ger.
193 J9 **Sedlo** *hill* Czech Rep.
158 E2 **Sedlyshche** Ukr.
150 D7 **Sedom** Israel
265 U7 **Sedona** *AZ* U.S.A.
Sedovo Ukr. *see* **Syedove**
227 G1 **Sédrata** Alg.
212 H4 **Sedrina** Italy
117 L4 **Sedulang** *Kalimantan* Indon.
160 G6 **Šeduva** Lith.
197 H4 **Sędziejowice** Pol.
196 G3 **Sędzin** Pol.
197 I5 **Sędziszów** Pol.
197 J5 **Sędziszów Małopolski** Pol.
200 H5 **See** *Salzburg* Austria
200 B5 **See** *Tirol* Austria
181 I4 **Sée** *r.* France
194 E4 **Seebach** *Baden-Württemberg* Ger.
191 J9 **Seebach** *Thüringen* Ger.
201 K7 **Seeberg** *pass* Austria/Slovenia
191 K9 **Seebergen** Ger.
201 I6 **Seeboden** Austria
195 M6 **Seebruck** Ger.
191 J7 **Seeburg** Ger.
190 J2 **Seedorf** *Schleswig-Holstein* Ger.
190 K3 **Seedorf** *Schleswig-Holstein* Ger.
195 K5 **Seefeld** *Bayern* Ger.
192 I5 **Seefeld** *Brandenburg* Ger.
190 F4 **Seefeld (Stadland)** Ger.
200 D5 **Seefeld in Tirol** Austria
169 G8 **Seefin** *hill* Ireland
195 J6 **Seeg** Ger.
193 G7 **Seegrehna** Ger.
192 I4 **Seehausen** *Brandenburg* Ger.
193 D6 **Seehausen** *Sachsen-Anhalt* Ger.
192 E5 **Seehausen (Altmark)** Ger.
195 K6 **Seehausen am Staffelsee** Ger.
234 C5 **Seeheim** Namibia
194 F2 **Seeheim-Jugenheim** Ger.
200 H4 **Seekirchen am Wallersee** Austria
236 G9 **Seekoegat** S. Africa
237 I6 **Seekoei** *r.* S. Africa
237 N3 **Seekoevlei Nature Reserve** S. Africa
245 M2 **Seela Pass** *Y.T.* Can.
194 D5 **Seelbach** Ger.
265 Q9 **Seeley** *CA* U.S.A.
286 R1 **Seelig, Mount** Antarctica
193 F9 **Seelingstädt** Ger.
192 J5 **Seelow** Ger.
191 I6 **Seelze** Ger.
195 M6 **Seeon** Ger.
212 F1 **Seerücken** *val.* Switz.
181 L4 **Sées** France
191 J7 **Seesen** Ger.
195 K6 **Seeshaupt** Ger.
201 J5 **Seetaler Alpen** *mts* Austria
201 I5 **Seethal** Austria
190 J4 **Seevetal** Ger.
201 I4 **Seewalchen am Attersee** Austria
201 L4 **Seewiesen** Austria
201 P4 **Seewinkel** *reg.* Austria
182 J5 **Séez** France
228 C4 **Sefadu** Sierra Leone
221 H4 **Seferihisar** Turkey
228 C3 **Séféto** Mali
144 C5 **Sefid, Kūh-e** *mt.* Iran
144 D6 **Sefid, Kūh-e** *mts* Iran
144 D5 **Sefid Dasht** Iran
144 I4 **Sefid Sang** Iran
235 E4 **Sefophe** Botswana
226 D2 **Sefrou** Morocco
103 E10 **Sefton, Mount** *South I.* N.Z.
185 I7 **Ségala** *reg.* France
228 C3 **Ségala** Mali
163 K6 **Segalstad bru** Norway
117 M2 **Segama** *r.* Malaysia
116 E3 **Segamat** Malaysia
202 E5 **Segangane** Morocco
219 L6 **Şegarcea** Romania
208 H4 **Segarra** *reg.* Spain
229 F4 **Ségbana** Benin
232 C3 **Segen Wenz** *watercourse* Eth.
233 C6 **Segera** Tanz.
115 A6 **Segeri** *Sulawesi* Indon.
198 G5 **Segesd** Hungary
156 F3 **Segezha** Rus. Fed.
227 F2 **Seggeur, Oued** *watercourse* Alg.
214 H2 **Seggiano** Italy
100 □6 **Seghe** *New Georgia Is* Solomon Is
145 N3 **Seghnān** Afgh.
143 L5 **Segiz, Ozera** *lakes* Kazakh.
212 H3 **Segl, Lago da** *l.* Switz.
180 E5 **Séglien** France
215 K4 **Segni** Italy
Segontia *Gwynedd, Wales* U.K. *see* **Caernarfon**
Segontium *Gwynedd, Wales* U.K. *see* **Caernarfon**
184 D4 **Segonzac** France
209 E8 **Segorbe** Spain
228 D3 **Ségou** Mali
228 D3 **Ségou** *admin. reg.* Mali
274 C3 **Segovia** Col.
Segovia *r.* Hond./Nic. *see* **Coco**
205 L7 **Segovia** Spain
205 L6 **Segovia** *prov.* Spain
156 F3 **Segozerskoye, Ozero** *resr* Rus. Fed.
181 J6 **Segré** France
208 F5 **Segre** *r.* Spain
181 J6 **Segréen** *reg.* France
208 G4 **Segrià** *reg.* Spain
181 L5 **Ségrie** France
244 D5 **Seguam Island** *AK* U.S.A.
245 □D5 **Seguam Pass** *sea channel AK* U.S.A.
229 I1 **Séguédine** Niger
228 D5 **Séguéla** Côte d'Ivoire
228 D3 **Séguéla** Mali
228 D4 **Séguélon** Côte d'Ivoire
228 E3 **Séguénéga** Burkina
285 G3 **Seguí** Arg.
261 G11 **Seguin** *TX* U.S.A.
245 □B5 **Segula Island** *AK* U.S.A.
285 F2 **Segundo** *r.* Arg.
183 B8 **Ségur** France
204 G9 **Segura** Port.
207 N4 **Segura** *r.* Spain
207 N5 **Segura, Sierra de** *mts* Spain
207 N4 **Segura de la Sierra** Spain
206 F4 **Segura de León** Spain
208 D6 **Segura de los Baños** Spain
205 K8 **Segurilla** Spain
144 E5 **Segzī** Iran
234 D4 **Sehithwa** Botswana
237 N5 **Sehlabathebe** Lesotho
237 N5 **Sehlabathebe National Park** Lesotho
191 J6 **Sehlde** Ger.
191 I6 **Sehnde** Ger.
115 D4 **Seho** *i.* Indon.
138 F8 **Sehore** *Madh. Prad.* India
145 L8 **Sehwan** Pak.
204 E8 **Seia** Port.
260 D6 **Seibert** *CO* U.S.A.
180 H6 **Seiche** *r.* France
181 K6 **Seiches-sur-le-Loir** France
126 A7 **Seidan** Japan
201 L5 **Seiersberg** Austria
162 K4 **Seierstad** Norway
193 K9 **Seifhennersdorf** Ger.
172 H2 **Seighford** *Staffordshire, England* U.K.
183 B8 **Seigne, Mont** *mt.* France
249 G3 **Seignelay** *r. Que.* Can.
178 G8 **Seignelay** France
212 B1 **Seignelégier** Switz.
185 B8 **Seignosse** France
126 C6 **Seika** Japan
118 B4 **Seikphyu** Myanmar
168 E10 **Seil** *i. Scotland* U.K.
162 Q1 **Seiland** *i.* Norway
184 H5 **Seilhac** France
261 F7 **Seiling** *OK* U.S.A.
183 J9 **Seillans** France
182 F3 **Seille** *r.* France
179 L5 **Seille** *r.* France
187 H8 **Seilles** Belgium
160 F7 **Šeimena** *r.* Lith.
180 B5 **Sein, Île de** *i.* France
126 G5 **Seinaiji** Japan
162 Q5 **Seinäjoki** Fin.
248 B3 **Seine** *r. Ont.* Can.
178 B5 **Seine** *r.* France
181 J3 **Seine, Baie de** *b.* France
182 F2 **Seine, Sources de la** France
178 F7 **Seine, Val de** *val.* France
178 F6 **Seine-et-Marne** *dept* France
Seine-Inférieure *dept* France *see* **Seine-Maritime**
178 A4 **Seine-Maritime** *dept* France
181 P4 **Seine-St-Denis** *dept* France
219 L3 **Seini** Romania
195 I2 **Seinsheim** Ger.
117 K5 **Seipinang** *Kalimantan* Indon.
197 L1 **Seira** *l.* Lith.
208 F3 **Seira** Spain
197 L1 **Seirijai** Lith.
197 L1 **Seirijis** *l.* Lith.
185 F9 **Seissan** France
Seistan *reg.* Iran *see* **Sīstān**
201 K3 **Seitenstetten** Austria
199 J5 **Şeitin** Romania
163 Q6 **Seitsemisen kansallispuisto** *nat. park* Fin.
282 G3 **Seival** Brazil
126 D7 **Seiwa** Japan
185 G10 **Seix** France
206 □ **Seixal** Madeira
206 A3 **Seixal** Port.
204 C5 **Seixas** Port.
206 B6 **Seixe** *r.* Port.
204 E8 **Seixo da Beira** Port.
117 L6 **Sejaka** *Kalimantan* Indon.
117 H4 **Sejangkung** *Kalimantan* Indon.
164 H6 **Sejerby** Denmark
164 H6 **Sejerø** *i.* Denmark
164 H6 **Sejerø Bugt** *b.* Denmark
197 L1 **Sejny** Pol.
117 I4 **Sekadau** *Kalimantan* Indon.
116 F5 **Sekanak, Teluk** *b.* Indon.
117 L3 **Sekatak Bengara** *Kalimantan* Indon.
116 E6 **Sekayu** *Sumatera* Indon.
199 K3 **Sekčov** *r.* Slovakia
Seke *Sichuan* China *see* **Sêrtar**
233 B5 **Seke** Tanz.
231 B6 **Seke-Banza** Dem. Rep. Congo
233 B6 **Sekenke** Tanz.
100 □4b **Sekeren Iap** *Pohnpei* Micronesia
126 E5 **Seki** *Gifu* Japan
126 D6 **Seki** *Mie* Japan
221 K6 **Seki** Turkey
221 K6 **Seki** *r.* Turkey
124 □B21 **Sekibi-sho** *i. Nansei-shotō* Japan
116 F7 **Sekicau, Gunung** *vol.* Indon.
126 E2 **Sekidō-san** *hill* Japan
126 D5 **Sekigahara** Japan
127 K3 **Sekijō** Japan
127 K3 **Sekiyado** Japan
234 D5 **Sekoma** Botswana
228 E5 **Sekondi** Ghana
232 C1 **Sek'ot'a** Eth.
197 J6 **Sękowa** Pol.
Sekseüil Kazakh. *see* **Saksaul'skiy**
145 I6 **Sekūheh** Iran
117 H4 **Sekura** *Kalimantan* Indon.
239 □2b **Sel, Pointe au** *pt Mahé* Seychelles
Şela Rus. Fed. *see* **Shali**
232 C2 **Şela Dingay** Eth.
116 D6 **Selagan** *r.* Indon.
262 D3 **Selah** *WA* U.S.A.
117 H4 **Selakau** *Kalimantan* Indon.
117 I3 **Selalang** *Sarawak* Malaysia
116 D3 **Selangor** *state* Malaysia
214 C9 **Selargius** *Sardegna* Italy
115 G8 **Selaru** *i. Maluku* Indon.
117 K7 **Selatan, Tanjung** *pt* Indon.
116 E4 **Selatpanjang** *Sumatera* Indon.
172 F2 **Selattyn** *Shropshire, England* U.K.
244 G2 **Selawik** *AK* U.S.A.
244 G2 **Selawik** *r. AK* U.S.A.
244 G2 **Selawik Lake** *AK* U.S.A.
244 H2 **Selawik National Wildlife Refuge** *nature res. AK* U.S.A.
205 M2 **Selaya** Spain
193 F10 **Selb** Ger.
200 G5 **Selbhorn** *mt.* Austria
193 E10 **Selbitz** Ger.
164 A2 **Selbjørnsfjorden** *sea chan.* Norway
162 K5 **Selbu** Norway
171 O6 **Selby** *North Yorkshire, England* U.K.
260 E3 **Selby** *SD* U.S.A.
244 I2 **Selby, Lake** *AK* U.S.A.
257 J10 **Selbyville** *DE* U.S.A.
213 R5 **Selce** Croatia
221 I5 **Selçuk** Turkey
260 E6 **Selden** *KS* U.S.A.
244 J4 **Seldovia** *AK* U.S.A.
115 G4 **Sele** *Papua* Indon.
215 N7 **Sele** *r.* Italy
115 G4 **Sele, Selat** *sea chan. Papua* Indon.
235 E4 **Selebi-Phikwe** Botswana
Selebi-Pikwe Botswana *see* **Selebi-Phikwe**
219 J9 **Selečka Planina** *mts* Macedonia
214 C8 **Selegas** *Sardegna* Italy
214 C6 **S'Elema** *r. Sardegna* Italy
122 F2 **Selemdzha** *r.* Rus. Fed.
122 G2 **Selemdzhinsk** Rus. Fed.
122 H2 **Selemdzhinskiy Khrebet** *mts* Rus. Fed.
221 J4 **Selendi** Turkey
128 J1 **Selenduma** Rus. Fed.

128 J1 Selenga r. Rus. Fed. alt. Selenge Mörön (Mongolia)
230 C5 Selenge Dem. Rep. Congo
128 H2 Selenge Mongolia
Selenge Mongolia see Ih-Uul
128 J2 Selenge prov. Mongolia
120 I1 Selenge Mörön r. Mongolia
128 J1 Selenge Mörön r. Mongolia alt. Selenga (Rus. Fed.)
220 A2 Selenicë Albania
190 J2 Selent Ger.
190 J2 Selenter See l. Ger.
133 F11 Sêlêpug Xizang China
179 N7 Sélestat France
116 □ Seletar Sing.
116 □ Seletar, Pulau i. Sing.
116 □ Seletar Reservoir Sing.
143 O1 Seletinskoye Kazakh.
Selety r. Kazakh. see Sileti
Seletyteniz, Oz. salt l. Kazakh. see Siletiteniz, Ozero
Seleucia Turkey see Silifke
Seleucia Pieria Turkey see Samandağı
199 K5 Seleuş Romania
160 L1 Seleznevo Rus. Fed.
161 O6 Selezni Rus. Fed.
162 □C2 Selfoss Iceland
260 E2 Selfridge ND U.S.A.
122 I4 Sel'gon Stantsiya Rus. Fed.
156 J3 Selib Rus. Fed.
228 B3 Sélibabi Maur.
161 R9 Selichnya Rus. Fed.
Selidovo Ukr. see Selydove
191 G10 Seligenstadt Ger.
161 Q4 Seliger, Ozero l. Rus. Fed.
265 T6 Seligman AZ U.S.A.
122 J3 Selikhino Rus. Fed.
230 D3 Sélim C.A.R.
151 D5 Selim Turkey
225 F4 Selîma Oasis Sudan
117 J4 Selimbau Kalimantan Indon.
221 I5 Selimiye Turkey
228 C4 Sélingué, Lac de l. Mali
228 C3 Selinnkegni Mali
220 D4 Selinountas r. Greece
258 B3 Selinsgrove PA U.S.A.
161 Q5 Selishche Rus. Fed.
157 H5 Selishchi Rus. Fed.
142 B4 Selitrennoye Rus. Fed.
117 G6 Seliu i. Indon.
161 Q5 Selizharovo Rus. Fed.
163 H5 Selje Norway
164 E2 Seljord Norway
164 E2 Seljordsvatnet l. Norway
193 D7 Selke r. Ger.
247 L5 Selkirk Man. Can.
168 K11 Selkirk Scottish Borders, Scotland U.K.
246 G4 Selkirk Mountains B.C. Can.
162 R1 Selkopp Norway
Şelkovski Rus. Fed. see Shelkovskaya
209 E10 Sella Spain
205 J2 Sella r. Spain
215 N5 Sella Canala pass Italy
215 P7 Sella Cessula pass Italy
215 M5 Sella del Perrone pass Italy
171 K5 Sellafield Cumbria, England U.K.
168 □N1 Sellafirth Shetland, Scotland U.K.
215 J2 Sellano Italy
258 E4 Sellersville PA U.S.A.
184 H1 Selles-St-Denis France
181 O7 Selles-sur-Cher France
107 K6 Sellheim r. Qld Austr.
220 F7 Sellia Kriti Greece
217 L6 Sellia Marina Italy
182 H3 Sellières France
192 I2 Sellin, Ostseebad Ger.
173 N5 Sellindge Kent, England U.K.
186 L3 Sellingen Neth.
Sellore Island Myanmar see Saganthit Kyun
200 D5 Sellrain Austria
265 U10 Sells AZ U.S.A.
199 G6 Sellye Hungary
191 D7 Selm Ger.
255 D9 Selma AL U.S.A.
264 M5 Selma CA U.S.A.
261 K8 Selmer TN U.S.A.
206 D4 Selmes Port.
197 K2 Selmęt Wielki, Jezioro l. Pol.
204 G3 Selmo r. Spain
190 K3 Selmsdorf Ger.
Selmunett, Gżejjer is Malta see San Pawl, Gżejjer ta'
178 B8 Selommes France
117 L9 Selong Lombok Indon.
182 G1 Selongey France
183 I8 Selonnet France
237 N1 Selonsrivier S. Africa
228 C4 Sélouma Guinea
245 N3 Selous, Mount Y.T. Can.
233 C7 Selous Game Reserve nature res. Tanz.
192 E3 Selow Ger.
144 I7 Selseleh-ye Pīr Shūrān mts Iran
171 M4 Selset Reservoir England U.K.
173 K6 Selsey West Sussex, England U.K.
173 K6 Selsey Bill hd England U.K.
190 H4 Selsingen Ger.
191 E9 Selters (Westerwald) Ger.
161 R8 Sel'tso Bryanskaya Oblast' Rus. Fed.
161 R8 Sel'tso Bryanskaya Oblast' Rus. Fed.
156 K4 Selty Rus. Fed.
179 P6 Seltz France
117 G2 Seluan i. Indon.
Selukwe Zimbabwe see Shurugwi
181 I4 Sélune r. France
282 E3 Selva Arg.
217 M2 Selva Italy
209 K8 Selva Spain
208 C3 Selva mt. Spain
208 K4 Selva reg. Spain
213 L2 Selva dei Molini Italy
213 K4 Selva di Progno Italy
200 E6 Selva di Val Gardena Italy
226 B3 Selvagens, Ilhas is Madeira
149 L5 Selvānā Iran
284 A6 Selva Obscura Chile
274 D6 Selvas reg. Brazil
213 L5 Selvazzano Dentro Italy
212 H4 Selvino Italy
280 B4 Selvíria Brazil
262 G3 Selway r. ID U.S.A.
247 J2 Selwyn Lake N.W.T./Sask. Can.
245 O2 Selwyn Mountains N.W.T./Y.T. Can.
106 G6 Selwyn Range hills Qld Austr.
158 E6 Selyatyn Ukr.
159 Q5 Selydove Ukr.
194 E2 Selz r. Ger.
201 J4 Selzthal Austria
185 I8 Sémalens France
220 A2 Seman r. Albania
116 F7 Semangka, Teluk b. Indon.
117 I8 Semarang Jawa Indon.
117 H4 Sematan Sarawak Malaysia
115 C9 Semau i. Indon.
117 L5 Semayang, Danau l. Indon.
183 D6 Sembadel France
117 L3 Sembakung r. Indon.
116 □ Sembawang Sing.
116 □ Sembawang, Sungai r. Sing.
230 B4 Sembé Congo
181 M6 Semblançay France
212 C3 Sembrancher Switz.
149 L5 Şemdinli Turkey
185 E9 Séméac France
182 D3 Sémelay France
225 H5 Semēnawī K'eyih Bahrī prov. Eritrea
Semendire Smederevo Serbia see Smederevo
231 C5 Semendua Dem. Rep. Congo
161 V4 Semendyayevo Rus. Fed.
219 K5 Semenic, Vârful mt. Romania
159 L1 Semenivka Chernihivs'ka Oblast' Ukr.
159 P5 Semenivka Kharkivs'ka Oblast' Ukr.
159 K3 Semenivka Kyivs'ka Oblast' Ukr.
159 M4 Semenivka Poltavs'ka Oblast' Ukr.
142 F1 Semenkino Rus. Fed.
159 T2 Semeno-Aleksandrovka Rus. Fed.
156 I4 Semenov Rus. Fed.
Semenovka Ukr. see Semenivka
161 S6 Semenovskoye Rus. Fed.
116 J9 Semeru, Gunung vol. Indon.
143 S2 Semey Kazakh.
146 D8 Semhar prov. Eritrea
159 S6 Semibalki Rus. Fed.
161 W4 Semibratovo Rus. Fed.
204 D8 Semide Port.
159 R2 Semidesyatnoye Rus. Fed.
244 H4 Semidi Islands AK U.S.A.
156 H4 Semigorodnyaya Rus. Fed.
157 H7 Semikarakorsk Rus. Fed.
157 G6 Semiluki Rus. Fed.
198 E1 Semily Czech Rep.
217 J7 Seminara Italy
182 H4 Semine r. France
262 K5 Seminoe Reservoir WY U.S.A.
261 D9 Seminole TX U.S.A.
255 E10 Seminole, Lake FL/GA U.S.A.
143 U2 Seminskiy Khrebet mts Rus. Fed.
161 X7 Semion Rus. Fed.
122 B2 Semiozernyy Rus. Fed.
Semipalatinsk Kazakh. see Semey
143 L1 Semipolka Kazakh.
114 C5 Semirara i. Phil.
114 C6 Semirara Islands Phil.
144 D6 Semīrom Iran
245 □B6 Semisopochnoi Island AK U.S.A.
117 I4 Semitau Kalimantan Indon.
143 R2 Semiyarka Kazakh.
143 P2 Semizbuga Kazakh.
Semizbughy Kazakh. see Semizbuga
161 V5 Semkhoz Rus. Fed.
Sem Kolodezey Ukr. see Lenine
218 I4 Semlac Romania
161 Q6 Semlevo Smolenskaya Oblast' Rus. Fed.
161 Q6 Semlevo Smolenskaya Oblast' Rus. Fed.
230 F4 Semliki r. Dem. Rep. Congo/Uganda
192 G2 Semlow Ger.
191 K6 Semmenstedt Ger.
144 E4 Semnān Iran
144 D4 Semnān prov. Iran
144 E5 Semnān va Dāmghaān reg. Iran
128 G8 Sêmnyi Qinghai China
187 G9 Semois r. Belgium
187 G9 Semois, Vallée de la val. Belgium/France
237 M5 Semonkong Lesotho
179 J7 Semoutiers-Montsaon France
212 E1 Sempach Switz.
212 E1 Sempacher See l. Switz.
201 I8 Šempeter Slovenia
117 M2 Semporna Sabah Malaysia
214 H2 Semproniano Italy
195 L5 Sempt r. Ger.
117 J9 Sempu i. Indon.
201 L5 Semriach Austria
199 K3 Šemša Slovakia
275 H6 Sem Tripa Brazil
161 Q9 Semtsy Rus. Fed.
182 E2 Semur-en-Auxois France
182 E4 Semur-en-Brionnais France
184 C4 Semussac France
Semyonovskoye Arkhangel'skaya Oblast' Rus. Fed. see Bereznik
Semyonovskoye Kostromskaya Oblast' Rus. Fed. see Ostrovskoye
156 I2 Semzha Rus. Fed.
119 G8 Sên, Stœng r. Cambodia
276 D2 Sena Bol.
144 D7 Senā Iran
199 K3 Seňa Slovakia
208 E4 Sena Spain
280 C2 Senador Canedo Brazil
278 F3 Senador Pompeu Brazil
225 H6 Senafe Eritrea
213 L3 Senaiga r. Italy
117 L1 Senaja Sabah Malaysia
151 D3 Senaki Georgia
213 J2 Senales Italy
213 J2 Senales, Val di val. Italy
214 C6 Senalonga, Punta mt. Italy
276 C2 Sena Madureira Brazil
136 G9 Senanayake Samudra l. Sri Lanka
231 D9 Senanga Zambia
117 I4 Senaning Kalimantan Indon.
178 C4 Senarpont France
183 G9 Sénas France
261 K8 Senatobia MS U.S.A.
209 K8 Sencelles Spain
159 M3 Sencha Ukr.
201 J7 Šenčur Slovenia
125 H15 Sendai Kagoshima Japan
124 R8 Sendai Miyagi Japan
125 H15 Sendai-gawa r. Japan
124 S8 Sendai-wan b. Japan
237 K2 Sendelingsfontein S. Africa
195 I5 Senden Bayern Ger.
191 D7 Senden Nordrhein-Westfalen Ger.
191 E7 Sendenhorst Ger.
204 H6 Sendim Bragança Port.
204 D6 Sendim Porto Port.
133 L11 Sêndo Xizang China
219 P5 Şendreni Romania
117 I5 Senduruhan Kalimantan Indon.
180 F6 Séné France
228 E5 Sene r. Ghana
116 D3 Senebui, Tanjung pt Indon.
198 G3 Senec Slovakia
250 F8 Seneca IL U.S.A.
260 G6 Seneca KS U.S.A.
262 E4 Seneca OR U.S.A.
256 F7 Seneca PA U.S.A.
256 I6 Seneca Lake NY U.S.A.
256 F10 Seneca Rocks WV U.S.A.
256 D9 Senecaville Lake OH U.S.A.
187 F7 Seneffe Belgium
228 B3 Senegal country Africa
228 A2 Sénégal r. Maur./Senegal
214 B7 Seneghe Sardegna Italy
122 J1 Seneka, Mys hd Rus. Fed.
237 L4 Senekal S. Africa
207 O6 Senes Spain
214 D7 Senes, Monte hill Italy
214 B4 Senetosa, Capu di c. Corse France
250 I3 Seney MI U.S.A.
250 H3 Seney National Wildlife Refuge nature res. MI U.S.A.
183 I9 Senez France
201 M3 Senftenberg Austria
193 J7 Senftenberg Ger.
233 B8 Senga Malawi
233 A7 Senga Hill Zambia
138 G6 Sengar r. India
117 L4 Sengata Kalimantan Indon.
133 E11 Sêngdoi Xizang China
195 K3 Sengenthal Ger.
233 B5 Sengerema Tanz.
280 C6 Sengés Brazil
156 J1 Sengeyskiy, Ostrov i. Rus. Fed.
157 J5 Sengiley Rus. Fed.
Sengirli, Mys pt Kazakh. see Syngyrli, Mys
133 G11 Sêngli Co l. Xizang China
185 F10 Sengouagnet France
201 J4 Sengsengebirge mts Austria
283 C7 Senguerr r. Arg.
235 F3 Sengwa r. Zimbabwe
146 D8 Senhit prov. Eritrea
206 E2 Senhora do Rosário Port.
278 E4 Senhor do Bonfim Brazil
198 G3 Senica Slovakia
198 G2 Senice na Hané Czech Rep.
213 O8 Senigallia Italy
284 C6 Senillosa Arg.
213 M6 Senio r. Italy
221 L4 Senirkent Turkey
214 B8 Senis Sardegna Italy
215 Q7 Senise Italy
210 E3 Senj Croatia
162 N2 Senja i. Norway
162 N2 Senjehopen Norway
126 C7 Senjōga-dake mt. Japan
127 H4 Senjōga-dake mt. Japan
124 □A21 Senkaku-shotō is Japan
149 K3 Şenkaya Turkey
156 J2 Sen'kina Rus. Fed.
228 C4 Senko Guinea
231 E9 Senkobo Zambia
159 Q4 Sen'kove Ukr.
161 N6 Sen'kovo Rus. Fed.
150 E2 Şenköy Turkey
236 H1 Senlac S. Africa
122 G7 Senlin Shan mt. Jilin China
178 E5 Senlis France
119 H8 Senmonorom Cambodia
126 B7 Sennan Japan
225 G6 Sennar Sudan
225 G6 Sennar state Sudan
214 B7 Sennariolo Sardegna Italy
159 Q8 Sennaya Rus. Fed.
191 G7 Senne reg. Ger.
182 F3 Sennecey-le-Grand France
182 G2 Sennecey-lès-Dijon France
172 □ Sennen Cornwall, England U.K.
248 E3 Senneterre Que. Can.
193 E7 Sennewitz Ger.
Senno Belarus see Syanno
127 I2 Sennokura-yama mt. Japan
214 B6 Sennori Sardegna Italy
212 G1 Sennwald Switz.
172 E4 Sennybridge Powys, Wales U.K.
199 I3 Senohrad Slovakia
178 F7 Sénonais reg. France
178 B6 Senonches France
179 M7 Senones France
214 C8 Senorbì Sardegna Italy
185 H8 Senouillac France
183 C6 Senouire r. France
201 L7 Senovo Slovenia
201 J8 Senožeče Slovenia
237 L6 Senqu r. Lesotho
178 F7 Sens France
180 H5 Sens-de-Bretagne France
178 F3 Sensée r. France
266 □O11 Sensuntepeque El Salvador
218 I5 Senta Vojvodina Serbia
185 F10 Sentein France
185 G10 Sentenac-d'Oust France
208 G3 Senterada Spain
201 M6 Šentilj Slovenia
265 S9 Sentinel AZ U.S.A.
215 N4 Sentinella, Colle della hill Italy
246 F4 Sentinel Peak B.C. Can.
286 S1 Sentinel Range mts Antarctica
Sentinum Italy see Sassoferrato
268 B4 Sentispac Mex.
201 L8 Šentjernej Slovenia
201 L7 Šentjur pri Celju Slovenia
116 □ Sentosa i. Sing.
179 I5 Senuc France
235 F4 Senwabarwana S. Africa
117 L4 Senyiur Kalimantan Indon.
199 K4 Sényő Hungary
151 C5 Senyurt Turkey
149 J5 Şenyurt Turkey
125 I12 Senzaki Japan
125 J14 Sen-zaki pt Japan
193 I6 Senzig Ger.
Seo de Urgell Spain see Le Seu d'Urgell
212 E1 Seon Switz.
138 I9 Seonath r. India
138 G6 Seondha Madh. Prad. India
138 G8 Seoni Madh. Prad. India
138 G8 Seoni Chhapara Madh. Prad. India
138 F8 Seoni-Malwa Madh. Prad. India
139 I9 Seorinarayan Chhattisgarh India
Seoul S. Korea see Sŏul
185 F7 Séoune r. France
117 K8 Sepanjang i. Indon.
102 G7 Separation Point South I. N.Z.
108 G7 Separation Well W.A. Austr.
144 B4 Separ Shāhābād Iran
117 L4 Sepasu Kalimantan Indon.
276 D1 Sepatini r. Brazil
117 I4 Sepauk Kalimantan Indon.
281 E5 Sepetiba, Baía de b. Brazil
113 J7 Sepik r. P.N.G.
117 M4 Sepinang Kalimantan Indon.
117 K3 Seping r. Malaysia
215 N5 Sepino Italy
123 E9 Sep'o N. Korea
196 F2 Sępólno Krajeńskie Pol.
196 E2 Sępolno Wielkie Pol.
139 O6 Sepon Assam India
277 F3 Sepotuba r. Brazil
139 N6 Seppa Arun. Prad. India
182 K1 Seppois-le-Bas France
219 J4 Şepreuş Romania
182 B3 Septaine reg. France
183 G10 Septèmes-les-Vallons France
178 C6 Septeuil France
185 H7 Septfonds France
249 H3 Sept-Îles Que. Can.
180 E4 Sept-Îles, Réserve Naturelle des nature res. France
249 H3 Sept-Îles-Port-Cartier, Réserve Faunique de nature res. Que. Can.
182 H4 Septmoncel France
204 H7 Sepulcro-Hilario Spain
205 M6 Sepúlveda Spain
234 D3 Sepupa Botswana
116 F7 Seputih r. Indon.
213 N3 Sequals Italy
255 E8 Sequatchie r. TN U.S.A.
285 I2 Sequeira Uru.
204 H7 Sequeros Spain
205 J5 Sequillo r. Spain
264 N5 Sequoia National Park CA U.S.A.
146 D8 Serae prov. Eritrea
151 B6 Şerafettin Dağları mts Turkey
157 H6 Serafimovich Rus. Fed.
178 H4 Seraincourt France
187 I7 Seraing Belgium
Sêraitang Qinghai China see Baima
115 F5 Seram i. Maluku Indon.
115 G5 Seram, Laut sea Indon.
182 H5 Séran r. France
116 G8 Serang Jawa Indon.
116 □ Serangoon, Pulau i. Sing.
116 □ Serangoon, Sungai r. Sing.
116 □ Serangoon Harbour b. Sing.
183 D9 Séranne, Montagne de la ridge France
183 J9 Séranon France
116 □ Serapong, Mount hill Sing.
117 H3 Serasan i. Indon.
117 H3 Serasan, Selat sea chan. Indon.
212 I8 Seravezza Italy
115 A8 Seraya i. Indon.
117 H3 Seraya i. Indon.
116 □ Seraya, Pulau reg. Sing.
218 I7 Serbia country Europe
218 I6 Serbia and Montenegro country Europe
133 I10 Sêrbug Co l. Xizang China
158 G4 Serbynivtsi Ukr.
133 L11 Sêrca Xizang China
151 B6 Serçelik Dağı mts Turkey
139 N8 Serchhip Mizoram India
213 I8 Serchio r. Italy
144 G2 Serdar Turkm.
214 C9 Serdiana Sardegna Italy
Serdica Bulg. see Sofiya
232 D2 Serdo Eth.
157 I5 Serdoba r. Rus. Fed.
157 I5 Serdobsk Rus. Fed.
156 K3 Serebryanka Rus. Fed.
159 M8 Serebryanka Ukr.
143 T3 Serebryansk Kazakh.
161 V7 Serebryanyye Prudy Rus. Fed.
199 G3 Sered' Slovakia
161 S6 Sereda Moskovskaya Oblast' Rus. Fed.
161 X4 Sereda Yaroslavskaya Oblast' Rus. Fed.
161 S7 Seredeyskiy Rus. Fed.
160 L3 Seredka Rus. Fed.
161 W6 Serednikovo Rus. Fed.
158 J7 Seredniy Kuyal'nyk r. Ukr.
228 C4 Sérédou Guinea
159 N1 Seredyna-Buda Rus. Fed.
158 B5 Seredyne Ukr.
148 F4 Şereflikoçhisar Turkey
199 H4 Seregélyes Hungary
212 G4 Seregno Italy
184 G4 Séreilhac France
178 G8 Serein r. France
116 D3 Seremban Malaysia
207 I3 Serena, Embalse de la resr Spain
233 B5 Serengeti National Park Tanz.
233 B5 Serengeti Plain Tanz.
231 F8 Serenje Zambia
180 F6 Sérent France
232 B4 Serere Uganda
158 E5 Seret r. Ukr.
156 H5 Serezha r. Rus. Fed.
161 N5 Serezha r. Rus. Fed.
200 C5 Serfaus Austria
156 L4 Ser'ga Rus. Fed.
156 I5 Sergach Rus. Fed.
161 X5 Sergeikha Rus. Fed.
129 N2 Sergelen Dornod Mongolia
Sergelen Mongolia see Tüvshinshiree
219 P9 Sergen Turkey
143 M2 Sergeyevka Akmolinskaya Oblast' Kazakh.
143 L1 Sergeyevka Severnyy Kazakhstan Kazakh.
159 S3 Sergeyevka Rus. Fed.
178 F7 Sergines France
152 H3 Sergino Rus. Fed.
278 F4 Sergipe state Brazil
161 V5 Sergiyev Posad Rus. Fed.
157 J5 Sergiyevsk Rus. Fed.
Sergiyevskiy Rus. Fed. see Fakel
161 V8 Sergiyevskoye Lipetskaya Oblast' Rus. Fed.
161 U9 Sergiyevskoye Orlovskaya Oblast' Rus. Fed.
212 H5 Sergnano Italy
Sergo Ukr. see Stakhanov
151 I3 Sergokala Rus. Fed.
128 F8 Serh Qinghai China
145 J4 Serhetabat Turkm.
159 L3 Serhiyivka Chernihivs'ka Oblast' Ukr.
159 N7 Serhiyivka Khersons'ka Oblast' Ukr.
158 J6 Serhiyivka Odes'ka Oblast' Ukr.
158 J7 Serhiyivka Odes'ka Oblast' Ukr.
159 N2 Serhiyivka Sums'ka Oblast' Ukr.
117 K2 Seria Brunei
117 I4 Serian Sarawak Malaysia
212 H4 Seriate Italy
116 G7 Seribu, Kepulauan is Indon.
116 C3 Seribudolok Sumatera Indon.
178 C5 Sérifontaine France
220 F5 Serifos Serifos Greece
220 F5 Serifos i. Greece
220 F5 Serifou, Steno sea chan. Greece
183 C10 Sérignan France
183 F8 Sérignan-du-Comtat France
249 G2 Sérigny r. Que. Can.
249 G2 Sérigny, Lac l. Que. Can.
221 M6 Serik Turkey
132 C7 Serikbuya Xinjiang China
115 E5 Serikkembelo Seram Indon.
212 H4 Serina Italy
235 □J3 Sèrinama Madag.
275 I6 Seringa, Serra da hills Brazil
108 G2 Seringapatam Reef W.A. Austr.
221 K5 Serinhisar Turkey
151 C7 Serinova Turkey
150 E2 Serinyol Turkey
212 H5 Serio r. Italy
212 H5 Serio, Parco del park Italy
Sêrkang Xizang China see Nyainrong
158 E2 Serkhiv Ukr.
227 G5 Serkout mt. Alg.
Serle atoll Arch. des Tuamotu Fr. Polynesia see Pukarua
178 D7 Sermaises France
179 I6 Sermaize-les-Bains France
214 C3 Sermano Corse France
115 F8 Sermata i. Maluku Indon.
115 F8 Sermata, Kepulauan is Maluku Indon.
219 K9 Sermenin Macedonia
243 L2 Sermersuaq glacier Greenland
243 M2 Sermersuaq glacier Greenland
213 K6 Sermide Italy
182 C3 Sermoise-sur-Loire France
215 K4 Sermoneta Italy
182 F3 Sermoyer France
160 I4 Sērmūkši Latvia
204 F7 Sernancelhe Port.
199 L3 Serne r. Ukr.
197 K4 Serniki Pol.
193 F7 Serno Ger.
157 J5 Sernovodsk Rus. Fed.
156 J4 Sernur Rus. Fed.
158 F2 Sernyky Ukr.
Sernyy Zavod Turkm. see Kükürtli
196 G2 Serock Kujawsko-Pomorskie Pol.
197 J3 Serock Mazowieckie Pol.
Sero Colorado Aruba see Seroe Colorado
285 G3 Serodino Arg.
271 □[9] Seroe Colorado Aruba
157 I7 Seroglazka Rus. Fed.
207 O6 Serón Spain
205 P6 Serón de Nájima Spain
205 L7 Serones, Embalse de resr Spain
234 D3 Seronga Botswana
186 E5 Serooskerke Neth.
208 F5 Seròs Spain
227 G4 Serouenout well Alg.
152 H4 Serov Rus. Fed.
234 E4 Serowe Botswana
206 D5 Serpa Port.
Serpa Pinto Angola see Menongue
249 G3 Serpent r. Que. Can.
228 C3 Serpent, Vallée du watercourse Mali
214 D9 Serpentara, Isola i. Sardegna Italy
109 C12 Serpentine r. W.A. Austr.
244 F2 Serpentine Hot Springs AK U.S.A.
104 B3 Serpentine Lakes salt flat S.A. Austr.
271 M9 Serpent's Mouth sea chan. Trin. and Tob./Venez.
161 S7 Serpeysk Rus. Fed.
204 D8 Serpins Port.
209 E10 Serpis r. Spain
158 I7 Serpneve Ukr.
161 U7 Serpukhov Rus. Fed.
179 K8 Serqueux France
181 M3 Serquigny France
281 G4 Serra Brazil
214 A6 Serra r. Italy
209 E8 Serra Spain
215 O4 Serracapriola Italy
205 K6 Serrada Spain
281 E5 Serra da Bocaina, Parque Nacional da nat. park Brazil
277 F5 Serra da Bodoquena, Parque Nacional da nat. park Brazil
280 D4 Serra da Canastra, Parque Nacional da nat. park Brazil
278 E4 Serra da Capivara, Parque Nacional da nat. park Brazil
276 D2 Serra da Cutia, Parque Nacional nat. park Brazil
204 E8 Serra da Estrela, Parque Natural da nature res. Port.
278 C5 Serra da Mesa, Represa resr Brazil
275 F4 Serra da Mociade, Parque Nacional da nat. park Brazil
278 E4 Serra das Confusões, Parque Nacional da nat. park Brazil
213 O8 Serra de'Conti Italy
215 Q6 Serra del Corvo, Lago di l. Italy
202 C3 Serra de São Mamede, Parque Natural da nature res. Port.
216 F9 Serradifalco Sicilia Italy
214 B4 Serra-di-Ferro Corse France
204 H9 Serradilla Spain
204 H7 Serradilla del Arroyo Spain
276 B2 Serra do Divisor, Parque Nacional da nat. park Brazil
275 H4 Serra do Navio Brazil
281 G2 Serra dos Aimorés Brazil
280 D3 Serra do Salitre Brazil
Sérrai Greece see Serres
214 B9 Serramanna Sardegna Italy
213 J7 Serramazzoni Italy
280 D4 Serrana Brazil
270 C6 Serrana Bank sea feature Caribbean Sea
275 E4 Serranía de la Neblina, Parque Nacional nat. park Venez.
270 D6 Serranilla Bank sea feature Caribbean Sea
205 K8 Serranillos Spain
285 F4 Serrano Arg.
283 B8 Serrano i. Chile
280 A3 Serranópolis Brazil
Serraria, Ilha i. Brazil see Queimada, Ilha
212 F6 Serra Riccò Italy
217 K6 Serra San Bruno Italy
213 O9 Serra San Quirico Italy
204 C9 Serras de Aire e Candeeiros, Parque Natural das nature res. Port.
278 F3 Serra Talhada Brazil
213 M8 Serravalle San Marino
215 J1 Serravalle di Chienti Italy
212 F6 Serravalle Scrivia Italy
178 F4 Serre r. France
215 O6 Serre Italy
182 H2 Serre, Massif de la hills France
183 J7 Serre-Chevalier France
204 I9 Serrejón Spain
214 B9 Serrenti Sardegna Italy
183 I8 Serre-Ponçon, Lac de l. France
Serrera, Pic de la mt. Andorra see Serrère, Pic de
208 I2 Serrère, Pic de mt. Andorra
183 H8 Serres France
220 E1 Serres Greece
185 D9 Serres-Castet France
238 □[1a] Serreta Terceira Azores
284 E2 Serrezuela Arg.
214 C8 Serri Sardegna Italy
214 B3 Serriera Corse France
182 G5 Serrière-de-Briord France
183 F6 Serrières France
194 B2 Serrig Ger.
278 F4 Serrinha Brazil
278 F3 Serrita Brazil
281 F3 Sêrro Brazil
205 J8 Serrota mt. Spain
184 E4 Sers France
211 B7 Sers Tunisia
217 L5 Sersale Italy
204 D9 Sertã Port.
278 F4 Sertânia Brazil
280 B5 Sertanópolis Brazil
280 A3 Sertão de Camapuã reg. Brazil
280 D4 Sertãozinho Brazil
130 C2 Sêrtar Sichuan China
150 B2 Sertavul Geçidi pass Turkey
229 H5 Serti Nigeria
161 N1 Sertolovo Rus. Fed.
115 G7 Serua vol. Maluku Indon.
116 C2 Seruai Sumatera Indon.
113 I7 Serui Papua Indon.
235 E4 Serule Botswana
117 H5 Serutu i. Indon.
117 J6 Seruyan r. Indon.
160 K7 Servach r. Belarus
179 M8 Servance France
183 C7 Serverette France
220 D2 Servia Greece
183 C10 Servian France
215 K1 Servigliano Italy
180 I5 Servon-sur-Vilaine France
182 J5 Servoz France
115 E8 Serwaru Maluku Indon.
128 D9 Sêrwolungwa Qinghai China
130 B2 Sêrxü Sichuan China
178 H4 Sery France
Seryítsi i. Limnos Greece see Sideritis
244 D2 Serykh Gusey, Ostrova is Rus. Fed.
122 F3 Seryshevo Rus. Fed.
208 E4 Sesa Spain
117 L3 Sesayap Kalimantan Indon.
117 L3 Sesayap r. Indon.
230 E4 Sese Dem. Rep. Congo
225 F4 Sese Sudan
248 B3 Seseganaga Lake Ont. Can.
251 N1 Sesekinika Ont. Can.
Sesel country Indian Ocean see Seychelles
205 M8 Seseña Spain
115 E4 Sesepe Maluku Indon.
234 B3 Sesfontein Namibia
136 F5 Seshachalam Hills India
161 Q8 Seshcha Rus. Fed.
231 E9 Sesheke Zambia
212 F5 Sesia r. Italy
206 A4 Sesimbra Port.
162 Q4 Seskar Furö i. Sweden
221 I6 Sesklio i. Greece
205 P4 Sesma Spain
124 □[1] Sesoko Okinawa Japan
124 □[1] Sesoko-jima i. Okinawa Japan
136 B6 Sesostris Bank sea feature India
209 H10 S'Espalmador i. Spain
209 I10 S'Espardell i. Spain
231 D8 Sessa Angola
215 L5 Sessa Aurunca Italy
215 O7 Sessa Cilento Italy
209 L9 Ses Salines Spain
212 E4 Sessera r. Italy
191 K10 Seßlach Ger.
212 H7 Sesta Godano Italy
209 K9 S'Estanyol de Migjorn Spain
205 O2 Sestao Spain
213 M8 Sestino Italy
213 M2 Sesto Italy
213 N4 Sesto al Reghena Italy
212 F4 Sesto Calende Italy
215 M5 Sesto Campano Italy
213 K8 Sesto Fiorentino Italy
197 L1 Šeštokai Lith.
213 J7 Sestola Italy
212 G4 Sesto San Giovanni Italy
161 U5 Sestra r. Rus. Fed.
212 B6 Sestriere Italy
212 G7 Sestri Levante Italy
160 M1 Sestroretsk Rus. Fed.
210 E3 Sestrunj i. Croatia
214 C9 Sestu Sardegna Italy
160 F6 Šešupė r. Lith./Rus. Fed.
210 F3 Sesvete Croatia
208 G4 Set r. Spain
118 H7 Set, Phou mt. Laos
124 Q4 Setana Japan
259 I3 Setauket NY U.S.A.
183 D10 Sète France
280 D6 Sete Barras Brazil
160 I6 Šetekšna r. Lith.
281 E3 Sete Lagoas Brazil
207 I7 Setenil Spain
162 O2 Setermoen Norway
164 D2 Setesdal val. Norway
124 □G18 Seteuchi Nansei-shotō Japan
190 J3 Seth Ger.
Seti Georgia see Mestia
138 H5 Seti r. Nepal
139 J6 Seti r. Nepal
Setia Italy see Sezze
227 G1 Sétif Alg.
205 Q7 Setiles Spain
225 G6 Setit r. Africa
126 F5 Seto Japan
125 J13 Seto-naikai sea Japan
126 A7 Seto-naikai Kokuritsu-kōen nat. park Japan
118 B6 Setsan Myanmar
213 K7 Setta r. Italy
226 D2 Settat Morocco
230 A5 Setté Cama Gabon
214 C9 Sette Fratelli, Monte dei mt. Sardegna Italy
212 E7 Settepani, Monte mt. Italy
212 D5 Settimo Torinese Italy
212 D4 Settimo Vittone Italy
171 M5 Settle North Yorkshire, England U.K.
106 G4 Settlement Creek r. Qld Austr.
238 □[2c] Settlement of Edinburgh Tristan da Cunha S. Atlantic Ocean
182 E2 Settons, Lac des l. France
281 F2 Setúbal r. Brazil
206 B3 Setúbal Port.
206 B4 Setúbal admin. dist. Port.
206 A4 Setúbal, Baía de b. Port.
285 G2 Setúbal, Laguna l. Arg.
281 F2 Setubinha Brazil
Seu i. Vanuatu see Hiu
195 L3 Seubersdorf in der Oberpfalz Ger.
184 C4 Seudre r. France
184 C4 Seugne r. France
214 C8 Seui Sardegna Italy
179 J6 Seuil-d'Argonne France
247 M5 Seul, Lac l. Ont. Can.
250 I4 Seul Choix Point MI U.S.A.
116 A2 Seulimeum Sumatera Indon.
191 J7 Seulingen Ger.
181 K3 Seulles r. France
214 C8 Seulo Sardegna Italy
182 G2 Seurre France
159 N1 Sev r. Rus. Fed.
208 J4 Seva Spain
151 F5 Sevan Armenia
Sevan, Lake Armenia see Sevana Lich
Sevan, Ozero l. Armenia see Sevana Lich
151 G5 Sevana Lich l. Armenia
151 G5 Sevani Lerrnashght'a hills Armenia/Azer.
276 D4 Sevaruyo Bol.
159 M9 Sevastopol' Ukr.
171 P5 Seven r. England U.K.
169 E9 Seven Heads Ireland
Seven Islands Que. Can. see Sept-Îles
249 I1 Seven Islands Bay Nfld and Lab. Can.
109 D7 Seven Mile Creek r. W.A. Austr.
237 O5 Sevenoaks S. Africa
173 M5 Sevenoaks Kent, England U.K.
172 E4 Seven Sisters Neath Port Talbot, Wales U.K.
172 □ Seven Stones is England U.K.
107 M8 Seventeen Seventy Qld Austr.
Seventy Mile House B.C. Can. see 70 Mile House
187 J6 Sevenum Neth.
258 B5 Seven Valleys PA U.S.A.
204 E6 Sever Port.
183 C8 Sévérac-le-Château France
204 D7 Sever do Vouga Port.
198 F6 Severin Croatia
279 B9 Severino Ribeiro Brazil
161 V6 Severka r. Rus. Fed.
105 M3 Severn r. N.S.W. Austr.
248 C2 Severn r. Ont. Can.
103 H9 Severn mt. South I. N.Z.
236 G2 Severn S. Africa
172 H4 Severn r. England/Wales U.K.
258 B6 Severn MD U.S.A.
256 H12 Severn NC U.S.A.
258 C7 Severn r. MD U.S.A.
258 B6 Severna Park MD U.S.A.
156 H2 Severnaya Dvina r. Rus. Fed.
156 L3 Severnaya Mylva r. Rus. Fed.
151 F2 Severnaya Osetiya-Alaniya, Respublika aut. rep. Rus. Fed.
152 H3 Severnaya Sos'va r. Rus. Fed.
153 L1 Severnaya Zemlya is Rus. Fed.
172 G4 Severn Beach South Gloucestershire, England U.K.
248 B2 Severn Lake Ont. Can.
157 K5 Severnoye Rus. Fed.
248 B2 Severn River Provincial Park Ont. Can.
159 P3 Severnyy Belgorodskaya Oblast' Rus. Fed.
161 U5 Severnyy Moskovskaya Oblast' Rus. Fed.
156 J1 Severnyy Nenetskiy Avtonomnyy Okrug Rus. Fed.
156 N2 Severnyy Respublika Komi Rus. Fed.
197 H1 Severnyy, Mys pt Rus. Fed.
122 L1 Severnyy, Zaliv b. Rus. Fed.
153 S3 Severnyy Anyuyskiy Khrebet mts Rus. Fed.
144 E2 Severnyy Aul Turkm.
160 L1 Severnyy Berezovyy, Ostrov i. Rus. Fed.
142 G4 Severnyy Chink Ustyurta esc. Kazakh.
143 M1 Severnyy Kazakhstan admin. div. Kazakh.
156 K4 Severnyy Kommunar Rus. Fed.
151 C2 Severnyy Priyut Rus. Fed.
Severnyy Suchan Rus. Fed. see Uglekamensk
156 L3 Severnyy Ural mts Rus. Fed.
121 I1 Severobaykal'sk Rus. Fed.
153 M4 Severo-Baykal'skoye Nagor'ye mts Rus. Fed.
132 H1 Severo-Chuyskiy Khrebet mts Rus. Fed.
Severodonetsk Ukr. see Syeverodonets'k
156 G2 Severodvinsk Rus. Fed.
Severo-Kazakhstanskaya Oblast' admin. div. Kazakh. see Severnyy Kazakhstan
153 Q4 Severo-Kuril'sk Kuril'skiye O-va Rus. Fed.
162 V2 Severomorsk Rus. Fed.
156 G3 Severoonezhsk Rus. Fed.
Severo-Osetinskaya A.S.S.R. aut. rep. Rus. Fed. see Severnaya Osetiya-Alaniya, Respublika
151 F3 Severo-Osetinskiy Zapovednik nature res. Rus. Fed.
122 M2 Severo-Sakhalinskaya Ravnina plain Rus. Fed.
153 L2 Severo-Sibirskaya Nizmennost' lowland Rus. Fed.
156 L3 Severoural'sk Rus. Fed.
153 K3 Severo-Yeniseyskiy Rus. Fed.
161 V7 Severo-Zadonsk Rus. Fed.
Seversk Ukr. see Sivers'k
157 G7 Severskaya Rus. Fed.
157 H7 Severskiy Donets r. Rus. Fed.
Severskiy Donets r. Ukr. see Sivers'kyy Donets'
180 I3 Sèves r. France
177 I4 Seveso Italy
212 G5 Seveso r. Italy
201 K1 Ševětín Czech Rep.
162 T2 Sevettijärvi Fin.
214 B3 Sevi, Col de pass France
265 T3 Sevier UT U.S.A.
265 T2 Sevier r. UT U.S.A.
265 U2 Sevier Bridge Reservoir UT U.S.A.
265 T2 Sevier Desert UT U.S.A.
265 S3 Sevier Lake UT U.S.A.
255 F8 Sevierville TN U.S.A.
180 G5 Sévignac France
185 D9 Sévignacq France
178 H4 Sévigny-Waleppe France
274 C3 Sevilla Col.
206 H6 Sevilla Spain
206 H5 Sevilla prov. Spain
205 L8 Sevilla la Nueva Spain
Seville Spain see Sevilla
205 K9 Sevilleja de la Jara Spain
285 I5 Sevingé Arg.
219 N7 Sevlievo Bulg.
Sevlyush Ukr. see Vynohradiv
210 E2 Sevnica Slovenia
218 H7 Sevojno Užice Serbia
184 A1 Sèvre Nantaise r. France
184 B3 Sèvre Niortaise r. France
182 I5 Sévrier France
182 G3 Sevron r. France
159 N1 Sevsk Rus. Fed.
133 I10 Sêwa Xizang China
136 D3 Sewand r. India
138 E5 Sewani Haryana India
245 J3 Seward AK U.S.A.
250 E7 Seward IL U.S.A.
260 G5 Seward NE U.S.A.
256 F8 Seward PA U.S.A.
245 L3 Seward Glacier Can./U.S.A.
286 T2 Seward Mountains Antarctica
244 F2 Seward Peninsula AK U.S.A.
258 E5 Sewell NJ U.S.A.
284 B4 Sewell (abandoned) Chile
245 N5 Sewell Inlet B.C. Can.
194 D5 Sexau Ger.
Sexi Spain see Almuñécar
246 G4 Sexsmith Alta Can.
266 G4 Sextín Mex.
266 G5 Sextín r. Mex.
127 J5 Seya Japan
145 J5 Seyah Band Koh mts Afgh.
152 I2 Seyakha Rus. Fed.
267 N8 Seybaplaya Mex.
239 □[2] Seychelles country Indian O
185 E6 Seyches France
193 G7 Seyda Ger.
221 M3 Seydi r. Turkey
145 J2 Seýdi Turkm.
148 E5 Seydişehir Turkey
162 □F1 Seyðisfjörður Iceland
180 H3 Seye r. France
148 G4 Seyfe Gölü salt flat Turkey
Seyhan Turkey see Adana
148 G5 Seyhan r. Turkey
150 D1 Seyhan Barajı resr Turkey
151 H5 Seyidlär Azer.
221 L3 Seyitgazi Turkey
221 K3 Seyitömer Turkey
159 Q2 Seym Rus. Fed.
159 N2 Seym r. Rus. Fed./Ukr.
153 Q3 Seymchan Rus. Fed.
221 J1 Seymen Turkey
105 J7 Seymour Vic. Austr.
237 K8 Seymour S. Africa
259 I2 Seymour CT U.S.A.
254 E6 Seymour IN U.S.A.
261 F9 Seymour TX U.S.A.
246 E5 Seymour Inlet B.C. Can.
106 D8 Seymour Range mts N.T. Au
183 I8 Seyne France
183 E8 Seynes France
182 I5 Seynod France
Seypan i. N. Mariana Is see Saipan
182 H5 Seyssel France
185 G8 Seysses France
182 F5 Seysseuel France
183 H6 Seyssins France
219 P9 Seytan r. Turkey
145 M4 Seyyedābād Afgh.
210 D3 Sežana Slovenia
178 G6 Sézanne France
237 O6 Sezela S. Africa
161 R6 Sezha r. Rus. Fed.
198 D2 Sezimovo Ústí Czech Rep.
215 K5 Sezze Italy
221 G7 Sfaka Kriti Greece
219 N5 Sfântu Gheorghe Covasna Romania
219 R6 Sfântu Gheorghe Tulcea Ro
219 R5 Sfântu Gheorghe, Braţul watercourse Romania
219 R6 Sfântu Gheorghe-Palade-P nature res. Romania
227 H2 Sfax Tunisia
220 D2 Sfendami Greece
214 D8 Sferracavallo, Capo c. Sarde Italy
220 D2 Sfikias, Limni resr Greece
Sfîntu Gheorghe Romania Sfântu Gheorghe
Sgiersch Pol. see Zgierz
168 D6 Sgiogarstaigh Western Isles, Scotland U.K.
168 F7 Sgorr Ruadh hill Scotland U.
186 G5 's-Gravendeel Neth.
186 F4 's-Gravenhage Neth.
187 E6 's-Gravenpolder Neth.
187 I7 's-Gravenvoeren Belgium
186 F5 's-Gravenzande Neth.
215 K4 Sgurgola Italy
168 F8 Sgurr a' Chaorachain mt. Scotland U.K.
168 G8 Sgurr a' Choire Ghlais mt. Scotland U.K.
168 D8 Sgurr Alasdair hill Scotland
168 G7 Sgurr a' Mhuilinn hill Scotla U.K.
168 F9 Sgurr Dhomhnuill hill Scotl U.K.
168 F8 Sgurr Fhuaran mt. Scotland
168 E7 Sgurr Mhòr hill Scotland U.
168 F7 Sgurr Mòr mt. Scotland U.K.
168 F8 Sgurr na Ciche mt. Scotland
151 G2 Shaami-Yurt Rus. Fed.
129 K9 Shaanxi prov. China
Shaartuz Tajik. see Shahrtuz
147 I3 Sha'b, Jabal ash hills Saudi A
145 L7 Shaban Pak.
Shabani Zimbabwe see Zvishavane
159 R9 Shabanovskoye Rus. Fed.
Shabbaz Uzbek. see Beruniy
232 E4 Shabeellaha Dhexe admin. Somalia
232 D4 Shabeellaha Hoose admin. Somalia
157 G7 Shabel'sk Rus. Fed.
144 A2 Shabestar Iran
219 Q7 Shabla Bulg.
219 Q7 Shabla, Nos pt Bulg.
161 S9 Shablykino Rus. Fed.
249 H2 Shabogamo Lake Nfld and Can.
230 E5 Shabunda Dem. Rep. Cong
146 H8 Shabwah Yemen
146 H8 Shabwah governorate Yemer
132 C7 Shache Xinjiang China
Shacheng Hebei China see Huailai
287 L1 Shackleton Coast Antarctic
287 M1 Shackleton Glacier Antarcti
287 G2 Shackleton Ice Shelf Antarc
286 V1 Shackleton Range mts Anta
146 E5 Shadād Saudi Arabia
130 G4 Shadaogou Hubei China
118 C5 Shadaw Myanmar
256 C9 Shade OH U.S.A.
144 C6 Shādegān Iran
258 D2 Shades Glen PA U.S.A.
145 L7 Shadihar Pak.
144 E7 Shādkām watercourse Iran
152 H4 Shadrinsk Rus. Fed.
Shadwan Island Egypt see Shākir, Jazīrat
256 G10 Shadwell VA U.S.A.
262 C5 Shady Grove OR U.S.A.
258 B7 Shady Side MD U.S.A.
256 D11 Shady Spring WV U.S.A.
250 H9 Shafer, Lake IN U.S.A.
287 K2 Shafer Peak Antarctica
144 G3 Shafī'ābād Iran
Shafirkan Uzbek. see Shofir
142 F1 Shafranovo Rus. Fed.
Shafrikan Uzbek. see Shofir
264 M6 Shafter CA U.S.A.
172 H5 Shaftesbury Dorset, England
103 E12 Shag r. South I. N.Z.
143 N1 Shagalalyteniz, Ozero l. Ka
248 C2 Shagamu r. Ont. Can.
229 F5 Shagamu Nigeria
142 G4 Shagan watercourse Kazakh.
143 R2 Shagan watercourse Kazakh.
129 L7 Shagedu Nei Mongol China
244 H3 Shageluk AK U.S.A.
146 C2 Shaghab oasis Saudi Arabia
Shaghan Kazakh. see Chaga
Shaghyray Üstirti plat. Kaza see Shagyray, Plato
142 H6 Shag'irlik Uzbek.
103 E12 Shag Point South I. N.Z.
273 G7 Shag Rocks is S. Georgia
142 G4 Shagyray, Plato plat. Kazakh
136 F4 Shahabad Andhra Prad. Ind
138 F4 Shahabad Haryana India
136 E4 Shahabad Karnataka India
138 F7 Shahabad Rajasthan India
138 H6 Shahabad Uttar Prad. India
Shāhābād Āzarbāyjān-e Gha Iran see Showt
144 G7 Shāhābād Kermān Iran
Shāhābād Kermānshāh Iran Eslāmābād-e Gharb
138 E9 Shahada Mahar. India
116 D3 Shah Alam Malaysia

Shahana Pak.
Shahapur Karnataka India
Shahapur Mahar. India
Shahbā' Syria
Shah Bandar Pak.
Shahbānū Faraḩ, Sadd-e Iran
Shahbaz Kalat Pak.
Shahbazpur sea chan. Bangl.
Shahbeg Pak.
Shah Bilawal Pak.
Shahdād Iran
Shahdad Kot Pak.
Shahdadpur Pak.
Shahdara Pak.
Shahdol Madh. Prad. India
Shahe Chongqing China
Shahe Shandong China
Sha He r. China
Shahejie Jiangxi China see Jiujiang
Shahepu Gansu China see Linze
Shahezhen Gansu China see Linze
Shahezhen Jiangxi China see Jiujiang
Shah Fuladi mt. Afgh.
Shahganj Uttar Prad. India
Shahgarh Madh. Prad. India
Shahgarh Rajasthan India
Shaḩḩāt Libya
Shah Hussain Pak.
Shahid, Ras pt Pak.
Shāhīn Dezh Iran see Sa'īndezh
Shah Ismail Afgh.
Shāh Jahān, Kūh-e mts Iran
Shahjahanpur Rajasthan India
Shahjahanpur Uttar Prad. India
Shāh Jūy Afgh.
Shāh Kūh mt. Iran
Shahmīrzād Iran
Shahousuo Liaoning China
Shāh Pasand Iran see Āzād Shahr
Shahpur Karnataka India
Shahpur Madh. Prad. India
Shahpur Madh. Prad. India
Shahpur Madh. Prad. India
Shahpur Madh. Prad. India
Shāhpūr Iran see Salmās
Shahpur Balochistan Pak.
Shahpur Punjab Pak.
Shahpur Sindh Pak.
Shahpura Madh. Prad. India
Shahpura Madh. Prad. India
Shahpura Rajasthan India
Shahr oasis Saudi Arabia
Shahrak Afgh.
Shāh Rakht Iran
Shahrān reg. Saudi Arabia
Shahr-e Bābak Iran
Shahr-e Kord Iran
Shahr-e Now Iran
Shahr-e Şafā Afgh.
Shahrezā Iran
Shahrig Pak.
Shahrihon Uzbek.
Shahrisabz Uzbek.
Shahriston Tajik.
Shahr Rey Iran
Shahr Sultan Pak.
Shahrtuz Tajik.
Shāhrūd Iran see Emāmrūd
Shāhrūd, Rūdkhāneh-ye r. Iran
Shāhrūd Bustām reg. Iran
Shāh Savārān, Kūh-e mts Iran
Shāh Taqī Iran see Emām Taqī
Shah Umar Pak.
Shaighalu Pak.
Shaikh Husain mt. Pak.
Shā'īr, Jabal mts Syria
Sha'īrah, Jabal mt. Egypt
Shaistaganj Bangl.
Shaj'ah, Jabal hill Saudi Arabia
Shajapur Madh. Prad. India
Shajianzi Liaoning China
Shakaga-dake mt. Japan
Shakar Bolāghī Iran
Shakaskraal S. Africa
Shakaville S. Africa
Shakawe Botswana
Shakespeare Island Ont. Can.
Shakh Khatlon Tajik. see Shoh
Shakhagach Azer. see Şahağac
Shakhbuz Azer. see Şahbuz
Shākhen Iran
Shakhovo Rus. Fed.
Shakhovskaya Rus. Fed.
Shakhrisabz Uzbek. see Shahrisabz
Shakhristan Tajik. see Shahriston
Shakhs, Ras pt Eritrea
Shakhtars'k Ukr.
Shakhtersk Ukr. see Shakhtars'k
Shakhterskoye Ukr. see Pershotravens'k
Shakhtinsk Kazakh.
Shakhty Kazakh.
Shakhty Respublika Buryatiya Rus. Fed. see Gusinoozersk
Shakhty Rostovskaya Oblast' Rus. Fed.
Shakhtyorsk Ukr. see Shakhtars'k
Shakhtyorskoye Ukr. see Pershotravens'k
Shakhun'ya Rus. Fed.
Shaki Nigeria
Shākir, Jazīrat i. Egypt
Shakopee MN U.S.A.
Shakotan-hantō pen. Japan
Shakotan-misaki c. Japan
Shakou Guangdong China
Shakshūk Libya
Shaktoolik AK U.S.A.
Shala Hāyk' l. Eth.
Shalakusha Rus. Fed.
Shalamzār Iran
Shalang Guangdong China
Shalbuzdag, Gora mt. Rus. Fed.
Shalday Kazakh.
Shalfleet Isle of Wight, England U.K.
Shalford Surrey, England U.K.
Shalginskiy Kazakh.
Shalgiya Kazakh. see Shalginskiy
Shali Rus. Fed.
Shaliangzi Qinghai China
Shalim Oman
Shaliuhe Qinghai China see Gangca
Shalkar Hima. Prad. India
Shalkar Aktyubinskaya Oblast' Kazakh.
Shalkar Kazakh. see Chelkar
Shalkar, Ozero salt l. Kazakh.
Shalkar Karashatau salt l. Kazakh.
Shalkarteniz, Solonchak salt marsh Kazakh.
Shalkar-Yega-Kara, Ozero l. Rus. Fed.
Shalkodesu Kazakh.
Shallow Bay N.W.T. Can.
Shalqar Aktyubinskaya Oblast' Kazakh. see Shalkar
Shalqar Zapadnyy Kazakhstan Kazakh. see Chelkar
Shalqar Köli salt l. Kazakh. see Shalkar, Ozero
Shalqīya Kazakh. see Shalginskiy
Shaltrak Iran
Shaluli Shan mts Sichuan China
Shaluni mt. Arun. Prad. India
Shalya Rus. Fed.
Shalyhyne Ukr.
Shām, Jabal mt. Oman
Shama r. Tanz.
Shamāl Sīnā' governorate Egypt
Shamalzā'ī Afgh.
Shamary Rus. Fed.
Shāmat al Akbād des. Saudi Arabia
Shamattawa Man. Can.
Shamattawa r. Ont. Can.
Shamava Belarus
Shambār Iran
Shambe Sudan
232 C2 Shambu Eth.
231 D6 Shambuanda Dem. Rep. Congo
131 □ Sham Chun r. Guangdong/H.K. China
138 E7 Shamgarh Madh. Prad. India
Shamgong Bhutan see Shemgang
144 G8 Shamīl Iran
151 H3 Shamil'kala Rus. Fed.
147 K4 Shamis U.A.E.
151 I2 Shamkhal Rus. Fed.
Shamkhor Azer. see Şämkir
146 F2 Shammar, Jabal reg. Saudi Arabia
258 B3 Shamokin PA U.S.A.
258 B3 Shamokin Dam PA U.S.A.
161 Q1 Shamoksha Rus. Fed.
158 I4 Shamrayivka Ukr.
261 E8 Shamrock TX U.S.A.
235 F3 Shamva Zimbabwe
237 K9 Shamwari Game Reserve nature res. S. Africa
118 D4 Shan state Myanmar
Shancheng Fujian China see Nanjing
Shancheng Shandong China see Shanxian
145 I6 Shand Afgh.
144 I7 Shāndak Iran
128 G7 Shandan Gansu China
128 G7 Shandan He r. Gansu China
129 O6 Shandian He r. China
144 H3 Shāndīz Iran
129 O8 Shandong prov. China
129 Q8 Shandong Bandao pen. China
159 K4 Shandra Ukr.
149 L7 Shandrūkh Iraq
145 O3 Shandur Pass Pak.
258 D4 Shanesville PA U.S.A.
235 F3 Shangani Zimbabwe
235 E3 Shangani r. Zimbabwe
130 B2 Shang Boingor Qinghai China
131 J2 Shangcai Henan China
130 G6 Shangchao Guangxi China
131 J3 Shangcheng Henan China
133 I12 Shang Chu r. China
131 I8 Shangchuan Dao i. Guangdong China
Shangchuankou Qinghai China see Minhe
129 M6 Shangdu Nei Mongol China
122 F5 Shangganling Heilong. China
131 J4 Shanggao Jiangxi China
131 M3 Shanghai Shanghai China
131 M3 Shanghai mun. China
131 K6 Shanghang Fujian China
129 O8 Shanghe Shandong China
123 D8 Shanghekou Liaoning China
Shangji Henan China see Xichuan
Shangjie Yunnan China see Yangbi
130 H2 Shangjin Hubei China
130 B2 Shang Kongma Qinghai China
129 Q1 Shangkuli Nei Mongol China
130 G2 Shangluo Shaanxi China
Shangmei Hunan China see Xinhua
130 H2 Shangnan Shaanxi China
231 D9 Shangombo Zambia
Shangpai Anhui China see Feixi
Shangpai Yunnan China see Fugong
Shangpaihe Anhui China see Feixi
129 N9 Shangqiu Henan China
131 K4 Shangrao Jiangxi China
132 F3 Shangsanshilipu Xinjiang China
131 J2 Shangshui Henan China
130 G7 Shangsi Guangxi China
Shangtang Zhejiang China see Yongjia
131 J6 Shangyou Jiangxi China
132 E6 Shangyou Shuiku resr China
131 M3 Shangyu Zhejiang China
130 A4 Shang Zayü Xizang China
122 E6 Shangzhi Heilong. China
Shangzhou Shaanxi China see Shangluo
129 P6 Shanhaiguan Hebei China
Shanhe Gansu China see Zhengning
122 E6 Shanhe Heilong. China
197 M3 Shani Belarus
229 I4 Shani Nigeria
151 F3 Shani, Mt'a Georgia/Rus. Fed.
173 J6 Shanklin Isle of Wight, England U.K.
130 G8 Shankou Guangxi China
131 H4 Shankou Hunan China
128 D5 Shankou Xinjiang China
102 J7 Shannon North I. N.Z.
169 E7 Shannon airport Ireland
169 E7 Shannon est. Ireland
169 E7 Shannon r. Ireland
237 K5 Shannon S. Africa
250 E7 Shannon IL U.S.A.
169 C7 Shannon, Mouth of the Ireland
109 D13 Shannon National Park W.A. Austr.
243 Q2 Shannon Ø i. Greenland
118 C4 Shan Plateau Myanmar
128 B5 Shanshan Xinjiang China
128 B5 Shanshanzhan Xinjiang China
Shansi prov. China see Shanxi
153 O4 Shantarskiye Ostrova is Rus. Fed.
131 □J7 Shan Tei Tong hill H.K. China
Shan Teng hill H.K. China see Victoria Peak
139 L8 Shantipur W. Bengal India
170 D5 Shantonagh Ireland
131 K7 Shantou Guangdong China
Shantung prov. China see Shandong
169 F4 Shanvus Ireland
131 J7 Shanwei Guangdong China
129 L7 Shanxi prov. China
129 O9 Shanxian Shandong China
161 S7 Shanya r. Rus. Fed.
130 G2 Shanyang Shaanxi China
129 M7 Shanyin Shanxi China
131 H5 Shaodong Hunan China
131 I6 Shaoguan Guangdong China
131 I5 Shaoshan Hunan China
131 K5 Shaowu Fujian China
131 M3 Shaoxing Zhejiang China
131 H5 Shaoyang Hunan China
131 H5 Shaoyang Hunan China
171 L4 Shap Cumbria, England U.K.
131 H8 Shapa Guangdong China
231 D6 Shapembe Dem. Rep. Congo
Shaping Sichuan China see Ebian
168 K4 Shapinsay i. Scotland U.K.
168 K4 Shapinsay Sound sea chan. Scotland U.K.
161 O2 Shapki Rus. Fed.
156 K2 Shapkina r. Rus. Fed.
159 L2 Shapovalivka Ukr.
161 R1 Shapsha Rus. Fed.
132 I1 Shapshal'skiy Khrebet mts Rus. Fed.
159 R9 Shapsugskaya Rus. Fed.
159 R9 Shapsugskoye Vodokhranilishche resr Rus. Fed.
160 M7 Shapyalyevichy Belarus
150 D5 Shaqīf, Qal'at ash tourist site Lebanon
132 I4 Shaqiuhe Xinjiang China
224 E6 Shaqq el Giefer, Wadi watercourse Sudan
224 E6 Shaqq el Khadir Sudan
146 G3 Shaqrā' Saudi Arabia
132 F4 Shaquanzi Xinjiang China
143 S3 Shar Kazakh.
146 B2 Shār, Jabal mt. Saudi Arabia
149 K8 Sharaf well Iraq
224 E6 Sharafa Sudan
149 L4 Sharaf-Khāneh Iran
129 J1 Sharalday Rus. Fed.
145 M5 Sharan Afgh.
156 K5 Sharan Rus. Fed.
156 I4 Sharanga Rus. Fed.
145 M6 Sharan Jogizai Pak.
161 U6 Sharapovo Rus. Fed.
150 G2 Sharaqraq Syria
160 H9 Sharashova Belarus
150 B10 Sharātīb, Ra's pt Egypt
169 G6 Sharavogue Ireland
150 E10 Sharawrā, Jabal hills Saudi Arabia
150 E10 Sharawrā', Qā' salt pan Saudi Arabia
Sharbaqty Kazakh. see Shcherbakty
147 M7 Sharbithāt, Ra's c. Oman
Sharbulag Mongolia see Dzavhan
143 S1 Sharchino Rus. Fed.
143 L7 Shardara Kazakh.
143 L7 Shardara, Step' plain Kazakh.
Shardara Bögeni resr Kazakh./Uzbek. see Chardarinskoye Vodokhranilishche
145 P4 Shardi Pak.
128 D3 Sharga Govĭ-Altay Mongolia
Sharga Mongolia see Tsagaan-Uul
Shargorod Ukr. see Sharhorod
143 L8 Sharg'un Uzbek.
158 H5 Sharhorod Ukr.
Sharhulsan Mongolia see Mandal-Ovoo
Shari r. Cameroon/Chad see Chari
124 V3 Shari Japan
149 L6 Shārī, Buḩayrat imp. l. Iraq
124 V3 Shari-dake vol. Japan
150 F4 Sharīfah Syria
150 C10 Sharīrah Pass Egypt
159 O3 Sharivka Kharkivs'ka Oblast' Ukr.
159 R4 Sharivka Luhans'ka Oblast' Ukr.
151 E3 Sharivtsek, Pereval pass Georgia/Rus. Fed.
Sharjah U.A.E. see Ash Shāriqah
133 J12 Sharka-leb La pass Xizang China
156 K4 Sharkan Rus. Fed.
160 K6 Sharkawshchyna Belarus
109 B8 Shark Bay W.A. Austr.
108 B8 Shark Bay Marine Park marine park Australia
114 B6 Shark Fin Bay Palawan Phil.
147 J8 Sharkhāt Yemen
107 K3 Shark Reef Coral Sea Is Terr. Austr.
259 G4 Shark River Hills NJ U.S.A.
Sharlawuk Turkm. see Şarlawuk
142 F1 Sharlyk Rus. Fed.
146 B1 Sharmah Saudi Arabia
225 G3 Sharm ash Shaykh Egypt
151 G2 Sharo-Argun r. Rus. Fed.
256 E7 Sharon PA U.S.A.
250 F7 Sharon WI U.S.A.
Sharon, Plain of Israel see HaSharon
260 E6 Sharon Springs KS U.S.A.
256 A9 Sharonville OH U.S.A.
151 G3 Sharoy Rus. Fed.
109 F12 Sharpe, Lake salt flat W.A. Austr.
247 M4 Sharpe Lake Man. Can.
245 M2 Sharp Mountain Y.T. Can.
172 H4 Sharpness Gloucestershire, England U.K.
Sharp Peak hill H.K. China see Nam She Tsim
256 H9 Sharpsburg MD U.S.A.
256 D9 Sharpsburg OH U.S.A.
Sharqat Iraq see Ash Sharqāţ
150 D5 Sharqī, Jabal ash mts Lebanon/Syria
142 H6 Sharqiy Ustyurt Chink esc. Uzbek.
145 P6 Sharqpur Pak.
258 C3 Shartlesville PA U.S.A.
Sharur Azer. see Şärur
128 E3 Shar Us Gol r. Mongolia
146 F2 Shary well Saudi Arabia
156 I4 Shar'ya Rus. Fed.
161 P2 Shar'ya r. Rus. Fed.
Sharyn Kazakh. see Charyn
143 R6 Sharyn r. Kazakh.
229 G5 Shasha Nigeria
235 E4 Shashe Botswana
235 F4 Shashe r. Botswana/Zimbabwe
235 E4 Shashe Dam resr Botswana
232 C3 Shashemenē Eth.
Shashi Hubei China see Jingzhou
143 P4 Shashubay Kazakh.
262 C6 Shasta, Mount vol. CA U.S.A.
262 C6 Shasta Lake CA U.S.A.
159 R2 Shatalovka Rus. Fed.
161 P7 Shatalovo Rus. Fed.
131 □J7 Sha Tau Kok Hoi inlet H.K. China
224 B3 Shāţi', Wādī ash watercourse Libya
151 G3 Shatili Georgia
Shatilki Belarus see Svyetlahorsk
131 □J7 Sha Tin H.K. China
131 □J7 Sha Tin Hoi b. H.K. China
157 I5 Shatki Rus. Fed.
150 G3 Shaţnat as Salmās, Wādī watercourse Syria
131 □J7 Sha Tong Hau Shan i. H.K. China
149 L2 Shatoy Rus. Fed.
157 H5 Shatsk Rus. Fed.
158 C2 Shats'k Ukr.
158 C2 Shats'kyy Natsional'nyy Park nat. park Ukr.
144 D7 Shaţţ, Ra's osh pt Iran
144 C7 Shaţţ al 'Arab r. Iran/Iraq
149 M8 Shaţţ al Gharrāf r. Iraq
261 F7 Shattuck OK U.S.A.
161 W6 Shatura Rus. Fed.
161 W6 Shaturtorf Rus. Fed.
Shaubak Jordan see Ash Shawbak
Shäüildir Kazakh. see Shaul'der
143 M6 Shaul'der Kazakh.
247 I5 Shaunavon Sask. Can.
162 U5 Shaverki Rus. Fed.
264 M4 Shaver Lake CA U.S.A.
256 F10 Shavers Fork r. WV U.S.A.
151 G3 Shavi Klde, Mt'a Georgia/Rus. Fed.
171 M7 Shavington Cheshire, England U.K.
245 K1 Shaviovik r. AK U.S.A.
285 H5 Shaw Arg.
108 E6 Shaw r. W.A. Austr.
171 M6 Shaw Greater Manchester, England U.K.
132 G4 Shawan Xinjiang China
258 B6 Shawan MD U.S.A.
259 G1 Shawangunk Kill r. NY U.S.A.
259 F2 Shawangunk Mountains hills NY U.S.A.
250 F5 Shawano WI U.S.A.
250 F5 Shawano Lake WI U.S.A.
146 C2 Shawāq well Saudi Arabia
168 C6 Shawbost Western Isles, Scotland U.K.
256 A10 Shawhan KY U.S.A.
261 G8 Shawnee OK U.S.A.
262 L5 Shawnee WY U.S.A.
256 E11 Shawsville VA U.S.A.
131 L5 Sha Xi r. China
131 K5 Shaxian Fujian China
143 M6 Shayan Kazakh.
131 I3 Shayang Hubei China
147 L4 Shaybah, 'Urūq ash des. Saudi Arabia
146 C3 Shaybārā i. Saudi Arabia
153 R3 Shayboveyem r. Rus. Fed.
108 F6 Shay Gap (abandoned) W.A. Austr.
Shaykh, Jabal ash mt. Lebanon/Syria see Hermon, Mount
150 B10 Shaykh, Wādī ash watercourse Egypt
149 M7 Shaykh Jūwī Iraq
150 E6 Shaykh Miskīn Syria
149 M7 Shaykh Sa'd Iraq
161 R7 Shaykovka Rus. Fed.
159 P6 Shaytanka r. Ukr.
150 E3 Shayzar Syria
144 C5 Shāzand Iran
132 L7 Shazaoyuan Gansu China
146 E2 Shaẕāẕ, Jabal mt. Saudi Arabia
145 O3 Shazud Tajik.
160 H8 Shchara r. Belarus
197 M3 Shcharchova Belarus
159 S5 Shchastya Ukr.
159 O9 Shchebetovka Ukr.
161 R9 Shcheglovka Rus. Fed.
161 U7 Shchekino Rus. Fed.
158 F3 Shchekychyn Ukr.
161 S7 Shchelkanovo Rus. Fed.
161 V6 Shchelkovo Rus. Fed.
156 K2 Shchel'yayur Rus. Fed.
Shcherbakov Rus. Fed. see Rybinsk
143 R1 Shcherbakty Kazakh.
159 K6 Shcherbani Ukr.
Shcherbinovka Ukr. see Dzerzhyns'k
156 G4 Shchetinskoye Rus. Fed.
157 G6 Shchigry Rus. Fed.
159 O8 Shcholkine Ukr.
160 K8 Shchomyslitsa Belarus
159 K2 Shchors Ukr.
159 N5 Shchors'k Ukr.
Shchuchin Belarus see Shchuchyn
143 N1 Shchuchinsk Kazakh.
159 T2 Shchuch'ye Rus. Fed.
160 H8 Shchuchyn Belarus
156 L2 Shchuger r. Rus. Fed.
158 C4 Shchyrets' Ukr.
160 L8 Shchytkavichy Belarus
275 G4 Shea Guyana
143 U2 Shebalino Rus. Fed.
250 D1 Shebandowan Lakes Ont. Can.
157 G6 Shebekino Rus. Fed.
232 E3 Shebelē Wenz, Wabē r. Eth.
232 D4 Shebelē Wenz, Wabē r. Somalia
145 K3 Sheberghān Afgh.
250 G6 Sheboygan WI U.S.A.
159 R9 Shebsh r. Rus. Fed.
229 H4 Shebshi Mountains Nigeria
122 L5 Shebunino Sakhalin Rus. Fed.
Shecheng Hebei China see Shexian
249 H4 Shediac N.B. Can.
246 E4 Shedin Peak B.C. Can.
151 B1 Shedok Rus. Fed.
169 H5 Sheelin, Lough l. Ireland
245 K2 Sheenjek r. AK U.S.A.
169 G2 Sheep Haven b. Ireland
237 O2 Sheepmoor S. Africa
265 Q5 Sheep Peak NV U.S.A.
186 J5 's-Heerenberg Neth.
173 M4 Sheering Essex, England U.K.
173 N5 Sheerness Kent, England U.K.
249 I4 Sheet Harbour N.S. Can.
150 D6 Shefar'am Israel
103 G10 Sheffield South I. N.Z.
171 O7 Sheffield South Yorkshire, England U.K.
255 D8 Sheffield AL U.S.A.
250 E8 Sheffield IL U.S.A.
256 F7 Sheffield PA U.S.A.
261 E10 Sheffield TX U.S.A.
249 J3 Sheffield Lake Nfld and Lab. Can.
173 L3 Shefford Bedfordshire, England U.K.
145 K6 Shegah Afgh.
138 F9 Shegaon Mahar. India
156 J2 Shegmas Rus. Fed.
251 M4 Sheguiandah Ont. Can.
232 D3 Shēh Husēn Eth.
130 E3 Shehong Sichuan China
169 D9 Shehy Mountains hills Ireland
Sheikh, Jebel esh mt. Lebanon/Syria see Hermon, Mount
Sheikh Othman Yemen see Ash Shaykh 'Uthman
145 P6 Sheikhupura Pak.
248 C3 Shekak r. Ont. Can.
144 F5 Shekār Āb Iran
145 M4 Shekārī, Darreh-ye r. Afgh.
145 M4 Shekārī, Darreh-ye r. Afgh.
138 E6 Shekhawati reg. India
Shekhem West Bank see Nāblus
159 T1 Shekhman' Rus. Fed.
Sheki Azer. see Şäki
131 □I7 Shekka Ch'ün-Tao is H.K. China
131 □I7 Shek Kwu Chau i. H.K. China
131 □I7 Shek Pik resr H.K. China
Shek Pik Reservoir H.K. China see Shek Pik
156 G4 Sheksna Rus. Fed.
156 G4 Sheksninskoye Vodokhranilishche resr Rus. Fed.
131 □J7 Shek Uk Shan mt. H.K. China
133 K11 Shela Xizang China
143 T1 Shelabolikha Rus. Fed.
145 I7 Shelag watercourse Afgh./Iran
153 S2 Shelagskiy, Mys pt Rus. Fed.
256 C11 Shelbiana KY U.S.A.
260 I6 Shelbina MO U.S.A.
254 D6 Shelburn IN U.S.A.
249 H5 Shelburne N.S. Can.
251 N5 Shelburne Ont. Can.
107 I1 Shelburne Bay Qld Austr.
257 M6 Shelburne Falls MA U.S.A.
250 H6 Shelby MI U.S.A.
261 J9 Shelby MS U.S.A.
262 I2 Shelby MT U.S.A.
255 G8 Shelby NC U.S.A.
256 C8 Shelby OH U.S.A.
260 K6 Shelbyville IL U.S.A.
254 E6 Shelbyville IN U.S.A.
260 I6 Shelbyville MO U.S.A.
255 D8 Shelbyville TN U.S.A.
260 K6 Shelbyville, Lake IL U.S.A.
237 J9 Sheldon S. Africa
260 H4 Sheldon IA U.S.A.
250 G9 Sheldon IL U.S.A.
250 D4 Sheldon WI U.S.A.
262 E6 Sheldon National Wildlife Refuge nature res. NV U.S.A.
244 F3 Sheldon Point AK U.S.A.
257 M4 Sheldon Springs VT U.S.A.
249 H3 Sheldrake Que. Can.
Shelek Kazakh. see Chilik
158 J6 Shelekhove Ukr.
153 Q3 Shelikhova, Zaliv g. Rus. Fed.
242 C4 Shelikof Strait AK U.S.A.
151 H2 Shelkovskaya Rus. Fed.
262 K4 Shell WY U.S.A.
168 C6 Shell, Loch inlet Scotland U.K.
247 J4 Shellbrook Sask. Can.
262 H5 Shelley ID U.S.A.
105 M6 Shellharbour N.S.W. Austr.
247 J4 Shell Lake Sask. Can.
250 C4 Shell Lake WI U.S.A.
109 I10 Shell Lakes salt flat W.A. Austr.
264 I1 Shell Mountain CA U.S.A.
160 N3 Shelon' r. Rus. Fed.
Shelter Bay Que. Can. see Port-Cartier
259 K2 Shelter Island NY U.S.A.
259 K2 Shelter Island i. NY U.S.A.
259 K2 Shelter Island Heights NY U.S.A.
259 K2 Shelter Island Sound str. NY U.S.A.
103 C14 Shelter Point Stewart I. N.Z.
259 I2 Shelton CT U.S.A.
262 C3 Shelton WA U.S.A.
156 F3 Sheltozero Rus. Fed.
Shelyakino Rus. Fed. see Sovetskoye
144 D3 Shem Iran
Shemakha Azer. see Şamaxı
229 H4 Shemankar r. Nigeria
161 R1 Shemenichi Rus. Fed.
139 M6 Shemgang Bhutan
151 D4 Shemok'medi Georgia
143 S2 Shemonaikha Kazakh.
156 J4 Shemordan Rus. Fed.
157 I5 Shemursha Rus. Fed.
157 I5 Shemysheyka Rus. Fed.
260 H5 Shenandoah IA U.S.A.
251 R9 Shenandoah PA U.S.A.
256 G10 Shenandoah VA U.S.A.
256 H9 Shenandoah r. VA U.S.A.
256 F10 Shenandoah Mountains VA/WV U.S.A.
256 G10 Shenandoah National Park VA U.S.A.
131 K7 Shen'ao Guangdong China
142 I3 Shenbertal Kazakh.
129 M7 Shenchi Shanxi China
229 H4 Shendam Nigeria
225 G5 Shendi Sudan
122 H5 Shending Shan hill Heilong. China
228 B5 Shenge Sierra Leone
143 Q5 Shengel'dy Almatinskaya Oblast' Kazakh.
142 I5 Shengel'dy Kyzylordinskaya Oblast' Kazakh.
143 M7 Shengel'dy Kazakh.
Shenggeldy Kazakh. see Shengel'dy
218 H9 Shëngjin Albania
131 J3 Shengli Hubei China
132 H5 Shengli Daban pass Xinjiang China
Shengli Feng mt. China/Kyrg. see Jengish Chokusu
132 D6 Shengli Qichang Xinjiang China
132 E6 Shengli Shibachang Xinjiang China
Shengrenjian Shanxi China see Pinglu
131 N3 Shengsi Zhejiang China
131 N3 Shengsi Liedao is China
Shengxian Zhejiang China see Shengzhou
131 M4 Shengzhou Zhejiang China
218 H9 Shënkoll Albania
156 H3 Shenkursk Rus. Fed.
129 L7 Shenmu Shaanxi China
130 H3 Shennongjia Hubei China
131 J2 Shenqiu Henan China
122 F5 Shenshu Heilong. China
Shensi prov. China see Shaanxi
173 I2 Shenstone Staffordshire, England U.K.
157 J5 Shentala Rus. Fed.
109 G10 Shenton, Mount hill W.A. Austr.
Shenxian Hebei China see Shenzhou
129 N8 Shenxian Shandong China
129 R6 Shenyang Liaoning China
131 J7 Shenzhen Guangdong China
131 □I7 Shenzhen Wan b. H.K. China
129 N8 Shenzhou Hebei China
138 D7 Sheoganj Rajasthan India
138 F7 Sheopur Madh. Prad. India
286 P2 Shepard Island Antarctica
158 G3 Shepetivka Ukr.
Shepetovka Ukr. see Shepetivka
256 A5 Shepherd MI U.S.A.
100 □5 Shepherd Islands Vanuatu
105 J7 Shepparton Vic. Austr.
173 L5 Shepperton Surrey, England U.K.
173 N5 Sheppey, Isle of i. England U.K.
258 C3 Sheppton PA U.S.A.
173 J2 Shepshed Leicestershire, England U.K.
159 M1 Sheptaky Ukr.
172 G5 Shepton Mallet Somerset, England U.K.
159 O2 Sheptukhovka Rus. Fed.
131 I2 Sheqi Henan China
230 E2 Sherab Sudan
Sherabad Uzbek. see Sherobod
243 J2 Sherard, Cape Nunavut Can.
145 I5 Sher Bakhsh Afgh.
237 I7 Sherborne S. Africa
172 G6 Sherborne Dorset, England U.K.
173 J5 Sherborne St John Hampshire, England U.K.
228 B5 Sherbro Island Sierra Leone
249 I4 Sherbrooke N.S. Can.
249 G4 Sherbrooke Que. Can.
171 N4 Sherburn Durham, England U.K.
257 J6 Sherburne NY U.S.A.
171 O6 Sherburn in Elmet North Yorkshire, England U.K.
169 I5 Shercock Ireland
224 C4 Sherda well Chad
143 T3 Sherdyayak Kazakh.
173 L5 Shere Surrey, England U.K.
225 G5 Shereiq Sudan
138 D6 Shergarh Rajasthan India
139 J7 Sherghati Bihar India
261 I8 Sheridan AR U.S.A.
262 K4 Sheridan WY U.S.A.
243 L1 Sheridan, Cape Nunavut Can.
171 O5 Sheriff Hutton North Yorkshire, England U.K.
104 E5 Sheringa S.A. Austr.
173 O2 Sheringham Norfolk, England U.K.
152 H3 Sherkaly Rus. Fed.
145 L7 Sher Khan Qala Afgh.
169 D10 Sherkin Island Ireland
108 D6 Sherlock r. W.A. Austr.
129 O1 Sherlovaya Gora Rus. Fed.
256 F6 Sherman NY U.S.A.
261 G9 Sherman TX U.S.A.
257 □Q3 Sherman Mills ME U.S.A.
265 Q1 Sherman Mountain NV U.S.A.
143 L9 Sherobod Uzbek.
161 O7 Sherovichi Rus. Fed.
139 M7 Sherpur Dhaka Bangl.
139 L7 Sherpur Rajshahi Bangl.
138 E1 Sher Qila Pak.
247 K4 Sherridon Man. Can.
172 H4 Sherston Wiltshire, England U.K.
Shertallai India see Cherthala
186 H5 's-Hertogenbosch Neth.
256 A7 Sherwood OH U.S.A.
103 E10 Sherwood Downs South I. N.Z.
171 O7 Sherwood Forest reg. England U.K.
247 K2 Sherwood Lake N.W.T. Can.
251 L4 Sheshegwaning Ont. Can.
144 G3 Sheshtamad Iran
245 O4 Sheslay B.C. Can.
245 N4 Sheslay r. B.C. Can.
156 J4 Shestakovo Kirovskaya Oblast' Rus. Fed.
159 T3 Shestakovo Voronezhskaya Oblast' Rus. Fed.
161 V4 Shestikhino Rus. Fed.
159 M6 Shestirnya Ukr.
260 H3 Shetek, Lake MN U.S.A.
247 L3 Shethanei Lake Man. Can.
168 □O2 Shetland admin. div. Scotland U.K.
166 G1 Shetland Islands Scotland U.K.
142 E5 Shetpe Kazakh.
259 K1 Shetucket r. CT U.S.A.
131 □J7 Sheung Shui H.K. China
131 □J7 Sheung Sze Mun sea chan. H.K. China
131 □J7 Sheung Yue Ho r. H.K. China
136 F7 Shevaroy Hills India
159 N5 Shevchenkivka Ukr.
Shevchenko Kazakh. see Aktau
142 I4 Shevchenko, Zaliv l. Kazakh.
159 K4 Shevchenkove Cherkas'ka Oblast' Ukr.
159 Q4 Shevchenkove Kharkivs'ka Oblast' Ukr.
159 M2 Shevchenkove Ukr.
Shevchenkovo Ukr. see Dolyns'ka
136 D3 Shevgaon Mahar. India
122 H1 Shevli r. Rus. Fed.
232 B3 Shewa Gīmīra Eth.
131 L4 Shexian Anhui China
129 M8 Shexian Hebei China
153 M3 Sheya Rus. Fed.
131 M2 Sheyang Jiangsu China
156 H4 Sheybukhta Rus. Fed.
260 F2 Sheyenne ND U.S.A.
260 G2 Sheyenne r. ND U.S.A.
161 O5 Sheykino Rus. Fed.
149 O8 Sheykkī Iran
139 I5 Shey Phoksundo National Park Nepal
144 F6 Sheyţūr Iran
142 C2 Shezhin II Kazakh.
168 D7 Shiant, Sound of str. Scotland U.K.
168 D7 Shiant Islands Scotland U.K.
153 Q5 Shiashkotan, Ostrov i. Kuril'skiye O-va Rus. Fed.
251 K6 Shiawassee r. MI U.S.A.
127 I5 Shibakawa Japan
147 I8 Shibām Yemen
128 D6 Shibandong Jing well China
128 F6 Shiban Jing well China
128 E7 Shibaocheng Gansu China
145 M4 Shībar, Kowtal-e pass Afgh.
124 Q9 Shibata Japan
127 L4 Shibayama Japan
126 D3 Shibayama-gata l. Japan
122 D2 Shibazhan Heilong. China
124 T2 Shibetsu Hokkaidō Japan
124 W3 Shibetsu Hokkaidō Japan
93 F3 Shibh Jazīrat Sīnā' pen. Egypt
225 F2 Shibīn al Kawm Egypt
130 G5 Shibing Guizhou China
248 B2 Shibogama Lake Ont. Can.
Shibotsu-jima i. Kuril'skiye O-va Rus. Fed. see Zelenyy, Ostrov
127 J3 Shibukawa Japan
125 I15 Shibushi Japan
125 I15 Shibushi-wan b. Japan
127 I2 Shibu-tōge pass Japan
127 J2 Shibutsu-san mt. Japan
Shicheng Fujian China see Zhouning
131 K5 Shicheng Jiangxi China
129 R7 Shicheng Dao i. China
127 H5 Shichimen-zan mt. Japan
124 S6 Shichinohe Japan
251 R8 Shickshinny PA U.S.A.
Shicun Shanxi China see Xiangfen
150 G7 Shidād al Mismā' hill Saudi Arabia
129 R8 Shidao Shandong China
129 R8 Shidao Wan b. China
143 P1 Shiderty r. Kazakh.
130 B6 Shidian Yunnan China
Shidian Yunnan China see Changning
125 L12 Shido Japan
Shidongsi Gansu China see Gaolan
145 N3 Shidud Afgh.
168 E9 Shiel, Loch l. Scotland U.K.
168 F8 Shiel Bridge Highland, Scotland U.K.
106 F2 Shield, Cape N.T. Austr.
168 E7 Shieldaig Highland, Scotland U.K.
171 J2 Shieldhill Falkirk, Scotland U.K.
Shīeli Kazakh. see Chiili
146 B1 Shifa, Jabal ash mts Saudi Arabia
130 E3 Shifang Sichuan China
172 H2 Shifnal Shropshire, England U.K.
127 G3 Shiga Nagano Japan
126 C5 Shiga Shiga Japan
126 C5 Shiga pref. Japan
138 E2 Shigar Pak.
126 D6 Shigaraki Japan
Shigatse Xizang China see Xigazê
136 D5 Shiggaon Karnataka India
132 L6 Shigong Gansu China
142 C1 Shigony Rus. Fed.
129 L6 Shiguai Nei Mongol China
Shiguaigou Nei Mongol China see Shiguai
147 K7 Shiḩan Yemen
147 K7 Shiḩan, Wādīal r. Oman
132 H4 Shihezi Xinjiang China
Shihkiachwang Hebei China see Shijiazhuang
232 E2 Shiikh Somalia
218 H9 Shijak Albania
Shijiao Guangdong China see Fogang
129 N7 Shijiazhuang Hebei China
131 L3 Shijiu Hu l. China
Shijiusuo Shandong China see Rizhao
126 E1 Shika Japan
124 R4 Shikabe Japan
248 B3 Shikag Lake Ont. Can.
130 G8 Shikang Guangxi China
145 J7 Shikar r. Pak.
136 D5 Shikarpur Karnataka India
145 M8 Shikarpur Pak.
131 I6 Shikengkong mt. Guangdong China
142 B1 Shikhany Rus. Fed.
127 K4 Shiki Japan
127 J7 Shikine-jima i. Japan
127 I4 Shikishima Japan
138 G6 Shikohabad Uttar Prad. India
125 K13 Shikoku i. Japan
125 J13 Shikoku-sanchi mts Japan
121 Q3 Shikotan, Ostrov i. Kuril'skiye O-va Rus. Fed.
Shikotan-tō i. Kuril'skiye O-va Rus. Fed. see Shikotan, Ostrov
124 S4 Shikotsu vol. Japan
124 R4 Shikotsu-Tōya Kokuritsu-kōen nat. park Japan
171 N3 Shilbottle Northumberland, England U.K.
142 H2 Shil'da Rus. Fed.
171 N4 Shildon Durham, England U.K.
156 I2 Shilega Rus. Fed.
129 P9 Shilianghe Shuiku resr China
139 L6 Shiliguri W. Bengal India
143 R6 Shilik r. Kazakh.
130 D6 Shilin Yunnan China
131 I3 Shilipu Hubei China
Shiliu Hainan China see Changjiang
138 G3 Shilla mt. Jammu and Kashmir India
168 B7 Shillay i. Scotland U.K.
169 I7 Shillelagh Ireland
251 N1 Shillington Ont. Can.
258 D4 Shillington PA U.S.A.
150 C6 Shillo r. Israel
139 M7 Shillong Meghalaya India
142 C2 Shil'naya Balka Kazakh.
258 E6 Shiloh NJ U.S.A.
256 C8 Shiloh OH U.S.A.
129 L8 Shilou Shanxi China
157 H5 Shilovo Ryazanskaya Oblast' Rus. Fed.
161 V8 Shilovo Tul'skaya Oblast' Rus. Fed.
128 E3 Shilüüstey Mongolia
126 E7 Shima Japan
127 I2 Shima spring Japan
125 H14 Shimabara Japan
125 H14 Shimabara-wan b. Japan
127 H6 Shimada Japan
126 D6 Shimagahara Japan
126 D7 Shima-hantō pen. Japan
124 R4 Shimamaki Japan
126 C6 Shimamoto Japan
125 J12 Shimane pref. Japan
125 J11 Shimane-hantō pen. Japan
122 E2 Shimanovsk Rus. Fed.
232 E2 Shimbiris mt. Somalia
232 D4 Shimbirre waterhole Kenya
131 H4 Shimen Hunan China
Shimen Yunnan China see Yunlong
130 D4 Shimian Sichuan China
126 D3 Shimizu Fukui Japan
124 T3 Shimizu Hokkaidō Japan
127 H5 Shimizu Shizuoka Japan
127 I5 Shimizu Shizuoka Japan
126 B7 Shimizu Wakayama Japan
138 F4 Shimla Hima. Prad. India
Shimminato Japan see Shinminato
126 F2 Shimo Japan
127 H5 Shimobe Japan
127 I6 Shimoda Japan
127 K3 Shimodate Japan
127 L4 Shimofusa Japan
136 D6 Shimoga Karnataka India
127 K1 Shimogō Japan
126 C7 Shimoichi Japan
127 G5 Shimojō Japan
124 T2 Shimokawa Japan
124 R5 Shimokita-hantō pen. Japan
126 C7 Shimokitayama Japan
125 G15 Shimo-Koshiki-jima i. Japan
233 C6 Shimoni Kenya
127 I3 Shimonita Japan
125 H13 Shimonoseki Japan
127 H3 Shimosuwa Japan
126 B7 Shimotsu Japan
127 K3 Shimotsuma Japan
126 F5 Shimoyama Japan
136 E6 Shimsha r. India
138 E1 Shimshal Pak.
161 N3 Shimsk Rus. Fed.
127 J3 Shin Japan
168 G6 Shin, Loch l. Scotland U.K.
Shināfīyah Iraq see Ash Shanāfīyah
Shinan Guangxi China see Xingye
127 H2 Shinano Japan
126 D5 Shin-asahi Japan
124 □H16 Shin-dake vol. Japan
145 J5 Shīndand Afgh.
128 F2 Shine-Ider Hövsgöl Mongolia
128 F4 Shinejinst Mongolia
173 K5 Shinfield Wokingham, England U.K.
231 F8 Shingana Dem. Rep. Congo
118 C1 Shingbwiyang Myanmar
118 C1 Shing-gai Myanmar
145 P3 Shinghshal Pass Pak.
256 G7 Shinglehouse PA U.S.A.
250 H3 Shingleton MI U.S.A.
Shing Mun Reservoir H.K. China see Ngan Hei Shui Tong
143 S4 Shingozha Kazakh.
125 N13 Shingū Japan
235 F4 Shingwedzi S. Africa
171 M7 Shining Tor hill England U.K.
251 M2 Shining Tree Ont. Can.
124 R8 Shinjō Japan
145 L6 Shīnkāy Afgh.
145 M5 Shīnkay Ghar mts Afgh.
126 F2 Shinminato Japan
125 I12 Shinnan-yō Japan
145 L6 Shin Narai Thana Afgh.
259 K3 Shinnecock Bay NY U.S.A.
168 H6 Shinness Lodge Highland, Scotland U.K.
256 E9 Shinnston WV U.S.A.
126 E6 Shino-jima i. Japan
127 H2 Shinonoi Japan
145 N4 Shinpokh Pak.
169 G7 Shinrone Ireland
126 E5 Shinsei Japan
150 E4 Shinshār Syria
126 F6 Shinshiro Japan
127 H2 Shinshūshin Japan
127 I3 Shintō Japan
124 T3 Shintoku Japan
127 L4 Shintone Japan
151 H6 Shinuhayr Armenia
233 B5 Shinyanga Tanz.
233 B5 Shinyanga admin. reg. Tanz.
126 E2 Shio Japan
127 K2 Shiobara Japan
124 S8 Shiogama Japan
127 G3 Shiojiri Japan
124 □B22 Shiokawa Nansei-shotō Japan
127 H4 Shiomi-dake mt. Japan
125 M13 Shiono-misaki c. Japan
127 K2 Shioya Japan
127 M1 Shioya-zaki pt Japan
127 I1 Shiozawa Japan
131 K3 Shipai Anhui China
257 K9 Ship Bottom NJ U.S.A.
270 E1 Ship Chan Cay i. Bahamas
219 N8 Shipchenski Prokhod pass Bulg.
161 V4 Shipilovo Rus. Fed.
130 D7 Shiping Yunnan China
133 D11 Shipki Pass China/India
173 K5 Shiplake Oxfordshire, England U.K.
171 N6 Shipley West Yorkshire, England U.K.
256 G11 Shipman VA U.S.A.
249 H4 Shippegan N.B. Can.
249 H4 Shippegan Island N.B. Can.
256 H8 Shippensburg PA U.S.A.
256 F7 Shippenville PA U.S.A.
126 E5 Shippō Japan
265 X5 Shiprock NM U.S.A.
265 X5 Shiprock Peak NM U.S.A.
173 I3 Shipston on Stour Warwickshire, England U.K.
171 O5 Shipton North Yorkshire, England U.K.
172 G2 Shipton Shropshire, England U.K.
173 I4 Shipton-under-Wychwood Oxfordshire, England U.K.
Shipu Shaanxi China see Huanglong
131 M4 Shipu Zhejiang China
153 R4 Shipunskiy, Mys hd Rus. Fed.
130 G5 Shiqian Guizhou China
Shiqiao Guangdong China see Panyu
Shiqizhen Guangdong China see Zhongshan
146 H7 Shiqqat al Kharītah des. Saudi Arabia
130 G2 Shiquan Shaanxi China
Shiquanhe Xizang China see Ali
138 G3 Shiquan He r. China conv. Indus
130 G2 Shiquan Shuiku resr China
146 F3 Shi'r, Jabal hill Saudi Arabia
168 F10 Shira r. Scotland U.K.
147 K3 Shirā'awh i. Qatar
144 C2 Shīrābād Iran
127 K6 Shirahama Chiba Japan
125 M13 Shirahama Wakayama Japan
126 D6 Shirai-san hill Japan
124 R5 Shirakami-misaki pt Japan
127 L1 Shirakawa Fukushima Japan
126 E3 Shirakawa Gifu Japan
126 F4 Shirakawa Gifu Japan
126 F3 Shirake-mine mt. Japan
127 L5 Shirako Japan
126 G5 Shirakura-yama mt. Japan
126 B7 Shirama-yama hill Japan
126 E3 Shiramine Japan
127 H4 Shirane Japan
127 H4 Shirane-san mt. Japan
127 I2 Shirane-san mt. Japan
127 J2 Shirane-san vol. Japan
124 V4 Shiranuka Japan
124 S4 Shiraoi Japan
127 J2 Shirasawa Japan
286 O1 Shirase Coast Antarctica
287 C2 Shirase Glacier Antarctica
124 U3 Shirataki Japan
233 B5 Shirati Tanz.
144 E7 Shīrāz Iran
148 E8 Shirbīn Egypt
233 B8 Shire r. Malawi
171 O7 Shirebrook Derbyshire, England U.K.
Shireet Mongolia see Bayandelger
144 B3 Shīreh Jīn Iran
172 G4 Shirenewton Monmouthshire, Wales U.K.
124 V3 Shiretoko-hantō pen. Japan
124 W2 Shiretoko Kokuritsu-kōen nat. park Japan
124 W2 Shiretoko-misaki c. Japan
145 K8 Shireza Pak.
143 M7 Shirin Uzbek.
145 L6 Shirinab r. Pak.
145 K3 Shirīn Tagāb Afgh.
124 R5 Shiriuchi Japan
124 S5 Shiriya-zaki c. Japan
142 G4 Shirkala reg. Kazakh.
171 O7 Shirland Derbyshire, England U.K.
259 J3 Shirley NY U.S.A.
207 □ Shirley Cove b. Gibraltar
127 L4 Shiroi Japan
124 R9 Shiroishi Japan
127 G5 Shirokura-yama mt. Japan
124 Q9 Shirone Japan
229 G4 Shiroro Reservoir Nigeria
126 E4 Shirotori Japan
126 G2 Shirouma-dake mt. Japan
127 J4 Shiroyama Japan
138 E9 Shirpur Mahar. India
128 E5 Shirten Holoy Gobi des. China
144 G3 Shīrvān Iran
128 B5 Shisanjianfang Xinjiang China
122 D3 Shisanzhan Heilong. China
237 P3 Shiselweni admin. dist. Swaziland
244 G5 Shishaldin Volcano AK U.S.A.
Shisha Pangma mt. Xizang China see Xixabangma Feng
125 L13 Shishikui Japan
Shishkaya Armenia see Geghamasar
244 F2 Shishmaref AK U.S.A.
244 F2 Shishmaref Inlet AK U.S.A.
131 I4 Shishou Hubei China
127 L4 Shisui Japan
131 K3 Shitai Anhui China
131 I6 Shitan Guangdong China

131 M4 **Shitang** *Zhejiang* China
128 J7 **Shitanjing** *Ningxia* China
126 G5 **Shitara** Japan
225 I1 **Shithāthah** Iraq
122 D7 **Shitoukoumen Shuiku** *resr Jilin* China
138 C6 **Shiv** *Rajasthan* India
153 R4 **Shiveluch, Sopka** *vol.* Rus. Fed.
138 F7 **Shivpuri** *Madh. Prad.* India
150 C8 **Shivta** *tourist site* Israel
265 S4 **Shivwits** *UT* U.S.A.
265 S5 **Shivwits Plateau** *AZ* U.S.A.
145 N3 **Shiwal** *l.* Afgh.
129 K8 **Shiwan** *Shaanxi* China
130 F8 **Shiwan Dashan** *mts* China
118 H3 **Shiwan Dashan** *mts* China
233 A7 **Shiwa Ngandu** Zambia
131 J6 **Shixing** *Guangdong* China
130 H2 **Shiyan** *Hubei* China
130 G4 **Shizhu** *Chongqing* China
131 L3 **Shizi** *Anhui* China
129 J9 **Shizi** *Gansu* China
Shizilu *Shandong* China *see* **Junan**
130 D6 **Shizong** *Yunnan* China
124 S8 **Shizugawa** Japan
128 J7 **Shizuishan** *Ningxia* China
128 J7 **Shizuishanzhan** *Ningxia* China
124 R7 **Shizukuishi** Japan
124 T4 **Shizunai** Japan
127 H6 **Shizuoka** Japan
127 H6 **Shizuoka** *pref.* Japan
218 I8 **Shkëlzenit, Maja e** *mt.* Albania
151 E3 **Shkhara** *mt.* Georgia/Rus. Fed.
158 C4 **Shklo** Ukr.
Shklov Belarus *see* **Shklow**
161 N7 **Shklow** Belarus
158 E3 **Shklyn'** Ukr.
151 E3 **Shk'meri** Georgia
218 H8 **Shkodër** Albania
Shkodrës, Liqeni i *l.* Albania/Montenegro *see* **Scutari, Lake**
218 H9 **Shkumbin** *r.* Albania
159 S7 **Shkurinskaya** Rus. Fed.
158 E2 **Shlapan'** Ukr.
161 R4 **Shlina** *r.* Rus. Fed.
161 Q4 **Shlino, Ozero** *l.* Rus. Fed.
161 O2 **Shlissel'burg** Rus. Fed.
153 K1 **Shmidta, Ostrov** *i.* Rus. Fed.
122 M1 **Shmidta, Poluostrov** *pen. Sakhalin* Rus. Fed.
160 L4 **Shmoylovo** Rus. Fed.
160 L6 **Sho, Vozyera** *l.* Belarus
105 L6 **Shoalhaven** *r. N.S.W.* Austr.
247 K5 **Shoal Lake** *Man.* Can.
247 K4 **Shoal Lake** *Sask.* Can.
254 D6 **Shoals** *IN* U.S.A.
107 M7 **Shoalwater Bay** *Qld* Austr.
125 K12 **Shōbara** Japan
125 L12 **Shōdo-shima** *i.* Japan
173 N4 **Shoeburyness** *Southend, England* U.K.
258 D3 **Shoemakersville** *PA* U.S.A.
142 K7 **Shofirkon** Uzbek.
126 F2 **Shōgawa** Japan
126 F2 **Shō-gawa** *r.* Japan
144 H3 **Shoghlābād** Iran
145 M3 **Shoh** *Khatlon* Tajik.
Shohi Pass Pak. *see* **Tal Pass**
258 F2 **Shohola** *PA* U.S.A.
124 S3 **Shokanbetsu-dake** *mt.* Japan
126 E3 **Shōkawa** Japan
124 U2 **Shokotsu-gawa** *r.* Japan
Shokpar Kazakh. *see* **Chokpar**
161 U1 **Shola** *r.* Rus. Fed.
143 M6 **Sholakkorgan** Kazakh.
142 K2 **Sholaksay** Kazakh.
Sholapur *Mahar.* India *see* **Solapur**
Sholaqorghan Kazakh. *see* **Sholakkorgan**
Sholaqsay Kazakh. *see* **Sholaksay**
108 C6 **Sholl Island** *W.A.* Austr.
156 F2 **Shomba** *r.* Rus. Fed.
142 H4 **Shomishkol'** Kazakh.
156 J3 **Shomvukva** Rus. Fed.
126 F2 **Shōmyō-gawa** *r.* Japan
168 E9 **Shona, Eilean** *i. Scotland* U.K.
288 J9 **Shona Ridge** *sea feature* S. Atlantic Ocean
139 M6 **Shongar** Bhutan
Shonzha Kazakh. *see* **Chundzha**
161 W4 **Shopsha** Rus. Fed.
170 E4 **Shoptown** *Northern Ireland* U.K.
142 G4 **Shoptykol'** *Aktyubinskaya Oblast'* Kazakh.
143 P2 **Shoptykol'** *Pavlodarskaya Oblast'* Kazakh.
Shoqpar Kazakh. *see* **Chokpar**
138 F3 **Shor** *Hima. Prad.* India
145 L7 **Shoran** Pak.
136 E7 **Shoranur** *Kerala* India
145 K9 **Shorap** Pak.
136 E4 **Shorapur** *Karnataka* India
145 K6 **Shorawak** *reg.* Afgh.
143 L9 **Sho'rchi** Uzbek.
259 G4 **Shore Acres** *NJ* U.S.A.
173 M5 **Shoreham** *Kent, England* U.K.
173 L6 **Shoreham-by-Sea** *West Sussex, England* U.K.
Shorghun Uzbek. *see* **Sharg'un**
145 O6 **Shorkot** Pak.
144 G1 **Shorkozakhly, Solonchak** *salt flat* Turkm.
145 P2 **Shorkŭl** *l.* Tajik.
Shornaq Kazakh. *see* **Chernak**
234 D3 **Shorobe** Botswana
143 N2 **Shortandy** Kazakh.
145 L3 **Shōr Tēpah** Afgh.
100 □6 **Shortland Island** Solomon Is
100 □6 **Shortland Islands** Solomon Is
256 H6 **Shortsville** *NY* U.S.A.
Shosambetsu Japan *see* **Shosanbetsu**
124 S2 **Shosanbetsu** Japan
161 T5 **Shosha** *r.* Rus. Fed.
265 P6 **Shoshone** *CA* U.S.A.
262 G5 **Shoshone** *ID* U.S.A.
262 J4 **Shoshone** *r. WY* U.S.A.
262 I4 **Shoshone Lake** *WY* U.S.A.
264 O2 **Shoshone Mountains** *NV* U.S.A.
265 P5 **Shoshone Peak** *NV* U.S.A.
234 E4 **Shoshong** Botswana
262 J5 **Shoshoni** *WY* U.S.A.
159 M2 **Shostka** Ukr.
159 M2 **Shostka** *r.* Ukr.
173 O4 **Shotley Gate** *Suffolk, England* U.K.
144 F5 **Shotoran, Chashmeh-ye** *well* Iran
145 K4 **Shotor Khūn** *pass* Afgh.
172 F1 **Shotton** *Flintshire, Wales* U.K.
168 I11 **Shotts** *North Lanarkshire, Scotland* U.K.
Shouchun *Anhui* China *see* **Shouxian**
129 P8 **Shouguang** *Shandong* China
131 K2 **Shouxian** *Anhui* China
129 M8 **Shouyang** *Shanxi* China
130 G2 **Shouyang Shan** *mt. Shaanxi* China
127 J2 **Shōwa** Japan
225 G6 **Showak** Sudan
265 V7 **Show Low** *AZ* U.S.A.
151 F6 **Showt** Iran
156 I2 **Shoyna** Rus. Fed.
157 H7 **Shpakovskoye** Rus. Fed.
159 K4 **Shpola** Ukr.
158 H5 **Shpykiv** Ukr.
158 I3 **Shpyli** Ukr.
Shqipërisë, Republika e *country* Europe *see* **Albania**
159 L3 **Shramkivka** Ukr.
256 C8 **Shreve** *OH* U.S.A.
261 I9 **Shreveport** *LA* U.S.A.
172 G2 **Shrewsbury** *Shropshire, England* U.K.
259 G4 **Shrewsbury** *NJ* U.S.A.
258 B5 **Shrewsbury** *PA* U.S.A.
173 I5 **Shrewton** *Wiltshire, England* U.K.
170 F5 **Shrigley** *Northern Ireland* U.K.
136 D3 **Shrigonda** *Mahar.* India
Shri Lanka *country* Asia *see* **Sri Lanka**
138 C6 **Shri Mohangarh** *Rajasthan* India
139 L8 **Shrirampur** *W. Bengal* India
173 I4 **Shrivenham** *Oxfordshire, England* U.K.
172 G2 **Shropshire** *admin. div. England* U.K.
259 H2 **Shrub Oak** *NY* U.S.A.
Shtefan-Vode Moldova *see* **Ştefan Vodă**
218 I10 **Shtërmen** Albania
218 J8 **Shtime** *Shtime* Kosovo
218 I8 **Shtiqën** Albania
159 M8 **Shtormove** Ukr.
143 O6 **Shu** Kazakh.
143 L5 **Shu** *r.* Kazakh.
147 K9 **Shu'ab, Ghubbat** *b. Suquṭrā* Yemen
147 K9 **Shu'ab, Ra's** *pt Suquṭrā* Yemen
149 M8 **Shu'aiba** Iraq
130 D2 **Shuajingsi** *Sichuan* China
151 D4 **Shuakhevi** Georgia
130 C6 **Shuangbai** *Yunnan* China
Shuangcheng *Fujian* China *see* **Zherong**
122 E6 **Shuangcheng** *Heilong.* China
131 I3 **Shuanghe** *Hubei* China
130 F3 **Shuanghechang** *Sichuan* China
122 G4 **Shuanghedagang** *Heilong.* China
133 H10 **Shuanghu** *Xizang* China
Shuanghuyu *Shaanxi* China *see* **Zizhou**
Shuangjiang *Guizhou* China *see* **Jiangkou**
Shuangjiang *Hunan* China *see* **Tongdao**
130 B7 **Shuangjiang** *Yunnan* China
Shuangjiang *Yunnan* China *see* **Eshan**
129 R5 **Shuangliao** *Jilin* China
131 H6 **Shuangpai** *Hunan* China
129 P6 **Shuangshanzi** *Hebei* China
Shuangshipu *Shaanxi* China *see* **Fengxian**
122 D7 **Shuangyang** *Jilin* China
122 G5 **Shuangyashan** *Heilong.* China
Shuangzhong *Jiangxi* China *see* **Hukou**
147 J7 **Shu'ayt, Wādī** *r.* Yemen
142 G3 **Shubarkudyk** Kazakh.
142 G3 **Shubarshi** Kazakh.
150 G8 **Shubayḩ** *well* Saudi Arabia
146 F3 **Shubayrimah** Saudi Arabia
245 K1 **Shublik Mountains** *AK* U.S.A.
140 C3 **Shubrā al Khaymah** Egypt
146 G3 **Shubrāmīyāh** Saudi Arabia
146 F4 **Shubrāmīyāh** *well* Saudi Arabia
131 K3 **Shucheng** *Anhui* China
274 C6 **Shucushuyacu** Peru
132 B7 **Shufu** *Xinjiang* China
118 A2 **Shuganu** *Manipur* India
145 N3 **Shughnon, Qatorkŭhi** *mts* Tajik.
Shugnanskiy Khrebet *mts* Tajik. *see* **Shughnon, Qatorkŭhi**
161 R2 **Shugozero** Rus. Fed.
152 H3 **Shugur** Rus. Fed.
129 P9 **Shu He** *r.* China
Shuicheng *Guizhou* China *see* **Lupanshui**
Shuiding *Xinjiang* China *see* **Huocheng**
Shuidong *Guangdong* China *see* **Dianbai**
Shuihu *Anhui* China *see* **Changfeng**
131 L5 **Shuiji** *Fujian* China
Shuiji *Shandong* China *see* **Laixi**
130 E2 **Shuijing** *Sichuan* China
133 J10 **Shuijingkuang** *Qinghai* China
131 J7 **Shuikou** *Guangdong* China
130 F7 **Shuikou** *Guangxi* China
131 H6 **Shuikou** *Hunan* China
131 I5 **Shuikoushan** *Hunan* China
Shuiluocheng *Gansu* China *see* **Zhuanglang**
128 I8 **Shuiquan** *Gansu* China
128 G7 **Shuiquanzi** *Gansu* China
130 C5 **Shuituo He** *r. Sichuan* China
Shuizhai *Guangdong* China *see* **Wuhua**
133 J8 **Shuizhan** *Qinghai* China
145 N7 **Shujaabad** Pak.
244 I2 **Shulakpachak Peak** *AK* U.S.A.
122 E6 **Shulan** *Jilin* China
132 C7 **Shule** *Xinjiang* China
132 M6 **Shulehe** *Gansu* China
128 C6 **Shule He** *r.* China
128 E7 **Shule Nanshan** *mts* China
159 T1 **Shul'gino** Rus. Fed.
159 R4 **Shul'hynka** Ukr.
129 L6 **Shulinzhao** *Nei Mongol* China
Shul'mak Tajik. *see* **Novobod**
Shulu *Hebei* China *see* **Xinji**
161 O2 **Shum** Rus. Fed.
244 G5 **Shumagin Islands** *AK* U.S.A.
159 P2 **Shumakovo** Rus. Fed.
142 H6 **Shumanay** Uzbek.
124 T2 **Shumarinai-ko** *l.* Japan
234 E3 **Shumba** Zimbabwe
219 O7 **Shumen** Bulg.
219 O7 **Shumensko Plato** *nat. park* Bulg.
156 I5 **Shumerlya** Rus. Fed.
152 H4 **Shumikha** Rus. Fed.
160 M6 **Shumilina** Belarus
153 Q4 **Shumshu, Ostrov** *i. Kuril'skiye O-va* Rus. Fed.
158 F3 **Shums'k** Ukr.
161 P8 **Shumyachi** Rus. Fed.
143 O4 **Shunak, Gora** *mt.* Kazakh.
150 D7 **Shūnat Nimrīn** Jordan
131 I7 **Shunde** *Guangdong* China
161 X4 **Shunga** Rus. Fed.
244 H2 **Shungnak** *AK* U.S.A.
258 B1 **Shunk** *PA* U.S.A.
Shunling *Hunan* China *see* **Ningyuan**
151 I3 **Shunudag, Gora** *mt.* Rus. Fed.
129 O6 **Shunyi** *Beijing* China
130 F7 **Shuolong** *Guangxi* China
Shuoxian *Shanxi* China *see* **Shuozhou**
129 M7 **Shuozhou** *Shanxi* China
146 G7 **Shuqqat Najrān** *depr.* Saudi Arabia
146 G9 **Shuqrah** Yemen
144 E7 **Shūr** *r.* Iran
144 F7 **Shūr** *r.* Iran
144 I4 **Shūr** *r.* Iran
144 I6 **Shūr** *r.* Iran
144 E7 **Shūr** *watercourse* Iran
144 F6 **Shūr** *watercourse* Iran
144 F8 **Shūr** *watercourse* Iran
144 H5 **Shur** *watercourse* Iran
144 E4 **Shūr, Chāh-e** *well* Iran
144 G6 **Shūr, Rūd-e** *watercourse* Iran
144 D5 **Shūrāb** *Chahār Maḩāll va Bakhtīārī* Iran
144 D4 **Shūr Āb** Iran
144 G5 **Shūrāb** *Khorāsān* Iran
144 F5 **Shūrāb** *Yazd* Iran
144 F6 **Shūr Āb** *watercourse* Iran
Shurab Tajik. *see* **Shŭrob**
144 E5 **Shureghestan** Iran
151 I6 **Shurestān** Iran
144 H7 **Shūr Gaz** Iran
151 I6 **Shūr Gol** Iran
124 □1 **Shuri** *Okinawa* Japan
144 E6 **Shūrjestān** Iran
156 J4 **Shurma** Rus. Fed.
145 N1 **Shŭrob** Tajik.
144 I7 **Shūrū** Iran
235 F3 **Shurugwi** Zimbabwe
149 L8 **Shuruppak** *tourist site* Iraq
144 I6 **Shūsf** Iran
144 C5 **Shūsh** Iran
Shusha Azer. *see* **Şuşa**
220 A2 **Shushicë** *r.* Albania
144 C5 **Shushtar** Iran
161 S6 **Shustikovo** Rus. Fed.
159 O2 **Shustovo** Rus. Fed.
246 G5 **Shuswap Lake** *B.C.* Can.
147 K4 **Shutfah, Qalamat** *well* Saudi Arabia
150 F7 **Shuwaysh, Tall ash** *hill* Jordan
161 Y5 **Shuya** *Ivanovskaya Oblast'* Rus. Fed.
156 F3 **Shuya** *Respublika Kareliya* Rus. Fed.
244 I4 **Shuyak Island** *AK* U.S.A.
129 P9 **Shuyang** *Jiangsu* China
156 H4 **Shuyskoye** Rus. Fed.
127 I6 **Shuzenji** Japan
161 U7 **Shvartsevskiy** Rus. Fed.
118 B5 **Shwebandaw** Myanmar
118 B3 **Shwebo** Myanmar
118 B5 **Shwedaung** Myanmar
118 B2 **Shwedwin** Myanmar
118 C6 **Shwegun** Myanmar
118 C6 **Shwegyin** Myanmar
118 B6 **Shwelaung** *r.* Myanmar
118 C3 **Shweli** *r.* Myanmar
118 C4 **Shwenyaung** Myanmar
118 C3 **Shweudaung** *mt.* Myanmar
158 F4 **Shybena** Ukr.
143 N5 **Shyganak** Kazakh.
Shyghanaq Kazakh. *see* **Chiganak**
Shyghys Qazaqstan Oblysy *admin. div.* Kazakh. *see* **Vostochnyy Kazakhstan**
Shyghys-Qongyrat Kazakh. *see* **Shygys Konyrat**
143 P4 **Shygys Konyrat** Kazakh.
143 M6 **Shymkent** Kazakh.
Shynggyrlaū Kazakh. *see* **Chingirlau**
Shyngqozha Kazakh. *see* **Shingozha**
142 E2 **Shyngyrlau** *r.* Kazakh.
143 R3 **Shyngystau, Khrebet** *mts* Kazakh.
138 E2 **Shyok** *r.* India
138 G2 **Shyok** *Jammu and Kashmir* India
159 Q4 **Shypuvate** Ukr.
159 M6 **Shyroke** *Dnipropetrovs'ka Oblast'* Ukr.
159 N8 **Shyroke** *Respublika Krym* Ukr.
159 N5 **Shyroke** *Zaporiz'ka Oblast'* Ukr.
159 K6 **Shyrokolanivka** Ukr.
159 Q6 **Shyrokyne** Ukr.
159 O6 **Shyrokyy Var** Ukr.
158 J6 **Shyryayeve** Ukr.
159 N4 **Shyshaky** Ukr.
160 K8 **Shyshchytsy** Belarus
113 H8 **Sia** *Maluku* Indon.
Siabost *Scotland* U.K. *see* **Shawbost**
116 C4 **Siabu** *Sumatera* Indon.
138 F2 **Siachen Glacier** India/Pak.
183 J9 **Siagne** *r.* France
145 J8 **Siahan Range** *mts* Pak.
144 A2 **Sīah Chashmeh** Iran
145 L3 **Siahgird** Afgh.
145 K5 **Siah Koh** *mts* Afgh.
145 I8 **Sīāh Kowr, Rūdkhāneh-ye** *watercourse* Iran
144 I6 **Sīāh Kūh** *l.* Iran
116 E4 **Siak** *r.* Indon.
116 E4 **Siak Sri Inderapura** *Sumatera* Indon.
145 P5 **Sialkot** Pak.
Siam *country* Asia *see* **Thailand**
214 B8 **Siamanna** *Sardegna* Italy
Sian *Shaanxi* China *see* **Xi'an**
Sianhala Côte d'Ivoire *see* **Sanhala**
165 M7 **Sianów** Pol.
116 G3 **Siantan** *i.* Indon.
275 E4 **Siapa** *r.* Venez.
144 I7 **Sīāreh** Iran
114 F7 **Siargao** *i.* Phil.
257 P7 **Siasconset** *MA* U.S.A.
114 C9 **Siasi** Phil.
114 C9 **Siasi** *i.* Phil.
220 C2 **Siatista** Greece
114 D7 **Siaton** *Negros* Phil.
115 D2 **Siau** *i.* Indon.
160 G6 **Šiauliai** Lith.
231 F9 **Siavonga** Zambia
114 C1 **Siayan** *i.* Phil.
Siazan' Azer. *see* **Siyäzän**
145 J8 **Sīb** Iran
147 N4 **Sīb** Oman
118 G7 **Si Bai, Lam** *r.* Thai.
144 C5 **Sībak** Iran
270 E3 **Sibanicú** Cuba
217 K4 **Sibari** Italy
Sibati *Xinjiang* China *see* **Xibet**
114 C6 **Sibay** *i.* Phil.
142 H1 **Sibay** Rus. Fed.
237 Q3 **Sibayi, Lake** S. Africa
287 L2 **Sibbald, Cape** Antarctica
191 I6 **Sibbesse** Ger.
163 R6 **Sibbo** Fin.
163 R6 **Sibbofjärden** *b.* Fin.
144 H5 **Sīb Chāh** Iran
210 E4 **Šibenik** Croatia
Siberia *reg.* Rus. Fed. *see* **Sibir'**
116 C5 **Siberut** *i.* Indon.
116 C5 **Siberut, Selat** *sea chan.* Indon.
116 C5 **Siberut, Taman Nasional** *nat. park* Indon.
145 L7 **Sibi** Pak.
113 J8 **Sibidiri** P.N.G.
116 A3 **Sibigo** Indon.
232 C4 **Sibiloi National Park** Kenya
93 G2 **Sibir'** *reg.* Rus. Fed.
122 H6 **Sibirtsevo** Rus. Fed.
152 I2 **Sibiryakova, Ostrov** *i.* Rus. Fed.
231 B5 **Sibiti** Congo
219 M5 **Sibiu** Romania
173 N4 **Sible Hedingham** *Essex, England* U.K.
260 H4 **Sibley** *IA* U.S.A.
115 B3 **Siboa** *Sulawesi* Indon.
116 C4 **Sibolga** *Sumatera* Indon.
116 C3 **Siborongborong** *Sumatera* Indon.
237 P2 **Sibowe** *r.* Swaziland
139 O6 **Sibsagar** *Assam* India
171 R7 **Sibsey** *Lincolnshire, England* U.K.
117 I3 **Sibu** *Sarawak* Malaysia
114 D8 **Sibuco** *Mindanao* Phil.
114 D8 **Sibuco Bay** *Mindanao* Phil.
114 D8 **Sibuguey** *r. Mindanao* Phil.
114 D8 **Sibuguey Bay** *Mindanao* Phil.
230 C3 **Sibut** C.A.R.
117 J2 **Sibuti** *Sarawak* Malaysia
114 B9 **Sibutu** *i.* Phil.
114 B9 **Sibutu Passage** Phil.
114 D5 **Sibuyan** *i.* Phil.
114 D5 **Sibuyan Sea** Phil.
219 L4 **Sic** Romania
246 G5 **Sicamous** *B.C.* Can.
114 C2 **Sicapoo** *mt. Luzon* Phil.
276 D4 **Sicasica** Bol.
114 D7 **Sicayac** *Mindanao* Phil.
Sicca Veneria Tunisia *see* **Le Kef**
104 G4 **Siccus** *watercourse S.A.* Austr.
144 E5 **Si Chah** Iran
Sicheng *Anhui* China *see* **Sixian**
Sicheng *Guangxi* China *see* **Lingyun**
119 D10 **Sichon** Thai.
130 D3 **Sichuan** *prov.* China
130 E4 **Sichuan Pendi** *basin Sichuan* China
183 H10 **Sicié, Cap** *c.* France
216 G8 **Sicilia** *admin. reg.* Italy
216 G7 **Sicilia** *i.* Italy
216 C9 **Sicilian Channel** Italy/Tunisia
Sicily *i.* Italy *see* **Sicilia**
196 E4 **Siciny** Pol.
258 F5 **Sicklerville** *NJ* U.S.A.
191 K6 **Sickte** Ger.
276 C3 **Sicuani** Peru
199 K5 **Şicula** Romania
216 E9 **Siculiana** *Sicilia* Italy
218 H5 **Šid** *Vojvodina* Serbia
199 I3 **Šíd** Slovakia
115 E3 **Sidangoli** *Halmahera* Indon.
172 F6 **Sidbury** *Devon, England* U.K.
186 K2 **Siddeburen** Neth.
138 D8 **Siddhapur** *Gujarat* India
Siddharthanagar Nepal *see* **Bhairawa**
136 F3 **Siddipet** *Andhra Prad.* India
163 P5 **Sideby** Fin.
115 A5 **Sidenreng, Danau** *l.* Indon.
162 O5 **Sidensjö** Sweden
228 D4 **Sidéradougou** Burkina
220 G2 **Sideritis** *i. Limnos* Greece
217 K7 **Siderno** Italy
221 H7 **Sideros, Akrotirio** *pt Kriti* Greece
236 G8 **Sidesaviwa** S. Africa
172 F6 **Sidford** *Devon, England* U.K.
145 O6 **Sidhai** Pak.
138 H6 **Sidhauli** *Uttar Prad.* India
138 H7 **Sidhi** *Madh. Prad.* India
Sidhirókastron Greece *see* **Sidirokastro**
Sidhpur *Gujarat* India *see* **Siddhapur**
227 F2 **Sidi Aïssa** Alg.
224 E2 **Sīdī Barrānī** Egypt
227 E2 **Sidi Bel Abbès** Alg.
226 C2 **Sidi Bennour** Morocco
Sidi Bou Sa'id Tunisia *see* **Sidi Bouzid**
227 H2 **Sidi Bouzid** Tunisia
227 H2 **Sidi El Hani, Sebkhet de** *salt pan* Tunisia
228 E2 **Sidi el Mokhtâr** *well* Mali
226 C3 **Sidi Ifni** Morocco
226 D2 **Sidi Kacem** Morocco
116 C3 **Sidikalang** *Sumatera* Indon.
227 G2 **Sidi Khaled** Alg.
227 E3 **Sidi Mannsour** *well* Alg.
226 B5 **Sidi Mhamed** *well* Western Sahara
227 G2 **Sidi Okba** Alg.
220 E1 **Sidirokastro** Greece
226 C2 **Sidi-Smaïl** Morocco
247 J2 **Sid Lake** *N.W.T.* Can.
168 J10 **Sidlaw Hills** *Scotland* U.K.
173 M6 **Sidley** *East Sussex, England* U.K.
286 P1 **Sidley, Mount** Antarctica
172 F6 **Sidmouth** *Devon, England* U.K.
107 I2 **Sidmouth, Cape** *Qld* Austr.
250 F3 **Sidnaw** *MI* U.S.A.
246 F5 **Sidney** *B.C.* Can.
260 H5 **Sidney** *IA* U.S.A.
262 L3 **Sidney** *MT* U.S.A.
260 D5 **Sidney** *NE* U.S.A.
257 J6 **Sidney** *NY* U.S.A.
256 A8 **Sidney** *OH* U.S.A.
255 F8 **Sidney Lanier, Lake** *GA* U.S.A.
236 I4 **Sidney-on-Vaal** S. Africa
228 D4 **Sido** Mali
115 B3 **Sidoan** *Sulawesi* Indon.
115 B3 **Sidoan** *Sulawesi* Indon.
117 J8 **Sidoarjo** *Jawa* Indon.
185 I8 **Sidobre** *reg.* France
118 B4 **Sidoktaya** Myanmar
Sidon Lebanon *see* **Saïda**
156 H4 **Sidorovo** Rus. Fed.
150 A9 **Sidr, Ra's as** *pt* Egypt
197 L2 **Sidra** *r.* Pol.
150 B10 **Sidrī, Wādī** *watercourse* Egypt
279 B7 **Sidrolândia** Brazil
237 P2 **Sidvokodvo** Swaziland
237 M7 **Sidwadweni** S. Africa
196 F5 **Sidzina** Pol.
162 Q2 **Siebe** Norway
162 Q2 **Siebejokka** *r.* Norway
186 J5 **Siebengewald** Neth.
193 H8 **Siebenlehn** Ger.
196 D4 **Siecieborzyce** Pol.
197 J4 **Sieciechów** Pol.
196 E2 **Siecino, Jezioro** *l.* Pol.
190 G5 **Siedenburg** Ger.
197 J5 **Siedlanka** Pol.
197 K3 **Siedlce** Pol.
196 E3 **Siedlec** Pol.
196 D2 **Siedlice** Pol.
196 D4 **Siedlisko** *Lubuskie* Pol.
196 E3 **Siedlisko** *Wielkopolskie* Pol.
197 L4 **Siedliszcze** *Lubelskie* Pol.
197 L4 **Siedliszcze** *Lubelskie* Pol.
191 D9 **Sieg** *r.* Ger.
191 D9 **Siegburg** Ger.
191 F9 **Siegen** Ger.
195 L4 **Siegenburg** Ger.
201 O4 **Siegendorf im Burgenland** Austria
201 N4 **Sieggraben** Austria
201 N3 **Sieghartskirchen** Austria
195 N6 **Siegsdorf** Ger.
190 J3 **Siek** Ger.
193 L8 **Siekierczyn** Pol.
197 L4 **Sielec** Pol.
199 I3 **Sielnica** Slovakia
193 J7 **Sielow** Ger.
197 L3 **Siemianówka** Pol.
197 L3 **Siemianówka, Jezioro** *l.* Pol.
197 K3 **Siemiatycze** Pol.
197 K4 **Siemień** Pol.
196 G4 **Siemkowice** Pol.
119 H7 **Siěmpang** Cambodia
119 F8 **Siěmréab** Cambodia
Siem Reap Cambodia *see* **Siěmréab**
196 D1 **Siemyśl** Pol.
Si'en *Guangxi* China *see* **Huanjiang**
213 K9 **Siena** Italy
213 K9 **Siena** *prov.* Italy
197 K5 **Sieniawa** Pol.
180 I3 **Sienne** *r.* France
197 J3 **Siennica** Pol.
197 J4 **Sienno** Pol.
162 Q3 **Sieppijärvi** Fin.
197 H6 **Siepraw** Pol.
189 J3 **Sieradowicki Park Krajobrazowy** Pol.
196 G4 **Sieradz** Pol.
196 G5 **Sieraków** *Śląskie* Pol.
196 E3 **Sieraków** *Wielkopolskie* Pol.
197 H3 **Sierakówek** Pol.
196 F1 **Sierakowice** Pol.
189 H2 **Sierakowski Park Krajobrazowy** Pol.
179 L5 **Sierck-les-Bains** France
133 K11 **Si'erdingka** *Xizang* China
179 N8 **Sierentz** France
190 K2 **Sierksdorf** Ger.
196 E2 **Sierczyno** Pol.
201 N3 **Sierndorf** Austria
201 J3 **Sierning** Austria
201 M4 **Sierningtal** *nature res.* Austria
196 F4 **Sieroszewice** Pol.
197 H3 **Sierpc** Pol.
197 H3 **Sierpienica** *r.* Pol.
283 D6 **Sierra, Punta** *pt* Arg.
205 J2 **Sierra, Punta de la** *pt* Spain
270 H4 **Sierra Bahoruco** *nat. park* Dom. Rep.
263 L11 **Sierra Blanca** *TX* U.S.A.
207 I4 **Sierra Boyer, Embalse de** *resr* Spain
285 G5 **Sierra Chica** Arg.
283 D6 **Sierra Colorada** Arg.
206 F5 **Sierra de Aracena y Picos de Aroche, Parque Natural de la** *nature res. Andalucía* Spain
207 N6 **Sierra de Baza, Parque Natural de la** *nature res. Andalucía* Spain
274 C4 **Sierra de Chiribiquette, Parque Nacional** *nature res.* Columbia
206 G2 **Sierra de Fuentes** Spain
207 I7 **Sierra de Grazalema, Parque Natural de la** *nature res. Andalucía* Spain
207 I5 **Sierra de Hornachuelos, Parque Natural de la** *nature res. Andalucía* Spain
274 D2 **Sierra de la Culata** *nat. park* Venez.
282 D4 **Sierra de las Quijadas, Parque Nacional** *nat. park* Arg.
Sierra del Gistral *mts* Spain *see* **Xistral, Serra do**
208 D3 **Sierra de Luna** Spain
207 J6 **Sierra de Yeguas** Spain
209 F7 **Sierra Engarcerán** Spain
283 D6 **Sierra Grande** Arg.
228 C4 **Sierra Leone** *country* Africa
288 H5 **Sierra Leone Basin** *sea feature* N. Atlantic Ocean
288 H5 **Sierra Leone Rise** *sea feature* N. Atlantic Ocean
264 L6 **Sierra Madre Mountains** *CA* U.S.A.
266 H4 **Sierra Mojada** Mex.
269 N9 **Sierra Morena** Mex.
274 D2 **Sierra Nevada, Parque Nacional** *nat. park* Venez.
207 M6 **Sierra Nevada, Parque Nacional de** *nat. park* Spain
207 L6 **Sierra Nevada, Parque Natural de** *nature res. Andalucía* Spain
274 C2 **Sierra Nevada de Santa Marta, Parque Nacional** *nat. park* Col.
285 G5 **Sierras Bayas** Arg.
207 N4 **Sierras de Cazorla, Segurla y Las Villas, Parque Natural de las** *park* Spain
264 L2 **Sierraville** *CA* U.S.A.
265 V10 **Sierra Vista** *AZ* U.S.A.
212 D3 **Sierre** Switz.
207 O6 **Sierro** Spain
207 O6 **Sierro** *r.* Spain
193 E7 **Siersleben** Ger.
160 F7 **Siesartis** *r.* Lith.
160 H6 **Siesartis** *r.* Lith.
209 D9 **Siete Aguas** Spain
205 J6 **Siete Iglesias de Trabancos** Spain
192 G4 **Sietow** Ger.
219 M3 **Şieu** Romania
219 M3 **Şieu** *r.* Romania
213 K8 **Sieve** *r.* Italy
192 F5 **Sieversdorf** Ger.
190 H1 **Sieverstedt** Ger.
162 R5 **Sievi** Fin.
197 H5 **Siewierz** Pol.
130 F7 **Sifang Ling** *mts* China
232 D1 **Sīfenī** Eth.
228 D5 **Sifié** Côte d'Ivoire
220 F5 **Sifnos** *i.* Greece
220 F5 **Sifnou, Steno** *sea chan.* Greece
227 E2 **Sig** Alg.
161 Q4 **Sig, Ozero** *l.* Rus. Fed.
147 K6 **Sigani** *well* Saudi Arabia
101 □7a **Sigatoka** *Viti Levu* Fiji
99 I3 **Sigave** Wallis and Futuna Is
183 B10 **Sigean** France
116 C5 **Sigep, Tanjung** *pt* Indon.
192 E4 **Siggelkow** Ger.
217 □ **Siġġiewi** Malta
171 Q6 **Sigglesthorne** *East Riding of Yorkshire, England* U.K.
243 M2 **Sigguup Nunaa** *pen.* Greenland
219 L3 **Sighetu Marmaţiei** Romania
219 M4 **Sighişoara** Romania
213 N9 **Sigillo** Italy
136 G9 **Sigiriya** Sri Lanka
151 J5 **Sığırlı** Azer.
116 □ **Siglap** Sing.
116 A2 **Sigli** *Sumatera* Indon.
162 □D1 **Siglufjörður** Iceland
114 D6 **Sigma** *Panay* Phil.
194 G5 **Sigmaringen** Ger.
194 G5 **Sigmaringendorf** Ger.
201 M2 **Sigmundsherberg** Austria
213 K8 **Signa** Italy
195 N3 **Signalberg** *hill* Ger.
187 J8 **Signal de Botrange** *hill* Belgium
183 H10 **Signal de la Ste-Baume** *mt.* France
183 C7 **Signal de Mailhebiau** *mt.* France
183 D7 **Signal de Randon** *mt.* France
182 F5 **Signal de St-André** *hill* France
184 G3 **Signal de Sauvagnac** *hill* France
184 H4 **Signal du Pic** *hill* France
181 K5 **Signal du Viviers** *hill* France
207 □ **Signal Hill** Gibraltar
265 R8 **Signal Peak** *AZ* U.S.A.
212 D2 **Signau** Switz.
183 H10 **Signes** France
178 H4 **Signy-l'Abbaye** France
178 H4 **Signy-le-Petit** France
237 M6 **Sigoga** S. Africa
184 D4 **Sigogne** France
116 C6 **Sigoisooinan** Indon.
185 E6 **Sigoulès** France
260 I5 **Sigourney** *IA* U.S.A.
288 C4 **Sigsbee Deep** *sea feature* G. of Mexico
165 N2 **Sigtuna** Sweden
267 P10 **Siguatepeque** Hond.
204 D3 **Sigüeiro** Spain
205 O6 **Sigüenza** Spain
185 H10 **Siguer** *r.* France
208 C2 **Sigües** Spain
228 C4 **Siguiri** Guinea
160 H4 **Sigulda** Latvia
265 U3 **Sigurd** *UT* U.S.A.
119 F9 **Sihanoukville** Cambodia
119 F9 **Sihanoukville, Chhâk** *b.* Cambodia
118 B3 **Sihaung Myauk** Myanmar
138 H9 **Sihawa** *Chhattisgarh* India
199 I2 **Sihelné** Slovakia
237 P1 **Sihhoya** Swaziland
212 F1 **Sihlsee** *l.* Switz.
131 L2 **Sihong** *Jiangsu* China
138 H8 **Sihora** *Madh. Prad.* India
138 G9 **Sihora** *Mahar.* India
Sihou *Shandong* China *see* **Changdao**
276 A2 **Sihuas** Peru
131 I7 **Sihui** *Guangdong* China
163 P6 **Siikainen** Fin.
162 R4 **Siikajoki** Fin.
162 R4 **Siikajoki** *r.* Fin.
162 S5 **Siilinjärvi** Fin.
Siipyy Fin. *see* **Sideby**
149 J5 **Siirt** Turkey
100 □4a **Siis** *i. Chuuk* Micronesia
145 M8 **Sijawal** Pak.
Sijjak Uzbek. *see* **Sijjaq**
143 N7 **Sijjaq** Uzbek.
187 D6 **Sijsele** Belgium
116 D5 **Sijunjung** *Sumatera* Indon.
Sikaka Saudi Arabia *see* **Sakākah**
116 D6 **Sikakap** Indon.
138 F6 **Sikandra** *Uttar Prad.* India
138 G6 **Sikandra Rao** *Uttar Prad.* India
246 F3 **Sikanni Chief** *B.C.* Can.
246 F3 **Sikanni Chief** *r. B.C.* Can.
138 E6 **Sikar** *Rajasthan* India
145 M4 **Sikaram** *mt.* Afgh.
228 D4 **Sikasso** Mali
228 D4 **Sikasso** *admin. reg.* Mali
118 C3 **Sikaw** Myanmar
Sikéa Greece *see* **Sykea**
115 B6 **Sikeli** *Sulawesi* Indon.
199 H4 **Sikenica** *r.* Slovakia
261 K7 **Sikeston** *MO* U.S.A.
199 H5 **Sík-hegy** *hill* Hungary
122 H7 **Sikhote-Alin'** *mts* Rus. Fed.
122 J6 **Sikhote-Alinskiy Zapovednik** *nature res.* Rus. Fed.
220 G6 **Sikinos** *i.* Greece
210 G3 **Sikirevci** Croatia
138 B8 **Sikka** *Gujarat* India
139 L6 **Sikkim** *state* India
199 H6 **Siklós** Hungary
244 E3 **Siknik Cape** *AK* U.S.A.
115 E3 **Siko** *i. Maluku* Indon.
231 D8 **Sikongo** Zambia
197 H3 **Sikórz** Pol.
162 N4 **Siksjö** Sweden
139 J6 **Sikta** *Bihar* India
129 R7 **Sikuaishi** *Liaoning* China
117 L1 **Sikuati** *Sabah* Malaysia
204 E4 **Sil** *r.* Spain
146 B2 **Şila'** *i.* Saudi Arabia
269 I8 **Silacayoapan** Mex.
114 E6 **Silago** *Leyte* Phil.
160 F6 **Šilalė** Lith.
213 J2 **Silandro** Italy
118 D5 **Si Lanna National Park** Thai.
214 B7 **Silanus** *Sardegna* Italy
268 F5 **Silao** Mex.
114 E5 **Sila Point** *Samar* Phil.
261 K10 **Silas** *AL* U.S.A.
136 F8 **Silavatturai** Sri Lanka
116 A2 **Silawaih Agam** *vol.* Indon.
114 D6 **Silay** *Negros* Phil.
213 R7 **Silba** Croatia
210 E3 **Silba** *i.* Croatia
213 R7 **Silbanski Kanal** *sea chan.* Croatia
190 H3 **Silberberg** *hill* Ger.
190 H1 **Silberstedt** Ger.
139 N7 **Silchar** *Assam* India
213 M4 **Sile** *r.* Italy
221 K1 **Şile** Turkey
173 J2 **Sileby** *Leicestershire, England* U.K.
171 K5 **Silecroft** *Cumbria, England* U.K.
160 J6 **Silene** Latvia
212 F2 **Silenen** Switz.
187 F8 **Silenrieux** Belgium
255 H8 **Siler City** *NC* U.S.A.
136 G4 **Sileru** *r.* India
207 N4 **Siles** Spain
196 E4 **Silesia** *reg.* Europe
227 G5 **Silet** Alg.
Sileti Kazakh. *see* **Seletinskoye**
143 O1 **Sileti** *r.* Kazakh.
143 O1 **Siletiteniz, Ozero** *salt l.* Kazakh.
180 E5 **Silfiac** France
Silgadi Nepal *see* **Silgarhi**
138 H5 **Silgarhi** Nepal
139 N6 **Silghat** *Assam* India
239 □2a **Silhouette** *i. Inner Islands* Seychelles
227 H1 **Siliana** Tunisia
211 B8 **Siliana** *admin. div.* Tunisia
148 F5 **Silifke** Turkey
214 B6 **Siligo** *Sardegna* Italy
Siliguri *W. Bengal* India *see* **Shiliguri**
231 E9 **Sililo** Zambia
199 K5 **Şilindia** Romania
133 I11 **Siling Co** *salt l.* China
138 F6 **Silipur** *Madh. Prad.* India
214 B9 **Siliqua** *Sardegna* Italy
214 B6 **Silis** *r.* Italy
100 □2 **Silisili, Mount** Samoa
Silistat Turkey *see* **Bozkır**
219 N6 **Siliştea** Romania
219 M6 **Siliştea Nouă** Romania
219 P6 **Silistra** Bulg.
Silistria Bulg. *see* **Silistra**
221 J1 **Silivri** Turkey
164 F2 **Siljan** Norway
163 M6 **Siljan** *l.* Sweden
165 K1 **Siljansnäs** Sweden
164 F5 **Silkeborg** Denmark
107 K4 **Silkwood** *Qld* Austr.
258 C2 **Silkworth** *PA* U.S.A.
200 D5 **Sill** *r.* Austria
209 E9 **Silla** Spain
160 K2 **Sillamäe** Estonia
212 I7 **Sillano** Italy
183 I9 **Sillans-la-Cascade** France
213 L6 **Sillaro** *r.* Italy
148 F5 **Sille** Turkey
204 D3 **Silleda** Spain
204 C4 **Silleiro, Cabo** *c.* Spain
181 K5 **Sillé-le-Guillaume** France
178 H5 **Sillery** France
228 E4 **Silli** Burkina
139 J8 **Silli** *Jharkhand* India
200 F6 **Sillian** Austria
138 E9 **Sillod** *Mahar.* India
180 E4 **Sillon de Talbert** *pen.* France
171 K4 **Silloth** *Cumbria, England* U.K.
196 E2 **Silnowo** Pol.
213 R5 **Silo** Croatia
261 H7 **Siloam Springs** *AR* U.S.A.
237 O2 **Silobela** S. Africa
206 F5 **Silos de Calañas** Spain
156 M2 **Silovayakha** *r.* Rus. Fed.
208 K4 **Sils** Spain
212 H3 **Sils** Switz.
261 H10 **Silsbee** *TX* U.S.A.
247 M4 **Silsby Lake** *Man.* Can.
171 N6 **Silsden** *West Yorkshire, England* U.K.
191 K7 **Silstedt** Ger.
162 S3 **Siltaharju** Fin.
160 J1 **Siltakylä** Fin.
224 B5 **Siltou** *well* Chad
117 H4 **Siluas** *Kalimantan* Indon.
145 I9 **Silūp** *r.* Iran
160 E6 **Šilutė** Lith.
237 O4 **Silutshana** S. Africa
160 G6 **Šiluva** Lith.
281 F5 **Silva Jardim** Brazil
149 J4 **Silvan** Turkey
280 C2 **Silvânia** Brazil
212 H3 **Silvaplana** Switz.
200 A7 **Silvaplaner See** *l.* Switz.
204 D6 **Silvares** *Braga* Port.
204 E8 **Silvares** *Castelo Branco* Port.
138 D9 **Silvassa** *Dadra* India
206 C3 **Silveiras** Port.
165 M4 **Silverån** *r.* Sweden
271 I3 **Silver Bank** *sea feature* Turks and Caicos Is
270 H3 **Silver Bank Passage** Turks and Caicos Is
250 C2 **Silver Bay** *MN* U.S.A.
263 J10 **Silver City** *NM* U.S.A.
264 M2 **Silver City** *NV* U.S.A.
245 M3 **Silver City (abandoned)** *Y.T.* Can.
256 F6 **Silver Creek** *NY* U.S.A.
265 V7 **Silver Creek** *r. AZ* U.S.A.
102 I3 **Silverdale** *North I.* N.Z.
171 L5 **Silverdale** *Lancashire, England* U.K.
258 E4 **Silverdale** *PA* U.S.A.
173 N4 **Silver End** *Essex, England* U.K.
102 J6 **Silverhope** *North I.* N.Z.
284 D3 **Silverio, Laguna** *l.* Arg.
250 F1 **Silver Islet** *Ont.* Can.
262 D5 **Silver Lake** *OR* U.S.A.
250 E5 **Silver Lake** *WI* U.S.A.
265 P6 **Silver Lake** *l. CA* U.S.A.
250 G3 **Silver Lake** *l. MI* U.S.A.
169 F7 **Silvermine Mountains** *hills* Ireland
169 F7 **Silvermines** Ireland
264 O4 **Silver Peak Range** *mts NV* U.S.A.
258 B7 **Silver Spring** *MD* U.S.A.
264 M2 **Silver Springs** *NV* U.S.A.
173 J3 **Silverstone** *Northamptonshire, England* U.K.
236 H4 **Silver Streams** S. Africa
246 E5 **Silverthrone Mountain** *B.C.* Can.
262 D2 **Silvertip Mountain** *B.C.* Can.
104 H4 **Silverton** *N.S.W.* Austr.
246 G5 **Silverton** *B.C.* Can.
172 F6 **Silverton** *Devon, England* U.K.
263 K8 **Silverton** *CO* U.S.A.
259 G4 **Silverton** *NJ* U.S.A.
261 E8 **Silverton** *TX* U.S.A.
251 L4 **Silver Water** *Ont.* Can.
275 G5 **Silves** Brazil
206 C6 **Silves** Port.
215 M2 **Silvi** Italy
274 B4 **Silvia** Col.
262 E5 **Silvies** *r. OR* U.S.A.
267 N8 **Silvituc** Mex.
212 I2 **Silvretta Gruppe** *mts* Switz.
200 B6 **Silvrettahorn** *mt.* Austria
151 J5 **Şilyan** Azer.
200 C5 **Silz** Austria
156 L5 **Sim** Rus. Fed.
156 L5 **Sim** *r.* Rus. Fed.
133 J11 **Sima** *Xizang* China
239 □3 **Sima** *Nzwani* Comoros
118 C2 **Sima** Myanmar
161 W5 **Sima** Rus. Fed.
214 B8 **Simala** *Sardegna* Italy
205 K5 **Simancas** Spain
199 K5 **Şimand** Romania
182 F3 **Šimandre** France
158 H2 **Simanichy** Belarus
220 E2 **Simantra** Greece
130 C7 **Simao** *Yunnan* China
278 F4 **Simão Dias** Brazil
114 D5 **Simara** *i.* Phil.
275 F3 **Simaraña** Venez.
248 E4 **Simard, Lac** *l. Que.* Can.
149 M7 **Şīmareh, Rūdkhāneh-ye** *r.* Iran
139 J7 **Simaria** *Jharkhand* India
138 H7 **Simaria** *Madh. Prad.* India
139 K7 **Simaria Ghat** *Bihar* India
115 B3 **Simatang** *i.* Indon.
209 E9 **Simat de la Valldigna** Spain
221 J3 **Simav** Turkey
221 J3 **Simav Dağları** *mts* Turkey
133 E8 **Simawat** *Xinjiang* China
214 B8 **Simaxis** *Sardegna* Italy
146 E7 **Sīmayr** *i.* Saudi Arabia
230 D4 **Simba** Dem. Rep. Congo
195 N4 **Simbach** Ger.
195 O5 **Simbach am Inn** Ger.
217 K6 **Simbario** Italy
Simbirsk Rus. Fed. *see* **Ul'yanovsk**
100 □6 **Simbo** *i. New Georgia Is* Solomon Is
215 K4 **Simbruini, Monti** *mts* Italy
161 T6 **Simbukhovo** Rus. Fed.
248 D5 **Simcoe** *Ont.* Can.
248 E4 **Simcoe, Lake** *Ont.* Can.
139 J8 **Simdega** *Jharkhand* India
163 N6 **Simeå** Sweden
225 H6 **Simēn** *mts* Eth.
232 C1 **Simēn Mountain National** Eth.
244 H5 **Simeonof Island** *AK* U.S.A.
219 N8 **Simeonovgrad** Bulg.
217 L6 **Simeri** *r.* Italy
219 L5 **Simeria** Romania
217 L6 **Simeri-Crichi** Italy
216 I9 **Simeto** *r. Sicilia* Italy
116 B3 **Simeulue** *i.* Indon.
159 N9 **Simferopol'** Ukr.
Sími *i.* Greece *see* **Symi**
199 L4 **Şimian** Romania
183 H9 **Šimiane-la-Rotonde** France
138 H5 **Simikot** Nepal
119 C10 **Similan, Ko** *i.* Thai.
200 C6 **Similaun** *mt.* Austria/Italy
230 D3 **Simindou** C.A.R.
199 J2 **Siminy** *mt.* Slovakia
219 L9 **Simitli** Bulg.
264 N7 **Simi Valley** *CA* U.S.A.
Simla *Hima. Prad.* India *see* **Shimla**
263 L7 **Simla** *CO* U.S.A.
164 J5 **Simlångsdalen** Sweden
219 K3 **Şimleu Silvaniei** Romania
139 K9 **Šimlipal National Park** Ind
212 D2 **Simme** *r.* Switz.
195 K2 **Simmelsdorf** Ger.
212 C2 **Simmental** *val.* Switz.
191 B9 **Simmerath** Ger.
194 D2 **Simmern (Hunsrück)** Ger.
261 J10 **Simmesport** *LA* U.S.A.
270 F2 **Simm's** *Long I.* Bahamas
262 I3 **Simms** *MT* U.S.A.
255 □2 **Simms Point** *New Prov.* Ba
160 G7 **Simnas** Lith.
162 R4 **Simo** Fin.
162 S3 **Simojärvi** *l.* Fin.
268 E1 **Simon** Mex.
246 G4 **Simonette** *r. Alta* Can.
139 O5 **Simong** *Arun. Prad.* India
247 K4 **Simonhouse** *Man.* Can.
199 K3 **Šimonka** *mt.* Slovakia
256 E7 **Simons** *OH* U.S.A.
172 E5 **Simonsbath** *Somerset, Engl* U.K.
190 G2 **Simonsberg** Ger.
236 C10 **Simon's Town** S. Africa
186 J1 **Simonszand** *i.* Neth.
199 H5 **Simontornya** Hungary
265 W9 **Simon Wash** *watercourse* A U.S.A.
246 E5 **Simoom Sound** *B.C.* Can.
Simoon Sound *B.C.* Can. *s* **Simoom Sound**
185 F9 **Simorre** France
116 F5 **Simpang** *Sumatera* Indon.
117 L1 **Simpang Mangayau, Tanju** Malaysia
187 I7 **Simpelveld** Neth.
278 E3 **Simplício Mendes** Brazil
212 E3 **Simplon** Switz.
212 E3 **Simplon Pass** Switz.
247 J5 **Simpson** *Sask.* Can.
262 I2 **Simpson** *MT* U.S.A.
258 E1 **Simpson** *PA* U.S.A.
106 F8 **Simpson Desert** *N.T.* Aust
104 G2 **Simpson Desert Conserva Park** *nature res. S.A.* Austr.
106 G8 **Simpson Desert National** *Qld* Austr.
104 F2 **Simpson Desert Regional Reserve** *nature res. S.A.* Aus
109 I9 **Simpson Hill** *W.A.* Austr.
250 G1 **Simpson Island** *Ont.* Can.
247 H2 **Simpson Islands** *N.W.T.* Ca
245 P1 **Simpson Lake** *N.W.T.* Can.
264 P2 **Simpson Park Mountains** U.S.A.
243 J3 **Simpson Peninsula** *Nunav* Can.
258 B6 **Simpsonville** *MD* U.S.A.
255 F8 **Simpsonville** *SC* U.S.A.
139 J6 **Simra** Nepal
165 K6 **Simrishamn** Sweden
116 B5 **Simuk** *i.* Indon.
116 C5 **Simulubek** Indon.
117 I4 **Simunjan** *Sarawak* Malays
114 B9 **Simunul** *i.* Phil.
153 Q5 **Simushir, Ostrov** *i. Kuril'sk O-va* Rus. Fed.
136 D4 **Sina** *r.* India
225 G2 **Sīnā', Shibh Jazīrat** *pen.* Eg
116 B3 **Sinabang** Indon.
201 M5 **Sinabelkirchen** Austria
116 C3 **Sinabung** *vol.* Indon.
232 E3 **Sina Dhaqa** Somalia
Sinai *pen.* Egypt *see* **Sīnā', Shibh Jazīrat**
178 H5 **Sinai, Mont** *hill* France
Sinai, Mount Egypt *see* **Mūsá, Jabal**
219 N5 **Sinaia** Romania
Sinai al Janûbîya *governor* Egypt *see* **Janūb Sīnā'**
Sinai ash Shamâlîya *gover* Egypt *see* **Shamāl Sīnā'**
119 D7 **Si Nakarin, Ang Kep Nam**
100 □6 **Sinalanggu** *Malaita* Solom
268 A2 **Sinaloa** *state* Mex.
213 L9 **Sinalunga** Italy
274 D2 **Sinamaica** Venez.
Sinancha Rus. Fed. *see* **Cheremshany**
123 D9 **Sinanju** N. Korea
220 A3 **Sinarades** *Kerkyra* Greece
209 C8 **Sinarcas** Spain
224 A2 **Sīnāwin** Libya
231 E9 **Sinazongwe** Zambia
118 B5 **Sinbaungwe** Myanmar
118 C2 **Sinbo** Myanmar
118 B4 **Sinbyugyun** Myanmar
151 I5 **Sincan** Azer.
148 H4 **Sincan** Turkey
221 L4 **Sincanlı** Turkey
274 C2 **Sincé** Col.
274 C2 **Sincelejo** Col.
178 F4 **Sinceny** France
Sinchu Taiwan *see* **T'aoyüa**
255 F9 **Sinclair, Lake** *GA* U.S.A.
103 I8 **Sinclair Head** *North I.* N.Z
246 F4 **Sinclair Mills** *B.C.* Can.
168 J5 **Sinclair's Bay** *Scotland* U.K
278 E5 **Sincora, Serra do** *hills* Braz
138 G6 **Sind** *r.* India
Sind *prov.* Pak. *see* **Sindh**
139 P4 **Sinda** *Xizang* China
122 J4 **Sinda** Rus. Fed.
233 A8 **Sinda** Zambia
164 G4 **Sindal** Denmark
114 D7 **Sindañgan** *Mindanao* Phil.
114 D7 **Sindangan Bay** *Mindanao*
116 G8 **Sindangbarang** *Jawa* Indo
230 A5 **Sindara** Gabon
138 C7 **Sindari** *Rajasthan* India
115 B8 **Sindeh, Teluk** *b. Flores* Ind
194 F4 **Sindelfingen** Ger.
136 E4 **Sindgi** *Karnataka* India
145 M9 **Sindh** *prov.* Pak.
136 E5 **Sindhnur** *Karnataka* India
Síndhos Greece *see* **Sindos**
139 J6 **Sindhuli Garhi** Nepal
Sindhulimadi Nepal *see* **Sindhuli Garhi**
160 H3 **Sindi** Estonia
138 G9 **Sindi** *Mahar.* India
214 B7 **Sindia** *Sardegna* Italy
269 J8 **Sindihui** Mex.
221 J3 **Sındırgı** Turkey
136 E3 **Sindkhed** *Mahar.* India
138 E9 **Sindkheda** *Mahar.* India
Sîndominic Romania *see* **Sândominic**
156 J3 **Sindor** Rus. Fed.
220 D2 **Sindos** Greece
228 D4 **Sindou** Burkina
136 E3 **Sindphana** *r.* India

K8 Sindri Jharkhand India
J8 Sindri Jharkhand India
N6 Sind Sagar Doab lowland Pak.
J4 Sinegor'ye Rus. Fed.
I2 Sinekçi Turkey
N3 Sinello r. Italy
Sinel'nikovo Ukr. see Synel'nykove
F4 Sinendé Benin
B3 Sine Ngayène and Wanar Stone Circles tourist site Gambia
B5 Sines Port.
B5 Sines, Cabo de c. Port.
R3 Sinettä Fin.
L8 Sineu Spain
R8 Sinezerki Rus. Fed.
D5 Sinfra Côte d'Ivoire
D4 Sing Myanmar
G6 Singa Sudan
H5 Singahi Uttar Prad. India
C4 Singaing Myanmar
□3a Singani Njazidja Comoros
F4 Singapore country Asia
□ Singapore Sing.
□ Singapore r. Sing.
□ Singapore, Strait of Indon./Sing.
Singapura country Asia see Singapore
Singapura Sing. see Singapore
H3 Singapuru Orissa India
K9 Singaraja Bali Indon.
G4 Singareni Andhra Prad. India
Singatoka Viti Levu Fiji see Sigatoka
Singave Wallis and Futuna Is see Sigave
E7 Sing Buri Thai.
F6 Singen (Hohentwiel) Ger.
Sîngeorgiu de Pădure Romania see Sângeorgiu de Pădure
Sîngeorz-Băi Romania see Sângeorz-Băi
H7 Sîngera Moldova
H6 Sîngerei Moldova
I5 Singgimtay Xinjiang China
N5 Singhampton Ont. Can.
E10 Singhofen Ger.
B6 Singida Tanz.
B6 Singida admin. reg. Tanz.
Singidunum Beograd Serbia see Beograd
Singim Xinjiang China see Singgimtay
B2 Singkaling Hkamti Myanmar
B6 Singkang Sulawesi Indon.
D5 Singkarak Sumatera Indon.
H4 Singkawang Kalimantan Indon.
F5 Singkep i. Indon.
B3 Singkil Sumatera Indon.
C4 Singkuang Sumatera Indon.
M5 Singleton N.S.W. Austr.
E6 Singleton N.T. Austr.
C7 Singleton, Mount hill N.T. Austr.
D10 Singleton, Mount hill W.A. Austr.
O1 Singö i. Sweden
E7 Singoli Madh. Prad. India
B3 Singon Myanmar
Singora Thai. see Songkhla
Sin'gosan N. Korea see Kosan
F4 Singou, Réserve Totale du nature res. Burkina
M7 Singra Assam India
B3 Singu Myanmar
I6 Singuilucan Mex.
N6 Singureni Romania
H8 Singwara Madh. Prad. India
E9 Sin'gye N. Korea
G6 Sinḩ, Jabal hill Saudi Arabia
Sinhala country Asia see Sri Lanka
G9 Sinharaja Forest Reserve nature res. Sri Lanka
D2 Sinhkung Myanmar
E8 Sinhŭng N. Korea
B8 Sini Sardegna Italy
C2 Siniatsiko mt. Greece
D6 Sinigo r. Italy
C4 Siniloan Luzon Phil.
Sining Qinghai China see Xining
A4 Sinio, Gunung mt. Indon.
D6 Siniscola Sardegna Italy
N9 Sini Vrŭkh mt. Bulg.
R2 Siniye Lipyagi Rus. Fed.
2 Siniy-Shikhan Rus. Fed.
F4 Sinj Croatia
B6 Sinjai Sulawesi Indon.
5 Sinjār Iraq
5 Sinjār, Jabal mt. Iraq
A3 Sīnji Iran
D6 Sinjil West Bank
H5 Sinkat Sudan
Sinkiang aut. reg. China see Xinjiang Uygur Zizhiqu
Sinkiang Uighur Autonomous Region aut. reg. China see Xinjiang Uygur Zizhiqu
E5 Sinking r. Ireland
B9 Sinking Spring OH U.S.A.
G1 Sinkyevichy Belarus
K6 Sinlabajos Spain
F3 Sin-le-Noble France
Sînmartin Romania see Sânmartin
D9 Sinmi-do i. N. Korea
F9 Sinn Ger.
10 Sinn r. Ger.
C9 Sinnai Sardegna Italy
H3 Sinnamary Fr. Guiana
D3 Sinnar Mahar. India
A9 Sinn Bishr, Jabal hill Egypt
D3 Sinne Ukr.
Sinneh Iran see Sanandaj
G7 Sinnemahoning PA U.S.A.
R7 Sinni r. Italy
Sînnicolau Mare Romania see Sânnicolau Mare
Sinoia Zimbabwe see Chinhoyi
Q6 Sinoie, Lacul lag. Romania
4 Sinole Latvia
G2 Sinop Brazil
G2 Sinop Turkey
Sinope Turkey see Sinop
7 Sinopoli Italy
D2 Sinoquipe Mex.
8 Sinp'a N. Korea
Sînpetru Mare Romania see Sânpetru Mare
8 Sinp'o N. Korea
9 Sinp'yŏng N. Korea
7 Sins Switz.
9 Sinsang N. Korea
3 Sinsheim Ger.
4 Sintang Kalimantan Indon.
□10 Sint Annabaai b. Curaçao Neth. Antilles
5 Sint Annaland Neth.
2 Sint Annaparochie Neth.
5 Sint Anthonis Neth.
□10 Sint Christoffelberg hill Curaçao Neth. Antilles
5 Sintea Mare Romania
4 Şinteu Romania
2 Sint Eustatius i. Neth. Antilles
7 Sint-Genesius-Rode Belgium
6 Sint-Gillis-Waas Belgium
6 Sint-Huibrechts-Lille Belgium
2 Sint Jacobiparochie Neth.
6 Sint Jansteen Neth.
6 Sint-Joris Belgium
6 Sint-Katelijne-Waver Belgium
Sint Kruis Curaçao Neth. Antilles see Santa Krus
6 Sint-Laureins Belgium
6 Sint-Lenaarts Belgium
4 Sint Maarten i. Neth. Antilles
5 Sint Maartensdijk Neth.
6 Sint-Margriete Belgium
7 Sint-Maria-Lierde Belgium
6 Sint-Martens-Latem Belgium
10 Sint Michiel Curaçao Neth. Antilles
9 Sint Nicolaas Aruba
3 Sint Nicolaasga Neth.
5 Sint-Niklaas Belgium
11 Sinton TX U.S.A.
186 G3 Sint Pancras Neth.
186 F5 Sint Philipsland Neth.
187 F7 Sint-Pieters-Leeuw Belgium
206 A3 Sintra Port.
202 B3 Sintra-Cascais, Parque Natural de nature res. Port.
213 L7 Sintria r. Italy
161 T5 Sintsovo Rus. Fed.
187 H7 Sint-Truiden Belgium
271 □10 Sint Willebrordus Curaçao Neth. Antilles
274 C2 Sinú r. Col.
123 D8 Sinŭiju N. Korea
232 F2 Sinujiif Somalia
244 F2 Sinuk AK U.S.A.
160 L4 Sinyaya r. Rus. Fed.
194 E4 Sinzheim Ger.
191 D9 Sinzig Ger.
195 M4 Sinzing Ger.
199 H5 Sió r. Romania
208 G4 Sió r. Spain
199 H5 Sióagárd Hungary
114 D8 Siocon Mindanao Phil.
199 H5 Siófok Hungary
231 D9 Sioma Zambia
231 D9 Sioma Ngwezi National Park Zambia
212 C3 Sion Switz.
168 F6 Sionascaig, Loch l. Scotland U.K.
151 G4 Sioni Georgia
169 H3 Sion Mills Northern Ireland U.K.
Sionmsheni Georgia see Sioni
243 K2 Siorapaluk Greenland
100 □6 Siota Solomon Is
182 C4 Sioule r. France
260 G4 Sioux Center IA U.S.A.
260 G4 Sioux City IA U.S.A.
260 G4 Sioux Falls SD U.S.A.
248 B3 Sioux Lookout Ont. Can.
267 N11 Sipacate Guat.
117 M2 Sipadan, Pulau i. Sabah Malaysia
114 D7 Sipalay Negros Phil.
210 F4 Šipan i. Croatia
117 I4 Sipang, Tanjung pt Malaysia
271 □7 Siparia Trin. and Tob.
118 C3 Sipein Myanmar
Siphaqeni S. Africa see Flagstaff
122 D7 Siping Jilin China
117 K2 Sipitang Sabah Malaysia
247 L4 Sipiwesk Man. Can.
247 L4 Sipiwesk Lake Man. Can.
286 P2 Siple, Mount Antarctica
286 N1 Siple Coast Antarctica
286 P2 Siple Island Antarctica
Sipolilo Zimbabwe see Guruve
Siponj Tajik. see Bartang
219 P3 Şipote Romania
210 F3 Šipovo Bos.-Herz.
194 G6 Sipplingen Ger.
261 K9 Sipsey r. AL U.S.A.
116 C6 Sipura i. Indon.
116 C6 Sipura, Selat sea chan. Indon.
150 A9 Sīq, Wādī as watercourse Egypt
147 L9 Siqirah Suquţrā Yemen
280 C5 Siqueira Campos Brazil
268 A2 Siqueiros Mex.
266 □Q11 Siquia r. Nic.
114 D7 Siquijor Phil.
114 D7 Siquijor i. Phil.
274 D2 Siquisique Venez.
145 M10 Sir r. Pak.
136 E6 Sira Karnataka India
164 C3 Sira Norway
164 C3 Sira r. Norway
147 L3 Şīr Abū Nu'āyr i. U.A.E.
183 I7 Sirac mt. France
119 E8 Si Racha Thai.
217 I9 Siracusa Sicilia Italy
217 I9 Siracusa prov. Sicilia Italy
Siraha Nepal see Sirha
139 L7 Sirajganj Bangl.
246 F4 Sir Alexander, Mount B.C. Can.
184 I6 Siran France
148 I3 Şiran Turkey
145 L9 Siranda Lake Pak.
138 H7 Sirathu Uttar Prad. India
229 F3 Sirba r. Burkina/Niger
150 B10 Sirbāl, Jabal mt. Egypt
147 K3 Şīr Banī Yās i. U.A.E.
Sircilla Andhra Prad. India see Sirsilla
149 N5 Sīrdān Iran
Sirdaryo r. Asia see Syrdar'ya
143 M7 Sirdaryo Uzbek.
143 M7 Sirdaryo admin. div. Uzbek.
Sirdaryo Wiloyati admin. div. Uzbek. see Sirdaryo
232 C2 Sīrē Oromīya Eth.
232 C2 Sīrē Oromīya Eth.
233 A6 Sire Tanz.
106 F3 Sir Edward Pellew Group is N.T. Austr.
250 B4 Siren WI U.S.A.
215 L3 Sirente, Monte mt. Italy
219 O3 Siret Romania
219 Q5 Siret r. Romania
Siret r. Ukr. see Seret
108 I2 Sir Graham Moore Islands W.A. Austr.
139 K6 Sirha Nepal
148 H8 Sirhān, Wādī an watercourse Saudi Arabia
150 F7 Sirḩān, Wādī as watercourse Jordan/Saudi Arabia
219 J4 Şiria Romania
144 G8 Sīrīk Iran
117 I3 Sirik, Tanjung pt Malaysia
118 E6 Siri Kit, Khuan Thai.
164 F2 Sirikjerka hill Norway
Sirína i. Greece see Syrna
119 D10 Sirinat National Park Thai.
145 M6 Siritoi r. Pak.
144 F6 Siriz Iran
145 I9 Sīrjā Iran
245 P3 Sir James MacBrien, Mount N.W.T. Can.
144 F7 Sīrjān Iran
144 F7 Sīrjān salt flat Iran
104 F6 Sir Joseph Banks Group Conservation Park nature res. S.A. Austr.
162 R3 Sirkka Fin.
138 F4 Sirmaur Hima. Prad. India
243 K2 Sirmilik National Park Nunavut Can.
213 J5 Sirmione Italy
Sirmium Vojvodina Serbia see Sremska Mitrovica
138 H7 Sirmour Madh. Prad. India
Sirmur Hima. Prad. India see Sirmaur
212 G1 Sirnach Switz.
149 K5 Şırnak Turkey
162 T4 Sirniö Fin.
201 J6 Sirnitz Austria
182 I3 Sirod France
138 D7 Sirohi Rajasthan India
199 J4 Sirok Hungary
199 J2 Široké Slovakia
232 B4 Siroko Uganda
213 P8 Sirolo Italy
116 B4 Sirombu Indon.
136 G3 Sironcha Mahar. India
115 C4 Sirong Sulawesi Indon.
138 F7 Sironj Madh. Prad. India
213 L3 Siròr Italy
Síros i. Greece see Syros
160 M6 Sirotsina Belarus
226 D3 Siroua, Jbel mt. Morocco
136 F3 Sirpur Andhra Prad. India
146 G3 Sirr, Nafūd as des. Saudi Arabia
146 E6 Sirrayn i. Saudi Arabia
232 D3 Sirrei Eth.
264 N6 Sirretta Peak CA U.S.A.
144 F9 Sīrrī, Jazīreh-ye i. Iran
138 E5 Sirsa Haryana India
246 G5 Sir Sandford, Mount B.C. Can.
136 D5 Sirsi Karnataka India
138 F7 Sirsi Madh. Prad. India
138 G5 Sirsi Uttar Prad. India
136 F3 Sirsilla Andhra Prad. India
Sirte Libya see Surt
Sirte, Gulf of Libya see Surt, Khalīj
104 B2 Sir Thomas, Mount hill S.A. Austr.
207 I3 Siruela Spain
136 E5 Siruguppa Karnataka India
263 J12 Sirupa r. Mex.
136 D4 Sirur Karnataka India
136 D3 Sirur Mahar. India
160 G6 Sirutiškis Lith.
149 K4 Şirvan Turkey
151 I5 Şirvan Düzü lowland Azer.
144 B1 Şirvan Düzü plain Azer.
151 J4 Şirvanovka Azer.
151 K6 Şirvan Qoruğu nature res. Azer.
136 F5 Sirvel Andhra Prad. India
197 K1 Širvinta r. Lith.
160 H6 Širvintos Lith.
146 G8 Şirwāḩ Yemen
149 L6 Sīrwān r. Iraq
246 G4 Sir Wilfrid Laurier, Mount B.C. Can.
107 I2 Sir William Thompson Range hills Qld Austr.
Sis Turkey see Kozan
145 L9 Sisa Creek inlet Pak.
210 F3 Sisak Croatia
118 G7 Sisaket Thai.
267 N7 Sisal Mex.
207 O2 Sisante Spain
204 C2 Sisargas, Illas is Spain
244 I2 Sischu Mountain AK U.S.A.
Siscia Croatia see Sisak
214 C2 Sisco Corse France
236 H3 Sishen S. Africa
128 J9 Sishilipu Gansu China
131 M5 Sishuang Liedao is China
151 H6 Sisian Armenia
151 G6 Sisiani Lerrnants'k pass Armenia/Azer.
228 E4 Sisili r. Ghana alt. Sissili (Burkina)
243 M3 Sisimiut Greenland
247 K4 Sisipuk Lake Man./Sask. Can.
250 F2 Siskiwit Bay MI U.S.A.
266 F4 Sisogúichic Mex.
119 F8 Sisŏphŏn Cambodia
264 L7 Sisquoc r. CA U.S.A.
212 D1 Sissach Switz.
260 G3 Sisseton SD U.S.A.
228 E4 Sissili r. Burkina alt. Sisili (Ghana)
257 □R1 Sisson Branch Reservoir N.B. Can.
178 G4 Sissonne France
256 D10 Sissonville WV U.S.A.
145 I6 Sistān reg. Iran
144 I8 Sīstān va Balūchestān prov. Iran
199 K5 Şiştarovăţ Romania
250 G4 Sister Bay WI U.S.A.
183 H8 Sisteron France
137 M7 Sisters is Andaman & Nicobar Is India
262 D4 Sisters OR U.S.A.
238 □2a Sisters Peak hill Ascension S. Atlantic Ocean
256 E9 Sistersville WV U.S.A.
215 K5 Sisto r. Italy
200 D5 Sistrans Austria
144 H8 Sīt Iran
161 U3 Sit' r. Rus. Fed.
233 A6 Sitalike Tanz.
139 J6 Sitamarhi Bihar India
138 E8 Sitamau Madh. Prad. India
235 □J3 Sitampiky Madag.
114 B9 Sitangkai Phil.
197 L5 Sitaniec Pol.
138 H6 Sitapur Uttar Prad. India
198 F2 Šitbořice Czech Rep.
221 H7 Siteia Kriti Greece
237 P2 Siteki Swaziland
208 I5 Sitges Spain
220 E2 Sithonias, Chersonisos pen. Greece
Sitía Kriti Greece see Siteia
128 D5 Sitian Xinjiang China
245 N1 Sitidgi Lake N.W.T. Can.
235 G4 Sitila Moz.
118 H2 Siting Guizhou China
278 D5 Sítio da Abadia Brazil
278 E5 Sítio do Mato Brazil
209 E7 Sitjar, Embalse de resr Spain
245 N4 Sitka AK U.S.A.
244 I4 Sitkalidak Island AK U.S.A.
245 N4 Sitka National Historical Park nat. park AK U.S.A.
244 I4 Sitkinak Island AK U.S.A.
244 I4 Sitkinak Strait AK U.S.A.
197 I5 Sitkówka-Nowiny Pol.
138 H7 Sitlaha Madh. Prad. India
218 I8 Sitnicë r. Kosovo
199 H3 Sitno mt. Slovakia
160 M4 Sitnya r. Rus. Fed.
224 E2 Sitrah oasis Egypt
160 M6 Sitsyenyets Belarus
Sittang r. Myanmar see Sittaung
187 I7 Sittard Neth.
118 B2 Sittaung Myanmar
118 C6 Sittaung r. Myanmar
190 I4 Sittensen Ger.
194 G6 Sitter r. Ger.
201 K6 Sittersdorf Austria
237 L9 Sittingbourne S. Africa
173 N5 Sittingbourne Kent, England U.K.
Sittoung r. Myanmar see Sittaung
118 A4 Sittwe Myanmar
117 K8 Situbondo Jawa Indon.
193 D9 Sitzendorf Ger.
201 M2 Sitzendorf an der Schmida Austria
193 G8 Sitzenroda Ger.
131 □I7 Siu A Chau i. H.K. China
115 C6 Siumpu i. Indon.
100 □2 Si'umu Samoa
266 □Q11 Siuna Nic.
163 R6 Siuntio Fin.
214 C8 Siurgus Donigala Sardegna Italy
139 K8 Siuri W. Bengal India
156 K4 Siva Rus. Fed.
199 I6 Sivac Vojvodina Serbia
136 F8 Sivaganga Tamil Nadu India
136 E8 Sivakasi Tamil Nadu India
122 E2 Sivaki Rus. Fed.
144 E6 Sivand Iran
148 H4 Sivas Turkey
221 K4 Sivaslı Turkey
228 B3 Sivé Maur.
148 I5 Siverek Turkey
160 K5 Sīvers l. Latvia
159 R5 Sivers'k Ukr.
161 N2 Siverskiy Rus. Fed.
Sivers'kyy Donets' r. Rus. Fed. see Severskiy Donets
159 S5 Sivers'kyy Donets' r. Ukr.
197 M6 Sivka-Voynylivs'ka Ukr.
156 M2 Sivomaskinskiy Rus. Fed.
148 I4 Sivrice Turkey
148 E4 Sivrihisar Turkey
187 F8 Sivry Belgium
179 J5 Sivry-sur-Meuse France
237 N2 Sivukile S. Africa
115 B5 Siwa Sulawesi Indon.
224 E2 Sīwah Egypt
224 E2 Sīwah, Wāḩāt oasis Egypt
138 F4 Siwalik Range mts India/Nepal
139 J6 Siwan Bihar India
138 D7 Siwana Rajasthan India
Siwa Oasis Egypt see Sīwah, Wāḩāt
151 H5 Şıxarx Azer.
271 □4 Six Cross Roads Barbados
183 H10 Six-Fours-les-Plages France
131 K2 Sixian Anhui China
250 I6 Six Lakes MI U.S.A.
169 E7 Sixmilebridge Ireland
169 H3 Sixmilecross Northern Ireland U.K.
182 J5 Sixt, Réserve Naturelle de nature res. France
182 J4 Sixt-Fer-à-Cheval France
245 L2 Sixtymile Y.T. Can.
237 N1 Siyabuswa S. Africa
151 H7 Siyah Rud Iran
Siyang Guangxi China see Shangsi
131 L2 Siyang Jiangsu China
237 M2 Siyathemba S. Africa
237 O1 Siyathuthuka S. Africa
151 K4 Siyäzän Azer.
129 K6 Siyitang Nei Mongol China
144 E5 Sīyunī Iran
206 A2 Sizandro r. Port.
173 P3 Sizewell Suffolk, England U.K.
Siziwang Qi Nei Mongol China see Ulan Hua
180 C5 Sizun France
156 K2 Sizyabsk Rus. Fed.
164 H7 Sjælland admin. reg. Denmark
164 H6 Sjælland i. Denmark
162 O3 Sjaunja naturreservat nature res. Sweden
218 I7 Sjenica Sjenica Serbia
163 J6 Sjoa Norway
165 J6 Sjöbo Sweden
162 I5 Sjøholt Norway
162 L3 Sjona sea chan. Norway
162 M4 Sjoutnäset Sweden
162 N2 Sjøvegan Norway
162 P4 Sjulsmark Sweden
162 □ Sjuøyane is Svalbard
162 L5 Skäckerfjällen mts Sweden
218 H8 Skadarsko Jezero nat. park Montenegro
159 L7 Skadovs'k Ukr.
164 H6 Skælsør Denmark
164 E6 Skærbæk Denmark
243 Q2 Skærfjorden inlet Greenland
243 Q3 Skaftafell nat. park Iceland
162 □E1 Skaftafell nat. park Iceland
162 □E2 Skaftárós r. mouth Iceland
162 □D1 Skagafjörður inlet Iceland
162 □C1 Skagaheiði reg. Iceland
164 G4 Skagen Denmark
164 G4 Skagen nature res. Denmark
165 K3 Skagern l. Sweden
164 E4 Skagerrak str. Denmark/Norway
262 C2 Skagit r. WA U.S.A.
246 F5 Skagit Mountain B.C. Can.
245 N4 Skagway AK U.S.A.
162 R1 Skaidi Norway
160 I7 Skaidiškės Lith.
168 J4 Skaill Orkney, Scotland U.K.
168 K5 Skaill Orkney, Scotland U.K.
221 H5 Skala Notio Aigaio Greece
220 D6 Skala Peloponnisos Greece
197 H5 Skała Pol.
221 H3 Skala Kallonis Lesvos Greece
162 N2 Skaland Norway
158 F5 Skala-Podil's'ka Ukr.
164 I5 Skälderviken b. Sweden
193 K9 Skalice Czech Rep.
151 B1 Skalistyy Khrebet reg. Rus. Fed.
199 H2 Skalité Slovakia
162 U1 Skallelv Norway
162 M4 Skalmodal Sweden
198 B1 Skalná Czech Rep.
164 F5 Skals r. Denmark
159 M9 Skalyste Ukr.
164 F5 Skanderborg Denmark
164 J6 Skåne county Sweden
165 J6 Skåne reg. Sweden
256 I6 Skaneateles NY U.S.A.
257 I6 Skaneateles Lake NY U.S.A.
164 B2 Skånevik Norway
164 B2 Skånevikfjorden sea chan. Norway
162 N4 Skansholm Sweden
220 F3 Skantzoura i. Greece
196 D3 Skąpe Pol.
164 J3 Skara Sweden
168 J4 Skara Brae tourist site Scotland U.K.
162 N2 Skarberget Norway
213 R7 Škarda i. Croatia
Skardarsko Jezero l. Albania/Montenegro see Scutari, Lake
107 I1 Skardon r. Qld Austr.
138 E2 Skardu Pak.
164 C2 Skare Norway
164 C3 Skåreheia mt. Norway
163 P7 Skärgårdshavets nationalpark nat. park Fin.
164 H4 Skärhamn Sweden
164 H1 Skarnes Norway
190 J1 Skarø i. Denmark
158 H2 Skarodnaye Belarus
165 N1 Skärplinge Sweden
163 L5 Skärsjövålen Sweden
163 J5 Skarstind mt. Norway
196 G1 Skarszewy Pol.
163 J5 Skarvedalseggen mt. Norway
162 N4 Skarvsjöby Sweden
197 J4 Skaryszew Pol.
158 F4 Skarzhyntsi Ukr.
197 I4 Skarżysko-Kamienna Pol.
164 I1 Skasberget hill Norway
164 I1 Skasen l. Norway
160 F6 Skaudvilė Lith.
162 P3 Skaulo Sweden
164 D1 Skaupsjøen-Hardangerjøkulen park Norway
164 E5 Skave Denmark
168 □O2 Skaw Shetland, Scotland U.K.
197 H5 Skawa r. Pol.
197 H6 Skawina Pol.
226 B4 Skaymat Western Sahara
165 O2 Skebobruk Sweden
165 L3 Skeda udde Sweden
165 O2 Skedviken l. Sweden
165 L2 Skedvisjön l. Sweden
245 O5 Skeena r. B.C. Can.
245 O4 Skeena Mountains B.C. Can.
171 R7 Skegness Lincolnshire, England U.K.
162 □E2 Skeiðarársandur sand area Iceland
168 □N2 Skeld Shetland, Scotland U.K.
168 □N2 Skelda Ness hd Scotland U.K.
190 I1 Skelde Denmark
234 B3 Skeleton Coast Game Park nature res. Namibia
162 P4 Skellefteå Sweden
162 P4 Skellefteälven r. Sweden
162 P4 Skelleftebukten b. Sweden
162 P4 Skelleftehamn Sweden
171 L6 Skelmersdale Lancashire, England U.K.
168 G11 Skelmorlie North Ayrshire, Scotland U.K.
171 P4 Skelton Redcar and Cleveland, England U.K.
Skelton-in-Cleveland England U.K. see Skelton
218 I8 Skenderaj Skenderaj Kosovo
172 G4 Skenfrith Monmouthshire, Wales U.K.
197 H3 Skępe Pol.
163 N5 Skeppshamn Sweden
236 G4 Skerpioenpunt S. Africa
168 H5 Skerray Highland, Scotland U.K.
169 J5 Skerries Ireland
172 E4 Sketty Swansea, Wales U.K.
158 B4 Skhidni Beskydy mts Pol./Ukr.
158 B4 Skhidni Karpaty mts Ukr.
197 L6 Skhidnytsya Ukr.
Skhimatárion Greece see Schimatari
227 H2 Skhira Tunisia
Skhíza i. Greece see Schiza
164 G2 Ski Norway
220 E3 Skiathos Greece
220 E3 Skiathos i. Greece
169 D9 Skibbereen Ireland
162 P2 Skibotn Norway
160 H8 Skidal' Belarus
171 K4 Skiddaw hill England U.K.
245 O5 Skidegate Mission B.C. Can.
Skidel' Belarus see Skidal'
258 C6 Skidmore MD U.S.A.
160 I6 Skiemonys Lith.
164 F2 Skien Norway
197 L5 Skierbieszów Pol.
197 I4 Skierniewice Pol.
163 P6 Skiftet sea chan. Fin.
227 G1 Skikda Alg.
160 K4 Škilbēni Latvia
220 B5 Skinari, Akrotirio pt Zakynthos Greece
165 L2 Skinnskatteberg Sweden
138 F3 Skio Jammu and Kashmir India
168 F11 Skipness Argyll and Bute, Scotland U.K.
258 E4 Skippack PA U.S.A.
171 Q6 Skipsea East Riding of Yorkshire, England U.K.
236 E10 Skipskop S. Africa
105 I7 Skipton Vic. Austr.
171 M6 Skipton North Yorkshire, England U.K.
258 C7 Skipton MD U.S.A.
171 Q6 Skirlaugh East Riding of Yorkshire, England U.K.
Skiropoúla i. Greece see Skyropoula
Skíros i. Greece see Skyros
164 F5 Skive Denmark
197 K3 Skiwy Duże Pol.
162 □E1 Skjálfandafljót r. Iceland
162 □E1 Skjálfandi b. Iceland
162 M3 Skjelatinden mt. Norway
162 L4 Skjellbreid Norway
164 G1 Skjellinhovde hill Norway
164 C1 Skjemmene mt. Norway
164 D3 Skjerkeknuten hill Norway
164 E6 Skjern Denmark
164 E6 Skjern r. Denmark
162 K4 Skjern Norway
162 M3 Skjerstadejorden inlet Norway
162 P1 Skjervøy Norway
163 I6 Skjolden Norway
190 J1 Skjoldnæs pen. Denmark
220 D3 Sklithro Greece
161 U4 Sknyatinovo Rus. Fed.
Skobelev Uzbek. see Farg'ona
143 O8 Skobeleva, Pik mt. Kyrg.
201 L8 Škocjan Slovenia
201 I8 Skocjanske jame tourist site Slovenia
196 G6 Skoczów Pol.
237 J10 Skoenmakerskop S. Africa
210 E2 Škofja Loka Slovenia
201 K8 Škofljica Slovenia
163 N6 Skog Sweden
162 R2 Skoganvarri Norway
162 T2 Skogfoss Norway
165 L5 Skoghult Sweden
172 B4 Skokholm Island Wales U.K.
196 F3 Skoki Pol.
250 G7 Skokie IL U.S.A.
142 I3 Skol' Kazakh.
158 C4 Skole Ukr.
165 L2 Sköllersta Sweden
197 J6 Skołyszyn Pol.
172 B4 Skomer Island Wales U.K.
196 G4 Skomlin Pol.
162 K3 Skomvær is Norway
237 K3 Skoonspruit r. S. Africa
220 E3 Skopelos Greece
220 E3 Skopelos i. Greece
220 G4 Skopelos i. Greece
220 G3 Skopia hill Limnos Greece
161 W8 Skopin Rus. Fed.
218 J9 Skopje Macedonia
Skoplje Macedonia see Skopje
166 D1 Skopunarfjørður sea chan. Faroe Is
196 G2 Skórcz Pol.
157 G6 Skorodnoye Rus. Fed.
196 F5 Skorogoszcz Pol.
196 F5 Skoroszyce Pol.
162 L4 Skorovatn Norway
166 J1 Skorpa i. Norway
164 F5 Skørping Denmark
197 K3 Skórzec Pol.
196 F3 Skorzęcińskie, Jezioro l. Pol.
220 E1 Skotoussa Greece
164 I2 Skotterud Norway
220 E1 Skoutari Greece
221 H3 Skoutaros Lesvos Greece
165 J3 Skövde Sweden
122 C2 Skovorodino Rus. Fed.
257 □P4 Skowhegan ME U.S.A.
164 F2 Skrimfjell hill Norway
160 I5 Skrīveri Latvia
210 D2 Škrlatica mt. Slovenia
197 J2 Skroda r. Pol.
162 P3 Skröven Sweden
160 F5 Skrunda Latvia
197 H3 Skrwa r. Pol.
197 H2 Skrwilno Pol.
161 N6 Skrydlyeva Belarus
196 E2 Skrzatusz Pol.
197 G6 Skrzyczne mt. Pol.
197 I4 Skrzyńsko Pol.
197 J6 Skrzyszów Pol.
164 B2 Skudeneshavn Norway
237 K1 Skuinsdrif S. Africa
245 N3 Skukum, Mount Y.T. Can.
235 F5 Skukuza S. Africa
162 O5 Skuleskogens nationalpark nat. park Sweden
265 P5 Skull Peak NV U.S.A.
265 T7 Skull Valley AZ U.S.A.
236 B6 Skulpfonteinpunt pt S. Africa
196 G3 Skulsk Pol.
165 M2 Skultuna Sweden
260 J5 Skunk r. IA U.S.A.
160 E5 Skuodas Lith.
161 U7 Skuratovskiy Rus. Fed.
164 J6 Skurup Sweden
219 L7 Skŭt r. Bulg.
165 N1 Skutskär Sweden
162 M2 Skutvik Norway
166 D1 Skúvoy i. Faroe Is
197 M6 Skvaryava Ukr.
158 I4 Skvyra Ukr.
245 J3 Skwentna r. AK U.S.A.
196 D3 Skwierzyna Pol.
199 H3 Skýcov Slovakia
220 D2 Skydra Greece
168 D8 Skye i. Scotland U.K.
164 C3 Skykula hill Norway
283 B9 Skyring, Seno b. Chile
220 F4 Skyropoula i. Greece
220 F4 Skyros Skyros Greece
220 F4 Skyros i. Greece
258 E2 Skytop PA U.S.A.
286 S1 Skytrain Ice Rise Antarctica
160 K6 Slabodka Belarus
197 I5 Słaboszów Pol.
258 C3 Slabtown PA U.S.A.
258 F4 Slack Woods NJ U.S.A.
Sládečkovce Slovakia see Močenok
159 R7 Sladkiy, Liman salt l. Rus. Fed.
166 D1 Slættaratindur hill Faroe Is
164 H6 Slagelse Denmark
186 K3 Slagharen Neth.
162 O4 Slagnäs Sweden
171 M6 Slaidburn Lancashire, England U.K.
168 I11 Slamannan Falkirk, Scotland U.K.
117 H8 Slamet, Gunung vol. Indon.
199 J3 Slaná r. Slovakia
245 L3 Slana AK U.S.A.
169 I5 Slane Ireland
199 K3 Slanec Slovakia
169 I8 Slaney r. Ireland
219 N5 Slănic Romania
219 O5 Slănic r. Romania
219 O4 Slănic Moldova Romania
199 K3 Slanské vrchy mts Slovakia
160 L2 Slantsy Rus. Fed.
198 D1 Slaný Czech Rep.
201 I7 Slap Slovenia
160 G6 Šlapaberžė Lith.
198 F2 Šlapanice Czech Rep.
210 E4 Slapovi Krke nat. park Croatia
157 H6 Slashchevskaya Rus. Fed.
107 K5 Slashers Reefs Qld Austr.
Śląsk reg. Europe see Silesia
196 F4 Śląska, Nizina lowland Pol.
197 G5 Śląska, Wyżyna hills Pol.
196 G5 Śląskie prov. Pol.
258 E3 Slateford PA U.S.A.
259 G2 Slate Hill NY U.S.A.
248 C3 Slate Islands Ont. Can.
108 J5 Slatey watercourse W.A. Austr.
210 F3 Slatina Croatia
219 M6 Slatina Romania
199 I3 Slatina r. Slovakia
219 K5 Slatina-Timiș Romania
258 D3 Slatington PA U.S.A.
198 G2 Slatinice Czech Rep.
256 E10 Slaty Fork WV U.S.A.
159 P3 Slatyne Ukr.
153 R3 Slautnoye Rus. Fed.
122 F2 Slava Rus. Fed.
246 H2 Slave r. Alta/N.W.T. Can.
229 F5 Slave Coast Africa
246 H4 Slave Lake Alta Can.
246 H2 Slave Point N.W.T. Can.
Slavgorod Belarus see Slawharad
143 R1 Slavgorod Rus. Fed.
Slavgorod Ukr. see Slavhorod
159 O5 Slavhorod Dnipropetrovs'ka Oblast' Ukr.
159 O3 Slavhorod Sums'ka Oblast' Ukr.
199 G2 Slavičín Czech Rep.
219 K7 Slavinja Pirot Serbia
160 M4 Slavkovichi Rus. Fed.
198 B1 Slavkovský les for. Czech Rep.
198 F2 Slavkov u Brna Czech Rep.
213 P4 Slavnik mt. Slovenia
161 T5 Slavnoye Rus. Fed.
Slavonia reg. Croatia see Slavonija
198 E3 Slavonice Czech Rep.
210 F3 Slavonija reg. Croatia
Slavonska Požega Croatia see Požega
210 G3 Slavonski Brod Croatia
199 J3 Slavošovce Slovakia
160 E6 Slavsk Rus. Fed.
158 F3 Slavuta Ukr.
158 J2 Slavutych Ukr.
Slavyanka Kazakh. see Myrzakent
122 G7 Slavyanka Rus. Fed.
219 M7 Slavyanovo Bulg.
Slavyansk Ukr. see Slov"yans'k
Slavyanskaya Rus. Fed. see Slavyansk-na-Kubani
157 G7 Slavyansk-na-Kubani Rus. Fed.
158 I2 Slavyechna r. Belarus
196 E4 Sława Pol.
197 L4 Sławatycze Pol.
196 F2 Sławęcin Pol.
161 O8 Slawharad Belarus
196 F2 Sławianowskie Wielkie, Jezioro l. Pol.
165 M7 Sławno Pol.
196 D2 Sławoborze Pol.
196 E4 Sławskie, Jezioro l. Pol.
196 E1 Sławsko Pol.
260 H4 Slayton MN U.S.A.
171 Q7 Slea r. England U.K.
171 Q7 Sleaford Lincolnshire, England U.K.
104 E6 Sleaford Bay S.A. Austr.
169 B8 Slea Head Ireland
168 E8 Sleat pen. Scotland U.K.
168 D8 Sleat, Point of Scotland U.K.
168 E8 Sleat, Sound of sea chan. Scotland U.K.
244 F2 Sledge Island AK U.S.A.
247 J4 Sled Lake Sask. Can.
171 P5 Sledmere East Riding of Yorkshire, England U.K.
138 H8 Sleemanabad Madh. Prad. India
186 K3 Sleen Neth.
248 E1 Sleeper Islands Nunavut Can.
250 H5 Sleeping Bear Dunes National Lakeshore nature res. MI U.S.A.
250 H5 Sleeping Bear Point MI U.S.A.
131 □J7 Sleep Island H.K. China
244 H3 Sleetmute AK U.S.A.
186 G5 Sleeuwijk Neth.
171 P5 Sleights North Yorkshire, England U.K.
117 I8 Sleman Indon.
197 H6 Ślemień Pol.
151 G2 Sleptsovskaya Rus. Fed.
196 G3 Ślesin Pol.
286 W1 Slessor Glacier Antarctica
196 E5 Ślęża hill Pol.
196 E4 Ślęża r. Pol.
198 F1 Ślężański Park Krajobrazowy Pol.
Slezsko reg. Europe see Silesia
199 I3 Sliač Slovakia
265 X3 Slick Rock CO U.S.A.
261 K10 Slidell LA U.S.A.
257 K7 Slide Mountain NY U.S.A.
163 J6 Slidre Norway
186 G5 Sliedrecht Neth.
217 □ Sliema Malta
169 B8 Slievanea hill Ireland
169 G4 Slieve Anierin hill Ireland
169 G7 Slieveardagh Hills Ireland
169 E6 Slieve Aughty Mountains hills Ireland
169 H4 Slieve Beagh hill Ireland/U.K.
169 E7 Slieve Bernagh hills Ireland
169 G7 Slieve Bloom Mountains hills Ireland
169 D7 Slievecallan hill Ireland
169 C4 Slieve Car hill Ireland
169 K4 Slieve Donard hill Northern Ireland U.K.
169 F7 Slievefelim Mountains hills Ireland
170 D4 Slieve Gallion hill Northern Ireland U.K.
Slieve Gamph hills Ireland see Ox Mountains
Slievekimalta h. Ireland see Keeper Hill
169 H3 Slievekirk hill Northern Ireland U.K.
169 B8 Slieve Mish Mountains hills Ireland
169 B9 Slieve Miskish Mountains hills Ireland
169 G4 Slievenakilla hill Ireland
169 G8 Slievenamon hill Ireland
170 B5 Slieve Rushen hill Northern Ireland U.K.
169 F3 Slieve Snaght hill Ireland
169 H2 Slieve Snaght hill Ireland
168 D8 Sligachan Highland, Scotland U.K.
Sligeach Ireland see Sligo
169 F4 Sligo Ireland
169 E4 Sligo county Ireland
256 F7 Sligo PA U.S.A.
169 E4 Sligo Bay Ireland
197 K2 Ślina r. Pol.
173 L5 Slinfold West Sussex, England U.K.
186 J4 Slinge r. Neth.
168 F7 Slioch hill Scotland U.K.
159 L4 Sliporid r. Ukr.
102 J4 Slipper Island North I. N.Z.
256 E7 Slippery Rock PA U.S.A.
165 O4 Slite Gotland Sweden
160 F4 Slīteres rezervāts nature res. Latvia
219 O8 Sliven Bulg.
219 L8 Slivnitsa Bulg.
219 O7 Slivo Pole Bulg.
196 G2 Śliwice Pol.
210 E3 Sljeme mt. Croatia
199 G3 Slňava l. Slovakia
265 Q6 Sloan NV U.S.A.
264 L2 Sloat CA U.S.A.
259 G2 Sloatsburg NY U.S.A.
158 I6 Slobidka Ukr.
156 I3 Sloboda Arkhangel'skaya Oblast' Rus. Fed.
Sloboda Respublika Komi Rus. Fed. see Ezhva
Sloboda Smolenskaya Oblast' Rus. Fed. see Przheval'skoye
157 H6 Sloboda Voronezhskaya Oblast' Rus. Fed.
159 M2 Sloboda Ukr.
156 J3 Slobodchikovo Rus. Fed.
161 R7 Slobodka Rus. Fed.
156 J4 Slobodskoy Rus. Fed.
Slobodzeya Moldova see Slobozia
158 I7 Slobozia Moldova
219 P6 Slobozia Romania
219 P5 Slobozia Bradului Romania
246 G5 Slocan B.C. Can.
186 K2 Slochteren Neth.
197 I5 Słomniki Pol.
160 I8 Slonim Belarus
159 Q3 Slonovka Rus. Fed.
196 D2 Słonowice Pol.
196 C3 Słońsk Pol.
186 G3 Slootdorp Neth.
186 I3 Sloten Neth.
186 I3 Slotermeer l. Neth.
173 K4 Slough Slough, England U.K.
173 K4 Slough admin. div. England U.K.
198 F2 Sloupnice Czech Rep.
159 M2 Slout Ukr.
199 I3 Slovakia country Europe
158 H2 Slovechna r. Ukr.
158 H2 Slovechne Ukr.
210 E2 Slovenia country Europe
Slovenija country Europe see Slovenia
210 E2 Slovenj Gradec Slovenia
210 E2 Slovenska Bistrica Slovenia
199 J2 Slovenská Ves Slovakia
210 E2 Slovenske gorice hills Slovenia
201 L7 Slovenske Konjice Slovenia
199 K3 Slovenské Nové Mesto Slovakia
199 I3 Slovenské rudohorie mts Slovakia
Slovensko country Europe see Slovakia
199 J3 Slovenský kras mts Slovakia
199 J3 Slovenský kras park Slovakia
199 J3 Slovenský raj nat. park Slovakia
199 J3 Slovinky Slovakia
197 M6 Slovita Ukr.
159 P5 Slov"yanka Ukr.
159 Q4 Slov"yanohirs'k Ukr.
159 R5 Slov"yanoserbs'k Ukr.
159 Q5 Slov"yans'k Ukr.
159 M8 Slov"yans'ke Ukr.
197 H4 Słowik Pol.
165 N7 Słowiński Park Narodowy nat. park Pol.
196 C3 Słubice Lubuskie Pol.
197 H3 Słubice Mazowieckie Pol.
160 K9 Sluch r. Belarus
158 F2 Sluch r. Ukr.
213 J2 Sluderno Italy
156 L4 Sludka Permskaya Oblast' Rus. Fed.
156 J4 Sludka Respublika Komi Rus. Fed.
187 D6 Sluis Neth.
187 E6 Sluiskil Neth.
198 D1 Šluknov Czech Rep.
198 G2 Slunečná hill Czech Rep.
119 H9 S'Lung, B'Nom mt. Vietnam
210 E3 Slunj Croatia
196 F3 Słupca Pol.
197 J5 Słupcza Pol.
197 H4 Słupia Łódzkie Pol.
197 H5 Słupia Świętokrzyskie Pol.
197 I4 Słupia Świętokrzyskie Pol.
165 M7 Słupia r. Pol.
197 H3 Słupno Pol.
165 N7 Słupsk Pol.
162 N4 Slussfors Sweden
196 G4 Słuszków Pol.
160 K8 Slutsk Belarus
160 F6 Šlyna r. Lith.
169 B6 Slyne Head Ireland
120 H1 Slyudyanka Rus. Fed.
261 I9 Smackover AR U.S.A.
184 B2 Smagne r. France
168 K11 Smailholm Scottish Borders, Scotland U.K.
165 K4 Småland reg. Sweden
164 H6 Smålandsfarvandet sea chan. Denmark
164 J4 Smålandsstenar Sweden
173 J2 Smalley Derbyshire, England U.K.
257 □P5 Small Point ME U.S.A.
249 H2 Smallwood Reservoir Nfld and Lab. Can.
161 N6 Smalowka Belarus
197 M3 Smalyanitsa Belarus
160 L7 Smalyavichy Belarus
197 I4 Smardzewice Pol.
196 D3 Smardzewo Pol.
196 D2 Smardzko Pol.
160 J7 Smarhon' Belarus
201 M7 Šmarje pri Jelšah Slovenia
201 L8 Šmarjeta Slovenia
201 L7 Šmartinsko jezero l. Slovenia
247 J2 Smart Lake N.W.T. Can.
201 K7 Šmartno Mozirje Slovenia
201 L7 Šmartno Slovenj Gradec Slovenia
236 H6 Smartt Syndicate Dam resr S. Africa
184 E2 Smarves France
247 J4 Smeaton Sask. Can.
193 J10 Smečno Czech Rep.
198 D1 Smědá r. Czech Rep.
165 M5 Smedby Sweden
218 I6 Smederevo Smederevo Serbia
218 I6 Smederevska Palanka Smederevska Palanka Serbia
219 O5 Smeeni Romania
173 N5 Smeeth Kent, England U.K.
Smela Ukr. see Smila
162 U1 Smelror Norway
256 G7 Smethport PA U.S.A.
173 I3 Smethwick West Midlands, England U.K.
196 G2 Smętowo Graniczne Pol.
198 E1 Smidary Czech Rep.
197 M4 Smidyn Ukr.
196 E3 Śmigiel Pol.
159 K4 Smila Ukr.
160 L8 Smilavichy Belarus
186 J3 Smilde Neth.
159 M3 Smile Ukr.
158 G3 Smilka r. Ukr.
196 E2 Śmiłowo Pol.
160 I4 Smiltene Latvia
160 F5 Smiltiņu kalns hill Latvia
162 M2 Smines Norway
198 E1 Smiřice Czech Rep.
143 M1 Smirnovo Kazakh.
Smirnovskiy Kazakh. see Smirnovo
122 M4 Smirnykh Sakhalin Rus. Fed.
246 H4 Smith Alta Can.
262 I3 Smith r. MT U.S.A.
256 F12 Smith r. VA U.S.A.
245 Q2 Smith Arm b. N.W.T. Can.
244 I1 Smith Bay AK U.S.A.
169 H4 Smithborough Ireland
260 F6 Smith Center KS U.S.A.
246 E4 Smithers B.C. Can.
246 E4 Smithers Landing B.C. Can.
237 K6 Smithfield S. Africa
255 H8 Smithfield NC U.S.A.
262 I6 Smithfield UT U.S.A.
256 I12 Smithfield VA U.S.A.
286 Q1 Smith Glacier Antarctica
286 T2 Smith Island Antarctica
243 K3 Smith Island Nunavut Can.
137 M6 Smith Island Andaman & Nicobar Is India
257 I10 Smith Island MD U.S.A.
257 J11 Smith Island VA U.S.A.
261 K7 Smithland KY U.S.A.
256 F11 Smith Mountain Lake VA U.S.A.
106 C1 Smith Point N.T. Austr.
245 P4 Smith River B.C. Can.
256 H9 Smithsburg MD U.S.A.
248 E4 Smiths Falls Ont. Can.
108 □1 Smithson Bight b. Christmas I.
243 K2 Smith Sound sea chan. Can./Greenland
105 J9 Smithton Tas. Austr.
105 N4 Smithtown N.S.W. Austr.
259 I3 Smithtown NY U.S.A.
259 G6 Smithville NJ U.S.A.
261 H8 Smithville OK U.S.A.
255 E8 Smithville TN U.S.A.
256 D9 Smithville WV U.S.A.
236 I9 Smitskraal S. Africa
199 J3 Smižany Slovakia
162 □F1 Smjörfjöll mts Iceland
264 M1 Smoke Creek Desert NV U.S.A.
245 P1 Smoking Mountains N.W.T. Can.
246 G3 Smoky r. Alta Can.
104 D5 Smoky Bay S.A. Austr.
104 D5 Smoky Bay b. S.A. Austr.
105 N4 Smoky Cape N.S.W. Austr.
106 G7 Smoky Creek watercourse Qld Austr.
248 D3 Smoky Falls Ont. Can.
260 E6 Smoky Hill r. KS U.S.A.
260 E6 Smoky Hill, North Fork r. KS U.S.A.
252 G3 Smoky Hills KS U.S.A.

260 F6 **Smoky Hills** *KS* U.S.A.
247 H4 **Smoky Lake** *Alta* Can.
262 G5 **Smoky Mountains** *ID* U.S.A.
162 I5 **Smøla** *i.* Norway
196 F1 **Smołdzino** Pol.
142 C2 **Smolenka** Rus. Fed.
161 P7 **Smolensk** Rus. Fed.
161 Q7 **Smolenskaya Oblast'** *admin. div.* Rus. Fed.
161 P7 **Smolensk-Moscow Upland** *hills* Rus. Fed.
Smolensk Oblast *admin. div.* Rus. Fed. *see* **Smolenskaya Oblast'**
Smolensko-Moskovskaya Vozvyshennost' *hills* Rus. Fed. *see* **Smolensk-Moscow Upland**
143 U1 **Smolenskoye** Rus. Fed.
Smolevichi Belarus *see* **Smalyavichy**
196 F4 **Smolice** Pol.
220 B2 **Smolikas** *mt.* Greece
159 K5 **Smoline** Ukr.
164 I2 **Smolmark** Sweden
192 K5 **Smolnica** Pol.
199 J3 **Smolník** Slovakia
219 M9 **Smolyan** Bulg.
122 H7 **Smolyoninovo** Rus. Fed.
248 D3 **Smooth Rock Falls** *Ont.* Can.
248 B3 **Smoothrock Lake** *Ont.* Can.
247 J4 **Smoothstone Lake** *Sask.* Can.
162 R1 **Smørfjord** Norway
Smorgon' Belarus *see* **Smarhon'**
161 P9 **Smotrova Buda** Rus. Fed.
158 F5 **Smotrych** Ukr.
159 L3 **Smotryky** Ukr.
198 G1 **Smrk** *mt.* Czech Rep.
193 L9 **Smrk** *mt.* Czech Rep.
159 K2 **Smyach** Ukr.
219 P7 **Smyadovo** Bulg.
164 J6 **Smygehamn** Sweden
158 E3 **Smyha** Ukr.
197 I4 **Smyków** Pol.
286 S2 **Smyley Island** Antarctica
Smyrna Turkey *see* **İzmir**
258 D6 **Smyrna** *DE* U.S.A.
255 E9 **Smyrna** *GA* U.S.A.
255 D8 **Smyrna** *TN* U.S.A.
258 D6 **Smyrna** *r. DE* U.S.A.
257 □Q2 **Smyrna Mills** *ME* U.S.A.
283 B8 **Smyth, Canal** *sea chan.* Chile
162 □F1 **Snæfell** *mt.* Iceland
170 I5 **Snaefell** *hill* Isle of Man
162 □B1 **Snæfellsjökull** *ice cap* Iceland
162 B1 **Snæfellsjökull** *nat. park* Iceland
162 □B1 **Snæfellsnes** *pen.* Iceland
245 L3 **Snag (abandoned)** *Y.T.* Can.
171 P5 **Snainton** *North Yorkshire, England* U.K.
171 O6 **Snaith** *East Riding of Yorkshire, England* U.K.
245 N2 **Snake** *r. N.W.T./Y.T.* Can.
260 E4 **Snake** *r. NE* U.S.A.
262 E3 **Snake** *r.* U.S.A.
106 B3 **Snake Creek** *r. N.T.* Austr.
265 R2 **Snake Range** *mts NV* U.S.A.
246 F3 **Snake River** *B.C.* Can.
262 G5 **Snake River Plain** *ID* U.S.A.
Snap Point *Andros* Bahamas *see* **Cistern Point**
246 G2 **Snare** *r. N.W.T.* Can.
246 H1 **Snare Lake** *N.W.T.* Can.
247 J3 **Snare Lake** *Sask.* Can.
Snare Lakes *N.W.T.* Can. *see* **Wekweêtì**
99 G6 **Snares Islands** N.Z.
162 L4 **Snåsa** Norway
162 L4 **Snåsvatn** *l.* Norway
256 B12 **Sneedville** *TN* U.S.A.
186 I2 **Sneek** Neth.
186 I2 **Sneekermeer** *l.* Neth.
169 C9 **Sneem** Ireland
236 D8 **Sneeuberg** *mt.* S. Africa
236 I7 **Sneeuberge** *mts* S. Africa
249 I2 **Snegamook Lake** *Nfld and Lab.* Can.
Snegurovka Ukr. *see* **Tetiyiv**
264 L4 **Snelling** *CA* U.S.A.
160 E5 **Snēpele** Latvia
173 N2 **Snettisham** *Norfolk, England* U.K.
161 T8 **Snezhed'** *r.* Rus. Fed.
152 J3 **Snezhnogorsk** Rus. Fed.
122 E1 **Snezhnogorskiy** Rus. Fed.
Snezhnoye Ukr. *see* **Snizhne**
198 E1 **Sněžka** *mt.* Czech Rep.
210 E3 **Snežnik** *mt.* Slovenia
197 J2 **Śniadowo** Pol.
197 J2 **Śniardwy, Jezioro** *l.* Pol.
Sniečkus Lith. *see* **Visaginas**
Snieżka *mt.* Czech Rep. *see* **Sněžka**
198 F1 **Śnieżnicki Park Krajobrazowy** Pol.
196 E5 **Śnieżnik** *mt.* Pol.
159 L6 **Snihurivka** Ukr.
199 L3 **Snina** Slovakia
173 I3 **Snitterfield** *Warwickshire, England* U.K.
159 M3 **Snityn** Ukr.
159 R5 **Snizhne** Ukr.
168 D7 **Snizort, Loch** *b. Scotland* U.K.
163 J5 **Snøhetta** *mt.* Norway
262 C3 **Snohomish** *WA* U.S.A.
164 C2 **Snønuten** *mt.* Norway
161 Q8 **Snopot'** *r.* Rus. Fed.
Snoul Cambodia *see* **Snuŏl**
159 K2 **Snov** *r.* Ukr.
159 P2 **Snova** *r.* Rus. Fed.
161 V9 **Snova** *r.* Rus. Fed.
Snovsk Ukr. *see* **Shchors**
160 J8 **Snow** Belarus
247 K2 **Snowbird Lake** *N.W.T.* Can.
244 I3 **Snowcap Mountain** *AK* U.S.A.
246 G5 **Snowcrest Mountain** *B.C.* Can.
103 C12 **Snowdon** *mt. South I.* N.Z.
172 D1 **Snowdon** *mt. Wales* U.K.
172 E2 **Snowdonia National Park** *Wales* U.K.
Snowdrift *N.W.T.* Can. *see* **Łutselk'e**
247 I2 **Snowdrift** *r. N.W.T.* Can.
265 V7 **Snowflake** *AZ* U.S.A.
257 J10 **Snow Hill** *MD* U.S.A.
255 I8 **Snow Hill** *NC* U.S.A.
247 K4 **Snow Lake** *Man.* Can.
104 G5 **Snowtown** *S.A.* Austr.
262 H6 **Snowville** *UT* U.S.A.
105 L7 **Snowy** *r. N.S.W./Vic.* Austr.
244 I4 **Snowy Mountain** *AK* U.S.A.
257 K5 **Snowy Mountain** *NY* U.S.A.
105 K7 **Snowy Mountains** *N.S.W.* Austr.
245 L2 **Snowy Peak** *AK* U.S.A.
105 L7 **Snowy River National Park** *Vic.* Austr.
160 K6 **Snudy, Vozyera** *l.* Belarus
270 G2 **Snug Corner** *Acklins I.* Bahamas
249 K2 **Snug Harbour** *Nfld and Lab.* Can.
251 N4 **Snug Harbour** *Ont.* Can.
119 H8 **Snuŏl** Cambodia
158 E5 **Snyatyn** Ukr.
261 F8 **Snyder** *OK* U.S.A.
261 E9 **Snyder** *TX* U.S.A.
258 A3 **Snyder County** *county PA* U.S.A.
258 D3 **Snyders** *PA* U.S.A.
236 E7 **Snyderspoort** *pass* S. Africa
161 T8 **Snykhovo** Rus. Fed.
158 H4 **Snyvoda** *r.* Ukr.
115 F5 **Soabuwe** *Seram* Indon.
235 □J3 **Soahany** Madag.
Soaigh *i. Western Isles, Scotland* U.K. *see* **Soay**
168 D10 **Soa Island** *Scotland* U.K.
204 D5 **Soajo** Port.
103 B12 **Soaker, Mount** *South I.* N.Z.
235 □J3 **Soalala** Madag.
204 D6 **Soalhães** Port.
204 F8 **Soalheira** Port.
235 □J4 **Soamanonga** Madag.
145 N5 **Soan** *r.* Pak.
212 D5 **Soana** *r.* Italy
235 □K3 **Soanierana-Ivongo** Madag.
123 E11 **Soan-kundo** *is* S. Korea
213 M9 **Soara** *r.* Italy
274 C3 **Soata** Col.
213 K5 **Soave** Italy
235 □J3 **Soavinandriana** Madag.
168 D8 **Soay** *i. Highland, Scotland* U.K.
168 □1 **Soay** *i. Western Isles, Scotland* U.K.
158 I5 **Sob** *r.* Ukr.
229 H4 **Soba** Nigeria
123 E11 **Sobaek-sanmaek** *mts* S. Korea
123 F10 **Sobaek-san National Park** S. Korea
231 C8 **Soba Matias** Angola
232 A2 **Sobat** *r.* Sudan
127 H5 **Sobatsubu-yama** *mt.* Japan
204 E4 **Sober** Spain
198 D2 **Soběslav** Czech Rep.
113 J7 **Sobger** *r. Papua* Indon.
138 G8 **Sobhapur** *Madh. Prad.* India
158 C2 **Sobiborski Park Krajobrazowy** Pol.
161 X6 **Sobinka** Rus. Fed.
161 V6 **Sobolevo** Rus. Fed.
197 J4 **Sobolew** Pol.
125 I14 **Sobo-san** *mt.* Japan
197 H3 **Sobota** Pol.
201 L6 **Soboth** Austria
198 G1 **Sobotín** Czech Rep.
198 G3 **Sobotište** Slovakia
198 E1 **Sobotka** Czech Rep.
196 E5 **Sobótka** *Dolnośląskie* Pol.
197 J5 **Sobótka** *Świętokrzyskie* Pol.
196 F4 **Sobótka** *Wielkopolskie* Pol.
196 G1 **Sobowidz** Pol.
204 G4 **Sobradelo** Spain
280 D1 **Sobradinho** Brazil
278 E4 **Sobradinho, Barragem de** *resr* Brazil
278 E4 **Sobrado** *Bahia* Brazil
275 H6 **Sobrado** *Pará* Brazil
204 D2 **Sobrado** *Galicia* Spain
204 D4 **Sobrado** *Galicia* Spain
274 D7 **Sobral** *Acre* Brazil
278 E2 **Sobral** *Ceará* Brazil
204 D8 **Sobral** Port.
206 E4 **Sobral da Adiça** Port.
206 A2 **Sobral de Monte Agraço** Port.
204 E8 **Sobral do Campo** Port.
199 L3 **Sobrance** Slovakia
138 E4 **Sobraon** *Punjab* India
208 E3 **Sobrarbe** *reg.* Spain
204 D6 **Sobreira** Port.
204 E9 **Sobreira Formosa** Port.
205 N3 **Sobrón, Embalse de** *resr* Spain
126 E5 **Sobue** Japan
190 J1 **Søby** Denmark
159 M2 **Sobych** Ukr.
Soča *r.* Italy *see* **Isonzo**
201 I7 **Soča** Slovenia
210 D3 **Soča** *r.* Slovenia
213 N3 **Socchieve** Italy
213 P5 **Sočerga** Slovenia
197 I3 **Sochaczew** Pol.
151 A2 **Sochi** Rus. Fed.
197 I3 **Sochocin** Pol.
123 E10 **Sŏch'ŏn** S. Korea
220 E2 **Sochos** Greece
101 □9 **Société, Archipel de la** *is* Fr. Polynesia
Society Islands Fr. Polynesia *see* **Société, Archipel de la**
199 K5 **Socodor** Romania
218 J6 **Socol** Romania
276 C6 **Socompa** Chile
199 L4 **Socond** Romania
Soconusco, Sierra de *mts* Mex. *see* **Madre de Chiapas, Sierra**
280 D5 **Socorro** Brazil
274 C3 **Socorro** Col.
263 K9 **Socorro** *NM* U.S.A.
252 D7 **Socorro, Isla** *i.* Mex.
274 B6 **Socota** Peru
Socotra *i.* Yemen *see* **Suquṭrá**
207 P4 **Socovos** Spain
119 H10 **Soc Trăng** Vietnam
207 N2 **Socuéllamos** Spain
264 M6 **Soda Lake** *CA* U.S.A.
265 P6 **Soda Lake** *CA* U.S.A.
162 S3 **Sodankylä** Fin.
133 D9 **Soda Plains** Aksai Chin
138 G8 **Sodarpur** *Madh. Prad.* India
262 I5 **Soda Springs** *ID* U.S.A.
127 K5 **Sodegaura** Japan
165 M5 **Söderåkra** Sweden
165 L1 **Söderbärke** Sweden
165 O1 **Söderboda** Sweden
165 N1 **Söderfors** Sweden
163 N6 **Söderhamn** Sweden
165 M3 **Söderköping** Sweden
165 M2 **Södermanland** *county* Sweden
190 J4 **Soderstorf** Ger.
165 N2 **Södertälje** Sweden
225 F6 **Sodiri** Sudan
236 H6 **Sodium** S. Africa
232 C3 **Sodo** Eth.
165 L1 **Södra Barken** *l.* Sweden
165 N2 **Södra Björkfjärden** *b.* Sweden
165 M3 **Södra Finnö** *i.* Sweden
162 P5 **Södra gloppet** *b.* Fin.
163 O6 **Södra Kvarken** *str.* Fin./Sweden
165 L4 **Södra Vi** Sweden
201 K8 **Sodražica** Slovenia
256 H5 **Sodus** *NY* U.S.A.
237 Q3 **Sodwana Bay** S. Africa
237 Q3 **Sodwana Bay National Park** S. Africa
115 D8 **Soë** *Timor* Indon.
236 B6 **Soebatsfontein** S. Africa
235 F4 **Soekmekaar** S. Africa
160 F3 **Soela väin** *sea chan.* Estonia
Soerabaia *Jawa* Indon. *see* **Surabaya**
187 I6 **Soerendonk** Neth.
191 F7 **Soest** Ger.
186 H4 **Soest** Neth.
190 E4 **Soeste** *r.* Ger.
237 K4 **Soetdoring Nature Reserve** S. Africa
236 D10 **Soetendalsvlei** *l.* S. Africa
220 D3 **Sofades** Greece
105 L5 **Sofala** *N.S.W.* Austr.
235 G4 **Sofala** Moz.
235 G3 **Sofala** *prov.* Moz.
235 G4 **Sofala, Baía de** *b.* Moz.
Sofia Bulg. *see* **Sofiya**
235 □J2 **Sofia** *r.* Madag.
220 E5 **Sofiko** Greece
219 L8 **Sofiya** Bulg.
Sofiyevka Ukr. *see* **Vil'nyans'k**
159 M5 **Sofiyivka** Ukr.
122 H2 **Sofiysk** *Khabarovskiy Kray* Rus. Fed.
122 K3 **Sofiysk** *Khabarovskiy Kray* Rus. Fed.
162 U4 **Sofporog** Rus. Fed.
221 H6 **Sofrana** *i.* Greece
161 U5 **Sofrino** Rus. Fed.
199 K5 **Şofronea** Romania
150 A2 **Şofta Kalesi** *tourist site* Turkey
125 R17 **Sōfu-gan** *i.* Japan
133 K11 **Sog** *Xizang* China
274 C3 **Sogamoso** Col.
151 A5 **Soğanlı Dağları** *mts* Turkey
151 B5 **Soğanlı Geçidi** *pass* Turkey
132 H6 **Sogat** *Xinjiang* China
122 H3 **Sogda** Rus. Fed.
190 E5 **Sögel** Ger.
145 M2 **Soghd** *admin. div.* Tajik.
133 E9 **Sogma** *Xizang* China
133 D10 **Sogmai** *Xizang* China
164 D3 **Søgne** Norway
163 H6 **Sognefjorden** *inlet* Norway
163 I6 **Sogn og Fjordane** *county* Norway
153 N2 **Sogo** Rus. Fed.
114 E6 **Sogod** *Leyte* Phil.
114 E6 **Sogod Bay** *Leyte* Phil.
232 C4 **Sogo Hills** Kenya
224 B6 **Sogolle** *well* Chad
133 K10 **Sog Qu** *r. Xizang* China
151 F6 **Soğuksu** Turkey
221 L2 **Söğüt** Turkey
221 J3 **Söğütcük** Turkey
221 K5 **Söğüt Dağı** *mts* Turkey
151 B7 **Söğütlü** Turkey
123 E12 **Sŏgwip'o** S. Korea
144 D5 **Soh** Iran
Sohâg *Sawhāj* Egypt *see* **Sūhāj**
138 G8 **Sohagpur** *Madh. Prad.* India
173 M3 **Soham** *Cambridgeshire, England* U.K.
113 L8 **Sohano** P.N.G.
Sohar Oman *see* **Şuḩār**
145 O5 **Sohawa** Pak.
187 H8 **Soheit-Tinlot** Belgium
139 I9 **Sohela** *Orissa* India
193 K8 **Sohland am Rotstein** Ger.
191 J6 **Söhlde** Ger.
138 F5 **Sohna** *Haryana* India
119 D7 **Sohng Gwe, Khao** *hill* Myanmar/Thai.
145 J8 **Sohrag** Pak.
194 C2 **Sohren** Ger.
178 H2 **Soignes, Forêt de** *for.* Belgium
187 F7 **Soignies** Belgium
130 A3 **Soila** *Xizang* China
199 L5 **Şoimi** Romania
182 H1 **Soing** France
181 O7 **Soings-en-Sologne** France
162 R5 **Soini** Fin.
191 I9 **Soisberg** *hill* Ger.
178 F5 **Soissons** France
284 D4 **Soitue** Arg.
178 G6 **Soizy-aux-Bois** France
125 K12 **Sōja** Japan
138 D7 **Sojat** *Rajasthan* India
138 D7 **Sojat Road** *Rajasthan* India
197 K5 **Sójkowa** Pol.
114 D7 **Sojoton Point** *Negros* Phil.
201 O6 **Söjtör** Hungary
157 J5 **Sok** *r.* Rus. Fed.
127 K4 **Sōka** Japan
158 D3 **Sokal'** Ukr.
123 F9 **Sokch'o** S. Korea
221 I5 **Söke** Turkey
231 E7 **Sokele** Dem. Rep. Congo
129 L2 **Sokhondo, Gora** *mt.* Rus. Fed.
128 I1 **Sokhor, Gora** *mt.* Rus. Fed.
Sokhós Greece *see* **Sochos**
151 C2 **Sokhumi** Georgia
151 C3 **Sokhumi-Babushara** *airport* Georgia
Sokiryany Ukr. *see* **Sokyryany**
125 G11 **Sŏkkuram Grotto** *tourist site* S. Korea
164 F1 **Sokna** Norway
162 K5 **Soknedal** Norway
219 J7 **Sokobanja** *Sokobanja* Serbia
229 F4 **Sokodé** Togo
Soko Islands *H.K.* China *see* **Shekka Ch'ün-Tao**
122 M5 **Sokol** *Sakhalin* Rus. Fed.
156 H4 **Sokol** *Vologodskaya Oblast'* Rus. Fed.
210 G4 **Sokolac** Bos.-Herz.
197 L2 **Sokolany** Pol.
158 J4 **Sokolivka** *Cherkas'ka Oblast'* Ukr.
197 M5 **Sokolivka** *L'vivs'ka Oblast'* Ukr.
197 L2 **Sokółka** Pol.
197 K1 **Sokółki** Pol.
201 O1 **Sokolnice** Czech Rep.
161 V7 **Sokol'niki** *Tul'skaya Oblast'* Rus. Fed.
161 R5 **Sokol'niki** *Tverskaya Oblast'* Rus. Fed.
228 D3 **Sokolo** Mali
159 N7 **Sokolohirne** Ukr.
198 B1 **Sokolov** Czech Rep.
159 N4 **Sokolova Balka** Ukr.
201 O7 **Sokolovac** Croatia
143 M1 **Sokolovka** Kazakh.
159 Q3 **Sokolovka** Rus. Fed.
143 U1 **Sokolovo** Rus. Fed.
159 S6 **Sokolovo-Kundryuchenskiy** Rus. Fed.
197 K5 **Sokołów Małopolski** Pol.
197 K3 **Sokołów Podlaski** Pol.
162 U3 **Sokolozero, Ozero** *l.* Rus. Fed.
156 H4 **Sokol'skoye** Rus. Fed.
197 K3 **Sokoły** Pol.
228 A3 **Sokone** Senegal
199 G4 **Sokorópátka** Hungary
162 T2 **Sokosti** *hill* Fin.
229 G3 **Sokoto** Nigeria
229 G4 **Sokoto** *r.* Nigeria
229 G3 **Sokoto** *state* Nigeria
228 C4 **Sokourala** Guinea
158 G5 **Sokyryany** Ukr.
197 K5 **Sól** Pol.
285 H3 **Sola** Arg.
270 E3 **Sola** Cuba
231 E6 **Sola** Dem. Rep. Congo
197 H6 **Soła** *r.* Pol.
Sola *i.* Tonga *see* **Ata**
138 F4 **Solan** *Hima. Prad.* India
264 O9 **Solana Beach** *CA* U.S.A.
206 F3 **Solana de los Barros** Spain
207 K4 **Solana del Pino** Spain
205 K7 **Solana de Rioalmar** Spain
103 A13 **Solander Island** *South I.* N.Z.
164 F1 **Sølandsfjellet** *mt.* Norway
285 H5 **Solanet** Arg.
114 C3 **Solano** *Luzon* Phil.
274 E4 **Solano** Venez.
136 D4 **Solapur** *Mahar.* India
217 I9 **Solarino** *Sicilia* Italy
214 C4 **Solaro** *Corse* France
214 B8 **Solarussa** *Sardegna* Italy
Solas *Scotland* U.K. *see* **Sollas**
162 N5 **Solberg** Sweden
165 K4 **Solberga** Sweden
219 N3 **Solca** Romania
199 H3 **Solčany** Slovakia
201 K7 **Solčava** Slovenia
213 J2 **Solda** Italy
213 J2 **Solda** *r.* Italy
274 C5 **Soldado Bartra** Peru
158 H6 **Şoldăneşti** Moldova
151 E1 **Soldato-Aleksandrovskoye** Rus. Fed.
151 E2 **Soldatskaya** Rus. Fed.
200 D6 **Sölden** Austria
208 I2 **Soldeu** Andorra
257 □Q1 **Soldier Pond** *ME* U.S.A.
245 J3 **Soldotna** *AK* U.S.A.
196 G2 **Solec Kujawski** Pol.
197 I5 **Solec-Zdrój** Pol.
285 G2 **Soledad** Arg.
270 F8 **Soledad** Col.
264 K5 **Soledad** *CA* U.S.A.
275 F2 **Soledad** Venez.
269 K6 **Soledad de Doblado** Mex.
268 G3 **Soledad Diez Gutierrez** Mex.
274 D6 **Soledade** *Amazonas* Brazil
279 B9 **Soledade** *Rio Grande do Sul* Brazil
159 R5 **Soledar** Ukr.
214 C9 **Soleminis** *Sardegna* Italy
163 K6 **Sølen** *mt.* Norway
157 H7 **Solenoye** Rus. Fed.
214 C4 **Solenzara** *Corse* France
228 D3 **Solenzo** Burkina
213 L5 **Solesino** Italy
178 F3 **Solesmes** *Nord-Pas-de-Calais* France
181 K6 **Solesmes** *Pays de la Loire* France
217 O3 **Soleto** Italy
185 C7 **Solférino** France
213 J5 **Solferino** Italy
162 L3 **Solfjellsjøen** Norway
165 L4 **Solgen** *l.* Sweden
156 H3 **Solginskiy** Rus. Fed.
149 J4 **Solhan** Turkey
213 J6 **Soliera** Italy
156 H4 **Soligalich** Rus. Fed.
184 G4 **Solignac** France
212 H6 **Solignano** Italy
213 M4 **Soligo** *r.* Italy
Soligorsk Belarus *see* **Salihorsk**
173 I3 **Solihull** *West Midlands, England* U.K.
156 L4 **Solikamsk** Rus. Fed.
142 F2 **Sol'-Iletsk** Rus. Fed.
211 C7 **Soliman** Tunisia
267 P8 **Solimón, Punta** *pt* Mex.
197 K6 **Solina** Pol.
191 D8 **Solingen** Ger.
197 K6 **Solinka** *r.* Pol.
197 K6 **Solińskie, Jezioro** *l.* Pol.
268 G6 **Solís** Mex.
268 G5 **Solís, Presa** *resr* Mex.
274 C4 **Solita** Col.
274 D2 **Solita** Venez.
103 B12 **Solitary, Mount** *South I.* N.Z.
208 H5 **Solivella** Spain
Sol-Karmala Rus. Fed. *see* **Severnoye**
201 J5 **Solker Tauern** *pass* Austria
201 I5 **Sölktäler** *nature res.* Austria
200 F4 **Söll** Austria
214 B4 **Sollacaro** *Corse* France
151 J4 **Şollar** Azer.
168 B7 **Sollas** *Western Isles, Scotland* U.K.
164 I3 **Sollebrunn** Sweden
162 N5 **Sollefteå** Sweden
201 N4 **Sollenau** Austria
165 N2 **Sollentuna** Sweden
209 K8 **Sóller** Spain
163 M6 **Sollerön** Sweden
190 L1 **Søllested** Denmark
193 G7 **Söllichau** Ger.
183 I10 **Solliès-Pont** France
183 I10 **Solliès-Ville** France
191 H7 **Solling** *hills* Ger.
191 K6 **Söllingen** Ger.
191 K8 **Sollstedt** Ger.
191 F9 **Solms** Ger.
161 T5 **Solnechnogorsk** Rus. Fed.
122 C1 **Solnechnyy** *Amurskaya Oblast'* Rus. Fed.
122 J3 **Solnechnyy** *Khabarovskiy Kray* Rus. Fed.
Solnechnyy *Khabarovskiy Kray* Rus. Fed. *see* **Gornyy**
198 F1 **Solnice** Czech Rep.
159 P2 **Solntsevo** Rus. Fed.
115 C5 **Solo** *r.* Indon.
117 J8 **Solo** *r.* Indon.
158 F4 **Solobkivtsi** Ukr.
157 I6 **Solodniki** Rus. Fed.
215 N6 **Solofra** Italy
178 D8 **Sologne** *reg.* France
116 D5 **Solok** *Sumatera* Indon.
151 A2 **Solokhaul** Rus. Fed.
158 D3 **Solokiya** *r.* Ukr.
267 N10 **Sololá** Guat.
151 F1 **Solomenskoye** Rus. Fed.
185 F8 **Solomiac** France
158 F4 **Solomna** Ukr.
244 F2 **Solomon** *AK* U.S.A.
265 W9 **Solomon** *AZ* U.S.A.
260 G6 **Solomon** *r. KS* U.S.A.
260 F6 **Solomon, North Fork** *r. KS* U.S.A.
260 F6 **Solomon, South Fork** *r. KS* U.S.A.
100 □6 **Solomon Islands** *country* S. Pacific Ocean
113 L8 **Solomon Sea** P.N.G./Solomon Is
129 Q3 **Solon** *Nei Mongol* China
257 □P4 **Solon** *ME* U.S.A.
159 N6 **Solona** *r.* Ukr.
159 P5 **Solona** *r.* Ukr.
159 N5 **Solone** Ukr.
143 U2 **Soloneshnoye** Rus. Fed.
250 C3 **Solon Springs** *WI* U.S.A.
216 H1 **Solopaca** Italy
115 C8 **Solor** *i.* Indon.
115 C8 **Solor, Kepulauan** *is* Indon.
205 P6 **Solorio, Sierra de** *mts* Spain
205 M2 **Solórzano** Spain
205 K7 **Solosancho** Spain
161 W7 **Solotcha** Rus. Fed.
212 D1 **Solothurn** Switz.
212 D1 **Solothurn** *canton* Switz.
158 D5 **Solotvyn** Ukr.
156 F2 **Solovetskiy** Rus. Fed.
156 F2 **Solovetskiye Ostrova** *is* Rus. Fed.
156 I4 **Solovetskoye** Rus. Fed.
158 I3 **Soloviyivka** Ukr.
161 X8 **Solovoye** Rus. Fed.
197 M4 **Solovychi** Ukr.
161 P7 **Solov'yevo** Rus. Fed.
129 N2 **Solov'yevsk** Mongolia
122 D1 **Solov'yevsk** Rus. Fed.
179 H3 **Solre-le-Château** France
208 I4 **Solsona** Spain
199 I5 **Solt** Hungary
210 F4 **Šolta** *i.* Croatia
144 G7 **Solṭānābād** Iran
144 H3 **Solṭānābād** *Khorāsān* Iran
144 H4 **Solṭānābād** Iran
144 D4 **Solṭānābād** *Tehrān* Iran
145 J5 **Soltān-e Bakva** Afgh.
144 D7 **Soltānī, Khowr-e** *b.* Iran
149 N5 **Solṭānīyeh** Iran
151 I6 **Soltanlı** Azer.
144 H3 **Solṭān Meydān** Iran
144 B5 **Solṭanqolī** Iran
190 I5 **Soltau** Ger.
190 K5 **Soltendieck** Ger.
199 I5 **Solti-síkság** *reg.* Hungary
143 V1 **Solton** Rus. Fed.
161 N3 **Sol'tsy** Rus. Fed.
199 I5 **Soltszentimre** Hungary
Soltüstik Qazaqstan Oblysy *admin. div.* Kazakh. *see* **Severnyy Kazakhstan**
199 I5 **Soltvadkert** Hungary
218 J9 **Solunska Glava** *mt.* Macedonia
182 F4 **Solutré-Pouilly** France
172 B4 **Solva** *Pembrokeshire, Wales* U.K.
172 B4 **Solva** *r. Wales* U.K.
264 L7 **Solvang** *CA* U.S.A.
257 I5 **Solvay** *NY* U.S.A.
165 K5 **Sölvesborg** Sweden
156 I3 **Sol'vychegodsk** Rus. Fed.
168 I13 **Solway Firth** *est. Scotland* U.K.
231 E8 **Solwezi** Zambia
124 R9 **Sōma** Japan
221 I3 **Soma** Turkey
235 F3 **Somabhula** Zimbabwe
Somabula Zimbabwe *see* **Somabhula**
178 F3 **Somain** France
232 E4 **Somalia** *country* Africa
289 H5 **Somali Basin** *sea feature* Indian Ocean
232 E2 **Somaliland** *physical area* Somalia
Somali Republic *country* Africa *see* **Somalia**
233 C7 **Somanga** Tanz.
229 E5 **Somanya** Ghana
Sombak'e *N.W.T.* Can. *see* **Yellowknife**
117 L3 **Sombang, Gunung** *mt.* Indon.
199 H5 **Somberek** Hungary
182 F2 **Sombernon** France
231 D7 **Sombo** Angola
218 H5 **Sombor** *Vojvodina* Serbia
191 H10 **Somborn** Ger.
187 G7 **Sombreffe** Belgium
268 D2 **Sombrerete** Mex.
271 L4 **Sombrero** *i.* Anguilla
283 C9 **Sombrero** Chile
137 M9 **Sombrero Channel** *Andaman & Nicobar Is* India
219 L3 **Şomcuţa Mare** Romania
138 D7 **Somdari** *Rajasthan* India
231 E6 **Somene** Dem. Rep. Congo
258 E5 **Somerdale** *NJ* U.S.A.
187 I6 **Someren** Neth.
163 Q6 **Somero** Fin.
255 □1 **Somerset** Bermuda
172 G5 **Somerset** *admin. div. England* U.K.
254 E7 **Somerset** *KY* U.S.A.
257 N7 **Somerset** *MA* U.S.A.
250 J7 **Somerset** *MI* U.S.A.
256 C9 **Somerset** *OH* U.S.A.
256 F9 **Somerset** *PA* U.S.A.
258 F3 **Somerset County** *county NJ* U.S.A.
237 J8 **Somerset East** S. Africa
255 □1 **Somerset Island** Bermuda
243 I2 **Somerset Island** *Nunavut* Can.
236 C10 **Somerset West** S. Africa
173 M3 **Somersham** *Cambridgeshire, England* U.K.
258 F6 **Somers Point** *NJ* U.S.A.
257 □O5 **Somersworth** *NH* U.S.A.
172 G5 **Somerton** *Somerset, England* U.K.
265 R9 **Somerton** *AZ* U.S.A.
160 J2 **Sõmeru** Estonia
258 F3 **Somerville** *NJ* U.S.A.
261 K8 **Somerville** *TN* U.S.A.
261 G10 **Somerville Reservoir** *TX* U.S.A.
219 K3 **Someş** *r.* Romania
102 □ **Somes, Point** *Chatham Is* S. Pacific Ocean
219 L4 **Someşan, Podişul** *plat.* Romania
219 L4 **Someşu Cald** *r.* Romania
219 L3 **Someşul Mare** *r.* Romania
219 K3 **Someşului, Câmpia** *plain* Romania
219 L3 **Someşu Mic** *r.* Romania
257 □Q4 **Somesville** *ME* U.S.A.
144 B5 **Someydeh** Iran
197 J3 **Somianka** Pol.
204 H2 **Somiedo, Parque Natural de** *nature res.* Spain
204 H2 **Somiedo, Puerto de** *pass* Spain
161 R2 **Somino** Rus. Fed.
196 F1 **Sominy** Pol.
237 Q4 **Somkele** S. Africa
198 G4 **Somlóvásárhely** Hungary
213 J5 **Sommacampagna** Italy
212 F4 **Somma Lombardo** Italy
212 D6 **Sommariva del Bosco** Italy
162 O2 **Sommarøy** Norway
216 F9 **Sommatino** *Sicilia* Italy
178 D4 **Somme** *dept* France
182 D3 **Somme** *r.* France
187 A8 **Somme** *r.* France
178 C3 **Somme, Baie de la** *b.* France
178 E4 **Somme, Canal de la** France
179 J5 **Sommedieue** France
187 H8 **Somme-Leuze** Belgium
165 K3 **Sommen** Sweden
165 L3 **Sommen** *l.* Sweden
178 I5 **Sommepy-Tahure** France
193 D8 **Sömmerda** Ger.
192 H5 **Sommerfeld** Ger.
193 D6 **Sommersdorf** Ger.
178 H5 **Somme-Soude** *r.* France
178 H6 **Sommesous** France
178 I5 **Somme-Suippe** France
249 G2 **Sommet, Lac du** *l. Que.* Can.
179 I7 **Sommevoire** France
183 E9 **Sommières** France
184 E3 **Sommières-du-Clain** France
138 C9 **Somnath** *Gujarat* India
198 G5 **Somogy** *county* Hungary
199 G5 **Somogyapáti** Hungary
199 G5 **Somogyi-dombság** *reg.* Hungary
199 G5 **Somogyjád** Hungary
199 G5 **Somogysárd** Hungary
198 G5 **Somogyszentpál** Hungary
198 G5 **Somogyszob** Hungary
250 F8 **Somonauk** *IL* U.S.A.
196 G1 **Somonino** Pol.
208 E3 **Somontano** *reg.* Spain
207 O6 **Somontín** Spain
205 M6 **Somosierra** *mts* Spain
205 M6 **Somosierra, Puerto de** *pass* Spain
101 □7 **Somosomo** *Taveuni* Fiji
266 □P11 **Somotillo** Nic.
266 □P11 **Somoto** Nic.
161 S9 **Somovo** *Orlovskaya Oblast'* Rus. Fed.
161 T8 **Somovo** *Tul'skaya Oblast'* Rus. Fed.
159 S2 **Somovo** *Voronezhskaya Oblast'* Rus. Fed.
137 I3 **Sompeta** *Andhra Prad.* India
196 G3 **Sompolno** Pol.
208 D2 **Somport, Col du** *pass* France/Spain
173 L6 **Sompting** *West Sussex, England* U.K.
178 H6 **Sompuis** France
219 J6 **Šomrda** *h.* Serbia
283 D6 **Somuncurá, Mesa Volcánica de** *plat.* Arg.
118 D1 **Somutu** Myanmar
136 D6 **Somvarpet** *Karnataka* India
187 F8 **Somzée** Belgium
139 J7 **Son** *r.* India
186 H5 **Son** Neth.
164 G2 **Son** Norway
213 J5 **Sona** Italy
266 □S14 **Soná** Panama
197 I3 **Sona** *r.* Pol.
Sonag *Qinghai* China *see* **Zêkog**
139 N6 **Sonai** *r.* India
139 N7 **Sonai** *r.* India
122 I3 **Sonakh** Rus. Fed.
138 F9 **Sonala** *Mahar.* India
139 K8 **Sonamukhi** *W. Bengal* India
139 I9 **Sonapur** *Orissa* India
139 O6 **Sonari** *Assam* India
122 G7 **Sŏnbong** N. Korea
212 C1 **Sonceboz** Switz.
123 D9 **Sŏnch'ŏn** N. Korea
205 M3 **Soncillo** Spain
212 H5 **Soncino** Italy
212 I3 **Sondalo** Italy
156 F3 **Sondaly** Rus. Fed.
164 F3 **Søndeled** Norway
164 E7 **Sønderå** *r.* Denmark
164 F7 **Sønderborg** Denmark
164 E6 **Sønder Omme** Denmark
191 K8 **Sondershausen** Ger.
164 G6 **Søndersø** Denmark
192 E1 **Sondersø** *l.* Denmark
164 F5 **Sønderup** Denmark
Søndre Strømfjord Greenland *see* **Kangerlussuaq**
Søndre Strømfjord *inlet* Greenland *see* **Kangerlussuaq**
Søndre Upernavik Greenland *see* **Upernavik Kujalleq**
212 H3 **Sondrio** Italy
212 H3 **Sondrio** *prov.* Italy
209 E8 **Soneja** Spain
136 E3 **Sonepet** *Mahar.* India
258 B2 **Sonestown** *PA* U.S.A.
230 A4 **Song** Gabon
117 J3 **Song** *Sarawak* Malaysia
229 I4 **Song** Nigeria
115 E4 **Songa** *Maluku* Indon.
138 C9 **Songadh** *Gujarat* India
Songbai *Hubei* China *see* **Shennongjia**
131 J3 **Songbu** *Hubei* China
119 I8 **Sông Câu** Vietnam
Songcheng *Fujian* China *see* **Xiapu**
118 G4 **Sông Đa, Hô** *resr* Vietnam
233 B7 **Songea** Tanz.
178 C4 **Songeons** France
123 E8 **Sŏnggan** N. Korea
122 E7 **Songhua Hu** *resr* China
122 D6 **Songhuajiang** *Jilin* China
122 D6 **Songhua Jiang** *r.* China
122 H5 **Songhua Jiang** *r.* China
Songjiachuan *Shaanxi* China *see* **Wubu**
122 F7 **Songjiang** *Jilin* China
131 M3 **Songjiang** *Shanghai* China
123 E7 **Songjianghe** *Jilin* China
Sŏngjin N. Korea *see* **Kimch'aek**
130 F4 **Songkan** *Guizhou* China
119 E11 **Songkhla** Thai.
118 G6 **Songkhram, Mae Nam** *r.* Thai.
143 P7 **Songköl** *l.* Kyrg.
129 P6 **Song Ling** *mts* China
118 D3 **Songlong** Myanmar
Songmai *Sichuan* China *see* **Dêrong**
130 D6 **Songming** *Yunnan* China
123 E10 **Sŏngnam** S. Korea
123 D9 **Songnim** N. Korea
123 E10 **Songni-san National Park** S. Korea
231 B6 **Songo** Angola
235 G2 **Songo** Moz.
231 B6 **Songololo** *Bas-Congo* Dem. Rep. Congo
Songololo *Bas-Congo* Dem. Rep. Congo *see* **Mbanza-Ngungu**
130 D2 **Songpan** *Sichuan* China
139 M7 **Songsak** *Meghalaya* India
123 E12 **Sŏngsan** S. Korea
128 H8 **Songshan** *Gansu* China
Songshan *Guizhou* China *see* **Ziyun**
129 M9 **Song Shan** *mt. Henan* China
130 G4 **Songtao** *Guizhou* China
131 L5 **Songxi** *Fujian* China
129 M9 **Songxian** *Henan* China
Songyang *Yunnan* China *see* **Songming**
Songyuan *Fujian* China *see* **Songxi**
122 D6 **Songyuan** *Jilin* China
131 H3 **Songzi** *Hubei* China
119 I9 **Sơn Hai** Vietnam
139 I8 **Sonhat** *Chhattisgarh* India
126 D6 **Soni** Japan
Sonid Youqi *Nei Mongol* China *see* **Saihan Tal**
Sonid Zuoqi *Nei Mongol* China *see* **Mandalt**
204 F5 **Sonim** Port.
138 F5 **Sonipat** *Haryana* India
138 F8 **Sonkach** *Madh. Prad.* India
156 D3 **Sonkajärvi** Fin.
Sonkël', Ozero *l.* Kyrg. *see* **Songköl**
161 U4 **Sonkovo** Rus. Fed.
118 F4 **Sơn La** Vietnam
145 L9 **Sonmiani** Pak.
145 L9 **Sonmiani Bay** Pak.
200 G5 **Sonnblick** *mt.* Austria
193 D10 **Sonneberg** Ger.
191 K9 **Sonneborn** Ger.
193 D10 **Sonnefeld** Ger.
200 F5 **Sonnenjoch** *mt.* Austria
193 I7 **Sonnewalde** Ger.
173 K4 **Sonning Common** *Oxfordshire, England* U.K.
215 K5 **Sonnino** Italy
200 A5 **Sonntag** Austria
201 K4 **Sonntagberg** Austria
281 E2 **Sono** *r.* Brazil
278 C4 **Sono** *r.* Brazil
126 B5 **Sonobe** Japan
265 T10 **Sonoita** Mex.
263 H11 **Sonoita** *watercourse* Mex.
265 V10 **Sonoita** *AZ* U.S.A.
264 J3 **Sonoma** *CA* U.S.A.
265 J3 **Sonoma, Lake** *resr CA* U.S.A.
237 L1 **Sonop** S. Africa
266 D3 **Sonora** *r.* Mex.
266 D3 **Sonora** *state* Mex.
264 L4 **Sonora** *CA* U.S.A.
261 E10 **Sonora** *TX* U.S.A.
265 T9 **Sonoran Desert** *AZ* U.S.A.
265 T9 **Sonoran Desert National Monument** *nat. park AZ* U.S.A.
264 M3 **Sonora Peak** *CA* U.S.A.
144 B4 **Sonqor** Iran
205 M9 **Sonseca** Spain
209 L8 **Son Servera** Spain
209 L8 **Son Servera, Badia de** *b.* Spain
197 I3 **Sońsk** Pol.
274 C3 **Sonsón** Col.
267 O11 **Sonsonate** El Salvador
113 H5 **Sonsorol Islands** Palau
236 G3 **Sonstraal** S. Africa
118 G4 **Sơn Tây** Vietnam
195 I5 **Sontheim** Ger.
195 I4 **Sontheim an der Brenz** Ger.
195 I6 **Sonthofen** Ger.
191 I8 **Sontra** Ger.
237 M7 **Sonwabile** S. Africa
159 O9 **Sonyachna Dolyna** Ukr.
238 □3c **Sóo** *Lanzarote* Canary Is
Soochow *Jiangsu* China *see* **Suzhou**
160 I2 **Soodla** *r.* Estonia
244 E3 **Sooghmeghat** *AK* U.S.A.
232 E2 **Sool** *admin. div.* Somalia
Soomaaliya *country* Africa *see* **Somalia**
194 D2 **Soonwald** *mts* Ger.
185 B8 **Soorts-Hossegor** France
285 I2 **Sopas** *r.* Uru.
208 G3 **Sopeira** Spain
255 F9 **Soperton** *GA* U.S.A.
183 K9 **Sophia-Antipolis** France
115 F2 **Sopi, Tanjung** *pt Maluku* Indon.
218 J9 **Sopište** Macedonia
230 E2 **Sopo** *watercourse* Sudan
219 M8 **Sopot** Bulg.
165 O7 **Sopot** Pol.
218 I6 **Sopot** *Sopot* Serbia
130 B10 **Sop Prap** Thai.
198 F4 **Sopron** Hungary
198 F4 **Soproni** *park* Hungary
198 F4 **Sopronkövesd** Hungary
143 O7 **Sopu-Korgon** Kyrg.
138 E2 **Sopur** *Jammu and Kashmir* India
115 D3 **Soputan, Gunung** *vol.* Indon.
100 □4a **Sopweru** *i. Chuuk* Micronesia
100 □4a **Sopweru, Mochun** *sea chan. Chuuk* Micronesia
159 N2 **Sopych** Ukr.
185 I8 **Sor** *r.* France
206 C3 **Sôr** *r.* Port.
204 E1 **Sor** *r.* Spain
215 L4 **Sora** Italy
201 J7 **Sora** *r.* Slovenia
136 D5 **Sorab** *Karnataka* India
137 I3 **Sorada** *Orissa* India
213 L3 **Soraga** Italy
212 I6 **Soragna** Italy
163 N5 **Söråker** Sweden
123 F9 **Sŏrak-san** *mt.* S. Korea
123 F9 **Sorak-san National Park** S. Korea
214 H2 **Sorano** Italy
276 C4 **Sorapa** Peru
213 M3 **Sorapis** *mt.* Italy
162 L3 **Sørarnøy** Norway
276 C3 **Sorata** Bol.
229 I4 **Sorau** Nigeria
164 D3 **Sør-Audnedal** Norway
151 J5 **Şorbaçı** Azer.
207 O6 **Sorbas** Spain
205 N7 **Sorbe** *r.* Spain
168 H13 **Sorbie** *Dumfries and Galloway, Scotland* U.K.
212 I6 **Sorbolo** Italy
179 K6 **Sorcy-St-Martin** France
185 B8 **Sorde-l'Abbaye** France
185 C7 **Sore** France
185 J10 **Sorède** France
243 K5 **Sorel** *Que.* Can.
105 K10 **Sorell** *Tas.* Austr.
150 C7 **Soreq** *r.* Israel
212 H5 **Soresina** Italy
100 □6 **Sorezaru Point** *New Georgia Is* Solomon Is
185 I9 **Sorèze** France
165 M2 **Sörfjärden** *l.* Sweden
164 C1 **Sørfjorden** *inlet* Norway
191 K7 **Sorge** Ger.
190 H2 **Sorge** *r.* Ger.
184 F5 **Sorges** France
214 C7 **Sorgono** *Sardegna* Italy
183 F8 **Sorgues** France
183 B9 **Sorgues** *r.* France
150 C2 **Sorgun** *İçel* Turkey
148 G4 **Sorgun** *Yozgat* Turkey
150 C2 **Sorgun** *r.* Turkey
205 P5 **Soria** Spain
205 O5 **Soria** *prov.* Spain
285 H3 **Soriano** Uru.
285 I3 **Soriano** *dept* Uru.
217 K6 **Soriano Calabro** Italy
215 I3 **Soriano nel Cimino** Italy
204 I8 **Sorihuela** Spain
207 M4 **Sorihuela del Gaudalimar** Spain
116 C4 **Sorikmarapi** *vol.* Indon.
213 R6 **Sorinj, Rt** *pt* Croatia
168 D9 **Sorisdale** *Argyll and Bute, Scotland* U.K.
162 □ **Sørkapp Land** *reg.* Svalbard
152 C2 **Sørkappøya** *i.* Svalbard
144 F5 **Sorkh, Kūh-e** *mts* Iran
144 E4 **Sorkheh** Iran
150 A1 **Sorkun** Turkey
197 J2 **Sorkwity** Pol.
162 L3 **Sørland** Norway
162 L4 **Sørli** Norway
162 P5 **Sörmjöle** Sweden
178 I4 **Sormonne** *r.* France
170 I2 **Sorn** *East Ayrshire, Scotland* U.K.
184 I4 **Sornac** France
194 C7 **Sorne** *r.* Switz.
164 H6 **Sorø** Denmark
139 K9 **Soro** *Orissa* India
216 H8 **Soro, Monte** *mt. Sicilia* Italy
158 H5 **Soroca** Moldova
280 D5 **Sorocaba** Brazil
161 U8 **Sorochinka** Rus. Fed.
142 E1 **Sorochinsk** Rus. Fed.
Soroki Moldova *see* **Soroca**
143 U1 **Sorokino** *Altayskiy Kray* Ru
160 M4 **Sorokino** *Pskovskaya Obla* Rus. Fed.
Sorokino Ukr. *see* **Krasnod**
113 J5 **Sorol** *atoll* Micronesia
229 I4 **Sorombéo** Cameroon
115 G4 **Sorong** *Papua* Indon.
275 F4 **Sororoca** Brazil
160 L4 **Sorot'** *r.* Rus. Fed.
232 B4 **Soroti** Uganda
162 Q1 **Sørøya** *i.* Norway
162 Q1 **Sørøysundet** *sea chan.* Nor
Sorp Turkey *see* **Reşadıye**
191 E8 **Sorpe Staubecken** *resr* Ger
214 B7 **Sorradile** *Sardegna* Italy
206 B2 **Sorraia** *r.* Port.
162 O2 **Sørreisa** Norway
215 M6 **Sorrento** Italy
162 S5 **Sorsakoski** Fin.
162 T3 **Sorsatunturi** *hill* Fin.
162 N4 **Sorsele** Sweden
214 B6 **Sorso** *Sardegna* Italy
114 E5 **Sorsogon** *Luzon* Phil.
162 **Sør-Spitsbergen Nasjonal** *nat. park* Svalbard
151 J6 **Şorsulu** Azer.
208 H3 **Sort** Spain
163 U6 **Sortavala** Rus. Fed.
204 F8 **Sortelha** Port.
217 I9 **Sortino** *Sicilia* Italy
162 M2 **Sortland** Norway
156 J3 **Sortopolovskaya** Rus. Fed.
225 F5 **Sortot** Sudan
162 K5 **Sør-Trøndelag** *county* Nor
165 N2 **Sorunda** Sweden
190 I1 **Sörup** Ger.
162 P1 **Sørvær** Norway
162 L3 **Sørvågen** Norway
Sõrve väin *sea chan.* Estonia/Latvia *see* **Irbe Str**
207 M7 **Sorvilán** Spain
185 E7 **Sos** France
123 E10 **Sŏsan** S. Korea
165 J5 **Sösdala** Sweden
208 C2 **Sos del Rey Católico** Spair
160 L3 **Sosedno** Rus. Fed.
161 S7 **Sosenskiy** Rus. Fed.
208 F4 **Soses** Spain
237 M1 **Soshanguve** S. Africa
197 M4 **Soshychne** Ukr.
216 E8 **Sosio** *r. Sicilia* Italy
161 S9 **Soskovo** Rus. Fed.
199 H4 **Sóskút** Hungary
161 V9 **Sosna** *r.* Rus. Fed.
284 C4 **Sosneado** *mt.* Arg.
196 E2 **Sośnica** Pol.
196 F4 **Sośnie** Pol.
158 D3 **Sosnivka** *L'vivs'ka Oblast'*
159 M2 **Sosnivka** *Sums'ka Oblast'*
158 E3 **Sosnivka** *Ternopils'ka Obla*
196 F2 **Sośno** Pol.
156 K3 **Sosnogorsk** Rus. Fed.
158 G3 **Sosnove** Ukr.
143 R2 **Sosnovka** Kazakh.
143 O6 **Sosnovka** Kyrg.
156 I3 **Sosnovka** *Arkhangel'skaya* Rus. Fed.
156 H2 **Sosnovka** *Murmanskaya C* Rus. Fed.
157 H5 **Sosnovka** *Tambovskaya Ob* Rus. Fed.
161 U3 **Sosnovka** *Vologodskaya Ob* Rus. Fed.
161 N1 **Sosnovo** Rus. Fed.
157 I5 **Sosnovoborsk** Rus. Fed.
121 J1 **Sosnovo-Ozerskoye** Rus.
156 F2 **Sosnovyy** Rus. Fed.
Sosnovyy Bor Belarus *see* **Sasnovy Bor**
160 M2 **Sosnovyy Bor** Rus. Fed.
197 L4 **Sosnowica** Pol.
197 H5 **Sosnowiec** Pol.
Sosnowitz Pol. *see* **Sosnow**
197 L4 **Sosnówka** Pol.
160 K9 **Sosny** Belarus
159 L2 **Sosnytsya** Ukr.
183 K9 **Sospel** France
230 B4 **Sosso** C.A.R.
185 F10 **Sost** France
201 L7 **Šoštanj** Slovenia
124 □1 **Sosu** *Okinawa* Japan
156 M3 **Sos'va** *Khanty-Mansiyskiy Avtonomnyy Okrug* Rus. Fe
152 H4 **Sos'va** *Sverdlovskaya Oblas* Rus. Fed.
159 S7 **Sosyka** *r.* Rus. Fed.
229 F4 **Sota** *r.* Benin
133 L11 **Sotang** *Xizang* China
284 B2 **Sotaquí** Chile
269 M7 **Soteapan** Mex.
276 D2 **Sotério** *r.* Brazil
206 F5 **Sotiel Coronada** Spain
206 I4 **Sotillo** *r.* Spain
205 K8 **Sotillo de la Adrada** Spain
205 O5 **Sotillo del Rincón** Spain
162 T4 **Sotkamo** Fin.
284 E2 **Soto** Arg.
271 □10 **Soto** *Curaçao* Neth. Antille
204 H1 **Soto** Spain
204 I4 **Soto de la Vega** Spain
205 M7 **Soto del Real** Spain
204 I2 **Soto de Ribera** Spain
269 I2 **Soto la Marina** Mex.
269 J2 **Soto La Marina** *r.* Mex.
269 J1 **Soto La Marina, Barra** *spi*
208 D3 **Sotonera, Embalse de** *resr*
205 M4 **Sotopalacios** Spain
205 P8 **Sotos** Spain
204 H8 **Sotoserrano** Spain
229 F4 **Sotouboua** Togo
204 I3 **Soto y Amio** Spain
205 K2 **Sotres** Spain
205 L3 **Sotresgudo** Spain
204 I2 **Sotrondio** Spain
159 R3 **Sotsgorodok** Rus. Fed.
Sotsgorodok Ukr. *see* **Hirn**
214 C4 **Sotta** *Corse* France
165 L2 **Sottern** *l.* Sweden
178 B5 **Sotteville-lès-Rouen** Fran
216 H8 **Sotto di Troina** *r. Sicilia* Ita
213 M5 **Sottomarina** Italy
190 H4 **Sottrum** Ger.
163 P6 **Sottunga** *Åland* Fin.
207 N2 **Sotuélamos** Spain
267 O7 **Sotuta** Mex.
178 I5 **Souain-Perthes-lès-Hurlu** France
185 I8 **Soual** France
230 B4 **Souanké** Congo
183 C9 **Soubès** France
228 D5 **Soubré** Côte d'Ivoire
103 H8 **Soucis, Cape** *South I.* N.Z.
178 F7 **Soucy** France
220 F7 **Souda** *Kriti* Greece
106 F6 **Soudan** *N.T.* Austr.
180 I6 **Soudan** France
220 F7 **Soudas, Ormos** *b. Kriti* Gre
258 E4 **Souderton** *PA* U.S.A.
Soúdha *Kriti* Greece *see* **Sc**
230 B2 **Soudio** Chad
185 F9 **Soueich** France
185 G10 **Soueix** France
181 P7 **Souesmes** France
179 O6 **Soufflenheim** France
221 H1 **Soufli** Greece
271 □2 **Soufrière** *vol.* Guadeloupe
271 □3 **Soufrière** St Lucia
271 □3 **Soufrière** *vol.* St Vincent
271 □2 **Soufrière Hills** Montserra
228 B4 **Souguéta** Guinea
185 G6 **Souillac** France
239 □1b **Souillac** Mauritius
179 J5 **Souilly** France
227 G1 **Souk Ahras** Alg.
211 A7 **Souk Ahras** *prov.* Alg.
226 D2 **Souk el Arbaâ du Rharb** M
202 D5 **Souk el Had el Rharbia** M
202 C5 **Souk Khemis du Sahel** Mo
229 F3 **Soukoukoutane** Niger
151 B2 **Souk'su, Konts'khi** *pt* Geo
202 D5 **Souk Tleta Taghramet** Mo
202 D5 **Souk-Tnine-de-Sidi-el-Yar** Morocco
123 E10 **Sŏul** S. Korea

B3 Soulabali Senegal
B4 Soulac-sur-Mer France
I7 Soulaines-Dhuys France
G10 Soulan France
J10 Soulatgé France
C9 Soule reg. France
J5 Soulgé-sur-Ouette France
H8 Soullans France
I3 Soulles r. France
O6 Soultz-sous-Forêts France
I7 Soumagne Belgium
D9 Soumoulou France
J3 Sound Beach NY U.S.A.
I4 Sounding Creek r. Alta Can.
Sounfat well Mali see Tessoûnfat
A4 Souni Cyprus
F5 Souniou, Ethnikos Drymos nat. park Greece
H2 Sountel well Niger
E7 Souppes-sur-Loing France
C8 Souprosse France
D5 Soûr Lebanon
J4 Sourdeval France
K3 Sourdough AK U.S.A.
C2 Soure Brazil
C8 Soure Port.
K5 Souris Man. Can.
I4 Souris P.E.I. Can.
L5 Souris r. Sask. Can.
Souriya country Asia see Syria
I10 Sournia France
F7 Souro Pires Port.
C2 Souroumelli well Maur.
D3 Sourpi Greece
C7 Sours France
E5 Sourzac France
C3 Sous, Oued watercourse Morocco
F3 Sousa Brazil
C6 Sousa r. Port.
Sousa Lara Angola see Bocoio
I6 Sousceyrac France
I5 Sousel Brazil
D3 Sousel Port.
D8 Souselas Port.
Sous le Vent reg. Réunion
Sous le Vent, Îles is Arch. de la Société Fr. Polynesia
H2 Sousse Tunisia
B8 Soustons France
B8 Soustons, Étang de l. France
C7 Sout r. S. Africa
E4 Sout watercourse S. Africa
B7 South r. MD U.S.A.
South Africa country Africa see South Africa, Republic of
E6 South Africa, Republic of country Africa
D2 South Alligator r. N.T. Austr.
Southam Warwickshire, England U.K.
South Amboy NJ U.S.A.
South America
Southampton Ont. Can.
Southampton Southampton, England U.K.
Southampton admin. div. England U.K.
M8 Southampton NY U.S.A.
Southampton, Cape Nunavut Can.
Southampton Island Nunavut Can.
Southampton Water est. England U.K.
M7 South Andaman i. Andaman & Nicobar Is India
H11 South Anna r. VA U.S.A.
South Anston South Yorkshire, England U.K.
Southard NJ U.S.A.
South Aulatsivik Island Nfld and Lab. Can.
South Australia state Austr.
South Australian Basin sea feature Indian Ocean
Southaven MS U.S.A.
South Ayrshire admin. div. Scotland U.K.
South Baldy mt. NM U.S.A.
South Bank Redcar and Cleveland, England U.K.
South Bass Island OH U.S.A.
South Bay FL U.S.A.
South Baymouth Ont. Can.
South Bend IN U.S.A.
South Bend WA U.S.A.
South Benfleet Essex, England U.K.
South Bight sea chan. Bahamas
South Bluff pt Acklins I. Bahamas
Southborough Kent, England U.K.
South Boston VA U.S.A.
South Brent Devon, England U.K.
Southbridge South I. N.Z.
Southbridge MA U.S.A.
South Brook Nfld and Lab. Can.
Southbroom S. Africa
South Burlington VT U.S.A.
Southburn South I. N.Z.
Southbury CT U.S.A.
South Canaan PA U.S.A.
South Carolina state U.S.A.
South Cave East Riding of Yorkshire, England U.K.
South Cerney Gloucestershire, England U.K.
South Chard Somerset, England U.K.
South Charleston OH U.S.A.
South Charleston WV U.S.A.
South China Karst tourist site China
South China Sea N. Pacific Ocean
South Coast Town Qld Austr. see Gold Coast
South Cousin Islet i. Inner Islands Seychelles see Cousine
South Dakota state U.S.A.
Southdean Scottish Borders, Scotland U.K.
South Deerfield MA U.S.A.
South Dennis NJ U.S.A.
South Dorset Downs hills England U.K.
South Downs hills England U.K.
South East Bay Ascension S. Atlantic Ocean
South East Cape Tas. Austr.
Southeast Cape AK U.S.A.
South East Forests National Park N.S.W. Austr.
Southeast Indian Ridge sea feature Indian Ocean
South-East Island Inner Islands Seychelles see Suète, Île du
South East Isles W.A. Austr.
Southeast Pacific Basin sea feature S. Pacific Ocean
Southeast Point Gt Inagua Bahamas
South East Reef S. Pacific Ocean
South East Rock i. Lord Howe I. Austr.
South Egg Harbor NJ U.S.A.
Southend Sask. Can.
Southend Argyll and Bute, Scotland U.K.
Southend admin. div. England U.K.
Southend-on-Sea Southend, England U.K.
South Entrance sea chan. Mauritius
Southern admin. dist. Botswana
Southern admin. reg. Malawi
Southern prov. Sierra Leone
Southern prov. Zambia
Southern Aegean admin. reg. Greece see Notio Aigaio
Southern Alps mts South I. N.Z.
Southern Central Aboriginal Reserve W.A. Austr.
Southern Cook Islands Cook Is
Southern Cross W.A. Austr.
Southern Darfur state Sudan
247 L3 Southern Indian Lake Man. Can.
230 F2 Southern Kordofan state Sudan
99 I3 Southern Lau Group is Fiji
231 D9 Southern Lueti watercourse Angola/Zambia
230 F3 Southern National Park Sudan
286 R3 Southern Ocean OCEAN World
255 H8 Southern Pines NC U.S.A.
Southern Rhodesia country Africa see Zimbabwe
273 G7 Southern Thule is S. Sandwich Is
168 G12 Southern Uplands hills Scotland U.K.
Southern Urals mts Rus. Fed. see Yuzhnyy Ural
263 K8 Southern Ute Indian Reservation res. CO U.S.A.
173 M2 Southery Norfolk, England U.K.
168 K9 South Esk r. Angus, Scotland U.K.
108 I5 South Esk Tableland reg. W.A. Austr.
247 J5 Southey Sask. Can.
237 L7 Southeyville S. Africa
260 J6 South Fabius r. MO U.S.A.
256 B6 Southfield MI U.S.A.
259 G2 Southfields NY U.S.A.
290 G7 South Fiji Basin sea feature S. Pacific Ocean
173 O5 South Foreland pt England U.K.
264 I1 South Fork CA U.S.A.
263 K8 South Fork CO U.S.A.
256 G8 South Fork PA U.S.A.
250 I4 South Fox Island MI U.S.A.
271 □2 South Friar's Bay St Kitts and Nevis
246 E5 Southgate r. B.C. Can.
173 L4 Southgate Greater London, England U.K.
287 H1 South Geomagnetic Pole (2009) Antarctica
273 G7 South Georgia terr. S. Atlantic Ocean
258 D1 South Gibson PA U.S.A.
250 E1 South Gillies Ont. Can.
259 J1 South Glastonbury CT U.S.A.
172 H4 South Gloucestershire admin. div. England U.K.
260 H6 South Grand r. MO U.S.A.
173 K6 South Harting West Sussex, England U.K.
139 M8 South Hatia Island Bangl.
250 H7 South Haven MI U.S.A.
173 K6 South Hayling Hampshire, England U.K.
102 I3 South Head North I. N.Z.
102 I3 South Head hd North I. N.Z.
247 L2 South Henik Lake Nunavut Can.
257 L4 South Hero VT U.S.A.
171 O4 South Hetton Durham, England U.K.
238 □2c South Hill hill Tristan da Cunha S. Atlantic Ocean
256 G12 South Hill VA U.S.A.
290 E3 South Honshu Ridge sea feature N. Pacific Ocean
232 C4 South Horr Kenya
247 L3 South Indian Lake Man. Can.
259 J1 Southington CT U.S.A.
108 □2 South Island Cocos Is
136 C7 South Island India
103 G11 South Island N.Z.
232 C4 South Island National Park Kenya
114 B7 South Islet rf Phil.
247 M5 South Junction Man. Can.
South Kazakhstan Oblast admin. div. Kazakh. see Yuzhnyy Kazakhstan
171 Q7 South Kelsey Lincolnshire, England U.K.
171 O6 South Kirkby West Yorkshire, England U.K.
233 C5 South Kitui National Reserve nature res. Kenya
139 J8 South Koel r. Jharkhand India
123 F11 South Korea country Asia
264 L3 South Lake Tahoe CA U.S.A.
168 I11 South Lanarkshire admin. div. Scotland U.K.
103 B12 Southland admin. reg. South I. N.Z.
173 N3 South Lopham Norfolk, England U.K.
260 F5 South Loup r. NE U.S.A.
233 A8 South Luangwa National Park Zambia
259 K2 South Lyme CT U.S.A.
245 N3 South Macmillan r. Y.T. Can.
287 J2 South Magnetic Pole (2009) Antarctica
135 □1 South Male Atoll Maldives
173 N4 Southminster Essex, England U.K.
172 E5 South Molton Devon, England U.K.
247 K4 South Moose Lake Man. Can.
258 A5 South Mountains hills PA U.S.A.
108 C6 South Muiron Island W.A. Austr.
246 D1 South Nahanni r. N.W.T. Can.
244 H4 South Naknek AK U.S.A.
270 □ South Negril Point Jamaica
168 □N2 South Nesting Bay Scotland U.K.
257 J6 South New Berlin NY U.S.A.
173 M4 South Ockendon Thurrock, England U.K.
259 K2 Southold NY U.S.A.
288 G10 South Orkney Islands S. Atlantic Ocean
South Ossetia reg. Georgia see Samkhret' Oset'i
173 L4 South Oxhey Hertfordshire, England U.K.
259 I3 South Oyster Bay NY U.S.A.
257 □O4 South Paris ME U.S.A.
109 B9 South Passage W.A. Austr.
100 □3a South Passage Kwajalein Marshall Is
255 G11 South Patrick Shores FL U.S.A.
172 G6 South Petherton Somerset, England U.K.
259 G3 South Plainfield NJ U.S.A.
260 E5 South Platte r. CO U.S.A.
270 F2 South Point Long I. Bahamas
271 □4 South Point Barbados
108 □1 South Point Christmas I.
238 □2a South Point Ascension S. Atlantic Ocean
286 T1 South Pole Antarctica
248 D3 South Porcupine Ont. Can.
107 N9 Southport Qld Austr.
105 K10 Southport Tas. Austr.
171 K6 Southport Merseyside, England U.K.
259 I2 Southport CT U.S.A.
255 H9 Southport NC U.S.A.
251 R7 Southport NY U.S.A.
257 □O5 South Portland ME U.S.A.
168 J11 South Queensferry Edinburgh, Scotland U.K.
104 □3 South Reef S. Pacific Ocean
251 O4 South River Ont. Can.
South Rona i. Highland, Scotland U.K. see Rona
168 K5 South Ronaldsay i. Scotland U.K.
257 M5 South Royalton VT U.S.A.
250 A5 South St Paul MN U.S.A.
288 H9 South Sandwich Islands S. Atlantic Ocean
288 H9 South Sandwich Trench sea feature S. Atlantic Ocean
264 J4 South San Francisco CA U.S.A.
247 J4 South Saskatchewan r. Alta/Sask. Can.
247 L3 South Seal r. Man. Can.
286 U2 South Shetland Islands Antarctica
288 E10 South Shetland Trough sea feature S. Atlantic Ocean
171 O3 South Shields Tyne and Wear, England U.K.
South Sinai governorate Egypt see Janūb Sīnā'
260 I5 South Skunk r. IA U.S.A.
290 F6 South Solomon Trench sea feature Pacific Ocean
169 D6 South Sound sea chan. Ireland
243 K3 South Spicer Island Nunavut Can.
258 E2 South Sterling PA U.S.A.
258 D3 South Tamaqua PA U.S.A.
102 I6 South Taranaki Bight b. North I. N.Z.
289 N8 South Tasman Rise sea feature Southern Ocean
265 U2 South Tent mt. UT U.S.A.
259 G5 South Toms River NJ U.S.A.
138 I7 South Tons r. India
265 V9 South Tucson AZ U.S.A.
232 B4 South Turkana Nature Reserve Kenya
248 E2 South Twin Island Nunavut Can.
249 K3 South Twin Lake Nfld and Lab. Can.
171 M4 South Tyne r. England U.K.
South Tyrol prov. Italy see Bolzano
168 B8 South Uist i. Scotland U.K.
262 C5 South Umpqua r. OR U.S.A.
168 J5 South Walls pen. Scotland U.K.
173 L5 Southwater West Sussex, England U.K.
171 P7 Southwell Nottinghamshire, England U.K.
106 G4 South Wellesley Islands Qld Austr.
South-West Africa country Africa see Namibia
255 □2 South West Bay New Prov. Bahamas
238 □2a South West Bay Ascension S. Atlantic Ocean
105 K10 South West Cape Tas. Austr.
103 B14 South West Cape Stewart I. N.Z.
244 E3 Southwest Cape AK U.S.A.
107 N6 South West Cay rf Coral Sea Is Terr. Austr.
105 J9 Southwest Conservation Area nature res. Tas. Austr.
107 M1 South West Entrance sea chan. P.N.G.
257 □Q4 Southwest Harbor ME U.S.A.
289 G7 Southwest Indian Ridge sea feature Indian Ocean
107 L4 South West Island Coral Sea Is Terr. Austr.
105 K10 South West National Park Tas. Austr.
291 I8 Southwest Pacific Basin sea feature S. Pacific Ocean
South-West Peru Ridge sea feature S. Pacific Ocean see Nazca Ridge
270 □ South West Point Jamaica
238 □2b South West Point St Helena
270 D5 Southwest Rock i. Jamaica
105 N4 South West Rocks N.S.W. Austr.
250 I8 South Whitley IN U.S.A.
261 F9 South Wichita r. TX U.S.A.
172 H5 Southwick Wiltshire, England U.K.
256 C11 South Williamson KY U.S.A.
251 R8 South Williamsport PA U.S.A.
257 □O5 South Windham ME U.S.A.
173 P3 Southwold Suffolk, England U.K.
173 N4 South Woodham Ferrers Essex, England U.K.
107 M9 Southwood National Park Qld Austr.
173 M2 South Wootton Norfolk, England U.K.
171 O7 South Yorkshire admin. div. England U.K.
256 C9 South Zanesville OH U.S.A.
204 G8 Souto Guarda Port.
204 D9 Souto Santarém Port.
204 E3 Souto Spain
204 E8 Souto da Casa Port.
237 K4 Soutpan S. Africa
235 F4 Soutpansberg mts S. Africa
226 B5 Souttouf, Adrar mts Western Sahara
182 C3 Souvigny France
164 C1 Sovarnuten mt. Norway
219 N4 Sovata Romania
219 O4 Soveja Romania
284 E4 Soven Arg.
217 L6 Soverato Italy
245 J3 Sovereign Mountain AK U.S.A.
214 C3 Soveria Corse France
217 K5 Soveria Mannelli Italy
143 N7 Sovet Kyrg.
145 M2 Sovet Tajik.
Sovetabad Uzbek. see Xonobod
Sovetashen Armenia see Zangakatun
160 E6 Sovetsk Kaliningradskaya Oblast' Rus. Fed.
156 J4 Sovetsk Kirovskaya Oblast' Rus. Fed.
161 U8 Sovetsk Tul'skaya Oblast' Rus. Fed.
151 C1 Sovetskaya Krasnodarskiy Kray Rus. Fed.
151 F1 Sovetskaya Stavropol'skiy Kray Rus. Fed.
122 L4 Sovetskaya Gavan' Rus. Fed.
Sovetskiy Kyrg. see Sovet
152 H3 Sovetskiy Khanty-Mansiyskiy Avtonomnyy Okrug Rus. Fed.
160 L1 Sovetskiy Leningradskaya Oblast' Rus. Fed.
156 N2 Sovetskiy Respublika Komi Rus. Fed.
156 J4 Sovetskiy Respublika Mariy El Rus. Fed.
Sovetskiy Tajik. see Sovet
159 S3 Sovetskoye Belgorodskaya Oblast' Rus. Fed.
Sovetskoye Chechenskaya Respublika Rus. Fed. see Shatoy
Sovetskoye Kabardino-Balkarskaya Respublika Rus. Fed. see Kashkhatau
Sovetskoye Respublika Dagestan Rus. Fed. see Khebda
142 B2 Sovetskoye Saratovskaya Oblast' Rus. Fed.
Sovetskoye Stavropol'skiy Kray Rus. Fed. see Zelenokumsk
210 F4 Soviči Bos.-Herz.
213 K9 Sovicille Italy
156 H2 Sovpol'ye Rus. Fed.
159 N8 Sovyets'kyy Ukr.
234 E4 Sowa Botswana
130 B4 Sowa Sichuan China
127 K3 Sōwa Japan
234 E4 Sowa Pan salt pan Botswana
171 O5 Sowerby North Yorkshire, England U.K.
171 N6 Sowerby Bridge West Yorkshire, England U.K.
237 L2 Soweto S. Africa
196 C2 Sowno Zachodniopomorskie Pol.
196 E1 Sowno Zachodniopomorskie Pol.
145 N2 So'x Tajik.
Sōya-kaikyō str. Japan/Rus. Fed. see La Pérouse Strait
267 M9 Soyaló Mex.
124 S1 Sōya-misaki c. Japan
156 H2 Soyana r. Rus. Fed.
123 E9 Soyang-ho l. S. Korea
184 E4 Soyaux France
124 S1 Sōya-wan b. Japan
182 I2 Soye France
195 M5 Soyen Ger.
Soylan Armenia see Vayk'
156 J2 Soyma r. Rus. Fed.
231 B6 Soyo Angola
183 F7 Soyons France
266 E3 Soyopa Mex.
151 G5 Soyuqbulaq Azer.
Sozaq Kazakh. see Suzak
161 N9 Sozh r. Europe
156 K4 Sozimskiy Rus. Fed.
219 P8 Sozopol Bulg.
187 I8 Spa Belgium
286 T2 Spaatz Island Antarctica
194 D2 Spabrücken Ger.
217 I7 Spadafora Sicilia Italy
190 E5 Spahnharrenstätte Ger.
194 F5 Spaichingen Ger.
202 E2 Spain country Europe
Spalato Croatia see Split
Spalatum Croatia see Split
104 G5 Spalding S.A. Austr.
173 L2 Spalding Lincolnshire, England U.K.
198 C2 Spálené Poříčí Czech Rep.
195 J3 Spalt Ger.
191 I8 Spangenberg Ger.
172 E5 Span Head hill England U.K.
249 K4 Spaniard's Bay Nfld and Lab. Can.
248 D4 Spanish Ont. Can.
248 D4 Spanish r. Ont. Can.
265 U1 Spanish Fork UT U.S.A.
Spanish Guinea country Africa see Equatorial Guinea
Spanish Netherlands country Europe see Belgium
271 □2 Spanish Point pt Antigua and Barbuda
255 □1 Spanish Point pt Bermuda
167 C5 Spanish Point Ireland
Spanish Sahara terr. Africa see Western Sahara
270 □ Spanish Town Jamaica
270 E1 Spanish Wells Eleuthera Bahamas
192 I3 Spantekow Ger.
216 D7 Sparagio, Monte mt. Italy
215 M5 Sparanise Italy
214 C5 Spargi, Isola i. Sardegna Italy
264 M2 Sparks NV U.S.A.
256 C6 Sparlingville MI U.S.A.
258 F2 Sparrow Bush NY U.S.A.
Sparta Greece see Sparti
217 J7 Spartà Sicilia Italy
255 F9 Sparta GA U.S.A.
250 I6 Sparta MI U.S.A.
256 D12 Sparta NC U.S.A.
258 F2 Sparta NJ U.S.A.
255 E8 Sparta TN U.S.A.
250 D6 Sparta WI U.S.A.
255 G8 Spartanburg SC U.S.A.
256 F7 Spartansburg PA U.S.A.
202 D5 Spartel, Cap c. Morocco
220 D5 Sparti Greece
214 B10 Spartivento, Capo c. Sardegna Italy
217 K8 Spartivento, Capo c. Italy
246 H5 Sparwood B.C. Can.
161 R7 Spas-Demensk Rus. Fed.
159 O5 Spas'ke Ukr.
161 X6 Spas-Klepiki Rus. Fed.
159 P5 Spas'ko-Mykhaylivka Ukr.
159 M5 Spasove Ukr.
161 S6 Spass Rus. Fed.
157 H5 Spassk Rus. Fed.
156 F3 Spasskaya Guba Rus. Fed.
161 O3 Spasskaya Polist' Rus. Fed.
122 H6 Spassk-Dal'niy Rus. Fed.
143 M1 Spasskoye Kazakh.
161 T8 Spasskoye-Lutovinovo Rus. Fed.
161 X7 Spassk-Ryazanskiy Rus. Fed.
161 U5 Spas-Ugol Rus. Fed.
220 E7 Spatha, Akrotirio pt Kriti Greece
220 D6 Spathi, Akrotirio pt Kythira Greece
246 D3 Spatsizi Plateau Wilderness Provincial Park B.C. Can.
191 E10 Spay Ger.
168 G9 Spean Bridge Highland, Scotland U.K.
260 D3 Spearfish SD U.S.A.
261 E7 Spearman TX U.S.A.
217 O4 Specchia Italy
257 K5 Speculator NY U.S.A.
173 J5 Speen West Berkshire, England U.K.
212 G1 Speer mt. Switz.
247 J4 Speers Sask. Can.
238 □2b Speery Island St Helena
194 B2 Speicher Ger.
201 H5 Speicher Sameralm l. Austria
195 L2 Speichersdorf Ger.
271 □4 Speightstown Barbados
201 L5 Speikkogel mt. Austria
233 B5 Speke Gulf Tanz.
191 D6 Spelle Ger.
215 J2 Spello Italy
168 E10 Spelve, Loch inlet Scotland U.K.
Spence Bay Nunavut Can. see Taloyoak
260 H4 Spencer IA U.S.A.
262 H4 Spencer ID U.S.A.
254 D6 Spencer IN U.S.A.
257 N6 Spencer MA U.S.A.
260 F4 Spencer NE U.S.A.
251 R7 Spencer NY U.S.A.
256 E12 Spencer VA U.S.A.
256 D10 Spencer WV U.S.A.
104 F6 Spencer, Cape S.A. Austr.
245 M4 Spencer, Cape AK U.S.A.
244 F2 Spencer, Point pt AK U.S.A.
234 B5 Spencer Bay Namibia
104 F6 Spencer Gulf est. S.A. Austr.
257 □O3 Spencer Lake ME U.S.A.
106 B3 Spencer Range hills N.T. Austr.
106 D2 Spencer Range hills N.T. Austr.
246 F5 Spences Bridge B.C. Can.
191 F6 Spenge Ger.
171 N4 Spennymoor Durham, England U.K.
103 G9 Spenser Mountains South I. N.Z.
220 D4 Spercheios r. Greece
193 H6 Sperenberg Ger.
164 G1 Sperillen l. Norway
Sperkhiós r. Greece see Spercheios
216 G8 Sperlinga Sicilia Italy
215 K5 Sperlonga Italy
219 M3 Spermezeu Romania
214 A10 Sperone, Capo c. Sardegna Italy
234 B5 Sperrgebiet National Park Namibia
169 H3 Sperrin Mountains hills Northern Ireland U.K.
256 G10 Sperryville VA U.S.A.
191 H11 Spessart reg. Ger.
258 C6 Spesutie Island MD U.S.A.
Spétsai i. Greece see Spetses
220 E5 Spetses Greece
220 E5 Spetses i. Greece
168 J7 Spey r. Scotland U.K.
168 J7 Spey Bay Moray, Scotland U.K.
194 E3 Speyer Ger.
271 □5 Speyside Trin. and Tob.
145 L7 Spezand Pak.
180 D5 Spézet France
215 Q8 Spezzano Albanese Italy
Spice Islands Indon. see Maluku
197 K4 Spiczyn Pol.
Spiddal Ireland see An Spidéal
195 O4 Spiegelau Ger.
190 E3 Spiekeroog Ger.
190 E3 Spiekeroog i. Ger.
201 K5 Spielberg bei Knittelfeld Austria
201 M6 Spielfeld Austria
194 C3 Spiesen-Elversberg Ger.
212 D2 Spiez Switz.
212 E6 Spigno Monferrato Italy
215 L5 Spigno Saturnia Italy
186 K2 Spijk Neth.
186 F5 Spijkenisse Neth.
245 L2 Spike Mountain AK U.S.A.
151 A6 Spikör Geçidi pass Turkey
213 K6 Spilamberto Italy
221 I4 Spil Dağı Milli Parkı nat. park Turkey
220 F7 Spili Kriti Greece
213 N3 Spilimbergo Italy
217 J6 Spilinga Italy
171 R7 Spilsby Lincolnshire, England U.K.
215 Q6 Spinazzola Italy
145 L6 Spīn Bōldak Afgh.
179 K5 Spincourt France
213 M5 Spinea Italy
215 L2 Spinetoli Italy
109 J9 Spinifex Aboriginal Reserve W.A. Austr.
258 E4 Spinnerstown PA U.S.A.
217 □ Spinola, Ix-Xatt ta' b. Malta
215 P7 Spinoso Italy
145 M7 Spintangi Pak.
199 L4 Spinuş Romania
145 N5 Spinwam Pak.
237 N4 Spioenkop Dam Nature Reserve S. Africa
260 H4 Spirit Lake IA U.S.A.
262 F2 Spirit Lake ID U.S.A.
247 J4 Spiritwood Sask. Can.
161 R4 Spirovo Rus. Fed.
198 G6 Špišić-Bukovica Croatia
200 B6 Spiss Austria
199 J2 Spišská Belá Slovakia
199 J3 Spišská Nová Ves Slovakia
199 J2 Spišská Stará Ves Slovakia
199 J3 Spišské Podhradie Slovakia
199 J3 Spišské Vlachy Slovakia
199 J3 Spišský Hrad Slovakia
199 J2 Spišský Štvrtok Slovakia
151 F5 Spitak Armenia
201 J4 Spital am Pyhrn Austria
201 M4 Spital am Semmering Austria
138 G4 Spiti r. India
108 E6 Spit Point W.A. Austr.
162 □ Spitsbergen i. Svalbard
236 G9 Spitskop mt. S. Africa
237 J7 Spitskopvlei S. Africa
160 K3 Spitsyno Rus. Fed.
201 H6 Spittal an der Drau Austria
168 J9 Spittal of Glenshee Perth and Kinross, Scotland U.K.
255 □1 Spittal Pond Bermuda
201 L3 Spitz Austria
Spitzbergen i. Svalbard see Spitsbergen
200 G6 Spitzkofel mt. Austria
212 G1 Spitzmeilen mt. Switz.
159 R4 Spivakivka Ukr.
173 O2 Spixworth Norfolk, England U.K.
164 E5 Spjald Denmark
210 F4 Split Croatia
247 L3 Split Lake Man. Can.
247 L3 Split Lake l. Man. Can.
212 G2 Spluga, Passo dello pass Italy/Switz.
212 G2 Splügen Switz.
158 H4 Spodakhy Ukr.
201 J7 Spodnja Idrija Slovenia
201 M6 Spodnje Hoče Slovenia
190 K1 Spodsbjerg Denmark
171 O6 Spofforth North Yorkshire, England U.K.
262 F3 Spokane WA U.S.A.
262 E3 Spokane r. WA U.S.A.
262 E3 Spokane Indian Reservation res. WA U.S.A.
151 C1 Spokoynaya Rus. Fed.
212 I2 Spöl r. Italy
Spoletium Italy see Spoleto
215 J2 Spoleto Italy
215 M3 Spoltore Italy
213 J2 Spondigna Italy
187 H8 Spontin Belgium
250 D9 Spoon r. IL U.S.A.
250 C4 Spooner WI U.S.A.
193 F8 Spora Ger.
192 E4 Spornitz Ger.
258 C4 Sporting Hill PA U.S.A.
270 D4 Spot Bay Cayman Is
212 E7 Spotorno Italy
259 G4 Spotswood NJ U.S.A.
256 H10 Spotsylvania VA U.S.A.
262 L4 Spotted Horse WY U.S.A.
251 L3 Spragge Ont. Can.
262 D5 Sprague r. OR U.S.A.
194 H4 Spraitbach Ger.
190 K5 Sprakensehl Ger.
246 F4 Spranger, Mount B.C. Can.
112 D5 Spratly Island S. China Sea
112 D4 Spratly Islands S. China Sea
262 E4 Spray OR U.S.A.
250 F4 Spread Eagle WI U.S.A.
210 G3 Spreča r. Bos.-Herz.
193 H5 Spree r. Ger.
193 I6 Spreenhagen Ger.
193 J7 Spreewald park Ger.
193 I6 Spreewald reg. Ger.
194 E7 Spreitenbach Switz.
193 J7 Spremberg Ger.
194 D2 Sprendlingen Ger.
213 M4 Spresiano Italy
212 H3 Spriana Italy
187 I7 Sprimont Belgium
261 H7 Spring r. MO U.S.A.
251 L4 Spring Bay Ont. Can.
236 B5 Springbok S. Africa
258 D4 Spring City PA U.S.A.
265 U2 Spring City UT U.S.A.
106 F5 Spring Creek r. N.T. Austr.
107 H8 Spring Creek watercourse Qld Austr.
260 E5 Spring Creek r. NE U.S.A.
249 K3 Springdale Nfld and Lab. Can.
261 H7 Springdale AR U.S.A.
191 I6 Springe Ger.
263 L8 Springer NM U.S.A.
265 W7 Springerville AZ U.S.A.
103 F10 Springfield South I. N.Z.
169 G4 Springfield Northern Ireland U.K.
261 D7 Springfield CO U.S.A.
255 G9 Springfield GA U.S.A.
262 H5 Springfield ID U.S.A.
260 K6 Springfield IL U.S.A.
254 E7 Springfield KY U.S.A.
257 M6 Springfield MA U.S.A.
257 □Q3 Springfield ME U.S.A.
260 H3 Springfield MN U.S.A.
261 I7 Springfield MO U.S.A.
256 B9 Springfield OH U.S.A.
262 C4 Springfield OR U.S.A.
258 E5 Springfield PA U.S.A.
255 D7 Springfield TN U.S.A.
257 M5 Springfield VT U.S.A.
256 G9 Springfield WV U.S.A.
237 J6 Springfontein S. Africa
275 G3 Spring Garden Guyana
259 G1 Spring Glen NY U.S.A.
258 B3 Spring Glen PA U.S.A.
265 V2 Spring Glen UT U.S.A.
250 D6 Spring Green WI U.S.A.
250 C6 Spring Grove MN U.S.A.
258 B5 Spring Grove PA U.S.A.
256 I11 Spring Grove VA U.S.A.
249 H4 Springhill N.S. Can.
255 F11 Spring Hill FL U.S.A.
168 I12 Springholm Dumfries and Galloway, Scotland U.K.
246 F5 Springhouse B.C. Can.
250 H6 Spring Lake MI U.S.A.
259 G4 Spring Lake Heights NJ U.S.A.
265 Q5 Spring Mountains NV U.S.A.
250 J7 Springport MI U.S.A.
237 M2 Springs S. Africa
259 K2 Springs NY U.S.A.
103 G9 Springs Junction South I. N.Z.
107 L8 Springsure Qld Austr.
258 E5 Springton Reservoir PA U.S.A.
107 H7 Springvale Qld Austr.
237 K8 Spring Valley S. Africa
264 P9 Spring Valley CA U.S.A.
250 B6 Spring Valley MN U.S.A.
259 G2 Spring Valley NY U.S.A.
250 B5 Spring Valley WI U.S.A.
260 F4 Springview NE U.S.A.
264 N5 Springville CA U.S.A.
256 G6 Springville NY U.S.A.
258 D1 Springville PA U.S.A.
265 U1 Springville UT U.S.A.
256 H6 Springwater NY U.S.A.
171 Q6 Sproatley East Riding of Yorkshire, England U.K.
191 D8 Sprockhövel Ger.
173 O2 Sprowston Norfolk, England U.K.
246 H4 Spruce Grove Alta Can.
256 F10 Spruce Knob mt. WV U.S.A.
265 X3 Spruce Mountain CO U.S.A.
265 R1 Spruce Mountain NV U.S.A.
258 F3 Spruce Run Reservoir NJ U.S.A.
186 G5 Sprundel Neth.
258 B5 Spry PA U.S.A.
217 L4 Spulico, Capo c. Italy
171 R6 Spurn Head England U.K.
244 I3 Spurr, Mount vol. AK U.S.A.
246 F5 Spuzzum B.C. Can.
197 J2 Spychowo Pol.
246 F5 Squamish B.C. Can.
246 F5 Squamish r. B.C. Can.
257 N5 Squam Lake NH U.S.A.
257 □Q2 Squapan Lake ME U.S.A.
213 K5 Squaranto r. Italy
257 □Q1 Square Lake ME U.S.A.
244 G5 Squaw Harbor AK U.S.A.
217 L6 Squillace Italy
217 L6 Squillace, Golfo di g. Italy
217 O3 Squinzano Italy
256 D11 Squire WV U.S.A.
109 I9 Squires, Mount hill W.A. Austr.
117 I8 Sragen Jawa Indon.
169 C6 Sraith Salach Ireland
Srbica Skenderaj Kosovo see Skenderaj
Srbija country Europe see Serbia
Srbinje Bos.-Herz. see Foča
Srbobran Bos.-Herz. see Donji Vakuf
218 H5 Srbobran Vojvodina Serbia
119 F9 Srê Âmběl Cambodia
210 G3 Srebrenica Bos.-Herz.
219 P6 Srebŭrna tourist site Bulg.
219 P8 Sredets Burgas Bulg.
Sredets Sofiya-Grad Bulg. see Sofiya
219 P8 Sredetska Reka r. Bulg.
153 Q4 Sredinnyy Khrebet mts Rus. Fed.
201 N7 Središče Slovenia
219 P7 Sredishte Bulg.
219 L8 Sredna Gora mts Bulg.
122 E3 Srednebelaya Rus. Fed.
153 Q3 Srednekolymsk Rus. Fed.
161 T7 Sredne-Russkaya Vozvyshennost' hills Rus. Fed.
153 M3 Sredne-Sibirskoye Ploskogor'ye plat. Rus. Fed.
162 U4 Sredneye Kuyto, Ozero l. Rus. Fed.
159 S2 Sredniy Ikorets Rus. Fed.
122 H3 Sredniy Urgal Rus. Fed.
213 Q5 Srednja Vrata, Kanal sea chan. Croatia
219 M8 Srednogorie Bulg.
157 I6 Srednyaya Akhtuba Rus. Fed.
119 H8 Sre Khtum Cambodia
196 F3 Śrem Pol.
218 H5 Srem reg. Serbia
218 H6 Sremska Mitrovica Vojvodina Serbia
119 G8 Srê Noy Cambodia
119 H8 Srêpok, Tônlé r. Cambodia
121 K1 Sretensk Rus. Fed.
117 I4 Sri Aman Sarawak Malaysia
159 L3 Sribne Ukr.
136 G6 Sriharikota Island India
136 F9 Sri Jayewardenepura Kotte Sri Lanka
137 I3 Srikakulam Andhra Prad. India
136 F6 Sri Kalahasti Andhra Prad. India
136 G9 Sri Lanka country Asia
138 E6 Sri Madhopur Rajasthan India
139 M7 Srimangal Bangl.
138 G4 Srinagar Uttaranchal India
138 E2 Srinagar Jammu and Kashmir India
136 D6 Sringeri Karnataka India
136 G9 Sri Pada mt. Sri Lanka
136 F7 Srirangam Tamil Nadu India
136 E6 Srirangapatna Karnataka India
136 F4 Srisailam Andhra Prad. India
136 E8 Srivaikuntam Tamil Nadu India
136 C3 Srivardhan Mahar. India
136 E8 Srivilliputtur Tamil Nadu India
210 F3 Srnetica mts Bos.-Herz.
210 G3 Srnice Bos.-Herz.
197 J1 Srockowo Pol.
196 E4 Środa Śląska Pol.
196 F3 Środa Wielkopolska Pol.
196 E3 Środkowy Kanał Obry canal Pol.
168 G8 Sròn a' Choire Ghairbh hill Scotland U.K.
143 U1 Srostki Rus. Fed.
218 I5 Srpska Crnja Vojvodina Serbia
Srpska Kostajnica Bos.-Herz. see Bosanska Kostajnica
Srpski Brod Bos.-Herz. see Bosanski Brod
218 I5 Srpski Itebej Vojvodina Serbia
137 H3 Srungavarapukota Andhra Prad. India
161 W9 Sselki Rus. Fed.
236 E3 Staansaam S. Africa
107 H4 Staaten r. Qld Austr.
107 I4 Staaten River National Park Qld Austr.
201 N2 Staatz Austria
162 R1 Stabbursdalen Nasjonalpark nat. park Norway
192 D2 Staberhuk c. Ger.
187 F6 Stabroek Belgium
Stabroek Guyana see Georgetown
198 C2 Stachy Czech Rep.
168 F6 Stac Pollaidh hill Scotland U.K.
Stac Polly hill Scotland U.K. see Stac Pollaidh
250 B4 Stacy MN U.S.A.
250 B6 Stacyville IA U.S.A.
190 H3 Stade Ger.
195 N6 Stadelhorn mt. Ger.
187 D7 Staden Belgium
190 K5 Stadensen Ger.
173 J4 Stadhampton Oxfordshire, England U.K.
Stadhlaigearraidh Scotland U.K. see Stilligarry
163 L6 Städjan-Nipfjällets naturreservat nature res. Sweden
201 I3 Stadl-Paura Austria
186 K3 Stadskanaal Neth.
186 K2 Stadskanaal canal Neth.
191 H9 Stadtallendorf Ger.
195 J5 Stadtbergen Ger.
191 H6 Stadthagen Ger.
193 D9 Stadtilm Ger.
191 C10 Stadtkyll Ger.
191 J10 Stadtlauringen Ger.
191 J9 Stadtlengsfeld Ger.
191 C7 Stadtlohn Ger.
191 I7 Stadtoldendorf Ger.
194 G2 Stadtprozelten Ger.
193 E9 Stadtroda Ger.
201 N5 Stadtschlaining Austria
193 E10 Stadtsteinach Ger.
190 H1 Stadum Ger.
212 F1 Stäfa Switz.
168 D10 Staffa i. Scotland U.K.
193 D10 Staffelberg hill Ger.
179 N8 Staffelfelden France
195 K6 Staffelsee l. Ger.
191 K10 Staffelstein Ger.
190 G5 Staffhorst Ger.
168 D7 Staffin Highland, Scotland U.K.
168 D7 Staffin Bay Scotland U.K.
213 O9 Staffolo Italy
212 G5 Staffora r. Italy
172 H2 Stafford Staffordshire, England U.K.
256 H10 Stafford VA U.S.A.
270 E1 Stafford Creek Andros Bahamas
172 H2 Staffordshire admin. div. England U.K.
237 N6 Stafford's Post S. Africa
257 M7 Stafford Springs CT U.S.A.
117 L6 Stagen Kalimantan Indon.
246 H2 Stagg Lake N.W.T. Can.
169 C4 Stags of Broad Haven is Ireland
195 P2 Šťáhlavy Czech Rep.
256 F8 Stahlstown PA U.S.A.
193 H6 Stahnsdorf Ger.
201 K7 Stahovica Slovenia
160 H4 Staicele Latvia
194 H5 Staig Ger.
215 O4 Staina r. Italy
201 J4 Stainach Austria
171 N4 Staindrop Durham, England U.K.
173 K5 Staines Surrey, England U.K.
171 M5 Stainforth North Yorkshire, England U.K.
171 O6 Stainforth South Yorkshire, England U.K.
171 Q5 Staintondale North Yorkshire, England U.K.
179 J6 Stainville France
201 L6 Stainz Austria
217 K8 Staìti Italy
199 L3 Stakčín Slovakia
168 G11 Stake, Hill of Scotland U.K.
159 R5 Stakhanov Ukr.
159 M8 Stakhanovka Ukr.
Stakhanovo Rus. Fed. see Zhukovskiy
172 H6 Stalbridge Dorset, England U.K.
212 D3 Stalden Switz.
190 L1 Ståldyb sea chan. Denmark
173 P2 Stalham Norfolk, England U.K.
Stalin Bulg. see Varna
Stalinabad Tajik. see Dushanbe
Stalingrad Rus. Fed. see Volgograd
Stalingradskaya Oblast' admin. div. Rus. Fed. see Volgogradskaya Oblast'
Staliniri Georgia see Ts'khinvali
Stalino Ukr. see Donets'k
Stalino Uzbek. see Shahrihon
Stalinogorsk Rus. Fed. see Novomoskovsk
Stalinogród Pol. see Katowice
Stalinsk Rus. Fed. see Novokuznetsk
200 H6 Stall Austria
165 N2 Stallarholmen Sweden
201 L5 Stallhofen Austria
171 M5 Stalling Busk North Yorkshire, England U.K.
195 N3 Stallwang Ger.
197 K5 Stalowa Wola Pol.
219 O5 Stâlpu Romania
237 L9 Stalwart Point S. Africa
171 M7 Stalybridge Greater Manchester, England U.K.
219 M8 Stamboliyski Bulg.
107 I6 Stamford Qld Austr.
173 L2 Stamford Lincolnshire, England U.K.
257 L7 Stamford CT U.S.A.
257 K6 Stamford NY U.S.A.
261 F9 Stamford TX U.S.A.
171 P6 Stamford Bridge East Riding of Yorkshire, England U.K.
171 N3 Stamfordham Northumberland, England U.K.
193 E10 Stammbach Ger.
195 K4 Stammham Ger.
Stampalia i. Greece see Astypalaia
234 C5 Stampriet Namibia
200 C5 Stams Austria
195 N3 Stamsried Ger.
162 L2 Stamsund Norway
169 J5 Stamullen Ireland
256 G10 Stanardsville VA U.S.A.
260 H5 Stanberry MO U.S.A.
286 W1 Stancomb-Wills Glacier Antarctica
246 H5 Standard Alta Can.
186 G5 Standdaarbuiten Neth.
237 N2 Standerton S. Africa
260 E3 Standing Rock Indian Reservation res. ND/SD U.S.A.
171 L6 Standish Greater Manchester, England U.K.
251 K6 Standish MI U.S.A.
173 M4 Standon Hertfordshire, England U.K.
170 J2 Stane North Lanarkshire, Scotland U.K.
219 M6 Stănești Romania
265 U9 Stanfield AZ U.S.A.
236 D10 Stanford S. Africa
254 E7 Stanford KY U.S.A.
262 I3 Stanford MT U.S.A.
173 M4 Stanford-le-Hope Thurrock, England U.K.
165 O4 Stånga Gotland Sweden
165 M4 Stångån r. Sweden
162 T1 Stáŋganasčohkka hill Norway
237 P5 Stanger S. Africa
162 J5 Stangvikfjorden inlet Norway
173 N2 Stanhoe Norfolk, England U.K.
171 M4 Stanhope Durham, England U.K.
258 F3 Stanhope NJ U.S.A.
219 Q4 Stănilești Romania
197 K4 Stanin Pol.
218 H5 Stanišić Vojvodina Serbia
Stanislav Ivano-Frankivs'ka Oblast' Ukr. see Ivano-Frankivs'k
159 L7 Stanislav Khersons'ka Oblast' Ukr.
197 M5 Stanislavchyk Ukr.
197 J3 Stanisławów Pol.
219 N3 Stânișoarei, Munții mts Romania
201 I8 Štanjel Slovenia
Stanke Dimitrov Bulg. see Dupnitsa
198 C2 Staňkov Czech Rep.
105 J9 Stanley Tas. Austr.
257 □S2 Stanley N.B. Can.
131 □J7 Stanley H.K. China
283 F8 Stanley Falkland Is
171 N4 Stanley Durham, England U.K.
168 J10 Stanley Perth and Kinross, Scotland U.K.
262 G4 Stanley ID U.S.A.
260 D1 Stanley ND U.S.A.
256 G10 Stanley VA U.S.A.
250 D5 Stanley WI U.S.A.
Stanley, Chutes waterfall Dem. Rep. Congo see Boyoma, Chutes
106 C7 Stanley, Mount hill N.T. Austr.
105 J9 Stanley, Mount hill Tas. Austr.
Stanley, Mount Dem. Rep. Congo/Uganda see Margherita Peak
Stanley Falls Dem. Rep. Congo see Boyoma, Chutes
136 E7 Stanley Reservoir India
Stanleyville Dem. Rep. Congo see Kisangani
235 F4 Stanmore Zimbabwe
Stann Creek Belize see Dangriga
171 N3 Stannington Northumberland, England U.K.
196 D2 Stanomino Pol.
220 C4 Stanos Greece
161 V9 Stanovaya Rus. Fed.
161 W8 Stanovaya Ryasa r. Rus. Fed.
193 G10 Stanovice, Vodní nádrž resr Czech Rep.
161 V9 Stanovoye Rus. Fed.
153 M4 Stanovoye Nagor'ye mts Rus. Fed.
153 N4 Stanovoy Khrebet mts Rus. Fed.
161 T9 Stanovoy Kolodez' Rus. Fed.
200 E5 Stans Austria
212 E2 Stans Switz.
104 F6 Stansbury S.A. Austr.
108 J6 Stansmore Range hills W.A. Austr.
173 M4 Stansted Mountfitchet Essex, England U.K.
105 M3 Stanthorpe Qld Austr.
173 N3 Stanton Suffolk, England U.K.
258 D5 Stanton DE U.S.A.
256 B11 Stanton KY U.S.A.
250 I6 Stanton MI U.S.A.
260 E2 Stanton ND U.S.A.
260 G5 Stanton NE U.S.A.
261 E9 Stanton TX U.S.A.
161 V9 Stantsiya Babarykino Rus. Fed.
161 U8 Stantsiya Skuratovo Rus. Fed.
Stantsiya-Yakkabag Uzbek. see Yakkabog'
173 N4 Stanway Essex, England U.K.
159 S5 Stanychno-Luhans'ke Ukr.
200 C5 Stanzach Austria
201 M5 Stanz im Mürztal Austria
190 K4 Stapel Ger.
191 K7 Stapelburg Ger.
190 J3 Stapelfeld Ger.
186 J3 Staphorst Neth.
173 J2 Stapleford Nottinghamshire, England U.K.
173 N5 Staplehurst Kent, England U.K.
260 H2 Staples MN U.S.A.
260 E5 Stapleton NE U.S.A.
197 I4 Stąporków Pol.
107 J5 Star r. Qld Austr.
161 R8 Star' Rus. Fed.
159 K3 Stara Basan' Ukr.
199 H2 Stará Bystrica Slovakia
158 G3 Stara Chortoryya Ukr.

197 J4 **Starachowice** Pol.
198 D2 **Stará Huť** Czech Rep.
159 M1 **Stara Huta** Ukr.
196 G2 **Stara Kiszewa** Pol.
197 K3 **Stara Kornica** Pol.
158 H3 **Stara Kotel'nya** Ukr.
196 E2 **Stara Łubianka** Pol.
199 J2 **Stará Ľubovňa** Slovakia
199 I6 **Stara Moravica** *Vojvodina* Serbia
213 R6 **Stara Novalja** Croatia
198 E1 **Stará Paka** Czech Rep.
218 I6 **Stara Pazova** *Vojvodina* Serbia
219 K7 **Stara Planina** *mts* Bulg./Yugo.
201 O8 **Stara Plošćica** Croatia
192 J5 **Stara Rudnica** Pol.
197 K6 **Stara Sil'** Ukr.
199 G3 **Stará Turá** Slovakia
158 G5 **Stara Ushytsya** Ukr.
201 M8 **Stara vas-Bizeljsko** Slovenia
158 D2 **Stara Vyzhivka** Ukr.
197 K5 **Stara Wieś** Pol.
Staraya Barda Rus. Fed. *see* **Krasnogorskoye**
159 T2 **Staraya Chigla** Rus. Fed.
159 S3 **Staraya Kalitva** Rus. Fed.
142 B1 **Staraya Kulatka** Rus. Fed.
142 B2 **Staraya Poltavka** Rus. Fed.
161 O4 **Staraya Russa** Rus. Fed.
161 O5 **Staraya Toropa** Rus. Fed.
157 J5 **Staraya Tumba** Rus. Fed.
219 N8 **Stara Zagora** Bulg.
158 E5 **Stara Zhadova** Ukr.
291 I6 **Starbuck Island** Kiribati
159 P6 **Starchenkove** Ukr.
219 O5 **Starchiojd** Romania
261 J9 **Star City** *AR* U.S.A.
250 H9 **Star City** *IN* U.S.A.
172 F6 **Starcross** *Devon, England* U.K.
159 M8 **Stare, Ozero** *l.* Ukr.
196 G5 **Stare Budkowice** Pol.
201 M1 **Stařeč** Czech Rep.
196 C2 **Stare Czarnowo** Pol.
196 D2 **Stare Dąbrowa** Pol.
197 K2 **Stare Dolistowo** Pol.
197 K3 **Stare Hołowczyce** Pol.
193 J9 **Staré Křečany** Czech Rep.
196 D3 **Stare Kurowo** Pol.
198 F1 **Staré Město** Czech Rep.
196 G3 **Stare Miasto** Pol.
197 H1 **Stare Pole** Pol.
158 D4 **Stare Selo** Ukr.
196 E4 **Stare Strącze** Pol.
Stargard in Pommern Pol. *see* **Stargard Szczeciński**
196 D2 **Stargard Szczeciński** Pol.
199 I3 **Star Huta** Slovakia
213 R6 **Starigrad** Croatia
218 E7 **Stari Grad Plain** *tourist site* Croatia
197 M4 **Stari Koshary** Ukr.
213 R4 **Stari Log** Slovenia
199 L2 **Starina, Vodná nádrž** *resr* Slovakia
158 J3 **Stari Petrivtsi** Ukr.
218 I7 **Stari Ras and Sopoćani** *tourist site* Serbia
213 Q4 **Stari Trg** Slovenia
161 R5 **Staritsa** Rus. Fed.
255 F11 **Starke** *FL* U.S.A.
193 F9 **Starkenberg** Ger.
256 F11 **Starkey** *VA* U.S.A.
102 □ **Star Keys** *is Chatham Is* S. Pacific Ocean
161 X6 **Starkovo** Rus. Fed.
261 K9 **Starkville** *MS* U.S.A.
257 J4 **Star Lake** *NY* U.S.A.
Starling Inlet *H.K.* China *see* **Sha Tau Kok Hoi**
195 K6 **Starnberg** Ger.
195 K6 **Starnberger See** *l.* Ger.
132 F1 **Staroaleyskoye** Rus. Fed.
Starobel'sk Ukr. *see* **Starobil's'k**
159 R6 **Starobesheve** Ukr.
159 R6 **Starobeshivs'ke Vodoskhovyshche** *resr* Ukr.
159 R4 **Starobil's'k** Ukr.
160 K9 **Starobin** Belarus
159 O6 **Starobohdanivka** Ukr.
159 R7 **Staroderevyankovskaya** Rus. Fed.
161 P9 **Starodub** Rus. Fed.
196 D2 **Starogard** Pol.
196 G2 **Starogard Gdański** Pol.
151 H2 **Starogladkovskaya** Rus. Fed.
Starokonstantinov Ukr. *see* **Starokostyantyniv**
158 G4 **Starokostyantyniv** Ukr.
158 I7 **Starokozache** Ukr.
161 W7 **Staroletovo** Rus. Fed.
159 S8 **Staroleushkovskaya** Rus. Fed.
157 G7 **Starominskaya** Rus. Fed.
159 P6 **Staromlynivka** Ukr.
219 J8 **Staro Nagoričane** *Staro Nagoričane* Macedonia
159 R8 **Staronizhestebliyevskaya** Rus. Fed.
219 P8 **Staro Oryakhovo** Bulg.
159 Q2 **Starooskol'skoye Vodokhranilishche** *resr* Rus. Fed.
219 M8 **Starosel** Bulg.
219 O7 **Staro Selo** Bulg.
161 X8 **Staroseslavino** Rus. Fed.
157 G7 **Staroshcherbinovskaya** Rus. Fed.
196 C4 **Starosiedle** Pol.
142 G1 **Starosubkhangulovo** Rus. Fed.
159 Q8 **Starotitarovskaya** Rus. Fed.
159 O4 **Starovirivka** Ukr.
197 H4 **Starowa Góra** Pol.
156 H4 **Staroye** Rus. Fed.
157 I5 **Staroye Drozhzhanoye** Rus. Fed.
161 Q6 **Staroye Istomino** Rus. Fed.
161 T5 **Staroye Melkovo** Rus. Fed.
161 T3 **Staroye Sandovo** Rus. Fed.
197 M3 **Staroye Syalo** *Brestskaya Voblasts'* Belarus
160 M6 **Staroye Syalo** *Vitsyebskaya Voblasts'* Belarus
157 H5 **Staroyur'yevo** Rus. Fed.
161 W7 **Starozhilovo** Rus. Fed.
197 H3 **Starożreby** Pol.
264 N1 **Star Peak** *NV* U.S.A.
172 E7 **Start Bay** *England* U.K.
171 N4 **Startforth** *Durham, England* U.K.
172 E7 **Start Point** *England* U.K.
Starve Island Kiribati *see* **Starbuck Island**
197 H2 **Stary Dzierzgoń** Pol.
199 L1 **Stary Dzików** Pol.
199 G2 **Starý Jičín** Czech Rep.
196 D4 **Stary Kisielin** Pol.
197 H3 **Stary Kobrzyniec** Pol.
197 K5 **Stary Majdan** Pol.
160 K7 **Starynki** Belarus
160 M6 **Starynovichy** Belarus
198 C2 **Starý Plzenec** Czech Rep.
197 I6 **Stary Sącz** Pol.
199 J2 **Starý Smokovec** Slovakia
197 J3 **Stary Szelków** Pol.
197 H2 **Stary Targ** Pol.
199 H3 **Starý Tekov** Slovakia
159 P3 **Starytsya** Ukr.
197 K4 **Stary Uścimów** Pol.
160 L8 **Staryya Darohi** Belarus
158 E2 **Staryy Chortoryys'k** Ukr.
161 X5 **Staryy Dvor** Rus. Fed.
Staryye Dorogi Belarus *see* **Staryya Darohi**
159 K1 **Staryye Yurkovichi** Rus. Fed.
142 H3 **Staryy Karabutak** Kazakh.
153 L2 **Staryy Kayak** Rus. Fed.
159 Q6 **Staryy Krym** *Donets'ka Oblast'* Ukr.
159 O8 **Staryy Krym** *Respublika Krym* Ukr.
151 E2 **Staryy Lesken** Rus. Fed.
152 I3 **Staryy Nadym** Rus. Fed.
158 E4 **Staryy Oleksynets'** Ukr.
157 G6 **Staryy Oskol** Rus. Fed.
158 G4 **Staryy Ostropil'** Ukr.
Staryy Salavan Rus. Fed. *see* **Novocheremshansk**
159 P3 **Staryy Saltiv** Ukr.
158 B4 **Staryy Sambir** Ukr.
Staryy Sambor Ukr. *see* **Staryy Sambir**
151 I2 **Staryy Terek** *r.* Rus. Fed.
196 G1 **Starzyno** Pol.
159 N4 **Stasi** Ukr.
193 E7 **Staßfurt** Ger.
197 J5 **Staszów** Pol.
256 H8 **State College** *PA* U.S.A.
261 K10 **State Line** *MS* U.S.A.
Staten Island Arg. *see* **Estados, Isla de los**
259 G3 **Staten Island** *NY* U.S.A.
255 F10 **Statenville** *GA* U.S.A.
255 G9 **Statesboro** *GA* U.S.A.
255 G8 **Statesville** *NC* U.S.A.
164 F2 **Stathelle** Norway
225 G4 **Station No. 6** Sudan
225 G5 **Station No. 10** Sudan
243 Q1 **Station Nord** Greenland
259 G3 **Statue of Liberty** *tourist site NJ* U.S.A.
201 L3 **Statzberg** *hill* Austria
201 M3 **Statzendorf** Austria
158 H6 **Stăuceni** Moldova
193 H8 **Stauchitz** Ger.
194 D6 **Staufen im Breisgau** Ger.
195 J5 **Staufersberg** *hill* Ger.
172 H4 **Staunton** *Gloucestershire, England* U.K.
256 F10 **Staunton** *VA* U.S.A.
193 I7 **Staupitz** Ger.
164 B3 **Stavanger** Norway
103 F10 **Staveley** *South I.* N.Z.
171 O7 **Staveley** *Derbyshire, England* U.K.
187 I8 **Stavelot** Belgium
192 G3 **Stavenhagen, Reuterstadt** Ger.
186 F5 **Stavenisse** Neth.
164 G3 **Stavern** Norway
219 M7 **Stavertsi** Bulg.
158 J6 **Stavkove** Ukr.
197 M4 **Stavky** Ukr.
199 L3 **Stavne** Ukr.
186 H3 **Stavoren** Neth.
221 G5 **Stavri, Akrotirio** *pt Naxos* Greece
220 C5 **Stavrodromi** Greece
157 H7 **Stavropol'** Rus. Fed.
143 L1 **Stavropolka** Kazakh.
Stavropol Kray *admin. div.* Rus. Fed. *see* **Stavropol'skiy Kray**
Stavropol'-na-Volge Rus. Fed. *see* **Tol'yatti**
157 H7 **Stavropol'skaya Vozvyshennost'** *hills* Rus. Fed.
151 E1 **Stavropol'skiy Kray** *admin. div.* Rus. Fed.
220 D2 **Stavros** *Kentriki Makedonia* Greece
220 E2 **Stavros** *Kentriki Makedonia* Greece
220 F7 **Stavros, Akrotirio** *pt Kriti* Greece
220 F1 **Stavroupoli** Greece
192 K5 **Staw** Pol.
161 O9 **Stawbun** Belarus
105 I7 **Stawell** *Vic.* Austr.
107 I6 **Stawell** *r. Qld* Austr.
197 I2 **Stawiguda** Pol.
197 K2 **Stawiski** Pol.
196 G4 **Stawiszyn** Pol.
189 I3 **Stawki, Park Krajobrazowy** Pol.
171 Q5 **Staxton** *North Yorkshire, England* U.K.
161 S8 **Stayki** Rus. Fed.
158 J3 **Stayky** Ukr.
251 N5 **Stayner** *Ont.* Can.
262 C4 **Stayton** *OR* U.S.A.
237 N4 **Steadville** S. Africa
264 M2 **Steamboat** *NV* U.S.A.
262 K6 **Steamboat Springs** *CO* U.S.A.
197 I2 **Stębark** Pol.
244 G3 **Stebbins** *AK* U.S.A.
159 K4 **Stebliv** Ukr.
197 L6 **Stebnyk** Ukr.
217 L6 **Steccato** Italy
198 D2 **Štěchovice** Czech Rep.
192 F5 **Stechow** Ger.
212 F1 **Steckborn** Switz.
190 E3 **Stedesdorf** Ger.
193 E8 **Stedten** Ger.
186 K2 **Stedum** Neth.
200 B5 **Steeg** Austria
236 I3 **Steekdorings** S. Africa
248 C3 **Steel** *r. Ont.* Can.
260 F2 **Steele** *ND* U.S.A.
245 L2 **Steele Creek** *AK* U.S.A.
286 T2 **Steele Island** Antarctica
104 □[1] **Steel's Point** Norfolk I.
258 B4 **Steelton** *PA* U.S.A.
260 J7 **Steelville** *MO* U.S.A.
246 G3 **Steen** *r. Alta* Can.
186 F5 **Steenbergen** Neth.
186 J4 **Steenderen** Neth.
237 O1 **Steenkampsberge** *mts* S. Africa
246 G3 **Steen River** *Alta* Can.
262 E5 **Steens Mountain** *OR* U.S.A.
Steenstrup Gletscher *glacier* Greenland *see* **Sermersuaq**
178 E2 **Steenvoorde** France
186 J3 **Steenwijk** Neth.
172 F5 **Steep Holm** *i. England* U.K.
171 R7 **Steeping** *r. England* U.K.
173 K4 **Steeple Claydon** *Buckinghamshire, England* U.K.
109 B9 **Steep Point** *W.A.* Austr.
245 K2 **Steese Highway** *AK* U.S.A.
171 N6 **Steeton** *West Yorkshire, England* U.K.
201 O8 **Štefanje** Croatia
198 G3 **Štefanov** Slovakia
220 D3 **Stefanovikeio** Greece
287 D2 **Stefansson Bay** Antarctica
243 H2 **Stefansson Island** *Nunavut* Can.
158 I7 **Ștefan Vodă** Moldova
219 P6 **Ștefan Vodă** Romania
212 D2 **Steffisburg** Switz.
161 V9 **Stegalovka** Rus. Fed.
195 J2 **Stegaurath** Ger.
164 I7 **Stege** Denmark
192 F1 **Stege Bugt** *b.* Denmark
193 E6 **Stegelitz** Ger.
192 F1 **Stege Nor** *lag.* Denmark
201 N5 **Stegersbach** Austria
186 J3 **Steggerda** Neth.
Stegi Swaziland *see* **Siteki**
197 H1 **Stegny** Pol.
161 O7 **Stegrimovo** Rus. Fed.
219 K4 **Ștei** Romania
201 L5 **Steiermark** *land* Austria
195 I2 **Steigerwald** *mts* Ger.
195 J2 **Steigerwald** *park* Ger.
237 P3 **Steilrand** S. Africa
190 H5 **Steimbke** Ger.
195 K3 **Stein** Ger.
187 I7 **Stein** Neth.
194 D6 **Stein** Switz.
194 E6 **Steina** *r.* Ger.
194 E5 **Steinach** *Baden-Württemberg* Ger.
195 N4 **Steinach** *Bayern* Ger.
193 D10 **Steinach** *Thüringen* Ger.
200 D5 **Steinach am Brenner** Austria
201 L3 **Steinakirchen am Forst** Austria
212 F1 **Stein am Rhein** Switz.
162 □D2 **Steinar** Iceland
190 G3 **Steinau** Ger.
191 H10 **Steinau an der Straße** Ger.
247 L5 **Steinbach** *Man.* Can.
193 H9 **Steinbach** Ger.
191 G10 **Steinbach (Taunus)** Ger.
201 I4 **Steinbach am Attersee** Austria
193 D10 **Steinbach am Wald** Ger.
201 J4 **Steinbach an der Steyr** Austria
191 K9 **Steinbach-Hallenberg, Kurort** Ger.
195 M3 **Steinberg** *Bayern* Ger.
190 I1 **Steinberg** *Schleswig-Holstein* Ger.
190 I1 **Steinbergkirche** Ger.
190 J3 **Steinburg** Ger.
201 J6 **Steindorf am Ossiacher See** Austria
194 D6 **Steinen** Ger.
200 G4 **Steinernes Meer** *mts* Austria
200 H6 **Steinfeld** Austria
194 H2 **Steinfeld** *Bayern* Ger.
194 E3 **Steinfeld** *Rheinland-Pfalz* Ger.
190 F5 **Steinfeld (Oldenburg)** Ger.
187 I9 **Steinfort** Lux.
191 D6 **Steinfurt** Ger.
195 J6 **Steingaden** Ger.
192 G2 **Steinhagen** *Mecklenburg-Vorpommern* Ger.
191 F6 **Steinhagen** *Nordrhein-Westfalen* Ger.
234 C4 **Steinhausen** Namibia
193 D10 **Steinheid** Ger.
191 H7 **Steinheim** Ger.
195 I4 **Steinheim am Albuch** Ger.
194 G4 **Steinheim an der Murr** Ger.
193 J6 **Steinhöfel** Ger.
195 M5 **Steinhöring** Ger.
190 J5 **Steinhorst** *Niedersachsen* Ger.
190 J3 **Steinhorst** *Schleswig-Holstein* Ger.
191 H6 **Steinhuder Meer** *l.* Ger.
190 H5 **Steinhuder Meer, Naturpark** *nature res.* Ger.
193 J8 **Steinigtwolmsdorf** Ger.
190 I3 **Steinkirchen** Ger.
162 K4 **Steinkjer** Norway
191 G10 **Steinkopf** *hill* Ger.
236 B5 **Steinkopf** S. Africa
193 K6 **Steinsdorf** Ger.
195 I3 **Steinsfeld** Ger.
164 B1 **Steinsland** Norway
194 D3 **Steinwenden** Ger.
193 D10 **Steinwiesen** Ger.
194 F6 **Steißlingen** Ger.
236 H7 **Stekaar** S. Africa
187 F6 **Stekene** Belgium
213 K8 **Stella** *r.* Italy
213 O4 **Stella** *r.* Italy
237 I2 **Stella** S. Africa
270 F2 **Stella Maris** *Long I.* Bahamas
239 □[1c] **Stella Matutina** Réunion
190 J4 **Stelle** Ger.
236 C9 **Stellenbosch** S. Africa
186 F5 **Stellendam** Neth.
245 L3 **Steller, Mount** *AK* U.S.A.
214 C2 **Stello, Monte** *mt. Corse* France
212 I3 **Stelvio, Parco Nazionale dello** *nat. park* Italy
212 I2 **Stelvio, Passo dello** *pass* Italy
190 I4 **Stemmen** Ger.
191 F6 **Stemshorn** Ger.
196 E5 **Stěnava** *r.* Pol.
179 J5 **Stenay** France
165 M4 **Stenbo** Sweden
192 E5 **Stendal** Ger.
160 F4 **Stende** Latvia
165 J4 **Stengårdshultasjön** *l.* Sweden
165 N2 **Stenhamra** Sweden
Stenhouse, Mount *hill H.K.* China *see* **Shan Tei Tong**
168 I10 **Stenhousemuir** *Falkirk, Scotland* U.K.
213 J3 **Stenico** Italy
164 I6 **Stenløse** Denmark
168 □M2 **Stenness** *Shetland, Scotland* U.K.
168 J4 **Stenness, Loch of** *l. Scotland* U.K.
220 D5 **Steno** Greece
195 O2 **Štěnovice** Czech Rep.
165 K6 **Stenshuvuds nationalpark** *nat. park* Sweden
164 I7 **Stensved** Denmark
168 K11 **Stenton** *East Lothian, Scotland* U.K.
162 N3 **Stenudden** Sweden
164 H3 **Stenungsund** Sweden
197 M5 **Stenyatyn** Ukr.
158 D3 **Stenzharychi** Ukr.
Steornabhagh *Western Isles, Scotland* U.K. *see* **Stornoway**
158 F2 **Stepan'** Ukr.
Stepanakert Azer. *see* **Xankändi**
151 F4 **Step'anavan** Armenia
159 L2 **Stepanivka** *Chernihivs'ka Oblast'* Ukr.
159 R6 **Stepanivka** *Donets'ka Oblast'* Ukr.
158 F3 **Stepanivka** *Khmel'nyts'ka Oblast'* Ukr.
159 N3 **Stepanivka** *Sums'ka Oblast'* Ukr.
159 O7 **Stepanivka Persha** Ukr.
161 V6 **Stepanshchino** Rus. Fed.
161 T5 **Stepantsevo** Rus. Fed.
169 J6 **Stepaside** Ireland
190 K3 **Stepenitz** *r.* Ger.
195 M6 **Stephanskirchen** Ger.
195 N4 **Stephansposching** Ger.
260 G1 **Stephen** *MN* U.S.A.
105 I5 **Stephens** *watercourse N.S.W.* Austr.
102 H7 **Stephens, Cape** *South I.* N.Z.
258 F3 **Stephensburg** *NJ* U.S.A.
256 G9 **Stephens City** *VA* U.S.A.
105 H4 **Stephens Creek** *N.S.W.* Austr.
245 O5 **Stephens Island** *B.C.* Can.
247 M3 **Stephens Lake** *Man.* Can.
250 G4 **Stephenson** *MI* U.S.A.
286 T2 **Stephenson, Mount** Antarctica
249 J3 **Stephenville** *Nfld and Lab.* Can.
261 F9 **Stephenville** *TX* U.S.A.
159 R8 **Stepnaya** Rus. Fed.
159 M1 **Stepne** Ukr.
259 I2 **Stepney** *CT* U.S.A.
196 C2 **Stepnica** Pol.
143 O1 **Stepnogorsk** Kazakh.
159 O6 **Stepnohirs'k** Ukr.
143 O6 **Stepnoy** Kyrg.
Stepnoy Rus. Fed. *see* **Elista**
142 I1 **Stepnoye** *Chelyabinskaya Oblast'* Rus. Fed.
142 B2 **Stepnoye** *Saratovskaya Oblast'* Rus. Fed.
151 F1 **Stepnoye** *Stavropol'skiy Kray* Rus. Fed.
143 N1 **Stepnyak** Kazakh.
218 I6 **Stepojevac** *Lazarevac* Serbia
100 □[2] **Steps Point** American Samoa
161 S5 **Stepurino** Rus. Fed.
197 K3 **Sterdyń-Osada** Pol.
220 E4 **Sterea Ellada** *admin. reg.* Greece
237 N4 **Sterkfontein Dam** *resr* S. Africa
237 L6 **Sterkspruit** S. Africa
237 K7 **Sterkstroom** S. Africa
197 J1 **Sterławki-Wielkie** Pol.
247 I1 **Sterlet Lake** *N.W.T.* Can.
142 F1 **Sterlibashevo** Rus. Fed.
236 F7 **Sterling** S. Africa
260 D5 **Sterling** *CO* U.S.A.
259 L1 **Sterling** *CT* U.S.A.
250 E8 **Sterling** *IL* U.S.A.
260 F6 **Sterling** *KS* U.S.A.
251 J5 **Sterling** *MI* U.S.A.
260 E2 **Sterling** *ND* U.S.A.
265 U2 **Sterling** *UT* U.S.A.
261 E10 **Sterling City** *TX* U.S.A.
251 K7 **Sterling Heights** *MI* U.S.A.
244 I3 **Sterling Landing** *AK* U.S.A.
142 F1 **Sterlitamak** Rus. Fed.
213 P5 **Sterna** Croatia
220 D5 **Sterna** Greece
192 E3 **Sternberg** Ger.
198 G2 **Šternberk** Czech Rep.
190 I1 **Sterup** Ger.
183 F10 **Stes Maries, Golfe des** *b.* France
183 E10 **Stes-Maries-de-la-Mer** France
196 E3 **Stęszew** Pol.
198 D1 **Štětí** Czech Rep.
159 L4 **Stetsivka** Ukr.
159 N2 **Stets'kivka** Ukr.
194 G5 **Stetten am kalten Markt** Ger.
Stettin Pol. *see* **Szczecin**
Stettiner Haff *b.* Ger. *see* **Oderhaff**
262 H1 **Stettler** *Alta* Can.
256 E8 **Steubenville** *OH* U.S.A.
201 J6 **Steuerberg** Austria
193 F7 **Steutz** Ger.
173 L4 **Stevenage** *Hertfordshire, England* U.K.
102 G7 **Stevens, Mount** *South I.* N.Z.
262 D4 **Stevenson** *WA* U.S.A.
104 E2 **Stevenson Creek** *watercourse S.A.* Austr.
244 I4 **Stevenson Entrance** *sea channel AK* U.S.A.
247 L4 **Stevenson Lake** *Man.* Can.
250 E5 **Stevens Point** *WI* U.S.A.
168 G11 **Stevenston** *North Ayrshire, Scotland* U.K.
245 J2 **Stevens Village** *AK* U.S.A.
258 C7 **Stevensville** *MD* U.S.A.
250 H7 **Stevensville** *MI* U.S.A.
251 R8 **Stevensville** *PA* U.S.A.
286 O1 **Steventon Island** Antarctica
164 I6 **Stevns Klint** *cliff* Denmark
107 I3 **Stewart** *r. Qld* Austr.
245 O5 **Stewart** *B.C.* Can.
245 M3 **Stewart** *r. Y.T.* Can.
264 U8 **Stewart** *NV* U.S.A.
106 E1 **Stewart, Cape** *N.T.* Austr.
283 C9 **Stewart, Isla** *i.* Chile
245 M3 **Stewart Crossing** *Y.T.* Can.
103 B14 **Stewart Island** N.Z.
103 B14 **Stewart Island** *nature res. Stewart I.* N.Z.
100 □[6] **Stewart Islands** Solomon Is
243 J3 **Stewart Lake** *Nunavut* Can.
168 G11 **Stewarton** *East Ayrshire, Scotland* U.K.
264 I3 **Stewarts Point** *CA* U.S.A.
169 I3 **Stewartstown** *Northern Ireland* U.K.
258 B5 **Stewartstown** *PA* U.S.A.
270 □ **Stewart Town** Jamaica
247 J5 **Stewart Valley** *Sask.* Can.
250 B6 **Stewartville** *MN* U.S.A.
249 I4 **Stewiacke** *N.S.* Can.
190 H5 **Steyerberg** Ger.
173 L6 **Steyning** *West Sussex, England* U.K.
237 L3 **Steynrus** S. Africa
237 J7 **Steynsburg** S. Africa
201 J3 **Steyr** Austria
201 J4 **Steyr** *r.* Austria
201 J3 **Steyregg** Austria
236 I9 **Steytlerville** S. Africa
197 J4 **Stężyca** *Lubelskie* Pol.
196 F1 **Stężyca** *Pomorskie* Pol.
213 L8 **Stia** Italy
199 H3 **Štiavnické vrchy** *mts* Slovakia
199 H3 **Štiavnické vrchy** *park* Slovakia
199 H2 **Štiavnik** Slovakia
172 D6 **Stibb Cross** *Devon, England* U.K.
171 M2 **Stichill** *Scottish Borders, Scotland* U.K.
171 R7 **Stickney** *Lincolnshire, England* U.K.
191 K7 **Stiege** Ger.
186 I2 **Stiens** Neth.
213 L6 **Stienta** Italy
Stif Alg. *see* **Sétif**
261 H8 **Stigler** *OK* U.S.A.
215 Q7 **Stigliano** Italy
217 K7 **Stignano** Italy
165 M3 **Stigtomta** Sweden
245 N4 **Stikine** *r. B.C.* Can.
245 O4 **Stikine Plateau** *B.C.* Can.
245 O4 **Stikine Ranges** *mts B.C.* Can.
246 D3 **Stikine River Provincial Park** *nature res. B.C.* Can.
164 G2 **Stikkvasskollen** *hill* Norway
236 F10 **Stilbaai** S. Africa
236 F10 **Stilbaai** *b.* S. Africa
250 F5 **Stiles** *WI* U.S.A.
237 K2 **Stilfontein** S. Africa
Stilís Greece *see* **Stylida**
168 B8 **Stilligarry** *Western Isles, Scotland* U.K.
171 O5 **Stillington** *North Yorkshire, England* U.K.
258 C6 **Still Pond** *MD* U.S.A.
250 B4 **Stillwater** *MN* U.S.A.
261 G7 **Stillwater** *OK* U.S.A.
262 J4 **Stillwater** *r. MT* U.S.A.
264 N2 **Stillwater National Wildlife Refuge** *nature res. NV* U.S.A.
264 N2 **Stillwater Range** *mts NV* U.S.A.
217 K7 **Stilo** Italy
217 L7 **Stilo, Punta** *pt* Italy
210 F4 **Štilt** *mt.* Bos.-Herz.
173 L3 **Stilton** *Cambridgeshire, England* U.K.
261 H8 **Stilwell** *OK* U.S.A.
Štimlje *Shtime* Kosovo *see* **Shtime**
195 I3 **Stimpfach** Ger.
287 E2 **Stinear, Mount** Antarctica
219 Q3 **Stînga Nistrului** *reg.* Moldova
261 E8 **Stinnett** *TX* U.S.A.
214 A6 **Stintino** *Sardegna* Italy
215 O7 **Stio** Italy
219 K9 **Štip** Macedonia
210 E3 **Stipanov Grič** *mt.* Croatia
179 M5 **Stiring-Wendel** France
106 D6 **Stirling** *N.T.* Austr.
251 Q5 **Stirling** *Ont.* Can.
168 I10 **Stirling** *Stirling, Scotland* U.K.
168 H10 **Stirling** *admin. div. Scotland* U.K.
259 G3 **Stirling** *NJ* U.S.A.
109 D11 **Stirling, Mount** *hill W.A.* Austr.
106 B4 **Stirling Creek** *r. N.T.* Austr.
104 F5 **Stirling North** *S.A.* Austr.
109 D13 **Stirling Range** *mts W.A.* Austr.
109 D13 **Stirling Range National Park** *W.A.* Austr.
212 I6 **Stirone** *r.* Italy
256 C11 **Stirrat** *WV* U.S.A.
172 B7 **Stithians** *Cornwall, England* U.K.
199 J3 **Štítnik** Slovakia
251 S4 **Stittsville** *Ont.* Can.
198 F2 **Štíty** Czech Rep.
213 Q6 **Štivan** Croatia
213 L4 **Stizzon** *r.* Italy
162 Q1 **Stjernøya** *i.* Norway
162 K5 **Stjørdalshalsen** Norway
168 G9 **Stob Choire Claurigh** *mt. Scotland* U.K.
168 G9 **Stob Ghabhar** *mt. Scotland* U.K.
197 J6 **Stobnica** *r.* Pol.
196 F5 **Stobrawa** *r.* Pol.
198 C1 **Stochov** Czech Rep.
173 M4 **Stock** *Essex, England* U.K.
179 M6 **Stock, Étang du** *l.* France
194 G6 **Stockach** Ger.
173 J5 **Stockbridge** *Hampshire, England* U.K.
251 J7 **Stockbridge** *MI* U.S.A.
190 K3 **Stockelsdorf** Ger.
201 I6 **Stockenboi** Austria
201 N3 **Stockerau** Austria
258 E3 **Stockertown** *PA* U.S.A.
193 D10 **Stockheim** Ger.
165 O2 **Stockholm** Sweden
165 N2 **Stockholm** *county* Sweden
257 □Q1 **Stockholm** *ME* U.S.A.
259 F2 **Stockholm** *NJ* U.S.A.
212 D2 **Stockhorn** *mt.* Switz.
105 K6 **Stockinbingal** *N.S.W.* Austr.
201 M6 **Stocking** Austria
171 M7 **Stockport** *Greater Manchester, England* U.K.
171 N7 **Stocksbridge** *South Yorkshire, England* U.K.
190 H5 **Stöckse** Ger.
171 N4 **Stocksfield** *Northumberland, England* U.K.
171 M5 **Stocks Reservoir** *England* U.K.
288 G6 **Stocks Seamount** *sea feature* S. Atlantic Ocean
194 G2 **Stockstadt am Main** Ger.
194 E2 **Stockstadt am Rhein** Ger.
264 K4 **Stockton** *CA* U.S.A.
250 D7 **Stockton** *IL* U.S.A.
260 F6 **Stockton** *KS* U.S.A.
261 I7 **Stockton** *MO* U.S.A.
258 F4 **Stockton** *NJ* U.S.A.
265 T1 **Stockton** *UT* U.S.A.
171 L7 **Stockton Heath** *Warrington, England* U.K.
250 D3 **Stockton Island** *WI* U.S.A.
245 K1 **Stockton Islands** *AK* U.S.A.
261 I7 **Stockton Lake** *MO* U.S.A.
171 O4 **Stockton-on-Tees** *Stockton-on-Tees, England* U.K.
171 O4 **Stockton-on-Tees** *admin. div. England* U.K.
261 D10 **Stockton Plateau** *TX* U.S.A.
257 □Q4 **Stockton Springs** *ME* U.S.A.
260 E5 **Stockville** *NE* U.S.A.
197 J3 **Stoczek** Pol.
197 J4 **Stoczek Łukowski** Pol.
198 C2 **Stod** Czech Rep.
163 N5 **Stöde** Sweden
161 P7 **Stodolishche** Rus. Fed.
119 G8 **Stœng Trêng** Cambodia
168 F6 **Stoer** *Highland, Scotland* U.K.
168 F6 **Stoer, Point of** *Scotland* U.K.
237 N1 **Stoffberg** S. Africa
218 I9 **Stogovo Planina** *mts* Macedonia
172 F5 **Stogursey** *Somerset, England* U.K.
201 M8 **Stojdraga** Croatia
201 M7 **Stojnci** Slovenia
173 K3 **Stoke Albany** *Northamptonshire, England* U.K.
173 O3 **Stoke Ash** *Suffolk, England* U.K.
173 N4 **Stoke-by-Nayland** *Suffolk, England* U.K.
173 O2 **Stoke Holy Cross** *Norfolk, England* U.K.
173 K4 **Stoke Mandeville** *Buckinghamshire, England* U.K.
173 K4 **Stokenchurch** *Buckinghamshire, England* U.K.
172 E7 **Stokenham** *Devon, England* U.K.
171 M7 **Stoke-on-Trent** *Stoke-on-Trent, England* U.K.
171 M7 **Stoke-on-Trent** *admin. div. England* U.K.
173 K4 **Stoke Poges** *Buckinghamshire, England* U.K.
172 H3 **Stoke Prior** *Worcestershire, England* U.K.
103 I8 **Stokes, Mount** *South I.* N.Z.
172 G3 **Stokesay** *Shropshire, England* U.K.
109 F12 **Stokes Inlet** *W.A.* Austr.
171 O5 **Stokesley** *North Yorkshire, England* U.K.
108 F12 **Stokes National Park** *W.A.* Austr.
105 I9 **Stokes Point** *Tas.* Austr.
106 C4 **Stokes Range** *hills N.T.* Austr.
172 F6 **Stoke St Mary** *Somerset, England* U.K.
172 G6 **Stoke sub Hamdon** *Somerset, England* U.K.
103 I8 **Stokes Valley** *North I.* N.Z.
158 E2 **Stokhid** *r.* Ukr.
190 L1 **Stokkemarke** Denmark
162 □C2 **Stokkseyri** Iceland
162 L3 **Stokkvågen** Norway
162 M2 **Stokmarknes** Norway
198 E2 **Štoky** Czech Rep.
219 K6 **Stol** *mt.* Serbia
201 H7 **Stol** *mt.* Slovenia
210 F4 **Stolac** Bos.-Herz.
191 K7 **Stolberg (Harz) Kurort** Ger.
191 B9 **Stolberg (Rheinland)** Ger.
143 U2 **Stolboukha** *Vostochnyy Kazakhstan* Kazakh.
143 U3 **Stolboukha** *Vostochnyy Kazakhstan* Kazakh.
152 G2 **Stolbovoy** *Novaya Zemlya* Rus. Fed.
153 O2 **Stolbovoy, Ostrov** *i. Novosibirskiye O-va* Rus. Fed.
Stolbtsy Belarus *see* **Stowbtsy**
196 F2 **Stołczno** Pol.
199 J3 **Stolica** *mt.* Slovakia
210 G3 **Stolice** *hill* Bos.-Herz.
158 F2 **Stolin** Belarus
193 G9 **Stollberg** Ger.
190 F3 **Stollhamm (Butjadingen)** Ger.
196 G2 **Stolno** Pol.
Stolp Pol. *see* **Słupsk**
192 J5 **Stolpe** *Brandenburg* Ger.
190 J2 **Stolpe** *Schleswig-Holstein* Ger.
193 J8 **Stolpen** Ger.
163 I6 **Stolsheimen** *park* Norway
163 J6 **Stolsvatnet** *l.* Norway
238 □[2c] **Stoltenhoff Island** *Tristan da Cunha* S. Atlantic Ocean
186 G5 **Stolwijk** Neth.
191 H5 **Stolzenau** Ger.
236 B8 **Stompneusbaai** S. Africa
215 Q1 **Stončica, Rt** *pt* Croatia
172 H4 **Stone** *Gloucestershire, England* U.K.
173 M5 **Stone** *Kent, England* U.K.
172 H2 **Stone** *Staffordshire, England* U.K.
256 E7 **Stoneboro** *PA* U.S.A.
162 □ **Stonebreen** *glacier* Svalbard
248 E4 **Stonecliffe** *Ont.* Can.
Stonecutters' Island *pen. H.K.* China *see* **Ngong Shuen Chau**
260 D5 **Stoneham** *CO* U.S.A.
258 F6 **Stone Harbor** *NJ* U.S.A.
168 L9 **Stonehaven** *Aberdeenshire, Scotland* U.K.
107 I8 **Stonehenge** *Qld* Austr.
173 I5 **Stonehenge** *tourist site England* U.K.
172 H4 **Stonehouse** *Gloucestershire, England* U.K.
168 I11 **Stonehouse** *South Lanarkshire, Scotland* U.K.
250 C4 **Stone Lake** *WI* U.S.A.
246 E3 **Stone Mountain Provincial Park** *B.C.* Can.
257 K7 **Stone Ridge** *NY* U.S.A.
256 F12 **Stoneville** *NC* U.S.A.
247 L5 **Stonewall** *Man.* Can.
261 G8 **Stonewall** *OK* U.S.A.
251 O6 **Stoney Creek** *Ont.* Can.
258 D4 **Stoney Creek Mills** *PA* U.S.A.
169 H7 **Stoneyford** Ireland
168 G13 **Stoneykirk** *Dumfries and Galloway, Scotland* U.K.
251 L7 **Stoney Point** *Ont.* Can.
237 M7 **Stoneyride** S. Africa
164 B2 **Stong** Norway
166 J1 **Stongfjorden** Norway
259 L2 **Stonington** *CT* U.S.A.
257 □Q4 **Stonington** *ME* U.S.A.
233 C5 **Stony Athi** Kenya
168 □M3 **Stonybreck** *Shetland, Scotland* U.K.
259 I3 **Stony Brook** *NY* U.S.A.
258 B5 **Stony Brook** *PA* U.S.A.
259 J2 **Stony Creek** *CT* U.S.A.
256 H12 **Stony Creek** *VA* U.S.A.
264 J2 **Stony Gorge Reservoir** *CA* U.S.A.
270 □ **Stony Hill** Jamaica
238 □[2c] **Stonyhill Point** *Tristan da Cunha* S. Atlantic Ocean
247 L3 **Stony Lake** *Man.* Can.
246 H4 **Stony Plain** *Alta* Can.
257 I5 **Stony Point** *NY* U.S.A.
247 J3 **Stony Rapids** *Sask.* Can.
244 H3 **Stony River** *AK* U.S.A.
173 K3 **Stony Stratford** *Milton Keynes, England* U.K.
201 O4 **Stoob** Austria
248 D2 **Stooping** *r. Ont.* Can.
201 L8 **Stopiče** Slovenia
197 J1 **Stopki** Pol.
197 I5 **Stopnica** Pol.
190 H3 **Stör** *r.* Ger.
164 E5 **Stora** *r.* Denmark
165 L2 **Storå** Sweden
165 M5 **Stora Alvaret** *pen.* Sweden
165 M4 **Stora Askö** *i.* Sweden
164 I2 **Stora Bör** *l.* Sweden
164 I2 **Stora Gla** *l.* Sweden
164 I4 **Stora Horredssjön** *l.* Sweden
164 H3 **Stora Le** *l.* Sweden
162 O3 **Stora Lulevatten** *l.* Sweden
165 P2 **Stora Nassa naturreservat** *nature res.* Sweden
162 N3 **Stora Sjöfallets nationalpark** *nat. park* Sweden
162 O4 **Storavan** *l.* Sweden
163 L6 **Storbäcken** Sweden
163 K6 **Storbekkfjellet** *mt.* Norway
163 L6 **Storbo** Sweden
164 B2 **Stord** *i.* Norway
162 I5 **Stordal** Norway
163 K6 **Store** *mt.* Norway
201 L7 **Štore** Slovenia
164 G6 **Store Bælt** *sea chan.* Denmark
164 B1 **Storebø** Norway
192 F1 **Store Damme** Denmark
164 I6 **Store Heddinge** Denmark
163 J6 **Store Jukleeggi** *mt.* Norway
243 Q2 **Store Koldewey** *i.* Greenland
162 P2 **Store Lenangstind** *mt.* Norway
162 Q1 **Storelv** Norway
162 T1 **Store Molvik** Norway
165 J4 **Store Moss nationalpark** *nat. park* Sweden
162 K5 **Støren** Norway
164 D2 **Store Nup** *mt.* Norway
190 J1 **Store Rise** Denmark
164 B1 **Store Sotra** *i.* Norway
164 D2 **Store Urevatnet** *l.* Norway
165 N1 **Storfjärden** *l.* Sweden
162 S1 **Storfjordbotn** Norway
162 □ **Storfjorden** *sea chan.* Svalbard
165 K2 **Storfors** Sweden
162 M3 **Storforshei** Norway
201 I8 **Štorje** Slovenia
162 M4 **Storjola** Sweden
162 M3 **Storjord** Norway
162 N4 **Storjuktan** *l.* Sweden
164 D3 **Storkarshei** *hill* Norway
243 H2 **Storkerson Peninsula** *Nunavut* Can.
193 I6 **Storkow** Ger.
190 J3 **Stormarn** *reg.* Ger.
105 K10 **Storm Bay** *Tas.* Austr.
237 K7 **Stormberg** S. Africa
237 K6 **Stormberg** *mt.* S. Africa
237 K6 **Stormberg** *r.* S. Africa
237 K7 **Stormberge** *mts* S. Africa
260 H4 **Storm Lake** *IA* U.S.A.
236 H9 **Stormsrivier** S. Africa
215 P5 **Stornara** Italy
215 P5 **Stornarella** Italy
168 D6 **Stornoway** *Western Isles, Scotland* U.K.
213 J4 **Storo** Italy
165 O2 **Storö-Bockö-Lökaöns naturreservat** *nature res.* Sweden
162 □ **Storøya** *i.* Svalbard
161 P1 **Storozhenskiy, Mys** *pt* Rus. Fed.
156 K3 **Storozhevsk** Rus. Fed.
161 P1 **Storozhno** Rus. Fed.
158 E5 **Storozhynets'** Ukr.
173 L6 **Storrington** *West Sussex, England* U.K.
164 E2 **Stor-Roan** *mt.* Norway
257 M7 **Storrs** *CT* U.S.A.
162 N4 **Storseleby** Sweden
164 H1 **Storsjøen** *l.* Norway
165 M1 **Storsjön** *l.* Sweden
162 M5 **Storsjön** *l.* Sweden
165 N2 **Storsjön** *l.* Sweden
162 J5 **Storskarhø** *mt.* Norway
162 M4 **Storskog** Sweden
162 P2 **Storslett** Norway
164 H7 **Storstrømmen** *sea chan.* Denmark
162 P4 **Storsund** Sweden
173 M4 **Stort** *r. England* U.K.
186 H2 **Stortemelk** *sea chan.* Neth.
162 N4 **Storuman** Sweden
162 N4 **Storuman** *l.* Sweden
162 L5 **Storvigelen** *mt.* Norway
165 M1 **Storvik** Sweden
162 N4 **Storvindeln** *l.* Sweden
164 G4 **Storvorde** Denmark
165 N2 **Storvreta** Sweden
262 K4 **Story** *WY* U.S.A.
218 I2 **Štós** Slovakia
283 B8 **Stosch, Isla** *i.* Chile
193 E8 **Stößen** Ger.
201 M3 **Stössing** Austria
173 L3 **Stotfold** *Bedfordshire, England* U.K.
195 J6 **Stötten am Auerberg** Ger.
193 D8 **Stotternheim** Ger.
258 C4 **Stouchsburg** *PA* U.S.A.
247 K5 **Stoughton** *Sask.* Can.
187 I8 **Stoumont** Belgium
119 G8 **Stoŭng, Stœng** *r.* Cambodia
172 I6 **Stour** *r. Dorset, England* U.K.
173 O4 **Stour** *r. Essex/Suffolk, England* U.K.
173 O5 **Stour** *r. Kent, England* U.K.
173 I3 **Stour** *r. Oxfordshire/Warwickshire, England* U.K.
172 H3 **Stourbridge** *West Midlands, England* U.K.
172 H3 **Stourport-on-Severn** *Worcestershire, England* U.K.
247 M4 **Stout Lake** *Ont.* Can.
168 K11 **Stow** *Scottish Borders, Scotland* U.K.
160 J8 **Stowbtsy** Belarus
258 D4 **Stowe** *PA* U.S.A.
196 F1 **Stowięcino** Pol.
173 N3 **Stowmarket** *Suffolk, England* U.K.
173 I4 **Stow-on-the-Wold** *Gloucestershire, England* U.K.
158 D3 **Stoyaniv** Ukr.
122 G2 **Stoyba** Rus. Fed.
197 K1 **Stożne** Pol.
213 M5 **Stra** Italy
193 G7 **Straach** Ger.
237 K1 **Straatsdrif** S. Africa
169 H3 **Strabane** *Northern Ireland* U.K.
197 L3 **Strabla** Pol.
168 K8 **Strachan** *Aberdeenshire, Scotland* U.K.
168 F10 **Strachur** *Argyll and Bute, Scotland* U.K.
197 M1 **Stračiūnai** Lith.
190 E4 **Strackholt (Großefehn)** Ger.
196 E2 **Strączno** Pol.
169 H6 **Stradbally** Ireland
173 O3 **Stradbroke** *Suffolk, England* U.K.
212 G5 **Stradella** Italy
201 M6 **Straden** Austria
173 N3 **Stradishall** *Suffolk, England* U.K.
169 H5 **Stradone** Ireland
173 M2 **Stradsett** *Norfolk, England* U.K.
191 B8 **Straelen** Ger.
105 J10 **Strahan** *Tas.* Austr.
265 U4 **Straight Cliffs** *ridge UT* U.S.A.
187 H9 **Straimont** Belgium
198 C2 **Strakonice** Czech Rep.
219 O8 **Straldzha** Bulg.
201 M5 **Strallegg** Austria
168 I9 **Straloch** *Perth and Kinross, Scotland* U.K.
192 H2 **Stralsund** Ger.
212 D5 **Strambino** Italy
187 I6 **Stramproy** Neth.
236 C10 **Strand** S. Africa
162 I5 **Stranda** Norway
164 D1 **Strandavatnet** *l.* Norway
190 J2 **Strande** Ger.
169 E4 **Strandhill** Ireland
255 H12 **Strangers Cay** *i.* Bahamas
169 K4 **Strangford** *Northern Ireland* U.K.
169 K4 **Strangford Lough** *inlet Northern Ireland* U.K.
165 N2 **Strängnäs** Sweden
215 K4 **Strangolagalli** Italy
106 D3 **Strangways** *r. N.T.* Austr.
106 E7 **Strangways Range** *mts N.T.* Austr.
199 G3 **Strání** Czech Rep.
169 J2 **Stranocum** *Northern Ireland* U.K.
169 G3 **Stranorlar** Ireland
168 F13 **Stranraer** *Dumfries and Galloway, Scotland* U.K.
216 D8 **Strasatti** *Sicilia* Italy
179 O6 **Strasbourg** France
192 I4 **Strasburg** Ger.
256 D8 **Strasburg** *OH* U.S.A.
258 C5 **Strasburg** *PA* U.S.A.
256 G10 **Strasburg** *VA* U.S.A.
158 H6 **Strășeni** Moldova
Strasheny Moldova *see* **Strășeni**
195 P2 **Strašice** Czech Rep.
194 G5 **Straßberg** *Baden-Württemberg* Ger.
193 D7 **Straßberg** *Sachsen-Anhalt* Ger.
201 J6 **Straßburg** Austria
Strassburg France *see* **Strasbourg**
187 J9 **Strassen** Lux.
201 L5 **Straßengel** Austria
191 E9 **Straßenhaus** Ger.
201 O3 **Strasshof an der Norbahn** Austria
195 N4 **Straßkirchen** Ger.
200 H4 **Straßwalchen** Austria
173 J5 **Stratfield Mortimer** *West Berkshire, England* U.K.
248 D5 **Stratford** *Ont.* Can.
102 I6 **Stratford** *North I.* N.Z.
169 I7 **Stratford** Ireland
264 M5 **Stratford** *CA* U.S.A.
259 I2 **Stratford** *CT* U.S.A.
261 D7 **Stratford** *TX* U.S.A.
250 D5 **Stratford** *WI* U.S.A.
173 I3 **Stratford-upon-Avon** *Warwickshire, England* U.K.
104 G6 **Strathalbyn** *S.A.* Austr.
168 H11 **Strathaven** *South Lanarksh* *Scotland* U.K.
170 I2 **Strathblane** *Stirling, Scotla*
168 K8 **Strathbogie** *reg. Scotland* U
168 G7 **Strathcarron** *val. Scotland*
287 G2 **Strathcona, Mount** Antarc
246 E5 **Strathcona Provincial Park** Can.
168 G7 **Strathconon** *val. Scotland*
168 H8 **Strath Dearn** *val. Scotland*
168 J8 **Strathdon** *Aberdeenshire, S* U.K.
168 H10 **Strath Earn** *val. Scotland* U
168 H6 **Strath Fleet** *val. Scotland* U
168 G8 **Strathglass** *val. Scotland* U
105 K10 **Strathgordon** *Tas.* Austr.
168 I6 **Strath Halladale** *val. Scotla* U.K.
246 H5 **Strathmore** *Alta* Can.
168 G5 **Strathmore** *r. Scotland* U.K
264 M5 **Strathmore** *CA* U.S.A.
246 F4 **Strathnaver** *B.C.* Can.
168 H6 **Strathnaver** *val. Scotland* U
168 I6 **Strath of Kildonan** *val. Sc* U.K.
168 G7 **Strathpeffer** *Highland, Sco* U.K.
251 M7 **Strathroy** *Ont.* Can.
168 I8 **Strathspey** *val. Scotland* U.
168 I9 **Strath Tay** *val. Scotland* U.K
168 I5 **Strathy** *Highland, Scotland*
168 H5 **Strathy Point** *Scotland* U.K
168 H10 **Strathyre** *Stirling, Scotland*
220 E2 **Stratoni** Greece
221 J5 **Stratonikeia** *tourist site* Tu
220 C4 **Stratos** Greece
172 C6 **Stratton** *Cornwall, Englan*
257 □O3 **Stratton** *ME* U.S.A.
257 M5 **Stratton Mountain** *VT* U.S
173 I4 **Stratton St Margaret** *Swin* *England* U.K.
195 N4 **Straubing** Ger.
162 M2 **Straume** Norway
162 M3 **Straumen** *Nordland* Norw
162 M3 **Straumen** *Nordland* Norw
162 □B1 **Straumnes** *pt* Iceland
193 J7 **Straupitz** Ger.
192 I5 **Strausberg** Ger.
191 K8 **Straußfurt** Ger.
258 C3 **Strausstown** *PA* U.S.A.
265 U7 **Strawberry** *AZ* U.S.A.
262 E4 **Strawberry Mountain** *OR*
265 U1 **Strawberry Reservoir** *UT* U
197 I5 **Strawczyn** Pol.
250 F9 **Strawn** *IL* U.S.A.
219 K8 **Straža** *mt.* Macedonia
219 N7 **Strazhitsa** Bulg.
198 D2 **Stráž nad Nežárkou** Czech
193 L9 **Stráž nad Nisou** Czech Re
201 I2 **Strážný** Czech Rep.
198 C2 **Strážov** Czech Rep.
199 H3 **Strážov** *mt.* Slovakia
193 K9 **Stráž pod Ralskem** Czech
199 K3 **Strážske** Slovakia
104 E5 **Streaky Bay** *S.A.* Austr.
104 E5 **Streaky Bay** *b. S.A.* Austr.
169 G6 **Streamstown** Ireland
173 J4 **Streatley** *West Berkshire, Er* U.K.
250 F8 **Streator** *IL* U.S.A.
198 D2 **Středočeský kraj** *admin. re* Czech Rep.
190 F4 **Streek** Ger.
172 G5 **Street** *Somerset, England* U
219 L6 **Strehaia** Romania
193 H8 **Strehla** Ger.
219 L5 **Strei** *r.* Romania
109 G11 **Streich Mound** *hill W.A.* Au
199 H4 **Strekov** Slovakia
198 C2 **Střela** *r.* Czech Rep.
219 M8 **Strelcha** Bulg.
159 R1 **Strelets** Rus. Fed.
159 P3 **Streletskoye** Rus. Fed.
198 F2 **Střelice** Czech Rep.
159 R2 **Strelitsa** Rus. Fed.
153 Q3 **Strelka** Rus. Fed.
161 R1 **Strelkovo** Rus. Fed.
108 E6 **Strelley** *W.A.* Austr.
108 E6 **Strelley** *r. W.A.* Austr.
108 E6 **Strelley Aboriginal Reserv** Austr.
156 G2 **Strel'na** *r.* Rus. Fed.
201 N5 **Strem** Austria
213 J3 **Strembo** Italy
193 F5 **Stremme** *r.* Ger.
158 H3 **Stremyhorod** Ukr.
160 I4 **Strenči** Latvia
201 K3 **Strengberg** Austria
200 B5 **Strengen** Austria
171 O5 **Strensall** *York, England* U.K
197 M5 **Streptiv** Ukr.
212 F4 **Stresa** Italy
171 M7 **Stretford** *Greater Manches* *England* U.K.
173 M3 **Stretham** *Cambridgeshire, England* U.K.
173 I2 **Stretton** *Staffordshire, Engl* U.K.
191 J10 **Streu** *r.* Ger.
191 K10 **Streufdorf** Ger.
166 D1 **Streymoy** *i.* Faroe Is
152 I3 **Strezhevoy** Rus. Fed.
198 B2 **Stříbro** Czech Rep.
168 L7 **Strichen** *Aberdeenshire, Sc* U.K.
113 J8 **Strickland** *r.* P.N.G.
213 L3 **Strigno** Italy
201 N6 **Štrigova** Croatia
186 G5 **Strijen** Neth.
159 P3 **Strilecha** Ukr.
198 E2 **Strimilov** Czech Rep.
220 E1 **Strimoniko** Greece
Strimonikón Greece *see* **Strimoniko**
170 G2 **Striven, Loch** *inlet Scotlan*
210 G3 **Strizivojna** Croatia
201 M8 **Strmec** Croatia
191 K7 **Ströbeck** Ger.
201 H4 **Strobl** Austria
283 E6 **Stroeder** Arg.
220 C5 **Strofades** *i.* Greece
195 L5 **Strogen** *r.* Ger.
159 M7 **Strohanivka** Ukr.
190 G5 **Ströhen** Ger.
158 H6 **Stroiești** Moldova
159 P3 **Stroitel'** Rus. Fed.
169 F5 **Strokestown** Ireland
192 I4 **Strom** *r.* Ger.
168 J5 **Stroma, Island of** *Scotland*
165 N1 **Strömaren** *l.* Sweden
163 N6 **Strömbacka** Sweden
194 D2 **Stromberg** Ger.
194 F3 **Stromberg-Heuchelberg, Naturpark** *nature res.* Ger.
217 I6 **Stromboli, Isola** *i. Isole Lip* Italy
217 I6 **Strombolicchio, Isola** *i. Is* *Lipari* Italy
168 E8 **Stromeferry** *Highland, Sco* U.K.
283 □ **Stromness** S. Georgia
168 J5 **Stromness** *Orkney, Scotlan*
163 N6 **Strömsbruk** Sweden
260 G5 **Stromsburg** *NE* U.S.A.
162 O2 **Strømsmoen** Norway
164 H3 **Strömstad** Sweden
162 M5 **Strömsund** Sweden
215 J3 **Stroncone** Italy
212 I5 **Strone** *r.* Italy
168 G11 **Strone** *Argyll and Bute, Sco* U.K.
261 I9 **Strong** *AR* U.S.A.
217 M5 **Strongoli** Italy
256 D7 **Strongsville** *OH* U.S.A.
196 E5 **Stronie Śląskie** Pol.
168 K4 **Stronsay** *i. Scotland* U.K.
168 K4 **Stronsay Firth** *sea chan. Scotland* U.K.
201 N2 **Stronsdorf** Austria
168 E9 **Strontian** *Highland, Scotla*
199 K2 **Stropkov** Slovakia

D3 Stropnice r. Czech Rep.
E5 Stroppiana Italy
C6 Stroppo Italy
H4 Stroud Gloucestershire, England U.K.
M5 Stroud Road N.S.W. Austr.
E3 Stroudsburg PA U.S.A.
Stroyentsy Moldova see Stroiești
H6 Stróża Pol.
E4 Strücklingen (Saterland) Ger.
E5 Struer Denmark
I9 Struga Macedonia
F3 Struga r. Pol.
M3 Strugi-Krasnyye Rus. Fed.
P8 Strugovskaya Buda Rus. Fed.
E10 Struis Bay S. Africa
E10 Struis Bay b. S. Africa
H3 Strule r. Northern Ireland U.K.
J2 Strullendorf Ger.
L9 Struma r. Bulg.
B3 Strumble Head Wales U.K.
E1 Strumeshnitsa r. Bulg.
K9 Strumica Macedonia
K9 Strumica r. Macedonia
G6 Strumień Pol.
L3 Strumkivka Ukr.
V5 Strunino Rus. Fed.
J1 Strunkovice nad Blanicí Czech Rep.
J8 Struth Ger.
E7 Struthers OH U.S.A.
M8 Stryama r. Bulg.
H5 Strydenburg S. Africa
J2 Strydpoort S. Africa
H4 Stryków Pol.
E2 Strymonas r. Greece
I6 Stryn Norway
K1 Strynø i. Denmark
E5 Strypa r. Ukr.
J6 Stryukove Ukr.
C4 Stryy Ukr.
D4 Stryy r. Ukr.
H4 Stryzhavka Ukr.
F3 Strzałkowo Pol.
G5 Strzebień Pol.
I3 Strzegocin Pol.
E5 Strzegom Pol.
E4 Strzegomka r. Pol.
I3 Strzegowo Pol.
H3 Strzelce Pol.
D3 Strzelce Krajeńskie Pol.
G5 Strzelce Opolskie Pol.
H4 Strzelce Wielkie Pol.
D6 Strzelecki, Mount hill N.T. Austr.
G3 Strzelecki Creek watercourse S.A. Austr.
G3 Strzelecki Regional Reserve nature res. S.A. Austr.
F5 Strzeleczki Pol.
F5 Strzelin Pol.
G3 Strzelno Pol.
G1 Strzepcz Pol.
J6 Strzyżów Pol.
J8 Sts-Geosmes France
G1 Stsvina r. Belarus
M9 Stuart r. Qld Austr.
G12 Stuart FL U.S.A.
H5 Stuart IA U.S.A.
F4 Stuart NE U.S.A.
E12 Stuart VA U.S.A.
D7 Stuart Bluff Range mts N.T. Austr.
L7 Stuartfield Aberdeenshire, Scotland U.K.
G3 Stuart Island AK U.S.A.
E4 Stuart Lake B.C. Can.
B12 Stuart Mountains South I. N.Z.
E3 Stuart Range hills S.A. Austr.
F10 Stuarts Draft VA U.S.A.
D5 Stubaier Alpen mts Austria
D5 Stubaital val. Austria
K5 Stubalpe mt. Austria
H1 Stubbæk Denmark
F1 Stubbekøbing Denmark
G4 Stubben Ger.
1 Stubbenkammer hd Ger.
□1 Stubbings Point Christmas I.
J6 Stubbington Hampshire, England U.K.
□3 Stubbs St Vincent
M5 Stubenberg Austria
7 Stubica Paracin Serbia
6 Stubline Obrenovac Serbia
K6 Stubno Pol.
Stuchka Latvia see Aizkraukle
D2 Stuchowo Pol.
Stučka Latvia see Aizkraukle
E2 Studená Czech Rep.
H5 Studena Ukr.
2 Studená Vltava r. Czech Rep.
7 Studenica tourist site Serbia
9 Studeničani Studeničani Macedonia
F5 Stüdenitz Ger.
H2 Studénka Czech Rep.
N9 Studen Kladenets, Yazovir resr Bulg.
Q1 Studenoye Rus. Fed.
G2 Studenytsya r. Ukr.
K4 Studham Bedfordshire, England U.K.
F11 Studholme Junction South I. N.Z.
G3 Studienka Slovakia
9 Studis S. Africa
6 Studland Dorset, England U.K.
3 Studley Warwickshire, England U.K.
N3 Studsvik Sweden
B3 Studsviken Sweden
D11 Study Butte TX U.S.A.
F1 Studzienice Pol.
M5 Stugun Sweden
G5 Stuhlfelden Austria
E6 Stühlingen Ger.
3 Stuhna r. Ukr.
G4 Stuhr Ger.
M4 Stull Lake Man./Ont. Can.
H6 Stülpe Ger.
N3 Stulpicani Romania
E5 Stumm Austria
L6 Stump Lake ND U.S.A.
Stung Treng Cambodia see Stœng Trêng
M4 Stupart r. Man. Can.
G3 Stupava Slovakia
V7 Stupino Rus. Fed.
Q1 Stupišće, Rt pt Croatia
2 Stupsk Pol.
E5 Stura r. Italy
C5 Stura di Ala r. Italy
D6 Stura di Demonte r. Italy
K6 Stura di Val Grande r. Italy
C5 Stura di Viù r. Italy
K2 Sturge Island Antarctica
E4 Sturgeon r. Ont. Can.
4 Sturgeon r. Sask. Can.
H4 Sturgeon r. MI U.S.A.
C1 Sturgeon, Lake Ont. Can.
L4 Sturgeon Bay b. Man. Can.
G5 Sturgeon Bay WI U.S.A.
4 Sturgeon Bay b. MI U.S.A.
G5 Sturgeon Bay Canal lake channel WI U.S.A.
E4 Sturgeon Falls Ont. Can.
P5 Sturgeon Lake Ont. Can.
B3 Sturgeon Lake Ont. Can.
D7 Sturgis KY U.S.A.
8 Sturgis MI U.S.A.
D3 Sturgis SD U.S.A.
G7 Sturla r. Italy
E3 Šturlić Bos.-Herz.
H6 Sturminster Newton Dorset, England U.K.
H4 Štúrovo Slovakia
D5 Sturry Kent, England U.K.
H3 Sturt, Mount hill N.S.W. Austr.
6 Sturt Bay S.A. Austr.
5 Sturt Creek W.A. Austr.
5 Sturt Creek watercourse W.A. Austr.
G7 Sturtevant WI U.S.A.
H3 Sturt National Park N.S.W. Austr.
D4 Sturt Plain N.T. Austr.
H3 Sturt Stony Desert Qld Austr.
179 O5 Sturzelbronn France
237 L8 Stutterheim S. Africa
194 G4 Stuttgart Ger.
194 H3 Stuttgart admin. reg. Ger.
261 J8 Stuttgart AR U.S.A.
Stutthof Pol. see Sztutowo
191 K9 Stützerbach Ger.
245 J1 Stuver, Mount AK U.S.A.
158 G2 Stvyha r. Ukr.
162 □B1 Stykkishólmur Iceland
159 Q6 Styla Ukr.
220 D4 Stylida Greece
158 F1 Styr r. Belarus/Ukr.
Styria land Austria see Steiermark
281 G3 Suaçuí Grande r. Brazil
115 D8 Suai East Timor
117 J3 Suai Sarawak Malaysia
274 C3 Suaita Col.
225 H5 Suakin Sudan
146 D6 Suakin Archipelago is Sudan
225 H5 Suakin Archipelago is Sudan
231 D6 Suana Dem. Rep. Congo
205 L2 Suances Spain
131 M6 Suao Taiwan
266 E3 Suaqui Grande Mex.
225 H5 Suara Eritrea
285 G2 Suardi Arg.
274 B4 Suárez Col.
151 L1 Suat Kazakh.
275 E2 Suata Venez.
100 □6 Suavanao Sta Isabel Solomon Is
160 H6 Subačius Lith.
117 G8 Subang Jawa Indon.
139 M6 Subankhata Assam India
133 L13 Subansiri r. India
139 K9 Subarnarekha r. W. Bengal India
144 C4 Sūbāshī Iran
221 J1 Subaşı İstanbul Turkey
221 I4 Subaşı İzmir Turkey
215 J1 Subasio, Monte mt. Italy
160 I5 Subate Latvia
147 H2 Subay reg. Saudi Arabia
146 F4 Subay, 'Irq des. Saudi Arabia
148 I8 Şubayḩah Saudi Arabia
146 G9 Şubayḩī reg. Yemen
213 L8 Subbiano Italy
219 N4 Subcetate Romania
132 L7 Subei Gansu China
Subeita tourist site Israel see Shivta
201 H3 Suben Austria
215 K4 Subiaco Italy
117 H3 Subi Besar i. Indon.
117 H3 Subi Kecil i. Indon.
196 G1 Subkowy Pol.
261 E7 Sublette KS U.S.A.
128 G5 Sub Nur l. Nei Mongol China
218 H4 Subotica Vojvodina Serbia
225 I6 Subucle mt. Eritrea
233 B5 Subugo mt. Kenya
199 H2 Sučany Slovakia
184 H5 Suc-au-May hill France
258 F3 Succasunna NJ U.S.A.
264 N5 Success, Lake CA U.S.A.
212 I7 Succiso, Alpi di mts Italy
219 O3 Suceava Romania
219 N3 Suceava r. Romania
180 H7 Sucé-sur-Erdre France
197 H6 Sucha Beskidzka Pol.
197 H1 Suchacz Pol.
199 G3 Suchá Loz Czech Rep.
196 D2 Suchań Pol.
Suchan Rus. Fed. see Partizansk
122 H7 Suchan r. Rus. Fed.
198 E2 Suchdol Czech Rep.
198 D3 Suchdol nad Lužnicí Czech Rep.
197 I4 Suchedniów Pol.
189 J3 Suchedniowsko-Oblęgorski Park Krajobrazowy Pol.
212 A2 Suchet, Mont mt. Switz.
268 D2 Suchil Mex.
197 L2 Suchowola Pol.
197 K3 Suchożebry Pol.
271 □1 Sucia, Bahía b. Puerto Rico
209 D12 Sucina Spain
274 B3 Sucio r. Col.
219 M3 Suciu de Sus Romania
169 F6 Suck r. Ireland
251 N3 Sucker Creek Landing Ont. Can.
245 L3 Suckling, Cape AK U.S.A.
192 E4 Suckow Ger.
276 D4 Sucre Bol.
274 C2 Sucre dept Col.
275 F2 Sucre state Venez.
274 D3 Sucuaro Col.
274 B5 Sucumbíos prov. Ecuador
275 G6 Sucunduri r. Brazil
280 B4 Sucuriú r. Brazil
Suczawa Romania see Suceava
229 H6 Sud prov. Cameroon
100 □5 Sud, Grand Récif du rf New Caledonia
239 □3a Sud, Pointe pt Njazidja Comoros
239 □2b Sud, Pointe du c. Mahé Seychelles
239 □3b Sud, Récif du rf Mayotte
257 L3 Sud, Rivière du r. Que. Can.
161 U2 Suda Rus. Fed.
161 U2 Suda r. Rus. Fed.
159 N9 Sudak Ukr.
127 H4 Sudama Japan
225 F6 Sudan country Africa
156 H4 Suday Rus. Fed.
146 G3 Sudayr reg. Saudi Arabia
149 L8 Sudayr, Sha'īb watercourse Iraq
161 U9 Sudbishchi Rus. Fed.
142 E1 Sud'bodarovka Rus. Fed.
248 D4 Sudbury Ont. Can.
173 I2 Sudbury Derbyshire, England U.K.
173 N3 Sudbury Suffolk, England U.K.
232 A3 Sudd swamp Sudan
191 D6 Suddendorf Ger.
275 G3 Suddie Guyana
190 K4 Sude r. Ger.
190 G2 Süden Ger.
190 I1 Süderbrarup Ger.
190 J5 Suderburg Ger.
190 J4 Südergellersen Ger.
190 H2 Süderhastedt Ger.
190 G1 Süderlügum Ger.
190 G2 Süderoog i. Ger.
190 F2 Süderoogsand i. Ger.
190 H2 Süderstapel Ger.
Sudest Island P.N.G. see Tagula Island
Sudetenland mts Czech Rep./Pol. see Sudety
196 D5 Sudety mts Czech Rep./Pol.
190 G2 Südfall i. Ger.
161 R8 Sudimir Rus. Fed.
161 Y4 Sudislavl' Rus. Fed.
231 F5 Sud-Kivu prov. Dem. Rep. Congo
258 D6 Sudlersville MD U.S.A.
191 C7 Südlohn Ger.
190 D5 Süd-Nord-Kanal canal Ger.
206 B6 Sudoeste Alentejano e Costa Vicentina, Parque Natural do nature res. Port.
161 X6 Sudogda Rus. Fed.
161 X5 Sudogda r. Rus. Fed.
198 G3 Sudoměřice Czech Rep.
160 M4 Sudomskiye Vysoty hills Rus. Fed.
161 Q9 Sudost' r. Rus. Fed.
229 H5 Sud-Ouest prov. Cameroon
239 □1b Sud Ouest, Pointe pt Mauritius
158 C4 Sudova Vyshnya Ukr.
201 N7 Sudovec Croatia
225 G2 Sudr Egypt
Südtirol prov. Italy see Bolzano
230 C4 Sud-Ubangi prov. Dem. Rep. Congo
151 I4 Sudur Azer.
151 B6 Suduragı Turkey
162 □B1 Suðurland constituency Iceland
162 B2 Suðurnes admin. div. Iceland
152 A3 Suðuroy i. Faroe Is
166 D1 Suðuroy i. Faroe Is
166 D1 Suðuroyarfjørður sea chan. Faroe Is
190 G5 Sudwalde Ger.
159 O2 Sudzha Rus. Fed.
159 O2 Sudzha r. Rus. Fed.
230 F3 Sue watercourse Sudan
209 E9 Sueca Spain
219 M8 Sŭedinenie Bulg.
214 C8 Suelli Sardegna Italy
239 □2b Suète, Île du i. Inner Islands Seychelles
205 J2 Sueva, Reserva Nacional de nature res. Spain
178 B8 Suèvres France
255 □1 Sue Wood Bay Bermuda
Suez Egypt see As Suways
Suez, Gulf of Egypt see Suways, Khalīj as
Suez Bay Egypt see Qulzum, Baḩr al
Suez Canal Egypt see Suways, Qanāt as
146 E4 Şufaynah Saudi Arabia
259 G2 Suffern NY U.S.A.
173 N3 Suffolk admin. div. England U.K.
256 I12 Suffolk VA U.S.A.
259 J3 Suffolk County county NY U.S.A.
144 A2 Sūfiān Iran
Sufi-Kurgan Kyrg. see Sopu-Korgon
151 E3 Sugan, Gora mt. Rus. Fed.
250 E7 Sugar r. WI U.S.A.
250 F4 Sugarbush Hill WI U.S.A.
256 C9 Sugar Grove OH U.S.A.
259 G2 Sugar Loaf NY U.S.A.
244 D3 Sugarloaf hill AK U.S.A.
169 C9 Sugarloaf Mountain hill Ireland
257 □O3 Sugarloaf Mountain ME U.S.A.
105 N5 Sugarloaf Point N.S.W. Austr.
238 □2b Sugar Loaf Point St Helena
258 D2 Sugar Notch PA U.S.A.
258 C1 Sugar Run PA U.S.A.
126 E7 Suga-shima i. Japan
114 F6 Sugbuhan Point Phil.
195 I2 Sugenheim Ger.
Süget Xinjiang China see Sogat
116 E4 Sugi i. Indon.
132 C7 Sugun Xinjiang China
117 L1 Sugut r. Malaysia
117 L1 Sugut, Tanjung pt Malaysia
219 N7 Suhaia Romania
132 K7 Suhai Hu l. Qinghai China
128 J6 Suhai Obo Nei Mongol China
128 I7 Suhait Nei Mongol China
225 F3 Sūhāj Sawhāj Egypt
201 K8 Suha krajina reg. Slovenia
147 M3 Şuḩār Oman
219 O2 Suharău Romania
218 I8 Suharekë Suharekë Kosovo
150 B8 Suhaymī, Wādī as watercourse Egypt
128 J1 Sühbaatar Mongolia
129 M3 Sühbaatar Mongolia
129 M3 Sühbaatar prov. Mongolia
136 C7 Suheli Par i. India
201 J8 Suhi vrh mt. Slovenia
191 K9 Suhl Ger.
190 K5 Suhlendorf Ger.
210 F3 Suhopolje Croatia
194 E7 Suhr Switz.
146 G4 Suhul reg. Saudi Arabia
147 K4 Suhūl al Kidan plain Saudi Arabia
228 E5 Suhum Ghana
221 L4 Şuhut Turkey
145 M7 Sui Pak.
119 D10 Sui, Laem pt Thai.
278 B4 Suiá Missur r. Brazil
Sui'an Fujian China see Zhangpu
122 G5 Suibin Heilong. China
131 L4 Suichang Zhejiang China
Suicheng Fujian China see Jianning
Suicheng Guangdong China see Suixi
131 J5 Suichuan Jiangxi China
Suid-Afrika country Africa see South Africa, Republic of
129 L8 Suide Shaanxi China
204 D3 Suído, Serra do mts Spain
Suidzhikurmsy Turkm. see Madaw
122 G6 Suifenhe Heilong. China
122 G7 Suifen He r. China
127 L2 Suifu Japan
138 C7 Suigam Gujarat India
126 C4 Suigetsu-ko l. Japan
127 L3 Suigō-Tsukuba Kokutei-kōen park Japan
122 E5 Suihua Heilong. China
130 D4 Suijiang Yunnan China
131 K4 Sui Jiang r. China
122 E5 Suileng Heilong. China
182 C2 Suilly-la-Tour France
168 F6 Suilven hill Scotland U.K.
130 H5 Suining Hunan China
131 K2 Suining Jiangsu China
130 E3 Suining Sichuan China
285 H4 Suipacha Arg.
276 D5 Suipacha Bol.
131 J2 Suiping Henan China
178 G5 Suippe r. France
178 I5 Suippes France
169 H8 Suir r. Ireland
Suisse country Europe see Switzerland
181 K4 Suisse Normande reg. France
126 C6 Suita Japan
151 L5 Suiti Burunu pt Azer.
258 B7 Suitland MD U.S.A.
131 K2 Suixi Anhui China
130 H8 Suixi Guangdong China
129 N9 Suixian Henan China
Suixian Hubei China see Suizhou
130 F5 Suiyang Guizhou China
129 N9 Suiyang Henan China
Suizhai Henan China see Xiangcheng
129 Q6 Suizhong Liaoning China
131 I3 Suizhou Hubei China
129 J5 Suj Nei Mongol China
138 E6 Sujangarh Rajasthan India
145 M9 Sujawal Pak.
Suk atoll Micronesia see Pulusuk
116 G8 Sukabumi Jawa Indon.
117 H5 Sukadana Kalimantan Indon.
116 F7 Sukadana Sumatera Indon.
117 H5 Sukadana, Teluk b. Indon.
127 L1 Sukagawa Japan
116 G8 Sukanegara Jawa Indon.
117 I6 Sukaraja Kalimantan Indon.
117 I6 Sukaramai Kalimantan Indon.
Sukarnapura Papua Indon. see Jayapura
Sukarno, Puntjak mt. Papua Indon. see Jaya, Puncak
117 M2 Sukau Sabah Malaysia
138 F7 Suket Rajasthan India
162 S5 Sukeva Fin.
122 H5 Sukhanovka Rus. Fed.
161 N8 Sukhary Belarus
161 S7 Sukhinichi Rus. Fed.
159 Q6 Sukhi Yaly r. Ukr.
197 M6 Sukhodil Ukr.
161 V8 Sukhodol'skiy Rus. Fed.
161 N1 Sukhodol'skoye, Ozero l. Rus. Fed.
161 S7 Sukhodrev r. Rus. Fed.
Sukhoivanovka Ukr. see Stepnohirs'k
151 G1 Sukhokumskiy Kanal canal Rus. Fed.
156 I3 Sukhona r. Rus. Fed.
118 D6 Sukhothai Thai.
122 E3 Sukhotino Rus. Fed.
161 S5 Sukhoverkovo Rus. Fed.
Sukhumi Georgia see Sokhumi
Sukhum-Kale Georgia see Sokhumi
159 Q5 Sukhyy Torets' r. Ukr.
159 K6 Sukhyy Yelanets' Ukr.
Sukkertoppen Greenland see Maniitsoq
156 F3 Sukkozero Rus. Fed.
145 M8 Sukkur Pak.
145 M8 Sukkur Barrage Pak.
136 G3 Sukma Chhattisgarh India
224 B2 Sūknah Libya
117 I8 Sukolilo Jawa Indon.
199 H5 Sükösd Hungary
192 E3 Sukow Ger.
122 J5 Sukpay Rus. Fed.
122 J5 Sukpay r. Rus. Fed.
138 D7 Sukri r. India
138 D7 Sukri r. India
161 R5 Sukromlya Rus. Fed.
161 T4 Sukromny Rus. Fed.
234 C4 Sukses Namibia
156 L4 Suksun Rus. Fed.
139 I9 Suktel r. India
125 J14 Sukumo Japan
125 J14 Sukumo-wan b. Japan
115 C8 Sukun i. Indon.
151 I6 Şükürbäyli Azer.
275 I5 Sul, Canal do sea chan. Brazil
281 F4 Sul, Pico do mt. Brazil
166 J1 Sula i. Norway
156 J2 Sula r. Rus. Fed.
159 L4 Sula r. Ukr.
115 D4 Sula, Kepulauan is Indon.
115 D5 Sulabesi i. Indon.
145 M6 Sulaiman Range mts Pak.
151 I2 Sulak Rus. Fed.
151 I2 Sulak r. Rus. Fed.
144 D6 Sūlār Iran
168 D4 Sula Sgeir i. Scotland U.K.
116 D5 Sulasih, Gunung vol. Indon.
117 L9 Sulat i. Indon.
114 E6 Sulat Samar Phil.
244 I2 Sulatna Crossing AK U.S.A.
115 B5 Sulawesi i. Indon.
115 A5 Sulawesi Barat prov. Indon.
115 A6 Sulawesi Selatan prov. Indon.
115 B4 Sulawesi Tengah prov. Indon.
115 C6 Sulawesi Tenggara prov. Indon.
115 D3 Sulawesi Utara prov. Indon.
149 L6 Sulaymān Beg Iraq
Sulaymānīyah Iraq see As Sulaymānīyah
146 G5 Sulayyimah Saudi Arabia
Sulci Sardegna Italy see Sant'Antioco
Sulcis Sardegna Italy see Sant'Antioco
214 B9 Sulcis reg. Sardegna Italy
164 C2 Suldalsvatnet l. Norway
196 D3 Sulechów Pol.
196 D3 Sulęcin Pol.
196 F3 Sulęcinek Pol.
196 F1 Sulęczyno Pol.
144 D3 Suledeh Iran
229 G4 Suleja Nigeria
197 H4 Sulejów Pol.
197 J3 Sulejówek Pol.
197 H4 Sulejowskie, Jezioro l. Pol.
117 M4 Suleman, Teluk b. Indon.
214 D6 Su Lernu r. Italy
168 H4 Sule Skerry i. Scotland U.K.
168 G4 Sule Stack i. Scotland U.K.
148 H5 Süleymanlı Kahramanmaraş Turkey
221 I4 Süleymanlı Manisa Turkey
116 D5 Suliki Sumatera Indon.
196 D4 Sulików Pol.
228 C5 Sulima Sierra Leone
219 R5 Sulina Romania
219 R5 Sulina, Braţul watercourse Romania
190 G5 Sulingen Ger.
128 D8 Sulin Gol r. Qinghai China
162 N3 Suliskongen mt. Norway
196 D2 Suliszewo Pol.
162 N3 Sulitjelma Norway
163 T6 Sulkava Fin.
145 I7 Sūlkī-ye Sangān Sīstān va Balūchestān Iran
197 H6 Sułkowice Pol.
151 H2 Sulla-Chubutla r. Rus. Fed.
274 A6 Sullana Peru
169 E9 Sullane r. Ireland
221 K4 Süller Turkey
173 L6 Sullington West Sussex, England U.K.
260 K6 Sullivan IL U.S.A.
254 D6 Sullivan IN U.S.A.
260 J6 Sullivan MO U.S.A.
246 E5 Sullivan Bay B.C. Can.
258 F1 Sullivan County county NY U.S.A.
258 B2 Sullivan County county PA U.S.A.
Sullivan Island Myanmar see Lanbi Kyun
247 I5 Sullivan Lake Alta Can.
168 □N2 Sullom Voe inlet Scotland U.K.
257 □P1 Sully Que. Can.
182 E2 Sully France
172 F5 Sully Vale of Glamorgan, Wales U.K.
178 D8 Sully-sur-Loire France
201 M6 Sulm r. Austria
197 H4 Sulmierzyce Łódzkie Pol.
196 F4 Sulmierzyce Wielkopolskie Pol.
Sulmo Italy see Sulmona
215 L3 Sulmona Italy
180 F6 Sulniac France
100 □6 Sulofoloa Malaita Solomon Is
219 O9 Süloğlu Turkey
197 H5 Sułoszowa Pol.
196 F4 Sułów Dolnośląskie Pol.
197 K5 Sułów Lubelskie Pol.
261 I10 Sulphur LA U.S.A.
261 G8 Sulphur OK U.S.A.
261 H9 Sulphur r. TX U.S.A.
261 D9 Sulphur Draw watercourse TX U.S.A.
261 H9 Sulphur Springs TX U.S.A.
261 E9 Sulphur Springs Draw watercourse NM/TX U.S.A.
248 D4 Sultan Ont. Can.
224 D2 Sultan Libya
145 J7 Sultan, Koh-i- mts Pak.
Sultanabad Andhra Prad. India see Osmannagar
Sultanabad Iran see Arāk
221 K2 Sultanbeyli Turkey
221 M4 Sultandağı Turkey
148 F4 Sultanhanı Turkey
221 J5 Sultanhisar Turkey
221 H2 Sultaniça Turkey
Sultanıye Turkey see Karapınar
138 I6 Sultanpur Uttar Prad. India
145 I1 Sultansandzharskoye Vodokhranilishche resr Turkm.
151 D1 Sultanskoye Rus. Fed.
231 E6 Sulu Dem. Rep. Congo
114 E6 Suluan i. Phil.
114 D8 Sulu Archipelago is Phil.
148 F4 Sülüklü Turkey
143 M8 Sülüktü Kyrg.
139 N6 Sulung Arun. Prad. India
224 D1 Suluntah Libya
224 D2 Sulūq Libya
136 G6 Suluru Andhra Prad. India
290 C5 Sulu Sea N. Pacific Ocean
151 J5 Sulut Azer.
249 F1 Suluvvaulik, Lac l. Que. Can.
159 K3 Sulymivka Ukr.
Sulyukta Kyrg. see Sülüktü
200 A5 Sulz Austria
195 K3 Sulz r. Ger.
195 I3 Sulzach r. Ger.
194 F5 Sulz am Neckar Ger.
195 O4 Sulzbach r. Ger.
194 G2 Sulzbach am Main Ger.
194 G3 Sulzbach an der Murr Ger.
194 H4 Sulzbach-Laufen Ger.
195 L2 Sulzbach-Rosenberg Ger.
194 C3 Sulzbach/Saar Ger.
200 A4 Sulzberg Austria
195 I6 Sulzberg Ger.
286 N1 Sulzberger Bay Antarctica
194 D6 Sulzburg Ger.
191 K10 Sulzdorf an der Lederhecke Ger.
195 K5 Sulzemoos Ger.
194 F3 Sulzfeld Baden-Württemberg Ger.
191 J10 Sulzfeld Bayern Ger.
195 I2 Sulzheim Ger.
191 J10 Sulzthal Ger.
126 B6 Suma Japan
274 B5 Sumaco, Volcán vol. Ecuador
218 I6 Šumadija reg. Serbia
147 N4 Sumāil Oman
115 C3 Sumalata Sulawesi Indon.
232 D3 Sumalē admin. reg. Eth.
282 E3 Sumampa Arg.
117 L1 Sumangat, Tanjung pt Malaysia
274 C4 Sumapaz, Parque Nacional nat. park Col.
144 A5 Sūmār Iran
186 J2 Sumar Neth.
116 C3 Sumatera i. Indon.
116 D5 Sumatera Barat prov. Indon.
116 E6 Sumatera Selatan prov. Indon.
116 C3 Sumatera Utara prov. Indon.
Sumatra i. Indon. see Sumatera
277 E1 Sumaúma Brazil
198 C2 Šumava mts Czech Rep.
198 C2 Šumava nat. park Czech Rep.
100 □1 Sumay Guam
115 B8 Sumba i. Indon.
230 C4 Sumba, Île i. Dem. Rep. Congo
115 A8 Sumba, Selat sea chan. Indon.
144 F3 Sumbar r. Turkm.
115 A8 Sumbawa i. Indon.
117 L9 Sumbawabesar Sumbawa Indon.
233 A6 Sumbawanga Tanz.
276 C3 Sumbay Peru
231 B7 Sumbe Angola
116 D6 Sumbing, Gunung vol. Indon.
231 F7 Sumbu Zambia
231 F7 Sumbu National Park Zambia
168 □N3 Sumburgh Shetland, Scotland U.K.
168 □N3 Sumburgh Head Scotland U.K.
228 C5 Sumbuya Sierra Leone
156 J4 Sumchino Rus. Fed.
133 D9 Sumdo Aksai Chin
130 C4 Sumdo Sichuan China
245 N4 Sumdum AK U.S.A.
245 N4 Sumdum, Mount AK U.S.A.
278 F3 Sumé Brazil
201 N8 Šumećani Croatia
117 G8 Sumedang Jawa Indon.
144 C3 Sume'eh Sarā Iran
198 G5 Sümeg Hungary
230 E2 Sumeih Sudan
183 D9 Sumène France
117 J8 Sumenep Jawa Indon.
138 D7 Sumerpur Rajasthan India
Sumgait Azer. see Sumqayıt
199 J3 Šumiac Slovakia
125 R15 Sumisu-jima i. Japan
212 D1 Sumiswald Switz.
Sümiyn Bulag Mongolia see Gurvandzagal
124 □G18 Sumiyō Nansei-shotō Japan
149 K5 Summēl Iraq
248 B2 Summer Beaver Ont. Can.
171 N5 Summer Bridge North Yorkshire, England U.K.
234 C4 Summerdown Namibia
249 K3 Summerford Nfld and Lab. Can.
169 I6 Summerhill Ireland
250 H4 Summer Island MI U.S.A.
168 E6 Summer Isles Scotland U.K.
246 G5 Summerland B.C. Can.
249 I4 Summerside P.E.I. Can.
256 E10 Summersville WV U.S.A.
256 E10 Summersville Lake WV U.S.A.
255 E8 Summerville GA U.S.A.
255 G9 Summerville SC U.S.A.
102 K7 Summit hill North I. N.Z.
245 J3 Summit AK U.S.A.
259 G3 Summit NJ U.S.A.
260 G3 Summit SD U.S.A.
258 D3 Summit Hill PA U.S.A.
246 E3 Summit Lake B.C. Can.
246 F4 Summit Lake B.C. Can.
245 K3 Summit Lake AK U.S.A.
265 P2 Summit Mountain NV U.S.A.
263 K8 Summit Peak CO U.S.A.
258 C3 Summit Station PA U.S.A.
201 M2 Šumná Czech Rep.
133 D9 Sumnal Aksai Chin
103 G10 Sumner South I. N.Z.
261 J9 Sumner MS U.S.A.
103 G9 Sumner, Lake South I. N.Z.
245 N4 Sumner Strait AK U.S.A.
127 J1 Sumon Japan
125 Q9 Sumon-dake mt. Japan
126 A7 Sumoto Japan
115 A6 Sumpangbinangae Sulawesi Indon.
198 F2 Šumperk Czech Rep.
118 C1 Sumprabum Myanmar
Sumpu Japan see Shizuoka
151 K5 Sumqayıt Azer.
151 K5 Sumqayıt r. Azer.
145 N8 Sumrahu Pak.
143 N7 Sumsar Kyrg.
159 M2 Sums'ka Oblast' admin. div. Ukr.
Sumskaya Oblast' admin. div. Ukr. see Sums'ka Oblast'
156 F2 Sumskiy Posad Rus. Fed.
190 K4 Sumte Ger.
255 G9 Sumter SC U.S.A.
138 F2 Sumur Jammu and Kashmir India
198 G2 Šumvald Czech Rep.
212 F2 Sumvitg Switz.
133 E9 Sumxi Xizang China
159 N3 Sumy Ukr.
Sumy Oblast admin. div. Ukr. see Sums'ka Oblast'
130 A4 Sumzom Xizang China
262 I3 Sun r. MT U.S.A.
156 J4 Suna Rus. Fed.
124 S3 Sunagawa Japan
138 F7 Sunaj Madh. Prad. India
138 E4 Sunam Punjab India
139 M7 Sunamganj Bangl.
126 E5 Sunami Japan
128 F7 Sunan Gansu China
123 D9 Sunan N. Korea
168 E9 Sunart, Loch inlet Scotland U.K.
199 J2 Šuňava Slovakia
147 L4 Şunaynah Oman
208 B1 Sunbilla Spain
144 A4 Sunbula Kuh mts Iran
262 I2 Sunburst MT U.S.A.
105 J7 Sunbury Vic. Austr.
173 L5 Sunbury Surrey, England U.K.
256 C8 Sunbury OH U.S.A.
251 R9 Sunbury PA U.S.A.
285 G2 Sunchales Arg.
195 M4 Sünching Ger.
277 E6 Suncho Corral Arg.
123 D9 Sunch'ŏn N. Korea
123 E11 Sunch'ŏn S. Korea
237 L1 Sun City S. Africa
265 T8 Sun City AZ U.S.A.
264 O8 Sun City CA U.S.A.
257 N5 Suncook NH U.S.A.
199 L5 Şuncuiuş Romania
160 D1 Sund Åland Fin.
116 F8 Sunda, Selat str. Indon.
Sunda Kalapa Jawa Indon. see Jakarta
262 L4 Sundance WY U.S.A.
139 L9 Sundarbans coastal area Bangl./India
139 L9 Sundarbans National Park Bangl./India
139 J8 Sundargarh Orissa India
138 F4 Sundarnagar Hima. Prad. India
289 L4 Sunda Shelf sea feature Indian Ocean
Sunda Strait Indon. see Sunda, Selat
Sunda Trench sea feature Indian Ocean see Java Trench
236 J9 Sundays r. Eastern Cape S. Africa
237 O4 Sundays r. KwaZulu-Natal S. Africa
108 G4 Sunday Strait W.A. Austr.
285 F4 Sundblad Arg.
164 B2 Sunde Hordaland Norway
162 J5 Sunde Sør-Trøndelag Norway
171 O4 Sunderland Tyne and Wear, England U.K.
191 F8 Sundern (Sauerland) Ger.
182 K1 Sundgau reg. France
191 K8 Sundhausen Ger.
221 L3 Sündiken Dağları mts Turkey
231 B6 Sundi-Mamba Dem. Rep. Congo
105 M3 Sundown National Park Qld Austr.
246 H5 Sundre Alta Can.
248 E4 Sundridge Ont. Can.
164 F5 Sunds Denmark
164 E2 Sundsli Norway
163 N5 Sundsvall Sweden
151 J5 Sündü Azer.
237 P5 Sundumbili S. Africa
129 L2 Sunduyka Rus. Fed.
138 F7 Sunel Rajasthan India
233 C6 Sunga Tanz.
116 E4 Sungaiapit Sumatera Indon.
117 I4 Sungai Ayak Kalimantan Indon.
116 E4 Sungaiguntung Sumatera Indon.
116 E4 Sungaikabung Sumatera Indon.
117 H5 Sungaikakap Kalimantan Indon.
116 G5 Sungailiat Sumatera Indon.
116 D6 Sungaipenuh Sumatera Indon.
116 D2 Sungai Petani Malaysia
117 H4 Sungaipinyuh Kalimantan Indon.
116 G6 Sungaiselan Indon.
116 □ Sungai Tuas Basin dock Sing.
Sungari r. China see Songhua Jiang
116 □ Sungei Seletar Reservoir Sing.
115 A6 Sungguminasa Sulawesi Indon.
225 F6 Sungikai Sudan
Sungkiang Shanghai China see Songjiang
131 □J7 Sung Kong i. H.K. China
235 G3 Sungo Moz.
Sungqu Sichuan China see Songpan
116 F6 Sungsang Sumatera Indon.
151 D4 Süngülü Turkey
219 O8 Sungurlare Bulg.
148 G3 Sungurlu Turkey
214 B7 Suni Sardegna Italy
210 F3 Sunja Croatia
143 O5 Sunkar, Gora mt. Kazakh.
139 L7 Sunkosh Chhu r. Bhutan
139 K6 Sun Kosi r. Nepal
159 L4 Sunky Ukr.
191 J9 Sünna Ger.
164 C1 Sunndal Norway
162 J5 Sunndalsøra Norway
164 J2 Sunne Sweden
163 H6 Sunnfjord reg. Norway
173 K5 Sunninghill Windsor and Maidenhead, England U.K.
265 V2 Sunnyside UT U.S.A.
262 E3 Sunnyside WA U.S.A.
264 J4 Sunnyvale CA U.S.A.
127 K6 Suno-saki pt Japan
250 E6 Sun Prairie WI U.S.A.
277 F4 Sunsas, Sierra de hills Bol.
264 □C12 Sunset Beach HI U.S.A.
246 G4 Sunset House Alta Can.
Sunset Peak hill H.K. China see Tai Tung Shan
Sunshine Island H.K. China see Chau Kung To
153 M3 Suntar Rus. Fed.
145 J9 Suntsar Pak.
232 C2 Suntu Eth.
262 G5 Sun Valley ID U.S.A.
123 D10 Sunwi-do i. N. Korea
122 E4 Sunwu Heilong. China
228 E5 Sunyani Ghana
151 H2 Sunzha r. Rus. Fed.
162 T2 Suojanperä Fin.
162 R5 Suolahti Fin.
156 E2 Suolijärvet l. Fin.
Suoločielgi Fin. see Saariselkä
162 Q2 Suoluvuobmi Norway
163 S6 Suomenniemi Fin.
250 E1 Suomi Ont. Can.
Suomi country Europe see Finland
160 G1 Suomusjärvi Fin.
162 T4 Suomussalmi Fin.
125 I13 Suō-nada b. Japan
162 S5 Suonenjoki Fin.
119 G9 Suŏng Cambodia
118 F5 Suong r. Laos
162 S5 Suontee Fin.
162 S5 Suontienselkä l. Fin.
156 F3 Suoyarvi Rus. Fed.
Suozhen Shandong China see Huantai
136 D5 Supa Karnataka India
265 T5 Supai AZ U.S.A.
139 K6 Supaul Bihar India
185 F10 Superbagnères France
178 G6 Superbe r. France
182 B5 Superbesse France
183 H7 Superdévoluy France
265 U8 Superior AZ U.S.A.
262 G3 Superior MT U.S.A.
260 F5 Superior NE U.S.A.
250 B3 Superior WI U.S.A.
269 M9 Superior, Laguna lag. Mex.
250 G2 Superior, Lake Can./U.S.A.
213 J5 Superiore, Lago l. Italy
183 B6 Superlioran France
213 R6 Supertarska Draga Croatia
210 F4 Supetar Croatia
119 E7 Suphan Buri Thai.
149 K4 Süphan Dağı mt. Turkey
215 K4 Supino Italy
113 I7 Supiori i. Papua Indon.
159 K4 Supiy r. Ukr.
199 L4 Suplacu de Barcău Romania
161 R8 Suponevo Rus. Fed.
191 K6 Süpplingen Ger.
286 V1 Support Force Glacier Antarctica
197 L2 Supraśl Pol.
197 K2 Supraśl r. Pol.
151 C3 Sup'sa r. Georgia
123 D8 Supung N. Korea
199 L4 Supur Romania
146 G7 Sūq al Inān Yemen
146 E5 Sūq ar Rubū' Saudi Arabia
149 M8 Sūq ash Shuyūkh Iraq
131 L2 Suqian Jiangsu China
146 D3 Sūq Suwayq Saudi Arabia
147 L9 Suquṭrá i. Yemen
195 N6 Sur r. Ger.
228 E4 Sur r. Ghana
199 H4 Súr Hungary
147 N4 Şūr Oman
264 K5 Sur, Point CA U.S.A.
285 I5 Sur, Punta pt Arg.
157 I5 Sura Rus. Fed.
142 B1 Sura r. Rus. Fed.
151 K5 Şuraabad Azer.
145 L7 Surab Pak.
117 J8 Surabaya Jawa Indon.
145 K7 Surai Pak.
139 I8 Surajpur Chhattisgarh India
144 H9 Sūrak Iran
117 I8 Surakarta Jawa Indon.
115 A4 Suramana Sulawesi Indon.
219 M5 Şura Mare Romania
182 G4 Suran r. France
145 I8 Sūran Iran
150 E3 Şūrān Syria
199 H3 Surany Slovakia
232 D3 Surar Eth.
275 F6 Surára Brazil
107 L9 Surat Qld Austr.
138 D9 Surat Gujarat India
138 D5 Suratgarh Rajasthan India
119 D10 Surat Thani Thai.
197 K3 Suraż Pol.
161 N6 Surazh Belarus
161 P8 Surazh Rus. Fed.
195 N6 Surberg Ger.
107 K7 Surbiton Qld Austr.
217 O3 Surbo Italy
149 L6 Sūrdāsh Iraq
219 P5 Surdila-Greci Romania
219 L3 Surduc Romania
219 K8 Surdulica Surdulica Serbia
194 B2 Sûre r. Ger./Lux.
187 I9 Sûre, Vallée de la val. Lux.
138 C8 Surendranagar Gujarat India
266 □R13 Suretka Costa Rica
264 L7 Surf CA U.S.A.
259 G5 Surf City NJ U.S.A.
173 L2 Surfleet Lincolnshire, England U.K.
138 D9 Surgana Mahar. India
184 C3 Surgères France
270 B2 Surgidero de Batabanó Cuba
152 I3 Surgut Rus. Fed.
186 J2 Surhuizum Neth.
Suri W. Bengal India see Siuri
208 I4 Súria Spain
136 F4 Suriapet Andhra Prad. India
125 □3 Suribachi-yama hill Iō-jima Japan
212 C4 Surier Italy
114 E7 Surigao Mindanao Phil.
114 E6 Surigao Strait Phil.
274 C4 Surimena Col.
119 F7 Surin Thai.
239 □1b Surinam Mauritius
Surinam country S. America see Suriname
275 G3 Suriname country S. America
275 H3 Suriname r. Suriname
119 C10 Surin Nua, Ko i. Thai.
274 D3 Suripá Venez.
149 P6 Surkhābād Iran
143 L9 Surkhandar'ya r. Uzbek.
Surkhandarya Oblast admin. div. Uzbek. see Surxondaryo
145 K6 Surkhduz Afgh.
138 H5 Surkhet Nepal
145 M2 Surkhob r. Tajik.
Surkhondaryo r. Uzbek. see Surkhandar'ya
Surkhondaryo Wiloyati admin. div. Uzbek. see Surxondaryo
144 E6 Sūrmaq Iran
178 G5 Surmelin r. France
149 J3 Sürmene Turkey
162 J5 Surnadalsøra Norway
219 N8 Sŭrnevo Bulg.
157 H6 Surovikino Rus. Fed.
245 N4 Surprise B.C. Can.
100 □5 Surprise, Île i. New Caledonia
245 N4 Surprise Lake B.C. Can.
146 F4 Surrah, Nafūd as des. Saudi Arabia
206 D2 Surrazala r. Port.
246 F5 Surrey B.C. Can.
270 □ Surrey reg. Jamaica
173 L5 Surrey admin. div. England U.K.
212 E1 Sursee Switz.
212 F2 Surselva reg. Switz.
159 N5 Surs'ko-Mykhaylivka Ukr.
157 I5 Surskoye Rus. Fed.
224 C2 Surt Libya
224 C2 Surt, Khalīj g. Libya
162 □C2 Surtsey i. Iceland
144 G8 Sūrū Hormozgan Iran
144 H9 Sūrū Sīstān va Balūchestān Iran
219 M5 Suru, Vârful mt. Romania
278 C2 Surubiú r. Brazil
148 I5 Suruç Turkey
232 E2 Surud, Raas pt Somalia
Surud Ad mt. Somalia see Shimbiris
127 H6 Suruga-wan b. Japan
116 E6 Surulangun Sumatera Indon.
275 F4 Surumú r. Brazil
114 F8 Surup Mindanao Phil.
244 I2 Survey Pass AK U.S.A.
178 E5 Survilliers France
190 E5 Surwold Ger.
143 L9 Surxondaryo admin. div. Uzbek.
Suryapet Andhra Prad. India see Suriapet
182 E5 Sury-le-Comtal France
180 F6 Surzur France
151 H6 Şuşa Azer.
164 H6 Suså r. Denmark
212 C5 Susa Italy
125 I12 Susa Japan
212 B5 Susa, Valle di val. Italy
210 F4 Sušac i. Croatia
Susah Tunisia see Sousse
213 Q6 Susak Croatia
210 E3 Susak i. Croatia
125 K13 Susaki Japan
125 M13 Susami Japan
Susamyr Kyrg. see Suusamyr
257 I11 Susan VA U.S.A.
144 C6 Sūsangerd Iran
122 L2 Susanino Khabarovskiy Kray Rus. Fed.
156 H4 Susanino Kostromskaya Oblast' Rus. Fed.
264 L1 Susanville CA U.S.A.
212 I2 Susch Switz.
158 G2 Suschany Ukr.
213 M4 Susegana Italy
148 I3 Suşehri Turkey
190 K2 Süsel Ger.
219 N7 Sushitsa Bulg.
129 L9 Sushui He r. China
198 C2 Sušice Czech Rep.
197 L5 Susiec Pol.
245 J3 Susitna r. AK U.S.A.
245 J3 Susitna, Mount AK U.S.A.
245 K3 Susitna Lake AK U.S.A.
160 L5 Šuškova Latvia
138 F8 Susner Madh. Prad. India
119 D11 Suso Thai.
205 O4 Suso, Monasterio de tourist site Spain
127 H2 Susobana-gawa r. Japan
131 K3 Susong Anhui China
127 I5 Susono Japan
208 K4 Susqueda, Pantà de resr Spain
257 J7 Susquehanna PA U.S.A.
251 R9 Susquehanna r. PA U.S.A.
256 I8 Susquehanna, West Branch r. PA U.S.A.
282 D1 Susques Arg.
194 H4 Süßen Ger.
249 H4 Sussex N.B. Can.
258 F2 Sussex NJ U.S.A.
256 H12 Sussex VA U.S.A.
258 F2 Sussex County county NJ U.S.A.
190 G5 Süstedt Ger.
187 I6 Susteren Neth.
268 D3 Susticacán Mex.
213 K5 Sustinente Italy
190 D5 Sustrum Ger.
246 E3 Sustut Provincial Park B.C. Can.
115 B5 Susua Sulawesi Indon.
100 □6 Susubona Sta Isabel Solomon Is
100 □6 Susuka Choiseul Solomon Is
117 L2 Susul Sabah Malaysia
153 P3 Susuman Rus. Fed.
115 E2 Susupu Halmahera Indon.
221 J3 Susurluk Turkey
151 E5 Susuz Turkey
160 G6 Šušvė r. Lith.
197 H2 Susz Pol.
138 F3 Sutak Jammu and Kashmir India
128 C3 Sutay Uul mt. Mongolia
221 L5 Sütçüler Turkey
216 F8 Sutera Sicilia Italy
105 M6 Sutherland N.S.W. Austr.
236 E8 Sutherland S. Africa
168 H6 Sutherland reg. Scotland U.K.
260 E5 Sutherland NE U.S.A.
256 H11 Sutherland VA U.S.A.
109 H9 Sutherland Range hills W.A. Austr.
210 G4 Sutjeska nat. park Bos.-Herz.
138 C5 Sutlej r. India/Pak.
160 G2 Sutlepa meri l. Estonia
150 B2 Sütlüce İçel Turkey
219 P9 Sütlüce Kırklareli Turkey
214 I3 Sutri Italy
264 K2 Sutter CA U.S.A.
264 L3 Sutter Creek CA U.S.A.
173 L2 Sutterton Lincolnshire, England U.K.
257 M3 Sutton Que. Can.
248 D2 Sutton r. Ont. Can.
103 E12 Sutton South I. N.Z.
173 M3 Sutton Cambridgeshire, England U.K.
245 J3 Sutton AK U.S.A.
260 G5 Sutton NE U.S.A.
256 E10 Sutton WV U.S.A.
173 M2 Sutton Bridge Lincolnshire, England U.K.
173 I2 Sutton Coldfield West Midlands, England U.K.
173 J4 Sutton Courtenay Oxfordshire, England U.K.
171 O7 Sutton in Ashfield Nottinghamshire, England U.K.
248 C2 Sutton Lake Ont. Can.
256 E10 Sutton Lake WV U.S.A.
171 O5 Sutton-on-the-Forest North Yorkshire, England U.K.
171 P7 Sutton on Trent Nottinghamshire, England U.K.
173 N5 Sutton Valence Kent, England U.K.

107 K6 Suttor r. Qld Austr.
124 R4 Suttsu Japan
244 H4 Sutwik Island AK U.S.A.
122 H3 Sutyr' r. Rus. Fed.
158 H4 Sutysky Ukr.
100 □6 Su'u Malaita Solomon Is
Suugant Mongolia see Guryansayhan
100 □6 Su'uholo Solomon Is
237 J7 Suurberg mt. S. Africa
237 J9 Suurberg mts S. Africa
236 E10 Suurbraak S. Africa
160 I3 Suure-Jaani Estonia
160 F3 Suuremõisa Estonia
160 F3 Suur katel b. Estonia
160 G2 Suur-Pakri i. Estonia
160 I2 Suurpea Estonia
160 G3 Suur väin sea chan. Estonia
143 O6 Suusamyr Kyrg.
101 □7a Suva Viti Levu Fiji
Suvalki Pol. see Suwałki
Suva Reka Suharekë Kosovo see Suharekë
151 F6 Suveren Turkey
214 F1 Suvereto Italy
215 Q10 Suvero, Capo c. Italy
213 K7 Suviano, Lago di l. Italy
Suvorov atoll Cook Is see Suwarrow
158 H8 Suvorov Moldova
161 T7 Suvorov Rus. Fed.
159 M6 Suvorove Dnipropetrovs'ka Oblast' Ukr.
158 H8 Suvorove Odes'ka Oblast' Ukr.
219 P7 Suvorovo Bulg.
Suvorovo Moldova see Ştefan Vodă
151 D1 Suvorovskaya Rus. Fed.
159 M8 Suvorovs'ke Ukr.
127 H3 Suwa Japan
127 H3 Suwa-ko l. Japan
117 K5 Suwakong Kalimantan Indon.
197 K1 Suwałki Pol.
118 F7 Suwannaphum Thai.
275 F11 Suwannee r. FL U.S.A.
124 □G17 Suwanose-jima i. Nansei-shotō Japan
117 L4 Suwaran, Gunung mt. Indon.
103 □2 Suwarrow atoll Cook Is
150 D6 Suwaylih Jordan
149 L7 Suwayqiyah, Hawr as imp. l. Iraq
149 J8 Suwayr well Saudi Arabia
225 G2 Suways, Khalīj as g. Egypt
225 G2 Suways, Qanāt as canal Egypt
150 C10 Suweihil pt Saudi Arabia
Suweilih Jordan see Suwaylih
Suweis, Khalig el g. Egypt see Suways, Khalīj as
123 E10 Suwŏn S. Korea
128 D7 Suxik Qinghai China
130 G7 Suxu Guangxi China
133 S3 Suykbulak Kazakh.
274 A6 Suyo Peru
Süyqbulaq Kazakh. see Suykbulak
146 F9 Suyūl Ḩanīsh i. Yemen
151 I1 Suyutkina Kosa Rus. Fed.
151 I1 Suyutkina Kosa, Mys pt Rus. Fed.
142 E7 Suz, Mys pt Kazakh.
144 G8 Sūzā Iran
143 M5 Suzak Kazakh.
127 H2 Suzaka Japan
161 X5 Suzdal' Rus. Fed.
178 F3 Suze-la-Rousse France
159 N1 Suzemka Rus. Fed.
131 K2 Suzhou Anhui China
Suzhou Gansu China see Jiuquan
131 M3 Suzhou Jiangsu China
123 D8 Suzi He r. China
125 O9 Suzu Japan
126 E6 Suzuka Japan
126 E6 Suzuka-gawa r. Japan
126 D5 Suzuka Kokutei-kōen park Japan
126 D6 Suzuka-sanmyaku mts Japan
125 O9 Suzu-misaki pt Japan
213 J6 Suzzara Italy
163 M6 Svabensverk Sweden
162 S1 Sværholthalvøya pen. Norway
162 □ Svalbard terr. Arctic Ocean
219 O7 Svalenik Bulg.
216 H9 Svallerup Denmark
158 B5 Svalyava Ukr.
165 O2 Svanberga Sweden
151 D3 Svanet'is K'edi hills Georgia
165 K5 Svängsta Sweden
162 Q3 Svanstein Sweden
159 N2 Svapa r. Rus. Fed.
162 P3 Svappavaara Sweden
161 P4 Svapushcha Rus. Fed.
198 C3 Švarcenberský kanál canal Czech Rep.
165 L1 Svärdsjö Sweden
164 F2 Svarstad Norway
160 I1 Svarta r. Fin.
165 K2 Svartå Sweden
165 K2 Svartälven r. Sweden
165 J2 Svartån r. Sweden
165 M2 Svartån r. Sweden
162 Q3 Svartbyn Sweden
Svartenhuk Halvø pen. Greenland see Sigguup Nunaa
164 C2 Svartevatn l. Norway
162 P3 Svartlå Sweden
162 P3 Svartlögafjärden b. Sweden
158 F2 Svarytsevychi Ukr.
193 G10 Svatava Czech Rep.
166 J1 Svatjell hill Norway
201 P2 Svatobořice-Mistřín Czech Rep.
159 R4 Svatove Ukr.
201 Q3 Svätuše Slovakia
198 G3 Svätý Jur Slovakia
199 H4 Svätý Peter Slovakia
119 G9 Svay Riĕng Cambodia
162 □ Sveagruva Svalbard
156 I4 Svecha Rus. Fed.
160 I6 Svėdasai Lith.
165 J5 Sveg Sweden
163 M5 Svegsjön l. Sweden
164 B2 Sveio Norway
160 J4 Sveki Latvia
160 E6 Švėkšna Lith.
163 H6 Svelgen Norway
162 J5 Svellingen Norway
159 N1 Sven' Rus. Fed.
160 I6 Švenčionėliai Lith.
160 I6 Švenčionys Lith.
160 J6 Svencionys Lith.
164 G6 Svendborg Denmark
164 J4 Svenljunga Sweden
162 □ Svenskøya i. Svalbard
165 M2 Svenstavik Sweden
197 L1 Šventežeris Lith.
160 F6 Šventoji r. Lith.
160 C2 Sverbeyevo Rus. Fed.
161 S6 Sverchkovo Rus. Fed.
157 I6 Sverdlovo Rus. Fed.
Sverdlovsk Rus. Fed. see Yekaterinburg
159 S5 Sverdlovs'k Ukr.
156 M4 Sverdlovskaya Oblast' admin. div. Rus. Fed.
Sverdlovsk Oblast admin. div. Rus. Fed. see Sverdlovskaya Oblast'
243 I2 Sverdrup Channel Nunavut Can.
243 I2 Sverdrup Islands Nunavut Can.
Sverige country Europe see Sweden
Svermovo Slovakia see Telgárt
159 M2 Svesa Ukr.
219 O7 Sveshtari, Tomb of tourist site Bulg.
210 E4 Sveta Andrija i. Croatia
201 O7 Sveta Marija Croatia
160 G5 Svėtė r. Lith.
213 R6 Sveti Damjan, Rt pt Croatia
213 R6 Sveti Grgur i. Croatia
Sveti Ivan Zelina Croatia see Zelina
210 F4 Sveti Jure mt. Croatia
219 J9 Sveti Nikole Macedonia
198 G1 Světlá Hora Czech Rep.
198 E2 Světlá nad Sázavou Czech Rep.
122 K5 Svetlaya Rus. Fed.
122 M4 Svetlodarskoye Sakhalin Rus. Fed.
Svetlogorsk Belarus see Svyetlahorsk
160 D7 Svetlogorsk Kaliningradskaya Oblast' Rus. Fed.
152 J3 Svetlogorsk Krasnoyarskiy Kray Rus. Fed.
157 H7 Svetlograd Rus. Fed.
156 K4 Svetlopolyansk Rus. Fed.
Svetlovodsk Ukr. see Svitlovods'k
160 D7 Svetlyy Kaliningradskaya Oblast' Rus. Fed.
142 I2 Svetlyy Orenburgskaya Oblast' Rus. Fed.
157 I6 Svetlyy Yar Rus. Fed.
160 L1 Svetogorsk Leningradskaya Oblast' Rus. Fed.
Svetogorsk Respublika Dagestan Rus. Fed. see Shamil'kala
Svetozarevo Jagodina Serbia see Jagodina
218 H5 Svetozar Miletić Vojvodina Serbia
160 H4 Svētupe r. Latvia
213 P5 Svetvinčenat Croatia
162 □E1 Sviahnúkar vol. Iceland
160 G3 Sviby Estonia
158 D4 Svicha r. Ukr.
199 K2 Svidník Slovakia
198 C2 Švihov Czech Rep.
210 F4 Svilaja mts Croatia
218 I6 Svilajnac Svilajnac Serbia
219 O9 Svilengrad Bulg.
219 K6 Svinecea Mare, Vârful mt. Romania
199 K2 Svinia Slovakia
199 H3 Svinná Slovakia
164 H6 Svinninge Denmark
Svinø i. Faroe Is see Svínoy
166 D1 Svínoy i. Faroe Is
160 J7 Svir Belarus
161 S1 Svir' r. Rus. Fed.
160 J7 Svir, Vozyera l. Belarus
161 P1 Sviritsa Rus. Fed.
161 P1 Svirskaya Guba b. Rus. Fed.
161 Q1 Svir'stroy Rus. Fed.
161 P1 Svirzh r. Ukr.
219 N7 Svishtov Bulg.
160 H8 Svislach Hrodzyenskaya Voblasts' Belarus
160 K8 Svislach Minskaya Voblasts' Belarus
197 M2 Svislach r. Belarus
160 L8 Svislach r. Belarus
Svislach r. Belarus see Svislach
199 J2 Svit Slovakia
198 F3 Svitava r. Czech Rep.
198 F2 Svitavy Czech Rep.
159 R5 Svitlodars'k Ukr.
159 N5 Svitlohirs'ke Ukr.
159 M4 Svitlovods'k Ukr.
197 L4 Svityaz' Ukr.
212 I2 Svizzer, Parc Naziunal nat. park Switz.
Svizzera country Europe see Switzerland
160 E7 Svoboda Kaliningradskaya Oblast' Rus. Fed.
159 P2 Svoboda Kurskaya Oblast' Rus. Fed.
198 E1 Svoboda nad Úpou Czech Rep.
122 F3 Svobodnyy Rus. Fed.
161 X5 Svobody Rus. Fed.
219 L8 Svoge Bulg.
160 L6 Svol'nya r. Belarus
162 M2 Svolvær Norway
198 F2 Svratka Czech Rep.
198 F2 Svratka r. Czech Rep.
199 H2 Svrčinovec Slovakia
219 K7 Svrljig Svrljig Serbia
219 K7 Svrljiške Planine mts Serbia
160 J7 Svyantsyanskiya Hrady hills Belarus
Svyatogorovskiy Rudnik Ukr. see Dobropillya
161 X6 Svyatoye, Ozero l. Rus. Fed.
161 P2 Svyatoy Nos, Mys c. Rus. Fed.
161 O9 Svyatsk Rus. Fed.
160 M8 Svyetlahorsk Belarus
159 M1 Svyha r. Ukr.
158 D3 Svynya r. Ukr.
159 T3 Svyten'ka r. Ukr.
145 O4 Swabi Pak.
173 I2 Swadlincote Derbyshire, England U.K.
237 J8 Swaershoek S. Africa
237 J8 Swaershoekpas pass S. Africa
173 N2 Swaffham Norfolk, England U.K.
107 N6 Swain Reefs Qld Austr.
275 G9 Swainsboro GA U.S.A.
99 I3 Swains Island atoll American Samoa
234 B4 Swakop watercourse Namibia
234 B4 Swakopmund Namibia
171 O5 Swale r. England U.K.
100 □6 Swallow Islands Santa Cruz Is Solomon Is
187 J6 Swalmen Neth.
136 E5 Swamihalli Karnataka India
249 G1 Swampy r. Que. Can.
109 C11 Swan r. W.A. Austr.
247 K4 Swan r. Man./Sask. Can.
248 D2 Swan r. Ont. Can.
170 C8 Swan Ireland
173 I6 Swanage Dorset, England U.K.
231 E7 Swana-Mume Dem. Rep. Congo
256 E10 Swandale WV U.S.A.
236 H9 Swanepoelspoort mt. S. Africa
110 J5 Swan Hill Vic. Austr.
246 H4 Swan Hills Alta Can.
Swan Islands is Caribbean Sea see Cisne, Islas del
245 O5 Swan Lake B.C. Can.
247 K4 Swan Lake l. Man. Can.
258 F1 Swan Lake NY U.S.A.
260 H3 Swan Lake l. MN U.S.A.
246 D4 Swan Lake Kispiox River Provincial Park res. Can.
173 M5 Swanley Kent, England U.K.
169 G4 Swanlinbar Ireland
103 G10 Swannanoa South I. N.Z.
255 I8 Swanquarter NC U.S.A.
255 I8 Swanquarter National Wildlife Refuge nature res. NC U.S.A.
104 G6 Swan Reach S.A. Austr.
247 K4 Swan River Man. Can.
250 A5 Swan River MN U.S.A.
170 D5 Swan's Cross Roads Ireland
105 L10 Swansea Tas. Austr.
172 E4 Swansea Swansea, Wales U.K.
172 E4 Swansea admin. div. Wales U.K.
172 E4 Swansea Bay Wales U.K.
257 □Q4 Swans Island ME U.S.A.
264 J4 Swanton CA U.S.A.
257 L4 Swanton VT U.S.A.
173 N2 Swanton Morley Norfolk, England U.K.
196 G1 Swarożyn Pol.
237 J8 Swartberg S. Africa
236 D10 Swartberg mt. S. Africa
237 I6 Swartbergpas pass S. Africa
236 F9 Swartdoorn r. S. Africa
258 E5 Swarthmore PA U.S.A.
237 L8 Swart Kei r. S. Africa
236 E6 Swartkolkvloer salt pan S. Africa
237 J9 Swartkops S. Africa
237 J9 Swartkops r. S. Africa
Swart Nossob watercourse Namibia see Black Nossob
237 K2 Swartplaas S. Africa
237 H4 Swartputs S. Africa
236 D2 Swartput se Pan salt pan Namibia
237 K1 Swartruggens S. Africa
237 K1 Swartruggens mts S. Africa
258 F2 Swartswood NJ U.S.A.
258 F2 Swartswood Lake NJ U.S.A.
237 P3 Swart Umfolozi S. Africa
257 K7 Swartz Creek MI U.S.A.
196 F3 Swarzędz Pol.
265 S2 Swasey Peak UT U.S.A.
251 N1 Swastika Ont. Can.
145 N4 Swat r. Pak.
258 B4 Swatara Creek r. PA U.S.A.
145 O4 Swat Kohistan reg. Pak.
Swatow Guangdong China see Shantou
170 D4 Swatragh Northern Ireland U.K.
173 I6 Sway Hampshire, England U.K.
237 P2 Swaziland country Africa
163 M6 Sweden country Europe
258 E5 Swedesboro NJ U.S.A.
106 G4 Sweers Island Qld Austr.
256 F11 Sweet Briar VA U.S.A.
262 C4 Sweet Home OR U.S.A.
256 E11 Sweet Springs WV U.S.A.
258 C2 Sweet Valley PA U.S.A.
261 E9 Sweetwater TX U.S.A.
262 K5 Sweetwater r. WY U.S.A.
262 J5 Sweetwater Station WY U.S.A.
236 E10 Swellendam S. Africa
237 L7 Swempoort S. Africa
197 I2 Świątki Pol.
196 G1 Świbno Pol.
197 J3 Świder r. Pol.
196 E5 Świdnica Dolnośląskie Pol.
196 D4 Świdnica Lubuskie Pol.
197 K4 Świdnik Pol.
196 E2 Świdwin Pol.
196 E5 Świebodzice Pol.
196 D3 Świebodzin Pol.
196 G2 Świecie Pol.
196 E5 Święciechowa Pol.
197 H2 Świecie nad Osą Pol.
193 K6 Świecko Pol.
197 H2 Świedziebnia Pol.
196 G2 Świekatowo Pol.
196 D5 Świeradów-Zdrój Pol.
197 I3 Świercze Pol.
196 F5 Świerczów Pol.
196 G5 Świerklaniec Pol.
196 D4 Świerzawa Pol.
196 E1 Świerzenko Pol.
196 C2 Świerzno Pol.
196 E1 Świeszyno Pol.
197 J2 Świętajno Warmińsko-Mazurskie Pol.
197 K1 Świętajno Warmińsko-Mazurskie Pol.
197 I5 Świętokrzyskie prov. Pol.
197 I5 Świętokrzyski, Góry hills Pol.
197 I5 Świętokrzyski Park Narodowy nat. park Pol.
244 H3 Swift r. AK U.S.A.
257 □O4 Swift r. ME U.S.A.
247 J5 Swift Current Sask. Can.
247 I5 Swiftcurrent Creek r. Sask. Can.
187 I3 Swifterbant Neth.
244 I3 Swift Fork r. AK U.S.A.
258 C3 Swiftwater PA U.S.A.
170 B4 Swilly r. Ireland
169 G2 Swilly, Lough inlet Ireland
173 I4 Swindon Swindon, England U.K.
173 I4 Swindon admin. div. England U.K.
171 P6 Swinefleet East Riding of Yorkshire, England U.K.
173 L2 Swineshead Lincolnshire, England U.K.
169 E5 Swinford Ireland
258 F1 Swinging Bridge Reservoir NY U.S.A.
196 G3 Świnice Warckie Pol.
237 J4 Swinkpan imp. l. S. Africa
197 H6 Świnna Pol.
196 C2 Świnoujście Pol.
168 L11 Swinton Scottish Borders, Scotland U.K.
171 O7 Swinton South Yorkshire, England U.K.
Swiss Confederation country Europe see Switzerland
212 G2 Swiss Tectonic Arena Sardona tourist site Switzerland
Świstocz r. Belarus see Svislach
212 E2 Switzerland country Europe
Swnt Enlli sea chan. Wales U.K. see Bardsey Sound
196 C2 Swobnica Pol.
169 J6 Swords Ireland
107 H6 Swords Range hills Qld Austr.
196 F5 Swornegacie Pol.
258 D2 Swoyerville PA U.S.A.
197 M2 Syalyava, Vozyera l. Belarus
197 M3 Syalyets Brestskaya Voblasts' Belarus
161 N8 Syalyets Mahilyowskaya Voblasts' Belarus
160 H9 Syalyets, Vodaskhovishcha resr Belarus
156 F3 Syamozero, Ozero l. Rus. Fed.
156 H3 Syamzha Rus. Fed.
139 I5 Syang Nepal
160 M7 Syanno Belarus
160 H8 Syarednenemanskaya Nizina lowland Belarus/Lith.
160 K8 Syarhyeyevichy Belarus
156 J3 Syas' r. Rus. Fed.
161 P1 Syas'troy Rus. Fed.
161 I4 Syava Rus. Fed.
169 B8 Sybil Point Ireland
237 M1 Sybrandskraal S. Africa
250 F8 Sycamore IL U.S.A.
161 P4 Sycewice Pol.
161 R6 Sychevka Rus. Fed.
161 T6 Sychevo Rus. Fed.
160 M8 Sychkava Belarus
196 F4 Syców Pol.
164 F6 Syddanmark admin. reg. Denmark
Sydenham atoll Gilbert Is Kiribati see Nonouti
105 M5 Sydney N.S.W. Austr.
249 I4 Sydney N.S. Can.
104 □1 Sydney Bay Norfolk I.
106 G4 Sydney Island Qld Austr.
Sydney Island Phoenix Is Kiribati see Manra
247 M5 Sydney Lake Ont. Can.
249 I4 Sydney Mines N.S. Can.
Sydzhak Uzbek. see Sijjaq
159 R6 Syedove Ukr.
150 A2 Syedra tourist site Turkey
159 R5 Syeverne Ukr.
159 S5 Syeverodonets'k Ukr.
159 C5 Syke Ger.
220 D6 Sykea Greece
258 B6 Sykesville MD U.S.A.
256 G7 Sykesville PA U.S.A.
220 E2 Sykia Greece
162 I5 Sykkylven Norway
156 J3 Syktyvkar Rus. Fed.
255 D9 Sylacauga AL U.S.A.
139 M7 Sylhet Bangl.
139 M7 Sylhet admin. div. Bangl.
196 G1 Syloga Rus. Fed.
160 H5 Sylt i. Ger.
190 F1 Sylt-Ost Ger.
156 L4 Sylva r. Rus. Fed.
254 F8 Sylva NC U.S.A.
109 E7 Sylvania W.A. Austr.
255 G9 Sylvania GA U.S.A.
256 B7 Sylvania OH U.S.A.
246 H4 Sylvan Lake Alta Can.
195 L6 Sylvensteinsee l. Ger.
255 F10 Sylvester GA U.S.A.
106 E5 Sylvester, Lake salt flat N.T. Austr.
245 O3 Sylvia, Mount B.C. Can.
221 I6 Symi Greece
221 I6 Symi i. Greece
168 I11 Symington South Lanarkshire, Scotland U.K.
159 N9 Synape Ukr.
115 D5 Syndicate Masbate Phil.
159 O5 Synel'nykove Ukr.
149 F5 Syngyrli, Mys pt Kazakh.
149 F5 Syngyrli, Mys pt Kazakh.
159 N3 Synivka Ukr.
153 N3 Synnagyn, Khrebet mts Rus. Fed.
163 J6 Synnfjell mt. Norway
108 H4 Synnott, Mount hill W.A. Austr.
108 H4 Synnott Range hills W.A. Austr.
173 D2 Synod Inn Ceredigion, Wales U.K.
143 T3 Syntas Kazakh.
156 L2 Synya Rus. Fed.
156 N2 Synya r. Rus. Fed.
158 J5 Synytsya r. Ukr.
158 J5 Synyukha r. Ukr.
Synzhera Moldova see Sîngerei
Synzherey Moldova see Sîngerei
259 H3 Syosset NY U.S.A.
287 C2 Syowa research stn Antarctica
197 J2 Sypniewo Mazowieckie Pol.
196 F2 Sypniewo Wielkopolskie Pol.
Syracusae Sicilia Italy see Siracusa
Syracuse Sicilia Italy see Siracusa
260 E6 Syracuse KS U.S.A.
257 I5 Syracuse NY U.S.A.
193 F9 Syrau Ger.
143 I4 Syrdar'ya r. Asia
Syrdar'ya Uzbek. see Sirdaryo
Syrdarya Oblast admin. div. Uzbek. see Sirdaryo
Syrdaryinskiy Uzbek. see Sirdaryo
195 I4 Syrgenstein Ger.
148 I6 Syria country Asia
Syrian Desert Asia see Bādiyat ash Shām
221 H6 Syrna i. Greece
161 N5 Syrokvashino Rus. Fed.
220 F5 Syros i. Greece
161 W9 Syrskiy Rus. Fed.
163 R6 Sysmä Fin.
156 J3 Sysola r. Rus. Fed.
159 Q1 Sysoyevo Rus. Fed.
171 O7 Syston Leicestershire, England U.K.
156 K3 Sytkivtsi Ukr.
156 K5 Syumsi Rus. Fed.
156 K5 Syun r. Rus. Fed.
122 L3 Syurkum Rus. Fed.
122 L3 Syurkum, Mys pt Rus. Fed.
159 O8 Syvash, Zatoka lag. Ukr.
159 N7 Syvas'ke Ukr.
163 T6 Syyspohja Fin.
159 M8 Syzivka Ukr.
142 C1 Syzran' Rus. Fed.
196 E5 Szabadhegy Hungary
199 H4 Szabadbattyán Hungary
199 H4 Szabadegyháza Hungary
Szabadka Vojvodina Serbia see Subotica
199 K5 Szabadkígyós Hungary
199 K5 Szabadkígyósi park Hungary
199 I5 Szabadszállás Hungary
199 L3 Szabolcs-Szatmár-Bereg county Hungary
196 G4 Szadek Pol.
197 I6 Szaflary Pol.
199 H5 Szajol Hungary
199 H5 Szakcs Hungary
199 J3 Szakmár Hungary
199 H4 Szákszend Hungary
199 H4 Szalaszend Hungary
199 I5 Szalkszentmárton Hungary
199 J3 Szalonna Hungary
196 G2 Szamocin Pol.
199 L3 Szamos r. Hungary
199 L3 Szamosszeg Hungary
199 E3 Szamotuły Pol.
199 E1 Szaniecki Park Krajobrazowy Pol.
199 J5 Szank Hungary
199 G4 Szany Hungary
199 J3 Szár Hungary
199 J5 Szarazér-Porgányi-főcsatorna canal Hungary
199 J4 Szarvas Hungary
199 J5 Szászberek Hungary
199 H5 Szászvár Hungary
199 L3 Szatmár-Beregi park Hungary
199 I5 Szatymaz Hungary
199 J4 Százhalombatta Hungary
196 E3 Szczaniec Pol.
197 K6 Szczawne Pol.
197 J6 Szczawnica Pol.
196 E5 Szczawno-Zdrój Pol.
197 K5 Szczebrzeszyn Pol.
196 C2 Szczecin Pol.
196 E2 Szczecinek Pol.
196 C2 Szczeciński, Zalew b. Pol.
192 K4 Szczeciński Park Krajobrazowy Pol.
197 J5 Szczekociny Pol.
197 H5 Szczepankowo Pol.
196 G5 Szczercÿw Pol.
197 J5 Szczucin Pol.
197 J5 Szczuczyn Pol.
196 G2 Szczurkowo Pol.
196 G2 Szczurowa Pol.
197 J5 Szczyrk Pol.
197 H6 Szczytna Pol.
196 E5 Szczytniki Pol.
197 J2 Szczytno Pol.
196 F2 Szczytno, Jezioro l. Pol.
Szechwan prov. China see Sichuan
199 I3 Szécsény Hungary
199 H5 Szederkény Hungary
199 J5 Szeged Hungary
199 K4 Szeghalom Hungary
199 J5 Szegvár Hungary
199 H4 Székesfehérvár Hungary
199 H5 Székkutas Hungary
199 H5 Szekszárd Hungary
197 I6 Szelag Wielki, Jezioro l. Pol.
199 J5 Szemud Pol.
199 J5 Szendehely Hungary
199 I3 Szendrő Hungary
199 I3 Szendrőlád Hungary
199 J5 Szentendre Hungary
198 G4 Szentgotthárd Hungary
199 H5 Szentgyörgyvölgyi park Hungary
199 J5 Szentistván Hungary
199 J4 Szentkirály Hungary
199 G5 Szentlászló Hungary
199 H5 Szentlőrinckáta Hungary
199 H4 Szentmártonkáta Hungary
199 G5 Szentőrinc Hungary
199 H5 Szentpéterfa Hungary
199 H5 Szentpéterszeg Hungary
198 F5 Szepetnek Hungary
199 G5 Szepietowo Pol.
199 K3 Szeremle Hungary
199 K3 Szerencs Hungary
199 K4 Szerep Hungary
199 K4 Szerzyny Pol.
197 K1 Szeska Góra hill Pol.
197 J2 Szestno Pol.
199 H4 Szigetbecse Hungary
199 H4 Szigethalom Hungary
199 H4 Szigetszentmiklós Hungary
199 H5 Szigetújfalu Hungary
199 G5 Szigetvár Hungary
199 H5 Szigliget Hungary
199 I4 Szihalom Hungary
199 J4 Szikszó Hungary
199 G4 Szil Hungary
199 K5 Szilvásvárad Hungary
197 I2 Szkaradowo Pol.
199 F5 Szklarska Poręba Pol.
199 J5 Szklary Górne Pol.
197 J2 Szklo r. Pol.
197 J6 Szkwa r. Pol.
197 J2 Szlichtyngowa Pol.
199 E4 Szob Hungary
199 H4 Szögliget Hungary
199 J3 Szolnok Hungary
199 J4 Szőlősgyörök Hungary
199 G5 Szombathely Hungary
199 G5 Szomolya Hungary
197 K5 Szówsko Pol.
196 D4 Szprotawa Pol.
196 D4 Szprotawa r. Pol.
197 J4 Szreniawa r. Pol.
197 J5 Szrenica mt. Czech Rep.
197 J1 Szreńsk Pol.
197 I1 Szropy Pol.
197 H2 Sztabin Pol.
199 J5 Szálinváros Hungary see Dunaújváros
199 H5 Sztum Pol.
197 H2 Sztutowo Pol.
197 I1 Szubin Pol.
196 F2 Szücsi Hungary
199 I4 Szügy Hungary
199 I3 Szuhogy Hungary
197 K3 Szulborze Wielkie Pol.
196 D3 Szumowo Pol.
197 K3 Szurdokpüspöki Hungary
199 I4 Szydłowiec Pol.
197 I2 Szydłowo Mazowieckie Pol.
196 E2 Szydłowo Wielkopolskie Pol.
197 J2 Szymonka Pol.
196 F4 Szymonków Pol.
196 G4 Szynkielów Pol.
197 L1 Szypliszki Pol.

T

228 D5 Taabo, Lac de l. Côte d'Ivoire
232 D2 Taagga Duudka reg. Somalia
103 □1 Taakoka i. Rarotonga Cook Is
114 C4 Taal, Lake Luzon Phil.
Taalabaya Lebanon
150 D5 Taalabaya Lebanon
101 □9a Taapuna Tahiti Fr. Polynesia
164 I6 Taastrup Denmark
199 H5 Tab Hungary
159 M9 Tabachne Ukr.
115 D4 Tabaco Luzon Phil.
144 H3 Tabādakān Iran
146 F2 Ţabah Saudi Arabia
277 E2 Tabajara Brazil
199 H4 Tabajd Hungary
146 F7 Tabakat well Mali
117 K9 Tabanan Bali Indon.
205 L4 Tabanera de Cerrato Spain
117 L4 Tabang Kalimantan Indon.
117 K4 Tabang r. Indon.
237 N6 Tabankulu S. Africa
Ţabaqah Ar Raqqah Syria see Madīnat ath Thawrah
148 I6 Ţabaqah Ar Raqqah Syria
271 □7 Tabaquite Trin. and Tob.
204 I5 Tábara Spain
113 L7 Tabar Islands P.N.G.
211 D7 Tabarka Tunisia
191 K9 Tabarz Ger.
144 G5 Ţabas Khorāsān Iran
160 H2 Tabasalu Estonia
268 E4 Tabasco Mex.
269 N8 Tabasco state Mex.
144 I5 Ţabas-e Masīnā Khorāsān Iran
144 G6 Tabāsīn Iran
144 I5 Tābask, Kūh-e mt. Iran
144 E5 Tabatinga Amazonas Brazil
276 D4 Tabatinga São Paulo Brazil
280 C4 Tabatinga, Serra da hills Brazil
278 D4 Tabayama Japan
127 I4 Tabayin Myanmar
118 B3 Tabayoo, Mount Luzon Phil.
114 C3 Tabbita N.S.W. Austr.
105 J5 Tabdi Hungary
199 I5 Tabédé well Chad
229 H3 Tabelbala Alg.
226 E3 Taber Alta Can.
247 H5 Taberg hill Sweden
227 G2 Tabernas Spain
165 K4 Tabernes de Valldigna Spain see Tavernes de la Valldigna
207 O6 Taberno Spain
207 O6 Tabet, Nam r. Myanmar
118 C2 Tabi Angola
231 B7 Tabia Tsaka salt l. China
133 G11 Tabiik i. Kwajalein Marshall Is
100 □3a Tabik Channel Kwajalein Marshall Is
100 □3a Tabik Channel Kwajalein Marshall Is
230 F4 Tabili Dem. Rep. Congo
117 M2 Tabin Wildlife Reserve nature res. Malaysia
116 E5 Tabir r. Indon.
99 H2 Tabiteuea atoll Gilbert Is Kiribati
160 J3 Tabivere Estonia
115 D5 Tablas i. Phil.
284 B2 Tablas, Cabo c. Chile
207 L2 Tablas de Daimiel, Parque Nacional de las nat. park Spain
114 C5 Tablas Strait Phil.
239 □1c Table, Pointe de la pt Réunion
236 C9 Table Bay S. Africa
102 L6 Table Cape North I. N.Z.
137 M6 Table Islands Andaman & Nicobar Is India
236 C9 Table Mountain hill S. Africa
245 L1 Table Mountain AK U.S.A.
236 C10 Table Mountain Nature Reserve S. Africa
114 B6 Table Point Palawan Phil.
261 I7 Table Rock Reservoir MO U.S.A.
229 F5 Tabligbo Togo
135 F3 Tablillas r. Spain
204 E3 Taboada Spain
275 F5 Tabocal Brazil
275 G5 Tabocal Brazil
275 F6 Tabocal r. Brazil
277 G4 Tabocó r. Brazil
118 C5 Tabong Myanmar
198 D2 Tábor Czech Rep.
233 B6 Tabora Tanz.
233 B6 Tabora admin. reg. Tanz.
199 I4 Táborfalva Hungary
145 M1 Taboshar Tajik.
285 H2 Tabossi Arg.
Tabost Scotland U.K. see Harbost
228 D5 Tabou Côte d'Ivoire
229 F2 Tabrichat well Mali
144 B2 Tabrīz Iran
178 B4 Tábua Port.
204 E6 Tabuaço Port.
291 I5 Tabuaeran atoll Kiribati
205 Q5 Tabuenca Spain
146 E2 Tabūk Saudi Arabia
146 E2 Tabūk prov. Saudi Arabia
105 N3 Tabulam N.S.W. Austr.
115 C4 Tabulan Sulawesi Indon.
143 R1 Tabuny Rus. Fed.
215 N5 Taburno, Monte mt. Italy
116 D4 Tabuyung Sumatera Indon.
101 □8a Tabwemasana hill Vanuatu
100 □5 Tabwémasana, Mount Vanuatu
165 O2 Täby Sweden
199 H4 Tác Hungary
275 H5 Tacaipu, Serra hills Brazil
274 B3 Tacalé Brazil
268 F6 Tacámbaro Mex.
267 N11 Tacaná, Volcán de vol. Mex.
266 □U13 Tacarcuna, Cerro mt. Panama
201 J7 Tacen Slovenia
132 G4 Tachakou Xinjiang China
229 F2 Tachdaït well Mali
132 F4 Tacheng Xinjiang China
195 N5 Tacherting Ger.
125 G14 Tachibana-wan b. Japan
127 J4 Tachikawa Tōkyō Japan
124 Q8 Tachikawa Yamagata Japan
195 N6 Tachinger See l. Ger.
272 C2 Táchira state Venez.
228 A3 Tachiumet well Libya
198 B2 Tachov Czech Rep.
217 L6 Tacina r. Italy
115 F5 Tacipi Sulawesi Indon.
276 D4 Taciuã, Lago l. Brazil
114 E6 Tacloban Leyte Phil.
276 C5 Tacna Col.
276 C4 Tacna Peru
276 C4 Tacna dept Peru
265 S9 Tacna AZ U.S.A.
262 C3 Tacoma WA U.S.A.
282 F2 Taco Pozo Arg.
208 □3a Tacoronte Tenerife Canary Is
282 G3 Tacuarembó Uru.
285 J3 Tacuarembó dept Uru.
282 G3 Tacuari Arg.
266 E3 Tacupeto Mex.
196 F4 Taczanów Drugi Pol.
125 Q9 Tadami Japan
125 Q9 Tadami-gawa r. Japan
214 B7 Tadasuni Sardegna Italy
171 O6 Tadcaster North Yorkshire, England U.K.
227 G5 Tadeïnte, Oued watercourse Alg.
229 G3 Tadélaka well Niger
226 F5 Tademaït, Plateau du Alg.
245 P1 Tadenet Lake N.W.T. Can.
100 □5 Tadin Îles Loyauté New Caledonia
227 H4 Tadjentourt hill Alg.
227 F5 Tadjeraout, Oued watercourse Alg.
Tadjikistan country Asia see Tajikistan
227 F4 Tadjmout Alg.
232 D1 Tadjourah Djibouti
232 D2 Tadjourah, Golfe de g. Djibouti
227 F2 Tadjrouna Alg.
173 J5 Tadley Hampshire, England U.K.
150 G4 Tadmur Syria
274 B3 Tadó Col.
126 E5 Tado Japan
123 E11 Tadohae Haesang National Park S. Korea
247 L3 Tadoule Lake Man. Can.
249 G3 Tadoussac Que. Can.
136 E5 Tadpatri Andhra Prad. India
227 H4 Tadrart hills Alg.
224 A3 Tadrart Acacus tourist site Libya
136 E3 Tadwale Mahar. India
173 L5 Tadworth Surrey, England U.K.
Tadzhikabad Tajik. see Tojikobod
Tadzhikskaya S.S.R. country Asia see Tajikistan
123 E10 T'aean Haean National Park S. Korea
123 E9 T'aebaek-sanmaek mts N. Korea/S. Korea
160 G3 Taebla Estonia
Taech'ŏn S. Korea see Poryŏng
123 D10 Taech'ŏng-do i. S. Korea
123 D9 Taedong-gang r. N. Korea
123 D10 Taedong-man b. N. Korea
123 F11 Taegu S. Korea
123 D11 Taehŭksan-kundo is S. Korea
123 E10 Taejŏn S. Korea
123 E12 Taejŏng S. Korea
123 F10 T'aepaek S. Korea
160 K3 Taevaskoja Estonia
172 D4 Taf r. Wales U.K.
99 I3 Tafahi i. Tonga
205 Q3 Tafalla Spain
227 H5 Tafassasset, Oued watercourse Alg./Niger
271 □10 Tafelberg hill Curaçao Neth. Antilles
237 J7 Tafelberg S. Africa
236 F8 Tafelberg mt. S. Africa
275 G4 Tafelberg mt. Suriname
275 G4 Tafelberg, Natuurreservaat nature res. Suriname
212 C2 Tafers Switz.
172 F4 Taff r. Wales U.K.
172 F4 Taff's Well Cardiff, Wales U.K.
Tafila Jordan see Aţ Ţafīlah
238 □3f Tafira Gran Canaria Canary Is
228 D4 Tafiré Côte d'Ivoire
282 D2 Tafí Viejo Arg.
163 I5 Tafjord Norway
226 C3 Tafraoute Morocco
144 D4 Tafresh Iran
144 F6 Taft Iran
264 M6 Taft CA U.S.A.
145 I7 Taftān, Kūh-e mt. Iran
150 E3 Taftanāz Syria
258 E2 Tafton PA U.S.A.
137 M9 Tafwap Andaman & Nicobar Is India
126 D5 Taga Japan
100 □2 Taga Samoa
208 J3 Taga mt. Spain
145 L5 Tagāb Afgh.
225 F5 Tagab Sudan
244 H2 Tagagawik r. AK U.S.A.
127 H4 Tagajō Japan
245 □D6 Tagalak Island AK U.S.A.
228 E2 Taganet Keyna well Mali
157 G7 Taganrog Rus. Fed.
159 R7 Taganrog, Gulf of Rus. Fed./Ukr.
Taganrogskiy Zaliv b. Rus. Fed./Ukr. see Taganrog, Gulf of
228 C2 Tagant admin. reg. Maur.
144 G2 Tagarev, Gora mt. Iran/Turkm.
118 C3 Tagaung Myanmar
125 H13 Tagawa Japan
157 I5 Tagay Rus. Fed.
229 G2 Tagaza well Niger
114 E6 Tagbilaran Bohol Phil.
173 F10 Tagchagpu Ri mt. Xizang China
Tagdempt Alg. see Tiaret
212 D8 Taggia Italy
228 E3 Taghin-Dassouri Burkina
Ţâghira Moldova see Ţighira
Taghmanant well Mali
226 D4 Taghmanant well Mali
245 N3 Tagish Y.T. Can.
245 N4 Tagish Lake B.C. Can.
213 K5 Tagliacozzo Italy
213 O4 Tagliamento r. Italy
214 C3 Taglio-Isolaccio Corse France
178 H5 Tagnon France
227 E5 Tagnout Chagguere well Mali
127 J1 Tagokura-ko resr Japan
115 E7 Tagoloan r. Mindanao Phil.
209 I9 Tagomago, Illa de i. Spain
228 D2 Tagouarâret well Maur.
144 H1 Tagta Turkm.
145 J4 Tagtabazar Turkm.
280 C1 Taguatinga Minas Gerais Brazil
278 D5 Taguatinga Tocantins Brazil
126 B7 Taguchi-zaki pt Japan
114 C3 Taguig Luzon Phil.
229 H2 Taguedoufat well Niger
Taguenout Haggueret well Mali see Tagnout Chagguere
99 F3 Tagula Island P.N.G.
114 E8 Tagum Mindanao Phil.
206 B3 Tagus r. Port./Spain alt. Tajo (Spain), alt. Tejo (Portugal)
226 B4 Tah, Sabkhat salt pan Morocco
129 S3 Taha Heilong. China
246 G5 Tahaetkun Mountain B.C. Can.
207 O6 Tahal Spain
114 A8 Tahan, Gunung mt. Malaysia
226 D3 Tahanaoute Morocco
101 □9 Tahanea atoll Arch. des Tuamotu Fr. Polynesia
Tahanroz'ka Zatoka b. Rus. Fed./Ukr. see Taganrog, Gulf of
126 F6 Tahara Japan
102 H2 Taharoa, Lake North I. N.Z.
101 □9a Taharuu r. Tahiti Fr. Polynesia
227 G5 Tahat, Mont mt. Alg.
Tahaurawe i. HI U.S.A. see Kaho'olawe
267 O7 Tahdzibichén Mex.
122 D2 Tahe Heilong. China
102 H2 Taheke North I. N.Z.
160 F3 Tahemaa Estonia
144 G8 Tāherū'ī Iran
227 G5 Tahifet Alg.
169 C9 Tahilla Ireland
Tahilt Mongolia see Tsogt
101 □9a Tahiti i. Fr. Polynesia
199 I4 Tahitótfalu Hungary
160 F2 Tahkuna nina pt Estonia
145 M8 Tahlab, Dasht-i- plain Pak.
Tahlab r. Iran/Pak.
261 H8 Tahlequah OK U.S.A.
264 G5 Tahltan B.C. Can.
264 L2 Tahoe, Lake CA U.S.A.
264 L2 Tahoe City CA U.S.A.
242 H3 Tahoe Lake Nunavut Can.
264 L2 Tahoe Vista CA U.S.A.
261 E9 Tahoka TX U.S.A.
102 I6 Tahora North I. N.Z.
267 N10 Tahorakuri North I. N.Z.
229 G3 Tahoua Niger
229 G3 Tahoua dept Niger
144 G7 Tahrūd Iran
144 H7 Tahrūd r. Iran
118 D4 Ta Hsai Myanmar
246 E5 Tahsis B.C. Can.
225 F3 Tahta Egypt
221 K5 Tahtaköprü Turkey
145 L8 Tahtalı Dağ mt. Turkey
246 E4 Tahtsa Peak B.C. Can.
276 D4 Tahua Bol.
276 D2 Tahuamanú r. Bol.
276 C2 Tahuamanú r. Peru
101 □9 Tahuata i. Fr. Polynesia
115 F4 Tahulandang i. Indon.
115 D2 Tahuna Sulawesi Indon.
228 D5 Taï Côte d'Ivoire
228 D5 Taï, Parc National de nat. park Côte d'Ivoire
139 L6 Taibabpur Bihar India
131 □17 Tai A Chau i. H.K. China
129 R6 Tai'an Liaoning China
129 O8 Tai'an Shandong China
101 □9a Taiarapu, Presqu'île de pen Fr. Polynesia
103 E12 Taiaroa Head South I. N.Z.
129 K8 Taibai Gansu China
129 J9 Taibai Shaanxi China
130 F2 Taibai Shan mt. Shaanxi China
Taibei Taiwan see T'aipei
227 G2 Taibet Alg.
207 O4 Taibilla r. Spain
209 C12 Taibilla, Canal del Spain
209 A11 Taibilla, Embalse de resr Spain
207 O4 Taibilla, Sierra de mts Spain
238 □3a Taibique El Hierro Canary Is
213 M3 Taibon Agordino Italy
Taibus Qi Nei Mongol China see Baochang
131 M6 T'aichung Taiwan
Taidong Taiwan see T'aitung
127 L4 Taiei Japan
103 E13 Taieri r. South I. N.Z.
103 E12 Taieri Ridge South I. N.Z.
Taigong Guizhou China see Taijiang
129 M8 Taigu Shanxi China
129 M8 Taihang Shan mts China
129 N7 Taihang Shan mts China
102 J6 Taihape North I. N.Z.
131 J2 Taihe Anhui China
Taihe Guangdong China see Qingxin
131 J5 Taihe Jiangxi China
Taihe Sichuan China see Shehong
Taihezhen Sichuan China see Shehong
124 □1 Taiho Okinawa Japan
131 □J7 Tai Ho Wan H.K. China
131 K3 Taihu Anhui China
131 M3 Tai Hu l. China
129 M7 Taihuai Shanxi China
125 M13 Taiji Japan
130 G5 Taijiang Guizhou China
129 S3 Taikang Heilong. China
129 N9 Taikang Henan China
129 U4 Taiki Japan
118 B6 Taikkyi Myanmar
126 B4 Taiko-yama hill Japan
115 D8 Tailaco East Timor
129 R3 Tailai Heilong. China
131 □J7 Tai Lam Chung Shui Tong H.K. China
116 C5 Taileleo Indon.
104 G6 Tailem Bend S.A. Austr.
131 □J7 Tai Long Wan b. H.K. China
Tailuge Taiwan see T'ailuko
131 M6 T'ailuko Taiwan
282 G4 Taim Brazil
145 J5 Taimani reg. Afgh.
131 □J7 Tai Mo Shan hill H.K. China
228 E4 Tain r. Ghana
168 H7 Tain Highland, Scotland U.K.
131 M7 T'ainan Taiwan
220 D6 Tainaro, Akrotirio pt Greece
182 C1 Taingy France
183 F6 Tain-l'Hermitage France
179 M7 Taintrux France
131 □I7 Tai O H.K. China
213 K3 Taio Italy
281 F1 Taiobeiras Brazil
115 B4 Taipa Sulawesi Indon.
102 H2 Taipa North I. N.Z.
131 □J7 Tai Pak Wan b. H.K. China
163 T6 Taipalsaari Fin.
131 M6 T'aipei Taiwan
131 I7 Taiping Guangdong China
Taiping Guangdong China see Shixing
Taiping Guangxi China see Chongzuo
130 H7 Taiping Guangxi China
116 D2 Taiping Malaysia
129 R4 Taipingchuan Jilin China
129 Q3 Taiping Ling mt. Nei Mongol China
131 □J7 Tai Po H.K. China
131 □J7 Tai Po Hoi b. H.K. China
Tai Poutini National Park South I. N.Z. see Westland National Park
278 G3 Taipu Brazil
139 O6 Taipudia Arun. Prad. India
129 N9 Taiqian Henan China
124 □1 Taira Okinawa Japan
126 E3 Taira Toyama Japan
124 R5 Tairadate-kaikyō sea chan. Japan
124 □G17 Taira-jima i. Nansei-shotō Japan
Tairbeart Western Isles, Scotland U.K. see Tarbert
119 D10 Tai Rom Yen National Park Thai.
129 N4 Tairua North I. N.Z.
144 A4 Tairuq Iran
116 E7 Tais Sumatera Indon.
124 Q4 Taisei Japan
124 T3 Taisetsu-zan mts Japan
127 J2 Taishaku-san mt. Japan
131 I6 Taishan Guangdong China
131 □J7 Tai Shek Mo hill H.K. China
127 L1 Taishin Japan
131 L5 Taishun Zhejiang China
131 □I7 Tai Siu Mo To is H.K. China
201 I3 Taiskirchen im Innkreis Austria
178 H5 Taissy France
233 C5 Taita Hills Kenya
116 D6 Taitaitanopo i. Indon.
131 □J7 Tai Tan Hoi Hap inlet H.K. China
283 B7 Taitao, Península de pen. Chile
283 B7 Taitao, Punta pt Chile
103 G10 Tai Tapu South I. N.Z.
232 B4 Taiti mt. Kenya
131 □J7 Tai Tau Tam H.K. China
127 L5 Taitō-zaki pt Japan
131 M7 T'aitung Taiwan
131 □J7 Tai Tung Shan hill H.K. China
131 M7 T'aitung Shan mts Taiwan
162 T4 Taivalkoski Fin.
162 R2 Taivaskero hill Fin.
163 Q6 Taivassalo Fin.
131 M7 Taiwan country Asia
Taiwan Haixia str. China/Taiwan see Taiwan Strait
Taiwan Shan mts Taiwan see Chungyang Shanmo
131 L7 Taiwan Strait China/Taiwan
Taixian Jiangsu China see Jiangyan
131 M2 Taixing Jiangsu China
Taiyetos Oros mts Greece see Taygetos
129 M8 Taiyuan Shanxi China
129 L8 Taiyue Shan mts China
182 F3 Taizé France
133 K11 Taizhao Xizang China
Taizhong Taiwan see T'aichung
131 L2 Taizhou Jiangsu China
131 M4 Taizhou Zhejiang China
131 M4 Taizhou Liedao i. China
131 M4 Taizhou Wan b. China
123 D8 Taizi He r. China
146 F9 Ta'izz Yemen
146 F9 Ta'izz governorate Yemen
125 I9 Tajamulco, Volcán de vol. Guat.
267 N10 Tajamulco, Volcán de vol. Guat.
224 B3 Tajarhī Libya
117 G6 Tajem, Gunung hill Indon.
144 D7 Tāj-e Malekī Iran
205 O7 Tajera, Embalse de la resr Spain
227 H2 Tajerouine Tunisia
145 M3 Tajikistan country Asia
126 F5 Tajima Japan
127 N2 Tajima Japan
128 F1 Tajiri Japan
266 C2 Tajitos Mex.
145 M8 Taj Mahal tourist site Uttar Prad. India
138 G6 Taj Mahal tourist site Uttar Prad. India
206 B3 Tajo r. Spain alt. Tejo (Portugal), conv. Tagus
139 P5 Tajobum Arun. Prad. India
207 O2 Tajo-Segura, Canal de Trasvase Spain
139 J7 Tajpur Bihar India
149 O6 Tajrīsh Iran

D5 Tajsara, Cordillera de mts Bol.
M8 Tajuña r. Spain
B1 Tājūra Libya
D6 Tak Thai.
B3 Takāb Iran
D4 Takabba Kenya
B7 Taka'Bonerate, Kepulauan atolls Indon.
B7 Taka Bonerate, Taman Nasional nat. park Indon.
G4 Takácsi Hungary
D2 Takadja C.A.R.
G4 Takagi Japan
M2 Takahagi Japan
E6 Takahama Aichi Japan
C5 Takahama Fukui Japan
F3 Takahara-gawa r. Japan
K12 Takahashi Japan
Q1 Takahe, Mount Antarctica
B6 Takaishi Japan
E1 Takaiwa-misaki pt Japan
G7 Takaka South I. N.Z.
F9 Takal Madh. Prad. India
C2 Takalaou Chad
C6 Takaloi well Tanz.
G5 Takalous, Oued watercourse Alg.
G3 Takama Guyana
□2b Takamaka Mahé Seychelles
E2 Takamatsu Ishikawa Japan
L12 Takamatsu Kagawa Japan
D7 Takami-yama mt. Japan
I14 Takamori Kumamoto Japan
G4 Takamori Nagano Japan
I14 Takanabe Japan
F3 Takane Gifu Japan
H4 Takane Yamanashi Japan
K2 Takanezawa Japan
R6 Takanosu Japan
F2 Takaoka Japan
K7 Takapau North I. N.Z.
M5 Takapau North I. N.Z.
I3 Takapuna North I. N.Z.
□G17 Takara-jima i. Nansei-shotō Japan
B6 Takarazuka Japan
A6 Takasago Japan
J3 Takasaki Japan
D5 Takashima Japan
E3 Takashōzu-yama mt. Japan
E4 Takasu Japan
H2 Takasuma-yama mt. Japan
M2 Takasuzu-san hill Japan
H4 Takatō Japan
E5 Takatokwane Botswana
E4 Takatomi Japan
C7 Takatori Japan
D4 Takatshwaane Botswana
C6 Takatsuki Ōsaka Japan
D5 Takatsuki Shiga Japan
J13 Takatsuki-yama mt. Japan
G4 Takatu r. Brazil/Guyana
C5 Takaungu Kenya
D4 Ta-Kaw Myanmar
F3 Takayama Gifu Japan
I2 Takayama Gunma Japan
I1 Takayanagi Japan
E11 Tak Bai Thai.
D4 Takefu Japan
J12 Takehara Japan
M4 Takeley Essex, England U.K.
B2 Takengon Sumatera Indon.
A4 Takeno Japan
Takeo Cambodia see Takêv
H13 Takeo Japan
K3 Tåkern l. Sweden
K3 Tåkern naturreservat nature res. Sweden
H3 Takeshi Japan
□H16 Take-shima i. Japan
Take-shima i. N. Pacific Ocean see Liancourt Rocks
C3 Takestān Iran
C5 Taketa Dem. Rep. Congo
I14 Taketa Japan
E6 Taketoyo Japan
G9 Takêv Cambodia
M2 Takfon Tajik.
L9 Takhādīd well Iraq
M3 Takhār prov. Afgh.
H8 Takhatpur Chhattisgarh India
G5 Takhemaret Alg.
Takhiatash Uzbek. see Taxiatosh
N3 Takhini r. Y.T. Can.
N3 Takhini Hotspring Y.T. Can.
E7 Ta Khli Thai.
G9 Ta Khmau Cambodia
H7 Takhta Rus. Fed.
Takhta Turkm. see Tagta
Takhta-Bazar Turkm. see Tagtabazar
L1 Takhtabrod Kazakh.
R9 Takhtamukay Rus. Fed.
Takhtamukayskiy Rus. Fed. see Takhtamukay
C5 Takht Apān, Kūh-e mt. Iran
E7 Takhteh Iran
K6 Takhteh Pol Afgh.
P9 Takht-e Jamshīd tourist site Iran
D3 Takht-e Soleymān mt. Iran
N6 Takht-i-Sulaiman mt. Pak.
E7 Taki Mie Japan
I11 Taki Shimane Japan
H3 Takiéta Niger
G3 Takikawa Japan
A6 Takino Japan
J2 Takinoue Japan
H4 Takisset, Oued watercourse Alg./Libya
K6 Takisung Kalimantan Indon.
B12 Takitimu Mountains South I. N.Z.
6 Täklä Azer.
6 Täklä Azer.
E4 Takla Lake B.C. Can.
E4 Takla Landing B.C. Can.
Takla Makan des. China see Taklimakan Shamo
Taklimakan Desert China see Taklimakan Shamo
E7 Taklimakan Shamo des. China
L4 Tako Japan
M2 Takob Tajik.
E5 Takoradi Ghana
H3 Takotna AK U.S.A.
H2 Takou Bay North I. N.Z.
K12 Takpa Shiri mt. Xizang China
G3 Takslesluk Lake AK U.S.A.
I4 Taksony Hungary
K4 Takta r. Hungary
K3 Taktaharkány Hungary
K3 Taktakenéz Hungary
C3 Taku B.C. Can.
J4 Taku r. Can./U.S.A.
H13 Taku Japan
J6 Takuan, Mount P.N.G.
D10 Takua Pa Thai.
D10 Takua Thung Thai.
H5 Takum Nigeria
C6 Takundi Dem. Rep. Congo
I2 Takutea i. Cook Is
2 Takuu Islands P.N.G.
J6 Takwa Malaita Solomon Is
8 Takyl, Mys pt Ukr.
8 Tal Madh. Prad. India
D4 Tal Pak.
F5 Tala Mex.
G4 Tala Uru.
7 Talab r. Iran/Pak.
C2 Talacasto Arg.
M7 Talachyn Belarus
D5 Talagang Pak.
G3 Talagante Chile
H10 Talaiassa hill Spain
8 Talaimannar Sri Lanka
I10 Talairan France
5 Talais France
F9 Talaja Gujarat India
G3 Talakan Amurskaya Oblast' Rus. Fed.
H4 Talakan Khabarovskiy Kray Rus. Fed.
9 Talala Gujarat India
M13 Talalayivka Ukr.
R13 Talamanca, Cordillera de mts Costa Rica
D5 Talamantes Spain

212 H3 Talamona Italy
214 G2 Talamone Italy
284 D1 Talampaya, Parque Nacional nat. park Arg.
214 C7 Talana Sardegna Italy
122 G4 Talandzha Rus. Fed.
116 D6 Talang, Gunung vol. Indon.
116 F6 Talangbatu Sumatera Indon.
116 F6 Talangbetutu Sumatera Indon.
285 F2 Tala Norte Arg.
182 G2 Talant France
139 O6 Talap Assam India
274 A6 Talara Peru
Talar-i-Band mts Pak. see Makran Coast Range
208 G3 Talarn, Embassament de resr Spain
207 I2 Talarrubias Spain
143 M5 Talas r. Kazakh./Kyrg.
143 O6 Talas Kyrg.
143 N6 Talas admin. div. Kyrg.
143 N6 Talas Ala-Too mts Kyrg.
113 L8 Talasea New Britain P.N.G.
161 P7 Talashkino Rus. Fed.
Talas Oblast admin. div. Kyrg. see Talas
Talas Range mts Kyrg. see Talas Ala-Too
Talasskaya Oblast' admin. div. Kyrg. see Talas
Talasskiy Alatau, Khrebet mts Kyrg. see Talas Ala-Too
115 B4 Talatakoh i. Indon.
150 D8 Tal'at al Jamā'ah, Rujm mt. Jordan
229 G3 Talata-Mafara Nigeria
150 E4 Ţal'at Mūsá mt. Lebanon/Syria
115 E1 Talaud, Kepulauan is Indon.
204 H9 Talaván Spain
207 P3 Talave, Embalse de resr Spain
205 K9 Talavera de la Reina Spain
206 F3 Talavera la Real Spain
106 H5 Talawanta Qld Austr.
118 C2 Talawgyi Myanmar
153 Q3 Talaya Rus. Fed.
114 E8 Talayan Mindanao Phil.
209 B12 Talayón hill Spain
204 I9 Talayuela Spain
209 C8 Talayuelas Spain
205 P9 Talayuelo mt. Spain
138 G7 Talbehat Uttar Prad. India
150 E4 Talbīsah Syria
109 I9 Talbot, Mount hill W.A. Austr.
258 C7 Talbot County county MD U.S.A.
243 K2 Talbot Inlet Nunavut Can.
247 L4 Talbot Lake Man. Can.
255 E9 Talbotton GA U.S.A.
105 L5 Talbragar r. N.S.W. Austr.
284 B4 Talca Chile
284 B3 Talca, Punta pt Chile
282 B5 Talcahuano Chile
284 A5 Talcamávida Chile
139 J9 Talcher Orissa India
122 D2 Taldan Rus. Fed.
161 U5 Taldom Rus. Fed.
143 O8 Taldyk, Pereval pass Kyrg.
143 R5 Taldykorgan Kazakh.
Taldy-Kurgan Kazakh. see Taldykorgan
Taldyqorghan Kazakh. see Taldykorgan
143 M3 Taldysay Kazakh.
Taldysu Kyrg. see Taldy-Suu
143 R6 Taldy-Suu Kyrg.
269 K8 Talea de Castro Mex.
136 D3 Talegaon Mahar. India
136 F2 Talegaon Mahar. India
144 C5 Taleh Zang Iran
138 F8 Talen Madh. Prad. India
185 C6 Talence France
237 M8 Taleni S. Africa
180 H5 Talensac France
209 E8 Tales Spain
Tālesh Gīlān Iran see Hashtpar
144 C3 Tālesh Gīlān Iran
161 T2 Talets, Ozero l. Rus. Fed.
108 E6 Talga r. W.A. Austr.
143 Q6 Talgar Kazakh.
143 Q6 Talgar, Pik mt. Kazakh.
172 D3 Talgarreg Ceredigion, Wales U.K.
172 F4 Talgarth Powys, Wales U.K.
225 G5 Talguharai Sudan
204 D7 Talhadas Port.
146 F7 Ţalḩah Saudi Arabia
104 E5 Talia S.A. Austr.
115 D4 Taliabu i. Indon.
183 I8 Taliard France
114 E6 Talibon Bohol Phil.
172 E3 Taliesin Ceredigion, Wales U.K.
206 E3 Táliga Spain
136 E4 Talikota Karnataka India
114 E8 Talikud i. Phil.
Talimardzhan Uzbek. see Tollimarjon
151 E5 T'alin Armenia
129 S3 Talin Hiag Heilong. China
226 D3 Taliouine Morocco
136 D6 Taliparamba Kerala India
232 A3 Tali Post Sudan
114 D6 Talisay Cebu Phil.
117 M4 Talisayan Kalimantan Indon.
114 E7 Talisayan Mindanao Phil.
151 J7 Talış Dağları mts Azer./Iran
115 D3 Talisei i. Indon.
168 D8 Talisker Highland, Scotland U.K.
284 E3 Talita Arg.
156 I4 Talitsa Kostromskaya Oblast' Rus. Fed.
161 V9 Talitsa Lipetskaya Oblast' Rus. Fed.
159 T1 Talitskiy Chamlyk Rus. Fed.
117 L9 Taliwang Sumbawa Indon.
160 L8 Tal'ka Belarus
190 K3 Talkau Ger.
245 J3 Talkeetna AK U.S.A.
245 J3 Talkeetna r. AK U.S.A.
245 J3 Talkeetna Mountains AK U.S.A.
213 L8 Talla Italy
104 D4 Tallacootra, Lake salt flat S.A. Austr.
168 F7 Talladale Highland, Scotland U.K.
255 D9 Talladega AL U.S.A.
149 K5 Tall 'Afar Iraq
169 J6 Tallaght Ireland
255 E10 Tallahassee FL U.S.A.
150 G2 Tall al Aḩmar Syria
105 K7 Tallangatta Vic. Austr.
169 I5 Tallanstown Ireland
255 D9 Tallapoosa r. AL U.S.A.
104 D3 Tallaringa Conservation Park nature res. S.A. Austr.
255 E9 Tallassee AL U.S.A.
225 H5 Talla Talla Seghir Island Sudan
149 J5 Tall Baydar Syria
185 B8 Taller France
109 C10 Tallering Peak hill W.A. Austr.
258 D5 Talleyville DE U.S.A.
160 H2 Tallinn Estonia
160 H2 Tallinna laht b. Estonia
150 E4 Tall Kalakh Syria
149 K5 Tall Kayf Iraq
149 K5 Tall Kūjik Syria
256 D7 Tallmadge OH U.S.A.
182 I5 Talloires France
214 D3 Tallone Corse France
204 C3 Tallós Spain
169 F8 Tallow Ireland
261 J9 Tallulah LA U.S.A.
149 K5 Tall 'Uwaynāt Iraq
Tallymerjen Uzbek. see Tollimarjon
219 M5 Tălmaciu Romania
258 C4 Talmage PA U.S.A.
182 G2 Talmay France
226 C3 Talmest Morocco
275 H4 Talmiã Brazil
168 H5 Talmine Highland, Scotland U.K.
184 C4 Talmont France
184 A3 Talmont-St-Hilaire France
158 J5 Tal'ne Ukr.
Tal'noye Ukr. see Tal'ne
138 D8 Talod Gujarat India
138 E9 Taloda Mahar. India
230 F2 Talodi Sudan

100 □1 Talofofo Guam
100 □1 Talofofo Bay Guam
261 F7 Taloga OK U.S.A.
145 K9 Taloi Range mts Pak.
249 H2 Talon, Lac l. Que. Can.
118 D4 Ta-long Myanmar
145 M3 Tāloqān Afgh.
214 C7 Talora r. Sardegna Italy
287 K2 Talos Dome ice feature Antarctica
118 F4 Ta Loung San mt. Laos
159 M5 Talova Balka Ukr.
142 D2 Talovaya Kazakh.
157 H6 Talovaya Rus. Fed.
151 H1 Talovka Rus. Fed.
243 I3 Taloyoak Nunavut Can.
268 C5 Talpa Mex.
145 O4 Tal Pass Pak.
229 H3 Talras well Niger
217 M3 Talsano Italy
Talshand Mongolia see Chandmanĭ
160 F4 Talsi Latvia
144 I7 Tal Sīyāh Iran
193 K8 Talsperre Quitzdorf Kollmer Höhen park Ger.
282 C2 Taltal Chile
247 H2 Taltson r. N.W.T. Can.
197 J2 Tałty, Jezioro l. Pol.
133 L11 Talu Xizang China
116 C4 Talu Sumatera Indon.
115 C3 Taludaa Sulawesi Indon.
115 F5 Taluti, Teluk b. Seram Indon.
213 K3 Talvera r. Italy
162 Q1 Talvik Norway
105 L3 Talwood Qld Austr.
157 H6 Taly Rus. Fed.
158 J5 Tal'yanky Ukr.
105 I5 Talyawalka r. N.S.W. Austr.
Talyshskiye Gory mts Azer./Iran see Talış Dağları
156 K2 Talyy Rus. Fed.
127 J4 Tama Japan
205 K2 Tama Spain
117 K3 Tama Abu, Banjaran mts Malaysia
Tamabo Range mts Malaysia see Tama Abu, Banjaran
118 B3 Tamadaw Myanmar
127 K4 Tama-gawa r. Japan
124 □1 Tamagusuku Okinawa Japan
118 D1 Tamai, Nam r. Myanmar
205 N6 Tamajón Spain
103 □4 Tamakautoga Niue
127 L1 Tamakawa Japan
126 E7 Tamaki Japan
102 I3 Tamaki Strait North I. N.Z.
109 B9 Tamala W.A. Austr.
157 H5 Tamala Rus. Fed.
274 C2 Tamalameque Col.
228 E4 Tamale Ghana
229 F3 Tamalelt well Mali
117 J5 Tamalung Kalimantan Indon.
204 H7 Tamames Spain
127 J3 Tamamura Japan
125 H14 Tamana Japan
99 H2 Tamana i. Gilbert Is Kiribati
226 C3 Tamanar Morocco
285 H6 Tamangueyú Arg.
224 B3 Tamanhint Libya
228 D3 Tamani Mali
116 E2 Taman Negara National Park Malaysia
125 K12 Tamano Japan
227 G5 Tamanrasset Alg.
227 F5 Tamanrasset, Oued watercourse Alg.
118 B2 Tamanthi Myanmar
269 H4 Tamapatz Mex.
258 D3 Tamaqua PA U.S.A.
139 J8 Tamar Jharkhand India
Tamar Syria see Tadmur
172 D7 Tamar r. England U.K.
229 F2 Tamaradant well Mali
125 I14 Tamarai Japan
127 L3 Tamari Japan
239 □1b Tamarin Mauritius
271 L9 Tamarindo Venez.
208 F4 Tamarite de Litera Spain
276 C4 Tamarugal, Pampa de plain Chile
235 E4 Tamasane Botswana
229 G2 Tamasgoï well Niger
197 L4 Tamashowka Belarus
199 H5 Tamási Hungary
219 P4 Tamaşi Romania
269 H4 Tamasopo Mex.
Tamatave Madag. see Toamasina
127 L3 Tamatsukuri Japan
269 H3 Tamaulipas state Mex.
269 I2 Tamaulipas, Sierra de mts Mex.
232 C3 Tama Wildlife Reserve nature res. Eth.
124 S7 Tamayama Japan
266 F5 Tamazula Durango Mex.
268 D6 Tamazula Jalisco Mex.
269 J8 Tamazulápam Mex.
269 I4 Tamazunchale Mex.
Tamba Japan see Tanba
232 B4 Tambach Kenya
191 K9 Tambach-Dietharz Ger.
228 B3 Tambacounda Senegal
Tamba-kōchi plat. Japan see Tanba-kōchi
115 B7 Tambalongang i. Indon.
117 I5 Tambangmunjul Kalimantan Indon.
116 E6 Tambangsawah Sumatera Indon.
237 P2 Tambankulu Swaziland
229 F3 Tambao Burkina
228 C3 Tambaoura, Falaise de esc. Mali
275 F6 Tambaqui Brazil
235 G3 Tambara Moz.
105 L4 Tambar Springs N.S.W. Austr.
280 D4 Tambau Brazil
229 G3 Tambawel Nigeria
115 B6 Tambea Sulawesi Indon.
116 G4 Tambelan, Kepulauan is Indon.
117 G4 Tambelan Besar i. Indon.
109 D13 Tambellup W.A. Austr.
284 C2 Tamberías Arg.
117 J8 Tamberu Jawa Indon.
284 C3 Tambillo, Cerro mt. Arg.
117 M2 Tambisan Sabah Malaysia
107 K8 Tambo Qld Austr.
105 K7 Tambo r. Vic. Austr.
276 C4 Tambo r. Peru
276 B3 Tambobamba Peru
276 A3 Tambo de Mora Peru
274 A6 Tambo Grande Peru
235 □I3 Tambohorano Madag.
115 B5 Tamboli Sulawesi Indon.
276 C3 Tambopata r. Peru
231 B9 Tambor Angola
266 G5 Tambor Mex.
117 L9 Tambora, Gunung vol. Sumbawa Indon.
285 I2 Tambores Uru.
278 E3 Tamboril Brazil
274 C5 Tamboryacu r. Peru
230 E3 Tamboura C.A.R.
157 H5 Tambov Rus. Fed.
151 E4 Tambovka Georgia
122 F3 Tambovka Rus. Fed.
Tambov Oblast admin. div. Rus. Fed. see Tambovskaya Oblast'
157 H5 Tambovskaya Oblast' admin. div. Rus. Fed.
204 C3 Tambre r. Spain
115 A3 Tambu, Teluk b. Indon.
117 M5 Tambulan Sulawesi Indon.
117 L2 Tambulanan, Bukit hill Malaysia
117 L2 Tambunan Sabah Malaysia
230 E3 Tambura Sudan
117 L1 Tambuyukon, Gunung mt. Malaysia
228 C2 Tâmchekket Maur.
142 G3 Tamdy Kazakh.
Tamdybulak Uzbek. see Tomdibuloq
274 D3 Tame Col.
204 D6 Tâmega r. Port.
283 C8 Tamel Aike Arg.
220 F5 Tamelos, Akrotirio pt Kea Greece
Tamenghest Alg. see Tamanrasset

139 N7 Tamenglong Manipur India
Tamerlanovka Kazakh. see Temirlanovka
229 G2 Tamesna reg. Niger
229 H2 Tamgak, Adrar mt. Niger
228 B3 Tamgué, Massif du mt. Guinea
138 G8 Tamia Madh. Prad. India
269 J4 Tamiahua Mex.
269 J4 Tamiahua, Laguna de lag. Mex.
255 G13 Tamiami Canal FL U.S.A.
116 C2 Tamiang r. Indon.
116 C2 Tamiang, Ujung pt Indon.
136 F7 Tamil Nadu state India
258 E2 Tamiment PA U.S.A.
117 K6 Taminglayang Kalimantan Indon.
212 G2 Tamins Switz.
128 H3 Tamirin Gol r. Mongolia
218 I6 Tamiš r. Serbia
278 B5 Tamitatoala r. Brazil
156 G2 Tamitsa Rus. Fed.
225 F2 Ţāmīyah Egypt
146 F3 Tamīyah, Jabal hill Saudi Arabia
229 H1 Tamjit well Niger
142 J3 Tamkamys Kazakh.
139 J6 Tamkuhi Uttar Prad. India
118 I7 Tam Ky Vietnam
226 E2 Tamlelt, Plaine de plain Morocco
139 K8 Tamluk W. Bengal India
194 G4 Tamm Ger.
215 N5 Tammaro r. Italy
247 K1 Tammarvi r. Nunavut Can.
160 G1 Tammela Etelä-Suomi Fin.
162 U4 Tammela Oulu Fin.
190 G1 Tammensiel Ger.
Tammerfors Fin. see Tampere
160 K1 Tammio i. Fin.
Tammisaaren Saariston Kansallispuisto nat. park Fin. see Ekenäskärgårds nationalpark
Tammisaari Fin. see Ekenäs
160 K3 Tammispää Estonia
165 N1 Tämnaren l. Sweden
218 I6 Tamnava r. Serbia
182 D2 Tamnay-en-Bazois France
204 E2 Támoga r. Spain
229 F3 Tamou Niger
229 F3 Tamou, Réserve Totale de Faune de nature res. Niger
255 F12 Tampa FL U.S.A.
255 F12 Tampa Bay FL U.S.A.
269 I4 Tampacán Mex.
269 I4 Tampamolón Mex.
116 F7 Tampang Sumatera Indon.
163 Q6 Tampere Fin.
269 J3 Tampico Mex.
269 J3 Tampico el Alto Mex.
116 E3 Tampin Malaysia
116 □ Tampines Sing.
116 □ Tampines, Sungai r. Sing.
115 C6 Tampo Sulawesi Indon.
119 I7 Tam Quan Vietnam
146 G5 Tamrah Saudi Arabia
129 O3 Tamsagbulag Mongolia
128 H6 Tamsag Muchang Nei Mongol China
160 J2 Tamsalu Estonia
274 C6 Tamshiyacu Peru
201 I5 Tamsweg Austria
118 B2 Tamu Myanmar
269 I4 Tamuín Mex.
100 □1 Tamuning Guam
139 K6 Tamur r. Nepal
207 J3 Tamurejo Spain
100 □4b Tamworohi Pohnpei Micronesia
105 M4 Tamworth N.S.W. Austr.
171 N8 Tamworth Staffordshire, England U.K.
143 Q3 Tan Kazakh.
Tana r. Fin./Norway see Tenojoki
232 D5 Tana r. Kenya
Tana Madag. see Antananarivo
245 L3 Tana r. AK U.S.A.
Tana i. Vanuatu see Tanna
Tana, Lake Eth. see T'ana Hāyk'
125 M13 Tanabe Japan
280 C4 Tanabi Brazil
162 T1 Tana Bru Norway
245 L3 Tanacross AK U.S.A.
162 T1 Tanafjorden inlet Norway
245 □C6 Tanaga vol. AK U.S.A.
245 □C6 Tanaga Island AK U.S.A.
245 □C6 Tanaga Pass sea channel AK U.S.A.
215 O6 Tanagro r. Italy
127 L1 Tanagura Japan
117 H8 Tanah, Tanjung pt Indon.
232 C2 T'ana Hāyk' l. Eth.
116 C5 Tanahbala i. Indon.
117 L5 Tanahgrogot Kalimantan Indon.
115 B7 Tanahjampea i. Indon.
116 C5 Tanahmasa i. Indon.
117 L3 Tanahmerah Kalimantan Indon.
116 E2 Tanah Merah Malaysia
116 D4 Tanahputih Sumatera Indon.
116 D2 Tanah Rata Malaysia
115 A6 Tanakeke i. Indon.
138 H5 Tanakpur Uttaranchal India
115 A5 Tanambung Sulawesi Barat Indon.
106 B5 Tanami N.T. Austr.
106 C5 Tanami Desert N.T. Austr.
119 H9 Tân An Vietnam
244 I2 Tanana AK U.S.A.
244 I2 Tanana r. AK U.S.A.
Tananarive Madag. see Antananarivo
235 □I4 Tanandava Madag.
147 I2 Tanāqīb, Ra's pt Saudi Arabia
212 F5 Tanaro r. Italy
172 F2 Tanat r. Wales U.K.
114 E6 Tanauan Leyte Phil.
214 D6 Tanaunella Sardegna Italy
101 □7a Tanavuso Point Viti Levu Fiji
126 B5 Tanba Japan
126 B5 Tanba-kōchi plat. Japan
107 H8 Tanbar Qld Austr.
129 P9 Tanbu Shandong China
181 L3 Tancarville France
Tancheng Fujian China see Pingtan
129 P9 Tancheng Shandong China
123 F8 Tanch'ŏn N. Korea
268 E6 Tancítaro Mex.
268 E6 Tancítaro, Cerro de mt. Mex.
269 N8 Tancochapa r. Mex.
228 E5 Tanda Côte d'Ivoire
138 E4 Tanda Punjab India
138 G5 Tanda Uttar Prad. India
139 I6 Tanda Uttar Prad. India
163 L6 Tandådalen Sweden
114 F7 Tandag Mindanao Phil.
219 P6 Ţăndărei Romania
231 C9 Tandaué Angola
117 L1 Tandek Sabah Malaysia
195 K5 Tandern Ger.
138 F3 Tandi Hima. Prad. India
285 H5 Tandil Arg.
285 H5 Tandil, Sierra del hills Arg.
230 C2 Tandjilé pref. Chad
145 M9 Tando Adam Pak.
145 M9 Tando Allahyar Pak.
145 M9 Tando Bago Pak.
145 M9 Tando Muhammad Khan Pak.
105 I5 Tandou Lake imp. l. N.S.W. Austr.
169 J4 Tandragee Northern Ireland U.K.
163 M6 Tandsjöborg Sweden
114 C9 Tandubatu i. Phil.
138 H9 Tandula r. India
136 E4 Tandur Andhra Prad. India
136 F3 Tandur Andhra Prad. India
145 L7 Tanduri Pak.
102 K5 Taneatua North I. N.Z.
124 □H16 Tanega-shima i. Japan
124 S6 Taneichi Japan
118 D5 Tanen Taunggyi mts Thai.
115 E4 Taneti i. Maluku Indon.
197 K5 Tanew r. Pol.
258 A5 Taneytown MD U.S.A.
227 E5 Tanezrouft reg. Alg./Mali
227 E5 Tanezrouft Tan-Ahenet reg. Alg.
150 G5 Ţanf, Jabal aţ hill Syria
144 H9 Tang Iran
170 B6 Tang Ireland
144 H9 Tang, Ra's-e pt Iran

129 L1 Tanga Rus. Fed.
233 C6 Tanga Tanz.
233 C6 Tanga admin. reg. Tanz.
102 I3 Tangaehe North I. N.Z.
139 L7 Tangail Bangl.
235 □J4 Tangainony Madag.
113 L7 Tanga Islands P.N.G.
136 G9 Tangalla Sri Lanka
268 E6 Tangamandapio Mex.
268 E6 Tangancícuaro de Arista Mex.
Tanganyika country Africa see Tanzania
231 E6 Tanganyika prov. Dem. Rep. Congo
233 A6 Tanganyika, Lake Africa
279 C8 Tangará Brazil
100 □6 Tangarare Guadalcanal Solomon Is
230 C2 Tangaray Chad
136 E8 Tangasseri Kerala India
130 D5 Tangdan Yunnan China
133 K11 Tangdê Xizang China
Tangdukou Hunan China see Shaoyang
149 P9 Tang-e Kalleh Iran
144 F3 Tangelī Iran
164 H1 Tangen Norway
287 D2 Tange Promontory hd Antarctica
226 D2 Tanger Morocco
202 D5 Tanger prov. Morocco
116 G8 Tangerang Jawa Indon.
193 E6 Tangerhütte Ger.
192 E5 Tangermünde Ger.
202 D5 Tanger-Tétouan prov. Morocco
144 H8 Tang-e Sarkheh Iran
128 F8 Tanggarma Qinghai China
133 J11 Tanggo Xizang China
130 D2 Tanggor Sichuan China
129 O7 Tanggu Tianjin China
128 C9 Tanggulashan Qinghai China
133 J10 Tanggula Shan mt. Qinghai/Xizang China
133 I10 Tanggula Shan mts Xizang China
133 J10 Tanggula Shankou pass Xizang China
133 G12 Tangguo Xizang China
129 O7 Tanghai Hebei China
131 I2 Tanghe Henan China
131 I2 Tang He r. China
145 N4 Tangi Pak.
Tangier Morocco see Tanger
257 I11 Tangier Island VA U.S.A.
102 J7 Tangimoana North I. N.Z.
115 B5 Tangkelemboko, Gunung mt. Indon.
116 F7 Tangkittebak, Gunung mt. Indon.
133 I13 Tang La pass Xizang China
118 A1 Tangla Assam India
130 B2 Tanglag Qinghai China
116 □ Tanglin Sing.
133 L11 Tangmai Xizang China
128 G9 Tangnag Qinghai China
126 B4 Tango Japan
107 J6 Tangorin Qld Austr.
144 F3 Tangrāh Iran
133 H11 Tangra Yumco salt l. China
116 A2 Tangse Sumatera Indon.
Tangshan Guizhou China see Shiqian
129 P7 Tangshan Hebei China
190 J3 Tangstedt Ger.
Tangsyq Kazakh. see Tansyk
118 C3 Tangte mt. Myanmar
114 D7 Tangub Mindanao Phil.
114 D6 Tangub Negros Phil.
229 F4 Tanguieta Benin
130 H5 Tangwan Hunan China
122 F4 Tangwanghe Heilong. China
122 F5 Tangwang He r. China
129 N7 Tangxian Hebei China
131 I3 Tangxianzhen Hubei China
118 D3 Tang-yan Myanmar
130 G4 Tangyan He r. China
129 N9 Tangyin Henan China
122 F5 Tangyuan Heilong. China
278 E5 Tanhaçu Brazil
162 S3 Tanhua Fin.
269 J4 Tanhuijo, Arrecife rf Mex.
119 G9 Tani Cambodia
130 A3 Taniantaweng Shan mts Xizang China
127 I2 Tanigawa-dake mt. Japan
126 E4 Tanigumi Japan
113 H8 Tanimbar, Kepulauan is Indon.
182 J4 Taninges France
Taninthari Myanmar see Tenasserim
Tanintharyi Myanmar see Tenasserim
Tanintharyi admin. div. Myanmar see Tenasserim
Taninthayi Myanmar see Tenasserim
115 F5 Taniwel Seram Indon.
125 H15 Taniyama Japan
Tanjah Morocco see Tanger
114 D7 Tanjay Negros Phil.
128 H8 Tanjiajing Gansu China
Tanjore Tamil Nadu India see Thanjavur
117 K6 Tanjung Kalimantan Indon.
116 F5 Tanjung Sumatera Indon.
116 C3 Tanjungbalai Sumatera Indon.
116 E4 Tanjungbalai Sumatera Indon.
115 E5 Tanjungbaliha Maluku Indon.
117 M3 Tanjungbatu Kalimantan Indon.
116 E4 Tanjungbatu Sumatera Indon.
117 M4 Tanjungbuayabuaya, Pulau i. Indon.
116 E6 Tanjungenim Sumatera Indon.
117 L6 Tanjunggaru Kalimantan Indon.
Tanjungkarang-Telukbetung Sumatera Indon. see Bandar Lampung
117 G6 Tanjungpandan Indon.
116 F4 Tanjungpinang Indon.
116 C3 Tanjungpura Sumatera Indon.
117 J6 Tanjung Puting, Taman Nasional nat. park Indon.
116 F6 Tanjungraja Sumatera Indon.
117 L3 Tanjungredeb Kalimantan Indon.
117 H5 Tanjungsaleh i. Indon.
117 H5 Tanjungsatai Kalimantan Indon.
117 L3 Tanjungselor Kalimantan Indon.
145 N5 Tank Pak.
138 C8 Tankara Gujarat India
162 S2 Tankavaara Fin.
138 D9 Tankhala Gujarat India
128 I1 Tankhoy Rus. Fed.
138 G2 Tanktse Jammu and Kashmir India
236 D8 Tankwa r. S. Africa
236 D8 Tankwa-Karoo National Park S. Africa
269 H4 Tanlacut Mex.
269 I4 Tanlajas Mex.
178 H8 Tanlay France
118 B5 Tanlwe r. Myanmar
195 N5 Tann Ger.
191 J9 Tann (Rhon) Ger.
193 E10 Tanna Ger.
100 □5 Tanna i. Vanuatu
168 K9 Tannadice Angus, Scotland U.K.
126 B5 Tannan Japan
163 L5 Tännäs Sweden
182 D2 Tannay Bourgogne France
179 I4 Tannay Champagne-Ardenne France
191 K7 Tanne Ger.
Tannenberg Pol. see Stębark
246 G5 Tanner, Mount B.C. Can.
183 J9 Tanneron France
258 E2 Tannersville PA U.S.A.
195 M2 Tännesberg Ger.
195 I4 Tannhausen Ger.
200 C5 Tannheim Austria
195 I6 Tannheim Ger.
200 B4 Tannheimer Gebirge mts Austria/Ger.
162 R4 Tannila Fin.
164 G4 Tannis Bugt b. Denmark
Tannoa i. Vanuatu see Tongoa
193 D9 Tannroda Ger.
107 M7 Tannum Sands Qld Austr.

128 B1 Tannu-Ola, Khrebet mts Rus. Fed.
Tannu Tuva aut. rep. Rus. Fed. see Tyva, Respublika
125 I15 Tano Japan
114 D7 Tañon Strait Phil.
138 C6 Tanot Rajasthan India
229 H3 Tanout Niger
196 C2 Tanowo Pol.
269 I4 Tanquian Mex.
139 I6 Tansen Nepal
131 M6 Tanshui Taiwan
228 D3 Tansilla Burkina
171 N7 Tansley Derbyshire, England U.K.
143 R4 Tansyk Kazakh.
225 F2 Ţanţā Egypt
118 C5 Tantabin Pegu Myanmar
118 B3 Tantabin Sagaing Myanmar
118 B6 Tantabin Yangôn Myanmar
226 C3 Tan-Tan Morocco
104 H7 Tantanoola S.A. Austr.
126 A5 Tantō Japan
179 L7 Tantonville France
192 J4 Tantow Ger.
269 I4 Tantoyuca Mex.
138 F6 Tantpur Uttar Prad. India
129 R3 Tantu Jilin China
136 G4 Tanuku Andhra Prad. India
127 K3 Tanuma Japan
106 E4 Tanumbirini N.T. Austr.
164 H3 Tanumshede Sweden
198 E1 Tanvald Czech Rep.
226 B5 Tanwakka, Sabkhat well Western Sahara
118 I3 Tanxu Guangxi China
159 R4 Tanyushivka Ukr.
233 B6 Tanzania country Africa
127 J5 Tanzawa-Ōyama Kokutei-kōen park Japan
245 O4 Tanzilla r. B.C. Can.
238 □3c Tao Lanzarote Canary Is
119 D9 Tao, Ko i. Thai.
Tao'an Jilin China see Taonan
Taobh Tuath Western Isles, Scotland U.K. see Northton
Taocheng Fujian China see Yongchun
Taocheng Guangdong China see Daxin
131 H6 Taochuan Hunan China
129 Q8 Taocun Shandong China
Taodeni Mali see Taoudenni
129 R4 Tao'er He r. China
128 H9 Tao He r. China
Taohong Hunan China see Longhui
Taohuajiang Hunan China see Taojiang
Taohuaping Hunan China see Longhui
131 I4 Taojiang Hunan China
Taolanaro Madag. see Tôlañaro
128 J7 Taole Ningxia China
129 R4 Taonan Jilin China
217 I8 Taormina Sicilia Italy
263 L8 Taos NM U.S.A.
229 F2 Taouârdeï well Mali
226 E5 Taoudenni Mali
226 D2 Taounate Morocco
227 E5 Taounnant well Mali
226 E2 Taourirt Morocco
226 D3 Taouz Morocco
131 K6 Taoxi Fujian China
Taoyang Gansu China see Lintao
131 H4 Taoyuan Hunan China
131 M6 T'aoyüan Taiwan
Taozhou Anhui China see Guangde
160 I2 Tapa Estonia
114 C9 Tapaan Passage Phil.
267 M10 Tapachula Mex.
100 □2 Tapaga Point Samoa
116 D2 Tapah Malaysia
275 H5 Tapajós r. Brazil
116 B3 Tapaktuan Sumatera Indon.
268 D6 Tapalpa Mex.
285 G5 Tapalqué Arg.
116 D6 Tapan Sumatera Indon.
Tapan Turkey see Mansurlu
275 H3 Tapanahoni r. Suriname
269 M9 Tapanatepec Mex.
116 C4 Tapanuli, Teluk b. Indon.
275 H5 Tapará, Ilha Grande do i. Brazil
275 H5 Tapara, Serra do hills Brazil
115 E4 Tapat i. Maluku Indon.
275 E6 Tapauá Brazil
275 E6 Tapauá r. Brazil
103 G8 Tapawera South I. N.Z.
279 B9 Tapera Rio Grande do Sul Brazil
275 F5 Tapera Roraima Brazil
283 C7 Tapera Chile
277 E3 Tapera Pesoe Brazil
278 F5 Taperoá Brazil
279 C9 Tapes Brazil
228 C5 Tapeta Liberia
195 J4 Tapfheim Ger.
138 D9 Tapi r. India
119 D10 Ta Pi, Mae Nam r. Thai.
277 F4 Tapia, Sierra de hills Bol.
204 G1 Tapia de Casariego Spain
283 C8 Tapi Aike Arg.
114 D8 Tapiantana i. Phil.
Tapiau Rus. Fed. see Gvardeysk
274 C6 Tapiche r. Peru
267 M9 Tapijulapa Mex.
117 I5 Tapinbini Kalimantan Indon.
199 J4 Tápió r. Hungary
199 I4 Tápióbicske Hungary
280 D2 Tapiocanga, Chapada do hills Brazil
199 I4 Tápiógyörgye Hungary
199 I4 Tápióság Hungary
199 I4 Tápiószecső Hungary
199 I4 Tápiószele Hungary
199 I4 Tápiószőlős Hungary
280 D3 Tapira Minas Gerais Brazil
280 A5 Tapira Paraná Brazil
278 D5 Tapiracanga Brazil
280 D5 Tapiraí Brazil
277 H2 Tapirapé r. Brazil
275 E4 Tapirapecó, Sierra mts Brazil/Venez.
277 F3 Tapirapuã Brazil
116 E2 Tapis, Gunung mt. Malaysia
266 E4 Tapisuelas Mex.
198 F4 Táplánszentkereszt Hungary
139 K6 Taplejung Nepal
131 □J7 Tap Mun Chau i. H.K. China
229 F3 Tapoa watercourse Burkina
230 B2 Tapol Chad
198 G5 Tapolca Hungary
118 D4 Ta-pom Myanmar
168 K8 Tap o' Noth hill Scotland U.K.
256 I11 Tappahannock VA U.S.A.
138 F5 Tappal Uttar Prad. India
117 M6 Tappalang Sulawesi Indon.
259 H2 Tappan NY U.S.A.
256 D8 Tappan Lake OH U.S.A.
144 D4 Tappeh, Kūh-e hill Iran
124 R5 Tappi-zaki pt Japan
151 H5 Tap Qaraqoyunlu Azer.
Taprobane country Asia see Sri Lanka
198 G5 Tapsony Hungary
122 B2 Taptugary Rus. Fed.
101 □8a Tapu, Motu i. Tonga
103 H8 Tapuaenuku mt. South I. N.Z.
114 C9 Tapul Phil.
114 C9 Tapul Group is Phil.
116 C4 Tapulonanjing mt. Indon.
116 D4 Tapung r. Indon.
275 F6 Tapurú Brazil
275 E5 Tapurucuara Brazil
100 □2 Taputapu, Cape American Samoa
Taputeouea atoll Gilbert Is Kiribati see Tabiteuea
146 G9 Taqar mt. Yemen
144 E6 Ţāqestān, Chāh-e well Iran
149 L6 Ţaqţaq Iraq
279 C9 Taquara Brazil
280 A1 Taquaral, Serra do hills Brazil
277 F4 Taquarí r. Brazil
277 F4 Taquarí, Pantanal do marsh Brazil
280 C4 Taquaritinga Brazil
280 C5 Taquarituba Brazil

280 A4 Taquaruçu r. Brazil
284 B5 Taquimilán Arg.
199 I4 Tar Hungary
169 G8 Tar r. Ireland
107 M9 Tara Qld Austr.
218 G7 Tara r. Bos.-Herz./Montenegro
218 H7 Tara nat. park Serbia
169 I5 Tara, Hill of Ireland
229 H4 Taraba r. Nigeria
229 H4 Taraba state Nigeria
280 B5 Tarabaí Brazil
276 D4 Tarabuco Bol.
224 B1 Ţarābulus Libya
205 N7 Taracena Spain
158 H8 Taraclia Moldova
276 C3 Taraco Peru
274 D4 Taracua Brazil
102 K6 Taradale North I. N.Z.
183 I10 Taradeau France
224 B3 Tarāghin Libya
128 H3 Taragt Mongolia
139 L6 Tarai reg. India
Taraíra r. Brazil see Traíra
276 E5 Tarairí Bol.
238 □3b Tarajalejo Fuerteventura Canary Is
117 L3 Tarakan Kalimantan Indon.
117 L3 Tarakan i. Indon.
145 L5 Tarakki reg. Afgh.
221 L2 Taraklı Turkey
Tarakliya Moldova see Taraclia
99 I3 Tarakua Fiji
105 L6 Taralga N.S.W. Austr.
124 □B22 Tarama-jima i. Nansei-shotō Japan
204 F2 Taramundi Spain
160 C7 Taran, Mys pt Rus. Fed.
138 F8 Tarana Madh. Prad. India
138 E5 Taranagar Rajasthan India
102 H6 Taranaki admin. reg. North I. N.Z.
102 I6 Taranaki, Mount vol. North I. N.Z.
205 N8 Tarancón Spain
159 L3 Tarandyntsi Ukr.
102 I2 Taranga Island North I. N.Z.
136 F7 Tarangambadi Tamil Nadu India
230 C2 Tarangara Chad
233 C6 Tarangire National Park Tanz.
Tarangul l. Kazakh. see Tarankol', Ozero
143 M1 Tarankol', Ozero l. Kazakh.
142 J1 Taranovskoye Kazakh.
168 B7 Taransay i. Scotland U.K.
217 M3 Taranto Italy
217 M2 Taranto prov. Italy
217 M3 Taranto, Golfo di g. Italy
198 G5 Tarany Hungary
276 C4 Tarapacá admin. reg. Chile
274 D5 Tarapacá Col.
100 □6 Tarapaina Malaita Solomon Is
274 B6 Tarapoto Peru
182 E5 Tarare France
285 I4 Tarariras Uru.
102 J7 Tararua Forest Park nature res. North I. N.Z.
103 J7 Tararua Range mts North I. N.Z.
Tarasaigh i. Scotland U.K. see Taransay
183 F9 Tarascon France
185 H10 Tarascon-sur-Ariège France
158 F5 Tarashany Ukr.
158 J4 Tarashcha Ukr.
144 G5 Tarasht Iran
159 M7 Tarasivka Khersons'ka Oblast' Ukr.
159 M7 Tarasivka Khersons'ka Oblast' Ukr.
159 L5 Tarasivka Kirovohrads'ka Oblast' Ukr.
159 R4 Tarasivka Luhans'ka Oblast' Ukr.
156 I2 Tarasovo Rus. Fed.
157 H6 Tarasovskiy Rus. Fed.
227 H4 Tarat Alg.
276 C4 Tarata Peru
276 C2 Tarauacá Brazil
274 D6 Tarauacá r. Brazil
101 □9a Taravao Tahiti Fr. Polynesia
101 □9a Taravao, Baie de b. Tahiti Fr. Polynesia
101 □9a Taravao, Isthme de isth. Tahiti Fr. Polynesia
213 P3 Taravisio, Foresta di Italy
214 B4 Taravo r. Corse France
99 H1 Tarawa atoll Kiribati
102 K6 Tarawera North I. N.Z.
102 K5 Tarawera, Lake North I. N.Z.
102 K5 Tarawera, Mount vol. North I. N.Z.
143 N6 Taraz Kazakh.
205 Q5 Tarazona Spain
207 P2 Tarazona de la Mancha Spain
143 S4 Tarbagatay Kazakh.
129 J1 Tarbagatay Rus. Fed.
143 S4 Tarbagatay, Khrebet mts Kazakh.
168 I7 Tarbat Ness pt Scotland U.K.
209 E10 Tárbena Spain
169 D7 Tarbert Ireland
168 E11 Tarbert Argyll and Bute, Scotland U.K.
168 F11 Tarbert Argyll and Bute, Scotland U.K.
168 C7 Tarbert Western Isles, Scotland U.K.
168 D11 Tarbert, Loch inlet Scotland U.K.
185 E9 Tarbes France
168 G10 Tarbet Argyll and Bute, Scotland U.K.
168 H11 Tarbolton South Ayrshire, Scotland U.K.
255 I8 Tarboro NC U.S.A.
199 L5 Tărcaia Romania
199 K3 Tarcal Hungary
199 L4 Tarcea Romania
213 O3 Tarcento Italy
104 E4 Tarcoola S.A. Austr.
105 K4 Tarcoon N.S.W. Austr.
104 D2 Tarcoonyinna watercourse S.A. Austr.
219 K5 Ţarcului, Munţii mts Romania
105 K6 Tarcutta N.S.W. Austr.
197 I4 Tarczyn Pol.
180 H4 Tard r. France
205 M4 Tardajos Spain
205 O5 Tardelcuende Spain
178 F5 Tardenois reg. France
184 J3 Tardes r. France
185 C9 Tardets-Sorholus France
208 D4 Tardienta Spain
184 E4 Tardoire r. France
122 K4 Tardoki-Yani, Gora mt. Rus. Fed.
105 N4 Taree N.S.W. Austr.
232 B2 Tareifing Sudan
105 I4 Tarella N.S.W. Austr.
162 Q3 Tärendö Sweden
268 F5 Tarengo Mex.
229 F2 Tarenkat well Mali
Tarentum Italy see Taranto
268 F6 Taretán Mex.
153 K2 Tareya Rus. Fed.
147 J4 Ţarfā', Baţn aţ depr. Saudi Arabia
146 F7 Ţarfā, Ra's aţ pt Saudi Arabia
226 B4 Tarfaya Morocco
168 K9 Tarfside Angus, Scotland U.K.
229 G2 Targa well Niger
Targan Heilong. China see Talin Hiag
Targan Kazakh. see Targyn
262 I4 Targhee Pass ID U.S.A.
185 D6 Targon France
219 N6 Târgovişte Romania
196 F3 Targowa Górka Pol.
219 P5 Târgu Bujor Romania
219 L6 Târgu Cărbuneşti Romania
219 O3 Târgu Frumos Romania
226 D2 Targuist Morocco
219 L5 Târgu Jiu Romania
219 L3 Târgu Lăpuş Romania
219 M4 Târgu Mureş Romania
219 O3 Târgu Neamţ Romania
219 O4 Târgu Ocna Romania
219 O4 Târgu Secuiesc Romania
133 G12 Targyailing Xizang China
143 T3 Targyn Kazakh.
144 B5 Tarhān Iran
226 D3 Tarhbalt Morocco
Tarhmanant well Mali see Taghmanant
199 K5 Tarhos Hungary

224 B1 **Tarhūnah** Libya
113 J8 **Tari** P.N.G.
129 K7 **Tarian Gol** *Nei Mongol* China
128 F2 **Tariat** Mongolia
146 F6 **Tarib, Wādī** *watercourse* Saudi Arabia
147 K3 **Tarif** U.A.E.
206 H8 **Tarifa** Spain
206 H8 **Tarifa, Punta de** *pt* Spain
114 D3 **Tarigtig Point** *Luzon* Phil.
276 D5 **Tarija** Bol.
276 D5 **Tarija** *dept* Bol.
136 D6 **Tarikere** *Karnataka* India
113 I7 **Tariku** *r. Papua* Indon.
132 F6 **Tarim** *Xinjiang* China
147 I7 **Tarīm** Yemen
Tarim Basin China *see* **Tarim Pendi**
233 B5 **Tarime** Tanz.
132 H6 **Tarim He** *r.* China
132 H6 **Tarim Liuchang** *Xinjiang* China
268 G5 **Tarimoro** Mex.
132 E7 **Tarim Pendi** *basin* China
132 H6 **Tarim Qichang** *Xinjiang* China
277 E5 **Taringuiti** Bol.
145 K5 **Tarīn Kowt** Afgh.
113 I7 **Taritatu** *r. Papua* Indon.
Taritipan *Sabah* Malaysia *see* **Tandek**
199 H4 **Tarján** Hungary
237 J8 **Tarka** *r.* S. Africa
229 G3 **Tarka, Vallée de** *watercourse* Niger
199 G4 **Tárkány** Hungary
237 K8 **Tarkastad** S. Africa
159 P8 **Tarkhan, Mys** *pt* Ukr.
159 L8 **Tarkhankut, Mys** *pt* Ukr.
151 I3 **Tarki** Rus. Fed.
260 H5 **Tarkio** *MO* U.S.A.
152 I3 **Tarko-Sale** Rus. Fed.
228 E5 **Tarkwa** Ghana
114 C4 **Tarlac** *Luzon* Phil.
114 C3 **Tarlac** *r. Luzon* Phil.
143 R4 **Tarlauly** Kazakh.
171 L6 **Tarleton** *Lancashire, England* U.K.
105 L6 **Tarlo River National Park** *N.S.W.* Austr.
256 C9 **Tarlton** *OH* U.S.A.
164 E6 **Tarm** Denmark
276 B2 **Tarma** *Junín* Peru
274 D5 **Tarma** *Loreto* Peru
139 L5 **Tarmar** *Xizang* China
190 H4 **Tarmstedt** Ger.
185 I8 **Tarn** *dept* France
183 B8 **Tarn** *r.* France
183 C8 **Tarn, Gorges du** France
199 I4 **Tarna** *r.* Hungary
205 J2 **Tarna, Puerto de** *pass* Spain
162 M4 **Tärnaby** Sweden
145 K6 **Tarnak** *r.* Afgh.
199 J3 **Tarnalelesz** Hungary
199 J4 **Tarnaméra** Hungary
199 J4 **Tarnaőrs** Hungary
199 J4 **Tarnaszentmiklós** Hungary
219 L4 **Târnava Mare** *r.* Romania
219 L4 **Târnava Mică** *r.* Romania
219 M4 **Târnăveni** Romania
197 K5 **Tarnawa Duża** Pol.
197 L5 **Tarnawatka** Pol.
185 G7 **Tarn-et-Garonne** *dept* France
197 K6 **Tarnica** *mt.* Pol.
197 J5 **Tarnobrzeg** Pol.
197 K5 **Tarnogród** Pol.
156 H3 **Tarnogskiy Gorodok** Rus. Fed.
199 H4 **Tárnok** Hungary
Tarnopol Ukr. *see* **Ternopil'**
185 B8 **Tarnos** France
197 L5 **Tarnoszyn** Pol.
199 K5 **Târnova** *Arad* Romania
219 K5 **Târnova** *Caraș-Severin* Romania
192 F3 **Tarnow** Ger.
196 C3 **Tarnów** *Lubuskie* Pol.
197 I5 **Tarnów** *Małopolskie* Pol.
197 J6 **Tarnowiec** Pol.
Tarnowitz Pol. *see* **Tarnowskie Góry**
196 E2 **Tarnówka** Pol.
196 E3 **Tarnowo Podgórne** Pol.
196 G5 **Tarnów Opolski** Pol.
196 G5 **Tarnowskie Góry** Pol.
138 E4 **Tarn Taran** *Punjab* India
162 M3 **Tårnvik** Norway
212 I6 **Taro** *r.* Italy
124 S7 **Tarō** Japan
133 F11 **Taro Co** *salt l.* China
144 F7 **Ţārom** Iran
159 N5 **Taroms'ke** Ukr.
185 D8 **Taron-Sadirac-Viellenave** France
107 L8 **Taroom** *Qld* Austr.
127 J2 **Tarō-san** *mt.* Japan
204 E6 **Tarouca** Port.
226 C3 **Taroudannt** Morocco
204 D6 **Tarouquela** Port.
190 H1 **Tarp** Ger.
199 L3 **Tarpa** Hungary
106 F5 **Tarpaulin Swamp** *N.T.* Austr.
104 H7 **Tarpeena** *S.A.* Austr.
255 F11 **Tarpon Springs** *FL* U.S.A.
171 L7 **Tarporley** *Cheshire, England* U.K.
197 L1 **Tarprubežiai** Lith.
270 E1 **Tarpum Bay** *Eleuthera* Bahamas
144 D5 **Ţarq** Iran
144 D6 **Tarqān** Iran
129 Q3 **Tarqi** *Nei Mongol* China
214 H3 **Tarquinia** Italy
214 H3 **Tarquinia Lido** Italy
Tarquinii Italy *see* **Tarquinia**
106 E5 **Tarrabool Lake** *salt flat N.T.* Austr.
Tarracina Italy *see* **Terracina**
Tarraco Spain *see* **Tarragona**
228 □ **Tarrafal** *Santiago* Cape Verde
208 H5 **Tarragona** Spain
208 G5 **Tarragona** *prov.* Spain
105 K10 **Tarraleah** *Tas.* Austr.
105 K5 **Tarran Hills** *N.S.W.* Austr.
106 G4 **Tarrant Point** *Qld* Austr.
103 D11 **Tarras** *South I.* N.Z.
Tarrasa Spain *see* **Terrassa**
208 H4 **Tàrrega** Spain
168 I7 **Tarrel** *Highland, Scotland* U.K.
200 C5 **Tarrenz** Austria
204 D2 **Tarrio** Spain
208 H4 **Tarroja de Segarra** Spain
259 H2 **Tarrytown** *NY* U.S.A.
164 H7 **Tårs** Denmark
215 Q8 **Tarsia** Italy
224 C4 **Tarso Ahon** *mt.* Chad
224 C4 **Tarso Emissi** *mt.* Chad
224 C4 **Tarso Kobour** *mt.* Chad
148 G5 **Tarsus** Turkey
150 C2 **Tarsus** *r.* Turkey
192 E1 **Tårs Vig** *b.* Denmark
133 K8 **Tart** *Qinghai* China
144 E1 **Tarta** Turkm.
282 E1 **Tartagal** *Salta* Arg.
282 F3 **Tartagal** *Santa Fé* Arg.
197 M5 **Tartakiv** Ukr.
151 H5 **Tärtär** Azer.
151 H5 **Tärtär** *r.* Azer.
151 I5 **Tärtär** *r.* Azer.
213 M5 **Tartaro** *r.* Italy
185 C8 **Tartas** France
160 J3 **Tartu** Estonia
150 D4 **Ţarţūs** Syria
150 E3 **Ţarţūs** *governorate* Syria
126 E5 **Tarui** Japan
Tarumae-san *vol.* Japan *see* **Shikotsu**
281 G3 **Tarumirim** Brazil
125 H15 **Tarumizu** Japan
151 H1 **Tarumovka** Rus. Fed.
118 C1 **Tarung Hka** *r.* Myanmar
161 U7 **Tarusa** Rus. Fed.
161 U7 **Tarusa** *r.* Rus. Fed.
147 J2 **Tārūt** Saudi Arabia
119 D11 **Tarutao, Ko** *i.* Thai.
119 D11 **Tarutao National Park** Thai.
116 C3 **Tarutung** *Sumatera* Indon.
158 I7 **Tarutyne** Ukr.
168 L8 **Tarves** *Aberdeenshire, Scotland* U.K.
171 L7 **Tarvin** *Cheshire, England* U.K.
213 P2 **Tarvisio** Italy
Tarvisium Italy *see* **Treviso**
277 E3 **Tarvo** Bol.
217 □ **Tarxien** Malta
128 F1 **Tarys-Arzhan** Rus. Fed.
144 G6 **Ţarz** Iran
143 O4 **Tasaral** Kazakh.
224 B3 **Tasāwah** Libya
142 K5 **Tasbuget** Kazakh.
212 D3 **Täsch** Switz.
248 E3 **Taschereau** *Que.* Can.
246 F5 **Taseko Mountain** *B.C.* Can.
227 F4 **Tasendjanet, Oued** *watercourse* Alg.
136 D4 **Tasgaon** *Mahar.* India
151 A5 **Taşgeçit** Turkey
159 N4 **Tashan'** *r.* Ukr.
Tashauz Turkm. *see* **Daşoguz**
Tashauzskaya Oblast' *admin. div.* Turkm. *see* **Daşoguz**
143 Q7 **Tash-Bashat** Kyrg.
158 H8 **Tashbunar** *r.* Ukr.
128 D6 **Tashi** *Gansu* China
Tashi Chho Bhutan *see* **Thimphu**
139 M6 **Tashigang** Bhutan
Tashino Rus. Fed. *see* **Pervomaysk**
151 F4 **Tashir** Armenia
144 E7 **Tashk, Daryācheh-ye** *l.* Iran
Tashkent Uzbek. *see* **Toshkent**
Tashkent Oblast *admin. div.* Uzbek. *see* **Toshkent**
143 O7 **Tash-Kömür** Kyrg.
Tash-Kumyr Kyrg. *see* **Tash-Kömür**
142 E2 **Tashla** Rus. Fed.
159 K4 **Tashlyk** Ukr.
Tāshqurghān Afgh. *see* **Kholm**
249 F1 **Tasialujjuaq, Lac** *l. Que.* Can.
248 F1 **Tasiat, Lac** *l. Que.* Can.
243 O3 **Tasiilap Karra** *c.* Greenland
Tasiilaq Greenland *see* **Ammassalik**
117 H8 **Tasikmalaya** *Jawa* Indon.
150 D6 **Tasīl** Syria
190 K1 **Tåsinge** *i.* Denmark
249 G1 **Tasiujaq** *Que.* Can.
243 M2 **Tasiusaq** Greenland
162 M4 **Tåsjö** Sweden
229 H3 **Task** *well* Niger
142 D2 **Taskala** Kazakh.
150 B1 **Taşkale** Turkey
151 E6 **Taşkapı** Turkey
150 A2 **Taşkent** Turkey
229 H3 **Tasker** Niger
143 S4 **Taskesken** Kazakh.
151 B5 **Taşkıran** Turkey
148 G3 **Taşköprü** Turkey
149 K4 **Taşlıçay** Turkey
151 E5 **Taşlıoğul** Turkey
103 H8 **Tasman** *South I.* N.Z.
103 G8 **Tasman** *admin. reg. South I.* N.Z.
103 E11 **Tasman** *r. South I.* N.Z.
103 E10 **Tasman, Mount** *South I.* N.Z.
290 F8 **Tasman Abyssal Plain** *sea feature* Austr.
289 O7 **Tasman Basin** *sea feature* Tasman Sea
103 H8 **Tasman Bay** *South I.* N.Z.
105 K10 **Tasman Head** *Tas.* Austr.
105 J10 **Tasmania** *state* Austr.
103 G8 **Tasman Mountains** *South I.* N.Z.
105 L10 **Tasman Peninsula** *Tas.* Austr.
99 H6 **Tasman Sea** S. Pacific Ocean
219 K3 **Tăşnad** Romania
143 O6 **Tasotkel'skoye Vodokhranilishche** *resr* Kazakh.
148 H3 **Taşova** Turkey
199 I4 **Tass** Hungary
170 D5 **Tassagh** *Northern Ireland* U.K.
229 G2 **Tassara** Niger
229 G2 **Tassa Takorat** *well* Niger
227 F4 **Tassedjefit, Erg** *des.* Alg.
182 F2 **Tasselot, Mont** *hill* France
229 F3 **Tasserest** *well* Mali
230 A5 **Tassi** Gabon
248 F1 **Tassialouc, Lac** *l. Que.* Can.
182 F5 **Tassin-la-Demi-Lune** France
208 F5 **Tastavíns** *r.* Spain
153 N3 **Tas-Tumus** Rus. Fed.
143 M5 **Tasty** Kazakh.
143 L2 **Tasty-Taldy** Kazakh.
245 N5 **Tasu** *B.C.* Can.
150 B2 **Taşucu** Turkey
144 A2 **Tasūj** Iran
153 M3 **Tas-Yuryakh** Rus. Fed.
199 G5 **Taszár** Hungary
199 H4 **Tát** Hungary
199 H4 **Tata** Hungary
226 D3 **Tata** Morocco
101 □9a **Tataa, Pointe** *pt Tahiti* Fr. Polynesia
115 C4 **Tataba** *Sulawesi* Indon.
199 H4 **Tatabánya** Hungary
199 I5 **Tataháza** Hungary
269 M7 **Tatahuicapan** Mex.
128 D8 **Tatalin Gol** *r. Qinghai* China
269 J9 **Tataltepec** Mex.
249 I4 **Tatamagouche** *N.S.* Can.
115 D8 **Tatamailau, Foho** *mt.* East Timor
100 □6 **Tatamba** *Sta Isabel* Solomon Is
139 K8 **Tatanagar** *Jharkhand* India
227 H2 **Tataouine** Tunisia
158 I8 **Tatarbunary** Ukr.
160 L8 **Tatarka** Belarus
159 O5 **Tatarka** *r.* Ukr.
221 L4 **Tatarlı** *Afyon* Turkey
150 E1 **Tatarlı** *Osmaniye* Turkey
138 F6 **Tatarpur** *Rajasthan* India
152 I4 **Tatarsk** *Novosibirskaya Oblast'* Rus. Fed.
161 O7 **Tatarsk** *Smolenskaya Oblast'* Rus. Fed.
Tatarskaya A.S.S.R. *aut. rep.* Rus. Fed. *see* **Tatarstan, Respublika**
122 L3 **Tatarskiy Proliv** *str.* Rus. Fed.
156 J5 **Tatarstan, Respublika** *aut. rep.* Rus. Fed.
Tatar Strait Rus. Fed. *see* **Tatarskiy Proliv**
199 I4 **Tatárszentgyörgy** Hungary
219 O3 **Tătăruși** Romania
101 □9a **Tatatua, Pointe** *pt Tahiti* Fr. Polynesia
117 J3 **Tatau** *Sarawak* Malaysia
144 A3 **Tatavi** *r.* Iran
151 I2 **Tatayurt** Rus. Fed.
107 I4 **Tate** *r. Qld* Austr.
127 K3 **Tatebayashi** Japan
126 D4 **Tateishi-misaki** *pt* Japan
127 K1 **Tateiwa** Japan
127 H3 **Tateshina** Japan
127 H3 **Tateshina-yama** *mt.* Japan
127 K6 **Tateyama** *Chiba* Japan
126 F2 **Tateyama** *Toyama* Japan
126 G2 **Tate-yama** *vol.* Japan
246 G2 **Tathlina Lake** *N.W.T.* Can.
146 F6 **Tathlīth** Saudi Arabia
146 G5 **Tathlīth, Wādī** *watercourse* Saudi Arabia
105 L7 **Tathra** *N.S.W.* Austr.
235 E4 **Tati** Botswana
228 B2 **Tâtîlt** *well* Maur.
190 G2 **Tating** Ger.
247 L2 **Tatinnai Lake** *Nunavut* Can.
142 A2 **Tatishchevo** Rus. Fed.
245 K3 **Tatitlek** *AK* U.S.A.
118 C4 **Tatkon** Myanmar
246 E5 **Tatla Lake** *B.C.* Can.
246 E5 **Tatla Lake** *l. B.C.* Can.
246 E3 **Tatlatui Provincial Park** *B.C.* Can.
246 E5 **Tatlayoko Lake** *B.C.* Can.
151 G4 **Tatlı** Azer.
247 N3 **Tatnam, Cape** *Man.* Can.
127 I4 **Tatomi** Japan
Tatra Mountains Pol./Slovakia *see* **Tatry**
133 G7 **Tatrang** *Xinjiang* China
199 J2 **Tatranská Javorina** Slovakia
199 J2 **Tatranský** *nat. park* Slovakia
197 H6 **Tatry** *mts* Pol./Slovakia
197 H6 **Tatrzański Park Narodowy** *nat. park* Pol.
245 M4 **Tatshenshini** *r. B.C.* Can.
246 B3 **Tatshenshini-Alsek Provincial Wilderness Park** *B.C.* Can.
157 H6 **Tatsinskiy** Rus. Fed.
125 L12 **Tatsuno** *Hyōgo* Japan
127 G4 **Tatsuno** *Nagano* Japan
126 E3 **Tatsunokuchi** Japan
126 E1 **Tatsuruhama** Japan
127 G6 **Tatsuyama** Japan
171 Q7 **Tattershall** *Lincolnshire, England* U.K.
143 O6 **Tatti** Kazakh.
Tatty Kazakh. *see* **Tatti**
102 I5 **Tatu** *hill North I.* N.Z.
280 D5 **Tatuí** Brazil
246 E4 **Tatuk Mountain** *B.C.* Can.
160 H5 **Tatula** *r.* Lith.
261 D9 **Tatum** *NM* U.S.A.
261 H9 **Tatum** *TX* U.S.A.
149 K4 **Tatvan** Turkey
100 □2 **Ta'u** *i.* American Samoa
164 B2 **Tau** Norway
101 □8a **Tau** *i.* Tonga
278 E3 **Taua** Brazil
100 □4b **Tauak Passage** *Pohnpei* Micronesia
275 F5 **Tauapeçaçu** Brazil
275 F6 **Tauariã** Brazil
281 E5 **Taubaté** Brazil
193 H8 **Taubenheim** Ger.
194 H2 **Tauber** *r.* Ger.
194 H2 **Tauberbischofsheim** Ger.
194 H3 **Taubergrund** *reg.* Ger.
193 F8 **Taucha** Ger.
193 J6 **Tauche** Ger.
142 D5 **Tauchik** Kazakh.
193 J7 **Tauer** Ger.
195 L5 **Taufkirchen** *Bayern* Ger.
195 M5 **Taufkirchen** *Bayern* Ger.
195 M5 **Taufkirchen (Vils)** Ger.
191 H9 **Taufstein** *hill* Ger.
102 K5 **Tauhara** *mt. North I.* N.Z.
102 I3 **Tauhoa** *North I.* N.Z.
275 G4 **Tauini** *r.* Brazil
143 P5 **Taukum, Peski** *des.* Kazakh.
180 D4 **Taulé** France
183 F8 **Taulignan** France
102 J5 **Taumarunui** *North I.* N.Z.
276 B2 **Taumaturgo** Brazil
277 G5 **Taunay** Brazil
237 I3 **Taung** S. Africa
118 C7 **Taungbon** Myanmar
118 B4 **Taungdwingyi** Myanmar
118 C4 **Taunggyi** Myanmar
118 C4 **Taunglau** Myanmar
118 C5 **Taung-ngu** Myanmar
118 C6 **Taungnyo Range** *mts* Myanmar
118 B4 **Taungtha** Myanmar
118 B5 **Taungup** Myanmar
145 N6 **Taunsa** Pak.
172 F5 **Taunton** *Somerset, England* U.K.
257 N7 **Taunton** *MA* U.S.A.
191 E10 **Taunus** *hills* Ger.
102 □ **Taupeka Point** *Chatham Is* S. Pacific Ocean
102 J4 **Taupiri** *North I.* N.Z.
201 J4 **Tauplitz** Austria
102 K5 **Taupo** *North I.* N.Z.
102 J5 **Taupo, Lake** *North I.* N.Z.
160 F6 **Tauragė** Lith.
160 E6 **Tauralaukis** Lith.
274 C3 **Tauramena** Col.
102 K4 **Tauranga** *North I.* N.Z.
Taurasia Italy *see* **Torino**
248 F4 **Taureau, Réservoir** *resr Que.* Can.
217 K7 **Taurianova** Italy
102 I2 **Taurikura** *North I.* N.Z.
184 G4 **Taurion** *r.* France
217 O4 **Taurisano** Italy
Tauriuiná *r.* Brazil *see* **Verde**
102 H2 **Tauroa Point** *North I.* N.Z.
Taurus Mountains Turkey *see* **Toros Dağları**
Taūshyq Kazakh. *see* **Tauchik**
208 C4 **Tauste** Spain
199 K5 **Tăuț** Romania
185 J10 **Tautavel** France
180 I3 **Taute** *r.* France
193 E9 **Tautenhain** Ger.
199 L4 **Tăuteu** Romania
101 □9a **Tautira** *Tahiti* Fr. Polynesia
182 B5 **Tauves** France
102 M5 **Tauwhareparae** *North I.* N.Z.
153 Q4 **Tauyskaya Guba** *g.* Rus. Fed.
Tauz Azer. *see* **Tovuz**
214 B3 **Tavaco** *Corse* France
213 O3 **Tavagnacco** Italy
218 H4 **Tavankut** *Vojvodina* Serbia
212 C1 **Tavannes** Switz.
181 L7 **Tavant** France
255 G11 **Tavares** *FL* U.S.A.
213 K8 **Tavarnelle Val di Pesa** Italy
221 K5 **Tavas** Turkey
Tavastehus Fin. *see* **Hämeenlinna**
182 G2 **Tavaux** France
152 H4 **Tavda** Rus. Fed.
204 D8 **Taveiro** Port.
183 F8 **Tavel** France
162 P4 **Tavelsjö** Sweden
173 O2 **Taverham** *Norfolk, England* U.K.
217 L5 **Taverna** Italy
182 E2 **Tavernay** France
214 I1 **Tavernelle** Italy
183 I9 **Tavernes** France
209 E9 **Tavernes de la Valldigna** Spain
172 C4 **Tavernspite** *Pembrokeshire, Wales* U.K.
178 D5 **Taverny** France
212 H7 **Taverone** *r.* Italy
208 J4 **Tavertet** Spain
101 □7 **Taveuni** *i.* Fiji
217 O4 **Taviano** Italy
214 D3 **Tavignano** *r. Corse* France
151 H7 **Tavil** Iran
145 N2 **Tavildara** Tajik.
215 O4 **Taviolere** *plain* Italy
206 D6 **Tavira** Port.
206 D6 **Tavira, Ilha de** *i.* Port.
251 N6 **Tavistock** *Ont.* Can.
172 D6 **Tavistock** *Devon, England* U.K.
215 M3 **Tavo** *r.* Italy
214 D6 **Tavolara, Isola** *i. Sardegna* Italy
143 Q1 **Tavolzhan** Kazakh.
204 E6 **Távora** *r.* Spain
119 D7 **Tavoy** Myanmar
119 D8 **Tavoy** *r. mouth* Myanmar
Tavoy Island Myanmar *see* **Mali Kyun**
119 D8 **Tavoy Point** Myanmar
143 T2 **Tavricheskoye** Kazakh.
Tavrīl Kazakh. *see* **Tavricheskoye**
159 M7 **Tavriys'k** Ukr.
221 K3 **Tavşanlı** Turkey
101 □7a **Tavua** *Viti Levu* Fiji
101 □7a **Tavua** *i.* Fiji
101 □7 **Tavuki** *Kadavu* Fiji
213 N8 **Tavullia** Italy
151 G4 **Tavush** *r.* Armenia
172 D7 **Tavy** *r. England* U.K.
172 D5 **Taw** *r. England* U.K.
146 G5 **Taw, Jabal at** *hill* Saudi Arabia
103 I8 **Tawa** *North I.* N.Z.
117 L2 **Tawai, Bukit** *mt.* Malaysia
261 H9 **Tawakoni, Lake** *TX* U.S.A.
106 E3 **Tawallah Range** *hills N.T.* Austr.
139 M6 **Tawang** *Arun. Prad.* India
100 □6 **Tawaraha** *San Cristobal* Solomon Is
126 C6 **Tawaramoto** Japan
100 □6 **Tawarogha** *San Cristobal* Solomon Is
251 K5 **Tawas Bay** *MI* U.S.A.
251 K5 **Tawas City** *MI* U.S.A.
117 L2 **Tawau** *Sabah* Malaysia
117 L2 **Tawau, Teluk** *b.* Malaysia
225 G3 **Ţawd** Egypt
Tawè Myanmar *see* **Tavoy**
172 E4 **Tawe** *r. Wales* U.K.
224 E6 **Taweisha** Sudan
194 B2 **Tawern** Ger.
102 K5 **Tawhiuau** *mt. North I.* N.Z.
138 E3 **Tawi** *r.* India
147 L3 **Ţawī Ḩafīr** *well* U.A.E.
224 E6 **Tawila** Sudan
146 A2 **Ţawīlah, Juzur** *is* Egypt
Tawîla Islands Egypt *see* **Ţawīlah, Juzur**
147 L3 **Ţawī Murra** *well* U.A.E.
114 B9 **Tawi-Tawi** *i.* Phil.
118 C2 **Tawmaw** Myanmar
131 M7 **Tawu** Taiwan
269 H7 **Taxco** Mex.
200 G5 **Taxenbach** Austria
142 H6 **Taxiatosh** Uzbek.
145 O5 **Taxila** *tourist site* Pak.
133 B8 **Taxkorgan** *Xinjiang* China
142 I6 **Taxtako'pir** Uzbek.
245 N3 **Tay** *r. Y.T.* Can.
168 J10 **Tay** *r. Scotland* U.K.
168 J10 **Tay, Firth of** *est. Scotland* U.K.
109 F12 **Tay, Lake** *salt flat W.A.* Austr.
168 H10 **Tay, Loch** *l. Scotland* U.K.
276 A2 **Tayabamba** Peru
114 C5 **Tayabas Bay** *Luzon* Phil.
117 I4 **Tayan** *Kalimantan* Indon.
144 I4 **Tāybād** Iran
156 F1 **Taybola** Rus. Fed.
232 E3 **Tayeeglow** Somalia
221 H2 **Tayfur** Turkey
152 J4 **Tayga** Rus. Fed.
144 D4 **Tāygān** Iran
Taygan Mongolia *see* **Delger**
220 D5 **Taygetos** *mts* Greece
168 E11 **Tayinloan** *Argyll and Bute, Scotland* U.K.
158 J7 **Tayirove** Ukr.
122 I1 **Taykanskiy Khrebet** *mts* Rus. Fed.
246 F3 **Taylor** *B.C.* Can.
244 F2 **Taylor** *AK* U.S.A.
265 V7 **Taylor** *AZ* U.S.A.
260 F5 **Taylor** *NE* U.S.A.
258 D2 **Taylor** *PA* U.S.A.
261 G10 **Taylor** *TX* U.S.A.
263 K7 **Taylor** *r. CO* U.S.A.
103 F10 **Taylor, Mount** *South I.* N.Z.
263 K9 **Taylor, Mount** *NM* U.S.A.
244 H3 **Taylor Mountains** *AK* U.S.A.
258 D6 **Taylors Bridge** *DE* U.S.A.
170 B7 **Taylor's Cross** Ireland
254 E6 **Taylorsville** *KY* U.S.A.
258 A6 **Taylorsville** *MD* U.S.A.
255 G8 **Taylorsville** *NC* U.S.A.
259 G3 **Taylortown** *NJ* U.S.A.
260 K6 **Taylorville** *IL* U.S.A.
146 D2 **Taymā'** Saudi Arabia
257 □S2 **Taymouth** *N.B.* Can.
153 K3 **Taymura** *r.* Rus. Fed.
153 L2 **Taymyr, Ozero** *l.* Rus. Fed.
153 J2 **Taymyr, Poluostrov** *pen.* Rus. Fed.
Taymyr Peninsula Rus. Fed. *see* **Taymyr, Poluostrov**
119 H9 **Tây Ninh** Vietnam
168 F10 **Taynuilt** *Argyll and Bute, Scotland* U.K.
268 B1 **Tayoltita** Mex.
142 D3 **Taypak** Kazakh.
Taypaq Kazakh. *see* **Taypak**
168 K10 **Tayport** *Fife, Scotland* U.K.
274 C2 **Tayrona, Parque Nacional** *nat. park* Col.
153 K4 **Tayshet** Rus. Fed.
128 E3 **Tayshir** Mongolia
142 E3 **Taysoygan, Peski** *des.* Kazakh.
Tayspun *tourist site* Iraq *see* **Ctesiphon**
221 J4 **Taytan** Turkey
114 C4 **Taytay** *Luzon* Phil.
114 B6 **Taytay** *Palawan* Phil.
114 B6 **Taytay Bay** *Palawan* Phil.
114 E6 **Taytay Point** *Leyte* Phil.
117 I8 **Tayu** *Jawa* Indon.
122 D3 **Tayuan** *Heilong.* China
170 F1 **Tayvallich** *Argyll and Bute, Scotland* U.K.
150 C10 **Ţayyib al Ism** Saudi Arabia
143 M1 **Tayynsha** Kazakh.
152 I3 **Taz** *r.* Rus. Fed.
226 E2 **Taza** Morocco
202 D5 **Taza-Al Hoceima-Taounate** *prov.* Morocco
Taza-Bazar Uzbek. *see* **Shumanay**
238 □3d **Tazacorte** *La Palma* Canary Is
151 H5 **Täzäkänd** Azer.
149 L6 **Tāza Khurmātū** Iraq
127 G3 **Tazawa** Japan
124 R7 **Tazawa-ko** *l.* Japan
118 B3 **Taze** Myanmar
144 B2 **Tazeh Kand** Azer.
151 I6 **Tāzeh Kand-e Angūt** Iran
226 D3 **Tazenakht** Morocco
256 B12 **Tazewell** *TN* U.S.A.
256 D11 **Tazewell** *VA* U.S.A.
244 I3 **Tazimina Lakes** *AK* U.S.A.
247 I2 **Tazin** *r. N.W.T./Sask.* Can.
247 I3 **Tazin Lake** *Sask.* Can.
224 D3 **Tāzirbū** Libya
224 D3 **Tazirbu Water Wells Field** Libya
229 H2 **Tazizilet** *well* Niger
199 I5 **Tázlár** Hungary
219 O4 **Tazlău** Romania
219 O4 **Tazlău** *r.* Romania
245 K3 **Tazlina** *AK* U.S.A.
245 K3 **Tazlina Lake** *AK* U.S.A.
211 C7 **Tazoghrane** Tunisia
229 H2 **Tazolé** *well* Niger
205 J1 **Tazones** Spain
227 E5 **Tazouikert** *hill* Mali
152 I3 **Tazovskaya Guba** *sea chan.* Rus. Fed.
152 I3 **Tazovskiy** Rus. Fed.
227 G5 **Tazrouk** Alg.
226 D3 **Tazzarine** Morocco
226 E2 **Tazzouguert** Morocco
Tbessa Alg. *see* **Tébessa**
151 F4 **T'bilisi** Georgia
157 H7 **Tbilisskaya** Rus. Fed.
229 I5 **Tchabal Gangdaba** *mt.* Cameroon
229 I5 **Tchabal Mbabo** *mt.* Cameroon
Tchad *country* Africa *see* **Chad**
229 F4 **Tchamba** Togo
229 F4 **Tchaourou** Benin
229 F5 **Tchetti** Benin
230 A5 **Tchibanga** Gabon
229 G2 **Tchidoutene** *watercourse* Niger
224 C5 **Tchié** *well* Chad
224 B4 **Tchigaï, Plateau du** Niger
231 B8 **Tchihepepe** Angola
231 C8 **Tchikala-Tcholohanga** Angola
230 C5 **Tchikapika** Congo
231 B8 **Tchindjenje** Angola
229 H3 **Tchin Garaguene** *well* Niger
229 G3 **Tchin-Tabaradene** Niger
229 I4 **Tchollíré** Cameroon
229 H2 **Tchou-m-Adegdeg** *well* Niger
165 O7 **Tczew** Pol.
119 H8 **Te, Prêk** *r.* Cambodia
274 E5 **Tea** *r.* Brazil
204 D4 **Tea** *r.* Spain
268 B3 **Teacapán** Mex.
109 F8 **Teague, Lake** *salt flat W.A.* Austr.
101 □9a **Teahupoo** *Tahiti* Fr. Polynesia
103 □3 **Te Aiti Point** *Rarotonga* Cook Is
168 K9 **Tealing** *Angus, Scotland* U.K.
103 B12 **Te Anau** *South I.* N.Z.
103 B12 **Te Anau, Lake** *South I.* N.Z.
259 G3 **Teaneck** *NJ* U.S.A.
102 I5 **Te Anga** *North I.* N.Z.
215 M5 **Teano** Italy
109 D8 **Teano Range** *mts W.A.* Austr.
Teanum Sidicinum Italy *see* **Teano**
267 M9 **Teapa** Mex.
102 M4 **Te Araroa** *North I.* N.Z.
218 J8 **Tearce** Macedonia
102 J4 **Te Aroha** *North I.* N.Z.
102 J4 **Te Aroha, Mount** *hill North I.* N.Z.
Teate Italy *see* **Chieti**
101 □9a **Teavaro** *Moorea* Fr. Polynesia
102 J5 **Te Awamutu** *North I.* N.Z.
207 J7 **Teba** Spain
205 P9 **Tebar** Spain
229 G3 **Tébarat** Niger
117 H4 **Tebas** *Kalimantan* Indon.
171 L5 **Tebay** *Cumbria, England* U.K.
117 I4 **Tebedu** *Sarawak* Malaysia
151 C2 **Teberda** Rus. Fed.
151 C2 **Teberda** *r.* Rus. Fed.
151 C2 **Teberdinskiy Zapovednik** *nature res.* Rus. Fed.
247 L2 **Tebesjuak Lake** *Nunavut* Can.
227 H2 **Tébessa** Alg.
227 H2 **Tébessa, Monts de** *mts* Alg.
277 F6 **Tebicuary** Para.
277 F6 **Tebicuary** *r.* Para.
116 C3 **Tebingtinggi** *Sumatera* Indon.
116 E6 **Tebingtinggi** *Sumatera* Indon.
116 E5 **Tebo** *r.* Indon.
211 B7 **Tébourba** Tunisia
211 B7 **Téboursouk** Tunisia
151 G3 **Tebulos Mt'a** Georgia/Rus. Fed.
268 D6 **Tecalitlán** Mex.
269 I6 **Tecamac** Mex.
269 J7 **Tecamachalco** Mex.
269 J7 **Tecamachalco Nogales** Mex.
266 A1 **Tecate** Mex.
150 C2 **Tece** Turkey
185 K10 **Tech** *r.* France
200 H6 **Techendorf** Austria
228 E5 **Techiman** Ghana
219 Q6 **Techirghiol** Romania
283 C6 **Tecka** Arg.
283 C6 **Tecka** *r.* Arg.
191 E6 **Tecklenburger Land** *reg.* Ger.
164 J6 **Teckomatorp** Sweden
269 I6 **Tecocomulca** Mex.
267 O7 **Tecoh** Mex.
268 C5 **Tecolotlán** Mex.
269 K5 **Tecolutla** Mex.
268 D7 **Tecomán** Mex.
269 H9 **Tecomate, Laguna** *lag.* Mex.
269 I7 **Tecomatlán** Mex.
265 P6 **Tecopa** *CA* U.S.A.
266 E3 **Tecoripa** Mex.
268 G8 **Técpan** Mex.
268 G8 **Tecpan** *r.* Mex.
268 B3 **Tecuala** Mex.
268 B5 **Tecuán** *Jalisco* Mex.
268 C6 **Tecuán** *Jalisco* Mex.
219 P5 **Tecuci** Romania
251 K8 **Tecumseh** *MI* U.S.A.
260 G5 **Tecumseh** *NE* U.S.A.
232 D3 **Ted** Somalia
170 C5 **Tedavnet** Ireland
224 C4 **Tédogora** *watercourse* Chad
126 D3 **Tedori-gawa** *r.* Japan
144 I3 **Tedzhenstroy** Turkm.
265 W5 **Teec Nos Pos** *AZ* U.S.A.
236 F8 **Teekloof Pass** S. Africa
Teel Mongolia *see* **Öndör-Ulaan**
132 J1 **Teeli** Rus. Fed.
169 G4 **Teemore** *Northern Ireland* U.K.
169 B9 **Teeranearagh** Ireland
171 O4 **Tees** *r. England* U.K.
171 O4 **Tees Bay** *England* U.K.
171 M4 **Teesdale** *val. England* U.K.
251 M5 **Teeswater** *Ont.* Can.
Teet'lit Zhen *N.W.T.* Can. *see* **Fort McPherson**
170 D6 **Teevurcher** Ireland
103 □1 **Te Fakanava** *i.* Tokelau
275 E5 **Tefé** Brazil
275 E5 **Tefé** *r.* Brazil
275 E5 **Tefé, Lago** *l.* Brazil
227 G4 **Tefedest** *mts* Alg.
221 K5 **Tefenni** Turkey
229 F2 **Téfoûlet** *well* Mali
117 H8 **Tegal** *Jawa* Indon.
192 H5 **Tegel** *airport* Ger.
187 J6 **Tegelen** Neth.
195 M3 **Tegernheim** Ger.
195 L6 **Tegernsee** Ger.
195 L6 **Tegernsee** *l.* Ger.
215 P7 **Teggiano** Italy
229 G4 **Tegina** Nigeria
116 F7 **Tegineneng** *Sumatera* Indon.
199 K4 **Téglás** Hungary
212 I3 **Teglio** Italy
213 M3 **Tegnàs** *r.* Italy
100 □5 **Tégua** *i.* Vanuatu
266 □P10 **Tegucigalpa** Hond.
238 □3a **Tegueste** *Tenerife* Canary Is
229 G2 **Teguidda-n-Tessoumt** Niger
238 □3c **Teguise** *Lanzarote* Canary Is
264 N6 **Tehachapi** *CA* U.S.A.
264 M7 **Tehachapi Mountains** *CA* U.S.A.
264 N6 **Tehachapi Pass** *CA* U.S.A.
102 I3 **Te Hana** *North I.* N.Z.
102 K6 **Te Hauke** *North I.* N.Z.
247 M1 **Tehek Lake** *Nunavut* Can.
Teheran Iran *see* **Tehrān**
247 M1 **Tehery Lake** *Nunavut* Can.
228 E4 **Téhini** Côte d'Ivoire
115 F5 **Tehoru** *Seram* Indon.
144 D4 **Tehrān** Iran
144 D4 **Tehrān** *prov.* Iran
Tehri *Madh. Prad.* India *see* **Tikamgarh**
269 J7 **Tehuacán** Mex.
269 L9 **Tehuantepec** *r.* Mex.
267 L10 **Tehuantepec, Golfo de** *g.* Mex.
Tehuantepec, Gulf of Mex. *see* **Tehuantepec, Golfo de**
269 M8 **Tehuantepec, Istmo de** *isth.* Mex.
291 M5 **Tehuantepec Ridge** *sea feature* N. Pacific Ocean
269 I7 **Tehuitzingo** Mex.
269 I9 **Tehuixtepec** Mex.
103 J8 **Te Humenga Point** *North I.* N.Z.
193 E7 **Teicha** Ger.
193 F9 **Teichwolframsdorf** Ger.
160 J5 **Teiču rezervāts** *nature res.* Latvia
238 □3a **Teide, Parque Nacional del** *nat. park Tenerife* Canary Is
238 □3a **Teide, Pico del** *vol. Tenerife* Canary Is
172 C3 **Teifi** *r. Wales* U.K.
172 E6 **Teign** *r. England* U.K.
172 F6 **Teignmouth** *Devon, England* U.K.
180 E7 **Teignouse, Passage de la** *str.* France
180 H6 **Teillay** France
185 I8 **Teillet** France
124 □1 **Teima** *Okinawa* Japan
195 N6 **Teisendorf** Ger.
229 F2 **Teïskot** *well* Mali
195 O3 **Teisnach** Ger.
183 B7 **Teissières-lès-Bouliès** France
191 J8 **Teistungen** Ger.
269 K9 **Teitipac** Mex.
219 N6 **Teiu** Romania
219 L4 **Teiuș** Romania
278 F3 **Teixeira** Brazil
Teixeira da Silva Angola *see* **Bailundo**
281 H2 **Teixeira de Freitas** Brazil
Teixeira de Sousa Angola *see* **Luau**
281 F4 **Teixeiras** Brazil
280 B6 **Teixeira Soares** Brazil
204 D2 **Teixeiro** Spain
204 F8 **Teixoso** Port.
204 F6 **Teja** *r.* Port.
205 Q8 **Tejadillos** Spain
205 P5 **Tejado** Spain
117 K9 **Tejakula** *Bali* Indon.
269 K6 **Tejar** Mex.
238 □3f **Tejeda** *Gran Canaria* Canary Is
204 I8 **Tejeda de Tiétar** Spain
207 L7 **Tejeda y Almijara, Sierra de** *nature res.* Spain
Tejen Turkm. *see* **Tejen**
144 I3 **Tejen** Turkm.
145 I3 **Tejen** *r.* Turkm.
139 M8 **Tejgaon** Bangl.
229 H3 **Tejira** *well* Niger
202 D1 **Tejo** *r.* Port. *alt.* **Tajo (Spain),** *conv.* **Tagus**
206 E1 **Tejo Internacional, Parque Natural do** *nature res.* Port.
268 D7 **Tejupan, Punta** *pt* Mex.
268 G7 **Tejupilco** Mex.
102 L4 **Te Kaha** *North I.* N.Z.
102 L4 **Te Kaha Point** *North I.* N.Z.
102 G1 **Te Kao** *North I.* N.Z.
103 E11 **Tekapo** *r. South I.* N.Z.
103 E10 **Tekapo, Lake** *South I.* N.Z.
139 J7 **Tekari** *Bihar* India
127 H5 **Tekari-dake** *mt.* Japan
103 J8 **Te Kaukau Point** *North I.* N.Z.
102 J4 **Te Kauwhata** *North I.* N.Z.
267 O7 **Tekax** Mex.
143 M6 **Teke** Kazakh.
219 O9 **Teke** *r.* Turkey
143 O1 **Teke, Ozero** *salt l.* Kazakh.
150 D2 **Tekebaşı** Turkey
142 I3 **Tekeli** *Aktyubinskaya Oblast'* Kazakh.
143 R5 **Tekeli** *Almatinskaya Oblast'* Kazakh.
132 E5 **Tekes** *Xinjiang* China
143 S6 **Tekes** Kazakh.
132 F5 **Tekes He** *r.* China
225 H6 **Tekezē Wenz** *r.* Eritrea/Eth.
133 E8 **Tekiliktag** *mt. Xinjiang* China
122 H4 **Tekin** Rus. Fed.
221 I2 **Tekirdağ** Turkey
221 I1 **Tekirdağ** *prov.* Turkey
221 L6 **Tekirova** Turkey
136 G3 **Tekka** *Mahar.* India
137 I3 **Tekkali** *Andhra Prad.* India
151 A5 **Tekke** Turkey
149 J4 **Tekman** Turkey
139 N9 **Teknaf** Bangl.
151 B5 **Tekneciler** Turkey
103 G9 **Tekoa, Mount** *South I.* N.Z.
116 □ **Tekong Kechil, Pulau** *i.* Sing.
250 J7 **Tekonsha** *MI* U.S.A.
102 H3 **Te Kopuru** *North I.* N.Z.
103 □3 **Te Kou** *hill Rarotonga* Cook Is
227 F5 **Tekouiat, Oued** *watercourse* Alg.
102 J4 **Te Kowhai** *North I.* N.Z.
224 D5 **Tékro** *well* Chad
150 H2 **Tektek Dağları** *hills* Turkey
115 C4 **Teku** *Sulawesi* Indon.
102 J5 **Te Kuiti** *North I.* N.Z.
139 I9 **Tel** *r.* India
231 F8 **Tela** Dem. Rep. Congo
266 □P10 **Tela** Hond.
103 □1 **Te Lafu** *i.* Tokelau
103 □1 **Te Lafu** *i.* Tokelau
227 E2 **Télagh** Alg.
197 K3 **Telaki** Pol.
116 F4 **Telan** *i.* Indon.
Telanaipura *Sumatera* Indon. *see* **Jambi**
133 K9 **Telashi Hu** *salt l. Qinghai* China
229 F2 **Télataï** Mali
197 L5 **Telatyn** Pol.
151 G4 **T'elavi** Georgia
150 C6 **Tel Aviv-Yafo** Israel
198 E2 **Telč** Czech Rep.
267 O7 **Telchac Puerto** Mex.
161 T8 **Tel'ch'ye** Rus. Fed.
219 M3 **Telciu** Romania
190 K4 **Teldau** Ger.
238 □3f **Telde** *Gran Canaria* Canary Is
230 D4 **Tele** *r.* Dem. Rep. Congo
228 E2 **Télé, Lac** *l.* Mali
219 N5 **Teleajen** *r.* Romania
218 H5 **Telečka** *Vojvodina* Serbia
117 J6 **Telegapulang** *Kalimantan* Indon.
216 E8 **Telegrafo, Pizzo** *hill* Italy
245 O4 **Telegraph Creek** *B.C.* Can.
199 J5 **Telekgerendás** Hungary
Telekhany Belarus *see* **Tsyelyakhany**
101 □8 **Teleki Tonga** *atoll* Tonga
101 □8 **Teleki Vavu'u** *atoll* Tonga
159 S1 **Telelyuy** Rus. Fed.
280 B6 **Telêmaco Borba** Brazil
164 E2 **Telemark** *county* Norway
284 E5 **Telén** Arg.
117 L4 **Telen** *r.* Indon.
Teleneshty Moldova *see* **Telenești**
158 H6 **Telenești** Moldova
144 I9 **Teleng** Iran
219 N7 **Teleorman** *r.* Romania
227 G4 **Telertheba, Djebel** *mt.* Alg.
264 O5 **Telescope Peak** *CA* U.S.A.
271 □6 **Telescope Point** Grenada
215 N5 **Telese** Italy
277 F1 **Teles Pires** *r.* Brazil
151 H3 **Teletl'** Rus. Fed.
108 G6 **Telfer Mining Centre** *W.A.* Austr.
172 H2 **Telford** *Telford and Wrekin, England* U.K.
258 E4 **Telford** *PA* U.S.A.
172 H2 **Telford and Wrekin** *admin. div. England* U.K.
200 D5 **Telfs** Austria
199 J3 **Telgárt** Slovakia
180 C5 **Telgruc-sur-Mer** France
191 E7 **Telgte** Ger.
204 E8 **Telhado** Port.
266 □P11 **Telica, Volcán** *vol.* Nic.
244 I3 **Telida** *AK* U.S.A.
226 E5 **Telîg** *well* Mali
228 B4 **Télimélé** Guinea
224 D5 **Télissour** *well* Chad
269 K8 **Telixtlahuaca** Mex.
224 E6 **Teljo, Jebel** *mt.* Sudan
246 E4 **Telkwa** *B.C.* Can.
179 K4 **Tellancourt** France
216 I10 **Tellaro** *r. Sicilia* Italy
Tell Atlas *mts* Alg. *see* **Atlas Tellien**
244 F2 **Teller** *AK* U.S.A.
Tell es-Sultan West Bank *see* **Jericho**
Tellicherry India *see* **Thalassery**
187 H8 **Tellin** Belgium
190 H2 **Tellingstedt** Ger.
151 C5 **Telli Tepe** *mt.* Turkey
274 C4 **Tello** Col.
158 J7 **Tellodar** Ukr.
149 M8 **Telloh** Iraq
263 K8 **Telluride** *CO* U.S.A.
159 R6 **Tel'manove** Ukr.
Tel'mansk Turkm. *see* **Gubadag**
150 D6 **Tel Megiddo** *tourist site* Israel
128 E2 **Telmen** Mongolia
128 E2 **Telmen Nuur** *salt l.* Mongolia
201 O1 **Telnice** Czech Rep.
116 C5 **Telo** Indon.
181 L6 **Teloché** France
204 E6 **Telões** Port.
269 H7 **Teloloapán** Mex.
Telo Martius France *see* **Toulon**
103 □1 **Te Loto** *i.* Tokelau
156 L3 **Telpoziz, Gora** *mt.* Rus. Fed.
283 D6 **Telsen** Arg.
160 F6 **Telšiai** Lith.
214 C6 **Telti** *Sardegna* Italy
193 H6 **Teltow** Ger.
Teluk Anson Malaysia *see* **Teluk Intan**
Telukbajur *Sumatera* Indon. *see* **Telukbayur**
117 H5 **Telukbatang** *Kalimantan* Indon.
116 D5 **Telukbayur** *Sumatera* Indon.
Telukbetung *Sumatera* Indon. *see* **Bandar Lampung**
116 B4 **Telukdalam** Indon.
116 D2 **Teluk Intan** Malaysia
116 D5 **Telukkuantan** *Sumatera* Indon.
117 H5 **Telukmelano** *Kalimantan* Indon.
116 G8 **Teluknaga** *Jawa* Indon.
117 H5 **Telukpakedai** *Kalimantan* Indon.
136 G9 **Telulla** Sri Lanka
161 U9 **Telyazh'ye** Rus. Fed.
229 F5 **Tema** Ghana
268 E4 **Temacapulín** Mex.
101 □9a **Temae, Lac** *l. Moorea* Fr. Polynesia
251 O2 **Temagami** *Ont.* Can.
248 E4 **Temagami Lake** *Ont.* Can.
117 H4 **Temaju** *i.* Indon.
103 □3 **Te Manga** *hill Rarotonga* Cook Is
117 I8 **Temanggung** *Jawa* Indon.
269 J4 **Temapache** Mex.
102 I6 **Te Mapou** *hill North I.* N.Z.
133 I10 **Têmarxung** *Xizang* China
269 K7 **Temascal** Mex.
268 G6 **Temascaltepec de González** Mex.
102 I4 **Te Mata** *North I.* N.Z.
101 □9 **Tematangi** *atoll Arch. des Tuamotu* Fr. Polynesia
267 O7 **Temax** Mex.
237 M1 **Temba** S. Africa
113 I7 **Tembagapura** *Papua* Indon.
237 Q2 **Tembe** *r.* Moz.
237 Q2 **Tembe Elephant Park** *nature res.* S. Africa
153 K3 **Tembenchi** *r.* Rus. Fed.
116 E5 **Tembesi** *r.* Indon.
116 E5 **Tembilahan** *Sumatera* Indon.
237 M2 **Tembisa** S. Africa
205 N9 **Tembleque** Spain
231 C6 **Tembo Aluma** Angola
231 C6 **Tembo Falls** Angola/Dem. Rep. Congo
Tembué Moz. *see* **Chifunde**
237 M7 **Tembuland** *reg.* S. Africa
233 B7 **Tembwe** Zambia
172 H3 **Teme** *r. England* U.K.
264 O8 **Temecula** *CA* U.S.A.
148 F4 **Temelli** Turkey
128 E1 **Temenchula, Gora** *mt.* Rus.
116 D2 **Temengor, Tasik** *resr* Malay
201 L8 **Temenica** *r.* Slovenia
218 H5 **Temerin** *Vojvodina* Serbia
116 E3 **Temerluh** Malaysia
116 E2 **Temiang, Bukit** *mt.* Malays
144 C5 **Temīleh** Iran
113 H7 **Teminabuan** *Papua* Indon.
142 G3 **Temir** *Aktyubinskaya Oblast* Kazakh.
Temir *Yuzhnyy Kazakhstan* Kazakh. *see* **Timur**
Temirlan Kazakh. *see* **Temirlanovka**
143 M6 **Temirlanovka** Kazakh.
143 O2 **Temirtau** Kazakh.
249 F3 **Témiscamie** *r. Que.* Can.
249 F3 **Témiscamie, Lac** *l. Que.* Ca
248 E4 **Témiscaming** *Que.* Can.
248 E4 **Témiscamingue, Lac** *l. Ont.* Can.
249 G4 **Témiscouata, Lac** *l. Que.* Ca
116 F4 **Temiyang** *i.* Indon.
161 R6 **Temkino** Rus. Fed.
105 J9 **Temma** *Tas.* Austr.
162 R4 **Temmes** Fin.
157 H5 **Temnikov** Rus. Fed.
214 A7 **Temo** *r. Sardegna* Italy
101 □9 **Temoe** *atoll Arch. des Tuamo* Fr. Polynesia
105 K6 **Temora** *N.S.W.* Austr.
266 F3 **Temósachic** Mex.
265 U8 **Tempe** *AZ* U.S.A.
115 A6 **Tempe, Danau** *l.* Indon.
106 D8 **Tempe Downs** *N.T.* Austr.
193 H6 **Tempelhof** *airport* Ger.
274 C5 **Tempestad** Peru
116 E5 **Tempino** *Sumatera* Indon.
214 C6 **Tempio Pausania** *Sardegna*
250 I5 **Temple** *MI* U.S.A.
258 D4 **Temple** *PA* U.S.A.
261 G10 **Temple** *TX* U.S.A.
178 H7 **Temple, Lac du** *resr* France
172 D3 **Temple Bar** *Ceredigion, Wal*
107 I2 **Temple Bay** *Qld* Austr.
145 M7 **Temple Dera** Pak.
169 F7 **Templederry** Ireland
173 O5 **Temple Ewell** *Kent, England*
169 D8 **Templeglantine** Ireland
169 G7 **Templemore** Ireland
169 C9 **Templenoe** Ireland
169 J3 **Templepatrick** *Northern Ire* U.K.
114 A6 **Templer Bank** *sea feature* P
171 L4 **Temple Sowerby** *Cumbria, England* U.K.
106 G6 **Templeton** *watercourse Qld*
103 G10 **Templeton** *South I.* N.Z.
172 C4 **Templeton** *Pembrokeshire, Wales* U.K.
264 L6 **Templeton** *CA* U.S.A.
169 G7 **Templetuohy** Ireland
178 F2 **Templeuve** France
192 I4 **Templin** Ger.
169 H4 **Tempo** *Northern Ireland* U.K
269 I4 **Tempoal** Mex.
269 I4 **Tempoal** *r.* Mex.
231 C8 **Tempué** Angola
128 F8 **Têmpung** *Qinghai* China
161 U5 **Tempy** Rus. Fed.
157 G7 **Temryuk** Rus. Fed.
157 G7 **Temryukskiy Zaliv** *b.* Rus. F
187 F6 **Temse** Belgium
219 K7 **Temska** *Pirot* Serbia
212 I3 **Temù** Italy
284 A6 **Temuco** Chile
103 F11 **Temuka** *South I.* N.Z.
Temuli *Sichuan* China *see* **Butuo**
100 □4b **Temwen** *i. Pohnpei* Microne
100 □4b **Temwetemwensekir** *hill Pol* Micronesia
142 H1 **Temyasovo** Rus. Fed.
274 B5 **Tena** Ecuador
208 E2 **Tena, Valle de** *val.* Spain
267 N7 **Tenabo** Mex.
264 P1 **Tenabo, Mount** *NV* U.S.A.
268 C6 **Tenacatita** Mex.
228 E3 **Ténado** Burkina
259 H3 **Tenafly** *NJ* U.S.A.
160 G1 **Tenala** Fin.
136 G4 **Tenali** *Andhra Prad.* India
268 C5 **Tenamaxtlán** Mex.
252 G7 **Tenancingo** Mex.
269 H6 **Tenango** *México* Mex.
269 L9 **Tenango** *Oaxaca* Mex.
101 □9 **Tenarunga** *atoll Arch. des Tu* Fr. Polynesia
119 D8 **Tenasserim** Myanmar
119 D8 **Tenasserim** *admin. div.* Mya
119 D8 **Tenasserim** *r.* Myanmar
182 H5 **Tenay** France
186 K2 **Ten Boer** Neth.
172 G3 **Tenbury Wells** *Worcestershir England* U.K.
172 C4 **Tenby** *Pembrokeshire, Wales*
251 K3 **Tenby Bay** *Ont.* Can.
183 E6 **Tence** France
199 I1 **Tenczyński Park Krajobraz** Pol.
232 D2 **Tendaho** Eth.
177 H4 **Tende** France
212 D7 **Tende, Col de** *pass* France/
137 M8 **Ten Degree Channel** *Anda Nicobar Is* India
225 F6 **Tendelti** Sudan
228 B2 **Te-n-Dghâmcha, Sebkhet** *salt marsh* Maur.
205 O7 **Tendilla** Spain
124 R8 **Tendō** Japan
226 E2 **Tendrara** Morocco
212 A2 **Tendre, Mont** *mt.* Switz.
159 K7 **Tendrivs'ka Kosa, Ostriv** *i.*
159 K7 **Tendrivs'ka Zatoka** *b.* Ukr.
181 O8 **Tendu** France
138 G8 **Tendukheda** *Madh. Prad.* In
151 E6 **Tendürek Dağı** *mt.* Turkey
228 C4 **Téné** *r.* Guinea
Tenedos *i.* Turkey *see* **Bozca**
127 L1 **Ten-ei** Japan
228 D3 **Ténenkou** Mali
160 E6 **Tenenys** *r.* Lith.
229 H2 **Ténéré, Erg du** *des.* Niger
229 H1 **Ténéré du Tafassâsset** *des.*
238 □3a **Tenerife** *i.* Canary Is
227 F1 **Ténès** Alg.
219 O8 **Tenevo** Bulg.
118 C5 **Teng, Nam** *r.* Myanmar
117 L8 **Tengah, Kepulauan** *is* Indo
116 □ **Tengah, Sungai** *r.* Sing.
115 C8 **Tengahdai** *Flores* Indon.
Tengcheng *Guangxi* China *see* **Tengxian**
130 B6 **Tengchong** *Yunnan* China
142 E6 **Tenge** Kazakh.
116 □ **Tengeh Reservoir** Sing.
199 H5 **Tengelic** Hungary
194 F6 **Tengen** Ger.
100 □6 **Te Nggano** *lag. Rennell* Solomon Is
117 L5 **Tenggarong** *Kalimantan* In
128 I8 **Tengger Els** *Nei Mongol* Ch
128 I7 **Tengger Shamo** *des. Nei M* China
116 E2 **Tenggul** *i.* Malaysia
143 M2 **Tengiz, Ozero** *salt l.* Kazak
130 G9 **Tengqiao** *Hainan* China
228 D4 **Tengréla** Côte d'Ivoire
157 H5 **Ten'gushevo** Rus. Fed.
130 H7 **Tengxian** *Guangxi* China
Tengxian *Shandong* China *see* **Tengzhou**
129 O9 **Tengzhou** *Shandong* China
183 J8 **Ténibre, Mont** *mt.* France/

E5 **Teniente Enciso, Parque Nacional** *nat. park* Para.
Teniente Jubany *research stn* Antarctica *see* **Jubany**
F6 **Teniente Origone** Arg.
F11 **Tenille** *FL* U.S.A.
D5 **Teningen** Ger.
A2 **Te-n-Ioubrar, Sebkhet** *salt marsh* Maur.
J5 **Tenixtepec** Mex.
K1 **Teniz, Ozero** *l.* Kazakh.
J4 **Tenk** Hungary
E8 **Tenkasi** *Tamil Nadu* India
C7 **Tenkawa** Japan
E7 **Tenke** Dem. Rep. Congo
P2 **Tenkeli** Rus. Fed.
J5 **Ten'ki** Rus. Fed.
E4 **Tenkodogo** Burkina
F8 **Ten Mile Lake** *salt flat W.A.* Austr.
J3 **Ten Mile Lake** *Nfld and Lab.* Can.
P9 **Tenna** *r.* Italy
E5 **Tennant Creek** *N.T.* Austr.
E5 **Tennenbronn** Ger.
H4 **Tennengau** *val.* Austria
H5 **Tennengebirge** *mts* Austria
G4 **Tennent** *NJ* U.S.A.
K7 **Tennessee** *r.* U.S.A.
B12 **Tennessee** *state* U.S.A.
K7 **Tennessee Pass** *CO* U.S.A.
I8 **Tenneville** Belgium
N2 **Tennevoll** Norway
L3 **Tennholmfjorden** *sea chan.* Norway
T3 **Tenniöjoki** *r.* Fin./Rus. Fed.
B4 **Teno** Chile
B4 **Teno** *r.* Chile
□3a **Teno, Punta de** *pt Tenerife* Canary Is
K6 **Tenochtitlán** Mex.
T1 **Tenojoki** *r.* Fin./Norway
K2 **Tenom** *Sabah* Malaysia
N9 **Tenosique** Mex.
E5 **Tenpaku** Japan
C6 **Tenri** Japan
G5 **Tenryū** *Nagano* Japan
G6 **Tenryū** *Shizuoka* Japan
G5 **Tenryū-gawa** *r.* Japan
G5 **Tenryū-Okumikawa Kokutei-kōen** *park* Japan
K4 **Ten Sleep** *WY* U.S.A.
B4 **Tenteno** *Sulawesi* Indon.
N5 **Tenterden** *Kent, England* U.K.
N3 **Tenterfield** *N.S.W.* Austr.
G13 **Ten Thousand Islands** *FL* U.S.A.
I4 **Ten Thousand Smokes, Valley of** *AK* U.S.A.
J2 **Tent Lake** *N.W.T.* Can.
B3 **Tentolomatinan, Gunung** *mt.* Indon.
G4 **Tentudia** *mt.* Spain
C8 **Tentúgal** Port.
H7 **Tenu** *r.* France
G4 **Tényő** Hungary
E4 **Teocaltiche** Mex.
K6 **Teocelo** Mex.
D5 **Teocuitatlán de Corona** Mex.
G4 **Teodelina** Arg.
D6 **Teodoro, Stagno di** *lag. Sardegna* Italy
A3 **Teodoro Beltrán** Mex.
A5 **Teodoro Sampaio** Brazil
A6 **Teodoro Schmidt** Chile
G2 **Teófilo Otôni** Brazil
F4 **Teofipol'** Ukr.
C8 **Teomabal** *i.* Phil.
□ **Te One** *Chatham Is* S. Pacific Ocean
H7 **Teonthar** *Madh. Prad.* India
M9 **Teopisca** Mex.
O6 **Teora** Italy
I6 **Teotihuacán** *tourist site* Mex.
J7 **Teotitlán** Mex.
K8 **Teotitlán del Valle** Mex.
E5 **Tepa** Ghana
F7 **Tepa** *Maluku* Indon.
E3 **Tepache** Mex.
G1 **Te Paki** *North I.* N.Z.
E6 **Tepalcatepec** Mex.
E7 **Tepalcatepec** *r.* Mex.
I7 **Tepalcingo** Mex.
□4 **Tepa Point** Niue
R3 **Tepasto** Fin.
H5 **Tepatepec** Mex.
E5 **Tepatitlán** Mex.
K4 **Tépe** Hungary
J7 **Tepeaca** Mex.
I6 **Tepeapulco** Mex.
D4 **Tepechitlán** Mex.
J1 **Tepecik** Turkey
J2 **Tepeguajes** Mex.
A1 **Tepehuaje** Mex.
G5 **Tepehuanes** Mex.
H6 **Tepeji** Mex.
Tepeköy Turkey *see* **Karakoçan**
B2 **Tepelenë** Albania
J8 **Tepelmeme de Morelos** Mex.
B2 **Tepelská vrchovina** *hills* Czech Rep.
F4 **Tepequem, Serra** *mts* Brazil
H2 **Tepere** Moz.
F4 **Tepetates** Mex.
D3 **Tepetengo** Mex.
G8 **Tepetixtla** Mex.
J4 **Tepetzintla** Mex.
J7 **Tepexi de Rodríguez** Mex.
J6 **Tepeyahualco** Mex.
L4 **Tepianlangsat** *Kalimantan* Indon.
C4 **Tepic** Mex.
F10 **Te Pirita** *South I.* N.Z.
B2 **Teplá** Czech Rep.
B1 **Teplá** *r.* Czech Rep.
C3 **Teplá Vltava** *r.* Czech Rep.
L4 **Teplaya Gora** Rus. Fed.
S5 **Teple** Ukr.
F3 **Tepli, Gora** *mt.* Rus. Fed.
C1 **Teplice** Czech Rep.
J3 **Teplička** Slovakia
M8 **Teplivka** Ukr.
K3 **Teplogorka** Rus. Fed.
V8 **Teploye** *Lipetskaya Oblast'* Rus. Fed.
U8 **Teploye** *Tul'skaya Oblast'* Rus. Fed.
I5 **Teplyk** Ukr.
C3 **Tepopa, Punta** *pt* Mex.
J8 **Teposcolula** Mex.
H7 **Tepoztlan** Mex.
J5 **Teppia** *r.* Italy
K4 **Te Puke** *North I.* N.Z.
K4 **Te Puna** *North I.* N.Z.
G6 **Tepuxtepec** Mex.
D5 **Tequila** Mex.
D5 **Tequila, Volcán de** *vol.* Mex.
L9 **Tequisistlán** Mex.
L9 **Tequisistlán** *r.* Mex.
H5 **Tequisquiapán** Mex.
J6 **Tequixquitla** Mex.
J7 **Tequixtépec** Mex.
F3 **Téra** Niger
C3 **Tera** *r.* Port.
I5 **Tera** *r.* Spain
G4 **Ter Aar** Neth.
J4 **Te Rahu** *North I.* N.Z.
D3 **Terai** Japan
A3 **Terakeka** Sudan
F2 **Teram Kangri** *mt.* China/Pak.
L2 **Teramo** Italy
L2 **Teramo** *prov.* Italy
I8 **Terang** *Vic.* Austr.
J4 **Te Rapa** *North I.* N.Z.
L3 **Ter Apel** Neth.
L5 **Teratyn** Pol.
I8 **Terawhiti, Cape** *North I.* N.Z.
F7 **Terbang Selatan** *i. Maluku* Indon.
F7 **Terbang Utara** *i. Maluku* Indon.
J5 **Terborg-Silvolde** Neth.
V9 **Terbuny** Rus. Fed.
Tercan *Erzincan* Turkey *see* **Otlukbeli**
J4 **Tercan** *Erzincan* Turkey
B6 **Tercan Barajı** *resr* Turkey
□1a **Terceira** *i.* Azores
F3 **Tercero** *r.* Arg.
185 B8 **Tercis-les-Bains** France
212 G5 **Terdoppio** *r.* Italy
161 S8 **Tereben'** Rus. Fed.
199 L4 **Terebești** Romania
158 C5 **Tereblya** *r.* Ukr.
158 E4 **Terebovlya** Ukr.
161 V7 **Terebush** Rus. Fed.
219 K5 **Teregova** Romania
Terek *r.* Georgia *see* **Tergi**
151 F2 **Terek** Rus. Fed.
149 M2 **Terek** *r.* Rus. Fed.
128 D1 **Tere-Khol'** Rus. Fed.
128 E1 **Tere-Khol', Ozero** *l.* Rus. Fed.
151 G1 **Terekli-Mekteb** Rus. Fed.
143 N7 **Terek-Say** Kyrg.
132 G1 **Terektinskiy Khrebet** *mts* Rus. Fed.
143 M3 **Terekty** *Karagandinskaya Oblast'* Kazakh.
143 U3 **Terekty** *Vostochnyy Kazakhstan* Kazakh.
199 J6 **Teremia Mare** Romania
206 E3 **Terena** Port.
157 J5 **Teren'ga** Rus. Fed.
116 E2 **Terengganu** *r.* Malaysia
116 E2 **Terengganu** *state* Malaysia
Terengözek Kazakh. *see* **Terenozek**
279 B7 **Terenos** Brazil
142 K5 **Terenozek** Kazakh.
142 H2 **Terensay** Rus. Fed.
117 H5 **Terentang** *Kalimantan* Indon.
117 L5 **Terentang, Pulau** *i.* Indon.
169 J6 **Terenure** Ireland
Teren-Uzyak Kazakh. *see* **Terenozek**
280 B6 **Teresa Cristina** Brazil
209 C9 **Teresa de Cofrentes** Spain
239 □2b **Térèse, Île** *i. Inner Islands* Seychelles
142 B2 **Tereshka** *r.* Rus. Fed.
197 I3 **Teresin** Pol.
278 E3 **Teresina** Brazil
274 D4 **Teresita** Col.
281 F5 **Teresópolis** Brazil
197 L3 **Terespol** Pol.
137 M8 **Teressa Island** *Andaman & Nicobar Is* India
158 C5 **Teresva** Ukr.
158 C6 **Teresva** *r.* Ukr.
197 K5 **Tereszpol-Zaorenda** Pol.
198 D1 **Terezín** Czech Rep.
198 G6 **Terezino Polje** Croatia
158 J4 **Terezyne** Ukr.
200 E5 **Terfens** Austria
203 F5 **Terga** Alg.
206 D5 **Terges** *r.* Port.
Tergeste Italy *see* **Trieste**
151 F3 **Tergi** *r.* Georgia
178 F4 **Tergnier** France
213 M5 **Tergola** *r.* Italy
214 B6 **Tergu** *Sardegna* Italy
128 D7 **Tergun Daba Shan** *mts Qinghai* China
186 G5 **Terheijden** Neth.
128 F2 **Terhiyn Tsagaan Nuur** *l.* Mongolia
156 F1 **Teriberka** Rus. Fed.
160 K3 **Terikeste** Estonia
133 I11 **Tering** *Xizang* China
143 L2 **Terisakkan** *r.* Kazakh.
226 B5 **Terjît** *well* Maur.
151 F3 **Terk** Rus. Fed.
197 K6 **Terka** Pol.
232 D3 **Terka Reba** Eth.
224 D5 **Terkezi** *well* Chad
213 K2 **Terlano** Italy
261 D11 **Terlingua Creek** *r. TX* U.S.A.
215 R5 **Terlizzi** Italy
225 I6 **Terma, Ras** *pt* Eritrea
158 I2 **Termakhivka** Ukr.
284 B5 **Termas de Chillán** Chile
284 B4 **Termas de Flaco** Chile
285 I2 **Termas del Arapey** Uru.
284 B6 **Termas de Pemehue** Chile
284 B2 **Termas de Socos** Chile
284 B6 **Termas de Tolhuaca** Chile
284 C3 **Termas de Villavicencio** Arg.
148 H3 **Terme** Turkey
215 P9 **Terme Luigiane** Italy
208 G4 **Térmens** Spain
185 J9 **Termes** France
221 L6 **Termessos Milli Parkı** *nat. park* Turkey
Termez Uzbek. *see* **Termiz**
183 J6 **Termignon** France
109 F13 **Termination Island** *W.A.* Austr.
178 C7 **Terminiers** France
216 F8 **Termini Imerese** *Sicilia* Italy
216 F7 **Termini Imerese, Golfo di** *b. Sicilia* Italy
215 J3 **Terminillo, Monte** *mt.* Italy
267 N8 **Términos, Laguna de** *lag.* Mex.
229 H2 **Termit** *well* Niger
229 H2 **Termit, Massif de** *hill* Niger
229 H3 **Termit-Kaoboul** Niger
143 L9 **Termiz** Uzbek.
215 N4 **Termoli** Italy
Termon Ireland *see* **An Tearmann**
Termonde Belgium *see* **Dendermonde**
170 E6 **Termonfeckin** Ireland
172 G2 **Tern** *r. England* U.K.
159 N3 **Tern** *r.* Ukr.
186 I2 **Ternaard** Neth.
115 E3 **Ternate** *Maluku* Indon.
115 E3 **Ternate** *i. Maluku* Indon.
239 □2b **Ternay, La Passe** *sea chan. Inner Islands* Seychelles
Ternay Pass *sea chan. Inner Islands* Seychelles *see* **Ternay, La Passe**
201 J4 **Ternberg** Austria
187 E6 **Terneuzen** Neth.
122 J6 **Terney** Rus. Fed.
215 J2 **Terni** Italy
215 I2 **Terni** *prov.* Italy
182 E3 **Ternin** *r.* France
201 N4 **Ternitz** Austria
159 P5 **Ternivka** *Dnipropetrovs'ka Oblast'* Ukr.
159 L6 **Ternivka** *Mykolayivs'ka Oblast'* Ukr.
159 M9 **Ternivka** *Respublika Krym* Ukr.
158 I5 **Ternivka** *Vinnyts'ka Oblast'* Ukr.
178 D3 **Ternois** *reg.* France
178 D3 **Ternoise** *r.* France
158 E4 **Ternopil'** Ukr.
Ternopil Oblast *admin. div.* Ukr. *see* **Ternopils'ka Oblast'**
158 E4 **Ternopils'ka Oblast'** *admin. div.* Ukr.
Ternopol' Ukr. *see* **Ternopil'**
Ternopol Oblast *admin. div.* Ukr. *see* **Ternopils'ka Oblast'**
Ternopol'skaya Oblast' *admin. div.* Ukr. *see* **Ternopils'ka Oblast'**
157 H6 **Ternovka** Rus. Fed.
Ternovka Ukr. *see* **Ternivka**
159 P6 **Ternuvate** Ukr.
159 Q4 **Terny** *Donets'ka Oblast'* Ukr.
159 M3 **Terny** *Sums'ka Oblast'* Ukr.
238 □3f **Teror** *Gran Canaria* Canary Is
104 G5 **Terowie** *S.A.* Austr.
122 N4 **Terpeniya, Mys** *c. Sakhalin* Rus. Fed.
122 N4 **Terpeniya, Poluostrov** *pen.* Rus. Fed.
122 M4 **Terpeniya, Zaliv** *g. Sakhalin* Rus. Fed.
256 F9 **Terra Alta** *WV* U.S.A.
264 M6 **Terra Bella** *CA* U.S.A.
280 A5 **Terra Boa** Brazil
281 F2 **Terra Branca** Brazil
246 D4 **Terrace** *B.C.* Can.
248 C3 **Terrace Bay** *Ont.* Can.
238 □1a **Terra Chã** *Terceira* Azores
215 K5 **Terracina** Italy
215 K5 **Terracina, Golfo di** *b.* Italy
Terradas Spain *see* **Terrades**
208 K3 **Terrades** Spain
208 G3 **Terradets, Pantà de** *resr* Spain
236 H1 **Terra Firma** S. Africa
162 L4 **Terråk** Norway
214 B8 **Terralba** *Sardegna* Italy
287 K1 **Terra Nova Bay** Antarctica
217 K4 **Terranova da Sibari** Italy
215 Q8 **Terranova di Pollino** Italy
249 K3 **Terra Nova National Park** *Nfld and Lab.* Can.
213 L8 **Terranuova Bracciolini** Italy
275 G6 **Terra Preta** Brazil
280 A5 **Terra Rica** Brazil
204 D5 **Terras do Bouro** Port.
216 E7 **Terrasini** *Sicilia* Italy
208 J4 **Terrassa** Spain
184 G5 **Terrasson-la-Villedieu** France
185 F8 **Terraube** France
217 L5 **Terravecchia** Italy
266 F3 **Terrazas** Mex.
Terre Adélie *reg.* Antarctica *see* **Adélie Land**
261 J11 **Terrebonne Bay** *LA* U.S.A.
271 □2 **Terre de Bas** *i.* Guadeloupe
271 □2 **Terre de Haut** *i.* Guadeloupe
254 D6 **Terre Haute** *IN* U.S.A.
258 C4 **Terre Hill** *PA* U.S.A.
261 G9 **Terrell** *TX* U.S.A.
179 K8 **Terre-Natale** France
269 J6 **Terrenate** Mex.
249 K4 **Terrenceville** *Nfld and Lab.* Can.
182 E2 **Terre Plaine** *plain* France
266 F3 **Terrero** Mex.
Terres Australes et Antarctiques Françaises *terr.* Indian Ocean *see* **French Southern and Antarctic Lands**
213 J8 **Terricciola** Italy
205 R8 **Terriente** Spain
207 I7 **Terril** *mt.* Spain
170 C6 **Terrin** Ireland
207 N3 **Terrinches** Spain
171 P5 **Terrington** *North Yorkshire, England* U.K.
173 M2 **Terrington St Clement** *Norfolk, England* U.K.
185 H6 **Terrou** France
206 A3 **Terrugem** *Lisboa* Port.
206 E3 **Terrugem** *Portalegre* Port.
262 L3 **Terry** *MT* U.S.A.
259 I1 **Terryville** *CT* U.S.A.
259 I3 **Terryville** *NY* U.S.A.
157 I6 **Tersa** *r.* Rus. Fed.
Tersakkan *r.* Kazakh. *see* **Terisakkan**
186 H2 **Terschelling** *i.* Neth.
Terskey Alatau, Khrebet *mts* Kyrg. *see* **Terskey Ala-Too**
143 Q7 **Terskey Ala-Too** *mts* Kyrg.
156 G2 **Terskiy Bereg** *coastal area* Rus. Fed.
151 F1 **Tersko-Kumskiy Kanal** *canal* Rus. Fed.
159 O6 **Tersyanka** Ukr.
214 D8 **Tertenia** *Sardegna* Italy
Terter Azer. *see* **Tärtär**
190 G2 **Tertius** *i.* Ger.
178 F4 **Tertry** France
209 C7 **Teruel** Spain
205 Q7 **Teruel** *prov.* Spain
160 H1 **Tervakoski** Fin.
219 P7 **Tervel** Bulg.
181 J8 **Terves** France
162 S5 **Tervo** Fin.
162 R3 **Tervola** Fin.
161 T5 **Teryayevo** Rus. Fed.
199 H4 **Tés** Hungary
128 D2 **Tes** Mongolia
213 M3 **Tesa** *r.* Italy
210 F3 **Tešanj** Bos.-Herz.
185 G7 **Tescou** *r.* France
269 L7 **Tesechoacán** *r.* Mex.
199 G3 **Tešedíkovo** Slovakia
238 □3b **Tesejerague** *Fuerteventura* Canary Is
225 H6 **Teseney** Eritrea
213 L3 **Tesero** Italy
157 H5 **Tesha** *r.* Rus. Fed.
244 I1 **Teshekpuk Lake** *AK* U.S.A.
229 E5 **Teshi** Ghana
124 V3 **Teshikaga** Japan
124 S2 **Teshio** Japan
124 T3 **Teshio-dake** *mt.* Japan
124 S2 **Teshio-gawa** *r.* Japan
124 S2 **Teshio-sanchi** *mts* Japan
266 E4 **Tesia** Mex.
219 J7 **Tešica** *Aleksinac* Serbia
213 K2 **Tesimo** Italy
213 L5 **Tesina** *r.* Italy
268 D5 **Tesistán** Mex.
128 C1 **Tesiyn Gol** *r.* Mongolia
205 M3 **Tesla, Sierra de la** *mts* Spain
210 F3 **Teslić** Bos.-Herz.
245 N3 **Teslin** *Y.T.* Can.
245 N3 **Teslin** *r. Y.T.* Can.
245 N3 **Teslin Lake** *B.C./Y.T.* Can.
219 M6 **Teslui** *r.* Romania
204 I6 **Teso Santo** *hill* Spain
279 B6 **Tesouro** Brazil
161 O3 **Tesovo-Netyl'skiy** Rus. Fed.
161 N3 **Tesovskiy** Rus. Fed.
190 J4 **Tespe** Ger.
227 F5 **Tessalit** Mali
229 G3 **Tessaoua** Niger
181 K4 **Tessé-la-Madeleine** France
187 H6 **Tessenderlo** Belgium
229 G2 **Tesséroukane** *well* Niger
192 F2 **Tessin** Ger.
Tessin *canton* Switz. *see* **Ticino**
235 G4 **Tessolo** Moz.
184 C4 **Tesson** France
227 F5 **Tessoûnfat** *well* Mali
181 I4 **Tessy-sur-Vire** France
173 J6 **Test** *r. England* U.K.
226 C3 **Test, Tizi-n-** *pass* Morocco
214 C5 **Testa, Capo** *c. Sardegna* Italy
215 Q4 **Testa del Gargano** Italy
216 H10 **Testa dell'Acqua** *Sicilia* Italy
204 D4 **Testeiro, Montes do** *mts* Spain
187 G6 **Testelt** Belgium
205 N9 **Testillos** *r.* Spain
227 H1 **Testour** Tunisia
185 K10 **Têt** *r.* France
199 G4 **Tét** Hungary
246 E4 **Tetachuck Lake** *B.C.* Can.
249 H4 **Tetagouche** *r. N.B.* Can.
276 C5 **Tetas, Punta** *pt* Chile
172 H4 **Tetbury** *Gloucestershire, England* U.K.
199 L4 **Țețchea** Romania
235 G3 **Tete** Moz.
235 G2 **Tete** *prov.* Moz.
183 J8 **Tête de l'Enchastraye** *mt.* France/Italy
183 J8 **Tête de l'Estrop** *mt.* France
183 I7 **Tête de Soulaure** *mt.* France
212 B6 **Tête des Toillies** *mt.* Italy
116 B4 **Tetehosi** Indon.
246 G4 **Tête Jaune Cache** *B.C.* Can.
102 K5 **Te Teko** *North I.* N.Z.
268 G8 **Tetela** Mex.
269 J6 **Tetela de Ocampo** Mex.
269 I7 **Tetela de Volcán** Mex.
100 □6 **Tetepare** *i. New Georgia Is* Solomon Is
186 G5 **Teteringen** Neth.
158 J2 **Teteriv** *r.* Ukr.
192 G3 **Teterow** Ger.
199 K4 **Tetétlen** Hungary
219 M8 **Teteven** Bulg.
171 Q7 **Tetford** *Lincolnshire, England* U.K.
214 C7 **Teti** *Sardegna* Italy
268 E2 **Tetillas** Mex.
Tetiyev Ukr. *see* **Tetiyiv**
158 I4 **Tetiyiv** Ukr.
159 N2 **Tetkino** Rus. Fed.
245 L3 **Tetlin** *AK* U.S.A.
245 L3 **Tetlin Junction** *AK* U.S.A.
245 L3 **Tetlin Lake** *AK* U.S.A.
245 L3 **Tetlin National Wildlife Refuge** *nature res. AK* U.S.A.
171 Q7 **Tetney** *Lincolnshire, England* U.K.
262 I3 **Teton** *r. MT* U.S.A.
262 I5 **Teton Range** *mts WY* U.S.A.
226 D2 **Tétouan** Morocco
202 D5 **Tétouan** *prov.* Morocco
218 I8 **Tetovo** Macedonia
156 G2 **Tetrino** Rus. Fed.
245 K1 **Tetsyeh Mountain** *AK* U.S.A.
193 D10 **Tettau** Ger.
190 E3 **Tettens** Ger.
194 H6 **Tettnang** Ger.
Tetuán Morocco *see* **Tétouan**
101 □9a **Tetufera** *mt. Tahiti* Fr. Polynesia
139 L6 **Tetulia** Bangl.
139 M8 **Tetulia** *sea chan.* Bangl.
192 K4 **Tetyń** Pol.
Tetyukhe Rus. Fed. *see* **Dal'negorsk**
Tetyukhe-Pristan' Rus. Fed. *see* **Rudnaya Pristan'**
157 J5 **Tetyushi** Rus. Fed.
195 M3 **Teublitz** Ger.
193 F8 **Teuchern** Ger.
Teuchezhsk Rus. Fed. *see* **Adygeysk**
125 G15 **Teuchi** Japan
282 E2 **Teuco** *r.* Arg.
234 C4 **Teufelsbach** Namibia
190 G4 **Teufelsmoor** *reg.* Ger.
212 G1 **Teufen** Switz.
201 J5 **Teufenbach** Austria
214 B10 **Teulada** *Sardegna* Italy
209 F10 **Teulada** Spain
214 B10 **Teulada, Capo** *c. Sardegna* Italy
214 B10 **Teulada, Golfo di** *b. Sardegna* Italy
268 D4 **Teul de González Ortega** Mex.
115 F7 **Teun** *vol. Maluku* Indon.
116 A2 **Teunom** *Sumatera* Indon.
116 A2 **Teunom** *r.* Indon.
195 M3 **Teunz** Ger.
193 I6 **Teupitz** Ger.
193 I6 **Teupitz-Köriser Seengebiet** *park* Ger.
124 S2 **Teuri-tō** *i.* Japan
193 D10 **Teuschnitz** Ger.
266 □Q11 **Teustepe** Nic.
191 F6 **Teutoburger Wald** *hills* Ger.
193 E8 **Teutschenthal** Ger.
163 P5 **Teuva** Fin.
199 H5 **Tevel** Hungary
213 M9 **Tevere** *r.* Italy
215 J1 **Teverone** *r.* Italy
150 D6 **Teverya** Israel
103 D12 **Teviot** *South I.* N.Z.
237 J7 **Teviot** S. Africa
168 L11 **Teviot** *r. Scotland* U.K.
168 K12 **Teviotdale** *val. Scotland* U.K.
168 K12 **Teviothead** *Scottish Borders, Scotland* U.K.
103 B13 **Te Waewae** *South I.* N.Z.
103 B13 **Te Waewae Bay** *South I.* N.Z.
117 J5 **Tewah** *Kalimantan* Indon.
Te Waiponamu *i.* N.Z. *see* **South Island**
235 E4 **Tewane** Botswana
107 N9 **Tewantin** *Qld* Austr.
117 K5 **Teweh** *r.* Indon.
102 I6 **Te Wera** *North I.* N.Z.
102 L5 **Te Wera** *North I.* N.Z.
102 K5 **Te Whaiti** *North I.* N.Z.
102 □ **Te Whanga Lagoon** *Chatham Is* S. Pacific Ocean
103 J8 **Te Wharau** *North I.* N.Z.
172 H4 **Tewkesbury** *Gloucestershire, England* U.K.
160 H9 **Tewli** Belarus
128 H9 **Têwo** *Gansu* China
130 D1 **Têwo** *Sichuan* China
168 D11 **Texa** *i. Scotland* U.K.
261 H9 **Texarkana** *AR* U.S.A.
261 H9 **Texarkana** *TX* U.S.A.
105 M3 **Texas** *Qld* Austr.
261 F10 **Texas** *state* U.S.A.
261 H11 **Texas City** *TX* U.S.A.
269 I6 **Texcoco** Mex.
186 G2 **Texel** *i.* Neth.
261 E7 **Texhoma** *OK* U.S.A.
269 M8 **Texistepec** Mex.
269 I6 **Texmelucan** Mex.
261 G9 **Texoma, Lake** *OK/TX* U.S.A.
237 L5 **Teyateyaneng** Lesotho
184 F4 **Teyjat** France
161 X5 **Teykovo** Rus. Fed.
173 N5 **Teynham** *Kent, England* U.K.
185 H6 **Teyssieu** France
182 E4 **Teyssonne** *r.* France
145 K5 **Teyvareh** Afgh.
156 H4 **Teza** *r.* Rus. Fed.
237 Q4 **Teza** S. Africa
269 J6 **Teziutlán** Mex.
269 J8 **Tezoatlán** Mex.
269 K7 **Tezonapa** Mex.
269 H5 **Tezontepec** Mex.
139 N6 **Tezpur** *Assam* India
139 P6 **Tezu** *Arun. Prad.* India
226 C4 **Tfaritiy** Western Sahara
118 E4 **Tha, Nam** *r.* Laos
247 M2 **Tha-anne** *r. Nunavut* Can.
237 N5 **Thabana-Ntlenyana** *mt.* Lesotho
237 K5 **Thaba Nchu** S. Africa
237 O3 **Thabankulu** *mt.* S. Africa
235 E6 **Thaba Putsoa** *mt.* Lesotho
237 L6 **Thaba Putsoa** *mts* S. Africa
237 M5 **Thaba-Tseka** Lesotho
235 E5 **Thabazimbi** S. Africa
118 C3 **Thabeikkyin** Myanmar
119 F7 **Thab Lan National Park** Thai.
118 F6 **Tha Bo** Laos
237 K3 **Thabong** S. Africa
183 J6 **Thabor, Mont** *mt.* France
118 C4 **Thabyedaung** Myanmar
118 G4 **Thac Ba, Hô** *l.* Vietnam
118 B5 **Thade** *r.* Myanmar
146 G3 **Thādiq** Saudi Arabia
119 D8 **Thagyettaw** Myanmar
Tha Hin Thai. *see* **Lop Buri**
118 H4 **Thai Binh** Vietnam
118 E6 **Thailand** *country* Asia
119 E9 **Thailand, Gulf of** Asia
119 D10 **Thai Muang** Thai.
118 G4 **Thai Nguyên** Vietnam
147 I2 **Thaj** Saudi Arabia
118 G6 **Thakèk** Laos
139 L6 **Thakurgaon** Bangl.
138 H9 **Thakurtola** *Chhattisgarh* India
191 J9 **Thal** Ger.
145 N5 **Thal** Pak.
227 H2 **Thala** Tunisia
Thalabarivat Cambodia *see* **Phumĭ Thalabârĭvăt**
119 D10 **Thalang** Thai.
136 D7 **Thalassery** *Puducherry* India
150 A8 **Thalāthah** Egypt
195 K3 **Thalbach** *r.* Ger.
145 N6 **Thal Desert** Pak.
193 D7 **Thale (Harz)** Ger.
194 D3 **Thaleischweiler-Fröschen** Ger.
194 B2 **Thalfang** Ger.
200 H4 **Thalgau** Austria
193 F7 **Thalheim** Ger.
201 J3 **Thalheim bei Wels** Austria
118 E6 **Tha Li** Thai.
Thaliparamba *Kerala* India *see* **Taliparamba**
105 L3 **Thallon** *Qld* Austr.
193 G8 **Thallwitz** Ger.
195 K3 **Thalmässing** Ger.
195 M4 **Thalmassing** Ger.
145 K7 **Thalo** Pak.
212 F1 **Thalwil** Switz.
224 C3 **Thamad Bū Hashīshah** *well* Libya
234 E5 **Thamaga** Botswana
146 H2 **Thāmām, 'Irq ath** *des.* Saudi Arabia
146 G9 **Thamar, Jabal** *mt.* Yemen
147 L7 **Thamarīt** Oman
173 K4 **Thame** *Oxfordshire, England* U.K.
173 J4 **Thame** *r. England* U.K.
251 L7 **Thames** *r. Ont.* Can.
102 J4 **Thames** *North I.* N.Z.
173 N5 **Thames** *est. England* U.K.
173 M5 **Thames** *r. England* U.K.
259 K2 **Thames** *r. CT* U.S.A.
102 J3 **Thames, Firth of** *b. North I.* N.Z.
Thamesdown *admin. div. England* U.K. *see* **Swindon**
251 N6 **Thamesford** *Ont.* Can.
251 M7 **Thamesville** *Ont.* Can.
191 K8 **Thamsbrück** Ger.
147 I7 **Thamūd** Yemen
Thamugadi *tourist site* Alg. *see* **Timgad**
138 C8 **Than** *Gujarat* India
Thana *Mahar.* India *see* **Thane**
138 F6 **Thana Ghazi** *Rajasthan* India
118 C6 **Thanatpin** Myanmar
118 C7 **Thanbyuzayat** Myanmar
118 C5 **Thandaung** Myanmar
138 E8 **Thandla** *Madh. Prad.* India
118 B5 **Thandwè** Myanmar
136 C3 **Thane** *Mahar.* India
173 O5 **Thanet, Isle of** *pen. England* U.K.
108 G5 **Thangoo** *W.A.* Austr.
107 M8 **Thangool** *Qld* Austr.
138 G3 **Thangra** *Jammu and Kashmir* India
118 G5 **Thanh Hoa** Vietnam
136 F7 **Thanjavur** *Tamil Nadu* India
119 D10 **Than Kyun** *i.* Myanmar
Thanlwin *r.* Myanmar *see* **Salween**
118 C6 **Thanlyin** Myanmar
179 N8 **Thann** France
195 I5 **Thannhausen** Ger.
145 L9 **Thano Bula Khan** Pak.
130 D8 **Than Uyên** Vietnam
234 D3 **Thaoge** *r.* Botswana
247 L2 **Thaolintoa Lake** *Nunavut* Can.
179 L7 **Thaon-les-Vosges** France
118 E6 **Tha Pla** Thai.
119 D10 **Thap Put** Thai.
Thapsacus Syria *see* **Dibsī**
119 D9 **Thap Sakae** Thai.
138 C8 **Thara** *Gujarat* India
119 D8 **Tharabwin** Myanmar
138 C7 **Tharad** *Gujarat* India
138 C7 **Tharad** *Gujarat* India
232 C5 **Tharaka** Kenya
193 I9 **Tharandt** Ger.
186 I4 **'t Harde** Neth.
138 B7 **Thar Desert** India/Pak.
107 I9 **Thargomindah** *Qld* Austr.
118 B6 **Tharrawaw** Myanmar
206 E5 **Tharsis** Spain
149 K7 **Tharthār, Buḩayrat ath** *l.* Iraq
149 K6 **Tharthār, Wādī ath** *r.* Iraq
147 L4 **Tharwānīyyah** U.A.E.
119 D10 **Tha Sala** Thai.
220 F2 **Thasopoula** *i.* Greece
220 F2 **Thasos** *Thasos* Greece
220 F2 **Thasos** *i.* Greece
173 J5 **Thatcham** *West Berkshire, England* U.K.
265 W9 **Thatcher** *AZ* U.S.A.
220 B2 **Thatë, Mali i** *mt.* Albania
118 H3 **Thât Khê** Vietnam
118 C6 **Thaton** Myanmar
145 L9 **Thatta** Pak.
183 D10 **Thau, Bassin de** *lag.* France
182 B3 **Thaumiers** France
118 B2 **Thaungdut** Myanmar
118 C6 **Thaungyin** *r.* Myanmar/Thai.
200 D5 **Thaur** Austria
118 G6 **Tha Uthen** Thai.
150 D9 **Thawr, Jabal** *mt.* Jordan
173 M4 **Thaxted** *Essex, England* U.K.
201 L2 **Thaya** Austria
201 M2 **Thaya** *r.* Austria/Czech Rep.
201 M2 **Thayatal, Nationalpark** *park* Austria/Czech Rep.
118 B6 **Thayawadi** Myanmar
119 C8 **Thayawthadangyi Kyun** *i.* Myanmar
118 B5 **Thayetmyo** Myanmar
118 C2 **Thayetta** Myanmar
212 F1 **Thayngen** Switz.
118 B5 **Thazi** *Magwe* Myanmar
118 C4 **Thazi** *Mandalay* Myanmar
245 K2 **Thazzik Mountain** *AK* U.S.A.
102 K3 **The Aldermen Islands** *North I.* N.Z.
270 □ **The Alley** Jamaica
265 T9 **Theba** *AZ* U.S.A.
Thebacha *N.W.T.* Can. *see* **Fort Smith**
Thebae *tourist site* Egypt *see* **Thebes**
253 K6 **The Bahamas** *country* West Indies
225 G3 **Thebes** *tourist site* Egypt
Thebes Greece *see* **Thiva**
270 E1 **The Bluff** *Eleuthera* Bahamas
238 □2b **The Briars** St Helena
173 P2 **The Broads** *nat. park England* U.K.
The Brothers *is* H.K. China *see* **Tai Siu Mo To**
The Brothers *is* Yemen *see* **Al Ikhwān**
171 L5 **The Calf** *hill England* U.K.
107 N1 **The Calvados Chain** *is* P.N.G.
171 M3 **The Cheviot** *hill England* U.K.
270 □ **The Cockpit Country** *hills* Jamaica
104 G6 **The Coorong** *inlet S.A.* Austr.
271 □4 **The Crane** Barbados
255 □1 **The Crawl** *pt* Bermuda
170 D7 **The Curragh** *lowland* Ireland
262 D4 **The Dalles** *OR* U.S.A.
260 E4 **Thedford** *NE* U.S.A.
170 D4 **The Diamond** *Northern Ireland* U.K.
190 H5 **Thedinghausen** Ger.
106 F1 **The English Company's Islands** *N.T.* Austr.
105 M5 **The Entrance** *N.S.W.* Austr.
236 D10 **Theewaterskloof Dam** *resr* S. Africa
168 □M1 **The Faither** *stack Scotland* U.K.
173 L2 **The Fens** *reg. England* U.K.
102 □ **The Forty Fours** *is Chatham Is* S. Pacific Ocean
228 A3 **The Gambia** *country* Africa
168 H12 **The Glenkens** *val. Scotland* U.K.
105 I7 **The Grampians** *mts Vic.* Austr.
106 C6 **The Granites** *hill N.T.* Austr.
The Great Oasis Egypt *see* **Khārijah, Wāḩāt al**
271 □3 **The Grenadines** *is* St Vincent
147 J1 **The Gulf** Asia
The Hague Neth. *see* **'s-Gravenhage**
169 J7 **The Harrow** Ireland
237 M8 **The Haven** S. Africa
102 □ **The Horns** *hill Chatham Is* S. Pacific Ocean
236 H7 **The Horseshoe** *mt.* S. Africa
103 E11 **The Hunters Hills** *South I.* N.Z.
181 P7 **Theillay** France
119 D9 **Theinkun** Myanmar
118 C6 **Theinzeik** Myanmar
193 F8 **Theißen** Ger.
180 F6 **Theix** France
103 B12 **The Key** *South I.* N.Z.
247 I2 **Thekulthili Lake** *N.W.T.* Can.
105 K7 **The Lakes National Park** *Vic.* Austr.
178 C5 **Thelle** *reg.* France
247 L1 **Thelon** *r. N.W.T./Nunavut* Can.
247 K1 **Thelon Game Sanctuary** *nature res. Nunavut* Can.
172 G2 **The Long Mynd** *hills England* U.K.
170 D4 **The Loup** *Northern Ireland* U.K.
107 J5 **The Lynd Junction** *Qld* Austr.
168 H13 **The Machars** *reg. Scotland* U.K.
169 K3 **The Maidens** *is Northern Ireland* U.K.
191 K9 **Themar** Ger.
236 I8 **Thembalesizwe** S. Africa
237 N3 **Thembalihle** S. Africa
168 D6 **The Minch** *sea chan. Scotland* U.K.
185 H6 **Thémines** France
169 B4 **The Mullet** *b.* Ireland
172 E4 **The Mumbles** *Swansea, Wales* U.K.
255 □1 **The Narrows** *sea chan.* Bermuda
271 □2 **The Narrows** *str.* St Kitts and Nevis
181 N8 **Thenay** France
The Naze *c.* Norway *see* **Lindesnes**
173 O4 **The Naze** *pt England* U.K.
103 C13 **The Neck** *pen. Stewart I.* N.Z.
173 I6 **The Needles** *stack England* U.K.
181 K8 **Thénezay** France
138 G8 **Theni** *Madh. Prad.* India
227 F2 **Theniet El Had** Alg.
184 G5 **Thenon** France
168 K4 **The North Sound** *sea chan. Scotland* U.K.
106 C6 **Theo, Mount** *hill N.T.* Austr.
168 D11 **The Oa** *pen. Scotland* U.K.
107 M8 **Theodore** *Qld* Austr.
247 K5 **Theodore** *Sask.* Can.
277 E1 **Theodore Roosevelt** *r.* Brazil
265 U8 **Theodore Roosevelt Lake** *AZ* U.S.A.
260 D2 **Theodore Roosevelt National Park** *ND* U.S.A.
Theodosia Ukr. *see* **Feodosiya**
104 D2 **The Officer Creek** *watercourse S.A.* Austr.
171 K5 **The Old Man of Coniston** *hill England* U.K.
181 P7 **Théols** *r.* France
183 J9 **Théoule-sur-Mer** France
169 D8 **The Paps** *hill* Ireland
247 K4 **The Pas** *Man.* Can.
238 □2a **The Peak** *hill Ascension* S. Atlantic Ocean
169 G8 **The Pike** Ireland
Thera *i.* Greece *see* **Santorini**
178 D5 **Thérain** *r.* France
103 C12 **The Remarkables** *mts South I.* N.Z.
191 J10 **Theres** Ger.
257 J4 **Theresa** *NY* U.S.A.
107 L7 **Theresa Creek** *r. Qld* Austr.
Thérèse Island *Inner Islands* Seychelles *see* **Térèse, Île**
168 F13 **The Rinns of Galloway** *pen. Scotland* U.K.
221 G2 **Therma** *Samothraki* Greece
220 D2 **Thermaïkos Kolpos** *g.* Greece
220 E2 **Thermi** Greece
220 C4 **Thermo** Greece
Thérmon Greece *see* **Thermo**
262 J5 **Thermopolis** *WY* U.S.A.
220 D4 **Thermopyles** Greece
105 K6 **The Rock** *N.S.W.* Austr.
207 □ **The Rock** *hill* Gibraltar
178 D2 **Thérouanne** France
270 □ **The Salt Ponds** *lakes* Jamaica
108 □1 **The Settlement** Christmas I.
169 B8 **The Seven Hogs** *is* Ireland
169 J3 **The Sheddings** *Northern Ireland* U.K.
242 F2 **Thesiger Bay** *N.W.T.* Can.
The Sisters *is Inner Islands* Seychelles *see* **Les Sœurs**
102 □ **The Sisters** *is Chatham Is* S. Pacific Ocean
244 G3 **The Sisters** *hill AK* U.S.A.
The Skaw *spit* Denmark *see* **Grenen**
169 A9 **The Skelligs** *is* Ireland
The Slot *sea chan.* Solomon Is *see* **New Georgia Sound**
168 □L2 **The Sneug** *hill Scotland* U.K.
173 J6 **The Solent** *str. England* U.K.
220 B3 **Thesprotiko** Greece
220 C3 **Thessalia** *admin. reg.* Greece
248 D4 **Thessalon** *Ont.* Can.
Thessalonica Greece *see* **Thessaloniki**
220 D2 **Thessaloniki** Greece
Thessaly *admin. reg.* Greece *see* **Thessalia**
173 N5 **The Stocks** *Kent, England* U.K.
168 D7 **The Storr** *hill Scotland* U.K.
173 N5 **The Swale** *sea chan. England* U.K.
173 N3 **Thet** *r. England* U.K.
114 B7 **The Teeth** *mt. Palawan* Phil.
170 F5 **The Temple** *Northern Ireland* U.K.
109 F10 **The Terraces** *hills W.A.* Austr.
173 N3 **Thetford** *Norfolk, England* U.K.
249 G4 **Thetford Mines** *Que.* Can.
103 E10 **The Thumbs** *mt. South I.* N.Z.
118 B7 **Thetkethaung** *r.* Myanmar
118 C2 **The Triangle** *mts* Myanmar
168 H10 **The Trossachs** *hills Scotland* U.K.
104 E4 **The Twins** *S.A.* Austr.
118 G5 **Theun** *r.* Laos
237 K4 **Theunissen** S. Africa
187 I7 **Theux** Belgium
Theva-i-Ra *rf* Fiji *see* **Ceva-i-Ra**
271 L4 **The Valley** Anguilla
104 D5 **Thevenard** *S.A.* Austr.
108 C6 **Thevenard Island** *W.A.* Austr.
249 G1 **Thévenet, Lac** *l. Que.* Can.
Theveste Alg. *see* **Tébessa**
173 M2 **The Wash** *b. England* U.K.
173 M5 **The Weald** *reg. England* U.K.
261 H10 **The Woodlands** *TX* U.S.A.
The Wrekin *admin. div. England* U.K. *see* **Telford and Wrekin**
185 D9 **Thèze** *Aquitaine* France
183 H8 **Thèze** *Provence-Alpes-Côte d'Azur* France
Thíamis *r.* Greece *see* **Kalamas**
179 K6 **Thiaucourt-Regniéville** France
181 L3 **Thiberville** France
178 H6 **Thibie** France
261 J11 **Thibodaux** *LA* U.S.A.
247 L4 **Thicket Portage** *Man.* Can.
178 I6 **Thiéblemont-Farémont** France
260 G1 **Thief River Falls** *MN* U.S.A.
Thiel Neth. *see* **Tiel**
212 B2 **Thielle** *r.* Switz.
259 G2 **Thiells** *NY* U.S.A.
286 R1 **Thiel Mountains** Antarctica
262 C5 **Thielsen, Mount** *OR* U.S.A.
Thielt Belgium *see* **Tielt**
213 K4 **Thiene** Italy
178 G4 **Thiérache** *reg.* France
195 J4 **Thierhaupten** Ger.
212 B2 **Thierrens** Switz.
182 D5 **Thiers** France
200 F4 **Thiersee** Austria
193 F10 **Thiersheim** Ger.
179 J5 **Thierville-sur-Meuse** France
228 A3 **Thiès** Senegal
214 B6 **Thiesi** *Sardegna* Italy
192 I2 **Thießow** Ger.
183 B6 **Thiézac** France
233 C5 **Thika** Kenya
Thikombia *i.* Fiji *see* **Cikobia**
136 C9 **Thiladhunmathi Atoll** Maldives
228 B3 **Thilogne** Senegal
Thimbu Bhutan *see* **Thimphu**
178 B6 **Thimert-Gâtelles** France
139 L6 **Thimphu** Bhutan
162 □C1 **Thingvallavatn (Þingvallavatn)** *l.* Iceland
162 □C1 **Thingvellir (Þingvellir)** Iceland
162 C1 **Thingvellir (Þingvellir)** *nat. park* Iceland
178 I4 **Thin-le-Moutier** France
100 □5 **Thio** New Caledonia
179 L5 **Thionville** France
Thira *i.* Greece *see* **Santorini**
220 G6 **Thirasia** *i.* Greece
171 K4 **Thirlmere** *resr England* U.K.
181 M5 **Thiron Gardais** France
178 B7 **Thironne** *r.* France
138 F4 **Thirrach** *Hima. Prad.* India
171 O5 **Thirsk** *North Yorkshire, England* U.K.
109 F12 **Thirsty, Mount** *hill W.A.* Austr.
247 L2 **Thirty Mile Lake** *Nunavut* Can.
136 E8 **Thiruvananthapuram** *Kerala* India
136 F7 **Thiruvarur** *Tamil Nadu* India
Thiruvattiyur *Tamil Nadu* India *see* **Tiruvottiyur**
182 I2 **Thise** France
220 F1 **Thissavros, Techniti Limni** *resr* Greece
164 E5 **Thisted** Denmark
162 □F1 **Thstilfjörður (Þistilfjörður)** *b.* Iceland
245 M3 **Thistle Creek** *Y.T.* Can.
104 F6 **Thistle Island** *S.A.* Austr.
247 I1 **Thistle Lake** *Nunavut* Can.
118 B3 **Thityabin** Myanmar
220 E4 **Thiva** Greece
Thívai Greece *see* **Thiva**
178 B7 **Thivars** France
184 F5 **Thiviers** France
182 E4 **Thizy** France
162 □C2 **Thjórsá (Þjórsá)** *r.* Iceland
247 M2 **Thlewiaza** *r. Nunavut* Can.
247 I2 **Thoa** *r. N.W.T.* Can.
183 I8 **Thoard** France
119 F10 **Thô Chu, Đao** *i.* Vietnam
118 D6 **Thoen** Thai.
118 E5 **Thoeng** Thai.
235 F4 **Thohoyandou** S. Africa
182 H4 **Thoirette** France
178 C6 **Thoiry** *Île-de-France* France
182 H4 **Thoiry** *Rhône-Alpes* France
182 F4 **Thoissey** France
182 E2 **Thoisy-la-Berchère** France
186 F5 **Tholen** Neth.
186 F5 **Tholen** *i.* Neth.
194 C3 **Tholey** Ger.
178 F7 **Tholon** *r.* France
109 D8 **Thomas** *r. W.A.* Austr.
106 F9 **Thomas, Lake** *salt flat S.A.* Austr.
190 K4 **Thomasburg** Ger.
260 I6 **Thomas Hill Reservoir** *MO* U.S.A.
243 I1 **Thomas Hubbard, Cape** *Nunavut* Can.
264 P8 **Thomas Mountain** *CA* U.S.A.
259 I1 **Thomaston** *CT* U.S.A.
255 E9 **Thomaston** *GA* U.S.A.
257 □P4 **Thomaston** *ME* U.S.A.
257 □R3 **Thomaston Corner** *N.B.* Can.
169 H7 **Thomastown** Ireland
255 D10 **Thomasville** *AL* U.S.A.
255 F10 **Thomasville** *GA* U.S.A.
255 G8 **Thomasville** *NC* U.S.A.
187 J8 **Thommen** Belgium
270 H4 **Thomonde** Haiti
247 L4 **Thompson** *Man.* Can.
246 F5 **Thompson** *r. B.C.* Can.
250 H4 **Thompson** *MI* U.S.A.
265 W3 **Thompson** *UT* U.S.A.
260 I6 **Thompson** *r. MO* U.S.A.
262 G3 **Thompson Falls** *MT* U.S.A.
263 L9 **Thompson Peak** *NM* U.S.A.
Thompson's Falls Kenya *see* **Nyahururu**
246 E5 **Thompson Sound** *B.C.* Can.
103 A12 **Thompson Sound** *inlet South I.* N.Z.
258 A3 **Thompsontown** *PA* U.S.A.
257 M7 **Thompsonville** *CT* U.S.A.
107 I8 **Thomson** *watercourse Qld* Austr.
255 F9 **Thomson** *GA* U.S.A.
250 D8 **Thomson** *IL* U.S.A.
103 C11 **Thomson Mountains** *South I.* N.Z.
119 E8 **Thon Buri** Thai.
138 F3 **Thondhe** *Jammu and Kashmir* India
182 I5 **Thônes** France
118 C6 **Thongwa** Myanmar
179 J7 **Thonnance-lès-Joinville** France
247 I1 **Thonokied Lake** *N.W.T.* Can.
182 I4 **Thonon-les-Bains** France
183 J8 **Thorame-Basse** France
183 J8 **Thorame-Haute** France
183 D7 **Thoras** France
185 I8 **Thoré** *r.* France
263 J9 **Thoreau** *NM* U.S.A.
181 M6 **Thoré-la-Rochette** France
183 J9 **Thorenc** France
182 I5 **Thorens-Glières** France
246 H4 **Thorhild** *Alta* Can.
178 F7 **Thorigny-sur-Oreuse** France
162 □D1 **Thórisvatn (Þórisvatn)** *l.* Iceland
201 L4 **Thörl** Austria
187 I6 **Thorn** Neth.
Thorn Pol. *see* **Toruń**
171 O4 **Thornaby-on-Tees** *Stockton-on-Tees, England* U.K.
250 I7 **Thornapple** *r. MI* U.S.A.
103 C13 **Thornbury** *South I.* N.Z.
172 G4 **Thornbury** *South Gloucestershire, England* U.K.
251 O3 **Thorne** *Ont.* Can.
171 P6 **Thorne** *South Yorkshire, England* U.K.
264 N3 **Thorne** *NV* U.S.A.
245 N5 **Thorne Bay** *AK* U.S.A.
173 L2 **Thorney** *Peterborough, England* U.K.
171 Q6 **Thorngumbald** *East Riding of Yorkshire, England* U.K.
168 I12 **Thornhill** *Dumfries and Galloway, Scotland* U.K.
170 I1 **Thornhill** *Stirling, Scotland* U.K.
258 D2 **Thornhurst** *PA* U.S.A.
171 O4 **Thornley** *Durham, England* U.K.
106 G5 **Thornton** *r. Qld* Austr.
168 J10 **Thornton** *Fife, Scotland* U.K.
171 L6 **Thornton** *Lancashire, England* U.K.
250 F5 **Thornton** *WI* U.S.A.
171 P5 **Thornton Dale** *North Yorkshire, England* U.K.
259 H2 **Thornwood** *NY* U.S.A.
251 O6 **Thorold** *Ont.* Can.
250 D5 **Thorp** *WI* U.S.A.
103 G8 **Thorpe** *South I.* N.Z.
173 O4 **Thorpe-le-Soken** *Essex, England* U.K.
173 O2 **Thorpe Market** *Norfolk, England* U.K.
173 P3 **Thorpeness** *Suffolk, England* U.K.
173 O2 **Thorpe St Andrew** *Norfolk, England* U.K.
246 H4 **Thorsby** *Alta* Can.
Thorshavn Faroe Is *see* **Tórshavn**
Thorshavnfjella *reg.* Antarctica *see* **Thorshavnheiane**
287 B2 **Thorshavnheiane** *reg.* Antarctica
162 □F1 **Thórshöfn (Þórshöfn)** Iceland
162 □E1 **Thorvaldsfell (Þorvaldsfell)** *vol.* Iceland
237 L5 **Thota-ea-Moli** Lesotho
181 K7 **Thouarcé** France
180 I7 **Thouaré-sur-Loire** France
184 D2 **Thouars** France
139 N7 **Thoubal** *Manipur* India
184 D1 **Thouet** *r.* France
108 E6 **Thouin, Cape** *pt W.A.* Austr.
178 E5 **Thourotte** France
Thourout Belgium *see* **Torhout**
251 R5 **Thousand Islands** Can./U.S.A.
265 U3 **Thousand Lake Mountain** *UT* U.S.A.
264 N7 **Thousand Oaks** *CA* U.S.A.
265 P8 **Thousand Palms** *CA* U.S.A.
256 B11 **Thousandsticks** *KY* U.S.A.
258 B6 **T. Howard Duckett Reservoir** *MD* U.S.A.
219 O9 **Thrace** *reg.* Turkey
Thraki *reg.* Turkey *see* **Thrace**
220 F2 **Thrakiko Pelagos** *sea* Greece
173 K3 **Thrapston** *Northamptonshire, England* U.K.
105 L7 **Thredbo** *N.S.W.* Austr.
258 F3 **Three Bridges** *NJ* U.S.A.
169 C10 **Three Castle Head** Ireland
Three Fathoms Cove *b.* H.K. China *see* **Kei Ling Ha Hoi**
262 I4 **Three Forks** *MT* U.S.A.
Three Gorges Reservoir *resr* China *see* **Sanxia Shuiku**
105 J9 **Three Hummock Island** *Tas.* Austr.
102 G1 **Three Kings Islands** *North I.* N.Z.
250 E4 **Three Lakes** *WI* U.S.A.
250 H8 **Three Oaks** *MI* U.S.A.
118 D7 **Three Pagodas Pass** Myanmar/Thai.
265 U9 **Three Points** *AZ* U.S.A.
228 E5 **Three Points, Cape** Ghana
264 N5 **Three Rivers** *CA* U.S.A.
250 I8 **Three Rivers** *MI* U.S.A.
261 F11 **Three Rivers** *TX* U.S.A.
236 H7 **Three Sisters** S. Africa
262 D4 **Three Sisters** *mt. OR* U.S.A.
100 □6 **Three Sisters Islands** Solomon Is
109 C10 **Three Springs** *W.A.* Austr.
171 K4 **Threlkeld** *Cumbria, England* U.K.
171 M5 **Threshfield** *North Yorkshire, England* U.K.
136 E7 **Thrissur** *Kerala* India
261 F9 **Throckmorton** *TX* U.S.A.
258 D2 **Throop** *PA* U.S.A.
171 N3 **Thropton** *Northumberland, England* U.K.
109 H9 **Throssell, Lake** *salt flat W.A.* Austr.

108 F6 Throssel Range hills W.A. Austr.
168 J6 Thrumster Highland, Scotland U.K.
172 H4 Thrupp Gloucestershire, England U.K.
107 K9 Thrushton National Park Qld Austr.
171 O7 Thrybergh South Yorkshire, England U.K.
233 D5 Thua watercourse Kenya
118 H6 Thuân An Vietnam
119 G10 Thư Ba Vietnam
118 I6 Thu Bôn, Sông r. Vietnam
247 I2 Thubun Lakes N.W.T. Can.
119 H9 Thu Dâu Môt Vietnam
105 L6 Thuddungra N.S.W. Austr.
119 H9 Thu Đuc Vietnam
185 I10 Thuès-entre-Valls France
183 E7 Thueyts France
187 F8 Thuin Belgium
191 E6 Thuine Ger.
185 J10 Thuir France
232 B2 Thul Sudan
232 A2 Thul watercourse Sudan
150 H3 Thulaythawāt Gharbī, Jabal hill Syria
191 I10 Thulba r. Ger.
Thule Greenland see Qaanaaq
235 F4 Thuli Zimbabwe
235 F4 Thuli r. Zimbabwe
Thulusdhoo N. Male Maldives see Thulusdhu
135 □1 Thulusdhu N. Male Maldives
193 G9 Thum Ger.
212 D2 Thun Switz.
107 I8 Thunda Qld Austr.
109 D10 Thundelarra W.A. Austr.
248 B3 Thunder Bay Ont. Can.
248 B3 Thunder Bay b. Ont. Can.
251 K4 Thunder Bay b. MI U.S.A.
247 J5 Thunder Creek r. Sask. Can.
270 C5 Thunder Knoll sea feature Caribbean Sea
173 N4 Thundersley Essex, England U.K.
212 D2 Thuner See l. Switz.
194 H2 Thüngen Ger.
194 H2 Thüngersheim Ger.
118 E6 Thung Salaeng Luang National Park Thai.
119 D10 Thung Song Thai.
119 D11 Thung Wa Thai.
118 D7 Thung Yai Naresuan Wildlife Reserve nature res. Thai.
179 N7 Thur r. France
212 F1 Thur r. Switz.
102 J7 Thuraua North I. N.Z.
171 O7 Thurcroft South Yorkshire, England U.K.
181 L8 Thuré France
182 C5 Thuret France
182 G3 Thurey France
212 G1 Thurgau canton Switz.
200 A5 Thüringen Austria
191 K8 Thüringen land Ger.
193 D8 Thüringer Becken reg. Ger.
191 J9 Thüringer Wald mts Ger.
191 K9 Thüringer Wald park Ger.
Thuringia land Ger. see Thüringen
Thuringian Forest mts Ger. see Thüringer Wald
182 F5 Thurins France
192 G3 Thürkow Ger.
173 L2 Thurlby Lincolnshire, England U.K.
169 G7 Thurles Ireland
193 G9 Thurm Ger.
195 O4 Thurmansbang Ger.
256 H9 Thurmont MD U.S.A.
200 F5 Thurn, Pass Austria
193 D10 Thurnau Ger.
171 O6 Thurnscoe South Yorkshire, England U.K.
173 M4 Thurrock admin. div. England U.K.
171 K4 Thursby Cumbria, England U.K.
107 I1 Thursday Island Qld Austr.
257 J3 Thurso Que. Can.
168 I5 Thurso Highland, Scotland U.K.
168 I5 Thurso r. Scotland U.K.
168 I5 Thurso Bay Scotland U.K.
173 N3 Thurston Suffolk, England U.K.
286 R2 Thurston Island Antarctica
Thurston Peninsula i. Antarctica see Thurston Island
173 O2 Thurton Norfolk, England U.K.
181 K4 Thury-Harcourt France
212 G2 Thusis Switz.
191 I6 Thüster Berg hill Ger.
182 H5 Thusy France
171 M5 Thwaite North Yorkshire, England U.K.
286 Q1 Thwaites Glacier Tongue Antarctica
164 E5 Thy reg. Denmark
Thyatira Turkey see Akhisar
164 E5 Thyborøn Denmark
182 J4 Thyez France
107 I9 Thylungra Qld Austr.
221 H5 Thymaina i. Greece
178 B6 Thymerais reg. France
233 B8 Thyolo Malawi
228 E4 Thyou Boulkiemde Burkina
Thyou Yatenga Burkina see Tiou
195 P4 Thyrnau Ger.
Thysville Dem. Rep. Congo see Mbanza-Ngungu
144 G8 Tīāb Iran
276 C4 Tiahuanaco Bol.
270 H8 Tía Juana Venez.
214 C7 Tiana Sardegna Italy
128 F6 Tiancang Gansu China
131 L2 Tianchang Anhui China
128 F7 Tiancheng Gansu China
Tiancheng Hubei China see Chongyang
129 J8 Tianchi Gansu China
Tianchi Sichuan China see Lezhi
130 F7 Tiandeng Guangxi China
Tiandiba Sichuan China see Jinyang
130 F7 Tiandong Guangxi China
130 F6 Tian'e Guangxi China
151 F3 T'ianet'i Georgia
131 K4 Tianfanjie Jiangxi China
228 B3 Tiângol Lougguéré watercourse Senegal
278 E2 Tianguá Brazil
269 I5 Tianguistengo Mex.
129 O7 Tianjin Tianjin China
129 O7 Tianjin mun. China
128 F8 Tianjun Qinghai China
228 B3 Tiankoye Senegal
130 F6 Tianlin Guangxi China
131 I3 Tianmen Hubei China
131 L3 Tianmu Shan mts China
122 F7 Tianqiaoling Jilin China
130 D3 Tianquan Sichuan China
129 Q5 Tianshan Nei Mongol China
Tian Shan mts China/Kyrg. see Tien Shan
123 D8 Tianshifu Liaoning China
128 I9 Tianshui Gansu China
128 J8 Tianshuibu Gansu China
133 D9 Tianshuihai Aksai Chin
132 L6 Tianshuijing Gansu China
131 M4 Tiantai Zhejiang China
129 O5 Tiantaiyong Nei Mongol China
Tiantang Anhui China see Yuexi
130 F7 Tianyang Guangxi China
Tianyi Nei Mongol China see Ningcheng
Tianzhen Shandong China see Gaoqing
129 N6 Tianzhen Shanxi China
Tianzhou Guangxi China see Tianyang
128 H8 Tianzhu Gansu China
130 G5 Tianzhu Guizhou China
101 □9a Tiarei Tahiti Fr. Polynesia
227 F2 Tiaret Alg.
227 H3 Tiaret well Tunisia
100 □5 Tiari New Caledonia
107 N8 Tiaro Qld Austr.
238 □3c Tías Lanzarote Canary Is
228 D5 Tiassalé Côte d'Ivoire
100 □2 Ti'avea Samoa
Tibabar Sabah Malaysia see Tambunan
280 B6 Tibagi Brazil
280 B5 Tibagi r. Brazil
Tibaji r. Brazil see Tibagi
149 K7 Tibal, Wādī watercourse Iraq
274 C3 Tibaná Col.
229 I5 Tibati Cameroon
145 N7 Tibba Pak.
168 I10 Tibbermore Perth and Kinross, Scotland U.K.
228 C4 Tibé, Pic de mt. Guinea
Tiber r. Italy see Tevere
227 F3 Tiberghamine Alg.
226 B5 Tiberguent well Maur.
Tiberias Israel see Teverya
262 I2 Tiber Reservoir MT U.S.A.
224 C4 Tibesti mts Chad
Tibet aut. reg. China see Xizang Zizhiqu
Tibet, Plateau of Xizang China see Qingzang Gaoyuan
209 D10 Tibi Spain
209 D11 Tibi, Embalse de resr Spain
229 G3 Tibiri Niger
219 M4 Țibleș, Vârful mt. Romania
275 G3 Tiboku Falls Guyana
199 J4 Tibolddaróc Hungary
105 I3 Tibooburra N.S.W. Austr.
199 L4 Tiborszállás Hungary
139 I5 Tibrikot Nepal
165 K3 Tibro Sweden
171 O7 Tibshelf Derbyshire, England U.K.
274 B3 Tibuga, Ensenada b. Col.
Tibur Italy see Tivoli
266 C3 Tiburón, Isla i. Mex.
114 D5 Ticao i. Phil.
173 M5 Ticehurst East Sussex, England U.K.
219 O7 Ticha r. Bulg.
219 K8 Tichak mt. Bulg.
Tichau Pol. see Tychy
251 R5 Tichborne Ont. Can.
249 F3 Tichégami r. Que. Can.
229 F2 Tichet well Mali
228 C2 Tîchît Maur.
228 C2 Tîchît, Dhar hills Maur.
226 D3 Tichka, Tizi-n- pass Morocco
226 B5 Tichla Western Sahara
212 G5 Ticino r. Italy/Switz.
212 F3 Ticino canton Switz.
Ticinum Italy see Pavia
171 O7 Tickhill South Yorkshire, England U.K.
219 L6 Țicleni Romania
257 L5 Ticonderoga NY U.S.A.
267 O7 Ticul Mex.
Ticumbia i. Fiji see Cikobia
165 J3 Tidaholm Sweden
165 K3 Tidan Sweden
165 J3 Tidan r. Sweden
118 A3 Tiddim Myanmar
190 K5 Tiddische Ger.
137 M9 Tiden Andaman & Nicobar Is India
172 G4 Tidenham Gloucestershire, England U.K.
227 F5 Tideridjaounine, Adrar mts Alg.
171 N7 Tideswell Derbyshire, England U.K.
227 F4 Tidikelt, Plaine du plain Alg.
256 F7 Tidioute PA U.S.A.
229 F2 Tidjerouene well Mali
228 C2 Tidjikja Maur.
212 H5 Tidone r. Italy
115 E3 Tidore i. Maluku Indon.
226 B5 Tidsit, Sabkhet salt pan Western Sahara
173 I5 Tidworth Wiltshire, England U.K.
185 A10 Tiebas Spain
228 D5 Tiébissou Côte d'Ivoire
224 C4 Tiéboro Chad
132 G3 Tiechanggou Xinjiang China
205 J5 Tiedra Spain
Tiefa Liaoning China see Diaobingshan
195 M4 Tiefenbach Bayern Ger.
195 N3 Tiefenbach Bayern Ger.
195 O4 Tiefenbach Bayern Ger.
194 F4 Tiefenbronn Ger.
212 H2 Tiefencastel Switz.
192 I5 Tiefensee Ger.
186 H5 Tiel Neth.
228 B3 Tiel Senegal
187 G6 Tielen Belgium
122 E5 Tieli Heilong. China
129 R5 Tieling Liaoning China
133 D9 Tielongtan Aksai Chin
187 D7 Tielt Belgium
228 D4 Tiémé Côte d'Ivoire
228 C5 Tiene Liberia
187 G7 Tienen Belgium
194 E6 Tiengen Ger.
132 C6 Tien Shan mts China/Kyrg.
Tien Shan Oblast admin. div. Kyrg. see Naryn
Tientsin Tianjin China see Tianjin
Tientsin mun. China see Tianjin
118 H4 Tiên Yên Vietnam
213 J6 Tiepido r. Italy
181 K6 Tiercé France
237 K4 Tierfontein S. Africa
205 Q5 Tierga Spain
165 N1 Tierp Sweden
282 C2 Tierra Amarilla Chile
263 K8 Tierra Amarilla NM U.S.A.
268 G4 Tierrablanca Mex.
269 K7 Tierra Blanca Mex.
274 C6 Tierra Blanca Peru
269 H8 Tierra Colorada Mex.
283 D9 Tierra del Fuego prov. Arg.
283 C9 Tierra del Fuego, Isla Grande de i. Arg./Chile
283 D9 Tierra del Fuego, Parque Nacional nat. park Arg.
274 B4 Tierradentro, Parque Arqueológico Nacional tourist site Col.
274 B2 Tierralta Col.
238 □3c Tierra Negra, Punta de pt Lanzarote Canary Is
268 G4 Tierranueva Mex.
205 Q7 Tierzo Spain
207 I5 Tiesa hill Spain
201 M6 Tieschen Austria
204 I9 Tiétar r. Spain
205 J8 Tiétar, Valle de val. Spain
280 D5 Tietê Brazil
280 B4 Tietê r. Brazil
104 D2 Tieyon S.A. Austr.
181 I7 Tiffauges France
256 B7 Tiffin OH U.S.A.
Tiflis Georgia see T'bilisi
115 E3 Tifore i. Maluku Indon.
255 F10 Tifton GA U.S.A.
115 E5 Tifu Buru Indon.
117 K2 Tiga i. Malaysia
100 □5 Tiga i. Îles Loyauté New Caledonia
244 F5 Tigalda Island AK U.S.A.
237 K2 Tigane S. Africa
219 N7 Țigănești Romania
116 E5 Tigapuluh, Pegunungan mts Indon.
142 D5 Tigen Kazakh.
144 I8 Tīgh Āb Iran
158 H8 Tigheciului, Dealurile hills Moldova
158 I7 Tighina Moldova
158 G6 Țîghira Moldova
168 F11 Tighnabruaich Argyll and Bute, Scotland U.K.
143 T2 Tigiretskiy Khrebet mts Kazakh./Rus. Fed.
139 J9 Tigiria Orissa India
213 J4 Tignale Italy
229 I5 Tignère Cameroon
182 J6 Tignes France
249 H4 Tignish P.E.I. Can.
161 O2 Tigoda r. Rus. Fed.
228 D2 Tigoumatene well Mali
Tigranocerta Turkey see Siirt
232 C1 Tigray admin. reg. Eth.
285 H4 Tigre Arg.
274 C6 Tigre r. Ecuador/Peru
269 J3 Tigre r. Mex.
269 H2 Tigre, Cerro del mt. Mex.
284 C2 Tigre, Sierra mts Arg.
149 M8 Tigris r. Asia
alt. Dicle (Turkey),
alt. Dijlah, Nahr (Iraq/Syria)
145 M3 Tigrovaya Balka Zapovednik nature res. Tajik.
227 F4 Tiguelguemine well Alg.
228 B2 Tiguent Maur.
226 C4 Tiguesmat hills Maur.
224 C5 Tigui Chad
229 G2 Tiguidit, Falaise de esc. Niger
228 D2 Tiguîguil well Maur.
227 H6 Tiguir well Niger
178 D8 Tigy France
226 C3 Tigzerte, Oued watercourse Morocco
225 G2 Tīh, Jabal at plat. Egypt
146 F7 Tihāmat 'Asīr reg. Saudi Arabia
199 G5 Tihany Hungary
199 G5 Tihany park Hungary
227 F4 Tihatimine well Alg.
227 G4 Tihodaïne, Erg des. Alg.
269 J5 Tihuatlán Mex.
276 D3 Tijamuchi r. Bol.
138 F6 Tijara Rajasthan India
238 □3d Tijarafe La Palma Canary Is
224 A1 Tījī Libya
226 B5 Tijirît reg. Maur.
186 I2 Tijnje Neth.
207 O6 Tíjola Spain
266 A1 Tijuana Mex.
279 C8 Tijucas Brazil
279 C8 Tijucas, Baía de b. Brazil
280 B3 Tijuco r. Brazil
Tika i. Îles Loyauté New Caledonia see Tiga
267 O9 Tikal tourist site Guat.
267 O9 Tikal, Parque Nacional nat. park Guat.
138 G7 Tikamgarh Madh. Prad. India
132 H6 Tikanlik Xinjiang China
244 H4 Tikchik Lakes AK U.S.A.
159 S3 Tikhaya Sosna r. Rus. Fed.
Tikherón Greece see Tychero
161 V3 Tikhmenevo Rus. Fed.
161 T7 Tikhonova Pustyn' Rus. Fed.
157 H7 Tikhoretsk Rus. Fed.
162 U4 Tikhtozero Rus. Fed.
161 Q2 Tikhvin Rus. Fed.
161 Q2 Tikhvinka r. Rus. Fed.
161 Q2 Tikhvinskaya Gryada ridge Rus. Fed.
291 K7 Tiki Basin sea feature Pacific Ocean
229 G2 Tikiktene well Niger
Tikirarjuaq Nunavut Can. see Whale Cove
102 M4 Tikitiki North I. N.Z.
101 □7a Tikituru mt. Viti Levu Fiji
162 R5 Tikkakoski Fin.
160 I1 Tikkurila Fin.
151 F6 Tīkmeh-ye Bālā Iran
102 K6 Tikokino North I. N.Z.
99 G3 Tikopia i. Solomon Is
149 K6 Tikrīt Iraq
138 F2 Tikse Jammu and Kashmir India
162 V3 Tikshozero, Ozero l. Rus. Fed.
153 N2 Tiksi Rus. Fed.
Tikumbia i. Fiji see Cikobia
Tikus i. Cocos Is see Direction Island
219 J9 Tikveš Ezero l. Macedonia
237 J3 Tikwana S. Africa
138 H5 Tila r. Nepal
139 J7 Tilaiya Reservoir India
284 B3 Tilama Chile
115 C3 Tilamuta Sulawesi Indon.
144 F3 Tilavar Iran
150 F2 Tilbeşar Ovasi plain Turkey
107 J9 Tilbooroo Qld Austr.
186 H5 Tilburg Neth.
251 L7 Tilbury Ont. Can.
173 M5 Tilbury Thurrock, England U.K.
282 D1 Tilcara Arg.
104 H3 Tilcha (abandoned) S.A. Austr.
104 H3 Tilcha Creek watercourse S.A. Austr.
182 G1 Til-Châtel France
261 F11 Tilden TX U.S.A.
219 K3 Tileagd Romania
173 J5 Tilehurst Reading, England U.K.
143 M2 Tilekey Kazakh.
229 G3 Tilemsès Niger
229 F2 Tîlemsi, Vallée du watercourse Mali
257 I10 Tilghman MD U.S.A.
185 C8 Tilh France
138 G6 Tilhar Uttar Prad. India
227 F4 Tilia, Oued watercourse Alg.
139 I5 Tilicho Lake l. Nepal
Tiligulo-Berezanka Ukr. see Berezanka
Tilimsen Alg. see Tlemcen
118 B4 Tilin Myanmar
284 E3 Tilisarao Arg.
171 M2 Till r. England U.K.
229 F3 Tillabéri Niger
229 F3 Tillabéri dept Niger
185 E9 Tillac France
262 C4 Tillamook OR U.S.A.
137 M8 Tillanchong Island Andaman & Nicobar Is India
182 G2 Tille r. France
193 D8 Tilleda (Kyffhäuser) Ger.
247 I5 Tilley Alta Can.
229 G2 Tillia Niger
168 I10 Tillicoultry Clackmannanshire, Scotland U.K.
178 B6 Tillières-sur-Avre France
178 I5 Tilloy-et-Bellay France
248 D5 Tillsonburg Ont. Can.
168 K8 Tillyfourie Aberdeenshire, Scotland U.K.
181 J3 Tilly-sur-Seulles France
229 F3 Tiloa Niger
Tilogne Senegal see Thilogne
276 C5 Tilomonte Chile
138 E6 Tilonia Rajasthan India
221 I6 Tilos i. Greece
139 J7 Tilothu Bihar India
105 J4 Tilpa N.S.W. Austr.
227 F2 Tilrhemt Alg.
160 K5 Tilsa r. Latvia
Tilsit Rus. Fed. see Sovetsk
171 L7 Tilston Cheshire, England U.K.
168 I9 Tilt r. Scotland U.K.
284 B3 Tiltil Chile
156 M2 Til'tim Rus. Fed.
257 N5 Tilton NH U.S.A.
115 B4 Tilu, Bukit mt. Indon.
160 K5 Tilža Latvia
157 G6 Tim Rus. Fed.
159 Q1 Tim r. Rus. Fed.
225 F3 Țimā Egypt
225 I6 Timā Yemen
116 □ Timah, Bukit hill Sing.
170 C8 Timahoe Ireland
136 C7 Timakara i. India
277 F5 Timane r. Para.
238 □3c Timanfaya vol. Lanzarote Canary Is
238 □3c Timanfaya, Parque Nacional de nat. park Lanzarote Canary Is
156 J2 Timanskiy Kryazh ridge Rus. Fed.
149 K4 Timar Turkey
103 F11 Timaru South I. N.Z.
142 D1 Timashevo Rus. Fed.
157 G7 Timashevsk Rus. Fed.
Timashevskaya Rus. Fed. see Timashevsk
213 O2 Timau Italy
Timbákion Kriti Greece see Tympaki
261 J11 Timbalier Bay LA U.S.A.
278 G3 Timbaúba Brazil
228 C2 Timbedgha Maur.
106 C3 Timber Creek N.T. Austr.
260 E3 Timber Lake SD U.S.A.
265 P4 Timber Mountain NV U.S.A.
256 G10 Timberville VA U.S.A.
274 B4 Timbiquí Col.
228 C4 Timbo Guinea
105 I8 Timboon Vic. Austr.
235 H3 Timbué, Ponta pt Moz.
Timbuktu Mali see Tombouctou
117 M2 Timbun Mata i. Malaysia
201 I3 Timelkam Austria
229 E2 Timétrine Mali
228 E2 Timétrine reg. Mali
Tímfi mts Greece see Tymfi
227 G2 Timgad tourist site Alg.
229 H2 Timia Niger
227 F5 Timiaouine Alg.
227 F3 Timimoun Alg.
220 F2 Timiou Prodromou, Akrotirio pt Greece
228 A2 Timirist, Râs pt Maur.
143 L1 Timiryazev Kazakh.
143 L1 Timiryazevo Kazakh.
199 K6 Timiș county Romania
219 I5 Timiș r. Romania
Timiskaming, Lake Ont./Que. Can. see Témiscamingue, Lac
218 J5 Timișoara Romania
218 I5 Timișului, Câmpia plain Romania
Timkovichi Belarus see Tsimkavichy
229 G2 Ti-m-Meghsoi watercourse Niger
200 D6 Timmelsjoch pass Austria/Italy
190 K3 Timmendorfer Strand Ger.
248 D3 Timmins Ont. Can.
250 D4 Timms Hill WI U.S.A.
Timoé atoll Arch. des Tuamotu Fr. Polynesia see Temoe
219 K6 Timok r. Serbia
161 T2 Timokhino Rus. Fed.
169 E9 Timoleague Ireland
278 E3 Timon Brazil
214 H3 Timone r. Italy
258 B6 Timonium MD U.S.A.
115 E8 Timor i. Indon.
98 C3 Timor Sea Austr./Indon.
Timor Timur country Asia see East Timor
161 T1 Timoshino Rus. Fed.
285 F4 Timote Arg.
281 F3 Timóteo Brazil
227 E3 Timoudi Alg.
115 D4 Timpaus i. Indon.
109 G8 Timperley Range hills W.A. Austr.
163 N5 Timrå Sweden
150 A8 Timsāḥ, Buḥayrat at l. Egypt
172 H5 Timsbury Bath and North East Somerset, England U.K.
255 D8 Tims Ford Lake TN U.S.A.
168 B6 Timsgearraidh Western Isles, Scotland U.K.
156 K3 Timsher Rus. Fed.
156 K3 Timsher r. Rus. Fed.
143 M6 Timur Kazakh.
138 F8 Timurni Muafi Madh. Prad. India
146 F2 Tīn, Jabal hill Saudi Arabia
224 D1 Tīn, Ra's at pt Libya
213 L2 Tina r. Italy
237 N7 Tina r. S. Africa
228 E2 Ti-n-Aba well Mali
150 G2 Tīnah Syria
150 A7 Ţīnah, Khalīj aṭ b. Egypt
170 E8 Tinahely Ireland
205 O8 Tinajas Spain
238 □3c Tinajo Lanzarote Canary Is
204 E9 Tinalhas Port.
224 A3 Tin Alkoum Libya
229 F2 Ti-n-Amâssine well Mali
227 G5 Tin Amzi, Oued watercourse Alg.
274 D2 Tinaquillo Venez.
229 F2 Ti-n-Azabo well Mali
226 C5 Ti-n-Bessaïs well Maur.
228 E2 Ti-n-Boukri well Mali
199 K5 Tinca Romania
107 N8 Tin Can Bay Qld Austr.
181 J4 Tinchebray France
227 E5 Ti-n-Didine well Mali
136 F6 Tindivanam Tamil Nadu India
226 C4 Tindouf Alg.
166 D1 Tindur hill Faroe Is
224 D6 Tiné Chad
228 E2 Ti-n-Echeri well Mali
228 E2 Ti-n-Edrine well Mali
183 K9 Tinée r. France
204 H2 Tineo Spain
229 F3 Ti-n-Eratilene well Mali
226 D3 Tinerhir Morocco
229 F2 Ti-n-Essako Mali
228 E2 Ti-n-Etissane well Mali
226 D3 Tinfouchy Alg.
173 J4 Tingewick Buckinghamshire, England U.K.
116 F3 Tinggi i. Malaysia
224 A2 Tingharat, Hammādat des. Libya
228 C4 Tingi Mountains Sierra Leone
Tingis Morocco see Tanger
131 K6 Ting Jiang r. China
118 C1 Tingkawk Sakan Myanmar
164 F7 Tinglev Denmark
276 B2 Tingo María Peru
Tingrela Côte d'Ivoire see Tengréla
133 H12 Tingri Xizang China
165 K5 Tingsryd Sweden
165 O4 Tingstäde Gotland Sweden
165 O4 Tingstädeträsk l. Gotland Sweden
268 E6 Tingüindín Mex.
284 B4 Tinguiririca Chile
284 B4 Tinguiririca, Volcán vol. Chile
164 D3 Tingvatn Norway
162 J5 Tingvoll Norway
168 J4 Tingwall Orkney, Scotland U.K.
Tingzhou Fujian China see Changting
278 F5 Tinharé, Ilha de i. Brazil
204 F6 Tinhela r. Port.
118 G5 Tinh Gia Vietnam
113 K4 Tinian i. N. Mariana Is
228 B2 Tiniéré well Maur.
274 C4 Tinigua, Parque Nacional nat. park Col.
Tini Heke is N.Z. see Snares Islands
102 L5 Tiniroto North I. N.Z.
210 G3 Tinja r. Bos.-Herz.
213 P5 Tinjan Croatia
117 K2 Tinjar r. Malaysia
116 F8 Tinjil i. Indon.
228 C4 Tinkisso r. Guinea
159 L4 Tin'ky Ukr.
103 H9 Tinline, Mount South I. N.Z.
227 H5 Ti-n-Merzouga des. Alg.
164 E2 Tinn Norway
164 F2 Tinne r. Norway
Tinnelvelly Tamil Nadu India see Tirunelveli
164 E2 Tinnsjo l. Norway
199 H4 Tinnye Hungary
212 H7 Tino, Isola del i. Italy
285 F2 Tinoco Arg.
282 D3 Tinogasta Arg.
115 B3 Tinompo Sulawesi Indon.
220 G5 Tinos Tinos Greece
220 G5 Tinos i. Greece
207 K6 Tiñosa mt. Spain
205 K7 Tiñosillos Spain
209 C12 Tiñoso, Cabo c. Spain
178 G5 Tinqueux France
227 G5 Ti-n-Rerhoh well Alg.
227 G3 Tinrhert, Hamada de Alg.
131 □I7 Tin Shui Wai H.K. China
229 F2 Ti-n-Srir well Mali
139 O6 Tinsukia Assam India
246 E4 Tintagel B.C. Can.
172 C6 Tintagel Cornwall, England U.K.
228 C2 Țințâne Maur.
227 G5 Ti-n-Tarabine well Alg.
227 G5 Ti-n-Tarabine, Oued watercourse Alg.
228 E2 Ti-n-Tehoun well Mali
227 F4 Tintejert, Adrar mt. Alg.
180 H5 Tinténiac France
172 G4 Tintern Parva Monmouthshire, Wales U.K.
229 F2 Ti-n-Tersi well Mali
187 I9 Tintigny Belgium
282 E2 Tintina Arg.
104 H6 Tintinara S.A. Austr.
206 F6 Tinto r. Spain
171 J2 Tinto hill Scotland U.K.
Tin Tounnant well Mali see Taounnant
103 K7 Tinui North I. N.Z.
159 M9 Tinyste Ukr.
229 F2 Ti-n-Zaouâtene Mali
260 D1 Tioga ND U.S.A.
256 H7 Tioga PA U.S.A.
256 H6 Tioga r. PA U.S.A.
258 A1 Tioga County county PA U.S.A.
116 F3 Tioman i. Malaysia
251 L1 Tionaga Ont. Can.
213 K5 Tione r. Italy
213 J3 Tione di Trento Italy
256 F7 Tionesta PA U.S.A.
228 C3 Tioribougou Mali
228 E3 Tiou Burkina
227 E5 Tiouararène well Mali
257 J6 Tioughnioga r. NY U.S.A.
227 F1 Tipasa Alg.
Tiphsah Syria see Dibsī
266 □P11 Tipitapa Nic.
250 F4 Tipler WI U.S.A.
254 D5 Tippecanoe r. IN U.S.A.
169 F8 Tipperary Ireland
169 G7 Tipperary county Ireland
139 K6 Tiptala Bhanjyang pass Nepal
264 M5 Tipton CA U.S.A.
260 J5 Tipton IA U.S.A.
260 I6 Tipton MO U.S.A.
265 R6 Tipton, Mount AZ U.S.A.
261 K7 Tiptonville TN U.S.A.
256 D11 Tiptop VA U.S.A.
248 C3 Tip Top Hill Ont. Can.
173 N4 Tiptree Essex, England U.K.
136 E6 Tiptur Karnataka India
Tipturi Karnataka India see Tiptur
276 C3 Tipuani Bol.
268 G7 Tiquicheo Mex.
274 D4 Tiquié r. Brazil
267 N10 Tiquisate Guat.
278 D3 Tiracambu, Serra do hills Brazil
227 F5 Tirahart, Oued watercourse Alg.
144 D5 Tīrān Iran
146 B2 Tīrān i. Saudi Arabia
Tirana Albania see Tiranë
218 H9 Tiranë Albania
183 D6 Tiranges France
212 I3 Tirano Italy
229 G2 Tiraouene well Niger
139 O6 Tirap Arun. Prad. India
146 F2 Ţirāq, Jāl aṭ hills Saudi Arabia
228 E2 Tiraraouine well Mali
104 G2 Tirari Desert S.A. Austr.
158 I7 Tiraspol Moldova
102 J4 Tirau North I. N.Z.
102 K7 Tiraumea North I. N.Z.
234 C5 Tiraz Mountains Namibia
221 I4 Tire Turkey
199 L4 Tiream Romania
168 C10 Tiree i. Scotland U.K.
227 F5 Tirek well Alg.
227 F5 Tirest well Mali
168 C7 Tirga Mòr hill Scotland U.K.
205 O3 Tirgo Spain
Tîrgoviște Romania see Târgoviște
Tîrgu Bujor Romania see Târgu Bujor
Tîrgu Cărbunești Romania see Târgu Cărbunești
Tîrgu Frumos Romania see Târgu Frumos
Tîrgu Jiu Romania see Târgu Jiu
Tîrgu Lăpuș Romania see Târgu Lăpuș
Tîrgu Mureș Romania see Târgu Mureș
Tîrgu Neamț Romania see Târgu Neamț
Tîrgu Ocna Romania see Târgu Ocna
Tîrgu Secuiesc Romania see Târgu Secuiesc
138 G3 Tiri Jammu and Kashmir India
145 L7 Tiri Pak.
145 N3 Tirich Mir mt. Pak.
207 O3 Tiriez Spain
208 F7 Tírig Spain
217 L6 Tiriolo Italy
268 F6 Tiripetío Mex.
227 H5 Tiririne, Oued watercourse Alg.
226 C5 Tiris Zemmour admin. reg. Maur.
160 F5 Tirkšliai Lith.
Tirlemont Belgium see Tienen
142 H1 Tirlyanskiy Rus. Fed.
136 E3 Tirna r. India
Tîrnăveni Romania see Târnăveni
Tírnavos Greece see Tyrnavos
Tîrnova Romania see Târnova
207 I3 Tiro hill Spain
138 G9 Tirodi Madh. Prad. India
200 D5 Tirol land Austria
205 O3 Tirón r. Spain
102 J4 Tironia North I. N.Z.
281 E3 Tiros Brazil
230 D2 Tiroungoulou C.A.R.
193 F10 Tirpersdorf Ger.
212 I8 Tirrenia Italy
Tirreno, Mare sea France/Italy see Tyrrhenian Sea
195 M2 Tirschenreuth Ger.
214 B8 Tirso r. Sardegna Italy
164 G5 Tirstrup Denmark
207 K3 Tirteafuera Spain
207 K3 Tirteafuera r. Spain
136 D6 Tirthahalli Karnataka India
139 K9 Tirtol Orissa India
136 F8 Tiruchchendur Tamil Nadu India
136 F7 Tiruchchirappalli Tamil Nadu India
136 E7 Tiruchengodu Tamil Nadu India
136 F7 Tirukkoyilur Tamil Nadu India
136 F8 Tirumangalam Tamil Nadu India
136 E8 Tirunelveli Tamil Nadu India
276 B1 Tiruntán Peru
136 F6 Tirupati Andhra Prad. India
136 F6 Tiruppattur Tamil Nadu India
136 F7 Tiruppattur Tamil Nadu India
136 E7 Tiruppur Tamil Nadu India
136 F6 Tiruttani Andhra Prad. India
136 F7 Tirutturaippundi Tamil Nadu India
136 F6 Tiruvallur Tamil Nadu India
136 F6 Tiruvannamalai Tamil Nadu India
136 F6 Tiruvettipuram Tamil Nadu India
136 G6 Tiruvottiyur Tamil Nadu India
108 H6 Tiru Well W.A. Austr.
220 E5 Tiryns tourist site Greece
160 J4 Tirza r. Latvia
219 J7 Tisa r. Serbia
alt. Tisza (Hungary),
alt. Tysa (Ukraine)
136 E8 Tisaiyanvilai Tamil Nadu India
165 L2 Tisaren l. Sweden
219 O5 Tisău Romania
172 H5 Tisbury Wiltshire, England U.K.
238 □3b Tiscamanita Fuerteventura Canary Is
207 M5 Tiscar, Puerto de pass Spain
247 J4 Tisdale Sask. Can.
261 G8 Tishomingo OK U.S.A.
197 I1 Tishono Rus. Fed.
193 K10 Tišice Czech Rep.
150 E6 Ţīsīyah Syria
227 H5 Tiska, Mont mt. Alg.
165 L3 Tisnaren l. Sweden
198 F2 Tišnov Czech Rep.
199 I3 Tisovec Slovakia
136 G9 Tissamaharama Sri Lanka
227 F2 Tissemsilt Alg.
214 B6 Tissi Sardegna Italy
139 L7 Tista r. India
199 J5 Tisza r. Hungary
alt. Tisa (Serbia),
alt. Tysa (Ukraine)
199 I5 Tiszaalpár Hungary
199 L3 Tiszabecs Hungary
199 L3 Tiszabezdéd Hungary
199 J4 Tiszabő Hungary
199 J4 Tiszabura Hungary
199 K4 Tiszacsege Hungary
199 J4 Tiszaderzs Hungary
199 K3 Tiszadob Hungary
199 K3 Tiszadobi arter nature res. Hungary
199 K3 Tiszaeszlár Hungary
199 J5 Tiszaföldvár Hungary
199 J4 Tiszafüred Hungary
199 J4 Tiszafüredi Madárrezervátum nature res. Hungary
199 J4 Tiszaigar Hungary
199 J4 Tiszajenő Hungary
199 K3 Tiszakarád Hungary
199 J5 Tiszakécske Hungary
199 L3 Tiszakerecseny Hungary
199 J4 Tiszakeszi Hungary
199 K3 Tiszalök Hungary
199 K3 Tiszalúc Hungary
199 K3 Tiszanagyfalu Hungary
199 J4 Tiszanána Hungary
199 J5 Tiszántúl reg. Hungary
199 J4 Tiszaörs Hungary
199 J4 Tiszapüspöki Hungary
199 J4 Tiszaroff Hungary
199 J5 Tiszasas Hungary
199 L3 Tiszaszentmárton Hungary
199 J5 Tiszasziget Hungary
199 K3 Tiszatelek Hungary
199 K3 Tiszatelek-Tiszabercel nature res. Hungary
199 J4 Tiszatenyő Hungary
199 J5 Tiszaug Hungary
199 K4 Tiszaújváros Hungary
199 K4 Tiszavasvári Hungary
227 F4 Tit Adrar Alg.
227 G5 Tit Tamanrasset Alg.
139 O6 Titabar Assam India
209 C8 Titaguas Spain
244 I1 Titaluk r. AK U.S.A.
287 K1 Titan Dome ice feature Antarctica
228 E3 Titao Burkina
159 T4 Titarevka Rus. Fed.
220 D3 Titarisios r. Greece
153 N2 Tit-Ary Rus. Fed.
Titawin Morocco see Tétouan
228 B4 Tite Guinea-Bissau
218 I5 Titel Vojvodina Serbia
215 M5 Titerno r. Italy
145 O4 Tithwal Pak.
276 C3 Titicaca, Lago l. Bol./Peru
Titicaca, Lake Bol./Peru see Titicaca, Lago
259 H2 Titicus CT U.S.A.
103 B14 Titi Islands Stewart I. N.Z.
103 □3 Titikaveka Rarotonga Cook Is
194 E6 Titisee Ger.
Tititea mt. South I. N.Z. see Aspiring, Mount
139 I9 Titlagarh Orissa India
212 E2 Titlis mt. Switz.
215 P6 Tito Italy
Titograd Podgorica Montenegro see Podgorica
210 E3 Titova Korenica Croatia
Titova Mitrovica Mitrovicë Kosovo see Mitrovicë
162 U2 Titovka r. Rus. Fed.
Titovo Užice Užice Serbia see Užice
Titovo Velenje Slovenia see Velenje
Titov Veles Macedonia see Veles
Titov Vrbas Vojvodina Serbia see Vrbas
162 J5 Titran Norway
106 D7 Ti Tree N.T. Austr.
251 K6 Tittabawassee r. MI U.S.A.
195 K4 Titting Ger.
195 O4 Tittling Ger.
195 N5 Tittmoning Ger.
219 N6 Titu Romania
205 M8 Titulcia Spain
230 E4 Titule Dem. Rep. Congo
255 G11 Titusville FL U.S.A.
256 F7 Titusville PA U.S.A.
131 □J7 Tiu Chung Chau i. H.K. China
168 D6 Tiumpan Head Scotland U.K.
233 C5 Tiva watercourse Kenya
138 D6 Tivari Rajasthan India
218 G8 Tivat Tivat Montenegro
165 K3 Tiveden nationalpark nat. park Sweden
208 G6 Tivenys Spain
251 M5 Tiverton Ont. Can.
172 F6 Tiverton Devon, England U.K.
Tivisa Spain see Tivissa
208 G5 Tivissa Spain
215 J4 Tivoli Italy
230 D2 Tiwal, Wadi watercourse Sudan
276 C4 Tiwanaku tourist site Bol.
147 N4 Ţīwī Oman
106 C1 Tiwi Aboriginal Land res. N.T. Austr.
115 C6 Tiworo, Selat sea chan. Indon.
267 O7 Tixkokob Mex.
269 H8 Tixtla Mex.
232 C2 Tiya tourist site Eth.
150 F4 Tiyās Syria
268 D5 Tizapán el Alto Mex.
269 I6 Tizayuca Mex.
267 O7 Tizimín Mex.
227 G1 Tizi Ouzou Alg.
133 C7 Tiznap He r. China
226 C3 Tiznit Morocco
266 H5 Tizoc Mex.
226 E2 Tiztoutine Morocco
214 B4 Tizzano Corse France
162 O3 Tjaktjajaure l. Sweden
165 L3 Tjällmo Sweden
162 O3 Tjåmotis Sweden
237 P1 Tjaneni Swaziland
162 O4 Tjappsåive Sweden
162 M4 Tjärmyrberget Sweden
162 P3 Tjautas Sweden
162 N3 Tjeggelvas l. Sweden
166 J1 Tjeldstø Norway
186 I3 Tjeukemeer l. Neth.
Tjirebon Jawa Indon. see Cirebon
109 H8 Tjirrkarli Aboriginal Reserve W.A. Austr.
Tjolotjo Zimbabwe see Tsholotsho
164 G2 Tjøme Norway
163 I7 Tjorhom Norway
164 H3 Tjörn i. Sweden
162 □E1 Tjörnes pen. Iceland
162 L4 Tjøtta Norway
Tjumen' Rus. Fed. see Tyumen'
165 K5 Tjurken l. Sweden
162 □ Tjuvfjorden b. Svalbard
Tkibuli Georgia see Tqibuli
Tkvarcheli Georgia see Tqvarch'eli
268 E4 Tlachichila Mex.
269 I5 Tlachichilo Mex.
269 I8 Tlacoapa Mex.
269 K9 Tlacolula Mex.
269 L9 Tlacolulita Mex.
269 L7 Tlacotalpán Mex.
269 H6 Tlacotenco Mex.
269 H8 Tlacotepec Mex.
268 G8 Tlacotepec, Cerro mt. Mex.
269 I5 Tlacuilotepec Mex.
266 H4 Tlahualilo Mex.
269 I6 Tlahuapan Mex.
268 D5 Tlajomulco Mex.
268 G7 Tlalchapa Mex.
269 J6 Tlalchichuca Mex.
269 K7 Tlalixcoyan Mex.
269 I8 Tlalixtaquilla Mex.
269 I6 Tlalmanalco Mex.
269 H6 Tlalnepantla Mex.
269 H6 Tlálpan Mex.
268 G6 Tlalpujahua Mex.
268 D4 Tlaltenango de Sánchez Román Mex.
269 H7 Tlaltizapan Mex.
269 I7 Tlancualpican Mex.
269 I8 Tlapa Mex.
269 J6 Tlapacoyan Mex.
269 I7 Tlapaneco r. Mex.
268 G7 Tlapehuala Mex.
268 D5 Tlaquepaque Mex.
269 J7 Tlaquilpa Mex.
269 I6 Tlaxcala Mex.
269 I6 Tlaxcala state Mex.
269 I6 Tlaxco Mex.
269 H5 Tlaxcoapán Mex.
269 J8 Tlaxiaco Mex.
245 O5 Tl'ell B.C. Can.
227 E2 Tlemcen Alg.
196 G2 Tleń Pol.
202 D5 Tleta Rissana Morocco
237 K2 Tlhabologang S. Africa
236 H4 Tlhakalatlou S. Africa
236 I2 Tlhakgameng S. Africa
237 M4 Tlholong S. Africa
199 H3 Tlmače Slovakia
151 H3 Tlokh Rus. Fed.
234 E5 Tlokweng Botswana
197 H3 Tłuchowo Pol.
195 O2 Tlučná Czech Rep.
158 E5 Tlumach Ukr.
196 F6 Tlumačov Czech Rep.
197 J3 Tłuszcz Pol.
151 H3 Tlyadal Rus. Fed.
151 H3 Tlyarata Rus. Fed.
159 S9 Tlyustenkhabl' Rus. Fed.
161 S5 T'ma r. Rus. Fed.
224 B3 Tmassah Libya
226 B5 Tmeïmîchât Maur.
119 G9 Tnaôt, Prêk r. Cambodia
158 G3 Tnya r. Ukr.
118 C6 To r. Myanmar
270 F3 Toa r. Cuba
271 □1 Toa Alta Puerto Rico
168 □N3 Toab Shetland, Scotland U.K.
271 □1 Toa Baja Puerto Rico
246 E3 Toad r. B.C. Can.
246 E3 Toad River B.C. Can.
114 □ Toagel Mlungui Palau
199 I4 Tóalmás Hungary
235 □K3 Toamasina Madag.
235 □K3 Toamasina prov. Madag.
169 E9 Toames Ireland
265 R1 Toana mts NV U.S.A.
213 J7 Toano Italy
256 I11 Toano VA U.S.A.
101 □9a Toanoano Tahiti Fr. Polynesia
116 □ Toa Payoh Sing.
256 E12 Toast NC U.S.A.
102 L5 Toatoa North I. N.Z.
225 G4 To Awai well Sudan
284 E5 Toay Arg.
130 A3 Toba Xizang China
191 K8 Toba Ger.
126 E7 Toba Japan
116 C3 Toba, Danau l. Indon.
Toba, Lake Indon. see Toba, Danau
145 L6 Toba and Kakar Ranges mts P
271 □5 Tobago i. Trin. and Tob.
246 E5 Toba Inlet B.C. Can.
235 F4 Tobane Botswana
207 P3 Tobarra Spain
282 E3 Tobas Arg.
145 O6 Toba Tek Singh Pak.
201 L6 Tobelbad Austria
115 E3 Tobelo Halmahera Indon.
169 E4 Tobercurry Ireland
169 I3 Tobermore Northern Ireland U
106 F7 Tobermorey N.T. Austr.
107 I9 Tobermory Qld Austr.
248 D4 Tobermory Ont. Can.
168 D9 Tobermory Argyll and Bute, Scotland U.K.
168 E10 Toberonochy Argyll and Bute, Scotland U.K.
124 S3 Tōbetsu Japan
113 H6 Tobi i. Palau
231 B7 Tobias Angola
278 F4 Tobias Barreto Brazil
243 Q2 Tobias Ø i. Greenland
125 □3 Tobiishi-hana c. Iō-jima Japa
108 H6 Tobin, Lake salt flat W.A. Aus
264 O1 Tobin, Mount NV U.S.A.
247 K4 Tobin Lake Sask. Can.
249 H4 Tobique r. N.B. Can.
126 E5 Tobishima Japan
124 Q7 Tobi-shima i. Japan
116 G6 Toboali Indon.
142 J1 Tobol Kazakh.
141 M2 Tobol r. Kazakh./Rus. Fed.
152 H4 Tobol'sk Rus. Fed.
100 □6 Tobona Island Solomon Is
114 D6 Toboso Negros Phil.
Tobruk Libya see Tubruq
156 K1 Tobseda Rus. Fed.
127 H3 Tōbu Japan
258 E2 Tobyhanna PA U.S.A.
Tobyl Kazakh. see Tobol
Tobyl r. Kazakh./Rus. Fed. see Tobol
Tobylzhan Kazakh. see Tavolz
156 J2 Tobysh r. Rus. Fed.
276 A2 Tocache Nuevo Peru
184 E5 Tocane-St-Apre France
278 D3 Tocantinópolis Brazil
275 G6 Tocantins r. Brazil
275 I5 Tocantins r. Brazil
278 C4 Tocantins state Brazil
255 F8 Toccoa GA U.S.A.
215 L3 Tocco da Casauria Italy
212 E4 Toce r. Italy
204 C8 Tocha Port.
145 N5 Tochi r. Pak.
127 K3 Tochigi Japan
127 J2 Tochigi pref. Japan
269 I7 Tochimizolco Mex.
125 P9 Tochio Japan
164 H2 Töcksfors Sweden
271 □7 Toco Trin. and Tob.
266 □P10 Tocoa Hond.
207 L6 Tocón Spain
276 C5 Tocopilla Chile
276 D5 Tocorpuri, Cerros de mts Bol./Chile
105 J6 Tocumwal N.S.W. Austr.
271 I8 Tocuyo de la Costa Venez.
197 K3 Toczna r. Pol.
246 G5 Tod, Mount B.C. Can.
127 K3 Toda Japan
138 F6 Toda Bhim Rajasthan India
138 E6 Toda Rai Singh Rajasthan In
285 G4 Todd Arg.
106 E8 Todd watercourse N.T. Austr.
173 K4 Toddington Bedfordshire, Eng U.K.
173 I4 Toddington Gloucestershire, England U.K.
257 □S2 Todd Mountain hill N.B. Can
109 I8 Todd Range hills W.A. Austr.
259 H2 Toddville NY U.S.A.
112 F7 Todeli Maluku Indon.
190 J3 Todesfelde Ger.
138 D7 Todgarh Rajasthan India
215 I2 Todi Italy
212 F2 Todi mt. Switz.
171 M6 Todmorden West Yorkshire, England U.K.
132 F4 Todog Xinjiang China
124 T7 Todoga-saki pt Japan
124 S5 Todohokke Japan
Todok Xinjiang China see To
281 G2 Todos os Santos r. Brazil
276 D4 Todos Santos Bol.
266 D6 Todos Santos Mex.
264 P10 Todos Santos, Isla i. Mex.
144 F8 Todrūyeh Iran
194 D6 Todtmoos Ger.
194 D6 Todtnau Ger.
169 D10 Toe Head Ireland
168 B7 Toe Head Scotland U.K.
126 G5 Tōei Japan
118 D7 Toe Jaga, Khao hill Thai.
204 E4 Toén Spain
228 E3 Toéni Burkina
103 C13 Toetoes Bay South I. N.Z.
246 H4 Tofield Alta Can.
246 E5 Tofino B.C. Can.
168 □N2 Toft Shetland, Scotland U.K.
165 L1 Toftan l. Sweden
250 D2 Tofte MN U.S.A.
165 K2 Toften l. Sweden
164 F6 Toftlund Denmark
101 □8 Tofua i. Tonga
126 F3 Toga Japan
256 G11 Toga VA U.S.A.
100 □5 Toga i. Vanuatu
127 L4 Tōgane Japan

E9 Togatax Xinjiang China
C3 Togbo C.A.R.
E2 Togdheer admin. reg. Somalia
G1 Toggenburg reg. Switz.
D9 Togher Cork Ireland
J5 Togher Louth Ireland
G6 Togher Offaly Ireland
E1 Togi Japan
G4 Togiak AK U.S.A.
G4 Togiak r. AK U.S.A.
G4 Togiak Bay AK U.S.A.
H4 Togiak Lake AK U.S.A.
G4 Togiak National Wildlife Refuge nature res. AK U.S.A.
B4 Togian i. Indon.
B4 Togian, Kepulauan is Indon.
N5 Töging am Inn Ger.
Togliatti Rus. Fed. see Tol'yatti
F4 Togo country Africa
F5 Tōgō Aichi Japan
I14 Tōgō Miyazaki Japan
A2 Togo MN U.S.A.
J7 Tograsay He r. China
H4 Tögrög Mongolia
Tögrög Mongolia see Manhan
M6 Togrog Ul Nei Mongol China
N3 Togston Northumberland, England U.K.
L6 Togtoh Nei Mongol China
K9 Togton He r. China
J4 Toguchin Rus. Fed.
H3 Togura Japan
D2 Tog Wajaale Somalia
I4 Togyz Kazakh.
H5 Tohamiyam Sudan
E5 Tohana Haryana India
X6 Tohatchi NM U.S.A.
J4 Tohenbatu mt. Malaysia
□9a Tohiea mt. Moorea Fr. Polynesia
U5 Tohmajärvi Fin.
U5 Tohmajärvi l. Fin.
D5 Tohoku Japan
R5 Toholampi Fin.
I6 Tohom Nei Mongol China
Töhöm Mongolia see Mandah
T9 Tohono O'Odham (Papago) Indian Reservation res. AZ U.S.A.
F5 Tohoun Togo
S5 Toi Hokkaidō Japan
I6 Toi Shizuoka Japan
□2 To'iave'a mt. Samoa
I11 Toiba Xizang China
M7 Toibalewe Andaman & Nicobar Is India
E2 Toide Japan
Q6 Toijala Fin.
C4 Toili Sulawesi Indon.
I15 Toi-misaki pt Japan
□6 Toimonapu P.N.G.
E5 Toin Japan
D9 Toineke Timor Indon.
E7 Toirano Italy
S5 Toivakka Fin.
□4 Toi Village Niue
O2 Toiyabe Range mts NV U.S.A.
B4 Toja Sulawesi Indon.
Tojikiston country Asia see Tajikistan
N2 Tojikobod Tajik.
K12 Tōjō Hiroshima Japan
B6 Tōjō Hyōgo Japan
E1 Tok r. Rus. Fed.
L3 Tok AK U.S.A.
U4 Tokachi-gawa r. Japan
E5 Tōkai Aichi Japan
M3 Tōkai Ibaraki Japan
K3 Tokaj Hungary
K3 Tokaj-Bodrog-Zug park Hungary
B4 Tokala, Gunung mt. Indon.
I1 Tōkamachi Japan
C13 Tokanui South I. N.Z.
H5 Tokar Sudan
E11 Tokarahi South I. N.Z.
□G18 Tokara-rettō is Japan
H6 Tokarevka Rus. Fed.
R1 Tokari Rus. Fed.
I5 Tokarnia Pol.
O8 Tokaryeve Ukr.
□E20 Tokasiki-jima i. Nansei-shotō Japan
H3 Tokat Turkey
H3 Tokatoka North I. N.Z.
I3 Tokatu Point North I. N.Z.
U2 Tokay r. Rus. Fed.
E10 Tŏkchŏk-to i. S. Korea
E9 Tŏkch'ŏn N. Korea
Tokdo i. N. Pacific Ocean see Liancourt Rocks
□1 Tokelau terr. S. Pacific Ocean
T'okhluja Armenia see Drakhtik
Tokhtamysh Tajik. see Tŭkhtamish
F5 Toki Japan
J3 Tokigawa Japan
E5 Toki-gawa r. Japan
Tokkuztara Xinjiang China see Gongliu
J2 Toklat AK U.S.A.
J2 Toklat r. AK U.S.A.
B6 Toklular Turkey
O6 Tokmachka r. Ukr.
Tokmak Kyrg. see Tokmok
O6 Tokmak Ukr.
P6 Tokmok Kyrg.
H4 Tokod Hungary
M5 Tokomaru Bay North I. N.Z.
E6 Tokoname Japan
J5 Tokoroa North I. N.Z.
V2 Tokoro-gawa r. Japan
J4 Tokorozawa Japan
D5 Tokou well Chad
C4 Tokounou Guinea
M2 Tokoza S. Africa
Tokrau watercourse Kazakh. see Tokyrau
F3 Toksook Bay AK U.S.A.
Toksu Xinjiang China see Xinhe
I5 Toksun Xinjiang China
Tok-tō i. N. Pacific Ocean see Liancourt Rocks
O7 Toktogul Kyrg.
Toktogul'skoye Vodokhranilishche resr Kyrg. see Toktogul Suu Saktagychy
O7 Toktogul Suu Saktagychy resr Kyrg.
Tokto-ri i. N. Pacific Ocean see Liancourt Rocks
T5 Tokty Kazakh.
I3 Tokū i. Tonga
□8 Tokulu atoll Tonga
□G19 Tokunoshima Nansei-shotō Japan
□F19 Toku-no-shima i. Nansei-shotō Japan
H2 Tokur Rus. Fed.
A7 Tokushima Japan
L13 Tokushima pref. Japan
I12 Tokuyama Japan
Tokwe r. Zimbabwe see Tugwi
K4 Tōkyō Japan
J5 Tōkyō mun. Japan
K4 Tōkyō-wan b. Japan
P4 Tokyrau watercourse Kazakh.
E11 Tokyu-san National Park S. Korea
L4 Tokzār Afgh.
□4a Tol i. Chuuk Micronesia
M5 Tolaga Bay North I. N.Z.
□J5 Tôlañaro Madag.
D2 Tolar, Cerro mt. Arg.
D6 Tolastadh Úr Western Isles, Scotland U.K.
K7 Tolbaños Spain
F1 Tolbazy Rus. Fed.
J2 Tolbert Neth.
B2 Tolbo Mongolia
Tolbukhin Bulg. see Dobrich
X4 Tolbukhino Rus. Fed.
D2 Tolbuzino Rus. Fed.
T1 Tolchin, Mount Antarctica
K3 Tolcsva Hungary
□S13 Tolé Panama
O6 Tole Bi Kazakh.
C6 Toledo Amazonas Brazil
279 B8 Toledo Paraná Brazil
282 C2 Toledo Chile
205 L9 Toledo Spain
205 L9 Toledo prov. Spain
260 I5 Toledo IA U.S.A.
260 K6 Toledo IL U.S.A.
256 B7 Toledo OH U.S.A.
262 C4 Toledo OR U.S.A.
205 K9 Toledo, Montes de mts Spain
261 I10 Toledo Bend Reservoir LA/TX U.S.A.
213 O9 Tolentino Italy
Toletum Spain see Toledo
214 H3 Tolfa Italy
107 J4 Tolga Qld Austr.
163 K5 Tolga Norway
284 B6 Tolhuaca, Parque Nacional nat. park Chile
132 F4 Toli Xinjiang China
235 □I4 Toliara Madag.
235 □J4 Toliara prov. Madag.
274 C4 Tolima dept Col.
268 D6 Tolimán Jalisco Mex.
269 H5 Tolimán Querétaro Mex.
115 B3 Tolitoli Sulawesi Indon.
190 I1 Tolk Ger.
152 J3 Tol'ka Rus. Fed.
164 I4 Tolken l. Sweden
165 P7 Tolkmicko Pol.
186 I3 Tollebeek Neth.
192 H3 Tollense r. Ger.
192 H4 Tollensesee l. Ger.
192 H4 Tollensesee-Becken park Ger.
173 N4 Tollesbury Essex, England U.K.
173 N4 Tolleshunt D'Arcy Essex, England U.K.
265 T8 Tolleson AZ U.S.A.
142 K8 Tollimarjon Uzbek.
215 M3 Tollo Italy
164 H6 Tølløse Denmark
160 M3 Tolmachevo Rus. Fed.
213 O3 Tolmezzo Italy
210 D2 Tolmin Slovenia
199 H5 Tolna Hungary
199 H5 Tolna county Hungary
199 H5 Tolnai-hegyhát hills Hungary
199 H5 Tolnanémedi Hungary
230 C5 Tolo Dem. Rep. Congo
266 □P10 Toloa Creek Hond.
Tolo Channel H.K. China see Chek Mun Hoi Hap
Tolochin Belarus see Talachyn
Tolo Harbour b. H.K. China see Tai Po Hoi
162 S2 Tolonen Fin.
115 F3 Tolonuu i. Maluku Indon.
Tolosa France see Toulouse
206 D2 Tolosa Port.
208 A1 Tolosa Spain
245 J2 Tolovana r. AK U.S.A.
207 J7 Tolox Spain
161 Y4 Tolpygino Rus. Fed.
123 E11 Tolsan-do i. S. Korea
251 K4 Tolsmaville Ont. Can.
168 D6 Tolsta Head Scotland U.K.
153 Q4 Tolstoy, Mys c. Rus. Fed.
283 B5 Toltén Chile
274 C2 Tolú Col.
269 H6 Toluca Mex.
208 G3 Tolva Spain
162 U3 Tolvand, Ozero l. Rus. Fed.
215 Q6 Tolve Italy
215 Q6 Tolve r. Italy
157 J5 Tol'yatti Rus. Fed.
185 E7 Tolzac r. France
122 E3 Tom' r. Rus. Fed.
228 E3 Toma Burkina
126 B7 Tomaga-shima i. Japan
126 A7 Tomagashima-suidō sea chan. Japan
250 D6 Tomah WI U.S.A.
250 E4 Tomahawk WI U.S.A.
159 N6 Tomakivka r. Ukr.
124 S4 Tomakomai Japan
264 J3 Tomales CA U.S.A.
124 S2 Tomamae Japan
117 K2 Tomani Sabah Malaysia
101 □7a Tomanivi mt. Viti Levu Fiji
275 F5 Tomar Brazil
204 D9 Tomar Port.
124 R3 Tomari Japan
122 M5 Tomari Sakhalin Rus. Fed.
151 E5 Tomarlı Turkey
220 B3 Tomaros mt. Greece
159 P3 Tomarovka Rus. Fed.
148 G4 Tomarza Turkey
276 D4 Tomás Barron Bol.
285 I2 Tomás Gomensoro Uru.
158 G2 Tomashhorod Rivnens'ka Oblast' Ukr.
158 G2 Tomashhorod Rivnens'ka Oblast' Ukr.
158 H5 Tomashpil' Ukr.
198 G3 Tomášov Slovakia
199 I3 Tomášovce Slovakia
197 L5 Tomaszów Lubelski Pol.
197 I4 Tomaszów Mazowiecki Pol.
168 I8 Tomatin Highland, Scotland U.K.
268 B6 Tomatlán Mex.
276 D5 Tomave Bol.
280 C5 Tomazina Brazil
278 E4 Tombador, Serra do hills Brazil
277 F3 Tombador, Serra do hills Brazil
239 □1b Tombeau Bay Mauritius
185 E6 Tombebœf France
255 D10 Tombigbee r. AL U.S.A.
237 N7 Tombo S. Africa
283 D7 Tombo, Punta pt Arg.
231 B6 Tomboco Angola
281 F4 Tombos Brazil
228 E2 Tombouctou Mali
228 E2 Tombouctou admin. reg. Mali
102 G1 Tom Bowling Bay North I. N.Z.
232 B4 Tombs of Buganda Kings tourist site Uganda
265 V10 Tombstone AZ U.S.A.
231 A8 Tombua Angola
235 E4 Tom Burke S. Africa
142 K7 Tomdibuloq Uzbek.
142 K7 Tomditov tog'lari hills Uzbek.
Tomditow Toghi hills Uzbek. see Tomditov tog'lari
282 B5 Tomé Chile
235 G4 Tome Moz.
115 C6 Tomea i. Indon.
165 J6 Tomelilla Sweden
207 M2 Tomelloso Spain
143 L6 Tomenaryk Kazakh.
199 L5 Tomeşti Hunedoara Romania
199 L6 Tomeşti Timiş Romania
Tomi Romania see Constanţa
197 H6 Tomice Pol.
124 □1 Tomigusuku Okinawa Japan
126 E5 Tomika Japan
251 O3 Tomiko Ont. Can.
276 D4 Tomina Bol.
228 B3 Tominé r. Guinea
105 L5 Tomingley N.S.W. Austr.
115 B4 Tomini, Teluk g. Indon.
228 D3 Tominian Mali
168 J8 Tomintoul Moray, Scotland U.K.
124 S9 Tomioka Fukushima Japan
127 I3 Tomioka Gunma Japan
127 L4 Tomisato Japan
210 F4 Tomislavgrad Bos.-Herz.
127 K5 Tomiura Japan
127 G5 Tomiyama Aichi Japan
127 K5 Tomiyama Chiba Japan
127 H5 Tomizawa Japan
259 H2 Tomkins Cove NY U.S.A.
104 B2 Tomkinson Ranges mts S.A. Austr.
164 E4 Tommerby Fjord l. Denmark
162 M3 Tømmerneset Norway
153 N4 Tommot Rus. Fed.
168 J8 Tomnavoulin Moray, Scotland U.K.
274 E4 Tomo Col.
274 E3 Tomo r. Col.
127 L3 Tomobe Japan
266 F3 Tomóchic Mex.
230 B4 Tomori C.A.R.
220 B2 Tomorit, Maja e mt. Albania
133 J7 Tomorlog Qinghai China
129 M6 Tomortei Nei Mongol China
199 I5 Tompa Hungary
115 B5 Tompira Sulawesi Indon.
115 A4 Tompo Sulawesi Indon.
153 O3 Tompo Rus. Fed.
108 D7 Tom Price W.A. Austr.
133 H11 Tomra Xizang China
259 G5 Toms r. NJ U.S.A.
145 L2 Tomshush Uzbek.
152 J4 Tomsk Rus. Fed.
108 □1 Tom's Ridge Christmas I.
257 K9 Toms River NJ U.S.A.
165 K4 Tomtabacken hill Sweden
153 P3 Tomtor Rus. Fed.
150 C2 Tömük Turkey
124 T3 Tomuraushi-yama mt. Japan
Tomur Feng mt. China/Kyrg. see Jengish Chokusu
151 F1 Tomuzlovka r. Rus. Fed.
245 L3 Tom White, Mount AK U.S.A.
159 L7 Tomyna Balka Ukr.
208 J4 Tona Spain
124 □E20 Tonaki-jima i. Nansei-shotō Japan
269 N9 Tonalá Chiapas Mex.
268 D5 Tonala Mex.
269 J8 Tonalá Oaxaca Mex.
269 M7 Tonalá Veracruz Mex.
269 H7 Tonalapa de Rio Mex.
213 J3 Tonale, Passo di pass Italy
126 E2 Tonami Japan
274 E5 Tonantins Brazil
214 C7 Tonara Sardegna Italy
262 E2 Tonasket WA U.S.A.
275 H3 Tonate Fr. Guiana
256 G5 Tonawanda NY U.S.A.
268 D6 Tonaya Mex.
Tonb-e Bozorg, Jazīreh-ye i. The Gulf see Greater Tunb
Tonb-e Küchek, Jazīreh-ye i. The Gulf see Lesser Tunb
173 M5 Tonbridge Kent, England U.K.
204 D7 Tonda Port.
126 C7 Tondabayashi Japan
115 D3 Tondano Sulawesi Indon.
204 D7 Tondela Port.
164 E7 Tønder Denmark
136 F8 Tondi Tamil Nadu India
144 I5 Tondī, Dagh-e imp. l. Afgh.
127 J2 Tone Gunma Japan
127 L4 Tone Ibaraki Japan
172 G5 Tone r. England U.K.
162 □ Tonefjellet hill Svalbard
127 M4 Tone-gawa r. Japan
286 Q1 Toney Mountain Antarctica
213 K4 Tonezza del Cimone Italy
229 H5 Tonga Cameroon
101 □8 Tonga country S. Pacific Ocean
232 A2 Tonga Sudan
237 P5 Tongaat S. Africa
131 L6 Tong'an Fujian China
231 E9 Tonga Plateau Zambia
102 I5 Tongaporutu North I. N.Z.
Tongareva atoll Cook Is see Penrhyn
102 J6 Tongariro vol. North I. N.Z.
102 J6 Tongariro National Park North I. N.Z.
101 □8a Tongatapu i. Tonga
101 □8a Tongatapu Group is Tonga
290 H7 Tonga Trench sea feature S. Pacific Ocean
131 I2 Tongbai Henan China
131 I2 Tongbai Shan mts China
131 K3 Tongcheng Anhui China
131 I4 Tongcheng Hubei China
Tongcheng Shandong China see Dong'e
123 E9 T'ongch'ŏn N. Korea
129 K9 Tongchuan Shaanxi China
Tongchuan Sichuan China see Santai
130 G5 Tongdao Hunan China
128 G9 Tongde Qinghai China
123 E10 Tongduch'ŏn S. Korea
187 H7 Tongeren Belgium
131 J4 Tonggu Jiangxi China
129 L9 Tongguan Shaanxi China
132 E7 Tongguzbasti Xinjiang China
130 H9 Tonggu Zui pt China
123 F10 Tonghae S. Korea
130 D6 Tonghai Yunnan China
122 F6 Tonghe Heilong. China
123 D8 Tonghua Jilin China
123 D8 Tonghua Jilin China
Tongi Bangl. see Tungi
122 H5 Tongjiang Heilong. China
130 F3 Tongjiang Sichuan China
122 C7 Tongjiangkou Liaoning China
123 E9 Tongjosŏn-man b. N. Korea
122 E5 Tongken He r. China
118 I4 Tongking, Gulf of China/Vietnam
115 B4 Tongko Sulawesi Indon.
168 H13 Tongland Dumfries and Galloway, Scotland U.K.
Tongle Guangxi China see Leye
129 R5 Tongliao Nei Mongol China
131 K3 Tongling Anhui China
131 K3 Tongling Anhui China
131 L4 Tonglu Zhejiang China
131 I5 Tongmu Jiangxi China
125 G11 Tongnae S. Korea
105 I4 Tongo N.S.W. Austr.
100 □5 Tongoa i. Vanuatu
235 □J4 Tongobory Madag.
284 B2 Tongoi, Bahía b. Chile
105 I4 Tongo Lake salt flat N.S.W. Austr.
284 B2 Tongoy Chile
Tongquan Yunnan China see Malong
114 C8 Tongquil i. Phil.
130 G5 Tongren Guizhou China
128 G9 Tongren Qinghai China
Tongres Belgium see Tongeren
139 M6 Tongsa Bhutan
Tongshan Jiangsu China see Xuzhou
Tongshi Hainan China see Wuzhishan
Tongshi Hainan China see Wuzhishan
118 D4 Tongta Myanmar
128 C9 Tongtian He r. Qinghai China
133 M10 Tongtian He r. Qinghai China
130 A2 Tongtian He r. China alt. Chang Jiang, alt. Jinsha Jiang, conv. Yangtze, long Yangtze Kiang
168 H6 Tongue Highland, Scotland U.K.
262 L3 Tongue r. MT U.S.A.
Tongue of Arabat spit Ukr. see Arabats'ka Strilka, Kosa
270 E1 Tongue of the Ocean sea chan. Bahamas
260 B3 Tongue River Reservoir MT U.S.A.
128 I9 Tongwei Gansu China
131 M3 Tongxiang Zhejiang China
128 I8 Tongxin Ningxia China
123 F11 T'ongyŏng S. Korea
129 R4 Tongyu Jilin China
129 O7 Tongzhou Beijing China
131 M2 Tongzhou Jiangsu China
130 F4 Tongzi Guizhou China
128 C3 Tonhil Mongolia
250 E8 Tonica IL U.S.A.
266 E3 Tónichi Mex.
268 D6 Tonila Mex.
230 F3 Tonj Sudan
230 F3 Tonj watercourse Sudan
138 E6 Tonk Rajasthan India
144 D3 Tonkābon Iran
261 G7 Tonkawa OK U.S.A.
244 J4 Tonki Cape AK U.S.A.
118 G4 Tonkin reg. Vietnam
156 I4 Tonkino Rus. Fed.
119 F8 Tônlé Sab l. Cambodia
Tonle Sap l. Cambodia see Tônlé Sab
172 E4 Tonna Neath Port Talbot, Wales U.K.
184 C4 Tonnay-Boutonne France
184 C4 Tonnay-Charente France
185 E7 Tonneins France
178 G8 Tonnerre France
178 H8 Tonnerrois reg. France
190 G2 Tönning Ger.
127 M1 Tōno Fukushima Japan
124 S7 Tōno Iwate Japan
100 □4a Tonoas i. Chuuk Micronesia
265 T8 Tonopah AZ U.S.A.
264 O3 Tonopah NV U.S.A.
127 M4 Tonoshō Chiba Japan
125 L12 Tonoshō Kagawa Japan
266 □S14 Tonosí Panama
133 C11 Tons r. India
164 G2 Tønsberg Norway
161 U2 Tonshalovo Rus. Fed.
245 K3 Tonsina AK U.S.A.
164 C3 Tonstad Norway
284 C2 Tontal, Sierra mts Arg.
236 E6 Tontelbos S. Africa
269 K7 Tonto r. Mex.
265 U8 Tonto Basin AZ U.S.A.
265 U8 Tonto Creek watercourse AZ U.S.A.
101 □8 Tonumea atoll Tonga
144 H4 Tonvarjeh Iran
158 G2 Tonyezh Belarus
172 F4 Tonyrefail Rhondda Cynon Taff, Wales U.K.
118 A3 Tonzang Myanmar
118 B2 Tonzi Myanmar
244 I3 Tonzona r. AK U.S.A.
105 L3 Toobeah Qld Austr.
228 C5 Toobli Liberia
109 D11 Toodyay W.A. Austr.
265 T1 Tooele UT U.S.A.
107 N9 Toogoolawah Qld Austr.
105 I6 Tooleybuc N.S.W. Austr.
104 E5 Tooligie S.A. Austr.
245 J1 Toolik r. AK U.S.A.
109 C9 Toolonga Nature Reserve W.A. Austr.
105 L7 Tooma r. N.S.W. Austr.
169 J3 Toome Northern Ireland U.K.
107 J9 Toompine Qld Austr.
105 K8 Toora Vic. Austr.
105 L4 Tooraweenah N.S.W. Austr.
236 I8 Toorberg mt. S. Africa
169 C9 Toormore Ireland
107 M9 Toowoomba Qld Austr.
232 F2 Tooxin Somalia
145 M4 Top Afgh.
285 I2 Topador Uru.
244 I1 Topagoruk r. AK U.S.A.
269 H7 Topalapa del Sur Mex.
161 T3 Topalki Rus. Fed.
219 M6 Topana Romania
207 O5 Topares Spain
239 □1a Topaze, Baie b. Rodrigues I. Mauritius
264 M3 Topaz Lake NV U.S.A.
143 T1 Topchikha Rus. Fed.
193 I6 Töpchin Ger.
159 N5 Topchyne Ukr.
171 O5 Topcliffe North Yorkshire, England U.K.
151 C6 Topçu Dağı mt. Turkey
151 D6 Top Dağı mt. Turkey
260 H6 Topeka KS U.S.A.
193 E10 Töpen Ger.
266 F5 Topia Mex.
215 J2 Topino r. Italy
161 V7 Topkanovo Rus. Fed.
152 J4 Topki Rus. Fed.
138 H8 Topla reg. Madh. Prad. India
199 K3 Topľa r. Slovakia
115 F5 Toplana, Gunung mt. Seram Indon.
246 E4 Topley B.C. Can.
246 E4 Topley Landing B.C. Can.
218 J7 Toplica r. Serbia
219 N4 Topliţa Harghita Romania
199 L6 Topliţa Hunedoara Romania
193 G6 Töplitz Ger.
201 I4 Toplitzsee l. Austria
238 □1c Topo São Jorge Azores
238 □1c Topo, Ilhéu do i. Azores
238 □1c Topo, Serra do mt. São Jorge Azores
284 A4 Topocalma, Punta pt Chile
265 R7 Topock AZ U.S.A.
199 H3 Topoľčany Slovakia
199 H3 Topoľčianky Slovakia
142 D4 Topoli Kazakh.
196 G3 Topólka Pol.
199 G2 Topolná Czech Rep.
219 M8 Topolnitsa r. Bulg.
266 E5 Topolobampo Mex.
219 Q6 Topolog Romania
219 M5 Topolog r. Romania
199 K6 Topolovăţu Mare Romania
219 N6 Topoloveni Romania
219 O8 Topolovgrad Bulg.
201 L7 Topolšica Slovenia
199 J2 Toporec Slovakia
196 D3 Toporów Pol.
158 F3 Topory Ukr.
158 H3 Toporyshche Ukr.
196 E2 Toporzyk Pol.
156 F2 Topozero, Ozero l. Rus. Fed.
262 D3 Toppenish WA U.S.A.
219 Q6 Topraisar Romania
151 D6 Toprakkale Ağrı Turkey
151 C5 Toprakkale Erzurum Turkey
150 E1 Toprakkale Osmaniye Turkey
151 B6 Topraklık Turkey
257 □R3 Topsfield ME U.S.A.
172 F6 Topsham Devon, England U.K.
151 C6 Toptepe Turkey
258 D3 Topton PA U.S.A.
102 I3 Topuni North I. N.Z.
276 C4 Toquepala Peru
Toqyraū watercourse Kazakh. see Tokyrau
232 B3 Tor Eth.
208 G3 Tor, Noguera de r. Spain
230 F4 Tora Dem. Rep. Congo
208 H4 Torá Spain
151 K5 Torağay Dağı hill Azer.
126 D5 Torahime Japan
204 I4 Toral de los Guzmanes Spain
204 G3 Toral de los Vados Spain
Toraman Turkey see Halilçavuş
128 B4 Toranggekuduk Xinjiang China
215 Q9 Torano Castello Italy
276 C4 Torata Peru
145 L6 Tor Baldak mt. Afgh.
221 I4 Torbalı Turkey
144 H4 Torbat-e Ḩeydarīyeh Iran
144 I4 Torbat-e Jām Iran
172 E7 Torbay admin. div. England U.K.
172 E7 Tor Bay England U.K.
109 D13 Torbay Bay W.A. Austr.
244 I3 Torbert, Mount AK U.S.A.
157 H5 Torbeyevo Respublika Mordoviya Rus. Fed.
161 R6 Torbeyevo Smolenskaya Oblast' Rus. Fed.
207 J7 Torcal de Antequera park Spain
208 C5 Torcas, Embalse de las resr Spain
247 K4 Torch r. Sask. Can.
215 O7 Torchiara Italy
217 O3 Torchiarolo Italy
161 X5 Torchino Rus. Fed.
158 E3 Torchyn Ukr.
205 L9 Torcón r. Spain
205 L9 Torcón, Embalse del resr Spain
182 E3 Torcy France
178 B4 Torcy-le-Petit France
199 H4 Tordas Hungary
205 J5 Tordehumos Spain
208 K4 Tordera Spain
205 K5 Tordesillas Spain
205 Q7 Tordesilos Spain
205 P9 Tórdiga, Puerto de pass Spain
215 L2 Tordino r. Italy
162 Q4 Töre Sweden
168 H7 Tore Highland, Scotland U.K.
165 K3 Töreboda Sweden
192 E1 Toreby Denmark
164 I5 Torekov Sweden
215 N4 Torella del Sannio Italy
209 D11 Torellano Spain
162 □ Torell Land reg. Svalbard
208 J3 Torelló Spain
186 I4 Torenberg hill Neth.
204 G3 Toreno Spain
115 C5 Toreo Sulawesi Indon.
102 L4 Torere North I. N.Z.
Toretam Kazakh. see Baykonyr
128 I1 Torey Rus. Fed.
159 R5 Torez Ukr.
172 F4 Torfaen admin. div. Wales U.K.
Torga i. Vanuatu see Toga
193 G7 Torgau Ger.
143 O2 Torgay Akmolinskaya Oblast' Kazakh.
192 J3 Torgelow Ger.
Torghay Kazakh. see Turgay
215 I1 Torgiano Italy
142 B2 Torgun r. Rus. Fed.
165 L5 Torhamn Sweden
187 D6 Torhout Belgium
158 E3 Torhovytsya Ukr.
160 H3 Tori Estonia
139 J8 Tori Jharkhand India
232 A3 Tori r. Sudan
127 L4 Toride Japan
127 H1 Torigakubi-misaki pt Japan
181 J3 Torigni-sur-Vire France
126 E3 Torigoe Japan
127 G4 Torii-tōge pass Japan
127 H3 Torii-tōge pass Japan
205 N7 Torija Spain
127 I2 Torikabuto-yama mt. Japan
210 G4 Torine pass Bos.-Herz.
212 D5 Torino Italy
212 D5 Torino prov. Italy
215 N3 Torino di Sangro Italy
125 R16 Tori-shima i. Japan
232 B3 Torit Sudan
217 L2 Toritto Italy
280 A2 Torixoréu Brazil
126 E2 Toriya Japan
144 B3 Torkamān Iran
145 J4 Torkestān, Band-e mts Afgh.
145 N5 Torkhan Pak.
161 N3 Torkovichi Rus. Fed.
208 E2 Torla Spain
160 J3 Torma Estonia
162 S2 Törmänen Fin.
108 G4 Torment, Point W.A. Austr.
204 H6 Tormes r. Spain
209 C7 Tormón Spain
168 F11 Tormore North Ayrshire, Scotland U.K.
205 K7 Tornadizos de Ávila Spain
246 H5 Tornado Mountain Alta/B.C. Can.
207 N5 Tornajuelos mt. Spain
199 J3 Tornaľa Slovakia
204 I8 Tornavacas Spain
204 I8 Tornavacas, Puerto de pass Spain
171 P6 Torne r. England U.K.
Torneå Fin. see Tornio
162 R4 Torneälven r. Sweden
207 K2 Torneros, Sierra de los mts Spain
190 I3 Tornesch Ger.
162 O2 Torneträsk Sweden
162 O2 Torneträsk l. Sweden
Torngat, Monts mts Nfld and Lab./Que. Can. see Torngat Mountains
249 H1 Torngat Mountains Nfld and Lab./Que. Can.
249 I1 Torngat Mountains National Park Reserve nat. park Nfld. and Lab. Can.
218 H7 Tornik mt. Serbia
162 R4 Tornio Fin.
199 I6 Tornjoš Vojvodina Serbia
212 G4 Torno Italy
205 R7 Tornos Spain
192 H4 Tornow Ger.
285 F6 Tornquist Arg.
199 L3 Tornyospálca Hungary
229 H4 Toro Nigeria
205 J5 Toro Spain
165 N3 Torö i. Sweden
283 B8 Toro, Lago del l. Chile
268 F1 Toro, Pico del mt. Mex.
284 B3 Toro, Punta pt Chile
115 C6 Torobuku Sulawesi Indon.
229 F3 Torodi Niger
199 H4 Törökbálint Hungary
199 J4 Törökszentmiklós Hungary
122 I1 Torom Rus. Fed.
248 E5 Toronto Ont. Can.
256 E8 Toronto OH U.S.A.
258 F1 Toronto Reservoir NY U.S.A.
201 O5 Torony Hungary
161 O5 Toropatsa Rus. Fed.
265 P8 Toro Peak CA U.S.A.
161 O5 Toropets Rus. Fed.
224 C6 Tororo Chad
232 B4 Tororo Uganda
148 F5 Toros Dağları mts Turkey
160 L4 Toroshino Rus. Fed.
205 K5 Torozos, Montes de reg. Spain
214 D6 Torpè Sardegna Italy
168 K8 Torphins Aberdeenshire, Scotland U.K.
172 D7 Torpoint Cornwall, England U.K.
279 B9 Torquato Severo Brazil
105 J8 Torquay Vic. Austr.
172 E7 Torquay Torbay, England U.K.
205 L4 Torquemada Spain
169 J2 Torr Northern Ireland U.K.
207 L2 Torralba de Calatrava Spain
214 B6 Torralba Sardegna Italy
205 P8 Torralba Spain
208 D4 Torralba de Aragón Spain
205 O5 Torralba de El Burgo Spain
205 R7 Torralba de los Sisones Spain
205 J9 Torralba de Oropesa Spain
264 N8 Torrance CA U.S.A.
206 C4 Torrão Port.
204 E8 Torre mt. Port.
215 M6 Torre Annunziata Italy
215 J5 Torre Astura cliff Italy
209 C7 Torrebaja Spain
205 O5 Torreblacos Spain
209 F7 Torreblanca Spain
266 B1 Torre Blanco, Cerro mt. Mex.
207 L5 Torreblascopedro Spain
215 N4 Torrebruna Italy
205 L7 Torrecaballeros Spain
207 J4 Torrecampo Spain
217 M2 Torre Canne Italy
207 M5 Torre-Cardela Spain
217 O2 Torre Cavallo, Capo di c. Italy
205 K2 Torrecerredo mt. Spain
214 G3 Torre Ciana, Punta di pt Italy
207 J7 Torrecilla mt. Spain
205 K9 Torrecilla de la Jara Spain
205 J6 Torrecilla de la Orden Spain
208 C6 Torrecilla del Rebollar Spain
205 O4 Torrecilla en Cameros Spain
204 I9 Torrecillas de la Tiesa Spain
215 N5 Torrecuso Italy
206 C3 Torre da Gadanha Port.
206 D2 Torre das Vargens Port.
207 K2 Torre de Abraham, Embalse de la resr Spain
208 I3 Torre de Cadí mt. Spain
204 F5 Torre de Dona Chama Port.
204 D7 Torredeita Port.
207 M3 Torre de Juan Abad Spain
206 H6 Torre del Águila, Embalse de la resr Spain
204 H3 Torre del Bierzo Spain
205 N7 Torre del Burgo Spain
207 L5 Torre del Campo Spain
215 M6 Torre del Greco Italy
212 I8 Torre della Meloria i. Italy
207 K7 Torre del Mar Spain
217 N4 Torre del Pizzo pt Italy
208 H5 Torredembarra Spain
206 F3 Torre de Miguel Sesmero Spain
204 F6 Torre de Moncorvo Port.
215 L3 Torre de'Passeri Italy
207 L5 Torredonjimeno Spain
204 F7 Torre do Terrenho Port.
204 H6 Torregamones Spain
208 G4 Torregrossa Spain
205 L6 Torreiglesias Spain
204 C7 Torreira Port.
204 H9 Torrejoncillo Spain
205 O8 Torrejoncillo del Rey Spain
205 N8 Torrejón de Ardoz Spain
205 N7 Torrejón del Rey Spain
204 I9 Torrejón el Rubio Spain
204 I9 Torrejón-Tajo, Embalse de resr Spain
204 I9 Torrejón-Tiétar, Embalse de resr Spain
208 C6 Torrelacarcel Spain
205 M7 Torrelaguna Spain
205 Q5 Torrelapaja Spain
205 L2 Torrelavega Spain
205 Q5 Torrellas Spain
208 I5 Torrelles de Foix Spain
205 J5 Torrelobatón Spain
205 M7 Torrelodones Spain
215 O4 Torremaggiore Italy
209 E10 Torremanzanas-La Torre de les Maçanes Spain
206 F3 Torremayor Spain
206 G3 Torremegía Spain
215 P4 Torre Mileto Italy
206 G2 Torremocha Spain
207 J7 Torremolinos Spain
209 F7 Torrenostra Spain
104 F4 Torrens, Lake imp. l. S.A. Austr.
107 J6 Torrens Creek Qld Austr.
107 J7 Torrens Creek watercourse Qld Austr.
282 F3 Torrent Arg.
209 E9 Torrent Spain
Torrente Valencia Spain see Torrent
208 F5 Torrente del Cinca Spain
207 M3 Torrenueva Spain
212 H9 Torre Nuovo Scalo Italy
266 H5 Torreón Mex.
206 G2 Torreorgaz Spain
215 O7 Torre Orsaia Italy
209 D12 Torre-Pacheco Spain
207 K5 Torreparedones hill Spain
212 C6 Torre Pellice Italy
207 M4 Torreperogil Spain
279 C9 Torres Brazil
266 D3 Torres Mex.
207 L5 Torres Spain
207 L5 Torres r. Spain
204 I1 Torres, Cabo c. Spain
205 M5 Torresandino Spain
217 O4 Torre San Giovanni Italy
215 L5 Torre Sant'Agostino cliff Italy
217 N3 Torre Santa Susanna Italy
207 N4 Torres de Albánchez Spain
208 C4 Torres de Berrellén Spain
205 N8 Torres de la Alameda Spain
204 I5 Torres del Carrizal Spain
283 B8 Torres del Paine, Parque Nacional nat. park Chile
208 G4 Torres de Segre Spain
100 □5 Torres Islands Vanuatu
204 I6 Torresmenudas Spain
206 B2 Torres Novas Port.
98 E2 Torres Strait Qld Austr.
206 A2 Torres Vedras Port.
215 P6 Torretta, Monte mt. Italy
208 E6 Torrevelilla Spain
209 D12 Torrevieja Spain
265 U3 Torrey UT U.S.A.
215 K4 Torrice Italy
217 N3 Torricella Italy
215 J3 Torricella in Sabina Italy
215 M3 Torricella Peligna Italy
215 L2 Torricella Sicura Italy
212 F3 Torricella Taverne Switz.
205 J9 Torrico Spain
206 F2 Torrico de San Pedro hill Spain
213 J4 Torri del Benaco Italy
172 D6 Torridge r. England U.K.
168 E7 Torridon Highland, Scotland U.K.
168 E7 Torridon, Loch b. Scotland U.K.
212 G6 Torriglia Italy
215 J3 Torri in Sabina Italy
209 D7 Torrijas Spain
205 Q6 Torrijo Spain
205 L9 Torrijos Spain
168 D8 Torrin Highland, Scotland U.K.
257 L7 Torrington CT U.S.A.
262 L5 Torrington WY U.S.A.
280 C5 Torrinha Brazil
214 H1 Torrita di Siena Italy
206 B4 Torroal Port.
208 L3 Torroella de Montgrí Spain
162 L5 Torrön l. Sweden
160 G1 Torronsuon kansallispuisto nat. park Fin.
207 L7 Torrox Spain
207 L7 Torrox, Punta de pt Spain
205 O9 Torrubia del Campo Spain
205 P5 Torrubia de Soria Spain
165 K2 Torrvarpen l. Sweden
139 L6 Torsa Chhu r. Bhutan
164 G1 Torsæterkampen hill Norway
190 H1 Tørsbøl Denmark
164 J1 Torsby Sweden
165 M2 Torshälla Sweden
166 D1 Tórshavn Faroe Is
165 J3 Torsö i. Sweden
162 O1 Torsvåg Norway
199 I4 Törtel Hungary
180 F3 Torteval Channel Is
265 U8 Tortilla Flat AZ U.S.A.
Törtkŏl Uzbek. see To'rtko'l
142 I7 To'rtko'l Uzbek.
143 P2 Tortkuduk Kazakh.
216 F8 Torto r. Sicilia Italy
271 K4 Tortola i. Virgin Is (U.K.)
205 N7 Tórtola de Henares Spain
205 L5 Tórtoles de Esgueva Spain
214 D8 Tortolì Sardegna Italy
219 Q6 Tortomanu Romania
212 F6 Tortona Italy
215 P8 Tortora Italy
215 L2 Tortoreto Italy
216 H7 Tortorici Sicilia Italy
208 G6 Tortosa Spain
204 E8 Tortozendo Port.
270 G3 Tortue, Île de la i. Haiti
205 Q7 Tortuera Spain
269 I3 Tortuga, Laguna l. Mex.
285 G3 Tortugas Arg.
266 □R12 Tortuguero, Parque Nacional nat. park Costa Rica
149 J3 Tortum Turkey
143 Q6 Toru-Aygyr Kyrg.
144 F4 Ţorūd Iran
115 B4 Torue Sulawesi Indon.
Torugart, Pereval pass China/Kyrg. see Turugart Pass
148 I3 Torul Turkey
196 G2 Toruń Pol.
160 I3 Tõrva Estonia
215 I4 Tor Vaianica Italy
171 K5 Torver Cumbria, England U.K.
207 M7 Torvizcón Spain
163 I5 Torvløysa mt. Norway
162 N4 Torvsjö Sweden
169 F2 Tory Island Ireland
199 J2 Torysa Slovakia
199 K3 Torysa r. Slovakia
169 F2 Tory Sound sea chan. Ireland
161 R5 Torzhkovskaya Gryada hills Rus. Fed.
161 R4 Torzhok Rus. Fed.
196 D3 Torzym Pol.
125 K13 Tosa Japan
213 J3 Tosa, Cima mt. Italy
125 J14 Tosashimizu Japan
125 K13 Tosa-wan b. Japan
125 K13 Tosa-yamada Japan
162 L4 Tosbotn Norway
236 H1 Tosca S. Africa
266 D5 Tosca, Punta pt Mex.
168 E8 Toscaig Highland, Scotland U.K.
213 K9 Toscana admin. reg. Italy
214 D2 Toscano, Arcipelago is Italy
213 J4 Toscolano-Maderno Italy
162 L4 Tosenfjorden inlet Norway
126 E6 Tōshi-jima i. Japan
127 J6 To-shima i. Japan
124 S6 Tōshima-yama mt. Japan
143 M7 Toshkent Toshkent Uzbek.
143 M7 Toshkent admin. div. Uzbek.
Toshkent Wiloyati admin. div. Uzbek. see Toshkent
161 N2 Tosno Rus. Fed.
128 E8 Toson Hu l. Qinghai China
128 F2 Tosontsengel Mongolia
128 G2 Tosontsengel Mongolia
212 F1 Töss r. Switz.
208 K4 Tossa Spain
185 B8 Tosse France
215 L2 Tossicia Italy
171 M5 Tosside Lancashire, England U.K.
282 E3 Tostado Arg.
160 G3 Tõstamaa Estonia
190 I4 Tostedt Ger.
204 B2 Tosto, Cabo c. Spain
125 H13 Tosu Japan
148 G3 Tosya Turkey
199 J4 Tószeg Hungary
196 G5 Toszek Pol.
209 C12 Totana Spain
136 G9 Totapola mt. Sri Lanka
103 E12 Totara South I. N.Z.
102 G7 Totaranui South I. N.Z.
268 D4 Totatiche Mex.
234 D4 Toteng Botswana
194 D5 Totenkopf hill Ger.
178 B4 Tôtes France
201 I4 Totes Gebirge mts Austria
100 □4a Totiw i. Chuuk Micronesia
173 I6 Totland Isle of Wight, England U.K.
156 H4 Tot'ma Rus. Fed.
172 E7 Totnes Devon, England U.K.
275 G3 Totness Suriname
269 K9 Totolapan Mex.
269 L9 Totolapilla Mex.
269 J7 Totoltepec Mex.
156 H4 Totomitsa Rus. Fed.
267 N10 Totonicapán Guat.
276 D4 Totora Bol.
284 D2 Totoral Arg.
282 C2 Totoral Chile
282 D3 Totoralejos Arg.
285 G3 Totoras Arg.
228 C5 Totota Liberia
268 E5 Tototlán Mex.
101 □7 Totoya i. Fiji
142 E1 Totskoye Rus. Fed.
127 K5 Totsuka Japan
126 C7 Totsukawa Japan
126 C8 Totsu-kawa r. Japan
198 F5 Tótszentmárton Hungary
198 F5 Tótszerdahely Hungary
173 J6 Totton Hampshire, England U.K.
125 L11 Tottori Japan
125 K11 Tottori pref. Japan
269 K6 Totutla Mex.
199 G4 Tótvázsony Hungary
229 G1 Touâret well Niger
228 D4 Touba Côte d'Ivoire
228 B3 Touba Senegal
226 D3 Toubkal, Jbel mt. Morocco
226 D3 Toubkal, Parc National du nat. park Morocco
229 I5 Touboro Cameroon
204 F6 Touça Port.
185 G8 Touch r. France
262 E3 Touchet r. WA U.S.A.
178 F8 Toucy France
128 I7 Toudaohu Nei Mongol China
226 B5 Toueïrma well Maur.
228 E2 Touérât well Mali
185 G7 Touffailles France
226 D4 Toufourine well Mali
228 E3 Tougan Burkina
185 F8 Touget France
227 G2 Touggourt Alg.
228 E3 Tougouri Burkina
229 G3 Tougoutaou well Niger
228 C4 Tougué Guinea
100 □5 Touho New Caledonia
228 C2 Touijinet well Maur.
228 C3 Touil Maur.
228 C3 Toukoto Mali
229 F4 Toukountouna Benin
179 K6 Toul France
228 C5 Toulépleu Côte d'Ivoire
228 E3 Toulfé Burkina
131 M7 Touliu Taiwan
180 D5 Toullaëron, Roc de hill France
249 G3 Toulnustouc r. Que. Can.
183 H10 Toulon France
250 E8 Toulon IL U.S.A.
182 C3 Toulon-sur-Allier France
182 E3 Toulon-sur-Arroux France
185 J10 Toulouges France
229 G2 Toulouk well Niger
185 G8 Toulouse France
229 G3 Toumbélaga well Niger
224 B4 Toummo well Niger
228 D5 Toumodi Côte d'Ivoire
228 D4 Touna Mali
226 D3 Tounassine, Hamada des. Alg.
229 G3 Tounfaminir well Niger
229 I4 Toungo Nigeria
130 H6 Toupai Guangxi China
181 L3 Touques France
181 L3 Touques r. France
228 D5 Toura, Monts mt. Côte d'Ivoire
184 E1 Touraine reg. France
181 L7 Touraine, Val de val. France
130 D9 Tourakom Laos
Tourane Vietnam see Đa Năng
226 C4 Tourassine well Maur.
224 B6 Tourba Chad
180 D5 Tourch France
178 F2 Tourcoing France
183 K9 Tourette-sur-Loup France
247 J1 Tourgis Lake Nunavut Can.
204 B2 Touriñán, Cabo c. Spain
220 D5 Tourkovigla, Akrotirio pt Greece
180 H2 Tourlaville France
Tourmakeady Ireland see Tuar Mhic Éadaigh
185 E10 Tourmalet, Col du pass France
182 E5 Tour Matagrin hill France
187 D7 Tournai Belgium
183 K8 Tournairet, Mont mt. France
178 E6 Tournan-en-Brie France
276 B2 Tournavista Peru
185 E9 Tournay France
227 H5 Tourndo, Oued watercourse Alg./Niger
185 F8 Tournecoupe France
185 G8 Tournefeuille France
185 F7 Tournon-d'Agenais France
181 M8 Tournon-St-Martin France
183 F6 Tournon-sur-Rhône France
182 F3 Tournus France
178 C5 Tourny France
204 E7 Touro Port.
279 A9 Touro Passo Brazil
278 G3 Touros Brazil
229 I4 Touroua Cameroon
181 M4 Tourouvre France
183 K9 Tourrette-Levens France
184 F1 Tours France
178 I4 Tourteron France
184 G5 Tourtoirac France
183 H10 Tourves France
178 C7 Toury France
209 D9 Tous, Embalse de resr Spain
228 D4 Toussiana Burkina
224 C4 Toussidé, Pic mt. Chad
230 D2 Toussoro, Mont mt. C.A.R.
122 D6 Toutai Heilong. China
206 E4 Toutalga r. Port.
104 □3 Toutcher, Cape S. Pacific Ocean
180 H8 Touvois France
236 F9 Touws r. S. Africa
236 E9 Touwsrivier S. Africa
198 B1 Toužim Czech Rep.
128 I3 Töv prov. Mongolia
198 G2 Tovačov Czech Rep.
274 D2 Tovar Venez.
161 S7 Tovarkovo Rus. Fed.
161 V8 Tovarkovskiy Rus. Fed.
199 K3 Tovarné Slovakia
210 G3 Tovarnik Croatia
173 K3 Tove r. England U.K.
200 C7 Tovel, Lago di l. Italy
Tovil'-Dora Tajik. see Tavildara
158 E5 Tovste Ukr.
101 □7 Tovu Fiji
151 G5 Tovuz Azer.
Tovuzçay r. Armenia see Tavush
259 G3 Towaco NJ U.S.A.
124 S6 Towada Japan

124 R7 Towada-Hachimantai Kokuritsu-kōen nat. park Japan
124 S6 Towada-ko l. Japan
102 I2 Towai North I. N.Z.
275 G3 Towakaima Guyana
244 F3 Towak Mountain hill AK U.S.A.
251 R8 Towanda PA U.S.A.
258 C1 Towanda Creek r. PA U.S.A.
265 X4 Towaoc CO U.S.A.
115 B6 Towari Sulawesi Indon.
173 K3 Towcester Northamptonshire, England U.K.
169 E9 Tower Ireland
250 B2 Tower MN U.S.A.
258 B3 Tower City PA U.S.A.
107 J7 Towerhill Creek watercourse Qld Austr.
Tower Island Islas Galápagos Ecuador see Genovesa, Isla
103 B13 Tower Peak South I. N.Z.
171 N4 Tow Law Durham, England U.K.
258 F7 Town Bank NJ U.S.A.
260 E1 Towner ND U.S.A.
168 I13 Townhead of Greenlaw Dumfries and Galloway, Scotland U.K.
168 J10 Townhill Fife, Scotland U.K.
106 E3 Towns r. N.T. Austr.
258 D6 Townsend DE U.S.A.
257 N6 Townsend MA U.S.A.
262 I3 Townsend MT U.S.A.
258 F6 Townsends Inlet NJ U.S.A.
107 M7 Townshend Island Qld Austr.
107 K5 Townsville Qld Austr.
115 B5 Towori, Teluk b. Indon.
232 B3 Towot Sudan
145 J4 Towraghondi Afgh.
145 N4 Towr Kham Afgh.
258 B6 Towson MD U.S.A.
115 B5 Towuti, Danau l. Indon.
172 E1 Towyn Conwy, Wales U.K.
Towyn Gwynedd, Wales U.K. see Tywyn
132 E6 Toxkan He r. China
264 N1 Toy NV U.S.A.
261 D10 Toyah TX U.S.A.
124 S4 Tōya-ko l. Japan
126 F2 Toyama Japan
126 F2 Toyama pref. Japan
126 F2 Toyama-wan b. Japan
128 G9 Toyêma Qinghai China
158 D2 Toykut Ukr.
125 K13 Tōyo Japan
126 F5 Toyoake Japan
127 G6 Toyoda Japan
125 K12 Toyohama Japan
126 F6 Toyohashi Japan
126 F6 Toyokawa Japan
126 F6 Toyo-kawa r. Japan
126 B6 Toyonaka Japan
126 G5 Toyone Japan
127 H2 Toyono Nagano Japan
126 B6 Toyono Ōsaka Japan
126 A4 Toyooka Hyōgo Japan
127 G4 Toyooka Nagano Japan
127 G6 Toyooka Shizuoka Japan
124 Q9 Toyosaka Japan
127 G3 Toyoshina Japan
126 F5 Toyota Japan
124 S1 Toyotomi Japan
126 E5 Toyoyama Japan
162 Q5 Töysä Fin.
143 M7 To'ytepa Uzbek.
Tozal del Orri mt. Spain see Orri, Tossal de l'
Tozanlı Turkey see Almus
133 F9 Tozê Kangri mt. Xizang China
227 H2 Tozeur Tunisia
245 J2 Tozi, Mount AK U.S.A.
244 I2 Tozitna r. AK U.S.A.
151 I4 Tpig Rus. Fed.
151 D3 Tqibuli Georgia
151 C3 Tqvarch'eli Georgia
204 F2 Trabada Spain
118 H4 Tra Ban, Đao i. Vietnam
204 H6 Trabanca Spain
204 H5 Trabazos Spain
216 F8 Trabia Sicilia Italy
196 G1 Trąbki Wielkie Pol.
150 D4 Trâblous Lebanon
201 K5 Traboch Austria
219 K9 Trabotivište Macedonia
214 A5 Trabuccato, Punta pt Sardegna Italy
149 I3 Trabzon Turkey
151 A5 Trabzon prov. Turkey
216 C10 Tracino Sicilia Italy
257 □S3 Tracy N.B. Can.
264 K4 Tracy CA U.S.A.
260 H3 Tracy MN U.S.A.
182 B2 Tracy-sur-Loire France
212 F4 Tradate Italy
191 G8 Traddelkopf hill Ger.
250 B4 Trade Lake WI U.S.A.
261 K7 Tradewater r. KY U.S.A.
248 B3 Trading r. Ont. Can.
162 L3 Træna i. Norway
162 L3 Trænfjorden sea chan. Norway
260 I4 Traer IA U.S.A.
206 G8 Trafalgar, Cabo c. Spain
245 O3 Traffic Mountain Y.T. Can.
205 Q8 Tragacete Spain
207 O4 Tragoncillo mt. Spain
221 G5 Tragonisi i. Greece
201 K3 Tragwein Austria
219 N7 Traian Romania
199 L6 Traian Vuia Romania
205 Q7 Traid Spain
284 A6 Traiguén Chile
208 F6 Traiguera Spain
246 G5 Trail B.C. Can.
261 F8 Trail OK U.S.A.
168 E11 Tràille, Rubha na pt Scotland U.K.
Traill Island Greenland see Traill Ø
243 P2 Traill Ø i. Greenland
195 L4 Train Ger.
178 F7 Traînel France
258 E5 Trainer PA U.S.A.
178 D8 Traînou France
278 F4 Traipu Brazil
274 D5 Traíra r. Brazil
280 D2 Trairas r. Brazil
278 F2 Trairi Brazil
201 M3 Traisen Austria
201 M3 Traisen r. Austria
201 N3 Traiskirchen Austria
201 M3 Traismauer Austria
195 N3 Traitsching Ger.
281 F5 Trajano de Morais Brazil
Trajectum Neth. see Utrecht
236 H9 Traka r. S. Africa
160 H7 Trakai Lith.
163 R9 Trakai nat. park Lith.
Trakiya reg. Turkey see Thrace
156 J3 Trakt Rus. Fed.
Trakya reg. Turkey see Thrace
169 C8 Tralee Ireland
169 C8 Tralee Bay Ireland
Trá Li Ireland see Tralee
205 Q8 Tramacastilla Spain
214 A6 Tramariglio Sardegna Italy
209 C7 Tramascastiel Spain
214 B7 Tramatza Sardegna Italy
213 L7 Tramazzo r. Italy
194 C7 Tramelan Switz.
185 E10 Tramezaïgues France
Trá Mhór Ireland see Tramore
256 C11 Trammel VA U.S.A.
200 G7 Tramonti, Lago dei l. Italy
213 N3 Tramonti di Sopra Italy
200 G7 Tramonti di Sotto Italy
169 H8 Tramore Ireland
209 J8 Tramuntana, Serra de mts Spain
215 P7 Tramutola Italy
165 K3 Tranås Sweden
164 G5 Tranbjerg Denmark
282 D2 Trancas Arg.
207 N4 Tranco de Beas, Embalse del resr Spain
281 H2 Trancoso Brazil
204 F7 Trancoso Port.
164 G6 Tranebjerg Denmark
164 J4 Tranemo Sweden
168 K11 Tranent East Lothian, Scotland U.K.
119 D11 Trang Thai.
113 H8 Trangan i. Indon.
105 K5 Trangie N.S.W. Austr.
215 Q5 Trani Italy
178 I7 Trannes France
118 F5 Trân Ninh, Cao Nguyên plat. Laos
235 □J5 Tranoroa Madag.
235 □J5 Tranovaho Madag.
205 Q6 Tranquera, Embalse de la resr Spain
282 G3 Tranqueras Uru.
284 B3 Tranquilla Chile
180 H5 Trans France
287 K2 Transantarctic Mountains Antarctica
247 H5 Trans Canada Highway Can.
Transcarpathian Oblast admin. div. Ukr. see Zakarpats'ka Oblast'
247 L5 Transcona Man. Can.
183 I9 Trans-en-Provence France
269 H6 Transfiguración Mex.
219 M4 Transilvaniei, Podişul plat. Romania
163 L6 Transtrand Sweden
Transylvanian Alps mts Romania see Carpaţii Meridionali
Transylvanian Basin plat. Romania see Transilvaniei, Podişul
168 I6 Trantlemore Highland, Scotland U.K.
119 G10 Tra Ôn Vietnam
216 D7 Trapani Sicilia Italy
216 D8 Trapani prov. Sicilia Italy
Trapezus Turkey see Trabzon
284 D3 Trapiche Arg.
258 E4 Trappe PA U.S.A.
190 J2 Trappenkamp Ger.
245 J3 Trapper Creek AK U.S.A.
262 G4 Trapper Peak MT U.S.A.
178 D6 Trappes France
279 B9 Trapua r. Brazil
105 K8 Traralgon Vic. Austr.
194 C2 Trarbach Ger.
165 J5 Traryd Sweden
228 B2 Trarza admin. reg. Maur.
215 L4 Trasacco Italy
219 L4 Trascăului, Munţii mts Romania
Trashigang Bhutan see Tashigang
214 I1 Trasimeno, Lago l. Italy
204 E4 Trasmiras Spain
204 F5 Trás-os-Montes reg. Port.
214 G2 Trasubbie r. Italy
205 P9 Trasvase, Canal de Spain
119 F8 Trat Thai.
214 B9 Tratalias Sardegna Italy
145 M7 Tratani r. Pak.
201 M6 Trate Slovenia
201 J3 Traun Austria
201 J3 Traun r. Austria
195 N5 Traun r. Ger.
195 N6 Traunreut Ger.
201 I4 Traunsee l. Austria
201 L3 Traunstein Austria
195 N6 Traunstein Ger.
160 H6 Traupis Lith.
201 O3 Trautmannsdorf an der Leitha Austria
213 R4 Trava Slovenia
212 I4 Travagliato Italy
245 O2 Travaillant Lake N.W.T. Can.
204 D8 Travanca do Mondego Port.
204 D7 Travassô Port.
204 E7 Travassós de Cima Port.
190 K3 Trave r. Ger.
105 I5 Travellers Lake imp. l. N.S.W. Austr.
190 K3 Travemünde Ger.
190 J3 Travenbrück Ger.
212 B2 Travers Switz.
103 G9 Travers, Mount South I. N.Z.
273 G7 Traversay Islands S. Sandwich Is
250 I5 Traverse City MI U.S.A.
244 H2 Traverse Peak hill AK U.S.A.
212 I6 Traversetolo Italy
281 G4 Travessão Brazil
213 L3 Travignolo r. Italy
119 H10 Tra Vinh Vietnam
261 F10 Travis, Lake TX U.S.A.
210 F3 Travnik Bos.-Herz.
214 C4 Travo r. Corse France
212 H6 Travo Italy
169 B4 Trawmore Bay Ireland
172 E2 Trawsfynydd Gwynedd, Wales U.K.
172 E2 Trawsfynydd, Llyn resr Wales U.K.
109 D11 Trayning W.A. Austr.
210 E2 Trbovlje Slovenia
119 G10 Tre, Hon i. Vietnam
Trean Ireland see An Trian
270 □ Treasure Beach Jamaica
100 □6 Treasury Islands Solomon Is
199 G3 Trebatice Slovakia
193 J6 Trebatsch Ger.
212 H5 Trebbia r. Italy
193 H6 Trebbin Ger.
210 G4 Trebebvić nat. park Bos.-Herz.
192 D5 Trebel Ger.
192 H3 Trebel r. Ger.
193 F8 Treben Ger.
198 C1 Třebenice Czech Rep.
192 I4 Trebenow Ger.
185 I9 Trèbes France
201 I6 Trebesing Austria
180 D4 Trébeurden France
198 E2 Třebíč Czech Rep.
210 G4 Trebinje Bos.-Herz.
217 L4 Trebisacce Italy
210 F4 Trebišnjica r. Bos.-Herz.
199 K3 Trebišov Slovakia
193 G7 Trebitz Ger.
210 F4 Trebižat r. Bos.-Herz.
Trebizond Turkey see Trabzon
210 E3 Trebnje Slovenia
285 F4 Trebolares Arg.
204 E3 Trebolle Spain
198 D2 Třeboň Czech Rep.
107 K5 Trebonne Qld Austr.
198 D2 Třeboňsko park Czech Rep.
180 C5 Tréboul France
193 G8 Trebsen Ger.
206 G7 Trebujena Spain
194 E2 Trebur Ger.
172 E4 Trecastle Powys, Wales U.K.
212 F5 Trecate Italy
215 P7 Trecchina Italy
213 K5 Trecenta Italy
172 F4 Tredegar Blaenau Gwent, Wales U.K.
173 I3 Tredington Warwickshire, England U.K.
213 L7 Tredozio Italy
170 C5 Treehoo Ireland
136 C7 Tree Island India
190 H2 Treene r. Ger.
Trefaldwyn Powys, Wales U.K. see Montgomery
Trefdraeth Wales U.K. see Newport
172 E2 Trefeglwys Powys, Wales U.K.
201 I6 Treffen Austria
180 C6 Treffiagat France
182 G4 Treffort-Cuisiat France
191 J8 Treffurt Ger.
Treffynnon Flintshire, Wales U.K. see Holywell
172 E1 Trefriw Conwy, Wales U.K.
Tref-y-clawdd Wales U.K. see Knighton
Trefynwy Monmouthshire, Wales U.K. see Monmouth
172 E3 Tregaron Ceredigion, Wales U.K.
180 D4 Trégastel France
213 K4 Tregnago Italy
250 C4 Trego WI U.S.A.
172 C7 Tregony Cornwall, England U.K.
180 E4 Trégorrois reg. France
107 M4 Tregosse Islets and Reefs Coral Sea Is Terr. Austr.
284 A5 Treguaco Chile
180 F5 Trégueux France
180 E4 Tréguier France
180 D6 Trégunc France
172 F2 Tregynon Powys, Wales U.K.
162 O5 Trehörningsjö Sweden
190 H1 Treia Ger.
213 O9 Treia Italy
168 G9 Treig, Loch l. Scotland U.K.
184 H4 Treignac France
182 C1 Treigny France
Treinta de Agosto Arg. see 30 de Agosto
282 G4 Treinta y Tres Uru.
191 D10 Treis Ger.
204 H2 Treisa, Peña mt. Spain
162 □ Tre Kroner mt. Svalbard
270 □ Trelawny parish Jamaica
181 K7 Trélazé France
172 D4 Trelech Carmarthenshire, Wales U.K.
283 D6 Trelew Arg.
184 F5 Trélissac France
180 G5 Trélivan France
164 J6 Trelleborg Sweden
178 H3 Trélon France
219 K7 Trem mt. Serbia
172 D2 Tremadog Gwynedd, Wales U.K.
172 D2 Tremadog Bay Wales U.K.
248 F4 Tremblant, Mont hill Que. Can.
180 I5 Tremblay France
178 B6 Tremblay-les-Villages France
239 □1c Tremblet Réunion
246 E4 Trembleur Lake B.C. Can.
205 Q7 Tremedal, Sierra del mts Spain
204 H6 Tremedal de Tormes Spain
187 G7 Tremelo Belgium
181 J7 Trémentines France
206 B2 Tremês Port.
180 D6 Tréméven France
212 G4 Tremezzo Italy
215 P3 Tremiti, Isole is Italy
160 M9 Tremlya r. Belarus
185 F6 Trémolat France
251 R9 Tremont PA U.S.A.
262 H6 Tremonton UT U.S.A.
198 C2 Třemošná Czech Rep.
198 E2 Třemošnice Czech Rep.
183 B8 Trémouilles France
208 G3 Tremp Spain
250 C5 Trempealeau r. WI U.S.A.
190 J3 Tremsbüttel Ger.
172 B7 Trenance Cornwall, England U.K.
250 H3 Trenary MI U.S.A.
249 F4 Trenche r. Que. Can.
199 H3 Trenčianska Turná Slovakia
199 G3 Trenčianske Stankovce Slovakia
199 H3 Trenčianske Teplice Slovakia
199 H3 Trenčiansky kraj admin. reg. Slovakia
199 H3 Trenčín Slovakia
191 H7 Trendelburg Ger.
285 E4 Trenel Arg.
119 F8 Trêng Cambodia
117 I9 Trenggalek Jawa Indon.
Trengganu state Malaysia see Terengganu
285 F4 Trenque Lauquén Arg.
185 C7 Trensacq France
192 H1 Trent Ger.
Trent Italy see Trento
171 P6 Trent r. Dorset, England U.K.
Trent r. England U.K. see Piddle
201 I7 Trenta Slovenia
185 F7 Trentels France
213 K3 Trentino-Alto Adige admin. reg. Italy
213 K3 Trento Italy
213 K3 Trento prov. Italy
215 M6 Trentola-Ducenta Italy
248 E4 Trenton Ont. Can.
255 F11 Trenton FL U.S.A.
255 E8 Trenton GA U.S.A.
260 I5 Trenton MO U.S.A.
255 I8 Trenton NC U.S.A.
260 E5 Trenton NE U.S.A.
258 F4 Trenton NJ U.S.A.
261 K8 Trenton TN U.S.A.
178 B6 Tréon France
172 E4 Treorchy Rhondda Cynon Taff, Wales U.K.
106 C1 Trepang Bay N.T. Austr.
249 K4 Trepassey Nfld and Lab. Can.
159 L5 Trepivka Ukr.
193 K6 Treppeln Ger.
182 G5 Trept France
217 O3 Trepuzzi Italy
214 H1 Trequanda Italy
212 F3 Tresa r. Italy
285 F4 Tres Algarrobas Arg.
212 H7 Tresana Italy
285 I3 Tres Arboles Uru.
285 G6 Tres Arroyos Arg.
280 B6 Três Bicos Brazil
285 H3 Tres Bocas Arg.
285 I3 Tres Bocas Uru.
275 F6 Três Casas Brazil
283 D8 Tres Cerros Arg.
258 D3 Tresckow PA U.S.A.
183 H8 Trescléoux France
172 □ Tresco i. England U.K.
281 E4 Três Corações Brazil
212 H4 Trescore Balneario Italy
282 D1 Tres Cruces Arg.
282 C3 Tres Cruces Chile
212 I3 Tresenda Italy
274 C4 Tres Esquinas Col.
285 I4 Tres Esquinas Uru.
Tres Forcas, Cabo c. Morocco see Trois Fourches, Cap des
168 D10 Treshnish Isles Scotland U.K.
213 L6 Tresigallo Italy
212 J3 Tre Signori, Corno dei mt. Italy
280 B4 Três Irmãos, Represa resr Brazil
282 E2 Tres Isletas Arg.
218 J8 Treska r. Macedonia
160 K4 Treski Estonia
280 B4 Três Lagoas Brazil
283 C8 Tres Lagos Arg.
285 F5 Tres Lomas Arg.
205 L2 Tres Mares, Pico mt. Spain
281 E3 Três Marias Brazil
281 E3 Três Marias, Represa resr Brazil
275 E2 Tres Matas Venez.
283 B7 Tres Montes, Península pen. Chile
214 B7 Tresnuraghes Sardegna Italy
205 N3 Trespaderne Spain
269 H9 Tres Palos Guerrero Mex.
269 I1 Tres Palos Tamaulipas Mex.
269 H9 Tres Palos, Laguna lag. Mex.
263 K12 Tres Picachos, Sierra mts Mex.
285 F6 Tres Picos Arg.
283 C6 Tres Picos mt. Arg.
267 M10 Tres Picos Mex.
285 G6 Tres Picos, Cerro mt. Arg.
269 N9 Tres Picos, Cerro mt. Mex.
263 L8 Tres Piedras NM U.S.A.
264 K5 Tres Pinos CA U.S.A.
281 E4 Três Pontas Brazil
280 C6 Tres Pontões, Pico mt. Brazil
284 C3 Tres Porteñas Arg.
282 C2 Tres Puentes Chile
283 D7 Tres Puntas, Cabo c. Arg.
280 D3 Três Ranchos Brazil
281 F5 Três Rios Brazil
168 I9 Tressait Perth and Kinross, Scotland U.K.
285 H4 Tres Sargentos Arg.
182 H5 Tresserve France
198 E2 Třešť Czech Rep.
215 N4 Treste r. Italy
161 Q4 Trestino Rus. Fed.
161 S4 Trestna Rus. Fed.
274 D6 Três Unidos Brazil
269 K7 Tres Valles Mex.
269 L7 Tres Zapotes tourist site Mex.
172 F4 Tretower Powys, Wales U.K.
183 H10 Trets France
163 K6 Tretten Norway
195 J4 Treuchtlingen Ger.
193 F9 Treuen Ger.
193 G6 Treuenbrietzen Ger.
164 E2 Treungen Norway
180 F5 Trévé France
207 M7 Trevélez Spain
207 M7 Trevélez r. Spain
283 C6 Trevelín Arg.
179 J6 Tréveray France
183 C8 Trèves France
Treves Ger. see Trier
215 J2 Trevi Italy
205 N3 Treviana Spain
181 J3 Trévières France
212 H4 Treviglio Italy
214 I3 Trevignano Romano Italy
182 J2 Trévillers France
205 O3 Treviño Spain
213 M4 Treviso Italy
213 M4 Treviso airport Italy
213 M4 Treviso prov. Italy
204 F6 Trevões Port.
Trevor Point pt Inner Islands Seychelles see Grande Barbe, Pointe
258 B3 Trevorton PA U.S.A.
258 F4 Trevose PA U.S.A.
172 B6 Trevose Head England U.K.
182 F5 Trévoux France
258 D3 Trexlertown PA U.S.A.
285 G2 Trezanos Pinto Arg.
182 D4 Trézelles France
219 K8 Trgovište Trgovište Serbia
198 D3 Trhové Sviny Czech Rep.
199 K3 Trhovište Slovakia
105 K10 Triabunna Tas. Austr.
204 F3 Triacastela Spain
258 A6 Triadelphia Reservoir MD U.S.A.
184 B3 Triaize France
106 F2 Trial Bay N.T. Austr.
151 F4 T'rialet'i Georgia
151 E4 T'rialet'is K'edi hills Georgia
119 H9 Tri An, Hô resr Vietnam
Triánda Rodos Greece see Trianta
256 H10 Triangle VA U.S.A.
235 F4 Triangle Zimbabwe
221 H6 Tria Nisia i. Greece
221 J6 Trianta Rodos Greece
145 N5 Tribal Areas admin. div. Pak.
213 R5 Tribalj Croatia
199 H3 Tribeč mts Slovakia
180 I3 Tribehou France
194 E5 Triberg im Schwarzwald Ger.
122 M1 Tri Brata, Gora hill Sakhalin Rus. Fed.
192 G2 Tribsees Ger.
107 J4 Tribulation, Cape Qld Austr.
260 E6 Tribune KS U.S.A.
284 B5 Tricao Malal Arg.
215 Q6 Tricarico Italy
217 O4 Tricase Italy
213 O3 Tricesimo Italy
213 M3 Trichiana Italy
Trichinopoly Tamil Nadu India see Tiruchchirappalli
220 C4 Trichonida, Limni l. Greece
Trichur India see Thrissur
178 E4 Tricot France
105 J5 Trida N.S.W. Austr.
Tridentum Italy see Trento
193 F10 Triebel r. Ger.
201 J4 Trieben Austria
193 F9 Triebes Ger.
178 C5 Trie-Château France
214 D7 Triei Sardegna Italy
194 E7 Triengen Switz.
194 B2 Trier Ger.
194 B2 Trierweiler Ger.
213 P4 Trieste Italy
213 P4 Trieste prov. Italy
Trieste, Golfo di g. Europe see Trieste, Gulf of
210 D3 Trieste, Gulf of Europe
213 O4 Trieste-Ronchi dei Legionari airport Italy
185 E9 Trie-sur-Baïse France
179 K5 Trieux France
180 E4 Trieux r. France
195 O5 Triftern Ger.
206 D4 Trigaches Port.
183 I9 Trigance France
217 L1 Triggiano Italy
201 I7 Triglav mt. Slovenia
210 D2 Triglavski narodni park nat. park Slovenia
192 F4 Triglitz Ger.
180 G7 Trignac France
215 N3 Trigno r. Italy
238 □1c Trigo, Monte hill São Jorge Azores
178 E8 Triguères France
206 F6 Trigueros Spain
205 K5 Trigueros del Valle Spain
220 C3 Trikala Greece
220 D3 Trikeriou, Diavlos sea chan. Greece
Tríkkala Greece see Trikala
Trikomo Cyprus see Trikomon
150 B3 Trikomon Cyprus
113 I7 Trikora, Puncak mt. Papua Indon.
220 D4 Trikorfo mt. Greece
210 F4 Trilj Croatia
285 F4 Trill Arg.
169 H4 Trillick Northern Ireland U.K.
205 O7 Trillo Spain
220 D5 Trilofo Greece
138 F3 Triloknath Hima. Prad. India
178 E6 Trilport France
169 I5 Trim Ireland
171 O4 Trimdon Durham, England U.K.
173 O4 Trimley St Mary Suffolk, England U.K.
212 H2 Trimmis Switz.
108 C6 Trimouille Island W.A. Austr.
172 D4 Trimsaran Carmarthenshire, Wales U.K.
266 D2 Trincheras Mex.
136 G8 Trincomalee Sri Lanka
280 C2 Trindade Brazil
206 D5 Trindade Beja Port.
204 F6 Trindade Bragança Port.
288 H7 Trindade, Ilha da i. S. Atlantic Ocean
199 H2 Třinec Czech Rep.
173 K4 Tring Hertfordshire, England U.K.
220 C3 Tringia mt. Greece
276 D3 Trinidad Bol.
270 D3 Trinidad Cuba
269 L8 Trinidad r. Mex.
271 □7 Trinidad i. Trin. and Tob.
285 I3 Trinidad Uru.
263 L8 Trinidad CO U.S.A.
283 B8 Trinidad, Golfo b. Chile
285 G6 Trinidad, Isla i. Arg.
271 M8 Trinidad and Tobago country West Indies
216 D8 Trinità, Lago della l. Sicilia Italy
214 B6 Trinità d'Agultu Sardegna Italy
215 Q5 Trinitapoli Italy
261 H10 Trinity TX U.S.A.
262 C6 Trinity r. CA U.S.A.
261 H11 Trinity r. TX U.S.A.
261 G9 Trinity, West Fork r. OK U.S.A.
107 J4 Trinity Bay Qld Austr.
249 K4 Trinity Bay Nfld and Lab. Can.
271 □7 Trinity Hills Trin. and Tob.
244 I4 Trinity Islands AK U.S.A.
264 M1 Trinity Range mts NV U.S.A.
137 M8 Trinkat Island Andaman & Nicobar Is India
146 C6 Trinkitat Sudan
212 E5 Trino Italy
200 D5 Trins Austria
204 F7 Trinta Port.
256 C8 Trinway OH U.S.A.
192 G2 Trinwillershagen Ger.
239 □1b Triolet Mauritius
205 K3 Triollo Spain
215 P4 Triolo r. Italy
217 L4 Trionto r. Italy
217 L4 Trionto, Capo c. Italy
212 D8 Triora Italy
184 I5 Triouzoune, Lac de la l. France
116 B3 Tripa r. Indon.
192 D4 Tripkau Ger.
220 D5 Tripoli Greece
Tripoli Lebanon see Trâblous
Tripoli Libya see Ţarābulus
Trípolis Greece see Tripoli
Tripolis Lebanon see Trâblous
224 B2 Tripolitania reg. Libya
220 C5 Tripotama Greece
194 D3 Trippstadt Ger.
193 E9 Triptis Ger.
136 E8 Tripunittura Kerala India
139 M8 Tripura state India
200 C5 Trisanna r. Austria
190 G2 Trischen i. Ger.
200 G6 Tristach Austria
238 □2c Tristan da Cunha i. S. Atlantic Ocean
228 B4 Tristao, Îles is Guinea
206 □ Tristão, Ponta do pt Madeira
200 H6 Tristenspitze mt. Austria
138 G4 Trisul mt. Uttaranchal India
249 K3 Triton Nfld and Lab. Can.
112 D3 Triton Island atoll Paracel Is
190 J3 Trittau Ger.
194 B2 Trittenheim Ger.
278 F3 Triunfo Pernambuco Brazil
276 D2 Triunfo Rondônia Brazil
266 □P11 Triunfo Hond.
Trivandrum Kerala India see Thiruvananthapuram
215 N4 Trivento Italy
212 E4 Trivero Italy
212 E6 Triversa r. Italy
215 P6 Trivigno Italy
183 B6 Trizac France
220 E5 Trizina Greece
199 G2 Trnava Czech Rep.
199 G3 Trnava Slovakia
199 H3 Trnavá Hora Slovakia
199 G3 Trnavský kraj admin. reg. Slovakia
201 N7 Trnovec Bartolovečki Croatia
201 I8 Trnovski gozd mts Slovenia
181 K3 Troarn France
193 H7 Tröbitz Ger.
113 L8 Trobriand Islands P.N.G.
194 G5 Trochtelfingen Ger.
246 H5 Trochu Alta Can.
163 N6 Trödje Sweden
204 C6 Trofa Port.
201 L5 Trofaiach Austria
162 L4 Trofors Norway
210 F4 Trogir Croatia
200 H6 Trogkofel mt. Austria/Italy
210 F4 Troglav mt. Croatia
164 H2 Trøgstad Norway
215 O5 Troia Italy
206 B4 Tróia Port.
216 H8 Troina Sicilia Italy
216 H8 Troina r. Sicilia Italy
191 D9 Troisdorf Ger.
179 N6 Troisfontaines France
226 E2 Trois Fourches, Cap des c. Morocco
249 G3 Trois-Pistoles Que. Can.
187 I8 Trois-Ponts Belgium
249 F4 Trois-Rivières Que. Can.
271 □2 Trois-Rivières Guadeloupe
185 G10 Trois Seigneurs, Pic des mt. France
178 D5 Troissereux France
182 C3 Trois-Vèvres France
187 J8 Troisvierges Lux.
152 H3 Troitsa Khanty-Mansiyskiy Avtonomnyy Okrug Rus. Fed.
161 X7 Troitsa Ryazanskaya Oblast' Rus. Fed.
142 I1 Troitsk Chelyabinskaya Oblast' Rus. Fed.
161 U6 Troitsk Moskovskaya Oblast' Rus. Fed.
159 Q2 Troitskiy Belgorodskaya Oblast' Rus. Fed.
Troitskiy Moskovskaya Oblast' Rus. Fed. see Troitsk
156 L3 Troitsko-Pechorsk Rus. Fed.
143 U1 Troitskoye Altayskiy Kray Rus. Fed.
122 J4 Troitskoye Khabarovskiy Kray Rus. Fed.
142 E1 Troitskoye Orenburgskaya Oblast' Rus. Fed.
142 G1 Troitskoye Respublika Bashkortostan Rus. Fed.
157 I7 Troitskoye Respublika Kalmykiya-Khalm'g-Tangch Rus. Fed.
270 □ Troja Jamaica
196 G5 Troja r. Pol.
201 K7 Trojane Slovenia
165 O7 Trójmiejski Park Krajobrazowy Pol.
286 X2 Troll research stn Antarctica
224 B6 Trolla well Chad
164 I3 Trollhättan Sweden
162 J5 Trollheimen park Norway
275 G5 Trombetas r. Brazil
239 □1 Tromelin, Île i. Indian Ocean
Tromelin Island Micronesia see Fais
212 F5 Tromello Italy
284 B5 Tromen, Volcán vol. Arg.
168 H8 Tromie r. Scotland U.K.
192 H1 Tromper Wiek b. Ger.
237 J6 Trompsburg S. Africa
162 O2 Troms county Norway
162 O2 Tromsø Norway
264 O6 Trona CA U.S.A.
283 C6 Tronador, Monte mt. Arg.
182 B3 Tronçais, Forêt de for. France
204 F5 Tronco Port.
268 E3 Troncoso Mex.
162 K5 Trondheim Norway
162 J5 Trondheimsfjorden sea chan. Norway
162 J5 Trondheimsleia sea chan. Norway
172 E6 Troney r. England U.K.
Trongsa Bhutan see Tongsa
139 M6 Trongsa Chhu r. Bhutan
215 L2 Tronto r. Italy
179 J6 Tronville-en-Barrois France
212 E5 Tronzano Vercellese Italy
181 M6 Troo France
150 A4 Troödos Cyprus
150 A4 Troödos, Mount Cyprus
150 A4 Troödos Mountains Cyprus
168 G11 Troon South Ayrshire, Scotland U.K.
220 C5 Tropaia Greece
161 S6 Troparevo Rus. Fed.
275 G6 Tropas r. Brazil
217 J6 Tropea Italy
278 D5 Tropeiros, Serra dos hills Brazil
265 T4 Tropic UT U.S.A.
169 G4 Trory Northern Ireland U.K.
156 K2 Trosh Rus. Fed.
161 S9 Trosna Rus. Fed.
193 G7 Trossin Ger.
194 F5 Trossingen Ger.
161 P9 Trostan' Rus. Fed.
169 J2 Trostan hill Northern Ireland U.K.
195 L1 Tröstau Ger.
195 N5 Trostberg Ger.
159 N3 Trostyanets' Sums'ka Oblast' Ukr.
158 I5 Trostyanets' Vinnyts'ka Oblast' Ukr.
158 E3 Trostyanets' Volyns'ka Oblast' Ukr.
168 D7 Trotternish hills Scotland U.K.
219 O4 Trotuş r. Romania
185 E10 Troumouse, Cirque de corrie France/Spain
168 L7 Troup Head Scotland U.K.
257 □S1 Trousers Lake N.B. Can.
246 E3 Trout r. B.C. Can.
246 G2 Trout r. N.W.T. Can.
171 L5 Troutbeck Cumbria, England U.K.
251 O4 Trout Creek Ont. Can.
250 E3 Trout Creek MI U.S.A.
256 D12 Trout Dale VA U.S.A.
246 H3 Trout Lake Alta Can.
246 F2 Trout Lake N.W.T. Can.
246 F2 Trout Lake l. N.W.T. Can.
247 M5 Trout Lake l. Ont. Can.
250 I3 Trout Lake MI U.S.A.
250 E3 Trout Lake l. WI U.S.A.
249 J3 Trout River Nfld and Lab. Can.
251 Q8 Trout Run PA U.S.A.
256 F11 Troutville VA U.S.A.
181 L3 Trouville-sur-Mer France
181 P7 Trouy France
204 D9 Troviscal Port.
172 H5 Trowbridge Wiltshire, England U.K.
105 J9 Trowutta Tas. Austr.
270 □ Troy Jamaica
Troy tourist site Turkey see Truva
255 E10 Troy AL U.S.A.
260 H6 Troy KS U.S.A.
251 K7 Troy MI U.S.A.
260 J6 Troy MO U.S.A.
262 G2 Troy MT U.S.A.
255 H8 Troy NC U.S.A.
257 M6 Troy NH U.S.A.
257 L6 Troy NY U.S.A.
256 A8 Troy OH U.S.A.
251 R8 Troy PA U.S.A.
219 M8 Troyan Bulg.
158 H3 Troyaniv Ukr.
158 J5 Troyanka Ukr.
161 V9 Troyekurovo Lipetskaya Oblast' Rus. Fed.
161 W8 Troyekurovo Lipetskaya Oblast' Rus. Fed.
161 U8 Troyekurovo Tul'skaya Oblast' Rus. Fed.
178 H7 Troyes France
159 R4 Troyits'ke Luhans'ka Oblast' Ukr.
158 J6 Troyits'ke Odes'ka Oblast' Ukr.
159 L6 Troyits'ko-Safonove Ukr.
264 P7 Troy Lake CA U.S.A.
179 J5 Troyon France
265 Q3 Troy Peak NV U.S.A.
198 G2 Tršice Czech Rep.
201 I8 Trstelj hill Slovenia
199 I2 Trstená Slovakia
218 J7 Trstenik Trstenik Serbia
199 G3 Trstice Slovakia
198 G3 Trstín Slovakia
106 F1 Truant Island N.T. Austr.
161 Q9 Trubchevsk Rus. Fed.
161 W9 Trubetchino Rus. Fed.
204 I2 Trubia Spain
204 I2 Trubia r. Spain
159 K3 Trubizh r. Ukr.
183 C7 Truc de la Garde mt. France
Truc Giang Vietnam see Bên Tre
204 H4 Truchas Spain
179 O6 Truchtersheim France
Trucial Coast country Asia see United Arab Emirates
Trucial States country Asia see United Arab Emirates
264 L2 Truckee CA U.S.A.
161 Q4 Trud Rus. Fed.
142 B5 Trudfront Rus. Fed.
Trudovoy Kazakh. see Novoishimskiy
Trudovoy Rus. Fed. see Yusta
122 H7 Trudovoye Rus. Fed.
161 U9 Trudy r. Rus. Fed.
106 C7 Truer Range hills N.T. Austr.
156 I2 Trufanovo Rus. Fed.
251 P2 Truite, Lac à la l. Que. Can.
206 G3 Trujillanos Spain
266 □Q10 Trujillo Hond.
276 A2 Trujillo Peru
206 H2 Trujillo Spain
274 D2 Trujillo Venez.
274 D2 Trujillo state Venez.
Trujillo, Monte mt. Dom. Rep. see Duarte, Pico
271 □1 Trujillo Alto Puerto Rico
Truk is Micronesia see Chuuk
194 D3 Trulben Ger.
172 F6 Trull Somerset, England U.K.
261 J8 Trumann AR U.S.A.
256 I6 Trumansburg NY U.S.A.
259 I2 Trumbull CT U.S.A.
265 S5 Trumbull, Mount AZ U.S.A.
116 B3 Trumon Sumatera Indon.
173 M3 Trumpington Cambridgeshire, England U.K.
219 K8 Trŭn Bulg.
181 L4 Trun France
212 F2 Trun Switz.
219 L8 Trŭna mt. Bulg.
105 K5 Trundle N.S.W. Austr.
118 H3 Trưng Khanh Vietnam
119 H10 Trưng Lơn, Hon i. Vietnam
119 H10 Trưng Nho, Hon i. Vietnam
Truong Sa is S. China Sea see Spratly Islands
249 I4 Truro N.S. Can.
172 B7 Truro Cornwall, England U.K.
117 K2 Trusan Sarawak Malaysia
117 K2 Trusan r. Malaysia
219 P3 Truşeşti Romania
191 J9 Trusetal Ger.
218 H9 Trush Albania
159 L4 Trushivtsi Ukr.
158 C4 Truskavets' Ukr.
169 F4 Truskmore hill Ireland
117 L2 Trus Madi, Gunung mt. Malaysia
219 M7 Trŭstenik Bulg.
246 F3 Trutch B.C. Can.
246 F3 Trutch Creek r. B.C. Can.
263 K10 Truth or Consequences NM U.S.A.
198 E1 Trutnov Czech Rep.
245 J4 Truuli Peak AK U.S.A.
221 H3 Truva tourist site Turkey
183 B7 Truyère r. France
183 B7 Truyère, Gorges de la France
161 S3 Truzhenik Rus. Fed.
219 N8 Tryavna Bulg.
220 C4 Tryfos Greece
190 K1 Tryggelev Denmark
220 C3 Trygona Greece
197 K5 Tryńcza Pol.
260 E5 Tryon NE U.S.A.
102 J3 Tryphena Harbour North I. N.Z.
220 F7 Trypiti, Akrotirio pt Kriti Greece
220 F3 Trypiti, Akrotirio pt Greece
163 L6 Trysil Norway
163 L6 Trysilelva r. Norway
163 L6 Trysilfjellet mt. Norway
160 F5 Tryškiai Lith.
210 E3 Tržac Bos.-Herz.
197 J3 Trzcianka Mazowieckie Pol.
196 E2 Trzcianka Wielkopolskie Pol.
197 K2 Trzcianne Pol.
196 D3 Trzciel Pol.
196 G4 Trzcinica Pol.
196 D1 Trzebiatów Pol.
196 C4 Trzebiel Pol.
196 F1 Trzebielino Pol.
197 K4 Trzebieszów Pol.
196 C2 Trzebież Pol.
197 H5 Trzebinia Pol.
196 F4 Trzebnica Pol.
197 K5 Trzebośnica r. Pol.
196 F3 Trzemeszno Pol.
196 D3 Trzemeszyno Lubuskie Pol.
197 L3 Trześcianka Pol.
197 J6 Trześniów Pol.
197 J5 Trześniówka r. Pol.
197 L5 Trzeszczany Pierwsze Pol.
210 E2 Tržič Slovenia
201 K7 Trzin Slovenia
196 C3 Trzrcińsko-Zdrój Pol.
197 H5 Trzyciąż Pol.
197 K5 Trzydnik Duży Pol.
128 A2 Tsagaannuur Bayan-Ölgiy Mongolia
Tsagaannuur Mongolia see Halhgol
128 D3 Tsagaan Nuur salt l. Mongolia
Tsagaan-Olom Mongolia see Tayshir
129 M2 Tsagaan-Ovoo Mongolia
Tsagaan-Ovoo Mongolia see Nariynteel
128 F2 Tsagaan-Uul Hövsgöl Mongolia
128 G1 Tsagaan-Üür Hövsgöl Mongolia
157 I7 Tsagan Aman Rus. Fed.
157 I7 Tsagan-Nur Rus. Fed.
151 D3 Ts'ageri Georgia
Tsaidam Basin China see Qaidam Pendi
151 I4 Tsakhur Rus. Fed.
151 B2 Tsakhvoa, Gora mt. Rus. Fed.
162 P2 Tsåktso mt. Sweden
151 D3 Tsalenjikha Georgia
230 B5 Tsama I Congo
239 □3a Tsangadjou Njazidja Comoros
162 M3 Tsangatjåkkå mt. Sweden
234 D4 Tsao Botswana
235 □J3 Tsaramandroso Madag.
235 □J3 Tsaratanana Madag.
235 □K2 Tsaratanana, Massif du mts Madag.
219 P8 Tsarevo Bulg.
161 R6 Tsarevo-Zaymishche Rus. Fe
Tsaribrod Dimitrovgrad Serbi
Dimitrovgrad
219 M8 Tsarimir Bulg.
Tsaritsyn Rus. Fed. see Volgo
159 N5 Tsarychanka Ukr.
157 I6 Tsatsa Rus. Fed.
237 M6 Tsatsana mt. S. Africa
131 □J7 Tsat Tsze Mui pt H.K. China
234 B5 Tsaukaib Namibia
233 C5 Tsavo Kenya
233 C5 Tsavo East National Park Ke
233 C5 Tsavo West National Park Ke
237 L7 Tsazo S. Africa
200 A5 Tschagguns Austria
193 K7 Tschernitz Ger.
234 E3 Tsebanana Botswana
151 C2 Tsebelda Georgia
128 D4 Tseel Mongolia
Tsefat Israel see Ẓefat
157 H7 Tselina Rus. Fed.
143 U1 Tselinnoye Rus. Fed.
142 I2 Tselinnyy Rus. Fed.
Tselinograd Kazakh. see Asta
Tselinogradskaya Oblast' admin. div. Kazakh. see Akmolinskaya Oblast'
Tsementnyy Rus. Fed. see Fok
128 A2 Tsengel Bayan-Ölgiy Mongol
Tsengel Mongolia see Tosontsengel
129 K3 Tsenhermandal Mongolia
156 I2 Tsenogora Rus. Fed.
219 M8 Tsentralen Balkan nat. park
161 P5 Tsentral'noolesnoy Zapovedn nature res. Rus. Fed.
156 J4 Tsentral'nyy Kirovskaya Oblas Rus. Fed.
Tsentral'nyy Moskovskaya Ob Rus. Fed. see Radovitskiy
161 W8 Tsentral'nyy Ryazanskaya Obl Rus. Fed.
161 N6 Tserkovishche Rus. Fed.
219 L7 Tserovo Bulg.
234 C5 Tses Namibia
128 C3 Tsetseg Mongolia
Tsetsegnuur Mongolia see Tsetseg
234 D4 Tsetseng Botswana
128 G2 Tsetserleg Arhangay Mongoli
128 G3 Tsetserleg Arhangay Mongoli
128 E2 Tsetserleg Hövsgöl Mongolia
131 □J7 Tseung Kwan O H.K. China
229 F5 Tsévié Togo
230 F4 Tsha Dem. Rep. Congo
234 D5 Tshabong Botswana
Tshad country Africa see Chad
231 D7 Tshala Dem. Rep. Congo
157 G7 Tshchikskoye Vodokhranilish resr Rus. Fed.
231 B6 Tshela Dem. Rep. Congo
231 C6 Tshene Dem. Rep. Congo
235 E4 Tshesebe Botswana
231 D6 Tshibala Dem. Rep. Congo
231 D6 Tshibuka Dem. Rep. Congo
231 D6 Tshibwika Dem. Rep. Congo
236 I1 Tshidilamolomo Botswana
231 D6 Tshikapa Dem. Rep. Congo
231 D6 Tshikapa r. Dem. Rep. Congo
231 D6 Tshilenge Dem. Rep. Congo
231 F6 Tshimbo Dem. Rep. Congo
231 D6 Tshimbulu Dem. Rep. Congo
237 K2 Tshing S. Africa
235 F4 Tshipise S. Africa
231 D6 Tshisenge Dem. Rep. Congo
231 D7 Tshitanzu Dem. Rep. Congo
231 D6 Tshitupa Dem. Rep. Congo
231 D6 Tshiumbe r. Angola/Dem. Rep. Congo
231 E6 Tshofa Dem. Rep. Congo
235 F5 Tshokwane S. Africa
235 E3 Tsholotsho Zimbabwe
231 E6 Tshongwe Dem. Rep. Congo
234 D4 Tshootsha Botswana
230 E4 Tshopo prov. Dem. Rep. Cong
230 D5 Tshuapa r. Dem. Rep. Congo
230 C5 Tshumbiri Dem. Rep. Congo
Tshwane S. Africa see Pretoria
235 □J3 Tsiazonano mt. Madag.
219 L7 Tsibritsa r. Bulg.
245 N2 Tsiigehtchic N.W.T. Can.
156 J2 Tsil'ma r. Rus. Fed.
160 J8 Tsimkavichy Belarus
157 H7 Tsimlyansk Rus. Fed.
157 H7 Tsimlyanskoye Vodokhranilishche resr Rus. F
122 K3 Tsimmermanovka Rus. Fed.
Tsinan Shandong China see Ji
236 H3 Tsineng S. Africa
Tsinghai prov. China see Qing
239 □3b Tsingoni Mayotte
131 □I7 Tsing Shan hill H.K. China
131 □I7 Tsing Shan Wan b. H.K. Chin
131 □J7 Tsing Shui Wan b. H.K. Chin
Tsingtao Shandong China see Qingdao
235 □J3 Tsingy de Bemaraha, Réserve nature res. Madag.
131 □J7 Tsing Yi i. H.K. China
239 □3a Tsinimouapanga Njazidja Comoros
Tsining Nei Mongol China see Jining
235 □J3 Tsinjomay mt. Madag.
234 C3 Tsintsabis Namibia
235 □J5 Tsiombe Madag.
151 E4 Tsip'a Georgia
235 □J3 Tsiroanomandidy Madag.
151 C4 Tsiskara Nakrdzali nature res. Georgia
Tsiteli Tskaro Georgia see Dedop'listsqaro
235 □J4 Tsitondroina Madag.
Tsitsihar Heilong. China see Qiqihar
236 H10 Tsitsikamma Forest and Coas National Park S. Africa
246 E4 Tsitsutl Peak B.C. Can.
151 C3 Ts'ivi r. Georgia
151 G4 Ts'ivi, Mt'a Georgia
156 I5 Tsivil'sk Rus. Fed.
Tskhakaia Georgia see Senaki
Tskhaltubo Georgia see Tsqalt
151 E3 Ts'khinvali Georgia
151 F4 Ts'khneti Georgia
160 K9 Tsna r. Belarus
157 H5 Tsna r. Rus. Fed.
161 R4 Tsna r. Rus. Fed.
161 W6 Tsna r. Rus. Fed.
151 G4 Tsnori Georgia
234 D3 Tsodilo Hills Botswana
128 E4 Tsogt Mongolia
128 I4 Tsogt-Ovoo Mongolia
128 I5 Tsogttsetsiy Mongolia
138 G3 Tsokar Chumo l. Jammu and Kashmir India
237 M7 Tsolo S. Africa
237 L8 Tsomo S. Africa
237 L8 Tsomo r. S. Africa
161 T9 Tson r. Rus. Fed.
Tsona Xizang China see Cona
221 G2 Tsopan hill Greece
220 C2 Tsotili Greece
151 G5 Tsovinar Armenia
151 D3 Tsqaltubo Georgia
126 E6 Tsu Japan
125 P9 Tsubame Japan
126 E2 Tsubata Japan
124 V3 Tsubetsu Japan
127 L3 Tsuchiura Japan
126 D6 Tsuchiyama Japan
151 I3 Tsudakhar Rus. Fed.
131 □J7 Tsuen Wan H.K. China
127 K3 Tsuga Japan
124 R5 Tsugarū-kaikyō str. Japan
Tsugaru Strait Japan see Tsugarū-kaikyō
126 C6 Tsuge Japan
126 G5 Tsugu Japan

F4 **Tsukechi** Japan
□[1] **Tsuken-jima** *i. Okinawa* Japan
D6 **Tsukigase** Japan
S3 **Tsukigata** Japan
I2 **Tsukiyono** Japan
L3 **Tsukuba** Japan
F6 **Tsukude** Japan
J4 **Tsukui** Japan
I13 **Tsukumi** Japan
Tsul-Ulaan Mongolia *see* **Bayannuur**
I2 **Tsumagoi** Japan
E3 **Tsuman'** Ukr.
C3 **Tsumeb** Namibia
I6 **Tsumeki-zaki** *pt* Japan
C4 **Tsumis Park** Namibia
D3 **Tsumkwe** Namibia
A7 **Tsuna** Japan
I1 **Tsunan** Japan
C4 **Tsunega-misaki** *pt* Japan
H12 **Tsuno-shima** *i.* Japan
H3 **Tsurib** Rus. Fed.
I4 **Tsuru** Japan
D4 **Tsuruga** Japan
C4 **Tsuruga-wan** *b.* Japan
E3 **Tsurugi** Japan
G2 **Tsurugi-dake** *mt.* Japan
L13 **Tsurugi-san** *mt.* Japan
Tsurukhaytuy Rus. Fed. *see* **Priargunsk**
J14 **Tsurumi-zaki** *pt* Japan
Q8 **Tsuruoka** Japan
E5 **Tsushima** Japan
G12 **Tsushima** *is* Japan
Tsushima-kaikyō *str.* Japan/S. Korea *see* **Korea Strait**
I12 **Tsuwano** Japan
L11 **Tsuyama** Japan
L9 **Tsvetino** Bulg.
K4 **Tsvitkove** Ukr.
L5 **Tsvitne** Ukr.
D4 **Tswaane** Botswana
J4 **Tswaraganang** S. Africa
J3 **Tswelelang** S. Africa
I4 **Tsybuliv** Ukr.
I9 **Tsyelyakhany** Belarus
K1 **Tsyerakhowka** Belarus
Tsygira Moldova *see* **Ţighira**
E5 **Ts'yl-os Provincial Park** B.C. Can.
O7 **Tsyomny Lyes** Belarus
V2 **Tsyp-Navolok** Rus. Fed.
N4 **Tsyr** *r.* Ukr.
L7 **Tsyurupyns'k** Ukr.
Tthedzeh Koe *N.W.T.* Can. *see* **Wrigley**
Tthenaagoo *N.W.T.* Can. *see* **Nahanni Butte**
C5 **Tua** Dem. Rep. Congo
F6 **Tua** *r.* Port.
F7 **Tua, Tanjung** *pt* Indon.
I4 **Tuakau** *North I.* N.Z.
H8 **Tual** *Maluku* Indon.
H6 **Tū 'Alī-ye Soflá** Iran
E5 **Tuam** Ireland
H8 **Tuamarina** *South I.* N.Z.
E7 **Tuamgraney** Ireland
□[9] **Tuamotu, Archipel des** *is* Fr. Polynesia
Tuamotu Islands Fr. Polynesia *see* **Tuamotu, Archipel des**
F4 **Tuân Giao** Vietnam
B3 **Tuangku** *i.* Indon.
□[4] **Tuapa** Niue
D13 **Tuapeka Mouth** *South I.* N.Z.
A1 **Tuapse** Rus. Fed.
L1 **Tuaran** *Sabah* Malaysia
D5 **Tuar Mhic Éadaigh** Ireland
□ **Tuas** Sing.
□[2] **Tuasivi** Samoa
B13 **Tuatapere** *South I.* N.Z.
D9 **Tuath, Loch** *sea chan. Scotland* U.K.
D6 **Tuath, Loch a'** *b. Scotland* U.K.
U5 **Tuba City** *AZ* U.S.A.
F4 **Tubalai** *i. Maluku* Indon.
J8 **Tuban** *Jawa* Indon.
C9 **Tubarão** Brazil
I8 **Tubarjal** Saudi Arabia
D6 **Ţūbās** West Bank
J3 **Tubau** *Sarawak* Malaysia
B7 **Tubbataha Reefs** Phil.
Tubbercurry Ireland *see* **Tobercurry**
K4 **Tubbergen** Neth.
B8 **Tubbrid** Ireland
D6 **Tubeya** Dem. Rep. Congo
C8 **Tubigan** *i.* Phil.
M3 **Tubilla del Agua** Spain
G4 **Tübingen** Ger.
H5 **Tübingen** *admin. reg.* Ger.
H1 **Tubinskiy** Rus. Fed.
F7 **Tubize** Belgium
C5 **Tubmanburg** Liberia
G4 **Tubo** *r.* Nigeria
D7 **Tubod** *Mindanao* Phil.
I3 **Tubou** Fiji
I2 **Tubre** Italy
C6 **Tubridgi Point** *W.A.* Austr.
D1 **Tubruq** Libya
L3 **Tubu** *r.* Indon.
□[9] **Tubuai** *i. Îs Australes* Fr. Polynesia
Tubuai Islands Fr. Polynesia *see* **Australes, Îles**
D2 **Tubutama** Mex.
I8 **Tucacas** Venez.
F5 **Tucandera** Brazil
E3 **Tucannon** *r. WA* U.S.A.
F4 **Tucano** Brazil
B5 **Tucapel** Chile
F4 **Tucavaca** Bol.
F4 **Tucavaca** *r.* Bol.
J10 **Tuchan** France
F4 **Tüchen** Ger.
F6 **Tuchheim** Ger.
O3 **Tuchitua** *Y.T.* Can.
T6 **Tuchkovo** Rus. Fed.
I10 **Tuchlovice** Czech Rep.
F3 **Tuchodi** *r. B.C.* Can.
F2 **Tuchola** Pol.
G2 **Tucholskie, Bory** *for.* Pol.
H2 **Tucholski Park Krajobrazowy** Pol.
F1 **Tuchomie** Pol.
J6 **Tuchów** Pol.
K4 **Tuchowicz** Pol.
F3 **Tuchyn** Ukr.
F6 **Tuckahoe** *NJ* U.S.A.
K3 **Tuckahoe** *NY* U.S.A.
F6 **Tuckahoe** *r. NJ* U.S.A.
D7 **Tuckahoe Creek** *r. MD* U.S.A.
E9 **Tuckanarra** *W.A.* Austr.
L2 **Tucker Glacier** Antarctica
□[1] **Tucker's Town** Bermuda
G5 **Tuckerton** *NJ* U.S.A.
D4 **Tuckerton** *PA* U.S.A.
Tucopia *i.* Solomon Is *see* **Tikopia**
K5 **Tucquegnieux** France
V9 **Tucson** *AZ* U.S.A.
U9 **Tucson Aqueduct** *canal* U.S.A.
U9 **Tucson Mountains** *AZ* U.S.A.
H1 **Tuctuc** *r. Que.* Can.
Tucumán Arg. *see* **San Miguel de Tucumán**
D2 **Tucumán** *prov.* Arg.
D8 **Tucumcari** *NM* U.S.A.
C2 **Tucunuco** Arg.
H6 **Tucuparé** Brazil
F2 **Tucupita** Venez.
C2 **Tucuracas** Col.
I5 **Tucuruí** Brazil
I6 **Tucuruí, Represa** *resr* Brazil
L4 **Tuczna** Pol.
E2 **Tuczno** Pol.
H6 **Tudeå** *r.* Denmark
Q4 **Tudela** Spain
K5 **Tudela de Duero** Spain
Tuder Italy *see* **Todi**
E2 **Tüdevtey** Mongolia
O3 **Tudora** Romania
P5 **Tudor Vladimirescu** Romania
Q5 **Tudovka** *r.* Rus. Fed.
J2 **Tudu** Estonia
K2 **Tudulinna** Estonia
H4 **Tudun-Wada** Nigeria
C2 **Tudweiliog** *Gwynedd, Wales* U.K.
209 C8 **Tuéjar** Spain
204 F5 **Tuela** *r.* Port.
131 □I7 **Tuen Mun** *H.K.* China
213 K3 **Tuenno** Italy
139 O6 **Tuensang** *Nagaland* India
275 I5 **Tueré** *r.* Brazil
204 I4 **Tuerto** *r.* Spain
161 X3 **Tufanovo** Rus. Fed.
147 I2 **Ţufayḩ** Saudi Arabia
181 M5 **Tuffé** France
113 K8 **Tufi** P.N.G.
291 J2 **Tufts Abyssal Plain** *sea feature* N. Pacific Ocean
Tuga *i.* Vanuatu *see* **Tégua**
237 P5 **Tugela** *r.* S. Africa
237 M4 **Tugela Falls** S. Africa
237 O4 **Tugela Ferry** S. Africa
Tūghyl Kazakh. *see* **Tugyl**
244 I4 **Tugidak Island** *AK* U.S.A.
133 K11 **Tuglung** *Xizang* China
114 E6 **Tugnug Point** *Samar* Phil.
130 C5 **Tuguancun** *Yunnan* China
115 A3 **Tuguan Maputi** *i.* Indon.
114 F8 **Tugubun Point** *Mindanao* Phil.
114 C3 **Tuguegarao** *Luzon* Phil.
122 J2 **Tugur** Rus. Fed.
122 J2 **Tugurskiy Zaliv** *b.* Rus. Fed.
235 F4 **Tugwi** *r.* Zimbabwe
143 U4 **Tugyl** Kazakh.
129 P8 **Tuhai He** *r.* China
116 B4 **Tuhemberua** Indon.
118 D1 **Tuhtong** Myanmar
204 C4 **Tui** Spain
276 D3 **Tuichi** *r.* Bol.
214 B8 **Tuili** *Sardegna* Italy
139 N8 **Tuilianpui** *r.* Bangl./India
238 □[3b] **Tuineje** *Fuerteventura* Canary Is
236 E5 **Tuins** *watercourse* S. Africa
160 H4 **Tūja** Latvia
144 G8 **Tūjak** Iran
Tujiabu *Jiangxi* China *see* **Yongxiu**
116 F5 **Tujuh, Kepulauan** *is* Indon.
117 L3 **Tujung** *Kalimantan* Indon.
142 G1 **Tukan** Rus. Fed.
115 C6 **Tukangbesi, Kepulauan** *is* Indon.
248 E1 **Tukarak Island** *Nunavut* Can.
232 E2 **Tukayel** Eth.
160 I9 **Tukhavichy** Belarus
147 I4 **Ţukhmān, Banī** *reg.* Saudi Arabia
158 C5 **Tukhol'ka** Ukr.
145 P3 **Tŭkhtamish** Tajik.
102 K6 **Tukituki** *r. North I.* N.Z.
244 H4 **Tuklung** *AK* U.S.A.
224 D1 **Tūkrah** Libya
245 N1 **Tuktoyaktuk** *N.W.T.* Can.
245 Q1 **Tuktut Nogait National Park** *N.W.T./Nunavut* Can.
160 G5 **Tukums** Latvia
117 I5 **Tukung, Bukit** *mt.* Indon.
122 E1 **Tukuringra, Khrebet** *mts* Rus. Fed.
151 G1 **Tukuy-Mekteb** Rus. Fed.
233 B7 **Tukuyu** Tanz.
100 □[2] **Tula** American Samoa
214 B6 **Tula** *Sardegna* Italy
232 C5 **Tula** *watercourse* Kenya
269 H5 **Tula** *Hidalgo* Mex.
269 H2 **Tula** *Tamaulipas* Mex.
269 H5 **Tula** *r.* Mex.
161 U7 **Tula** Rus. Fed.
Tulach Mhór Ireland *see* **Tullamore**
100 □[6] **Tulaghi** Solomon Is
133 K8 **Tulagt Ar Gol** *r.* China
284 B2 **Tulahuén** Chile
128 F7 **Tulai** *Qinghai* China
128 E7 **Tulai Nanshan** *mts* China
128 E7 **Tulai Shan** *mts* China
145 J5 **Tulak** Afgh.
287 D2 **Tula Mountains** Antarctica
269 I5 **Tulancingo** Mex.
116 F7 **Tulangbawang** *r.* Indon.
Tula Oblast *admin. div.* Rus. Fed. *see* **Tul'skaya Oblast'**
264 M5 **Tulare** *CA* U.S.A.
264 M6 **Tulare Lake Bed** *CA* U.S.A.
263 L10 **Tularosa** *NM* U.S.A.
136 H3 **Tulasi** *mt. Madh. Prad./Orissa* India
190 K5 **Tülau** Ger.
197 I2 **Tuławki** Pol.
236 D9 **Tulbagh** S. Africa
201 N3 **Tulbing** Austria
199 K5 **Tulca** Romania
274 B4 **Tulcán** Ecuador
196 F3 **Tulce** Pol.
219 Q5 **Tulcea** Romania
Tul'chin Ukr. *see* **Tul'chyn**
158 H5 **Tul'chyn** Ukr.
269 I7 **Tulcingo** Mex.
264 M5 **Tule** *r. CA* U.S.A.
270 G8 **Tulé** Venez.
Tuléar Madag. *see* **Toliara**
144 E4 **Tuleh** Iran
115 F5 **Tulehu** *Maluku* Indon.
262 D6 **Tulelake** *CA* U.S.A.
247 L2 **Tulemalu Lake** *Nunavut* Can.
129 Q4 **Tule Mod** *Nei Mongol* China
183 F8 **Tulette** France
198 F5 **Tulfás** *r.* Hungary
200 E5 **Tulfes** Austria
219 N4 **Tulgheș** Romania
261 E8 **Tulia** *TX* U.S.A.
129 Q1 **Tulihe** *Nei Mongol* China
244 E5 **Tulik Volcano** *AK* U.S.A.
196 G3 **Tuliszków** Pol.
136 E3 **Tuljapur** *Mahar.* India
150 D6 **Ţūlkarm** West Bank
169 E7 **Tulla** Ireland
169 F4 **Tullaghan** Ireland
255 D8 **Tullahoma** *TN* U.S.A.
105 K5 **Tullamore** *N.S.W.* Austr.
169 H6 **Tullamore** Ireland
170 C8 **Tullaroan** Ireland
184 H5 **Tulle** France
190 K1 **Tullebølle** Denmark
105 K5 **Tullibigeal** *N.S.W.* Austr.
183 G6 **Tullins** France
201 N3 **Tulln** Austria
201 M3 **Tullner Feld** *plain* Austria
264 L4 **Tullock Lake** *CA* U.S.A.
261 I10 **Tullos** *LA* U.S.A.
169 I7 **Tullow** Ireland
107 K4 **Tully** *Qld* Austr.
169 G4 **Tully** *Northern Ireland* U.K.
169 H4 **Tully** *Northern Ireland* U.K.
169 J5 **Tullyallen** Ireland
169 G4 **Tullybrack** *hill Northern Ireland* U.K.
169 I8 **Tullycanna** Ireland
107 J4 **Tully Falls** *Qld* Austr.
169 I3 **Tullyhogue** *Northern Ireland* U.K.
258 F4 **Tullytown** *PA* U.S.A.
169 H4 **Tullyvin** Ireland
169 F3 **Tullyvoos** Ireland
219 O5 **Tulnici** Romania
162 V2 **Tuloma** *r.* Rus. Fed.
162 U5 **Tulos** Rus. Fed.
197 I3 **Tułowice** *Mazowieckie* Pol.
196 F5 **Tułowice** *Opolskie* Pol.
156 L3 **Tulpan** Rus. Fed.
162 T3 **Tulppio** Fin.
261 H7 **Tulsa** *OK* U.S.A.
245 N4 **Tulsequah** *B.C.* Can.
138 I5 **Tulsipur** Nepal
169 F5 **Tulsk** Ireland
161 U8 **Tul'skaya Oblast'** *admin. div.* Rus. Fed.
151 B1 **Tul'skiy** Rus. Fed.
274 B3 **Tuluá** Col.
232 C2 **Tulu Bolo** Eth.
219 Q5 **Tulucești** Romania
232 C3 **Tulu Dīmtu** *mt.* Eth.
244 G3 **Tuluksak** *AK* U.S.A.
150 F6 **Tulūl al Ashāqif** *hills* Jordan
267 P7 **Tulum** *tourist site* Mex.
284 C2 **Tulum, Valle de** *val.* Arg.
120 H1 **Tulun** Rus. Fed.
117 I9 **Tulungagung** *Jawa* Indon.
Tulusdu *N. Male* Maldives *see* **Thulusdhu**
275 F4 **Tulu-Tuloi, Serra** *hills* Brazil
232 B2 **Tulu Welel** *mt.* Eth.
156 K4 **Tulva** *r.* Rus. Fed.
197 M4 **Tulychiv** Ukr.
159 M2 **Tulyholove** Ukr.
266 □Q11 **Tuma** *r.* Nic.
161 X6 **Tuma** Rus. Fed.
274 B4 **Tumaco** Col.
237 L2 **Tumahole** S. Africa
133 J10 **Tumain** *Xizang* China
142 C4 **Tumak** Rus. Fed.
144 I4 **Tūmān Āqā** Iran
Tuman-gang *r.* Asia *see* **Tumen Jiang**
Tumannaya *r.* Asia *see* **Tumen Jiang**
156 F1 **Tumannyy** Rus. Fed.
161 R6 **Tumanovo** Rus. Fed.
153 S3 **Tumanskiy** Rus. Fed.
Tumasik Sing. *see* **Singapore**
275 G3 **Tumatumari** Guyana
161 R1 **Tumazy** Rus. Fed.
128 G8 **Tumba** *Qinghai* China
231 D5 **Tumba** Dem. Rep. Congo
165 N2 **Tumba** Sweden
230 C5 **Tumba, Lac** *l.* Dem. Rep. Congo
117 J5 **Tumbangmiri** *Kalimantan* Indon.
117 J5 **Tumbangsamba** *Kalimantan* Indon.
117 J5 **Tumbangsenamang** *Kalimantan* Indon.
117 I5 **Tumbangtiti** *Kalimantan* Indon.
114 E8 **Tumbao** *Mindanao* Phil.
214 A5 **Tumbarino, Punta** *pt Sardegna* Italy
105 L6 **Tumbarumba** *N.S.W.* Austr.
274 A5 **Tumbes** Peru
274 A5 **Tumbes** *dept* Peru
268 E7 **Tumbiscatio** Mex.
246 F4 **Tumbler Ridge** *B.C.* Can.
Tumbou Fiji *see* **Tubou**
104 F6 **Tumby Bay** *S.A.* Austr.
162 U3 **Tumcha** *r.* Fin./Rus. Fed.
Tumd Youqi *Nei Mongol* China *see* **Salaqi**
Tumd Zuoqi *Nei Mongol* China *see* **Qasq**
122 F7 **Tumen** *Jilin* China
130 H2 **Tumen** *Shaanxi* China
122 G7 **Tumen Jiang** *r.* Asia
275 F3 **Tumeremo** Venez.
275 F3 **Tumereng** Guyana
114 B9 **Tumindao** *i.* Phil.
281 G3 **Tumiritinga** Brazil
136 E6 **Tumkur** *Karnataka* India
139 K6 **Tumlingtar** Nepal
168 I9 **Tummel, Loch** *l. Scotland* U.K.
168 H9 **Tummel Bridge** *Perth and Kinross, Scotland* U.K.
224 B4 **Tummo, Mountains of** Libya/Niger
122 L4 **Tumnin** *r.* Rus. Fed.
100 □[1] **Tumon Bay** Guam
145 J8 **Tump** Pak.
117 K5 **Tumpah** *Kalimantan* Indon.
116 E1 **Tumpat** Malaysia
119 F8 **Tumpôr, Phnum** *mt.* Cambodia
115 C4 **Tumpu, Gunung** *mt.* Indon.
115 C4 **Tumputiga, Gunung** *mt.* Indon.
138 G9 **Tumsar** *Mahar.* India
228 E4 **Tumu** Ghana
275 G4 **Tumucumaque, Serra** *hills* Brazil
137 H3 **Tumudibandh** *Orissa* India
204 H9 **Tumuja** *r.* Spain
276 D3 **Tumupasa** Bol.
Tumur Kazakh. *see* **Timur**
132 E6 **Tumushuke** *Xinjiang* China
276 D5 **Tumusla** Bol.
105 L6 **Tumut** *N.S.W.* Austr.
156 K5 **Tumutuk** Rus. Fed.
228 E4 **Tuna** Ghana
271 □[1] **Tuna, Punta** *pt* Puerto Rico
114 E8 **Tuna Bay** *Mindanao* Phil.
165 L1 **Tuna-Hästberg** Sweden
271 □[7] **Tunapuna** Trin. and Tob.
276 D4 **Tunari, Parque Nacional** *nat. park* Bolivia
270 D3 **Tunas de Zaza** Cuba
Ţunb al Kubrá *i.* The Gulf *see* **Greater Tunb**
Ţunb aş Şughrá *i.* The Gulf *see* **Lesser Tunb**
173 M5 **Tunbridge Wells, Royal** *Kent, England* U.K.
221 K3 **Tunçbilek** Turkey
148 I4 **Tunceli** Turkey
151 A6 **Tunceli** *prov.* Turkey
130 H9 **Tunchang** *Hainan* China
151 D4 **Tunçoluk** Turkey
105 N5 **Tuncurry** *N.S.W.* Austr.
133 D13 **Tundla** *Uttar Prad.* India
225 F5 **Tundubai** *well* Sudan
233 B7 **Tunduma** Tanz.
233 C7 **Tunduru** Tanz.
219 O9 **Tundzha** *r.* Bulg.
164 I6 **Tune** Denmark
Tunes Tunisia *see* **Tunis**
229 H4 **Tunga** Nigeria
168 D6 **Tunga** *Western Isles, Scotland* U.K.
136 F5 **Tungabhadra** *r.* India
136 E5 **Tungabhadra Reservoir** India
232 A2 **Tungaru** Sudan
114 D8 **Tungawan** *Mindanao* Phil.
131 □I7 **Tung Chung** *H.K.* China
131 □I7 **Tung Chung Wan** *b. H.K.* China
139 M8 **Tungi** Bangl.
117 M2 **Tungku** *Sabah* Malaysia
266 □Q11 **Tungla** Nic.
131 □J7 **Tung Lung Chau** *i. H.K.* China
Tung Lung Island *H.K.* China *see* **Tung Lung Chau**
162 □D1 **Tungnaá** *r.* Iceland
122 M2 **Tungor** *Sakhalin* Rus. Fed.
162 U4 **Tungozero** Rus. Fed.
131 □J7 **Tung Pok Liu Hoi Hap** *sea chan. H.K.* China
245 O3 **Tungsten (abandoned)** *N.W.T.* Can.
156 F2 **Tunguda** Rus. Fed.
117 J4 **Tungun, Bukit** *mt.* Indon.
131 □J7 **Tung Wan** *b. H.K.* China
137 H4 **Tuni** *Andhra Prad.* India
144 H5 **Tūnī, Chāh-e** *well* Iran
261 J8 **Tunica** *MS* U.S.A.
194 F5 **Tuningen** Ger.
251 N1 **Tunis** *Ont.* Can.
227 H1 **Tunis** Tunisia
227 H1 **Tunis, Golfe de** *g.* Tunisia
227 H2 **Tunisia** *country* Africa
274 C3 **Tunja** Col.
258 D1 **Tunkhannock** *PA* U.S.A.
266 □Q11 **Tunki** Nic.
129 M8 **Tunliu** *Shanxi* China
250 D5 **Tunnel City** *WI* U.S.A.
109 E8 **Tunnel Creek** *watercourse W.A.* Austr.
256 F9 **Tunnelton** *WV* U.S.A.
164 E1 **Tunnhovd** Norway
164 E1 **Tunnhovdfjorden** *l.* Norway
162 L4 **Tunnsjøen** *l.* Norway
161 X4 **Tunoshna** Rus. Fed.
173 O3 **Tunstall** *Suffolk, England* U.K.
195 M6 **Tuntenhausen** Ger.
162 T3 **Tuntsa** Fin.
244 G3 **Tuntutuliak** *AK* U.S.A.
249 H1 **Tunulic** *r. Que.* Can.
244 F3 **Tununak** *AK* U.S.A.
249 I1 **Tunungayualok Island** *Nfld and Lab.* Can.
284 C3 **Tunuyán** Arg.
284 D4 **Tunuyán** *r.* Arg.
284 C3 **Tunuyán, Sierra de** *mts* Arg.
284 D3 **Tunuyán, Travesía** *des.* Arg.
Tunxi *Anhui* China *see* **Huangshan**
199 L4 **Tunyogmatolcs** Hungary
Tuodian *Yunnan* China *see* **Shuangbai**
131 K2 **Tuo He** *r.* China
Tuojiang *Hunan* China *see* **Fenghuang**
Tuojiang *Hunan* China *see* **Jianghua**
130 E4 **Tuo Jiang** *r. Sichuan* China
119 G9 **Tuŏl Khpos** Cambodia
264 L4 **Tuolumne** *CA* U.S.A.
264 K4 **Tuolumne** *r. CA* U.S.A.
264 M4 **Tuolumne Meadows** *CA* U.S.A.
214 H1 **Tuoma** *r.* Italy
130 E6 **Tuoniang Jiang** *r. Guangxi* China
Tuoputiereke *Xinjiang* China *see* **Jeminay**
213 M9 **Tuoro sul Trasimeno** Italy
Tuotuoheyan *Qinghai* China *see* **Tanggulashan**
143 R6 **Tüp** Kyrg.
280 B4 **Tupã** Brazil
280 C3 **Tupaciguara** Brazil
144 B3 **Tūp Āghāj** Iran
Tupai *i.* Fr. Polynesia *see* **Motu Iti**
275 F5 **Tupanaóca** Brazil
279 B9 **Tupanciretã** Brazil
261 K8 **Tupelo** *MS* U.S.A.
198 G2 **Tupesy** Czech Rep.
275 G5 **Tupinambarama, Ilha** *i.* Brazil
280 B4 **Tupi Paulista** Brazil
277 H2 **Tupiratins** Brazil
276 D5 **Tupiza** Bol.
142 D5 **Tupkaragan, Mys** *pt* Kazakh.
196 C4 **Tuplice** Pol.
246 F4 **Tupper** *B.C.* Can.
257 K4 **Tupper Lake** *NY* U.S.A.
257 K4 **Tupper Lake** *l. NY* U.S.A.
Tüpqaraghan Tübegi *pen.* Kazakh. *see* **Mangyshlak, Poluostrov**
284 C3 **Tupungato** Arg.
284 C3 **Tupungato, Cerro** *mt.* Arg./Chile
149 L9 **Tuqayyid** *well* Iraq
129 Q4 **Tuquan** *Nei Mongol* China
274 B4 **Túquerres** Col.
219 K2 **Tur** *r.* Romania
133 H8 **Tura** *Xinjiang* China
199 I4 **Tura** Hungary
139 M7 **Tura** *Meghalaya* India
153 L3 **Tura** Rus. Fed.
146 F1 **Turabah** *Ḩā'īl* Saudi Arabia
146 E5 **Turabah** *Makkah* Saudi Arabia
146 F4 **Turabah, Wādī** *watercourse* Saudi Arabia
275 E3 **Turagua, Serranía** *mt.* Venez.
136 F7 **Turaiyur** *Tamil Nadu* India
102 J7 **Turakina** *North I.* N.Z.
102 J7 **Turakina** *r. North I.* N.Z.
103 I8 **Turakirae Head** *North I.* N.Z.
144 G4 **Turan** Iran
122 G3 **Turana, Khrebet** *mts* Rus. Fed.
102 J5 **Turangi** *North I.* N.Z.
142 G8 **Turan Lowland** Asia
215 J3 **Turano** *r.* Italy
Turanskaya Nizmennost' *lowland* Asia *see* **Turan Lowland**
150 G5 **Ţurāq al 'Ilab** *hills* Syria
143 N6 **Turar Ryskulov** Kazakh.
158 G1 **Turaw** Belarus
148 I8 **Ţurayf** Saudi Arabia
147 I2 **Ţurayf** *well* Saudi Arabia
150 G7 **Ţurayf, Kutayfat** *vol.* Saudi Arabia
160 H2 **Turba** Estonia
274 C2 **Turbaco** Col.
197 I6 **Turbacz** *mt.* Pol.
156 J3 **Turbanovo** Rus. Fed.
145 J8 **Turbat** Pak.
212 F1 **Turbenthal** Switz.
268 F5 **Turbio** *r.* Mex.
158 H4 **Turbiv** Ukr.
274 B2 **Turbo** Col.
258 B2 **Turbotville** *PA* U.S.A.
200 H5 **Türchlwand** *mt.* Austria
204 I3 **Turcia** Spain
199 H3 **Turčianske Teplice** Slovakia
179 N7 **Turckheim** France
276 C4 **Turco** Bol.
219 L4 **Turda** Romania
161 U8 **Turdey** Rus. Fed.
182 F5 **Turdine** *r.* France
109 D7 **Turee Creek** *r. W.A.* Austr.
205 L6 **Turégano** Spain
144 C4 **Tūreh** Iran
196 G3 **Turek** Pol.
160 H1 **Turenki** Fin.
196 E3 **Turew** Pol.
Turfan *Xinjiang* China *see* **Turpan**
Turfan Depression China *see* **Turpan Pendi**
142 J3 **Turgay** *Kostanayskaya Oblast'* Kazakh.
142 J4 **Turgay** *r.* Kazakh.
142 J3 **Turgayskaya Dolina** *val.* Kazakh.
142 I2 **Turgayskaya Stolovaya Strana** *reg.* Kazakh.
128 B2 **Türgen Uul** *mt.* Mongolia
128 B2 **Türgen Uul** *mts* Mongolia
248 E3 **Turgeon** *r. Ont./Que.* Can.
219 O7 **Tŭrgovishte** Bulg.
148 E4 **Turgut** *Konya* Turkey
221 J5 **Turgut** *Muğla* Turkey
221 I3 **Turgutalp** Turkey
221 I4 **Turgutlu** Turkey
221 I6 **Turgutreis** Turkey
148 H3 **Turhal** Turkey
159 M9 **Turhenyevka** Ukr.
160 I3 **Türi** Estonia
217 M2 **Turi** Italy
209 E9 **Turia** *r.* Spain
278 D2 **Turiaçu** Brazil
278 D2 **Turiaçu** *r.* Brazil
278 D2 **Turiaçu, Baía de** *b.* Brazil
271 J8 **Turiamo** Venez.
233 C6 **Turiani** Tanz.
199 H2 **Turie** Slovakia
199 H3 **Turiec** *r.* Slovakia
247 H5 **Turin** *Alta* Can.
Turin Italy *see* **Torino**
152 H4 **Turinsk** Rus. Fed.
209 D9 **Turís** Spain
158 D2 **Turiya** *r.* Ukr.
122 G6 **Turiy Rog** Rus. Fed.
158 D2 **Turiys'k** Ukr.
198 G5 **Türje** Hungary
121 I1 **Turka** Rus. Fed.
158 C4 **Turka** Ukr.
232 B4 **Turkana, Lake** *salt l.* Eth./Kenya
221 I2 **Türkeli** Turkey
221 I2 **Türkeli Adası** *i.* Turkey
195 K5 **Türkenfeld** Ger.
143 M6 **Turkestan** Kazakh.
145 L2 **Turkestan Range** *mts* Asia
199 J4 **Túrkeve** Hungary
148 G4 **Turkey** *country* Asia/Europe
256 B11 **Turkey** *KY* U.S.A.
260 J4 **Turkey** *r. IA* U.S.A.
108 J4 **Turkey Creek** *W.A.* Austr.
195 J5 **Türkheim** Ger.
157 H6 **Turki** Rus. Fed.
Türkistan Kazakh. *see* **Turkestan**
145 J2 **Türkmenabat** *Lebapskaya Oblast'* Turkm.
Turkmen Adasy *i.* Turkm. *see* **Ogurjaly Adasy**
Türkmen Aylagy *b.* Turkm. *see* **Türkmen Aýlagy**
144 E2 **Türkmen Aýlagy** *b.* Turkm.
144 E1 **Türkmenbaşy** Turkm.
144 E2 **Türkmenbaşy Aýlagy** *b.* Turkm.
144 E2 **Türkmenbaşy Döwlet Gorugy** *nature res.* Turkm.
221 L3 **Türkmen Dağı** *mt.* Turkey
145 J3 **Türkmengala** Turkm.
144 H1 **Turkmenistan** *country* Asia
Turkmeniya *country* Asia *see* **Turkmenistan**
Turkmen-Kala Turkm. *see* **Türkmengala**
145 J4 **Turkmenkarakul'** Turkm.
Türkmenostan *country* Asia *see* **Turkmenistan**
Turkmenskaya S.S.R. *country* Asia *see* **Turkmenistan**
148 H5 **Türkoğlu** Turkey
160 L6 **Turkova** Belarus
270 H3 **Turks and Caicos Islands** *terr.* West Indies
270 H3 **Turks Island Passage** Turks and Caicos Is
270 H3 **Turks Islands** Turks and Caicos Is
163 Q6 **Turku** Fin.
232 C4 **Turkwel** *watercourse* Kenya
205 M9 **Turleque** Spain
264 L4 **Turlock** *CA* U.S.A.
264 L4 **Turlock Lake** *CA* U.S.A.
169 D6 **Turlough** *Clare* Ireland
169 D5 **Turlough** *Mayo* Ireland
281 F2 **Turmalina** Brazil
146 F2 **Turmus, Wādī at** *watercourse* Saudi Arabia
245 P4 **Turnagain** *r. B.C.* Can.
102 K7 **Turnagain, Cape** *North I.* N.Z.
151 A5 **Turnalı** Turkey
199 J3 **Turňa nad Bodvou** Slovakia
201 L4 **Turnau** Austria
168 G12 **Turnberry** *South Ayrshire, Scotland* U.K.
103 C12 **Turnbull, Mount** *South I.* N.Z.
265 V8 **Turnbull, Mount** *AZ* U.S.A.
267 P9 **Turneffe Islands** *atoll* Belize
108 J4 **Turner** *W.A.* Austr.
108 E6 **Turner** *r. W.A.* Austr.
109 E8 **Turner** *watercourse W.A.* Austr.
251 K5 **Turner** *MI* U.S.A.
173 L5 **Turners Hill** *West Sussex, England* U.K.
228 B5 **Turner's Peninsula** Sierra Leone
246 H5 **Turner Valley** *Alta* Can.
187 G6 **Turnhout** Belgium
201 N6 **Turnišče** Slovenia
201 M4 **Türnitz** Austria
247 I3 **Turnor Lake** *Sask.* Can.
247 I3 **Turnor Lake** *l. Sask.* Can.
198 E1 **Turnov** Czech Rep.
Tŭrnovo Bulg. *see* **Veliko Tŭrnovo**
219 M7 **Turnu Măgurele** Romania
Turnu Severin Romania *see* **Drobeta-Turnu Severin**
197 K5 **Turobin** Pol.
105 L5 **Turon** *r. N.S.W.* Austr.
207 J7 **Turón** *r.* Spain
Turones France *see* **Tours**
210 E3 **Turopolje** *plain* Croatia
197 J2 **Turośl** *Podlaskie* Pol.
197 J2 **Turośl** *Warmińsko-Mazurskie* Pol.
156 H4 **Turovets** Rus. Fed.
161 U7 **Turovo** Rus. Fed.
197 K4 **Turów** Pol.
160 L6 **Turowlya** Belarus
196 E2 **Turowo** Pol.
132 I5 **Turpan** *Xinjiang* China
132 I5 **Turpan Pendi** *depr.* China
132 I5 **Turpan Zhan** *Xinjiang* China
206 B2 **Turquel** Port.
201 I6 **Turrach** Austria
201 I6 **Turracher Höhe** *pass* Austria
207 P6 **Turre** Spain
266 □R13 **Turrialba** Costa Rica
183 I8 **Turriers** France
168 L7 **Turriff** *Aberdeenshire, Scotland* U.K.
Turris Libisonis *Sardegna* Italy *see* **Porto Torres**
149 L7 **Tursāq** Iraq
217 K3 **Tursi** Italy
158 D2 **Turs'kyy Kanal** *canal* Ukr.
219 L3 **Turț** Romania
250 D3 **Turtle Flambeau Flowage** *resr WI* U.S.A.
247 I4 **Turtleford** *Sask.* Can.
107 M4 **Turtle Island** *Coral Sea Is Terr.* Austr.
Turtle Island Fiji *see* **Vatoa**
114 B8 **Turtle Islands** Phil.
228 B5 **Turtle Islands** Sierra Leone
247 I4 **Turtle Lake** *l. Sask.* Can.
250 B4 **Turtle Lake** *WI* U.S.A.
162 Q3 **Turtola** Fin.
143 P7 **Turugart Pass** China/Kyrg.
Turugart Shankou *pass* China/Kyrg. *see* **Turugart Pass**
152 J3 **Turukhansk** Rus. Fed.
199 M4 **Turulung** Romania
275 G4 **Turuna** *r.* Brazil
150 D1 **Turunçlu** Turkey
221 L6 **Turunçova** Turkey
136 E5 **Turuvanur** *Karnataka* India
280 B2 **Turvelândia** Brazil
279 C9 **Turvo** Brazil
280 B2 **Turvo** *r.* Brazil
280 C3 **Turvo** *r.* Brazil
280 C5 **Turvo** *r.* Brazil
199 L3 **Tur"ya** *r.* Ukr.
199 L3 **Tur"ya-Bystra** Ukr.
151 I5 **Türyançay** Azer.
151 I5 **Türyançay** *r.* Azer.
151 I5 **Türyançay Qoruğu** *nature res.* Azer.
199 L3 **Tur"ya-Polyana** Ukr.
158 C4 **Tur"ye** Ukr.
199 L3 **Tur"yi Remety** Ukr.
158 D3 **Turynka** Ukr.
142 G5 **Turysh** Kazakh.
197 I2 **Turza Wielka** Pol.
199 H2 **Turzovka** Slovakia
144 H3 **Ţus** Iran
207 O4 **Tús** *r.* Spain
216 G8 **Tusa** *Sicilia* Italy
216 G7 **Tusa** *r. Sicilia* Italy
265 T6 **Tusayan** *AZ* U.S.A.
255 D9 **Tuscaloosa** *AL* U.S.A.
214 H3 **Tuscania** Italy
Tuscany *admin. reg.* Italy *see* **Toscana**
256 D8 **Tuscarawas** *r. OH* U.S.A.
258 C3 **Tuscarora** *PA* U.S.A.
256 H8 **Tuscarora Mountains** *hills PA* U.S.A.
260 K6 **Tuscola** *IL* U.S.A.
261 F9 **Tuscola** *TX* U.S.A.
255 D8 **Tuscumbia** *AL* U.S.A.
260 I6 **Tuscumbia** *MO* U.S.A.
144 G4 **Tusharīk** Iran
159 P2 **Tuskar'** *r.* Rus. Fed.
255 E9 **Tuskegee** *AL* U.S.A.
219 N4 **Tușnad** Romania
195 J5 **Tussenhausen** Ger.
256 G8 **Tussey Mountains** *hills PA* U.S.A.
195 N5 **Tüßling** Ger.
250 I5 **Tustin** *MI* U.S.A.
245 J3 **Tustumena Lake** *AK* U.S.A.
197 J5 **Tuszów Narodowy** Pol.
197 J5 **Tuszyma** Pol.
197 H4 **Tuszyn** Pol.
144 F5 **Tūt** Iran
149 K4 **Tutak** Turkey
144 H8 **Tūtān** Iran
161 W4 **Tutayev** Rus. Fed.
173 I2 **Tutbury** *Staffordshire, England* U.K.
Tutera Spain *see* **Tudela**
145 N5 **Tutia Khel** Pak.
136 F8 **Tuticorin** *Tamil Nadu* India
117 K3 **Tutoh** *r.* Malaysia
117 K2 **Tutong** Brunei
219 P4 **Tutova** *r.* Romania
192 H3 **Tutow** Ger.
219 O6 **Tutrakan** Bulg.
172 G4 **Tutshill** *Gloucestershire, England* U.K.
260 G6 **Tuttle Creek Reservoir** *KS* U.S.A.
258 F2 **Tuttles Corner** *NJ* U.S.A.
194 F6 **Tuttlingen** Ger.
243 P2 **Tuttut Nunaat** *reg.* Greenland
115 E8 **Tutuala** East Timor
233 B6 **Tutubu** Tanz.
100 □[2] **Tutuila** *i.* American Samoa
102 I2 **Tutukaka** *North I.* N.Z.
235 E4 **Tutume** Botswana
274 B3 **Tutunendo** Col.
276 C4 **Tutupaca, Volcán** *vol.* Peru
103 J8 **Tuturumuri** *North I.* N.Z.
244 G2 **Tututalak Mountain** *AK* U.S.A.
269 J9 **Tututepec** Mex.
195 K6 **Tutzing** Ger.
192 H3 **Tützpatz** Ger.
128 I2 **Tuul Gol** *r.* Mongolia
160 H1 **Tuulos** Fin.
123 E8 **Tuun-bong** *mt.* N. Korea
162 U5 **Tuupovaara** Fin.
162 T5 **Tuusniemi** Fin.
163 R6 **Tuusula** Fin.
Tuva *aut. rep.* Rus. Fed. *see* **Tyva, Respublika**
99 H2 **Tuvalu** *country* S. Pacific Ocean
99 I4 **Tuvana-i-Colo** *i.* Fiji
99 I4 **Tuvana-i-Ra** *i.* Fiji
Tuvana-i-Tholo *i.* Fiji *see* **Tuvana-i-Colo**
164 H4 **Tuve** Sweden
286 S2 **Tuve, Mount** *hill* Antarctica
Tuvinskaya A.S.S.R. *aut. rep.* Rus. Fed. *see* **Tyva, Respublika**
129 L3 **Tüvshinshiree** *Sühbaatar* Mongolia
101 □[7a] **Tuvutau** *mt. Viti Levu* Fiji
117 L4 **Tuwau** *r.* Indon.
146 G2 **Tuwayq, Jabal** *hills* Saudi Arabia
146 G5 **Tuwayq, Jabal** *mts* Saudi Arabia
146 D3 **Ţuwayrah** Saudi Arabia
150 D9 **Ţuwayyil al Ḩājj** *mt.* Jordan
150 E8 **Ţuwayyil ash Shihāq** *mt.* Jordan
146 D4 **Tuwwal** Saudi Arabia
268 D6 **Tuxcacuesco** Mex.
259 G2 **Tuxedo Park** *NY* U.S.A.
200 E5 **Tuxer Gebirge** *mts* Austria
171 P7 **Tuxford** *Nottinghamshire, England* U.K.
268 D6 **Tuxpan** *Jalisco* Mex.
268 B4 **Tuxpan** *Nayarit* Mex.
269 J5 **Tuxpan** *Veracruz* Mex.
269 J4 **Tuxpan, Arrecife** *rf* Mex.
267 M9 **Tuxtla Gutiérrez** Mex.
Túy *Galicia* Spain *see* **Tui**
271 K8 **Tuy** *r.* Venez.
245 O4 **Tuya Lake** *B.C.* Can.
119 H8 **Tuy Đức** Vietnam
118 G4 **Tuyên Quang** Vietnam
151 D5 **Tuygun** Turkey
119 I8 **Tuy Hoa** Vietnam
157 K5 **Tuymazy** Rus. Fed.
144 C4 **Tūysarkān** Iran
Tŭytepa Uzbek. *see* **To'ytepa**
143 R6 **Tuyyk** Kazakh.
Tuz, Lake *salt l.* Turkey *see* **Tuz Gölü**
268 G7 **Tuzantla** *r.* Mex.
148 F4 **Tuz Gölü** *salt l.* Turkey
219 N8 **Tŭzha** Bulg.
156 I4 **Tuzha** Rus. Fed.
218 H8 **Tuzi** *Podgorica* Montenegro
149 L6 **Tuz Khurmātū** Iraq
210 G3 **Tuzla** Bos.-Herz.
219 Q6 **Tuzla** Romania
148 G5 **Tuzla** Turkey
149 J4 **Tuzla** *r.* Turkey
157 H7 **Tuzlov** *r.* Rus. Fed.
151 E5 **Tuzluca** Turkey
201 N7 **Tužno** Croatia
118 B2 **Tuzu** *r.* Myanmar
224 C4 **Tuzugu** *well* Libya
164 I4 **Tvååker** Sweden
162 O4 **Tvärålund** Sweden
198 F2 **Tvarožná** Czech Rep.
164 E3 **Tvedestrand** Norway
164 B1 **Tveitakvitingen** *mt.* Norway
161 S5 **Tver'** Rus. Fed.
Tver Oblast *admin. div.* Rus. Fed. *see* **Tverskaya Oblast'**
151 A1 **Tverskaya** Rus. Fed.
161 S4 **Tverskaya Oblast'** *admin. div.* Rus. Fed.
161 S5 **Tvertsa** *r.* Rus. Fed.
166 D1 **Tvøroyri** Faroe Is
160 L3 **Tvorozhkovo** Rus. Fed.
201 O2 **Tvrdonice** Czech Rep.
199 I2 **Tvrdošín** Slovakia
219 N8 **Tvŭrditsa** Bulg.
264 L3 **Twain Harte** *CA* U.S.A.
196 F4 **Twardogóra** Pol.
168 J4 **Twatt** *Orkney, Scotland* U.K.
251 Q5 **Tweed** *Ont.* Can.
171 M2 **Tweed** *r. England/Scotland* U.K.
168 J11 **Tweeddale** *val. Scotland* U.K.
186 K3 **Tweede Exloërmond** Neth.
105 N3 **Tweed Heads** *N.S.W.* Austr.
247 I4 **Tweedie** *Alta* Can.
171 M2 **Tweedmouth** *Northumberland, England* U.K.
168 J11 **Tweedsmuir** *Scottish Borders, Scotland* U.K.
246 E4 **Tweedsmuir Provincial Park** *B.C.* Can.
236 D8 **Tweefontein** S. Africa
237 M3 **Tweeling** S. Africa
234 C5 **Twee Rivier** Namibia
236 E2 **Twee Rivieren** Botswana
237 L5 **Tweespruit** S. Africa
186 J4 **Twello** Neth.
186 K4 **Twente** *reg.* Neth.
186 J4 **Twentekanaal** *canal* Neth.
265 P7 **Twentynine Palms** *CA* U.S.A.
230 C5 **Tweya** Dem. Rep. Congo
249 K3 **Twillingate** *Nfld and Lab.* Can.
264 L3 **Twin Bridges** *CA* U.S.A.
262 H4 **Twin Bridges** *MT* U.S.A.
261 E10 **Twin Buttes Reservoir** *TX* U.S.A.
249 H2 **Twin Falls** *Nfld and Lab.* Can.
262 G5 **Twin Falls** *ID* U.S.A.
231 F7 **Twingi** Zambia
108 I6 **Twin Heads** *hill W.A.* Austr.
244 G4 **Twin Hills** *AK* U.S.A.
258 F2 **Twin Lakes** *PA* U.S.A.
257 N4 **Twin Mountain** *NH* U.S.A.
244 H3 **Twin Mountain** *AK* U.S.A.
264 L2 **Twin Peak** *CA* U.S.A.
109 D13 **Twin Peaks** *hill W.A.* Austr.
256 D7 **Twinsburg** *OH* U.S.A.
104 G3 **Twins Creek** *watercourse S.A.* Austr.
262 D2 **Twisp** *WA* U.S.A.
190 D5 **Twist** Ger.
191 G8 **Twiste (Twistetal)** Ger.
190 G5 **Twistringen** Ger.
264 L6 **Twitchen Reservoir** *CA* U.S.A.
245 O2 **Twitya** *r. N.W.T.* Can.
103 E11 **Twizel** *South I.* N.Z.
238 □[2a] **Two Boats Village** *Ascension* S. Atlantic Ocean
261 D6 **Two Butte Creek** *r. CO* U.S.A.
250 C2 **Two Harbors** *MN* U.S.A.
247 I4 **Two Hills** *Alta* Can.
170 B8 **Two Mile Borris** Ireland
169 H6 **Two Mile Bridge** Ireland
250 G5 **Two Rivers** *WI* U.S.A.
196 G5 **Tworóg** Pol.
234 B4 **Twyfelfontein Rock Engravings** *tourist site* Namibia
173 J5 **Twyford** *Hampshire, England* U.K.
173 K5 **Twyford** *Wokingham, England* U.K.
168 H13 **Twynholm** *Dumfries and Galloway, Scotland* U.K.
Tyachev Ukr. *see* **Tyachiv**
158 C5 **Tyachiv** Ukr.
159 M7 **Tyahynka** Ukr.
Tyan' Shan' *mts* China/Kyrg. *see* **Tien Shan**
Tyanshanskaya Oblast' *admin. div.* Kyrg. *see* **Naryn**
118 A3 **Tyao** *r.* India/Myanmar
159 L4 **Tyasmyn** *r.* Ukr.
124 X2 **Tyatya, Vulkan** *vol.* Rus. Fed.
221 H1 **Tychero** Greece
196 E2 **Tychówko** Pol.
196 E2 **Tychowo** Pol.
196 G5 **Tychy** Pol.
197 K6 **Tyczyn** Pol.
162 K5 **Tydal** Norway
Tyddewi *Pembrokeshire, Wales* U.K. *see* **St David's**
256 F10 **Tygart Valley** *WV* U.S.A.
122 E2 **Tygda** Rus. Fed.
122 E2 **Tygda** *r.* Rus. Fed.
169 I4 **Tyholland** Ireland
163 J6 **Tyinkrysset** Norway
159 L2 **Tykhonovychi** Ukr.
197 K2 **Tykocin** Pol.
197 J6 **Tylawa** Pol.
261 H9 **Tyler** *TX* U.S.A.
261 J10 **Tylertown** *MS* U.S.A.
158 K7 **Tylihul** *r.* Ukr.
122 I2 **Tyl'skiy Khrebet** *mts* Rus. Fed.
122 M3 **Tym'** *r. Sakhalin* Rus. Fed.
197 I6 **Tymbark** Pol.
159 L4 **Tymchenky** Ukr.
220 B2 **Tymfi** *mts* Greece
196 D1 **Tymień** Pol.
159 R4 **Tymonove** Ukr.
159 L1 **Tymonovychi** Ukr.
159 O6 **Tymoshivka** Ukr.
122 M3 **Tymovskoye** *Sakhalin* Rus. Fed.
196 E4 **Tymowa** Pol.
220 F7 **Tympaki** *Kriti* Greece
186 K2 **Tynaarlo** Neth.
170 D5 **Tynan** *Northern Ireland* U.K.
153 N4 **Tynda** Rus. Fed.
260 G4 **Tyndall** *SD* U.S.A.
Tyndinskiy Rus. Fed. *see* **Tynda**
168 G10 **Tyndrum** *Stirling, Scotland* U.K.
168 K10 **Tyne** *r. Scotland* U.K.
171 O4 **Tyne and Wear** *admin. div. England* U.K.
198 E1 **Týnec nad Labem** Czech Rep.
198 D2 **Týnec nad Sázavou** Czech Rep.
171 O3 **Tynemouth** *Tyne and Wear, England* U.K.
257 N6 **Tyngsboro** *MA* U.S.A.
165 J1 **Tyngsjö** Sweden
198 F1 **Týniště nad Orlicí** Czech Rep.
158 J4 **Tynivka** Ukr.
198 D2 **Týn nad Vltavou** Czech Rep.
158 F2 **Tynne** Ukr.
163 K5 **Tynset** Norway
245 K3 **Tyone** *r. AK* U.S.A.
Tyr Lebanon *see* **Soûr**
Tyras Ukr. *see* **Bilhorod-Dnistrovs'kyy**
197 K6 **Tyrawa Wołoska** Pol.
Tyre Lebanon *see* **Soûr**
286 S1 **Tyree, Mount** Antarctica
170 F5 **Tyrella** *Northern Ireland* U.K.
165 O2 **Tyresö** Sweden
165 O2 **Tyresta nationalpark** *nat. park* Sweden
164 G1 **Tyrifjorden** *l.* Norway
195 N5 **Tyrlaching** Ger.
122 H3 **Tyrma** Rus. Fed.
122 G3 **Tyrma** *r.* Rus. Fed.
162 R4 **Tyrnävä** Fin.
220 D3 **Tyrnavos** Greece
161 W7 **Tyrnovo** Rus. Fed.
151 D2 **Tyrnyauz** Rus. Fed.
Tyrol *land* Austria *see* **Tirol**
169 H3 **Tyrone** *county Northern Ireland* U.K.
263 J10 **Tyrone** *NM* U.S.A.
256 G8 **Tyrone** *PA* U.S.A.
105 I6 **Tyrrell** *r. Vic.* Austr.
105 I6 **Tyrrell, Lake** *dry lake Vic.* Austr.
247 J2 **Tyrrell Lake** *N.W.T.* Can.
169 H6 **Tyrrellspass** Ireland
211 C5 **Tyrrhenian Sea** France/Italy
Tyrus Lebanon *see* **Soûr**
158 A5 **Tysa** *r.* Ukr. *alt.* **Tisa (Serbia),** *alt.* **Tisza (Hungary)**
158 D5 **Tysmenytsya** Ukr.
164 B2 **Tysnesøy** *i.* Norway
265 R8 **Tyson Wash** *watercourse AZ* U.S.A.
164 B1 **Tysse** Norway
166 J1 **Tyssebotnen** Norway
164 C1 **Tyssedal** Norway
164 H6 **Tystrup-Bavelse** *nature res.* Denmark
197 L5 **Tyszowce** Pol.
172 E5 **Tythegston** *Bridgend, Wales* U.K.
186 I2 **Tytsjerk** Neth.
160 G6 **Tytuvėnai** Lith.
151 I2 **Tyube** Rus. Fed.
153 P3 **Tyubelyakh** Rus. Fed.
151 L1 **Tyub-Karagan, Poluostrov** *pen.* Kazakh.
152 I4 **Tyukalinsk** Rus. Fed.
Tyuleniy, Mys *pt* Azer. *see* **Suiti Burunu**
151 I1 **Tyuleniy, Ostrov** *i.* Rus. Fed.
142 G1 **Tyul'gan** Rus. Fed.
156 L4 **Tyul'kino** Rus. Fed.
152 H4 **Tyumen'** Rus. Fed.
Tyumen'-Aryk Kazakh. *see* **Tomenaryk**
143 S1 **Tyumentsevo** Rus. Fed.
153 N3 **Tyung** *r.* Rus. Fed.
142 K1 **Tyuntyugur** Kazakh.
Tyup Kyrg. *see* **Tüp**
Tyuratam Kazakh. *see* **Baykonyr**
162 V2 **Tyuva-Guba** Rus. Fed.
145 I1 **Tyuyamuyunskoye Vodokhranilishche** *resr* Turkm./Uzbek.
128 E1 **Tyva, Respublika** *aut. rep.* Rus. Fed.
158 H4 **Tyvriv** Ukr.
196 C2 **Tywa** *r.* Pol.
172 C7 **Tywardreath** *Cornwall, England* U.K.
172 D4 **Tywi** *r. Wales* U.K.
172 D2 **Tywyn** *Gwynedd, Wales* U.K.
235 F4 **Tzaneen** S. Africa
220 F5 **Tzia** *i.* Greece
267 O7 **Tzucacab** Mex.
186 I2 **Tzummarum** Neth.

U

275 F3 **Uacauyén** Venez.
Uaco Congo Angola *see* **Waku-Kungo**
100 □[2] **Uafato** Samoa
101 □[9] **Ua Huka** *i.* Fr. Polynesia
274 D4 **Uainambi** Brazil
Ualan *atoll* Micronesia *see* **Kosrae**
Ūālīkhanov Kazakh. *see* **Valikhanovo**
231 D9 **Uamanda** Angola
235 H3 **Uape** Moz.
Ua Pou *i.* Fr. Polynesia *see* **Ua Pu**
101 □[9] **Ua Pu** *i.* Fr. Polynesia
275 E5 **Uara** Brazil
Uarc, Ras *c.* Morocco *see* **Trois Fourches, Cap des**
275 G6 **Uari** Brazil
275 E5 **Uarini** Brazil
109 C7 **Uaroo** *W.A.* Austr.
274 D4 **Uaruma** Brazil
275 E3 **Uasadi-jidi, Sierra** *mts* Venez.
275 F4 **Uatatás** *r.* Brazil
275 G5 **Uatumã** *r.* Brazil
278 F4 **Uauá** Brazil
274 E5 **Uaupés** Brazil
274 E4 **Uaupés** *r.* Brazil
267 O9 **Uaxactún** Guat.
146 G5 **U'ayfirah** *well* Saudi Arabia
150 G8 **U'aylī, Wādī al** *watercourse* Saudi Arabia
146 G1 **U'aywij** *well* Saudi Arabia
149 K9 **U'aywij, Wādī al** *watercourse* Saudi Arabia
218 I6 **Ub** *Ub* Serbia
281 F4 **Ubá** Brazil
191 B9 **Übach-Palenberg** Ger.
142 K1 **Ubagan** *r.* Kazakh.
281 E2 **Ubaí** Brazil
224 E6 **Ubaid** *well* Sudan
278 F5 **Ubaitaba** Brazil
146 F8 **'Ubāl** Yemen
230 C5 **Ubangi** *r.* C.A.R./Dem. Rep. Congo
Ubangi-Shari *country* Africa *see* **Central African Republic**
281 F3 **Ubaporanga** Brazil
158 H1 **Ubarts'** *r.* Belarus
274 C3 **Ubate** Col.
281 E5 **Ubatuba** Brazil
145 M7 **Ubauro** Pak.
183 I8 **Ubaye** *r.* France
149 K7 **Ubayyiḍ, Wādī al** *watercourse* Iraq/Saudi Arabia
125 I13 **Ube** Japan
207 M4 **Úbeda** Spain
233 C6 **Ubenazomozi** Tanz.
280 D3 **Uberaba** Brazil
280 C4 **Uberaba** *r.* Brazil
194 B3 **Überherrn** Ger.
280 C3 **Uberlândia** Brazil
194 G6 **Überlingen** Ger.
194 G6 **Überlinger See** *l.* Ger.
195 M6 **Übersee** Ger.
116 □ **Ubin, Pulau** *i.* Sing.
204 I2 **Ubiña, Peña** *mt.* Spain
159 R9 **Ubinskaya** Rus. Fed.
152 J4 **Ubinskoye, Ozero** *l.* Rus. Fed.
280 A6 **Ubiratâ** Brazil
251 L6 **Ubly** *MI* U.S.A.

159 Q2 Ublya r. Rus. Fed.
118 F6 Ubolratna, Ang Kep Nam Thai.
237 Q3 Ubombo S. Africa
230 E5 Ubondo Dem. Rep. Congo
118 G7 Ubon Ratchathani Thai.
230 F3 Ubori Sudan
158 G2 Ubort' r. Ukr.
122 I6 Ubovka Rus. Fed.
183 J9 Ubraye France
207 I7 Ubrique Spain
194 F3 Ubstadt-Weiher Ger.
230 E5 Ubundu Dem. Rep. Congo
285 F3 Ucacha Arg.
145 J2 Üçajy Turkm.
151 I5 Ucar Azer.
150 A2 Uçarı Turkey
276 B2 Ucayali dept Peru
274 C6 Ucayali r. Peru
214 B3 Ucciani Corse France
187 F7 Uccle Belgium
205 N7 Uceda Spain
183 E7 Ucel France
205 N5 Ucero Spain
205 N5 Ucero r. Spain
145 N7 Uch Pak.
204 C5 Ucha Port.
Üchajy Turkm. see Üçajy
144 D3 Üchān Iran
143 S4 Ucharal Kazakh.
183 F8 Uchaux France
127 M1 Uchigō Japan
127 L3 Uchihara Japan
125 J13 Uchiko Japan
127 H3 Uchimura-gawa r. Japan
126 E2 Uchinada Japan
125 I15 Uchinoura Japan
126 B7 Uchita Japan
125 O9 Uchiura Japan
124 R4 Uchiura-wan b. Japan
127 I3 Uchiyama-tōge pass Japan
276 A2 Uchiza Peru
182 F3 Uchizy France
151 D2 Uchkeken Rus. Fed.
Uchkuduk Uzbek. see Uchquduq
151 D2 Uchkulan Rus. Fed.
142 J6 Uchquduq Uzbek.
143 L7 Uchquloch Uzbek.
Uchsay Uzbek. see Uchsoy
142 H6 Uchsoy Uzbek.
191 G6 Uchte Ger.
192 E5 Uchte r. Ger.
191 J10 Üchtelhausen Ger.
192 E5 Uchtspringe Ger.
153 O4 Uchur r. Rus. Fed.
205 L4 Ucieza r. Spain
179 L5 Uckange France
192 J2 Ückeritz Ger.
192 I4 Uckermark reg. Ger.
173 M6 Uckfield East Sussex, England U.K.
193 I7 Uckro Ger.
205 O9 Uclés Spain
246 E5 Ucluelet B.C. Can.
151 B6 Üçpınar Erzincan Turkey
150 A1 Üçpınar Konya Turkey
262 K4 Ucross WY U.S.A.
128 J7 Ud Nei Mongol China
122 I1 Uda r. Rus. Fed.
159 P4 Uda r. Ukr.
151 G4 Udabno Georgia
151 G4 Udabno, Mt'a hill Georgia
157 I7 Udachnoye Rus. Fed.
153 M3 Udachnyy Rus. Fed.
136 E7 Udagamandalam Tamil Nadu India
138 D7 Udaipur Rajasthan India
138 E6 Udaipur Rajasthan India
139 M8 Udaipur Tripura India
138 G8 Udaipura Madh. Prad. India
139 K6 Udaipur Garhi Nepal
197 L4 Udal r. Pol.
139 N6 Udalguri Assam India
196 E4 Udanin Pol.
139 I9 Udanti r. India/Myanmar
285 H5 Udaquilla Arg.
151 D1 Udarnyy Rus. Fed.
199 K3 Udava r. Slovakia
199 K3 Udavské Slovakia
136 G9 Uda Walawe Reservoir Sri Lanka
159 M3 Uday r. Ukr.
136 F5 Udayagiri Andhra Prad. India
137 I3 Udayagiri Orissa India
147 I4 'Udaynān well Saudi Arabia
165 J1 Uddeholm Sweden
186 I4 Uddel Neth.
164 H3 Uddevalla Sweden
170 I2 Uddingston South Lanarkshire, Scotland U.K.
168 I11 Uddington South Lanarkshire, Scotland U.K.
162 N4 Uddjaure l. Sweden
151 D4 Ude Georgia
147 J3 'Udeid, Khōr al inlet Qatar
186 I5 Uden Neth.
186 H5 Udenhout Neth.
191 J8 Uder Ger.
200 E5 Uderns Austria
191 C10 Üdersdorf Ger.
136 E3 Udgir Mahar. India
Udhagamandalam Tamil Nadu India see Udagamandalam
138 E3 Udhampur Jammu and Kashmir India
199 H2 Udiča Slovakia
156 I3 Udimskiy Rus. Fed.
213 O3 Udine Italy
213 N3 Udine prov. Italy
138 D6 Udit Rajasthan India
249 I2 Udjuktok Bay Nfld and Lab. Can.
Udmalaippettai Tamil Nadu India see Udumalaippettai
Udmurtia aut. rep. Rus. Fed. see Udmurtskaya Respublika
Udmurtskaya A.S.S.R. aut. rep. Rus. Fed. see Udmurtskaya Respublika
156 K4 Udmurtskaya Respublika aut. rep. Rus. Fed.
151 C1 Udobnaya Rus. Fed.
153 M4 Udokan, Khrebet mts Rus. Fed.
161 S4 Udomlya Rus. Fed.
127 J7 Udone-jima i. Japan
118 F6 Udon Thani Thai.
196 F1 Udorpie Pol.
100 □4a Udot i. Chuuk Micronesia
204 C4 Udra, Cabo c. Spain
197 L5 Udrycze Pol.
122 I1 Udskoye Rus. Fed.
136 E7 Udumalaippettai Tamil Nadu India
136 D6 Udupi Karnataka India
159 P3 Udy Ukr.
122 K2 Udyl', Ozero l. Rus. Fed.
Udzharma Georgia see Ujarma
Udzhary Azer. see Ucar
Uéa atoll Îles Loyauté New Caledonia see Ouvéa
193 H7 Uebigau Ger.
115 B4 Uëbonti Sulawesi Indon.
192 J3 Uecker r. Ger.
192 J3 Ueckermünde Ger.
127 H3 Ueda Japan
195 J2 Uehlfeld Ger.
191 K6 Uehrde Ger.
115 B4 Uekuli Sulawesi Indon.
230 D3 Uele r. Dem. Rep. Congo
153 U3 Uelen Rus. Fed.
153 T3 Uel'kal' Rus. Fed.
191 C6 Uelsen Ger.
190 K5 Uelzen Ger.
127 I3 Ueno Gunma Japan
126 D6 Ueno Mie Japan
127 J4 Uenohara Japan
230 E4 Uere r. Dem. Rep. Congo
212 D2 Uetendorf Switz.
190 I3 Uetersen Ger.
194 H2 Uettingen Ger.
191 J6 Uetze Ger.
156 K5 Ufa Rus. Fed.
156 L5 Ufa r. Rus. Fed.
172 F6 Uffculme Devon, England U.K.
195 I2 Uffenheim Ger.
195 K6 Uffing am Staffelsee Ger.
215 O5 Ufita r. Italy
191 K7 Uftrungen Ger.
156 I3 Uftyuga r. Rus. Fed.
234 B4 Ugab watercourse Namibia
244 H4 Ugaiushak Island AK U.S.A.
244 I4 Ugak Bay AK U.S.A.
244 I4 Ugak Island AK U.S.A.
160 F4 Ugāle Latvia
233 A6 Ugalla r. Tanz.
233 A6 Ugalla River Game Reserve nature res. Tanz.
232 B4 Uganda country Africa
244 I4 Uganik AK U.S.A.
210 F3 Ugar r. Bos.-Herz.
205 O2 Ugarana Spain
284 C3 Ugarteche Arg.
244 H4 Ugashik AK U.S.A.
172 E7 Ugborough Devon, England U.K.
190 H1 Uge Denmark
217 O4 Ugento Italy
164 B1 Uggdal Norway
164 G4 Uggerby r. Denmark
217 O3 Uggiano la Chiesa Italy
229 G5 Ughelli Nigeria
237 M7 Ugie S. Africa
Ugi Island Solomon Is see Uki Island
207 M7 Ugíjar Spain
144 I8 Ūgīnak Iran
182 I5 Ugine France
122 M4 Uglegorsk Sakhalin Rus. Fed.
122 H7 Uglekamensk Rus. Fed.
156 L4 Ugleural'skiy Rus. Fed.
161 V4 Uglich Rus. Fed.
210 E3 Ugljan i. Croatia
161 Q3 Uglovka Rus. Fed.
122 F3 Uglovoye Amurskaya Oblast' Rus. Fed.
122 H7 Uglovoye Primorskiy Kray Rus. Fed.
143 S2 Uglovskoye Rus. Fed.
199 G4 Ugod Hungary
Ugodskiy Zavod Rus. Fed. see Zhukovo
153 P3 Ugol'noye Rus. Fed.
Ugolnyy Rus. Fed. see Beringovskiy
151 E2 Ugol'nyy Rus. Fed.
153 S3 Ugol'nyye Kopi Rus. Fed.
161 R7 Ugra Rus. Fed.
161 T7 Ugra r. Rus. Fed.
128 I2 Ugtaaltsaydam Mongolia
219 M7 Ugŭrchin Bulg.
221 G2 Uğurlu Gökeada Turkey
152 I3 Ugut Rus. Fed.
199 K3 Uh r. Slovakia
205 Q3 Uharte-Arakil Spain
201 O2 Uherčice Czech Rep.
129 L6 Uher Hudag Nei Mongol China
197 L4 Uherka r. Pol.
198 G2 Uherské Hradiště Czech Rep.
199 G2 Uherský Brod Czech Rep.
194 H4 Uhingen Ger.
198 C2 Úhlava r. Czech Rep.
194 G6 Uhldingen Ger.
198 E2 Uhlířské Janovica Czech Rep.
193 D9 Uhlstädt Ger.
158 C3 Uhniv Ukr.
256 D8 Uhrichsville OH U.S.A.
199 H3 Uhrovec Slovakia
159 O3 Uhroyidy Ukr.
193 D6 Uhrsleben Ger.
193 K8 Uhyst Ger.
278 E4 Uibaí Brazil
Uibhist a' Deas i. Scotland U.K. see South Uist
Uibhist a' Tuath i. Scotland U.K. see North Uist
193 E8 Uichteritz Ger.
168 D7 Uig Highland, Scotland U.K.
231 B6 Uíge Angola
231 B6 Uíge prov. Angola
101 □8 'Uiha Tonga
123 E10 Ŭijŏngbu S. Korea
123 D8 Ŭiju N. Korea
142 F3 Uil Kazakh.
151 E3 Uilpata, Gora mt. Rus. Fed.
162 U5 Uimaharju Fin.
265 S5 Uinkaret Plateau AZ U.S.A.
156 L4 Uinskoye Rus. Fed.
262 J6 Uinta r. CO U.S.A.
265 W1 Uintah and Ouray Indian Reservation res. UT U.S.A.
262 I6 Uinta Mountains UT U.S.A.
234 B4 Uis Mine Namibia
237 J9 Uitenhage S. Africa
186 G3 Uitgeest Neth.
186 G4 Uithoorn Neth.
186 K2 Uithuizen Neth.
186 K2 Uithuizermeeden Neth.
236 C5 Uitkyk S. Africa
236 E3 Uitsakpan salt pan S. Africa
236 D8 Uitspankraal S. Africa
249 I1 Uivak, Cape Nfld and Lab. Can.
199 J6 Uivar Romania
151 G4 Ujarma Georgia
197 H4 Ujazd Łódzkie Pol.
196 G5 Ujazd Opolskie Pol.
199 G2 Újezd Czech Rep.
198 F2 Újezd u Brna Czech Rep.
199 K4 Újfehértó Hungary
138 G6 Ujhani Uttar Prad. India
199 I4 Újhartyán Hungary
126 C6 Uji Japan
126 C6 Uji-gawa r. Japan
125 G15 Uji-guntō is Japan
127 K2 Ujiie Japan
126 C6 Ujitawara Japan
Ujiyamada Japan see Ise
138 E8 Ujjain Madh. Prad. India
199 L3 Újkenéz Hungary
198 F4 Újkér Hungary
199 K5 Újkígyós Hungary
199 K4 Újléta Hungary
117 K4 Ujohbilang Kalimantan Indon.
108 □2 Ujong Tanjong pt Cocos Is
199 H6 Újpetre Hungary
196 E2 Ujście Pol.
197 H6 Ujsoły Pol.
199 K5 Újszalonta Hungary
199 J4 Újszász Hungary
199 J5 Újszentiván Hungary
199 K4 Újszentmargita Hungary
199 I4 Újszilvás Hungary
199 K4 Újtikos Hungary
198 F5 Újudvar Hungary
116 F8 Ujung Kulon, Taman Nasional nat. park Indon.
Ujung Pandang Sulawesi Indon. see Makassar
Újvidék Vojvodina Serbia see Novi Sad
124 □1 Uka Okinawa Japan
138 D9 Ukal Sagar l. India
229 G4 Ukata Nigeria
126 F1 Ukawa Japan
146 G2 'Ukayrishah well Saudi Arabia
124 □G19 Uke-jima i. Nansei-shotō Japan
233 B5 Ukerewe Island Tanz.
237 N5 uKhahlamba-Drakensberg Park nat. park S. Africa
149 K7 Ukhaydir tourist site Iraq
146 G7 Ukhdūd tourist site Saudi Arabia
Ukhimath Uttaranchal India see Okhimath
157 H5 Ukholovo Rus. Fed.
197 M4 Ukhovets'k Ukr.
139 O7 Ukhrul Manipur India
Ukhta Respublika Kareliya Rus. Fed. see Kalevala
156 K3 Ukhta Respublika Komi Rus. Fed.
156 K3 Ukhta r. Rus. Fed.
160 M7 Ukhvala Belarus
105 N3 Uki N.S.W. Austr.
264 I2 Ukiah CA U.S.A.
262 E4 Ukiah OR U.S.A.
100 □6 Uki Island Solomon Is
233 B6 Ukimbo Tanz.
243 M2 Ukkusissat Greenland
196 D2 Ukleja r. Pol.
160 H6 Ukmergė Lith.
161 S8 Ukolitsa Rus. Fed.
244 G5 Ukolnoi Island AK U.S.A.
158 K4 Ukraine country Europe
Ukrainka Kyivs'ka Oblast' Ukr. see Ukrayinka
Ukrainka Respublika Krym Ukr. see Ukrayinka
Ukrainskaya S.S.R. country Europe see Ukraine
Ukrainskoye Ukr. see Ukrayins'ke
Ukrayina country Europe see Ukraine
158 J3 Ukrayinka Kyivs'ka Oblast' Ukr.
159 N9 Ukrayinka Respublika Krym Ukr.
159 L3 Ukrayins'ke Ukr.
210 F3 Ukrina r. Bos.-Herz.
231 B7 Uku Angola
125 G13 Uku-jima i. Japan
231 B8 Ukuma Angola
234 D4 Ukwi Botswana
133 C11 Ul r. India
160 M6 Ula Belarus
160 M6 Ula r. Belarus
197 M1 Ūla r. Lith.
221 J5 Ula Turkey
128 J3 Ulaanbaatar Mongolia
128 J3 Ulaanbaatar mun. Mongolia
129 L5 Ulaanbadrah Mongolia
Ulaan-Ereg Mongolia see Bayanmönh
128 C2 Ulaangom Mongolia
Ulaanhudag Mongolia see Erdenesant
128 H4 Ulaan Nuur salt l. Mongolia
Ulaan-Uul Mongolia see Öldziyt
Ulaan-Uul Mongolia see Erdene
244 E4 Ulakaia Hill AK U.S.A.
245 □C6 Ulak Island AK U.S.A.
105 L5 Ulan N.S.W. Austr.
129 K7 Ulan Nei Mongol China
128 F8 Ulan Qinghai China
Ulan Bator Mongolia see Ulaanbaatar
143 N5 Ulanbel' Kazakh.
128 J6 Ulan Buh Shamo des. China
157 I7 Ulan Erge Rus. Fed.
Ulanhad Nei Mongol China see Chifeng
129 R3 Ulanhot Nei Mongol China
129 L6 Ulan Hua Nei Mongol China
158 H4 Ulaniv Ukr.
157 I7 Ulan-Khol Rus. Fed.
132 H5 Ulanlinggi Xinjiang China
197 K4 Ulan-Majorat Pol.
128 I7 Ulan Mod Nei Mongol China
159 N2 Ulanove Ukr.
197 K5 Ulanów Pol.
128 I6 Ulan Suhai Nei Mongol China
129 K6 Ulansuhai Nur l. China
128 G6 Ulan Tohoi Nei Mongol China
120 I1 Ulan-Ude Rus. Fed.
133 J9 Ulan Ul Hu l. China
284 D2 Ulapes Arg.
284 D2 Ulapes, Sierra mts Arg.
148 H4 Ulaş Sivas Turkey
221 I1 Ulaş Tekirdağ Turkey
214 D8 Ulassai Sardegna Italy
132 H5 Ulastai Xinjiang China
100 □6 Ulawa Island Solomon Is
233 C6 Ulaya Tanz.
146 H4 Ulayyah reg. Saudi Arabia
143 T2 Ul'ba Kazakh.
122 J2 Ul'banskiy Zaliv b. Rus. Fed.
262 K3 UL Bend National Wildlife Refuge nature res. MT U.S.A.
Ülbi Kazakh. see Ul'ba
160 H5 Ulbroka Latvia
168 J6 Ulbster Highland, Scotland U.K.
171 Q6 Ulceby North Lincolnshire, England U.K.
123 F10 Ulchin S. Korea
218 H9 Ulcinj Ulcinj Montenegro
236 I4 Ulco S. Africa
164 F6 Uldum Denmark
Uldz Mongolia see Norovlin
129 N2 Uldz r. Mongolia
Uleåborg Fin. see Oulu
Ulebsechel i. Palau see Auluptagel
164 F2 Ulefoss Norway
100 □5 Uléi Vanuatu
207 O6 Uleila del Campo Spain
128 I1 Ulekchin Rus. Fed.
160 J3 Ülenurme Estonia
129 M1 Ulety Rus. Fed.
197 K4 Ułęż Pol.
164 E5 Ulfborg Denmark
164 E5 Ulfborg Vind nature res. Denmark
Ulflingen Lux. see Troisvierges
186 J5 Ulft Neth.
129 P4 Ulgain Gol r. China
171 N3 Ulgham Northumberland, England U.K.
143 L2 Ul'gili Kazakh.
136 C3 Ulhasnagar Mahar. India
197 L5 Ulhówek Pol.
151 G4 Ulianovka Georgia
129 O4 Uliastai Nei Mongol China
128 E3 Uliastay Mongolia
Uliatea i. Arch. de la Société Fr. Polynesia see Raiatea
199 L3 Ulič Slovakia
187 G6 Ulicoten Neth.
Ulie atoll Micronesia see Woleai
100 □3b Uliga i. Majuro Marshall Is
230 E5 Ulindi r. Dem. Rep. Congo
156 F1 Ulita r. Rus. Fed.
113 I4 Ulithi atoll Micronesia
Uljanovsk Rus. Fed. see Ul'yanovsk
142 J3 Ul'kayak r. Kazakh.
143 R6 Ul'ken Aksu Kazakh.
143 T3 Ul'ken Boken Kazakh.
143 N1 Ul'ken-Karoy, Ozero salt l. Kazakh.
143 U3 Ul'ken Naryn Kazakh.
Ülkenözen r. Kazakh./Rus. Fed. see Bol'shoy Uzen'
143 P6 Ul'ken Sulutor Kazakh.
Ülken Vladīmīrovka Kazakh. see Bol'shaya Vladimirovka
204 C3 Ulla r. Spain
105 M6 Ulladulla N.S.W. Austr.
168 F7 Ullapool Highland, Scotland U.K.
164 I4 Ullared Sweden
162 P3 Ullatti Sweden
276 C3 Ulla Ulla, Parque Nacional nat. park Bol.
109 D7 Ullawarra Aboriginal Reserve W.A. Austr.
208 F6 Ulldecona Spain
208 G5 Ulldemolins Spain
164 G6 Ullerslev Denmark
199 I5 Üllés Hungary
171 O6 Ulleskelf North Yorkshire, England U.K.
286 S1 Ullmer, Mount Antarctica
276 C4 Ulloma Bol.
162 O2 Ullsfjorden sea chan. Norway
171 L4 Ullswater l. England U.K.
151 J3 Ulluchay r. Rus. Fed.
123 G10 Ullŭng-do i. S. Korea
194 H5 Ulm Ger.
122 F3 Ul'ma r. Rus. Fed.
191 H10 Ulmbach Ger.
206 B2 Ulme r. Port.
191 C10 Ulmen Ger.
219 O6 Ulmeni Călărași Romania
219 L3 Ulmeni Maramureș Romania
210 G4 Ulog Bos.-Herz.
235 G2 Ulongue Moz.
104 G2 Uloowaranie, Lake salt flat S.A. Austr.
171 K5 Ulpha Cumbria, England U.K.
164 J4 Ulricehamn Sweden
201 I2 Ulrichsberg Austria
191 H9 Ulrichstein Ger.
186 J2 Ulrum Neth.
123 F11 Ulsan S. Korea
162 J5 Ulsberg Norway
168 □N1 Ulsta Shetland, Scotland U.K.
164 G4 Ulsted Denmark
162 H5 Ulsteinvik Norway
169 H3 Ulster reg. Ireland/U.K.
251 R8 Ulster PA U.S.A.
259 G1 Ulster County county NY U.S.A.
270 □ Ulster Spring Jamaica
105 I6 Ultima Vic. Austr.
276 B1 Ultraoriental, Cordillera mts Peru
205 Q3 Ultzama r. Spain
208 B1 Ultzama, Valle de val. Spain
115 D2 Ulu Sulawesi Indon.
232 B2 Ulu Sudan
266 □P10 Ulúa r. Hond.
151 C5 Ulubağ Turkey
221 J2 Ulubat Gölü l. Turkey
221 K4 Ulubey Turkey
221 L4 Uluborlu Turkey
221 K2 Uludağ mt. Turkey
221 K2 Uludağ Milli Parkı nat. park Turkey
Ulugqat Xinjiang China see Wuqia
116 D3 Ulu Kali, Gunung mt. Malaysia
151 C7 Ulukaya Turkey
242 G2 Ulukhaktok N.W.T. Can.
148 G5 Ulukışla Turkey
221 L4 Uluköy Turkey
237 P4 Ulundi S. Africa
132 H3 Ulungur He r. China
132 H3 Ulungur Hu l. China
264 □E13 'Ulupalakua HI U.S.A.
116 □ Ulu Pandan Sing.
Uluqsaqtuua N.W.T. Can. see Ulukhaktok
106 C8 Uluru hill N.T. Austr.
106 C8 Uluru-Kata Tjuta National Park N.T. Austr.
221 J3 Ulus Dağı mt. Turkey
Ulutau Kazakh. see Ulytau
117 K2 Ulu Temburong National Park Brunei
168 D10 Ulva i. Scotland U.K.
Ulvéah i. Vanuatu see Lopévi
162 □ Ulvebreen glacier Svalbard
164 B2 Ulvenåso mt. Norway
186 G5 Ulvenhout Neth.
171 K5 Ulverston Cumbria, England U.K.
105 K9 Ulverstone Tas. Austr.
164 C1 Ulvik Norway
163 N5 Ulvsjön Sweden
161 U3 Ul'yanikha Rus. Fed.
161 V6 Ul'yanino Rus. Fed.
159 K6 Ulyanivka Mykolayivs'ka Oblast' Ukr.
159 N3 Ulyanivka Sums'ka Oblast' Ukr.
Ūl'yanov Kazakh. see Ul'yanovskiy
161 N2 Ul'yanovka Rus. Fed.
158 J5 Ul'yanovka Kirovohrads'ka Oblast' Ukr.
159 L3 Ul'yanovka Poltavs'ka Oblast' Ukr.
160 F7 Ul'yanovo Kaliningradskaya Oblast' Rus. Fed.
161 S8 Ul'yanovo Kaluzhskaya Oblast' Rus. Fed.
157 J5 Ul'yanovsk Rus. Fed.
157 I5 Ul'yanovskaya Oblast' admin. div. Rus. Fed.
143 O2 Ul'yanovskiy Kazakh.
Ulyanovsk Oblast admin. div. Rus. Fed. see Ul'yanovskaya Oblast'
Ul'yanovskoye Kazakh. see Ul'yanovskiy
129 O1 Ulyatuy Rus. Fed.
261 E7 Ulysses KS U.S.A.
256 C11 Ulysses KY U.S.A.
143 L3 Ulytau Kazakh.
143 L4 Ulytau, Gory mts Kazakh.
142 J3 Uly-Zhylanshyk r. Kazakh.
122 B2 Uma Rus. Fed.
210 D3 Umag Croatia
245 □D6 Umak Island AK U.S.A.
276 D4 Umala Bol.
122 H3 Umaltinskiy Rus. Fed.
'Umān country Asia see Oman
267 O7 Umán Mex.
100 □4a Uman i. Chuuk Micronesia
158 J5 Uman' Ukr.
282 C3 Umango, Cerro mt. Arg.
145 K7 Umarao Pak.
150 E7 'Umarī, Qā' al salt pan Jordan
138 H8 Umaria Madh. Prad. India
136 E3 Umarkhed Mahar. India
136 H3 Umarkot Orissa India
145 N7 Umarkot Pak.
145 M9 Umarkot Pak.
104 G2 Umaroona, Lake salt flat S.A. Austr.
138 D9 Umarpada Gujarat India
100 □1 Umatac Guam
262 E4 Umatilla OR U.S.A.
114 E7 Umayan r. Mindanao Phil.
146 G9 'Umayrah, Khawr al b. Yemen
147 M5 'Umayrī, Wādī watercourse Oman
156 F2 Umba Rus. Fed.
257 □N4 Umbagog Lake NH U.S.A.
106 F2 Umbakumba N.T. Austr.
106 D8 Umbeara N.T. Austr.
230 E2 Umbelasha watercourse Sudan
115 C5 Umbele i. Indon.
172 E6 Umberleigh Devon, England U.K.
213 M9 Umbertide Italy
113 K8 Umboi i. P.N.G.
103 D12 Umbrella Mountains South I. N.Z.
270 □ Umbrella Point Jamaica
213 M9 Umbria admin. reg. Italy
217 L5 Umbriatico Italy
237 P5 Umdloti Beach S. Africa
235 F3 Ume r. Zimbabwe
162 P5 Umeå Sweden
162 P5 Umeälven r. Sweden
115 F4 Umera Maluku Indon.
157 H5 Umet Rus. Fed.
237 Q4 Umfolozi r. S. Africa
237 P4 Umfolozi Game Reserve nature res. S. Africa
162 M4 Umfors Sweden
247 M5 Umfreville Lake Man./Ont. Can.
Umfuli r. Zimbabwe see Mupfure
237 O6 Umgababa S. Africa
237 P5 Umgeni r. S. Africa
147 H1 Umgharah Kuwait
237 P5 Umhali S. Africa
200 C5 Umhausen Austria
237 P5 Umhlanga Rocks S. Africa
237 Q4 Umhlatuzi Lagoon S. Africa
204 C3 Umia r. Spain
245 I1 Umiat AK U.S.A.
127 G1 Umi-gawa r. Japan
243 N3 Umiiviip Kangertiva inlet Greenland
264 □F14 'Umikoa HI U.S.A.
242 H3 Umingmaktok (abandoned) Nunavut Can.
248 E1 Umiujaq Que. Can.
194 D5 Umkirch Ger.
237 O6 Umkomaas S. Africa
237 O6 Umkomaas r. S. Africa
244 F3 Umkumiut AK U.S.A.
237 O5 Umlazi S. Africa
149 L8 Umma tourist site Iraq
150 D6 Umm ad Daraj, Jabal mt. Jordan
150 F4 Umm al 'Amad Syria
146 D4 Umm al Birak Saudi Arabia
150 D9 Umm al Hashīm, Jabal mt. Jordan
146 G2 Umm al Jamājim well Saudi Arabia
147 L3 Umm al Qaywayn U.A.E.
Umm al Qaiwain U.A.E. see Umm al Qaywayn
146 E2 Umm al Qulbān Saudi Arabia
192 H2 Ummanz i. Ger.
150 F9 Umm ar Raqabah, Khabrat imp. l. Saudi Arabia
147 L5 Umm as Samīm salt flat Oman
147 L4 Umm az Zumūl well Oman
147 J3 Umm Bāb Qatar
224 E6 Umm Badr Sudan
224 F6 Umm Bel Sudan
150 B10 Umm Bujmah Egypt
225 F6 Umm Dam Sudan
194 H5 Ummendorf Ger.
224 C2 Umm Farud Libya
225 G4 Umm Gerifat waterhole Sudan
146 C2 Umm Ḥarb Saudi Arabia
230 F2 Umm Heitan Sudan
224 E6 Umm Keddada Sudan
146 C3 Umm Lajj Saudi Arabia
150 C9 Umm Mafrūḍ, Jabal mt. Egypt
146 D4 Umm Mukhbār, Jabal hill Saudi Arabia
150 G9 Umm Nukhaylah hill Saudi Arabia
150 D10 Umm Nukhaylah well Saudi Arabia
149 M8 Umm Qaşr Iraq
225 F5 Umm Qurein well Sudan
146 B2 Umm Quşūr i. Saudi Arabia
225 G5 Umm Rumeila well Sudan
225 F6 Umm Ruwaba Sudan
224 E2 Umm Sa'ad Libya
147 J3 Umm Sa'id Qatar
225 F6 Umm Saiyala Sudan
147 J3 Umm Şalāl 'Alī Qatar
146 D4 Umm Samā Saudi Arabia
150 D9 Umm Saysabān, Jabal mt. Jordan
150 E9 Umm Shaitiya well Jordan
150 B10 Umm Shawmar, Jabal mt. Egypt
225 F6 Umm Shugeira Sudan
150 A10 Umm Tināşşib, Jabal mt. Egypt
146 C3 Umm Urūmah i. Saudi Arabia
150 G7 Umm Wa'āl hill Saudi Arabia
146 G4 Umm Wazīr well Saudi Arabia
150 A10 Umm Zanātīr mt. Egypt
244 E5 Umnak Island AK U.S.A.
244 E5 Umnak Pass sea channel AK U.S.A.
118 D7 Um Phang Wildlife Reserve nature res. Thai.
235 H2 Umpilua Moz.
262 B5 Umpqua r. OR U.S.A.
231 C8 Umpulo Angola
221 M3 Umraniye Turkey
138 G9 Umred Mahar. India
136 C1 Umreth Gujarat India
Umtali Zimbabwe see Mutare
237 O7 Umtamvuna r. S. Africa
237 O6 Umtentweni S. Africa
229 G5 Umuahia Nigeria
280 A5 Umuarama Brazil
151 H5 Umudlu Azer.
151 C5 Umudum Turkey
221 H2 Umurbey Turkey
221 J3 Umurlar Turkey
102 J7 Umutoi North I. N.Z.
237 P5 Umvoti r. S. Africa
Umvukwes Zimbabwe see Mvurwi
Umvuma Zimbabwe see Mvuma
237 N7 Umzimhlava r. S. Africa
237 N6 Umzimkulu S. Africa
237 O6 Umzimkulu r. S. Africa
237 N7 Umzimvubu r. S. Africa
Umzingwani r. Zimbabwe see Mzingwani
237 O6 Umzinto S. Africa
237 O6 Umzumbe S. Africa
161 N6 Una Belarus
210 F3 Una r. Bos.-Herz./Croatia
279 F5 Una Brazil
278 G4 Una r. Brazil
138 F4 Una Hima. Prad. India
205 Q8 Uña Spain
103 G9 Una, Mount South I. N.Z.
150 E9 'Unāb, Jabal al hill Jordan
150 E8 'Unāb, Wādī al watercourse Jordan
210 F3 Unac r. Bos.-Herz.
204 H4 Uña de Quintana Spain
257 J6 Unadilla NY U.S.A.
257 J6 Unadilla r. NY U.S.A.
280 D2 Unaí Brazil
127 M4 Unakami Japan
244 G3 Unalakleet AK U.S.A.
244 G3 Unalakleet r. AK U.S.A.
244 F5 Unalaska AK U.S.A.
244 F5 Unalaska Island AK U.S.A.
233 B8 Unango Moz.
198 F3 Únanov Czech Rep.
168 F6 Unapool Highland, Scotland U.K.
162 R3 Unari Fin.
115 B4 Unauna i. Indon.
158 J3 Unava r. Ukr.
150 D8 'Unayzah Jordan
146 F2 'Unayzah Saudi Arabia
148 I7 'Unayzah, Jabal hill Iraq
126 G2 Unazuki Japan
208 C3 Uncastillo Spain
138 H7 Unchahra Madh. Prad. India
265 X3 Uncompahgre Plateau CO U.S.A.
107 J5 Undara Volcanic National Park Qld Austr.
165 K3 Unden l. Sweden
237 N5 Underberg S. Africa
105 H6 Underbool Vic. Austr.
162 L5 Undersåker Sweden
260 E2 Underwood ND U.S.A.
194 G5 Undingen Ger.
157 J5 Undory Rus. Fed.
115 B9 Undu, Tanjung pt Sumba Indon.
185 B10 Undués de Lerda Spain
115 G5 Undur Seram Indon.
160 E3 Undva Estonia
172 G4 Undy Monmouthshire, Wales U.K.
161 P9 Unecha Rus. Fed.
161 O9 Unecha r. Rus. Fed.
275 E5 Uneiuxi r. Brazil
244 G5 Unga AK U.S.A.
244 G5 Unga Island AK U.S.A.
244 G2 Ungalik AK U.S.A.
244 G2 Ungalik r. AK U.S.A.
105 K5 Ungarie N.S.W. Austr.
104 F6 Ungarra S.A. Austr.
Ungava, Baie d' b. Que. Can. see Ungava Bay
243 K3 Ungava, Péninsule d' pen. Que. Can.
249 H1 Ungava Bay Que. Can.
Ungava Peninsula Que. Can. see Ungava, Péninsule d'
Ungeny Moldova see Ungheni
195 I5 Ungerhausen Ger.
158 G6 Ungheni Moldova
219 M4 Ungheni Romania
235 G4 Unguana Moz.
Unguja i. Tanz. see Zanzibar Island
Unguja North admin. reg. Tanz. see Zanzibar North
Unguja South admin. reg. Tanz. see Zanzibar South
Unguja West admin. reg. Tanz. see Zanzibar West
219 M3 Ungurași Romania
144 H2 Unguz, Solonchakovyye Vpadiny salt flat Turkm.
144 H1 Üngüz Angyrsyndaky Garagum des. Turkm.
Ungvár Ukr. see Uzhhorod
233 D5 Ungwana Bay Kenya
204 E8 Unhais da Serra Port.
204 E8 Unhais-o-Velho Port.
193 J10 Unhošť Czech Rep.
156 J4 Uni Rus. Fed.
276 C2 União Acre Brazil
280 B3 União Minas Gerais Brazil
278 E3 União Piauí Brazil
279 C8 União da Vitória Brazil
275 F5 União do Mararé Brazil
278 G4 União dos Palmares Brazil
138 F7 Uniara Rajasthan India
238 □2a Unicorn Point Ascension S. Atlantic Ocean
198 G2 Uničov Czech Rep.
196 G4 Uniejów Pol.
183 E6 Unieux France
213 Q6 Unije Croatia
210 E3 Unije i. Croatia
244 F5 Unimak Bight b. AK U.S.A.
244 F5 Unimak Island AK U.S.A.
244 F5 Unimak Pass sea channel AK U.S.A.
198 G3 Unín Slovakia
275 F5 Unini r. Brazil
276 B2 Unini Peru
284 E4 Unión Arg.
277 F6 Unión Para.
257 □P4 Union ME U.S.A.
260 J6 Union MO U.S.A.
259 G3 Union NJ U.S.A.
262 F4 Union OR U.S.A.
255 G8 Union SC U.S.A.
256 E11 Union WV U.S.A.
283 E5 Unión, Bahía b. Arg.
265 T7 Union, Mount AZ U.S.A.
259 G4 Union Beach NJ U.S.A.
258 A5 Union Bridge MD U.S.A.
256 A8 Union City OH U.S.A.
256 F7 Union City PA U.S.A.
261 K7 Union City TN U.S.A.
259 G3 Union County county NJ U.S.A.
258 A3 Union County county PA U.S.A.
236 H9 Uniondale S. Africa
258 E1 Union Dale PA U.S.A.
270 C2 Unión de Reyes Cuba
268 C6 Unión de Tula Mex.
169 D9 Unionhall Ireland
269 M9 Unión Hidalgo Mex.
271 □3 Union Island St Vincent
258 E6 Union Lake NJ U.S.A.
255 E9 Union Springs AL U.S.A.
256 I6 Union Springs NY U.S.A.
255 D9 Uniontown AL U.S.A.
256 F9 Uniontown PA U.S.A.
239 □1b Union Vale Mauritius
264 L3 Union Valley Reservoir CA U.S.A.
259 J1 Unionville CT U.S.A.
251 K6 Unionville MI U.S.A.
260 I5 Unionville MO U.S.A.
264 N1 Unionville NV U.S.A.
258 F2 Unionville NY U.S.A.
258 D5 Unionville PA U.S.A.
256 H10 Unionville VA U.S.A.
196 G2 Unisław Pol.
147 K4 United Arab Emirates country Asia
United Arab Republic country Africa see Egypt
167 G4 United Kingdom country Europe
United Provinces state India see Uttar Pradesh
252 G3 United States of America country N. America
243 L1 United States Range mts Nunavut Can.
213 M7 Uniti r. Italy
247 I4 Unity Sask. Can.
262 E4 Unity OR U.S.A.
258 B2 Unityville PA U.S.A.
205 Q8 Universales, Montes reg. Spain
234 B4 Unjab watercourse Namibia
138 D8 Unjha Gujarat India
191 D9 Unkel Ger.
200 G4 Unken Austria
194 H5 Unlingen Ger.
191 E7 Unna Ger.
138 H6 Unnao Uttar Prad. India
191 E9 Unnau Ger.
126 E2 Unoke Japan
123 D9 Ŭnp'a N. Korea
285 E2 Unquillo Arg.
123 D8 Unsan N. Korea
123 E9 Ŭnsan N. Korea
151 E7 Ünseli Turkey
168 □O1 Unst i. Scotland U.K.
171 O7 Unstone Derbyshire, England U.K.
193 E8 Unstrut r. Ger.
193 E8 Unstrut-Trias-Land park Ger.
124 □1 Unten Okinawa Japan
219 O3 Unțeni Romania
212 F1 Unterägeri Switz.
195 K6 Unterammergau Ger.
191 I9 Unterbreizbach Ger.
195 J6 Unterdießen Ger.
195 N5 Unterdietfurt Ger.
192 F5 Untere Havel park Ger.
212 I2 Unter Engadin reg. Switz.
192 J5 Unteres Odertal, Nationalpark nat. park Ger.
192 J5 Unteres Odertal, Nationalpark nat. park Ger.
193 E8 Unteres Saaletal, Naturpark park Ger.
191 I10 Unterfranken admin. reg. Ger.
195 P4 Untergriesbach Ger.
195 L5 Unterhaching Ger.
200 D5 Unter Inn Thal val. Austria
212 E1 Unterkulm Switz.
201 N6 Unterlamm Austria
190 J5 Unterlüß Ger.
191 J9 Untermaßfeld Ger.
195 J5 Untermeitingen Ger.
191 K10 Untermerzbach Ger.
194 H3 Untermünkheim Ger.
195 N5 Unterneukirchen Ger.
195 I2 Unterpleichfeld Ger.
195 M5 Unterreit Ger.
212 F2 Unterschächen Switz.
195 L5 Unterschleißheim Ger.
195 I4 Unterschneidheim Ger.
194 G6 Untersee l. Ger./Switz.
191 K10 Untersiemau Ger.
193 E10 Untersteinach Ger.
195 J6 Unterthingau Ger.
192 I4 Unterueckersee l. Ger.
201 K3 Unterweißenbach Austria
193 D9 Unterwellenborn Ger.
195 M6 Unterwössen Ger.
151 H3 Untsukul' Rus. Fed.
275 E4 Unturán, Sierra de mts Venez.
245 O4 Unuk r. Can./U.S.A.
128 B9 Unuli Horog Qinghai China
178 B7 Unverre France
156 L3 Un'ya r. Rus. Fed.
125 H14 Unzen-Amakusa Kokuritsu-kōen nat. park Japan
156 I4 Unzha Rus. Fed.
205 Q3 Unzué Spain
124 □A21 Uoturi-shima i. Nansei-shotō Japan
126 F2 Uozu Japan
198 E1 Úpa r. Czech Rep.
161 T7 Upa r. Rus. Fed.
265 V1 Upalco UT U.S.A.
139 J8 Upar Ghat reg. Chhattisgarh India
275 F2 Upata Venez.
173 I5 Upavon Wiltshire, England U.K.
231 E7 Upemba, Lac l. Dem. Rep. Congo
231 E7 Upemba, Parc National de l' nat. park Dem. Rep. Congo
139 K8 Uperbada Orissa India
243 M2 Upernavik Greenland
243 M2 Upernavik Kujalleq Greenland
190 D3 Upgant-Schott Ger.
114 E8 Upi Mindanao Phil.
274 C3 Upía r. Col.
198 F1 Úpice Czech Rep.
236 F4 Upington S. Africa
163 R6 Upinniemi Fin.
264 O7 Upland CA U.S.A.
138 C9 Upleta Gujarat India
151 F4 Up'lists'ikhe Georgia
172 G6 Uplyme Devon, England U.K.
244 H3 Upnuk Lake AK U.S.A.
102 J6 Upokongaro North I. N.Z.
162 U3 Upoloksha Rus. Fed.
100 □2 'Upolu i. Samoa
264 □F13 'Upolu Point HI U.S.A.
151 C1 Upornaya Rus. Fed.
262 D6 Upper Alkali Lake CA U.S.A.
256 B8 Upper Arlington OH U.S.A.
246 G5 Upper Arrow Lake B.C. Can.
Upper Austria land Austria see Oberösterreich
169 J3 Upper Ballinderry Northern Ireland U.K.
168 D6 Upper Bayble Western Isles, Scotland U.K.
258 E3 Upper Black Eddy PA U.S.A.
168 J6 Upper Camster Highland, Scotland U.K.
172 F3 Upper Chapel Powys, Wales U.K.
Upper Chindwin Myanmar see Mawlaik
173 J5 Upper Clatford Hampshire, England U.K.
258 C5 Upper Crossroads MD U.S.A.
106 C3 Upper Daly Aboriginal Land res. N.T. Austr.
258 E5 Upper Darby PA U.S.A.
228 E4 Upper East admin. reg. Ghana
246 F4 Upper Fraser B.C. Can.
173 J4 Upper Heyford Oxfordshire, England U.K.
103 J8 Upper Hutt North I. N.Z.
250 C6 Upper Iowa r. IA U.S.A.
244 G3 Upper Kalskag AK U.S.A.
257 □R2 Upper Kent N.B. Can.
262 D5 Upper Klamath Lake OR U.S.A
168 J8 Upper Knockando Moray, Scotland U.K.
169 I3 Upperlands Northern Ireland U
245 O3 Upper Liard Y.T. Can.
169 G4 Upper Lough Erne l. Northern Ireland U.K.
248 A3 Upper Manitou Lake Ont. Car
271 □7 Upper Manzanilla Trin. and T
258 B7 Upper Marlboro MD U.S.A.
251 Q5 Upper Mazinaw Lake Ont. Ca
262 J3 Upper Missouri Breaks Natio Monument nat. park MT U.S.A
232 B2 Upper Nile state Sudan
259 H2 Upper Nyack NY U.S.A.
116 □ Upper Peirce Reservoir Sing.
250 E9 Upper Preoria Lake IL U.S.A.
260 H1 Upper Red Lake MN U.S.A.
256 B8 Upper Sandusky OH U.S.A.
257 K4 Upper Saranac Lake NY U.S.A
Upper Seal Lake Que. Can. see Iberville, Lac d'
103 G8 Upper Takaka South I. N.Z.
173 I2 Upper Tean Staffordshire, England U.K.
Upper Tunguska r. Rus. Fed. s Angara
Upper Volta country Africa see Burkina
136 D6 Uppinangadi Karnataka India
173 K2 Uppingham Rutland, England U
165 N2 Uppland reg. Sweden
165 N1 Upplanda Sweden
165 N2 Upplands-Väsby Sweden
165 N2 Uppsala Sweden
165 N1 Uppsala county Sweden
139 I8 Uprara Chhattisgarh India
244 D3 Upright, Cape AK U.S.A.
248 B3 Upsala Ont. Can.
138 F3 Upshi Jammu and Kashmir In
250 D3 Upson WI U.S.A.
107 K5 Upstart, Cape Qld Austr.
107 K5 Upstart Bay Qld Austr.
172 H6 Upton Dorset, England U.K.
257 N6 Upton MA U.S.A.
172 H4 Upton St Leonards Gloucestershire, England U.K.
172 H3 Upton upon Severn Worcestershire, England U.K.
150 D8 'Uqayqah, Wādī watercourse Jordan
150 F3 'Uqayribāt Syria
149 M9 'Uqlat al 'Udhaybah well Iraq
146 F3 'Uqlat aş Şuqūr Saudi Arabia
Uqsuqtuq Nunavut Can. see Gjoa Haven
Uqturpan Xinjiang China see Wushi
149 M8 Ur tourist site Iraq
274 B2 Urabá, Golfo de b. Col.
Uracas vol. N. Mariana Is see Farallon de Pajaros
Urad Qianqi Nei Mongol Chir see Xishanzui
Urad Zhongqi Nei Mongol Ch see Haliut
144 G6 Ūrāf Iran
168 □N2 Urafirth Shetland, Scotland U.
127 K6 Uraga-suidō sea chan. Japan
127 H1 Uragawara Japan
212 H4 Urago d'Oglio Italy
162 V2 Ura-Guba Rus. Fed.
124 U4 Urahoro Japan
280 B5 Uraí Brazil
198 F4 Uraiújfalu Hungary
124 T4 Urakawa Japan
105 K5 Ural hill N.S.W. Austr.
142 D4 Ural r. Kazakh./Rus. Fed.
105 M4 Uralla N.S.W. Austr.
Ural Mountains Rus. Fed. see Ural'skiy Khrebet
122 F2 Uralovka Rus. Fed.
142 D2 Ural'sk Kazakh.
Ural'skaya Oblast' admin. div. Kazakh. see Zapadnyy Kazakhs
Ural'skiye Gory mts Rus. Fed. Ural'skiy Khrebet
156 L2 Ural'skiy Khrebet mts Rus. Fe
233 B6 Urambo Tanz.
136 C3 Uran Mahar. India
105 K6 Urana N.S.W. Austr.
105 K6 Urana, Lake N.S.W. Austr.
106 G6 Urandangi Qld Austr.
278 E5 Urandi Brazil
247 I3 Uranium City Sask. Can.
105 K6 Uranquinty N.S.W. Austr.
106 E3 Urapunga N.T. Austr.
106 E4 Urapunga Aboriginal Land re N.T. Austr.
106 E7 Urapuntja N.T. Austr.
275 F4 Uraricoera Brazil
275 F4 Uraricoera r. Brazil
Urartu country Asia see Armen
214 B8 Uras Sardegna Italy
124 □1 Urasoe Okinawa Japan
Ura-Tyube Tajik. see Ŭroteppa
136 E5 Uravakonda Andhra Prad. Ind
265 X3 Uravan CO U.S.A.
152 H3 Uray Rus. Fed.
127 K4 Urayasu Japan
150 C8 'Urayf an Nāqah, Jabal hill Eg
147 I3 Uray'irah Saudi Arabia
146 F3 'Urayq, Nafūd al des. Saudi Arabia
146 G2 'Urayq ad Duḥūl des. Saudi Arabia
146 H2 'Urayq Sāqān des. Saudi Arabi
196 E4 Uraz Pol.
157 I5 Urazovka Rus. Fed.
157 G6 Urazovo Rus. Fed.
191 E9 Urbach Ger.
260 K5 Urbana IL U.S.A.
250 I9 Urbana IN U.S.A.
256 B8 Urbana OH U.S.A.
213 N8 Urbania Italy
278 E2 Urbano Santos Brazil
191 E10 Urbar Ger.
205 P3 Urbasa, Sierra de mts Spain
212 F7 Urbe Italy
205 M4 Urbel r. Spain
105 N3 Urbenville N.S.W. Austr.
194 F2 Urberach Ger.
213 N8 Urbino Italy
214 C3 Urbino, Étang d' lag. Corse Fr
Urbinum Italy see Urbino
205 O4 Urbión mt. Spain
205 O4 Urbión, Picos de mts Spain
213 O9 Urbisaglia Italy
182 D4 Urbise France
Urbs Vetus Italy see Orvieto
198 G2 Určice Czech Rep.
276 C3 Urcos Peru
185 B9 Urcuit France
142 B3 Urda Kazakh.
207 L2 Urda Spain
285 G5 Urdampolleta Arg.
208 B1 Urdax-Urdazuli Spain
Ur'devarri hill Fin./Norway se Urtivaara
285 H3 Urdinarrain Arg.
156 J3 Urdoma Rus. Fed.
194 E7 Urdorf Switz.
185 C10 Urdos France
128 G3 Urd Tamir Gol r. Mongolia
205 O3 Urduña Spain
151 L1 Urdyuk, Mys pt Kazakh.
156 J2 Urdyuzhskoye, Ozero l. Rus.
143 S4 Urdzhar Kazakh.
171 O5 Ure r. England U.K.
160 K9 Urechcha Belarus
219 P4 Urechești Romania
156 I4 Uren' Rus. Fed.
152 I3 Urengoy Rus. Fed.
164 D2 Urenosi mt. Norway
102 I5 Urenui North I. N.Z.
100 □5 Uréparapara i. Vanuatu
185 B9 Urepel France
266 D3 Ures Mex.
126 D6 Ureshino Japan
186 J2 Ureterp Neth.
102 L5 Urewera National Park North I. N.Z.
Urfa Turkey see Şanlıurfa

1 B9 Urft r. Ger.
Urga Mongolia see Ulaanbaatar
2 H3 Urgal r. Rus. Fed.
I7 Urganch Uzbek.
I4 Urganlı Turkey
8 H4 Urgell, Canal d' Spain
Urgench Uzbek. see Urganch
8 G4 Ürgüp Turkey
3 L8 Urgut Uzbek.
2 G3 Urho Xinjiang China
2 S2 Urho Kekkosen kansallispuisto nat. park Fin.
4 B6 Uri Sardegna Italy
8 E2 Uri Jammu and Kashmir India
2 F2 Uri canton Switz.
3 F9 Uriah, Mount South I. N.Z.
5 O3 Uribarri-Ganboa, Embalse de resr Spain
4 C2 Uribia Col.
5 F5 Uriburu Arg.
8 L8 Urie r. Scotland U.K.
2 G4 Uril Rus. Fed.
9 L7 Uriménil France
8 E6 Uripitijuata, Cerro mt. Mex.
6 F4 Urique Mex.
3 K13 Urique r. Mex.
2 F2 Uri-Rotstock mt. Switz.
5 I3 Urisino N.S.W. Austr.
9 R1 Uritskoye Rus. Fed.
2 C1 Urī Wenz r. Eth.
7 L3 Urizura Japan
3 Q6 Urjala Fin.
6 I3 Urk Neth.
2 D1 Urkan Rus. Fed.
2 E2 Urkan r. Rus. Fed.
1 I3 Urkarakh Rus. Fed.
9 G4 Úrkút Hungary
2 D4 Urkut Somalia
1 H4 Urla Turkey
9 O6 Urlați Romania
9 G7 Urlingford Ireland
9 N7 Urlui r. Romania
9 J1 Urluk Rus. Fed.
0 E2 Urmā aş Şughrá Syria
3 H11 Urmai Xizang China
0 E6 'Urmān Syria
6 I5 Urmary Rus. Fed.
M2 Urmetan Tajik.
2 I4 Urmi r. Rus. Fed.
Urmia Iran see Orūmīyeh
Urmia, Lake salt l. Iran see Orūmīyeh, Daryācheh-ye
9 O3 Urmitz Ger.
1 M7 Urmston Greater Manchester, England U.K.
1 □I7 Urmston Road sea chan. H.K. China
2 G1 Urnäsch Switz.
8 A1 Urola r. Spain
9 G5 Uromi Nigeria
Uroševac Ferizaj Kosovo see Ferizaj
6 F3 Urosozero Rus. Fed.
M2 Ŭroteppa Tajik.
N8 Urozhayne Ukr.
1 F2 Urozhaynoye Rus. Fed.
5 P3 Urquilla, Sierra de mts Spain
5 N4 Urquiza, Embalse de resr Spain
6 E2 Urra Port.
8 E5 Urrea de Gaén Spain
8 C4 Urrea de Jalón Spain
4 E6 Urre Lauquén, Laguna l. Arg.
5 B10 Urriés Spain
4 F6 Urros Port.
5 R3 Urroz Spain
3 H11 Urru Co salt l. China
5 A9 Urrugne France
5 O3 Urrúnaga, Embalse de resr Spain
Ursat'yevskaya Uzbek. see Xovos
5 I5 Ursberg Ger.
5 L3 Ursensollen Ger.
1 X6 Urshel'skiy Rus. Fed.
9 I3 Úrsulo Galván Mex.
9 K6 Ursulo Galván Mex.
5 B9 Ursuya, Mont hill France
7 L4 Urszulin Pol.
5 B9 Urt France
Urt Mongolia see Gurvantes
2 H1 Urtazym Rus. Fed.
2 C1 Urtenen Switz.
2 Q2 Urtivaara hill Fin./Norway
3 K8 Urt Moron Qinghai China
8 C8 Urt Moron r. Qinghai China
6 E4 Uruáchic Mex.
8 C5 Uruaçu Brazil
7 H3 Uruana Brazil
3 F11 Uruapan Baja California Mex.
8 E6 Uruapan Michoacán Mex.
6 B3 Urubamba Peru
5 E5 Urubaxi r. Brazil
5 G5 Urubu r. Brazil
0 B4 Urubupungá, Salto do waterfall Brazil
5 G5 Urucara Brazil
1 Q9 Uruch'ye Rus. Fed.
5 F6 Urucu r. Brazil
8 D3 Uruçuí Brazil
8 D4 Uruçuí, Serra do hills Brazil
1 E2 Urucuia Brazil
1 E2 Urucuia r. Brazil
8 D3 Uruçui Preto r. Brazil
7 F4 Urucum Brazil
5 G5 Urucurituba Brazil
5 J5 Urueña Spain
6 G5 Urugi Japan
5 H3 Uruguai r. Brazil alt. Uruguay (Arg./Uru.)
F3 Uruguaiana Brazil
9 B8 Uruguay r. Arg./Uru. alt. Uruguai (Brazil)
2 G4 Uruguay country S. America
Uruk tourist site Iraq see Erech
1 F2 Urukh r. Rus. Fed.
4 □ Urukthapel i. Palau
Urumchi Xinjiang China see Ürümqi
2 H5 Ürümqi Xinjiang China
Urundi country Africa see Burundi
5 N4 Urunga N.S.W. Austr.
0 □1 Uruno Point Guam
1 C2 Urup Rus. Fed.
1 C1 Urup r. Rus. Fed.
3 Q5 Urup, Ostrov i. Kuril'skiye O-va Rus. Fed.
7 E2 Urupá r. Brazil
5 Q1 Uru Pass China/Kyrg.
0 C4 Urupês Brazil
Urupskaya Rus. Fed. see Sovetskaya
5 O4 Ururi Italy
2 C1 Urusha Rus. Fed.
2 C2 Urusha r. Rus. Fed.
1 G2 Urus-Martan Rus. Fed.
7 K5 Urussu Rus. Fed.
0 C2 Urutaí Brazil
2 I5 Uruti North I. N.Z.
3 K8 Uruti Point North I. N.Z.
A6 Uruwira Tanz.
5 L5 Urūzgān prov. Afgh.
1 E2 Urvan' Rus. Fed.
0 H2 Urville Nacqueville France
4 S3 Uryū Japan
4 S3 Uryū-gawa r. Japan
2 B2 Uryumkan r. Rus. Fed.
2 B2 Uryupino Rus. Fed.
7 H6 Uryupinsk Rus. Fed.
6 C5 Urza hill Port.
7 K5 Urzędów Pol.
8 □1c Urzelina São Jorge Azores
Ürzhar Kazakh. see Urdzhar
6 J4 Urzhum Rus. Fed.
9 O6 Urziceni Ialomița Romania
9 L4 Urziceni Satu Mare Romania
9 Q7 Urzuf Ukr.
4 D7 Urzulei Sardegna Italy
2 C2 Urzy France
0 L8 Usa r. Belarus
5 I13 Usa Japan
2 C1 Usa r. Rus. Fed.
6 L2 Usa r. Rus. Fed.
4 C9 Usada i. Phil.
6 G4 Usagre Spain
1 K4 Uşak Turkey
1 K4 Uşak prov. Turkey
4 B4 Usakos Namibia
233 C6 Usambara Mountains Tanz.
233 B7 Usangu Flats plain Tanz.
287 K2 Usarp Mountains Antarctica
283 F8 Usborne, Mount hill Falkland Is
218 I7 Ušće Kraljevo Serbia
191 I8 Uschlag (Staufenberg) Ger.
197 J6 Uście Gorlickie Pol.
197 I5 Uście Solne Pol.
212 G7 Uscio Italy
192 I3 Usedom Ger.
192 J3 Usedom i. Ger.
109 B9 Useless Loop W.A. Austr.
214 B8 Usellus Sardegna Italy
232 B5 Usengi Kenya
209 E7 Useras Spain
146 D5 Usfān Saudi Arabia
160 I8 Usha r. Belarus
160 L8 Usha r. Belarus
Ushachi Belarus see Ushachy
160 L6 Ushachy Belarus
152 I1 Ushakova, Ostrov i. Rus. Fed.
143 T3 Ushanovo Kazakh.
Ushant i. France see Ouessant, Île d'
Üsharal Kazakh. see Ucharal
143 N6 Usharal Kazakh.
171 N4 Ushaw Moor Durham, England U.K.
146 G3 Ushayqir Saudi Arabia
146 E5 'Ushayrah Saudi Arabia
151 D2 Ushba, Mt'a Georgia
160 M6 Ushcha r. Rus. Fed.
161 O9 Ushcherp'ye Rus. Fed.
127 M4 Ushibori Japan
125 H14 Ushibuka Japan
127 L3 Ushiku Japan
126 C8 Ushimawashi-yama mt. Japan
233 A5 Ushirombo Tanz.
159 N6 Ushkalka Ukr.
156 M3 Ushma Rus. Fed.
142 E6 Ushtagan Kazakh.
143 Q5 Ushtobe Kazakh.
Ush-Tyube Kazakh. see Ushtobe
283 C9 Ushuaia Arg.
158 G5 Ushytsya r. Ukr.
160 F4 Uši Latvia
278 B3 Usina Brazil
191 G10 Usingen Ger.
214 B6 Usini Sardegna Italy
156 L2 Usinsk Rus. Fed.
172 G4 Usk Monmouthshire, Wales U.K.
172 G4 Usk r. Wales U.K.
139 I6 Uska Uttar Prad. India
160 K8 Uskhodni Belarus
Uskoplje Bos.-Herz. see Gornji Vakuf
172 E4 Usk Reservoir Wales U.K.
221 K1 Üsküdar Turkey
219 P9 Üsküp Turkey
191 I7 Uslar Ger.
198 C2 Úslava r. Czech Rep.
160 F4 Usma Latvia
161 W9 Usman' Rus. Fed.
161 W9 Usman' r. Rus. Fed.
160 F4 Usmas ezers l. Latvia
143 L8 Usmat Uzbek.
Usmet Uzbek. see Usmat
161 O6 Usmyn' Rus. Fed.
284 D2 Usno Arg.
205 J9 Uso r. Spain
156 J3 Usogorsk Rus. Fed.
233 B6 Usoke Tanz.
156 L4 Usol'ye Rus. Fed.
120 H1 Usol'ye-Sibirskoye Rus. Fed.
210 G3 Usora r. Bos.-Herz.
198 G2 Úsov Czech Rep.
159 N1 Usozha r. Rus. Fed.
159 O1 Usozha r. Rus. Fed.
284 C3 Uspallata Arg.
159 P6 Uspenivka Ukr.
143 Q1 Uspenka Kazakh.
159 R6 Uspenka Donets'ka Oblast' Ukr.
159 M5 Uspenka Kirovohrads'ka Oblast' Ukr.
159 M2 Uspenka Sums'ka Oblast' Ukr.
122 E2 Uspenovka Rus. Fed.
143 O3 Uspenskoye Kazakh.
157 H7 Uspenskoye Krasnodarskiy Kray Rus. Fed.
161 N5 Uspenskoye Pskovskaya Oblast' Rus. Fed.
156 H4 Uspen'ye Rus. Fed.
186 K2 Usquert Neth.
214 C9 Ussana Sardegna Italy
214 C8 Ussassai Sardegna Italy
183 K6 Usseglio Italy
183 B6 Ussel Auvergne France
184 I4 Ussel Limousin France
182 H5 Usses r. France
184 F3 Usson-du-Poitou France
183 D6 Usson-en-Forez France
122 I4 Ussuri r. Rus. Fed.
122 G7 Ussuriysk Rus. Fed.
156 I4 Usta r. Rus. Fed.
Ust'-Abakanskoye Rus. Fed. see Abakan
156 I3 Ust'-Alekseyevo Rus. Fed.
145 M7 Usta Muhammad Pak.
185 B9 Ustaritz France
Ust'-Balyk Rus. Fed. see Nefteyugansk
121 I1 Ust'-Barguzin Rus. Fed.
156 L4 Ust'-Dolgaya Rus. Fed.
160 M5 Ust'-Dolyssy Rus. Fed.
157 H7 Ust'-Donetskiy Rus. Fed.
151 C1 Ust'-Dzheguta Rus. Fed.
Ust'-Dzhegutinskaya Rus. Fed. see Ust'-Dzheguta
198 C1 Ústecký kraj admin. reg. Czech Rep.
198 D1 Úštěk Czech Rep.
212 F1 Uster Switz.
164 D1 Ustevatn l. Norway
216 E6 Ustica Sicilia Italy
216 E6 Ustica, Isola di i. Sicilia Italy
153 L4 Ust'-Ilimsk Rus. Fed.
153 L4 Ust'-Ilimskiy Vodokhranilishche resr Rus. Fed.
129 M1 Ust'-Ilya Rus. Fed.
156 L3 Ust'-Ilych Rus. Fed.
198 D1 Ústí nad Labem Czech Rep.
198 F2 Ústí nad Orlicí Czech Rep.
Ustinov Rus. Fed. see Izhevsk
Ustirt plat. Kazakh./Uzbek. see Ustyurt Plateau
165 M7 Ustka Pol.
143 T1 Ust'-Kalmanka Rus. Fed.
153 R4 Ust'-Kamchatsk Rus. Fed.
143 T3 Ust'-Kamenogorsk Kazakh.
132 G1 Ust'-Kan Rus. Fed.
122 A2 Ust'-Karsk Rus. Fed.
132 G1 Ust'-Koksa Rus. Fed.
156 K3 Ust'-Kulom Rus. Fed.
153 L4 Ust'-Kut Rus. Fed.
153 O2 Ust'-Kuyga Rus. Fed.
157 G7 Ust'-Labinsk Rus. Fed.
Ust'-Labinskaya Rus. Fed. see Ust'-Labinsk
122 B2 Ust'-Lubiya Rus. Fed.
160 L2 Ust'-Luga Rus. Fed.
156 L2 Ust'-Lyzha Rus. Fed.
156 M3 Ust'-Man'ya Rus. Fed.
153 O3 Ust'-Maya Rus. Fed.
Ust'-Mongunay Rus. Fed. see Primorskiy
152 J3 Ust'-Munduyka Rus. Fed.
156 K3 Ust'-Nem Rus. Fed.
153 P3 Ust'-Nera Rus. Fed.
156 J3 Ust'-Ocheya Rus. Fed.
153 M2 Ust'-Olenek Rus. Fed.
153 P3 Ust'-Omchug Rus. Fed.
120 H1 Ust'-Ordynskiy Rus. Fed.
185 G10 Ustou France
152 J3 Ust'-Port Rus. Fed.
219 O8 Ustrem Bulg.
196 G6 Ustroń Pol.
196 D1 Ustronie Morskie Pol.
197 K6 Ustrzyki Dolne Pol.
161 Q1 Ust'-Sara Rus. Fed.
156 H3 Ust'-Shonosha Rus. Fed.
156 K2 Ust'-Tsil'ma Rus. Fed.
132 H1 Ust'-Ulagan Rus. Fed.
156 L3 Ust'-Uls Rus. Fed.
122 H3 Ust'-Umalta Rus. Fed.
156 L3 Ust'-Unya Rus. Fed.
156 I3 Ust'-Ura Rus. Fed.
122 H3 Ust'-Urgal Rus. Fed.
122 B2 Ust'-Urov Rus. Fed.
156 L2 Ust'-Usa Rus. Fed.
142 J1 Ust'-Uyskoye Kazakh.
156 H3 Ust'-Vayen'ga Rus. Fed.
156 L2 Ust'-Voya Rus. Fed.
156 I3 Ust'-Vyyskaya Rus. Fed.
156 H3 Ust'ya r. Rus. Fed.
153 O2 Ust'-Yansk Rus. Fed.
161 O5 Ust'ye Tverskaya Oblast' Rus. Fed.
156 G4 Ust'ye Vologodskaya Oblast' Rus. Fed.
156 H4 Ust'ye Vologodskaya Oblast' Rus. Fed.
161 W4 Ust'ye Yaroslavskaya Oblast' Rus. Fed.
161 W4 Ust'ye r. Rus. Fed.
161 S3 Ust'ye-Kirovskoye Rus. Fed.
158 D3 Ustyluh Ukr.
159 L6 Ustynivka Ukr.
Ustyurt, Plato plat. Kazakh./Uzbek. see Ustyurt Plateau
142 G6 Ustyurt Plateau Kazakh./Uzbek.
Ustyurt Platosi plat. Kazakh./Uzbek. see Ustyurt Plateau
161 S3 Ustyutskoye Rus. Fed.
161 T3 Ustyuzhna Rus. Fed.
132 G4 Usu Xinjiang China
115 C9 Usu i. Indon.
127 H3 Usuda Japan
151 I4 Usukhchay Rus. Fed.
125 I13 Usuki Japan
266 □O11 Usulután El Salvador
267 M8 Usumacinta r. Guat./Mex.
Usumbura Burundi see Bujumbura
117 K3 Usun Apau, Dataran Tinggi plat. Malaysia
208 A1 Usurbil Spain
197 H6 Úšust mt. Pol.
237 Q2 Usutu r. Africa
156 L4 Us'va Rus. Fed.
161 N6 Usvyaty Rus. Fed.
160 M7 Usvyeyka r. Belarus
197 I6 Uszew Pol.
199 H5 Uszód Hungary
197 I5 Uszwica r. Pol.
113 I7 Uta Papua Indon.
115 F3 Uta i. Maluku Indon.
214 B9 Uta Sardegna Italy
265 U2 Utah state U.S.A.
265 U1 Utah Lake UT U.S.A.
162 S4 Utajärvi Fin.
117 L9 Utan Sumbawa Indon.
126 C7 Utano Japan
190 D3 Utarp Ger.
Utashinai Kuril'skiye O-va Rus. Fed. see Yuzhno-Kuril'sk
128 H1 Utata Rus. Fed.
101 □8 'Uta Vava'u Vava'u Gp Tonga
146 E4 'Utaybah reg. Saudi Arabia
150 E5 'Utaybah, Buḩayrat al imp. l. Syria
150 B10 Utayrtīr ad Dahamī, Jabal mt. Egypt
147 I2 Utayyiq Saudi Arabia
164 B2 Utbjoa Norway
208 D4 Utebo Spain
261 D8 Ute Creek r. NM U.S.A.
183 K9 Utelle France
231 D9 Utembo r. Angola
265 X4 Ute Mountain Indian Reservation res. CO/NM U.S.A.
160 I6 Utena Lith.
122 B1 Uteni Rus. Fed.
138 C7 Uterlai Rajasthan India
190 F1 Utersum Ger.
233 C7 Utete Tanz.
138 F6 Utgir Rajasthan India
118 E7 Uthai Thani Thai.
145 L9 Uthal Pak.
191 K8 Uthleben Ger.
190 G4 Uthlede Ger.
150 F4 'Uthmānīyah Syria
119 D7 U Thong Thai.
118 G7 Uthumphon Phisai Thai.
277 F3 Utiariti Brazil
251 K7 Utica MI U.S.A.
261 J9 Utica MS U.S.A.
257 J5 Utica NY U.S.A.
256 C8 Utica OH U.S.A.
209 C8 Utiel Spain
246 H4 Utikuma Lake Alta Can.
266 □P9 Utila Hond.
278 E5 Utinga r. Brazil
163 I6 Utladalen park Norway
165 L5 Utlängan i. Sweden
237 J3 Utlwanang S. Africa
159 N7 Utlyuts'kyy Lyman b. Ukr.
125 H14 Uto Japan
165 O3 Utö i. Sweden
106 E7 Utopia N.T. Austr.
244 I2 Utopia AK U.S.A.
284 E5 Utracán Arg.
197 I3 Utrata r. Pol.
138 I6 Utraula Uttar Prad. India
186 H4 Utrecht Neth.
186 H4 Utrecht prov. Neth.
237 O3 Utrecht S. Africa
206 H6 Utrera Spain
206 F4 Utrera, Peña hill Spain
208 D6 Utrillas Spain
199 I6 Utrine Vojvodina Serbia
160 L4 Utroya r. Rus. Fed.
164 A2 Utsira Norway
162 S2 Utsjoki Fin.
162 M2 Utskor Norway
127 G4 Utsugi-dake mt. Japan
127 K2 Utsunomiya Japan
157 I7 Utta Rus. Fed.
136 F6 Uttangarai Tamil Nadu India
118 E6 Uttaradit Thai.
Uttarakhand state India see Uttaranchal
138 G4 Uttaranchal state India
138 G4 Uttarkashi Uttaranchal India
138 G6 Uttar Pradesh state India
200 H3 Uttendorf Oberösterreich Austria
200 G5 Uttendorf Salzburg Austria
195 K2 Uttenreuth Ger.
194 H5 Uttenweiler Ger.
190 L1 Utterslev Denmark
195 K5 Utting am Ammersee Ger.
173 I2 Uttoxeter Staffordshire, England U.K.
Uttranchal state India see Uttaranchal
Utu Xinjiang China see Miao'ergou
271 □1 Utuado Puerto Rico
132 H3 Utubulak Xinjiang China
244 G1 Utukok r. AK U.S.A.
101 □9a Utuofai Tahiti Fr. Polynesia
100 □6 Utupua i. Santa Cruz Is Solomon Is
192 H3 Utzedel Ger.
160 H3 Uulu Estonia
243 L2 Uummannaq Avanersuaq Greenland
243 M2 Uummannaq Kitaa Greenland
243 M2 Uummannaq Fjord inlet Greenland
Uummannarsuaq c. Greenland see Nunap Isua
243 P2 Uunartoq Qeqertoq i. Greenland
162 R5 Uurainen Fin.
128 B1 Üüreg Nuur salt l. Mongolia
128 G1 Üür Gol r. Mongolia
Uusikaarlepyy Fin. see Nykarleby
163 P6 Uusikaupunki Fin.
234 B3 Uutapi Namibia
274 D4 Uva r. Col.
156 K4 Uva Rus. Fed.
218 H7 Uvac r. Bos.-Herz./Yugo.
261 F11 Uvalde TX U.S.A.
198 D1 Úvaly Czech Rep.
161 N9 Uvaravichy Belarus
161 S6 Uvarovka Rus. Fed.
157 H6 Uvarovo Rus. Fed.
Uvéa atoll Îles Loyauté New Caledonia see Ouvéa
142 I1 Uvel'ka r. Rus. Fed.
161 R3 Uver' r. Rus. Fed.
183 J8 Uvernet-Fours France
233 A6 Uvinza Tanz.
231 F5 Uvira Dem. Rep. Congo
161 Y5 Uvod' r. Rus. Fed.
237 O6 Uvongo S. Africa
128 C2 Uvs prov. Mongolia
128 C1 Uvs Nuur salt l. Mongolia
125 J13 Uwa Japan
125 J13 Uwajima Japan
125 J13 Uwa-kai b. Japan
147 M4 'Uwayfī Oman
146 E3 'Uwayja well Saudi Arabia
224 B2 'Uwaynāt Wannīn Libya
146 C2 'Uwayriḍ, Ḩarrat al lava field Saudi Arabia
150 G8 Uwaysiţ well Saudi Arabia
224 E4 Uweinat, Jebel mt. Sudan
233 B7 Uwemba Tanz.
116 G4 Uwi i. Indon.
251 O5 Uxbridge Ont. Can.
173 L4 Uxbridge Greater London, England U.K.
182 E3 Uxeau France
191 C10 Üxheim Ger.
129 K7 Uxin Ju Nei Mongol China
Uxin Qi Nei Mongol China see Dabqig
275 H6 Uxituba Brazil
267 O7 Uxmal tourist site Mex.
269 M8 Uxpanapa r. Mex.
132 H5 Uxxaktal Xinjiang China
142 J1 Uy r. Rus. Fed.
244 I4 Uyak AK U.S.A.
Uyaly, Ozero l. Kazakh. see Koshkarkol', Ozero
151 A7 Uyandık Turkey
128 H3 Uyanga Övörhangay Mongolia
153 K4 Uyar Rus. Fed.
Üydzin Mongolia see Manlay
168 □O1 Uyea i. Scotland U.K.
168 □O1 Uyeasound Shetland, Scotland U.K.
229 G5 Uyo Nigeria
128 C3 Üyönch Mongolia
128 B4 Üyönch Gol r. China
233 A6 Uyowa Tanz.
142 I1 Uyskoye Rus. Fed.
118 B2 Uyu Chaung r. Myanmar
143 N6 Uyuk Kazakh.
147 I3 Uyun Saudi Arabia
276 D5 Uyuni Bol.
276 D5 Uyuni, Salar de salt flat Bol.
159 M8 Uyutne Ukr.
185 B7 Uza France
142 A1 Uza r. Rus. Fed.
149 L6 'Uẕaym, Nahr al r. Iraq
142 I6 Uzbekistan country Asia
Ŭzbekiston country Asia see Uzbekistan
Uzbekskaya S.S.R. country Asia see Uzbekistan
Uzbek S.S.R. country Asia see Uzbekistan
151 K6 Uzboy Azer.
144 F2 Uzboý Turkm.
160 K8 Uzda Belarus
180 F5 Uzel France
Uzen' Kazakh. see Kyzylsay
183 E7 Uzer France
184 H5 Uzerche France
183 E8 Uzès France
Uzgen Kyrg. see Özgön
158 B5 Uzh r. Ukr.
158 J2 Uzh r. Ukr.
161 Q7 Uzha r. Rus. Fed.
Uzhgorod Ukr. see Uzhhorod
158 B5 Uzhhorod Ukr.
158 B5 Uzhok Ukr.
Užhorod Ukr. see Uzhhorod
218 H7 Užice Užice Serbia
161 V8 Uzlovaya Rus. Fed.
160 K6 Uzmyony Belarus
156 H4 Uzola r. Rus. Fed.
143 R7 Üzöngü Toosu mt. China/Kyrg.
151 A6 Üzümlü Erzincan Turkey
221 K6 Üzümlü Muğla Turkey
143 M8 Uzun Uzbek.
221 H4 Uzun Ada i. Turkey
143 Q6 Uzunagach Almatinskaya Oblast' Kazakh.
151 C6 Uzunark Turkey
132 G4 Uzunbulak Xinjiang China
132 I6 Uzun Bulak spring Xinjiang China
150 B2 Uzuncaburç Turkey
151 C5 Uzundere Turkey
151 B5 Uzungöl Turkey
221 H1 Uzunköprü Turkey
159 P8 Uzunlars'ke, Ozero l. Ukr.
151 J4 Uzunoba Azer.
151 B6 Uzunsavat Turkey
151 J6 Uzuntäpä Azer.
160 F6 Užventis Lith.
161 O6 Uzvoz Rus. Fed.
158 J4 Uzyn Ukr.
143 Q6 Uzynagash Almatinskaya Oblast' Kazakh.
Uzynaghash Kazakh. see Uzunagach
142 K1 Uzynkol' Kostanayskaya Oblast' Kazakh.

V

135 □1 Vaadhu i. S. Male Maldives
135 □1 Vaadhu Channel Maldives
135 □1 Vaagali i. S. Male Maldives
156 D3 Vaajakoski Fin.
237 H5 Vaal r. S. Africa
162 S4 Vaala Fin.
237 M3 Vaal Dam S. Africa
237 M2 Vaal Dam Nature Reserve S. Africa
190 H3 Vaale Ger.
237 M1 Vaalplass S. Africa
187 J7 Vaals Neth.
187 J7 Vaalserberg hill Neth.
235 F5 Vaalwater S. Africa
160 K4 Vaartsi Estonia
181 L6 Vaas France
162 P5 Vaasa Fin.
186 I4 Vaassen Neth.
135 □1 Vaataru i. N. Male Maldives
160 H6 Vabalninkas Lith.
160 M8 Vabich r. Belarus
161 Q9 Vablya r. Rus. Fed.
185 I8 Vabre France
183 B9 Vabres-l'Abbaye France
199 I4 Vác Hungary
217 K7 Vacale r. Italy
281 E4 Vacaré r. Brazil
279 C9 Vacaria Brazil
281 F2 Vacaria r. Brazil
279 B7 Vacaria r. Brazil
279 C9 Vacaria, Campo da plain Brazil
279 B7 Vacaria, Serra hills Brazil
264 K3 Vacaville CA U.S.A.
236 F10 Vacca, Cape S. Africa
183 F9 Vaccarès, Étang de lag. France
217 K4 Vaccarizzo Albanese Italy
212 H5 Vaccheli, Canale canal Italy
191 J9 Vacha Ger.
156 H5 Vacha Rus. Fed.
199 I4 Váchartyán Hungary
182 J4 Vacheresse France
239 □2b Vaches, Île aux i. Inner Islands Seychelles
151 I3 Vachi Rus. Fed.
165 K5 Väckelsång Sweden
239 □1b Vacoas Mauritius
195 P3 Vacov Czech Rep.
183 F8 Vacqueyras France
219 O3 Văculeşti Romania
156 I5 Vad Rus. Fed.
157 H5 Vad r. Rus. Fed.
136 C3 Vada Mahar. India
136 D7 Vadakara Kerala India
160 F5 Vadakste r. Latvia/Lith.
219 M7 Vădăstrița Romania
164 E6 Vadehavet nature res. Denmark
164 E6 Vadehavet sea chan. Denmark
219 P5 Vădeni Romania
158 H6 Vădeni, Dealul hill Moldova
164 H3 Väderöarna is Sweden
166 J1 Vadheim Norway
136 C5 Vadi Mahar. India
157 H5 Vadinsk Rus. Fed.
212 E7 Vado, Capo di c. Italy
205 N6 Vado, Embalse del resr Spain
205 M5 Vadocondes Spain
138 D8 Vadodara Gujarat India
212 E7 Vado Ligure Italy
162 T1 Vadsø Norway
165 K3 Vadstena Sweden
219 K4 Vadu Crişului Romania
194 H7 Vaduz Liechtenstein
192 E1 Væggerløse Denmark
162 L3 Værøy i. Norway
156 H3 Vaga r. Rus. Fed.
163 J6 Vågåmo Norway
210 E3 Vaganski Vrh mt. Croatia
166 D1 Vágar i. Faroe Is
136 G4 Vagavaram Andhra Prad. India
162 T2 Vaggatem Norway
165 K4 Vaggeryd Sweden
100 □6 Vaghena i. Solomon Is
220 E4 Vagia Greece
213 K8 Vaglia Italy
215 P6 Vaglio Basilicata Italy
212 I7 Vagli Sotto Italy
179 M7 Vagney France
165 N3 Vagnhärad Sweden
204 C7 Vagos Port.
162 O4 Vägsele Sweden
162 N2 Vågsfjorden sea chan. Norway
199 H4 Váh r. Slovakia
162 Q5 Vähäkyrö Fin.
144 G7 Vahhābī Iran
191 H7 Vahlbruch Ger.
283 □ Vahsel, Cape S. Georgia
163 Q6 Vahto Fin.
99 H2 Vaiaku Funafuti Tuvalu
206 E2 Vaiamonte Port.
213 K8 Vaiano Italy
160 H2 Vaida Estonia
261 K9 Vaiden MS U.S.A.
136 F8 Vaigai r. India
181 K5 Vaiges France
194 F4 Vaihingen an der Enz Ger.
101 □9a Vaihiria, Lac l. Tahiti Fr. Polynesia
136 D3 Vaijapur Mahar. India
136 E8 Vaikam Kerala India
160 J3 Väike Emajõgi r. Estonia
160 J2 Väike-Maarja Estonia
160 G2 Väike-Pakri i. Estonia
162 O3 Vaikijaur Sweden
260 B6 Vail CO U.S.A.
168 □M2 Vaila i. Scotland U.K.
178 G5 Vailly-sur-Aisne France
182 B2 Vailly-sur-Sauldre France
100 □2 Vailoa Samoa
259 G2 Vails Gate NY U.S.A.
160 K4 Väimela Estonia
160 G3 Väinameri b. Estonia
101 □8a Vaini Tongatapu Tonga
160 E5 Vaiņode Latvia
136 F8 Vaippar r. India
179 K7 Vair r. France
215 M5 Vairano Patenora Italy
215 M5 Vairano Scalo Italy
101 □9a Vairao Tahiti Fr. Polynesia
183 J9 Vaire r. France
138 E4 Vairowal Punjab India
204 C8 Vais Port.
183 G8 Vaison-la-Romaine France
185 H7 Vaïssac France
100 □2 Vaitogi American Samoa
99 H2 Vaitupu i. Tuvalu
100 □2 Vaiusu Samoa
182 I1 Vaivre-et-Montoille France
199 L4 Vaja Hungary
Vajrakarur Andhra Prad. India see Kanur
199 G6 Vajszló Hungary
199 H5 Vajta Hungary
230 D2 Vakaga pref. C.A.R.
230 D2 Vakaga r. C.A.R.
136 G8 Vakarai Sri Lanka
145 O3 Vakhan Tajik.
159 R5 Vakhrusheve Ukr.
145 M3 Vakhsh Tajik.
145 M3 Vakhsh r. Tajik.
Vakhstroy Tajik. see Vakhsh
156 I4 Vakhtan Rus. Fed.
144 G7 Vakīlābād Iran
144 H7 Vakīlābād Iran
164 B1 Vaksdal Norway
199 H4 Vál Hungary
122 M2 Val Rus. Fed.
163 U6 Valaam Rus. Fed.
136 G9 Valachchenai Sri Lanka
162 L5 Vålådalen Sweden
162 L5 Vålådalen naturreservat nature res. Sweden
204 D4 Valadares Port.
204 F1 Valadouro mts Spain
212 D3 Valais canton Switz.
199 K3 Valaliky Slovakia
156 K4 Valamaz Rus. Fed.
219 K9 Valandovo Macedonia
181 J7 Valanjou France
205 R4 Valareña Spain
199 I3 Valaská Slovakia
162 P5 Valassaaret-Björkögrund nature res. Fin.
199 G2 Valašská Polanka Czech Rep.
199 H2 Valašské Klobouky Czech Rep.
199 G2 Valašské Meziříčí Czech Rep.
220 F4 Valaxa i. Greece
251 S3 Val-Barrette Que. Can.
183 J8 Valberg France
213 Q5 Valbiska Croatia
165 N1 Valbo Sweden
209 D7 Valbona Spain
212 I3 Valbondione Italy
183 H7 Valbonnais France
183 K9 Valbonne France
205 O4 Valbornedo, Embalse de resr Spain
205 L5 Valbuena de Duero Spain
199 H2 Valča Slovakia
219 N5 Vâlcănești Romania
219 K5 Vâlcanului, Munții mts Romania
199 L4 Valcău de Jos Romania
183 J6 Val-Cenis France
283 D6 Valcheta Arg.
208 F5 Valcuerna r. Spain
213 K4 Valdagno Italy
182 I2 Valdahon France
Valdai Hills Rus. Fed. see Valdayskaya Vozvyshennost'
213 M2 Valdaora Italy
205 L4 Valdavia r. Spain
161 Q4 Valday Rus. Fed.
161 P5 Valdayskaya Vozvyshennost' hills Rus. Fed.
161 Q3 Valdayskoye, Ozero l. Rus. Fed.
208 E5 Valdealgorfa Spain
207 J3 Valdeazogues r. Spain
183 K8 Valdeblore France
207 I2 Valdecaballeros Spain
204 J9 Valdecañas, Embalse de resr Spain
204 I9 Valdecañas de Tajo Spain
205 J7 Valdecarros Spain
205 L3 Valdecebollas mt. Spain
205 M2 Valdecilla Spain
205 R8 Valdecuenca Spain
206 G2 Valdefuentes Spain
207 P2 Valdeganga Spain
205 K4 Valdeginate r. Spain
207 P5 Valdeinfierno, Embalse de resr Spain
204 I7 Valdelacasa Spain
205 J9 Valdelacasa de Tajo Spain
206 F5 Valdelamusa Spain
208 D7 Valdelinares Spain
205 R7 Valdellosa mt. Spain
212 F5 Val del Ticino, Parco della park Italy
207 J3 Valdemanco del Esteras Spain
181 P4 Val-de-Marne dept France
160 F4 Valdemārpils Latvia
165 M3 Valdemarsvik Sweden
205 Q8 Valdemeca Spain
206 G3 Valdemedé r. Spain
205 Q10 Valdemembra r. Spain
205 L7 Valdemorillo Spain
205 M8 Valdemoro Spain
205 Q8 Valdemoro-Sierra Spain
205 N7 Valdenoches Spain
285 I4 Valdense Uru.
204 H8 Valdeobispo Spain
204 H8 Valdeobispo, Embalse de resr Spain
207 M3 Valdepeñas Spain
207 L5 Valdepeñas de Jaén Spain
205 J3 Valdepiélago Spain
205 I5 Valderaduey r. Spain
205 J4 Valderas Spain
178 B5 Val-de-Reuil France
216 D7 Valderice Sicilia Italy
185 I7 Valderiès France
208 F6 Valderrobres Spain
205 K3 Valderrueda Spain
250 G5 Valders WI U.S.A.
285 G4 Valdés Arg.
283 E6 Valdés, Península pen. Arg.
205 L8 Val de Santo Domingo Spain
251 S4 Val-des-Bois Que. Can.
205 K6 Valdestillas Spain
208 F6 Valdetormo Spain
206 G3 Valdetorres Spain
205 J9 Valdeverdeja Spain
204 I4 Valdevimbre Spain
245 K3 Valdez AK U.S.A.
Valdgeym Ukr. see Dobropillya
212 I3 Valdidentro Italy
205 L7 Valdihuelo mt. Spain
205 N8 Valdilecha Spain
183 J6 Val-d'Isère France
212 I3 Valdisotto Italy
283 B5 Valdivia Chile
274 C3 Valdivia Col.
184 F2 Valdivienne France
180 I5 Val-d'Izé France
213 L4 Valdobbiadene Italy
179 M8 Valdoie France
178 D5 Val-d'Oise dept France
248 E3 Val-d'Or Que. Can.
205 N5 Valdosa mt. Spain
255 F10 Valdosta GA U.S.A.
163 J6 Valdres val. Norway
183 H7 Valdrôme France
205 J4 Valdunquillo Spain
180 F3 Vale Channel Is
151 D4 Vale Georgia
262 F4 Vale OR U.S.A.
219 K3 Valea lui Mihai Romania
219 M4 Valea Lungă Alba Romania
219 N5 Valea Lungă Dâmbovița Romania
206 D6 Vale da Rosa Port.
206 C2 Vale das Mós Port.
206 D5 Vale de Açor Beja Port.
206 D2 Vale de Açor Portalegre Port.
204 D7 Vale de Cambra Port.
206 B2 Vale de Cavalos Port.
204 G8 Vale de Espinho Port.
204 F7 Vale de Estrela Port.
206 B2 Vale de Figueira Port.
206 C4 Vale de Gaio, Barragem de resr Port.
206 C4 Vale de Guiso Port.
204 F8 Vale de Prazeres Port.
206 C4 Vale de Reis Port.
204 F5 Vale de Salgueiro Port.
206 B2 Vale de Santarém Port.
206 E5 Vale de Vargo Port.
206 D5 Vale do Guadiana, Parque Natural do nature res. Port.
206 D3 Vale do Pereiro Port.
206 D2 Vale do Peso Port.
204 C7 Válega Port.
213 J5 Valeggio sul Mincio Italy
246 G4 Valemount B.C. Can.
278 F5 Valença Brazil
204 C4 Valença Port.
278 E3 Valença do Piauí Brazil
184 H1 Valençay France
185 F7 Valence Midi-Pyrénées France
183 F7 Valence Rhône-Alpes France
185 I7 Valence-d'Albigeois France
185 E8 Valence-sur-Baïse France
209 E9 Valencia Spain
209 D9 Valencia aut. comm. Spain
209 D9 Valencia prov. Spain
271 □7 Valencia Trin. and Tob.
274 E2 Valencia Venez.
209 F9 Valencia, Golfo de g. Spain
206 E2 Valencia de Alcántara Spain
204 I4 Valencia de Don Juan Spain
206 G4 Valencia de las Torres Spain
206 E4 Valencia del Mombuey Spain
206 G4 Valencia del Ventoso Spain
169 B9 Valencia Island Ireland
Valenciana, Comunidad aut. comm. Spain see Valencia
178 G3 Valenciennes France
219 O5 Vălenii de Munte Romania
183 H9 Valensole France
183 I9 Valensole, Plateau de France
214 H2 Valentano Italy
269 K6 Valente Díaz y La Loma Mex.
Valentia Spain see Valencia
182 J2 Valentigney France
122 I7 Valentin Rus. Fed.
185 F9 Valentine France
260 E4 Valentine NE U.S.A.
263 L11 Valentine TX U.S.A.
260 E4 Valentine National Wildlife Refuge nature res. NE U.S.A.
212 F5 Valenza Italy
217 L1 Valenzano Italy
114 C4 Valenzuela Luzon Phil.
207 K5 Valenzuela Spain
207 L3 Valenzuela de Calatrava Spain
172 F5 Vale of Glamorgan admin. div. Wales U.K.
164 H1 Våler Norway
274 D2 Valera Venez.
205 P9 Valera de Arriba Spain
183 H8 Valernes France
206 E5 Vales Mortos Port.
281 H2 Vale Verde Brazil
215 J1 Valfabbrica Italy
208 E4 Valfarta Spain
179 L7 Valfroicourt France
212 I3 Valfurva Italy
160 J4 Valga Estonia
Valga Spain see Ponte Valga
160 I2 Valgejõgi r. Estonia
183 E7 Valgorge France
212 E3 Val Grande, Parco Nazionale della nat. park Italy
212 E3 Valgrande e Monte Mottac, Riserva Naturale nature res. Italy
212 C4 Valgrisenche Italy
216 G9 Valguarnera Caropepe Sicilia Italy
259 H2 Valhalla NY U.S.A.
246 G5 Valhalla Provincial Park B.C. Can.
204 F8 Valhelhas Port.
205 Q7 Valhermoso Spain
185 G10 Valier, Mont mt. France
143 N1 Valikhanovo Kazakh.
214 B4 Valinco, Golfe de b. Corse France
280 D5 Valinhos Brazil
208 H3 Valira r. Andorra/Spain
218 H6 Valjevo Valjevo Serbia
208 F6 Valjunquera Spain
160 J4 Valka Latvia
163 R6 Valkeakoski Fin.
187 I7 Valkenburg Limburg Neth.
186 F4 Valkenburg Zuid-Holland Neth.
187 H6 Valkenswaard Neth.
197 M1 Valkininkai Lith.
160 I2 Valkla Estonia
160 J1 Valko Fin.
199 I4 Valkó Hungary
Valkoni Fin. see Valko
159 O4 Valky Ukr.
287 C1 Valkyrie Dome ice feature Antarctica
138 C9 Vallabhipur Gujarat India
183 F9 Vallabrègues France
209 D10 Vallada Spain
267 O7 Valladolid Mex.
205 K5 Valladolid Spain
205 K5 Valladolid prov. Spain
209 C12 Valladolises Spain
179 J7 Vallage reg. France
199 L4 Vállaj Hungary
214 C5 Vall'Alta, Cala b. Sardegna Italy
209 C7 Vallanca Spain
249 G2 Vallard, Lac l. Que. Can.
183 K9 Vallauris France
168 B7 Vallay i. Scotland U.K.
162 I5 Valldal Norway
209 E7 Vall d'Alba Spain
209 K8 Valldemossa Spain
274 B4 Valle dept Col.
164 D2 Valle Norway
205 L2 Valle Spain
215 L2 Valle Castellana Italy
267 J4 Vallecillos Mex.
284 D2 Vallecito Arg.
271 I9 Vallecito Venez.
268 F8 Vallecitos Guerrero Mex.
268 G1 Vallecitos Nuevo León Mex.
215 K5 Vallecorsa Italy
212 C4 Valle d'Aosta admin. reg. Italy
284 E5 Valle Daza Arg.
207 J7 Valle de Abdalajís Spain
268 B5 Valle de Banderas Mex.
268 G6 Valle de Bravo Mex.
268 E4 Valle de Guadalupe Mex.
275 E2 Valle de la Pascua Venez.
206 H3 Valle de la Serena Spain
206 F4 Valle de Matamoros Spain
266 F4 Valle de Olivos Mex.
263 K13 Valle de Rosario Mex.
206 F4 Valle de Santa Ana Spain
268 F5 Valle de Santiago Mex.
266 G4 Valle de Zaragoza Mex.
213 M3 Valle di Cadore Italy
216 F8 Valledolmo Sicilia Italy
214 B6 Valledoria Sardegna Italy
274 C2 Valledupar Col.
178 F3 Vallée de la Scarpe et de l'Escaut park France
239 □2a Vallée de Mai tourist site Seychelles
212 A2 Vallée du Doubs nature res. Switz.
249 G4 Vallée-Jonction Que. Can.
284 C2 Valle Fértil, Sierra de mts Arg.
276 D4 Valle Grande Bol.
238 □3a Vallehermoso La Gomera Canary Is
267 K5 Valle Hermoso Mex.
182 H4 Valleiry France
268 G2 Vallejo Mex.
264 J3 Vallejo CA U.S.A.
212 G4 Valle Lambro, Parco della park Italy
216 F8 Vallelunga Pratameno Sicilia Italy
212 E4 Valle Mosso Italy
162 N5 Vallen Sweden
269 K8 Valle Nacional Mex.
282 C3 Vallenar Chile
191 E10 Vallendar Ger.
178 I7 Vallentigny France
165 O2 Vallentuna Sweden
183 D8 Valleraugue France
214 B9 Vallermosa Sardegna Italy
215 L4 Vallerotonda Italy
238 □3f Valleseco Gran Canaria Canary Is
180 I7 Vallet France
217 □ Valletta Malta
247 L5 Valley r. Man. Can.
195 L6 Valley Ger.
172 C1 Valley Isle of Anglesey, Wales U.K.
264 O8 Valley Center CA U.S.A.
260 F2 Valley City ND U.S.A.
262 D5 Valley Falls OR U.S.A.
258 E4 Valley Forge PA U.S.A.
114 D3 Valley Head hd Luzon Phil.
256 E10 Valley Head WV U.S.A.
169 I6 Valleymount Ireland
225 G3 Valley of the Kings tourist site Egypt
264 L3 Valley Springs CA U.S.A.
254 E6 Valley Station KY U.S.A.
259 H3 Valley Stream NY U.S.A.
246 G4 Valleyview Alta Can.
258 B3 Valley View PA U.S.A.
208 H4 Vallfogona de Riucorb Spain
Vallgrund i. Fin. see Raippaluoto
184 I4 Vallières France
208 H5 Vallmoll Spain
215 O7 Vallo della Lucania Italy
183 I6 Valloire France
182 B3 Vallon-en-Sully France
183 E8 Vallon-Pont-d'Arc France
212 A2 Vallorbe Switz.
182 J4 Vallorcine France
183 I7 Vallouise France
208 H5 Valls Spain
165 K4 Vallsjön l. Sweden
163 N6 Vallsta Sweden
212 G4 Valmadrera Italy
208 D5 Valmadrid Spain
247 J5 Val Marie Sask. Can.
Valmaseda Spain see Balmaseda
207 K4 Valmayor r. Spain
205 L7 Valmayor, Embalse de resr Spain
160 I4 Valmiera Latvia
205 L8 Valmojado Spain
181 M2 Valmont France
215 J4 Valmontone Italy
183 I6 Valmorel France
178 I5 Valmy France
205 M2 Valnera mt. Spain
180 I2 Valognes France
178 E5 Valois reg. France
Valona Albania see Vlorë
206 D2 Valongo Portalegre Port.
204 D6 Valongo Porto Port.
207 M7 Válor Spain
205 K5 Valoria la Buena Spain
160 J7 Valozhyn Belarus
204 F5 Valpaços Port.
208 D3 Valpalmas Spain
248 E3 Val-Paradis Que. Can.
136 E7 Valparai Tamil Nadu India
280 B4 Valparaíso Brazil
284 B3 Valparaíso Chile
284 B3 Valparaíso admin. reg. Chile
268 D3 Valparaíso Mex.
267 P2 Valparaiso FL U.S.A.
254 D5 Valparaiso IN U.S.A.
204 H5 Valparaíso, Embalse de resr Spain
182 K5 Valpelline Italy
212 C4 Valpelline val. Italy
212 D5 Valperga Italy
136 D5 Valpoi Goa India
210 G3 Valpovo Croatia
183 C10 Valras-Plage France
183 F8 Valréas France
207 K2 Valronquillo hill Spain
183 C10 Valros France
237 K3 Vals r. S. Africa
212 G2 Vals Switz.
113 I8 Vals, Tanjung c. Papua Indon.
138 D9 Valsad Gujarat India
212 C4 Valsavarenche Italy
212 C4 Valsavarenche val. Italy
192 E1 Vålse Denmark
205 L6 Valseca Spain
238 □3f Valsequillo Gran Canaria Canary Is
207 I4 Valsequillo Spain
182 H4 Valserine r. France
265 T10 Valshui Wash watercourse AZ U.S.A.
217 K3 Valsinni Italy
162 M4 Valsjöbyn Sweden
183 E7 Vals-les-Bains France
237 I3 Valspan S. Africa
237 M4 Valsrivier S. Africa
213 L4 Valstagna Italy
213 K2 Valsura r. Italy
182 F2 Val-Suzon France
156 I2 Val'tevo Rus. Fed.
183 J6 Val-Thorens France
198 F3 Valtice Czech Rep.
205 M6 Valtiendas Spain
205 Q4 Valtierra Spain
162 T5 Valtimo Fin.
239 □1b Valton Mauritius
215 J1 Valtopina Italy

220 C3 Valtou *mts* Greece
212 D4 Valtournenche Italy
212 B6 Val Troncea, Parco Naturale *nature res.* Italy
213 P6 Valtura Croatia
Valua *i.* Vanuatu *see* Mota Lava
183 B6 Valuéjols France
213 Q6 Valun Croatia
159 R3 Valuy *r.* Rus. Fed.
161 Q9 Valuyets Rus. Fed.
157 H7 Valuyevka Rus. Fed.
157 G6 Valuyki Rus. Fed.
151 K4 Välväläçay *r.* Azer.
238 □3c Valverde *El Hierro* Canary Is
Valverde Dom. Rep. *see* Mao
284 F6 Valverde de Burguillos Spain
205 P9 Valverde de Júcar Spain
206 F5 Valverde del Camino Spain
206 F3 Valverde de Leganés Spain
204 G8 Valverde del Fresno Spain
206 H4 Valverde de Llerena Spain
205 N6 Valverde de los Arroyos Spain
206 G3 Valverde de Mérida Spain
200 C8 Valvestino, Lago di *l.* Italy
162 M3 Valvika Norway
160 L5 Valyasy Belarus
213 L9 Vama *Satu Mare* Romania
219 N3 Vama *Suceava* Romania
198 F1 Vamberk Czech Rep.
119 H9 Vam Co Đông *r.* Vietnam
119 H9 Vam Co Tây *r.* Vietnam
164 F6 Vamdrup Denmark
233 D7 Vamizi, Ilha *i.* Moz.
163 Q6 Vammala Fin.
199 I4 Vámosgyörk Hungary
199 H4 Vámosmikola Hungary
199 K4 Vámospércs Hungary
199 K3 Vámosújfalu Hungary
163 Q6 Vampula Fin.
137 I3 Vamsadhara *r.* India
221 H4 Vamvakas, Akrotirio *pt Chios* Greece
149 K4 Van Turkey
151 E7 Van *prov.* Turkey
Van, Lake *salt l.* Turkey *see* Van Gölü
151 F5 Vanadzor Armenia
163 R6 Vanajavesi *l.* Fin.
160 K4 Vana-Koiola Estonia
163 L6 Vanån *r.* Sweden
Vananchal *state* India *see* Jharkhand
219 Q5 Vânători *Galaţi* Romania
219 M4 Vânători *Mureş* Romania
178 I6 Vanault-les-Dames France
153 L3 Vanavara Rus. Fed.
261 H8 Van Buren *AR* U.S.A.
250 I9 Van Buren *IN* U.S.A.
257 □R1 Van Buren *ME* U.S.A.
261 J7 Van Buren *MO* U.S.A.
Van Buren *OH* U.S.A. *see* Kettering
119 I8 Văn Canh Vietnam
257 □R3 Vanceboro *ME* U.S.A.
256 B10 Vanceburg *KY* U.S.A.
Vanch Tajik. *see* Vanj
Vanchskiy Khrebet *mts* Tajik. *see* Vanj, Qatorkŭhi
256 B11 Vancleve *KY* U.S.A.
259 H2 Van Cortlandtville *NY* U.S.A.
246 F5 Vancouver *B.C.* Can.
262 C4 Vancouver *WA* U.S.A.
109 E13 Vancouver, Cape *W.A.* Austr.
244 F3 Vancouver, Cape *AK* U.S.A.
245 M3 Vancouver, Mount Can./U.S.A.
246 E5 Vancouver Island *B.C.* Can.
199 K4 Váncsod Hungary
Vanda Fin. *see* Vantaa
260 K6 Vandalia *IL* U.S.A.
256 A9 Vandalia *OH* U.S.A.
151 I5 Vandam Azer.
200 A5 Vandans Austria
136 F6 Vandavasi *Tamil Nadu* India
247 K3 Vandekerckhove Lake *Man.* Can.
208 G5 Vandellós Spain
182 D3 Vandenesse France
182 F2 Vandenesse-en-Auxois France
237 L2 Vanderbijlpark S. Africa
250 J4 Vanderbilt *MI* U.S.A.
256 F8 Vandergrift *PA* U.S.A.
246 E4 Vanderhoof *B.C.* Can.
237 I6 Vanderkloof Dam *resr* S. Africa
106 F3 Vanderlin Island *N.T.* Austr.
106 C1 Van Diemen, Cape *N.T.* Austr.
106 G4 Van Diemen, Cape *Qld* Austr.
106 D1 Van Diemen Gulf *N.T.* Austr.
Van Diemen's Land *state* Austr. *see* Tasmania
258 E1 Vandling *PA* U.S.A.
179 L6 Vandœuvre-lès-Nancy France
212 L3 Vandoies Italy
160 I3 Vändra Estonia
215 M4 Vandra *r.* Italy
237 N2 Vandyksdrif S. Africa
160 G6 Vandžiogala Lith.
160 F5 Vāne Latvia
Väner, Lake Sweden *see* Vänern
164 I3 Vänerborgsviken *b.* Sweden
164 J2 Vänern *l.* Sweden
164 I3 Vänersborg Sweden
205 L3 Vañes Spain
286 T2 Vang, Mount Antarctica
233 C6 Vanga Kenya
235 □J4 Vangaindrano Madag.
160 H5 Vangaži Latvia
119 I8 Van Gia Vietnam
151 H5 Vängli Azer.
149 K4 Van Gölü *salt l.* Turkey
164 I1 Vangsvatnet *l.* Norway
162 N2 Vangsvik Norway
247 J5 Vanguard *Sask.* Can.
100 □6 Vangunu *i. New Georgia Is* Solomon Is
100 □6 Vangunu, Mount *New Georgia Is* Solomon Is
186 I2 Van Harinxmakanaal *canal* Neth.
263 L11 Van Horn *TX* U.S.A.
151 D3 Vani Georgia
248 F4 Vanier *Ont.* Can.
100 □6 Vanikoro Islands *Santa Cruz Is* Solomon Is
212 C2 Vanil Noir *mt.* Switz.
113 J7 Vanimo P.N.G.
154 O4 Vanino Rus. Fed.
122 L4 Vanivilasa Sagara *resr* India
136 F6 Vaniyambadi *Tamil Nadu* India
145 N2 Vanj Tajik.
145 N2 Vanj, Qatorkŭhi *mts* Tajik.
162 O4 Vänjaurträsk Sweden
219 K6 Vânju Mare Romania
153 T3 Vankarem Rus. Fed.
163 R6 Vankavesi *l.* Fin.
248 F4 Vankleek Hill *Ont.* Can.
256 B8 Vanlue *OH* U.S.A.
162 □ Van Mijenfjorden *inlet* Svalbard
162 O5 Vännäs Sweden
178 F7 Vanne *r.* France
180 F6 Vannes France
249 H2 Vannes, Lac *l. Que.* Can.
Vannovka Kazakh. *see* Turar Ryskulov
162 O1 Vannøya *i.* Norway
162 O1 Vanntinden *mt.* Norway
213 L4 Vanoi *r.* Italy
183 J6 Vanoise, Massif de la *mts* France
183 J6 Vanoise, Parc National de la *nat. park* France
237 N4 Van Reenen S. Africa
113 I7 Van Rees, Pegunungan *mts Papua* Indon.
236 C7 Vanrhynsdorp S. Africa
107 H4 Vanrook *Qld* Austr.
107 H4 Vanrook Creek *r. Qld* Austr.
138 D9 Vansada *Gujarat* India
256 C11 Vansant *VA* U.S.A.
165 K1 Vansbro Sweden
164 C3 Vanse Norway
108 H2 Vansittart Bay *W.A.* Austr.
243 J3 Vansittart Island *Nunavut* Can.
164 G2 Vansjø *l.* Norway
237 L5 Vanstadensrus S. Africa
186 J2 Van Starkenborgh Kanaal *canal* Neth.
163 R6 Vantaa Fin.
160 H1 Vantaa *r.* Fin.
109 G9 Van Truer Tableland *reg. W.A.* Austr.
237 O4 Vant's Drift S. Africa
99 I3 Vanua Balavu *i.* Fiji
100 □5 Vanua Lava *i.* Vanuatu
101 □7 Vanua Levu *i.* Fiji
101 □7a Vanua Levu Barrier Reef Fiji
Vanua Mbalavu *i.* Fiji *see* Vanua Balavu
100 □5 Vanuatu *country* S. Pacific Ocean
Vanua Valavo *i.* Fiji *see* Vanua Balavu
178 I8 Vanvey France
260 M5 Van Wert *OH* U.S.A.
236 F9 Van Wyksdorp S. Africa
236 F6 Vanwyksvlei S. Africa
236 F6 Vanwyksvlei *l.* S. Africa
199 I4 Vanyarc Hungary
212 E4 Vanzone Italy
236 G2 Van Zylsrus S. Africa
100 □5 Vao New Caledonia
103 □1 Vao Tokelau
204 F4 Vao, Embalse de *resr* Spain
185 H7 Vaour France
198 G1 Vápenná Czech Rep.
158 H5 Vapnyarka Ukr.
206 D6 Vaqueiros Port.
183 I10 Var *dept* France
183 K9 Var *r.* France
160 J3 Vara Estonia
212 H7 Vara *r.* Italy
164 I3 Vara Sweden
136 E5 Varada *r.* India
207 O2 Vara del Rey Spain
270 C2 Varadero Cuba
181 I7 Varades France
199 L5 Vărădia de Mureş Romania
183 H9 Varages France
138 C8 Varahi *Gujarat* India
185 H7 Varaire France
212 D6 Varaita *r.* Italy
160 J5 Varakļāni Latvia
228 E4 Varalé Côte d'Ivoire
199 H5 Varalja Hungary
212 E4 Varallo Italy
144 D4 Varāmīn Iran
139 I7 Varanasi *Uttar Prad.* India
156 L1 Varandey Rus. Fed.
162 T2 Varangerbotn *Finnmark* Norway
162 T1 Varangerfjorden *sea chan.* Norway
162 T1 Varangerhalvøya *pen.* Norway
215 P4 Varano, Lago di *lag.* Italy
212 H6 Varano de'Melegari Italy
160 K6 Varapayeva Belarus
145 L4 Varas Afgh.
207 J4 Varas *r.* Spain
144 E8 Vāravī Iran
210 F2 Varaždin Croatia
201 N7 Varaždinske Toplice Croatia
212 F7 Varazze Italy
164 I4 Varberg Sweden
160 G3 Varbla Estonia
199 J3 Varbó Hungary
183 H6 Varces-Allières-et-Risset France
144 C5 Varcheh Iran
199 L5 Vârciorog Romania
220 C4 Varda Greece
136 F4 Vardannapet *Andhra Prad.* India
218 K9 Vardar *r.* Macedonia *alt.* Axios (Greece)
220 D1 Vardar *r.* Macedonia
164 E6 Varde Denmark
164 E6 Varde *r.* Denmark
151 G5 Vardenis Armenia
151 G5 Vardenisi Lerr *mt.* Armenia
151 F6 Vardenisi Lerrnashght'a *mts* Armenia
151 G4 Vardisubani Georgia
163 P6 Vårdö *Åland* Fin.
162 U1 Vardø Norway
199 H5 Várdomb Hungary
220 D4 Vardousia *mts* Greece
160 F5 Varduva *r.* Lith.
161 W4 Varegovo Rus. Fed.
190 F4 Varel Ger.
284 D4 Varela Arg.
228 A3 Varela Guinea-Bissau
160 H7 Varėna Lith.
160 H7 Varėnė *r.* Lith.
178 A4 Varengeville-sur-Mer France
159 Q8 Varenikovskaya Rus. Fed.
151 F1 Varenikovskiy Rus. Fed.
178 B4 Varenne *r.* France
178 E8 Varennes-Changy France
179 J5 Varennes-en-Argonne France
182 G4 Varennes-St-Sauveur France
182 C4 Varennes-sur-Allier France
182 C2 Varennes-Vauzelles France
159 S6 Varenovka Rus. Fed.
210 G3 Vareš Bos.-Herz.
212 F4 Varese Italy
212 F4 Varese *prov.* Italy
212 F4 Varese, Lago di *l.* Italy
212 H7 Varese Ligure Italy
184 G5 Varetz France
122 H6 Varfolomeyevka Rus. Fed.
199 L5 Vârfuraşu, Vârful *mt.* Romania
199 L5 Vârfurile Romania
164 I3 Vårgårda Sweden
284 C4 Vargas Arg.
274 E2 Vargas *admin. dist.* Venez.
274 B5 Vargas Guerra Peru
278 F4 Vargem *r.* Brazil
281 G4 Vargem Alta Brazil
278 E2 Vargem Grande Brazil
280 D4 Vargem Grande do Sul Brazil
281 E4 Varginha Brazil
164 B3 Varhaug Norway
199 J5 Variaş Romania
185 H9 Varilhes France
199 H2 Varín Slovakia
165 L2 Väringen *l.* Sweden
284 D4 Varita, Pampa de la *plain* Arg.
Varkana Iran *see* Gorgān
162 S5 Varkaus Fin.
160 M6 Varkhi Belarus
191 I8 Varlosen (Niemetal) Ger.
162 □D1 Varmahlíð Iceland
164 I2 Varmeln *l.* Sweden
164 I2 Värmland *county* Sweden
164 I2 Värmland *reg.* Sweden
164 I3 Värmland naturreservat *nature res.* Sweden
164 J3 Värmlandsnäs *i.* Sweden
165 J2 Värmlandsskärgårdens naturreservat *nature res.* Sweden
219 P7 Varna Bulg.
136 D4 Varna *r.* India
213 L2 Varna Italy
142 I1 Varna Rus. Fed.
165 K4 Värnamo Sweden
164 J1 Värnäs Sweden
156 I4 Varnavino Rus. Fed.
159 R8 Varnavinskoye Vodokhranilishche *resr* Rus. Fed.
160 F6 Varniai Lith.
160 K3 Varnja Estonia
Várnjárg *pen.* Norway *see* Varangerhalvøya
198 D1 Varnsdorf Czech Rep.
255 G9 Varnville *SC* U.S.A.
160 J7 Varnyany Belarus
160 K6 Varonka Belarus
199 I5 Városföld Hungary
Varosha Cyprus *see* Varosia
150 B3 Varosia Cyprus
210 F3 Varoška Rijeka Bos.-Herz.
199 G4 Városlőd Hungary
162 S5 Varpaisjärvi Fin.
199 H4 Várpalota Hungary
190 G5 Varrel Ger.
162 T3 Värriön luonnonpuisto *nature res.* Fin.
184 E4 Vars *Poitou-Charentes* France
183 J7 Vars *Provence-Alpes-Côte d'Azur* France
183 J7 Vars, Col de *pass* France
219 N4 Vărşag Romania
145 N3 Varsaj Afgh.
221 L6 Varsak Turkey
218 J4 Vărşand Romania
199 I3 Varsány Hungary
156 I2 Varsh, Ozero *l.* Rus. Fed.
212 H6 Varsi Italy
163 Q6 Varsinais-Suomi *reg.* Fin.
160 K4 Värska Estonia
186 J5 Varsseveld Neth.
165 N2 Vårsta Sweden
Vartashen Azer. *see* Oğuz
162 I5 Vartdalsfjorden *inlet* Norway
164 H2 Varteig Norway
220 C5 Vartholomio Greece
149 J4 Varto Turkey
219 L6 Vârtop Romania
219 K4 Vârtop, Pasul *pass* Romania
170 E8 Vartry *r.* Ireland
170 E7 Vartry Reservoir Ireland
151 D3 Varts'ikhe Georgia
162 U5 Värtsilä Fin.
159 L3 Varva Ukr.
284 B5 Varvarco Campos, Lago *l.* Arg.
159 O5 Varvarivka *Dnipropetrovs'ka Oblast'* Ukr.
159 Q3 Varvarivka *Kharkivs'ka Oblast'* Ukr.
158 F3 Varvarivka *Khmel'nyts'ka Oblast'* Ukr.
159 R3 Varvarovka Rus. Fed.
199 L3 Vary Ukr.
158 D3 Varyazh Ukr.
152 I3 Var'yegan Rus. Fed.
144 E5 Varzaneh Iran
144 B2 Varzaqān Iran
278 F3 Várzea Alegre Brazil
281 E2 Várzea da Palma Brazil
278 E3 Várzea Grande Brazil
212 G6 Varzi Italy
156 G1 Varzino Rus. Fed.
212 E3 Varzo Italy
145 M2 Varzob Tajik.
156 G2 Varzuga Rus. Fed.
182 C2 Varzy France
198 F4 Vas *county* Hungary
Vasa Fin. *see* Vaasa
278 F4 Vasa Barris *r.* Brazil
199 I4 Vasad Hungary
136 C3 Vasai *Mahar.* India
160 H2 Vasalemma Estonia
160 H2 Vasalemma *r.* Estonia
215 I3 Vasanello Italy
199 H5 Vásárosdombó Hungary
199 L3 Vásárosnamény Hungary
206 D5 Vascão *r.* Port.
219 K4 Vaşcău Romania
156 I2 Vashka *r.* Rus. Fed.
158 E5 Vashkivtsi Ukr.
151 H4 Vashlovanis Nakrdzali *nature res.* Georgia
Vasht Iran *see* Khāsh
219 K9 Vasilevo *Vasilevo* Macedonia
220 E2 Vasilika Greece
220 B4 Vasiliki *Lefkada* Greece
197 M2 Vasilishki Belarus
Vasilkov Ukr. *see* Vasyl'kiv
Vasilkovka Ukr. *see* Vasyl'kivka
156 I4 Vasil'sursk Rus. Fed.
158 I1 Vasilyevichy Belarus
157 H6 Vasil'yevka Rus. Fed.
156 I3 Vasil'yevo Rus. Fed.
160 K4 Vasil'yevo Rus. Fed.
161 S4 Vasil'yevskiy Mokh Rus. Fed.
161 N8 Vas'kavichy Belarus
160 F1 Vaskijärven luonnonpuisto *nature res.* Fin.
163 Q5 Vaskivesi Fin.
160 K2 Vasknarva Estonia
158 H2 Vas'kovychi Ukr.
199 H5 Vaskút Hungary
184 D2 Vasles France
219 P4 Vaslui Romania
165 K1 Väsman *l.* Sweden
199 K3 Vasmegyer Hungary
230 C2 Vassako-Bolo, Réserve Nationale Intégrale de la *nature res.* C.A.R.
251 K6 Vassar *MI* U.S.A.
163 L6 Vassbo Sweden
163 I6 Vassenden Norway
164 F1 Vassfaret og Vidalen *park* Norway
183 G7 Vassieux-en-Vercors France
184 H4 Vassivière, Lac de *l.* France
198 F4 Vas-Soproni-síkság *hills* Hungary
281 F5 Vassouras Brazil
181 J4 Vassy France
198 F4 Vasszécseny Hungary
Vastan Turkey *see* Gevaş
162 N5 Västana Sweden
160 F1 Västanfjärd Fin.
162 N4 Västansjö Sweden
160 I3 Vastemõisa Estonia
162 N3 Vastenjaure *l.* Sweden
165 M2 Västerås Sweden
162 M4 Västerbotten *county* Sweden
163 M6 Västerdalälven *r.* Sweden
162 N3 Västerfjäll Sweden
164 J4 Västergötland *reg.* Sweden
165 O2 Västerhaninge Sweden
162 N5 Västernorrland *county* Sweden
165 M4 Västervik Sweden
165 L2 Västlandasjön *l.* Sweden
165 L2 Västmanland *county* Sweden
215 N3 Vasto Italy
190 K4 Vastorf Ger.
164 J2 Västra Ämtervik Sweden
164 J4 Västra Fegen *l.* Sweden
164 I3 Västra Götaland *county* Sweden
162 P5 Västra Kvarken *sea chan.* Sweden
162 N4 Västra Ormsjö Sweden
164 I2 Västra Silen *l.* Sweden
160 J3 Vastse-Kuuste Estonia
198 F4 Vasvár Hungary
159 L5 Vasylivka *Kirovohrads'ka Oblast'* Ukr.
159 N3 Vasylivka *Sums'ka Oblast'* Ukr.
159 O6 Vasylivka *Zaporiz'ka Oblast'* Ukr.
158 J3 Vasyl'kiv Ukr.
159 P5 Vasyl'kivka Ukr.
197 M6 Vasyuchyn Ukr.
159 L4 Vasyutyntsi Ukr.
199 G4 Vaszar Hungary
199 L5 Vaţa de Jos Romania
184 H1 Vatan France
165 O4 Väte *Gotland* Sweden
Vaté *i.* Vanuatu *see* Éfaté
168 C7 Vaternish Point *Scotland* U.K.
168 A9 Vatersay *Western Isles, Scotland* U.K.
168 A9 Vatersay *i. Scotland* U.K.
195 L5 Vaterstetten Ger.
220 D6 Vatheia Greece
Vathi Greece *see* Ithaki
Vathí Greece *see* Vathy
221 H5 Vathy *Voreio Aigaio* Greece
221 I6 Vati *Rodos* Greece
101 □7a Vatia Point *Viti Levu* Fiji
215 I4 Vatican City Europe
217 J6 Vaticano, Capo *c.* Italy
Vaticano, Città del Europe *see* Vatican City
100 □6 Vatilau *i.* Solomon Is
Vatiu *i.* Cook Is *see* Atiu
162 □E1 Vatnajökull *ice cap* Iceland
162 □E1 Vatnajökull National Park Iceland
162 I5 Vatne Norway
99 I3 Vatoa *i.* Fiji
235 □K3 Vatomandry Madag.
221 H3 Vatoussa *Lesvos* Greece
219 N3 Vatra Dornei Romania
199 J4 Vatta Hungary
Vätter, Lake Sweden *see* Vättern
165 K3 Vättern *l.* Sweden
165 N1 Vattholma Sweden
163 N6 Vattrång Sweden
101 □7a Vatu-i-Cake *i.* Fiji
101 □7a Vatu-i-Ra Channel Fiji
Vatu-i-Thake *i.* Fiji *see* Vatu-i-Cake
101 □7a Vatukoula *Viti Levu* Fiji
101 □7 Vatulele *i.* Fiji
181 J3 Vaubadon France
179 J6 Vaubecourt France
178 G7 Vauchassis France
182 D2 Vauclaix France
183 G8 Vaucluse *dept* France
183 G9 Vaucluse, Monts de *mts* France
182 H1 Vauconcourt-Nervezain France
179 K6 Vaucouleurs France
212 B2 Vaud *canton* Switz.
179 L7 Vaudémont France
178 G7 Vaudeurs France
106 C7 Vaughan Springs *N.T.* Austr.
263 L9 Vaughn *NM* U.S.A.
182 F5 Vaugneray France
182 D1 Vault-de-Lugny France
182 F5 Vaulx-en-Velin France
182 G5 Vaulx-Milieu France
274 D4 Vaupés *dept* Col.
274 D4 Vaupés *r.* Col.
248 E2 Vauquelin *r. Que.* Can.
183 H9 Vauvenargues France
183 E9 Vauvert France
179 L8 Vauvillers France
182 D2 Vaux, Étang de *l.* France
179 J5 Vaux-devant-Damloup France
247 H5 Vauxhall *Alta* Can.
178 E6 Vaux-le-Pénil France
184 B4 Vaux-sur-Mer France
187 I9 Vaux-sur-Sûre Belgium
138 C7 Vav *Gujarat* India
235 □K3 Vavatenina Madag.
99 I3 Vava'u *i.* Tonga
101 □8 Vava'u Group *is* Tonga
179 J6 Vavincourt France
Vavitao *i. Îs Australes* Fr. Polynesia *see* Raivavae
228 D5 Vavoua Côte d'Ivoire
156 J4 Vavozh Rus. Fed.
136 G8 Vavuniya Sri Lanka
160 K7 Vawkalata Belarus
161 N8 Vawkavichy Belarus
160 H8 Vawkavysk Belarus
160 H8 Vawkavyskaye Wzvyshsha *hills* Belarus
165 O2 Vaxholm Sweden
165 K5 Växjö Sweden
119 F10 Vay, Đao *i.* Vietnam
136 F6 Vayalpad *Andhra Prad.* India
Vayenga Rus. Fed. *see* Severomorsk
152 G2 Vaygach, Ostrov *i.* Rus. Fed.
136 E7 Vayittiri *Kerala* India
151 G6 Vayk' Armenia
162 S2 Väylä Fin.
184 H6 Vayrac France
184 F4 Vayres France
280 D2 Vazante Brazil
Vazáš Sweden *see* Vittangi
151 G5 Vazashen Armenia
199 I2 Važec Slovakia
161 R1 Vazhinka *r.* Rus. Fed.
151 G4 Vaziani Georgia
235 □J3 Vazobe *mt.* Madag.
285 G6 Vázquez Arg.
161 R6 Vazuza *r.* Rus. Fed.
161 R6 Vazuzskoye Vodokhranilishche *resr* Rus. Fed.
198 D3 Včelná Czech Rep.
Veaikevárri Sweden *see* Svappavaara
119 F8 Veal Vêng Cambodia
182 E5 Veauche France
164 J6 Veberöd Sweden
162 P4 Vebomark Sweden
183 D8 Vebron France
212 I8 Vecchiano Italy
199 K3 Vechec Slovakia
191 J6 Vechelde Ger.
186 J3 Vecht *r.* Neth. *alt.* Vechte (Germany)
190 F5 Vechta Ger.
191 C5 Vechte *r.* Ger. *alt.* Vecht (Neth.)
238 □3f Vecindario *Gran Canaria* Canary Is
204 I7 Vecinos Spain
191 K7 Veckenstedt Ger.
191 I8 Veckerhagen (Reinhardshagen) Ger.
160 G5 Vecmiķeļi Latvia
199 I4 Vecsés Hungary
198 E2 Vectec *hill* Czech Rep.
160 H5 Vecumnieki Latvia
Vedana Rus. Fed. *see* Vedeno
136 F7 Vedaranniyam *Tamil Nadu* India
136 E7 Vedasandur *Tamil Nadu* India
164 I4 Veddige Sweden
219 M6 Vedea *Argeş* Romania
219 N7 Vedea *Giurgiu* Romania
219 N7 Vedea *r.* Romania
213 M4 Vedelago Italy
183 F9 Vedène France
151 H3 Vedeno Rus. Fed.
165 L2 Vedevåg Sweden
151 F6 Vedi Armenia
285 G4 Vedia Arg.
156 F3 Vedlozero Rus. Fed.
159 S5 Vedmezha *r.* Ukr.
204 D3 Vedra Spain
209 H10 Vedrà, Illa de es *i.* Spain
183 C6 Védrines-St-Loup France
158 J1 Vedrych *r.* Belarus
159 S2 Veduga *r.* Rus. Fed.
186 K2 Veendam Neth.
186 I4 Veenendaal Neth.
186 J2 Veenhuizen Neth.
190 D4 Veenhusen Ger.
186 K3 Veenoord Neth.
168 □N2 Veensgarth *Shetland, Scotland* U.K.
186 I2 Veenwouden Neth.
186 E5 Veere Neth.
190 H4 Veerse *r.* Ger.
186 E5 Veerse Meer *resr* Neth.
162 L4 Vefsnfjord *sea chan.* Norway
162 K4 Vega *i.* Norway
261 D8 Vega *TX* U.S.A.
271 □1 Vega Alta Puerto Rico
271 □1 Vega Baja Puerto Rico
204 I3 Vegacervera Spain
269 K5 Vega de Alatorre Mex.
204 G3 Vega de Espinareda Spain
204 F2 Vegadeo Spain
205 M2 Vega de Pas Spain
238 □3f Vega de San Mateo *Gran Canaria* Canary Is
204 I6 Vega de Tirados Spain
204 G3 Vega de Valcarce Spain
205 J5 Vega de Valdetronco Spain
205 M6 Veganzones Spain
245 □B6 Vega Point *pt AK* U.S.A.
164 E3 Vegar *l.* Norway
204 H3 Vegarienza Spain
164 E3 Vegarshei Norway
205 J3 Vegas del Condado Spain
205 L7 Vegas de Matute Spain
186 I5 Veghel Neth.
217 N3 Veglie Italy
220 C2 Vegoritida, Limni *l.* Greece
181 K6 Vègre *r.* France
247 H4 Vegreville *Alta* Can.
276 A2 Végueta Peru
145 O6 Vehari Pak.
160 K1 Vehkalahti Fin.
192 F4 Vehlow Ger.
163 P6 Vehmaa Fin.
145 N6 Vehowa Pak.
145 N6 Vehowa *r.* Pak.
162 S1 Veidneset Norway
181 M7 Veigné France
182 I4 Veigy-Foncenex France
191 K10 Veilsdorf Ger.
Veinticinco de Mayo *Buenos Aires* Arg. *see* 25 de Mayo
Veinticinco de Mayo *La Pampa* Arg. *see* 25 de Mayo
Veinticinco de Mayo *Mendoza* Arg. *see* 25 de Mayo
Veinticinco de Mayo Uru. *see* 25 de Mayo
275 H5 Veiros Brazil
206 D3 Veiros Port.
145 M9 Veirwaro Pak.
160 G7 Veisiejai Lith.
197 L1 Veisiejis *l.* Lith.
195 J2 Veitsbronn Ger.
201 M4 Veitsch Austria
201 L4 Veitsch *mt.* Austria
194 H2 Veitshöchheim Ger.
162 R4 Veitsiluoto Fin.
160 E6 Veiviržas *r.* Lith.
214 I3 Vejano Italy
164 F6 Vejen Denmark
206 H8 Vejer de la Frontera Spain
195 O2 Vejprnice Czech Rep.
198 C1 Vejprty Czech Rep.
190 J1 Vejsnæs Nakke *pt* Denmark
274 C1 Vela, Cabo de la *c.* Col.
138 D9 Velachha *Gujarat* India
205 K9 Velada Spain
210 F4 Vela Luka Croatia
205 O6 Velamazán Spain
266 H5 Velardena Mex.
238 □1c Velas *São Jorge* Azores
266 □Q12 Vèlas, Cabo *c.* Costa Rica
269 I3 Velasco Mex.
282 D3 Velasco, Sierra de *mts* Arg.
135 □1 Velassary *i. S. Male* Maldives
199 K3 Veľaty Slovakia
183 G9 Velaux France
210 E3 Vela Vrata, Kanal *sea chan.* Croatia
183 D6 Velay *reg.* France
144 E8 Velāyat Iran
282 G4 Velázquez Uru.
191 D8 Velbert Ger.
195 L3 Velburg Ger.
219 K8 Velbŭzhdki Prokhod *pass* Macedonia
236 C8 Velddrif S. Africa
187 D6 Veldegem Belgium
195 L2 Velden *Bayern* Ger.
195 M5 Velden *Bayern* Ger.
187 J6 Velden Neth.
201 J6 Velden am Wörther See Austria
187 H6 Veldhoven Neth.
136 E5 Veldurti *Andhra Prad.* India
210 E3 Velebit *mts* Croatia
210 E3 Velebitski Kanal *sea chan.* Croatia
207 O6 Velefique Spain
219 P8 Veleka *r.* Bulg.
191 C7 Velen Ger.
199 H4 Velence Hungary
199 H4 Velencei-tó *l.* Hungary
210 E2 Velenje Slovenia
219 J9 Veles Macedonia
218 H9 Velës, Mali i *mt.* Albania
198 D3 Velešín Czech Rep.
213 Q6 Vele Srakane *i.* Croatia
207 M6 Veleta, Pico *mt.* Spain
210 F4 Velež *mts* Bos.-Herz.
274 C3 Vélez Col.
207 O5 Vélez-Blanco Spain
207 M7 Vélez de Benaudalla Spain
207 K7 Vélez-Málaga Spain
207 O5 Vélez-Rubio Spain
162 L4 Velfjorden *inlet* Norway
192 G2 Velgast Ger.
280 D3 Velhas *r.* Brazil
281 E2 Velhas *r.* Brazil
Velibaba Turkey *see* Aras
157 I7 Velichayevskoye Rus. Fed.
218 J7 Velika Drenova *Trstenik* Serbia
210 F3 Velika Gorica Croatia
210 E3 Velika Kapela *mts* Croatia
210 E3 Velika Kladuša Bos.-Herz.
210 F3 Velika Mlaka Croatia
218 J6 Velika Morava *canal* Serbia
198 G6 Velika Pisanica Croatia
218 J6 Velika Plana *Velika Plana* Serbia
201 K8 Velika Račna Slovenia
201 K7 Velika Rogatec *mt.* Slovenia
156 J4 Velikaya Rus. Fed.
156 J4 Velikaya *r.* Rus. Fed.
153 S3 Velikaya *r.* Rus. Fed.
160 L4 Velikaya *r.* Rus. Fed.
156 F3 Velikaya Guba Rus. Fed.
122 J6 Velikaya Kema Rus. Fed.
Velikaya Novoselka Ukr. *see* Velyka Novosilka
159 L1 Velikaya Topal' Rus. Fed.
201 K8 Velike Lašče Slovenia
210 F4 Veliki Drvenik *i.* Croatia
198 G6 Veliki Grđevac Croatia
218 J7 Veliki Jastrebac *mts* Serbia
219 O7 Veliki Preslav Bulg.
210 E3 Veliki Risnjak *mt.* Croatia
219 J7 Veliki Šiljegovac *Kruševac* Serbia
219 K8 Veliki Strešer *mt.* Serbia
218 I6 Veliki Šturac *mt.* Serbia
161 N5 Velikiye Luki Rus. Fed.
161 O3 Velikiy Novgorod Rus. Fed.
156 I3 Velikiy Ustyug Rus. Fed.
159 T3 Velikoarkhangel'skoye Rus. Fed.
161 X6 Velikodvorskiy Rus. Fed.
159 Q3 Velikomikhaylovka Rus. Fed.
136 F5 Velikonda Range *hills* India
161 Q4 Velikooktyabr'skiy Rus. Fed.
198 F6 Veliko Trojstvo Croatia
219 N7 Veliko Tŭrnovo Bulg.
151 D4 Veliköy Turkey
161 T2 Velikoye *Vologodskaya Oblast'* Rus. Fed.
161 W4 Velikoye *Yaroslavskaya Oblast'* Rus. Fed.
161 X6 Velikoye, Ozero *l. Ryazanskaya Oblast'* Rus. Fed.
161 T4 Velikoye, Ozero *l. Tverskaya Oblast'* Rus. Fed.
208 F4 Velilla de Cinca Spain
208 E5 Velilla de Ebro Spain
Velilla de Guardo Spain *see* Velilla del Río Carrión
205 K3 Velilla del Río Carrión Spain
207 L6 Velillas *r.* Spain
210 E3 Veli Lošinj Croatia
218 G8 Velimlje *Nikšić* Montenegro
185 E6 Vélines France
228 B3 Vélingara *Kolda* Senegal
228 B3 Vélingara *Louga* Senegal
219 M8 Velingrad Bulg.
215 J2 Velino *r.* Italy
215 K3 Velino, Monte *mt.* Italy
160 G6 Veliuona Lith.
161 O6 Velizh Rus. Fed.
198 F2 Velká Bíteš Czech Rep.
198 D1 Velká Dobrá Czech Rep.
199 K2 Veľká Domaša, Vodná nádrž *resr* Slovakia
199 H3 Veľká Fatra *mts* Slovakia
199 I3 Veľká Fatra *park* Slovakia
198 G2 Velká Haná *r.* Czech Rep.
195 N2 Velká Hleďsebe Czech Rep.
199 G3 Velká Javořina *hill* Czech Rep./Slovakia
199 K2 Veľká Javorina *mt.* Slovakia
199 H3 Veľká Lehota Slovakia
199 H2 Veľká Lúka *mt.* Slovakia
199 I3 Veľká nad Ipľom Slovakia
199 H2 Velká Polom Czech Rep.
Veľká Rača *mt.* Pol./Slovakia *see* Wielka Racza
198 F3 Velké Bílovice Czech Rep.
193 J9 Velké Březno Czech Rep.
199 L3 Veľké Kapušany Slovakia
199 H2 Velké Karlovice Czech Rep.
201 P2 Veľké Leváre Slovakia
198 G1 Velké Losiny Czech Rep.
199 H3 Veľké Lovce Slovakia
199 H4 Veľké Ludince Slovakia
198 F2 Velké Meziříčí Czech Rep.
198 F3 Velké Němčice Czech Rep.
198 F3 Velké Pavlovice Czech Rep.
199 G3 Veľké Rípňany Slovakia
199 L3 Veľké Trakany Slovakia
199 H3 Veľké Uherce Slovakia
160 E1 Velkua Fin.
199 J3 Veľký Blh Slovakia
199 H3 Veľký Ďur Slovakia
199 H2 Veľký Javorník *mt.* Slovakia
199 I2 Veľký Kriváň *mt.* Slovakia
199 I3 Veľký Krtíš Slovakia
199 H3 Veľký Kýr Slovakia
199 G3 Velký Lopeník *hill* Czech Rep.
199 G4 Veľký Meder Slovakia
199 K2 Veľký Šariš Slovakia
199 H3 Veľký Tribeč *hill* Slovakia
198 G2 Velký Týnec Czech Rep.
198 B2 Velký Zvon *hill* Czech Rep.
201 J6 Vellach *r.* Austria
100 □6 Vella Gulf *sea chan. New Georgia Is* Solomon Is
190 K4 Vellahn Ger.
100 □6 Vella Lavella *i. New Georgia Is* Solomon Is
136 F7 Vellar *r.* India
194 H3 Vellberg Ger.
204 E4 Velle, Encoro de *resr* Spain
215 J4 Velletri Italy
182 J2 Vellevans France
182 H1 Vellexon-Queutrey-et-Vaudey France
164 J6 Vellinge Sweden
205 O8 Vellisca Spain
191 I8 Vellmar Ger.
136 F6 Vellore *Tamil Nadu* India
208 F2 Vellos *r.* Spain
153 K3 Vel'mo *r.* Rus. Fed.
220 D5 Velo Greece
179 J4 Velosnes France
187 H7 Velp *r.* Belgium
186 I5 Velp Neth.
191 K6 Velpke Ger.
156 H3 Vel'sk Rus. Fed.
Velsuna Italy *see* Orvieto
156 J1 Vel't Rus. Fed.
192 H5 Velten Ger.
191 K6 Veltheim (Ohe) Ger.
198 D1 Veltrusy Czech Rep.
213 L2 Velturno Italy
186 H4 Veluwe *reg.* Neth.
186 I4 Veluwemeer *l.* Neth.
186 I4 Veluwezoom, Nationaal Park *nat. park* Neth.
260 E1 Velva *ND* U.S.A.
198 D1 Velvary Czech Rep.
220 D2 Velventos Greece
161 P4 Vel'ye, Ozero *l.* Rus. Fed.
159 L4 Velyka Andrusivka Ukr.
159 P4 Velyka Babka Ukr.
159 M4 Velyka Bahachka Ukr.
158 E4 Velyka Berezovytsya Ukr.
159 N6 Velyka Bilozerka Ukr.
159 N6 Velyka Bilozerka *r.* Ukr.
159 L4 Velyka Burimka Ukr.
158 J3 Velyka Dymerka Ukr.
158 E2 Velyka Hlusha Ukr.
197 L6 Velyka Horozhanka Ukr.
158 H5 Velyka Kisnytsya Ukr.
159 P4 Velyka Komyshuvakha Ukr.
199 M3 Velyka Kopanya Ukr.
159 K7 Velyka Korenykha Ukr.
159 M6 Velyka Kostromka Ukr.
159 M6 Velyka Lepetykha Ukr.
158 I6 Velyka Mykhaylivka Ukr.
159 P6 Velyka Novosilka Ukr.
159 M6 Velyka Oleksandrivka Ukr.
158 F2 Velyka Ozera Ukr.
159 O3 Velyka Pysarivka Ukr.
159 N4 Velyka Rublivka Ukr.
159 L5 Velyka Severynka Ukr.
158 G3 Velyka Tsvilya Ukr.
159 J5 Velyka Vys' *r.* Ukr.
159 K5 Velyka Vyska Ukr.
159 N6 Velyka Znam"yanka Ukr.
199 L3 Velyki Kom"yaty Ukr.
159 L7 Velyki Kopani Ukr.
158 H4 Velyki Korovyntsi Ukr.
159 M4 Velyki Krynky Ukr.
158 E4 Velyki Kunynets' Ukr.
199 L3 Velyki Luchky Ukr.
158 D3 Velyki Mosty Ukr.
159 M3 Velyki Sorochyntsi Ukr.
159 L4 Velykiy Khutir Ukr.
158 J7 Velykiy Kuyal'nyk *r.* Ukr.
159 K2 Velykiy Lystven Ukr.
158 C4 Velykiy Lyubin' Ukr.
159 M2 Velykiy Sambir Ukr.
158 J7 Velykodolyns'ke Ukr.
159 O5 Velykomykhaylivka *Dnipropetrovs'ka Oblast'* Ukr.
159 P6 Velykomykhaylivka *Dnipropetrovs'ka Oblast'* Ukr.
159 O5 Velykooleksandrivka Ukr.
159 K6 Velykoserbulivka Ukr.
158 B5 Velykyy Bereznyy Ukr.
159 Q3 Velykyy Burluk Ukr.
158 D6 Velykyy Bychkiv Ukr.
Velykyy Tokmak Ukr. *see* Tokmak
156 K3 Vel'yu *r.* Rus. Fed.
136 F3 Vemalwada *Andhra Prad.* India
288 J8 Vema Seamount *sea feature* S. Atlantic Ocean
289 I5 Vema Trench *sea feature* Indian Ocean
136 E8 Vembanad Lake India
199 H5 Véménd Hungary
122 M5 Vemor'ye *Sakhalin* Rus. Fed.
136 F5 Vempalle *Andhra Prad.* India
164 I6 Ven *i.* Sweden
214 C3 Venaco *Corse* France
268 F3 Venado Mex.
266 □R12 Venado, Isla del *i.* Nic.
269 I5 Venados *r.* Mex.
285 G3 Venado Tuerto Arg.
215 M5 Venafro Italy
275 F3 Venamo *r.* Venez. *alt.* Wenamu (Guyana)
275 F3 Venamo, Cerro *mt.* Venez.
180 H8 Venansault France
182 E1 Venarey-les-Laumes France
212 D5 Venaria Italy
215 K2 Venarotta Italy
183 K7 Venasca Italy
208 G2 Venasque, Port de *pass* France/Spain
183 K9 Vence France
275 F6 Vencedor Brazil
280 C5 Venceslau Bráz Brazil
205 M6 Vencías, Embalse de las *resr* Spain
160 H7 Venciūnai Lith.
213 L5 Venda, Monte *hill* Italy
206 A3 Venda do Pinheiro Port.
281 G4 Venda Nova Brazil
204 E5 Venda Nova, Barragem de *resr* Port.
183 D9 Vendargues France
206 B3 Vendas de Azeitão Port.
206 C3 Vendas Novas Port.
182 C4 Vendat France
184 B5 Vendays-Montalivet France
180 I8 Vendée *dept* France
184 C3 Vendée *r.* France
179 O6 Vendenheim France
181 L8 Vendeuvre-du-Poitou France
178 H7 Vendeuvre-sur-Barse France
217 I10 Vendicari, Isola *i. Sicilia* Italy
156 I3 Vendinga Rus. Fed.
206 D4 Vendinha Port.
181 N8 Vendœuvres France
178 B8 Vendôme France
206 G4 Vendoval *r.* Spain
Vendrell Spain *see* El Vendrell
158 G5 Vendychany Ukr.
274 C4 Venecia Col.
268 G2 Venegas Mex.
183 G9 Venelles France
185 I8 Vénès France
213 M5 Veneta, Laguna *lag.* Italy
Venetia Italy *see* Venezia
245 K2 Venetie *AK* U.S.A.
245 K2 Venetie Landing *AK* U.S.A.
213 L5 Veneto *admin. reg.* Italy
161 V7 Venev Rus. Fed.
213 M5 Venezia Italy
213 N4 Venezia *prov.* Italy
Venezia, Golfo di *g.* Europe *see* Venice, Gulf of
275 E3 Venezuela *country* S. America
274 D2 Venezuela, Golfo de *g.* Venez.
288 E4 Venezuelan Basin *sea feature* S. Atlantic Ocean
136 C5 Vengurla *Mahar.* India
186 H3 Venhuizen Neth.
204 I6 Venialbo Spain
244 H4 Veniaminof Volcano *AK* U.S.A.
Venice Italy *see* Venezia
255 F12 Venice *FL* U.S.A.
261 K11 Venice *LA* U.S.A.
210 D3 Venice, Gulf of Europe
212 H3 Venina *r.* Italy
182 F5 Vénissieux France
178 F5 Venizel France
163 L6 Venjan Sweden
136 F6 Venkatagiri *Andhra Prad.* India
136 G3 Venkatapalem *Orissa* India
136 G3 Venkatapuram *Andhra Prad.* India
187 J6 Venlo Neth.
164 D3 Vennesla Norway
164 E5 Venø Bugt *b.* Denmark
215 P6 Venosa Italy
215 P5 Venosa *r.* Italy
213 I2 Venosta, Val *val.* Italy
178 G8 Venoy France
186 I5 Venray Neth.
200 C6 Vent Austria
101 □9 Vent, Îles du *is Arch. de la Sociét*[é] Fr. Polynesia
160 F5 Venta *r.* Latvia/Lith.
160 F5 Venta Lith.
183 G9 Ventabren France
183 K9 Ventabren, Mont *mt.* France
205 L5 Venta de Baños Spain
207 K4 Venta del Charco Spain
209 C9 Venta del Moro Spain
207 M4 Venta de los Santos Spain
204 I1 Venta las Ranas Spain
285 F6 Ventana, Sierra de la *hills* Arg.
282 E5 Ventana, Sierra de la *mts* Arg.
280 B6 Ventania Brazil
204 G2 Venta Nueva Spain
207 L6 Ventas de Huelma Spain
207 K7 Ventas de Zafarraya Spain
183 H8 Ventavon France
237 L4 Ventersburg S. Africa
237 K2 Ventersdorp S. Africa
237 L2 Venterskroon S. Africa
237 J6 Venterstad S. Africa
183 D7 Venteuges France
214 C5 Ventilegne, Golfe de *b. Corse* France
212 D8 Ventimiglia Italy
214 C4 Ventiseri *Corse* France
283 C6 Ventisquero *mt.* Arg.
173 J6 Ventnor *Isle of Wight, England* U.K.
259 G6 Ventnor City *NJ* U.S.A.
215 K6 Ventotene, Isola *i.* Italy
183 G8 Ventoux, Mont *mt.* France
192 E3 Ventschow Ger.
160 E4 Ventspils Latvia
275 E3 Ventuari *r.* Venez.
264 M7 Ventura *CA* U.S.A.
101 □9a Vénus, Pointe *pt Tahiti* Fr. Polynesia
105 J8 Venus Bay *Vic.* Austr.
Venusia Italy *see* Venosa
268 D6 Venustiano Mex.
269 N9 Venustiano Carranza *Chiapas* Mex.
269 J5 Venustiano Carranza *Puebla* Mex.
267 I4 Venustiano Carranza, Presa *re*[sr] Mex.
214 C3 Venzolasca *Corse* France
213 O3 Venzone Italy
198 F4 Vép Hungary
159 N3 Vepryk Ukr.
161 R1 Vepsovskaya Vozvyshennost' *h*[ills] Rus. Fed.
282 E3 Vera Arg.
207 P6 Vera Spain
277 F6 Verá, Lago *l.* Para.
276 D2 Vera Cruz *Amazonas* Brazil
280 C5 Vera Cruz *São Paulo* Brazil
269 K6 Veracruz Mex.
Vera Cruz Mex. *see* Veracruz
269 J5 Veracruz *state* Mex.
206 D4 Vera Cruz Port.
258 E3 Vera Cruz *PA* U.S.A.
208 D2 Veral *r.* Spain
279 C9 Veranópolis Brazil
138 C9 Veraval *Gujarat* India
285 G2 Vera y Pintado Arg.
158 E3 Verba *Rivnens'ka Oblast'* Ukr.
158 D3 Verba *Volyns'ka Oblast'* Ukr.
212 F4 Verbania Italy
259 H1 Verbank *NY* U.S.A.
212 E3 Verbano-Cusio-Ossola *prov.* It[aly]
178 E5 Verberie France
215 P8 Verbicaro Italy
212 C3 Verbier Switz.
161 U5 Verbilki Rus. Fed.
159 L5 Verblyuzhka Ukr.
159 O6 Verbove Ukr.
158 E4 Verbovets' Ukr.
157 H5 Verbovskiy Rus. Fed.
159 N7 Verby Ukr.
212 G3 Verceia Italy
212 E5 Vercelli Italy
212 E5 Vercelli *prov.* Italy
182 I2 Vercel-Villedieu-le-Camp Fra[nce]
192 G3 Verchen Ger.
183 G7 Vercors *reg.* France
183 G7 Vercors, Parc Naturel Régiona[l] du *nature res.* France
Vercovicium *tourist site Englan*[d] U.K. *see* Housesteads
201 J8 Verd Slovenia
161 X8 Verda *r.* Rus. Fed.
183 I8 Verdaches France
162 K5 Verdalsøra Norway
283 D6 Verde *r.* Arg.
280 B2 Verde *r.* Brazil
280 B3 Verde *r.* Brazil
280 B4 Verde *r.* Brazil
280 C3 Verde *r.* Brazil
280 D2 Verde *r.* Brazil
281 E4 Verde *r.* Brazil
278 E4 Verde *r.* Brazil
277 F3 Verde *r.* Brazil
277 G2 Verde *r.* Brazil
268 D5 Verde *r. Aguascalientes/Jalisco* Mex.
266 F4 Verde *r. Chihuahua/Durango* M[ex.]
269 I9 Verde *r. Guerrero/Oaxaca* Mex.
269 H4 Verde *r.* Mex.
269 J10 Verde *r.* Mex.
277 F5 Verde *r.* Para.
207 L7 Verde *r.* Spain
207 M6 Verde *r.* Spain
265 U8 Verde *r. AZ* U.S.A.
Verde, Cabo *c.* Senegal *see* Vert, Cap
285 F6 Verde, Península *pen.* Arg.
281 F1 Verde Grande *r.* Brazil
114 C5 Verde Island Passage Phil.
190 H5 Verden (Aller) Ger.
278 E5 Verde Pequeno *r.* Brazil
264 M2 Verdi *NV* U.S.A.
261 H8 Verdigris *r. KS* U.S.A.
220 C3 Verdikoussa Greece
280 B2 Verdinho *r.* Brazil
280 B3 Verdinho, Serra do *mts* Brazil
269 H2 Verdolaga Mex.
183 H9 Verdon *r.* France
183 H9 Verdon, Basses Gorges du Fra[nce]
183 I9 Verdon, Grand Canyon du *gor*[ge] France
204 C4 Verdugo *r.* Spain
179 J5 Verdun France
185 G8 Verdun-sur-Garonne France
182 G3 Verdun-sur-le-Doubs France
216 E9 Verdura *r. Sicilia* Italy
197 L1 Verebiejai Lith.
237 L2 Vereeniging S. Africa
159 L4 Veremiyivka Ukr.
237 N1 Verena S. Africa
248 E4 Vérendrye, Réserve Faunique [de] la *nature res. Que.* Can.
199 I4 Veresegyház Hungary
156 K4 Vereshchagino Rus. Fed.
159 K2 Veresoch Ukr.
161 T4 Verestovo, Ozero *l.* Rus. Fed.
161 T6 Vereya Rus. Fed.
161 W6 Vereyka Rus. Fed.
185 H7 Verfeil *Midi-Pyrénées* France
185 H8 Verfeil *Midi-Pyrénées* France
228 B4 Verga, Cap *c.* Guinea
285 I4 Vergara Arg.
Vergara Spain *see* Bergara
282 G4 Vergara Uru.
213 K7 Vergato Italy
179 M6 Vergaville France
236 I1 Vergeleë S. Africa
107 I8 Vergemont Creek *watercourse Qld* Austr.
257 L4 Vergennes *VT* U.S.A.
208 L3 Verges Spain

E9 Vergèze France
M8 Verghereto Italy
G8 Vergigny France
D2 Vergina Greece
B3 Vergio, Col de *pass* France
C6 Vergongheon France
F5 Vergt France
L4 Verhuny *Cherkas'ka Oblast'* Ukr.
M4 Verhuny *Poltavs'ka Oblast'* Ukr.
Véria Greece *see* Veroia
V5 Verigino Rus. Fed.
F5 Verín Spain
G5 Veringenstadt Ger.
Verin T'alin Armenia *see* T'alin
K3 Veriora Estonia
C3 Veríssimo Brazil
Veríssimo Sarmento Angola *see* Camissombo
K4 Verkeerdevlei S. Africa
N5 Verkhivtseve Ukr.
G1 Verkhne-Avzyan Rus. Fed.
Q9 Verkhnebakanskiy Rus. Fed.
T2 Verkhneberezovskiy Kazakh.
Verkhnedneprovsk Ukr. *see* Verkhn'odniprovs'k
Q7 Verkhnedneprovskiy Rus. Fed.
J3 Verkhneimbatsk Rus. Fed.
L2 Verkhnekolvinsk Rus. Fed.
S6 Verkhneruzskoye Vodokhranilishche *resr* Rus. Fed.
I4 Verkhnespasskoye Rus. Fed.
U2 Verkhnetulomskiy Rus. Fed.
U2 Verkhnetulomskoye Vodokhranilishche *resr* Rus. Fed.
R2 Verkhneturovo Rus. Fed.
H1 Verkhneural'sk Rus. Fed.
N3 Verkhnevilyuysk Rus. Fed.
P4 Verkhnevolzhskoye Vodokhranilishche *resr* Rus. Fed.
K5 Verkhneyarkeyevo Rus. Fed.
U4 Verkhneye Kuyto, Ozero *l.* Rus. Fed.
F1 Verkhnezeysk Rus. Fed.
Q3 Verkhniy At-Uryakh Rus. Fed.
D2 Verkhniy Baksan Rus. Fed.
I6 Verkhniy Baskunchak Rus. Fed.
P4 Verkhniy Byshkyn Ukr.
F2 Verkhniye Achaluki Rus. Fed.
Verkhniye Kholokhory Moldova *see* Halahora de Sus
O6 Verkhniye Koshevichi Rus. Fed.
O6 Verkhniye Mokhovichi Rus. Fed.
F3 Verkhniy Fiagdon Rus. Fed.
Verkhniy Karabulag Georgia *see* Zemo Qarabulakhi
V9 Verkhniy Lomovets Rus. Fed.
H6 Verkhniy Mamon Rus. Fed.
Verkhniy Naur Rus. Fed. *see* Lakkha-Nevre
N6 Verkhniy Rohachyk Ukr.
J1 Verkhniy Shar Rus. Fed.
K1 Verkhniy Shergol'dzhin Rus. Fed.
K4 Verkhniy Tatyshly Rus. Fed.
P6 Verkhniytokmak Ukr.
M2 Verkhniy Ul'khun Rus. Fed.
F2 Verkhniy Vyalozerskiy Rus. Fed.
N5 Verkhn'odniprovs'k Ukr.
J5 Verkhnyachka Ukr.
M6 Verkhnya Lypytsya Ukr.
N3 Verkhnya Syrovatka Ukr.
O5 Verkhnya Tersa *r.* Ukr.
C5 Verkhnya Vysots'ke Ukr.
L3 Verkhnya Vyznytsya Ukr.
E2 Verkhnyaya Balkariya Rus. Fed.
L2 Verkhnya Yablun'ka Ukr.
Q2 Verkhnyaya Grayvoronka Rus. Fed.
M2 Verkhnyaya Inta Rus. Fed.
G6 Verkhnyaya Khava Rus. Fed.
D2 Verkhnyaya Mara Rus. Fed.
R3 Verkhnyaya Pakhachi Rus. Fed.
T2 Verkhnyaya Plavitsa Rus. Fed.
K2 Verkhnyaya Taymyra *r.* Rus. Fed.
C2 Verkhnyaya Teberda Rus. Fed.
T2 Verkhnyaya Tishanka Rus. Fed.
T2 Verkhnyaya Toyda Rus. Fed.
I3 Verkhnyaya Toyma Rus. Fed.
U4 Verkhnyaya Troitsa Rus. Fed.
Verkhnyaya Tunguska *r.* Rus. Fed. *see* Angara
C4 Verkhnye Syn'ovydne Ukr.
J4 Verkhoramen'ye Rus. Fed.
M9 Verkhorichchya Ukr.
J4 Verkhoshizhem'ye Rus. Fed.
N3 Verkhosulka Ukr.
Z1 Verkhovazh'ye Rus. Fed.
Verkhovina Ukr. *see* Verkhovyna
U9 Verkhov'ye Rus. Fed.
D5 Verkhovyna Ukr.
N2 Verkhoyanskiy Khrebet *mts* Rus. Fed.
T2 Verkhuba Kazakh.
N4 Verkhy Ukr.
H7 Verknė *r.* Lith.
I3 Verkola Rus. Fed.
N3 Verkykerskop S. Africa
G7 Verl Ger.
H7 Verlaine Belgium
E8 Verlatekloof *pass* S. Africa
□ Verlegenhuken *pt* Svalbard
J5 Verma Norway
F10 Vermaaklikheid S. Africa
F4 Vermand France
F4 Vermandois *reg.* France
B5 Vermelha, Serra *hills* Brazil
C3 Vermelho *r.* Brazil
D3 Vermelho *r.* Brazil
H3 Vermelho *r.* Brazil
G8 Vermenton France
J5 Vermeș Romania
J3 Vermiglio Italy
I4 Vermilion *Alta* Can.
C7 Vermilion *OH* U.S.A.
E8 Vermilion *r. IL* U.S.A.
J11 Vermilion Bay *LA* U.S.A.
T5 Vermilion Cliffs *esc. AZ* U.S.A.
T4 Vermilion Cliffs *esc. UT* U.S.A.
H8 Vermilion Cliffs National Monument *nat. park AZ* U.S.A.
B2 Vermilion Lake *MN* U.S.A.
B2 Vermilion Range *hills MN* U.S.A.
G4 Vermillion *SD* U.S.A.
G4 Vermillion *r. SD* U.S.A.
G4 Vermillion, East Fork *r. SD* U.S.A.
M5 Vermillion Bay *Ont.* Can.
K2 Vermillon *r. Que.* Can.
C2 Vermio *mt.* Greece
G7 Vermiosa Port.
C9 Vermoil Port.
□3 Vermont St Vincent
M4 Vermont *state* U.S.A.
T2 Vernadsky *research stn* Antarctica
J2 Vernago, Lago di *l.* Italy
H10 Vernajoul France
J6 Vernal *UT* U.S.A.
D7 Vernante Italy
L7 Vernantes France
C3 Vernayaz Switz.
J6 Vern-d'Anjou France
D4 Verner *Ont.* Can.
D1 Verneřice Czech Rep.
G9 Vernet France
I10 Vernet-les-Bains France
M4 Verneuil-sur-Avre France
G4 Verneuil-sur-Vienne France
F5 Verneuk Pan *salt pan* S. Africa
A3 Vernier Switz.
K7 Vernio Italy
H9 Verniolle France
C2 Verno *mt.* Greece
O3 Vernole Italy
G5 Vernon *B.C.* Can.
B5 Vernon France
K9 Vernon *AL* U.S.A.
E6 Vernon *IN* U.S.A.
G2 Vernon *NJ* U.S.A.
F8 Vernon *TX* U.S.A.
T1 Vernon *UT* U.S.A.
E8 Vernon, Mount *hill W.A.* Austr.
C2 Vernon Islands *N.T.* Austr.
B6 Vernouillet France
F7 Vernoux-en-Vivarais France
F3 Vernoy *NJ* U.S.A.
F3 Vernoye Rus. Fed.
180 H5 Vern-sur-Seiche France
179 L5 Verny France
Vernyy Kazakh. *see* Almaty
214 B3 Vero *Corse* France
208 F4 Vero *r.* Spain
255 G12 Vero Beach *FL* U.S.A.
199 I4 Verőcemaros Hungary
220 D2 Veroia Greece
212 I5 Verolanuova Italy
215 K4 Veroli Italy
178 F7 Véron France
213 J5 Verona Italy
213 K5 Verona *prov.* Italy
256 F10 Verona *VA* U.S.A.
250 E7 Verona *WI* U.S.A.
285 I4 Verónica Arg.
182 E4 Verosvres France
199 J4 Verpelét Hungary
259 H2 Verplanck *NY* U.S.A.
104 F5 Verran *S.A.* Austr.
212 D4 Verres Italy
184 F3 Verrières France
215 M4 Verrino *r.* Italy
212 E6 Versa *r.* Italy
212 G5 Versa *r.* Italy
213 O4 Versa *r.* Italy
178 D6 Versailles France
254 E6 Versailles *IN* U.S.A.
254 E6 Versailles *KY* U.S.A.
260 I6 Versailles *MO* U.S.A.
256 A8 Versailles *OH* U.S.A.
276 E3 Versalles Bol.
Versec *Vojvodina* Serbia *see* Vršac
160 H7 Verseka *r.* Lith.
182 H3 Vers-en-Montage France
159 L4 Vershatsi Ukr.
191 F6 Versmold Ger.
212 A3 Versoix Switz.
183 B9 Versols-et-Lapeyre France
181 K3 Verson France
183 F9 Vers-Pont-du-Gard France
185 C7 Vert France
185 G6 Vert *r.* France
228 A3 Vert, Cap *c.* Senegal
249 G3 Vert, Île *i. Que.* Can.
182 C5 Vertaizon France
184 E5 Verteillac France
278 C4 Vertentes *r.* Brazil
199 H4 Vértesacsa Hungary
199 H4 Vértesboglár Hungary
199 H4 Vertesi *park* Hungary
185 E7 Verteuil-d'Agenais France
184 E4 Verteuil-sur-Charente France
184 C5 Vertheuil France
270 D3 Vertientes Cuba
159 K2 Vertiyivka Ukr.
285 F4 Vertiz Arg.
178 C3 Verton France
213 J2 Vertona, Cima *mt.* Italy
180 I7 Vertou France
178 H6 Vertus France
213 M8 Verucchio Italy
237 P5 Verulam S. Africa
Verulamium *Hertfordshire, England* U.K. *see* St Albans
187 I7 Verviers Belgium
178 G4 Vervins France
200 A5 Verwallgruppe *mts* Austria
Verwoerdburg S. Africa *see* Centurion
247 J5 Verwood *Sask.* Can.
173 I6 Verwood *Dorset, England* U.K.
Veryína Greece *see* Vergina
181 J6 Verzée *r.* France
178 H5 Verzenay France
217 L5 Verzino Italy
212 C6 Verzuolo Italy
178 H5 Verzy France
162 S5 Vesanto Fin.
214 C3 Vescovato *Corse* France
212 I5 Vescovato Italy
187 I7 Vesdre *r.* Belgium
198 G5 Vése Hungary
152 G4 Veselaya, Gora *mt.* Rus. Fed.
159 N6 Vesele Ukr.
161 T6 Veselevo Rus. Fed.
219 N7 Veselina *r.* Bulg.
198 D2 Veselí nad Lužnicí Czech Rep.
198 G3 Veselí nad Moravou Czech Rep.
159 L6 Veselivka *Kirovohrads'ka Oblast'* Ukr.
158 H3 Veselivka *Zhytomyrs'ka Oblast'* Ukr.
159 R6 Veselo-Voznesenka Rus. Fed.
157 H7 Veselovskoye Vodokhranilishche *resr* Rus. Fed.
143 S2 Veseloyarsk Rus. Fed.
159 R3 Veseloye Rus. Fed.
159 K3 Veselynivka Ukr.
159 K6 Veselynove Ukr.
157 H7 Veselyy Rus. Fed.
142 K1 Veselyy Podol Kazakh.
122 I7 Veselyy Yar Rus. Fed.
178 B6 Vesgre *r.* France
157 H6 Veshenskaya Rus. Fed.
156 H2 Veshkoma Rus. Fed.
163 R6 Vesijärvi *l.* Fin.
212 E6 Vesime Italy
178 F5 Vesle *r.* France
156 K3 Veslyana *r.* Rus. Fed.
Vesontio France *see* Besançon
182 I1 Vesoul France
212 F5 Vespolate Italy
187 H6 Vessem Neth.
164 D3 Vest-Agder *county* Norway
162 L2 Vesterålen *is* Norway
162 L2 Vesterålsfjorden *sea chan.* Norway
190 L1 Vesterby Denmark
192 E1 Vestermark Denmark
190 I1 Vester Sottrup Denmark
162 S1 Vestertana Norway
162 □B1 Vestfirðir *constituency* Iceland
164 E2 Vestfjorddalen *val.* Norway
162 L3 Vestfjorden *sea chan.* Norway
164 G2 Vestfold *county* Norway
287 F2 Vestfold Hills Antarctica
162 □ Vestfonna *ice cap* Svalbard
280 B4 Véstia Brazil
166 D1 Vestmanna Faroe Is
162 □C2 Vestmannaeyjar *is* Iceland
162 I5 Vestnes Norway
212 I4 Vestone Italy
162 T1 Vestre Jakobselv Norway
286 X2 Veststraumen Glacier Antarctica
162 □B1 Vesturland *constituency* Iceland
162 L2 Vestvågøy *i.* Norway
183 K9 Vésubie *r.* France
215 M6 Vesuvio *vol.* Italy
215 M6 Vesuvio, Parco Nazionale del *nat. park* Italy
Vesuvius *vol.* Italy *see* Vesuvio
161 U3 Ves'yegonsk Rus. Fed.
198 G4 Veszkény Hungary
199 G4 Veszprém Hungary
198 G4 Veszprém *county* Hungary
199 G4 Veszprémvarsány Hungary
199 K5 Vésztő Hungary
237 J3 Vet *r.* S. Africa
101 □7 Vetauua *i.* Fiji
162 Q5 Veteli Fin.
247 I4 Veteran *Alta* Can.
218 H5 Veternik *Vojvodina* Serbia
178 C5 Vétheuil France
199 L4 Vetiș Romania
165 L4 Vetlanda Sweden
163 I6 Vetlefjorden Norway
156 I4 Vetluga Rus. Fed.
156 I4 Vetluga *r.* Rus. Fed.
152 F4 Vetluzhskiy *Kostromskaya Oblast'* Rus. Fed.
156 I4 Vetluzhskiy *Nizhegorodskaya Oblast'* Rus. Fed.
158 E2 Vetly Ukr.
161 Q8 Vet'ma *r.* Rus. Fed.
219 O7 Vetovo Bulg.
214 I3 Vetralla Italy
219 P8 Vetren Bulg.
219 Q4 Vetrișoaia Romania
198 D3 Větřní Czech Rep.
193 J7 Vetschau Ger.
162 S2 Vetsikko Fin.
162 P3 Vettasjärvi Sweden
191 D9 Vettelschoss Ger.
212 I7 Vetto Italy
215 K2 Vettore, Monte *mt.* Italy
181 L7 Veude *r.* France
181 M2 Veules-les-Roses France
181 M2 Veulettes-sur-Mer France
187 C6 Veurne Belgium
254 E6 Vevay *IN* U.S.A.
218 J9 Vevčani *Vevčani* Macedonia
232 B3 Veveno *r.* Sudan
212 B3 Vevey Switz.
212 C3 Vex Switz.
178 C5 Vexin Français *reg.* France
178 B5 Vexin Normand *reg.* France
157 G6 Veydelevka Rus. Fed.
182 F4 Veyle *r.* France
183 H7 Veynes France
182 D3 Veynon *r.* France
265 S4 Veyo *UT* U.S.A.
182 C5 Veyre-Monton France
182 I5 Veyrier-du-Lac France
144 C6 Veys Iran
160 E6 Vėžaičiai Lith.
182 D2 Vézelay France
179 L7 Vézelise France
183 E8 Vézénobres France
184 F6 Vézère *r.* France
156 K3 Vezhayu Rus. Fed.
219 M8 Vezhen *mt.* Bulg.
181 J7 Vezins France
183 B8 Vézins-de-Lévézou France
221 K2 Vezirhan Turkey
148 G3 Vezirköprü Turkey
179 L6 Vezouze *r.* France
212 I3 Vezza d'Oglio Italy
200 E7 Vezzana, Cima della *mt.* Italy
214 C3 Vezzani *Corse* France
213 K3 Vezzano Italy
228 C5 Via *r.* Liberia
276 C4 Viacha Bol.
213 J6 Viadana Italy
204 E5 Viade de Baixo Port.
183 K9 Vial, Mont *mt.* France
183 B8 Viala du Tarn France
Vialar Alg. *see* Tissemsilt
183 D8 Vialas France
285 G2 Viale Arg.
279 C9 Viamao Brazil
285 F3 Viamonte *Córdoba* Arg.
283 D9 Viamonte *Tierra del Fuego* Arg.
231 B7 Viana Angola
281 G4 Viana *Espírito Santo* Brazil
278 D2 Viana *Maranhão* Brazil
205 P3 Viana Spain
205 K5 Viana de Cega Spain
Viana del Bollo Spain *see* Viana do Bolo
206 D4 Viana do Alentejo Port.
204 F4 Viana do Bolo Spain
204 C5 Viana do Castelo Port.
204 D5 Viana do Castelo *admin. dist.* Port.
187 J9 Vianden Lux.
183 B9 Viane France
186 H5 Vianen Neth.
118 F6 Viangchan Laos
118 E4 Viangphoukha Laos
185 E7 Vianne France
221 G7 Viannos *Kriti* Greece
204 D2 Viaño Pequeno Spain
280 C2 Vianópolis Brazil
207 O3 Vianos Spain
206 H5 Viar *r.* Spain
212 I8 Viareggio Italy
178 D5 Viarmes France
183 C10 Vias France
204 C6 Viatodos Port.
207 O7 Viator Spain
185 H7 Viaur *r.* France
185 I6 Viazac France
215 P7 Vibonati Italy
207 K5 Víboras *r.* Spain
Viborg Rus. Fed. *see* Vyborg
217 K6 Vibo Valentia Italy
217 K6 Vibo Valentia *prov.* Italy
181 M5 Vibraye France
208 J4 Vic Spain
184 H5 Vic, Roche de *hill* France
266 D4 Vicam Mex.
207 N7 Vícar Spain
216 F8 Vicari *Sicilia* Italy
170 C7 Vicarstown Ireland
213 K8 Vicchio Italy
185 H10 Vicdessos France
185 H10 Vicdessos *r.* France
Viçe Turkey *see* Fındıklı
Vicecomodoro Marambio *research stn* Antarctica *see* Marambio
185 E9 Vic-en-Bigorre France
264 N8 Vicente, Point *CA* U.S.A.
285 H4 Vicente Casares Arg.
284 D4 Vicente Dupuy Arg.
266 A2 Vicente Guerrero *Baja California* Mex.
268 D2 Vicente Guerrero *Durango* Mex.
269 N7 Vicente Guerrero *Tabasco* Mex.
269 I6 Vicente Guerrero *Tlaxcala* Mex.
269 K7 Vicente y Camalote Mex.
213 L4 Vicenza Italy
213 K4 Vicenza *prov.* Italy
185 E8 Vic-Fezensac France
Vich Spain *see* Vic
274 D3 Vichada *dept* Col.
274 E3 Vichada *r.* Col.
282 G3 Vichadero Uru.
269 I3 Vichinchijol Nuevo Mex.
156 H4 Vichuga Rus. Fed.
284 A4 Vichuquén Chile
182 C4 Vichy France
261 F7 Vici *OK* U.S.A.
208 E3 Vicién Spain
171 K5 Vickerstown *Cumbria, England* U.K.
265 S8 Vicksburg *AZ* U.S.A.
250 I7 Vicksburg *MI* U.S.A.
261 J9 Vicksburg *MS* U.S.A.
258 B3 Vicksburg *PA* U.S.A.
182 C5 Vic-le-Comte France
214 B3 Vico *Corse* France
214 I3 Vico, Lago di *l.* Italy
215 P4 Vico del Gargano Italy
215 M6 Vico Equense Italy
212 D7 Vicoforte Italy
215 K4 Vico nel Lazio Italy
205 Q6 Vicort, Sierra de *mts* Spain
278 F4 Viçosa *Alagoas* Brazil
281 F4 Viçosa *Minas Gerais* Brazil
215 J3 Vicovaro Italy
219 N3 Vicovu de Sus Romania
181 P8 Vicq-Exemplet France
184 G4 Vicq-sur-Breuilh France
178 F5 Vic-sur-Aisne France
183 B7 Vic-sur-Cère France
179 M6 Vic-sur-Seille France
287 C2 Victor, Mount Antarctica
190 D4 Victorbur (Südbrookmerland) Ger.
104 G6 Victor Harbor *S.A.* Austr.
285 G3 Victoria Arg.
285 H3 Victoria *r.* Arg.
106 C3 Victoria *r. N.T.* Austr.
105 J7 Victoria *state* Austr.
Victoria Cameroon *see* Limbe
246 F5 Victoria *B.C.* Can.
284 A6 Victoria *Araucanía* Chile
283 C9 Victoria *Magallanes y Antártica Chilena* Chile
271 □6 Victoria Grenada
266 □P10 Victoria Hond.
Victoria Malaysia *see* Labuan
217 □ Victoria *Gozo* Malta
268 G4 Victoria Mex.
114 C4 Victoria *Luzon* Phil.
219 P6 Victoria *Brăila* Romania
219 M5 Victoria *Brașov* Romania
239 □2b Victoria *Mahé* Seychelles
271 □7 Victoria *county* Trin. and Tob.
261 G11 Victoria *TX* U.S.A.
256 G12 Victoria *VA* U.S.A.
283 B7 Victoria, Isla *i.* Chile
232 B4 Victoria, Lake Africa
104 H5 Victoria, Lake *N.S.W.* Austr.
Victoria, Mount *Viti Levu* Fiji *see* Tomanivi
118 A4 Victoria, Mount Myanmar
103 G9 Victoria, Mount *South I.* N.Z.
113 K8 Victoria, Mount P.N.G.
243 K2 Victoria and Albert Mountains *Nunavut* Can.
231 E9 Victoria Falls *waterfall* Zambia/Zimbabwe
234 E3 Victoria Falls Zimbabwe
234 E3 Victoria Falls National Park Zimbabwe
243 N1 Victoria Fjord *inlet* Greenland
103 G8 Victoria Forest Park *nature res.* *South I.* N.Z.
Victoria Harbour *sea chan.* *H.K.* China *see* Hong Kong Harbour
239 □2b Victoria Harbour *b. Mahé* Seychelles
242 H2 Victoria Island *N.W.T./Nunavut* Can.
249 J3 Victoria Lake *Nfld and Lab.* Can.
287 K2 Victoria Land *coastal area* Antarctica
131 □J7 Victoria Peak *hill H.K.* China
104 □3 Victoria Point S. Pacific Ocean
103 G9 Victoria Range *mts South I.* N.Z.
106 C3 Victoria River *N.T.* Austr.
106 C4 Victoria River Downs *N.T.* Austr.
102 H2 Victoria Valley *North I.* N.Z.
249 G4 Victoriaville *Que.* Can.
236 H7 Victoria West S. Africa
284 E5 Victorica Arg.
274 E4 Victorino Venez.
268 E3 Víctor Rosales Mex.
264 O7 Victorville *CA* U.S.A.
199 K6 Victor Vlad Delamarina Romania
256 I5 Victory *NY* U.S.A.
106 D8 Victory Downs *N.T.* Austr.
284 B2 Vicuña Chile
284 E3 Vicuña Mackenna Arg.
204 H9 Vid, Río de la *r.* Spain
204 E5 Vidago Port.
206 A2 Vidais Port.
283 B8 Vidal, Isla *i.* Chile
261 J10 Vidalia *LA* U.S.A.
265 R7 Vidal Junction *CA* U.S.A.
160 G9 Vidamlya Belarus
208 C2 Vidángoz Spain
183 I10 Vidauban France
214 B6 Viddalba *Sardegna* Italy
164 E5 Videbæk Denmark
279 C8 Videira Brazil
285 G2 Videla Arg.
219 N6 Videle Romania
201 N6 Videm *Gornja Radgona* Slovenia
201 K8 Videm *Grosuplje* Slovenia
204 F7 Videmonte Port.
219 K8 Viden *mt.* Bulg.
Viderø *i.* Faroe Is *see* Viðoy
197 K1 Vidgirių kalnas *hill* Lith.
206 D4 Vidigueira Port.
219 N8 Vidima *r.* Bulg.
219 K7 Vidin Bulg.
199 I3 Vidiná Slovakia
204 H1 Vidio, Cabo *c.* Spain
138 F8 Vidisha *Madh. Prad.* India
168 □N2 Vidlin *Shetland, Scotland* U.K.
161 P1 Vidlitsa Rus. Fed.
164 D2 Vidmyr *nature res.* Norway
198 G1 Vidnava Czech Rep.
161 U6 Vidnoye Rus. Fed.
165 J4 Vidöstern *l.* Sweden
183 E9 Vidourle *r.* France
210 F4 Vidova Gora *hill* Croatia
201 N7 Vidovec Croatia
166 D1 Viðoy *i.* Faroe Is
199 L5 Vidra Romania
Vidreras Spain *see* Vidrieres
208 K4 Vidrieres Spain
162 P4 Vidsel Sweden
160 F6 Viduklė Lith.
210 G4 Viduša *mts* Bos.-Herz.
160 I5 Vidzemes centrālā augstiene *hills* Latvia
160 J6 Vidzy Belarus
180 H8 Vie *r.* France
181 K3 Vie *r.* France
195 N3 Viechtach Ger.
197 M1 Viečiūnai Lith.
237 M7 Viedgesville S. Africa
283 E6 Viedma Arg.
283 B8 Viedma, Lago *l.* Arg.
201 K2 Viehberg *mt.* Austria
183 C6 Vieille-Brioude France
180 I8 Vieillevigne France
204 C9 Vieira de Leiria Port.
204 D5 Vieira do Minho Port.
268 C2 Viejo *r.* Mex.
266 C2 Viejo, Cerro *mt.* Mex.
160 F5 Viekšniai Lith.
192 D4 Vielank Ger.
208 G2 Vielha Spain
185 D8 Viella France
Viella Spain *see* Vielha
185 E10 Vielle-Aure France
185 B8 Vielle-St-Girons France
185 I8 Vielmur-sur-Agout France
187 I8 Vielsalm Belgium
182 G2 Vielverge France
191 K7 Vienenburg Ger.
Vienna Austria *see* Wien
255 F9 Vienna *GA* U.S.A.
261 K7 Vienna *IL* U.S.A.
257 J10 Vienna *MD* U.S.A.
260 J6 Vienna *MO* U.S.A.
258 F3 Vienna *NJ* U.S.A.
256 D9 Vienna *WV* U.S.A.
182 F5 Vienne France
181 L8 Vienne *dept* France
184 E1 Vienne *r.* France
179 I5 Vienne-le-Château France
Vientiane Laos *see* Viangchan
284 B5 Viento, Cordillera del *mts* Arg.
207 I7 Viento, Puerto del *pass* Spain
271 □1 Vieques *i.* Puerto Rico
179 I6 Vière *r.* France
192 J3 Viereck Ger.
162 S5 Vieremä Fin.
195 J2 Viereth-Trunstadt Ger.
195 K5 Vierkirchen Ger.
186 I5 Vierlingsbeek Neth.
191 K9 Viernau Ger.
194 F2 Viernheim Ger.
192 J4 Vierraden Ger.
191 B8 Viersen Ger.
181 J3 Vierville-sur-Mer France
212 E1 Vierwaldstätter See *l.* Switz.
184 I1 Vierzon France
266 H5 Viesca Mex.
192 F4 Viesecke Ger.
193 D9 Vieselbach Ger.
160 I5 Viesīte Latvia
215 Q4 Vieste Italy
160 F6 Viešvilės rezervatas *nature res.* Lith.
162 O3 Vietas Sweden
Viet Nam *country* Asia *see* Vietnam
118 G5 Vietnam *country* Asia
118 G3 Việt Quang Vietnam
215 P6 Vietri di Potenza Italy
215 N6 Vietri sul Mare Italy
118 G4 Việt Tri Vietnam
185 B8 Vieux-Boucau-les-Bains France
271 □2 Vieux-Bourg Guadeloupe
183 I7 Vieux Chaillol *mt.* France
182 J1 Vieux-Charmont France
248 E2 Vieux Comptoir, Lac du *l. Que.* Can.
178 G3 Vieux-Condé France
249 J3 Vieux-Fort *Que.* Can.
271 □2 Vieux-Fort Guadeloupe
271 □3 Vieux Fort St Lucia
271 □2 Vieux-Fort, Pointe de *pt* Guadeloupe
271 □2 Vieux-Habitants Guadeloupe
249 I3 Vieux Poste, Pointe du *pt Que.* Can.
160 H7 Vievis Lith.
170 I2 Viewpark *North Lanarkshire, Scotland* U.K.
285 I4 Vieytes Arg.
183 H6 Vif France
160 H3 Vigala *r.* Estonia
114 C3 Vigan *Luzon* Phil.
213 K6 Vigarano Mainarda Italy
213 J5 Vigasio Italy
200 H4 Vigaun Austria
184 H5 Vigeois France
212 F5 Vigevano Italy
214 B4 Viggianello *Corse* France
215 Q8 Viggianello Italy
215 P7 Viggiano Italy
212 F4 Viggiù Italy
278 C2 Vigia Brazil
206 C5 Vigia *hill* Port.
206 D3 Vigia, Barragem da *resr* Port.
283 D8 Vigía, Cabo *c.* Arg.
267 P8 Vigía Chico Mex.
199 I3 Vígľaš Slovakia
215 K4 Viglio, Monte *mt.* Italy
178 D3 Vignacourt France
212 E5 Vignale Monferrato Italy
215 I3 Vignanello Italy
185 D10 Vignemale *mt.* France
179 K6 Vigneulles-les-Hattonchâtel France
182 H3 Vignoble *reg.* France
213 K7 Vignola Italy
214 C5 Vignola *r.* Italy
214 C5 Vignola Mare l'Agnata *Sardegna* Italy
179 J7 Vignory France
178 C5 Vigny France
204 C4 Vigo Spain
204 C4 Vigo, Ría de *est.* Spain
213 M3 Vigo di Cadore Italy
200 E7 Vigo di Fassa Italy
212 C6 Vigone Italy
213 L5 Vigonza Italy
213 J3 Vigo Rendena Italy
108 E7 Vigors, Mount *W.A.* Austr.
164 E4 Vigsø Bugt *b.* Denmark
212 F6 Viguzzolo Italy
179 L5 Vigy France
162 R4 Vihanti Fin.
184 C1 Vihiers France
199 L3 Vihorlat *mt.* Slovakia
199 L3 Vihorlat *park* Slovakia
199 K3 Vihorlatské vrchy *mts* Slovakia
160 G2 Vihterpalu *r.* Estonia
163 R6 Vihti Fin.
163 Q6 Viiala Fin.
199 L4 Viile Satu Mare Romania
Viipuri Rus. Fed. *see* Vyborg
162 S3 Viirinkylä Fin.
199 L4 Viișoara Romania
162 R5 Viitasaari Fin.
160 K4 Viitka Estonia
138 D5 Vijainagar *Rajasthan* India
138 D8 Vijapur *Gujarat* India
136 C4 Vijayadurg *Mahar.* India
Vijayanagar *Karnataka* India *see* Hampi
136 E8 Vijayapati *Tamil Nadu* India
136 G4 Vijayawada *Andhra Prad.* India
162 □D2 Vík Iceland
162 L4 Vik Norway
162 S3 Vikajärvi Fin.
136 E4 Vikarabad *Andhra Prad.* India
165 M3 Vikbolandet *pen.* Sweden
164 B2 Vikedal Norway
Vikeke East Timor *see* Viqueque
165 K3 Viken *l.* Sweden
164 F2 Vikersund Norway
164 B2 Vikevåg Norway
161 O7 Vikhra *r.* Rus. Fed.
219 L9 Vikhren *mt.* Bulg.
247 I4 Viking *Alta* Can.
162 K4 Vikna *i.* Norway
199 I2 Vikolínec Slovakia
220 B3 Vikou-Aoou, Ethnikos Drymos *nat. park* Greece
163 I6 Vikøyri Norway
162 O2 Vikran Norway
197 L1 Viktarinas Lith.
158 J6 Viktorivka Ukr.
Viktorovka Kazakh. *see* Taranovskoye
193 D7 Viktorshöhe *hill* Ger.
204 D5 Vila Spain
Vila Vanuatu *see* Port Vila
Vila Alferes Chamusca Moz. *see* Guija
206 D4 Vila Alva Port.
Vila Arriaga Angola *see* Bibala
206 □ Vila Baleira Madeira
274 D5 Vila Bittencourt Brazil
204 G8 Vila Boa Port.
206 E3 Vila Boim Port.
275 G6 Vila Braga Brazil
Vila Bugaço Angola *see* Camanongue
Vila Cabral Moz. *see* Lichinga
204 D6 Vila Caiz Port.
Vila Caldas Xavier Moz. *see* Muende
276 D4 Vilacaya Bol.
204 C6 Vila Chã Port.
204 E7 Vila Chã de Sá Port.
204 D6 Vila Chão do Marão Port.
Vila Coutinho Moz. *see* Ulongue
204 E7 Vila Cova à Coelheira Port.
204 D6 Vila Cova da Lixa Port.
208 I3 Vilada Spain
208 L3 Viladamat Spain
Vila da Ponte Angola *see* Kuvango
204 E5 Vila da Ponte Port.
238 □1a Vila da Praia da Vitória *Terceira* Azores
228 □ Vila da Ribeira Brava Cape Verde
Vila de Aljustrel Angola *see* Cangamba
Vila de Almoster Angola *see* Chiange
208 J5 Viladecans Spain
204 D3 Vila de Cruces Spain
Vila de João Belo Moz. *see* Xai-Xai
Vila de Junqueiro Moz. *see* Gurué
285 F1 Vila de María Arg.
Vilademat Spain *see* Viladamat
204 D9 Vila de Rei Port.
235 G3 Vila de Sena Moz.
Vila de Trego Morais Moz. *see* Chókwé
206 B6 Vila do Bispo Port.
204 C6 Vila do Conde Port.
228 □ Vila do Maio Cape Verde
208 J4 Viladrau Spain
209 E7 Vilafamés Spain
208 K3 Vilafant Spain
206 E3 Vila Fernando Port.
238 □3a Vilaflor *Tenerife* Canary Is
204 F6 Vila Flor Port.
Vila Fontes Moz. *see* Caia
238 □1b Vila Franca, Ilhéu de *i.* Azores
204 F7 Vila Franca das Naves Port.
209 L8 Vilafranca de Bonany Spain
208 I5 Vilafranca del Penedès Spain
206 B3 Vila Franca de Xira Port.
238 □1b Vila Franca do Campo *São Miguel* Azores
204 C3 Vilagarcía de Arousa Spain
235 G5 Vila Gomes da Costa Moz.
Vila Gouveia Moz. *see* Catandica
204 D2 Vilagudín, Encoro de *resr* Spain
180 G6 Vilaine *r.* France
208 L3 Vilajuiga Spain
160 K4 Viļaka Latvia
204 E2 Vilalba Spain
208 J3 Vilallonga Spain
Vila Luísa Moz. *see* Marracuene
Vila Marechal Carmona Angola *see* Uíge
204 F4 Vilamartín Spain
209 D8 Vilamarxant Spain
284 A5 Vila Mercedes Chile
Vila Miranda Moz. *see* Macaloge
206 B2 Vila Moreira Port.
206 C6 Vilamoura Port.
276 D2 Vila Murtinho Brazil
204 B2 Vilán, Cabo *c.* Spain
235 □J3 Vilanandro, Tanjona *pt* Madag.
235 G4 Vilanculos Moz.
160 J5 Viļāni Latvia
206 A3 Vila Nogueira de Azeitão Port.
Vila Nova Angola *see* Tchikala-Tcholohanga
238 □1a Vila Nova *Terceira* Azores
204 F2 Vilanova Spain
206 C4 Vila Nova da Baronia Port.
235 G3 Vila Nova da Fronteira Moz.
209 F7 Vilanova d'Alcolea Spain
204 C8 Vila Nova de Anços Port.
204 C3 Vilanova de Arousa Spain
Vilanova de Castelló Spain *see* Villanueva de Castellón
204 C5 Vila Nova de Cerveira Port.
204 C6 Vila Nova de Famalicão Port.
204 F6 Vila Nova de Foz Coa Port.
204 C6 Vila Nova de Gaia Port.
208 H4 Vilanova de L'Aguda Spain
208 H4 Vilanova de Meià Spain
204 C9 Vila Nova de Ourém Port.
204 E7 Vila Nova de Paiva Port.
204 D8 Vila Nova de Poiares Port.
206 E5 Vila Nova de São Bento Port.
Vila Nova do Seles Angola *see* Uku
208 I5 Vilanova i la Geltrú Spain
228 □ Vila Nova Sintra Cape Verde
Vila Paiva de Andrada Moz. *see* Gorongosa
Vila Pery Moz. *see* Chimoio
204 E8 Vila Pouca da Beira Port.
204 E5 Vila Pouca de Aguiar Port.
204 C5 Vila Praia de Âncora Port.
204 F7 Vilar, Barragem de *resr* Port.
204 F5 Vilarandelo Port.
204 E4 Vilarchao Spain
204 D5 Vilar da Veiga Port.
204 C6 Vilar de Andorinho Port.
204 E4 Vilar de Barrio Spain
204 E4 Vilar de Santos Spain
204 F5 Vilardevós Spain
204 E6 Vila Real Port.
204 E5 Vila Real *admin. dist.* Port.
206 E6 Vila Real de Santo António Port.
204 F5 Vilarelho da Raia Port.
204 G7 Vilar Formoso Port.
204 F6 Vilarinho da Castanheira Port.
204 C8 Vilarinho do Bairro Port.
204 F4 Vilariño de Conso Spain
208 H5 Vila-rodona Spain
206 D4 Vila Ruiva Port.
Vilas *i. S. Male* Maldives *see* Velassary
Vila Salazar Angola *see* N'dalatando
Vila Salazar Zimbabwe *see* Sango
151 J6 Viläşçay *r.* Azer.
204 C5 Vila Seca Port.
208 H5 Vilaseca de Solcina Spain
Vila Teixeira de Sousa Angola *see* Luau
285 G2 Vila Trinidad Arg.
136 E8 Vilavankod *Tamil Nadu* India
275 I4 Vila Velha *Amapá* Brazil
281 G4 Vila Velha *Espírito Santo* Brazil
204 E9 Vila Velha de Ródão Port.
204 D5 Vila Verde *Braga* Port.
204 C8 Vila Verde *Coimbra* Port.
204 E6 Vila Verde *Vila Real* Port.
204 F5 Vila Verde da Raia Port.
206 E5 Vila Verde de Ficalho Port.
206 E3 Vila Viçosa Port.
276 B3 Vilcabamba, Cordillera *mts* Peru
276 C3 Vilcanota, Cordillera de *mts* Peru
158 I2 Vil'cha Ukr.
152 H1 Vil'cheka, Zemlya *i. Zemlya Frantsa-Iosifa* Rus. Fed.
207 M4 Vilches Spain
284 A6 Vilcun Chile
156 I3 Viled' *r.* Rus. Fed.
285 H4 Vilela Arg.
Vileyka Belarus *see* Vilyeyka
156 L3 Vil'gort *Permskaya Oblast'* Rus. Fed.
156 J3 Vil'gort *Respublika Komi* Rus. Fed.
162 N4 Vilhelmina Sweden
277 E3 Vilhena Brazil
Viligili *i. N. Male* Maldives *see* Vilingli
159 M9 Viline Ukr.
135 □1 Vilingli *i. N. Male* Maldives
135 □1 Vilingli *i. N. Male* Maldives
160 I7 Viliya *r.* Belarus/Lith.
158 F3 Viliya *r.* Ukr.
160 I3 Viljandi Estonia
236 D10 Viljoenshof S. Africa
237 K3 Viljoenskroon S. Africa
160 G7 Vilkaviškis Lith.
159 S5 Vil'khova *r.* Ukr.
160 G6 Vilkija Lith.
152 I2 Vil'kitskogo, Ostrov *i.* Rus. Fed.
153 K2 Vil'kitskogo, Proliv *str.* Rus. Fed.
276 D5 Villa Abecia Bol.
284 C2 Villa Aberastain Arg.
215 J4 Villa Adriana *tourist site* Italy
266 F2 Villa Ahumada Mex.
285 F6 Villa Alba Arg.
284 B4 Villa Alegre Chile
284 B3 Villa Alemana Chile
269 K8 Villa Alta Mex.
270 H4 Villa Altagracia Dom. Rep.
282 F3 Villa Ana Arg.
285 G3 Villa Ángela Arg.
282 E2 Villa Ángela Arg.
268 G5 Villa Apaseo El Alto Mex.
285 F6 Villa Atlántica Arg.
284 D4 Villa Atuel Arg.
269 J5 Villa Ávila Camacho Mex.
269 L7 Villa Azueta Mex.
213 K5 Villa Bartolomea Italy
216 E7 Villabate *Sicilia* Italy
276 D2 Villa Bella Bol.
Villa Bens Morocco *see* Tarfaya
282 E2 Villa Berthet Arg.
206 E6 Villablanca Spain
204 H3 Villablino Spain
208 A1 Villabona Spain
205 J5 Villabrágima Spain
205 J6 Villabuena del Puente Spain
184 G5 Villac France
285 G4 Villa Cañás Arg.
205 N9 Villacañas Spain
212 I4 Villa Carcina Italy
284 E2 Villa Carlos Paz Arg.
207 M4 Villacarrillo Spain
285 F5 Villa Castelar Arg.
217 M2 Villa Castelli Italy
205 L7 Villacastín Spain
201 I6 Villach Austria
214 B9 Villacidro *Sardegna* Italy
205 O5 Villaciervos Spain
Villa Cisneros Western Sahara *see* Ad Dakhla
Villa Cisneros, Ría de *b.* Western Sahara *see* Río de Oro, Bahía de
267 M10 Villa Comaltitlán Mex.
285 F2 Villa Concepción del Tío Arg.
205 N8 Villaconejos Spain
205 P8 Villaconejos de Trabaque Spain
285 G3 Villa Constitución Arg.
268 D5 Villa Corona Mex.
266 G4 Villa Coronado Mex.
267 M9 Villa Corzo Mex.
284 E2 Villa Cura Brochero Arg.
285 G3 Villada Arg.
205 K4 Villada Spain
212 H4 Villa d'Almè Italy
268 D6 Villa de Álvarez Mex.
268 E2 Villa de Cos Mex.
274 E2 Villa de Cura Venez.
267 N8 Villa de Guadalupe *Campeche* Mex.
268 G2 Villa de Guadalupe *San Luis Potosí* Mex.
284 E3 Villa del Carmen Arg.
205 L8 Villa del Prado Spain
268 G5 Villa del Pueblito Mex.
207 K5 Villa del Río Spain
285 F2 Villa del Rosario Arg.
284 C2 Villa del Salvador Arg.
285 E2 Villa del Totoral Arg.
204 H5 Villadepera Spain
268 F3 Villa de Ramos Mex.
268 G4 Villa de Reyes Mex.
209 C9 Villa de Ves Spain
285 G3 Villa Diego Arg.
205 L3 Villadiego Spain
284 E2 Villa Dolores Arg.
285 H3 Villa Domínguez Arg.
213 L5 Villadose Italy
212 E3 Villadossola Italy
208 C5 Villadoz Spain
284 C6 Villa El Chocón Arg.
205 K3 Villaeles de Valdavia Spain
285 H3 Villa Elisa Arg.
285 G3 Villa Eloisa Arg.
268 F6 Villa Escalante Mex.
205 O9 Villaescusa de Haro Spain
205 N4 Villaescusa la Sombría Spain
204 I5 Villafáfila Spain
205 R6 Villafeliche Spain
267 M9 Villa Flores Mex.
205 J6 Villaflores Spain
277 F6 Villa Florida Para.
205 Q4 Villafranca Spain
212 E6 Villafranca d'Asti Italy
207 J5 Villafranca de Córdoba Spain
204 G3 Villafranca del Bierzo Spain
208 C6 Villafranca del Campo Spain
208 E7 Villafranca del Cid Spain
206 G3 Villafranca de los Barros Spain
207 M2 Villafranca de los Caballeros Spain
Villafranca del Penedès Spain *see* Vilafranca del Penedès
213 J5 Villafranca di Verona Italy
212 H7 Villafranca in Lunigiana Italy
205 N4 Villafranca-Montes de Oca Spain
217 I7 Villafranca Tirrena *Sicilia* Italy
213 J5 Villafranca Veronese *airport* Italy
206 G6 Villafranco del Guadalquivir Spain
216 E8 Villafrati *Sicilia* Italy
205 J5 Villafrechos Spain
205 M5 Villafruela Spain
205 L5 Villafuerte Spain
Villagarcía de Arosa Spain *see* Vilagarcía de Arousa
205 J5 Villagarcía de Campos Spain
206 G4 Villagarcía de la Torre Spain
207 P2 Villagarcía del Llano Spain
284 D3 Villa General Roca Arg.
285 I5 Villa Gesell Arg.
217 L5 Villagio Mancuso Italy
206 G3 Villagonzalo Spain
285 G3 Villa Governador Gálvez Arg.
269 H1 Villagrán Mex.
214 D8 Villagrande Strisaili *Sardegna* Italy
285 H2 Villaguay Arg.
268 D4 Villa Guerrero Mex.
282 F3 Villa Guillermina Arg.
207 J4 Villaharta Spain
277 F6 Villa Hayes Para.
267 M8 Villahermosa Mex.
207 N3 Villahermosa Spain
209 E7 Villahermosa del Río Spain
285 H2 Villa Hernandarias Arg.
205 L4 Villaherreros Spain
268 E4 Villa Hidalgo *Jalisco* Mex.
268 B4 Villa Hidalgo *Nayarit* Mex.
268 G3 Villa Hidalgo *San Luis Potosí* Mex.
263 J11 Villa Hidalgo *Sonora* Mex.
205 M4 Villahizán Spain
205 M4 Villahoz Spain
284 E4 Villa Huidobro Arg.
178 I8 Villaines-en-Duesmois France
181 K5 Villaines-la-Juhel France
181 K6 Villaines-sous-Malicorne France
266 D5 Villa Insurgentes Mex.
285 F6 Villa Iris Arg.
209 E10 Villajoyosa-La Vila Joíosa Spain
268 E3 Villa Juárez Mex.
268 B4 Villa Juárez *Nayarit* Mex.
268 G3 Villa Juárez *San Luis Potosí* Mex.
213 K4 Villa Lagarina Italy
215 L4 Villalago Italy
205 J5 Villalar de los Comuneros Spain
215 L4 Villa Latina Italy
269 M7 Villa La Venta Mex.
269 J5 Villa Lázaro Cárdenas Mex.
216 F8 Villalba *Sicilia* Italy
271 □1 Villalba Puerto Rico
205 M5 Villalba de Duero Spain
205 K3 Villalba de Guardo Spain
206 G6 Villalba del Alcor Spain
205 P8 Villalba de la Sierra Spain
205 K4 Villalba de los Alcores Spain
206 F3 Villalba de los Barros Spain
205 O8 Villalba del Rey Spain
208 F5 Villalba dels Arcs Spain
205 O3 Villalba de Rioja Spain
204 H5 Villalcampo Spain
204 H6 Villalcampo, Embalse de *resr* Spain
205 K4 Villalcázar de Sirga Spain
267 I4 Villaldama Mex.
205 Q6 Villalengua Spain
207 O2 Villalgordo del Júcar Spain
205 P9 Villalgordo del Marquesado Spain
285 H4 Villa Lía Arg.
285 H3 Villa Lila Arg.
215 M5 Villa Literno Italy
205 J5 Villalobos Spain
205 J4 Villalón de Campos Spain
283 E5 Villalonga Arg.
209 E10 Villalonga Spain
205 J5 Villalpando Spain
207 P2 Villalpardo Spain
205 M8 Villaluenga de la Sagra Spain
205 K4 Villalumbroso Spain
268 F6 Villa Madero Mex.
269 H1 Villa Mainero Mex.
207 P2 Villamalea Spain
204 I4 Villamañán Spain
204 I4 Villamandos Spain
207 N3 Villamanrique Spain
206 G6 Villamanrique de la Condesa Spain
205 L8 Villamanta Spain
214 B8 Villamar *Sardegna* Italy
Villamarchante Spain *see* Vilamarxant
285 G4 Villa María Arg.
285 F3 Villa María *Córdoba* Arg.
285 G2 Villa María *Entre Ríos* Arg.
285 H1 Villa María Grande Arg.
276 D5 Villa Martín Bol.
206 H7 Villamartín Spain
205 K4 Villamartín de Campos Spain
214 B9 Villamassargia *Sardegna* Italy
282 E2 Villa Matoque Arg.
204 I7 Villamayor Spain
207 K3 Villamayor de Calatrava Spain
205 J5 Villamayor de Campos Spain
205 O9 Villamayor de Santiago Spain
205 L4 Villamayor de Treviño Spain
184 F5 Villambard France
205 L4 Villamediana Spain
205 P4 Villamediana de Iregua Spain
204 H3 Villamejil Spain
284 C2 Villa Mercedes Arg.
284 E3 Villa Mercedes *San Luis* Arg.
206 H2 Villamesías Spain
204 G8 Villamiel Spain
212 I7 Villa Minozzo Italy
276 E5 Villa Montes Bol.
204 I6 Villamor de los Escuderos Spain
268 F5 Villa Morelos Mex.
205 M9 Villamuelas Spain
205 L5 Villamuriel de Cerrato Spain
185 D7 Villandraut France
217 N2 Villanova Italy
212 E7 Villanova d'Albenga Italy
212 D6 Villanova d'Asti Italy
215 O5 Villanova del Battista Italy
214 C8 Villanovafranca *Sardegna* Italy
214 A6 Villanova Monteleone *Sardegna* Italy
214 B8 Villanova Truschedu *Sardegna* Italy
214 C8 Villanova Tulo *Sardegna* Italy
212 G5 Villanterio Italy
208 D2 Villanúa Spain
205 K5 Villanubla Spain
285 F3 Villa Nueva *Córdoba* Arg.
284 C3 Villa Nueva *Mendoza* Arg.
274 C2 Villanueva Col.

268 E3 Villanueva Mex.
Villanueva Spain see Vilanova
205 O9 Villanueva de Alcardete Spain
Villanueva de Alcolea Spain see Vilanova d'Alcolea
205 P7 Villanueva de Alcorón Spain
207 K6 Villanueva de Algaidas Spain
205 M4 Villanueva de Argaño Spain
Villanueva de Arosa Spain see Vilanova de Arousa
205 M9 Villanueva de Bogas Spain
205 O4 Villanueva de Cameros Spain
209 E9 Villanueva de Castellón Spain
207 J4 Villanueva de Córdoba Spain
208 D4 Villanueva de Gállego Spain
205 K7 Villanueva de Gómez Spain
205 M8 Villanueva de la Cañada Spain
207 J7 Villanueva de la Concepción Spain
207 N3 Villanueva de la Fuente Spain
207 P2 Villanueva de la Jara Spain
207 L4 Villanueva de la Reina Spain
207 M4 Villanueva del Arzobispo Spain
206 E5 Villanueva de las Cruces Spain
206 H3 Villanueva de la Serena Spain
204 H8 Villanueva de la Sierra Spain
207 M5 Villanueva de las Torres Spain
205 J8 Villanueva de la Vera Spain
205 J5 Villanueva del Campo Spain
207 J4 Villanueva del Duque Spain
206 E4 Villanueva del Fresno Spain
206 E5 Villanueva de los Castillejos Spain
207 N3 Villanueva de los Infantes Spain
207 I4 Villanueva del Rey Spain
209 C11 Villanueva del Río Segura Spain
206 H5 Villanueva del Río y Minas Spain
207 K7 Villanueva del Rosario Spain
207 K6 Villanueva del Trabuco Spain
207 L3 Villanueva de San Carlos Spain
207 I6 Villanueva de San Juan Spain
207 K6 Villanueva de Tapia Spain
205 N3 Villanueva de Valdegovia Spain
Villanueva-y-Geltrú Spain see Vilanova i la Geltrú
205 K3 Villanuño de Valdavia Spain
199 H6 Villány Hungary
199 H6 Villányi-hegység ridge Hungary
282 F3 Villa Ocampo Arg.
266 G4 Villa Ocampo Mex.
283 B8 Villa O'Higgins Chile
282 E3 Villa Ojo de Agua Arg.
277 F6 Villa Oliva Para.
Villa O. Pereyra Mex. see Villa Orestes Pereyra
213 P4 Villa Opicina Italy
266 G4 Villa Orestes Pereyra Mex.
276 D4 Villa Oropeza Bol.
207 N3 Villapalacios Spain
214 B9 Villaperuccio Sardegna Italy
263 J12 Villa Pesqueira Mex.
217 K4 Villapiana Italy
217 K4 Villapiana Lido Italy
213 K6 Villa Poma Italy
182 D3 Villapourçon France
284 B4 Villa Prat Chile
214 D9 Villaputzu Sardegna Italy
204 I4 Villaquejida Spain
204 I3 Villaquilambre Spain
276 D4 Villar Bol.
204 I6 Villaralbo Spain
207 J4 Villaralto Spain
285 G3 Villa Ramírez Arg.
205 M3 Villarcayo Spain
183 I6 Villar-d'Arêne France
183 H6 Villard-Bonnot France
183 H6 Villard-de-Lans France
207 P3 Villar de Chinchilla Spain
204 G7 Villar de Ciervo Spain
204 H5 Villardeciervos Spain
205 J5 Villardefrades Spain
209 D8 Villar del Arzobispo Spain
204 G7 Villar de la Yegua Spain
204 H6 Villar del Buey Spain
205 Q8 Villar del Cobo Spain
205 Q9 Villar del Humo Spain
204 G3 Villar de los Barrios Spain
208 C5 Villar de los Navarros Spain
205 J9 Villar del Pedroso Spain
206 F2 Villar del Rey Spain
205 R7 Villar del Salz Spain
205 P8 Villar de Olalla Spain
204 H6 Villar de Peralonso Spain
206 H2 Villar de Rena Spain
205 O4 Villar de Torre Spain
207 K5 Villardompardo Spain
209 E8 Villareal Spain
Villareal de los Infantes Spain see Villareal
285 F3 Villa Reducción Arg.
284 D6 Villa Regina Arg.
205 O9 Villarejo de Fuentes Spain
205 K9 Villarejo de Montalbán Spain
204 I4 Villarejo de Orbigo Spain
205 N8 Villarejo de Salvanés Spain
213 J3 Villa Rendena Italy
205 J3 Villarente Spain
204 I6 Villares de la Reina Spain
277 F6 Villa Rey Para.
284 E3 Villa Reynolds Arg.
207 L5 Villargordo Spain
204 H6 Villarino de los Aires Spain
208 D6 Villarluengo Spain
216 G9 Villa Romana del casale tourist site Italy
216 G8 Villarosa Sicilia Italy
208 C6 Villarquemado Spain
205 K4 Villarramiel Spain
208 C5 Villarreal de Huerva Spain
284 A6 Villarrica Chile
277 F6 Villarrica Para.
284 A6 Villarrica, Lago l. Chile
284 B6 Villarrica, Parque Nacional nat. park Chile
204 I5 Villarrín de Campos Spain
207 N2 Villarrobledo Spain
207 N4 Villarrodrigo Spain
205 P4 Villarroya Spain
208 D6 Villarroya de los Pinares Spain
207 L2 Villarrubia de los Ojos Spain
205 N9 Villarrubia de Santiago Spain
205 O9 Villarrubio Spain
285 H4 Villars Arg.
184 F5 Villars Aquitaine France
183 E6 Villars Rhône-Alpes France
183 J7 Villar-St-Pancrace France
205 P9 Villars del Saz Spain
182 J2 Villars-lès-Blamont France
182 G5 Villars-les-Dombes France
183 K9 Villars-sur-Var France
207 P2 Villarta Spain
207 J2 Villarta de los Montes Spain
207 M2 Villarta de San Juan Spain
258 F6 Villas NJ U.S.A.
Villasalazar Zimbabwe see Sango
214 C9 Villasalto Sardegna Italy
202 E1 Villasana de Mena Spain
205 L4 Villasandino Spain
217 J7 Villa San Giovanni Italy
285 H3 Villa San José Arg.
Villa Sanjurjo Morocco see Al Hoceima
285 H3 Villa San Marcial Arg.
282 D3 Villa San Martin Arg.
215 M4 Villa Santa Maria Italy
284 D2 Villa Santa Rita de Catuna Arg.
284 C2 Villa Santa Rosa Arg.
205 N2 Villasante de Montija Spain
213 N3 Villa Santina Italy
284 E4 Villa Sarmiento Arg.
205 L4 Villasarracino Spain
285 F4 Villa Sauze Arg.
185 I9 Villasavary France
205 O6 Villasayas Spain
285 I3 Villasboas Uru.
204 G6 Villasbuenas Spain
204 H6 Villasdardo Spain
204 H3 Villaseca de Laciana Spain
205 M9 Villaseca de la Sagra Spain
204 H6 Villaseco de los Gamitos Spain
204 H6 Villaseco de los Reyes Spain
204 I6 Villaseco del Pan Spain
205 M9 Villasequilla de Yepes Spain
276 D4 Villa Serrano Bol.
214 D9 Villasimius Sardegna Italy
217 I9 Villasmundo Sicilia Italy
214 B9 Villasor Sardegna Italy
214 B9 Villaspeciosa Sardegna Italy
204 G8 Villasrubias Spain
209 C7 Villastar Spain
205 N4 Villasur de Herreros Spain
205 N9 Villatobas Spain
205 J7 Villatoro Spain
209 C9 Villatoya Spain
285 E2 Villa Tulumba Arg.
205 J3 Villaturiel Spain
205 K4 Villaumbrales Spain
282 C3 Villa Unión Arg.
267 I3 Villa Unión Coahuila Mex.
268 C2 Villa Unión Durango Mex.
268 A2 Villa Unión Sinaloa Mex.
214 B8 Villaurbana Sardegna Italy
285 G2 Villa Urquiza Arg.
284 E4 Villa Valeria Arg.
215 L4 Villavallelonga Italy
270 H4 Villa Vasquez Dom. Rep.
205 O4 Villavelayo Spain
238 □3b Villaverde Fuerteventura Canary Is
214 B8 Villa Verde Sardegna Italy
207 N4 Villaverde de Guadalimar Spain
206 H5 Villaverde del Río Spain
209 A8 Villaverde y Pasaconsol Spain
212 F6 Villavernia Italy
274 C3 Villavicencio Col.
205 J2 Villaviciosa Spain
205 J1 Villaviciosa, Ría de inlet Spain
207 I4 Villaviciosa de Córdoba Spain
205 M8 Villaviciosa de Odón Spain
268 D7 Villa Victoria Mex.
209 E8 Villavieja Spain
205 M6 Villavieja del Lozoya Spain
204 H7 Villavieja de Yeltes Spain
276 D4 Villa Viscarra Bol.
205 L5 Villaviudas Spain
204 G2 Villayón Spain
205 K3 Villazanzo de Valderaduey Spain
268 G3 Villa Zaragoza Mex.
276 D5 Villazon Bol.
179 N7 Villé France
182 G5 Villebois France
184 E5 Villebois-Lavalette France
185 G8 Villebrumier France
185 E9 Villecomtal-sur-Arros France
182 G1 Villecomte France
183 I9 Villecroze France
183 B10 Villedaigne France
181 I7 Villedieu-la-Blouère France
180 I4 Villedieu-les-Poêles France
181 O8 Villedieu-sur-Indre France
214 C2 Ville-di-Pietrabugno Corse France
181 M6 Villedômer France
178 G5 Ville-en-Tardenois France
184 E3 Villefagnan France
182 G5 Villefontaine France
183 D8 Villefort France
178 F8 Villefranche Bourgogne France
185 F9 Villefranche Midi-Pyrénées France
185 I8 Villefranche-d'Albigeois France
182 B4 Villefranche-d'Allier France
185 I10 Villefranche-de-Conflent France
185 H9 Villefranche-de-Lauragais France
184 E6 Villefranche-de-Lonchat France
183 B8 Villefranche-de-Panat France
185 I7 Villefranche-de-Rouergue France
185 G6 Villefranche-du-Périgord France
181 O7 Villefranche-sur-Cher France
183 K9 Villefranche-sur-Mer France
182 F5 Villefranche-sur-Saône France
185 B9 Villefranque France
205 L4 Villegas Spain
209 C7 Villel Spain
268 G4 Villela Mex.
183 G9 Villelaure France
178 E8 Villemandeur France
251 O2 Ville-Marie Que. Can.
Ville-Marie Que. Can. see Montréal
178 G7 Villemaur-sur-Vanne France
251 P1 Villemontel Que. Can.
178 H7 Villemorien France
185 I9 Villemoustaussou France
185 H8 Villemur-sur-Tarn France
209 D10 Villena Spain
178 G6 Villenauxe-la-Grande France
185 C6 Villenave-d'Ornon France
185 I7 Villeneuve Midi-Pyrénées France
183 H9 Villeneuve Provence-Alpes-Côte d'Azur France
182 F4 Villeneuve Rhône-Alpes France
212 B3 Villeneuve Switz.
178 G7 Villeneuve-au-Chemin France
183 C6 Villeneuve-d'Allier France
178 F2 Villeneuve-d'Ascq France
183 F7 Villeneuve-de-Berg France
185 D8 Villeneuve-de-Marsan France
185 F9 Villeneuve-de-Rivière France
185 H10 Villeneuve-d'Olmes France
185 H9 Villeneuve-du-Paréage France
178 F7 Villeneuve-la-Guyard France
178 G7 Villeneuve-l'Archevêque France
183 F9 Villeneuve-lès-Avignon France
183 C10 Villeneuve-lès-Béziers France
183 D9 Villeneuve-lès-Maguelone France
183 K9 Villeneuve-Loubet France
178 F5 Villeneuve-St-Germain France
182 C3 Villeneuve-sur-Allier France
185 F7 Villeneuve-sur-Lot France
178 F7 Villeneuve-sur-Yonne France
185 G8 Villeneuve-Tolosane France
185 H9 Villenouvelle France
185 I9 Villepinte France
261 I10 Ville Platte LA U.S.A.
181 M2 Villequier France
183 B7 Villercomtal France
185 F6 Villeréal France
182 E5 Villerest France
182 E5 Villerest, Barrage de dam France
205 K5 Villerías Spain
183 B10 Villerouge-Termenès France
181 J3 Villers-Bocage Basse-Normandie France
178 D4 Villers-Bocage Picardie France
178 E4 Villers-Bretonneux France
178 E4 Villers-Carbonnel France
178 F5 Villers-Cotterêts France
178 A4 Villers-Écalles France
179 I5 Villers-en-Argonne France
182 I1 Villersexel France
182 H2 Villers-Farlay France
187 H7 Villers-le-Bouillet Belgium
182 J2 Villers-le-lac France
179 L6 Villers-lès-Nancy France
178 F3 Villers-Outréaux France
187 B10 Villers-St-Paul France
178 I4 Villers-Semeuse France
212 C2 Villers-sur-Glâne Switz.
181 K3 Villers-sur-Mer France
179 J5 Villers-sur-Meuse France
179 K5 Villerupt France
181 L3 Villerville France
178 H7 Villery France
178 H6 Villeseneux France
183 G8 Villes-sur-Auzon France
179 I5 Ville-sur-Tourbe France
277 F6 Villeta Para.
215 L4 Villetta Barrea Italy
182 G5 Villette-d'Anthon France
182 F5 Villeurbanne France
183 D9 Villeveyrac France
183 F6 Villevocance France
284 C2 Villicun, Sierra mts Arg.
182 F4 Villié-Morgon France
237 M3 Villiers S. Africa
181 J6 Villiers-Charlemagne France
236 D9 Villiersdorp S. Africa
179 I6 Villiers-en-Lieu France
184 C3 Villiers-en-Plaine France
178 D5 Villiers-le-Bel France
179 J7 Villiers-le-Sec France
178 F8 Villiers-St-Benoît France
178 F6 Villiers-St-Georges France
169 G8 Villierstown Ireland
182 G5 Villieu-Loyes-Mollon France
194 E5 Villingen Ger.
194 F5 Villingendorf Ger.
191 F10 Villmar Ger.
205 K4 Villoldo Spain
205 Q9 Villora Spain
205 Q9 Villora r. Spain
213 M4 Villorba Italy
212 G4 Villoresi, Canale canal Italy
205 J7 Villoria Spain
205 J6 Villoruela Spain
179 J6 Villotte-sur-Aire France
207 H1 Villuercas, Sierra de las mts Spain
136 F7 Villupuram Tamil Nadu India
192 I2 Vilm i. Ger.
199 K3 Vilmány Hungary
247 I4 Vilna Alta Can.
Vilna Lith. see Vilnius
166 J1 Vilnesfjorden inlet Norway
160 I7 Vilnius Lith.
159 N5 Vil'nohirs'k Ukr.
159 O6 Vil'nyans'k Ukr.
208 K4 Viloví d'Onyar Spain
163 R5 Vilppula Fin.
200 C4 Vils Austria
195 L3 Vils r. Ger.
195 O4 Vils r. Ger.
160 E3 Vilsandi i. Estonia
160 E3 Vilsandi rahvuspark nature res. Estonia
195 M5 Vilsbiburg Ger.
195 L2 Vilseck Ger.
159 K4 Vil'shana Cherkas'ka Oblast' Ukr.
159 L3 Vil'shana Chernihivs'ka Oblast' Ukr.
159 Q4 Vil'shana Kharkivs'ka Oblast' Ukr.
158 J5 Vil'shanka Kirovohrads'ka Oblast' Ukr.
158 H5 Vil'shanka Vinnyts'ka Oblast' Ukr.
158 H3 Vil'shanka Zhytomyrs'ka Oblast' Ukr.
195 O4 Vilshofen Ger.
164 E5 Vilsund Vest Denmark
Viluppuram Tamil Nadu India see Villupuram
160 K4 Viluste Estonia
204 G6 Vilvestre Spain
187 F7 Vilvoorde Belgium
160 J7 Vilyeyka Belarus
160 K7 Vilyeyskaye Vodaskhovishcha l. Belarus
153 N3 Vilyuy r. Rus. Fed.
153 M3 Vilyuyskoye Vodokhranilishche resr Rus. Fed.
231 F8 Vimbe mt. Zambia
208 H5 Vimbodi Spain
206 A2 Vimeiro Port.
212 G4 Vimercate Italy
178 C3 Vimeu reg. France
204 B2 Vimianzo Spain
206 D3 Vimieiro Port.
204 G5 Vimioso Port.
165 L4 Vimmerby Sweden
178 E8 Vimory France
181 L4 Vimoutiers France
162 Q5 Vimpeli Fin.
198 C2 Vimperk Czech Rep.
229 I5 Vina r. Cameroon
264 J2 Vina CA U.S.A.
208 D5 Vinaceite Spain
284 B3 Viña del Mar Chile
212 C7 Vinadio Italy
208 G5 Vinaixa Spain
270 B2 Viñales Cuba
270 E4 Viñales Valley tourist site Cuba
257 □Q4 Vinalhaven ME U.S.A.
257 Q4 Vinalhaven Island ME U.S.A.
209 D11 Vinalopó r. Spain
235 □K2 Vinanivao Madag.
193 J10 Vinařice Czech Rep.
100 □6 Vinarori, Mount New Georgia Is Solomon Is
208 F7 Vinaròs Spain
Vinaroz Spain see Vinaròs
183 C10 Vinassan France
183 G6 Vinay France
269 J5 Vinazco r. Mex.
185 J10 Vinça France
249 F2 Vincelotte, Lac l. Que. Can.
239 □1c Vincendo Réunion
254 D6 Vincennes IN U.S.A.
287 H2 Vincennes Bay Antarctica
104 □1 Vincent, Point Norfolk I.
258 F5 Vincentown NJ U.S.A.
274 B5 Vinces r. Ecuador
179 L7 Vincey France
215 N5 Vinchiaturo Italy
282 C3 Vinchina Arg.
276 B3 Vinchos Peru
213 J8 Vinci Italy
190 J1 Vindeballe Denmark
162 O5 Vindelälven r. Sweden
162 M3 Vindelfjällens naturreservat nature res. Sweden
162 O4 Vindeln Sweden
164 E5 Vinderup Denmark
138 E8 Vindhya Range hills Madh. Prad. India
Vindobona Austria see Wien
208 G5 Vinebre Spain
258 E6 Vineland NJ U.S.A.
181 N6 Vineuil Centre France
181 O8 Vineuil Centre France
237 K6 Vineyard S. Africa
218 J4 Vinga Romania
218 J4 Vingăi, Câmpia plain Romania
165 L2 Vingåker Sweden
182 G2 Vingeanne r. France
185 J10 Vingrau France
118 G5 Vinh Vietnam
204 G5 Vinhais Port.
204 G5 Vinhas Port.
118 G3 Vinh Loc Vietnam
119 G9 Vinh Long Vietnam
118 H4 Vinh Thực, Đao i. Vietnam
118 G4 Vinh Yên Vietnam
201 N7 Vinica Croatia
219 K9 Vinica Macedonia
199 I3 Vinica Slovakia
198 G3 Viničné Slovakia
201 O1 Viničné Šumice Czech Rep.
205 O4 Viniegra de Arriba Spain
261 H7 Vinita OK U.S.A.
138 B8 Vinjhan Gujarat India
Vînju Mare Romania see Vânju Mare
158 G4 Vin'kivtsi Ukr.
210 G3 Vinkovci Croatia
Vinland i. Nfld and Lab. Can. see Newfoundland
199 K3 Vinné Slovakia
160 J2 Vinni Estonia
194 D3 Vinningen Ger.
Vinnitsa Ukr. see Vinnytsya
Vinnitsa Oblast admin. div. Ukr. see Vinnyts'ka Oblast'
Vinnitskaya Oblast' admin. div. Ukr. see Vinnyts'ka Oblast'
161 R1 Vinnitsy Rus. Fed.
158 G5 Vinnyts'ka Oblast' admin. div. Ukr.
158 H4 Vinnytsya Ukr.
Vinnytsya Oblast admin. div. Ukr. see Vinnyts'ka Oblast'
204 I6 Vino, Tierra del reg. Spain
199 H3 Vinodol Slovakia
Vinogradov Ukr. see Vynohradiv
161 V6 Vinogradovo Rus. Fed.
199 G3 Vinohrady nad Váhom Slovakia
165 L2 Vinön i. Sweden
183 H9 Vinon-sur-Verdon France
183 G8 Vinsobres France
286 S1 Vinson Massif mt. Antarctica
163 J6 Vinstra Norway
114 C2 Vintar Luzon Phil.
260 I4 Vinton IA U.S.A.
207 K7 Viñuela, Embalse de la resr Spain
205 N7 Viñuelas Spain
205 O5 Vinuesa Spain
136 F4 Vinukonda Andhra Prad. India
231 B5 Vinza Congo
192 E5 Vinzelberg Ger.
190 H1 Viöl Ger.
208 D3 Violada, Llanos de la plain Spain
182 E5 Violay France
183 F8 Violès France
Violeta Cuba see Primero de Enero
108 I4 Violet Valley Aboriginal Reserve W.A. Austr.
183 D9 Viols-le-Fort France
236 B4 Vioolsdrif S. Africa
180 I6 Vioreau, Grand Réservoir de resr France
178 D5 Viosne r. France
201 I8 Vipava Slovenia
201 I8 Vipava r. Slovenia
233 B8 Viphya Mountains Malawi
213 K2 Vipiteno Italy
192 G4 Vipperow Ger.
115 E8 Viqueque East Timor
210 E3 Vir i. Croatia
201 K7 Vir Slovenia
114 E5 Virac Phil.
114 E5 Virac Point Phil.
280 C4 Viradouro Brazil
138 D8 Viramgam Gujarat India
149 I5 Viranşehir Turkey
136 D6 Virarajendrapet Karnataka India
145 N9 Virawah Pak.
160 M6 Virawlya Belarus
185 E6 Virazeil France
160 G5 Vircava r. Latvia/Lith.
108 D6 Virchow, Mount hill W.A. Austr.
Virdáánjarga Fin. see Virtaniemi
247 K5 Virden Man. Can.
181 J4 Vire France
181 I3 Vire r. France
231 B8 Virei Angola
178 I3 Vireux-Molhain France
178 I3 Vireux-Wallerand France
178 H7 Virey-sous-Bar France
281 F2 Virgem da Lapa Brazil
200 F5 Virgen Austria
207 O6 Virgen, Puerto de la pass Spain
205 Q5 Virgen, Sierra de la mts Spain
283 C9 Vírgenes, Cabo c. Arg.
200 F5 Virgental val. Austria
256 G12 Virgilina VA U.S.A.
265 R5 Virgin r. AZ U.S.A.
251 O1 Virginatown Ont. Can.
271 K4 Virgin Gorda i. Virgin Is (U.K.)
169 H5 Virginia Ireland
237 K4 Virginia S. Africa
250 B2 Virginia MN U.S.A.
256 G11 Virginia state U.S.A.
257 J12 Virginia Beach VA U.S.A.
262 I4 Virginia City MT U.S.A.
264 M2 Virginia City NV U.S.A.
245 P3 Virginia Falls N.W.T. Can.
173 K5 Virginia Water Surrey, England U.K.
271 K4 Virgin Islands (U.K.) terr. West Indies
271 K4 Virgin Islands (U.S.A.) terr. West Indies
265 R5 Virgin Mountains AZ U.S.A.
281 F3 Virginópolis Brazil
182 G4 Viriat France
182 G6 Virieu France
182 H5 Virieu-le-Grand France
182 E5 Virigneux France
182 H5 Virignin France
183 G6 Viriville France
160 H1 Virkkala Fin.
162 S5 Virmasvesi l. Fin.
119 H8 Virôchey Cambodia
187 G8 Viroin r. Belgium
163 S6 Virolahti Fin.
250 D6 Viroqua WI U.S.A.
210 F3 Virovitica Croatia
160 F4 Virpe Latvia
163 Q5 Virrat Fin.
165 L4 Virserum Sweden
162 T2 Virtaniemi Fin.
187 I9 Virton Belgium
160 G3 Virtsu Estonia
276 A2 Virú Peru
275 F4 Viruá, Parque Nacional do nat. park Brazil
136 E8 Virudhunagar Tamil Nadu India
230 F5 Virunga, Parc National des nat. park Dem. Rep. Congo
160 F5 Virvytė r. Lith.
182 H4 Viry Franche-Comté France
182 I4 Viry Rhône-Alpes France
178 F4 Viry-Noureuil France
210 F4 Vis Croatia
210 F4 Vis i. Croatia
183 C9 Vis, Gorges de la France
160 J6 Visaginas Lith.
Visakhapatnam Andhra Prad. India see Vishakhapatnam
100 □6 Visale Guadalcanal Solomon Is
264 M5 Visalia CA U.S.A.
183 F8 Visan France
219 P5 Vişani Romania
136 D3 Visapur Mahar. India
138 C9 Visavadar Gujarat India
114 E6 Visayan Islands Phil.
114 D6 Visayan Sea Phil.
190 F5 Visbek Ger.
190 G1 Visby Denmark
165 O4 Visby Gotland Sweden
281 F4 Visconde do Rio Branco Brazil
243 H2 Viscount Melville Sound sea chan. N.W.T./Nunavut Can.
187 I7 Visé Belgium
210 G4 Višegrad Bos.-Herz.
213 N7 Viserba Italy
278 D2 Viseu Brazil
204 E7 Viseu Port.
204 E7 Viseu admin. dist. Port.
219 M3 Vişeu r. Romania
219 M3 Vişeu de Sus Romania
213 R5 Viševica mt. Croatia
137 H4 Vishakhapatnam Andhra Prad. India
219 O9 Vishegrad hill Bulg.
156 K3 Vishera r. Rus. Fed.
156 L4 Vishera r. Rus. Fed.
161 O3 Vishera r. Rus. Fed.
157 H5 Vishnevoye Rus. Fed.
Vishnevoye Ukr. see Vyshneve
160 J7 Vishnyeva Belarus
208 C6 Visiedo Spain
160 K4 Visikums Latvia
156 L4 Visim Rus. Fed.
219 N6 Vişina Romania
165 K3 Visingsö i. Sweden
164 I4 Viskan r. Sweden
160 J5 Višķi Latvia
210 F4 Viški Kanal sea chan. Croatia
165 K5 Vislanda Sweden
138 D8 Visnagar Gujarat India
201 K8 Višnja Gora Slovenia
193 L9 Višňová Czech Rep.
198 F3 Višňové Czech Rep.
199 H2 Višňové Slovakia
212 C6 Viso, Monte mt. Italy
207 L3 Viso del Marqués Spain
210 G4 Visoko Bos.-Herz.
212 F6 Visone Italy
199 J4 Visonta Hungary
212 D3 Visp Switz.
237 J7 Visrivier S. Africa
183 D6 Vissac-Auteyrac France
136 G4 Vissannapeta Andhra Prad. India
165 L5 Visselfjärda Sweden
190 I5 Visselhövede Ger.
165 K5 Vissjön l. Sweden
215 K2 Visso Italy
212 D3 Vissoie Switz.
264 O8 Vista CA U.S.A.
259 H2 Vista NY U.S.A.
274 D4 Vista Alegre Amazonas Brazil
274 D6 Vista Alegre Amazonas Brazil
275 F6 Vista Alegre Amazonas Brazil
277 F4 Vista Alegre Mato Grosso do Sul Brazil
275 F4 Vista Alegre Roraima Brazil
209 E7 Vistabella del Maestrazgo Spain
284 C3 Vista Flores Arg.
269 J2 Vista Hermosa Mex.
264 M6 Vista Lake CA U.S.A.
164 J2 Visten l. Sweden
220 G1 Vistonida, Limni lag. Greece
Vistula r. Pol. see Wisła
197 K1 Vištyčio ežeras l. Lith./Rus. Fed.
160 F7 Vištytis Lith.
159 L6 Visun' r. Ukr.
139 O7 Viswema Nagaland India
199 J4 Visznek Hungary
219 M7 Vit r. Bulg.
274 E3 Vita r. Col.
216 D8 Vita Sicilia Italy
214 E2 Vita, Capo c. Italy
145 M7 Vitakri Pak.
218 G7 Vitao mt. Montenegro
199 J3 Vít'az Slovakia
Vitebsk Belarus see Vitsyebsk
Vitebskaya Oblast' admin. div. Belarus see Vitsyebskaya Voblasts'
Vitebsk Oblast admin. div. Belarus see Vitsyebskaya Voblasts'
214 I3 Viterbo Italy
214 H3 Viterbo prov. Italy
179 L6 Viterne France
210 F3 Vitez Bos.-Herz.
210 G4 Vitez pass Bos.-Herz.
218 J8 Viti Viti Kosovo
276 D5 Vitichi Bol.
204 H6 Vitigudino Spain
101 □7a Viti Levu i. Fiji
121 K1 Vitim r. Rus. Fed.
121 J1 Vitimskoye Ploskogor'ye plat. Rus. Fed.
Vitina Viti Kosovo see Viti
201 L2 Vitis Austria
199 G2 Vítkov Czech Rep.
201 O4 Vitnyéd Hungary
100 □6 Vito P.N.G.
219 J9 Vitolište Macedonia
218 I8 Vitomiricë Pejë Kosovo
276 C4 Vitor Peru
276 B4 Vitor r. Peru
214 I3 Vitorchiano Italy
281 G4 Vitória Espírito Santo Brazil
275 H5 Vitória Pará Brazil
Vitoria Spain see Vitoria-Gasteiz
205 O3 Vitoria airport Spain
205 O3 Vitoria, Montes de mts Spain
279 E5 Vitória da Conquista Brazil
205 O3 Vitoria-Gasteiz Spain
288 G7 Vitória Seamount sea feature S. Atlantic Ocean
219 L8 Vitosha nat. park Bulg.
217 M5 Vitravo r. Italy
180 I5 Vitré France
179 K8 Vitrey-sur-Mance France
183 G10 Vitrolles France
178 E3 Vitry-en-Artois France
178 I6 Vitry-en-Perthois France
178 H6 Vitry-la-Ville France
178 I6 Vitry-le-François France
182 D3 Vitry-sur-Loire France
178 D6 Vitry-sur-Seine France
158 I2 Vits' r. Belarus
161 N6 Vitsyebsk Belarus
160 L6 Vitsyebskaya Voblasts' admin. div. Belarus
162 P3 Vittangi Sweden
182 F2 Vitteaux France
179 K7 Vittel France
216 H10 Vittoria Sicilia Italy
Vittoriosa Malta see Birgu
213 M4 Vittorio Veneto Italy
215 M5 Vitulazio Italy
159 Q8 Vityazevo Rus. Fed.
159 Q8 Vityazevskiy Liman lag. Rus. Fed.
193 E8 Vitzenburg Ger.
209 E8 Viuda, Rambla de la r. Spain
182 I4 Viuz-en-Sallaz France
183 E7 Vivarais, Monts du mts France
214 C3 Vivario Corse France
159 R4 Vivcharove Ukr.
204 E1 Viveiro Spain
204 E1 Viveiro, Ría de est. Spain
208 D6 Vivel del Río Martín Spain
209 D8 Viver Spain
285 F4 Vivero Arg.
Vivero Spain see Viveiro
183 D6 Viverols France
212 E5 Viverone, Lago di l. Italy
207 N3 Viveros Spain
261 I9 Vivian LA U.S.A.
179 I4 Vivier-au-Court France
183 F8 Viviers France
185 I6 Viviez France
183 E9 Viv-le-Fesq France
235 F4 Vivo S. Africa
201 K7 Vivodnik mt. Slovenia
184 E3 Vivonne France
285 I5 Vivoratá Arg.
266 □R10 Vivorillo, Cayos is Hond.
178 I8 Vix Bourgogne France
184 C3 Vix Pays de la Loire France
197 M5 Viynytsya Ukr.
159 O5 Viys'kove Ukr.
158 F4 Viytivtsi Ukr.
Vizagapatam Andhra Prad. India see Vishakhapatnam
266 C4 Vizcaíno, Desierto de des. Mex.
266 B4 Vizcaíno, Sierra mts Mex.
205 O2 Vizcaya prov. Spain
148 C3 Vize Turkey
152 I2 Vize, Ostrov i. Rus. Fed.
182 E5 Vizézy r. France
156 I2 Vizhas Rus. Fed.
156 I2 Vizhas r. Rus. Fed.
197 L6 Vizhomlya Ukr.
137 H3 Vizianagaram Andhra Prad. India
183 H6 Vizille France
213 P5 Vižinada Croatia
156 J3 Vizinga Rus. Fed.
219 P5 Viziru Romania
199 G2 Vizovice Czech Rep.
199 I3 Vizslás Hungary
199 K3 Vizsoly Hungary
216 H9 Vizzini Sicilia Italy
276 C3 V. J. José Perez Bol.
220 A2 Vjosë r. Albania
187 G7 Vlaams-Brabant prov. Belgium
186 F5 Vlaardingen Neth.
220 B4 Vlachata Kefallonia Greece
220 D5 Vlachokerasia Greece
201 I1 Vlachovo Březí Czech Rep.
199 L5 Vlădeasa, Munţii mts Romania
219 K4 Vlădeasa, Vârful mt. Romania
219 K8 Vladičin Han Vladičin Han Serbia
151 F2 Vladikavkaz Rus. Fed.
122 I7 Vladimir Primorskiy Kray Rus. Fed.
161 X5 Vladimir Vladimirskaya Oblast' Rus. Fed.
199 K5 Vladimirescu Romania
122 H7 Vladimiro-Aleksandrovskoye Rus. Fed.
Vladimir Oblast admin. div. Rus. Fed. see Vladimirskaya Oblast'
142 K1 Vladimirovka Kostanayskaya Oblast' Kazakh.
142 D2 Vladimirovka Zapadnyy Kazakhstan Kazakh.
122 M3 Vladimirovka Sakhalinskaya Oblast' Rus. Fed.
151 F1 Vladimirovka Stavropol'skiy Kray Rus. Fed.
219 L7 Vladimirovo Bulg.
122 M4 Vladimirovo Rus. Fed.
Vladimirovskiy Kazakh. see Vladimirovka
161 X6 Vladimirskaya Oblast' admin. div. Rus. Fed.
161 Q6 Vladimirskiy Tupik Rus. Fed.
Vladimir-Volynskiy Ukr. see Volodymyr-Volyns'kyy
198 E2 Vladislav Czech Rep.
122 G7 Vladivostok Rus. Fed.
156 G4 Vladychnoye Rus. Fed.
186 L2 Vlagtwedde Neth.
219 N4 Vlăhiţa Romania
219 J8 Vlajna mt. Serbia
Vlakhokerassía Greece see Vlachokerasia
210 G3 Vlasenica Bos.-Herz.
218 H6 Vlašić Planina mts Serbia
198 D2 Vlašim Czech Rep.
159 M4 Vlasivka Ukr.
219 K8 Vlasotince Vlasotince Serbia
Vlasova-Ayuta Rus. Fed. see Ayutinskiy
161 W6 Vlasovo Rus. Fed.
122 L2 Vlas'yevo Rus. Fed.
161 P8 Vlazovichi Rus. Fed.
199 G3 Vlčany Slovakia
186 J3 Vledder Neth.
236 F10 Vleesbaai b. S. Africa
236 F9 Vleiland S. Africa
186 H4 Vleuten Neth.
186 G2 Vlieland i. Neth.
186 H5 Vlijmen Neth.
187 E6 Vlissingen Neth.
220 A2 Vlorë Albania
220 A2 Vlorës, Gjiri i b. Albania
191 G6 Vlotho Ger.
Vlotslavsk Pol. see Włocławek
198 D1 Vltava r. Czech Rep.
201 J7 Vnanje Gorice Slovenia
161 T2 Vnina r. Rus. Fed.
142 K7 Vobkent Uzbek.
193 F7 Vockerode Ger.
201 I3 Vöcklabruck Austria
201 H3 Vöcklamarkt Austria
199 G3 Voderady Slovakia
221 J6 Vodi, Akrotirio pt Rodos Greece
213 Q5 Vodice Istra Croatia
210 E4 Vodice Šibenik Croatia
156 G3 Vodlozero, Ozero l. Rus. Fed.
198 D2 Vodňany Czech Rep.
210 D3 Vodnjan Croatia
Vodopyanovo Rus. Fed. see Donskoye
168 □N2 Voe Shetland, Scotland U.K.
237 J9 Voël r. S. Africa
191 C7 Voerde (Niederrhein) Ger.
187 I7 Voerendaal Neth.
164 G4 Voerså Denmark
229 F5 Vogan Togo
186 G4 Vogelenzang Neth.
179 O7 Vogelgrun France
Vogelkop Peninsula Papua Indon. see Doberai, Jazirah
229 H4 Vogel Peak Nigeria
192 H4 Vogelsang Ger.
191 G10 Vogelsberg hills Ger.
193 I6 Vogelsdorf Ger.
179 O7 Vogelsheim France
194 D3 Vogelweh Ger.
212 G6 Voghera Italy
213 L6 Voghiera Italy
151 H6 Voghji r. Armenia
162 J5 Vognill Norway
210 G4 Vogošća Bos.-Herz.
194 H6 Vogt Ger.
195 M6 Vogtareuth Ger.
193 F10 Vogtland reg. Ger.
183 E7 Vogüé France
100 □5 Voh New Caledonia
195 L4 Vohburg an der Donau Ger.
Vohémar Madag. see Iharaña
195 M2 Vohenstrauß Ger.
Vohibinany Madag. see Ampasimanolotra
235 □J4 Vohilava Fianarantsoa Madag.
235 □K4 Vohilava Fianarantsoa Madag.
Vohimarina Madag. see Iharaña
235 □J5 Vohimena, Tanjona c. Madag.
235 □J4 Vohipeno Madag.
235 □K4 Vohitrandriana Madag.
191 G8 Vöhl Ger.
160 I3 Võhma Estonia
194 E5 Vöhrenbach Ger.
194 F5 Vöhringen Baden-Württemberg Ger.
195 I5 Vöhringen Bayern Ger.
233 C5 Voi Kenya
179 K6 Void-Vacon France
193 D8 Voigtstedt Ger.
163 S6 Voikoski Fin.
179 I6 Voillecomte France
219 L5 Voineasa Romania
219 P3 Voineşti Romania
228 C4 Voinjama Liberia
161 T8 Voin Pervyy Rus. Fed.
183 H6 Voiron France
178 C6 Voise r. France
249 I1 Voisey's Bay Nfld and Lab. Can.
182 H3 Voiteur France
201 L5 Voitsberg Austria
199 K3 Vojčice Slovakia
164 F6 Vojens Denmark
162 N4 Vojmsjön l. Sweden
Vojnice Slovakia see Bátorove Kosihy
201 L7 Vojnik Slovenia
218 H5 Vojvodina prov. Serbia
160 K2 Voka Estonia
199 H6 Vokány Hungary
156 I4 Vokhma Rus. Fed.
162 U4 Voknavolok Rus. Fed.
229 I4 Voko Cameroon
156 K3 Vol' r. Rus. Fed.
198 C3 Volary Czech Rep.
Volaterrae Italy see Volterra
262 L4 Volborg MT U.S.A.
282 D1 Volcán Arg.
276 D5 Volcán, Cerro vol. Bol.
284 B2 Volcán, Cerro del vol. Chile
285 H5 Volcán, Sierra del hills Arg.
266 □R13 Volcán Barú, Parque Nacional nat. park Panama
Volcano Bay Japan see Uchiura-wan
264 □F14 Volcano House HI U.S.A.
Volcano Islands N. Pacific Ocean see Kazan-rettō
183 B6 Volcans d'Auvergne, Parc Naturel Régional des nature res. France
Volchansk Ukr. see Vovchans'k
161 O8 Volchas r. Belarus
143 S1 Volchikha Rus. Fed.
161 S4 Volchina r. Rus. Fed.
161 P1 Volchiy Nos, Mys pt Rus. Fed.
159 T1 Volchki Rus. Fed.
163 I5 Volda Norway
156 K3 Vol'dino Rus. Fed.
195 P2 Volduchy Czech Rep.
186 H4 Volendam Neth.
256 F12 Volens VA U.S.A.
161 V4 Volga Rus. Fed.
161 V4 Volga r. Rus. Fed.
Volga Upland hills Rus. Fed. see Privolzhskaya Vozvyshennost'
157 H7 Volgodonsk Rus. Fed.
157 I6 Volgograd Rus. Fed.
Volgograd Oblast admin. div. Rus. Fed. see Volgogradskaya Oblast'
157 I6 Volgogradskaya Oblast' admin. div. Rus. Fed.
157 I6 Volgogradskoye Vodokhranilishche resr Rus. Fed.
161 Y4 Volgorechensk Rus. Fed.
Volhynia admin. div. Ukr. see Volyns'ka Oblast'
158 I7 Volintiri Moldova
221 G4 Volissos Chios Greece
101 □7a Volivoli Point Viti Levu Fiji
195 I2 Volkach Ger.
195 I2 Volkach r. Ger.
201 K6 Völkermarkt Austria
194 F6 Volkertshausen Ger.
212 F1 Volketswil Switz.
161 P2 Volkhov Rus. Fed.
161 P1 Volkhov r. Rus. Fed.
161 P1 Volkhovskaya Guba b. Rus. Fed.
161 O3 Volkhovskiy Rus. Fed.
194 B3 Völklingen Ger.
191 H8 Volkmarsen Ger.
Volkovichi Belarus see Vawkavichy
161 N7 Volkovo Rus. Fed.
Volkovysk Belarus see Vawkavysk
Volkovyskiye Vysoty hills Belarus see Vawkavyskaye Wzvyshsha
237 N3 Volksrust S. Africa
193 E7 Volkstedt Ger.
190 D4 Völlen Ger.
186 I3 Vollenhove Neth.
190 G4 Vollersode Ger.
182 D5 Vollore-Montagne France
179 N5 Volmunster France
182 F2 Volnay France
Vol'nogorsk Ukr. see Vil'nohirs'k
122 G7 Vol'no-Nadezhdinskoye Rus. Fed.
159 Q6 Volnovakha Ukr.
143 N1 Vol'noye Rus. Fed.
Vol'nyansk Ukr. see Vil'nyans
153 K2 Volochanka Rus. Fed.
122 I4 Volochayevka-Vtoraya Rus. F
Volochisk Ukr. see Volochys'k
158 F4 Volochys'k Ukr.
158 I4 Volodarka Ukr.
197 J1 Volodarovka Rus. Fed.
159 Q6 Volodars'ke Ukr.
142 C4 Volodarskiy Rus. Fed.
Volodarskoye Kazakh. see Saumalkol'
158 H3 Volodars'k-Volyns'kyy Ukr.
158 F2 Volodymyrets' Ukr.
159 L6 Volodymyrivka Ukr.
158 D3 Volodymyr-Volyns'kyy Ukr.
156 G4 Vologda Rus. Fed.
Vologda Oblast admin. div. Rus. Fed. see Vologodskaya Oblast'
179 M7 Vologne r. France
161 Y2 Vologodskaya Oblast' admin Rus. Fed.
159 Q3 Volokhivka Ukr.
159 P4 Volokhiv Yar Ukr.
161 S5 Volokolamsk Rus. Fed.
157 G6 Volokonovka Rus. Fed.
156 J2 Volokovaya Rus. Fed.
183 I8 Volonne France
236 G4 Volop S. Africa
220 D3 Volos Greece
197 L6 Voloshcha Ukr.
159 S5 Voloshino Rus. Fed.
156 H3 Voloshka Rus. Fed.
159 Q4 Volos'ka Balakliya Ukr.
159 P4 Volos'ka Balakliyka r. Ukr.
160 M2 Volosovo Rus. Fed.
199 L3 Volosyanka Ukr.
161 N4 Volot Rus. Fed.
159 R3 Volotovo Rus. Fed.
158 C5 Volovets' Ukr.
157 G5 Volovo Lipetskaya Oblast' Rus. Fed.
161 V8 Volovo Tul'skaya Oblast' Rus.
199 J3 Volovské vrchy mts Slovakia
161 R7 Voloye Rus. Fed.
Volozhin Belarus see Valozhy
200 F8 Volpago del Montello Italy
212 F6 Volpedo Italy
212 D5 Volpiano Italy
193 D6 Völpke Ger.
200 D5 Völs Austria
192 H3 Völschow Ger.
214 H2 Volsini, Monti mts Italy
Volsinii Italy see Orvieto
142 B1 Vol'sk Rus. Fed.
236 H9 Volstruisleegte S. Africa
236 G6 Volstruispoort pass S. Africa
229 F5 Volta admin. reg. Ghana
229 F5 Volta r. Ghana
229 F5 Volta, Lake resr Ghana
108 H3 Voltaire, Cape W.A. Austr.
Volta Noire r. Africa see Black Volta
281 E5 Volta Redonda Brazil
Volta Rouge r. Burkina/Ghan see Nazinon
213 J9 Volterra Italy
191 E6 Voltlage Ger.
205 K6 Voltoya r. Spain
215 O5 Volturara Appula Italy
216 H2 Volturara Irpina Italy
215 O5 Volturino Italy
215 P7 Volturino, Monte mt. Italy
215 L5 Volturno r. Italy
226 D2 Volubilis tourist site Morocco
219 O6 Voluntari Romania
283 F8 Volunteer Point Falkland Is
259 L1 Voluntown CT U.S.A.
220 E2 Volvi, Limni l. Greece
182 C5 Volvic France
183 H9 Volx France
197 L3 Volya Belarus
159 S2 Volya Rus. Fed.
156 M3 Vol'ya r. Rus. Fed.
197 L6 Volya Arlamivs'ka Ukr.
198 C2 Volyně Czech Rep.
198 C2 Volyňka r. Czech Rep.
159 L2 Volynka Ukr.
Volyn Oblast admin. div. Ukr. see Volyns'ka Oblast'
158 D2 Volyns'ka Oblast' admin. div. Ukr.
Volynskaya Oblast' admin. di Ukr. see Volyns'ka Oblast'
158 F4 Volytsya Ukr.
158 F4 Volytsya Druha Ukr.
156 J5 Volzhsk Rus. Fed.
142 D1 Volzhskiy Samarskaya Oblast Rus. Fed.
157 I6 Volzhskiy Volgogradskaya Ob Rus. Fed.
101 □7a Voma mts Viti Levu Fiji
215 M2 Vomano r. Italy
101 □7a Vomo i. Fiji
200 E5 Vomp Austria
100 □6 Vonavona i. New Georgia Is Solomon Is
247 J4 Vonda Sask. Can.
156 I4 Vondanka Rus. Fed.
235 □J4 Vondrozo Madag.
244 I3 Von Frank Mountain AK U.S.
156 H2 Vonga Rus. Fed.
182 G2 Vonges France
220 B4 Vonitsa Greece
182 F4 Vonnas France
160 K3 Võnnu Estonia
161 R1 Vonozero Rus. Fed.
136 G5 Vontimitta Andhra Prad. India
198 G5 Vonyarcvashegy Hungary
186 F4 Voorburg Neth.
257 L6 Voorheesville NY U.S.A.
186 F4 Voorschoten Neth.
186 J4 Voorst Neth.
186 I4 Voorthuizen Neth.
160 G2 Voosi kurk sea chan. Estonia
161 P7 Vop' r. Rus. Fed.
162 □F1 Vopnafjörður Iceland
162 □F1 Vopnafjörður b. Iceland
162 Q5 Vörå Fin.
201 K4 Voralm mt. Austria
160 L6 Voran' Belarus
160 I7 Voranava Belarus
200 A5 Vorarlberg land Austria
156 J4 Vorchanka Rus. Fed.
201 I3 Vorchdorf Austria
186 J4 Vorden Neth.
201 K4 Vordernberg Austria
212 H1 Vorderrhein r. Switz.
164 H6 Vordingborg Denmark
191 K6 Vordorf Ger.
218 H9 Vorë Albania
220 B2 Voreia Pindos mts Greece
220 B4 Voreies Echinades i. Greece
220 E3 Voreies Sporades is Greece
221 G3 Voreio Aigaio admin. reg. Gre
220 E4 Voreios Evvoïkos Kolpos sea chan. Greece
156 F3 Vorenzha Rus. Fed.
183 H6 Voreppe France
183 D6 Vorey France
161 P8 Vorga Rus. Fed.
156 M2 Vorgashor Rus. Fed.
Voriai Sporádhes is Greece se Voreies Sporades
Voría Píndhos mts Greece see Voreia Pindos
288 J1 Voring Plateau sea feature N. Atlantic Ocean
139 O5 Vorjing mt. Arun. Prad. India
156 N2 Vorkuta Rus. Fed.
164 H1 Vorma r. Norway
164 C2 Vormedalsheia park Norway
160 G2 Vormsi i. Estonia
164 H1 Vormsund Norway
161 W9 Vorob'yevka Lipetskaya Oblas Rus. Fed.
157 H6 Vorob'yevka Voronezhskaya Oblast' Rus. Fed.
159 M1 Vorob"yivka Ukr.
159 M8 Vorobyove Ukr.
152 J3 Vorogovo Rus. Fed.
158 D5 Vorokhta Ukr.
219 O3 Vorona Romania

H6 Vorona r. Rus. Fed.
G6 Voronezh Rus. Fed.
W9 Voronezh r. Rus. Fed.
Voronezh Oblast admin. div. Rus. Fed. see Voronezhskaya Oblast'
H6 Voronezhskaya Oblast' admin. div. Rus. Fed.
G6 Voronezhskiy Zapovednik nature res. Rus. Fed.
S2 Voronezhskoye Vodokhranilishche resr Rus. Fed.
M2 Voronizh Ukr.
M3 Voron'ky Ukr.
F2 Voron'ky Ukr.
L1 Voronok Rus. Fed.
H2 Voronov, Mys pt Rus. Fed.
P1 Voronov, Mys pt Rus. Fed.
U6 Voronovo Rus. Fed.
H4 Voronovytsya Ukr.
H6 Vorontsovka Rus. Fed.
L4 Vorontsovo Rus. Fed.
Vorontsovo-Aleksandrovskoye Rus. Fed. see Zelenokumsk
D4 Voronyaky hills Ukr.
H4 Voron'ye Rus. Fed.
Voroshilov Rus. Fed. see Ussuriysk
Voroshilovgrad Ukr. see Luhans'k
Voroshilovsk Rus. Fed. see Stavropol'
Voroshilovsk Ukr. see Alchevs'k
H6 Vorotan r. Armenia
Q6 Vorot'kovo Rus. Fed.
I4 Vorotynets Rus. Fed.
T7 Vorotynsk Rus. Fed.
D1 Vorovskolesskaya Rus. Fed.
N2 Vorozhba Sums'ka Oblast' Ukr.
N3 Vorozhba Sums'ka Oblast' Ukr.
G2 Vorpommersche Boddenlandschaft, Nationalpark nat. park Ger.
B2 Vorposten Peak Antarctica
K2 Vorra Ger.
M5 Vorsau Austria
G6 Vorselaar Belgium
F6 Vorskla r. Rus. Fed.
O3 Vorsklitsa r. Rus. Fed./Ukr.
H6 Vorst Belgium
H1 Vorstershoop S. Africa
L5 Vorța Romania
B2 Vørterkaka Nunatak mt. Antarctica
I3 Võrtsjärv l. Estonia
K4 Võru Estonia
N2 Vorukh Tajik.
H4 Vorwerk Ger.
R7 Vorya r. Rus. Fed.
J3 Vorzel' Ukr.
M4 Vosa Belarus
G6 Vosburg S. Africa
M3 Vose Tajik.
N3 Vösendorf Austria
L7 Vosges dept France
M8 Vosges mts France
O6 Vosges du Nord, Parc Naturel Régional des nature res. France
W4 Voshchazhnikovo Rus. Fed.
G4 Voskevan Armenia
N8 Voskhod Ukr.
V6 Voskresensk Rus. Fed.
L6 Voskresens'ke Ukr.
V8 Voskresenskoye Lipetskaya Oblast' Rus. Fed.
I4 Voskresenskoye Nizhegorodskaya Oblast' Rus. Fed.
G1 Voskresenskoye Respublika Bashkortostan Rus. Fed.
U7 Voskresenskoye Tul'skaya Oblast' Rus. Fed.
U2 Voskresenskoye Vologodskaya Oblast' Rus. Fed.
U4 Voskresenskoye Yaroslavskaya Oblast' Rus. Fed.
F2 Vosne-Romanée France
I6 Voss Norway
G6 Vosselaar Belgium
N1 Vossinansari, Ostrov i. Rus. Fed.
G1 Vostochnaya Litsa Rus. Fed.
Vostochno-Kazakhstanskaya Oblast' admin. div. Kazakh. see Vostochnyy Kazakhstan
Vostochno-Kounradskiy Kazakh. see Shygys Konyrat
M3 Vostochno-Sakhalinskiy Gory mts Sakhalin Rus. Fed.
P2 Vostochno-Sibirskoye More sea Rus. Fed.
F2 Vostochnoye Munozero Rus. Fed.
K4 Vostochnyy Kirovskaya Oblast' Rus. Fed.
M4 Vostochnyy Sakhalin Rus. Fed.
Q8 Vostochnyy, Liman l. Rus. Fed.
U3 Vostochnyy Kazakhstan admin. div. Kazakh.
F1 Vostochnyy Sayan mts Rus. Fed.
I5 Vostok Primorskiy Kray Rus. Fed.
Vostok Sakhalin Rus. Fed. see Neftegorsk
I6 Vostretsovo Rus. Fed.
I3 Vostroye Rus. Fed.
I2 Võsu Estonia
D2 Votice Czech Rep.
K4 Votkinsk Rus. Fed.
K4 Votkinskoye Vodokhranilishche resr Rus. Fed.
E1 Votna r. Norway
D5 Votorantim Brazil
P6 Votrya r. Rus. Fed.
□5 Vot Tandé i. Vanuatu
□7 Votua Vanua Levu Fiji
C4 Votuporanga Brazil
I3 Voueize r. France
Vouga Angola see Cunhinga
C7 Vouga r. Port.
F2 Vougeot France
H4 Vouglans, Lac de l. France
D3 Vouillé Poitou-Charentes France
E2 Vouillé Poitou-Charentes France
E5 Voula Greece
I8 Voulaines-les-Templiers France
E7 Voulx France
E2 Vouneuil-sous-Biard France
M8 Vouneuil-sur-Vienne France
A5 Voungou Gabon
C2 Vourinos mt. Greece
D1 Voutenay-sur-Cure France
G5 Voutezac France
C2 Vouvant France
M7 Vouvray France
B3 Vouvry Switz.
D7 Vouzela Port.
I5 Vouziers France
D8 Vouzon France
O5 Vovcha r. Ukr.
P3 Vovcha r. Ukr.
P3 Vovchans'k Ukr.
M3 Vovchyk Ukr.
C7 Voves France
G4 Vovk r. Ukr.
F3 Vovkoshiv Ukr.
G4 Vovkovyntsi Ukr.
E3 Vovodo r. C.A.R.
G9 Vowchyn Belarus
M6 Voxna Sweden
N6 Voxnan r. Sweden
J4 Voya r. Rus. Fed.
I1 Voyageurs National Park MN U.S.A.
K5 Voyevods'ke Ukr.
U4 Voynitsa Rus. Fed.
M6 Voynyliv Ukr.
Vöyri Fin. see Vörå
K2 Voyvozh Respublika Komi Rus. Fed.
K3 Voyvozh Respublika Komi Rus. Fed.
□6 Voza Choiseul Solomon Is
T5 Vozdvizhenskoye Moskovskaya Oblast' Rus. Fed.
V5 Vozdvizhenskoye Moskovskaya Oblast' Rus. Fed.
W7 Vozha r. Rus. Fed.
G3 Vozhe, Ozero l. Rus. Fed.
156 H3 Vozhega Rus. Fed.
156 J2 Vozhgora Rus. Fed.
205 Q5 Vozmediano Spain
143 N1 Voznesenka Kazakh.
159 K6 Voznesens'k Ukr.
151 C1 Voznesenskaya Krasnodarskiy Kray Rus. Fed.
151 F2 Voznesenskaya Respublika Ingushetiya Rus. Fed.
159 K6 Voznesens'ke Ukr.
157 H5 Voznesenskoye Rus. Fed.
161 Y5 Voznesen'ye Ivanovskaya Oblast' Rus. Fed.
161 S1 Voznesen'ye Leningradskaya Oblast' Rus. Fed.
142 H5 Vozrojdenie Uzbek.
142 H5 Vozrozhdenya Island pen. Uzbek.
159 L6 Vozsiyats'ke Ukr.
143 N1 Vozvyshenka Kazakh.
Vozvyshenskiy Kazakh. see Vozvyshenka
122 F3 Vozzhayevka Rus. Fed.
164 F4 Vrå Denmark
219 M8 Vrabevo Bulg.
199 H3 Vráble Slovakia
220 B5 Vrachionas hill Zakynthos Greece
220 C4 Vrachnaiika Greece
164 E2 Vrådal Norway
158 J6 Vradiyivka Ukr.
Vrakhiónas Óros hill Zakynthos Greece see Vrachionas
Vrakhnaíika Greece see Vrachnaiika
210 F4 Vran mt. Bos.-Herz.
219 O7 Vrana r. Bulg.
218 I9 Vraneštica Vraneštica Macedonia
122 H7 Vrangel' Rus. Fed.
122 K1 Vrangelya, Mys pt Rus. Fed.
153 T2 Vrangelya, Ostrov i. Rus. Fed.
164 H4 Vrångö naturreservat nature res. Sweden
210 G3 Vranjak Bos.-Herz.
219 J8 Vranje Vranje Serbia
219 K8 Vranjska Banja Vranje Serbia
198 E3 Vranov, Vodní nádrž resr Czech Rep.
201 O2 Vranovice Czech Rep.
199 K3 Vranov nad Topľou Slovakia
201 K7 Vransko Slovenia
213 Q6 Vransko Jezero l. Croatia
218 D7 Vransko Jezero l. Croatia
218 I9 Vrapčište Macedonia
220 F2 Vrasidas, Akrotirio pt Greece
219 K7 Vratarnica Zaječar Serbia
219 O8 Vratnik pass Bulg.
219 L7 Vratsa Bulg.
210 F3 Vrbanja r. Bos.-Herz.
210 F3 Vrbas r. Bos.-Herz.
218 H5 Vrbas Vojvodina Serbia
199 J5 Vrbica Vojvodina Serbia
213 R5 Vrbnik Croatia
198 G1 Vrbno pod Pradědem Czech Rep.
199 J2 Vrbov Slovakia
198 G3 Vrbovce Slovakia
199 G3 Vrbové Slovakia
210 F3 Vrbovec Croatia
210 E3 Vrbovsko Croatia
198 E1 Vrchlabí Czech Rep.
179 K7 Vrécourt France
237 N3 Vrede S. Africa
237 L2 Vredefort S. Africa
191 C6 Vreden Ger.
236 B8 Vredenburg S. Africa
236 C7 Vredendal S. Africa
236 D3 Vredeshoop Namibia
275 G3 Vreed-en-Hoop Guyana
186 H4 Vreeland Neth.
190 E5 Vrees Ger.
204 E6 Vreia de Jales Port.
218 I8 Vrellë Istog Kosovo
201 J8 Vremščica mt. Slovenia
187 G9 Vresse Belgium
210 E3 Vrhnika Slovenia
136 F7 Vriddhachalam Tamil Nadu India
186 K2 Vries Neth.
186 K4 Vriezenveen Neth.
165 K4 Vrigstad Sweden
182 B1 Vrille r. France
133 C13 Vrindavan Uttar Prad. India
145 N3 Vrist Afgh.
165 J3 Vristulven l. Sweden
178 I5 Vrizy France
218 I7 Vrnjačka Banja Vrnjačka Banja Serbia
236 D9 Vrolijkheid Nature Reserve S. Africa
178 C3 Vron France
186 K4 Vroomshoop Neth.
220 B3 Vrosina Greece
198 C1 Vroutek Czech Rep.
186 E5 Vrouwenpolder Neth.
218 H9 Vrrin Albania
218 J5 Vršac Vojvodina Serbia
213 P5 Vrsar Croatia
201 I8 Vrtojba Slovenia
237 I2 Vryburg S. Africa
237 O3 Vryheid S. Africa
195 O2 Všeruby Czech Rep.
193 K10 Všetaty Czech Rep.
199 G2 Vsetín Czech Rep.
244 E5 Vsevidof, Mount vol. AK U.S.A.
161 N1 Vsevolozhsk Rus. Fed.
159 O4 Vshyva r. Ukr.
161 R7 Vskhody Rus. Fed.
199 H3 Vtáčnik mt. Slovakia
199 H3 Vtáčnik mts Slovakia
182 H4 Vuache, Montagne de mt. France
101 □7 Vuaqava i. Fiji
130 E8 Vu Ban Vietnam
219 M9 Vŭcha r. Bulg.
210 G3 Vučica r. Croatia
Vučitrn Vushtrri Kosovo see Vushtrri
219 J8 Vučje Leskovac Serbia
186 H5 Vught Neth.
159 Q6 Vuhledar Ukr.
159 R5 Vuhlehirs'k Ukr.
210 G3 Vuka r. Croatia
210 G3 Vukovar Croatia
156 L3 Vuktyl' Rus. Fed.
237 N3 Vukuzakhe S. Africa
246 H5 Vulcan Alta Can.
219 L5 Vulcan Romania
158 H8 Vulcănești Moldova
Vulcan Island P.N.G. see Manam Island
216 H7 Vulcano, Isola i. Isole Lipari Italy
219 L7 Vŭlchedrŭm Bulg.
219 P7 Vŭlchi Dol Bulg.
215 O4 Vulgano r. Italy
118 G5 Vu Liêt Vietnam
Vulkaneshty Moldova see Vulcănești
159 O8 Vulkanivka Ukr.
104 G4 Vulkathuna-Gammon Ranges National Park S.A. Austr.
215 P6 Vulture, Monte mt. Italy
265 S8 Vulture Mountains AZ U.S.A.
119 H9 Vung Tau Vietnam
101 □7a Vunidawa Viti Levu Fiji
Vunindawa Viti Levu Fiji see Vunidawa
160 J1 Vuohijärvi Fin.
163 S6 Vuohijärvi l. Fin.
162 T4 Vuokatti Fin.
160 N1 Vuoksa r. Rus. Fed.
160 M1 Vuoksa, Ozero l. Rus. Fed.
160 L1 Vuoksi r. Fin.
162 S4 Vuolijoki Fin.
162 P3 Vuollerim Sweden
162 O3 Vuolvojaure l. Sweden
162 S3 Vuostimo Fin.
162 S2 Vuotso Fin.
100 □6 Vuranimala Solomon Is
219 O8 Vŭrbitsa Bulg.
219 M5 Vurpær Romania
219 L7 Vŭrshets Bulg.
218 I8 Vushtrri Vushtrri Kosovo
160 K6 Vustsye Belarus
219 P4 Vutcani Romania
136 G4 Vuyyuru Andhra Prad. India
201 L6 Vuzenica Slovenia
158 D3 Vuzlove L'vivs'ka Oblast' Ukr.
158 B5 Vuzlove Zakarpats'ka Oblast' Ukr.
160 J7 Vuzlyanka r. Belarus
142 J1 Vvedenka Kazakh.
161 Y5 Vveden'ye Rus. Fed.
233 B7 Vwawa Tanz.
233 B7 Vwaza Game Reserve nature res. Malawi
159 P7 Vyacheslavka Ukr.
197 M2 Vyalikaya Byerastavitsa Belarus
160 H8 Vyalikaya Mazheykava Belarus
160 M8 Vyalikiya Bortniki Belarus
160 J8 Vyalikiya Zhukhavichy Belarus
161 N2 Vyal'ye, Ozero l. Rus. Fed.
138 D9 Vyara Gujarat India
161 N6 Vyarechcha Belarus
160 G9 Vyarkhovichy Belarus
Vyarkhowye Belarus see Ruba
160 L9 Vyatchyn Belarus
Vyatka Rus. Fed. see Kirov
156 J5 Vyatka r. Rus. Fed.
156 J4 Vyatskiye Polyany Rus. Fed.
161 X4 Vyatskoye Rus. Fed.
160 M5 Vyaz Rus. Fed.
122 I5 Vyazemskiy Rus. Fed.
161 R6 Vyaz'ma Rus. Fed.
161 Q6 Vyaz'ma r. Rus. Fed.
156 H4 Vyazniki Rus. Fed.
157 I6 Vyazovka Astrakhanskaya Oblast' Rus. Fed.
142 A2 Vyazovka Saratovskaya Oblast' Rus. Fed.
142 B1 Vyazovka Saratovskaya Oblast' Rus. Fed.
157 H6 Vyazovka Volgogradskaya Oblast' Rus. Fed.
161 W8 Vyazovo Rus. Fed.
159 P2 Vyazovoye Rus. Fed.
160 L1 Vyborg Rus. Fed.
160 L1 Vyborgskiy Zaliv b. Rus. Fed.
156 I3 Vychegda r. Rus. Fed.
156 I3 Vychegodskiy Rus. Fed.
199 I2 Východná Slovakia
199 L2 Východné Karpaty park Slovakia
197 M1 Vydeniai Lith.
197 N4 Vyderta Ukr.
197 M4 Vydranytsya Ukr.
128 I1 Vydrino Rus. Fed.
197 M4 Vydrychi Ukr.
161 O8 Vyeramyeyki Belarus
160 K6 Vyerkhnyadzvinsk Belarus
161 O9 Vyetka Belarus
160 L6 Vyetryna Belarus
161 R8 Vygonichi Rus. Fed.
156 F3 Vygozero, Ozero l. Rus. Fed.
158 E1 Vyhanashchy Belarus
199 H3 Vyhne Slovakia
157 H5 Vyksa Rus. Fed.
182 I1 Vy-lès-Lure France
158 I8 Vylkove Ukr.
158 B5 Vylok Ukr.
156 J3 Vym' r. Rus. Fed.
158 D4 Vynnyky Ukr.
158 C5 Vynohradiv Ukr.
159 M5 Vynohradivka Ukr.
159 K6 Vynohradne Ukr.
159 L7 Vynohradove Khersons'ka Oblast' Ukr.
159 M8 Vynohradove Respublika Krym Ukr.
136 E7 Vypin Island India
161 Q4 Vypolzovo Rus. Fed.
159 M3 Vyrishal'ne Ukr.
161 N2 Vyritsa Rus. Fed.
172 F2 Vyrnwy, Lake Wales U.K.
159 N2 Vyry Ukr.
157 G7 Vyselki Rus. Fed.
158 J3 Vyshcha Dubechnya Ukr.
159 Q4 Vyshche Solone Ukr.
159 N6 Vyshchetarasivka Ukr.
161 X7 Vyshgorod Rus. Fed.
160 K4 Vyshgorodok Rus. Fed.
158 J3 Vyshhorod Ukr.
158 B5 Vyshka Ukr.
161 O9 Vyshkov Rus. Fed.
161 S4 Vyshkovo Rus. Fed.
158 C5 Vyshkovo Ukr.
159 M5 Vyshneve Dnipropetrovs'ka Oblast' Ukr.
158 J3 Vyshneve Kyivs'ka Oblast' Ukr.
161 R5 Vyshnevolotskaya Gryada ridge Rus. Fed.
161 R4 Vyshnevolotskoye Vodokhranilishche resr Rus. Fed.
159 Q1 Vyshneye-Ol'shanoye Rus. Fed.
197 M4 Vyshniv Ukr.
158 E4 Vyshnivets' Ukr.
161 R4 Vyshniy-Volochek Rus. Fed.
158 C4 Vyshnya r. Ukr.
159 M4 Vyshnyaky Ukr.
161 N4 Vyskod' Rus. Fed.
198 G2 Vyškov Czech Rep.
199 K2 Vyšný Mirošov Slovakia
199 K2 Vyšný Orlík Slovakia
198 E2 Vysočina admin. reg. Czech Rep.
198 D3 Vysoká mt. Czech Rep.
198 G3 Vysoká hill Slovakia
158 H3 Vysoka Pich Ukr.
198 F3 Vysoká pri Morave Slovakia
160 G9 Vysokaye Brestskaya Voblasts' Belarus
161 N7 Vysokaye Vitsyebskaya Voblasts' Belarus
159 M7 Vysoke Ukr.
198 F2 Vysoké Mýto Czech Rep.
161 T7 Vysokinichi Rus. Fed.
122 K3 Vysokogorniy Rus. Fed.
159 Q5 Vysokopillya Donets'ka Oblast' Ukr.
159 O4 Vysokopillya Kharkivs'ka Oblast' Ukr.
159 M6 Vysokopillya Khersons'ka Oblast' Ukr.
161 V4 Vysokovo Rus. Fed.
161 T5 Vysokovsk Rus. Fed.
Vysokoye Belarus see Vysokaye
161 R5 Vysokoye Rus. Fed.
160 L1 Vysotsk Rus. Fed.
158 F2 Vysots'k Ukr.
201 J2 Vyšší Brod Czech Rep.
158 I2 Vystupovychi Ukr.
161 T1 Vytegra Rus. Fed.
153 R3 Vyvenka Rus. Fed.
156 I3 Vyya r. Rus. Fed.
158 D2 Vyzhivka r. Ukr.
158 E5 Vyzhnytsya Ukr.
160 I6 Vyžuona r. Lith.
197 I1 Vzmor'ye Rus. Fed.

W

229 F4 W, Parcs Nationaux du nat. park Niger
228 E4 Wa Ghana
190 I1 Waabs Ger.
232 D4 Waajid Somalia
191 J7 Waake Ger.
195 L6 Waakirchen Ger.
195 J6 Waal Ger.
186 G5 Waal r. Neth.
187 H6 Waalre Neth.
186 H5 Waalwijk Neth.
106 F5 Waanyi/Garawa Aboriginal Land res. N.T. Austr.
186 G3 Waarland Neth.
187 E6 Waarschoot Belgium
187 F6 Waasmunster Belgium
232 B2 Waat Sudan
113 J8 Wabag P.N.G.
248 B3 Wabakimi Lake Ont. Can.
248 B3 Wabakimi Provincial Park Ont. Can.
147 M4 Wabal well Oman
246 H4 Wabamun Alta Can.
246 H4 Wabamun Lake Alta Can.
246 H3 Wabasca r. Alta Can.
246 H4 Wabasca-Desmarais Alta Can.
254 E5 Wabash IN U.S.A.
256 A8 Wabash OH U.S.A.
260 K7 Wabash r. IN U.S.A.
250 B5 Wabasha MN U.S.A.
248 C3 Wabassi r. Ont. Can.
251 J1 Wabatongushi Lake Ont. Can.
250 F4 Wabeno WI U.S.A.
191 H8 Wabern Ger.
248 A3 Wabigoon Lake Ont. Can.
247 L4 Wabowden Man. Can.
147 H2 Wabrah well Saudi Arabia
196 G2 Wąbrzeźno Pol.
131 K2 Wabu Anhui China
248 C2 Wabuk Point Ont. Can.
249 H2 Wabush Nfld and Lab. Can.
249 H2 Wabush Lake Nfld and Lab. Can.
255 H9 Waccamaw r. SC U.S.A.
255 H8 Waccamaw, Lake NC U.S.A.
255 F11 Waccasassa Bay FL U.S.A.
257 J11 Wachapreague VA U.S.A.
201 L3 Wachau reg. Austria
194 E3 Wachenheim an der Weinstraße Ger.
126 B5 Wachi Japan
232 C3 Wach'īlē Eth.
192 G5 Wachow Ger.
187 E6 Wachtebeke Belgium
191 H10 Wächtersbach Ger.
257 N6 Wachusett Reservoir MA U.S.A.
190 H2 Wacken Ger.
195 M3 Wackersdorf Ger.
249 H3 Waco Que. Can.
261 G10 Waco TX U.S.A.
260 F6 Waconda Lake KS U.S.A.
250 B5 Wacouta MN U.S.A.
127 L5 Wada Japan
224 E6 Wada'a Sudan
126 B6 Wada-misaki pt Japan
127 H3 Wada-tōge pass Japan
106 F3 Wada Wadalla Aboriginal Land res. N.T. Austr.
126 A5 Wadayama Japan
224 E6 Wad Banda Sudan
105 L7 Wadbilliga National Park N.S.W. Austr.
224 C2 Waddān Libya
224 B2 Waddān, Jabal hills Libya
265 T8 Waddell Dam AZ U.S.A.
186 G2 Waddeneilanden is Neth.
Wadden Islands Neth. see Waddeneilanden
186 G3 Waddenzee sea chan. Neth.
173 K4 Waddesdon Buckinghamshire, England U.K.
190 K4 Waddeweitz Ger.
104 F5 Waddikee S.A. Austr.
171 P7 Waddington Lincolnshire, England U.K.
246 E5 Waddington, Mount B.C. Can.
169 I8 Waddingtown Ireland
186 G4 Waddinxveen Neth.
107 N8 Waddy Point Qld Austr.
172 C6 Wadebridge Cornwall, England U.K.
232 B2 Wadega Sudan
247 K5 Wadena Sask. Can.
260 H2 Wadena MN U.S.A.
140 C7 Wad en Nail Sudan
212 F1 Wädenswil Switz.
194 B2 Wadern Ger.
191 F7 Wadersloh Ger.
255 G8 Wadesboro NC U.S.A.
106 B3 Wadeye N.T. Austr.
136 C3 Wadgaon Mahar. India
138 F9 Wadgaon Mahar. India
194 B3 Wadgassen Ger.
145 L8 Wadh Pak.
225 G5 Wad Hamid Sudan
230 E2 Wad Hassib Sudan
173 M5 Wadhurst East Sussex, England U.K.
138 C8 Wadhwan Gujarat India
Wadhwan Gujarat India see Surendranagar
136 E4 Wadi Karnataka India
131 I2 Wadian Henan China
150 D7 Wādī as Sīr Jordan
150 B10 Wādī Fayrān Egypt
Wâdi Gimâl Island Egypt see Wādī Jimāl, Jazīrat
225 F4 Wadi Halfa Sudan
146 E4 Wādī Ḩammah Saudi Arabia
146 B3 Wādī Jimāl, Jazīrat i. Egypt
150 D8 Wādī Mūsá Jordan
258 G5 Wading r. NJ U.S.A.
259 J3 Wading River NY U.S.A.
197 H4 Wadlew Pol.
225 G6 Wad Medani Sudan
124 □F19 Wadomari Nansei-shotō Japan
197 H6 Wadowice Pol.
197 J5 Wadowice Górne Pol.
264 M2 Wadsworth NV U.S.A.
256 D7 Wadsworth OH U.S.A.
Wadu i. S. Male Maldives see Vaadhu
Wadu Channel Maldives see Vaadhu Channel
236 E10 Waenhuiskrans S. Africa
286 P1 Waesche, Mount Antarctica
129 R7 Wafangdian Liaoning China
230 D5 Wafania Dem. Rep. Congo
Wafra Kuwait see Al Wafrah
124 S7 Waga-gawa r. Japan
138 E4 Wagah Punjab India
196 G3 Waganiec Pol.
190 G5 Wagenfeld Ger.
190 K5 Wagenhoff Ger.
186 I5 Wageningen Neth.
275 G3 Wageningen Suriname
243 J3 Wager Bay Nunavut Can.
105 K6 Wagga Wagga N.S.W. Austr.
138 D9 Waghai Gujarat India
194 F3 Waghäusel Ger.
109 D12 Wagin W.A. Austr.
195 N6 Waging am See Ger.
195 N6 Waginger See l. Ger.
212 F1 Wägitaler See l. Switz.
246 D4 Waglisla B.C. Can.
278 E5 Wagner Brazil
260 F4 Wagner SD U.S.A.
261 H7 Wagoner OK U.S.A.
263 L8 Wagon Mound NM U.S.A.
200 H5 Wagrain Austria
190 J2 Wagrien reg. Ger.
196 F3 Wągrowiec Pol.
145 O5 Wah Pak.
115 F5 Wahai Seram Indon.
229 F5 Wahala Togo
224 D2 Wāḩāt Jālū Libya
230 F2 Wahda state Sudan
249 G2 Wahemen, Lac l. Que. Can.
264 □C12 Wahiawā HI U.S.A.
147 N5 Wahībah, Ramlat al des. Oman
162 □ Wahlenbergfjorden inlet Svalbard
191 I8 Wahlhausen Ger.
193 H7 Wahlsdorf Ger.
190 J3 Wahlstedt Ger.
260 G5 Wahoo NE U.S.A.
260 G2 Wahpeton ND U.S.A.
Wahran Alg. see Oran
190 K5 Wahrenholz Ger.
265 S3 Wah Wah Mountains UT U.S.A.
136 C4 Wai Mahar. India
264 □D12 Waiāhole HI U.S.A.
264 □E13 Waiakoa HI U.S.A.
264 □B11 Wai'ale'ale mt. HI U.S.A.
264 □C12 Wai'ale'e HI U.S.A.
264 □C12 Waialua HI U.S.A.
264 □C12 Waialua Bay HI U.S.A.
264 □C12 Wai'anae HI U.S.A.
264 □C12 Wai'anae Range mts HI U.S.A.
102 M4 Waiapu r. North I. N.Z.
102 K7 Waiaruhe North I. N.Z.
103 H9 Waiau South I. N.Z.
102 L5 Waiau r. North I. N.Z.
103 B13 Waiau r. South I. N.Z.
103 H9 Waiau r. South I. N.Z.
194 G4 Waiblingen Ger.
194 F3 Waibstadt Ger.
195 N2 Waidhaus Ger.
195 K4 Waidhofen Ger.
201 L2 Waidhofen an der Thaya Austria
201 K4 Waidhofen an der Ybbs Austria
115 F4 Waigama Papua Indon.
115 G4 Waigeo i. Papua Indon.
195 I2 Waigolshausen Ger.
103 E11 Waihao Downs South I. N.Z.
102 H1 Waiharara North I. N.Z.
102 J4 Waiharoa North I. N.Z.
102 J3 Waiheke Island North I. N.Z.
102 J4 Waihi North I. N.Z.
102 J4 Waihi Beach North I. N.Z.
102 K4 Waihi Estuary North I. N.Z.
103 E13 Waihola, Lake South I. N.Z.
102 J4 Waihou r. North I. N.Z.
102 L6 Waihua North I. N.Z.
230 E5 Waika Dem. Rep. Congo
115 A8 Waikabubak Sumba Indon.
103 C12 Waikaia South I. N.Z.
103 C12 Waikaia r. South I. N.Z.
103 D12 Waikaka South I. N.Z.
103 J7 Waikanae North I. N.Z.
264 □D12 Waikāne HI U.S.A.
264 □E13 Waikapu HI U.S.A.
102 J4 Waikare, Lake North I. N.Z.
102 L5 Waikareiti, Lake North I. N.Z.
102 K5 Waikaremoana, Lake North I. N.Z.
102 I4 Waikaretu North I. N.Z.
103 G9 Waikari South I. N.Z.
102 I4 Waikato admin. reg. North I. N.Z.
102 I4 Waikato r. North I. N.Z.
103 D13 Waikawa South I. N.Z.
102 L4 Waikawa Point North I. N.Z.
102 J5 Waikeria North I. N.Z.
104 G6 Waikerie S.A. Austr.
264 □F14 Waiki'i HI U.S.A.
264 □D12 Waikīkī Beach HI U.S.A.
102 K5 Waikirikiri North I. N.Z.
115 C8 Waiklibang Flores Indon.
103 D13 Waikoikoi South I. N.Z.
102 L6 Waikokopa North I. N.Z.
103 E12 Waikouaiti South I. N.Z.
101 □7a Wailotua Viti Levu Fiji
264 □B11 Wailua HI U.S.A.
264 □E13 Wailua HI U.S.A.
264 □E13 Wailuku HI U.S.A.
103 C13 Waimahake South I. N.Z.
103 G10 Waimakariri r. South I. N.Z.
102 L5 Waimana North I. N.Z.
264 □D12 Waimānalo HI U.S.A.
264 □D12 Waimānalo Beach HI U.S.A.
103 F8 Waimangaroa South I. N.Z.
102 K6 Waimarama North I. N.Z.
103 F8 Waimarie South I. N.Z.
103 F11 Waimate South I. N.Z.
102 H2 Waimatenui North I. N.Z.
102 I3 Waimauku North I. N.Z.
264 □B12 Waimea HI U.S.A.
264 □C12 Waimea HI U.S.A.
264 □F13 Waimea HI U.S.A.
264 □C12 Waimea Bay HI U.S.A.
115 B5 Waimenda Sulawesi Indon.
187 J8 Waimes Belgium
195 I5 Wain Ger.
256 F6 Wainfleet Ont. Can.
171 R7 Wainfleet All Saints Lincolnshire, England U.K.
136 F3 Wainganga r. India
115 B8 Waingapu Sumba Indon.
103 J7 Waingawa North I. N.Z.
172 C6 Wainhouse Corner Cornwall, England U.K.
275 G2 Waini Point Guyana
103 F11 Wainono Lagoon South I. N.Z.
247 I4 Wainwright Alta Can.
244 H1 Wainwright AK U.S.A.
102 L5 Waioeka r. North I. N.Z.
102 I2 Waiotira North I. N.Z.
102 J6 Waiouru North I. N.Z.
102 J4 Waipa r. North I. N.Z.
103 D13 Waipahi South I. N.Z.
264 □C12 Waipahu HI U.S.A.
102 L5 Waipaoa r. North I. N.Z.
103 C13 Waipapa Point South I. N.Z.
103 G10 Waipara South I. N.Z.
102 K6 Waipawa North I. N.Z.
102 I4 Waipipi North I. N.Z.
102 I2 Waipu North I. N.Z.
102 K6 Waipukurau North I. N.Z.
102 K5 Wairakei North I. N.Z.
103 J8 Wairarapa, Lake North I. N.Z.
103 I8 Wairau r. South I. N.Z.
103 H8 Wairau Valley South I. N.Z.
102 L6 Wairoa North I. N.Z.
102 I3 Wairoa r. North I. N.Z.
102 L6 Wairoa r. North I. N.Z.
115 C8 Wairunu Flores Indon.
115 G4 Waisai Papua Indon.
195 K2 Waischenfeld Ger.
131 L4 Waishe Zhejiang China
102 K5 Waitahanui North I. N.Z.
103 D12 Waitahuna South I. N.Z.
102 J4 Waitakaruru North I. N.Z.
103 F11 Waitaki South I. N.Z.
103 F11 Waitaki r. South I. N.Z.
102 □ Waitangi Chatham Is S. Pacific Ocean
103 E10 Waitangitaona r. South I. N.Z.
102 I5 Waitara North I. N.Z.
103 E12 Waitati South I. N.Z.
104 □3 Waite, Mount hill S. Pacific Ocean
106 E7 Waite River N.T. Austr.
102 J4 Waitoa North I. N.Z.
102 J5 Waitomo Caves North I. N.Z.
102 I6 Waitotara North I. N.Z.
102 I6 Waitotari r. North I. N.Z.
262 E3 Waitsburg WA U.S.A.
102 I4 Waiuku North I. N.Z.
103 D13 Waiwera South South I. N.Z.
115 F5 Waiya Seram Indon.
131 L5 Waiyang Fujian China
101 □7 Waiyevo Taveuni Fiji
201 I3 Waizenkirchen Austria
146 G6 Wajīd, Jabal al hills Saudi Arabia
125 L13 Wajiki Japan
125 N9 Wajima Japan
232 D4 Wajir Kenya
230 D4 Waka Équateur Dem. Rep. Congo
230 D5 Waka Équateur Dem. Rep. Congo
115 B8 Waka Flores Indon.
230 A5 Waka, Parc National de la nat. park Ngounié Gabon
115 E5 Waka, Tanjung pt Indon.
251 L2 Wakami Lake Ont. Can.
103 H8 Wakapuaka South I. N.Z.
125 L11 Wakasa Japan
126 C4 Wakasa-wan b. Japan
126 C4 Wakasa-wan Kokutei-kōen park Japan
103 C12 Wakatipu, Lake South I. N.Z.
115 C6 Wakatobi, Taman Nasional nat. park Indon.
251 K3 Wakatoma Lake Ont. Can.
247 J4 Wakaw Sask. Can.
101 □7 Wakaya i. Fiji
106 F5 Wakaya Aboriginal Land res. N.T. Austr.
126 B7 Wakayama Japan
126 B8 Wakayama pref. Japan
124 S8 Wakayanagi Japan
Wake Atoll N. Pacific Ocean see Wake Island
260 F6 WaKeeney KS U.S.A.
251 S4 Wakefield Que. Can.
270 □ Wakefield Jamaica
103 H8 Wakefield South I. N.Z.
171 N6 Wakefield West Yorkshire, England U.K.
250 E3 Wakefield MI U.S.A.
256 B10 Wakefield OH U.S.A.
258 C5 Wakefield PA U.S.A.
257 N7 Wakefield RI U.S.A.
256 I12 Wakefield VA U.S.A.
Wakeham Que. Can. see Kangiqsujuaq
97 F2 Wake Island N. Pacific Ocean
118 B6 Wakema Myanmar
145 O3 Wakhan reg. Afgh.
125 L12 Waki Japan
124 R5 Wakinosawa Japan
146 D8 Wakiro watercourse Eritrea
232 B4 Wakiso Uganda
124 S1 Wakkanai Japan
237 O3 Wakkerstroom S. Africa
105 J6 Wakool N.S.W. Austr.
105 I6 Wakool r. N.S.W. Austr.
249 H2 Wakuach, Lac l. Que. Can.
231 B7 Waku-Kungo Angola
124 S8 Wakuya Japan
248 D3 Wakwayowkastic r. Ont. Can.
100 □6 Walade Solomon Is
108 F7 Walagunya Aboriginal Reserve W.A. Austr.
136 F6 Walajapet Tamil Nadu India
193 D6 Walbeck Ger.
173 P3 Walberswick Suffolk, England U.K.
196 E5 Wałbrzych Pol.
191 I8 Walburg Ger.
105 M4 Walcha N.S.W. Austr.
195 K6 Walchensee l. Ger.
200 F4 Walchsee Austria
200 F4 Walchsee l. Austria
190 D5 Walchum Ger.
262 K6 Walcott WY U.S.A.
108 H4 Walcott Inlet W.A. Austr.
187 F8 Walcourt Belgium
196 E2 Wałcz Pol.
194 G6 Wald Baden-Württemberg Ger.
195 M3 Wald Bayern Ger.
194 F7 Wald Switz.
194 F5 Waldachtal Ger.
201 K3 Waldaist r. Austria
194 D2 Waldböckelheim Ger.
191 D9 Waldbreitbach Ger.
191 E9 Waldbröl Ger.
194 H2 Waldbrunn Ger.
191 F9 Waldbrunn-Lahr Ger.
194 H6 Waldburg Ger.
109 D8 Waldburg Range mts W.A. Austr.
193 I7 Walddrehna Ger.
191 H8 Waldeck Ger.
201 N4 Waldegg Austria
259 G1 Walden NY U.S.A.
194 G4 Waldenbuch Ger.
194 H3 Waldenburg Baden-Württemberg Ger.
193 G9 Waldenburg Sachsen Ger.
Waldenburg Pol. see Wałbrzych
212 D1 Waldenburg Switz.
195 M3 Walderbach Ger.
195 M2 Waldershof Ger.
173 N5 Walderslade Medway, England U.K.
194 D3 Waldfischbach-Burgalben Ger.
201 L2 Waldhausen Austria
201 K3 Waldhausen im Strudengau Austria
193 H8 Waldheim Ger.
201 J3 Walding Austria
191 I8 Waldkappel Ger.
194 D5 Waldkirch Ger.
195 P4 Waldkirchen Ger.
195 M5 Waldkraiburg Ger.
194 F2 Wald-Michelbach Ger.
194 C3 Waldmohr Ger.
195 N3 Waldmünchen Ger.
255 F11 Waldo FL U.S.A.
250 G6 Waldo WI U.S.A.
257 □P4 Waldoboro ME U.S.A.
172 D6 Waldon r. England U.K.
256 I10 Waldorf MD U.S.A.
196 G2 Wałdowo-Szlacheckie Pol.
262 B4 Waldport OR U.S.A.
194 B2 Waldrach Ger.
261 H8 Waldron AR U.S.A.
250 J8 Waldron MI U.S.A.
287 H2 Waldron, Cape Antarctica
193 F10 Waldsassen Ger.
194 E6 Waldshut Ger.
212 G1 Waldstatt Switz.
194 H4 Waldstetten Baden-Württemberg Ger.
195 I5 Waldstetten Bayern Ger.
195 M2 Waldthurn Ger.
201 L3 Waldviertel reg. Austria
115 C4 Walea, Selat sea chan. Indon.
115 C4 Waleabahi i. Indon.
115 C4 Waleakodi i. Indon.
109 D11 Walebing W.A. Austr.
130 C4 Walêg Sichuan China
212 G1 Walenstadt Switz.
172 E3 Wales admin. div. U.K.
244 E2 Wales AK U.S.A.
228 E4 Walewale Ghana
187 J9 Walferdange Lux.
105 L4 Walgett N.S.W. Austr.
286 Q1 Walgreen Coast Antarctica
250 H6 Walhalla MI U.S.A.
260 G1 Walhalla ND U.S.A.
255 F8 Walhalla SC U.S.A.
145 M7 Walhar Pak.
230 F5 Walikale Dem. Rep. Congo
145 J5 Walima Afgh.
109 C10 Walkaway W.A. Austr.
192 G3 Walkendorf Ger.
191 K7 Walkenried Ger.
106 E2 Walker r. N.T. Austr.
106 D8 Walker watercourse N.T. Austr.
250 I6 Walker MI U.S.A.
260 H2 Walker MN U.S.A.
264 N3 Walker r. NV U.S.A.
236 D10 Walker Bay S. Africa
255 H12 Walker Cay i. Bahamas
107 H4 Walker Creek r. Qld Austr.
247 L4 Walker Lake l. Man. Can.
264 N3 Walker Lake NV U.S.A.
244 I2 Walker Lake AK U.S.A.
264 N3 Walker Lake l. NV U.S.A.
286 R2 Walker Mountains Antarctica
264 N3 Walker River Indian Reservation res. NV U.S.A.
256 H9 Walkersville MD U.S.A.
256 E10 Walkersville WV U.S.A.
251 M5 Walkerton Ont. Can.
250 H8 Walkerton IN U.S.A.
259 G1 Walker Valley NY U.S.A.
260 D3 Wall SD U.S.A.
109 D7 Wall, Mount hill W.A. Austr.
109 B10 Wallabi Group is W.A. Austr.
107 H3 Wallaby Island Qld Austr.
262 F3 Wallace ID U.S.A.
255 I8 Wallace NC U.S.A.
260 E5 Wallace NE U.S.A.
256 C12 Wallace VA U.S.A.
248 D5 Wallaceburg Ont. Can.
103 C13 Wallacetown South I. N.Z.
108 F5 Wallal Downs W.A. Austr.
109 D11 Wallambin, Lake salt flat W.A. Austr.
105 M3 Wallangarra Qld Austr.
104 F5 Wallaroo S.A. Austr.
171 K7 Wallasey Merseyside, England U.K.
107 M8 Wallaville Qld Austr.
262 E3 Walla Walla WA U.S.A.
194 F3 Walldorf Baden-Württemberg Ger.
194 F1 Walldorf Hessen Ger.
191 J9 Walldorf Thüringen Ger.
194 G2 Walldürn Ger.
236 B6 Wallekraal S. Africa
105 L6 Wallendbeen N.S.W. Austr.
193 D10 Wallenfels Ger.
258 E2 Wallenpaupack, Lake PA U.S.A.
212 G1 Wallensee l. Switz.
195 N4 Wallerfing Ger.
201 O4 Wallern im Burgenland Austria
195 N4 Wallersdorf Ger.
200 H4 Wallersee l. Austria
195 I4 Wallerstein Ger.
195 K6 Wallgau Ger.
195 I3 Wallhausen Baden-Württemberg Ger.
194 D2 Wallhausen Rheinland-Pfalz Ger.
102 K7 Wallingford North I. N.Z.
173 J4 Wallingford Oxfordshire, England U.K.
259 J2 Wallingford CT U.S.A.
257 M5 Wallingford VT U.S.A.
Wallis canton Switz. see Valais
99 I3 Wallis, Îles is Wallis and Futuna Is
99 I3 Wallis and Futuna Islands terr. S. Pacific Ocean
194 F7 Wallisellen Switz.
Wallis et Futuna, Îles terr. S. Pacific Ocean see Wallis and Futuna Islands
Wallis Islands Wallis and Futuna Is see Wallis, Îles
259 G1 Wallkill NY U.S.A.
259 H1 Wallkill r. NY U.S.A.
257 J11 Wallops Island VA U.S.A.
262 F4 Wallowa OR U.S.A.
262 F4 Wallowa Mountains OR U.S.A.
168 □M2 Walls Shetland, Scotland U.K.
190 H1 Wallsbüll Ger.
171 N4 Wallsend Tyne and Wear, England U.K.
105 K9 Walls of Jerusalem National Park Tas. Austr.
192 D5 Wallstawe Ger.
191 F10 Walluf Ger.
262 E3 Wallula WA U.S.A.
107 L9 Wallumbilla Qld Austr.
173 O5 Walmer Kent, England U.K.
247 I2 Walmsley Lake N.W.T. Can.
171 K5 Walney, Isle of i. England U.K.
250 E8 Walnut IL U.S.A.
256 H8 Walnut Bottom PA U.S.A.
264 J4 Walnut Creek CA U.S.A.
260 F6 Walnut Creek r. KS U.S.A.
264 K3 Walnut Grove CA U.S.A.
258 D3 Walnutport PA U.S.A.
261 J7 Walnut Ridge AR U.S.A.
139 P5 Walong Arun. Prad. India
193 K7 Wałowice Pol.
195 L5 Walpertskirchen Ger.
109 D13 Walpole W.A. Austr.
257 M5 Walpole NH U.S.A.
100 □5 Walpole, Île i. New Caledonia
197 J2 Wałpusza r. Pol.
244 E4 Walrus Island AK U.S.A.
244 G4 Walrus Islands AK U.S.A.
200 G4 Wals Austria
173 I2 Walsall West Midlands, England U.K.
195 J2 Walsdorf Ger.
263 L8 Walsenburg CO U.S.A.
107 I4 Walsh r. Qld Austr.
261 D7 Walsh CO U.S.A.
192 G5 Walsleben Ger.
173 M2 Walsoken Cambridgeshire, England U.K.
190 I5 Walsrode Ger.
197 H1 Wałsza r. Pol.
137 H4 Waltair Andhra Prad. India
195 I6 Waltenhofen Ger.
255 G9 Walterboro SC U.S.A.
255 E10 Walter F. George Reservoir AL/GA U.S.A.
261 F8 Walters OK U.S.A.
191 K9 Waltershausen Ger.
105 J3 Walter's Range hills Qld Austr.
261 K9 Walthall MS U.S.A.
251 R4 Waltham Que. Can.
171 Q6 Waltham North East Lincolnshire, England U.K.
257 N6 Waltham MA U.S.A.
257 □Q4 Waltham ME U.S.A.
173 M4 Waltham Abbey Essex, England U.K.
173 K2 Waltham on the Wolds Leicestershire, England U.K.
195 K4 Walting Ger.
250 H9 Walton IN U.S.A.
257 J6 Walton NY U.S.A.
256 D10 Walton WV U.S.A.
270 D5 Walton Bank sea feature Jamaica
173 L5 Walton-on-Thames Surrey, England U.K.
173 O4 Walton on the Naze Essex, England U.K.
Walvisbaai Namibia see Walvis Bay
234 B4 Walvis Bay Namibia
234 B4 Walvis Bay b. Namibia
288 I8 Walvis Ridge sea feature S. Atlantic Ocean
109 E11 Walyahmoing hill W.A. Austr.
145 N4 Wama Afgh.
232 A4 Wamala, Lake Uganda
231 E6 Wamaza Dem. Rep. Congo
230 D5 Wamba Équateur Dem. Rep. Congo
230 E4 Wamba Orientale Dem. Rep. Congo
231 C5 Wamba r. Dem. Rep. Congo
229 H4 Wamba Nigeria
205 K5 Wamba Spain
106 C3 Wambardi Aboriginal Land res. N.T. Austr.
260 G6 Wamego KS U.S.A.
113 I7 Wamena Papua Indon.
233 C6 Wami r. Tanz.
115 E5 Wamlana Buru Indon.
106 E4 Wampaya Aboriginal Land res. Qld Austr.
266 □Q10 Wampusirpi Hond.
262 K6 Wamsutter WY U.S.A.
115 E5 Wamulan Buru Indon.
145 M5 Wana Pak.
105 J3 Wanaaring N.S.W. Austr.
103 D11 Wanaka South I. N.Z.
103 D11 Wanaka, Lake South I. N.Z.
259 G4 Wanamassa NJ U.S.A.
258 C2 Wanamie PA U.S.A.
131 J5 Wan'an Jiangxi China
248 D4 Wanapitei Lake Ont. Can.
259 G2 Wanaque NJ U.S.A.
259 G2 Wanaque Reservoir NJ U.S.A.
115 C6 Wanasabari Sulawesi Indon.
104 H6 Wanbi S.A. Austr.
130 C5 Wanbi Yunnan China
103 E12 Wanbrow, Cape South I. N.Z.
255 J8 Wanchese NC U.S.A.
115 C6 Wanci Sulawesi Indon.
282 G2 Wanda Arg.
109 C10 Wandana Nature Reserve W.A. Austr.
122 H6 Wanda Shan mts China
247 H4 Wandering River Alta Can.
191 K9 Wandersleben Ger.
190 H1 Wanderup Ger.
130 B6 Wanding Yunnan China
Wandingzhen Yunnan China see Wanding
Wandiwash Tamil Nadu India see Vandavasi
103 H9 Wandle Downs South I. N.Z.
192 H5 Wandlitz Ger.
123 E11 Wando S. Korea
107 L9 Wandoan Qld Austr.
173 L5 Wandsworth Greater London, England U.K.
201 L3 Wang Austria
118 D6 Wang, Mae Nam r. Thai.
230 F4 Wanga Dem. Rep. Congo
102 J6 Wanganui North I. N.Z.
102 I6 Wanganui r. North I. N.Z.
103 E10 Wanganui r. South I. N.Z.
105 K7 Wangaratta Vic. Austr.
104 E6 Wangary S.A. Austr.
130 F2 Wangcang Sichuan China
131 I4 Wangcheng Hunan China
129 Q8 Wangcun Shandong China
Wangda Xizang China see Zogang
133 I12 Wangdain Xizang China
139 L6 Wangdi Phodrang Bhutan
129 N7 Wangdu Hebei China
191 I7 Wangelnstedt Ger.
190 K2 Wangels Ger.
212 D1 Wangen Switz.
194 H6 Wangen im Allgäu Ger.
190 E3 Wangerooge Ger.
190 E3 Wangerooge i. Ger.
115 B9 Wanggamet, Gunung mt. Sumba Indon.
128 E8 Wang Gaxun Qinghai China
Wanggezhuang Shandong China see Jiaonan
130 E2 Wangguan Gansu China
212 F1 Wängi Switz.
115 C6 Wangiwangi i. Indon.
131 K3 Wangjiang Anhui China
129 K8 Wangjiawan Shaanxi China
266 □Q10 Wangkibila Hond.
122 E5 Wangkui Heilong. China
200 C5 Wängle Austria
Wang Mai Khon Thai. see Sawankhalok
130 G7 Wangmao Guangxi China
130 F6 Wangmo Guizhou China
Wangolodougou Côte d'Ivoire see Ouangolodougou
122 F7 Wangqing Jilin China
Wangying Jiangsu China see Huaiyin
246 G4 Wanham Alta Can.
275 H3 Wanhatti Suriname

118 D4 Wan Hsa-la Myanmar
230 E4 Wanie-Rukula Dem. Rep. Congo
106 C3 Wanimiyn Aboriginal Land res. N.T. Austr.
109 F9 Wanjarri Nature Reserve W.A. Austr.
138 C8 Wankaner Gujarat India
190 J2 Wankendorf Ger.
Wankie Zimbabwe see Hwange
232 E4 Wanlaweyn Somalia
190 G3 Wanna Ger.
109 J10 Wanna Lakes salt flat W.A. Austr.
109 C11 Wanneroo W.A. Austr.
131 K4 Wannian Jiangxi China
130 H9 Wanning Hainan China
126 E5 Wanouchi Japan
186 I5 Wanroij Neth.
129 L9 Wanrong Shanxi China
130 G5 Wanshan Guizhou China
131 I8 Wanshan Qundao is Guangdong China
193 E8 Wansleben am See Ger.
102 K7 Wanstead North I. N.Z.
173 J4 Wantage Oxfordshire, England U.K.
259 H3 Wantagh NY U.S.A.
251 N3 Wanup Ont. Can.
Wanxian China see Wanzhou
130 G2 Wanyuan Sichuan China
131 J4 Wanzai Jiangxi China
187 H7 Wanze Belgium
Wanzhi Anhui China see Wuhu
130 G3 Wanzhou Chongqing China
256 A8 Wapakoneta OH U.S.A.
247 J4 Wapawekka Lake Sask. Can.
186 J4 Wapenveld Neth.
197 H2 Wąpiersk Pol.
248 B3 Wapikaimaski Lake Ont. Can.
248 B2 Wapikopa Lake Ont. Can.
246 G4 Wapiti r. Alta Can.
197 I2 Waplewo Pol.
196 D2 Wapnica Pol.
196 F3 Wapno Pol.
115 E5 Wapotih Buru Indon.
261 J7 Wappapello Lake resr MO U.S.A.
259 H1 Wappinger Creek r. NY U.S.A.
259 H1 Wappingers Falls NY U.S.A.
260 J5 Wapsipinicon r. IA U.S.A.
243 I4 Wapusk National Park Man. Can.
130 D2 Waqên Sichuan China
150 E7 Waqf aş Şawwān, Jibāl hills Jordan
149 K8 Wāqişah well Iraq
147 I4 Waqr well Saudi Arabia
146 G7 Waqr Maryamah well Yemen
256 D11 War WV U.S.A.
126 F4 Wara Japan
230 F2 Warab Sudan
230 F2 Warab state Sudan
127 K4 Warabi Japan
232 D4 Waradi waterhole Kenya
145 L8 Warah Pak.
232 E3 Warandab Eth.
136 F4 Warangal Andhra Prad. India
138 H9 Waraseoni Madh. Prad. India
105 J9 Waratah Tas. Austr.
147 I1 Warbah, Jazīrat i. Iraq
191 K6 Warberg Ger.
173 L3 Warboys Cambridgeshire, England U.K.
107 I8 Warbreccan Qld Austr.
246 H4 Warburg Alta Can.
191 H8 Warburg Ger.
191 H8 Warburger Börde reg. Ger.
105 J7 Warburton Vic. Austr.
109 I9 Warburton W.A. Austr.
104 F2 Warburton watercourse S.A. Austr.
237 O2 Warburton S. Africa
109 I9 Warburton Aboriginal Reserve W.A. Austr.
247 I2 Warburton Bay N.W.T. Can.
109 I8 Warburton Range hills W.A. Austr.
145 O5 Warcha Pak.
187 I8 Warche r. Belgium
171 M4 Warcop Cumbria, England U.K.
179 K5 Warcq France
107 K9 Ward watercourse Qld Austr.
103 I8 Ward South I. N.Z.
286 T2 Ward, Mount Antarctica
103 B12 Ward, Mount South I. N.Z.
103 D10 Ward, Mount South I. N.Z.
145 M4 Wardag prov. Afgh.
104 F6 Wardang Island S.A. Austr.
232 D4 Wardeglo waterhole Kenya
237 M3 Warden S. Africa
190 F4 Wardenburg Ger.
138 G9 Wardha Mahar. India
136 F3 Wardha r. India
168 J5 Ward Hill Scotland U.K.
217 □ Wardija, Il-Ponta tal- pt Gozo Malta
217 □ Wardija Ridge Malta
173 J3 Wardington Oxfordshire, England U.K.
168 □N2 Ward of Bressay hill Scotland U.K.
192 F3 Wardow Ger.
171 L5 Ward's Stone hill England U.K.
246 E3 Ware B.C. Can.
173 L4 Ware Hertfordshire, England U.K.
257 M6 Ware MA U.S.A.
187 D7 Waregem Belgium
172 H6 Wareham Dorset, England U.K.
257 O7 Wareham MA U.S.A.
187 H7 Waremme Belgium
192 G3 Waren Ger.
191 E7 Warendorf Ger.
186 K2 Warffum Neth.
Wargili i. S. Male Maldives see Vaagali
107 M7 Warginburra Peninsula Qld Austr.
Wargla Alg. see Ouargla
173 K5 Wargrave Wokingham, England U.K.
232 E2 War Gunbi waterhole Somalia
105 M3 Warialda N.S.W. Austr.
145 L10 Wari Creek inlet Pak.
107 M1 Wari Island P.N.G.
192 E3 Warin Ger.
118 G7 Warin Chamrap Thai.
244 G2 Waring Mountains AK U.S.A.
169 J4 Waringstown Northern Ireland U.K.
171 M3 Wark Northumberland, England U.K.
197 J4 Warka Pol.
102 I3 Warkworth North I. N.Z.
171 N3 Warkworth Northumberland, England U.K.
232 E2 War Idaad Somalia
Warli Sichuan China see Walêg
173 L5 Warlingham Surrey, England U.K.
178 E3 Warloy-Baillon France
196 G2 Warlubie Pol.
247 J4 Warman Sask. Can.
234 C6 Warmbad Namibia
195 L2 Warmensteinach Ger.
178 H5 Warmeriville France
236 D3 Warmfontein Namibia
165 Q7 Warmia reg. Pol.
243 P2 Warming Island i. Greenland
173 J3 Warmington Warwickshire, England U.K.
197 I2 Warmińsko-Mazurskie prov. Pol.
172 H5 Warminster Wiltshire, England U.K.
258 E4 Warminster PA U.S.A.
186 G4 Warmond Neth.
191 G6 Warmsen Ger.
265 P3 Warm Springs NV U.S.A.
256 F10 Warm Springs VA U.S.A.
262 D4 Warm Springs Indian Reservation res. OR U.S.A.
236 E9 Warmwaterberg S. Africa
236 E9 Warmwaterberg mts S. Africa
192 F2 Warnemünde Ger.
247 H5 Warner Alta Can.
257 N5 Warner NH U.S.A.
262 E5 Warner Lakes OR U.S.A.
262 D6 Warner Mountains CA U.S.A.
255 F9 Warner Robins GA U.S.A.
264 P8 Warner Springs CA U.S.A.
277 E4 Warnes Bol.
187 C7 Warneton Belgium
195 L6 Warngau Ger.
173 L5 Warnham West Sussex, England U.K.
196 C2 Warnice Zachodniopomorskie Pol.
192 K5 Warnice Zachodniopomorskie Pol.
196 E2 Warnino Pol.
192 E3 Warnow Ger.
192 F2 Warnow r. Ger.
186 J4 Warnsveld Neth.
136 E3 Waronda Mahar. India
109 C12 Waroona W.A. Austr.
138 G9 Warora Mahar. India
190 H5 Warpe Ger.
107 M9 Warra Qld Austr.
106 E6 Warrabri Aboriginal Land res. N.T. Austr.
105 I7 Warracknabeal Vic. Austr.
105 M6 Warragamba Reservoir N.S.W. Austr.
105 J8 Warragul Vic. Austr.
104 G3 Warrakalanna, Lake salt flat S.A. Austr.
259 I1 Warramaug, Lake CT U.S.A.
104 E5 Warramboo S.A. Austr.
109 D10 Warramboo hill W.A. Austr.
105 K4 Warrambool r. N.S.W. Austr.
104 F2 Warrandirinna, Lake salt flat S.A. Austr.
105 J7 Warrandyte Vic. Austr.
108 F6 Warrawagine W.A. Austr.
105 J4 Warrego r. N.S.W./Qld Austr.
107 J8 Warrego Range hills Qld Austr.
105 K4 Warren N.S.W. Austr.
109 C13 Warren r. W.A. Austr.
251 N3 Warren Ont. Can.
261 I9 Warren AR U.S.A.
250 E7 Warren IL U.S.A.
250 I9 Warren IN U.S.A.
251 K7 Warren MI U.S.A.
260 G1 Warren MN U.S.A.
256 E7 Warren OH U.S.A.
256 F7 Warren PA U.S.A.
258 F3 Warren County county NJ U.S.A.
259 G5 Warren Grove NJ U.S.A.
Warren Hastings Island Palau see Merir
245 N5 Warren Island AK U.S.A.
245 N1 Warren Point pt N.W.T. Can.
169 J4 Warrenpoint Northern Ireland U.K.
250 D5 Warrens WI U.S.A.
260 I6 Warrensburg MO U.S.A.
257 L5 Warrensburg NY U.S.A.
258 B2 Warrensville PA U.S.A.
237 I4 Warrenton S. Africa
255 F9 Warrenton GA U.S.A.
260 J6 Warrenton MO U.S.A.
255 H7 Warrenton NC U.S.A.
256 H10 Warrenton VA U.S.A.
229 G5 Warri Nigeria
109 D10 Warriedar hill W.A. Austr.
104 F3 Warriners Creek watercourse S.A. Austr.
103 E12 Warrington South I. N.Z.
171 L7 Warrington Warrington, England U.K.
171 L7 Warrington admin. div. England U.K.
255 D10 Warrington FL U.S.A.
104 G4 Warriota watercourse S.A. Austr.
105 I8 Warrnambool Vic. Austr.
260 H1 Warroad MN U.S.A.
104 E6 Warrow S.A. Austr.
105 L4 Warrumbungle National Park N.S.W. Austr.
106 D1 Warruwi N.T. Austr.
105 H3 Warry Warry watercourse Qld Austr.
Warsaw Pol. see Warszawa
250 C9 Warsaw IL U.S.A.
254 E5 Warsaw IN U.S.A.
254 E6 Warsaw KY U.S.A.
260 I6 Warsaw MO U.S.A.
256 G6 Warsaw NY U.S.A.
256 I11 Warsaw VA U.S.A.
201 J4 Warscheneck mt. Austria
232 E4 Warshiikh Somalia
190 D4 Warsingsfehn Ger.
171 N7 Warslow Staffordshire, England U.K.
191 F8 Warstein Ger.
197 J3 Warszawa Pol.
196 E1 Warszkowo Pol.
196 G4 Warta Pol.
196 C3 Warta r. Pol.
196 D4 Warta Bolesławiecka Pol.
196 G3 Warta-Gopło, Kanał canal Pol.
201 J4 Wartberg an der Krems Austria
255 E7 Wartburg TN U.S.A.
193 B9 Wartburg, Schloss tourist site Ger.
193 B9 Wartburg Schloß tourist site Ger.
195 L5 Wartenberg Ger.
191 H9 Wartenberg-Angersbach Ger.
200 B5 Warth Austria
194 H5 Warthausen Ger.
192 J4 Wartin Ger.
197 H4 Wartkowice Pol.
191 I10 Wartmannsroth Ger.
171 L5 Warton Lancashire, England U.K.
117 L5 Waru Kalimantan Indon.
138 G9 Warud Mahar. India
106 E5 Warumungu Aboriginal Land res. N.T. Austr.
105 N3 Warwick Qld Austr.
173 I3 Warwick Warwickshire, England U.K.
258 D6 Warwick MD U.S.A.
259 G2 Warwick NY U.S.A.
257 N7 Warwick RI U.S.A.
171 L4 Warwick Bridge Cumbria, England U.K.
106 F3 Warwick Channel N.T. Austr.
173 I3 Warwickshire admin. div. England U.K.
130 C4 Warzhong Sichuan China
246 H5 Wasa B.C. Can.
251 N5 Wasaga Beach Ont. Can.
229 G4 Wasagu Nigeria
265 U2 Wasatch Range mts UT U.S.A.
237 O4 Wasbank S. Africa
190 I2 Wasbek Ger.
168 J4 Wasbister Orkney, Scotland U.K.
191 K6 Wasbüttel Ger.
247 J5 Wascana Creek r. Sask. Can.
194 H4 Wäschenbeuren Ger.
264 M6 Wasco CA U.S.A.
250 C3 Wascott WI U.S.A.
260 I3 Waseca MN U.S.A.
247 I3 Wasekamio Lake Sask. Can.
197 J3 Wąsewo Pol.
275 G3 Washado Suriname
145 J8 Washap Pak.
250 E9 Washburn IL U.S.A.
257 □Q2 Washburn ME U.S.A.
260 E2 Washburn ND U.S.A.
256 B12 Washburn TN U.S.A.
250 D3 Washburn WI U.S.A.
126 E4 Washiga-take mt. Japan
138 F9 Washim Mahar. India
284 E3 Washington Arg.
171 N4 Washington Tyne and Wear, England U.K.
259 I1 Washington CT U.S.A.
258 A7 Washington DC U.S.A.
255 F9 Washington GA U.S.A.
260 J5 Washington IA U.S.A.
250 E9 Washington IL U.S.A.
254 D6 Washington IN U.S.A.
260 G6 Washington KS U.S.A.
256 B10 Washington KY U.S.A.
255 I8 Washington NC U.S.A.
257 M5 Washington NH U.S.A.
258 F3 Washington NJ U.S.A.
256 E8 Washington PA U.S.A.
265 S4 Washington UT U.S.A.
256 G10 Washington VA U.S.A.
262 D3 Washington state U.S.A.
287 L2 Washington, Cape Antarctica
257 N4 Washington, Mount NH U.S.A.
256 B9 Washington Court House OH U.S.A.
258 F4 Washington Crossing NJ U.S.A.
259 I1 Washington Depot CT U.S.A.
258 A6 Washington Grove MD U.S.A.
250 H4 Washington Island WI U.S.A.
250 H4 Washington Island i. WI U.S.A.
243 L2 Washington Land reg. Greenland
259 G2 Washingtonville NY U.S.A.
258 B2 Washingtonville PA U.S.A.
145 J5 Washir Afgh.
261 G8 Washita r. OK U.S.A.
105 N3 Washpool National Park N.S.W. Austr.
262 E3 Washtucna WA U.S.A.
145 K8 Washuk Pak.
136 D3 Wasi Mahar. India
147 H3 Wasīʻ Saudi Arabia
147 J4 Wasīʻ well Saudi Arabia
178 H4 Wasigny France
197 L2 Wasilków Pol.
242 D3 Wasilla AK U.S.A.
229 F4 Wasinmi Nigeria
115 E7 Wasiri Maluku Indon.
115 E5 Wasisi Buru Indon.
150 C9 Wāsiţ Egypt
149 L7 Wāsiţ governorate Iraq
149 M7 Wasit tourist site Iraq
147 M4 Wāsiţ Oman
146 D4 Wāsiţah Saudi Arabia
248 E3 Waskaganish Que. Can.
247 L3 Waskaiowaka Lake Man. Can.
246 H4 Waskatenau Alta Can.
244 H4 Waskey, Mount AK U.S.A.
196 E4 Wąsosz Dolnośląskie Pol.
197 K2 Wąsosz Podlaskie Pol.
196 E3 Wąsowo Pol.
266 □Q10 Waspán Nic.
186 G5 Waspik Neth.
171 O5 Wass North Yorkshire, England U.K.
228 B3 Wassadou Senegal
124 T2 Wassamu Japan
187 H7 Wasseiges Belgium
179 N6 Wasselonne France
212 F2 Wassen Switz.
186 F4 Wassenaar Neth.
191 B8 Wassenberg Ger.
234 C5 Wasser Namibia
195 I4 Wasseralfingen Ger.
195 M5 Wasserburg am Inn Ger.
191 I10 Wasserkuppe hill Ger.
191 K7 Wasserleben Ger.
194 B2 Wasserliesch Ger.
191 J10 Wasserlosen Ger.
195 J3 Wassertrüdingen Ger.
178 G3 Wassigny France
228 B4 Wassou Guinea
264 N3 Wassuk Range mts NV U.S.A.
179 I6 Wassy France
146 D4 Wasta Saudi Arabia
171 K5 Wast Water l. England U.K.
191 J9 Wasungen Ger.
248 E3 Waswanipi, Lac l. Que. Can.
251 N1 Watabeag Lake Ont. Can.
115 B4 Watambayoli Sulawesi Indon.
115 B6 Watampone Sulawesi Indon.
245 J3 Watana, Mount AK U.S.A.
115 A6 Watansoppeng Sulawesi Indon.
247 I4 Watapi Lake Sask. Can.
126 E7 Watarai Japan
127 K3 Watarase-gawa r. Japan
106 C8 Watarrka National Park N.T. Austr.
127 H2 Watauchi Japan
256 C12 Watauga r. TN U.S.A.
118 D5 Wat Chan Thai.
172 F5 Watchet Somerset, England U.K.
171 L5 Watchgate Cumbria, England U.K.
259 L2 Watch Hill Point RI U.S.A.
Watenstadt-Salzgitter Ger. see Salzgitter
173 M3 Waterbeach Cambridgeshire, England U.K.
234 C4 Waterberg Namibia
234 C4 Waterberg Plateau Game Park nature res. Namibia
257 L7 Waterbury CT U.S.A.
257 M4 Waterbury VT U.S.A.
247 J3 Waterbury Lake Sask. Can.
270 E2 Water Cays i. Bahamas
251 O6 Waterdown Ont. Can.
255 G9 Wateree r. SC U.S.A.
245 N5 Waterfall AK U.S.A.
104 □3 Waterfall Lake S. Pacific Ocean
169 H8 Waterford Ireland
169 G8 Waterford county Ireland
237 J9 Waterford S. Africa
264 L4 Waterford CA U.S.A.
259 K2 Waterford CT U.S.A.
256 F7 Waterford PA U.S.A.
169 I8 Waterford Harbour Ireland
258 F5 Waterford Works NJ U.S.A.
172 B7 Watergate Bay England U.K.
247 J4 Waterhen r. Sask. Can.
247 L4 Waterhen Lake Man. Can.
106 D3 Waterhouse r. N.T. Austr.
106 D8 Waterhouse Range mts N.T. Austr.
186 F4 Wateringen Neth.
187 E6 Waterland-Oudeman Belgium
106 B4 Waterloo N.T. Austr.
187 F7 Waterloo Belgium
248 D5 Waterloo Ont. Can.
228 B4 Waterloo Sierra Leone
271 □7 Waterloo Trin. and Tob.
260 I4 Waterloo IA U.S.A.
260 J6 Waterloo IL U.S.A.
258 B6 Waterloo MD U.S.A.
256 I6 Waterloo NY U.S.A.
250 F6 Waterloo WI U.S.A.
173 J6 Waterlooville Hampshire, England U.K.
250 F8 Waterman IL U.S.A.
259 K3 Watermill NY U.S.A.
171 K2 Water of Leith r. Scotland U.K.
168 G9 Water of Tulla r. Scotland U.K.
173 I2 Water Orton Warwickshire, England U.K.
235 F4 Waterpoort S. Africa
169 H3 Waterside Northern Ireland U.K.
250 E3 Watersmeet MI U.S.A.
246 H5 Waterton Lakes National Park B.C. Can.
246 H5 Waterton Park Alta Can.
259 I1 Watertown CT U.S.A.
257 J5 Watertown NY U.S.A.
260 G3 Watertown SD U.S.A.
250 F6 Watertown WI U.S.A.
237 M2 Waterval r. S. Africa
237 O1 Waterval Boven S. Africa
104 G5 Watervale S.A. Austr.
261 K8 Water Valley MS U.S.A.
169 B9 Waterville Ireland
257 □P4 Waterville ME U.S.A.
256 B7 Waterville OH U.S.A.
262 D3 Waterville WA U.S.A.
257 L6 Watervliet NY U.S.A.
117 I8 Wates Indon.
251 M7 Watford Ont. Can.
173 L4 Watford Hertfordshire, England U.K.
260 D2 Watford City ND U.S.A.
247 K3 Wathaman r. Sask. Can.
247 K3 Wathaman Lake Sask. Can.
109 D11 Watheroo W.A. Austr.
109 C11 Watheroo National Park W.A. Austr.
246 G4 Watino Alta Can.
150 C9 Watīr, Wādī watercourse Egypt
256 I6 Watkins Glen NY U.S.A.
255 F9 Watkinsville GA U.S.A.
Watling Island Bahamas see San Salvador
173 J4 Watlington Oxfordshire, England U.K.
261 F8 Watonga OK U.S.A.
115 F3 Watowato, Bukit mt. Halmahera Indon.
247 J5 Watrous Sask. Can.
263 L9 Watrous NM U.S.A.
230 F4 Watsa Dem. Rep. Congo
250 G9 Watseka IL U.S.A.
230 D5 Watsi Kengo Dem. Rep. Congo
107 H2 Watson r. Qld Austr.
247 J4 Watson Sask. Can.
286 P1 Watson Escarpment Antarctica
245 O3 Watson Lake Y.T. Can.
258 B2 Watsontown PA U.S.A.
264 K5 Watsonville CA U.S.A.
109 I9 Watt, Mount hill W.A. Austr.
178 D2 Watten France
168 J6 Watten Highland, Scotland U.K.
168 J6 Watten, Loch l. Scotland U.K.
190 J2 Wattenbek Ger.
200 E5 Wattens Austria
212 D2 Wattenwil Switz.
247 L2 Watterson Lake Nunavut Can.
178 H3 Wattignies-la-Victoire France
104 F3 Wattiwarriganna watercourse S.A. Austr.
169 H4 Wattlebridge Northern Ireland U.K.
192 F3 Wattmannshagen Ger.
173 N2 Watton Norfolk, England U.K.
173 L4 Watton at Stone Hertfordshire, England U.K.
178 F2 Wattrelos France
255 E8 Watts Bar Lake resr TN U.S.A.
256 F6 Wattsburg PA U.S.A.
212 G1 Wattwil Switz.
113 H7 Watubela, Kepulauan is Indon.
115 B5 Watuwila, Bukit mt. Indon.
191 G9 Watzenborn-Steinberg Ger.
113 K8 Wau P.N.G.
230 E3 Wau Sudan
230 E3 Wau watercourse Sudan
260 G3 Waubay Lake SD U.S.A.
105 N4 Wauchope N.S.W. Austr.
106 E6 Wauchope N.T. Austr.
255 G12 Wauchula FL U.S.A.
115 A4 Waukara, Gunung mt. Indon.
108 F6 Waukarlycarly, Lake salt flat W.A. Austr.
250 F6 Waukau WI U.S.A.
250 G7 Waukegan IL U.S.A.
250 F6 Waukesha WI U.S.A.
250 C6 Waukon IA U.S.A.
250 E6 Waunakee WI U.S.A.
260 E5 Wauneta NE U.S.A.
250 E5 Waupaca WI U.S.A.
250 F6 Waupun WI U.S.A.
259 L1 Wauregan CT U.S.A.
261 G8 Waurika OK U.S.A.
250 E5 Wausau WI U.S.A.
250 G4 Wausaukee WI U.S.A.
256 A7 Wauseon OH U.S.A.
250 E5 Wautoma WI U.S.A.
106 C4 Wave Hill N.T. Austr.
173 P3 Waveney r. England U.K.
102 I6 Waverley North I. N.Z.
260 I4 Waverly IA U.S.A.
256 I6 Waverly NY U.S.A.
256 C9 Waverly OH U.S.A.
255 D7 Waverly TN U.S.A.
256 H11 Waverly VA U.S.A.
187 G7 Wavre Belgium
178 E2 Wavrin France
118 C6 Waw Myanmar
248 C4 Wawa Ont. Can.
229 G4 Wawa Nigeria
248 E3 Wawagosic r. Que. Can.
115 C5 Wawalalindu Sulawesi Indon.
224 C3 Wāw al Kabīr Libya
224 C3 Wāw an Nāmūs waterhole Libya
259 G1 Wawarsing NY U.S.A.
250 I8 Wawasee, Lake IN U.S.A.
Wāwāwahi Waka l. South I. N.Z. see Alabaster, Lake
196 F5 Wąwelno Pol.
115 B5 Wawo Sulawesi Indon.
113 J8 Wawoi r. P.N.G.
197 K4 Wąwolnica Pol.
115 C5 Wawotebi Sulawesi Indon.
196 D3 Wawrów Pol.
197 I5 Wawrzeńczyce Pol.
261 G9 Waxahachie TX U.S.A.
128 H9 Waxü Gansu China
191 B10 Waxweiler Ger.
132 H7 Waxxari Xinjiang China
109 F9 Way, Lake salt flat W.A. Austr.
101 □7a Waya i. Fiji
115 F2 Wayabula Maluku Indon.
115 G3 Wayag i. Papua Indon.
Waya Lailai i. Fiji see Wayasewa
115 F3 Wayamli Halmahera Indon.
Wayaobu Shaanxi China see Zichang
101 □7a Wayasewa i. Fiji
255 F10 Waycross GA U.S.A.
115 D4 Wayhaya Maluku Indon.
116 F7 Way Kambas, Taman Nasional nat. park Indon.
115 D4 Waykilo Maluku Indon.
256 C11 Wayland KY U.S.A.
250 I7 Wayland MI U.S.A.
250 C9 Wayland MO U.S.A.
256 H6 Wayland NY U.S.A.
251 K7 Wayne MI U.S.A.
260 G4 Wayne NE U.S.A.
259 G3 Wayne NJ U.S.A.
258 E4 Wayne PA U.S.A.
256 C10 Wayne WV U.S.A.
258 E1 Wayne County county PA U.S.A.
255 F9 Waynesboro GA U.S.A.
261 K10 Waynesboro MS U.S.A.
256 H9 Waynesboro PA U.S.A.
255 D8 Waynesboro TN U.S.A.
256 G10 Waynesboro VA U.S.A.
256 E9 Waynesburg PA U.S.A.
261 I7 Waynesville MO U.S.A.
255 F8 Waynesville NC U.S.A.
261 F7 Waynoka OK U.S.A.
229 I4 Waza Cameroon
118 C2 Waza Myanmar
229 I4 Waza, Parc National de nat. park Cameroon
178 F3 Waziers France
145 M5 Wazi Khwa Afgh.
145 P5 Wazirabad Pak.
126 C6 Wazuka Japan
196 G2 Wda r. Pol.
189 I2 Wdecki Park Krajobrazowy Pol.
Wdig Pembrokeshire, Wales U.K. see Goodwick
196 F2 Wdzydze, Jezioro l. Pol.
189 H1 Wdzydzki Park Krajobrazowy Pol.
100 □5 We Îles Loyauté New Caledonia
116 A2 We, Pulau i. Indon.
248 B2 Weagamow Lake Ont. Can.
171 O4 Wear r. England U.K.
257 N5 Weare NH U.S.A.
106 F4 Wearyan r. N.T. Austr.
107 J3 Weary Bay Qld Austr.
261 F8 Weatherford OK U.S.A.
261 G9 Weatherford TX U.S.A.
258 D3 Weatherly PA U.S.A.
171 L7 Weaverham Cheshire, England U.K.
247 L4 Weaver Lake Man. Can.
262 C6 Weaverville CA U.S.A.
108 J7 Webb, Mount hill W.A. Austr.
248 D4 Webbwood Ont. Can.
248 C2 Webequie Ont. Can.
102 K7 Weber North I. N.Z.
262 H6 Weber r. UT U.S.A.
245 O5 Weber, Mount B.C. Can.
289 M5 Weber Basin sea feature Indon.
286 T2 Weber Inlet Antarctica
257 N6 Webster MA U.S.A.
258 C5 Webster MD U.S.A.
260 G3 Webster SD U.S.A.
250 B4 Webster WI U.S.A.
260 I4 Webster City IA U.S.A.
256 E10 Webster Springs WV U.S.A.
232 B4 Webuye Kenya
187 G6 Wechelderzande Belgium
191 K9 Wechmar Ger.
246 H2 Wecho r. N.W.T. Can.
246 H2 Wecho Lake N.W.T. Can.
193 G8 Wechselburg Ger.
115 E3 Weda Halmahera Indon.
115 F3 Weda, Teluk b. Halmahera Indon.
186 L2 Wedde Neth.
286 V2 Weddell Abyssal Plain sea feature Southern Ocean
283 E8 Weddell Island Falkland Is
286 V2 Weddell Sea Antarctica
105 I7 Wedderburn Vic. Austr.
105 K5 Weddin Mountains National Park N.S.W. Austr.
103 E12 Wedderburn South I. N.Z.
190 H2 Weddingstedt Ger.
190 I3 Wedel (Holstein) Ger.
162 □ Wedel Jarlsberg Land reg. Svalbard
246 F5 Wedge Mountain B.C. Can.
172 G5 Wedmore Somerset, England U.K.
172 H2 Wednesbury West Midlands, England U.K.
255 E9 Wedowee AL U.S.A.
262 C6 Weed CA U.S.A.
190 J3 Weede Ger.
173 J3 Weedon Bec Northamptonshire, England U.K.
256 G7 Weedville PA U.S.A.
115 G4 Weeim i. Papua Indon.
258 F5 Weekstown NJ U.S.A.
187 G6 Weelde Belgium
105 L3 Weemelah N.S.W. Austr.
237 O4 Weenen S. Africa
237 O4 Weenen Nature Reserve S. Africa
190 D4 Weener Ger.
200 E5 Weerberg Austria
186 K4 Weerselo Neth.
187 I6 Weert Neth.
190 I1 Wees Ger.
212 G1 Weesen Switz.
186 H4 Weesp Neth.
105 K5 Weethalle N.S.W. Austr.
105 L4 Wee Waa N.S.W. Austr.
191 B7 Weeze Ger.
193 D6 Weferlingen Ger.
191 B8 Wegberg Ger.
236 F4 Wegdraai S. Africa
193 D7 Wegeleben Ger.
193 D6 Wegenstedt Ger.
194 E7 Weggis Switz.
196 D4 Węgliniec Pol.
197 J1 Węgorzewo Pol.
196 D2 Węgorzyno Pol.
197 K3 Węgrów Pol.
196 D3 Węgrzynice Pol.
197 I3 Węgrzynowo Pol.
201 L4 Wegscheid Austria
195 P4 Wegscheid Ger.
190 G3 Wehdel Ger.
186 J2 Wehe-den Hoorn Neth.
186 J5 Wehl Neth.
Wehlau Rus. Fed. see Znamensk
232 C1 Wehnī Eth.
194 D6 Wehr Ger.
190 G5 Wehrbleck Ger.
191 G10 Wehrheim Ger.
195 J5 Wehringen Ger.
191 D10 Weibern Ger.
194 G2 Weibersbrunn Ger.
129 O6 Weichang Hebei China
195 K4 Weichering Ger.
195 K5 Weichs Ger.
193 F9 Weida Ger.
193 F9 Weida r. Ger.
195 J3 Weidenbach Ger.
195 L2 Weidenberg Ger.
195 M2 Weiden in der Oberpfalz Ger.
194 H4 Weidenstetten Ger.
194 D3 Weidenthal Ger.
195 N3 Weiding Ger.
Weidongmen Heilong. China see Qianjin
194 C2 Weiersbach Ger.
129 P8 Weifang Shandong China
193 K8 Weigersdorf Ger.
258 B5 Weiglestown PA U.S.A.
129 R8 Weihai Shandong China
129 N8 Wei He r. Henan China
129 L9 Wei He r. Shaanxi China
129 P8 Wei He r. Shandong China
195 J3 Weihenzell Ger.
195 M2 Weiherhammer Ger.
195 M4 Weihmichl Ger.
129 N9 Weihui Henan China
122 E7 Weihu Ling mts China
201 O3 Weikendorf Austria
194 H3 Weikersheim Ger.
195 J5 Weil Ger.
194 D6 Weil am Rhein Ger.
194 G2 Weilbach Ger.
191 F10 Weilburg Ger.
194 F4 Weil der Stadt Ger.
200 A5 Weiler Austria
194 H6 Weiler Ger.
194 D3 Weilerbach Ger.
191 C9 Weilerswist Ger.
194 E6 Weilheim Ger.
194 H4 Weilheim an der Teck Ger.
195 K6 Weilheim in Oberbayern Ger.
105 K3 Weilmoringle N.S.W. Austr.
191 F10 Weilmünster Ger.
193 D9 Weimar Ger.
191 H8 Weimar (Ahnatal) Ger.
129 K9 Weinan Shaanxi China
191 F10 Weinbach Ger.
193 I8 Weinböhla Ger.
212 G1 Weinfelden Switz.
194 H6 Weingarten Ger.
194 F3 Weingarten (Baden) Ger.
194 F2 Weinheim Ger.
130 E5 Weining Guizhou China
194 G3 Weinsberg Ger.
201 K2 Weinsberger Wald for. Austria
194 D2 Weinsheim Rheinland-Pfalz Ger.
191 B10 Weinsheim Rheinland-Pfalz Ger.
194 G4 Weinstadt Ger.
201 N3 Weinviertel reg. Austria
107 H2 Weipa Qld Austr.
Weiqu Shaanxi China see Chang'an
105 L3 Weir r. Qld Austr.
109 D9 Weiragoo Range hills W.A. Austr.
128 I9 Weirong Gansu China
247 M3 Weir River Man. Can.
256 E8 Weirton WV U.S.A.
193 F10 Weischlitz Ger.
168 □N2 Weisdale Shetland, Scotland U.K.
192 E4 Weisen Ger.
195 J2 Weisendorf Ger.
262 F4 Weiser ID U.S.A.
262 F4 Weiser r. ID U.S.A.
129 O9 Weishan Shandong China
130 C6 Weishan Yunnan China
129 O9 Weishan Hu l. China
129 N9 Weishi Henan China
194 B2 Weiskirchen Ger.
193 D10 Weismain Ger.
195 L6 Weißach r. Ger.
200 H6 Weißbriach Austria
193 E8 Weiße Elster r. Ger.
195 L3 Weiße Laber r. Ger.
200 C5 Weißenbach am Lech Austria
193 K8 Weißenberg Ger.
191 J8 Weißenborn Hessen Ger.
193 H9 Weißenborn Sachsen Ger.
191 J7 Weißenborn-Lüderode Ger.
193 D10 Weißenbrunn Ger.
195 J3 Weißenburg in Bayern Ger.
193 E8 Weißenfels Ger.
195 I5 Weißenhorn Ger.
194 H6 Weißensberg Ger.
201 H6 Weißensee l. Austria
193 D8 Weißensee Ger.
193 E10 Weißenstadt Ger.
201 I6 Weißenstein Austria
191 D10 Weißenthurm Ger.
193 D10 Weißer Main r. Ger.
195 N3 Weißer Regen r. Ger.
193 K8 Weißer Schöps r. Ger.
212 D3 Weisshorn mt. Switz.
193 I8 Weißig Ger.
193 K8 Weißkeißel Ger.
201 J3 Weißkirchen an der Traun Austria
201 K5 Weißkirchen in Steiermark Austria
193 J8 Weißkollm Ger.
200 C6 Weißkugel mt. Austria/Italy
255 E8 Weiss Lake AL U.S.A.
212 E3 Weissmies mt. Switz.
234 C5 Weissrand Mountains Namibia
193 K7 Weißwasser Ger.
201 K3 Weistrach Austria
187 J8 Weiswampach Lux.
194 D5 Weisweil Ger.
179 O6 Weitbruch France
191 E9 Weitefeld Ger.
201 L3 Weiten Austria
201 L6 Weitendorf Austria
192 H2 Weitenhagen Ger.
201 J6 Weitensfeld Austria
201 M2 Weitersfeld Austria
194 F2 Weiterstadt Ger.
186 L3 Weiteveen Neth.
195 I6 Weitnau Ger.
201 K2 Weitra Austria
191 K10 Weitramsdorf Ger.
247 J3 Weitzel Lake Sask. Can.
193 I8 Weixdorf Ger.
130 B5 Weixi Yunnan China
129 N8 Weixian Hebei China
130 E5 Weixin Yunnan China
128 D6 Weiya Xinjiang China
128 I9 Weiyuan Gansu China
Weiyuan Qinghai China see Huzhu
Weiyuan Yunnan China see Jinggu
130 C7 Weiyuan Jiang r. Yunnan China
201 M5 Weiz Austria
128 J8 Weizhou Ningxia China
Weizhou Sichuan China see Wenchuan
130 G8 Weizhou Dao i. China
129 R6 Weizi Liaoning China
165 O7 Wejherowo Pol.
142 I9 Wekilbazar Turkm.
247 L4 Wekusko Man. Can.
247 L4 Wekusko Lake Man. Can.
246 H1 Wekweêtì N.W.T. Can.
197 H2 Wel r. Pol.
118 D1 Welatam Myanmar
237 K5 Welbedacht Dam S. Africa
104 E2 Welbourn Hill S.A. Austr.
256 D11 Welch WV U.S.A.
257 □O4 Weld ME U.S.A.
109 G10 Weld, Mount hill W.A. Austr.
195 J5 Welden Ger.
232 C2 Weldiya Eth.
173 K3 Weldon Northamptonshire, England U.K.
109 D9 Weld Range hills W.A. Austr.
107 I8 Welford National Park Qld Austr.
187 I7 Welkenraedt Belgium
232 C2 Welk'īt'ē Eth.
237 K3 Welkom S. Africa
186 J5 Well Neth.
251 O7 Welland Ont. Can.
173 L2 Welland r. England U.K.
251 O6 Welland Canal Ont. Can.
193 G7 Wellaune Ger.
136 G9 Wellawaya Sri Lanka
190 I4 Welle Ger.
187 H7 Wellen Belgium
194 F5 Wellendingen Ger.
173 I3 Wellesbourne Warwickshire, England U.K.
251 N6 Wellesley Ont. Can.
106 G4 Wellesley Islands Qld Austr.
106 G4 Wellesley Islands Aboriginal Reserve Qld Austr.
245 M3 Wellesley Lake Y.T. Can.
257 O7 Wellfleet MA U.S.A.
195 K4 Wellheim Ger.
187 H8 Wellin Belgium
191 D10 Welling Ger.
173 K3 Wellingborough Northamptonshire, England U.K.
105 L5 Wellington N.S.W. Austr.
104 G6 Wellington S.A. Austr.
251 Q6 Wellington Ont. Can.
103 I8 Wellington North I. N.Z.
103 J8 Wellington admin. reg. North I. N.Z.
236 C9 Wellington S. Africa
172 F6 Wellington Somerset, England U.K.
172 G2 Wellington Telford and Wrekin, England U.K.
262 L6 Wellington CO U.S.A.
261 G7 Wellington KS U.S.A.
264 M3 Wellington NV U.S.A.
256 C7 Wellington OH U.S.A.
261 E8 Wellington TX U.S.A.
265 V2 Wellington UT U.S.A.
283 B8 Wellington, Isla i. Chile
169 I8 Wellingtonbridge Ireland
106 D2 Wellington Range hills N.T. Austr.
109 F9 Wellington Range hills W.A. Austr.
246 F4 Wells B.C. Can.
172 G5 Wells Somerset, England U.K.
262 G6 Wells NV U.S.A.
109 G9 Wells, Lake salt flat W.A. Austr.
256 H7 Wellsboro PA U.S.A.
256 E8 Wellsburg WV U.S.A.
102 I3 Wellsford North I. N.Z.
246 F4 Wells Gray Provincial Park B.C. Can.
173 N2 Wells-next-the-Sea Norfolk, England U.K.
250 I5 Wellston MI U.S.A.
256 H6 Wellsville NY U.S.A.
256 E8 Wellsville OH U.S.A.
258 B4 Wellsville PA U.S.A.
265 R9 Wellton AZ U.S.A.
196 E3 Wełna r. Pol.
173 M2 Welney Norfolk, England U.K.
197 L4 Wełnianka r. Pol.
264 □F14 Welokā HI U.S.A.
201 J3 Wels Austria
194 B2 Welschbillig Ger.
192 J4 Welse r. Ger.
172 L4 Welsh Newton Herefordshire, England U.K.
172 F2 Welshpool Powys, Wales U.K.
193 H7 Welsickendorf Ger.
193 E7 Welsleben Ger.
171 Q7 Welton Lincolnshire, England U.K.
191 E7 Welver Ger.
232 E3 Welwel Eth.
Welwitschia Namibia see Khorixas
173 L4 Welwyn Hertfordshire, England U.K.
173 L4 Welwyn Garden City Hertfordshire, England U.K.
194 H4 Welzheim Ger.
194 H4 Welzheimer Wald hills Ger.
193 J7 Welzow Ger.
172 G2 Wem Shropshire, England U.K.
230 D5 Wema Dem. Rep. Congo
172 F5 Wembdon Somerset, England U.K.
233 B6 Wembere r. Tanz.
237 N5 Wembesi S. Africa
246 G4 Wembley Alta Can.
195 J4 Wemding Ger.
186 F5 Wemeldinge Neth.
232 D3 Wemel Shet' r. Eth.
248 E2 Wemindji Que. Can.
168 G11 Wemyss Bay Inverclyde, Scotland U.K.
270 E1 Wemyss Bight Eleuthera Bahamas
275 F3 Wenamu r. Guyana alt. Venamo (Venezuela)
262 D3 Wenatchee WA U.S.A.
262 D3 Wenatchee Mountains WA U.S.A.
130 H9 Wenchang Hainan China
Wenchang Sichuan China see Zitong
131 M5 Wencheng Zhejiang China
228 E5 Wenchi Ghana
232 C2 Wench'īt Shet' r. Eth.
Wenchow Zhejiang China see Wenzhou
130 D3 Wenchuan Sichuan China
191 J6 Wendeburg Ger.
194 E2 Wendelsheim Ger.
195 K3 Wendelstein Ger.
195 M6 Wendelstein mt. Ger.
191 E9 Wenden Ger.
Wenden Latvia see Cēsis
265 S8 Wenden AZ U.S.A.
129 R8 Wendeng Shandong China
173 M3 Wendens Ambo Essex, England U.K.
190 J4 Wendisch Evern Ger.
192 F4 Wendisch Priborn Ger.
193 J6 Wendisch Rietz Ger.
192 D4 Wendland reg. Ger.
194 G4 Wendlingen am Neckar Ger.
232 C3 Wendo Eth.
228 B4 Wéndou Mbôrou Guinea
173 K4 Wendover Buckinghamshire, England U.K.
262 G6 Wendover UT U.S.A.
172 B7 Wendron Cornwall, England U
187 D6 Wenduine Belgium
251 K2 Wenebegon Lake Ont. Can.
Wenfeng Jiangxi China see Ji'a
130 E1 Wenfengzhen Gansu China
230 D4 Wenge Dem. Rep. Congo
212 D2 Wengen Switz.
191 D6 Wengsel (Isterberg) Ger.
130 B4 Wengshui Yunnan China
131 J6 Wengyuan Guangdong China
129 P9 Wen He r. China
Wenhua Yunnan China see Weishan
130 E4 Wenjiang Sichuan China
131 I5 Wenjiashi Hunan China
Wenlan Yunnan China see Mer
Wenlin Sichuan China see Renshou
131 M4 Wenling Zhejiang China
107 H2 Wenlock r. Qld Austr.
172 G3 Wenlock Edge ridge England U
274 □ Wenman, Isla i. Islas Galápag Ecuador
191 F8 Wenne r. Ger.
191 I6 Wennigsen (Deister) Ger.
171 L5 Wenning r. England U.K.
190 F1 Wenningstedt Ger.
200 C5 Wenns Austria
100 □4a Weno Chuuk Micronesia
100 □4a Weno i. Chuuk Micronesia
250 E8 Wenona IL U.S.A.
257 J10 Wenona MD U.S.A.
Wenping Yunnan China see Ludian
130 G3 Wenquan Chongqing China
130 F4 Wenquan Guizhou China
Wenquan Hubei China see Yingshan
128 F9 Wenquan Qinghai China
133 J10 Wenquan Qinghai China
132 E4 Wenquan Xinjiang China
131 J4 Wenquanzhen Hubei China
130 E7 Wenshan Yunnan China
130 F4 Wenshui Guizhou China
171 N5 Wensley North Yorkshire, Englc U.K.
171 M5 Wensleydale val. England U.K.
132 E6 Wensu Xinjiang China
173 O2 Wensum r. England U.K.
171 P6 Went r. England U.K.
190 J3 Wentorf Ger.
190 J4 Wentorf bei Hamburg Ger.
105 H6 Wentworth N.S.W. Austr.
255 H7 Wentworth NC U.S.A.
257 N5 Wentworth NH U.S.A.
250 C3 Wentworth WI U.S.A.
129 L9 Wenxi Shanxi China
130 E2 Wenxian Gansu China
Wenxing Hunan China see Xiangyin
129 L8 Wenyu He r. China
195 M3 Wenzenbach Ger.
131 M5 Wenzhou Zhejiang China
193 F6 Wenzlow Ger.
172 G3 Weobley Herefordshire, Englan U.K.
237 L5 Wepener S. Africa
187 G8 Wépion Belgium
138 F6 Wer Rajasthan India
194 H2 Werbach Ger.
192 I5 Werbellin Ger.
192 I5 Werbellinsee l. Ger.
193 J7 Werben Ger.
192 E5 Werben (Elbe) Ger.
193 H7 Werbig Ger.
197 L5 Werbkowice Pol.
187 I8 Werbomont Belgium
234 D5 Werda Botswana
193 F9 Werdau Ger.
232 E3 Werdēr Eth.
193 G6 Werder Brandenburg Ger.
192 H3 Werder Mecklenburg-Vorpomm Ger.
191 E8 Werdohl Ger.
190 E3 Werdum Ger.
173 M2 Wereham Norfolk, England U.K
200 H5 Werfen Austria
186 I2 Wergea Neth.
115 G5 Werinama Seram Indon.
191 E7 Werl Ger.
190 E5 Werlte Ger.
191 D8 Wermelskirchen Ger.
193 G8 Wermsdorf Ger.
193 G8 Wermsdorfer Forst park Ger.
191 I10 Wern r. Ger.
194 G4 Wernau Ger.
201 I6 Wernberg Austria
195 M2 Wernberg-Köblitz Ger.
201 M6 Werndorf Austria
191 E7 Werne Ger.
193 B11 Werneck Ger.
245 M2 Wernecke Mountains Y.T. Can
192 I5 Werneuchen Ger.
191 K7 Wernigerode Ger.
191 J9 Wernshausen Ger.
232 C2 Werota Eth.
190 E5 Werpeloh Ger.
191 I8 Werra r. Ger.
191 G6 Werre r. Ger.
105 N4 Werrikimbe National Park N.S Austr.
104 H6 Werrimull Vic. Austr.
105 M4 Werris Creek N.S.W. Austr.
195 I6 Wertach Ger.
195 J5 Wertach r. Ger.
194 H2 Wertheim Ger.
194 E7 Werthenstein Switz.
191 K8 Werther Ger.
191 F6 Werther (Westfalen) Ger.
195 J4 Wertingen Ger.
186 H3 Wervershoof Neth.
187 D7 Wervik Belgium
115 F8 Werwaru Maluku Indon.
191 C7 Wesel Ger.
191 C7 Wesel-Datteln-Kanal canal Ge
192 G4 Wesenberg Ger.
190 K5 Wesendorf Ger.
186 J4 Wesepe Neth.
191 F4 Weser r. Ger.
190 F3 Weser sea chan. Ger.
191 G6 Wesergebirge hills Ger.
260 E6 Weskan KS U.S.A.
232 B3 Weska Weka Eth.
261 G12 Weslaco TX U.S.A.
251 Q4 Weslemkoon Lake Ont. Can.
237 L9 Wesley S. Africa
257 □R4 Wesley ME U.S.A.
249 K3 Wesleyville Nfld and Lab. Can.
256 E6 Wesleyville PA U.S.A.
197 J3 Wesoła Pol.
106 F1 Wessel, Cape N.T. Austr.
190 G2 Wesselburen Ger.
191 C9 Wesseling Ger.
106 F1 Wessel Islands N.T. Austr.
190 H2 Wesseln Ger.
237 K3 Wesselsbron S. Africa
236 H3 Wesselsvlei S. Africa
237 N2 Wesselton S. Africa
187 I6 Wessem Neth.
260 F3 Wessington Springs SD U.S.A.
195 K5 Weßling Ger.
195 K6 Wessobrunn Ger.
245 P1 West r. N.W.T. Can.
258 C7 West r. MD U.S.A.
104 E5 Westall, Point S.A. Austr.
106 D2 West Alligator r. N.T. Austr.
250 F6 West Allis WI U.S.A.
286 P1 West Antarctica reg. Antarctica
259 G6 West Atlantic City NJ U.S.A.
171 N4 West Auckland Durham, England U.K.
289 K6 West Australian Basin sea feat Indian Ocean
259 I3 West Babylon NY U.S.A.
106 C3 West Baines r. N.T. Austr.
138 C8 West Banas r. India
150 D7 West Bank terr. Asia
249 J2 West Bay Nfld and Lab. Can.
270 C4 West Bay Cayman Is
261 K11 West Bay b. LA U.S.A.
255 E10 West Bay inlet FL U.S.A.

F6 **West Bend** *WI* U.S.A.
K8 **West Bengal** *state* India
N4 **West Bergholt** *Essex, England* U.K.
J5 **West Berkshire** *admin. div. England* U.K.
F5 **West Berlin** *NJ* U.S.A.
B9 **Westboro** *OH* U.S.A.
J5 **West Branch** *MI* U.S.A.
J2 **West Bridgford** *Nottinghamshire, England* U.K.
I2 **West Bromwich** *West Midlands, England* U.K.
K2 **Westbrook** *CT* U.S.A.
□O5 **Westbrook** *ME* U.S.A.
F1 **Westbrookville** *NY* U.S.A.
N4 **West Burke** *VT* U.S.A.
West Burra *i. Scotland* U.K. *see* **Burra**
K9 **Westbury** *Tas.* Austr.
H5 **Westbury** *Wiltshire, England* U.K.
D6 **Westby** *WI* U.S.A.
G3 **West Caicos** *i.* Turks and Caicos Is
I11 **West Calder** *West Lothian, Scotland* U.K.
B3 **West Cameron** *PA* U.S.A.
A12 **West Cape** *South I.* N.Z.
D13 **West Cape Howe** *W.A.* Austr.
F7 **West Cape May** *NJ* U.S.A.
E5 **West Caroline Basin** *sea feature* N. Pacific Ocean
D5 **West Chester** *PA* U.S.A.
H2 **Westchester County** *county NY* U.S.A.
L7 **Westcliffe** *CO* U.S.A.
E9 **West Coast** *admin. reg. South I.* N.Z.
C9 **West Coast National Park** S. Africa
G6 **West Coker** *Somerset, England* U.K.
B5 **West Concord** *MN* U.S.A.
L5 **Westcott** *Surrey, England* U.K.
G5 **West Creek** *NJ* U.S.A.
C12 **West Dome** *mt. South I.* N.Z.
E6 **Westdorpe** Neth.
K4 **West Duck Island** *Ont.* Can.
G11 **West Dunbartonshire** *admin. div. Scotland* U.K.
H12 **West End** *Gd Bahama* Bahamas
J6 **West End** *NY* U.S.A.
C6 **Westende** Belgium
F5 **Westendorf** Austria
H12 **West End Point** *Gd Bahama* Bahamas
J3 **Westenholte** Neth.
I2 **Westensee** Ger.
I2 **Westensee** *l.* Ger.
K5 **Westerbeck (Sassenburg)** Ger.
G5 **Westerberg** S. Africa
K3 **Westerbork** Neth.
E9 **Westerburg** Ger.
I6 **Westerdale** *Highland, Scotland* U.K.
D7 **Westeregeln** Ger.
D4 **Westerende-Kirchloog (Ihlow)** Ger.
F10 **Westerfield** *South I.* N.Z.
K6 **Westergate** *West Sussex, England* U.K.
J4 **Westergellersen** Ger.
K4 **Westerhaar** Neth.
Westerhall Grenada *see* **Westerhall Point**
□6 **Westerhall Point** Grenada
M5 **Westerham** *Kent, England* U.K.
D7 **Westerhausen** Ger.
H4 **Westerheim** *Baden-Württemberg* Ger.
I5 **Westerheim** *Bayern* Ger.
D3 **Westerholt** Ger.
I3 **Westerhorn** Ger.
H6 **Westerhoven** Neth.
F1 **Westerland** Ger.
G6 **Westerlo** Belgium
L2 **Westerly** *RI* U.S.A.
I7 **Western** *watercourse Qld* Austr.
E5 **Western** *admin. reg.* Ghana
D8 **Western** *prov.* Zambia
B4 **Western Area** *admin. div.* Sierra Leone
F8 **Western Australia** *state* Austr.
E3 **Western Bahr el Ghazal** *state* Sudan
E9 **Western Cape** *prov.* S. Africa
D6 **Western Darfur** *state* Sudan
Western Desert Egypt *see* **Aş Şaḩrā' al Gharbīyah**
B5 **Western Desert Aboriginal Land** *res. N.T.* Austr.
Western Dvina *r.* Europe *see* **Zapadnaya Dvina**
F3 **Western Equatoria** *state* Sudan
D5 **Western Ghats** *mts* India
C6 **Western Isles** *admin. div. Scotland* U.K.
F2 **Western Kordofan** *state* Sudan
Western Lesser Sunda Islands *prov.* Indon. *see* **Nusa Tenggara Barat**
J8 **Western Port** *b. Vic.* Austr.
Western Province *prov.* Zambia *see* **Copperbelt**
□ **Western Reef** *is Chatham Is* S. Pacific Ocean
□ **Western Rocks** *is England* U.K.
D3 **Western Sahara** *terr.* Africa
Western Samoa *country* S. Pacific Ocean *see* **Samoa**
Western Sayan Mountains *reg.* Rus. Fed. *see* **Zapadnyy Sayan**
H1 **Wester-Ohrstedt** Ger.
I12 **Wester Parkgate** *Dumfries and Galloway, Scotland* U.K.
F7 **Wester Ross** *reg. Scotland* U.K.
D6 **Westerschelde** *est.* Neth.
E4 **Westerstede** Ger.
H4 **Westerstetten** Ger.
C8 **Westerville** *OH* U.S.A.
I5 **Westervoort** Neth.
E10 **Westerwald** *hills* Ger.
H8 **Westewitz** Ger.
E8 **West Falkland** *i.* Falkland Is
G2 **West Fargo** *ND* U.S.A.
K5 **West Fayu** *atoll* Micronesia
Q7 **West Fen** *reg. Lincolnshire, England* U.K.
N6 **Westfield** *East Sussex, England* U.K.
M6 **Westfield** *MA* U.S.A.
□R2 **Westfield** *ME* U.S.A.
G3 **Westfield** *NJ* U.S.A.
F6 **Westfield** *NY* U.S.A.
H7 **Westfield** *PA* U.S.A.
E6 **Westfield** *WI* U.S.A.
West Flanders *prov.* Belgium *see* **West-Vlaanderen**
□P3 **West Forks** *ME* U.S.A.
G4 **West Freehold** *NJ* U.S.A.
H3 **West Friesland** *reg.* Neth.
West Frisian Islands Neth. *see* **Waddeneilanden**
J1 **Westgat** *sea chan.* Neth.
K9 **Westgate** *Qld* Austr.
M4 **Westgate** *Durham, England* U.K.
H2 **West Glacier** *MT* U.S.A.
□R3 **West Grand Lake** *ME* U.S.A.
L6 **West Grinstead** *West Sussex, England* U.K.
D5 **West Grove** *PA* U.S.A.
J3 **West Haddon** *Northamptonshire, England* U.K.
C10 **West Hamlin** *WV* U.S.A.
J3 **Westhampton** *NY* U.S.A.
G5 **West Harptree** *Bath and North East Somerset, England* U.K.
J1 **West Hartford** *CT* U.S.A.
I4 **Westhausen** Ger.
J2 **West Haven** *CT* U.S.A.
H2 **West Haverstraw** *NY* U.S.A.
D3 **West Hazleton** *PA* U.S.A.
L8 **Westhill** *Aberdeenshire, Scotland* U.K.

194 E2 **Westhofen** Ger.
179 N6 **Westhoffen** France
260 E1 **Westhope** *ND* U.S.A.
287 F2 **West Ice Shelf** Antarctica
271 L4 **West Indies** N. America
168 □O1 **Westing** *Shetland, Scotland* U.K.
West Irian *prov.* Indon. *see* **Papua Barat**
106 F3 **West Island** *N.T.* Austr.
108 □2 **West Island** Cocos Is
137 M6 **West Island** *Andaman & Nicobar Is* India
259 I3 **West Islip** *NY* U.S.A.
256 B9 **West Jefferson** *OH* U.S.A.
186 D5 **Westkapelle** Neth.
West Kazakhstan Oblast *admin. div.* Kazakh. *see* **Zapadnyy Kazakhstan**
168 G11 **West Kilbride** *North Ayrshire, Scotland* U.K.
257 N7 **West Kingston** *RI* U.S.A.
171 K7 **West Kirby** *Merseyside, England* U.K.
171 P5 **West Knapton** *North Yorkshire, England* U.K.
254 D5 **West Lafayette** *IN* U.S.A.
West Lamma Channel *H.K.* China *see* **Sai Pok Liu Hoi Hap**
107 I7 **Westland** *Qld* Austr.
256 B6 **Westland** *MI* U.S.A.
100 □3b **West Landing** *i. Majuro* Marshall Is
103 E10 **Westland National Park** *South I.* N.Z.
173 I5 **West Lavington** *Wiltshire, England* U.K.
258 D4 **West Lawn** *PA* U.S.A.
237 L3 **Westleigh** S. Africa
173 P3 **Westleton** *Suffolk, England* U.K.
256 B11 **West Liberty** *KY* U.S.A.
256 B8 **West Liberty** *OH* U.S.A.
168 J11 **West Linton** *Scottish Borders, Scotland* U.K.
168 C6 **West Loch Roag** *b. Scotland* U.K.
168 E11 **West Loch Tarbert** *inlet Scotland* U.K.
246 H4 **Westlock** *Alta* Can.
172 D7 **West Looe** *Cornwall, England* U.K.
248 D5 **West Lorne** *Ont.* Can.
168 I11 **West Lothian** *admin. div. Scotland* U.K.
172 H6 **West Lulworth** *Dorset, England* U.K.
231 E8 **West Lunga** *r.* Zambia
231 E8 **West Lunga National Park** Zambia
106 D7 **West MacDonnell National Park** *N.T.* Austr.
West Malaysia *pen.* Malaysia *see* **Malaysia, Semenanjung**
187 G6 **Westmalle** Belgium
173 M5 **West Malling** *Kent, England* U.K.
Westman Islands Iceland *see* **Vestmannaeyjar**
107 L9 **Westmar** *Qld* Austr.
290 E4 **West Mariana Basin** *sea feature* Pacific Ocean
169 H5 **Westmeath** *county* Ireland
261 J8 **West Memphis** *AR* U.S.A.
173 J5 **West Meon Hut** *Hampshire, England* U.K.
102 I6 **Westmere** *North I.* N.Z.
173 N4 **West Mersea** *Essex, England* U.K.
173 I3 **West Midlands** *admin. div. England* U.K.
259 G2 **West Milford** *NJ* U.S.A.
251 K8 **West Millgrove** *OH* U.S.A.
256 A9 **West Milton** *OH* U.S.A.
258 B2 **West Milton** *PA* U.S.A.
258 B5 **Westminster** *MD* U.S.A.
172 F5 **West Monkton** *Somerset, England* U.K.
261 I9 **West Monroe** *LA* U.S.A.
173 I6 **West Moors** *Dorset, England* U.K.
106 G4 **Westmoreland** *Qld* Austr.
270 □ **Westmoreland** Jamaica
260 G6 **Westmoreland** *KS* U.S.A.
265 Q8 **Westmorland** *CA* U.S.A.
258 C2 **West Nanticoke** *PA* U.S.A.
168 J4 **Westness** *Orkney, Scotland* U.K.
171 K4 **Westnewton** *Cumbria, England* U.K.
235 F4 **West Nicholson** Zimbabwe
261 F11 **West Nueces** *r. TX* U.S.A.
259 H2 **West Nyack** *NY* U.S.A.
237 O2 **Westoe Dam** S. Africa
117 K2 **Weston** *Sabah* Malaysia
103 E12 **Weston** *South I.* N.Z.
172 H6 **Weston** *Dorset, England* U.K.
172 H2 **Weston** *Staffordshire, England* U.K.
259 I2 **Weston** *CT* U.S.A.
256 B7 **Weston** *OH* U.S.A.
256 E9 **Weston** *WV* U.S.A.
237 L2 **Westonaria** S. Africa
172 G5 **Weston-super-Mare** *North Somerset, England* U.K.
172 G5 **Westonzoyland** *Somerset, England* U.K.
257 J10 **Westover** *MD* U.S.A.
255 G12 **West Palm Beach** *FL* U.S.A.
West Papua *prov.* Indon. *see* **Papua Barat**
West Passage Palau *see* **Toagel Mlungui**
261 J7 **West Plains** *MO* U.S.A.
105 J9 **West Point** *pt Tas.* Austr.
238 □2c **West Point** *pt Tristan da Cunha* S. Atlantic Ocean
264 L3 **West Point** *CA* U.S.A.
250 G9 **Westpoint** *IN* U.S.A.
261 K9 **West Point** *MS* U.S.A.
260 G5 **West Point** *NE* U.S.A.
257 L7 **West Point** *NY* U.S.A.
256 E8 **West Point** *OH* U.S.A.
256 I11 **West Point** *VA* U.S.A.
245 K2 **West Point** *mt. AK* U.S.A.
255 E9 **West Point Lake** *resr AL/GA* U.S.A.
251 R5 **Westport** *Ont.* Can.
103 F8 **Westport** *South I.* N.Z.
169 C5 **Westport** Ireland
264 I2 **Westport** *CA* U.S.A.
259 I2 **Westport** *CT* U.S.A.
257 L4 **Westport** *NY* U.S.A.
169 C5 **Westport Quay** Ireland
271 □10 **Westpunt** *Curaçao* Neth. Antilles
171 N4 **West Rainton** *Durham, England* U.K.
247 K4 **Westray** *Man.* Can.
168 J4 **Westray** *i. Scotland* U.K.
168 J4 **Westray Firth** *sea chan. Scotland* U.K.
259 I2 **West Redding** *CT* U.S.A.
248 D4 **Westree** *Ont.* Can.
194 C3 **Westrich** *reg.* Ger.
246 F4 **West Road** *r. B.C.* Can.
168 K11 **Westruther** *Scottish Borders, Scotland* U.K.
257 L5 **West Rutland** *VT* U.S.A.
264 K3 **West Sacramento** *CA* U.S.A.
256 C8 **West Salem** *OH* U.S.A.
251 P7 **West Seneca** *NY* U.S.A.
West Siberian Plain Rus. Fed. *see* **Zapadno-Sibirskaya Ravnina**
105 K8 **West Sister Island** *Tas.* Austr.
173 P2 **West Somerton** *Norfolk, England* U.K.
257 N4 **West Stewartstown** *NH* U.S.A.
173 L5 **West Sussex** *admin. div. England* U.K.
186 H2 **West-Terschelling** Neth.
257 M4 **West Topsham** *VT* U.S.A.
173 K6 **West Town** *Hampshire, England* U.K.
258 F2 **Westtown** *NY* U.S.A.
250 J5 **West Twin Lake** *MI* U.S.A.
250 C7 **West Union** *IA* U.S.A.
256 B10 **West Union** *OH* U.S.A.
256 E9 **West Union** *WV* U.S.A.
262 I6 **West Valley City** *UT* U.S.A.
250 H8 **Westville** *IN* U.S.A.
261 H8 **Westville** *OK* U.S.A.
256 E10 **West Virginia** *state* U.S.A.

187 C7 **West-Vlaanderen** *prov.* Belgium
264 M3 **West Walker** *r. NV* U.S.A.
172 D5 **Westward Ho!** *Devon, England* U.K.
173 I6 **West Wellow** *Hampshire, England* U.K.
168 J10 **West Wemyss** *Fife, Scotland* U.K.
171 R8 **West Winch** *Norfolk, England* U.K.
107 M7 **Westwood** *Qld* Austr.
264 L1 **Westwood** *CA* U.S.A.
259 G3 **Westwood** *NJ* U.S.A.
105 K5 **West Wyalong** *N.S.W.* Austr.
173 K4 **West Wycombe** *Buckinghamshire, England* U.K.
168 □N1 **West Yell** *Shetland, Scotland* U.K.
262 I4 **West Yellowstone** *MT* U.S.A.
258 B5 **West York** *PA* U.S.A.
171 M6 **West Yorkshire** *admin. div. England* U.K.
186 G4 **Westzaan** Neth.
115 F7 **Wetan** *i. Maluku* Indon.
115 E7 **Wetar** *i. Maluku* Indon.
115 E8 **Wetar, Selat** *sea chan.* Indon.
246 H4 **Wetaskiwin** *Alta* Can.
231 E6 **Wete** Dem. Rep. Congo
233 C6 **Wete** Tanz.
193 E8 **Wethau** Ger.
171 L4 **Wetheral** *Cumbria, England* U.K.
171 O6 **Wetherby** *West Yorkshire, England* U.K.
259 J1 **Wethersfield** *CT* U.S.A.
103 A12 **Wet Jacket Arm** *inlet South I.* N.Z.
197 K6 **Wetlina** Pol.
250 H3 **Wetmore** *MI* U.S.A.
286 T2 **Wetmore Glacier** Antarctica
190 F5 **Wetschen** Ger.
191 G10 **Wetter** *r.* Ger.
191 G9 **Wetter (Hessen)** Ger.
191 D8 **Wetter (Ruhr)** Ger.
191 G10 **Wetterau** *reg.* Ger.
187 E6 **Wetteren** Belgium
193 F8 **Wetterzeube** Ger.
193 E7 **Wettin** Ger.
212 E1 **Wettingen** Switz.
191 D6 **Wettringen** Ger.
190 E5 **Wettrup** Ger.
195 K4 **Wettstetten** Ger.
255 D9 **Wetumpka** *AL* U.S.A.
118 C3 **Wetwun** Myanmar
212 F1 **Wetzikon** Switz.
191 G9 **Wetzlar** Ger.
187 D7 **Wevelgem** Belgium
244 F1 **Wevok** *AK* U.S.A.
255 E10 **Wewahitchka** *FL* U.S.A.
113 J7 **Wewak** P.N.G.
190 H3 **Wewelsfleth** Ger.
261 G8 **Wewoka** *OK* U.S.A.
169 J8 **Wexford** Ireland
169 I7 **Wexford** *county* Ireland
169 J8 **Wexford Bay** Ireland
169 J8 **Wexford Harbour** *b.* Ireland
247 J4 **Weyakwin** *Sask.* Can.
195 L6 **Weyarn** Ger.
250 F5 **Weyauwega** *WI* U.S.A.
173 L5 **Weybridge** *Surrey, England* U.K.
247 K5 **Weyburn** *Sask.* Can.
191 E9 **Weyerbusch** Ger.
201 K4 **Weyer Markt** Austria
179 O6 **Weyersheim** France
191 K6 **Weyhausen** Ger.
190 G5 **Weyhe** Ger.
249 H4 **Weymouth** *N.S.* Can.
172 H6 **Weymouth** *Dorset, England* U.K.
257 O6 **Weymouth** *MA* U.S.A.
258 F5 **Weymouth** *NJ* U.S.A.
107 I2 **Weymouth, Cape** *Qld* Austr.
186 J4 **Wezep** Neth.
102 L4 **Whakaari** *i. North I.* N.Z.
Whaka a Te Wera *inlet Stewart I.* N.Z. *see* **Paterson Inlet**
102 L6 **Whakaki** *North I.* N.Z.
102 J5 **Whakamaru** *North I.* N.Z.
102 L5 **Whakapunake** *hill North I.* N.Z.
Whakaraupō *inlet South I.* N.Z. *see* **Lyttelton Harbour**
102 K5 **Whakarewarewa Forest Park** *nature res. North I.* N.Z.
102 K4 **Whakatane** *North I.* N.Z.
Whakatipu Kā Tuka *r. South I.* N.Z. *see* **Hollyford**
Whakatipu Waitai *l. South I.* N.Z. *see* **McKerrow, Lake**
105 L3 **Whalan Creek** *r. N.S.W.* Austr.
Whale *r. Que.* Can. *see* **Baleine, Rivière à la**
245 N4 **Whale Bay** *AK* U.S.A.
270 E1 **Whale Cay** *i.* Bahamas
247 M2 **Whale Cove** *Nunavut* Can.
Whale Island *North I.* N.Z. *see* **Moutohora Island**
245 N4 **Whale Pass** *AK* U.S.A.
237 N7 **Whale Rock** *i.* S. Africa
171 N7 **Whaley Bridge** *Derbyshire, England* U.K.
256 I12 **Whaleyville** *VA* U.S.A.
168 □O2 **Whalsay** *i. Scotland* U.K.
171 N3 **Whalton** *Northumberland, England* U.K.
116 □ **Whampoa, Sungai** *r.* Sing.
102 J7 **Whangaehu** *r. North I.* N.Z.
102 J4 **Whangamata** *North I.* N.Z.
103 H8 **Whangamoa** *South I.* N.Z.
102 I6 **Whangamomona** *North I.* N.Z.
102 G7 **Whanganui Inlet** *South I.* N.Z.
102 I6 **Whanganui National Park** *North I.* N.Z.
102 I3 **Whangaparaoa** *North I.* N.Z.
102 L4 **Whangaparaoa Bay** *North I.* N.Z.
102 I3 **Whangaparaoa Head** *North I.* N.Z.
102 H2 **Whangape Harbour** *North I.* N.Z.
102 M5 **Whangara** *North I.* N.Z.
102 I2 **Whangarei** *North I.* N.Z.
102 H2 **Whangaroa Bay** *North I.* N.Z.
102 I2 **Whangaruru Harbour** *b. North I.* N.Z.
173 L2 **Whaplode** *Lincolnshire, England* U.K.
248 E2 **Whapmagoostui** *Que.* Can.
103 I8 **Wharanui** *South I.* N.Z.
103 K7 **Whareama** *North I.* N.Z.
171 O6 **Wharfe** *r. England* U.K.
171 N5 **Wharfedale** *val. England* U.K.
251 K3 **Wharncliffe** *Ont.* Can.
256 D11 **Wharncliffe** *WV* U.S.A.
258 F3 **Wharton** *NJ* U.S.A.
261 G11 **Wharton** *TX* U.S.A.
247 L1 **Wharton Lake** *Nunavut* Can.
103 E10 **Whataroa** *South I.* N.Z.
246 G2 **Whatî** *N.W.T.* Can.
168 H13 **Whauphill** *Dumfries and Galloway, Scotland* U.K.
264 K2 **Wheatland** *CA* U.S.A.
262 L5 **Wheatland** *WY* U.S.A.
251 L7 **Wheatley** *Ont.* Can.
250 F8 **Wheaton** *IL* U.S.A.
260 G3 **Wheaton** *MN* U.S.A.
172 H2 **Wheaton Aston** *Staffordshire, England* U.K.
258 A6 **Wheaton-Glenmont** *MD* U.S.A.
104 □2 **Wheatsheaf Island** *Lord Howe I.* Austr.
172 E5 **Wheddon Cross** *Somerset, England* U.K.
261 E8 **Wheeler** *TX* U.S.A.
250 C4 **Wheeler** *WI* U.S.A.
246 H2 **Wheeler Lake** *N.W.T.* Can.
255 D8 **Wheeler Lake** *resr AL* U.S.A.
263 L8 **Wheeler Peak** *NM* U.S.A.
265 R3 **Wheeler Peak** *NV* U.S.A.
256 C10 **Wheelersburg** *OH* U.S.A.
264 M7 **Wheeler Springs** *CA* U.S.A.
256 E8 **Wheeling** *WV* U.S.A.
285 G3 **Wheelwright** Arg.
171 M5 **Whernside** *hill England* U.K.
173 J5 **Wherwell** *Hampshire, England* U.K.
171 N4 **Whickham** *Tyne and Wear, England* U.K.
172 E6 **Whiddon Down** *Devon, England* U.K.
169 D9 **Whiddy Island** Ireland
108 D6 **Whim Creek** *W.A.* Austr.
172 F6 **Whimple** *Devon, England* U.K.

104 C2 **Whinham, Mount** *S.A.* Austr.
259 G3 **Whippany** *NJ* U.S.A.
102 K5 **Whirinaki Forest Park** *nature res. North I.* N.Z.
247 K3 **Whiskey Jack Lake** *Man.* Can.
264 J3 **Whispering Pines** *CA* U.S.A.
106 E6 **Whistleduck Creek** *watercourse N.T.* Austr.
246 F5 **Whistler** *B.C.* Can.
249 K4 **Whitbourne** *Nfld and Lab.* Can.
168 I11 **Whitburn** *West Lothian, Scotland* U.K.
251 P6 **Whitby** *Ont.* Can.
171 P5 **Whitby** *North Yorkshire, England* U.K.
173 K4 **Whitchurch** *Buckinghamshire, England* U.K.
172 F4 **Whitchurch** *Cardiff, Wales* U.K.
173 J5 **Whitchurch** *Hampshire, England* U.K.
172 G2 **Whitchurch** *Shropshire, England* U.K.
251 O6 **Whitchurch-Stouffville** *Ont.* Can.
103 E10 **Whitcombe, Mount** *South I.* N.Z.
248 C3 **White** *r. Ont.* Can.
245 M3 **White** *r.* Can./U.S.A.
270 □ **White** *r.* Jamaica
253 H4 **White** *r. AR* U.S.A.
261 J9 **White** *r. AR* U.S.A.
265 W1 **White** *r. CO* U.S.A.
254 D6 **White** *r. IN* U.S.A.
250 H6 **White** *r. MI* U.S.A.
265 R5 **White** *r. NV* U.S.A.
260 F4 **White** *r. SD* U.S.A.
257 M5 **White** *r. VT* U.S.A.
250 D3 **White** *r. WI* U.S.A.
265 V8 **White** *watercourse AZ* U.S.A.
261 E9 **White** *watercourse TX* U.S.A.
254 D6 **White, East Fork** *r. IN* U.S.A.
106 B6 **White, Lake** *salt flat N.T.* Austr.
261 I7 **White, North Fork** *r. MO* U.S.A.
171 M2 **Whiteadder Water** *r. Scotland* U.K.
249 J3 **White Bay** *Nfld and Lab.* Can.
260 D2 **White Butte** *mt. ND* U.S.A.
265 V4 **White Canyon** *UT* U.S.A.
169 E9 **Whitechurch** *Cork* Ireland
169 G8 **Whitechurch** *Waterford* Ireland
105 I4 **White Cliffs** *N.S.W.* Austr.
250 I6 **White Cloud** *MI* U.S.A.
103 D12 **Whitecoomb** *mt. South I.* N.Z.
168 J12 **White Coomb** *hill Scotland* U.K.
246 H4 **Whitecourt** *Alta* Can.
168 J11 **Whitecraig** *East Lothian, Scotland* U.K.
169 J4 **Whitecross** *Northern Ireland* U.K.
258 B2 **White Deer** *PA* U.S.A.
260 H2 **White Earth Indian Reservation** *res. MN* U.S.A.
250 B2 **Whiteface Lake** *MN* U.S.A.
257 L4 **Whiteface Mountain** *NY* U.S.A.
257 N4 **Whitefield** *NH* U.S.A.
251 M3 **Whitefish** *Ont.* Can.
245 P2 **Whitefish** *r. N.W.T.* Can.
262 G2 **Whitefish** *MT* U.S.A.
250 H4 **Whitefish** *r. MI* U.S.A.
250 G5 **Whitefish Bay** *WI* U.S.A.
247 J2 **Whitefish Lake** *N.W.T.* Can.
250 E1 **Whitefish Lake** *Ont.* Can.
244 I3 **Whitefish Lake** *AK* U.S.A.
250 J3 **Whitefish Point** *MI* U.S.A.
258 C5 **Whiteford** *MD* U.S.A.
169 F7 **Whitegate** *Clare* Ireland
169 F9 **Whitegate** *Cork* Ireland
169 D9 **White Hall** Ireland
169 H7 **Whitehall** Ireland
168 K4 **Whitehall** *Orkney, Scotland* U.K.
260 J6 **White Hall** *IL* U.S.A.
258 B5 **White Hall** *MD* U.S.A.
250 H6 **Whitehall** *MI* U.S.A.
262 H4 **Whitehall** *MT* U.S.A.
257 L5 **Whitehall** *NY* U.S.A.
256 C9 **Whitehall** *OH* U.S.A.
258 B2 **White Hall** *PA* U.S.A.
258 E3 **Whitehall** *PA* U.S.A.
250 C5 **Whitehall** *WI* U.S.A.
171 J4 **Whitehaven** *Cumbria, England* U.K.
258 D2 **White Haven** *PA* U.S.A.
169 K3 **Whitehead** *Northern Ireland* U.K.
249 I4 **White Hill** *N.S.* Can.
173 K5 **Whitehill** *Hampshire, England* U.K.
168 K7 **Whitehills** *Aberdeenshire, Scotland* U.K.
245 J1 **White Hills** *AK* U.S.A.
245 N3 **Whitehorse** *Y.T.* Can.
258 F4 **White Horse** *NJ* U.S.A.
173 I4 **White Horse, Vale of** *val. England* U.K.
270 □ **White Horses** Jamaica
258 F3 **Whitehouse** *NJ* U.S.A.
258 F3 **White House Station** *NJ* U.S.A.
287 D2 **White Island** Antarctica
White Island *North I.* N.Z. *see* **Whakaari**
237 L8 **White Kei** *r.* S. Africa
109 F8 **White Lake** *salt flat W.A.* Austr.
248 C3 **White Lake** *l. Ont.* Can.
248 E4 **White Lake** *l. Ont.* Can.
258 F1 **White Lake** *NY* U.S.A.
261 I11 **White Lake** *l. LA* U.S.A.
250 H6 **White Lake** *l. MI* U.S.A.
105 L9 **Whitemark** *Tas.* Austr.
258 E1 **White Mills** *PA* U.S.A.
244 G2 **White Mountain** *AK* U.S.A.
264 N4 **White Mountain Peak** *CA* U.S.A.
245 K2 **White Mountains** *AK* U.S.A.
257 N4 **White Mountains** *NH* U.S.A.
107 J6 **White Mountains National Park** *Qld* Austr.
252 G1 **Whitemouth** *r. Man.* Can.
247 M5 **Whitemouth Lake** *Man.* Can.
246 G3 **Whitemud** *r. Alta* Can.
168 G5 **Whiten Head** *Scotland* U.K.
225 G6 **White Nile** *state* Sudan
225 G6 **White Nile** *r.* Sudan/Uganda *alt.* **Abiad, Bahr el,** *alt.* **Jebel, Bahr el**
225 G6 **White Nile Dam** Sudan
234 C4 **White Nossob** *watercourse* Namibia
256 B11 **White Oak** *KY* U.S.A.
248 B3 **White Otter Lake** *Ont.* Can.
245 N4 **White Pass** Can./U.S.A.
250 I8 **White Pigeon** *MI* U.S.A.
250 E3 **White Pine** *MI* U.S.A.
265 Q3 **White Pine Range** *mts NV* U.S.A.
259 H2 **White Plains** *NY* U.S.A.
168 L8 **Whiterashes** *Aberdeenshire, Scotland* U.K.
248 C3 **White River** *Ont.* Can.
265 W8 **Whiteriver** *AZ* U.S.A.
260 E4 **White River** *SD* U.S.A.
257 M5 **White River Junction** *VT* U.S.A.
261 J8 **White River National Wildlife Refuge** *nature res. AR* U.S.A.
265 Q3 **White River Valley** *NV* U.S.A.
265 R3 **White Rock Peak** *NV* U.S.A.
White Russia *country* Europe *see* **Belarus**
246 E4 **Whitesail Lake** *B.C.* Can.
262 D4 **White Salmon** *WA* U.S.A.
246 H2 **Whitesand** *r. Alta/N.W.T.* Can.
247 K5 **Whitesand** *r. Sask.* Can.
263 K10 **White Sands National Monument** *nat. park NM* U.S.A.
258 F6 **Whitesboro** *NJ* U.S.A.
257 J5 **Whitesboro** *NY* U.S.A.
256 C11 **Whitesburg** *KY* U.S.A.
White Sea Rus. Fed. *see* **Beloye More**
247 M5 **Whiteshell Provincial Park** *Man.* Can.
245 M2 **Whitestone** *r. Y.T.* Can.
257 I11 **White Stone** *VA* U.S.A.
262 I3 **White Sulphur Springs** *MT* U.S.A.
256 E11 **White Sulphur Springs** *WV* U.S.A.
258 E1 **Whites Valley** *PA* U.S.A.
256 D11 **Whitesville** *WV* U.S.A.
237 P4 **White Umfolozi** *r.* S. Africa
255 H8 **Whiteville** *NC* U.S.A.

228 E4 **White Volta** *watercourse* Burkina/Ghana *alt.* **Nakambé,** *alt.* **Nakanbe,** *alt.* **Volta Blanche**
228 E4 **White Volta** *r.* Ghana
264 P8 **White Water** *CA* U.S.A.
265 X3 **Whitewater** *CO* U.S.A.
250 F7 **Whitewater** *WI* U.S.A.
263 J10 **Whitewater Baldy** *mt. NM* U.S.A.
248 B3 **Whitewater Lake** *Ont.* Can.
104 C4 **White Well** *S.A.* Austr.
260 E6 **White Woman Creek** *r. KS* U.S.A.
107 I6 **Whitewood** *Qld* Austr.
247 K5 **Whitewood** *Sask.* Can.
105 K7 **Whitfield** *Vic.* Austr.
173 O5 **Whitfield** *Kent, England* U.K.
172 F1 **Whitford** *Flintshire, Wales* U.K.
172 D4 **Whitford Point** *Wales* U.K.
168 H13 **Whithorn** *Dumfries and Galloway, Scotland* U.K.
102 J3 **Whitianga** *North I.* N.Z.
257 □R4 **Whiting** *ME* U.S.A.
259 G5 **Whiting** *NJ* U.S.A.
250 E5 **Whiting** *WI* U.S.A.
168 F12 **Whiting Bay** *North Ayrshire, Scotland* U.K.
172 C4 **Whitland** *Carmarthenshire, Wales* U.K.
171 O3 **Whitley Bay** *Tyne and Wear, England* U.K.
255 E7 **Whitley City** *KY* U.S.A.
258 E5 **Whitman Square** *NJ* U.S.A.
255 G8 **Whitmire** *SC* U.S.A.
237 M7 **Whitmore** S. Africa
286 Q1 **Whitmore Mountains** Antarctica
173 I3 **Whitnash** *Warwickshire, England* U.K.
251 P4 **Whitney** *Ont.* Can.
261 G10 **Whitney, Lake** *TX* U.S.A.
264 N5 **Whitney, Mount** *CA* U.S.A.
257 J6 **Whitney Point** *NY* U.S.A.
172 D7 **Whitsand Bay** *England* U.K.
173 O5 **Whitstable** *Kent, England* U.K.
107 L6 **Whitsunday Group** *is Qld* Austr.
107 L6 **Whitsunday Island** *Qld* Austr.
107 L6 **Whitsunday Island National Park** *Qld* Austr.
107 L6 **Whitsunday Passage** *Qld* Austr.
Whitsun Island Vanuatu *see* **Pentecost Island**
251 K5 **Whittemore** *MI* U.S.A.
245 J3 **Whittier** *AK* U.S.A.
264 N8 **Whittier** *CA* U.S.A.
171 N3 **Whittingham** *Northumberland, England* U.K.
172 F2 **Whittington** *Shropshire, England* U.K.
106 D5 **Whittington Range** *hills N.T.* Austr.
105 J7 **Whittlesea** *Vic.* Austr.
237 K8 **Whittlesea** S. Africa
173 L2 **Whittlesey** *Cambridgeshire, England* U.K.
250 D4 **Whittlesey** *WI* U.S.A.
250 D3 **Whittlesey, Mount** *hill WI* U.S.A.
105 K6 **Whitton** *N.S.W.* Austr.
107 H8 **Whitula** *watercourse Qld* Austr.
171 M6 **Whitworth** *Lancashire, England* U.K.
247 J2 **Wholdaia Lake** *N.W.T.* Can.
265 T9 **Why** *AZ* U.S.A.
104 F5 **Whyalla** *S.A.* Austr.
Whydah Benin *see* **Ouidah**
118 D6 **Wiang Kosai National Park** Thai.
118 D5 **Wiang Pa Pao** Thai.
118 E5 **Wiang Sa** Thai.
197 K6 **Wiar** *r.* Pol.
197 J2 **Wiartel** Pol.
248 D4 **Wiarton** *Ont.* Can.
228 E4 **Wiasi** Ghana
196 F3 **Wiatrowo** Pol.
228 E5 **Wiawso** Ghana
168 B8 **Wiay** *i. Scotland* U.K.
196 F5 **Wiązów** Pol.
262 L3 **Wibaux** *MT* U.S.A.
232 C2 **Wich'alē** Eth.
187 E6 **Wichelen** Belgium
261 G7 **Wichita** *KS* U.S.A.
261 F8 **Wichita** *r. TX* U.S.A.
261 F9 **Wichita Falls** *TX* U.S.A.
261 F8 **Wichita Mountains** *OK* U.S.A.
261 F8 **Wichita Mountains National Wildlife Refuge** *nature res. OK* U.S.A.
168 J6 **Wick** *Highland, Scotland* U.K.
172 H5 **Wick** *South Gloucestershire, England* U.K.
172 E5 **Wick** *Vale of Glamorgan, Wales* U.K.
173 K6 **Wick** *West Sussex, England* U.K.
168 J6 **Wick** *r. Scotland* U.K.
191 E7 **Wickede** *airport* Ger.
191 E8 **Wickede (Ruhr)** Ger.
265 T8 **Wickenburg** *AZ* U.S.A.
109 D12 **Wickepin** *W.A.* Austr.
261 H8 **Wickes** *AR* U.S.A.
173 N4 **Wickford** *Essex, England* U.K.
108 D6 **Wickham** *W.A.* Austr.
106 C4 **Wickham** *r. N.T.* Austr.
173 J6 **Wickham** *Hampshire, England* U.K.
105 I8 **Wickham, Cape** *Tas.* Austr.
106 B4 **Wickham, Mount** *hill N.T.* Austr.
173 O3 **Wickham Market** *Suffolk, England* U.K.
261 K7 **Wickliffe** *KY* U.S.A.
169 J7 **Wicklow** Ireland
169 J6 **Wicklow** *county* Ireland
169 K7 **Wicklow Head** Ireland
169 I7 **Wicklow Mountains** Ireland
169 J6 **Wicklow Mountains National Park** Ireland
196 F1 **Wicko** Pol.
165 M7 **Wicko, Jezioro** *lag.* Pol.
172 H4 **Wickwar** *South Gloucestershire, England* U.K.
258 B3 **Wiconisco** *PA* U.S.A.
258 B3 **Wiconisco Creek** *r. PA* U.S.A.
196 G4 **Widawa** Pol.
196 E4 **Widawa** *r.* Pol.
197 G4 **Widawka** *r.* Pol.
107 N8 **Wide Bay** *Qld* Austr.
172 E6 **Widecombe in the Moor** *Devon, England* U.K.
168 J4 **Wide Firth** *sea chan. Scotland* U.K.
109 K8 **Wide Gum** *watercourse S.A.* Austr.
287 B2 **Widerøe, Mount** Antarctica
173 M4 **Widford** *Hertfordshire, England* U.K.
107 J9 **Widgeegoara** *watercourse Qld* Austr.
109 F11 **Widgiemooltha** *W.A.* Austr.
115 F4 **Widi, Kepulauan** *is Maluku* Indon.
212 H1 **Widnau** Switz.
171 L7 **Widnes** *Halton, England* U.K.
123 E11 **Wi-do** *i.* S. Korea
196 C2 **Widuchowa** Pol.
196 F2 **Więcbork** Pol.
192 G2 **Wieck am Darß** Ger.
197 I2 **Wieczfnia Kościelna** Pol.
196 G2 **Wieczno, Jezioro** *l.* Pol.
191 D10 **Wied** *r.* Ger.
191 K7 **Wieda** Ger.
193 G9 **Wiederau** Ger.
193 F8 **Wiederitzsch** Ger.
217 □ **Wied Il-Għajn** Malta
193 J8 **Wiednitz** Ger.
190 F4 **Wiefelstede** Ger.
193 D8 **Wiehe** Ger.
191 F6 **Wiehengebirge** *hills* Ger.
191 E9 **Wiehl** Ger.
192 H1 **Wiek** Ger.
196 G5 **Większyce** Pol.
197 I2 **Wielbark** Pol.
196 E3 **Wieleń** Pol.
195 K6 **Wielenbach** Ger.
197 H3 **Wielgie** Pol.
196 E3 **Wielichowo** Pol.
197 I6 **Wieliczka** Pol.
197 K2 **Wieliczki** Pol.
196 E2 **Wielimie, Jezioro** *l.* Pol.
196 G2 **Wielka Nieszawka** Pol.

199 H2 **Wielka Racza** *mt.* Pol./Slovakia
197 K6 **Wielka Rawka** *mt.* Pol.
196 E5 **Wielka Sowa** *mt.* Pol.
197 L5 **Wielkie Oczy** Pol.
197 H2 **Wielkie Partęczyny, Jezioro** *l.* Pol.
196 G1 **Wielki Klincz** Pol.
196 F4 **Wielkopolska, Nizina** *lowland* Pol.
196 F3 **Wielkopolskie** *prov.* Pol.
196 F3 **Wielkopolskie, Pojezierze** *reg.* Pol.
196 E3 **Wielkopolski Park Narodowy** *nat. park* Pol.
197 J6 **Wielopole Skrzyńskie** Pol.
196 G5 **Wielowieś** Pol.
187 D7 **Wielsbeke** Belgium
196 G4 **Wieluń** Pol.
190 I3 **Wiemersdorf** Ger.
201 N3 **Wien** Austria
201 N3 **Wien** *land* Austria
201 L4 **Wienerbruck** Austria
201 N3 **Wiener Neudorf** Austria
201 N4 **Wiener Neustadt** Austria
201 N3 **Wiener Wald** *mts* Austria
190 J5 **Wienhausen** Ger.
197 I4 **Wieniawa** Pol.
196 G3 **Wieniec** Pol.
245 J2 **Wien Lake** *AK* U.S.A.
201 L3 **Wiensberg** *mt.* Austria
192 D5 **Wiepke** Ger.
197 H6 **Wieprz** Pol.
197 J4 **Wieprz** *r.* Pol.
165 M7 **Wieprza** *r.* Pol.
197 L4 **Wieprz-Krzna, Kanał** *canal* Pol.
197 K3 **Wiercień Duży** Pol.
186 K4 **Wierden** Neth.
190 K5 **Wieren** Ger.
186 G3 **Wieringermeer Polder** Neth.
186 H3 **Wieringerwerf** Neth.
194 F4 **Wiernsheim** Ger.
196 G4 **Wieruszów** Pol.
197 L4 **Wierzbica** *Lubelskie* Pol.
197 J4 **Wierzbica** *Mazowieckie* Pol.
196 F4 **Wierzbica Górna** Pol.
196 D2 **Wierzbięcin** Pol.
196 G3 **Wierzbinek** Pol.
196 F5 **Wierzbnik** Pol.
197 L2 **Wierzchlesie** Pol.
196 G3 **Wierzchosławice** *Kujawsko-Pomorskie* Pol.
197 I5 **Wierzchosławice** *Małopolskie* Pol.
196 E2 **Wierzchowo** *Zachodniopomorskie* Pol.
196 E2 **Wierzchowo** *Zachodniopomorskie* Pol.
196 E2 **Wierzchowo, Jezioro** *l.* Pol.
196 G1 **Wierzchucino** Pol.
196 G2 **Wierzyca** *r.* Pol.
201 L6 **Wies** Austria
195 J6 **Wies** Ger.
193 G9 **Wiesa** Ger.
195 M2 **Wiesau** Ger.
191 F10 **Wiesbaden** Ger.
194 D6 **Wiese** *r.* Ger.
201 L3 **Wieselburg** Austria
201 N4 **Wiesen** Austria
191 H10 **Wiesen** Ger.
212 H2 **Wiesen** Switz.
193 K6 **Wiesenau** Ger.
193 F6 **Wiesenburg** Ger.
195 N3 **Wiesenfelden** Ger.
194 H4 **Wiesensteig** Ger.
195 M3 **Wiesent** Ger.
195 K2 **Wiesent** *r.* Ger.
195 K2 **Wiesenthau** Ger.
195 I2 **Wiesentheid** Ger.
195 K2 **Wiesenttal** Ger.
200 E5 **Wiesing** Austria
190 H4 **Wiesle** *r.* Ger.
194 F3 **Wiesloch** Ger.
201 N4 **Wiesmath** Austria
190 E4 **Wiesmoor** Ger.
258 D3 **Wiessport** *PA* U.S.A.
190 D5 **Wietmarschen** Ger.
197 I5 **Wietrzychowice** Pol.
190 I5 **Wietze** Ger.
191 I5 **Wietze** *r.* Ger.
190 H5 **Wietzen** Ger.
190 I5 **Wietzendorf** Ger.
165 O7 **Wieżyca** *hill* Pol.
171 L6 **Wigan** *Greater Manchester, England* U.K.
195 I6 **Wiggensbach** Ger.
261 K10 **Wiggins** *MS* U.S.A.
224 C3 **Wīgh, Ramlat al** *des.* Libya
167 G6 **Wight, Isle of** *i. England* U.K.
197 L1 **Wigierski Park Narodowy** *nat. park* Pol.
172 G3 **Wigmore** *Herefordshire, England* U.K.
247 J2 **Wignes Lake** *N.W.T.* Can.
197 L1 **Wigry, Jezioro** *l.* Pol.
173 J2 **Wigston** *Leicestershire, England* U.K.
171 K4 **Wigton** *Cumbria, England* U.K.
168 H13 **Wigtown** *Dumfries and Galloway, Scotland* U.K.
168 H13 **Wigtown Bay** *Scotland* U.K.
186 I5 **Wijchen** Neth.
162 □ **Wijdefjorden** *inlet* Svalbard
196 E4 **Wijewo** Pol.
186 J4 **Wijhe** Neth.
186 G4 **Wijk aan Zee** Neth.
186 H5 **Wijk bij Duurstede** Neth.
186 H5 **Wijk en Aalburg** Neth.
187 G6 **Wijnegem** Belgium
186 J2 **Wijnjewoude** Neth.
265 S7 **Wikieup** *AZ* U.S.A.
232 C1 **Wik'ro** Eth.
251 M4 **Wikwemikong** *Ont.* Can.
212 G1 **Wil** Switz.
197 H6 **Wilamowice** Pol.
260 G5 **Wilber** *NE* U.S.A.
103 F10 **Wilberforce** *r. South I.* N.Z.
106 F1 **Wilberforce, Cape** *N.T.* Austr.
262 E3 **Wilbur** *WA* U.S.A.
195 I3 **Wilburgstetten** Ger.
261 H8 **Wilburton** *OK* U.S.A.
105 I4 **Wilcannia** *N.S.W.* Austr.
256 G7 **Wilcox** *PA* U.S.A.
Wilczek Land *i. Zemlya Frantsa-Iosifa* Rus. Fed. *see* **Vil'cheka, Zemlya**
197 H1 **Wilczęta** Pol.
196 G3 **Wilczogóra** Pol.
196 G3 **Wilczyn** Pol.
201 K4 **Wildalpen** Austria
201 L4 **Wildalpener Salzatal** *nature res.* Austria
193 I6 **Wildau** Ger.
194 F4 **Wildberg** *Baden-Württemberg* Ger.
192 G5 **Wildberg** *Brandenburg* Ger.
192 H3 **Wildberg** *Mecklenburg-Vorpommern* Ger.
247 K4 **Wildcat Hill Provincial Wilderness Park** *nature res. Sask.* Can.
264 P3 **Wildcat Peak** *NV* U.S.A.
237 N7 **Wild Coast** S. Africa
191 J9 **Wildeck-Obersuhl** Ger.
191 J9 **Wildeck-Richelsdorf** Ger.
191 J7 **Wildemann** Ger.
201 N2 **Wildendürnbach** Austria
193 G9 **Wildenfels** Ger.
236 G9 **Wilderness** S. Africa
256 H10 **Wilderness** *VA* U.S.A.
236 G10 **Wilderness National Park** S. Africa
190 F5 **Wildeshausen** Ger.
191 I10 **Wildflecken** Ger.
250 E1 **Wild Goose** *Ont.* Can.
246 G4 **Wildhay** *r. Alta* Can.
212 C3 **Wildhorn** *mt.* Switz.
263 L11 **Wild Horse Draw** *r. TX* U.S.A.
260 E5 **Wild Horse Hill** *mt. NE* U.S.A.
201 M6 **Wildon** Austria
195 I6 **Wildpoldsried** Ger.
260 G2 **Wild Rice** *r. MN* U.S.A.
260 G2 **Wild Rice** *r. ND* U.S.A.
250 B3 **Wild Rice Lake** *MN* U.S.A.
200 G5 **Wildseeloder** *mt.* Austria
200 G3 **Wildshut** Austria
200 C6 **Wildspitze** *mt.* Austria
246 H4 **Wildwood** *Alta* Can.

255 F11 **Wildwood** *FL* U.S.A.
258 F7 **Wildwood** *NJ* U.S.A.
258 F7 **Wildwood Crest** *NJ* U.S.A.
260 D6 **Wiley** *CO* U.S.A.
256 G9 **Wiley Ford** *WV* U.S.A.
197 J4 **Wilga** Pol.
197 J4 **Wilga** *r.* Pol.
237 M3 **Wilge** *r. Free State* S. Africa
237 N1 **Wilge** *r.* S. Africa
104 E4 **Wilgena** *S.A.* Austr.
113 J8 **Wilhelm, Mount** P.N.G.
275 G4 **Wilhelmina Gebergte** *mts* Suriname
186 H6 **Wilhelmina Kanaal** *canal* Neth.
162 □ **Wilhelmøya** *i.* Svalbard
Wilhelm-Pieck-Stadt Ger. *see* **Guben**
201 M3 **Wilhelmsburg** Austria
192 I3 **Wilhelmsburg** Ger.
194 G6 **Wilhelmsdorf** Ger.
190 F3 **Wilhelmshaven** Ger.
234 C4 **Wilhelmstal** Namibia
193 D10 **Wilhelmsthal** Ger.
201 J3 **Wilhering** Austria
195 J3 **Wilhermsdorf** Ger.
135 □2 **Wilingili** *i. Addu Atoll* Maldives
193 G9 **Wilkau-Haßlau** Ger.
258 D2 **Wilkes-Barre** *PA* U.S.A.
255 G7 **Wilkesboro** *NC* U.S.A.
287 I2 **Wilkes Coast** Antarctica
287 I2 **Wilkes Land** *reg.* Antarctica
247 I4 **Wilkie** *Sask.* Can.
256 F8 **Wilkinsburg** *PA* U.S.A.
286 T2 **Wilkins Coast** Antarctica
286 T2 **Wilkins Ice Shelf** Antarctica
104 D3 **Wilkinson Lakes** *salt flat S.A.* Austr.
169 I5 **Wilkinstown** Ireland
197 K4 **Wilkołaz Pierwszy** Pol.
197 J4 **Wilków** *Lubelskie* Pol.
196 F4 **Wilków** *Opolskie* Pol.
196 D3 **Wilkowo** Pol.
245 O4 **Will, Mount** *B.C.* Can.
262 C4 **Willamette** *r. OR* U.S.A.
172 F6 **Willand** *Devon, England* U.K.
105 J5 **Willandra Billabong** *watercourse N.S.W.* Austr.
105 J5 **Willandra National Park** *N.S.W.* Austr.
262 B3 **Willapa Bay** *WA* U.S.A.
266 D3 **Willard** Mex.
263 K9 **Willard** *NM* U.S.A.
256 C7 **Willard** *OH* U.S.A.
257 J10 **Willards** *MD* U.S.A.
171 K7 **Willaston** *Cheshire, England* U.K.
265 W9 **Willcox** *AZ* U.S.A.
265 W9 **Willcox Playa** *salt flat AZ* U.S.A.
191 H7 **Willebadessen** Ger.
187 F6 **Willebroek** Belgium
237 L4 **Willem Pretorius Game Reserve** *nature res.* S. Africa
186 F5 **Willemstad** Neth.
271 □10 **Willemstad** *Curaçao* Neth. Antilles
106 C3 **Willeroo** *N.T.* Austr.
247 I3 **William** *r. Sask.* Can.
105 I7 **William, Mount** *Vic.* Austr.
109 C7 **Williambury** *W.A.* Austr.
104 F3 **William Creek** *S.A.* Austr.
247 L4 **William Lake** *Man.* Can.
109 D12 **Williams** *W.A.* Austr.
107 H6 **Williams** *r. Qld* Austr.
109 D12 **Williams** *r. W.A.* Austr.
265 T6 **Williams** *AZ* U.S.A.
264 J2 **Williams** *CA* U.S.A.
260 I5 **Williamsburg** *IA* U.S.A.
256 A12 **Williamsburg** *KY* U.S.A.
250 I5 **Williamsburg** *MI* U.S.A.
256 A9 **Williamsburg** *OH* U.S.A.
256 G8 **Williamsburg** *PA* U.S.A.
256 I11 **Williamsburg** *VA* U.S.A.
270 □ **Williamsfield** Jamaica
270 D1 **Williams Island** Bahamas
246 F4 **Williams Lake** *B.C.* Can.
249 H1 **William Smith, Cap** *c. Que.* Can.
256 H5 **Williamson** *NY* U.S.A.
256 C11 **Williamson** *WV* U.S.A.
254 D5 **Williamsport** *IN* U.S.A.
256 B9 **Williamsport** *OH* U.S.A.
251 Q8 **Williamsport** *PA* U.S.A.
251 J7 **Williamston** *MI* U.S.A.
255 I8 **Williamston** *NC* U.S.A.
257 L6 **Williamstown** *MA* U.S.A.
258 F5 **Williamstown** *NJ* U.S.A.
257 J5 **Williamstown** *NY* U.S.A.
258 B3 **Williamstown** *PA* U.S.A.
256 D9 **Williamstown** *WV* U.S.A.
191 C8 **Willich** Ger.
271 □2 **Willikies** Antigua and Barbuda
257 M7 **Willimantic** *CT* U.S.A.
259 K1 **Willimantic** *r. CT* U.S.A.
258 F4 **Willingboro** *NJ* U.S.A.
173 M6 **Willingdon** *East Sussex, England* U.K.
191 G8 **Willingen (Upland)** Ger.
173 M3 **Willingham** *Cambridgeshire, England* U.K.
Willingili *i. N. Male* Maldives *see* **Vilingli**
191 H9 **Willingshausen** Ger.
173 I2 **Willington** *Derbyshire, England* U.K.
212 E1 **Willisau** Switz.
107 M4 **Willis Group** *atolls Coral Sea Is Terr.* Austr.
283 □ **Willis Islands** S. Georgia
236 E7 **Williston** S. Africa
255 F11 **Williston** *FL* U.S.A.
260 D1 **Williston** *ND* U.S.A.
255 G9 **Williston** *SC* U.S.A.
246 F4 **Williston Lake** *B.C.* Can.
172 F5 **Williton** *Somerset, England* U.K.
264 I2 **Willits** *CA* U.S.A.
260 H3 **Willmar** *MN* U.S.A.
246 G4 **Willmore Wilderness Provincial Park** *Alta* Can.
104 F4 **Willochra** *watercourse S.A.* Austr.
171 R7 **Willoughby** *Lincolnshire, England* U.K.
256 D7 **Willoughby** *OH* U.S.A.
257 M4 **Willoughby, Lake** *VT* U.S.A.
246 F4 **Willow** *r. B.C.* Can.
245 J3 **Willow** *AK* U.S.A.
265 R6 **Willow Beach** *AZ* U.S.A.
247 J5 **Willow Bunch** *Sask.* Can.
246 H5 **Willow Creek** *r. Alta* Can.
245 K3 **Willow Creek** *AK* U.S.A.
262 C6 **Willow Creek** *CA* U.S.A.
262 D4 **Willow Creek** *r. OR* U.S.A.
265 W1 **Willow Creek** *r. UT* U.S.A.
258 D6 **Willow Grove** *DE* U.S.A.
258 E4 **Willow Grove** *PA* U.S.A.
256 H8 **Willow Hill** *PA* U.S.A.
246 G2 **Willow Lake** *N.W.T.* Can.
246 F2 **Willowlake** *r. N.W.T.* Can.
236 H9 **Willowmore** S. Africa
106 D6 **Willowra** *N.T.* Austr.
Willowra Aboriginal Land Trust *res. N.T.* Austr. *see* **Wirliyajarrayi Aboriginal Land Trust**
250 E4 **Willow Reservoir** *WI* U.S.A.
264 J2 **Willows** *CA* U.S.A.
261 J7 **Willow Springs** *MO* U.S.A.
258 C5 **Willow Street** *PA* U.S.A.
237 M8 **Willowvale** S. Africa
108 J6 **Wills, Lake** *salt flat W.A.* Austr.
106 H7 **Wills Creek** *watercourse Qld* Austr.
194 D4 **Willstätt** Ger.
104 G6 **Willunga** *S.A.* Austr.
255 E10 **Wilma** *FL* U.S.A.
192 I4 **Wilmersdorf** *Brandenburg* Ger.
193 J7 **Wilmersdorf** *Brandenburg* Ger.
104 G5 **Wilmington** *S.A.* Austr.
258 D5 **Wilmington** *DE* U.S.A.
255 I8 **Wilmington** *NC* U.S.A.
256 B9 **Wilmington** *OH* U.S.A.
257 M6 **Wilmington** *VT* U.S.A.
255 G9 **Wilmington Island** *GA* U.S.A.
171 M7 **Wilmslow** *Cheshire, England* U.K.
186 G4 **Wilnis** Neth.
Wilno Lith. *see* **Vilnius**
191 F9 **Wilnsdorf** Ger.
186 J4 **Wilp** Neth.

136 G8 Wilpattu National Park Sri Lanka
104 G4 Wilpena S.A. Austr.
104 G4 Wilpena watercourse S.A. Austr.
193 I8 Wilsdruff Ger.
190 I4 Wilseder Berg hill Ger.
192 I4 Wilsickow Ger.
108 J4 Wilson r. W.A. Austr.
107 I9 Wilson watercourse Qld Austr.
Wilson atoll Micronesia see Ifalik
260 F6 Wilson KS U.S.A.
250 C6 Wilson MN U.S.A.
255 I8 Wilson NC U.S.A.
256 G5 Wilson NY U.S.A.
258 E3 Wilson PA U.S.A.
243 J3 Wilson, Cape Nunavut Can.
263 K8 Wilson, Mount CO U.S.A.
265 R3 Wilson, Mount NV U.S.A.
262 D4 Wilson, Mount OR U.S.A.
106 C5 Wilson Creek watercourse N.T. Austr.
287 K2 Wilson Hills Antarctica
264 N5 Wilsonia CA U.S.A.
255 D8 Wilson Lake resr AL U.S.A.
256 H11 Wilsons VA U.S.A.
105 K8 Wilson's Promontory pen. Vic. Austr.
105 K8 Wilson's Promontory National Park Vic. Austr.
190 H4 Wilstedt Ger.
190 H3 Wilster Ger.
190 C5 Wilsum Ger.
201 O2 Wiltersdorf Austria
193 J8 Wilthen Ger.
194 B2 Wiltingen Ger.
106 E3 Wilton r. N.T. Austr.
173 I5 Wilton Wiltshire, England U.K.
259 I2 Wilton CT U.S.A.
257 □O4 Wilton ME U.S.A.
260 E2 Wilton ND U.S.A.
257 N6 Wilton NH U.S.A.
172 I5 Wiltshire admin. div. England U.K.
187 I9 Wiltz Lux.
109 F9 Wiluna W.A. Austr.
172 F5 Wimbleball Lake England U.K.
102 K7 Wimbledon North I. N.Z.
173 M2 Wimblington Cambridgeshire, England U.K.
173 I6 Wimborne Minster Dorset, England U.K.
178 C2 Wimereux France
193 E7 Wimmelburg Ger.
105 H7 Wimmera r. Vic. Austr.
212 D2 Wimmis Switz.
201 N4 Wimpassing Austria
Wina r. Cameroon see Vina
254 D5 Winamac IN U.S.A.
232 B5 Winam Gulf Kenya
107 J9 Winbin watercourse Qld Austr.
237 L4 Winburg S. Africa
236 G3 Wincanton S. Africa
172 H5 Wincanton Somerset, England U.K.
173 I4 Winchcombe Gloucestershire, England U.K.
173 N6 Winchelsea East Sussex, England U.K.
257 M6 Winchendon MA U.S.A.
194 A2 Wincheringen Ger.
257 J3 Winchester Ont. Can.
103 F11 Winchester South I. N.Z.
173 J5 Winchester Hampshire, England U.K.
260 J6 Winchester IL U.S.A.
254 E5 Winchester IN U.S.A.
256 A11 Winchester KY U.S.A.
257 M6 Winchester NH U.S.A.
255 D8 Winchester TN U.S.A.
256 G9 Winchester VA U.S.A.
187 I8 Wincrange Lux.
245 N2 Wind r. Y.T. Can.
262 J5 Wind r. WY U.S.A.
197 J1 Winda Pol.
104 F4 Windabout, Lake salt flat S.A. Austr.
195 K5 Windach Ger.
Windau Latvia see Ventspils
256 G8 Windber PA U.S.A.
260 D4 Wind Cave National Park SD U.S.A.
190 I2 Windeby Ger.
255 F9 Winder GA U.S.A.
171 L5 Windermere Cumbria, England U.K.
171 L5 Windermere l. England U.K.
194 D2 Windesheim Ger.
258 E3 Windgap PA U.S.A.
191 D9 Windhagen Ger.
245 N4 Windham AK U.S.A.
259 K1 Windham CT U.S.A.
256 D7 Windham OH U.S.A.
191 J7 Windhausen Ger.
234 C4 Windhoek Namibia
109 G9 Windidda Aboriginal Reserve W.A. Austr.
243 I4 Windigo r. Ont. Can.
248 B2 Windigo Lake Ont. Can.
201 L2 Windigsteig Austria
195 M2 Windischeschenbach Ger.
201 J4 Windischgarsten Austria
168 K11 Windlestraw Law hill Scotland U.K.
170 D7 Windmill Ireland
207 □ Windmill Hill Flats Gibraltar
263 L10 Wind Mountain NM U.S.A.
260 H4 Windom MN U.S.A.
107 I8 Windorah Qld Austr.
195 O4 Windorf Ger.
265 W6 Window Rock AZ U.S.A.
250 G7 Wind Point WI U.S.A.
256 E9 Wind Ridge PA U.S.A.
262 J5 Wind River Indian Reservation res. WY U.S.A.
262 J5 Wind River Range mts WY U.S.A.
173 J4 Windrush r. England U.K.
287 G2 Winds, Bay of Antarctica
195 J3 Windsbach Ger.
105 M5 Windsor N.S.W. Austr.
249 H4 Windsor N.S. Can.
248 D5 Windsor Ont. Can.
249 F4 Windsor Que. Can.
173 K5 Windsor Windsor and Maidenhead, England U.K.
257 M7 Windsor CT U.S.A.
255 I7 Windsor NC U.S.A.
258 F4 Windsor NJ U.S.A.
257 J6 Windsor NY U.S.A.
258 B5 Windsor PA U.S.A.
256 I12 Windsor VA U.S.A.
257 M5 Windsor VT U.S.A.
173 K5 Windsor and Maidenhead admin. div. England U.K.
257 M6 Windsor Dam MA U.S.A.
257 M7 Windsor Locks CT U.S.A.
236 I4 Windsorton S. Africa
107 H9 Windula watercourse Qld Austr.
271 □³ Windward Grenada
271 M6 Windward Islands Caribbean Sea
Windward Islands Arch. de la Société Fr. Polynesia see Vent, Îles du
270 F4 Windward Passage Cuba/Haiti
244 I3 Windy Fork r. AK U.S.A.
109 C13 Windy Harbour W.A. Austr.
247 I4 Winefred Lake Alta Can.
255 D9 Winfield AL U.S.A.
261 G7 Winfield KS U.S.A.
256 D10 Winfield WV U.S.A.
172 G5 Winford North Somerset, England U.K.
173 K4 Wing Buckinghamshire, England U.K.
171 O4 Wingate Durham, England U.K.
106 C3 Wingate Mountains hills N.T. Austr.
259 H1 Wingdale NY U.S.A.
105 M4 Wingen N.S.W. Austr.
187 D6 Wingene Belgium
179 N6 Wingen-sur-Moder France
191 J8 Wingerode Ger.
105 N4 Wingham N.S.W. Austr.
248 D5 Wingham Ont. Can.
173 O5 Wingham Kent, England U.K.
178 E3 Wingles France
190 H3 Wingst Ger.
195 N5 Winhöring Ger.
115 D8 Wini East Timor
108 G7 Winifred, Lake salt flat W.A. Austr.
285 E5 Winifreda Arg.
100 □⁴ᵃ Winion, Mochun sea chan. Chuuk Micronesia
248 C2 Winisk r. Ont. Can.
248 C2 Winisk (abandoned) Ont. Can.
248 C2 Winisk Lake Ont. Can.
248 C2 Winisk River Provincial Park Ont. Can.
118 C7 Winkana Myanmar
236 D8 Winkelhaaks r. S. Africa
195 K3 Winkelhaid Ger.
265 V9 Winkelman AZ U.S.A.
237 K3 Winkelpos S. Africa
190 G5 Winkelsett Ger.
173 K5 Winkfield Bracknell Forest, England U.K.
195 M3 Winklarn Ger.
172 E6 Winkleigh Devon, England U.K.
247 L5 Winkler Man. Can.
200 G6 Winklern Austria
201 J5 Winklern bei Oberwölz Austria
262 C3 Winlock WA U.S.A.
106 C8 Winnalls Ridge N.T. Austr.
228 E5 Winneba Ghana
260 H4 Winnebago MN U.S.A.
250 F5 Winnebago, Lake WI U.S.A.
260 G4 Winnebago Indian Reservation res. NE U.S.A.
106 C5 Winnecke Creek watercourse N.T. Austr.
250 F5 Winneconne WI U.S.A.
262 F6 Winnemucca NV U.S.A.
264 M1 Winnemucca Lake NV U.S.A.
194 G4 Winnenden Ger.
260 E4 Winner SD U.S.A.
173 K5 Winnersh Wokingham, England U.K.
190 H2 Winnert Ger.
262 J3 Winnett MT U.S.A.
261 I10 Winnfield LA U.S.A.
260 H2 Winnibigoshish, Lake MN U.S.A.
197 I3 Winnica Pol.
261 H11 Winnie TX U.S.A.
109 C7 Winning W.A. Austr.
191 E10 Winningen Rheinland-Pfalz Ger.
193 D7 Winningen Sachsen-Anhalt Ger.
247 L5 Winnipeg Man. Can.
247 L5 Winnipeg r. Man./Ont. Can.
247 L5 Winnipeg, Lake Man. Can.
247 L5 Winnipegosis Man. Can.
247 K4 Winnipegosis, Lake Man. Can.
257 N5 Winnipesaukee, Lake NH U.S.A.
261 J9 Winnsboro LA U.S.A.
255 G8 Winnsboro SC U.S.A.
261 H9 Winnsboro TX U.S.A.
194 D2 Winnweiler Ger.
265 U6 Winona AZ U.S.A.
250 F3 Winona MI U.S.A.
250 C5 Winona MN U.S.A.
261 J7 Winona MO U.S.A.
261 K9 Winona MS U.S.A.
257 L4 Winooski VT U.S.A.
257 L4 Winooski r. VT U.S.A.
186 L2 Winschoten Neth.
172 G5 Winscombe North Somerset, England U.K.
190 I5 Winsen (Aller) Ger.
190 J4 Winsen (Luhe) Ger.
171 L7 Winsford Cheshire, England U.K.
196 E4 Wińsko Pol.
172 H5 Winsley Wiltshire, England U.K.
173 K4 Winslow Buckinghamshire, England U.K.
265 V6 Winslow AZ U.S.A.
257 □P4 Winslow ME U.S.A.
258 F5 Winslow NJ U.S.A.
257 L7 Winsted CT U.S.A.
171 N4 Winston Durham, England U.K.
255 G7 Winston-Salem NC U.S.A.
186 I2 Winsum Friesland Neth.
186 K2 Winsum Groningen Neth.
250 C4 Winter WI U.S.A.
191 G8 Winterberg Ger.
237 K8 Winterberg mts S. Africa
172 G4 Winterbourne South Gloucestershire, England U.K.
172 G6 Winterbourne Abbas Dorset, England U.K.
192 D5 Winterfeld Ger.
257 □Q4 Winter Harbor ME U.S.A.
255 G11 Winter Haven FL U.S.A.
194 G5 Winterlingen Ger.
255 G11 Winter Park FL U.S.A.
257 □Q4 Winterport ME U.S.A.
264 K3 Winters CA U.S.A.
261 F10 Winters TX U.S.A.
193 F8 Wintersdorf Ger.
260 H5 Winterset IA U.S.A.
258 C6 Winters Run r. MD U.S.A.
258 B5 Winterstown PA U.S.A.
186 K5 Winterswijk Neth.
212 F1 Winterthur Switz.
237 N4 Winterton S. Africa
171 P6 Winterton North Lincolnshire, England U.K.
237 M1 Winterveld S. Africa
257 □Q2 Winterville ME U.S.A.
259 K2 Winthrop CT U.S.A.
257 □P4 Winthrop ME U.S.A.
107 I7 Winton Qld Austr.
255 □² Winton New Prov. Bahamas
103 C13 Winton South I. N.Z.
171 M5 Winton Cumbria, England U.K.
255 I7 Winton NC U.S.A.
194 B2 Wintrich Ger.
179 N7 Wintzenheim France
173 L3 Winwick Cambridgeshire, England U.K.
191 I7 Winzenburg Ger.
201 N4 Winzendorf Austria
195 O4 Winzer Ger.
193 D8 Wipper r. Ger.
191 K8 Wipperdorf Ger.
191 D8 Wipperfürth Ger.
190 D5 Wippingen Ger.
193 D7 Wippra Kurort Ger.
200 D5 Wipptal val. Austria
116 F6 Wiralaga Sumatera Indon.
190 D4 Wirdumer (Wirdum) Ger.
191 E10 Wirges Ger.
171 N7 Wirksworth Derbyshire, England U.K.
106 D6 Wirliyajarrayi Aboriginal Land Trust res. N.T. Austr.
104 G5 Wirrabara S.A. Austr.
171 K7 Wirral pen. England U.K.
104 F4 Wirraminna S.A. Austr.
104 H7 Wirrega S.A. Austr.
104 E3 Wirrida, Lake salt flat S.A. Austr.
104 E5 Wirrulla S.A. Austr.
193 E10 Wirsberg Ger.
100 □⁴ᵃ Wisas i. Chuuk Micronesia
173 M2 Wisbech Cambridgeshire, England U.K.
257 □P4 Wiscasset ME U.S.A.
190 H3 Wischhafen Ger.
250 C6 Wisconsin r. WI U.S.A.
260 K3 Wisconsin state U.S.A.
250 E6 Wisconsin, Lake WI U.S.A.
250 E6 Wisconsin Dells WI U.S.A.
250 E5 Wisconsin Rapids WI U.S.A.
256 C12 Wise VA U.S.A.
245 J2 Wiseman AK U.S.A.
168 I11 Wishaw North Lanarkshire, Scotland U.K.
260 F2 Wisher ND U.S.A.
232 F3 Wisil Dabarow Somalia
171 O5 Wiske r. England U.K.
197 I3 Wiskitki Pol.
196 G6 Wisła Pol.
165 O7 Wisła r. Pol.
165 P7 Wiślana, Mierzeja spit Pol.
165 P7 Wiślany, Zalew b. Pol.
197 I5 Wiślica Pol.
197 K5 Wisłok r. Pol.
197 J5 Wisłoka r. Pol.
192 D3 Wismar Ger.
192 D2 Wismarbucht b. Ger.
261 J10 Wisner LA U.S.A.
197 K3 Wiśniew Pol.
197 I2 Wiśniewo Pol.
197 I6 Wiśniowa Pol.
178 C2 Wissant France
179 O5 Wissembourg France
191 E9 Wissen Ger.
250 C5 Wissota Lake WI U.S.A.
172 G3 Wistanstow Shropshire, England U.K.
246 E4 Wistaria B.C. Can.
171 M7 Wistaston Cheshire, England U.K.
190 I4 Wistedt Ger.
197 K6 Wisznia r. Pol.
196 F4 Wisznia Mała Pol.
197 L4 Wisznice Pol.
237 N1 Witbank S. Africa
234 C5 Witbooisvlei Namibia
236 E2 Witdraai S. Africa
173 N4 Witham Essex, England U.K.
173 M2 Witham r. England U.K.
257 L4 Witherbee NY U.S.A.
172 E6 Witheridge Devon, England U.K.
171 R6 Withernsea East Riding of Yorkshire, England U.K.
245 K3 Witherspoon, Mount AK U.S.A.
255 F10 Withlacoochee r. FL U.S.A.
255 F11 Withlacoochee r. FL U.S.A.
104 E2 Witjira National Park S.A. Austr.
237 N3 Witkoppies mt. S. Africa
196 F3 Witkowo Wielkopolskie Pol.
196 D2 Witkowo Zachodniopomorskie Pol.
237 J7 Witkransnek pass S. Africa
173 K5 Witley Surrey, England U.K.
186 H2 Witmarsum Neth.
237 J8 Witmos S. Africa
237 M1 Witnek S. Africa
173 J4 Witney Oxfordshire, England U.K.
196 C3 Witnica Lubuskie Pol.
196 C3 Witnica Zachodniopomorskie Pol.
197 H3 Witonia Pol.
196 F2 Witosław Pol.
236 I5 Witput S. Africa
237 P1 Witrivier S. Africa
178 H5 Witry-lès-Reims France
236 G4 Witsand Nature Reserve S. Africa
190 F1 Wittdün Ger.
236 G9 Witteberg mt. Eastern Cape S. Africa
237 M4 Witteberg mt. Free State S. Africa
237 L6 Witteberg mts S. Africa
236 E9 Witteberge mts S. Africa
179 N8 Wittelsheim France
191 D8 Witten Ger.
194 G7 Wittenbach Switz.
Wittenberg Ger. see Lutherstadt Wittenberg
250 E5 Wittenberg WI U.S.A.
192 E5 Wittenberge Ger.
192 D3 Wittenburg Ger.
192 D3 Wittenförden Ger.
192 H2 Wittenhagen Ger.
179 N8 Wittenheim France
108 E7 Wittenoom W.A. Austr.
Wittenoom Gorge W.A. Austr. see Wittenoom
190 I2 Wittensee l. Ger.
271 □⁸ Witte Pan salt l. Bonaire Neth. Antilles
173 L2 Wittering Peterborough, England U.K.
193 G9 Wittgensdorf Ger.
117 L2 Witti, Banjaran mts Malaysia
195 N5 Wittibreut Ger.
193 J8 Wittichenau Ger.
194 H2 Wittighausen Ger.
190 K5 Wittingen Ger.
195 I4 Wittislingen Ger.
194 B2 Wittlich Ger.
258 C7 Wittman MD U.S.A.
191 K6 Wittmar Ger.
190 E3 Wittmund Ger.
171 N4 Witton Gilbert Durham, England U.K.
192 H1 Wittow pen. Ger.
192 F4 Wittstock Ger.
233 D5 Witu Kenya
113 K7 Witu Islands P.N.G.
234 C4 Witvlei Namibia
237 L2 Witwatersberg mts S. Africa
237 K2 Witwatersrand mts S. Africa
191 I8 Witzenhausen Ger.
190 J3 Witzhave Ger.
192 E3 Witzin Ger.
190 G2 Witzwort Ger.
172 F5 Wiveliscombe Somerset, England U.K.
173 N4 Wivenhoe Essex, England U.K.
107 N9 Wivenhoe, Lake Qld Austr.
197 K1 Wiżajny Pol.
178 D2 Wizernes France
197 K2 Wizna Pol.
197 I3 Wkra r. Pol.
196 G3 Władysławów Pol.
165 O7 Władysławowo Pol.
196 D4 Wleń Pol.
197 H3 Włocławek Pol.
197 L4 Włodawa Pol.
197 L4 Włodawka r. Pol.
197 H5 Włodowice Pol.
196 F5 Włodzienin Pol.
197 H4 Włodzimierzów Pol.
196 E4 Włoszakowice Pol.
197 H5 Włoszczowa Pol.
192 E4 Wöbbelin Ger.
Wobkent Uzbek. see Vobkent
257 □O3 Woburn Que. Can.
173 K4 Woburn Bedfordshire, England U.K.
173 K3 Woburn Sands Milton Keynes, England U.K.
105 K7 Wodonga Vic. Austr.
197 J3 Wodynie Pol.
197 H4 Wodzierady Pol.
197 I5 Wodzisław Pol.
196 G5 Wodzisław Śląski Pol.
186 G4 Woerden Neth.
179 O6 Wœrth France
179 J5 Wœvre, Forêt de for. France
179 K5 Woëvre, Plaine de la plain France
186 H3 Wognum Neth.
230 F3 Wohko watercourse Sudan
212 E1 Wohlen Aargau Switz.
212 C2 Wohlen Bern Switz.
193 D8 Wohlmirstedt Ger.
287 A2 Wohlthat Mountains Antarctica
190 J3 Wohltorf Ger.
191 G9 Wohra r. Ger.
190 H2 Wöhrden Ger.
197 K4 Wohyń Pol.
130 B2 Woinbo Sichuan China
179 L5 Woippy France
197 J6 Wojaszówka Pol.
197 J5 Wojciechowice Pol.
197 K4 Wojcieszków Pol.
196 D5 Wojcieszów Pol.
196 G3 Wójcin Pol.
100 □³ᵇ Woje Majuro i. Majuro Marshall Is
Wōjjā atoll Marshall Is see Wotje
197 H5 Wojkowice Pol.
197 I6 Wojnicz Pol.
196 F2 Wojnowo Pol.
197 L5 Wojsławice Pol.
197 L5 Wojsławka r. Pol.
113 H8 Wokam i. Indon.
122 F5 Woken He r. China
139 O6 Wokha Nagaland India
173 K5 Woking Surrey, England U.K.
107 I7 Wokingham watercourse Qld Austr.
173 K5 Wokingham Wokingham, England U.K.
173 K5 Wokingham admin. div. England U.K.
105 M4 Woko National Park N.S.W. Austr.
192 H4 Wokuhl Ger.
197 H3 Wola Pol.
197 J4 Wola Mysłowska Pol.
197 I4 Wolanów Pol.
197 L4 Wola Uhruska Pol.
197 I3 Wola Wierzbowska Pol.
201 I6 Wolayersee und Umgobung nature res. Austria
197 H4 Wolbórz Pol.
197 H5 Wolbrom Pol.
259 J1 Wolcott CT U.S.A.
250 G9 Wolcott IN U.S.A.
256 I5 Wolcott NY U.S.A.
257 M4 Wolcott VT U.S.A.
250 I8 Wolcottville IN U.S.A.
196 G4 Wołczyn Pol.
192 I4 Woldegk Ger.
186 L2 Woldendorp Neth.
171 Q5 Wold Newton East Riding of Yorkshire, England U.K.
Wolea atoll Micronesia see Woleai
113 J5 Woleai atoll Micronesia
230 A4 Woleu-Ntem prov. Gabon
245 N3 Wolf r. Y.T. Can.
261 J8 Wolf r. TN U.S.A.
250 F5 Wolf r. WI U.S.A.
274 □ Wolf, Volcán vol. Islas Galápagos Ecuador
194 E5 Wolfach Ger.
262 H3 Wolf Creek MT U.S.A.
262 C5 Wolf Creek OR U.S.A.
261 F7 Wolf Creek r. OK U.S.A.
244 G3 Wolf Creek Mountain hill AK U.S.A.
263 K8 Wolf Creek Pass CO U.S.A.
257 □N5 Wolfeboro NH U.S.A.
194 H6 Wolfegg Ger.
251 R5 Wolfe Island Ont. Can.
193 F7 Wolfen Ger.
191 K6 Wolfenbüttel Ger.
191 G10 Wölfersheim Ger.
201 H4 Wolfgangsee l. Austria
191 H8 Wolfhagen Ger.
191 K9 Wölfis Ger.
Wolf Island Islas Galápagos Ecuador see Wenman, Isla
245 O3 Wolf Lake Y.T. Can.
250 H6 Wolf Lake MI U.S.A.
244 I2 Wolf Mountain AK U.S.A.
201 L3 Wolfpassing Austria
262 L2 Wolf Point MT U.S.A.
195 J3 Wolframs-Eschenbach Ger.
195 K6 Wolfratshausen Ger.
201 K6 Wolfsberg Austria
191 K6 Wolfsburg Ger.
194 D2 Wolfstein Ger.
249 H4 Wolfville N.S. Can.
192 I2 Wolgast Ger.
212 E1 Wolhusen Switz.
197 L5 Wolica r. Pol.
196 C2 Wolin Pol.
196 C2 Wolin i. Pol.
196 C2 Woliński Park Narodowy nat. park Pol.
197 H3 Wólka Kujawsko-Pomorskie Pol.
197 K4 Wólka Lubelskie Pol.
197 L3 Wólka Dobryńska Pol.
193 H9 Wolkenstein Ger.
201 O3 Wolkersdorf Austria
191 K8 Wolkramshausen Ger.
173 K3 Wollaston Northamptonshire, England U.K.
283 D9 Wollaston, Islas is Chile
247 K3 Wollaston Lake Sask. Can.
247 K3 Wollaston Lake l. Sask. Can.
242 G3 Wollaston Peninsula N.W.T./Nunavut Can.
105 M5 Wollemi National Park N.S.W. Austr.
212 F1 Wollerau Switz.
192 I4 Wolletzsee l. Ger.
105 M6 Wollongong N.S.W. Austr.
237 J3 Wolmaransstad S. Africa
193 D7 Wolmirsleben Ger.
193 E6 Wolmirstedt Ger.
195 L4 Wolnzach Ger.
197 J3 Wołomin Pol.
130 D3 Wolong Reserve nature res. China
196 E4 Wołów Pol.
115 B8 Wolowaru Flores Indon.
194 H3 Wolpertshausen Ger.
194 H6 Wolpertswende Ger.
191 H6 Wölpinghausen Ger.
191 K6 Wolsdorf Ger.
104 H7 Wolseley S.A. Austr.
236 D9 Wolseley S. Africa
260 F3 Wolsey SD U.S.A.
171 N4 Wolsingham Durham, England U.K.
243 K3 Wolstenholme, Cap c. Que. Can.
173 J3 Wolston Warwickshire, England U.K.
196 E3 Wolsztyn Pol.
193 H6 Woltersdorf Brandenburg Ger.
193 I6 Woltersdorf Brandenburg Ger.
192 D5 Woltersdorf Niedersachsen Ger.
191 I7 Woltershausen Ger.
186 J3 Wolvega Neth.
172 H2 Wolverhampton West Midlands, England U.K.
245 O1 Wolverine r. N.W.T. Can.
250 J4 Wolverine MI U.S.A.
237 I9 Wolwefontein S. Africa
237 J4 Wolwespruit S. Africa
116 A2 Wolya r. Indon.
201 J5 Wölzer Tauern mts Austria
172 H2 Wombourne Staffordshire, England U.K.
171 O6 Wombwell South Yorkshire, England U.K.
258 C4 Womelsdorf PA U.S.A.
244 I4 Womens Bay AK U.S.A.
186 I2 Wommels Neth.
194 C2 Womrather Höhe hill Ger.
106 F5 Wonarah N.T. Austr.
145 M4 Wonay, Kowtal-e pass Afgh.
107 M9 Wondai Qld Austr.
187 E6 Wondelgem Belgium
237 N1 Wonderfontein S. Africa
237 L3 Wonderkop S. Africa
237 L4 Wonderkop mt. S. Africa
237 K1 Wondermere S. Africa
195 M1 Wondreb r. Ger.
105 J4 Wongalarroo Lake salt l. N.S.W. Austr.
109 D11 Wongan Hills W.A. Austr.
230 A5 Wonga Wongué, Réserve de nature res. Gabon
139 L6 Wong Chhu r. Bhutan
131 □J7 Wong Chuk Hang H.K. China
131 □J7 Wong Leng hill H.K. China
131 □J7 Wong Wan Chau i. H.K. China
123 E10 Wŏnju S. Korea
117 I8 Wonogiri Jawa Indon.
117 I8 Wonosari Indon.
117 H8 Wonosobo Jawa Indon.
246 F3 Wonowon B.C. Can.
115 E8 Wonreli Maluku Indon.
123 E9 Wŏnsan N. Korea
195 K2 Wonsees Ger.
173 J5 Wonston Hampshire, England U.K.
105 J8 Wonthaggi Vic. Austr.
109 E8 Wonyulgunna, Mount hill W.A. Austr.
173 K4 Wooburn Buckinghamshire, England U.K.
104 F4 Woocalla S.A. Austr.
245 J2 Wood r. AK U.S.A.
285 F6 Wood, Isla i. Arg.
245 L3 Wood, Mount Y.T. Can.
106 F2 Woodah, Isle i. N.T. Austr.
255 G10 Woodbine GA U.S.A.
258 A6 Woodbine MD U.S.A.
258 F6 Woodbine NJ U.S.A.
250 E4 Woodboro WI U.S.A.
103 H8 Woodbourne South I. N.Z.
258 F1 Woodbourne NY U.S.A.
173 O3 Woodbridge Suffolk, England U.K.
259 I2 Woodbridge CT U.S.A.
259 G3 Woodbridge NJ U.S.A.
256 H10 Woodbridge VA U.S.A.
246 H3 Wood Buffalo National Park Alta Can.
105 N3 Woodburn N.S.W. Austr.
250 J8 Woodburn IN U.S.A.
262 C4 Woodburn OR U.S.A.
259 I1 Woodbury CT U.S.A.
250 I7 Woodbury MI U.S.A.
258 E5 Woodbury NJ U.S.A.
258 E5 Woodbury Heights NJ U.S.A.
245 L2 Woodchopper Creek AK U.S.A.
106 E5 Woodcock, Mount hill N.T. Austr.
173 J4 Woodcote Oxfordshire, England U.K.
105 N3 Wooded Bluff hd N.S.W./Qld Austr.
105 N3 Woodenbong N.S.W. Austr.
169 J7 Woodenbridge Ireland
199 J2 Wooden Churches tourist site Slovakia
105 J7 Woodend Vic. Austr.
103 C13 Woodend South I. N.Z.
103 G10 Woodend South I. N.Z.
162 □ Woodfjorden inlet Svalbard
271 □⁶ Woodford Grenada
169 F6 Woodford Ireland
264 M3 Woodfords CA U.S.A.
171 Q7 Woodhall Spa Lincolnshire, England U.K.
173 L6 Woodingdean Brighton and Hove, England U.K.
247 K4 Wood Lake Sask. Can.
264 M5 Woodlake CA U.S.A.
264 K3 Woodland CA U.S.A.
257 □R3 Woodland ME U.S.A.
262 C4 Woodland WA U.S.A.
258 B7 Woodland Beach MD U.S.A.
247 M5 Woodland Caribou Provincial Park Ont. Can.
263 L7 Woodland Park CO U.S.A.
116 □ Woodlands Sing.
113 L8 Woodlark Island P.N.G.
258 B6 Woodlawn MD U.S.A.
173 K5 Woodley Wokingham, England U.K.
258 E5 Woodlyn PA U.S.A.
171 Q6 Woodmansey East Riding of Yorkshire, England U.K.
104 F2 Woodmurra Creek watercourse S.A. Austr.
171 L6 Woodplumpton Lancashire, England U.K.
247 L5 Woodridge Man. Can.
258 F1 Woodridge NY U.S.A.
106 G6 Woodroffe watercourse N.T. Austr.
104 C2 Woodroffe, Mount S.A. Austr.
262 I6 Woodruff UT U.S.A.
250 E4 Woodruff WI U.S.A.
106 D4 Woods, Lake salt flat N.T. Austr.
252 H1 Woods, Lake of the Can./U.S.A.
256 D9 Woodsfield OH U.S.A.
257 O7 Woods Hole MA U.S.A.
105 K8 Woodside Vic. Austr.
258 D6 Woodside DE U.S.A.
105 L5 Woodstock N.S.W. Austr.
107 K5 Woodstock Qld Austr.
249 H4 Woodstock N.B. Can.
248 D5 Woodstock Ont. Can.
173 J4 Woodstock Oxfordshire, England U.K.
250 F7 Woodstock IL U.S.A.
256 G10 Woodstock VA U.S.A.
257 M5 Woodstock VT U.S.A.
237 N4 Woodstock Dam resr S. Africa
169 H8 Woodstown Ireland
258 E5 Woodstown NJ U.S.A.
257 M4 Woodsville NH U.S.A.
173 O3 Woodton Norfolk, England U.K.
169 I5 Woodtown Ireland
251 P5 Woodville Ont. Can.
102 J7 Woodville North I. N.Z.
261 J10 Woodville MS U.S.A.
256 B7 Woodville OH U.S.A.
261 H10 Woodville TX U.S.A.
261 F7 Woodward OK U.S.A.
264 L4 Woodward Reservoir CA U.S.A.
264 N6 Woody CA U.S.A.
237 K9 Woody Cape Nature Reserve S. Africa
244 I4 Woody Island AK U.S.A.
172 G3 Woofferton Shropshire, England U.K.
113 I7 Wooi Papua Indon.
172 H6 Wool Dorset, England U.K.
172 D5 Woolacombe Devon, England U.K.
106 E2 Woolen r. N.T. Austr.
171 M2 Wooler Northumberland, England U.K.
107 I6 Woolgar r. Qld Austr.
105 N4 Woolgoolga N.S.W. Austr.
105 N3 Wooli N.S.W. Austr.
106 D7 Woolla Downs (abandoned) N.T. Austr.
286 W1 Woollard, Mount Antarctica
104 G4 Wooltana S.A. Austr.
256 E12 Woolwine VA U.S.A.
109 F12 Woolyeenyer Hill W.A. Austr.
104 F4 Woomera S.A. Austr.
104 D3 Woomera Prohibited Area S.A. Austr.
257 N6 Woonsocket RI U.S.A.
260 F3 Woonsocket SD U.S.A.
107 L8 Woorabinda Qld Austr.
109 C8 Wooramel r. W.A. Austr.
256 D8 Wooster OH U.S.A.
173 K3 Wootton Bedfordshire, England U.K.
173 I4 Wootton Bassett Wiltshire, England U.K.
232 D2 Woqooyi Galbeed admin. reg. Somalia
123 F10 Worak-san National Park S. Korea
212 D2 Worb Switz.
107 H2 Worbody Point Qld Austr.
236 D9 Worcester S. Africa
172 H3 Worcester Worcestershire, England U.K.
257 N6 Worcester MA U.S.A.
257 K6 Worcester NY U.S.A.
172 H3 Worcestershire admin. div. England U.K.
201 N3 Wördern Austria
172 H2 Worfield Shropshire, England U.K.
200 F5 Wörgl Austria
195 I6 Woringen Ger.
113 H8 Workai i. Indon.
171 J4 Workington Cumbria, England U.K.
171 O7 Worksop Nottinghamshire, England U.K.
186 H3 Workum Neth.
262 K4 Worland WY U.S.A.
193 F7 Wörlitz Ger.
187 J9 Wormeldange Lux.
186 G4 Wormer Neth.
178 D2 Wormhout France
168 K10 Wormit Fife, Scotland U.K.
194 E2 Worms Ger.
172 D4 Worms Head Wales U.K.
195 J4 Wörnitz r. Ger.
228 D4 Worofla Côte d'Ivoire
173 K5 Worplesdon Surrey, England U.K.
190 G4 Worpswede Ger.
194 E2 Wörrstadt Ger.
201 J4 Wörschach Austria
187 G6 Wortel Belgium
200 G5 Wörth Austria
195 L5 Wörth Ger.
173 L5 Worth West Sussex, England U.K.
194 G2 Wörth am Main Ger.
194 E3 Wörth am Rhein Ger.
195 M3 Wörth an der Donau Ger.
195 M4 Wörth an der Isar Ger.
201 J6 Wörther See l. Austria
173 L6 Worthing West Sussex, England U.K.
260 H4 Worthington MN U.S.A.
256 B8 Worthington OH U.S.A.
258 C6 Worton MD U.S.A.
115 E4 Wosi Halmahera Indon.
115 B5 Wosu Sulawesi Indon.
196 D2 Woświn, Jezioro l. Pol.
108 G4 Wotjalum Aboriginal Reserve W.A. Austr.
290 G6 Wotje atoll Marshall Is
172 H4 Wotton-under-Edge Gloucestershire, England U.K.
115 B5 Wotu Sulawesi Indon.
186 H4 Woudenberg Neth.
186 G5 Woudrichem Neth.
186 I3 Woudsend Neth.
173 K3 Woughton on the Green Milton Keynes, England U.K.
260 D4 Wounded Knee SD U.S.A.
224 B4 Wour Chad
229 H5 Wouri r. Cameroon
179 N5 Woustviller France
186 F5 Wouw Neth.
107 M7 Wowan Qld Austr.
115 C6 Wowoni i. Indon.
115 C5 Wowoni, Selat sea chan. Indon.
197 H5 Woźniki Pol.
Wozrojdeniye Oroli pen. Uzbek. see Vozrozhdenya Island
171 Q7 Wragby Lincolnshire, England U.K.
Wrangel Island Rus. Fed. see Vrangelya, Ostrov
245 N4 Wrangell AK U.S.A.
244 □A5 Wrangell, Cape AK U.S.A.
245 K3 Wrangell, Mount AK U.S.A.
245 N4 Wrangell Island AK U.S.A.
244 H4 Wrangell Mountains AK U.S.A.
245 L3 Wrangell-St Elias National Park and Preserve AK U.S.A.
171 R7 Wrangle Lincolnshire, England U.K.
168 F5 Wrath, Cape Scotland U.K.
260 D5 Wray CO U.S.A.
173 J2 Wreake r. England U.K.
108 □² Wreck Point Cocos Is
270 □ Wreck Point Jamaica
236 A4 Wreck Point S. Africa
Wrecsam Wrexham, Wales U.K. see Wrexham
196 G5 Wręczyca Wielka Pol.
192 G4 Wredenhagen Ger.
171 P5 Wrelton North Yorkshire, England U.K.
190 G3 Wremen Ger.
255 F9 Wrens GA U.S.A.
190 K5 Wrestedt Ger.
191 G7 Wrexen (Diemelstadt) Ger.
172 G1 Wrexham Wrexham, Wales U.K.
172 G1 Wrexham admin. div. Wales U.K.
103 C13 Wreys Bush South I. N.Z.
190 J4 Wriedel Ger.
192 J5 Wriezen Ger.
114 E6 Wright Samar Phil.
262 L5 Wright WY U.S.A.
137 M7 Wrightmyo Andaman & Nicobar Is India
261 H9 Wright Patman Lake TX U.S.A.
265 V10 Wrightson, Mount AZ U.S.A.
258 F4 Wrightstown PA U.S.A.
250 F5 Wrightstown WI U.S.A.
255 F9 Wrightsville GA U.S.A.
258 B4 Wrightsville PA U.S.A.
264 O7 Wrightwood CA U.S.A.
245 Q3 Wrigley N.W.T. Can.
256 B10 Wrigley KY U.S.A.
286 P2 Wrigley Gulf Antarctica
172 G5 Wrington North Somerset, England U.K.
190 I3 Wrist Ger.
173 M4 Writtle Essex, England U.K.
196 G4 Wróblew Pol.
196 F4 Wrocław Pol.
190 H2 Wrohm Ger.
197 K1 Wronki Warmińsko-Mazurskie Pol.
196 E3 Wronki Wielkopolskie Pol.
197 K3 Wrotnów Pol.
173 I4 Wroughton Swindon, England U.K.
196 G3 Wrząielka Pol.
197 J4 Wrzelowiec Pol.
196 F1 Wrzeście Pol.
196 F3 Września Pol.
196 F3 Wrześnica r. Pol.
196 D1 Wrzosowo Pol.
197 J5 Wschodnia r. Pol.
196 E4 Wschowa Pol.
Wu'an Fujian China see Changtai
129 N8 Wu'an Hebei China
Wubalawun res. N.T. Austr. see Wubawalum Aboriginal Land
106 D3 Wubawalum Aboriginal Land res. N.T. Austr.
109 D11 Wubin W.A. Austr.
129 L8 Wubu Shaanxi China
129 Q3 Wuchagou Nei Mongol China
122 E6 Wuchang Heilong. China
Wuchang Hubei China see Jiangxia
131 L4 Wucheng Anhui China
Wucheng Anhui China see Wuwei
Wuchow Guangxi China see Wuzhou
130 H8 Wuchuan Guangdong China
130 F4 Wuchuan Guizhou China
129 L6 Wuchuan Nei Mongol China
Wuda China see Ud
122 E4 Wudalianchi Heilong. China
147 M4 Wuḏām 'Alwā Oman
129 P5 Wudan Nei Mongol China
130 G2 Wudang Shan mts China
129 Q7 Wudao Liaoning China
122 E3 Wudaogou Heilong. China
128 C9 Wudaoliang Qinghai China
147 H7 Wuday'ah well Saudi Arabia
129 O8 Wudi Shandong China
229 H4 Wudil Nigeria
130 D6 Wuding Yunnan China
129 L8 Wuding He r. China
104 E5 Wudinna S.A. Austr.
130 H3 Wufeng Hubei China
Wufeng Yunnan China see Zhenxiong
128 I8 Wufo Gansu China
130 H5 Wugang Hunan China
129 K9 Wugong Shaanxi China
128 J7 Wuhai Nei Mongol China
131 J3 Wuhan Hubei China
131 K2 Wuhe Anhui China
131 L3 Wuhu Anhui China
131 L3 Wuhu Anhui China
131 J7 Wuhua Guangdong China
133 D10 Wüjang Xizang China
130 G8 Wujia Guangxi China
131 M3 Wujiang Jiangsu China
130 F4 Wu Jiang r. China
Wujin Sichuan China see Xinjin
Wukang China see Deqing
229 H5 Wukari Nigeria
129 Q8 Wuleidao Wan b. China
193 E7 Wulfen Ger.
192 F4 Wulfersdorf Ger.
191 J10 Wülfershausen an der Saale Ger.
190 J4 Wulfsen Ger.
191 J7 Wulften Ger.
128 C9 Wuli Qinghai China
130 D4 Wulian Feng mts Yunnan China
130 C6 Wuliang Shan mts Yunnan China
113 H8 Wuliaru i. Indon.
130 G8 Wuli Jiang r. China
244 F2 Wulik r. AK U.S.A.
130 G4 Wuling Shan mts China
192 F5 Wulkau Ger.
201 N2 Wullersdorf Austria
130 F4 Wulong Chongqing China
129 Q8 Wulong He r. China
Wulongji Henan China see Huaibin
197 I2 Wulpińskie, Jezioro l. Pol.
190 G4 Wulsbüttel Ger.
115 F7 Wulur Maluku Indon.
229 H5 Wum Cameroon
133 J11 Wumatang Xizang China
130 D5 Wumeng Shan mts Guizhou/Yunnan China
130 G7 Wuming Guangxi China
190 G4 Wümme r. Ger.
137 O2 Wundwin Myanmar
130 C3 Wungda Sichuan China
131 J4 Wuning Jiangxi China
191 G7 Wünnenberg Ger.
248 B2 Wunnummin Lake Ont. Can.
230 F2 Wun Rog Sudan
193 F9 Wünschendorf Ger.
193 H6 Wünsdorf Ger.
230 F2 Wun Shwai Sudan
193 F10 Wunsiedel Ger.
191 H6 Wunstorf Ger.
232 B2 Wuntau Sudan
118 B3 Wuntho Myanmar
265 U6 Wupatki National Monument nat. park AZ U.S.A.
131 K6 Wuping Fujian China
191 D8 Wuppertal Ger.
236 D8 Wuppertal S. Africa
129 K8 Wuqi Shaanxi China
132 B7 Wuqia Xinjiang China
132 B7 Wuqia Xinjiang China
129 N7 Wuqiang Hebei China
129 O8 Wuqiao Hebei China
129 O7 Wuqing Tianjin China
Wuquan Henan China see Wuyang
109 D10 Wuranga W.A. Austr.
195 K5 Würm r. Ger.
195 N5 Wurmannsquick Ger.
194 F5 Wurmlingen Ger.
229 G3 Wurno Nigeria
106 F3 Wurralibi Aboriginal Land res. N.T. Austr.
191 B9 Würselen Ger.
259 G1 Wurtsboro NY U.S.A.
193 E10 Wurzbach Ger.
194 H2 Würzburg Ger.
193 G8 Wurzen Ger.
130 G3 Wushan Chongqing China
128 I9 Wushan Gansu China
130 H3 Wu Shan mts China
130 F3 Wusheng Sichuan China
130 G8 Wushi Guangdong China
132 D6 Wushi Xinjiang China
192 F5 Wust Ger.
191 H8 Wüstegarten hill Ger.
194 G3 Wüstenrot Ger.
192 F5 Wusterhausen Ger.
192 I2 Wusterhusen Ger.
192 G5 Wustermark Ger.
193 F6 Wusterwitz Ger.
191 J8 Wüstheuterode Ger.
192 G5 Wustrau-Altfriesack Ger.
192 G4 Wustrow Mecklenburg-Vorpommern Ger.
192 D5 Wustrow Niedersachsen Ger.
192 E2 Wustrow, Halbinsel spit Ger.
192 F2 Wustrow, Ostseebad Ger.
Wusuli Jiang r. Rus. Fed. see Ussuri
194 E6 Wutach r. Ger.
129 M7 Wutai Shanxi China
132 F4 Wutai Xinjiang China
129 M7 Wutaishan Shanxi China
129 M7 Wutai Shan mts China
131 H4 Wutan Hunan China
191 J9 Wutha Ger.
128 F6 Wutonggou Nei Mongol China
132 I6 Wutonggou Xinjiang China
122 G5 Wutong He r. China
128 D5 Wutongwozi Quan well Xinjiang China
187 G6 Wuustwezel Belgium
113 J7 Wuvulu Island P.N.G.
131 K3 Wuwei Anhui China
128 H8 Wuwei Gansu China
130 G3 Wuxi Chongqing China
130 H4 Wuxi Hunan China
Wuxi Hunan China see Qiyang
131 M3 Wuxi Jiangsu China
Wuxia Chongqing China see Wushan
129 M8 Wuxiang Shanxi China
Wuxing Zhejiang China see Huzhou
130 G7 Wuxu Guangxi China
130 G7 Wuxuan Guangxi China
131 J4 Wuxue Hubei China
Wuyang Guizhou China see Zhenyuan
131 I2 Wuyang Henan China
129 M8 Wuyang Shanxi China
Wuyang Zhejiang China see W[illegible]
131 L4 Wuyi Zhejiang China
122 F4 Wuyiling Heilong. China
131 L5 Wuyishan Fujian China
131 K6 Wuyi Shan mts China
131 L5 Wuyi Shan tourist site Fujian China
131 K4 Wuyuan Jiangxi China
129 K6 Wuyuan Nei Mongol China
Wuyuan Zhejiang China see Haiyan
Wuyun Zhejiang China see Jinyun
129 L7 Wuzhai Shanxi China
131 H3 Wuzhen Hubei China
129 M9 Wuzhi Henan China
130 G9 Wuzhishan Hainan China
130 G9 Wuzhishan Hainan China
130 G9 Wuzhi Shan mts China
128 J8 Wuzhong Ningxia China
131 H7 Wuzhou Guangxi China
107 H4 Wyaaba Creek r. Qld Austr.
250 C9 Wyaconda r. MO U.S.A.
109 D11 Wyalkatchem W.A. Austr.
251 R8 Wyalusing PA U.S.A.
251 K7 Wyandotte MI U.S.A.
107 J9 Wyandra Qld Austr.
250 E8 Wyanet IL U.S.A.
105 L5 Wyangala Reservoir N.S.W. Austr.
105 J3 Wyara, Lake salt flat Qld Austr.
173 L2 Wyberton Lincolnshire, England U.K.
105 I7 Wycheproof Vic. Austr.
259 G2 Wyckoff NJ U.S.A.
196 F2 Wyczechy Pol.
197 K2 Wydminy Pol.
173 N5 Wye Kent, England U.K.
171 N7 Wye r. Derbyshire, England U.K.
172 G4 Wye r. England/Wales U.K.
109 E10 Wyemandoo hill W.A. Austr.
258 C7 Wye Mills MD U.S.A.
250 D5 Wyeville WI U.S.A.
199 I1 Wygoda Pol.
196 D2 Wygon Pol.
194 D5 Wyhl Ger.
193 F8 Wyhra r. Ger.
190 G1 Wyk auf Föhr Ger.
196 F3 Wylatowo Pol.
256 G12 Wylliesburg VA U.S.A.
109 D7 Wyloo W.A. Austr.
173 I5 Wylye Wiltshire, England U.K.
173 I5 Wylye r. England U.K.
190 D4 Wymeer Ger.
193 L7 Wymiarki Pol.
173 O2 Wymondham Norfolk, England U.K.
260 G5 Wymore NE U.S.A.
104 D4 Wynbring S.A. Austr.
108 J3 Wyndham W.A. Austr.
103 C13 Wyndham South I. N.Z.
105 J7 Wyndham-Werribee Vic. Austr.
261 J8 Wynne AR U.S.A.
242 G2 Wynniatt Bay N.W.T. Can.
105 J9 Wynyard Tas. Austr.
247 J5 Wynyard Sask. Can.
250 E6 Wyocena WI U.S.A.
104 C3 Wyola Lake salt flat S.A. Austr.
258 D6 Wyoming DE U.S.A.
250 E8 Wyoming IL U.S.A.
250 I7 Wyoming MI U.S.A.
262 K5 Wyoming state U.S.A.
258 C1 Wyoming County county PA U.S.A.
262 I5 Wyoming Peak WY U.S.A.
262 I5 Wyoming Range mts WY U.S.A.
258 D4 Wyomissing PA U.S.A.
105 M5 Wyong N.S.W. Austr.
106 F2 Wyonga r. N.T. Austr.
104 I6 Wyperfeld National Park Vic. Austr.
168 K4 Wyre i. Scotland U.K.
171 L6 Wyre r. England U.K.
197 L4 Wyryki-Połód Pol.
196 F2 Wyrzysk Pol.
197 I4 Wyśmierzyce Pol.
196 D3 Wysoka Lubuskie Pol.
197 J6 Wysoka Podkarpackie Pol.
196 F2 Wysoka Wielkopolskie Pol.
196 C2 Wysoka Kamieńska Pol.
196 D5 Wysoka Kopa mt. Pol.
197 K5 Wysokie Lubelskie Pol.
197 K2 Wysokie Warmińsko-Mazurskie Pol.
197 K3 Wysokie Mazowieckie Pol.
197 J6 Wysowa Pol.
251 R8 Wysox PA U.S.A.
197 K3 Wyszki Pol.
197 J3 Wyszków Pol.
197 I3 Wyszogród Pol.

3 I13 **Wythall** Worcestershire, England U.K.
6 D12 **Wytheville** VA U.S.A.
7 L4 **Wytyczno** Pol.
7 J4 **Wyżnica** r. Pol.
5 P7 **Wzniesienie Elbląskie, Park Krajobrazowy** Pol.

X

2 F2 **Xaafuun** Somalia
2 F2 **Xaafuun, Raas** pt Somalia
2 F2 **Xabo** Somalia
3 M11 **Xabyai** Xizang China
1 I5 **Xaçınçay** r. Azer.
1 J4 **Xaçmaz** Azer.
4 D4 **Xade** Botswana
7 □ **Xagħra** Gozo Malta
3 K12 **Xagjang** Xizang China
3 E10 **Xagnag** Xizang China
3 I11 **Xago** Xizang China
3 K11 **Xagquka** Xizang China
3 D8 **Xaidulla** Xinjiang China
3 E5 **Xaignabouli** Laos
9 L7 **Xaintois** reg. France
3 I11 **Xainza** Xizang China
3 I12 **Xaitongmoin** Xizang China
5 G5 **Xai-Xai** Moz.
2 D7 **Xakur** Xinjiang China
7 O7 **Xal, Cerro de** hill Mex.
9 K6 **Xalapa** Mex.
1 I5 **Xaldan** Azer.
2 F2 **Xalin** Somalia
4 B3 **Xallas** r. Spain
2 H6 **Xalqobod** Uzbek.
1 J5 **Xaltan** Azer.
9 H8 **Xaltianguis** Mex.
1 D9 **Xamavera** Angola
9 J6 **Xamba** Nei Mongol China
8 C3 **Xambioa** Brazil
0 A5 **Xambrê** Brazil
3 G4 **Xam Nua** Laos
1 C7 **Xá-Muteba** Angola
3 F5 **Xan** r. Laos
4 D2 **Xanceda** Spain
8 H6 **Xangd** Nei Mongol China
Xangda Qinghai China see **Nangqên**
9 L5 **Xangdin Hural** Nei Mongol China
3 E10 **Xangdoring** Xizang China
1 B9 **Xangongo** Angola
3 G6 **Xangxoy, Xé** r. Laos
3 L11 **Xangzha** Xizang China
9 I8 **Xanh, Cu Lao** i. Vietnam
9 K9 **Xanica** Mex.
1 H6 **Xankändi** Azer.
1 H5 **Xanlar** Azer.
1 H6 **Xanlıq** Azer.
1 B7 **Xanten** Ger.
0 F1 **Xanthi** Greece
3 D5 **Xanthos-Letoon** tourist site Turkey
9 B8 **Xanxerê** Brazil
5 C2 **Xapuri** Brazil
5 C2 **Xapuri** r. Brazil
4 C2 **Xaraba Şǝhǝr Sayı** i. Azer.
3 F8 **Xarag** Qinghai China
2 E3 **Xarardheere** Somalia
1 K6 **Xärä Zirä Adası** is Azer.
3 G12 **Xarba La** pass Xizang China
Xar Burd Nei Mongol China see **Bayan Nuru**
3 G11 **Xardong** Xizang China
4 F4 **Xares** r. Spain
9 N4 **Xar Hudag** Nei Mongol China
9 L5 **Xar Moron** r. China
9 Q5 **Xar Moron** r. China
6 C4 **Xarrama** r. Port.
0 B3 **Xarrë** Albania
9 K5 **Xarru** Xizang China
Xarsingma Xizang China see **Yadong**
1 C7 **Xassengue** Angola
1 G4 **Xatınlı** Azer.
9 D10 **Xàtiva** Spain
Xatl'o Dehe N.W.T. Can. see **Hay River**
4 E4 **Xau, Lake** Botswana
4 D3 **Xaudum** watercourse Botswana/Namibia
0 C5 **Xavantes, Represa de** resr Brazil
8 C5 **Xavantes, Serra dos** hills Brazil
3 F10 **Xaxa** Xizang China
8 F4 **Xay** Laos
2 F6 **Xayar** Xinjiang China
2 H3 **Xazgat** Xinjiang China
7 P8 **Xcalak** Mex.
7 P7 **X-Can** Mex.
2 D6 **Xegil** Xinjiang China
2 C7 **Xekar** Xinjiang China
8 H7 **Xêkong** Laos
6 B9 **Xenia** OH U.S.A.
3 I11 **Xênkyêr** Xizang China
1 C9 **Xequessa** Angola
9 E9 **Xeraco** Spain
9 E9 **Xeresa** Spain
5 F5 **Xeriuini** r. Brazil
4 E2 **Xermade** Spain
Xero Potamos r. Cyprus see **Xeros**
0 A4 **Xeros** r. Cyprus
8 G6 **Xerta** Spain
9 L7 **Xertigny** France
7 □ **Xewkija** Gozo Malta
Xhora S. Africa see **Elliotdale**
4 E4 **Xhorodomo Pan** salt pan Botswana
4 E4 **Xhumo** Botswana
2 C7 **Xia Awat** Xinjiang China
Xiabancheng Hebei China see **Chengde**
2 C7 **Xia Bazar** Xinjiang China
2 D3 **Xiabole Shan** mt. China
2 G6 **Xiachengzi** Heilong. China
1 I8 **Xiachuan Dao** i. Guangdong China
Xiacun Shandong China see **Rushan**
8 F9 **Xia Dawo** Qinghai China
8 D6 **Xiadong** Gansu China
Xiaguan Yunnan China see **Dali**
8 I9 **Xiaguanying** Gansu China
8 H9 **Xiahe** Gansu China
Xiajiang Jiangxi China see **Baqiu**
Xiajiang Xizang China see **Xagjang**
9 O8 **Xiajin** Shandong China
0 A2 **Xialaxiu** Qinghai China
0 A4 **Xia Lingka** Xizang China
8 D5 **Xiamaya** Xinjiang China
1 L6 **Xiamen** Fujian China
8 I8 **Xi'an** Ningxia China
9 K9 **Xi'an** Shaanxi China
0 G4 **Xianfeng** Hubei China
1 I2 **Xiangcheng** Henan China
1 J2 **Xiangcheng** Henan China
0 B4 **Xiangcheng** Sichuan China
Xiangcheng Yunnan China see **Xiangyun**
1 I2 **Xiangfan** Hubei China
9 L9 **Xiangfen** Shanxi China
Xiangfeng Hubei China see **Laifeng**
Xianggang H.K. China see **Hong Kong**
Xianggang Tebie Xingzhengqu special admin. reg. China see **Hong Kong**
0 B5 **Xianggelila** Yunnan China
Xianghuang Qi Nei Mongol China see **Xin Bulag**
Xiangjiang Jiangxi China see **Huichang**
1 I4 **Xiang Jiang** r. China
8 F5 **Xiangkhoang** Laos
Xiangkou Chongqing China see **Wulong**
9 L9 **Xiangning** Shanxi China
8 E9 **Xiangride** Qinghai China
Xiangshan Yunnan China see **Menghai**
131 M4 **Xiangshan** Zhejiang China
131 M4 **Xiangshan Gang** b. Zhejiang China
129 P9 **Xiangshui** Jiangsu China
130 G5 **Xiangshuiba** Hunan China
131 I5 **Xiangtan** Hunan China
131 I5 **Xiangxiang** Hunan China
Xiangyang Hubei China see **Xiangfan**
131 I2 **Xiangyang** Hubei China
133 I9 **Xiangyang Hu** l. Xizang China
131 I4 **Xiangyin** Hunan China
130 C6 **Xiangyun** Yunnan China
130 G7 **Xiangzhou** Guangxi China
131 M4 **Xianju** Zhejiang China
131 J4 **Xianning** Hubei China
Xiannümiao Jiangsu China see **Jiangdu**
Xianshui Sichuan China see **Dawu**
130 C3 **Xianshui He** r. Sichuan China
Xiantang Guangdong China see **Dongyuan**
131 I3 **Xiantao** Hubei China
131 K5 **Xianxia Ling** mts China
129 O7 **Xianxian** Hebei China
129 K9 **Xianyang** Shaanxi China
131 L6 **Xianyou** Fujian China
Xiaoba Ningxia China see **Qingtongxia**
129 N6 **Xiaochang** Hebei China
131 I3 **Xiaochang** Hubei China
130 E2 **Xiaochuan** Gansu China
130 G7 **Xiaodong** Guangxi China
129 R2 **Xiao'ergou** Nei Mongol China
Xiaofan Hebei China see **Wuqiang**
131 I3 **Xiaogan** Hubei China
132 G4 **Xiaoguai** Xinjiang China
129 J8 **Xiaoguan** Gansu China
132 D7 **Xiaohaizi Shuiku** resr Xinjiang China
122 E3 **Xiao Hinggan Ling** mts China
Xiaojiang Guangxi China see **Pubei**
129 J9 **Xiaojin** Gansu China
130 D3 **Xiaojin** Sichuan China
129 M9 **Xiaolangdi Shuiku** resr Henan/Shanxi China
131 L5 **Xiaomei** Zhejiang China
Xiaonan Gansu China see **Dongxiangzu**
128 D9 **Xiaonanchuan** Qinghai China
Xiaopu Hunan China see **Jiangyong**
133 L8 **Xiao Qaidam** Qinghai China
129 P8 **Xiaoqing He** r. China
131 I6 **Xiaosanjiang** Guangdong China
131 M3 **Xiaoshan** Zhejiang China
129 L9 **Xiao Shan** mts China
130 E4 **Xiaoshi** Sichuan China
130 A2 **Xiao Surmang** Qinghai China
131 K6 **Xiaotao** Fujian China
129 N7 **Xiaowutai Shan** mt. Hebei China
Xiaoxi Fujian China see **Pinghe**
129 O9 **Xiaoxian** Anhui China
130 D4 **Xiaoxiang Ling** mts Sichuan China
Xiaoyi Henan China see **Gongyi**
129 L8 **Xiaoyi** Shanxi China
132 E4 **Xiaoyingpan** Xinjiang China
131 M5 **Xiapu** Fujian China
130 C5 **Xiaqiaotou** Yunnan China
Xiaqiong Sichuan China see **Batang**
Xiashan Guangdong China see **Zhanjiang**
128 H7 **Xiasifen** Gansu China
267 O8 **Xiatil** Mex.
129 L9 **Xiaxian** Shanxi China
Xiayang Hunan China see **Yanling**
Xiayanjing Xizang China see **Yanjing**
Xiayingpan Guizhou China see **Lupanshui**
130 C2 **Xia Zanggor** Qinghai China
130 C3 **Xiazhai** Sichuan China
Xiazhen Shandong China see **Weishan**
130 B4 **Xibdê** Sichuan China
132 I3 **Xibet** Xinjiang China
131 L5 **Xibing** Fujian China
Xibu Fujian China see **Dongshan**
130 G8 **Xichang** Guangxi China
130 D5 **Xichang** Sichuan China
Xicheng Hebei China see **Yangyuan**
130 E7 **Xichou** Yunnan China
131 H2 **Xichuan** Henan China
269 J6 **Xico** Mex.
269 I2 **Xicohténcatl** Mex.
269 J5 **Xicotepec de Juárez** Mex.
130 D4 **Xide** Sichuan China
Xidu Hunan China see **Hengyang**
274 E4 **Xié** r. Brazil
Xiejiaji Shandong China see **Qingyun**
131 H3 **Xiemahe'** Hubei China
Xieng Khouang Laos see **Xiangkhoang**
118 G5 **Xiêng Lam** Vietnam
130 G8 **Xieyang Dao** i. China
131 K2 **Xifei He** r. China
130 F5 **Xifeng** Guizhou China
122 D7 **Xifeng** Liaoning China
Xifeng China see **Qingyang**
Xifengzhen Gansu China see **Qingyang**
128 J7 **Xi Ganqu** r. China
133 I12 **Xigazê** Xizang China
130 F2 **Xihan Shui** r. Gansu China
130 E2 **Xihe** Gansu China
129 Q6 **Xi He** r. Liaoning China
130 F3 **Xi He** r. Sichuan China
132 L6 **Xihu** Gansu China
131 J2 **Xihua** Henan China
Xihuachi Gansu China see **Heshui**
232 E2 **Xiis** Somalia
128 I9 **Xiji** Ningxia China
131 I7 **Xi Jiang** r. Guangdong China
128 E6 **Xijian Quan** well Gansu China
130 G7 **Xijin** Guangxi China
128 B9 **Xijir** Qinghai China
133 J9 **Xijir Ulan Hu** salt l. China
128 H8 **Xijishui** Gansu China
122 B2 **Xikouzi** Nei Mongol China
129 M5 **Xil** Nei Mongol China
Xilaganí Greece see **Xylagani**
129 Q4 **Xilaotou Shan** mt. Nei Mongol China
132 K7 **Xiliangzi** Qinghai China
129 R5 **Xiliao He** r. China
Xiligou Qinghai China see **Ulan**
130 E6 **Xilin** Guangxi China
129 O5 **Xilinhot** Nei Mongol China
Xilinji Heilong. China see **Mohe**
Xilin Qagan Obo Nei Mongol China see **Qagan Obo**
269 I4 **Xilitla** Mex.
151 K6 **Xıllı** Azer.
151 J5 **Xilmilli** Azer.
Xilókastron Greece see **Xylokastro**
Xilópolis Greece see **Xyloupoli**
130 B7 **Ximeng** Yunnan China
128 G6 **Ximiao** Nei Mongol China
129 K7 **Xin** Nei Mongol China
151 J4 **Xınalıq** Azer.
Xin'an Anhui China see **Lai'an**
Xin'an Guizhou China see **Anlong**
Xin'an Hebei China see **Anxin**
129 M9 **Xin'an** Henan China
129 P8 **Xin'an** Shandong China
Xin Barag Youqi Nei Mongol China see **Altan Emel**
Xin Barag Zuoqi Nei Mongol China see **Amgalang**
123 D8 **Xinbin** Liaoning China
153 M5 **Xin Bulag** Nei Mongol China
129 P2 **Xin Bulag Jin** Nei Mongol China
131 J2 **Xincai** Henan China
Xinchang Jiangxi China see **Yifeng**
131 M4 **Xinchang** Zhejiang China
Xincheng Fujian China see **Gutian**
Xincheng Guangdong China see **Xinxing**
130 G6 **Xincheng** Guangxi China
129 K8 **Xincheng** Shaanxi China
Xincheng Shanxi China see **Yuanqu**
Xincheng Sichuan China see **Zhaojue**
128 G7 **Xinchengzi** Gansu China
132 G4 **Xinchepaizi** Xinjiang China
Xincun Yunnan China see **Dongchuan**
131 H7 **Xindi** Guangxi China
Xindi Hubei China see **Honghu**
129 S3 **Xindian** Heilong. China
131 H7 **Xindu** Guangxi China
Xindu Sichuan China see **Luhuo**
130 E3 **Xindu** Sichuan China
130 C3 **Xinduqiao** Sichuan China
131 J6 **Xinfeng** Guangdong China
131 J6 **Xinfeng** Jiangxi China
131 J7 **Xinfengjiang Shuiku** resr China
130 H6 **Xing'an** Guangxi China
131 J5 **Xingan** Jiangxi China
129 Q7 **Xingangzhen** Liaoning China
Xingba China see **Lhünzê**
Xingcheng Hebei China see **Qianxi**
129 Q6 **Xingcheng** Liaoning China
132 H6 **Xingdi** Xinjiang China
231 C7 **Xinge** Angola
Xingguo Gansu China see **Qin'an**
131 J5 **Xingguo** Jiangxi China
128 F9 **Xinghai** Qinghai China
122 D2 **Xinghua** Heilong. China
131 L2 **Xinghua** Jiangsu China
131 L6 **Xinghua Wan** b. China
122 H6 **Xingkai** Heilong. China
Xingkai Hu l. China/Rus. Fed. see **Khanka, Lake**
129 O6 **Xinglong** Hebei China
122 D3 **Xinglong** Heilong. China
122 E5 **Xinglong** Heilong. China
131 J6 **Xingning** Guangdong China
131 I6 **Xingning** Hunan China
131 I3 **Xingou** Hubei China
129 K9 **Xingping** Shaanxi China
130 E6 **Xingren** Guizhou China
128 I8 **Xingrenbu** Ningxia China
128 G9 **Xingsagoinba** Qinghai China
Xingshan Guizhou China see **Majiang**
130 H3 **Xingshan** Hubei China
129 N8 **Xingtai** Hebei China
129 N7 **Xingtang** Hebei China
275 H5 **Xingu** r. Brazil
278 B4 **Xingu, Parque Indígena do** res. Brazil
129 M7 **Xinguangwu** Shanxi China
278 C3 **Xinguara** Brazil
130 E4 **Xingwen** Sichuan China
129 L7 **Xingxian** Shanxi China
128 D6 **Xingxingxia** Xinjiang China
129 M9 **Xingyang** Henan China
130 G7 **Xingye** Guangxi China
130 E6 **Xingyi** Guizhou China
131 K4 **Xingzi** Jiangxi China
129 N8 **Xinhe** Hebei China
132 F6 **Xinhe** Xinjiang China
129 N5 **Xin Hot** Nei Mongol China
Xinhua Guangdong China see **Huadu**
131 H5 **Xinhua** Hunan China
Xinhua Yunnan China see **Qiaojia**
Xinhua Yunnan China see **Funing**
130 G5 **Xinhuang** Hunan China
129 P5 **Xinhui** Nei Mongol China
128 G8 **Xining** Qinghai China
129 N8 **Xinji** Hebei China
Xinji Henan China see **Xinxian**
131 J4 **Xinjian** Jiangxi China
129 L9 **Xinjiang** Shanxi China
Xinjiang aut. reg. China see **Xinjiang Uygur Zizhiqu**
131 K4 **Xin Jiang** r. China
Xinjiangkou Hubei China see **Songzi**
128 B5 **Xinjiang Uygur Zizhiqu** aut. reg. China
129 K7 **Xinjie** Nei Mongol China
130 B6 **Xinjie** Yunnan China
130 D7 **Xinjie** Yunnan China
Xinjin Liaoning China see **Pulandian**
130 D3 **Xinjin** Sichuan China
Xinjing Guangxi China see **Jingxi**
129 R5 **Xinkai He** r. China
122 D7 **Xinlicheng Shuiku** resr Jilin China
Xinling Hubei China see **Badong**
122 E3 **Xinlitun** Heilong. China
130 C3 **Xinlong** Sichuan China
129 M9 **Xinmi** Henan China
Xinmian Sichuan China see **Shimian**
122 E4 **Xinmin** Heilong. China
129 R6 **Xinmin** Liaoning China
129 L7 **Xinminzhen** Shaanxi China
Xinning Gansu China see **Ningxian**
Xinning Guangxi China see **Fusui**
130 H5 **Xinning** Hunan China
Xinning Jiangxi China see **Wuning**
Xinning Sichuan China see **Kaijiang**
130 C6 **Xinping** Yunnan China
122 F4 **Xinqing** Heilong. China
131 K6 **Xinquan** Fujian China
Xinshan Jiangxi China see **Anyuan**
131 H5 **Xinshao** Hunan China
Xinshi Hubei China see **Jingshan**
Xinshiba Sichuan China see **Ganluo**
129 O9 **Xintai** Shandong China
131 J4 **Xintanpu** Hubei China
131 I6 **Xintian** Hunan China
122 D3 **Xintian** Nei Mongol China
131 J3 **Xinxian** Henan China
Xinxian Shanxi China see **Xinzhou**
129 M9 **Xinxiang** Henan China
131 I7 **Xinxing** Guangdong China
131 J2 **Xinyang** Henan China
131 M2 **Xinyang Gang** r. China
131 I2 **Xinye** Henan China
131 H7 **Xinyi** Guangdong China
129 P9 **Xinyi** Jiangsu China
129 P9 **Xinyi He** r. China
130 G9 **Xinying** Hainan China
Xinying Taiwan see **Hsinying**
131 J5 **Xinyu** Jiangxi China
Xinyuan Qinghai China see **Tianjun**
132 F5 **Xinyuan** Xinjiang China
129 Q1 **Xinzhangfang** Nei Mongol China
129 M9 **Xinzheng** Henan China
Xinzhou Guangxi China see **Longlin**
Xinzhou Guizhou China see **Huangping**
131 J3 **Xinzhou** Hubei China
129 M7 **Xinzhou** Shanxi China
Xinzhu Taiwan see **Hsinchu**
204 E4 **Xinzo de Limia** Spain
Xiongshan Fujian China see **Zhenghe**
Xiongzhou Guangdong China see **Nanxiong**
276 D2 **Xipamanu** r. Bol./Brazil
131 H2 **Xiping** Henan China
131 J2 **Xiping** Henan China
128 G9 **Xiqing Shan** mts China
128 H7 **Xiqu** Gansu China
278 E4 **Xique Xique** Brazil
151 K5 **Xırdalan** Azer.
209 E9 **Xirivella** Spain
220 E4 **Xiro** hill Greece
221 H5 **Xirokampo** Greece
274 E6 **Xiruá** r. Brazil
Xisa Yunnan China see **Xichou**
129 K6 **Xishanzui** Nei Mongol China
130 C7 **Xishuangbanna** reg. Yunnan China
Xishuanghe Shandong China see **Kenli**
130 F4 **Xishui** Guizhou China
131 J3 **Xishui** Hubei China
204 E2 **Xistral, Serra do** mts Spain
133 K8 **Xi Taijnar Hu** l. Qinghai China
128 D8 **Xitieshan** Qinghai China
269 K9 **Xitla** Mex.
228 B4 **Xitole** Guinea-Bissau
Xiucaiwan Chongqing China see **Fengdu**
Xiugu Jiangxi China see **Jinxi**
Xi Ujimqin Qi Nei Mongol China see **Bayan Ul Hot**
131 L4 **Xiuning** Anhui China
130 G4 **Xiushan** Chongqing China
Xiushan Yunnan China see **Tonghai**
131 J4 **Xiushui** Jiangxi China
131 J4 **Xiu Shui** r. China
130 F5 **Xiuwen** Guizhou China
129 M9 **Xiuwu** Henan China
129 R6 **Xiuyan** Liaoning China
Xiuyan Shaanxi China see **Qingjian**
130 H8 **Xiuying** Hainan China
142 I7 **Xiva** Uzbek.
Xiwanzi Hebei China see **Chongli**
130 A2 **Xiwu** Qinghai China
133 G12 **Xixabangma Feng** mt. Xizang China
131 H2 **Xixia** Henan China
128 J7 **Xixia** Ningxia China
131 J2 **Xixian** Henan China
129 L8 **Xixian** Shanxi China
130 F2 **Xixiang** Shaanxi China
Xixiu Guizhou China see **Anshun**
Xixón Spain see **Gijón-Xixón**
129 M8 **Xiyang** Shanxi China
131 M5 **Xiyang Dao** i. China
130 E6 **Xiyang Jiang** r. Yunnan China
128 H8 **Xiying** Gansu China
Xizang aut. reg. China see **Xizang Zizhiqu**
Xizang Gaoyuan plat. Xizang China see **Qingzang Gaoyuan**
130 A3 **Xizang Zizhiqu** aut. reg. China
129 Q7 **Xizhong Dao** i. China
151 K5 **Xızı** Azer.
133 L11 **Xobando** Xizang China
151 H6 **Xocalı** Azer.
151 I6 **Xocavänd** Azer.
269 L8 **Xochiapa** Mex.
269 I5 **Xochiatiapan** Mex.
269 H7 **Xochicalco** tourist site Mex.
269 H6 **Xochimilco** Mex.
269 I9 **Xochistlahuaca** Mex.
221 H6 **Xodoto, Akrotirio** pt Greece
Xoi Xizang China see **Qüxü**
142 J8 **Xo'jadavlat** Uzbek.
141 J2 **Xo'japiryox tog'i** mt. Uzbek.
142 H6 **Xo'jayli** Qoraqalpog'iston Respublikasi Uzbek.
133 K12 **Xoka** Xizang China
237 L8 **Xolobe** S. Africa
151 J6 **Xol Qarabucaq** Azer.
269 H6 **Xonacatlán** Mex.
143 O7 **Xonobod** Uzbek.
142 I7 **Xonqa** Uzbek.
Xonrupt France see **Xonrupt-Longemer**
179 M7 **Xonrupt-Longemer** France
237 L7 **Xonxa Dam** S. Africa
130 B4 **Xo Qu** r. Sichuan China
142 I7 **Xorazm** admin. div. Uzbek.
132 J7 **Xorkol** Xinjiang China
133 G8 **Xortang** Xinjiang China
151 I5 **Xosrov** Azer.
204 E1 **Xove** Spain
143 M7 **Xovos** Uzbek.
131 L3 **Xuancheng** Anhui China
130 G3 **Xuan'en** Hubei China
130 F3 **Xuanhan** Sichuan China
129 N6 **Xuanhua** Hebei China
119 H9 **Xuân Lôc** Vietnam
130 E5 **Xuanwei** Yunnan China
Xuanzhou Anhui China see **Xuancheng**
204 D4 **Xubín** Spain
131 I2 **Xuchang** Henan China
121 J5 **Xuchang** Henan China
Xucheng Guangdong China see **Xuwen**
151 J4 **Xudat** Azer.
232 D3 **Xuddur** Somalia
232 E2 **Xudun** Somalia
133 K12 **Xueba** Xizang China
Xuefeng Fujian China see **Mingxi**
130 G5 **Xuefeng Shan** mts China
129 L9 **Xuehua Shan** hill Shanxi China
129 L7 **Xuejiawan** Nei Mongol China
130 B5 **Xue Shan** mts Yunnan China
128 D9 **Xugin Gol** r. Qinghai China
128 H6 **Xugui** Nei Mongol China
128 D9 **Xugui** Qinghai China
Xuguit Qi Nei Mongol China see **Yakeshi**
Xujiang Jiangxi China see **Guangchang**
Xulun Hobot Qagan Qi Nei Mongol China see **Qagan Nur**
Xulun Hoh Qi Nei Mongol China see **Dund Hot**
130 D6 **Xundian** Yunnan China
Xungba Xizang China see **Xangdoring**
133 I11 **Xungmai** Xizang China
133 K11 **Xung Qu** r. Xizang China
133 G12 **Xungru** Xizang China
122 E4 **Xunhe** Heilong. China
122 F4 **Xun He** r. China
130 G2 **Xun He** r. China
128 H9 **Xunhua** Qinghai China
130 H7 **Xun Jiang** r. China
122 F4 **Xunke** Heilong. China
204 E4 **Xunqueira de Ambía** Spain
131 J6 **Xunwu** Jiangxi China
129 N9 **Xunxian** Henan China
130 G2 **Xunyang** Shaanxi China
129 K9 **Xunyi** Shaanxi China
130 H5 **Xupu** Hunan China
205 P8 **Xúquer, Riu** r. Spain
128 D9 **Xurgan** Qinghai China
133 H11 **Xuru Co** salt l. China
129 N7 **Xushui** Hebei China
130 H8 **Xuwen** Guangdong China
Xuyang Sichuan China see **Rongxian**
131 L2 **Xuyi** Jiangsu China
130 E4 **Xuyong** Sichuan China
129 O9 **Xuzhou** Jiangsu China
221 G2 **Xylagani** Greece
220 D4 **Xylokastro** Greece
220 E2 **Xyloupoli** Greece

Y

107 M7 **Yaamba** Qld Austr.
130 D3 **Ya'an** Sichuan China
105 I6 **Yaapeet** Vic. Austr.
115 E4 **Yaba** Maluku Indon.
Yabanabat Turkey see **Kızılcahamam**
229 H5 **Yabassi** Cameroon
100 □3a **Yabbenohr** i. Kwajalein Marshall Is
232 C3 **Yabēlo** Eth.
232 C3 **Yabēlo Wildlife Sanctuary** nature res. Eth.
230 D4 **Yabia** Dem. Rep. Congo
219 M7 **Yablanitsa** Bulg.
219 O8 **Yablanovo** Bulg.
159 S2 **Yablochnoye** Rus. Fed.
159 T1 **Yablonovets** Rus. Fed.
159 R9 **Yablonovskiy** Rus. Fed.
129 K1 **Yablonovyy Khrebet** mts Rus. Fed.
158 H3 **Yablunets'** Ukr.
158 D5 **Yabluniv** Ukr.
159 K4 **Yablunivka** Ukr.
229 G3 **Yabo** Nigeria
128 H7 **Yabrai Shan** mts China
128 H7 **Yabrai Yanchang** Nei Mongol China
147 I4 **Yabrīn** reg. Saudi Arabia
150 E5 **Yabrūd** Syria
126 A5 **Yabu** Japan
271 □1 **Yabucoa** Puerto Rico
271 □1 **Yabucoa, Puerto** b. Puerto Rico
127 L1 **Yabuki** Japan
122 F6 **Yabuli** Heilong. China
274 C5 **Yabuyanos** Peru
127 J3 **Yabuzukahon** Japan
Yacha Hainan China see **Baisha**
130 G9 **Yacheng** Hainan China
130 F5 **Yachi He** r. China
127 L4 **Yachimata** Japan
127 L4 **Yachiyo** Chiba Japan
127 K3 **Yachiyo** Ibaraki Japan
279 A8 **Yaciretá, Isla** i. Para.
105 K7 **Yackandandah** Vic. Austr.
276 E5 **Yacuiba** Bol.
274 E3 **Yacurai** Venez.
282 F2 **Yacyretá Apipé, Embalse** resr Arg./Para.
230 B3 **Yadé, Massif du** mts C.A.R.
136 E4 **Yadgir** Karnataka India
136 E5 **Yadiki** Andhra Prad. India
255 G8 **Yadkin** r. NC U.S.A.
255 G7 **Yadkinville** NC U.S.A.
133 I13 **Yadong** Xizang China
156 I5 **Yadrin** Rus. Fed.
101 □7 **Yadua** i. Fiji
124 □A22 **Yaeyama-rettō** is Japan
Yafa Israel see **Tel Aviv-Yafo**
224 B1 **Yafran** Libya
228 E4 **Yagaba** Ghana
Yagaing state Myanmar see **Arakan**
124 □1 **Yagaji-jima** i. Okinawa Japan
125 G14 **Yagami** Japan
128 H6 **Yagan** Nei Mongol China
221 I3 **Yağcılı** Turkey
Yağda Turkey see **Erdemli**
288 E9 **Yaghan Basin** sea feature S. Atlantic Ocean
126 C5 **Yagi** Japan
124 S2 **Yagishiri-tō** i. Japan
150 D1 **Yağızlar** Turkey
128 F8 **Yagkêng** Qinghai China
151 E5 **Yağlıca Dağı** mt. Turkey
156 E3 **Yaglyayarvi** Rus. Fed.
144 F2 **Yagman** Turkm.
151 E6 **Yağmurlu** r. Turkey
161 U3 **Yagnitsa** Rus. Fed.
268 B4 **Yago** Mex.
219 N8 **Yagoda** Bulg.
142 A2 **Yagodnaya Polyana** Rus. Fed.
161 S8 **Yagodnoye** Kaluzhskaya Oblast' Rus. Fed.
153 P3 **Yagodnoye** Magadanskaya Oblast' Rus. Fed.
122 K3 **Yagodnyy** Rus. Fed.
Yagotin Ukr. see **Yahotyn**
229 I4 **Yagoua** Cameroon
133 F11 **Yagra** Xizang China
128 D9 **Yagradagzê Shan** mt. Qinghai China
270 D2 **Yaguajay** Cuba
Yaguarón r. Brazil/Uru. see **Jaguarão**
274 D5 **Yaguas** r. Peru
119 E11 **Yaha** Thai.
126 E6 **Yahagi-gawa** r. Japan
230 D4 **Yahila** Dem. Rep. Congo
246 G5 **Yahk** B.C. Can.
158 I6 **Yahorlyk** r. Ukr.
159 K3 **Yahotyn** Ukr.
268 E4 **Yahualica** Mex.
230 D4 **Yahuma** Dem. Rep. Congo
140 D2 **Yahyalı** Turkey
145 M6 **Yahya Wana** Afgh.
119 D8 **Yai, Khao** mt. Thai.
127 K2 **Yaita** Japan
238 □3c **Yaiza** Lanzarote Canary Is
127 H6 **Yaizu** Japan
130 C3 **Yajiang** Sichuan China
230 C3 **Yaka** C.A.R.
150 E2 **Yakacık** Turkey
245 □C6 **Yakak, Cape** AK U.S.A.
150 D2 **Yakapınar** Turkey
132 H7 **Yakatograk** Xinjiang China
145 K5 **Yak Dar** Afgh.
126 G3 **Yake-dake** vol. Japan
129 Q2 **Yakeshi** Nei Mongol China
144 G4 **Yakhab** waterhole Iran
145 K6 **Yakhehal** Afgh.
158 F4 **Yakhivtsi** Ukr.
159 M3 **Yakhnyky** Ukr.
161 U5 **Yakhroma** Rus. Fed.
262 D3 **Yakima** WA U.S.A.
262 E3 **Yakima** r. WA U.S.A.
262 D3 **Yakima Indian Reservation** res. WA U.S.A.
144 E5 **Yakinish** Iran
143 L8 **Yakkabog'** Uzbek.
145 J7 **Yakmach** Pak.
228 E3 **Yako** Burkina
245 M4 **Yakobi Island** AK U.S.A.
230 D3 **Yakoma** Dem. Rep. Congo
219 L8 **Yakoruda** Bulg.
159 P4 **Yakovenkove** Ukr.
122 H6 **Yakovlevka** Rus. Fed.
159 P3 **Yakovlevo** Rus. Fed.
156 K4 **Yakshur-Bod'ya** Rus. Fed.
124 R4 **Yakumo** Japan
126 A5 **Yakuno** Japan
124 □H16 **Yaku-shima** i. Japan
245 M4 **Yakutat** AK U.S.A.
245 L4 **Yakutat Bay** AK U.S.A.
153 N3 **Yakutsk** Rus. Fed.
159 O7 **Yakymivka** Ukr.
228 E4 **Yala** Ghana
232 B4 **Yala** Kenya
136 G9 **Yala** Sri Lanka
119 E11 **Yala** Thai.
133 H12 **Yalai** Xizang China
130 C3 **Yalakan** Sichuan China
221 K2 **Yalakdere** Turkey
151 J4 **Yalama** Azer.
150 A2 **Yalan Dünya Mağarası** tourist site Turkey
104 C4 **Yalata Aboriginal Lands** res. S.A. Austr.
103 G10 **Yaldhurst** South I. N.Z.
246 F5 **Yale** B.C. Can.
251 L6 **Yale** MI U.S.A.
230 E4 **Yaleko** Dem. Rep. Congo
228 E3 **Yalgo** Burkina
109 D10 **Yalgoo** W.A. Austr.
221 I5 **Yalıkavak** Turkey
219 Q9 **Yalıköy** Turkey
151 C6 **Yalınca** Turkey
230 D3 **Yalinga** C.A.R.
160 M8 **Yalizava** Belarus
267 O7 **Yalkubul, Punta** pt Mex.
270 □ **Yallahs** Jamaica
107 J8 **Yalleroi** Qld Austr.
109 C12 **Yallingup** W.A. Austr.
228 E3 **Yallo** Burkina
105 K8 **Yallourn** Vic. Austr.
151 D5 **Yalnızçam Dağları** mts Turkey
261 J9 **Yalobusha** r. MS U.S.A.
Yalogo Burkina see **Yalgo**
230 C3 **Yaloké** C.A.R.
130 C5 **Yalong Jiang** r. Sichuan China
221 K2 **Yalova** Turkey
219 R10 **Yalova** prov. Turkey
Yaloven' Moldova see **Ialoveni**
106 D7 **Yalpirakinu Aboriginal Land** res. N.T. Austr.
158 H8 **Yalpuh, Ozero** l. Ukr.
Yalpukh r. Moldova see **Ialpug**
159 Q7 **Yalta** Donets'ka Oblast' Ukr.
159 N9 **Yalta** Respublika Krym Ukr.
158 G5 **Yaltushkiv** Ukr.
159 N9 **Yaltyns'kyy Zapovidnyk** nature res. Ukr.
129 R3 **Yalu He** r. China
123 D8 **Yalu Jiang** r. China/N. Korea
230 D5 **Yalusaka** Dem. Rep. Congo
152 H4 **Yalutorovsk** Rus. Fed.
221 M4 **Yalvaç** Turkey
146 G7 **Yām** reg. Saudi Arabia
Yama Ukr. see **Sivers'k**
127 M4 **Yamada** Chiba Japan
124 S7 **Yamada** Iwate Japan
126 F2 **Yamada** Toyama Japan
125 H13 **Yamaga** Japan
127 L2 **Yamagata** Ibaraki Japan
124 S6 **Yamagata** Iwate Japan
127 G3 **Yamagata** Nagano Japan
124 R8 **Yamagata** Yamagata Japan
124 Q8 **Yamagata** pref. Japan
126 G4 **Yamaguchi** Nagano Japan
125 I12 **Yamaguchi** Yamaguchi Japan
125 I12 **Yamaguchi** pref. Japan
127 J5 **Yamakita** Japan
152 H2 **Yamal, Poluostrov** pen. Rus. Fed.
122 I2 **Yam-Alin', Khrebet** mts Rus. Fed.
Yamal Peninsula Rus. Fed. see **Yamal, Poluostrov**
126 D3 **Yamanaka** Japan
127 I5 **Yamanaka-ko** l. Japan
127 I4 **Yamanashi** Japan
127 H4 **Yamanashi** pref. Japan
Yamankhalinka Kazakh. see **Makhambet**
127 I5 **Yamanokako** Japan
127 H2 **Yamanouchi** Japan
128 C6 **Yamansu** Xinjiang China
126 F5 **Yamaoka** Japan
129 L1 **Yamarovka** Rus. Fed.
125 L11 **Yamasaki** Japan
126 C6 **Yamashiro** Japan
126 E4 **Yamato** Gifu Japan
127 L3 **Yamato** Ibaraki Japan
127 J5 **Yamato** Kanagawa Japan
124 □G18 **Yamato** Nansei-shotō Japan
127 I1 **Yamato** Niigata Japan
126 C6 **Yamato-Aogaki Kokutei-kōen** park Japan
126 C6 **Yamato-Kōriyama** Japan
126 C6 **Yamatotakada** Japan
127 L2 **Yamatsuri** Japan
126 D6 **Yamazoe** Japan
105 N3 **Yamba** N.S.W. Austr.
105 I8 **Yambacoona** Tas. Austr.
247 I1 **Yamba Lake** N.W.T. Can.
106 C3 **Yambarran Range** hills N.T. Austr.
230 B2 **Yamba Tchangsou** Chad
228 B4 **Yambéring** Guinea
274 D4 **Yambi, Mesa de** hills Col.
230 F3 **Yambio** Sudan
219 O8 **Yambol** Bulg.
274 B6 **Yambrasbamba** Peru
113 H8 **Yamdena** i. Indon.
125 H13 **Yame** Japan
118 C4 **Yamethin** Myanmar
114 C1 **Y'ami** i. Phil.
127 L2 **Yamizo-san** mt. Japan
136 D4 **Yamkanmardi** Karnataka India
Yamkhad Syria see **Ḥalab**
160 M4 **Yamkino** Rus. Fed.
160 L3 **Yamm** Rus. Fed.
107 H9 **Yamma Yamma, Lake** salt flat Qld Austr.
159 O3 **Yamne** Ukr.
228 D5 **Yamoussoukro** Côte d'Ivoire
159 K5 **Yampil'** Cherkas'ka Oblast' Ukr.
158 F4 **Yampil'** Khmel'nyts'ka Oblast' Ukr.
159 M2 **Yampil'** Sums'ka Oblast' Ukr.
158 H5 **Yampil'** Vinnyts'ka Oblast' Ukr.
Yampol' Cherkas'ka Oblast' Ukr. see **Yampil'**
Yampol' Khmel'nyts'ka Oblast' Ukr. see **Yampil'**
Yampol' Sums'ka Oblast' Ukr. see **Yampil'**
Yampol' Vinnyts'ka Oblast' Ukr. see **Yampil'**
138 H7 **Yamuna** r. India
138 F4 **Yamunanagar** Haryana India
133 J12 **Yamzho Yumco** l. China
229 H4 **Yana** Nigeria
153 O2 **Yana** r. Rus. Fed.
104 H7 **Yanac** Vic. Austr.
276 B2 **Yanachaga-Chemillen, Parque Nacional** nat. park Peru
125 K13 **Yanadani** Japan
124 R9 **Yanagawa** Japan
124 □1 **Yanaha-jima** i. Okinawa Japan
125 J13 **Yanai** Japan
136 H4 **Yanam** Puducherry India
129 K8 **Yan'an** Shaanxi China
276 C3 **Yanaoca** Peru
Yanaon Puducherry India see **Yanam**
156 K4 **Yanaul** Rus. Fed.
161 N6 **Yanavichy** Belarus
274 C5 **Yanayacu** Peru
130 C5 **Yanbian** Yunnan China
146 C3 **Yanbu, Sharm** b. Saudi Arabia
146 D3 **Yanbu' al Baḥr** Saudi Arabia
146 D3 **Yanbu' an Nakhl** reg. Saudi Arabia
255 H7 **Yanceyville** NC U.S.A.
129 L8 **Yanchang** Shaanxi China
131 M2 **Yancheng** Jiangsu China
Yancheng Shandong China see **Qihe**
Yancheng Sichuan China see **Jingyan**
109 C11 **Yanchep** W.A. Austr.
129 J8 **Yanchi** Ningxia China
128 D5 **Yanchi** Xinjiang China
132 H3 **Yanchi** Xinjiang China
132 L7 **Yanchiwan** Gansu China
129 L8 **Yanchuan** Shaanxi China
159 P6 **Yanchur** r. Ukr.
105 K6 **Yanco** N.S.W. Austr.
105 J6 **Yanco Creek** r. N.S.W. Austr.
105 H4 **Yanco Glen** N.S.W. Austr.
105 J4 **Yanda** watercourse N.S.W. Austr.
104 H4 **Yandama Creek** watercourse S.A. Austr.
131 M5 **Yandang Shan** mts China
Yandao Sichuan China see **Yingjing**
108 E6 **Yandeyarra Aboriginal Reserve** W.A. Austr.
108 E7 **Yandicoogina Mine** W.A. Austr.
109 E9 **Yandil** W.A. Austr.
107 N9 **Yandina** Qld Austr.
100 □6 **Yandina** Solomon Is
230 C5 **Yandja** Dem. Rep. Congo
118 B6 **Yandoon** Myanmar
Yandua i. Fiji see **Yadua**
128 D5 **Yandun** Xinjiang China
161 Q1 **Yanega** Rus. Fed.
228 C4 **Yanfolila** Mali
230 D3 **Yangalia** C.A.R.
230 E4 **Yangambi** Dem. Rep. Congo
133 L11 **Ya'ngamdo** Xizang China
133 L11 **Ya'ngamdo** Xizang China
228 D3 **Yangasso** Mali
133 J11 **Yangbajain** Xizang China
130 B6 **Yangbi** Yunnan China
Yangcheng Guangdong China see **Yangshan**
129 M9 **Yangcheng** Shanxi China
Yangchuan Guizhou China see **Suiyang**
131 H7 **Yangchun** Guangdong China
131 J7 **Yangcun** Guangdong China
Yangcun Tianjin China see **Wuqing**
132 I7 **Yangdaxkak** Xinjiang China
123 E9 **Yangdok** N. Korea
131 H8 **Yangdong** Guangdong China
129 M6 **Yanggao** Shanxi China
129 N8 **Yanggu** Shandong China
Yanghe Ningxia China see **Yongning**
129 N6 **Yang He** r. China
133 G9 **Yang Hu** l. Xizang China
142 I7 **Yangiariq** Uzbek.
Yangibazar Kyrg. see **Jangy-Bazar**
133 D9 **Yangi Davan** pass Aksai Chin/China
142 K8 **Yangi Nishon** Uzbek.
145 M3 **Yangī Qal'ah** Afgh.
143 L7 **Yangiqishloq** Uzbek.
142 K7 **Yangirabot** Uzbek.
143 M7 **Yangiyo'l** Uzbek.
129 K8 **Yangjialing** Shaanxi China
131 H8 **Yangjiang** Guangdong China
129 P8 **Yangkou** Shandong China
118 C6 **Yangôn** Myanmar
137 O4 **Yangôn** admin. div. Myanmar
131 H3 **Yangping** Hubei China
129 M8 **Yangquan** Shanxi China
129 L8 **Yangquanqu** Shanxi China
131 I6 **Yangshan** Guangdong China
130 H6 **Yangshuo** Guangxi China
119 I8 **Yang Sin, Chư** mt. Vietnam
118 F6 **Yang Talat** Thai.
130 C6 **Yangtouyan** Yunnan China
Yangtze r. Qinghai China see **Tongtian He**
131 M3 **Yangtze** r. China alt. **Chang Jiang,** alt. **Jinsha Jiang,** alt. **Tongtian He,** long **Yangtze Kiang**
Yangtze, Mouth of the China see **Changjiang Kou**
130 E1 **Yanguan** Gansu China
205 P4 **Yanguas** Spain
232 D2 **Yangudi Rassa National Park** Eth.
129 P9 **Yangweigang** Jiangsu China
131 H8 **Yangxi** Guangdong China
130 F2 **Yangxian** Shaanxi China
123 F9 **Yangyang** S. Korea
129 N6 **Yangyuan** Hebei China
131 L2 **Yangzhou** Jiangsu China
Yangzhou Shaanxi China see **Yangxian**
130 G4 **Yanhe** Guizhou China
129 L8 **Yan He** r. China
132 I5 **Yanhu** Xinjiang China
133 F10 **Yanhu** Xizang China
104 E5 **Yaninee, Lake** salt flat S.A. Austr.
156 F3 **Yanishpole** Rus. Fed.
162 U5 **Yanis"yarvi, Ozero** l. Rus. Fed.
122 F7 **Yanji** Jilin China
129 N9 **Yanjin** Henan China
130 E4 **Yanjin** Yunnan China
Yanjing Sichuan China see **Yanyuan**
130 B4 **Yanjing** Xizang China
Yanjing Yunnan China see **Yanjin**
229 H4 **Yankari National Park** Nigeria
160 L6 **Yankavichy** Belarus
Yankou Sichuan China see **Wusheng**
260 G4 **Yankton** SD U.S.A.
260 F4 **Yankton Indian Reservation** res. SD U.S.A.
151 D1 **Yankul'** Rus. Fed.
151 D1 **Yankul'** r. Rus. Fed.
129 N9 **Yanling** Henan China
131 I5 **Yanling** Hunan China
Yannina Greece see **Ioannina**
153 P2 **Yano-Indigirskaya Nizmennost'** lowland Rus. Fed.
161 P7 **Yanovo** Rus. Fed.
152 J3 **Yanov-Stan** Rus. Fed.
136 G8 **Yan Oya** r. Sri Lanka
132 H5 **Yanqi** Xinjiang China
129 N6 **Yanqing** Beijing China
147 M4 **Yanqul** Oman
109 C7 **Yanrey** r. W.A. Austr.
129 O7 **Yanshan** Hebei China
131 K4 **Yanshan** Jiangxi China
130 E7 **Yanshan** Yunnan China
129 O6 **Yan Shan** mts China
129 M9 **Yanshi** Henan China
133 K10 **Yanshiping** Qinghai China
122 F6 **Yanshou** Heilong. China
153 O2 **Yanskiy Zaliv** g. Rus. Fed.
105 J3 **Yantabulla** N.S.W. Austr.
144 C2 **Yantagh** Iran
129 Q8 **Yantai** Shandong China
283 B6 **Yántales, Cerro** mt. Chile
159 N8 **Yantarne** Ukr.
160 C7 **Yantarnyy** Rus. Fed.
259 K1 **Yantic** r. CT U.S.A.
130 E3 **Yanting** Sichuan China
122 E7 **Yantongshan** Jilin China
131 M4 **Yantou** Zhejiang China
219 N7 **Yantra** r. Bulg.
101 □7a **Yanuca** i. Fiji
146 F4 **Yanūfī, Jabal al** hill Saudi Arabia
Yanutha i. Fiji see **Yanuca**
130 B5 **Yanwa** Yunnan China
130 H4 **Yanxi** Hunan China
Yany-Kurgan Kazakh. see **Zhanakorgan**
130 C5 **Yanyuan** Sichuan China
129 O9 **Yanzhou** Shandong China
126 C6 **Yao** Japan
130 C6 **Yao'an** Yunnan China
129 K8 **Yaodian** Shaanxi China
Yaodu Anhui China see **Dongzhi**
Yaojie Gansu China see **Honggu**
131 K4 **Yaoli** Jiangxi China
128 E7 **Yaoquanzi** Gansu China
126 F5 **Yaotsu** Japan
229 H6 **Yaoundé** Cameroon
Yaoxian Shaanxi China see **Yaozhou**
119 D10 **Yao Yai, Ko** i. Thai.
129 L7 **Yaozhen** Shaanxi China
129 K9 **Yaozhou** Shaanxi China
113 I5 **Yap** i. Micronesia
274 E4 **Yapacana, Parque Nacional** nat. park Venez.
276 D3 **Yapacani** r. Bol.
228 E4 **Yapei** Ghana
113 I7 **Yapen** i. Papua Indon.
113 I7 **Yapen, Selat** sea chan. Papua Indon.
282 F3 **Yapeyú** Arg.
259 J3 **Yaphank** NY U.S.A.
107 H5 **Yappar** r. Qld Austr.
173 K6 **Yapton** West Sussex, England U.K.
290 E5 **Yap Trench** sea feature N. Pacific Ocean
275 G4 **Yapukarri** Guyana
109 I9 **Yapuparra Aboriginal Reserve** W.A. Austr.
266 D4 **Yaqui** r. Mex.
156 K4 **Yar** Rus. Fed.
270 E3 **Yara** Cuba
274 D2 **Yaracal** Venez.
274 D2 **Yaracuy** state Venez.
Yaradzha Turkm. see **Ýarajy**
144 G2 **Ýarajy** Turkm.
107 J8 **Yaraka** Qld Austr.
Yarangüme Turkey see **Tavas**
156 I4 **Yaransk** Rus. Fed.
Yardan Uzbek. see **Yordon**
104 E5 **Yardea** S.A. Austr.
221 L6 **Yardımcı Burnu** pt Turkey
151 J7 **Yardımlı** Azer.
258 F4 **Yardley** PA U.S.A.
133 J12 **Yardoi** Xizang China
258 F4 **Yardville** NJ U.S.A.
Yardymly Azer. see **Yardımlı**
173 P3 **Yare** r. England U.K.
156 K3 **Yarega** Rus. Fed.
158 D5 **Yaremcha** Ukr.
99 G2 **Yaren** Nauru
156 J3 **Yarenga** r. Rus. Fed.
269 K8 **Yareni** Mex.
156 J3 **Yarensk** Rus. Fed.
159 M4 **Yares'ky** Ukr.
Yargara Moldova see **Iargara**
274 C5 **Yari** r. Col.
126 G3 **Yariga-take** mt. Japan
146 G8 **Yarīm** Yemen
Yarımca Turkey see **Körfez**
106 G6 **Yaringa** watercourse Qld Austr.
275 H4 **Yaripo** Brazil
229 G3 **Yaris** well Niger
271 I8 **Yaritagua** Venez.
Yarkand Xinjiang China see **Shache**
Yarkant Xinjiang China see **Shache**
133 D7 **Yarkant He** r. China
251 R5 **Yarker** Ont. Can.
145 O3 **Yarkhun** r. Pak.
109 K11 **Yarle Lakes** salt flat S.A. Austr.
219 L8 **Yarlovo** Bulg.
133 L12 **Yarlung Zangbo** r. China alt. **Dihang (India),** alt. **Jamuna (Bangladesh),** conv. **Brahmaputra**
171 O4 **Yarm** Stockton-on-Tees, England U.K.
158 F4 **Yarmolyntsi** Ukr.

249 H5 Yarmouth N.S. Can.
173 J6 Yarmouth Isle of Wight, England U.K.
Yarmouth Norfolk, England U.K. see Great Yarmouth
257 □O5 Yarmouth ME U.S.A.
150 D6 Yarmuk r. Asia
265 T7 Yarnell AZ U.S.A.
173 J4 Yarnton Oxfordshire, England U.K.
161 X9 Yarok Rus. Fed.
161 N6 Yaromina Belarus
159 M3 Yaroshivka Ukr.
159 M2 Yaroslavets' Ukr.
161 R1 Yaroslavichi Rus. Fed.
161 W4 Yaroslavl' Rus. Fed.
Yaroslavl Oblast admin. div. Rus. Fed. see Yaroslavskaya Oblast'
151 B1 Yaroslavskaya Rus. Fed.
161 W4 Yaroslavskaya Oblast' admin. div. Rus. Fed.
122 H6 Yaroslavskiy Rus. Fed.
107 J4 Yarrabah Aboriginal Reserve Qld Austr.
107 I3 Yarraden Qld Austr.
105 J7 Yarra Junction Vic. Austr.
106 C4 Yarralin Aboriginal Land res. N.T. Austr.
108 C6 Yarraloola W.A. Austr.
105 K8 Yarram Vic. Austr.
107 M9 Yarraman Qld Austr.
105 J7 Yarrawonga Vic. Austr.
109 C10 Yarra Yarra Lakes salt flat W.A. Austr.
108 F6 Yarrie W.A. Austr.
107 J9 Yarronvale Qld Austr.
107 J6 Yarrowmere Qld Austr.
139 N5 Yartö Tra La pass Xizang China
152 J3 Yartsevo Krasnoyarskiy Kray Rus. Fed.
161 P6 Yartsevo Smolenskaya Oblast' Rus. Fed.
133 H12 Yaru r. China
274 C3 Yarumal Col.
128 E2 Yaruu Mongolia
130 B3 Yarwa Sichuan China
151 H2 Yaryk-Aul Rus. Fed.
130 A4 Yarzhong Xizang China
Yaş Romania see Iaşi
231 D5 Yasa Dem. Rep. Congo
137 J1 Yasai r. W. Bengal India
126 B4 Yasaka Kyōto Japan
127 G3 Yasaka Nagano Japan
127 L3 Yasato Japan
101 □7 Yasawa i. Fiji
101 □7 Yasawa Group is Fiji
158 D5 Yasen' Ukr.
159 R7 Yaseni r. Rus. Fed.
219 O7 Yasenkovo Bulg.
157 G7 Yasenskaya Rus. Fed.
157 H7 Yashalta Rus. Fed.
229 G3 Yashi Nigeria
229 F4 Yashikera Nigeria
145 O3 Yashilkŭl l. Tajik.
124 R7 Yashima Japan
125 J13 Ya-shima i. Japan
127 H2 Yashira Japan
126 A6 Yashiro Japan
125 J13 Yashiro-jima i. Japan
157 K5 Yashkino Rus. Fed.
157 I7 Yashkul' Rus. Fed.
138 D1 Yasin Pak.
Yasinovataya Ukr. see Yasynuvata
158 D5 Yasinya Ukr.
160 K9 Yaskavichy Belarus
151 K5 Yaşma Azer.
151 K5 Yaşma Adası i. Azer.
219 P8 Yasna Polyana Bulg.
161 U7 Yasnogorsk Rus. Fed.
159 Q5 Yasnohirka Ukr.
158 J3 Yasnohorodka Ukr.
122 F2 Yasnyy Amurskaya Oblast' Rus. Fed.
142 H2 Yasnyy Orenburgskaya Oblast' Rus. Fed.
118 G7 Yasothon Thai.
105 L6 Yass N.S.W. Austr.
105 L6 Yass r. N.S.W. Austr.
Yassı Burnu c. Cyprus see Plakoti, Cape
221 K5 Yassıhüyük Turkey
161 N4 Yasski Rus. Fed.
151 C6 Yastıktepe Turkey
159 Q2 Yastrebovka Rus. Fed.
159 N2 Yastrubyne Ukr.
126 D5 Yasu Japan
125 K13 Yasuda Japan
125 K11 Yasugi Japan
144 D6 Yāsūj Iran
274 C5 Yasuní, Parque Nacional nat. park Ecuador
127 G5 Yasuoka Japan
99 G3 Yasur vol. Vanuatu
127 H1 Yasuzuka Japan
158 F1 Yasyel'da r. Belarus
159 Q5 Yasynuvata Ukr.
229 I1 Yat well Niger
276 D2 Yata r. Bol.
230 D2 Yata r. C.A.R.
221 J5 Yatağan Turkey
229 F3 Yatakala Niger
230 D2 Yata-Ngaya, Réserve de Faune de la nature res. C.A.R.
233 C5 Yata Plateau Kenya
100 □5 Yaté New Caledonia
172 H4 Yate South Gloucestershire, England U.K.
173 K5 Yateley Hampshire, England U.K.
246 H2 Yates r. Alta/N.W.T. Can.
261 H7 Yates Center KS U.S.A.
247 L2 Yathkyed Lake Nunavut Can.
105 J5 Yathong Nature Reserve N.S.W. Austr.
269 I5 Yatipan Mex.
230 E4 Yatolema Dem. Rep. Congo
126 E5 Yatomi Japan
Yatou Shandong China see Rongcheng
209 D9 Yátova Spain
158 J5 Yatran' r. Ukr.
127 H4 Yatsuga-take vol. Japan
127 H3 Yatsuga-take-Chūshin-kōgen Kokutei-kōen park Japan
126 F2 Yatsuo Japan
125 H14 Yatsushiro Japan
125 H14 Yatsushiro-kai b. Japan
150 D7 Yaṭṭa West Bank
172 G5 Yatton North Somerset, England U.K.
276 B3 Yauca Peru
276 B3 Yauca r. Peru
271 □1 Yauco Puerto Rico
276 A2 Yauli Peru
274 D5 Yauna Maloca Col.
276 C3 Yauri Peru
276 B3 Yauricocha Peru
269 H7 Yautepec Morelos Mex.
269 K9 Yautepec Oaxaca Mex.
131 □J7 Yau Tong b. H.K. China
276 B3 Yauyos Peru
266 □P11 Yauyupe Hond.
Yavan Tajik. see Yovon
274 D6 Yavari r. Brazil/Peru alt. Javari
266 E4 Yávaros Mex.
138 G9 Yavatmal Mahar. India
276 B3 Yavero r. Peru
275 E3 Yaví, Cerro mt. Venez.
159 L6 Yavkyne Ukr.
143 M1 Yavlenka Kazakh.
197 L6 Yavora Ukr.
158 D5 Yavoriv Ivano-Frankivs'ka Oblast' Ukr.
158 C4 Yavoriv L'vivs'ka Oblast' Ukr.
162 U2 Yavr r. Fin./Rus. Fed.
150 F2 Yavuzlu Turkey
126 C6 Yawata Japan
125 J13 Yawatahama Japan
133 F8 Yawatongguz He r. China
133 F8 Yawatongguzlangar Xinjiang China
118 B4 Yaw Chaung r. Myanmar
118 C4 Yawng-hwe Myanmar
267 N9 Yaxchilan tourist site Guat.
Yaxian Hainan China see Sanya
173 L2 Yaxley Cambridgeshire, England U.K.
151 C7 Yaygın Turkey
151 A6 Yaylabaşı Turkey
150 E3 Yayladağı Turkey
151 B6 Yayladere Turkey
151 D6 Yayladüzü Turkey
156 L4 Yayva Rus. Fed.
118 B3 Yazagyo Myanmar
144 F6 Yazd Iran
144 F6 Yazd prov. Iran
144 I5 Yazdān Iran
144 E6 Yazd-e Khvāst Iran
Yazgulemskiy Khrebet mts Tajik. see Yazgulom, Qatorkŭhi
145 N2 Yazgulom, Qatorkŭhi mts Tajik.
161 P3 Yazhelbitsy Rus. Fed.
148 I4 Yazıhan Turkey
221 J5 Yazıkent Turkey
221 I6 Yazıköy Turkey
221 L5 Yazır Turkey
261 J9 Yazoo r. MS U.S.A.
261 J9 Yazoo City MS U.S.A.
127 L2 Yazukami Japan
156 L3 Yaz'va r. Rus. Fed.
224 B4 Ybakoura well Chad
Y Bala Gwynedd, Wales U.K. see Bala
201 L3 Ybbs r. Austria
201 L3 Ybbs an der Donau Austria
201 K4 Ybbsitz Austria
277 F6 Ybycuí Para.
185 C7 Ychoux France
184 I5 Ydes France
220 E5 Ydra Greece
220 E5 Ydra i. Greece
220 E5 Ydras, Kolpos sea chan. Greece
Y Drenewydd Powys, Wales U.K. see Newtown
118 C7 Ye Myanmar
118 C7 Ye r. Myanmar
171 N6 Yeadon West Yorkshire, England U.K.
172 E7 Yealmpton Devon, England U.K.
Yebaishou Liaoning China see Jianping
118 B2 Yebawmi Myanmar
224 C4 Yebbi-Bou Chad
224 C4 Yebbi-Souma Chad
205 L9 Yébenes, Sierra de mts Spain
224 C4 Yebigué, Enneri watercourse Chad
205 O8 Yebra Spain
208 E3 Yebra de Basa Spain
133 C8 Yecheng Xinjiang China
209 C10 Yecla Spain
204 H7 Yecla de Yeltes Spain
266 E3 Yécora Mex.
269 K6 Yecuautla Mex.
118 C5 Yedashe Myanmar
232 C3 YeDebub Bihēroch Bihēreseboch na Hizboch admin. reg. Eth.
221 K6 Yedi Burun Başı pt Turkey
Yedintsy Moldova see Edineţ
Yedisa Georgia see Edisa
151 B6 Yedisu Turkey
150 D3 Yeditepe Turkey
156 I3 Yedoma Rus. Fed.
224 C4 Yedri well Chad
161 Q4 Yedrovo Rus. Fed.
232 D3 Yeed Eth.
108 G4 Yeeda River W.A. Austr.
255 G12 Yeehaw Junction FL U.S.A.
104 E6 Yeelanna S.A. Austr.
161 R2 Yefimovskiy Rus. Fed.
161 V8 Yefremov Rus. Fed.
Yêgainnyin Qinghai China see Henan
229 I2 Yeggueba well Niger
151 G6 Yeghegis r. Armenia
151 G6 Yeghegnadzor Armenia
151 F5 Yeghvard Armenia
143 P2 Yegindy Kazakh.
143 Q3 Yegindybulak Kazakh.
143 M2 Yegindykol' Kazakh.
157 H7 Yegorlyk r. Rus. Fed.
157 H7 Yegorlykskaya Rus. Fed.
122 J6 Yegorova, Mys pt Rus. Fed.
161 Q6 Yegor'ye Rus. Fed.
161 W6 Yegor'yevsk Rus. Fed.
207 K4 Yeguas r. Spain
207 K4 Yeguas, Embalse del resr Spain
207 I6 Yeguas, Sierra de las hills Spain
284 B4 Yeguas, Volcán vol. Chile
229 F4 Yégué Togo
232 A3 Yei Sudan
232 A3 Yei r. Sudan
131 J3 Yeji Anhui China
228 E4 Yeji Ghana
Yejiaji Anhui China see Yeji
152 H4 Yekaterinburg Rus. Fed.
Yekaterinodar Rus. Fed. see Krasnodar
151 F2 Yekaterinogradskaya Rus. Fed.
Yekaterinoslav Ukr. see Dnipropetrovs'k
122 F3 Yekaterinoslavka Rus. Fed.
161 V9 Yekaterinovka Lipetskaya Oblast' Rus. Fed.
159 R6 Yekaterinovka Rostovskaya Oblast' Rus. Fed.
157 I5 Yekaterinovka Saratovskaya Oblast' Rus. Fed.
Yekaterinovskaya Rus. Fed. see Krylovskaya
Yekhegnadzor Armenia see Yeghegnadzor
143 P2 Yekibastuz Kazakh.
161 Q7 Yekimovichi Rus. Fed.
230 D4 Yekokora r. Dem. Rep. Congo
122 I4 Yelabuga Khabarovskiy Kray Rus. Fed.
156 J5 Yelabuga Respublika Tatarstan Rus. Fed.
157 H6 Yelan' Rus. Fed.
157 H6 Yelan' r. Rus. Fed.
157 H6 Yelan' r. Rus. Fed.
159 K6 Yelanets' Ukr.
105 M3 Yelarbon Qld Austr.
157 H5 Yelat'ma Rus. Fed.
144 I2 Yelbarsli Turkm.
221 J4 Yeleğen Turkey
Yelenovka Ukr. see Zoryns'k
Yelenovskiye Kar'yery Ukr. see Dokuchayevs'k
161 S8 Yelenskiy Rus. Fed.
161 V9 Yelets Rus. Fed.
156 N2 Yeletskiy Rus. Fed.
161 Q3 Yeligovo Rus. Fed.
128 H9 Yeliguan Gansu China
228 C3 Yélimané Mali
161 W7 Yelino Rus. Fed.
159 N5 Yelizarove Ukr.
Yelizavetgrad Ukr. see Kirovohrad
159 R7 Yelizavetovka Rostovskaya Oblast' Rus. Fed.
159 T3 Yelizavetovka Voronezhskaya Oblast' Rus. Fed.
153 P4 Yelizavety, Mys c. Sakhalin Rus. Fed.
153 Q4 Yelizovo Rus. Fed.
157 J5 Yelkhovka Rus. Fed.
168 □N1 Yell i. Scotland U.K.
104 D4 Yellabina Regional Reserve nature res. S.A. Austr.
136 G4 Yellandu Andhra Prad. India
136 D5 Yellapur Karnataka India
136 E3 Yellareddi Andhra Prad. India
250 D6 Yellow r. WI U.S.A.
109 E11 Yellowdine W.A. Austr.
258 F3 Yellow Frame NJ U.S.A.
246 G4 Yellowhead Pass Alta/B.C. Can.
258 D4 Yellow House PA U.S.A.
246 H2 Yellowknife N.W.T. Can.
246 H2 Yellowknife r. N.W.T. Can.
105 K5 Yellow Mountain hill N.S.W. Austr.
Yellow River r. China see Huang He
290 D3 Yellow Sea N. Pacific Ocean
256 B9 Yellow Springs OH U.S.A.
260 D2 Yellowstone r. MT U.S.A.
262 I4 Yellowstone Lake WY U.S.A.
262 I4 Yellowstone National Park U.S.A.
168 □N1 Yell Sound str. Scotland U.K.
261 I7 Yellville AR U.S.A.
262 C3 Yelm WA U.S.A.
207 N4 Yelmo mt. Spain
157 H5 Yel'niki Rus. Fed.
161 Q7 Yel'nya Rus. Fed.
156 K4 Yelovo Rus. Fed.
151 G6 Yelp'in Armenia
158 I2 Yel'sk Belarus
143 S4 Yel'tay Kazakh.
204 H7 Yeltes r. Spain
161 Q5 Yel'tsy Rus. Fed.
266 □Q10 Yelucá mt. Nic.
156 J3 Yelva r. Rus. Fed.
243 J1 Yelverton Bay Nunavut Can.
229 G4 Yelwa Kebbi Nigeria
229 H4 Yelwa Plateau Nigeria
159 P6 Yelyseyivka Ukr.
159 L5 Yelyzavethradka Ukr.
128 D7 Yema Nanshan mts China
132 L7 Yema Shan mts China
128 E9 Yematan Qinghai China
128 F8 Yematan Qinghai China
232 C2 Yembo Eth.
205 Q9 Yémeda Spain
143 S4 Yemel' r. Kazakh.
146 G8 Yemen country Asia
156 H3 Yemetsk Rus. Fed.
158 G3 Yemil'chyne Ukr.
Yemişenbükü Turkey see Taşova
Yemmiganur Andhra Prad. India see Emmiganuru
156 H3 Yemtsa Rus. Fed.
156 J3 Yemva Rus. Fed.
229 I6 Yen Cameroon
162 U3 Yena Rus. Fed.
229 G5 Yenagoa Nigeria
159 R5 Yenakiyeve Ukr.
Yenakiyevo Ukr. see Yenakiyeve
118 B4 Yenangyat Myanmar
118 B4 Yenangyaung Myanmar
118 B5 Yenanma Myanmar
118 G4 Yên Bai Vietnam
143 Q3 Yenbek Kazakh.
143 M7 Yenbekshi Kazakh.
118 G4 Yên Châu Vietnam
105 K6 Yenda N.S.W. Austr.
229 E4 Yendi Ghana
Yêndum Xizang China see Zhag'yab
231 B5 Yénéganou Congo
231 C6 Yenga-Lusundji Dem. Rep. Congo
118 C4 Yengan Myanmar
230 D5 Yenge r. Dem. Rep. Congo
144 B3 Yengejeh Iran
228 C4 Yengema Sierra Leone
132 C7 Yengisar Xinjiang China
132 G6 Yengisar Xinjiang China
132 H6 Yengisu Xinjiang China
230 B4 Yengo Congo
105 M5 Yengo National Park N.S.W. Austr.
151 B6 Yenibaşlar Turkey
157 F8 Yeniçağa Turkey
221 I3 Yenice Çanakkale Turkey
150 D2 Yenice İçel Turkey
221 K2 Yeniceköy Turkey
148 F4 Yeniceoba Turkey
221 I2 Yeniçiftlik Çanakkale Turkey
221 I1 Yeniçiftlik Tekirdağ Turkey
151 B7 Yenidal Turkey
Yenidamlar Turkey see Demirtaş
221 J5 Yenidere r. Turkey
221 H4 Yenifoça Turkey
151 G5 Yeni Göyçä Azer.
Yenıhan Turkey see Yıldızeli
221 I5 Yenihisar Turkey
Yenije-i-Vardar Greece see Giannitsa
151 H5 Yenikänd Azer.
151 J5 Yenikänd Azer.
150 E2 Yeniköy Hatay Turkey
221 I4 Yeniköy İzmir Turkey
221 J3 Yeniköy Kütahya Turkey
221 K4 Yeniköy Kütahya Turkey
221 H2 Yenimuhacirköy Turkey
221 J5 Yenipazar Aydın Turkey
221 L2 Yenipazar Bilecik Turkey
221 I4 Yenişakran Turkey
Yeniséa Greece see Genisea
Yenişehir Greece see Larisa
221 K2 Yenişehir Turkey
153 J2 Yenisey r. Rus. Fed.
153 K4 Yeniseysk Rus. Fed.
153 K4 Yeniseyskiy Kryazh ridge Rus. Fed.
152 I2 Yeniseyskiy Zaliv inlet Rus. Fed.
128 E9 Yeniugou Qinghai China
128 F7 Yeniugou Qinghai China
Yeniyol Turkey see Borçka
118 G3 Yên Minh Vietnam
182 H5 Yenne France
157 I7 Yenotayevka Rus. Fed.
245 J3 Yentna r. AK U.S.A.
172 E6 Yeo r. England U.K.
138 E9 Yeola Mahar. India
109 H9 Yeo Lake salt flat W.A. Austr.
109 H10 Yeo Lake Nature Reserve W.A. Austr.
Yeotmal Mahar. India see Yavatmal
105 L5 Yeoval N.S.W. Austr.
172 G6 Yeovil Somerset, England U.K.
172 G5 Yeovilton Somerset, England U.K.
Yeo Yeo r. N.S.W. Austr. see Bland
266 E3 Yepachi Mex.
205 M9 Yepes Spain
161 V8 Yepifan' Rus. Fed.
107 M7 Yeppoon Qld Austr.
Yerakaroú Greece see Gerakarou
157 H5 Yerakhtur Rus. Fed.
Yeráki, Ákra pt Zakynthos Greece see Gerakas, Akrotirio
Yerákion Greece see Geraki
Yeraliyev Kazakh. see Kuryk
268 F2 Yerbabuena Mex.
144 H2 Yerbent Turkm.
153 L3 Yerbogachen Rus. Fed.
136 F7 Yercaud Tamil Nadu India
151 F5 Yerevan Armenia
143 O2 Yereymentau Kazakh.
143 O2 Yereymentau, Gory hills Kazakh.
151 J4 Yerfi Azer.
136 E4 Yergara Karnataka India
157 I7 Yergeni hills Rus. Fed.
Yergoğu Romania see Giurgiu
Yeriho West Bank see Jericho
109 F10 Yerilla W.A. Austr.
264 M3 Yerington NV U.S.A.
221 J5 Yerkesik Turkey
150 A1 Yerköprü Mağarası tourist site Turkey
148 G4 Yerköy Turkey
136 D4 Yerla r. India
Yermak Kazakh. see Aksu
122 E2 Yermakovo Rus. Fed.
292 A1 Yermak Plateau sea feature Arctic Ocean
Yermentau Kazakh. see Yereymentau
157 H5 Yermish' Rus. Fed.
156 K2 Yermitsa Rus. Fed.
266 G4 Yermo Mex.
264 P7 Yermo CA U.S.A.
161 Y4 Yermolino Rus. Fed.
122 B2 Yerofey Pavlovich Rus. Fed.
Yeropótamos r. Kriti Greece see Geropotamos
178 B7 Yerre r. France
178 D6 Yerres r. France
156 K2 Yersa r. Rus. Fed.
186 F6 Yerseke Neth.
151 F3 Yersh Rus. Fed.
161 R7 Yershi Rus. Fed.
161 P8 Yershichi Rus. Fed.
142 C2 Yershov Rus. Fed.
160 L4 Yershovo Rus. Fed.
Yertis r. Kazakh./Rus. Fed. see Irtysh
161 X1 Yertsevo Rus. Fed.
150 C8 Yeruḥam Israel
276 A2 Yerupaja mt. Peru
Yerushalayim Israel/West Bank see Jerusalem
142 B2 Yeruslan r. Rus. Fed.
181 M2 Yerville France
159 T3 Yeryshevka Rus. Fed.
Yerzhar Uzbek. see Gagarin
208 C2 Yesa Spain
208 C2 Yesa, Embalse de resr Spain
142 D3 Yesbol Kazakh.
161 R4 Yesenovichi Rus. Fed.
Yeshera Georgia see Eshera
143 Q6 Yesik Kazakh.
143 L2 Yesil' Kazakh.
150 E2 Yeşil Turkey
221 K5 Yeşildere Burdur Turkey
150 F2 Yeşildere Gaziantep Turkey
150 B1 Yeşildere Karaman Turkey
148 G4 Yeşilhisar Turkey
148 H3 Yeşilırmak r. Turkey
150 F1 Yeşilkent Turkey
221 K3 Yeşilköy Turkey
221 K5 Yeşilova Burdur Turkey
Yeşilova Yozgat Turkey see Sorgun
221 L5 Yeşilyayla Turkey
221 J4 Yeşilyurt Turkey
221 K5 Yeşilyuva Turkey
161 W5 Yesiplevo Rus. Fed.
142 E4 Yeskene Kazakh.
161 O6 Yes'kovo Rus. Fed.
168 J4 Yesnaby Orkney, Scotland U.K.
285 H2 Yeso Arg.
284 B4 Yeso, Cerro mt. Chile
143 P6 Yespe Kazakh.
151 D1 Yessentuki Rus. Fed.
151 D1 Yessentukskaya Rus. Fed.
153 L3 Yessey Rus. Fed.
207 O4 Yeste Spain
172 D6 Yes Tor hill England U.K.
150 D5 Yesud HaMa'ala Israel
207 O4 Yetas de Abajo Spain
Yêtatang Xizang China see Baqên
105 M3 Yetman N.S.W. Austr.
118 B3 Ye-U Myanmar
180 G8 Yeu, Île d' i. France
159 S3 Yevdakovo Rus. Fed.
Yevdokimovskoye Rus. Fed. see Krasnogvardeyskoye
Yevlakh Azer. see Yevlax
159 Q1 Yevlanovo Rus. Fed.
151 I5 Yevlax Azer.
159 M8 Yevpatoriya Ukr.
159 M8 Yevpatoriys'kyy, Mys pt Ukr.
182 A2 Yèvre r. France
122 H4 Yevreyskaya Avtonomnaya Oblast' admin. div. Rus. Fed.
161 O6 Yevseyevka Rus. Fed.
159 S3 Yevstratovka Rus. Fed.
159 S5 Yevsuh r. Ukr.
131 I2 Yexian Henan China
Yexian Shandong China see Laizhou
157 G7 Yeya r. Rus. Fed.
133 F8 Yeyik Xinjiang China
157 G7 Yeysk Rus. Fed.
159 R7 Yeyskiy Liman inlet Rus. Fed.
159 R7 Yeyskoye Ukreplenie Rus. Fed.
132 G6 Yeyungou Xinjiang China
160 N6 Yezerishche, Ozero l. Belarus/Rus. Fed.
Yezhou Hubei China see Jianshi
156 I2 Yezhuga r. Rus. Fed.
Yezo i. Japan see Hokkaidō
160 M6 Yezyaryshcha Belarus
Y Fali Wales U.K. see Valley
Y Fenni Monmouthshire, Wales U.K. see Abergavenny
180 F5 Yffiniac France
Y Fflint Flintshire, Wales U.K. see Flint
277 G6 Ygatimí Para.
Y Gelli Gandryll Wales U.K. see Hay-on-Wye
185 C8 Ygos-St-Saturnin France
182 B3 Ygrande France
277 G6 Yhú Para.
285 I3 Yí r. Uru.
Yialí i. Greece see Gyali
Yialousa Cyprus see Aigialousa
122 D5 Yi'an Heilong. China
Yianisádha i. Greece see Gianisada
Yiannitsá Greece see Giannitsa
146 E6 Yibā, Wādī watercourse Saudi Arabia
130 E4 Yibin Sichuan China
130 E4 Yibin Sichuan China
133 H10 Yibug Caka salt l. China
131 H3 Yichang Hubei China
Yicheng Henan China see Zhumadian
131 I3 Yicheng Hubei China
129 L9 Yicheng Shanxi China
129 M9 Yichuan Henan China
129 L9 Yichuan Shaanxi China
122 F5 Yichun Heilong. China
131 J5 Yichun Jiangxi China
Yidu Shandong China see Qingzhou
130 B3 Yidun Sichuan China
131 J4 Yifeng Jiangxi China
Yiggêtang Qinghai China see Sêrwolungwa
130 A2 Yiggêtang Qinghai China
221 M2 Yığılca Turkey
151 A6 Yiğitler Turkey
150 E2 Yiğityolu Turkey
100 □1 Yigo Guam
Yigu Guam see Yigo
128 E5 Yihatuoli Gansu China
129 M9 Yi He r. Henan China
129 P9 Yi He r. Shandong China
131 K5 Yihuang Jiangxi China
Yijiang Jiangxi China see Yiyang
129 K9 Yijun Shaanxi China
129 S2 Yilaha Heilong. China
122 F5 Yilan Heilong. China
Yilan Taiwan see Ilan
151 B5 Yıldırım Turkey
148 C3 Yıldız Dağları mts Turkey
148 H4 Yıldızeli Turkey
122 C3 Yilehuli Shan mts China
130 D6 Yiliang Yunnan China
130 E5 Yiliang Yunnan China
133 K8 Yiliping Qinghai China
109 D12 Yilliminning W.A. Austr.
122 D5 Yilong Heilong. China
130 F3 Yilong Sichuan China
Yilong Yunnan China see Shiping
130 D7 Yilong Hu l. China
129 O6 Yimatu He r. China
118 F2 Yimen Yunnan China
122 F6 Yimianpo Heilong. China
129 P2 Yimin He r. China
122 B2 Yimuhe Nei Mongol China
129 P9 Yinan Shandong China
118 C6 Yinbaing Myanmar
Yincheng Jiangxi China see Dexing
128 J7 Yinchuan Ningxia China
109 G11 Yindarlgooda, Lake salt flat W.A. Austr.
106 C4 Yingawunarri Aboriginal Land res. N.T. Austr.
131 I3 Yingcheng Hubei China
122 D7 Yingchengzi Jilin China
131 I6 Yingde Guangdong China
130 G9 Yinggehai Hainan China
Yinggen Hainan China see Qiongzhong
131 K2 Ying He r. China
130 A6 Yingjiang Yunnan China
130 D4 Yingjing Sichuan China
139 O5 Yingkiong Arun. Prad. India
Yingkou Liaoning China see Dashiqiao
129 R6 Yingkou Liaoning China
128 I8 Yingpanshui Ningxia China
131 J3 Yingshan Hubei China
130 F3 Yingshan Sichuan China
131 K2 Yingshang Anhui China
131 K4 Yingtan Jiangxi China
129 N9 Yingtaoyuan Shandong China
229 H5 Yingui Cameroon
129 M7 Yingxian Shanxi China
Yining Jiangxi China see Xiushui
132 E5 Yining Xinjiang China
132 E5 Yining Xinjiang China
106 B6 Yiningarra Aboriginal Land res. N.T. Austr.
130 G5 Yinjiang Guizhou China
131 J5 Yinkeng Jiangxi China
118 B3 Yinmabin Myanmar
122 D6 Yinma He r. China
118 C6 Yinnyein Myanmar
129 K6 Yin Shan mts China
Yinxian Zhejiang China see Ningbo
129 M8 Yin Xu tourist site China
Yiófiros r. Kriti Greece see Giofyros
133 L11 Yi'ong Nongchang Xizang China
133 L11 Yi'ong Zangbo r. Xizang China
Yioúra i. Greece see Gioura
130 C6 Yipinglang Yunnan China
221 L4 Yıprak Turkey
Yiquan Guizhou China see Meitan
281 E5 Yira Chapéu, Monte mt. Brazil
133 K10 Yiran Co l. Qinghai China
232 C3 Yirga Alem Eth.
232 C3 Yirga Ch'efē Eth.
232 A3 Yirol Sudan
106 F2 Yirrkala N.T. Austr.
129 P3 Yirshi Nei Mongol China
132 I6 Yirtkuq Bulak spring Xinjiang China
Yirxie Nei Mongol China see Yirshi
Yisa Yunnan China see Honghe
Yishan Guangxi China see Yizhou
Yishan Jiangsu China see Guanyun
129 P8 Yi Shan mt. Shandong China
129 P8 Yi Shan mts China
129 P9 Yishui Shandong China
116 □ Yishun Sing.
229 I1 Yi Tchouma well Niger
Yíthion Greece see Gytheio
Yitiaoshan Gansu China see Jingtai
122 D7 Yitong Jilin China
122 D6 Yitong He r. China
118 C3 Yi Tu, Nam r. Myanmar
128 C5 Yiwanquan Xinjiang China
128 D5 Yiwu Xinjiang China
130 C8 Yiwu Yunnan China
129 Q6 Yiwulü Shan mts China
131 K4 Yixian Anhui China
129 N7 Yixian Hebei China
129 Q6 Yixian Liaoning China
122 D2 Yixiken Heilong. China
131 L3 Yixing Jiangsu China
129 O6 Yixun He r. China
131 I4 Yiyang Hunan China
131 K4 Yiyang Jiangxi China
129 P8 Yiyuan Shandong China
131 I6 Yizhang Hunan China
131 L2 Yizheng Jiangsu China
130 G6 Yizhou Guangxi China
Yizhou Hebei China see Yixian
Yizhou Liaoning China see Yixian
Yizra'el country Asia see Israel
162 R5 Ylä-Keitele l. Fin.
163 T6 Ylämaa Fin.
163 Q6 Yläne Fin.
100 □1 Ylig Bay Guam
162 Q5 Ylihärmä Fin.
162 R4 Yli-Ii Fin.
162 R4 Yli-Kärppä Fin.
162 S4 Ylikiiminki Fin.
162 T3 Yli-Kitka l. Fin.
162 Q5 Ylistaro Fin.
162 Q3 Ylitornio Fin.
162 R4 Ylivieska Fin.
162 R3 Ylläs hill Fin.
172 E2 Y Llethr hill Wales U.K.
163 Q6 Ylöjärvi Fin.
243 P2 Ymer Nunatak Greenland
243 P2 Ymer Ø i. Greenland
178 C7 Ymonville France
165 J3 Ymsen l. Sweden
156 K3 Yndin Rus. Fed.
165 M3 Yngaren l. Sweden
165 K2 Yngen l. Sweden
165 N2 Yngern l. Sweden
143 N3 Yntaly Kazakh.
153 O3 Ynykchanskiy Rus. Fed.
Ynys Enlli i. Wales U.K. see Bardsey Island
Ynys Môn i. Wales U.K. see Anglesey
261 G11 Yoakum TX U.S.A.
229 H4 Yobe state Nigeria
124 R3 Yobetsu-dake vol. Japan
232 D2 Yoboki Djibouti
125 G13 Yobuko Japan
225 H5 Yob Wildlife Reserve nature res. Eritrea
126 B6 Yodo-gawa r. Japan
160 K6 Yody Belarus
258 B5 Yoe PA U.S.A.
283 C9 Yogan, Cerro mt. Chile
269 K9 Yogana Mex.
126 D4 Yogo Japan
224 C5 Yogoum well Chad
117 I8 Yogyakarta Indon.
117 I9 Yogyakarta admin. dist. Indon.
246 G5 Yoho National Park B.C. Can.
124 R3 Yoichi Japan
124 S3 Yoichi-dake mt. Japan
133 M9 Yoigilanglêb r. Qinghai China
266 □P10 Yojoa, Lago de l. Hond.
123 E10 Yŏju S. Korea
126 A5 Yōka Japan
229 I6 Yokadouma Cameroon
125 J13 Yokagawara Japan
126 D5 Yōkaichi Japan
127 M4 Yōkaichiba Japan
124 □F18 Yokate-jima i. Nansei-shotō Japan
126 B6 Yokawa Japan
126 E6 Yokkaichi Japan
229 I5 Yoko Cameroon
124 S5 Yokohama Aomori Japan
127 K5 Yokohama Kanagawa Japan
127 I3 Yokokawa Japan
127 L4 Yokoshiba Japan
127 K5 Yokosuka Japan
125 K11 Yokota Japan
124 R7 Yokote Japan
124 R5 Yokotsu-dake mt. Japan
127 J4 Yokoze Japan
138 F3 Yol Hima. Prad. India
229 I4 Yola Nigeria
266 □Q12 Yolaina, Cordillera de mts Nic.
264 J1 Yolla Bolly Middle Eel Wilderness nature res. CA U.S.A.
264 K3 Yolo CA U.S.A.
230 D5 Yolombo Dem. Rep. Congo
Yolöten Turkm. see Ýolöten
145 J3 Ýolöten Turkm.
269 J9 Yolotepec Mex.
269 K8 Yolox Mex.
269 I9 Yoloxóchitl Mex.
267 P7 Yoluk Mex.
118 E7 Yom, Mae Nam r. Thai.
125 □2 Yome-jima i. Japan
127 M1 Yomogida-dake hill Japan
228 C5 Yomou Guinea
151 A5 Yomra Turkey
139 N6 Yomtam Arun. Prad. India
184 B2 Yon r. France
100 □1 Yona Guam
124 □1 Yona Okinawa Japan
124 □1 Yonabaru Okinawa Japan
125 K11 Yonago Japan
124 □A22 Yonaguni-jima i. Nansei-shotō Japan
124 □1 Yonaha-dake hill Okinawa Japan
123 E10 Yŏnan N. Korea
124 R6 Yoneshiro-gawa r. Japan
127 I1 Yone-yama hill Japan
124 R9 Yonezawa Japan
104 G5 Yongala S.A. Austr.
123 E11 Yŏng-am S. Korea
Yong'an Chongqing China see Fengjie
131 K6 Yong'an Fujian China
Yongbei Yunnan China see Yongsheng
128 G7 Yongchang Gansu China
131 K2 Yongcheng Henan China
123 F11 Yŏngch'ŏn S. Korea
130 E4 Yongchuan Chongqing China
131 L6 Yongchun Fujian China
130 B6 Yongde Yunnan China
128 H8 Yongdeng Gansu China
131 K6 Yongding Fujian China
Yongding Yunnan China see Yongren
Yongding Yunnan China see Fumin
129 O7 Yongding He r. China
123 F10 Yŏngdŏk S. Korea
131 J5 Yongfeng Jiangxi China
Yongfeng Jiangxi China see Guangfeng
132 H5 Yongfeng Xinjiang China
130 G6 Yongfu Guangxi China
123 E11 Yŏnggwang S. Korea
129 L8 Yonghe Shanxi China
123 E9 Yŏnghŭng N. Korea
123 E9 Yŏnghŭng-man b. N. Korea
125 G11 Yŏngil-man b. S. Korea
122 E7 Yongji Jilin China
131 M4 Yongjia Zhejiang China
128 H9 Yongjing Gansu China
Yongjing Guizhou China see Xifeng
Yongjing Liaoning China see Xifeng
123 F10 Yŏngju S. Korea
130 B6 Yongkang Yunnan China
131 M4 Yongkang Zhejiang China
130 C3 Yonglaxi Sichuan China
Yongle Shaanxi China see Zhen'an
Yongle Sichuan China see Jiuzhaigou
123 D8 Yongling Liaoning China
129 N8 Yongnian Hebei China
130 G7 Yongning Guangxi China
Yongning Jiangxi China see Tonggu
128 J7 Yongning Ningxia China
Yongning Sichuan China see Xuyong
130 B6 Yongping Yunnan China
Yongqing Gansu China see Qingshui
130 C5 Yongren Yunnan China
123 E11 Yŏngsan-gang r. S. Korea
130 D4 Yongshan Yunnan China
130 C5 Yongsheng Yunnan China
129 K9 Yongshou Shaanxi China
130 G4 Yongshun Hunan China
131 L6 Yongtai Fujian China
123 F10 Yŏngwol S. Korea
Yongxi Guizhou China see Nayong
131 J5 Yongxin Jiangxi China
131 I5 Yongxing Hunan China
129 L7 Yongxing Shaanxi China
131 J4 Yongxiu Jiangxi China
131 H5 Yongzhou Hunan China
257 L8 Yonkers NY U.S.A.
178 G8 Yonne dept France
178 E7 Yonne r. France
228 B3 Yonoféré Senegal
229 I2 Yoo Baba well Niger
274 C3 Yopal Col.
132 C7 Yopurga Xinjiang China
266 F4 Yoquivo Mex.
143 N7 Yordon Uzbek.
138 E3 Yordu Jammu and Kashmir India
268 F6 Yoricostío Mex.
127 J3 Yorii Japan
109 D11 York W.A. Austr.
251 O6 York Ont. Can.
247 M4 York r. Man. Can.
171 O6 York York, England U.K.
171 O6 York admin. div. England U.K.
261 K9 York AL U.S.A.
260 G5 York NE U.S.A.
258 B5 York PA U.S.A.
255 G8 York SC U.S.A.
107 I1 York, Cape Qld Austr.
York, Kap c. Greenland see Innaanganeq
171 N5 York, Vale of val. England U.K.
258 B5 York County county PA U.S.A.
107 I2 York Downs Qld Austr.
104 F6 Yorke Peninsula S.A. Austr.
104 F6 Yorketown S.A. Austr.
258 B4 York Haven PA U.S.A.
244 F2 York Mountains AK U.S.A.
171 M5 Yorkshire Dales National Park England U.K.
171 P6 Yorkshire Wolds hills England U.K.
258 A4 York Springs PA U.S.A.
247 K5 Yorkton Sask. Can.
256 I11 Yorktown VA U.S.A.
259 H2 Yorktown Heights NY U.S.A.
248 B5 Yorkville IL U.S.A.
266 □P10 Yoro Hond.
126 E5 Yōrō Japan
126 E7 Yoroi-zaki pt Japan
124 □G18 Yoro-jima i. Nansei-shotō Japan
115 F4 Yoronga i. Maluku Indon.
124 □F19 Yoron-tō i. Nansei-shotō Japan
128 J2 Yöröö Gol r. Mongolia
228 D3 Yorosso Mali
264 M4 Yosemite National Park CA U.S.A.
264 M4 Yosemite Village CA U.S.A.
125 J13 Yoshida Ehime Japan
125 J12 Yoshida Hiroshima Japan
127 J3 Yoshida Saitama Japan
127 H6 Yoshida Shizuoka Japan
125 H13 Yoshii Fukuoka Japan
127 I3 Yoshii Gunma Japan
125 L12 Yoshii-gawa r. Japan
127 H1 Yoshikawa Japan
127 M1 Yoshima Japan
126 C7 Yoshino Japan
126 E3 Yoshinodani Japan
126 C7 Yoshino-gawa r. Japan
125 L12 Yoshino-gawa r. Japan
126 D8 Yoshino-Kumano Kokuritsu-kōen nat. park Japan
156 I4 Yoshkar-Ola Rus. Fed.
128 H3 Yösöndzüyl Mongolia
Yos Sudarso i. Papua Indon. see Dolok, Pulau
123 E11 Yŏsu S. Korea
277 E4 Yotau Bol.
124 R4 Yōtei-zan mt. Japan
127 L4 Yotsukaidō Japan
127 M1 Yotsukura Japan
150 D9 Yotvata Israel
232 E3 Yoube well Eth.
246 E5 Youbou B.C. Can.
133 J7 Youdunzi Qinghai China
169 G9 Youghal Ireland
169 F9 Youghal Bay Ireland
130 G7 You Jiang r. China
171 N7 Youlgreave Derbyshire, England U.K.
230 C5 Youmba Congo
105 L6 Young N.S.W. Austr.
109 F12 Young r. W.A. Austr.
285 I3 Young Uru.
265 V7 Young AZ U.S.A.
102 □ Young, Cape Chatham Is S. Pacific Ocean
104 F4 Younghusband, Lake salt flat S.A. Austr.
104 G6 Younghusband Peninsula S.A. Austr.
287 K2 Young Island Antarctica
102 L5 Young Nicks Head North I. N.Z.
103 D11 Young Range mts South I. N.Z.
247 I5 Youngstown Alta Can.
256 E7 Youngstown OH U.S.A.
256 F7 Youngsville PA U.S.A.
264 J3 Yountville CA U.S.A.
133 J7 Youshashan Qinghai China
130 H4 You Shui r. China
226 C2 Youssoufia Morocco
228 D3 Youvarou Mali
131 L5 Youxi Fujian China
131 I5 Youxian Hunan China
130 G4 Youyang Chongqing China
122 G5 Youyi Heilong. China
132 H2 Youyi Feng mt. China/Rus. Fe
129 M7 Youyu Shanxi China
145 M2 Yovon Tajik.
105 J3 Yowah watercourse Qld Austr.
109 E8 Yowereena Hill W.A. Austr.
173 I2 Yoxall Staffordshire, England U
173 P3 Yoxford Suffolk, England U.K.
148 G4 Yozgat Turkey
277 G5 Ypé-Jhú Para.
181 L2 Yport France
162 R4 Yppäri Fin.
Ypres West-Vlaanderen Belgiu see Ieper
251 K7 Ypsilanti MI U.S.A.
262 C6 Yreka CA U.S.A.
Yrghyz Kazakh. see Irgiz
142 J3 Yrgyz r. Kazakh.
Yr Wyddfa mt. Wales U.K. see Snowdon
Yr Wyddgrug Flintshire, Wales U.K. see Mold
172 E3 Ysbyty Ystwyth Ceredigion, Wales U.K.
178 E2 Yser r. France alt. IJzer (Belgium)
186 I6 Ysselsteyn Neth.
183 E6 Yssingeaux France
165 J6 Ystad Sweden
172 E4 Ystalyfera Neath Port Talbot, Wales U.K.
172 F1 Ystrad r. Wales U.K.
172 E4 Ystradgynlais Powys, Wales U.
172 D3 Ystwyth r. Wales U.K.
143 P6 Ysyk-Ata Kyrg.
Ysyk-Köl Kyrg. see Balykchy
143 R7 Ysyk-Köl admin. div. Kyrg.
143 Q6 Ysyk-Köl salt l. Kyrg.
168 L8 Ythan r. Scotland U.K.
Y Trallwng Powys, Wales U.K. s Welshpool
164 C1 Ytre Samlen b. Norway
Ytre Vinje Norway see Åmot
153 O3 Ytyk-Kyuyel' Rus. Fed.
115 F4 Yu i. Maluku Indon.
150 B8 Yu'alliq, Jabal mt. Egypt
131 H3 Yuan'an Hubei China
129 P5 Yuanbaoshan Nei Mongol Chi
130 G6 Yuanbao Shan mt. Guangxi Ch
131 I4 Yuanjiang Hunan China
130 C7 Yuanjiang Yunnan China
130 H4 Yuan Jiang r. Hunan China
130 D7 Yuan Jiang r. Yunnan China
Yuanjiazhuang Shaanxi China Foping
131 M6 Yüanli Taiwan
129 Q2 Yuanlin Nei Mongol China
130 H4 Yuanling Hunan China
Yuanma Yunnan China see Yuanmou
130 C6 Yuanmou Yunnan China
129 M7 Yuanping Shanxi China
129 L9 Yuanqu Shanxi China
Yuanquan Gansu China see An
Yuanshan Guangdong China s Lianping
128 F7 Yuanshanzi Gansu China
Yuanyang Yunnan China see Xinjie
130 D7 Yuanyang Yunnan China
126 B7 Yuasa Japan
146 B2 Yub'ā i. Saudi Arabia
264 K2 Yuba City CA U.S.A.
124 S3 Yūbari Japan
124 T3 Yūbari-dake mt. Japan
124 T3 Yūbari-sanchi mts Japan
130 F4 Yubei Chongqing China
124 U2 Yūbetsu Japan
124 U2 Yūbetsu-gawa r. Japan
230 E3 Yubu Sudan
264 O7 Yucaipa CA U.S.A.
267 N8 Yucatán pen. Mex.
267 O7 Yucatán state Mex.
267 P6 Yucatan Channel Cuba/Mex.
265 R7 Yucca AZ U.S.A.
265 P5 Yucca Lake NV U.S.A.
265 P7 Yucca Valley CA U.S.A.
151 C7 Yücetepe Turkey
129 N9 Yucheng Henan China
129 O8 Yucheng Shandong China
Yucheng Sichuan China see Ya
Yuci Shanxi China see Jinzhon
276 D3 Yucumo Bol.
161 U5 Yudino Moskovskaya Oblast' Rus. Fed.
156 J5 Yudino Respublika Tatarstan Rus. Fed.
156 G4 Yudino Yaroslavskaya Oblast' Rus. Fed.
122 B2 Yudi Shan mt. China
153 O4 Yudoma r. Rus. Fed.
131 J6 Yudu Jiangxi China
Yuecheng Sichuan China see Yuexi
130 F3 Yuechi Sichuan China
Yuelai Heilong. China see Huachuan
129 R4 Yueliang Pao l. China
106 C7 Yuendumu N.T. Austr.
106 C7 Yuendumu Aboriginal Land re N.T. Austr.
131 □J7 Yuen Long H.K. China
131 M4 Yueqing Zhejiang China
131 K3 Yuexi Anhui China
130 D4 Yuexi Sichuan China
131 I4 Yueyang Hunan China
131 I4 Yueyang Hunan China
Yueyang Sichuan China see Any
156 L4 Yug Rus. Fed.
156 I3 Yug r. Rus. Fed.
131 K4 Yugan Jiangxi China
127 J5 Yugawara Japan
133 L9 Yuge Qinghai China
150 B1 Yuğluk Dağı mts Turkey
156 K4 Yugo-Kamskiy Rus. Fed.
Yugo-Osetinskaya Avtonomna Oblast' aut. reg. Georgia see Samkhret' Oset'i
152 H3 Yugorsk Rus. Fed.
156 M1 Yugorskiy Poluostrov pen. Rus. Fed.
156 M2 Yugud-Vayskiy Natsional'nyy Park nat. park Rus. Fed.
131 M3 Yuhang Zhejiang China
129 M7 Yu He r. China
Yuhu Yunnan China see Eryuan
131 M4 Yuhuan Zhejiang China
129 O8 Yuhuang Ding mt. Shandong China
127 I5 Yui Japan
109 D9 Yuin W.A. Austr.
131 K4 Yujiang Jiangxi China
130 H7 Yu Jiang r. China
Yujin Sichuan China see Qianw
153 Q3 Yukagirskoye Ploskogor'ye pla Rus. Fed.
156 K4 Yukamenskoye Rus. Fed.
151 F7 Yukarı Balçıklı Turkey
221 I3 Yukarıbey Turkey
151 B5 Yukarıcanören Turkey
151 D4 Yukarıgündeş Turkey
151 E5 Yukarıkaragüney Turkey
221 M3 Yukarı Sakarya Ovaları plain Turkey
151 D5 Yukarısarıkamış Turkey
148 G4 Yukarısarıkaya Turkey
160 L5 Yukhavichy Belarus
157 J5 Yukhmachi Rus. Fed.
161 S7 Yukhnov Rus. Fed.
161 N5 Yukhovo Rus. Fed.
231 C5 Yuki Dem. Rep. Congo
125 K12 Yuki Japan
127 K3 Yūki Japan
244 H2 Yuki r. AK U.S.A.
245 F3 Yukon r. Can./U.S.A.
245 L2 Yukon-Charley Rivers Nationa Preserve nature res. AK U.S.A.
245 M3 Yukon Crossing (abandoned) Y.T. Can.
244 F3 Yukon Delta AK U.S.A.
244 G3 Yukon Delta National Wildlif Refuge nature res. AK U.S.A.

5 K2 Yukon Flats National Wildlife Refuge nature res. AK U.S.A.
5 N3 Yukon Territory admin. div. Can.
9 L5 Yüksekova Turkey
5 H13 Yukuhashi Japan
6 C8 Yulara N.T. Austr.
2 G1 Yuldybayevo Rus. Fed.
8 E6 Yule r. W.A. Austr.
7 L9 Yuleba Qld Austr.
5 G10 Yulee FL U.S.A.
2 H6 Yuli Xinjiang China
1 M7 Yüli Taiwan
0 H7 Yulin Guangxi China
0 G9 Yulin Hainan China
9 K7 Yulin Shaanxi China
0 C5 Yulong Xueshan mt. Yunnan China
5 R9 Yuma AZ U.S.A.
0 D5 Yuma CO U.S.A.
5 R9 Yuma Desert AZ U.S.A.
2 G1 Yumaguzino Rus. Fed.
4 D4 Yumbarra Conservation Park nature res. S.A. Austr.
2 A4 Yumbe Uganda
4 A5 Yumbel Chile
0 C5 Yumbi Bandundu Dem. Rep. Congo
0 E5 Yumbi Maniema Dem. Rep. Congo
4 B4 Yumbo Col.
3 G11 Yumco Xizang China
8 E6 Yumen Gansu China
Yumen Gansu China see Laojunmiao
8 E7 Yumendongzhan Gansu China
2 K6 Yumenguan Gansu China
Yumenzhen China see Yumen
2 F3 Yumin Xinjiang China
8 E4 Yumt Uul mt. Mongolia
0 D2 Yumurtalık Turkey
9 C10 Yuna W.A. Austr.
0 I4 Yuna r. Dom. Rep.
8 E4 Yunak Turkey
9 O2 Yunakivka Ukr.
1 H7 Yunan Guangdong China
1 I7 Yun'an Guangdong China
4 E5 Yunaska Island AK U.S.A.
6 D5 Yunchara Bol.
9 N9 Yuncheng Shandong China
9 L9 Yuncheng Shanxi China
1 C5 Yüncüler Turkey
9 G10 Yundamindera W.A. Austr.
1 I7 Yunfu Guangdong China
6 D4 Yungas reg. Bol.
6 C6 Yungay Antofagasta Chile
4 A5 Yungay Biobío Chile
6 C4 Yungayo Peru
0 D6 Yungui Gaoyuan plat. Guizhou/Yunnan China
Yunhe Jiangsu China see Pizhou
Yunhe Yunnan China see Heqing
1 L4 Yunhe Zhejiang China
Yunjinghong Yunnan China see Jinghong
0 H7 Yunkai Dashan mts China
6 C7 Yunkanjini Aboriginal Land res. N.T. Austr.
Yunling Fujian China see Yunxiao
0 B5 Yun Ling mts Yunnan China
0 B6 Yunlong Yunnan China
1 I3 Yunmeng Hubei China
0 C6 Yunnan prov. China
9 R5 Yunokomunarivs'k Ukr.
7 J1 Yunotani Japan
5 J11 Yunotsu Japan
7 J7 Yunquera Spain
5 N7 Yunquera de Henares Spain
1 I3 Yun Shui r. China
4 G5 Yunta S.A. Austr.
0 A2 Yunt Dağı mt. Turkey
5 M1 Yuntut National Park Y.T. Can.
1 K3 Yunuslar Turkey
1 H7 Yunwu Shan mts China
0 H2 Yunxi Hubei China
Yunxi Sichuan China see Yanting
0 H2 Yunxian Hubei China
0 C6 Yunxian Yunnan China
1 K7 Yunxiao Fujian China
6 M2 Yun'yakha r. Rus. Fed.
0 G3 Yunyang Chongqing China
1 I2 Yunyang Henan China
Yupin Yunnan China see Pingbian
Yuping Guizhou China see Libo
0 G5 Yuping Guizhou China
1 L3 Yuqian Zhejiang China
0 F5 Yuqing Guizhou China
6 D5 Yura Bol.
6 D5 Yura r. Bol.
6 B8 Yura Japan
6 C4 Yura Peru
4 B6 Yuracyacu Peru
6 B5 Yura-gawa r. Japan
4 R4 Yūrappu-dake mt. Japan
9 S3 Yurasovka Rus. Fed.
0 I7 Yuratsishki Belarus
8 I2 Yuravichy Belarus
5 N3 Yuraygir National Park N.S.W. Austr.
3 H9 Yurba Co l. Xizang China
9 Q4 Yurchenkove Ukr.
8 E5 Yurécuaro Mex.
0 D2 Yürekli Turkey
2 J4 Yurga Rus. Fed.
4 B6 Yurimaguas Peru
6 I4 Yurino Rus. Fed.
8 F5 Yuriria Mex.
8 F5 Yuriria, Laguna l. Mex.
1 H1 Yurkovka Rus. Fed.
6 K4 Yurla Rus. Fed.
9 T1 Yurlovka Rus. Fed.
6 I2 Yuroma Rus. Fed.
9 Q8 Yurovka Rus. Fed.
1 I2 Yürük Turkey
3 E7 Yurungkax He r. China
4 W3 Yururi-jima i. Japan
6 J4 Yur'ya Rus. Fed.
6 K2 Yur'yakha r. Rus. Fed.
Yuryev Estonia see Tartu
6 H4 Yur'yevets Ivanovskaya Oblast' Rus. Fed.
1 X5 Yur'yevets Vladimirskaya Oblast' Rus. Fed.
1 W5 Yur'yev-Pol'skiy Rus. Fed.
9 P5 Yur"yivka Dnipropetrovs'ka Oblast' Ukr.
9 P7 Yur"yivka Zaporiz'ka Oblast' Ukr.
6 □P11 Yuscarán Hond.
1 L5 Yushan Fujian China
1 L4 Yushan Jiangxi China
1 M7 Yü Shan mt. Taiwan
1 M4 Yushan Liedao is China
9 M8 Yushe Shanxi China
6 K1 Yushino Rus. Fed.
6 F2 Yushkozero Rus. Fed.
2 E6 Yushu Jilin China
0 A2 Yushu Qinghai China
2 H5 Yushugou Xinjiang China
6 J4 Yushut r. Rus. Fed.
7 I7 Yusta Rus. Fed.
9 J3 Yusufeli Turkey
5 K13 Yusuhara Japan
6 K4 Yus'va Rus. Fed.
9 O9 Yutai Shandong China
Yutan Hunan China see Ningxiang
7 K5 Yutaza Rus. Fed.
9 O7 Yutian Hebei China
3 E8 Yutian Xinjiang China
9 P5 Yutiangao Nei Mongol China
6 G6 Yūtō Japan
Yutpundji Djindiniwirritj res. N.T. Austr. see Roper Bar Aboriginal Land
5 F5 Yutuyaco Arg.
7 F6 Yuty Para.
9 L5 Yutz France
1 K6 Yuva Turkey
1 A5 Yuvacık Turkey
4 □G18 Yuwan-dake hill Nansei-shotō Japan
8 J8 Yuwang Ningxia China
1 I5 Yuxarı Garabağ Kanalı canal Azer.
1 G4 Yuxarı Salahlı Azer.
151 H4 Yuxarı Tala Azer.
Yuxi Guizhou China see Daozhen
131 H3 Yuxi Hubei China
130 D6 Yuxi Yunnan China
130 H3 Yuxiakou Hubei China
129 N7 Yuxian Hebei China
129 M7 Yuxian Shanxi China
131 L3 Yuxikou Anhui China
131 H3 Yuyangguan Hubei China
131 M3 Yuyao Zhejiang China
Yuyue Hubei China see Jiayu
124 Q7 Yuza Japan
124 R7 Yuzawa Japan
151 F5 Yüzbaşılar Turkey
156 H4 Yuzha Rus. Fed.
159 K7 Yuzhne Ukr.
Yuzhno-Alichurskiy, Khrebet mts Tajik. see Alichuri Janubí, Qatorkŭhi
122 M5 Yuzhno-Kamyshovyy Khrebet ridge Sakhalin Rus. Fed.
Yuzhno-Kazakhstanskaya Oblast' admin. div. Kazakh. see Yuzhnyy Kazakhstan
121 Q3 Yuzhno-Kuril'sk Kuril'skiye O-va Rus. Fed.
153 M4 Yuzhno-Muyskiy Khrebet mts Rus. Fed.
122 M5 Yuzhno-Sakhalinsk Sakhalin Rus. Fed.
151 G1 Yuzhno-Sukhokumsk Rus. Fed.
157 E7 Yuzhnoukrayinsk Ukr.
142 I1 Yuzhnoural'sk Rus. Fed.
143 T1 Yuzhnyy Altayskiy Kray Rus. Fed.
197 I1 Yuzhnyy Kaliningradskaya Oblast' Rus. Fed.
Yuzhnyy Respublika Kalmykiya-Khalm'g-Tangch Rus. Fed. see Adyk
157 H7 Yuzhnyy Rostovskaya Oblast' Rus. Fed.
153 Q4 Yuzhnyy, Mys hd Rus. Fed.
143 V3 Yuzhnyy Altay, Khrebet mts Kazakh.
Yuzhnyy Bug r. Ukr. see Pivdennyy Buh
143 M6 Yuzhnyy Kazakhstan admin. div. Kazakh.
142 G1 Yuzhnyy Ural mts Rus. Fed.
128 I9 Yuzhong Gansu China
Yuzhou Hebei China see Yuxian
129 M9 Yuzhou Henan China
Yuzkuduk Uzbek. see Yuzquduq
Yuzovka Ukr. see Donets'k
142 J6 Yuzquduq Uzbek.
126 A7 Yuzuruha-yama hill Japan
180 G5 Yvel r. France
178 C6 Yvelines dept France
212 B2 Yverdon Switz.
181 M2 Yvetot France
180 G5 Yvignac France
187 G8 Yvoir Belgium
182 I4 Yvoire France
212 B2 Yvonand Switz.
118 B4 Ywamun Myanmar
118 C5 Ywathit Myanmar
Y Waun Wales U.K. see Chirk
165 M4 Yxern l. Sweden
165 M3 Yxningen l. Sweden
165 M3 Yxnö i. Sweden
236 C9 Yzerfontein S. Africa
236 C9 Yzerfonteinpunt pt S. Africa
182 C3 Yzeure France
181 M8 Yzeures-sur-Creuse France

Z

226 E2 Za, Oued r. Morocco
269 K9 Zaachila Mex.
236 H9 Zaaimansdal S. Africa
Zaamin Uzbek. see Zomin
187 E6 Zaamslag Neth.
186 G4 Zaandam Neth.
186 G4 Zaandijk Neth.
219 O5 Zăbala r. Romania
218 I5 Žabalj Vojvodina Serbia
149 K5 Zāb al Kabīr, Nahr az r. Iraq
144 G4 Zabānābād Iran
146 C4 Zabarjad, Jazīrat i. Egypt
149 K6 Zāb aş Şaghīr, Nahr az r. Iraq
129 O2 Zabaykal'sk Rus. Fed.
121 K1 Zabaykal'skiy Kray admin. div. Rus. Fed.
217 □ Żabbar Malta
198 F2 Žabčice Czech Rep.
144 A4 Zab-e Kuchek r. Iran
193 I8 Zabeltitz-Treugeböhla Ger.
230 E4 Zabia Dem. Rep. Congo
197 I3 Żabia Wola Pol.
213 Q4 Zabiče Slovenia
146 F8 Zabīd Yemen
146 F8 Zabīd, Wādī watercourse Yemen
197 J2 Zabiele Pol.
197 J3 Ząbki Pol.
196 E5 Ząbkowice Śląskie Pol.
218 H7 Žabljak Žabljak Montenegro
197 L4 Zabłocie Pol.
197 L2 Zabłudów Pol.
201 O8 Žabno Croatia
197 I5 Żabno Pol.
210 E2 Zabok Croatia
199 H2 Žabokreky Slovakia
145 I6 Zābol Iran
145 I8 Zābolī Iran
158 E5 Zabolotiv Ukr.
158 D2 Zabolottya Ukr.
160 K4 Zabolova Latvia
189 H2 Zaborski Park Krajobrazowy Pol.
161 S2 Zabor'ye Rus. Fed.
192 K4 Żabów Pol.
196 D2 Żabowo Pol.
133 H11 Zabqung Xizang China
219 J4 Zăbrani Romania
151 K5 Zabrat Azer.
228 E4 Zabré Burkina
198 F2 Zábřeh Czech Rep.
196 G5 Zabrze Pol.
145 L5 Zābul prov. Afgh.
142 D4 Zaburun'ye Kazakh.
158 I3 Zabuyannya Ukr.
158 C2 Zabuzhzhya Ukr.
229 F4 Zabzugu Ghana
267 O10 Zacapa Guat.
269 J6 Zacapoaxtla Mex.
268 F6 Zacapu Mex.
268 G7 Zacapuato Mex.
278 C4 Zacarias r. Brazil
267 N8 Zacatal Mex.
268 E3 Zacatecas Mex.
268 E2 Zacatecas state Mex.
266 □O11 Zacatecoluca El Salvador
269 I6 Zacatelco Mex.
269 H7 Zacatepec Morelos Mex.
269 J9 Zacatepec Oaxaca Mex.
269 L8 Zacatepec Oaxaca Mex.
269 J6 Zacatlán Mex.
142 D2 Zachagansk Kazakh.
220 C5 Zacharo Greece
196 F2 Zacharzyn Pol.
195 O4 Zachenberg Ger.
159 O4 Zachepylivka Ukr.
196 D2 Zachodniopomorskie prov. Pol.
268 D5 Zacoalco Mex.
269 H7 Zacualpán Mex.
268 B4 Zacualpan Nayarit Mex.
269 I5 Zacualpan Veracruz Mex.
269 I5 Zacualtipán Mex.
Zacynthus i. Greece see Zakynthos
197 L3 Zaczopki Pol.
226 D2 Zad, Col du pass Morocco
210 E3 Zadar Croatia
210 E3 Zadarski Kanal sea chan. Croatia
158 J2 Zaderiyivka Ukr.
119 D9 Zadetkale Kyun i. Myanmar
119 D10 Zadetkyi Kyun i. Myanmar
119 C7 Zadi Myanmar
133 L10 Zadoi Qinghai China
161 V9 Zadonsk Rus. Fed.
205 O3 Zadorra r. Spain
145 M5 Zadran reg. Afgh.
161 N6 Zadubrowye Belarus
199 G2 Zádveřice Czech Rep.
161 N6 Zadzyetuni Belarus
225 G2 Za'farānah Egypt
150 A9 Za'farānah, Ra's pt Egypt
207 K7 Zafarraya Spain
145 P5 Zafarwal Pak.
Zafer Adaları is Cyprus see Kleides Islands
Zafer Burnu c. Cyprus see Apostolos Andreas, Cape
217 I8 Zafferana Etnea Sicilia Italy
216 F7 Zafferano, Capo c. Sicilia Italy
206 G4 Zafra Spain
205 O9 Zafra de Záncara Spain
205 Q8 Zafrilla Spain
205 Q8 Zafrilla, Sierra de mts Spain
226 C3 Zag Morocco
201 H7 Žaga Slovenia
196 D4 Żagań Pol.
160 G5 Žagarė Lith.
215 J4 Zagarolo Italy
Zagazig Ash Sharqīyah Egypt see Az Zaqāzīq
151 F4 Zages Georgia
144 G4 Zaghdeh well Iran
144 D4 Zāgheh Iran
144 B4 Zāgheh-ye Bālā Iran
227 H1 Zaghouan Tunisia
211 C7 Zaghouan admin. div. Tunisia
197 I5 Zagnańsk Pol.
219 O5 Zagon Romania
220 E3 Zagora Greece
226 D3 Zagora Morocco
201 M7 Zagorje reg. Croatia
213 Q4 Zagorje Slovenia
210 E2 Zagorje ob Savi Slovenia
196 F3 Zagórów Pol.
Zagorsk Rus. Fed. see Sergiyev Posad
197 K6 Zagórz Pol.
207 K6 Zagra Spain
219 M9 Zagrazhden Bulg.
210 E3 Zagreb Croatia
196 D4 Zagrodno Pol.
144 B4 Zagros, Kūhhā-ye mts Iran
Zagros Mountains Iran see Zagros, Kūhhā-ye
219 J6 Žagubica Žagubica Serbia
Zagunao Sichuan China see Lixian
133 I11 Za'gya Zangbo r. Xizang China
199 J4 Zagyva r. Hungary
199 J4 Zagyvarékas Hungary
158 I3 Zahal'tsi Ukr.
235 □K3 Zahamena, Parc National de nature res. Madag.
207 I7 Zahara Spain
206 H8 Zahara de los Atunes Spain
207 I7 Zahara-El Gastor, Embalse de resr Spain
197 M3 Zaharoddzye reg. Belarus
144 E7 Zāhedān Fārs Iran
144 I7 Zāhedān Sīstān va Balūchestān Iran
206 F4 Zahinos Spain
145 N7 Zahir Pir Pak.
150 D5 Zahlé Lebanon
151 G5 Zähmätkänd Azer.
145 J3 Zähmet Turkm.
193 G7 Zahna Ger.
199 L3 Záhony Hungary
199 G2 Záhorovice Czech Rep.
198 F3 Záhorská Ves Slovakia
146 F7 Zahrān Saudi Arabia
145 L7 Zahri Nur Gama Pak.
160 K4 Zaiceva Latvia
205 Q6 Zaida, Laguna de resr Spain
208 F4 Zaidín Spain
160 G6 Žaiginys Lith.
146 G5 Zā'in, Jabal hill Saudi Arabia
Zainlha Sichuan China see Xiaojin
Zainsk Rus. Fed. see Novyy Zay
Zair Uzbek. see Zoir
Zaire country Africa see Congo, Democratic Republic of the
231 B6 Zaire prov. Angola
Zaïre r. Congo/Dem. Rep. Congo see Congo
218 I9 Zajas Macedonia
219 K7 Zaječar Zaječar Serbia
195 P2 Zaječov Czech Rep.
196 D2 Zajezierze Pol.
235 F4 Zaka Zimbabwe
128 H1 Zakamensk Rus. Fed.
198 F5 Zákány Hungary
199 I5 Zákányszek Hungary
158 C5 Zakarpats'ka Oblast' admin. div. Ukr.
Zakarpatskaya Oblast' admin. div. Ukr. see Zakarpats'ka Oblast'
Zakataly Azer. see Zaqatala
Zakháro Greece see Zacharo
161 W7 Zakharovo Rus. Fed.
158 D3 Zakhidnyy Buh r. Ukr.
149 K5 Zākhō Iraq
Zakhodnyaya Dzvina r. Europe see Zapadnaya Dvina
156 G1 Zakhrebetnoye Rus. Fed.
144 A2 Zakī, Kūh-e mt. Iran
Zákinthos i. Greece see Zakynthos
197 I6 Zakliczyn Pol.
197 K5 Zaklików Pol.
197 H6 Zakopane Pol.
230 C2 Zakouma Chad
230 C2 Zakouma, Parc National de nat. park Chad
221 H7 Zakros Kriti Greece
197 K5 Zakrzew Lubelskie Pol.
197 J4 Zakrzew Mazowieckie Pol.
196 G3 Zakrzewo Kujawsko-Pomorskie Pol.
196 F2 Zakrzewo Wielkopolskie Pol.
197 K5 Zakrzówek-Wieś Pol.
198 D1 Zákupy Czech Rep.
246 F5 Zakwaski, Mount B.C. Can.
220 B5 Zakynthos Zakynthos Greece
220 B5 Zakynthos i. Greece
220 B5 Zakynthou, Porthmos sea chan. Greece
231 B6 Zala Angola
133 L11 Zala Xizang China
198 F5 Zala county Hungary
218 F4 Zala r. Romania
198 G5 Zalaapáti Hungary
198 F5 Zalaegerszeg Hungary
198 F5 Zalai-domsag hills Hungary
198 G5 Zalakaros Hungary
198 G5 Zalakomár Hungary
198 F5 Zalalövő Hungary
206 H3 Zalamea de la Serena Spain
206 F5 Zalamea la Real Spain
229 H4 Zalanga Nigeria
129 R3 Zalantun Nei Mongol China
198 G5 Zalaszántó Hungary
198 F5 Zalaszentbalázs Hungary
198 G5 Zalaszentgrót Hungary
198 F5 Zalaszentiván Hungary
198 F5 Zalaszentmihály Hungary
219 L3 Zalău Romania
199 L4 Zalău r. Romania
198 G5 Zalavár Hungary
160 J7 Zalavas Lith.
197 J4 Załazy Pol.
210 E2 Žalec Slovenia
189 I3 Załęczański Park Krajobrazowy Pol.
161 T9 Zalegoshch' Rus. Fed.
196 F3 Zalesie Kujawsko-Pomorskie Pol.
197 L3 Zalesie Lubelskie Pol.
256 C9 Zaleski OH U.S.A.
161 T3 Zales'ye Rus. Fed.
197 H2 Zalewo Pol.
146 F4 Zalim Saudi Arabia
224 D6 Zalingei Sudan
158 E5 Zalishchyky Ukr.
158 E5 Zalissya Ukr.
159 P6 Zaliznychne Ukr.
159 L7 Zaliznyy Port Ukr.
158 E4 Zaliztsi Ukr.
224 B3 Zallāf, Wādī az watercourse Libya
146 D2 Zalmā, Jabal az mt. Saudi Arabia
196 F2 Zalno Pol.
224 A1 Zalţan Libya
224 C2 Zaltan, Jabal hills Libya
186 H5 Zaltbommel Neth.
197 L1 Žaltytis l. Lith.
161 O4 Zaluch'ye Rus. Fed.
158 D2 Zalukhiv Ukr.
151 E2 Zalukokoazhe Rus. Fed.
137 N4 Zalun Myanmar
160 L8 Zaluzhzha Belarus
197 M2 Zal'vyanka r. Belarus
199 L5 Zam Romania
127 J5 Zama Japan
229 F3 Zama Niger
246 G3 Zama City Alta Can.
147 H7 Zamakh Saudi Arabia
237 N3 Zamani S. Africa
148 G4 Zamanti r. Turkey
199 G5 Zamárdi Hungary
196 F2 Zamarte Pol.
114 C4 Zambales Mountains Luzon Phil.
198 F1 Žamberk Czech Rep.
231 D8 Zambeze r. Africa alt. Zambezi
231 D7 Zambezi r. Africa alt. Zambeze
231 D8 Zambezi Zambia
235 H3 Zambézia prov. Moz.
231 E9 Zambezi Escarpment Zambia/Zimbabwe
234 E3 Zambezi National Park Zimbabwe
231 E8 Zambia country Africa
114 D8 Zamboanga Mindanao Phil.
114 D8 Zamboanga Peninsula Mindanao Phil.
114 D7 Zamboanguita Negros Phil.
205 O3 Zambrana Spain
270 F9 Zambrano Col.
197 K3 Zambrów Pol.
235 F2 Zambue Moz.
206 A4 Zambujal de Cima Port.
206 B5 Zambujeira do Mar Port.
196 D2 Zamęcin Pol.
229 G3 Zamfara state Nigeria
229 G3 Zamfara watercourse Nigeria
145 J6 Zamīndāvar reg. Afgh.
Zamkog Sichuan China see Zamtang
226 B4 Zamlat Amagraj hills Western Sahara
160 K3 Zamogil'ye Rus. Fed.
199 H4 Zámoly Hungary
274 B6 Zamora Ecuador
274 B5 Zamora r. Ecuador
204 I5 Zamora Spain
204 I5 Zamora prov. Spain
268 E6 Zamora de Hidalgo Mex.
197 L5 Zamość Lubelskie Pol.
197 J2 Zamość Mazowieckie Pol.
Zamost'ye Pol. see Zamość
159 Q6 Zamozhne Ukr.
Zampa-misaki hd Okinawa Japan see Zanpa-misaki
151 D5 Zamp Dağı mt. Turkey
200 C5 Zams Austria
130 C2 Zamtang Sichuan China
274 D2 Zamuro, Punta pt Venez.
275 F3 Zamuro, Sierra del mts Venez.
224 B2 Zamzam, Wādī watercourse Libya
274 B6 Zaña Peru
230 B5 Zanaga Congo
269 M9 Zanatepec Mex.
151 K5 Zänbil Adası i. Azer.
205 N10 Záncara r. Spain
Zancle Sicilia Italy see Messina
133 D11 Zanda Xizang China
235 G5 Zandamela Moz.
275 H3 Zanderij Suriname
187 G6 Zandhoven Belgium
193 J9 Žandov Czech Rep.
187 F6 Zandvliet Belgium
186 G4 Zandvoort Neth.
244 H2 Zane Hills AK U.S.A.
256 C9 Zanesville OH U.S.A.
151 G6 Zangakatun Armenia
228 D3 Zangasso Mali
Zangelan Azer. see Zängilan
151 G6 Zangezuri Lerrnashghtʼa mts Armenia/Azer.
133 D8 Zangguy Xinjiang China
151 H6 Zängilan Azer.
138 F3 Zangla Jammu and Kashmir India
133 G9 Zangsêr Kangri mt. Xizang China
129 N8 Zanhuang Hebei China
230 F4 Zani Dem. Rep. Congo
145 M7 Zani Pak.
196 F3 Zaniemyśl Pol.
144 C3 Zanjān Iran
144 C3 Zanjān prov. Iran
149 M5 Zanjān Rūd r. Iran
284 D3 Zanjitas Arg.
147 K3 Zannah, Jabal az hill U.A.E.
215 K6 Zannone, Isola i. Italy
124 □[1] Zanpa-misaki hd Okinawa Japan
138 F2 Zanskar r. India
138 F3 Zanskar reg. Jammu and Kashmir India
138 F2 Zanskar Mountains India
Zante i. Ionioi Nisoi Greece see Zakynthos
Zante i. Ionioi Nisoi Greece see Zakynthos
109 G11 Zanthus W.A. Austr.
228 D4 Zantiébougou Mali
233 C6 Zanzibar Tanz.
233 C6 Zanzibar Channel Tanz.
233 C6 Zanzibar Island Tanz.
233 C6 Zanzibar North admin. reg. Tanz.
233 C6 Zanzibar South admin. reg. Tanz.
233 C6 Zanzibar West admin. reg. Tanz.
287 H1 Zaohe Jiangsu China
161 U7 Zaokskiy Rus. Fed.
211 C7 Zaonia Mornag Tunisia
205 P7 Zaorejas Spain
230 C3 Zaoro-Songou C.A.R.
129 K9 Zaosheng Gansu China
131 I3 Zaoshi Hubei China
131 I5 Zaoshi Hunan China
161 Q1 Zaostrov'ye Rus. Fed.
227 H4 Zaouatallaz Alg.
Zaouet el Kahla Alg. see Bordj Omer Driss
227 E4 Zaouiet Kounta Alg.
131 I2 Zaoyang Hubei China
131 I2 Zaoyangzhan Hubei China
132 H4 Zaoyuan Xinjiang China
124 R8 Zaō-zan vol. Japan
159 M8 Zaozerne Ukr.
143 N1 Zaozernyy Kazakh.
153 K4 Zaozernyy Rus. Fed.
161 V4 Zaozer'ye Rus. Fed.
129 O9 Zaozhuang Shandong China
149 K5 Zap r. Turkey
218 J7 Zapadna Morava r. Serbia
161 P5 Zapadnaya Dvina r. Europe alt. Daugava (Latvia), alt. Zakhodnyaya Dzvina, conv. Western Dvina
161 P5 Zapadnaya Dvina Rus. Fed.
219 L9 Zapadni Rodopi mts Bulg.
Zapadno-Kazakhstanskaya Oblast' admin. div. Kazakh. see Zapadnyy Kazakhstan
122 M3 Zapadno-Sakhalinskiy Khrebet mts Rus. Fed.
Zapadno-Sibirskaya Nizmennost' plain Rus. Fed. see Zapadno-Sibirskaya Ravnina
152 J3 Zapadno-Sibirskaya Ravnina plain Rus. Fed.
143 P6 Zapadnyy Alamedin, Pik mt. Kyrg.
160 L1 Zapadnyy Berezovyy, Ostrov i. Rus. Fed.
142 F7 Zapadnyy Chink Ustyurta esc. Kazakh.
149 Q3 Zapadnyy Chink Ustyurta esc. Kazakh.
142 D3 Zapadnyy Kazakhstan admin. div. Kazakh.
156 F1 Zapadnyy Kil'din Rus. Fed.
120 E1 Zapadnyy Sayan reg. Rus. Fed.
158 G4 Zapadyntsi Ukr.
284 B6 Zapala Arg.
284 B3 Zapallar Chile
197 K5 Zapałów Pol.
205 J6 Zapardiel r. Spain
284 C3 Zapata Arg.
261 F12 Zapata TX U.S.A.
270 C2 Zapata, Península de pen. Cuba
274 C3 Zapatoca Col.
206 F3 Zapatón r. Spain
274 C2 Zapatoza, Ciénaga de l. Col.
191 K10 Zapfendorf Ger.
276 C4 Zapiga Chile
Zápio Greece see Zappeio
160 M3 Zaplyus'ye Rus. Fed.
219 P4 Zăpodeni Romania
196 G4 Zapolice Pol.
162 U2 Zapolyarnyy Murmanskaya Oblast' Rus. Fed.
156 M2 Zapolyarnyy Respublika Komi Rus. Fed.
160 M3 Zapol'ye Pskovskaya Oblast' Rus. Fed.
161 T2 Zapol'ye Vologodskaya Oblast' Rus. Fed.
268 D5 Zapopan Mex.
159 O6 Zaporizhzhya Ukr.
Zaporizhzhya Oblast admin. div. Ukr. see Zaporiz'ka Oblast'
159 O6 Zaporiz'ka Oblast' admin. div. Ukr.
Zaporozhskaya Oblast' admin. div. Ukr. see Zaporiz'ka Oblast'
161 N1 Zaporozhskoye Rus. Fed.
Zaporozh'ye Ukr. see Zaporizhzhya
Zaporozhye Oblast admin. div. Ukr. see Zaporiz'ka Oblast'
268 D6 Zapotiltic Mex.
268 D6 Zapotitlán Jalisco Mex.
269 J6 Zapotitlán Puebla Mex.
269 J7 Zapotitlán Salinas Mex.
268 D5 Zapotlanejo Mex.
122 H7 Zapovednyy Rus. Fed.
220 D3 Zappeio Greece
193 E7 Zappendorf Ger.
215 P5 Zapponeta Italy
210 E3 Zaprešić Croatia
161 U5 Zaprudnya Rus. Fed.
160 H9 Zaprudy Belarus
133 E10 Zapug Xizang China
197 M6 Zapytiv Ukr.
151 H4 Zaqatala Azer.
151 H4 Zaqatala Qoruğu nature res. Azer.
Zaqāzīq Egypt see Az Zaqāzīq
133 L10 Zaqên Qinghai China
224 C2 Zaqqui Libya
130 A3 Za Qu r. Qinghai China
133 I10 Zaqungngomar mt. Xizang China
Zara Xizang China see Moinda
Zara Croatia see Zadar
148 H4 Zara Turkey
Zarafshan Uzbek. see Zarafshon
145 M2 Zarafshon Tajik.
145 M2 Zarafshon r. Tajik.
142 K7 Zarafshon Uzbek.
143 J8 Zarafshon r. Uzbek.
145 L2 Zarafshon, Qatorkŭhi mts Tajik.
274 C3 Zaragoza Col.
267 I3 Zaragoza Coahuila Mex.
269 H2 Zaragoza Nuevo León Mex.
269 J6 Zaragoza Puebla Mex.
208 D4 Zaragoza Spain
205 R5 Zaragoza prov. Spain
208 D7 Zaragozana mt. Spain
144 G6 Zarand Kermān Iran
144 D4 Zarand Markazī Iran
199 K5 Zărand Romania
219 K4 Zarandului, Munții hills Romania
133 D11 Zarang Xizang China
145 I6 Zaranj Afgh.
196 D2 Zarańsko Pol.
160 J6 Zarasai Lith.
151 K5 Zarat Azer.
205 O2 Zaratamo Spain
205 K5 Zaratán Spain
285 H4 Zárate Arg.
208 A1 Zarautz Spain
161 V7 Zaraysk Rus. Fed.
275 E2 Zaraza Venez.
143 M7 Zarbdor Uzbek.
207 P5 Zarcilla de Ramos Spain
145 K7 Zard Pak.
151 I5 Zärdab Azer.
144 C5 Zard Kūh mts Iran
197 J2 Zaręby Pol.
197 K3 Zaręby-Kościelne Pol.
156 E2 Zarechensk Rus. Fed.
158 E1 Zarechka Belarus
156 L3 Zarechka Rus. Fed.
161 W8 Zarechnyy Rus. Fed.
161 X7 Zarech'ye Rus. Fed.
144 C4 Zāreh Iran
245 N4 Zarembo Island AK U.S.A.
160 F6 Žarėnai Lith.
146 E2 Zarghat Saudi Arabia
145 M5 Zarghūn Shahr Afgh.
145 L6 Zargun mt. Pak.
145 L4 Zari Afgh.
229 G4 Zaria Nigeria
Zariaspa Afgh. see Balkh
199 L3 Zaricheve Ukr.
159 N8 Zarichne Respublika Krym Ukr.
158 F2 Zarichne Rivnens'ka Oblast' Ukr.
144 F6 Zarīgān Iran
144 A3 Zarīneh Rūd r. Iran
197 H5 Żarki Pol.
196 C4 Żarki Wielkie Pol.
145 J5 Zarmardan Afgh.
151 J5 Zarnava Azer.
144 B5 Zarneh Iran
219 N5 Zărnești Romania
199 H3 Žarnovica Slovakia
197 I4 Żarnów Pol.
197 H5 Żarnowiec Pol.
165 O7 Żarnowieckie, Jezioro l. Pol.
196 E5 Żarów Pol.
190 K3 Zarpen Ger.
Zarqā' Jordan see Az Zarqā'
150 D6 Zarqā', Nahr az r. Jordan
150 D7 Zarqā' Mā'īn, Wādī r. Jordan
144 E7 Zarqān Iran
151 J4 Zärqava Azer.
187 C6 Zarren Belgium
190 K3 Zarrentin Ger.
144 F5 Zarrīn Iran
197 K6 Zarszyn Pol.
144 E6 Zarū Iran
161 Q3 Zarubino Novgorodskaya Oblast' Rus. Fed.
122 G7 Zarubino Primorskiy Kray Rus. Fed.
127 H5 Zaruga-dake mt. Japan
196 D4 Żary Pol.
142 G3 Zarya Oktyabrya Kazakh.
207 I3 Zarza Capilla Spain
206 G3 Zarza de Alange Spain
204 H8 Zarza de Granadilla Spain
205 N8 Zarza de Tajo Spain
207 P5 Zarzadilla de Totana Spain
227 H3 Zarzaïtine Alg.
274 B3 Zarzal Col.
204 G9 Zarza la Mayor Spain
197 K6 Zarzecze Pol.
227 H2 Zarzis Tunisia
205 L7 Zarzuela del Monte Spain
205 L6 Zarzuela del Pinar Spain
204 C2 Zas Spain
160 I5 Zasa Latvia
162 U3 Zasheyek Rus. Fed.
Zaskar reg. Jammu and Kashmir India see Zanskar
160 L6 Zaskarki Belarus
199 I2 Žaškov Slovakia
160 K8 Zaslawskaye Vodaskhovishcha resr Belarus
160 K7 Zaslawye Belarus
198 E2 Zásmuky Czech Rep.
159 R3 Zasosna Rus. Fed.
197 J5 Zasów Pol.
151 B1 Zassovskaya Rus. Fed.
158 E5 Zastavna Ukr.
237 L6 Zastron S. Africa
197 K3 Zaszków Pol.
150 E6 Za'tarī, Wādī az watercourse Jordan
198 C1 Žatec Czech Rep.
151 G1 Zaterechnyy Rus. Fed.
142 J1 Zatobol'sk Kazakh.
158 J7 Zatoka Ukr.
199 G1 Zátor Czech Rep.
197 H6 Zator Pol.
197 J3 Zatory Pol.
158 D3 Zaturtsi Ukr.
158 I6 Zatyshshya Ukr.
193 G6 Zauche reg. Ger.
269 J6 Zautla Mex.
199 M2 Zavadka Ukr.
199 I3 Závadka nad Hronom Slovakia
287 F2 Zavadovskiy Island Antarctica
285 G4 Zavalía Arg.
285 G3 Zavalla Arg.
261 H10 Zavalla TX U.S.A.
158 J5 Zavallya Ukr.
144 E5 Zavāreh Iran
212 G6 Zavattarello Italy
187 F7 Zaventem Belgium
157 H7 Zavetnoye Rus. Fed.
122 L4 Zavety Il'icha Rus. Fed.
210 G3 Zavidovići Bos.-Herz.
161 T5 Zavidovskiy Zapovednik nature res. Rus. Fed.
Zavitaya Rus. Fed. see Zavitinsk
122 F3 Zavitinsk Rus. Fed.
159 N8 Zavit-Lenins'ky Ukr.
198 G3 Závod Slovakia
197 M5 Zavods'ke L'vivs'ka Oblast' Ukr.
158 E4 Zavods'ke Ternopils'ka Oblast' Ukr.
143 U1 Zavodskoy Altayskiy Kray Rus. Fed.
Zavodskoy Respublika Mordoviya Rus. Fed. see Komsomol'skiy
151 F3 Zavodskoy Respublika Severnaya Osetiya-Alaniya Rus. Fed.
219 K7 Zavojsko Jezero resr Serbia
156 H4 Zavolzhsk Rus. Fed.
Zavolzh'ye Rus. Fed. see Zavolzhsk
235 G5 Závora, Ponta pt Moz.
159 K3 Zavorychi Ukr.
160 L6 Zavutstsye Belarus
160 L6 Zavyachellye Belarus
153 Q4 Zav'yalova, Ostrov i. Rus. Fed.
143 S1 Zav'yalovo Rus. Fed.
197 L6 Zavydovychi Ukr.
128 G8 Zawa Qinghai China
133 D8 Zawa Xinjiang China
197 H4 Zawada Łódzkie Pol.
197 L5 Zawada Lubelskie Pol.
196 D4 Zawada Lubuskie Pol.
196 F5 Zawada Opolskie Pol.
197 H5 Zawada Śląskie Pol.
197 K2 Zawady Pol.
196 G5 Zawadzkie Pol.
118 C4 Zawgyi r. Myanmar
197 J5 Zawichost Pol.
196 D4 Zawidów Pol.
197 H3 Zawidz Kościelny Pol.
197 H5 Zawiercie Pol.
224 B3 Zawīlah Libya
150 E3 Zāwīyah, Jabal az hills Syria
224 D2 Zāwiyat Masūs Libya
148 C8 Zāwiyat Shammās pt Egypt
147 L5 Zawlīyah, Jiddat az plain Oman
197 H6 Zawoja Pol.
196 F4 Zawonia Pol.
147 I2 Zawr, Ra's az pt Saudi Arabia
133 J11 Zaxoi Xizang China
156 J5 Zay r. Rus. Fed.
201 O2 Zaya r. Austria
151 G5 Zäyäm Azer.
151 G4 Zäyämçay r. Azer.
144 E5 Zāyandeh Rūd r. Iran
150 E6 Zaydī, Wādī az watercourse Syria
161 N6 Zaykava Belarus
143 U4 Zaysan Kazakh.
Zaysan, Lake Kazakh. see Zaysan, Ozero
143 T3 Zaysan, Ozero l. Kazakh.
159 R5 Zaytseve Ukr.
160 L4 Zaytsevo Rus. Fed.
130 A4 Zayü Xizang China
Zayü Xizang China see Gyigang
130 A4 Zayü Xizang China
151 E2 Zayukovo Rus. Fed.
130 A4 Zayü Qu r. China/India
Zayyr Uzbek. see Zoir
235 □J4 Zazafotsy Madag.
229 G3 Zazagawa Nigeria
227 G6 Zazir, Oued watercourse Alg.
199 I2 Zázrivá Slovakia
158 E4 Zbarazh Ukr.
196 D3 Zbąszyn Pol.
196 D3 Zbąszynek Pol.
196 D3 Zbąszyńskie, Jezioro l. Pol.
197 H2 Zbiczno Pol.
196 G4 Zbiersk Pol.
195 P2 Zbiroh Czech Rep.
196 G2 Zblewo Pol.
197 I5 Zbludowice Pol.
197 J2 Zbójna Pol.
197 H2 Zbójno Pol.
218 H7 Zborište mt. Serbia
158 E4 Zboriv Ukr.
199 K2 Zborov Slovakia
196 F6 Zborovice Czech Rep.
201 N1 Zbraslav Czech Rep.
198 E2 Zbraslavice Czech Rep.
158 F5 Zbruch r. Ukr.
198 C2 Zbůch Czech Rep.
197 K3 Zbuczyn Poduchowny Pol.
159 L7 Zbur"yivka Ukr.
201 N1 Zbýšov Czech Rep.
198 G5 Ždala Croatia
201 P1 Ždánice Czech Rep.
198 F2 Ždánický les for. Czech Rep.
193 L9 Žďár Czech Rep.
198 E2 Žďar nad Sázavou Czech Rep.
198 E2 Žďárské vrchy hills Czech Rep.
198 E2 Zdárské vrchy park Czech Rep.
199 J2 Ždiar Slovakia
198 C2 Zdíkov Czech Rep.
198 E2 Ždírec nad Doubravou Czech Rep.
158 F3 Zdolbuniv Ukr.
Zdolbunov Ukr. see Zdolbuniv
198 G2 Zdounky Czech Rep.
196 G4 Zduńska Wola Pol.
197 H3 Zduny Łódzkie Pol.
196 F4 Zduny Wielkopolskie Pol.
158 J2 Zdvyzh r. Ukr.
197 J6 Zdynia Pol.
196 G4 Zdziechowice Opolskie Pol.
197 K5 Zdziechowice Podkarpackie Pol.
196 G5 Zdzieszowice Pol.
197 K5 Zdziłowice Pol.
197 N3 Zdzitava Belarus
Zealand i. Denmark see Sjælland
145 N3 Zēbāk Afgh.
283 C7 Zeballos mt. Arg.
246 E5 Zeballos B.C. Can.
149 L5 Zēbār Iraq
217 □ Żebbiegħ Malta
217 □ Żebbuġ Gozo Malta
217 □ Żebbuġ Malta
Zebirget Island Egypt see Zabarjad, Jazīrat
196 G5 Zębowice Pol.
195 P2 Žebrák Czech Rep.
204 F9 Zebreira Port.
196 D4 Zebrzydowa Pol.
196 G6 Zebrzydowice Dolne Pol.
255 E9 Zebulon GA U.S.A.
256 C11 Zebulon KY U.S.A.
255 H8 Zebulon NC U.S.A.
213 Q6 Zeča i. Croatia
192 G4 Zechlin Dorf Ger.
192 G4 Zechlinerhütte Ger.
186 J5 Zeddam Neth.
214 B8 Zeddiani Sardegna Italy
187 D6 Zedelgem Belgium
201 I5 Zederhaus Austria
199 I6 Žednik Vojvodina Serbia
187 D6 Zeebrugge Belgium
105 J9 Zeehan Tas. Austr.
186 I5 Zeeland Neth.
186 E5 Zeeland prov. Neth.
250 H7 Zeeland MI U.S.A.
150 C7 Ze'elim Israel
237 K1 Zeerust S. Africa
193 I6 Zeesen Ger.
187 D6 Zeeuwsch-Vlaanderen reg. Neth.
186 I4 Zeewolde Neth.
150 D6 Zefat Israel
144 E5 Zefreh Iran
208 A2 Zegama Spain
197 I6 Żegiestów Pol.
197 I6 Żegocina Pol.
197 J3 Zegrzyńskie, Jezioro l. Pol.
192 H5 Zehdenick Ger.
192 F3 Zehna Ger.
193 H8 Zehren Ger.
106 D7 Zeil, Mount N.T. Austr.
191 K10 Zeil am Main Ger.
195 N5 Zeilarn Ger.
160 H5 Žeimelis Lith.
201 N3 Zeiselmauer Austria
186 H4 Zeist Neth.
193 H8 Zeithain Ger.
195 M3 Zeitlarn Ger.
191 I10 Zeitlofs Ger.
193 F8 Zeitz Ger.
217 □ Żejtun Malta
128 G9 Zêkog Qinghai China
132 F5 Zekti Xinjiang China
Zela Turkey see Zile
196 G4 Żelazków Pol.
187 F6 Zele Belgium
197 I4 Żelechlinek Pol.
197 J4 Żelechów Pol.
158 F5 Zelena Chernivets'ka Oblast' Ukr.
158 D5 Zelena Ivano-Frankivs'ka Oblast' Ukr.
158 D5 Zelena Ivano-Frankivs'ka Oblast' Ukr.
210 F4 Zelena Gora mt. Bos.-Herz.
198 G2 Zelená hora tourist site Czech Rep.
143 P1 Zelenaya Roshcha Kazakh.
151 C2 Zelenchukskaya Rus. Fed.
193 K10 Zeleneč Czech Rep.
199 G3 Zeleneč Slovakia
159 P6 Zelene Pole Ukr.
210 G4 Zelengora mts Bos.-Herz.
219 J9 Zelenikovo Zelenikovo Macedonia
159 L7 Zelenivka Ukr.
159 N4 Zelenkivka Ukr.
156 I3 Zelennik Rus. Fed.
162 V3 Zelenoborskiy Rus. Fed.
156 J5 Zelenodol'sk Rus. Fed.
159 M6 Zelenodol's'k Ukr.
160 M1 Zelenogorsk Rus. Fed.
161 U5 Zelenograd Rus. Fed.
160 D7 Zelenogradsk Rus. Fed.
158 J6 Zelenohirs'ke Ukr.
151 E1 Zelenokumsk Rus. Fed.
156 I4 Zelentsovo Rus. Fed.
121 Q3 Zelenyy, Ostrov i. Kuril'skiye O-va Rus. Fed.
143 N2 Zelenyy Gay Kazakh.
201 O1 Želešice Czech Rep.
198 E2 Železný Ruda Czech Rep.
199 I3 Železné Slovakia
198 E2 Železné hory hills Czech Rep.
201 J7 Železniki Slovenia
198 E1 Železný Brod Czech Rep.
186 J4 Zelhem Neth.
256 E8 Zelienople PA U.S.A.
199 H3 Želiezovce Slovakia
210 F3 Zelina Croatia
128 E8 Zelinggou Qinghai China
198 E2 Želivka r. Czech Rep.
198 E2 Želivka, Vodní nádrž resr Czech Rep.
218 I7 Željin mt. Serbia
197 K3 Żelków-Kolonia Pol.
193 E10 Zell Ger.
191 D10 Zell (Mosel) Ger.
191 K9 Zella-Mehlis Ger.
194 E5 Zell am Harmersbach Ger.
200 G5 Zell am See Austria
200 E5 Zell am Ziller Austria
201 I3 Zell an der Pram Austria
201 M2 Zellerndorf Austria
201 L4 Zellerrain pass Austria
200 G5 Zeller See l. Austria
201 H4 Zellersee l. Austria
194 G6 Zellersee l. Ger.
194 D6 Zell im Wiesental Ger.
194 H2 Zellingen Ger.
201 J7 Zell-Pfarre Austria
199 I3 Želovce Slovakia
197 H4 Zelów Pol.
194 C2 Zeltingen-Rachtig Ger.
160 J4 Zeltiņi Latvia
201 K5 Zeltweg Austria
160 H8 Zel'va Belarus
197 M2 Zel'vyenskaye Vodaskhovishcha resr Belarus
187 E6 Zelzate Belgium
160 E6 Žemaičių Naumiestis Lith.
160 E5 Žemaitijos nacionalinis parkas nat. park Lith.
199 H3 Žemberovce Slovakia
160 L7 Zembin Belarus
220 B2 Zemblak Albania
197 K3 Zembrów Pol.
197 H6 Zembrzyce Pol.
219 K8 Zemen Bulg.
219 O4 Zemeș Romania
157 H5 Zemetchino Rus. Fed.
199 G4 Zemianska Oľča Slovakia
230 E3 Zémio C.A.R.
192 I3 Zemitz Ger.
159 R2 Zemlyansk Rus. Fed.
194 B2 Zemmer Ger.
151 C3 Zemo Barghebi Georgia
151 E4 Zemo Khveduret'i Georgia
230 E3 Zémongo, Réserve de Faune de nature res. C.A.R.
151 F4 Zemo Qarabulakhi Georgia
199 L3 Zemplénagárd Hungary
199 K3 Zempleni park Hungary
199 K3 Zempléni-hegység hills Hungary
199 L3 Zemplínska šírava l. Slovakia
199 K3 Zemplínska Teplica Slovakia
199 L3 Zemplínske Hámre Slovakia
269 I6 Zempoala Hidalgo Mex.
269 K6 Zempoala Veracruz Mex.
269 L8 Zempoaltépetl, Nudo de mt. Mex.
187 F7 Zemst Belgium
161 P5 Zemtsy Rus. Fed.
218 I6 Zemun Beograd Serbia
130 A2 Zênda Sichuan China
131 I7 Zengcheng Guangdong China
122 F7 Zengfeng Shan mt. China
199 H5 Zengő hill Hungary
210 F3 Zenica Bos.-Herz.
150 C8 Zenifim watercourse Israel
195 J2 Zenn r. Ger.
172 □ Zennor Cornwall, England U.K.
Zenta Vojvodina Serbia see Senta
125 K12 Zentsūji Japan
145 M4 Zenyeh Afgh.
227 F2 Zenzach Alg.
269 J9 Zenzontepec Mex.
210 G3 Žepče Bos.-Herz.
192 I5 Zepernick Ger.
264 M2 Zephyr Cove NV U.S.A.
255 F11 Zephyrhills FL U.S.A.
133 C7 Zepu Xinjiang China
230 C2 Zérab, Ouadi watercourse Chad
232 A2 Zeraf, Bahr el r. Sudan
Zeravshan Tajik. see Zarafshon
Zeravshan r. Tajik. see Zarafshon
Zeravshan r. Uzbek. see Zarafshon
Zeravshanskiy Khrebet mts Tajik. see Zarafshon, Qatorkŭhi
193 F7 Zerbst Ger.
145 I6 Zereh, Gowd-e depr. Afgh.
145 J7 Zereh, Gowd-e depr. Afgh.
143 M1 Zerendy Kazakh.
194 B2 Zerf Ger.
227 G2 Zeribet el Oued Alg.
199 K5 Zerind Romania
196 F3 Żerków Pol.
212 D3 Zermatt Switz.
212 I2 Zernez Switz.
190 K4 Zernien Ger.
192 F5 Zernitz Ger.
157 H7 Zernograd Rus. Fed.
Zernovoy Rus. Fed. see Zernograd

213 M4 Zero r. Italy
192 I5 Zerpenschleuse Ger.
192 J4 Zerrenthin Ger.
189 I2 Zespół Nadwiślanskich Parków Krajobrazowych Pol.
189 I2 Zespół Nadwiślanskich Parków Krajobrazowych Pol.
Zestafoni Georgia see Zestap'oni
151 E3 Zestap'oni Georgia
208 A1 Zestoa Spain
139 L5 Zêsum Xizang China
218 H8 Zeta r. Montenegro
201 M7 Žetale Slovenia
133 J12 Zêtang Xizang China
219 N4 Zetea Romania
190 E4 Zetel Ger.
193 E9 Zeulenroda Ger.
193 I6 Zeuthen Ger.
190 H4 Zeven Ger.
186 J5 Zevenaar Neth.
186 G5 Zevenbergen Neth.
186 J2 Zevenhuizen Neth.
150 A4 Zevgari, Cape Cyprus
220 D5 Zevgolatio Greece
213 K5 Zevio Italy
122 E2 Zeya Rus. Fed.
122 E3 Zeya r. Rus. Fed.
144 F7 Zeydābād Iran
145 J8 Zeydī Iran
144 G7 Zeynālābād Iran
122 E1 Zeyskiy Zapovednik nature res. Rus. Fed.
122 G3 Zeysko-Bureinskaya Vpadina depr. Rus. Fed.
122 E1 Zeyskoye Vodokhranilishche resr Rus. Fed.
Zeytin Burnu c. Cyprus see Elaia, Cape
221 I4 Zeytindağ Turkey
220 B2 Zezë, Maja e mt. Albania
204 D10 Zêzere r. Port.
129 M9 Zezhou Shanxi China
150 D4 Zgharta Lebanon
197 H4 Zgierz Pol.
197 I6 Zgłobice Pol.
201 J7 Zgornje Bitnje Slovenia
201 J7 Zgornje Jezersko Slovenia
201 M6 Zgornji Duplek Slovenia
196 D4 Zgorzelec Pol.
158 G5 Zgurița Moldova
158 D1 Zhabinka Belarus
158 H5 Zhabokrychka Ukr.
Zhabye Ukr. see Verkhovyna
158 H3 Zhad'ky Ukr.
159 L1 Zhadove Ukr.
Zhaggo Sichuan China see Luhuo
130 B2 Zhaglag Sichuan China
130 A3 Zhag'yab Xizang China
Zhahti Koe N.W.T. Can. see Fort Providence
142 I2 Zhailma Kazakh.
143 L2 Zhaksy Kazakh.
143 M3 Zhaksy-Kon watercourse Kazakh.
142 I4 Zhaksykylysh Kazakh.
142 I4 Zhaksykylysh, Ozero salt l. Kazakh.
Zhaksy Sarysu watercourse Kazakh. see Sarysu
Zhalaghash Kazakh. see Dzhalagash
143 R6 Zhalanash Almatinskaya Oblast' Kazakh.
Zhalanash Kostanayskaya Oblast' Kazakh. see Damdy
Zhalgyztöbe Kazakh. see Zhangiztobe
142 C3 Zhalpaktal Kazakh.
Zhalpaqtal Kazakh. see Zhalpaktal
143 M2 Zhaltyr Akmolinskaya Oblast' Kazakh.
143 Q2 Zhaltyr Pavlodarskaya Oblast' Kazakh.
142 D4 Zhaltyr, Ozero l. Kazakh.
160 H8 Zhaludok Belarus
142 J3 Zhamanakkol', Ozero salt l. Kazakh.
142 E4 Zhamansor Kazakh.
143 N4 Zhambyl Karagandinskaya Oblast' Kazakh.
Zhambyl Zhambylskaya Oblast' Kazakh. see Taraz
Zhambyl Oblast admin. div. Kazakh. see Zhambylskaya Oblast'
143 O5 Zhambylskaya Oblast' admin. div. Kazakh.
Zhamo Xizang China see Bomi
143 M4 Zhanabas (abandoned) Kazakh.
143 S3 Zhana Kanay Kazakh.
143 L6 Zhanakorgan Kazakh.
142 I5 Zhanakurylys Kazakh.
133 J12 Zhanang Xizang China
143 P4 Zhanaortalyk Kazakh.
142 E6 Zhanaozen Kazakh.
143 R6 Zhanatalan Kazakh.
143 M6 Zhanatas Kazakh.
142 I5 Zhanay Kazakh.
142 D4 Zhanbay Kazakh.
122 E4 Zhanbei Heilong. China
Zhangaözen Kazakh. see Zhanaozen
Zhangaqazaly Kazakh. see Ayteke Bi
Zhanga Qazan Kazakh. see Novaya Kazanka
Zhangaqorghan Kazakh. see Zhanakorgan
Zhangatas Kazakh. see Zhanatas
129 N6 Zhangbei Hebei China
Zhangcheng Fujian China see Yongtai
131 K2 Zhangcunpu Anhui China
Zhangdian Shandong China see Zibo
Zhanggu Sichuan China see Danba
122 F5 Zhangguangcai Ling mts China
129 R5 Zhanggutai Liaoning China
129 N8 Zhang He r. China
Zhanghua Taiwan see Changhua
130 G8 Zhanghuang Guangxi China
143 S3 Zhangiztobe Kazakh.
130 F1 Zhangjiachuan Gansu China
130 H4 Zhangjiajie Hunan China
129 N6 Zhangjiakou Hebei China
Zhangjiang Hunan China see Taoyuan
Zhangjiapan Shaanxi China see Jingbian
122 C2 Zhangling Heilong. China
131 K2 Zhanglou Anhui China
131 K6 Zhangping Fujian China
131 K6 Zhangpu Fujian China
129 R5 Zhangqiangzhen Liaoning China
129 O8 Zhangqiu Shandong China
131 J4 Zhangshu Jiangxi China
Zhangwan Hubei China see Xiangyang
129 O7 Zhangwei Xinhe r. China
129 R5 Zhangwu Liaoning China
128 I9 Zhangxian Gansu China
128 G7 Zhangye Gansu China
131 K6 Zhangzhou Fujian China
129 M8 Zhangzi Shanxi China
Zhanhe Heilong. China see Zhanbei
122 F4 Zhan He r. China
129 P8 Zhanhua Shandong China
142 B3 Zhanibek Kazakh.
Zhänibek Kazakh. see Zhanibek
130 H8 Zhanjiang Guangdong China
Zhansügirov Kazakh. see Dzhansugurov
142 F4 Zhanterek Kazakh.
130 D6 Zhanyi Yunnan China
131 K7 Zhao'an Fujian China
122 D5 Zhaodong Heilong. China
Zhaoge Henan China see Qixian
130 D4 Zhaojue Sichuan China
131 I4 Zhaoliqiao Hubei China
130 H6 Zhaoping Guangxi China
131 I7 Zhaoqing Guangdong China
Zhaoren Shaanxi China see Changwu
132 E5 Zhaosu Xinjiang China
129 R5 Zhaosutai He r. China
130 D5 Zhaotong Yunnan China
129 N8 Zhaoxian Hebei China
129 O9 Zhaoyang Hu l. China
122 D6 Zhaoyuan Heilong. China
129 Q8 Zhaoyuan Shandong China
Zhaozhen Sichuan China see Jintang
Zhaozhou Hebei China see Zhaoxian
122 D6 Zhaozhou Heilong. China
131 H8 Zhapo Guangdong China
Zhaqsy Kazakh. see Zhaksy
158 H4 Zhar r. Ukr.
143 T4 Zharbulak Kazakh.
160 K7 Zhardzyazhzha Belarus
133 G11 Zhari Namco salt l. China
142 G4 Zharkamys Kazakh.
143 S5 Zharkent Kazakh.
161 P6 Zharkovskiy Rus. Fed.
142 E6 Zharma Mangistauskaya Oblast' Kazakh.
143 S3 Zharma Vostochnyy Kazakhstan Kazakh.
142 E5 Zharmysh-Ondy Kazakh.
143 S4 Zharsuat (abandoned) Kazakh.
Zharyk Kazakh. see Saken Seyfullin
143 S3 Zharyk Kazakh.
158 J4 Zhashkiv Ukr.
Zhashkov Ukr. see Zhashkiv
130 G2 Zhashui Shaanxi China
Zhaslyk Uzbek. see Jasliq
161 P8 Zhastkovo Rus. Fed.
Zhaxi Yunnan China see Weixin
133 G10 Zhaxi Co salt l. China
133 D10 Zhaxigang Xizang China
133 I12 Zhaxigang Xizang China
130 A3 Zhaxizê Xizang China
133 H12 Zhaxizong Xizang China
143 N3 Zhayrem Kazakh.
130 B4 Zhayü Xizang China
Zhayylma Kazakh. see Zhailma
Zhayyq r. Kazakh./Rus. Fed. see Ural
159 O5 Zhdanivka Ukr.
Zhdanov Ukr. see Mariupol'
161 Q4 Zhdanovo Rus. Fed.
Zhdanovsk Azer. see Beyläqan
159 M3 Zhdany Ukr.
Zhdenevo Ukr. see Zhdeniyevo
158 C5 Zhdeniyevo Ukr.
129 N9 Zhecheng Henan China
Zhedao Yunnan China see Lianghe
130 C3 Zhêhor Sichuan China
131 M4 Zhejiang prov. China
143 P3 Zhekezhal Kazakh.
131 J7 Zhelang Guangdong China
152 H2 Zhelaniya, Mys c. Novaya Zemlya Rus. Fed.
160 K3 Zhelcha r. Rus. Fed.
143 P1 Zhelezinka Kazakh.
160 E7 Zheleznodorozhnyy Kaliningradskaya Oblast' Rus. Fed.
Zheleznodorozhnyy Respublika Komi Rus. Fed. see Yemva
Zheleznodorozhnyy Uzbek. see Qo'ng'irot
161 S9 Zheleznogorsk Rus. Fed.
151 E1 Zheleznovodsk Rus. Fed.
161 U7 Zheleznya Rus. Fed.
Zhelou Guizhou China see Ceheng
143 P5 Zheltorangy Kazakh.
Zheltyye Vody Ukr. see Zhovti Vody
161 T3 Zhelyabova, imeni Rus. Fed.
159 N8 Zhelyabovka Ukr.
219 O8 Zhelyu Voyvoda Bulg.
Zhem Kazakh. see Emba
142 E4 Zhem r. Kazakh.
130 G2 Zhen'an Shaanxi China
130 F2 Zhenba Shaanxi China
130 E6 Zhenfeng Guizhou China
130 F4 Zheng'an Guizhou China
129 N7 Zhengding Hebei China
131 L5 Zhenghe Fujian China
Zhengjiakou Hebei China see Gucheng
Zhengjiatun Jilin China see Shuangliao
Zhengkou Hebei China see Gucheng
Zhenglan Qi Nei Mongol China see Dund Hot
128 H8 Zhenglubu Gansu China
129 K9 Zhengning Gansu China
Zhengxiangbai Qi Nei Mongol China see Qagan Nur
131 J2 Zhengyang Henan China
129 M9 Zhengzhou Henan China
131 M4 Zhenhai Zhejiang China
131 L2 Zhenjiang Jiangsu China
130 D2 Zhenjiangguan Sichuan China
Zhenkang Yunnan China see Fengwei
130 B7 Zhenkang Yunnan China
129 R4 Zhenlai Jilin China
130 E5 Zhenning Guizhou China
130 G3 Zhenping Shaanxi China
Zhenwudong Shaanxi China see Ansai
130 E5 Zhenxiong Yunnan China
Zhenyang Henan China see Zhengyang
129 J9 Zhenyuan Gansu China
130 G5 Zhenyuan Guizhou China
130 C7 Zhenyuan Yunnan China
130 H3 Zhenziling Hubei China
157 H6 Zherdevka Rus. Fed.
161 T8 Zherdevo Rus. Fed.
158 F5 Zherdya Ukr.
159 R5 Zherebets' r. Ukr.
158 I2 Zheriv r. Ukr.
158 I3 Zheriv r. Ukr.
131 L5 Zherong Fujian China
156 J3 Zheshart Rus. Fed.
161 U5 Zhestylevo Rus. Fed.
Zhetibay Kazakh. see Zhetybay
Zhetikara Kazakh. see Zhitikara
Zhetisay Kazakh. see Zhetysay
142 E6 Zhetybay Kazakh.
142 I2 Zhetykol', Ozero l. Rus. Fed.
143 M7 Zhetysay Kazakh.
143 R5 Zhetysuskiy Alatau mts China/Kazakh.
133 H11 Zhêxam Xizang China
131 H4 Zhexi Shuiku resr China
143 L3 Zhezdy Kazakh.
143 L4 Zhezkazgan Karagandinskaya Oblast' Kazakh.
143 L4 Zhezkazgan Karagandinskaya Oblast' Kazakh.
Zhezqazghan Kazakh. see Zhezkazgan
Zhicheng Shandong China see Qingzhou
Zhicheng Zhejiang China see Changxing
161 O6 Zhichitsy Rus. Fed.
129 K8 Zhidan Shaanxi China
133 L10 Zhidoi Qinghai China
153 N3 Zhigansk Rus. Fed.
129 P9 Zhigou Shandong China
142 C1 Zhigulevsk Rus. Fed.
133 J11 Zhigung Xizang China
130 G5 Zhijiang Hunan China
130 E5 Zhijin Guizhou China
161 V7 Zhilevo Rus. Fed.
161 T8 Zhilino Orlovskaya Oblast' Rus. Fed.
159 S4 Zhilino Voronezhskaya Oblast' Rus. Fed.
Zhilong Guangdong China see Yangxi
129 K9 Zhiluozhen Shaanxi China
Zhilyanka Kazakh. see Kargalinskoye
157 I6 Zhirnovsk Rus. Fed.
Zhirnovskiy Rus. Fed. see Zhirnovsk
Zhirnoye Rus. Fed. see Zhirnovsk
161 Q8 Zhiryatino Rus. Fed.
Zhitarovo Bulg. see Vetren
142 I1 Zhitikara Kazakh.
Zhitkovichi Belarus see Zhytkavichy
160 M1 Zhitkovo Rus. Fed.
157 I6 Zhitkur Rus. Fed.
220 A2 Zhitom Albania
Zhitomir Ukr. see Zhytomyr
Zhitomir Oblast admin. div. Ukr. see Zhytomyrs'ka Oblast'
Zhitomirskaya Oblast' admin. div. Ukr. see Zhytomyrs'ka Oblast'
149 M6 Zhīvār Iran
161 R8 Zhizdra Rus. Fed.
161 T7 Zhizdra r. Rus. Fed.
161 O5 Zhizhitsa Rus. Fed.
161 O5 Zhizhitskoye, Ozero l. Rus. Fed.
130 B5 Zhiziluo Yunnan China
161 N9 Zhlobin Belarus
Zhmerinka Ukr. see Zhmerynka
158 H4 Zhmerynka Ukr.
145 M6 Zhob Pak.
145 M5 Zhob r. Pak.
160 L7 Zhodzina Belarus
153 Q2 Zhokhova, Ostrov i. Novosibirskiye O-va Rus. Fed.
Zholkva Ukr. see Zhovkva
143 T3 Zholnuskau Kazakh.
143 N2 Zholymbet Kazakh.
Zhong'an Yunnan China see Fuyuan
131 J7 Zhongba Guangdong China
Zhongba Sichuan China see Jiangyou
133 G12 Zhongba Xizang China
Zhongcheng Sichuan China see Xingwen
Zhongcheng Yunnan China see Suijiang
Zhongduo Chongqing China see Youyang
Zhongguo country Asia see China
Zhongguo Renmin Gongheguo country Asia see China
Zhonghe Chongqing China see Xiushan
129 N9 Zhongmou Henan China
128 I8 Zhongning Ningxia China
Zhongping Yunnan China see Huize
128 H8 Zhongpu Gansu China
287 F2 Zhongshan research stn Antarctica
131 I7 Zhongshan Guangdong China
131 H6 Zhongshan Guangxi China
Zhongshan Guizhou China see Lupanshui
Zhongsha Qundao sea feature Paracel Is see Macclesfield Bank
Zhongshu Yunnan China see Luliang
Zhongshu Yunnan China see Luxi
Zhongtai Gansu China see Lingtai
129 L9 Zhongtiao Shan mts China
128 I8 Zhongwei Ningxia China
130 G3 Zhongxian Chongqing China
131 J6 Zhongxin Guangdong China
Zhongxin Yunnan China see Huaping
131 K3 Zhongxing Anhui China
Zhongxing Jiangsu China see Siyang
130 B1 Zhongxinzhan Qinghai China
129 L8 Zhongyang Shanxi China
122 D3 Zhongyaozhan Heilong. China
130 D6 Zhongyicun Yunnan China
130 H9 Zhongyuan Hainan China
Zhong Yunhe canal China see Jinghang Yunhe
Zhong Yunhe canal China see Jinghang Yunhe
130 E2 Zhongzhai Gansu China
131 N4 Zhongzhai Zhejiang China
Zhongzhou Chongqing China see Zhongxian
197 L4 Zhorany Ukr.
Zhosaly Kyzylordinskaya Oblast' Kazakh. see Dzhusaly
129 O9 Zhoucheng Shandong China
130 F3 Zhou He r. China
128 H7 Zhoujiajing Gansu China
130 F2 Zhoujiaping Shaanxi China
131 J2 Zhoukou Henan China
Zhoukou Sichuan China see Peng'an
129 N7 Zhoukoudian tourist site China
131 L5 Zhouning Fujian China
131 N3 Zhoushan Zhejiang China
131 N3 Zhoushan Dao i. China
131 N3 Zhoushan Qundao is China
129 K9 Zhouzhi Shaanxi China
158 C3 Zhovkva Ukr.
159 M6 Zhovta r. Ukr.
159 M5 Zhovte Ukr.
158 J6 Zhovten' Ukr.
159 M5 Zhovti Vody Ukr.
159 L2 Zhovtneve Ukr.
159 Q4 Zhovtneve Kharkivs'ka Oblast' Ukr.
159 N4 Zhovtneve Poltavs'ka Oblast' Ukr.
159 N3 Zhovtneve Sums'ka Oblast' Ukr.
197 M5 Zhovtneve Volyns'ka Oblast' Ukr.
129 R7 Zhuanghe Liaoning China
128 I9 Zhuanglang Gansu China
143 M5 Zhuantobe Kazakh.
130 A2 Zhubgyügoin Qinghai China
158 G2 Zhubrovychi Ukr.
129 P9 Zhucheng Shandong China
Zhudong Taiwan see Chutung
128 F8 Zhugkyung Qinghai China
133 K11 Zhugla Xizang China
130 E2 Zhugqu Gansu China
131 I7 Zhuhai Guangdong China
131 M4 Zhuji Zhejiang China
129 L7 Zhujia Chuan r. China
131 I7 Zhu Jiang r. Guangdong China
131 M3 Zhujing Shanghai China
131 I7 Zhukeng Guangdong China
161 P5 Zhukopa r. Rus. Fed.
161 Q8 Zhukovka Rus. Fed.
161 T6 Zhukovo Rus. Fed.
161 V6 Zhukovskiy Rus. Fed.
158 J3 Zhukyn Ukr.
129 N7 Zhulong He r. China
131 J2 Zhumadian Henan China
142 D4 Zhumysker Kazakh.
129 N6 Zhuolu Hebei China
Zhuoyang Henan China see Suiping
129 M8 Zhuozhang He r. China
129 O7 Zhuozhou Hebei China
129 M6 Zhuozi Nei Mongol China
Zhuozishan Nei Mongol China see Zhuozi
218 I8 Zhur Prizren Kosovo
159 T3 Zhuravka Rus. Fed.
159 O8 Zhuravky Ukr.
143 M2 Zhuravlevka Kazakh.
158 D4 Zhuravno Ukr.
159 S8 Zhuravskaya Rus. Fed.
159 L1 Zhurbin Rus. Fed.
159 K3 Zhurivka Ukr.
160 K6 Zhurki Belarus
142 G3 Zhuryn Kazakh.
143 O5 Zhusandala, Step' plain Kazakh.
Zhushan Hubei China see Xuan'en
130 H2 Zhushan Hubei China
130 G2 Zhuxi Hubei China
Zhuyang Sichuan China see Dazhu
131 I5 Zhuzhou Hunan China
131 I5 Zhuzhou Hunan China
197 M5 Zhvyrka Ukr.
158 D4 Zhydachiv Ukr.
142 E2 Zhympity Kazakh.
142 D5 Zhyngyldy Kazakh.
197 N1 Zhyrmuny Belarus
197 N2 Zhyrovichy Belarus
197 M4 Zhyrychi Ukr.
158 G1 Zhytkavichy Belarus
158 H3 Zhytomyr Ukr.
Zhytomyr Oblast admin. div. Ukr. see Zhytomyrs'ka Oblast'
158 G3 Zhytomyrs'ka Oblast' admin. div. Ukr.
158 I4 Zhyvka r. Ukr.
160 I8 Zhyzhma r. Belarus
228 C4 Ziama mt. Guinea
144 D3 Ziārān Iran
144 G3 Ziārat Iran
145 L6 Ziarat Pak.
199 H3 Žiar nad Hronom Slovakia
150 G8 Zibā salt pan Saudi Arabia
149 K5 Zībār Iraq
212 I5 Zibello Italy
129 P8 Zibo Shandong China
206 B2 Zibreira Port.
214 C4 Zicavo Corse France
129 K8 Zichang Shaanxi China
Zicheng Guangdong China see Zijin
195 P3 Žichovice Czech Rep.
192 D5 Zichtauer Berge und Klötzer Forst park Ger.
192 D3 Zickhusen Ger.
268 F7 Zicuirán Mex.
201 L7 Zidani Most Slovenia
144 G3 Zīdar Iran
145 M2 Ziddí Tajik.
145 L8 Zidi Pak.
159 P4 Zid'ky Ukr.
196 F5 Ziębice Pol.
192 E4 Ziegendorf Ger.
193 E9 Ziegenrück Ger.
193 H8 Ziegra Ger.
Ziel, Mount N.T. Austr. see Zeil, Mount
197 L4 Zielawa r. Pol.
196 D1 Zieleniewo Zachodniopomorskie Pol.
196 D2 Zieleniewo Zachodniopomorskie Pol.
193 E6 Zielitz Ger.
197 I3 Zielkowice Pol.
197 H2 Zielona Pol.
196 F2 Zielona Chocina Pol.
196 D4 Zielona Góra Lubuskie Pol.
196 E3 Zielona Góra Wielkopolskie Pol.
197 J3 Zielonka Pol.
197 H2 Zieluń Pol.
160 F4 Ziemelkursas augstiene hills Latvia
160 K4 Ziemeri Latvia
195 J5 Ziemetshausen Ger.
160 E5 Ziemupe Latvia
191 H8 Zierenberg Ger.
186 E5 Zierikzee Neth.
201 M2 Ziersdorf Austria
192 E4 Zierzow Ger.
193 F6 Ziesar Ger.
225 F2 Ziftá Egypt
118 A4 Zigaing Myanmar
151 A5 Zigana Geçidi pass Turkey
133 J10 Zigê Tangco l. China
224 D3 Zīghan Libya
213 N4 Zignago, Valle lag. Italy
118 B5 Zigon Myanmar
130 E4 Zigong Sichuan China
224 B6 Ziguey Chad
Zigui Hubei China see Guojiaba
130 H3 Zigui Hubei China
228 A3 Ziguinchor Senegal
160 K4 Žīguri Latvia
129 P8 Zi He r. China
198 C1 Žihle Czech Rep.
268 F7 Zihuaquio Mex.
268 F8 Zihuatanejo Mex.
131 J7 Zijin Guangdong China
186 J4 Zijpenberg hill Neth.
Ziketan Qinghai China see Xinghai
161 R8 Zikeyevo Rus. Fed.
150 C6 Zikhron Ya'aqov Israel
142 G1 Zilair Rus. Fed.
160 I4 Zilaiskalns Latvia
148 G3 Zile Turkey
157 L5 Zilim r. Rus. Fed.
199 H2 Žilina Slovakia
197 M1 Žilinai Lith.
199 I2 Žilinský kraj admin. reg. Slovakia
224 C2 Zillah Libya
200 E5 Ziller r. Austria
200 E5 Zillertal val. Austria
200 E5 Zillertaler Alpen mts Austria
212 G2 Zillis Switz.
191 K7 Zilly Ger.
193 K6 Ziltendorf Ger.
160 L5 Zilupe Latvia
120 H1 Zima Rus. Fed.
199 K5 Zimandu Nou Romania
269 H5 Zimapán Mex.
269 K9 Zimatlán Mex.
231 E9 Zimba Zambia
235 F4 Zimbabwe country Africa
Zimbabwe tourist site Zimbabwe see Great Zimbabwe National Monument
144 A4 Zīmkān, Rūdkhāneh-ye r. Iran
Zimmerbude Rus. Fed. see Svetlyy
194 F5 Zimmern ob Rottweil Ger.
191 H8 Zimmersrode (Neuental) Ger.
228 C5 Zimmi Sierra Leone
219 N7 Zimnicea Romania
156 G2 Zimniy Bereg coastal area Rus. Fed.
157 H7 Zimovniki Rus. Fed.
148 G6 Zimrīn Syria
150 D7 Zin watercourse Israel
269 M8 Zinapa r. Mex.
268 F5 Zináparo Mex.
268 G6 Zinapécuaro Mex.
235 G4 Zinave, Parque Nacional de nat. park Moz.
221 L4 Zindan Mağarası tourist site Turkey
145 N6 Zindawar Pak.
229 H3 Zinder Niger
229 H3 Zinder dept Niger
130 C3 Zindo Sichuan China
229 H4 Zing Nigeria
233 C7 Zinga Mulike Tanz.
192 G2 Zingst reg. Ger.
192 G2 Zingst am Darß, Ostseebad Ger.
228 E3 Ziniaré Burkina
128 I7 Zinihu Nei Mongol China
146 G9 Zinjibār Yemen
159 N3 Zin'kiv Ukr.
195 O3 Žinkovy Czech Rep.
237 P5 Zinkwazi Beach S. Africa
192 I2 Zinnowitz Ger.
161 X5 Zinovo Rus. Fed.
Zinoyevsk Ukr. see Kirovohrad
130 B3 Zin Qu r. Sichuan China
228 D3 Zinzana Mali
271 □2 Zion St Kitts and Nevis
250 G7 Zion IL U.S.A.
258 D5 Zion MD U.S.A.
258 C3 Zion Grove PA U.S.A.
265 S4 Zion National Park UT U.S.A.
248 B3 Zionz Lake Ont. Can.
133 M10 Zi Qu r. Qinghai China
130 A2 Ziqudukou Qinghai China
144 E3 Zīrāb Iran
268 G7 Zirándaro Mex.
201 K5 Zirbitzkogel mt. Austria
199 G4 Zirc Hungary
192 J3 Zirchow Ger.
151 D6 Zirekli Turkey
201 J7 Žiri Slovenia
210 E4 Žirje i. Croatia
262 K6 Zirkel, Mount CO U.S.A.
147 K3 Zirkūh i. U.A.E.
200 D5 Zirl Austria
195 J3 Zirndorf Ger.
139 N6 Ziro Arun. Prad. India
201 L1 Žirovnice Czech Rep.
145 I7 Zirreh Afgh.
144 D7 Zīr Rūd Iran
131 I4 Zi Shui r. China
201 O2 Zistersdorf Austria
268 G6 Zitácuaro Mex.
199 H4 Zitava r. Slovakia
218 I5 Žitište Vojvodina Serbia
278 D2 Zitiua r. Brazil
130 E3 Zitong Sichuan China
219 J7 Žitorađa Žitorađa Serbia
193 K9 Zittau Ger.
193 K9 Zittauer Gebirge park Ger.
200 A5 Zitterklapfen mt. Austria
193 F6 Zitz Ger.
245 J2 Zitziana r. AK U.S.A.
149 L5 Zīveh Iran
210 G3 Živinice Bos.-Herz.
232 C2 Ziway Hāyk' l. Eth.
131 K5 Zixi Jiangxi China
131 I6 Zixing Hunan China
129 O7 Ziya He r. China
Ziyamet Cyprus see Leonarisson
142 G2 Ziyanchurino Rus. Fed.
Ziyang Jiangxi China see Wuyuan
130 G2 Ziyang Shaanxi China
130 E3 Ziyang Sichuan China
144 G8 Ziyārat Iran
150 C2 Ziyaret Dağı hill Turkey
151 A5 Ziyaret Dağı mt. Turkey
130 H5 Ziyuan Guangxi China
130 F6 Ziyun Guizhou China
226 D3 Ziz, Oued watercourse Morocco
212 H2 Zizers Switz.
130 E4 Zizhong Sichuan China
129 L8 Zizhou Shaanxi China
208 A1 Zizurkil Spain
201 N7 Zlatar Croatia
218 H7 Zlatar mts Serbia
201 N7 Zlatar-Bistrica Croatia
199 H3 Zlatá Studňa mt. Slovakia
198 G1 Zlaté Hory Czech Rep.
199 H3 Zlaté Moravce Slovakia
219 K6 Zlaten Rog Bulg.
218 H7 Zlatibor mts Serbia
218 I5 Zlatica r. Serbia
219 L4 Zlatna Romania
219 Q7 Zlatni Pyasŭtsi nat. park Bulg.
219 N9 Zlatograd Bulg.
152 G4 Zlatoust Rus. Fed.
159 M6 Zlatoustivka Dnipropetrovs'ka Oblast' Ukr.
159 Q6 Zlatoustivka Donets'ka Oblast' Ukr.
122 H2 Zlatoustovsk Rus. Fed.
199 J3 Zlatý Stôl mt. Slovakia
196 G2 Zławieś Wielka Pol.
158 F3 Zlazne Ukr.
201 K8 Žlebič Slovenia
199 G2 Zlín Czech Rep.
199 G2 Zlínský kraj admin. reg. Czech Rep.
224 B1 Zlīṭan Libya
198 D2 Zliv Czech Rep.
196 E2 Złocieniec Pol.
196 G4 Złoczew Pol.
193 J10 Zlonice Czech Rep.
197 I4 Złota Pol.
196 G3 Złotniki Kujawskie Pol.
196 D4 Złotoryja Pol.
196 F2 Złotów Pol.
196 E5 Złoty Stak Pol.
198 C1 Žlutice Czech Rep.
157 E5 Zlynka Rus. Fed.
159 K5 Zlynka Ukr.
143 T2 Zmeinogorsk Rus. Fed.
196 E4 Żmigród Pol.
213 P5 Žminj Croatia
Zmiyev Ukr. see Zmiyiv
161 T9 Zmiyevka Rus. Fed.
219 S5 Zmiyinyy, Ostriv i. Ukr.
159 P4 Zmiyiv Ukr.
159 M7 Zmiyivka Ukr.
197 L4 Żmudź Pol.
143 R2 Znamenka Kazakh.
143 R1 Znamenka Altayskiy Kray Rus. Fed.
161 S9 Znamenka Orlovskaya Oblast' Rus. Fed.
161 R7 Znamenka Smolenskaya Oblast' Rus. Fed.
Znamenka Ukr. see Znam"yanka
197 J1 Znamensk Rus. Fed.
161 W8 Znamenskoye Lipetskaya Oblast' Rus. Fed.
161 S8 Znamenskoye Orlovskaya Oblast' Rus. Fed.
159 L5 Znam"yanka Ukr.
159 L5 Znam"yanka Druha Ukr.
Znauri Georgia see Qornisi
196 F3 Żnin Pol.
159 M1 Znobivka r. Ukr.
159 M1 Znob-Novhorods'ke Ukr.
198 F3 Znojmo Czech Rep.
212 G7 Zoagli Italy
236 F9 Zoar S. Africa
144 B4 Zobeyrī Iran
235 G2 Zóbuè Moz.
200 C6 Zoccola, Lago di l. Italy
133 E10 Zoco Xizang China
151 E3 Zodi Georgia
Zodi-Qornisi Georgia see Zodi
186 H5 Zoelen Neth.
187 G6 Zoersel Belgium
229 H6 Zoétélé Cameroon
186 F4 Zoetermeer Neth.
186 F4 Zoeterwoude Neth.
212 D1 Zofingen Switz.
Zogainrawar Qinghai China see Huashixia
130 A4 Zogang Xizang China
212 H4 Zogno Italy
130 B2 Zogqên Sichuan China
220 E5 Zografou Greece
144 A4 Zohāb Iran
198 F3 Zohor Slovakia
144 C6 Zohreh r. Iran
133 I10 Zoidê Lhai Xizang China
130 D2 Zoigê Sichuan China
142 H6 Zoir Uzbek.
233 C6 Zoissa Tanz.
138 E2 Zoji La pass Jammu and Kashmir India
237 K8 Zola S. Africa
213 K6 Zola Predosa Italy
187 H6 Zolder Belgium
213 M3 Zoldo Alto Italy
151 E1 Zolka r. Rus. Fed.
197 K5 Żółkiewka-Osada Pol.
192 E3 Zölkow Ger.
212 C1 Zollikofen Switz.
212 F1 Zollikon Switz.
195 L5 Zolling Ger.
Zolochev Kharkivs'ka Oblast' Ukr. see Zolochiv
Zolochev L'vivs'ka Oblast' Ukr. see Zolochiv
159 O3 Zolochiv Kharkivs'ka Oblast' Ukr.
158 D4 Zolochiv L'vivs'ka Oblast' Ukr.
158 E5 Zolota Lypa r. Ukr.
122 E1 Zolotaya Gora Rus. Fed.
159 R5 Zolote Ukr.
159 O8 Zolote Pole Ukr.
197 K6 Zolotkovychi Ukr.
158 E4 Zolotnyky Ukr.
159 L4 Zolotonosha Ukr.
142 A2 Zolotoye Rus. Fed.
Zolotoye Ukr. see Zolote
157 G5 Zolotukhino Rus. Fed.
158 E5 Zolotyy Potik Ukr.
196 E2 Zółtnica Pol.
197 K5 Żołynia Pol.
235 □J4 Zomandao r. Madag.
199 H5 Zomba Hungary
233 B8 Zomba Malawi
Zombor Vojvodina Serbia see Sombor
187 E6 Zomergem Belgium
143 M8 Zomin Uzbek.
284 C2 Zonda Arg.
128 E8 Zongjiafangzi Qinghai China
230 C3 Zongo Dem. Rep. Congo
269 K7 Zongolica Mex.
148 E3 Zonguldak Turkey
221 M1 Zonguldak prov. Turkey
131 K3 Zongyang Anhui China
130 B4 Zongza Sichuan China
128 F7 Zongzhai Gansu China
187 H7 Zonhoven Belgium
187 C7 Zonnebeke Belgium
217 □ Żonqor, Il-Ponta taż- pt Malta
144 A2 Zonūz Iran
214 C4 Zonza Corse France
229 I2 Zoo Baba well Niger
269 K8 Zoogocho Mex.
216 H8 Zoppo, Portella dello pass Italy
269 I6 Zoquiapán y Anexas, Parque Nacional nat. park Mex.
269 J7 Zoquitlán Mex.
196 F5 Żórawina Pol.
193 F7 Zörbig Ger.
151 E6 Zor Dağ mt. Turkey
191 K7 Zorge Ger.
228 E3 Zorgho Burkina
Zorgo Burkina see Zorgho
Zorinsk Ukr. see Zoryns'k
206 H2 Zorita Spain
205 L7 Zorita r. Spain
208 E6 Zorita del Maestrazgo Spain
159 N8 Zorkine Ukr.
145 O3 Zorkŭl l. Afgh./Tajik.
219 P4 Zorleni Romania
219 J5 Zorlențu Mare Romania
179 P6 Zorn r. France
195 L5 Zorneding Ger.
194 E2 Zornheim Ger.
219 O8 Zornitsa Bulg.
Zornotza País Vasco Spain see Amorebieta
274 A5 Zorritos Peru
196 G5 Żory Pol.
159 R5 Zoryns'k Ukr.
228 C5 Zorzor Liberia
193 H6 Zossen Ger.
187 E7 Zottegem Belgium
228 C5 Zouan-Hounien Côte d'Ivoire
224 C4 Zouar Chad
129 O9 Zoucheng Shandong China
226 B5 Zouérat Maur.
228 D2 Zouina well Maur.
128 F7 Zoulang Nanshan mts China
129 O8 Zouping Shandong China
220 E5 Zourvas, Akrotirio pt Greece
131 H4 Zoushi Hunan China
186 J2 Zoutkamp Neth.
187 H7 Zoutleeuw Belgium
Zouxian Shandong China see Zoucheng
144 E5 Zovār Iran
160 L3 Zovka Rus. Fed.
269 J5 Zozocolco de Hidalgo Mex.
201 L7 Zreče Slovenia
218 I5 Zrenjanin Vojvodina Serbia
201 O7 Zrinski Topolovac Croatia
210 E3 Zrmanja r. Croatia
219 K9 Zrnovci Zrnovci Macedonia
195 O2 Zruč Czech Rep.
198 E2 Zruč nad Sázavou Czech Rep.
199 K5 Zsadány Hungary
199 K4 Zsáka Hungary
199 H4 Zsámbék Hungary
199 I4 Zsámbok Hungary
199 I5 Zsana Hungary
193 H8 Zschaitz Ger.
193 H9 Zschopau Ger.
193 H8 Zschopau r. Ger.
193 F8 Zschortau Ger.
199 G5 Zselic hills Hungary
199 G5 Zselicsegi park Hungary
145 N3 Zu Afgh.
275 E3 Zuata r. Venez.
213 P5 Zub, Rt pt Croatia
149 K9 Zubālah, Birkat waterhole Saudi Arabia
146 F8 Zubayr, Jazā'ir az i. Yemen
199 I2 Zuberec Slovakia
202 E4 Zubia Spain
205 O2 Zubiaur Spain
212 E5 Zubiena Italy
208 B1 Zubieta Spain
208 A1 Zubieta Spain
285 F5 Zubillaga Arg.
205 Q3 Zubiri Spain
161 T8 Zubkovo Rus. Fed.
157 H5 Zubova Polyana Rus. Fed.
157 J5 Zubovka Rus. Fed.
161 S7 Zubovo Kaluzhskaya Oblast' Rus. Fed.
161 T1 Zubovo Vologodskaya Oblast' Rus. Fed.
158 C4 Zubria r. Ukr.
196 D3 Żubrów Pol.
161 R5 Zubtsov Rus. Fed.
209 E7 Zucaina Spain
212 F3 Zucchero, Monte mt. Switz.
194 D7 Zuchwil Switz.
200 D6 Zuckerhütl mt. Austria
247 J2 Zucker Lake N.W.T. Can.
205 P3 Zudaire Spain
192 H2 Zudar Ger.
228 D5 Zuénoula Côte d'Ivoire
208 D4 Zuera Spain
147 L7 Ẓufār admin. reg. Oman
206 G5 Zufre Spain
206 G5 Zufre, Embalse de resr Spain
212 F1 Zug Switz.
212 F1 Zug canton Switz.
208 B1 Zugarramurdi Spain
151 C3 Zugdidi Georgia
212 E1 Zuger See l. Switz.
200 C5 Zugspitze mt. Austria/Ger.
229 G4 Zugu Nigeria
205 O3 Zuhatzu-Kuartango Spain
207 K5 Zuheros Spain
159 R5 Zuhres Ukr.
186 F5 Zuid-Beijerland Neth.
Zuider Zee l. Neth. see IJsselmeer
186 F5 Zuid-Holland prov. Neth.
186 J2 Zuidhorn Neth.
186 G4 Zuid-Kennemerland Nationaal Park nat. park Neth.
186 K2 Zuidlaardermeer l. Neth.
186 F5 Zuidland Neth.
186 K2 Zuidlaren Neth.
186 I6 Zuid-Willemsvaart canal Neth.
186 J3 Zuidwolde Neth.
187 D6 Zuienkerke Belgium
Zuitai Gansu China see Kangxia
Zuitaizi Gansu China see Kangxian
Zuitou Shaanxi China see Taiba
207 N5 Zújar Spain
207 H2 Zújar r. Spain
207 I3 Zújar, Embalse del resr Spain
197 L4 Żuków Lubelskie Pol.
197 I3 Żuków Mazowieckie Pol.
196 D4 Żukowice Pol.
165 O7 Żukowo Pol.
274 D2 Zulia state Venez.
128 I8 Zuli He r. Gansu China
198 G1 Žulová Czech Rep.
191 C9 Zülpich Ger.
187 D7 Zulte Belgium
208 A1 Zumaia Spain
208 A1 Zumarraga Spain
274 B6 Zumba Ecuador
201 L8 Žumberačka Gora mts Croatia
235 F2 Zumbo Moz.
250 B5 Zumbro r. MN U.S.A.
250 B5 Zumbrota MN U.S.A.
207 O4 Zumeta r. Spain
269 H7 Zumpahuacán Mex.
269 H6 Zumpango Mex.
269 H8 Zumpango del Río Mex.
187 G6 Zundert Neth.
229 G4 Zungeru Nigeria
217 J6 Zungri Italy
129 P6 Zunhua Hebei China
265 X6 Zuni NM U.S.A.
265 W7 Zuni watercourse AZ/NM U.S.A.
263 J9 Zuni Mountains NM U.S.A.
129 N1 Zun-Torey, Ozero l. Rus. Fed.
130 F5 Zunyi Guizhou China
130 F5 Zunyi Guizhou China
205 R3 Zunzarren Spain
118 I3 Zuo Jiang r. China/Vietnam
129 M8 Zuoquan Shanxi China
129 M7 Zuoyun Shanxi China
212 H2 Zuoz Switz.
210 G3 Županja Croatia
146 E6 Zuqāq i. Saudi Arabia
156 K4 Zura Rus. Fed.
149 L4 Zūrābād Āzarbāyjān-e Gharbī Ir
142 G9 Zūrābād Iran
145 I4 Zūrābād Khorāsān Iran
144 B5 Zurbāṭīyah Iraq
207 O6 Zúrgena Spain
212 F1 Zürich Switz.
212 F1 Zürich canton Switz.
212 F1 Zürichsee l. Switz.
145 M5 Zurmat reg. Afgh.
151 H5 Zurnabad Azer.
201 P4 Zurndorf Austria
219 P7 Zŭrnevo Bulg.
197 H2 Żuromin Pol.
192 E3 Zurow Ger.
217 □ Żurrieq Malta
229 G4 Zuru Nigeria
212 E1 Zurzach Switz.
Zurzuna Turkey see Çıldır
195 J4 Zusam r. Ger.
161 T8 Zusha r. Rus. Fed.
127 K5 Zushi Japan
195 J5 Zusmarshausen Ger.
192 E3 Züsow Ger.
192 I3 Züssow Ger.
187 I7 Zutendaal Belgium
186 J4 Zutphen Neth.
237 J9 Zuurberg National Park S. Afri
197 L1 Žuvintas l. Lith.
160 G7 Žuvinto rezervatas nature res. Lith.
224 B1 Zuwārah Libya
159 N8 Zuya r. Ukr.
178 D1 Zuydcoote France
156 J4 Zuyevka Rus. Fed.
109 C9 Zuytdorp Nature Reserve W.A. Austr.
144 H4 Zūzan Iran
201 K8 Žužemberk Slovenia
218 I8 Zveçan Zveçan Kosovo
Zvečan Zveçan Kosovo see Zveça
160 H4 Zvejniekciems Latvia
161 T6 Zvenigorod Rus. Fed.
Zvenigorodka Ukr. see Zvenyhorodka
158 J4 Zvenyhorodka Ukr.
159 T5 Zverevo Rus. Fed.
219 L7 Zverino Bulg.
142 K1 Zverinogolovskoye Rus. Fed.
220 B2 Zvezdë Albania
210 G3 Zvijezda mts Bos.-Herz.
235 F4 Zvishavane Zimbabwe
199 I3 Zvolen Slovakia
219 K8 Zvonce Babušnica Serbia
210 G3 Zvornik Bos.-Herz.
197 M5 Zvynyache Ukr.
186 J2 Zwaagwesteinde Neth.
201 L6 Zwaring Austria
236 F6 Zwarkop S. Africa
186 J3 Zwartewater l. Neth.
186 J3 Zwartsluis Neth.
228 C5 Zwedru Liberia
186 K3 Zweeloo Neth.
194 C3 Zweibrücken Ger.
212 C2 Zweisimmen Switz.
236 D9 Zweletemba S. Africa
237 L8 Zwelitsha S. Africa
193 F8 Zwenkau Ger.
201 M3 Zwentendorf an der Donau Austria
193 H7 Zwethau Ger.
201 L2 Zwettl Austria
201 L2 Zwettl r. Austria
187 D7 Zwevegem Belgium
187 D6 Zwevezele Belgium
193 G9 Zwickau Ger.
193 G8 Zwickauer Mulde r. Ger.
194 G5 Zwiefalten Ger.
196 D3 Zwierzyn Pol.
197 K5 Zwierzyniec Pol.
195 O3 Zwiesel Ger.
195 N6 Zwiesel mt. Ger.
187 F6 Zwijndrecht Belgium
186 G5 Zwijndrecht Neth.
212 D1 Zwingen Switz.
194 F2 Zwingenberg Ger.
190 F4 Zwischenahner Meer l. Ger.
200 A5 Zwischenwasser Austria
193 F8 Zwochau Ger.
197 J4 Zwoleń Pol.
186 J3 Zwolle Neth.
193 G9 Zwönitz Ger.
193 F10 Zwota Ger.
156 K4 Zyablovo Rus. Fed.
160 L6 Zyal'ki Belarus
159 N8 Zybyny Ukr.
197 H3 Żychlin Pol.
196 F3 Żydowo Wielkopolskie Pol.
196 E1 Żydowo Zachodniopomorskie Pol
197 M3 Zyelyanyevichy Belarus
150 B4 Zygi Cyprus
196 G4 Zygry Pol.
197 M5 Zymne Ukr.
Zymogor'ye Ukr. see Zymohir"y
159 R5 Zymohir"ya Ukr.
159 M8 Zymyne Ukr.
197 I3 Żyrardów Pol.
Zyryan Kazakh. see Zyryanovsk
153 Q3 Zyryanka Rus. Fed.
152 J3 Zyryanovo Rus. Fed.
143 U3 Zyryanovsk Kazakh.
197 K4 Żyrzyn Pol.
197 K1 Żytkiejmy Pol.
197 H5 Żytno Pol.
197 H6 Żywiec Pol.
199 I2 Żywiecki Park Krajobrazowy Pol.
196 F5 Żywocice Pol.
Zyyi Cyprus see Zygi

ACKNOWLEDGEMENTS

Maps, design and origination by
Collins Geo, HarperCollins Publishers, Glasgow

The publishers would like to thank all National Survey Departments, Road, Rail and National Park authorities, Statistical Offices and national place name committees throughout the World for their valuable assistance, and in particular the following:

Antarctic Place-Names Committee, FCO, London, UK

Australian Surveying & Land Information Group, Belconnen, Australia

Automobile Association of South Africa, Johannesburg, Republic of South Africa

British Antarctic Survey, Cambridge, UK

BP Amoco PLC, London, UK

British Geological Survey, Keyworth, Nottingham, UK

Chief Directorate: Surveys and Mapping, Mowbray, Republic of South Africa

Commission de toponymie du Québec, Québec, Canada

Dr John Davies, The Royal Observatory, Edinburgh

Defence Geographic and Imagery Intelligence Agency, Geographic Information Group, Tolworth, UK

Federal Survey Division, Lagos, Nigeria

Food and Agriculture Organization of the United Nations, Rome, Italy

Foreign and Commonwealth Office, London, UK

Mr P J M Geelan, London, UK

General Directorate of Highways, Ankara, Turkey

Hydrographic Office, Ministry of Defence, Taunton, UK

Institut Géographique National, Brussels, Belgium

Institut Géographique National, Paris, France

Instituto Brasileiro de Geografia e Estatistica, Rio de Janeiro, Brazil

Instituto Geográfico Nacional, Lima, Peru

Instituto Geográfico Nacional, Madrid, Spain

Instituto Portugués de Cartografia e Cadastro, Lisbon, Portugal

International Atomic Energy Agency, Vienna, Austria

International Boundary Research Unit, University of Durham, UK

International Hydrographic Organization, Monaco

International Union for the Conservation of Nature, Gland, Switzerland and Cambridge, UK

Kort- og Matrikelstyrelsen, Copenhagen, Denmark

Land Information New Zealand, Wellington, New Zealand

Lands and Surveys Department, Kampala, Uganda

H A G Lewis OBE

National Geographic Society, Washington DC, USA

National Library of Scotland, Edinburgh, UK

National Mapping and Resources Information Authority (NAMRIA), Manila, Philippines

National Oceanic and Atmospheric Administration, USA

Permanent Committee on Geographical Names, London, UK

Royal Geographical Society, London, UK

Royal Scottish Geographical Society, Glasgow, UK

Scientific Committee on Antarctic Research, Cambridge, UK

Scott Polar Research Institute, Cambridge, UK

Scottish Office Development Department, Edinburgh, UK

SNCF French Railways, London, UK

Statens Kartverket, Hønefoss, Norway

Survey Department, Singapore

Survey of India, Dehra Dun, India

Survey of Israel, Tel Aviv, Israel

Survey of Kenya, Nairobi, Kenya

Surveyor General, Harare, Zimbabwe

Surveyor General, Ministry of Lands and Natural Resources, Lusaka, Zambia

Surveys and Mapping Branch, Natural Resources, Ottawa, Canada

Surveys and Mapping Division, Dar-es-Salaam, Tanzania

Terralink New Zealand Ltd, Wellington, New Zealand

The Meteorological Office, Bracknell, Berkshire, UK

The National Imagery and Mapping Agency (NIMA), Bethesda, Maryland, USA

The Stationery Office, London, UK

The United States Board on Geographic Names, Washington DC, USA

The United States Department of State, Washington DC, USA

The United States Geological Survey,

Earth Science Information Center, Reston, Virginia, USA

United Nations, specialized agencies, New York, USA

Marcel Vârlan, University 'Al. I. Cuza', Iași, Romania

MAPS AND DATA

All mapping in this atlas is generated from Collins Bartholomew digital databases. Collins Bartholomew, the UK's leading independent geographical information supplier, can provide a digital, custom, and premium mapping service to a variety of markets. For further information:
Tel: +44 (0) 141 306 3752
e-mail: collinsbartholomew@harpercollins.co.uk
www.collinsbartholomew.com

Data acknowledgements
Pages 50–51
Köppen classification map: Kottek, M., J. Grieser, C. Beck, B. Rudolf, and F. Rubel, 2006: World Map of the Köppen-Geiger climate classification updated. *Meteorol. Z.*, **15**, 259–263. http://koeppen-geiger.vu-wien.ac.at

Pages 52–53
Land cover map: © ESA / ESA GlobCover Project, led by MEDIAS-France.
Olivier Arino, Patrice Bicheron, Frederic Achard, John Latham, Ron Witt, Jean-Louis Weber, November 2008, GLOBCOVER. The most detailed portrait of Earth. *ESA Bulletin* **136**, pp25–31
Available at
www.esa.int/esapub/bulletin/bulletin136/bul136d_arino.pdf

Pages 56–57
Population map: Center for International Earth Science Information Network (CIESIN), Columbia University; International Food Policy Research Institute (IFPRI); and World Resources Institute (WRI). 2000. Gridded Population of the World (GPW), Version 3. Palisades, NY: CIESIN, Columbia University. Available at
http://sedac.ciesin.columbia.edu/plue/gpw

Pages 286–287
Antarctic Digital Database (versions 1 and 2),
© Scientific Committee on Antarctic Research (SCAR), Cambridge (1993, 1998)
Bathymetric data: The GEBCO Digital Atlas published by the British Oceanographic Data Centre on behalf of IOC and IHO, 1994

IMAGES AND PHOTOS

Illustrations created by HarperCollins Publishers unless otherwise stated.

Cover
Sun glinting on the Golfo de Penas, Pacific Ocean, Chile. Image courtesy of the Image Science and Analysis Laboratory, NASA Johnston Space Center. http://eol.jsc.nasa.gov

Pages 19–31
Blue Marble: Next Generation
NASA's Earth Observatory

Pages 32–33
NRSC Ltd/Science Photo Library and Blue Marble: Next Generation. NASA's Earth Observatory

Pages 34–35
Taylor Valley, Antarctica: NASA image created by Jesse Allen, using data provided courtesy of NASA/GSFC/METI/ERSDAC/JAROS, and U.S./Japan ASTER Science Team.

Pages 36–37
New Caledonia: NASA image created by Jesse Allen, using Landsat data provided by the USGS.

Pages 38–39
Grand Coulee Dam, Washington State USA: NASA image created by Jesse Allen, using Landsat data provided by the USGS.

Pages 40–41
Palm Islands, Dubai: NASA/GSFC/METI/ERSDAC/JAROS, and U.S./Japan ASTER Science Team
Palm Jumeirah 2002–2004: IKONOS satellite imagery courtesy of GeoEye

Pages 42–43
Paris: IKONOS satellite imagery courtesy of GeoEye/Telespazio. Copyright 2009.

Pages 44–45
The Sun: Jisas/Lockheed/Science Photo Library
Asteroid: NASA/Science Photo Library
Mercury: NASA/Science Photo Library
Venus: NASA/Science Photo Library
Earth: Photo Library International/Science Photo Library
Mars: US Geological Survey/Science Photo Library
Jupiter: NASA/Science Photo Library
Saturn: Space Telescope ScienceInstitute/NASA/
Science Photo Library
Uranus: NASA/Science Photo Library
Neptune: NASA/Science Photo Library
Pluto and Charon: Space Telescope Science Institute/
NASA/Science Photo Library

Pages 46–47
Big Island, Hawaii: © George Burba/Shutterstock

Pages 48–49
1: WHF Smith, US National Oceanic and Atmospheric Administration (NOAA), USA
3: CLS/DOS, Ramonville St-Agne, France. TOPEX/POSEIDON
4: Science Photo Library

Pages 50–51
3, 4: *Climate Change 2007: Impacts, Adaptation and Vulnerability, summary for Policymakers*, Intergovernmental Panel on Climate Change.

Pages 52–53
1: © ESA / ESA GlobCover Project, led by MEDIAS-France
2: Global Footprint Network
3: Adapted with permission from maps by Philippe Rekacwicz, Le Monde diplomatique, Paris
4: *Our Land Our Future* FAO 1996. *GEO-3: Global Environment Outlook* UNEP 2002
Saudi Arabia images reproduced by kind permission of UNEP

Pages 54–55
1: UNEP-WCMC
2: Millennium Ecosystem Assessment, 2005. *Ecosystems and Human Well-Being: Biodiversity Synthesis.* World Resources Institute, Washington D.C.
4: WWF and ZSL, 2006 *Living Planet Report 2006*
5: LandScanTM Global Population Database. Oak Ridge, TN: Oak Ridge National Laboratory Modified and updated from: 2004 IUCN *Red List of Threatened Species: A Global Species Assessment*
6: UNEP-WCMC and World Database on Protected Areas for terrestrial ecoregions as identified by the World Wide Fund for Nature (WWF). www.unep-wcmc.org/wdpa
Sea Around Us Project (L. Wood, 2007), University of British Columbia Fisheries Centre, in collaboration with UNEP-WCMC and WWF, for large marine ecosystems. www.mpaglobal.org

Page 62
Telecommunications traffic: TeleGeography a division of PriMetrica, Inc. 1909 K Street NW, Suite 380, Washington DC 2006 USA. T. +1 202 741 0020, F. +1 202 741 0021
www.telegeography.com

Pages 64–65
1: © British Museum, London, UK
2: The British Library, London, UK
3: Bridgeman Art Library
4: Hereford Cathedral/Bridgeman Art Library
5: The Art Archive/The British Library
6: The British Library, London, UK
7 and 8: Reproduced by permission of the Trustees of the National Library of Scotland, Edinburgh, UK
9: Alan Collinson Design/Geoinnovations, Llandudno, UK

Pages 66–67
3: Flinders River: MODIS/NASA
4: IKONOS satellite image courtesy of GeoEye www.geoeye.com
5: © Leif Skoogfors/CORBIS
6: Richland County, South Carolina GIS www.richlandmaps.com, www.carto.net
7: Courtesy of Garmin Ltd www.garmin.com

Page 68
Puncak Jaya: Alpine Ascents International Inc.
New Guinea: NASA/Goddard Space Flight Center/USGS
Darling river: Image courtesy of Earth Sciences and Image Analysis Laboratory, NASA Johnson Space Center. STS099-719-87 http://eol.jsc.nasa.gov
Lake Eyre: NASA
Mt Everest: © Pal Teravagimov/Shutterstock
Borneo: NASA/Goddard Space Flight Center/USGS
Chang Jiang: Earth Satellite Corporation/Science Photo Library
Aral Sea: U.S. Geological Survey, EROS Data Center, Sioux Falls, SD, USA

Page 69
El'brus: © scodaru/Shutterstock
Great Britain: M-SAT LTD/Science Photo Library
Volga: CNES, 1996 Distribution SPOT Image/Science Photo Library
Caspian Sea: MODIS/NASA
Kilimanjaro: © enote/Shutterstock
Madagascar: MODIS/NASA
Nile: MODIS/NASA
Lake Victoria: MODIS/NASA

Pages 70–71
Mt McKinley: © Brian Brazil/Shutterstock
Greenland: MODIS/NASA
Mississippi: ASTER/NASA
Lake Superior: Image courtesy of MODIS Rapid Response Project at NASA/GSFC
Cerro Aconcagua: Andes Press Agency
Isla Grande de Tierra del Fuego: MODIS/NASA
Amazonas: NASA
Lago Titicaca: NASA
Vinson Massif: B. Storey/British Antarctic Survey

242–243
244–245
246–247
248–249
250–251
NORTH AMERICA
240-241
264–265
San Francisco
263
Los Angeles
263
Chicago
250
New York
259
258–259
Washington
259
256–257
262–263
266–267
Bermuda
255
260–261
254–255
New Providence
255
270–2
268–269
Mexico
269
252–253
266